Encyclopedia of the
AMERICAN CIVIL WAR
A Political, Social, and Military History

Encyclopedia of the
AMERICAN CIVIL WAR
A Political, Social, and Military History

David S. Heidler and Jeanne T. Heidler
Editors

Foreword by
James M. McPherson

David J. Coles
Associate Editor

Gary W. Gallagher
James M. McPherson
Mark E. Neely, Jr.
Editorial Board

Cartography by
Donald Frazier
Richard J. Thompson, Jr.

W. W. Norton & Company
New York   London

Copyright © 2000 by David S. Heidler and Jeanne T. Heidler

Published by arrangement with ABC-CLIO

Library of Congress Cataloging-in-Publication Data

Encyclopedia of the American Civil War : a political, social, and military history / David S. Heidler and Jeanne
T. Heidler, editors ; foreword by James M. McPherson ; David J. Coles, associate editor ; Gary W. Gallagher,
James M. McPherson, Mark E. Neely, Jr., editorial board.
p. cm.
Combines into one v. original 5 v. work published by ABC-CLIO, Santa Barbara, Calif. in 2000.
Includes bibliographical references and index.
ISBN 0-393-04758-X
1. United States—History—Civil War. 1861–1865—Encyclopedias. I. Heidler, David Stephen, 1955–II.
Heidler, Jeanne T. III. Coles, David J.

E468 .E53 2002
973.7'03—dc21   2002070280

W. W. Norton & Company, Inc., 500 Fifth Avenue, New York, N.Y. 10110
www.wwnorton.com

W. W. Norton & Company Ltd., Castle House, 75/76 Wells Street, London W1T 3QT

1 2 3 4 5 6 7 8 9 0

To

Thomas A. Belser, Jr.
Joseph H. Harrison, Jr.
Robert R. Rea

Our Great Triumvirate

CONTRIBUTORS

Gretchen A. Adams
University of New Hampshire

Frank Alduino
Anne Arundel Community College

Donald Altschiller
Mugar Memorial Library, Boston
   University

William L. Anderson
Western Carolina University

Byron Andreasen
University of Illinois at Urbana—
   Champaign

Brad Arnold
Virginia Military Institute

Steven M. Avella
Marquette University

Rolando Avila
The University of Texas—Pan American

Catherine O. Badura
Valdosta State University

Anne J. Bailey
Georgia College & State University

Jean Harvey Baker
Goucher College

Daniel P. Barr
Kent State University

Christopher Bates
University of California—Los Angeles

James S. Baugess
Columbus State Community College

Harry M. Bayne
Brewton Parker College

Jonathan M. Beagle
University of New Hampshire

Terry L. Beckenbaugh
University of Arkansas

W. Robert Beckman
Illinois State University

James R. Belpedio
Becker College

Robert Patrick Bender
University of Arkansas

Kurt O. Berends
Calvin College

Jennifer L. Bertolet
George Washington University

Eugene H. Berwanger
Colorado State University

Paul M. Bessell
George Washington Masonic National
   Memorial

Alexander M. Bielakowski
Kansas State University

Andrew Paul Bielakowski
University of Toronto

Louis Bielakowski
Independent scholar

Judith Bielecki
Washburn-Norlans Foundation

John David Bladek
University of Washington

Frederick J. Blue
Youngstown State University

Arnold D. Blumberg
Johns Hopkins University

Kenneth J. Blume
Albany College of Pharmacy

Eric L. Bobo
University of Southern Mississippi

Lori Bogle
United States Naval Academy

Ray E. Boomhower
Indiana Historical Society

Lincoln Bramwell
University of Utah

Russell K. Brown
Groveton, Georgia

William H. Brown
North Carolina State Archives

Gary L. Browne
University of Maryland—Baltimore
   County

Judkin Jay Browning
Independent scholar

Susannah U. Bruce
Kansas State University

Stephen P. Budney
University of Mississippi

Robert W. Burg
Purdue University

Frank J. Byrne
The Ohio State University

Lauren Cooke Burgess
Independent scholar

Mike Butler
University of Mississippi

Chris M. Calkins
Petersburg National Battlefield

Bill Cameron
United States Army (Retired)

Heidi Campbell-Shoaf
Independent scholar

Jack J. Cardoso
State University College at Buffalo

Rosemarie S. Cardoso
Art Education, Clarence, New York

David Carlson
Georgia Military College

Stephen A. Carney
Kent State University

Ruth C. Carter
University of Pittsburgh Library System
   (Retired)

Joan E. Cashin
The Ohio State University

JoAnn E. Castagna
University of Iowa

Albert Castel, Emeritus
Western Michigan University

Adrienne Caughfield
Texas Christian University

Mark R. Cheathem
Mississippi State University

H. Lee Cheek, Jr.
Lee University

Robert H. Churchill
Rutgers University

Paul A. Cimbala
Fordham University

Mary Lynn Cluff
University of Phoenix

Thomas Burnell Colbert
Marshalltown Community College

David J. Coles
Longwood College

Michael J. Connolly
St. Anselm College

Rory Cornish
Northeast Louisiana University

Janet L. Coryell
Western Michigan University

Karen L. Cox
Independent scholar

Lynda Lasswell Crist
Rice University

Edward R. Crowther
Adams State College

Thomas F. Curran
Saint Louis University

Enrico Dal Lago
National University of Ireland, Galway

C. David Dalton
College of the Ozarks

Michael S. Davis
Kansas State University

William C. Davis
Independent scholar

Thomas A. DeBlack
Arkansas Tech University

Christine Dee
Harvard University

Kenneth A. Deitreich
West Virginia University

Frank E. Deserino
University College, London

Charles Ellis Dickson
Independent scholar

Richard Digby-Junger
Western Michigan University

Laurent Ditmann
Spelman College

James G. Downhour
Southern Illinois University

Alan C. Downs
Georgia Southern University

Dorothy L. Drinkard
East Tennessee State University

Hubert F. Dubrulle
University of Puget Sound

Russell Duncan
University of Copenhagen

John P. Dunn
Valdosta State University

R. Blake Dunnavent
Lubbock Christian University

Robert N. Dykstra
SUNY—Albany

Gary T. Edwards
University of Memphis

David P. Eldridge
Mississippi State University

Stephen D. Engle
Florida Atlantic University

Paul D. Escott
Wake Forest University

Nicole Etcheson
University of Texas at El Paso

Damon R. Eubank
Campbellsville University

Warner D. Farr
U.S. Army Special Operations Command

Carol Faulkner
Pamona College

William B. Feis
Buena Vista University

Eric Fettmann
Independent scholar

Phyllis F. Field
Ohio University

Roy E. Finkenbine
University of Detroit Mercy

Steven Fisher
University of Denver

Jane Flaherty
Texas A & M University

Chris E. Fonvielle, Jr.
University of North Carolina—
    Wilmington

Franklin Forts
University of Georgia

Buck T. Foster
Mississippi State University

Daniel L. Fountain
University of Mississippi

Lisa Tendrich Frank
University of Florida

Donald S. Frazier
McMurry University

John C. Fredriksen
Independent scholar

Derek W. Frisby
University of Alabama

Gary W. Gallagher
University of Virginia

J. Matthew Gallman
Gettysburg College

Douglas G. Gardner
Miami University

Samantha Jane Gaul
Virginia Tech

Peter S. Genovese
Bowling Green State University

David J. Gerleman
Southern Illinois University

Charles Dana Gibson
Independent scholar

William Gillette
Rutgers University

James M. Gillispie
University of Mississippi

Lesley J. Gordon
University of Akron

Mark R. Grandstaff
Brigham Young University

Jennifer L. Gross
University of Georgia

Carl J. Guarneri
St. Mary's College of California

K. R. Constantine Gutzman
John Jay College—CUNY

Richard C. Halseth
Independent scholar

Ron Hamilton
Indiana University—Indianapolis

Edward John Harcourt
Vanderbilt University

William C. Harris
North Carolina State University

Jennifer Harrison
North Carolina Wesleyan College

Lowell H. Harrison
Western Kentucky University

Dale F. Harter
The Library of Virginia

William T. Hartley
University of Tennessee

Charles L. Heath, Jr.
Institute for Historical and Cultural
    Research, East Carolina University

David S. Heidler
Independent scholar

Jeanne T. Heidler
United States Air Force Academy

David C. R. Heisser
Daniel Library, The Citadel

Earl J. Hess
Lincoln Memorial University

Wallace C. Hettle
University of Northern Iowa

Bernard Hirschhorn
Independent scholar

Wolfgang C. Hochbruck
University of Stuttgart, Germany

Randolph Hollingsworth
University of Kentucky

Peter C. Holloran
New England Historical Association

James V. Holton
Polk County Historical Museum, Bartow,
    Florida

Ari Hoogenboom
Brooklyn College and Graduate Center
    City University of New York

Charles F. Howlett
Amityville (NY) Public Schools /
    University College, Adelphi University

Leonne M. Hudson
Kent State University

James L. Isemann
Southeast Community College, Lincoln,
    NE

Kathryn Allamong Jacob
Schlesinger Library, Harvard University

James Robbins Jewell
West Virginia University

Robert W. Johannsen
University of Illinois at Urbana-
    Champagne

Charles Thomas Johnson
Valdosta State University

Timothy D. Johnson
Lipscomb University

Trevor M. Jones
Early American Museum, Mahomet, IL

Mauriel P. Joslyn
Independent scholar

Jerry Keenan
Independent scholar

Christian B. Keller
Pennsylvania State University

Jeff Kinard
Independent scholar

Charles E. Kinzer
Longwood College

James C. Klotter
Georgetown College

Willard Carl Klunder
Wichita State University

Joe Knetsch
Florida Department of Environmental
    Protection

Paul E. Kuhl
Winston Salem University

Alan K. Lamm
Mount Olive College

Scott M. Langston
Southwest Baptist University

Lisa Lauterbach Laskin
Harvard University

Mark A. Lause
University of Cincinnati

Dennis S. Lavery
Department of the Army

Elizabeth D. Leonard
Colby College

Kevin M. Levin
St. Anne's—Belfield School

Frank R.Levstik
Kentucky Department of Libraries and
    Archives

Daniel Liestman
Kansas State University Libraries

Brad D. Lookingbill
Columbia College

Richard D. Loosbrock
Chadron State College

M. Philip Lucas
Cornell College

Kenneth L. Lyftogt
University of Northern Iowa

Sharon S. MacDonald
Illinois State University

Ronald G. Machoian
Independent scholar

Bruce D. Mactavish
Washburn University

Brock Magoon
Independent scholar

Dane Magoon
Southern Illinois University

Jonathan L. Mahaffey
Appalachian State University

Sr. Mary Denis Maher, CSA
Ursuline College

Wayne Mahood, Emeritus
SUNY—Genesee

Jo Ann Manfra
Worcester Polytechnic Institute

John F. Marszalek
Mississippi State University

James Marten
Marquette University

Bruce E. Matthews
Auburn University

John Mayfield
Samford University

Joseph M. McCarthy
Suffolk University

James L. McDonough
Auburn University

David McGee
University of Georgia

Stanley S. McGowen
Sam Houston State University

John E. McKay
Independent scholar

Brian D. McKnight
Mississippi State University

James H. Meredith
United States Air Force Academy

Nathan R. Meyer
Eureka, Illinois

Christopher C. Meyers
Georgia Military College

Carl H. Moneyhon
University of Arkansas at Little Rock

James M. Morris
Christopher Newport University

Malcolm Muir, Jr.
Austin Peay State University

Earl F. Mulderink III
Southern Utah University

William H. Mulligan, Jr.
Murray State University

R. Boyd Murphree
Florida State Archives

Diane Neal
University of Central Oklahoma

Frank Nickell
Southeast Missouri State University

Alan T. Nolan
Indiana Historical Society

David A. Norris
Independent scholar

Greg O'Brien
University of Southern Mississippi

Broeck N. Oder
Santa Catalina School, Monterey, CA

Matthew Pacer
Kansas State University

Dave Page
Independent scholar

Christopher M. Paine
Indiana University Southeast

William A. Pannapacker
Harvard University

Sue C. Patrick
University of Wisconsin—Barron
County

Donald K. Pickens
University of North Texas

Michael D. Pierce
Tarleton State University

Walter E. Pittman
University of West Alabama

Brian C. Pohanka
Independent scholar

W. Scott Poole
University of South Carolina—Aiken

David A. Powell
Independent scholar

J. Tracy Power
South Carolina Department of Archives
and History

Thomas Lynwood Powers
University of South Carolina Sumter

Dorothy O. Pratt
University of Notre Dame

James M. Prichard
Kentucky Department of Libraries &
Archives

David A. Proctor
North Florida Community College

Jeffery S. Prushankin
University of Arkansas

Ethan S. Rafuse
University of Missouri—Kansas City

Edward Ragan
Syracuse University

Steven J. Ramold
University of Nebraska—Lincoln

Chad A. Reisig
Claremont Graduate University

Kent D. Richards, Emeritus
Central Washington University

Curtis Richardson
Northern Illinois University

William H. Roberts
The Ohio State University

James I. Robertson, Jr.
Virginia Polytechnic Institute & State
University

Glenn Robins
University of Southern Mississippi

Junius P. Rodriguez
Eureka College

Alicia E. Rodriquez
California State University, Bakersfield

Charles P. Roland
University of Kentucky

Todd Anthony Rosa
George Washington University

Michael A. Ross
Loyola University New Orleans

Anne Sarah Rubin
American University

Susan Sessions Rugh
Brigham Young University

Robert D. Sampson
University of Illinois at Urbana-
Champaign

Charles W. Sanders, Jr.
Kansas State University

Stanley Sandler
Virginia Military Institute

Richard A. Sauers
Superior (WI) Public Museums

Robert Saunders, Jr.
Troy State University Dothan

Elizabeth D. Schafer
Independent scholar

Jane E. Schultz
Indiana University-Purdue University

Angela Schwarz
University of Duisberg, Germany

Mark E. Scott
Independent scholar

Paul Searls
University of Vermont

Philip Lee Secrist
Kennesaw State University

Peter J. Sehlinger
Indiana University, Indianapolis

Edward Sharp
University of North Carolina at
Greensboro

William L. Shea
University of Arkansas at Monticello

Dana B. Shoaf
Independent scholar

Rae Sikula
Cudahy Library, Loyola University of
Chicago

Larry C. Skogen
Independent scholar

James L. Sledge III
Truett-McConnell College

Adam I. P. Smith
Queen Mary and Westfield College,
University of London

Duane A. Smith
Fort Lewis College

Elbert B. Smith, Emeritus
University of Maryland

G. Judson Smith, Jr.
Alexander H. Stephens State Historic
Park

Gene A. Smith
Texas Christian University

Gerald J. Smith
Paine College

Michael Thomas Smith
Louisburg College

Timothy B. Smith
Mississippi State University

Mark Snell
Shepherd College

Irvin D. Solomon
Florida Gulf Coast University

Richard J. Sommers
Independent scholar

Ian M.Spurgeon
Kansas State University

Kenneth R. Stevens
Texas Christian University

Christopher S. Stowe
The University of Toledo

Reginald C. Stuart
St. Bonaventure University

David M. Sullivan
Independent scholar

Stephen C. Svonavec
Francis Marion University

Katherine L. Swimm
University of Mississippi

Wiley Sword
Independent scholar

Craig L. Symonds
United States Naval Academy

John Syrett
Trent University

Bruce Tap
Independent scholar

Robert A. Taylor
Florida Institute of Technology

Teresa A. Thomas
Fitchburg State College

J. Mark Thompson
University of North Carolina at
Pembroke

William A. Tidwell
Independent scholar

Eric Tscheschlok
Auburn University

Adam-Max Tuchinsky
University of North Carolina at Chapel
Hill

Spencer C. Tucker
Virginia Military Institute

Minoa Uffelman
Austin Peay State University

David J. Ulbrich
Kansas State University

Gregory J. W. Urwin
Temple University

Antoinette G. Van Zelm
Independent scholar

Wendy Hamand Venet
Georgia State University

Eric H. Walther
University of Houston

Matthew S. Warshauer
Central Connecticut State University

Zack C. Waters
Independent scholar

Tim J. Watts
Kansas State University

Clive Webb
University of Sussex at Brighton

Jim Weeks
Pennsylvania State University

William Weisberger
Independent scholar

Stephen G. Weisner
Springfield Technical Community
College

Mark A. Weitz
Auburn University—Montgomery

David P. Werlich
Southern Illinois University—
Carbondale

Kristy Armstrong White
Northeast Mississippi Museum
Association

Clay Williams
Old Capitol Museum, Jackson, MS

David Williams
Valdosta State University

Teresa C. Williams
Valdosta State University

Brian S. Wills
University of Virginia's College at Wise

Mary Ellen Wilson
Middle Georgia College

Thomas A. Wing
Fort Smith National Historic Site

Robert S. Wolff
Central Connecticut State University

Thomas E. Woods, Jr.
Suffolk Community College

Eddie Woodward
The Library of Virginia

CONTRIBUTORS

Robert Wooster
Texas A&M University—Corpus Christi

Susan Wyly-Jones
Harvard University

Ben Wynne
University of Mississippi

Mitchell Yockelson
National Archives

Duane C. Young
De Montford University

David T. Zabecki
American Military University

Kathleen R. Zebley
University of North Carolina at Pembroke

Qingsong Zhang
Independent scholar

Gregory R. Zieren
Austin Peay State University

CONTENTS

ENCYCLOPEDIA OF THE AMERICAN CIVIL WAR
A Political, Social, and Military History

LIST OF ENTRIES

FOREWORD

By *James M. McPherson*

An advertising slogan popular during the years of my youth was: "When better cars are built, Buick will build them." The clear message was that, while there were many makes of automobiles on the market, Buick was the best.

That slogan comes to mind when reading the *Encyclopedia of the American Civil War.* Readers can choose from several reference works on the Civil War, but this one is the best. Comprehensive, authoritative, well written, cross-referenced, its 1600+ articles range from a column to several pages in length, covering every conceivable subject and significant person connected with the causes, course, and consequences of the war—from the Free Soil Party and the Wilmot Proviso to the Freedmen's Bureau and the Thirteenth Amendment; from John C. Calhoun and George Fitzhugh to Duncan Kenner and the Confederacy's last-ditch effort to enlist African-American soldiers; from the firing on *Star of the West* in January 1861 to the CSS *Shenandoah*'s rampage among American whalers in the Pacific during the summer of 1865.

Even the most learned and dedicated Civil War aficionados will find something here that they did not know before. Test yourself: What do you know about the battles of Alleghany Mountain, Glasgow, Greenbrier River, Ware Bottom Church, or Yellow Bayou? You can read about them in these pages. Can you identify Gaetano Bedini, Virginia Caroline Tunstall Clay-Clopton, Xavier Blanchard De Bray, Antonia Ford, Cordelia Perrine Harvey, or William Holland Thomas? Look them up in this encyclopedia and you will be prepared to win the Civil War *Jeopardy* sweepstakes. Most readers of this foreword know something of Braxton Bragg, but how many are familiar with Edward Stuyvesant Bragg and Thomas Bragg? How many can describe the Charleston (Illinois) Riot or Phelps's Raid? Can you explain the issues at stake in the case of

Lemmon v. People and relate them to the causes of the war? With this encyclopedia in hand, you can answer all of these questions and many, many more. Arranged alphabetically, the entries cover a broad range of categories: persons; states; military campaigns and battles; the names of ships; the various armies (of Northern Virginia, of the Potomac, etc.); famous units like the Stonewall Brigade and the Iron Brigade; important legislation and proclamations; names of newspapers and magazines; names of important organizations; prisoner-of-war camps; key events such as the Centralia Massacre, the burning of Columbia, the assassination of Lincoln; and categories such as casualties; class conflict (C.S.A. and U.S.A.); United States Colored Troops; African-American Soldiers (C.S.A.); photography; the Underground Railroad; armories, arsenals, and foundries; and scores of others. In short, nothing of importance or interest is left out. Cross-references and a brief bibliography at the end of each article refer the reader to other relevant articles in this encyclopedia and to outside sources for further research. Another valuable feature are the documents that provide a primary-source accompaniment to many of the articles. These documents give a sense of immediacy to the subjects of the articles; they also suggest sources and ideas for further reading and research.

For good reason, the Civil War is the most written-about subject in American history. Northern victory assured the survival of the United States as one nation, indivisible, and ended the anomaly of slavery in a country founded on a charter of freedom. A blend of triumph and tragedy, courage and cowardice, heroes and knaves, selfless sacrifice and selfish profiteering, the war shaped and defined the America that has emerged in the 135 years since the guns fell silent. This reference work will broaden and deepen the knowledge of this titanic conflict for novice and expert alike.

PREFACE

We have sought with this encyclopedia to fashion a comprehensive source for a boundless subject. At most for both serious scholars and interested amateurs, we hope to provide a reference of first resort for those seeking information either on broad areas or specific topics. More than 1,600 essays describe and explain a myriad of aspects that cover the coming of the war, its conduct, and its consequences in a political, military, and social context. In addition to full biographies of major and minor military, political, diplomatic, and cultural figures, these essays include descriptions of more than sixty major engagements as well as important skirmishes and their role in the larger military setting. We have also tried to cover broad areas such as strategy and tactics, social trends, and technological innovations. Primary documents are provided in a separate section, maps depict military aspects, and illustrations furnish both portraiture and vivid scenes from the period. Appendices supply the executive officers of both the United States and Confederate States, general officers of each army, a glossary of terms unique to military usage or peculiar to the period, and an extensive bibliography.

We are grateful to our editorial board for guidance and advice. Our associate editor, David J. Coles, provided insightful assistance in identifying potential contributors and reviewing work once it came to hand. While indebted to all our contributors, we are especially appreciative of those whose special exertions materially advanced this project to its completion. Albert Castel, Warner Farr, Dave Sullivan, Spencer Tucker, and Dave Zabecki were among those who took time from busy schedules to read material and offer suggestions for its improvement. Elizabeth Leonard not only made a significant contribution herself, she introduced us to several scholars whose expertise proved invaluable in deepening the texture of this work. Jane Schultz and Wendy Venet number among those contributors whose special command of areas in the field helped us round out our list and bring it to a conclusion. Jack Davis was an early friend to the project, as were Paul Cimbala, John Marszalek, Greg Urwin, and David Williams, all of whom made valuable suggestions for additions to the list and provided introductions to scholars who could write on specialized subjects. Many contributors gave us leads to illustrations, and Judith Bielecki, JoAnn Castagna, Paul Cimbala, Paul Kuhl, David Williams, and Dave Zabecki even went so far as to send camera-ready prints or negatives with permissions. Don Frazier's cartography again proved peerless and his timing flawless. We could not have completed the enterprise without John Fredriksen's valuable and timely contributions, and we owe special thanks to Jean Harvey Baker and Richard J. Sommers for their extraordinary efforts as much as for their impeccable work. Finally, we are humbled by the professionalism and high consideration of several authors who made their valuable contributions to the project in spite of dire health crises. Wishing to preserve their privacy, we have thanked them privately, painfully aware that our acknowledgments both public and private are inadequate notice of their splendid sacrifices and pale expressions of our deep appreciation.

The support of friends and family was so ample that it eludes the proper expression of thanks. Cyrus K. Heidler was always standing by to help ease the weariness of long labors. Friends like Kathryn E. Holland Braund, Steve Engle, and Reg Stuart had kind words ready when such were sorely needed. And Joseph and Sarah Twiggs have been in this, as in all things, wise and witty, and though at some remove, always near when needed and always cheerful wherever.

—*David S. Heidler and Jeanne T. Heidler*

INTRODUCTION

More than any other event, the American Civil War went far in defining a United States that had been imperfectly and incompletely shaped by its first seventy years. For seven decades, the presence of slavery in a republic founded upon principles of human freedom increasingly befuddled the political system and unraveled the social fabric. Although slavery in the South had given rise to antislavery movements in the North as early as the American Revolution, notably among religious groups such as the Quakers, a fresh vigor characterized abolitionist activities in the 1830s. Although the abolitionists divided along radical and moderate lines and argued among themselves about the viability of political solutions to the moral blight of slavery, the abolitionists became a moral force of growing influence and gradually made a deep impression on Northern sentiments. The movement also provoked a proslavery reaction from Southern whites that enlarged the breach between North and South. Southerners came to feel beleaguered and isolated as moderate Northerners increasingly exhibited the attitude that slavery was wrong and at least should not be extended to the nation's western territories.

Arguments over these western territories goaded the country into a series of disruptive crises. Each was settled with an unsatisfying compromise that left most Southerners feeling materially cheated and many Northerners morally embarrassed. In 1854, efforts to organize the vast Midwest region called the Nebraska Territory led to the ill-conceived Kansas-Nebraska Act. It was a project designed to secure Southern support for the organization of what by prior agreement would have been a free territory. Two territories, Kansas and Nebraska, would be created from the region under the principal of popular sovereignty, which was to say that each territory would decide for itself whether to admit or prohibit slavery. This cynical calculation for Southern endorsement was apparent from the start. Kansas, the southernmost section of the region, was obviously supposed to become a slave state, while Nebraska to the north would apparently become a free state. The plan instantly went awry, however, when the fate of Kansas became a point of occasionally violent contention between armed antislavery and proslavery factions that went far in turning the territory into a battleground.

Antislavery Northerners were enraged while Southerners took Northern reaction as another instance of bad faith. Consequently, all previous compromises on the slavery issue were imperiled, and any future compromises were preemptively questionable. The party system was immediately altered. Democrats began to drift into Northern and Southern wings, sometimes hostile and always suspicious of each other. The Whig Party simply disintegrated with much of its Northern element forming into the new Republican Party. This new party's initial reason for existence was to mount a robust objection to slavery, but within two years its program would expand to attract Northern yeomen farmers and businessmen as well as antislavery advocates. Although it was an exclusively sectional party, it contended successfully against Northern Democrats in state and local contests, became a powerful force in Congress, and mounted a serious bid for the presidency in 1856.

Democrat James Buchanan won the 1856 election, but he had been in office only two days when the Supreme Court made a ruling in the *Dred Scott* Case on 6 March 1857. Scott was a slave who sued for his freedom on the basis that his owner had taken him to live for five years in the free state of Illinois and the free Wisconsin Territory. In addition to denying Scott his freedom, Chief Justice Roger Taney's comprehensive decision went further to declare that Congress had no authority to prohibit slavery in the territories, even if territorial inhabitants desired such a prohibition. The ruling seriously eroded the power of popular sovereignty to exclude slavery from any territories in the Union, thus depriving Northern Democrats of a convenient way to sidestep confrontations with their Southern wing over slavery. Republicans decried the decision and condemned the Court, thus giving Southerners additional evidence that the North would not respect any measures—even Supreme Court decisions—that did not assail slavery.

The most disruptive issue distracting the Buchanan administration, however, was the ongoing controversy over Kansas. When Buchanan attempted to obtain statehood for the troubled territory, proslavery forces at Lecompton, Kansas, drafted a constitution that not only reflected their views on slavery but also removed the possibility of a territorial referendum excluding it from the new state. Illinois senator Stephen A. Douglas, leading Democrat in Congress and a proponent of popular sovereignty, objected to the Lecompton Constitution so strenuously that he earned the lasting enmity of President Buchanan. Douglas was forced to defend his Senate seat in 1858 against the Republican challenger Abraham Lincoln, doing so in a series of joint appearances across Illinois that would be immortalized as the Lincoln-Douglas Debates. Douglas kept his Senate seat, but Lincoln's declarations on slavery struck such a sympathetic chord among Northerners that he would emerge from the contest a national figure. Stating a

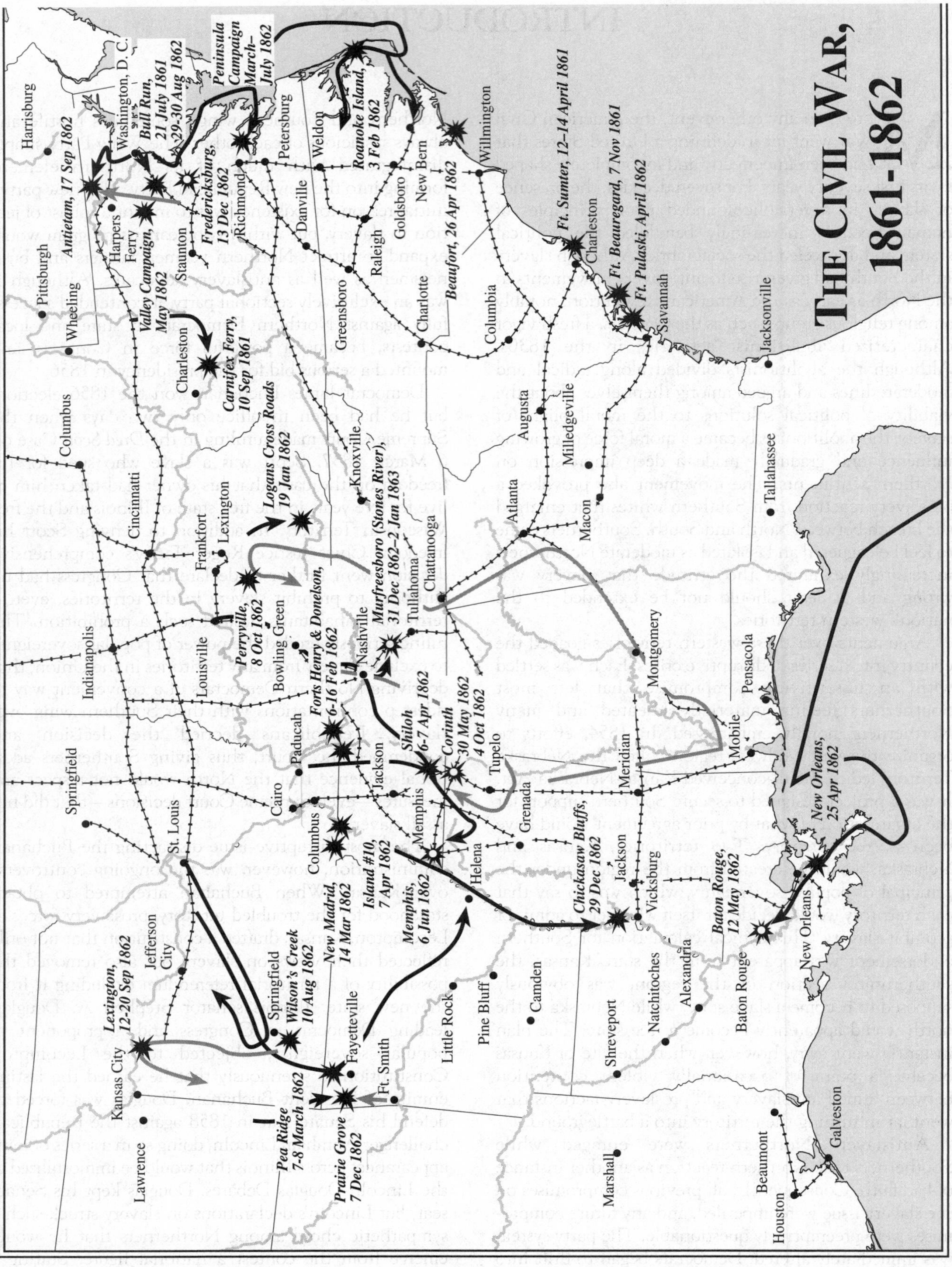

THE CIVIL WAR, 1861-1862

Harrisburg

Washington, D. C.

Bull Run,
21 July 1861
29-30 Aug 1862

Peninsula
Campaign
March–
July 1862

Pittsburgh

Wheeling

Antietam, 17 Sep 1862

Harpers Ferry

Fredericksburg,
13 Dec 1862

Petersburg

Weldon

Roanoke Island,
3 Feb 1862

Willmington

Ft. Sumter, 12–14 April 1861

Columbus

Valley Campaign,
May 1862

Staunton

Richmond

Danville

Greensboro

New Bern

Beaufort, 26 Apr 1862

Charleston

Ft. Beauregard, 7 Nov 1861

Ft. Pulaski, April 1862

Charleston

Carnifex Ferry,
10 Sep 1861

Raleigh

Goldsboro

Charlotte

Columbia

Savannah

Jacksonville

Cincinnatti

Knoxville

Logans Cross Roads
19 Jan 1862

Augusta

Milledgeville

Tallahassee

Frankfort

Lexington

Atlanta

Macon

Perryville,
8 Oct 1862

Murfreesboro (Stones River),
31 Dec 1862–2 Jan 1863

Chattanooga

Tullahoma

Indianapolis

Louisville

Bowling Green

Forts Henry & Donelson,
6-16 Feb 1862

Nashville

Montgomery

Springfield

Paducah

Cairo

Jackson

Shiloh
6-7 Apr 1862

Corinth
30 May 1862
4 Oct 1862

Tupelo

Meridian

Mobile

Pensacola

St. Louis

Columbus

Memphis

Island #10,
7 Apr 1862

Memphis,
6 Jun 1862

Helena

Grenada

Jackson

Vicksburg

Chickasaw Bluffs,
29 Dec 1862

Baton Rouge,
12 May 1862

New Orleans,
25 Apr 1862

Jefferson
City

Lexington,
12-20 Sep 1862

Springfield

Wilson's Creek
10 Aug 1862

New Madrid,
14 Mar 1862

Fayetteville

Little Rock

Pine Bluff

Camden

Natchitoches

Alexandria

Baton Rouge

New Orleans

Kansas City

Ft. Smith

Pea Ridge
7-8 March 1862

Prairie Grove
7 Dec 1862

Lawrence

Shreveport

Marshall

Beaumont

Houston

Galveston

moderate antislavery position, Lincoln insisted that slavery could not be molested where it existed, but it must not be allowed to spread to areas where it did not; even as he condemned slavery, he refused to denounce slaveholders. Prominent members of the Republican Party began taking Lincoln's measure as a possible presidential candidate for 1860.

Moderation of Lincoln's type reflected the majority opinion in the North, but the increasing tensions of the sectional dispute saw dramatic and extreme occurrences overwhelm the demeanor of such moderation. Ultimately, Southerners were unable to distinguish between temperate opposition to slavery and radical abolitionism. The most notorious episode of the latter was John Brown's October 1859 raid on the federal armory at Harper's Ferry in western Virginia. Brown intended to mount an invasion of the South, arming liberated slaves to commit insurrection and bring about the violent destruction of slavery. The raid failed, but Brown's subsequent trial revealed that some prominent Northern abolitionists had backed the scheme. For Southerners, such a revelation was bad enough, yet worse was the mantle of martyrdom that many Northerners settled on Brown's shoulders even as the hangman was placing the noose around his neck. Pealing bells and cannon salutes provided the backdrop for large gatherings that heard Brown compared to Christ, his gallows likened to the cross.

The election of 1860 was held in the shadow of these ominous events. The Democrats soon found themselves divided over both a candidate and a platform, and an abortive convention in Charleston, South Carolina, and then a discordant one in Baltimore, Maryland, failed to mend the rift. Instead, two Democratic Party candidates would emerge from the brawl, Stephen A. Douglas and John C. Breckinridge, the latter bearing the onus of being the "Southern" candidate. Whigs and other disaffected political strays, untethered by the roiling sectional dispute, cobbled together a Constitutional Union Party to nominate John Bell, touted as a candidate who would avoid the distracting slavery controversy to restore the Union to amity. And the Republicans on the third ballot of their convention in Chicago nominated Abraham Lincoln, who in November 1860 became the sixteenth president-elect of the United States.

The outcome of the 1860 election triggered a grave crisis. Four days after Abraham Lincoln's election, South Carolina's legislature unanimously called a special convention that met in Charleston. On 20 December 1860, the convention unanimously chose to secede from the Union, and six additional Deep South states had followed by early February 1861. That month representatives from these states met at Montgomery, Alabama, to form the Confederate States of America and choose their president, former U.S. Senator Jefferson Davis of Mississippi, and vice president, Alexander H. Stephens of Georgia. Basic American ideals of self-determination as manifested in the Declaration of Independence guided the Southerners toward secession and in their mind justified them in the act. Southern secessionists drew parallels from the American Revolution's defiance of the British Empire in 1776. Furthermore, to the secessionists the Union that was formed in the aftermath of the Revolution was a voluntary formation that could be voluntarily disbanded. Separated from Northern assaults on its "peculiar institution" of slavery, the South would seek to forge its own fate, confident that it would do so more agreeably as a separate nation.

Meanwhile, Lincoln would not take office until 4 March 1861, and elderly President James Buchanan confronted the emergency. Unswerving in his loyalty to the Union, Buchanan rejected the idea that secession was legal. Yet, he also insisted that the Constitution did not empower the president to employ force to preserve the Union. In any event, the United States's small peacetime army was widely scattered and mainly occupied with policing the western frontier. Buchanan was not alone in hoping that compromise and reconciliation would avert the storm. Indeed, the specter of war was a powerful incentive for compromise, and serious efforts for reconciliation were played out in Washington in tandem with the secession crisis. One was the set of initiatives sponsored by Kentucky senator John J. Crittenden as proposed constitutional amendments protecting slavery and thus designed to accommodate Southern apprehensions. This compromise effort failed in part because Lincoln declared his opposition to it on the grounds that its provisions would violate Republican promises to halt the spread of slavery into the territories. The other major effort was the Washington Peace Conference, a meeting attended mainly by fading luminaries of another time—former president John Tyler was its presiding officer—and whose informal appellation of "The Old Gentlemen's Convention" indicated the futility of its labors.

Even after his inauguration, Lincoln remained hopeful that reconciliation was still possible, and he fundamentally continued Buchanan's policy of watchful waiting. Yet political compromises fashioned to postpone a final reckoning became at the end only another source of confusion and dissatisfaction themselves, and the final reckoning loomed as the republic remained divided. And Lincoln could not wait forever. Federal authority over forts in the South brought the secession crisis to its conclusion. Seceding states had taken over almost all U. S. property within their borders so that when Lincoln became president, there were only two important garrisons in the South still in federal possession. One was lightly manned Fort Sumter in Charleston Harbor, whose supplies would be exhausted by mid-

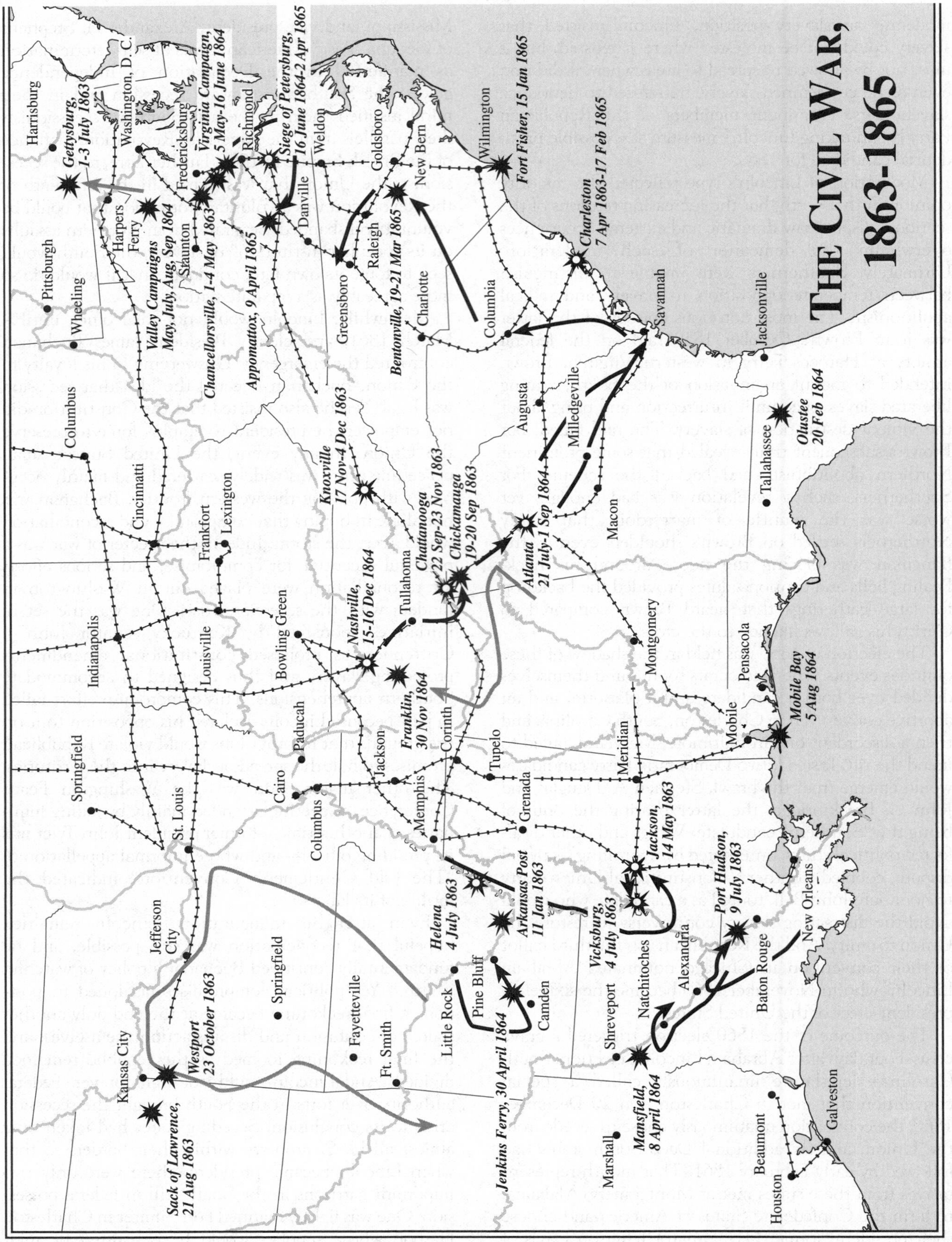

THE CIVIL WAR, 1863-1865

Harrisburg

Washington, D.C.

Gettysburg, 1-3 July 1863

Pittsburgh

Wheeling

Harpers Ferry

Fredericksburg

Virginia Campaign, 5 May-16 June 1864

Richmond

Siege of Petersburg, 16 June 1864-2 Apr 1865

Weldon

Goldsboro

New Bern

Wilmington

Fort Fisher, 15 Jan 1865

Staunton

Valley Campaigns May, July, Aug, Sep 1864

Chancellorsville, 1-4 May 1863

Appomattox, 9 April 1865

Danville

Greensboro

Raleigh

Bentonville, 19-21 Mar 1865

Charlotte

Columbia

Charleston 7 Apr 1863-17 Feb 1865

Savannah

Jacksonville

Columbus

Cincinnatti

Frankfort

Lexington

Knoxville 17 Nov-4 Dec 1863

Chattanooga

Chattanooga 22 Sep-23 Nov 1863

Chickamauga 19-20 Sep 1863

Augusta

Milledgeville

Atlanta 21 July-1 Sep 1864

Macon

Olustee 20 Feb 1864

Tallahassee

Indianapolis

Louisville

Bowling Green

Nashville, 15-16 Dec 1864

Tullahoma

Franklin, 30 Nov 1864

Corinth

Montgomery

Mobile

Pensacola

Mobile Bay 5 Aug 1864

Springfield

St. Louis

Paducah

Cairo

Jackson

Columbus

Memphis

Tupelo

Grenada

Meridian

Jackson, 14 May 1863

Port Hudson, 9 July 1863

Baton Rouge

New Orleans

Jefferson City

Springfield

Fayetteville

Ft. Smith

Helena 4 July 1863

Arkansas Post 11 Jan 1863

Little Rock

Pine Bluff

Camden

Vicksburg, 4 July 1863

Natchitoches

Alexandria

Westport 23 October 1863

Kansas City

Sack of Lawrence, 21 Aug 1863

Jenkins Ferry, 30 April 1864

Shreveport

Mansfield, 8 April 1864

Marshall

Houston

Beaumont

Galveston

April. Buchanan's attempt to reinforce Sumter in January had failed when batteries drove off the *Star of the West*. Now, after giving up the dim hope that force would not be necessary, Lincoln ultimately elected to hold the fort and informed South Carolina authorities that an expedition would supply though not reinforce it. The Confederate government deemed the gesture as aggression, and on 12 April 1861 batteries opened fire on Fort Sumter, an act that many Northerners found so provocative that it gave Lincoln a significant psychological advantage in both the domestic and foreign arenas. By making the South appear to be the aggressor against the Union, Lincoln was able to summon patriots to protect the flag. On 15 April he called on the states for 75,000 men to suppress the rebellion. On 19 April, Lincoln proclaimed a blockade of Southern seaports, extending its range on 27 April. Young men gathered into armies, and brothers braced to strike down brothers. The Civil War had begun.

For the next four years, the country would test the limits of its endurance and the durability of its central ideas. The remarkable will and resolution of both sides prolonged a contest that became a horrifying nightmare from the first shots. Every day of those four years marked the delivery to countless firesides of doleful messages announcing that the boy who had gone away to fight would never be coming home.

From the Southern perspective, Lincoln's call for volunteers amounted to unprovoked aggression against the Confederacy. Soon Virginia, Arkansas, Tennessee, and North Carolina joined the Confederacy, although they did so with considerable anxiety and debate. The western counties of Virginia, in fact, refused to join the state in secession and themselves seceded from Virginia in mid-1861, eventually to become the state of West Virginia. Furthermore, the border states of Missouri, Kentucky, Maryland, and Delaware did not secede. The Confederacy was thus deprived of border state factories, horses, and mules as well as control of strategic waterways such as the Ohio River. From the Ohio, the Cumberland and Tennessee Rivers would provide avenues of invasion for Union gunboats. Lincoln adopted a deft balance of inducement and force in dealing with the border states. To protect the capital, he imposed martial law in parts of Maryland. He was careful about Kentucky, but he sent troops to western Virginia and Missouri to aid Unionists in protecting their regions for the Union. These areas of vague and tenuous loyalty would experience an especially ugly aspect of the Civil War when guerrilla warfare erupted and preyed on civilian as well as military targets. Missouri would be especially plagued with tragic atrocities and grisly retribution.

In the coming conflict, the Confederacy had the advantage of interior lines, and the Union faced the hard task of conquering and occupying an immense amount of territory. If it could endure long enough to discourage the North, the Confederacy could win by surviving. In the face of Northern invasion, Southerners also would be spurred by the need to protect hearth and home. Also during the war, Confederate commerce raiders such as the notorious *Alabama* plied global waters to capture or destroy more than 250 Northern ships, an accomplishment that so damaged the American merchant marine that it would not recover for the remainder of the century.

Northern advantages, however, especially derived from a war of attrition. With only a marginal manufacturing capability, the South would experience serious shortages of the most basic items that would diminish the Confederate ability to wage war. The South's substandard railroad system caused chronic supply problems, and logistical difficulties would only compound when invading Union armies destroyed what railroad lines existed. The North contained not only ample farms but also a diversified and large manufacturing potential. The United States would build a large navy that effectively blockaded Southern ports even as it protected grain exports abroad and facilitated imports from European factories. The Union's larger population of about 22 million to the Confederacy's 9 million people (including about 3.5 million slaves) would be bolstered by European immigrants, many of whom immediately enlisted in Union armies.

Eventually, these Northern advantages would prove irresistible, but at the outset of the conflict Southern victory was a definite possibility. Many thought it would be a short war, and many young men rushed to the colors in both the North and South, fearful that the glorious conflict would conclude before they could see action. Lincoln's initial call for volunteers had anticipated that they would be needed for only ninety days. At the end of May, the Confederate government relocated its capital from Montgomery, Alabama, to Richmond, Virginia—a move that would have profound strategic implications for the coming war—and Northerners, eagerly expecting a swift settlement with one big battle, entreated their raw soldiers to march "On to Richmond!"

The hastily raised Union army of about 30,000 men was hardly ready to go on the offensive, but under pressure from newspapers and the public, Lincoln decided the army should move against a smaller Confederate army near Bull Run and Manassas Junction, about thirty miles southwest of Washington. The resulting battle of First Bull Run (there would another battle at the same place thirteen months later) on 21 July 1861 was a Confederate victory that ended with many Union soldiers in panicked flight. Yet Confederate forces were too fatigued to pursue and exploit their triumph. Worse, the victory at Bull Run amplified Southerners' conceit

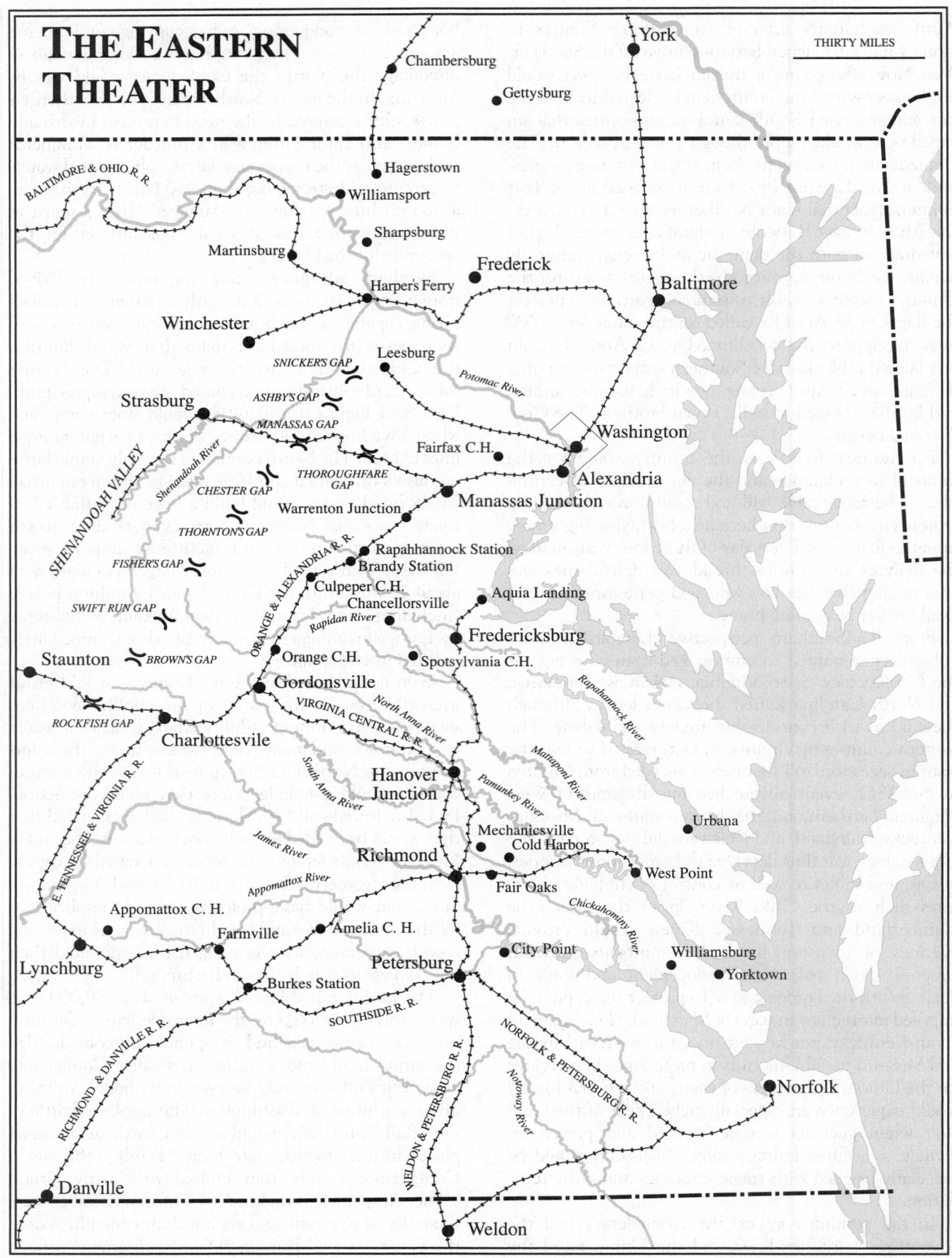

THE EASTERN THEATER

THIRTY MILES

York

Chambersburg

Gettysburg

BALTIMORE & OHIO R. R.

Hagerstown

Williamsport

Sharpsburg

Martinsburg

Frederick

Harper's Ferry

Baltimore

Winchester

Leesburg

Potomac River

SNICKER'S GAP

ASHBY'S GAP

MANASSAS GAP

Strasburg

Fairfax C.H.

Washington

THOROUGHFARE GAP

SHENANDOAH VALLEY

Shenandoah River

CHESTER GAP

Warrenton Junction

Manassas Junction

Alexandria

THORNTON'S GAP

Rapahhannock Station

FISHER'S GAP

Brandy Station

Culpeper C.H.

Chancellorsville

Aquia Landing

SWIFT RUN GAP

Rapidan River

Fredericksburg

ORANGE & ALEXANDRIA R. R.

Staunton

BROWN'S GAP

Orange C.H.

Spotsylvania C.H.

Rapahannock River

Gordonsville

VIRGINIA CENTRAL R. R.

North Anna River

ROCKFISH GAP

Charlottesville

South Anna River

Mattaponi River

Hanover Junction

Pamunkey River

James River

Urbana

Mechanicsville

Cold Harbor

E. TENNESSEE & VIRGINIA R. R.

Richmond

Fair Oaks

West Point

Appomattox River

Chickahominy River

Appomattox C. H.

Farmville

Amelia C. H.

City Point

Williamsburg

Lynchburg

Burkes Station

Petersburg

Yorktown

SOUTHSIDE R. R.

NORFOLK & PETERSBURG R. R.

RICHMOND & DANVILLE R. R.

WELDON & PETERSBURG R. R.

Nottoway River

Norfolk

Danville

Weldon

about their superiority over the "mongrel" hordes of the North. With many believing that the war was won, enlistments decreased and preparations for a lengthy contest no longer seemed necessary. In the North the fantasy of a quick end to this crisis died at Bull Run, and the Lincoln administration dedicated the country's resources to the towering job of winning the war.

Eventually Union strategy would be honed to embrace something resembling a modern, coordinated war effort. Aging General Winfield Scott had been ridiculed in the press for his proposal of the so-called Anaconda Plan, and Lincoln himself had thought the idea envisioned a needlessly protracted war. Yet a modification of Scott's idea was in due time implemented. The Union was already planning to choke the South with the blockade, and its fixation on capturing the Confederate capital at Richmond remained a constant. Yet the strategy would also move to cut the Confederacy in half by controlling the Mississippi River and at the end would further fragment the rebellion by invading Georgia and the Carolinas. Finally, under the strategic vision of Ulysses S. Grant, the North would apply its inexhaustible resources in men and materiel to engage the South simultaneously on as many fronts as possible to pulverize it into capitulation.

Immediately after First Bull Run, though, Lincoln had to restore confidence and rehabilitate the main Union army that had returned to Washington a shattered mob. In the hopes that competent and charismatic leadership would rebuild this force and bring order to the entire military organization, Lincoln turned to West Point graduate Major General George B. McClellan. Eventually made general-in-chief of all Union armies, McClellan was young, energetic, and confident. The newspapers dubbed him "The Young Napoleon," and his flair for organization and meticulous attention to detail soon whipped the force he renamed the Army of the Potomac into impressive fighting trim. The men loved him, but he became so cautious about their welfare that he became too attentive to risks. When Lincoln pressed him to action, McClellan adopted a contemptuous manner toward the president that was beyond inappropriate. Lincoln nonetheless was resolved to be charitable if McClellan could win the war.

Mistaken in his belief that Confederate forces in northern Virginia outnumbered his own, McClellan resolved to avoid a direct confrontation and instead planned a waterborne approach to Richmond. The Peninsula campaign was the ambitious result in the spring of 1862. McClellan's large army of almost 100,000 men was ferried to the end of Virginia's York Peninsula from whence it moved slowly up toward Richmond. McClellan would claim that Lincoln's insistence on keeping back forces to protect the capital hopelessly subverted the Peninsula campaign. Yet Lincoln was adamant, especially when Thomas "Stonewall" Jackson's epic maneuvers in the Shenandoah Valley seemed to imperil Washington. When Confederate general Joseph E. Johnston attacked McClellan in the battle of Seven Pines, it was an indecisive engagement that nonetheless rattled the Young Napoleon even as it left Johnston seriously wounded. General Robert E. Lee, given command of the forces he named the Army of Northern Virginia, soon launched a series of furious attacks known as the Seven Days' battles (25 June–1 July 1862). Lee drove McClellan away from Richmond, and Lincoln gave up on the Peninsula campaign and at least temporarily cast aside McClellan.

The Western theater offered more encouraging events for the Union, especially as they led to the emergence of an able general in Ulysses S. Grant. Although Grant was not a prepossessing figure and his prewar career both in military and civilian pursuits had branded him a failure, his audacity, ingenuity, and determination soon revealed him to be a unique commodity among Union general officers. In February 1862, his capture of Fort Henry on the Tennessee River and Fort Donelson on the Cumberland River pierced the Confederate defense of the entire region, especially Tennessee. Emboldened by such success, Grant brashly moved on the important railroad junction at Corinth, Mississippi, and was handed a stunning setback when Confederate forces under Albert Sidney Johnston nearly destroyed his army at the battle of Shiloh on 6 April 1862. Yet Johnston was mortally wounded at Shiloh, a loss that many regarded as a crippling blow to the Confederacy. For his part, Grant was able to hold on until reinforcements allowed him to turn the tide the next day. Nonetheless, the near disaster at Shiloh was a mistake that had some calling for Grant's hide. Lincoln would have none of it, and he refused to act on stories that labeled Grant a drunkard. The country was too much in need of generals who fought and, even better, won. Lincoln would not discard any who did so.

Other Union successes in the West were heartening as well. In the spring of 1862, David G. Farragut's naval forces conducted a joint operation with the army to capture New Orleans. Soon much of the Mississippi River was crawling with Union gunboats, and the Confederacy anxiously sought to protect a cramped region between Vicksburg and Port Hudson to keep available the imperative supplies of livestock and stores in Louisiana and Texas. In the fall of 1862, a Confederate invasion of Kentucky ended at the muddled battle of Perryville, which at least had the effect of requiring Southern forces to retreat into east Tennessee.

In the East, Lincoln supplanted George McClellan with a general who had won in the West. General John Pope had waged a successful assault against Island No. 10 on the Mississippi River, and in the wake of the

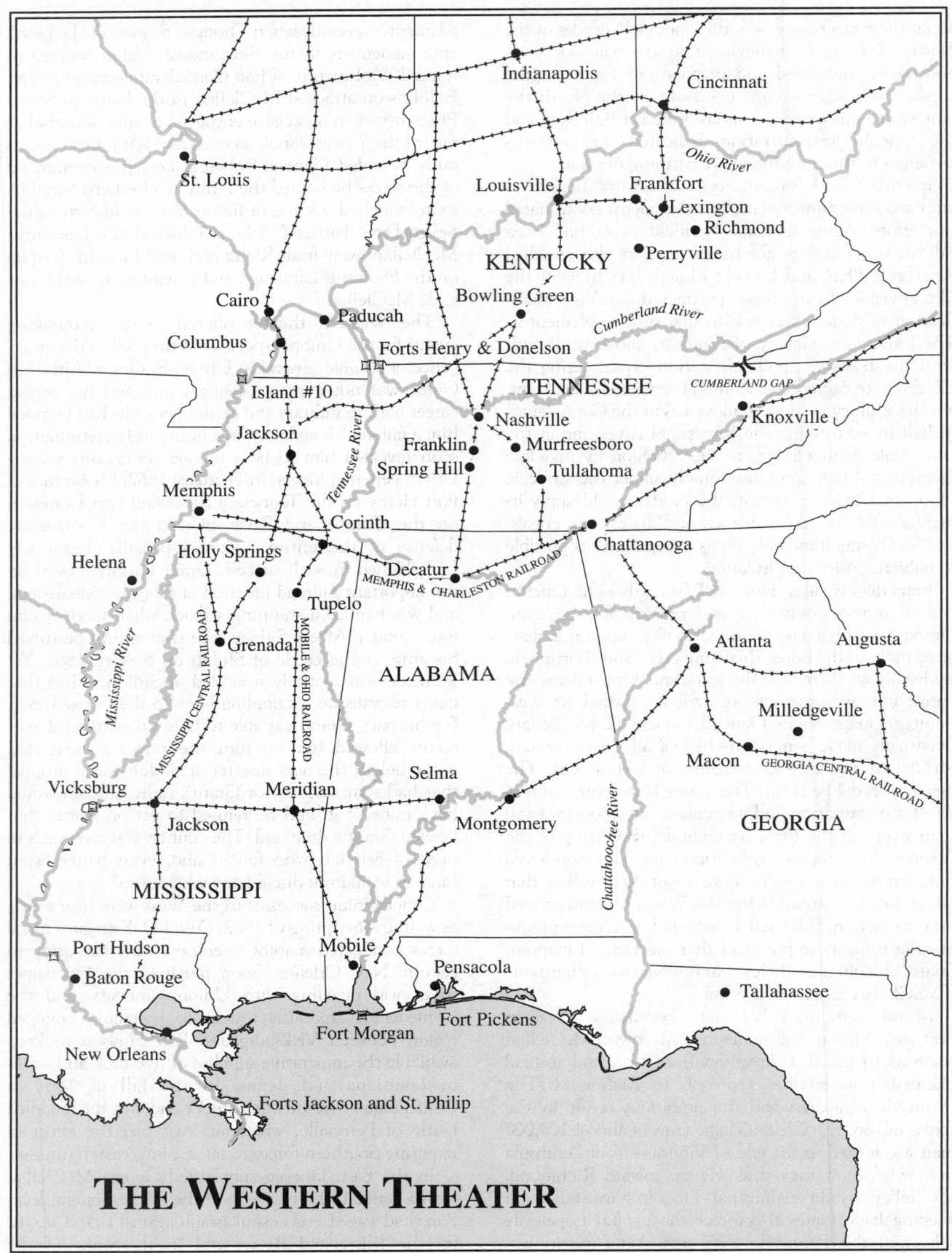

Indianapolis

Cincinnati

Ohio River

St. Louis

Louisville

Frankfort

Lexington

Richmond

Perryville

KENTUCKY

Bowling Green

Cumberland River

Cairo

Paducah

Columbus

Forts Henry & Donelson

CUMBERLAND GAP

Island #10

TENNESSEE

Knoxville

Jackson

Nashville

Tennessee River

Franklin

Murfreesboro

Spring Hill

Tullahoma

Memphis

Corinth

Chattanooga

Helena

Holly Springs

Decatur

MEMPHIS & CHARLESTON RAILROAD

Tupelo

Mississippi River

Grenada

MISSISSIPPI CENTRAL RAILROAD

MOBILE & OHIO RAILROAD

ALABAMA

Atlanta

Augusta

Milledgeville

Macon

GEORGIA CENTRAL RAILROAD

Vicksburg

Meridian

Selma

Chattahoochee River

GEORGIA

Jackson

Montgomery

MISSISSIPPI

Port Hudson

Mobile

Pensacola

Tallahassee

Baton Rouge

Fort Pickens

Fort Morgan

New Orleans

Forts Jackson and St. Philip

THE WESTERN THEATER

Peninsula disappointment, Lincoln tapped him to command a new Federal army to march on Richmond. Yet Pope proved more boastful than resourceful, and Robert E. Lee handed him and his army a sundering defeat at the battle of Second Bull Run on 29–30 August 1862. In the wake of this disaster, Lincoln reluctantly reinstated McClellan as the army's principal commander.

In the autumn of 1862, Lee hoped that by moving north of the Potomac River he would advance not only Confederate military fortunes, but also Confederate diplomatic efforts to secure foreign recognition. The possibility of foreign intervention on the Confederacy's behalf promised the surest path to ultimate victory. Many in Europe's ruling classes were repelled by American democracy and consequently intrigued by Southern chivalry with its aristocratic pretensions.

At the outset of Lee's invasion of western Maryland, McClellan, with characteristic caution, made only tentative moves to counter it until a copy of Lee's battle plans was found by Union soldiers and delivered to headquarters. Moving with unusual dispatch, McClellan descended on the hastily congregated Southern army at Antietam Creek on 17 September 1862 and fought there for twelve hours to produce the bloodiest single day of the war. Although Antietam ended in a stalemate, it did produce conclusive consequences. Immediately, Lee was forced to move back across the Potomac, his invasion a failure and its objectives unrealized. McClellan's failure to exploit fully the remarkable advantage handed him in the discovery of Lee's lost order, and the subsequent return of his habitual caution, led Lincoln again to remove him from command, this for the last time.

And in a larger sense, the battle of Antietam was truly decisive. The Confederacy would never again be so near the chance of obtaining British and French recognition, a diplomatic achievement that might have led to indispensable military alliances. After Antietam, Britain rightly had second thoughts about the potential for Confederate military success. British reservations were also reinforced when Lincoln used the modest Union success at Antietam as a reason to announce the preliminary Emancipation Proclamation on 23 September 1862. In this preliminary document, Lincoln promised that should the rebellion continue, on 1 January 1863 emancipation would become final. Thus the Civil War became not only a moral crusade, it also became a revolution growing out of the exercise to suppress a rebellion.

The effect of the proclamation on the diplomatic situation was instantly telling. The South had counted on British dependence on cotton to sway the working class of England to support the Confederacy. Yet, the great abundance of southern cotton yields in the years before the war had glutted British warehouses. Eighteen months into the war, British cotton reserves would begin to dwindle, but then the strong antislavery sentiments among British common folk made them violently oppose official intervention on behalf of the South, and the British government accordingly took heed. The moral imperative of the Emancipation Proclamation both bolstered and sealed this British attitude toward the Union. Although Anglo-American relations were occasionally vexed by incidents such as the *Trent* Affair and the construction in British shipyards of Confederate commerce raiders and possible warships, the adroit U.S. minister Charles Francis Adams was able to maintain civil, if not always congenial, relations with his British hosts.

Napoleon III of France followed the British lead in ultimately refusing to recognize the Confederacy. Instead Napoleon took advantage of American preoccupations to establish a puppet regime in Mexico under Austrian Archduke Maximilian. The venture certainly excited American displeasure, but until the war ended, there was little the United States could do. In 1865, however, the armies that had recently defeated the Confederacy were prepared to march into Mexico, and Napoleon equivocated as long as he could before abruptly abandoning Maximilian in 1867 to his fate before a Mexican firing squad.

Domestically, the Emancipation Proclamation changed almost everything, even as its limited scope of freeing slaves only in those areas in rebellion changed almost nothing, at least right away. For one thing, it paved the way for the enlistment of significant numbers of African-Americans into the U.S. military. At first, however, public reactions to the proclamation were mixed. Many abolitionists protested that Lincoln had issued a meaningless manifesto, while many ordinary Northerners, reflecting the racism of the time, grumbled that the war was to preserve the Union, not to end slavery. A significant number of Union soldiers deserted, and the 1862 congressional elections seemed to repudiate the administration's call for emancipation. Yet in spite of all that, Lincoln's gesture moved the war from a limited political goal of preserving the Union to its larger meaning as a fight for representative democracy and human freedom. Its participants consequently found themselves engulfed in and overwhelmed by a drama as profoundly affecting as any that has ever impinged on the American experience. Some understood and accepted this great change better than others, but the country as well as the world would eventually see the moral imperative of emancipation as a shining moment in the history of human affairs. The Civil War, in the doing of it, would mark the country's most tragic time, but the war, in the meaning of it, became its finest hour.

Emancipation and all its ramifications were played out in the context of striving for Union victory. Lincoln's search for a general to win the war continued,

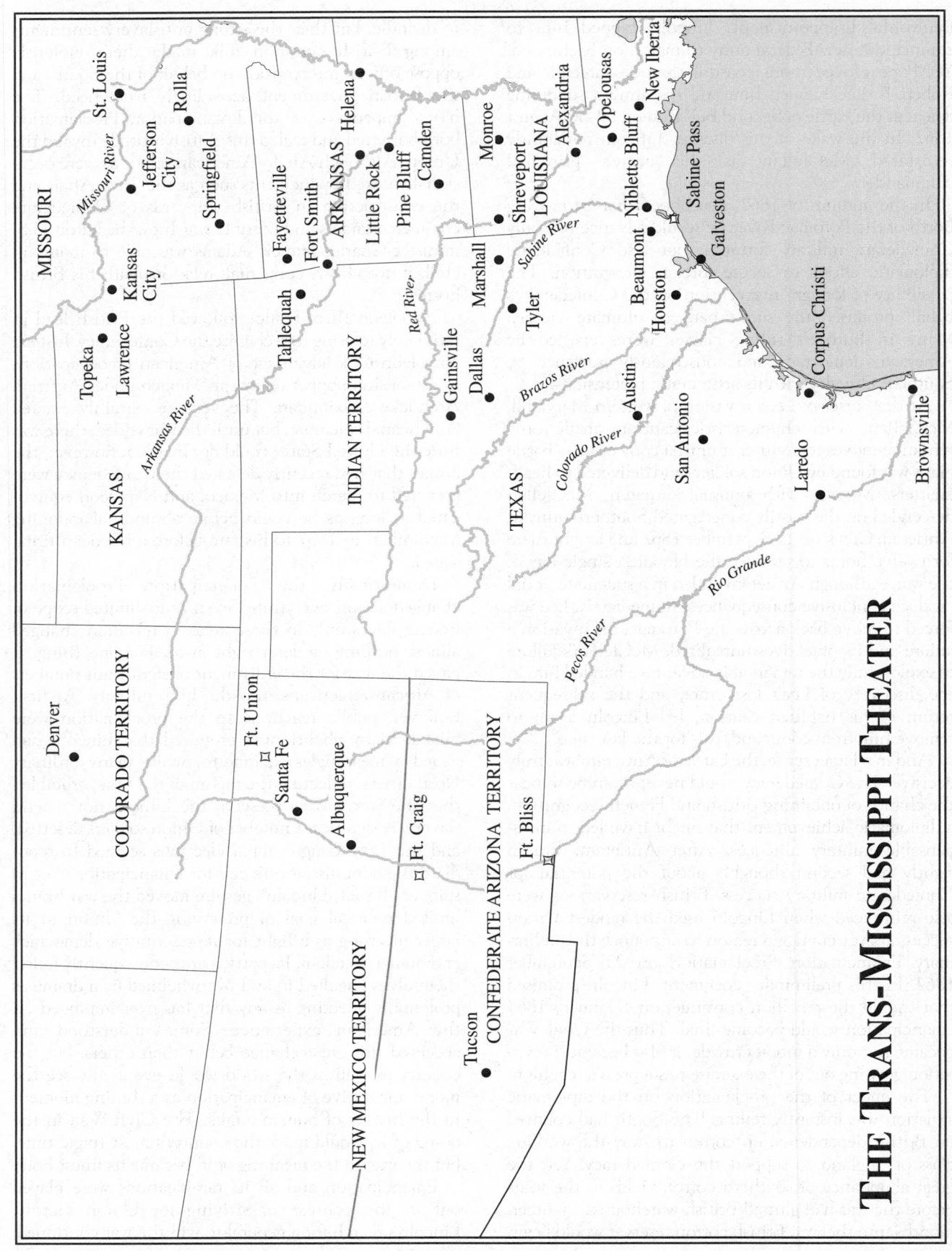

THE TRANS-MISSISSIPPI THEATER

with gruesome results on the battlefield. After McClellan's disappointing indecision following Antietam, General Ambrose E. Burnside replaced him as commander of the Army of the Potomac. At Fredericksburg, Virginia, on 13 December 1862, Burnside used up more than 10,000 Union soldiers with repeated assaults against Lee's unassailable position. Lincoln was never more forlorn than during the bleak Christmas that followed this ghastly engagement. After Burnside staged another, though less costly, misadventure, Joseph Hooker replaced him. Hooker resembled McClellan in his flair for organization as well as insubordination, yet Hooker was aggressive, at least to a point. When he tried to force Lee out of his stronghold at Fredericksburg, Hooker brought on the battle of Chancellorsville on 2–4 May 1863. Lee seized the initiative by dividing his numerically inferior force, sending "Stonewall" Jackson to attack the Union right flank, a move that caught "Fighting Joe" Hooker completely by surprise. Often described as Lee's most dazzling victory, Chancellorsville nonetheless was a tragic business for the Confederacy because during the battle Jackson's own men mistook him for the enemy and mortally wounded him.

The loss of Stonewall Jackson was a dire blow. More than ever, Lee believed another invasion of the North was necessary to win a conclusive victory on Union soil that would secure Southern independence and end the war. During this perilous period, Lincoln again was faced with the necessity of replacing the commander of the Army of the Potomac. Hooker had become quarrelsome, difficult, and apparently ineffective after his humiliation at Chancellorsville. Consequently, the president selected General George Gordon Meade, even as Lee was moving briskly into Pennsylvania. Chance and opportunity rather than deliberate design threw the two armies together at the small seminary village of Gettysburg, Pennsylvania. During the first three days of July 1863, Lee repeatedly tried to dislodge Meade from strong positions south of Gettysburg along Cemetery Ridge. On the last day, 3 July 1863, the most famous assault of the war occurred. What would become known as Pickett's Charge sent about 15,000 Confederates directly against the Union line, a majestically brave gesture the failure of which broke the back of the Army of Northern Virginia. Lee was forced to retreat south of the Potomac River.

At the same time as the titanic clash at Gettysburg, a more prolonged but equally significant military drama was ending in the West. Vicksburg, Mississippi, had rightly gained the label "The Gibraltar of the Confederacy" because of its impregnable situation on the Mississippi River. The city protected the Confederacy's only remaining route to its western regions with their indispensable supplies. Ulysses S.

Grant had the chore of capturing Vicksburg, a task that presented such strategic and tactical problems that his management of the campaign produced a military masterpiece. Still, the operations were lengthy, ultimately necessitating a siege of Vicksburg that featured a nerve-shattering bombardment of the city's starving population. On 4 July 1863, the day after Lee's defeat in Pennsylvania, Vicksburg and its entire garrison of irreplaceable Confederate troops surrendered. When Port Hudson fell on 9 July, the Mississippi River was completely in federal hands.

Beyond their military significance, the twin victories at Gettysburg and Vicksburg produced political consequences of the first order. Peace movements in the North that were bolstered by the lack of Union military success were quieted, at least for a time. The Union reaped benefits abroad as well. The British government seized warships apparently slated for delivery to the Confederate navy, and Napoleon III halted the Confederacy's plans to purchase naval vessels from France.

That fall at Gettysburg, Lincoln delivered a brief address at dedication ceremonies for a national cemetery. In the most eloquent pronouncement of the war, the president praised the soldiers whose deaths had marked "the last full measure of devotion" to liberty and pledged the country to finish the work and secure "a new birth of freedom." Thus, as 1863 drew to a close, the Confederacy was to be stalked continually by the specter of impending defeat. Southern armies would fight on for another sixteen months, however, compelling the Union to adopt a fully coordinated and relentless policy of military engagement and destruction.

In one of 1863's few bright spots for the South, that fall Confederate forces under Braxton Bragg defeated Union forces at Chickamauga, Georgia. The whipped Union army was very nearly annihilated, but elements of it under George H. Thomas held a key position long enough to allow the remainder to flee into Chattanooga. Bragg was besieging the city, and the Union army was trapped there when Lincoln ordered Grant to take charge in east Tennessee. Aided by reinforcements rapidly transported toward Chattanooga by railroad, Grant was able to score signal victories in November at Missionary Ridge and Lookout Mountain. Not only was the siege of Chattanooga thus raised, but also Bragg was forced to retreat into north Georgia, his veteran army badly shaken by the inability to exploit its hard-won victory at Chickamauga. As the Union laid plans to invade Georgia, Bragg's troubled tenure as commander of the Confederate Army of Tennessee ended when Jefferson Davis replaced him with Joseph E. Johnston.

Lincoln also made some command changes. Convinced that he had found the man who could win the war in the hard-driving Grant, the president

appointed him general-in-chief and summoned him to Washington. Although Meade remained in command of the Army of the Potomac, many, including Lincoln, were dissatisfied with his caution after Gettysburg. Grant proved himself willing to use all the weapons in the North's arsenal, including its vast economic, material, and manpower resources. It this last, Grant would demonstrate an unswerving determination to endure enormous casualties in applying remorseless pressure against all points of the Confederate military. Set upon all at once, the South's armies would fall prey to the numerical superiority of Union forces and be destroyed in detail. Grant, like Lincoln, realized that the destruction of the Confederate military presence would end the war, not the mere occupation of selected regions or particular cities.

As part of this coordinated strategy, William Tecumseh Sherman would invade Georgia, first to seize the important rail center at Atlanta. During the spring and summer of 1864, Sherman's forces commenced a deft game of maneuver and deadly confrontation with Johnston's forces in the mountains and passes of northern Georgia. Yet as Johnston continued to retreat toward Atlanta in a search for ground that would allow him to halt Sherman's advance, Jefferson Davis impatiently replaced him with John Bell Hood. The aggressive and impetuous Hood tried to stop Sherman with direct confrontation, a design that badly mauled the Confederate army and allowed Sherman to capture Atlanta in September 1864.

It was a crucial victory, for it occurred in time to affect positively Lincoln's chances in the presidential election of 1864. As the fall elections loomed, Lincoln had despaired that the bleak military picture would cause his defeat and bring to office the Democratic Party nominee, George B. McClellan. Lincoln's fears were not without foundation, for Grant's overland move against Lee's army, begun in the spring of 1864, had produced shocking losses. With more than 100,000 men, Grant had repeatedly struck Lee at a cost to the Union army of almost 50,000 casualties. This devil's arithmetic was calculated on the certainty that Lee's losses, proportionately similar, would remain gaping holes in the Army of Northern Virginia, while Grant could replace his with a steady stream of new recruits and draftees. On 3 June 1864, a Union assault at Cold Harbor left almost 7,000 Union soldiers killed or wounded in a matter of minutes. Though his attack at Cold Harbor was a mistake rather than a deliberate expenditure—Grant, who would always regret his decision to attack at Cold Harbor, thought that Lee's army was more brittle than it obviously was—Northerners were dismayed by the butchery. As Grant besieged Lee at Petersburg just southeast of Richmond, a considerable sentiment arose during that summer's intense presidential campaign that Lincoln and his general had managed only a bloody stalemate. Sherman's victory in Atlanta helped to diminish that attitude, and Lincoln won a second term in November. It was the final blow to any hope in the Confederacy of ending the war on Southern terms.

And in its final, anguished months, parts of the Confederacy would suffer a terrible fate. By living off the countryside, Sherman was able to move far away from his line of supply and cut a wide swath through Georgia all the way to Savannah on the coast. On this March to the Sea, Sherman's "bummers" not only stripped the land of foodstuffs, they destroyed anything that could be of military value to the Confederacy. Gutted buildings and ruined railroads lay in the wake of an army that, as Sherman put it, was committed to making the South feel the hard fist of war. Hearing of such destruction, Southern soldiers far from their homes began to leave their posts and head for their families. After his capture of Savannah, Sherman marched northward into South Carolina to commence a campaign of destruction that visited upon the seat of secession an almost biblical retribution. Meanwhile, in Virginia's Shenandoah Valley, Union practitioners of the hard war policy smashed one of Lee's most important sources of supply. A force under Philip Sheridan was so destructive that he claimed a crow flying over the Shenandoah Valley would have to carry its own supplies.

In the spring of 1865, Grant's overwhelming preponderance broke Lee's lines at Petersburg and finally gave the Army of the Potomac the prize of Richmond. As Jefferson Davis and the remnants of the Confederate government fled, Lee tried to run westward, but he was trapped near Appomattox Court House in Virginia. On 9 April, Lee formally surrendered the Army of Northern Virginia to Grant, who followed Lincoln's instructions for leniency, the first step as Lincoln saw it to an amicable restoration of the nation. In the weeks that followed, other Confederate forces in the field also surrendered. The Civil War, or at least the fighting of it, was over.

In a sense, though, the most important work lay before the country. At this pivotal moment, an assassin's bullet struck down Lincoln even before the last Southern armies had surrendered. To bind up wounds, to forget scars, and to allay antagonisms would now be all the harder. The fate of emancipated slaves would depend on political uncertainties and suffer under the weight of ancient prejudices in both the North and the South. The legions of dead soldiers would remain as ghosts in memory, compelling some to preserve old allegiances and promote outmoded ideas. The country would stumble through the years of Reconstruction only partially realizing the vision of those who saw an opportunity to remake both the North and the South into places of racial and social equality. Indeed, that work yet continues.

Yet, by ultimately reaffirming and reanimating their

commitment to liberty and Union, those who survived the incredible ordeal emerged transformed by the experience, as was their country. Both Northerners and Southerners, both white and black, would, in a new birth of freedom, continue to redefine that country. They would people its vast reaches, contract its continent by lacing it with steel rails, and look beyond its borders to weigh the burdens of global power. Having survived what Lincoln called the "fiery trial" and a "mighty scourge," in the end, they were all Americans, and there was nothing they could not do.

Encyclopedia of the
AMERICAN CIVIL WAR
A Political, Social, and Military History

After the war he returned to the Corps of Engineers and his regular rank of major. Commanding an engineer battalion at Willett's Point, New York, gave him the chance to establish the Engineer School of Application. He became a ubiquitous presence on commissions and boards, traveled extensively, and retired from the army in August 1895 as a colonel, respected by his colleagues and honored by Congress with promotion to brigadier general, retired.

Abbot continued his engineering career as a consultant and took rank with the successful minority on the board that recommended the construction of locks for the Panama Canal. When he died on 1 October 1927, he left a legacy of engineering innovations marked, in part, by exemplary service in the Civil War.

—*David S. Heidler and Jeanne T. Heidler*

See also Petersburg Campaign.
For further reading:
Abbot, C. G. *Biographical Memoir of Henry Larcom Abbot, 1831–1927* (1930).

ABBOT, HENRY LARCOM
(1831–1927)
Union officer

Born 31 August 1831 in Beverly, Massachusetts, to Joseph H. and Fanny Larcom Abbot, Henry L. Abbot was descended from notable Revolutionary War veterans. The recipient of an excellent preparatory education in Boston, he graduated from West Point in 1854, second in his class of forty-six. He was a promising addition to the Army Corps of Engineers, surveying railroad routes in California and Oregon and contributing to innovative methods of flood control and dredging on the Mississippi River.

At the start of the Civil War, Abbot was attached to General Irvin McDowell's headquarters as a first lieutenant of topographical engineers. He was wounded at First Bull Run, earning a brevet, and he participated in McClellan's Peninsula campaign, winning another brevet at Yorktown. As a captain in June 1862, Abbot briefly served as General John G. Barnard's aide during the construction of Washington's defenses, and afterward accompanied General Nathaniel Banks's expedition to New Orleans as its chief topographical engineer.

In January 1863 Abbot was breveted to colonel and placed in command of the 1st Connecticut Heavy Artillery in defense of Washington. He and the 1st Connecticut remained at this post until the Virginia campaign. Beginning in March 1864, Abbot commanded Ulysses S. Grant's siege artillery, including the celebrated "Dictator," a massive mortar that could hurl a shot more than two miles.

By the time he mustered out of the Volunteer forces in September 1865, Abbot had won seven brevets for merit and bravery and stood at the rank of major general.

ABBOTT, HENRY LIVERMORE
(1842–1864)
Union officer

Born in Lowell, Massachusetts, on 21 January 1842, Henry Abbott grew up in a large, prosperous, and well-educated family. His father, Josiah Gardner Abbott, was a successful attorney and politically active member of the Democratic Party, and his mother, Caroline, was a member of the socially prominent Livermore family. Henry, the third of eleven children, proved to be something of a prodigy and enrolled in Harvard at age fourteen with his older brother Edward in 1856. He graduated in 1860 and was reading law in his father's office when the Civil War broke out.

Abbott did not immediately follow his older and younger brothers to war when they joined the 2d Massachusetts Infantry as officers. Instead he waited, and, after serving a brief stint in the militia, he followed his friend Oliver Wendell Holmes, Jr., in signing up with the 20th Massachusetts on 10 July 1861. Abbott became a second lieutenant in the regiment at the end of August and accompanied it, when he was healthy, for the remainder of his service in the war. He thus participated in the Union catastrophe that October at Ball's Bluff, where he distinguished himself by demonstrating remarkable composure under fire as the regiment suffered staggering losses (almost 30 percent killed or wounded and 37 percent captured). Promoted to first lieutenant on 8 November 1861, he was with the regiment in the Peninsula campaign, fighting at Fair Oaks and later protecting General George McClellan's retreat to the James River during the Seven Days. At Glendale,

Abbott suffered a serious wound in his right arm that compelled his recuperation at home.

Although he had rejoined the 20th Massachusetts before the battle of Antietam, he nevertheless missed the Maryland campaign when he was hospitalized at Frederick, Maryland, because of a combination of typhoid fever and grief over his brother, who had been killed at Cedar Mountain. By the end of the year, he was back in action, courageously leading his regiment during the vicious fighting to occupy Fredericksburg, Virginia, and on 13 December he participated in the Union assault on Marye's Heights. Apparently charmed after his injury at Glendale, Abbott survived unscathed and was promoted to captain on 28 December.

The following spring he fought at the second battle of Fredericksburg, which coincided with the Chancellorsville campaign, and in July on the third day at Gettysburg, his regiment helped to repulse the Confederate attack. This last action so eviscerated the 20th Massachusetts that command of it devolved on Abbott, the senior of the three officers who had emerged uninjured from the fight. He would remain in this command until his death. On 10 October 1863, he was promoted to major, and four days later fought in the sharp action at Bristoe Station. With the onset of Ulysses S. Grant's overland march on Richmond in the spring of 1864, Abbott's luck was exhausted. He was mortally wounded in the Wilderness on 6 May.

Abbott's service and exploits had been distinguished enough to earn him some notoriety, so news of his death caused consternation at the highest levels of command. He was soon memorialized with a brevet promotion to brigadier general of volunteers, antedated to the day he was killed. His burial in his hometown of Lowell, Massachusetts, was especially somber, for, as Oliver Wendell Holmes, Jr., would later remark, Abbott was a friend whose death "seemed to end a portion of our life also."

—David S. Heidler and Jeanne T. Heidler

See also Holmes, Oliver Wendell, Jr.
For further reading:
Scott, Robert Garth, ed. *Fallen Leaves: The Civil War Letters of Major Henry Livermore Abbott* (1991).

ABERCROMBIE, JOHN JOSEPH
(1798–1877)
Union general

John J. Abercrombie's origins, beginning with both the place and date of his birth, have been the source of considerable confusion. He may have been a native of Maryland, born on 4 March 1798 in Baltimore, or he may have been born in Tennessee on 24 March 1798. Though he was later related by marriage to celebrated people, such as father-in-law General Robert Patterson (for whom he served as aide-de-camp in the Mexican-American War) and his brother-in-law Brigadier General Francis E. Patterson, much of Abercrombie's early life remains unknown.

Abercrombie attended West Point, graduating thirty-seventh of forty in the class of 1822, and served at posts in various regions of the country during the 1820s. In the ensuing years, he fought in the Black Hawk War, the Second Seminole War, and the Mexican-American War, in which he was wounded. Having earned a brevet in both the Seminole and Mexican-American conflicts, he had reached the rank of colonel in the 7th U.S. Infantry as of 25 February 1861. He saw action in the Civil War's earliest engagements. On 20 June 1861, he was placed in command of the 6th Brigade, 2d Division of the Department of Pennsylvania, and led his brigade at Falling Waters on 2 July 1861. He then commanded the 2d Brigade in Nathaniel Banks's division in the Shenandoah Valley from mid-July to mid-August 1861.

Promoted to brigadier general of volunteers on 31 August 1861, Abercrombie was part of General Charles Stone's disastrous reconnaissance at Ball's Bluff in October 1861. In that operation, his 1st Brigade of Volunteers crossed from the Maryland side of the Potomac River opposite Edward's Ferry and fought a brief engagement there on 21 October before recrossing the river the following day. During an otherwise tragic series of events, Abercrombie demonstrated initiative and competence in placing his people and repulsing a Confederate attack. He praised his men, but noted that "there were instances when the officers exhibited less zeal than the men," especially when it was discovered that some officers had "absented themselves and were found on the Maryland side when their regiments were recalled."

In the spring of 1862, Abercrombie commanded the 2d Brigade, 1st Division of V Corps, headquartered at Warrenton Junction. Demonstrating a sense of the enemy more astute than that of George McClellan's intelligence operatives, Abercrombie conducted a reconnaissance on the Rappahannock River to ascertain Confederate strength there. He estimated that reports of 7,000 rebels in the area were likely an exaggeration that doubled their actual numbers.

In the Peninsula campaign, he led the 2d Brigade at Fair Oaks on 31 May–1 June 1862 and ably protected the Union right flank. Although wounded at Fair Oaks, Abercrombie was present on the crest of Malvern Hill in support of the Union left. At the height of the battle, he rode to his batteries to direct them personally to increase their elevation for the protection of the men in his front.

After the Peninsula campaign, Abercrombie's field service was limited to directing operations from various headquarters situated in the environs of Washington or northern Virginia. Doubtless his age (he was 65 in 1863)

John Abercrombie (*Library of Congress*)

and his wounds, the latest from Fair Oaks, dictated his reduced activity in the field. At the close of his service in 1864, he commanded the depot at White House supporting Ulysses S. Grant's march on Richmond. On 20 June 1864, the day that he relinquished this command to Brigadier General George W. Getty, Abercrombie fended off an attack mounted by Wade Hampton's legion. It was Abercrombie's last combat of the war; he was mustered out of the U.S. volunteers four days later.

In March 1865, Abercrombie was awarded a final brevet to brigadier general in the regular army, an honor that marked the nation's gratitude as he neared retirement. Leaving the army on 12 June 1865, Abercrombie took up residence in Roslyn, Long Island, where he died on 3 January 1877.

—*David S. Heidler and Jeanne T. Heidler*

See also Patterson, Robert.
For further reading:
The War of the Rebellion: A Compilation of the Official Records of the Union and Confederate Armies (1880–1901).

ABOLITIONIST MOVEMENT

The abolitionist movement, or abolitionism, flourished in the United States between 1830 and 1865. Its aim was the immediate emancipation of the slaves in the American South. For most of its history, abolitionism was a movement at the margins of American politics, and abolitionists were a dissenting minority. Abolitionism is distinguished from a more general antislavery attitude, which characterized a much larger group of people, and which focused on preventing the expansion of slavery into the western territories of the United States.

Abolitionism had its historical roots in the Enlightenment's doctrine of human rights and in the evangelical attack on the morality of slavery that characterized the Great Awakening of the 1730s and 1740s. Early abolitionists included the Quakers, who, throughout the eighteenth century, engaged in an uncompromising battle against slavery, which they saw as a moral abomination in opposition to God's plans for human progress. Eighteenth-century abolitionism gained momentum during the revolutionary period and reached its peak between 1784 and 1804, when slavery was abolished in the Northern states and many slaves were manumitted in the South. After 1804, the new economic opportunities brought by the cotton boom and increasing fears of slave rebellion made Southern slaveholders tighten their control over their slaves.

By 1810 this early wave of militant abolitionism had died out and opposition to slavery had embraced the idea of gradual, compensated emancipation. In 1816 a group of antislavery advocates, who sought the end of slavery, but at the same time feared the consequences of emancipation for the white population, formed the American Colonization Society with the aim of transporting free blacks to Africa. Although racist in principle, the movement received widespread support from Christian antislavery advocates throughout the late 1810s and 1820s, and served as an important forum for meeting and discussion on the subject of slavery for future abolitionists, such as William Lloyd Garrison.

In the 1820s America was undergoing tremendous transformation. In the North, early industrialization, improvement in the communication system, and the spread of mass culture and popular publications influenced almost every aspect of social life. As people strove to make sense of these momentous transformations, several morally committed individuals dedicated themselves to showing Americans the contradictions of the society in which they lived and called for a variety of

social reforms. Especially in New England, where change brought by early industrialization was more pronounced, organized movements for reform, such as temperance, affected a large part of the population.

Related to the reformist ferment, a new evangelical revival swept across America in the 1820s; preachers like Charles G. Finney and Lyman Beecher urged individuals to abandon their sinful lives and look for God's salvation through contribution to the moral improvement of society. Evangelical ministers and evangelical converts touched by the new revivalist wave effectively constituted the most important influence on the abolitionist movement; several abolitionist leaders were educated in New England by evangelical preachers, who gave them a strong sense of moral and religious commitment and a will to fight moral degradation and the evil represented by sin, such as the one of owning slaves.

While white abolitionism was not yet an active force in the 1820s, black abolitionism was gaining ground. African-American abolitionists rejected the plans for colonization as racist and considered the idea of gradual emancipation as a way of postponing the solution of the problem posed by the existence of slavery in the South. In 1829, David Walker, a former slave from North Carolina living in Boston, published his "Appeal to the Colored Citizens of the World," in which he denounced colonization and urged slaves to take up arms and rebel against their masters. Two years later, Nat Turner's rebellion in Virginia caused Southern slaveholders to suspect that Walker's pamphlet had managed to circulate among the slaves.

The conventional date for the beginning of the renewed abolitionist movement in antebellum America is January 1831, when William Lloyd Garrison started the publication of the antislavery journal, *The Liberator*, which soon became as influential as David Walker's "Appeal." Garrison published his paper from his native Boston, where he had been influenced by evangelical preachers and had been involved in numerous antislavery activities. In time, he had become convinced that the only possible solution to the problem of the existence of slavery in the South was its immediate abolition. From the pages of the *Liberator*, Garrison repeatedly denounced slavery as a scandal and a sin, condemned colonization, and urged Americans to embrace the cause of "immediate, unconditional, uncompensated emancipation." In 1832 in Boston, Garrison and twelve friends, who were equally committed to abolitionism, founded the New England Anti-Slavery Society; the organization was devoted to immediatism and, unlike earlier antislavery societies founded in the post-Revolutionary era, included both whites and blacks.

Between 1831 and 1833, abolitionist groups sprang up in two other areas of the North, apart from New England. One group was based in New York, where their main representatives were Arthur and Lewis Tappan, both wealthy merchants and committed evangelicals, and Joshua Leavitt. The other group was based in upstate New York and northeastern Ohio and included James G. Birney, Elizur Wright, and Theodore D. Weld, who was a disciple of evangelical preacher Charles G. Finney. In 1833 sixty-two representatives of the three abolitionist groups gathered in Philadelphia and founded the American Anti-Slavery Society, the first national organization whose aim was the immediate emancipation of slaves in the South. Its "Declaration of Sentiments," written by Garrison, endorsed the Christian attitude of nonviolent resistance and condemned slavery as a violation of the principles stated in the Declaration of Independence and as a sin in the eyes of God. At the same time, the "Declaration of Sentiments" urged abolitionists to persuade citizens in the Northern states to endorse the abolition of slavery through the tactic of "moral suasion" and the spread of antislavery literature. A year after its foundation, the American Anti-Slavery Society, controlled by the wealthy New York–based Tappan brothers, started publishing its own periodical, *The Emancipator*, which was circulated nationally; several other periodicals, such as the *Anti-Slavery Reporter* and the *Anti-Slavery Standard*, joined the *Emancipator* in an impressive flow of publications, which also included pamphlets and books aimed at showing Americans the evils of slavery.

As early as 1833, abolitionists confronted mobs of hostile Northerners, who assaulted them and attempted to silence them. Typically, the mobs included professionals, such as lawyers, physicians, and businessmen, whom abolitionists called "gentlemen of property and standing," and who considered the call for immediate emancipation of the Southern slaves as socially disruptive and revolutionary. In 1835, after the American Anti-Slavery Society launched a postal campaign for the spreading of abolitionist literature, anti-abolitionist violence increased dramatically throughout the North; riots were reported in Utica, Cincinnati, Philadelphia, and Boston, where William Lloyd Garrison was dragged through the city streets. Anti-abolitionist violence reached its peak in 1837, when a mob killed antislavery newspaper editor Elijah P. Lovejoy at Alton, Illinois, and subsided after 1838. Meanwhile, angry Southerners pressed the president and Congress to censor abolitionist literature, which flooded the postal offices of both North and South. In 1837, in response to Southern requests, Congress adopted the "gag rule," according to which antislavery petitions would not be taken into consideration. Even though the rule remained valid until 1844, it did not prevent abolitionists from continuing their campaign, which by 1838 registered a total of 415,000 petitions sent to the capital.

After 1835, in spite of a successful record in the influence of public opinion, abolitionists manifested signs of deep ideological divisions within the American Anti-Slavery Society, as they realized that immediatism and moral suasion had not achieved the aim of changing the national attitude against slavery. In the debates about the implementation of new tactics, Garrison and his followers emerged as radical supporters of doctrines of nonresistance and moral revolution. "Garrisonians" thought that American values were the expression of the nation's profound corruption and that reform was needed in several spheres to bring about a new society. Consequently, they did not restrict themselves to the battle against slavery, but became involved in other movements for social reform—and they kept a general attitude of questioning accepted authority, whether it came from husbands, religious ministers, or government officials.

Garrisonians welcomed women within the abolitionist movement and encouraged them to join the American Anti-Slavery Society. Some of the best-known female abolitionists were Lydia Maria Child and Angelina and Sarah Grimké. Hundreds of others were actively involved in the society's activities, especially in the 1837 petitions campaign. In the late 1830s and 1840s, they started to merge the fight against slavery with the battle for women's rights and equality. While Garrisonians supported their battle as part of the necessary moral revolution of society, anti-Garrisonians, mainly including abolitionists from New York, considered the movement for women's rights extraneous to abolitionism and unnecessary, given that American society was fundamentally sound, apart from the flaws related to the existence of slavery.

Between 1838 and 1840, Garrisonians and anti-Garrisonians confronted each other not just over women's rights, but also on the equally important issue of political action. While Garrisonians continued to show an antigovernment attitude and rely on moral suasion, anti-Garrisonians went as far as conceiving the possibility of a third party based on abolitionist principles. At the 1840 meeting of the American Anti-Slavery Society, anti-Garrisonians were defeated in the elections of the executive committee by the Garrisonian faction and abandoned the organization; most of them ended up in the American and Foreign Anti-Slavery Society, founded by Arthur and Lewis Tappan. Garrisonians remained in control of the original American Anti-Slavery Society, which, even though greatly diminished in numbers, remained a far more radical organization in its principles.

With the split of 1840, the abolitionist movement lost both its unity and its momentum. Within the Garrisonian faction, women became increasingly convinced that they needed their own organization to be able to fight effectively for their rights; in 1848, a group of female abolitionists, headed by Garrisonians Elizabeth Cady Stanton and Susan B. Anthony, gathered at Seneca Falls, New York, and started the first women's rights movement in American history. They demanded equal participation with men in professional activities and the right to vote. Although they continued to be supported by Garrisonian abolitionists, women had started to follow a distinct trajectory from their initial participation in the American Anti-Slavery Society.

By 1848, African-American abolitionists had become disillusioned and convinced that their goals did not fully coincide with the goals of the American Anti-Slavery Society, which they had enthusiastically supported throughout the 1830s. Even though Garrisonians had made a genuine effort at fighting racial prejudice, several African-Americans felt that white abolitionists tended to patronize them. After 1843, black activists organized in a Negro National Convention Movement to fight discrimination and promote the advancement of the free people of color. African-Americans could count among themselves some of the most famous abolitionists, such as Frederick Douglass, Harriet Tubman, and Sojourner Truth, who toured the Northern cities and gave public lectures on their experience in slavery.

In 1840 at Albany, New York, a small group of abolitionists founded the Liberty Party, a political organization dedicated to the cause of immediate emancipation, and elected as candidate for the forthcoming elections James G. Birney. As a political force, the Liberty Party was never able to challenge the hegemony of Democrats and Whigs in Congress, and, after garnering a record of 60,000 votes in the 1844 elections, gradually disappeared from the scene. Several anti-Garrisonian abolitionists ended up reluctantly voting for the Free-Soil Party and then for the Republican Party. Garrisonians, instead, continued to be skeptical about political involvement throughout the crisis of the 1850s. However, the effects of the 1850 Fugitive Slave Act and the internecine fighting in Kansas convinced most of them to abandon the doctrine of moral suasion and support active resistance of the slaves toward slaveowners.

Most abolitionists applauded John Brown's revolutionary attack on Harper's Ferry, and, after the election of Lincoln and the secession of the Southern states, sided with the Union. However, as soon as it became clear that the Republican government had not started a war for the destruction of slavery, they denounced the Lincoln administration and increased their demands for immediate emancipation. After the Emancipation Proclamation of 1863, abolitionists began a campaign for securing the achievement of emancipation through a constitutional amendment. In July 1865, after the passage of the Thirteenth Amendment, which prohibited the existence of slavery, Garrison abandoned the American Anti-Slavery Society, declaring that it had fulfilled its aim. The organization continued to exist under the direction of Wendell Phillips until 1870, after the passage of the Fourteenth and Fifteenth Amendment, which guaranteed the protection of the rights of black citizens in the United States.

—Enrico Dal Lago

See also Abolitionists; Emancipation Proclamation; Free Soil Party; Fugitive Slave Act; Republican Party; Thirteenth Amendment; Underground Raiload.

For further reading:
Aptheker, Herbert. *Abolitionism: A Revolutionary Movement* (1989).
Goodman, Paul. *Of One Blood: Abolitionists and the Origins of Racial Equality* (1998).
Stewart, James B. *Holy Warriors: The Abolitionists and American Slavery* (1996).
Walters, Ronald. *The Antislavery Appeal: American Abolitionism after 1830* (1978).

ABOLITIONISTS

Although they were never large in number, abolitionists exerted extraordinary influence in catalyzing debates and issues that brought on the American Civil War. These individuals differed from others who opposed slavery because they favored immediately ending slavery without compensating slave owners for the loss of their "property" and without relocating freed slaves outside the United States. Free blacks, manumitted slaves, slaves who had escaped bondage, and whites of both sexes joined the cause of immediate abolitionism, and they constantly argued over means and ends. Black abolitionists, for example, did not find compelling the white abolitionist strategy of moral suasion. In 1843 at a convention in Buffalo, New York, and again in 1850, they encouraged Southern slave revolts that they pledged to join once they were under way. Slowly, their arguments made inroads on the consciousness of white abolitionists, who increasingly favored direct action or political activism by the end of the 1850s. Indeed, an association of abolitionists styling itself the "Secret Six" supported John Brown's seizure of the U.S. arsenal at Harper's Ferry in 1859.

The posture of moral suasion embraced by white abolitionists rooted itself in the soil of reform, especially in New England and New York after the War of 1812. Animated by evangelicalism and its emphasis on individual moral responsibility, abolitionists tried to show that slaveholding was a sin in the eyes of God, and immediate repentance offered the only remedy. Since such moral appeals had resulted in countless religious conversions and seemed to be effective in related reform movements such as temperance, white abolitionists clung to persuasion until the 1850s.

Abolitionists tended to eschew partisan politics, too, because political parties inclined toward corruption and moved toward solutions by compromise. To the abolitionists, since slaveholding was a sin, it could not be the subject of mediation. Beginning around 1840, some abolitionists did move toward formal politics and associated themselves with the Liberty Party in 1840, with the Free Soil Party in 1848, and, after 1854, with the Republican Party, but abolitionists did not play a determining role in shaping policy or platforms.

Abolitionists did fashion organizations to spread their ideas. In December 1833, leading abolitionists such as William Lloyd Garrison, Arthur Tappan, and Lewis Tappan established the American Anti-Slavery Society, which labored to organize local antislavery societies, to produce antislavery publications, and to convert ministers to abolitionism. Although the society focused most of its labors in the free states, it did disseminate abolitionist literature through the mails to the Southern states.

By 1840, the American Anti-Slavery Society had fractured. Those who followed Garrison and Abby Kelly believed that the abolition of slavery was just one of a myriad of reforms that needed to be undertaken. This group tended to favor women's rights and included those abolitionists who favored social and legal equality for emancipated slaves. The other faction, led by the Tappans, believed that society was basically healthy and that the emancipation of slaves was the last remaining hurdle needed to redeem the promise of the United States. They did not link abolitionism to other reforms or to further attempts to ameliorate the conditions of African-Americans.

This division among whites reflected some differences between whites and blacks over the goals of abolitionism. For many of the Tappan faction, once slavery was ended, the work was done. Black abolitionists understood that freedom from slavery did not mean the ending of white racism, and they tended to endorse other reforms, including guarantees of voting rights. Black abolitionists also found frustrating the condescension of white abolitionists and the difficulty white abolitionists had in appraising slavery and racism as systems rather than as the moral failings of individuals.

An African-American organization offered one solution to the racial divide in abolitionism. Founded in 1830, the National Negro Convention not only worked for abolitionism, it also crusaded against Northern racism. Like African-American churches in the North, this organization, run by blacks, helped to harbor runaway slaves and offered blacks a community largely free from white interference.

Yet black and white abolitionists could and did work together, such as when they pursued the release and repatriation of African slaves taken into custody by the U.S. Navy after they had seized control of the slave ship *Amistad*. Although white abolitionists did not embrace

Seven noted abolitionsists depicted in *Pioneers of Freedom*, an 1866 carte-de-viste photograph. (*Library of Congress*)

violence, they believed that the Africans in this instance had acted appropriately to effect their freedom. And the *Amistad* mutiny and aftermath allowed abolitionists who employed moral suasion, legal arguments, or direct action to play important and interrelated parts in a saga that actually resulted in real freedom for persons held in bondage.

In the 1850s, abolitionists continued to occupy the fringes of Northern society and Northern opinion, although antislavery, as opposed to abolitionism, became an increasingly mainstream point of view. The Republican Party embraced an antislavery theme, but abolitionists did not believe attempts to confine slavery to the Southern states would lead to its quick end. Abolitionists proved willing to endorse slave violence and other forms of direct action to end slavery. Garrison even hoped that Northern states, weary of the power Southern states wielded in national counsels, would themselves secede from the Union, leaving the South to

contend with slaves who, according to Garrison, would rebel and earn their freedom. Others, like Lysander Spooner, a Boston attorney, encouraged non-slave-holding whites and Southern slaves to make common cause and overthrow the slave regime.

Spooner's discourses, along with the links between abolitionists and John Brown, illustrate how abolitionists contributed to the coming of the Civil War. No one acted on Spooner's call, and Brown's raid failed. Yet repeated efforts at agitation might have one day provoked the slave rebellion that Southern whites feared. Mainstream Northerners' disavowals of abolitionists could not diminish the growing Southern belief that abolitionists were more than a fringe element. Worse for Southerners was the possibility that the new abolitionist message of direct action might attract enough converts to effect emancipation, even as their message of moral suasion had not done so in the previous thirty years. As the South perceived that possibility becoming more likely, the destruction of the Union and the war that followed it did so as well.

—*Edward R. Crowther*

See also Abolitionist Movement; Brown, John; Garrison, William Lloyd; Tappan, Lewis.

For further reading:

Dillon, Merton L. *The Abolitionists: The Growth of a Dissenting Minority* (1974).

———. *Elijah P. Lovejoy, Abolitionist Editor* (1961).

———. *Slavery Attacked: Southern Slaves and their Allies, 1619–1865* (1990).

Friedman, Lawrence J. *Gregarious Saints: Self and Community in American Abolitionism, 1830–1870* (1982).

Kraditor, Aileen S. *Means and Ends in American Abolitionism: Garrison and His Critics on Strategy and Tactics, 1834–1850* (1969).

Renehan, Edward J., Jr. *The Secret Six: The True Tale of the Men Who Conspired with John Brown* (1995).

Stewart, James Brewer. *Holy Warriors: The Abolitionists and American Slavery* (1997).

ACOUSTIC SHADOWS

An acoustic shadow is an area where sound from nearby locations is prevented from reaching because of atmospheric phenomena or terrain features. On several occasions in the Civil War, acoustic shadows had important effects on major battles. Some nineteenth-century writers referred to these cases as "silent battles." Commanders depended on the sounds of battle to know where to send troops or respond to threats to their lines, and acoustic shadows contributed to several disastrous command decisions.

There are four major causes of acoustic shadows: wind direction; absorption of sound by woods or other obstacles; variation in the temperature of the air at different altitudes; and differences in wind speed at different altitudes. Most acoustic shadows are due to wind direction or the absorption of sound. Sound carries better downwind than it does upwind. Sound absorption by thick woods, hills, or mountains can significantly affect the audibility of sound.

Sound travels faster in warm air than in cool air. Usually, the air gets cooler at higher altitudes. Sound waves near the ground, therefore, travel faster than they would at a higher altitude. If anything makes part of a sound wave travel faster than another part, it causes the entire sound wave to change direction. This phenomenon is called refraction. Refraction often causes a sound wave to move upward, away from the hearing of people on the ground. However, if there is a temperature inversion, the air is warmer at a higher altitude than a lower one. This causes the opposite of normal refraction, and sends sound waves toward the ground, making them carry farther than normal.

Changes in wind speed also cause acoustic shadows. Winds tend to blow faster as they get higher from the ground, away from friction caused by trees and other obstacles. Higher wind speeds increase the velocity of the upper part of a sound wave and push it back toward the ground. It is possible for a sound wave to bounce upward after hitting the ground, and sometimes repeatedly bounce up and down, causing alternating areas of sound or silence to people listening on the ground.

Acoustic shadows were reported as having affected the battles at Fort Donelson, Seven Pines, Gaines's Mill, Perryville, Iuka, Chancellorsville, Gettysburg, and Five Forks, among others.

At Iuka on 18 September 1862, a force under Confederate major general Sterling Price attacked Brigadier General William Rosecrans. Rosecrans's men barely managed to hold their own until the fighting broke off at dark. More Union forces under Major General Edward Ord were only four miles away in Price's rear, upwind from the battle. Rosecrans was furious about Ord's failure to reinforce him, which he felt would have enabled him to crush Price's army. Ord saw smoke rising from the battle, which he thought was only Rosecrans burning captured materiel, because no noise of the battle reached his position.

At Chancellorsville on 2 May 1863, "Stonewall" Jackson's surprise attack shattered Union general Joseph Hooker's right flank, only three miles from his headquarters. Hooker heard little or none of the battle and knew nothing of the collapse of his right until the first panic-stricken soldiers streamed into view near his headquarters.

Acoustic shadows were also noted during naval battles. Witnesses of the battle between the *Monitor* and the *Virginia* on 9 March 1862 had a plain view of the action from the shore but heard nothing. An extreme example of acoustic shadowing was reported after the battle of Port Royal on 7 November 1861. Union soldiers aboard a transport ship upwind of the fighting saw the

flashes and smoke of the naval bombardment but heard nothing except during brief times when the steady wind slowed down. On the other hand, residents of St. Augustine, Florida, heard the same bombardment 150 miles away in the other direction.

Acoustic shadows played a major role in the battle of Five Forks on 1 April 1865. Confederate major generals George Pickett and Fitzhugh Lee left their commands to attend a shad bake held by Brigadier General Thomas Rosser. While Pickett was away, his men were hit by a strong Union assault led by Major General Philip Sheridan. The weakened Confederate lines reeled under the impact, and they needed the authority of a division commander to meet the crisis. Pickett and Lee, separated from the front lines by only a mile and a half of thick pine forest, heard nothing of the fighting until it was too late. The loss of the rebel right flank that day forced the abandonment of Petersburg and Richmond and led to the surrender at Appomattox on 9 April.

—*David A. Norris*

See also Chancellorsville, Battle of; Five Forks, Battle of; Iuka, Battle of.

For further reading:
De Motte, John B. "The Cause of a Silent Battle." In *Battles and Leaders of the Civil War* (1887).
Koerner, Brendan I. "The Battle Was Lost in a Zone of Silence: Acoustics Helps Explain Civil War Blunders." *U.S. News and World Report* (1998).
Ross, Charles. "Ssh! Battle in Progress." *Civil War Times Illustrated* (1996).
Suhr, Robert Collins. "Small But Savage Battle of Iuka." *America's Civil War* (1999).

ADAMS, CHARLES FRANCIS
(1807–1886)

U.S. minister to Great Britain

On 25 November 1863 Charles Francis Adams, America's minister to the Court of St. James, wrote to his son: "The war has done us much good. It has cured us of much of the spirit of vaunting and braggadocio which peace and prosperity had pampered, and has left us moderate but firm." Then, in analyzing his contribution, he continued: "The prejudices and distrust that prevailed here at the outset against every act of the Administration are slowly yielding to the conviction that it deserves confidence. All the little that I have contributed to this result has been to nourish by a steady and uniform bearing, as well under adverse as under favorable circumstances, the growth of this opinion in the British Cabinet. I believe that now it is firmly planted there. If our arms favor us in any moderate degree for the future, I think we may hope to steer clear of farther trouble in this kingdom." In his best self-deprecating style, Charles Francis Adams modestly summed up a great achievement. His steady and firm course had helped keep the two nations from war and the British government from assisting the Southern cause of independence in any decisive fashion.

Charles Francis Adams, the son of President John Quincy Adams and Louisa Catherine (Johnson) Adams, was born on 18 August 1807. His early life took him to St. Petersburg, Russia, where his father was serving, and there young Adams learned French, German, and Russian, preferring to speak French to his native English. His father's duties in Belgium and France also afforded young Charles exposure to European politics during the exciting "Hundred Days," when Napoleon briefly reclaimed his throne in 1815. John Quincy Adams's appointment to the Court of St. James meant that Charles would attend English public schools, a not altogether pleasant experience. Although his academic performance did not always please his parents, the young scholar had a chance to mature and learn much about English public life. Upon returning to the United States during his father's tenure as secretary of state, Charles was placed in the Boston Latin School and later Harvard University, graduating from the latter in 1825, at the young age of eighteen.

After spending three years in Washington while his father was president, Charles decided to settle down and study law under the brief tutelage of Daniel Webster. He was admitted to the practice of law in January 1829. He married his beloved Abigail, the daughter of the influential Peter C. Brooks of Boston (whose other sons-in-law were Reverend Nathaniel Frothingham and Edward Everett), on 5 September 1829. Aside from his law practice, Charles assumed the care of most of his father's property, alleviating the elder statesman from the woes of financial management while he served eighteen years in the United States Congress. Charles also found time to write some articles for the *North American Review*, the leading literary magazine of the day.

During this time Charles wrote pamphlets on national topics and became interested in the abolitionist cause. His interest in politics got him elected to the Massachusetts legislature in 1840 as a Whig. He served three years in the state house of representatives and two in the senate. Along with Stephen Phillips, Charles Sumner, and others, he helped to establish the Boston *Whig*, which became the voice of the "Conscience Whigs," those who strongly opposed slavery and the so-called Southern policy of the "Cotton Whigs." With such divisions besetting the Whig Party, Adams was soon attracted to the new Free Soil Party and was actually named its vice presidential candidate in 1848. The failure of this party to materialize into a more permanent organization led Adams and others to join the newly formed Republican Party. In 1858 Adams was nominated for his father's seat in the United States Congress and was easily elected over two rival candidates. In

Congress he became aligned with his friend William Seward and took to the campaign trail with him in the 1860 presidential election. Although he preferred Seward for the Republican nomination, Adams joined the majority in backing Abraham Lincoln for the post and worked hard throughout the Northeast for his election. Adams's own reelection to Congress put him into a leadership position and made his role pivotal in the negotiations to prevent the South from leaving the Union. Adams's controversial policy of moderation in these negotiations led some, such as Charles Sumner, to think of him as weak and break off social and political relations with him.

Seward's appointment as secretary of state, a post some thought Adams deserved, soon placed Adams in the forefront of events. His old friend nominated him for the post of minister to the Court of St. James. Adams had few illusions about the difficulty of representing the United States in Great Britain. It was already known that Prime Minister Lord Palmerston had no love for the young republic and that many in the British ministry, including William Gladstone, were pro-Southern in sympathy. These men and Foreign Minister Lord John Russell would have to be met on their own terms and under trying conditions. Even prior to presenting his credentials, Adams learned that Great Britain had already granted belligerent status to the Confederacy. Although this gesture by the British was designed primarily to preserve their neutral status in shipping, Seward and many in America took it as a direct insult to the United States. Belligerent status, however, did not confer official recognition and thereby sovereignty. It only instituted the right to realize certain defined goals within the international community. At the same time, the British declared their neutrality in the American conflict, and this in effect recognized the Union's blockade of Southern ports. Adams handled this situation with directness and firmness and soon earned not only the respect of Lord Russell but also established an informal understanding with him. In his first extended meeting with Russell, Adams complained that the British recognition of Confederate belligerency encouraged a government that actually lacked an organized military or naval establishment. Adams's steady handling of the affair won Russell's admiration and achieved something of a diplomatic triumph. Russell from then on kept representatives of the Confederacy at arm's length.

Much of Adams's anxiety during his tenure as minister resulted from Union reverses on the battlefield. He wrote to his son on 7 September 1861: "The feeling here which at one time was leaning our way has been very much changed by the disaster at Bull's run, and by the steady operation of the press against us. Great Britain always looks to her own interest as a paramount law of her action in foreign affairs. She might deal quite summarily with us, were it not for the European complications which are growing more and more embarrassing." Major Union victories inspired the opposite feelings, and although each victory elated him, Adams was careful to maintain a level posture. After the fall of Vicksburg, he noted, "I tried to bear up under the intelligence with a suitable degree of moderation. I ventured to indulge a slight sense of satisfaction."

Aside from the vicissitudes caused by uncertain battles, Adams had to handle several delicate situations. The most notable was the *Trent* Affair. In this case, the Union vessel *San Jacinto* intercepted the British mail-packet *Trent* and seized its two Confederate passengers, John Slidell and James M. Mason, special commissioners on their way to Europe to procure supplies, arms, and if possible, allies. The capture of the two envoys by Captain Charles Wilkes caused an international uproar. Adams, who believed that British neutrality had been violated, nevertheless obeyed Seward's commands and presented the Union case to the British government. The British demanded that the prisoners be released and that the United States formally apologize for its violation of the rights of neutrals. After postponing a response to let matters cool, Adams finally notified the British that Wilkes had acted without orders and that the prisoners would be released. Yet he also noted that the United States government held that neutrals who knowingly carried enemy envoys with their contraband dispatches were subject to seizure under the laws of nations and that such captures should be adjudicated before an international tribunal. This response, while capitulating to British demands for the surrender of the prisoners and an admission of a wrongful act, saved face for Seward and Lincoln by asserting a justification for the seizure that was recognized by international law. At the same time Adams's reply assuaged British ire by recognizing long-held British principles concerning the rights of blockading nations. Indeed, as one historian has observed, "The *Trent* Affair served to underline the importance of a naval blockade as England's most formidable offensive weapon."

Adams also had to deal with problems arising from the construction and release of Confederate raiders, such as the *Alabama*, and the Laird rams. In the former case, Adams failed to stop the release, and the *Alabama*'s career of destruction became a persistent source of Anglo-American irritation that lingered for years after the war. In the latter case, steady pressure from Adams and Lord Russell's willingness to lessen tensions led to a unique solution. The British government purchased the rams instead of releasing them to their putative buyers in Egypt. Such an indication of British sympathy toward the Northern cause greatly lessened the strain between the two countries.

In addition to ships being built for the Confederacy in Britain, there was the problem of vessels under British registry trading with the South. The Bahamas and Bermuda were regular stops for ships engaged in this trade. These ports also carried on a regular trade with Southern blockade runners. The running of contraband arms and goods through Mexico, especially at Matamoros, disturbed Adams and the State Department. Here an old legal doctrine known as "continuous voyage" came into play when the United States seized the *Peterhoff*, which had been plying this trade. The principle of continuous voyage did not deem shipment by land as part of a "voyage." In this case, the announcement by Lloyds of London that they would no longer underwrite such voyages brought this potentially dangerous situation under control.

Adams displayed poise and reserve that played well with his British hosts. He also benefitted from European turmoil in the early 1860s. Concern about the aims of Napoleon III, the rise of German nationalism, uprisings in Poland, reform in Russia, and its own colonial ventures, did not give the British government the freedom to act as the British public sometimes demanded. It was also not lost on the British government that Canada was essentially a hostage to the United States. An expected cotton shortage in Britain was not the factor the South believed it would be to bring the British to their aid. As it turned out, a surplus of cotton from the 1860 harvest had augmented British reserves, and by the time those were expended the harvests from India began to fill the void. Meanwhile, Adams's contacts with Richard Cobden, John Bright, and others kept him well informed about the mood in Manchester, Lancaster, and Liverpool.

Although tending to modesty, Charles Francis Adams's evaluation of his tenure was accurate. It was his calm, steady, and firm demeanor that impressed the British Cabinet, especially Lord Russell, and members of Parliament on both sides of the aisle.

Adams's contributions to American diplomacy continued after the war with the signing of the Treaty of Washington in 1871. In this episode Adams led the campaign to reject the concept of "indirect damages" resulting from the *Alabama* claims. Again he ran afoul of his former colleague, Charles Sumner, who had insisted on their inclusion in any settlement. That the final treaty reflected Adams's ideas gives silent witness to his solid judgment. Moreover, without the acceptance of Adams's counsel, the final arbitration of the *Alabama* claims may never have taken place or may have been inordinately delayed.

Weary of public life, Adams avoided a movement to have him run against Ulysses S. Grant for the presidency and spent the remainder of his days editing his father's diary and other family papers. He died on 21 November 1886.

—Joe Knetsch

See also Adams, Charles Francis, Jr.; Adams, Henry Brooks; *Alabama* Claims; *Alabama*, CSS; Diplomacy, U.S.A.; Great Britain.
For further reading:
Crook, D. P. *Diplomacy during the American Civil War* (1975).
Duberman, Martin. *Charles Francis Adams, 1807–1886* (1968).
Ford, W. C., ed. *A Cycle of Adams Letters, 1861–1865* (1920).

ADAMS, CHARLES FRANCIS, JR.
(1835–1915)
Union officer

Born in Boston, the son of Charles Francis and Abigail Brooks Adams, Charles Francis Adams, Jr., graduated from Harvard in 1856. After a brief career as a lawyer, during which time he established a hearty reputation as a partygoing patrician with regular attendance at Boston's Tiger Ball, Adams abandoned his legal career for the grand tour of Europe. In 1860 he traveled across America, making several valuable political contacts, including a brief meeting with Lincoln. Adams took up journalism and wrote an economic critique of Southern cotton producers entitled "King Cotton" for the *Atlantic* magazine in 1861.

Although a member of the Massachusetts Militia, Adams did not leap into military service. Instead, he busied himself drafting a diplomatic strategy on the cotton issue for his father to use in negotiating with the British after Lincoln appointed the elder Adams minister to London. Yet Adams joined the 1st Massachusetts Cavalry by December 1861. He was stationed on the Sea Islands, later the site of the Port Royal experiment, and found the area populated by thousands of former slaves. There was little armed resistance from the Confederates, though, and little of Adams's early service involved combat. As the war intensified and tactics changed, Union cavalry correspondingly saw more activity. In the June 1862 battle at Johns Island, South Carolina, Adams was forced to retreat, but in a letter home he assured his father that the retreat was orderly and that "we should have whipped them dreadfully had they followed us."

The 1st Massachusetts suffered severe losses at Antietam and the following summer, in July 1863, Adams escorted infantry on a forty-mile forced march to Gettysburg, Pennsylvania, reaching that place in less than twenty-four hours. Determined to "bear up the reeling fortunes" of the Union, he upon the next morning witnessed the scene of "twenty thousand fellow creatures wounded or dead around us … yet the elements seemed electrified with a certain magnetic influence of victory, as the great army sank down overwearied in its tracks." Later that month, however, Adams soberly wrote, "I no longer believe in a collapse of the rebellion."

In 1864 Adams became an officer in the 5th Massachusetts Cavalry, the first black cavalry regiment from that state. Although the descendent of generations of antislavery advocates, including Presidents John Adams and John Quincy Adams, the latter of whom had acted as defense counsel in the *Amistad* case, Charles Francis Adams, Jr., never evinced the same confidence in his regiment's black soldiers as did some others. He had no doubt that the "one good to result from this war must be the freedom and regeneration of the African race," but he firmly believed that black troops required different treatment than did white soldiers. He observed, "Patience, kindness, and self-control have not been my characteristics as an officer." However, after months in command he wrote that he hoped "to see the Army become for the black race a school of skilled labor and of self reliance, as well as an engine of war."

Adams's health began a precipitous decline in spring 1865 as he suffered from malarial fevers. He saw little active duty until his regiment occupied Richmond. Despite a brief incident involving horse theft by some of his regiment—an episode that nearly got Adams arrested and court-martialed—he finished out the war and returned home in June 1865, weighing barely 130 pounds, distressed by the carnage he had witnessed, and disheartened by Lincoln's assassination. Adams gradually recovered his health and eventually married Mary Hone Ogden and fathered five children.

Charles Francis Adams's career was filled with contradictions. He was a crusading journalist against the powerful railroad combinations and then an investor in, and later president of, the Union Pacific Railroad, in which position he made a substantial fortune. He attempted a second career as a reformer in the 1890s by employing his writing talent to support the Anti-Imperialist League. He wrote and lectured on the Civil War, served as an overseer of Harvard College, and became president of the Massachusetts Historical Society. Adams resided in Quincy and Lincoln, Massachusetts, until his death in 1915. Leaving his autobiography to be published posthumously, he managed to ignite yet another controversy from the grave. When the book appeared in 1916 it included blunt criticism of General Joseph Hooker and other Union officers.

—Teresa Thomas

See also Adams, Charles Francis; Adams, Henry Brooks.
For further reading:
Adams, Charles F., Jr. *The Double Anniversary: '76 and '63. A Fourth of July Address Delivered at Quincy, Massachusetts, by Charles F. Adams, Jr.* (1869).
Adams, Charles F., Jr. *Charles Francis Adams, 1835–1915: An Autobiography* (1916).
Crowninshield, Benjamin W. *A History of the First Regiment of Massachusetts Cavalry Volunteers* (1891).
Ford, Worthington Chauncey, ed. *A Cycle of Adams Letters 1861–1865* (1920).
Kirkland, Edward Chase. *Charles Francis Adams Junior 1835–1915: The Patrician at Bay* (1965).

ADAMS, DANIEL WEISIGER
(1821–1872)
Confederate general

Born to George Adams and Anna Weisiger Adams in Frankfort, Kentucky, Daniel Adams moved with his family to Natchez, Mississippi, as a child. Before being admitted to the Mississippi bar, Adams attended the University of Virginia. After a brief stint in Mississippi politics, he moved to Louisiana. As the secession crisis loomed, Adams was active in efforts to prevent Louisiana from seceding. When these efforts failed and Louisiana joined the Confederacy, however, Adams actively helped prepare his adopted state for war.

Governor Thomas E. Moore appointed Adams to a three-member commission to make defensive and offensive preparations. Following his service on this body, Adams began his military service as a lieutenant colonel of the 1st Louisiana Regulars. On 30 October 1861 he became the colonel of the regiment. His promotion occurred while Adams was stationed at Pensacola, Florida. He divided his time between this city and Mobile, Alabama, during the first months of the war.

Adams moved north in early 1862 and commanded the 1st Brigade, 2d Division, II Corps, at Shiloh after its commander, Brigadier General Adley H. Gladden, was mortally wounded early in the battle. Adams lost his right eye in the attack on the Federal center and was temporarily left for dead. For his service in this battle Adams was promoted to brigadier general on 23 May 1862.

After recovering from his wounds, Adams served under William J. Hardee as the commander of the 2d Louisiana Brigade at Perryville. A few months later at Stones River, Adams commanded the 1st Brigade, 1st Division of Hardee's Corps. Once again Adams suffered serious wounds (this time in the left arm) that knocked him out of action for several months.

In September 1863 Adams commanded a brigade of Breckinridge's Division of D. H. Hill's Corps. During the battle, he was seriously wounded in the arm, and after most of his possessions were stolen by Northern soldiers, he was captured by a Union officer. By summer 1864 he had been exchanged. He then commanded a cavalry brigade guarding railroads out of Alabama, before being given command of the District of Central Alabama on 24 September. With Confederate commands disintegrating in early 1865, Adams's authority gradually widened, until on 11 March 1865 he received command of all forces in Alabama above the Department of the Gulf. His limited resources kept him from preventing the raids by Union cavalry Brigadier General James Wilson against Selma, Alabama, on 2 April 1865, and Montgomery, Alabama, on 16 April 1865.

After surrendering in May 1865, Adams received his parole at Meridian, Mississippi, on 9 May 1865. Following a brief trip to England after the war, Adams returned to New Orleans, where he practiced law until his death in 1872. Adams was the younger brother of fellow Confederate general William Wirt Adams.

—David S. Heidler and Jeanne T. Heidler

See also Adams, William Wirt; Chickamauga, Battle of; Hardee, William J.; Wilson, James Harrison; Wilson's Selma Raid.

For further reading:
Cozzens, Peter. *No Better Place to Die: The Battle of Stones River* (1991).
———. *This Terrible Sound; The Battle of Chickamauga* (1992).
Tourgee, Albion. *The Story of a Thousand, Being a History of the Services of the One Hundred Fifth Ohio Volunteer Infantry, in the War for the Union* (1896).
Watts, T. H. "To the People of Alabama." *Montgomery Weekly Mail* (1865).

ADAMS, HENRY BROOKS
(1838–1918)
Intellectual and historian

Henry Adams was the great grandson of John Adams, the second president of the United States, and the grandson of John Quincy Adams, the sixth president. His father was Charles Francis Adams, Sr., who married the youngest daughter of Peter Chardon Brooks, thought to be the wealthiest man in Boston at the time. A member of the Boston Brahmin aristocracy, Adams was born into one of the most dominant political families in the first hundred years of the American republic.

After graduating from Harvard University in 1858, Adams took the Brahmin obligatory Grand Tour of Europe, where he studied for two years, mainly in Berlin. Returning to America after finishing his studies, Adams found the United States, in the months before the 1860 elections, teetering toward civil war. Charles Francis Adams, a Republican in the House of Representatives, joined William Seward of New York in campaigning for their fellow Republican Abraham Lincoln. Henry Adams voted for Lincoln on 6 November, and his father won reelection by a sizable margin. He joined his father in Washington, D.C., by early December, and for a time he served both as his father's private secretary and covertly as the Washington correspondent of the Boston newspaper *Daily Advertiser*, which had strong Republican affiliations.

Adams served his father in Washington until the congressman was appointed envoy extraordinary and minister plenipotentiary to England on 20 March 1861. Adams eventually accompanied his father to England, serving as the elder Adams's private secretary. Unbeknownst to his father, Adams also served as a foreign correspondent for the *New York Times* in violation of State Department regulations.

When the minister delayed his departure to London

for six weeks until his eldest son, John Quincy, was married, the Confederate diplomats to England took the opportunity to influence England's Proclamation of Neutrality in the American civil conflict. The England that Adams was visiting in the early 1860s was at its apogee of economic and military power and thus was more concerned about protecting its position and wealth than it was concerned with moral imperatives. Because of England's prominence in the world, the American diplomatic ministry in London was the most critical one, especially since Confederate cotton was a vital component of the British textile industry.

At the heart of the Union's foreign relationship with England was the contention that the Confederate cause was nothing more than a rebellion and any foreign emissary from those rebelling states was illegitimate and should not be recognized by the British foreign ministry. Charles F. Adams, Sr., found, however, that the British government and people were at best indifferent not only to this Union argument but to their overall cause as well. Compounding the complexity of the situation was Secretary of State Seward's impetuous involvement in diplomatic affairs with England, manifested especially in his aggressive memorandum that practically declared war on any European power that recognized Confederate legations. As he would prove to do throughout his service in London, Adams's father always managed to avoid completely rupturing relations with the British, which proved a difficult proposition as the Union army bungled through one military defeat after another until Antietam. The claim of a victory there gave Lincoln the opportunity to issue the Emancipation Proclamation in 1862, which was to prove a major turning point in Anglo-American relations.

Later victories at Vicksburg and Gettysburg discouraged the British from ever providing aid to the Confederate cause and further cemented the relations between the U.S. government and England. When the most intense pressure was off the Union ministry, Adams found life in London pleasurable, as he enjoyed the association with prominent Englishman and Americans alike. Adams's experiences as his father's secretary during the United States' most turbulent period and his life in London, which was the English-speaking world's intellectual capital, proved to be influential to his later writings, especially in his masterpiece *The Education of Henry Adams*, which was privately published in September 1918 and won the Pulitzer Prize posthumously.

In *The Education*, Adams wrote about the complexity of his feelings during this time in his life, "Of the year 1862 Henry Adams could never think without a shudder. The war alone did not greatly distress him; already in his short life he was used to seeing people wade in blood, and he could plainly discern in history,

that man from the beginning had found his chief amusement in bloodshed; but the ferocious joy of destruction at its best requires that one should kill what one hates, and young Adams neither hated nor wanted to kill his friends the rebels, while he wanted nothing so much as to wipe England off the earth."

Adams's memoirs remain a classic in American literature.

—*James H. Meredith*

See also Adams, Charles Francis; Adams, Charles Francis, Jr.; Diplomacy, U.S.A.; Great Britain.
For further reading:
Adams, Henry. *The Education of Henry Adams, Henry Adams: Novels, Mont Saint Michel, and The Education* (1983).
———. *Henry Adams: Selected Letters* (1992).
Samuels, Ernest. *Henry Adams* (1989).

ADAMS, JOHN
(1825–1864)
Confederate general

Born to Irish immigrant parents in Nashville, Tennessee, Adams moved with his family to Pulaski, Tennessee, while still a child. He lived there until entering the United States Military Academy in 1841. He graduated five years later, twenty-fifth of fifty-nine in the Class of 1846. He received a commission in the 1st Dragoons and was sent immediately to Mexico to serve in the war that erupted there. During the Mexican War, Adams received a brevet promotion to first lieutenant for bravery at the battle of Santa Cruz de Rosales. Following the war, he served in several frontier posts in California, New Mexico, and Minnesota. In the midst of these moves around the frontier, Adams married Georgia McDougal and started what would become a family of six children.

When the Civil War began, Adams was in command of Fort Crook, California, as a captain. Hearing of Tennessee's secession, Adams immediately resigned his commission and boarded a steamer for New York City, arriving there in late summer 1861. General Winfield Scott recommended to Secretary of State William Henry Seward that Adams be arrested as a political prisoner before he could join the Confederate army. Adams made his way south, however, and received an appointment as a captain in the Confederate cavalry.

Adams commanded briefly at Memphis where his main duty was housing and feeding prisoners of war. He then served in western Kentucky and subsequently in Mississippi. Adams was promoted to colonel in May 1862 and commanded a brigade of William Wing Loring's division during the Vicksburg campaign the following year. After Vicksburg, he commanded a brigade under Joseph Johnston at Jackson, Mississippi. Upon the organization of Johnston's Army of Tennessee in December 1863, Adams commanded a brigade in Leonidas Polk's division and fought in northern Mississippi and Alabama before rejoining the main Army of Tennessee in the attempt to stop William T. Sherman's Atlanta campaign.

In the Atlanta campaign, Adams was commended for bravery for his actions at Rocky Face Ridge and Resaca, but he failed to prevent the federal crossing of the Chattahoochee River in July 1864. After Atlanta fell Adams commanded a brigade in John Bell Hood's march into Tennessee. At the battle of Franklin on 30 November 1864, a wounded right arm did not deter Adams from leading a cavalry charge on the Union breastworks. Union soldiers, awed by his bravery, did not shoot at him until he grabbed a set of Union colors. Struck nine times, he died atop the Union works. He was buried near his home in Pulaski, Tennessee.

—David S. Heidler and Jeanne T. Heidler

See also Army of Tennessee; Franklin, Battle of.
For further reading:
McDonough, James L., and Thomas L. Connelly. *Five Tragic Hours: The Battle of Franklin* (1983).
Sword, Wiley. *Embrace an Angry Wind: The Confederacy's Last Hurrah; Spring Hill, Franklin and Nashville* (1992).

ADAMS, WILLIAM WIRT
(1819–1888)
Confederate general

Born in Frankfort, Kentucky, to George Adams and Anna Weisiger Adams, William Wirt Adams (generally called Wirt Adams throughout his life) moved briefly to Texas as a young man, where he served in the army of the Republic of Texas in 1839. From Texas he moved to Mississippi, where he became a prominent banker, planter, and state legislator. Adams became active in the secession movement in Mississippi, and after that state's secession, the governor sent Adams as part of a commission to urge Louisiana to secede.

Following the formation of the Confederate States of America, Confederate president Jefferson Davis offered Adams the position of postmaster general, but he refused. Instead, Adams raised and became the colonel of the 1st Mississippi Cavalry. Adams and his men guarded part of the Confederate retreat from Kentucky in spring 1862 and fought at Shiloh. Shortly afterward Adams became Major General Earl Van Dorn's chief of artillery and in that capacity fought at Iuka in September, where he was commended for a trap he set for Union soldiers. October 1862 found him again in command of his cavalry regiment, and he fought at Corinth in Frank Armstrong's cavalry brigade. In 1863 Adams fought in the Vicksburg campaign, particularly in the failed effort to repulse Colonel Benjamin H. Grierson's raid in April and May. He was involved in several skirmishes outside

Vicksburg in June, and on 25 September received a promotion to brigadier general for his actions in the campaign. Throughout the late summer and fall of 1863, Adams operated throughout Mississippi.

Serving under Nathan Bedford Forrest for the remainder of the war, Adams saw action in the weak Confederate attempt to prevent William T. Sherman from taking Meridian, Mississippi, in February 1864. During Sherman's Atlanta campaign, Adams commanded a cavalry division guarding rail lines out of Mississippi and Alabama. In fall 1864 he commanded the Northern District of Mississippi.

Adams surrendered in May 1865 and was paroled. He lived the remainder of his life in Vicksburg and Jackson, Mississippi. He served in state government and as the postmaster of Jackson. In 1888 a Jackson newspaper editor with whom Adams had been feuding killed him in a fight in Jackson.

—David S. Heidler and Jeanne T. Heidler

See also Forrest, Nathan Bedford; Grierson's Raid; Meridian Campaign; Van Dorn, Earl.
For further reading:
Bearss, Margie Riddle. *Sherman's Forgotten Campaign: The Meridian Expedition* (1987).
Brown, D. Alexander. *Grierson's Raid: A Cavalry Adventure of the Civil War* (1954).

AFRICAN-AMERICAN SAILORS

In 1861, faced with the daunting task of blockading hundreds of miles of Confederate coast with a minuscule force, the United States Navy turned to African-Americans to fill their ranks. As the navy rapidly acquired ships to carry out the blockade, a shortage of sailors became a critical problem. African-American seamen proved the solution. Not only did large numbers of African-Americans possess maritime skills, but also black sailors had a tradition of service with the navy going back to the Revolutionary War. African-American sailors had served with distinction in all of America's previous wars and represented a small percentage of the navy's manpower in 1861. Blacks were also numerous in the antebellum merchant marine's manpower, filling jobs in a disreputable occupation considered beneath the dignity of most Americans.

The number of African-Americans who enlisted in the Union navy is subject to debate. The total number of navy enlistments (regardless of race) is estimated at roughly 118,000. The first research into African-American Civil War sailors in the late 1940s fixed the percentage of black sailors at 25 percent (about 32,000) of the navy's total enlisted force. Later research in the 1970s guessed the number of enlistees at 9 percent (roughly 10,000). Contemporary research conducted by the National Park Service estimates the number of African-Americans in the Union navy at about 24,000

(16 percent). The number of black Union sailors will probably never be known for certain as navy documents generally did not classify sailors by race, a remarkable fact in a highly race-conscious era.

The recruitment of African-American sailors was markedly different from the enlisting of black soldiers into the Union armies. First, African-American sailors had served the United States from the start. Northern racists initially opposed the enlistment of black soldiers because the war was a conflict over the Union, not slavery. But African-American sailors had a long tradition of service to the nation and their entrance into the navy in large numbers caused little stir. While pubic pressure and federal policy kept black soldiers out of the war, African-American sailors fought for the Union. Second, naval service was not considered socially elevating. While soldiers were usually held in low esteem by the general public, at least some generals (such as George Washington or Andrew Jackson) had risen to the presidency and the army enjoyed a modicum of social standing. Sailors, however, were considered the dregs of society. Thus, the public objected to black soldiers as the elevation of an inferior people to a minimal status with whites. Slaves and seaman, however, shared a common low social standing. Also, whereas the states recruited the army's volunteer regiments, the navy retained its recruiting responsibilities unto itself. Thus, the states had no say in the recruiting of African-American sailors at federal installations, and the enlistment of black sailors occurred out of sight of the general public.

Lastly, the African-American sailors who enlisted in the navy represented an almost opposite demographic background than did black soldiers. Black soldiers were overwhelmingly rural southern slaves who fled from slavery to enlist in the Union army. African-American sailors, however, were mostly urban northern free blacks. While the largest demographic group of African-Americans in the Union army comprised slaves from the Mississippi River valley, a common African-American sailor was a skilled laborer from New York or Boston. Also, unique to African-American sailors, large numbers of foreign-born blacks came to the United States to enlist in the navy. Nearly one in eight African-American sailors came from a foreign land.

Once enlisted in the service, African-American sailors had a much different experience than their counterparts in the army. First, African-American sailors fought from the very first days of the war. While the army resisted black recruits in large numbers until 1863, black sailors served the nation from the opening shots to the bitter end. Second, while the army segregated its black troops into separate "colored" units, the navy fully integrated African-American sailors into its ship crews. This was not an attempt at social equalization; rather it was simply impracticable to segregate African-American sailors into specific portions of a vessel or onto vessels manned only by black seamen. The integration of crews generated less overt racism than in the army. Living side by side on crowded vessels and sharing common dangers led black and white sailors to at best learn respect for each other or at least keep their prejudices to themselves. The army did little to quell racism in its ranks, but the navy enjoyed relatively harmonious race relations.

The navy also paid its black sailors equal wages to its white crewmen in sharp contrast to the army. For most of the war white army privates received $13 per month in pay along with free uniforms. Until 1864, however, black soldiers received only $10 per month plus a $3 deduction to pay for uniforms and food. The navy, however, always paid the same wages. Along with fair wages, African-American sailors also shared equally in prize moneys when Confederate merchant ships and blockade-runners were captured. Prize money was so lucrative a sailor lucky to participate in a rich capture could receive several years' wages in a matter of hours. The navy provided other benefits in equal portions. For instance, many black army regiments received substandard weapons, uniforms, and food, leading to unnecessary deaths from combat, disease, and exposure. The fully integrated navy crews, however, enjoyed not only a common standard of equipment, clothing, and sustenance, but also a superior supply system that provided replenishment on a fairly regular schedule.

Navy medical care also surpassed its army equivalent. The army chronically lacked physicians, especially to support its black regiments. The navy enjoyed a much larger medical service, however, and smaller percentage of African-American sailors died by disease than black soldiers. The army in general lost roughly one in every fifteen recruits to disease and one in every seven black soldiers to various ailments. Navy doctors, operating with better facilities, drugs, and equipment, limited deaths to disease to one in every forty recruits with relatively minor differences between white and African-American sailors.

African-American sailors shared in the dangers of combat alongside their white shipmates. In many instances the army relegated black troops to relatively unimportant supporting roles such as felling trees, digging trenches, and building roads because the army derided their skills as soldiers. African-American sailors, integrated among navy crews, received every opportunity to demonstrate their bravery under fire. Eight African-American sailors received the Medal of Honor during the Civil War.

Lastly, the navy equally applied its criminal justice system to its African-American recruits. Often the army unjustly prosecuted black soldiers or ignored injustices inflicted upon them by white officers and men. The navy, however, equally applied its criminal justice procedures to both punish and protect African-American sailors. Whites who assaulted or abused black sailors faced navy justice equal to crimes against white personnel. While blacks in the North enjoyed few legal privileges, the navy permitted African-American sailors to testify in court against white defendants or, if charged with an offense, to cross-examine white witnesses. The navy, eager to preserve its source of manpower, even granted beneficial treatment to black sailors accused of violations. When charged with a crime, African-American sailors generally received less severe punishment than white sailors in the form of shorter prison sentences, lower fines, and a higher acquittal rate. Fewer African-American sailors received the death penalty or life sentences in prison relative to their percentage of the navy population.

The Union navy achieved its Civil War goals only with the assistance of African-American sailors. Filling the manpower gap at a time when the navy desperately needed skilled personnel, African-Americans proved their worth to the Union. Whether fighting on river or sea, African-American sailors demonstrated that courage, loyalty, and ability knew no race.

—*Steven J. Ramold*

See also African-American Soldiers, C.S.A.; Navy, U.S.A..

For further reading:

Canney, Donald L. *Lincoln's Navy: The Ships, Men, and Organization, 1861–1865* (1998).

Quarles, Benjamin. *The Negro in the Civil War* (1989).

Ramold, Steven J. "Valuable Men for Certain Kinds of Duty: African-Americans in the Civil War Navy" (Ph.D. dissertation, 1999).

Valuska, David L. "The Negro in the Union Navy, 1861–1865" (Ph.D. dissertation, 1973).

AFRICAN-AMERICAN SOLDIERS, C.S.A.

Throughout the Civil War, the Confederate government and military were increasingly preoccupied with obtaining new white recruits to fill depleted ranks. At the national level, legislation such as the Conscription Acts of 1862 and 1864 tried to deal with this problem. Within the army measures were implemented to remove whites from regimental support roles such as teamsters, cooks, and musicians, and to detail them to front line duty. Body servants or free blacks often filled the resulting vacancies. Slave labor and conscripted free blacks were also utilized extensively in the Confederate military to perform duties such as building fortifications, expanding river defenses, repairing rail networks, and assisting in the manufacture of armaments. All such measures were designed to free up whites for service in the Confederate army.

The burdens of the Civil War greatly strained the relations between the southern states and their central government. The logistics of fielding and equipping an army became the paramount concern, not just for the national government, but for the state governments as well. Throughout the war the state governments, particularly those most vulnerable to Union invasion, acted according to their individual needs, insisting that their primary obligation was the protection and defense of their citizens, even when that conflicted with Confederate policy. For instance, when Tennessee and Louisiana seceded, their governors saw no other option than to enlist or draft all able bodied men of fighting age, whether white or black, into home guards, militias, and state defense forces. These groups were separate from other state forces incorporated into the Confederate army, and their training and supply were somewhat inferior to that of the Regular Army. Yet it remains that over time Southern states realized that tapping slave and free black populations was the only way to replenish depleted manpower. No specific Confederate law prohibited the practice, but ironically these state actions threatened the very foundation of the Confederacy's reason for existence.

For this reason, the Confederacy found it difficult to assign a meaningful role to slaves and free blacks in the war. Racism and the stigma of slavery were traditions built over centuries, and they continued to dictate white Southerners' perceptions of African-Americans. An extensive legal framework defined African-Americans as property. Although the Confederate government refused to enlist blacks as soldiers, they were often put to other tasks. Measures such as the Negro Musicians Bill in 1863, and the Regimental Cooks Bills of 1862 and 1863, allowed the government to move whites from support functions to the front lines. Going any further in the use of African-Americans was unthinkable to the majority of white Southerners. The Confederate Congress would not even discuss the matter because to contemplate black southern combat soldiers made meaningless for the planter class the very foundation for secession. On the facade, the Confederate Congress—constantly aware of its labor problems—claimed that the issue of black soldiers was not for debate, as they saw this as an affront to the very reason for secession from the Union. Howell Cobb of Georgia, a former member of the Confederate Congress, was so vehemently against the arming of black Southerners that even as the war drew to a close he wrote, "the day you make them soldiers would be the beginning of the end of the revolution."

Nonetheless, there are numerous examples of slaves and free blacks being utilized in the war effort as military support staff. In the early months of the war, some free blacks joined military companies such as Harvey's Scouts (who rode with Nathan Bedford Forrest) and the 3d Georgia Infantry Regiment. In addition, some free blacks from New Orleans also offered their services to the Confederacy. Besides free blacks, slaves also served and

African-American laborers on the James River, Virginia (*National Archives*)

occasionally bore arms as body servants. These were slaves whose prewar career did not generally involve working in the fields, but in the plantation house. Often they grew up with the children of their masters and had close, though often ambivalent, relationships with them, and so when the war began it was a natural consequence for them to accompany their masters into the military whether they wanted to or not.

Several of the Confederate state governments specifically targeted their black population for use in state defense. With its pivotal position as an inland gateway to the Deep South, Tennessee would be a prime target for the Union. The people of Tennessee were divided in their loyalties, as the eastern half of the state generally supported the Union, while elites in the western half supported the Confederacy. Shortly after its secession from the Union, Tennessee's state legislature tried to meet the problems of defense by authorizing Governor Isham G. Harris, "to accept into the armed forces of the state all male persons of color." The number of recruits that were obtained is not known, but some of these men did apply for and receive black Confederate pensions in the postwar period.

The state of Louisiana, with its own unique geographic, social, and governmental systems, held the largest Creole and free black communities in the South. Here, Governor Thomas O. Moore in 1861, and his successor, Henry W. Allen in 1864, specifically authorized the use of black Southerners as soldiers. Although Moore was thinking of their use as more of a supportive role, he did allow the organization of the Native Guards in 1861, but Allen went so far as to make a request to the Confederate secretary of war James A. Seddon, for the immediate organization of black regiments. Best known of these were the Native Guards, a regiment that was both officered and manned by the free black population of New Orleans. This occurred prior to the official enlistment of blacks in the Union army. Ironically, following the fall of New Orleans in 1862, many of the members of the Native Guards would join the Union army as part of the early Northern efforts to recruit blacks.

Another example of the utilization of black Southerners in the early part of the war can be seen in South Carolina. South Carolina's planter class were uncompromising on the crucial issues of slavery and states rights, but this did not deter groups of slaves and free blacks from participating in that state's regiments. Members from the state's free black communities in Columbia and Charleston petitioned Governor Francis

Pickens to allow them to "render service where we can be most useful." Pickens ordered one such group to assist with the artillery barrage of Fort Sumter after they said "they would be ready whenever called upon to assist in preparing the State a defense against any action that may be brought against her." However, as in Tennessee, South Carolina also encompassed geographical and cultural distinctions where the influence of low and upcountry elites impinged on governmental policy towards the state's black population.

A more serious attempt to directly enlist black Southerners into the army as soldiers occurred in January 1864. Major General Patrick Cleburne, an Irish-born division commander in the Army of Tennessee, circulated a document calling for the enlistment of slaves. Cleburne proposed "that we immediately commence training a large reserve of the most courageous of our slaves, and further that we guarantee freedom within a reasonable time to every slave in the South who shall remain true to the Confederacy in this war." Cleburne stressed the Confederacy's need for additional troops, and added: "[w]e can only get a sufficiency [of numbers] by making the negro share the danger and hardships of the war."

While Jefferson Davis would not consider the plan at that time, military necessity eventually ended his reluctance. In late 1864, Secretary of State Judah Benjamin also called for the enlistment of slaves, and in January 1865, Robert E. Lee added his support for the immediate employment of black soldiers. "We must decide," the general wrote, "whether slavery shall be extinguished by our enemies and the slave be used against us, or use them ourselves at the risk of the effects which may be produced upon our social institutions."

On 13 March 1865, the Confederate Congress finally authorized the recruitment of "Negro Soldiers." In exchange for their "loyal service," a loosely defined emancipation would be their reward with the defeat of the Union. In Richmond, Majors James W. Pegram and Thomas P. Turner were the first to recruit the city's slaves into military companies. A Richmond newspaper noted in late March that the black recruits "move with evident pride and satisfaction to themselves" and that "the knowledge of the military art they already exhibit was something remarkable." During the retreat from Richmond, some of the black soldiers were involved in a rear guard action on 5 April, near Paineville, while others were seen constructing earthworks the following day. The remnants of these companies were evidently disbanded or captured before the final capitulation, as the only known blacks listed on the Appomattox surrender rolls are a handful of cooks, teamsters, and musicians.

When considering the issue of African-American soldiers in Confederate service, the question of numbers remains inconclusive, a natural consequence when considering that many Southern records were lost or destroyed at the war's conclusion. Aside from the service of the Louisiana Native Guards at the outbreak of the war, and the several companies of African-Americans organized in Richmond in March 1865, there is little documentation indicating that blacks served as combat soldiers in southern armies in anything but the most negligible numbers. Their main role in the Confederate military was that of support staff, servants, cooks, teamsters, and musicians. The most contentious question of why black Southerners might support the Confederacy remains a riddle. The majority of these participants were either conscripted, coerced, or in a few cases saw the war as a means of economic advancement. Yet, perhaps the answer in part also lies in the same motives of many Southern whites who went to war. They wanted to protect their families and their communities. In the case of some body servants, there was the paternalistic relationship between master and slave. But obviously absent from such motives was any loyalty to the Confederacy or to its peculiar institution.

—*Frank E. Deserino*

See also African-American Sailors; African-American Suffrage; Cleburne, Patrick Ronayne; Slaves; United States Colored Troops.

For further reading:
Berlin, Ira, ed. *Freedom: A Documentary History of Emancipation, 1861-1867. Series II: The Black Military Experience* (1982).
Brewer, James H. *The Confederate Negro: Virginia's Craftsmen and Military Laborers, 1861-1865* (1969).
Durden, Robert F. *The Gray and the Black* (1972).
Helsley, Alexia J. *South Carolina's African-American Confederate Pensioners 1923-1925* (1998).
Jordan, Ervin L., Jr. *Black Confederates and Afro-Yankees in Civil War Virginia* (1995).
McPherson, James M. *The Negro's Civil War: How American Negroes Felt and Acted During the War for the Union* (1965).
Trudeau, Noah Andre. *Like Men of War: Black Troops in the Civil War, 1862-1865* (1998).

AFRICAN-AMERICAN SOLDIERS, U.S.A.
See United States Colored Troops

AFRICAN-AMERICAN SUFFRAGE

The issue of extending to African-Americans the right to vote tested the egalitarian meaning of the Civil War. In 1861 less than one-tenth of African-Americans in the North lived in states where they could legally vote. These states were Maine, Massachusetts, New Hampshire, New York (where a discriminatory $250 property qualification applied), Rhode Island, and Vermont. Exclusion from the ballot box generally reflected a belief, reiterated by the Supreme Court in its decision in the *Dred Scott* Case (1857), that African-Americans could not be citizens because of inherent racial differences. Abolitionists had persistently challenged this idea, arguing not only that all men should be free but that they should enjoy freedom equally—that is, without civil or political disabilities based on race. Even with the emergence of a sectional northern Republican Party in the 1850s, egalitarians made little headway. While Republican legislators in several states pushed to equalize suffrage, popular referenda in the decade before the war in New York, Michigan, Iowa, and Wisconsin defeated their proposals by large margins. Only in areas settled by New Englanders did the suffrage issue fail to divide Republican voters seriously.

When African-Americans served the Union cause during the war as guides, scouts, cooks, teamsters, laborers, nurses, and, above all, as soldiers, they challenged existing stereotypes about their race. Wartime hostility toward the South and its institutions also diminished open defenses of racism by moderate Republicans, especially as captured African-American soldiers faced execution or enslavement at Confederate hands. Abolitionists meanwhile argued that the North's wartime suffering would be meaningless unless the nation repented the sin of slavery and pledged itself to freedom and equality for all. Thus, wartime conditions facilitated moves toward not only emancipation of Southern slaves but also equal rights.

In 1862 Attorney General Edward Bates delivered an opinion that contradicted the *Dred Scott* decision by declaring that African-Americans were citizens. The right to establish qualifications to vote, however, rested with the individual states. Although some abolitionists doubted that newly freed slaves were prepared to vote, Wendell Phillips and Frederick Douglass argued that the freedmen were no less capable than the impoverished immigrants currently entering the electorate in the North; possession of the ballot would be essential for blacks to achieve equal access to education and economic opportunity. Because white Southerners were unlikely to embrace African-American suffrage, abolitionists and their radical Republican allies favored the idea that the Southern states, by seceding, had lost their rights as states, which would permit Congress to regulate their suffrage until these rights were regained.

In 1864 radicals, led principally by Senator Charles Sumner, tested sentiment in Congress on African-American suffrage. Attempts to remove the term *white* from the suffrage provisions for Montana Territory and the District of Columbia went down to defeat. Democrats, recognizing the ability of the race issue to divide Republicans, stressed it incessantly. They accused Republicans of pursuing equality to perpetuate their own political power and predicted a race war endangering the Republic if equal rights prevailed. Acknowledging the existence of prejudice, President Abraham Lincoln's Ten Per Cent Plan for reconstruction permitted white Southerners who pledged future loyalty to the United States to reorganize state governments. Petitioned by representatives of New Orleans's large free black community, however, Lincoln privately inquired of Louisiana governor Michael Hahn whether African-Americans who had served in the Union army or owned property might not vote. Even a qualified suffrage for African-Americans, however, was anathema to most Southern whites.

Radical Republicans, deploring Lincoln's deference to former Rebels, articulated a different approach to Reconstruction in the Wade-Davis Bill. Fearful of the race issue, its sponsors proposed granting political power to whites who had never supported the Confederacy, but not African-Americans. Lincoln's pocket veto of the Wade-Davis Bill angered radicals, some of whom joined a movement to secure a more radical Republican candidate for president in 1864. Wendell Phillips tirelessly toured the country, proclaiming that there could be no peace without justice for African-Americans and that they deserved to participate in a government they defended with their lives. Phillips and other radicals, including Frederick Douglass and Elizabeth Cady Stanton, promoted John C. Frémont as the nominee of a radical Democratic Party. Many abolitionists (including powerful antislavery editors William Lloyd Garrison and Theodore Tilton) refused to abandon Lincoln, however, despite his perceived ideological shortcomings.

At the end of the war, the suffrage issue remained unresolved. Despite Garrison's recommendation that the American Antislavery Society disband upon the passage of the Thirteenth Amendment abolishing slavery, Phillips's supporters within the society voted to continue the quest for equal rights. Radical Republicans in Wisconsin, Minnesota, and Connecticut prepared for referenda to revise their state suffrage provisions to permit African-Americans to vote. Although all would fail, as had the prewar referenda, the war had heightened a partisanship that soon would be harnessed on behalf of African-American suffrage. The nation's ultimate commitment to African-American suffrage in the Fifteenth Amendment (1870), however, would owe as much to political calculations as an acceptance of ideals of equality.

—*Phyllis F. Field*

See also Bates, Edward; Douglass, Frederick; *Dred Scott* Case; Emancipation Proclamation; Freedmen's Bureau; Frémont, John C.; Garrison, William Lloyd; Hahn, Michael; Lincoln's Reconstruction Policy; Phillips, Wendell; Thirteenth Amendment; Wade-Davis Bill.

For further reading:

Dykstra, Robert R. *Bright Radical Star: Black Freedom and White Supremacy on the Hawkeye Frontier* (1993).

McPherson, James M. *The Struggle for Equality: Abolitionists and the Negro in the Civil War and Reconstruction* (1964).

Voegeli, V. Jacque. *Free But Not Equal: The Midwest and the Negro During the Civil War* (1967).

ALABAMA

Alabama was established as a separate territory in 1817 and was admitted into the Union as the twenty-second state in 1819. By 1820 Alabama's population was more than 125,000, including about 500 free African-Americans. By 1830 there were 300,000 residents, 38 percent of them slaves, and cotton was the principal money crop. Agriculture dominated Alabama, and Mobile was second to only New Orleans as a cotton port. Until the Civil War, domestic politics centered on removal of the Indians, land policy, the banking system, and the question of slavery.

The state suffered severely for almost a decade in the economic depression that followed the panic of 1837. During the late 1840s and 1850s efforts were made to create a more modern, industrialized economy. Coal and iron were boated out of the mountains because Alabama, lagging far behind other states, had only 165 miles of railroad track as late as 1852. By 1860 that had increased to 743 miles; however, the mountain regions remained unpenetrated, and the northern and southern portions of the state were not linked for lack of a standard gauge. In the mineral district before the Civil War, only seventeen forges, nine primitive furnaces, and one crude rolling mill were engaged in ironmaking. Until the Civil War, the vast majority of investment remained in cotton and slaves. The population was almost 1 million, with nearly half that number African-American. All but 5 percent of the population lived in rural areas.

By the late 1850s, slavery and other sectional issues had long been important in Alabama politics; however, the state was still secure in the Union. Andrew Barry Moore, a moderate Democrat, was elected governor without any opposition and was reelected two years later. A series of events, beginning with John Brown's raid in Virginia in October 1859, drove Alabamians toward the radical Southern rights stance of William Lowndes Yancey.

On 24 February 1860, the legislature called for a state convention in the event of a Republican presidential victory. Within a year, events on the national level made secession inevitable in Alabama. Alabama delegates walked out of the Democratic National Convention at Charleston when supporters of Illinois senator Stephen A. Douglas would not accept a platform protecting slavery in the territories. The presidential campaign of 1860 brought Alabama to the point of secession. In the general election, Kentuckian John C. Breckinridge won the state with 48,000 votes. Union-minded Democrats supported Douglas, who received 13,000 votes, and Whigs cast 27,000 votes for Constitutional Union candidate, John Bell of Tennessee.

With Lincoln's election, Governor Moore—now a secessionist—called for the election of delegates to a 7 January 1861 state convention. Moore sent commis-sioners to other slave states to counter Union supporters or "cooperationists" who advocated pan-Southern action. Voters elected a clear majority of "immediate secessionists" (fifty-four) over cooperationists (forty-six). The cooperationists, largely from northern Alabama, were vulnerable to invasion in the event of war, and their livelihood did not center on slavery.

At the state convention—under the leadership of Yancey and Thomas Hill Watts—secessionists claimed that Alabama, as a sovereign state, had the right to secede. On 11 January, Alabama was voted out of the Union, followed by a petition inviting other Southern states to send delegates to a 4 February convention in Montgomery. The vote on the secession ordinance was sixty-nine to thirty-one. Many cooperationists refused to sign the official copy of the secession ordinance, though most of them recognized secession as legal and binding. Among farmers from the north part of the state, there was talk of seceding from Alabama and inviting neighboring citizens in Georgia and Tennessee to join them in forming a free state under the Indian name of Nickajack.

By the end of January, six lower states had cut their ties with the Union. Montgomery hosted the convention that created the Confederate States of America. It was chosen due largely to its central location and convenient railroad and river facilities. Thirty-seven delegates began secret deliberation on 4 February. Within days a provisional constitution was drafted and a vice president, Alexander Hamilton Stephens of Georgia, and a president, Jefferson Davis of Mississippi, were elected.

The Provisional Constitution provided that until otherwise decided Montgomery would serve as the capital of the Confederacy. Yet Montgomery's inadequate accommodations and hot climate were a source of constant complaint, and Virginia's entry into the Confederacy soon prompted a move to Richmond. Some argued for the move on the grounds that Virginia's security and consequently that of the entire Confederacy was dependent on situating the capital in Richmond. Others concluded that Virginia would be the scene of crisis, and the government needed to be there to offer logistical, as well as political support for Virginians who would bear the brunt of campaigning.

Montgomery nevertheless remained important. The city was a stop on a major railroad line, and thousands of troops passed through each month. The city included seven military hospitals and served as a major supply depot.

Confederate volunteers in Alabama, like those in other Southern states, anticipated a short war. Loyalists in the hill country who took a position of neutrality were threatened in those counties that lagged in filling their ranks of volunteers for the Confederacy. To deal with this, the state legislature passed a conscription act in

1862 and appropriated several million dollars for military operations and for the support of the families of soldiers. As a result, neutralists hardened into Unionists and many joined the Union army. Historians disagree on the extent of Unionism in Alabama, but statistics show that 2,578 white Alabamians joined the Union army. Otherwise, 75,000 whites served in the Confederate army. In addition, 10,000 African-American Alabamians fought for the Union.

Alabama saw its share of fighting toward the end of the Civil War, including the largest naval engagement of the war in Mobile Bay in August 1864. Mobile was the leading port on the Gulf Coast after the fall of New Orleans in 1862. Blockade runners shipped cotton to Havana in exchange for military supplies and other items. Union admiral David Glasgow Farragut began his attack in Mobile Bay running past Forts Morgan and Gaines on 5 August. All but one of eighteen Union gunboats passed safely into the bay, leading to Fort Morgan's capitulation on 23 August. Though Mobile Bay was under Union control, Mobile's citizens held out until the end of the war and made it the last coastal city in the Confederacy to fall. Two of the last land battles of the Civil War took place at Fort Blakeley and Spanish Fort on the eastern side of Mobile Bay, between 27 March and 9 April 1865.

In early 1865, Union general James Harrison Wilson attacked the Confederacy's second largest arsenal in Selma, Alabama. Selma produced cannon, cartridges, shovels, uniforms, and other war materiel in machine shops, iron mills, and cotton mills. By the time of Wilson's attack, Confederate opposition consisted mainly of old men and boys, and Federal troops easily took control of the town, setting fire to its public buildings, storehouses, business district, and more than a hundred private homes. Selma was left with more damage than all other Alabama towns combined. On 4 May 1865, General Richard Taylor surrendered remaining Confederate forces at Citronell.

Following the collapse of the Confederacy and the refusal of the state legislature to ratify the Fourteenth Amendment to the U.S. Constitution, Alabama in 1867 was placed under military rule. In 1868 the state ratified a new constitution that protected the civil rights of African-Americans, and Alabama was readmitted to the Union. Moreover, the Civil War dealt a mortal blow to Alabama's feudal society. Planters were forced to substitute tenant farming or peonage for slavery; however, they never recovered completely from the emancipation of their labor force. Soybeans and cattle supplanted the production of cotton.

From 1868 to 1874 Alabama was in political turmoil. To many whites, the Reconstruction period was tragic; to many blacks, it was a period of opportunity and hope. Among white Alabamians, a struggle ensued between those who defied the notion of African-Americans having political rights and power and those willing to cooperate with African-Americans and their Northern allies. African-Americans demanded access to education and were given it, but most whites insisted that schools be racially separate. Although African-Americans participated in the constitutional conventions and in the state legislatures, their political power was not as strong as that of African-Americans in South Carolina, Mississippi, or Louisiana. In 1874 the white Democrats of Alabama, most of whom had been supporters of the Confederacy, regained control of the state political machinery. African-Americans were left with little political power until the Civil Rights movement of the 1960s.

—*Kevin M. Levin*

See also Army of Mobile; Blakely, Alabama, Battle of; Mobile Bay; Mobile Campaign; Selma, Alabama; Wilson's Selma Raid.

For further reading:
Fleming, Walter L. *Civil War and Reconstruction in Alabama* (1905).
McMillan, Malcolm C. *Constitutional Development in Alabama, 1798–1901* (1955).
Rogers, William W., Robert D. Ward, and Leah R. Atkins. *Alabama: The History of a Deep South State* (1994).

ALABAMA CLAIMS

During the Civil War, in addition to procuring certain supplies for the war effort, the Confederate States of America also purchased ships in Great Britain and then took those ships to other ports for outfitting as warships. Confederate purchasing agent James D. Bulloch was the most successful at this practice, and two of the ships he purchased, the CSS *Alabama* and the CSS *Florida*, did serious damage to the U.S. merchant fleet during the war. Other vessels purchased later, like the CSS *Shenandoah*, also caused serious losses to U.S. shippers.

While these purchases were taking place, the U.S. minister to Great Britain, Charles Francis Adams, protested vigorously to the British government that allowing such practices to take place violated British neutrality in the conflict. At times the British government seemed to agree and even made an unsuccessful attempt to prevent the *Alabama* from leaving Great Britain. Off and on throughout the war, however, the Confederacy was able to procure such ships, and the damage to U.S. shipping continued.

During the war, Adams made a formal claim to the British government that the United States should be paid for damage to American shipping as a result of the activities of the *Alabama*. As a result of that claim, which was rejected, all subsequent claims made by the United States for damages inflicted by all of the other British-built ships have generally been lumped together as the "*Alabama* claims."

After the war, the British government of Lord Palmerston refused to negotiate the continued claims of the United States and refused to submit the matter to arbitration by neutral parties. Many other men in the British government, however, saw such a stand as short-sighted. They argued that Palmerston's position established the precedent that neutral powers like the United States could allow Britain's enemies to purchase warships in those neutral ports. To give weight to that argument, the U.S. Congress made it plain after the war that such purchases would be allowed.

The British government changed in 1866, and President Andrew Johnson's secretary of state, William Henry Seward, immediately opened negotiations with Great Britain regarding the *Alabama* claims. When the two governments reached an agreement in 1868, Seward's efforts were thwarted in the Senate by the chairman of the Senate Committee on Foreign Relations, Charles Sumner. Sumner argued that the monetary settlement was not large enough (he demanded that since so much long-term damage had been done to American merchant shipping that the British government should pay for half the cost of the Civil War) and that the British should include an apology in the agreement. Sumner's ultimate goal apparently was to secure Canada in payment of the *Alabama* claims.

The incoming Ulysses S. Grant administration took up the negotiations. Grant's secretary of state, Hamilton Fish, opened negotiations with British emissary John Rose in 1870. The British government still believed that it was to its advantage to settle with the United States and, as part of a settlement, to have a statement agreed upon by both countries that neutrality would prevent either nation from allowing the enemies of either from outfitting warships in the neutral country.

Fish and Rose reached an agreement in early 1871 to submit the *Alabama* claims as well as other matters of dispute between the two countries to a commission of five representatives from each country. Thrown into the negotiations were New England fishing rights along the Canadian coast and U.S. navigation rights on the St. Lawrence River. The joint commission negotiated the Treaty of Washington in the spring of 1871, and the treaty was ratified by the U.S. Senate on 24 May 1871.

The Treaty of Washington contained a statement of regret from the British government regarding the damage done by the Confederate ships, and a statement by both nations that neither side would allow such an occurrence in the future. The treaty also allowed for temporary fishing rights for New Englanders and navigation of the St. Lawrence. As for the monetary claims regarding the damage done by the *Alabama* and the other ships, the claims were submitted to a commission of one representative from the United States, one from Great Britain, and one each from Switzerland, Brazil, and Italy. Charles Francis Adams was the American representative. Caleb Cushing, former U.S. attorney general, served as counsel for the United States regarding legal matters of the settlement. The commission reached an agreement that the United States should be paid $15,500,000 in gold for damages caused by the Confederate ships. The British made the payment in 1873, thus ensuring that the United States as a neutral power would never give material aid to enemies of Great Britain.

—*David S. Heidler and Jeanne T. Heidler*

See also Adams, Charles Francis; *Alabama*, CSS; Bulloch, James Dunwody; Diplomacy, U.S.A.; *Florida*, CSS; *Shenandoah*, CSS.

For further reading:
Cook, Adrian. *The Alabama Claims: American Politics and Anglo-American Relations, 1865–1872* (1975).

ALABAMA, CSS
Confederate commerce raider

On 1 August 1861, Confederate purchasing agent James D. Bulloch contracted for a ship with John Laird & Sons at Liverpool, England. First identified as Hull No. 290, she was launched on 15 May 1862 as the *Enrica*. United States diplomats in Britain learned she was intended for the Confederacy and brought pressure on the British government to impound her, but Bulloch managed to get her to sea on 30 July, before she could be seized. Rendezvousing with two other ships, she received her ordnance and other supplies at the Portuguese island of Terceira in the Azores. There her captain, Raphael Semmes, joined her and on 24 August placed her into commission as the *Alabama*.

A sleek, three-masted, bark-rigged sloop of oak with a copper hull, the *Alabama* was probably the finest cruiser of her class in the world. She weighed 1,050 tons and was 220 feet in length overall, 31 feet 9 inches in beam, and 14 feet in depth of hold. She had a screw propeller that could be detached so that she might make faster speed under sail alone. She could make 13 knots under steam and sail and 10 knots under sail. Captain Semmes characterized her as "a very perfect ship of her class." A well-built vessel, she survived several bad storms, including a hurricane.

The *Alabama* had a fully equipped machine shop to enable her crew to make all ordinary repairs themselves and could carry coal sufficient for eighteen days of continuous steaming. Semmes preferred to rely on sail where possible. In fact, all but about a half dozen of her subsequent captures were taken under sail alone. If able to provision from captured prizes, the *Alabama* could remain at sea a long time.

The *Alabama* mounted eight guns: six 32-pounders in broadside and two pivot-guns (a 7-inch, 110-

The CSS *Alabama*, from an undated print (*Library of Congress*)

pounder rifled Blakeley, and a smoothbore 8-inch, 68-pounder) amidships. She had a 120-man crew and twenty-four officers.

The *Alabama* first cruised in the Azores and took a number of prizes. She then sailed to the Newfoundland Banks where she was also quite successful. Semmes then took her into the Caribbean, where she intercepted and took the *Ariel*, her most important prize. The *Alabama* then sailed to Galveston, Texas, where on 11 January 1863 she lured out, engaged, and then sank the Union warship *Hatteras*.

Captain Semmes then returned the *Alabama* to the West Indies. She next spent several months off the coast of Latin America, where she took additional prizes before sailing for South Africa. Learning that the more powerful U.S. Navy steamer *Vanderbilt* was searching for him, Semmes then took the *Alabama* into the Pacific, hopeful of inflicting serious damage on U.S.-Asian trade. She sailed all the way to India but took few prizes because U.S. merchant captains, having been warned of her presence, stayed in port. Semmes was also experiencing increasing disciplinary problems with his crew, and the ship herself badly needed an overhaul in a modern shipyard.

The *Alabama* sailed to France by way of Cape Town, dropping anchor at Cherbourg on 11 June 1864. Since her commissioning, she had sailed 75,000 miles, taken sixty-six prizes, and sunk a Union warship. Twenty-five Union warships had searched for her, costing the Federal

government over $7 million. Her exploits had also been a considerable boost to Confederate morale.

On 19 June 1864 after the French denied him access to a dry dock, Semmes took the *Alabama* out to engage the Union warship *Kearsarge*, which had taken up position off the harbor. The ensuing battle was one of the most spectacular Civil War naval engagements. Superior Union gunnery, chain armor aboard the *Kearsarge*, and poor cannon powder on the *Alabama* all spelled disaster for the Confederate commerce raider. Having been repeatedly holed, the *Alabama* went down. She suffered forty-one casualties: Nine were killed and twenty wounded in the engagement, and twelve others subsequently drowned.

In 1984 the French navy located the *Alabama*'s resting place. Although she is within French territorial waters, British preservationist groups want the wreck, if raised, to be displayed at Birkenhead where she was built. The United States government had asserted ownership, however, and in 1989 Congress passed the CSS *Alabama* Preservation Act. The fight over the *Alabama* continues.

—*Spencer C. Tucker*

See also Bulloch, James Dunwody; *Kearsarge*, USS; Navy, C.S.A.; Semmes, Raphael.
For further reading:
Robinson, Charles M., III. *Shark of the Confederacy. The Story of the CSS Alabama* (1995).
Semmes, Raphael. *Memoirs of Service Afloat During the War Between the States* (1987).

Silverstone, Paul H. *Warships of the Civil War Navies* (1989).
Sinclair, Arthur. *Two Years on the Alabama* (1895).
Summersell, Charles G. *CSS Alabama: Builder, Captain, and Plans* (1985).
Tucker, Spencer C. *Raphael Semmes and the Alabama* (1996).

ALBEMARLE, CSS

One of the Confederate navy's most successful ironclads, the *Albemarle* played a key role in the capture of Plymouth, North Carolina, on 17–20 April 1864. The *Albemarle*'s contractor was Gilbert Elliott, a nineteen-year-old shipbuilder and engineer. The designer and supervisor of construction was John L. Porter, who had worked on the conversion of the *Merrimack* into the CSS *Virginia*. The *Albemarle* was built in a former cornfield on the Roanoke River at Edwards Ferry, North Carolina. Construction, begun in spring 1863, was painfully slow. The remote yard had to compete with other ironclads for workers, transportation of supplies, and other resources. Elliott scrounged railroad rails and even scrap nuts and bolts to be rolled into armor plate.

The *Albemarle* was 152 feet long, with a beam of 45 feet and a draft of 8 feet. Built of solid 8-by-10 pine timbers, and covered with 4-inch planks and two layers of 2-inch thick iron plating, the vessel was powered by two 200-horsepower engines. Her armament consisted of two 6.4-inch Brooke rifles, mounted at the bow and stern. An 18-foot oak prow, also covered with iron plates, could be used as a ram.

The Confederate navy assigned Commander James W. Cooke to the *Albemarle*. Early in 1864, Brigadier General Robert F. Hoke planned an attack on the nearby Union-held town of Plymouth, and persuaded Cooke to bring the still unfinished *Albemarle* down the river to help him. Hoke surrounded Plymouth on 17 April 1864, and began his attack, which continued the next day. When Cooke ordered the *Albemarle* to cast off late on 17 April, workmen still labored aboard the vessel. The rudder broke during the trip, and the engines broke down, resulting in hours of delay. It was 2:30 A.M. on 19 April when the *Albemarle* reached Plymouth and steered for the Union gunboats, *Miami* and *Southfield*. Commander C. W. Flusser had stretched chains and spars between the two gunboats to snag the *Albemarle* between them. Cooke avoided this trap and rammed the *Southfield*, which sank quickly. The *Albemarle* and the *Miami* dueled at close range until a Federal shell bounced off the *Albemarle*'s armor and exploded on the deck of the *Miami*, killing Flusser. The

Battle between the *Sassacus* and the *Albermarle*, May 1864, from an undated painting (*National Archives*)

Miami and two smaller Union vessels retreated down the river.

Plymouth held out until 10 A.M. on 20 April, when Brigadier General W. H. Wessells surrendered. Perhaps the *Albemarle* was the deciding factor in Hoke's victory, for she had deprived the Federals of the protection of the Union navy's heavy guns while adding her own 100-pounders to Hoke's field artillery. The fall of Plymouth threatened Union control of all of eastern North Carolina. In nearby Washington, the Union garrison looted and set fire to the town before fleeing to New Bern. Hoke followed and began an attack on New Bern in early May.

Cooke and Hole planned to have the *Albemarle* steam to New Bern to help in the attack. On 5 May 1864 Cooke found his way blocked by seven Union gunboats in Albemarle Sound. After a two-and-a-half-hour battle, the *Albemarle* and the Federal flotilla fought to a draw. The combined Union flotilla failed to destroy the ram, but the *Albemarle* was damaged and unable to push past the Union vessels. Hoke was soon ordered to break off his operations and rejoin Lee in Virginia.

The *Albemarle* remained a threat to the Union navy. Lieutenant William B. Cushing was chosen to lead a raid against the ram. Cushing designed a special boom tipped with a torpedo and fitted onto a steam launch. On the night of 27 October 1864 Cushing and his twenty-five men steamed into the Roanoke River and neared the *Albemarle*. At the last minute, a sleeping sentinel was awakened by his barking dog. Cushing came under musket fire from shore, and a bonfire lit to reveal the raiders also showed a protective log boom surrounding the *Albemarle*. Cushing steamed full speed to jump the boat over the boom and detonated the torpedo against the ironclad's hull, sinking her in eight feet of water. Cushing and one other man escaped; two drowned, and the rest were captured.

Thus, the *Albemarle* became the only Confederate ironclad to be destroyed by enemy action—the others were either captured or scuttled to avoid capture. Without the *Albemarle*, Plymouth fell to the Union again on 31 October. The Confederates never again had a chance to regain control of the sounds of North Carolina.

The *Albemarle* was raised in 1865, towed to the Norfolk Navy Yard, and sold at auction in 1867.

—*David A. Norris*

See also Albemarle Sound; Cushing, William Barker; Plymouth, Battle of.
For further reading:
Barrett, John G. *The Civil War in North Carolina* (1963).
Cushing, W. B. "The Destruction of the *Albemarle*." In *Battles and Leaders of the Civil War*, vol. 4.
Elliott, Gilbert. "The First Battle of the Confederate Ram *Albemarle*." In *Battles and Leaders of the Civil War*, vol. 4.
Elliott, Robert G. *Ironclad of the Roanoke* (1994).
Holden, Edgar. "The *Albemarle* and the *Sassacus*." In *Battles and Leaders of the Civil War*, vol. 4.
Official Record. Naval Records. Series I, vols. 9–10.
Still, William N., Jr. *Iron Afloat: The Story of the Confederate Armorclads* (1985).

ALBEMARLE SOUND
(5 May 1864)

Plymouth, North Carolina, was captured on 20 April 1864 by three Confederate brigades under Brigadier General Robert F. Hoke, aided by the CSS *Albemarle*. Hoke intended to follow up his victory by mounting an attack on New Bern, where most of the remaining Union forces in North Carolina were. Commander James W. Cooke, captain of the *Albemarle*, planned to bring his vessel again to help Hoke in the attempt to take New Bern.

Bringing the *Albemarle* to New Bern would be difficult for Cooke. The Rebel ram faced a long trip steaming across the rough waters of the Albemarle, Croatan, and Pamlico sounds. The final leg of the journey was a trip up the Neuse River, dodging Federal obstructions, before joining the fighting at New Bern. Cooke also knew that whatever gunboats could be sent by the Union navy would be waiting for him.

Hoke was already embroiled in the attack on New Bern when the *Albemarle* left Plymouth on 5 May 1864. The ram was accompanied by two smaller steamers, the *Bombshell* and the *Cotton Plant*. The *Bombshell* had been an Erie Canal boat before being added to the Union navy. The vessel had been sunk during the battle of Plymouth, but had been raised and repaired by the Confederates. The *Bombshell* carried coal and supplies, and the *Cotton Plant* towed several launches loaded with soldiers.

Cooke soon learned that his way to New Bern was blocked off Sandy Point, North Carolina, by a force of seven Union vessels under Captain Melancton Smith. Smith had four double-enders, the *Mattabesett*, *Sassacus*, *Wyalusing*, and *Miami*, and three smaller steamers, the *Whitehead*, *Ceres*, and *Commodore Hull*. Although none of Smith's vessels was an ironclad—Union ironclads drew too much water to pass through the inlets along North Carolina's coast—he massed sixty guns against the *Albemarle*'s two.

The *Albemarle* opened fire at about 5 P.M. Cooke's first two shots smashed the *Mattabesset*'s launch, tore through her rigging, and wounded six men. The *Albemarle* then tried to ram the *Sassacus*, but the Confederate ship was difficult to steer and missed. The *Sassacus* unloaded a full broadside at the *Albemarle*, but the shots bounced harmlessly off the ram's armor. Cooke had ordered his tenders to steam upriver to safety; the *Cotton Plant* did, but the *Bombshell* for some reason did not and was captured by the *Sassacus*.

After taking the *Bombshell*, the *Sassacus* was about a mile from the ram. Lieutenant Commander F. A. Roe

ordered the *Sassacus* to run full steam to ram the *Albemarle*. The *Sassacus* struck the *Albemarle* with a great crash that threatened to capsize the ram. The *Sassacus's* bow remained entangled with the *Albemarle*. The Rebel gunners fired a 100-pounder shot that tore through the *Sassacus*, exploding her starboard boiler and filling the ship's interior with scalding steam. The *Sassacus* finally parted from the *Albemarle* and drifted downstream without steam power, continuing to fire at the *Albemarle* until out of range.

The fighting continued until about 7:30 P.M., although none of the Federal fleet engaged the *Albemarle* as aggressively as the *Sassacus*. Cooke then steered for Plymouth. The *Albemarle* had taken many hits from the Union vessels, had run out of fuel, and had suffered damage to her steering. Her stern Brooke rifle was broken off at the muzzle. The smokestack was torn with so many shot holes that it could not provide enough draft for the engines to work efficiently. Bacon, lard, and butter had to be used as fuel to get up enough steam for the *Albemarle* to return to Plymouth.

Although Smith failed to capture the *Albemarle*, his flotilla prevented her from reaching New Bern to join Hoke. At any rate, news soon reached Plymouth that Hoke had been ordered to break off his attack on New Bern and return with his men to Virginia to join Robert E. Lee's army, which was facing a spring offensive.

The *Albemarle* remained a threat to the Union navy until she was sunk at her moorings in Plymouth in a raid led by Lieutenant William B. Cushing on 27 October 1864. With the *Albemarle* gone, the Federals once again took control of the sound and the region around it. The smokestack of the *Albemarle*, bearing holes from the battle of 5 May, is on display at the North Carolina Museum of History in Raleigh.

—*David A. Norris*

See also *Albemarle*, CSS.

For further reading:

Elliott, Robert G. *Ironclad of the Roanoke* (1994).
Holden, Edgar. "The 'Albemarle' and the 'Sassacus.'" In *Battles and Leaders of the Civil War*, vol. 4.
Nichols, Roy F., ed. "Fighting in North Carolina Waters." *North Carolina Historical Review* (1963).
Official Records. Naval Records Series I:9.
Still, William N., Jr. *Iron Afloat: The Story of the Confederate Armorclads* (1985).

ALBERT, PRINCE
(1819–1861)

Royal consort to Queen Victoria

As Queen Victoria's husband and advisor, Prince Albert played a significant role in bringing the *Trent* Affair to a peaceful resolution. Asked by his wife to read and emend a draft of the British Cabinet's demand for redress from the American government, Albert softened its wording. His emendations probably did not prove decisive in preventing the outbreak of war; nonetheless, they made British demands easier for the Americans to swallow.

Born on 26 August 1819 at Rosenau, his father's residence near Coburg in present-day Germany, Albert was the second son of Duke Ernest of Saxe-Coburg-Gotha, and Louise, daughter of Duke Augustus of Saxe-Gotha-Altenburg. Starting in 1836, King Leopold I of Belgium arranged several meetings between his nephew Albert and his niece, Princess Victoria of England. After several elaborately staged encounters, Victoria grew enamored of Albert. In 1840 Albert and Victoria, now Queen Victoria, were married in London.

Albert's official and unofficial position in Britain proved difficult to settle, particularly as Britain had never before had a prince consort. The government could not decide whether Albert was merely a private person who had married the queen or whether it should recognize him as a public figure with public duties of his own. Many British politicians sought to limit what they saw as a foreign influence on the queen, while others advocated that the talents of the well-educated prince could contribute to the public good. Albert's personality—intelligent, disciplined, ambitious, and serious—rubbed many British acquaintances the wrong way. His interest in administrative efficiency and desire to expand the role of the monarchy antagonized British statesmen who saw him as an interloper. As a foreign prince from a minor German state, Albert never enjoyed much popularity in the country at large. Not until 1857 would an act of Parliament officially make Albert the prince consort, thereby recognizing his position as a public figure and the queen's advisor.

Very close in private life, Victoria and Albert formed an intimate political partnership. Although Albert was better educated, Victoria often possessed a better understanding of the British mood. While Victoria acted as the queen, Albert served as her private secretary and main advisor. Albert had many interests and exerted his influence in a number of areas (for instance, he took the lead in organizing the Great Exhibition of 1851). In particular, he constantly advised Victoria on foreign policy. It was in this capacity that he played an important role in the American Civil War.

On 27 November 1861 the British mail steamer *Trent* reached Southampton, England, bearing news of its famous encounter with the USS *San Jacinto*. Anticipating that this type of crisis would arise, Prime Minister Lord Palmerston had already consulted the law officers of the Crown about whether the Federals could seize the Confederate commissioners from a British vessel. The law officers had described such an act as a violation of international law. Nevertheless, Palmerston invited them to deliver their opinion again at a Cabinet meeting on 29 November. Presented with this legal opinion, the Cabinet decided to demand an apology and the restoration of the Confederate commissioners. If the U.S. government refused, the British would recall Lord Lyons, their minister in Washington, D.C.

The Cabinet reconvened on 30 November to write the official dispatch that Lyons would give to Henry Seward, the American secretary of state. The fourteen members of the Cabinet who attended the meeting offered a number of revisions to the draft submitted by Lord John Russell, the foreign secretary. That night, Russell forwarded a new draft of the dispatch to Queen Victoria for her comments. Victoria entrusted the draft to Albert, who had just fallen ill with typhoid fever. Initially, the *Trent* Affair had outraged the prince consort. Given time to consider the matter, however, he concluded that Britain probably would not attain its ends by threatening the United States. Writing in the Queen's name, Albert jotted down a note to the Cabinet, in which he described the Cabinet draft as "somewhat meagre." Borrowing the idea from a *London Times* editorial, Albert advised that the dispatch to the United States express the hope that "the American captain [of the USS *San Jacinto*] did not act under instructions, or, if he did, that he misapprehended them." Albert hoped that by framing the communication in this way, the British government would allow the United States to back down without losing face. Both Palmerston and Russell agreed that softening the dispatch in this manner would prove useful and make British demands more palatable. Having amended the dispatch accordingly, the Cabinet sent it to Lyons.

It is unlikely that Albert's revisions to the British note prevented war between the United States and Great Britain. Other members of the Cabinet also had a hand in softening the dispatch. Russell, for instance, advised Lyons to avoid menacing Seward. Nevertheless, Albert's dramatic intervention had a palpable impact. After reading the British dispatch, Seward told Lyons that its "courteous and friendly" wording would make it easier for him to convince the American Cabinet and public to accept British demands.

After writing his note, Albert confessed he felt so weak that he could barely hold his pen. He never wrote another political memorandum. His illness took a turn for the worse, and he declined precipitously. On 14 December 1861, he died at Windsor.

—*Hubert F. Dubrulle*

See also Adams, Charles Francis; Diplomacy, U.S.A.; Great Britain; Lyons, Richard Bickerton Pemell; *Trent* Affair.

For further reading:
Bennett, Daphne. *King without a Crown* (1983).
Bolitho, Hector. *Albert, Prince Consort* (1964).
Hobhouse, Hermione. *Prince Albert, His Life and Work* (1983).
James, Robert Rhodes. *Albert, Prince Consort: A Biography* (1983).
Martin, Theodore. *The Life of His Royal Highness the Prince Consort* (1880).
Pound, Reginald. *Albert: A Biography of the Prince Consort* (1973).
Weintraub, Stanley. *Uncrowned King: The Life of Prince Albert* (1997).

ALCOTT, LOUISA MAY
(1832–1888)
Author

Best known as the author of the classic *Little Women* (1868), Louisa May Alcott incorporated the Civil War into her writing in numerous ways. The daughter of Bronson Alcott, Louisa was reared in Concord, Massachusetts, where the Hawthornes were good friends and Henry David Thoreau was one of her teachers.

Alcott began publishing in literary and women's magazines before she turned twenty. Eventually she graduated to such respected journals as *The Atlantic Monthly* and *The Commonwealth*. In addition to her stories and articles about domesticity, she created mystery thrillers under pseudonyms such as A. M. Barnard, and contributed regularly to magazines for children such as *The Little Pilgrim*, *Youth's Companion*, *Our Young Folks*, and *Merry's Museum*, which she edited for a time in the late 1860s.

Not surprisingly given her background, Alcott was sympathetic to the abolitionist cause. After John Brown was hanged for his attack on Harper's Ferry, she published a poem in the abolitionist newspaper *The Liberator* entitled "With a Rose, That Bloomed on the Day of John Brown's Martyrdom." As befitting a member of the reform-minded, activist New England elite, she contributed to the Union war effort by sewing uniforms and acting in amateur theatricals to raise money for the United States Sanitary Commission. She became a nurse late in 1862 at the Union Hotel Hospital in Georgetown, just in time to help receive the casualties from the battle of Fredericksburg. After a few weeks, she developed typhoid and was rushed back to Concord. Her active participation in the Civil War was over (although she joined the League of Loyal Women) and she would be a semi-invalid for the rest of her life.

Alcott spent the next several years writing books, articles, and stories about the Civil War. She placed some of her domestic thrillers in Civil War settings, but much better known were the books she published under her own name. She reworked letters she had written while serving at the hospital into a series of stories featuring a character called Nurse Tribulation Periwinkle. These were collected in the book *Hospital Sketches* in 1863. More war stories followed in *On Picket Duty, and Other Tales*, and in incidental pieces she wrote for adult, as well as juvenile, magazines. One of her wartime stories, "Nelly's Hospital," appeared just as the war ended in a new children's periodical called *Our Young Folks*. It told the story of a little girl who, animated by sympathy for her wounded brother, decides to create her own hospital in which she will treat all the "wounded" animals she finds in the neighborhood. Aided by the gardener's son, she gathers mice, spiders, birds, and insects into her "U.S. Sanitary Commission" wagon and nurses them back to health. "Nelly's Hospital" captured perfectly the ways in which Civil War–era children incorporated the war into their own lives through play and support for family members in the army.

The same determination to show the domestic side of the Civil War appeared in Alcott's most famous work, *Little Women*. Although its account of Meg, Jo, Beth, and Amy ranged far beyond the Civil War home front—linking, as one modern critic argues, "the cause of domestic reform to patriotism and abolition"—it also offered a moving portrayal of a Northern family whose comfortable lives have been disrupted by the patriarch's absence. The girls make do with sparse Christmases and restricted opportunities, and Mrs. March busies herself with long hours of work for the local branch of the Sanitary Commission. In an early scene that reflected one of the realities of the Civil War home front, the family huddles near a fire for the ceremonial reading of a letter from Mr. March. Such letters were full of news about camp life, the next campaign, hopeful assurances that the war would soon be over, and earnest advice from absent fathers. "Very few letters written in those hard times were not touching, especially those which fathers sent home," wrote Alcott.

Alcott's chief contribution to the Civil War effort did not come from her brief stint as an army nurse. Rather, it came in the form of her deep understanding of the ways that the war affected every element of life on the Northern home front. Never out of print since its publication, *Little Women* remains one of the most telling portrayals of the Civil War experience of Northern families.

—*James Marten*

For further reading:
Alcott, Louisa May. *Little Women* (1868–1869).
Elbert, Sarah. *A Hunger for Home: Louisa May Alcott and "Little Women"* (1984).
Saxton, Martha. *Louisa May: A Modern Biography of Louisa May Alcott* (1977).
Stein, Madeleine B. *Louisa May Alcott: A Biography* (1996).

ALDIE, VIRGINIA, BATTLE OF
(17 June 1863)

In June 1863, Robert E. Lee moved the Army of Northern Virginia out of its works near Fredericksburg to begin a second invasion of the North in as many years. Joseph Hooker, chastened by the defeat at Chancellorsville, kept the Army of the Potomac massed across the Rappahannock River at Falmouth until he could discern Lee's plans.

Hooker gave his cavalry commander General Alfred Pleasonton the job of finding out Lee's purpose. Lee needed to postpone such a discovery as long as possible, so he directed General Jeb Stuart's cavalry to screen the army as it headed north. Pleasonton, emboldened by his surprise of Stuart at Brandy Station on 9 June, undertook his probing with enthusiasm. Stuart, still stinging from Brandy Station, saw his assignment of shielding Lee's army as a way to redeem himself. The result was a series of violent cavalry clashes in the third week of June, beginning at Aldie, Virginia.

Lee wanted to get the bulk of his army west of the Blue Ridge as quickly as possible. On his right, James Longstreet's I Corps trudged north from Culpeper toward Snicker's Gap. Stuart also rambled north, east of Longstreet, between the Northern and Southern armies. He deployed Beverly Robertson, Fitz Lee, and W. F. H. "Rooney" Lee's brigades (this last commanded by John Chambliss in the stead of the wounded Lee) across a broad front. On 17 June, part of Fitz Lee's brigade commanded by Colonel Thomas Munford was scouting near Aldie. Munford posted pickets outside the town and then led the bulk of the troopers to forage on the Snicker's Gap road to the west. In the early afternoon, General H. Judson Kilpatrick's brigade, riding ahead of David M. Gregg's division, stumbled into Munford's pickets and began what Alfred Pleasonton described as "a pretty sharp fight."

Thomas Rosser first heard the musket fire back at Aldie. He wheeled the 5th Virginia toward the guns and soon came upon the field where Kilpatrick was driving back the gray pickets. Rosser now did some driving of his own, pushing Kilpatrick back through Aldie and hastily setting up a defensive line. Munford soon returned and managed a skillful mix of charges and retrogrades that badly mauled the persistent Kilpatrick. At the end of four hours, the Rebel line had stalled the Federal advance, but Kilpatrick was being reinforced. Moreover, Stuart, several miles to the west at Middleburg, called Munford back because he was surrounding Alfred Duffié's Rhode Island cavalry regiment there. So Munford pulled away from Aldie in the late afternoon along the Snicker's Gap Road. The Confederates had suffered about 100 casualties; Kilpatrick's brigade, approximately 300, a jolt that gave David Gregg pause and consequently doomed Duffié's Rhode Islanders.

Pleasonton had ordered Alfred Duffié's 1st Rhode Island Cavalry to ride through Thoroughfare Gap toward Middleburg, there to join with Gregg's division, which was supposed to be moving west from Aldie. With Gregg engaged at Aldie, however, Duffié soon found himself alone in a neighborhood teeming with Confederates. He had brushed against Chambliss's pickets as he came through Thoroughfare, so he knew that a Confederate brigade was trailing his rear. Chambliss kept his distance, however, and because Duffié expected to meet Gregg any minute, Duffié was unalarmed. Following his instructions, he swung north and reached Middleburg at 4:00 P.M. Stuart and his staff were in Middleburg, and Stuart was initially surprised by the sudden appearance of Union cavalry. Duffié drove into the town and pushed Stuart out of it, an embarrassment that the Confederate cavalry would avenge with a will. Duffié found himself virtually surrounded in Middleburg with Chambliss and Robertson joined in overwhelming numbers that grew with the arrival of Munford from Aldie. Duffié sent calls for help toward Aldie, but his couriers fell to capture. After suffering three bludgeoning assaults, he extricated himself from the town he had three hours earlier resolved to hold at all costs. Of the 275 men of the 1st Rhode Island, he was able to fight his way out with only 31, fleeing across Little River to the northeast. About 100 of those that Duffié had left behind would eventually make their way back to Union lines, but it remained obvious that Duffié had essentially lost his entire regiment at Middleburg. "I cannot understand Duffié's conduct," said Pleasonton.

On 18 June, Pleasanton belatedly sent Colonel J. Irwin Gregg of the 16th Pennsylvania with a brigade to Duffié's relief at Middleburg. After a heated contest, Gregg gained possession of the town for all of three hours before he responded at 6:00 P.M. to an order to return to Aldie. He had half-executed that order when it was countermanded, so he camped halfway between the two towns. The next day, Gregg again took Middleburg after a violent action that consumed much of the day and cost him about 100 casualties.

Stuart had to pull back toward the Shenandoah, however, as he faced an increasingly determined press by Pleasonton's cavalry. On the morning of 20 June, Pleasonton learned from a captured Confederate that Longstreet had finally moved through Ashby's Gap into the Shenandoah Valley, apparently leaving Stuart alone east of the Blue Ridge. Pleasonton wanted to take his entire corps "and throw it on Stuart's whole force, and cripple it up." Accordingly, on the next day, David Gregg's division pressured Wade Hampton and Beverly Robertson out of their lines at Goose Creek. They retired toward Upperville. Farther north, John Buford threatened to turn Stuart's entire left flank and thus forced Chambliss and "Grumble" Jones to fall back toward Upperville as well, with Buford in pursuit. Thus on 21 June, the last collision of a four-day cavalry contest played out as scattered Union and Confederate forces concentrated at Upperville, the Union intention now being to "cripple up" Stuart as much as it had been to discover Lee's intentions. After putting up a stout resist-

ance, Stuart remained mindful of the need to keep his screen intact, so he pulled back again to stronger positions at Ashby's Gap.

The clashes at Aldie, Middleburg, and Upperville allowed Lee to move north screened as much by the gray cavalry as by the Blue Ridge. Pleasonton, however, was able to tell Hooker that Lee was in the Shenandoah Valley obviously headed for the Potomac and beyond. In the longer view, Stuart was able to persuade Lee to consent to detaching his cavalry from the main Confederate column as it moved into southern Pennsylvania. Aware of Lee's instruction that his cavalry rejoin the army once Hooker also crossed the Potomac, Stuart struck out toward the east in another of his famous raids. This raid, however, would prove more costly to his own army than to the Federals. When Union and Confederate forces collided at Gettysburg, Lee's indispensable cavalry would not be there.

—*David S. Heidler and Jeanne T. Heidler*

See also Cavalry, C.S.A.; Cavalry, U.S.A.; Duffié, Alfred; Gregg, David McMurtrie; Kilpatrick, Hugh Judson; Munford, Thomas Taylor; Pleasonton, Alfred; Rosser, Thomas Lafayette; Stuart, James Ewell Brown.

For further reading:
O'Neill, Robert F. *The Cavalry Battles of Aldie, Middleburg and Upperville: Small but Important Riots, June 10–27, 1863* (1993). Starr, Stephen Z. *The Union Cavalry in the Civil War* (1979–1985).

ALEXANDER, EDWARD PORTER
(1835–1910)
Confederate general

Edward Porter Alexander was born to Leopold Alexander and Sarah Gilbert Alexander in Washington, Georgia. Porter entered the U.S. Military Academy and graduated third of thirty-eight in the class of 1857. During Porter's time as a cadet, Robert E. Lee served as superintendent. Commissioned an engineering officer, Porter taught briefly at the academy before going west to participate in the Mormon expedition. Before reaching Albert Sidney Johnston's army, Porter learned of the termination of the expedition and returned to West Point to teach. During his time at the academy, Alexander participated in a number of weapons' experiments and was charged with developing a flag signal system for the U.S. Army. The system he arrived at would be used by both the Union and Confederacy during the Civil War.

In 1860 Alexander was sent to the Pacific Northwest, where he served briefly in Washington before being sent to San Francisco. While there in early 1861, Alexander heard of the secession of Georgia and resigned his commission. Upon his return east, he accepted a captain's commission in the Confederate engineers.

Alexander's first important assignment in the

E. Porter Alexander (*Library of Congress*)

Confederate Army was to organize and train a Confederate signal service. While still in the process of training his new recruits, he was ordered in July 1861 to report to Major General P. G. T. Beauregard at Manassas Junction, Virginia. Arriving a short time before the beginning of the battle of First Bull Run, Alexander supervised the erection of his signal towers, placed his men, and prepared for battle. During the engagement on 21 July 1861, Porter's signals had a direct impact on the movement of Confederate troops to meet the Northern attack.

During the fall of 1861, Alexander served under Joseph Johnston in northern Virginia as acting chief of artillery. He was also active in intelligence gathering, dealing extensively with spies operating around Washington.

Promoted to major, Alexander was chief of ordnance under Johnston during the early phases of the Peninsula campaign in the spring of 1862. Though charged with distributing weapons and ammunition, he fought at the battle of Williamsburg on 5 May 1862 and was commended by James Longstreet for his actions there.

Continuing as chief of ordnance under Robert E. Lee in the Army of Northern Virginia, Alexander distributed ammunition to the widely dispersed units in preparation for the Seven Days' battles. Most of his work done and

his interest in intelligence gathering unabated, Alexander volunteered to go up in a hot air balloon at Gaines' Mill on 27 June. He ascended several times over the next several days, bringing down valuable information regarding the positions of George McClellan's army.

Still chief of ordnance through the fall of 1862, Alexander was at Second Bull Run and in the invasion of Maryland. Promoted to major in November, Alexander was given an artillery battalion to command. A colonel by the time of the battle of Fredericksburg in December 1862, Alexander had command of the batteries on Marye's Heights and was largely responsible for the resounding Confederate victory.

Not accompanying his corps commander Longstreet to North Carolina in the spring of 1863, Alexander traveled around Joseph Hooker's flank with Stonewall Jackson at Chancellorsville. After the initial attack that pushed back Hooker's lines upon one another and after Jackson had been wounded reconnoitering his lines, Alexander spent the entire night into the following morning finding the right location for the guns to commence the attack at dawn.

After Hooker's retreat, Alexander was fairly inactive, but at the beginning of what would become the Gettysburg campaign, Longstreet gave him command of the I Corps' reserve artillery. Alexander was quite busy during 2 and 3 July at this pivotal battle. On 2 July his artillery supported that part of the I Corps' attack through the Peach Orchard. The following day Alexander would see his greatest test of the war.

Called upon to command the artillery barrage that would attempt to knock out Federal guns in preparation for the charge that would bear George Pickett's name, Alexander gathered as much ammunition as possible, spent the predawn hours of 3 July finding the best locations for his guns, and began the firing at 1:00 P.M. For about half an hour, the two sides exchanged almost continuous fire. Shortly before 1:30, Alexander sent word to Pickett to begin the advance while the artillery still had sufficient ammunition to support the charge. A few minutes later the Union guns slackened, and hoping that perhaps some had been knocked out, Alexander again urged Pickett to hurry. The ill-fated charge failed, largely because the Federal guns were still firmly in place waiting only for the charge to commence.

In the late summer of 1863, Alexander followed Longstreet to Georgia, where he arrived too late to participate at Chickamauga, but served as Longstreet's chief of artillery in the Knoxville campaign and in the Department of East Tennessee in early 1864. Promoted brigadier general in February 1864, Alexander returned with Longstreet to Virginia in the spring of 1864 and served as chief of artillery, I Corps, Army of Northern Virginia, for the remainder of the war. He fought in all the major battles opening Ulysses S. Grant's Virginia campaign. When Grant attempted to move across the James River to assault Petersburg, Alexander was able to move his artillery quickly through the lines and had his guns in place when the main attack commenced.

During the siege of Petersburg, Alexander worked constantly to devise ways to use his artillery effectively from the trenches. He experimented with various types of mortars to some effect. As June wore on, Alexander also became convinced that Union forces were tunneling in an attempt to break the Confederate lines. Before acting on this belief, however, he was hit in the arm by a sharpshooter. As he departed to convalesce, he informed Lee of his suspicion, and unsuccessful efforts were made to thwart the Union plan. Upon recovery, Alexander returned to the army, primarily supervising the defense of Richmond along the James River. He joined the retreat of the Army of Northern Virginia in April 1865 and surrendered at Appomattox Court House.

After the war, Alexander engaged in various pursuits. He served briefly as a college professor before devoting most of the rest of his life to different business ventures, including one in the railroad industry. He became a wealthy planter on islands off the coast of South Carolina but spent much of his time in Savannah, Georgia. He also wrote, most notably, a memoir of the war that became a classic military analysis of Confederate successes and failures.

—*David S. Heidler and Jeanne T. Heidler*

See also Artillery; Balloons; Chancellorsville, Battle of; Fredericksburg, Battle of; Gettysburg, Battle of; Petersburg Campaign.

For further reading:

Alexander, Edward Porter. *Fighting for the Confederacy: The Personal Recollections of General Edward Porter Alexander* (1989).

———. *Military Memoirs of a Confederate: A Critical Narrative* (1907).

Golay, Michael. *To Gettysburg and Beyond: The Parallel Lives of Joshua Lawrence Chamberlain and Edward Porter Alexander* (1994).

Klein, Maury. *Edward Porter Alexander* (1971).

ALEXANDRIA, LOUISIANA, DESTRUCTION OF
(May 1864)

Situated in central Louisiana on the Red River opposite Pineville, Alexandria suffered almost total devastation during Nathaniel Banks's Red River campaign of 1864. When initially occupied by Federal forces under Brigadier General A. J. Smith along with a flotilla of gunboats under Admiral David D. Porter, the town was looted by Smith's rough westerners and Porter's sailors. Banks arrived four days later, stopped the plundering, and tried to secure the region by adminis-

tering loyalty oaths and recruiting from the local population with substantial bounties as enticements.

After his defeat by Richard Taylor at Mansfield on 8 April 1864, Banks fought a defensive engagement at Pleasant Hill and then retreated to Alexandria, reaching there on 26 April. Banks would have preferred to continue his retreat toward the Mississippi, but he had to await the arrival of Porter's fleet that had ranged up the river as far as Blair's Landing. The gunboats did not arrive until 28 April, and both Banks and Porter could have been in serious trouble had Taylor's force remained at full strength. Instead, General Edmund Kirby Smith had detached parts of it for operations in Arkansas, and by the time he sent it back to Louisiana, the Federals were beyond reach and Alexandria was in ruins. For the time being, the best Taylor could do was harass Banks with skirmishes around the town.

When Porter finally did arrive, his gunboats had been badly beaten up by raking fire from the banks as he moved down the river. The main problem once he reached Alexandria was the Red River. Its level had fallen so quickly and considerably that an impassable rapids prevented the gunboats from moving any farther down the river. As news came that Taylor was working to seal off Banks's avenues of retreat, Porter became concerned that the army would abandon him.

Lieutenant Colonel Joseph Bailey, 4th Wisconsin Cavalry and acting engineer of the 19th Army Corps, had anticipated this problem during the retreat. Even before the engagement at Pleasant Hill, he had submitted a plan to build a dam at Alexandria to raise the level of the water so Porter's vessels could pass. When it was learned that Porter had scuttled the iron-clad *Eastport* after it had grounded on a snag, Bailey was dispatched to help the admiral raise the vessel and relate to him the plan for the dam at Alexandria. When the flotilla reached Alexandria, Bailey examined the falls and, after some effort, persuaded Banks to authorize the construction. Banks remained dubious, however, and with good reason. At the point Bailey proposed to place his dam, the river was 758 feet wide, 4 to 6 feet deep, and with a strong current running about 10 miles per hour. Nonetheless, Bailey put details from a dozen different regiments (prominently including the 97th and 99th Colored Infantry) to work with materials stripped from Alexandria and the nearby woods. Confederate brigadier general St. John Liddell, who occupied the bank opposite this construction site, would later be criticized by Taylor for allowing the work to proceed fairly unimpeded, but Liddell claimed that there was little he could do without artillery. Bailey built not only the dam at the base of the falls, but completed two wing dams on each side of the river at their head. Moreover, he was able to complete the dam in an astonishing ten days to raise the Red River at the base of the falls more than five feet and more than a foot at their head. It was enough to float Porter's eight remaining gunboats free and allow the army to proceed south to safety. In June, Congress voted a resolution of thanks to Colonel Bailey for his work on the Red River that had rescued Porter's vessels "from imminent peril."

As the army evacuated Alexandria on 13 May, Andrew J. Smith's men set fire to it. In this action, which was taken with considerable planning and care about where to place combustibles, they continued a practice of looting and destruction that had marked their retreat during the campaign. They had laid waste to Grand Ecore while passing through it, and now they did such a thorough job of razing Alexandria that, after the fires had burned out, there were reportedly only two houses left standing. Banks did nothing to stop the destruction, although some of his soldiers before departing tried to save some homes. Smith's command had served under Sherman, and their behavior in this campaign, especially at Alexandria, has been attributed to the hard war policy they learned under him and that he would make even more infamous during his campaign in Georgia later that year.

—*David S. Heidler and Jeanne T. Heidler*

See also Bailey, Joseph; Banks, Nathaniel Prentice; Mansfield, Louisiana, Battle of; Pleasant Hill, Louisiana, Battle of; Porter, David Dixon; Red River Campaign; Smith, Andrew Jackson; Taylor, Richard.

For further reading:
Johnson, Ludwell H. *Red River Campaign: Politics and Cotton in the Civil War* (1958).
Parrish, T. Michael. *Richard Taylor: Soldier Prince of Dixie* (1992).
Taylor, Richard. *Destruction and Reconstruction: Personal Experiences of the Late War* (1879; reprint, 1983).

ALGER, RUSSELL ALEXANDER
(1836–1907)
Union officer

Born on 27 February 1836 in the Western Reserve of Ohio, Russell A. Alger exemplified a certain type of American during the Civil War era. He began life in a log cabin, fended largely for himself in his youth, was drawn to the law, but made a fortune in timber. He was also of the prime age to be swept into the Civil War. He willingly thrust himself into the conflict, but almost three decades after it, he would have to endure a public controversy about the way he had left it.

Alger's main service was as colonel of the 5th Michigan Cavalry, part of George Armstrong Custer's celebrated 2d Cavalry Brigade of the Army of the Potomac. Custer's unit sustained more losses than any other mounted force during the war, and the 5th Michigan was second only to the 1st Michigan Cavalry in casualties. Alger participated in the advance from the Rappahannock River to the Rapidan River in September 1863, seeing action near Culpeper and Raccoon Ford.

During the early part of 1864 he was in Washington, where as a special commissioner he became involved in plans for the distribution of Abraham Lincoln's December 1863 Amnesty Proclamation. Alger suggested that cavalry units carry the proclamation directly to the enemy to encourage desertion by speeding its proliferation among war-weary Confederates.

In May 1864, Alger and the 5th Michigan crossed the Rapidan River at Ely's Ford as part of Ulysses S. Grant's Richmond campaign. He saw action at Todd's Tavern, where his regiment assisted in driving rebel forces from the field. The 5th Michigan helped destroy Confederate supplies and transportation facilities by tearing up sections of the Richmond & Fredericksburg Railroad. At Yellow Tavern on 11 May, Alger's regiment took heavy losses, and he reportedly was nearby when a sharpshooter mortally wounded Jeb Stuart. At the end of June, Alger fought at Trevilian Station, where his pursuit of fleeing Confederates left him and about forty of his men separated from their brigade with a large Confederate force in between. He fought his way back into Union lines near Louisa Court House.

The 5th Michigan joined Philip Sheridan's raid of the Shenandoah Valley in the summer of 1864, and it was this service under Sheridan that tarnished Alger's reputation. He already had been ill earlier in the year when sickness had required his handing over the command of the regiment during late May. In August 1864, the illness became so serious that it put Alger into an infirmary and required his reassignment to light administrative duties in Washington. He resigned from the army on 20 September 1864, receiving an honorable discharge and eventually the award for bravery of two brevet ranks to major general of volunteers. Alger moved to Detroit and began a political carrier that made him Michigan's governor in 1884 and saw him mentioned for president in the 1888 Republican convention. He became commander in chief of the Grand Army of the Republic in 1889.

Nevertheless, during the presidential race of 1892, newspaper allegations implied that he had been dismissed from the army for dereliction. The accounts cited charges lodged in 1864 by George A. Custer and apparently supported by Sheridan. After the war Alger had given $10,000 to a financially embarrassed Sheridan, and the generosity did not help appearances.

Although Alger enjoyed the support of many influential defenders, the matter remained unresolved to linger as an unsubstantiated blemish. In spite of the charges, William McKinley appointed Alger secretary of war in 1897. During his tenure, the War Department published the monumental *The War of the Rebellion: A Compilation of the Official Records of the Union and Confederate Armies.*

When the foibles of the war with Spain in 1898 were laid at Alger's door, he resigned under pressure from the president in 1899. Elected by the Michigan legislature to the Senate in 1902, he died in office on 24 January 1907.

—*David S. Heidler and Jeanne T. Heidler*

See also The War of the Rebellion: A Compilation of the Official Records of the Union and Confederate Armies.

For further reading:
Bell, Rodney Ellis. "A Life of Russell Alexander Alger, 1836–1907" (Ph.D. dissertation, 1957).

ALLATOONA, BATTLE OF
(5 October 1864)

After Major General William T. Sherman's successful capture of Atlanta in September 1864, the Confederate Army of Tennessee was forced to change its very fighting nature. Jefferson Davis, having finally lost confidence in General Joseph E. Johnston during the battle for the city, replaced him with the more aggressive John Bell Hood on 17 July. This change to a more aggressive officer did little to alter either the inevitable loss of Atlanta or the overall campaign. Having ingeniously maneuvered and fought his way through rugged northwest Georgia, Sherman seemed unassailable in Atlanta; nothing could dislodge him, except for defeat in open battle or the severing of his supply lines.

The Confederates could no longer engage the massive Union force in open battle, especially since they no longer had the defensive advantages of north Georgia's mountainous terrain at their disposal. And except for foolhardiness, they had no reason to fight a major engagement because they had already lost Atlanta, the one thing worth defending in that area. Hood, therefore, moved his troops back northward through Georgia, attempting to disrupt Sherman's vital supply line and in the hopes of drawing small Union forces out of Atlanta to defend their rear where he could defeat them piecemeal.

The initial strategy called for Hood's men almost to retrace the route Sherman had taken during his advance from Chattanooga to Atlanta, keeping the main body of his meager forces west of the Western and Atlantic rail line. Hood intended to destroy critical bridges, passes, and supply centers north toward Tennessee. On 29 September, Hood's army forded the Chattahoochee River and began to tear up railroad track from Big

Allatoona Pass, Georgia, *ca.* 1864 (Photograph by Mathew Brady Studio / *Library of Congress*)

Shanty to Acworth. Because of its initial surprise, Hood's plan worked well, destroying more than eight miles of track and taking more than 600 prisoners. Flush with success, Hood ordered Confederate Lieutenant General Alexander P. Stewart's troops to capture the large Union supply center at Allatoona Pass, a 180-foot deep gash through the Allatoona Mountain range northwest of Atlanta. Stewart gave Major General Samuel G. French's division, a force of 3,276 men, the assignment first to take the pass and then to destroy the railroad bridge over the Etowah River.

Aware that Hood was on the move, Sherman hurriedly moved his troops. In his memoirs Sherman wrote: "[L]earning that heavy masses of infantry, artillery, and cavalry, had been seen from Kenesaw (marching north), I inferred that Allatoona was their objective." He also observed that the objective contained more than a million rations of bread. Sherman sent Brigadier General John M. Corse to reinforce this vulnerable supply center, which action provided a total of 2,025 soldiers to defend what was already a highly defensible position. That many of Corse's troops were using Henry repeating rifles did not hurt his situation as well.

With the element of surprise gone and an almost equivalence in firepower between the two opposing forces, French's soldiers were walking into a far more difficult situation than they could ever have imagined. After exchanging messages concerning French's request for Corse's surrender, the Confederates attacked from the west and north, mounting a furious assault against the determined Union defenders. By midday, they had managed to push the Federals back into the mountaintop fort and were seemingly making significant progress in forcing a capitulation until Federal troops rallied. French, finally recognizing the futility of his position, withdrew to regroup with Hood's main force. The battle for Allatoona Pass was over.

In the end, Corse's casualties were 706, while French lost 897. Unfit for a major battle, Hood's army moved westward toward the Coosa and Oostenaula rivers and later toward Gadsden, Alabama.

Although Sherman later denied it, he was supposed to have sent a message to Corse stating: "Hold the Fort; I am coming." Whether it is true or not, this phrase became part of the refrain for the revival hymn "Hold the Fort" by Phillip B. Bliss. By this stage in the war, whatever Sherman did seemed to carry with it legendary implications.

—*James Meredith*

For further reading:
O'Connor, Richard. *Hood: Cavalier General* (1949).
Scaife, William R. "Hood's March to Tennessee: October–December 1864." In *The Civil War Battlefield Guide* (1998).
Sherman, William T. *Memoirs of William T. Sherman* (1990).

ALLEGHANY MOUNTAIN, [WEST] VIRGINIA, BATTLE OF
(13 December 1861)

In late November 1861, the Confederate Army of the Northwest withdrew eastward from Camp Bartow on the Greenbrier River to the mountaintop garrison known as Camp Alleghany (sometimes spelled Allegheny). From there, a large portion of the army under Major General William W. Loring continued on, uniting with Jackson's Army of the Valley at Winchester. Colonel Edward Johnson, with six regiments of infantry, two batteries of artillery, and a detachment of cavalry, some 1,200 in all, remained on the mountain to hold the Confederate line.

Brigadier General Robert H. Milroy had recently replaced Joseph J. Reynolds as commander of the Union garrison at Cheat Mountain. Possibly inspired by Loring's departure, Milroy determined to move against his Southern counterparts at Camp Alleghany, fifteen miles to the east, and at dawn on 13 December 1861 he did so. Milroy's plan divided his army in two. One column consisting of about 930 men under Colonel Gideon C. Moody, would march twelve miles, turning the Confederate left flank. The other column, numbering around 830 men and under Milroy's supervision, traveled only five miles, turning the Confederate right and rear. Moody was to attack at the sound of Milroy's guns.

Difficult terrain, however, put Moody's brigade hours behind. Consequently, when Milroy ran into Confederate pickets, Moody was not in place and the planned simultaneous assault had to be aborted. The firing on their right alerted the Southerners, and Johnson ordered elements of his various regiments to occupy the crest of the mountain on the right or eastern edge of the camp.

The morning was clear and cold, the frost thick and white on the ground. The Southerners almost froze in the piercing wind awaiting the attack. The Union troops advanced, gaining a foothold in the timbers that skirted the mountain summit. The Confederates counterattacked and pushed the Federals back into the woods, thus inaugurated an indeterminable amount of charges and countercharges. The fighting was largely hand to hand and "the roar of the musketry was incessant and deafening." The opposing forces could scarcely see one another for the smoke. Command control was lost and units became intermingled. "The men fought on their own hook, each loading and firing as fast as possible...."

And in the middle of it all was Edward Johnson. Although Johnson sustained no wounds or injuries, by the end of the battle his clothes were riddled with holes. When his men were nearly out of ammunition, Johnson and his forces made a determined rush, and amid deafening shouts the Southerners drove the Federals, inflicting severe losses. Years later, John S. Robson of the

52d Virginia, recalled that, in the final charge in this sector, Johnson with a musket in one hand and "swinging a big club in the other…led his line right up among the enemy, driving them headlong down the mountain, killing and wounding many with the bayonet and capturing a large number of prisoners."

The lack of anticipated cooperation by Moody's column on the Confederate left had a demoralizing effect on the Federals. By the time Moody's unit came up, the Southerners were waiting for them. After repulsing Milroy on his right, Johnson, with the advantage of interior lines, quickly moved the bulk of his force to the left. Moody's men formed their lines and quickly advanced. When the Federals got to within 200 yards of the Confederate entrenchments, the fire became so hot that the Northerners were compelled to make for the shelter of logs, trees, and whatever protection could be found. As opposed to the earlier charge and countercharge on the Confederate right, this portion of the battle was a firefight, lasting approximately five hours, the Southerners firing from the cover of their entrenchments, and the Federals firing from under the cover of the fallen timbers.

In the end, Southern leadership, determination, and firepower, combined with the plunging morale of the Northern soldiers, brought the same result on the Confederate left. "They were met on both points with the most determined heroism," wrote Johnson, "and, after a contest lasting from 7:00 A.M. until near 2:00 P.M., repulsed with great loss." The Federals returned to Cheat Mountain, according to Sergeant Major Ambrose Bierce, "a beaten, dispirited and exhausted force, feeble from fatigue and savage from defeat." The Southerners did not pursue and remained at Camp Alleghany through the winter.

Confederate losses amounted to 20 killed, 98 wounded, and 28 missing. The Federals lost 20 killed, 107 wounded, and 10 missing.

Johnson was lauded for his personal bravery. According to the 17 December 1861 *Daily Dispatch*, Edward Johnson "covered himself with glory, and is entitled to the appellation of the Hero of the Alleghany." One month later, Edward "Alleghany" Johnson was elevated to brigadier general, effective 13 December 1861.

—*Eddie Woodward*

See also Army of the Northwest; Johnson, Edward.
For further reading:
Bierce, Ambrose. "On a Mountain." In *Collected Works* (1909–1912).
Driver, Robert J. *52d Virginia Infantry* (1986).
Hamilton, W.D. "Camp Baldwin Expedition." In *History of the Thirty-Second Regiment, Ohio Veteran Volunteer Infantry* (1896).
———. *Recollections of a Cavalryman of the Civil War after Fifty Years, 1861–1865* (1915).
Hotchkiss, J., ed. *Virginia. Confederate Military History* (1899; reprint, 1987).
Lessor, W. Hunter, Kim A. McBride, and Janet G. Brasher. "Cheat Summit Fort and Camp Allegheny: Early Civil War Encampments in West Virginia." In *Look to the Earth: Historical Archaeology and the American Civil War* (1994).
Robson, John S. *How a One-Legged Rebel Lives* (1898).
Woodward, Edward V. "Holding the Alleghany Line: Edward Johnson, the Army of the Northwest, and the Battle of Alleghany Summit." (Thesis, 1998).

ALLEN, HENRY WATKINS
(1820–1866)
Confederate general; governor of Louisiana

Born in Virginia to Thomas Allen, a physician, and Ann Watkins Allen, Henry Watkins Allen moved to Missouri as a child with his parents. He eventually moved to Mississippi, was admitted to the bar, traveled briefly to the Republic of Texas, and finally returned to Mississippi to become a planter. A restless spirit, however, took him to Louisiana, where he wrote extensively and became involved in state politics. He traveled extensively, spending a brief time in Massachusetts during which he attended classes at Harvard Law School. In 1859 Allen went to Italy, hoping to enlist in Garibaldi's revolutionary force, only to find the insurrection over when he arrived.

Returning to the United States just as the Civil War began, Allen immediately enlisted in the Confederate army, rising quickly from private to colonel of the 4th Louisiana Regiment. Initially, the regiment garrisoned coastal fortifications in Louisiana, but in February 1862 it was summoned north to reinforce Albert Sidney Johnston's army as it retreated into northern Mississippi. Allen commanded the 4th Louisiana Regiment at the battle of Shiloh, in which he was wounded in the face in an attack on the Hornet's Nest, and at Baton Rouge on 5 August 1862, where he was wounded again, this time more severely.

In the failed Confederate attempt to retake Baton Rouge, Allen commanded the Louisiana Brigade. He was wounded in both legs, the damage to the right leg being so severe that Allen would never again walk without crutches. He remained in active service, though, first as the military governor of Jackson, Mississippi, and then as a brigadier general beginning on 19 August 1863 under Edmund Kirby Smith. In 1864, however, Allen was elected governor of Louisiana and left military service.

As governor, Allen proved tremendously effective in rebuilding Louisiana's shattered economy. Working to keep both the military forces and civilians supplied with necessities, Allen opened trade with Mexico, particularly utilizing the state's large supply of cotton. He also established state-run supply points for civilians and encouraged industry with state funds and incentives. Concerned about the defense of the state, he sent out a call on 16 March 1864 to all able-bodied Louisiana males to be ready at a moment's notice to defend the state. He also reorganized the militia to make it more responsive to emergencies and suggested to the Confederate War Department the enlistment of black men. The United States Army was using black soldiers against the Confederacy, he argued, so the Confederate army should also use the resource.

As the war drew to a close, Allen used his influence to bring about the surrender of the trans-Mississippi Confederate forces to save his state from any further destruction. He attended a conference in May 1865 in Marshall, Texas, with the governors of Texas, Arkansas, and Missouri to urge the surrender of remaining Confederate military forces in the region. Following capitulation, Allen moved to Mexico and started an American newspaper in Mexico City. He died there in 1866, and his body was returned to Baton Rouge for burial.

—*David S. Heidler and Jeanne T. Heidler*

See also Baton Rouge, Battle of; Louisiana.
For further reading:
Cassidy, Vincent H. *Henry Watkins Allen of Louisiana* (1964).
Chandler, Luther Edward. "The Career of Henry Watkins Allen." (Ph.D. dissertation, 1940).
Dorsey, Sarah A. *Recollections of Henry Watkins Allen* (1866).

ALLEN, WILLIAM WIRT
(1835–1894)
Confederate general

William Wirt Allen was born in New York City to Wade Hampton Allen and Eliza Sayre Allen. Wade Allen was a successful businessman and had agricultural interests in the South. William Allen was educated in Alabama before being sent to Princeton, from which he graduated in 1854. On graduation he became an Alabama planter. Opposing secession, Allen nevertheless became a first lieutenant in the 1st Montgomery Mounted Rifles.

In 1862 Allen achieved the rank of major in the same unit and, after fighting bravely at Shiloh, was promoted to colonel of the 1st Alabama Cavalry. He commanded this regiment in Braxton Bragg's invasion of Kentucky in fall 1862 and was wounded at Perryville. Back in command in December at Stones River, Allen led a brigade and again suffered serious wounds.

In February 1864 Allen was promoted to brigadier general and commanded one of Joseph Wheeler's cavalry brigades. As a part of the Army of Tennessee, he fought to defend Atlanta in the summer of 1864. During the early months of 1865, he commanded a division of Joseph Johnston's army in the Carolinas and was promoted to major general on 4 March 1865. He surrendered his force in May 1865 at Concord, North Carolina, and was paroled from Charlotte, North Carolina.

Following the war, Allen returned to planting and served in Alabama state government as a U.S. marshal. He died at Sheffield, Alabama.

—*David S. Heidler and Jeanne T. Heidler*

See also Wheeler, Joseph.
For further reading:
Barrett, John G. *Sherman's March through the Carolinas* (1996).
Glatthaar, Joseph T. *The March to the Sea and Beyond: Sherman's Troops in the Savannah and Carolinas Campaigns* (1985).

ALTON FEDERAL MILITARY PRISON

With Union prison facilities in St. Louis overtaxed by the end of the war's first year, Adjutant General Lorenzo Thomas authorized Major General Henry Halleck to seek the permission of Illinois governor Richard Yates to utilize the condemned and abandoned Alton State Penitentiary, northeast of St. Louis near the Mississippi River. Yates agreed, and the Alton Prison received its first military prisoners on 9 February 1862.

Within three days the facility experienced overcrowding. When opened in 1831, the state penitentiary had a maximum capacity of 800 inmates. In its second career as a military prison, it usually housed between 1,000 and 1,500 persons at any given time, and at one point held almost 1,900 prisoners.

As was true of all Civil War prisons, Alton remained overcrowded, unsanitary, and disease-ridden throughout the conflict. Although Alton primarily housed captured soldiers, its inmates consisted of some political prisoners, including about two dozen women.

—*Thomas F. Curran*

See also Andersonville Prison; Belle Isle Prison; Camp Chase Prison; Camp Douglas Prison; Camp Morton Prison; Elmira Prison; Fort Delaware Prison; Fort Warren Prison; Gratiot Street and Myrtle Street Prisons; Johnson's Island Prison; Libby Prison; Old Capitol Prison; Prisoner Exchanges; Prisoner Paroles; Prisoners of War; Prisons, C.S.A.; Prisons, U.S.A.; Rock Island Prison; Salisbury Prison; Yates, Richard.
For further reading:
Frost, Griffin. *Camp and Prison Journal.* (1867; reprint 1994).
Hesseltine, William B. *Civil War Prisons: A Study in War Psychology* (1930).
Speers, Lonnie R. *Portals to Hell: Military Prisons of the Civil War* (1997).

AMELIA COURT HOUSE/JETERSVILLE
(3–5 April 1865)

The near-confrontation at Jetersville, Virginia, on 5 April 1865 capped the initial segment of the retreat of the Army of Northern Virginia from Richmond and Petersburg to Appomattox. Having concentrated his army at Amelia Court House, a rail station thirty-nine miles southwest of Richmond,

General Robert E. Lee began a march toward Danville along the Richmond & Danville Railroad. As the Confederates approached the next station, at Jetersville, they discovered a strong Federal force under General Philip Sheridan entrenched across the railroad. Deciding not to risk an open engagement, Lee ordered a night march farther west to Farmville, where supplies awaited and from whence he still hoped to proceed south and ultimately rendezvous with Confederate forces under General Joseph Johnston.

After the disaster at Five Forks and the loss of the Southside Railroad at Sutherland Station on 1–2 April, Lee ordered a withdrawal of some 55,000 Confederate troops from the 28-mile front held during the siege of Petersburg and Richmond. His first objective was to concentrate his army, and he chose to do so at Amelia Court House, a station on the Danville Railroad roughly equidistant from all points on the defense line. Aware that Lee intended to march to Danville, and concerned that he might unite with Johnston's Army of Tennessee, General Ulysses S. Grant immediately sent a Federal contingent of about 63,000 troops under Generals Sheridan, George G. Meade, and Ord in pursuit from Petersburg westward along the Southside Railroad. Grant hoped to secure Burkeville, the junction between the Southside Railroad and the Richmond & Danville Railroad, before the Confederates arrived there and thus cut Lee's intended route of retreat.

Making an all-night march on 2–3 April along three main routes, the Confederates reached Amelia generally unmolested, although rearguard actions did include a cavalry engagement at Namozine Church between the Confederate forces under Major General W. H. F. "Rooney" Lee and the Federals under Major General George Custer. Before the evacuation, Robert E. Lee had requisitioned 350,000 food rations to be sent from Richmond to Amelia, but upon arrival at the station the commander was dismayed to find that confusion in the transmission of the orders had resulted instead in a delivery of ordnance stores. The mistake proved costly because Lee was compelled to spend all of 4 April in bivouac at Amelia to let his troops forage for food. The fleeting opportunity to turn south ahead of the Union pursuit was lost.

While Lee's men foraged, the Federal Army of the Shenandoah, a cavalry force under Major General Philip Sheridan, moved rapidly to the west along a route just south of the Confederate position. By 5:00 P.M. on 4 April, Sheridan had gained footing on the Richmond & Danville Railroad north of Burkeville at Jetersville, a station about seven miles below Amelia. Sheridan was soon reinforced by the II and V Infantry Corps from Meade's Army of the Potomac. These troops spent the morning and early afternoon of 5 April digging entrenchments in a front facing northeast and

extending ultimately about two miles on either side of the railroad.

The Confederate forage wagons returned to Amelia early on 5 April with little for the troops to eat. Lee's army was hungry and had lost its day's lead on the Federals. Lee would later term this delay "fatal." At 1:00 P.M. he directed the Army of Northern Virginia to take up the march for Danville along the railroad with Lieutenant General James Longstreet's I Corps in the van.

Hearing skirmish fire as they neared Jetersville, Lee and Longstreet halted the Confederate column and conferred with the commander's son, Rooney Lee, whose cavalry had discovered Sheridan's forces. Longstreet readied three divisions for battle, but Lee, advised that more Federal infantry were soon to arrive, judged the enemy position too strong to warrant an attack. Here Lee changed his original plans, deciding to make another night march around the Union left flank and west about 20 miles to Farmville. There he could obtain supplies and rations, then turn south and reach the Danville Railroad at Keysville. The orders were given and the Confederate column withdrew.

Sheridan and Meade remained entrenched through the night of 5 April. The Federals had been unable to mount an offensive during the day, as Meade's VI Corps did not reach the field until about 6:00 P.M. Leaving his reserve force, Ord's Army of the James, at Burkeville, General Grant arrived in Jetersville by 10:30 P.M. The next morning the Federals advanced up the railroad only to find the enemy gone. When the trailing elements of Lee's column were observed heading west across nearby Flat Creek, however, the Union infantry quickly changed front behind it and the chase was resumed.

—*Charles E. Kinzer*

See also Appomattox Court House; Farmville/High Bridge, Battle of; Five Forks, Battle of; Namozine Church; Sayler's Creek/Harper's Farm, Battle of.
For further reading:
Calkins, Chris M. *The Appomattox Campaign: March 29–April 9, 1865* (1997).

AMERICAN PARTY

The American Party (or the Know-Nothings, as members were commonly known), played a key role in the transformation of the second American political party system during the mid-1850s. Originally founded as a secret nativist society, by 1854 the Know-Nothings had supplanted the Whigs as the major opposition party to the Democrats. In their meteoric rise they threatened to overwhelm the newly formed Republican Party and even to capture the presidency. By the end of 1856, however, the American Party had all but vanished as a political power, sacrificed on the alter of sectionalism and destroyed by the chaos of political realignment.

The Know-Nothings grew out of a nativist organization in New York City called the Order of the Star Spangled Banner. It was a secret society devoted to denying political participation to Catholics and the foreign born, and to defeating the old, corrupt Whig and Democratic Parties, which the society accused of catering to the immigrant vote. Energized by unrest over the waves of primarily Irish and German immigrants pouring into the United States (2.9 million immigrants entered the country between 1845 and 1854), the Know-Nothings spread throughout much of the eastern and border states in 1853 and 1854, gradually moving into politics in support of their anti-Catholic, antiforeign, and antiparty agenda. Still unknown by much of the population, the Know-Nothing Party was catapulted into prominence through the silent campaign of its initiates in the autumn elections of 1854. Its most amazing victories came in Massachusetts, where members waged a "dark lantern" crusade, voting for fellow Know-Nothings not even listed on the ballot. Seemingly out of nowhere the party managed to capture all but three seats in the state legislature and the entire congressional delegation, and to elect the governor and a United States senator. Know-Nothings earned less spectacular, but still significant, victories in New York, Pennsylvania, Maryland, and Ohio. Thus, the Know-Nothings stood on the verge of national power.

In 1854 the Know-Nothings officially became the American Party, and Northern and Southern members convened at the party's first convention in Philadelphia in June 1855. In a meeting marked by the chaos that was to become so familiar to Americans during the political breakdown of the 1850s, Northern and Southern Know-Nothings battled over the party's platform. While in agreement over their nativist and antiparty beliefs, the issue of slavery proved divisive. The main controversy concerned the recently adopted Kansas-Nebraska Act, which opened up the old Louisiana Purchase territory to so-called popular sovereignty. This was an old idea that now threatened to allow slavery into the territories where it was previously restricted by the Missouri Compromise of 1820. The American Party had three major divisions over slavery. Many of the Northern men were free-soil adherents. Led by Henry Wilson of Massachusetts, they attempted to force the party to take a stand against the Kansas-Nebraska Act. A group of Southerners, convinced by the previous month's loss in Virginia's gubernatorial race in which they had been savaged by Democrat Henry Alexander Wise for being secret abolitionists, believed that the party had to take a strong stand defending slavery in the territories. A third group of both Northern and Southern moderates, centered on Kenneth Rayner of North Carolina and

Henry Fuller of Pennsylvania, tried to steer a middle road in the vain hope of removing slavery from the political arena. This struggle over the platform effectively split the party, as Wilson and his backers bolted the convention after passage of a plank that failed to meet their demands for a restoration of the Missouri Compromise. This left the proslavery Southerners and moderates to control the party. The nativist tenets upon which the American Party had been founded had not been strong enough to hold the Know-Nothings together.

Following this breakup, the Know-Nothings tried on several occasions to reunite, but a disastrous two-month battle in the U.S. House of Representatives over the election of the Speaker in 1855–1856, and the nomination of the old Whig Millard Fillmore for president in February 1856 fractured the party forever. Southerners largely stayed with Fillmore, a New Yorker, but the majority of Northerners deserted and joined the Republicans over the summer of 1856. In the 1856 election Fillmore finished third behind Democrat James Buchanan and Republican John C. Frémont, capturing only Maryland. By this time the nativist party of 1854 had become a shell of its former self, controlled by old Whigs and little resembling the party that had so amazed Americans two years earlier. Following the 1856 election the American Party survived for a year in a few Southern states, and then died. Its remnants were awakened from the dead in 1860 in the form of the Constitutional Union Party, but it too had little in common with the old Know-Nothings and the nativism responsible for the American Party's initial popularity.

—*John David Bladek*

See also Democratic Party; Popular Sovereignty; Republican Party.

For further reading:

Anbinder, Tyler. *Nativism and Slavery: The Northern Know Nothings and the Politics of Slavery* (1992).

Baker, Jean H. *Ambivalent Americans: The Know-Nothing Party in Maryland* (1977).

Bladek, John David. "Virginia is Middle Ground: The Know Nothing-Party and the Virginia Gubernatorial Election of 1855." *Virginia Magazine of History and Biography* (1998).

Cantrell, Greg. "Southern and Nativist: Kenneth Rayner and the Ideology of 'Americanism.'" *North Carolina Historical Review* (1992).

Holt, Michael F. *The Rise and Fall of the American Whig Party: Jacksonian Politics and the Onset of the Civil War* (1999).

AMERICAN RED CROSS

The American Red Cross did not officially exist during the Civil War, but the origins of the American chapter stem from the incidents of war, especially those involving Clara Barton, numerous women's organizations (mainly relief oriented), and the U.S. Sanitary Commission. The idea behind the American Red Cross began with local aid organizations

such as the Women's Central Association of Relief, various local organizations that sought to meet the needs of Union armies, the Catholic Sisters of Mercy, the Sisters of the Holy Cross, and others. In addition, the horrors of the Austro-Prussian War and the activities of Florence Nightingale during the Crimean War impressed many people in the United States, who thus became aware of the need to create better conditions for wounded and encamped soldiers.

The Women's Central Association of Relief pressured the federal government early in the war to create a sanitary commission to care for the soldiers' needs. President Lincoln and army officials initially thought that such an organization would prove to be either useless or a hindrance. Public pressure, though, forced the hand of government, and in June 1861 the federal government sanctioned the U.S. Sanitary Commission. Under the supervision of the Army Medical Service, the commission inspected hospitals and camps, suggesting improvements to the Army Medical Service.

The Sanitary Commission, however, was only one step toward the formation of the American Red Cross. Clara Barton also played a vital role that led to the creation of the American Red Cross. Appalled by the ravages of war, Barton strove to help wounded soldiers and locate those who were missing, especially after seeing the casualty figures from the first battle of Bull Run. She found, however, that the authorities did not want her help. When she contacted the governor of Massachusetts, he resisted her idea of working on the front lines.

Undeterred, Barton went directly to Washington. She already possessed supplies and had assistants to help her distribute them on the front lines. All she needed was official approval to do so. She approached Colonel Daniel Rucker, a member of the Quartermaster Corps, who was intrigued by her knowledge and impressed with the supplies already at her disposal. Her preparation convinced him to allow her and her assistants access to the front. Her first direct experience with the war occurred at Fredericksburg, Virginia, during the Peninsula campaign in 1862, when officers and soldiers welcomed her help, and her supplies were quickly distributed. She also began administering medicine, cleaning wounds, applying fresh dressings, or simply speaking a few words of comfort to a dying soldier. Convinced that some organization such as the International Red Cross was needed to care for soldiers, Clara committed herself to the establishment of an American version after the war.

All local relief organizations, the Sanitary Commission, Clara Barton, and other individuals contributed to the creation of the American Red Cross after the Civil War. Their combined experiences, as well as the destruction of the war, helped establish the American organization, but it was Barton who took the final steps. On 21 May 1881, she founded the American Association of the Red Cross, and in March 1882 the U.S. government approved the organization. It then officially became the American Red Cross.

Barton also lectured and lobbied for the U.S. government's support of the 1864 Geneva Convention, a treaty that stipulated fair treatment of wounded soldiers and prisoners.

The American chapter of the Red Cross operated under the articles of the 1864 convention that had established the International Red Cross. Accordingly, it was affiliated with the International Red Cross and the League of Red Cross Societies. Today, the Red Cross plays a large role in relief activities, caring for victims of war and natural disasters.

—Matthew Pacer

See also Barton, Clara; Blackwell, Elizabeth; Disease; Medicine; United States Christian Commission; United States Sanitary Commission.

For further reading:

Barton, Clara. *The Red Cross* (1898).
Burton, David H. *Clara Barton: In the Service of Humanity* (1995).
Dulles, Foster R. *The American Red Cross: A History* (1950).

AMES, ADELBERT
(1835–1933)
Union general

Adelbert Ames served in the Union army during the American Civil War and established an outstanding record while rising from second lieutenant to brevet brigadier general. As governor of Mississippi during Reconstruction, he battled unsuccessfully to establish a democratic society. At his death in 1933, he was the last surviving Civil War officer.

The son of a prosperous clipper ship captain, Ames was born in Rockland, Maine, on 31 October 1835. He entered West Point in July 1856 and graduated in May 1861 near the top of his class. During the course of the Civil War, Ames fought in seven major military campaigns and sixteen battles, including First Bull Run, the Peninsula campaign, Gaines's Mill, Malvern Hill, Antietam, Fredericksburg, Chancellorsville, Gettysburg, Petersburg, Cold Harbor, and Fort Fisher. He earned a reputation as a stern disciplinarian who led by example and often joined his troops in the heat of battle. He began the war as a second lieutenant in the U.S. Artillery Corps and ended as commander of the Tenth Army Corps with the rank of brevet major general.

After the Confederate surrender, Ames was stationed in South Carolina, where he experienced the hatred of Southern whites while working to halt widespread violence against former slaves. In 1868, Ames took

Adelbert Ames (*Library of Congress*)

charge of Union occupational forces at Vicksburg, Mississippi, and in 1869 President Grant appointed him provisional governor of Mississippi and commander of the Fourth Military District. Governor Ames used his political and military authority to establish and protect the political, economic, and social rights of freedmen and freedwomen. He favored racial equality, universal manhood suffrage, and a system of state-supported schools for all children. Ames responded to frequent racial violence in Mississippi by using troops to protect black citizens, directing military commissions to convict perpetrators, and removing from office state and local officials who violated the rights of black Mississippians. The Republican-controlled state legislature appointed Ames senator in 1870, a position he held until 1873. In 1874, Ames once again became governor of Mississippi after a hard-fought victory over James Lusk Alcorn. His inaugural address emphasized his continued commitment to full economic rights for all Mississippians. Such ideals brought Ames into direct conflict with the rising tide of Democratic political terrorism sweeping the state. Lacking the assistance of Federal troops, he was unable to stop the organized campaign of violence, intimidation, and assassination that brought Redeemer Democrats into office. The Democratic-controlled legislature fabricated a series of charges against Ames and in 1876 moved to impeach him. Exhausted from struggling against political violence and fed up with the absence of a federal commitment to racial equality and the protection of political rights, Ames resigned the governorship on 28 March 1876.

During the second half of his long life, Ames amassed a sizable fortune from business interests in flour milling, textile manufacturing, and real estate. He frequently attended military reunions and died in 1933, immensely proud of his military, political, and business careers.

—*Bruce D. Mactavish*

See also Fort Fisher.
For further reading:
Ames, Blanch. *Adelbert Ames, 1835–1933: General, Senator, Governor* (1964).
Current, Richard N. *Three Carpetbag Governors* (1967).
Harris, William C. *The Day of the Carpetbagger: Republican Reconstruction in Mississippi* (1979).

AMMEN, JACOB
(1807–1894)
Union general

Born to David Ammen and Sally Houtz Ammen in Fincastle, Virginia, Jacob Ammen moved with his family to Ohio when he was ten years old. He was educated locally before receiving an appointment to the U.S. Military Academy in 1827. He graduated twelfth of thirty-three from the class of 1831. Commissioned an artillery officer, Ammen resigned from the army after six years, serving most of that time as an instructor at West Point but also a short time from 1832 to 1833 as an artillery officer in Charleston Harbor. For the next 18 years, Ammen spent most of his time teaching at various universities including what would become Transylvania University and Indiana University.

Immediately before the Civil War, Ammen made his living as a civil engineer. With Abraham Lincoln's call for volunteers on 15 April 1861, Ammen organized a company of the 12th Ohio and became its captain. Two months later Ammen was made the colonel of the 24th Ohio.

For the first months of the war, the 24th served in the campaign in western Virginia. In November 1861 the 24th was transferred to the Army of the Ohio. On the second day of the battle of Shiloh, 7 April, Ammen commanded the 10th Brigade of the 4th Division, protecting the extreme left flank of Don Carlos Buell's army. He was commended by both his division commander, Brigadier General William Nelson, and Major General Buell for his actions there.

Ammen continued to command the 10th Brigade during the siege of Corinth. He was promoted to brigadier general in July 1862, but was forced to take a leave of absence that fall as a result of ill health. For the remainder of the war, Ammen held a variety of jobs, primarily staff or desk jobs, because of the feebleness of his health.

In the spring of 1863, he assumed command of Camp Douglas, a prisoner-of-war camp in Chicago. By the summer, Ammen was transferred to East Tennessee, where he participated in Ambrose Burnside's campaign there. At the end of the year, Ammen was given command of the District of Central Kentucky. In the spring of 1864, Ammen was given command of the 4th Division, XXIII Corps, commanded by Major General John Schofield and headquartered in Knoxville, Tennessee. The primary job of the division in the spring was to combat against raids perpetrated by Confederate cavalryman Joseph Wheeler. The following fall, while still in East Tennessee, Ammen guarded Federal positions against the campaign of John C. Breckinridge.

In January 1865, citing failing business interests but probably as much a result of his bad health, Ammen resigned from the army. After the war he worked as a civil engineer and a Maryland farmer. He traveled to Central America in 1874 as part of a government-appointed commission to look at possible canal locations. He retired to Lockland, Ohio, in 1891 and died there on 6 February 1894.

—*David S. Heidler and Jeanne T. Heidler*

See also Corinth, Battle of; Shiloh, Battle of.

For further reading:
Wessen, Ernest James, ed. *Papers of Brigadier General Jacob Ammen* (1957).

ANACONDA PLAN

When South Carolinians fired on Fort Sumter on 12 April 1861, the U.S. Army, numbering some 16,000 men, was suddenly expected to subdue the rebellious South, a region measuring 750,000 square miles and inhabited by 9 million people. Initially, many Northerners, including President Abraham Lincoln, expected that the conflict would be over in a few months. However, U.S. Army General-in-Chief Winfield Scott saw the magnitude of the future conflict more clearly. In 1861, he predicted that the Civil War would last more than two years, require 300,000 Union soldiers, and cost 100,000 casualties as a result of both combat and disease. Aside from insufficient manpower and material, the Union's military and political leaders did not possess a coherent plan for victory. As part of his responsibilities as general-in-chief, Scott made a significant contribution to the Union's cause by formulating the so-called Anaconda Plan, a grand strategic or political plan for the subjugation of the Confederacy. Something of a misnomer, the term "Anaconda" came into use after 1861 among Union leaders and skeptical Union press to describe Scott's strategy.

Born in 1786, Winfield Scott started his military career in 1808 as a captain of artillery and served with distinction in the War of 1812. He rose to the rank of brigadier general by the age of thirty and fought in several battles and wars against Indians. In 1835, his three-volume *Infantry Tactics* appeared. Scott took part in diplomatic missions to England and Canada in 1838, and he was promoted to general-in-chief of the army in 1841. During the Mexican-American War, he brilliantly commanded the U.S. landing at Vera Cruz and the subsequent campaign in 1847. In Mexico, he clearly demonstrated intelligent leadership, a knack for organization, an appreciation for logistics, and a comprehension of strategic and political issues. Scott accepted the Whig Party's presidential nomination in 1852. Consequently, Winfield Scott brought more than fifty years of experience in domestic, foreign, and military affairs to the situation facing the Union army in the Civil War's early months.

For Scott, war was a game of chess. Opposing armies would maneuver to bring each other into checkmate and obtain victories without necessarily destroying all the enemy forces or losing all their own forces. The overall political or grand strategic goal of victory could be achieved by limited means. Scott's strategic thinking was consistent with his strategy employed in the Mexican-American War. Using the continent as a chessboard, Scott designed his Anaconda Plan to accomplish a political goal: forcing the Confederacy into peace negotiations rather than the purely military goal of defeating its armed forces on the battlefield. Scott favored conciliation with the Confederacy rather than its destruction in a total war.

Scott's plan was influenced by the moderate strategic theories of Baron Antoine Henri Jomini, a Swiss military thinker who had served with both Napoleon's French forces and the opposing Russian forces. Jomini's interpretation of Napoleonic warfare influenced U.S. military leaders during the mid-nineteenth century. Jomini did not want needlessly bloody battles. Instead, he advocated the use of interior lines and control of geography to allow a preponderance of force to be exerted against an enemy's weak points.

Scott's Anaconda Plan called for the Union army and navy to exert constant pressure on the South and gradually strangle it to death. It consisted of two main parts. First, exploiting its great advantage in number of ships and experienced leaders, the Union fleet would impose a naval blockade, causing economic hardship in the South. As the South's commercial activities decreased, its valuable cash crops such as tobacco and cotton could not be used to trade with the Europeans. Second, the Union naval and land forces would open the Mississippi and other Southern rivers and split the South into two parts. Controlling these rivers would deprive the Confederate army of its interior lines of communication and transportation as well as allow the Union army to employ these same lines of communication and trans-

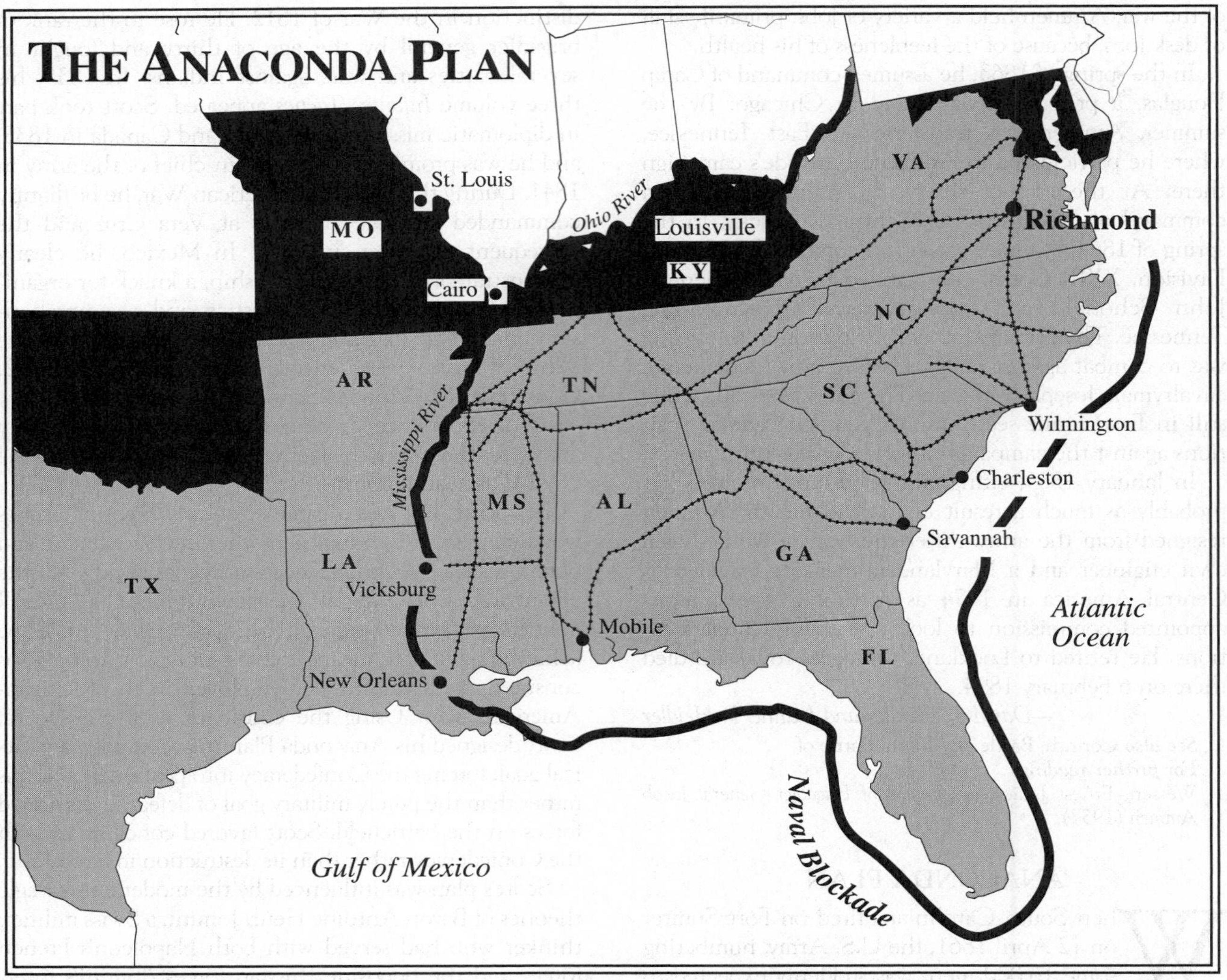

THE ANACONDA PLAN

Map showing the Anaconda Plan, labeled with states MO, KY, VA, NC, SC, AR, TN, MS, AL, GA, LA, TX, FL; cities St. Louis, Louisville, Cairo, Richmond, Wilmington, Charleston, Savannah, Vicksburg, Mobile, New Orleans; the Ohio River, Mississippi River, Naval Blockade, Gulf of Mexico, and Atlantic Ocean.

portation. Consequently, a war of attrition would take its toll as the isolated and enveloped Confederacy lost its logistical capabilities.

Contemporaries scoffed at Scott and his Anaconda Plan. The North's public and their representatives impatiently clamored for a dramatic military confrontation culminating in a Confederate defeat. Naysayers believed that Scott's grand strategy was too passive and too elaborate. The plan did have some weaknesses and shortcomings. For example, its implementation would not have directly damaged the South's will to fight. Moreover, the Anaconda Plan did not strike any blows against the Confederacy's agricultural base in the Deep South. Lastly, the plan did not anticipate occupation and control of conquered Confederate territory. Ultimately, four years of bloody battles and bitter occupations were also needed to achieve the political goal of victory by means of a strategy of annihilation. The Confederacy's military forces had to be bludgeoned into

submission in a methodical, destructive, total war.

These weaknesses and shortcomings notwithstanding, Winfield Scott's Anaconda Plan did indeed influence the strategy that the Union military eventually used to win the Civil War. The Union's naval blockade handicapped the Confederacy's commercial activities. With the capture of New Orleans in April 1862 and Vicksburg in July 1863, Union control of the Mississippi split the South into two parts.

—David Ulbrich

See also Scott, Winfield.
For further reading:
Eisenhower, John S. D. *Agent of Destiny: The Life and Times of General Winfield Scott* (1997).
Johnson, Timothy D. *Winfield Scott: The Quest for Military Glory* (1998).
Marszalek, John F. "Where Did Winfield Scott Find His Anaconda?" *Lincoln Herald* (1987).
Ropp, Theodore. "Anacondas Anyone?" *Military Affairs* (1963).
Scott, Winfield. *Memoirs of Lieutenant-General Scott, LL. D.* (1864; reprint, 1970).

ANDERSON, GEORGE THOMAS
(1824–1901)
Confederate general

Born in Covington, Georgia, to Joseph Stewart Anderson and Lucy Cunningham Anderson, George Thomas Anderson was educated at Emory College. At the outbreak of the Mexican War in 1848 he received a commission as a second lieutenant in the Georgia Mounted Volunteers and served in Winfield Scott's Mexico City campaign. Anderson returned to his family's home after the war. In 1855 he decided to return to the military and accepted a captain's commission in the 1st United States Cavalry. He served for three years, resigning his commission in 1858 and again returning home to the family plantation.

At the outbreak of the Civil War, Anderson helped to raise the 11th Georgia Regiment and was made the regiment's colonel. During the summer of 1861 Anderson took his regiment to Virginia, where it served without seeing combat for the remainder of the year. In February 1862 Anderson was given command of a brigade that included the 11th and was composed entirely of Georgia troops. Initially, the brigade was part of the division commanded by Major General Gustavus W. Smith, but during the early phases of the Peninsula campaign it was placed under Major General David R. Jones. As part of a force under the overall command of John B. Magruder, Anderson and his men occupied the Confederate works at Yorktown in an effort to delay Union general George B. McClellan's movement up the Peninsula. Anderson and his brigade also fought during the Seven Days' battles, being especially conspicuous at Malvern Hill.

Upon the organization of the Army of Northern Virginia into two corps, Anderson and his brigade came under the command of James Longstreet. In late August 1862 Anderson led his brigade at Second Bull Run where he was slightly injured. He was back in command by mid-September, however, in time to fight in the defense of Turner's Gap at South Mountain and then at Antietam. Anderson was commended for his actions in the latter battle.

In November 1862 Anderson was formally promoted to brigadier general. He had commanded a brigade for almost a year. At Fredericksburg a month later, he continued to command the same brigade in the division under John Bell Hood. In spring 1863, along with much of Longstreet's corps, Anderson went to Suffolk, Virginia, but was back with the Army of Northern Virginia in time to begin the invasion of the North that would culminate in the battle of Gettysburg.

As was the case with the remainder of Longstreet's corps, Anderson arrived too late to fight on the first day of the battle of Gettysburg. Anderson and his brigade were part of Hood's division that attacked the Union left on the afternoon of 2 July. In the fierce fighting in the Devil's Den at the base of Little Roundtop Anderson was seriously wounded.

After a convalescence of several months, in October 1863 Anderson was sent to Tennessee to join much of the remainder of Longstreet's corps. He distinguished himself in the Knoxville campaign. In the spring he returned with the corps to command his brigade in the Wilderness campaign and all the subsequent battles of Ulysses S. Grant's campaign against Robert E. Lee. At the end of June he settled into the trenches of Petersburg with his brigade where he would spend much of the remainder of the war.

In the meantime Anderson had entered into a dispute with the governor of Georgia, Joseph Brown. In spring 1864 Anderson and the officers of his brigade took offense at the efforts of Brown to withhold troops and supplies from the Confederate government. When Brown called the state legislature into session to acquiesce in his efforts, Anderson and his officers circulated a petition among the soldiers of the brigade, who were all from Georgia units, protesting Brown's actions. Anderson then forwarded the petition to Brown with the assurance that virtually every soldier in the brigade had signed it. Brown fired back, angrily accusing Anderson of trying to gain the favor of the Richmond government to secure a promotion to major general. In the intensity of preparations for the coming campaign the dispute ended there, although the episode provided a clear example of the damage done to morale when soldiers learn of the failure of home governments to support their efforts in the field. Anderson ended the war by surrendering with what was left of the Army of Northern Virginia at Appomattox Court House.

After the war Anderson returned to Georgia, where he tried to rebuild his fortunes. Landless, he accepted a number of positions, including working for the Georgia Railroad in Atlanta. He became somewhat prominent in civic affairs in the city and served briefly as the boom town's chief of police. In his later years he moved to Anniston, Alabama, where he also occupied several civic offices. He died in Anniston on 4 April 1901.

—*David S. Heidler and Jeanne T. Heidler*

See also Georgia; Gettysburg, Battle of.
For further reading:
Boney, F. N. *Rebel Georgia* (1997).
Pfanz, Harry W. *Gettysburg, The Second Day* (1987).

ANDERSON, JAMES PATTON
(1822–1872)
Confederate general; congressman

James Patton Anderson was the son of William Preston Anderson and Margaret Adair Anderson. He was born in Winchester, Tennessee, in 1822. His father having died when James was still a boy, Anderson

was brought up by his grandfather, who had him educated at Jefferson College in Pennsylvania. As a young man, Anderson moved to Mississippi where he became a physician and county sheriff. While engaged in these occupations, Anderson studied law and was admitted to the Mississippi bar. In 1847 he raised the 1st Battalion Mississippi Rifles to fight in the Mexican War and became the unit's lieutenant colonel and then colonel.

Upon his return to the United States, Anderson became involved in Mississippi politics, served in the state legislature, and became a protege of Jefferson Davis. After losing his bid for reelection to the state legislature, Anderson was appointed by President Franklin Pierce—probably at the urging of the president's secretary of war, Jefferson Davis—to serve as U.S. marshal in the Washington Territory and to take the territorial census. Anderson became so popular in Washington that he was selected as the territory's congressional delegate. He served in that position from 1855 to 1857. When offered the position of territorial governor by President James Buchanan, however, Anderson refused because of his desire in the midst of the sectional crisis to return to the South.

Anderson moved to Florida to manage the plantation of an elderly aunt and there became involved in Florida politics. Jefferson County, Florida, sent him as one of its delegates to the secession convention and then as a congressman to the Provisional Confederate Congress.

Within a few months, however, Anderson resigned his seat to join the 1st Florida Regiment stationed under Braxton Bragg at Pensacola. In February 1862 he received a promotion to brigadier general. He led a brigade at Shiloh and in defense of Corinth. In Bragg's invasion of Kentucky, he temporarily commanded a division that constituted the left of Bragg's morning attack on 8 October 1862 at Perryville. At Stones River he was again in command of his brigade when he captured a portion of the Union artillery. Leading a division the following year at Chickamauga, Georgia, Anderson was commended for his bravery there, and a few months later he led the same division at Chattanooga, Tennessee.

In February 1864 Anderson received a promotion to major general and was placed in charge of the District of Florida. In summer 1864 John Bell Hood summoned him from Florida after replacing Joseph Johnston in the defense of Atlanta. Anderson fought at Ezra Church and Utoy Creek before suffering a severe wound at Jonesboro. Physicians judged that his injuries would preclude further service, but as Sherman made his way through the Carolinas in the early months of 1865, Anderson ignored this advice and returned to the army. He surrendered at Greensboro, North Carolina, but stubbornly refused a parole.

Following the war Anderson worked as the editor of an agricultural newspaper and as a tax collector in Tennessee.

—*David S. Heidler and Jeanne T. Heidler*

See also Perryville, Battle of; Stones River, Battle of.

For further reading:
Anderson, James Patton. "Autobiography." (Transcript, Southern Historical Collection, University of North Carolina).
Hoffman, John. *The Confederate Collapse at the Battle of Missionary Ridge: The Reports of James Patton Anderson and His Brigade Commanders* (1985).

ANDERSON, JOSEPH REID
(1813–1892)
Confederate general; industrialist

Joseph Reid Anderson was born in Virginia to William Anderson and Anne Thomas Anderson. He graduated fourth of forty-nine in the United States Military Academy Class of 1836. Upon graduation, he entered the 3d Artillery but within months transferred to the Army Corps of Engineers. In less than a year, however, he resigned this commission to work as an engineer for the state of Virginia. In 1841 he opened his own engineering firm and became the superintendent of the Tredegar Iron Works. Over the next decade and a half, Anderson gradually gained financial control of the iron works until he owned it outright by 1858.

In addition to his business pursuits, Anderson became involved in Virginia politics. Originally a Whig, he became a Democrat in 1857 and served in the Virginia House of Delegates. Although he was not a radical, he did strongly support efforts to organize Southern commercial ventures before the war. Once Virginia seceded, he used these commercial connections to supply the Confederacy with war materiel.

To further support the war effort, Anderson accepted a commission as a major of artillery in the Confederate army in August 1861. A month later he received a promotion to brigadier general and a transfer to Wilmington, North Carolina. Concern that his absence would hurt the Tredegar Iron Works prompted the Confederate War Department to make his field command contingent on the iron works' smooth operation. Even while in North Carolina, Anderson remained apprehensive about the safety of Virginia and sent suggestions to the Confederate War Department about the best ways to block the James River to Union gunboats.

In early 1862 Anderson briefly commanded the District of Cape Fear and the District of North Carolina before bringing the Third North Carolina Brigade to the York Peninsula to join in the defense of Richmond. As Union general Irvin McDowell's army moved south from Washington in May 1862, Anderson commanded the

Joseph Reid Anderson (*Library of Congress*)

Army of the Rappahannock guarding the crossings around Fredericksburg, Virginia. During the Seven Days' battles, he commanded the 3d Brigade of A. P. Hill's division until he was wounded at Frayser's Farm on 30 June 1862. Because of his injury and the need to maximize the output from the Tredegar Works, Anderson resigned his commission in July 1862.

For the remainder of the war, Anderson dedicated all of his time to the operation of the iron works, keeping it at full production almost to the moment the Union army entered Richmond. The ammunition and artillery pieces produced there became an essential part of the Confederate war effort. Upon Richmond's surrender, the federal government confiscated the facility and did not relinquish it until 1867.

After the iron works returned to his ownership, Anderson spent much of the rest of his life managing it. He also remained active in Richmond affairs and efforts to industrialize the South. He died in New Hampshire in 1892, and his body was returned to Richmond for burial.

—*David S. Heidler and Jeanne T. Heidler*

See also Tredegar Iron Works; Wilmington, North Carolina.
For further reading:
Dew, Charles B. *Ironmaker to the Confederacy: Joseph R. Anderson and the Tredegar Iron Works* (1966).

ANDERSON, RICHARD HERON
(1821–1879)
Confederate general

Born to William Wallace Anderson and Mary Jane MacKenzie Anderson in South Carolina, Richard Anderson graduated fortieth of fifty-six in the 1842 class of the United States Military Academy. During the Mexican-American War, he fought in Winfield Scott's campaign to take Mexico City. He received a brevet to first lieutenant for his actions in this campaign. During the 1850s, Anderson served in a number of frontier posts and was promoted to captain in 1855. From 1858 to 1859, he served as a member of Colonel Albert Sidney Johnston's Utah expedition, following which he was stationed in Nebraska Territory. When he heard of the secession of his home state of South Carolina, Anderson resigned his commission and accepted a major's commission in the Confederate army.

Initially assigned to the Department of South Carolina and Florida, Anderson served under P. G. T. Beauregard in Charleston, South Carolina, during the Fort Sumter crisis and was present when that fort surrendered. When Beauregard moved from Charleston to assume command of the Confederate forces at Manassas Junction during the summer of 1861, Anderson assumed command at Charleston. He received a promotion to brigadier general in July 1861.

In early 1862 Anderson transferred to Richmond, where he commanded a brigade under James Longstreet in the Peninsula campaign and earned a promotion to the rank of major general. He remained a part of the Army of Northern Virginia for the remainder of the war, fighting in every major engagement of that army.

During the Peninsula campaign, Anderson commanded the guard for the Confederate retreat from Yorktown and held the Union army briefly at Williamsburg. Anderson moved north after this action to guard the Rappahannock River crossings from Irvin McDowell's move south from Washington. He left that position just in time to participate on 31 May 1862 in Joseph Johnston's attack on McClellan at Fair Oaks. James Longstreet commended Anderson for his actions there and during the Seven Days' battles.

Anderson received a promotion to major general in July 1862. After McClellan's retreat to the James River, Lee sent Jackson and Longstreet north to engage the Union army under John Pope. Anderson was temporarily left behind to guard Richmond against any renewal of hostilities by McClellan. When it became apparent that McClellan had no intention of attacking, Anderson joined General Longstreet's corps in time for the descent on Pope at Second Bull Run.

Lee followed this victory with his first invasion of the North, and Anderson's division was temporarily

detached to join with Stonewall Jackson's capture of Harper's Ferry in western Virginia. That goal accomplished, Anderson's division departed for the rendezvous with Lee's army at Sharpsburg. Anderson arrived at 7 A.M. on 17 September 1862, in time to participate in the early phases of the battle. He was wounded early in the day, however, and did not lead his men in their support of D. H. Hill at the sunken road. At the battle of Fredericksburg, Anderson commanded the Confederate far left and as a result had little part in the fighting. When Longstreet was sent to the Carolinas following Fredericksburg, Anderson's division remained with Lee. He moved out of Fredericksburg on 29 April 1863 to protect the approaches from Chancellorsville. He remained in that position, digging in for several days, and prevented Hooker from moving forward while Jackson moved around the Union army. Lee commended Anderson for his actions during the battle of Chancellorsville in May 1863.

With Stonewall Jackson's death at the battle of Chancellorsville, Anderson's division was moved to A. P. Hill's Corps. On the second day of the fighting at Gettysburg, Anderson and his division, temporarily attached to Longstreet, attacked the Union right of Daniel Sickles's corps that had moved off of Cemetery Ridge. The following day, part of Anderson's division participated in Pickett's Charge.

In May 1864 Anderson temporarily rose to the rank of lieutenant general and corps commander when James Longstreet was severely wounded at the battle of the Wilderness. In command of Longstreet's corps, Anderson was ordered by Lee to move out of Confederate lines to Spotsylvania Court House before General Grant could reach that point. Anderson managed to move his men to the position earlier and with greater speed than Lee had anticipated, but Anderson was nonetheless barely ahead of the lead elements of the Union army.

When Longstreet returned to command of his corps in October 1864, Anderson was moved to help supervise Richmond's defenses. When Confederate forces evacuated their entrenchments at Petersburg, Anderson commanded the right of the retreat. Most of his command was either devastated or scattered at Sayler's Creek, and the remainder was put under Longstreet and John B. Gordon. Absent a command, Anderson received permission to return home. He departed for South Carolina on 7 April 1865, two days before Lee's surrender on 9 April at Appomattox.

The period after the war was difficult for Anderson. His failure at several endeavors left him dying in virtual poverty in Beaufort, South Carolina.

—*David S. Heidler and Jeanne T. Heidler*

See also Sayler's Creek, Battle of.
For further reading:
Elliott, Joseph Cantey. *Lieutenant General Richard Heron Anderson: Lee's Noble Soldier* (1985).
Walker, Cornelius Irvine. *The Life of Lieutenant General Richard Heron Anderson, of the Confederate States Army* (1917).

ANDERSON, ROBERT
(1805–1871)
Union officer

Robert Anderson was born near Louisville, Kentucky, the son of a Revolutionary War officer. He graduated from West Point, fifteenth in a class of thirty-seven, in 1825, and was commissioned a lieutenant with the 3d U.S. Artillery. Anderson went on to distinguish himself by fighting in the Black Hawk War of 1832, winning a brevet promotion to captain; he also earned praise for his performance against the Seminole Indians from 1836 to 1838.

Anderson subsequently served as assistant adjutant general in the Eastern Division, 1838–1841, where he rose to captain. During the Mexican-American War, he campaigned under Winfield Scott throughout the advance upon Mexico City in 1847. Valorous behavior at Molino del Rey brought him a second brevet promotion to major and a severe wound. After the war, Anderson fulfilled a number of routine assignments without fanfare, and sought to supplement his meager income by translating several French artillery texts for the army. By 1857 he had risen to the rank of major and gained a reputation as a deeply religious, highly conscientious soldier. In 1845 he married Elizabeth Bayard Clinch of Georgia and came into possession of several slaves. Moreover, like many officers of Southern birth (his family was originally Virginian), he espoused pro-slavery and pro-Southern sympathies. As events would prove, the slight, nondescript Anderson was also possessed of an unimpeachable sense of loyalty and devotion to the United States.

By November 1860, the escalating tide of secession emboldened Southern resentment toward the North, and isolated army garrisons became objects of derision. Such was the state of affairs around Charleston, South Carolina, when the War Department ordered Anderson to take charge of the three small forts in the harbor. His appointment was a calculated move, for they anticipated that a pro-Southern officer would use tact and discretion in dealing with Charleston authorities. Although he accepted the assignment, Anderson keenly felt the weight of his predicament and was determined not to initiate any moves that might precipitate a war.

In his dealings with local authorities, Anderson proved polite, even sympathetic, but to no avail. He also believed that it was only a matter of time before the government ordered him to hand his post over to the Southerners. However, attitudes hardened toward the presence of a Union garrison after 20 December 1860, when an ordinance of secession was passed. Anderson at this point deemed his position untenable, and on the night of 26 December he abandoned Fort Moultrie and Castle Pinckney, spiking the guns. He then relocated the 137 men of his command to Fort Sumter, an unfinished work on an island in the middle of Charleston harbor. The beleaguered garrison set about fortifying their position while awaiting further instructions from Washington.

As events unfolded, the administration of James Buchanan proved unable to handle the growing secession crisis. They ignored or overlooked Anderson's pleas for both reinforcements and supplies throughout the winter and early spring of 1861. Bereft of orders, Anderson took it upon himself to maintain the status quo as long as his possession of Fort Sumter was not compromised. He politely rebuffed Confederate demands for his surrender, but in a most conciliatory fashion. His determination to avoid provoking hostilities was underscored on 9 January 1861, when Confederate shore batteries fired upon and drove off the much-needed supply ship *Star of the West*. This greatly exacerbated his logistical problems, and he went so far as to advise Southern emissaries that he would be forced to capitulate on 15 April 1861 if supplies were not forthcoming.

It fell upon the newly installed administration of Abraham Lincoln to break the impasse. The president probably realized that Anderson's garrison was doomed in the event of war, so he orchestrated a scheme to maximize political benefit from their demise. He thereupon declared that an expedition was being mounted for the express purpose of resupplying Fort Sumter and not reinforcing it. If the Confederates had the audacity to violate this humane mission, he expected Southern aggression to mobilize and unify his Northern political base.

Lincoln's reasoning proved correct. Unwilling to tolerate a Union garrison further, and determined to prevent its being supplied, on 12 April 1861 General Pierre G. T. Beauregard sent an ultimatum to Anderson demanding his immediate surrender. Anderson, unmoved as always, politely declined. One hour later, at 4:30 A.M., Confederate gunners fired the first shots of the Civil War. Discarding his past deference, Anderson replied in kind and allowed his subordinate, Captain Abner Doubleday, the honor of returning the first Union shot. The ensuing 36-hour bombardment severely damaged Fort Sumter before Anderson struck his colors on 14 April 1861. The garrison then surrendered with honors of war and was paroled and allowed to leave. Miraculously, Union forces sustained only two fatalities—a gunner who died when his cannon exploded as it fired a salute to the lowering American flag and another soldier mortally wounded by the explosion. But, as Lincoln anticipated, the Confederates were tarred as aggressors and bolstered Northern sentiment for war.

Anderson's stand at Fort Sumter made him a national hero overnight, and he was promoted to brigadier general on 15 May 1861. He subsequently commanded the Department of Kentucky (later the Department of the Cumberland) for several months as the neutrality of that essential border state hung in the balance. Anderson worked carefully on behalf of the federal government until his health gave out and he was replaced by General William T. Sherman on 8 October 1861. He saw no further action until April 1865, when he donned the uniform of a brevet major general of volunteers and hoisted the American flag over Fort Sumter after the Confederate surrender. Anderson then relocated to Europe in an attempt to improve his health; he died in Nice, France, and was interred at West Point.

—*John C. Fredriksen*

See also Doubleday, Abner; Fort Sumter.
For further reading:
Garrison, Webb S. *Lincoln's Little War* (1997).
Klein, Maury. *Days of Defiance: Sumter, Secession, and the Coming of the Civil War* (1997).

ANDERSON, WILLIAM "BLOODY BILL" (1839–1864)

Confederate guerrilla leader

Born in Kentucky in 1839, the oldest of six children born to William Anderson, Sr., and Martha Anderson, William, Jr., migrated with his family from Missouri to his father's land claim east of Council Grove, Kansas, in 1857. By the time he reached 21 he had acquired a land claim of his own and was accompanying wagon trains west on the Santa Fe Trail and apparently engaging in selling stolen ponies and horses. With the outbreak of the Civil War he began a career in banditry, first with pro-Union, antislavery Jayhawkers, then with pro-Confederate, proslavery Bushwhackers. In both cases his object was financial. Like other such irregular forces operating in Kansas, they were enriched themselves under the guise of fighting for liberty.

After his father died the victim of a shotgun blast to the chest over a matter of "family honor"—his mother had died in 1860 when struck by lightning—Bill and his brother Jim took the remainder of the family back to Missouri but not before mortally wounding the object of the family's "dishonor" in July 1862. Here in western Missouri they resumed their guerrilla warfare, now against pro-Unionists in the area, especially along the Santa Fe Trail. Bill eventually headed up his own 30-to-40-man guerrilla band as its "captain."

Anderson's notoriety as a guerrilla began in 1863 when he joined the band led by William Clarke Quantrill. This move was triggered by the death of his 14-year-old sister Josephine and injuries to his 16-year-

old sister Mary Ellen and 10-year-old sister Janie in the collapse of a temporary Union jail in Kansas City on 13 August 1863. The jail was a three-story brick building being used to house women suspected of aiding the pro-Confederate guerrillas. It collapsed when a weakened adjoining building fell in on it. Believing that the Union soldiers had deliberately weakened the structure and acting out of revenge with some 450 other partisans, Anderson (along with Frank James, Cole Younger, and others) played a leading role in Quantrill's retaliatory raid on Lawrence, Kansas, on 21 August of that year. Quantrill's last order to his men was to "Kill every man big enough to carry a gun." Close to 200 unarmed men and boys were killed—Anderson personally killing fourteen—and the business district of the town was put to the torch.

In Texas that winter Anderson got married and broke with Quantrill. In the spring of 1864 led about 50 guerrillas back to Missouri, there to burn, loot, and slaughter Union soldiers and pro-Union civilians in the central part of the state. This orgy of violence climaxed on 27 September 1864, at the little town of Centralia when Anderson's gang, joining with those of Thomas Todd, Si Gordon, and others, first looted the town and held up a stagecoach. They then stopped a North Missouri train a mile out of town, stripped 24 unarmed Union soldiers of their uniforms and shot them down in cold blood (except for Sergeant Tom Goodman, whom they spared to exchange for one of their men captured four days before). When a Union force chasing them fell into their trap three miles southeast of Centralia, Anderson's men killed over 100 soldiers, mutilating some. The guerrillas thereafter returned to Centralia to kill more soldiers before riding off.

Anderson and his guerrillas then went on to serve with Confederate generals Sterling Price and Joseph Shelby in their unsuccessful raid into Missouri that ended decisively at Westport on 23 October. Caught in a Union ambush outside of Albany, Missouri, on 7 October 1864, Anderson, now referred to as "the blood-drenched savage," was cut down by two shots to the head as he led his guerrilla column into the fray. The next day his body was placed on public exhibition in nearby Richmond and photographed with his head propped up, wearing a "guerrilla shirt," and with pistols in both hands. It was also reported that he was decapitated by Unionist militiamen, his head stuck atop of a pole, his body dragged through town behind a horse.

Thus ended the short and violent career of the Confederacy's most noted and brutal guerrilla partisan other than William Quantrill. Anderson claimed to have tied a knot in a silken cord for every man he killed (the knots totaling 54 by his death) and to have decorated the bridle of his horse with the scalps of Federal soldiers. He was buried that day in an unmarked grave in the Richmond cemetery. Today an incorrectly dated headstone marks his grave.

—*James M. Morris*

See also Centralia Massacre; Guerrilla Warfare; Lawrence, Kansas; Missouri; Quantrill, William Clarke.

For further reading:

Brownlee, Richard S. *Gray Ghosts of the Confederacy: Guerrilla Warfare in the West, 1861–1865* (1958).

Castel, Albert, and Thomas Goodrich. *Bloody Bill Anderson: The Short, Savage Life of a Civil War Guerrilla* (1998).

Goodrich, Thomas. *Black Flag: Guerrilla Warfare on the Western Border, 1861–1865* (1995).

Harris, Charles F. "Catalyst for Terror: The Collapse of the Women's Prison in Kansas City." *Missouri Historical Review* (1995).

Leslie, Edward. *The Devil Knows How to Ride: The True Story of William Clarke Quantrill and His Confederate Raiders* (1996).

Monaghan, Jay. *Civil War on the Western Border, 1854–1865* (1955).

Schultz, Duane. *Quantrill's War: The Life and Times of William Clarke Quantrill, 1837–1865* (1996).

ANDERSONVILLE
(1864–1865)
Confederate military prison

Construction of Andersonville prison, officially known as Camp Sumter, began in southern Georgia in January 1864. Between February 1864 and May 1865, 45,613 United States prisoners were held at Andersonville, and nearly 13,000 men died there.

Filth, vermin, disease, malnutrition, exposure to the elements, and a stench that was said to cause prisoners to vomit upon entering the grounds characterized Andersonville prison. Conditions such as these were endemic to many hastily constructed Civil War military penitentiaries, but Andersonville's reputation for its exceptionally brutal conditions has made it the best known of all Civil War prisons.

Until 1863 prisoners of war were exchanged under a cartel between the Confederate and United States governments. After the agreement collapsed, the need to construct large military prison camps developed. The site for Andersonville, selected by Confederate captain W. Sidney Winder, was chosen because of its distance from battle lines, access to railroad lines, and its ample supply of pure water and lumber in the Georgia pine forest.

Although plans dictated that barracks be built at the prison, the inflated price of lumber meant that Confederate officials could not afford to purchase the board feet needed for such construction. Instead, a stockade that surrounded 16.5 acres of land enclosed the prisoners beneath the open sky. Built with slave labor, the stockade was constructed of pine logs cut to a length of 25 feet. Logs hewn to a thickness of 12 inches were placed into the ground at a depth of 5 feet, leaving a wall

View from the main gate of prisoners drawing rations at Andersonville, 17 August 1864
(Photograph by A. J. Riddle / *National Archives*)

of 15 feet surrounding the grounds. A stream about five feet wide flowed through the prison and supplied the inmates with water.

The first prisoners arrived at Andersonville on 25 February 1864, before construction of the facility was completed. In June 1864, while the prison held over 23,000 men, the stockade was enlarged to enclose a total of 26 acres of land. With no buildings in which inmates could take shelter, captives were exposed to the elements. Using scraps of lumber, logs, blankets, and whatever materials they could scavenge, prisoners built crude structures, which they called "shebangs," that served as inadequate housing.

A lack of sanitary practices and overcrowding plagued the prison. Workers in the prison bakery, which was located upstream of the stockade, discarded refuse into the stream, thus contaminating the water supply before it reached the inmates. Men bathing and defecating in

and near the stream were another source of contamination. The prison was built to accommodate 10,000 men; however, by the end of July 1864, Confederate officials crowded over 31,000 prisoners into the stockade. In August 1864 Andersonville's inmate population reached its high of nearly 33,000. Such a high population taxed limited facilities and resources. Prisoners standing and walking near the stream eroded its banks and created a three-and-a-half-acre swamp in the center of the prison. The swamp, which served as a toilet area, resulted not only in a portion of land rendered uninhabitable, but also created an unbearable stench and a source of disease where maggots were said to breed 15 to 18 inches deep.

Many prisoners who arrived at Andersonville sickly and weak found conditions at the prison camp compounded their misery. Meager, nutritionally inadequate, and uncooked rations resulted in a variety of illnesses and contributed to the deaths of many inmates.

A burial party at Andersonville prison, 17 August 1864. (Photograph by A. J. Riddle / *National Archives*)

Scurvy, which was widespread in the camp, as well as malnutrition, intensified the suffering of thousands of men who were plagued with and died from respiratory ailments and from various intestinal tract disorders and diseases, including diarrhea and dysentery.

Along with disease, violence perpetrated by prison guards, as well as by inmates resulted in many deaths. Guards were known to kill prisoners who made the unfortunate mistake of venturing too close to the stockade's deadline.

The degree to which Confederates deliberately brutalized Union prisoners, however, has been debated. Because of a shortage of Confederate soldiers available to serve as guards, Andersonville's prison guards were posted only to ensure that inmates would not escape, and not necessarily to maintain order. As a result, inmates terrorized, stole from, and killed fellow prisoners. The largest and most notorious of these raiders was a band of men that arrived in April 1864 under the leadership of William "Mosby" Collins of Pennsylvania.

After suffering the attacks of Mosby's raiders for some months, inmates appealed to the commander of the prison for relief. He eventually decided to allow prisoners to organize themselves, and to arrest and try the suspected criminals.

In July the so-called Regulators arrested twenty-four members of the raider gang. A jury made up of twelve inmates heard evidence against the raiders and brought a sentence of death against six of the ringleaders. On 11 July, the guilty men were executed by hanging. The eighteen who were not convicted were forced to run a gauntlet of their fellow prisoners armed with clubs. Three men died from the beatings they received.

In early September 1864, as Unions troops advanced deeper into the South and closer to Andersonville, Confederate officials transferred most of the camps' inmates to other Southern penitentiaries. By December 1864 only 1,359 prisoners who were too sick to travel remained in Andersonville. Additional men, however, were transferred to the prison in late December. On 4

May 1865 Colonel George C. Gibbs, who had taken command of the prison in October 1864, paroled the remaining inmates.

Noteworthy among Andersonville's prison officials was Captain Henry Wirz, who commanded the interior of the prison. In the aftermath of the war, Wirz, a native of Switzerland, was arrested and tried by a military court for crimes connected to his service at Andersonville. It appears that much of testimony of former prisoners against Wirz, who was hated by inmates, lacked credibility. Wirz did not receive a fair trial. Nevertheless, he was found guilty and sentenced to death. On 10 November 1865, he was hanged in Washington, D.C.

Today, the prison grounds and the adjoining cemetery are part of the 395-acre Andersonville National Historic Site.

—Alicia Rodriquez

See also Prisoner Exchanges; Prisoner Paroles; Prisoners of War; Prisons, C.S.A.; Wirz, Henry.

For further reading:

Hesseltine, William Best. *Civil War Prisons: A Study in War Psychology* (1998).

Marvel, William. *Andersonville: The Last Depot* (1994).

Speer, Lonnie R. *Portals to Hell: Military Prisons of the Civil War* (1997).

ANDREW, JOHN ALBION
(1818–1867)
Governor of Massachusetts

John A. Andrew was born in Windham, Maine, on 31 May 1818, the son of a farmer and merchant. After graduating from Bowdoin College in 1837, he studied law in Boston and was admitted to the Massachusetts bar in 1840. As a young lawyer, Andrew was an active abolitionist opponent of the war with Mexico and the Fugitive Slave Act. As a Conscience Whig allied with Charles Francis Adams, Charles Sumner, and Theodore Parker, Andrew moved easily to the Free Soil Party in 1848 and was an organizer of the Republican Party in 1856. Elected as a Republican state legislator from Boston in 1857, Andrew became prominent as a defender of John Brown. His legal defense efforts led a U.S. Senate committee investigating the Harper's Ferry raid to summon Andrew to Washington. In 1860 he was chairman of the Massachusetts delegation at the Republican Convention in Chicago and was instrumental in switching many votes from Seward to Lincoln. Later that year, Andrew was elected governor by the largest popular majority of the era.

Upon taking office, Governor Andrew obtained an emergency appropriation from the legislature to expand the state militia before the attack on Fort Sumter. Despite Andrew's distrust of the new administration and Secretary of War Simon Cameron, Massachusetts was the first state to respond to Lincoln's call for volunteers in April 1861. The 6th Massachusetts Regiment battled a Baltimore mob on 19 April while boarding trains to defend Washington, D.C. The zealous Andrew became one of the strongest and most effective wartime governors and was reelected to five terms spanning 1861 to 1866.

Perhaps his chief achievement was in persuading Secretary of War Edwin M. Stanton to authorize African-American troops. When enlistments of black troops in Massachusetts proved inadequate, Andrew's agents recruited in other states despite the objections of Stanton, General Ulysses S. Grant, and some governors. By May 1863, the 54th Massachusetts Regiment became the first regular army regiment of black soldiers (led by Colonel Robert Gould Shaw and other white officers) in the Union army. Andrew championed the 178,000 African-American soldiers who served in the Union army when Stanton ruled that they were not entitled to a Federal enlistment bounty and were paid less than white troops. In this imbroglio, the clearsighted Andrew also opposed the War Department's action authorizing Massachusetts general Benjamin F. Butler to recruit six regiments in the New England states (called the Department of New England) while the region's governors recruited troops at the same time with subsequent confusion and expense. When Stanton replaced Cameron in January 1862, Andrew persuaded the War Department to abolish the Department of New England and ended his quarrel with General Butler.

Andrew also defended another despised minority when he adopted a pro-Catholic stance in 1862. By showing his support for Irish Catholic soldiers, he won a following among Catholic and anti-nativist voters. Andrew patiently resolved disputes in the 9th Massachusetts Volunteer Infantry and other Irish units and persuaded the legislature to repeal discriminatory laws aimed at Irish immigrants and passed with Know-Nothing and Republican Party support in 1857–1859. Consequently, Colonel Patrick R. Guiney, commanding the 9th Massachusetts, broke with most Irish Catholics in the state to support Andrew and other Republican candidates.

Governor Andrew encountered other problems from an unexpected quarter, the 20th Massachusetts Volunteer Infantry, dubbed the "Harvard Regiment" because so many officers were Harvard graduates, including Oliver Wendell Holmes, Jr., and the grandson of Paul Revere. The 20th was also labeled the "Copperhead Regiment" because of the antiabolitionist views of many of its Harvard-educated officers even though two of its companies were made up of abolitionist Germans.

In 1865 Andrew honored the 54th Regiment's heroic service at Fort Wagner, South Carolina, on 18 July 1863 by appointing the committee that authorized the Shaw

Memorial unveiled on Boston Common on Decoration Day 1897. This monumental bronze relief of Shaw and his black troops, sculpted by Augustus Saint-Gaudens, was the first significant public celebration of African-American service in the Civil War.

Governor Andrew presided over the first national convention of the Unitarian Church and retired from public office. His farewell address in January 1866 included his support for a lenient reconstruction policy. Returning to his law practice, he continued his interests in temperance, divorce, and usury reforms. But exhausted by the war years, Andrew died suddenly in Boston on 30 October 1867 and was buried at Mount Auburn Cemetery in Cambridge and later interred in Hingham, Massachusetts.

John Andrew's skill in coping with the conflicting demands of Garrisonian abolitionists, pro-war and Copperhead Democrats, African-American leaders, a vigilant local press, the patronage pressures in commissioning officers, the public welfare needs on the home front, and an often inefficient and inconstant War Department is, perhaps, his great legacy.

—*Peter C. Holloran*

See also Butler, Benjamin Franklin; Parker, Theodore; Shaw, Robert Gould; Sumner, Charles.

For further reading:

Chandler, Peleg W. *Memoir of the Hon. John Albion Andrew* (1880).

Hamrogue, John M. "John A. Andrew, Abolitionist Governor, 1861–1865" (Ph.D. dissertation, 1974).

O'Connor, Thomas H. *Civil War Boston: Homefront and Battlefield* (1997).

Pearson, Henry Greenleaf. *The Life of John A. Andrew, Governor of Massachusetts, 1861–1865* (1904).

Samito, Christian G. *Commanding Boston's Irish Ninth: The Civil War Letters of Colonel Patrick R. Guiney, Ninth Massachusetts Volunteer Infantry* (1998).

ANDREWS, GEORGE LEONARD
(1828–1899)
Union general

George Leonard Andrews was born to Manasseh Andrews and Harriet Leonard Andrews in Bridgewater, Massachusetts. He attended the State Normal School at Bridgewater before accepting an appointment to the U.S. Military Academy, from which he graduated first of forty-two in the class of 1851. After commissioning in the Corps of Engineers, Andrews served on the Fort Warren project in Boston and as an instructor at West Point before resigning his commission in 1855. Before the Civil War, he worked as a civil engineer.

At the outbreak of hostilities, Andrews accepted a commission as the lieutenant colonel of the 2d Massachusetts. During the Shenandoah Valley campaign of the spring of 1862, Andrews commanded the 2d under Nathaniel Prentiss Banks. Andrews was promoted to colonel of the regiment on 13 June 1862 and led it at the battles of Cedar Mountain and Antietam. At the latter engagement, the 2d Massachusetts supported Major General Joseph Hooker on the Union right.

On 10 November 1862, Andrews was promoted to brigadier general and assigned to Banks's Louisiana expedition. He was sent by Banks to New York City in December 1862 to prepare the transports for shipment of the army. Upon his arrival in New Orleans in early 1863, Andrews was made Banks's chief of staff.

During the summer of 1863, Andrews participated in the siege and capture of Port Hudson, and upon its surrender on 9 July 1863, Andrews was placed in command. The following day, he was given command of the Corps d'Afrique, a unit of African-American soldiers. At the same time that Andrews was charged with raising this new unit from surrounding plantations, he commanded the District of Baton Rouge and Port Hudson, headquartered at Port Hudson. Until February 1865 he held this command, during which he sent out parties to outlying plantations on and near the Mississippi River to recruit young male slaves for African-American units.

In February 1865 Andrews was relieved from his command at Port Hudson and ordered to report to New Orleans. He was made provost-marshal general of the Army of the Gulf, a position he held until the end of the war. He fought in the Mobile campaign of the spring of 1865, for which he was commended by Major General Edward R. S. Canby.

Andrews was one of the commissioners appointed by Canby in May 1865 to receive the surrender of Lieutenant General Richard Taylor. Andrews became Canby's chief of staff in June and spent the next weeks supervising the paroling of prisoners at Shreveport, Louisiana.

Andrews left the army in August 1865 and spent the next two years as a Mississippi planter. He returned to Massachusetts in 1867 where he worked for several years as a U.S. marshal. He became a professor of French at the U.S. Military Academy in 1871, a position he occupied for over twenty years. He retired to Brookline, Massachusetts, where he died on 4 April 1899. His remains were taken to Arlington National Cemetery for burial.

—*David S. Heidler and Jeanne T. Heidler*

See also African-American Soldiers, C.S.A.; Banks, Nathaniel Prentiss; Mobile Campaign; Port Hudson.

For further reading:

Hollingsworth, Harold M. "George Andrews—Carpetbagger." *Tennessee Historical Quarterly* (1969).

ANDREWS, JAMES
See Andrews's Raid

ANDREWS'S RAID
(12 April 1862)

Both Union and Confederate troops sabotaged railroads to impede enemy supply and troop transport. The Andrews's Raid, popularly known as the "Great Locomotive Chase," was one of the best-known attempts at railroad destruction during the Civil War. The Civil War was the first U.S. war in which railroads were used. Because tracks linked major cities, control of the railroad provided a strategic advantage.

In the spring of 1862, the Confederate defense line stretched from Richmond, Virginia, to Corinth, Mississippi. General Joseph E. Johnston was at Richmond, relying on railroads to connect with forces in the Deep South that were commanded by General P. G. T. Beauregard. The rail line between Richmond and Memphis, passing through east Tennessee, was the quickest route. From Memphis, supplies could be diverted to or received from such major centers as New Orleans, Mobile, Montgomery, Charleston, and Savannah. Union strategists realized that controlling the Tennessee railroad would hinder Confederate troops in Virginia. Brigadier General Ormsby M. Mitchel planned to move Union troops from western Tennessee to the eastern part of the state, expelling Confederates from Chattanooga. From there, he planned to launch an assault against Virginia and defeat the Confederacy. To achieve this, he wanted to damage the rail lines from Atlanta to Chattanooga.

Previously, an effort to destroy the Western & Atlantic Railroad's bridges in Georgia had failed because the operatives did not show up as planned in Atlanta. On 7 April 1862, Mitchel asked James J. Andrews, a furtive character with a mysterious past, to recruit volunteers for a second attempt. Andrews had admirably performed spying missions for General Don Carlos Buell and had also smuggled quinine to Union troops. Mitchel ordered Andrews to steal a train to burn railroad bridges, destroy tracks, and cut telegraph lines along the Georgia State Railroad south of Chattanooga. At the same time, Mitchel planned to secure Huntsville, Alabama, and move east to meet up with Andrews and his men behind Federal lines in Chattanooga. (The Andrews's Raiders are sometimes also referred to as the Mitchel's Raiders.) Twenty-two Ohio soldiers from General Joshua W. Sill's brigade accepted Andrews's invitation. Traveling from Shelbyville, Tennessee, wearing civilian clothes, they walked through rain and mud in small groups to Chattanooga where they boarded a southbound train. By midnight on 11 April, the raiders reached Marietta, Georgia, where they rendezvoused with Andrews. Several of the volunteers were delayed by the weather, and two had been impressed into the Confederate army. The next morning, they bought tickets to Big Shanty (Kennesaw), Georgia, twenty-five miles north of Atlanta. When they arrived,

they discovered that a Confederate camp was located by the tracks, a fact that Andrews had been unaware of, and he told his men to proceed cautiously.

While the train's crew and passengers ate breakfast at a restaurant, the Union raiders separated the steam locomotive named the General, the tender, and three boxcars from the train and opened the throttle to leave the station. A Confederate sentry observed the train thieves, but was unsure if they were railroad employees or saboteurs. When he realized that they were stealing the engine, he was unable to notify other stations because Big Shanty did not have a telegraph. Inside the restaurant, the General's conductor, Captain William A. Fuller, and crew heard the train and rushed outside to see the engine departing while Confederate soldiers fired rifles at it. Fuller, engineer Jeff Cain, and shop foreman Anthony Murphy began running after the General, and two miles up the track, they found a handcar. The handcar derailed at a spot where the raiders had broken the rails. Placing the handcar back on the tracks, the train crew reached Etowah, Georgia, where they found the engine Yonah sitting on a siding. The raiders had not stopped to disable the Yonah because they feared it would raise suspicions. While the train crew steamed up the Yonah, the raiders stopped to cut telegraph wires at several places so that any pursuers could not warn stations up the tracks. Andrews had obtained a timetable for the railroad and put the General on a siding at Kingston, Georgia, so that a scheduled southbound express train could pass. However, two more trains arrived that were not listed on the timetable, and an anxious Andrews insisted that he be allowed to pass, stating that he had orders to deliver a trainload of gunpowder to Confederate General P. G. T. Beauregard. When Andrews demanded to know the cause of the delay, the station agent told him that General Mitchel had captured Huntsville and Confederate train traffic had been diverted to the Georgia route.

After sixty-five minutes of waiting, the raiders were permitted to continue. Five minutes later, Fuller and his men were stopped by the three southbound trains. They abandoned the Yonah on a siding and traveled to a junction two miles north of Kingston where they took the engine named William L. Smith, but were halted by broken rails that the raiders had thrown on the tracks. Fuller and Murphy raced on foot, stopping the engine Texas at Adairsville and then pursuing the General in reverse. The raiders released two boxcars to block the Texas. When they tried to burn bridges, the rain-soaked wood refused to catch fire, and they left a boxcar aflame on one bridge. After pushing the boxcars onto a siding, the Texas began a pursuit that reached speeds of sixty miles per hour, with the pursuers catching glimpses of the General. Depleted of wood and water, the General lost steam two miles north of Ringgold, just south of the Tennessee border. The approximately ninety-mile chase ended with the raiders abandoning the General and running into the woods.

Search parties located and captured most of the raiders within days and placed them in jails at Chattanooga and Atlanta. Two raiders floated down the Chattahoochee and Apalachicola rivers to the coast, and others who eluded capture headed north to rejoin their regiments. Andrews and seven men were tried as spies and hanged in Atlanta in June. If they had worn uniforms, they would have been considered prisoners of war. Six raiders were exchanged for Confederate prisoners and were awarded the U.S. Army's first Medal of Honor in March 1863. The remaining raiders, except Andrews, later received Medals of Honor, including posthumous presentations.

The surviving Andrews's Raiders wrote articles and books about their adventures, attended anniversary celebrations of the raid, and were honored guests at Grand Army of the Republic conventions. The General was displayed at the 1888 national grand encampment in Columbus, Ohio. The Confederate pursuers joined the raiders to speak to audiences about the chase. In May 1891, several raiders also attended dedication services for the Ohio Monument at the National Cemetery in Chattanooga. Topped by a bronze replica of the General, the monument was placed next to the graves of the executed raiders. Historical markers were placed at significant Andrews's Raid sites in Tennessee and Georgia. In April 1962, a steam engine reenacted the chase for the Civil War Centennial, and President John F. Kennedy hosted ceremonies at the White House for the raiders' descendants. The General toured the United States before being housed at the Big Shanty Museum in Kennesaw. The Texas was displayed in the lobby of the Atlanta Cyclorama. Embellished as a folk legend, the Andrews's Raid was the subject of books and movies, including Walt Disney's *The Great Locomotive Chase* (1956).

—*Elizabeth D. Schafer*

See also Covert Activities, C.S.A.; Espionage; Railroads, C.S.A.; Railroads, U.S.A..
For further reading:
Epstein, Samuel, and Beryl Epstein. *The Andrews Raid or the Great Locomotive Chase April 12, 1862* (1956).
Gregg, Frank M. *Andrews Raiders* (1891).
O'Neill, Charles. *Wild Train: The Story of the Andrews Raiders* (1956).
Pittenger, William. *Daring and Suffering: A History of the Great Railroad Adventure* (1863).
Wilson, John A. *Adventures of Alf. Wilson: A Thrilling Episode of the Dark Days of the Rebellion* (1897).

"ANNALS OF THE WAR"

Considered by many historians to be one of the finest postwar series of recollections by veterans of the Civil War, the "Annals of the War" was the brainchild of Philadelphia journalist Alexander K. McClure. An active Republican politician, McClure

owned the Philadelphia *Times*, a daily paper in the city. To increase circulation, McClure contacted Civil War generals and civilian leaders and asked them to contribute to a series about the war that he wished to publish in a new paper.

The new paper, the Philadelphia *Weekly Times*, began publication on 3 March 1877. Each weekly issue featured the series "Annals of the War" on the front page. The first issue included an article written by Gideon Welles entitled "The First Ironclad." Contributors from the Union side included James H. Wilson, William B. Franklin, Andrew A. Humphreys, Samuel W. Crawford, Noble D. Preston, and David H. Strother. To balance the perspectives, McClure made sure that former Confederates wrote articles for the Annals. These men included John E. Cooke, Henry B. McClellan, Armistead L. Long, James Longstreet, Walter H. Taylor, Henry Heth, and John H. Reagan.

Subjects included the controversies surrounding the battle of Gettysburg, the fighting at Bristoe Station, the Knoxville campaign, Chancellorsville, Second Manassas, Petersburg, and a wide array of other battles and campaigns. Some writers delved into the subject of blacks in Confederate armies; others wrote of amazing adventures of scouts behind the lines. Boston Corbett wrote of the death of John Wilkes Booth, and Matoaca Gay penned a short piece about social life in Richmond during the war.

In 1879, McClure published a hardbound book that contained fifty-five of the articles included thus far in the series. The series continued to attract a wide reading audience but a planned second volume was never published. "Annals of the War" finally ground to a halt in 1888. The entire series included more than 800 contributions, ranging in size from an entire page to a single column. The series proved to be a valuable contribution to the history of the Civil War as seen by men and women who took part in this great epic of U.S. history.

—*Richard A. Sauers*

See also National Tribune.
For further reading:
McClure, Alexander K., ed. *The Annals of the War Written by Leading Participants North and South* (1879; reprint 1994).

ANTHONY, SUSAN BROWNELL
(1820–1906)
Abolitionist; suffragist

Susan Brownell Anthony was born in Adams, Massachusetts, the daughter of Daniel and Lucy Anthony. Anthony's early career was as a schoolteacher, but when she left home in 1852 to run her family's farm in Center Falls, New York, she became interested in the temperance, antislavery, and women's rights movements. Anthony met Elizabeth Cady Stanton in 1851, a meeting that began a close working and personal relationship that would last for both their lives. Anthony attended her first women's rights convention in 1852 in Syracuse, New York, and threw herself into her work as a reformer for the rest of the 1850s.

Beginning in 1856, she lectured for the American Anti-Slavery Society throughout New York state and in January 1861, with tensions over slavery and the sectional conflict mounting, she was mobbed when speaking in Albany and Buffalo. Anthony's continued commitment was clear when she wrote Martha Coffin Wright, reformer and sister of Lucretia Mott, "There was a more determined union to put down a speech, not to the mind of the masses—but we must face it through."

Anthony and other women's rights supporters halted their conventions for the duration of the Civil War, but remained interested in the abolition of slavery. Disappointed with the limited nature of President Lincoln's Emancipation Proclamation, Anthony founded the Women's National Loyal League with Stanton on 14 May 1863 in New York City. Anthony served as the secretary, while Stanton held the office of president. The goals of the League were to collect a million signatures on a petition calling for the abolition of slavery throughout the United States, a petition that they later revised to call for a constitutional amendment: "believing slavery the great cause of the present rebellion, and an institution fatal to the life of Republican government, earnestly pray your honorable bodies to immediately abolish it throughout the United states; and to adopt measures for so amending the Constitution, as forever to prohibit its existence in any portion of our common country." The League collected 400,000 signatures by the summer of 1864. Anthony also opposed Lincoln's reelection in 1864, supporting the more avowedly antislavery candidate, John C. Frémont.

After the war, Anthony continued her agitation on behalf of rights for women and African-Americans, joining the American Equal Rights Association. In 1867 she and Stanton headed to Kansas, where both women's and African-American suffrage were to be put to a referendum. Anthony and Stanton could not gain the support of the Republican Party or their fellow abolitionists in agitating for the passage of the women's suffrage referendum. The relationship between Stanton and Anthony and the Equal Rights Association grew worse in 1869, when the Association endorsed the Fifteenth Amendment, even though it did not include a provision for women's suffrage. Stanton and Anthony broke with the Association to form the National Woman Suffrage Association later that year.

In 1870 financial woes forced Anthony to give up the *Revolution*, the paper she, Stanton, and George Francis Train began after the Kansas campaign. Anthony embarked on a lecture tour until 1876 to pay off debts

from this paper. She also continued her work for the National Woman Suffrage Association, campaigning for a federal amendment for women's suffrage and aiding state campaigns. With Stanton and Matilda Joslyn Gage, she compiled the multivolume *History of Woman Suffrage*, published between 1881 and 1885.

When the divided women's rights movement reunited in 1890 to form the National American Woman Suffrage Association, Anthony served first as vice president and then in 1892 she began a term as president that lasted until 1900. Anthony also worked throughout her career on behalf of working women's rights and coeducation. When she moved permanently to Rochester, New York, in 1890, she became a trustee of the State Industrial School and encouraged the University of Rochester to admit women. Anthony became the most famous nineteenth-century suffragist. Though criticized and mocked early in her career for lacking the charm or oratorical ability of Elizabeth Cady Stanton, she was much admired at the time of her death for her devotion to the cause of women's rights.

—*Carol Faulkner*

See also African-American Suffrage; Election of 1864; Frémont, John C.; Mott, Lucretia; Stanton, Elizabeth Cady.
For further reading:
Anthony, Susan B., Matilda Joslyn Gage, and Elizabeth Cady Stanton, eds. *A History of Woman Suffrage* (1970).
DuBois, Ellen Carol. *Feminism and Suffrage: The Emergence of an Independent Women's Movement in America 1848–1861* (1978).
Gordon, Ann D. *The Selected Papers of Elizabeth Cady Stanton and Susan B. Anthony: In the School of Anti-Slavery 1840–1866* (1997).
Sherr, Lynn. *Failure Is Impossible: Susan B. Anthony in Her Own Words* (1996).
Venet, Wendy Hamand. *Neither Ballots nor Bullets: Women Abolitionists and the Civil War* (1991).

ANTIETAM, BATTLE OF
(17 September 1862)

The battle of Antietam, outside Sharpsburg, Maryland, on 17 September 1862, was America's bloodiest day. Combined, Union and Confederate soldiers inflicted upon one another 22,719 casualties: 12,401 for Major General George McClellan's Army of the Potomac and 10,318 for General Robert E. Lee's Army of Northern Virginia. Although his forces were vastly superior in numbers, General McClellan spent the days both before and after the battle convinced that Lee possessed unseen divisions that awaited any false step. The result at Antietam, as at the battle of South Mountain, was that McClellan never committed his forces thoroughly to the fight. Rather than attack Lee's positions simultaneously, he fought them piecemeal. Reserve troops, numbering some 20,000, were kept out of the fight to meet these phantom divisions of

Confederate soldiers. While McClellan lacked resolve during the battle, Lee had resolve to spare, so much so that historians question the wisdom of giving battle in the first place. With but one means of escape, Lee stood ground against an army he knew to be vastly superior in size to his own.

Even contemporaries, however, understood that the meaning of the battle was somehow more than could be gleaned from the wisdom or folly of the commanders on that day. For the troops who fought, Antietam was the place that invested everyday names like "the cornfield" or "the west woods" with images of battlefield chaos and horror. In October, Mathew Brady opened his exhibition of photographs entitled "The Dead of Antietam" in New York City. A writer for the *New York Times* noted, "Mr. Brady has done something to bring home to us the terrible reality and earnestness of war. If he has not brought bodies and laid them in our door-yards and along the streets, he has done something very like it...."

Lee's army had crossed into Maryland just ten days earlier, beset by straggling and relegated to a diet of green apples and raw corn. Confederate leaders believed that a major victory, in the wake of the battle of Second Bull Run and occurring on Northern soil, might convince Britain and France to recognize Confederate independence. Continued victories might also encourage Northern voters to reject Republican candidates in favor of peace Democrats during the fall congressional elections. There were important tactical reasons as well. By taking the fight to the North, Lee was able to provision his troops from a region untouched by the war and guarantee that any battles would scar Northern farms rather than Southern ones. If he were successful at severing rail lines at Harper's Ferry and Harrisburg, the eastern states would be cut off from their western counterparts, at least temporarily. Finally, Confederate leaders—both political and military—wanted to boost Southern morale by going on the offensive. It is sometimes also argued that Lee also hoped to raise the rebellion in western Maryland. Confederate troops sang "Maryland, My Maryland" as they crossed the Potomac River, and Lee pointedly encouraged Marylanders to throw off their

Middle Bridge, photographed shortly after the battle (Photograph by Alexander Gardner / *Library of Congress*)

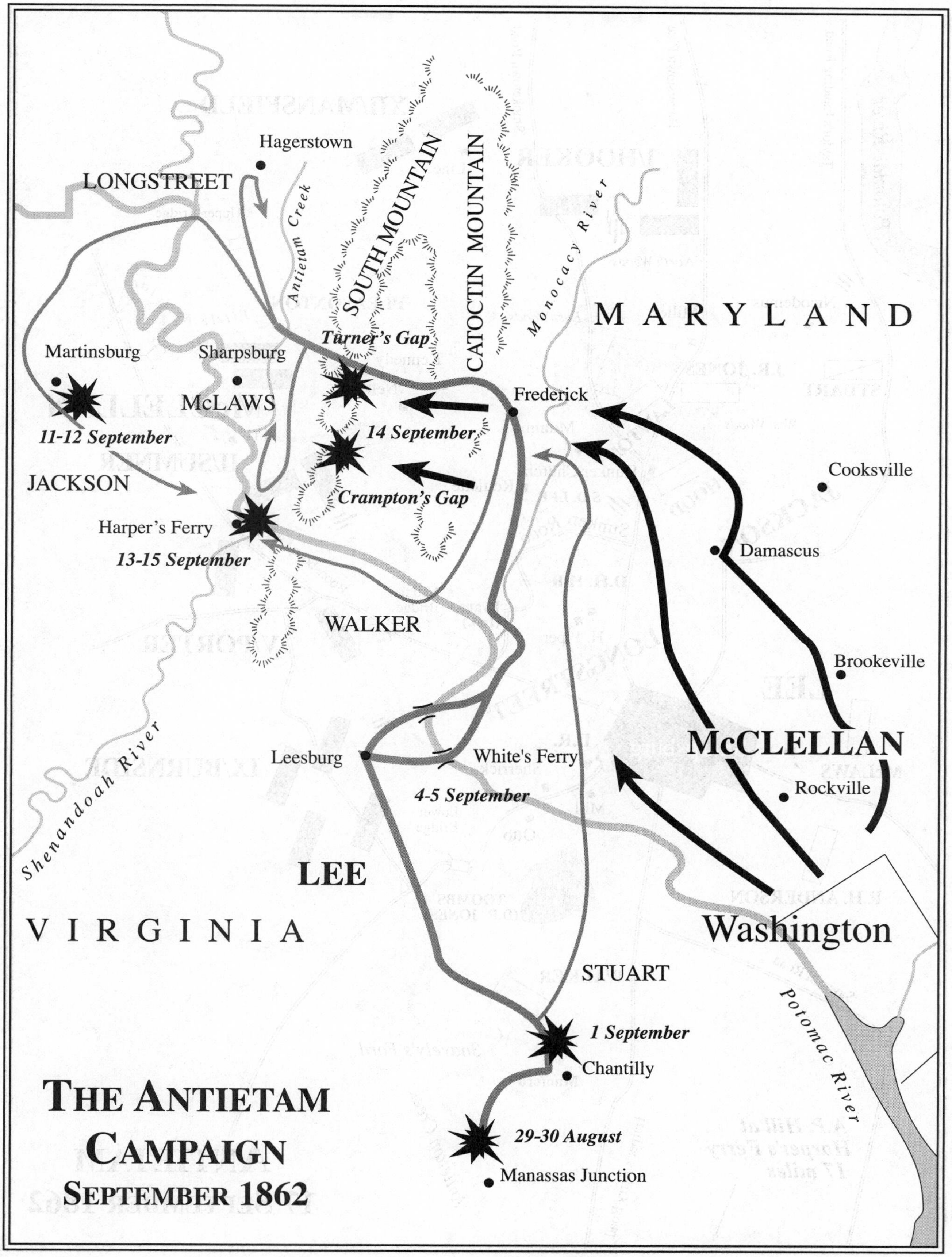

Hagerstown

LONGSTREET

SOUTH MOUNTAIN

CATOCTIN MOUNTAIN

Antietam Creek

Monocacy River

MARYLAND

Martinsburg

Sharpsburg

Turner's Gap

McLAWS

Frederick

11-12 September

14 September

Crampton's Gap

Cooksville

JACKSON

Harper's Ferry

13-15 September

Damascus

WALKER

Brookeville

Shenandoah River

Leesburg

White's Ferry

McCLELLAN

4-5 September

Rockville

LEE

VIRGINIA

Washington

STUART

Potomac River

1 September

Chantilly

THE ANTIETAM CAMPAIGN
SEPTEMBER 1862

29-30 August

Manassas Junction

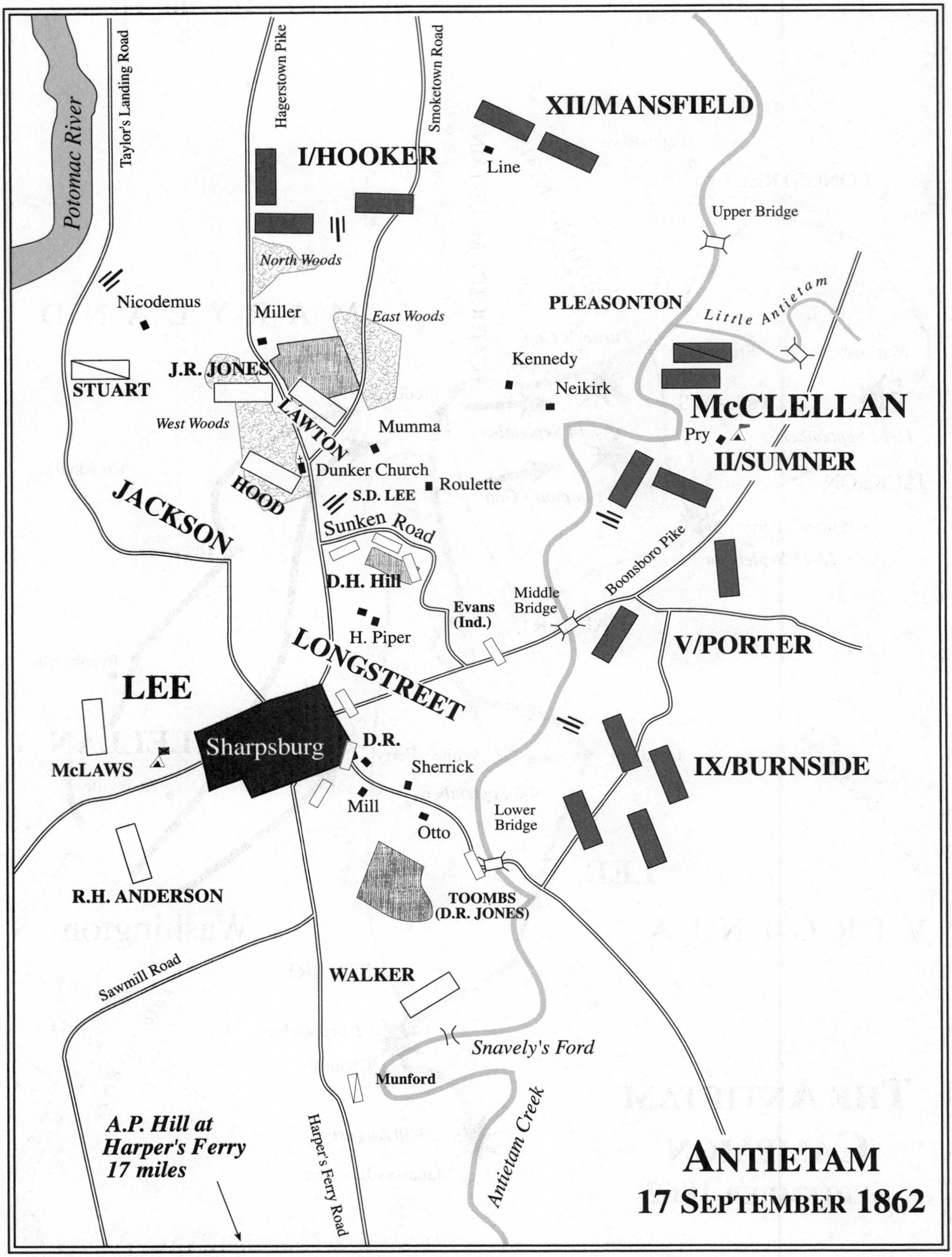

Potomac River

Taylor's Landing Road

Hagerstown Pike

Smoketown Road

XII/MANSFIELD

I/HOOKER

Line

North Woods

Nicodemus

Miller

East Woods

PLEASONTON

Little Antietam

Upper Bridge

STUART

J.R. JONES

Kennedy

Neikirk

McCLELLAN

West Woods

LAWTON

Mumma

Pry

II/SUMNER

JACKSON

HOOD

Dunker Church

Roulette

S.D. LEE

Sunken Road

Boonsboro Pike

D.H. Hill

Evans
(Ind.)

Middle
Bridge

V/PORTER

H. Piper

LONGSTREET

LEE

Sharpsburg

D.R.

Sherrick

IX/BURNSIDE

McLAWS

Mill

Otto

Lower
Bridge

R.H. ANDERSON

Sawmill Road

**TOOMBS
(D.R. JONES)**

WALKER

Snavely's Ford

Munford

Harper's Ferry Road

*A.P. Hill at
Harper's Ferry
17 miles*

Antietam Creek

**ANTIETAM
17 SEPTEMBER 1862**

Confederate dead along the Hagerstown road (Photograph by Alexander Gardner / *Library of Congress*)

"foreign yoke." Privately, however, Lee reported to Confederate president Jefferson Davis that western Maryland farmers would not fight to support slave-holding states because they had no slaves themselves. Unbeknown to Lee and Davis, President Abraham Lincoln awaited a Union victory to issue his proclamation freeing all slaves in the Confederacy if Southern states did not return to the Union by the end of the year.

The battle of Antietam was the result of a chain of circumstance that began shortly after Lee's 43,000 troops entered Maryland. Having detached troops under Major General T. J. "Stonewall" Jackson, Major General Lafayette McLaws, and Brigadier General John G. Walker to subdue the Federal garrison at Harper's Ferry, Lee accompanied the remainder under Major General James Longstreet and Major General D. H. Hill to capture Boonsboro. These plans were detailed in Special Order 191, dated on 9 September, calling for all forces to converge on Harper's Ferry and Boonsboro several days later. On 13 September in a field outside Frederick, two Indiana soldiers discovered a copy of those orders, reportedly wrapped around three cigars. The discovery of Lee's plans allowed McClellan to pursue the Confederate force, which was already a day behind its plans. At the battle of South Mountain on 14 September, Lee's forces fought a delaying action that allowed him to entrench his forces outside Sharpsburg.

Meanwhile, the Harper's Ferry garrison—more than 12,000 Federal troops—surrendered the following day under the punishing fire from the surrounding hills.

The stage was set for the battle of Antietam as Lee entrenched his troops in a bend of the Potomac River between the town of Sharpsburg and Antietam Creek. The creek and the ridges surrounding it provided a strong natural fortification. Three bridges—the Upper, Middle, and Rohrbach's (later known as Burnside's)—spanned the creek. On the 15th, 70,000 Federal troops arrived, taking positions opposite the ridge fortified by Lee. Although D. H. Hill, Longstreet, and Jackson (who had marched directly from Harper's Ferry) could field only 26,000 troops, McClellan estimated Lee's Army of Northern Virginia at 120,000 troops total. On the 16th, the forces exchanged artillery fire while McClellan, in his customarily cautious fashion, surveyed the terrain and planned the battle for the following day. McClellan himself later recounted more than one version of his battle plans, so it is impossible to know how far the events of the 17th deviated from his plan. One thing is certain: McClellan intended the first blow to fall on the Confederate left.

Late in the afternoon on the 16th, McClellan sent Major General Joseph Hooker's I Corps of 8,600 men across the Antietam via the Upper Bridge. From there they swung north, bivouacking near the Hagerstown turnpike in preparation for a dawn assault on the Confederate left. Around midnight, Major General Joseph K. F. Mansfield's XII Corps followed Hooker, establishing a position from which he could support the I Corps on the following day. These moves did not go unnoticed; overnight Lee reinforced his left, bringing its strength to 7,700 men. Thus McClellan's forces allowed Lee precious time to amass his forces to receive the blow.

The battle of Antietam occurred in three stages on 17 September as McClellan sent his troops in successive attacks against the Confederate left, center, and right. Beginning at dawn, Hooker's troops advanced toward their objectives, crossing the Hagerstown turnpike and seizing the plateau upon which sat a whitewashed church belonging to a German Baptist sect known locally as the Dunkers. In Hooker's plan of attack, Brigadier General Abner Doubleday's 1st Division would march south on the turnpike while Brigadier General James B. Ricketts's 2d Division would advance through the East Woods and the Miller farm's thirty-acre cornfield. Brigadier General George G. Meade's 3d Division would form the center, providing support for Doubleday and Ricketts while advancing through the East Woods. To meet the Federal force, Stonewall Jackson had spread two divisions under Brigadier General Alexander R. Lawton and Brigadier General John R. Jones from the West Woods across the turnpike, running just south of the Miller cornfield to the Mumma farm. Four reserve brigades waited inside the West Woods to stage a counterattack. Confederate artillery near the Dunker Church and on Nicodemus Hill, flanking the approach along the turnpike, completed Jackson's preparations.

At dawn, Meade's 1st Brigade of Pennsylvanians under Brigadier General Truman Seymour began to advance through the East Woods, exchanging fire with Colonel James A. Walker's brigade of Alabama, Georgia, and North Carolina troops. No sooner had Walker's men forced back their opponents than the first of Ricketts's infantry advanced into Miller's field. Confederate artillery directed by Colonel Stephen Lee near the Dunker Church inflicted heavy casualties on the advancing troops. Around 6:00 A.M., Brigadier General Abram Duryea's brigade (the 97th, 104th, and 105th New York and the 107th Pennsylvania) marched through the standing corn directly into volleys from Colonel Marcellus Douglass's brigade of the 13th, 26th, 31st, 38th, 60th, and 61st Georgia Regiments. Firing upon one another at a range of 250 yards, both sides were so badly mauled that the firing simply stopped with neither side achieving an advantage. Some of Walker's troops, the 12th and 21st Georgia as well as the 21st North Carolina, managed to find a position from which to put Duryea's forces under flanking fire, but only at the cost of receiving fire from Meade's men in the East Woods. Duryea had endured enough, however. When

reinforcements failed to materialize, he ordered his troops to withdraw back through the cornfield.

Those reinforcements, brigades under Brigadier General George L. Hartstuff and Colonel William A. Christian, advanced haphazardly. A shell wounded Hartstuff while Christian fled the line in terror. Colonel Richard Coulter rallied Hartstuff's men, but they emerged from the East Woods and the cornfield into the same fire as previous troops had encountered with the added hazard that Colonel Lee's artillery had ranged the field in the previous engagement. Despite their losses, Federal forces outnumbered their opponents, whose line began to buckle. Lawton then threw in Brigadier General Harry T. Hays's Louisiana "Tiger" brigade, forcing the Federals back to the East Woods and inflicting on the 12th Massachusetts 67 percent casualties, the highest casualty rate of any unit that day.

Brigadier General John Gibbon's 4th Brigade in Doubleday's division advanced down the turnpike, pushing Jackson's men east of the turnpike back behind the edge of the cornfield. Troops from the 7th Wisconsin and the 19th Indiana crossed the turnpike and advanced toward the West Woods. Yet as his remaining regiments, the 6th and 7th Wisconsin, cleared the edge of the cornfield, they came under a withering fire from Rebels that had been concealed in a pasture. The Federal advance was completely halted, however, by a charge of 1,150 troops under Brigadier General William E. Starke from the West Woods. By taking up positions just west of the turnpike, Starke's troops could fire upon Doubleday's men easily but were themselves exposed. After Starke was mortally wounded, his forces withdrew.

Fortunately for Confederate forces, two divisions under Major General Lafayette McLaws and Major General Robert H. Anderson arrived just after 7:00 A.M., having completed a night march from Harper's Ferry. Around 7:15, Lee then ordered Colonel George T. Anderson to move his Georgia brigade from the army's right to reinforce Jackson's left. For Hooker's men, the battle on the Confederate left was proceeding at great cost, but still forcing Jackson's corps backward slowly. At 7:00 A.M., Brigadier General John Bell Hood's division of 2,300 men advanced through the West Woods, gathered other Confederate troops, and pushed Federal forces back through the cornfield again. The assault cost Hood's units dearly: 60 percent were casualties, but the dramatic charge prevented Confederate lines from rupturing. Two hours and 2,500 casualties later, Hooker's troops were back where they had begun. Of the cornfield, later Hooker wrote that "every stalk in the northern and greater part of the field was cut as closely as could have been done with a knife."

Hooker called for support from Mansfield's XII Corps of 7,200 men to support his retreating line. Hood had

Bodies of Confederate dead gathered for burial (Photograph by Alexander Gardner / *Library of Congress*)

also called for reinforcement during his advance, but none arrived in time to secure his position. When later asked where his troops were, Hood replied, "Dead on the field." Brigadier General Roswell S. Ripley's brigade did shift from the Confederate center in time to prevent a complete rout. Hood's forces, uniting with Ripley's, formed a new line, one that was quickly reinforced when D. H. Hill sent two additional divisions under Brigadier General Alfred H. Colquitt and Colonel D. K. McRae to their assistance. Together, these troops were more than a match for Mansfield's 1st Division, half of whom were new recruits. Mansfield himself was mortally wounded in one exchange, leaving command of the corps to Brigadier General Alpheus S. Williams. McRae's men, however, broke under the advance of Brigadier General George Sears Greene's 2d Division on their flank. Hill worked frantically to pull his men back through the cornfield before they were overrun. Hood did the same. Outnumbered, they regrouped in the West Woods, where they had begun the day.

The assault on the Confederate left began to lurch into the center after Hill committed McRae and Colquitt's troops to the battle. Major General Edwin V.

Sumner received the order to send two of his divisions into battle at 7:20 A.M., when word of Hood's counterattack reached McClellan. Major General John Sedgwick's 2d Division led the way, fording Antietam Creek between the Upper and Middle bridges. On the battlefield, Williams's XII Corps was stretched by then from the West Woods across the road to the East Woods. Sumner led Sedgwick's men through the East Wood with all intention of crossing the turnpike, turning left, and forcing Confederate troops into the Union right wing of Major General Ambrose Burnside's IX Corps. But Sumner's lead division advanced without Brigadier General William H. French's 3d Division, which had become separated at the East Woods. Having lost contact with Sumner, French ordered his men to reinforce the XII Corps troops around the East Woods, while Sedgwick's men advanced alone.

Sumner's incautious plan—he apparently failed to gather sufficient intelligence on the field from I and XII Corps commanders—led his troops to disaster. Marching in three parallel lines across what Sumner assumed was clear ground, Sedgwick's 5,400 men were exposed to a flanking attack from their left shortly after

Mass burial of Confederate dead in a rifle pit (Photograph by Alexander Gardner / *Library of Congress*)

9:00 A.M. First, Major John Pelham's Virginia horse artillery commenced fire on the advancing soldiers from behind the West Woods. Jackson then seized the opportunity that Sumner presented to him. With 3,000 troops of McLaws's division joining the 1,400 remaining troops of Brigadier General Jubal A. Early's Virginia brigade and Brigadier General Maxcy Gregg's South Carolina brigade, rebel soldiers slammed into the left and rear of Sedgwick's division, scattering some of his men back across the turnpike while cornering the rest in the West Woods. Finding themselves under fire from three directions, those troops trapped in the woods beat a retreat to the north. Even so, another flanking attack by Brigadier General Paul J. Semmes's Georgia and Virginia troops from the west, as well as continued artillery fire, introduced a sense of sheer panic into the retreating Federal forces. At the North Woods, however, I Corps troops and artillery stopped the Confederate advance, but all ground gained west of the turnpike that day had been lost.

Both sides took this chance to reinforce their troops and renew the offensive. Brigadier General Alpheus S. Williams, now in command of the XII Corps, sent the 2d Massachusetts and the 13th New Jersey into the fray. Lee had earlier ordered Brigadier General John G. Walker's division, composed primarily of North Carolina soldiers, from the Confederate right to reinforce Jackson and McLaws. These new forces clashed around 10:00 A.M. in the area between the cornfield and the West Woods, but shortly thereafter Walker's men were forced backward by two brigades of Brigadier General George S. Greene's 2d Division. Again, Federal troops surged forward, seizing ground in the West Woods.

Meanwhile, as Sumner directed Sedgwick's division on the Federal right, French's division, unable to locate Sumner and Sedgwick, had taken up positions facing the Rebel center. With Greene's men on his right, and Major General Israel B. Richardson's 1st Division of Sumner's corps on his left, French confronted Major General D. H. Hill's men entrenched in a sunken road that branched

Unburied dead near the Dunker church (Photograph by Alexander Gardner / *Library of Congress*)

off the Hagerstown turnpike. Hill commanded roughly 2,500 men, less than half the number of French's forces, but Hill's men were concealed in the sunken road, ready to fire down a gradual ridge at any advancing Federal troops. The first Federal brigade to approach—the 1st Delaware, 5th Maryland, and 4th New York—were cut down. The second, composed of the 14th Connecticut, 108th New York, and 130th Pennsylvania, came under heavy fire as well, but beat off a counterattack by the Alabama brigade of Brigadier General Robert E. Rodes. The third brigade—the 8th Ohio, 14th Indiana, and 7th West Virginia—advanced only to meet the same hail of fire directed from the sunken road. Of French's 5,700 men, 1,750 became casualties in less than an hour.

Richardson's division, numbering 4,000 men, was ordered forward to continue the assault on the Confederate center. For his part, Lee sent his final

reserve of Major General Richard H. Anderson's division, some 3,400 men, to reinforce Hill. Richardson's first assault, that of Brigadier General Thomas F. Meagher's "Irish Brigade" and the 29th Massachusetts, met the same fate as the previous three attempts. A fatal error by Confederate troops on the right of the sunken road then transformed their defensive haven into a shooting gallery. Richardson's second brigade, under Brigadier General John C. Caldwell, began a gradual flanking move on the sunken road position that, at that point, was swollen with reinforcements. As Colonel Carnot Posey ordered his Mississippi troops to fall back to ease the overcrowding on the right of the line, others sensed in this movement the beginnings of a general retreat. A similar disaster occurred on the left-hand side of the sunken road. Lieutenant Colonel J. N. Lightfoot of the 6th Alabama misinterpreted an order for his own troops to shift position and relayed an order of withdrawal throughout Rodes's command. The remaining Confederate troops were then exposed to fire from three directions, transforming the sunken road into "Bloody Lane." Those who could escape the trench fled headlong toward Sharpsburg, but many were cut down before they had the chance.

Elsewhere on the battlefield, Federal troops under George Sears Greene that had seized ground near the Dunker Church advanced, unaware that Sedgwick's division, which Greene assumed was protecting his right, had been routed earlier. Suddenly, the 49th North Carolina appeared on Greene's right, while a counterattack planned by Longstreet to relieve the pressure on Hill caught him unawares on the left. Longstreet's relief force, a composite command of 675 men under Colonel John R. Cooke, helped to scatter Greene's men back across the turnpike and then staged a counterattack against Federal troops in the center. This effort failed, but Cooke's men easily repelled an ill-conceived charge toward the Dunker Church by Colonel William H. Irwin's brigade of New York and Maine troops from VI Corps. Still outnumbered, the collapse of the center was stemmed by Hill himself, who led one brief counterattack of perhaps 200 men. These battles in and around Bloody Lane cost the Confederate command 2,600 casualties. Although the assaults by Cooke and Hill provided time for artillery units to seal the breech in the line, the remaining troops were scattered and disorganized. Had further pressure from the Federals been forthcoming, the line would have broken.

The only portent of battle on the Confederate right was the exchange of artillery and skirmishing fire between Burnside's IX Corps and Longstreet's troops. Confederate infantry was positioned on the opposite side of Rohrbach's Bridge, a triple-arched, stone bridge over Antietam Creek. From their position, they could shoot down the ridge at any forces trying to cross the river. Burnside's orders were to cross the creek, capture Sharpsburg, and seize the only serviceable ford (Boteler's) across the Potomac available to Lee's troops if they were forced to retreat. The defenses had been staffed at dawn by the divisions of Brigadier General David R. Jones and Brigadier General John G. Walker. Yet by 10:00 A.M., when Burnside finally received the order to advance, Lee had already pulled out all of Walker's men and Colonel George T. Anderson's Georgia brigade to reinforce other positions. When the attack finally came, Jones had but 3,000 men of whom the 400 men of the 2d and 20th Georgia in the command of Brigadier General Robert Toombs defended Rohrbach's Bridge itself. The opposing force, Burnside's corps of 12,500 infantry, outnumbered their adversaries, but suffered disadvantages due to the terrain. The road approaching the bridge ran parallel to Antietam Creek;

thus forces approaching by the clearest path were exposed to the greatest fire.

Around 10:00 A.M., Burnside and Brigadier Jacob D. Cox received the order to advance. Colonel Henry W. Kingsbury's 11th Connecticut Regiment led the way to provide covering fire for the advance of Colonel George Crook's Ohio brigade of the Kanawha division. This attack failed as advancing troops were picked off from the opposite shore. Meanwhile, Brigadier General Isaac P. Rodman's 3d Division, plus the remaining Kanawha brigade of Ohioans, struggled downstream through thick brush in search of Snavely's Ford, by which they hoped to outflank Jones's position. The ford, however, was difficult to locate; it proved to be two miles downstream. A second assault directed at the bridge by one of Brigadier General Samuel D. Sturgis's brigades, led by the 2d Maryland and 6th New Hampshire, was cut down by Confederate rifle and artillery fire. Finally Cox ordered Sturgis's other brigade under Brigadier General Edward Ferrero to charge directly downhill to take the bridge. At 12:30 P.M., the 51st New York and 51st Pennsylvania plunged downhill toward the bridge, taking up positions on the east side. The Georgia troops opposite, now running low on ammunition, yielded just enough ground for the two Federal regiments to charge across the bridge. Shortly after 1:00 P.M., Burnside's forces, including Rodman's division, converged on the west side of what after the battle was known as Burnside's Bridge.

At this point, a dispute between Sumner and Major General William B. Franklin occurred about whether to press the attack against Hill's troops in the Confederate center. Franklin had arrived on the scene with five brigades of his VI Corps, eager to join Sumner's troops in a final assault. Sumner refused, arguing that his troops were already too close to the breaking point. When McClellan sent a courier with a message suggesting he pursue the attack, an exasperated Sumner replied, "Go back, young man, and tell General McClellan I have no command! Tell him my command, Banks' command, and Hooker's command are all cut up and demoralized. Tell him General Franklin has the only organized command on this part of the field." After reviewing the situation, McClellan sided with Sumner, and the attack was postponed.

Lee, on the other hand, had asked Stonewall Jackson around noon to fashion a counterattack that would relieve the pressure on the center. Jackson planned a two-prong attack in which 5,000 infantry and cavalry under Major General J. E. B. Stuart would try to outflank the right wing of McClellan's forces while the 48th North Carolina from John G. Walker's division would push forward from the West Woods. This effort failed to achieve Jackson's objective of unraveling the Federal right wing because Federal I Corps batteries heavily

Soldiers at Antietam, September 1862 (*Library of Congress*)

outgunned Stuart's artillery. After a two-hour delay in bringing ammunition and supporting troops across the bridge, 8,000 troops from Burnside's IX Corps at 3:00 P.M. advanced on the remnants of Jones's men, now numbering perhaps 2,800. The Federal plan was to outflank the weakened Confederate right and cut Lee off from Boteler's Ford. Outnumbered, Jones's forces were slowly pushed backward despite the assistance of artillery that poured rounds into the advancing Union troops. Colonel Harrison S. Fairchild's brigade of New York soldiers pushed all the way to the outskirts of Sharpsburg, whereupon the Army of Northern Virginia received a reprieve from certain defeat.

Having left Harper's Ferry at 6:30 A.M., A. P. Hill arrived with 3,000 troops after a punishing seventeen-mile march. Hill's troops, some wearing captured Federal uniforms from the Harper's Ferry garrison, slammed into the 16th Connecticut on Burnside's left shortly after 3:30 P.M. These troops were part of Colonel Edward Harland's brigade, like Fairchild's, a part of Rodman's division. Having demolished that force, Hill's men then dispatched the 4th Rhode Island and Colonel Hugh Ewing's brigade of Ohio soldiers from the Kanawha division in fierce fighting near the Otto family cornfield. The sudden pressure on their flank forced Burnside's men (including those that had begun to enter

Lincoln visits the Antietam battlefield, 3 October 1862 (Photograph by Alexander Gardner / *Library of Congress*)

Sharpsburg) to retreat from the pursuit of Confederates under the command of A. P. Hill, Toombs, and Longstreet. Federal troops finally regrouped on a ridge with their backs to Antietam Creek. The third stage of the battle was complete.

On the morning of 18 September, Lee's battered forces were drawn up, prepared to meet a Federal offensive that never came. Throughout the night of the 17th, both sides had tended to their wounded, but nothing could be done for those trapped between the lines. Many survivors remembered the cries of agony that punctuated the night. On the 18th, an improvised truce held while the two sides exchanged their wounded and began the ghastly task of burying the dead. Outside the makeshift field hospitals, rows of bodies grew steadily throughout the day, but a more macabre sight were the burial pits given over solely to the amputated limbs of the wounded. By afternoon, Lee had given orders to fall back across the Potomac under cover of night. To the occasional and improvised refrain of "Damn My Maryland," the Army of Northern Virginia departed.

McClellan's men suffered 12,401 casualties, including 2,108 dead, 9,540 wounded, and 753 missing. Lee's men lost 10,318, including 1,546 dead, 7,752 wounded, and 1,108 missing. According to historian Stephen Sears, these figures amount to 25 percent of the overall Federal force and 31 percent of the Confederate. On no day before or since have U.S. military forces fallen in such numbers.

At the battle of Antietam, Union and Confederate forces fought to a tactical draw because Lee's line outside Sharpsburg held. McClellan never delivered the final blow that would have scattered Confederate troops into the Potomac. Later, Generals Burnside and Cox both testified before a congressional committee that Burnside had offered to take the remaining troops of IX Corps (numbering roughly 9,000–9,500) and attack the Confederate right at dawn on the 18th if McClellan could supply an additional 5,000 men. These numbers could have been drawn from I, II, and XII Corps troops that had fought the previous day or from V and VI Corps that had seen little action. Sears estimates that the I, II, IX, and XII Corps combined had approximately 30,000 infantrymen available on the morning of the 18th. Another 20,300 were available from V and VI Corps because only one brigade of twelve had seen significant action the day before. In addition, the 1st Division of IV Corps, under Major General Darius N. Couch, arrived midday on the 18th from Crampton's Gap, bringing an additional 6,000 experienced troops. Earlier that morning, Brigadier Andrew A. Humphreys had also arrived with 6,000 newly recruited Pennsylvania troops for V Corps. All told, McClellan commanded 50,000 combat-ready soldiers at dawn with an additional 12,000 arriving by the middle of the day, yet no attempt was made to assault Lee's battered line.

McClellan's failure to pursue his numerical advantage is often ascribed to his continued belief in Lee's phantom reserve. McClellan had significant battlefield advantages that make his hesitation incomprehensible. The natural barrier of Antietam Creek no longer protected the Confederate right. Moreover, Lee's line had been pushed back so far that he risked catastrophe; if Lee's position was overrun, McClellan's forces could threaten his only escape at Boteler's Ford long before his troops could retreat across the Potomac. Lee's decision to remain in Maryland, courting absolute disaster not just for the Army of Northern Virginia but for the Confederacy itself, is similarly inexplicable.

For more than a month, from 17 September to 26 October, McClellan declined to pursue Lee across the Potomac. Urged on by prodding from both Major General Henry W. Halleck, general-in-chief of the U.S. Army, and President Abraham Lincoln, McClellan dithered, citing shortages of equipment and the fear of overextending his forces. In his official report on the Maryland campaign, Halleck wrote, "The long inactivity of so large an army in the face of a defeated foe, and during the most favorable season for rapid movements and a vigorous campaign, was a matter of great disappointment and regret." For McClellan, however, Antietam was his greatest victory. That the Army of Northern Virginia escaped his grasp McClellan attributed to the cowardly surrender of the Harper's Ferry garrison. Had Federal forces there held out one day longer, McClellan wrote in his official report of 15 October, he could have captured the Confederates that had seized Maryland Heights above the town, preventing the garrison's surrender. Thereby he would have been able to tie up the Confederate troops besieging the town from Loudoun and Bolivar Heights. "I would have had," he wrote, "35,000 or 40,000 less men to encounter at Antietam, and must have captured or destroyed all opposed to me. As it was, I had to engage an army fresh from a recent and to them a great victory, and to reap the disadvantages of their being freshly and plentifully supplied with ammunition and supplies." Having

inflated his opponent's numbers, McClellan similarly inflated the casualties inflicted by his men, reporting to Halleck that he had inflicted some 30,000 casualties, nearly three times those suffered by Lee's forces at Antietam. In November, McClellan was relieved of command by Halleck and Secretary of War Edwin Stanton in favor of Ambrose Burnside.

The battle of Antietam was, however, a tremendous strategic success for the Union army. The battle had cost the Union army dearly, and Confederate forces more so. McClellan had inadvertently demonstrated that the path to strategic victory would not lie solely in brilliant tactics or battlefield heroism, but in the slow attrition of men that the more populous North could afford but the South could not. On 23 September, Lincoln published his Emancipation Proclamation, threatening to abolish slavery in all areas loyal to the Confederacy. Antietam, then, became the moment when the "war between the states" became "a battle for freedom."

—*Robert S. Wolff*

See also Emancipation Proclamation; Gaines's Mill, Battle of; Lee, Robert E.; Maryland; McClellan, George B.; South Mountain, Battle of.

For further reading:

Foote, Shelby. *The Civil War: A Narrative. Fort Sumter to Perryville* (1958).

Frassanito, William A. *Antietam: The Photographic Legacy of America's Bloodiest Day* (1978).

Gallagher, Gary W., ed. *Antietam: Essays on the 1862 Maryland Campaign* (1989).

Sears, Stephen W. *Landscape Turned Red: The Battle of Antietam* (1983).

APPOMATTOX COURT HOUSE

The small Virginia town of Appomattox Court House, ninety miles east of Richmond, was the site of the surrender of the Army of Northern Virginia to Federal forces on 9 April 1865. A twelve-day campaign drew both armies away from the metropolitan area of the Confederate capital, before the Confederate army finally gave in to increasing Federal pressure and superior numbers. The Confederate surrender was the end of the Civil War in Virginia and marked the beginning of the end of the war across the South.

The Federal forces that gathered for the spring campaign in 1865 numbered just over 76,000 and were under the overall command of Lieutenant General Ulysses S. Grant. Grant's army consisted of the Army of the Potomac, under Major General George G. Meade, the Army of the Shenandoah, under Major General Philip H. Sheridan, and the Army of the James, under Major General E. O. C. Ord. The Confederate forces of approximately 57,800 were led by General Robert E. Lee and his Army of Northern Virginia. The Confederate ranks also included soldiers from the Department of Richmond, under Lieutenant General Richard S. Ewell,

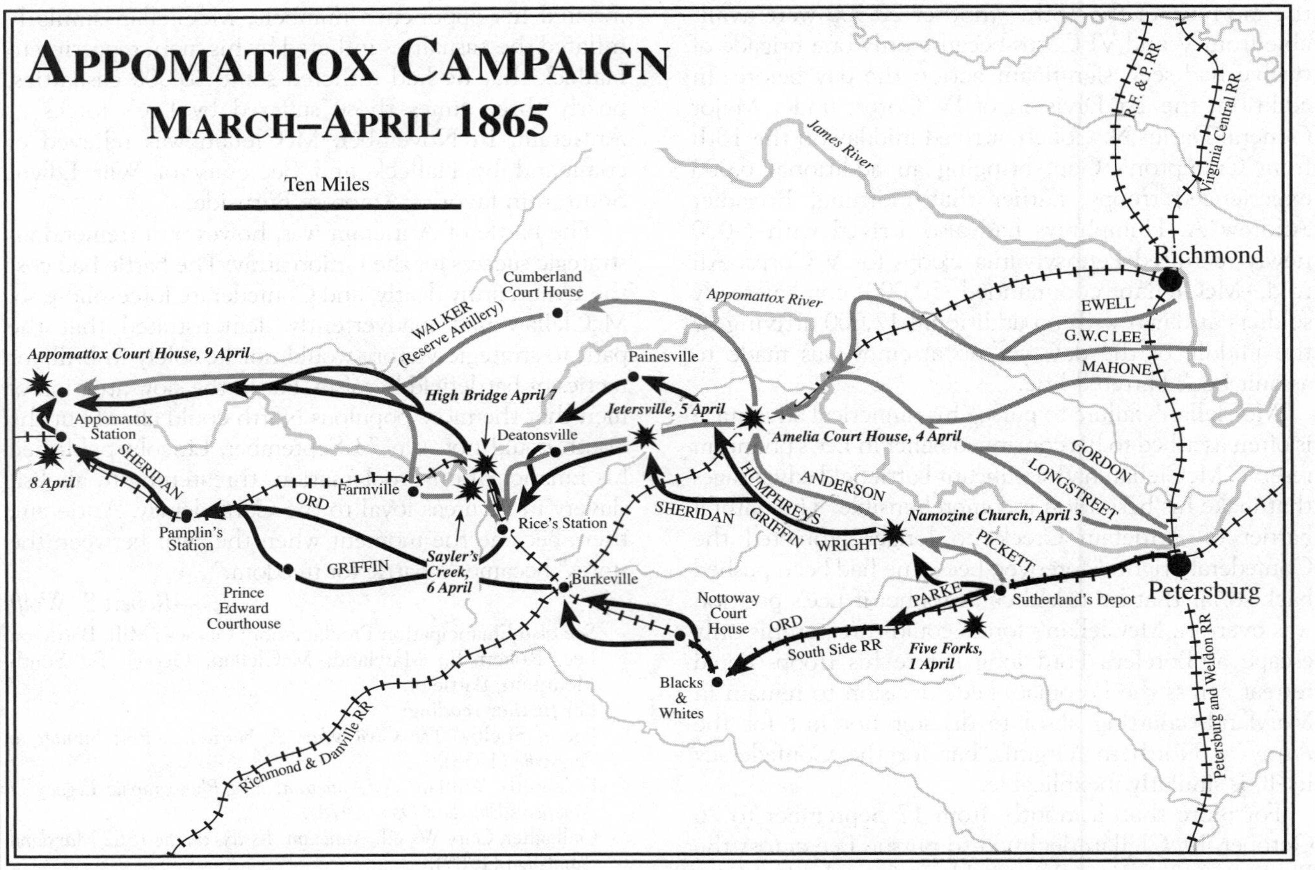

APPOMATTOX CAMPAIGN
MARCH–APRIL 1865

Ten Miles

Map showing locations including Richmond, Petersburg, Appomattox Court House (9 April), Appomattox Station, High Bridge April 7, Jetersville 5 April, Amelia Court House 4 April, Namozine Church April 3, Five Forks 1 April, Sayler's Creek 6 April, Farmville, Burkeville, with commanders marked: WALKER (Reserve Artillery), SHERIDAN, ORD, GRIFFIN, HUMPHREYS, WRIGHT, ANDERSON, GORDON, LONGSTREET, PICKETT, PARKE, MAHONE, EWELL, G.W.C LEE, and railroads including R.F. & P. RR, Virginia Central RR, Petersburg and Weldon RR, South Side RR, Richmond & Danville RR.

and the Department of North Carolina and Southern Virginia, under Brigadier General Henry Wise.

The Campaign —The Appomattox campaign began on 29 March 1865. Federal and Confederate forces had been entrenched around Petersburg since late spring 1864, but both sides expected decisive action in 1865.

The immediate goal of the Federal army at this time was to capture the Southside Railroad to cut off Petersburg from its major supply route. The larger objective of the campaign was to force Lee to stretch his thin forces to the point where the Confederates would have to abandon Petersburg and Richmond. Accordingly, Grant sent infantry and cavalry forces to the southwest of Petersburg, planning to flank and draw the Confederate forces out of their entrenchments. In the final days of March, several actions took place at Quaker Road, White Oak Road, and Dinwiddie Court House, all of which were preliminary to the decisive battle at Five Forks on 1 April.

The Confederate defeat at Five Forks left Petersburg and Richmond vulnerable to the strong Federal forces that now circled the two cities from the south. Lee advised President Jefferson Davis that the Confederate government should abandon the capital immediately,

and on 2 April, a stream of political and civilian refugees began to pour out of the city. Petersburg was also evacuated that day, and Federal forces occupied both cities on 3 April. As for the Confederate army, its best hope was to move southwest out of Virginia and attempt to join Joseph Johnston's forces in North Carolina. With this goal, Lee's forces began a westward retreat, trying to stay ahead of the rapidly advancing Federal army.

In addition to meeting up with Johnston, Lee had the more immediate problem of feeding and supplying his troops. Over the next three days, the army moved west, toward Amelia Court House, engaging with Federal forces at Sutherland Station, Namozine Church, and Jetersville. Supplies were to be sent from Richmond to meet the army at Amelia. When the army arrived on 4 April however, there was no food waiting—ordnance and other supplies had been sent instead. The delay caused by this error cost Lee his small lead on the Federal forces. He was forced to redirect his army toward the next potential supply depot, Farmville.

On 6 April, as Lee's army neared Farmville another fierce battle took place at Sayler's Creek, culminating in another Confederate defeat. Some soldiers did receive rations at Farmville on 7 April, but the appearance of

Federal troops at Appomattox Court House, April 1865 (Photograph by Timothy O'Sullivan / *Library of Congress*)

Federal troops forced the Confederates to move on, abandoning their supplies. Lee hoped that by crossing the Appomattox River and destroying the bridges he could cut off the Federal pursuit. One bridge was not destroyed in time however, and the Federals were able to maintain their chase across the river. The Confederates had to keep going, fighting a holding action at Cumberland Church and making a hard night march toward their next supply stop, Appomattox Station. Meanwhile, fast-moving Federal cavalry remained south of the river and kept moving west to head off the Confederate forces.

By 7 April, Grant had begun to think that the Confederates might consider surrendering. He was told that the captured General Ewell claimed that the Confederates should have surrendered earlier, when they could have negotiated better terms. By the 7th, Grant had also been informed of Sheridan's intention to capture several Confederate supply trains waiting at

Appomattox Station. As a result of this information, Grant opened communications with Lee by sending a note requesting the surrender of his army, since further Confederate resistance appeared futile.

Lee was also considering his options, which were few and difficult. Ten days into this campaign, Lee's army was rapidly losing its effectiveness. Lack of proper nourishment and hard marching were taking their toll physically, and men began literally to drop from exhaustion. Morale was plummeting; the precarious position of the Confederacy had to have been evident to soldiers with the loss of Richmond, the flight of the government, and the Army's own difficult campaign all combining to present a bleak prospect for their future. Soldiers began to desert in large numbers.

Surrender was a painful choice, but Lee's other options were hardly more palatable. Should they not get through to North Carolina, the Army of Northern Virginia could engage in one final bloody battle that would probably destroy it completely; alternatively, soldiers could be ordered to return to their states to carry on the war by other means. That night, Lee responded to Grant's note, saying only that in the interest of avoiding more bloodshed, he would like to know what terms Grant would offer.

Grant's next communication, received by Lee on 8 April, stated that the only condition upon which he would insist was that soldiers be disqualified from taking up arms against the U.S. government until properly exchanged. In this message, Grant offered to meet with Lee or a representative to arrange the surrender.

Despite the formidable realities of his situation, Lee replied to Grant that perhaps the Federal commander had misunderstood; he still did not think that "the emergency has risen to call for the surrender of this Army" and had not proposed to arrange a surrender with his last note. However, he was willing to discuss peace terms generally and offered to meet with Grant the following morning at 10:00 A.M. Grant's response, received on the morning of 9 April, was brief—he was not authorized to treat generally for peace, only for the surrender of the army, so there would be no point in meeting unless it was to discuss surrender.

On the night of 8 April, Lee and his corps commanders decided to make one final attempt to break through the next morning. In their front, General John Gordon's Confederate infantry division, supported by Fitzhugh Lee's cavalry, faced only Federal cavalry and would make the initial assault. A breakthrough here was considered the only feasible option. James Longstreet's corps held the Confederate rear.

Unknown to the Confederates, however, Federal infantry was marching hard through that night to join Sheridan's cavalry and reinforce their precarious position. More Federal infantry rapidly approached the Confederate rear guard. Once the forces were engaged very early on 9 April, Gordon sent word back to Lee that he did not think he could hold his position without support.

While waiting for the expected 10:00 A.M. meeting with Grant, Lee informally polled some of his commanders for their opinions on the situation. Longstreet and William Mahone counseled surrender. E. Porter Alexander opposed that view and encouraged Lee to disperse his forces and to carry on the fight however possible. Lee responded that to allow that would be to let loose on the countryside an undisciplined mob of soldiers who would rob and plunder to support themselves. Such actions would certainly bring retaliation from the enemy, and he could not allow such a state of affairs to develop. Later that morning, Lee received Grant's note turning down the proposed meeting, yet the grim news from Gordon had left him little room to negotiate. Now with his forces pressed in on one another, there appeared to be no other option but to request explicitly a surrender conference, which Lee did in a final note.

The response at Grant's headquarters was subdued. Only a feeble cheer and some tears greeted the news that Lee would meet to discuss surrender, although Grant did declare that his migraine headache had miraculously disappeared. Further communications proposed that Lee and his staff should find a location; Grant would meet them where they indicated. White truce flags went out from both sides. As the news of the truce took time to disseminate, there was some disagreement whether particular units should surrender directly to one another or wait for orders. By the early afternoon of 9 April, much of the fighting had stopped in Virginia. It is estimated that at this time the Confederates had approximately 10,000 effective soldiers in the field; Union forces numbered more than 60,000.

The Surrender —At midday, Lee and his aide Colonel Charles Marshall rode out on the road to Appomattox Court House. The first white civilian they encountered was local resident Wilmer McLean, who, when asked, initially offered a nearby outbuilding for the conference. When the shabby, unfurnished structure was declared unsuitable, McLean proffered his own, more comfortable home. What Marshall and Lee probably did not know is that McLean's reluctance may have been a result of his earlier war experiences. By a remarkable coincidence, the McLean family had left a previous home after the house had served as a Confederate hospital and General P. G. T. Beauregard's headquarters during First Bull Run, the first battle of the war in Virginia. Hoping to avoid the rest of the war, McLean had moved his family to Appomattox Court House in 1863.

A half-hour after Lee and Marshall arrived, Grant and his staff arrived at the McLean house at approximately 2:00 P.M. By all accounts, the contrast between the two commanders was extraordinary. Lee presented a dignified figure, tall and dressed in his best uniform, with a fine sword. In comparison, Grant was muddy from his long ride, wearing a simple soldier's coat with only three-star shoulder straps to indicate his rank, and was swordless. While only Marshall accompanied Lee, Grant had a small entourage of staff and officers. These included Sheridan and Ord, as well as J. A. Rawlins, Rufus Ingalls, M. R. Morgan, Robert T. Lincoln (the president's son), Adam Badeau, Orville Babcock, Horace Porter, Seth Williams, Theodore Bowers, and Ely Parker. There is some debate about other Federal officers and journalists who may or may not have been in the parlor during the conference.

After brief conversation about their mutual service in Mexico, Lee called Grant's attention to the matter at hand by requesting his terms for surrender. Grant replied that they were as he had stated earlier: men and officers who surrendered were to be paroled and could not take up arms again until properly exchanged. Their arms and

The McLean House, Appomattox, April 1865 (Photograph by Timothy O'Sullivan / *Library of Congress*)

supplies were to be turned over as captured property. Lee asked Grant to write out the terms. In the written proposal, Grant added that officers would not have to surrender side arms and may also keep their horses. Grant also stated that soldiers could go home and would not be disturbed by U.S. authority as long as they maintained their parole.

With this last condition, Grant exceeded his charter of negotiating only the surrender of the army. He effectively said that Confederate soldiers would not be treated as traitors by the U.S. government. Although Lincoln would probably have endorsed this decision, it was not Grant's to make.

Lee commented that the terms would have a most happy effect on his army, but noted that in the Confederate army all cavalry and artillery horses were privately owned (as opposed to the army-owned Federal horses); did the terms mean that only officers could keep their horses? Grant considered, and he agreed that, as

horses would be necessary in the coming months to the many small farmers in the ranks, they could be retained by all who claimed ownership. Marshall drafted a note of agreement, which Lee signed. Copies of the surrender terms and agreement were made, signed, and distributed. Marshall commented afterward: "There was no theatrical display about it. It was in itself perhaps the greatest tragedy that ever occurred in the history of the world, but it was the simplest, plainest, and most thoroughly devoid of any attempt at effect, that you can imagine."

After the signing, the meeting began to dissolve into individual conversations between the officers present. Lee and Grant discussed the return of Federal prisoners, and the provision of rations by the well-supplied Federal army to the starving Confederate forces. There was no discussion of Lee's surrendering his sword, despite popular myth to the contrary. Lee met the other officers in the room, shaking hands with each before leaving the

McLean house at approximately 3:00 P.M. Lee's ride back to his camp through Confederate lines brought throngs of soldiers to the roadside, a few cheers, some tears, and much disbelief that the four years of intense combat had ended so abruptly.

After Grant left the McLean house, Federal officers descended upon it, buying and taking the furniture as souvenirs. McLean tried to prevent the chaos, but his parlor was left a shambles. Grant cabled the news to Washington at 4:30 P.M. As word of the surrender spread through Federal lines, great rejoicing commenced, culminating in the firing of artillery salutes. Grant, sensitive to the proximity of his vanquished foe, quickly ordered the excessive exultation stopped.

The formal surrender ceremony took place on 12 April. General Joshua Chamberlain was given the honor of receiving the surrender, in this final encounter between the two armies. As the Confederate soldiers marched between the two lines of Federal soldiers, Chamberlain ordered his troops to display a carry arms salute. Confederate general John Gordon responded with an order in kind—"honor answering honor." Confederate arms were stacked, banners laid on the ground, and the Southern soldiers began to go home. Approximately 28,000 Confederate soldiers surrendered at Appomattox. This number is higher than the effective number in the field at the truce because of the return of stragglers and deserters in the days between the cessation of hostilities and the surrender ceremony.

The surrender that took place at Appomattox Court House is remarkable for its lack of rancor between the two previously bitter enemies and for the dignity of the proceedings. Upon the appearance of flags of truce on the morning of the 9th, Confederate and Federal officers met between the lines to exchange greetings, information, and flasks. After the surrender, Federal soldiers freely shared the contents of their haversacks with their hungry Confederate counterparts. The surrender ceremony was marked by a profound respect on both sides. The choices made by the commanders of the two armies reflected an awareness of the long-term effects of the war on the nation. Grant could have treated the defeated Confederates far more harshly and deprived them of the basic necessities for starting their civilian lives again. Lee could have allowed his army to become a guerrilla fighting force, a decision that would have further embittered the two sides. Both commanders strove to set examples for their armies and their country to follow.

Other forces remained in the field, and it would be another year before Andrew Johnson could proclaim the insurrection at an end. Nonetheless, the end of the war in Virginia signaled the beginning of the end of the Confederate States of America.

—*Lisa Lauterbach Laskin*

See also Amelia Court House/Jetersville; Farmville/High Bridge; Grant, Ulysses S.; Lee, Robert E.; McLean, Wilmer; Namozine Church; Richmond, Surrender of; Sayler's Creek/Harper's Farm, Battle of.

For further reading:
Adams, Charles Francis. "Lee at Appomattox." In *Lee at Appomattox and Other Papers* (1902).
Calkins, Chris M. *The Appomattox Campaign: March 29–April 9, 1865* (1997).
Cauble, Frank P. *The Surrender Proceedings: April 9, 1865, Appomattox Court House* (1987).
Chamberlain, Joshua Lawrence. *The Passing of the Armies: An Account of the Final Campaign of the Army of the Potomac, Based upon Personal Reminiscences of the Fifth Army Corps* (1915; reprint, 1994).
Grant, U.S. *Personal Memoirs of U.S. Grant* (1885).
Marshall, Charles. *An Aide-de-Camp of Lee: Being the Papers of Colonel Charles Marshall, Sometime Aide-de-Camp, Military Secretary, and Assistant Adjutant General on the Staff of Robert E. Lee, 1862–1865* (1927).

ARCHER, JAMES JAY
(1817–1864)
Confederate general

Born to John Archer and Ann Stump Archer in Harford County, Maryland, James Archer was educated at Princeton, and at Bacon College in Kentucky, before studying law and opening a practice in Maryland. At the outbreak of the Mexican-American War, Archer accepted a captain's commission, commanding a company of Maryland volunteers. He fought with distinction during the Mexico City campaign, earning a brevet promotion to major for his actions during the taking of Chapultepec.

After seven years in civilian life as a lawyer, Archer decided to return to the army and became a captain in the 9th Infantry in 1855. He saw service primarily in the Pacific Northwest. At the outbreak of the Civil War, Archer's sympathies lay with the South, and in May 1861 he resigned his commission. In the fall of 1861, he was commissioned colonel of the 5th Texas Infantry as part of the Texas Brigade of John Bell Hood.

He commanded the 5th in the early days of the Peninsula campaign in the spring of 1862 and was recognized for gallantry during the battle of Seven Pines on 31 May 1862. On 3 June 1862 he was promoted brigadier general and commander of the Texas Brigade that became known as Archer's brigade.

As part of A. P. Hill's division, Archer commanded his brigade at the Seven Days' battles, during which he was especially conspicuous at Mechanicsville and Gaines' Mill. In August 1862, Archer fought at Cedar Mountain and Second Bull Run and led his brigade in Robert E. Lee's invasion of Maryland in September 1862, going as part of A. P. Hill's division to take Harper's Ferry and then marching quickly to Antietam. Archer became ill on the march, and temporarily relinquished command of his brigade. He fought at Fredericksburg and Chancellorsville before leading his brigade north again as part of A. P. Hill's corps into Pennsylvania.

At Gettysburg, Archer's brigade was a part of the division commanded by Major General Henry Heth. On the first day of the battle, 1 July, Archer led his brigade against the center of the Federal line on Seminary Ridge, pushing forward so quickly that his brigade was virtually enveloped before they could be supported by other parts of the division. Archer was captured.

Transported to Johnson's Island in Ohio, Archer was held there until June 1864 when he was transferred to Fort Delaware and then finally exchanged in August 1864. During his imprisonment, Archer's health had suffered, but he was determined to return to active command. Given command of his former brigade, Archer received orders on 9 August to report to the Army of the Tennessee under John Bell Hood in Atlanta. Ten days later this order was revoked, possibly as a result of Archer's bad health, and he was ordered to report to the Army of Northern Virginia in Petersburg, Virginia. Archer's health continued to deteriorate, however, and he died in Richmond on 24 October 1864.

—*David S. Heidler and Jeanne T. Heidler*

See also Gettysburg, Battle of; Harper's Ferry; Hood, John Bell.
For further reading:
Craig, David R. "James J. Archer: The Little Gamecock" (M.A. thesis, 1983).
Schoeberlein, Robert W. "A Marylander at the Northwest Frontier." *Maryland Historical Magazine* (1995).

ARKANSAS

Arkansas seceded from the Union on 6 May 1861, following months of bitter debate among its people. Like other border states, many citizens held strong Union sympathies. They successfully blocked the efforts of delegates to the first secession convention (3–18 March 1861) to secede, but Lincoln's call for troops following the capture of Fort Sumter broadened support for secession and led to the state's leaving the Union. In the next four years, Arkansas contributed as many as 60,000 men to the Confederate cause. Its forty-six infantry regiments, seventeen cavalry regiments, and thirteen batteries of artillery fought in every theater of action.

For both the Confederacy and the Union, Arkansas possessed considerable strategic value. Its location made it important for carrying out Confederate ambitions in Missouri and the Indian Territory. For the United States government, its occupation was essential for protecting Missouri and St. Louis. As a result, northern Arkansas became an immediate focus of military activity.

In summer 1861 Governor Henry Rector ordered troops there. These troops fought under General Ben McCulloch on 10 August 1861 at Oak Hills, Missouri. That bloody battle temporarily halted the Federal effort to push Confederate forces out of Missouri.

Following Oak Hills, Confederate forces fell back into Arkansas. The Federals reorganized, and before the end of 1861 their Army of the Southwest under General Samuel R. Curtis had pushed into northwestern Arkansas. On 7 March 1862, General Earl Van Dorn's Confederate forces attacked Curtis at Pea Ridge. The two-day battle failed to dislodge Curtis, and Van Dorn, responding to requests by General Albert S. Johnston for reinforcements, removed his army east of the Mississippi River.

After regrouping, Curtis's army reentered Arkansas on the White River on 29 April 1862. His goal was Little Rock. Van Dorn's move had left Arkansas unprotected, but the state's new military commander, Major General Thomas C. Hindman, scraped up a force to resist Curtis. A combination of low water on the White River and a lucky shot by Confederate artillery that sank the USS *Mound City* at St. Charles on 17 June and turned back a Federal flotilla moving up-river to join Curtis thwarted Federal plans. Curtis's column moved overland to the Mississippi and occupied the town of Helena on 12 July.

With Curtis out of the way, Hindman hoped to regain control of northwestern Arkansas. His plan was approved by General Theophilus Holmes, who had replaced him because of civilian complaints about harsh measures, such as declaring martial law, and Hindman marched back into northwest Arkansas in the autumn of 1862. Determined not to allow the Confederates to return, General Curtis ordered the Federal Army of the Frontier to deal with Hindman. The two forces collided at Prairie Grove on 7 and 8 December. Neither side defeated the other on the field, but Hindman's badly supplied army retreated south. After Prairie Grove, the Confederates never reoccupied the northwest, although small-unit operations continued there until the war's end, and Confederate raids into Missouri passed through in 1863 and 1864.

After Prairie Grove, the Confederate effort in Arkansas became unfocused, and their authorities lacked clear strategic goals. They made decisions that accomplished little and squandered men. Brigadier General Thomas J. Churchill decided to build up a small fort on the Arkansas River to threaten Federal operations on the Mississippi River, but the Federals responded with a massive force that captured Fort Hindman and most of its inadequate garrison on 11 June 1863. On 4 July 1863, General Holmes attacked the Federals at Helena, hoping to divert men from the siege of Vicksburg. The battle was ill timed—Vicksburg surrendered that day—and badly planned. The Confederates were driven back with severe losses.

Federal strategy appeared to have clearer goals, especially following the victory at Vicksburg. The Federals sought control over the Arkansas River as an avenue into the Indian Territory and to serve as a barrier to Confederate operations north of the river. They also had the resources to achieve these goals. On 1 September 1863, General James G. Blunt captured the river town of Fort Smith as a part of his operations in the Indian Territory. On 10 September, Major General Frederick Steele occupied Little Rock in a virtually unopposed march from Helena. Four days later the Federals occupied the city of Pine Bluff.

The Union occupation of Little Rock, Helena, and Fort Smith encouraged local Unionists to reorganize a loyal state government in Arkansas. Following a January 1864 state convention endorsed by President Abraham Lincoln, the Unionists held an election and chose as governor Isaac Murphy, one of the delegates to the 1861 convention who had refused to support secession. The Federal occupation also encouraged many civilians to switch sides. By the end of the war, 8,289 whites had enlisted in the Union army. The Federal presence also effectively ended slavery behind Union lines, and some 6,000 freedmen from Arkansas also joined the Union army.

After the capture of Little Rock, General Steele's primary mission was to hold the Arkansas River and he did little to disturb the Confederates who had fled into southwestern Arkansas. Only orders to cooperate with General Nathaniel Banks's Red River expedition in the spring of 1864 led him in that direction. Steele got as far as Camden, but after the defeat of Banks's army in Louisiana at Mansfield and Pleasant Hill on 8 and 9 April 1864, his advance halted. Following attacks upon his supply lines at Poison Springs on 17 April and Marks' Mills on 25 April, he retreated toward Little Rock. A major battle at Jenkins' Ferry on 28 April stopped Confederate pursuit and allowed him to escape back to the capital city.

Confederate authorities never despaired completely and from the fall of Little Rock to the end of the war they probed Federal lines, even mounting an unsuccessful attack on Pine Bluff shortly after its occupation in September 1863. After the Red River campaign they used southwestern Arkansas as a base from which General Sterling Price carried out his raid into Missouri in the summer of 1864. Nonetheless, they found they could do little to change the military situation. They did not have enough men to challenge the Federal occupation and, increasingly, they had to deal with internal problems produced by defeat and the collapse of the domestic economy. Confederate conscription in spring 1862 had hastened the disillusionment, and opposition to Confederate authority developed to the point of requiring military force to suppress it.

When the Confederacy's eastern armies surrendered in April 1865, most Arkansas soldiers and civilians had no desire to continue the war. Despite official efforts to stop it, desertion quickly depleted Confederate units in the state. Civilians plundered military warehouses. When E. Kirby Smith formally surrendered forces in the Trans-Mississippi District on 2 June 1865, little of the Confederacy remained intact within Arkansas.

—*Carl H. Moneyhon*

See also Arkansas Post, Battle of; Curtis, Samuel R.; Fort Smith, Arkansas; Helena, Arkansas, Battle of; Hindman, Thomas C.; Holmes, Theophilus; McCulloch, Ben; Pea Ridge, Battle of; Poison Spring, Battle of; Prairie Grove, Battle of; Rector, Henry M.; Steele, Frederick; Van Dorn, Earl.

For further reading:

Christ, Mark, ed. *Rugged and Sublime: The Civil War in Arkansas* (1994).

Dougan, Michael. *Confederate Arkansas: The People and Policies of a Frontier State in Wartime* (1976).

Moneyhon, Carl H. *The Impact of the Civil War and Reconstruction: Persistence in the Midst of Ruin* (1994).

Shea, William L., and Earl J. Hess. *Pea Ridge: Civil War Campaign in the West* (1992).

Thomas, David Y. *Arkansas in War and Reconstruction, 1861–1874* (1926).

ARKANSAS, CSS

The *Arkansas* was the most successful Confederate ironclad on the Mississippi. She contributed greatly to the revival of Southern fortunes in the west in the summer of 1862. In her twenty-three-day career, the *Arkansas* was undefeated by Union forces but ultimately was wrecked by her own unsophisticated technology.

On 16 August 1861 the Confederate Congress appropriated $160,000 to construct two ironclads at Memphis to defend the Mississippi. Similar in appearance to the CSS *Virginia*, the rams were smaller, but still measured 165 feet in length and 35 feet in width. When loaded the *Arkansas* drew at least 14 feet of water. Contractor John T. Shirley intended to have both rams finished in four months, but a shortage of trained laborers and materials prevented him from meeting this deadline. By April 1862, when Memphis was captured by Union forces, neither ironclad was finished. One was burned, while the other, the *Arkansas*, was towed down the Mississippi and up the Yazoo River to be completed. On 26 May 1862 Lieutenant Isaac Newton Brown took command. When he arrived, work on the *Arkansas* was at a standstill. The Yazoo River had overflowed its banks, and the *Arkansas* was moored to a submerged levy four miles from dry land.

Brown demonstrated enormous energy and creativity. He had the *Arkansas* towed to Yazoo City. Local planters provided laborers and forges. A sunken barge loaded with railroad rails for the *Arkansas*'s armor was raised. The rails were bolted to the superstructure, with alternating rails reversed, so that bulbs and flanges interlocked for maximum strength. Brown's workers were unable to curve the rails to conform to the shape of the *Arkansas*'s stern and quarter, so they bolted thinner boiler plates there. Armament consisted of ten guns of mixed calibers. Henry K. Stevens, the first lieutenant, drew plans for the gun carriages from memory and had them constructed from unseasoned cypress wood. Gunpowder had to be produced locally from sulphur, saltpeter, and charcoal.

An iron ram extended ten feet forward of the *Arkansas*'s bow. She was powered by 450-horsepower short-stroke screw engines salvaged from a sunken steamer. They drove two screws, but Brown quickly discovered that if one engine stopped, the remaining screw could only propel the Arkansas in a circle. Work with the ill-tempered engines was made more difficult by the lack of insulating material; temperatures in the fire-room reached 130 degrees.

Short of her intended complement of 200 men, the *Arkansas* boasted only 100 sailors, although they were experienced, having served on Confederate gunboats. Sixty soldiers were recruited from the army to work the guns, but the *Arkansas* was still undermanned when she sailed into battle. Nonetheless, on 12 July 1862 Brown took the *Arkansas* downstream toward the Mississippi. The Yazoo had fallen to fifteen feet and would soon trap the *Arkansas*, but by 15 July Brown was ready to enter the Mississippi and move downstream to the Confederate fortress of Vicksburg.

Between the *Arkansas* and Vicksburg were the combined fleets of Admiral David Farragut, who had captured New Orleans and run past the fortifications at Vicksburg, and Captain Charles H. Davis, whose river gunboats had conquered the upper Mississippi. Warned by deserters that the "Arkansas Traveler" was coming out, three Union ships had been sent up the Yazoo to reconnoiter. At first mistaking the *Arkansas* for an ordinary steamer, the Union vessels ran back for the fleet under fire from the Confederate ironclad. The ironclad *Carondelet* was badly damaged and forced ashore. The gunboat *Tyler* was cut up badly, and the ram *Queen of the West* ran away without attempting a collision. The firing was heard by the rest of the Union flotilla, but they believed that they were hearing only the *Tyler* firing on Confederate shore positions. When they realized that the monster ironclad was coming, most Union ships were unprepared to move.

Brown hove in close to the line of anchored ships and fired broadsides as fast as his guns could be loaded. As the *Arkansas* ran through the fleet, she received hits as fast as she dealt them out. The sixteen Union warships suffered smashed boilers and cut steam lines, but one-eighth of the *Arkansas*'s crew was also struck down. Her smokestack was riddled and the draft failed. Losing power, she slid past the last ships and rounded for Vicksburg.

Farragut was beside himself with fury and embarrass-

ment. Not only had his command been surprised, but the *Arkansas* was now between him and New Orleans. Worried about falling water levels in the Mississippi, Farragut determined to run back past Vicksburg while he could. The *Arkansas*'s position was marked, and Farragut's fleet began to sail past Vicksburg as dusk fell. As each ship passed the *Arkansas*'s anchorage, it fired broadsides at the ironclad; Brown, however, had shifted his anchor and thus escaped what would have been certain destruction.

On 22 July Davis tried again to sink the *Arkansas* with the ironclad *Essex* and ram *Queen of the West*. The *Essex* exchanged fire with the *Arkansas*, but got the worst of the exchange and drifted without power down the Mississippi. The *Queen of the West* slammed into the *Arkansas*, dislocating her temperamental engines but doing no other damage. Farragut towed the disabled *Essex* to Baton Rouge for repairs and left for deeper waters.

Brown commenced repairs on the badly damaged *Arkansas* before departing for a much-needed leave. Soon after his departure, Stevens was ordered to take the ironclad downriver to support the land attack on Baton Rouge. Leaving Vicksburg on 3 August, the *Arkansas* reached Baton Rogue two days later, just as her starboard engine broke down. After she had run aground, the ironclad's crew worked desperately to repair the engine. Early on 6 August, they spotted the *Essex* coming up to fight. As the *Arkansas* moved out into the river, one of her propeller shafts broke, and the ironclad again circled helplessly until it ran aground. Fearing that the *Essex* would pour fire into the lightly armored stern, Stevens ordered the *Arkansas* abandoned and then blew her up.

—Tim J. Watts

See also Ironclads; Riverine Warfare.
For further reading:
Coleman, S. B., and Paul Stevens. "A July Morning with the Rebel Ram *Arkansas*." *U.S. Naval Institute Proceedings* (1962).
Flynt, David. "Run the Fleet: The Career of the C.S. Ram *Arkansas*." *Journal of Mississippi History* (1989).
Huffstot, Robert S. "The Brief, Glorious Career of the CSS *Arkansas*." *Civil War Times Illustrated* (1968).
Parrish, Tom Z. *The Saga of the Confederate Ram Arkansas: The Mississippi Valley Campaign, 1862* (1987).
Still, William N., Jr. "Confederate Shipbuilding in Mississippi." *Journal of Mississippi History* (1968).

ARKANSAS POST, BATTLE OF
(11 January 1863)

In late 1862 Confederate forces at Vicksburg controlled navigation on the Mississippi River. One-hundred miles to the north, Confederate supremacy was not as certain. In September 1862 Major General Theophilus H. Holmes, commander of the Trans-Mississippi Department, ordered Colonel John W.

Dunnington to ensure Confederate control of the Arkansas and White rivers. Rebel engineers chose a site twenty-five miles above the mouth of the Arkansas River and 117 miles below Little Rock to construct an earthen fort. By the middle of November 1862 the Post of Arkansas (as the Confederates called it) or Fort Hindman (as it was known to the Federals) was nearly complete.

When completed, Arkansas Post formed a hollow square, 190 feet on each side with a bastion at each corner, surrounded by a ditch 20 feet wide and 8 feet deep. Artillery firepower consisted of four 10-pounder Parrott rifles, four 6-pounder smoothbores, and three 9-inch Columbiads. The fort was on a bluff 25 feet above the Arkansas River, 50 miles from its mouth. Inside the fort were some 5,000 Confederates under the command of General Thomas J. Churchill. Arkansas Post not only defended the Arkansas and White rivers, but also disrupted Federal commerce on those rivers. In late December 1862, just a month after construction was completed, the Union steamer *Blue Wing* was forced to surrender to Confederate artillery fire from the Arkansas shore and was taken to Arkansas Post. The Federal army had to capture Arkansas Post to protect its commerce.

The man to do this was Major General John A. McClernand, a political general (one who gained his commssion through political position or connections) from Illinois. McClernand had spent the first year of the war as General Ulysses S. Grant's second in command, and badly wanted an independent command. September 1862 saw him in Washington, D.C., meeting with cabinet officials and President Lincoln in an attempt to get a separate command. His friendship with the president helped him acquire his independent status. In October 1862 McClernand was authorized to recruit an army in the Midwest and use it against Vicksburg. The general wished to capture Arkansas Post, however, before turning his attention to Vicksburg.

After several delays, General McClernand assumed command of his force, which he called the Army of the Mississippi, on 2 January 1863. This Federal army numbered approximately 32,000 men and was divided into two army corps. General George W. Morgan commanded the First Corps and General William T. Sherman the Second. Accompanying the army was a naval flotilla under the command of Admiral David D. Porter. On 4 January, McClernand, Sherman, and Porter met at Milliken's Bend to determine the army's movements. At this council of war, the three men agreed to reduce Arkansas Post.

Their plan called for an expedition to sail up the Mississippi until it met the White River, then continue up that river. From there the flotilla was to move up the Arkansas River, which ran into the White. At a suitable place below the fort the troops would disembark.

Morgan's 1st Corps would form the left wing and Sherman's 2d Corps the right. Sherman's men were to march behind the fort, linking up with the Arkansas River above the bastion. Morgan's troops would establish a line below the fort connecting with Sherman's men and the Arkansas River. This would encircle the fortress, forcing its surrender.

By 8 January, the Federal expedition had reached the White River undetected. At about 5 P.M. on 9 January, the flotilla landed about three miles from Arkansas Post and the soldiers disembarked. Late that afternoon, Confederate general Churchill received word that a large Federal fleet was approaching. Churchill ordered his men to draw ammunition and prepare three days' rations—his troops were to be prepared for action at a minute's notice. Meanwhile, the Federal army spent 10 January getting into position. As the moon rose on the tenth, Admiral Porter commenced a naval bombardment of the fort in preparation for the next day's assault.

On 11 January, the navy began the assault by again bombarding the fortress at about 1 P.M. A half hour later the infantry moved in. As the Federal lines advanced, the heavily outnumbered Confederates poured a destructive fire into the blue columns. Admiral Porter's gunboats passed by the fort and opened a reverse fire upon the enemy. By 3:30 P.M. the Union attackers were within 100 yards of the fort, and artillery fire from within it had ceased. As the Yankee assault bore down upon the fortress, it was obvious that further resistance was futile, and white flags of surrender appeared.

The Federal expedition netted almost 5,000 prisoners, seven enemy flags, seventeen pieces of artillery, thousands of small arms, and a great deal of ammunition. The Union casualties numbered 134 killed, 898 wounded, and 29 missing. Along with preserving Federal commerce on the Arkansas River, this victory also provided a much-needed victory that rejuvenated the Federal army and boosted Union morale.

—*Christopher C. Meyers*

See also Army of Mississippi; Holmes, Theophilus; McClernand, John A.; Morgan, George W.; Porter, David Dixon; Sherman, William Tecumseh.

For further reading:
Bearss, Edwin. "The Battle of the Post of Arkansas." *The Arkansas Historical Quarterly* (1959).
Coleman, Roger. *The Arkansas Post Story* (1987).
Walker, John W. *Excavation of the Arkansas Post Branch of the Bank of the State of Arkansas* (1971).

ARLINGTON

The Civil War was Arlington National Cemetery's *raison d'etre*. Hundreds of Confederate dead and thousands of Union dead lie in Arlington, the largest of the nation's burial grounds. In April 1861 these acres on the Virginia heights overlooking the Potomac

Brigadier General Gustavus A. DeRussey (*third from left*) and staff on the portico of Arlington House, May 1864
(*Library of Congress*)

River and Washington, D.C., were not planted with the dead, but with crops. Robert E. Lee was doing his best to make his wife's estate a model farm.

Mary Anne Custis Lee inherited Arlington in 1857 upon the death of her father, George Washington Parke Custis, the adopted grandson of George Washington. She grew up in Arlington House. After her wedding there in 1831 to Robert E. Lee, scion of an equally august Virginia family, she continued to live at Arlington while Lee was stationed throughout the west. Six of their seven children were born in the house. Mrs. Lee's pride was her beautiful rose garden to the east of the mansion.

When he resigned his commission in the United States Army in April 1861 and left for Richmond, Lee urged his wife to prepare to follow him. He was certain that Arlington, so strategically located, would soon be occupied by Union soldiers. Within weeks, Mrs. Lee received

word that Federal troops would soon arrive. Taking away whatever family relics she could and storing the rest in the attic and cellar, she and her daughters headed south. Neither she nor her husband would ever again set foot in Arlington House, their home of thirty years.

In 1862, Congress levied taxes on real estate in the "insurrectionary" districts. Because the real goal was confiscation of Southerners' property rather than raising revenue, tax collectors refused to accept payment from anyone but the owner himself or herself. When Mrs. Lee, who was an invalid confined to a wheelchair, sent a cousin with her payment, it was refused. With uncommon speed, the 1,100-acre Arlington estate went on the auction block for default of taxes and was sold to the United States government for $26,800.

By the time the government became the owner of Arlington, the war had already created an urgent need for national cemeteries, especially in Washington. After each major battle in the surrounding countryside, the dead and dying were brought into the capital. Scores of Union soldiers and captured Confederates died every week in the makeshift hospitals that filled the city. Authority for military cemeteries rested with Quartermaster General Montgomery C. Meigs. Although he was raised in Georgia and owed his promotions to Southern friends in Congress, once the war began, Meigs turned virulently anti-Southern. He saved his deepest hatred for his old commander, Robert E. Lee. When in 1864 Secretary of War Edwin Stanton ordered Meigs to create a national cemetery near Washington, Meigs ordered no surveys of other sites, but immediately recommended that the 200 acres of the Arlington estate closest to the house be transformed into a burying ground for the Union dead.

Meigs ordered the first soldiers' graves dug in Mrs. Lee's rose garden in May 1864. By the end of 1864, over 7,000 graves spread across the area known as the Field of the Dead. Among them was the grave of Meigs's son, John Rodgers Meigs, killed by Confederate guerrillas. By the war's end, more than 16,000 Union graves surrounded Arlington House on three sides. The markers above the majority of them are inscribed simply "Unknown U.S. Soldier."

Immediately after the war, Meigs ordered a huge vault dug in what was left of Mrs. Lee's rose garden. Into the enormous pit went the skeletal remains of all the unidentified war dead gathered up from Bull Run and other battlefields near Washington. Though Meigs was loath to admit it, among the skeletons of the 2,111 or more bodies in the common grave under the huge granite marker intended to honor the Union's "army of martyrs" some Confederate bones were almost certainly commingled.

By the end of the war, several hundred Confederate dead, mostly prisoners of war who died in local hospitals, lay in graves scattered about Arlington. Meigs refused their relatives entry to the cemetery. On the first Decoration Day (now Memorial Day) in 1868, Meigs ordered that the Southern women who came to decorate the Confederate graves be turned away. Not until a new generation of leaders took up the reins of power and another war intervened would the Confederate dead at Arlington be recognized.

In 1898 President William McKinley, speaking in Atlanta, extolled the many Confederate veterans who had rallied to the flag and fought side by side with former Union men in the Spanish-American War. Old differences should be buried, McKinley told the crowd, and the bravery and sacrifice of all the dead should be recognized. In 1900 Congress authorized a Confederate section within Arlington National Cemetery. More than 400 Confederate dead were gathered from all over the cemetery and from graves in Alexandria and at the Soldiers' Home and were reinterred in the new Confederate section. In 1906 the United Daughters of the Confederacy won permission to erect a memorial in the midst of the Southern dead. Sculpted by Moses Ezekiel, himself a Confederate veteran, and dedicated in 1914, the Confederate Monument, the largest memorial in the cemetery, takes its theme from the verse from Isaiah carved around the pedestal: "They shall beat their swords into plowshares, and their spears into pruning hooks."

Among the 200,000 veterans of America's wars and their dependents buried at Arlington National Cemetery, 20,000 are the Civil War dead. The more than four million tourists who visit the cemetery each year traverse sixteen miles of roads, most named for heroes of the Civil War—Grant, Sherman, Sheridan, McClellan, McPherson, Farragut. This cemetery that was created as an act of revenge upon Robert E. Lee by Montgomery Meigs, who is also buried there and for whom a drive is named, has become the most hallowed ground in America.

—*Kathryn Allamong Jacob*

For further reading:
Ashabranner, Brent. *A Grateful Nation: The Story of Arlington National Cemetery* (1990).
Hinkle, John Vincent. *Arlington: Monument to Heroes* (1970).

ARMISTEAD, LEWIS ADDISON
(1817–1863)
Confederate general

Lewis A. Armistead was born in New Bern, North Carolina, on 18 February 1817 to General Walker Keith and Elizabeth Armistead. Armistead's ancestors, originally named Armstädt, came from Hessen-Darmstädt, now a part of Germany. The Armistead name early became prominent in U.S. military circles. Lewis's father and five brothers served during the War of 1812. One of them, Major George Armistead, was the commander of Fort McHenry during the British attack on the installation. The Armisteads were also related to four U.S. presidents: James Monroe, William Henry Harrison, John Tyler, and Benjamin Harrison.

Lewis Armistead entered West Point in 1834, but left in 1836. Two versions of the story regarding his departure exist. In one, he was dismissed after an altercation with Jubal Early during which he broke a plate over Early's head. A second version cites poor grades as reason for dismissal. Three years later Armistead joined the army as a second lieutenant, beginning a military career that would take him from the swamps of Florida, to the hills of Mexico City, and finally to the farmlands of Pennsylvania. During the Seminole Wars of 1835–1842,

Armistead fought under the command of his father Walker Keith Armistead and shortly thereafter was promoted to first lieutenant, a rank he held when the war with Mexico broke out in 1846. Armistead was decorated for heroism three times during the war, most notably for his actions at Chapultepec were he was "the first to leap into the Great Ditch." For his service that day he was brevetted to the rank of major. After the war, Armistead served on the western frontier, earning a reputation as a casual, friendly, but highly disciplined officer who believed that "obedience to duty was the first qualification of a soldier." During this time he cultivated many lasting friendships, most significant of which was his close association with Winfield Scott Hancock of Pennsylvania.

The outbreak of Civil War in the spring of 1861 left Armistead with a difficult choice. He had developed strong friendships with men like Hancock and others who chose to remain loyal to the Union. In the end, however, his devotion to his home state took precedence, and on 26 May 1861 he resigned his commission in the U.S. Army. Armistead, who by now was a widower and older than most of his comrades, accepted a colonelcy in the Confederate army and command of the 57th Virginia Infantry. Less than a year later, on 1 April 1862 he was promoted to brigadier general in the Army of Northern Virginia. In Armistead's first action, the battle of Seven Pines, he served with distinction and his brigade quickly won a reputation as one of the toughest units in the Army of Northern Virginia. Later, at the battle of Malvern Hill, Armistead would "charge with a yell" and help to turn the tide in favor of the Confederacy. His toughness extended beyond the battlefield. Soldiers either straggling or caught in dereliction of duty were disciplined by their superior officer who himself was directly responsible for their actions. Armistead believed that the private must answer to the officer, but the officer to him. This devotion to discipline was tempered by his soft-spoken manner, creating a blend that made him one of the most popular officers in the Army of Northern Virginia.

During the Antietam campaign, Armistead served as provost marshal for Lee's army. Later, he participated in the battles of Fredericksburg and Chancellorsville. Armistead's roles in these engagements, however, were minor compared with the immortality he would gain at Gettysburg. On the third day of the battle, 3 July 1863, Armistead led one of General George Pickett's brigades in the charge against the Union center commanded by Armistead's close friend Winfield Scott Hancock. With his hat on the point of his sword and uttering "Men! Remember what you are fighting for—your homes, your friends, and your sweethearts!" Armistead moved forward. Eventually he and a handful of men succeeded in reaching and scaling the stone wall that protected a battery of Union guns. It was while taking these guns, that Armistead fell mortally wounded. After the battle he was removed to a Federal field hospital where he died on 5 July 1863. On his deathbed he requested that his watch and other valuables be given to his friend Hancock who had also been wounded that day, though he would survive the war. Shortly after his death, Lewis Armistead's body was claimed by friends and taken to Baltimore, where he was buried in the family cemetery plot at St. Paul's Church.

—*Charles Thomas Johnson*

See also Gettysburg, Battle of.
For further reading:
Poindexter, James E. "General Armistead's Portrait Presented." *Southern Historical Society Papers* (1909).
Schuricht, Herrmann. *History of the German Element in Virginia* (1898–1900).

ARMORIES, ARSENALS, AND FOUNDRIES

An elaborate complex of armories, arsenals, foundries, laboratories, and depots provided the North and South with the weapons, ammunition, and equipment necessary to wage the Civil War. The functions of armories and arsenals were not strictly distinctive during the war, for both armories and arsenals not only stored arms, but both in some instances were capable of producing them as well. Laboratories were both research and production facilities, and depots were repositories for distributing ordnance.

The United States military listed the following extant armories and arsenals in 1859: Allegheny Arsenal, Pittsburgh, Pennsylvania; Augusta Arsenal, Georgia; Baton Rouge Arsenal, Louisiana; Benicia Arsenal, California; Charleston Arsenal, South Carolina; Detroit Arsenal, Dearbornville, Michigan; Fayetteville Arsenal, North Carolina; Fort Monroe Arsenal, Old Point Comfort, Virginia; Frankford Arsenal, Philadelphia, Pennsylvania; Harper's Ferry Armory, Virginia; Kennebec Arsenal, Augusta, Maine; Little Rock Arsenal, Arkansas; Mount Vernon Arsenal, Alabama; New York Arsenal, Governor's Island, New York; Pikesvilee Arsenal, Maryland; Saint Louis Arsenal, Missouri; San Antonio Arsenal, Texas; Springfield Armory, Massachusetts; Vancouver Arsenal, Washington Territory; Washington Arsenal, Washington, D.C.; Watertown Arsenal, Massachusetts; and Watervliet Arsenal, New York.

The combined inventory of these armories and arsenals included a total of 561,400 muskets and 48,862 rifles. James Buchanan's secretary of war during the secession crisis, the Virginian John B. Floyd, was later accused of ordering a controversial series of transfers that moved weapons from Northern armories and arsenals to Southern ones. Yet such a stratagem would have had little effect in the long term. In arms production and maintenance, as in everything else, the

Ruins of the federal arsenal at Harper's Ferry, Virginia, October 1862 (Photograph by S. A. Holmes / *Library of Congress*)

Confederate States could not match the potential of the North. From 1 January 1861 to 30 June 1866, Union arsenals and foundries supplied a prodigious amount of weaponry and equipment, including 7,892 cannon, 11,787 artillery carriages, 4,022,130 small arms, 1,022,176,474 cartridges for small arms, 1,220,555,435 percussion caps, 2,862,177 rounds of fixed artillery ammunition, 14,507,682 cannon primers and fuses, 12,875,294 pounds of artillery projectiles, 26,440,054 pounds of gunpowder, 6,395,152 pounds of potassium nitrate, and 90,416,295 pounds of lead. The U.S. Ordnance Department also produced an enormous amount of parts for repairing damaged items or replacing those lost or destroyed.

As for the South, records of production are not as complete, but the circumstantial evidence of Confederate armies relatively well supplied with arms indicates a titanic achievement by the Confederacy's

Ordnance Department. Federal arsenals in the South were among the Federal property seceding states immediately seized. The Confederacy would superintend the operation of these facilities during the war with astounding results, considering the Ordnance Department had to cope with dire shortages. In addition to arsenals at Charleston, Fayetteville, Augusta, Mount Vernon, Baton Rouge, Little Rock, and San Antonio, there were also the large Tredegar Irons Works in Richmond and arsenals in Apalachicola, Florida, and Selma, Alabama, the last of which came on line later in the war (1863). The Tredegar plant was the principal foundry for the Confederacy and the only one capable of casting the largest guns, although it did not have the Rodman technique. In Alabama, in addition to Selma's arsenal, the facilities there included a naval ordnance works, ten iron foundries, eight machine-shops, a shovel factory, a card factory for carding cotton, two wagon factories, a horseshoe factory, and a large rolling-mill. With abundant iron and coal mines only forty-five miles away at Montevallo and linked by the Alabama & Tennessee Railroad, Selma could produce almost anything, including 7- and 6-inch rifled cannon. At the Augusta Arsenal, Gabriel W. Rains produced heavy artillery and field pieces, and in February 1862, the War Department reported that government armories at Richmond (augmented by equipment taken down from Harper's Ferry) and Fayetteville were supplying 1,500 muskets and rifles per month. As a testament to the chronic dearth of manpower, authorities calculated that the rate of supply could have been doubled had they possessed enough skilled labor. The government competed with private workshops for workmen in their arsenals and foundries, but the high priority given to arms production prompted the Confederacy to grant wholesale draft exemptions to persons working in foundries.

Foundries, establishments that could cast metals, were an integral part of arms production. Foundries were part of an arsenal's manufacturing plant, but in the North and South, scores of private firms received government contracts. The Union and Confederacy contracted with private foundries to cast heavy artillery as well as cooking utensils, railroad spikes, tools, and nails. At the outbreak of the war, the biggest three foundries in the North were the Fort Pitt Foundry directed by Charles Knap, the West Point Foundry Association directed by Robert Parrott, and the South Boston Foundry directed by Cyrus Anger.

In the South, the arsenal and foundry eventually became vulnerable military targets, so they continued to operate until Federal military conquests either put them out of operation by occupation or deprived them of areas that provided imperative raw materials. Facilities in western Virginia were the objectives of frequent raids, while the Harper's Ferry Armory's workshops were burned and the site was mainly used as an ordnance depot. The Little Rock Arsenal would be occupied by Federals troops, and foundries in Atlanta and in Rome, Georgia, would invite destruction by Sherman's forces as he advanced to the sea. When Sherman moved into the Carolinas, his forces destroyed the Fayetteville Arsenal. In Alabama, Selma not only was an important weapons manufacturer, it was also the repository for all the iron and coal distributed through Georgia, Alabama, and Mississippi, so it became a prime target for James H. Wilson's sweeping cavalry raid in March–April 1865.

—*David S. Heidler and Jeanne T. Heidler*

See also *Artillery; Fayetteville Arsenal; Rifles; Small Arms; Springfield Armory; Springfield Rifle.*

For further reading:

Albaugh, William A., and Edward N. Simmons. *Confederate Arms* (1957; reprint, 1987).
Davis, Carl L. *Arming the Union: Small Arms in the Civil War* (1973).
Downey, Fairfax. *The Sound of the Guns: The Story of the American Artillery* (1955).
Edwards, William B. *Civil War Guns: The Complete Story of Federal and Confederate Small Arms: Design, Manufacture, Identification, Procurement, Issue, Employment, Effectiveness, and Postwar Disposal* (1997).
McKee, W. Reid, and M.E. Mason, Jr. *Civil War Projectiles II: Small Arms & Artillery* (1980).
Murphy, John M., and Howard M. Madaus. *Confederate Rifles & Muskets: Infantry Small Arms Manufactured in the Southern Confederacy, 1861–1865* (1996).
Naisawald, L. Van Loan, *Grape and Canister: The Story of the Field Artillery of the Army of the Potomac* (1983).
Olmstead, Edwin, Wayne Stark, and Spencer Tucker. *The Big Guns. Civil War Siege, Seacoast and Naval Cannon* (1997).
Peterson, Harold L. *Round Shot and Rammers: An Introduction to Muzzle-loading Land Artillery in the United States* (1969).
Tucker, Spencer C. *Arming the Fleet: U.S. Navy Ordnance in the Muzzle-loading Era.* (1989)
Wilson, Eugene K. "James H. Burton and the Development of the Confederate Small Arms Industry" (Thesis, 1976).

ARMSTRONG, FRANK CRAWFORD
(1835–1909)
Confederate general

Frank Crawford Armstrong was born to Frank W. Armstrong, an army officer, and Anne Millard Armstrong in Indian Territory (present-day Oklahoma) in 1835. While still a boy, he suffered the loss of his father, and his mother remarried General Persifor F. Smith. Armstrong went to Massachusetts to school, and upon the completion of his education, chose a military career. He received a commission as a second lieutenant of cavalry. Before the Civil War, he served at a number of frontier military posts and was a part of Albert Sidney Johnston's expedition to Utah to subdue the Mormons.

At the beginning of the Civil War, Armstrong did not immediately resign his commission. Promoted to captain in June 1861, he fought as a Union officer at the battle of First Bull Run. He resigned his commission on 13 August 1861 and accepted a commission in the Confederate army. The Confederate War Department sent him to the western theater, where he served as aide to Brigadier General Ben McCulloch at the battle of Wilson's Creek in August 1861. In December 1861 Armstrong fought at the battle of Chustenahlah in the Cherokee Nation. His connection with the Cherokees from his upbringing in Indian Territory made him useful in bringing many of those people to the Confederate side.

By early 1862 Armstrong was serving as Brigadier General McCulloch's adjutant general headquartered at Fort Smith. He was standing nearby when McCulloch was killed by Union sharpshooters at the battle of Pea

Ridge on 7 March 1862. After this battle, Armstrong briefly served as the colonel of the 3d Louisiana Infantry. In June 1862 he received a promotion to acting brigadier general with command of Major General Sterling Price's cavalry.

On 25 July 1862 Armstrong attacked the Union position at Courtland, Alabama, taking over 150 prisoners and Union supplies with the loss of only eight casualties. General Price commended Armstrong for his actions at Courtland. On 1 September 1862, while commanding 1,600 cavalry, he defeated another Union force at Bolivar, Tennessee, capturing seventy-one prisoners. He also cut part of Union communications in the area by destroying railroad track and bridges. Price again commended him in the strongest terms. Armstrong commanded Price's cavalry later in September 1862 at Iuka and in October at Corinth.

In January 1863, after fighting in the battle of Stones River, Armstrong received a permanent promotion to brigadier general. In March 1863 he fought at the battle of Spring Hill and as the commander of the 1st Brigade of Nathan Bedford Forrest's cavalry at the battle of Brentwood, Tennessee.

Armstrong temporarily commanded a division at Chickamauga, Georgia, but was back in command of a cavalry brigade attached to Leonidas Polk during the Atlanta campaign. He moved with John Bell Hood into Tennessee in the fall of 1864, fought at Franklin, and guarded the Confederate army's retreat from Nashville in December 1864. Armstrong was captured during Wilson's Raid on Selma, Alabama, on 2 April 1865.

After the war Armstrong lived in Texas and the Indian Territory, working for the government in various Indian posts. He died in Bar Harbor, Maine, in 1909.

—David S. Heidler and Jeanne T. Heidler

See also Brentwood, Tennessee; Cherokee Indians.

ARMY OF KANSAS

The Army of Kansas was composed of forces within a geographical area that included Kansas, the Indian Territory west of Arkansas, and the Nebraska, Dakota, and Colorado territories.

Created on 9 November 1861, the Department of Kansas was commanded by Major General David Hunter and consisted of five newly formed regiments of Kansas and Wisconsin infantry and five new cavalry regiments from Kansas and Ohio. Three regiments each of infantry and cavalry from the regular establishment rounded out the forces. The department was merged into the Department of the Mississippi on 11 March 1862, but was recreated on 2 May 1862 with Brigadier General James G. Blunt commanding.

In August 1862 forces were organized into three brigades commanded by Brigadier General Frederick Salomon (1st Brigade), Colonel William Weer (2d Brigade), and Colonel W. F. Cloud (3d Brigade). When the department again was subsumed on 19 September 1862, this time into the Department of Missouri, these brigades were reformed with forces of the Department of Missouri into the Army of the Frontier under Brigadier General John M. Schofield.

The Department of Kansas was yet again revived on 1 January 1864 under Major General Samuel R. Curtis. That summer five districts (North Kansas, South Kansas, Upper Arkansas, Nebraska, and Colorado) were established and remained in place until war's end in April 1865. Meanwhile, the Department of Kansas was merged into the Department of Missouri on 30 January 1865.

In spite of all these organizational changes, the soldiers in the region were frequently described as the Army of Kansas, even in those times when no such entity officially existed.

—David S. Heidler and Jeanne T. Heidler

See also Departments, Military; Kansas.
For further reading:
Miller, Edward A. *Lincoln's Abolitionist General: The Biography of David Hunter* (1997).

ARMY OF KENTUCKY

There were three embodiments of a Union military force known either officially or informally as the Army of Kentucky. The first was created from recruits collected by Lovell H. Rousseau near Danville, Kentucky, during the state's early neutrality. That neutrality guided Federal behavior, constraining it to the creation of a Department of Kentucky under Kentucky native Brigadier General Robert Anderson. The breaching of Kentucky's neutrality in the summer of 1861, however, saw the forces of Rousseau and those similarly recruited by William Nelson organized into the Army of Kentucky on 25 August 1861. The army was placed under Major General Gordon Granger and consisted of two brigades commanded by Brigadier Generals Mahlon D. Manson and Charles Cruft. This Army of Kentucky was routed and much of it captured at the battle of Richmond, Kentucky, on 30 August 1861, thus ending the first army's existence.

The second Army of Kentucky had only a brief existence. It consisted of three divisions under Stephen G. Burbridge (later under Andrew Jackson Smith), Green Clay Smith (later under Quincy A. Gillmore), and Absalom Baird. When this second Army of Kentucky was dismantled by reassignments to other forces and departments, a third Army of Kentucky, as it was informally called, came into being in February 1863. It was essentially a reorganization of Baird's division with his two brigades from the second Army of Kentucky being joined by William P. Reed's brigade from the District of Western Kentucky and George Crook's from West

Virginia. Baird's division formed the nucleus for Gordon Granger's reserve corps that became until October 1863 part of the Army of the Cumberland.

The third "Army of Kentucky" that fought with such distinction at Chickamauga was composed of elements of Baird's division by then under the command of James Steedman. During the critical stage of the battle's second day, Granger had three brigades of his reserve corps protecting the Union flank near McAffee's Church. He boldly moved two of them into the fray and managed to save the Union position from complete collapse. Some accounts refer to these brigades as the reserve corps and others as the Army of the Kentucky, the latter likely because Gordon Granger's original command remained so closely identified with him.

A Confederate Army of Kentucky existed, beginning in late August 1862. It was the force Edmund Kirby Smith led into Kentucky simultaneous to Braxton Bragg's invasion of the state. The army was composed of divisions under C. L. Stevenson, Henry Heth, Patrick Cleburne, and Thomas J. Churchill. John Hunt Morgan led its cavalry. It was this Confederate Army of Kentucky that ironically met and routed the first Union Army of Kentucky at the battle of Richmond. It would later join with Bragg's forces for the indecisive but critical battle of Perryville.

—*David S. Heidler and Jeanne T. Heidler*

See also Baird, Absalom; Chickamauga, Battle of; Granger, Gordon S.; Kentucky; Richmond, Kentucky, Battle of.

For further reading:

Baird, John A. *Profile of a Hero: The Story of Absalom Baird, His Family, and the American Military Tradition* (1977).

Coulter, E. Merton. *The Civil War and Readjustment in Kentucky* (1926).

Falaise, Louis De. "General Stephen Gano Burbridge's Command in Kentucky." *Register of the Kentucky Historical Society* (1971).

Hafendorfer, Kenneth A. *Perryville: Battle for Kentucky* (1981).

Harrison, Lowell H. *The Civil War in Kentucky* (1975).

Lambert, D. Warren. *When the Ripe Pears Fell: The Battle of Richmond, Kentucky* (1995).

McDonough, James Lee. *War in Kentucky: From Shiloh to Perryville* (1994).

ARMY OF MIDDLE TENNESSEE

The Confederate Army of Middle Tennessee was organized on 28 October 1862 by combining the approximately 4,000 men of Major General John C. Breckinridge's corps with Nathan Bedford Forrest's cavalry operating in the region for which the force was named. Breckinridge's corps had already seen considerable service. Organized in March 1861, it was originally under the command of George B. Crittenden, already under a cloud for his role in the Confederate disaster at Logan's Cross Roads the previous January. At the end of March, Breckinridge replaced Crittenden as corps commander because of charges of the latter's chronic drunkenness. Under Breckinridge, the outfit fought at Shiloh, Corinth, and Baton Rouge before returning to middle Tennessee in the fall of 1862.

Headquartered at Murfreesboro, Breckinridge's task was to guard against additional Federal encroachment while Braxton Bragg and Edmund Kirby Smith carried out their invasions of Kentucky. Therefore Forrest's cavalry, with two batteries assigned, was given the job of watching the approaches to Murfreesboro from Nashville. He was to place his cavalry close to Nashville to exploit any chances to harass the Union troops in the area. Mainly, though, Breckinridge wanted the Confederate cavalry to watch for any Federal moves toward the army's position from anywhere east or west of Nashville or from the Tennessee River. In November, Joseph Wheeler assumed command of the Army of Middle Tennessee's cavalry.

The Army of Middle Tennessee's infantry was formed into three brigades. The 1st Brigade was commanded by Colonel R. W. Hanson and consisted of the 2d, 4th, 6th, and 9th Kentucky Regiments as well as two batteries. Acting as a reserve, it was placed on the Shelbyville road near that town. The 2d Brigade was commanded by Colonel John B. Palmer and consisted of the 18th and 32d Tennessee, 32d Alabama, 4th Florida, and two batteries. It formed the right wing of the army and was encamped to protect the Lebanon and Nashville turnpike. The 3d Brigade, commanded by Colonel F. M. Walker, consisted of the 20th, 28th, and 45th Tennessee, the 60th North Carolina, and two batteries. It formed the left wing of the army and guarded the ground between the road leading to Nashville and the one leading to Franklin.

After failing to win a decisive victory at Perryville and thus failing in his invasion of Kentucky, Bragg returned to Murfreesboro, where the Army of Middle Tennessee was absorbed into the Army of Tennessee as the 1st Division of William Hardee's II Corps. It thus ceased to exist as an organizational entity. As part of II Corps, it consisted of four brigades commanded by Gideon Pillow, William Preston, Daniel W. Adams, and R. W. Hanson. During the Stones River campaign, it numbered about 7,000 men.

—*David S. Heidler and Jeanne T. Heidler*

See also Army of Tennessee; Breckinridge, John C.; Tennessee.

ARMY OF MISSISSIPPI

The Army of Mississippi was not a continuous classification throughout the Civil War. Many armies such as the Union Army of the Tennessee, Confederate Army of Northern Virginia, and Confederate Army of Tennessee had definite dates of origin and lasted throughout the war. The Army of Mississippi was not so resilient, however. Actually, three

Confederate Armies of (the) Mississippi existed in the Civil War. The first, the progenitor of the Confederacy's great western army, the Army of Tennessee, was created by General P. G. T. Beauregard on 5 March 1862 from troops in the Western Department (or Department No. 2). The force initially consisted of the two corps led by Major Generals Leonidas Polk and Braxton Bragg. On 29 March, the Central Army of Kentucky directly under General Albert Sydney Johnston, the department commander, reinforced the Army of the Mississippi. Johnston on this date took charge of the Army of the Mississippi, with Beauregard relegated to second-in-command.

The troops that would constitute the Army of Mississippi were widely scattered over the western Confederacy. Soldiers of Leonidas Polk's Corps were spread from Columbus, Kentucky, to Memphis along the great river as well as into the interior of the Confederate heartland. Braxton Bragg's men defended the Gulf Coast, principally at Pensacola, Mobile, and New Orleans. During the closing days of March 1862, the army concentrated in northeastern Mississippi, a major effort made possible by the steamboat, railroad, and telegraph. However, the army was green; probably 80 percent of the men had never heard a gun fired in anger. Bragg referred to the army as a mob.

The first action of this army, so designated by official representation, came at Shiloh on 6–7 April 1862. As the army assembled at Corinth, Mississippi, it was reorganized and its principal units renamed. Polk's troops, initially dubbed the First Grand Division, became after 29 March the I Corps, Bragg commanded II Corps and Major General William Hardee III Corps. The Reserve Corps was initially placed under George Crittenden, but he relinquished command on 31 March to Brigadier General John C. Breckinridge.

In personnel, the Army of Mississippi at Shiloh officially numbered 44,699. Its main strength was situated in its line infantry of the volunteer state regiments raised almost entirely in areas west of the Appalachians. On 6 April, the army listed in its order of battle 76 infantry regiments or battalions from the following states: Alabama, 10; Arkansas, 10; Florida, 1; Kentucky, 5; Louisiana, 12; Mississippi, 9; Missouri, 1; Tennessee, 26; and Texas, 2. Also present were two regiments and one battalion of the small regular Confederate army. The infantry was equipped with a wide array of weaponry, from shotguns to state-of-the-art British .577 Enfield rifles that had been run through the blockade.

In artillery, Johnston's army could muster 22 batteries and companies from the following states: Alabama, 3; Arkansas, 5; Georgia, 1; Kentucky, 2; Louisiana, 2; Mississippi, 4; and Tennessee, 5. Many of the artillery pieces in the Army of the Mississippi were guns of Southern origin, made at Nashville, Memphis, or New Orleans.

In cavalry, Johnston counted 9 regiments, squadrons, and other units of varying size from the following states: Alabama, 1; Georgia, 1; Kentucky, 2; Mississippi, 3; Tennessee, 1; and Texas, 1. The Army of Mississippi was the source of some of the finest cavalrymen that the war produced, including Nathan Bedford Forrest, John Hunt Morgan, and Joseph Wheeler.

Lacking time for training, the army embarked almost immediately on an offensive to destroy the Army of the Tennessee under Major General Ulysses S. Grant at Pittsburg Landing. The resulting battle of Shiloh, one of the greatest bloodlettings of the war, showed that the Confederate army would fight bravely, if not especially skillfully. Lacking more than a veneer of experienced officers, the army paid a terrible price for its callowness. Its losses at Shiloh totaled 10,694. Among the casualties was the army's commander, Albert Sidney Johnston, the only four-star American ever killed in action.

Under Johnston's replacement, P. G. T. Beauregard, the Army of Mississippi fell back to Corinth, and pressed heavily by Union forces in May, retreated to Tupelo, Mississippi. Disappointed in the apparent passivity of its commander, President Jefferson Davis replaced Beauregard temporarily on 27 June with Bragg and then on 5 July with William Hardee who moved the army to Chattanooga. On 15 August, command passed back to Bragg, who reorganized the force. Bragg left the forces in Mississippi under Major Generals Earl Van Dorn and Sterling Price. The second Confederate force called the Army of Mississippi was formed on 7 December 1862 out of Major General Earl Van Dorn's Army of West Tennessee and the corps (sometimes called the Army of the West) commanded by Major General Sterling Price. Prior to its designation as the Army of Mississippi (the label would lie idle for several months), the force was troubled by the lack of cooperation between Van Dorn and Price. Price fought the interesting yet unimportant battle of Iuka on 19 September 1862. Eventually, Jefferson Davis himself rectified the command situation in Mississippi. He gave Van Dorn command of the 22,000-man army, and the Confederates subsequently attacked and lost at Corinth on 3–4 October 1862. Van Dorn was relieved and replaced by Lieutenant General John C. Pemberton who commanded the army through the Vicksburg campaign, although in January 1863 he reorganized his forces and dropped the designation Army of Mississippi. The forces fought its largest and most important battle at Champion's Hill on 16 May, where Grant defeated Pemberton and sealed Vicksburg's fate. Most of the army, 28,000 strong, withdrew and subsequently surrendered with the city on 4 July 1863. Most of the army was paroled and exchanged, which put the units back into the ranks by 1864. Lieutenant General Leonidas Polk took command of the forces in Mississippi and endeavored to thwart Major General William T. Sherman's Meridian campaign in February 1864.

Thus a third Army of Mississippi came into existence under Polk. It joined the Army of Tennessee on 12 May 1864 during the Atlanta campaign. Following Polk's death in action on 14 June at Pine Mountain, Georgia, the organization was renamed on 26 July as Stewart's Corps to reflect more accurately its size (about 20,000) and its new commander Lieutenant General Alexander P. Stewart.

While little continuity emerges regarding the various names, a definite pattern exists regarding geography and units that made up the army. A history of the Army of Mississippi can be used loosely to describe the western-most portion of the Western theater. For instance, when General Braxton Bragg split the Confederate army at Tupelo, Mississippi, in July 1862 and moved to Tennessee for his subsequent march into Kentucky, he split the Western theater into two parts. The Army of Tennessee fought the remainder of the war in the east-ernmost portion of the Western theater, while the Army of Mississippi fought the western battles. This split in the Western theater remained until May 1864, when the two armies again united into the Army of Tennessee, the Army of Mississippi becoming the third corps. Thus, from July 1862 to May 1864, the Army of Mississippi fought on its own in its own theater. Many historians argue convincingly that it was in this west-ernmost area of the Western theater that the war was won and lost, making the operations of the Army of Mississippi highly significant.

Historians have pointed out that the Army of Mississippi is frequently mentioned in the *Official Records* as the Army of the Mississippi. Several Union organizations (under John McClernand, John Pope, William S. Rosecrans, Ulysses S. Grant, and William T. Sherman) also bore the name Army (or Division) of the Mississippi.

—*Malcolm Muir and Timothy B. Smith*

See also Champions Hill, Battle of; Corinth, Battle of; Departments, Military, C.S.A.; Departments, Military, U.S.A.; Iuka, Battle of; Shiloh, Battle of; Vicksburg Campaign.

For further reading:

Bearss, Edwin C. *The Vicksburg Campaign* (1985).

Bearss, Margie Riddle. *Sherman's Forgotten Campaign: The Meridian Expedition* (1987).

Cozzens, Peter. *The Darkest Days of the War: The Iuka Corinth Campaign* (1997).

Sword, Wiley. *Shiloh: Bloody April* (1974).

ARMY OF MISSOURI

The Confederate Army of Missouri began with at least 12,000 men, but the short-lived, largely blue-coated army relied so heavily on foraging men, as well as uniforms and supplies, that its commanders likely had only a vague idea how large it was at any given point. Passing through Federally occupied territory during Price's Missouri Raid, the army surely added thousands to its ranks, but the army's itinerary surely caused it to lose thousands who simply went home as the certainty of defeat loomed so largely. Although 20,000 men probably passed through its ranks, the army rarely had more than 12,000 at any one time and regularly functioned with far fewer effectives.

In August 1864, Confederate Trans-Mississippi commander General Edmund Kirby Smith authorized General Sterling Price, heading the Department of Arkansas, to organize its cavalry division with supplemental forces into this new army. From 16 to 18 September, Price reorganized the mounted Confederate forces in Arkansas into three divisions.

General Joseph O. Shelby commanded the smallest division of nearly 3,400 men. Within it, Colonel David Shanks commanded Shelby's old "Iron Brigade" with Colonel Sidney D. Jackman taking another, and Colonel Charles H. Tyler slated to organize a new brigade to be raised in Missouri.

The largest division of almost 5,100 men was commanded by Brigadier General James F. Fagan, an infantry commander who was promoted to a mounted command over experienced cavalrymen. Fagan's division had four brigades, including the largest in Price's army, that of Brigadier General William Lewis Cabell, who had served the Richmond government well before going west. Colonels William Slemmons, Archibald S. Dobbins, and Thomas H. McCray commanded the other three brigades.

The final 3,800-man division was commanded by Brigadier General John S. Marmaduke, who had earned a reputation as "the cavalier general" for his two 1863 mounted raids into Missouri. His most reliable brigade belonged to Brigadier General John Bullock Clark, Jr., the son of a Missouri politician expelled from the U.S. Congress in 1861. Marmaduke's other brigade belonged to Colonel Thomas R. Freeman.

Among the ranks of Price's army were such distinguished figures as Thomas C. Reynolds, exiled governor of Missouri's Confederate state government; Trusten Polk, who had been expelled from the U.S. Senate; and Brigadier General Merriwether Jeff Thompson, the former mayor of St. Joseph, who had recently been paroled after a year's captivity. Many of these officers and men had served alongside each other, and their official hope was to liberate what they saw as a Confederate state.

While Price's officers were accomplished leaders, the bitter legacy of guerrilla war and reprisals that had raged in the state predisposed the Army of Missouri to be avengers rather than liberators. Of the five Missouri brigadiers, Jackman and Freeman had both led guerrillas themselves. As regimental commanders, Colonels John Truesdale Coffee and William O. Coleman had fought

primarily as irregulars, and DeWitt Clinton Hunter had actually participated in the Baxter Springs Massacre. Others with ties to partisan warfare included Colonels John Q. A. Burbridge, Colton Green, David Shanks, Moses W. Smith, Alonzo Slayback, Benjamin Elliott, Sol Kitchen, William L. Jeffries, Robert R. Lawther, J. A. Schnable, and Timothy Reeves (also spelled Reves).

This army, then, was not merely a Trans-Mississippi version of the eastern Confederate forces. Viewing Missouri as a seceded state, the Army of Missouri readily "conscripted" thousands of unwilling civilians as recruits and rarely recognized lines between civilians and combatants or between prisoners of war and active enemies. No Confederate army of comparable size and importance so persistently left in its wake a trail of murdered civilians and prisoners, particularly African-Americans and Germans.

Problems of logistics and poor management crippled the Army of Missouri. In a region where adult white men carried arms in peacetime, the complaints of Confederate officers that the army had not armed their men likely meant not that they remained unarmed but that the lack of standardized arms meant an unmanageably wild variety of ammunition. Later recruits, of course, would have only what arms they could bring to the army. More seriously, Price had been unable to mount the entire command, and those few on foot—fewer than 200 in Shelby's division—slowed the entire column to the pace of infantry. Still worse, confiscations continued to swell the size of Price's supply train to 500 wagons. Price usually ran the army from the back of an ambulance owing to malaria or—if his critics were to be believed—the bottle. All bode very poorly for an army dependent on speed for its success.

Arguably, the achievements of the Army of Missouri were politically self-defeating, and its military successes depended most directly on the ineptness of Federal generalship.

—*Mark A. Lause*

See also Price, Sterling; Price's Missouri Raid.

For further reading:
Hinton, Richard J. *Rebel Invasion of Missouri and Kansas, and the Campaign of the Army of the Border against General Sterling Price, in October and November 1864* (1865).
Monaghan, Jay. *Civil War on the Western Border* (1955).
Sallee, Scott E. "Missouri! One Last Time: Sterling Price's 1864 Missouri Expedition, 'A Just and Holy Cause.'" *Blue and Gray Magazine* (1991).

ARMY OF MOBILE

Prior to the creation of the Army of Mobile, troops in the vicinity of that city were commanded by Brigade General Jones M. Withers and were designated as the District of Alabama (October 1861) in Braxton Bragg's Department of Alabama and West Florida. On 20 December 1861, Withers's area of responsibility was extended westward to include Pascagoula Bay and the part of Mississippi east of the Pascagoula River. On 27 January 1862, Withers's command officially became the Army of Mobile and was charged with the defense of the Gulf Coast between the Pascagoula and Perdido rivers. The army consisted of 10,056 men with 9,278 present for duty. It contained the 2d, 18th, 19th, 20th, 21st, 22d, 23d, 24th, and 25th Alabama Infantry Regiments, the 2d Alabama Battalion, a company of Alabama infantry, a battalion of Mississippi volunteers, a company of Mississippi infantry, six companies of the Alabama Mounted Volunteers, the 1st Battalion of Alabama Artillery, and the 2d Battalion of Alabama Light Artillery.

Authorities consistently calculated the army as undermanned and its capabilities limited, not only by a paucity of resources but also because of a rapid turnover in its command. Withers was relieved in February 1861, when he and elements of the Army of Mobile were shifted to the 2d Division of Bragg's II Corps, Army of Mississippi, in which they would fight at Shiloh. Meanwhile Brigadier General Samuel Jones, commanding from Pensacola, absorbed Mobile's department, and temporary commanders of lesser rank supervised the Army of Mobile. Colonel John B. Villepeague took command on 28 February 1862, but was soon relieved for duty with the Army of Mississippi. His replacement was Colonel W. L. Powell, commander of the 2d Brigade, who was himself replaced at the end of April 1862 by Brigadier General James E. Slaughter. At roughly the same time, Major General John H. Forney succeeded Samuel Jones as commander of what now was designated as the District of the Gulf. Forney established his headquarters in Mobile.

By the fall of 1862 the Army of Mobile was still being reported in Confederate returns, but it had been reduced to nearly half its original size by detachments to other armies and postings to nearby garrisons. Ultimately, in June 1863 the District of the Gulf came under its final commander, Major General Dabney H. Maury. By this time, the organizational entity labeled the Army of Mobile had been subsumed by the patchwork collection of troops that remained in defense of the city. They were generally referred to as the Mobile garrison.

—*David S. Heidler and Jeanne T. Heidler*

ARMY OF NEW MEXICO

The Confederate Army of New Mexico was actually a glorified brigade of less than 4,000 men under the command of Brigadier General Henry Hopkins Sibley that was given the task of conquering the New Mexico Territory (now Arizona and New Mexico). Confederate interest in New Mexico, spurred by dreams

of access to California gold and Pacific ports, originated in July 1861, when John R. Baylor led the 2d Texas Mounted Rifles into New Mexico and captured the 700-man Union garrison of Fort Fillmore. At this time, Henry Hopkins Sibley, just resigned from Federal army service in New Mexico, persuaded Confederate president Jefferson Davis of the feasibility of conquering the area. Commissioned brigadier general, Sibley organized and proclaimed the Army of New Mexico (also known as Sibley's Arizona Brigade, Sibley's New Mexico Brigade, or simply Sibley's Brigade) at Fort Bliss, Texas, on 14 December 1861. The army consisted of the 4th, 5th, and 7th Regiments of Texas Volunteer Cavalry, Baylor's command, and assorted support units—an aggregate of approximately 3,700 men.

Relatively well trained for that stage of the war, but plagued by logistical shortages, Sibley's force was largely ill clothed, chronically low on food for both man and mount, and short of appropriate weapons (two companies carried only revolvers and nine-foot lances). Hoping to live off the land and captured Federal stores, the Army of New Mexico pushed northward into New Mexico in January 1862. By mid-February 1862, Sibley's force confronted approximately 3,800 Federals under Colonel Edward R. S. Canby at Fort Craig. Canby commanded about 1,200 regulars, most of the remainder being New Mexico and Colorado volunteers and militia in disparate states of discipline. Having left garrisons at several locations, Sibley took only 2,600 men into battle at Valverde near Fort Craig on 21 February 1862. The day-long battle was furious, and Sibley, who was ill or intoxicated, turned over command to Colonel Thomas Green, who drove the Unionists back to Fort Craig with a final furious assault near sunset.

Having suffered approximately 200 casualties, Sibley then bypassed Fort Craig, moving up the Rio Grande Valley toward the bountiful supply depots at Albuquerque and Santa Fe. With little enthusiasm for fighting, significant numbers had deserted the Union forces, and Sibley's campaign seemed poised for complete success, as Confederate forces spread as far west as Tucson, Arizona. However, quick-thinking Federal quartermasters in Albuquerque and Santa Fe destroyed or evacuated virtually all supplies, so the capture of these locations on 4 and 23 March, respectively, hardly alleviated the Army of New Mexico's dire logistics. Additionally, the Confederates had become progressively dispersed by garrisoning captured areas, so that only 600 men actually occupied Santa Fe. Conversely, Canby received modest but steady reinforcements that allowed him to move northward with his own forces at Fort Craig, while also directing 1,300 men from Fort Union (northeast of Santa Fe) to move on the Confederate-held territorial capital.

On 26 through 28 March 1862, 600 Confederates under W. R. Scurry clashed with 1,300 Federals under John Slough and John Chivington at the battle of Glorieta Pass, twenty miles southeast of Santa Fe. Although driven from the main field, the Unionists captured the Confederate supply train and killed hundreds of horses and mules, leaving the Army of New Mexico virtually bereft of supplies and mounts.

In Santa Fe, the just-arrived Sibley surveyed the remains of his army and learned that Canby and 1,200 Federals were now approaching Albuquerque. Sibley concentrated his depleted force at Albuquerque and contemplated three options: starvation in Albuquerque, an attack on Canby's now-united forces that outnumbered him two to one, or retreat down the Rio Grande River.

On 12 April 1862, the Army of New Mexico left Albuquerque, moving down the west bank of the Rio Grande, shadowed on the east bank by Canby. Although in constant visual contact, only desultory skirmishing resulted, for Canby's supply situation precluded taking prisoners. Thus "escorted," Sibley's men suffered terribly, water shortages causing some to slaughter their few animals and drink the blood. By early May, Sibley and 1,700 survivors staggered back to Fort Bliss in Texas and eventually on to San Antonio. Hopes of renewing the campaign ended when the Union's "California Column" reached New Mexico.

Its ambitions dashed, the Army of New Mexico later fought as Sibley's Brigade and Green's Brigade, but its greatest days lay behind, in the Union-held Rio Grande Valley. If successful, the Army of New Mexico's exploits might have ranked with Scott's 1847 Mexico campaign, but, in failure, it remains a quixotic sidelight of the war.

—*Broeck N. Oder*

See also Baylor, John Robert; Canby, Edward R. S.; Fort Craig, Battle of; Glorieta Pass, Battle of; New Mexico; Sibley, Henry Hopkins; Val Verde, Battle of.

For further reading:

Frazier, Donald S. *Blood and Treasure: Confederate Empire in the Southwest* (1995).

Hall, Martin H. *The Confederate Army of New Mexico* (1978).

———. *Sibley's New Mexico Campaign* (1960).

Johnson, Robert U., and Clarence C. Buel. *Battles and Leaders of the Civil War*, vol. 2 (1956).

Josephy, Alvin M. *The Civil War in the American West* (1991).

Thompson, Jerry. *Henry Hopkins Sibley: Confederate General of the West* (1987).

ARMY OF NORTHERN VIRGINIA

The most famous and most successful of all the Confederate armies had its origins in the Department of Alexandria, a command created in April 1861 encompassing most of northern Virginia and also known as the Department of the Potomac. After P. G. T. Beauregard took command of the department in June, its field army became known as the Army of the

Potomac. This army, merged with Joseph E. Johnston's Army of the Shenandoah, won the first major battle of the war at First Bull Run in July, and the combined force, under Johnston's command, kept its new name in the Department of the Potomac.

When a new Department of Northern Virginia was created in October 1861, Johnston was assigned to command it, with department headquarters at Manassas and the Army of the Potomac as its principal army. After Johnston was seriously wounded at Fair Oaks/Seven Pines in May 1862, Robert E. Lee left his position as military advisor to President Jefferson Davis to take command of the army and the department, a post he would hold for the rest of the war.

Within a month the renamed Army of Northern Virginia would drive the Federal Army of the Potomac, under George B. McClellan, from the outskirts of Richmond in the Seven Days' battles (25 June–1 July 1862). Though Confederate casualties were heavy, and Lee's complicated and ambitious plans often went astray on the battlefield, the campaign helped save the capital and gave a much-needed boost to Southern morale.

It also marked the beginning of a remarkable ten-month period in which Lee took the initiative from the Federals in the East and his army fought a series of battles that transformed it into one of the greatest armies in American military history. Lee soon reorganized the Army of Northern Virginia to reflect his strategic and tactical vision, transferring or shifting generals and units, and settled on two infantry wings under James Longstreet and Thomas J. "Stonewall" Jackson, a large cavalry division under James E. B. "Jeb" Stuart, and artillery batteries assigned to specific brigades or divisions.

Lee soon took his army north to oppose the Army of Virginia, a new Federal force under John Pope that had been organized to operate between Richmond and Washington. He took a bold gamble by dividing his force in the face of Pope's large army. After Jackson captured or destroyed a huge cache of Union supplies at Manassas Junction, his wing was attacked by Pope on the old Manassas battlefield. The Confederates held their position until Longstreet arrived to help deliver a crushing blow to the Federals, whose retreat turned into a rout toward Washington late on the second day of the battle of Second Bull Run/Second Manassas (29–30 August 1862).

This victory helped convince Lee, Davis, and other authorities in Richmond that the time was right for an invasion of Maryland, to carry the war into Northern territory and perhaps to encourage foreign intervention on behalf of the Confederacy. The Army of Northern Virginia crossed the Potomac River in early September with its ranks reduced by widespread straggling and weakened by its losses during the summer. Lee, still willing to take enormous risks, separated his forces again, sending Jackson to capture the arsenal and garrison at Harper's Ferry while the rest of the army faced the Army of the Potomac, once again under McClellan. He concentrated his forces at the town of Sharpsburg, on the banks of Antietam Creek, and endured the bloodiest single day of the entire war at Antietam/Sharpsburg (17 September 1862). The Confederates held off a succession of piecemeal Federal assaults until timely reinforcements arrived on the field at a critical moment, saving the Army of Northern Virginia from almost certain destruction. The battle ended in a draw, though Lee's withdrawal back across the Potomac and the army's appalling losses gave some Southerners cause for concern if not alarm.

There was a significant lull in the Eastern theater after Antietam as both major armies there spent the fall of 1862 recuperating from several months of hard campaigning and looking toward their next battle, which many believed would not come until spring. Lee took advantage of the opportunity to organize his army into two permanent infantry corps, the first under Longstreet and the second under Jackson, and a cavalry corps, under Stuart.

By December 1862 the Army of the Potomac, this time under Ambrose E. Burnside, attempted another advance toward Richmond, this time by way of Fredericksburg, a town on the Rappahannock River between the two capitals. The Army of Northern Virginia established a strong defensive position along the river and easily repulsed wave after wave of Federal attacks launched against its lines in the remarkably one-sided battle of Fredericksburg (11–13 December 1862).

By the spring of 1863, Lee and the Army of Northern Virginia confronted a revitalized Army of the Potomac under new commander Joseph Hooker, who confidently predicted victory. The two armies met west of Fredericksburg in the Wilderness, a nearly impenetrable forest dense with thickets and underbrush. Lee boldly divided his army in two and pinned the Federals in place with a third of his force while Jackson, with the rest of the army, marched around Hooker's flank and launched a slashing attack that threatened to rout almost half of the Army of the Potomac. After heavy fighting, in which Hooker never committed all his troops, the Federals withdrew across the Rappahannock River. The four-day battle of Chancellorsville (1–4 May 1863) was the army's most impressive victory, marred only by the death of Jackson, who was accidentally wounded by his own men. Soon afterward, a confident Lee wrote to one of his generals, "there never were such men in an army before. They will go anywhere and do anything if properly led." One of his soldiers claimed at about the same time, "This is the best army in the world I expect. We are all satisfied with General Lee and he is always ready for a fight." That confidence would cost Lee and his men dearly in their next campaign.

Lee now proposed another invasion of the North—this time advancing as far as Pennsylvania—which would take the war out of Virginia and into Northern territory once again, and perhaps winning a smashing victory that would end the war. He also realized that it was not feasible to continue operating with an army split into two large and unwieldy corps and decided to reorganize it. Longstreet retained the I Corps, Richard S. Ewell was promoted to command Jackson's old II Corps, and A. P. Hill was promoted to command a new III Corps, created from units in the I and II Corps. The army's artillery had already been reorganized in the months before Chancellorsville, with the creation of battalions assigned to each corps.

The Army of Northern Virginia, about 75,000 strong, crossed over the Potomac River in mid-June and by the end of the month was scattered among several towns in southern Pennsylvania. By then the Confederates faced an Army of the Potomac numbering about 95,000 and commanded by yet another new general, George G. Meade. Lee concentrated his force near Gettysburg, a town at the center of an extensive road network in southern Pennsylvania.

The three days of battle at Gettysburg (1–3 July 1863) have often been called "the High Water Mark of the Confederacy," an assessment more justified after 1865 than it was in the summer of 1863. The Confederates launched a fierce attack on the first day, pushing the Federals through the streets of Gettysburg and eventually to Cemetery Ridge due south of the town, where Meade rallied his troops and established a strong defensive position that evening. Heavy fighting on the second day, in the area between Cemetery Ridge and the Confederate position on Seminary Ridge, also lasted until nightfall but accomplished little, as the Federals managed to hold their ground under intense pressure from repeated assaults. Lee, who still believed that the Army of the Potomac would break if he sent enough troops against it at the right place, planned a massive frontal assault against Meade's center, on Cemetery Ridge, for the afternoon of 3 July. The attack, known to history as "Pickett's Charge," had little if any chance of success and was a bloody failure that ended the battle. After suffering enormous casualties—more than a third of its officers and men killed, wounded, or captured in three days—the army soon withdrew from Pennsylvania and recrossed the Potomac into Virginia. Though Lee, his soldiers, the Confederate authorities, and the Southern people were naturally disappointed by the outcome, they were still confident that the Army of Northern Virginia would still help win the Confederacy's independence.

The army fought no pitched battles for the rest of 1863 and, except for minor clashes at Bristoe Station,

Rappahannock Station, and Mine Run, spent its time waiting for an opportunity to resume the offensive the next spring. Lee did send Longstreet and I Corps to reinforce Braxton Bragg's Army of Tennessee, and, although this detached force participated in the Confederate victory at Chickamauga (19–20 September 1863) and the Knoxville campaign (November–December 1863), it accomplished little before returning to Virginia the following April.

By that time, the Army of the Potomac would be directed by Ulysses S. Grant, who had just been promoted to command all the armies of the United States. Although the army was still officially under Meade, Grant established his headquarters in the field with it and became Lee's principal opponent for the remainder of the war. When Grant made a move toward Richmond and entered the same Wilderness where Lee had been so successful against Hooker the year before, the Confederates attacked. Two days of battle in the Wilderness (5–6 May 1864), characterized by fierce but inconclusive combat in which neither side held an advantage for long, ended in a draw. This first phase of the Overland campaign marked a change in Lee's generalship, as he would thereafter take a more defensive stance than he preferred in the hope of preventing unnecessary losses that could not be replaced.

Grant now made an attempt to get the Army of the Potomac between Lee and Richmond, but the Army of Northern Virginia blocked his path at Spotsylvania Court House. Several days of bloody battle there at Spotsylvania (8–19 May 1864), most notably in an incredible hand-to-hand battle for the center of the Confederate lines that lasted for almost twenty-four hours on 12 May, resulted in staggering losses for both armies but did little to slow the momentum of the Army of the Potomac.

Within two weeks the Army of Northern Virginia would find itself in essentially the same position as it held when Lee took command in June 1862: facing the Army of the Potomac within sight of Richmond. At Cold Harbor both armies dug makeshift entrenchments, and two days of preliminary fighting there convinced Grant that the Confederates were demoralized by being maneuvered so close to their capital. He ordered a frontal assault against a strong Confederate position on the morning of 3 June, hoping to break Lee's lines and open the way to Richmond. The Army of Northern Virginia held its lines, easily repulsing the Federals and inflicting heavy casualties on the attackers. Three days of fighting at Cold Harbor (1–3 June 1864) ended with the Army of the Potomac no closer to its goal.

In just under a month of almost daily combat from the Wilderness to Cold Harbor, major and minor actions had now killed, wounded, or made prisoners of about 30,000 Confederates in the Army of Northern Virginia.

Thirty-seven of Lee's general officers—most notably Longstreet, seriously wounded by his own men at the Wilderness, and Stuart, mortally wounded at Yellow Tavern—were among these losses. These casualties, in officers and among the rank and file, would soon prove to be catastrophic.

Grant, realizing that he could not break Lee's lines by sheer force, now used his superior numbers in conjunction with other Federal forces to try and force the Confederates to choose between saving Richmond or saving Petersburg, a vital railroad center south of the capital. When the Army of the Potomac and the Army of Northern Virginia constructed an elaborate system of earthworks and trenches facing each other around Petersburg in mid-June, they initiated a siege that would last for the next ten months (June 1864–April 1865).

The remarkable battle of the Crater (30 July 1864), in which the Federals exploded four tons of gunpowder under Lee's army, was an excellent opportunity to break through his lines and capture Petersburg. Grant's assault, however, was decisively defeated by a fierce Confederate counterattack and actually had little real impact on the siege. The stalemate continued throughout the summer, fall, and winter, and would do so with few major breaks until the spring of 1865. The two armies, within yards of each other, occupied an extensive line of trenches, rifle pits, and batteries, and spent most of their days waiting for the decisive battle that never came.

Lee, hoping to take some pressure off the Army of Northern Virginia and to save the vital Shenandoah Valley for the Confederacy, sent his II Corps, under Jubal A. Early, to the valley in June. Early, facing a Federal army under Philip H. Sheridan, was soundly defeated in three battles that fall—at Winchester (19 September 1864), Fisher's Hill (22 September 1864), and Cedar Creek (19 October 1864)—and the remnants of his corps returned to Lee in December.

The sharp decline in Confederate morale that followed the fall of Atlanta, Early's crushing defeats in the Shenandoah Valley, Lincoln's reelection, the March to the Sea, and the twin disasters at Franklin and Nashville only confirmed to many that the Army of Northern Virginia was indeed, in the words of one of its officers, "the last hope of the South." Many of Lee's soldiers, however, whether veterans or conscripts, began to desert in greater numbers throughout the fall and into the winter of 1864–1865 as it became more and more evident that the Confederacy was dying. Lee's appointment to the position of general in chief of the Confederate armies, made in February 1865, might have had some impact if it had made earlier in the war but was by that point an empty gesture.

The spring campaign was mercifully short. Lee made one last desperate attempt to break through Grant's lines near Petersburg at Fort Stedman (25 March 1865). That assault, the last serious offensive move undertaken by the Army of Northern Virginia, was repulsed with heavy casualties. A week later, at Five Forks (1 April 1865), Grant defeated a third of Lee's army, capturing or driving it from the crossroads. A Federal assault all along the lines at Petersburg on the morning of 2 April broke Lee's defenses in several places and forced the evacuation of Richmond by the next morning. "If we, the Army of Northern Virginia, are defeated, all is lost," one of Lee's gloomy soldiers wrote in his diary that night. Lee retreated southwest, hoping to somehow reach Joseph E. Johnston and the remnants of the Army of Tennessee in North Carolina, but was so closely pursued by Grant that escape was impossible. Within days, Federals captured or scattered about a quarter of his entire army at Sayler's Creek/Harper's Farm (6 April 1865). When the Army of Northern Virginia reached the small town of Appomattox Court House, Lee found Federal cavalry blocking his retreat to the west with Grant's infantry close behind him. He met Grant at Wilmer McLean's house on Palm Sunday, 9 April, and finally surrendered the Army of Northern Virginia—about 28,000 officers and men, according to best estimates—to the Army of the Potomac.

Though Lee's surrender to Grant did not technically end the Civil War, it deprived the Confederacy of its last viable fighting force and its best general. In the years to come, the name "Appomattox" would eventually come to signify the end of the war.

—*J. Tracy Power*

See also Anderson, Richard Heron; Antietam, Battle of; Appomattox Court House; Brandy Station; Bull Run, First Battle of; Bull Run, Second Battle of; Cedar Creek; Cedar Mountain; Chambersburg Raid; Chancellorsville, Battle of; Cold Harbor; Crater, Battle of the; Early, Jubal Anderson; Ewell, Richard Stoddert; Fisher's Hill; Five Forks; Fort Stedman; Fredericksburg, First Battle of; Fredericksburg, Second Battle of; Gaines's Mill; Gettysburg, Battle of; Glendale, Battle of; Gordon, John Brown; Groveton, Virginia, Battle of; Hampton, Wade; Hill, Ambrose Powell; Jackson, Thomas Jonathan; Knoxville Campaign; Lee, Fitzhugh; Lee, Robert Edward; Longstreet, James; Malvern Hill; Mechanicsville; Mine Run Campaign; Petersburg Campaign; Rappahannock Station; Savage's Station; Sayler's Creek; Seven Days'; Shenandoah Valley Campaign (1862); Shenandoah Valley Campaign (1864-1865); South Mountain, Battle of; Spotsylvania; Stonewall Brigade; Stuart, James Ewell Brown; Stuart's Dumfries Raid; Stuart's Ride Around McClellan; Wilderness, Battle of the; Winchester, Second Battle of; Winchester, Third Battle of; Yellow Tavern.

For further reading:

Alexander, Edward Porter. *Fighting for the Confederacy: The Personal Recollections of General Edward Porter Alexander* (1989).

———. *Military Memoirs of a Confederate: A Critical Narrative* (1907).

Allen, William. *The Army of Northern Virginia in 1862* (1892).

Casler, John O. *Four Years in the Stonewall Brigade* (1971).

Freeman, Douglas Southall. *Lee's Lieutenants: A Study in Command* (1942–1944).

Gallagher, Gary W. *Lee and His Generals in War and*

Memory (1998).

———, ed. *Lee the Soldier* (1996).

Hattaway, Herman, and Archer Jones. *How the North Won: A Military History of the Civil War* (1983).

Hewitt, Janet B., et al., eds. *Supplement to the Official Records of the Union and Confederate Armies* (1994–2000).

Lee, R. E. *Lee's Dispatches: Unpublished Letters of General Robert E. Lee, C.S.A. to Jefferson Davis and the War Department of The Confederate States of America 1862–1865* (1957).

———. *The Wartime Papers of R. E. Lee* (1961).

McCarthy, Carlton. *Detailed Minutiae of Soldier Life in the Army of Northern Virginia 1861–1865* (1882).

McMurry, Richard M. *Two Great Rebel Armies: An Essay in Confederate Military History* (1989).

Power, J. Tracy. *Lee's Miserables: Life in the Army of Northern Virginia from the Wilderness to Appomattox* (1998).

Taylor, Walter H. *Four Years With General Lee* (1877).

———. *General Lee: His Campaigns in Virginia 1861–1865 with Personal Reminiscences* (1906).

U.S. War Department. *The War of the Rebellion: A Compilation of the Official Records of the Union and Confederate Armies* (1880–1901).

Woodworth, Steven E. *Davis and Lee at War* (1995).

ARMY OF TENNESSEE

This hard-bitten army was the Confederacy's military mainstay in the Southern heartland. That it ultimately failed to withstand an ever-increasing and resilient Union opponent reflected more the flaws in the army's leadership than it revealed any absence of resolution or valor on the part of its soldiers. Created in late November 1862 by combining the Army of Kentucky and the Army of Mississippi, it would fight major engagements at Stones River and Chickamauga, unsuccessfully lay siege to occupied Chattanooga, and then execute a skillful retrograde through the mountains of North Georgia to fight a series of battles in the defense of Atlanta. After the fall of Atlanta, the army moved north into Tennessee to fight at Franklin and Nashville. By then it was a badly mauled shadow of its former self, stumbling as much as marching toward its surrender near Durham, North Carolina, an event that occurred fifteen days after Lee's Army of Northern Virginia had surrendered at Appomattox Court House.

The Army of Tennessee's creation grew from the failure of Braxton Bragg and Edmund Kirby Smith's invasion of Kentucky in the fall of 1862. The two distinct southern armies that had fought together at Perryville in September were designated as the Army of Tennessee upon their return to that state. Bragg was placed in command. The army was organized into two corps under Lieutenant General Leonidas Polk and Lieutenant General William J. Hardee and four brigades of cavalry, commanded by Brigadier Generals Joseph Wheeler (the overall cavalry commander), Alexander Buford, John Pegram, and John Wharton. Almost immediately after its formation, the army was reduced by the need to send Carter Stevenson's division of 10,000 men

to Vicksburg, so Polk's corps consisted of two divisions under Major Generals B. F. Cheatham and Jones M. Withers, while Hardee's contained three divisions under Major Generals John C. Breckinridge, Patrick R. Cleburne, and John P. McCown, this last part of the original Army of Kentucky or Kirby Smith's Corps as it was also known. It was in this configuration and at a strength of less than 40,000 that the army fought the furious and stalemated battle of Stones River at the end of the year.

Retreating to Tullahoma after Stones River, the Army of Tennessee was reinforced and by the summer of 1863 numbered 43,700 men, a figure that included Nathan Bedford Forrest's cavalry division. After William S. Rosecrans's campaign of maneuver had displaced Bragg from his positions in middle Tennessee, James Longstreet's Corps was detached from the Army of Northern Virginia to reinforce the Army of Tennessee. It was also bolstered by the arrival from Mississippi of brigades under John Gregg and Evander McNair, and a brigade under Major General W. H. T. Walker, who was placed in command of the Reserve Corps. These arrivals accounted for a considerable addition to the army and required its significant reorganization. It was formed into a Right Wing under Polk (D. H. Hill's corps and Walker's Reserve Corps) and a Left Wing under Longstreet (Simon Bolivar Buckner's corps and Longstreet's corps under John Bell Hood). The infantry numbered almost 48,000 men, and Wheeler's corps with Forrest's division accounted for nearly 15,000 cavalry.

It was thus with confidence that Bragg tried to exploit the scattered nature of Rosecrans's Army of the Cumberland as it moved through the mountainous terrain of the Tennessee-Alabama-Georgia border. The attempt to cut up Rosecrans in detail, however, brought on the concentration of the armies at Chickamauga on 19–20 September where the Army of Tennessee won its greatest victory. Bragg's failure to exploit this victory with a decisive blow squandered his greatest opportunity and enraged his subordinates. His unhappy facility for blaming his staff for his failures shook the army to its roots when it brought about another major reorganization. The personal intervention of President Jefferson Davis, who visited the army's gloomy headquarters after Chickamauga, hastened the rearrangement. Leonidas Polk was relieved of command and in late October was transferred to the command of the Department of Alabama, Mississippi, and East Louisiana. Buckner's request for reassignment was swiftly granted, and on 14 December he was detached to command the District of the Gulf in Mobile. D. H. Hill's outspoken criticism of Bragg and his insistence that Bragg be removed so irritated the president that he relieved Hill instead. As it was then reconstituted after Chickamauga, the Army of Tennessee consisted of three corps under Longstreet,

Hardee, and Breckinridge, but even this arrangement proved temporary. In November, Longstreet was detached to lay siege to Ambrose Burnside's occupation of Knoxville.

Bragg's failure at Chattanooga indicated how low the army's morale had sunk following such carping, command dislocation, impermanence. On 25 November, the army's center was routed at Missionary Ridge and the whole of it streamed south toward Dalton, Georgia, where on 2 December Bragg finally was relieved of command to be replaced by Joseph E. Johnston. The army's new commander left much of its organization in place and tried to repair the damage of the post-Chickamauga contretemps. Hardee remained in command of Polk's former I Corps, Hood commanded II Corps, and Polk fatefully rejoined the army with his Army of Mississippi that became III Corps, Army of Tennessee. He would be killed at Pine Mountain on 14 June.

Under Johnston's skillful management, the army executed a series of complicated retrogrades through the mountains of north Georgia as William T. Sherman began his inexorable advance on Atlanta, but criticism of Johnston's defensive withdrawal led Davis to replace his with the impetuous Hood on 18 July 1864. There had never been any doubt that the Army of Tennessee would fight—just if Johnston would—so Hood rushed it to combat in a rash but unsuccessful effort to drive Sherman from the environs of Atlanta. In this way, Hood went far in breaking his army as an effective combat force and then completed the job by taking it into Tennessee where it would fight George H. Thomas's army at Franklin and Nashville. After the latter battle, Hood asked to be relieved of command and was briefly replaced by Richard Taylor. Finally on 25 February 1865, Joseph E. Johnston resumed command of the shattered remnants of the Army of Tennessee.

Depleted now by abominable morale as well as casualties and at less than half its fighting size, the army was joined by all available troops in the Department of South Carolina, Georgia, and Florida, more to trail Sherman's march through the Carolinas than effectively oppose it. Johnston's command comprised a geographical expanse of considerable dimension, but his manpower was a pitiful testimony to the final limitations and fatal weariness of the Confederacy. With less than 20,000 effectives, he forlornly reorganized the Army of Tennessee again on 9 April, the day that Lee was surrendering at Appomattox. Hardee, Alexander P. Stewart, and Stephen D. Lee commanded ragged corps and Wade Hampton led the cavalry, but the war was over. A cease-fire on 18 April was the prelude to Johnston's surrender of the Army of Tennessee to Sherman at Bennett's House on 26 April 1865.

—David S. Heidler and Jeanne T. Heidler

See also Atlanta Campaign; Bragg, Braxton; Carolinas Campaign; Chattanooga Campaign; Chickamauga, Battle of; Hood, John Bell; Johnston, Joseph E.; Stones River, Battle of; Tullahoma Campaign

For further reading:
Connelly, Thomas. *Autumn of Glory: The Army of Tennessee, 1862–1865* (1971).
Cumming, Kate. *A Journal of Hospital Life in the Confederate Army of Tennessee* (1866).
Horn, Stanley. *The Army of Tennessee* (1952).
Madaus, Howard M. *The Battle Flags of the Confederate Army of Tennessee* (1976).
McWhiney, Grady. *Braxton Bragg and Confederate Defeat* (1969).
Sykes, E. T. "Walthall's Brigade—A Cursory Sketch with Personal Experiences of Walthall's Brigade, Army of Tennessee, C.S.A., 1862–1865." *Publications of the Mississippi Historical Society* (1917).

ARMY OF THE CUMBERLAND

Union general Don Carlos Buell's Army of the Ohio became the Army of the Cumberland on 24 October 1862, when General Order No. 168, Adjutant General's Office, reorganized the Department of the Cumberland. The new department included east Tennessee from the Tennessee River and the parts of Alabama and Georgia that would come under Federal control by military occupation. The Army of the Ohio had already seen hard action at Shiloh in April and Perryville in October. In October 1861 its official classification became XIV Corps. Yet from the start the army was also called the Army of the Cumberland, possibly because it contained in part elements of the force that had operated in the old Department of the Cumberland (15 August–9 November 1861) under Robert Anderson and William T. Sherman.

William S. Rosecrans took command of the Army of the Cumberland on 30 October 1862. On 19 December under General Order No. 41, the army was arranged into three wings, with the right wing commanded by Alexander McCook, the left wing by Thomas L. Crittenden, and the center wing by George H. Thomas. The cavalry was commanded by Brigadier General David Stanley. It was in this arrangement that the army would fight the fierce engagement at Stone's River at the end of 1862.

The Army of the Cumberland was reorganized into three corps on 9 January 1863 with Thomas commanding XIV Corps; McCook, XX Corps; and Crittenden, XXI Corps. Rosecrans in June created the Reserve Corps from the Army of Kentucky commanded by Major General Gordon Granger. During June 1863, the army conducted the Tullahoma campaign, a skillful series of maneuvers and skirmishes against Braxton Bragg in middle Tennessee that kept Bragg from reinforcing besieged Vicksburg. Yet on 20 September, the Army of the Cumberland suffered a stunning defeat at

Headquarters of the Army of the Cumberland, Missionary Ridge (Photograph by Mathew Brady Studio / *National Archives*)

Chickamauga and retreated into Chattanooga where XI and XII Corps from the Army of the Potomac would reinforce it. The army was again reorganized on 9 October when XX and XXI Corps were merged with the Reserve Corps to create a new IV Corps under Gordon Granger. The most important change came at the army's head. Rosecrans's calamitous performance in the fall of 1863 prompted Ulysses S. Grant to replace him with George H. Thomas on 20 October. Thomas, with William T. Sherman's Army of the Tennessee and under the personal direction of Grant, would lift the siege of Chattanooga at the end of November, setting the stage for the 1864 Atlanta campaign.

In April 1864, the Army of the Cumberland revived XX Corps by merging the Army of the Potomac's XI and XII Corps and placing the new unit under Joseph Hooker. Also in that month, Granger was replaced at the head of IV Corps by Oliver O. Howard, and the army's cavalry was organized into four divisions of three brigades each. At the outset of the Atlanta campaign, the army was composed of IV, XIV, and XX Corps, totaling close to 61,000 men and boasting artillery that numbered 130 guns. Howard would command IV Corps until he assumed command of the Army of the Tennessee on 27 July, when the corps devolved upon David Stanley. John M. Palmer commanded XIV Corps until 7 August, when General Richard W. Johnson succeeded him. Johnson was in turn succeeded by brevet Major General Jefferson C. Davis on 22 August. Hooker was followed in command of XX Corps by Brigadier General Alpheus S. Williams on 28 July, and Williams was replaced on 27 August by General Henry W. Slocum.

From the spring of 1864 to the fall of Atlanta in September, the Army of the Cumberland would see some of its hardest fighting, suffering almost 23,000 casualties, of whom more than 3,000 were killed. After the Atlanta campaign, the army was essentially dismantled. Thomas took what was still designated as the Army of the Cumberland but actually was only its IV Corps and the 4th Division of XX Corps to harry John Bell Hood's advance into Tennessee. In November and December 1864, the Army of the Cumberland with XXIII Corps (John Schofield's Army of the Ohio) defeated Hood at Franklin and Nashville. Meanwhile, XIV and XX Corps (again under Williams) were placed under Slocum and formed Sherman's right wing in the epic March to the Sea. These two corps would be officially constituted as Slocum's Army of Georgia on 28 March 1865.

—*David S. Heidler and Jeanne T. Heidler*

See also Rosecrans, William Starke; Thomas, George Henry.
For further reading:
Cist, Henry M. *The Army of the Cumberland* (1882).
Van Horne, Thomas B. *History of the Army of the Cumberland: Its Organization, Campaigns, and Battles, Written at the Request of Major-General George H. Thomas Chiefly from His Private Military Journal and Official and Other Documents Furnished by Him* (1875).

ARMY OF THE GULF

The Union Department of the Gulf was organized on 23 February 1862 to span the Gulf Coast west of Pensacola, Florida, and into the interior as it was occupied by Federal troops. Forces in the department were frequently and somewhat loosely described as the Army of

the Gulf. Originally, it comprised Benjamin F. Butler's New Orleans Expeditionary Corps. Butler commanded the department and stirred controversy during the initial occupation of New Orleans where the department's headquarters were situated. On 17 December 1862, Nathaniel P. Banks succeeded him and remained in command until 23 September 1864, when Stephen G. Hurlbut took charge. At war's end, Banks resumed command briefly from 22 April until 3 June 1865, when Edward R. S. Canby was placed in command. The department had been embraced by the Military Division of West Mississippi on 7 May 1864 and remained there until 17 May 1865, but even during that time it had continued to function as a discrete organizational entity.

Upon the establishment of the Defenses of New Orleans on 16 December 1862, a major reorganization of the Army of the Gulf followed early the following year. Most of its regiments became part of XIX Corps (organized on 5 January 1863 to date from 14 December 1862) under Banks. From then to its discontinuance as a part of the department on 7 November 1864, XIX Corps formed the heart of the body troops called the Army of the Gulf. After Banks the corps was commanded by Major General William B. Franklin (21 August 1863–2 May 1864), Brigadier General William H. Emory (2 May–2 July 1864), Brigadier General Benjamin S. Roberts (2 July–6 July 1864), Brigadier General Michael K. Lawler (6 July–7 July 1864), and finally Major General John J. Reynolds to 7 November 1864.

Shortly after its organization the corps consisted of four divisions and seven unattached regiments at Brashear City, Key West, Tortugas, and West Florida. Among its unique features were six newly organized regiments of Louisiana African-American troops. It boasted nineteen batteries of light artillery, a regiment of heavy artillery, and five regiments of cavalry. Returns for the corps totaled 55,229, with 44,832 present, and 35,670 present for duty.

This force participated in the campaigns against Port Hudson, the Texas Coast, and—joined by XIII, XVI, and XVII Corps—in Banks's abortive Red River campaign of 1864 during his tenure as commander of the department. After the Red River campaign, the 1st and 2d Divisions of XIX Corps departed for Virginia to participate in the Shenandoah Valley campaign. The balance of the corps remained in Louisiana, and with XIII and XVI Corps fought in Canby's assault on Fort Blakely, Spanish Fort, and Mobile in the spring of 1865.

—David S. Heidler and Jeanne T. Heidler

See also Departments, Military, U.S.A.; Mobile Campaign; New Orleans, Capture of; Port Hudson Campaign; Red River Campaign.

For further reading:
Gregg, Jo Chandler. *Life in the Army in the Departments of Virginia, and the Gulf, including Observations in New Orleans: With an Account of the Author's Life and Experience in the Ministry* (1866).

ARMY OF THE JAMES

This Union force was created in April 1864 to assist in General Ulysses S. Grant's overland campaign against Richmond. The Army of the James was in the Department of Virginia and North Carolina, which had been created on 15 July 1863 by combining the separate departments of the two states. At the time of the establishment of the Army of the James, the department was under the command of Major General Benjamin F. Butler, who also commanded the army.

The Army of the James was composed of the X and XVIII Corps and a cavalry division under August V. Kautz. The X Corps was a celebrated outfit, originally organized on 3 September 1862 as the Department of the South. Under General Quincy A. Gillmore, it had participated in the failed attack on Fort Wagner outside Charleston, South Carolina, on 18 July 1863 with the 54th Massachusetts leading the assault. The XVIII Corps had been organized in the Department of North Carolina on 24 December 1862. By the time it was transferred to Virginia in spring 1864, it had absorbed the VII Corps when that unit was discontinued on 1 August 1863. When the X and XVIII Corps assembled at Yorktown in April 1864, they totaled 33,898 officers and men and boasted eighty-two artillery pieces.

Brigadier General Alfred H. Terry briefly commanded the X Corps until Gillmore resumed command on 4 May 1864. Terry commanded the corps four additional times, stepping in each time to fill voids created by the departure of other officers. He would be the corps's last commander when its white troops were merged into the new XXIV Corps and its African-American troops into the new XXV Corps. The other commanders of X Corps were W. T. H. Brooks (21 June–18 July 1864), David B. Birney (28 July–10 October 1864), and Adelbert Ames (4 November–18 November 1864).

Major General William F. Smith commanded the XVIII Corps as part of the Army of the James from 2 May to 10 July 1864. He was succeeded by Brigadier General J. H. Martindale (10 July–21 July 1864), Major General E. O. C. Ord (21 July–4 September 1864), and Major General John Gibbon (4 September–22 September 1864). Ord returned to command on 22 September and remained until the end of the month when Brigadier General Charles A. Heckman briefly commanded (29 September–1 October 1864). Finally Brevet Major General Godfrey Weitzel took command on 1 October and continued in charge until the corps's discontinuance on 3 December 1864. Like the X Corps, the XVIII Corps's white troops were moved to XXIV Corps, Ord commanding, and its African-Americans to XV Corps, Weitzel commanding.

The army's cavalry division was modest in number—Philip Sheridan described it as "Kautz's small cavalry division"—and never numbered more than about 2,300. In participating in raids and skirmishes during the Bermuda Hundred campaign, it performed some marginal service.

The Army of the James fought well, but it was badly led from the top. Butler was occasionally impetuous and frequently inept, so the army's career was mainly checkered and its people generally unhappy. In October 1864 Assistant Adjutant General Edward W. Smith chastised officers for their "laziness and inattention" in failing to file timely reports. Butler often meted out equally harsh discipline for both small and serious matters. Consequently, the army did not fulfill many of Grant's expectations. It offered little assistance on his southern flank as the Army of the Potomac began the march on Richmond from the north. Instead, the Army of the James suffered such severe defeats in the Bermuda Hundred campaign that Grant detached considerable parts of it to aid the Army of the Potomac in the main advance on the Army of Northern Virginia. Parts of the X and the entire XVIII Corps fought at Cold Harbor with dreadful losses. Returning to Bermuda Hundred, these detached elements again functioned as the Army of the James in the Petersburg campaign.

The reorganization of the Army of the James on 3 December 1864 formed the army into the XXIV and XXV Corps. Butler led detachments from the XXIV Corps on a failed expedition to take Fort Fisher, North Carolina, but a second foray on 15 January 1865 under Terry was successful. The units detached to form Terry's expedition—the 2d Division and Abbot's Brigade of XXIV Corps and Paine's (African-American) Brigade of XXV corps—stayed in North Carolina and became part of a restored X Corps.

Ord replaced the discredited Butler as commander of the Army of the James in January 1865. The Army of the James assisted in the final assault on Richmond in April, and African-American troops of the XXV Corps were the first to enter the captured city. As part of the Union pursuit of the Army of Northern Virginia, XXIV Corps was engaged on the morning of Lee's surrender and reportedly fired the last infantry volley in the campaign. After the war, the XXV Corps formed part of the Army of Occupation in Texas, remaining at that duty until January 1866, when the corps was discontinued.

—*David S. Heidler and Jeanne T. Heidler*

See also Bermuda Hundred Campaign; Butler, Benjamin Franklin; Departments, Military, U.S.A.; Petersburg Campaign.

For further reading:
Longacre, Edward G. *Army of Amateurs: General Benjamin F. Butler and the Army of the James, 1863–1865* (1997).
Smith, William Farrar. *From Chattanooga to Petersburg under Generals Grant and Butler; A Contribution to the History of the War and a Personal Vindication* (1893).

ARMY OF THE KANAWHA

Confederate forces in the Kanawha Valley region of western Virginia were organized into the Army of the Kanawha in the first months of the war. Former Virginia governor Henry A. Wise had been given command on 6 June 1861 of troops he had raised and others from the Confederate Provisional Army. Styling itself Wise's Legion, the unit was only marginally structured with militia and provisional army soldiers mingled in fluidly shifting companies. The Legion was badly supplied, ravaged by disease, especially measles, and depleted by desertion when local men ran away after being ordered out of the Kanawha to protect, for instance, the Virginia Central Railroad. At most the outfit numbered only about 1,800 men.

To bolster this meager military presence, former governor John B. Floyd was authorized to raise troops and was given overall command of the Army of the Kanawha on 11 August. Floyd's army consisted of the 45th and 50th Virginia Infantry and the 8th Cavalry Regiment. Efforts to meld Wise's Legion into the Army of the Kanawha, however, foundered because of Wise's ego and Floyd's tactlessness. The two had never like one another, and now these political rivals found themselves military ones as well. Only the Federals would profit.

By the time Floyd came into the region, Wise had already been forced to retreat from the Kanawha as Jacob D. Cox's Federals moved into the valley and occupied Charleston. Situated in Lewisburg at the time of Floyd's appointment, Wise gave only a formal nod to his new superior's status. Moreover, he commenced a series of complaints about his belief that Floyd intended "to destroy my command, and not only transfer to himself the State volunteers and militia, but by constant detachments of my Legion, to merge it also in his brigade, to be commanded by his field officers, and be torn to pieces by maladministration, and to sink me, the second in command, even below his majors and captains."

The Army of the Kanawha was under the overall command of the Northwest Army under Robert E. Lee with headquarters at Valley Mountain. It was to this authority that Wise directed his pleas that his command remain an independent one, and it was from that remove that Lee tried to cope with the Wise-Floyd antagonism that threatened to endanger the entire region. Lee wanted Wise and Floyd to cooperate against William S. Rosecrans's positions at Gauley Bridge, but even his legendary tact could not resolve the discord. "Feeling assured of the patriotism and zeal of the officers and men composing the Army of the Kanawha," he wrote to Wise, "I have never apprehended any embarrassment or interference in the execution of their respective duties believing they would make everything yield to the welfare of the republic.

Nonetheless, Lee was compelled to delineate the lines

of command, which he did on 21 August by directing that Colonel C. Q. Tompkins's 22d Virginia and Colonel John McCausland's 36th Virginia would be assigned to Floyd. The Wise Legion was by the same order placed under the "immediate command" of Henry Wise, but everybody would be subject to the orders of the commanding general of the Army of the Kanawha, which meant John B. Floyd. It was to no avail, and Floyd remained undermanned, bereft of any meaningful cooperation from the Wise Legion. On 10 September, the Army of the Kanawha barely managed to hold its positions when Rosecrans attacked it at Carnifex Ferry. That night Floyd had to withdraw.

President Jefferson Davis, the War Department, and Lee finally threw up their hands in the face of Wise's recalcitrance. On 12 September, Adjutant and Inspector General Samuel Cooper conveyed Davis's order that Lee had the authority to transfer Wise's Legion to any command other than General Floyd's. It was an admission that the two men would never work together. Accordingly to make up for the absence of Wise's Legion, Colonel William Phillips's Georgia Legion and Colonel D. R. Russell's 20th Mississippi Infantry reinforced Floyd. The resolution of the Army of the Kanawha's command problems came too late to salvage the military situation in the region.

Wise's Legion was subsequently sent to Norfolk and from there to North Carolina to help defend Roanoke. The Army of the Kanawha itself soon ceased to be when Floyd took the 20th Mississippi, 36th Virginia, and 50th Virginia to Bowling Green, Kentucky. There these units and the 51st and 56th Virginia were incorporated into William J. Hardee's Central Army of Kentucky as its 3d Division. By year's end, only two regiments of the old Army of the Kanawha remained at Lewisburg: Colonel Henry Heth's 45th Virginia and Tompkins's 22d Virginia.

—*David S. Heidler and Jeanne T. Heidler*

See also Carnifex Ferry, Battle of; Floyd, John Buchanan; Wise, Henry Alexander.

For further reading:
Simpson, Craig M. *A Good Southerner: The Life of Henry A. Wise of Virginia* (1985).

ARMY OF THE NORTHWEST, CONFEDERATE
(June 1861–May 1862)

On 8 June 1861, the Southern troops operating in northwestern Virginia, near what would become the border of present-day Virginia and West Virginia, were designated the Confederate Army of the Northwest and placed under the command of Brigadier General Robert S. Garnett. The army's ominous 11 July 1861 debut against Union Generals George B. McClellan and William S. Rosecrans resulted in a Confederate defeat at Rich Mountain and included the surrender of a large portion of the Southern army under Colonel John Pegram. While evacuating his position at Laurel Hill on 13 July, Garnett's retreating army was again attacked at Carrick's Ford on the Cheat River. Garnett was killed in that engagement, the first general on either side to die in battle. Brigadier General Henry Rootes Jackson temporarily took charge of the shattered army. On 21 July Major General William W. Loring officially took command.

Although the size and regiments were continually fluctuating, in general the Army of the Northwest was separated into two components: the Monterey Division on the western front and the Huntersville Division in the rear defending transportation, communications, and the interior.

In late July, General Robert E. Lee, commander of all Virginia forces, traveled personally to this sector to oversee operations. Late summer and fall 1861 were an unusually cold and damp season in this mountainous region. Snow fell in late August. Frozen or thawing roads made transportation nearly impossible. Soldiers struggled to survive as military operations and campaigning became all but impossible. For this and other reasons, Loring remained inactive. After considerable prompting by Lee and a favorable change in the weather, Loring advanced, and on 12–13 September the army again suffering a severe setback with the ill-fated Cheat Mountain campaign. A few days later, Lee traveled to the nearby Army of the Kanawha to mediate between his two feuding generals, John B. Floyd and Henry Wise. Soon after, Loring and five regiments of the Army of the Northwest followed Lee for a combined movement against the Federal forces in the Sewell Mountain campaign. (Unfortunately for the Confederacy, Lee chose to deal with these two commands piecemeal instead of uniting them in one coordinated effort.) Henry R. Jackson and the rest of the Army of the Northwest remained at Camp Bartow on the Greenbrier River.

On 3 October 1861, Federal forces under the command of Brigadier General Joseph J. Reynolds attacked the Confederates at Camp Bartow. The advance was repulsed and the Federal army retreated to their garrison at Cheat Mountain. Both sides seemed to settle down into winter quarters.

In late November, Loring's forces returned and again the Army of the Northwest was divided. Loring, under orders from the Army of the Northwest's departmental commander Major General Thomas J. Jackson, took the majority of the army to Winchester and then on to Romney. This would result in the infamous Loring-Jackson confrontation, concluding in Loring's transfer out of the department on 9 February 1862. This division never returned to the Army of the Northwest, being absorbed into the Army of the Valley.

The remainder of the Army of the Northwest (the

Monterey Division) withdrew to the mountain pass, where the Staunton and Parkersburg Turnpike crossed the summit of Alleghany Mountain. Command of the small mountain garrison fell to Colonel Edward Johnson. There, at Camp Alleghany, Johnson and his 1,800 men were again attacked by the Union garrison at Cheat Mountain, this time under Brigadier General Robert H. Milroy. And again, the Federal forces were repulsed.

This action concluded campaigning in the region for the winter of 1861–1862. Except for a raid on Huntersville in early January and scouting or occasional skirmishing, both sides remained inactive. In early spring, newly appointed Brigadier General Edward Johnson and his six regiments, still designated as the Army of the Northwest, gradually moved eastward toward a union with Jackson's Army of the Valley.

On 8 May 1862, with Johnson directing the Confederate operations, the combined two armies won a victory at McDowell, again over Milroy. Near the end of the engagement, Edward Johnson received a serious ankle wound. The wound was so serious that he was unable to remain with his small army. Subsequently, Johnson's army, the last of the northwestern command, was incorporated into Jackson's Army of the Valley and the Confederate Army of the Northwest ceased to exist.

—*Eddie Woodward*

See also Johnson, Edward.

For further reading:

Freeman, Douglas Southall. *Lee's Lieutenants: A Study in Command* (1942–1944).

Hall, James E. *Diary of a Confederate Soldier* (1961).

Hotchkiss, Jed. *Virginia. Confederate Military History.* vol. IV (1899; reprint, 1987).

Pryor, Shepherd Green. *A Post of Honor: The Pryor Letters, 1861–63* (1989).

Woodward, Edward V. "Holding the Alleghany Line: Edward Johnson, the Army of the Northwest, and the Battle of Alleghany Summit" (Thesis, 1998).

ARMY OF THE OHIO

Some confusion surrounds what constituted the body of soldiers known as the Union Army of the Ohio at any given time during the Civil War. The force was nominally a creation of the large Department of the Ohio, which went through several reorganizations during the war's first year. It is therefore useful to review those reorganizations to describe the initial creation of the Army of the Ohio as well as its subsequent reincarnation.

The Department of the Ohio was created on 3 May 1861 to embrace Illinois, Indiana, and Ohio. Six days later, portions of what is now West Virginia and Pennsylvania were added to it, as was Missouri on 6 June 1861. Illinois was transferred to the Western Department on 3 July. The Department of the Ohio's boundaries were again readjusted on 19 September 1861 to embrace Ohio, Indiana, and the area of Kentucky

within fifteen miles of Cincinnati. Finally on 9 November, it took on the final shape of its first existence to include Ohio, Michigan, Indiana, and Kentucky east of the Cumberland River.

The department's new commander was Brigadier General Don Carlos Buell, who took over from Brigadier General Ormsby Mitchell on 15 November 1861. Buell's force would be designated as the Army of the Ohio. General in Chief George B. McClellan resisted the idea of organizing the Union armies into corps, so army structure consisted of divisions numbered according to when they were formed. Although eastern armies abandoned this structure in favor of corps organization in the spring of 1862, it remained in the western armies until the following December. Consequently, the Army of the Ohio had several numbered divisions, each with three numbered brigades. It was under this rudimentary and unsatisfactory organization that the Army of the Ohio fought at Shiloh in April 1862. This structure would remain in place until corps organization was introduced in 1863 for the western armies.

In March 1862, the Department of the Ohio ceased to exist when it was divided between the Department of the Mississippi and the Mountain Department. The department was revived on 19 August 1862, but in the interim the troops in Buell's Army of the Ohio had operated under William S. Rosecrans as part of Rosecrans's new Department of the Cumberland. This new incarnation of the Cumberland department came into being on 24 October 1862 and should not be confused with the original Department of the Cumberland under Robert Anderson and then William T. Sherman. With this change, the Army of the Ohio officially became XIV Corps. Yet because it now contained some elements from the earlier Department of the Cumberland and because of its association with the new department of the same name, XIV Corps (or the original Army of the Ohio) was frequently referred to as the Army of the Cumberland. The army fought at Stones River under this appellation.

The Department of the Ohio was recreated on 19 August 1862 under Major General Horatio Wright. It embraced Illinois, Indiana, Ohio, Michigan, briefly Wisconsin, and Kentucky east of the Tennessee River, including Cumberland Gap. By then, troops of the original Army of the Ohio were scattered geographically and organizationally. Some elements, for instance, made up the whole of the Army of the Kentucky that performed with high distinction at Chickamauga. When Ambrose Burnside assumed command of the department on 25 March 1863, IX Army Corps was dispatched from the east to participate in operations in east Tennessee. Eventually IX Corps was merged with regiments from Kentucky under George L. Hartsuff to form XXIII Corps, which would capture Knoxville and then withstand James Longstreet's siege of that city.

Placed under John Schofield on 4 April 1864, XXIII Corps, numbering about 12,800 men, was the Army of the Ohio that participated in the Atlanta campaign. It was sharply engaged at Resaca, Kennesaw Mountain, and Utoy Creek. As Sherman began his March to the Sea, the Army of the Ohio, numbering about 10,000 men, joined with George H. Thomas's army to fight in the battle of Franklin. It mainly formed the reserve at the battle of Nashville. In these operations, the Army of the Ohio in its last embodiment had scored its most memorable accomplishments.

After campaigning in Tennessee with Thomas, the bulk of Schofield's Army of the Ohio (officially still XXIII Corps) was transferred to the east. Original plans called for it to join the Army of the Potomac's siege at Petersburg, Virginia, but it finally wound up in North Carolina to assist in William T. Sherman's advance northward from Savannah. There it would remain, forming the core of the Department of North Carolina. Considerably diminished by regiments mustering out, it was discontinued on 1 August 1865.

—*David S. Heidler and Jeanne T. Heidler*

See also Atlanta Campaign; Buell, Don Carlos; Franklin, Battle of; Kennesaw Mountain, Battle of; Resaca, Battle of; Schofield, John M.; Utoy Creek, Battle of.

For further reading:

Castel, Albert E.. *Decision in the West: The Atlanta Campaign of 1864* (1992).

Fry, James B. *Operations of the Army Under Buell from June 10th to October 30th, 1862 and the "Buell Commission"* (1884).

McDonough, James L. *Schofield: Union General in the Civil War and Reconstruction* (1972).

Schofield, John McAllister. *Forty Six Years in the Army* (1897).

Weigley, Russell F. "The Military Thought of John M. Schofield." *Military Affairs* (1959).

ARMY OF THE PENINSULA

The Confederate government placed Virginia's York Peninsula in the Department of the Peninsula on 26 May 1861. John Bankhead Magruder was put in command of the department, and from his headquarters at Yorktown he commanded a scattered group of garrisons and camps that was labeled the Army of the Peninsula. This force has the distinction of having fought at Big Bethel on 10 June 1861, reportedly the first land engagement of the war in the east.

By January 1862, the Army of the Peninsula consisted of two divisions. The 1st Division, under Brigadier General Gabriel J. Rains, posted at Yorktown and Ship Point. The 13th Alabama, 2d Florida, 6th Georgia, 23d Georgia, 14th Louisiana, a Louisiana Zouave battalion, 2d Mississippi, 15th North Carolina, 32d Virginia (2 companies), 53d Virginia (8 companies), 115th Virginia Militia, Maurin's Louisiana battery, Nelson's battery, and the 1st Virginia Artillery (3 companies) embodied the division, as well as six independent companies of heavy artillery.

The 2d Division, under Brigadier General Lafayette McLaws, included the 8th Alabama, Cobb's Legion, 10th Georgia, 16th Georgia, Greenville Guards, 2d Louisiana, 5th Louisiana, 10th Louisiana, 14th Virginia, 32d Virginia, one company of the 53d Virginia, four companies of Virginia Cavalry, and five companies of 1st Virginia Artillery at Mulberry Point. The 6th Virginia, 9th Virginia Militia, 21st Virginia Militia, 87th Virginia Militia, one company of the 3d Virginia Cavalry, and one company of the 1st Virginia Artillery were at Gloucester Point with four batteries of heavy artillery. Encamped at Williamsburg were the 1st Louisiana Battalion, two companies of the 32d Virginia, and one company of the 53d Virginia, while the 61st Virginia Militia and a company of Virginia Cavalry were stationed in Matthews County. Six companies of the 3d Virginia Cavalry were at Lebanon Church and around Yorktown, and the 52d Virginia Militia, one company of the 1st Virginia Artillery, and two independent companies of Virginia Artillery were at Jamestown Island. The returns for the army listed its effective strength at about 11,000 men.

These were the forces that were fated to face the first phase of George B. McClellan's Peninsula campaign in the spring of 1862. On 27 March, Richmond dispatched the 14th and 26th Alabama (the latter without arms) to Yorktown, and on 11 April, 4,000 additional men under D. H. Hill joined the Army of the Peninsula to bring its aggregate strength up to about 31,000. Magruder warned that number would not be nearly enough to oppose the vast blue host assembling in his front. He calculated that he had about 23,000 effective men on a 14-mile front to resist what he estimated to be between 100,000 and 200,000 enemy troops.

Even though Magruder's estimation of enemy strength was somewhat exaggerated, his appraisal of the situation was not. Confederate forces swiftly consolidated to face McClellan's offensive, and one result was the incorporation of the Army of the Peninsula into Joseph E. Johnston's main force. Thus, on 26 April 1862, the Army of the Peninsula ceased to exist as an organizational entity. Thereafter it would be referred to as Johnston's Right Wing.

—*David S. Heidler and Jeanne T. Heidler*

See also Big Bethel, Battle of; Magruder, John B.; Peninsula Campaign.

For further reading:

Casdorph, Paul D. *Prince John Magruder: His Life and Campaigns* (1996).

ARMY OF THE POTOMAC

After the defeat of Union arms at the battle of Bull Run (First Manassas) in July 1861, George B. McClellan was placed in command of Union forces in and around Washington, D.C., and immediately threw himself into the task of building an army. As

Officers of the 1st Massachusetts Cavalry at Army of the Potomac headquarters, August 1864 (*Left to right*) unknown; Captain Edward A. Flint; Captain Charles Francis Adams, Jr.; Lieutenant George H. Teague (*Library of Congress*)

regiments poured into Washington, McClellan established a system by which they would be organized into provisional brigades and receive instruction. By 4 August 1861, twelve brigades had been organized and were rigorously training under McClellan's direction. Two weeks later, McClellan formally conferred upon his command the name it would carry through the hardest fighting of the Civil War, the Army of the Potomac.

In November 1861 McClellan replaced Winfield Scott as general in chief of all the Union armies, but did not relinquish command of the Army of the Potomac. On 15 October he had organized the army into twelve divisions and remained deeply involved in its training as he worked to organize the rest of the Union war machine. On 20 November McClellan displayed his work in a spectacular grand review of the Army of the Potomac at Munson's Hill, Virginia, but shortly thereafter decided to postpone the commencement of operations until spring 1862.

Frustration with military inactivity led Congress in December to establish the Joint Committee on the Conduct of the War (JCCW). The JCCW was dominated by radical Republicans who were ignorant of, and had nothing but contempt for, military science, and who

demanded a hard war against the South. It did not take long for the members of the JCCW to develop a powerful distaste for McClellan and his "pets" in the Army of the Potomac high command, a sentiment that was fully reciprocated. To the radicals, these officers were too conservative in their politics and generalship. Throughout the war, the JCCW would be a thorn in the side of the Army of the Potomac, as the radicals used its investigative powers to promote generals who shared their views on strategy, tactics, and politics, and to make life difficult for any officer who did not.

As the JCCW pursued its investigations in early 1862, the issue of organizing the Army of the Potomac into corps emerged as a major source of tension between McClellan and the politicians. Skeptical of the senior division commanders, the leading candidates for corps command who proved all too willing to cooperate with the JCCW, McClellan resisted calls for the organization of corps. His uneasiness about organizing corps was exacerbated when he submitted his plan for operating against Richmond from the lower Chesapeake Bay to a council of war in March. Of the four senior division commanders, Irvin McDowell, Edwin Sumner, and Samuel Heintzelman opposed the plan, while Erasmus

Keyes only conditionally approved it. The other division commanders endorsed the plan. Lincoln, who was beginning to have reservations about McClellan, accepted the vote of the majority, but then issued orders mandating the organization of corps with McDowell, Sumner, Heintzelman, and Keyes as their commanders. Three days later the president removed McClellan as general in chief so that he could focus exclusively on the Army of the Potomac.

During the Peninsula campaign, McClellan managed to secure permission to organize two new corps, which he gave to his friends Fitz John Porter and William Franklin. The army reached the outskirts of Richmond in late May 1862. Then, at the battle of Fair Oaks (Seven Pines), the Confederate commander, Joseph E. Johnston, was wounded and replaced by Robert E. Lee. Lee's strategic and tactical brilliance would make the road to Union victory a long, bloody, and frustrating ordeal.

When Lee drove McClellan from the gates of Richmond in the Seven Days' battles, Lincoln organized the Army of Virginia under John Pope for operations along the direct overland route from Washington to Richmond. In August Lincoln and his new general in chief, Henry W. Halleck, ordered McClellan's army back to northern Virginia to cooperate with Pope. Friction between Pope, a favorite of the Radical Republicans, and McClellan plagued the operation from the outset and helped Lee defeat Pope's army at the second battle of Bull Run (Manassas). Pope blamed an Army of the Potomac "cabal" for his failure and, backed by the Radical Republicans and the Lincoln administration, engineered an unfair court-martial to cashier Fitz John Porter from the service for disobedience of orders.

After Second Bull Run, Lincoln placed McClellan in command of Pope's army and the Army of the Potomac and directed him to deal with Lee's invasion of Maryland. McClellan immediately abolished the Army of Virginia as an independent force and integrated its units into the Army of the Potomac. Then, for the push westward into Maryland, he organized the army into three wings commanded by Franklin, Sumner, and Ambrose Burnside. Although he successfully turned back Lee's invasion, McClellan infuriated Lincoln by failing to destroy Lee's army or recross the Potomac until over a month after the battle of Antietam. Lincoln removed him from command in November 1862.

McClellan's replacement, Burnside, organized the army into three "grand" divisions under Sumner, Franklin, and Joseph Hooker. Burnside, however, proved inept as an army commander, and under his leadership the Army of the Potomac suffered its worst defeat of the war at Fredericksburg on 13 December 1862. This disaster was followed in January by an attempt to flank Lee that bad weather transformed into a miserable "Mud March." Morale plunged, desertion became rampant,

and several generals implored Lincoln to replace Burnside before the army melted away. Impressed by his acceptance of full responsibility for the Fredericksburg debacle, Lincoln chose to sustain Burnside until, in an effort to stamp out dissension, the general drafted orders removing several officers from their posts or cashiering them from the service altogether. Endorse the orders, Burnside told the president, or accept his resignation. Lincoln did neither, although he did relieve Burnside from command of the Army of the Potomac.

As Burnside's replacement, Lincoln chose Hooker, a hard fighter of high ambition but low character. During Burnside's tenure in command, Hooker had actively intrigued against him, as he had against almost anyone else who stood between Hooker and command of the Army of the Potomac. He earlier had also cultivated a positive relationship with the Radical Republicans by criticizing and firmly establishing his independence from McClellan and the rest of the army high command.

By the time Hooker assumed command, Lincoln and Halleck had fundamentally reoriented Union strategy. They accepted McClellan's argument that the prospects for success operating along the overland route from Washington to Richmond were not great and the most effective way to attack the Confederate capital was via the Peninsula. But to do the latter meant either dividing Union forces in Virginia or uncovering Washington. Lincoln and Halleck were unwilling to do either. Consequently, they decided to keep the Army of the Potomac concentrated on the overland route from Washington to Richmond, where they were to make Lee's army the target of their operations. Lincoln and Halleck recognized that Lee's ability, geography, logistics, and the strength of the tactical defensive made it highly unlikely that a decisive victory could be achieved by following the new "headquarters doctrine." Yet Lee's aggressive generalship and demonstrated preference for operating as far north as possible might well, they surmised, produce an opportunity to catch the Confederate army far from its base and deliver a crippling blow. Along with the change in strategy, there had been tremendous turnover in the Army of the Potomac high command by the time Hooker took over. Not only had McClellan and Burnside come and gone, but all six of the original corps commanders were no longer with the army. John Reynolds now commanded the 1st Corps, Darius Couch commanded the 2d, Dan Sickles commanded the 3d, George Meade commanded the 5th, and John Sedgwick commanded the 6th. (The 4th Corps had been left in garrison on the Peninsula the previous summer.) Also now with the army were Oliver Otis Howard's 11th Corps and Henry Slocum's 12th Corps. Despite this turnover, with the exception of Hooker, his chief of staff Daniel Butterfield, and Sickles, the army high command was still dominated by

Army of the Potomac near Falmouth, Virginia, as sketched by Alfred R. Waud (*Library of Congress*)

conservative McClellanites like Reynolds, Couch, Meade, Sedgwick, Gouverneur K. Warren, and Winfield Scott Hancock.

Whatever skepticism greeted Hooker's ascension to command quickly dissipated as a result of his spectacular success restoring the army's fighting spirit. He improved the soldiers' diets by adding fresh vegetables and soft bread to their rations, instituted liberal furlough policies, improved sanitation, built hospitals, and made sure the men received their pay. Hooker also abandoned Burnside's grand division scheme and returned to corps organization. To promote unit pride and facilitate control on the battlefield, he instituted a system of corps and division badges: a circle for the 1st Corps, trefoil for the 2d, lozenge for the 3d, Maltese cross for the 5th, cross for the 6th, crescent for the 11th, and star for the 12th. Within each corps, the 1st Division's patch was red, the 2d's white, and the 3d's blue.

By April 1863 the army was again ready for action. Unfortunately, at the battle of Chancellorsville in May Hooker lost his nerve and the army suffered yet another humiliating defeat. Hooker's subsequent actions in response to Lee's decision to undertake another invasion

of the North did little to restore confidence in his generalship. Consequently, to the delight of the majority of the corps commanders and the dismay of the radicals, Lincoln replaced Hooker with Meade on 28 June.

In the three days of fighting at Gettysburg in the week that followed, Meade's leadership, mistakes by the enemy, and the inspiration that came from fighting on Northern soil enabled the army to win its first clear and unambiguous battlefield victory over Lee. Meade, however, frustrated Lincoln by failing to pursue Lee's army with the vigor the president hoped for. Then in November Meade further antagonized the politicians, but won the hearts of his army, when he refused to assault an impregnable Rebel position at Mine Run.

Political discontent with Meade contributed to an ugly imbroglio that illustrated and exacerbated tensions between the JCCW and the Army of the Potomac and within the Army's high command. Radical favorite Sickles instigated the controversy by accusing Meade of wanting to surrender the field at Gettysburg to the Confederates (which was patently false) and claiming that his own actions (which in fact nearly lost the battle) had saved the army by preventing Meade from

A group of scouts and guides for the Army of the Potomac at Berlin (now Brunswick), Maryland, October 1862
(Photograph by Alexander Gardner / *National Archives*)

doing this. Relishing the opportunity to diminish Meade, a conservative West Pointer, the JCCW zealously pursued the matter in spring 1864, seeking out testimony from officers hostile to Meade and sympathetic to Sickles. The JCCW also undertook an investigation of Chancellorsville that was designed to rehabilitate Hooker by pinning the blame for the defeat on Sedgwick, a McClellan loyalist.

As the Army spent the winter of 1863–1864 encamped in the vicinity of Culpeper, Virginia, the beleaguered Meade decided to reorganize his command. He abolished the 1st and 3d Corps (the 11th and 12th had been sent to Tennessee the previous September) and assigned their units to one of the three remaining corps: Hancock's 2d; Warren's 5th; and Sedgwick's 6th. Aided by his chief of staff, Andrew A. Humphreys, Meade also implemented reforms that dramatically improved the army's administration. Better living conditions, an array of inducements offered by the government, and a determination to see the war through to the end helped convince over half of the thousands of veterans whose enlistments were scheduled to expire in 1864 to reenlist.

When Ulysses S. Grant became general in chief of the Federal armies in the spring of 1864, many speculated that he would replace Meade as the commander of the Army of the Potomac. Grant did choose to accompany the Army on its final campaign, but he technically left Meade in place as the army's commander. These 1864 spring and summer campaigns introduced the Army of the Potomac to a brutal, unrelenting form of war unprecedented in the American experience. Over 60,000 men fell in continuous fighting and bad weather that made the army's drive from the Wilderness to Petersburg an unceasing horror. Combat effectiveness plummeted as experienced veterans fell and were replaced by garrison soldiers, conscripts, and substitutes. Then, after a useless assault at Cold Harbor, even experienced officers and men began to exhibit what became known as Cold Harbor syndrome, a reluctance to assault entrenchments. Nonetheless, they remained determined to fight on until victory was won. Although they still retained a powerful affection for McClellan, in the November 1864 election the Army of the Potomac expressed this determination by voting overwhelmingly for Lincoln.

By the time the siege of Petersburg began, Grant was exercising almost complete control over the army. Under Grant, the Army maintained a bulldog grip on

Petersburg until April 1865, when Lee abandoned the town and Richmond. The army vigorously pursued Lee and managed to cut off his retreat near Appomattox Court House. There Lee surrendered on 9 April 1865, bringing an end to four years of war. Its mission accomplished, on 23 May the North's greatest army marched down Pennsylvania Avenue in the Grand Review. Shortly thereafter, the Army of the Potomac was officially disbanded and the men whose courage, skill, and determination on the battlefields of Virginia, Maryland, and Pennsylvania had preserved the Union returned to their homes to build modern America.

—*Ethan S. Rafuse*

See also Antietam, Battle of; Appomattox Court House; Army of Virginia; Burnside, Ambrose E.; Chancellorsville, Battle of; Fredericksburg, Battle of; Gettysburg, Battle of; Grand Review; Grant, Ulysses S.; Heintzelman, Samuel Peter; Hooker, Joseph; Joint Committee on the Conduct of the War; Keyes, Erasmus Darwin; McClellan, George B.; McDowell, Irvin; Meade, George Gordon; Petersburg Campaign; Sickles, Daniel; Sumner, Edwin V.

For further reading:

———. *The Army of the Potomac: Glory Road* (1952).

Catton, Bruce. *Mr. Lincoln's Army* (1951).

———. *A Stillness at Appomattox* (1953).

Grant, Ulysses S. *Personal Memoirs of U. S. Grant* (1885).

Hattaway, Herman, and Archer Jones. *How the North Won: A Military History of the Civil War* (1983).

McClellan, George B. *McClellan's Own Story: The War for the Union, the Soldiers Who Fought It, the Civilians Who Directed It, and His Relations to It and to Them* (1887).

Meade, George Gordon. *Life and Letters of George Gordon Meade, Major-General United States Army* (1913; reprint, 1994).

Tap, Bruce. *Over Lincoln's Shoulder: The Committee on the Conduct of the War* (1998).

U.S. War Department. *The War of the Rebellion: A Compilation of the Official Records of the Union and Confederate Armies* (1880–1901).

ARMY OF THE SHENANDOAH, C.S.A.

Virginia State troops had already been gathering for a month in the Shenandoah Valley when Colonel Thomas J. Jackson was placed in command of them on 28 April 1861. Jackson continued recruiting activities, and on 24 May 1861, Major General Joseph E. Johnston took command of the force designated as the Army of the Shenandoah. By the end of June 1861 it consisted of four infantry brigades and the 1st Virginia Cavalry, 334 strong, under Colonel J. E. B. Stuart.

Colonel T. J. Jackson's 1st Brigade included the 2d, 4th, 5th, 27th Virginia Infantry, and Pendleton's battery for a strength of 2,256 officers and men. Colonel F. S. Bartow's 2d Brigade included the 7th, 8th, 9th Georgia Infantry, Duncan's and Pope's Kentucky Battalions, and Alburtis's battery for a strength of 2,608. Brigadier General Bernard E. Bee's 3d Brigade included the 4th

Alabama Infantry, 2d Mississippi Infantry, 11th Mississippi Infantry, 1st Tennessee Infantry, and Imboden's battery for a strength of 2,882. And Colonel Arnold Elzey's 4th Brigade included the 1st Maryland Battalion of Infantry, 3d Tennessee Infantry, 10th Virginia Infantry, 13th Virginia Infantry, and Grove's battery for a strength of 2,311. The 33d Virginia Infantry was not brigaded but would fight with Jackson's division at First Bull Run. The aggregate strength of the Army of the Shenandoah was 10,057.

This force fought at Falling Waters on 2 July and subsequently was engaged at Bunker Hill and Charles Town before slipping from the valley to join P. G. T. Beauregard's Confederate Army of the Potomac to fight at First Bull Run on 21 July 1861. By then, Colonel Elzey's brigade had been placed under the command of Edmund Kirby Smith. The arrival of the Army of the Shenandoah on the Confederate left helped to turn the course of the battle for the South, and it was Jackson's Virginians who were described by Bee as standing like a stone wall, thus giving Jackson the most famous nickname of the war.

After the battle of First Bull Run, the Army of the Shenandoah was incorporated into the Confederate Army of the Potomac, which the following spring Robert E. Lee would name the Army of Northern Virginia.

—*David S. Heidler and Jeanne T. Heidler*

See also Bull Run, First Battle of; Falling Waters; Jackson, Thomas J.; Johnston, Joseph E.; Smith, Edmund Kirby.

For further reading:

Downs, Alan Craig. "Gone Past All Redemption? The Early War Years of General Joseph Eggleston Johnston" (Ph.D. dissertation, 1991).

Henderson, G. F. R. *Stonewall Jackson and the American Civil War* (1898).

Johnston, Joseph E. *Narrative of Military Operations Directed during the Late War between the States* (1874; reprint, 1959).

Robertson, James I., Jr. *Stonewall Jackson: The Man, The Soldier, The Legend* (1997).

Symonds, Craig L. *Joseph E. Johnston: A Civil War Biography* (1992).

Woodward, Harold R., Jr. *Defender of the Valley. Brigadier General John Daniel Imboden, C.S.A.* (1996).

ARMY OF THE SHENANDOAH, U.S.A.

In the summer of 1864, Union general in chief Ulysses S. Grant reorganized forces in the East to make command structures more efficient. He merged the Department of the Susquehanna, the Middle Department, the Department of Washington, and the Department of West Virginia into the Middle Military Division and named Brigadier General Philip Sheridan as temporary commander on 5 August. Given the task of clearing Confederate forces under Jubal Early from the Shenandoah Valley, Sheridan took command of the Army of the Shenandoah, which consisted of the Army

of the Potomac's VI Corps under Major General Horatio G. Wright and the 1st and 2d Divisions (commanded by Brigadier Generals William Dwight and Cuvier Grover) of XIX Corps under Brigadier General William H. Emory. The VI Corps included divisions under Brigadier Generals David A. Russell, George W. Getty, and James B. Ricketts. Major General George Crook's Army of West Virginia, designated as VIII Corps, was also part of the army. Colonel Joseph Thoburn and Isaac Duval commanded its divisions. The army boasted twelve batteries of artillery.

Sheridan brought with him from the Army of the Potomac Wesley Merritt's 1st and James H. Wilson's 3d Cavalry Divisions. Brigadier General Alfred Torbert took command of the cavalry forces in the Army of the Shenandoah, which were soon bolstered by two additional divisions under Alfred N. Duffié and William Woods Averell from the Army of West Virginia. The total strength of the army was about 40,000 men when it began the Shenandoah Valley campaign of 1864.

The army's activities in the Shenandoah Valley gave the Union a series of brilliant victories marked by hard-won fights at Opequon, Fisher's Hill, and Cedar Creek. Sharp skirmishes were a constant feature of the campaign, and total casualties were heavy in both the infantry and cavalry. General David Russell was killed at Opequon, and James Ricketts was seriously wounded at Cedar Creek.

After successfully concluding the Shenandoah Valley campaign, the Army of the Shenandoah was dismantled by the return of detached elements to the Army of the Potomac. It remained to be mentioned, however, as the name occasionally applied to Merritt's cavalry corps, which was sometimes referred to as the cavalry of the Army of the Shenandoah. Upon its return to service in the siege of Petersburg, this corps consisted of Thomas C. Devin's and George A. Custer's divisions with the addition of Crooks's division. In the final campaign of 1865 it had thirty-seven regiments of cavalry for a strength of about 13,800, and distinguished itself in actions from Five Forks to Appomattox.

—*David S. Heidler and Jeanne T. Heidler*

See also Cedar Creek, Battle of; Early, Jubal; Fisher's Hill, Battle of; Merritt, Wesley; Shenandoah Valley Campaign (August 1864–March 1865); Sheridan, Philip H.; Torbert, Alfred T. A.; Winchester (Opequon), Third Battle of.

For further reading:

Bushong, Millard K. *Old Jube: A Biography of General Jubal A. Early* (1988).

Heatwole, John L. *The Burning: Sheridan in the Shenandoah Valley* (1998).

Morris, Roy, Jr. *Sheridan: The Life and Wars of General Phil Sheridan* (1992).

Osborne, Charles C. *Jubal: The Life and Times of General Jubal A. Early, C.S.A., Defender of the Lost Cause* (1992).

Sheridan, Philip Henry. *Personal Memoirs of P. H. Sheridan, General, U. S. Army. New and Enl. Ed. With an Account of his Life from 1871 to His Death, in 1888, by Brigadier-General Michael V. Seridan* (1904).

Stackpole, Edward J. *Sheridan in the Shenandoah: Jubal Early's Nemesis* (1992).

ARMY OF THE TENNESSEE

Union brigadier general Ulysses S. Grant commanded the forerunner of the Department and Army of the Tennessee from 1 August 1861 to 14 February 1862, when he was succeeded by Brigadier General William T. Sherman. During this time it was designated as the Military District of Cairo (Kentucky) and included Cairo, Bird's Point, and Cape Girardeau, Missouri, as well as assorted other posts.

On 16 October 1862, the Department of the Tennessee was created and embraced Cairo, Forts Henry and Donelson, northern Mississippi, and the regions of Kentucky and Tennessee that lay west of the Tennessee River. Grant was placed in command, and all troops in the department were organized into XIII Army Corps on 24 October 1862. This massive organization constituted the entire Army of the Tennessee and was thus too unwieldy. On 18 December 1862, XIII Corps was consequently arranged into four new corps, designated as XIII, XV, XVI, and XVII Corps. General John A. McClernand was placed in command of XIII Corps; General William T. Sherman, of XV Corps; Major General Stephen A. Hurlbut, of XVI Corps; and Major General James B. McPherson, of XVII Corps. On 24 October 1863, Grant was succeeded in command by Sherman, who in turn was succeeded on 26 March 1864 by McPherson, who was killed during the Atlanta campaign on 22 July 1864. Major General John A. Logan commanded the army for five days until Major General O. O. Howard took command and remained in that position until 19 May 1865. Logan resumed command until 1 August 1865, when the organization was discontinued.

The Army of the Tennessee was a large force whose separate components were often detached for service in various operations. As a result, it is easy to confuse both the organizational structure of the army and its nomenclature. For instance, Sherman early took the right wing of McClernand's XIII Corps with parts of his XV Corps on the Yazoo expedition that included the failed attack at Chickasaw Bluffs. And in January 1863, McClernand assailed Arkansas Post with part of his XIII Corps and Sherman's XV Corps, although he referred to these detached forces of the Army of the Tennessee as I and II Corps of the Army of the Mississippi.

The Army of the Tennessee was actively engaged in the lengthy Vicksburg campaign of 1863. During that campaign, McClernand's bravado so irritated Grant that he relieved him from command of XIII Corps, replacing him with General E. O. Ord. After the fall of Vicksburg, the corps was briefly stationed at Jackson, Mississippi, and then was moved to New Orleans. Detachments scattered it along the Gulf from Texas to Louisiana, and parts of the corps would participate in the Red River Expedition of April 1864.

As for XV Corps, after Vicksburg the bulk of it would move to Memphis and from there to Chattanooga to participate in the raising of the Confederate siege in November 1863. By then Sherman's promotion on 27 October to command the Army of the Tennessee had placed General Frank P. Blair in charge of XV Corps. After Chattanooga, it advanced on Knoxville to assist Ambrose Burnside's resistance to James Longstreet's siege there. The corps arrived after Longstreet had already retreated. Under General John A. Logan, XV Corps with two divisions of XVI Corps and XVII Corps (minus two divisions left in the Mississippi Valley) took part in the Atlanta campaign as the Army of the Tennessee.

With Howard in command, the Army of the Tennessee formed the right wing of Sherman's March to the Sea. During this operation it consisted of XV and XVII Corps with the two divisions of XVI Corps that had participated in the Atlanta campaign integrated into them. After occupying Savannah, Sherman's force began its march through the Carolinas on 1 February. The Army of the Tennessee thus was part of the force present when Joseph E. Johnston surrendered on 26 April 1865 at Bennett House near Durham, North Carolina. The army participated in the Grand Review in Washington and was discontinued in August 1865.

—David S. Heidler and Jeanne T. Heidler

See also Atlanta Campaign; Carolinas Campaign; Chattanooga Campaign; Sherman's March to the Sea; Vicksburg Campaign.

For further reading:
Cannan, John. *The Atlanta Campaign, May–November, 1864* (1991).

Castel, Albert E. *Decision in the West: The Atlanta Campaign of 1864* (1992).

Cozzens, Peter. *The Civil War in the West: From Stones River to Chattanooga* (1996).

———. *The Shipwreck of Their Hopes: The Battles for Chattanooga* (1994).

Glatthaar, Joseph T. *The March to the Sea and Beyond: Sherman's Troops in the Savannah and Carolinas Campaigns* (1985).

Meyers, Christopher C. " 'Two Generals Cannot Command This Army': John A. McClernand and the Politics of Command in Grant's Army of the Tennessee." *Columbiad* (1998).

Miers, Earl Schenck. *The Web of Victory: Grant at Vicksburg* (1955; reprint, 1983).

ARMY OF THE WEST

A creation of Brigadier General Nathaniel Lyon, the Army of the West survived little longer than did the general himself. In June 1861 Federal forces took the field in Missouri, pursuing the pro-Southern forces of Governor Claiborne Jackson into southwest Missouri. Arriving in Springfield, Missouri, on 13 July, Brigadier General Lyon took command of the Union forces there, designating them the Army of the West. Within a month, Lyon led this army at Wilson's Creek.

In June 1861 Lyon had sent two columns from St. Louis to capture Southern supporters within Missouri. The newly enlisted Missouri volunteer regiments, which overwhelmingly consisted of German and German-American volunteers, made up the majority of Lyon's forces. Lyon led one column to Jefferson City, defeated Jackson's forces at Boonville, and pursued the Confederates south. The second column headed south to secure southwest Missouri for the Union. Lyon took command of both columns when they assembled in Springfield, Missouri. On 24 July he reorganized these columns into four brigades and designated them the Army of the West.

As July wore on, grave problems plagued the army as it camped near Springfield. It faced critical supply shortages, and Lyon's appeals for supplies and reinforcements seemed to fall on deaf ears. Additionally, most of the troops, consisting of three-month volunteers, were reaching the end of their enlistments. Meanwhile, rumors circulated that Southern forces were moving north toward Springfield. Lyon chose to march out and face them.

Lyon led the army south out of Springfield on 1 August. The next day they encountered the Southern forces at Dug Springs, Missouri, and drove the Confederates back. Having won the initial engagement, Lyon pushed on to Curran Post Office. The army's lack of food and the danger of being cut off by the enemy, however, forced Lyon to return to Springfield, arriving on 6 August. The Confederates under Generals Sterling Price and Benjamin McCulloch also moved north and encamped at Wilson's Creek, ten miles south of Lyon's position.

The army's situation had become serious. Lyon still had not received support from St. Louis. He felt the enemy to his front made any retreat dangerous, but he feared that he could not defend Springfield with his forces, as discharges continued to eat away at his ranks. By 9 August Lyon had decided to risk a withdrawal, but after consulting with Colonel Franz Sigel, he chose to attack instead.

Lyon divided the army of 5,400 effectives into two columns for the attack. Lyon commanded the northern column and was to strike the Confederate camp from the northwest with three brigades. The first, Major Samuel Sturgis's brigade, consisted of Plummer's battalion of regulars, a battalion of the 2d Missouri Infantry, Kansas Rangers, Company B, 1st U.S. Cavalry, and Battery F, 2d U.S. Artillery. Lieutenant Colonel George Andrews commanded the 2d Brigade that included Steele's

battalion of regulars, the 1st Missouri Volunteers, and DuBois's battery. Colonel George W. Deitzler led the 3d Brigade containing the 1st and 2d Kansas Volunteers. In addition, Lyon's force included the 1st Iowa and two units of home guard cavalry.

While Lyon attacked the Confederates from the northeast, Sigel was to strike the Confederates from the southwest with his brigade. It included the 3d and 5th Missouri Volunteers, Backoff's battalion of Missouri Artillery, Carr's Cavalry, Company I, 1st U.S. Artillery, and Company C, 2d U.S. Dragoons. The two columns were to catch the Confederates between them.

The Army of the West marched out of Springfield on 9 August. The next morning, both columns struck the Confederates. Lyon's troops fought well for most of the morning, however, the Confederates routed Sigel's brigade, driving it from the field. The northern column fought on, unaware of Sigel's fate. Late in the morning, Lyon was killed leading a charge. Command passed to Sturgis, who called a retreat, leading the column back to Springfield.

As senior officer, Sigel took command of the army in Springfield and withdrew toward Rolla on 11 August. Along the march, however, Sturgis regained command when a number of officers, criticizing Sigel's performance at Wilson's Creek, called for his removal. Reaching Rolla on 19 August, the Army of the West returned by rail to St. Louis where General John C. Frémont chose to disband it and shifted its forces to northern Missouri. Although the army existed less than a month, its actions at Wilson's Creek aided the Union forces in retaining control of Missouri.

—James G. Downhour

See also Lyon, Nathaniel; Wilson's Creek.
For further reading:
Bearss, Edwin C. *The Battle of Wilson's Creek* (1992).
Welcher, Frank J. *The Union Army, 1861–1865: Organization and Operations* (1989).

ARMY OF VIRGINIA

The Federal Army of Virginia was formed on 26 June 1862 by the consolidation of three independent departments–the Mountain Department, the Department of the Shenandoah, and the Department of the Rappahannock. Major General John Pope was given command of this new army. Pope had connections with Mary Todd Lincoln's family, and had received an early appointment to brigadier general. He was in charge of the forces that captured Island No. 10 and then commanded the left wing of the Union army that captured Corinth, Mississippi, in May 1862.

Pope's new command consisted of three corps. The I Corps was led by Major General John C. Frémont, and was composed of troops that had been in the Mountain Department of western Virginia. Frémont, Pope's senior

in rank, refused to serve and was soon replaced by Major General Franz Sigel, a German-born soldier, who, though inept in the field, was a symbol of support for the war effort. His division commanders were Robert C. Schenck, Adolph von Steinwehr, and Carl Schurz. Brigadier General Robert H. Milroy led an independent brigade, and a cavalry brigade under the command of Colonel John Beardsley completed the corps organization.

Major General Nathaniel P. Banks led II Corps, formerly the Department of the Shenandoah. Banks was a political general from Massachusetts who had served as both governor and Speaker of the House of Representatives. Although ill suited for military success, Banks was an ardent supporter of the Lincoln administration. His troops had been defeated by Stonewall Jackson in May and had been driven across the Potomac River into Maryland. Brigadier Generals Alpheus S. Williams and James Cooper (soon replaced by Christopher C. Augur), led the two divisions of infantry. Brigadier General John P. Hatch (later replaced by John Buford) commanded the cavalry attached to II Corps.

Major General Irvin McDowell was in charge of the army's III Corps. McDowell was the general defeated at First Bull Run and thereafter was a corps commander and placed in command of the Department of the Rappahannock. His two four-brigade divisions were led by Brigadier Generals Rufus King and James B. Ricketts. Brigadier General George D. Bayard commanded the cavalry brigade.

Pope's army numbered some 51,000 troops. Lincoln hoped that this army would move south to threaten Southern communications and draw off troops from Richmond, allowing McClellan's Army of the Potomac a chance to attack the Confederate capital. However, McClellan's withdrawal during the Seven Days' battles forced Pope to scrap any offensive plans and remain in northern Virginia, waiting for the Army of the Potomac to reinforce him. With the strength of these combined forces, Pope could attack Richmond from the north.

Pope took active command and issued orders that included permission for his troops to provision themselves off the country through which they passed, and one designed to hold citizens responsible for acts of Confederate irregulars behind the lines. Another order allowed Pope's officers to arrest all male citizens suspected of disloyalty.

After McClellan retreated to Harrison's Landing, Lee sent Jackson's corps north to watch Pope. Seeing an opportunity to attack, Jackson crossed the Rapidan River and headed for Culpeper to strike Banks's corps. Banks attacked first at Cedar Mountain on 9 August. After a hard battle Banks was repulsed, but Federal reinforcements prohibited a Confederate advance, and Jackson retreated south.

When McClellan's corps began to move north by water to Aquia Creek to join Pope, Lee and Longstreet's Corps joined Jackson to attack Pope. Lee planned a rapid forward march and crossing of the Rapidan on 18 August to force Pope to withdraw westward, but Pope learned of the advance and quickly withdrew behind the Rappahannock River. Reinforcements from the Army of the Potomac here joined the Army of Virginia. To breach this line, Jackson's corps made a circuitous march behind Pope's right flank and destroyed his supply base at Manassas Junction.

Jackson then withdrew to the old battlefield of Manassas and managed to hide his divisions while waiting for Longstreet to join him. Pope, blinded by his misuse of cavalry, retreated to catch Jackson. On 28 August Jackson struck at Rufus King's division at Brawner's Farm. The next day, Pope's troops began assaulting Jackson's line even as Longstreet's troops arrived on the battlefield. On 30 August Longstreet struck Pope's exposed left flank and drove the Union army from the field. A sharp engagement at Chantilly on 1 September essentially ended the Second Bull Run campaign as the defeated Union armies withdrew to Washington.

Here, Pope was replaced and McClellan placed in command of the defenses of the city. Pope's three corps were merged into the Army of the Potomac. Sigel's command became the XI Army Corps. Banks was replaced and his corps became the XII Army Corps. Joseph Hooker replaced McDowell, and his corps was renumbered the I Army Corps.

—*Richard A. Sauers*

See also Bull Run, Second Battle of; Pope, John.

For further reading:

Gordon, George H. *History of the Campaign of the Army of Virginia, Under John Pope: From Cedar Mountain to Alexandria, 1862* (1879).

Hennessy, John J. *Return to Bull Run: The Campaign and Battle of Second Manassas* (1993).

Ropes, John C. *The Army Under Pope* (1881).

ARMY OF WEST TENNESSEE

The Army of West Tennessee was the official designation of a Confederate force that existed for about two months at the end of 1862. It was also the name applied to the Union army under the command of Major General Ulysses S. Grant, starting in February 1862, that fought at Shiloh in April. Actually, the Union army derived its name from the fact that it was under the District of West Tennessee, a geographical setting that by September 1862 embraced several other forces as well. For instance, the Districts of Jackson and Corinth became the 3d Division of the district, Memphis the 1st Division, and Mississippi the 4th Division. (On 26 October 1863, these would be incorporated into the District of Tennessee, XIII Army Corps.)

In any case, the Union Army of West Tennessee was much more substantial in comparison to the Confederate force. Reflecting the absence of corps organizations in the western Union armies before December 1862, it consisted of six divisions of three brigades each. The 1st Division was commanded by John McClernand except for a brief period in May and early June. Major General C. F. Smith originally commanded the 2d Division, but at Shiloh the division was under Brigadier General W. H. L. Wallace, who was mortally wounded. Ultimately it was placed under Major General Edward O. C. Ord. Major General Lewis Wallace commanded the 3d Division, Brigadier General Stephen A. Hurlbut commanded the 4th, Brigadier General William T. Sherman commanded the 5th, and Brigadier General Benjamin Prentiss commanded the 6th.

The Confederate Army of West Tennessee was created by merging Sterling Price's Army of the West with Earl Van Dorn's troops from Mississippi and eastern Louisiana. As constituted on 28 September 1862, the army operated somewhat like two corps, although the force was cobbled together so quickly that its parts retained separate identities. Price's Army of the West was designated as Price's corps and included the 1st Division, four brigades strong, under Brigadier General Louis Hébert, and Brigadier General Dabney Maury's division. Brigadier General Mansfield Lovell commanded the troops officially called the District of Mississippi. Colonel William H. Jackson led the cavalry, and Van Dorn was in overall command. This Confederate Army of West Tennessee made the furious but failed assault at Corinth on 3–4 October, ironically attacking William S. Rosecrans's 2d Division of the Union Army of West Tennessee.

Corinth was this Confederate army's largest engagement. Not until 16 October was it officially named the Army of West Tennessee, and then the attempt was made to place it into the structure of two actual corps. Yet discipline in the force was bad and relations between its general officers was worse. On 22 November, the War Department in Richmond asked in some exasperation what the army intended to call itself. Neither Price's persistent Army of the West nor Van Dorn's Army of West Tennessee seemed appropriate, given the outfit's situation following the retreat from Corinth. The War Department suggested "Army of Northern Mississippi." Two days later, Adjutant General Samuel Cooper curtly observed that all other names aside from I and II Corps of the Department of Mississippi were "improper."

On 7 December 1862, two days after elements of the Army of West Tennessee had fought a skirmish at Coffeeville, its brief existence came to an end. The secretary of war directed that the army would consist of two corps, designated I and II Corps, to be commanded

respectively by Van Dorn and Price. Mansfield Lovell was relieved and was instructed to await further orders.
—*David S. Heidler and Jeanne T. Heidler*

See also Corinth, Battle of; Lovell, Mansfield; Price, Sterling; Shiloh, Battle of; Van Dorn, Earl.

ARMY ORGANIZATION, C.S.A.

At first glance, a Confederate field army looked indistinguishable from its Northern opponent. Like the Federal army, a Southern army was built on infantry regiments, grouped into brigades, with those brigades grouped into divisions. Artillery was also initially not organized or grouped above the battery level, and was usually attached to infantry brigades on a one-battery-per-brigade basis.

Subtle differences distinguished the armies, however. Some of those differences proved to be advantages and contributed significantly to early Southern victories over more numerous enemies, while others were liabilities that remained uncorrected. The Confederacy overall raised fewer regiments than did the Union and made an effort to keep those regimental ranks filled up with draftees and recruits. The result was that Confederate units at the tactical level were often as strong or stronger then their foes, despite a significant, overall Union advantage in numbers. With fewer subordinates to command, the job of a Confederate brigade or divisional commander was less complicated. More Southern manpower could be brought to bear in a fight than might be the case for a Northern army. Regimental strengths remained relatively strong until the last year of the war, when the depletion of Southern manpower simply meant that there were no more troops to send forward. Confederate regiments had eroded to mere fragments by the end of the war.

The Confederacy was also much quicker to mass artillery into battalions of four batteries each and attach them to the divisional and corps level. Robert E. Lee's Army of Northern Virginia had reorganized most of its artillery by mid-1862, and the value of this organization proved its worth at both Second Bull Run and Antietam, where the timely intervention of Confederate artillery battalions helped stem powerful Union attacks. The Federals always had more—and usually better—cannon, but the superior Confederate organization meant that Southern artillery would not be dominated by those enemy advantages. The Confederates also formed an artillery reserve, but, unlike their Northern foes, rarely used it to its greatest advantage. By 1863 the Confederacy had done away with the idea of a central army artillery reserve entirely, preferring instead to mass more guns at the corps level.

The South did not formally adopt the army corps model as quickly as the Federals did, but in practice used it all the time. The western Confederate armies under Braxton Bragg created a logical and sensible corps structure soon after the battle of Shiloh in 1862. In Virginia, the Confederates relied on "wings," informal groupings of divisions that were de facto corps. Here the South relied on the superiority of its senior leadership, for both these wings were much larger than the normal Federal corps, with four or five divisions to command instead of the Union's two or three. As long as superior leaders such as James Longstreet and Thomas J. Jackson were present, this system worked well, but with Jackson's death in 1863, General Lee realized that the structure was too large for most commanders, and revised the army into three corps of three divisions each. In the west, with a much smaller infantry force to work with, the Confederate Army of Tennessee usually contained two corps of two or three divisions each. Only for the Atlanta campaign, when all available force was gathered to defend the Deep South, did the Army of Tennessee's strength increase to three corps.

At the divisional and brigade level, other distinguishing Southern characteristics may be noted. Confederate brigades were more likely to contain regiments all from the same state, an idea that Confederate president Davis felt fostered more esprit de corps and had some political advantages back home. Further, Confederate divisions tended to be larger then their Union counterparts, with four or five brigades instead of two or three. This difference meant that a Confederate division was likely to have twice as many men as a Union one, and sometimes a single Confederate division might be as strong as a Union corps. Hence, while weaker in numbers overall, the available Confederate strength was better concentrated at the vanguard.

Confederate cavalry was brigaded much earlier than Federal cavalry, another massing of force that helped contribute significantly to the early Southern dominance by that arm. Also, Confederates more liberally recruited the mounted arm than did their Northern opponents. For example, throughout much of 1863, the Army of Tennessee boasted more cavalry than did the Federal Army of the Cumberland. By the latter part of the war, however, the imbalance was reversed. In the last year of the war, the Confederacy could not find sufficient horses to mount a large portion of its troops, could not arm them with repeaters and breechloading carbines to match Federal firepower, and suffered from serious desertion problems. All added up to a Union dominance in cavalry operations not previously seen.

In the East, Confederate cavalry was also hampered by the fact that no formal corps structure was created to command the expanded force, meaning that J. E. B. Stuart had to manage the affairs of 10,000 men in up to seven brigades without any intermediate commanders. This decided liability was not remedied until the spring of 1864.

In the west, the exact opposite problem arose. By 1863 the Army of Tennessee had no less than two cavalry corps, commanded by Generals Joseph Wheeler and Nathan B. Forrest, with no sole commander of all mounted troops. A more logical situation would have been to merge the two corps into a single entity, but Forrest, for one, was politically difficult and refused to serve under Wheeler's command. This unfortunate situation allowed the most significant advantage the Army of Tennessee possessed—its superiority in the mounted arm—to be rendered largely useless in practical terms. General Bragg, for instance, was badly surprised at both Tullahoma and at the crossing of the Tennessee River in 1863.

—David A. Powell

See also Army Organization, U.S.A.

For further reading:

Beringer, Richard E., Herman Hattaway, Archer Jones, and William N. Still, Jr. *Why the South Lost the Civil War* (1986).
Hattaway, Herman, and Archer Jones. *How the North Won: A Military History of the Civil War* (1983).

ARMY ORGANIZATION, U.S.A.

The basic building block of the Civil War army was the infantry regiment. Recruited initially by the states, each regiment numbered about 1,000 men organized into ten companies. Most regiments received at least some recruits during the war, and so ended up with between 1,500 to 2,000 men on their rolls by war's end. In reality, however, disease and combat kept up a continual attrition, so that regiments rarely numbered more than 500 men, and often less than 200. Cavalry regiments were similarly recruited, with an initial strength of about 1,200 men. Artillery, while nominally organized in regiments, was most often recruited and deployed by battery, a unit ranging between four to six guns and approximately eighty to 120 men.

At the start of the war, Union army organization was primitive at best. Four regiments were grouped together into brigades, and two to three brigades were assigned to divisions. Initially, the division was the largest subunit organized, meaning that an army commander could expect to command five or six such divisions directly. When only the initial rush of recruits was available, this structure proved adequate to manage the approximately 35,000 to 40,000 men who filled a typical Federal army in 1861.

Cavalry and artillery initially were adjuncts to the infantry. Cavalry was rarely even brigaded, but instead was usually superintended directly by the army commander. Artillery was most often assigned to an infantry brigade one battery at a time. Consequently, it was difficult to mass either branch on a battlefield, as these units were scattered all throughout the army.

By 1862, however, the Union armies were simply too large to abide such informality. In March of that year, the Union Army of the Potomac numbered over 100,000 men in twelve infantry divisions and thus defied management by one man. The situation required the creation of army corps. Corps were the relatively permanent grouping of two to four divisions into a single tactical and administrative unit, putting into place a middle management between the army commander and his divisions and brigades. Some artillery was assigned to a central reserve, but most of it was still parceled out at the brigade or division level. Cavalry remained informally assigned directly to the corps or remained under the army commander's direct supervision, but formal brigade or divisional groupings for the mounted arm remained a distant development.

Organizational development in the west tended to lag behind that in the east. Smaller-sized forces were committed there in the first two years of the war, and the much greater distances in the west necessitated dispersion rather than concentration. Hence, western armies tended to number 40,000 to 60,000 men, remaining easier to manage with less formal organizational structure.

The year 1863 saw little change to the main structure of the army, but significant changes did occur in the way the supporting arms—cavalry and artillery—were arranged. Union general John Pope, much maligned for his mishandling of the Second Bull Run campaign, took a significant step when he forged several Union cavalry regiments into three formal mounted brigades in the fall of 1862. Yet it was General Joseph E. Hooker who finally placed the mounted arm into a discrete cavalry corps in 1863. With the creation of an independent cavalry corps, massing approximately 12,000 mounted men together for the first time, Hooker created an instrument that later commanders would use to great effect. No longer would Federal cavalry always be outnumbered and outfought.

Similarly, artillery batteries were removed from direct divisional or brigade control and assigned directly to corps commanders in their own brigades. This step allowed the corps commander to mass the five or six batteries in his corps into a single force, and use it where most needed at rapid notice. In the east, Union practice continued to include a significant artillery reserve directly under the army commander, a useful practice for reinforcing any particularly threatened corps or massing for an attack. Together, these three steps: the infantry corps, the cavalry corps, and the artillery brigades and reserve all constituted the final form of Union army organization. It was an effective, flexible structure that allowed the army commander to focus on fighting his opponent rather than overwhelming him with administrative detail.

The western armies eventually adopted all the innovations of the Federals in Virginia, though not as quickly. For instance, at Chickamauga in September

1863, artillery batteries were most often still assigned at the brigade level, though nominally they were grouped into battalions under division command. No independent artillery reserve existed. By 1864, however, there was virtually no difference in organization between theaters.

One significant drawback to the Union organization was the failure to maintain the strength of infantry regiments in the field. Given the political nature of how these units were first raised, state politicians often found it more advantageous to raise new units (which meant more political appointments of high rank) rather than send recruits to existing units in the field. As the war dragged on, veteran units dwindled in size to mere shadows of their initial strength. To maintain brigades at anything like a reasonable strength, these skeleton units were often merged into one brigade, meaning that a single brigade might number eight or ten regiments by late 1864. This duplicated the administrative difficulties that the corps structure was supposed to alleviate, although at an admittedly smaller scale. Newly arrived units, still large due to their lack of time in service, often outnumbered the rest of their new brigade put together. Far better from a tactical standpoint would have been to fill up existing veteran units with a steady stream of recruits.

By contrast, the basic Union staff organization remained superior to that of its opponents throughout the war. In the Army of the Potomac, for example, the army staff evolved into a quite modern organization of several hundred men, including a military intelligence section that, from 1863 on, did a splendid job of keeping the Union army commander informed of his opponent's organization and strength. Confederate staffs remained much more informal, to the detriment of their commanders.

—*David A. Powell*

See also Army Organization, C.S.A.
For further reading:
Beringer, Richard E., Herman Hattaway, Archer Jones, and William N. Still, Jr. *Why The South Lost the Civil War* (1986).
Hattaway, Herman, and Archer Jones. *How the North Won: A Military History of the Civil War* (1983).

ARMY, UNITED STATES
(1861–1865)

When the Civil War began, the army of the United States was scattered around the country in numerous small posts. A mere 12,698 men, not including officers, were authorized by Congress to hold down three million square miles of territory. The army consisted then of ten regiments of infantry, five of cavalry (including "Dragoons" and "Mounted Rifles"), and three of artillery. The artillery found in the west, however, was often acting either as ad

hoc cavalry or infantry. One hundred eighty-three companies (or batteries) of the total of 198 available garrisoned seventy-nine outposts on the frontier. The remaining fifteen were allotted to Atlantic coastal fortresses, twenty-three Federal arsenals, and the line of the Canadian border. The largest formation at any post, and then rarely seen, was a battalion of a few companies.

However, the North possessed a huge advantage over the South in human and material resources in early 1861, an advantage that would eventually prove decisive. In manufactures the North enjoyed marked advantages in the ability to produce the goods needed for war, possessing as it did "close to 90 percent of the nation's industrial capacity." Additionally, the Union outnumbered the South by nearly four to one in potential military manpower.

Data from the 1860 Census shows that the populations of the two sections of the country contrasted sharply. The South contained 5,447,220 whites, 132,760 free blacks, and 3,521,110 black slaves, for a total of 9,103,332 persons. Of these, only 1,064,193 white men between the ages of eighteen and forty-five constituted the military population of the South. In contrast, the population of the loyal states and territories was 21,475,373 whites, 355,310 free blacks, and 432,650 black slaves, for a total of 22,339,989 persons. Of these, 4,559,872 white men aged eighteen to forty-five constituted the military population of the North. The North's population advantage of nearly 2.5:1 would be telling for agriculture and manufacturing, but its advantage of 4.28:1 in military population was overwhelming, with 2,494,592 whites serving in the army and 101,207 more serving as sailors and marines. The total of 2,595,799 made up 57 percent of the total Northern population of military age.

In April 1861 President Lincoln resorted to the only measure available to him under the Law of 1795 and called out 75,000 militia for three months. However, following the fiasco at Bull Run, this was rarely done again. Continuing a trend begun after the War of 1812, the North's new regiments were largely made up by calling out "Volunteers" for longer periods of service, and not by either calling out large numbers of militia or increasing appreciably the size of the regular forces. In May 1861 Lincoln did increase the regular army to 22,714 men by adding nine regiments of infantry, one of artillery, and one of cavalry, but after that little was done for them. He also called for 42,000 three-year Volunteers, the first of many such calls.

In July 1861 the North began to convert its manpower advantage into a huge army of Volunteer regiments, which compared favorably with any fielded by European industrial powers at the time. Congress legalized President Lincoln's increase in the regular establishment and his call for the first three-year Volunteers, and then called for 500,000 additional Volunteers. Following the pattern set as early as the American Revolution, this manpower was organized into regiments of infantry, cavalry, and artillery, nominally of 1,000 men each—but always far fewer in reality, especially after active campaigning. Each regiment in turn usually consisted of ten companies, or artillery batteries, and a small headquarters termed a "Field and Staff." The regiments of artillery were administrative only, and batteries served independently attached to larger formations.

There were exceptions to the general organization in the regular army that played havoc with attempts at homogeneity in drill and tactics. The regular cavalry was increased to twelve companies, as was the artillery. While the ten original infantry regiments were organized, as were the Volunteers, with ten companies, the nine new infantry regiments raised in 1861 were organized with twenty-four companies divided into three battalions, or nominally 2,400 men. However, the disruption this multiplicity of organization caused was often alleviated in practice. Lone regular regiments or battalions were often employed as General Officer's Escorts, such as the battalion of the 4th U.S. Cavalry in Major General James H. Wilson's Cavalry Corps in 1865. Groups of regiments were organized into discrete brigades of Regulars, such as the 1st and 2d Brigades of the 2d Division, V Corps, at Gettysburg in 1863.

The army was not a static force. The exertions of campaigning and attrition through casualties, desertions, and disease reduced the initial force quickly, so that as the war dragged on, more calls for Volunteers were needed. In July 1862 Congress called for an additional 300,000 Volunteers. The results were disappointing, and to redress the shortfall, in August a "draft" for 300,000 men was levied on state militias for a term of nine months' service. States responded even less enthusiastically. However, the use of federal, state, and local bounties, or cash incentives to induce enlistment, filled most of the original call out. Given this history, the Enrollment Act was passed on 3 March 1863, the first compulsory citizen conscription in U.S. history. Inequities in the system, such as allowing the hiring of substitutes and the payment of $300 directly to the government for exemptions, led to the notion that the struggle was becoming a rich man's war and a poor man's fight. Draft riots also erupted, notably in New York City during the summer. Still, the scheme raised only 10 percent of the total manpower enlisted for the war: 86,724 men paid the $300 commutation and were exempted, while only 118,010 substitutes were enlisted, and only 52,068 men were actually drafted.

One of President Lincoln's more successful war measures was the Emancipation Proclamation. This document cut the bonds of Southern blacks to the South and spurred the recruiting of black troops. Of the 178,975 "Colored Troops" that served in the Union army, 99,337 were recruited in the South, thus diminishing Southern resources because most blacks were engaged in agricultural pursuits. Black troops made up nearly 12 percent of the Union army in service in 1864 and 1865, and could be justly proud of their record. One in three were casualties. They served in 449 engagements, including thirty-nine major battles. They were organized into 120 regiments of infantry, seven of cavalry, twelve of heavy artillery, and ten batteries of light artillery. One entire corps—the XXV Corps organized on 3 December 1864 under Major General Godfrey Weitzel—was composed of black troops previously belonging to X and XVIII Corps. The black troops of Kautz's division of XXV Corps were the first to enter Richmond after its fall.

The total Union force organized by war's end amounted to 272 regiments, forty-five separate battalions, and seventy-eight independent companies of cavalry; sixty-one regiments, eight battalions, and thirty-six companies of heavy artillery; nine battalions and 432 batteries of light artillery; thirteen regiments, one battalion, and seven companies of engineers; four regiments, three battalions, and thirty-five companies of "Sharp Shooters"; and a staggering 2,144 regiments, sixty battalions, and 351 companies of infantry. This amounted to a grand total of 3,559 independent units. By the war's end, when the Confederacy could muster barely 180,000 men under arms, the Union still had over one million of these men in uniform. From the over 2.5 million men who served the Union under all enlistment terms, 110,070 died in battle, while 249,458 more died from disease or other causes.

—*Duane C. Young*

See also Army of Mississippi; Army of the Gulf; Army of the James; Army of the Kanawha; Army of the Northwest Confederate; Army of the Ohio; Army of the Peninsula; Army of the Potomac; Army of the Shenandoah (U.S.A); Army of the Tennessee; Army of the West; Army of Virginia; Army Organization, U.S.A.; Artillery.

For further reading:
Cornish, Dudley Taylor. *The Sable Arm: Negro Troops in the Union Army, 1861–1865* (1966).
Dyer, Frederick H. *A Compendium of the War of the Rebellion* (1908).
Fox, William F. *Regimental Losses in the American Civil War, 1861–1865* (1889).
Ganoe, William A. *The History of the United States Army* (1942; reprint, 1964).
McPherson, James M. *Ordeal by Fire: The Civil War and Reconstruction* (1992).
Randall, James G., and David Herbert Donald. *The Civil War and Reconstruction* (1969).
Segal, David R. *Recruiting For Uncle Sam: Citizenship and Military Manpower Policy* (1989).
Shannon, Fred A. *The Organization and Administration of the Union Army, 1861–1865* (1928).
United States Department of the Census. *Population of the United States in 1860* (1864).

ART OF THE CIVIL WAR

To consider the art of the Civil War is to accept that the North had an embarrassment of riches. With a larger population, some art organizations, and burgeoning art schools, the North had a greater number of men and women practicing art. More European artists immigrated to the major cities of the North, where wealthy patrons lived, and more young artists traveled to European capitals for academic training. More publishing houses flourished, and printing firms employed and trained many engravers and lithographers.

The South had a smaller, more agrarian population and relatively fewer trained artists. Before the war, graphic images were obtained from the North and Europe or from small publishing houses in Baltimore or New Orleans.

Once the North tightened the noose of the blockade, paper, printing ink, canvas, and art materials became scarce. With all able Southern men joining the Confederate army, the Southern government had difficulty finding engravers to print Confederate money, postage stamps, and notes, to say nothing of newspaper illustrations and prints.

Southerners did not lack an appreciation for prints and artwork. However, during the war and after, their energies had to focus on survival. During the postwar period, Civil War prints, paintings, and sculpture would help heal the divisive wounds and glorify the leaders and combatants of both the North and South.

The immediacy of the sketches, engravings, and photographs from the front lines served the purpose of bringing the war to the public as soon as possible. It would be later in comfortable studios, often with the service of paid models, that the large oil paintings of notables and battle scenes would be completed.

At the start of the Civil War, the art and illustrations that Americans saw were derivative and often poorly executed. In the North, publications such as *Harper's Weekly, Frank Leslie's Illustrated Newspaper,* and the *New York Illustrated News* hired talented combat artists who followed the armies, witnessed the bloody battles, camped with the soldiers and lived in the heart of the war. However, their talent was poorly served by the primitive printing process of the day.

In the field, artists would sketch and draw what they objectively saw in pencil, crayon, watercolor, and pen and ink. These drawings would be rushed to the editorial offices in New York using whatever mode was available—horse, train, boat, messenger, or bribery. In New York, wood engravers, often less skilled, would quickly copy the drawing on a thick block of wood and carve away the negative areas, leaving the raised surfaces to carry the ink to the newsprint. The sensitive line of pencil and pen, as well as significant detail and information, would often be lost in the transfer to the cruder medium of wood engraving.

At that time, the technique for reproducing photographs did not exist. It was long after the war that photographs were studied by artists and were used to produce paintings, drawings, lithographs, and wood engravings of a higher artistic level.

The most complete visual history of the war was published by the editors of *Century Magazine* in 1887–1888. Called *Battles and Leaders of the Civil War,* this four-volume set is considered to be the definitive account of the war and has the richest collection of illustrations. *Century* editors used seventy artists who created over 1,000 pictures from their field sketches; former soldiers who became artists after the war; and professional illustrators who used artists' sketch books. Also used were photographs by Mathew Brady and Alexander Gardner and the oral descriptions by veterans to produce accurate and skillful representations of the war era.

The artists joined the journalists to risk dysentery, gunfire, deprivation, and the ire of commanders to make a graphic portrayal of war for the rest of the country. Most of the more accomplished artists were from Eastern Seaboard cities, and many had received classical training in the artistic capitals of Europe. After the battles, the artists and journalists enjoyed being considered part of the rakish Bohemian Brigade. They shared information, and often the artists drew maps and diagrams for the writers.

Since salaries were meager (from $15 to $35 a week), only Winslow Homer, the best known of the artists, would receive $60 dollars for a double-page spread. The war provided tremendous impetus to Homer's career. He had completed an apprenticeship in lithography in 1857 when he was twenty-one. At the start of the war he was attending night school at the National Academy of Design in New York. He had published some drawings in *Ballou's Pictorial* and in *Harper's Weekly.* In 1861 the latter commissioned him to make drawings of Lincoln's inauguration. He was then sent to cover the Peninsula campaign when the war began. He sketched countless scenes of battle and the soldier's life in the field. He returned to New York and began work on paintings such as *Sharpshooter on Picket Duty, Rations,* and *Home Sweet Home.* Some of these works were exhibited at the National Academy in 1863. He continued with his Civil War themes, with his *Prisoners from the Front* being perhaps his best work. It was exhibited at the Paris International Exposition of 1867 and is now in the collections of the Metropolitan Museum of Art in New York. After travel in Europe, Homer shifted his art to sea and marine scenes, returning only briefly in 1878 to painting of "negro life" in Virginia in a work called *Visit from the Old Mistress,* which was exhibited in the Paris

A *Harper's Weekly* depiction of their artist, Alfred R. Waud, at work (*Library of Congress*)

Exhibition of 1878 and is now in the National Gallery of Art in Washington, D.C.

Many artists, however, were not paid when their work was not published. Artists were also responsible for travel and accommodations. Many artists carried letters of introduction to commanders. The artists moved about all fronts of the war. For example, Theodore R. Davis of *Harper's Weekly* accompanied General Sherman's march through Georgia and was considered the artist who saw more of the war than any other.

By 1861, Henri Lovi of Cincinnati estimated that he had ridden horseback 1,000 miles in three months. He complained to the editors at *Frank Leslie's Illustrated Newspaper,* "Riding from ten to fifteen miles daily through mud and underbrush and then working until midnight by the dim light of a tallow dip…I am nearly 'played out' and as soon as the Pittsburg landing is worked up and Corinth settled, I must beg a furlough for

rest and repairs. I am deranged about the stomach, ragged, unkempt and unshorn, and need the co-joined skill and services of the apothecary, the tailor and the barber and above all the attentions of home…."

Some artists, such as Alfred R. Waud, were gifted writers as well. Waud accompanied General Custer on a raid, and his article "A Day in Camp" was as skillful as his line and wash drawings portraying the scene. Some of the hundreds of Civil War artists became famous after the war. Winslow Homer, George Caleb Bingham, Eastman Johnson, William Morris Hunt, Albert Bierstadt, Thomas Moran, and Thomas Nast are familiar names of artists who covered the Union at war.

Naval artists also had their part. The navies of the North and South launched ingenious warships in the form of gunboats and odd submarines. Xanthus Smith and other maritime artists painted dramatic pictures of fierce battles on the seas and rivers. Unlike life with the armies and access to all the battles, on the seas the artists found a less than hospitable terrain. With close quarters and firm discipline, naval ships did not often carry journalists, photographers, or artists.

On 8 March 1862, at Hampton Roads off Newport News, Virginia, the ironclad Confederate vessel CSS *Virginia* (formerly the USS *Merrimack*), a massive mound of deadly power, shelled and rammed the wooden ships of the Union navy. Xanthus Russell Smith, who had served on a wooden frigate, later painted the 9 March battle between the *Virginia* and the USS *Monitor*. In the painting, the stately wooden ships were a background for the squat and deadly steam-driven ironclads. Julian O. Davidson, who had been to sea, showed marine paintings with close attention to the technical details of the new line of ironclad vessels. Davidson produced a variety of naval illustrations that the Boston-based Louis Prang Company printed in a chromolithography series of Civil War prints. These artists, regardless of their training—classical European or naive primitive—painted large military battles in oil or quick pencil sketches, often drawn in the noisy fury of battle, and brought a dimension of emotion, humanity, and heroic drama of the tragic epic.

More dominant and immediate was the work of photographers. Mathew B. Brady's name is synonymous with photographs of President Lincoln and the Civil War, but he was a single player. While Brady had received permission from the president to privately document the impending war, many anonymous photographers were in the field with the Confederate armies as well.

Brady's colleague was Alexander Gardner. Scottish by birth, he probably met Brady during the 1851 World's Fair, as Gardner was one of the early experts in wet-plate photography. In 1856 Gardner sailed for New York City, his fare paid by Brady. He was Brady's closest associate during the war.

Gardner entered Brady's world of photography when Brady was nationally known as photographer to politicians, millionaires, and visiting royalty. His ornate studios in New York and Washington were hung with a who's who of reigning celebrities. In 1858, Alexander Gardner was manager of Brady's Washington studio. With the start of war in 1861, Brady, "the Lincoln photographer," convinced Lincoln and the war department that it was imperative to record the history of the war as it happened by means of photography. Disappointed at having to finance the venture himself, he believed that it would be a profitable investment.

Photographic technology was only twenty-two years old when the Civil War began. On 21 July 1861, at the battle of First Bull Run there appeared strange-looking hooded black wagons drawn by horses. Called "what's-its" by the soldiers, these black-hooded laboratories were ingenious, efficient photo processing laboratories manned by Brady's photographic artists. Photography in the middle of a battlefield was a daunting task. A photographer would set up the heavy studio camera on the tripod and view the objects to be filmed. In the wagon, the assistant would coat a sheet of clean glass with the liquid collodian, let it dry, then dip it in silver nitrate. These tasks had to be done in near darkness so as not to expose the plate. The glass plate was placed into a lightproof holder, rushed to the photographer, and slotted into the back of the camera. Then the black cloth was pulled over the camera and the photographer's head, and the plate was exposed for approximately ten seconds, then rushed back to the wagon for developing. Dust, humidity, and timing were all obstacles to be overcome by those Civil War photographers. The entire procedure had to be accomplished within ten to twenty minutes or the image would be lost. Alexander Gardner worked in one of those Brady wagons and reportedly took three-quarters of the photographs of the Army of the Potomac. However, Brady's name appears as the photographer.

Brady had no taste for the war and after a short time at the Bull Run debacle he returned to his New York portrait studio. The cost of supplying and photographing the war, coupled with his poor business practices, caused his financial ruin, resulting in his bankruptcy by 1873. His hope of reaping riches from his Civil War photographs was dashed by a glut of pictures. More than a million exposures were made, and the public could not get enough of the war pictures, but by the end of the horrific conflict the Americans had no desire to see the painful images.

Alexander Gardner left Brady in 1863 and set up a studio similar to Brady's in Washington where, for the remainder of the war, he sporadically photographed battles and the tragic aftermaths. Gardner photographed Lincoln's funeral and the famous pictures of the hanging of the assassination conspirators.

Gardner closed his studio and became a field photographer for the Union Pacific Railroad. His black laboratory wagon followed the covered wagons on the Chisolm Trail into the western frontier. He became famous for some of the best photographs of the western frontier.

Southern photographers were also on hand at the start of the war. F. K. Houston of Charleston, South Carolina, photographed the vanquished Fort Sumter; he was followed by James Osburn and F. E. Durbec. Perhaps because of limited supplies, they did not continue to photograph Civil War subjects.

Brady's failing eyesight led him to relegate the camera work to his talented staff. The bulk of the photos were taken by Gardner, his son James, Timothy O'Sullivan, William Pywell, George N. Barnard, David Woodbury, E. Guy Fox, and others. Gardner's and O'Sullivan's work developed into true art, and they left Brady when he denied them credit for their work. The only official government photographer working for the U.S. Military Railroad was a Captain A. J. Russell, who is credited with work of high quality. These were artists who captured the static scenes of scarred and blasted fields littered with broken equipment, although they would frequently move bodies to improve the composition of a photograph and add drama to the scene. They took thousands of *carte de viste* photos of young, smartly dressed recruits and grizzled veterans in rag-tag uniforms. They captured homey scenes of encampments, barbers working outdoors, cooks stirring pots, soldiers playing cards at their leisure in front of their tents, the dead and dying in field hospitals, and generals whose names are now a part of the American pageant. The results of their work often had an ignominious end. When the demand for Civil War photographs waned, thousands of the glass-plate negatives were sold for use as windows in greenhouses. As the seasons changed, the captured faces in the glass—the corpse-strewn battlefields of Antietam, Fredericksburg, Vicksburg, Gettysburg; the sunken gunboats; the ruined cities; and the heroic and battle-weary soldiers—were burned away by the rays of the sun. These negatives became the ghostly pentimento of this tragic civil war.

To produce lithographs, the artist would draw on smooth stone slabs with a grease pencil. It offered a more sensitive surface for detail and shading than woodcut engraving, but it was time-consuming, as the stone required inking with a brayer for each print. After several hundred prints the original image would fade.

Engravings on copper or steel plates were the most demanding of skill and time. The artist was required to scratch and carve incised lines into hard sheets of treated copper with engraving tools. Ink would be rubbed into these lines, excess ink would be wiped away, and the plate would be placed into a press with a sheet of dampened paper. The plate and paper, sandwiched between felt blankets, would be drawn through the press, forcing the damp paper into the incised lines and creating a richly detailed engraving.

Among the most popular and accessible American art forms—priced for as little as twenty-five cents and sold in general stores and on street corners—were prints by Currier and Ives. This company, started in 1835, achieved great success through mass-producing familiar American scenes as well as Civil War battle prints. Rare was the household that did not have a Currier and Ives print on the wall.

Established artists would sell paintings to the firm, which then had them copied on lithographic stones and printed as black-and-white prints. In the New York City factory, the prints would move down an assembly line, where workers would dab bright colors on the print through a stencil. Although Currier and Ives prints were

not always historically accurate, they filled a demand by the masses for Civil War art. By the mid-1880s, the Louis Prang Company of Boston and the firm of Kurz and Allison of Chicago had also printed a series of battle scenes that are still used today as graphic illustrations for book covers.

None of the art produced during the Civil War was officially sponsored by the governments of either side. It did not occur to these mid–nineteenth-century administrations to utilize art as propaganda, nor could they afford it. Initially it was the artists and the few patrons who documented the war. After the war, the growing number of veterans' organizations continued to stimulate and encourage the creation of Civil War art. Other factors also contributed to these efforts, such as a curiosity about the war by those who had not experienced it directly, and a desire to honor those who had fought.

One defining image from all the art produced for and about the Confederacy is an engraving called *The Burial of Latane*. William DeHartburn Washington, an artist from Richmond, Virginia, completed an oil painting in 1864 portraying the burial of a young doctor who was killed as his unit repulsed the Union forces just north of Richmond. Captain Latane, sword drawn and charging the retreating forces, was killed by a fusillade of gunfire. His brother, a comrade in arms, transported his body to a nearby plantation, where the mistress of the plantation, with the help of the slaves and other women, tenderly put the young officer to rest as if he were one of their beloved sons. Reported by the press and memorialized in a widely read poem, the incident moved the artist to paint the burial scene with the women and girls performing the service and mourning the unknown soldier. This image would strike the heart of all those Southerners who lost a loved one far from home and among strangers. Ironically, it was a Northern engraver, A. G. Campbell, working from a photograph, and a New York City publishing house that produced the print that evoked such an unparalleled response, particularly among the women of the South. Universal sorrow, the skill of the engraver, and active promotion and marketing of the print created a symbol of the Lost Cause. *The Burial of Latane* portrayed a woman's view of the war, sustained the Southern identity, and became an enduring image for decades after the war.

From 1785 to 1903, military cyclorama paintings were a popular art form in the great capitals of Europe. Brought to the United States in 1790, this kind of touring painting was displayed on the interior walls of specially constructed round buildings. Stretching up to fifty feet in height and encircling the viewer for nearly four hundred feet in length, the canvas would envelop the viewer in an immense painting in the round. At first, experienced European artists did the research, visited

battle sites, and interviewed the soldiers and officers. Teams of painters would work for months to create the battle scene vistas that would draw millions of viewers in American cities. They paid between twenty-five and fifty cents for admission. Many major battles—Antietam, Second Bull Run, Shiloh, the clash of the *Monitor* and the *Virginia*, and others—were the subject matter of these colossal canvasses. Few have survived, and those that have are rarely exhibited.

Around 1882, Paul Philippoteaux, a Frenchman who had worked on European cycloramas, came to Gettysburg to do research on the battle. With a team of five artists he completed the first of four cycloramas of the battle of Gettysburg. He exhibited the first work to great acclaim in Chicago in 1883. One of Philippoteaux's Gettysburg cycloramas is on display at the Gettysburg National Military Park. Another cyclorama, *The Battle of Atlanta,* by William Wehner and his team of European artists, was restored in 1982 and is on view in modern facilities near the Atlanta battleground.

As an art form the cyclorama never attained the level of museum quality. As a spectacle it was hyped and promoted in the florid language of the time. The sheer size and weight of the canvas, the need for a special building, and the growing distaste among Americans for the illustrated carnage doomed this once-popular kind of painting. The arrival of new technology heralded by D. W. Griffith's movie *The Birth of a Nation* in 1915 closed the door on the cyclorama, a unique form of artistic storytelling.

For decades after the war, to heal the wounds, confront the terrible losses, and glorify the survivors of this national cataclysm, thousands of statues, obelisks, plaques, busts, tombs, canons, and pillars were carved and constructed in twenty-five states and the District of Columbia. In almost every hamlet, town, and city that sent soldiers to the war there are examples of sculpture in parks, town squares, cemeteries, and battle sites. The National Park Service and numerous other organizations maintain and administrate various buildings and battlegrounds throughout these states.

The largest and most imposing of all Civil War sculpture is carved into the granite of a mountain near Atlanta called Stone Mountain. The equestrian figures of Robert E. Lee, "Stonewall" Jackson, and Jefferson Davis were conceived and begun by Gutzon Borglum, who later designed and created Mount Rushmore. This impressive sculpture, later completed by Walker Hancock, measures 90 feet high by 190 feet long. It is a spectacular feat of engineering and carving.

Augustus Saint-Gaudens was commissioned to create a sculptural monument for Boston honoring Colonel Robert Gould Shaw, the leader of the 54th Massachusetts, the black regiment that stormed Fort Wagner. A masterpiece, this bas relief took fourteen years to complete. It depicts Shaw on horseback accompanied by a column of his men and is sculpted with attention to detail and honest realism. Saint-Gaudens's equestrian statue of General William T. Sherman being led by the winged female figure of American victory was placed on New York's Fifth Avenue near the entrance to Central Park. The figure of the horse and rider and the striding Victory create an unmistakable feeling of forward movement and progress. This gilded statue rides high above pedestrians, taxis, and hansom cabs on one of the busiest, most affluent, and modern city corners in the world.

The nation's capital, with a wealth of sculpture, is home to one of America's most familiar monuments, the Lincoln Memorial. The white marble sculpture of the seated Abraham Lincoln by America's acknowledged leading sculptor, Daniel Chester French, is a powerful symbol for all Americans. From within the stone emerges the sad but rugged character of the man who held the country together through its bloody struggle.

The Hudson River school of painting, rooted in European themes, was the predominant style of painting in the period before the war. English-born Thomas Cole was painting in this manner in 1825. The majestic American landscape was painted as a vision from a palette arranged by God.

By the 1850s a more natural and realistic style emerged as artists like George Caleb Bingham portrayed the reality of American life and work in everyday scenes. Unlike the Europeans, who had a long art history of military themes, the antimilitary American artists were more likely to paint idyllic landscapes and upon these arcadian backgrounds superimpose the war scene. An example would be a painting by Albert Bierstadt entitled *Guerilla Warfare (Picket Duty in Virginia)* (1862), in which five Union soldiers fire upon Confederate troops in the distance. The rolling hills bathed in summer haze, the carefully painted lush grasses, and beautifully rendered trees provide a theatrical set upon which the soldiers casually play at war.

Conrad Wise Chapman, an ardent son of Virginia, returned from Italy at age nineteen to fight as well as record scenes of camp life. After recovery from a head wound, he was transferred in October 1863 to Charleston, South Carolina. Later, he was to paint a series of thirty-one oils of the harbor during the siege. These landscapes and seascapes are peaceful depictions of the harbor watched over by the lone sentry at his post atop the ramparts. His work, in the Museum of the Confederacy, is considered the most important of the Confederacy.

John Ross Key, who also painted a work called *The Bombardment of Fort Sumter* in 1864, fell victim to the same philosophy that so many Civil War painters employed. They sought to reduce the carnage and

destruction to a lovely landscape that just happened to be a background for columns of marching soldiers and prancing horses. Critics were no better in the assessment of these works of Civil War art, much of which was sentimental, idealized, and sanitized views of a horrific national explosion. The artists Gilbert Gaul, Peter F. Rothermel, William B. T. Trego, Walton Taber, and Thure de Thulstrup seemed to portray the battle scenes with more visual realism, honesty, and artistic skill than others.

Winslow Homer, considered the greatest of the Civil War painters, after his brief sojourn to the front for *Harper's Weekly*, almost exclusively concentrated his paintings' subject matter on genre scenes of the soldiers' life in camp. He had no interest in being a painter of military battles; his forte was being a painter of the people. Perhaps if we strip away the pretensions of glory formed in the idealized portraits of military leaders, the carefully painted rows of nameless soldiers marching to their deaths, the stiff and static generals astride their foaming steeds, safely behind the lines, we would accept Lincoln's observation that it was "the people's war."

—Rosemarie S. Cardoso

See also *Battles and Leaders of the Civil War*; Brady, Mathew B.; Cyclorama; *Frank Leslie's Illustrated Newspaper*; Gardner, Alexander; *Harper's Weekly*; Homer, Winslow; Nast, Thomas; Photography; Waud, Alfred Rudolph.

For further reading:

Blay, John S. *The Civil War A Pictorial Profile* (1958).
Gardner, Alexander. *Gardner's Photographic Sketchbook of the Civil War* (1959).
Holzer, Harold, and Mark E. Neely, Jr. *Mine Eyes Have Seen the Glory* (1993).
Jacobson, Doranne. *The Civil War in Art: A Visual Odyssey* (1996).
Ketchum, Richard M., ed. *The American Heritage Picture History of the Civil War* (1960).
McSpadden, J. Walker. *Famous Sculptors of America* (1968).
Neely, Mark E. Jr., Harold Holzer, and Gabor S. Boritt. *The Confederate Image: Prints of the Lost Cause* (1987).
Sears, Stephen W. *The American Heritage Century Collection of Civil War Art* (1974).
Starr, Louis M. *Bohemian Brigade: Civil War Newsmen in Action* (1987).
Ward, Geoffrey C., et al. *The Civil War: An Illustrated History* (1990).
Williams, Herman Warner, Jr. *The Civil War: The Artists' Record* (1961).

ARTILLERY

Land-based artillery was typed variously by its design, projectile, trajectory, deployment, and bore. The two most general classifications were *heavy*, massive large caliber cannons used in garrison, siege, and seacoast roles, and *light*, mobile horse-drawn weapons used most often with infantry in the field. A cannon's trajectory—the arc of its projectile's flight—and basic design provided more specific classifications.

Guns were long-barreled weapons capable of firing heavy projectiles in relatively flat trajectories. Howitzers had shorter barrels, a powder chamber smaller in diameter than the bore of the piece, and achieved a higher trajectory than guns. Mortars had very short, thick-walled barrels and lobbed large caliber projectiles at an extremely high trajectory. Columbiads were the heaviest weapons, usually deployed in garrison, siege, and seacoast roles, and were capable of firing tremendous projectiles great distances.

Both rockets and hand grenades also saw limited use. Some evidence supports the view that the Confederates used British-designed Congreve rockets early in the war. However, they found the Congreves, which resembled very large bottle rockets, so highly inaccurate that they soon abandoned them. The Union army fielded the spin-stabilized Hale rocket in both 6- and 16-pound weights. Although the Hale could achieve a maximum range of about 2,200 yards, it, like the Congreve, was far from accurate, and carried an insufficient warhead to inflict significant damage.

Numerous hand grenade patents also emerged during the war, but the Ketcham was the most commonly used hand-thrown ordnance. Significant numbers of Ketchams were manufactured by the Federal arsenals in 1-, 2-, 3-, and 5-pound weights. The Ketcham was stabilized by cardboard fins and detonated by a percussion fuse in its nose. Other types of grenades included the Adams and Excelsior patents, as well as common 6-pound spherical cannon balls that were lit and either rolled or thrown at nearby enemy positions.

Both smoothbore and rifled weapons saw extensive use during the war. The majority were muzzle loading, although a limited number of breech-loading pieces were also fielded. Smoothbore cannons fired spherical projectiles attached by tinned iron straps to wooden bases called *sabots*. This arrangement, when attached to a powder bag, was what was known as fixed ammunition. Fixed ammunition afforded smoothbore gunners a speed advantage over their rifled-gun counterparts, who usually had to load their powder charge and projectile separately.

Smoothbore ammunition classifications included solid shot, common shell, case shot, canister, and grapeshot. Solid shot consisted of solid-cast iron balls used for battering down brick or masonry fortifications. The tendency of solid shot to carom across hard ground also proved particularly deadly for long-range antipersonnel purposes. Common shells were hollow iron projectiles filled with a bursting charge, detonated by either time or impact fuses and designed to explode into numerous fragments. Case shot, also known as shrapnel for its English inventor, Henry Shrapnel, was also a hollow iron sphere but with thinner walls and filled with iron or lead balls designed to scatter upon detonation. It too was fuse detonated.

An eight-inch Parrot gun (*foreground*), with a Rodman gun beyond; Battery Rogers at Hunting Creek and the Potomac, Alexandria, Virginia. (*Library of Congress*)

A canister round was a tinned iron can filled with iron or lead balls sealed with a heavy iron plate at either end and nailed to a wooden sabot. In effect a huge shotgun cartridge, canister was particularly effective against attacking infantry and cavalry at close ranges. In many instances gunners loaded "double canister" when threatened with being overrun. Grapeshot was typically fired from the larger garrison, siege, and seacoast artillery. A stand of grapeshot, as the projectile was called, consisted of nine large iron balls arranged in three tiers and held in place by two heavy iron plates at either end with two iron rings around the middle. A long bolt passing through the middle of the stand through each end plate secured the projectile until it was fired. When fired, the bolt would bend or fracture, thus releasing the stand's deadly components with an effect similar to canister but on a larger scale. Grapeshot was particularly effective in wrecking ships' rigging as well as against personnel.

Rifled cannon projectiles were most commonly cylindrical, and resembled modern artillery ordnance in appearance. Rather than a wooden sabot, rifled projectiles were usually cast with integral lead, copper, or brass expansion rings designed to grip the bore's rifling upon firing. The advent of rifled artillery sparked a rush to the U.S. Patent Office as inventors submitted scores of designs for "improved" projectiles and their various components, including fuses and sabots. Capable of greater range and accuracy than smoothbore weapons,

A modified 12-pounder breech-loading Whitworth gun, location unknown (*Library of Congress*)

rifled artillery was most effective firing case shot and shell, as well as—to a limited extent—solid shot, also known as bolts. Bolts were most useful against armored and masonry targets but relatively ineffective against infantry, owing to their tendency to bury themselves in the earth rather than bounce along the ground in the manner of spherical solid shot. The spin afforded by rifled barrels also tended to make grapeshot and canister impractical, because of their tendency to sling their components in unpredictable patterns.

Explosive shell and case projectiles relied on either time or percussion fuses to ignite their bursting charges. The simplest time fuse consisted of a 2-inch paper tube of compressed gunpowder inserted into either a wooden or metal fuse adapter that in turn was fitted into a hole in the projectile. Time fuses of various patents were fitted to both spherical and rifled shell and case shot. The paper fuses were color coded to indicate their various burning times and were ignited by the cannon's firing. The Borman time fuse was a threaded soft metal disc filled with an internal powder train graduated from one to five seconds burning time. Preparatory to loading, the gunner punched a hole into the fuse at the appropriate second

mark indicated on its face. This exposed the powder trail to the flames generated by the cannon's ignition.

As their detonation relied on direct impact with a target, percussion fuses were impractical for use with spherical ammunition, as round balls tended to spin unpredictably after firing. Screwed into the nose of the projectile and designed to explode on impact, percussion fuses were best suited to rifled artillery. Their basic principle relied on a sliding powder-filled plunger that, through inertia, would fly forward on impact against the front of the fuse. The impact would then explode a percussion cap very similar to those used on percussion muskets. There were several varieties of percussion fuses and some combined both time and percussion characteristics. Parrott, Hotchkiss, and Schenkl were three of the most widely used percussion patents.

As a general rule the Union, with its superior manufacturing capabilities, produced ammunition more reliable than the ordnance in the Confederates' limber chests. But owing to the many variables inherent in its manufacture, components, and use, explosive ammunition used by both sides was always subject to malfunction. Despite the often ingenious efforts of their inventors, explosive shells were prone either to explode before leaving the muzzle of the cannon or not explode at all.

Field artillery usually consisted of 12-pounder smoothbores and 10- and sometimes 20-pounder rifled guns. Their two-wheeled "stock trail" field carriages were most typically constructed of wood with iron fittings. The Model 1841 bronze 6-pounder guns and 12-pounder howitzers were already obsolete in 1861, and as the war progressed were eventually removed from Federal service. The ordnance-starved Confederacy, however, continued to field both until the war's end. Although seeing rather limited use, the 12-pounder mountain howitzer was designed for easy disassembly for transport on muleback in difficult terrain. At only 37 inches in length and weighing a diminutive 220 pounds, the mountain howitzer shared the same bore size and thus the same ammunition as its larger 12-pounder cousins. The mountain howitzer's short barrel precluded long-range accuracy, but by virtue of its design it could be deployed in areas inaccessible to conventional artillery.

By far the most popular field cannon among gunners of both sides was the bronze 12-pounder smooth-bore Model 1857 Napoleon. Namesake of Napoleon III, under whose auspices it was originally designed for the French army, the Model 1857 was a hybrid gun-howitzer, being somewhat smaller and lighter than the earlier model 12-pounder, yet taking the same powder charge. In Federal service it replaced both the 6-pounder and the 12-pounder howitzer. The South relied heavily on

captured Napoleons and also manufactured simplified Napoleons cast without the muzzle swell found on Federal models. The Napoleon fired shot, shell, case, and canister with equal ease.

Some debate arose among gunners concerning the relative merits and liabilities between smoothbore and rifled artillery. The Napoleon was unsurpassed as a relatively short-range antipersonnel weapon. Firing fixed ammunition, it was somewhat faster to load than rifled field guns. Also, its projectile was some two pounds heavier, allowing for a significantly stronger blasting charge. The Napoleon's 4.62-inch smooth bore was particularly well suited to the use of canister, and it was more effective than rifled guns in heavily wooded terrain. In addition, many contemporary observers noted that rifled projectiles tended to bury themselves and explode harmlessly in the earth upon impact, thus negating their effectiveness. The smoothbores' spherical projectiles, however, tended to bounce across the ground, causing considerable destruction before detonating. For their part, the rifles' proponents viewed such drawbacks a small price to pay for their pieces' far superior accuracy and range.

The two most commonly used rifled field artillery pieces were the 3-inch, 10-pounder Parrotts and Ordnance Rifles. Patented in 1861 by Robert P. Parrott, superintendent of the West Point Foundry of Cold Spring, New York, the Parrott was originally produced in 2.9-inch caliber, but later models were standardized as 3-

The "Dictator," a flatcar-mounted mortar, was used during the siege of Petersburg.
(Photograph by David Knox / *Library of Congress*)

inch weapons. Parrotts are easily distinguished by the wrought-iron reinforcing band around the breech of their inherently brittle cast-iron tubes. The reinforcing band did much to improve the Parrott's reliability, but throughout the war Parrotts managed to explode with annoying and often dangerous regularity. Still, the Parrott was accurate and relatively inexpensive to produce. Two models of Parrott rifles were produced during the war—the Model 1861, easily identified by its muzzle swell, and the simpler Model 1863, cast without a muzzle swell. The Parrott design sufficiently impressed Confederate ordnance officers to prompt them to produce their own copies at Richmond's Tredegar Works. Twenty-pounder (3.67-inch) Parrotts also saw field service.

Adopted by the Federal Ordnance Department in 1861, the wrought-iron 3-inch Ordnance Rifle, often mistakenly referred to as the Rodman, was originally patented by John Griffen in 1855. The majority of the Ordnance Rifles were manufactured at the Phoenix Iron Company of Phoenixville, Pennsylvania. The foundry's president, Samuel J. Reeves, received his own patent in 1862 for additional improvements in the weapon's production. The Ordnance Rifle, with its strikingly modern, streamlined appearance, accuracy, and reliability, was considered the best muzzle-loading rifled field gun of the day. Ordnance Rifles made up 41 percent of the Federal guns at Gettysburg. The Ordnance Rifle most often fired projectiles of the Hotchkiss and Schenkl patents, but would also accept 3-inch Parrott ammunition. Confederate inventors also produced a number of unique designs, such as the Archer, Mullane, Reed, and Reed-Braun patents, for use in captured Ordnance Rifles.

The James Rifles saw rather less use during the war. Designed by General Charles T. James of the Rhode Island militia to accept his own unique patented projec-

Army engineers remove an 8-inch Columbiad gun from Fort McAllister, Savannah, Georgia, in December 1864. (*Library of Congress*)

A 12-pounder howitzer captured from the Confederates by Butterfield's Brigade near Hanover Court House, 27 May 1862
(*Library of Congress*)

tile, the 14-pounder (3.8-inch) James Rifles were cast by the Ames Manufacturing Company of Chicopee, Massachusetts. The James, however, exhibited a number of drawbacks, and after 1862 became an increasing rarity in the field. The James patent projectile with its soft lead sabot proved the first culprit in the gun's demise. Early in the war gunners delivering covering fire over the heads of their own infantry found that their ammunition tended to fling off its lead sabot upon leaving the muzzles of their guns. The resulting casualties among their own troops caused by this rain of deadly shrapnel from the rear understandably cost the James much in the way of reputation. Although the ammunition problem was remedied by the substitution of Hotchkiss pattern projectiles, the material of its manufacture eventually doomed the James. Despite sharing a similar appearance to the Ordnance Rifle, the James was of the softer cast bronze, rather than wrought iron. Its rifling, therefore, tended to erode quickly after heavy use with a consequent loss in accuracy.

Two breech-loading rifles were introduced during the war. Both the Armstrong and Whitworth rifles were designed and manufactured in England and were imported in limited numbers. The majority saw use in Confederate service. Despite their advanced designs, neither the Armstrong nor Whitworth's breech-loading mechanisms afforded any significant advantage in their speed of loading. Crews often found them overly complicated, difficult to operate, and prone to fouling and breakage. In addition, neither weapon employed fixed ammunition. Both weapons, however, won reputations for unsurpassed range and accuracy.

The Armstrong employed a projectile either fitted with three rows of small brass studs intended to mate with its bore's rifling or lead driving bands. Armstrongs were manufactured in a number of calibers, the most common being 3-inch 10-pounder weapons. The weapons developed by the prolific English weapons designer Sir Joseph Whitworth were also produced in a number of calibers, the most common probably the 12-pounder (2.75-inch) models with a few large caliber Whitworths also seeing some action. Although some Whitworths were manufactured as muzzle-loading weapons, all shared their inventor's unique twisting hexagonal bore and corresponding ammunition. The efficiency of the Whitworth system allowed gunners to

Parrot gun at an unknown location, early 1860s (*Library of Congress*)

achieve ranges of almost six miles—an advantage often lost in practical use owing to the era's primitive aiming. The Whitworth's streamlined, hexagonal projectiles also shared the disadvantage of most rifled field gun projectiles in that they were not large enough to accommodate a significant blasting charge. They were most effective firing bolts that could be delivered accurately at high velocity in much flatter trajectories than conventional artillery. Troops noted that the Whitworth projectiles' hexagonal shape, coupled with its high rate of speed, lent it an unnerving high-pitched whine that added much to its fearsome reputation.

Classified as heavy artillery, siege and garrison cannons were of heavier caliber and less mobile than field artillery. Siege artillery, however, was usually mounted on relatively mobile wooden carriages similar in design to the field artillery's. The great weight of the more permanently fixed garrison and seacoast weapons necessitated that their carriages be constructed of heavy timber or iron. The two most common types of mounts were the casement and the barbette carriages. The tracked casement carriage was similar to naval carriages, as it was used primarily in older, permanent masonry forts with gun ports. Its design facilitated the limited movement necessary to retract the cannon into the fort for loading. The more common barbette carriages were most often employed in open earthen or masonry fortifications. Their design employed small wheels on tracks and either a front or center pivot or *pintle*. This arrangement allowed gunners to traverse their weapons for a wide angle of fire.

Some of the most common seacoast smoothbores were the iron Model 1829 32-pounder and the Model 1831 42-pounder guns. Both weapons were typically mounted on wooden, front pintle, barbette carriages for garrison use. Experiences early in the war quickly led artillerists to the conclusion that rifled weapons, with their higher velocities, were far superior to the older smoothbore cannons against masonry targets. As a result, some smoothbore guns were rifled to accept James projectiles.

The West Point Foundry also produced its famous Parrott rifles in massive 6.4-inch (100-pound), 8-inch (200-pound), and 10-inch (250–300-pound) versions. Mounted on wrought iron, front pintle, barbette carriages, these huge weapons shared not only the accuracy of the smaller Parrotts, but, unfortunately, their propensity to burst during firing. The bursting of such larger guns was an ongoing concern for weapons designers of the era, owing to the comparatively primitive metallurgy of the day and the volatility of black powder propellant charges. One solution was the "built-up" gun—a cannon manufactured of separate components fused together to provide added strength. The Parrott was an example of the built-up gun, but other designs proved more successful, including the British-designed Blakely and Armstrong rifles and the Confederate-designed Brooke rifles.

A few 5-inch (80-pound) Whitworth rifles also saw service in Confederate coastal defenses.

First developed by American Colonel George Bomford and introduced in 1811, the cast-iron smoothbore Columbiads were some of the largest cannons to see service in the war. Primarily a seacoast weapon, the Columbiad combined various aspects of the gun and howitzer. Early Columbiads shared a similar powder chamber to the howitzer and all were capable of firing in both high howitzer and low gun trajectories. The Columbiad's design underwent a number of modifications both before and during the war, resulting in a wide variety of types and calibers. The Models of 1844 and 1858 were cast in 8-inch (65-pound) and 10-inch (128-pound) calibers, as was the Model 1861 Rodman, which was also cast in a 15-inch (428-pound) version. At least one 20-inch Rodman was produced in 1864. Named for their inventor, Thomas Jefferson Rodman, these innovative weapons introduced a number of improvements in casting and overall design and both Union and Confederate foundries produced them in significant numbers. Most Columbiads were mounted on massive wrought-iron, center pintle, barbette carriages.

Mortars were classified as siege, garrison, and seacoast artillery and were cast in a number of sizes. They fired heavy spherical time-fused shell and case ammunition. The Coehorn, named for its inventor, the seventeenth-century Dutch artillerist Baron van Menno Coehoorn,

was the smallest weapon of this class and saw wide use. The standard 24-pound Coehorn consisted of a short 16.32-inch bronze tube mounted on a simple wooden bed with four handles. Weighing a mere 296 pounds, the Coehorn could be carried by as few as two men. It was particularly well suited for trench warfare, owing to its mobility and ability to throw projectiles in a high arc into opposing earthworks. The Confederates produced somewhat simplified iron Coehorns in both 24- and 12-pound models. The iron Model 1841 8- and 10-inch siege models were much heavier mortars than the Coehorns, and in 1861 were augmented by still more massive weapons, the 10- and 13-inch seacoast mortars. The tube of the largest of these, the 13-inch seacoast mortar, weighed 17,120 pounds and could hurl a 220-pound projectile 4,325 yards at a 45 degree elevation. Owing partially to transportation difficulties, few of these mortars were actually installed in seacoast fortifications by war's end. They did, however, see use on special mortar boats operating along the Mississippi River, and the most famous mortar of all, the "Dictator," was mounted on a special railroad flatcar for use during the siege of Petersburg.

—*Jeff Kinard*

See also Armories, Arsenals, and Foundries; Dahlgren Guns; Ordnance, Naval; Rodman Gun; Springfield Armory; Tredegar Iron Works.

For further reading:
Coggins, Jack. *Arms and Equipment of the Civil War* (1989).
Peterson, Harold L. *Round Shot and Rammers: An Introduction to Muzzle-loading Land Artillery in the United States* (1969).
Thomas, Dean S. *Cannons* (1985).

ASBOTH, ALEXANDER SANDOR
(1811–1868)
Union general

A veteran of the Hungarian Revolution of 1848, Alexander Sandor Asboth fled to the United States, befriended powerful politicians, and rose rapidly in rank at the outbreak of the Civil War. He led divisions at the battle of Pea Ridge and during the advance on Corinth in early 1862, before questions about his competence relegated him to minor commands for the remainder of the war.

Born in Keszthely, Hungary, on 18 December 1811, Asboth studied engineering and worked as a civil servant, before participating in the unsuccessful 1848 revolt against Austria as an aide to Louis Kossuth. He fled his homeland after the uprising's failure, traveling first to Turkey, before receiving asylum in the United States. Upon his arrival Asboth continued to work for Hungarian independence, establishing several factories in New York to produce supplies for the continued struggle.

During the 1850s Asboth remained in New York,

where he fortuitously befriended John C. Frémont. Upon the outbreak of the Civil War, the famed Pathfinder appointed the dashing, militarily experienced Hungarian as his chief of staff with the rank of brigadier general. This appointment, however, would not be confirmed until early 1862.

Asboth's first serious engagement was at the battle of Pea Ridge in March 1862, where he commanded the 2d Division of Samuel Curtis's Army of the Southwest. Suffering a serious arm wound in the battle, the Hungarian performed erratically, urging Curtis to withdraw from the field after the first day's fighting. Asboth next led troops in the Union advance on Corinth, Mississippi, which was followed successively by garrison duty in Mississippi, as commander of fortifications at Memphis, and, in early 1863, as commander of the District of Columbus in western Kentucky. In the latter position he strove to defend the supply lines of Ulysses Grant's army against attacks from Confederate guerrillas. Asboth's actions again led to questions about his competence. He often bombarded his superiors with exaggerated or pessimistic reports, and asked for reinforcements after noting that he had driven Confederate forces from his district.

Ultimately, in August 1863 the Hungarian was relieved of his command. He briefly commanded a division in William Sherman's XVI Corps, before being transferred to Edward Ord's XIII Corps, and eventually to Nathaniel Banks's Department of the Gulf. In November 1863, Banks finally placed Asboth in command of the District of West Florida, with his headquarters at Fort Barrancas, near Pensacola. Asboth would spend the remainder of the war in this remote location. Despite his eagerness to return to a more active theater, Asboth generally performed well in his new position. He worked to organize a regiment of cavalry from Unionist refugees, encouraged black enlistments, and mounted a number of raids into the Confederate-held interior.

The only significant military engagement in which Asboth participated while in Florida was the 27 September 1864 raid on Marianna. With 700 men from the 2d Maine Cavalry, 1st Florida Infantry, and the 82d and 86th United States Colored Infantry, Asboth left Barrancas on 18 September, with the objectives of capturing isolated Confederate outposts, recruiting men for his black and Unionist regiments, and collecting supplies and mounts for his command. Upon reaching Marianna, the Federals fought a heated engagement with a small Rebel force composed primarily of a home guard company referred to as the Cradle and the Grave. Asboth's troops captured the town, killing or capturing most of the defenders, but while leading a charge their commander suffered two serious wounds, one breaking his cheekbone and the other his left arm.

After several months' recuperation, Asboth returned to his command in early 1865. He received a major general's brevet in March, and was mustered out of volunteer service five months later. His postwar career proved tragically brief. Though still suffering from his Marianna wound, Asboth was appointed minister to Argentina in early 1866. While in Buenos Aires he attempted to mediate an end to a war that pitted Paraguay against Argentina, Brazil, and Uruguay. Despite failing health, Asboth was appointed minister to Uruguay in October 1867. Over the next several months his condition deteriorated, and he died on 21 January 1868 in Buenos Aires.

—David J. Coles

See also Immigrants; Pea Ridge, Battle of.
For further reading:
Hess, Earl J. "Alexander Asboth: One of Lincoln's Hungarian Heroes?" *Lincoln Herald* (1982).
Shea, William L., and Earl J. Hess. *Pea Ridge: Civil War Campaign in the West* (1992).
Vasvary, Edmund. *Lincoln's Hungarian Heroes: The Participation of Hungarians in the Civil War, 1861–1865* (1939).

ASHBY, TURNER
(1828–1862)
Confederate officer

Born on 23 October 1828, in Fauquier County, Virginia, Turner Ashby was from a wealthy Virginia planter family. His grandfather, Captain "Jack" Ashby, had earned fame in the American Revolutionary War. Taught by his mother and hired tutors, Ashby had little formal education. After the early death of his father, he and his brothers managed the family farm, Rose Hill.

As sectional tensions heightened, Ashby formed a volunteer cavalry company, his reputation as a horseman attracting many recruits. Following John Brown's 1859 raid at Harper's Ferry, Ashby took his company there, and subsequently it patrolled the Potomac River crossings to prevent other such raids.

Following the secession of Virginia, Ashby's company became part of Colonel Angus W. McDonald's 7th Virginia Cavalry Regiment. McDonald knew a fighter when he saw one and on 25 June 1861, he recommended Ashby for promotion to lieutenant colonel. The next day, Ashby's brother Richard, out searching for a Northern sympathizer, was mortally wounded by a Union patrol. Turner came upon the scene before his brother died and was convinced that Richard had been stabbed after he had fallen. He vowed vengeance.

Ashby soon developed a reputation for reckless bravery in battle equalled by few other commanders, North or South, yet he was reportedly so soft-spoken, mild mannered, and gentlemanly when not in a fight,

Turner Ashby (*Library of Congress*)

that those who met him could not remember anything he had said. When rheumatism forced McDonald to retire, Ashy became colonel of the regiment and exercised virtually independent command in the region west of Harper's Ferry. Ashby was a poor disciplinarian, however, and his units had a reputation for going their own way and looting.

On 16 October 1861 Ashby planned to attack Federal troops active in the vicinity of his camp on Bolivar Heights near Harper's Ferry. With no more than 550 men, of whom 300 were militia, and two artillery pieces, he drove Union troops from the vicinity. Ashby performed a variety of other missions until the spring of 1862 when Major General Thomas J. "Stonewall" Jackson gave him command of his cavalry. Ashby speedily built up this force to twenty-one companies. Ashby played a key role in Jackson's Shenandoah Valley campaign, securing vital intelligence on Union forces and masking Jackson's weakness.

After participating in the withdrawal from Winchester, Virginia, on 11 March, Ashby reported to Jackson ten days later the mistaken impression that Federal troops were retiring northward and only a meager Union presence remained in that city. This faulty information contributed to Jackson's decision to attack and to his subsequent repulse in the battle of Kernstown

on 23 March 1862. Afterward, some of Ashby's cavalry became demoralized. Discipline was lax and the companies operated as semi-independent commands with control exercised by individual captains, some of whom were incompetent. Federal troops captured one company of sixty men and mounts, and they came on another company hors de combat ("out of the fight") on applejack and quickly scattered it.

Under pressure from Richmond and believing Ashby a poor disciplinarian who attached little importance to drill, Jackson dispersed Ashby's cavalry within his command. An angry Ashby then threatened to resign. Despite Ashby's shortcomings, Jackson could ill afford to lose him. He was invaluable in scouting in front or commanding the rear guard, only he could hold the diverse cavalry units together, and his bravery in battle was an important example for the army. Ashby's men boasted that within a single month he had engaged the Federals on twenty-eight separate occasions. So, following a private meeting between the two men on 24 April 1862, Jackson relented and restored the whole of the cavalry to Ashby's command. Having promised Jackson that he would discipline his men, Ashby now fought harder than ever, and Jackson was instrumental in securing his promotion to brigadier general on 23 May.

Late in the afternoon on 6 June, two miles south of Harrisonburg, Virginia, Ashby was leading several companies of infantry on foot in a rear-guard action against Union troops. He had just shouted, "Forward, my brave men!" when he was struck and killed by a Union bullet. Jackson, who received the news at Port Republic, was visibly shaken by it. He later observed of Ashby, "As a partisan officer I never knew his superior; his daring was proverbial; his powers of endurance almost incredible; his tone of character heroic; and his sagacity almost intuitive in divining the purpose and movements of the enemy." Ashby's death was indeed a heavy blow to Jackson's army.

—*Spencer C. Tucker*

See also Cavalry, C.S.A.; Jackson, Thomas J.; Kernstown, Battle of; Shenandoah Valley Campaign.
For further reading:
Freeman, Douglas Southall. "Manassas to Malvern Hill." In *Lee's Lieutenants: A Study in Command*, vol. 1 (1942–1944).

ASHLEY, JAMES MITCHELL
(1824–1896)
U.S. congressman

Born to John C. Ashley and Mary Kilpatrick Ashley in Allegheny County, Pennsylvania, James Mitchell Ashley received no formal schooling. His father was a circuit minister, and by traveling with his father into the upper South, the younger Ashley saw slavery firsthand. As a teenager, he left home for life aboard a steamboat on the Ohio River, first as a crew member and then as a clerk for the company. After leaving that job, he traveled throughout the South, where he developed a strong abhorrence of the institution of slavery. He frequently spoke out against the institution during his travels, a habit that caused him to be forced out of the state of Virginia.

Returning north, Ashley took up residence in Ohio, where he became a printer and then a journalist. At the same time, Ashley began the study of law and entered into several business pursuits. His antislavery views also led him into Ohio politics, starting as a Democrat, then as a member of the Free Soil Party, and soon after its founding, as a member of the Republican Party. He served as an Ohio delegate in 1856 to the first Republican National Convention, where he supported the candidacy of John C. Frémont. In 1858, Ashley was elected from Toledo to the U.S. House of Representatives.

Ashley served five consecutive terms in Congress during which time he introduced a number of controversial measures and gained a reputation as one of that body's more eccentric members. Early in his congressional career he took up the unpopular issue of civil rights for African-Americans, believing that the best place for the federal government to address this issue was in the territories. Eventually rising to the position of chairman of the Committee on Territories, he used that forum to urge legislation on that issue.

From the very beginning of the Civil War, Ashley championed treating the seceded states harshly as punishment for rebelling against the legal government. Many of the measures he advocated for the reconstruction of the Union were embodied in the Wade-Davis Bill in 1864 and later enacted in the Reconstruction Acts of 1867.

During the war, Ashley quickly became a vocal part of that group of congressional representatives known as the Radical Republicans. He saw the war as an opportunity to end the evil of slavery and worked tirelessly during the conflict to bring about that goal. In the spring of 1862, he helped sponsor the bill that ultimately abolished slavery in Washington, D.C., and was a guiding force behind what would become the Thirteenth Amendment to the Constitution, which abolished slavery in the United States. Ashley was also an early advocate of African-American suffrage and worked to make such a measure a part of the reconstruction legislation introduced in Congress in 1864.

During the war, Ashley frequently corresponded with those officers he considered right-minded on the political issues of the day. He supported the resolution of Congress that recommended that officers not be required to return runaway slaves. He also sought to determine through his contacts in the army how many officers supported the issues espoused by the Radical Republicans and what preponderance of George McClellan supporters the army still contained, particularly in later phases of the war.

After the war, Ashley quickly became a vocal opponent of the new president, Andrew Johnson. Ashley developed a theory that indicated that Johnson had been directly involved in the assassination of Abraham Lincoln. He based this supposition on his belief that every previous vice president who had become president because of the death of a president had been involved in that death. To him John Tyler had conspired to kill William Henry Harrison, Millard Fillmore had been involved in the death of Zachary Taylor, and therefore it followed that Andrew Johnson was implicated in the death of Abraham Lincoln. Besides the fact that Ashley opposed Johnson's lenient reconstruction plan for the South, he believed that Johnson was a conspirator in murder as well.

In December 1866, before the new, more radical Congress that had been elected the month before took its seat, Ashley introduced a resolution in Congress that a committee be appointed to determine charges for impeachment of Andrew Johnson. Though the measure failed at that time, Ashley was among that group of Radical Republicans who were determined to return articles of impeachment against Johnson as soon as the new Congress was seated. Perhaps the most dogged of the group, Ashley introduced the early measures that resulted in the articles that brought Johnson to trial in the Senate.

Ashley's singlemindedness on this issue discredited him somewhat in the eyes of his constituents when Johnson was acquitted, and Ashley was defeated for reelection in 1868. His loyalty to that cause, however, was rewarded in 1869 when the new president, Ulysses S. Grant, appointed Ashley territorial governor of Montana. Early in Grant's administration, however, Ashley openly criticized some of the president's decisions and was removed from his governorship in 1870. His opposition to Grant led him to join the Liberal Republicans in 1872 and attend as a delegate that group's convention the same year. This participation was his last major political activity. He returned to business pursuits in Toledo, where he became one of the founders and ultimately president of the Toledo, Ann Arbor & Northern Michigan Railroad. Ashley retired in 1893 and died in Toledo on 16 September 1896.

—*David S. Heidler and Jeanne T. Heidler*

See also Congress, U.S.A.; Radical Republicans; Wade-Davis Bill.

For further reading:
Horowitz, Robert F. *The Great Impeacher: A Political Biography of James M. Ashley* (1979).
Trefousse, Hans Louis. *Impeachment of a President; Andrew Johnson, the Blacks, Reconstruction* (1975).

ATCHISON, DAVID RICE
(1807–1886)
United States senator

David Rice Atchison left his native state of Kentucky shortly after graduating from Transylvania University in 1825 to practice law in Liberty, Missouri. During the 1830s and early 1840s, Atchison gained prominence as a Democratic state legislator, circuit court judge, and militia officer. In 1843 he was appointed to fill a vacancy in the U.S. Senate and continued to represent Missouri there for the next thirteen years.

In Congress, Atchison rose to a position of power and influence. He was highly regarded by his colleagues, who elected him president pro tempore of the Senate sixteen times between 1846 and 1854. An advocate of territorial expansion, Atchison pushed for American annexation of Texas in 1845 and occupation of the Oregon Country in 1846, and he supported President James K. Polk's expansionist aims during the Mexican-American War. He likewise advocated the extension of slavery, insisting that Southern slaveholders had a constitutional right to carry their peculiar institution into the nation's territorial possessions. Thus, he strenuously opposed the Wilmot Proviso, which was intended to outlaw slavery in the Mexican Cession. He also objected to the Compromise of 1850, seeing in it no sufficient guarantees for Southern slave property in the territories. Amid these controversies, Atchison gravitated to the militant Southern rights movement led by John C. Calhoun, with its doctrine of unobstructed slavery expansion. Following Calhoun's death, Atchison emerged as the most outspoken champion of Southern rights in the Senate.

The territorial issue divided the Democratic Party in Missouri and provided the backdrop for the state's 1850 Senate race, which pitted Atchison against his hated rival, Thomas Hart Benton. Though Benton had long reigned as chief potentate of Missouri's Democracy, he had lost popular support after the Mexican-American War by favoring congressional restrictions against slavery in the territories. Running on the strength of his Southern rights credentials, Atchison was able to win the election and deny his nemesis a sixth term in the Senate.

In Washington Atchison was part of an influential bloc of Southern senators that included Andrew P. Butler of South Carolina and Virginians James M. Mason and Robert M. T. Hunter. Dubbed the "F Street Mess" because they lodged in the same boardinghouse on F Street, the foursome composed the Capitol's most formidable proslavery phalanx. In 1853–1854 Atchison and his messmates led Southern opposition to the organization of Nebraska Territory as free soil. As a precondition for organization they demanded unimpeded access for slaveowners through the repeal of the Missouri Compromise (which would have banned slavery from the territory). Thus, Atchison had a key role in framing the provisions of the Kansas-Nebraska Act that rescinded the 36 degree 30 minute parallel of latitude restriction on slavery, while opening the new territories to slaveholders on the basis of popular sovereignty.

Thereafter Atchison labored intensively to bring Kansas into the Union as a slave state. In 1855–1856 (while still a member of the Senate), he had a direct hand in fomenting violent confrontation in "Bleeding Kansas" as the head the Missouri border ruffians, proslavery posses who rode across the Kansas border to bully and harass free-soil settlers there. These guerrilla bands also used fraud and intimidation to rig elections, hoping to create a proslavery territorial government, despite the free-soil sentiments of most Kansas residents. When free-soil elements ultimately prevailed, Atchison left politics and retired to his Missouri home and farm.

With the advent of the Civil War, Atchison warmly embraced the Confederate cause and was active in the failed secession movement led by Missouri's governor, Claiborne F. Jackson. When Jackson established a rump secessionist government loyal to the Confederacy, Atchison acted as an intermediary with Confederate authorities, appealing to President Jefferson Davis—a former colleague in the Senate—for official recognition of the state's pro-Southern government. After the battle of Pea Ridge, Arkansas, in March 1862, which left Missouri under firm Union control, Atchison moved to Grayson County, Texas. There he spent the balance of the war in relative obscurity. He returned to Missouri in 1867, settling in Clinton County. Aside from taking part in occasional speaking engagements, Atchison made no effort to revive his public career in postbellum years. He neither sought political office nor resumed his law practice, preferring instead to devote his energies solely to agricultural pursuits.

—*Eric Tscheschlok*

See also Kansas; Kansas-Nebraska Act; Missouri; Popular Sovereignty.

For further reading:

Parrish, William E. *David Rice Atchison of Missouri, Border Politician* (1961).

Potter, David M. *The Impending Crisis, 1848–1861* (1976).

Rawley, James A. *Race and Politics: "Bleeding Kansas" and the Coming of the Civil War* (1969).

ATLANTA CAMPAIGN
(May–September 1864)

In the early spring of 1864, Union major general William Tecumseh Sherman saw that Georgia, and Atlanta specifically, held the key to bringing the war to an end. Confederate General Robert E. Lee's forces in Virginia, the main focus of the war to that point, were able to hold the Union forces away from Richmond

Fortifications at Atlanta, 1864 (*Library of Congress*)

largely because of the supplies that flowed steadily up from the transportation and logistical center of Atlanta.

With Lieutenant General Ulysses S. Grant's blessing, Sherman set about building an overwhelming force from his headquarters in Chattanooga, Tennessee, a little more than 100 miles northwest of Atlanta. Other Union commands were asked to supply what men they could spare, and by late April 1864, three grand armies with more than 98,000 men stood ready to invade Georgia. A steady stream of reinforcements brought this force to more than 112,000 by June. To oppose him stood Confederate general Joseph Eggleston Johnston with but a single grand army of just two corps' strength, numbering just under 50,000 men. Reinforcements from Alabama, including Major General Leonidas Polk's entire corps and other commands not then under direct siege, bolstered Johnston's total strength to three corps with just under 65,000 men by late June.

Besides being understaffed and underequipped, Johnston faced an equally serious situation. His own combatant forces would be forced to protect the railroads leading to and from Atlanta and keep their own supply lines intact. One key factor lay in their favor, however: Johnston was a master of defensive strategy, rarely successful in the advance, but almost supernatural in his ability to know the exact moment to withdraw, just at the point where fierce resistance would damage his enemy the most while keeping his own forces intact. Unusual for a combat commander, he was also a humanist who deeply cared about his men and sought to minimize casualties even at the advantage of the enemy. Johnston had another serious disadvantage, the enmity of Confederate president Jefferson Davis, who blamed him for the loss of Vicksburg the previous summer and all too readily listened to whomever had a complaint about his tactics.

On 7 May 1864, the Union forces marched out of Chattanooga and the Ringgold area toward the southeast, through Tunnel Hill and just to the west of Dalton. The Atlanta campaign would consist of nine individual battles or local campaigns, as well as nearly five months of unbroken skirmishes and small actions.

About thirty miles southeast of Chattanooga, Dalton was shielded from a direct advance by a long, shear cliff face locally known as Rocky Face Ridge and called the "Georgian Gibraltar" by Union troops. Three gaps in the otherwise foreboding mountain ridge were large enough to allow an army to pass through in a reasonable amount of time, but they could be easily blockaded with a relatively small force of infantry and artillery.

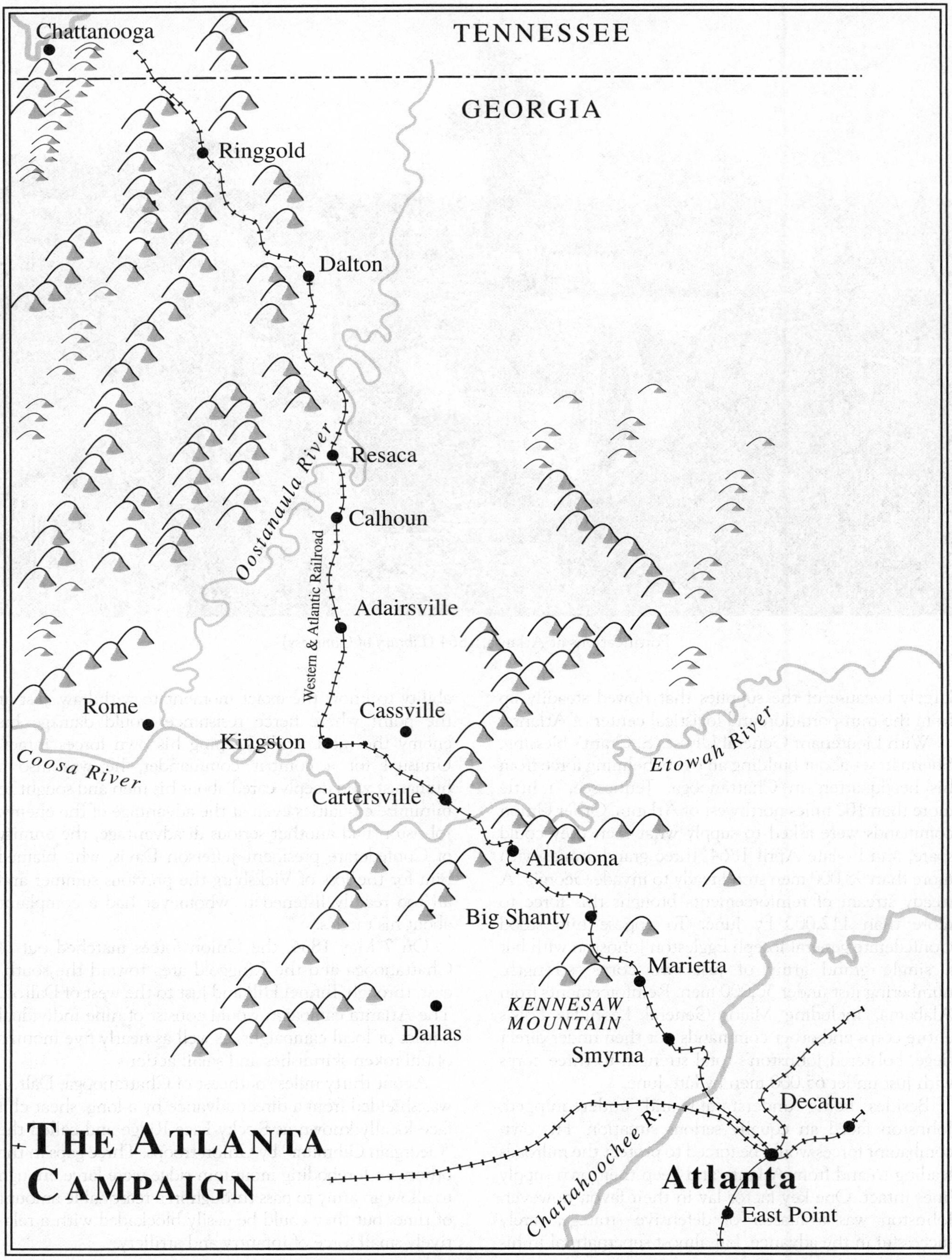

TENNESSEE

GEORGIA

Chattanooga

Ringgold

Dalton

Resaca

Calhoun

Oostanaula River

Western & Atlantic Railroad

Adairsville

Rome

Cassville

Kingston

Coosa River

Cartersville

Etowah River

Allatoona

Big Shanty

Marietta

KENNESAW MOUNTAIN

Dallas

Smyrna

Decatur

Chattahoochee R.

THE ATLANTA CAMPAIGN

Atlanta

East Point

Sherman had explored most of this area while on detached duty in Marietta in 1844 and recalled the lay of the land in great detail. Johnston's army could be trapped by the rocky ridge that was then their refuge if Union forces could get to the level open ground between it and Atlanta. Sherman sent two of his armies to distract Johnston by a strong direct assault at the northernmost gap, Mill Creek, while his third army slipped through the southernmost gap, Snake Creek, to cut off Johnston's retreat to Resaca.

Johnston expected that Sherman would merely feint toward Dalton and then race south to try and cut Confederate forces off from the rail line to Atlanta. Consequently, Johnston ordered preparation of defensive works on "good ground" seventeen miles south, just north and west of Resaca. In addition, he ordered a series of "military roads" prepared between the two positions, so that he could rapidly shuttle his troops into the new positions when Sherman made his move.

On 8 May 1864, having received notice from his cavalry scouts that Sherman's forces were on the march toward him, Johnston positioned Lieutenant General John Bell Hood's army corps on top of the ridgeline and across Crow Valley to Pickett Top and refused southward over Hamilton Mountain directly north of Dalton. William J. Hardee's corps took up positions just to the west of Dalton, directly on top of the impressive ridgeline. The Confederate line here snaked along roughly five miles of hill and valley, forming an almost fishhook shape with Rocky Face Ridge as the shank and Dalton just below the point. A detached division guarded the railway just to the northeast of Dalton, and a smaller detachment took up post above Dug Gap, two miles below the city.

Union major general George H. Thomas's Army of the Cumberland moved down the railway from Ringgold on 8 May and took up a position just to the west of Mill Creek Gap, while Major General John M. Schofield's Army of the Ohio moved in from the north and took up a position across Crow Valley. The distraction caused by these highly visible movements and the ridgeline screening him from the Confederate positions allowed Union major general James Birdseye McPherson to march the Army of the Tennessee quickly south through Snake Creek Gap.

Later that day, two small demonstrations were mounted by the Union troops against the strong Confederate position just south of Mill Creek Gap and against the weaker position at Dug Gap. The attack at Mill Creek nearly turned into a full battle, with part of Oliver O. Howard's IV Army Corps actually making it to the top of the northern end of the ridgeline before being violently repulsed. Both attacks were ultimately unsuccessful, though the attack at Dug Gap degenerated at one point into hand-to-hand combat, actually a compar-

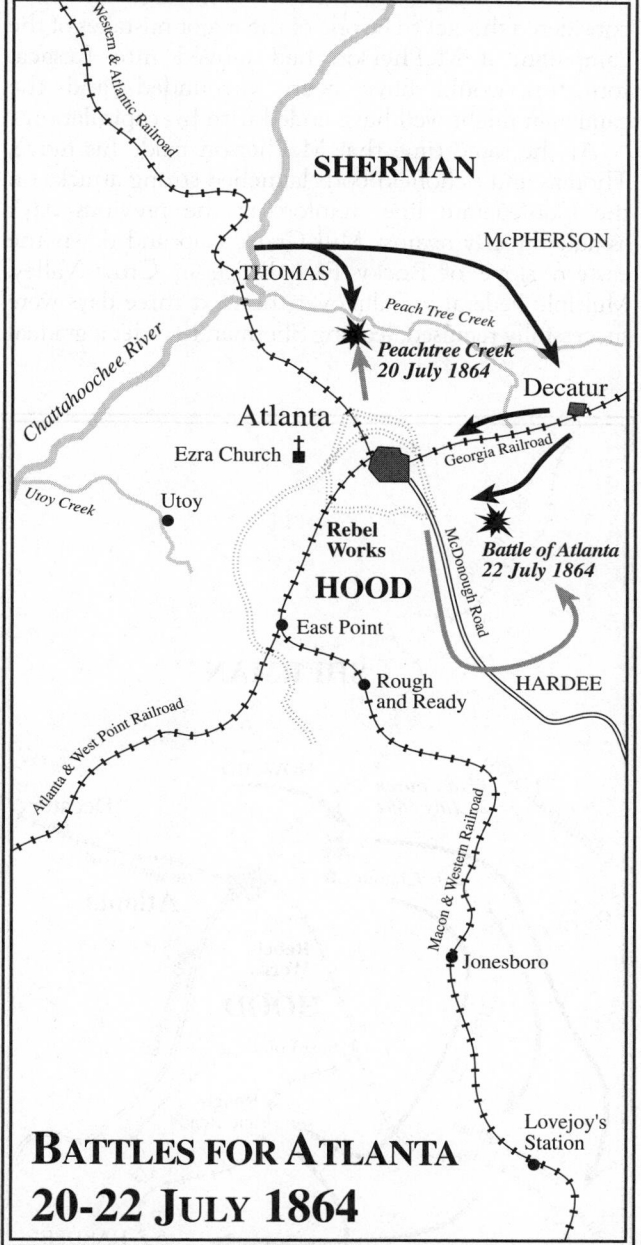

BATTLES FOR ATLANTA 20-22 JULY 1864

atively rare event during the war, and featured the Confederates at one point rolling large boulders down the steep mountainside at the onrushing Union force.

Early in the morning of 9 May, McPherson's men emerged from Snake Creek Gap and marched quickly toward Resaca, but the sight of Confederate cavalry and infantry troops in the area along with the well-prepared roads gave McPherson pause. Afraid that he would be caught in the open ground and unsure just how strong a force he was facing at that moment (less than one division of infantry and a few cavalry), McPherson became unusually cautious and elected to withdraw and

entrench at the mouth of Snake Creek Gap. Sherman considered this act to be one of the major mistakes of the campaign; if McPherson had moved into Resaca, Johnston would have been surrounded, and the campaign might well have ended with his capitulation.

At the same time that McPherson made his move, Thomas and Schofield both launched strong attacks on the Confederate line, reinforcing the previous day's assault directly against Mill Creek Gap and down the eastern slope of Rocky Face Ridge in Crow Valley. Multiple Federal assaults over the next three days were successfully repulsed, leading Sherman to order a gradual

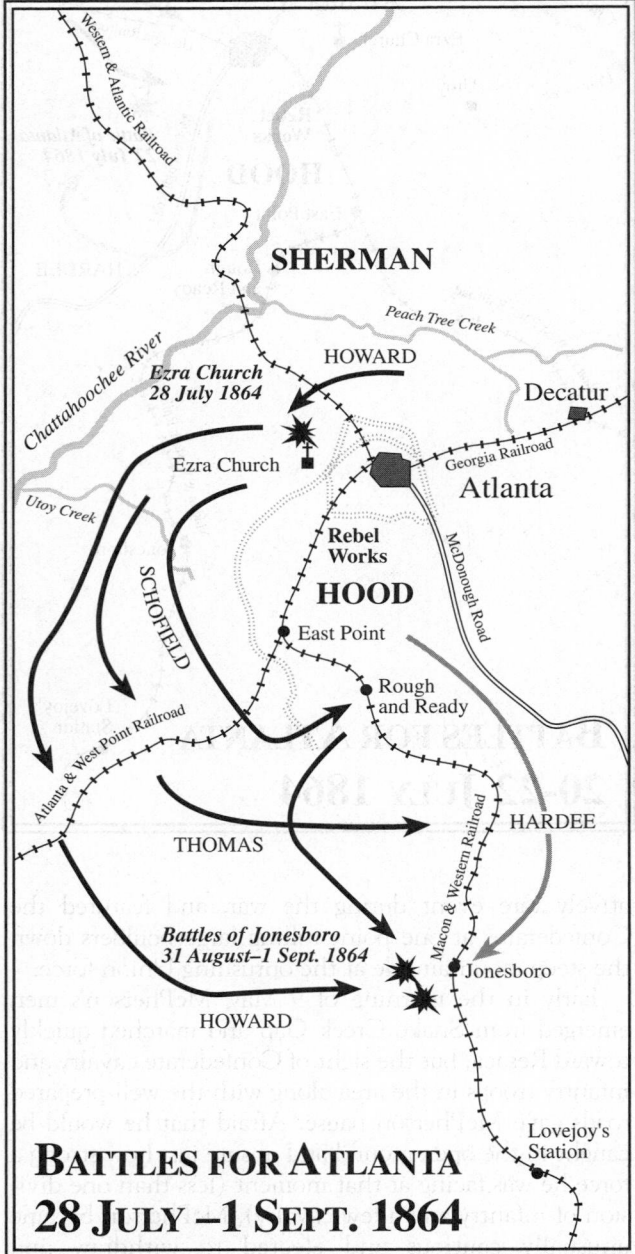

BATTLES FOR ATLANTA
28 JULY –1 SEPT. 1864

withdrawal of forces from the fight to follow McPherson's route down to Resaca. Johnston fully expected this, and by the afternoon of 11 May, while the battle was still fully under way, he began ordering his units also to break off gradually and march to their prepared positions outside Resaca. By midnight on the 12th, nearly all his army had moved south, staying intact as fighting units and taking all their supplies with them.

Resaca was the only site of the campaign, where all the armies of both sides clashed at the same battle-ground. The small hamlet of Resaca straddled a single rail line running almost due north-south. Johnston was tied to the railroad both by the need to protect his avenue of supply and to prevent Sherman from acquiring a speedy approach to Atlanta.

The area around Resaca was primarily farm fields and other open areas surrounded by thick woods with an abundance of entangling underbrush. Johnston's defensive position had two major weaknesses. First, to the rear of his lines was the Oostanaula River, making a hasty withdrawal nearly impossible. Second, the railroad he had to defend lay nearly underfoot and all along the Confederate line, also limiting his chances for tactical maneuver. His advantage was chiefly that his forces were in close proximity and well protected on his flanks by the river.

Sherman placed his forces in a semicircle that was anchored by the river on the right and curved around to face the northernmost Confederates directly. His position had little immediate advantage over the Confederate line, but units traveling through Snake Creek Gap quickly reinforced it.

Johnston's plan—to defend the river and rail line from heavily fortified positions—was clear. Sherman's purpose was less so. Starting early on the afternoon of 13 May, Union forces mounted uncoordinated and seemingly random attacks against the Confederate left, right, center, and the right again on the morning of the 15th. The incredibly rough terrain before the Confederate lines blunted most of these assaults as much as armed resistance did. On the afternoon of 14 May, an attack on the bend of the Confederate line was Brigadier General Henry M. Judah's 2d Division, XIII Corps, and Brigadier General Absalom Baird's 3d Division, XIV Corps, nearly annihilated by coordinated artillery and long-range rifle fire. It had only taken a few minutes for the Federals to lose more than 600 men even before they could move through the muck. Judah was dismissed from the army four days later for his alleged incompetence during the battle.

The unsuccessful Union assaults failed to push back the Confederate line at all. Several divisions of Hood's army corps stepped out on the late afternoon of 15 May in a counterattack on the Union left, but were withdrawn after Johnston learned of the only Union success of the

Camp of the 2d Massachusetts Infantry on the grounds of the Atlanta City Hall, 1864
(Photograph by George N. Barnard / *Library of Congress*)

battle: Brigadier General Thomas W. Sweeney's 2d Division (Major General Grenville M. Dodge's XVI Army Corps) had crossed the Oostanaula River a few miles south at Lay's Ferry and was threatening to cut the railroad and block the Confederate line of retreat. Within hours Johnston had evacuated his forces intact across the river and was marching south toward Cassville, destroying all bridges behind him. The last, the railroad bridge just below Resaca, was set afire at 3:30 A.M.

Johnston, ever the wily strategist, came up with a unique plan while pulling back from Resaca on the night of 15 May. He would send Hardee's corps with most of the army's supply wagons and ambulances straight through Adairsville to Kingston, fifteen miles down the main road. Meanwhile, Hood's and Polk's corps moved down a little-used route to the small town of Cassville, just ten miles away. To ensure the safety of the supply train, Major General Benjamin F. Cheatham's division was placed across the road about three miles north of Adairsville. Hood and Polk were ordered to march rapidly and "tightly"—to give the appearance that only a small force had passed down their path—and to be ready to launch a sudden counterattack when the unsuspecting Union forces appeared.

Sherman followed Johnston southward, delayed by the long river crossings necessary for his large force and by an almost comical spat between Schofield and Major General Joseph Hooker over which one had the right of way on the narrow roads. The Union forces had not paused to regroup after raking the Resaca battleground. They headed south with McPherson's Army of the Tennessee wide to the Union right, Thomas's Army of the Cumberland marching straight down the railway, and Schofield's Army of the Ohio (also known as and consisting only of the XXIII Army Corps) wide to the left. Expecting Johnston to make a stand at Adairsville, Sherman ordered his widely separated columns to close together just north of the small crossroads town. The lead elements of the Union force arrived in Adairsville after a brief but spirited skirmish with Cheatham's division on the morning of 18 May.

Sherman was apparently deceived by the Confederate diversionary tactic. Eager to engage Johnston before the Confederate force reached good defensive ground south of the Etowah River, Sherman hastily pushed all his units except Hooker's XX and Schofield's XXIII Army Corps down the single road to Kingston. These two corps were ordered down the road to Cassville, to protect the flank of the main Union column.

Just to the west of the main Union line of advance, a single infantry division commanded by Union brigadier general Jefferson C. Davis (2d Division, XIV Army Corps) and supported by Brigadier General Kenner Garrard's 2d Cavalry Division marched in and captured the important industrial center of Rome on 18 May after a one-day battle with Confederate major general Samuel G. French's division.

At Cassville, Johnston ordered Polk to place his corps across the road about one-half mile northeast of the town square, with Hood's corps positioned about one mile east and parallel to the road, so as to hit the Union flank as it approached. On the morning of 19 May, just as Schofield's corps was walking into the trap, a small unit of Union cavalry led from the east by Brigadier General Edward M. McCook stumbled into Hood's troops and a brief skirmish erupted. Fearful that McCook was supported by infantry, Hood suddenly pulled back from his ambush position to one facing east, supporting Polk's right. Johnston believed that the chance for surprise was lost and ordered both corps to a low range of hills southeast of the town.

Hood defended his overreaction to the end of his life, insisting that he had infantry to his rear and that he would have been unable to launch his attack on the main column of Union troops on the Cassville road. Surprisingly enough, he was partly correct; close behind McCook were two brigades of Union infantry supported by a single battery of horse artillery wandering around lost. They were looking for a road leading into the east side of Cassville when they ran into the rear column of Hood's corps.

On the Confederate left, Hardee put up a stiff resistance against the massed Union forces near Kingston, but shortly after the Cassville disaster, and at the urging of Hood and Polk, Johnston ordered all forces to disengage and withdraw south of the Etowah River and into the Allatoona Mountains. Johnston's forces finally halted about eleven miles southeast of Cassville and set up a strong defensive position around the railroad gap at Allatoona Pass, just northwest of the small town of Acworth. As usual, Johnston ordered the railroad bridge across the Etowah burned as they retreated. Sherman moved in and occupied Cassville and Kingston, giving his men a few days to rest while he studied the ground ahead.

Sherman had ridden the area around Allatoona extensively as a young officer assigned to Marietta; he knew the potential for making the gap into a natural fortress. Changing tactics, he abandoned his line of march straight down the railroad and moved westward, toward the small town of Dallas. It is not clear whether he was trying to pull Johnston behind him into more open terrain (which is doubtful) or whether he was trying to take a more western approach into Atlanta. The real danger for Sherman was that, by abandoning the railroad, he was lengthening his own supply column, making it more vulnerable to a rear attack by Johnston's troops and cavalry.

Ordered up and out by buglers on the morning of 22 May, the three grand armies moved out of camp at Cassville and Kingston in their usual three columns. Thomas and Schofield moved nearly due south while McPherson swung far to the right in order to approach Dallas from due west. The huge columns of massed Union infantry in a front nearly twenty miles wide were hard to conceal, and the move west was soon discovered by Confederate major general Joseph Wheeler's cavalry corps. By the afternoon of 23 May, Johnston ordered Hardee to good defensive ground just east of Dallas and Polk at a tiny crossroads nearby called New Hope. Hood remained entrenched at Allatoona Pass overnight and then was ordered to New Hope when Johnston realized that all the Union forces were headed toward Dallas. On his arrival, Polk shifted his men slightly to the west, tying in with Hardee and forming a strong defensive line nearly four miles long from directly south of Dallas to one mile east of New Hope.

Hood scurried into line just before the forward Union skirmishers and scouts came into view. Confederate major general Carter L. Stevenson's division set up on the right, Major General Thomas C. Hindman's division set up on the higher ground on the left, and Major General Alexander P. Stewart's division deployed directly in front of the small, log New Hope Church in the center. Just before 10:00 A.M. on 25 May, Confederate skirmishers encountered the forward elements of Hooker's XX Army Corps rapidly marching toward New Hope. They attempted to burn a bridge over Pumpkinvine Creek to set up a delaying action, but were quickly overrun by Union brigadier general John W. Geary's 2d Division.

Warned that action was imminent, Stewart deployed his men in line astride the crossroads, ordering them to dig in as rapidly as possible. Brigadier General Marcellus Stovall's Georgia Brigade was positioned on an open hilltop in the church's graveyard and was unable or unwilling to dig in at all, but Brigadier General Henry D. Clayton's and Brigadier General Alpheus Baker's Alabama Brigades in the center and right of the line threw up hasty works of felled trees and earthen embankments. Sixteen guns from Captain McDonald Oliver's Eufaula Alabama and Captain Charles E. Fenner's Louisiana Batteries were massed within Stewart's roughly one-half mile front.

Sherman ordered Hooker to push through what he believed was a small force and march directly on to Dallas, remarking that "There haven't been twenty rebels there today" to the front of him. Just before 4:00 P.M., a severe thunderstorm started to blow in over the New Hope area. Marching steadily on through the mounting wind and pounding thunder came Geary's 2d Division, with Major General Daniel Butterfield's 3d

Federal soliders relax in a captured Confederate fort near Atlanta, 1864
(Photograph by George N. Barnard / *Library of Congress*)

Battery M, 5th U.S. Artillery, manning a captured Confederate fort near Atlanta, 1864 (*Library of Congress*)

Division to his left and Brigadier General Alpheus S. Williams's 1st Division on his right, all spread across a one-half mile front in column formation and unknowingly beating down directly on the massed Confederate front of Stewart's division.

Just after 5:00 P.M., as Geary's skirmishers drove back Hood's, Union buglers sounded out the call to go forward double-quick. Stumbling and falling through the thick brush and unable to see what lay ahead, the men from Ohio, Pennsylvania, and New York hoped to brush straight through what they believed was a weak line of Confederate militia and detached infantry brigades. Just as the monsoon-force rains began, Williams's men broke out of the thickest part of the woods and rushed straight for the Confederate line.

Stewart had wisely ordered the artillery to load with double-canister and had positioned his 4,000 men nearly shoulder to shoulder on a very tight front, anticipating quite accurately that Hooker would be compacted in heavy infantry formations on his approach. As lightning crackled all around and sheets of rain poured down, the shouting mass of more than 16,000 blue-coated infantry burst into sight less than 100 feet in front of Stewart's lines. Immediately the Confederate line opened up and disappeared again in a thick cloud of bluish gray rifle and cannon smoke. Williams's men took the brunt of the concentrated fire, losing most of their more than 800 casualties in the first ten minutes of battle.

For more than three hours, this one-sided slaughter went on, into the dark and stormy evening. Geary, Butterfield, and Williams all ordered repeated assaults, trying to break through what was obviously the main Confederate army line, only to be thrown back each time by murderous artillery and rifle fire. Stewart's Confederate forces started running out of ammunition, the sixty round per man standard issue being depleted in as little as thirty minutes in some cases. Stewart brought his reserve forces in line primarily for their ammunition supply, and runners searched the wounded and dead for any extra cartridges. Hooker finally admitted defeat about 7:30 P.M., pulling his men back a short distance to dig in for the night.

Throughout the long night, as Union men dug in with shovels, bayonets, tin cups, or bare hands, sporadic rifle and artillery fire broke out, but no further assaults by either side were mounted. Hooker's command lost more than 1,600 men in the short fight. (Most references support this figure, but one source claims less than 700.) Confederate losses amounted to "between 300 and 400" as reported by Stewart. One bitter Union infantryman remarked that Hooker had sent them into a "hell hole;" the name sticks as a common reference to the brutal fight there and at Pickett's Mill.

After the blow he received at New Hope Church, Sherman returned to his standard tactic of rapid flanking maneuver and ordered three divisions under the direct

command of Howard to the far left in an attempt to turn the Confederate right. Johnston soon learned of the flanking attempt and ordered two divisions to shift to the right of Hood's line, covering the probable Union line of attack. To the far right of the newly extended Confederate line was one of Johnston's best, Major General Patrick R. Cleburne's division, taking up positions on a hilltop overlooking the small settlement of Pickett's Mill.

Although his scouts reported fresh earthworks and Howard himself rode forward and observed gray-uniformed troops moving in on the hill before them, the Union commander was somewhat convinced that he had reached the flank or rear of the Confederate line of battle and possibly believed that only a small picket outpost was entrenching. His uncertainty is obvious in a message sent about 3:30 P.M., "I am now turning the enemy's right flank, I think." Just after noon on 27 May, Howard brought his three divisions in line of attack on a hilltop just north of the small mill community, again forming the men into the same narrow, deep, heavy infantry formations that had failed so miserably two days earlier at New Hope Church.

At this point, the Confederate line curved to the east following the ridgeline atop a low rounded hill overlooking a steep, densely overgrown ravine. As the battle unfolded, two brigades of Cleburne's force were shifted to the far right of the line, refusing at right angles to the line to prevent any possibility of being flanked.

At 4:30 P.M. the Union line, or at least most of it, stepped off into the thick, entangling underbrush. There were serious communication and land navigation problems, and one brigade ended up marching completely away from the growing sounds of battle, "to get rations." That particular brigade's commander, Brigadier General Nathaniel McLean of Kentucky, was a political enemy of Howard and on this day chose a particularly poor way of demonstrating his contempt.

Howard's leading brigade, Brigadier General William B. Hazen's 2d Brigade (Brigadier General Thomas J. Wood's 3d Division, Howard's IV Army Corps), easily drove away the Confederate pickets and moved into the ravine. The growth was so thick that the colors had to be encased to prevent them from being torn to pieces, and Hazen was forced to resort to his compass to stay moving in the right direction. Emerging suddenly in an open field, his troops first encountered a weak skirmish line of about 1,000 dismounted cavalrymen from Confederate brigadier general John Kelly's and Brigadier General William Hume's cavalry divisions, who they mistook as unentrenched infantry. Steadily overpowering the cavalrymen, Hazen's men rushed cheering across the open ground upward to what they thought was an undefended rocky ridgeline. Just before the Union infantry gained the heights, Confederate brigadier

general Hiram M. Granbury's Texas Brigade suddenly stood up and began pouring a galling fire into the face of the onrushing line.

Hazen's men kept up the pressure, although suffering appalling casualties from a two-gun battery (Confederate captain Thomas J. Key's Arkansas battery) to their right at the point of the ravine and from two more regiments rushing in to support Granbury, Colonel George Baucum's 8th Brigade, 19th Arkansas Consolidated Regiment, to his left and Brigadier General Mark P. Lowrey's Alabama-Mississippi Brigade to his right. Hazen managed to stay in the fight for about fifty minutes before being forced to withdraw, leaving his more than 500 wounded and dead in place in the open ravine.

As Hazen withdrew, Union colonel William H. Gibson's 1st Brigade advanced over nearly the same ground and met the same fate. Far from hitting a weakened Confederate line, as 3d Division commander Brigadier General Thomas J. Wood had hoped, Gibson's men advanced as far as the Confederate line itself before being thrown violently back. Roughly an hour of combat resulted in nothing more than an additional 687 Union casualties. Another brigade, Union colonel Frederick Knefler's 3d, was sent in about 6:30 P.M. to cover Gibson's retreat and to recover as many wounded as possible. They too were subjected to intense, nearly point-blank fire from the Confederate positions as soon as they entered the entangled ravine.

The major assaults ended by 7:00 P.M., but occasional firefights erupted until 10:00 P.M., when Granbury was ordered to "clear his front." The Texans fixed bayonets and with wild rebel yells charged forward into the darkened ravine, killing or capturing many of the remaining Union troops. The remaining Union troops either "skedaddled" or "retreated in good order, with no pursuit [by the Texans] even being attempted," depending on whose account you read. Both sides encamped for the night after the firing died down about 11:00 P.M., their attention still fixed on the body-strewn battleground eerily lit up by dead pine trees set afire during the hot exchange.

Total Union losses for the day's action totaled 1,689 killed, wounded, captured, or missing; Cleburne reported 398 killed or wounded. This failed action so upset Sherman that he apparently "forgot" to mention it in both his official report and his postwar memoirs.

The following day, 28 May 1864, Sherman finally decided that this westward flanking movement was getting him nowhere. Short on rations, his lines stretched nearly to the breaking point trying to hold the entire five-mile line of battle from south of Dallas to northeast of Pickett's Mill, as well as the lines of communication necessary to protect the supply line back to the railroad north of Allatoona. He ordered a gradual shifting motion of the line back east toward

Kennesaw and Marietta and sent his cavalry to capture Allatoona Pass itself. Johnston soon learned of this movement and ordered an attack on the Union right, straight toward Dallas itself, but was repulsed with no positive effects on the Union movement, and at the cost of more than 600 casualties.

By 1 June, Sherman had begun massing his armies at Big Shanty (now called Kennesaw) and made preparations to strike straight for the Chattahoochee River. Between stood the twin peaks of Kennesaw Mountain and Johnston's entire combat force. Johnston initially arranged his 65,000 troops in a thin, ten-mile-long line of battle that stretched from Brushy Mountain on the east to Lost Mountain on the west, about three miles northwest of Kennesaw Mountain itself. This line was known as both the "Lost Mountain" and "First Kennesaw" line.

In the late morning of 14 June 1864, Johnston, accompanied by Hardee, Polk, and several other general officers, climbed to the crest of Pine Mountain, roughly in the center of the line. While observing their lines, they were spotted by a Union artillery battery, posted less than a half-mile away, which immediately opened fire. The first round scattered the distinguished crowd; the aging and slow General Leonidas Polk was struck directly in the chest by the second Parrott shot and killed instantly.

After heavy attacks on 14, 15, and 17 June, Johnston realized that his men were spread much too thin and withdrew quietly during the pitch black night and heavy rains of 18 June two miles to the southeast. There he heavily entrenched from the railroad to the right, up across Kennesaw Mountain, Little Kennesaw Mountain, and Pigeon Hill, and left over a low ridge later know as Cheatham Hill. This strong, compact six-mile-long "Kennesaw," or "Second Kennesaw," line was reinforced by artillery batteries placed on the heights and cavalry placed on both flanks. One Union officer noted that the natural barricade of the mountain seemed purposefully made to stop any attacking army. The sides facing the Union troops were steep and boulder-strewn, and most of the rest was covered with thick scrub. Confederate engineers cleared the peaks of trees and brush to serve as signal and artillery stations. The main entrenchments were at the proper military crests, with a series of screening entrenchments and fire pits before them at the mountain base.

Cannon were hauled by hand up the steep slopes, 100 men per gun pulling, tugging, and cursing all the way. Eventually, two four-gun batteries were established on Pigeon Hill, one four-gun battery on the north end of Big Kennesaw, another nearly on the peak, and nine guns atop Little Kennesaw. Before they were emplaced completely, firing erupted between them and newly arriving Union batteries. This was followed by a series of probing and skirmish actions by scattered Union infantry units.

Impatient as ever, Sherman soon saw that these probing actions were gaining nothing, so again he returned to his classic flanking moves. Hooker's XX and Schofield's XXIII Army Corps were sent on a sweeping movement to the south of the Kennesaw line to attempt to gain Marietta and cut off the Confederate line of retreat. Johnston's near supernatural ability to read Sherman's intentions came to his aid once again; through a pounding thunderstorm on the night of 21 June, Hood's entire corps marched from the far right of the line to the far left, consolidating and entrenching across the path of the approaching Union troops on Powder Springs Road, just west of Marietta.

As the Union troops probed and advanced down that road on the afternoon of 22 June, Hood suddenly decided to abandon his fairly strong defensive position and risk it all on a full-force assault. Hindman's division into the north and Stevenson's division on the left suddenly burst out of the thick woods into an open plain near the Kolb farm, straight into the massed rim of more than forty Union artillery pieces. The attack gained nothing, falling apart nearly before coming within rifle range of the hastily dug Union lines. The shattered remnants of Stevenson's division attempted to take refuge in a shallow creek bed, where they were continuously raked by artillery fire until able to pull back after dark.

With his probing actions indecisive and his flanking maneuver halted at Kolb farm, Sherman chose yet another tactic. Tiring of the constant way Johnston slipped out of his flanking attacks, and possibly hoping to destroy the Confederate Army of Tennessee in one huge battle, he issued the order for a direct assault on the entrenchments of the Kennesaw line itself, to begin at 8:00 A.M. on 27 June. McPherson was ordered to attack the southern side of the mountain, Thomas was ordered to attack south of the Dallas road in support of McPherson, and Schofield was directed to feint south of the Kolb farm area as a diversion.

At 9:00 A.M., three brigades of McPherson's corps stepped off, moving up into the steep slopes of Pigeon Hill, straight into the rocky fortifications. Surprisingly, some made it far enough to engage in hand-to-hand combat atop the entrenchments before being forced back under heavy artillery fire. Union losses in this futile attack were more than 850, with Confederate losses described as "about 250."

Thomas chose to attack a salient in the Confederate line nearly three miles south of Pigeon Hill, later famous as the Dead Angle. Believing that one mighty push would drive out the heavily entrenched Confederates of Cheatham's division, Thomas decided to use heavy infantry formations. The five attacking brigades each spread out across a 200-yard front (1,500 to 2,000 yards

The Atlanta railroad depot, 1864 (Photograph by George N. Barnard / *Library of Congress*)

was more nearly normal), with about ten yards between each brigade. The overwhelming fire from the Confederate line proved so intense that the ten-yard interval gradually closed until all five brigades ended up attacking as a single mass twelve ranks deep. An absolute slaughter ensued as every artillery piece and rifle within range concentrated on the 1,000-yard front line.

By nightfall, most Union units had been completely thrown back, those few left under some protection of the hilly terrain would stay within rock-throwing distance for the next six days and keep up a constant sniping harassment. The only gain of the entire day's action, ironically, was Schofield's diversionary attack to the south, which managed to get between Johnston's line and the Chattahoochee River while the Confederate forces were distracted by the main attack. Sherman was enraged over the failure to break the Confederate lines,

however, and seriously contemplated ordering further attacks the next day. Thomas brought him back to reality by informing him that "one or two more such assaults would use up this army." Sherman finally reported in a cable to Washington that night that his attack had failed and that he had suffered "about 3,000 casualties." Several reports dispute this figure, placing it closer to 7,000 or even 7,500. Confederate losses for the day were placed at just under 1,000.

After his stunning defeat at Kennesaw Mountain, Sherman required more than a week just to regroup and resupply his demoralized soldiers. On 1 July, he abandoned for good his frontal assault tactics on entrenchments and planned another flanking maneuver to the south and east, to try once again to bypass Johnston and gain Marietta. Johnston's scouts observed the huge army getting under way before any real progress could be made. With no real natural defensive barrier to help stop the numerically superior Union army, Johnston decided to abandon Marietta and fall back across the wide, shallow Chattahoochee River, burning or destroying whatever supplies and equipment Sherman might find useful along the way.

By the afternoon of 2 July, Johnston set up a new line of defense at the small town of Smyrna, just northwest of the Chattahoochee, while his main body crossed to the south bank. This line collapsed in less than a day of heavy skirmishing with forward elements of the Union line, and by the next afternoon Johnston pulled back to his last line of entrenchments north of the river.

Finding nearly all the ferries and pontoon bridges out due to the high water caused by weeks of heavy rains, and what bridges remaining either heavily defended or burned, Sherman was running out of options to find a crossing that would not result in losing most of his army in the muddy water. Garrard's 2d Division Cavalry (Brigadier General Washington Elliott's Cavalry Corps, Schofield's XXIII Army Corps) was sent about fifteen miles to the north and quickly captured the small town of Roswell, overlooking the Chattahoochee River. He found the bridge there burned, but discovered several spots nearby where the river could be safely forded. With Union major general George Stoneman's cavalry division ranging as far south as Sandtown, McPherson's corps feinting to the right, and Thomas's corps keeping the pressure on the river line, Schofield's corps was quickly moved up river on 8 July to find the best crossing site.

In the early afternoon of 9 July, finding a 300-yard-wide, relatively shallow spot over a submerged fish dam near Sope Creek (Soap Creek on some maps), Union colonel Daniel Cameron's 103d Ohio Infantry swam across to establish a beachhead. Encountering no opposition, Schofield then ordered a crossing in force at 3:30 that afternoon. Led by a combat amphibious assault by the 12th Kentucky Regiment under Union lieutenant colonel Laurence H. Rousseau, part of Colonel Robert K. Boyd's 3d (Kentucky) Brigade (the same brigade that had "withdrawn for rations" at Pickett's Mill), the crossing was an outstanding success. The only Confederates in the area were part of a small picket outpost, who got off only a single volley before running away.

By nightfall the entire division was across, and with the news of the Union on the south bank, Johnston decided that his only recourse was to retreat again. Abandoning the river line to Sherman, Johnston pulled his forces back south of Peachtree Creek, on the very doorstep of Atlanta itself. Without further resistance to his river crossing, Sherman paused only long enough to rebuild pontoon and railroad bridges before striking south again. On 11 July, McPherson was sent eastward toward Decatur and Stone Mountain, with orders to cut the railway between Atlanta and Augusta. Sherman's greatest fear at this point was that Johnston would receive reinforcements by rail from Lee's Army of Northern Virginia. Thomas was sent south toward Peachtree Creek, with Schofield marching just to his right headed toward Buckhead.

Johnston carefully noted the Union approach and planned to wait until close contact was established and then attack the gap between Thomas and Schofield before they were deployed for the fight. Before he could carry out this attack, Jefferson Davis carried out one of the worst decisions made during the war and fired Johnston. Late in the afternoon of 17 July, Hood was promoted to general and given command of the entire Army of Tennessee.

The day after Hood took command, Union infantrymen of Palmer's XIV Army Corps advanced through heavy resistance mounted by Wheeler's cavalry to the northern banks of Peachtree Creek, near Howell Mill Road. At just about the same time, Garrard's cavalry, supported by McPherson's infantry, reached the Georgia Railroad and captured the railroad depot at Stone Mountain, fifteen miles east of Atlanta. On 19 July, three brigades of Palmer's XIV Army Corps forced a crossing of Peachtree Creek toward Moore's Mill, followed by other crossings under fire by elements of Howard's IV Army Corps near Peachtree Road and Hooker's XX Army Corps near Collier Road. By nightfall the Union forces formed a solid line of blue-coated infantry on the south banks of Peachtree Creek itself, facing due south toward the Confederate line arranged atop low hills about one-half mile away.

Pleased with the progress of his subordinates, Sherman ordered Thomas to cross Peachtree Creek and engage Hood, Schofield to capture Decatur, and McPherson to advance toward Atlanta, tearing up the railroad tracks along the way. Obsessed with detail, Sherman sent word on exactly how he wanted the tracks torn up: "Pile the ties into shape for a bonfire, put the rails across and when red hot in the middle, let a man at each end twist the bar so that its surface becomes spiral."

Hood had a reputation as a battlefield brawler, and he wasted little time going on the offensive. A general attack was ordered at about 1:00 P.M. on 20 July, intended to drive the dug-in Union infantry back across the creek and as far as the banks of the Chattahoochee River. Before the attack could commence, Hood ordered the entire line to shift a little under one mile to the east to protect his right flank from counterattack. Although this movement threw the whole line into disarray and caused a general confusion about where to advance, Hood ordered the attack to begin at 4:00 P.M.

At about 2:45 P.M., Confederate major general William W. Loring's division (Stewart's corps) stepped off, almost immediately encountering Union infantry and mistakenly initiating battle in the center of the line.

Confederate major general William B. Bate's division of Hardee's corps, ordered to begin the general assault on the extreme right of the Confederate lines, did not actually move out until nearly one-half hour later. The rest of the two-mile-long line followed in piecemeal, advancing more in small groups and masses rather than well-formed lines, a result of the uneven terrain and thick underbrush.

The only real success of the entire assault was made by Confederate brigadier general Thomas M. Scott's brigade (Stewart' corps) of mostly Alabama troops, who advanced through the Tanyard Branch and Collier Road vicinity, attacking, driving off, and capturing the flag of Union colonel Patrick H. Jones's 33d New Jersey Infantry Regiment (Geary's 2d Division, Hooker's XX Army Corps), as well as a four-gun artillery battery. Scott's men were soon forced to withdraw, as no other unit was able to break through to support them on either flank.

No other unit made even that little of a success, and the entire attack was over with all units back in their original positions by 6:00 P.M. that evening. The well-positioned Union forces had badly mauled the advancing Confederates. Although the numbers engaged were fairly even with 21,450 Federals to 18,450 Confederates, casualties were much more one-sided, 1,780 Union to 4,800 Confederate. Hood's first outing as an army commander was a unqualified disaster.

To add insult to injury, shortly before noon of 20 July, four 20-pounder Parrott rifles of Union captain Francis De Gress set up and began firing the first of thousands of artillery shells into the Gate City itself. The first shell exploded at the intersection of Ivy and East Ellis Streets, killing a young girl who had been walking with her parents past Frank P. Rice's lumber dealership on the northwest corner. Shelling would continue for several weeks at the rate of one round every fifteen minutes. The bombardment posed more as a harassment and reminder of the siege than it did an attempt at destruction.

Before the fighting even died down at Peachtree Creek, Sherman was massing his forces for the next assault. McPherson's three corps were set in motion down the Georgia Railroad to attack Atlanta from the east, while Thomas and Schofield were ordered to close up and keep as much pressure on the Confederates as possible. By late in the day on 20 July, forward elements of Union major general Frank P. Blair's XVII Army Corps engaged Wheeler's dismounted cavalry on a small hilltop two miles to the east of Atlanta. Heavy combat erupted as the two lines collided, until the cavalrymen were overwhelmed and withdrew about midnight.

Realizing the tactical importance of the small hill, in the early morning of 21 July Blair sent in Union brigadier general Mortimer D. Leggett's 3d Division and Brigadier General Giles A. Smith's 4th Division against Cleburne's division, which had replaced the decimated cavalrymen. Cleburne's men spent the night reinforcing the hilltop position, but were unable to stop the Union assault. The Confederates withdrew slightly and then spent most of the rest of the day attempting to retake the hill. While the battle raged on, Blair ordered up his artillery and set the guns into newly reversed entrenchments, bringing Atlanta itself within good artillery range for the first time. In honor of his men's heroics, the hilltop was renamed Leggett's Hill, a name that the area still bears on some maps today.

Hood had no intention of pursuing the same sort of well-planned, but plodding and slow retreat that Johnston used. Instead he thought he saw an opportunity for offensive action against McPherson. Withdrawing Stewart's corps and the Georgia Militia to the strongly fortified positions in the outer ring of defenses around Atlanta, Hood ordered Hardee's corps on an all-night forced march. Moving due south down Peachtree Street through the middle of town (and panicking the civilians, who believe that their entire army was deserting them), they swung eastward toward Decatur, attempting to get behind Blair's corps lines before moving north into the line of battle. Cleburne's division withdrew with some difficulty from the action on Leggett's Hill and joined Hardee's march. At the same time, two divisions of Wheeler's cavalry were sent around the Union left flank, to attempt a strike at Federal supply wagons in Decatur.

Unknown to the Confederates, McPherson was worried that they would attempt this exact movement and had ordered his lines extended and turned to the south. Dodge's XVI Army Corps was ordered to Blair's left, facing southeast, where the men entrenched, as had become the norm. At McPherson's urging, Blair's men also heavily entrenched and blocked lanes of approach before them.

By the morning of 22 July, Hardee's men had trudged down the McDonough Road south of Atlanta and then turned to the northeast on the Fayetteville Road toward Decatur. Still trying to make up the time lost on the rest stops, Hardee ordered Cleburne's and Brigadier General George E. Maney's divisions to begin deploying to the left when they reached Bouldercrest Road, while Bate's and Major General William H. T. Walker's divisions continued on up the road before turning left on what is today called Wilkinson Drive. Both of these moves into line were short of their original goals.

Soon running into a large mill pond that their guides had repeatedly warned them about, Walker's and Bate's divisions wandered around in the thick forest for nearly an hour trying to sort themselves out and get into line of battle. As Walker roundly cursed their guides, grumbling that they must be "traitors" to allow him to get himself

in such a fix, he raised his field glasses to try to figure out his next move. A nearby Union picket spotted Walker and killed him with a single well-aimed shot.

Walker's command was taken over by Brigadier General Hugh W. Mercer, and the planned dawn attack commenced at about 12:15 P.M. after more confusion and shifting of troops. On advancing to the planned line of departure, the Confederates discovered to their horror that, far from being in the Union rear, they were advancing straight into a heavily invested front-line position. Pressing forward under intense fire from Sweeney's 2d Division (Dodge's XVI Army Corps), they immediately were raked by fire from two well-sited artillery positions, one six-gun Napoleon battery (Lieutenant Andrew T. Blodgett's 1st Missouri Light Battery) and one six-gun three-inch ordnance rifle battery (Captain Jerome M. Burrows 14th Ohio Light Battery, noted as being replaced in command by Lieutenant Seith M. Laird in a few accounts).

About thirty minutes later, Cleburne's and Maney's divisions launched their attack to the left of the ongoing fight, straight into the bend of the Union line held by Giles Smith's 4th Division (Blair's XVII Army Corps). This attack was much more successful, driving the Union line all the way north to Leggett's Hill and capturing an entire infantry regiment (Lieutenant Colonel Addison H. Sander's 16th Iowa), as well as eight artillery pieces.

McPherson had been eating lunch with his staff and corps commanders less than a mile away when he heard the sudden crash of artillery fire. He hastily mounted his horse and rode south with a small group of officers to check on the situation, pausing atop a nearby hill. From there he could see that Sweeney's division was holding up well, but he could not see the situation on the other end of the line. Striking out immediately for the spot between the two Confederate assaults, he realized that his line was not continuous in that area and quickly ordered up more troops to fill the gap. Riding through the unmanned gap toward Giles Smith's position, his party suddenly burst out of the heavy forest into a clearing, coming face to face with the advancing 5th Confederate Regiment (Captain Richard Beard's Tennessee). The Confederates called on him to surrender, but attempting to escape, he wheeled his horse around, raised his hat in salute, and attempted to make the tree line. A single shot fired by Corporal Robert F. Coleman tore through McPherson's lungs, killing him instantly.

Hood finally realized that the Union left flank was engaged, not the rear as planned, and ordered Cheatham's corps out of the east Atlanta defense line and to assault the entrenched Union main line. At the same time, Maney's division was ordered to break off and move to Cleburne's left, where they could support Cheatham's attack. Maney's division started their assault at about 3:30 P.M. Cheatham's corps moved out one-half hour later, possibly as a result of confusion over orders. Once again, Leggett's Hill was in the center of much of the action, but the repeated Confederate assaults failed to regain control of it.

The general assault found a weak spot at the position held by Union brigadier general Joseph Lightburn's 2d Brigade (Brigadier General Morgan L. Smith's 2d Division, Logan's XV Army Corps). Confederate brigadier general Arthur M. Manigault's brigade (Cheatham's corps) led the assault, pushing through the railroad cut (near the present-day Inman Park MARTA Station) and capturing a four-gun artillery battery that had been cutting them to pieces (De Gress's 1st Illinois Light Battery H, consisting of four 20-pounder Parrott rifles); it then turned left and battered four Ohio regiments (the 47th, 54th, 37th, and 53d, in turn). More Confederate units poured through the opening, capturing another two-gun artillery battery, and forced a total of four Union brigades to retreat from a nearly half-mile front.

Sherman, observing from his headquarters about three-fourths of a mile to the northwest, ordered Schofield to mass all his artillery (twenty guns) at the Confederate breach and ordered Logan to collect eight brigades to fill in the gap. Between the massed artillery and Logan's strong counterattack, the Confederates were soon forced back into their original positions at a heavy loss. Wheeler's cavalry strike at Decatur met with more success, driving back two regiments of infantry and capturing 225 prisoners and an artillery piece, but Wheeler was ordered back to the west to support Hardee before he could capture or destroy the Union supply train, his main goal.

The day was another unqualified disaster for the Confederate Army of Tennessee. Total casualties ran more than 5,000 (Sherman claimed more than 8,000, but this was no doubt exaggerated) for no gain other than twelve briefly captured artillery pieces that could not even be withdrawn in the retreat, as all the caisson horses had been killed in the action. The Union Army of the Tennessee fared little better, giving up no territory but losing 3,722 killed, wounded, or missing.

Four days after the indecisive battle of Atlanta, on 26 July Union major general Oliver O. Howard took over McPherson's Army of the Tennessee and immediately began moving to the west along the northern arc of Atlanta's defenses. The targets this time were the last two open railroads leading into the besieged city, the Macon and Western and the Atlanta and West Point.

Hood soon learned of the Union movement and decided that this would be a good opportunity to launch an offensive action. He sent his old corps, now under command of Lieutenant General Stephen D. Lee, along with Stewart's corps west down Lick Skillet Road (now Gordon Road) to confront Howard at the small crossroads where Ezra Methodist Church stands and to arrive before the Union troops could reach the vital railway.

This was in itself not a bad plan, the only problem being that Howard's corps had already reached the crossroads, was aware of Hood's intent, and was entrenching before Lee's corps ever left the city. Lee did not know this when his corps marched out of the Atlanta defenses about 10:00 A.M. on 28 July, with Brigadier General John

C. Brown's and Major General Henry D. Clayton's divisions leading the column line of march. Within a mile or so, Brown encountered elements of Confederate brigadier general William H. Jackson's cavalry division, who inform him of the entrenched Yankee lines ahead. Lee made a poor decision and ordered Brown's and Clayton's men to move straight ahead and assault without additional support.

Brown's division hastily formed in line of battle directly opposite three Union brigades and part of a

Federal encampment on Decatur Street, Atlanta, 1864 (Photograph by George N. Barnard / *Library of Congress*)

Shell damage to the Potter house, Atlanta, 1864
(Photograph by George N. Barnard / *Library of Congress*)

fourth of Morgan Smith's 2d Division (Logan's XV Army Corps) and then moved forward about 12:30 P.M. Clayton's division lagged a bit behind, moving through thick forest over to Brown's right flank. Clayton formed up and moved forward about 10 minutes later, also into the same four Union brigades. Both Confederate divisions were assaulting uphill into a barricaded, entrenched line of heavily supplied infantry (the Union troops had been issued 100 rounds per man before the battle, about 40 percent more than usual) and were being thrown into the headlong fight piecemeal as they arrived. In addition, the forest in this area was so thick that the assaulting Confederates could not see the Union entrenchment until they were nearly on them.

Only one unit managed to break through the Union barricade, Colonel William F. Brantley's Mississippi brigade on the extreme left of the Confederate line of assault, but it was pushed back by a strong counterattack before its troops could invest the trench lines. The rest of the Confederate line melted away under rifle fire so intense that "no mortal could stand," as put by Union colonel Hugo Wangelin (3d Brigade commander, Smith's 1st Division, Logan's corps).

Stewart's corps fared no better on their attempt. Leading the way was Confederate major general Edward C. Walthall's division over the same ground that Brown had charged through. Stumbling over the dead and wounded Confederates in the thick forest, his line was repulsed in quick order, and his dead and wounded lay side by side with Brown's. Sporadic skirmishing and sniper fire continued until dark, when the Confederates withdrew back into the Atlanta defenses, carrying as many wounded as the exhausted men were able to drag behind them.

For the third time in less than ten days, Hood had wrecked part of his once hardened and capable army by sending them against superior forces who were well-entrenched. Total casualty figures for the brief attack are difficult to assess accurately, as few Confederate records exist, but somewhere between 2,500 and 5,000 were killed, wounded, or missing. The Union lost about 600.

Both sides gained and lost something as a result of the ten-day, three-battle campaign around the Atlanta defenses. Sherman failed to take the city proper, but did inflict serious damage on the Confederate Army of Tennessee. Hood failed to cripple or even drive back any of the three Union grand armies before him, but he did manage to hold the city and two of the four railroads supplying it.

After the battle at Ezra Church, Sherman turned to his cavalry corps to try to cut Hood's supply line. On 27 July, McCook's 1st Division Cavalry with about 3,500 horsemen moved around the western flank of Atlanta's defenses, bound for Lovejoy Station about twenty-five miles south of the city. Later the same day, Garrard's 2d Division Cavalry and Stoneman's cavalry division moved around the eastern line of defense with about 5,000 horsemen toward the same destination. The plan was to tear up the last remaining railway supplying Atlanta, along with its accompanying telegraph line, and then proceed to the Macon and Andersonville prisoner-of-war camps to release the more than 30,000 Union prisoners.

Sherman did not have to wait long for word of his "great cavalry raid." By 30 July, McCook's division had been thoroughly routed near Newnan by two cavalry brigades under Wheeler's personal command, assisted by several infantry units. The next day, Stoneman's entire force was captured, killed, or scattered at Sunshine Church just north of Macon. Stoneman not only failed to liberate the Union prisoners at Macon and Andersonville, he suffered the ignobility of joining their ranks at Macon's Camp Oglethorpe.

The "great raid" was not only a spectacular Confederate victory, but so many cavalry horses were captured that an entire brigade was able to be mounted. Sherman, noted for his extravagant prose in victory, was somewhat more terse in defeat, writing: "On the whole the cavalry raid is not deemed a success."

Sherman grew increasingly more frustrated with his inability to pound or starve Hood's troops out of the city and ordered yet another attack on the single remaining railroad to try to force the Confederates out in the open where they could be finally destroyed. On 4 August, Schofield's XXIII and Palmer's XIV Army Corps were ordered to swing around to the southwest and strike toward the two remaining railroad tracks near East Point. Another squabble between officers—this time between Palmer and Schofield over who was the senior officer—delayed the movement for nearly two full days.

Hood got word on 5 August of the Union movement and ordered a new line of emplacements built along the Sandtown Road and staffed by Bate's division of Hardee's corps reinforced by a two-gun artillery battery, a brigade of the Georgia Militia, and Confederate brigadier general Lawrence S. Ross's Texas Cavalry Brigade.

At dawn on 6 August, Union brigadier general Jacob D. Cox's 3d Division (Schofield's XXIII Army Corps) advanced with a 2,500-man front against the now heavily entrenched Confederate left. This attack got within thirty yards of the Confederate line before being broken up with severe loss and thrown back. Several other multibrigade assaults were attempted with the same result, and nearly 400 casualties.

In the midst of all this action, still upset over his argument with Schofield, Union major general John M. Palmer tendered his resignation and quit his command. Brigadier General Richard W. Johnson hastily took command and ordered an immediate assault on the right of the Confederate line. They were no more successful, suffering 200 more casualties for no gain. Total Confederate losses for the day were about 200, included those captured in their forward skirmish positions in the early part of the battle. Sherman described the action as "a noisy but not bloody battle."

Frustrated with his inability to cut the rail lines, Sherman pondered his next move. A direct assault on the Atlanta fortifications was completely out of the question. An interlocking series of artillery batteries and infantry parapets ringed the city a little over a mile out from its center, reinforced by as many as four rows of abatis and long lines of chevaux-de-frise. In those works were the tired, hungry, and undersupplied but highly experienced Confederate Army of Tennessee supplemented by the Georgia State Line, Georgia Militia, and other irregular troops. Planned and constructed by Georgia's chief military engineer, Confederate captain Lemuel P. Grant, using slave labor from nearby plantations, the fortress city was "too strong to assault and too extensive to invest," according to Sherman's own chief of engineers, Captain Orlando M. Poe. Sherman decided simply to bombard the city into submission.

On 1 August, Sherman had ordered Schofield's artillery to increase their rate of fire, and after the disaster at Utoy Creek, he sent for large artillery guns and plenty of ammunition. Two 30-pounder Parrott rifles were brought in from Chattanooga, specifically to demolish buildings, and eight huge 4.5-inch siege guns were in place by 8 August. On 9 August, Sherman ordered every battery within range to open fire, "and make the inside of Atlanta too hot to be endured." That day alone more than 5,000 shells slammed into the city's heart.

Sherman kept the intense bombardment up for more than two weeks, gradually wearing away the strength and endurance of the hollow-eyed soldiers within the city fortifications. Then, suddenly, on 25 August all the guns fell silent. Hood hoped for a moment that Sherman had given up and was withdrawing, but his hopes were dashed when word came of yet another Union flanking attempt. Thomas's entire Army of the Cumberland and Howard's Army of the Tennessee moved around the right of Atlanta and swept down on the Atlanta and West Point Railroad, nine miles southwest of East Point. Hood could not hope to muster any sort of force to stop them, but pulled nearly his entire army out of Atlanta to try to protect the last remaining railway, leaving Stewart's corps and Smith's Georgia Militia to hold the city lines.

Realizing that Sherman intended to strike at Jonesboro and cut the railway, after dark on 30 August, Hood ordered Hardee's and Lee's corps to move hastily to defend the small town. Encountering Union pickets about 3:00 A.M. and not wanting to risk a night battle, the two Confederate corps moved slightly to the east, not arriving in line at Jonesboro until just after noon on the 31st. Hood was almost frantic to defend his railroad, sending Hardee repeated messages to attack "as soon as you can get your troops up."

At 3:00 P.M. that afternoon the order came to fix bayonets and drive the Yankees from their trenches. The Confederate assault, two corps wide, advancing through open fields and against concentrated artillery cannister fire never made it closer than sixty yards at any point before withdrawing. Losses were staggeringly one-sided, at least 1,700 Confederate versus 179 Union soldiers killed or wounded.

At the same time, Schofield's Army of the Ohio, reinforced by Union Major General David S. Stanley's IV Army Corps, moved around the southern Atlanta defenses and struck the Macon & Western Railroad near Rough & Ready. Quickly overwhelming the small dismounted cavalry unit stationed there, the Union troops ripped up the tracks and moved north toward East Point.

At 6:00 P.M. that evening, Hood ordered Lee's corps back to help defend Atlanta against the new attack, leaving Hardee alone in Jonesboro facing three full Union corps. At midnight, Hardee sent a message by courier to Hood (the telegraph wire having been cut about 2:00 P.M.) advising that the attack had failed and Atlanta should be abandoned. Through the rest of the long hot night, Hardee's forces shifted around to cover the gaps left by Lee's departure and dug in as best they could. All knew that their real job was to hold the main Union armies long enough for Hood to get the rest of the forces out of Atlanta.

At 4:00 P.M. on 1 September the Union attack began, led by two brigades of Brigadier General William P. Carlin's 1st Division (Brevet Major General Jefferson C. Davis's XIV Army Corps). They were quickly followed by brigade after brigade, division after division, until three full corps were engaged in the assault. Amazingly, although one side of his line caved in and 865 prisoners and two full batteries of artillery were captured, Hardee managed to hold until the attack ended after nightfall. About midnight, he withdrew his three remaining divisions south to Lovejoy Station, leaving behind about 1,400 dead and wounded. The Union force fared little better, losing a total of 1,272, but at last taking and cutting the railway line they had sought for so long.

On the morning of 1 September, having received Hardee's dreadful message, Hood at long last ordered the evacuation of the doomed city. With the railway cut, it was impossible to take much in the way of supplies with them, so warehouses were ordered opened up for the civilians. Stewart's corps and Smith's Militia began marching out around 5:00 P.M., with French's divisional pickets acting as a rearguard and withdrawing about 11:00 P.M. Sappers and engineers hastily prepared the abandoned military supplies for destruction. About midnight, a thunderous roar announced the end for a large ammunition train that Hood was unable to withdraw. Sherman heard the blast fifteen miles away in his headquarters at Jonesboro and knew he now had the city.

On 3 September 1864, Sherman telegraphed Major General Henry W. Halleck in Washington: "So Atlanta is ours, and fairly won." Hood managed to slip away with what remained of his forces, more or less intact after blowing up his large ammunition train and abandoning warehouses full of supplies. No complete records exist, but somewhere nearly 30,000 starving and ill-equipped troops were left to carry out Hood's desperate plan to strike at the Union rear. Well over 81,000 troops were still available to Sherman, who decided not to follow and finish off the badly mauled Confederate force. Instead he would simply rest and resupply within the fortifications of Atlanta.

Between Dalton and the gates of Atlanta lie the graves of 4,423 Union and 3,044 Confederate soldiers. During the four-month campaign, 22,822 Union and 18,952 Confederates were wounded, and a total of 17,335 on both sides were captured or disappeared.

—*John E. McKay*

See also Atlanta Campaign; Dallas, Georgia, Battle of; Ezra Church; Jonesboro; Kennesaw Mountain; Peachtree Creek; Resaca, Battle of; Rocky Face Ridge, Battle of; Stoneman's Raid (July 1864); Utoy Creek.

For further reading:

Cannan, John. *The Atlanta Campaign, May–November, 1864* (1991).

Castel, Albert E. *Decision in the West: The Atlanta Campaign of 1864* (1992).

Crompton, James. "The Second Division of the 16th Corps in the Atlanta Campaign." In *The Atlanta Papers* (1980).

Evans, David. *Sherman's Horsemen: Union Cavalry Operations in the Atlanta Campaign* (1996).

ATLANTA, GEORGIA

Atlanta's importance as a railroad, industrial, and distribution center, and its symbolism as the South's "second capital," made the city a focal point during the Civil War. The city began inauspiciously as the small settlement known as Terminus. Incorporated in 1843 as Marthasville (named for the governor's daughter), the town changed its name again to Atlanta in 1847. Before the war, Atlanta remained important principally for its railroads. Four railroads converged in the city: the Georgia Railroad, the Atlanta & West Point, and the Macon & Western, in addition to the Western & Atlantic. By the late 1850s, calling itself the "Gate City of the South," Atlanta boasted the largest and grandest passenger depot in the region. Its population of 10,000 included many prosperous merchants, industrialists, and professionals who built fine homes, although the city had few paved streets and had problems with gambling and prostitution.

With its railroad and commercial interests, Atlanta did not support secession before 1860. In the presidential contest in that year, the city gave a majority of its votes to Unionist candidate John Bell. However, Abraham Lincoln's election moved public opinion toward secession, Atlanta fire-eaters burned the president-elect in effigy, and unionism gave way to support for Confederate nationhood. Several thousand Atlanta men joined the Confederate armies, while women volunteered their time with the Ladies' Soldiers' Relief Society or the Atlanta Hospital Association. Nevertheless, throughout the war, a minority of Atlantans continued to support the Union. Most of city's Unionists were merchants. They visited the city's prison, which housed three hundred Federal soldiers, and smuggled provisions to these men. Occasionally they acted as spies. Nervous Confederates, fearing plots to liberate slaves and prisoners, harassed and occasionally imprisoned Unionists.

The war hindered commerce in Atlanta, just as it did in other cities of the Confederacy. Early in the war, the city's merchants still managed to import some supplies from New York by way of Memphis and other towns along the Mississippi River. When Federal military success closed this commercial avenue, Atlanta's merchants hoped to import goods from Europe. Although several Atlantans founded blockade-running companies, this activity carried its own hazards.

While commerce foundered, industry flourished. Atlanta's wartime factories produced a wide range of consumer goods, ranging from saddles and plows to soap, buttons, and porcelain teeth. The city became best known as an ordnance center. Its factories manufactured a wide array of military goods, including knives, swords, cannon, pistols, and naval armor plate for the famous ironclad *Merrimack*. Atlanta's most important factory was the Confederate government arsenal, run by

Colonel Moses H. Wright. Opened in the spring of 1862, after arsonists burned an earlier Confederate facility in Nashville, the arsenal produced harnesses and saddles, percussion caps, rifle cartridges, and artillery shells. Employing nearly 5,500 men and women, it would be Atlanta's biggest employer of the nineteenth century. The city also housed the Quartermaster's Depot, commanded by Major G. W. Cunningham. It produced shoes, along with underclothing, shirts, pants, jackets, and hats for the Confederate army, hiring dozens of shoemakers and tailors, along with three thousand seamstresses. Atlanta's contributions to the war effort, along with the city's importance as a rail center, made it an obvious target for the Union military.

With its economic success the city's population grew to nearly 22,000. But Atlanta's situation began to decline even before the arrival of General William T. Sherman's army. The city's factories suffered from a lack of raw materials. Skilled labor was in short supply. With the city's rapid wartime population growth and lack of sanitation, Atlanta was not a very healthy place to live. A smallpox epidemic beginning in December 1862 afflicted at least 100 city residents. Atlantans suffered from the inflation that bedeviled the entire Confederate South. As the war stretched on, price gouging, food scarcities, and lawlessness increased. On 18 March 1863, a group of Confederate war widows, angered by the high cost of food, rioted by breaking into stores on Whitehall Street and stealing flour, bacon, and other items. The city marshal arrived quickly and reestablished order with no serious injuries. Similar riots occurred in other Georgia cities, as well as in the Confederate capital of Richmond. Although the city attempted to offer "poor relief" to its indigent residents through special grocery stores, free medical care, and paid burial, there was never enough money to help all of those in need.

Although city residents once considered themselves safe from Yankee invasion because they believed the Union army could never negotiate the north Georgia mountains, the Federal army shattered their complacency by breaking through Confederate lines at Chattanooga in November 1863. By May 1864, with Sherman pushing his way south, many Atlantans began to leave the city, seeking refuge in safer locations. Others stayed even when Sherman's bombardment of the city began on 20 July. They sought shelter in makeshift pits dug in back yards and covered with metal sheeting or railroad ties. Twenty civilians died in the six-week siege, including, ironically, a free African-American man who operated a barbershop in a local hotel and who was killed by a shell fragment. On 2 September 1864, after Sherman's army had flanked the Confederates south of the city, Mayor James Calhoun surrendered Atlanta. Sherman ordered the city's evacuation before beginning the systematic destruction of railroads and all war industries. The ensuing fires claimed between 4,000 and 5,000 buildings, including many residential structures.

In November 1864, after an occupation of two months, General Sherman and his army left Atlanta, with Savannah as their next goal. Like the ancient phoenix it adopted as its new symbol, the city of Atlanta would quickly begin to rise again, eventually establishing itself as the center of the postwar New South.

—*Wendy Hamand Venet*

See also Atlanta Campaign.
For further reading:
Dyer, Thomas G. *Secret Yankees: The Union Circle in Confederate Atlanta* (1999).
Rose, Michael. *Atlanta: A Portrait of the Civil War* (1999).
Russell, James Michael. *Atlanta 1847–1890: City Building in the Old South and the New* (1988).

AUGUR, CHRISTOPHER COLUMBUS
(1821–1898)
Union general

Born to Ammon Augur and Annis Wellman Augur in Kendall, New York, Christopher Augur moved to Michigan with his mother after his father's death. In 1839 he received an appointment to the U.S. Military Academy, from which he graduated in the class of 1843, sixteenth of thirty-nine. At the outbreak of the Mexican-American War, he fought in northern Mexico under Zachary Taylor and served as an aide to two of Taylor's generals. After the war, Augur served on garrison duty in the Pacific Northwest and fought in several of the Indian wars there. At the outbreak of the Civil War he was commandant of cadets at the U.S. Military Academy.

Promoted to brigadier general of volunteers in November 1861, Augur managed the outlying defenses of Washington, D.C. In March 1862, he was part of the initial advance south toward Richmond and led the force that captured Fredericksburg, Virginia, in April 1862. He occupied the town until July, when his division was made part of John Pope's Army of Virginia. He fought at Cedar Mountain on 9 August. At approximately 7:00 P.M. he was severely wounded and had to leave the field. He was promoted major general of volunteers for his bravery at Cedar Mountain.

Augur's injury prevented him from returning to duty until November 1862. His first assignment was to serve as Nathaniel P. Banks's second-in-command for Banks's Louisiana campaign. For the first four months of the campaign, Augur commanded the District of Baton Rouge in Banks's Department of the Gulf. In May 1863 Augur took command of the attack made on Port Hudson on 21 May and then oversaw the left of the siege works until the surrender. By that point, Augur's health, aggravated by his earlier wound, forced him to ask for a

leave of absence. He was unable to exercise a field command for the remainder of the war.

From October 1863 until August 1866, Augur commanded the Department of Washington. Along with maintaining the defenses of the city, Augur engaged in a variety of activities during his command in Washington. During Ulysses S. Grant's campaign against Robert E. Lee that commenced in the spring of 1864 and lasted until Lee surrendered in April 1865, Augur was charged with equipping and moving Grant's replacement troops through Washington down to the front as quickly as possible. Augur managed this monumental task while also guarding the city during the summer of 1864 against Jubal Early's raid and remaining vigilant through the fall of 1864 and into the early months of 1865 against the activities of other Confederate raiders like John Singleton Mosby. During these hectic times, Philip Sheridan commended Augur for the assistance he rendered him during the latter's Shenandoah Valley campaign.

After the war, Augur's duties in Washington hardly tapered off. He was charged with keeping the streets cleared during the various troop reviews after the Confederate surrenders and was instructed to oversee the execution of Andersonville commandant Henry Wirz in November 1865.

When the remainder of the volunteers were mustered out of service in 1866, Augur became the colonel of the 12th Infantry. He was promoted to brigadier general in 1869. He served in the various Indian wars of the post–Civil War era and for a time in 1876 commanded the Department of the Gulf during the last days of Reconstruction. Augur retired at the rank of brigadier general in 1885. He died in the District of Columbia on 16 January 1898.

—*David S. Heidler and Jeanne T. Heidler*

See also Cedar Mountain, Battle of; Port Hudson Campaign; Washington, D.C.

For further reading:
Men of the Time; Being Biographies of Generals Halleck, Pope, Siegel, Corcoran, Prentiss, Kearney, Hatch and Augur (1862).

AVERASBORO (AVERASBOROUGH), BATTLE OF
(16 March 1865)

The battle near Averasboro, North Carolina, was the first of two engagements fought during the third stage of Union major general William T. Sherman's Carolinas campaign in 1865. This engagement, which was fought between the Black and Cape Fear rivers, represented the initial Confederate attempt to monitor the Federal advance northward from Fayetteville, North Carolina.

The arrival of General Sherman's two armies at Fayetteville, North Carolina, on 11 March 1865 signaled the beginning the third stage of the Federal raid northward through the Carolinas. Sherman now prepared to move overland to Goldsboro, North Carolina, where he expected to link up with additional reinforcements and supplies. Within a hundred miles of Sherman, Confederate general Joseph E. Johnston worked to concentrate his scattered forces to form an army to stop the Federal advance. One of those forces was the provisional corps of two divisions under the command of Lieutenant General William J. Hardee, which was encamped on the old Plank Road north of Fayetteville, North Carolina. General Hardee's corps consisted of garrison troops that were displaced by General Sherman's march through Georgia and South Carolina. As his troops rested near the Smith plantation, General Hardee soon received orders from General Johnston to conduct a delaying action to determine whether Goldsboro or Raleigh was Sherman's next objective. The information would be vital to Johnston, so that he would be able to organize an attack on one of the two Union columns. General Hardee deployed his forces in three positions to receive Sherman's advance. His first two lines were manned by brigades from Brigadier General William B. Taliaferro's division, and the third line was occupied by Major General Lafayette McLaws's division in front of the intersection of the Goldsboro and Raleigh roads.

On 15 March 1865, elements of General Sherman's left wing brushed into skirmishers of Colonel Alfred Rhett's brigade on the old Plank Road. This Union column consisted of four infantry divisions of both XIV and XX Army Corps under the command of Major General Henry Slocum and brevet Major General Judson Kilpatrick's 3d Cavalry Division. The initial contact came from General Kilpatrick's troopers pushing down the old Plank Road. They quickly discovered Rhett's brigade was entrenched and supported by artillery. A general engagement commenced on both sides of the road, during which Colonel Rhett was captured by Federal scouts. Rhett's brigade began to probe the Union cavalry, and soon Union infantry was brought up to reinforce General Kilpatrick's men.

The next morning (16 March 1865), General Kilpatrick again attempted to clear the road and soon found his troopers fighting with Confederate infantry supported by artillery fire. The Union situation became worse, when rebel infantry began to press Kilpatrick's flanks. General Slocum quickly ordered up the two divisions of XX Corps into line to reinforce the Federal line, and called up his artillery to shell the Confederates. While this pressure was maintained on Rhett's brigade, Colonel Henry Case's brigade from the 3d Division, XX Corps, swung around the Confederate right flank and unhinged the position. Rhett's brigade soon retreated northward after abandoning two cannon.

The survivors of Rhett's brigade fell back on Brigadier General Stephen Elliott's brigade, which was deployed a couple of miles to the north. With General Sherman now on the field, the Union commanders pushed forward to clear the road. With the deployment of another division from XIV Corps, General Elliott soon found his brigade pressed on three sides by Union forces. He quickly pulled his regiments back to General McLaws's position. General Slocum's advancing troops, who were attempting to probe the rebel flanks, quickly discovered this line. Unlike the first two positions, this line was anchored on both the Black and Cape Fear rivers by Confederate cavalry, and its center was reinforced with artillery and infantry. After several failed attempts to turn the position, the Federal infantry was soon settled into heavy skirmishing with McLaws's division until nightfall.

During the night of 16 March, General Hardee received orders to move his troops to the north and rejoin General Johnston's army near Smithfield, North Carolina. General Johnston now needed to get his army united, so that a plan could be developed to attack General Sherman. At the same time, Sherman prepared to send portions of XV Corps to assist Slocum's advance. By 17 March the Confederates had abandoned their defensive lines, and Sherman saw the opportunity to push his forces eastward to avoid any further Confederate contact.

—*William H. Brown*

See also Carolinas Campaign.

For further reading:
Barrett, John G. *The Civil War in North Carolina* (1963).
———. *Sherman's March through the Carolinas* (1956; reprint, 1996).
Long, E. B. *The Civil War Day By Day: An Almanac* (1971).
U.S. War Department. *War of the Rebellion: A Compilation of the Official Records of the Union and Confederate Armies* (1880–1901).

AVERELL, WILLIAM WOODS
(1832–1900)
Union general

William Woods Averell was born on 5 November 1832 in the small town of Cameron, New York. The son of a farmer and minor political figure, Averell began attending the U.S. Military Academy at West Point in December 1850. His academic career was less than stellar, and upon graduation in 1855 he ranked in the lower third of his class. Yet, Averell was a natural at horsemanship. It was as a horseman that he gained his prominence and enjoyed much success.

In 1857 Averell was sent to the New Mexico Territory, where his skills as a cavalryman were invaluable in scouting operations. In 1859, however, a serious leg wound sent him home to convalesce, and for the next two years he lived at his family's residence in Bath, New York. It was there that Averell learned of the attack on Fort Sumter in 1861.

Yearning for a return to military service, Averell presented himself for duty on 16 April 1861. He was ordered to Fort Arbuckle, situated west of Arkansas, to relay an order to the commander, who had lost communication with Washington, to destroy all property, retreat north, and prepare for war. This journey took Averell deep into Southern territory, but he survived it and returned to Washington to help muster volunteers. Eventually he was later assigned as assistant adjutant general to Colonel Andrew Porter.

After fighting at Bull Run, Averell moved briefly to the staff of the provost marshal in Washington, D.C. Since horsemanship was Averell's true passion, however, he was not happy serving as an administrative officer, and he soon sought a field appointment. On 7 October 1861, Averell's hope was realized when he assumed command of the 3d Pennsylvania Cavalry. By June 1862, he had transformed his unit of green cavalrymen into accomplished horsemen, and by August, Averell had attained the rank of brigadier general. The next two years revealed Averell to be an adept commander who was skilled at handling his men. He was moved into West Virginia to help aid in that infant state's separation from Virginia and to conduct raids against various strategic targets. Starting in August 1863 through May 1864, Averell's raids into western Virginia scored the most success in distracting Confederate forces in the region and harrying the Army of Northern Virginia's lines of supply out of east Tennessee.

In August 1864, Averell's command was placed under Philip Sheridan, who was about to start his destructive raid of the Shenandoah Valley. Averell would serve under Sheridan into September 1864, but after the battle of Fisher's Hill on 21–22 September 1864, Averell lost his command when Sheridan accused him of incompetence.

Averell's postwar career proved to be profitable. In October 1865, Averell became involved in the Averill Coal and Oil Company. In 1866, he learned that he was to receive the appointment of consul general to British North America at Montreal. In the fall of 1870, Averell's interest in the new mineral asphalt led by 1880 to his becoming president of The American Asphalt Company. Though the company split within two years, Averell was rewarded with nearly $700,000. Exhibiting a remarkable penchant for invention, Averell went on to design an underground electrical conduit for use in telegraphic, telephonic, and lighting.

In 1888, Averell was appointed assistant inspector general of Soldiers Homes. He died in 1900.

—*Chad A. Reisig*

William W. Averell (*seated*) (*Library of Congress*)

See also Averell's Raids; Fisher's Hill, Battle of.
For further reading:
Amato, Nicholas J., and Edward Eckert, eds. *Ten Years in the Saddle: The Memoir of William Woods Averell: 1851–1862* (1978).
Pond, George E. *The Shenandoah Valley in 1864* (1883).

AVERELL'S RAIDS
(August 1863–May 1864)

During the second half of 1863 and into the spring of 1864, Union operations in West Virginia were aimed at destroying railroads and depriving the Confederacy of valuable resources such as lead and salt mines in southwestern Virginia. Four raids mounted or participated in by Brigadier General William W. Averell tried to accomplish these goals and achieved mixed results.

The first raid occurred in August 1863 and had as its principal purpose clearing out Confederate forces from the area around Huntersville so that a subsequent operation could be mounted against Staunton and the Virginia & Tennessee Railroad. Averell was also instructed to seize the Virginia Court of Appeals law library at Lewisburg. The library had been purchased for the western counties and was thus deemed the property of West Virginia. In any event, the new state's judges needed it to hold court.

Departing from Winchester on 5 August, Averell's command consisted of four companies of West Virginia cavalry, the 14th Pennsylvania Cavalry, three regiments of mounted infantry, Gibson's Independent Battalion, and a battery of artillery. After a short skirmish on 6 August with elements of John Imboden's command, the Union force arrived at Moorefield, where it stayed for two days. Although Averell was short of supplies, he headed south again on 9 August, but stopped in Petersburg until he could at least have his horses shod. Partially supplied on 17 August, but still lacking adequate ammunition, he elected to proceed. He pushed south toward Monterey, destroying a saltpeter works near Franklin en route. On 20 August, he entered Monterey and arrested the officers of the quarterly court in session there. He also heard of plans being hatched by Imboden and Major General Samuel Jones to counter the Federal raid.

The Confederate response to the raid was hampered by ignorance of Averell's real intentions. Major General Samuel Jones, the Commander of the Department of Western Virginia, persisted in the belief that the Union raid was directed at Staunton and the vital Virginia & Tennessee Railroad. He directed forces under his command to respond accordingly and requested from Robert E. Lee that detachments from the Army of Northern Virginia move to defend Staunton. Instead of heading toward Staunton, Averell in accordance with his orders pushed toward Huntersville, the only resistance being the annoyance of snipers lurking in the scrub. He skirmished on 22 August outside of Huntersville with elements of Colonel William "Mudwall" Jackson's scattered command, outflanking and forcing them to retire southeastward toward Warm Springs. The 8th West Virginia pursued, overran the Confederate bivouac at Camp Northwest, and destroyed it and its stores. Reinforced on 23 August by the 10th and part of the 2d West Virginia as well as another battery, Averell drove toward Warm Springs the next day to skirmish again with Jackson and force him eastward toward Millborough.

Averell hoped that his march toward Warm Springs, east of Huntersville and consequently in the direction of Staunton, had misled the Confederates into thinking that the town really was his objective. The next day, he compounded the ruse by sending the 10th West Virginia back to Huntersville while he resumed his southerly march toward Callaghan's, smashing another saltpeter works on the way at Jackson's River. From Callaghan's, Union scouts ranged east to Covington and as far south as Sweet Springs, capturing rebel wagons and torching another saltpeter facility.

Although Jackson would later claim that he had

deduced Averell's actual objective to be Lewisburg and had tried to notify Jones of it, it was not until Averell showed up in Callaghan's that Jones came to a realistic conclusion about Union movements. He recalled Colonel George S. Patton, commanding the 1st Brigade, from his march toward Warm Springs and directed him to White Sulphur Springs, about halfway between Lewisburg and Callaghan's. Since Averell had run Jackson out of Pocahontas County, on 26 August he now turned to Lewisburg, moving over the difficult road from Callaghan's that crossed two mountain ranges in the space of ten miles. As his advanced parties were debouching from a long defile, they ran into Patton's soldiers who had executed a night march to reach White Sulphur Springs almost at the same time as Averell did. The two forces, growing to their full strengths with ensuing arrivals, stubbornly contested the ground for the remainder of the day and held their positions that night. The next morning, Averell attempted to renew the fight, but his dwindling ammunition prompted him to break off the attack at midmorning and fall back toward Huntersville in good order. By felling trees behind him on roads that ran through ravines, he was able to impede the Confederate pursuit. Jones's hope that John Imboden was moving down from Monterey with enough speed to cut off Averell at Huntersville also proved forlorn, so the Union raiders safely reached Beverly, northeast of Huntersville, by the end of the month. Averell's losses were a little more than 200, mostly from the engagement at White Sulphur Springs. Jackson had lost not more than 20 men in the skirmishing around Huntersville and Warm Springs, and Patton's losses at White Sulphur were about 200.

The Federal effort had been only half realized and ultimately pointless at that. Rebel forces soon reoccupied Pocahontas County with Jackson's command headquartered at Mill Point. Averell remained in Beverly until undertaking the second of his raids in November. This effort had as its objective the capture of Lewisburg with an operation that had Averell advancing south from Beverly while Brigadier General Alfred Duffié moved east from Charleston in the Kanawha Valley. Infantry would occupy Lewisburg while all mounted troops pushed forward by way of Union to the Dublin Depot of the Virginia & Tennessee Railroad. Nearby they would destroy the railroad's New River Bridge. On 1 November, Averell left Beverly on the Staunton Pike heading toward Bartow with two regiments of infantry, four mounted regiments, an independent battalion of cavalry, and two light batteries. Two days later, Duffié pulled out of Charleston commanding a detachment of Brigadier General Eliakim P. Scammon's Third Division consisting of two regiments of infantry, two mounted regiments, and a section of artillery.

Averell moved through Greenbank toward

Huntersville and approached Mill Point on 5 November, where he skirmished with Jackson's outposts. Badly outnumbered, Jackson judiciously withdrew to a formidable position on Droop Mountain over which ran the main Lewisburg road. From there Jackson called for reinforcements from Brigadier General John Echols who hurried up from Lewisburg. By the time Averell was moving on Jackson's position on the morning of 6 November, a fourteen-mile march had brought Echols into position and swelled the rebel numbers on the crest to about 1,700 men. They mounted a stout defense against the superior Union force, but the defensive advantages of mountainous terrain also proved treacherous, for Averell was able to mask his movements behind rolling hills and in deep ravines. Gradually aware of a Federal effort to turn his left and mindful of Duffié's column advancing from the west, Echols elected to withdraw rather than risk being surrounded. The four miles of road along the crest of Droop Mountain, however, proved perilous, and a general panic was only barely averted as the rebels began their retreat. Some of Echols's people ran, though, and it was this element of the withdrawal that apparently created a rumor that he had been routed after a catastrophic defeat that left the whole region open to Averell's designs. As a result, Major General Jones was in dread for two days and made no secret of it to Richmond.

Actually, Echols was in fairly good shape, except he was most alarmed over the chance that Duffié would cut off his retreat at Lewisburg. For his part, Duffié had been only lightly engaged in skirmishes along his route—one at Little Sewell Mountain on the same day as Droop Mountain and another just west of Lewisburg at Muddy Creek the following day. Realizing the need for haste if he was to bag Echols, he left his infantry at Little Sewell Mountain and raced toward Lewisburg, but when he arrived at midmorning on 7 November, the rebels had slipped the noose, passing through the town and heading farther south toward Union the previous night. Duffié later uncharitably claimed that, had Averell been less aggressive at Droop Mountain, Echols would not have been so rapid in his retreat, and the Kanawha column would have had time to close the trap at Lewisburg. The two men never got along afterward.

Averell arrived in Lewisburg late in the afternoon on 7 November to find the business of destroying Confederate stores and ordnance well under way. The question now was what to do next. Averell's orders left it to his discretion about the practicability of proceeding with his mission to the Virginia & Tennessee Railroad, and at the end of the following day he would exercise his option to break off the operation and go home. He and Duffié sallied forth with their troopers southward early on 8 November, but Echols had made a thorough job of blocking the roads with felled trees. And then the blue

troopers ran into Echols's rearguard at Second Creek about fifteen miles south of Lewisburg. Duffié declared that his people could not proceed. He had only a day's rations, and his infantry, able to make only ten miles a day, would be starving if they did not get home. Averell was loaded down with prisoners and materiel from Droop Mountain, so everybody went back to Lewisburg and from there parted ways, Duffié to the west, Averell's infantry north to Beverly, and Averell with his troopers to the east toward Callaghan's and the Valley of the South Branch.

Haste urged the Yankee troopers. By then, every Confederate in the region was alerted. John Imboden had left his headquarters near Bridgewater, Virginia, early on 5 November and raced toward Goshen. From there he had moved toward Covington on the assumption that Averell intended to destroy the forges and furnaces in the area or perhaps make for Staunton; and it was there, between Callaghan's and Covington, on 10 November that Averell brushed against Imboden's pickets before abruptly turning north and racing up Back Creek as fast as he could move. Imboden was content to watch him, still suspicious that he would strike east and do some more destruction somewhere, so Averell was able to reach Petersburg by 14 November and his destination at New Creek three days later. By then, Duffié had been back in Charleston four days, his only problem upon his return being the weather: five inches of new snow had blocked the roads across Little Sewell Mountain.

This second raid into Confederate-occupied West Virginia had not reached the railroad, but it had demonstrated the vulnerability of the region to swift incursion. Casualties for the raiders were rather light—a little more than a hundred, and most of those from the fight at Droop Mountain—yet they were as light for the defenders, in spite of Jones's initial alarm. Echols counted almost 300 of his command missing, but most of those had run during the brief panic of the retreat. What had to be more alarming to Richmond, however, was the ease with which Federal troopers could move through the region even when encountering organized Confederate resistance, and the reflexive response of Jones to cry for help from the overburdened Army of Northern Virginia the moment a bluecoat appeared south of Huntersville. The Federal perspective was also alloyed, for Averell had failed to exploit his rather easy advance to Lewisburg.

Nonetheless, Averell had barely returned to his lines when a third raid was planned for December. It would be the most ambitious and complicated yet, relying on two elaborate feints to draw attention away from the main objective, which was the Virginia & Tennessee Railroad bridge, either at Bonsack's Station or Salem, Virginia. On 8 December, Averell's entire command moved out of New Creek, headed toward Petersburg, and then to

Franklin and Monterey. He was accompanied by two regiments of infantry and artillery that left his column at Monterey to head east toward McDowell, Virginia, and from there not only guard Averell's line of retreat but also to threaten Staunton and tie down Imboden as well as Jubal Early and Fitzhugh Lee. In case the Confederates remained unimpressed by that menace, all of Brigadier General Jeremiah Sullivan's 1st Division Cavalry, two infantry regiments, and a battery would ride up the Shenandoah Valley from Harper's Ferry to occupy Harrisonburg and also threaten Staunton from the north. Simultaneous to Averell's sortie on 8 December, Brigadier General Scammon's 3d Division set forth from Charleston toward Lewisburg as the 28th Ohio Cavalry and two infantry regiments advanced from Beverly toward Droop Mountain to support Scammon's maneuver. From Lewisburg, Scammon was supposed to head south toward Union and then act as though he were threatening the New River Bridge some twenty-five miles south of Salem. All the activity aimed at perfectly plausible targets would, it was hoped, so confuse and distract the Confederate defenders that Averell would be able slip unmolested into the Roanoke region and do some major tearing up of the railroad there.

It was, as it turned out, wise for the Union plan to employ more than enough complications because some of them simply did not work. Scammon's part of the project was no help at all because skirmishes at Big Sewell Mountain and Meadow Bluff on 11 December apparently convinced him that Lewisburg was indefensible. Rather than joining the forces coming from Droop Mountain—where Jackson's tattered command had again been put to flight—and then demonstrating toward the New River Bridge, Scammon pulled back to the west. Only Alfred Duffié's cavalry and some artillery remained in Lewisburg, and that only briefly. Scammon, alarmed that guerrilla's were threatening his rear and gray regulars were increasing on his front, simply went home. When Colonel Augustus Moor leading the forces down from Droop Mountain tried to communicate with Scammon, he made the puzzling discovery that Confederates were still in Lewisburg and the alarming one that they were beginning to people the roads to his rear. He hastily headed back to Beverly, and the entire western part of the operation collapsed just as Averell was approaching his target.

It did not matter, although it would make Averell's escape adventurous. Yet Confederate resources were stretched so thin by the end of 1863, even the failures of this raid accounted for its principal success. The Federal threat to Staunton at first preoccupied the only significant forces in the region, so, as Averell came down a little-known road on Back Creek, he was able to surprise even Jackson's rear guard retreating from Droop Mountain. When he reached Callaghan's, he heard that

Federals were in Lewisburg—Scammon had not yet been spooked out of it—so he made a move east toward Covington in case anybody was watching before racing southwest to Sweet Springs. He then learned about Scammon's inexplicable retreat from Lewisburg and must have taken pause. Word was that Echols was near Union, but Averell took heart when a captured Rebel revealed that nobody knew that bluecoats were south of Lewisburg. He switched back to the southeast, moved through New Castle, and descended on Salem. His arrival there on 16 December was such a surprise to everyone, including the residents, that he found the town's considerable supply depot completely unguarded. Moreover, he was able to send parties out on the railroad miles to the east and west, destroying five bridges and tearing up sections of rails.

Averell had shelled a train of Confederates trying to get into Salem, so his hours of destroying rail lines and burning supplies in the town were borrowed ones. At 4:00 P.M. that afternoon, he headed back north along the same route of his advance, now concerned about getting out of the hornet's nest he had stirred up. Samuel Jones was advancing from the west and Fitzhugh Lee, out of his camp near Charlottesville two days earlier, was moving southward toward Averell's line of retreat. Jubal Early had raced out of Hanover Junction on 15 December and in forty-eight hours was in Millborough, from whence he would register an unanswered demand for Averell's surrender on the 20th. As perilous as this closing snare was, darkness and exhaustion were even more immediate enemies. Averell's people had been in the saddle for more than a day riding hard for the better part of a hundred miles, so he had to stop near Salem and give his men and animals some rest.

Rain began to fall hard and continued through the night of 16 December into the next day. Craig's Creek in Averell's front became a cataract, and he was barely able to get his wagons and artillery across it. By the time the bedraggled raiders reached New Castle on 18 December, both they and their sodden ammunition were almost useless. By now, Jones was closing on the Sweet Springs Road, and Fitz Lee was in Fincastle, a stone's throw from the Yankee raiders. At 9:00 P.M., Averell feinted toward Lee at Fincastle and then whirled on Jones with such fury that he drove his pickets back a dozen miles. The Yankee troopers then stoked up fires and promptly abandoned them to creep north toward Covington on a back road.

Now, the main obstacle to escape was Jackson's River, swollen and running fast with broken ice on its surface. The Confederates had made arrangements to burn the bridges should Averell try to use them, but the defense of them had been entrusted to hapless "Mudwall" Jackson, whose impediments to Averell's escape would prove completely ineffective. When Averell appeared, the bridge fires could not be set. Also a captured message from General Jones to Jubal Early revealed to Averell all the plans of his pursuers. As a sharp fight for control of the bridges developed, the Yankees crossed and burned them so quickly that Averell's rearguard was trapped on the south bank. Most of them swam the icy river. Gathering up at Callaghan's, the raiders raced northwest through frozen passes. When they camped at the northern base of Droop Mountain on 21 December, their clothes were in shreds and they had no rations. Finally, they rode into Beverly on Christmas Eve.

It had been an arduous journey that left Averell's people badly used and minus almost 200 casualties, but they had finally done extensive damage to the Virginia & Tennessee Railroad, although it was quickly repaired. Yet, the raid had revealed again the permeable nature of Confederate defenses in the region. As for the gray defenders, the principal casualty of this last Federal sortie was Samuel Jones's career. In spite of Jones's attempts to lay blame elsewhere and claim vigilance where none had really been demonstrated—Jones as late as 11:00 P.M. on 15 December suspected that Averell was heading toward Fincastle rather than Salem—both Jefferson Davis and Robert E. Lee became so disenchanted with Jones that he was replaced. In March 1864, Major General John C. Breckinridge would become the new commander of the Department of Western Virginia. Soon he too would have to face another and, as it happened, the final of Averell's West Virginia raids.

Jones's Federal counterpart, Brigadier General Benjamin F. Kelley, was replaced in March as well, a victim of Union failures to secure the upper valley and make any dent in southwestern Virginia. Major General Franz Sigel became the new commander of the Department of West Virginia, and one of the changes he made was to make Averell the commander of a unit designated as the 2d Cavalry Division composed of Duffié's brigade, the 14th Pennsylvania, the 8th Ohio, and the 1st, 5th, and 7th West Virginia. When Lieutenant General Ulysses S. Grant actively formulated a grand, coordinated campaign to end the war, it included another move on the Virginia & Tennessee Railroad with the goal of making it useless for the movement of men and supplies between East Tennessee and the Army of Northern Virginia. Ultimately this task fell to Brigadier General George C. Crook, nominally under Sigel, but virtually independent in his command of the Kanawha Valley. Crook devised a plan to take a column of 6,000 infantry to destroy the New River Bridge while Averell led his cavalry to Saltville. The main column of Union infantry marched along the Kanawha River and headed south toward Rocky Gap, fought at Cloyd's Mountain, captured Dublin, and destroyed the Virginia & Tennessee Railroad bridge at New River. Meanwhile, Averell's cavalry on 5 May moved out from Logan Court House toward Wyoming Court House, skirmishing there with elements of the 8th Virginia Cavalry out of Saltville. Moving over rough and unmarked terrain through Abb's Valley, the Union troopers emerged to skirmish again with the 8th Virginia and then some Kentuckians near Tazewell Court House. As he approached Saltville, however, Averell despaired over news that the town had been fortified by Brigadier Generals John Morgan and W. E. "Grumble" Jones, a testament to the importance that Richmond assigned to the salt works there.

Electing to seek a more vulnerable target and keep Confederate forces from assailing Crook, Averell headed toward the lead works at Wytheville, but Morgan and Jones arrived there before him and assumed strong positions in Rocky Gap. Averell was fought to a standstill there on 10 May in a four-hour engagement that cost him 114 casualties. That night he withdrew toward Dublin, where he arrived next evening in a heavy rain that drenched his command and turned the New River, now bereft of its bridges thanks to Crook's work, into a nearly impassable torrent. Averell was just barely able to ford the river ahead of the pursuing Jones and Morgan. Reaching Christianburg, he received instructions from Crook to tear up as much of the Virginia & Tennessee Railroad as he could, but he soon learned of Confederates bearing in from the west by train. Heading north toward Crook's column, Averell led his troopers over some of the most terrifying terrain any could remember, especially since the rains had made the narrow mountain paths all the more perilous. Confederate attempts to block his progress proved fruitless, so he finally made it to Crook's column in Union on 15 May.

This last of Averell's raids in the region was much like the previous three. It had accomplished little of tangible strategic value except to prevent a concentration of Confederate strength against Crook's main initiative. Yet, Averell had shown a Federal presence in a region whose Unionist sympathies were vulnerable to unchallenged Confederate occupation. The raids also demonstrated Averell's uncanny talent for evasion that used terrain, rapid movement, and surprise to their best advantages. As spotty as his achievements in the mountains of West Virginia were, they had their moments of intrepid execution. Confederate soldiers did not like to hear that he was in the area. It was a compliment.

—*David S. Heidler and Jeanne T. Heidler*

See also Averell, William Woods; Cavalry, C.S.A.; Cavalry, U.S.A.; Cloyd's Mountain, Virginia; Jones, Samuel; Kelley, Benjamin Franklin; West Virginia.

For further reading:
Duncan, Richard R. *Lee's Endangered Left: The Civil War in Western Virginia, Spring of 1864* (1998).
Eckert, Edward K., and Nicholas J. Amatos, eds. *Ten Years in the Saddle: Memoir of William Woods Averell, 1851–1862* (1978).

AYRES, ROMEYN BECK
(1825–1888)
Union general

Romeyn Ayres was born in East Creek, Montgomery County, New York. He received an appointment to the U.S. Military Academy and graduated twenty-second of thirty-eight in the class of 1847. Upon commissioning, he went to Mexico, where the fighting had ceased before his arrival. He served for the remainder of the year on garrison duty in Mexico before being sent to a variety of posts in the West and South before the Civil War. At the outbreak of that conflict, Ayres was a captain in the 5th Artillery.

Ayres's battery was attached to William T. Sherman's brigade at First Bull Run. Still a captain of artillery the following year, Ayres commanded the artillery of the 2d Division, IV Corps, at the siege of Yorktown and the battle of Williamsburg and was commended by Brigadier General Erasmus Keyes for his actions. Ayres participated in the raid up the Pamunkey River on 17 May 1862 and fought in the remaining actions of the Peninsula campaign.

During the late summer of 1862, Ayres participated in George McClellan's pursuit of Robert E. Lee, fighting at Crampton's Gap and Antietam. For the latter battle, he was commended by Colonel William H. Irwin. In November 1862, Ayres was promoted to brigadier general of volunteers and was made acting chief of artillery for the IV Corps, a position he occupied during the battle of Fredericksburg.

Because general officers seldom commanded artillery units, Ayres was moved to the infantry in early 1863. At Chancellorsville he commanded Sykes's division of the V Corps. Commanding the same division at Gettysburg,

Ayres fought on Little Round Top on the afternoon of 2 July. Ayres left the army shortly after the end of the battle to use his division to patrol the congressional districts of New York to prevent additional draft riots. In the fall of 1863 he fought at Bristoe Station and in the Mine Run campaign.

In March 1864 Ayres was given command of the 1st Brigade, 1st Division, V Corps. He crossed the Rapidan River on 4 May as part of Ulysses S. Grant's campaign against Robert E. Lee. At the beginning of the battle of the Wilderness the following day, Ayres noticed that the right flank of his brigade was unsupported by any other unit. Knowing that the Confederate corps under Richard Ewell was in position to attack him there, Ayres complained that he needed reinforcements on his flank. Before any action could be taken, he was attacked and his brigade decimated. He fought gamely with what he had, but was forced to withdraw. For his actions he was given command of the 2d Division, V Corps on 5 June. He continued in this command during the siege of Petersburg until he was wounded in January 1865. He returned to command in time to fight at Five Forks on 1 April and was commended for his actions there.

After the war, Ayres was promoted to lieutenant colonel in the regular army and served in garrisons in Arkansas, Louisiana, and Florida before being promoted to colonel of 2d Artillery in 1879. He died on active duty on 4 December 1888 at Fort Hamilton, New York. He was buried in Arlington National Cemetery.

—David S. Heidler and Jeanne T. Heidler

See also Five Forks; Wilderness, Battle of the.
For further reading:
Rhea, Gordon C. *The Battle of the Wilderness, May 5–6, 1864* (1994).
———. *The Battles for Spotsylvania Court House and the Road to Yellow Tavern, May 7–12, 1864* (1997).

B

BABCOCK, ORVILLE ELIAS
(1835–1884)
Union officer

An 1861 graduate of West Point who rose quickly in the ranks of Union officers during the Civil War, Orville E. Babcock is notable for his military success and for his close association with Ulysses S. Grant. Babcock served in a variety of capacities as a trusted aide. He was "a man in whom I have great confidence," Grant wrote later. After Grant became president, he demonstrated his confidence in Babcock by publicly defending him against charges of corruption, an act that reflected badly on Grant and his administration.

Orville Elias Babcock was born to Elias Babcock, Jr. and Clara Olmstead Babcock at Franklin, Vermont, on 25 December 1835. Upon graduation from West Point in 1861, the newly commissioned second lieutenant was given command of a company of engineers. In November 1861, he was assigned to the Army of the Potomac, and in April 1862, he was appointed a staff officer to General W. B. Franklin. Later that year, General George B. McClellan, commander of the Army of the Potomac, cited Babcock for work "splendidly done" and recommended that he be promoted. Babcock was subsequently cited for "meritorious service" in the defense of Knoxville and for "gallant conduct" at Fort Sanders, the battle of the Wilderness, and Petersburg. In 1864, Babcock was appointed acting chief for the Department of the Ohio and shortly thereafter joined General Grant's staff as an aide-de-camp.

In April 1865, when the Army of Northern Virginia moved west of Petersburg, Grant sent Babcock behind Confederate lines to deliver the terms of surrender to Robert E. Lee. Babcock reported that he discovered Lee

about a half mile from Appomattox lying on the ground under an apple tree by the side of the road. One of Lee's staff officers took the summons from Babcock and handed it to Lee. After reading it, the general announced that he would accompany Babcock to meet with Grant, but Lee asked that Babcock first notify General George Meade of his decision to avoid any resumption of hostilities. Babcock agreed, asking Meade to hold back until he received orders from Grant. Lee and his secretary then rode with Babcock to Appomattox Court House, where Lee formally submitted his surrender to Grant.

On 6 June 1865, Orville Babcock was promoted to brigadier general by brevet. On 8 November 1866, Babcock married Annie Eliza Campbell at Galena, Illinois. After Grant's inauguration as president on 4 March 1869, Grant appointed Babcock his private secretary. In this capacity, Babcock became a friend of John McDonald, a supervisor of internal revenue at St. Louis. Because of their friendship, and because he and his wife had accepted expensive gifts from McDonald, Babcock was investigated and later indicted by a St. Louis grand jury for conspiracy to commit fraud. McDonald was indicted, along with other officials, as a member of the infamous Whiskey Ring. Grant shielded Babcock, protesting that Babcock was innocent of the charges, an act that caused much criticism of the president. In February 1876, Babcock was found not guilty and, for a short time, returned to his duties at the White House. But the publicity surrounding the affair, along with other scandals that were revealed, further tainted the Grant administration, and Babcock retired to private life, becoming superintendent of buildings and grounds for Washington, D.C. He later became chief engineer for lighthouse establishment in Florida, assuming responsibility for the construction of a lighthouse at Mosquito Inlet. However, on 2 June 1884, before construction could begin, Babcock was drowned when a shorebound schooner he was on overturned and sank. He was forty-nine.

—*James R. Belpedio*

See also Grant, Ulysses S.
For further reading:
Grant, Ulysses S. *Personal Memoirs of U.S. Grant* (1885).

BAGBY, GEORGE WILLIAM
(1828–1883)
Southern journalist

Born in Buckingham County, Virginia, to George Bagby and Virginia Young Evans Bagby, George William attended a variety of boarding schools and colleges before graduating in 1849 from the University of Pennsylvania Medical School. He practiced medicine only briefly, however, before entering the field of journalism. Before the Civil War he edited the Lynchburg

Virginian and the Lynchburg *Express*. Besides his editorial chores, Bagby also served as a Washington correspondent for a number of southern newspapers as well as writing numerous articles for the *Southern Literary Messenger*. For his correspondent work and the articles for the *Messenger*, Bagby was paid by the article, giving him the incentive to become one of the most prolific journalists in the South.

In 1860 Bagby took the position of editor of the *Southern Literary Messenger*. He served in that capacity for most of the war. Though Bagby wrote about the war in general, he was a Virginian, who when he was not reporting news from the front and the government, wrote primarily about Virginia for Virginians. Therefore his literary efforts were not read much beyond his own state. His most famous series during the war consisted of articles he penned under the name of Mozis Adduma, a homespun, comedic philosopher.

Because Bagby lived and worked in Richmond throughout the war, his insights were hungrily sought by a news-starved Confederacy. Therefore he served as a correspondent for several southern newspapers. He wrote for the Charleston *Mercury* under the pseudonym of "Hermes," for the Mobile *Register* as "Gamma," and the Columbus (Georgia) *Sun* as "Pan." Because of the many connections he cultivated within the Confederate government, he also wrote for newspapers in Richmond.

Bagby's reporting style was direct and often critical of the military and the Confederate government. His numerous confidential sources in the government kept him informed not only of troop movements, but also of important decisions made by President Jefferson Davis. Early in the war, Bagby became an outspoken critic of Davis and often of Davis's generals. His antagonism toward Davis's policies only grew as the war progressed. Eventually, he openly sided with Confederate vice president Alexander Stephens in the vice president's feud with Davis.

In his articles on the military, Bagby wrote mostly about the eastern theater. He became an ardent supporter of Robert E. Lee, although he was critical of the general's early actions in 1861 in what would become West Virginia. Bagby was effusive in his praise for J. E. B. Stuart when the flamboyant cavalry commander rode around George McClellan's army on the Peninsula in the spring of 1862, but was quick to criticize Stuart when the general was surprised at Brandy Station a year later. In the latter part of the war, Bagby rode the trenches outside Petersburg to observe the struggle there. The articles he wrote from the siege of that city were in high demand throughout the South.

Besides his journalistic endeavors, Bagby was technically in the Confederate army from 1861 until 1864, although his weak health kept him out of combat. He briefly served as a clerk on P. G. T. Beauregard's staff at First Bull Run, but apparently had no other serious military duties for the next three years. He left the army in 1864, the same year he resigned as the editor of the *Southern Literary Messenger*. In that year he became the associate editor of the Richmond *Whig*. His articles for the *Whig* were increasingly critical of President Davis's conduct of the war.

After the war, Bagby temporarily moved to New York City but soon returned to Virginia where he made his living as a lecturer, author, and editor. From 1870 to 1878, he also held the position of state librarian in Richmond. He became involved in Virginia politics and opposed reforms to the state government. In spite of failing eyesight, he remained a prolific author, although his works were seldom read outside his native state.

—*David S. Heidler and Jeanne T. Heidler*

See also Newspapers; *Southern Literary Messenger*.

For further reading:
Andrews, J. Cutler. *The South Reports the Civil War* (1970).
King, Joseph Leonard. *Dr. William Bagby: A Study of Virginia Literature* (1927).

BAILEY, JOSEPH
(1825–1867)
Union general

Born in Pennsville, Ohio, Joseph Bailey went with his family to Illinois while he was still a child. As an adult he moved to Wisconsin, where he became a civil engineer before the war. At the outbreak of the Civil War, Bailey was commissioned a captain in the 4th Wisconsin Cavalry.

After being mustered into federal service, the regiment went to Washington, D.C. Seeing little action in the early months of the war, Bailey and his regiment were sent to the Gulf of Mexico in the early months of 1862 to participate in the reduction of New Orleans. Once the city had fallen, Bailey became the acting chief defensive engineer for the city. In May 1863, Bailey was promoted to major; in July 1863, to lieutenant colonel. Though still a member of the 4th Wisconsin, Bailey served most of his time as an engineering officer.

As an engineer officer, Bailey was sent to Port Hudson in the summer of 1863, helping in the reduction of the town. In the spring of 1864, again on detached service from the 4th Wisconsin, Bailey accompanied the Nathaniel P. Banks's Red River expedition. Upon the retreat during this campaign, Banks and the fleet of thirty-three boats accompanying him discovered to their dismay that the water level of the river had fallen since their earlier passage and that the boats could not move over the shoaled areas. While most of the engineers on the trip believed the situation hopeless and that the boats would have to be destroyed, Bailey convinced the senior officers to allow him to construct wing dams to raise the water level at the shoals. Using several thousand soldiers as laborers, Bailey constructed the dams and was able to save the boats. For his actions, Congress voted Bailey its thanks, one of only fifteen officers to receive such an honor. In May 1864 Bailey was promoted colonel of the 4th Wisconsin.

He did not have the opportunity to enjoy his new command for he was again detached and made the commander of the Engineering Brigade of XIX Corps, Department of the Gulf. He commanded this brigade, made up almost entirely of African-American troops, in the Mobile Bay campaign of September 1864. Bailey was commended for his bravery and initiative in this campaign.

In October 1864, Bailey was the commander of the District of West Florida and then briefly commanded the District of Baton Rouge at the end of the year before finally being given command of a cavalry division in the Department of the Gulf. In November 1864 Bailey was promoted to brigadier general. Several times, however, in the last months of the war, Bailey's engineering skills gained him detached duty as an engineer.

In May 1865, Bailey fulfilled his last important military duty. As the commander of the 2d Brigade of the 2d Cavalry Division, Department of the Gulf, Bailey and his division were sent from Alabama to Baton Rouge. During this ride, Bailey and his men were to determine the extent, if any, of continued Confederate military activity in that area and the attitude of the civilian population. Bailey's determination was that there was no longer any military activity in the area and that the civilian morale was so low that they could present no threat to Union authority.

Bailey resigned his volunteer commission on 7 July 1865 and returned to civilian life. He moved to Missouri, where he became the sheriff of Vernon County in 1866. He was killed near Nevada, Missouri, by two miscreants he had arrested on 21 March 1867.

—David S. Heidler and Jeanne T. Heidler

See also Mobile Bay; Red River Campaign.
For further reading:
Cron, Frederick William. "Colonel Bailey's Red River Dams." In The Military Engineer (1937).

BAILEY, THEODORUS
(1805–1877)
Union naval officer

In his nearly fifty-year career in the U.S. Navy, Theodorus Bailey rose from midshipman to rear admiral and served in a wide variety of assignments before, during, and after the Civil War. He is perhaps best remembered for his role in the capture of New Orleans—and particularly as one of two officers sent to demand the city's surrender—and subsequently as commander of the one of the navy's wartime blockading squadrons.

Bailey was born near Plattsburgh, New York, on 12 April 1805 and was educated at Plattsburgh Academy. His father was a judge and his mother was prominent in local society. In addition, Bailey's uncle had served in both the U.S. House of Representatives and the Senate. These political and social connections enabled him to receive a midshipman's commission in January 1818.

The young officer first served on the Cyane off Africa and in the West Indies before being assigned to the Pacific Squadron's Franklin in 1821. During the next forty years he served on a number of ships and in different positions ashore. These included duty on board the schooner Shark in the West Indies, on the receiving ship Fulton, and aboard the warships Natchez and Vincennes. While serving on the latter vessel, Bailey rounded Cape Horn, stopped at various Pacific islands, and eventually circumnavigated the globe.

After recruiting duty and service at the New York Navy Yard, Bailey sailed on the USS Constellation in the East Indies Squadron. During the Mexican-American War he commanded the Lexington as it transported troops to California and conducted blockade duty. Having previously risen to the rank of lieutenant, Bailey was promoted to commander in 1849 and to captain six years later. Bailey would subsequently command the St. Mary's and serve in the Pacific Squadron until 1856, when he began a five-year leave of absence. His distinguished antebellum career had earned Bailey a reputation as one of the more experienced and capable officers in the U.S. Navy.

Upon the outbreak of the Civil War, Captain Bailey took command of the frigate Colorado, which was assigned to the West Gulf Blockading Squadron. His ship helped defend Union-occupied Fort Pickens near Pensacola, Florida, and Bailey organized an expedition to capture a Confederate privateer in Pensacola Bay. In the spring of 1862, after commanding the Colorado while it performed blockade duty near the mouth of the Mississippi, Bailey was selected by David Farragut to assist in the Union attack against Forts Jackson and St. Philip, below New Orleans. The Colorado drew too much water to cross over the bar at the mouth of the Mississippi, so Bailey transferred his flag to the gunboat Cayuga. He led Farragut's 1st Division during the 24 April 1862 attack that successfully breached a chain barrier across the river, passed the forts, and dueled with a small fleet of Confederate gunboats. His ships then bombarded the Southern batteries at Chalmette and, by the morning of 25 April, had reached New Orleans with the rest of Farragut's fleet. Early that afternoon, Farragut sent Bailey ashore to receive the city's surrender. A large, pro-Confederate crowd had assembled at the wharf and hurled insults at Bailey and another Union officer who had accompanied him when they stepped ashore. The two officers, "unguarded and alone, looking not to the right or to left, never frowning, never flinching, while

the mob screamed in their ears," walked to City Hall, where they demanded the city's surrender. "It was one of the bravest deeds I ever saw done" commented a southern onlooker.

After the surrender of New Orleans, Farragut sent Bailey to Washington, D.C., to convey the reports of his operations against the city. In failing health, Bailey recuperated while in command of the naval station at Sackets Harbor, New York. In November 1862, Bailey received an appointment as acting rear admiral and was assigned to command of the East Gulf Blockading Squadron (EGBS), which was responsible for the blockade of Florida from Cape Canaveral on the Atlantic coast to St. Andrew's Bay in the Gulf of Mexico. The veteran officer remained in this position, with his headquarters at Key West, until August 1864. Florida's long, shallow coastline and its proximity to Cuba and the Bahamas presented a number of difficulties for the Union blockading fleet. While the EGBS could often maintain fewer than 20 ships on patrol, it still managed to capture or destroy 283 Confederate vessels attempting to run the blockade. Of these, 150 were taken during Bailey's tenure. The EGBS also conducted numerous raids along the coast to destroy rebel saltworks, provided supplies to Florida unionists, and assisted in the formation of a regiment known as the 2d Florida Union Cavalry.

Assigned in September 1864 to command of the Portsmouth Navy Yard, Bailey saw no further active service during the war. He was formally promoted to rear admiral in July 1866, and, in poor health, he retired three months later. In his retirement, the veteran naval officer lived in Washington, D.C., and served on a number of naval boards. He died on 10 February 1877.

—*David J. Coles*

See also Blockade of C.S.A.; New Orleans, Capture of.

For further reading:
Buker, George E. *Blockaders, Refugees, & Contrabands: Civil War on Florida's Gulf Coast, 1861–1865* (1993).
Coles, David J. "Unpretending Service: The *James L. Davis*, the *Tahoma*, and the East Gulf Blockading Squadron." *Florida Historical Quarterly* (1992).
Hearn, Chester G. *The Capture of New Orleans, 1862* (1995).
Katcher, Philip R.N. "Union Captain Theodorus Bailey Faced Down an Angry Southern Mob to Take Command of New Orleans." In *America's Civil War* (2000).

BAIRD, ABSALOM
(1824–1905)
Union general

Born to William Baird and Nancy Mitchell Baird in Washington, Pennsylvania, Absalom Baird was educated at Washington College, after which he accepted an appointment to the United States Military Academy in 1845. He graduated ninth of forty-three in the class of 1849. Upon graduation he was commissioned into the artillery and sent to Florida during the difficulties there that preceded the Third Seminole War. Upon leaving Florida, he returned to West Point where he served as an instructor. Following his stint at the Academy, Baird was transferred to the Department of Texas.

The outbreak of the Civil War found him in Washington, D.C., as a lieutenant, 1st Artillery, where he accepted the position of adjutant general to Brigadier General Daniel Tyler. He served in that capacity with Tyler's division at Blackburn's Ford on 18 July 1861 and a few days later at First Bull Run.

In November 1861 Baird was promoted to major and made assistant inspector general. In that job he was responsible for mustering into United States service many of the volunteers who made their way to Washington. In preparation for the Peninsula campaign in the spring of 1862, Baird became chief of staff and inspector general for IV Corps, Army of the Potomac, commanded by Erasmus Keyes.

Baird traveled to the Peninsula where he participated in the siege of Yorktown and the subsequent battle of Williamsburg. In the midst of the campaign, on 28 April 1862, he was promoted to brigadier general. Shortly thereafter he was transferred to the Army of the Ohio to take a field command.

In command of the 27th Brigade Baird was part of the force in June 1862 that took control of Cumberland Gap. He remained at Cumberland Gap through the summer. Following evacuation from that position in September, Baird was sent to the Army of Kentucky, where he commanded a brigade under Gordon Granger in the campaign against Braxton Bragg. He remained there, using his brigade to guard strategic points against Confederate cavalry, until February 1863 when he was sent to Nashville, Tennessee. Later in the spring he took command of a division in the Army of the Cumberland.

Baird commanded the reserve division in the Tullahoma campaign, after which he was given command of a division in the Army of the Cumberland's XIV Corps commanded by George H. Thomas. He commanded that division during the Chickamauga campaign, where he occupied a strategic point on the Horseshoe Ridge. His division suffered very heavy casualties on 19 September. The following day Baird and his depleted division held their ground against furious Confederate assaults and remained to guard the withdrawal of the remainder of the corps. The army's commander, William S. Rosecrans, and Thomas commended him for the gallantry he displayed during the battle, and Rosecrans recommended his promotion to major general of volunteers.

During the Chattanooga campaign in October–November 1863 Baird displayed the same courage and initiative that had won him recognition at Chickamauga. On 25 November 1863 Baird and his division participated in the attack on Missionary Ridge. Again George Thomas commended his courage, and Ulysses S. Grant recommended his promotion to major general of volunteers.

In early 1864 Baird commanded his division in north Georgia where he fought at the demonstration against Dalton, Georgia, 22–27 February. He continued to skirmish with Confederates in north Georgia through the early spring of 1864 and then led his division in the Atlanta campaign.

Baird fought in all the major engagements of the Atlanta campaign, especially distinguishing himself at Resaca, Kennesaw Mountain, and Peachtree Creek. Toward the end of the campaign at the battle of Jonesboro, Baird led a successful brigade charge against a heavily defended Confederate position. In 1896 he received the Medal of Honor for his actions in that battle.

After the fall of Atlanta, Baird led his division in pursuit of John Bell Hood before returning to Atlanta to participate in William T. Sherman's March to the Sea. He continued in command of his division through the Carolina campaign and was present at the surrender of Joseph Johnston. In June 1865 George Thomas again recommended Baird for promotion to major general of volunteers, but though he had been breveted to that rank in September 1864, none of the many recommendations for his actual promotion were acted on.

During the immediate postwar period, Baird served in the Freedmen's Bureau. Upon being mustered out of the volunteer army, he reverted to major and again took up the duties of an assistant adjutant general. Over the next nineteen years he served at a variety of posts in the role of inspector general, gradually rising in rank. In 1885 he became inspector general of the army at the rank of brigadier general. He traveled to France in 1887 to observe that country's army on maneuvers. He retired to his home in Relay, Maryland, a year later. Baird lived quietly in retirement, dying at home on 14 June 1905. His remains were interred at Arlington.

—*David S. Heidler and Jeanne T. Heidler*

See also Chickamauga; Jonesboro; Missionary Ridge.

For further reading:

Baird, John A. *Profile of a Hero: The Story of Absalom Baird, His Family, and the American Military Tradition* (1977).

Bowers, John. *Chickamauga and Chattanooga: The Battles That Doomed the Confederacy* (1994).

Cozzens, Peter. *This Terrible Sound: The Battle of Chickamauga* (1992).

BAKER, EDWARD DICKINSON
(1811–1861)
U.S. senator and officer

Edward Baker was born in London, England. His family moved to the United States in 1815, and Baker spent the next ten years of his life in Philadelphia before his family moved to Indiana and then Illinois. While still a teenager, Baker studied law and was admitted to the Illinois bar at the age of nineteen. At twenty-four, Baker moved to Springfield, Illinois, where he became over the next seventeen years a prominent attorney and political figure. During his time in Springfield, Baker became close friends with another rising young lawyer, Abraham Lincoln. Abraham and Mary Lincoln named their second son after their close friend Baker.

In his early political life, Baker was a Whig, although he did not always follow the party line. At the age of twenty-six, Baker entered the Illinois legislature and served two terms in the lower house before moving to the state senate in 1840. In 1844 he defeated his good friend Lincoln for the district's Whig nomination to the U.S. House of Representatives and won the election. While in the House beginning in 1845, Baker broke party ranks by supporting the expansionist policies of President James K. Polk.

At the outbreak of the Mexican-American War, Baker traveled from Washington to Illinois to raise a regiment. He became colonel of the regiment and took it to serve under Zachary Taylor in northern Mexico. Baker returned briefly to Congress at the end of 1846 and, wearing his uniform, urged the Congress to vote more funds for the maintenance of soldiers at the front.

Shortly after the beginning of 1847, Baker resigned his congressional seat and joined Winfield Scott's Mexico City campaign. From April through September 1847, Baker fought in all the major battles of the war and commanded a brigade at one point.

After the Mexican-American War, Baker returned to Illinois, where he moved to another congressional district and was elected to Congress. In 1851 Baker left Congress and the following year moved to California. Baker's Whig and then Republican affiliations meant that he would have little political future in heavily Democratic California. He became, however, a popular local attorney in San Francisco and, in spite of his politics, was much in demand as a public speaker.

His political future bleak in California, Baker accepted the invitation of Oregon Republicans to move to that state and run for the U.S. Senate in 1860. Baker did so and won the election. As senator-elect from Oregon and the only Republican senator from the West Coast, Baker made it a personal crusade to encourage those states, particularly California, to stay in the Union. Some people later credited him with saving the heavily Democratic state for the United States.

On his way to Washington after his visit to California, Baker stopped in Springfield to meet with President-elect Lincoln. Over the next several months, Baker made several stirring speeches urging support for the Union. He refused the offer of a brigadier general's commission because any commission at the general rank

would require him to resign his Senate seat. Therefore, when offered the colonelcy of the 71st Pennsylvania (sometimes referred to as the 1st California because of Baker's ties to the West Coast), he accepted. Throughout the summer of 1861, Baker divided his time between training his regiment and serving in the U.S. Senate.

In August 1861, Baker commanded a brigade along the Potomac, though he remained at the rank of colonel. On 28 September 1861, Baker commanded his brigade at a skirmish near Munson's Hill, Virginia. A week earlier he had been offered a major general's commission but was apparently still considering it and had made no reply.

On 21 October, Baker's commander Brigadier General Charles P. Stone ordered Baker to demonstrate against Confederates across the Potomac near Poolesville. At Ball's Bluff, without careful reconnaissance, Baker moved across the river into a trap. He was killed, and most of his command were killed or captured. He had never replied to the offer of a major general's commission.

The president deeply mourned the loss of his friend, but the most lasting impact of the debacle was the persecution of Charles Stone. Many blamed Stone for the popular Baker's death. That Stone was a Democrat did not help his cause. He was called before the Committee on the Conduct of the War and eventually arrested without charge. He was imprisoned for 189 days and never held an important command for the remainder of the war.

—*David S. Heidler and Jeanne T. Heidler*

See also Ball's Bluff; California; Joint Committee on the Conduct of the War; Stone, Charles Pomeroy.

For further reading:
Blair, Harry C., and Rebecca Tarshis. *The Life of Colonel Edward D. Baker, Lincoln's Constant Ally, Together with Four of His Great Orations* (1960).
Farwell, Byron. *Ball's Bluff: A Small Battle and Its Long Shadow* (1990).

BAKER, LA FAYETTE CURRY
(1826–1868)
Union general

Born in Stafford, New York, the son of Remember Baker, La Fayette Curry Baker moved with his family to Michigan while still a child. As an adult, he traveled the country as a handyman, living for a time in San Francisco, where he claimed later to have served as one of the city's famous vigilantes. At the outbreak of the Civil War, Baker lived in New York, but quickly offered his services to the government in Washington as a spy.

U.S. commanding general Winfield Scott employed Baker in the summer of 1861, sending him to Richmond to spy on the Confederate government. While there, Baker apparently convinced Confederate officials that he would spy on the Federal government for them. His audacity won him a place in the Union government as a detective.

In the fall of 1861, Baker investigated suspected disloyal persons in Maryland, Pennsylvania, and New York. In October he traveled to Niagara Falls to prevent the movement of Confederates from across the border in Canada into the United States.

Over the next year, Baker engaged in a variety of spy and courier missions for the Union government. Given Baker's penchant for embellishing or even fabricating his role in most activities, it is still difficult to separate fact from fiction in his own writings.

The trust that high-ranking officials such as William Henry Seward and Edwin Stanton placed in Baker encouraged him to usurp power. In February 1862, Baker asked permission to arrest Senator Jesse Bright of Indiana should the Senate expel the contentious Democrat. It does seem certain that during the war—especially starting in 1862 when he was appointed special provost marshal for the War Department—Baker began to take bribes for looking the other way on certain matters. Consequently, he became one of the most corrupt government officials in Washington, which was no mean feat in a city known for widespread corruption.

On 5 May 1863, Baker received a colonel's commission with command of the 1st District of Columbia Cavalry. While still engaged in spy missions, Baker also patrolled the periphery of the city to detect Confederate raids. In October 1863, his regiment skirmished with John Singleton Mosby's Raiders near Fairfax Court House.

In July 1864, Baker traveled west to St. Louis to investigate suspected disloyal persons there. The city had experienced a rash of arson, and to make matters worse for the government, a counterfeit ring was apparently operating in the area. Baker reported back to Washington that he believed an organization existed in the western states bent on the overthrow of the Federal government by destroying Federal property and undermining the currency.

The following year, when Abraham Lincoln was assassinated, Baker was in New York. He received an urgent telegram from Secretary of War Stanton on 15 April asking him to return to Washington to apprehend the assassin. Baker took command of a 25-man contingent to track down the killer or killers and was personally in command when John Wilkes Booth was located and killed. Baker was promoted to brigadier general dating from 26 April, the date of Booth's death.

By that time, Baker's effective tracking of Booth and the apprehension of the other alleged conspirators could not blunt congressional alarm that Baker had become a power unto himself, and a corrupt one. For that reason, Congress reduced Baker's reward for the death of Booth and the capture of the other conspirators to $3,750 from

$17,500. Baker's fortunes continued to slide when he was fired by President Andrew Johnson.

Baker tried to exact some revenge on Johnson by testifying at the impeachment hearings, but could produce no evidence against the president. In 1867 Baker published his memoirs, but it is difficult to discern what is true in this very colorful account of his adventures. He died the following year on 3 July 1868 in Philadelphia, but by then he had provided an even more enduring and dubious legacy. During Johnson's impeachment controversy, Baker embarrassed the government by revealing the existence of the diary that had been taken from Booth after his capture. The small notebook, which had been in Stanton's possession, was now produced with several pages missing. Conspiracy theorists eventually would use the allegedly expurgated Booth diary to bolster their claims that the U.S. government was behind the Lincoln assassination.

—*David S. Heidler and Jeanne T. Heidler*

See also Espionage; Lincoln Assassination.
For further reading:
Mogelever, Jacob. *Death to Traitors; The Story of General Lafayette C. Baker, Lincoln's Forgotten Secret Service Chief* (1960).
Orrmont, Arthur. *Mr. Lincoln's Master Spy: Lafayette Baker* (1966).

BALDWIN, JOHN BROWN
(1820–1873)
Confederate officer and congressman

John Baldwin was born to Briscoe G. Baldwin and Martha Brown Baldwin near Staunton in Augusta County, Virginia, and educated at the Staunton Military Academy and the University of Virginia before studying law and opening a practice in Staunton. Besides practicing law, Baldwin was an active Whig in Virginia politics. He served one term in the Virginia House of Delegates.

As the sectional crisis intensified in 1860, Baldwin opposed secession. As a member of the Virginia convention, he voted against the ordinance of secession and served as delegate to Washington to confer with Abraham Lincoln regarding a peaceful solution to the crisis. When Virginia seceded after the Sumter crisis and Lincoln's subsequent call for volunteers, Baldwin offered his services to the state.

Appointed by Governor John Letcher to be inspector general of Virginia with the rank of colonel in May 1861, Baldwin's primary duty was the supervision of the mustering in of Virginia troops. Later in the summer, he was made the commander of the 52nd Virginia Infantry, which became part of the Confederate Army of Northwestern Virginia. Stationed at Alleghany Mountain, Baldwin complained bitterly in the fall about the difficulty of obtaining supplies in the area. He even

took the liberty of bypassing the military chain of command by writing directly to Secretary of War Judah Benjamin about his men's plight. Baldwin commanded the 52nd through the fall, seeing some action, but ill health led him to accept the candidacy from Augusta County for its seat in the Confederate Congress. Baldwin won the election and resigned his commission to take his seat.

Serving in the First and Second Confederate Congresses, Baldwin, although considering himself a strong supporter of the war effort and early on in his career there accepting most of the recommendations of President Jefferson Davis, increasingly came to object to what he saw as violations of states' rights and personal property rights by the Confederate government. In November 1862, he complained about the seizure of civilian flour by the army. Temporarily mollified by the explanation that the price paid for the flour in question had been agreed to by the millers and the officers on the scene, Baldwin remained for the most part an administration supporter during his first term in Congress.

Baldwin's second term, however, was another matter. He joined a growing chorus of critics who believed that the government was putting an unnecessary burden on the civilian population through excessive seizures of foodstuffs, and he also criticized the government for the repeated suspension of the writ of habeas corpus in certain areas. Still his main concern remained food, particularly in Virginia. He argued that the government could more efficiently use requisitioned slave labor in harvesting food rather than in building military fortifications, and he warned that if the government continued to take civilian food, riots and civil unrest would result.

After the war, Baldwin returned to Staunton and his practice, but also retained his interest in politics. He was elected by his district to the Virginia House of Delegates in 1865 and served as that body's speaker and the architect of its rules of procedure. He continued to be active in state and national politics, serving as a Virginia delegate to the 1868 Democratic National Convention. Increasingly poor health caused him to withdraw from public life, and he died near Staunton on 30 September 1873.

—*David S. Heidler and Jeanne T. Heidler*

See also Congress, C.S.A.; Habeas Corpus, Writ of (C.S.A.).
For further reading:
Curry, Charles. *John Brown Baldwin: Lawyer, Soldier, Statesman* (1928).

BALLOONS

Both Union and Confederate forces used balloons for observation and intelligence gathering during the early part of the Civil War. Ballooning was an established practice before the Civil War. A regular balloon unit, the Ier Compagnie d'Aerostiers, was created during the French Revolution, and balloons were used for military reconnaissance during the battle of Fleurus in 1794. President Washington attended a balloon ascent in 1793 by French aeronaut Jean Blanchard.

With clear signs of approaching hostilities, several individuals approached the U.S. War Department in early 1861, suggesting the formation of a balloon corps that would use their balloons for battlefield observations. Principal among these aspiring military aeronauts were Thaddeus Lowe, John Wise, and John La Mountain.

Thaddeus Sobieski Constantine Lowe became interested in using balloons for military intelligence gathering. Lowe had been ballooning for several years and on 20 April 1861, while practicing for an Atlantic crossing, set a distance record of more than 900 miles in nine hours when he left Cincinnati, Ohio, and ended near Unionville, South Carolina. After being jailed twice by Carolinians who thought he was a Yankee spy, Lowe luckily received aid from some local academic admirers and made his way by train back to Ohio.

Lowe had previously solicited the aid of the Smithsonian Institution in sponsoring him in his endeavors to cross the Atlantic. A committee of Philadelphians had written the secretary of the Smithsonian, Professor Joseph Henry, in December 1860 requesting "aid and advice" for Lowe in his attempt to cross the Atlantic.

On 5 June 1861, Lowe took his balloon, the *Enterprise*, to Washington and again solicited the aid of Professor Henry to convince the government of its military usefulness. Henry had several communications with President Lincoln, Secretary of War Simon Cameron, and several senior officers of the Topographical Engineers, recommending Lowe's balloon for military use. On 18 June 1861, with the help of Henry, Lowe demonstrated his balloon by lifting off from the Columbian Armory in Washington. The balloon was inflated with "street gas" from one of the gas mains on the armory grounds, and Lowe made several ascensions from the armory, the Smithsonian grounds, and the south lawn of the White House. Lowe was equipped with telegraphic equipment and an operator provided by the American Telegraph Company. Lowe telegraphed to President Lincoln:

Balloon Enterprise, June 1[8], 1861
To the President of the United States:
Sir;
This Point of observation commands an area nearly 50 miles in diameter. The city, with its girdle of encampments, presents a superb scene. I have pleasure in sending you this first dispatch ever telegraphed from an aerial station, and in acknowledging indebtedness for your encouragement for the

opportunity of demonstrating the availability of the science of aeronautics in the military service of the country.

On 21 June, Professor Henry sent a report of the trial to Secretary Cameron detailing the technical aspects. He included the facts that the balloon could stay inflated for three days, be towed by a few men over fields, be let up by ropes, and serve as a platform for telegraphic communications. Henry also commented that Lowe's balloon could only be used in a city where "street gas" could be obtained. Otherwise, it would require a device for generating gas if the balloon was to be deployed at a distance beyond that to which it could be towed. Henry also requested that Lowe be reimbursed $250 for his expenses to conduct the trials. The same day Henry filed his report, Captain A. W. Whipple, Topographical Engineers, directed Lowe by telegram to take his balloon to Arlington. Lowe complied and later moved the balloon to Falls Church where he made a number of observations. The balloon was also used to send several engineering officers aloft and some panoramic sketches were made of the surrounding countryside.

On 26 June, Lowe was distressed to hear that Whipple had decided to order a balloon from John Wise because Wise's estimate for construction was $200 less than that proposed by Lowe. Whipple indicated that Lowe might be retained to operate the balloon, but Lowe was indignant and told Whipple that he would not be willing to risk his life by using a machine "made by a person in whom I had no confidence."

John Wise was an experienced aeronaut from Lancaster, Pennsylvania, who had made his first flight in 1835. Wise received a contract from Whipple to provide a balloon for use by the Bureau of Topographical Engineers. Lowe attempted to obtain gas for his balloon to move it toward the impending battle on his own accord. When the director of the gas company informed Lowe that Wise's balloon was to be used instead, Lowe removed his balloon from the gas pipes. Major Albert Myer, chief signal officer of the army, transported the Wise balloon toward the battle with a detachment of twenty men from the 26th Pennsylvania Infantry. Due to Myer's impatience once he heard the sounds of the battle, the balloon was attached directly to a wagon and the mules whipped to a trot. The balloon soon became tangled in trees and was abandoned. Whipple later directed Lowe to move his balloon to Manassas where he made significant observations of troop positions after the battle.

Lowe's other significant competitor was John La Mountain from Troy, New York. La Mountain had teamed with John Wise in 1859 and had taken a trip in a balloon named the *Atlantic*, departing from St. Louis and landing near Henderson, New York, in less than

The balloon *Intrepid* being inflated during the battle of Fair Oaks, Virginia, 31 May 1862. (*National Archives*)

twenty-four hours. The feat had set a distance record for a nonstop flight, but it had also resulted in the end of the partnership between Wise and La Mountain.

La Mountain, like Lowe, had contacted the War Department offering his services as an aeronaut. La Mountain did not receive an initial response, but in June 1861 he was invited to demonstrate his balloon at Fort Monroe by Major General George Benjamin Butler. La Mountain made several flights from Fort Monroe in his balloon *Atlantic*, and after a flight on August 10 he reported to Butler:

I attained an altitude of 3,500 feet, and made observations as follows: About 5 or 6 miles northwest of Hampton I discovered an encampment of the enemy, but owing to the misty state of the atmosphere, caused by the recent rain, I was unable to form a correct idea of their numerical force, but should judge from 4,000 to 5,000. There were no vessels or encampments of any kind either at York or Back Rivers or at New Market Bridge.

La Mountain later made an ascent in his balloon from the Union ship *Fanny* at Hampton Roads to observe Confederate batteries on Sewell's Point, Virginia.

La Mountain continued making observations without an official sponsorship, but he entered into an acrimonious relationship with Lowe after Lowe was given an official position. The two battled in the media and through their various military champions. At one point, Lowe was directed by the Topographical Engineers to surrender one of his balloons for La Mountain's use. The dispute ended on 19 February 1862, when Major General McClellan ordered that La Mountain's services would no longer be used.

On 29 June 1861 Whipple wrote Lowe that he should repair his balloon and the Topographical Engineers would employ his services for $30 per day on the days that he went aloft. Lowe replied that he would serve for $10 per day if the army would instruct him to construct a new balloon designed specifically for military purposes. On 2 August Whipple complied and directed Lowe to construct a balloon that contained at least 25,000 cubic feet of gas, made of the "best India silk." Lowe completed construction of his new balloon on 28 August, and the balloon went aloft the next day. Lowe made observations of the Confederates building earthworks on Munson's Hill and Clark's Hill. Lowe's balloon quickly became popular with senior officers and several went aloft with Lowe, including Brigadier Generals Fitz John Porter and

Irvin McDowell. On 7 September Major General George McClellan went up and examined the enemy's works.

On 25 September, Lowe received an order for four more balloons and gas generators for use by the Army of the Potomac. Two of the balloons were to be smaller because Lowe had recommended smaller balloons for bad weather. He received $1,500 each for the larger ones and $1,200 for the smaller versions. They were constructed from silk and coated with varnish. The larger ones, *Intrepid* and *Union*, were filled with "coal gas" and the smaller ones, *Washington* and *Constitution*, were filled with hydrogen.

In March 1862 the responsibility for Lowe's balloons was transferred from the Topographical Engineers to the Quartermaster Department. Lowe was ordered to transport his balloons to Fort Monroe to support operations on the peninsula, and he shipped his balloon to Fort Monroe on the steamer *Hugh Jenkins*. Lowe's balloons were used frequently to make observations of the Confederates at Yorktown. Numerous general officers

Thaddeus S. Lowe observing the battle of Fair Oaks from the *Intrepid*. (*National Archives*)

and their staffs and guests, including the Comte de Paris, ascended in the balloons for observations. Brigadier General Fitz John Porter made over one hundred such flights. Lowe recalled in his report that Porter made one flight by himself aided on the ground by one of Lowe's assistants. Instead of the three or four ropes Lowe normally used, a single rope tethered the general. When that rope broke, Porter in free flight released all the gas in his eagerness to get down. The deflated balloon descended like a parachute, but the experience left Porter wary of future flights in Lowe's balloons.

Lowe frequently used the telegraph to relay his observations from the balloon without descending. On the morning of 4 May Lowe telegraphed McClellan that Yorktown had been evacuated by the Confederates. Lowe made numerous flights from the banks of the Chickahominy River and on several occasions took Brigadier General George Stoneman aloft for observations. Lowe and Stoneman could see Richmond from the Chickahominy and later learned that the citizens of Richmond had observed the balloon. A Richmond paper reported:

> The enemy are fast making their appearance on the banks of the Chickahominy. Yesterday they had a balloon in the air the whole day, it being witnessed by many of our citizens from the streets and house tops. They evidently discovered something of importance to them, for at about 4 P.M. a brisk cannonading was heard at Mechanicsville and the Yankees now occupy that place.

Lowe continued to make frequent flights during the Peninsula campaign. The Balloon Department's services were particularly noteworthy during the battle of Fair Oaks. At one point, Lowe attempted to ascend in the small balloon *Constitution*, but the weight of his telegraph equipment would not allow him to obtain the proper height. He descended and attempted to inflate the larger balloon *Intrepid*. Faced with losing more than an hour to inflating the large balloon, Lowe seized upon the idea of transferring gas from the *Constitution* to the *Intrepid*. After instructing soldiers to cut the bottom out of a camp kettle, Lowe used it to connect the two balloons and transferred the gas, thus allowing him to make a timely ascent to a sufficient height in the *Intrepid*.

The Confederates were less successful in their attempts to use balloons for observations. The first attempt was a hot air balloon constructed by a novice. A more successful attempt was the "Silk Dress Balloon." This balloon was constructed of multicolored bolts of dress silk. The only gas available for this balloon was in Richmond, so it had to be towed inflated to the battlefield. It was captured by a Federal gunship on 4 July 1862 while tethered to a barge on the James River. A second

"Silk Dress Balloon" was tethered over Richmond until it was lost in a storm.

During the Peninsula campaign, Lowe became ill in late June with malaria and remained incapacitated until early September. He continued to support the Army of the Potomac under its subsequent commanders performing numerous observations at Fredericksburg under Major General Ambrose Burnside. Lowe also played a significant role at Chancellorsville supporting Major General Joseph Hooker, but he never gained the favor with Burnside and Hooker that he had enjoyed with McClellan. A review of the correspondence by Hooker concerning the Balloon Corps during 1862 reveals a general mistrust of the service on his part. The demise of the Balloon Department began with its transfer from the Quartermaster Department to the Corps of Engineers. Captain C. E. Comstock, Corps of Engineers, was placed in control of the "Balloon Establishment" and became Lowe's immediate supervisor.

One of Comstock's first actions was to reduce Lowe's compensation from $10 to $6 per day. Lowe was incensed and protested in a letter to the chief of staff, Major General Daniel Butterfield, only to be rebuked for not using the chain of command, which meant sending his complaint through Comstock. Lowe had previously experienced difficulties in accounting for supplies and equipment and his civilian status had caused him difficulties in the Army of the Potomac. The pay reduction, and Comstock's dismissal of Lowe's father, who had worked for him since the Peninsula campaign, was the last straw. He served until the end of the battle of Chancellorsville and then resigned his position on 8 May 1863.

James and Ezra Allen, who had worked for Lowe as assistants, replaced him for a time. The Allens had similar difficulties with lack of authority and complained to Lowe in a letter shortly before the Balloon Department was disbanded:

Since you left the army of the Potomac, we have endeavored as you requested, to make this branch of the service as efficient as possible, but to accomplish what was done when you were in charge is simply impossible under the present management, and I fear that things will soon be in such a condition that when an important observation is wanted, it cannot be had.

In July 1863 control of the Balloon Corps was offered to Colonel Albert Myer, Chief Signal Officer, but he declined it. The Balloon Corps was disbanded in August 1863. Balloons eventually reentered service in 1892 when the Signal Corps purchased a balloon for observation from a French company. It was christened the *General Myer* in honor of the first chief signal officer who happened to be the officer responsible for snagging the army's first balloon in the trees en route to the Bull Run battlefield.

—*Bill Cameron*

See also Lowe, Thaddeus.
For further reading:
Brown, J. Willard. *The Signal Corps, U.S.A. in the War of the Rebellion* (1896).
Evans, Charles M. "Air War Over Virginia." *Civil War Times* (1996).
Haydon, F. Stansbury. *Aeronautics in the Union and Confederate Armies with a Survey of Military Aeronautics Prior to 1861* (1941).
Lowe, T. S. C. "The Balloons with the Army of the Potomac." In *The Photographic History of the Civil War*, vol. 4 (1987).
———. "Report of Operations." Official Records, Series III, vol. I.
Raines, Rebecca Robbins. *Getting the Message Through, A Branch History of the U.S. Army Signal Corps* (1996).
Scheips, Paul J. "Union Signal Communications: Innovation and Conflict." *Civil War History* (1963).

BALL'S BLUFF, BATTLE OF
(21 October 1861)

Ball's Bluff was a small battle by the standards of the Civil War, but it had ramifications far beyond its size. It was only the second significant battle in the east, and received a great deal of attention in both North and South. Edward Baker, a senator from Oregon and close personal friend and political ally of President Lincoln, was killed during the battle and became a martyr to those who took a hard line against the Confederacy. Perhaps most importantly, the defeat spurred the creation of the Joint Committee on the Conduct of the War by Congress; the Committee became a persecutor of those who were considered to be soft on defeating the Confederacy and destroying slavery.

George McClellan took command of Union forces around Washington, D.C., in the wake of the defeat at Bull Run in July 1861. He immediately set about training and improving the state of his army. As the good campaigning weather of fall 1861 passed, however, he began to feel pressure to advance on the Rebel forces just across the Potomac River from Washington. Probes and raids by Yankee forces over the Potomac combined intelligence gathering with training. On 19 October McClellan ordered General George McCall to conduct a reconnaissance toward the village of Dranesville, Virginia, covering a topographical survey in the area. McClellan alerted neighboring commander General Charles P. Stone of the movement and told him to keep a vigilant watch on the town of Leesburg; if the Rebels evacuated it, he could move in. A "light demonstration" on Stone's part would help move them on.

Stone moved one brigade to the Potomac opposite Leesburg. When an inexperienced scouting party crossed into Virginia during the night of 20 October, it mistook

Death of Colonel Edward Baker at Ball's Bluff, from an 1862 engraving (*Library of Congress*)

shadows for an unguarded Confederate camp. Stone ordered Colonel Charles Devens and 300 men to make a dawn attack. If no other Confederate forces were found, Devens was to stay on the Virginia side and conduct a further reconnaissance. When Devens found no camp, he pushed on to Leesburg, which he found empty of enemy troops. Devens requested reinforcements so that he could hold Leesburg.

When Stone ordered additional troops to join Devens, only three boats were available to ferry soldiers to the Virginia side and so movement was slow. Colonel Edward Baker was ordered to take command of the larger force, totaling 1,640 men. Baker was an inexperienced soldier, but he was also an old Illinois friend of President Abraham Lincoln. Lincoln, in fact, had named his second son after Baker. After he had moved west, Baker was elected senator from Oregon. He had turned down a commission as brigadier general, because it would require his resignation from the Senate. An outspoken enemy of any who would compromise with the slaveholding South, he looked forward to an opportunity to prove his point in battle.

Baker ordered his men to form a line of battle in a clearing near the river. Immediately in the rear of his position was the 100-foot Ball's Bluff; a single narrow path led down to the Potomac. More experienced officers worried about a wooded ridge immediately in front of Baker's line. Confederates on that height would be able to shoot down at the Union soldiers in the clearing below.

Actually, Confederate units under the command of Colonel Nathan "Shanks" Evans were slowly arriving on the battlefield and exchanging shots with the Yankees. At 3:00 P.M. the Confederates launched a general assault on the four Union regiments at Ball's Bluff. Soon, Evans's 1,600 Rebel soldiers in wooded cover were pouring shot into Baker's forces in the open. For three and one-half hours, the Union soldiers held on. Baker was killed around 5:00 P.M. Unable to stand the fire and unable to retreat in an orderly manner, the Yankee formation began to crumble. Some leaped off the bluff in an attempt to reach the river, and many were killed or injured by the fall. Others climbed safely down Ball's Bluff, but the few boats were swamped by the numbers trying to regain the Maryland side. As the Confederates fired down from the top of the bluff, boats sank and scores drowned in the river. By 7:00 P.M. the battle was virtually over and most Federal survivors were prisoners.

Union losses totaled 49 killed, 158 wounded, and 714 captured or wounded. Confederate casualties amounted to 33 killed, 115 wounded, and one man missing. The obvious disparity in losses was clear to all and trumpeted by the Confederates, while the defeat having occurred so near to Washington ensured that newspaper reporters would quickly spread the news to the rest of the country.

The effects were quickly felt in the North. For Lincoln, Baker's death was a personal blow. When informed, Lincoln stood stunned and silent for several minutes. He walked slowly back to the executive mansion with bystanders noting tears rolling down his face. Baker was buried in a state funeral attended by the president, vice president, congressional leaders, and the Supreme Court. He immediately became a martyr to the cause of the Union, despite the fact that his inexperience had contributed to the disaster.

Nonetheless, the political establishment was intent on discovering darker motives for the disaster. Although many regular officers blamed Baker, Republicans who favored a hard war policy and the destruction of slavery blamed McClellan and Stone. On 20 December, Congress created the Joint Committee on the Conduct of the War. Representatives from both the Senate and the House of Representatives thus formed a permanent committee to inquire into and investigate how the war was being directed. Investigations were conducted in secret, and the committee was soon persecuting those suspected of having Southern sympathies.

Their first victim was General Charles P. Stone. Witnesses denounced Stone, alleging that he secretly communicated with unnamed Southerners and returned runaway slaves to their owners. He was also blamed for failing to reinforce Baker at Ball's Bluff. The Committee took their findings to Secretary of War Edwin M. Stanton, who ordered Stone relieved of command and arrested on 8 February 1862. Stone was never tried, but enough testimony was released to the newspapers to paint him as a traitor. Stone was released from prison in August 1862, and though he served again, his military career was virtually at an end. Stone's experience remained an example and warning to Union commanders throughout the remainder of the war.

—*Tim J. Watts*

See also Joint Committee on the Conduct of the War; Stone, Charles P.

For further reading:
Farwell, Byron. *Ball's Bluff: A Small Battle and Its Long Shadow* (1990).
Grimsley, Mark. "The Definition of Disaster." *Civil War Times Illustrated* (1989).
Holien, Kim Bernard. *Battle at Ball's Bluff* (1985).
Sears, Stephen W. "The Ordeal of General Stone." *MHQ: The Quarterly Journal of Military History* (1995).
Tap, Bruce. *Over Lincoln's Shoulder: The Committee on the Conduct of the War* (1998).

BALTIMORE, MARYLAND

The first disruptions in Baltimore associated with the Civil War began in October 1860, when the city's trade with its largest geographic market, the South, began a precipitous decline. Bankruptcies and massive unemployment followed Lincoln's election as president in November. Baltimore's voters had given 46 percent of their votes to the Democratic Party candidate, John Breckinridge, who was widely perceived as a secessionist. John Bell, of the Constitutional Union Party, hastily formed in May in Baltimore's First Presbyterian Church, had claimed 45 percent of the vote, and 6.5 percent went to Union Democrat Stephen Douglas. Supporters of President-elect Lincoln had numbered only 2.5 percent of the vote, but they held their first pro-Union meeting on 6 December.

Three of the city's four major newspapers—the *Baltimore Clipper*, the *Baltimore American*, and the *Baltimore Sun*—supported Unionist activity in the city, and on 7 January 1861, both the *Clipper* and the *American* published a list of Unionist Baltimoreans consisting of more than one thousand names. The *Baltimore Republican*, published by the father-and-son team of Beale and Francis Richardson, supported the secession of six states during January and early February, the formation of the Confederate States of America on 4 February, and Jefferson Davis's election as the Confederate president five days later. The loud intensity of Baltimore's prosecessionists was the main reason for Lincoln's clandestine passage in the middle of the night of 22 February through Baltimore on his way to Washington, D.C., to assume the presidency.

Baltimore's proximity to the nation's capital established the city's importance to the Union. Against the wishes of his military advisors, Lincoln insisted that the nation's government would remain in Washington, rather than withdraw to Philadelphia. Almost all railroad and telegraph traffic between Washington and points north passed through Baltimore. The city was a transportation and communication hub and, from Lincoln's point of view, a bottleneck that secessionists could not be allowed to control. Even the physical arrangement of the city's railroad depots compounded the problem. There was no through traffic, and different railroad companies owned the different depots. Most people coming from the north en route to Washington arrived at the Calvert Street Station or the Bolton Street Station in the north of the city or the President Street Station on the southeastern side of the city. They would then either have to walk or take the city's streetcars to the Camden Street Station on the southwestern side of Baltimore, which linked the city with Washington via the Baltimore & Ohio Railroad.

Baltimore's status during the war was determined by events between March and November 1861.

Baltimore under federal occupation, 28 July 1863 (*Library of Congress*)

Baltimoreans responded to the failure of the Washington Peace Conference, the firing on Fort Sumter, and Lincoln's call for volunteers in various ways. At first, both the *Sun* and the *American* took a pro-Union but antiwar stand, while prowar Unionists formed the so-called Minute Men and secessionists formed the National Volunteers. Both groups met more or less continuously, but news of Virginia's secession on 17 April tipped the balance in favor of secessionists. Lieutenant John Thompson Mason Barnes, commissioned by Confederate president Davis, had already been recruiting Baltimoreans for the Confederate army, and the trickle of men leaving on steamboats for Norfolk, Charleston, and Savannah now turned into a flood. Most of the University of Maryland's Medical School physicians resigned to join the Confederate army. People commonly carried South Carolina palmetto flags and talked of the need for a Southern rights convention in the city and for resistance to the passage of Union troops through Baltimore. In this atmosphere occurred the infamous riot of Friday, 19 April 1861, in which civilians attacked the 6th Massachusetts Regiment as it marched from the President Street Station to the Camden Street Station, en route to Washington, D.C. Twenty-six men were killed and more than a hundred wounded in the riot. An estimated three to four hundred Unionist families left Baltimore over the following weekend. The pro-secessionist Maryland Guard began actively drilling, a new secessionist newspaper, *The South*, edited by Thomas W. Hall, appeared on Monday, 22 April, as did Governor Thomas Hicks's announcement that he was convening a special session of the state legislature on the twenty-sixth. James Ryder Randall wrote the poem/song, "Maryland, My Maryland," that was soon being published throughout the South, and there was a run on the Savings Bank of Baltimore. On Wednesday, 24 April, John Thompson Mason, chief of the Baltimore customs house and the organizer of Baltimore's States Rights Party, led the attempt to elect secessionists to vacated seats in the legislature. On Saturday, 27 April, the day after the state legislature convened, Lincoln suspended the writ of habeas corpus in the region between Washington and Philadelphia.

The die was now cast. As Washington's back door to

the North, Baltimore would have to be kept in the Union. The first Union troops—in the beginning numbering only about 1,200 under General Benjamin Butler—arrived in Baltimore on 13 May to begin the military occupation of the city that would last throughout the war. More soldiers arrived and constructed fortifications. Homes vacated by Baltimoreans who had joined the Confederacy were confiscated and turned into hospitals, while additional, new hospitals were built. Baltimore increasingly resembled an armed camp. The Union naval ship, *Harriet Lane*, was docked at the Calvert Street wharf, its guns trained—like those of General Butler's men on Federal Hill overlooking Baltimore's inner harbor—on the city's business district. Although Butler's command lasted only three days, his actions were a harbinger of what would come: he confiscated weapons and searched private property; he arrested Baltimoreans on the charge of treason; and, as provost marshall, he forbade all expressions of support for, or sympathy with, secession. In late June, Baltimore's prosecessionist city marshall, George P. Kane, was arrested with three civilian members of the Police Board. Meanwhile, the Union Relief Association was established to furnish food, reading material, and entertainment to the growing Union army garrison that now numbered about 40,000 men.

All this activity intensified after the first battle of Bull Run in mid-July 1861 that made Washington vulnerable to Confederate attack. In a memorandum of 26 July, Lincoln instructed, "Let Baltimore be held as now, with a gentle but firm and certain hand." The firm and certain hand revealed itself to be less gentle as time wore on. The War Department began its censorship of the news under the 57th Article of War in August 1861, and on 11 September, Secretary of War Simon Cameron warned Governor Hicks that any act of secession by the Maryland legislature must be prevented. He threatened to arrest all or any of the members who supported secession. A week later, on 17 September, he acted on his own advice and ordered the arrest of Baltimore's mayor, George William Brown, and various members of the city council. Frank Key Howard and Thomas W. Hall, editors of the *Baltimore Exchange* and *The South*, respectively, were also arrested. Civilian government virtually ceased to operate in the city, but under military guidance, support for the Union was encouraged with less coercive measures. General John A. Dix informed Provost Marshall Dodge in November 1861 that Maryland could be controlled by force, but it would better to control it through opinion.

Union officials spent the remainder of the war doing that through censorship of the press and public opinion and through advancing such organizations as the Union League. The Federal government contracted with Baltimore's merchants and industrialists for a wide variety of goods and services, all the while restricting political participation only to those loyal to the Union. Demonstrations of patriotism such as displaying the Union flag were required and on-going, and the threat of military arrest was ever present, but the war gradually changed Baltimore society as emancipation became increasingly central to its purpose. African-Americans were actively recruited beginning in July 1863 at the Bureau of Colored Troops, and by the end of the year many of Maryland's leading politicians publicly advocated emancipation. Maryland became the first slave state to abolish slavery and rewrite its constitution. When the last Union troops left Baltimore in July 1865, the city had become a very different commercial and social community from what it had been in 1860.

—*Gary L. Browne*

See also Baltimore Riot; Hicks, Thomas H.; Maryland; Washington Peace Conference.

For further reading:
Browne, Gary. *Baltimore in the Civil War* (1986).
Catton, William Bruce. "The Baltimore Business Community and the Secession Crisis, 1860–61" (Master's thesis, 1952).
Pruzan, Jeffrey S. "Shadows of Civil War Baltimore." *Civil War Illustrated* (1995).
Sheads, Scott S., and Daniel C. Toomey. *Baltimore During the Civil War* (1997).

BALTIMORE & OHIO RAILROAD

Geography and leadership account for the Baltimore & Ohio (B&O) Railroad's crucial role during the Civil War. Its Washington, D.C., branch was a single track running from Camden Station in Baltimore, Maryland, through the Washington junction (frequently called Relay), then through the Annapolis junction (a spur line to Maryland's state capitol), to its Washington, D.C., depot at New Jersey Avenue and Second Street, N.W. (now a corner of Capitol Park). It alone connected the nation's capital with the Northern states. The western portions of Maryland and Virginia were dependent upon the B&O to reach eastern markets. At the outbreak of the Civil War in 1861, the B&O comprised 236 locomotives, 128 coaches, 3,451 cars, and 513 miles of line, much of it in slave territory. The railroad was crucial to the Union and, hence, a target for destruction by Confederate forces.

This was the dilemma confronted by John Work Garrett, the railroad's president, who was not afraid to change his mind. Garrett assumed the presidency of the B&O in November 1858. He reorganized management to make the road more profitable and presided over its transportation of troops to capture John Brown and his raiders at Harper's Ferry a year later. In that context, he announced that the B&O was a "Southern line . . . and will prove the great bulwark of the border, and a sure agency for home defense." But directly following

President Lincoln's call for volunteers fourteen months later, Garrett immediately arranged transportation for them to Washington.

Beginning on 17 April 1861 Garrett supported the Union, which in turn protected his road from competitors, chiefly the Northern Central owned by Secretary of War Simon Cameron, who was determined to establish a through-line through Baltimore. If Garrett had not acted, the Northern Central would have replaced the B&O as the northern connection to the nation's capital. Furthermore, the B&O would not have made the same huge wartime profits that his competitors did.

These profits proved essential in keeping the road in operation when Confederate forces raided B&O property 143 times over the course of the war. In the words of Archibald W. Campbell, Unionist editor of Wheeling's newspaper, the *Intelligencer*, "This road [the B&O] in its geographical position, is to be deeply sympathized with. . . . At Harper's Ferry it is completely under military despotism, and every train has to run the gauntlet of cannon and armed espionage." In 1861 alone, for example, twenty-three railroad bridges were burned; 102 miles of telegraph wire were cut; thirty-six and one-half miles of track torn up, stolen, or destroyed; forty-two locomotives and 386 cars stolen or destroyed; and the company's depot, hotel on Queen Street, machine shop, stone bridge, and roundhouses at Martinsburg, Virginia, were destroyed. More destruction followed every year, especially when Robert E. Lee crossed into Maryland in 1862, when he crossed through Maryland into Pennsylvania in 1863, and when General Jubal Early raided the region in 1864. The list of losses is staggering, and the principal figure behind the B&O's ability to

restore itself was William Prescott Smith, the master of transportation throughout the war.

Troops, animals, food for both, and military supplies of nearly every description were shipped over the road. The railroad seemed be in a state of permanent construction, not only because of damage from the Confederate forces, but because cars frequently had to be altered to carry the different kinds of freight. Also, their sequencing from point to point required meticulous planning. All the elements of modern management—planning, organizing, controlling, coordinating, and directing—that made the Civil War the first modern industrial war were present in Garrett and Smith's administration. Perhaps a single instance that made everyone recognize the new industrial way of war and the importance of the railroads to it was Secretary of War Edwin M. Stanton's bold decision to ship 20,000 troops and materiel from General George Gordon Meade's Army of the Potomac in the eastern theater to General William S. Rosecrans's Army of the Cumberland, then at Chattanooga, Tennessee, in the fall of 1863. Stanton called Garrett and Smith of the B&O, Samuel M. Felton of the Philadelphia, Wilmington & Baltimore Railroad, and Thomas A. Scott of the Pennsylvania Railroad to Washington, where they planned and executed the all-rail, 1,200-mile transfer of the troops from Virginia, north through Washington, D.C., west to Indiana, and south to Bridgeport, Alabama, on the Tennessee River, in approximately five days. Such experiences as this enabled Garrett and Smith to expand capacity quickly when circumstances required it.

In June and July 1865 the end of the war saw the B&O move 233,300 troops, 2,000 tons of baggage, and

The Baltimore & Ohio railroad line opposite Harper's Ferry, (West) Virginia (*Library of Congress*)

27,000 mules northward out of their Washington depot. From Baltimore to West Virginia they also transferred 96,796 troops and 9,896 animals.

Garrett always remembered Stonewall Jackson's destruction of the B&O's properties at Martinsburg, Virginia, in June 1861, and he admired how Confederate colonel Thomas R. Sharpe, with just thirty-five men comprising six machinists, ten teamsters, and twelve laborers, had moved fourteen of his big locomotives—including a Hayes Camal 198, a Mason locomotive, and a "dutch waggon"—over forty miles of dirt roads from Martinsburg to Strasburg, Virginia. When the indispensable William Prescott Smith died prematurely at age forty-seven in 1872, Garrett hired Sharpe to replace him as master of transportation.

—Gary L. Browne

See also Railroads, U.S.A.

For further reading:
Bain, William E. B&O in the Civil War: From the Papers of Wm. Prescott Smith. (1966).
Hungerford, Edward. The Story of the Baltimore & Ohio Railroad, 1827–1927 (1928).
Lawrence W. Sagle Collection. The B&O Railroad Museum, Ellicott City, Maryland.
Stover, John F. History of the Baltimore and Ohio Railroad (1987).
Summers, Festus P. The Baltimore and Ohio in the Civil War (1939).
Turner, George Edgar. Victory Rode the Rails (1953).

BALTIMORE RIOT
(19 April 1861)

The Baltimore riot that began about 11 A.M. on Friday, 19 April 1861, pushed Baltimoreans so close to supporting Maryland's secession that Federal authorities took military action to prevent it going further, an action that changed the city forever by forcing it to support the Union.

Baltimore's identification with secession was well known. Just 2,294 of the city's voters—2.5 percent of the total vote—cast their votes for Abraham Lincoln in the November 1860 presidential election. Instead, 46 percent of Baltimore's voters had supported John Breckinridge, the South's Democratic Party candidate. The winter following had been a tense one. As Southern states cascaded into secession and formed the Confederate States of America during the winter and early spring, Baltimore's primary market was disrupted and the city's economy fell into bankruptcy and mass unemployment. Pro-Union and larger prosecession rallies vied with the Workingmen's Aid Association for the attention of the unemployed before Lincoln had even departed Illinois to assume the presidency.

Lincoln received a letter threatening him with assassination in Baltimore on his trip to Washington, D.C., Samuel Felton, president of the Philadelphia,

Wilmington & Baltimore Railroad, on which Lincoln was to ride to Baltimore, had heard of the plot and hired Allan Pinkerton, a detective already working for him, to investigate. Felton and Pinkerton had good reason to worry; there were no through railroads in Baltimore. All the railroads terminated in depots scattered around the city. Two of these, the Calvert Street Station and the Bolton Street Station, were in the northern part of the city. The President Street Station, the terminal for Felton's road, lay on the eastern side of the harbor, while the Camden Station, depot for the Baltimore & Ohio Railroad Company and the only link to Washington, lay on the western side of the harbor. Everyone traveling from Pennsylvania through Baltimore to Washington had to get off the train at one of the three depots and then travel by foot or streetcar to the Camden Station. Lincoln himself did so on the night of 22 February 1861. In disguise in the middle of the night, the president-elect traveled in a closed, horse-drawn streetcar from the President Street to the Camden Station, doing so against the advice of his military advisors. Lincoln had personal knowledge of the problem that Baltimore posed.

Trouble intensified during the next month and a half. Peace efforts failed, Fort Sumter was fired upon, Lincoln issued his call for volunteers on Monday, 15 April, and Virginia announced its secession the following Wednesday. The entire week of 15 through 19 April, punctuated by these last two events, marked a defining moment for Baltimore. On 13 April, Unionists organized themselves into "Minute Men" and secessionists into "National Volunteers." They were milling in the streets on the 15th when Lincoln's call for volunteers caused many of the Unionists to enlist. The Confederate army recruiting office in Marsh Market closed, and the National Volunteers both condemned Lincoln's resort to force and called on citizens to resist the passage of Union troops through Baltimore.

The news of Virginia's secession just as suddenly swung the pendulum the other way. Baltimore's secessionists called for a Southern rights convention, while many intent on enlisting in Confederate armies left in steamboats bound for Norfolk, Charleston, and Savannah. Other National Volunteer groups marched in the streets. Events on Thursday, 18 April, further polarized the city. Over 700 National Volunteers met in Monument Square in the morning and walked to Bolton Station, where Pennsylvania volunteers had arrived en route to Camden Station and ultimately, Washington, D.C. The Baltimoreans screamed insults at the Pennsylvanians and threw bricks and paving stones at them. Later that afternoon they tried—unsuccessfully, in the face of Unionist resistance—to raise a Confederate flag on Federal Hill. Finally, that evening they attended a Southern rights convention led by Thomas Parkin Scott whose main topic was resistance to Union invasion.

The Baltimoreans were ready the next morning when the 6th Massachusetts Regiment arrived at the President Street Station. The 6th Massachusetts was organized into eleven companies and had left Boston on Wednesday, 17 April. Samuel Felton had warned the regiment's commander, Colonel Edward Jones, to expect trouble, and Jones had ordered his men to march from the President Street Station along Pratt Street to the Camden Station with arms ready. They were not to fire unless fired upon, however, and then only after their officers had ordered them to do so.

The train arrived a little after 10 A.M. The men disembarked to board the Pratt Street streetcars that would take them the mile and a half to Camden Station. Baltimore's secessionists gathered to hurl insults and then bricks and paving stones. As the crowd grew larger, it became more violent. By the time the seventh of the eleven companies had reached Camden, sand had been dumped on the streetcar rails, and ship anchors dragged over them, all as the rain of cobblestones, bottles, and other things continued. Mayor George William Brown and City Marshall George P. Kane led Baltimore's entire police force of about fifty men to shield the remaining troops and escort them to Camden. They doubled their pace to a quick jog, but both sides began shooting. By the time the beleaguered soldiers had reached Camden Station, four of their number were dead and thirty-six wounded. Twelve Baltimoreans lay dead and over a hundred wounded. The rioters then turned on Baltimore's Unionists among Pratt Street's business establishments, looting and destroying property and stealing weapons.

From Camden, the troops proceeded to Washington, and all were gone by early afternoon when Mayor Brown and Governor Thomas H. Hicks called for a citywide meeting in Monument Square. A crowd of approximately 10,000 met about 3:30 P.M. There, Brown, Hicks, several members of the city council, and Severn Teackle Wallis, a prominent secessionist, assessed Baltimore's situation and agreed that the city must oppose any additional Union troops moving through its streets. Unionists began leaving the city that night, and over the weekend an estimated three hundred to four hundred families fled. City officials and volunteers cut telegraph wires and stopped the mails between Baltimore and Washington and points to the north. They also burned railroad bridges north of the city, stopped food and medical supplies from leaving Baltimore, raised money from the banks, and contracted for muskets and cannon from Confederate military forces in Virginia. Meanwhile, they overwhelmingly elected states' rights supporters to the special session of Maryland's legislature called by Governor Hicks. With secession threatening in Baltimore, Lincoln suspended the writ of habeas corpus a week later, which allowed the Union military to arrest and hold suspected Confederates.

Those arrests began shortly after Union troops arrived on 13 May. Over the next six months, all expressions of support for secession and the Confederacy were outlawed, and people expressing such opinions were arrested, regardless of office or standing. City officials such as City Marshall George P. Kane, Mayor Brown, and several members of the city council, as well as Federal office holders and even judges found themselves imprisoned in Fort McHenry. Prosecession newspapers were shut down, and their editors were also imprisoned. News was censored and churches were required to fly the Stars and Stripes. Thus was the city physically secured for the Union.

—*Gary L. Browne*

See also Hicks, Thomas H.; Maryland.
For further reading:

Brown, George William. *Baltimore and the Nineteenth of April: A Study of the War* (1887).
Clark, Charles B. "Baltimore and the Attack on the 6th Massachusetts Regiment, April 19, 1861." *Maryland Historical Magazine* (1961).
Ellenberger, Matthew. "Whigs in the Streets? Baltimore Republicanism in the Spring of 1861." *Maryland Historical Magazine* (1991).
Towers, Frank. "A Vociferous Army of Howling Wolves: Baltimore's Civil War Riot of April 19, 1861." *The Maryland Historian* (1992).

BANKS, NATHANIEL PRENTISS
(1816–1894)
Union general

The son of a cotton mill worker, Nathaniel Banks was born in Waltham, Massachusetts, in 1816, worked in the mills as a child, and later earned the nickname "the Bobbin Boy of Massachusetts" for his early trade. He never attended college but spent considerable time educating himself in languages, oratory, and the law. After being admitted to the bar in the late 1830s, Banks dabbled in newspaper work and in 1849 was elected to the state legislature as a Democrat. The 1851 Free-Soil–Democrat coalition that sent Charles Sumner to the U.S. Senate also made Banks Speaker of the Massachusetts House. An able politician and orator, Banks soon became a major force in state politics and in 1853 was elected to the U.S. Congress.

Never a loyal party member, Banks switched allegiance to the upstart Know-Nothings in 1854 and two years later was chosen Speaker of the U.S. House. In 1857, the Free-Soil Banks was elected governor of Massachusetts as a Republican over Know-Nothing incumbent Henry Gardner. A highly effective and popular executive, Banks left office in 1860 to become vice president of the Illinois Central Railroad, succeeding George B. McClellan. When the Civil War began, Banks returned to Massachusetts and, although he had no military experience, was commissioned a major general and sent to Maryland. Because Banks was a prominent antislavery Republican from a crucial Northern state, Lincoln could not afford to leave him out of the war effort. In so doing, Banks became the quintessential "political general"—politically connected but militarily incompetent.

More concerned with military pomp than preparation, Banks quickly developed a reputation as an ineffectual commander better suited for parade grounds than for battlefields. Confederate general Thomas "Stonewall" Jackson proved his greatest nemesis. During McClellan's Peninsula campaign in the spring of 1862, Lee sent Jackson to the Shenandoah Valley to threaten Washington, D.C., divert Federal troops, and prevent any reinforcement of McClellan. Banks, commanding a sizable army near Harper's Ferry, advanced down the valley but was visiting Washington when his troops defeated Jackson at the battle of Kernstown in late March. Upon his return to the field, Banks cautiously followed the Confederates farther into the valley. Jackson meanwhile defeated a small Federal force at McDowell in western Virginia, turned toward Banks, and routed his left flank at Front Royal on 23 May. In danger of being cut off, the Federal army quickly retreated to Winchester and was again attacked by Jackson on 25 May. Beaten and weary, Banks's troops fled across the Potomac River. Over a third of his army had been lost in the Valley campaign and so many supplies were captured by Jackson that the Confederates dubbed the Massachusetts general "Commissary Banks." In three months, Jackson had prevented McClellan's reinforcement by feigning a threat to Washington and soundly defeated the overmatched Banks.

The two met again during the Second Bull Run campaign of August 1862. Commanding a corps of John Pope's Army of Virginia, Banks boldly attacked Jackson's forces at the battle of Cedar Mountain and nearly defeated the larger Confederate army. Outnumbered and bloodied, his corps was forced to retreat toward Washington, where he took command of the city's defenses. Twice beaten, Banks was transferred to New Orleans in November 1862 to direct the Department of the Gulf, succeeding fellow Massachusetts political general Benjamin F. Butler. Banks would never again command troops in the East.

Although President Lincoln wanted to begin the reconstruction of Louisiana, General Banks continued his military operations and began moving north to help open the Mississippi River. While Grant targeted Vicksburg, Banks aimed at capturing Port Hudson, a well-defended bluff-fortress above Baton Rouge. To allow Admiral David Farragut's small flotilla passage north of the fortress, thereby helping isolate both

Nathaniel Banks (Photograph by Mathew Brady Studio / *Library of Congress*)

Vicksburg and Port Hudson, Banks's army planned to feign a land attack from the south. His attack was late, however, and the navy barely escaped total destruction as they scrambled past the fortress in mid-March 1863. In May and June, Banks surrounded the fort and began a series of unsuccessful bloody attacks on the entrenched Confederates. His force suffered 4,000 casualties and lost another 7,000 soldiers to disease. Five days after the Vicksburg surrender on 4 July, Port Hudson also capitulated, giving Banks his first victory as a military commander.

Banks's military exploits were not finished, however. In March 1864, he was given overall command of the Red River expedition, a land-sea operation aimed to gain wider control of Louisiana, Texas, and Arkansas. Supported heavily by Lincoln, the plan was strongly opposed by Banks, Grant, and Farragut. Driving toward Shreveport, Banks battled Confederate forces under General Richard Taylor at Sabine's Crossroads and

Pleasant Hill on 8 and 9 April, but was forced to retreat. As a result of low water levels on the Red River, the Union navy was nearly trapped and slowly moved south with the army. Banks ended his military career with this complete Union disaster, which could have been much worse.

Meanwhile, Banks the politician remained busy "reconstructing" Louisiana. Instead of helping write a new constitution, Banks simply kept the antebellum document and deleted the sections relating to slavery. In addition, he called for statewide elections for the winter of 1864 to bring Louisiana back into the Union as a loyal state. This move angered many Radical Republicans by not promoting the suffrage rights of ex-slaves or engineering the exclusion of the old planters who had dominated state government before 1860. Complicating matters, Banks used the army to force ex-slaves away from "vagrancy" and back into plantation work, sustaining the state economy and gaining allies among the influential planter elite. Radicals thought Banks's governing too conservative, and he left New Orleans in 1865 to return to Washington and help lobby for the moderates' Reconstruction program.

Mustered out of service in August 1865, Banks returned to his native Massachusetts and immediately returned to his political roots. Elected as a Republican to the U.S. Congress, he chaired the Committee on Military Affairs and served until a feud with President Grant and his advocacy of Horace Greeley's presidential campaign caused his defeat for reelection in 1872. Banks returned to Congress in 1874 as a Democrat, but switched again to the Republican Party in 1876 and retired from Congress two years later. After ten years as a U.S. Marshal, he was elected to Congress as a Republican in 1888 and served until his death in mid-1894 at the age of seventy-eight.

Twice a Republican, twice a Democrat, and once a Know-Nothing, Nathaniel Banks, the crafty politician, always pictured himself a president, but never moved above the governor's chair or the Congress. A powerful voice in antebellum Republican politics and in the Reconstruction debate, he was less successful as a military commander, clearly outgeneraled by the likes of Jackson, Lee, and even Richard Taylor. His appointment, however, served an important political purpose. As the first Republican Speaker of the House and an important antislavery leader from a crucial state, his generalship doubled as a necessary political alliance for a president desperately seeking to unite a divided North. Like the appointments of John McClernand and Benjamin F. Butler, Banks, the "political general," served as a leader of men on the battlefield and a leader of opinion at home.

—*Michael J. Connolly*

See also American Party; Bull Run, Second Battle of; Free Soil Party; Front Royal, Battle of; Kernstown, First Battle of; Port Hudson Campaign; Red River Campaign; Winchester, First Battle of.

For further reading:
Donald, David Herbert. *Lincoln* (1995).
Harrington, Fred Harvey. *The Fighting Politician: Major General N.P. Banks* (1948; reprint, 1970).
Hattaway, Herman, and Archer Jones. *How the North Won: A Military History of the Civil War* (1983).
Hollandsworth, James G. *Pretense of Glory: The Life of General Nathaniel P. Banks* (1998).

BARKSDALE, ETHELBERT
(1824–1893)
Journalist and Confederate congressman

The brother of United States congressman and Confederate general William Barksdale, Ethelbert Barksdale was born in Smyrna, Tennessee, the youngest child of William and Nancy Hervey Lester Barksdale. Their parents deceased, the four Barksdale brothers settled in Yazoo County, Mississippi, in 1837. Ethelbert Barksdale first edited the *Yazoo City Democrat* (1845–1850), before taking the reins of the state Democratic Party organ, the *Jackson Mississippian* (1850–1861), later called the *Clarion* (1867–1882). In 1843 he married Alice, daughter of Claiborne and Dianna Boone Harris of Holmes County, Mississippi. They had three children: Harris, Edwin, and Ethel.

Barksdale was a strong proponent of states' rights during the Compromise of 1850 crisis and worked for the election of Jefferson Davis as the State Rights Democratic gubernatorial nominee in 1851, but was not an original secessionist. Walking out of the Democratic convention in 1860 with his fellow Southerners, he campaigned instead for John C. Breckinridge. After Lincoln's election, Barksdale favored secession.

In the Confederate Congress Barksdale was viewed as a nationalist and a supporter of the Davis administration on many controversial issues: suspending the writ of habeas corpus, imposing martial law, conscription, tax increases, using slaves in the army, and negotiations for peace. Between congressional sessions he functioned as the president's eyes and ears in Mississippi, reporting directly on military and political affairs.

During the postwar period Barksdale was at first a cooperationist, even advocating black enfranchisement, but soon was a vocal and vigorous foe of Reconstruction Governor Adelbert Ames, consistently advocating the governor's removal from office. Finally, Barksdale became best known as a champion of small farmers in their disputes with the conservatives who controlled the state Democratic Party after 1875. For example, one of his House speeches, published as a pamphlet in 1885, was entitled, "No Taxation to Create Sinecures for the Benefit of Privileged Classes."

A fellow editor described him as "by all odds the

ablest editor of the state, [who] dealt the Republicans more sledge-hammer blows than any editor of his time. His writing was heavy, strong and powerful." From his vantage point as editor of the *Mississippian* and *Clarion* for nearly three decades, Barksdale exercised considerable influence on party policies. He was equally effective as a debater in public forums and as a congressman, appreciated not only for his encyclopedic knowledge of state politics, but also for his sociability and his often sarcastic and sharp verbal skills. A contemporary recalled, "Some of his paragraphs were electric batteries, which produced a shock from which only those victims who were blessed with strong nerves and great recuperative powers could recover. In person he was small, and his manner was grave and dignified. He rarely laughed, and there was something in his smile which indicated more of malice than of mirth."

A delegate to Democratic national conventions in 1860, 1868, 1872, and 1880, Barksdale served on the national platform committee five times, was a presidential elector in 1876, president of the state electoral college, and chairman of the state executive committee, 1877–1879. In 1890 he was defeated in his run for Congress as the Alliance Party candidate, and likewise lost his bid for a Senate seat in 1890. After his retirement from Congress, he tended his Oak Valley plantation in Yazoo County and wrote occasionally on agricultural subjects for various newspapers. He died at Oak Valley and was buried in Greenwood Cemetery, Jackson.

—*Lynda Lasswell Crist*

See also Barksdale, William; Congress, C.S.A.

For further reading:

Barksdale, Ethelbert. "Reconstruction in Mississippi." In *Why the Solid South?* (1890).

Davis, Reuben. *Recollections of Mississippi and Mississippians* (1890).

Halsell, Willie D. "Democratic Dissensions in Mississippi, 1878–1882." *Journal of Mississippi History* (1940).

Henry, Robert Hiram. *Editors I Have Known since the Civil War* (1922).

Peterson, Owen. "Ethelbert Barksdale in the Democratic National Convention of 1860." *Journal of Mississippi History* (1952).

Yearns, Wilfred Buck. *The Confederate Congress* (1960).

BARKSDALE, WILLIAM E.
(1821–1863)
Confederate general

William E. Barksdale was born to William Barksdale and Nancy Hervey Lester Barksdale in Smyrna, Tennessee. After being educated in Tennessee, the young William moved to Mississippi where he studied and briefly practiced law. Not finding that profession to his liking, he turned to the newspaper business and became the editor of the

Columbus (Mississippi) *Democrat*. He used his paper to espouse strong states' rights views.

When war with Mexico broke out in 1846, Barksdale became a captain in the 2d Mississippi Volunteers. After that war he entered politics and was elected to the United States House of Representatives in 1853. He served in that body until he resigned on the secession of Mississippi in January 1861. During his congressional career he urged United States expansion into Latin America. As the sectional crisis worsened in the country, he became a strong proponent of Southern secession.

In March 1861, rather than continue his political career in the Confederacy, he enlisted in state forces and became the quartermaster general of Mississippi. Shortly thereafter, craving a more active role in the upcoming conflict, Barksdale accepted a post as colonel of the 13th Mississippi Regiment. His brother was Confederate congressman, Ethelbert Barksdale.

Barksdale's regiment was sent to Virginia, where it participated in the battle of First Bull Run. Barksdale developed a reputation early in the war for being eager to fight, and was commended for his actions on the Potomac River in October 1861. He continued to command the 13th during the Peninsula campaign in the spring and summer of 1862. During the Seven Days' battles he assumed command of the 3d Brigade of Magruder's Division when his brigade commander, Brigadier General Richard Griffith, was mortally wounded on 29 June at Savage's Station. Two days later at the battle of Malvern Hill, Barksdale distinguished himself and the brigade that would quickly become known as Barksdale's Mississippi Brigade. Barksdale was promoted to brigadier general on 12 August 1862.

Barksdale and his brigade did not arrive on the field at the battle of Antietam, 17 September 1862, until about 9 A.M., after the fighting was well underway. Because of his men's forced march, many had fallen by the wayside from exhaustion, and Barksdale was forced to enter the fighting on the Confederate left with only part of his brigade. Nevertheless, he and his men distinguished themselves in the heavy fighting that morning.

A few months later, Barksdale requested and received the duty of delaying the Union movement across the Rappahannock River at Fredericksburg, Virginia. As the Union forces prepared to assemble their pontoon bridges across the river, Barksdale's brigade moved down into Fredericksburg from the heights above the town to slow the work of the bridge assemblers. Using the brick walls of the many structures near the waterside, Barksdale's men so harassed the Northern workmen that Union general Ambrose Burnside was forced to order a large contingent of men to cross in boats to dislodge the riflemen. Barksdale then fought a delaying action against the Federal troops through the streets of the city.

During the Chancellorsville campaign in April and

May 1863, Barksdale's brigade remained behind in Fredericksburg as part of the force intended to delay any Federal crossing from that quarter. When the crossing occurred, Barksdale and his men delayed the Federal advance against overwhelming odds.

As part of Longstreet's corps, Barksdale participated in the attack on the Federal left on the second day at Gettysburg (2 July 1863). Again eager to be a part of the fighting, Barksdale champed at the bit as Longstreet meticulously arranged his forces for the attack on the Round Tops. When Barksdale was finally sent in, witnesses claimed to have seen his flowing white hair from a great distance as he led his brigade into the Peach Orchard. There his conspicuous appearance made him an easy target for Federal riflemen, and he was shot in both legs and the chest. Because of his condition, his men had to leave him behind when they were pushed back by a Federal counterattack. Union forces captured the general, and he died the next morning from his wounds.

—*David S. Heidler and Jeanne T. Heidler*

See also Fredericksburg, Battle of; Gettysburg, Battle of.
For further reading:
Barksdale, John A. *Barksdale Family History and Genealogy* (1940).
Hawley, Steve Carl. *Brigadier General William Barksdale, C.S.A.: A Study in the Generalship of a Volunteer Officer* (Master's thesis, Texas A & M University 1992).
McKee, James Willette. "William Barksdale: The Intrepid Mississippian." (Ph.D. dissertation, 1973).

BARLOW, FRANCIS CHANNING
(1834–1896)
Union general

Born to David Hatch Barlow and Almira Penniman Barlow in Brooklyn, New York, Francis Channing Barlow moved with his family to Brookline, Massachusetts, when he was a small child. He graduated from Harvard before embarking on the practice of law in New York City. At the outbreak of the Civil War, Barlow enlisted as a private in a three-month regiment, the 12th New York Volunteers.

The regiment traveled to Washington, D. C., where it became a part of the capital's defenses. Shortly after arrival Barlow was promoted to the rank of first lieutenant. Upon the mustering out of the regiment in August 1861, Barlow returned home to New York to help raise a long-term regiment. In November 1861 he was commissioned lieutenant colonel in the 61st New York Regiment. Upon arrival in Washington, the regiment became a part of the Army of the Potomac.

In preparation for the Peninsula campaign, Barlow and his regiment were sent to Fort Monroe in March 1862. In April, at the commencement of the campaign,

Barlow was promoted to colonel of the regiment. He and his regiment fought in most of the engagements of the Peninsula campaign, and he especially distinguished himself at the battle of Seven Pines. In August he was given command of a brigade of XI Corps, which he commanded at the battle of Antietam. In that battle he was seriously wounded when struck in the groin by a ball from a Confederate case shot. He was forced to leave the field and recuperated for several months before resuming command of his brigade. During his convalescence he was promoted to brigadier general of volunteers.

Barlow was unable to return to active duty until early 1863. He took command of his old brigade in XI Corps, now under the command of Oliver O. Howard, in April. Unfortunately for Barlow, he resumed command just in time to be a part of the rout of Howard's corps at Chancellorsville in early May. He was given command of 1st Division, XI Corps, in the move north in June in pursuit of Robert E. Lee's Army of Northern Virginia.

On the first day of the battle of Gettysburg, 1 July 1863, XI Corps was rushed forward to support I Corps north and west of town. As Barlow positioned his men north of town, the Confederate corps of Richard Ewell slammed into his lines. Barlow was shot through the body, the bullet exiting his back near his spinal cord. His fleeing men, assuming he was dead, left him on the field as they fell back to Cemetery Hill. As the Confederates pursued, Barlow was discovered by Confederate brigadier general John B. Gordon. Gordon gave the still conscious Barlow some of his water and had him taken to a nearby house, where Confederate doctors tended his wounds. For a brief time, Barlow was paralyzed from his wound. At the end of the three-day battle, the Confederates could not transport even their own most seriously wounded soldiers, so like them, Barlow was left behind. His wife traveled from New York to nurse him, and after a number of months in the hospital and on convalescent leave, Barlow returned to duty.

Initially unable to accept a field command, Barlow was sent in December 1863 to Springfield, Illinois, to oversee the draft depot there. By spring he felt fit enough to return to the Army of the Potomac, and at the end of March 1864 was given command of 1st Division, II Corps, under Winfield Scott Hancock. He commanded his division at the Wilderness, and then at Spotsylvania he was hand-picked by Hancock to lead part of the assault on 12 May against the Bloody Angle. In the attack the Federals captured over 3,000 Confederate prisoners, two general officers, almost two dozen artillery pieces, and thirty stands of colors. Hancock recommended that Barlow receive a brevet promotion to major general for his actions in the offensive. Shortly thereafter George

Gordon Meade, commander of the Army of the Potomac, made a similar recommendation. In August 1864 Barlow received the brevet promotion to major general.

Barlow fought at Cold Harbor and in the early engagements around Petersburg in June and July 1864. In mid-August 1864 he led his division in the battle at Deep Bottom Run, but shortly after the battle was forced to take an extended sick leave. His health had never fully recovered, and he was allowed to take a trip to Europe in an attempt to recover his strength. He returned in time to take part in the final phases of the campaign against Lee. He commanded 2d Division, II Corps, in reserve at Sayler's Creek and then was part of the Union capture of the bridge over the Appomattox River at Farmville on 7 April that allowed the continued pursuit of Lee's army.

Following the war, Barlow was promoted to major general of volunteers and briefly commanded II Corps before resigning his commission in November 1865 to return to his law practice in New York. He quickly became involved in New York politics and was elected the state's secretary of state before the end of the year. Over the next decade he held a number of positions, including another term as secretary of state, state attorney general, and United States marshal. He was also one of the commissioners charged with investigating the presidential election of 1876. By that time he had all but retired from public life to devote himself to his law practice. He remained active in New York's legal circles until his death on 11 January 1896. His remains were returned to his childhood home of Brookline, Massachusetts, for burial.

—*David S. Heidler and Jeanne T. Heidler*

See also Farmville/High Bridge; Gettysburg, Battle of; Spotsylvania, Battle of.

For further reading:
Abbot, Edwin Hale. *Francis Channing Barlow* (1983).
New York State Monuments Commission. *In Memoriam. Francis Channing Barlow* (1923).

BARNARD, GEORGE NORMAN
(1819–1902)
Photographer

George N. Barnard, a well-known and respected photographer in nineteenth-century America, ranges among the most important of his profession, due to his artistic sophistication, originality, and technical expertise. During his remarkably long career he dealt with a great variety of themes, including portrait art, news photography, American landscape, and the life of African-Americans after 1865. He is most noted for his pictures of the Civil War, especially for those of General William T. Sherman's campaigns. Because only

a few published statements exist and even fewer personal documents have survived, knowledge of Barnard is fragmentary. Yet as biographer Keith Davis has shown, Barnard's life need not remain a mystery.

George Norman Barnard was born on 23 December 1819 in Coventry, Connecticut, a village about eighteen miles east of Hartford. Barnard started out to live the life of a farmer's child, but things changed after the death of his father in 1826, when the family moved to live with relatives in nearby towns. Barnard's adolescent years were spent in family businesses, creating or amplifying in him a strong faith in personal improvement and material social progress. The overall atmosphere of this formative period apparently was progressive and literate.

In 1845, two years after his marriage, George Barnard and his wife moved to Oswego, New York, where he became the town's first full-time daguerreotypist after a one-year interim in the hotel business. He had been introduced to the technique by friends several years before, and itinerant daguerreotypists in Oswego possibly rekindled his interest in photography and its business potential. With low prices and high quality images, Barnard made his gallery a success well into the 1850s, allowing him to lead an upper-middle-class life. Because of the complicated process, the majority of daguerreotypes were produced in studios, though there are a few notable exceptions. On the night of 5 July 1853, a mill on the east side of the Oswego River caught fire, and the blaze quickly spread to adjacent buildings. Barnard preserved the spectacle in at least two memorable views, perhaps the earliest news photographs taken in America.

In December 1853 Barnard moved his studio to Syracuse, New York, where he was increasingly involved with the New York State Daguerreian Association, a self-regulatory body dealing with mounting competitive pressure among the rapidly expanding group of professional daguerreotypists. Due to the poor economy, Barnard was at last forced to close his studio in 1857. He went to work for Edward Anthony and produced stereographs depicting urban views and landscapes for a new mass market. He was even sent to take photographs in Cuba in 1860. He also worked for Alexander Gardner and for Mathew Brady at his Washington gallery, where he earned notice in 1861 for his photographs of Abraham Lincoln's inauguration and his cartes-de-visite of prominent persons in the capital.

As many other daguerreotypists had done when the process became obsolete in the late 1850s, Barnard adopted a new technique called the collodion, or wet-plate process. His earliest known collodion photographs are of the Civil War, taken in 1862 on the battlegrounds of First Bull Run for either Anthony or Brady. The following year, however, he returned to the battlegrounds as official photographer of the Military

George Barnard's photographic equipment southeast of Atlanta in 1864, photograhed by Barnard himself (*National Archives*)

Division of the Mississippi and the campaigns of General William T. Sherman.

In late December 1863 Barnard began the work for which he is best known. He started to duplicate maps for the Topographical Branch of the Department of Engineers and photographed rail links, buildings, camps, and the area around Nashville. Later, when he accompanied Sherman on his advance on Atlanta, he recorded a unique series of images of war-torn Georgia and of the captured city of Atlanta being demolished by Union troops in November 1864. While in devastated Charleston in March 1865, he took pictures of the ruins of Fort Sumter and the burned district of the port city. Other images were taken in Columbia, South Carolina, in March or early April 1865, and afterwards in North Carolina.

After the war, Barnard published some of his wartime photographs in an expensive collectors' edition, the *Photographic Views of Sherman's Campaign* (1866), with a separately issued thirty-two-page booklet written by Theodore R. Davis to explain the scenes depicted. Barnard operated a studio in Charleston, South Carolina, together with Charles Quinby, and another in Chicago, though the latter was destroyed during the great fire of 1871—a catastrophe whose destructive force Barnard systematically documented as soon as he could obtain new equipment and materials.

From 1873 onwards, Barnard concentrated on producing portraits in his gallery in Charleston and took hundreds of stereographs of outdoor scenes and posed artistic shots. In 1880 he sold the business and returned to Rochester, New York, where he adapted to yet another revolution in photographic technique, the dry-plate process. For several years, Barnard worked as a promoter of the new plates for George Eastman. He resumed studio work between 1884 and 1888 in Painesville, Ohio, and then retired. In late 1892 or early 1893, George Barnard moved to Cedarville, New York, where he died on 4 February 1902.

—*Angela Schwarz*

See also Brady, Mathew B.; O'Sullivan, Timothy; Photography.
For further reading:
Barnard, George N. *Photographic Views of Sherman's Campaign* (1977).
Davis, Keith F. *George N. Barnard: Photographer of Sherman's Campaign* (1990).
McCaslin, Richard B. *Portraits of Conflict. A Photographic History of South Carolina in the Civil War* (1994).

BARNARD, JOHN GROSS
(1815–1882)
Union general

Born to Robert Foster Barnard and Augusta Porter Barnard in Sheffield, Massachusetts, John Gross Barnard was educated locally before cousin John Buel Porter, John Quincy Adams's secretary of war, gained him an appointment to the U.S. Military Academy. Barnard graduated second of forty-three in the class of 1833.

Commissioned in the Corps of Engineers, Barnard spent the next twenty-five years engaged primarily in the construction of coastal defenses. Most of the country's coastal fortifications dated to the Revolutionary War era and, as a result, the Corps undertook a lengthy modernization effort. Barnard was an important part of this effort.

In addition, Barnard undertook to supervise the improvement of U.S. harbors and inland waterways. His most extensive project, which extended to the post–Civil War years, was the improvement of navigation near the mouth of the Mississippi River. He wrote extensively on the subject, and time would eventually bear out the logic of his approach.

During the Mexican-American War, Barnard served under Winfield Scott. Along with supervising the construction of fortifications, Barnard made reports on the various battles, especially those around Mexico City. In the pre–Civil War period, Barnard also served one year, 1855–1856, as superintendent of the U.S. Military Academy. He also wrote extensively about his various engineering assignments, a habit that would carry over into the post–Civil War period, and he wrote about his various interests in scientific pursuits. The latter interest would lead to his being one of the founding members of the National Academy of Sciences.

At the outbreak of the Civil War, Barnard's reputation as a superior military engineer led to his being brought to Washington, D.C., to improve the capital's defenses. His field experience, however, led Major General Irvin McDowell to ask for his services in the first major campaign of the war at Manassas Junction, Virginia. Barnard designed much of the campaign. Despite the Union defeat at First Bull Run—the plan's execution had not been very good—McDowell commended him for his efforts.

When George McClellan arrived in Washington to assume command of the Army of the Potomac, he made Barnard that army's chief engineer. As a result, on 23 September 1861 Barnard was promoted from major in the regular army to brigadier general of volunteers.

In the spring of 1862, Barnard traveled with the Army of the Potomac to the York Peninsula, where he directed the siege of Yorktown and supervised field works at

John G. Barnard (Photograph by Mathew Brady Studio / *Library of Congress*)

Williamsburg and the battles of the Seven Days. McClellan's dissatisfaction with Barnard led to his being relieved of duty as chief engineer, Army of the Potomac, on 14 August and returned to his former post as the chief engineer of Washington, D.C., charged with directing the defense of the city. He remained in this position, with some detached duty to surrounding areas, until June 1864.

During his time in Washington, Barnard served as an advisor to the War Department on more than the capital's defenses. Because of his wide prewar experience with fortifications, he made recommendations on the defense of other areas as well. In addition, Barnard traveled to outlying areas, such as Harper's Ferry, to recommend changes to enhance their defense.

During the spring of 1864, Ulysses S. Grant began consulting Barnard on the best approaches to Richmond. Grant formalized the relationship on 5 June 1864 when he made Barnard the chief engineer of the Armies in the Field. Barnard traveled to Grant's army, then near Cold Harbor, and for the remainder of the war, with brief interruptions, remained until Robert E. Lee's surrender.

Those interruptions were occasioned by the need for Barnard's presence elsewhere. For instance, later in the

summer of 1864, Barnard returned to Washington to deal with the emergency of Jubal Early's raid on the outlying defenses of the capital. Later in 1864, Grant sent Barnard to Savannah, Georgia, to confer with William T. Sherman on the best northward approach for Sherman's army.

During the war, Barnard continued to write, primarily publishing his views on the various campaigns in which he had been involved. After the war, he remained in the Corps of Engineers, rising to the regular rank of colonel. He also continued his prolific writing on various engineering and scientific subjects. His activities in the Corps continued to revolve around coastal defense, and to that end he traveled to Europe to study the best ways to improve U.S. fortifications in the wake of the development of armored vessels and rifled navy artillery. He retired from the service in 1881 and died on 14 May 1882 in Detroit, Michigan.

—*David S. Heidler and Jeanne T. Heidler*

See also Peninsula Campaign; Petersburg Campaign; Washington, D.C.; Yorktown.

For further reading:
Abbot, Henry Larcom. *Biographical Memoir of John Gross Barnard, 1815–1882* (1905).

BARNES, JOSEPH K.
(1817–1883)
Union surgeon general

Born the son of Joseph Barnes in Philadelphia, Pennsylvania, Joseph K. Barnes was educated in Massachusetts and attended Harvard University before choosing a career in medicine. In 1838 he graduated from the medical school of the University of Pennsylvania. In 1840 he entered the U.S. Army as a member of the medical corps. Serving first in Florida in the latter phases of the Second Seminole War, Barnes was next attached to Zachary Taylor in the Mexican-American War when the Army of Observation became the Army of Occupation as it crossed the Rio Grande River. Barnes was next transferred to Winfield Scott's command and accompanied Scott's army on the Mexico City Campaign.

After the Mexican-American War, Barnes served in a variety of frontier posts and was in the Northwest when the Civil War erupted. He transferred to the Department of Kansas, where he served as medical director. In April 1862, Major Barnes moved to the Department of the Mississippi and then to Washington, D.C.

For the next year and one-half, Barnes performed his duties so diligently, attending the thousands of wounded soldiers sent to Washington, that he gained the attention of the Secretary of War, Edwin Stanton. Barnes was promoted to lieutenant colonel in February 1863 and colonel in August 1863. Stanton was not pleased with the performance of Surgeon General William A. Hammond and replaced him with Barnes in September 1863. Barnes held the title of acting surgeon general until August 1864, when he became surgeon general and was promoted to brigadier general.

In this last year of the war, Barnes faced a number of challenges. As the war ranged in various theaters, it was his job to learn of engagements as quickly as possible to arrange for the establishment of field hospitals. Along with this heavy responsibility came the necessity of caring for large numbers of Rebel prisoners as the Confederacy collapsed. Barnes's department had to minister to these men as well as injured Union soldiers.

During Barnes's tenure as surgeon general he recruited as many highly qualified physicians as possible and worked to preserve the experience and knowledge gained for the medical profession by the war. After the war, his work came to fruition with the publication of the *Medical and Surgical History of the War of the Rebellion*. He also established the library that would become the Army Medical Library.

Perhaps Barnes's most difficult duty came in the last days of the war when he had to minister to the mortally wounded Abraham Lincoln. After Lincoln died, Barnes went to Secretary of State William Henry Seward's home. As part of the same conspiracy, another assassin had seriously injured the secretary the previous evening.

After the war, Barnes remained surgeon general, serving in the position until his retirement in 1882. Before he left the job, he had the unenviable task of attending to President James Garfield when that president was mortally wounded by an assassin. Barnes died in Washington, D.C., on 5 April 1883.

—*David S. Heidler and Jeanne T. Heidler*

See also Lincoln Assassination; Medicine.
For further reading:
Brevet Major General Joseph K. Barnes, Surgeon General of the United States Army, 1864–1882 (1904).

BARRINGER, RUFUS
(1821–1895)
Confederate general

Born to Paul Barringer and Elizabeth Brandon Barringer at their family home, Poplar Grove, near Concord, North Carolina, Rufus Barringer graduated from the University of North Carolina, studied law, and became a prominent attorney in the state before the war. He also entered North Carolina politics as a Whig. As the sectional crisis worsened, Barringer opposed secession for his state and supported the Constitutional Union candidate, John Bell, for president in 1860. When North Carolina seceded, however, Barringer raised his own cavalry company, which eventually became a part of the Army of Northern Virginia.

Barringer fought at the Seven Days, Second Bull Run, Antietam, and Fredericksburg. He was seriously wounded in the battle of Brandy Station on 9 June 1863, which prevented him from participating in the Gettysburg campaign. He was promoted to major on 26 August 1863 and, in October of the same year, to lieutenant colonel. In June 1864 he received a promotion to brigadier general and commanded a brigade in the division of William Henry Fitzhugh (Rooney) Lee, R. E. Lee's son. Barringer's brigade consisted of all North Carolina cavalry regiments. He briefly commanded a division at the battle of Reams's Station, 25 August 1864.

In April 1865, again as part of Lee's cavalry division, Barringer's brigade guarded the retreat of the Army of Northern Virginia. At the battle of Sayler's Creek, 3 April 1865, Barringer's brigade was decimated, and he was captured near Namozine Church. He remained a prisoner of war at Fort Delaware until July 1865.

After the war, Barringer became active in the Republican Party in North Carolina. He also resumed his law practice and wrote extensively about the war.

—*David S. Heidler and Jeanne T. Heidler*

See also Reams's Station, Battle of; Sayler's Creek, Battle of.

For further reading:

Barringer, Rufus. *Civil War Diary of General Rufus Barringer, PACS from Concord, North Carolina, April 1 Through August 8, 1865 from a Photocopy of the Original Manuscript given by Osmond Long "Bugs" Barringer, Jr., to the Southern Historical Collection, University of North Carolina, Chapel Hill, North Carolina* (1998).

Trudeau, Noah Andre. *Out of the Storm; the End of the Civil War, April–June 1865* (1994).

BARRY, WILLIAM FARQUHAR
(1818–1879)
Union general

William Farquhar Barry was born in New York City on 18 August 1818. His father died when Barry was young, but his mother hired a tutor to enhance his education, and the bright boy entered West Point and graduated seventeenth in his class in 1838. He joined the 2d U.S. Artillery and saw his first service along the Canadian border. While engaged in this duty he married Kate McNight in 1840.

During the Mexican-American War, Barry traveled with the 2d Artillery to Mexico, became quite ill, and was assigned to staff work upon his recovery. After the conflict, Barry endured the humdrum peacetime army until he was promoted to captain in 1852. After service against the Seminoles in Florida and in strife-torn Kansas in 1857 and 1858, Barry was recalled to Washington to write a tactical manual for U.S. artillery units.

The outbreak of the Civil War found Barry helping to defend Fort Pickens as a major in the 5th U.S. Artillery. By July, Barry had traveled north to become Brigadier General Irvin McDowell's chief of artillery. He fought at Bull Run after being with McDowell's force for only three days.

Under McDowell's orders, Barry placed two of his batteries on Henry Hill, even though infantry did not properly support them. Although Barry did try to find infantry to bolster the position, his gunners were overrun by a Confederate attack that proved to be the turning point of the battle. Yet Barry's career was little harmed by this, for many Union officers were culpable for the debacle. In August 1861 he became a brigadier general of volunteers. Major General George B. McClellan then appointed him chief of artillery for the Peninsula campaign.

Considering the vaunted reputation of the Army of the Potomac's artillery, it is strange that Barry is not better known for his vital role in developing this arm. When Barry came to Washington in July 1861, he commanded thirty guns, 400 horses, and 650 men. By March 1862 McClellan had 520 cannon, 11,000 horses, and 12,500 gunners for his campaign—an increase Barry did much to facilitate.

After operations on the peninsula, Barry received a transfer to Washington to become the inspector of artillery for the U.S. Army and the chief of artillery of the Washington defenses. Camp Barry, an artillery marshalling camp in this vicinity, was named in his honor. Barry also tirelessly served on boards dedicated to improving Federal ordnance and fortifications, and coauthored a book in 1863 on McClellan's engineer and artillery detachments during the Peninsula campaign.

Barry's good service gained him a lieutenant colonelcy in the regular army in August 1863. Fellow officers were impressed with the bearing and cultured nature of the tall, handsome artillery officer. One peer wrote that he found Barry to be a "gentleman of cultivated tastes and a soldier." Other fellow officers marveled at Barry's classical knowledge and his ability to play the flute.

In the spring of 1864 Barry again took to the field, this time in the western theater serving as Major General Ulysses S. Grant's chief of artillery. He maintained this position under Major General William T. Sherman after Grant's promotion. During Sherman's Atlanta campaign, Barry kept his scattered batteries in good repair and well supplied with ordnance.

Barry relished serving under the successful Sherman, and Sherman returned the sentiments. In his Atlanta campaign report, Sherman lauded Barry as an officer of "enlarged capacity and great experience, [who] has filled the office of chief of artillery to perfection." On 1 September 1864, Barry gained a brevet promotion to major general of volunteers and colonel in the regular army.

After Barry fought in the campaign to drive

Confederate general John B. Hood from northeast Georgia, he received the dual brevets of brigadier and major general in the regular service on 13 March 1865. The capable artillerist then participated in Sherman's rugged push from Savannah through the Carolinas that resulted in the Army of Tennessee's surrender on 26 April 1865.

On 11 December 1865 Barry was promoted to full colonel and rejoined the 2d U.S. Artillery. By 1866 he was again on duty along the Canadian border, this time monitoring the Fenian situation. In the fall of 1867 he transferred to Fort Monroe, Virginia, to run the military's artillery school, a post he held for ten years.

In 1877 Barry took command of Fort McHenry, dying there on 18 July 1879. The old soldier is buried with his wife in Buffalo's Forest Lawn Cemetery.

—*Dana B. Shoaf*

See also Artillery.

For further reading:
Barnard, John Gross, and William F. Barry. *Report of the Engineer and Artillery Operations of the Army of the Potomac, From its Organization to the Close of the Peninsula Campaign* (1863).
Hitchcock, Henry. *Marching With Sherman; Passages From the Letters and Campaign Diaries of Henry Hitchcock, Major and Assistant Adjutant General of Volunteers. November 1864–May 1865* (1927).

BARTLETT, JOSEPH JACKSON
(1834–1893)
Union general

Born in Binghamton, New York, Joseph Jackson Bartlett studied law as a young man and started to practice in 1858. Upon the outbreak of the Civil War he enlisted in the 27th New York Volunteers and was elected a company captain. Shortly thereafter, however, he was chosen one of the regiment's majors.

After traveling to Washington, D.C., the regiment was made a part of Irvin McDowell's expedition to dislodge the Confederates occupying Manassas Junction. In the resulting battle of First Bull Run, Bartlett assumed temporary command of the regiment when its commander was wounded. He was commended for his bravery and credited with keeping the regiment in the battle when panic threatened. In September 1861 he was promoted to colonel and commander of the regiment, which by then was a part of the Army of the Potomac.

During the Peninsula campaign the following spring and summer, Bartlett, still at the rank of colonel, was given command of a brigade. He led his brigade during the Seven Days' battles and was commended for his actions at Gaines' Mill.

During the Maryland campaign he commanded his brigade at Crampton's Pass on 14 September as part of

William B. Franklin's VI Corps. Finally, in October 1861 he received the long-awaited promotion to brigadier general, one month before his twenty-eighth birthday. His promotion was not confirmed by the Senate in the requisite amount of time and expired the following March. It was resubmitted for the next session and confirmed.

In the meantime, Bartlett fought at Fredericksburg against Stonewall Jackson's Corps on the Confederate right. In the subsequent Chancellorsville campaign in May 1863, Bartlett, as part of VI Corps, remained opposite Fredericksburg while the remainder of the Army of the Potomac moved to flank Robert E. Lee's position. The corps crossed the Rappahannock after the bulk of Lee's army had left its works, took Marye's Heights and moved toward Lee's army from Fredericksburg. Bartlett fought at Salem Church before retreating back across the river with the remainder of the army.

During the Gettysburg campaign, Bartlett continued to command 2d Brigade, 1st Division, VI Corps, but on the evening of 2 July was given command of an extra brigade along with his own. He commanded both brigades the following day in the effort to dislodge the Confederate forces from the areas at the foot of the Roundtops. Following the battle, Bartlett temporarily assumed command of 3d Division, VI Corps, although he was back in command of his brigade by early August 1863.

In early September 1863 Bartlett nearly fell into Confederate hands. Headquartered with his brigade at New Baltimore, Virginia, Bartlett was unaware that his rather exposed position was known to Confederate cavalry general J. E. B. Stuart. Stuart, determined to bag Bartlett as a trophy of war, sent a small raiding party to New Baltimore to capture the Union general. The Confederates arrived in the middle of the night, but made enough noise that Bartlett was alerted to their presence before they found him. He was forced to flee his headquarters in his underclothes, something Stuart made great fun of in his final report.

In November 1863 Bartlett was transferred to V Corps and temporarily given command of 1st Division. He commanded that division at Rappahannock Station on 7–8 November and during the Mine Run campaign. Then in January 1864 he took his men into quarters at Rappahannock Station. He remained there through February 1864.

During Ulysses S. Grant's campaign against Robert E. Lee in the spring of 1864, Bartlett reverted to brigade command. He led 3d Brigade, 1st Division, V Corps at the Wilderness, Spotsylvania, and Cold Harbor. In July 1864, in the early phases of the Siege of Petersburg, Bartlett again temporarily succeeded to the command of 1st Division but was back in command of his brigade by August. In that month he received a brevet promotion to major general of volunteers. He continued to command the same brigade throughout the siege of

Petersburg into the early stages of the Appomattox campaign. On 1 April 1865 he again was made commander of 1st Division, V Corps, which he commanded until the surrender of Lee. When Lee's men marched out on 12 April 1865, Bartlett commanded the Union detachment that accepted the stacked Confederate arms.

A week and a half after the surrender Bartlett was transferred to IX Corps, where he briefly commanded 2d Division. He remained in the army until mustered out with most of the volunteers in 1866.

Following the war Bartlett entered into a diplomatic and government career. He served from 1867 to 1869 as United States minister to Sweden and Norway. Upon his return, he resumed the practice of law before accepting an appointment as a deputy pension commissioner. In his later years, Bartlett lived in Baltimore, Maryland, where he died on 14 January 1893. His remains were interred at Arlington.

—*David S. Heidler and Jeanne T. Heidler*

See also Appomattox Court House.

For further reading:

Trudeau, Noah Andre. *The Last Citadel: Petersburg, Virginia, June 1864–April 1865* (1991).

———. *Out of the Storm: The End of the Civil War, April–June 1865* (1994).

BARTLETT, WILLIAM FRANCIS
(1840–1876)

Union general

Born in Haverhill, Massachusetts, William Francis Bartlett was educated locally before enrolling in Harvard in 1858. When he learned of the surrender of Fort Sumter in April 1861, he left school to enlist in the army as a private in a ninety-day unit, the 4th Massachusetts. After being mustered out at the expiration of the unit's term, Bartlett later in the summer joined the 20th Massachusetts Infantry and was elected his company's captain.

In the early fall of 1861, the 20th Massachusetts became a part of the Army of the Potomac. In October 1861 Bartlett led his company in the disastrous Union defeat at Ball's Bluff. In the spring of 1862, Bartlett and the 20th traveled to the York Peninsula in Virginia to participate in the Peninsula campaign. In the fighting during the siege of Yorktown, Bartlett was struck in the leg by enemy fire and lost the limb to amputation.

Bartlett returned home, where he recuperated and received his degree from Harvard that summer. Rather than return to the 20th upon his recovery, he opted instead to raise a regiment on his own, and in November 1862 he was commissioned the colonel of the 49th Massachusetts. Upon being mustered into Federal service, the 49th was sent to Louisiana to

become part of the Army of the Gulf under the command of Nathaniel P. Banks.

Bartlett led his regiment in the battles for and the siege of Port Hudson. During the fighting in the spring and summer of 1863 he received two wounds and as a result could not move about the battlefield except on horseback. Even though he presented quite a target for his Confederate opponents, Confederates later claimed that their admiration for Bartlett's bravery prevented them from firing at him.

After the Port Hudson campaign, Bartlett again, because of his wounds, was forced to temporarily return home. After recovering through the summer and fall of 1863, he began to raise yet another regiment for Federal service.

Bartlett became the colonel of the 57th Massachusetts just in time for Ulysses S. Grant's Virginia campaign against Robert E. Lee. The 57th became a part of IX Corps commanded by Ambrose Burnside. Commanding his regiment in the opening battle of the campaign at the Wilderness, Bartlett was again seriously wounded. In June 1864 he was promoted to brigadier general of volunteers, and when he returned to duty in July, he was given command of 1st brigade, 1st division, IX Corps. His division commander was James H. Ledlie.

In July, Bartlett led his brigade in some of the early engagements around Petersburg. As part of IX Corps, he was also involved in the planning of the tunnel under the Confederate works that would result in the battle of the Crater. On 30 July he led his brigade forward after the initial explosion but was slightly wounded and had his prosthetic leg shot off. Unable to retreat with his men, Bartlett was captured by the Confederates. Ambrose Burnside commended Bartlett for his bravery at the Crater.

Bartlett spent several months in Richmond's Libby Prison before a special exchange could be arranged. Upon his release he returned to his brigade. Before the war was over he commanded a division of IX Corps at age twenty-four. In March 1865 he received a brevet promotion to major general for gallantry. After Lee's surrender, Bartlett remained in the army until being mustered out with most of the volunteers in 1866.

After leaving the army, Bartlett accepted a position with the Tredegar Iron Works in Richmond. The company had been confiscated by the U.S. government. Within a few years, homesick and in very poor health due to his many wounds received during the war, Bartlett returned to Massachusetts and settled in Pittsfield. He never regained his health and died in Pittsfield at the age of thirty-six on 17 December 1876.

—*David S. Heidler and Jeanne T. Heidler*

See also Crater, Battle of the; Port Hudson; Wilderness, Battle of the.

For further reading:

Palfrey, Francis Winthrop. *Memoir of William Francis Bartlett* (1881).

BARTON, CLARA
(1821–1912)
Union relief worker

The Civil War was a proving ground for Clarissa Harlowe Barton. Named for Samuel Richardson's eighteenth-century fictional heroine whose filial bonds could not protect her from the world of men, the Massachusetts native spent the war years navigating the treacherous waters of independent relief work and looking for allies among soldiers and government officials. In the first year and a half of the war, Barton brought food and supplies to thousands wounded at Second Manassas, Antietam, and Fredericksburg, before the Army Medical Department and other philanthropists had coordinated relief efforts. So adept was Barton at arriving at the moment of greatest need that she became known as the Army of the Potomac's "angel of the battlefield," and soldiers named their daughters after her. She was also adept at promoting her battlefield stories; postwar audiences had little idea that the legendary woman of steel suffered acutely from depression and lack of confidence throughout the war.

As the youngest of five, whose older siblings held parental authority over her, Barton was traditionally reared to keep house and respect her elders. From her father Stephen, who had fought Indians in Michigan Territory and was fond of regaling his young daughter with tales of his prowess, Clara inherited a love of nation and things military. Before she was out of adolescence, she was a skilled marksman and rider, and proficient—thanks to her mother Sarah—in the domestic arts. Starting in her eleventh year, Barton nursed her brother David for two years after he was seriously injured in a fall. She worked briefly in the family's satinet mill, then found her calling as a teacher late in the 1830s. A charismatic educator, Clara and her brother Stephen helped bring educational reform to North Oxford, Massachusetts, in the 1840s.

Only five feet tall in adulthood, Clara was determined to overcome her family's diminutive expectations for her future. In 1850 she began studies at the Clinton (New York) Liberal Institute in the hope of becoming something more than a New England schoolmarm. After her mother's death in 1851, Barton moved to school chum Mary Norton's home in New Jersey and found work in Cedarville. When opportunity arose to open a free school in Bordentown, Clara became a principal and built the student body from six to six hundred pupils in just one year. Soon the community hired a man to assume Barton's position, believing a woman unsuited to such responsibility, and Barton resigned rather than accept demotion. By 1854 she had secured one of the first jobs open to women in the U.S. Civil Service, as a Patent Office copyist in Washington. The target of male clerks' ire because she earned a salary equal to theirs and greatly surpassed their productivity, Barton worked under stress until 1857 when the Buchanan administration terminated her. After three years of nursing her ailing father in Massachusetts, Barton returned to the Patent Office under the Lincoln administration, but at a reduced salary, which felt like a slap in the face to her.

Initially uneasy about the prospect of becoming a relief worker—Barton believed that her reputation would suffer if she cast her lot with soldiers—she solicited supplies from friends in North Oxford in 1861 and began distributing them among Massachusetts boys stationed in Washington. As she stockpiled goods in her three-room flat at Seventh and Pennsylvania, Barton was called away to her father's deathbed. It was he who encouraged her to engage more actively in work at the front. With the help of Colonel Daniel Rucker in the Quartermaster's Office, she got permission and the wagons to carry her supplies to Culpeper Court House and, after Second Bull Run in August 1862, to Fairfax Station. When, years later, Barton confessed that she had brought only five cups, two buckets, one kettle, four knives, and two lanterns to serve several thousand men, she was quick to add that she "was never caught so again."

Barely three weeks later, Barton and four teamsters raced with provisions toward Sharpsburg, Maryland, on the eve of the battle of Antietam. Working in a farmhouse on a line of wounded that extended for five miles, Barton stopped for only a catnap between Saturday and Tuesday. During this time she extracted a bullet from the cheek of a soldier and helped surgeon James Dunn (whom she had assisted at Second Bull Run) perform amputations without flinching. Here also bullets passed through the sleeve of her dress, killing a man she was tending. After six weeks of hard service, Barton developed typhoid and returned to Washington. By December, she was literally back in the saddle with IX Army Corps, as Ambrose Burnside tried to outflank Robert E. Lee at Fredericksburg. In bitter weather, with 12,000 dead and thousands more wounded, Barton completed her first and best year of the war. Never again would so much authority to act on soldiers' behalf be given to her. The Sanitary Commission, which had little tolerance for women in charge, effectively put Barton and countless other independent relief workers out of business by the end of 1862.

The year 1863 was a low point in Barton's nursing career. Assigned to the Sea Islands during the siege of Charleston, she felt like an intruder on turf already contested by Sanitary Commission agents, Freedmen's Relief workers, and uncooperative staff officers. Even the presence of Barton's brother David in the Quartermaster's Office did little to shield her from "surgeons bristling like porcupines" at the prospect of civilian help and female nurses who compromised Barton's claim to center stage. Two friendships from this period were significant: Abolitionist and woman's rights advocate Frances Dana Gage challenged Barton intellectually and provided unstinting moral support; and Colonel John Elwell, whom Barton called "whole, solid, and deep," became her cavalier and lover, joining her at dawn for horseback rides on the beach.

Barton left Port Royal on the last day of 1863, having celebrated her forty-second birthday on Christmas. Back in Washington, she sank into severe depression, alleviated somewhat by an invitation to join the Army of the Potomac at Belle Plain in late spring. She was on hand for the battles of the Wilderness in May 1864 and the slaughter of 7,000 Union troops at Cold Harbor in June. In late June Benjamin Butler invited Barton to join his men at Point of Rocks, Virginia. She told her friends that she had been appointed superintendent of nursing for Butler's Army of the James, but she exaggerated: she worked in a "flying" or mobile field hospital staffed by nurses of equal responsibility. Never easy about relinquishing her diva status, Barton sparred with New Yorker Adelaide Smith until a surgeon, fearing Barton's ultimatums, sent Smith packing. In the fall General Butler helped Barton secure the release of her brother Stephen from a Union prison camp in Norfolk; Stephen had established mills in North Carolina in 1856 and was reviled as a Northern sympathizer when the war began.

By early 1865 Barton began to hatch a new plan in conjunction with Union prisoners of war released to Annapolis. She was determined to create a bureau of missing soldiers, hoping to provide desperate mothers and wives with information about their sons and husbands. Having no funds for starting up—her Patent Office job had long since stagnated and she was never on a nursing payroll—she sought President Lincoln's help. After a protracted struggle during which Barton called on such men of influence as Butler, Senator Henry Wilson, and Secretary of War Edwin Stanton for help, she learned that Captain James Moore had been appointed head of the U.S. Burial Bureau. Again, a man had been chosen to do what Barton knew she could do better; the particular choice was galling because Moore had stolen her thunder during the July 1865 expedition to identify missing soldiers at Andersonville prison. These events, coupled with the deaths of Stephen and her twenty-four-year-old nephew, Irving Vassal, in the spring, devastated her.

By December, Barton felt friendless. "I make up my mind more and more," she wrote, "that I must be and do by myself and alone, of all that I have helped no one who has strength is ready to help me, my affairs are as bad as they can be." But as she had done before, she made new plans—this time to capitalize on her war exploits from the podium. From 1866 to 1868, Barton gave more than 300 lectures in towns across the East and Midwest, sometimes earning $100 for an appearance. Years later, after

Barton's genius for relief had been realized in the American Red Cross (ARC) and she had retired from twenty-three years at its head, she told a G.A.R. encampment celebrating the fiftieth anniversary of the firing on Fort Sumter, "Under the guns our love grew up, under the sod it shall remain." Though Barton's work with the Red Cross made hers a household name by the 1880s, she always retained her keenest sense of connection with the soldiers she had cared for during the war. She continued to honor them long after her ARC leadership had begun to founder and she retired to Glen Echo, Maryland, in 1904. Here Barton spent her last years, promoting disaster relief, women's suffrage, and pay equity until her death at age ninety-one.

—*Jane E. Schultz*

See also American Red Cross; Nurses; United States Sanitary Commission.

For further reading:

Barton, Clara. Collection. Manuscript Division, Library of Congress, Washington, D.C.

Burton, David H. *Clara Barton: In the Service of Humanity* (1995).

Norton, Mary. Papers. Perkins Library, Duke University, Durham, North Carolina.

Oates, Stephen. *A Woman of Valor: Clara Barton and the Civil War* (1994).

Pryor, Elizabeth Brown. *Clara Barton, Professional Angel* (1987).

BARTON, SETH MAXWELL
(1829–1900)
Confederate general

Born in Fredericksburg, Virginia, the son of Thomas Bowerbank Barton, Seth Barton was admitted to the United States Military Academy at West Point at the age of fifteen. He graduated twenty-eighth in a class of forty-three in 1849. After serving briefly in New York Harbor, Barton was transferred to New Mexico. For the next eleven years, he served in a variety of frontier posts, achieving the rank of captain before resigning his commission on 11 June 1861 while stationed at Fort Leavenworth, Kansas Territory.

Following his return to Virginia, Barton offered his services to the Confederate army and received a captain's commission. In July 1861 he was offered the position of lieutenant colonel of the 3d Arkansas Regiment and traveled to western Virginia where that regiment was serving. He fought at Cheat Mountain under Robert E. Lee in September 1861. Later in the year, his engineering talents came to the attention of Confederate general Stonewall Jackson, and from the end of 1861 to early 1862, Barton served as Jackson's chief engineer.

On 11 March 1862 Barton was promoted to brigadier general and transferred to east Tennessee to serve under

E. Kirby Smith. Barton's primary task in the spring and summer of 1862 was to prevent Union movement through the Cumberland Gap. In the fall his brigade moved into Tennessee with the remainder of Kirby Smith's army to participate in Braxton Bragg's Kentucky campaign. In December 1862 Barton and his brigade were transferred to the defenses of Vicksburg, Mississippi.

In the Vicksburg campaign, Barton and his brigade fought in most of the major engagements, including Chickasaw Bayou, Chickasaw Bluffs, and the battle of Champion's Hill, where Barton lost 42 percent of his brigade. Barton surrendered with Confederate forces at Vicksburg in July 1863 and was paroled with the bulk of that army. After being exchanged shortly thereafter, Barton was sent to Petersburg, Virginia, to take command of the late Lewis Armistead's brigade of George Pickett's division. In the Confederate attack on New Bern, North Carolina, in January 1864, Barton became embroiled in a dispute with Pickett about the failure of that campaign. Shortly after this dispute, Barton was transferred to Major Robert Ransom's division in Virginia. After fighting at the Wilderness and Drewry's Bluff, Barton was this time criticized as incompetent by his new commander. Ransom removed Barton from command of his brigade on 10 May.

Over the next several weeks, Barton repeatedly requested that a court of inquiry be convened on his behalf, but although one was scheduled for 7 June, it was canceled at the last minute. Even though Barton's subordinate officers signed a letter attesting to his fitness for command, he did not return to active service until the fall of 1864 and then only in temporary command of a brigade. He did not regain permanent command of a brigade until January 1865. Barton was captured with most of his brigade at Sayler's Creek on 6 April and imprisoned in Fort Warren until July 1865.

Virtually nothing is known of Barton's life after the war except that he died in Washington, D.C., in 1900.

—*David S. Heidler and Jeanne T. Heidler*

See also Ransom, Robert, Jr.; Sayler's Creek, Battle of.

BARTOW, FRANCIS STEBBINS
(1816–1861)
Confederate congressman and officer

Born to Theodosius Bartow and Frances Lloyd Stebbins Bartow in Savannah, Georgia, Francis Bartow was educated at Franklin College in Georgia and Yale Law School before returning to Georgia to become a practicing attorney. In the years before the outbreak of the Civil War, Bartow became a very influential lawyer and active Whig politician. He served as both a senator and representative in the Georgia legislature. As the sectional crisis intensified in the 1850s, Bartow became increasingly associated with strong states' rights factions in the state. Following the election of Abraham Lincoln to the presidency, Bartow was selected a delegate to the Georgia secession convention as an advocate for secession.

Following the secession of the state, Bartow represented Georgia as one of the provisional congressmen to Montgomery, Alabama, where the Confederate States of America was formed. In Montgomery, Bartow was part of the Howell Cobb faction and supported Cobb for president of the Confederacy. He was one of the signers for Georgia of the Confederate Constitution.

Bartow served on several committees of the provisional Confederate Congress, including the Flag Committee. On that committee, Bartow urged that the new Confederate flag not stray too far from the appearance of the United States flag. Bartow also served as the chairman of the Military Affairs Committee of the Provisional Confederate Congress. In this position, he often conferred with President Jefferson Davis on the military preparedness of the new nation and on the proper military response to the continued presence of United States troops on Confederate soil. Bartow was anxious that, should a conflict occur, the Confederate States Army should be properly organized and supplied so that it could react quickly. Therefore, he urged the Confederate Congress and Davis to organize the army before any conflict occurred. Once the organizational process began, Bartow was instrumental in the selection of gray as the color for Confederate uniforms.

Once the war broke out at Fort Sumter in April 1861, Bartow resigned from the Confederate Congress to join the Confederate army. Before the war, he had been a captain in the Oglethorpe Light Infantry militia unit in Savannah, Georgia, and pictured himself as somewhat of a military expert. He raised and accepted the colonelcy of the 8th Georgia Regiment in the spring of 1861 and participated almost immediately in the seizure of Fort McAllister. Shortly thereafter, Bartow's regiment was transferred to Virginia, where he took command of a brigade at Manassas.

Although never promoted to brigadier general, Bartow commanded his brigade at First Bull Run. He fought alongside Bernard Bee's brigade on the north side of the Warrenton Turnpike and retreated with that officer and his brigade to Henry House Hill after the Federal offensive. Along with Bee, Bartow led a counterattack against the Union forces and was killed in that action.

—*David S. Heidler and Jeanne T. Heidler*

See also Bull Run, First Battle of; Cobb, Howell; Congress, C.S.A.; Georgia.
For further reading:
Confederate States of America. Congress. *Proceedings of the Congress on the Announcement of the Death of Colonel Francis S. Bartow of the Army of the Confederate States, and Late a Delegate in the Congress, from the State of Georgia* (1861).

BATE, WILLIAM BRIMAGE
(1825–1905)
Confederate general

Born to James Henry Bate and Amanda Weathered Bate in Bledsoe's Lick, Tennessee, William Bate was educated in Tennessee before becoming a steamboat clerk as a young man. At the outset of the Mexican-American War in 1846, he enlisted in the 3d Tennessee Volunteers as a private and rose to the rank of first lieutenant by the end of the war two years later. Following the Mexican-American War he became a newspaper editor for the *Tenth Legion* in Gallatin, Tennessee. He also entered politics as an active member of the Democratic Party and served in the Tennessee legislature from 1849 to 1851. While engaged in politics, Bate studied law at Lebanon University and opened an office after graduation in 1852. Bate had a private practice from 1852 until 1854, when he received an appointment as the attorney general for the Nashville District. He remained active in Democratic politics and became a strong advocate of states' rights. In 1860 he was selected as a Breckinridge elector for the presidential election and upon Lincoln's election, he supported Tennessee's secession from the Union.

After Tennessee seceded, Bate enlisted as a private to serve in that rank until receiving a colonel's appointment in the 2d Tennessee Regiment. He led his regiment at Shiloh where he saw his younger brother, Captain Humphrey Bate, commander of one of the Second Tennessee's companies, killed. He himself was severely wounded in the left leg. When doctors proposed amputating the limb, Bate held a gun on them to prevent it. He kept the leg, but he never walked again without a crutch.

During his recuperation, Bate was stationed at Huntsville, Alabama. While there on 3 October 1862, he received a promotion to brigadier general. By the end of the year, he was again commanding his brigade. He fought at Stones River and then in the Tullahoma campaign at the end of June 1863, at Chickamauga in September 1863, and led a division at Missionary Ridge in November 1863. In 1863 he was courted as a potential governor of Tennessee, but refused to leave the field. On 23 February 1864, he was promoted to major general and commanded a division of Hardee's Corps in the Atlanta campaign. He was commended for his actions at Resaca.

Like most of the Confederate army, he went with John Bell Hood into Tennessee following the fall of Atlanta, and was commended for bravery for his actions at Franklin. He fought tenaciously at Nashville in December 1864 and then joined Lieutenant General Joseph E. Johnston in the Carolinas in early 1865. He surrendered what was left of his division at Greensboro, North Carolina, in April 1865.

Though barred from voting or running for office during Reconstruction, Bate remained active in Democratic politics in Tennessee. With the return to Democratic domination of the state, he was elected governor in 1882. He remained in that office until elected to the United States Senate in 1886. As a United States senator, Bate sponsored a bill, passed in 1893, that removed the last federal controls over local elections remaining from the Reconstruction period. Bate died in office as a U.S. Senator in Washington, D.C., in 1905.

Wounded three times during the war, Bate was known as something of a martinet, although one who could inspire his men to perform tremendous feats of bravery.

—*David S. Heidler and Jeanne T. Heidler*

See also Missionary Ridge; Nashville, Battle of; Resaca, Battle of.
For further reading:
Bate, William B. "The Campaign in Tennessee: Official Report of Major-General William B. Bate of the Operations of His Division at Franklin, Murfreesboro and Nashville." *Annals of the Army of Tennessee and Early Western History* (1878).
Marshall, Park. *A Life of William B. Bate, Citizen, Soldier and Statesman* (1908).

BATES, EDWARD
(1793–1869)
U.S. attorney general

Edward Bates was born on 4 September 1793 in Goochland County, Virginia, to Quaker parents. His family was thrust into debt when, during the Revolutionary War, the British destroyed their plantation, a situation not fully rectified when his father died in 1805. The responsibility for rearing Bates, the youngest of twelve children, was assumed by his older brother Frederick. Over his mother's objections, Bates volunteered for service in the War of 1812. In 1814 he departed for St. Louis, where Frederick had established a successful law practice.

Bates read law for two years under the guidance of Rufus Eaton and received his license in 1816. While his brother and Eaton made their fortunes settling land dispute cases, Bates accepted the less lucrative cases involving the personal and professional affairs of politicians and members of the business community of St. Louis. Bates cut his political teeth on the campaign for Missouri statehood, developing a resentment for federal interference in states' rights. In 1826 he was elected as a Whig to serve in the Twentieth Congress, where he opposed U.S. occupation of Oregon. Losing the race for reelection to the House, Bates returned to Missouri, hoping to capture a vacant U.S. Senate seat, but was defeated by Thomas Hart Benton, one of Missouri's leading Democrats. Bates returned to practicing law and became the state's most prominent Whig.

Bates gained national recognition as the presiding officer at the 1847 River and Harbor Commission convention held in Chicago. He advocated increased funding for a series of internal improvements to develop the western states. Thereafter his opinion was sought regarding national political issues. He became a leading opponent of the extension of slavery into the territories, yet believed that the federal government must not meddle with the "peculiar institution" in states where it was established legally.

Bates acted as president of the last Whig convention in 1856. He remained suspicious of the new Republican Party because of its strong abolitionist element, but his anti-Lecompton stance in 1858 enamored many Republicans to him. A "Bates for President" drive launched by conservative Republicans before the 1860 convention flattered him, but suspicion of his Southern roots, advocacy of states' rights, and support for Millard Fillmore's campaign in 1856 stymied his candidacy. When the Chicago convention rallied around Abraham Lincoln, Bates graciously accepted defeat and agreed to join the president-elect's cabinet. His status as the most prominent border state politician in the cabinet gave him influence in the early days of the administration. He advocated strengthening the military presence along the Mississippi, forethought that reaped great benefit to the Union army during the war. Bates cheered the president's removal of General John C. Frémont from command in Missouri and provided legal justification for Lincoln's controversial suspension of the writ of habeas corpus.

Bates's habitual equivocation, as seen during the *Trent* Affair, caused him problems within the cabinet. Initially he applauded the detention of the Confederate diplomats, but pressure from Secretary of State William H. Seward, who feared a war with Great Britain, compelled Bates to reverse his position. Bates's conservative opinions became increasingly unpopular among his Republican colleagues. He opposed the admission of West Virginia as a state, believing this action assailed the Constitution to expedite emancipation. He publicly disagreed with the president over having the freedmen serve in the Union army and increased his criticism of congressional plans for rapid emancipation of the slaves. Bates opined repeatedly that the radicals in Congress were attempting to undermine the power of the executive branch and urged the president to be more decisive. Bates believed that the army was abusing the "military necessity" doctrine and posed a threat to the rights of civilians in occupied Confederate territory. As his influence on the president waned, Bates scrapped more openly with his colleagues. Tired of feuding with fellow cabinet members and with his health impaired, Bates resigned on 30 November 1864. He hoped that the president would reward his service by naming him chief justice of the Supreme Court to replace the deceased Roger Taney. Bates was bitterly disappointed when Salmon P. Chase was chosen instead.

Bates returned to Missouri where Radical Republicans dominated the state government. He objected to the new state constitution and lobbied for an end to the military influence in the government. Disheartened by the course of events in his state and the national Reconstruction policy fashioned by the Radical Republicans in Congress, Bates's health deteriorated further until his death on 25 March 1869.

—Jane Flaherty

See also Election of 1860; Habeas Corpus, Writ of (U.S.A.); Missouri; *Trent* Affair.

For further reading:
Beale, Howard K., ed. *The Diary of Edward Bates, 1859–1866* (1930; reprint, 1971).
Cain, Marvin R. *Lincoln's Attorney General: Edward Bates of Missouri* (1965).

BATON ROUGE, BATTLE OF
(5 August 1862)

The August 1862 engagement at Baton Rouge, Louisiana, marked a period of joint army-navy operations by both antagonists. The 3,200 Federal troops who occupied Baton Rouge had been landed there by Federal ships commanded by Rear Admiral David G. Farragut after the failed July 1862 attack on Vicksburg. U.S. brigadier general Thomas Williams concentrated his garrison on the city's eastern side, with a detachment on the north and gunboats on the river anchoring the western flank.

Major General Earl Van Dorn, Confederate commander at Vicksburg, sought to exploit Farragut's defeat by seizing Port Hudson, which lay 25 miles north of Baton Rouge and between Baton Rouge and Vicksburg. In 1862, Vicksburg was the key to the Confederacy's Mississippi River defense.

Van Dorn assigned Major General John C. Breckinridge to lead the attack with 4,000 men of the Vicksburg garrison. The CSS *Arkansas*, the last of the Confederate ironclads, was assigned to provide artillery support and to fight Union gunboats that supported the city's western flank.

On 4 August, on the eve of the battle, almost half of the city's garrison was hors de combat due to fever. Many of the sick left their beds to join the defense.

Breckinridge's force of almost equal strength was stricken by fever. Breckinridge divided his force into two units under Brigadier General Daniel Ruggles and Brigadier General Charles Clark.

The first shots were fired early on the morning of 5 August. While Confederate attackers threw themselves at the city's eastern defenses, a smaller artillery-supported detachment attacked the Federal north flank and was turned back. General Clark's men arrived and reinforced the initial Confederate attack, eventually pushing the Federal left flank toward the eastern defenders. Fog added to the confusion of the battle, and Federal troops were routed westward into the city, pursued by vengeful civilians.

General Williams fell while trying to put together a counterattack. Union naval artillery intervened to prevent Breckinridge from exploiting his advance. The exhausted Federal troops remained in the city for the next several days while Ruggles's troops fortified Port Hudson. Clark was wounded on the battlefield and captured. Two weeks after the battle, Federal troops evacuated the city and returned to New Orleans. Union casualties were approximately 400 killed, wounded, and missing; Confederate losses were approximately 450 dead, wounded, and missing.

The battle at Baton Rouge marked the end of the CSS *Arkansas*. Its commander, Captain Isaac Newton Brown, was away on sick leave, and his replacement, Lieutenant Henry Kennedy Stevens, received orders to weigh anchor and support Breckinridge's attack. Since repairs had not been completed, the orders were ill advised. In addition, the *Arkansas*'s experienced chief engineer was left ashore due to sickness.

The *Arkansas* was not ready for action when the fighting on land started. The ship's engines failed several times, including once while the *Arkansas* was in front of Federal ships. On 6 August, the drifting and unmaneuverable *Arkansas* was scuttled by fire and sank.

—*James V. Holton*

See also *Arkansas*, CSS; Breckinridge, John Cabell.
For further reading:
Luraghi, Raimondo. *A History of the Confederate Navy* (1996).

"BATTLE HYMN OF THE REPUBLIC"

The "Battle Hymn of The Republic" by Julia Ward Howe is more identified with the American Civil War than any other piece of music. Sung to the tune of an old Methodist camp meeting song, it drew upon the musical legacy of African-American spirituals as well as that of the Protestant "Second Great Awakening." In response to the hanging of John Brown in October 1859, anonymous admirers who shared his vision of slave liberation began using the old tune:

John Brown's body lies a-mouldering in the grave,
John Brown's body lies a-mouldering in the grave,
John Brown's body lies a-mouldering in the grave,
But his soul goes marching on.
Glory, glory, hallelujah!
Glory, glory, hallelujah!
Glory, glory, hallelujah!
His soul goes marching on.

Thrice acknowledging that "John Brown's Body lies a-mouldering in the grave," it closed with the ominous warning that his dream of slave liberation marched on. Easily learned and used, the song spread quickly through the antislavery movement, the Republican Party, and, in 1861, the volunteer units of the Federal army.

However, the song's very simplicity inspired not only many verses but also more elaborate and less repetitive lyrics. "The John Brown Song," for example, related that

He captured Harper's Ferry with his nineteen men so true,
They frightened old Virginia 'til she trembled through and through.
They hanged him for a traitor, they themselves the traitor crew,
But his truth is marching on.

With the outbreak of the war, the volunteer units of the Federal army, particularly those with antislavery leaderships, took up the refrain. Clearly, until the formal adoption of emancipation as a war goal in late 1862, the singing of these verses represented a musical appeal to expand the political and social purposes of the war.

In October 1861, the newly arrived 14th Massachusetts sang "John Brown's Body" as it slogged its way through Washington during a driving rainstorm. Its commander, Colonel William B. Greene, was a radical Transcendentalist who, unusually, had been to West Point and provided a vital link between New England abolitionist leaders and the emerging military hierarchy. Assigned to build and garrison the fortifications adjacent to Washington in northern Virginia, the regiment frequently hosted official and quasiofficial visitors with its singing of "John Brown's Body."

In November, Governor John Andrew of Massachusetts brought a party across the Potomac to visit the regiment at Fort Albany. Julia Ward Howe was among the visitors. On the way back, Andrew remarked to Julia Ward Howe that the song might better employ its lines. On her return to Washington, Howe penned "The Battle Hymn of the Republic":

Mine eyes have seen the glory of the coming of the Lord:
He is trampling out the vintage where the grapes of wrath are stored;
He hath loosed the fateful lightning of His terrible swift sword:
His truth is marching on.

The title alone spoke volumes. The "Battle Hymn of the Republic" sings of a faith that history represented the unfolding of the divine will for human justice, that the American republic represented such progress, and that

the ordeal of civil strife remained part of this ultimately benevolent process. Like its author, it continued to be identified with the range of social reforms that emerged from the Civil War, ranging from black rights to women's suffrage and the labor movement. It has, in the process, remained one of the most popular of the nation's patriotic "hymns."

—*Mark A. Lause*

See also Brown, John; "Dixie"; Howe, Julia Ward; Music.

For further reading:
Crawford Richard, comp. *The Civil War Songbook* (1977).
Roe, Alfred S., and Charles Nutt. *History of the First Regiment of Heavy Artillery Massachusetts Volunteers, Formerly the Fourteenth Regiment of Infantry, 1861–1865* (1917).
Silber, Irwin. *Songs of the Civil War* (1960).
Silverman, Jerry. *Ballads and Songs of the Civil War* (1993).

BATTLES AND LEADERS OF THE CIVIL WAR

Published as a four-volume book set in 1887, although some of the material was originally printed in *The Century* magazine in the preceding years, *Battles and Leaders of the Civil War* compiled the written recollections from men who survived the war. The editors of the book edition note that the genesis of this material began with the publication of two opposing views on the John Brown raid. From November 1884 to November 1887, *The Century* published its Civil War series, and circulation soared from 127,000 to 225,000 in the first six months alone. The book version expanded the material taken from the magazine publications.

In the introduction to the book, the editors state that their chief motive was "strict fairness to the testimony of both sides" and that their chief endeavors were "to prove every important statement by the *Official Records* and other trustworthy documents, and to spare no pains in the interest of elucidation and accuracy." Both sides of the conflict were thus scrupulously represented. The book was also richly illustrated.

The material in *Battles and Leaders* helped inform a whole generation of Americans, particularly those born immediately after the Civil War, about the bloody conflict. Some participants even used the opportunity to clarify or defend a particular matter of controversy they may have been involved in during the war. For example, Major General Oliver O. Howard explains his perspective of the embarrassing rout and retreat of his regiment by General Thomas J. "Stonewall" Jackson during the battle of Chancellorsville. Howard ends his account with a tribute to his rival:

Stonewall Jackson was victorious. Even his enemies praise him; but, providentially for us, it was the last battle that he waged against American Union. For, in bold planning, in energy of execution, which he had the power to diffuse, in indefatigable activity and moral ascendancy, Jackson stood head and shoulders above his conferees, and after his death General Lee could not replace him.

Another interesting recollection is that of General James Longstreet, which engendered extreme controversy in its assessment of Lee's performance at Gettysburg, especially in ordering Pickett's fateful charge. About his role in the decision, Longstreet writes:

It has been said that I should have exercised discretion and should not have sent Pickett on his charge. It has been urged that I had exercised discretion on previous occasions. It is true that at times when I saw a certainty of success in another direction, I did not follow the orders of my general, but that was when he is away, you have a right to exercise discretion; but if he sees everything that you see, you have no right to disregard his positive and repeated orders. I never exercised discretion after discussing with General Lee the points of his orders, *and* when, after discussion, he had ordered the execution of his policy. I had offered my objections to Pickett's battle and had been overruled, and I was in the immediate presence of the commanding general when the order was given for Pickett to advance.

That day at Gettysburg was one of the saddest of my life.

Responding to Longstreet's self-exculpatory explanation, Colonel William Allan, formerly of the C.S.A., answered what many perceived to be Longstreet's heretical criticism of the beloved Lee:

Pickett was overwhelmed not by troops in front but by those on his flanks, especially by those on his right flank.... Yet Longstreet did not use any part of Hood's and McLaw's divisions to support Pickett, or to make a diversion in his favor, or to occupy the troops on his flank which finally defeated him.... Longstreet, in a word, sent forward one-third of his corps to the attack, but the remainder of his troops did not cooperate. And yet he reproaches Lee for the result!

Allan here is opening the insinuation that Longstreet, sulking over Lee's disregard of his advice and other perceived grievances, sabotaged the assault by not doing all he could to support an action with which he did not agree.

This four-volume treasure (a one-volume edition, selected and edited by Ned Bradford, also exists) of personal accounts of the most important period of American history is a rich and valuable contribution to the understanding of the war. However, care must be taken in accepting all of its insights at face value, since by their very nature these accounts are personal and subjective.

—*James H. Meredith*

See also Chancellorsville, Battle of; Jackson, Thomas Jonathan; Longstreet, James.

For further reading:

Bradford, Ned, ed. *Battles and Leaders of the Civil War* (1957).
Johnson, Robert Underwood, and Clarence Clough Buel, eds. *Battles and Leaders of the Civil War: Being for the Most Part Contributions by Union and Confederate Officers* (1887–1888).

BAXTER SPRINGS, BATTLE OF
(6 October 1863)

Among the violent altercations that characterized the guerrilla fighting along the Kansas-Missouri border during the Civil War was the battle of Baxter Springs, Kansas, in early October 1863. The battle, perhaps more correctly classified as a massacre, came about as an unintended consequence of Confederate partisan William Clarke Quantrill's bloody attack on the town of Lawrence, Kansas, on 21 August 1863. After butchering some 150 innocent citizens and setting the town ablaze, Quantrill and his force of 450 Confederate partisans managed to evade Union military units for more than a month. By 1 October, however, Quantrill found it necessary to move his force south to evade Federal patrols and take refuge for the winter in Confederate-controlled Texas. During the journey, Quantrill's band happened upon a small Federal military post located along the Texas road at Baxter Springs in southeastern Kansas.

Quantrill thought the fort an easy target and decided to attack the isolated outpost. He divided his command into two columns and approached the fort from either side of the Texas road. The column approaching from the north, under the command of one of Quantrill's lieutenants, David Poole, soon encountered a unit of the 2d Kansas Colored Infantry on the road outside the fort. After a brief skirmish, Poole's partisans drove the Federals back into the log and earthen structure. Although the Union troops suffered heavy casualties during Poole's surprise attack, Quantrill lost the element of surprise and was forced to attempt a half-hearted siege. The small Union garrison, consisting of the remainder of the 2d Kansas Colored Infantry and two companies of the 3d Wisconsin Cavalry, was able to hold off Quantrill's assault, thanks mainly to their use of a light howitzer and the reluctance of Quantrill's men to assault a fortified position.

At approximately the same time, Union general James G. Blunt was approaching the post at Baxter Springs from the north. Blunt, who was in the process of transferring his headquarters from Fort Scott in Kansas to the recently occupied Fort Smith in Arkansas, was burdened by several wagons carrying his personal effects and accompanied by only a small detachment, comprised mostly of clerks, staff officers, and members of his regimental band. Unaware of Quantrill's presence in the area, Blunt's column stumbled onto the scene just as the Confederates were leaving the fort. Quantrill's partisans, who had adopted the habit of wearing blue coats and carrying a United States flag, were mistaken by Blunt for a detachment from the outpost sent to escort him. Blunt realized his mistake too late as Quantrill's partisans opened fire on the confused Union column at close range, scattering the Federals in all directions and touching off a chaotic melee. When the rout ended, seventy of Blunt's 100-man detachment had been killed, many of them ridden down and shot by the Confederates even as they tried to surrender, and all of his wagons and supplies had been captured. Blunt and the remaining third of his force managed to escape the massacre and then outrace the pursuing Confederates, eventually reaching the safety of Fort Smith to the southeast.

Disappointed at having failed to capture or kill Blunt, Quantrill and his command resumed their trek towards Texas, randomly attacking frontier homesteads and Indian villages along their path, while the humiliated Blunt was temporarily relieved of command by Union general John M. Schofield for his role in the fiasco. Blunt would later regain his command, but the stinging defeat he experienced at Baxter Springs remained a dark blot on his military resume.

—*Daniel P. Barr*

See also Blunt, James G.; Guerrilla Warfare; Kansas; Quantrill, William.

For further reading:

Castel, Albert E. *Civil War Kansas: Reaping the Whirlwind* (1958; reprint, 1997).
Josephy, Alvin M. *The Civil War in the American West* (1991).
Monaghan, Jay. *Civil War on the Western Border, 1854–1865* (1955).

BAYLOR, JOHN ROBERT
(1822–1894)

Confederate officer and politician; governor of Arizona Territory

Born in Kentucky, John Robert Baylor moved west with his family when his father assumed the post of assistant surgeon with the 7th U.S. Infantry at Fort Gibson in Indian Territory. Baylor returned east, attending school in Cincinnati, but the pull of the West was strong. When word reached Cincinnati of the Texas Revolution in 1835, Baylor ran away and tried to make his way to war. A concerned traveler intervened, returning the thirteen-year-old boy to his school.

After the death of his father, Baylor, still keen for adventure, abandoned his formal education and settled on the farm of his uncle near LaGrange, Texas, in 1840. Baylor participated in some of the Texan campaigns against Mexico, but always just missed actual combat. In 1842, the restless Baylor returned to Fort Gibson, where he taught school at the Creek agency. A year later he fled to Texas after authorities implicated him as an accomplice in the murder of a trader.

After this traumatic event, the young drifter began to settle down. In 1844 in Marshall, Texas, Baylor married Emily Hanna, with whom he raised seven sons and three daughters. The couple moved back to Fayette County, Texas, near his uncle, where Baylor raised livestock. In the early 1850s, Baylor was admitted to the bar, served a successful term in the state legislature, and received appointment as agent to the Comanche Reservation on the Clear Fork of the Brazos River. Controversy plagued his time in that post, and the state removed him for financial irregularities and for his propensity to argue with his superiors. Baylor, along with his brother George Wythe Baylor, subsequently became one of the leading persecutors of the Indians, ultimately leading partisan groups that forced the reservation Indians to relocate to Indian Territory.

Baylor was active during the Texas secession crisis of 1861. A member of the Knights of the Golden Circle, he raised prosecession forces that helped bring about the surrender of the U.S. Army's Department of Texas to state authorities in February. Baylor received the rank of lieutenant colonel for his services and helped organize the 2d Texas Mounted Rifles in March and April. He led a battalion of that organization west along the San Antonio to San Diego mail route, seizing abandoned U.S. army posts along the way.

After arriving at Fort Bliss near present-day El Paso, Texas, Baylor launched what is arguably the first Confederate offensive of the war in July. With approximately 200 troops from his regiment, Baylor moved into Mesilla, New Mexico Territory, and later captured nearby Fort Fillmore along with most of the 7th U.S. Infantry. Shortly thereafter, he organized the Confederate Territory of Arizona, with himself as governor. On 15 December, Baylor advanced to the rank of colonel in the Confederate army.

Baylor suffered a rocky tenure in office. A shortage of revenue, and an abundance of troubles with Apaches and U.S. troops plagued him, as did poor relations with his superior, Confederate general Henry Hopkins Sibley, who arrived in Mesilla with his reinforcing army from Texas at the end of 1861. Early the next year, Baylor left Arizona, determined to raise an army of his own in Texas and return to the desert southwest and complete its conquest. He traveled through the South, building financial and political support for his scheme before laying it before the Confederate government in Richmond.

President Jefferson Davis cut short Baylor's ambitions. Although the Confederate Congress had conferred upon Baylor the rank of brigadier general, the Confederate executive stripped him of that rank, and his position as governor, because of controversy involving his treatment of Indians in Arizona. Refusing to be disgraced, Baylor returned to Texas and volunteered to fight in the battle of Galveston on 31 December 1862 as a private of artillery.

Baylor was not through serving the Confederacy. In 1863, he parlayed his battlefield exploits into a seat in the second Confederate Congress, where he served on the Patents and Indian Affairs committees. In March 1865, the rift between Davis and Baylor had partially healed. That month, with the Confederacy crumbling around them, the president again authorized Baylor to raise a brigade of mounted Texans to liberate Confederate Arizona and restored him to the rank of colonel. Baylor was on his way home to pursue this errand when the war ended.

Baylor moved his family to San Antonio after the war and in 1873 made a serious but unsuccessful run for the Democratic nomination for governor. He continued to be politically active until 1878, when at age fifty-six Baylor moved his family to a sizable ranch at Montell, Texas, northwest of Uvalde. He continued in his confrontational ways, reportedly killing a man over a livestock issue in the 1880s. He died at home on 6 February 1894.

—*Donald S. Frazier*

See also Sibley, Henry Hopkins; Texas.
For further reading:

Baylor, George Wythe. *John Robert Baylor* (1966).
Finch, L. Boyd. *Confederate Pathway to the Pacific: Major Sherod Hunter and Arizona Territory, C.S.A.* (1996).
Frazier, Donald S. *Blood and Treasure: Confederate Empire in the Southwest* (1995).
Thompson, Jerry Don. *Colonel John Robert Baylor* (1971).

BAYONET

The bayonet is a device attached to the barrel of muskets for close combat. Developed and widely used in European warfare, the bayonet was an important weapon on the battlefield.

The most widely used bayonets in the Civil War were socket and sword bayonets. The socket bayonet was developed to fit around the front of the muzzle to allow continuous firing until a bayonet charge was ordered. The socket bayonet was a steel weapon ranging from fourteen to eighteen inches long. The shaft was triangular in shape and projected to a point. The purpose of the socket bayonet was not to slash at an opponent, but to stab and thrust. The shape of the socket bayonet would produce holes rather than cuts, much like a spear. The drill maneuvers practiced by infantrymen focused on thrusting motions to impale opponents. Bayonet wounds could be ghastly. After stabbing the victim, drill procedure called for twisting the gun to enlarge the wound.

Sword bayonets were shaped much like their name suggests. These larger bayonets attached to the side of the barrel and extended up to two feet past the muzzle. Unlike the socket bayonet, sword bayonets were equipped with a handle and were shaped with a sharp edge. These weapons could be used for stabbing or cutting. However, sword bayonets were considerably larger than socket bayonets and many soldiers found them unwieldy. Civil War muskets were heavy pieces of equipment without the bayonet, and the extension of two feet of steel increased the difficulty of musket movement and aiming.

Sword bayonets and socket bayonets were not interchangeable. Certain muskets required particular bayonets. The popular Springfield and Enfield rifles required their own socket bayonets, whereas the Model 1841 rifle and 1855 rifle were fitted with sword bayonets.

The bayonet saw limited action in the Civil War compared with that in previous European wars. Bayonet charges were not common occurrences and bayonet wounds were very rare. Many field surgeons confessed to never treating bayonet wounds. But bayonets continued to be part of the soldier's armament.

Some officers have defended the use of the bayonet in the Civil War. The bayonet served a deeper purpose than creating horrible wounds. It could be used as a shock weapon. In infantry drill, the command "Charge, bayonet!" was answered by the forward thrust of the musket and a collective yell from the ranks. A line of bayonets would be an impressive sight to an opposing army. The gleam of the "cold steel" and the surge of a mass body of troops could unnerve an opponent. Therefore, the bayonet served as a psychological weapon to disrupt enemy formations without actual contact.

The bayonet could also be used for defensive measures. When the call for bayonets was issued in desperate situations, soldiers knew that they must hold. One classic case involved Colonel Joshua L. Chamberlain's 20th Maine on Little Round Top at the battle of Gettysburg in 1863. Without sufficient ammunition, or the option to fall back, Chamberlain's bayonet charge prevented a Confederate key flanking maneuver and contributed to the Union victory.

The use of the bayonet in the American Civil War was limited on the battlefield. Most soldiers found the bayonet to be a nuisance, just one more piece of equipment to carry. Soldiers got the most use out of their bayonets as camp tools, candle holders, or digging uten-

sils. It was also necessary in the practice of stacking arms. Stacking arms was the interlocking of bayonets to prop the muskets off the ground. The psychological effect of bayonets on the battlefield can only be speculated. The number of wounds from bayonets were minimal, yet the bayonet continued to be issued to soldiers in all armies well into the twentieth century as a tool for hand-to-hand combat.

—*Ian M. Spurgeon*

See also Rifles; Springfield Rifle.
For further reading:
Griffith, Paddy. *Battle Tactics of the Civil War* (1989).
Lord, Francis A. *Civil War Collector's Encyclopedia* (1995).
Wiley, Bell I. *The Life of Johnny Reb: The Common Soldier of the Confederacy* (1978; reprint, 1997).

BAYOU DE GLAIZE
(May 1864)
See Yellow Bayou, Louisiana

BAYOU TECHE, LOUSIANA
(January 1863)
See Irish Bend

BEALE, RICHARD LEE TURBEVILLE
(1819–1893)
Confederate general

Born in Westmoreland County on Virginia's Northern Neck to Robert Beale and Martha Felicia Turbeville Beale, Richard Beale graduated in 1838 from the University of Virginia. After studying law, he began a private practice in Hague, Virginia. Also active in state Democratic politics, Beale was elected to the United States House of Representatives in 1847. After one term, he refused to stand for a second. He continued to be active, however, in the state party, participating in state constitutional reform and serving in the state senate from 1858 to 1860.

On the secession of Virginia from the Union, Beale received a commission in a cavalry unit known as Lee's Light Horse. In July 1861 he was promoted to captain and later in the year to major. The unit's main job was to patrol northern Virginia, particularly along the Potomac River. He commanded Camp Lee in his home of Westmoreland County in fall 1861. In this capacity he became concerned for the loyalty of the poor of his county and wrote to the Confederate War Department that the government needed to court the loyalty of the people by ensuring that adequate supplies reached the region. In spring 1862 his unit became a part of the 9th Virginia Cavalry regiment, and in April 1862 Beale was promoted to lieutenant colonel. With the creation of the

Richard Lee Beale (*Library of Congress*)

for the retreating Army of Northern Virginia out of Pennsylvania. In September 1863 he was wounded in a small skirmish and spent several months convalescing.

By January 1864, Beale was back in command of the 9th patrolling eastern Virginia, looking for food and reconnoitering Northern movements. In early March a part of the 9th took up the pursuit of Colonel Ulric Dahlgren in his retreat after the failed Kilpatrick-Dahlgren raid. Dahlgren was killed and Beale forwarded to the Confederate government what would become the controversial Dahlgren papers outlining a plot to kill Jefferson Davis and his cabinet.

Beale received a promotion to brigadier general in August 1864, although misplacement of the paperwork delayed his confirmation in that rank until early 1865. Nevertheless, throughout the fall of 1864, he commanded a brigade as part of W. H. F. Lee's cavalry division until the surrender of the Army of Northern Virginia in April 1865.

Following the war, Beale returned to Westmoreland County, where he was a planter and lawyer. After Reconstruction he served one term in the United States House of Representatives before returning to his law practice. He also spent much of the latter part of his life writing a history of the 9th Virginia Regiment. He died in Hague, Virginia.

—*David S. Heidler and Jeanne T. Heidler*

See also Kilpatrick-Dahlgren Raid; Stoneman's Raid (April–May 1863).
For further reading:
Beale, Richard Lee Turbeville. *History of the Ninth Virginia Cavalry* (1899).

BEAN'S STATION, TENNESSEE, ENGAGEMENT AT
(15 December 1863)

On 4 December 1863, after his failure to drive Ambrose Burnside from Knoxville, James Longstreet withdrew eastward on the road running north of the Holston River. Three days later, elements of the Army of the Ohio under Major General John G. Parke moved out of Knoxville on the same route to follow the retreating Confederates. By 9 December, the Union infantry was at Rutledge some twenty miles northeast of Knoxville and the cavalry was another five miles beyond at Bean's Station. The best that Yankee reconnaissance could determine was that Longstreet was stopped somewhere between Bean's Station and Rogersville, at most about ten miles farther on the same road toward Kingsport. Longstreet had superior numbers, so the Federals waited and watched—or at least they tried to.

Longstreet's rear guard stood firm enough to fight a series of brisk skirmishes beginning on the afternoon of 9

Army of Northern Virginia, the 9th Virginia became a part of the cavalry division of that army that eventually became a separate corps under the command of J. E. B. Stuart.

As a member of the 9th Virginia, Beale fought in the Peninsula campaign, Second Bull Run, and Antietam. Though always praised by his commanders, Beale apparently chafed under the restrictions of taking orders from others and three times tried to resign from the army, requesting permission to raise a troop of independent rangers. Each time, his resignation was refused. In October 1862, he was promoted to colonel of the 9th Virginia.

As the Union army moved down from Sharpsburg, Maryland, in the fall of 1862, it became the job of the 9th to patrol the area north of the Rappahannock River to hinder the Army of the Potomac's progress. Beale fought at Fredericksburg and in April 1863 was a part of W. H. F. Lee's cavalry brigade that engaged Major General George Stoneman in his raid during the Chancellorsville campaign.

Beale fought at Brandy Station before the Gettysburg campaign, at Gettysburg, and was part of the rear guard

December and continuing for the next several days. From these encounters the Rebels determined that their pursuers were not nearly as strong as first suspected, especially since William Sherman was returning to Chattanooga and Gordon Granger's IV Corps was being held near Knoxville. Consequently, on 15 December Longstreet whirled and drove upon Bean's Station, pushed back the Union forces there, and took possession of the crossroads that led south to Morristown and north to Tazewell. Longstreet hoped to trap the Federal cavalry by sending two brigades of troopers under William E. "Grumble" Jones around the Clinch Mountains to Bean's Station Gap while William T. Martin took four brigades south of the Holston to pinch the Yankee retreat from the south.

Martin was late, and the Federal cavalry and mounted infantry absorbed the shock and fell back, taking 115 casualties. The Federal retreat finally stopped about ten miles outside Knoxville at Blain's Crossroads and was there reinforced with Granger's IV Corps and everybody else available. Longstreet did not press the attack, however. The weather was ghastly, and winter quarters beckoned, so he again turned toward the mountains, moving off as Federal cavalry rode out to nip at the edges of his tattered army. As late as 29 December, blue and gray troopers were still sparring on Mossy Creek near Dandridge while Longstreet slipped into the mountains.

—*David S. Heidler and Jeanne T. Heidler*

See also Longstreet, James; Nashville, Battle of; Nashville, Tennessee; Parke, John Grubb; Tennessee.

For further reading:
Sheridan, Don. *The Battle of Bean's Station: A Spirited Conflict, December 14–16, 1863* (1997).

BEATTY, SAMUEL
(1820–1885)
Union general

Born in Mifflin County, Pennsylvania, Samuel Beatty moved to Stark County, Ohio, with his family when he was a small boy. He was educated locally and as a young man helped with the family farm. At the outbreak of the Mexican-American War, Beatty helped to raise a volunteer company, becoming a lieutenant in the 3d Ohio. He returned to his farm at the end of the war. When the Civil War started, Beatty was the county sheriff in addition to running the family farm.

News of Fort Sumter prompted Beatty to raise a company for Federal service. He was elected captain, and his company became a part of the 19th Ohio Infantry. By the end of May 1861 he had been selected colonel of the regiment. Later in the year, the regiment became a part of the Army of the Ohio.

In the spring of 1862, Beatty led his regiment south into Tennessee as part of Don Carlos Buell's effort to join

Ulysses S. Grant at Pittsburg Landing. Arriving at Shiloh aboard the steamboat *Planet* the night of the first day of the battle, 6 April, Beatty and his men saw serious action the following day in the Union repulse of the Confederate forces. During the advance on Corinth, Mississippi, the following month, Beatty was given command of the 19th's brigade.

Beatty commanded the same brigade that fall in the campaign against Braxton Bragg in Kentucky and fought with distinction at Perryville. He continued in command of the same unit during the battle of Stones River in December 1862, but, still at the rank of colonel, he succeeded to command of the division when its commander, Horatio P. Van Cleve, was wounded on 31 December. He was promoted to brigadier general of volunteers in early 1863 with a date of rank of 29 November 1862. He had been recommended for the promotion by William Rosecrans for his performance at Stones River.

With the recovery of Van Cleve, Beatty reverted to command of his brigade and led them effectively during the Tullahoma campaign in June 1863. In July 1863, he and his brigade were stationed in Manchester, Tennessee, guarding the army's supply train. In September he moved to join his division for the Chickamauga campaign. Both Van Cleve and the corps commander, Thomas L. Crittenden, commended Beatty for his actions at Chickamauga even though the overall performance of XXI Corps was poor.

After Chickamauga, Beatty moved to the command of 3d Brigade, 3d Division (commanded by Thomas J. Wood), IV Corps (commanded by Gordon Granger), Army of the Cumberland. During the Chattanooga campaign, Beatty was again conspicuous for his bravery, particularly in the Union attack on Missionary Ridge. He was commended by Granger for his part in that attack.

After the Chattanooga campaign, Beatty remained in Tennessee, primarily leading his brigade in reconnaissance missions scouting Confederate positions. In the spring he began to prepare his brigade for the upcoming Atlanta campaign, but when the army was about to move, he became seriously ill and had to relinquish command. He was unable to return to duty until the following fall, and hence missed the entire campaign.

By the time Beatty resumed command of his brigade, it had returned to Tennessee to meet the threat of John Bell Hood's invasion. He fought at the battle of Franklin. After the battle, Wood became commander of IV Corps, and Beatty was given command of the division. He commanded the division through the Nashville campaign at the end of the year and was commended by Major General George Thomas for his actions in that campaign. After the battle, Beatty led his division in pursuit of what was left of Hood's army. He remained in command of the 3d Division until March 1865, when he returned to his brigade command.

In early April 1865, Beatty and his brigade were given what at the time seemed like a very important assignment. Having heard of Robert E. Lee's evacuation of his lines at Petersburg and the abandonment of Richmond, Union forces in Tennessee expected the Army of Northern Virginia to move west, perhaps into Tennessee, before turning toward Joseph Johnston's force in North Carolina. For that reason Beatty was ordered to take his brigade to Jonesborough, Tennessee, and to send scouts from there to determine Lee's movements. After learning of Lee's surrender to Grant, Beatty's superiors ordered him back to his headquarters at Greeneville, Tennessee.

In May 1865, George Thomas, commander of the Army of the Cumberland, wrote a special recommendation to the War Department urging that Beatty be promoted to major general of volunteers for his gallantry at Chickamauga, Chattanooga, Missionary Ridge, and Nashville and for the pursuit of Hood after the battle of Nashville. He received a brevet promotion to that rank instead.

After being mustered out of the volunteer service in 1866, Beatty returned to his farm in Ohio. He lived there quietly until his death on 26 May 1885.

—*David S. Heidler and Jeanne T. Heidler*

See also Chattanooga, Tennessee; Missionary Ridge; Nashville, Tennessee.

For further reading:
Cozzens, Peter. *The Shipwreck of Their Hopes: The Battles for Chattanooga* (1994).
Sword, Wiley. *Embrace an Angry Wind: The Confederacy's Last Hurrah—Spring Hill, Franklin, and Nashville* (1992).

BEAUREGARD, PIERRE GUSTAVE TOUTANT
(1818–1893)
Confederate general

Certainly the most recognized and admired Southern general at the outset of the war, and arguably the most flamboyant, Pierre Gustave Toutant Beauregard never fulfilled his military aspirations or the hopes placed upon him by the Confederate public and political leadership. Embodying the paradoxes and travails of the Confederate high command, he was seen by some as an expert strategist betrayed by political enemies and by others as a vainglorious, inept officer undeserving of the high charges he received.

The scion of a powerful family of French, Welsh, and Italian extraction, Beauregard was born in the parish of Saint-Pierre near New Orleans on 28 May 1818. He was educated in the language of his Gallic forbears at the French School of New York City. It was at this institution that he familiarized himself with the life and

campaigns of Napoleon Bonaparte, whose demeanor and tactics he purported to emulate throughout his military career. Over his parents' objections, he was admitted to the U.S. Military Academy at West Point in 1834. He rapidly distinguished himself as a highly intelligent, poised, and reflective cadet of great promise. He graduated second in the class of 1838, which included future Confederate officers Richard S. Ewell and Jubal A. Early, as well as Irvin McDowell, whom he was to face on the field of battle. Like his idol Napoleon, Beauregard was interested in gunnery, so upon graduation he elected to serve in the Army Corps of Engineers. He spent a few months redesigning fortifications in Rhode Island and Florida and was then reassigned to his native Louisiana for topographic and hydrographic work.

Beauregard fastidiously worked on these projects until the outbreak of the Mexican-American War, when he was sent to Tampa, Florida, to rebuild fortifications. Upon completion of what he considered an inglorious task, he requested to be sent to Mexico. Along with, among others, Captain Robert E. Lee and Lieutenant George B. McClellan, he was assigned to General Winfield Scott's staff. An active member of this chosen retinue of elite artillerists and engineers, he played a significant part in the successful siege of Vera Cruz. He later saw action at the battles of Contreras and Churubusco and played no small role in the strategy that led to the storming of the Chapultepec citadel and concomitant capturing of Mexico City. Beauregard, however, believed that he did not receive adequate accolades for his service in Mexico, a complaint that would later echo in his diatribes against his commanders during the Civil War. Further embittered by the lack of opportunities offered by the peacetime army—he tried to no avail to secure promotions in the artillery and infantry—he returned to New Orleans to enhance the accessibility and navigability of the Mississippi River.

Between 1853 and 1860, he served as New Orleans's superintendent engineer of U.S. Customs' installations. During this period, he was also somewhat active in politics, writing much on behalf of Democratic candidate Franklin Pierce in the 1852 presidential election and running for mayor of New Orleans in 1858 against a more successful Know-Nothing candidate. In September 1841, he had married Marie Laure Villeré, who died while giving birth to their second child in March 1850. He then married Catherine Deslonde, also a Creole aristocrat and sister-in-law of U.S. senator and political power broker John Slidell.

On 23 January 1861, thanks in no small part to Slidell's support, Beauregard was appointed superintendent of West Point. However, only five days later, having publicly admitted that he would follow Louisiana if the state seceded from the Union, he was forced to leave his new assignment. He resigned his Federal commission on 20 February 1861 to receive a brigadier generalship in the Confederate army on 1 March. Ostensibly planning to become head of the Louisiana state army, he was handed his first disappointment of the war when this command was given to his nemesis-to-be, North Carolinian Braxton Bragg. Capitalizing on what he hoped to be a close advisorial relationship with President Jefferson Davis, Beauregard was then dispatched to Charleston, South Carolina, to coordinate the siege of Fort Sumter. He took command on 6 March in spite of the suspicions of South Carolinians toward a French-speaking Louisianian, and he skillfully marshaled the artillery resources made available to him. The first shot of the conflict was fired on 12 April 1861 with the fort surrendering on 14 April. Beauregard allowed Union troops under his erstwhile West Point artillery instructor Robert Anderson to evacuate Sumter with full military honors.

Beauregard was summoned to Montgomery and given a welcome befitting the "Hero of Sumter." He was also given the command of Confederate forces then mustered for the defense of the Mississippi River from Vicksburg to the Tennessee-Kentucky border. He kept this assignment for only a brief time, receiving orders to proceed to the new Confederate capital of Richmond, Virginia, on 28 May 1861. While he developed a good rapport with Robert E. Lee, at the time commander of state troops, the first signs of friction with Jefferson Davis rapidly appeared. Beauregard fully expected to dictate Confederate strategy, its centerpiece being the creation of a sizable army concentrated in northern Virginia and dedicated to a northward invasion of Maryland and capture of Washington. Judged unclear and unrealistic, his plan, however, was rejected by Davis, much to Beauregard's chagrin.

With Richmond apparently committed to a defensive strategy, Beauregard abandoned the initiative to his Federal opponent Irvin McDowell, who moved South in mid-July 1861. During the ensuing battle of First Bull Run on 21 July 1861, Beauregard showed much bravery under fire, but also inefficiency and poor tactical control of front-line units. Only McDowell's ineptitude and Joseph E. Johnston's composure were to save the day and ensure a Federal debacle. Nonetheless, Beauregard was promoted to general in the regular Confederate army on 31 August 1861. He hoped to return to Louisiana, but on 22 October he and his Army of the Potomac were placed under the control of Johnston, who had been made commander of the Department of Northern Virginia. By the time this area again became an object of military contention the following spring, Beauregard was no longer there.

In January 1862, Beauregard was transferred to the western theater of operations. He was placed under General Albert Sidney Johnston, who gave him command of the corps constituting his left wing, an assignment that Beauregard understood as giving him quasi-autonomy. Confronted with the Federal capture of Forts Pillow and Donelson, Beauregard again succumbed to his tendency for overreaching, Napoleonic plans, designing a major offensive into Tennessee and that could possibly lead to an advance on St. Louis. He took official command of his self-styled Army of the Mississippi on 5 March 1862 and planned to connect with Johnston's main body near Corinth, Mississippi.

What followed was a battle with Federal forces that was one of the bloodiest fights of the war, the battle of Shiloh on 6–7 April 1862. Supported by able division commanders such as Leonidas Polk, William J. Hardee, and John C. Breckinridge, Johnston pushed the Federals almost back into the Tennessee River, but he was fatally wounded during the first day of the battle. Beauregard then assumed command of the whole Confederate army. His attack the following day could not break reinforced Federal lines, and he ordered a general withdrawal, which raised the ire of his subordinates, especially Braxton Bragg. After he evacuated Corinth under questionable circumstances, Beauregard clearly found himself the object of Davis's enmity. When Beauregard relinquished command to Bragg in June 1862 for the duration of a sick leave, the move was motivated as much by politics as by his compromised health.

Strong political backing for Beauregard's return to the West could not persuade Davis to relent, so in September 1862, Beauregard returned to Charleston to assume command of the Confederacy's coastal defenses. Compensating for the scarcity of troops with technological innovations such as ironclads, floating mines, and even a prototype submarine, he managed to repulse several assaults on the Charleston fortifications of Forts Sumter and Moultrie in April 1863 and Battery Wagner in July 1863. He also spent much time providing unsolicited advice on the conduct of the war (for instance, in the form of a plan for a major campaign to recapture New Orleans), thus doing little to placate the Confederate political and military leadership. Beauregard seems to have been genuinely distressed by what he considered Davis's military and political blunders and even spoke of leaving the Confederacy to offer his services to European nations. The death of his second wife in March 1864 further disheartened him.

Yet his star was destined to shine anew. After the Confederate disasters in the summer of 1863, Beauregard, who had repulsed yet another round of assaults on Charleston in August, was perceived by some as a reliable, fighting, and technically undefeated commander. Such at least was the opinion of officers such as James Longstreet. In late April 1864, Beauregard was consequently dispatched to the Department of North Carolina, which included Virginia south of the

James River. He knew that the region would be subjected to a Federal offensive in support of Ulysses S. Grant's overland thrust toward Richmond, and it came in the form of Benjamin Butler's landing at Bermuda Hundred on 5 May 1864.

Adroitly mustering limited assets, Beauregard held the Richmond-Petersburg line and defeated Benjamin Butler's forces at Drewry's Bluff on 15–16 May, a victory for which he received little credit. He again assisted Robert E. Lee successfully in the defense of Petersburg on 15–18 June 1864. Yet, his expectation of being placed on equal footing with the Virginian never materialized. Instead, his command was then placed in the Army of Northern Virginia. When Grant's failure to destroy Confederate forces in the field turned the Overland campaign into the siege of Petersburg, Beauregard's claim of mastery in defensive warfare caused another quarrel with Davis and Bragg, by then Davis's principal military advisor, that even Lee could not resolve.

In the fall of 1864, Beauregard was therefore sent to Georgia. After the fall of Atlanta, the Confederacy's accelerating collapse necessitated the creation of a new Department of the West including Georgia and the Carolinas. With misgivings but having little choice, Davis gave the command to Beauregard. Davis forbade Beauregard, however, from taking the field, so the only army in the area remained under the command of John Bell Hood. Unable to reverse a rapidly deteriorating situation after Hood's debacle at Nashville on 15–16 December, Beauregard oversaw the evacuation and retreat of Southern troops from Columbia and Charleston in the early spring of 1865. As a final humiliation, he again had to relinquish command to Johnston on 22 February 1865. On 1 May, shortly after Johnston's surrender to William T. Sherman, Beauregard left for New Orleans, reaching his hometown on 21 May.

Pardoned by President Andrew Johnson, Beauregard spent time in Europe on behalf of the New Orleans, Jackson, and Great Northern Railroad Company of which he served as president. Like many other Confederate officers, he was considered for military command abroad, but negotiations with Brazil, Rumania, and Egypt fizzled. Beauregard remained negligibly involved in Democratic Party politics, but was mostly active in 1872 in the ill-fated Reform Party, which sought to integrate freed slaves into Southern political life and to lure them away from the Republican Party.

A fairly wealthy man, Beauregard lent his name and credit to numerous endeavors, not all of them successful. Along with former classmate Jubal Early, he was thus seriously criticized for his supervision of the questionable Louisiana lottery between 1877 and 1893. Under the influence of Thomas Jordan, his former chief-of-staff, he wrote and published articles on the war, generally in response to Joseph Johnston's published recollections, *Narrative of Military Operations* (1874). Beauregard assisted his long-time friend Alfred Roman in the 1884 publication *of Military Operations of General Beauregard*, a work of self-vindication that he saw as paramount in molding his historical reputation. In 1879 he was appointed adjutant general of Louisiana and in 1888 was elected commissioner of public works.

Beauregard died on 18 February 1893 of heart failure. Mourned by an imposing delegation of Confederate veterans led by Edmund Kirby Smith, he was buried in the Métairie Cemetery, a few paces away from an equestrian statue of Albert Sidney Johnston.

—*Laurent Ditmann*

See also Bermuda Hundred Campaign; Bull Run, First Battle of; Drewry's Bluff, Battle of; Fort Sumter, Bombardment of; Shiloh, Battle of.

For further reading:

Basso, Hamilton. *Beauregard, the Great Creole* (1933).

Williams, T. Harry. *P.G.T. Beauregard: Napoleon in Gray* (1955).

Woodworth, Steven E., ed. *Leadership and Command in the American Civil War* (1995).

BEDINI, GAETANO
(1806–1864)
Roman Catholic cardinal, diplomat

Born in Sinigaglia, Italy (the hometown of Pope Pius IX), in May 1806, Gaetano Bedini served as secretary to the papal nuncio in Vienna in the late 1830s and in 1845 was appointed papal representative to Brazil, where he gained fame for his aggressive defense of the rights of German immigrants. Two years later, he returned to Italy and was appointed papal governor of Bologna. When Austrian troops brutalized and executed Bolognese revolutionaries in 1849, European liberals condemned Governor Bedini as a reactionary even though his influence with the Austrian authorities was relatively limited. Pius IX appointed him titular archbishop of Thebes and papal nuncio to Brazil in 1852, but also asked him to travel to the United States and inspect the Church there. Besides investigating the feasibility of an American nuncio, Bedini was to help settle a wide variety of Church problems with parish trustees, public schools, and the growing specter of anti-Catholicism. An accomplished diplomat and politician, he seemed an excellent choice to arbitrate Church difficulties in the United States.

Unfortunately for Bedini, the ex-priest and Italian revolutionary Alessandro Gavazzi preempted his visit, toured America, and for months assailed the prelate as the "Bloody Butcher of Bologna." In particular, he held Bedini responsible for the 1849 death of Father Ugo Bossi. Bossi, a Barnabite father, ally of Italian nationalist

Giuseppe Garibaldi, and well-known radical priest, was captured outside Venice by Austrian troops and executed. According to Gavazzi, the antiliberal Bedini had Bossi killed, subjugated Italian liberty in 1849, and was about to do the same to the United States. Gavazzi maintained that the visit of the ex–papal governor was not a diplomatic mission, but part of a greater papist plan to institute Catholic monarchism in the United States.

Archbishop Bedini's seven-month visit was a disaster, punctuated with riots, an assassination attempt, and a dramatic increase in anti-Catholic feeling. Arriving in New York on 30 June 1853, he was welcomed by New York bishop John Hughes and traveled to Washington, D.C., where he met with President Franklin Pierce and attended Georgetown University's commencement. Joined again by Hughes, he visited Milwaukee, the Indian Territory, and Detroit, offering Mass and speaking with American Catholics. While in Detroit, press criticism of Bedini's use of a Great Lakes military steamer began to sour his visit. The Bishop's three-week hiatus in Canada did not dampen protests, and details emerged of a foiled assassination plot planned by Sardinian revolutionaries in New York. Although frightened for his life, he remained in the United States through the fall and was convinced by Bishop Hughes to make an extended tour of the Midwest and South.

The decision to stay was a huge mistake. Bedini was accosted by nativists in Pittsburgh, riots broke out as he visited Cincinnati during Christmas week, mobs jeered him in Wheeling, Virginia (now West Virginia), and he was forced to cancel a trip to New Orleans over rumors of more violence. In cities across the country, he was burned in effigy and denounced as an enemy of American republicanism. After a last visit to Washington, he secretly took a train to New York and began to plan his departure for Europe. New York officials could not guarantee his safety and begged him to leave the country quickly and quietly. On 4 February 1854, Bishop Bedini and his assistants quietly took a rowboat off Staten Island and boarded a ferry steamer captained by a U.S. Marshal deputy. As a mob searched in vain for the Catholic prelate on the docks, Bedini boarded a British bound ship far out in New York harbor.

The visit not only set back Vatican diplomatic initiatives to America—an apostolic delegate was not sent to the United States until 1893—but effectively ended Bedini's career as a diplomat. In 1856, he was made secretary of the Sacred Congregation of Propaganda Fide and five years later was appointed cardinal-archbishop of Viterbo-Toscanella. He died at that post on 6 September 1864.

By instigating U.S. anti-Catholicism, the ill-timed Bedini visit of 1853–1854 helped destroy the Jacksonian party system in place since the 1830s. His U.S. tour factored in the emergence of the nativist Know-Nothing Party, the overthrow of the Whigs, and the creation of a new national Republican Party in 1856.

—*Michael J. Connolly*

See also American Party; Catholics.
For further reading:
Billington, Ray Allen. *The Protestant Crusade 1800–1860: A Study of the Origins of American Nativism* (1938).
Connelly, James F. *The Visit of Archbishop Bedini to the United States of America* (1960).
Guilday, Peter. "Gaetano Bedini: An Episode in the Life of Archbishop John Hughes." *Historical Records and Studies* (1933).
Shaw, Richard. *Dagger John: The Unquiet Life and Times of Archbishop John Hughes of New York* (1977).

BEE, BARNARD ELLIOTT
(1824–1861)
Confederate general

The son of Barnard E. Bee, born in Charleston, South Carolina, moved as a boy with his family to Texas. His father became prominent in the government of the Republic of Texas. In spite of the elder Bee's citizenship in that foreign country, he was able to secure his son an at-large appointment to the United States Military Academy at West Point. Bee graduated thirty-third of the forty-one members in the class of 1845.

Bee fought in the Mexican-American War (1846–1848), in which he received two brevet promotions and was wounded once. After the war he served in several frontier posts, rising to the rank of captain in the 10th Infantry. Bee resigned his commission on 3 March 1861 and received a major's commission in the Confederate infantry. Shortly thereafter, he was promoted to lieutenant colonel in the 1st South Carolina Artillery. Along with several other Confederate officers, including Thomas J. Jackson, he received a promotion to brigadier general on 17 June 1861.

Dispatched to the Shenandoah Valley in Virginia to become a part of Major General Joseph E. Johnston's growing army at Winchester, Bee took command of Johnston's 3d Brigade. Bee accompanied Johnston to Manassas Junction on 20 July 1861 to join forces with P. G. T. Beauregard's army there.

When Union forces under Irvin McDowell began their attack the following day, Bee was sent with his brigade to reinforce the Confederate left. Convinced that the primary fighting of the day would be on the Confederate right, Bee was angry about being removed from the scene of battle. Little did he realize that McDowell's main attack not only would come on the left, but would be in progress as Bee put his men into position.

As the Union attack unfolded, Bee and the other Confederate commanders north of the Warrenton

Turnpike quickly found their positions untenable. As they began falling back, the green troops' retreat turned into a rout, and the entire Confederate left threatened to collapse.

In the meantime, Thomas J. Jackson's brigade, more recently arriving on the left, had taken up a position along a ridge line called Henry House Hill. His men remained on the protected side of the hill as the retreating Confederates streamed by them. Bee fought desperately to rally his men when he spotted Jackson's brigade in its protected position. Different versions exist of what he said, but in effect Bee exclaimed, "There stands Jackson like a stone wall!"—apparently to urge his men to emulate that brigade's example. At least one witness later claimed, however, that Bee was criticizing Jackson for not coming to the aid of the retreating Confederates. Whatever Bee meant, he was responsible for one of he most enduring nicknames in American military history.

Bee never had the chance to explain what he had meant that afternoon on that hill. After the Confederates had stemmed the tide of the Union attack, Bee led an attack of his own, directly into Union artillery fire. He was mortally wounded and died the next day. Beauregard's report of the battle lamented Bee's death.

—*David S. Heidler and Jeanne T. Heidler*

See also Bull Run, First Battle of; Jackson, Thomas J.

For further reading:

McKissick, J. Rion. *General Barnard Elliott Bee: An Address* (1939).

BEECHER, HENRY WARD
(1813–1887)
Religious leader

The son of prominent minister Lyman Beecher and brother of author Harriet Beecher Stowe, Henry Ward Beecher became one of the most influential ministers of nineteenth-century America. Although never a radical abolitionist, he opposed slavery and advocated civil disobedience to the 1850 Fugitive Slave Law. He was an ardent supporter of the Union cause during the Civil War, yet promoted a moderate position on Reconstruction policy. On these issues and others, Beecher reflected Northern white middle-class attitudes even as he shaped them.

Henry Ward Beecher attended Amherst College, where he was known more for his athleticism and practical jokes than his scholarship. He followed his father's wishes and entered Lane Seminary in Cincinnati, Ohio, to prepare for the ministry upon graduation from Amherst, but had little attraction to the severe Calvinist religion of his father's church. His exposure to the militant abolitionist students whose activities caused a crisis between Lane—which his father headed—and the white

Henry Ward Beecher (*Library of Congress*)

population of Cincinnati in 1835 and 1836 convinced him that persuasion, rather than militancy, was more suited to his temperament. He married Eunice White Bullard, whom he courted at Amherst in 1837 and accepted a call to a small Presbyterian Church in Lawrenceburg, Indiana, in that year.

Success in the frontier district parish brought him to the attention of the Second Presbyterian Church in Indianapolis, where he accepted a position in 1839. In Indianapolis he assisted in the creation of a school for the deaf and the blind and gave a series of lectures in 1843 published as *Lectures to Young Men*. In these immensely popular lectures he emphasized the maintenance of moral values with colorful examples of the types of sin to be avoided.

On the issue of slavery Beecher chose a course that condemned slavery itself as sinful but did not challenge prevailing racial attitudes. In this, as in other issues, he believed that the public mood should dictate a minister's response. Beecher's moderation and emphasis on ethical values attracted the notice of New York merchants, who established the Plymouth Church in Brooklyn specifically to attract Beecher to the pulpit. In 1847 Brooklyn was growing quickly due to immigration and the older residents embraced the new social imperatives of respectability and order as a method of distinguishing themselves from lower classes and immigrants. This environment was well suited to Beecher's favorite themes, which he further refined and popularized during his forty-year tenure at Plymouth Church. His sermons did not challenge his middle-class congregation but rather reaffirmed their values and opinions. Beecher's philosophy of reform was aimed toward the enhancement of the existing social order and strengthening the family. More radical abolitionists like Theodore Weld and William Lloyd Garrison did the initial work of linking abolition with moral sensibilities, and by 1848 Beecher saw that the moment had come to join the abolitionists' fight. His relentless advocacy of barring slavery from the territories, especially in Kansas during the 1850s, resulted in the label "Beecher's Bibles" being given to the Sharps rifles carried by antislavery proponents in that territory.

Beecher's sermons emphasized the moral degeneracy of slavery, both for the slave and the surrounding free society. This was always linked to its impact on his central tenets of a Victorian-era faith in virtue, industry, thrift, and order. Slavery's deleterious effects were often exemplified in these sermons by its depressing effect on white social and economic mobility. As the middle-class white Northerner became more incensed by the moral dilemma of slavery, Beecher found that he was swept along. By the time of the Civil War, Beecher believed that war would purify society by reestablishing norms of order and morality in American culture. Patriotism itself was the expression of this commitment to national regeneration as Beecher linked the destiny of the nation to God's will. The man who earlier avoided controversy and contention thus became a militant supporter of the Union war effort.

After the Civil War, Beecher's views on the newly freed slaves retreated to his old position of moral suasion. His public and vocal stand against Federal protection of freedmen's rights and desire to rely instead upon public opinion to encourage the former slave states to recognize political rights for freedmen gradually as they became educated, and even civilized, brought him severe public criticism. Alienating the public (through newspaper reprints of his comments), his congregation, and even his family with such views, it was clear that Beecher's practiced fingers momentarily slipped off the pulse of public opinion. This public humiliation would not be forgotten as he focused on moral reform as a foundation of social stability with more domestic issues and continued to refine his position as a national religious leader. One project was the publication of *Evolution and Religion* in 1885 within which he reconciled scientific Darwinism with God's role in the universe.

In 1874 editor Theodore Tilton's public accusation of adultery between his wife and Beecher challenged Henry Ward Beecher's reputation as a moral authority. At this moment, probably no one in America was more linked with morality than Beecher, and the trial itself created a crisis of confidence in the idea of middle-class moral values. The trial was a staple of the tabloid-style newspapers of the day and commanded national interest. Ultimately, the jury, and later his own church's investigatory committee, were unable to reach a verdict on the charge.

Beecher's enduring cultural significance came from his superior oratorical skills and brilliant ability to articulate the mood of the most influential segment of American society almost before they themselves recognized their own shifts in opinion. His ability to preach familiar and orthodox Protestant doctrines that appealed to a large variety of mainstream congregants, his delivery of these homely truths liberally sprinkled with humorous and pointed illustrations, and his amazing ability to create an atmosphere of intimate conversation to an audience of several thousand were his most remarkable achievements. Although the scandal in his last years sullied his reputation, his popularity remained largely untouched, as evidenced by the over forty thousand mourners who attended his wake after his death from a cerebral hemorrhage in 1887.

—*Gretchen A. Adams*

See also: Abolitionists; Religion.
For further reading:
Abbott, Lyman. *Henry Ward Beecher* (1904).
Clark, Clifford E., Jr. *Henry Ward Beecher: Spokesman for Middle-Class America* (1978).

BELKNAP, WILLIAM WORTH
(1829–1890)
Union general

William Worth Belknap was the son of Brevet Brigadier General William G. Belknap, a career army officer who earned distinction in the Mexican-American War and who died in 1848. Belknap studied law in New Jersey and became a practicing attorney in the District of Columbia in 1851.

Belknap went to Keokuk, Iowa, in 1853 as a law partner of Ralph P. Lowe, a future governor of the state. He was an ambitious citizen, active in local politics. He was elected, as a Democrat, to the Seventh General Assembly in 1857, the first Iowa Assembly to meet in the new capital of Des Moines, and the first to meet under the authority of the new state constitution of 1857.

Belknap confronted Southern secession as a "War Democrat" and during the winter of 1860–1861 actively recruited, and was elected captain, of a local company of volunteers prepared to offer their services to the Union in case of war.

The town of Keokuk served as Iowa's military assembly and mustering center during the summer and fall of 1861, and Belknap's company was sworn into service as Company B, 15th Iowa Volunteer Infantry, in September 1861. The rest of the regiment was organized and mustered into service throughout the fall and winter, becoming fully organized by the end of February 1862, with Belknap commissioned as major in November 1861.

Belknap, due to his family's military tradition, was familiar with military drill and tradition and served as the regimental drill master while the volunteers were encamped in Keokuk.

Despite being in service for many months, the regiment did not receive its first weapons, uniforms, or true military drill until March 1862, when it shipped out from Keokuk to Benton Barracks, Missouri. The regiment was not long at Benton Barracks. Few of the soldiers had time to learn how to use their new rifles before they were sent to St. Louis in preparation for joining General Ulysses S. Grant's army in Tennessee.

On the morning of 6 April 1862, the green troops were transported to Pittsburg Landing, Tennessee, just as the battle of Shiloh was beginning.

The first day of the Shiloh battle was a disaster for the Union forces. The 15th Iowa fought as hard, and suffered

as much, as most other regiments in the army—of 760 men engaged, the regiment lost 188 men killed, wounded, or missing. Belknap suffered a shoulder wound.

On 27 April 1862, the 15th Iowa became part of Marcellus M. Crocker's Iowa Brigade and served in that unit for the rest of the war.

In August 1862, Belknap was promoted to lieutenant colonel and on 3 and 4 October led the regiment at the battle of Corinth. The regiment lost 85 men and Belknap won praise from Colonel Crocker for his bravery and ability to lead his men.

Belknap was promoted to full colonel in April 1863 and, with the exception of a few months when he served as a staff officer of XVII Corps, led the 15th Iowa during the Vicksburg campaign. At the close of the year, with their original terms of service nearly complete, Belknap and three-fourths of the regiment chose to reenlist. After returning from their veteran's furlough, Belknap and the other veterans of the Iowa Brigade joined William Sherman's army as it advanced across Georgia to Atlanta. From Kennesaw Mountain to the battles for the city itself, Belknap and the Iowa Brigade participated in virtually every engagement of the Atlanta campaign.

Belknap's greatest battlefield moment came on 22 July in the battle of Atlanta. Confederate troops seemed to attack from every side, and the fighting was so fierce that the Iowa troops were forced to fight first on one side of their trenches and then on the other side. Belknap, a large, red-bearded man who was often described as looking like a Viking warrior in battle, took advantage of the close-quarters combat to leap over the earthworks and grab an Alabama colonel and private as personal prisoners. Sherman rewarded his gallantry by appointing him brigadier general in August 1864 and giving him command of the Iowa Brigade.

Belknap served under Sherman throughout the March to the Sea and campaigns through the Carolinas. By the spring of 1865 he was in command of XVII Corps of Sherman's army with the rank of brevet major general.

At the end of the war he was offered a commission in the regular army, but he turned the offer down and returned to Keokuk, Iowa, and reopened his law practice. His service in the war caused him to abandon the Democratic Party and become a Republican, and, in 1869, on the personal recommendation of General Sherman, President U.S. Grant appointed him secretary of war, a position he held until 1876.

Belknap's political career ended in disgrace, one part of the corruption scandals that plagued the Grant administration. In March 1876 he was accused of malfeasance in office, charged with accepting bribes from an Indian post trader seeking political favors. Belknap resigned his office, in part to protect the reputation of his wife, who was also implicated in the scandal. President Grant accepted the resignation, but, even though he was

William W. Belknap (*Library of Congress*)

no longer in office, Belknap was formally impeached and subjected to a Senate trial. He was acquitted by the Senate but never again held a position in the Grant administration.

After his trial he returned to civilian law practice in Philadelphia and Washington, D.C. He remained popular with veteran soldiers and often returned to Iowa to serve as the presiding officer of the annual postwar reunions of the Iowa Brigade.

—Kenneth L. Lyftogt

See also Atlanta Campaign; Kennesaw Mountain, Battle of; Shiloh, Battle of.

For further reading:
Brigham, Johnson. *Iowa: Its History and Its Foremost Citizens* (1916).
Gue, Benjamin F. *A History of Iowa* (1903).
Iowa Adjutant General's Office. *Roster and Record of Iowa Soldiers in the War of the Rebellion* (1910).
Lewis, Lloyd. *Sherman: Fighting Prophet* (1932).
Sage, Leland L. *A History of Iowa* (1974).
Stuart, Captain A.A. *Iowa Colonels and Regiments: Being a History of Iowa Regiments in the War of the Rebellion* (1891).
Throne, Mildred, ed. *The Civil War Diary of Cyrus F. Boyd: 15th Iowa Infantry, 1861–1863* (1977).
———. "Iowans and the Civil War." *Palimpsest* (1969).

BELL, JOHN
(1796–1869)
Tennessee Unionist

John Bell was born in Mill Creek, Tennessee, on 18 February 1796, the son of Samuel Bell, a farmer and blacksmith, and Margaret Edminston. He graduated from Cumberland College in Nashville in 1814 and soon set his sights on a career in law. In 1816 he began his practice in Franklin, Tennessee. A year later he won a seat in the state senate. After a single term, Bell returned to his law practice and his new bride, Sally Dickinson, whom he had married in 1818. The couple had five children before Sally's death in 1832.

In 1822 the Bell family settled in Nashville, where Bell steadily built his reputation as an able, hard-working lawyer. In 1827 he won the first of seven consecutive terms in the U.S. House of Representatives. Although Andrew Jackson had backed Bell's opponent in the race, Bell pledged his allegiance to the popular Tennessee general when he became president in 1828. Bell disapproved of Jackson's war on the U.S. National Bank, but broke openly with the president only after Jackson ordered the removal of federal deposits from the bank in 1833. In 1834, Bell challenged Jacksonian loyalist and home state rival, James K. Polk, for the House Speaker's chair. Bell won the speakership and the bitter enmity of Tennessee Jacksonians, who exulted when Polk reclaimed the Speaker's chair from Bell in 1835. Bell contested Polk unsuccessfully for the speaker-

ship again in 1837 and lost narrowly to Robert M. T. Hunter of Virginia in 1839.

In 1835 Bell threw himself behind the presidential candidacy of Tennessee senator Hugh Lawson White, who was one of three candidates of the fledgling Whig opposition to challenge Vice President Martin Van Buren in the 1836 election. White carried Tennessee and Georgia, but his candidacy had little influence outside the South, where Whig voters supported either William Henry Harrison or Daniel Webster. Against a divided opposition, Van Buren captured the White House, and Bell's breach with the Democratic Party was complete.

Bell labored diligently for Harrison's 1840 presidential campaign, although he had originally supported Henry Clay's claim to the Whig nomination. The Whigs' "log cabin and hard cider" campaign earned the party its first presidential victory. Bell was rewarded with an appointment as secretary of war. When Harrison died a month after taking office, Vice President John Tyler assumed the reins of the administration. Tyler soon alienated Whig leaders in Congress when he proved implacably opposed to the Whig economic program. In 1841, at Clay's strong urging, nearly the entire cabinet, including Bell, resigned in protest.

Bell was elected to the Tennessee legislature in 1847 and was soon elevated to the U.S. Senate. He quickly became embroiled in the controversy over the status of slavery in the new territories acquired by the United States in 1848 as a result of the Mexican-American War. Southerners were outraged by Northern attempts to exclude slavery from the new lands and particularly opposed the plan of President Zachary Taylor to admit California as a free state. Clay attempted to break the sectional impasse with his Compromise package, which tied the admission of California to several other pro-Southern conditions. Bell opposed Clay's plan and urged instead the division of Texas into at least two slave states to appease Southern interests. Clay's omnibus bill failed, but its provisions eventually passed the Senate one by one. Bell belatedly endorsed the Compromise, sensing its popularity at home.

Bell and the disintegrating Whig Party faced another sectional controversy in 1854. The Kansas-Nebraska Act repealed the line between slavery and freedom that had been established in the 1820 Missouri Compromise, theoretically opening up the Kansas and Nebraska territories to slavery's expansion. Northern Whigs were outraged, and Southern Whigs such as Bell initially opposed the bill, arguing that it would provoke sectional hostility without delivering tangible benefits to the South. Once opposition to the bill became equated with antislavery sentiment, however, Southerners then rushed to endorse it. In the end, Bell cast the only Southern vote in the Senate against the bill; only seven

Southern Whigs followed his lead in the House. In 1858, after a bloody battle between antislavery and proslavery settlers, Kansas sought admission to the Union as a slave state under the controversial Lecompton constitution. Again, Bell broke with his region in opposing admission and was denounced by Southern Democrats as a traitor.

Bell's unsuccessful efforts to quell sectional tensions and prevent the collapse of the Whig Party in the 1850s won him praise from Northerners and conservative ex-Whigs. In 1860, a group of former Whigs nominated Bell as the presidential candidate of a new Constitutional Union Party and selected Edward Everett of Massachusetts for the vice presidential slot. Reserved in demeanor, Bell lacked the charisma of an effective candidate for national office; he also was hobbled by his party's refusal to address the slavery controversy. His only hope was for the Republicans to lose enough states in the North, and for Southern Democrats to divide their votes between Stephen A. Douglas and John C. Breckinridge, so that the election would be thrown into the House of Representatives. In the end, however, Bell carried only Tennessee, Virginia, and Kentucky, and Lincoln swept the North to win decisive electoral victory.

As the momentum of secession moved rapidly forward after Lincoln's election, Bell was characteristically cautious. He refused an urgent request from Mississippi conservatives to visit that state, instead issuing a public statement urging moderation and denouncing secession as an illegitimate solution to the South's grievances. In a major speech to a Nashville audience in January 1861, Bell reiterated his belief that the Republicans posed no immediate danger to the South, although he expressed a hope that Tennessee and Kentucky would join forces in a "Central Confederacy" if the Union dissolved. Bell's speech helped stay secession furor in Tennessee—on 9 February, voters voted overwhelmingly against a secession convention. In April, Bell traveled to Washington to confer with the new president and returned convinced that Lincoln's policy would be conciliatory.

Lincoln's decision to resupply Fort Sumter and his subsequent call for 75,000 troops reignited secession sentiment in the South. Bell reluctantly accepted that Tennessee would side with the Confederacy. His reversal on secession outraged some of his conservative allies, who thought Bell had cowed to popular opinion, but Tennessee's overwhelming vote for secession in June 1861 proved that little could have been done to keep the state in the Union.

Bell had no direct involvement in the Southern war effort, although he was certainly affected by wartime dislocation and destruction of property. Union forces invaded middle Tennessee in early 1862, damaging Bell's extensive iron and coal works, which he had obtained through his second marriage to Jane Erwin Yeatman in 1835. As Union troops approached Nashville, Bell moved his family southward to Alabama and then to Georgia. After the war, he returned to Tennessee and attempted to rebuild his mines and mills in Stewart County; there he lived out the final years of his life.

Unrelentingly, Bell clung to the belief that compromise was possible on the slavery issue and blamed extremists in both sections for escalating tensions. His unsuccessful efforts to hold the Union together epitomized the tragic failure of moderation as the nation hurtled toward civil war.

—*Susan Wyly-Jones*

See also Election of 1860.
For further reading:
Atkins, Jonathan M. *Parties, Politics, and the Sectional Conflict in Tennessee, 1832–1861* (1997).
Bergeron, Paul H. *Antebellum Politics in Tennessee* (1982).
Crofts, Daniel W. *Reluctant Confederates: Upper South Unionists in the Secession Crisis* (1989).
Parks, Joseph H. *John Bell of Tennessee* (1950).

BELLE ISLE
Confederate military prison

An island in the James River connected to Richmond by a footbridge, Belle Isle was used as a day resort by the people of Richmond before the war. During the early months of the war, the island was used to drill new troops for the Confederate army. Because of the difficulty of swimming the rapids around the island, it was deemed an ideal place to house prisoners in tents once other facilities in Richmond became overcrowded.

Until the Peninsula campaign of the spring and summer of 1862, the buildings used as prisons within the city were adequate for the needs of the army. However, by April 1862 the number of Federal soldiers housed in the city had seriously overtaxed the available facilities. Therefore a company of cavalry was allocated to serve as guards, and in June the first Federal soldiers were brought to the island.

Used only for privates and noncommissioned officers, Belle Isle was intended only as a holding facility until more adequate prisons were available. As a result no buildings were erected, and the first prisoners were issued tents for their shelter. The men were confined to a 6-acre site surrounded by an earthwork that they were not allowed to cross. The first commandant of the prison was Captain Norris Montgomery, who was considered rather lenient with the men. Captain Henry Wirz replaced him in August 1862 and revoked all the privileges granted by his predecessor. Part of the reason for Wirz's seeming cruelty was that the numbers of prisoners in the stockade had swollen to 5,000 in areas that had been designed for 3,000. Wirz believed that such overcrowding and his limited number of guards dictated that captives be kept closely confined. Soon after Wirz took command, however, an exchange agreement emptied the grounds, and the prison was closed in September 1862.

Belle Isle opened again briefly in January 1863 following the battle of Fredericksburg and then again in May 1863 in response to the surplus of prisoners from the battle of Chancellorsville. Then Lieutenant Virginius Bossieux commanded the camp. His tenure as commandant was characterized by some of the worst conditions endured there. During the summer Belle Isle's average occupancy was double its 3,000-man capacity, and there were only 300 tents, which at best could sleep ten men each. The remaining half of the men had to sleep in the open, sometimes in holes they dug to provide some shelter.

By fall 1863 conditions had worsened, with as many as 8,000 men sometimes confined in the small enclosure. Word naturally leaked North of these conditions, and the situation at Belle Isle soon became one of the major sources of Northern propaganda regarding Southern cruelty to prisoners. General Neal Dow, a prisoner of war at Libby Prison in Richmond, was allowed to go to Belle Isle to distribute blankets that had been sent by the United States government, and following that visit he was able to slip out a report to the North on the conditions there. However, his intelligence did little, if anything, to improve the conditions at the camp. During the extremely hard winter of 1863–1864, the camp continued to be overcrowded, and some nights as many as fourteen men froze to death.

Conditions at the camp made disease rampant. To add to the misery of the prisoners, their swelling numbers drove up the price of food in Richmond and consequently caused a cut in their rations. During early 1864 the average ration consisted of a square of cornbread and thin soup that the men complained was full of bugs.

At the same time that conditions at the camp worsened, concerns increased that its proximity to Richmond made the prison a target for Union raiders hoping to liberate the inmates. As a result, in February 1864 the process of gradually removing the prisoners and shipping them by rail to Andersonville and other prisons farther south began. By the end of March, Belle Isle was again empty.

With the beginning of Ulysses S. Grant's campaign against Robert E. Lee in May of 1864, however, the need for prison facilities in Richmond again grew. Belle Isle was opened again in June 1864, and 6,000 prisoners were put there. They remained through the summer of 1864, but fears of attempts to liberate them caused their shipment south in October and caused the closure of the camp. It never opened again.

—David S. Heidler and Jeanne T. Heidler

See also Prisoners of War; Prisons, C.S.A.

For further reading:
Abbott, Horace R. *My Escape from Belle Isle* (1889).
Coburn, Jacob Osborn. *Hell on Belle Isle: Diary of a Civil War POW: Journal of Sgt. Jacob Osborn Coburn* (1997).
Goss, Warren Lee. *The Soldier's Story of His Captivity at Andersonville, Belle Isle and Other Rebel Prisons* (1867).
Hesseltine, William B. *Civil War Prisons: A Study in War Psychology* (1930; reprint 1998).
Robinson, Daniel W. "Belle Isle: Prison in the James, 1862–1865" (Master's thesis, 1980).
Speer, Lonnie R. *Portals to Hell: Military Prisons of the Civil War* (1997).

BELMONT, BATTLE OF
(7 November 1861)

On 1 September 1861, Union brigadier general Ulysses S. Grant took command of the District of Southeast Missouri, with headquarters at Cairo, Illinois. Charged with overseeing Union operations in southeastern Missouri, his responsibilities increased when Confederate forces under Major General Leonidas Polk and Brigadier General Gideon Pillow invaded neutral Kentucky and captured Columbus, a key position atop the bluffs along the east bank of the Mississippi. Polk fortified Columbus and made it the anchor of the Confederacy's main defensive line in the west. Across from Columbus lay Belmont, Missouri, an old ferry landing occupied by a small Southern garrison and renamed Camp Johnston. Until the Federals seized Columbus (called "the Gibraltar of the West" by Confederates), a large stretch of the Mississippi River would remain under Confederate control. Strategically located across the river from Columbus, Belmont was, to Grant, a logical place from which to start the process of capturing the fortress, something he had longed to do since early September.

On the evening of 6 November 1861 three thousand Union troops boarded transports at Cairo and steamed downriver toward Belmont. Escorted by the Union gunboats *Tyler* and *Lexington*, Grant's expeditionary force consisted of two infantry brigades, two cavalry companies, and a battery of artillery. In conjunction with the attack on Belmont, Union major general Charles F. Smith at Paducah was to send a force to demonstrate against Columbus. Early on 7 November, Grant's troops disembarked at Hunter's Farm, three miles above Belmont, and marched toward the Confederate camp. Under the overall command of Confederate colonel James C. Tappan, Camp Johnston was occupied by one regiment of infantry, a cavalry battalion, and an artillery battery. Once the attack commenced, Polk, hearing the gunfire, sent four more infantry regiments (2,500 men) under Pillow across the river to defend the outpost. As this force arrived to even the odds, Grant pressed his attack. After heavy fighting in a cornfield

The battle of Belmont, from an undated engraving (*Library of Congress*)

west of the camp, Pillow's line collapsed. Although orderly at first, Pillow's retreat soon lapsed into chaos as panic gripped his men, some of whom found themselves under fire from different directions. Some Southern units lost all cohesion as Grant's men, smelling blood, advanced toward the camp. The Federals continued to drive the Confederates toward the river and finally captured Camp Johnston. With victory in their grasp and exhilarated by their first taste of combat, many pursuing Union soldiers laid down their arms and began looting the camp, despite the desperate pleas of their officers to remain in the ranks. As Pillow's men huddled along the bank or fled upriver, the Union pursuit lost momentum. Men fell out to ransack tents, musicians struck up the "Star-Spangled Banner," and politician-officers, including John A. McClernand, gave patriotic speeches to commemorate the occasion.

On the opposite bank, Smith's demonstration failed to convince Polk for very long that the Belmont attack was only a diversion for the main attack against Columbus. Once Polk concluded that Smith was not a threat, he ordered the Columbus guns to open on the Federals milling about Camp Johnston and dispatched more reinforcements (five regiments) under Brigadier General Frank Cheatham to rescue the beleaguered Pillow. Glimpsing transports loaded with Southern

soldiers heading his way, Grant ordered his men back to the boats, but it took time to get them reorganized and underway. Meanwhile, the Confederates, buttressed by Cheatham's arrival, began a dogged and deadly pursuit of Grant's retreating columns. Some Federal units had to cut their way out and Grant himself barely escaped capture. Under fire from the shoreline, the Union steamers finally slipped away and returned to Cairo. The Federals suffered 607 casualties (including 120 dead) out of approximately 2,500 engaged, while the Confederates suffered 641 casualties (including 105 dead) out of approximately 5,000 engaged.

Grant claimed victory at Belmont, although contemporaries and historians alike have questioned this assessment, especially since his chaotic retreat left the enemy in possession of the field and because the battle accomplished few worthwhile results. Despite Grant's hope that he would achieve much more with his attack, Belmont and Columbus remained in Confederate hands until Forts Henry and Donelson fell in February 1862. The capture of these two important points shattered the Confederacy's western defensive line, and not until then did Polk abandon the Confederate Gibraltar of the West.
—*William B. Feis*

See also Cheatham, Benjamin Franklin; Grant, Ulysses S.; McClernand, John A.; Pillow, Gideon; Polk, Leonidas.

For further reading:
Feis, William B. "Grant and the Belmont Campaign: A study in intelligence and command." In *The Art of Command in the Civil War*. Edited by Steven E. Woodworth (1998).
Hughes, Nathaniel Cheairs, Jr. *The Battle of Belmont: Grant Strikes South* (1991).

BENJAMIN, JUDAH PHILIP
(1811–1884)

U.S. senator; Confederate attorney general, secretary of war, and secretary of state

Judah Benjamin was raised the son of Sephardic Jews in Charleston, South Carolina. His education included a brief period when he attended Fayetteville Academy in North Carolina, and in 1825 Benjamin entered Yale College. For reasons not entirely clear, he left Yale two years later without graduating. Benjamin soon thereafter moved to New Orleans, a cosmopolitan city with a religiously diverse population that included a sizable Jewish community. He found employment as a clerk in a commercial house, and he supplemented his income by giving English lessons. It was in his capacity as a tutor that he met and fell in love with Natalie St. Martin, the daughter of a wealthy and prominent Catholic family. After their marriage in 1833, Judah and Natalie's relationship was at the least peculiar; Natalie was terribly unhappy, and soon she and their daughter, Ninette, moved to Paris. Although the marriage lasted for over fifty years, Natalie spent most of those years in France.

Meanwhile, Benjamin was admitted to the Louisiana bar, where he displayed considerable skill at forcefully and successfully representing his many clients. He was considered by many people to be New Orleans's finest attorney. One of the more significant cases with which Benjamin was associated involved a slave mutiny aboard the ship *Creole*. He was hired by a New Orleans insurance company to argue that the ship owners were not due remuneration because the mutiny occurred in international waters. Benjamin's arguments in this case are fascinating and might lead one to conclude that he opposed Southern slavery as a cruel and inhumane institution. It is important to remember, however, that Benjamin merely presented the most forceful argument he could muster as a well-paid advocate, and his briefs in no manner reflected his personal views regarding slavery. In fact, Benjamin's foremost ambition seems to have been to join the ranks of Louisiana's elite planter class. Indeed, his success at the bar afforded him sufficient income to purchase a sugar plantation of several hundred acres, complete with nearly 150 slaves.

As the successful owner of a sugar estate, Benjamin circulated in upper-crust planter society, and he began courting prominent individuals in hopes of gaining political office. No relationship proved more valuable than his friendship with John Slidell, a New Orleans Whig whose political machine virtually ran the state. In 1842 Benjamin was elected as a Whig representative to the state legislature, and in 1848 he was a presidential elector from Louisiana. Benjamin was elected by his fellow Whigs as a U.S. senator in 1852, but his affiliation with the Whig Party was short-lived; he joined the Democratic Party in 1856 as a staunch Buchanan supporter. Benjamin served in the U.S. Senate until 1860, and during that period he developed a strong friendship with Jefferson Davis of Mississippi. This relationship did not begin cordially; during one heated exchange between the two senators regarding military appropriations, tempers flared nearly to the point of a duel. Yet Davis quickly realized that he had insulted Benjamin without warrant and he apologized openly on the floor of the Senate. From that time on the two were close friends who deeply respected one another.

On New Years' Eve 1860, Benjamin addressed a packed gallery in the Senate to deliver his farewell speech. The secession crisis had earlier prompted South Carolinians to withdraw their state from the Union, and after a secession convention in Louisiana was similarly productive, Benjamin promptly tendered his resignation.

Judah P. Benjamin (*Library of Congress*)

His farewell speech, though rife with caustic invective for Northern extremists, nevertheless was as eloquent as it was forceful in imploring Northerners to allow the South to depart the Union in peace.

As President Jefferson Davis assembled his cabinet for the fledgling Confederate government, he turned at once to Judah Benjamin to fill the post of attorney general, a position that required him to be the Confederacy's chief prosecutor. Although his duties involved purely civilian affairs, Benjamin regularly offered his opinion on military matters. His counsel was sound in a time when reason seemed wanting in many quarters. Davis soon relied on his attorney general as his principal adviser. By the time the government relocated to Richmond, Virginia, in late spring 1861, Davis and Benjamin had developed a close relationship based on Benjamin's unswerving loyalty to the president and Davis's profound trust in Benjamin. No person, perhaps with the exception of his wife Varina, advised Jefferson Davis more closely than did Judah Benjamin.

Soon after the first battle of Bull Run, when the Davis administration suffered harsh criticism for not pursuing Union general Irvin McDowell's fleeing army, Davis requested Secretary of War Leroy Walker's resignation. Walker had not been an especially efficient administrator, and his removal opened the way for Davis to appoint Benjamin as his replacement. Although seemingly illogical to appoint a person, such as Benjamin, with absolutely no prior military experience to such a highly important post within the Confederacy's military, Davis needed an individual who would unquestionably carry out directives. The fact was that Jefferson Davis believed himself most fit to run the War Department, and he thus appointed Benjamin to avoid the inevitable conflicts that would arise if a career military officer had been named. Benjamin had an almost obsessive commitment to efficient office management, and his organizational skills were at once beneficial.

Benjamin was a tireless worker who regularly spent ten to fifteen hours each day at his desk or in conference with the president. He rarely complained, was a most congenial person, and was ever the optimist, even during the darkest days of the war. Benjamin's high, full cheeks gave him the appearance of wearing a perpetual smile and having a carefree disposition that Davis seemed to appreciate, especially as the Confederacy's fortunes grew bleak. Not everyone, though, appreciated Judah Benjamin, and soon after assuming his duties at the War Department he was involved in disputes with some of the Confederacy's leading generals. P. G. T. Beauregard, for example, sent a letter to Benjamin requesting that he be placed in command of all Confederate armies in the eastern theater. When Benjamin refused this request, Beauregard wrote a scathing letter to Davis in which he referred to the war secretary as that "functionary at his desk." Davis was eventually able to placate Beauregard's delicate ego, but many well-trained officers resented following directives from a nonmilitary head of the War Department. A second dispute arose between Benjamin and Thomas J. "Stonewall" Jackson when the secretary ordered Stonewall to regroup his dangerously scattered armies in the Shenandoah Valley. Jackson complied with the order, but he obviously resented the unwarranted intrusion. Jackson offered his resignation, and once again Davis had to heal a breach between a popular general and his most loyal secretary.

As these disputes became public, and as Union armies made considerable military gains in the western theater, Benjamin's once sound reputation quickly evaporated. Newspapers throughout the South expressed doubts about his ability to lead the War Department, and not a few shamelessly suggested that as a Jew, Benjamin's loyalty should not only be questioned but closely scrutinized. Such attacks displayed an inherent prejudice against Jews, and Benjamin was a convenient target for disgruntled generals, ambitious politicians, and discontented newspaper editors.

Verbal attacks against the war secretary reached a crescendo after the fall of Roanoke Island in February 1862. The 2,500 Confederate soldiers garrisoned there under General Henry Wise were running desperately short of supplies as a superior Union force threatened to overtake them. Wise sent several letters pleading for more men and materiel, but Benjamin simply had little to send; about all that he could do was hope that the island's meager defenses would hold until supplies could be obtained. On 8 February 1862 Union forces numbering over 19,000 men stormed ashore and successfully seized the Confederate stronghold. General Wise's son, Jennings, was among the Confederate dead at Roanoke, and Benjamin suffered tremendous criticism from throughout the South. Calls for his resignation were universal, as were demands that Davis dismiss Benjamin, should the latter refuse to step down.

Robert M. T. Hunter of Virginia resigned as Confederate secretary of state in March 1862 after having a heated exchange of words with Davis. With his war secretary under assault for the Roanoke debacle, Davis felt it wise to remove Benjamin from the War Department and to name him as Hunter's replacement. Many people could not understand Davis's unwillingness to fire Benjamin outright; some even began referring to Benjamin as Mr. Davis's "pet Jew." Nevertheless, as the newly appointed secretary of state, Benjamin was in a role far more suitable to his talents and skills. It was becoming ever more imperative that the Confederate government cajole England and France into granting the Richmond government full diplomatic recognition. Such a pronouncement would have lent considerable validity to the South's quest for independence and an aura of illegality to Lincoln's war against it. Benjamin thus redirected his energies away from creating an efficient war department and toward gaining recognition from England and France.

Confederate diplomacy to mid-1863 had been driven largely by the deluded belief among many within the Richmond government that England's demands for Southern cotton would force recognition and perhaps prompt British intervention in the war to break the Union blockade. By 1862, however, it was apparent that such reasoning had been fallacious and that European powers were not going to enter the war to save cotton. Many Southerners—Benjamin among them—became convinced that recognition was not granted because of the South's determination to hold onto slavery. England had abolished the institution in 1833, and sentiment there was clearly against the South's labor system. After the disaster at Gettysburg in July 1862, Benjamin reasoned that recognition would be possible only if the Confederacy abolished slavery and showed the Palmerston government in England that the war was being fought more for Southern independence than for slavery. The problem for Benjamin was that, for the present at least, President Davis was not interested in freeing the slaves or even in entertaining the subject.

By summer 1864, when Lee's haggard and increasingly weakened army was entrenched at Petersburg staving off Grant's massive forces, the Confederacy's dark fate seemed all but certain without some dramatic shift in foreign policy. Although Benjamin had already concluded that emancipation was the South's only hope for independence, it was not until Lincoln's reelection in November 1864 that Davis agreed to discuss emancipation options. Benjamin proposed that emancipation should occur in two stages: first, Duncan Kenner, a Louisiana congressman who had favored emancipation since early in the war, should be dispatched to Europe and offer a promise of emancipation in return for recognition. Once Kenner's mission was complete, Benjamin proposed that Davis should declare all slaves free.

The problem with Benjamin's daring plan were the political risks involved. After all, did the president of a confederacy have authority to abolish an institution fundamentally protected by state authority? Secondly, Davis was concerned whether the troops would fight if slavery were abolished. Would the troops remain with the armies or simply return home demoralized? These uncertainties led Davis to move slowly on the emancipation issue. He did, however, consent to secretly send Kenner to Europe with authority to bargain on terms that included emancipation. Benjamin and Kenner then planned the latter's mission to Europe. Unfortunately for the Confederacy, Kenner's mission was initiated far too late in the war to sway either Napoleon III in France or Lord Palmerston in Britain. On 2 April 1865, when Lee notified the government that his army was retreating from Petersburg and that Richmond would have to be evacuated, Benjamin hurriedly packed the State Department's papers. He joined his colleagues within the administration for the train ride to Danville, Virginia, with the hope that some miracle could save the Confederacy.

Abraham Lincoln was assassinated on 14 April 1865. It was soon discovered that two of the coconspirators had maintained close ties to Benjamin, and he was at once suspected of plotting to kill the U.S. president. Although Benjamin had had nothing to do with Lincoln's death, his ties to the Surratt family were undeniable, and he knew that in the highly emotional atmosphere generated by Lincoln's death, he most assuredly would be tried and hanged.

Benjamin thus resolved to flee the country for England. After a harrowing four-month escape that took him to Florida, Bimini, Nassau, Havana, and, finally, Southampton, Benjamin was safe in England and resolute about putting the war behind him. He decided to pursue a new career as an attorney at the British bar, and after but five months of studying the intricacies of English law, Benjamin was permitted to practice in English courts. Perhaps Benjamin's most noteworthy and far reaching accomplishment during this period was his writing of the *Treatise on the Law of Sale of Personal Property*, a well-received textbook that for many years remained the standard work on sales contracts. He continued to practice law in England with great success, and he visited Natalie and Ninette in France on occasion. Benjamin suffered a heart attack in 1882 and was forced into retirement. He died in Paris in 1884.

From 1865 until his death, Judah Benjamin rarely spoke of his services to the Confederacy, perhaps preferring to forget those terrible four years. Though he served in three high-level positions, Benjamin's most influential role was as Jefferson Davis's closest friend and adviser. It actually mattered little which position Benjamin held, for Davis would have relied similarly on his advice in whatever capacity. As the Confederacy's fortunes turned bleak with each military loss, and as criticism of the Richmond government reached fever pitch, it was often Judah Benjamin who bore the brunt of the verbal attacks. And he did so while maintaining his characteristic pleasant demeanor and optimism.

—*Robert Saunders, Jr.*

See also Davis, Jefferson; Diplomacy, C.S.A.; Jews.
For further reading:
Butler, Pierce. *Judah P. Benjamin* (1981).
Evans, Eli N. *Judah P. Benjamin, The Jewish Confederate* (1988).
Meade, Robert D. *Judah P. Benjamin, Confederate Statesman* (1975).

BENNETT HOUSE

Owned by James Bennett (frequently spelled Bennitt) and his wife Nancy, the unassuming Bennett farmhouse in Orange County, North Carolina (near present-day Durham), was the site of the largest surrender of the American Civil War, on 26 April 1865. Bennett, his wife, and three children lived on 325 acres, raising hogs and growing potatoes, corn, wheat, and oats. Bennett was also a resourceful entrepreneur, serving as a tailor, cobbler, and broker of horse feed, tobacco plugs, and distilled liquor. Before the surrender negotiations, Bennett and his wife had been directly touched by the war, as their sons and son-in-law died during the conflict.

In March 1865, 60,000 Federal troops under the command of General William Tecumseh Sherman entered North Carolina south of Fayetteville. In an effort to check Sherman's advance, Robert E. Lee called General Joseph E. Johnston out of his retirement in Lincolnton, North Carolina, and gave him command of what was left of the Army of Tennessee and the Department of South Carolina, Georgia, and Florida. The two forces clashed near the small town of Bentonville on 19 March in what proved to be the largest battle on North Carolina soil. Forced to withdraw his army, Johnston moved north to Smithfield, then through Raleigh and west to Hillsborough. Sherman followed slowly, entering the North Carolina capital on 13 April and establishing his headquarters in the governor's mansion.

When rumors of Lee's surrender at Appomattox filtered into the Confederate encampment at Hillsborough, Johnston knew that the end was in sight. Not only did he face the imminent threat of Sherman's seemingly unstoppable force, but now the massive Army of the Potomac could conceivable join in the pursuit. Johnston made his opinion known to President Jefferson Davis when the two conferred in Greensboro, and on 14 April the Confederate commander wrote to Sherman asking for "a temporary suspension of active operations." Sherman agreed, and the two generals and their escorts met on the Hillsborough Road on 17 April, midway between their opposing armies.

After exchanging cordial greetings, Johnston suggested that the two parties proceed to the nearby Bennett farmhouse. Bennett gave his pro forma permission for the generals to confer in his house while their respective staffs remained outside lounging against his rail fence and under the blooming cherry trees. Before discussing terms, Sherman informed Johnston of Lincoln's assassination and watched as "the perspiration came out in large drops" on the stunned general's forehead. Johnston responded that this was "the greatest possible calamity to the South" and was reassured by Sherman that he did not hold the Confederate military

responsible for the tragedy. Sherman was prepared to offer Johnston the same terms and conditions that were made by General Ulysses S. Grant to Lee eight days earlier. Johnston, however, wanted to go one step further and work out terms for a permanent peace. Sherman agreed to meet again the next day if Johnston could secure the approval of the Confederate politicos and be permitted to negotiate for all the Confederate armies remaining in the field.

At 2:00 in the afternoon on 18 April, Sherman and Johnston reconvened at the Bennett house, prepared to work out an agreement for peace. After some preliminary negotiating, both parties agreed to very broad terms that provided for demobilizing all Confederate armies, depositing arms in state arsenals, recognizing state governments, establishing new federal courts, and restoring political and civil rights as long as laws were obeyed. In short, the war was to cease followed by a general amnesty. President Davis readily agreed to such liberal terms, but the federal government rejected them outright and instructed General Grant to direct Sherman to renegotiate terms strictly along the lines of those established with Lee at Appomattox on 9 April.

Accordingly, on 26 April, Johnston and Sherman met at the Bennett house for the third and last time and signed an agreement that conformed to Grant's guidelines. The document effectively ended the war in the Carolinas, Georgia, and Florida and demobilized and disarmed the 89,270 men still under Johnston's overall command.

—*Alan C. Downs*

See also Bentonville, Battle of; Carolinas Campaign; Johnston, Joseph Eggleston; Sherman, William Tecumseh.
For further reading:
Barrett, John G. *The Civil War in North Carolina* (1963).
Marszalek, John F. *Sherman: A Soldier's Passion for Order* (1994).

BENNETT, JAMES GORDON
(1795–1872)
Journalist, editor, and publisher

James Gordon Bennett became a dominant force in newspaper publishing during the middle of the nineteenth century. The Civil War especially encouraged the innovative Bennett to take advantage of a climactic event that would allow him to beat a fierce competition. What set him apart from his rivals was his adherence to basic principles of journalism, not the least of which was "if it bleeds, it leads." He also saw the need to put out as complete a paper as possible. This meant that cultural events, books, music, theater, and human interest, would share with crime and politics. His editorial policy was daring and courageous, often to the point of being dangerous to himself. Bennett had no fear of being physically attacked by someone whose interests he had criticized in his paper. He knew full well too that the reading public was too prone to regard "yesterday's news" too literally; therefore, any contradictions in the paper required few retractions. His *New York Herald* covered commerce, shipping, and business generally, but it was the sensational story that challenged for readership. Bennett came to his perception of what a real newspaper should be by hard experience. This experience taught him that independence meant that he and his paper would be beholden to no one.

Bennett was born a Catholic in intensely Protestant Scotland. He received a classical education of Greek, Latin, mathematics, history, and the Bible, all of which, and especially the last, were reinforced at home. He was set on a path to the priesthood, which he rejected after four years at Blair's College in Aberdeen. For five years until 1819 he traveled throughout Scotland and decided to go to the Americas with $25 in his pocket.

He landed in Nova Scotia, but it was not the America he had read about in books such as Benjamin Franklin's *Autobiography*. His classical education fitted him for everything and nothing. He taught bookkeeping in Halifax but the suffocating English atmosphere pushed him south to Portland. He did some teaching and absorbed something of the independent outlook of the people. He moved on to Boston and was repelled by the arrogance and snobbishness of the city. To him Bostonians seemed to represent a nation within a nation and they preferred their own. Religion was also a problem in Boston, as it seemed too much like that of the rigid Scot Presbyterians. He worked in a bookshop and printery, a job that allowed him to read extensively. His employers found him to be a good worker, but customers commented on his speech, ungainly manners, and especially his disconcerting crossed eyes. He was assigned to the print shop as a proofreader where he astutely absorbed the craft of printing for a commercial market. He stayed until 1823, when he moved to New York.

In New York, Bennett again did proofreading and bookkeeping and was hired at $5 a week, translating Spanish and French news for the *Charleston (South Carolina) Courier*. He spent ten months in the South and was impressed with the culture and pride of the city and the intelligence of the people working with him. He was quick to discover, however, that ideas and wit were secondary to appearances. His withdrawn behavior prevented him from participating fully in social settings. New York seemed to be more suited to him.

After writing freelance articles and editorials for various papers, he became an editor for Mordecai Noah's *Enquirer*, concentrating on politics in Albany and Washington. When the paper joined with James Watson Webb's *Courier*, Bennett went along to write on both politics and banking. His editorials targeted the recharter bill of Nicholas Biddle's Second National Bank. The *Courier and Enquirer* was a powerful and prosperous paper that changed its beliefs on the bank after President Andrew Jackson vetoed the recharter. Bennett suspected the bank's influence, so he left. He himself had played a duplicitous game with Biddle by requesting underwriting to allow him to buy into the paper while maintaining contacts with the Jackson people. Rebuffed by the bank, Bennett heaped scorn on the bank as a "vast and corrupt political machine...buying and selling votes...bribing officials and editors."

Bennett tried without success to buy a paper in both New York and Washington and found work as editor for a Democratic Party daily, the *Pennsylvanian* in Philadelphia. He lasted two years and again returned to New York, where he was intrigued by the newest paper in town, the *New York Sun*, which was a penny paper that was sold directly by carriers who swarmed the streets with the little dailies. It was a paper designed for the common people and proved to be successful. Bennett saw possibilities for a more sophisticated penny daily.

Horace Greeley, who had his own ups and downs with dailies and weekly papers until he got political underpinning for his *Tribune*, referred Bennett to two printers he knew. Bennett started his paper in a basement room at 20 Wall Street on a couple of planks laid across some barrels. He named it the *Herald* with the first issue appearing on 6 May 1835. He worked from eight in the morning until ten in the evening, doing everything, from the work of editor to that of distributor. He structured his time to fit every facet of the paper, an organizational impulse that was to sustain him throughout his career and make his paper the most dominant media force in the nation by 1865.

His sharp wit and acerbic language poked and prodded the pretentious, the politician, the reformers, business promoters, and usurious bankers. All became targets. He invented the idea of attribution to anonymous sources for stories of his own creation. He prowled the streets seeking story ideas. He described dead people in gruesome detail, a practice he used when reviewing photographic exhibitions by Mathew Brady of battlefield casualties. He printed personal interviews with question-answer confrontations. He followed fire engines and police wagons and even hearses to get a story. The *Herald* soon became the one paper bought by New Yorkers. His paper was constantly threatened with lawsuits for slander and libel, and he was often attacked. His former employer, Webb, beat him up two times, and each time Bennett greeted his reading public with a full accounting, much to the dismay of Webb. The pen was mightier than the sword. Words and ideas were his answer to physical threats. Critics were relentless and unprincipled in their attacks. The success of the paper enraged his enemies, especially his former associates Webb and Noah.

After Bennett's marriage in 1840, Webb and Noah questioned the chastity of the bride, and when a son was born, they challenged Bennett's fatherhood. Bennett filed a lawsuit, and Noah was assessed a $250 fine. The harassment continued, however, and Bennett's wife chose to spend much of her time in Paris or on cruises. Bennett hewed to the task of putting out the best paper with the most stories. Money was devoted to expansion and to hiring more journalists. He gave them bylines and underwrote expenses. He hired vessels to meet foreign shipping at sea before they got to port in order to get the story first. He employed translators and sent correspondents to cover European events such as the Crimean War.

His paper was a great concern to political parties because its policy could often become mercurial. Generally conservative in criticism of abolitionists and its calls for the hanging of John Brown, it nevertheless insisted on crushing the Confederacy once war began, much to the disappointment of Southerners, who had appreciated his empathy for their interests before the war. The paper generally supported Democrats, except it went for John Charles Frémont in 1856. It did not support Lincoln in either election, though Lincoln was an avid reader of the *Herald*, even going so far as to offer Bennett an ambassadorship to France—which was declined by Bennett. Bennett had as many as sixty-five correspondents in the combat zones of the Civil War and kept a battery of columnists in Washington at a cost of $200 a week. Circulation grew from 100,000 to 123,000 in the first six months of 1862. William Russell, who had set the standard for combat correspondents in the Crimean War while writing for the *London Times*, became subject for a *Herald* story, which crowed in 1861 that it had bettered Russell in "truthfulness, graphic power and bravery of its reporters."

Nothing was spared in reporting the war. Shaping stories for public consumption was standard. Only the enemy had deserters, shirkers, stragglers, and cowards. Combat always ended decisively and genius of leadership became a given in news articles. Some reporters had insinuated themselves within military units, and Union commanders were uncertain about their status. T. W. Knox, a reporter for the *Herald*, was court-martialed by General William Tecumseh Sherman as a suspected spy; other reporters were mobbed by soldiers and run out of camps in ball and chain. For $15 to $50 a week and all the danger and excitement required, the reporters fed the appetite for news. Lincoln's people's war was guaranteed to be public by Bennett and his *Herald*.

The competition was left far behind by the speed, depth, and breadth of the *Herald*'s war coverage. Dailies in other cities around the nation picked stories from the *Herald* to run in their own papers. Bennett had expended almost $750,000 in telegraph costs to cover the war. He even donated a sloop outfitted with cannon in return for a commission as lieutenant for his son, James, Jr., who promptly resigned his commission two years later when the ship was taken out of service in 1864. By this time, he was being groomed to take over the firm, which had grown to a dozen editors and almost 500 employees.

Though never a champion of Lincoln, Bennett used the *Herald* to ennoble him after his death. The martyrdom of Lincoln was assured by the paper, and those involved in the conspiracy were condemned with all the vituperative power for which the *Herald* was noted.

James Gordon Bennett turned control of the paper over to his son in 1867. He was certainly unsure of the ability of his dilettante son to continue the progress that had been made. Staying on top of technology, insisting on a cash-and-carry advertising practice, and stressing broad coverage of stories with a personal side were *Herald* hallmarks that eventually the Joseph Pulitzers and the William Randolph Hearsts parlayed into successes of their own. Virtually alone, as his wife preferred to stay in Europe, Bennett, Sr. had a stroke that paralyzed him from the waist down, and on 1 June 1872 he died with no family in attendance. On his deathbed he renewed his Catholic faith, calling upon the archbishop to take his confession and administer the last sacrament. His wife died in Germany the following year, also alone.

The *Herald* continued as a viable but declining force, as it was running on inertia alone. The son was not a hands-on manager, and by 1877 he was an expatriate in Paris after an embarrassing social gaffe that made him unacceptable in polite society. He remained in Paris for forty years, though he continued to manage the paper via trans-Atlantic cable messages. He maintained an expensive lifestyle with a large estate and a yacht. He also created the *Paris Herald*, which he steadfastly kept publishing during World War I. He died in 1918, and two years later the *Herald* was sold to Whitelaw Reid and the *New York Tribune* with the stipulation that "*Herald*" would appear first on any masthead. The younger Bennett's underwriting of the British explorer Henry M. Stanley's expedition to find the English explorer David Livingstone was a dramatic stroke that even the father might have approved.

—*Jack J. Cardoso*

See also New York Tribune; Newspapers.

For further reading:

Carlson, Oliver. *The Man Who Made the News* (1942).

Crouthamel, James L. *Bennett's* New York Herald *and the Rise of the Popular Press* (1989).

Cutler, Andrew J. *The North Reports the Civil War* (1955).

Fermer, Douglas. *James Gordon Bennett and the* New York Herald: *A Study of Editorial Opinion in the Civil War Era, 1854–1867* (1986).

Herd, Harold. *Seven Editors* (1955; reprint, 1977).

Kluger, Richard. *The Paper: The Life and Death of the* New York Herald (1986).

Schudson, Michael. *Discovering the News: A Social History of American Newspapers* (1981).

Seitz, Don C. *The James Gordon Bennetts: Father and Son* (1928).

Tebbell, John, and Sarah Miles Watts. *The Press and the Presidency* (1985).

BENNING, HENRY LEWIS
(1814–1875)
Confederate general

Born to Pleasant Moon Benning and Matilda Meriwether White Benning in Columbia County, Georgia, Henry Lewis Benning graduated from Franklin College (later the University of Georgia) in 1834 and began immediately to study law. He became a prominent attorney in Columbus, Georgia, and was active in state Democratic politics. In 1850 Benning was selected one of the state's delegates to the Nashville Convention, where he distinguished himself as a strong proponent of states' rights. From 1853 to 1859 he served as a judge on Georgia's supreme court. In April 1860 Benning served as a delegate to the Democratic National Convention in Charleston, South Carolina, and when that body adjourned to Baltimore in June 1860, Benning served as the vice president of the convention.

After the election of Abraham Lincoln, Benning became an ardent supporter of secession and served as a delegate to Georgia's secession convention. Following Georgia's secession, the convention sent him to Virginia to urge that state's secession.

In August 1861 Benning received a commission as the colonel of the 17th Georgia Regiment. His regiment was placed in the brigade of Brigadier General Robert Toombs and moved north to Virginia with him in the spring of 1862. Benning's regiment fought in the Peninsula campaign, especially distinguishing itself at Malvern Hill.

When General Toombs temporarily took command of a division at Second Bull Run, Benning assumed command of the brigade there and continued in that command at Antietam in September 1862. As the commander of Toombs's brigade at Antietam, Benning's primary responsibility was to resist the crossing of Antietam Creek by Union general Ambrose Burnside's corps at what would become known as Burnside's Bridge. The brigade gained a great deal of distinction that day by delaying the movement of Burnside across the creek and allowing time for reinforcements to be brought to the Confederate right. Benning continued in command of the brigade at Fredericksburg but took little part in the battle because of the brigade's placement in the second line of battle.

On 17 January 1863 Benning was promoted to brigadier general and placed in command of a brigade in John Bell Hood's division. He remained with that division through 1863. At Gettysburg, Benning and his brigade saw their heaviest action on the Confederate right in the Devil's Den on 2 July 1863.

Following Gettysburg, Benning was part of Longstreet's corps that was detached for temporary duty with Bragg's Army of Tennessee. On the way south, Benning's brigade allegedly destroyed the newspaper office of the Raleigh *Standard* because it was not as loyal to the war effort as the brigade thought it should be. Benning was not present during the riot.

Once with Bragg's army, the brigade was soon engaged in the battle of Chickamauga. A few weeks later Benning and his men fought again at the failed Confederate night attack at Wauhatchie, Tennessee. By early 1864, however, Benning was sent back to the Virginia theater where his brigade was placed in the division of Major General Charles William Fields. At the battle of the Wilderness, Benning suffered such a severe wound in his arm that he had to leave the army until the spring of 1865. He returned to his brigade in time to command it in the last few engagements of the war and was present at the surrender at Appomattox.

After the war Benning returned to his law practice and died one of Columbus's most successful attorneys in 1875. Fort Benning, outside Columbus, Georgia, is named for him.

—*David S. Heidler and Jeanne T. Heidler*

See also Antietam, Battle of
For further reading:
Gardner, David Tytus. "Henry Lewis Benning: Confederate General" (Master's thesis, 1998).
Kerrison, Marie W. "Henry Lewis Benning: States' Rights Advocate and Soldier" (Master's thesis, 1937).

BENTONVILLE, BATTLE OF
(19–21 March 1865)

Fought 25 miles southwest of Goldsboro, North Carolina, the battle of Bentonville was the largest battle ever fought in the state and the only significant attempt to arrest Union general William Tecumseh Sherman's advance through the Carolinas in the spring of 1865. Sherman, having left Savannah, Georgia, with 60,000 troops in late January, moved north in two wings of approximately 30,000 men each. Facing little resistance as his army advanced through South Carolina, Sherman concluded that Confederate troops in the area were too widely scattered to pose any real threat to his operation. His goal was first to reach Goldsboro, North Carolina, and link up with Federal forces under Generals Alfred E. Terry and John M. Schofield advancing westward from the coast. Achieving that objective, Sherman would continue northward toward Petersburg, Virginia, to aid Ulysses

The battle of Bentonville, from an undated engraving (*Library of Congress*)

S. Grant and his effort to crush Robert E. Lee and the Army of Northern Virginia.

With the fall of Fort Fisher on 15 January and the subsequent evacuation of Wilmington, North Carolina, on 22 February, the last open port of the Confederacy and the last major supply line to Virginia were in Federal hands. Desperately hoping to forestall a juncture of Sherman and Grant, Lee called General Joseph E. Johnston out of retirement in Lincolnton, North Carolina, with instructions to "concentrate all available forces and drive back Sherman." While duty and honor swayed him to accept the charge, personally Johnston recognized the futility of the task. He embraced the command, he later wrote, in hopes of achieving "fair terms of peace."

On 8 March, Sherman's army entered North Carolina and concentrated on capturing Fayetteville. Confederate cavalry led by Lieutenant General Wade Hampton struck their Federal counterparts under Brigadier General Hugh Judson Kilpatrick at Monroe's Crossroads on 10 March but were eventually driven back. Federal troops entered Fayetteville on 11 March and destroyed the arsenal and mills located in and around the city. Leaving Fayetteville on 15 March, Sherman's next planned stop was Goldsboro, where he would find fresh troops and supplies and be linked by rail to the coast.

While Sherman's two wings continued moving northward, Johnston was busy assembling a fighting force out of four commands: the remnants of the Army of Tennessee under Lieutenant General Alexander P. Stewart; Major General Robert F. Hoke's division from the defense of the North Carolina coast; Lieutenant General William J. Hardee's corps from Georgia and South Carolina; and Hampton's cavalry. Lacking sufficient numbers to engage Sherman's entire army, Johnston's hope was to concentrate his disparate troops at Smithfield, situated roughly midway between Goldsboro and the state capital of Raleigh, and then move to strike one of Sherman's two wings at a point when each was beyond supporting distance of the other. Uncertainty over Sherman's destination led Johnston to deploy Hardee's 6,455 men near a road junction at Averasboro to determine if the Federal objective was Goldsboro or Raleigh. A brief but intense battle ensued on 16 March between Hardee's command and elements of the Federal left wing under Major General Henry W. Slocum. Although Hardee eventually withdrew that evening toward Smithfield, the indecisive battle served to slow Slocum's column, further separating it from Sherman's right wing, which was advancing under the command of Major General Oliver Otis Howard.

Johnston recognized that he now had the opportunity he had been looking for. Accordingly, on the evening of 18 March, the Confederate general began positioning his troops in the formation of a scythe-like trap across the Goldsboro Road at Willis Cole's plantation near the community of Bentonville. The following morning, lead elements of Brigadier General William P. Carlin's division of Slocum's XIV Corps encountered Confederate troops as they were deploying. Expecting light resistance, Carlin's men pressed on, only to discover entrenched Confederate troops concealed in the thick underbrush. Johnston launched an attack, smashing Carlin's division, but was finally halted by a Federal counterattack led by Brigadier General William Cogswell. The two forces grappled with each other well into the evening until Johnston ordered a withdrawal back to his original position at the Cole plantation around midnight.

Johnston's plan for the following day was to establish a strong defensive perimeter while he removed his wounded to Smithfield. The Confederate commander also hoped that the Federals would decide to attack, thereby giving Johnston a defensive advantage. On 20 March, while Johnston worked to extricate his wounded and waited for Sherman to attack, Howard's column began to arrive on the field. The union of his two wings gave Sherman close to 60,000 men, three times the number of Johnston's force before the battle. Yet Sherman chose to avoid a general engagement.

On 21 March, a Federal reconnaissance of the Confederate left led by Brigadier General Joseph A. Mower wound up penetrating well into the Confederate rear and threatening Johnston's only avenue of withdrawal: the bridge across flooded Mill Creek. Confederate infantry and cavalry managed to stem the advance and reestablish a perimeter, but Johnston knew that he could no longer afford to hold his ground at Bentonville. That night, guided by torchlight, the Confederate army abandoned its position and crossed over Mill Creek toward Smithfield. Sherman chose not to pursue, deciding instead to continue on to Goldsboro.

The battle of Bentonville cost Johnston 240 killed, 1,700 wounded, and 1,500 missing. Sherman's casualties were 194 killed, 1,112 wounded, and 221 missing. The message to Lee was clear. Ever mindful of the Confederate general-in-chief's earlier directive to "drive back Sherman," Johnston wrote on March 23, "I can do no more than annoy him."

—*Alan C. Downs*

See also Averasboro, Battle of; Carolinas Campaign; Johnston, Joseph Eggleston; Sherman, William Tecumseh.
For further reading:
Barrett, John G. *The Civil War in North Carolina* (1963).
Hughes, Nathaniel Cheairs, Jr. *Bentonville* (1996).

BERDAN, HIRAM
(1823–1893)
Union general

Born in Phelps, New York, Hiram Berdan was educated as an engineer. Before the outbreak of the Civil War he worked as a mechanical engineer, primarily in New York City. He was also a competitive recreational rifleman and had won the honor of calling himself the best shot in the country for fifteen years. In addition to his own competitive shooting, he also had developed his own method of teaching marksmanship.

When the war began, Berdan wrote the commanding general of the army, Winfield Scott, offering his services in organizing a regiment of sharpshooters for the U.S. Army. Berdan met with Scott and so impressed the old general with his confidence that Scott gave approval for Berdan to establish a recruiting and training camp outside New York City.

Berdan spent the summer and most of the fall at his encampment attracting young men from all over the country to become part of his elite regiment. In the fall he began using his own method to train them to become crack shots at great distances. By October, the War Department was becoming somewhat impatient with the time it was taking to prepare the men for duty, and began sending Berdan letters urging him to bring his regiment to Washington. He did so in November 1861, and the regiment was dubbed the 1st U.S. Sharpshooters, and Berdan was commissioned its colonel. While in camp outside Washington, Berdan and his men quickly gained a reputation for considering themselves more important than other units and for engaging in many unmilitary extracurricular activities. The medical department also expressed concern that their camp sanitary conditions were anything but optimal.

The regiment saw its first major actions during the Peninsula campaign the following spring. Berdan was commended for his and his men's actions during the siege of Yorktown and at Hanover Court House a month later. They fought in the Seven Days and, after the retreat to Harrison's Landing, were summoned back to Washington in August to become a part of John Pope's Army of Virginia.

At Second Bull Run, Berdan and his men were used as skirmishers but were accused after the battle of not moving out enough in front of the other units to be effective. Berdan weathered the criticism to fight with distinction at South Mountain in the Maryland campaign and to suffer heavy casualties at Antietam. Berdan and his sharpshooters were also particularly useful in the engagement at Blackford's Ford in the pursuit of Robert E. Lee after Antietam.

Under Ambrose Burnside before and during the

battle of Fredericksburg, Berdan and his men became dissatisfied with their situation. Before the battle, the supply situation caused shortages of rations and, more importantly to Berdan, ammunition. Attached to V Corps as they had been since the Peninsula campaign, the sharpshooters might have expected, like the rest of the corps, to be heavily engaged at Fredericksburg but were held in reserve during the heaviest fighting on 13 December. They did not cross the Rappahannock until 14 December and were then used to guard the retreat of the rest of the army.

Berdan and his men remained in camp for much of the winter of 1863. With Joseph Hooker's reorganization of the Army of the Potomac, they were moved to III Corps under Daniel Sickles. Before that occurred, there was some discussion between the War Department and the leadership of the Army of the Potomac about elevating Berdan to a larger command and promoting him to brigadier general. Such a plan was abandoned because of the fear that if Berdan did not command the sharpshooters, they would not be as effective. Instead he was given command of the 1st and 2d U.S. Sharpshooters, a group that increasingly became known as Berdan's Brigade.

During the battle of Chancellorsville, Berdan actually succeeded temporarily to a real brigade command when Sickles placed him in charge of 3d Brigade, 3d Division of the corps. This brigade included his sharpshooters. During the battle, Berdan and his men were heavily engaged, suffering heavy casualties. Again it fell to the sharpshooters to guard the retreat of much of the army.

In early June, back in command of the 1st and 2d Sharpshooters, Berdan scouted the movements of Lee's Army of Northern Virginia. Still a part of III Corps in the brigade commanded by Brigadier General J. H. Hobart Ward, Berdan's sharpshooters saw some of their heaviest fighting on the second day of the battle of Gettysburg. Initially charged with guarding the flanks of the division as it moved on orders from Sickles down off Cemetery Ridge, later in the day Berdan succeeded to the command of the brigade when Ward was elevated to division command. The following day the sharpshooters spent much of their time clearing Devil's Den of remaining Confederates.

In the fall, in pursuit of Lee's army, Berdan and his men were heavily engaged at Kelly's Ford on 7 November 1863 and then again in the Mine Run campaign. Berdan, however, by no means a modest man, had become increasingly dissatisfied with his role in the Army of the Potomac and perhaps with his failure to advance. The glory and fame he had sought with the formation of the sharpshooters had simply not been forthcoming. In early 1864 he resigned his commission and returned to his engineering career. The units that he had created continued to bear his name for the remainder of the war.

Back in civilian life, Berdan turned to inventing, particularly arms and related devices, using his wartime experience as his guide to what armies needed. He invented the Berdan breechloading rifle and then traveled to Europe to demonstrate it to foreign governments. Most were very favorably impressed. He also invented a range finder with six-mile accuracy and a mechanical artillery shell fuse that increased control over when a shell would explode. Along with these activities, Berdan also worked with veterans groups, especially survivors of his old units. He attended reunions of the sharpshooters and worked with them to have a monument to them erected at Gettysburg. Because some of the states had already established monuments to the sharpshooter companies that represented their states, it became impossible to raise the necessary money to build a monument to the two regiments. Berdan died in New York in 1893 with his dream unrealized.

—*David S. Heidler and Jeanne T. Heidler*

See also Chancellorsville, Battle of; Gettysburg, Battle of; Rifles; Sharpshooters.

For further reading:

Fahle, Michael L. *The Best the Union Could Muster: The True Story of Berdan's U.S. Sharpshooters at the Battle of Gettysburg* (1998).

Marcot, Roy M. *Civil War Chief of Sharpshooters Hiram Berdan: Military Commander and Firearms Inventor* (1989).

Sword, Wiley. *Sharpshooter: Hiram Berdan, His Famous Sharpshooters, and Their Sharps Rifles* (1988).

BERMUDA HUNDRED CAMPAIGN
(May–June 1864)

In 1864 General Ulysses S. Grant, general in chief of the Armies of the United States, devised a plan consisting of a two-pronged attack to crush the Confederate armies, thus drawing the Civil War to a close. This plan featured a drive on the Confederate capital of Richmond, Virginia, by Grant, while General William T. Sherman crushed the heart of the Confederacy in his now infamous March to the Sea. As a component of the overall assault on Richmond, Grant sanctioned a smaller campaign on the Southern capital via the James River. Brigadier General Benjamin F. Butler, a political general with relatively little field experience, was to lead this campaign as the commander of the newly formed Army of the James. Butler, former commander of the Department of Virginia and North Carolina, selected Bermuda Hundred Landing in Chesterfield County, Virginia, as his base of operations. Bermuda Hundred Landing, located at the confluence of the James and Appomattox rivers, was only sixteen miles to the south of Richmond and eight miles north of Petersburg. What ensued was the Bremuda Hundred campaign, which lasted from May to June of 1864.

The Army of the James was created in April 1864

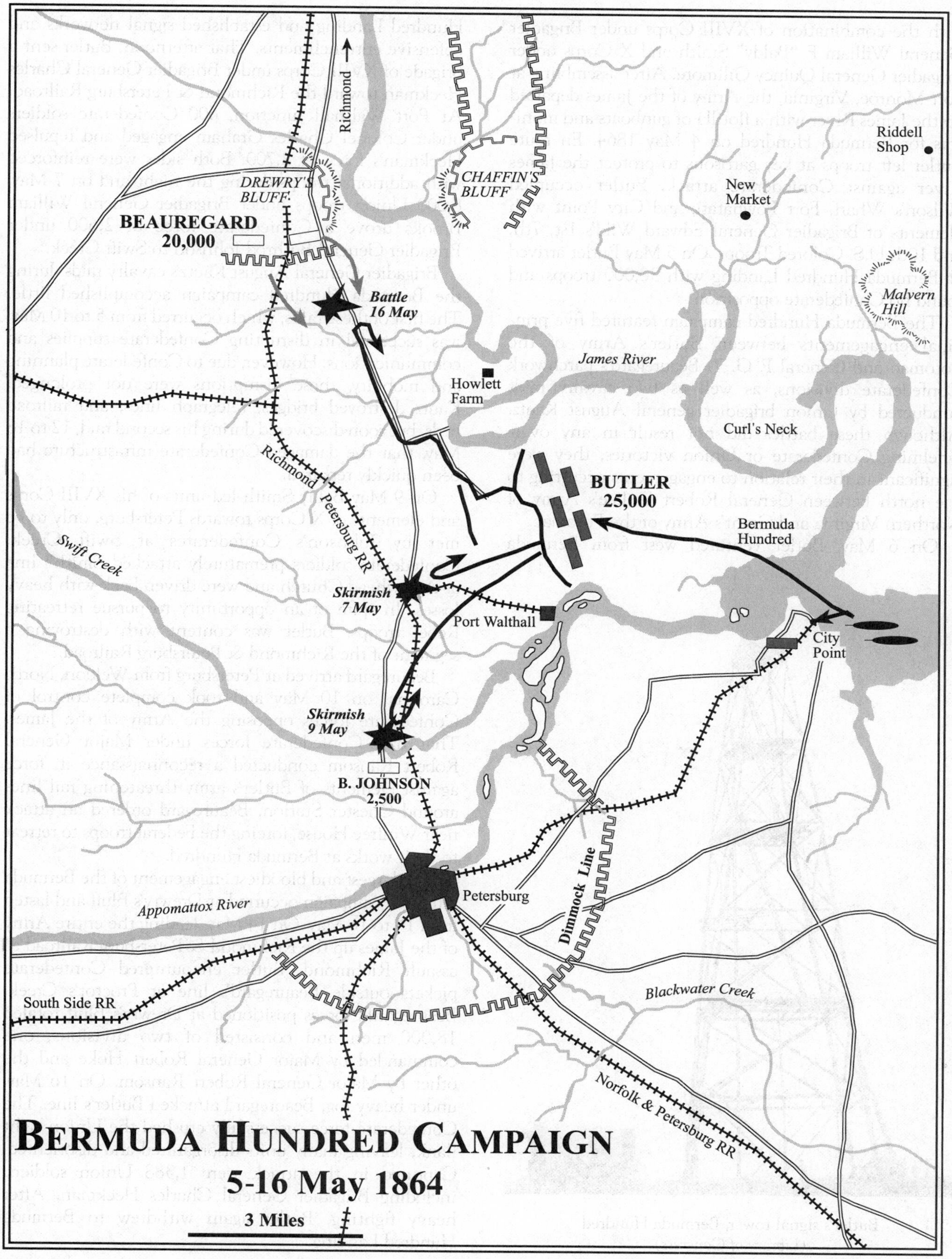

Richmond →

DREWRY'S
BLUFF

CHAFFIN'S
BLUFF

BEAUREGARD
20,000

Riddell
Shop ●

New
Market

*Malvern
Hill*

★ *Battle
16 May*

James River

Howlett
Farm ■

Curl's Neck

Richmond Petersburg RR

BUTLER
25,000

Bermuda
Hundred

Swift Creek

★ *Skirmish
7 May*

Port Walthall ■

City
Point

★ *Skirmish
9 May*

B. JOHNSON
2,500

Dimmock Line

Appomattox River

Petersburg

South Side RR

Blackwater Creek

Norfolk & Petersburg RR

BERMUDA HUNDRED CAMPAIGN
5-16 May 1864

3 Miles

with the combination of XVIII Corps under Brigadier General William F. "Baldy" Smith and X Corps under Brigadier General Quincy Gillmore. After assembling at Fort Monroe, Virginia, the Army of the James departed up the James River with a flotilla of gunboats and monitors for Bermuda Hundred on 4 May 1864. En route Butler left troops at key garrisons to protect the James River against Confederate attack. Butler occupied Wilson's Wharf, Fort Powhatan, and City Point with elements of Brigadier General Edward Wild's 1st, 7th, and 10th U.S. Colored Troops. On 5 May Butler arrived at Bermuda Hundred Landing with 30,000 troops and found no Confederate opposition.

The Bermuda Hundred campaign featured five principal engagements between Butler's Army of the Potomac and General P. G. T. Beauregard's patchwork Confederate divisions, as well as two cavalry raids conducted by Union brigadier general August Kautz. Although these battles did not result in any overwhelming Confederate or Union victories, they were significant in their relation to engagements occurring to the north between General Robert E. Lee's Army of Northern Virginia and Grant's Army of the Potomac.

On 6 May, Butler ventured west from Bermuda

Butler's signal tower, Bermuda Hundred
(*Library of Congress*)

Hundred Landing and established signal networks and defensive entrenchments. That afternoon, Butler sent a brigade of XVIII Corps under Brigadier General Charles Heckman toward the Richmond & Petersburg Railroad. At Port Walthall Junction, 600 Confederate soldiers under Colonel Charles Graham engaged and repulsed Heckman's force of 2,700. Both sides were reinforced with additional troops during the night and on 7 May, 8,000 Union troops under Brigadier General William Brooks drove a Confederate force of 2,600 under Brigadier General Bushrod Johnson to Swift Creek.

Brigadier General August Kautz's cavalry raids during the Bermuda Hundred campaign accomplished little. The first of these raids, which occurred from 5 to 10 May, was successful in disrupting Confederate supplies and communications. However, due to Confederate planning and mobility, these disruptions were not prolonged. Kautz destroyed bridges, telegraph lines, and railroad beds, but soon discovered during his second raid, 12 to 18 May, that the damaged Confederate infrastructure had been quickly repaired.

On 9 May Baldy Smith led units of his XVIII Corps and elements of X Corps towards Petersburg, only to be met by Johnson's Confederates at Swift Creek. Confederate soldiers prematurely attacked Smith's line at Arrowhead Church and were driven back with heavy losses. In spite of an opportunity to pursue retreating Rebel troops, Butler was content with destroying a segment of the Richmond & Petersburg Railroad.

Beauregard arrived at Petersburg from Weldon, North Carolina, on 10 May and took complete control of Confederate forces opposing the Army of the James. That day, Confederate forces under Major General Robert Ransom conducted a reconnaissance in force against elements of Butler's army threatening rail lines around Chester Station. Beauregard ordered an attack near Winfree House, forcing the Federal troops to retreat to their works at Bermuda Hundred.

The largest and bloodiest engagement of the Bermuda Hundred campaign occurred at Drewry's Bluff and lasted from 14 to 16 May. On 14 May, leading the entire Army of the James up the Richmond & Petersburg Railroad to assault Richmond, Butler encountered Confederate pickets outside Beauregard's line at Proctor's Creek. Beauregard's forces positioned at Drewry's Bluff totaled 18,000 men and consisted of two divisions, one commanded by Major General Robert Hoke and the other by Major General Robert Ransom. On 16 May, under heavy fog, Beauregard attacked Butler's line. The Confederate force successfully crushed the Union right flank, leaving many units disorganized and disoriented. Captured in the attack were 1,388 Union soldiers, including Brigadier General Charles Heckman. After heavy fighting, Butler again withdrew to Bermuda Hundred Landing.

Beauregard immediately pursued the Army of the James to its defensive lines at Bermuda Hundred. On 20 May, Confederates attacked the advanced Union positions at Ware Bottom Church and drove back the divisions of Adelbert Ames and Alfred Howe Terry. After considerable fighting throughout the day, Union forces regained their original positions, enabling the construction of the Howlett Line. This containment action bottled up the Army of the James, however, resulting in Butler's nickname, "Bottled-Up Ben." Troops remained at their respective lines until 16 June, when dawn broke and Federal troops found Beauregard had withdrawn his forces to protect Petersburg.

Butler's main objectives in the Bermuda Hundred campaign were to disrupt Confederate supply and communication networks, delay and detain Confederate reinforcements from joining Lee's Army of Northern Virginia, threaten Petersburg, and ultimately to aid in the assault on Richmond. While many of these objectives were in part accomplished, the lasting legacy of the Bermuda Hundred campaign rests with Butler's nickname of "Bottled-Up Ben." General Beauregard's construction of the Howlett Line effectively trapped Butler's larger Army of the James at Bermuda Hundred Landing, causing the campaign to be assessed overall as a stalemate.

—*Brock A. Magoon*

See also Army of the James; Butler, Benjamin Franklin; Drewry's Bluff; Kautz, August V.; Petersburg Campaign; Ware Bottom Church.

For further reading:

Humphreys, Andrew. *The Virginia Campaign of 1864 and 1865. The Army of the Potomac and the Army of the James* (1883).

Longacre, Edward G. *Army of Amateurs: General Benjamin F. Butler and the Army of the James, 1863–1865* (1997).

Robertson, William Glenn. *Back Door to Richmond: The Bermuda Hundred Campaign, April–June 1864* (1987).

Schiller, Herbert M. *The Bermuda Hundred Campaign* (1988).

BERRY, HIRAM GREGORY
(1824–1863)
Union general

Born to Jeremiah Berry and Frances Gregory Berry in Rockland, Maine, Berry was educated locally and worked at various jobs as a young man including carpentry. Eventually able to start his own business, Berry eventually went into banking and became a bank president. He was also interested in Maine Democratic politics and served in the Maine state legislature and as mayor of Rockland. He also served as an officer in the state militia.

At the outbreak of the Civil War, Berry raised, and became the colonel of, the 4th Maine Infantry. He led his regiment to Virginia, where he fought at First Bull Run in July 1861. The following year, as part of the

Army of the Potomac, Berry became a brigadier general in March and later in the spring participated in the Peninsula campaign. He led his brigade at the siege of Yorktown and the battles of Williamsburg, Seven Pines, and the Seven Days and was commended for his actions in most of these engagements. After this campaign, however, illness forced him to take an extended sick leave back to Maine. He returned to the Army of the Potomac in the fall of 1862 and was promoted to major general.

In spite of his promotion, Berry still commanded a brigade at Fredericksburg. Commended for his actions there, he even received praise for his brigade's discipline from Confederate major general A. P. Hill. In the engagement, Confederate artillery pinned down Berry's brigade and forced it to lie on the ground under Rebel batteries for two days.

In February 1863, Berry was given command of the 2d Division of the Daniel Sickles's Corps (III Corps). He led this division across the Rapidan River in the beginning days of the Chancellorsville campaign at the end of April 1863 and was partially responsible for re-forming Union lines on the morning of 3 May after the near disaster of Stonewall Jackson's charge of the evening before. In the midst of leading a countercharge against Confederate forces at 7:00 A.M. on 3 May, Berry was shot. He died approximately one-half hour later. His body was taken home for burial.

Though possessing virtually no military experience before the war, Berry earned the regard of superiors and subordinates for his integrity and ability to master the rudiments of military leadership.

—*David S. Heidler and Jeanne T. Heidler*

See also Chancellorsville, Battle of; Fredericksburg, Battle of.

For further reading:

Lemke, William. *A Pride of Lions: Joshua Chamberlain and Other Maine Civil War Heroes* (1997).

BERRYVILLE, VIRGINIA
(13 June 1863)

As Robert E. Lee began moving the Army of Northern Virginia behind the Blue Ridge to invade the North, he planned to have Richard Ewell's corps move on Major General Robert Milroy's 2d Division, VIII Corps, at Winchester, Virginia. To accompany that maneuver, he directed Ewell to detach Major General Robert E. Rodes's division and General Albert G. Jenkins's cavalry brigade to drive out Federal forces occupying Berryville. Rodes was then to cut Winchester's line of communication to Harper's Ferry by marching on Martinsburg.

The 3d Brigade under Colonel Andrew T. McReynolds had been in Berryville since late March, scouting from there to watch Snicker's and Ashby's Gaps through the Blue Ridge and Snicker's and Berry's Fords across the Shenandoah River. McReynolds was also guarding the line of communication to Harper's Ferry. His command consisted of the 6th Maryland Volunteer Infantry, 67th Pennsylvania Infantry, 1st New York Cavalry, and Captain F. W. Alexander's "Baltimore" Battery. His numbers were about 1,800, far inferior to those approaching him. Milroy had instructed McReynolds that if the 3d Brigade was needed at Winchester, about ten miles to the west, he would signal with four reports from the main fort's heavy guns.

Ewell on 10 June was near Brandy Station, where he had belatedly arrived to support Jeb Stuart the previous day. From Culpeper Court House, he proceeded by way of Gaines' Crossroads and Flint Hill to cross the branches of the Shenandoah near Front Royal. He reached Cedar Hill in two days and from there moved on to Winchester after detaching Rodes's division and some 1,600 of Jenkins's cavalry. From Cedar Hill, Rodes enlisted the service of John McCormack as guide and headed north on a back road toward Millwood. Jenkins meanwhile took the main road through Nineveh and White Post, also toward Millwood. The evening of 12 June found the division camped near Stone Bridge, and Rodes apparently expected Jenkins to be in Millwood screening the infantry's movements. Yet Jenkins did not reach Millwood on the night of the 12th, so when Rodes started toward Berryville the next morning, his advance was soon discovered, and McReynolds made arrangements to evacuate the town.

The problem was that Jenkins's cavalry potentially could cut the direct road to Winchester—precisely, in fact, what Rodes wanted it to do. With rebel forces not more than four miles away, McReynolds sent out his supply train northwest toward Bunker Hill escorted by a company of infantry and cavalry. He then sent the bulk of the 3d Brigade toward Summit Point, from where it would double back the twenty-three miles to Winchester. It was a substantial detour that more than doubled the distance the brigade would have to cover to reach Winchester, but it promised a better chance of avoiding the Confederate cavalry.

Avoiding Jenkins proved easier than either McReynolds or Rodes had expected. In fact, almost nothing went right for the Confederates. Once discovered, Rodes tried to hurry toward Berryville, but by the time he brought all his people up, he was meeting a determined resistance from what he deduced was McReynold's entire brigade. Actually it was only a rear guard of four Maryland infantry companies, part of Alexander's battery, and 150 troopers from the 1st New York. Their defensive positions were strong enough, however, to allow them to stall Rodes for almost an hour before they too moved off and revealed the ruse. Rodes sent Jenkins pounding after them, but the cavalry again

proved feckless. Only Major J. W. Sweeney's battalion found the retreating Federals at Opequon Creek, and his numbers were too small to accomplish anything other than a brief skirmish that left him badly wounded and from which he withdrew. The best Rodes could do was trudge after McReynolds toward Summit Point. As Ewell wryly observed, "Jenkins failed from some cause to overtake the enemy."

McReynolds reached Winchester about 9:00 P.M. Later that night, Milroy chose to move his division into the town's fortifications west of town where he planned to make a stand against the advancing Confederate column. Accordingly, the 3d Brigade took up positions in the Star Fort just north of the main bastion and awaited the arrival of Ewell's force looming from the south.

Later McReynolds would declare that the entire division, the 3d Brigade included, should have retreated to Harper's Ferry on 13 June rather than holing up at Winchester. Milroy's disastrous stand at Winchester seemed to bear out the claim, but that was hindsight. As a court of inquiry would later rule, the 3d Brigade might have been more imperiled had it moved independently from the main force.

—David S. Heidler and Jeanne T. Heidler

See also Jenkins, Albert Gallatin; Martinsburg, Virginia; Milroy, Robert H.; Winchester, Second Battle of.

For further reading:

Adams, Owen E. "Confederate Major General Robert E. Rodes: A Civil War Biography" (M.A. thesis, 1995).
Johnson, Freddie L., III. "Mountain Warrior: The Political and Military Career of Albert Gallatin Jenkins" (Thesis, 1993).
Steward, Michelle Lee. "Robert E. Rodes: Lee's Forgotten General" (M.A. thesis, 1997).

BIBB, HENRY
See Refugee Home Society

BICKERDYKE, MARY ANN BALL
(1817–1901)

Union Army nurse

She began with the war, knows all about cooking, and can cook forty things at once. I never saw such a worker; she stirs round the cookhouse with a big meat fork or ladle upraised, and looks as if she would annihilate them all." Thus Union nurse Mary Phinney von Olnhausen described Mary Ann "Mother" Bickerdyke when they met in North Carolina in 1865. Arguably the most influential nurse of the Civil War era, Bickerdyke loved common soldiers and gave their officers reasons to fear her wrath. Generals Ulysses S. Grant and William T. Sherman were known to defer to her wisdom in sanitary matters. Soldiers solicited her opinion about romantic prospects during the war and later asked her to testify in their behalf when they sought pensions. The respect and reverence her name inspired among patients were the result of her fearlessness before military authority and her success at putting the health and comfort of soldiers above all else.

Mary Ann Ball was born on a farm in central Ohio. Her mother died before she was two, and although her father remarried within several years, Ball spent her formative years living with grandparents and her maternal uncle's family. At age sixteen, she moved to Oberlin, where she claimed to have studied botanic medicine. Several years later she joined her uncle's family near Cincinnati and earned her keep by nursing cholera patients in a local hospital. Here she met and married English widower James Bickerdyke in 1847. The couple moved to Galesburg, Illinois, in 1856. However, by 1860 Mary Ann Bickerdyke had lived a life of transience, prematurely losing her mother, husband, and a daughter—a family portrait all too common in nineteenth-century America.

Supporting her remaining children by selling herbal remedies in Galesburg, Bickerdyke decided in June 1861 to help other mothers' sons by carrying church-donated supplies to typhoid patients in camp at Cairo. So abysmal were the conditions she encountered that she cleaned and cooked around the clock until the sick were made comfortable. This take-charge attitude, rendered even more effective when she could deputize others, characterized Bickerdyke's approach to work throughout the war. Matron of the Cairo hospital by the time wounded from the battle of Belmont arrived in November, Bickerdyke deferred only to her patients. When she suspected surgeons of pilfering delicacies meant for convalescents, she baked an emetic into a peach cobbler and left it on the counter for revenge. Bickerdyke also reported surgeons for graft, negligence, and drunkenness until they towed the line or were fired. Their appeals to higher authority, including to General Sherman, were fruitless. When another surgeon at Cairo wished to remove Bickerdyke early in 1862, she left it to a voice vote of the rank and file, who unanimously decided the referendum in her favor.

After the siege of Forts Henry and Donelson in February 1862, Bickerdyke and Mary Jane Safford, a diminutive Cairo resident who would go on to study medicine in Europe after the war, helped evacuate the wounded on hospital transports. When a Northern journalist publicized Bickerdyke's solitary late-night trip to the battlefield to ascertain if any of the fallen were still alive, she became a national celebrity. By the time the battle of Shiloh took place in April, the Sanitary Commission had made her its agent. At Savannah, Tennessee, in mid-April, she met Wisconsin governor Louis Harvey, who was so

impressed with her that he left her five tons of unused supplies to distribute. After spending seven months in tent hospitals and proving her mettle to General Grant, Bickerdyke—now the Commission's hot commodity—was sent by Mary Livermore on a fund-raising tour of several Northern states.

Early in 1863 the Commission asked Bickerdyke to bring sanitary order to Union hospitals in Memphis. At this time, Superintendent of Nursing Dorothea Dix, fearing a competitor, wrote the powerful Western nurse "on the chance of opening a communication with you." As matron of the Gayoso, Bickerdyke imported washing machines, purchased with money from her speaking tour, and hired contraband women to do laundry. Unhappy with the unwholesome hospital cuisine, she collected a herd of livestock and a thousand chickens in Illinois and floated them down the Mississippi. From Memphis, she rejoined General Grant outside Vicksburg in July, then in September marched more than 400 miles to Chattanooga with Sherman's army. During the march, she put to work a fleet of black orderlies, who are said to have washed up to 2,000 pieces of laundry per day. The lone female nurse on hand for the battles of Missionary Ridge and Lookout Mountain in late November, Bickerdyke again made headlines when she burned defunct breastworks as kindling so that wounded soldiers would not freeze to death. When military police asked her under whose authority she had acted, she is reported to have said, "Under the authority of the Lord God Almighty. Have you got anything better than that?" Bickerdyke remained in the Chattanooga area for ten more months, aided by Eliza Chappell Porter who had shadowed her after Shiloh. Both women accompanied the XV Army Corps as it moved through Confederate territory toward Atlanta and attended soldiers at Resaca and Marietta. When Atlanta fell to Union forces in September, Bickerdyke and Porter began the two-month process of evacuating the sick and wounded to Northern hospitals. After a second speaking tour, Bickerdyke carried supplies meant for Sherman's troops outside Savannah, Georgia, to the needier troops returning from Andersonville prison to Wilmington, North Carolina, in early 1865.

After a brief trip to Washington for the Grand Review of the Union army in May, Mother Bickerdyke traveled to Camp Butler in Springfield, Illinois, where she helped in the mustering-out process and fought to have the barracks converted into soldiers' homes. In March 1866, she moved on to Chicago, collected her sons, and spent one year as matron of the Home for the Friendless. Working to raise money for soldiers' relief, she secured land in Kansas in the hope of helping veterans finance homes. Though the plan never materialized, Bickerdyke did open a boardinghouse in Salina, on the Kansas-Pacific Railroad line. By 1870, Bickerdyke was working in New York for the city board of missions and traveling periodically to Washington to testify in pension cases. In 1874, Bickerdyke moved back to Kansas to join her sons, but two years later, relocated to San Francisco for her health, where war friend and senator, General John Logan, helped get her a job at the U.S. Mint. The Woman's Relief Corps (WRC), established to aid aging nurses, took an interest in her in the 1880s, inviting her to speak at their functions. In 1886 one of the WRC's members, Margaret Burton Davis, published a one-dollar biography (*Mother Bickerdyke: The Woman Who Battled for the Boys in Blue*) to benefit the by-now legendary nurse. In the same year, Bickerdyke's service was honored with a $25 monthly pension—-more than twice as much as nurses would receive when legislation was enacted in 1892. In 1887 she returned to Kansas to be with family as her health declined. While the spirit of sentimental reunion swept the United States, a Mother Bickerdyke Home and Hospital opened in Ellsworth, Kansas, in the 1890s. Bickerdyke died in nearby Bunker Hill several years later. The city of Galesburg dedicated a monument to her in 1906, where her likeness may still be seen in the court-house square.

—*Jane E. Schultz*

See also Dix, Dorothea; Nurses; Women.

For further reading:

Baker, Nina Brown. *Cyclone in Calico: The Story of Mary Ann Bickerdyke* (1952).

Bickerdyke, Mary Ann Ball. Collection. Manuscript Division, Library of Congress, Washington, D.C.

Brockett, Linus P., and Mary C. Vaughan. *Woman's Work in the Civil War* (1867).

Holland, Mary Gardner. *Our Army Nurses* (1897).

Moore, Frank. *Women of the War: Their Heroism and Self-Sacrifice* (1866).

BICKLEY, GEORGE WASHINGTON LEIGH
(1819–1867)
Confederate officer

An antebellum adventurer with a dubious reputation, George W. L. Bickley was born in Louisa County, Virginia, in 1819. In 1851 he migrated from Tazewell County, Virginia, to Cincinnati, Ohio, where, after falsely claiming to be a graduate of the University of London medical school, he gained some measure of respectability as a physician, scholar, and journalist. Bickley married a wealthy widow and made liberal use of her fortune to finance a number of fruitless schemes. His wife, poorer but wiser, soon left him. Yet he saved himself from complete ruin by becoming the self-proclaimed champion of Southern expansionism.

With this venture, Bickley shrewdly manipulated the spirit of Manifest Destiny that swept the nation after the Mexican-American War. Throughout the turbulent decade before the Civil War, American adventurers known as filibusters participated in illegal military expeditions that attempted to liberate Cuba or seize territory in Mexico and Central America. In 1854, Bickley founded the American Legion of the Knights of the Golden Circle, a secret paramilitary organization that sought to "regenerate Spanish America" through conquest and/or colonization by a "superior Anglo-American civilization." Seeking Southern support, President-General Bickley promised to restore the sectional balance of power by acquiring new territories for the expansion of slavery.

Little is known about the early activities of the organization. However the outbreak of civil war in Mexico in 1859, combined with Bickley's efforts to elude his creditors, sparked a major publicity campaign. Bickley toured several eastern cities before establishing his headquarters in Washington. Armed with a sixty-three page manifesto entitled *Rules, Regulations and Principles of the Knights of the Golden Circle*, Bickley vowed to "fight the battles of the South on Mexican soil." After a convention held at White Sulphur Springs, Virginia, on 8 August 1859, he prepared to take active operations. His followers were ordered in early 1860 to rendezvous in Texas for an advance into Mexico.

Both Texas governor Sam Houston and President James Buchanan had initially advocated U.S. intervention to restore order in Mexico. However, Houston was unwilling to lend support to Bickley's efforts to extend slavery south of the Rio Grande. On 21 March 1860, Houston issued a proclamation condemning the activities of the Knights. Houston's opposition coupled with Bickley's failure to deliver promised reinforcements led the Texas Knights to abandon the venture. Convinced that Bickley was a charlatan, they expelled him from the organization at a meeting in New Orleans in early April. Bickley promptly summoned a grand convention at Raleigh, North Carolina, on 7 May that reinstated him as head of the national organization.

On 18 July 1860, in an open letter published in the Richmond *Daily Whig*, Bickley called for another invasion of Mexico. Boasting that Mexico's liberal party would welcome the Knights as allies, he urged his followers to concentrate at Fort Ewen, Texas, on 15 September. The "Americanization" of Mexico, he assured Southerners, would silence abolitionists, remove the South's "bothersome" free black population, and cause cotton production to soar. Bickley established his headquarters in San Antonio on 10 October; however, the secession movement that swept the South after Abraham Lincoln's election to the presidency forced him to abandon his latest scheme. Although he did not abandon his dreams of empire, Bickley made the establishment of a Southern

Confederacy the next goal of his organization.

Bickley left Texas in late 1860 and spent the spring and summer of 1861 promoting secession in the crucial border state Kentucky. Vilified by Kentucky's pro-Union press, Bickley boasted in an open letter that more than 8,000 Kentucky "Knights" had rallied to his banner and threatened that the Confederate flag would soon fly over the state capitol. Publicly calling for volunteers on 29 June, he afterward established a recruiting camp just over the state line at Clarksville, Tennessee. However, Bickley was forced to disband his followers after a clash with Confederate leaders in the late summer of 1861.

The "General's" fortunes afterward sank like a stone. After his offer to raise a regiment of Kentucky cavalry was rejected by Confederate authorities in the fall of 1861, he repaired to the mountains of southwestern Virginia, where he spent the balance of 1862 in a futile effort to obtain authority from the governor to raise a mounted command. In a final plea for a commission, he boasted on 14 September 1862 that he had "built up practical secession and inaugurated the greatest war of modern times." Assigned to duty as surgeon in the Army of Tennessee, he deserted the Confederate cause on 6 July 1863. Making his way through the lines, he was arrested in Indiana shortly afterward and imprisoned by Federal authorities. Efforts to connect Bickley to Copperhead societies in the North proved futile and he was finally released on 14 October 1865. Sinking into obscurity, he reportedly died a broken man in Baltimore on 3 August 1867.

Although he sought to portray himself as a great filibuster chieftain, Bickley was a mere charlatan compared with bold adventurers such as William Walker. Furthermore, Bickley's Knights of the Golden Circle apparently had no connection with the similarly named secret, antiwar society that arose in the North during the Civil War. Rather, his organization was more properly connected with the sectional discord and expansionism that marked the 1850s. Yet, despite the farcical aspects of Bickley's career, his efforts to promote the extension of slavery and secession convinced many Northerners that he represented the South's true ambitions. In this respect, Bickley contributed significantly to the sectional crisis that led to war.

—*James M. Prichard*

See also Knights of the Golden Circle; Order of American Knights.

For further reading:

Crenshaw, Ollinger. "The Knights of the Golden Circle: The Career of George Bickley." *American Historical Review* (1941).

Klement, Frank J. *Dark Lanterns: Secret Political Societies, Conspiracies, and Treason Trials in the Civil War* (1984).

May, Robert E. *The Southern Dream of a Caribbean Empire, 1834–1861* (1973).

BIERCE, AMBROSE GWINETT
(1842–ca. 1913)
Union officer and author

Ambrose Bierce's sardonic and often macabre short stories based on his Civil War military experiences are classics of their genre. Born in Meigs County, Ohio, in 1842, Bierce was among the ten children of a poor farming family and purportedly educated himself from his parent's meager stock of books. When Bierce was six, his family relocated to Warsaw, Indiana. He was working in an Elkhart, Indiana, store when the Civil War began.

Eighteen-year-old Bierce enlisted as a private in the 9th Indiana infantry on 19 April 1861. The green regiment went to rugged western Virginia, where it participated in actions around Philippi. By July the regiment was back in Indiana and discharged. The 9th reorganized for three-year service with Bierce again in its ranks, this time as a sergeant. He soon became a sergeant major.

In early 1862 Bierce's regiment was placed in Brigadier General William B. Hazen's brigade of the Army of the Ohio. This began Bierce's friendly association with Hazen. While Bierce would excoriate other officers in his writings, he had only praise for Hazen.

Bierce fought at Shiloh—an experience he later recorded in the nonfiction "What I Saw of Shiloh"—and took part in the siege of Corinth. By December 1862 he had been promoted to second lieutenant. After fighting in the battle of Stones River, Bierce became a first lieutenant and joined Hazen's staff as a topographical engineer. In this capacity he saw service from Chickamauga to Missionary Ridge.

During the 1864 Atlanta campaign, Bierce's brigade experienced vicious fighting. At the battle of Pickett's Mill on 27 May, sheltered Confederates gunned down Hazen's men as they made a futile attack down a ravine. The engagement so outraged Bierce that he made it the subject of "The Crime at Pickett's Mill."

On 23 June near Kennesaw Mountain, Bierce was struck in the skull by a bullet. The round, wrote Hazen, "caused a very dangerous and complicated wound" and remained lodged in Bierce's head until surgically removed. Partially healed, Bierce returned to duty on the staff of Brigadier General Samuel Beatty to fight at Franklin and Nashville in the winter of 1864. In January 1865 Bierce, still in pain from his wound, asked for and received a discharge.

After the war, Bierce moved to San Francisco, where his newspaper writing career first blossomed. He married Mary Day in 1871, and they lived in England until 1876. While abroad, Bierce wrote for British publications. He returned to San Francisco to write for Bay City newsheets. By 1887 William Randolph Hearst had employed him as a writer for the *Examiner*, and Bierce authored a Sunday column entitled "Prattle." His acerbic writing style earned him the nicknames "Bitter Bierce," and the "Literary Dictator of the West Coast."

In 1891 Bierce published *Tales of Soldiers and Civilians*, a collection of short stories based on his military career. These gore-tinged writings shocked readers of the era. This passage, for example, is from "Chickamauga" and describes a woman killed by a stray round: "[T]he long dark hair in tangles and full of blood. The greater part of the forehead was torn away, and from the jagged hole the brain protruded ... a frothy mass of gray, crowned with crimson bubbles." The slain woman is found by her deaf-mute son, who in abject horror at the sight of his mangled mother, begins uttering screams described as "something between the chattering of an ape and the gobbling of a turkey." Clearly, Bierce had seen his share of carnage during the war.

Bierce was in Washington, D.C., by 1876, working for another newspaper. In 1906, he published the *Devil's Dictionary*, a collection of satiric phrases coined by the author.

Bierce's death is shrouded in mystery. Many believe that he died in Mexico in 1913 while helping to cover the exploits of Pancho Villa. Just before leaving, he wrote a letter to friends that predicted his death in a characteristically sarcastic manner. The missive ended: "Goodbye, if you hear of my being stood up against a Mexican stone wall and being shot to rags please know that I think it is a pretty good way to depart this life. It beats old age, disease, or falling down the stairs. To be a *gringo* in Mexico—ah, that is euthanasia!" Some historians contend, however, that Bierce died in an accident in the Grand Canyon.

Whatever caused his death, Ambrose Bierce ranks among the highest of those authors who based writings on their wartime experiences.

—*Dana B. Shoaf*

For further reading:
Joshi, S. J., and David E. Schultz. *Ambrose Bierce: A Sole Survivor/Bits of Autobiography* (1999).
McCann, William, ed. *Ambrose Bierce's Civil War* (1956).
Morris, Roy, Jr. *Ambrose Bierce: Alone in Bad Company* (1999).

BIG BETHEL, BATTLE OF
(10 June 1861)

Big Bethel is regarded by many as the first battle of the Civil War. Union major general Benjamin F. Butler, in charge of the Department of Virginia and North Carolina, established his headquarters early in the war at Fort Monroe, one of the few points in Virginia that remained in Federal hands. He soon occupied the nearby towns of Hampton and Newport News and began sending his men out into the surrounding countryside to look for Rebel troops. Colonel John B. Magruder commanded the Confederate forces in the area. The nearest Confederate troops to Fort Monroe were only a few miles away. One outpost was at Bethel Church, and its nearby namesake, the village of Big Bethel; the other was at a smaller church known as Little Bethel.

After some minor skirmishes in early June 1861, Butler ordered a major attack against Little Bethel and Big Bethel. His men marched from their camps on the night of 9 June 1861. Under the command of Brigadier General Ebenezer Pierce, the Union force of about 4,400 men consisted of the 1st, 2d, 3d, 5th, and 7th New York Regiments; detachments from the 4th Massachusetts and the 1st Vermont; and an eleven-man detachment with two guns from the 2d U.S. Artillery. Pierce's men marched in two columns, one starting from Fort Monroe and the other from Newport News. The two columns were to unite near Little Bethel, and then attack the enemy there and at Big Bethel. Pierce's night march was plagued with bad luck and inept handling of his green troops. Near Little Bethel (which the Rebels had abandoned), the two Union columns mistook each other for the enemy and opened fire, causing twenty-one casualties.

The 1,400 Confederate troops near Big Bethel, under the command of Colonel Magruder, were Colonel Daniel H. Hill's 1st North Carolina Volunteers; 208 men of the 3d Virginia Infantry; Major E. B. Montague's Virginia Battalion; and Major George W. Randolph's Howitzer Battalion. They were deployed in earthworks around the road from Fort Monroe to Yorktown, at a bridge across the northwest branch of the Back River. The Confederate right, held by the 3d Virginia and one howitzer, was anchored on a hill south of the river. Most of the Confederates were entrenched north of the river. Thick woods and swamps protected much of their flanks.

The Rebel pickets were driven in about 8 A.M. on 10 June, and the main Union force marched into sight around 9 A.M. After two hours of skirmishing and artillery fire, Colonel Abram Duryee's 5th New York Zouaves and Colonel Frederick Townsend's 3d New York advanced toward the Confederate right. The Rebel troops holding the works had to abandon their position after a broken priming wire accidentally spiked their howitzer. The Zouaves rushed in to occupy the works. Instead of reinforcing the Zouaves, Townsend ordered a retreat when he saw what he thought was a body of enemy troops threatening his left. The "enemy" troops were only a company of Townsend's that been had separated from the main force. His mistake left the Zouaves unsupported. Colonel Hill ordered a counterattack, which drove the Yankees out of the captured works. Some of the Zouaves fell back from the Rebel works to a nearby building, from which they fired at the Confederates. Five men of the 1st North Carolina volunteered to charge the building and burn it. The Zouaves drove them back with a volley that mortally wounded Private Henry L. Wyatt.

Townsend and Duryee did not renew their attack. Major Theodore Winthrop led one last Union attack against the Rebel left north of the river. Leading part of the 1st Vermont and the 4th Massachusetts, Winthrop was shot dead. His death unnerved his men and squelched the attack.

After the repulse of Winthrop's charge, Pierce ordered a withdrawal. It was about 1 P.M. The retreat was disorganized and badly managed, but there was little pursuit and they returned safely to their camps.

The Union casualties were shocking for a country unprepared for war: eighteen dead, fifty-three wounded, and five missing. The Confederates lost only one man killed and seven wounded. A statue of the one dead Confederate, nineteen-year-old Private Henry L. Wyatt, stands today on the grounds of North Carolina's capitol in Raleigh. Wyatt was the first Southern soldier to die in a battle during the war. Wyatt's 1st North Carolina Volunteers, and its successor, the 11th North Carolina Infantry, proudly bore the nickname of the Bethel Regiment ever afterward.

The fight at Big Bethel brought shock and dismay to the North, and joy and confidence to the South. In terms of the number of troops involved and the strategic results, the battle was perhaps only a large skirmish that was soon overshadowed by the first battle of Bull Run. To many of the green soldiers of 1861, Big Bethel was their first battle, and it seemed for a time to have been a great one.

The site of the battle of Big Bethel today lies under the waters of the Big Bethel Reservoir, a man-made lake.

—*David A. Norris*

See also Bull Run, First Battle of; Butler, Benjamin F.; Zouaves.

For further reading:
Chapman, Craig S. *More Terrible Than Victory: North Carolina's Bloody Bethel Regiment 1861–65* (1998).
Hale, Edward. "The 'Bethel' Regiment." In *Histories of the Several Regiments and Battalions from North Carolina in the Great War 1861–65. Written by Members of their Respective Commands.* Edited by Walter Clark (1901).
U.S. War Department. *The War of the Rebellion: A Compilation of the Official Records of the Union and Confederate Armies.*

BIG BLACK RIVER, FIRST BATTLE OF
(17 May 1863)

On 16 May 1863, Ulysses S. Grant's army fought the largest and most significant battle of the Vicksburg campaign. The result of this Union victory at the battle of Champion's Hill was a Confederate retreat west in the direction of Vicksburg. Located twelve miles east of Vicksburg and ten miles west of the battlefield of Champion's Hill is the Big Black River. Upon reaching the Big Black River on the evening of 16 May, Lieutenant General John C.

Pemberton chose to defend a bridgehead on the east bank of the river. This action allowed a Confederate division, which became separated from Pemberton, to rejoin the army. Unbeknownst to Pemberton, Major General William W. Loring's "lost" division was marching in another direction, attempting to unite with the forces of General Joseph E. Johnston.

The Confederates built an entrenchment line in a north-south direction, across a one-mile neck of land formed by a loop in the river. The river and the bridges were to the rear, or west, of the Rebel position, which was anchored at each extremity near the river. The Rebels constructed a strong defense line of earth-covered cotton bales, with its flanks protected by the Big Black River. That evening Pemberton ordered General John Bowen to defend the bridgehead until the arrival of Loring's division. Under his command, Bowen had between 4,500 and 5,000 soldiers and eighteen artillery pieces rendered immobile when the horses were sent towards Vicksburg. He knew that he would soon be heavily outnumbered and that sooner or later would be forced to retreat to the safety of the west bank of the Big Black River, three-quarters of a mile to his rear.

Union general Eugene Carr's division of Major General John A. McClernand's XIII Corps resumed the pursuit of Pemberton's forces around 5:00 A.M. on the morning of 17 May. Within thirty minutes, McClernand's forces made contact with the Confederate position and halted to prepare for deployment. A frontal attack against such a fortified position would cost the Union many casualties. Not only because of the actual defenses, but because of the waist-deep bayou and marshy ground in front of the Confederate position. Flanking the Rebel position would be impossible because of the river at each end.

Brigadier General Michael Lawler's brigade did not fight in the previous day's battle and therefore did not share in the glory of the Union victory. Well-rested and ready for action, Lawler's brigade was at the spearhead of the Union advance. Lawler received orders from Carr, his division commander, to advance cautiously and reconnoiter the Rebel left. One of his regimental commanders reported back that a section where the Confederates had placed obstructions had been washed away by the recent heavy rains. Using this sheltered depression, a column of four abreast could reach the enemy's works relatively unnoticed.

Lawler ordered four regiments to take part in the attack on the Confederate left. He used the 21st and 23d Indiana in the lead, while having the 11th Wisconsin in close support and the 22d Iowa as a general reserve. As the 21st and 23d Indiana regiments were advancing over their respective avenues, he would use a diversionary force further to the south to confuse the defenders. The advance began around 9:00 A.M.

The attack on the Confederate left caught Bowen by

Big Black River Station, February 1864 (Photograph by William R. Pywell / *Library of Congress*)

surprise. The 23d Indiana charged out of the depression, through the marshy ground, and over the enemy's defensive works. They were able to break through the defense line and fired a deadly enfilading fire up and down the Confederate line causing the Rebels to scatter. As the 23d Indiana caused havoc on the Rebel left, the 21st Indiana and 11th Wisconsin charged across less concealed terrain to get to the defensive works. They had to leap into the stagnant bayou water in front of the Rebel position and make their way towards the breastworks. Upon reaching the Confederates, they too were able to create and exploit a breach in the defensive line.

Three Union regiments quickly exploited the breach and were able to roll up the Confederate line. The 22d Iowa, once through the opening, turned right and proceeded to push the Confederates toward the river, causing many either to flee or surrender. The 49th and 69th Indiana regiments turned to the South and rolled up the Confederate line, causing the center of the Rebel position to collapse. By 10:00 A.M. the Confederate defense was hopeless and Pemberton ordered a retreat to Vicksburg. Pemberton's forces did manage to destroy the bridges across the Big Black River, causing the Union army's pursuit to be delayed. Pemberton, still afraid that Grant would find a way to get between his forces and Vicksburg, ordered his army to retreat all the way to Vicksburg instead of establishing a line of defense in the hills west of the Big Black River. Now the path to Vicksburg would lay unhindered for Grant's army.

Elements of McClernand's Corps were the only Union forces engaged during the battle of Big Black River. The Union forces numbered around 10,000, while the Confederates numbered around 4,500. The casualties for the battle included 1,751 Confederates killed, wounded and captured and Union losses of 279 killed, wounded and missing. The Union also captured eighteen artillery pieces.

—*James L. Isemann*

See also Champion's Hill, Battle of; Pemberton, John Clifford; Vicksburg Campaign.

For further reading:

Arnold, James R. *Grant Wins the War: Decision at Vicksburg* (1997).

Miers, Earl Schenck. *The Web of Victory: Grant at Vicksburg* (1955; reprint; 1983).

Welcher, Frank J. *The Union Army, 1861–1865: Organization and Operations* (1989).

BIG BLACK RIVER, SECOND BATTLE OF

(February 1864)

See Meridian Campaign

BIGELOW, JOHN

(1817–1911)

U.S. consul general to Paris

For more than seven decades, as journalist, author, diplomat, and statesman, John Bigelow played a vital and virtually unparalleled role in American public life, enjoying considerable success in each of his chosen fields. Although only the controversial—and still debated—defeat of his close friend, Samuel Tilden, in the 1876 presidential race kept him from realizing the crowning achievement of serving as secretary of state, Bigelow came to be known as "First Citizen of the Republic." The historian Allan Nevins notes that Bigelow was "prominent in almost every great civic undertaking in New York in the last half-century of his life."

But Bigelow's place in history was best secured by his diplomatic service as American consul general in Paris during the Civil War, when he almost single-handedly blocked French intervention on behalf of the South and stymied Confederate plans to build a European-based naval fleet. Few members of the U.S. diplomatic service served their country as well as he.

Admitted to the New York bar in 1838, he fell in with a literary/political circle of prominent and soon-to-be-prominent men and began contributing essays to the *Democratic Review* and editorials to William Cullen Bryant's *New York Evening Post*. Taken by his obvious talent, Bryant in 1848 offered Bigelow a one-third share of the paper in hopes of grooming him as a possible successor. Over the next dozen years, Bigelow specialized in political journalism and his pieces on the free-soil and abolition movements attracted wide attention. He joined Bryant in helping to form the new Republican Party: in 1856, Bigelow wrote the official campaign biography of its first presidential candidate, John Frémont. Two years later, he covered the Illinois senatorial election for the *Evening Post*, and was greatly impressed by the Republican candidate, Abraham Lincoln.

Having made a considerable fortune at the *Evening Post*, Bigelow left the paper soon after the 1860 election, determined to spend his time on writing several biographies. But when he heard that the job of consul general at Paris was available, he lobbied intensely for it and beat out *New York Times* publisher Henry Raymond for the post. He arrived in France in August 1861.

Bigelow's assignment was critical: the South had three agents, led by William L. Yancey, already working in Paris to secure British and French support for the Confederate cause—specifically, military aid in breaking the Northern blockade, which, the Southerners declared, would resume the shipment of cotton to Europe. Bigelow was to head off such action—or any French and British intervention, for that matter—and to ensure that the European press remained favorable towards the North.

Arriving first in London, Bigelow used his formidable journalistic contacts to press home the argument that British military involvement on behalf of an aristocracy that practiced slavery would result in a social revolution in England. But British sentiment, fueled by the pro-Southern battle reports from William Russell of the *Times of London*, remained largely with the Confederates.

Similarly, in France government officials, with a few exceptions, greeted Bigelow coldly.

Bigelow's first success came in the wake of the *Trent Affair*, which enraged British public opinion against the North and in favor of immediate military intervention. Bigelow cannily wrote a studied defense of the American government's actions and arranged for it to appear in print. Because he was a diplomatic official, publishing it under his own name would have been considered a breach of protocol. So, Bigelow got General Winfield Scott to agree to sign it. The article, which was widely reprinted in both England and France, was later called "the most successful bit of propaganda in the whole war."

Almost immediately after, Bigelow was called on to counter another piece of Southern propaganda when charges appeared in the French press that the North had callously destroyed Charleston Harbor. Bigelow published letters in the French press demonstrating that no permanent damage had been done.

But the Northern blockade remained Bigelow's most formidable diplomatic obstacle. Thousands of British and French workers had been laid off because of its effects. Bigelow pressed Secretary of State William Seward to lift the blockade, citing the immense propaganda value that would result. "Such a proposal from our govt. would remove all pretext for recognizing the South," he wrote, and "would win for our govt. the esteem & gratitude of the continent." Happily for Bigelow's efforts, the Confederate government miscalculated: It arrogantly declared a virtual embargo, prohibiting its cotton from being sold to any nation that refused to recognize its legitimacy. Seward, through Bigelow, warned France that if it acceded to the South's demands, it might face a similar embargo on Northern wheat—and France had just suffered its worst grain harvest in three decades.

For the rest of the war, Bigelow found himself countering the propaganda efforts of John Slidell, one of the Confederate agents involved in the *Trent* Affair, and of Edwin de Leon, who came to Paris with $25,000 in Southern funds to be used "for the special purpose of enlightening public opinion." The Confederate agents' primary mission was arranging for French firms to build ships secretly—particularly ironclads and corvettes—with which the South might break the blockade. Bigelow tirelessly tracked down all the contracts and presented them to the French government, along with a vigorous diplomatic protest over the flagrant violation of neutrality laws. As a result of his efforts—which included bringing about a shift in French press opinion in favor of the North—the ships never sailed.

After the war, Bigelow rendered further service in Paris by preserving Franco-American friendship during the controversy over the Mexican emperor Maximilian's attempted empire building. Returning to the United States, Bigelow enlisted in the political career of his longtime friend, Samuel Tilden, serving as secretary of state for New York and then as principal advisor and strategist during the ill-fated 1876 campaign. He remained politically active for the remaining thirty-five years of his life, as a celebrated author—publishing biographies of Tilden and Benjamin Franklin—and as publicist for good-government causes. When Bigelow died in 1911, John Jay Chapman wrote that he "stands as a monument of old-fashioned sterling culture and accomplishment—a sort of beacon to the present age of ignorance and pretense, and to a 'land where all things are forgotten.'"

—Eric Fettmann

See also Blockade of C.S.A; Chicago *Tribune*; DeLeon, Edwin; Diplomacy, U.S.A.; Newspapers; Slidell, John; *Trent* Affair
For further reading:
Bigelow, John, Jr. *Retrospections of an Active Life* (1909).
Clapp, Margaret. *Forgotten First Citizen: John Bigelow* (1947).
Nevins, Allan. *The Evening Post: A Century of Journalism* (1922).

BIRNEY, DAVID BELL
(1825–1864)
Union general

Born in Huntsville, Alabama, the son of future abolitionist James G. Birney, David Bell Birney moved with his family while still a child to Cincinnati, Ohio. Birney was educated at Andover. Upon graduation, he lived briefly in Cincinnati before moving to Upper Saginaw, Michigan. He studied law there and practiced briefly before moving to Philadelphia, where he worked in business before admission to the Pennsylvania bar. Before the war, Birney became a prominent Philadelphia citizen and an officer in the local militia. At the outbreak of hostilities, Birney raised the 23d Pennsylvania. He led his regiment to Washington, where they patrolled along the Potomac River. Birney was promoted to brigadier general in February 1862.

Birney fought at the siege of Yorktown and at the battle of Williamsburg. Serving in Phil Kearny's division, Birney led his brigade at Seven Pines, where he was accused of not bringing his men up in time to participate in the battle. (A court-martial later exonerated him.) Birney fought in the Seven Days battles before returning to Washington, where Kearny's division became part of John Pope's Army of Virginia. At the battle of Chantilly on 1 September 1862, Birney took temporary command of the division when Kearny was killed.

Given command of the division though not yet the rank to go with it, Birney led his men at the battle of Fredericksburg, where they were trapped under Confederate artillery for two days after the battle was over. General George Stoneman commended Birney for his actions at Fredericksburg. At Chancellorsville,

David Bell Birney (*Library of Congress*)

Birney commanded the 1st Division of Daniel Sickles' corps (III Corps). After the battle, on 20 May 1863, Birney was promoted to major general.

Birney led his division forward into Pennsylvania in June 1863 and on the second day of the battle of Gettysburg took command of III Corps when Sickles was wounded. Birney too was wounded, but did not leave the field during the battle.

Back in command of his division at Bristoe Station and Mine Run, Birney again temporarily commanded III Corps in February 1864. After the reorganization of the Army of the Potomac, he commanded the 3d Division of Winfield Scott Hancock's corps (II Corps). Birney temporarily commanded the corps in July 1864, and in late July 1864 Birney was given command of X Corps.

At the time Birney took command of X Corps, he was already feeling the effects of malaria that he had contracted during the Petersburg campaign. After temporarily commanding the Army of the James in September 1864, his condition worsened. In early October he went home to recuperate, but the trip only exacerbated his illness. He died on 18 October 1864, only a week after returning home. His brother was Union brigadier general William Birney.

—*David S. Heidler and Jeanne T. Heidler*

See also Chantilly, Battle of; Fredericksburg, Battle of; Gettysburg, Battle of.
For further reading:
Davis, Oliver Wilson. *Life of David Bell Birney, Major-General United States Volunteers* (1867; reprint, 1987).

BIRNEY, WILLIAM
(1819–1907)
Union general

Born to James G. Birney and Agatha McDowell Birney in Madison County, Alabama, William Birney moved with his family to Cincinnati, Ohio, after his father rejected the institution of slavery and determined that he would work for its abolition. James G. Birney became an important advocate for abolition and no doubt influenced his son's views on the subject.

In Cincinnati, William Birney became an attorney. In the late 1840s Birney traveled to Europe and was in France during the revolutions of 1848. He was deeply affected by the events of that year and determined to stay to see the experiment in government to its conclusion. While there, he studied literature, taught in one of the nation's universities, and contributed articles for American newspapers about events in Europe. Enjoying the journalistic life, upon his return to the United States, Birney established the *Philadelphia Register*.

News of Fort Sumter motivated him to raise a New Jersey volunteer company that became a part of the 1st New Jersey. He commanded his company at First Bull Run. In September 1861, he was promoted to major in the 4th New Jersey. Birney was captured during the Peninsula campaign the following spring; upon his exchange in August 1862, he was promoted to lieutenant colonel of the 4th New Jersey.

At Fredericksburg on 13 December 1862, Birney and the 38th spent much of the day supporting some of the Federal batteries before advancing late in the day as part of John Reynolds's I Corps. In January 1863, Birney was promoted to colonel. He commanded his regiment at Chancellorsville, but since he and his men were detailed to guard the supply train, they saw no action during the battle.

Shortly after the battle of Chancellorsville, Birney's association with abolitionist causes brought about his promotion to brigadier general of volunteers and his appointment to recruit African-American soldiers. Through the summer of 1863 he was attached to the Department of Washington while recruiting his brigade. In the fall he moved his recruiting efforts to Benedict, Maryland, where he remained until early 1864. One of his sources for recruits was the slave prison in Baltimore.

In the spring of 1864, Birney was sent with his brigade to South Carolina. Shortly after his arrival, he was sent to command the District of Florida, headquartered at Jacksonville. From there he operated into the interior, destroying supplies, capturing Confederate soldiers on furlough, and destroying rail lines. Probably most active during July 1864, Birney skirmished with Confederates outside Jacksonville at Trout Creek in the middle of the month and made a raid on the railroad at Baldwin, Florida, from 23 to 28 July. During his time in Florida, a large part of the northeastern part of the state came firmly under Federal control. At the end of the month, however, he was recalled to Virginia to assume command of a brigade of the 3d Division, a largely African-American unit of X Corps of Benjamin F. Butler's Army of the James.

Upon assuming command of his brigade, Birney wasted no time before seeing action at Deep Bottom Run from 13 to 20 August. He was commended for his actions during that battle, and on 25 August he assumed command of the 3d Division. He continued to command this division through November 1864, and in December he assumed command of the 2d Division, XXV Corps under Godfrey Weitzel. Birney commanded this division through the last stages of the siege of Petersburg and the Appomattox campaign. He was present with his men at Robert E. Lee's surrender at Appomattox Court House. Toward the end of the war, in March 1865, Birney received a brevet promotion to major general of volunteers for his service during the conflict.

After the war, Birney did not remain in the volunteer service beyond the summer of 1865. Mustered out in August, he moved to Florida for several years but, failing to make an adequate living there, he relocated to Washington, D.C. Initially he opened a private practice but eventually accepted an appointment as U.S. Attorney for the District. He also served as a correspondent on Washington affairs for the *New York Examiner*. In his later years, Birney also wrote extensively on such diverse topics as religion, political affairs, and his father. He retired to a house outside the capital at Forest Glen, Maryland, where he died on 14 August 1907.

—*David S. Heidler and Jeanne T. Heidler*

See also Florida; United States Colored Troops.
For further reading:
Birney, William. *General William Birney's Answer to Libels Clandestinely Circulated by James Shaw, Jr., Late Colonel of the Seventh U.S. Colored Troops* (1878).

BLACKFORD'S (BOTELER'S) FORD
(19–20 September 1862)

The Army of Northern Virginia retreated south after the battle of Antietam in September 1862 by crossing the Potomac at Blackford's (or Boteler's) Ford. By 19 September, two days after the battle, the Confederate army was back in Virginia and some forty-

four guns of Lee's reserve artillery were covering the ford to prevent Federal pursuers from coming too close. The job was given to Brigadier General William N. Pendleton, Lee's chief of artillery, who was able to place all but eleven of the guns on points covering the ford. Lee instructed Pendleton to hold the ford through the nineteenth, if possible, to give his army time to put some distance between itself and the Army of the Potomac.

At 8:00 A.M. on 19 September, Union forces appeared on the bank opposite the ford. They were elements of Fitz John Porter's V Corps, and soon they had brought up about seventy pieces of artillery to pound the Confederate position. Pendleton had two brigades of infantry to help cover the ford, but he was to learn that their numbers had been much diminished by the battle at Antietam. Withering fire from Union sharpshooters presently joined the heavy artillery barrage as the riflemen moved to the banks of the Chesapeake and Ohio Canal. Pendleton not only saw his foremost artillery become impossible to man, he also found it hard to find 200 infantry to put forward to repel the Federal advance.

After a lull the Yankees renewed their attack in the late afternoon. Pendleton's ammunition was running low, so he weighed the choice of retiring against the risk of losing his guns. Trying to have it both ways, he instructed batteries to withdraw only if they could do so under cover. He hoped, forlornly as it happened, that the piecemeal retrograde would deceive the bluecoats at least until the day had passed. By sunset, though, the Confederates were being hard pressed, and by dark it became apparent that the Federal force meant to cross and assail his position. Just then, Pendleton's 200 infantry broke.

The river at Blackford's Ford was about 300 yards wide and only about three feet deep, so neither it nor the Confederates on the Virginia bank posed much trouble to the two Union brigades coming across. Under overall command of Brigadier General Charles Griffin, 2d Brigade, 1st Division, the party also included Colonel James Barnes's 1st Brigade. As the Yankees gained the crest of the high ground on the Virginia side, Pendleton worried that they might make a headlong rush that would likely see them capture the entire reserve artillery. He later claimed, however, that he could deduce from the range of their continuing barrage that such was unlikely—and it was. Only four Confederate guns fell to the Yankees. Nonetheless, at the time Pendleton was nearly frantic, so much so that he rushed to the rear and personally sought out Lee. Awakening the commanding general, Pendleton blurted out that all his guns had been taken. Lee told him to calm down; they would take stock of the situation the next morning.

At dawn the next day, 20 September, Lee told Stonewall Jackson to take care of the Union advance, so

Jackson sent A. P. Hill's Light Division toward Blackford's Ford. About a half mile from the river, Hill formed six brigades into two lines of battle, the first consisting of Dorsey Pender, Maxcy Gregg, and Edward L. Thomas. The second line contained the dead Lawrence O'Bryan Branch's brigade under the command of Colonel James Lane, James J. Archer's brigade, and Colonel John M. Brockenbrough commanding the wounded Charles M. Field's brigade. Gregg and Archer coordinated the two lines in an advance that was, in Hill's characteristic fashion, both unceremonious and grimly businesslike. It was hot work, for the Confederates moved into a nasty fire from the 70 guns across the river, as well as what remained of the two brigades atop the high ground on the Virginia side. Gregg easily collapsed the Federal right and center, but the left proved stubborn. In fact, Pender nearly got in trouble until Archer reinforced and extended his left flank to continue the push toward the river. The Federals commenced a general retreat, but confusion temporarily disorganized the maneuver, and the 118th Pennsylvania Regiment suffered heavy casualties. The regiment stumbled down the steep bluff to an exposed position on the river, where they were little more than targets for Confederate rifles above. Hill, hardened to such sights, nevertheless viewed this slaughter as remarkable; the Potomac, he said, was "blue with the floating bodies of our foe."

Casualties were about the same for blue and gray alike—almost 300 for Hill and little more than that for the Federals. After the carnage at Antietam earlier in the week, such losses possibly did not have the power to shock. Yet it was, as Hill noted, a stern lesson for the Army of the Potomac. The 118th Pennsylvania alone had lost 272 men, 3 officers included. That was what happened, Hill declared, when a retreating army was pressed too closely.

—*David S. Heidler and Jeanne T. Heidler*

See also Antietam, Battle of; Pendleton, William Nelson.

For further reading:
Lee, Susan Pendleton. *Memoirs of William Nelson Pendleton, D. D.* (1893).

BLACKWELL, ELIZABETH
(1821–1910)
Physician

In 1861, at the start of the Civil War, Dr. Elizabeth Blackwell led a group of elite white women in their efforts to found the Women's Central Relief Association (WCRA) in New York City, an institute that trained female nurses for the war. By September the WCRA had become one of the numerous local aid societies to come under the organizational banner of the U.S. Sanitary Commission (USSC). Many of the socially prominent women who were trained in nursing

by Blackwell through the WCRA served temporarily as volunteers aboard hospital ships like the *Daniel Webster*, the *Ocean Queen*, and the *Spaulding*, and later as army nurses and relief workers. Through their experiences as volunteer nurses in the war, these women traversed the narrow confines of Victorian gender boundaries to work in the public sphere as was the custom for many white and a few free African-American women involved in antebellum reform. The women in the WCRA did so by emphasizing how gender traits associated with the feminine and domestic, such as the nurturing capacity of women, were well suited for nursing. Elizabeth Blackwell, their teacher, had already broken through one of the strongest barriers to women in the professions when she became the first woman to receive a degree from a U.S. medical school.

After being rejected by a number of major medical schools because of her sex, Elizabeth Blackwell was accepted by Geneva Medical College, a "country school" in upstate New York in 1847. Geneva was not being progressive in accepting a woman into their school. Her acceptance was a farcical gesture on the part of the faculty, who turned over to the student body—a reputedly "rude [and] boisterous" bunch—the decision of whether or not to admit Blackwell. Believing her application to be a hoax from a rival school, the students accepted it, expecting her to fail or be intimidated into leaving. Instead, she graduated in 1849 at the head of her class. Although this did not lead immediately to more liberal admission policies for women among existing medical schools, it did lead more women to take up the challenge.

Born in Bristol, England, in 1821, Blackwell moved with her family to New York in 1832 after a fire destroyed her father's business. When financial misfortune struck with the Panic of 1837 the family moved from New York City to Cincinnati, Ohio, that same year. Blackwell's father, Samuel, died in 1838 before he was able to recover financially, and left his wife and nine children practically destitute. With few other economic options available to them, Blackwell, her mother, and older sisters opened a school. Blackwell took other jobs teaching for several more years before she decided to go into the medical profession.

The source of Blackwell's interest in medicine and her ambition to get a medical degree against all odds are subjects of speculation, especially considering that she practiced medicine for only a short time before going into administration and then into public health and sanitation reform. Like her four sisters, none of whom ever married, Blackwell was emotionally and temperamentally unsuited for Victorian marriage. She may have sought a career in medicine as a means of caring for herself financially and thereby avoiding marriage, which in the absence of extenuating circumstances was expected of women in the antebellum era.

She also may have seen medicine as one of the most legitimate and credible avenues into social reform, an endeavor to which she was naturally drawn. Blackwell came from a family of reformers. Her father was a religious dissenter in England and became involved in both the abolitionist and temperance movements after he moved to the United States. Two brothers married women well known for their reform activism. Lucy Stone, noted abolitionist and women's rights and suffrage activist, and Antoinette Brown, one of the first women preachers to be ordained and have her own recognized ministry, were Elizabeth's sisters-in-law.

Whatever her motives for pursuing a medical degree, Blackwell recognized the need for women to have women doctors. A story she tells in her autobiography reveals, at least in part, one reason she chose to pursue the medical degree. Victorian etiquette and prudery too often made guarding their timidity a greater virtue for women than guarding their health. Male medical students in training received detailed instruction in how not to offend their female patients' modesty, including a reminder to keep the lights dim—even though such a practice could result in accidental mutilations of mothers and newborn infants. Dr. Charles D. Meigs, noted professor of women's medicine at Jefferson Medical College in Philadelphia, explained to his students the reason why they should never challenge their patients' timidity. His words attest to the strength of Victorian moral values. "It is perhaps best, upon the whole," Meigs wrote, "that this great degree of modesty should exist even to the extent of putting a bar to researches, without which no very clear and understandable notions can be obtained of the sexual disorders. I confess I am proud to say that in this country generally there are women who prefer to suffer the extremity of danger and pain rather than wave those scruples of delicacy which prevent their maladies from being explored. I say it is fully an evidence of the dominion of a fine morality in our society." Blackwell's consciousness of the cost of such standards was awakened when a friend who was apparently dying of uterine cancer told her, "If I could have been treated by a lady doctor, my worst sufferings would have been spared me." Accordingly, Blackwell saw women's entry into the medical profession as part of a "moral crusade," and she pursued the course until she broke a number of barriers to making this dream reality.

Blackwell's acceptance into, and completion of, medical school were only the beginning of her struggles. Finding a place to practice proved just as trying. After being barred from New York hospitals and dispensaries and then ostracized and ignored by male colleagues when she practiced in area clinics, Blackwell started a hospital, fully staffed by women to serve women and children only. Blackwell and her sister,

Emily, who had recently graduated from Cleveland Medical College in 1854 and finished postgraduate medical work in Europe, established the New York Infirmary for Women and Children in 1857. Dissatisfied with the caliber of training her staff of female physicians were receiving in the all-female medical schools most of them were forced to attend, Elizabeth and Emily founded the Medical College of the New York Infirmary for Women and Children in 1868. Thanks to the Blackwell sisters, who insisted that their college not merely meet but exceed existing standards of excellence in medical colleges, their school was ahead of its time with its higher-than-average standards of admission. The required entrance exam for applicants to the Medical College of the New York Infirmary was ten years ahead of a New York state requirement for medical schools. And the three-year program that the Blackwells' school required (as opposed to the customary two-year program) was the only one of its kind among medical colleges in the country. (Harvard's was not established until 1871.) As a final measure to ensure the competence of its graduates, the Blackwell sisters appointed an examining board of independent physicians. Elizabeth Blackwell returned to England in 1869 to help found the London School of Medical Medicine for Women, the first female medical college for women in Great Britain. She remained in England for the rest of her life.

In recent studies of Elizabeth Blackwell, feminists have noted some of the particularly progressive insights she held in spite of her opposition to openly feminist causes like the women's rights movement started in Seneca Falls, New York, in 1848. Blackwell's open and, among her peers, practically lone, criticism of "radical objectivity and scientific reductionism" in medicine was one that "foreshadow[ed] the maternalist strain of thinking among contemporary feminist philosophers and thinkers." Furthermore, given the trend in medicine at the end of the twentieth century toward holistic approaches that include homeopathic as well as allopathic treatments, Blackwell's perspective merits even more consideration. With regard to human sexuality, although Blackwell herself never married and apparently avoided intimate relationships with men altogether, she believed, unlike the majority of her Victorian male colleagues, that women had an even greater capacity for sexual passion than did men. Equally as consequential, she disagreed with the one-sex model of classical theory then prevalent that the male body was the norm. Agreeing with the scientific and resulting societal theory of complementarity to explain differences between the two sexes, Blackwell held nonetheless that it was the female, not the male, who was the norm upon which human sexuality was based.

—Catherine O. Badura

See also American Red Cross; Barton, Clara; Medicine; Nurses; United States Sanitary Commission.

For further reading:

Blackwell, Elizabeth. *Medicine and Society in America: Essays in Medical Sociology* (1972).

———. *Pioneer Work in Opening the Medical Profession to Women: Autobiographical Sketches by Dr. Elizabeth Blackwell* (1977).

Drachman, Virginia G. "The Loomis Trial: Social Mores and Obstetrics in the Mid-Nineteenth Century." In *Women and Health in America*, edited by Judith Walzer Leavitt (1984).

Krug, Kate. "Women Ovulate, Men Spermate: Elizabeth Blackwell as a Feminist Physiologist." *Journal of the History of Sexuality* (1996).

Monteiro, Lois A. "On Separate Roads: Florence Nightingale and Elizabeth Blackwell." *Signs: Journal of Women in Culture and Society* (1984).

Morantz-Sanchez, Regina. "Feminism, Professionalism, and Germs: The Thought of Mary Putnam Jacobi, and Elizabeth Blackwell." *American Quarterly* (1982).

———. "Feminist Theory and Historical Practice: Rereading Elizabeth Blackwell." *History and Theory* (1992).

Ross, Kristie. "Arranging a Doll's House: Refined Women as Union Nurses." In *Divided Houses: Gender and the Civil War*, edited by Catherine Clinton and Nina Silber (1992).

Rossi, Alice S. "The Blackwell Clan." In *The Feminist Papers: From Adams to de Beauvoir* (1973).

Scholten, Catherine M. "'On the Importance of the Obstetrick Art': Changing Customs of Childbirth in America, 1760–1825." In *Women and Health in America*, edited by Judith Walzer Leavitt (1984).

Wilson, Dorothy Clarke. *Lone Woman: The Story of Elizabeth Blackwell, the First Woman Doctor* (1970).

BLAINE, JAMES GILLESPIE
(1830–1893)
U.S. congressman

Born to Ephraim Lyon Blaine and Louise Gillespie Blaine in West Brownsville, Pennsylvania, James Gillespie Blaine was educated at Washington College. After graduation he tried school teaching but decided on the study of law instead. In 1854 he moved to Augusta, Maine, home to his wife's family, and began a career in journalism. As part owner and editor of the *Kennebec Journal* and editor for the *Portland Advertiser*, Blaine took a keen interest in politics. Although Blaine was originally a Whig, the passage of the Kansas-Nebraska Act in 1854 and Blaine's realization that Maine's population opposed the expansion of slavery caused him to identify with the new Republican Party, and he became a founding member of the party in Maine.

Blaine quickly became a party leader in the state. In 1856 he was selected one of the state's delegates to the Republican National Convention, where he unsuccessfully supported the nomination of John McLean of Ohio. Three years later he became chairman of the state party committee, a position he held for twenty-two years. In addition to his party activities, Blaine also served in the

state legislature beginning with his election in 1858. In the same year, Blaine traveled to the Midwest, where he covered the congressional elections for his paper. There he witnessed one of the debates between Abraham Lincoln and Stephen Douglas and came away inspired by Lincoln. Even though he was not a delegate, in 1860 he went to the Republican National Convention in Chicago, where he worked behind the scenes to help Lincoln win the nomination. Afterwards he spent much of the summer campaigning for Lincoln. During the elections of 1860, Blaine was reelected to the lower house of Maine's legislature, and, after the legislature convened, he was chosen its speaker.

With the outbreak of the Civil War, in addition to his position in the legislature, Blaine served as the military agent for Governor Israel Washburn. In this capacity Blaine supervised recruitment and supplying of Maine's quota of volunteers. Ironically, when threatened with conscription later, Blaine hired a substitute rather than serve in the army.

In 1862, Blaine was elected to the U.S. House of Representatives. The first committees for the freshman congressman were the Committee on Post Offices and Post Roads and the Committee on Militia—not terribly inspiring assignments, but Blaine approached them with a sense of opportunity. He quickly gained a name for himself by pushing through legislation to authorize railroad cars for the U.S. Mail that allowed sorting en route and sped mail delivery. Blaine's first major speech in Congress also gained him a great deal of attention. In "The Ability of the American People to Suppress the Rebellion," Blaine delivered an inspirational call for greater efforts on the part of the people. The speech was subsequently printed in pamphlet form and distributed throughout the country.

Blaine as a congressman was careful to avoid issues that could make him dangerous political enemies. As a result, he seemed a friend to most members and was quite popular from the very beginning of his service. However, after his easy reelection in 1864, he inadvertently became embroiled in what would become a lifelong feud with Representative Roscoe Conkling of New York. The quarrel between the two became one of the most bitter in congressional history. Out of it grew the two factions of the Republican Party during the Ulysses S. Grant administration known as the Stalwarts (Conkling) and the Half-Breeds (Blaine).

During the Lincoln administration, Blaine's activities in Congress showed him to be a strong supporter of the president. After Lincoln's death, however, Blaine fell more into the camp of the Radical Republicans, particularly on the issue of Reconstruction. Because he disagreed with some of the most extreme Radical proposals, however, he was seen primarily as a moderate by the end of Reconstruction. His ability to work with all sides secured him election as Speaker of the House in 1869.

In 1876, Blaine was seen as a strong presidential candidate for the Republican Party. The exposure of some suspicious dealings with the Little Rock and Fort Smith Railroad put him under suspicion of corruption and ruined his chances for the nomination. Blaine, however, entered a new phase of his political career in 1876 when he was appointed to fill an unexpired term in the U.S. Senate. He served in the senate until he was appointed secretary of state by President James Garfield in 1881.

Blaine took a strong interest in foreign affairs during his brief tenure as secretary. The assassination of Garfield, bringing Conkling supporter Chester Arthur to the presidency, caused Blaine to resign at the end of the 1881. For the next few years, Blaine wrote what would be the first volume of his memoirs, *Twenty Years of Congress*. In 1884 he was somewhat vindicated in the party when he received the nomination for the presidency.

Blaine lost the election to Grover Cleveland and once again withdrew from public life. He completed his memoirs and traveled in Europe. In 1889 President Benjamin Harrison appointed him secretary of state. During the next three years, Blaine devoted himself to the foreign affairs of the United States, working most notably on cementing ties between the United States and Latin America. By the spring of 1892, however, he found himself increasingly at odds with the president and resigned his post in June 1892.

By the fall of 1892, Blaine's health began to fail. He became seriously ill and bedridden by early 1893 and died quietly in his sleep at his home in Washington, D.C., on 27 January 1893.

—*David S. Heidler and Jeanne T. Heidler*

See also Congress, U.S.A.; Conkling, Roscoe.

For further reading:
Blaine, James Gillespie. *Twenty Years of Congress* (1884–1886).
Russell, Charles Edward. *Blaine of Maine; His Life and Times* (1931).

BLAIR, AUSTIN
(1818–1894)
Governor of Michigan

Born to George Blair and Rhoda Blackman Mann Blair in Tompkins County, New York, Austin Blair attended Cazenovia Seminary and Hamilton College before enrolling in Union College, from which he graduated in 1837. Blair's parents were ardent abolitionists, and they no doubt influenced him along that same path as a young man. After his graduation from college, Blair studied law. After his admission to the bar in New York, he moved to Jackson, Michigan, where he established his practice in 1841.

In addition to his law practice, Blair took a strong

interest in Michigan Whig politics. In 1844 he was elected to the Michigan state legislature, where he was a strong supporter of African-American rights in the state. He served in the legislature until 1849 and there encouraged the passage of a law that would grant suffrage to African-American adult males and a Michigan personal liberty law designed to prevent the enforcement of federal fugitive slave legislation in the state.

Not finding the Whig Party in Michigan sufficiently antislavery in its official positions, Blair in 1848 joined the Free Soil Party. Six years later he participated in the meeting in Jackson that organized the Republican Party. The following year he was elected as a Republican to the Michigan state senate.

A strong supporter of William Henry Seward for the Republican presidential nomination in 1860, Blair chaired the Michigan delegation to the Republican National Convention in Chicago that year. When Abraham Lincoln was nominated instead, Blair pledged his support for the ticket and agreed to accept the state party's nomination for governor for the November election. He was elected governor and began his term in January 1861.

As governor of Michigan for most of the war (he was reelected for a second term in November 1862), Blair was a strong supporter of the Lincoln administration and worked tirelessly to raise troops and money for the war effort. After Lincoln's call for volunteers in April 1861, Blair convened a meeting of the state's leadership to address the most efficient methods possible for raising Michigan's quota. After this meeting, he called a special session of the state legislature for that body to appropriate the money to raise and equip ten regiments of Michigan volunteers. The state was in a rather precarious situation financially because of graft in the state treasury during the previous administration. Blair's quick response to the president's call and efficient recruiting methods gave Michigan the honor, however, of having its first recruited regiment reach Washington before any other volunteers.

Throughout the war, Blair corresponded frequently with the War Department regarding recruiting issues. Although he generally had little difficulty meeting the state's quotas during the war and enthusiastically approached those responsibilities, he had difficulties with the War Department bureaucracy in procuring the necessary arms for Michigan recruits before they left the state. He also received frequent and sometimes frantic requests from individual generals for additional troops in times of emergency. This was especially the case during the Confederate invasion of Kentucky in the late summer and fall of 1862 and in 1864 when rumors abounded that Confederates were amassing on the other side of the U.S.-Canadian border. Blair met all the requests that were within his power and gained the repu-

tation throughout his governorship as one of the staunchest supporters of the administration.

Along with his efforts to help raise troops and money for the war, Blair also took a very active interest in the activities of Michigan troops during the war. In the spring of 1862, after the battle of Shiloh, he traveled to Pittsburg Landing, Tennessee, to visit with the Michigan troops who had fought in that momentous battle and to encourage them in their future endeavors for the Union cause. He received frequent reports from Michigan officers regarding the behavior of Michigan troops in various engagements throughout the war. When those units were depleted by injuries and deaths, he worked tirelessly to recruit replacements so that Michigan units would not have to be combined with those of any other states.

In the spring of 1864 Blair traveled to Washington to confer with the president and the War Department about the progress of the war and Michigan's part in it. He came away satisfied that the end was in sight and that Michigan was still doing its part to bring about a successful conclusion to the war. Tired from his exertions during the conflict, he determined to retire from the governor's chair at the end of his second term.

After the war, Blair lived quietly while trying to reestablish his law practice. The call of politics proved too much, however, and he stood for a seat in the U.S. House of Representatives in the fall of 1866. Blair was elected and served three successive terms in Congress. A dispute with the party leadership in Michigan over the U.S. Senate nomination in 1871 caused Blair to join the reform wing of the party in 1872 and campaign for Horace Greeley for president. Blair returned to the regular party in the 1880s but never enjoyed much political success in his remaining years. Instead he devoted his time to his law practice and died quietly in retirement on 6 August 1894.

—*David S. Heidler and Jeanne T. Heidler*

See also Election of 1860; Republican Party.
For further reading:
Harris, Robert Charles. "Austin Blair of Michigan: A Political Biography" (Ph.D. dissertation, 1969).

BLAIR, FRANCIS PRESTON
(1791–1876)

Newspaper editor and presidential adviser

Francis Preston Blair was born in Abingdon, Virginia, the son of James Blair, attorney general of Kentucky, and Elizabeth Smith. Reared in Frankfort, Kentucky, Blair in 1811 graduated with honors from Transylvania University. In 1812 he married Eliza Gist, daughter of frontiersman Nathaniel Gist. For 64 years Eliza was Blair's equal partner in every endeavor. He enlisted in the army during the War of 1812 but had to be sent home from Indiana because of bleeding lungs.

As circuit court clerk of Franklin County from 1813 to 1830, Blair was deeply involved in local and state politics, and he coedited the *Argus*, a highly partisan local paper. After the depression of 1819, the Kentucky legislature passed controversial bankruptcy laws and created a bank to help debtors, which the state supreme court declared unconstitutional. The legislature then created a new supreme court that validated the same laws, and a bitter struggle ensued between the old and new courts. Blair served as clerk of the new court and president of the new bank. Ultimately, the old court won. In 1824 Blair supported Henry Clay for president, but in 1828 he helped Andrew Jackson carry Kentucky. In 1830 the grateful president made Blair editor of a new Washington paper dedicated to Jackson and his policies.

Blair's highly readable paper, *The Globe*, idealized democracy and made Jackson its symbol. Democratic Party newspapers nationwide reprinted Blair's editorials, and did much to spread the concept of America as a great experiment in democracy and a beacon of freedom for the world. Because the Bank of the United States exercised uncontrolled power over the American economy and enjoyed financial ties to various members of Congress and the Whig Party, Blair attacked the Bank as a threat to democracy and glorified both Jackson's veto of the bill renewing it and his transfer of the national treasury to state banks. When South Carolina tried to nullify the tariff laws, Blair portrayed this as an effort to destroy the national Union and pictured Jackson's threat of military force as a noble act of supreme wisdom. He was an adviser in Jackson's "kitchen cabinet," helped organize the Democratic Party into a national institution, and wielded great power in the dispensation of government jobs.

In 1840, when Martin Van Buren was defeated by Whig William Henry Harrison, *The Globe* opposed Whig efforts to recreate the Bank of the United States and raise tariffs. Harrison soon died, however, and his successor John Tyler vetoed the policies of the party that had elected him. Blair supported Tyler's vetoes and worked for the renomination and election of Van Buren in 1844.

In 1844 the major issue was the annexation of Texas, which had recently separated from Mexico. Many Northerners feared the addition of a vast new slave area, and Texas was claiming a huge section of Mexico that had never been part of Texas. Blair and Van Buren feared that annexation before a settlement of the Texas boundaries and an agreement between North and South with regard to slavery's extension would bring war with Mexico and eventually provoke an American civil war. This cost Van Buren the nomination, and even though the Democratic Party platform and its candidate, James K. Polk, advocated immediate annexation, Blair opposed it, although he did support Polk and win a $22,000 bet on his election. Polk, however, forced Blair to sell *The Globe* to a new editor more amenable to party discipline.

Blair retired to his Silver Spring plantation, but remained highly influential through his reputation and friendships. In 1848, although he owned a few slaves, he strongly supported Van Buren's free-soil presidential candidacy. He was certain that slavery should not go to the territories taken from Mexico and believed that Southern radicals led by John C. Calhoun were misrepresenting the issue to promote disunion. In 1850, like President Zachary Taylor, Blair opposed Henry Clay's compromise Omnibus Bill that tied the different slavery expansion issues into one bill, but approved the bills that finally passed one at a time. In 1852 he wrote pamphlets supporting the candidacy of Franklin Pierce, but was bitterly disappointed when Pierce gave much of the federal patronage to radical Southerners and promoted the Kansas-Nebraska Act, which repealed the Missouri Compromise and opened the western territories to slavery. He helped organize the new Republican Party that opposed the expansion of slavery, and when the abolitionist senator Charles Sumner was caned, Blair brought him to Silver Spring for recuperation. In 1856 Blair chaired the first Republican National Convention and was instrumental in securing the nomination of John C. Frémont for president. In a widely distributed pamphlet, "A Voice from the Grave of Jackson," he urged northwestern Democrats to vote for Frémont and argued that if Jackson were alive he would be a Republican.

Blair's son Montgomery was the attorney for Dred Scott when the Supreme Court ruled that the Missouri Compromise was unconstitutional, and his son Frank was a congressman from Missouri who made eloquent speeches advocating abolition and repatriation of the slaves to Latin America. Father and sons were influential delegates at the 1860 Republican Convention and were rewarded when Lincoln appointed Montgomery Blair postmaster general. Throughout Lincoln's presidency, Lincoln and Francis P. Blair were close friends and confidants. Blair argued passionately with Lincoln for reinforcing Fort Sumter, and Montgomery Blair was at first the only cabinet member opposed to its surrender. The Blairs persuaded Lincoln to make Frémont the western commander, and helped get Frémont relieved when he proved incompetent and rebellious. Frank Blair performed heroically as a general under Sherman, but returned to Congress briefly in 1864 to make speeches that destroyed Salmon P. Chase's effort to supplant Lincoln as the 1864 candidate. The Emancipation Proclamation did not apply to Maryland, but Blair immediately freed his slaves and supported the emancipation movement in Maryland.

By supporting Lincoln's cautious approach to abolition and reconstruction, the Blairs by 1864 had acquired

numerous enemies. In September, at Blair's suggestion, his son Montgomery resigned from Lincoln's cabinet as part of the price for Frémont's withdrawal as a radical presidential candidate, but the Blairs and Lincolns remained close. In December 1864, with Lincoln's approval, Blair went to Richmond twice to implore Jefferson Davis to accept abolition and make peace. He brought back valuable information and his efforts led to a subsequent conference between Lincoln and Confederate vice president Alexander H. Stephens at Hampton Roads, Virginia. Blair's daughter Elizabeth Lee remained with Mary Lincoln almost night and day for a month after her tragic bereavement.

After the war, the Blairs favored an easy reconstruction process that would not threaten states' rights or white supremacy, and they soon broke with the Republicans. In 1868 Frank Blair was the Democratic vice presidential candidate and in 1871 he was elected to the Senate. In 1875, however, Frank died, and his broken-hearted father followed a year later on 18 October.

As a partisan editor, Blair exaggerated both the egalitarianism of the Democrats and the elitism of the Whigs, but by glorifying democracy as the national ideal and by identifying the immensely popular Jackson with a coherent democratic philosophy, he contributed to the national spirit that enabled Lincoln to save the Union in 1861. On the Texas issue he sacrificed personal advantage for principle, and he worked tirelessly and effectively to prevent the expansion of slavery and preserve the American Union. His Pennsylvania Avenue home in Washington, D.C., still serves as a guest house for visiting foreign dignitaries.

—*Elbert B. Smith*

See also Blair, Francis Preston, Jr.; Blair, Montgomery.

For further reading:

Laas, Virginia J., ed. *Wartime Washington: The Civil War Letters of Elizabeth Blair Lee* (1991).
Smith, Elbert B. *Francis Preston Blair* (1980).
Smith, William E. *The Francis Preston Blair Family in Politics* (1933; reprint, 1969).

BLAIR, FRANCIS PRESTON, JR.
(1821–1875)

Union general; U.S. congressman, senator, and vice presidential candidate.

The youngest and most spectacular son of Francis P. Blair, Francis Preston (Frank) Blair, Jr., was born at Lexington, Kentucky, on 19 February 1821. Extremely energetic, spoiled, and rebellious, he was expelled from Yale and the University of North Carolina for misconduct, and he finished at Princeton in 1841 without graduating because of a wild party during his final week. Through the intervention of Joseph Henry,

the degree was granted a year later. In 1842, after studying law at Transylvania University, Francis joined his brother Montgomery in St. Louis as another protege of Senator Thomas Hart Benton, who dubbed him the "Young Ajax." He was traveling in the Rocky Mountains when the Mexican-American War began and was at Bent's Fort in New Mexico when the area was conquered bloodlessly by General Stephen Kearny. Appointed by Kearny to be attorney general for the territory, he helped write a legal code and successfully prosecuted numerous criminals, as well as a handful of Mexican leaders convicted of treason for stirring up a final resistance.

In 1847 he married Apolline Alexander, who ultimately produced eight children and patiently endured his extravagance and constant financial misfortunes. In 1848 he established a free-soil newspaper in St. Louis and supported Martin Van Buren for president, despite the opposition of Benton. In 1849, when Blair was working for Benton's reelection, an assassin fired at him on a dark street. Serving in the Missouri legislature, 1852–1856, he vigorously opposed the extension of slavery, although he owned a handful of house servants, and in 1856 he supported the Republican John C. Frémont for president and was the only free-soil advocate elected to the U.S. Congress from a slave state. In Congress he urged the South to abolish slavery gradually, and argued that North and South should cooperate in a program of deportation and colonization of the slaves in Central America. In a widely published speech, "The Destiny of the Races on this Continent," he argued that while the Africans were a social and political burden to white society in the United States, they would raise the level of political life in Latin America because of their previous association with the democracy of the United States. Above all, he insisted, while slavery must go, miscegenation and the inevitable domination of the freedmen by whites would also threaten American democracy. Blair echoed the racial prejudice that dominated the thinking of most Americans, both North and South, but he at least recognized slavery and racial adjustment as national problems to be solved by sectional cooperation rather than merely a sin to be eliminated by the South with no assistance in the process.

Defeated by proslavery Democrats in 1858, Blair began organizing Union supporters in St. Louis. In 1860 he campaigned tirelessly for Lincoln and was again elected to Congress, where he became chairman of the Military Affairs Committee. Dividing his time between St. Louis and Washington, he and General Nathaniel Lyon organized Missouri's pro-Union forces and rescued the Federal arsenal that was being threatened by Confederate sympathizers.

His efforts were a major factor in keeping Missouri from seceding. He helped persuade Lincoln to make his long-time friend John C. Frémont the western commander with headquarters in St. Louis, but when the inexperienced Frémont proved ineffective, Blair contributed to and supported Lincoln's decision to relieve him.

In 1862 Blair recruited seven regiments in Missouri and was appointed brigadier general. Ulysses S. Grant and William T. Sherman were usually contemptuous of political generals, but Blair won their respect and high praise as a fearless and effective leader at Vicksburg and other battles. He was promoted to major general and was a top commander for Sherman on the latter's March through Georgia.

At one point in 1864 Blair resigned from the army long enough to make a blistering speech in Congress against the congressional radicals and the presidential ambitions of Treasury Secretary Salmon P. Chase. Having forced Chase to reaffirm his loyalty to Lincoln, Blair resumed his commission and rejoined Sherman in Georgia.

After the war, Blair supported Andrew Johnson's efforts to prevent a radical Reconstruction. He opposed black suffrage, the disfranchising of Southern whites, and the establishment of military governments in the Southern states. He failed to win control of the Missouri Republican Party from the radicals and switched back to the Democratic Party. In 1868 he was the Democratic candidate for vice president. Horatio Seymour, the presidential candidate, tried to soft-pedal the issue of Reconstruction, but Blair probably lost votes for the party by publicly demanding a complete reversal of the ongoing Reconstruction process.

In 1869 Blair forged an alliance between Missouri Democrats and liberal Republicans that won control of the Missouri state government. He was elected to the state legislature and in 1870 was chosen to fill an unexpired term in the U.S. Senate. In 1872, however, he was defeated for reelection. He was preparing for future battles, but suffered a stroke and did not recover. He learned to write painfully with his left hand, and continued his political efforts, but slowly lost ground and died on 9 July 1875.

Except for his widely shared racial attitudes, Frank Blair was a strong force for American democracy. His political campaigns invariably gave the voters clear-cut and unmistakable alternatives. Representing a slave-holding state, he fearlessly called for the abolition of slavery and the preservation of the Union. By keeping Missouri in the Union, supporting Lincoln against all comers, and serving with great military ability, he contributed significantly to the emergence of a better America, even though he opposed the developments his own efforts had helped make inevitable.

—*Elbert B. Smith*

See also Blair, Francis Preston; Blair, Montgomery; Election of 1864.

For further reading:
Laas, Virginia J., ed. *Wartime Washington: The Civil War Letters of Elizabeth Blair Lee* (1991).
Parrish, William E. *Frank Blair: Lincoln's Conservative* (1998).
Smith, Elbert B. *Francis Preston Blair* (1980).
Smith, William E. *The Francis Preston Blair Family in Politics* (1933; reprints 1969).

BLAIR, MONTGOMERY
(1813–1883)
U.S. postmaster general

Eldest son of Francis P. Blair and postmaster general in the cabinet of Abraham Lincoln, Montgomery Blair was born in Franklin County, Kentucky, on 10 May 1813, and grew to manhood thoroughly imbued with his father's democratic political principles. When his father moved to Washington in 1830 to edit Andrew Jackson's official party newspaper, Montgomery was enthralled by Jackson, who persuaded him to attend West Point. There he did well academically, but he disliked the academy intensely because of what he considered its favoritism, the low demands made upon its cadets, and the lazy and immoral habits of his fellow students.

He graduated in 1835 and served for a few months during the Second Seminole War in Florida, but then resigned from the army and studied law at Transylvania University. In 1837 he began practicing law in St. Louis as a protegé of Senator Thomas Hart Benton. His law practice and investments prospered, and he easily assumed the role of financial adviser to his father and brothers, none of whom possessed his business acumen. He served as U.S. district attorney for Missouri (1839–1841), mayor of St. Louis (1842–1843), and judge of the Court of Common Pleas (1845–1849). In 1848 he defied Benton and supported the Free Soil Party presidential candidacy of Martin Van Buren.

In 1844 his first wife, Elizabeth Buckner, died in childbirth, and in 1846 he married Mary Elizabeth Woodbury, daughter of former Treasury Secretary Levi Woodbury. In 1853 he moved back to the Washington area, where his law practice soon gained a national reputation. In 1857 he wrote a forty-page brief and argued brilliantly, though unsuccessfully, for Dred Scott's freedom in the famous Supreme Court case that resulted in a verdict denying either the Federal government or any territorial government the right to prevent slavery in any territory.

In 1856 Blair strongly supported the presidential campaign of John C. Frémont and the free-soil Republican Party. Earlier he had done much to straighten out Frémont's financial affairs. Frémont was defeated, but the Blairs played an important role in bringing former Jacksonian Democrats into the new party.

In 1860 the Blairs helped nominate Abraham Lincoln and were rewarded with Montgomery's appointment as postmaster general. Lincoln's immediate problem was how to retain the major Federal forts situated in the seceded Southern states. Fort Sumter, located in Charleston Harbor, was particularly vulnerable and highly symbolic. At first every cabinet member except Blair urged that Lincoln abandon it rather than risk a war. Blair, however, argued that only a show of firm strength could prevent a war, and cited the example of Jackson's victory over Nullification in 1832. He brought his brother-in-law, Gustavus Fox, a former naval officer, to Lincoln with an elaborate plan for reinforcing the fort. Lincoln agreed and Fox sailed for Charleston, but the Confederates attacked the fort before Fox's expedition could enter the harbor.

Lincoln's cabinet was bitterly divided between radicals like Chase and Stanton, who wanted immediate emancipation, and moderates like Blair, Welles, and Seward, who argued that the war must be won first by avoiding policies that might induce the border slave states to secede. The Blairs had originally persuaded Lincoln to give the western command to John C. Frémont, the radicals' favorite general, but they ultimately recommended his dismissal for incompetence and because, without authority, he had issued an emancipation proclamation for Missouri. When Lincoln relieved Frémont, the radicals were furious.

When the Union army was demoralized by the defeat of General John Pope at Second Bull Run, only Blair supported Lincoln's decision that George McClellan was the best hope for restoring morale. Blair considered McClellan the best commander from a political viewpoint, but ultimately agreed with Lincoln that McClellan lacked the aggressiveness needed for military success.

When Lincoln first informed his cabinet that an emancipation proclamation would be forthcoming, Blair approved, but urged a delay until after the upcoming elections. Lincoln did wait two more months, but, as Blair had feared, the proclamation cost the administration heavily in the northwestern state elections.

For Lincoln, Blair's supreme virtue was unselfish loyalty. In 1864 the Radical Republicans nominated Frémont for president, while the Democrats chose General McClellan and a platform calling for a negotiated peace. A Frémont vote large enough to give some key states to McClellan was a real possibility. Aware of the bitter personal animosity felt toward himself by Frémont and the radicals, Blair privately offered to resign if it would help induce Frémont to withdraw. Assuring Blair of his personal respect and gratitude, Lincoln accepted the offer, and Blair's resignation was an important part of Frémont's decision to withdraw. Blair's affection and support for Lincoln never wavered.

The office of postmaster general has usually been that of political manager, with subordinates actually managing the department. Montgomery Blair, however, took personal charge. He originated new practices such as requiring postage from the sender, free mail delivery, the sorting of mail on railway cars, the return-receipt system of accountability, and the money order system, which he developed as a means for soldiers to send and receive money. He organized a highly efficient postal system for the army and navy, and abolished the franking privilege for postmasters. In 1863 he sponsored the first International Postal Congress at Paris. The modern postal system was in large part his creation.

After the Civil War, Blair supported President Andrew Johnson's efforts to maintain Southern white supremacy and avoid harsh measures against the South. He agitated unsuccessfully for colonization of the freedmen. After the disputed presidential election of 1876, Blair established a newspaper to support Democrat Samuel J. Tilden's claim to the presidency, and represented Tilden before the electoral commission appointed to render the verdict. He was elected to the Maryland House of Delegates in 1878, but was defeated for Congress in 1882. He died on 27 July 1883.

—*Elbert B. Smith*

See also Blair, Francis Preston; Blair, Francis Preston, Jr.; Election of 1864.

For further reading:
Laas, Virginia J., ed. *Wartime Washington: The Civil War Letters of Elizabeth Blair Lee* (1991).
Monroney, Rita. *Montgomery Blair: Postmaster General* (1963).
Smith, Elbert B. *Francis Preston Blair* (1980).
Smith, William E. *The Francis Preston Blair Family In Politics* (1933; reprint, 1969).

BLAKELY, ALABAMA, BATTLE OF
(9 April 1865)

The Federal assault on Mobile, Alabama, began in August 1864 with David Farragut's victory in Mobile Bay. While that action effectively closed the port, the city itself remained in Confederate hands until the end of the war. Situated on the upper west side of Mobile Bay, the city of Mobile was protected on the west by heavy fortifications and across the bay to the east by Batteries Huger and Tracy and two fortifications, Spanish Fort and Fort Blakely.

In spring 1865, Ulysses S. Grant's coordinated offensive envisioned pressing the Confederacy at as many points as possible and thus a sizeable Federal army commanded by Major General E. R. S. Canby again seriously menaced Mobile. With the intention of reducing the Confederate forts on the east side of Mobile Bay and thus opening the Tensas and Alabama rivers, Canby hoped also to force Mobile's surrender.

Two columns would mount the attack. The main one moved by water and had Spanish Fort as its objective. The second, a smaller force under Major General Frederick Steele, moved out of Pensacola on 19 March, ultimately to head for Fort Blakely. First, however, Steele sent part of his command north to threaten Montgomery and Selma, while it covered cavalry units tearing up railroads. Steele had to cope with bad weather that plagued the early stages of the entire operation. Finally, low on supplies and sodden from heavy rains, his entire command turned west, reached Stockton, and from that place headed south to join operations on the east side of the bay.

On 1 April, Lieutenant Colonel Andrew B. Spurling's cavalry clashed with Confederates of the 46th Mississippi Infantry about five miles from Blakely at Sibley's Mills. Reinforced with additional cavalry and a regiment of African-American troops from Brigadier General John B. Hawkins's division, Spurling drove the Confederates out of their positions, losing only two men to the Confederate losses of seventy-five. One of the Federal casualties had been the result of a land mine exploding beneath a horse and rider. Steele compelled his prisoners "to dig up those remaining in this road." The next morning a Confederate attempt to retake the position failed when the African-American regiment resolutely held. The Confederates then withdrew into their works at Blakely.

By 5 April, an extended Federal line had invested both Blakely and Spanish Fort. The following day the siege at Blakely was pressed with skirmishing all along the Confederate works. The Union right was especially annoyed by enfilading barrages directed from the CSS *Nashville* stationed in the mouth of the Raft River. As for the defenders at Blakely, Brigadier General St. John R. Liddell knew that his 4,000 men could not long resist a force three times larger. When Spanish Fort fell on 8 April and Canby was able to shift guns and men from that place to Blakely, Liddell's cause became hopeless. He surveyed a Federal line of 45,000 men that was four miles long. On its right was Hawkins's division of African-Americans, then two brigades of Brigadier General Christopher C. Andrews's division spanning to James C. Veatch's division, which was linked to Kenner Garrard on the far left. A division of XIII Corps and two from XVI Corps supported the flanks, and an abundance of siege guns and field pieces were put into position.

Late on the afternoon of 9 April an assault conducted by 16,000 men got underway. It took twenty minutes to overwhelm the nine redoubts, rifle pits, and palisades that constituted the defenses of Fort Blakely. The bluecoats stumbled over broken ground obstructed by telegraph wire entanglements and made more treacherous by buried land mines. The action cost them more than 600 casualties, a hundred of whom were killed and thus would never know that they had fallen the day Robert E. Lee surrendered at Appomattox. In the last desperate moments, Liddell led a tattered group of refugees to the shore of the bay as Lieutenant John W. Bennett brought in the *Nashville* to rescue as many Confederates as he could. Boats could only collect about 200 from the water, however, before Union sharpshooters drove them off. Liddell remained on shore and was captured along with more than 3,000 of his garrison.

Batteries Huger and Tracy were abandoned, and finally Federal troops occupied Mobile, one of the last cities of the Confederacy to fall. In less than a month, Richard Taylor would surrender those of the city's garrison who had escaped northward. They had the distinction of having tried to resist the last joint Federal operation of the American Civil War.

—*David S. Heidler and Jeanne T. Heidler*

See also Canby, Edward R. S.; Garrard, Kenner; Hawkins, John Parker; Mobile Bay; Mobile Campaign; Spanish Fort, Battle of; Steele, Frederick.

For further reading:

Hearn, Chester G. *Mobile Bay and the Mobile Campaign: The Last Great Battles of the Civil War* (1993).

Heyman, Max L. *Prudent Soldier: A Biography of Major General E. R. S. Canby, 1817–1873* (1959).

Maury, Dabney H. *Recollections of a Virginian in the Mexican, Indian, and Civil Wars* (1894).

Parker, Prescott A. *Story of the Tensaw: Blakely, Spanish Fort, Jackson Oaks, Fort Mims* (1922).

BLOCKADE OF THE C.S.A.

On 19 April 1861, President Abraham Lincoln announced a blockade of South Carolina, Georgia, Florida, Alabama, Mississippi, Louisiana, and Texas. Implementation began seven days later, as the Union navy began its blockading operations. On 27 April 1861, Lincoln extended the blockade to Virginia and North Carolina.

In implementing the blockade, the Union grappled with a fundamental contradiction. The North maintained throughout the war that the Confederate States of America did not exist—that the Federal government faced merely a domestic insurrection. If that was indeed the case, foreign governments had no justification for recognizing or aiding the Confederacy. But at the same time, if the Confederate States did not exist, could the Union legally blockade its own southern coastline? Secretary of the Navy Gideon Welles, taking such legal complications seriously, personally opposed initiating a blockade, favoring instead a policy of "closing" Southern ports, a traditional technique in times of domestic insurrection. Yet for practical military, political, and diplomatic advantages, President Lincoln and Secretary of State William H. Seward chose to ignore the legal technicalities of the issue and continued to maintain both positions—that the Confederate States did not in fact exist but that the Union could blockade the coastline anyway—throughout the war.

Lincoln's proclamation of the blockade created practical problems for both the Union and Confederate governments. With only a handful of ships available to blockade 3,000 miles of coastline, the Union faced the challenge of turning a paper blockade into a real one. At breakneck speed, therefore, Secretary of the Navy Gideon Welles proceeded to create a massive fleet by buying or commandeering virtually every vessel available—including ferry boats—and beginning a shipbuilding program that was to bear fruit later in the war. In addition, four blockading fleets were created: the North Atlantic, South Atlantic, East Gulf, and West Gulf blockading squadrons.

For the Confederacy, the problem was how to break a blockade without a fleet. The solution was to take advantage of the new technologies of naval warfare, such as rifled guns, armored vessels, commerce destruction, and submarine weapons.

Blockade running was triangular, with its three main corners at the South, the West Indies, and Europe (or sometimes even the North itself). Because of its proximity to the Confederacy, Nassau, Bahamas, was the headquarters of blockade-running operations. Other common destinations included Bermuda, St. Thomas, Havana, Jamaica, and Nova Scotia.

Nassau, in particular, grew wealthy because of the wartime trade with the Confederacy, in part because British colonial officials permitted blockade running to thrive, and indeed encouraged it. On rare occasions when the local government acted to stop a blockade runner, the action was half-hearted at best. The trade out of Nassau continued at full strength until the late fall of 1864, when Havana became the primary port and most of the trade began to head for Gulf ports. Major Confederate ports for blockade runners included Wilmington, North Carolina; Charleston, South Carolina; Savannah, Georgia; Mobile, Alabama; and, especially in the last year of the war when other ports had been closed, Galveston, Texas.

About 92 percent of all the attempts to run the blockade succeeded. (From a Northern perspective, then, the blockade was only about 8 percent effective.) However, the rate of success for blockade running declined significantly as the war progressed and the blockade itself became more effective. Some 300 steamers tested the blockade during four years of war. Of 1,300 attempts, 1,000 were successful. The average career of a blockade-running vessel was typically only about two round trips, but because of high profits there was always capital to construct new vessels. Innovative designs were developed for vessels constructed specifically for the purpose; a typical blockade runner was small and low with a shallow draft, equipped with collapsible funnels, and capable of considerable speed. Whenever possible it used clean-burning anthracite coal

Although Secretary of the Navy Welles had originally opposed the blockade, he implemented the policy vigorously and encouraged aggressive naval actions that resulted in diplomatic conflicts. Union naval officers were sometimes overzealous in pursuing their blockading duty, and insensitive to issues of belligerent and neutral rights, so that Union naval interference with neutral shipping was a source of friction with both shippers and foreign governments. Not only zeal, but the vagueness of their instructions from Welles, frequently saw Union officers failing to observe the niceties of international law. They sometimes entered colonial ports without permission or sometimes hovered beyond the three-mile limit outside colonial ports, waiting for Confederate blockade runners or cruisers. Such practices in effect established an illegal blockade of a neutral port. In other instances, Union warships harassed or detained neutral ships suspected of having the Confederacy as their ultimate destination. Union warships often acted before checking the requirements of international law and occasionally fired on foreign merchant vessels, not all of which were carrying contraband to the Confederacy. The problem continued throughout the war, despite efforts after mid-1863 to be more scrupulous in observing neutral rights.

Enforcement of the blockade, in short, presented many practical challenges for the Union. The State Department had two goals, which occasionally conflicted with each other: halting or curtailing Confederate blockade running and cruiser activity, and avoiding diplomatic conflict with other nations. Thus, electing to institute and maintain a blockade was one thing, but making it work was another. One of the main difficulties was simply how to tell a blockade runner from a legitimate vessel. One method was the "rule-of-thumb" approach, a combination of intuition and physical and circumstantial evidence. Although it was not foolproof, captures under the "rule of thumb" usually stood the tests of prize courts.

Standard shipping regulations and new rules imposed by the United States in reaction to blockade running provided some basic standards for judging a voyage's legitimacy. Clues to illegal intentions included an incorrect type of license, the lack of appropriate papers (sometimes a vessel had been robbed of its papers), forged clearance papers, or papers whose evident purpose was to hide the origin or ultimate destination of a vessel. If a ship flew a Confederate flag there was no question, but if it flew a neutral flag, the Union navy had to determine if the flag itself was legitimate or simply an ensign hoisted temporarily to avoid capture. Such tasks fell, according to accepted international law, under the legitimate rights of a belligerent warship.

Despite the occasionally excessive energy with which Union squadrons enforced the blockade, their efforts were never enough to stem completely the flow of cotton out of the Confederacy or manufactured goods into it. Vessels broke the blockade throughout the war, but statistics suggest that the blockade became increasingly effective as the war progressed. In addition, the blockade's very existence probably dissuaded some shippers from even attempting to reach the Confederacy.

Successful blockade runners got Southern products to their international markets and brought in some of the materials that the South desperately needed. Typical cargoes on inward-bound runs were arms, ammunition, and other essential war products, in addition to luxury goods for wealthy Southerners. In exchange, Confederate traders were able to provide tobacco and, especially, cotton to other countries. In all, the trade was very profitable, and because Confederate cruisers and commerce raiders posed a more direct threat to Northern security, restricting those activities was more important to the Union war effort than was the ending of blockade running.

In the end, however, the blockade was significant for military, diplomatic, and economic reasons. Enforcing the blockade took Union warships away from other naval activity. Enforcement also made diplomatic conflict almost inevitable, particularly with Great Britain. In effect, the blockade and blockade running increased the difficulty of maintaining Anglo-American stability, the goal of both the United States and Great Britain throughout the war. From an economic perspective, the blockade—regardless of how many vessels did or did not manage to break it—choked the South. The Confederacy was not a self-sufficient nation and desperately needed the economic contacts with the outside world that the blockade made increasingly difficult. On the other hand, from the Northern perspective, the blockade contributed to economic woes by the disruption of normal shipping that characterized the war years.

—*Kenneth J. Blume*

See also Blockade Runners; Diplomacy, U.S.A.; Great Britain; Navy, U.S.A.; Prize Cases.

For further reading:

Bradlee, Francis B. C. *Blockade Running During the Civil War and the Effect of Land and Water Transportation on the Confederacy* (1925).

Dalzel, George W. *The Flight from the Flag: The Continuing Effect of the Civil War upon the American Carrying Trade* (1940).

Silverstone, Paul H. *Warships of the Civil War Navies* (1989).

Soley, James Russell. *The Blockade and the Cruisers* (1887).

Wise, Stephen R. *Lifeline of the Confederacy. Blockade Running During the Civil War* (1988).

BLOCKADE RUNNERS

Blockade runners were ships that attempted to elude the Union naval blockade of the South. The most successful and famous were swift, shallow-draft steamers, many of which were specially built in Britain. Lacking an industrial base, the South was dependent on weapons, ammunition, machinery, cloth, medicine, and food run through the blockade. In Confederate soldiers' slang, "running the blockade" also referred to slipping in or out of camp without permission.

President Lincoln proclaimed a Union blockade of Southern ports on 19 April 1861, and the first capture of a blockade runner seems to have been made by the USS *Cumberland* off Virginia on 24 April. Yet until the Union could recall ships in foreign ports and buy or build new naval vessels, the blockade existed mostly on paper. An unofficial Southern boycott of cotton exports to Europe both failed to induce foreign intervention and lost the South valuable opportunities for importing necessities before the blockade tightened.

Early blockade runners were a motley collection of sloops, schooners, and small steamers that set out from many Southern ports. The racing yacht *America*, namesake of the America's Cup, was a blockade runner early in the war. Sailing vessels were soon replaced by steamships everywhere, except they retained some use in the Gulf of Mexico and as smuggling vessels on the East Coast. The first steam blockade runner to reach the South was the Fraser, Trenholm and Company's *Bermuda*, which entered Savannah from Liverpool on 18 September 1861. Her military cargo included four large seacoast guns. Much of the cargo was sold at auction. The *Bermuda* left Savannah on 29 October, and its cargo of 2,000 bales of cotton was sold in Britain at a fantastic profit.

Pointing to their great risks, owners of blockade runners such as the *Bermuda* charged tremendous prices. Cotton could be bought in the South and sold for ten times the cost in England. Freight charges and profits on outgoing cotton and incoming luxury merchandise could pay for a fine new steamer in one trip. Although private Southern and foreign firms owned many blockade runners, the Confederate government and the states of North Carolina and Georgia also bought their own ships. Major blockade-running firms included Fraser, Trenholm and Company and the related firm of John Fraser and Company, as well as Crenshaw and Collie and Company, and Edward Lawrence and Company. Yet many blockade runners were owned by small companies that held only one or two ships. Later in the war, the Confederacy regulated blockade running and required all vessels to reserve half their cargo space for government shipments at a set rate.

The South's major blockade-running ports were the Atlantic ports of Wilmington and Charleston, and the Gulf of Mexico ports of Mobile and Galveston. Other major ports were blocked or captured by Union forces early in the war. Some blockade runners used St. Mark's, Florida, and other minor ports. Charleston was the major port until the fall of Morris Island in summer 1863 exposed the harbor entrance to Union artillery fire. Most operations shifted to Wilmington for the rest of the

Wreck of the British-built blockade runner *Ruby*, run aground on Folly Island, South Carolina, 10–11 June 1863
(*Library of Congress*)

war. Wilmington, on the Cape Fear River, was admirably suited as a blockade-running port because Smith Island and the long and dangerous Frying Pan Shoals divided the mouth of the Cape Fear. Runners had two major approaches to the port, requiring the Union to maintain two separate blockading squadrons. Fort Fisher (the strongest fortification in the South) and other posts armed with long-range rifled guns kept the blockaders a considerable distance out to sea and saved many a blockade runner.

Blockade runners from Wilmington and Charleston typically tried to reach Nassau, Bahamas, or St. George, Bermuda. Goods brought from Europe in large deep-draft ships were transferred to fast shallow-draft vessels for the final dash to the South. Some trips were made to Halifax, Nova Scotia, during an outbreak of yellow fever in 1864. Blockade runners from the Gulf ports nearly always ran to Havana.

As the Union blockade tightened, blockade running companies began to purchase better ships. "Clyde steamers," modern coastal passenger boats built on Scotland's Clyde River, were popular by 1862. Companies soon built specially designed blockade runners. They usually were long, low, narrow-beamed and shallow-draft ships. They were painted dull white or light gray for camouflage, their masts were often hinged or set into sockets so they could be quickly lowered, and

the ships' boats were kept below the gunwales. They burned smokeless coal to avoid detection, and had special pipes for blowing off steam underwater. Staterooms were torn out and cargo space was expanded as much as possible. Outgoing runners might carry 600 to 800 bales of tightly pressed cotton, crammed into every space and piled high atop the decks. Although the Confederate government pressed for the importation of military supplies, medicines, food, and other necessities, private companies preferred to bring in highly profitable luxury items. Cigars, pepper, soap, laces, silks, and fine liquors and wines were popular imports.

Many crewmen were British or Irish, and the officers ranged from Confederate naval officers to British merchant ship or naval officers. Captured Confederates faced long spells in Northern prisons, but British subjects were usually released quickly. Pay rates reflected the high profits. Civilian captains could earn $5,000 in gold for a successful run from the Carolina ports, and even crewmen earned $250 or more per round trip. Officers could carry goods to sell on their own account. Confederate naval personnel on blockade runners received their regular monthly pay, but in gold.

Blockade runners usually departed on moonless nights. With their low profiles, smokeless coal, and camouflage paint, a blockade runner could slip by an

The USS *Fort Donelson* (the former Confederate blockade runner *Robert E. Lee*) at Norfolk, Virginia, December 1864
(*Library of Congress*)

enemy ship as little as a hundred yards away. Their speed enabled them to outrun nearly all pursuers except blockade runners that had been captured and put into Union service. Union sailors were eligible for prize money for capturing blockade runners. Some captured ships were added to the Union navy, while others were sold to private interests, which often put them back into blockade running. Under international law, a "neutral" blockade runner could not fire a shot in its defense without making its crew guilty of piracy and subject to hanging. Captures of blockade runners increased later in the war.

The Union navy's efficiency was increased by adding the swiftest blockade runners to its fleet. Pilots, needed to negotiate the intricate and dangerous shoals at Wilmington and Charleston, became scarce, as captured ones were never exchanged. Wilmington was lost to blockade running with the fall of Fort Fisher on 15 January 1865, and Charleston was evacuated on 17 February. Blockade running shifted to Galveston and the Gulf ports for a few final months. The last steam blockade runner to leave a Southern port, the *Lark*, left Galveston on 24 May 1865. President Johnson officially lifted the blockade on 23 June.

During the war, about 300 steamers attempted to run the blockade. Of these, 136 were captured and 85 were destroyed. Altogether about 1,000 out of 1,300 attempted runs were successful. The *Syren* held the

record with thirty-three successful round trips; the *Denbigh* with twenty-six was second. One of the last surviving blockade runners, the *Chicora*, operated as a Great Lakes excursion boat until 1919.

Supplies run through the blockade were crucial to the South's war effort. The Army of Northern Virginia was so dependent on imports of food and munitions through Wilmington that Lee said his army could not survive if that port fell. Blockade runners brought in about 60 percent of the South's modern small arms; a third of their lead; and two-thirds of their saltpeter necessary for gunpowder production. Uniforms, cloth, artillery pieces and ammunition, medicine, and great amounts of food also came through the blockade. Sales of cotton brought the Confederacy much-needed money and credit from Britain and France.

—*David A. Norris*

See also Blockade of C.S.A.
For further reading:
Hobart-Hampden, C. Augustus. *Never Caught: Personal Adventures Connected with Twelve Successful Trips in Blockade-Running During the American Civil War, 1863–4* (1900; reprint, 1967).
Taylor, Thomas E. *Running the Blockade* (1995).
Vandiver, Frank E., ed. *Confederate Blockade Running through Bermuda 1861-1865: Letters and Cargo Manifests* (1947).
Wilkinson, John. *The Narrative of a Blockade-Runner* (1877; reprint, 1984).
Wise, Stephen R. *Lifeline of the Confederacy Blockade Running During the Civil War* (1988).

BLUNT, JAMES GILPATRICK
(1826–1881)
Union general

Blunt was a leader of Union forces in the Trans-Mississippi and played a significant role in the battles of Old Fort Wayne, Cane Hill, Honey Springs, Prairie Grove, and Westport.

Blunt was born on 21 July 1826 in Trenton, Maine. Drawn to the sea at age fifteen, Blunt rose to the rank of captain in the merchant marine after five years. Eventually, Blunt moved to Columbus, Ohio, where he earned a degree from Starling Medical College in 1849. He set up a practice in New Madison, Ohio, before moving west and settling in Greeley, Kansas, in 1856. An ardent abolitionist, he aided John Brown in helping escaped slaves make their way to Canada. In Greeley, Blunt became active in Kansas politics. He participated in the Wyandotte Constitutional Convention in 1859, chairing the committee on militia.

Blunt's military career began as a Jayhawker, commanding cavalry in Senator James H. Lane's "Kansas Brigade." Blunt was commissioned a lieutenant colonel in the 3d Kansas Infantry in July 1861. After promotion to brigadier general of U.S. Volunteers on 8 April 1861, Blunt headed the Department of Kansas from 15 May to 19 September 1862 and defeated a mixed Confederate–Native American force under Colonel (later Brigadier General) Douglas H. Cooper at Old Fort Wayne, Indian Territory, in October 1862.

After Blunt's assignment to command of the 1st Division of the Army of the Frontier in October, he defeated Brigadier General John S. Marmaduke in a sharp action at Cane Hill, Arkansas, on 28 November 1862. Blunt, who was promoted to major general the day after his victory, vigorously pursued Marmaduke and dangerously isolated his command from the 2d and 3d Divisions of the Army of the Frontier that were located in Springfield, Missouri, more than 100 miles away. Confederate major general Thomas C. Hindman saw an opportunity for his I Corps, Army of the Trans-Mississippi, to crush Blunt's isolated division and then possibly invade Missouri and defeat the remainder of the Union army. Hindman's plans were foiled by the superhuman efforts of the 2d and 3d Divisions commanded by Brigadier General Francis J. Herron, who marched his troops a remarkable 110 miles in three days to reach Prairie Grove, Arkansas, to join Blunt. Hindman, fearful of Herron eight miles in his rear, ordered a night flanking march against him. Fighting erupted between Herron and Hindman on the afternoon of 7 December 1862. Hearing cannon fire, Blunt immediately marched to the sound of the guns. His timely arrival saved Herron's command. Tactically, the battle of Prairie Grove was a draw. Strategically,

however, the battle was a Union victory, as Confederate forces withdrew the next day over the Boston Mountains to Van Buren, Arkansas. Characteristically, Blunt aggressively hounded Hindman's forces to the Arkansas River and captured Van Buren shortly thereafter.

Blunt led the Army of the Frontier into Indian Territory in June 1863 and defeated a combined Indian-Confederate force led by Cooper at Honey Springs in early July. Blunt's military career suffered two successive jolts in October 1863, when William C. Quantrill's raiders surprised him and his headquarters staff outside Baxter Springs, Kansas. Because many of the Confederate bushwhackers were wearing captured blue uniforms, Blunt mistook them for Union soldiers. Blunt's group scattered and, of the roughly 100-man retinue, nearly 70 were hunted down and killed. Blunt managed to escape, but quarrels with his superior, Department of the Missouri head Brigadier General John M. Schofield, resulted in Blunt's being relieved of command.

Blunt's career seemed over as he bounced from one assignment to another until early 1864, when Major General Samuel R. Curtis was appointed to command the Department of Kansas. Curtis, who respected Blunt's military abilities and sympathized with his political leanings, placed him in command of the District of Southern Kansas. Blunt played a significant role under Curtis's command in the Army of the Border on 21–23 October 1864 during the battle of Westport, Missouri, which was part of Major General Sterling Price's Missouri Raid of 1864. After the Union victory, Blunt led an active pursuit of Price's forces. He mustered out of the service on 29 July 1865.

Blunt returned to Kansas after the war and resumed his medical practice. In 1869 he moved to Washington, D.C., where he became a solicitor of claims. Blunt, along with several others, was charged in 1873 by the Department of Justice with conspiracy to defraud the Cherokee Indians. The case was later dropped. Blunt was committed to a hospital for the mentally insane before he finally died on 27 July 1881. His remains were interred at Fort Leavenworth, Kansas.

For one who had no formal military training, Blunt was a remarkably successful army officer. He was aggressive to the point of recklessness, and at times this placed his command in precarious situations. While Blunt was aggressive, he was also lucky. At Prairie Grove, the remarkable march by Herron's troops rescued him from a difficult situation. Blunt may not have faced the top Confederate generals, but he deserves more credit than he is given. He served in the Trans-Mississippi, an under-staffed military backwater that Richmond seemed to abandon after the first year of the war. Blunt's aggressive personality and his politics sometimes made relations with his superiors difficult, but he did as well as could be expected with the resources and the men, including large numbers of African-Americans and Native Americans, allotted him.

—Terry L. Beckenbaugh

See also Baxter Springs; Cane Hill, Battle of; Honey Springs, Battle of; Prairie Grove, Battle of; Westport, Battle of.

For further reading:

Banasik, Michael E. *Embattled Arkansas: The Prairie Grove Campaign of 1862* (1996).

Castel, Albert E. *A Frontier State at War: Kansas, 1861–1865* (1958).

Josephy, Alvin M. *The Civil War in the American West* (1991).

Starr, Stephen Z. *Jennison's Jayhawkers: A Civil War Cavalry Regiment and Its Commander* (1973).

BONDS

The governments of both the Confederate States of America and the United States used bonds to finance their war efforts. The sale of bonds, which relies heavily on the investors' confidence in the strength of the government, fluctuated greatly depending on victories or defeats in the field.

Confederate States of America — The Confederacy's wealth was derived from land, the commodities produced on that land, and slaves. This financial structure, which lacks liquidity, proved to be incapable of meeting the sudden increase in expenses of a wartime economy. The Southerners had hoped that sales of their cotton and agricultural goods would provide ample fuel for the war machine, but the increasing effectiveness of the Union's blockade impeded trade; consequently, the flow of specie into Confederate coffers dwindled.

Within three weeks of the formation of the government, the Confederate Congress authorized the first sale of bonds. Dubbed the "bankers' loan," this initial issue represented $15 million worth of ten-year bonds that paid 8 percent interest. This loan was fully subscribed, primarily through sales to banks and other financial institutions. It became apparent to Secretary of the Treasury Christopher Memminger that the dearth of specie available in the Confederacy could stifle future bond sales, so another device would have to be employed.

In May 1861, the Confederate government unveiled a new issue of $50 million in bonds that sold for "specie, military stores, or from the proceeds of sales of raw produce or manufactured articles." This "produce loan" opened the bond market to planters who were cotton rich, but capital poor. The issue was expanded to $100 million in August, and another $250 million in April 1862, but sales of the bonds lagged. As the price of cotton rose, planters preferred to hold their cotton,

hoping for greater future profits, rather than exchange it for the fixed value of a bond.

As the fiscal problems of the Confederacy grew, Memminger decided to look abroad for money. A Confederate agent in France negotiated the Erlanger loan in March 1863, a $15 million bond issue that was sold in European cities. The bonds were convertible for discounted cotton. The initial enthusiasm for this loan soured after Confederate defeats in Vicksburg and Gettysburg. Undaunted, Memminger tried to launch another $250 million bond issue in England in April 1863. The "cotton loan" comprised twenty-year bonds that paid 6 percent interest and were redeemable in discounted cotton or coin. The British showed great interest in these bonds until the Union's financial agent in London, the highly regarded Robert J. Walker, spread the rumor that Confederate president Jefferson Davis had been involved in a failed bond issue during the 1840s in which hundreds of British investors had lost money. Thereafter, Confederate bonds sold poorly in Europe.

Desperate for revenue, in 1864 the Confederate government announced a funded loan called the "One Billion Dollar" issue. These bonds were redeemable in twenty years, paid 6 percent interest that was tax free, and would be funded with a 5 percent tax on all property and mandatory contributions from each of the Confederate states. To encourage sales, public auctions were held throughout the Confederacy, but few investors materialized. Most regarded the announcement of this loan as an admission of bankruptcy. The Confederate treasury collapsed months before Lee's surrender at Appomattox.

In total, bonds paid for 23 percent of the Confederate finances during the war. The total funded debt accumulated by the Confederate states amounted to $712 million. All the bonds purchased by investors lost their value with the dissolution of the Confederate government after the South's defeat. All state bonds issued during the war were repudiated as one provision of the Fourteenth Amendment and readmission to the United States.

United States — The Union government faced a similar crisis in meeting the immediate expenses of the war. Unlike the Confederate states, the North had a better financial infrastructure upon which Secretary of the Treasury Salmon P. Chase could draw.

Chase strove to keep interest rates low, fearing that a massive debt would be laid for future generations. In his first loan negotiations, Chase alienated the banking community with his demands for specie and inflexibility regarding the terms of the bonds. When the need for a second issue arose in February 1862, Chase requested a $500 million issue of bonds bearing 6 percent interest, redeemable after five years and payable in twenty years. By the following December, only $23.7 million of the "5–20s" had been sold. As the unpaid requisitions accumulated and bankers continued to rebuff the secretary's calls for support, Chase took the unconventional step of turning to a sales agent to market the bonds directly to the American people. Chase hired Jay Cooke, a Philadelphia banker and financier, in October 1862. Cooke established a nationwide marketing system and sold $400 million of the 5–20s by December 1863.

Cooke's success did not alleviate the Union's financial problems. In March 1863, a $900 million loan was approved, $300 for the current fiscal year and $600 for the following year. The bonds paid no more than 6 percent interest and were redeemable in 10 years and payable in 40 years. Sensitive to congressional criticism of his cozy relationship with Cooke, Chase did not employ Cooke's services to sell the "10–40s." Instead, he tried to sell the issue through the new national banking system. Only $73 million of this issue was sold. Chase was forced to use the 10–40s to pay requisitions as well as the salaries for the troops.

In March 1864, another issue of the 5–20s was floated; concerned about the mounting debt, Chase tried selling the new bonds at a 5 percent interest rate. This strategy failed. Three months later, Chase resigned his position as secretary and was replaced by William Pitt Fessenden, a fiscal conservative. Fessenden was shocked by the state of the Treasury and resolved to rectify the financial crisis. He rehired Cooke and raised interest rates; immediately bond sales improved and fresh money flowed into the Treasury.

At the end of the war, the Union's debt amounted to $2.7 billion. Both the interest on the bonds and their redeemable value were to be paid in gold according to a provision of the initial legislation authorizing the bonds. With the depreciation of the greenbacks during the war and the rise in the price of gold, the value of the North's war bonds increased sharply. Whether to honor the bonds in gold, as stipulated originally, or redeem them in greenbacks became one of the most divisive political issues in the immediate postwar years.

—*Jane Flaherty*

See also Chase, Salmon P.; Cooke, Jay; Diplomacy, C.S.A.; Fessenden, William Pitt; Financing, C.S.A.; Financing, U.S.A.; Greenbacks; Memminger, Christopher.

For further reading:
Dewey, Davis R. *Financial History of the United States* (1939).
Gentry, Judith Fenner. "A Confederate Success in Europe: The Erlanger Loan." *Journal of Southern History* (1970).
Richardson, Heather Cox. *The Greatest Nation of the Earth: Republican Economic Policies during the Civil War* (1997).
Schwab, John C. *The Confederate States of America, 1861–65; A Financial and Industrial History of the South during the Civil War* (1901; reprint, 1968).
Todd, Richard Cecil. *Confederate Finance* (1954).

BONHAM, MILLEDGE LUKE
(1813–1890)
Confederate general; congressman and governor of South Carolina

Milledge Luke Bonham was born to James Bonham and Sophia Smith Bonham in Edgefield District, South Carolina. He was educated locally and at South Carolina College before studying law and opening a practice near his childhood home. Along with his successful law practice, Bonham also displayed an early interest in politics and the military. He took a brigade of South Carolina troops to Florida and fought during the Second Seminole War. Upon his return, he remained active in the state militia. With the outbreak of the Mexican-American War, Bonham accepted a commission as a lieutenant colonel and fought under volunteer officer Brigadier General Franklin Pierce.

Between these two wars, Bonham served in the South Carolina legislature. After the Mexican-American War, Bonham served as solicitor for the district court of southern South Carolina until 1857. In that year, he was selected to fill the unexpired congressional term of his deceased cousin Preston Brooks, who was notorious for his caning of Massachusetts senator Charles Sumner. Bonham, who like his cousin was a strong supporter of states' rights, remained in Congress until Abraham Lincoln's election in the fall of 1860.

After the secession of South Carolina, Bonham traveled to Mississippi to arrange cooperation between that state and South Carolina. Returning home, Bonham, with the rank of major general, became the commander of all South Carolina troops. The arrival of P. G. T. Beauregard in Charleston signaled Confederate command of all troops besieging Fort Sumter and caused Bonham to place himself under Beauregard and accept the rank of brigadier general in the Confederate army.

After the surrender of Fort Sumter, Bonham led South Carolina troops north with Beauregard to Virginia. Bonham commanded his brigade first around Richmond before moving north to Fairfax and Alexandria and then to Manassas Junction. He commanded his brigade defending the center of the Confederate line at First Bull Run.

In November 1861, Bonham allowed his name to be put forward as a candidate for the Confederate Congress from South Carolina. Already in a dispute with the Jefferson Davis administration over its policy of using previous service in the U.S. Army to determine seniority in the Confederate army, Bonham was probably already contemplating leaving the army. Upon his election, he used the seniority dispute as an excuse to resign his commission on 27 January 1862.

In the Confederate Congress, Bonham held to his states' rights views, particularly regarding the removal of state troops to far away places within the Confederacy. However, realizing the need for a strong central government in time of war, Bonham believed that the government should be granted exceptional powers regarding economic issues. Later that year, Bonham was elected governor of South Carolina, necessitating his resignation from Congress in January 1863 to assume his new duties.

As governor of South Carolina, Bonham's early concerns centered on the coastal defense of the state, particularly at Charleston. He worked closely with the Confederate army there, especially during the summer of 1863 when the Federal forces launched a campaign to take the city. He vigorously requisitioned the use of slaves to construct defenses around the city.

At the end of his term as governor in January 1865, Bonham, in the midst of William T. Sherman's invasion of the state, again offered his services to the Confederate army. Given a commission as a brigadier general of cavalry under Joseph E. Johnston, Bonham led his brigades in Johnston's fighting retreat through the Carolinas and surrendered with that army in April 1865.

After his parole, Bonham returned to South Carolina and his law practice. He was elected to the South Carolina legislature and served two years there. In 1868 he represented South Carolina at the Democratic National Convention. After the end of Reconstruction, Bonham worked with Governor Wade Hampton to restore white South Carolinian control of the state. For the remainder of his life, Bonham served as a state railroad commissioner. He died suddenly of a stroke on 27 August 1890.

—*David S. Heidler and Jeanne T. Heidler*

See also Bull Run, First Battle of; South Carolina.
For further reading:
"Papers of Francis W. Pickens and Milledge L. Bonham, 1837–1920." Library of Congress.

BOONEVILLE, MISSISSIPPI, BATTLE OF
(1 July 1862)

The little-known battle of Booneville, Mississippi, resulted from three months of Union activity in north Mississippi after the narrow Union victory at Shiloh in April 1862. The brisk Union victory at Booneville caused Confederate major general Braxton Bragg to proceed with caution as he tried to retake the important railroad junction at Corinth, Mississippi. It was also at this battle that Union colonel Philip Sheridan began to earn his reputation for boldness, aggressiveness, and tenaciousness. His "brilliant affair of our cavalry" led Major General Henry W. Halleck to recommend him for promotion to brigadier general.

The little town of Booneville, roughly twenty miles south of Corinth, lay near the Corinth-Chattanooga railroad line. After the battle of Shiloh, Confederate

brigadier general P. T. G. Beauregard slowly withdrew to Tupelo, Mississippi. Bragg assumed overall command and made plans to retake the important railroad junction at Corinth. A Union cavalry brigade under the command of Brigadier General Washington L. Elliot sought to cut the line of retreat for Beauregard's army during the month after the battle of Shiloh. Although this expedition lasted only a few days, Federal forces destroyed part of the railroad, burned military stores, and captured 1,000 men. During this activity, Halleck learned that the enemy had released all its prisoners captured at Shiloh due to food shortages. This information encouraged Halleck to order Federal cavalry to advance. In late June, Halleck ordered a general movement south. Union scouts and Confederate deserters reported Bragg preparing an advance using Beauregard's army. Sheridan established a fortified position at Booneville on 28 June and braced for an attack.

Four thousand seven hundred troopers under the immediate command of Confederate brigadier general James R. Chalmers merged a few miles southwest of Booneville from the towns of Tupelo and Saltillo. Confederate scouts made contact with Sheridan's pickets three and a half miles southwest of Booneville. On 1 July Federal pickets fell back, straddling where the Tupelo and Saltillo roads converged. Federal forces repelled Chalmers's initial charge due to good positions and the new Colt revolving rifle. Sheridan's pickets could not hold their ground against Chalmers's lead elements and withdrew again toward a secondary position about one and a half miles closer to town. Sheridan's advance guard arrived to support his pickets shortly thereafter.

Confederate forces tried to turn the Federal left flank, but the arrival of Sheridan's main force thwarted this attempt. Despite overwhelming odds, Sheridan made the bold move of ordering Captain Russell Alexander Alger's 2d Michigan cavalry to attack the Southern rear. The 2d Iowa cavalry, commanded by Lieutenant Colonel Edward Hatch, supported the attack by engaging the Southern left flank and part of its rear. The remaining Federal troops fought a holding action until Chalmers sounded the retreat around 3:30 P.M. Sheridan rallied his troops and pursued Chalmers for four miles before swampy terrain and fatigue stopped the Federals.

The battle lasted roughly eight hours, from 8:30 A.M. to 3:30 P.M. Confederate records for the engagement are scarce; of the 4,700 Confederates participating, Sheridan counted no fewer than 65 dead. Of the 728 Federal troops involved, there were 41 casualties: 1 killed, 24 wounded, and 16 missing.

The actual battle of Booneville was a small affair. It was part of a larger effort on the part of the Confederacy to recapture Corinth, an important railroad junction in the northern part of the Confederacy. Chalmers's defeat

caused Bragg to reevaluate his offensive plans, and gave time for Halleck to consolidate his forces for future operations. The battle was also a glimpse into the fighting abilities of Sheridan.

—David P. Eldridge

See also Corinth, Battle of; Corinth, Mississippi; Sheridan, Philip Henry.

For further reading:
Hutton, Paul A. *Phil Sheridan and His Army* (1985).
Robinson, Virgil, comp. *Booneville, Mississippi, in the Civil War: A Compilation of Information from Many Sources* (1998).
Sheridan, Philip. *Personal Memoirs of Philip Henry Sheridan, General of the U.S. Army.New and Enl. Ed. With an Account of his Life from 1871 to His Death, in 1888, by Brigadier-General Michael V. Sheridan* (1904).

BOONVILLE, MISSOURI, BATTLE OF
(17 June 1861)

After Union volunteers had secured St. Louis, Missouri, the prosecessionist governor of Missouri, Claiborne F. Jackson, called for 50,000 volunteers to form the so-called Missouri State Guard. Rather than encamping in or near the capital at Jefferson City, the Guard's commanding general, former Governor Sterling Price, decided to bivouac near Boonville, a village strategically situated on the Missouri River about fifty miles from Jefferson City. Jackson issued a call to the leaders of the militia districts to assemble their troops, and additional volunteers from the surrounding slaveholding counties swelled the numbers present to about 1,500 by 15 June 1861. Most of these men were poorly trained and armed. Also, most of their artillery was twenty miles farther south under Brigadier General Mosby Parsons.

Responding fast to the possibility that Jackson and Price might consolidate a stronger military force, Union general Nathaniel Lyon quickly and decisively moved about 2,000 soldiers upriver from his base in St. Louis, occupied Jefferson City on 15 June and, after leaving a detachment under Colonel Henry Boernstein in the city, attacked the militia in Camp Bacon near Boonville on 17 June. The Union forces moved by boat again, and much to Lyon's surprise they were allowed to land near the camp without meeting any opposition.

Jackson and his nephew, Colonel John S. Marmaduke, had formed a line of defense, but they had no artillery present to counter the two field pieces of Union captain James Totten, who quickly disposed of some sharpshooters in a house in his front. The Union infantry—most of Francis Blair's 1st Missouri and Company B, and Peter J. Osterhaus's 2d Missouri Rifle Battalion—drove the Missouri State Guard from the field in less than twenty minutes. Almost simultaneously, two companies from the 1st Missouri, covered by a steamboat with a field piece on board, took the camp

itself. Losses were comparatively light, with only three dead and about ten wounded on each side, and sixty Guardsmen captured. The Missouri State Guard was scattered, however, and many of its arms and provisions were lost.

The immediate military effect of the lightly won Union victory was that the remnants of Jackson's forces fled south. Sterling Price, who had been ill on his farm in Chariton at the time of the Boonville fight, evacuated Lexington, Missouri, and also moved south with another column of assembled militia and volunteers to unite with Confederate forces from Arkansas and Texas. The retreat of these prosecessionist Missouri forces not only returned the counties along the Missouri to Federal control for the duration of the war, but also seriously weakened the political authority of Claiborne Jackson. Many inhabitants of Missouri with pro-Southern leanings decided to remain submissive for the time being. The effect on Confederate recruiting efforts and in the long run on the morale of Missouri forces from the northern part of the state was negative.

Although a comparatively small engagement, the fight at Boonville received no small attention. Exaggerated claims about Union losses and Missouri State Guard resistance made the rounds in Southern papers; in New York a theater play, *The Battle of Boonville*, based on a report by a *New York Herald* correspondent who had accompanied Lyon, attracted a sizable audience.

—Wolfgang Hochbruck

For further reading:
Hinze, David C., and Karen Farnham. *The Battle of Carthage. Border War in Southwest Missouri* (1998).
Pollard, Edward A. *The Lost Cause: A New Southern History of the War of the Confederates* (1866).
Snead, Thomas L. "The First Year of the War in Missouri." In *Battles & Leaders of the Civil War*, vol. 1. (1956).

BOOTH, JOHN WILKES
(1838–1865)

Assassin of Abraham Lincoln

Born on 10 May 1838 near Bel Air, Harford County, Maryland, John Wilkes Booth was the son of Junius Brutus Booth and Mary Ann Holmes. Abandoning his wife, the elder Booth, a promising British actor, sailed for America with his young mistress, Mary Ann, in 1821. Junius Brutus Booth exploded onto the American stage and became one of the young republic's foremost actors. Plagued by alcoholism and fits of insanity, the "Mad Tragedian" died on tour in 1851.

Young John, who was raised on the remote family farm, Tudor Hall, received a sporadic education at local academies. Following in the footsteps of his late father and elder brother, Edwin, seventeen-year-old John made his stage debut on 14 August 1855 in Baltimore. An undisciplined but fiery performer, he subsequently appeared in popular plays and Shakespearean classics in Philadelphia and Richmond. The darkly handsome young actor made women swoon, while one contemporary claimed he possessed the same élan and oddness seen in his celebrated father.

Booth was widely regarded as a rising star by 1860, and he successfully toured the North and South as the nation drifted toward war. However, the young Marylander regarded himself primarily as a Southern actor, and he particularly sought the acclaim of Southern audiences. Unlike his father, who detested the institution, John defended slavery and denounced Northern abolitionists during the growing sectional crisis.

In the aftermath of the attempted insurrection at Harper's Ferry, Booth left the stage in Richmond, Virginia, and joined the Richmond Grays, a local militia unit. The uniformed actor was among the troops present when John Brown was executed on 2 December 1859. During the same period he also joined the Knights of the Golden Circle, a secret pro-Southern society that promoted secession and the expansion of slavery.

Yet, despite his devotion to the Southern cause, Booth did not take up arms with the outbreak of hostilities. Although he continued to pursue a career that took him through many Northern cities, Booth did not hesitate to denounce Lincoln and the Federal government openly. In late 1862, the fiery actor was arrested in St. Louis for declaring that he "wished the whole damn government would go to hell." He hinted to family members that he secretly assisted the Confederate cause by furnishing supplies and money, adding, "My soul, life and possessions are for the South."

By the fall of 1864, Booth had apparently grown weary of being a mere stage hero and armchair rebel. Unwilling to become just another soldier in the ranks, he sought the spotlight by leading a foray into Washington to capture President Lincoln. Booth was convinced that his masterstroke would either end the war or provide the Confederacy with a hostage to negotiate the release of all Confederate prisoners of war.

The actor-turned-conspirator continued to make theater appearances as he secretly put his grandiose plans in motion. After recruiting Samuel Arnold and Michael O'Laughlin, two old schoolmates and former Confederate soldiers, Booth traveled to Canada in October 1864. Historians have traditionally portrayed Booth as acting alone. At least one recent study, however, contends that Booth was already acting in concert with Rebel agents and that his kidnapping plot was supported by the Confederate secret service.

Booth subsequently returned to Washington and took up residence at the National Hotel. He then recruited John H. Surratt, whose widowed mother, Mary E. Surratt

John Wilkes Booth (*Library of Congress*)

ran a boarding house. By March 1865, his followers, who made Mrs. Surratt's rooms their headquarters, had grown to include David E. Herold, George A. Atzerodt, and a Confederate deserter named Lewis Paine (whose real name was Lewis Thornton Powell).

On 20 March, Booth's band of misfits prepared to kidnap Lincoln as he rode to a matinee performance for wounded soldiers at Campbell Hospital. Yet, the president attended another function, and Booth's dispirited followers, thinking the authorities knew of their plans, were thrown into a panic. Arnold, O'Laughlin, and Surratt promptly scattered, leaving Booth and the others to carry on alone.

The fall of Richmond and Lee's surrender at Appomattox forced Booth to abandon his original plans. On 11 April 1865, Booth was present when Lincoln gave what proved to be his last public address. The actor was enraged, however, by the president's references to limited black suffrage. "Now, by God, I'll put him through," he reportedly snarled.

Acting on his own accord, Booth apparently hatched a new plot in which he and his remaining followers would avenge the South by assassinating Lincoln, Vice President Andrew Johnson, and Secretary of State William H. Seward in one swift stroke. On the morning of 14 April 1865 Booth learned that Lincoln planned to attend the evening performance of *Our American Cousin*

at Ford's Theater. He quickly sought out his accomplices and prepared to strike that very night.

After carefully inspecting the scene of attack earlier in the day, Booth returned to Ford's Theater shortly after 10 P.M. and slipped into the presidential box. After firing one fatal bullet into the back of Lincoln's head, Booth stabbed the president's companion, a Union officer, and leapt over the balcony to the stage below. The desperate assassin reportedly shouted, "Sic semper tyrannis!", a Latin phrase meaning, "Thus always to tyrants!" Although he broke his left leg in the eleven-foot fall, Booth fled the theater, jumped on his horse, and escaped into the night.

As for the other conspirators, George Atzerodt lost his nerve and slunk away without making an attempt on the life of Vice President Johnson. Although Lewis Powell, alias Paine, brutally attacked Secretary of State Seward at his residence, he failed to inflict a fatal wound. David Herold overtook Booth somewhere outside Washington, and the pair fled through Maryland into Virginia.

On 26 April, Union cavalry surrounded the fugitives in a tobacco barn near Bowling Green in Caroline County, Virginia. Herold promptly surrendered, yet Booth, who vowed never to surrender, defiantly stood his ground until he fell mortally wounded. After initial interment at the Washington arsenal, his remains were exhumed in 1869 and buried in Green Mount Cemetery in Baltimore.

Many Southerners initially hailed Booth's "one mad act." In *The End of an Era*, John S. Wise of Virginia recalled that "among the thoughtless, the desperate, and the ignorant, it was hailed as a sort of retributive justice." A poetic tribute to Booth entitled "Our Brutus," sometimes attributed to Judge Alexander W. Terrell of Texas, reportedly circulated in the South after the assassin's death. Some of it was set to music in 1868, and in 1913 the *Confederate Veteran's Magazine* published a rendition of the poem.

However, as Lincoln's legend grew and many former Confederates came to recognize his death as a tragedy for the South, Booth was damned in the pages of American history as a misguided fanatic.

—*James M. Pritchard*

See also Lincoln Assassination.
For further reading:
Bryan, George S. *The Great American Myth: The True Story of Lincoln's Murder* (1990).
Kimmel, Stanley. *The Mad Booths of Maryland* (1940).
Rhodehamel, John, and Louise Taper, eds. *"Right or Wrong, God Judge Me": The Writings of John Wilkes Booth* (1997).
Smith, Gene. *American Gothic: The Story of America's Legendary Theatrical Family—Junius, Edwin and John Wilkes Booth* (1992).
Tidwell, William A., James O. Hall, and David Winfred Gaddy. *Come Retribution: The Confederate Secret Service and the Assassination of Lincoln* (1988).
Turner, Thomas Reed. *Beware the People Weeping: Public Opinion and the Assassination of Abraham Lincoln* (1982).

BORDER STATES

Border states were Southern in their sanctioning of slavery but were particularly ambivalent about the destruction of the Union. They charted courses characterized by shifting and contradictory allegiances.

The definition of a "border state" shifted somewhat during the course of the Civil War. By February 1861, seven slave states had seceded and formed the Confederacy, but eight had flatly declined to join them. From February into the late spring, North Carolina, Virginia, Tennessee, and Arkansas were considered border states along with Maryland, Kentucky, and Missouri, as well as Delaware, where the outcome was never in serious doubt. By June, when four more of these states seceded, the term came to refer rather narrowly to Maryland, Kentucky, and Missouri. Precisely in such areas did loyalists form their own Union Leagues.

Strategies for dealing with the border shifted accordingly. During that initial period from February into April 1861, the Unionists prevailed. The Confederates sought success by orienting to the existing political leadership in these states and by issuing dire warnings predicting their tyrannical "coercion" by the United States. In contrast, the Union, under both lame-duck Democratic president James Buchanan and incoming Republican president Abraham Lincoln, generally avoided any confrontation that would give substance to such fears of coercion that might push the border toward secession. The Lincoln administration amended this approach to take greater pains to avoid the further cession of Federal installations in areas now claiming to constitute the Confederacy. In this first phase, Unionist strategy successfully retained the loyalties of all eight slaveholding states that had not already seceded.

During the next phase, from April into September 1861, the Union and the Confederacy each obtained four of the eight slaveholding states that had not earlier seceded. The outbreak of open hostilities at Fort Sumter in Charleston Harbor and Lincoln's call for the states to supply the government with volunteer troops clearly presaged Federal "coercion." Given the imminence of an armed conflict, Southern state governments that had not wanted to secede would either have to do so anyway or render assistance to the U.S. authorities. Secession followed in Virginia (17 April), Arkansas (6 May), Tennessee (7 May), and North Carolina (20 May). Delaware, Maryland, Kentucky, and Missouri did not secede but did not necessarily embrace cooperation with the Federal authorities either.

Securing these border states imposed the most trying ordeal on the new Lincoln administration, elected with the weakest popular mandate of any presidency. However, the government succeeded through pragmatic approaches combining diverse strategies that varied considerably from state to state. Even afterward, though, its concern over the possible responses of these slave-holding states retarded the Federal expansion of its war goals to include emancipation.

Securing the nation's capital in the District of Columbia required a virtual military seizure of power in Maryland. In the weeks after the war's outbreak, secessionist officials sought to deny Federal transit to Washington, leading to attacks on Massachusetts volunteers passing through Baltimore (19 April) and resulting in a U.S. military occupation. With the suspension of the writ of habeas corpus (27 April), martial law largely superseded civilian authority in the state. This placed Maryland legislators under threat of immediate arrest when they voted to repudiate secession (29 April).

To a lesser extent, securing Washington also meant clearing the Confederates from the Potomac opposite Maryland. The Federals broke the Chesapeake blockade in small naval actions at Sewell's Point (18–19 May) and Aquia Creek (29 May–1 June), while also occupying the adjacent heights in Virginia at Arlington and Alexandria (24 May).

In the transmountain counties of western Virginia, differences over secession tapped a deep-seated tension between the local authorities and the tidewater political machines governing from Richmond. Just as Maryland straddled the rail lines north from Washington, the course of the Baltimore & Ohio between the capital and the Ohio valley passed through western Virginia. Virginians at Wheeling and other communities protested secession. When Federal troops, including Virginians, routed a Confederate force at Philippi (3 June), it marked the beginning of a successful Union campaign in the mountains. Under Washington's protection, an independent Unionist government of Virginia later established the new state of West Virginia.

In contrast to military occupation in Maryland or the fostering of local revolutionary movements in Virginia, the Lincoln administration simply left Kentucky alone. Badly divided between a Unionist legislature and a secessionist governor, the state authorities simply postponed a crisis by declaring Kentucky's neutrality (20 May). Because both sides sought to avoid toppling Kentucky into the enemy camp, they generally accepted this arrangement.

In Missouri, local federal officials gladly fostered the internal civil war that broke out in that state, as loyal citizens rose against the secessionist state government. Loyal citizens of St. Louis, mainly German immigrants, surrounded and forced the surrender of Camp Jackson (10 May), while secessionist units attacked Unionist encampments like Camp Cole (18 June) in the center of the state. When the de facto truce ended (11 June), Federal volunteers moved west from St. Louis into the interior against the state capital, Jefferson City. Union victory at Boonville (17 June) did not end the seces-

sionist threat, but it allowed for a state convention to reassemble (22 July), establishing a provisional military government. Despite decisive Confederate victories at Wilson's Creek (10 August) and Lexington (12–20 September), Federal reinforcements continued to pour into the state for some months. In the end, the Unionists wielded an unquestioned authority through much of the state.

Kentucky's neutrality broke when the Confederate forces moved north to occupy Columbus (3 September) in hopes of fortifying the Mississippi River, a movement that largely tipped the state toward the Union. Federal forces based at Cairo, Illinois, crossed to Paducah (6 September) as defenders of the state's sovereignty against rebel aggression and troops from both sides formed a long and very porous line of garrisons and outposts across the state.

Just as the opening of hostilities in western Virginia created dual governments in that nominally secessionist state, it had the same results in nominally loyal places. Claiming a quorum, the secessionists in the Missouri legislature reassembled at Neosho and voted for secession (28 October), ratifying the action later at Cassville (31 October). Placed in a similar position by the Federal army, pro-secessionist Kentucky officials, together with state militia officers, established their own legislature at Russellville and voted that state out of the Union (18 November).

It should also be noted that secession created the tumultuous conditions characteristic of the border state in some of the western territories. Although a territorial convention of transplanted Texans at Mesilla (16 March) also laid claim to much of present southern New Mexico and Arizona, the secessionist project simply stalled during these critical three months. Indian Territory, which later became Oklahoma, was occupied by the autonomous nation-states, the "Five Civilized Tribes." Their leaders early preferred neutrality, but Texas troops crossed the Red River in April to encourage the Choctaw and the Chickasaw to abrogate their treaties with the United States and make new treaties with the Confederacy that obligated every adult male to military service at the executive order of the president. The secessionists bypassed principal chiefs among the Creeks and Seminoles to make similar treaty arrangements with their internal rivals. The Cherokees managed to resist a treaty until August, but Confederate authority, on paper at least, extended to the Quapaws, Euchees, Delawares, Wichitas, Caddos, and even the Osage in Kansas. Their course, however, provoked little consistent concern in either Richmond or Washington, and rival factions allied to both sides emerged.

Militarily, the first year of the war centered on the fate of these border states. The struggle brought into play some of the principal commanders of the war. George B.

McClellan, Robert E. Lee, and Joseph Johnston first took their own troops into the fields of western Virginia. Operations to secure the river areas of Missouri and Kentucky shaped the early successes of Ulysses S. Grant and William T. Sherman. McClellan alternately denounced and assumed credit for the achievements of his subordinates, establishing his reputation for strong generalship early in the region. In contrast, Grant had a rather lackluster career in Missouri, although he was not so widely viewed as a failure as was Lee based on his losses in western Virginia.

By March 1862, however, Federal forces in the Virginia mountains had pushed beyond the trans-Allegheny counties that became West Virginia into the Shenandoah Valley. Union armies had pushed through Kentucky into Tennessee and through Missouri into Arkansas. That month, the Federals also turned back a bold Rebel effort in the New Mexico Territory.

Thereafter, Union authority was secure in these areas, though never so completely as in the North. Through eastern Maryland, an ongoing trafficking through the lines maintained its ties to the Confederacy; in the western part of the state, Confederate armies invaded at several points in the war. So, too, incursions by small Confederate columns and an ongoing guerrilla war continued to contest Union control in the interior of western Virginia. Kentucky and Missouri also experienced periodic invasions.

More innovatively, of course, the early military settlement of affairs in these states left a large number of secessionists behind Union lines, joined by growing numbers of captured and paroled Confederate prisoners. As the Federal armies pushed farther south, they required longer and increasingly vulnerable lines of supply going through such areas. From northern Virginia to Indian Territory, these border conditions inspired a unique type of hit-and-run guerrilla warfare that blurred lines between soldiers and civilians for both the combatants and their targets. The brutality of this fighting grew worse to the west, as did the vulnerability of civilian populations. In Missouri, civilians were as likely as not to be the targets of military operations, which left virtually no county records intact south of the Missouri River. Along the Missouri-Kansas border, entire towns were abandoned and burned, with thousands of desperate refugees camped among the charred ruins. Control changed hands so frequently in northwestern Arkansas, and especially in Indian Territory, that the areas became virtually depopulated.

Nevertheless, with even nominal Federal ascendancy, the authorities sought to maintain or develop loyal civilian mechanisms of power. The population generally took little active interest in the overthrow of the Union. In the end, the Confederacy simply faced a virtually impossible task even in those border states that joined it.

Most of the people of Kentucky and Missouri opposed secession, however much they dreaded or disliked Federal occupation. Neither North Carolina nor Arkansas held plebiscites on secession, even ones of dubious value like those held in Virginia and Tennessee. The military reversals in the war's first year quickly chilled the early war fever in such areas, and the Confederate imposition of conscription after spring 1862 failed to rekindle it.

In the end, the type of dual governments that first appeared along the border also pointed the course toward Federal victory and, ultimately, the reestablishment of loyal governments in the South. By November 1861, such competing governments vied in Virginia, Missouri, and Kentucky, as well as territorial administrations in the Southwest. By spring 1863, rival chiefs and grand councils contested for the loyalties of the divided Creek, Seminole, and Cherokee Nations. By the end of the war, Unionists in Louisiana, Tennessee, Arkansas, North Carolina, and Texas also formed governments allied to Washington.

—*Mark A. Lause*

See also Arkansas; Guerrilla Warfare; Indian Territory; Kentucky; Maryland; Missouri; West Virginia.

For further reading:

Coulter, E. Merton. *The Civil War and Readjustment in Kentucky* (1926).

Fellman, Michael. *Inside War: The Guerrilla Conflict in Missouri during the American Civil War* (1989).

Monaghan, Jay. *Civil War on the Western Border, 1854–1865* (1955).

Parrish, William E. *Turbulent Partnership: Missouri and the Union, 1861–1865* (1963).

BOTTS, JOHN MINOR
(1802–1869)

Virginia Unionist

I could not willingly take up arms against a Union that I have been taught and accustomed to adore, as indispensable to my own liberties, and I never will raise my hand against my native State, although her arm had ever been against me and mine." Written on 29 April 1861, John Minor Botts's letter to Attorney General Edward Bates revealed the anguish and conflict of conscience wrought by secession. Dismayed over his home state of Virginia's decision to secede, Botts implored Bates to call a National Convention and recognize the independence of those states that desired to leave the Union. It was the only way, Botts argued, to "save the unnecessary effusion of brothers' blood."

Botts earnestly believed that his plan would ultimately reunite the Union. After a trial separation, he hoped that the Southern states would understand the "hour of madness" that had rushed them to secession and, after reasoned deliberation, they would return to the

Union. To Botts, such a plan was exceedingly moderate compared with the threat of armed conflict. Botts's political career, in fact, revealed a consistently moderate course in the dispute between the North and South over slavery and its extension.

Born in Dumfries, Virginia, in 1802, Botts entered politics in 1831 as a Whig candidate for the Virginia legislature and was elected in 1833 to serve until 1839, when he entered Congress. He represented the Richmond District until 1843 and served again from 1847 to 1849. During his time in Washington, Botts was equally disdainful of abolitionists and those who attempted to usurp their constitutional right of petition through the 1836 "Gag Rule." He opposed the annexation of Texas and the Mexican-American War, but helped to bring the war to a successful conclusion by serving as the chairman of the Committee on Military Affairs. After leaving the House in 1849, he returned to Washington at the request of Henry Clay to help with the measures that led to the Compromise of 1850. Botts deplored both the repeal of the Missouri Compromise and the 1858 attempted statehood of Kansas under the Lecompton Constitution. In all of these actions, Botts displayed a sincere reverence for his duty to the nation and a respect for the spirit of political moderation and compromise.

John M. Botts was not, however, without passion. As the dispute between the North and South grew, he unleashed his ire at John C. Calhoun and radical, conspiratorial minded "Democratic bosses" who clamored for disunion. In a speech entitled "Union or Disunion," delivered before a crowd in Lynchburg, Virginia, on 18 October 1860, Botts argued that the Democratic Party had deliberately split its 1860 ticket between Stephen Douglas and John Breckinridge "to make the election of Lincoln sure, and thus get up agitation and excitement at the South." Moreover, Botts characterized Virginia governor Henry A. Wise as "The Unwise Henry A." for using John Brown's attack on Harper's Ferry to further the secession conspiracy.

Continuing the moderate course that had guided his path through the sectional dispute, Botts assured his listeners that Lincoln was not an abolitionist and that even if he were intent on usurping Southern rights he would first have to bypass Congress and the Supreme Court.

When Virginia ultimately called a convention to debate secession, Botts was nominated as a representative but, he argued, defeated by fraud. It was shortly after Virginia seceded that Botts wrote the letter to Attorney General Bates. When Bates refused to consider a National Convention, Botts retired to his farm near Culpeper Court House, unable to fight either the Union he revered or his home state. Still intent on proving a Democratic secession conspiracy, he began a book on the causes of the war. Shortly thereafter, on 1 March 1862, Jefferson Davis declared martial law, and the next morning 100 soldiers under the command of a General Winder arrested Botts and searched for the manuscript, which had been given to the French Minister Count de Mercier for safekeeping. Incarcerated for eight weeks in a jail usually set aside for African-Americans, Botts was paroled only after a new Confederate secretary of war, Judah Benjamin, was appointed. Botts returned to his farm and waited out the end of the war.

In 1866, Botts published his "secret" work, *The Great Rebellion: Its Secret History, Rise, Progress, and Disastrous Failure*. That year he proposed a plan of reconstruction, which was rejected, and led the Virginia delegation to the Convention of Southern Loyalists held in Philadelphia. And though he criticized Jefferson Davis for his part in the secession conspiracy, and even called the Confederate president "the most unscrupulous despot since the days of Nero," Botts was among those who signed Davis's bail bond, proving again his ability to steer toward the moderate path.

—*Matthew S. Warshauer*

See also Civil Liberties, C.S.A.; Southern Unionism; Virginia.
For further reading:

Botts, John Minor. "Union or Disunion. The Union Cannot Be Dissolved. Mr. Lincoln Not an Abolitionist." Speech of the Hon. John M. Botts, Lynchburg, Virginia, October 18, 1860.
Lapidus, Robert D. "A Southern Enigma: The Unwavering Unionism of John Minor Botts" (M.A. thesis, 1972).
Webster, Clyde Cannon. "John Minor Botts: Anti-secessionist." Richmond College Historical Papers (1915).

BOUDINOT, ELIAS CORNELIUS
(1835–1890)

Cherokee Confederate officer and congressman

Born in the Cherokee Nation (present-day Georgia) to mixed-blood Cherokee leader Elias Boudinot, Elias Cornelius was just over four months old when his father signed the Treaty of New Echota, which would remove the Cherokees to Indian Territory. As a result of his action, three years later the elder Boudinot was assassinated. In turn, their white mother's family in New England raised his children.

Well educated in the east, Elias Cornelius returned to the west in the 1850s. He studied law in Fayetteville, Arkansas, where he eventually practiced law, engaged in civic activities, became active in the Democratic Party, and edited the *Fayetteville Arkansian*. Establishing himself as a notable supporter of Senator Robert Johnson, he was chosen as the first chairman of the Arkansas Democratic Central Committee. Quarrels within the Democratic Party in Arkansas between Robert Johnson and Representative Thomas Hindman led Boudinot to edit the *Little Rock True Democrat*.

When secession loomed, Boudinot considered himself a Unionist, as did many in northwest Arkansas. When his Unionist friend Judge David Walker was elected president of the Arkansas Secession Convention, Boudinot was chosen as secretary. The delegates initially opted against secession, but when fighting began they voted to secede.

After finishing his work for the secession convention, Boudinot joined his uncle Stand Watie, a leading Confederate supporter in the Cherokee Nation. Boudinot helped Watie raise a Cherokee Confederate regiment. They also put pressure on Principal Chief John Ross to sign a treaty of alliance with the Confederacy, which Ross did reluctantly.

When Ross led the Cherokee Nation into the Confederacy, Watie, Boudinot, who had been elected major, and the regiment had already seen action at the battle of Wilson's Creek in Missouri. Then in late 1861 in Indian Territory, Boudinot led his men against neutral-minded Creeks fleeing to Kansas in the battle of Chustenahlah. The following March he fought in the battle of Pea Ridge. In July, at the battle of Locust Grove, he again distinguished himself for bravery. By then, Boudinot had advanced to the rank of lieutenant colonel.

In mid-1862, Ross allowed himself to be captured and, with many followers, headed north with Federal troopers to Kansas, where he switched sides. The Southern Cherokees then elected Watie as principal chief and chose Boudinot as their delegate to the Confederate Congress.

Boudinot entered the Congress as one of the two youngest members. He had several close acquaintances in the Congress, including Robert Johnson. However, he did not have the right to vote and could speak only on Indian concerns. Boudinot nonetheless energetically engaged in pursuing Indian matters, and he eventually received the right to introduce legislation pertaining to Indian policy.

Concerned about the scarcity of Confederate soldiers in Indian Territory, Boudinot proposed that whites be offered Indian land if they enlisted in Cherokee forces. The idea of giving land to whites angered a majority of the Southern Cherokees. They rejected the proposal, and some sought to have Boudinot removed from the Congress. However, many endorsed his efforts to have the Indian Territory made a separate command. Boudinot also lobbied for Watie's promotion, and in May of 1864, Watie became a brigadier general. Thereafter, Boudinot turned his attention to the plight of Cherokee refugees and convinced the Congress to appropriate $100,000 for the Cherokee Nation.

With the defeat of the Confederacy, Boudinot played a significant role in representing the Cherokees in treaty negotiations. He and his fellow former Confederate Cherokees almost secured a treaty that would have split the Cherokee Nation between Southern and Union elements. However, a dying John Ross prevailed in getting a treaty that maintained tribal unity.

In the following years, Boudinot continued to be a controversial member of the Cherokee Nation. Although he served for a while on the official Cherokee delegation to Washington, D.C., he would venture on his own course—often at odds with a majority of his fellow Cherokees and other tribespeople in Indian Territory. He promoted opening unsettled parts of Indian Territory to white settlers, bringing in railroads, establishing federal courts, and making Cherokees citizens of the United States. In pursuing such goals, he spent most of his years after the Civil War as a lawyer, lobbyist, professional orator on Indian issues, and newspaperman.

Boudinot died in 1890 in Fort Smith, Arkansas, where he was practicing law and operating a farm in the Cherokee Nation.

—*Thomas Burnell Colbert*

See also Cherokee Indians; Ross, John; Watie, Stand.

For further reading:
Colbert, Thomas Burnell. "Prophet of Progress: The Life and Times of Elias Cornelius Boudinot" (Ph.D. dissertation, 1982).
Dale, Edward Everett, and Gaston Litton, eds. *Cherokee Cavaliers: Forty Years of Cherokee History as Told in the Correspondence of the Ridge-Watie-Boudinot Family* (1939).
Wilson, T. Paul. "Delegates of the Five Civilized Tribes to the Confederate Congress." *Chronicles of Oklahoma* (1975).
Wright, Marcus J. "Colonel Elias C. Boudinot." *Southern Bivouac* (1884).

BOUNTY SYSTEM

Bounties were payments made by the various governments of the Union and the Confederacy to induce men to enlist in the military. Even though volunteers initially supplied all the men needed on both sides, the tradition of using bounties was so strong that Congress passed a law only a month after Fort Sumter to enable the Federal government to pay a bounty of up to $300. The more hard-pressed Confederacy also passed an allocation for its bounty system in December 1861. The provision was for a $50 payment at the end of three years or more of service. As the need for men became more desperate in 1864, the Confederate bounty increased to $100. Yet the sum was in Confederate money, which in 1864 had little real value. Bounties in the Confederacy, therefore, never carried the weight they did in the North.

The U.S. Congress continued to adjust the bounty provisions throughout the war by specifying how much the bounty should be, when the bounty should be paid, and to whom it would devolve if the volunteer died in battle. In addition, states and local areas also added to the bounty pool. Local, state, and Federal agencies scraped together money by taxation, bond issues, and solicited donations. Because pay for soldiers throughout the war was low and sporadic, bounties enabled families at home to survive and added to the ability of returning soldiers to return to civilian life.

The draft changed the bounty system in both the North and the South. The Confederacy resorted to a draft in 1862. The Union also needed men that early, but the Lincoln administration was hesitant about instituting national conscription. Lincoln relied instead on allocating quotas to the states, a practice that shifted the burden of raising men to local areas. To forestall any move toward a national draft, states acted quickly. They subdivided their quotas regionally and increased their state bounties to encourage volunteers. In turn, the subdivided sections also increased their bounties. Theoretically, a volunteer might then benefit from three or four separate bounties when enlisting. Although the increased bounties helped in 1862, by 1863 none of these plans was sufficient and the Federal government instituted a draft.

Reactions to the draft were negative in both the Union and the Confederacy. The Northern draft gave the draftee five days after notice before reporting for induction. During those five days the draftee had the option of volunteering for the army and receiving a bounty. Being conscripted imparted a social stigma and carried no bounty, so it is surprising that some men actually remained drafted instead of volunteering.

As the availability of young, healthy men diminished and quotas increased, bounties from all sources soared dramatically. By January 1865, the *New York Tribune* quoted the local county bounty alone at $1,000. Such large sums enticed unscrupulous men to become bounty jumpers. They would claim bounties by volunteering, desert before reaching the front lines, and move onto the next locality to claim another and perhaps even larger bounty. Because a draftee/volunteer did not have to be a resident of the area, competition between counties and states became intense as draftable men shopped for the most lucrative bounties. Also, governments relied on brokers to provide eligible men, who were often garnered from some distance. Brokers from various states recruited immigrants disembarking from boats in New York and Boston to fill their quotas. These brokers took a cut of the bounty and added to an increasing corruption by intensifying competition for men and therefore enlarging the size of bounties. As the war progressed and bounties increased, indignation surfaced in the men who had earned earlier—and smaller—bounties. Resentment also arose in localities understandably envious of wealthier regions that could pay larger sums. Procedural differences further contributed to tensions.

Most historians agree that the draft worked during the Civil War. Yet the success of the draft must be balanced by the inducement proffered by bounty payments. And though bounties mainly accomplished what they were supposed to, both the immediate and long-term consequences of the system were negative. At the end of the war, Provost Marshall General James B. Fry wrote a report on the draft in which he castigated the bounty system as inviting corruption. His criticism was sufficient to ensure opposition to bounties in World War I.

—*Dorothy O. Pratt*

See also Conscription, C.S.A.; Conscription, U.S.A.; Pay, C.S.A.; Pay, U.S.A.

For further reading:

Geary, James W. *We Need Men: The Union Draft in the Civil War* (1991).

Moore, Albert B., ed. *Conscription and Conflict in the Confederacy Southern Classics Series* (1924; reprint, 1996).

Murdock, Eugene C. *One Million Men: The Civil War Draft in the North* (1971).

BOUTWELL, GEORGE SEWALL
(1818–1905)
Commissioner of internal revenue

George S. Boutwell distinguished himself as one of the Radical Republicans serving in the U.S. House of Representatives during the Civil War.

Boutwell began life humbly in Brookline, Massachusetts. During his teens he worked in a store in Lunenberg and attended school. He demonstrated an early interest in politics by writing commentaries for the local newspaper. In 1842 he commenced eight years of service in the Massachusetts legislature as a Democrat representing the town of Groton. Boutwell helped forge the union between antislavery Democrats and Free Soilers that overturned the Whig dominance of Massachusetts politics. This alliance supported his candidacy for governor in 1850 and Boutwell held two one-year terms. When he left the governorship, Boutwell studied law until 1862, when he was admitted to the bar.

Boutwell served on the Massachusetts Board of Education from 1855 to 1861, during which time he helped organize the Republican Party in the Bay State. Between 1862 and 1863, Boutwell was appointed to his first federal position, commissioner of internal revenue. In one year Boutwell organized the office that would soon supersede the Treasury Department in the number of employees. He wrote and published in 1863 *A Manual of the Direct and Excise Tax System of the United States*, which outlined how to comply with the complex new system.

Boutwell was elected to the House of Representatives during the turbulent years between 1863 and 1869. He became a secondary leader of the Radical Republicans behind the "tyrant" Thaddeus Stevens. He helped draft the Fourteenth and Fifteenth Amendments to the Constitution and lobbied extensively to counter the

hesitancy many Republicans harbored about granting full suffrage for the freedmen. "Next to the restoration of the Union and the abolition of slavery, the recognition of universal suffrage is the most important result of the war," he wrote in his autobiography. Boutwell created an early draft of the Reconstruction plan that formed the basis of congressional Reconstruction. Boutwell was selected as chairman of the managers in President Andrew Johnson's impeachment trial.

In 1869 Boutwell accepted President Ulysses S. Grant's offer to become secretary of the treasury. He strove to reduce the massive public debt accumulated during the war, rid the department of corruption and its bloated payroll, and systematized the revenue collection apparatus. He is best remembered for thwarting the efforts of Jay Gould and James Fiske, Jr. to corner the gold market on "Black Friday," 24 September 1869, by releasing $4 million worth of the Treasury Department's gold to help stabilize its price. Boutwell's unabashed enthusiasm for the gold standard contributed to the "Crime of 1873" in which silver was demonetized for a brief period.

Boutwell represented Massachusetts in the Senate from 1873 to 1877. His most memorable contribution as a senator entailed chairing the committee that investigated the 1875 election in Mississippi in which the African-American vote was suppressed with astonishing brutality. The whole affair appalled Boutwell, who confided to his journals that he feared the outbreak of a second civil war if these outrages were allowed to continue.

After his failed reelection bid, Boutwell served in a variety of government positions, including chairman of the committee to revise the U.S. statutes and counsel for the government in defense of French citizens' claims for losses during the Civil War. Although Boutwell abhorred corruption, throughout his career he both dispensed and received the benefits of the patronage system that lay at the heart of the political baseness of the Gilded Age.

Late in the nineteenth century, Boutwell grew increasingly leery of the expansionist policies advocated by Republicans. He openly disagreed with President William McKinley's policy in the Philippines and eventually withdrew from the party. He served as president of the Anti-Imperialist League until his death in 1905.

—*Jane Flaherty*

See also Financing, U.S.A.; Lincoln's Reconstruction Policy; Radical Republicans; Wade-Davis Bill.

For further reading:
Benedict, Michael Les. *A Compromise of Principle: Congressional Republicans and Reconstruction* (1974).
Boutwell, George S. *Reminiscences of Sixty Years in Public Affairs* (1902; reprint, 1968).
Brown, Thomas H. *George Sewall Boutwell: Human Rights Advocate* (1989).

BOWEN, JOHN STEVENS
(1830–1863)
Confederate general

Born to William Parker Bowen and Ann Elizabeth Wilkins Bowen in Savannah, Georgia, Bowen attended the United States Military Academy, from which he graduated thirteenth of fifty-one in the class of 1853. He served in various frontier posts as a mounted rifleman until 1856, when he resigned his commission. Shortly afterward he moved to St. Louis, Missouri, where he worked as an architect until the outbreak of the Civil War. During his years in St. Louis he was a neighbor and friendly acquaintance of Ulysses S. Grant.

At the outbreak of the war, Bowen went with the Missouri militia forces that supported the Confederacy. Captured by Union forces under the command of Nathaniel Lyon at Camp Jackson, Bowen received his parole, but was later accused of violating it by accepting a commission as colonel of the 1st Missouri Confederate regiment on 11 June 1861. He served under Brigadier General Daniel M. Frost early in the war, before taking his regiment to Kentucky, where he served under Leonidas Polk.

Bowen was promoted to brigadier general on 14 March 1862 and commanded a brigade under John C. Breckinridge at Shiloh. He was wounded the first day there and did not see any further serious actions until the battle of Corinth in October 1862. As a result of that engagement Bowen entered into a dispute with Earl Van Dorn about that officer's movements during and following the battle. Van Dorn was vindicated in the subsequent investigation.

From the beginning of the Vicksburg campaign, Bowen was very active as one of General John C. Pemberton's best subordinates. On 1 May 1863 he held Port Gibson for almost 24 hours against three times his number and then destroyed key bridges in his retreat. For his actions at Port Gibson, Bowen was promoted to major general.

Bowen commanded a division in the battles outside Vicksburg and withdrew with the rest of Pemberton's army at the beginning of the siege. During the siege Bowen became seriously ill with dysentery, but continued in command and participated in the surrender negotiations. Some hope arose among the senior Confederate leadership in Vicksburg that Bowen's prewar acquaintance with General Grant would facilitate talks and perhaps lead to a lenient surrender, but Grant refused even to meet with Bowen.

Following the Confederates surrender, Bowen, like most of the officers received a parole, although there was some opposition because of his supposed violation of parole back in 1861. It probably mattered little to

Bowen; the dysentery he contracted during the siege had so weakened him that he died on 13 July 1863.

—*David S. Heidler and Jeanne T. Heidler*

See also Port Gibson.

For further reading:

"Proceedings of a Court of inquiry: Held at Abbeville, Mississippi on Charges Preferred by Brigadier General John S. Bowen, P.A.C.S., against Major General Earl Van Doren, P.A.C.S., from 15th to 22nd November, 1862." *Mobile (Alabama) Daily Register* (1862).

BOYCE, WILLIAM WATERS
(1818–1890)
Confederate congressman

Born to Robert Boyce and Lydia Waters Boyce in Charleston, South Carolina, William Waters Boyce was educated in local schools before attending South Carolina College and then studying law at the University of Virginia. He began his law practice in 1839 in Winnsboro, South Carolina, where he also owned a small plantation. Through the 1840s, Boyce became increasingly interested in South Carolina politics as a staunch defender of states' rights. In 1850 he was elected to represent his district in the state legislature partly because of his strong stance against the Compromise of 1850 and support for Southern rights. Two years later, he was elected to the U.S. House of Representatives again as a strong proponent of states' rights.

In Congress Boyce made numerous speeches on Southern rights and those issues that he believed threatened those rights. Very vocal on the issues of slavery in the territories, the protective tariff, and the acquisition of Cuba, Boyce also frequently expanded his speeches into lengthy pamphlets for distribution at home, no doubt wanting to assure his constituents and other Southerners as to his vigilance in protecting their rights.

While certainly not a fire-eater, Boyce believed that the election of Abraham Lincoln in 1860 justified Southern secession and supported that move for South Carolina. Before the convention met in that state, he was one of the prominent South Carolinians who wrote to President James Buchanan that the Federal forts in South Carolina would not be attacked until after secession and then only if a negotiated settlement could not be reached. After the war, he claimed that he had expected during the first weeks after secession that a compromise would be reached and that the seceded states would reenter the Union. Whether that statement was merely an effort to gain the good graces of the conquering government cannot be determined, but Boyce did not hesitate to accept a seat in the Provisional Confederate Congress in February 1861 and actively participate in the formation of the Confederate States of America.

During the creation of the Confederate government, Boyce served on several committees including the Drafting Committee of the executive portion of the Confederate Constitution; the Postal Committee; and after the selection of Jefferson Davis as provisional president, the Inauguration Committee. During that selection process, however, Boyce had endorsed the candidacy of Howell Cobb for president. Boyce's opposition to Jefferson Davis would continue for the remainder of the Confederacy's existence.

In the fall of 1861, Boyce was elected to the first regular Confederate Congress. From the beginning of that Congress's first session, Boyce became one of the most vocal critics of the method by which the Davis administration conducted the war. Initially Boyce supported a strong aggressive military policy and voted for spending measures that he believed would bring about such a policy. At the same time, however, he opposed the conscription measures taken by the Confederate Congress in early 1862 and strongly advocated steps be taken to improve local defense.

In committee work both in the First and Second Confederate Congresses, Boyce was very active, serving on the Currency, Ways and Means, and Naval Affairs Committees. He used these forums to become increasingly critical of Davis and to advocate that Congress take a more active role in directing the military affairs of the country. He recommended that the Confederate Congress create the position of commanding general of the army so that Davis would have less direct impact on military policy.

By the end of 1863, Boyce increasingly came to see the military situation as hopeless and began advocating opening negotiations with the United States. Davis's increasing use of the power to suspend the writ of habeas corpus alarmed him, not only because he did not trust Davis, but also because he feared that the independent Confederacy would become a dictatorship. His vocal advocacy of peace in 1864 began to wear on his constituents, who had not felt the full brunt of the war as yet and still believed that victory was possible. He became increasingly unpopular at home as well as with the Davis administration. He remained in his congressional seat until the end of the war, but was increasingly seen by other representatives as somewhat of a crank.

After the war, Boyce returned to Winnsboro, where he was greeted with less than enthusiasm by some of his neighbors. He had lost most of his property, but sought to rebuild his political fortunes by courting the Republican government in Washington. In July 1865, he wrote to Secretary of State William Henry Seward asserting his loyalty to the U.S. government and claiming that he had wanted compromise in 1860 and 1861 and that he had opposed Jefferson Davis throughout the war. Boyce asked

Seward that if he were elected to the U.S. Congress he be allowed to take his seat.

Boyce was being optimistic about his political chances in South Carolina; his peace efforts in the latter part of the war had made him unpopular throughout the state. Once he determined that, he moved to Washington, D.C., in 1866 and opened a law practice there. Over the next twenty years he developed a prosperous practice and was able to retire to an estate he purchased in Fairfax County, Virginia. He died there on 3 February 1890. His remains were taken back to Winnsboro for burial.

—*David S. Heidler and Jeanne T. Heidler*

See also Congress, C.S.A.

For further reading:
Taylor, Rosser Howard, ed. "The Boyce-Hammond Correspondence." *Journal of Southern History* (1937).

BOYD, MARIA ISABELLA "BELLE"
(1843–1900)
Confederate spy

Probably the most famous among the hundreds of women who performed espionage and resistance activity on behalf of the armies of the Civil War, Belle Boyd was born near Martinsburg, Virginia (now West Virginia), in 1843. By the time the war broke out, the teenaged Boyd had developed a bold and uncompromising stance in favor of her native South and had dedicated herself to doing whatever she could to serve the Confederate cause. Boyd began her career as a pro-Southern activist by shooting and killing a Yankee soldier who, as part of the Union forces occupying Martinsburg in July 1861, tried to hoist a Union flag above the Boyd family home. Although they did not arrest her for shooting the soldier, Union officials reportedly scolded Boyd roundly and temporarily placed a guard at her door to prevent similar demonstrations of her secessionism in the future.

Boyd responded to such cautions with disdain and soon began a regular routine of gathering and transmitting information to Confederate authorities on Union fortifications, troop movements, and battle plans. Considered extremely attractive and beguiling to men, Boyd made shrewd use of all her charms to serve the Southern cause. Even in her own time, a legend developed that Boyd could compel even apparently invulnerable men in blue to disclose precious military secrets. Indeed, some accused her of prostituting herself, literally, for the sake of the Confederacy. Although Boyd herself wrote candidly in her memoir, *Belle Boyd in Camp and Prison*, about her ability to entice enemy soldiers into revealing important information, she denied this baser charge with vehemence, and indeed, the evidence fails to support convincingly any such claim against her.

The espionage work for which Boyd is best known was her timely delivery of crucial information to General Thomas J. "Stonewall" Jackson during his May 1862 campaign to hold Virginia's Shenandoah Valley for the South. The previous March, frustrated by their inability to control Boyd's behavior, Federal officials in Martinsburg had sent Boyd about forty miles south to Front Royal, Virginia. There Boyd regularly eavesdropped on conversations and solicited information from Federal soldiers and officers as yet unfamiliar with either her face or her reputation. By the end of May, she had compiled a cache of information that she then transmitted personally on 23 May to Jackson's headquarters several miles outside of town. When he later recalled Boyd's daring horseback ride to convey the information she had collected, Confederate major Henry Kyd Douglas spoke nostalgically of the "romantic maiden" who had heeded "neither weeds nor fences . . . as she came on" to inform him that Union general Nathaniel Banks's forces were sufficiently few in number as to permit Jackson's easy victory over them, should Jackson move quickly. Tradition has it that the information Boyd brought that day was instrumental in allowing Jackson to drive Banks's forces back across the Potomac towards Washington, and Jackson's brief written statement acknowledging Boyd's courage and expressing his gratitude became one of her most treasured possessions.

Boyd did not avoid arrest for the entire course of the war. Indeed, twice before the events at Front Royal Boyd had been taken into custody, but only very briefly, in part because enduring traditions of chivalry made it difficult to hold her, and also, more practically, because of the dearth of prison facilities for women on either side during the war. Some weeks after her Front Royal adventure, however, Federal officials reached a breaking point over the troublesome Boyd, who seemed to be able to travel with complete freedom and to gather masses of important information, regardless of her growing reputation or repeated admonitions to cease and desist. Thus, when Boyd was captured again in late July 1862 following an expedition to carry dispatches, Federal officials held her for about a month at the Old Capitol Prison in Washington, D.C. There she earned the respect and admiration of many of her fellow inmates and even her jailers for her unrelenting dedication to the South.

Released at the end of August, Boyd resumed her espionage work, only to be arrested again the following summer and imprisoned for three months. Upon her next release, Boyd decided to exchange the work she had been performing for a new job of bearing dispatches from the Confederacy to its supporters in England. Accordingly, in May 1864 she boarded a blockade runner called the *Greyhound* and set sail for Europe. Before it had fairly got out to sea, however, the *Greyhound*—and its most famous passenger—were captured, and Boyd's spying career was finally brought to a close.

After the war Boyd took her wartime story to the stage, performing in England and America, and supplementing her theater performances with lectures to veterans' gatherings across America. Boyd also wrote her memoirs, married three times, bore three children, and collapsed for a brief period of time in a mental hospital in Stockton, California. She died in 1900 in Kilbourne, Wisconsin, apparently from a heart attack.

—*Elizabeth D. Leonard*

See also Espionage; Shenandoah Valley Campaign; Women.
For further reading:
Davis, Curtis Carroll, ed. *Belle Boyd in Camp and Prison, Written by Herself* (1968).
Douglas, Henry Kyd. *I Rode With Stonewall Being Chiefly the War Experiences of the Youngest Member of Jackson's Staff from the John Brown Raid to the Hanging of Mrs. Surratt* (1940).
Leonard, Elizabeth D. *All the Daring of the Soldier: Women of the Civil War Armies* (1999).
Scarborough, Ruth. *Belle Boyd: Siren of the South* (1983).
Sigaud, Louis. *Belle Boyd: Confederate Spy* (1944).

BRADFORD, AUGUSTUS WILLIAMSON
(1806–1881)
Governor of Maryland

Born to Samuel Bradford and Jane Bond Bradford in Bel Air, Maryland, Augustus Williamson Bradford was educated locally before enrolling in St. Mary's College. He graduated from that institution in 1824 after which he studied law and began his practice in Bel Air. Over the next two decades he divided his time between Bel Air and Baltimore. Along with his law practice, Bradford also became involved in Maryland Whig politics, though he became somewhat disillusioned with politics when Henry Clay was defeated for the presidency in 1844. While still respected in Maryland political circles, Bradford spent most of the time before the outbreak of the Civil War building his legal practice.

During the secession crisis in early 1861, Governor Thomas Hicks asked Bradford to represent the state at the Washington Peace Conference. An ardent supporter of the Union, Bradford at the meetings of the conference spoke strongly in favor of its preservation. Upon his return home, his name was mentioned increasingly as a candidate for governor on the state's new Union Party ticket. Bradford won the election handily, though accusations would be made later that Democratic voters had been intimidated into staying away from the polls. Although he was a demonstrated supporter of the Union, Bradford nevertheless tried without success to prevent the use of U.S. troops at polling places during future elections.

Governor Bradford had one of the most difficult jobs of any U.S. governor during the war. As the governor of a border state with strong support for the Confederacy (his son William Bradford enlisted in the Confederate army), Bradford, a very principled person, had to walk a fine line between support for the Union and violation of the Maryland citizens' civil rights. In frequent contact with the U.S. attorney general's office and sometimes directly with the president, Bradford worked for the release of members of the state legislature who had been imprisoned early in the war for expressing secessionists views and the prevention the use of troops in the domestic concerns of the state. At the same time, Bradford realized that conscription would be unpopular in a state as divided as Maryland and requested that the War Department supply troops whenever a draft was held.

The defense of Maryland increasingly became a concern in the late summer of 1862 and would remain a focus of Bradford's efforts until the fall of 1864. During each emergency, beginning with Robert E. Lee's invasion in September 1862, Bradford summoned state forces and called for extra volunteers to protect the threatened areas. Because many of the Southern sympathizers in the state viewed such activity as helping the U.S. Army, Bradford had to resort to a state draft on several occasions to meet the defensive demands of the state. During the last of the Confederate invasions in the summer of 1864, Bradford's home outside Baltimore was burned by a party of Confederate raiders, and all the contents of the house were destroyed. Bradford was singled out for this action because of his support for the Union and because Union general David Hunter had destroyed Virginia governor John Letcher's home the previous spring.

Bradford's efforts to keep as many citizens loyal to the Union as possible were complicated early in the war by the increasing numbers of runaway slaves after the commencement of hostilities. These slaves naturally saw the war as an opportunity to gain their freedom, but the reluctance of neighboring states to enforce the Fugitive Slave Act once the war started made it difficult for Bradford to convince the state's slave owners that the war was not about slavery. When many of the slaves also began taking refuge in Washington, D.C., and Federal officers there took no effort to return them to the state, Bradford's job became even more difficult. Ultimately Bradford, who did not own slaves, saw the inevitability of emancipation and used his influence to bring about the end of the institution in Maryland in a new constitution in 1864.

After leaving the governor's chair in 1866, Bradford served several years as the surveyor of Baltimore's port. After leaving that position in 1869, Bradford spent most of his time in his law practice. Disapproving of the direction of the Republican Party, of which he was now a member, during the first Ulysses S. Grant administration, Bradford joined the reform wing of the party and was chosen an elector for Horace Greeley in the presidential election of 1872. After that election, Bradford

took little interest in public life and lived quietly outside Baltimore until his death on 1 March 1881.

—*David S. Heidler and Jeanne T. Heidler*

See also Maryland; Civil Liberties, U.S.A.

For further reading:
Cottom, Robert I., Jr., and Mary Ellen Hayward. *Maryland in the Civil War: A House Divided* (1994).

BRADLEY, AMY MORRIS
(1823–1904)
Union army nurse

Amy Morris Bradley was like other successful relief workers in her organizational genius and understanding of how to cut red tape without breaching military etiquette—a code of conduct she referred to as her "peace method." When she left the service in 1865, she had worked as a transport nurse, brought order to Alexandria's Convalescent Camp "Misery," helped hundreds of soldiers obtain discharges and back pay, and won praise from surgeons, hospital administrators, and soldiers as a woman "possessed of superior executive ability."

With a history of respiratory illnesses and weighing just over a hundred pounds, this native of East Vassalboro, Maine, was an unlikely candidate for war service when she arrived at Camp Franklin, Virginia, in September 1861. As a young child, Bradley lost her mother and was raised by her married sisters. At sixteen, she went to work teaching, a career she parlayed into administrative positions in the 1840s. By 1850 she was suffering from acute bronchitis and resigned her job in the hope of recovering in a brother's Charleston home. When Bradley returned to New England in 1851 and fell ill again, doctors advised her to relocate permanently. In 1853 she jumped at an opportunity to work in Central America as a governess. She moved to San Jose in November, and in a matter of months, had opened Costa Rica's first international school. Its principal until 1857, the thirty-eight-year-old spinster, now fluent in Spanish, accepted a job translating documents for a glass company in East Cambridge, Massachusetts.

From East Cambridge, she wrote to the 3d Maine Volunteers in 1861, asking for a position as a nurse. Regimental surgeons G. S. Palmer and George E. Brickett attempted to dissuade her, but Bradley insisted that she was equal to the rigors of camp life and started as matron on 1 September. With hard physical labor, Bradley's health actually improved; she would always prefer work in the field to that in poorly ventilated general hospitals. So adept was she in bringing order to the regimental hospital that by late fall, General Henry Slocum gave her charge of medical arrangements for his brigade. Near Camp Franklin she fitted out the Powell and Octagon houses to accommodate sick and wounded men. After the brigade

left for Centreville in the spring, the hospitals were closed. After several weeks of transience Bradley went to Washington to seek employment with the Sanitary Commission, which was then equipping hospital boats in anticipation of McClellan's spring campaigns.

In retrospect, Bradley's move from the Army of the Potomac to the Sanitary Commission was not fortunate. Although commissioners like Frederick Knapp enthusiastically enlisted her aid, Bradley was snubbed by elite transport workers, who believed—erroneously—that she drew a salary. After conducting 1,000 wounded from Fortress Monroe to New York on the *Ocean Queen*, Bradley was left to manage the cleanup, a formidable task of flushing the decks of mud and effluvia and laundering bloody uniforms left behind. From the battle of Fair Oaks in May 1862, until McClellan's forces vacated the Peninsula at the end of the summer, Bradley served as custodial supervisor on seven ships, while "the Aristocracy of the Commission"—New York blue bloods like Katharine Wormeley, Georgeanna Woolsey, and Ellie (Mrs. George Templeton) Strong—managed to secure more desirable assignments. On board the *Knickerbocker* in June, Bradley met Michigan's Annie Etheridge, whose sterling work ethic and lack of pretense were more to Bradley's liking.

No sooner had Bradley helped evacuate men from the Peninsula to Aquia Creek than she was summoned to Washington to revive the Soldiers' Home on North Capitol, a facility that offered soldiers a free bed and food when they made the transition from the hospital to their regiments. After putting the home in order—accomplished chiefly through hiring three women to do the cooking, laundry, and chamber work—Bradley began to seek other venues for her organizational zeal. By December 1862 she began to clean up the dismal Convalescent Camp in Alexandria by establishing a hospital, bath house, cook house, and regular laundry service. Bradley also put into place procedures to help soldiers obtain back pay and discharge papers and to rescind desertion charges if they had been hospitalized. In a year's time, nearly 112,000 men went through the camp, hundreds of whom Bradley personally escorted through the military bureaucracy.

Early in 1864 the government sent inmates of the camp to area hospitals and reorganized it as Camp Distribution (later Rendezvous of Distribution). So grateful to Bradley were the convalescents, that a delegation honored her with a gold watch. Without its sick and wounded, Camp Distribution now served as a way station for soldiers awaiting assignment to new regiments. In the interest of disseminating information about furloughs, medical discharges, and sanitary procedures, Bradley created the *Soldiers' Journal* in February 1864, which ultimately boasted 20,000 subscribers, including President Lincoln and General Grant. For

eighteen months, the journal was published weekly at five cents per copy; its profits of over $2,000 went to an orphanage after the war. On her last day of service in August 1865, Bradley was nearly killed when a driver lost control of her carriage and left her to fend for herself from the back seat. The irony of spending four years exposed to bullets and disease only to be killed by a runaway horse was not lost on Bradley, who managed to stop the animal before it vaulted over a cliff.

Bradley traveled to Wilmington, North Carolina, in late summer, where she turned her attention back to school administration. Under the auspices of the Soldiers' Memorial Association, she opened a free school, which became the seed for Wilmington's public schools later in the century. Bradley maintained her roles as teacher and administrator until her retirement in 1891. She died thirteen years later at the age of eighty.

—*Jane E. Schultz*

See also Etheridge, Annie; Nurses.

For further reading:

Bradley, Amy Morris. Diaries and Letterbooks. Perkins Library, Duke University.

Brockett, Linus P., and Mary C. Vaughan. *Woman's Work in the Civil War* (1867).

Cashman, Diane Cobb. *Headstrong: The Biography of Amy Morris Bradley* (1990).

Moore, Frank. *Women of the War: Their Heroism and Self-Sacrifice* (1866).

BRADY, MATHEW B.
(ca. 1823–1896)
Photographer

Little is known about Mathew Brady's early life except that he was born in Warren County, New York, to Andrew and Julia Brady around 1823. Afflicted with an eye inflammation as a teen, Brady

Brady's photographic outfit near Petersburg, Virginia, *ca.* 1864 (*Library of Congress*)

Mathew Brady (*center, in hat*) and troops under fire before Petersburg, Virginia, 21 June 1864
(Photograph by Mathew Brady Studios / *National Archives*)

traveled to Albany and Saratoga in search of a cure. During his time in Saratoga, Brady probably met portrait painter William Page. Through this acquaintance, he most likely met Samuel F. B. Morse, who in the 1830s was experimenting with the new medium of daguerreotypy, an early form of photography. As Morse was offering lessons in the new art at the time, most scholars believe that this is where Brady first learned what was to become his trade.

In 1843 Brady was living in New York City and manufacturing cases to house daguerreotypes, jewelry, and painted miniature portraits. By April 1844 Brady had opened his first studio, the Daguerrean Miniature Gallery, on Broadway. In October of the same year, he exhibited his work at the American Institute's annual fair and won the premium (or highest) award, which he won again in 1845, 1846, 1849, and 1857.

Shortly thereafter, Brady began his lifelong endeavor of collecting images of notable Americans. He opened a studio in Washington, D.C., in 1849 so that he could obtain portraits of the important political personages in the city. To this end, he made daguerreotypes of Henry Clay, Daniel Webster, John C. Calhoun, Zachary Taylor, and Millard Fillmore. In 1850 Brady published his collection in a book entitled *The Gallery of Illustrious Americans*, which sold for $15 a copy. At around the same date, Brady married Juliette Handy.

Brady's work continued to win the praise of others working with daguerreotypy. In 1851 he won a medal at the Fair of All Nations in London, England, and in 1854 he won a bronze medal at the New York Industrial Exhibition at the Crystal Palace for his daguerreotypes.

By 1858 Brady had two studios on Broadway, the largest with twenty-six employees. One of these employees was a Scottish immigrant named Alexander Gardner. When Brady decided to open a new studio in Washington, D.C., to replace the earlier studio that had eventually failed, the photographer chose Gardner to manage it. Brady's National Photographic Art Gallery, on Pennsylvania Avenue, enabled him to acquire photographs of the politicians in the city, including presidential candidates Stephen A. Douglas and Abraham Lincoln, as well as all the members of the House of Representatives, some of whom would become notable for their roles in the Confederate cause.

By the outbreak of the Civil War, Brady's business was near its peak. The advent of carte de visite cameras enabled a photographer to take multiple pictures simultaneously. Exposed on paper and mounted on card stock, these new photographs provided inexpensive likenesses for a wider portion of the public and thus expanded Brady's business in both New York and Washington. At the same time, his photographers were in the field with the Union army, recording the events of the war.

Brady's photographic gallery, at the corner of Broadway and Tenth Street, New York
(*Frank Leslie's Illustrated Newspaper* / *Library of Congress*)

Engravings based on Alexander Gardner's photographs of the aftermath of Antietam were the first graphic images of battlefield dead and were published in *Harper's Weekly*. The original photographs, on display at Brady's New York studio, caused an outcry of horror among his patrons.

Throughout his career, though he had many wealthy and influential friends and was able to amass property and investments, Brady could not manage his finances. Constantly in debt, he managed to procure loans on his good name and artistic talent. By the end of the Civil War, however, Brady was in serious financial difficulty. The photographic medium that he helped make popular, the carte de visite, undermined the attraction of his New York and Washington galleries. Now that the images of famous personages could be reproduced in quantity and sold to the public, individuals could collect their own small portrait galleries.

At the end of the war, Brady negotiated to sell his massive archive of photographs to the prestigious New York Historical Society. The profits of the sale were intended to pay off his outstanding debts. To his great disappointment, the deal fell through. In 1870, Brady then traveled to Washington to try to sell his collection to the federal government. His debts too large to ignore, in 1872 Brady sold his opulent New York studio and filed for bankruptcy. Finally, in 1875 the U.S. Congress bought the title to the Brady collection for $25,000. The embattled photographer was then able to pay off his debts.

Brady remained in Washington and worked with his nephew Levin Handy, also a photographer. Though his enthusiasm for the art had waned, Brady continued to take portraits of notable people, though he no longer pursued them with as much vigor as he had twenty years earlier.

After his wife's death in 1887, Brady's health deteriorated, exacerbated by alcohol and depression. He managed to open his last studio in 1890 in Washington, where, instead of his portraits, he was the main attraction. As the only survivor of the many photographers who recorded the Civil War, Brady became popular among journalists interested in the great upheaval of the previous generation. Regaining some of his interest in the promotion of his work, he began compiling a slide lecture of his old photographs. In 1895, a traffic accident aborted his plans and left him with a broken leg. He never fully recovered from the injury and died a year later, on 16 January 1896 in New York.

Brady was ever popular with the former soldiers of the

"Brady, the Photographer, Returned from Bull Run,"
22 July 1861 (*Library of Congress*)

Civil War and with the New York art world, and his funeral was financed by artists and the veterans of the New York 7th Regiment Veterans Association. He was buried beside his wife in Congressional Cemetery in Washington, D.C.

—*Heidi Campbell-Shoaf*

See also Photography.
For further reading:
Panzer, Mary. *Mathew Brady and the Image of History* (1994).
Sullivan, George. *Mathew Brady: His Life and Photographs* (1994).

BRAGG, BRAXTON
(1817–1876)
Confederate general

The acerbic, easily agitated Confederate commander Braxton Bragg, who was probably the most ill-suited general to lead a large army in the war, was born in Warrenton, North Carolina, on 21 March 1817.

Bragg's brother, Thomas, would serve as Confederate attorney general. A strict disciplinarian in an army that caviled at strict discipline, few other commanders earned such severe rebukes from his subordinates than Bragg. Although he never proved himself competent in leading a large force, he was given this responsibility in several key campaigns. Even counting the one major victory he could claim at Chickamauga, he mismanaged them all.

He graduated fifth of fifty in his 1837 class at West Point and served in both the Second Seminole War and the Mexican-American War. Serving under General Zachary Taylor in Mexico, he was promoted three times for extraordinary service, yet two assassination attempts were reportedly made on his life by fellow soldiers, an early indication of his ability to make enemies. He later served with Colonel Albert Sidney Johnston in his Utah expedition before Bragg resigned his commission as a brevet lieutenant colonel in 1856. In the time between then and the beginning of the Civil War, Bragg lived as a sugar planter in Louisiana. In 1861, he was appointed brigadier general and was assigned to coastal defense in Pensacola, Florida, where he quickly took charge of various navy assets and fortifications. Subsequently, he was given command over the whole Gulf Coast defense and was promoted to major general before he and his troops were sent to reinforce General Albert Sidney Johnston in Corinth, Mississippi. Before the battle of Shiloh, Bragg served as Johnston's chief of staff, helping to organize an army almost in shambles. During the battle, Bragg acted gallantly as he directed attacks at the center of the conflict; he had two horses shot out from under him. After Johnston's death on the battlefield, Bragg was elevated to second in command by General P. G. T. Beauregard, whose subsequent ill health led him to depart the army and leave Bragg in command. Bragg quickly began establishing strict discipline for his troops and reorganizing the damaged army. Eventually abandoning Corinth, Mississippi, he shifted his command to Chattanooga, Tennessee.

From Chattanooga, Bragg began planning and organizing an offensive north through central Tennessee into Kentucky. During these preparations, Bragg applied what became a habit of purging officers he thought inferior. He also began exhibiting the effects of stress, a condition that tended to further diminish his ineffectiveness as a commander. Nonetheless, when Bragg advanced, he pushed Union general Don Carlos Buell out of Tennessee without fighting a battle. By 15 September, Bragg's men were marching to Munfordville, Kentucky, and received the surrender of the Union garrison there. Although he was now in a position to break Buell's lines of communication, Bragg allowed Buell to reach Louisville. His efforts to recruit Kentuckians for the rebel cause proved unsuccessful as well. As the Confederate invasion of Kentucky turned into a muddle, its fortunes were finally settled at the battle of Perryville, where a stalemate forced the Confederates south. The failure of the Kentucky invasion revealed Bragg's inability to control army operations, even to the point that he began to run out of provisions. Moreover, his failure in Kentucky caused considerable disappointment throughout the Confederacy, so in October he was summoned to Richmond to answer critics in the government. President Jefferson Davis allowed him to keep his job, however, which would prove to be one of the most crucial mistakes of his presidency.

By Christmas 1862, Bragg's army was encamped in Murfreesboro, Tennessee, where from Nashville the new Union commander General William S. Rosecrans would oppose it. Rosecrans was under pressure to advance on Bragg, so on 31 December, the armies were in place for battle near Stones River. Lacking the strength and the imagination to exploit the success of an early Confederate assault, Bragg managed only a series of attacks against a firm Union line during the next two days. Bragg had thought Rosecrans would retreat to fortifications in Nashville, but when the Federals remained in place, it was the Confederate army that retreated as rain threatened to put Stones River out of its banks. Rosecrans did not follow, but the campaign was a strategic defeat for Bragg, and it left his army badly mauled. Total casualties from the battle were staggering at almost 25,000 men.

Historians have generally been critical of Bragg for his lack of imagination at Stones River. Although his experience at Shiloh and Perryville had made him aware of the futility of such frontal assaults, he persisted in them at Stones River. Bragg's tactical management of battles hence followed a distinctive and deadly pattern. Initial success would occur, often in spite of Bragg's muddled understanding of the tactical picture, and then that success would lose momentum until Bragg was unable to deliver a final decisive blow.

After Stones River, Bragg retreated to Tullahoma and awaited Rosecrans's inevitable advance, although the Federal force would not begin another campaign until June. Because Bragg was preparing to send reinforcements to embattled Vicksburg, Rosecrans finally accelerated his offensive. A demonstration against one of Bragg's divisions at Shelbyville set the stage for General George H. Thomas to attack another at Manchester. With other Union forces moving to outflank his positions around Tullahoma, Bragg ignominiously retreated to Chattanooga, giving up central Tennessee without fighting a battle for it.

In mid-August 1863, Rosecrans again tried to beguile Bragg into giving up ground without a fight. Dividing his Army of the Cumberland into three parts, Rosecrans threw Bragg into a confused belief that he was about to be outflanked again. Fearful that he would be separated

from the important city of Atlanta, Bragg gave up Chattanooga without a fight, but he soon discovered that Rosecrans had kept the Union army divided. Bragg concentrated his own forces to attack the most exposed part of Rosecrans's scattered advance. Yet when he failed to destroy the Union army piecemeal, Rosecrans recognized his peril and quickly regrouped. On 18 September, the Union and Confederate armies faced one another across Chickamauga Creek, unaware of the other's exact location. Bragg wanted to get between Rosecrans and Chattanooga, and the endeavor brought on a full-scale engagement at Chickamauga. Again early success gave way to a series of stalled attacks, this time against George H. Thomas's stubborn stand on Snodgrass Hill. Although Rosecrans despondently retreated to Chattanooga, there was some irony in that Bragg's objective of reclaiming that city had resulted in driving the Federal army into it. Furthermore, while Bragg could claim the field at Chickamauga with a sound defeat of the enemy, he had done nothing to make his victory meaningful. Instead, he had allowed the shattered Union forces to limp away and dig in.

It was a mistake that was compounded later by his poor troop placement around Chattanooga. Also, his chronic inability to get along with subordinates, especially the more talented ones, finally reached a critical level after Chickamauga. Jefferson Davis tried to intervene in October with a personal visit to Bragg's headquarters, but the beleaguered president tried to placate everyone, with the result that the situation was only worsened. On the other side, Ulysses S. Grant had acted decisively to replace Rosecrans with Thomas. The stage was set in November 1863 for Bragg's final humiliation.

On 23 November, Thomas began breaking Bragg's siege of Chattanooga by advancing on Orchard Knob, a rise below Missionary Ridge where most Confederate forces were in place. Sherman attacked Bragg's right, and General Joseph Hooker assailed Confederates on Lookout Mountain. When the center of the Union attack spontaneously charged up Missionary Ridge and routed the Confederates there, Bragg had to flee the city's environs. He barely made it into Dalton, Georgia. While reliable Patrick Cleburne fended off Federal attempts to destroy the retreating army, Bragg reformed his shattered force the best he could. As Rosecrans had similarly done after the battle of Chickamauga, Bragg braced himself for the consequence of this last dismal failure.

Davis accepted Bragg's resignation and replaced him with General Joseph E. Johnston. Bragg's days of field command were over, but his military career continued when his loyal friend President Davis brought him to Richmond as his military adviser. By then, the Confederacy's military fortunes were to enter such a rapid decline that Bragg's influence for good or ill in this new position would be hard to calculate. Some would

insist, however, that he again blundered by letting the Union capture the last remaining open Confederate port at Wilmington, North Carolina. Fleeing with the Davis party upon the evacuation of Richmond, Bragg and his wife were captured in Georgia. After the war, he pursued a career in civil engineering and became a railroad executive. He died in Galveston, Texas, in 1876 and was buried in Mobile, Alabama.

Bragg's reputation has never recovered from the series of tactical blunders he began during his 1862 invasion of Kentucky and concluded with his mismanagement at Chattanooga the following year. Unable to cultivate talent on his staff and with a penchant for alienating his most gifted subordinates, Bragg was audacious when he should have been careful and timid when he should have been bold. Certainly as much as any individual, he was responsible for Confederate defeat.

—James H. Meredith

See also Army of Mississippi; Buell, Don Carlos; Chattanooga Campaign; Chickamauga, Battle of; Davis, Jefferson; Kentucky; Munfordville, Battle of; Perryville, Battle of; Rosecrans, William Starke; Shiloh, Battle of; Stones River, Battle of; Tullahoma Campaign.

For further reading:
Buell, Thomas B. *The Warrior Generals: Combat Leadership in the Civil War* (1997).
Coffey, David. *John Bell Hood and the Struggle for Atlanta* (1998).
McWhiney, Grady. *Braxton Bragg and Confederate Defeat* (1969).
Snow, William P. *Lee and His Generals* (1982).

BRAGG, EDWARD STUYVESANT
(1827–1912)
Union general

Born to Joel Bragg and Margaretha Kohl Bragg in Unadilla, New York, Edward Bragg was educated locally and at what would become Hobart College before reading law and being admitted to the bar in 1848. Two years later he moved to Fond du Lac, Wisconsin, where he became a prominent attorney and Democratic leader.

In the election of 1860, Bragg supported the presidential candidacy of Stephen Douglas and traveled to Charleston, South Carolina, in the spring of 1860 as a Wisconsin delegate to the Democratic National Convention. Upon the election of Abraham Lincoln in the fall of 1860 and the outbreak of the Civil War in the spring of 1861, Bragg organized a company and became a captain in the 6th Wisconsin Infantry. The 6th Wisconsin would become one of the regiments composing the famous Iron Brigade. Bragg was promoted major in September 1861.

For the first year of the war, the 6th did garrison duty in Washington, D.C. During that time, in June 1862, Bragg was promoted to lieutenant colonel. In July 1862 the 6th became part of John Pope's Army of Virginia and

marched out of the city. It saw its first action at Cedar Mountain in August 1862. By the end of the month, Bragg was in temporary command of the regiment after its colonel was injured at Gainesville, Virginia, on 28 August during the Second Bull Run campaign.

Bragg continued to command the 6th at South Mountain and Antietam and fought at Fredericksburg. He was promoted colonel and commander of the regiment in March 1863 and led those troops into battle as part of I Corps under the command of John Reynolds at Chancellorsville. Because of illness, Bragg did not participate in the Gettysburg campaign.

The following fall, however, still part of I Corps, the regiment and the Iron Brigade fought at Bristoe Station and the Mine Run campaign. During the spring of 1864, Bragg led the 6th in the opening stages of Ulysses S. Grant's campaign against Robert E. Lee. At the Wilderness, Bragg assumed command of the Iron Brigade, and a month later he was recommended for promotion to brigadier general by George Gordon Meade and was promoted on 25 June 1864. Bragg led his men in the attempt to cut the Weldon Railroad at Globe Tavern in August 1864 and Hatcher's Run in October 1864.

Bragg took a short leave of absence in January 1865 and in February 1865 went with what was left of his brigade to Baltimore to help with the organization and transport of new troops. He would see no major action for the remainder of the war and was mustered out of the volunteers in October 1865.

After the war, Bragg returned to Wisconsin, his law practice, and Democratic politics. He served in the state legislature and was elected to the U.S. House of Representatives in 1876. As a delegate to the 1884 Democratic National Convention, Bragg coined the phrase, in referring to the nomination of Grover Cleveland, "We love him for the enemies he has made!" Later in life Bragg served as consul general to Hong Kong during the Theodore Roosevelt administration. Bragg died on 20 June 1912 at home in Fond du Lac, Wisconsin.

—David S. Heidler and Jeanne T. Heidler

See also Globe Tavern; Hatcher's Run; Iron Brigade.
For further reading:
Farnum, George R. "Edward S. Bragg: Soldier, Lawyer and Diplomat." *American Bar Association Journal* (1944).

BRAGG, THOMAS
(1810–1872)
Confederate attorney general

Born in Warrenton, North Carolina, to Thomas Bragg and Margaret Crossland Bragg, the younger Bragg was educated locally before being sent as a youth to a military school in Connecticut.

Upon his return to North Carolina, Bragg studied law and began his own practice in 1833. Over the years before the outbreak of the Civil War, Bragg became one of the most respected attorneys in the state. During this time Bragg also became active in North Carolina Democratic politics. He was slow to advance in party circles, however, because he lived in a largely Whig area of the state. He served two terms in the state legislature in the 1840s before gaining the attention of state Democratic leaders and won the governorship of the state in 1854. He won reelection in 1856. Judged a very able governor by his contemporaries, Bragg was also viewed as a moderate on secession. Although he believed that secession was a perfectly legitimate response to violations of Southern rights, Bragg did not believe that that remedy was the best solution for the South. His excellent handling of state affairs during his four years in office caused his election to the United States Senate in 1859.

In the Senate, Bragg continued his moderate stand regarding secession and affirmed his strong belief in the limited powers of the federal government. Although he still did not believe that secession was in the best interest of the South or of North Carolina, he supported his state when it seceded in May 1861. For a brief time he served as an assistant to Governor John W. Ellis, until the governor's death in July 1861. In November 1861 he accepted appointment by Confederate president Jefferson Davis as Confederate attorney general.

During his brief tenure as attorney general, Bragg was considered a close adviser of Jefferson Davis. Bragg worked hard to protect civilian rights and to insist that the military adequately compensate civilians for requisitioned supplies. He received numerous requests for the release of civilian prisoners. Confederate policies were becoming increasingly unpopular in Bragg's native state of North Carolina, so in March 1862 Bragg resigned his cabinet post and returned home to act as a spokesman for the Confederate government against the increasingly strong peace movement in North Carolina.

Over the next few years Bragg worked tirelessly to offset the criticisms leveled at Jefferson Davis by states' right advocates such as Governor Zebulon Vance. Some people in the state credited him with moderating some of Vance's extremist views. In March 1864 Bragg became the North Carolina commissioner for the Confederate law suspending the writ of habeas corpus, an onerous duty in a fractious state. From 1864 to 1865, Bragg edited the North Carolina *State Journal*.

Following the war, Bragg returned to his legal practice. In 1870, the legislature hired him as one of its attorneys in the impeachment of Governor William Holden. He died in Raleigh two years later. Bragg was the brother of Confederate general Braxton Bragg.

—*David S. Heidler and Jeanne T. Heidler*

See also North Carolina.

For further reading:
Bragg, Thomas. Thomas Bragg Diary, 1861–1862. Southern Historical Collection of the University of North Carolina Library at Chapel Hill.
Cowper, Pulaski. *Sketch of the Life of Governor Thomas Bragg: To which is Appended an Account of First Joint Discussion Between Gov. Thomas Bragg and Hon. John A. Gilmer, at Murphy, Cherokee County, in 1856* (1891).
Peele, W. J. *Lives of Distinguished North Carolinians with Illustrations and Speeches* (1898).
Snow, William Parker. *Lee and His Generals* (1982).

BRAMLETTE, THOMAS ELLIOTT
(1817–1875)
Union officer; Kentucky governor

Thomas Elliott Bramlette was born on 3 January 1817 to Colonel Ambrose S. and Sarah Bramlette in Cumberland (now Clinton) County, Kentucky. After education in the common schools, he studied law and was admitted to the bar in 1837. That year he married Sallie Travis with whom he had two children. After her death in 1872, he married Mrs. Mary E. Graham Adams in 1874. Bramlette was elected to the Kentucky House of Representatives in 1841 but did not seek reelection. Appointed commonwealth attorney in 1848, he resigned in 1850 and moved to Columbia, Kentucky. In 1856 he won election as a judge of the Sixth Judicial District.

A staunch Unionist Democrat, Bramlette resigned his judgeship in 1861 to raise and command the 3d Kentucky Volunteer Infantry Regiment. When he resigned in 1862 over a command dispute, Lincoln appointed him United States district attorney for Kentucky, and he moved to Louisville. Commissioned a major general in 1863, he was raising a division when the Union Democrats nominated him for the governorship. He won easily over Charles A. Wickliffe. In his 1 September 1863 inaugural address, Bramlette promised to make every effort to preserve the Union and the Constitution, but soon he demonstrated that even a strong Unionist could differ with the administration's policies.

While the Emancipation Proclamation did not apply to Kentucky, Bramlette accused Lincoln of breaking his promise not to interfere with slavery in the states that had it. His protests increased when the Union moved to enlist black soldiers. He threatened to use force to halt enlistments in Kentucky, but he led a delegation to Washington that got some concessions from Lincoln. The black soldiers, and later their families, gained freedom by military service, and before the war ended some 71 percent of Kentucky's African-Americans had become free.

Bramlette clashed frequently with overzealous military commanders who violated civil rights and interfered with elections. In a scathing 3 September 1864 letter to Lincoln, Bramlette complained that "We are dealt with, as though Kentucky was a rebellious and conquered province. . . . I am opposed to your reelection and regard a change of policy as essential to the salvation of the country." The governor helped the Democratic presidential candidate, George B. McClellan, carry Kentucky by a wide margin in 1864. He was much incensed in 1864 when Major General Stephen Gano Burbridge expelled Lieutenant Governor Richard T. Jacob to the Confederacy. Lincoln, who had not been consulted, allowed Jacob to return to Kentucky.

Toward the end of the war Bramlette was bedeviled by increased guerrilla activities in his state. On 4 January 1864 he issued a drastic proclamation that held Rebel sympathizers responsible for guerrilla raids, but later he quarreled with General Stephen Gano Burbridge for excessive enforcement of the orders. Bramlette helped secure Burbridge's reassignment in early 1865, but his differences continued with Major General John M. Palmer.

Lincoln could not persuade Kentucky to accept some form of gradual compensated emancipation, but Bramlette saw that slavery was doomed. He recommended that the legislature ratify the Thirteenth Amendment, provided that adequate compensation was paid to owners of slaves. Both Houses rejected his advice.

After Lincoln's assassination, Bramlette set aside a day for state mourning and admitted in a public address that the president had been correct in his views. The Democrats carried the state elections easily in August 1865, and in December Bramlette eased the return of former Confederates by promising a general pardon to those indicted in state courts. He furiously opposed the introduction of the Freedmen's Bureau into the state. While the legislature conferred some civil rights upon the new freedmen, Bramlette successfully opposed ratification of the Fourteenth and Fifteenth Amendments. (In 1976 Kentucky ratified the Civil War Amendments.)

When he left office in 1867, Bramlette lauded the state's prosperity and called for an end to sectional hatred. By then Kentucky had become part of the solid Democratic South. Bramlette resumed his law practice in Louisville, where he was active in civic affairs. After a brief illness he died there on 12 January 1875.

—*Lowell H. Harrison*

See also Kentucky.

For further reading:

Basler, Roy P., ed. *The Collected Works of Abraham Lincoln* (1953–1955).

Clift, G. Glenn. *Governors of Kentucky, 1792–1942* (1942).

Coulter, E. Merton. *The Civil War and Readjustment in Kentucky* (1926).

Webb, Ross A. Thomas Elliott Bramlette. In *Kentucky's Governors, 1792–1985* (1985).

BRANCH, LAWRENCE O'BRYAN
(1820–1862)
Confederate general

Born to Joseph Branch and Susan Simpson O'Bryan Branch, Lawrence O'Bryan Branch was brought up by his uncle John Branch, who was governor of North Carolina. His wealthy uncle saw that Lawrence was well educated (for example, his tutor was future secretary of the treasury and chief justice of the Supreme Court Salmon P. Chase). Lawrence attended the University of North Carolina before transferring to Princeton, from which he graduated in 1838. He studied law and dabbled in journalism in Tennessee before moving to Florida. He fought briefly in the Second Seminole War and practiced law in Florida before moving back to North Carolina in 1848.

In North Carolina Branch managed his plantations and became active in railroad promotion in the state. He served for three years as the president of the Raleigh & Gaston Railroad and became active in the 1850s in North Carolina politics. An active Democrat, he was chosen as a Franklin Pierce elector in the election of 1852 and in 1854 was himself elected to the United States House of Representatives. He served in that body until the secession of North Carolina. He was considered to be a moderate supporter of states' rights but not an advocate of secession. He served on the Committee on Territories, where he advocated the distribution of moneys from the sale of public lands to the states. He strongly supported the policies of President James Buchanan but refused an appointment as secretary of the treasury upon Georgian Howell Cobb's resignation in January 1861. After the firing on Fort Sumter and the subsequent call by President Abraham Lincoln for Federal volunteers, Branch changed his views regarding North Carolina's secession and advocated the state's departure from the Union.

After North Carolina's seceded, Branch offered his services to the state as a private, but the governor appointed him the quartermaster and paymaster general of North Carolina. He resigned this position shortly, however, to accept a commission as the colonel of the 33d North Carolina Regiment. In November 1861 he was made a brigadier general in the Confederate army, commanding forces around New Bern, North Carolina. Upon the assault on this position in March 1862 by an overwhelming Federal force under Ambrose Burnside, Branch successfully led his men in retreat to the York Peninsula.

In June 1862 Branch was transferred to Stonewall Jackson's corps. He commanded a brigade of A. P. Hill's division, Jackson's corps at the battles of the Seven Days', Cedar Run, Second Bull Run, and Ox Hill before moving with his brigade as part of Robert E. Lee's first invasion of Northern territory in September 1862. As part of Jackson's corps, Branch led his men to Harper's Ferry and participated in the taking of that Union position before moving with Hill's division to Sharpsburg to link up with the remainder of Lee's army as it prepared for an assault by George McClellan. In the resulting battle of Antietam, Branch arrived late with the remainder of Hill's division, which had been left behind by Jackson to mop up in Harper's Ferry. Branch did not arrive on the battlefield until late in the day on 17 September 1862. Hill's arrival had caused a retreat by the Union left. Riding ahead of his men to exhort them to pursue more rapidly, Branch was shot in the head and killed instantly.

—*David S. Heidler and Jeanne T. Heidler*

See also Harper's Ferry; New Bern, Battle of.
For further reading:
Brawley, James S. "The Public and Military Career of Lawrence O'Bryan Branch" (Master's thesis, 1951).

BRANDY STATION, BATTLE OF
(9 June 1863)

The largest cavalry clash of the Civil War, the battle of Brandy Station took place as Robert E. Lee began to move his army north for the invasion of Pennsylvania in 1863. Although the battle was technically a Confederate victory, it demonstrated how much the Union cavalry had closed the gap against its Southern counterpart since the beginning of the war.

After his brilliant victory at Chancellorsville in May 1863, Lee began to plan another invasion of the North. By the end of the month, he began to draw his forces together near Culpeper for a march northward. Lee placed General J. E. B. Stuart and his formidable cavalry at Brandy Station, just east of Culpeper, to screen the rest of Lee's army as it began to head to the Blue Ridge Mountains on its way to Pennsylvania. On 5 June, Stuart staged a grand review to boost morale and show

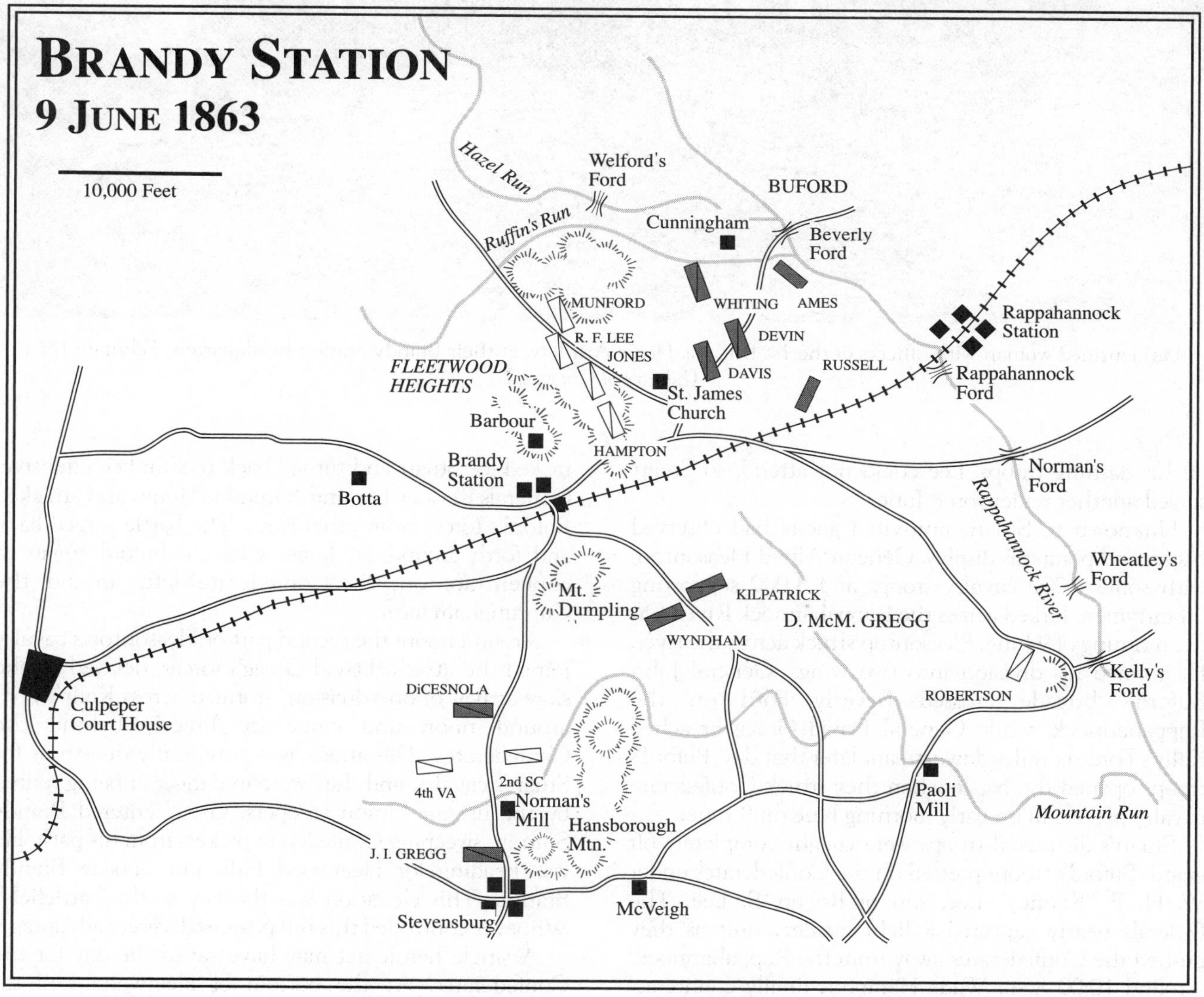

BRANDY STATION
9 JUNE 1863

10,000 Feet

Hazel Run
Ruffin's Run
Welford's Ford
BUFORD
Cunningham
Beverly Ford
MUNFORD
WHITING
AMES
R. F. LEE
JONES
DEVIN
Rappahannock Station
DAVIS
RUSSELL
FLEETWOOD HEIGHTS
St. James Church
Rappahannock Ford
Barbour
HAMPTON
Brandy Station
Botta
Norman's Ford
Rappahannock River
Wheatley's Ford
Mt. Dumpling
KILPATRICK
D. McM. GREGG
WYNDHAM
Kelly's Ford
DiCESNOLA
ROBERTSON
Culpeper Court House
4th VA
2nd SC
Norman's Mill
Hansborough Mtn.
Paoli Mill
Mountain Run
J. I. GREGG
Stevensburg
McVeigh

Unidentified woman with officers of the 1st Brigade, Horse Artillery, at their Brandy Station headquarters, February 1864
(*Library of Congress*)

off his dashing troops. Lee could not attend, so Stuart staged another review on 8 June.

Unknown to Stuart, uninvited guests had observed his second pompous display. General Alfred Pleasonton, with some 8,000 cavalry troops and 3,000 supporting infantrymen, lurked across the Rappahannock River. On the morning of 9 June, Pleasonton struck across the river. He formed his division into two wings. General John Buford's brigade crossed Beverly Ford on the Rappahannock, while General David Gregg breached Kelly's Ford six miles downstream later that day. Buford's troops opened the battle when they struck Confederate cavalry pickets in an early morning haze on 9 June.

Stuart's distracted troops were caught completely off guard. Buford's troops pressed on the Confederates under W. H. F. "Rooney" Lee, son of Robert E. Lee. The Federals nearly captured a light artillery unit as they pushed the Confederates away from the Rappahannock. Around 10:00 A.M., Wade Hampton finally counterat-

tacked for Stuart and turned back the Yankee offensive. Generals Rooney Lee and "Grumble" Jones also attacked Buford's forces from other sides. The battle surged back and forth around St. James Church. Buford began to concentrate on the Confederate left, around the Cunningham farm.

Around noon, the second part of Pleasonton's cavalry joined the attack. David Gregg's forces, delayed by the slow arrival of one division, stormed across Kelly's Ford around noon and came in directly behind the Confederates. The attack was potentially disastrous for Stuart's cavalry, and they were in danger of being routed by the upstart Union troopers. Gregg entered Brandy Station, sweeping Confederate pickets from his path. He was heading for Fleetwood Hill, just outside Brandy Station. This elevation was the key to the battlefield. Whoever controlled this hill possessed a great advantage.

A single heroic act may have saved the day for the Confederates. At the bottom of Fleetwood Hill sat

Rufus Ingalls and officers at the Army of the Potomac headquarters, Brandy Station, April 1864
(Photograph by Timothy O'Sullivan / *Library of Congress*)

Lieutenant John Carter with a six-pound cannon, left there for want of ammunition. Major Henry McClellan, Stuart's aide, frantically signaled Carter to bring the gun to the crest of Fleetwood Hill. Carter quickly unlimbered the gun and hauled it to the top of the hill where he packed it with bits of metal and substandard shells. There was enough powder for only one shot.

Meanwhile, Gregg was leading his troops towards Fleetwood Hill. As his forces began to ride up the hill, Carter fired the one blast his cannon had. It hit nothing, but it stopped the Yankees in their tracks. Colonel Percy Wyndham, the leader of the Federal column, suspected that the shot came from a line of guns set just over the top of the hill. He paused his men to wait for Gregg and the rest of the force. The ploy bought critical time for the Confederates. McClellan summoned part of Jones's brigade toward Fleetwood Hill. A frantic, hand-to-hand struggle for the hill ensued. The two sides literally charged through each other, and the summit of the hill changed hands numerous times.

Five miles south of Brandy Station yet another battle was raging. Colonel Alfred Duffié had split from Gregg's wing to cover the Union left flank. He encountered two regiments from Hampton's division and soundly defeated the rebels. Duffié then rode toward Brandy Station on a route that would have brought him directly into the Confederate rear. The move might have won the battle for the Union, but Duffié received an order to rejoin Gregg. This forced his men to backtrack several miles, and it effectively took them out of the action. They were the only division in Pleasonton's cavalry that could not embroider "Brandy Station" on its flag.

Back at Fleetwood Hill, the action continued. Buford's men, pinned down by the triple Confederate attack earlier, now surged ahead when the Confederates had to turn their attention toward Gregg's attack from

A canvas pontoon boat (50th New York Engineers) at Brandy Station, winter 1863–1864
(Photograph by Timothy O'Sullivan / *Library of Congress*)

the far right. This Union advance only fueled the chaos of the battle. The day saw many spectacular cavalry charges and saber fights as well as intense combat by dismounted troops. Fighting continued until the late afternoon, and the Confederates finally controlled Fleetwood Hill. Both sides were exhausted.

The Union cavalry evacuated the battlefield by the early evening after an intense ten-hour engagement. Because the Confederates held the field, Stuart could call it a victory. The Confederates inflicted some 935 casualties while sustaining 525. But most observers realized what had happened. The Union cavalry had surprised the Southerners and matched them blow for blow for the first time during the war. It removed the sense of inferiority that had haunted the Federal troopers in previous engagements. The huge psychological advantage that the Confederate cavalry had enjoyed throughout the war was lost in a single day. With a new sense of confidence, the Union cavalry fought well in succeeding battles. At Gettysburg, it fought Stuart's troops to a standstill as the Confederates tried to disrupt Union lines from the rear. Stuart's troops held Brandy Station, but were embarrassed by the tremendous difficulty they had in breaking even.

—*Richard D. Loosbrock*

See also Buford, John; Cavalry, C.S.A.; Cavalry, U.S.A.; Gregg, David M.; Hampton, Wade; Lee, William Henry Fitzhugh; Pleasonton, Alfred; Stuart, J. E. B.

For further reading:

Carter, Samuel, III. *The Last Cavaliers: Confederate and Union Cavalry in the Civil War* (1979).

Downey, Fairfax Davis. *Clash of Cavalry: The Battle of Brandy Station, June 9, 1863* (1959).

Nofi, Albert A. *The Gettysburg Campaign: June and July, 1863* (1986).

BRANNAN, JOHN MILTON
(1819–1892)
Union general

Born in Washington, D.C., John Milton Brannan as a teenager worked as a messenger in the House of Representatives. He became popular with the representatives and used his influence to secure an appointment to the U.S. Military Academy. He gradu-

John M. Brannan (*Library of Congress*)

ated twenty-third of fifty-two in the class of 1841. Commissioned a second lieutenant of artillery, Brannan served at several posts before the outbreak of the Mexican-American War. During that conflict, he was a member of the 1st Artillery and participated in Winfield Scott's Mexico City campaign. Brannan was wounded at Belen Gate and was brevetted to captain during the war.

After the Mexican-American War, Brannan served at a variety of frontier posts and fought briefly in Florida during the Third Seminole War. As tensions escalated between North and South in the early months of 1861, Brannan commanded Fort Taylor at Key West, Florida, as a captain of the 1st Artillery. He had only forty-four men at the post, and after Florida seceded in January 1861, he became increasingly concerned about secessionists trying to take the fort.

Brannan continued unmolested at the fort for the remainder of the year, during which he was made brigadier general of volunteers in September 1861. On 11 January 1862 the Department of Key West was created, which included all of Florida north from Key West to Cape Canaveral on the east coast and the Appalachicola River on the west coast. He remained in command there until August 1862, when he received command of the District of Beaufort, South Carolina.

On 3 September 1862, he received temporary command of the Department of the South headquartered at Hilton Head, South Carolina.

From Beaufort and the area around Hilton Head, Brannan organized an expedition down the coast at the end of September directed at St. John's Bluff near Jacksonville, Florida. A few weeks later, on 22–23 October, Brannan commanded an expedition against the plantations near Pocotaligo, South Carolina.

In the spring of 1863, Brannan was transferred to the Army of the Cumberland. He initially commanded the 1st Division of XXI Corps before being transferred to command the 3d Division of XIV Corps, commanded by Major General George Thomas. In this command he fought in the Tullahoma campaign and in September 1863 at Chickamauga.

At Chickamauga, the 3d, commanded by Brannan, engaged in one of the preliminary skirmishes with Nathan Bedford Forrest's cavalry on 19 September, and then on the 20th Brannan and the 3d Division served as one of the bulwarks of the defense of Horseshoe Ridge on the extreme left of Thomas's corps. Brannan retreated with the remainder of the corps in the late afternoon.

On 10 October 1863, Brannan was relieved of command of the 3d Division and became the chief of artillery for the Army of the Cumberland. He served in that capacity during the Chattanooga campaign and at Missionary Ridge. The following spring he became the chief of artillery for the Atlanta campaign. In all the engagements of that campaign through the surrender of the city, Brannan commanded the Union artillery.

With the commencement of William T. Sherman's March to the Sea, Brannan reverted to the command of the artillery for the Army of the Cumberland and returned to Tennessee, where for the remainder of the year he lent his expertise in combating John Bell Hood's campaign there.

After the war, Brannan returned to the rank of major in the 1st Artillery. For a short time after the war, Brannan commanded the Department of Georgia that included Fort Pulaski, the place of imprisonment for many high-ranking former Confederates. He was promoted to lieutenant colonel in 1877 and colonel in 1881. During his postwar service, he was stationed at a variety of posts in New York, Florida, and Pennsylvania. He retired in 1882 and died on 16 December 1892 in New York City.

—*David S. Heidler and Jeanne T. Heidler*

See also Atlanta Campaign; Chickamauga, Battle of; Florida; Jacksonville, Florida.

For further reading:

Bowers, John. *Chickamauga and Chattanooga; The Battles That Doomed the Confederacy* (1994).
Cozzens, Peter. *This Terrible Sound; The Battle of Chickamauga* (1992).

BRATTON, JOHN
(1831–1898)
Confederate general

General John Bratton of South Carolina was one of only a few men who enlisted in the Confederate army as a private, rose to the rank of brigadier general, and fought in both Eastern and Western theaters of action. Born in Winnsboro, South Carolina, to Dr. John Bratton and his second wife Isabella on 7 March 1831, the future general spent his formative years in the Palmetto State. As an adult John Bratton followed in his father's footsteps. He pursued a career in medicine. After graduating from South Carolina College in 1850 Bratton attended Charleston College for his medical training. He started his own practice in Winnsboro in 1853 and continued in that profession until the Civil War broke out in 1861.

When the Civil War started, John Bratton volunteered in Summerville, South Carolina, for twelve months. The doctor became a 30-year-old private in what later became the 6th South Carolina Infantry Regiment. On 25 June 1861, only twelve days after enlisting, Bratton was appointed second lieutenant. The 6th South Carolina moved in mid-July 1861 from Charleston to Richmond, Virginia. Arriving on 21 July, Bratton and his comrades marched immediately to the Manassas battlefield, which they reached in the afternoon of the battle. Although not engaged the sights of war impressed the new lieutenant. The regiment saw no action during the rest of 1861 and the end of the year found Bratton at Centreville, Virginia.

The next year was far more eventful for both the regiment and Bratton, starting with his appointment as colonel of the unit in April. He held the rank of colonel until promoted brigadier general in May 1864. In early 1862 the 6th South Carolina was part of General Richard H. Anderson's brigade of General James Longstreet's Second Division in the Army of Northern Virginia. Bratton commanded the regiment in the engagements at Williamsburg and Seven Pines, where he was wounded in the left arm and captured by Federal forces on 31 May 1862. Following his capture Colonel Bratton was transported to Fort Monroe, Virginia, where he stayed until exchanged on 31 August 1862. He rejoined the regiment in October.

Winter set in and Federal general Ambrose Burnside determined to launch a December attack on the Confederate army at Fredericksburg. Ostensibly part of General Micah Jenkins's brigade of General George Pickett's division in General James Longstreet's I Corps, Colonel Bratton's regiment was placed at various points in the Confederate line in the days leading up to the battle. The 6th South Carolina was in the center of Longstreet's corps for several days before being moved to the flank. Here it served to connect Longstreet's and General Thomas J. Jackson's corps. During the battle Bratton's men saw no action, which he described in a letter to his wife on 16 December: "We were not called upon to do anything but stand a little shelling, by which we lost one man wounded."

Though his participation in the battle of Fredericksburg was scant, John Bratton was recommended for promotion to brigadier general in January 1863. The recommendation came from General Micah Jenkins, passed through General Richard Anderson and General Longstreet before Robert E. Lee forwarded it to the Confederate War Department for approval. Unfortunately for Bratton there were no openings available, so the recommendation was denied.

In the fall of 1863 Bratton's 6th South Carolina, still in Micah Jenkins's Brigade, accompanied Longstreet's Corps to the West. General Jenkins's brigade did not arrive in time to fight in the battle of Chickamauga, however. During the battle General John B. Hood was seriously wounded and Longstreet put Jenkins in command of Hood's division. Colonel Bratton was then elevated to command Jenkins's Brigade. In this capacity Bratton led a night attack on Federal forces at Wauhatchie on 28–29 October, 1863. In this engagement Bratton had the 1st, 2d, 5th, and 6th South Carolina Regiments and Hampton's Legion at his disposal. Opposing him were the 109th and 111th Pennsylvania Regiments along with the 137th and 149th New York Regiments, commanded by General John W. Geary. After a fight of several hours the Confederates were forced to withdraw, and Bratton reported 356 casualties.

Colonel Bratton returned to Virginia when General Longstreet was ordered to rejoin General Lee's army. When Micah Jenkins was killed on 6 May 1864 during the battle of the Wilderness, Bratton was promoted to brigadier general. He led the brigade through the rest of the war, suffering a shoulder wound in October 1864. At Appomattox, Bratton's brigade was the largest in the Army of Northern Virginia, numbering about 1,500 effectives.

Following the war John Bratton entered politics. In 1866 he was elected to the South Carolina state legislature and served one term. Ten years later he chaired the South Carolina delegation that attended the Democratic National Convention. In 1884 Bratton was elected to the U.S. House of Representatives and served one term. His final act in South Carolina politics was his defeat in the gubernatorial election in 1890 at the hands of Ben "Pitchfork" Tillman. General John Bratton died on 12 January 1898 in Winnsboro, South Carolina, and is buried there.

—*Christopher C. Meyers*

See also Wauhatchie, Battle of.

For further reading:
Bratton, John. *Letters.* Southern Historical Society Collection, University of North Carolina at Chapel Hill.
Freeman, Douglas Southall. *Lee's Lieutenants: A Study in Command* (1942–1944).
Pickenpaugh, Roger. *Rescue By Rail: Troop Transfer and the Civil War in the West, 1863* (1998).

BRECKINRIDGE, JOHN CABELL
(1821–1875)

Confederate general and secretary of war

Born on 16 January 1821, near Lexington, Kentucky, John Cabell Breckinridge grew to maturity in a family that expected greatness. The only son of the six children of Mary Clay Smith and Joseph Cabell Breckinridge, he learned early that his paternal grandfather had been a U.S. senator and attorney general under Thomas Jefferson and was the man who in the 1790s introduced the Kentucky Resolutions stressing states' rights. Breckinridge's father died when the boy was only two, but in his thirty-five years had been speaker of the Kentucky House and then the commonwealth's secretary of state. John's grandfather, on his mother's side, had been president of the College of New Jersey at Princeton and had married a daughter of a signer of the Declaration of Independence. When John C. Breckinridge attended Centre College, where he received his degree in 1838, his brother-in-law served as the school's president. Breckinridge's favorite uncle held the Presbyterian Church's highest national office and won accolades as the father of the public school system in Kentucky. In short, almost everywhere young John turned, he had powerful examples of family achievement, models of leadership, and useful supporting allies.

A college graduate before the age of eighteen, Breckinridge spent part of a year as a resident graduate at Princeton and then enrolled in legal classes at Transylvania University, where he received his law degree in 1841. He moved to Iowa to practice his profession, but in two years returned to his home state and married Mary Cyrene Burch in December 1843. That happy union produced six children over the next decade. His wife's family ties added to Breckinridge's network and included cousin George W. Johnson, later the first governor of Confederate Kentucky.

In June 1847, as a young attorney Breckinridge gave an eloquent and powerful speech concerning the Mexican-American War, then raging. Soon the handsome, witty, charming, and charismatic Breckinridge won wide acclaim. He followed that with service in the conflict, as a major, but saw no real action in Mexico. However, the experience did give him insight into battle and war, and the costs.

Returning to Kentucky after the war, Breckinridge soon entered the political world and was repeatedly successful. Although his closest influences had been Whig, he soon joined the Democratic Party, as part of its Young America. At age twenty-eight, he won a seat in the Kentucky legislature; in 1851, at age thirty, he went to the United States House Representatives and won reelection by defeating a former Kentucky governor. In 1856, he ran for national office as the vice presidential candidate with James Buchanan, and on election became the youngest in the nation's history to serve in that position. Before the unhappy term ended, the state legislature selected him to be U.S. senator, beginning in March 1861.

But the presidency beckoned as well before then. During the 1850s, Breckinridge had fashioned a political philosophy based on a belief in a limited government with a strict interpretation of the Constitution. Regarding slavery, for instance, though he held a few slaves at various times, he apparently did not by 1860, and yet he defended the institution, supported the *Dred Scott* decision, and argued for the constitutional right to hold slaves as property. But he remained far removed from the fire-eating secessionists. That moderate stance brought him the presidential nomination for the Southern Democrats in 1860, after the Northern branch selected Stephen A. Douglas. With John Bell leading the Constitutional Unionists, and Abraham Lincoln (whose wife Breckinridge had known back in Lexington) heading the Republicans, Breckinridge found himself in a four-candidate race. Viewed in the North as the slaveholder's candidate, Breckinridge tried to show his moderation and wide appeal, but found only limited success. His support indicated, in fact, that his greatest allies in the South came from rural Democratic areas more than from slaveholding ones. But in 1861, as vice president, he had the duty to announce Lincoln elected with 170 electoral votes to his own 72, with Bell and Douglas dividing the other 51. At age forty, Breckinridge had suffered his first and only political defeat.

As a senator, Breckinridge followed a somewhat strange course over the next months. He stressed the right of secession, saw state after Southern state leave the Union, and watched as Kentucky declared neutrality. Had he joined the Confederacy early, he might have been an important figure in its political circles. Breckinridge had widespread appeal and support. As it was, he remained in Washington, attacked the Republicans for what he stressed were their unconstitutional actions, and called for a peaceful separation. But as the fighting continued, his obvious Southern sympathies became evident, and politicians termed him a traitor in their midst. Throwing off neutrality, Kentucky declared itself Union in September 1861. That same

month, fearing arrest, Breckinridge left the commonwealth and joined the Confederate army: "I exchange, with proud satisfaction, a term of six years in the Senate of the United States for the musket of a soldier." The most prominent Kentuckian to fight for the South, he would not be able to return to his native state for more than seven years.

Made a brigadier general in November 1861, despite his lack of combat experience and West Point training, Breckinridge first led what became known as the famous Orphan Brigade. While never a military strategist, he did prove a successful general overall. Displaying some of the characteristics that made people follow him in politics, Breckinridge seemed a natural leader. He showed courage and coolness during battles, inspired the troops at key times, and impressed them as a man who cared. And he did. A humane person, Breckinridge never became reconciled to the killing that war brought.

During the conflict, Breckinridge served as a subordinate commander in six major battles—Shiloh, Stone's River, Chickamauga, Chattanooga, Cold Harbor, and Winchester—and as an independent commander at Port Hudson and in southwest Virginia and the Shenandoah Valley. In his first major battle, as a division commander at Shiloh in April 1862, he made mistakes, as did so many officers leading large numbers of soldiers in battles beyond the scope of anything they had seen. His unit, however, did fight well, with terrible losses—368 killed, 1,682 wounded, 165 missing, a total of 34.7 percent of the force.

Promoted to major general after that fight, Breckinridge led troops toward Baton Rouge in an attempt to retake the city. Despite malaria and heat prostration, his men drove the Union troops back, but gunboats prevented further advances. He did occupy Port Hudson, which would remain a key Confederate post after that. That attack took Breckinridge away from the army, now led by Braxton Bragg, that invaded Kentucky in the fall of 1862. Ordered to join that campaign, he learned of the defeat at Perryville before reentering Kentucky. Disappointed, some thirty-miles from his home state, he turned back.

A long conflict then began between Breckinridge and Bragg. The commanding general blamed the Kentuckian for not having joined him sooner; the popular Breckinridge had little regard for Bragg as a leader, or man. When Bragg ordered the execution of a Kentuckian deserter who had gone home to help his starving family and had been retaken as he returned to the army, Breckinridge had protested in vain and had grown physically ill at the killing. Soon those disagreements grew.

At Stones River in December 1862 and January 1863, Breckinridge did not initially move his unit into place, as per General Bragg's plan, as quickly as he should have.

Nor did others. In an attempt to break Union lines, Bragg then ordered Breckinridge to attack a well-defended Federal position. Anticipating huge losses in an assault that few thought could succeed, the Kentuckian vehemently protested, but carried out the orders. The bloody repulse had the expected effect and Breckinridge saw many of his men, and personal friends, die. Bragg's report, critical of Breckinridge's role in the battle, brought Breckinridge to request a court of inquiry, but none resulted.

In the battle of Chickamauga in September 1863, Breckinridge's division fought well, suffered losses of nearly a third of the unit, and contributed to the Confederate victory. However, two months later as a corps commander at Chattanooga, Breckinridge was ordered to send a portion of his troops to another part of the battlefield and his thinned ranks proved little match for the sizable Union forces before him. That battle ended Bragg's career in the West, but, as usual, he blamed others for the defeat, particularly Breckinridge, charging him with drunkenness. As William C. Davis and other authors have noted, although Breckinridge certainly enjoyed one of Kentucky's best-known products, the charges of overindulgence do not withstand scrutiny and are not supported by others.

After several months of leave in late 1863 and early 1864, Breckinridge became commander of the almost forgotten Western Department of Virginia theater. There he generally did well under difficult circumstances. His worst moment of the war may have come in October 1864 at the battle of Saltville, where—without his knowledge—Confederates began massacring the African-American Union soldiers they encountered. By the time he ordered that to end, the worst of the military murders had already occurred. On the other hand, his victory at the battle of New Market in May 1864 had been his finest day as a general. Outnumbered and forced to use the Virginia Military Institute cadets from his reserves, Breckinridge handled his artillery well, made hard decisions, and won a complete victory, inflicting considerable Union losses. Confederates praised him as a "New Jackson in the Valley." Transferred to the east, his division fought at Cold Harbor in June, and then he joined Jubal Early in his advance on Washington. Breckinridge got close enough to see the Capitol dome, then a retreat followed. The ensuing battle of Winchester proved to be his last military battle.

On 6 February 1865, Confederate president Jefferson Davis made Breckinridge the last, as it turned out, Confederate secretary of war. Breckinridge's efforts in that office showed the strengths that he might have brought to the government had he been made a part of it earlier. Confident enough to challenge Davis, Breckinridge operated as a powerful secretary, relieving General Lucius Northrop as commissary general, devising a better supply plan, advising on strategy, and working closely with General Robert E. Lee. But by then, the cause was lost and within months the armies were surrendering.

Breckinridge supervised the evacuation of Richmond, advised General Joseph E. Johnston regarding his negotiations with General William T. Sherman, and, perhaps most important, presented President Davis with his thoughts on how to proceed. As debate raged on whether to continue to fight, in some guerrilla-type warfare, the secretary of war advanced arguments made earlier, that the Confederacy "should not disband like bandits" but rather should surrender with dignity and respect: "this had been a magnificent epic; in God's name, let it not terminate in a farce." Breckinridge realized the reality—the war was over and the killing should stop. For him personally, however, flight was his future. Fearing arrest as a traitor, Breckinridge made a tortuous and somewhat heroic escape through Florida, to Cuba, and then to Europe. Over the next few years, he remained in exile, traveling, waiting. Then, with a pardon from the president, Breckinridge and his family returned to the United States, arriving back in Lexington in March 1869.

Over the next six years, Breckinridge served as a defense and corporate attorney, as well as president of both a railroad company and an insurance company. In one of his few public stances, he denounced the Ku Klux Klan and supported the admission of black testimony in the courts. On 17 May 1875, at the age of fifty-four, John Cabell Breckinridge died. Although he had achieved in many different areas, the war had dictated that his bright promise remained not fully realized.

—*James C. Klotter*

See also Early's Washington Raid; Election of 1860; Kentucky; New Market, Battle of; Orphan Brigade.

For further reading:

Davis, William C. *Breckinridge: Statesman, Soldier, Symbol* (1974).

Heck, Frank H. *Proud Kentuckian: John C. Breckinridge, 1821–1875* (1976).

Klotter, James C. *The Breckinridges of Kentucky, 1760–1981* (1986).

BRECKINRIDGE, ROBERT JEFFERSON
(1800–1871)

Presbyterian minister and abolitionist

Born on 8 March 1800, Robert J. Breckinridge was the son of Mary Breckinridge and John Breckinridge, the legislator who in 1798 introduced what came be known as the Kentucky Resolutions. Robert attended Princeton and Yale and graduated from Union College in New York in 1819. In 1823 he married his cousin, Ann Sophonisba Preston,

with whom he would have eleven children. By 1825, Breckinridge had began his life's work as a Kentucky politician-farmer. When his wife died, he married another cousin, the widow Virginia Hart Shelby, and they had three more children.

In 1832 Breckinridge was ordained in the Presbyterian Church and served in Baltimore, Maryland, and Lexington, Kentucky. After a stormy year as president of Jefferson College in Pennsylvania, he returned to Kentucky, where he took the appointment of superintendent of public instruction. Under his reforms, Kentucky school attendance increased almost tenfold in four years. He found his niche as a professor at Danville Theological Seminary in Kentucky, where he published his two largest theological works.

Breckinridge was an active stump speaker, never hesitating to support his controversial stances on compensated emancipation and colonization, Know-Nothingism, and Unionism. He led the drive for the 1833 Non-Importation Law, which limited the number of slaves imported into Kentucky. In the 1840s he went from Clay Whiggism to the American Party, where he complained about the effects of immigrants and the Catholic faith on the morals of native white Americans. He helped form the Friends of Emancipation, a society whose members promised to free their slaves' children when the children reached the age of twenty-one.

On the steps of the courthouse in Lexington, Kentucky, on 4 January 1861, Breckinridge gave a powerful speech, "The Day of National Humiliation," which verbalized the Unionist beliefs of many in the border states. On 4 July of that year, his eldest son, Robert Jr., led the Ashland Rifles out of Lexington to form the first organized Kentucky volunteers for the C.S.A. A few months later, his nephew, John C. Breckinridge, former vice president of the United States, left to become a Confederate brigadier general. A year later his second son, Willie, left to join the South, as did two sons-in-law. Two of his youngest sons and three other sons-in-law joined the U.S. Army, thus exemplifying the horrors of "the Brothers' War."

When President Abraham Lincoln issued his Preliminary Emancipation Proclamation in 1862, Breckinridge objected strenuously. He believed it unconstitutional and even immoral, but most importantly, it undermined the Unionist cause in Kentucky that he espoused. The president's decision to use African-American troops Breckinridge saw as even more dangerous. However, upon the threat of Kentucky governor Thomas E. Bramlette's issuing a nullification proclamation of the federal draft of African-Americans, Breckinridge led a caucus that persuaded the governor to issue a more moderate message to Kentuckians and to persuade them to accept the U.S. recruiting efforts. Ultimately, even though the

Emancipation Proclamation never affected Kentucky, more than 23,000 black Kentuckians earned their freedom by joining the Union forces.

Though committed to public support for the Union, Breckinridge continued in his role as a slave owner. In July 1864 he went to the Federal headquarters at Camp Nelson, Kentucky, and demanded that General Speed Fry return to him seventeen women and children who had run away from his farm to join their male relatives stationed at the camp.

That summer, as Kentucky's Union Democratic Party split, Breckinridge led those who were "Unconditional Unionists." He stumped across the state, openly opposing such conservative Union Democrats as Governor Bramlette, Lieutenant Governor Richard Jacob, and *Louisville Journal* editor George Prentice. Unconditional Unionist delegates chose Breckinridge to represent them at the 1864 Baltimore convention, where he served as temporary chairman. The Kentucky delegation then called upon President Lincoln, who had just been renominated, and, with Breckinridge as their spokesperson, they protested especially against the military power of Governor Bramlette and also against the draft in Kentucky for home defense.

Between 20 and 25 July 1864, the Unconditional Unionists gave to the military the names of their political competitors to be arrested for treason and thereby secured their own election. In early October, over the course of two weeks while convalescing after a fall from his horse, Breckinridge met with elite groups of Unionists, including the military commander of Kentucky, General Stephen G. Burbridge. These meetings became widely known, and Breckinridge was labeled as the leader of a "Secret Inquisition." According to a Kentucky newspaper, Burbridge's local advisors used him "as a mere instrument to satiate their own cravings for human blood."

As the war drew to a close, Breckinridge feared the continued vigilantism and guerrilla warfare. By 1865 he reversed his position on black troops and advocated stationing more blacks in the state. This stance, along with his past association with the hated General Burbridge and President Lincoln, made him extremely unpopular.

The Union lost Kentucky after the Civil War. Breckinridge watched in dismay as the various parts of the Republican platform were rejected. He envisioned doom and destruction for his state and nation. He could not even halt the split in the Kentucky Synod of the Presbyterian Church in 1866.

Breckinridge's second wife had died in 1859, and at the age of sixty-eight Breckinridge married the young widow Margaret Faulkner White in 1868. He resigned from the Danville Theological Seminary as a result of ill health in October 1869, and he died two years later on 27 December 1871.

—*Randolph Hollingsworth*

See also Kentucky.
For further reading:
Collins, Lewis. *Collins' Historical Sketches of Kentucky: History of Kentucky* (1874; reprint, 1966).
Gilliam, William D., Jr. "Robert J. Breckinridge." *Register of the Kentucky Historical Society* (1971).
Howard, Victor B. *Black Liberation in Kentucky: Emancipation and Freedom, 1862–1884* (1983).
Kelley, Ruth E. "Robert Jefferson Breckinridge: His Political Influence and Leadership during 1849 and the Civil War" (M.A. thesis, 1948).
Klotter, James C. *The Breckinridges of Kentucky, 1760–1981* (1986).

BRENTWOOD, TENNESSEE
(25 March 1863)

As Ulysses S. Grant commenced plans to move on Vicksburg during early 1863, farther to the east Union and Confederate forces clashed around Nashville and the outlying region. South of Nashville, about halfway to Franklin, Lieutenant Colonel Edward Bloodgood guarded the Harpeth River Bridge of the Nashville & Columbia Railroad. Bloodgood had about 520 men of the 22nd Wisconsin Infantry camped to protect the forks of the Wilson and Franklin pikes as well as a nearby rail facility. He had placed 230 men of the 19th Michigan Infantry under Captain E. B. Bassett at a stockade a mile and a half south of Brentwood near the railroad bridge. Nathan Bedford Forrest moved upon this place early on 25 March to capture the garrison and its supplies, as well as destroy the Harpeth River Bridge.

Forrest intended to reduce both the stockade and Brentwood simultaneously by sending Colonel James W. Starnes's 2d Brigade to cross the Harpeth six miles east of Franklin. Starnes was to cut the telegraph and tear up the railroad before moving on the stockade. Meanwhile, Forrest would accompany Brigadier General Frank C. Armstrong's 1st Brigade with the 10th Tennessee Cavalry attached to assail Bloodgood at Brentwood.

Everything got underway before dawn on 25 March, and brushes with Union pickets over a wide area alerted the Federals that something was afoot. Telegraphed warnings to Bloodgood, however, were blocked when the Confederates cut the wires. Bloodgood would not know about the large force bearing down on him until it arrived. Forrest was having his own troubles. He had difficulty getting his artillery across the Harpeth and consequently was late in arriving at Brentwood. Alone near the stockade and increasingly bewildered about what might have gone wrong, Starnes finally moved around to the Hillsborough Pike. News of Starnes's presence had been enough, however, to convince Bloodgood that the stockade was under attack and the bridge was being wrecked. He tried to advance to help Bassett, but he promptly ran into Forrest who had finally arrived. It was

now between 7 and 8 A.M. Forrest had posted a squadron of the 10th Tennessee to watch his rear and another to cut any Federal retreat toward Nashville, while watching out for Federal reinforcements from that direction. He then took ten companies of the 10th to the right while Armstrong took his brigade and the artillery to the left.

Bloodgood's desperation was not alleviated when he discovered his telegraph dead. He tried to send couriers for help, but only one got out, and Forrest captured him. Soon Bloodgood had a note demanding his surrender, to which he replied that Forrest would have to come in and get him. It was an empty boast, of course—the Confederate force outnumbered his ten to one—but he hoped that a little time would allow him to get away toward Nashville. Bloodgood did not have even a little time, however. Six companies of the 10th Tennessee had already dismounted to begin the attack when Bloodgood found that the road to Nashville was blocked. He surrendered. It had all taken about half an hour.

While the business went on of gathering up prisoners and materiel and destroying what they could not carry, Forrest swung south with the 4th Mississippi Cavalry, 10th Tennessee Cavalry, and artillery to finish the job at the stockade on the Harpeth. It was even shorter work. One round from the Confederate artillery convinced Bassett to capitulate. Forrest counted more than 200 prisoners from the stockade including eleven wagons and three ambulances. He demolished the railroad bridge, destroyed what he could not carry, and moved away with what he could toward Hillsborough. For good and precautionary measure, he hurled skirmishers toward Nashville to drive in pickets there to within three miles of the city.

By now the Federal command was alert to what was going on. Gordon Granger sent Brigadier General Green Clay Smith with about 700 troopers of the 2d Michigan, 9th Pennsylvania, 4th Kentucky, and 6th Kentucky to relieve Brentwood. Arriving early in the afternoon, Smith found the smoldering wreckage that always marked a finished Forrest project. The Federal cavalry was game, though, so Smith rode in hard pursuit of the scattered Confederates lumbering off to the west laden with their prisoners, wagons, and mules. He found the rear of them three and a half miles outside of Brentwood. It was Starnes, and suddenly there was a nasty little fight as Smith's troopers fell upon him with a will. Starnes was driven back about six miles, abandoning wagons, mules, and supplies along the way, before making a stand near the Little Harpeth River. Forrest reappeared to move on Smith's left while Brigadier General John A. Wharton's cavalry brigade circled to the right. All the Yankees could do was fall back to Brentwood. They had reclaimed some men and materiel, but Forrest was free to proceed toward Spring Hill, while most of his 700 prisoners, still in hand, were escorted to Columbia.

The cavalry action on the Little Harpeth provided something for the Federals to praise in an otherwise discouraging episode. For their part, Bloodgood and Bassett came under harsh criticism for what was regarded as their unseemly haste in surrendering. Granger noted that had these "milk and water soldiers" held out for even an hour, Union cavalry might have arrived in time to cut up Forrest.

—David S. Heidler and Jeanne T. Heidler

For further reading:
Fulcher, Richard Carlton. Brentwood, Tennessee: The Civil War Years (1993).

BREVET RANK

Brevet rank was usually an honorary rank awarded to an officer for valor in battle or for meritorious service. The tradition of brevet rank began in the British army before the Revolutionary War, and this tradition was continued in the U.S. Army. In the years after the Revolutionary War, Congress wrote legislation that specified the circumstances under which brevet ranks could be awarded and defined the actual amount of authority that brevet ranks gave to the awardee. In general, brevet ranks were higher than the individual's official rank, but held none of the authority or the pay of that higher rank.

The Civil War created a situation in which the awarding of brevet ranks became very commonplace. More than 1,700 officers and at least one enlisted man were awarded brevet ranks during the war, the majority of these ranks being awarded at the end of the war as a gesture of thanks. Unfortunately, the awarding of brevet ranks became so commonplace and overused that it was often difficult to determine the legitimate rank of an officer. An officer could simultaneously hold a state militia rank, a rank in the U.S. Volunteers, a rank in the U.S. Army, and a brevet rank. Though the regulations of the Confederate army provided for the awarding of brevet ranks, there is no evidence of a brevet rank ever being awarded.

After the Civil War, the awarding of brevet ranks became less and less common, though several were awarded during the Spanish-American War. The last brevet rank to be awarded by the United States was given to Tasker H. Bliss in 1918. Bliss, who held the rank of lieutenant general in the U.S. Army, was awarded the brevet rank of full general in order for him to be considered an equal of the European delegates at the Paris Peace Conference.

—Alexander M. Bielakowski

For further reading:
Boatner, Mark Mayo III. Army Lore and the Customs of the Service (1954).
———. Military Customs and Traditions (1956).

BRICE'S CROSS ROADS/GUNTOWN, BATTLE OF
(10 June 1864)

On 10 June 1864, Confederate forces under Major General Nathan Bedford Forrest routed a numerically superior Union force commanded by Brigadier General Samuel D. Sturgis at the northeastern Mississippi battle of Brice's Cross Roads (also known as Guntown and Tishomingo Creek). Although the Union's goal of preventing Forrest from disrupting General William Tecumseh Sherman's supply line in middle Tennessee was achieved, the battle also stands as the foremost victory in Forrest's notorious career. Confederate forces inflicted heavy casualties and captured sixteen pieces of artillery and significant supplies.

As Sherman moved into northern Georgia, he grew increasingly concerned about the vulnerability of his supply and communication lines in middle Tennessee. In late May 1864, Sherman instructed Union forces in Memphis to hunt down and defeat Forrest's cavalry. Major General Cadwallader C. Washburn, Union commander at Memphis, planned and organized an effort to carry out an attack 100 or more miles into northern Mississippi. At the heart of this plan was chief of cavalry General Sturgis. Sturgis's force included three brigades of infantry led by Colonel William L. McMillen totalling 5,000 men, two brigades of cavalry commanded by Brigadier General Benjamin H. Grierson totalling 3,300 troops, twenty-two pieces of artillery, and 250 wagons loaded with three weeks of food and ammunition. An African-American division held additional motivation to punish Forrest. The 55th and 59th U.S. Colored Troops had pledged to revenge Forrest's horrific and cowardly massacre of several dozen black soldiers after they had surrendered at Fort Pillow, Tennessee, only eight weeks before. Union troops departed Memphis on 1 June and immediately encountered the first of seven days of rain storms and the start of many miles of muddy roads. Progress was slow and exhausting. In one week, Sturgis had covered only fifty miles as they arrived at the small town of Ripley.

Sherman was correct in anticipating Forrest's intention of attacking middle Tennessee. Forrest was camped at the Tennessee River in northern Alabama preparing for such an assault. He quickly returned to Mississippi when he received word of Sturgis's move into Mississippi. Forrest positioned his 4,800 men along the Mobile & Ohio Railroad so that he could respond to a Union advance on either Corinth or Tupelo. On 8 June, when he received a report that Sturgis was advancing toward Tupelo, Forrest selected the spot for the field of fight to be at the intersection of two roads, a place known to locals as Brice's Cross Roads. The narrow road (muddy from heavy rain), dense woods, and thick brush was just the terrain Forrest needed to execute his aggressive plan. His strategy called for fighting the numerically superior Union forces in two phases. The Union cavalry, moving ahead of the infantry, would be destroyed first. As fighting broke out, Union infantry would rush in the June heat to the battle, arrive exhausted, and be an easy target for Confederates. Forrest and his men executed this plan to perfection.

At 5:30 A.M. Grierson's 3,300 cavalry troopers rode out of camp and advanced southeastward along Ripley Road. An hour and a half later, Colonel William L. McMillen and 5,000 soldiers followed. By 10:00 A.M. fighting between dismounted cavalry units had begun. In heavy fighting, the outnumbered rebels charged several times, and on each occasion they were repulsed. The intense June heat became a factor as Federal cavalry were near collapse and Union infantry arrived exhausted from their five-mile race to join the fight. The battle was unfolding according to Forrest's plan.

After a brief lull in fighting, Forrest organized his men for a series of coordinated assaults. At 1:30 P.M., Colonel Tyree H. Bell's 2,800 men hit the Union right. Yankee soldiers halted this attack and mounted a brief counterattack. The next rebel advance, this time on the Union left, was stopped as well. The fight was now six hours old, when Forrest sent his right, his left, and a small group at the Union rear, forward at once. This massive assault crushed Union lines and brought a complete collapse. The Union retreat quickly became a scene of chaos and slaughter as overturned wagons clogged the escape route and Confederate cannons took aim at the panicked mob. Led primarily by black Union troops, a brief, but spirited attempt to hold off Forrest's advance failed, and Union soldiers rushed desperately from advancing rebels.

The Confederate pursuit continued into the night and the next day. Greatly fatigued and embarrassed, Union forces reached the safety of Memphis on 13 June. A tally sheet provides clear evidence of the magnitude of Forrest's victory. Federal losses included 223 killed, 394 wounded, 1,623 captured, 16 pieces of artillery, 176 wagons, and a significant amount of ammunition and arms. Forrest's loses were 96 killed and 396 wounded. After the battle of Brice's Cross Roads, Union frustration with its inability to destroy General Forrest grew. In August 1864, an even larger Union force under General Andrew J. Smith failed to defeat the illusive target. But Forrest was never able to slow Sherman's advance through Georgia with a successful attack on his Tennessee supply lines.

—*Bruce D. Mactavish*

See also Forrest, Nathan Bedford; Sturgis, Samuel Davis; United States Colored Troops.
For further reading:
Bearss, Edwin C. *Forrest at Brice's Cross Roads and in North Mississippi in 1864* (1979).
Wills, Brian Steel. *A Battle from the Start: The Life of Nathan Bedford Forrest* (1992).

BRIGHT, JESSE DAVID
(1812–1875)
U.S. senator

Born to David Graham Bright and Rachel Bright in Norwich, New York, Jesse David Bright moved to Madison, Indiana, with his family when he was a small child. He was educated locally in New York and Indiana. As a young man, he became active in Indiana Democratic politics. He rose quickly in state party circles, serving first as a probate judge, then as a marshal of the district court and as a state senator, and then as lieutenant governor by the age of thirty-one. His wide political experience at such a young age gave him a great deal of influence over the pro-Southern wing of the Indiana Democratic Party. This influence brought him election in 1845 by the state legislature as U.S. senator from Indiana. During Bright's time in the Senate, he purchased a farm in Kentucky and owned a few slaves who worked on that farm.

In the U.S. Senate, Bright was a strong proponent of national expansion and accommodation of Southern concerns regarding the territories. He also used the organization skills he had honed in Indiana politics, using patronage and other methods, to build a large bloc of support. He quickly became a powerful member of the Senate. In 1850 he served on the committee that drew up the proposals that would become the Compromise of 1850, and in 1854 he was a very influential supporter of the Kansas-Nebraska Bill. During the maneuvering before the Democratic National Convention in 1856, Bright became a strong supporter of the candidacy of James Buchanan and worked with a number of other prominent Democrats to secure Buchanan's nomination and then election. Bright was naturally a strong supporter of the administration and opponent of the Stephen Douglas faction of the Democratic Party on such issues as the Lecompton Constitution for Kansas. Douglas's break with Buchanan on this issue caused the president's supporters such as Bright to begin planning early to block Douglas's nomination for the presidency in 1860.

The Democratic Convention in Charleston promised to be the most contentious in party history, and Bright and other Buchanan administration operatives certainly contributed to the acrimony by doing everything within their power to block the nomination of Stephen Douglas. This combination with opposition to Douglas of most Southern delegations succeeded in blocking the Little Giant's nomination in Charleston and forced the convention to Baltimore, where it became irreparably divided.

With the election of Abraham Lincoln in the fall of 1860 and the subsequent secession of the lower South, Bright became a part of the Democratic opposition to the Lincoln administration in Congress. Over the years, Bright's rather highhanded political maneuvering and obvious sympathy for the South had offended many of his colleagues in the Senate. In the spring of 1861, those enemies found the ammunition they needed to attack Bright's loyalty to the Union. In March, Bright wrote a letter of introduction for an acquaintance who was traveling to Montgomery, Alabama. The letter was addressed to Jefferson Davis and referred to Davis as the president of the Confederated States. To Bright's enemies, this form of address in effect recognized the legitimacy of Davis's title. As a Kentucky slave owner and strong supporter of the previous administration, Bright's loyalty was already suspect, but this action proved to be too much for some of the other senators.

Over the summer and fall of 1861, this opposition to Bright became organized and in early 1862 brought charges against Bright in the Senate with the goal of bringing about his expulsion. Bright tried to defend himself by arguing that the letter had been written before a war had erupted, but after almost three weeks of debate, the Senate voted on 5 February, 32 to 14 to expel Bright from the Senate. His expulsion was attributed by many to the fact that he had made so many political enemies among Republicans and some Democrats. Some War Democrats, though, fretted that the action might embolden Republicans to take similar actions against other Democrats.

Two days before Bright was expelled from the Senate, Lincoln administration special security agent Lafayette Baker wrote to Secretary of State William Henry Seward suggesting that Bright would probably move to the Confederacy after his expulsion and that he should probably be arrested before he could leave. Seward refused to act on the suggestion. Upon his return home, Bright tried to secure reelection, but even to most Indiana Democrats he had become too much of a political liability. After sixteen years in the U.S. Senate and as one of the nation's leading behind-the-scenes political operatives, Bright went to his farm in Kentucky in disgrace. He lived there quietly until after the war, when he again entered public life.

Bright remained in Kentucky after the war, returning briefly to politics as a member of the Kentucky state legislature. He also became active in Kentucky business activities including the growing coal mining industry there. In the last year of his life he moved to Baltimore, Maryland, where he died on 20 May 1875.

—*David S. Heidler and Jeanne T. Heidler*

See also Congress, U.S.A.; Democratic Party; Election of 1860.
For further reading:
Smith, Vickey Dee. "The Expulsion of Jesse D. Bright from the United States Senate" (M.A. thesis, 1974).

Thornbrough, Emma Lou. *Indiana in the Civil War Era, 1850–1880* (1965).

Van Der Weele, Wayne J. "Jesse David Bright: Master Politician from the Old Northwest" (Ph.D. dissertation, 1958).

BRIGHT, JOHN
(1811–1889)
British statesmen

The most prominent of Britain's parliamentary radicals, John Bright waged a public battle against British intervention in the American Civil War. Linking the abolition of slavery to the rights of labor in this public campaign, he sought to mobilize British working-class support for the North. Although historians continue to debate whether he succeeded in this respect, Bright's campaign seems to have forged an alliance between radicalism and trade union leaders that proved highly significant for British politics after the Civil War.

Born at Rochdale in Lancashire on 16 November 1811, John was the second child of Jacob Bright, a cotton mill owner, and Martha Wood. As a Quaker, John obtained his education at a variety of schools associated with the Society of Friends in Lancashire and Yorkshire. His education completed by 1827, John assisted his father in overseeing the family cotton mill business.

Bright first entered local politics in the 1830s, when he became involved in a dispute that started when Dissenters in Rochdale sought to prevent the Church of England from imposing a compulsory rate on the town. Bright took a leading role in opposing the rate and achieved some local prominence. Shortly thereafter, he joined the Anti-Corn Law League, which sought to abolish the tariffs that protected domestic agriculture. Bright's activities on behalf of the League, a powerful pressure group, made him a household name throughout Britain and associated him with Richard Cobden, with whom he would form a long-lasting political partnership.

In 1847, a year after the repeal of the Corn Laws, Bright won a seat in the House of Commons representing Manchester. Associated with the parliamentary radicals in the Commons, he pushed for free trade, reductions in public expenditures, extension of suffrage, and a less aggressive foreign policy. He vigorously opposed the Crimean War, a stance that cost him a great deal of popularity. In the late 1850s he launched a public campaign to extend the franchise, but met with little response. He did play a major role, however, in backing the free trade treaty that Cobden negotiated with France in 1860.

Bright had long admired the United States as a shining example of what a middle-class democracy could accomplish. Bright believed that if Britain enjoyed a greater degree of social and political democracy, Britons would come to possess the liberty and prosperity that seemed to characterize the United States. In fact, he and Cobden referred so frequently to America in their speeches that they became known in the House of Commons as the "members for the United States."

With the outbreak of the American Civil War in 1861, Bright immediately threw his support behind the North. As a Quaker, he had a strong moral objection to slavery and believed (well before most Britons) that a Northern victory would culminate in the destruction of that "peculiar institution." He also supported the North because he believed it represented the best part of the American experiment. In his eyes, Northern democracy had safeguarded the liberty that allowed people to live up to their potential.

Nominally committed to supporting Lord Palmerston's coalition government, Bright and his fellow radicals took the lead in attempting to prevent the administration from intervening in the conflict. They knew that Palmerston was ill disposed toward the United States, and they feared that his tendency toward aggressive foreign policy moves might culminate in war. Bright, however, did not have much of a following in the House of Commons, nor did he exert much influence on the Cabinet. Consequently, he took his message to the public in an attempt to educate British opinion on the American conflict.

During the *Trent* Affair, Bright publicly argued that instead of sending an ultimatum, Britain should take its case against the United States before international arbitration. He and Cobden urged moderation upon the North. Bright also deployed what influence he could upon Charles Villiers and Thomas Milner-Gibson, the two radicals in the Cabinet.

With the peaceful resolution of the *Trent* Affair, Bright sought to achieve two related ends. First, he wanted to prevent the British government from offering its good offices to mediate the conflict, because such a move could only benefit the South. Second, he sought at all costs to prevent the government from officially recognizing the Confederacy. In pursuit of these objectives, he frequently spoke about the war in public, appealing mainly to working-class audiences. Perhaps his most important tactic consisted of linking the cause of abolition to the rights of labor. Historians have long disputed the effectiveness of Bright's oratory in attracting British working-class support for the North. It seems clear, however, that a number of important labor leaders entered radical politics during the Civil War because of their opposition to slavery. During the conflict, then, Bright began forming the basis of the alliance between radicalism and trade unionism that eventually played a large role in the politics that led up to the extension of the franchise in 1867.

Because of his wholehearted support of the Union, his politics, and his reputation as the representative of the working man, Bright won the gratitude of the North.

Although his activities may not have played a pivotal role in preventing the British government from intervening in the conflict, they provided comfort for Northerners who came to see that not all Britons proved hostile to the United States.

After the war ended, Bright took advantage of the alliance between labor and radicalism that he had formed and pressed again for the extension of suffrage. Although the Liberal reform act of 1866 failed and the government fell, Bright had popularized reform to such an extent that the Conservatives, who subsequently came to office, felt compelled to introduce a sweeping reform measure to expand suffrage in Britain.

When the Liberals returned to power in 1868, Bright joined the Cabinet as president of the Board of Trade, but resigned after suffering a breakdown in 1870. He returned to the Cabinet as the chancellor of the Duchy of Lancaster in 1873, holding the post until the administration fell in 1874. He held the office again from 1880 until 1882, when he resigned because he opposed Gladstone's Irish Home Rule bill.

In May 1888 Bright fell ill, suffering from a combination of diabetes and Bright's disease. After lingering for some months, he died at One Ash, the family home in Rochdale, on 27 March 1889.

—*Hubert F. Dubrulle*

See also Diplomacy, U.S.A.; Great Britain; Palmerston, Viscount; *Trent* Affair.
For further reading:
Ausubel, Herman. *John Bright, Victorian Reformer* (1966).
Read, Donald. *Cobden and Bright: A Victorian Political Partnership* (1967).
Robbins, Keith. *John Bright* (1979).
Trevelyan, George Macaulay. *The Life of John Bright* (1913).

BRISTOE STATION, BATTLE OF
(14 October 1863)

The Bristoe campaign began 10 October 1863. General Robert E. Lee had learned that the Army of the Potomac's 6th and 7th Corps were headed west to participate in the Chattanooga campaign. Though outnumbered almost two to one, Lee auda-

The Army of the Potomac near Bristoe Station, October 1863 (*Library of Congress*)

ciously decided to interpose his troops between the Federal army and Washington, analogous to what he had done at Second Bull Run.

By 13 October, the Confederates, moving north, had passed Warrenton, west of Manassas Junction. However, the Army of the Potomac, commanded by Major General George G. Meade, who had intercepted Confederate signals, was already retreating up the Orange & Alexandria Railroad, intending to mass at Centreville.

The battle of Bristoe Station was actually two battles on the same day, 14 October 1863, with the first occurring near Auburn, just northeast of Bristoe. As the Union 2d Corps, commanded by Major General Gouverneur K. Warren, attempted to cross Cedar Run, it was attacked by ex-U.S. congressman and now Confederate colonel Thomas Ruffin's 1st North Carolina Cavalry. Warren faced a dilemma: "to halt was to await annihilation, and to move as prescribed" took him into a valley, "above which loomed Confederates."

Brigadier General Alexander Hays, Warren's 3d Division commander, sent out skirmishers who repulsed Ruffin's cavalry and mortally wounded Ruffin. Then, along with Brigadier General John C. Caldwell's division, Hays's men drove away the remainder of Lieutenant General J. E. B. Stuart's cavalrymen. With St. Stephens Road now open, the Union 2d Corps hurried toward Bristoe Station to catch up with Major General George Sykes's 5th Corps.

Lee, acutely aware of a golden opportunity to cut Meade's army into pieces and destroy it piecemeal, advanced Lieutenant General A. P. Hill's corps up the Warrenton Turnpike. Hill spied Sykes's 5th Corps waiting to ford Broad Run, a swift-moving stream just east of Bristoe. Mistakenly thinking that this was the rear of the whole Union column, Hill smelled blood and moved in for the kill. He impetuously ordered a coordinated attack by Brigadier General Henry Heth's Division and Major William T. Poague's artillery battalion on the unsuspecting Union corps.

The initial shelling forced Sykes's men to clamber wildly across Broad Run. Encouraged, Heth ordered the brigades of Brigadier Generals John Walker, William W. Kirkland, and John R. Cooke to attack around 4 P.M. To Hill's and Heth's surprise, however, Warren's 2d Corps was waiting to cross the stream, with Hays's column in the lead. Realizing that Heth's Division was now in danger from a rear attack, Hill halted Cooke's men and sent out two companies of the 27th North Carolina as skirmishers to test the Union strength.

Warren's corps, the smallest of the Union troops and greatly outnumbered, headed for an opening extending on both sides of the railroad tracks that rose to a gentle hill occupied by two lines of Heth's Confederates. Then it was a race for a deep cut by the far side of the railroad, where the embankment facing the Confederates could serve as a breastwork.

The Union troops quickly occupied the cut, repulsed the first Confederate attack, and prepared for the second line. It came with what a Union captain labeled a "mad rush." Yet the Union fire, lasting possibly twenty minutes, forced many of Heth's men to huddle behind a house. With nowhere to go, the Confederates began to retreat toward the hill from whence they had come, all the while ducking Union fire. Union skirmishers were immediately ordered after them, capturing those who had tried to find safety in the small house and then their guns, which were left unprotected during the withdrawal.

The battle of Bristoe Station would be refought in accounts thereafter, with Hill and Lieutenant General Richard Ewell blamed for failing to annihilate the Union 2d Corps. The main criticisms were that not only had Hill and Ewell outnumbered Warren, Hill also had enjoyed plenty of time to survey the land from the high ground above Bristoe, which was near Ewell's prewar home. A melancholy Lee could only say to Hill that dreary night, "Bury these poor men, and let us say no more about it." Bury they did, for the Confederates had suffered approximately 1,400 casualties, "roughly one man lost every two seconds of the engagement." By contrast, the Union II Corps lost a total of 546 killed, wounded, and missing, with almost 40 percent of the casualties sustained by Hays's division.

Although Lee had failed to cut off Meade's withdrawal, and the battle would be considered insignificant, the Army of Northern Virginia had temporarily destroyed a key railroad and had forced the Army of the Potomac back 40 miles.

—*Wayne Mahood*

See also Caldwell, John C.; Hays, Alexander; Hill, Ambrose Powell; Warren, Gouverneur K.

For further reading:

Fleming, George T., ed. *The Life and Letters of Alexander Hays* (1919).
Henderson, William D. *The Road to Bristoe Station: Campaigning With Lee and Meade, August 1–October 20, 1863* (1987).
Robertson, James I., Jr. *A.P. Hill: The Story of a Confederate Warrior* (1987).
Walker, Francis. *History of the Second Army Corps of the Army of the Potomac* (1891).

BROOKE, JOHN MERCER
(1826–1906)

Confederate naval officer; ordnance designer

John Mercer Brooke's father, George Mercer Brooke, entered the U.S. Army in 1808 and ended the War of 1812 as a major with the brevet rank of colonel. In 1824 he constructed Fort Brooke on the site of present-day Tampa, Florida. There, on 18 December 1826, John Mercer Brooke was born.

Young Brooke joined the U.S. Navy as a midshipman in 1841 and graduated from the Naval Academy in 1847. Promoted to lieutenant in 1855, Brooke's intellectual curiosity and scientific bent led to useful inventions, including deep-sea sounding leads that eventually made possible the laying of an Atlantic cable. Later he led major explorations of the north Pacific and the coast of Japan. He also escorted the first Japanese diplomatic mission to the United States.

On 20 April 1861, three days after the secession of Virginia, Brooke resigned his commission in the U.S. Navy. His wife and close friends seem to have been the key factors in the decision. Future admiral David Dixon Porter stated that he only regretted the loss of two men from the U.S. Navy: Catesby ap R. Jones and Brooke.

Commissioned a lieutenant in the Virginia navy on 23 April, Brooke was made naval aide to the commander of Virginia forces, General Robert E. Lee. When it was clear that Virginia would be linked to the Confederacy, Brooke applied for a commission in the Confederate navy. On 2 May 1861 Confederate secretary of the navy Stephen R. Mallory informed him that he had been granted a commission as a lieutenant.

In a June meeting with Mallory, Brooke assured the secretary that the South could build its own ironclads. Mallory then transferred Brooke to the naval ordnance office, where he supervised work on armor and guns for the CSS *Virginia*, the former USS *Merrimack*. Scuttled by the Federals when they abandoned the Gosport (Norfolk) Navy Yard, she had been raised and was undergoing conversion into an ironclad.

Brooke's ordnance achievements were remarkable, particularly given his lack of experience in what he undertook. Brooke was responsible for the *Virginia*'s slanted armor casemate, subsequently copied in other Confederate ironclads, as well as the idea of her bow and stern extensions under water. Yet friction between Brooke and constructor John D. Porter, who claimed credit for the *Virginia*'s design, contributed to Brooke's subsequent lack of interest in the ironclad program. Promoted to commander in September 1862, Brooke in March 1863 was named chief of the Confederate Bureau of Ordnance and Hydrography, which post he held until the end of the war.

Brooke designed a variety of guns for the Confederacy, including 8- and 9-inch smoothbores, 10- and 11-inch double-banded smoothbores, and the 11-inch triple-banded smoothbore. He is, however, best known for his double- and triple-banded rifled guns, produced in 6.4-inch, 7-inch, and 8-inch bore sizes. They were probably the finest rifled navy guns on either side in the war. As with his Union counterpart, John A. Dahlgren, Brooke understood that a hemisphere offered the strongest cap for a cylindrical pressure vessel. He also

understood, as did Union founder Robert P. Parrott, the gain in strength afforded by a wrought-iron band around the breech of a cast-iron gun.

Brooke-designed guns are identified, with few exceptions, by a fully hemispheric breech contour; layers of welded-on reinforcing bands; a plain tapered chase extending from the reinforcing bands to the muzzle; unturned rough exteriors; and, save in the smoothbores, 7-groove rifling of right-hand twist.

After the war Brooke joined the Virginia Military Institute faculty as professor of astronomy, meteorology, and geography. He served in that position from 1865 until 1899. Brooke died in Lexington, Virginia, on 14 December 1906.

—*Spencer C. Tucker*

See also Dalhgren, John Adolph Bernard; Mallory, Stephen R.; Ordnance, Naval; *Virginia*, CSS.
For further reading:
Brooke, George M., Jr. *John M. Brooke. Naval Scientist and Educator* (1980).
Brooke, John M. "The *Virginia* or *Merrimack*: Her Real Projector." *Southern Historical Society Papers* (1891).
Olmstead, Edwin, Wayne Stark, and Spencer Tucker. *The Big Guns. Civil War Siege, Seacoast and Naval Cannon* (1997).

BROOKE, JOHN RUTTER
(1838–1926)
Union general

John Brooke was born on his family's farm near Pottstown, Pennsylvania. He received his early education at local schools, but this sturdy six-foot-tall farm boy was described as "not especially fond of books, uncouth in manner, and participating but seldom in the social doings of the young people of the neighborhood" and his stentorian voice was characterized as "uninviting by reason of its depth and brusqueness." Brooke was sent away to schools in New Jersey and West Chester, Pennsylvania, and then he went west and lived for a time with an uncle who served in the army. He then returned to the farm and was essentially managing it when war began in 1861.

When a local militia company was reorganized, Brooke was selected as its captain. This company joined the 4th Pennsylvania and served for three months. Brooke then returned home, obtained a colonel's commission from Governor Andrew G. Curtin, and organized the 53d Pennsylvania, becoming its colonel.

Brooke's regiment was assigned to the 1st Division, II Army Corps, and went to the Peninsula with the Army of the Potomac. The 53d first engaged the enemy at Fair Oaks on 1 June 1862, suffering heavy casualties. After fighting at Gaines's Mill and the Peach Orchard during the Seven Days' battles, Brooke's regiment went north when the army withdrew from the Peninsula. Brooke's men fought at Antietam and then at Fredericksburg, where the 53d again sustained heavy losses.

Brooke was then placed in command of the 4th Brigade, 1st Division, II Corps, and ably directed his men at Chancellorsville and Gettysburg. After leading his brigade through the wheatfield at Gettysburg on 2 July 1863, Brooke was wounded in the ankle and assisted off the field. He returned to active duty the following spring, after commanding a convalescent camp at Harrisburg. During the 1864 Virginia campaign, Brooke's men were actively engaged in the Wilderness, Spotsylvania, and Cold Harbor. In this latter battle, on 3 June, Brooke was seriously wounded and incapacitated for any further active duty. Promoted to brigadier general effective from 12 May 1864 and then to major general on 1 August, Brooke sat on courts-martial until the spring of 1865, when he received command of a division in Winfield S. Hancock's new corps, which occupied the Shenandoah Valley.

After returning home in 1865, Brooke accepted a commission as lieutenant colonel in the regular army and was assigned to the 37th Infantry, which was stationed in New Mexico. Brooke thereafter served in the army until his retirement in 1902. He was successively promoted to major general and served in a number of various posts, including stints in Colorado, Mississippi, Louisiana, Alabama, Montana, Massachusetts, and New York. Brooke also was in command of the Departments of the Platte, Dakota, and Missouri.

When war with Spain was declared in 1898, Brooke took command of both I Army Corps and Camp Thomas on the Chickamauga battlefield. He accompanied the expedition to Puerto Rico, where he remained as military governor after the end of hostilities. Brooke then was transferred to Cuba and served as governor of the island until 1900, when he was placed in command of the Department of the East.

Reaching the mandatory retirement age in 1902, Brooke left the army. The general was twice married; his first wife died during childbirth in 1867, and he remarried ten years later. He died in 1926 and is buried in Arlington National Cemetery.

—*Richard A. Sauers*

See also: Cold Harbor.
For further reading:
Auge, M. *Lives of the Eminent Dead and Biographical Notices of Prominent Living Citizens of Montgomery County, Pa.* (1879).
"General John R. Brooke." *Philadelphia Public Ledger* (1898).
"Major General John R. Brooke." *New York Herald* (1898).

BROOKS, PRESTON SMITH
(1819–1857)
U.S. congressman

Preston Brooks was born on 6 August 1819 in Edgefield, South Carolina. He attended South Carolina College but left without a degree in 1839. In 1842 he was admitted to the South Carolina bar,

where he practiced law until he was called to public service shortly thereafter. During 1842–1844 he served as aide-de-camp to South Carolina governor James Henry Hammond. When Hammond's term as governor expired in 1844, Brooks ran for and won a seat in the South Carolina house, where he served only a single two-year term. He returned to public service in 1853, when he was elected to the U.S. House of Representatives.

A man of unquestioned loyalty but limited judgment, Brooks's public career was marked from its earliest days by violence. Brooks engaged in an argument with Louis Wigfall in 1840 over Hammond's gubernatorial bid. Wigfall, who supported Hammond's opponent, had already fought two duels with members of Brooks's family, killing one of Brooks's relatives. Soon enough Brooks and Wigfall were fighting a duel of their own. Both missed their first shots, but Brooks's second shot struck Wigfall's leg as Wigfall seriously wounded Brooks in the hip. Brooks carried the bullet and required the use of a cane for the remainder of his life.

As a representative of South Carolina in Congress, Brooks was said to have possessed great but underutilized oratorical skills. Although his oratory may have been exceptional, it was his temper that has made him most remembered to history. It was during this time that the Senate took up the issue of Kansas. Massachusetts senator and ardent abolitionist Charles Sumner on 19 and 20 May 1856 delivered a two-day long speech entitled, "The Crime against Kansas," in which he denounced the old and infirm Senator Andrew P. Butler of South Carolina. Butler, who was Preston Brooks's cousin, was ill and absent from the proceedings. Brooks took it upon himself to defend his cousin's honor. Claiming later that he waited two days for an apology, Brooks searched out Sumner on 22 May 1856 and found him seated at his desk on the floor of the Senate shortly after it had recessed for the day. After the briefest exchange, Brooks began to beat Sumner on the head with a gutta-percha cane until it was in splinters. Only then was he restrained. During the attack, Sumner had been held fast by his desk bolted to the floor until he managed to wrench it loose and collapse. Sumner's recovery would take several years, while Brooks was lionized by Southerners as a hero and defender of liberty.

In dealing with what amounted to a case of battery, Congress had to act on behalf of Sumner. An investigating committee from the House voted in favor of expelling Brooks, but a vote along party lines saved him from the necessary two-thirds majority. After taking the floor of the House to explain his reasons for the attack, Brooks resigned his seat and returned to South Carolina. His constituents immediately returned him to the House of Representatives.

The Brooks-Sumner incident further expanded the already gaping sectional rift, illustrating to Southerners that Northerners were cowardly abolitionists and to Northerners that Southerners were violent hatemongers. Within a month of the attack, Massachusetts representative Anson Burlingame spoke to the House to label Brooks a coward who lacked the ethics of fairness. Brooks responded by challenging Burlingame to a duel. In accordance with the *code duello*, Burlingame chose the location, selecting the Canadian side of Niagara Falls so that Brooks would have to travel through the heart of the North. When Brooks refused to go, it was triumphantly reported throughout the North as evidence of his cowardice. Nonetheless, during the months that followed the attack on Sumner, Brooks received countless canes from Southerners with laudatory notes and inscriptions encouraging future beatings.

Brooks would not live to see the war that he had a small role in foreshadowing. Within a year of the beating incident, he died at Brown's Hotel in Washington on 27 January 1857. Although obviously possessing a temper, Brooks was said to have been a kind and gentle man capable of great generosity. Evidently during the months after the attack, Brooks understood the detrimental effects for the South caused by his reckless attack on Sumner.

—*Brian D. McKnight*

See also Butler, Andrew Pickens; Kansas-Nebraska Act; Sumner, Charles.

For further reading:
Campbell, J.E. "Sumner, Brooks, Burlingame, or the Last of the Great Challenges." *Ohio Archaeological and Historical Society* (1925).
Heidler, David S. *Pulling the Temple Down: The Fire-eaters and the Destruction of the Union* (1994).
Nevins, Allan. *Ordeal of the Union* (1947).
Walther, Eric H. *The Fire-eaters* (1992).

BROOKS, WILLIAM THOMAS HARBAUGH
(1821–1870)
Union general

Born in New Lisbon, Ohio, William Thomas Harbaugh Brooks received an appointment to the U.S. Military Academy in 1837 at age sixteen. He graduated forty-sixth of fifty-two in the class of 1841. Commissioned into the 3d U.S. Infantry, Brooks was sent immediately to Florida, where he fought in the final phases of the Second Seminole War. The end of that conflict saw him bouncing from post to post before the outbreak of the Mexican-American War had him traveling to Texas to serve in Zachary Taylor's Army of Occupation. After serving in northern Mexico under Taylor, Brooks was transferred to Winfield Scott's army and participated in the Mexico City campaign. He served under Captain Robert E. Lee during that campaign. During the Mexican-American War, Brooks received two brevet promotions for bravery.

After the end of that conflict, Brooks joined the staff of Brigadier General David E. Twiggs. He served as that officer's adjutant general and then as Twiggs's aide-de-camp while Twiggs commanded the Department of Texas. At the end of the 1850s, Brooks served in New Mexico, where he engaged in campaigns against the Navajo Indians. During that time, he contracted a series of illnesses that would plague him for the remainder of his life.

At the outbreak of the Civil War, Brooks was a captain in the 3d U.S. Infantry. His extensive military experience, however, gained him rapid advancement, and in September 1861 he became brigadier general of volunteers. Commanding a brigade in William F. Smith's division, Army of the Potomac, Brooks saw little action in the fall of 1861 and the winter of 1861–1862. In early 1862, however, he privately complained to friends about the arrest of Charles P. Stone for the Ball's Bluff fiasco. Word of Brooks's complaints reached some Radical Republicans, who marked him as a potential disloyal officer.

During the spring of 1862, Brooks led his brigade in the Peninsula campaign. He distinguished himself during the siege of Yorktown, the battle of Williamsburg, and the Seven Days. In the latter series of engagements, Brooks was wounded at the battle of Savage's Station. In command of the same brigade, 2d Division, VI Corps, Brooks fought in the Maryland campaign at Crampton's Gap on 14 September and at Antietam on 17 September 1862. In the latter engagement he marched his men to the battlefield from Crampton's Gap the morning of the battle and brought them immediately into the fray. He was wounded during the battle.

After Antietam, Brooks and his division were headquartered at Hagerstown, Maryland. While there on 18 October, he was given command of 1st Division, VI Corps. He commanded that division in the battle of Fredericksburg. Like so many officers in the Army of the Potomac, Brooks disapproved of the battle plan for Fredericksburg and believed the results of the battle vindicated his judgment. The subsequent attempt to flank Robert E. Lee's position in the infamous Mud March only further confirmed him in the opinion that Ambrose Burnside was unfit for command. Brooks, like other officers (Joseph Hooker most conspicuous among them), made no secret of his disdain for Burnside. Before his dismissal as commander of the Army of the Potomac, Burnside dismissed Brooks from the army for complaining about government policy. Burnside took this action at the same time that he tried to dismiss Hooker for similar offenses. The dismissals had to have the final approval of the president, and Abraham Lincoln, who was about to appoint Hooker as Burnside's successor, declined to approve the dismissals. However, again Brooks had criticized policy and was again marked as a potential troublemaker.

Brooks continued to command his division in the Chancellorsville campaign, but in late May 1863 he was transferred to the Department of the Monongahela, headquartered in Pittsburgh, Pennsylvania. Ironically one of Brooks's first duties was to cooperate with Ambrose Burnside's Army of the Ohio in the repulse of John Hunt Morgan's Ohio Raid. For the most part, however, Brooks confined himself to recruiting duty, primarily recruiting three-month units used for emergencies like the Morgan raid. Brooks had been promoted in June 1863 to major general of volunteers, but the Senate never approved the promotion, and it expired the following spring.

In April 1864, Brooks was ordered back east to assume command of the 1st Division, XVIII Corps. He fought with his division at Drewry's Bluff and Cold Harbor. On 18 June he was given command of X Corps, Army of the James. His health, however, was deteriorating quickly, and he did not know then whether he would be able to continue in a field command. Brooks also was in the middle of a dispute with the commanding general of the U.S. Army, Ulysses S. Grant. When Brooks's promotion to major general had expired, he had expected to have his name resubmitted, as had happened with officers in similar circumstances. Neither Grant nor the president had raised the issue, and Brooks was angry. When Grant refused to address his concerns in July 1864, Brooks resigned both his volunteer and regular commissions, and Grant accepted.

After the war, Brooks moved to Huntsville, Alabama, where he bought a farm. During his few remaining years, he made many friends among his former enemies, and became one of the most well-liked men in the community. His death on 19 July 1870 was mourned greatly by his new friends, who buried him in the local cemetery.

—*David S. Heidler and Jeanne T. Heidler*

See also Burnside, Ambrose; Crampton's Gap.

For further reading:
Gallagher, Gary W., ed. *The Fredericksburg Campaign: Decision on the Rappahannock* (1995).
Trudeau, Noah Andre. *Bloody Roads South: The Wilderness to Cold Harbor, May–June 1864* (1989).

BROUGH, JOHN
(1811–1865)
Governor of Ohio

Born to John Brough, an English immigrant, and Jane Garnet Brough in Marietta, Ohio, the younger John Brough received a local education, but the death of his parents when he was a child led him to enter the printing trade and eventually journalism. He used his skills in this area to work his way through Ohio University. He studied law after graduation and became active in Ohio Democratic politics. He served in the lower house of the state legislature where he demonstrated great administrative abilities as the chairman of the banking and currency committee. This experience led to his appointment as state auditor. During his time in office, he removed many of the abuses within the state tax system.

Returning to the newspaper business in the 1840s and his law practice, he used the profits from both to invest in railroad projects. He served as the president of several railroad companies in the years before the outbreak of the Civil War.

Unlike many Ohio Democrats, Brough was a strong supporter of a vigorous prosecution of the war. He used his influence with the state's railroads to speed the movement of troops and equipment. The growth of opposition in his state, led by such Copperheads as Clement Vallandigham, caused Brough to begin speaking out publicly about the need for support from all citizens. These speaking engagements became so popular and influential that the Republican Party of Ohio approached Brough in 1863 to run for governor. He agreed and won an overwhelming victory over Vallandigham.

Brough began his term as governor in January 1864 and immediately demonstrated his strong support for the war effort by a renewed push for recruiting in the state and his insistence that officers of state forces be promoted based on merit. Somewhat discouraged by the lackluster recruiting in the state, he wrote to the War Department within two months of taking office, suggesting that bounties be suspended as useless and that the draft be increased.

While Brough advocated widespread conscription, he was also tremendously concerned about the physical condition of Ohio troops. He worked tirelessly to improve military hospitals in the state and wrote to the War Department frequently urging better and more numerous supplies for Ohio troops. He also worked diligently to obtain federal reimbursement to the state for the damage done during the summer of 1863 by the raid conducted by John Hunt Morgan.

Along with these activities Brough took an active interest in the war in all theaters. He frequently corresponded with Ohio officers regarding the performance of Ohio troops in battle and the state of the war throughout the country. In addition, he proposed and entertained creative solutions to various problems facing the state, including recruiting. One of the major impediments to recruiting by 1864 was the shortage of men to work the many farms in the state. For that reason, he was intrigued by a proposal put forth by Major General George Thomas that Confederate deserters be sent to states such as Ohio to work as agricultural laborers. He also suggested to Secretary of War Edwin Stanton that federal recruiting be conducted in occupied areas of the South to take advantage of what he believed to be the large loyal population there.

The military readiness and defense of Ohio were also among Brough's major concerns. Morgan's raid in 1863 left the state shaken and left many people, including Brough, convinced that, given the opportunity, Confederate raiders would raid again. To protect against such a possibility, Brough increased the efficiency of home guard units. At the same time, he proposed to the War Department that new recruits and draftees be retained in border fortifications, freeing more veteran troops to move to the various fronts. He also took Stanton's advice in the summer of 1864 to establish regular patrols of the Ohio River by state recruited boats.

During his first year in office, Brough returned a large measure of efficiency to the state government and the state's military preparations. Yet, he also offended a large number of defenders of the status quo and those people who had made a great deal of money or gained advancement because of the war. Because of what he deemed the emergency nature of the situation, he also was less than politic in some of his dealings with important people in the state. Because of this mounting opposition and his failing health, he decided not to seek reelection in 1865. As it happened, he would have been unable to serve a second term. He died on 29 August 1865, four months before his term expired.

—David S. Heidler and Jeanne T. Heidler

See also Vallandigham, Clement.
For further reading:
Reid, Whitelaw. *Ohio in the War: Her Statesmen, Her Generals, and Soldiers* (1868).

BROWN, ALBERT GALLATIN
(1813–1880)
Confederate congressman

Born in Chester District, South Carolina, on 31 May 1813, Albert Gallatin Brown moved to Copiah County, Mississippi, when he was ten years old. He attended Mississippi College and Jefferson College. He was admitted to the bar, but in 1835 he began an impressive political career. Before the Civil War, Brown served as a state legislator, state circuit court judge, governor for two terms, and congressman (1839–1841, 1847–1853). He represented Mississippi in the U.S. Senate from 1854 until 14 January 1861, when he withdrew upon the secession of his state.

A Democrat, Brown was a strict constructionist and an opponent of banks. The Compromise of 1850 and the rise of the Republican Party after 1854 made him a fervent Southern nationalist, and his rhetoric became increasingly belligerent. He defended slavery as a blessing for all whites and blacks and advocated the acquisition of Cuba and the admission of Kansas as a slave state. Brown consistently protected the interests of nonslaveholders and advocated fair taxation and free public education. He

was successful in influencing the yeomen farmers' "triple prejudices against large slaveholders, against [blacks], but most of all, against the North."

With Lincoln's election, Brown urged the immediate secession of the slave states. After his resignation from the Senate, he organized a company in the 18th Mississippi Infantry and participated in First Bull Run. Brown was cited for bravery at Ball's Bluff in October 1861. Mississippi then elected Brown to the Confederate Senate, and he took his seat on 18 February 1862. As chair of the Committee on Naval Affairs, Brown worked well with Secretary Stephen R. Mallory.

Brown's commitment to Southern nationalism never wavered during the war. The preservation of the Confederacy took precedence over states' rights. He encouraged government intervention to reduce cotton and tobacco production and to increase foodstuffs. An ardent defender of conscription, Brown opposed practically all exemption and substitute laws. He railed against the rich and speculators who both avoided service and undermined the war effort. He favored suspending the writ of habeas corpus so the government could better enforce the draft and preserve the nation. Never a defeatist, Brown rejected pursuing all peace negotiations and in February 1865 proposed legislation emancipating slave soldiers if they proved loyal. To him, Southern nationhood ultimately was much more important than slavery.

After the war, Brown returned to farming and occasionally practiced law. Although mostly retired from politics, he unsuccessfully urged Mississippi Democrats to educate and incorporate African-Americans into the party. He criticized white violence against blacks but to no avail. He died at his farm near Terry in Hinds County on 12 June 1880 and is buried in Jackson.

—M. Philip Lucas

See also Congress, C.S.A.; Conscription, C.S.A.; Mallory, Stephen R.; Mississippi.
For further reading:
Alexander, Thomas Benjamin, and Richard E. Beringer. *The Anatomy of the Confederate Congress; A Study of the Influences of Member Characteristics on Legislative Voting Behavior, 1861–1865* (1972).
Rable, George C. *The Confederate Republic: A Revolution against Politics* (1994).
Ranck, James Byrne. *Albert Gallatin Brown: Radical Southern Nationalist* (1937).

BROWN, ISAAC NEWTON
(1817–1889)
Confederate naval officer

Born in Livingston County, Kentucky, the son of Samuel Brown, Isaac Newton Brown moved to Mississippi when he was a child. He entered the U.S. Navy as a cadet at the age of seventeen. He served his first years in the navy in the West Indies and on the

rivers of Florida during the Second Seminole War. He received his full commission in 1840. During the Mexican-American War, Brown served in the Gulf of Mexico and during the siege of Vera Cruz. After the war, he served on Pacific station, made a trip to Australia, and made two circumnavigations of the world. When not on sea duty, he served a stint at the U.S. Naval Observatory and doing coastal surveys. Immediately preceding the outbreak of the Civil War, Brown was executive officer on the USS *Niagara*, the ship that took the first Japanese ministry back to Japan. When Brown and the *Niagara* returned to the United States, the Confederate States of America had been formed.

Brown resigned his lieutenant's commission and offered his services to the Confederacy. He was commissioned a lieutenant in the Confederate States Navy in June 1861 and in the fall of 1861 was sent west to aid in the defense of the Mississippi and other western rivers. Before leaving the East, however, Brown arranged for the shipment of fifty guns from the Norfolk shipyard. He also made preparations to have material shipped west with which he could construct mines to defend many of the western rivers. With the limited Confederate shipbuilding capabilities, Brown believed that mines would be an integral part of Confederate river defense.

Upon arrival in the West, Brown's work converting private vessels to ironclads was interrupted in early 1862 when he was hurriedly sent to Nashville to prepare boats to protect the Cumberland River. All of these preparations came too late, however, to prevent U.S. Army and Navy forces from taking Forts Henry and Donelson and bringing about the evacuation of Nashville.

Brown was then sent to New Orleans, where, until Union forces took possession of the city, he supervised construction of gunboats. He left with his workers at the approach of the Federals and traveled up the Mississippi to Vicksburg. On 9 May 1862, Brown took command of the Confederate ironclad ram, CSS *Arkansas*. The vessel was used in defense of Vicksburg through the summer of 1862, especially on 15 July 1862, when he defeated a larger Union force. For his actions on that day he was promoted to commander on 25 August 1862. At that time, Brown was on an extended sick leave, and in his absence the *Arkansas* was destroyed by its crew to prevent its capture after running aground.

Upon his return to duty, Brown, now without a ship, supervised the mining of western rivers, particularly concentrating on the Yazoo. His efforts were responsible for the destruction of two Federal ironclad boats. He also supervised shipbuilding during this time at Yazoo City. In command of a land force comprising a mix of sailors and soldiers, Brown participated in the defense of Vicksburg in the spring and early summer of 1863.

Not present at the surrender of Vicksburg, having been sent east, Brown assumed command in early 1864

of the CSS *Charleston* at Charleston, South Carolina. He served there until the Federal army occupied Charleston. The government in Richmond then sent him west again to take command of what naval forces remained. During his overland journey, he heard of the collapse of the Confederacy and surrendered himself to Federal authorities at Montgomery, Alabama. Brown was paroled on 22 May 1865 and allowed to return to his plantation in Mississippi. For the remainder of his life, Brown lived quietly at his home in Mississippi and on land he acquired in Corsicana, Texas, after the war.

—*David S. Heidler and Jeanne T. Heidler*

See also *Arkansas*, CSS; Navy, C.S.A.

For further reading:
Carroll, John M., ed. *Register of Officers of the Confederate States Navy, 1861–1865* (1983).
Gretchell, Charles Munro. "Defender of the Inland Waters: The Military Career of Isaac Newton Brown, Commander, Confederate States Navy, 1861–1865" (M.A. thesis, 1978).
Luraghi, Raimondo. *A History of the Confederate Navy* (1996).
Scharf, J. Thomas. *History of the Confederate States Navy: From Its Organization to the Surrender of Its Last Vessel* (1877; reprint, 1996).

BROWN, JOHN
(1800–1859)
Abolitionist

Born in Torrington, Connecticut, and raised in Ohio, John Brown was the third of six children of Owen and Ruth Mills Brown. The Brown family held deep religious convictions and solid antislavery beliefs. Owen Brown provided his children with a strong Calvinist foundation, and he raised them in an environment in which slavery was considered unacceptable and unjust. It was from his father that John Brown inherited his abhorrence of slavery and his commitment to religion.

In 1820, Brown married Dianthe Lusk in Hudson, Ohio. Six years later, the couple sold their farm and moved to Pennsylvania, where Brown opened his own tannery, the first of his many failed business ventures. Brown farmed, operated a tannery, raised sheep, drove cattle, served as a wool company agent, and was involved in land speculation at various times in his life, but he was wholly unsuccessful in all of these pursuits. He experienced serious financial problems by age thirty-one and declared bankruptcy at age forty-two. By the time he was fifty-six, he had accumulated in six states a string of twenty failed businesses, which ultimately contributed to the filing of twenty-one lawsuits against him.

Although Brown had always opposed slavery, he was not committed to the cause until he attended an abolitionist meeting in Cleveland in 1837. Upon the conclusion of this meeting, Brown swore that he would dedicate his life to the abolition of slavery. Nonconformist and radical in his approach, Brown never joined an antislavery society, he demanded immediate emancipation for slaves, and he was not averse to the use of violence. His commitment to the destruction of slavery was unwavering.

By 1848, Brown had grown increasingly militant in his opposition to slavery. The previous year when he first met Frederick Douglass, Brown revealed to Douglass his plan for freeing the slaves. Brown believed that the Alleghany Mountains were the "hills to freedom" and that they were the best place from which to launch an attack on slavery. Brown told Douglass that he hoped to start an insurrection with twenty-five of his own men who would quickly be joined by slaves. After the meeting, Douglass wrote in his newspaper, the *North Star*, that Brown, "though a white gentleman, [was] in sympathy, a black man, and as deeply interested in [the black] cause, as though his own soul had been pierced with the iron of slavery."

In 1855, after a temporary move to Kansas, Brown continued his fight against slavery. The passage of the Kansas-Nebraska Act in 1854 had drawn several of Brown's sons to the newly organized Kansas Territory. After living in Kansas for a few months, the sons informed Brown of the tension that existed between proslavery and antislavery forces in the area. Subsequently, Brown left his wife and younger children in New York and traveled with his son Oliver and his son-in-law Henry Thompson to join the others in Kansas. Years later, Brown admitted that he had moved to Kansas to fight, not to settle permanently.

In May 1856, as tensions in Kansas continued to rise, Brown, five of his sons, and Thompson joined the Pottawatomie Rifles in the free-soil defense of Lawrence, Kansas. By the time the group reached Lawrence, however, proslavery forces had already sacked the town and U.S. troops had restored order. Brown was furious with the proslavery forces and the failure of the Lawrence men to defend their town. Consequently, he persuaded several men to accompany him to Pottawatomie Creek. Brown, determined to exact revenge, wanted to "sweep the creek of all proslavery men." Armed with broadswords, the party approached three houses in the area and killed five men, including John Doyle and two of his sons, Allen Wilkinson and William Sherman. Throughout the rest of his life, Brown remained vague about his role at Pottawatomie. He was never legally punished for the crimes.

The Pottawatomie massacre of 24–25 May 1856 helped trigger guerrilla warfare in Kansas that lasted throughout the fall. Coupled with the recent sack of Lawrence on 21 May and the caning of Charles Sumner on the floor of the Senate on 22 May, the massacre led many in Kansas to believe that the Civil War had begun. At this time, John Brown made the fight to end slavery his full-time career. Throughout the remainder of the

An early portrait of John Brown (*Library of Congress*)

year, Brown and his sons fought in Kansas and Missouri. In August, Brown organized a company of "Kansas Regulars" and headed for Osawatomie, Kansas. On 30 August, proslavery Border Ruffians from Missouri raided free-state Osawatomie. In the process, they burned and looted the town and killed Brown's son Frederick. After the battle of Osawatomie, Brown vowed, "I will die fighting for this cause. There will be no more peace in this land until slavery is done for." Henceforth, this symbol of the antislavery crusade was known as "Old Osawatomie Brown."

In October 1856, Brown returned to the East, where he soon began a speaking tour to raise money for his military company. By this time, Brown had nearly finalized his plans for a future attack on the federal arsenal at Harper's Ferry, Virginia. He lacked only the money necessary to carry out the plan.

In 1858, Brown briefly returned to Kansas and launched an invasion of Missouri in which a slave owner was killed and eleven slaves were freed. After the invasion, Brown continued his speaking tour, although there was a $200 bounty on his head.

On Sunday, 16 October 1859, John Brown led his men in the failed attack on Harper's Ferry. Less than thirty-six hours later, a company of U.S. Marines under

the leadership of Colonel Robert E. Lee and Lieutenant J. E. B. Stuart halted the assault and killed ten of Brown's men, including his sons Oliver and Watson. Brown was seriously wounded and captured. On 2 November, he was convicted of treason, murder, and insurrection, and he was sentenced to death. On 2 December 1859, John Brown, who had failed at almost everything he had tried, and who believed that as an abolitionist he had carried out the will of God, was hanged in Charlestown, Virginia. He died convinced that he was "worth inconceivably more to hang than for any other purpose."

—*Jennifer L. Bertolet*

See also Abolitionist Movement; Abolitionists; Harper's Ferry; Kansas.

For further reading:
Abels, Jules. *Man on Fire: John Brown and the Cause of Liberty* (1971).
Oates, Stephen B. *To Purge This Land with Blood: A Biography of John Brown* (1970).
Villard, Oswald Garrison. *John Brown 1800–1859: A Biography Fifty Years After* (1910; reprint, 1966).

BROWN, JOHN CALVIN
(1827–1889)
Confederate general

Born in Giles County, Tennessee, to Duncan Brown and Margaret Smith Brown, the younger Brown graduated from Jackson College, studied law upon graduation and quickly became a prominent attorney in Pulaski, Tennessee. Before the war, Brown was more devoted to his law practice than politics, although he was a member of the Whig Party. He opposed secession and served as an elector for John Bell's Constitutional Union Party candidacy for president in the 1860 elections. However, upon the secession of Tennessee after Fort Sumter was fired upon, Brown enlisted in the Confederate army as a private.

Brown served at that rank only briefly before being named colonel of the 3d Tennessee Infantry in May 1861. In early 1862 he temporarily commanded a brigade at Fort Donelson and was part of the ill-fated garrison there that surrendered in February 1862. Exchanged in August 1862, he was promptly promoted to brigadier general.

Brown commanded his brigade at Perryville in October 1862 and was wounded there. A year later while commanding a brigade of Major General Alexander P. Stewart's division at Chickamauga, he received a second wound. Within two months, he was again leading his brigade, and at Missionary Ridge his actions merited commendation for bravery. Brown commanded a division of John Bell Hood's corps during the Atlanta campaign and again received notice for his actions at Dalton. On 4 August 1864, his acting divisional command became official with his promotion to major general.

Brown accompanied Hood's army as it moved into Tennessee in the fall of 1864. An exploding shell severely wounded him at Franklin, an event that threatened to remove him permanently from the war. After a slow convalescence, he joined Joseph E. Johnston's army in North Carolina on 2 April, just weeks before Johnston's surrender. Brown was paroled from Greensboro, North Carolina.

Following the war, Brown resumed his lucrative law practice and became a prominent businessman. In 1870 and 1872, he was elected governor of Tennessee. He died in Red Boiling Springs, Tennessee, in 1889.

—*David S. Heidler and Jeanne T. Heidler*

See also Fort Donelson.
For further reading:
Butler, Margaret. "The Life of John C. Brown" (Master's thesis, 1936).

BROWN, JOSEPH EMERSON
(1821–1894)
Georgia governor

Joseph E. Brown, governor of Georgia throughout the Civil War, was a brilliant politician whose career revealed the social and ideological fault lines within the Confederacy. Displaying acute political instincts, Brown registered the discontents of Southern society and then channeled them to advance his public career. Although not a constructive statesman, Brown was a sensitive barometer of trouble and a vigorous, resourceful foe of President Jefferson Davis and the policies of the Confederate central government.

Brown burst onto the political scene in 1857 when the convention of Georgia's Democratic Party deadlocked. Nominated as a dark horse candidate for governor, he defeated Benjamin H. Hill of the American Party and thereafter held onto center stage in Georgia politics until his retirement from the U.S. Senate in 1890. In his first term as governor, Brown showed a perceptive grasp of class issues in politics. Though he was rapidly becoming rich, Brown's background was that of a country lawyer, and he took strong Jacksonian stands against the banks, which appealed to rural voters. In his second term he emphasized military preparedness and states' rights, anticipating the effective appeals that he soon would make to the elite.

Throughout the Civil War Brown stressed two powerful political themes: strict adherence to states' rights and social equity in the sacrifices made by Georgia's people. As the champion of states' rights and state sovereignty, Brown repeatedly lambasted the Davis administration and appealed to an increasingly disaffected elite. As an innovator in social welfare policies, Brown demonstrated concern for the suffering of the common people and brought them tangible measures of relief. In both ways his actions advanced his renown and strengthened his position, even as the fortunes of the Confederacy declined.

Brown signaled his extreme states' rights views even before Georgia joined the Confederacy. As soon as the state seceded from the United States, he sent a representative abroad with instructions to seek diplomatic recognition from Queen Victoria, Napoleon III, and the king of Belgium. More strong steps were soon to follow. He jealously kept all his state's guns under his own control and threatened to disarm Georgia volunteers when they left the state to fight for the Confederacy. Next he began a practice of offering the Confederacy "skeleton" regiments—units that had a full complement of officers (appointed by Brown up through the level of colonel) but only a scattering of enlisted men. To win the favor of Georgia's voters, he frequently insisted that units of the army actually were militia and therefore entitled to elect their officers.

In the conscription law Brown found his preeminent states' rights cause. The governor objected almost immediately to the Confederate Congress's first conscription law, passed in April 1862, and thus became a leader of opposition to the Davis administration. Denying the necessity of the law, he demanded a long list of exemptions, denounced conscription as a power to "destroy the civil government of each State," and ordered his state's enrolling officers not to cooperate with Confederate officials. A few weeks later he sent President Davis a long attack on the law, calling conscription "subversive of [Georgia's] sovereignty, and at war with all the principles for the support of which Georgia entered into this revolution." Among his turgid arguments was the assertion that the Confederacy could not draft the militia of the states, which he defined as "the whole arms-bearing population of the State who are not enlisted in the regular armies of the Confederacy."

This letter prompted an exchange on constitutional theories, in which Brown took delight in pillorying Jefferson Davis as more of a broad constructionist than Alexander Hamilton. When the Confederate Congress passed a second conscription act in September 1862, Brown thundered that this law "strikes down" Georgia's "sovereignty at a single blow," destroyed the state's militia, and left his citizens defenseless against any slave uprising. These protests undermined unity and support for the central government. Even Jefferson Davis admitted publicly that "unexpected criticism" had "impaired" the government's efforts to raise an army, and other politicians and newspapers took up the cry against the administration. Eventually Brown allowed conscription to go forward, as court cases repeatedly upheld the authority of Congress, but his actions kept more than 8,000 Georgians out of the army and weakened support for the cause.

As he became the champion for states' rights theorists, Brown also won gratitude from thousands of ordinary citizens by ministering to their needs. When shortages of salt foreshadowed the greater suffering that would follow, Governor Brown ordered seizures of salt throughout his state and sold this vital preservative at bargain prices to soldiers' wives and destitute widows. To supply the common people and his state's troops, Brown also found funds to manufacture salt in Virginia. With impressive energy he arranged the manufacture of cotton cards, so that people could make cloth, and bought blankets, shoes, and other supplies for soldiers. He fought to suppress the distilling of scarce grain and from the legislature obtained appropriations as large as $10 million for relief. At times he denounced conscription officers as dragging off hundreds of men who left helpless families behind them. In all of his efforts he put the poorest citizens, ordinary soldiers, and their families first. Arguing that "the poor have generally paid their part . . . in military service, exposure, fatigue and blood, the rich, who have been in a much greater degree exempt from these, should meet the money demands of the Government," he won the gratitude and support of the poor.

Reelected twice during the Civil War, Brown took his opposition to the Confederate government to a new level in the spring of 1864. Resentment of the suspension of the writ of habeas corpus and a yearning for peace were growing in Georgia. In concert with Alexander and Linton Stephens, Brown assailed the central government and promoted the idea of peace negotiations. First Brown addressed a special session of the state legislature, condemned the Congress for authorizing Jefferson Davis to make "illegal and unconstitutional arrests," and asserted that only negotiations could end the fighting. Linton Stephens and his more prominent brother followed with vigorous denunciations of the suspension of the writ and other essential war measures. Their supporters then introduced resolutions calling on the people to act "through their state organizations and popular assemblies" to end the war. All these proposals tapped strong emotions in war-weary Georgia, but others were dismayed at the prospect of Confederate disunity and state-initiated disintegration. Supporters of the government managed to pass resolutions supporting Jefferson Davis and the war effort along with the peace resolutions.

Joe Brown ended his Confederate career as he had started it—a foe of the central government and a hindrance to its war effort, but a popular politician who knew how to appeal to both rich and poor. His shrewdness and insight kept him in high political office through a checkered, but long and successful, postwar career.

—*Paul D. Escott*

See also Georgia
For further reading:
Candler, Allen D., ed. *The Confederate Records of the State of Georgia* (1910).

Escott, Paul D. *After Secession: Jefferson Davis and the Failure of Confederate Nationalism* (1977).

Hill, Louise Biles. *Joseph E. Brown and the Confederacy* (1939).

Parks, Joseph H. *Joseph E. Brown of Georgia* (1977).

Richardson, James D., comp. *A Compilation of the Messages and Papers of the Confederacy* (1906).

U.S. War Department. *The War of the Rebellion: A Compilation of the Official Records of the Union and Confederate Armies* (1880–1901).

Yearns, W. Buck. *The Confederate Governors* (1985).

BROWN, WILLIAM WELLS
(ca. 1814–1884)

African-American abolitionist and author

William Wells Brown was born near Lexington, Kentucky. In a narrative of his life as a slave, he wrote about his enslaved mother, Elizabeth, who told him that she was a daughter of Daniel Boone and a slave lover. She told him his father was a white slave owner, George W. Higgins. The family moved to St. Louis, where Brown was hired out because of his embarrassing resemblance to his master's white nephew. In 1830 Brown worked for the abolitionist Elijah P. Lovejoy at the St. Louis *Times*. Later he was sold to a merchant and then to a riverboat captain.

Brown escaped in 1834 to Ohio, where a Quaker by the name of Wells Brown helped him. After reaching Cleveland, Brown became part of the antislavery movement, attended Black National Conventions, and began teaching himself to read and write. He married Elizabeth (Betsey) Schooner in that same year. Of their three children only two survived, Clarissa (born in 1836) and Josephine (born in 1839). Brown's most successful business venture was stewarding for lake steamers, and he eventually settled his young family in Buffalo, New York. In one year he helped sixty fugitives reach Canada.

In 1847 Brown and his wife separated and he moved to Boston with his two daughters. There he published his story of his life as a slave, *Narrative of William W. Brown, a Fugitive Slave*, first published in 1847 and expanded the next year to sell 8,000 copies in two years.

He went as one of several American representatives to the World Peace Congress in Paris in 1849. There he established his renown as a nonviolent Garrisonian by emphasizing the role of the threat and use of violence by slave owners. He asserted, "The dissemination of the principles of peace would be the means of emancipation." He remained in Europe for the next five years, researching in the archives of England and France and also visiting the West Indies. He also helped to found and run in 1852 the London newspaper *The Anti-Slavery Advocate*.

Out of this period in his life came the first novel published by an African-American. Published in 1853, *Clotel; or, the President's Daughter: A Narrative of Slave Life in the United States* was a politically charged narrative of slave life in the Southern states. By putting at the center of this novel the black offspring of President Thomas Jefferson, Brown put in print what the Hemmings family alleged for so many years.

Although he wrote many plays, only one was published: *The Escape; or, A Leap for Freedom*, published in Boston in 1858. The five-act drama is generally acknowledged to be the first play published by an African-American author. The other plays he presented as dramatic readings in place of the usual antislavery lecture while on tours. His journalist talent can be found in his contributions to the *London Daily News*; *The Liberator*; Frederick Douglass' paper; and *The National Anti-Slavery Standard*. His most important books were history books written during and after the Civil War.

After the election of Abraham Lincoln and as the secession crisis grew, Brown continued making his money from his antislavery publications, even serializing a revised portion of his novel *Clotel* under the name of "Miranda; or The Beautiful Quadroon" in the *Weekly Anglo-African* (1 December 1860–6 March 1861). He discouraged black enlistments until blacks had won equality of treatment in the military. In September 1862, President Lincoln issued his preliminary Emancipation Proclamation and few Northern blacks rejoiced; many saw the move as a cautious war measure, even callous rather than humanitarian in motive. Brown said at that time, "The colored people of the country rejoice in what Mr. Lincoln has done for them, but they all wish that General Frémont had been in his place." (U.S. general John C. Frémont had on 30 August 1861 established martial law in Missouri and freed the slaves of all traitors.)

At a meeting of black activists held in Liberty Hall, New Bedford, on 18 February 1863, Brown gave an address that reversed his position. He described at length the heroic heritage of black Americans and how they had already made progress in the integration of America. He said they "had poets and preachers; it was time to have a hero on the battlefield....The time had come...for the black man to vindicate his own character." In March, President Lincoln sent Adjutant General Lorenzo Thomas to the Mississippi Valley with the authority to raise black troops. Brown joined Massachusetts governor John Andrews's "Black Committee" that worked to encourage and recruit black men into the 54th and 55th Massachusetts Infantry and the 5th Massachusetts Cavalry. General Orders No. 143, dated 22 May 1863, established the Bureau for Colored Troops with the authority to supervise organizing black units and examine candidates seeking commissions in them. This was a milestone in the history of blacks in the Civil War: they now fought officially for the United States and not just for a state or individual. However, in Massachusetts, only whites could join the militia and no blacks could be commissioned as officers. "Equality first, guns afterward," posited Brown.

That year, while living in Cambridgeport, Massachusetts, Brown published *The Black Man*, a set of historical and literary essays that traced the African origins of black Americans. This publication was a heroic effort to explode current myths of blacks' "natural inferiority." Brown included fifty-three biographical sketches of artists, teachers, actors, poets, preachers, lawyers, rebel slave leaders, and rulers of Haiti and Liberia. He showed that he had fully broken with the nonviolence of Garrisonianism by portraying Nat Turner as the model for black action needed in the South during the Civil War. This book went through ten printings in three years.

In the summer of 1863, whites in New York City rioted ostensibly in protest of the draft, but from 13 to 17 July they expressed their frustrations and hatred against Americans of African descent. More than eleven African-American citizens were killed, hundreds wounded, thousands left homeless and destitute. Brown was there recruiting blacks for the Massachusetts regiments and recorded the heroic efforts of men and women during those violent times.

In October 1864 in Syracuse, New York, Brown attended the National Convention of Colored Citizens of the United States, organized by Frederick Douglass. There he helped draft "Declarations of Wrong and Rights." He also revised his novel *Clotel* that year and reissued it under the name *Clotelle: A Tale of Southern States*, adding more dramatic scenes and references to actual newspaper accounts and historical facts of the horrors of slavery in the South. Clotelle was the name of his two-year-old daughter; he had married in 1860 Annie Elizabeth Gray. Also in 1864 Brown began treating patients in the Boston area, and thereafter he added M.D. after his name.

In 1867 he published *The Negro in the American Rebellion; His Heroism and His Fidelity.* He wanted to give historical proof of what African-American men had contributed to the building of the nation that debated whether to give them basic civil rights. Though the book began with the deeds of the military man of African descent in the American Revolution and continued with the War of 1812, more than half of the book was devoted to the last two years of the Civil War. It was the first published historical analysis of the black role in the Civil War. It was not a popular book and did not sell well; many copies were burned in the great Boston fire of 1872.

After the war, Brown continued to give lectures on black history, but he redirected his abolitionist energies toward temperance work and medicine. In 1880 he published his last and most popular book, *My Southern Home; or The South and Its People.* He urged black self-respect, hard work, and self-improvement, recom-mending emigration from the South. He foreshadowed W. E. B. DuBois's *Souls of Black Folks* (1903) when he appealed to his fellow African-Americans: "Don't be ashamed to show your colors, and to own them." Brown died on 6 November 1884 in Chelsea, Massachusetts, from a tumor of the bladder and was buried in an unmarked grave.

—*Randolph Hollingsworth*

See also Abolitionist Movement; African-American Soldiers, C.S.A.; Douglass, Frederick; Emancipation Proclamation; Garrison, William Lloyd; Underground Railroad; United States Colored Troops.

For further reading:

Brown, Josephine. *Biography of an American Bondman, by His Daughter* (1856).

Brown, William Wells. *The Black Man: His Antecedents, His Genius, and His Achievements* (1863).

———. *My Southern Home; or The South and Its People* (1880).

———. *The Negro in the American Rebellion* (1867).

Candela, Gregory L. "William Wells Brown." In *Afro-American Writers before the Harlem Renaissance,* vol. 50 of *Dictionary of Literary Biography* (1986).

Dunnigan, Alice Allison. *The Fascinating Story of Black Kentuckians: Their Heritage and Traditions* (1982).

Farrison, William Edward. *William Wells Brown: Author and Reformer* (1969).

Lucas, Marion B. *From Slavery to Segregation, 1760–1891. A History of Blacks in Kentucky,* vol. 1 (1992).

Mabee, Carleton. *Black Freedom: The Nonviolent Abolitionists from 1830 through the Civil War* (1970).

BROWNING, ORVILLE HICKMAN
(1806–1881)
Union politician

Orville H. Browning was a friend and political associate of Abraham Lincoln. Browning's increasingly conservative wartime views, however, conflicted with Lincoln's emancipation policy and other administration war measures, and in the postwar years Browning drifted away from the Republican Party that he had helped to shape in antebellum Illinois. His diary and correspondence are important primary sources for Civil War–era history.

Browning, like Lincoln, was a native Kentuckian, born on 10 February 1806 near Cynthiana in Harrison County. He attended Augusta College and then read law with an uncle. He passed the bar and moved to Quincy, Illinois, in 1831. The next year he served briefly as a militiaman in the Black Hawk War. He married in 1836 and entered politics the same year, winning election to the state senate as a Whig. In 1843 he lost a race for the U.S. Congress to Democrat Stephen A. Douglas. In 1850 and 1852 he was again unsuccessful in congressional elections. During these prewar years Browning gained a reputation as an able attorney and influential public figure, though he was sometimes considered aloof

and somewhat conceited. He was noted for his stately manner and his old style ruffled shirts and cuffs.

Browning believed slavery was wrong in the abstract, and he opposed its extension beyond the states where it already existed. He was not sure, however, that there was any better system for relations between the races in America. He favored proposals to colonize freed blacks outside the country. In 1845 he became the vice president of the Illinois Colonization Society. Throughout his life he never abandoned a common belief of his time that blacks were inferior to whites.

The Kansas-Nebraska Act of 1854 roused his anger. He joined the newly formed Republican Party, and in 1856 and 1858 he drafted state party platforms that helped attract like-minded conservatives to the Illinois Republican banner. In the presidential election of 1860 Browning actually favored the Missouri conservative Edward Bates, but as an Illinois delegate to the Chicago convention he did his part to help his friend Lincoln obtain the nomination. Lincoln followed Browning's suggestion to soften some strident language in his first inaugural address, replacing a threat to "reclaim" captured Federal property with a less bellicose resolution to "hold, occupy and possess" Federal positions. Browning let Lincoln know of his desire to become a U.S. Supreme Court justice, but with the sudden death of Stephen Douglas in June 1861, the Republican governor of Illinois, Richard Yates, appointed Browning to finish Douglas's term in the U.S. Senate.

The onset of a shooting war radicalized Browning for a time. As a senator, he declared the North should treat the seceded states as conquered territories; he voted for the First Confiscation Act; he supported General John C. Frémont's proclamation freeing the slaves in Missouri; he defended the administration against criticism for arbitrary arrests of Northern citizens; and he voted to emancipate slaves in Washington, D.C.

By late spring 1862, however, Browning began reverting to his characteristic conservatism. First, he opposed the Second Confiscation Act. Then he broke unequivocally with the Radical Republicans by condemning Lincoln's preliminary Emancipation Proclamation as unconstitutional and unwise. He persisted in admonishing Lincoln to abandon emancipation right up until the policy officially took effect on 1 January 1863. Browning became so alienated by the course of events that in the 1864 presidential election he refrained from supporting Lincoln's reelection. Though his political relations with Lincoln became strained, the two men and their wives maintained cordial personal relations. The Brownings had been of particular comfort to the grieving Lincolns on the death of their son Willie in 1862, and Browning served as a pallbearer at the president's funeral.

Democrats won control of the Illinois legislature in the 1862 elections, so Browning did not retain his U.S. Senate seat. He remained in Washington, however, where as a lobbyist he used his connections with Lincoln and other government leaders to obtain favors for his clients. During the last months of the war he was apparently involved in a failed scheme to make money trading in Confederate commodities.

After the war, Browning was a strong critic of the Radical Republicans in Congress and their reconstruction policies. He even participated in an unsuccessful attempt to form a new conservative political party. President Andrew Johnson appointed him secretary of the interior in 1866. Browning stood by the president in his impeachment battle with Congress, serving in a dual capacity as attorney general during the impeachment trial. When President Grant took office in 1869, Browning returned to Illinois where he prospered as an attorney for the Chicago, Burlington & Quincy Railroad. He also finally reached the Supreme Court— but in the capacity of an attorney arguing for railroad interests in one of the Granger cases. He died in Quincy on 10 August 1881 at the age of seventy-five.

—Byron Andreasen

For further reading:
Baxter, Maurice. *Orville H. Browning: Lincoln's Friend and Critic* (1957).

BROWNLOW, WILLIAM GANNAWAY
(1805–1877)

Tennessee Unionist

Born 25 August 1805 in Wythe County, Virginia, William Brownlow came of age with, and helped to shape, the evangelical world of the antebellum South. A Unionist, his religion and politics illustrate the complexity of Southern proslavery and secession views. Orphaned at age eleven, Brownlow worked for ten years as a carpenter and laborer before being converted to evangelical Christianity at a camp meeting. With no formal education, he became a circuit rider for the Methodist Episcopal Church, preaching repentance and damnation in western Virginia, North Carolina, and eastern Tennessee. He married in 1836 and settled in Elizabethton, Tennessee.

A man of fiery temper and fiercely committed to religious and political truth, Brownlow found an outlet for his contentious personality through editing a newspaper, the *Whig*, which he published in Knoxville from 1849 to 1862. Despite the convention that ministers were not to meddle in partisan politics, Brownlow was a vocal champion of Henry Clay and the Whig Party's program of economic development. He loathed Democrats and increasingly focused his political vitriol on Andrew Johnson, the leading Democrat in eastern Tennessee.

Brownlow also represented the truth of evangelical

Christianity as he understood it. He wrote book-length diatribes denouncing Catholicism as contrary to scripture and, during the 1850s, defended the Methodist Church from charges leveled against it by James Robinson Graves, a Baptist editor in Nashville, Tennessee. Graves characterized Methodism as "a great iron wheel" because its polity rolled over congregational liberty. Brownlow responded with two tomes, *The Great Iron Wheel Examined; or its False Spokes Extracted* and *The Little Iron Wheel Enlarged: or Elder Graves.*

Brownlow also loathed abolitionism. He referred to Harriet Beecher Stowe as "ugly as Original Sin." He considered abolitionism as contrary to the Bible and to the Constitution, which made slaves "a lawful species of property." He concluded that "those who feed and clothe them well, and instruct them in religion, are better friends to them than those who set them at liberty." In these exchanges, Brownlow relied on ad hominem arguments and liberal interpretation of scripture. He pointed out that the biblical Cain had nullified God's law in slaying Abel, and suggested that throughout the Bible, nullification equaled sin.

Apart from a personal devotion to his deity, Brownlow's special loyalty was to the Union. During the secession crisis, he urged people to pray for "grace to perceive the right path, which. . . leads from the camps of Southern mad-caps and Northern fanatics." He rejected the notion that secession was an appropriate remedy for Lincoln's election and counseled moderation. At the same time, Brownlow displayed a United States flag over his house and announced that he would support secession and join the Democratic Party only "when man forgets to be selfish, or Democrats lose their inclination to steal." He pledged that he would "fight the Secession leaders until Hell freezes over, and then fight them on the ice."

Brownlow's pro-Union invective had a supportive audience in eastern Tennessee, but it also invited the ire of the Confederate government. Anxious to avoid provocation, it did not move against Brownlow or other Unionists until Brownlow's increasingly vehement editorials in his newspaper, the Knoxville *Whig,* became impossible to ignore. After a brief incarceration, Brownlow was permitted to flee to the North, where he published an account of his experiences during the early days of secession and civil war.

Lionized in the North as the embodiment of the quintessential loyal Southerner, Brownlow toured Northern cities before returning to Tennessee behind the Union army. He resumed publishing his newspaper in November 1863. He labored alongside Andrew Johnson, his antebellum archfoe, to obtain Tennessee's restoration to the Union. Brownlow supported Johnson's efforts, and quasi-legal machinations, to get some sort of approval for the abolition of slavery and a government organized along the lines of Lincoln's Proclamation of Amnesty and Reconstruction. When Johnson became Lincoln's vice president, Brownlow succeeded Johnson as wartime Reconstruction governor.

Conservative Unionists abandoned Brownlow at this point because they feared that wartime Reconstruction would lead to the political equality of freedmen. They hoped to regain control of their state and to keep former slaves out of politics. Brownlow had initially supported this position, but rather than lose office, he supported Federal efforts to register black voters, courted their support, and won reelection in 1867. Although he doubtless recognized that the forces of Redemption and the Ku Klux Klan would be ultimately irresistible, Brownlow had the legislature elect him to the United States Senate in 1868, and he served out his full term. He died on 29 April 1877.

—*Edward R. Crowther*

For further reading:
Brownlow, William G. *Sketches of the Rise, Progress, and Decline of Secession; with a Narrative of Personal Adventures among the Rebels* (1862).
Coulter, E. Merton. *William G. Brownlow: Fighting Parson of the Southern Highlands* (1937).
Harris, William C. *With Charity for All: Lincoln and the Restoration of the Union* (1997).

BROWNSVILLE, TEXAS

Sixty-five miles up the Rio Grande from its mouth on the Gulf of Mexico, Brownsville was the site of one of the first Confederate successes in the war when the small Union garrison evacuated nearby Fort Brown after a show of force by Texas troops in early 1861. Brownsville became a significant trading center because of its proximity to Matamoros, Mexico, just across the river. Although the president of Mexico, Benito Juarez, favored the Union, the governor of Tamaulipas Province, Santiago Vidaurri, maintained friendly relations with Confederate Texans. As a result, as other Confederate ports were shut down by the Union blockade and as the Mississippi was closed to Confederate traffic, Brownsville became the center of a bustling trade between Southern cotton growers and English, French, and even Yankee merchants. Confederate and Texas authorities tried without effect to control the indiscriminate trade between Southerners and Northerners. From late 1861 until the end of the war, thousands of ox-drawn wagons laden with cotton wound their way through south Texas to Brownsville from as far away as Louisiana and Arkansas. A Texan who served as a teamster on one of those wagons recalled years later that the trail stretching north from Brownsville "became a broad thorofare along which continuously moved two vast unending trains of wagons"—one southbound, piled high with cotton; and

Confederates evacuating the town of Brownsville (*Harper's Weekly* / *Library of Congress*)

the other northbound, crammed with military and civilian supplies. By mid-1863 the Brownsville *Flag* could announce that "the town is crowded with merchants and traders from all parts of the world, and the side-walks are blocked up with goods." Northern traders eagerly bought all the cotton they could get from Mexican intermediaries acting on behalf of Texas cotton speculators; Southerners then used the profits to buy "all manner of explosive and destructive things" to sell to the Confederate military. Because of its economic prosperity, which benefitted not only the few men who became millionaires trading in cotton, but also skilled and manual laborers, the town's wartime population swelled to 25,000, while Matamoros soared to 40,000 and the makeshift town of Bagdad on the Rio Grande to 15,000. The cotton trade naturally attracted the attention of the United States government, which mounted the Rio Grande campaign to shut it down. Brownsville served as the headquarters of the Union 8th Corps when it occupied parts of the Rio Grande Valley and Texas Gulf Coast between November 1863 and July 1864. Union troops in occupied Brownsville set up housekeeping in the courthouse and other public buildings, published their own newspaper, the *Loyal National Union Journal*, held the occasional review or military ball, and enjoyed

the illicit attractions of both Brownsville and Matamoros. Brownsville also served as "capital" to the new provisional governor of Texas, the former Congressman and Texas Unionist Brigadier General A. J. Hamilton. Along with other well-known Unionist refugees like former U.S. District Court Judge Thomas H. DuVal and Hamilton's former law partner John Hancock, Hamilton attempted to establish a government loyal to the United States. They established a chapter of the Union League, a national Republican organization, and recruited a few hundred troops for the Union's 1st and 2d Texas Cavalry.

Brownsville was also the scene of much intrigue related to Mexican politics, after Mexico itself was thrown into civil war by the French invasion of 1862. Competing armies fought on behalf of the French, for the Mexican president, Juarez, or for powerful borderland opportunists like Juan Cortinas, a Mexican-Texan rancher who in 1859 had briefly occupied Brownsville during a dispute with local law officers. Matamoros changed hands several times during the course of the war; the defeated factions would often retreat across the river to Brownsville to lick their wounds and plan their next attack. Union troops actually crossed over to Matamoros during the fighting one night in 1864 to protect the U.S. consulate. When much of the Federal occupation force was transferred to Louisiana in the summer of 1864, Confederate troops under Colonel John "Rip" Ford began pushing Union detachments out of the Rio Grande Valley in June and July. Skirmishes at Ebonal on 22 July and on the outskirts of Brownsville on 25 July convinced the disorganized Yankees to evacuate the city on 29 July. It remained a Confederate stronghold in south Texas for the remainder of the war. The Rebel force, again under the command of Ford, that won the last land battle of the Civil War at Palmito Ranch rode out of Fort Brown. The city and its neighboring fort were finally reoccupied by Union soldiers in late May 1865.

—*James Marten*

See also Blockade of C.S.A.; Hamilton, Andrew Jackson; Matamoros, Mexico; Palmito Ranch, Battle of; Rio Grande Campaign.

For further reading:

Daddysmith, James W. *The Matamoros Trade: Confederate Commerce, Diplomacy, and Intrigue* (1984).

Hunter, John Warren. "The Fall of Brownsville on the Rio Grande, November 1863" (n.d.).

Kerby, Robert L. *Kirby Smith's Confederacy: The Trans-Mississippi South, 1863–1865* (1972).

Marten, James. "For the Army, the People, and Abraham Lincoln: A Yankee Newspaper in Occupied Texas." *Civil War History* (1993).

BRYANT, WILLIAM CULLEN
(1794–1878)
Poet

William Cullen Bryant was born on 3 November 1794 in Cummington, Massachusetts, the son of Peter Bryant, a physician, and Sarah Snell. Bryant's early start with books came from his parents. He attended Williams College in Williamstown, Massachusetts, from 1810 to 1811. He then studied law privately, was admitted to the bar in 1815, and practiced law in Plainfield and Great Barrington for ten years. Moving to New York in 1825, he became associate editor of the *New York Evening Post* from 1826 to 1829 and editor-in-chief from 1829 to 1878. In 1836, he became half-owner of the journal.

An ardent believer in human rights and liberty, Bryant, speaking on 4 July 1820 at Stockbridge, Massachusetts, had already evinced an abhorrence of slavery. He found reprehensible the Missouri Compromise of 1820, which extended slavery in the Louisiana Purchase territory south of latitude 36°30' and in Missouri, north of the line. In 1836, angered by antiabolition violence in Cincinnati to stop James G. Birney from publishing his abolitionist newspaper, Bryant defended the right to bring the slavery issue into the public arena. He became outraged again in 1837

when Reverend Elijah P. Lovejoy, editor of an antislavery paper in Alton, Illinois, was murdered by a mob.

Bryant wove the Civil War into his poetry. "The Antiquity of Freedom" (1842), was a forerunner of his later verses: "...nor yet, O Freedom! close thy lids/In slumber; for thine enemy [Tyranny] never sleeps,/And thou must watch and combat till the day/Of the new earth and heaven." In April 1844, Bryant's articles raised the issue whether Texas should join the Union as a slave-holding territory from which other states could be created. Sincerely devoted to the Wilmot Proviso (1846), which would have barred slavery in any territory acquired from Mexico, Bryant urged Congress in 1847 to prohibit slavery expansion into New Mexico and California. In the presidential election of 1848, antislavery Democrats, antislavery Whigs, and the Liberty Party combined to nominate a "Free Soil" ticket, headed by Martin Van Buren, who now had approved of the exclusion of slavery from new territories. Bryant supported Van Buren, but the Free Soilers did not win a single state. Bryant's *Evening Post*, a Free-Soil Democratic newspaper, objected to the Compromise of 1850 that, by abandoning the Wilmot Proviso, opened the Mexican cession to slavery. Though the Democratic Convention of 1852 expressed its loyalty to the Compromise of 1850, Bryant, wanting to remain affiliated with Democratic Free Soilers, accepted their presidential nominee, Franklin Pierce.

The Kansas-Nebraska Act of 1854, which repealed the prohibition of slavery north of 36°30' in the Louisiana Purchase territory, caused Bryant to work industriously on the formation of the Republican Party, which stood for resisting the extension of slavery. In 1856, he threw the increasingly influential *Evening Post* solidly behind their presidential candidate, John C. Frémont. Bryant, who had written many editorials denouncing the Kansas-Nebraska Act, called attention in 1856 to the violence of slaveholders attempting to establish their control over free-state Kansas. He also reprimanded newly elected President James Buchanan for his proslavery policy, believing that Buchanan was contributing greatly to the disruption of the Democratic Party. And in 1857, when Chief Justice Roger B. Taney ruled that Congress never had the right to exclude slavery from a territory, Bryant complained that the "peculiar institution" had become a Federal institution.

In late 1858, Bryant sensed the emergence of Abraham Lincoln as a prominent national figure and, with other leading New York Republicans, brought about his historic visit to the Cooper Institute on 27 February 1860. Bryant introduced the speaker, praising him for his involvement in the Frémont campaign of 1856. After Lincoln's nomination for the presidency three months later, Bryant unhesitatingly and vigorously supported his candidacy, committing the *Evening Post* to work strenuously to elect him.

The restoration of the Union became the *Evening Post*'s editorial policy and, throughout the war, the editors rejected any compromise with the South. Bryant, who in a 12 November 1860 editorial declared that peaceable secession was an "absurdity," advised the president-elect in his letter of 25 December 1860 to be resolute on the questions of slavery and secession. In "Not Yet" (July 1861), Bryant expressed optimism: "Shall traitors lay that greatness low?/No,/and of Hope and Blessing, No!" In "Our Country's Call," written shortly thereafter (1861), he implored workaday men to take up arms: "…we/Must beat the banded traitors back."

A diligent advocate of immediate and universal emancipation by 1862 in editorials and in speeches at abolitionist rallies, Bryant arguably had rebuked Lincoln for rescinding General Frémont's proclamation of 31 August 1861, which had freed the slaves of rebellious Missourians. Later, in a speech on 2 October 1863, Bryant made a particularly robust statement opposing the president's policy of gradual emancipation. Further, arguably questioning Lincoln's leadership, he visited the president in August 1862, counseling him to pursue the war forcefully if the Union cause was not to be lost. Immediately after the horrendous Union defeat at Fredericksburg, Bryant in his editorial of 18 December 1862, asked with a sense of hopelessness, "How long is such intolerable and wicked blundering to continue? What does the President wait for?"

To counteract the growing peace movement in the North fueled by the Copperhead press, Bryant in 1863 helped direct an organized effort aimed to rally public support for continuing the war. In his 6 September 1864 editorial, "No Negotiations With the Rebel Government," he insisted on no peace without the abolition of slavery. In that same month, Bryant became confident of Lincoln's reelection, and his paper firmly supported the chief executive. In "The Death of Lincoln" (April 1865), the sorrowful Bryant wrote of the president's compassion and strength: "Oh, slow to smite and swift to spare,/Gentle and merciful and just:/Who, in the fear of God, didst bear/the sword of power, a nation's trust!" A year later, in "Death of Slavery" (May 1866), he recalled the cruelties imposed on the slaves and, addressing the slaveholders, exclaimed: "Well was thy doom deserved…."

Bryant, who was a founder and devoted worker for the National Freedmen's Relief Association (1863), declared in his Cooper Institute address of 26 February 1864 that the major challenge of reconstruction was to provide assistance to the four million slaves in their transition to freedom. Generally in agreement with Johnson's views on reconstruction, he strongly favored a conciliatory policy after the war: for example, his readiness to accept state approval (rather than a congressional act) for the abolition of slavery. Bryant insisted, however, on federal protection of the freed people's civil rights and on their omission from the population count (to determine representation in Congress) until they were granted the right of suffrage. In 1868 he supported Grant's candidacy for the presidency; but only reluctantly, because of the administration's policies, did he support Grant's reelection campaign. Bryant, a civic leader in New York City, was an early supporter of public parks (one in Manhattan was renamed Bryant Park in 1884) and a participant in the formation of the Metropolitan Museum of Art in 1870. Bryant died in New York City on 12 June 1878.

—*Bernard Hirschhorn*

See also Abolitionist Movement; Free Soil Party.

For further reading:
Brown, Charles H. *William Cullen Bryant: A Biography* (1971).
Bryant, William Cullen II, and Thomas G. Voss, eds. *The Letters of William Cullen Bryant* (1984, 1992).
McDowell, Tremaine. *William Cullen Bryant: Representative Selections with Introduction, Bibliography and Notes* (1935).
McLean, Jr., Albert F. *William Cullen Bryant* (1989).
Nevins, Allan. *The Evening Post: A Century of Journalism* (1922).

BUCHANAN, FRANKLIN
(1800–1874)
Confederate admiral

After a distinguished forty-five-year career in the U.S. Navy, Franklin Buchanan went south in 1861 and commanded both of the Confederate Navy's famous ironclads—the CSS *Virginia* (nee *Merrimack*) and the CSS *Tennessee*—in the process earning the distinction of being the Confederacy's only full admiral.

Buchanan was born at Auchentorlie, a family estate near Baltimore, on 17 September 1800, the fifth child and third son of Dr. George Buchanan, a physician, and Laetitia McKean, the daughter of a prominent Philadelphia family. He obtained a U.S. Navy midshipman's warrant at the age of fourteen during the War of 1812, but the war ended before he could report for duty. Most of his early naval service was in the Mediterranean on the frigate *Java* and the ship-of-the-line *Franklin*, and in the Caribbean where the U.S. Navy pursued pirates and slavers in smaller craft. Promoted to lieutenant on 13 January 1825 and to commander on 8 September 1841, Buchanan obtained his first command in September 1842 as captain of the sloop *Vincennes*. He married the former Ann Catherine (Nannie) Lloyd, a member of a prominent family on Maryland's Eastern Shore, with whom he had nine children.

Highlights of Buchanan's pre–Civil War career include his role as the founding superintendent of the U.S. Naval Academy in 1845–1846, and his command of the sloop *Germantown* in the War with Mexico (1847–1848) in which capacity he twice led shore expe-

Franklin Buchanan (*Library of Congress*)

ditions to capture Mexican fortifications. In 1853–1854, he was the captain of Matthew C. Perry's flagship during the expedition to Japan and conducted the negotiations that eventually led to a rapprochement between the U.S. and Japan.

Promoted to captain in 1855, Buchanan was posted to the command of the Washington Navy Yard in 1859. He was there on 19 April 1861 when a Massachusetts regiment passing through Baltimore on its way to Washington in anticipation of civil war was assailed by a civilian mob.

The troops opened fire, and when it was over four soldiers and twelve civilians lay dead. This event provoked Buchanan to tender his resignation from the Navy in the full expectation that Maryland would soon secede and join the Confederacy. When that did not happen, he sought to recall his resignation. But Secretary of the navy Gideon Welles did not want half-hearted patriots in his navy and informed Buchanan that his name was to be struck from the Navy list.

Buchanan's sympathies for the South derived in part from his close association with his slave-holding in-laws, the Lloyds of Wye House. Even so, he delayed several weeks before deciding to join the Confederacy. Not until after the battle of Bull Run (21 July 1861) did he leave his home on Maryland's Eastern Shore and cross the Potomac to offer his services to the Confederate navy. Serving briefly in an administrative capacity as Chief of the Bureau of Orders and Detail, he was posted in February 1862 to the command of the newly reconstituted ironclad steamer *Virginia,* created from the scorched hull of the frigate *Merrimack.*

On 8 March 1862, Buchanan led the *Virginia* out of its Gosport Navy Yard berth and down the Elizabeth River into Hampton Roads on its maiden voyage. He immediately attacked the two U.S. Navy warships lying off Newport News Point, sinking the sloop *Cumberland* with his iron ram, and shelling the frigate *Congress* into submission. Irritated when Federal troops on shore fired at the boarding party that was attempting to secure the surrendered *Congress,* Buchanan took up a musket himself and fired back. His bravado made him a target for the Federal troops as well, and he received a serious wound through his upper thigh. That wound kept him from being in command when the *Virginia* dueled the *Monitor* the next day.

Promoted to the rank of full admiral, Buchanan's next command after he recovered from his wound was in Mobile Bay. There the Confederacy could not convert existing ships into ironclads; it had to construct them from the raw materials. This proved a daunting task.

Nevertheless, after months of effort, marred by difficulties in obtaining iron plate and engine parts, guns and a crew, Buchanan could finally boast in May 1864 that a fully armed and manned ironclad floated in Mobile Bay, the CSS *Tennessee.*

On 5 August, the Federal fleet offshore under the command of Rear Admiral David G. Farragut, got underway with the clear intention of fighting its way into Mobile Bay. Buchanan conned the *Tennessee* into the channel off Fort Morgan and prepared to attack the Federal warships one by one as they entered. The first of them, however, the ironclad monitor *Tecumseh,* struck a mine and exploded spectacularly, going to the bottom in just 25 seconds and taking 93 men with it. Farragut's other ships steamed into the bay and Buchanan moved forward to engage. The slow speed of his ironclad (6 knots) made it impossible for him to use his ram, but he engaged in a furious gun duel with the entire Federal fleet as his own vessel was rammed three times by three different Federal warships. He was again wounded when flying debris from a Federal shell smashed his leg. Not long thereafter, it became evident that he would have to surrender: with the *Tennessee's* steering chains cut, the vessel could no longer maneuver, several of her guns were out of order, and she could not effectively defend itself.

Buchanan was a prisoner of war in Fort Lafayette (New York) for several months before he was exchanged in April of 1865. He arrived back in Mobile just as the war ended. After the war, Buchanan served for a year as president of Maryland Agricultural College (later the University of Maryland) and as secretary for the Life Assurance Association of America. He died quietly at his home, the Rest, on Maryland's Eastern Shore on 11 May 1874 survived by his wife and nine children.

—*Craig L. Symonds*

See also Farragut, David Glasgow; Mobile Bay; *Monitor* versus *Virginia*; Navy, C.S.A.; *Tecumseh*, USS; *Tennessee*, CSS.

For further reading:

Brown, John William. "Franklin Buchanan, Naval Leader" (M.A. thesis, 1948).
Lewis, Charles Lee. *Admiral Franklin Buchanan, Fearless Man of Action* (1929).
Still, William N., Jr. "The Confederate States Navy at Mobile, 1861 to August 1864." *Alabama Historical Quarterly* (1968).
Symonds, Craig L. *Confederate Admiral: The Life and Wars of Franklin Buchanan* (1999).
Walter, Francis X. *The Naval Battle of Mobile Bay, August 5, 1864; & Franklin Buchanan on the* Tennessee, *A Portrait of the Admiral of the Confederate Fleet in Mobile Bay* (1993).

BUCHANAN, JAMES
(1791–1868)

Fifteenth president of the United States

Born near Memersburg, Pennsylvania, James Buchanan graduated from Dickinson College in 1809, studied law at Lancaster, and amassed a large fortune. In 1819 his fiancee died suddenly, and he vowed to remain a bachelor. This may have affected his political outlook, because in Washington later he shared bachelor quarters with Southerners who became his closest friends.

After 1824 he became a Jacksonian Democrat. As a U.S. representative (1821–1831) and senator (1834–1845), he voted with the Southern planters against tariffs, federal support for homesteads, river and harbor improvements, and land grants for schools. He was minister to Russia in 1832–1833. As Polk's secretary of state (1845–1849), he advocated limited annexations during the Mexican War, but later opposed the peace treaty because it did not annex enough territory. While minister to England (1852–1857), he coauthored the Ostend Manifesto, which urged the annexation of Cuba, by force if necessary, to prevent Cuba's abolition of slavery.

As president from 1857–1861, Buchanan alienated many Northerners and strengthened the new free-soil Republican Party by advocating proslavery policies. In 1857 he influenced and urged compliance with the Supreme Court's *Dred Scott* decision, which declared the Missouri Compromise limitation on western slavery to be unconstitutional. When a small pro-Southern minority in Kansas wrote the Lecompton Constitution approving slavery, Buchanan unsuccessfully pressured Congress to admit Kansas as a slave state.

During 1857–1858 the United States suffered a brief recession for which Buchanan offered no solutions. This helped cause the off-year elections of 1858 to go heavily Republican, which angry Southerners interpreted as opposition to slavery. Senator Stephen A. Douglas was the only Democrat strong enough to maintain the party coalition of South and northwest, but Buchanan disliked Douglas and gave the political patronage in the northwest to the senator's proslavery enemies.

At the Democratic Presidential Convention in 1860, the only candidate with a significant following in both North and South was Douglas, who was clearly no enemy of slavery. Supported by the president, however, the radical Southerners countered the moderation of Douglas with the "Alabama Platform," demanding Federal protection for slavery in all territories. No Northern delegate could support this principle and it was defeated. As a result, seven Southern states bolted the convention and later nominated Vice President John C. Breckinridge, while the Northern Democrats nominated Douglas. The Buchanan White House served as campaign headquarters for Breckinridge, and the Democratic split helped elect Lincoln with less than 40 percent of the popular vote.

With Lincoln elected and seven Southern states preparing to secede, Buchanan's annual message blamed the crisis entirely upon the North. He denounced secession as unconstitutional, but defended the reasons for secession, announced his unwillingness to coerce seceding states, and asked for Northern concessions that every Southerner knew would never be granted. This probably influenced those Southerners still debating secession. He also strongly supported various efforts to frame an acceptable compromise. Even without the seceded Southerners, Congress did pass a thirteenth amendment denying Congress any right to deal with slavery, but the battle of Fort Sumter intervened before it could be ratified.

Despite his personal sympathies, Buchanan rejected Southern demands for the Federal Forts Pickens, Taylor, and Sumter. He strengthened the first two and they remained intact. Sumter, however, was inside Charleston Harbor and very vulnerable. The army's chief, General Winfield Scott, urged Buchanan to strengthen the forts, pointed out that no forces were available for doing it, announced that a Union that could be preserved only by force was not worth saving, and suggested that the United States should be divided into four separate nations. When Buchanan ordered the warship *Brooklyn* to reinforce Sumter, Scott persuaded him to substitute the unarmed sidewheeler *Star of the West*. Confederate guns repulsed the ship and Scott later blamed Buchanan for not sending the *Brooklyn*, although the decision had been made by Scott. Four ships prepared to defend Sumter were already assembled in New York when Lincoln took office. To his credit, Buchanan handed the fort to Lincoln intact.

While the sectional conflict dominated Buchanan's attention, he also advocated very aggressive foreign policies, most of which were prevented by Congress. He sent an army against the Utah Mormons, and only skilled intervention by Thomas L. Kane prevented serious bloodshed. He offered to buy Alaska for the Mormons, but the Russians refused his tentative $10 million offer. He successfully opposed British expansion in Central America and won a dispute over the U.S-Canadian border in Puget Sound. In trying to stop the African slave trade, the British were searching suspicious-looking vessels. The United States was committed by treaty to assist this effort, but Buchanan ordered every available vessel to protect American ships from search or detention. When William Walker invaded Nicaragua with a Southern army, he was arrested by Commodore Paulding and an American fleet. Buchanan, however, ordered Walker released and reprimanded Paulding for invading Nicaraguan territory.

When France threatened Mexico, Buchanan asked Congress for money to buy northern Mexico, and he later asked for authority to invade Mexico to obtain "indemnity for the past and security for the future." In 1859 his congressional friends tried to get $30 million to buy Cuba. When a Paraguayan sniper killed an American sailor, Buchanan sent nineteen warships carrying 200 guns and 2,500 men to seek redress. Paraguay paid $10,000, apologized, and signed a useless trade treaty. Perhaps Buchanan was merely trying to unite the North and South against some common enemy, but his proposals indicated a readiness to annex everything from the Rio Grande to Colombia.

In retirement, Buchanan was unfairly harassed by charges that he had sacrificed Fort Sumter and sabotaged war efforts. Congress abolished his franking privileges and his portrait was removed from the Capitol. Buchanan, however, supported the war and opposed the peace plank in the 1864 Democratic presidential platform. He opposed the Emancipation Proclamation, however, and wanted to allow the Confederates to "return to the Union just as they were when they left it." He published letters that demolished General Scott's false charges, and his well-documented 1868 memoirs established his innocence of wrongdoing, but his belief that Northern fanatics had provoked the war unnecessarily remained strong. He died on 1 June 1868.

—*Elbert B. Smith*

See also Democratic Party; Election of 1856.
For further reading:
Auchampaugh, Philip G. *James Buchanan and His Cabinet on the Eve of Secession* (1926).

Buchanan, James. Mr. *Buchanan's Administration on the Eve of the Rebellion* (1866).
Curtis, George T. *Life of James Buchanan* (1883).
Klein, Philip Shriver. *President James Buchanan: A Biography* (1962).
Moore, John Bassett. *The Works of James Buchanan: Comprising His Speeches, State Papers, and Private Correspondence.* (1908–1911; reprint, 1960).
Smith, Elbert B. *The Presidency of James Buchanan* (1975).

BUCHANAN, ROBERT CHRISTIE
(1811–1878)
Union officer

Although best remembered as a military martinet, Robert C. Buchanan was in reality an officer of distinguished accomplishments in forty years of service. He was born in Baltimore on 1 March 1811, to an established old Maryland family; his mother's sister was Mrs. John Quincy Adams. He graduated from West Point in 1830, was assigned to the 4th Infantry Regiment, saw service in the Black Hawk War, and fought at the battle of Lake Okeechobee in the Second Seminole War.

In 1845 Buchanan's regiment went to Texas with Zachary Taylor's Army of Observation, and Buchanan, by now a captain, fought in the engagements at Palo Alto and Resaca de la Palma in May 1846, winning a brevet promotion to major, and at the battle of Monterrey, Mexico, that September. In November 1846 he was selected to lead the Baltimore and Washington Battalion of Volunteers and held that position until the volunteers were mustered out of service in May 1847. Returning to the 4th Infantry, Buchanan marched to Mexico City with Winfield Scott's army, participating in the battles at Churubusco, Molino del Rey (for which he was breveted to lieutenant colonel), and Chapultepec. After the war he served on the frontier and in California, where he commanded Fort Humboldt in 1854 and the District of Southern Oregon and Northern California in 1856. In 1855 he was made a major in the 4th Infantry.

Buchanan was promoted to lieutenant colonel of his regiment in September 1861 and commanded it in the defenses of Washington, D.C., from November 1861 to March 1862, at which time it was made a part of the Army of the Potomac. In May 1862, still a lieutenant colonel, Buchanan became commander of one of the two regular brigades making up Sykes's division of Fitz John Porter's V Corps. Buchanan led the brigade until March 1863, fighting in McClellan's Peninsula campaign, being promoted by brevet to colonel for his part in the engagement at Gaines' Mill, the Seven Days' battles, the Second Bull Run campaign, the Maryland campaign of 1862, and the battle of Fredericksburg. In November 1862 he received a recess appointment as brigadier general of U.S. Volunteers, but when Congress convened the following March, he was not confirmed and the commission expired.

Buchanan saw no more field duty. He was briefly commander of Fort Delaware, then chief of recruiting in New Jersey for a year. He was promoted to colonel of the 1st Infantry in February 1864 and commanded his regiment in the garrison at New Orleans from November 1864 to August 1865. At war's end he received the regular army brevet promotions of brigadier general for the battle of Malvern Hill and major general for participation in Second Bull Run and Fredericksburg.

For two years following the war, Buchanan served on commissions and with the Freedman's Bureau. From March 1868 to March 1869 he commanded in Louisiana, overseeing and administering the volatile mix of Reconstruction politics in that state. He then returned to command of his regiment and retired from active duty in December 1870. He died in Washington on 29 November 1878.

Buchanan was the quintessential regular army officer. He administered evenhanded discipline in the ranks, while instilling respect, and his men affectionately called him "Old Buck." To civilians, his imperious manner suggested arrogance and the local settlers of northern California referred to him as "Jesus Christ Jr." It has been implied that Buchanan's strict attitude drove the despondent Ulysses S. Grant, who served under him at Fort Humboldt, out of the service in 1854. Yet John R. Kenly wrote that Buchanan had "a remarkable equanimity of temperament," suitable for dealing with a volunteer compound. Aside from his meritorious conduct on the field of battle, Buchanan's finest hour was in Louisiana in 1868 where by his "wisdom, firmness and moderation," he prevented bloodshed, restored order, and ended military rule. Joseph G. Dawson wrote of Buchanan that he was "perhaps the most objective and fair-minded commander to serve in the state during the post-war years."

—*Russell K. Brown*

See also Freedmen's Bureau; Louisiana.
For further reading:
Coffman, Edward M. *The Old Army: A Portrait of the American Army in Peacetime, 1784–1898* (1986).
Cullum, George W. *Biographical Register of the Officers and Graduates of the U.S. Military Academy at West Point, New York, from its Establishment, in 1802, to 1890; With the Early History of the United States Military Academy* (1891).
Dawson, Joseph G., III. *Army Generals and Reconstruction: Louisiana, 1862–1877* (1994).
Kenly, John R. *Memoirs of a Maryland Volunteer* (1873).

BUCK AND BALL

The buck and ball was a cartridge or other loading consisting of one standard caliber round ball topped by three smaller buckshot. In rare instances, cartridges topped with four buckshot have been observed. Although sometimes used in shotguns and caliber 0.58 and 0.577 rifled muskets, buck and ball was most commonly used as a caliber 0.69 smoothbore musket loading. In effect a miniature grapeshot load, buck and ball was capable of inflicting horrendous wounds in all four weapons at close range. Its scatter effect, however, rendered the buck and ball most effective in extending the killing range of the notoriously inaccurate caliber 0.69 smoothbores to approximately 200 yards. Although phased out by many frontline units by midwar, buck and ball cartridges have been recovered in Confederate campsites that date from late April 1865.

—*Jeff Kinard*

See also Minié Ball; Rifles; Smoothbores; Springfield Rifle.
For further reading:
Lord, Francis A. *Civil War Collector's Encyclopedia* (1995).
McKee, W. Reid, and M. E. Mason, Jr. *Civil War Projectiles II: Small Arms & Artillery* (1980).

BUCKINGHAM, WILLIAM ALFRED
(1804–1875)
Governor of Connecticut

Born to Samuel Buckingham and Joanna Matson Buckingham in Lebanon, Connecticut, William Alfred Buckingham was educated locally. As a young man, he taught school for a while before learning the surveying trade and then entering the dry goods business. He eventually purchased his own store in Norwich, Connecticut. Using his profits from the store to invest in a variety of enterprises, Buckingham ultimately became a wealthy man when he became involved in the infant rubber industry.

Buckingham was active in Connecticut politics. He served two terms as the mayor of Norwich, the first time as a Whig and the second as a Republican. He received the Republican nomination for governor in 1858. He was elected for the first of eight one-year terms as a moderate Republican.

With the election of Abraham Lincoln as president in 1860, Buckingham became a strong supporter of the administration. Even before the outbreak of the Civil War, he wrote to Lincoln offering his support in the crisis. He began the early stages of military mobilization of the state as early as January 1861, but at the same time believed it incumbent upon him to pursue all avenues for peace and sent representatives from the state to the Washington Peace Conference. He made it clear before these delegates departed, however, that there could be no compromise on the issue of slavery in the territories.

Once the war began, Buckingham worked tirelessly to recruit Connecticut's quota of volunteers for Federal service. In fact, the recruitment of Federal soldiers would occupy much of his time for the next four years. Along with recruitment, Buckingham also selected the commanders of the regiments that were raised in the state. Initially some of his appointments were criticized as not representing a geographic balance in the state. As a result, he appointed war committees throughout the state to make recommendations to him, thus ending much of the criticism. Ultimately Connecticut, largely due to Buckingham's efforts, furnished one of the largest per capita percentages of volunteers of all Union states.

Once Connecticut citizens were recruited for Federal service, Buckingham believed it his duty to see to their welfare as best he could. He traveled to recruiting camps to inspect the facilities and talk with the soldiers about their needs. He also traveled to the fronts to meet with the Connecticut soldiers who had seen action during the war. He corresponded frequently with Connecticut officers to learn not only about the performance of Connecticut troops in battle but also to determine their needs while serving away from home. As part of his efforts to protect the welfare of Connecticut soldiers, Buckingham also expanded the hospital facilities of the state and worked to bring home seriously wounded men so that they might recover near their families.

Besides his concern for the interests of Connecticut troops, Buckingham also took an active interest in the military affairs of the entire Union. He wrote to the president and the War Department, offering advice about what he viewed as the vital military interests of the country and where the military could most usefully be deployed. Unlike many of his eastern counterparts, he believed that the West held part of the key to Confederate defeat. He urged the president to put resources into the conquest of Texas so that the loyal people of that state could be used to help the Union while the Confederacy would be deprived of the food resources of that area.

While engaging in all of these activities, Buckingham also had to stand for reelection every year. Doing so no doubt provided some distractions from his primary duties, especially because he was not even free from criticism within his own party. Not considered radical enough by some Connecticut Republicans, these men criticized Buckingham for not urging African-American recruitment with the Federal government. Democrats also criticized him, though for other reasons. That he was forced to use a draft to meet some Federal quotas gave Democrats some ammunition among those voters who did not wholeheartedly support the war effort. Buckingham's strongest Democratic challenger during the war was the popular Thomas H. Seymour, but the governor was able to weather all threats to his position and retained the governorship through the war.

Buckingham was considered one of the most loyal of the Northern war governors and certainly one of the hardest working. In 1866 he considered his job done, and he declined to run for reelection for a ninth term.

He lived quietly for two years before accepting election to the U.S. Senate. He brought to the Senate the same work habits and dedication to his constituents and the nation that had made him such a popular governor. He died in office on 5 February 1875.

—*David S. Heidler and Jeanne T. Heidler*

See also Seymour, Thomas.
For further reading:
Niven, John. *Connecticut for the Union: The Role of the State in the Civil War* (1965).

BUCKNER, SIMON BOLIVAR
(1823–1914)
Confederate general; governor of Kentucky

Simon Bolivar Buckner, the longest surviving Confederate general of lieutenant general rank, was born 1 April 1823 at the family estate in Hart County, Kentucky. Both parents, Aylett Hartswell and Elizabeth Ann (Morehead) Buckner, were of Virginia ancestry. The boy attended schools in Greenville and Hopkinsville, then received an appointment to West Point in 1840. Six feet tall, handsome, possessed of a powerful physique, he graduated eleventh in a class of twenty-five in 1844. After routine garrison duty, he taught at West Point in 1845 and 1846 before joining the American army in Mexico, where General Winfield Scott became his hero. Buckner resumed teaching at West Point after the Mexican-American War but left because he objected to compulsory Sunday chapel. On 2 May 1850, he married Mary Jane Kingsbury, daughter of an army officer who had extensive real estate investments in Chicago. Buckner resigned his commission in 1855 and joined his father-in-law in business until 1858, when he returned to Kentucky.

Buckner reorganized the moribund Kentucky militia and became its inspector general in 1860. As the Civil War started, Governor Beriah Magoffin used Buckner in efforts to secure acceptance of Kentucky's neutrality from Union and Confederate officials. In August 1861 Buckner refused a Union commission as brigadier general; he accepted that rank in the Confederate army in September. When Kentucky's unusual neutrality ended in early September, Buckner occupied Bowling Green and probed northward. A fatal error by Albert Sidney Johnston who did not withdraw troops from Fort Donelson, and a comedy of command errors led to Buckner surrendering Donelson and its troops to his friend Ulysses S. Grant on 16 February 1862.

Exchanged in August 1862, Buckner was promoted to major general and assigned to Braxton Bragg's army. He commanded a division in William J. Hardee's corps during the summer 1862 invasion of Kentucky. At Munfordville, Union colonel John R. Wilder sought Buckner's advice on whether he should surrender some

4,000 troops. At Perryville on 8 October 1862 Buckner's division made gains against the Union left flank, but the Confederates soon withdrew from the state. In December 1862 Buckner assumed command of the Department of the Gulf, but in May 1863, he was shifted to the Department of East Tennessee, which in August became part of Bragg's Department of Tennessee. Buckner led a corps at Chickamauga, but, disgusted with Bragg's leadership, he participated in efforts to get Bragg removed from command. Bragg reduced Buckner to divisional command and ordered him to East Tennessee, but Buckner's illness blocked that transfer.

In February 1864 Buckner took command of John Bell Hood's division and again was assigned to the Department of East Tennessee. Then he learned on 2 May 1864 that he had been transferred to the Trans-Mississippi Department. General Edmund Kirby Smith secured Buckner's promotion to lieutenant general and gave him command of the District of West Louisiana; on 19 April 1865 he was assigned the enlarged District of Arkansas. Buckner became Kirby Smith's chief of staff on 9 May 1865, and it was he who surrendered the Trans-Mississippi Department on 26 May.

Buckner was a competent, dependable general who never attained great military success. His active involvement in the anti-Bragg cabal hurt his reputation in administrative circles.

Ordered to remain in New Orleans, Buckner wrote for a newspaper, became a commission merchant, then president of an insurance company. He was allowed to return home in early 1868, and litigation recovered much of his prewar property. His wife died in 1874. In 1885 he married twenty-eight-year-old Delia Claiborne. Their son, Simon Bolivar Buckner, Jr., was born in 1886.

Elected governor of Kentucky as a Democrat in 1887, Buckner gave the state an honest, efficient administration. The conservative legislature usually checked his occasionally liberal policies. When Treasurer James W. "Honest Dick" Tate absconded with the state's funds in 1888, Buckner loaned the state enough money to keep it solvent until taxes were collected. At the end of his term Buckner retired to a quiet life at Glen Lily, near Munfordville. Threatened with blindness, he memorized five of Shakespeare's plays so he could "read Shakespeare in the dark." Cataract operations were successful. In 1895, he failed in a bid to be elected U.S. Senator. Unable to accept William Jennings Bryan's money policies, Buckner ran for vice president in 1896 on the Gold Democrat ticket with Union general John M. Palmer.

Buckner enjoyed attending Confederate encampments, and in 1909 he made a nostalgic trip to Mexican War battlefields. He was delighted when his son was admitted to West Point in 1904. The Sage of Glen Lily died at home on 8 January 1914 and was buried in Frankfort.

—*Lowell H. Harrison*

See also Bragg, Braxton; Fort Donelson; Kentucky; Smith, Edmund Kirby.
For further reading:
Connelly, Thomas L. *Army of the Heartland: The Army of Tennessee, 1861–1862* (1967).
———. *Autumn of Glory: The Army of Tennessee, 1862–1865* (1971).
Harrison, Lowell H. "Simon Bolivar Buckner." In *Kentucky's Governors, 1792–1985*, edited by Lowell H. Harrison (1985).
Hewitt, Lawrence L. "Simon Bolivar Buckner." In *The Confederate General*, edited by William C. Davis (1991).
Stickles, Arndt M. *Simon Bolivar Buckner: Borderland Knight* (1940).

BUELL, DON CARLOS
(1818–1898)
Union general

Born on 23 March 1818, Don Carlos Buell spent the first years of his life on a small farm in Lowell, Ohio, on the Muskingum River. His father died when Buell was young, and the boy was sent to live with his uncle in Lawrenceburg, Indiana. In 1837 he was appointed to West Point and graduated in 1841, ranking thirty-second of fifty-two, which caused him to be appointed to the 3d Infantry. He served briefly in the Second Seminole War. In 1843 he was court-martialed for severely reprimanding a private, but was acquitted. He served gallantly in the Mexican-American War, participating in numerous campaigns and battles, including the battle of Churubusco, and won brevets to captain and major. Severely wounded at Churubusco, he was soon transferred from line to staff duties, serving in the adjutant general's department for the next thirteen years. He was posted in several military departments, including those in Texas, Missouri, Utah, and New York.

In 1859 Secretary of War John B. Floyd assigned Buell to the War Department, and the following year he sent Buell on a secret mission to observe the mood in Charleston, South Carolina, and the condition of Robert Anderson's garrison in Fort Moultrie. After a brief stay, Buell was convinced that the military situation was so pressing that he left instructions with Anderson to move his garrison to Fort Sumter if Anderson had tangible evidence that South Carolina would threaten his force. He was afterwards sent to San Francisco, where he spent the remainder of the Great Secession winter as well as the spring and summer of 1861. Prior to his departure from Washington, he was commissioned brigadier general of volunteers on 17 May 1861. In September 1861, at the urging of George B. McClellan, Buell was assigned to the Army of the Potomac. In November, McClellan appointed Buell to replace William T. Sherman as commander of the newly designated Department of the Ohio, whose army was headquartered in Louisville, Kentucky.

It was McClellan's intention for Buell to lead the Army of the Ohio into eastern Tennessee to liberate the loyal residents in that region from Confederate oppression. Because of the lack of roads and with winter fast approaching, Buell urged an alternative advance over the Cumberland and Tennessee rivers or over the railroad to Nashville. Despite the opposition of civil and military superiors, the river campaign was carried out with only slight modification and resulted in the river victories at Fort Henry and Fort Donelson in February 1862. Ulysses S. Grant's victories enabled Buell to march overland unopposed to Nashville, which surrendered on 26 February 1862. In the campaign to Corinth, Mississippi, that March and April, Buell arrived at Pittsburg Landing and helped turn what was almost certain defeat into victory by counterattacking the second day at the battle of Shiloh. Buell then served under Henry W. Halleck (appointed overall commander of the West in March 1862) in the campaign to take Corinth, an operation that lasted until 30 May 1862, when Confederate commander P. G. T. Beauregard abandoned the railroad junction.

In June 1862 Halleck ordered Buell east toward Chattanooga, Tennessee, with instructions to repair the Memphis & Charleston Railroad as he advanced. Buell's army was continually harassed by Confederate cavalrymen John Hunt Morgan and Nathan Bedford Forrest. In August Confederate commander Braxton Bragg reached Chattanooga before Buell and then took his army into Kentucky, hoping to entice Kentuckians to join the Confederacy. In September, Buell marched his army into Kentucky and reached Louisville in late September before Bragg. On 8 October 1862 part of the Army of the Ohio engaged Bragg's army in the bloody but indecisive battle of Perryville. Bragg gave up the field to Buell and retired into eastern Kentucky and Tennessee, but Buell pursued too slowly. As a result, Lincoln removed him from command and replaced him with William S. Rosecrans.

Critics accused Buell of being out of touch with the Union's war aims and of being too sympathetic with the Southern cause. Shortly after being relieved, Buell demanded a trial to clear his reputation. Secretary of War Edwin M. Stanton agreed and after five months of testimony the court acquitted Buell of any wrongdoing or mismanagement of his army. Although Grant recommended that Buell be restored to duty, the Lincoln administration concluded that the commander was too much of a political liability, particularly because Buell refused to fight a war for emancipation. He resigned his commission in June 1864.

After the war Buell spent his life in Kentucky operating an ironworks and a coal mine. In 1885 President Grover Cleveland patronized the veteran with a short-term civil service position as a government pension agent.

During the war Buell ignored political considerations. He was reserved in manner and was thought to be unfriendly to the administration. Though he was an administrator and organizer of ability, his political liabilities and refusal to wage anything but a limited war proved too costly for the administration. He died on 19 November 1898 in Airdrie near Paradise, Kentucky, and was buried in Bellefontaine Cemetery, St. Louis.

—*Stephen D. Engle*

See also Corinth, Mississippi; Fort Sumter; Perryville/Chaplin Hills, Battle of; Shiloh, Battle of.

For further reading:

Chumney, James. "Gentleman General: Don Carlos Buell" (Ph.D. dissertation, 1964).

Engle, Stephen D. *Don Carlos Buell: Most Promising of All* (1999).

BUFORD, ABRAHAM
(1820–1884)
Confederate general

Born to William B. Buford and Frances Walker Kirtley Buford in Woodford County, Kentucky, Abraham Buford attended Centre College briefly before receiving an appointment to the United States Military Academy at West Point. He graduated fifty-first of a class of fifty-two in 1841. As a member of the 1st Dragoons upon graduation, Buford served in a variety of frontier posts before being promoted to first lieutenant at the beginning of the Mexican War in 1846. He received a brevet promotion to captain for his actions at the battle of Buena Vista in February 1847. Following that war, he was stationed in New Mexico before being transferred to the army's cavalry school at Carlisle, Pennsylvania. He resigned his commission in 1854 to return to Kentucky and pursue the family business of cattle and horse breeding.

Upon the outbreak of the Civil War and after much soul searching, Buford decided to side with the Confederacy. In 1862 he offered his military services to the Confederate army. On 2 September 1862 he accepted a commission as a brigadier general and joined Braxton Bragg's Kentucky campaign. During Bragg's retreat from Kentucky, Buford's Kentucky cavalry brigade guarded the army's withdrawal to Knoxville, Tennessee. Buford commanded his brigade at the battle of Stones River. Shortly after Stones River, Buford's brigade was placed under the command of Major General William W. Loring. As part of Loring's division, Buford participated in the Vicksburg campaign. He remained in Loring's division until spring 1864 when he received command of one of Nathan Bedford Forrest's cavalry divisions. At Tupelo in July 1864 his division was considered the most heavily engaged of all Confederate divisions present. He was wounded late in the year and did not return to active service until the war was almost over.

After the war, he returned to Kentucky and became one of the nation's most important breeders of thoroughbred horses. By the 1870s, personal and financial tragedies began to take their toll. His only son died in 1872 and his wife shortly thereafter. His business interests suffered and bankruptcy lost him his home. He committed suicide in Indiana in 1884. His cousin was Union general John Buford.

—*David S. Heidler and Jeanne T. Heidler*

See also Tupelo, Battle of.

BUFORD, JOHN
(1826–1863)
Union general

John Buford was born on 4 March 1826, in Woodford County, Kentucky, but migrated with his family to Rock Island, Illinois. He was born into a prominent family. Both his grandfather and great-uncle had been officers in Virginia regiments during the American Revolution. His father was a prominent Democratic politician in Illinois and a political opponent to Whig politician Abraham Lincoln. After attending Knox College in Galesburg, Illinois, for one year, Buford entered the U.S. Military Academy at West Point, New York, and graduated near the middle of his class in 1848. Such had become something of a family tradition. His half-brother Napoleon Bonaparte Buford, who would become a Union major general, entered West Point in 1827; his cousin Abraham Buford, who would become a Confederate brigadier general, did so in 1841. Buford was commissioned a second lieutenant in the 1st Dragoon Regiment. A year later he was transferred to the 2d Dragoon Regiment, where he spent the remainder of his prewar career. He fought against the Sioux, helped to keep the peace in Kansas, served in Texas and the Southwest, and participated in the abortive Mormon War in 1858.

When the Civil War began, Buford was a captain in the 2d Dragoon Regiment. Promoted to major on 12 November 1861, he was given the position of assistant inspector general of the defenses of Washington, D.C. After Major General John Pope arrived in Washington to take command of the newly formed Army of the Virginia in June 1862, however, Buford was promoted to brigadier general of volunteers on 27 July 1862 and given command of the Cavalry Brigade, II Corps, Army of the Virginia. Buford rightly recognized that the main roles of cavalry in the Civil War would be as mounted infantry and as reconnaissance for higher commands. He used his own cavalry for these two purposes expertly during the war.

During the battle of Second Bull Run, Buford performed well before being wounded in the knee during the Army of the Potomac's withdrawal and was initially reported as killed in action by Union newspapers. After recovering from his wounds, Buford became the chief of cavalry of the Army to the Potomac under Major General George B. McClellan during the Maryland campaign and under Major General Ambrose E. Burnside at the battle of Fredericksburg. After Major General Joseph Hooker's appointment as commander of the Army of the Potomac, the cavalry was reorganized and Buford found himself in command of the Reserve Brigade, Cavalry Corps. With Major General George Stoneman in command of the newly formed Cavalry Corps, Army of the Potomac, Buford was one of only a few people to receive any praise for their actions during Stoneman's unsuccessful raids in the Chancellorsville campaign.

During the battle of Gettysburg, Buford gained his greatest fame and performed his greatest feat of the Civil War. On 1 July 1863, Buford, who had been promoted to major general of volunteers on 1 June 1863 and was now commanding the 1st Division of the Cavalry Corps, encountered elements of the Army of Northern Virginia outside Gettysburg, Pennsylvania. With only one man per yard of ground, Buford ordered his men to dismount to oppose the advance of Confederate lieutenant general A. P. Hill's III Corps along the Chambersburg Pike toward Gettysburg. This delaying action allowed Union major general John Reynolds to deploy his I Corps to meet the Confederates outside Gettysburg, therefore, denying them the defensive value of the town itself.

In the autumn of 1863, Buford was stricken with typhoid fever and went on sick leave in November 1863. Already weakened by his years of hard campaigning, which included a poor diet, exposure, lack of sleep, and too much stress, he died on 16 December 1863 and was buried at West Point. His promotion to major general in the regular army was presented to him on his deathbed, though it was backdated to the first day of the battle of Gettysburg.

—*Alexander M. Bielakowski*

See also Buford, Abraham; Cavalry, U.S.A.; Gettysburg, Battle of.
For further reading:
Longacre, Edward G. *Cavalry at Gettysburg: A Tactical Study of Mounted Operations during the Civil War's Pivotal Campaign 9 June–14 July 1863* (1986).
———. *General John Buford: A Military Biography* (1995).
———. *Mounted Raids of the Civil War* (1975).

BUFORD, NAPOLEON BONAPARTE
(1807–1883)
Union general

Born to John Buford and Nancy Hickman Buford in Woodford, Kentucky, Napoleon Bonaparte Buford was educated locally before receiving an appointment to the United States Military Academy in 1823. He graduated sixth of thirty-eight in the class of 1827.

Buford was commissioned an artillery officer and served at a variety of posts in the east and on the frontier over the next four years. In 1831 he was granted a leave of absence to study law at Harvard. Following his studies there, he returned briefly to West Point as an instructor before resigning his commission in 1835.

Upon leaving the army, Buford worked for a while as an engineer in Kentucky and then moved to Illinois, where he became involved in a variety of business enterprises, including banking. At the outbreak of the Civil War Buford raised a regiment of volunteers and became its colonel when it was mustered into Federal service as the 27th Illinois.

Buford and the 27th were placed under the command of Brigadier General Ulysses S. Grant headquartered at Cairo, Illinois. Buford led his regiment in its first major action under Grant at Belmont, Missouri, on 7 November 1861. He distinguished himself in the battle and was commended for his bravery in action. Due to the negligence of senior officers, he and his men were almost captured, but Buford was able to extricate them from the field. For the remainder of the year Buford and his regiment served in garrison duty in Cairo.

In early 1862 Buford and the 27th were transferred to the command of John Pope and the Army of the Mississippi. Buford participated in the occupation of Columbus, Kentucky, in early March and temporarily commanded the garrison there until called to command the so-called Flotilla Brigade in Pope's assault on Island No. 10. Buford's brigade was transported aboard Andrew Foote's gunboats. During the siege, Buford led his brigade on a raid to Union City, Tennessee, which netted Pope's army some much-needed supplies. For this action he would later in the spring be promoted to brigadier general of volunteers.

Following the surrender of Island No. 10, Buford briefly commanded the fortifications there. Later in the spring, after his promotion to brigadier general, Buford commanded a brigade in the advance on Corinth. During the late summer Buford came under the command of William Rosecrans at Corinth. He participated in the defense of the town in the fall of 1862, but on the second day of the battle fell dangerously ill from sunstroke and had to be hospitalized. His immediate superior, Brigadier General Charles S. Hamilton, commended Buford for his actions at Corinth. Once he was able to assume desk duty, Buford was sent east to serve on court-martial duty.

Upon his arrival in Washington, Buford was made a member of the court that heard the case of Fitz John Porter. Like some other members of the court, Buford had ties to the case in that he had served under Porter's accuser, John Pope, in the west. This duty done in early 1863, Buford, whose health was still precarious, was sent to command the garrison at Cairo, Illinois. Buford remained in command at Cairo through summer of 1863. During that time, one of his primary responsibilities was to direct the various recruited and drafted units to points throughout the Western theater. During the summer of 1863 these routine duties were interrupted when a raid by Confederate John Hunt Morgan threatened southern Illinois. Buford saw to the defense of the area as best he good with his limited garrison and the raw recruits stationed there.

In September 1863, Buford was sent to Helena, Arkansas, to command the District of Eastern Arkansas. He commanded this post until February 1865. During that year and a half, Buford experienced everything from the boredom of a remote post to periodic raids and sabotage by Confederate forces and sympathizers. To deal with the raids he knew that he needed cavalry, but it was difficult to persuade other nearby commanders to relinquish any. When he finally received some cavalry support in the spring of 1864, it was not nearly as much as he had requested.

Besides Buford's problems acquiring the cavalry he needed, he complained that most of the new troops he received were African-American recruits. The previous year Buford, while still in Cairo, had been accused of not doing enough to help refugee former slaves because he disagreed with abolition. He denied the charges, arguing that he had expended a great deal of his resources helping the unfortunate refugees. In 1864 when he complained about having to rely on African-American soldiers, he explained that the reason he preferred white soldiers was that they were generally better trained and less subject to bushwhackers in the area who resented the presence of African-Americans in uniform.

Receiving no satisfactory answer to these complaints and suffering ever-failing health, Buford became very dissatisfied with his assignment. In addition, feeling ignored by his superiors, he found himself occupied more and more with annoying administrative duties. Along with protecting his position, he had to supervise the sale of cotton being shipped north from occupied areas, to prevent smuggling, and to oversee the food and shelter needs of an ever-increasing number of refugee slaves. In dealing with the latter situation, he silenced his critics by creating a model program for providing for the immediate and long-term needs of the former slaves. By early 1865, however, he no longer felt physically able to continue and requested to be relieved. His request was granted in early March 1865, after which he was brevetted a major general of volunteers. After being relieved, Buford was granted a leave of absence until mustered out of the army in August 1865.

Following the war, Buford engaged in a variety of business activities in Colorado and Illinois. He retired to Chicago, where he died on 28 March 1883. He was the older half-brother of Union general John Buford, who died during the war.

—*David S. Heidler and Jeanne T. Heidler*

See also Arkansas; Belmont, Battle of.

For further reading:
Hughes, Nathaniel Cheairs, Jr. *The Battle of Belmont: Grant Strikes South* (1991).

BULL RUN, FIRST BATTLE OF
(21 July 1861)

Manassas Junction, Virginia, was the magnet that attracted the armies of North and South to the banks of Bull Run in July 1861. There two railroads, the Manassas Gap and the Orange & Alexandria, connected thirty miles southwest of Washington, D.C. The Orange & Alexandria was a natural line of advance for a Union army marching southward from Washington, while the Manassas Gap was important because Confederate forces in northern Virginia were divided. Eleven thousand men under Joseph E. Johnston guarded the Shenandoah Valley, while Pierre G. T. Beauregard had 22,000 men at Manassas, Centreville, and Fairfax Court House. The Manassas Gap linked these two armies and made it possible for the South to concentrate its forces wherever the threat was greatest.

The commanding general of the Union army, Winfield Scott, opposed an offensive into Virginia. Such a move, Scott feared, would only exacerbate sectional tensions. He also had little faith in the ninety-day volunteers that had been gathering around Washington since April. President Abraham Lincoln, however, believed a quick offensive against Manassas was worth a try and ordered Union general Irvin McDowell to organize a 35,000-man army for an operation against Manassas. McDowell shared Scott's apprehensions over the reliability of his untrained army, but received little sympathy from Lincoln, who admonished, "You are green it is true, but they are green also."

On 16 July, McDowell's army began its march out of Washington, but did not reach Fairfax Court House until the evening of the seventeenth, giving the Rebels time to evacuate their advanced outpost there. McDowell's lead division, under Daniel Tyler, reached Centreville the following day and found Beauregard had already evacuated the town to concentrate behind Bull Run. Tyler then pushed on toward the Bull Run crossings, provoking a sharp skirmish at Blackburn's Ford, in which the Confederates thrashed Tyler's force and forced it to withdraw back to Centreville.

Beauregard's army was now positioned in an eight-mile line that was strong on the right, where the Orange & Alexandria Railroad crossed Bull Run and a series of fords—Mitchell's, Blackburn's, and McLean's—provided convenient crossing points. Alone at the far left was Nathan G. Evans's brigade overlooking a stone bridge where the Warrenton Turnpike crossed Bull Run.

After the setback at Blackburn's Ford and reconnaissances demonstrated that Beauregard's right was too strong to be attacked, McDowell learned that Sudley Ford, a few miles upstream from the stone bridge, was weakly defended and offered a convenient route around the Confederate left. So on 20 July he drew up a battle plan that called for Tyler to march his division west along the Warrenton Turnpike from Centreville toward the stone bridge, followed by David Hunter's and Samuel Heintzelman's divisions. Tyler would make a demonstration at the bridge to make Beauregard think the main attack would come there, while Heintzelman and Hunter turned north and moved to Sudley Ford. There they would cross the run at 7:00 and then march south along the Manassas-Sudley Road to crush Beauregard's left and rear.

It was a good plan. However, its success, like McDowell's entire campaign, depended upon whether Robert Patterson's army in the Valley could prevent Johnston from reinforcing Beauregard. Unfortunately for McDowell, Patterson failed, and on 19 July units from Johnston's army began boarding railroad cars bound for Manassas.

To make matters worse for McDowell, his plan began unraveling from the minute he awoke his men at 2:00 A.M. on 21 July. First, it took an hour for Tyler to get on the road toward the stone bridge. His division then marched at a snail's pace through the pitch black night until it finally reached the stone bridge at 5:30 A.M. Yet the flanking force had only just begun moving north toward Sudley Ford. At 6 A.M. Tyler began his demonstration by firing an artillery shell across Bull Run; Hunter's lead brigade under Union general Ambrose Burnside was three miles from Sudley Ford. To make matters worse, Burnside found the road leading to their crossing point was little more than a cart path. Not until 9:30 A.M.—over two hours behind schedule—did the 13,000-man Union flanking force begin crossing Bull Run.

By 8 A.M. Evans had begun to suspect that Tyler's force at the stone bridge was in fact a feint, a suspicion that was confirmed by a warning from a Confederate signal station: "Look out for your left, you are turned." Leaving 200 men to watch Tyler, Evans led 900 men north to Matthews Hill. By midmorning, the Confederate force on Matthews Hill had swelled to 2,800 with the arrival of Francis Bartow's and Barnard Bee's brigades. Their goal was simply to slow down the Federal army and buy time for Beauregard and Johnston to shift forces north to save the Confederate flank.

They bought an hour and a half. By 11:30 A.M. McDowell's flanking force had crushed the Confederate

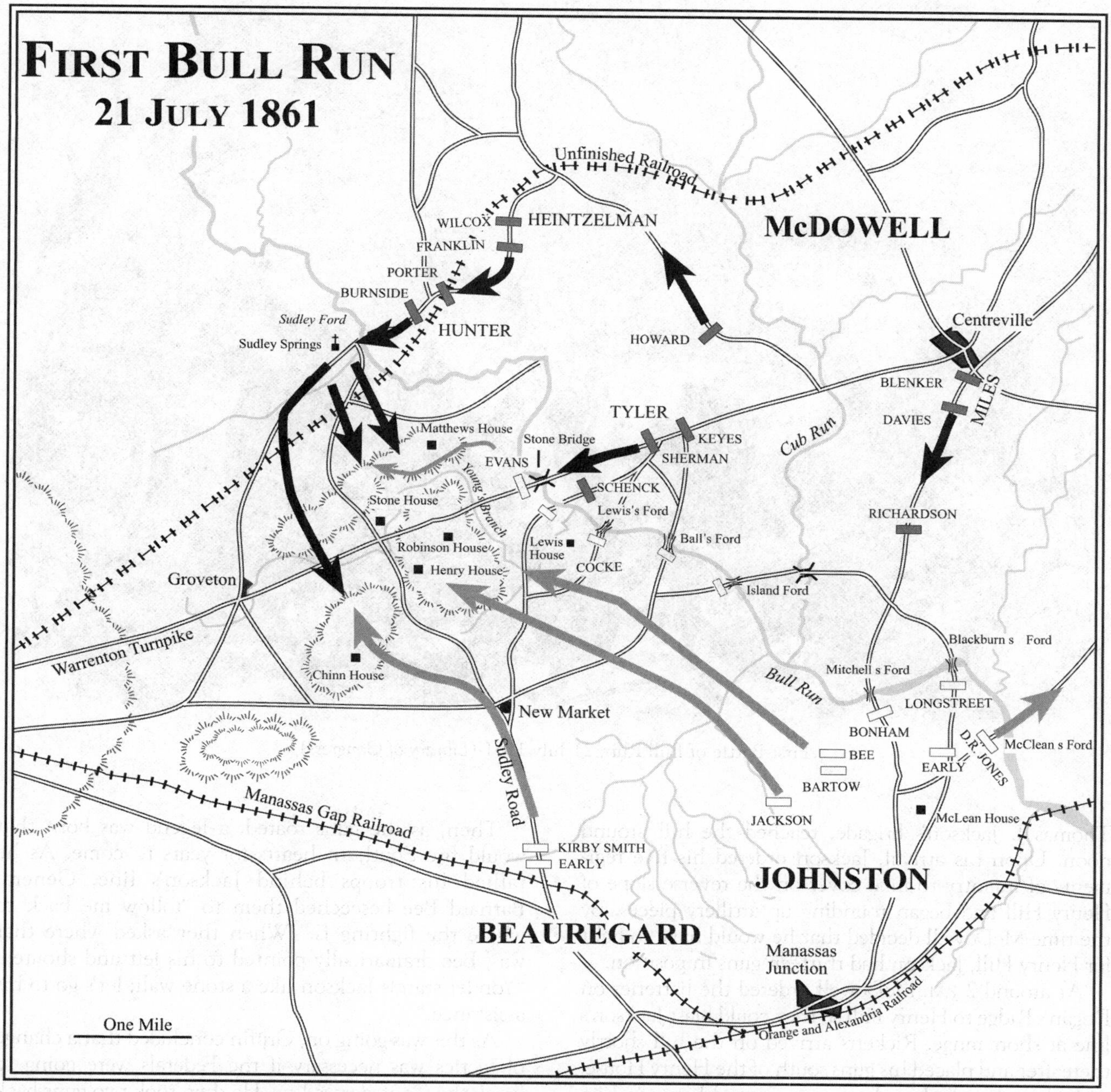

FIRST BULL RUN
21 JULY 1861

Unfinished Railroad

WILCOX — HEINTZELMAN

FRANKLIN

PORTER

BURNSIDE

Sudley Ford

Sudley Springs — HUNTER

McDOWELL

HOWARD

Centreville

BLENKER

DAVIES

MILES

Matthews House

TYLER

Stone Bridge — KEYES

EVANS — SHERMAN

SCHENCK

Stone House

Lewis's Ford

Cub Run

RICHARDSON

Young's Branch

Robinson House

Lewis House — COCKE

Henry House

Ball's Ford

Groveton

Island Ford

Warrenton Turnpike

Chinn House

Blackburn's Ford

Mitchell's Ford

LONGSTREET

New Market

BONHAM

BEE

EARLY

D. R. JONES

McClean's Ford

Bull Run

BARTOW

Sudley Road

JACKSON

McLean House

Manassas Gap Railroad

KIRBY SMITH
EARLY

JOHNSTON

BEAUREGARD

Manassas
Junction

One Mile

Orange and Alexandria Railroad

line on Matthews Hill and sent the Rebels fleeing southward. "Victory! Victory!" an ecstatic McDowell shouted to his men on Matthews Hill. "The day is ours."

This was not how Beauregard had expected the battle to develop. He had massed his forces on the right so he could attack McDowell's left and rear and won the approval of Johnston, who had arrived at Manassas on 19 July to assume overall command, for the scheme. Yet, the complex and confusing orders Beauregard issued for the operation and the crisis on Matthews Hill compelled the Southern commanders to abandon this plan and begin shifting forces northward.

Henry Hill, approximately a mile and a half south of Matthews Hill and six miles north of Manassas Junction, would be the key to the battle. If McDowell could capture it, his victory would be complete. But instead of immediately pushing his 18,000 men southward to drive the beaten and disorganized remnants of Evans's, Bartow's, and Bee's commands off Henry Hill, McDowell decided to have only James B. Ricketts's and Charles Griffin's batteries fire at the hill from Dogan's Ridge.

Beauregard and Johnston took full advantage of McDowell's generosity and began moving reinforcements to Henry Hill. The most important to arrive,

First Battle of Bull Run, 21 July 1861 (*Library of Congress*)

Thomas J. Jackson's brigade, reached the hill around noon. Upon his arrival, Jackson ordered his five regiments of infantry to take cover on the reverse slope of Henry Hill and began rounding up artillery pieces. By the time McDowell decided that he would have to fight for Henry Hill, Jackson had thirteen guns in position.

At around 2 P.M. McDowell ordered the batteries on Dogan's Ridge to Henry Hill so they could blast Jackson's line at short range. Ricketts arrived on the hill shortly thereafter and placed his guns south of the Henry House, with three hundred yards of open ground between him and Jackson. Griffin's battery then arrived on Ricketts's left and a massive duel commenced between their eleven guns and Jackson's artillery.

The Confederates got the better of the exchange. The Federals were now within range of Jackson's smoothbore cannon, which they had not been on Dogan's Ridge, and began taking significant casualties. At the same time, the Confederate line was now too close for the rifled Federal guns to be effective and most of their shells sailed harmlessly over the heads of the Confederates. To make matters worse, McDowell's efforts to push up infantry support to Ricketts and Griffin were unsuccessful, while Jackson's line grew stronger by the minute.

Then, as the guns roared, a legend was born that would fire Southern hearts for years to come. As he rallied his troops behind Jackson's line, General Barnard Bee beseeched them to "follow me back to where the fighting is." When they asked where that was, Bee dramatically pointed to his left and shouted, "Yonder stands Jackson like a stone wall; let's go to his assistance."

As this was going on, Griffin concluded that a change of tactics was necessary if the Federals were going to break the Confederate line. He then took two guns back to the Sudley Road, turned south, swung around Ricketts's guns, and positioned them on a slight rise to Ricketts's right. From here, Griffin hoped to hit Jackson's line with a destructive enfilade fire.

At approximately 3 P.M. Griffin observed an unidentified force moving toward his new position from the right. Although a number of men in this force were wearing blue uniforms, Griffin deduced that it was hostile and ordered his men to load their guns with canister. Just then, McDowell's chief of artillery, William Barry, told Griffin: "Don't fire there. Those are your battery support." Griffin disagreed. "They are Confederates," he protested, "as certain as the world." Barry was adamant:

View of the battlefield, First Battle of Bull Run, July 1861 (*Library of Congress*)

"I know they are your battery support." Griffin reluctantly yielded to the judgment of his superior.

The unidentified force was in fact Confederate William Smith's battalion of Virginia troops. Seventy yards from Griffin's position they stopped, lowered their muskets, and fired a devastating volley at the Federal gunners. Smith and Arthur Cummings's 33d Virginia Infantry Regiment then charged and captured Griffin's guns. Sensing the tide had turned, Jackson then ordered two of his regiments to charge Ricketts's battery. Soon Ricketts's guns were in Rebel hands as well.

Just then McDowell finally managed to get infantry up to his beleaguered artillerymen and a desperate struggle ensued in which the guns changed hands several times. The Federal effort was fatally compromised, however, by McDowell's failure to commit fully

his superior numbers and the fact that, although McDowell managed to get fifteen regiments into the battle, not once did more than two join the fight together. Finally, at around 4 P.M. a spirited charge by two regiments from Confederate colonel Phillip St. George Cocke's brigade pushed the last Union forces off Henry Hill.

As the battle raged on Henry Hill, McDowell ordered Oliver O. Howard's brigade to Chinn Ridge. If Howard could seize the ridge, he would be on the western flank of Henry Hill and in an ideal position from which to deliver a decisive stroke against the Confederate line. Just then, however, Arnold Elzey's and Jubal Early's brigades, the last Confederate reinforcements from the Shenandoah Valley, reached the battlefield. At 4 P.M. they arrived on Chinn Ridge and crushed Howard's

Federal soldiers at Confederate forticifications near Manassas, March 1862
(Photograph by George Barnard / *Library of Congress*)

command. Beauregard then ordered his entire line forward. This convinced McDowell that his army had had enough for one day, and at 4:30 P.M. the Federal retreat began.

With their army "more disorganized by victory than that of the United States by defeat," the Confederate high command was unable to organize an effective pursuit. The Federals were thus able to recross Bull Run well enough, but then a Confederate artillery shell capsized a wagon on the Cub Run Bridge, creating a bottleneck on their line of retreat. Whatever order had existed until then evaporated as panic gripped the exhausted Union troops and the civilians who had come out to Centreville to watch the battle. The retreat degenerated into a chaotic flight back to Washington, and what had been a closely fought battle became a decisive Southern victory. Altogether, nearly 900 men had been killed and over 2,700 wounded, numbers that would pale in comparison to later battles, but nonetheless shocked a nation that had naively expected a relatively bloodless war.

Southerners had anticipated that one victory such as Bull Run would persuade the North to abandon the effort to restore the Union by force. Lincoln, however, made it clear after the battle that he would continue the fight by organizing new armies for the long war to come.

Thirteen months later the men in blue and gray would meet again in battle on the plains of Manassas.

—*Ethan S. Rafuse*

See also Bartow, Francis S.; Beauregard, P. G. T.; Bee, Barnard; Jackson, Thomas J.; Johnston, Joseph E.; McDowell, Irvin.

For further reading:

Davis, William C. *Battle at Bull Run: A History of the First Major Campaign of the Civil War* (1977).

Freeman, Douglas Southall. *Lee's Lieutenants: A Study in Command,* vol. 1 (1942–1944).

Hennessy, John. *The First Battle of Manassas: An End to Innocence July 18–21, 1861* (1989).

Johnson, Robert Underwood, and Clarence Clough Buel, eds. *Battles and Leaders of the Civil War: Being for the Most Part Contributions by Union and Confederate Officers* (1887–1888).

U.S. War Department. *War of the Rebellion: A Compilation of the Official Records of the Union and Confederate Armies* (1880–1901).

BULL RUN, SECOND BATTLE OF
(29–30 August 1862)

Following the end of the Peninsula campaign, General Robert E. Lee sent Stonewall Jackson north with 24,000 men to watch the new Federal Army of Virginia, led by Major General John Pope. Consisting of three corps (commanded by generals Franz Sigel, Nathaniel P. Banks, and Irvin McDowell), Pope's

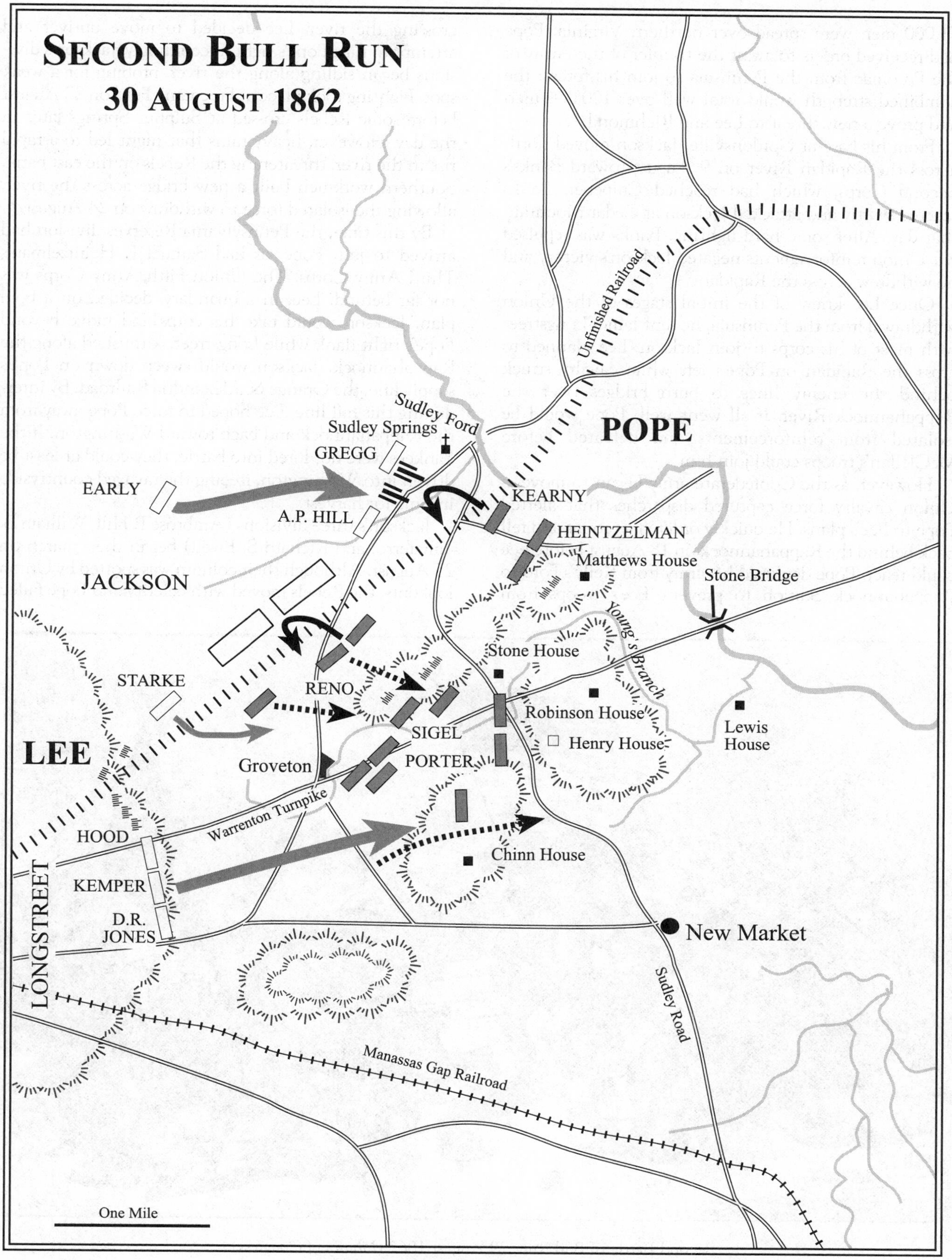

SECOND BULL RUN
30 AUGUST 1862

Unfinished Railroad

POPE

Sudley Ford

Sudley Springs

GREGG

KEARNY

EARLY

A.P. HILL

HEINTZELMAN

Matthews House

JACKSON

Stone House

Stone Bridge

Young's Branch

STARKE

RENO

SIGEL

Robinson House

Lewis House

Groveton

PORTER

Henry House

LEE

Warrenton Turnpike

Chinn House

HOOD

KEMPER

New Market

D.R. JONES

Sudley Road

LONGSTREET

Manassas Gap Railroad

One Mile

51,000 men were spread over northern Virginia. Pope had received orders to await the transfer of the Army of the Potomac from the Peninsula to join his forces; the combined strength would total well over 100,000 men and prove a new threat to Lee and Richmond.

From his base at Gordonsville, Jackson moved north across the Rapidan River on 9 August toward Banks's Second Corps, which had reached Culpeper. Banks reacted swiftly and attacked Jackson at Cedar Mountain that day. After some hard fighting, Banks was repulsed but Union reinforcements negated Jackson's victory and he withdrew across the Rapidan.

Once Lee knew of the initial stages of the Union withdrawal from the Peninsula, he sent James Longstreet with most of his corps to join Jackson. Lee planned to cross the Rapidan on Pope's left while cavalry struck behind the enemy lines to burn bridges over the Rappahannock River. If all went well, Pope would be isolated from reinforcements and defeated before McClellan's troops could join him.

However, as the Confederate army began to move, a Union cavalry force captured dispatches that alerted Pope to Lee's plans. He quickly ordered a retreat and fell back behind the Rappahannock on 18 August before Lee could react. Pope deployed his army from Kelly's Ford to Rappahannock Station to prevent Lee's troops from crossing the river. Lee decided to move upriver and attempt to turn Pope's right. Accordingly, Jackson's divisions began sidling along the river, probing for a weak spot. Fighting took place at Freeman's Ford on 22 August before some Rebels crossed at Sulphur Springs later in the day. However, heavy rains that night led to a rapid rise in the river, threatening the Rebels on the east bank. Southern workmen built a new bridge across the river, allowing the isolated force to withdraw on 24 August.

By this time, the Pennsylvania Reserves division had arrived to join Pope, as had Samuel P. Heintzelman's Third Army Corps. The Union Fifth Army Corps was not far behind. Lee, in a quandary, decided on a bold plan. Jackson would take his corps and move beyond Pope's right flank while Longstreet skirmished along the Rappahannock. Jackson would sweep down on Pope's supply line, the Orange & Alexandria Railroad. By interdicting this rail line, Lee hoped to force Pope away from the Rappahannock and back toward Washington. If the Yankees were not lured into battle, they could at least be driven into Washington, freeing the ravaged countryside in time for harvest.

Jackson's three divisions (Ambrose P. Hill, William B. Taliaferro, and Richard S. Ewell) began their march on 25 August. Although their column was spotted by Union lookouts, the Rebels moved with celerity and Pope failed

Second Battle of Bull Run, 29 August 1862 (*Library of Congress*)

Men of Company C, 41st New York Infantry, at Manassas (Photograph by Timothy O'Sullivan / *Library of Congress*)

to grasp the significance of the route of march. Jackson's column headed to Salem, then through Thoroughfare Gap across the Bull Run Mountains to Gainesville. Late on 26 August, Confederate horsemen captured Bristoe Station, then, followed by infantry, moved north along the railroad to Manassas Junction, the site of Pope's massive supply depot. Easily scattering the few defenders, Jackson's men took possession of the junction after dark.

Although surprised by the enemy in his rear, Pope realized that Lee's army was separated in two parts. If he moved quickly, his men could overwhelm Jackson before Longstreet could arrive. Early on 27 August, Pope abandoned the Rappahannock and turned his army toward Manassas. After repelling the attack of a New Jersey brigade from the Union Sixth Army Corps, moving from Alexandria, Jackson's men destroyed whatever supplies they could not take with them. In the meantime, Joseph Hooker's division of the Third Army Corps encountered Ewell's Division at Kettle Run, near Bristoe Station. Ewell managed to hold off the attacking Yankees before rejoining Jackson at Manassas later in the day.

Jackson was aware that Lee and Longstreet were at Salem that night. After his men burned the Union supplies, he withdrew to a position he selected near the old Manassas battlefield of July 1861. Throughout the night and into the morning of 28 August, Jackson's men abandoned Manassas Junction and moved into position behind an unfinished railroad cut north of the Warrenton Turnpike. Hidden by the embankment and wooded terrain, Jackson's tired soldiers settled down to await events. Stonewall hoped to avoid detection until Longstreet's men arrived via Thoroughfare Gap, ten miles to the west. If, perchance, Union troops continued to block the way, Jackson could still withdraw northward.

Throughout the day on 28 August, Union troops converged on Manassas Junction, only to find Jackson gone. The Union division of James B. Ricketts moved to Thoroughfare Gap, encountering the van of Longstreet's column already moving through the gap. Ricketts deployed and contested the enemy advance, but was outnumbered and forced to withdraw. Meanwhile, Pope was confused and issued contradictory orders to his troops

Soldiers with damaged rolling stock of the Orange & Alexandria Railroad, Manassas Junction, August 1862
(Photograph by Timothy O'Sullivan / *Library of Congress*)

as he attempted to locate the enemy. Wrongfully believing that Jackson had moved toward Centreville, Pope issued orders for his scattered divisions to move in that direction.

Rufus King's division of McDowell's corps moved along the Warrenton Turnpike across the front of Jackson's hidden corps. Jackson spied the Yankee column and decided to attack in order to expose his position to Pope's view, knowing that Longstreet would join him the next day. The Confederates moved forward as the day was drawing to a close and attacked John Gibbon's brigade at the Brawner Farm. Both sides fed troops into the savage close fighting that continued well after dark. The bloody stalemate resulted in heavy casualties for both sides before King withdrew his bloodied division.

Pope, thinking that King had encountered a retreating Jackson, issued attack orders for his converging divisions. Franz Sigel's First Corps of the Army of Virginia moved into position on Jackson's front on 29 August and began a series of piecemeal assaults on the railroad cut. John Reynolds's Pennsylvania Reserves soon joined the fray. As Major General Fitz John Porter's Fifth Army Corps, Army of the Potomac, marched

toward the field, Pope issued orders for Porter to move west to take position between Jackson and Longstreet. But Pope did not know that even as Sigel launched his first attacks, Longstreet was already beginning to deploy on Jackson's right. Porter's skirmishers encountered these new arrivals; the Union general halted his movement and spent most of the day vacillating.

Meanwhile, Heintzelman's corps reached the field and joined in the attacks on Jackson's line. Troops from Major General Jesse L. Reno's Ninth Army Corps came onto the field, as did McDowell's two divisions. Pope failed to coordinate their attacks, and, as a result, although individual Union brigades briefly gained ground and pierced Jackson's line, each attack was eventually repulsed. By the end of 29 August, Jackson held his position and Longstreet was deployed to his right, extending the Confederate line south of the Warrenton Turnpike. Lee wanted Longstreet to attack, but the general demurred, claiming that he faced an unknown number of Yankees to his front and right. The day ended with Longstreet launching a limited advance to discover what lay in his front. His men encountered King's divi-

Pontoon bridge across Bull Run, 1862 (*National Archives*)

sion and some confused fighting took place after dark until Longstreet recalled his brigades, which returned to their original positions.

At daylight on 30 August, Pope still believed that the enemy was retreating, even though he knew Longstreet was on the field. Skirmishing along Jackson's front revealed that the enemy was yet on the field, and Pope spent the morning undecided what to do. Finally, with the skirmishing along Jackson's front providing all the evidence that the enemy was still there, Pope decided to launch a massive attack on Jackson. Porter was to mass his corps on the left and assail the enemy line.

Porter began his attack shortly after 3:00 P.M. His men, though brave, were unable to pierce the enemy line. Enfiladed by Longstreet's artillery, the attackers were repelled at every point and Porter withdrew. With the repulse of Pope's largest attack, Lee ordered Longstreet forward. His divisions surged ahead, thrashing Colonel G. K. Warren's small brigade, then mauling a brigade of Pennsylvania Reserves. The oncoming Rebels rolled forward and met the next Union line on Chinn Ridge, where a mixed force of troops from two corps managed to hold long enough for another line to take position on Henry House Hill.

By this time, Pope had ordered a retreat by the entire army. Throughout the late afternoon and evening hours, the Federals fell back across Bull Run and headed toward Centreville. Longstreet's men seized Henry House Hill after the Yankees withdrew, but with their organization disrupted and darkness coming on, further pursuit was not possible. Pope continued to retreat to the Washington defenses. On 1 September, Jackson's troops collided with the retreating Union armies at Chantilly. In a confused battle in the rain, Jackson was repelled and the campaign soon ended. The Union army suffered a loss of 16,054 officers and men—1,724 killed, 8,372 wounded, and 5,958 missing. Lee reported a loss of 1,481 killed, 7,627 wounded, and only 89 missing, a total of 9,197.

—*Richard A. Sauers*

See also Army of Virginia; Pope, John
For further reading:
Gaff, Alan D. *Brave Men's Tears: The Iron Brigade at Brawner Farm* (1985).
Hennessy, John J. *Return to Bull Run: The Campaign and Battle of Second Manassas* (1993).
———. "The Second Battle of Manassas." *Blue & Gray Magazine* (1992).
Kelly, Dennis. "Second Manassas: The Battle and Campaign." *Civil War Times Illustrated* (1983).

BULLOCH, JAMES DUNWODY
(1823–1901)
Confederate diplomat

Born into a prominent Georgia family, James Dunwody Bulloch was the son of James Stephens Bulloch and Hester Amarinthia Elliott Bulloch. The younger Bulloch's sister, Martha Bulloch, married Theodore Roosevelt, Sr., and became the mother of future president Theodore Roosevelt.

Born and reared in Savannah, Georgia, James Bulloch developed an interest in the sea at an early age. At age 16 he accepted a midshipman's berth in the U.S. Navy. He served on several vessels, including the USS *United States*, USS *Decatur*, and USS *Delaware*, and on several stations, including Latin America, the Mediterranean, and the Pacific, before receiving his first command with the mail steamship *Georgia*. The U.S. government engaged in this activity to give young officers experience commanding steam vessels, but Bulloch, like so many others, used this experience to find civilian employment as a steamer captain and left the service in 1854.

With Georgia's secession, Bulloch returned home to provide naval assistance to his native state. The start of the Civil War caused Bulloch to offer his services to Confederate secretary of the navy, Stephen Mallory. Given the rank of commander, Bulloch hoped to command a Confederate warship, but his expertise in commanding various types of vessels caused the Confederate government to detail him to Europe, where he was charged with procuring ships for the new nation.

Over the next four years, Bulloch became an invaluable Confederate agent, contracting for numerous ships, but also involved in the acquisition of other essential supplies for the Confederacy and arranging for their transport through the Union blockade. By July 1861, Bulloch had already purchased in Great Britain ten ships suitable for commerce raiding and was being watched closely by U.S. agents in Europe.

After seeing the purchase and beginning of the construction of what would become the CSS *Florida* and CSS *Alabama*, Bulloch purchased a large number of war supplies and personally escorted them back through the blockade and then returned to Great Britain in February 1862.

When pressure from U.S. diplomats made it increasingly difficult for Bulloch to purchase ships and supplies in Great Britain, Bulloch moved his operation to France in early 1863. Receiving regular payments from the Confederate treasury to finance his operation, as late as the fall of 1863, Bulloch was still shipping necessary items back to the Confederacy and working to outfit commerce raiders. His tireless efforts during the war exceeded those of all other Confederate purchasing agents and have been credited with prolonging the war.

After the war, Bulloch, believing he could not expect a pardon from the U.S. government and having grown fond of his European surroundings decided to live in Liverpool and go into the shipping business there. He was often consulted in his adopted home on matters of maritime law. In his spare time, he wrote about some of his activities during the war in what became *The Secret Service of the Confederate States in Europe*. He died in Liverpool, England, on 7 January 1901.

—*David S. Heidler and Jeanne T. Heidler*

See also Diplomacy, C.S.A.; Navy, C.S.A.

For further reading:

Nuckols, Jack Randall. "A Confederate Agent in Europe: The Life and Career of Commander James Dunwody Bulloch" (M.A. thesis, 1982).

Young, Michael T. "A Study of the Activities of James Dunwody Bulloch: Confederate Naval Agent in Great Britain" (M.A. thesis, 1968).

BUMMERS

The term *bummers* is a derisive term describing foragers operating out of Major General William T. Sherman's Army of Georgia and Army of the Tennessee during the Savannah campaign of 1864 (March to the Sea) and the Carolinas campaign. Many times, this term is a negative one referring to the abuses of this foraging system on the populations of Georgia, South Carolina, and North Carolina. This word *bummer* still brings out strong emotional feelings in the Southern United States relating to the conduct of the war by General Sherman.

Bummer is a reference to the detailed soldier who goes out independently to obtain food for his parent unit. Knowing that his columns would be cut off from supply during the march to Savannah, Georgia, General Sherman ordered his two armies to institute a system of obtaining food from the countryside to enable the columns to continue to advance without any concern over wagon-based or rail-based supply. In Special Order 120 on 9 November 1864, Sherman established the guidelines for foraging. Sherman desired that brigade commanders would organize foraging parties, which would consist of officers commanding a detachment of soldiers from each regiment of the brigade. This detachment would leave the camps in the morning to forage along the skirts of the columns and obtain enough food to keep the wagons filled for at least ten days. General Sherman desired these forager detachments to move out on foot and return to the camps with horses and mules.

Despite Sherman's intentions, the art of foraging took on a life of its own. The system of foraging would become more decentralized with more detachments ranging across the countryside. Soon, these detachments would become permanently mounted with horses and mules from Southern farms, and detachments would start to

travel farther from their parent units to find food. By the time of the Carolinas campaign, many of these detachments were also operating as a form of cavalry by screening columns and racing ahead to capture important locations. The greater mobility gave rise to competition between detachments for choice locations for forage. Many foraging parties would race each other to the nearest town to secure it for their own unit. A classic example was the intense rivalry between the forager detachments of XIV and XX Army Corps in South Carolina. In some cases, these ad hoc units would fight each other more than the Confederate cavalry and militia units.

The greatest problem with these forager detachments was the different levels of discipline found in these units. Some detachments were tightly controlled by both divisional and brigade-level officers in an attempt to control any abuses. On the other hand, some detachments were allowed to range freely over the country and take items that were not considered forage. In addition, a number of soldiers took the opportunity to leave their regiments to conduct their own forage trips. It was to these unauthorized foragers that the term *bummer* originally applied. These bummers, along with army deserters and Confederate cavalry units foraging in the same area, had a truly devastating effect on the civilian populations of Georgia, South Carolina, and North Carolina.

A week into the Savannah campaign, many corps and divisional commanders were issuing orders to curb the destruction of mainly abandoned homes along the march route. This destruction of abandoned houses increased tenfold during the march through South Carolina. In addition to abandoned homes, occupied dwellings would be in danger of destruction, especially if Union soldiers were killed in the area. Confederate cavalry and civilians began to attack forager detachments, and in many cases no quarter was given to the Union soldiers. Detachments started to limit their foraging areas to routes where they could get support from the main columns in case of an attack. By mid-February 1865, correspondence was began between Union and Confederate generals to curb the killing of Union soldiers, but no resolution was ever made.

By the time General Sherman's two armies were entering North Carolina in March 1865, most forager detachments were led by a permanently assigned officer with a select group of noncommissioned officers and privates. This system provided more forage for the column and also ensured more control over the actions of the detachment. By the time of the occupation of Goldsboro, North Carolina, on 24 March 1865, the foraging system was discontinued in Sherman's two armies. By this point, the Union armies faced an organized Confederate army with superbly led cavalry. Any detachments going out would find themselves almost constantly open to Confederate cavalry attacks. Finally, a supply line was opened to New Bern, North Carolina, and Sherman's forces did not need a foraging system to keep the army fed.

—*William H. Brown*

See also Carolinas Campaign; Sherman, William Tecumseh; Sherman's March to the Sea.
For further reading:
Barrett, John G. *Sherman's March through the Carolinas* (1956).
Faust, Patricia. *Historical Times Illustrated Encyclopedia of the Civil War* (1986).
Glatthaar, Joseph T. *The March to the Sea and Beyond: Sherman's Troops in the Savannah and Carolinas Campaigns* (1985).
Grimsley, Mark. *The Hard Hand of War: Union Military Policy Toward Southern Civilians, 1861–1865* (1995).
Marszalek. John F. *Sherman: A Soldier's Passion for Order* (1994).

BURBRIDGE, STEPHEN GANO
(1831–1894)
Union general

Born on 31 August 1831 in Scott County, Kentucky, Stephen G. Burbridge was the son of Captain Robert Burbridge, a War of 1812 veteran, and Eliza Ann Barnes. After completing studies at Georgetown College from 1845 to 1847, he attended the Frankfort (Kentucky) Military Institute. Young Burbridge subsequently studied law but chose the life of a merchant and farmer.

With the outbreak of the war, Burbridge left his Logan County farm and raised the 26th Kentucky Infantry for the Union cause. Commissioned colonel on 27 August 1861, he was too ill to command at Shiloh. Promoted to brigadier general of volunteers on 9 June 1862, he subsequently served ably at Chickasaw Bayou, Arkansas Post, and the Vicksburg campaign.

On 15 February 1864, Burbridge was placed in temporary command of the District of Kentucky. At the request of Governor Thomas Bramlette and other prominent Kentuckians, the command became permanent on 14 March. Although largely Unionist in sentiment, Kentucky bitterly opposed any measure that threatened the existence of slavery. Within this volatile political climate, the new commander was forced to contend with the frequent threat of guerrilla depredations and large-scale enemy cavalry raids

Burbridge served ably in the field and was breveted major general of volunteers on 4 July 1864 for shattering John Hunt Morgan's command during the noted raider's last foray into the state. Although Burbridge's advance into southwestern Virginia was halted at Saltville on 2 October 1864, he subsequently participated in Major General George Stoneman's successful raid into the vital region from 10 to 21 December 1864. Although a slave owner, Burbridge vigorously supported the organization of black troops in the state. Praised for his efforts by Adjutant General Lorenzo Thomas, Burbridge was hailed by the men of the 5th and 6th U.S. Colored Cavalry regiments as the "pioneer of freedom for the slaves of Kentucky."

After Lincoln's 5 July 1864 proclamation declaring martial law and suspending the writ of habeas corpus in Kentucky, Burbridge assumed extensive civil and military powers. In his zeal to crush dissent, he ordered the arbitrary arrest of "disloyal" citizens, including several prominent critics of the Lincoln administration, and suppressed those newspapers he considered "rebel sheets." Burbridge's bayonets also controlled the polls during state elections and the presidential contest of 1864. While praised by Kentucky "radicals," conservative Unionists loudly condemned him as a tyrant. Governor Bramlette became his bitter foe and in late 1864 bombarded Lincoln, Grant, and Sherman with demands for Burbridge's removal.

Burbridge's extreme measures to rout out the guerrilla menace proved the most controversial aspect of his career. Issued on 16 July 1864, his General Orders No. 59 decreed that four guerrilla prisoners would henceforth be publicly executed for every Unionist murdered by irregulars. Scores of men fell before his firing squads in the months that followed. Historians have overlooked that Confederate forces operating in Kentucky frequently shot Union irregulars out of hand. However, it is undeniable that the victims of Burbridge's policy were executed without trial for crimes they did not commit. Outraged Kentuckians damned Burbridge as a butcher—a charge that would haunt him for the rest of his days.

Burbridge's bitter feud with Bramlette and his alienation of Kentucky's conservative majority cost him the support of both Grant and Lincoln. After a conference between the president and a delegation of prominent Kentuckians in Washington, Burbridge was relieved of command on 23 February 1865. Although initially ordered to report to General George H. Thomas at Nashville, Burbridge spent the remainder of the war without a command. He subsequently resigned his commission on 1 December 1865.

Burbridge remained a controversial figure for years after the conflict. Vilified by Kentucky's Democratic press as a "despot" and "butcher," he was frequently forced to defend his war record publicly. Although warmly defended by many wartime comrades and Republican leaders, Burbridge failed to obtain any further military position or government office. Virtually ostracized, he lamented in 1867 that "my services to my country have caused me to be exiled from my home." He afterward left Kentucky and established a successful legal practice in Washington, D.C. He retired from the legal profession in 1879 and accepted a position with a Philadelphia real estate firm. He died in Brooklyn, New York, on 2 December 1894 and was buried in Arlington National Cemetery.

A victim of partisan politics both during and after the conflict, Burbridge claimed, rightly in most cases, that he merely followed the orders of his superiors. Nevertheless, he never shrank from carrying out ruthless measures nor did he exhibit the judgment and skill necessary to command in a politically turbulent district. He remains to this day one of the most controversial figures in Kentucky history.

—*James M. Prichard*

See also Bramlette, Thomas E; Kentucky; Morgan, John Hunt; Morgan's Raids.

For further reading:
Coulter, E. Merton. *The Civil War and Readjustment in Kentucky* (1926).
Falaise, Louis De. "General Stephen Gano Burbridge's Command in Kentucky." *Register of the Kentucky Historical Society* (1971).
Louisville *Commercial* (9 January 1882; 5 February 1882).
Louisville *Courier-Journal* (7 and 8 December 1894).

BURNETT, HENRY LAWRENCE
(1838–1916)
Union general

Born to Henry Burnett and Nancy Jones Burnett in Youngstown, Ohio, Henry Lawrence Burnett was educated at Chester Academy before embarking on the study of law. He opened a practice in Warren, Ohio, in 1859. Upon the firing on Fort Sumter, Burnett addressed Union meetings in and around Warren trying to encourage support for the Union and recruiting for the U.S. Army. When he was criticized for not being in the army himself, he enlisted in a volunteer regiment that became the 2d Ohio Cavalry. In August 1861 he was elected captain of his company.

In the fall of 1861 the 2d Ohio was sent to Missouri, where it saw considerable action. The following year Burnett's regiment served in Kansas and during the repulse of Braxton Bragg from Kentucky. As part of the Army of the Ohio, Burnett and the regiment participated in the engagements of that force through the summer of 1863. In August of that year, Burnett was promoted to major and was chosen by the army's commander, Ambrose Burnside, to serve as the judge advocate for the Army of the Ohio. Burnside, frustrated in dealings with potentially disloyal persons like Clement Vallandigham, sought to regularize the procedures for dealing with civilian political prisoners. During his early time in his position, Burnett gained a great deal of experience in trying political prisoners, experience that would stand him in good stead for the remainder of the war and beyond.

In 1864, Indiana governor Oliver P. Morton requested assistance from the army in prosecuting suspected disloyal persons. Burnett was sent to the governor's assistance to prosecute before military tribunals alleged members of the Knights of the Golden Circle. Burnett also traveled to Illinois, where he successfully prosecuted individuals involved in a conspiracy to free the Confederate prisoners at Camp Douglas outside Chicago. He also investigated and prosecuted individuals involved in attempts to incite draft riots in the Midwest.

Burnett's growing experience made him a valuable member of the legal team that prepared the military prosecution of Lamdin P. Milligan at the end of 1864. He offered one of the opinions that it was perfectly justified to try the case in a military court even though the civil courts of Indiana were functioning. Of course it would be the very fact that the civil courts were operational that brought about the overturning by the Supreme Court of Milligan's conviction in *Ex parte Milligan* after the war.

In early 1865, Burnett was transferred to Washington, D.C., to work directly under Joseph Holt in the judge advocate general's office. In March he was brevetted to colonel and later the same month to brigadier general. With the Lincoln assassination in April 1865, Burnett would see his greatest responsibility.

As assistant judge advocate to Holt, Burnett was given the responsibility of conducting much of the investigation of the assassination and collecting evidence against those suspected of being involved in the conspiracy. During one point in his investigation, his experience with the Knights of the Golden Circle and his conviction that the group was involved in so many conspiracies convinced him that that group had masterminded the Lincoln assassination. He later changed his view somewhat to believe that Confederate government officials had planned the assassination.

During the trial, Burnett served as Holt's special assistant. His primary duty was to organize the evidence against the defendants for presentation to the panel of military judges. Although he did not openly disagree with Holt, Burnett questioned some of his chief's methods, particularly the strict secrecy regarding much of the trial. Burnett wrote privately to Secretary of War Edwin Stanton complaining of some of his misgivings but was instructed by Stanton that he was to be governed in all aspects of the trial by Holt.

With the trials complete, Burnett was mustered out of the volunteer service. He returned to Ohio, where he practiced law in Cincinnati. He moved to New York City in 1869, where he entered into partnership with a number of prominent attorneys and soon gained a reputation as one of the most important corporate lawyers in the nation. At different times during his career, he represented the Erie Railroad, British concerns in the Emma Mine case, and the Rutland Railroad Company. He was also very active in behind-the-scenes activities of the Republican Party and served as an unofficial advisor to William McKinley. When McKinley became president he appointed Burnett one of New York's federal district attorneys. In his later life, Burnett wrote extensively while living much of the time on his estate near Goshen, New York. He died in New York City on 4 January 1916 from complications of pneumonia.

—*David S. Heidler and Jeanne T. Heidler*

See also *Ex parte Milligan*; Knights of the Golden Circle; Lincoln Assassination.

For further reading:
Burnett, Henry Lawrence. "Assassination of President Lincoln and the Trials of the Assassins." In *History of the Ohio Society of New York, 1885–1905* (1906).

———. "The Controversy between President Johnson and Judge Holt." In *Some Incidents in the Trial of President Lincoln's Assassins* (1891).

Turner, Thomas Reed. *Beware the People Weeping; Public Opinion and the Assassination of Abraham Lincoln* (1982).

BURNS, ANTHONY
(ca. 1834–1862)
Fugitive slave

No single event galvanized the antislavery contingent in Boston and Massachusetts like the capture and return of Anthony Burns. On 24 May 1854, as Burns, an escaped slave, walked home from work, a deputy marshal arrested him, detaining him in Boston's municipal courthouse. This event was explosive because it coincided with passage of the Kansas-Nebraska Act, repealing the 1820 Missouri Compromise prohibiting slavery in certain areas of the country. Northerners, particularly abolitionists, interpreted the Kansas-Nebraska Act as another assault on freedom, another victory for Southern slaveholders' power.

As word spread, members of Boston's Vigilance Committee organized a meeting for 26 May at Faneuil Hall. Thousands clamored to listen to fiery orations by abolitionists. Some decided to attempt to free Burns. After gathering axes, a battering ram, pistols, and knives, a crowd of 500 milled around the courthouse. When the door burst, Reverand Thomas Wentworth Higginson and another stormed in, grappling with deputies. In the melee a deputy was fatally stabbed. Burns remained behind bars. Though state and federal governments would attempt to prosecute the rowdies, no convictions resulted.

While attorneys Richard H. Dana and Charles M. Ellis labored to prevent their client's return to slavery, others raised money to purchase Burns from his owner, Virginian Charles F. Suttle, who requested $1,200. When the parties met to conclude the sale, U.S. district attorney Benjamin F. Hallett, forbid it, declaring that the Fugitive Slave Law had to be obeyed. This 1850 law required special U.S. commissioners to conduct hearings, grant arrest warrants, and issue documents returning slaves to owners. Hallett feared that, if Burns were sold, the federal government would not reimburse Boston for debts incurred in apprehending and confining Burns.

Newspaper accounts of Burns put his age between twenty and thirty years. Not even Burns knew his exact age, but his tombstone bears the date 31 May 1834. He was the youngest of thirteen children, and his owner, Suttle, hired him out to various employers. Burns enjoyed a measure of independence, running errands and working in a grocery store, a tavern, and a sawmill. He underwent religious conversion and preached to slaves, ministering and performing marriages. In 1854, Burns worked for a Richmond apothecary who permitted Burns to find other odd jobs. Burns found work along the docks and stowed aboard a Boston-bound ship, landing in February. Later, the scarcely literate Burns penned a letter to his brother in Virginia that was intercepted by Suttle, who rushed to Boston.

After hearings and motions, the commissioner ruled on 2 June that Suttle owned Burns and ordered the fugitive returned to Virginia. That afternoon an estimated 50,000 people lined the streets waiting to catch a glimpse of Burns. Businesses closed and people hung black shawls and fabric out of windows and hoisted over the street a large black coffin bearing the word "Liberty." Surrounded by sixty volunteer guards and marine and infantry companies, Burns walked to the ship returning him to the South. He was transported to Norfolk, Jamestown, and finally Richmond, where he was kept handcuffed and chained at the ankles in a six- by eight-foot room for four months.

In November, Suttle sold Burns to a North Carolina slave owner for $905. In 1855, Boston acquaintances purchased Burns's freedom from his new owner for $1,300. Burns spoke in Northern cities about his travails and later enrolled at Oberlin College and Cincinnati's Fairmont Theological Seminary. Burns moved to St. Catherine's, Ontario, in late 1860 to minister at the black Baptist church there. After a brief tenure, he died of tuberculosis on 27 July 1862.

In the sensational case's wake, Massachusetts's voters shunned the Democratic and Whig parties in fall elections in 1854. The nascent Know-Nothing, or American, Party triumphed in the gubernatorial election as well as in the state house and in congressional races. Democrats lost because voters identified the party with Stephen Douglas's Kansas-Nebraska Act and President Franklin Pierce's eagerness to enforce the Fugitive Slave Law. Although the Know-Nothing Party espoused anti-Catholic and anti-immigrant policies, it did pass the most comprehensive Personal Liberty Law, hoping to prevent another incident like the Burns case. Burns was the last fugitive slave returned from Boston.

—*Kathleen R. Zebley*

See also Abolitionist Movement; Abolitionists; Dana, Richard Henry; Emerson, Ralph Waldo; Fugitive Slave Act; Higginson, Thomas Wentworth; Parker, Theodore; Personal Liberty Laws; Thoreau, Henry David.

For further reading:

Maginnes, David R. "The Case of the Court House Rioters in the Rendition of the Fugitive Slave Anthony Burns, 1854." *Journal of Negro History* (1971).

Pease, Jane H., and William H. Pease. *The Fugitive Slave Law and Anthony Burns: A Problem in Law Enforcement* (1975).

Shapiro, Samuel. "The Rendition of Anthony Burns." *Journal of Negro History* (1959).

Von Frank, Albert J. *The Trials of Anthony Burns: Freedom and Slavery in Emerson's Boston* (1998).

BURNS, JOHN LAWRENCE
(1793–1872)
Gettysburg citizen

Enshrined as the "hero of Gettysburg" in American popular mythology, John Burns remains one of the most famous human-interest stories of the Civil War. Born John Lawrence Burns in Burlington, New Jersey, on 5 September 1793, he was the son of an immigrant from Aberdeenshire, Scotland. Although Burns was a cobbler by trade, it appears that his true aspirations were always for a military life. Burns was said to have served in the army during the War of 1812, having fought in the battle of Lundy's Lane, and was "in camp in

John Burns at his home following the battle of Gettysburg (*Library of Congress*)

preparation for the Mexican War," being at that time a resident of Gettysburg, Pennsylvania. When the Civil War broke out, he tried twice to join local volunteer units, but was rejected because of his age. Supposedly, he managed to circumvent this obstacle by finding work for a while as a Union wagoneer in Washington.

In the lapses between wars, local records indicate that Burns played a visible part in the public life of the community. In 1853 he was appointed the Gettysburg borough constable, winning election to the office in 1855 under the Know-Nothing ticket. He was again appointed constable in 1856 when the leading vote candidate declined the position. The following year Burns won victory as an anti-Buchanan candidate by a single vote. Not on the ballot in 1858 and 1859, he was defeated in 1860 when he ran as an independent Democrat. When he ran as constable for the last time in 1862, he was listed as a Union Party candidate.

The record of his political activities before the battle of Gettysburg suggests that Burns was essentially a Democrat and a nationalist who had little use for abolitionist sentiment or the pro-Southern posture advocated by the Democratic Party in the 1850s. Given this political sentiment and his prior military experience, it is not surprising that, when the war reached Gettysburg in July 1863, Burns went out to meet it.

Over the years Burns's story has become so riddled with myth and legend that it has become almost impossible to discern fact from fiction. The fact remains, however, that on 1 July 1863, the first day of the battle, Burns, dressed in civilian clothes and armed with an antiquated musket, left his home on the west side of town and joined the Union troops on McPherson's Ridge. According to eyewitnesses, Burns approached Major Thomas Chamberlain of the 150th Pennsylvania Infantry, offering his assistance. Accepted into the unit, he engaged the enemy for a while on the skirmish line about fifty yards ahead of where his monument stands today. Soon afterward he moved into the ranks of the 7th Wisconsin Infantry. During a lull in the fighting, Lieutenant A. D. Rood, Company K, led him to Colonel John B. Callis, who, fearing the old man's capture and execution as a guerilla or bushwhacker, had him sworn in as a volunteer soldier, thus dispelling the myth that Burns was the only civilian per se to fight in the battle. By the time the day's fighting was done and outflanked Union forces had retreated back through Gettysburg to take up a defensive position on Cemetery Hill, Burns had been wounded at least three times, in the arm and calf of the leg. Left behind in the retreat, Burns was caught by the Confederates, who bandaged his wounds and carried him to his home.

News of Burns's participation in the battle quickly spread through the ranks. On 5 July he was visited at his home by the lieutenant who had met and encouraged him at the firing line and had taken him before Colonel Callis of the 7th Wisconsin. After the battle, Burns was serenaded by army bands. Even Abraham Lincoln sought him out after delivering his Gettysburg speech, and they attended church together. Burns also profited financially from his 1 July adventures. He was awarded a pension by a special act of Congress, and he received thousands of dollars in contributions from all over after the battle. After selling his home to the Springs Hotel Company as a potential tourist attraction, his last days were spent near a little farm that he owned at Bonneauville, Pennsylvania, where he died on 4 February 1872.

—*Samantha Jane Gaul*

See also Gettysburg, Battle of.

For further reading:
Burns, John, File. Adams County Historical Society.
Burns, John, Vertical File V8-28. Library, Gettysburg National Military Park.
Coco, Gregory A. *On the Bloodstained Field: 130 Human Interest Stories of the Campaign and Battle of Gettysburg* (1987).
Craven, Wayne. *The Sculptures at Gettysburg* (1982).
Johnston, John W. *The True Story of John Burns* (1916).
The National Cyclopaedia of American Biography (1921).
Patterson, John S. "John Burns and Jennie Wade: The Hero and Heroine of Gettysburg?" Paper Presented at American Folklore Society Meeting, Philadelphia (1989).
Pennsylvania at Gettysburg: Ceremonies at the Dedication of the Monuments Erected by the Commonwealth of Pennsylvania to Major General George C. Meade, Major General Winfield S. Hancock, Major General John F. Reynolds and to Mark the Positions of the Pennsylvania Commands Engaged in the Battle (1904).
Presbyterian Church, Gettysburg, Pennsylvania. *Presentation and Unveiling of the Memorial Tablets Commemorating the Lincoln and Burns Event (November 19, 1863) Held at the Presbyterian Church, Gettysburg, Pa., Nov. 19th, 1914* (1916).
Sifakis, Stewart. *Who Was Who in the Civil War* (1988).

BURNSIDE, AMBROSE EVERETT
(1824–1881)
Union general

Born in Indiana, Ambrose Burnside received his early education at Liberty Seminary before being apprenticed to a tailor after his mother died. Always interested in the military, Burnside secured an appointment to West Point and graduated eighteenth of twenty in the class of 1847. Commissioned a lieutenant in the artillery, Burnside was sent to Mexico, where the shooting had stopped before his arrival in Vera Cruz.

Burnside was assigned to Captain Braxton Bragg's battery of the 3d Artillery, which was then stationed at Fort Adams, Newport, Rhode Island. In 1849, the battery was transferred to the New Mexico territory, where Burnside was slightly wounded during a skirmish with Apache warriors.

After a brief assignment to Jefferson Barracks, St. Louis, Burnside was part of the survey party of the U.S.-

Mexican boundary. In 1852, he was sent to Fort Adams, where he married Mary Bishop Richmond and worked on perfecting a breech-loading carbine that he had invented. Burnside resigned from military service in 1852 to devote his full energies to developing this weapon. Although government boards liked the carbine, Secretary of War John B. Floyd essentially demanded a bribe to secure a contract. Personally honest, Burnside rejected the offer and his firm went bankrupt. The disillusioned Burnside went west in search of work and was hired by his friend, George B. McClellan, to a position in the Illinois Central Railroad. In 1861, Burnside was the rail line's treasurer, with an office in New York.

Burnside was commissioned colonel of the 1st Rhode Island and led a brigade at First Bull Run, where he committed his troops piecemeal and did not provide outstanding service. However, Burnside was promoted to brigadier general of volunteers on 6 August and placed in command of the training of provisional brigades of the new Army of the Potomac. A simple, honest man, Burnside stood six feet tall, his face adorned by magnificent muttonchop whiskers. "The very beau ideal of a soldier," wrote one newspaper correspondent.

In the fall of 1861, McClellan assigned Burnside to command the Coast Division, a three-brigade unit assigned to conduct coastal operations in support of the Army of the Potomac. Burnside assembled 15,000 men and a motley array of gunboats and transport vessels at Annapolis, Maryland. In early January, the fleet put to sea and arrived at Hatteras Inlet, North Carolina, where it sustained few casualties while riding out two major storms. Finally, the fleet, supported by naval warships, headed north and attacked Roanoke Island on 7–8 February 1862. Overwhelmed by Federal troops and ships, the 2,500-troop garrison was cornered and forced to surrender.

After wiping out the small North Carolina naval squadron at Elizabeth City on 10 February, Burnside moved most of his infantry toward Newbern, fighting with Southern defenders on 14 March a pitched battle that resulted in another victory. After capturing the city, Burnside dispatched a brigade to besiege Fort Macon, guarding Beaufort harbor. After a day's bombardment, the fort surrendered on 26 April. Thereafter, Burnside's troops conducted raids along the Carolina coast and waited for further orders, hampered by lack of reinforcements.

As a result of the failure of the Peninsula campaign, Burnside brought many of his troops to reinforce McClellan. Now promoted to major general (to rank from 18 March), Burnside was placed in command of the new IX Army Corps, which went to Fredericksburg to reinforce John Pope's Army of Virginia. Burnside remained in Fredericksburg directing troop movements and was not involved in the defeat at Second Manassas.

The general, in command of both his IX Corps and Joseph Hooker's I Corps, moved with the reorganized army and fought at South Mountain on 14 September and at Antietam on 17 September 1862. In the war's bloodiest day, Burnside was ordered to seize the lower stone bridge over Antietam Creek. A series of assaults finally carried "Burnside's Bridge," but it was too late in the day and, even though IX Corps advanced, Southern reinforcements blunted its late afternoon attack on Lee's right flank.

On 10 November, despite his protestations, Burnside replaced McClellan in command of the army. He devised a plan to move the army quickly to Fredericksburg and outflank Lee, but a series of mishaps forced the army to remain opposite the city while waiting for pontoon bridges. The delay allowed Lee time to entrench his army behind the city, and Burnside, doggedly pursuing his original plan, crossed his army and fought a battle on 13 December, suffering more than 12,000 casualties in failed assaults. As a result of this defeat and the January 1863 Mud March, several officers literally revolted, and Burnside was removed from army command.

Lincoln, still respecting the general, assigned Burnside to command of the Department of the Ohio. The general became involved in political imbroglios when he suppressed newspapers suspected of sedition and arrested Ohio politician Clement Vallandigham on charges of treason. Burnside supervised the extension of Union power into eastern Tennessee, culminating with the capture of Knoxville and then a successful November 1863 defense against James Longstreet's Confederates.

In the spring of 1864, IX Corps was brought back to Virginia and took part in Grant's offensive against Lee. Burnside initially reported directly to Grant because he outranked Meade, but when events proved this system too clumsy, Burnside consented to serve under Meade for the good of the service. The general's last combat action occurred on 30 July, when he supervised the debacle at the Crater. Meade and Burnside got into a heated argument that day and, as a result of the defeat, a court of inquiry made Burnside the scapegoat. Having gone on leave after the Crater fiasco, the general resigned from the service in April 1865.

After the war, the affable Burnside returned to Rhode Island and was thrice elected governor. During the Franco-Prussian War, Burnside served as a mediator in an effort to end the hostilities. From 1878 until his death in 1881, Burnside served as a U.S. senator from Rhode Island. He is buried in Swan Point Cemetery, Providence, Rhode Island.

—*Richard A. Sauers*

See also Antietam, Battle of; Crater, Battle of the; Fredericksburg, Battle of; Mud March; Vallandigham, Clement L.
For further reading:
Marvel, William. *Burnside* (1991).
Poore, Ben Perley. *The Life and Public Services of Ambrose E. Burnside, Soldier-Citizen-Statesman* (1882).
Sauers, Richard A. *"A Succession of Honorable Victories": The Burnside Expedition in North Carolina* (1996).

BUTLER, ANDREW PICKENS
(1796–1857)
U.S. senator

Born on 18 November 1796 to Revolutionary War veteran William Butler and Behethland Foote Moore, Andrew Pickens Butler grew up in the revolutionary tradition of independence. His mother's midnight ride to warn American troops, in a fashion similar to that of Paul Revere, had brought about the meeting between her and William Butler. After receiving his early education at Moses Waddell's academy in Abbeville District, the same school that had produced Senators John C. Calhoun and George McDuffie, Andrew Butler went on to South Carolina College, where he graduated in 1817. During the two years after his graduation, Butler studied law and was admitted to the South Carolina bar in 1819. He settled in Edgewood at "Stonelands," and his practice thrived. His reputation grew, aiding his election in 1824 to the South Carolina lower house, where he served until 1831. In 1832 he was elected to the South Carolina senate. Butler was a moderate by antebellum South Carolina standards, but he nevertheless successfully aligned himself with Calhoun and became an outspoken proponent of nullification. The year 1833 proved to be one of change for Butler. He resigned his newly gained seat in the Senate upon his election as judge of the court of general sessions and common pleas.

By 1846, Butler was growing bored with judicial work. He resigned his judgeship and his position as trustee of South Carolina College, a position that he had held since 1829, and chose to serve out the remainder of retiring George McDuffie's U.S. Senate term. Running unopposed in 1848, Butler was elected on his own and was reelected in 1854. Serving the early part of his term alongside of John C. Calhoun, Butler benefited from Calhoun's friendship and influence. Although he could never rival Calhoun in the Senate, Butler was not intimidated by the elder statesman and vigorously attacked some of his more radical work. Yet Butler, noted for his skill in debate, was a devoted servant to his slaveholding constituency, opposing the admission of California and supporting the Fugitive Slave Act. Perhaps he is most remembered for his part in igniting the infamous Brooks-Sumner incident in the U.S. Senate. Butler's impassioned speech on the Kansas question apparently helped to provoke Charles Sumner to make his "The Crime against Kansas" speech in 1856. Sumner verbally attacked several Southern politicians, including Butler, then absent from the Senate as a result of illness. On 22 May 1856, Preston Brooks, Butler's cousin and a member of Congress, sought to defend his family's honor by thrashing Sumner with a cane on the floor of the Senate. Butler, who had been suffering from ill health for some time, died just over a year later on 25 May 1857 at his home in Edgefield.

While Andrew Pickens Butler enjoyed a hugely successful public life, his personal life was filled with misfortune. He lost his first wife, Susan Anne Simkins, only months after their marriage. In 1832, he married Harriet Hayne, who died after their second year of marriage, leaving Butler to raise their infant daughter Nancy, who later married Confederate general Johnson Hagood. Throughout the turbulent years of Butler's personal life, his mother was his most trusted companion, helping to raise Nancy and keeping house for him until her death in 1851.

—*Brian D. McKnight*

See also Brooks, Preston Smith; Sumner, Charles
For further reading:
Aldrich, Alfred P. *Memoir of Judge Andrew Pickens Butler* (1878).
Perry, Benjamin Franklin. *Reminiscences of Public Men* (1883).

BUTLER, BENJAMIN FRANKLIN
(1818–1893)
Union general

The general perhaps reviled the most by Confederates was born in Deerfield, New Hampshire, on 5 November 1818 to Captain John Butler and Charlotte Ellison Butler. Only five months old when his father died of yellow fever, Benjamin and his siblings lived with relatives until they moved to Lowell, Massachusetts, where his mother began keeping a boardinghouse in 1828. Graduating from Lowell high school in 1834, Butler matriculated at Waterville College in Maine (now Colby College). Contrary to his mother's hopes of a career for him in the ministry, Benjamin was intrigued by the physical sciences and he disdained the college's religious atmosphere. Butler's fervent wish to attend West Point went unfulfilled. However, before graduating in 1838, he watched attorney Jeremiah Mason argue a case, moving Butler to study law, and in 1840 he was admitted to the bar.

The young lawyer joined the Masonic Order and enlisted in the Lowell City Guards. Many of his cases were police court cases, and he specialized in criminal law, winning a high percentage of verdicts. By the 1850s, the five-foot-four, redheaded, barrel-chested, and cross-eyed native of New Hampshire boasted New England's largest criminal practice.

Butler pursued other interests with the same zeal as he pursued law. He pressed for reforms in police court procedures and in currency and banking, and he sought ten-hour days for factory workers. Interest in reform and Democratic politics led him to win a seat in the Massachusetts state house in 1853 and in the state

senate in 1859. He lobbied to reduce the usual fourteen-hour workday to a ten-hour day, whereupon corporations voluntarily moved to eleven hours. Butler's reputation spread in law, politics, and business when he purchased a majority interest in the Middlesex Corporation, Lowell's first woolen mill.

While Butler refused to endorse the Fugitive Slave Law, his maverick streak led him to agree with fellow "Hunker" Democrats that the Constitution protected slavery. Butler further enraged Massachusetts Democrats at the Charleston Democratic Convention in 1860 by casting 57 ballots in favor of Jefferson Davis for president, instead of Stephen Douglas. The convention splintered and some delegates agreed to meet in Baltimore. Democrats who refused to support Douglas nominated John C. Breckinridge for president. Butler had vested personal interests because he was selected as candidate for Massachusetts governor on the Breckinridge ticket.

After Republican Abraham Lincoln's election as president in 1860, South Carolina seceded and several Southern states followed. Alarmed by looming civil war, Butler joined a political foe, Republican Massachusetts governor John Andrew, to urge preparations for war. Militia brigadier general Butler informed the governor that the state militia needed woolen overcoats, and Andrew placed the order with Butler's Middlesex Company. Setting aside previous squabbles, Andrew and other politicians recognized Butler's value; namely, this faithful Democratic operative placed his country above party loyalty, regarding secession as treason, and he might entice other Democrats to support the Union.

Brigadier General Butler led the 8th Massachusetts Militia to Maryland, where a tense situation held. Maryland's proximity to Washington meant that it must remain Unionist so that the nation's capital was not exposed. Butler's bold proclamations quelled any thought Marylanders had of seceding, but irritated General in Chief Winfield Scott. Butler vowed to arrest all Maryland legislators if they passed an ordinance of secession. Furthermore, Butler confiscated Maryland's great seal; thus, if state leaders passed a secession ordinance, they could not affix a seal making it legal. On 25 April 1861, Winfield Scott ordered Butler to command the Department of Annapolis and keep open the rail line between Annapolis and Washington. With characteristic impetuousness, Butler occupied Baltimore without Scott's knowledge, and Scott ordered the Massachusetts general to Fort Monroe. Lincoln softened the blow by making Butler the first major general of volunteers.

Initially dismayed at his new assignment, Butler turned to innovative spying techniques and war machines. Learning of a volunteer balloonist, Butler used the man's services to spy on Confederate troops, camps, and ships. Butler was also the first to use the new Gatling guns. Butler established a precedent when he classified as contraband slaves who escaped to Federal lines for safety. He employed former slaves on fortifications, refusing to return them to their Southern owners.

Still, Butler longed for active military engagement and his chance came when he acquired maps of Richmond through a private source. In June 1861, Butler believed he could lead an invasion by way of the James River and seize the Confederate capital. On his own initiative, Butler aimed for Big Bethel, heading straight for disaster. His own confused colonels fired on comrades; Confederate batteries opened up, shooting many Federal soldiers at close range, and Butler's men beat a hasty retreat. This failure forced Lincoln to relieve Butler of his command at Fort Monroe and in the Senate almost cost Butler his commission.

Butler turned his attention to recruiting young Democrats in New England into the army. He kept a high profile, shuttling between Massachusetts and Washington, hoping for a new opportunity to showcase his skills. When troops were to join Admiral David Farragut and Comander David Dixon Porter in attacking New Orleans, Butler accompanied as army commander.

On 1 May 1862, Farragut transferred command of New Orleans to Butler. His troops subdued the largely pro-Confederate population of 168,000, which greeted soldiers with jeers and wishes that yellow fever would wipe them out. Butler declared that citizens had to respect the Federal government and remove signs of Confederate allegiance. When gambler William Mumford tore down the U.S. flag and dragged it through the streets, Butler hung him. What is less known is that in later years Butler assisted Mumford's widow in finding employment. Butler ordered that civil officers, attorneys, and even clergy take oaths of allegiance to the Union. Butler's most infamous act, General Order No. 28, proclaimed that any woman who insulted Federal troops would "be treated as a woman of the town plying her avocation." This threat served its purpose and Butler never had to enforce it.

Butler's New Orleans tenure proved controversial, especially concerning business transactions with his brother, Colonel Andrew Jackson Butler. General Butler fined merchants and entrepreneurs not engaging in trade. Washington and New Orleans officials grew suspicious as Andrew Butler gained trade permits allowing steamboats through enemy lines to sell contraband items such as salt and medicine, returning with cotton and sugar, which fetched premium prices in New York. Although General Butler cannot be directly linked to violating the law, the affair appeared unseemly when coupled with rumors of the confiscation of private property and the stealing of silver spoons, charges the general never could put to rest.

Butler's iron-fisted civic control prevented the usual outbreak of yellow fever. Butler ordered ships arriving from infected ports quarantined. He enforced rules of cleanliness and organized wagons to pick up and dispose of refuse. Still, this could not redeem the man Jefferson Davis branded a felon and outlaw deserving execution. Lincoln and Secretary of State William Henry Seward received numerous complaints from foreign consuls stationed in New Orleans about Butler's behavior. In late 1862, Lincoln removed Butler, replacing him with Nathaniel Banks.

Butler returned to Lowell, remaining away from the war for almost a year. In November 1863, he assumed command of the Departments of Virginia and North Carolina and busied himself with trying to exchange military prisoners. In May 1864, he attempted to prove his leadership qualities by assisting Ulysses S. Grant's assault toward Richmond. Butler was to lead troops from Fort Monroe along the James, marching toward Richmond's rear. Butler's Army of the James was to prevent Confederate soldiers from bolstering Lee's army. On 5 May, Butler and 12,000 soldiers occupied City Point and Bermuda Hundred. Eight days later, Butler assaulted enemy lines at Drewry's Bluff, but was quickly repulsed. On 16 May, rebel general P. G. T. Beauregard pushed Butler's men back to the Bermuda Hundred neck and cut Union soldiers off from the city and railroads. Butler's troops had nowhere to go and gradually they were detailed to assist Grant. Again, Butler's quest for military greatness evaporated.

After this debacle, Butler returned to administrative duties, cleaning up Norfolk to prevent yellow fever outbreaks. Treasury Secretary Salmon P. Chase noticed Butler's political value and offered Butler the post of vice president on his ticket. Lincoln sought him too, to replace Hannibal Hamlin. Butler flatly refused both offers, preferring to continue as major general. Instead, on election day in 1864, Butler and several thousand troops in ferry boats surrounded Manhattan and prepared to squelch any riots such as the ones in 1863.

As commander of the Virginia and North Carolina military department, Butler wished to seize Wilmington, North Carolina closing the Confederate port. His strategy involved detonating 300 tons of powder aboard a tugboat positioned near Fort Fisher, guarding the city's entrance. With the fort neutralized, Federals would land and capture it. Butler proposed this scheme in the fall of 1864 and coordinated the attack with the navy, which only added to the confusion in December 1864. Unbeknown to Butler, the navy ordered the explosion, doing minimal damage to the fort. When Butler learned of it, he landed his troops, only to watch them repulsed. In early January 1865, Lincoln removed Butler from command. Butler later learned of the successful second expedition to Fort Fisher.

After the war ended, Butler returned to politics in 1866, now as a congressman. In Washington he championed controversial causes such as civil rights, assistance for freed people and impoverished whites, women's suffrage, greenback currency, and eight-hour workdays for government workers, and he chaired the House Committee on Reconstruction.

Never far from the spotlight, Butler served as a prosecutor in President Andrew Johnson's impeachment trial and vociferously argued for conviction only to be outraged by the not-guilty verdict of the Senate. Butler shepherded the Ku Klux Klan Bill through Congress, goading colleagues to vote for the bill by waving the bloody shirt of a carpetbagger savagely beaten in Mississippi. The bill, passed in April 1871, was one of Butler's most prized accomplishments.

Butler served three consecutive terms in Congress from 1867 to 1875, losing in 1874 but elected in 1876 for a final term. In 1878, disillusioned with the Republican Party, he returned to his Democratic roots. Still, one office had repeatedly eluded him: the post of governor of Massachusetts. In 1881, the Democratic and National Greenback and Labor state conventions nominated Butler and he was elected in 1882, serving only one term. Butler's defeat for reelection permitted him to accept the 1884 presidential nomination of both the Anti-Monopoly and Greenback Parties. His last political battle failed and Butler faded away. He continued his legal practice and wrote his memoirs in 1891. Two years later, on 11 January 1893, Butler died in Washington.

—*Kathleen R. Zebley*

See also Army of the James; Bermuda Hundred Campaign; Drewry's Bluff; Election of 1864; Fort Fisher.

For further reading:
Butler, Benjamin F. *Autobiography and Personal Reminiscences of Major-General Benjamin F. Butler* (1892).
Capers, Gerald M., Jr. "Confederates and Yankees in Occupied New Orleans, 1862–1865." *Journal of Southern History* (1964).
Holzman, Robert S. "Ben Butler in the Civil War." *New England Quarterly* (1957).
———. *Stormy Ben Butler* (1961).
Trefousse, Hans Louis. *Ben Butler: The South Called Him Beast!* (1957).
West, Richard S., Jr. *Lincoln's Scapegoat General: A Life of Benjamin F. Butler, 1818–1893* (1965).

BUTLER, MATTHEW CALBRAITH
(1836–1909)
Confederate general

Born in Greenville, South Carolina, the son of William Butler and Jane Tweedy Perry Butler, the younger Butler grew up in a privileged, well-connected family (his uncle was Senator Andrew Pickens Butler). After attending college, Butler studied law, and after admission to the bar he began what would become a prominent practice in Edgefield. He married the daughter of Governor Francis W. Pickens, further

cementing his position in South Carolina society. Butler also became involved in South Carolina politics and was elected to the state legislature in 1860.

On the formation of the Confederacy, however, Butler resigned from the legislature to become the captain of the Edgefield Hussars. In May 1861, he accepted a commission in Hampton Legion. The Legion traveled to Virginia where it took part in the battle of First Bull Run. Shortly thereafter, Butler was promoted to major for his actions at Bull Run.

Butler continued with the Legion in the Peninsula campaign and for his actions there, particularly at the battle of Williamsburg in May 1862, was promoted to colonel of the 2d South Carolina Cavalry Regiment. He commanded the regiment at the battles of Second Bull Run and Antietam in Virginia, and the cavalry raid on Chambersburg, Pennsylvania, in October 1862. Following the battle of Fredericksburg, Butler led the 2d South Carolina in the Confederate cavalry raid on the Federal position at Occoquan, Virginia, and was able to make off with much-needed supplies for the Army of Northern Virginia.

In June 1863 severe wounds inflicted on him at the battle of Brandy Station cost Butler his right foot to amputation. His slow convalescence kept him from the Gettysburg campaign. He returned to the Army of Northern Virginia in September 1863, and at the same time was promoted to brigadier general.

In the spring of 1864, Butler commanded a brigade of Hampton's division and was cited for his bravery at the battles of the Wilderness and Spotsylvania Court House. His exploits won him promotion to major general in September 1864. In January 1865, as the winter fighting in Virginia ground to a halt, Butler's division was detached to the Carolinas to aid in the campaign against Union general William T. Sherman. Butler participated in all of Joseph Johnston's delaying actions and was involved in the preliminary negotiations for the surrender of Johnston's army.

Following the surrender, Butler returned to his law practice in Edgefield, South Carolina. He also reentered politics and became very active in trying to return the Democratic Party to power. He served in the state legislature and from 1876 until 1894 was United States Senator from South Carolina. When the Spanish-American War broke out in 1898 he received an appointment as a major general of volunteers and served on the settlement commission in Cuba after the war ended. He then became a prominent businessman and died in Washington, D.C., in 1909.

—*David S. Heidler and Jeanne T. Heidler*

See also Butler, Andrew P.; South Carolina.

For further reading:

Brooks, Ulysses Robert. *Butler and His Cavalry in the War of Secession* (1909).
Cumming, Joseph B. *True Lovers: Remarks Made by Joseph B. Cumming, Introducing General Matthew Calbraith Butler, Orator of the Day, On the Occasion of Decorating Confederate Soldiers' Graves at the Augusta Cemetery, Memorial Day, 1895* (1895).

BUTLER'S PROCLAMATION
(15 May 1862)

A lawyer and politician in his native Massachusetts, Brigadier General Benjamin F. Butler took command of the city of New Orleans on 1 May 1862. Only recently taken by Federal troops, the city's sentiments were divided, and Butler's abrasive nature did nothing to close the chasm. In the first days of his command, he further alienated the hostile New Orleans populace by confiscating an entire hotel when its pro-Southern proprietor refused to serve him breakfast.

Particularly troublesome to Butler's forces were the women of New Orleans. Determined to do all they could to oppose the Union general's authority, the city's women protested in a number of ways. Butler's men were insulted, spat upon, and even showered with the contents of second-story chamber pots. For more than two weeks he and his troops endured the insults. Understanding that arresting the women would only fill the jails and further anger the perpetrators, he sought an alternative. Butler settled on a method of controlling them in his Order No. 28, also referred to as "the Woman Order." Issued on 15 May, his order stated:

> As the officers and soldiers of the United States have been subject to repeated insults from the women (calling themselves ladies) of New Orleans, in return for the most scrupulous non-interference and courtesy on our part, it is ordered that hereafter when any female shall, by word, gesture, or movement, insult or show contempt for any officer or soldier of the United States, she shall be regarded and held liable to be treated as a woman of the town plying her avocation.

Butler's order further evidenced the perceived callous disrespect Federal men had for women and sent shock waves throughout the entire nation. Northerners and Southerners alike were outraged that the Union commander was not protecting the women of New Orleans. The British press even interpreted the order as authorization for Federal troops to rape.

Although Butler's Order No. 28 made him increasingly unpopular, it was effective in curbing overt acts of insult on his troops. The remainder of Butler's time in New Orleans continued to be stormy, and he was removed from command in December 1862. Still with some political power, he continued to be a thorn in the side of Abraham Lincoln's administration until Lincoln could afford to relieve himself of Butler toward the end of the war.

—*Brian D. McKnight*

See also Butler, Benjamin Franklin; New Orleans.
For further reading:
Butler, Benjamin F. Private and Official Correspondence of Benjamin F. Butler (1917).
Hearn, Chester G. When the Devil Came Down to Dixie: Ben Butler in New Orleans (1997).

BUTTERFIELD, DANIEL
(1831–1901)
Union general

Born to John Butterfield and Malinda Harriet Baker Butterfield in Utica, New York, Daniel Butterfield was educated locally and at Union College before entering the business world. He used his father's connections to become superintendent of the American Express Company's eastern division. Before entering into business, Butterfield had traveled the country, particularly the South, and had come to the conclusion that conflict was inevitable over the issue of slavery. In the years before the Civil War he was active in the New York militia, becoming the colonel of the 12th New York Militia.

At the outbreak of the war with the firing on Fort Sumter, Butterfield was on a business trip in Washington, D.C., and briefly became the first sergeant of the Clay Guards, a makeshift citizens' militia organized in the event of a Southern attack on the city. With the threat ended, he returned to New York City to prepare the 12th for induction into Federal service, an event that was accomplished on 2 May 1861. Butterfield was commissioned the regiment's colonel. Leaving Washington on 24 May 1861, the 12th New York Militia became the first Union regiment to enter the state of Virginia.

Butterfield and the 12th spent the first months of the war serving in western Virginia under Major General Robert Patterson at Martinsburg. In fall 1861 Butterfield was summoned back to Washington, where he was promoted to brigadier general of volunteers. He received a regular commission as a lieutenant colonel on 14 May. Butterfield was given command of a brigade in the Army of the Potomac and became a part of the Peninsula campaign in the spring of 1862. With the organization of the army into corps, his brigade became a part of Fitz John Porter's V Corps.

During the early phases of the Peninsula campaign, Butterfield led his brigade during the siege of Yorktown and even commanded the Federal operations on 27–28 April as general of the trenches. During the Seven Days' battles, Butterfield distinguished himself, especially at the battle of Gaines' Mill, where he personally seized a fallen regimental flag to rally his men and succeeded in leading them forward. He was seriously wounded in the engagement and in 1892 received the Medal of Honor for his actions on that day.

Butterfield returned to duty in time for the Second Bull Run campaign, where he once again served under Fitz John Porter. He fought at Antietam, and a month later was given command of a division of V Corps. He became the corps commander when Fitz John Porter was relieved in November 1862 to face the court-martial that would eventually remove him from the army. Butterfield commanded V Corps in the battle of Fredericksburg, leading it against the stone wall at the base of Marye's Heights. Butterfield had been promoted to major general with a date of rank of 29 November 1862.

With Ambrose Burnside's replacement by Joseph Hooker as commander of the Army of the Potomac at the end of January 1863, Butterfield became Hooker's chief of staff. In this role, he handled routine communications between Hooker and the other generals and aided the reorganization of the Army of the Potomac from Burnside's grand divisions to strictly an organization composed of corps. One of the most famous things that Butterfield did as chief of staff of the Army of the Potomac was to design the corps badges that Hooker envisioned to increase unit pride among the men, an idea originated by the late Phil Kearny.

Daniel Butterfield (*Library of Congress*)

Butterfield served as Hooker's chief of staff during the chaotic battle of Chancellorsville and remained in that position under Hooker's successor, George Gordon Meade. On 3 July 1863 Butterfield was seriously wounded during the artillery duel that preceded Pickett's Charge at Gettysburg. Following the battle he became involved in a heated dispute with Meade over whether Meade had seriously contemplated retreat on 2 July 1863. Butterfield said he had; Meade said he had not. As a result of the dispute, Butterfield transferred to the Army of the Cumberland to serve under his old commander, Joseph Hooker, who commanded XX Corps.

At Chattanooga, Butterfield became Hooker's chief of staff, a position he held during the battle of Lookout Mountain through the following spring and the commencement of the Atlanta campaign. Early in that campaign, however, Butterfield was given command of the 3d Division of Hooker's corps. He commanded that division through the early engagements of the campaign, but became seriously ill in early July 1864 and had to leave his command. He never sufficiently recovered to hold another field command in the war but did sit on court-martial duty.

Following the war Butterfield remained in the army, supervising recruiting in New York City and commanding the harbor forces there. He resigned his commission in 1870 when promised an appointment by President Ulysses S. Grant as New York City's U.S.

subtreasurer. He left that position to return to the business world. At various times for the remainder of his life, he had interests in the railroad, steamboat, hotel, and banking industries. He was also quite active in veterans organizations and causes, organizing a number of reunions and parades of veterans, including the funeral of William T. Sherman. He became famous after the war for having composed "Taps" while the Army of the Potomac was encamped at Harrison's Landing, Virginia, during the summer of 1862. He died on 17 July 1901 at Cold Spring, New York.

—*David S. Heidler and Jeanne T. Heidler*

See also Fredericksburg, Battle of; Gaines' Mill, Battle of; Music.

For further reading:
Butterfield, Julia Lorrilard Safford. *A Biographical Memorial of General Daniel Butterfield including Many Addresses and Military Writings* (1904).

BUTTERNUTS
See Uniforms, Ensignia, and Equipment

BUZZARD ROOST
(February 1864)
See Dalton, Georgia, First Battle of

C

CADWALADER, GEORGE
(1806–1879)
Union general

George Cadwalader was born in Philadelphia on 16 May 1806, one of three sons of General Thomas Cadwalader and Mary Biddle Cadwalader. He attended the University of Pennsylvania, where he read law, and was admitted to the bar. His progenitors were among the first families of the Penn land grant and were familiars of statesmen and presidents. As was the case with many of the Northern participants in the Civil War, Cadwalader had close family connections in the South. His wife, Frances (also known as Fanny) Butler Mease, whom he married in 1830, was a granddaughter of U.S. senator Pierce Butler of South Carolina.

Cast in this mold, by 1826 he was a member of the already significant 1st City Troop (1st Troop, Philadelphia City Cavalry) and was captain of the Philadelphia Greys in 1832. Cadwalader was commissioned brigadier general of the 1st Brigade, 1st Division, Pennsylvania militia, and commanded forces in the streets during the divisive nativist riots that erupted from the activities of the American, or Know-Nothing, Party in 1844. After spending a few years administering to his private affairs, Cadwalader returned to public duty at the beginning of the Mexican-American War and was commissioned a brigadier general of volunteers in the regular army in March 1847. Brevetted major general for gallantry in the Chapultepec fighting, he also served briefly as the governor of the state of Toluca. Philadelphia welcomed him as a hero in 1848 on his return.

Cadwalader practiced estate law, maintained his military interests, and became a trustee of the Mutual Assurance Company, an early underwriter of policies against domestic loss due to fire, and popularly known in Philadelphia as the Green Tree. He would become chairman of that board and continue to serve in that capacity until his death.

At the outbreak of the Civil War, Cadwalader, then fifty-five, was appointed a major general of volunteers and commanded the whole of the 1st Division under General Robert Patterson, chief commander of the Pennsylvania troops. In this capacity Cadwalader also served on boards of inquiry, in garrison commands, as advisor to the president and the secretary of war, and on various military commissions.

The lawyer-general became embroiled in the constitutional challenges that characterized the early part of the war. In an attempt to deal with the Copperheads, or Peace Democrats, on 27 April 1861 Lincoln had issued a proclamation that suspended the writ of habeas corpus covering the line from Philadelphia to Washington. It allowed the army to imprison anyone who threatened its operations and keep them in jail as long as they were deemed a threat. No judge could demand the release of the prisoners so the civil courts could try them.

In a matter of weeks, scores of individuals were arrested and transported to military prisons. One of these men was John Merryman, lieutenant of a secessionist drill company at Cockeysville, Maryland. Caught burning railroad bridges and recruiting for the South, he was imprisoned in Fort McHenry in Baltimore. The day after the incident, Chief Justice Roger B. Taney issued a writ of habeas corpus, which ordered that Merryman be tried before a regular court or released. Taney had it served on Cadwalader, who was commander at Fort McHenry. When Cadwalader refused to accept the writ, Taney believed that he had no alternative but to rule that the chief executive had acted unlawfully. Citing Cadwalader for contempt of court, Taney then wrote an opinion about the section of the U.S. Constitution that allows the suspension of habeas corpus, arguing that Congress, not the president, had the power to suspend habeas corpus. However, unable to make an argument for broad presidential war powers, Lincoln merely ignored Taney's opinion and adhered to the writ's suspension throughout the Civil War. The man at the center of the controversy, John Merryman, was nearly forgotten in the public debate. Later, he was released from imprisonment.

From August 1863 until the end of the war, General Cadwalader commanded the post at Philadelphia. With the end of hostilities, Cadwalader gave his resignation on 1 July 1865 and again returned to private life, devoting himself to his private interests. Cadwalader died at home on 3 February 1879 and was buried in Christ Church Cemetery with honors.

—*Samantha Jane Gaul*

See also Merryman, John.
For further reading:
Baltzell, E. Digby. *Philadelphia Gentlemen* (1979).
Burt, Nathaniel. *The Perennial Philadelphians* (1975).
Garvan, Anthony N. B., and Carol A. Wojtowicz. *Catalogue of the Green Tree Collection* (1977).
Leffingwell, Edward G. "'A Fine Animal': Portraits of General George Cadwalader of Philadelphia" (M.A. thesis, 1984).
Taylor, Frank H. *Philadelphia in the Civil War, 1861–1865* (1913).
Warner, Ezra J. *Generals in Blue, Lives of Confederate Generals* (1959; reprint, 1964).
Weigley, Russell F., ed. *Philadelphia, A 300-Year History* (1982).

CAIRO, U.S.S.

While the most famous ironclad warships of the Civil War fought in coastal operations, many smaller ironclads performed distinguished service on southern rivers. Subject to ambushes along narrow river channels, ironclads proved invaluable in saving their crews from hostile fire. Early in the war, both sides of the conflict constructed makeshift armored vessels using wood, thin metal shielding, or even bales of cotton. In January 1862, however, the Union unveiled its first class of purpose-designed riverine ironclads constructed at Mound City, Illinois.

Often referred to as the City class, the seven ironclads (*Cairo, Carondelet, Cincinnati, Louisville, Mound City, Pittsburgh,* and *St. Louis*) were designed by Samuel B. Pook and constructed under the direction of James B. Eads. Essentially armored rafts fitted with a bow ram, the *Cairo* and its sister ships were propelled by a stern paddle wheel, although the two and a half inches of armor plate also covered the paddle wheel, making the ships appear to be propeller driven. Unfortunately, the heavy armor limited "Pook's Turtles," as the ships became known, to a top speed of only five knots. The ships were armed with thirteen guns (four on each broadside, three facing forward, and two firing to the rear).

The *Cairo* enjoyed an active but unfortunately brief career. Like its sister ships, the *Cairo*'s construction was funded by the Union army, and the vessels operated under army control until transferred to the navy's new Mississippi Squadron in the summer of 1862. The *Cairo* itself took part in only three major engagements. The first, in May 1862, found the *Cairo* providing gunfire support for the Federal assault on Fort Pillow, Tennessee. Surprised by a force of eight Confederate rams, the *Cairo* assisted other Union warships in driving off the attackers. The Union suffered severe damage to two gunboats, but the *Cairo* itself was undamaged. One month later, as part of the wider Union effort to capture Memphis, Tennessee, the *Cairo* and other Union

The USS *Cairo* (*Library of Congress*)

gunboats destroyed the only significant Confederate naval force on the Mississippi River.

In December 1862, the *Cairo*, under the command of Lieutenant Commander Thomas O. Selfridge, moved into the Yazoo River to support Union assaults on Vicksburg, Mississippi. Union forces under the command of General William T. Sherman attempted to approach Vicksburg through its northern waterways, and navy gunboats were instrumental in forcing the advance upriver. Ignoring warnings of Confederate torpedoes (underwater mines) in the area, Selfridge rashly ordered the *Cairo* past other Union warships acting as minesweepers to respond to Confederate fire from the shore. Before the *Cairo* could return fire, two torpedoes, detonated by Confederate troops hidden ashore, exploded in rapid succession and the Union ship immediately began to list to port. Nothing could be done to save the ship, which sank in six fathoms of water. Fortunately, the *Cairo*'s stout armor absorbed most of the blast, the ship sank slowly, and the entire crew escaped without loss of life. The *Cairo* earned the dubious distinction of become the first ship to be sunk by an electrically detonated torpedo.

Immediate salvage of the wreck was minimal, essentially limited to the ship's guns. Buried in a sandy grave, the *Cairo* remained forgotten until the National Park Service began a search for the wreck in 1956. The *Cairo* was raised from the Yazoo River in 1965 and after extensive restoration was installed at the Vicksburg National Military Park in 1977 as a permanent exhibit alongside a museum featuring artifacts collected from the wreck site.

—*Steven J. Ramold*

See also Carondelet; Eads, James B.; Fort Pillow, Massacre; Ironclads; Navy, U.S.A.; Pook's "Turtles"; Riverine Warfare, U.S.N.; Vicksburg Campaign; Yazoo Expedition.

For further reading:
Canney, Donald L. *The Old Steam Navy. Volume Two: The Ironclads, 1842–1885* (1993).
Fowler, William M., Jr. *Under Two Flags: The American Navy in the Civil War* (1990).
Selfridge, Thomas O. *Memoirs of Thomas O. Selfridge, Jr., Rear Admiral, U.S.N.* (1900).
Silverstone, Paul H. *Warships of the Civil War Navies* (1989).

CALDWELL, JOHN CURTIS
(1833–1912)
Union general

Born in Lowell, Vermont, John Curtis Caldwell was educated at Amherst College before embarking on a career in education. Not long before the outbreak of the Civil War, he had accepted a position as a principal at Washington Academy in Maine, and so it was in that state that he helped to raise a volunteer regiment for Federal service. In November 1861, he was commissioned colonel of the 11th Maine Volunteers.

John Curtis Caldwell (*Library of Congress*)

The regiment departed Maine for Washington, D.C., on 13 November 1861.

Upon arrival in Washington, Caldwell and his regiment became a part of the defenses of Washington. They remained there until May 1862, when the 11th became a part of the Army of the Potomac and were sent to the York Peninsula in Virginia. After the battle of Seven Pines, in which their brigade commander, Oliver O. Howard, was seriously wounded, Caldwell was given command of the 1st Brigade, 1st Division, of II Corps, which was commanded by Edwin Sumner. He commanded that brigade through the Seven Days' campaign.

During the Maryland campaign, Caldwell continued in command of his brigade, of which the 11th Maine was a part. Briefly during the battle of Antietam, he assumed command of the 1st Division when its commander, Israel B. Richardson, fell mortally wounded. However, after directing the operations of the division for a short time against the Bloody Lane, Caldwell was superseded in command by Winfield Scott Hancock, who had been sent personally by George McClellan to take command of the division. Corps commander Sumner commended Caldwell for his actions in the battle.

Hancock remained in command of the division after Antietam, and in October he directed the reconnaissance activities of Caldwell and his brigade out of Harper's Ferry. In one such mission from 16 to 17

October 1862, Caldwell and his men scouted the area between Harper's Ferry and Charles Town and skirmished heavily with Confederate forces there. The following month, Caldwell led his men in the Army of the Potomac's move toward the Rappahannock River.

In the battle of Fredericksburg, Caldwell led his brigade against the heavily defended Confederate position on Marye's Heights. Very early in the advance, the brigade came under heavy fire, and Caldwell had difficulty rallying his men for the offensive. While in the midst of trying to turn a fleeing regiment, he was struck in the side by a Confederate bullet. He remained in command, however, and continued to urge his men on. As they pushed forward, he was hit again, this time in the left shoulder, and was forced to leave the field. Hancock commended Caldwell for his bravery in the battle.

Returning to duty in February 1863, Caldwell commanded his brigade in the battle of Chancellorsville, after which he was given command of the division when Hancock was elevated to II Corps commander. In the battle of Gettysburg, although Hancock had been sent ahead by George Gordon Meade to assess the situation in Gettysburg, the remainder of the corps, including Caldwell and his division, did not arrive on the field until early on 2 July. When Hancock was wounded the next day, Caldwell temporarily assumed command of the corps. He returned to his division when Gouverneur K. Warren assumed command of the corps. Periodically for the remainder of the year, Caldwell would assume command of the corps when Warren was away from headquarters.

In October 1863, Warren commended Caldwell for the thankless job he had done in guarding the corps' advance at Bristoe Station and then guarding the corps' retreat. Late in the year, Caldwell commanded his men in the Mine Run campaign. In early 1864, he led his men in demonstrations along the Rapidan River.

In March 1864, during the reorganization of the Army of the Potomac in anticipation of Ulysses S. Grant's campaign against Robert E. Lee, Caldwell was unceremoniously relieved of his divisional command and sent to Washington to serve on military boards. He engaged in that type of duty for the remainder of the war. In April 1865 he was selected as one of the officers to escort Abraham Lincoln's body back to Springfield, Illinois. Caldwell remained in the army until being mustered out of the volunteer service in 1866.

After the war, Caldwell returned to Maine, where he practiced law briefly. After serving as the adjutant general for the state, he embarked on a diplomatic career when he was appointed consul to Valparaiso, Chile. In 1874 he was appointed U.S. minister to Uruguay. He returned to the United States in 1882. He lived in Kansas for more than a decade before accepting another diplomatic post in 1897 as consul to Costa Rica. He

remained there for twelve years before retiring in 1909. He died on 31 August 1912 in Calais, Maine.

—*David S. Heidler and Jeanne T. Heidler*

See also Antietam, Battle of; Bristoe Station, Battle of; Fredericksburg, Battle of.

For further reading:

Brady, Robert. *The Story of One Regiment: The Eleventh Maine Infantry Volunteers in the War of the Rebellion* (1896).

Maxfield, Albert. *Roster and Statistical Record of Company D of the Eleventh Regiment Maine Infantry Volunteers: With a Sketch of Its Services in the War of the Rebellion* (1890).

CALHOUN, JOHN CALDWELL
(1782–1850)

U.S. senator, cabinet member, presidential candidate

John Caldwell Calhoun was born in 1782 near Abbeville, South Carolina. Calhoun's educational opportunities were limited, although they were advanced by the occasional tutelage offered by his brother-in-law, Reverend Moses Waddel. After his parents' death and a period of self-education, Calhoun entered Yale College, studying under the arch-Federalist Dr. Timothy Dwight. He proceeded to study law for two years under Judge Tapping Reeve at the Litchfield Law School, the most prominent institution devoted to legal training during this period. Returning to his native South Carolina to practice law, a pursuit he considered "both dry and laborious," Calhoun was married and served two terms in the South Carolina legislature before being elected to the U.S. House of Representatives in 1811. As a congressman, Calhoun continued to embody republican principles and acquired a reputation as a moral statesman who regarded republicanism and patriotism as synonymous: he supported the War of 1812; he revised James Madison's original national bank proposal and backed limited internal improvements; and he continued to praise a free economy and a regime founded on "reason and equity" that was surrounded by a world of "fraud, violence or accident."

As many have noted, Calhoun supported "national" legislation during his early career, encouraging scholars to inappropriately divide his life into stages based on his perceived degree of attachment to a centralized political order. The rising protectionist spirit in America would also affirm Calhoun's wisdom in supporting the 1816 tariff, even though he held subsequent tariffs in disdain. In 1817, President Monroe asked Calhoun to assume the helm at the War Department, where he served until 1825.

Calhoun was generally considered too philosophical for such a practical post, but he accepted the appointment out of a republican sense of duty. In the course of two terms in office, Calhoun completely reorganized and revitalized the War Department and its staff, resolved its financial problems resulting from the War of 1812, and demonstrated a new, more compassionate approach to Native American affairs. Calhoun also began reforming West Point through a new spirit of openness in terms of admissions and administrative procedures. Calhoun has been described as the ablest war secretary the government had before Jefferson Davis in 1853.

A broad spectrum of supporters encouraged Calhoun's candidacy for president in 1824 against his fellow cabinet members William H. Crawford and John Quincy Adams, Speaker of the House Henry Clay, and war hero and newly elected senator Andrew Jackson. Initially entering the presidential field, Calhoun realized he lacked adequate support and withdrew after Pennsylvania nominated Andrew Jackson. Accepting the vice-presidential nomination, Calhoun was elected by a large majority. The results in the presidential contest between Jackson and Adams were inconclusive in terms of the electoral and popular vote, and the election was thrown into the House of Representatives, where Jackson's nemesis Clay served as speaker. In an unusual series of events, Clay came to Adams's aid, with the House vote securing the election for Adams. The president-elect proceeded to appoint Clay secretary of state. Many Americans considered the supposed arrangement between Clay and Adams a "corrupt bargain." Calhoun believed the "corrupt bargain" had disrupted the balance between preserving liberty and assuming power explicitly reserved to the people; "improperly acquired" power would doubtless be "improperly used," he opined. Calhoun and either Adams or his representative engaged in a pseudonymous debate about the sources of political power. Calhoun began to separate himself from what he considered to be Adams's abuses of office, and he supported General Andrew Jackson in 1828. It was as part of this ticket, later known as the Democratic Party, that Calhoun was elected vice president in 1828.

The falling apart of the political union between Calhoun and Jackson is one of the most remarkable events in American politics. Calhoun had hoped Jackson would assume the republican political mantle, but his expectations were not fulfilled. Several controversies were ignited that raised questions about the corruptibility of the administration. The most important of these concerned Mrs. Margaret Eaton, wife of Jackson's dear friend and secretary of war, John H. Eaton. Out of a sense of propriety, Mrs. Calhoun and most ladies in Washington refused to receive her into their homes. After John Eaton made the controversy public, Calhoun was forced to respond; he stated that his wife's actions amounted to a moral stance and not an act of snobbery, as it had been called.

As a result of the dispute with Jackson over the protective tariff, Calhoun resigned as vice president and was elected to the Senate. In an attempt to moderate the crisis posed by tariff-related concerns and the "Force Bill" in 1832, Calhoun questioned the prospect of preserving the union by force, and not relying on the "harmonious aggregate of the States." Up to this point in his career as a statesman, Calhoun had made few statements regarding slavery. Troubled by the increasing influence of abolitionism and the rise of sectional conflict, Calhoun would devote the remainder of his life to defending the South and attempting to avoid conflict. Retiring from the Senate in 1843, he unsuccessfully pursued the presidency for the last time. In 1844, Calhoun was appointed secretary of state.

Returning to the Senate in 1845, Calhoun served as a thoughtful critic of the war with Mexico, and he suggested that the conflict would encourage disharmony between the North and South. In 1844, Calhoun had helped contain the truly revolutionary Bluffton movement, composed of his fellow South Carolinians. Many leading South Carolina politicians threatened drastic responses to a troublesome new tariff and the questionable status of Texas. Calhoun's success at moderating the conflict demonstrated both his restraint in a crisis situation and his lack of control over the politicians often described as "Calhounites" due to their intimate ties to the statesman.

Published after his death, Calhoun's two treatises on political theory and American constitutionalism, *Disquisition* and *Discourse*, demonstrate his hope that America could avoid the pending conflict. Calhoun's persistent concern about the unequal treatment of the South would, he feared, lead to increased regional tensions and to civil war. His last years were spent attempting to unify the South and avoid strife. On 31 March 1850, Calhoun died in Washington, D.C. In death, Calhoun became a source of inspiration for the Confederate government, its leaders, and the South. Calhoun's understanding, albeit imperfect, of restraint within political order remains one of the most important characteristics of his political thought and his achievement as a statesman. In Calhoun's interpretation, the interposing and amending power of the states implicit in the Constitution could only augment authentic popular rule by allowing for a greater diffusion of authority. Calhoun's purpose was the preservation of the original balance of authority and the fortification of the American political system against the obstacles it faced.

—*H. Lee Cheek, Jr.*

See also South Carolina.
For further reading:
Wilson, Clyde N. *John C. Calhoun: A Bibliography* (1990).
Wiltse, Charles M. *John C. Calhoun: Sectionalist, 1840–1850* (1951).

CALIFORNIA

Californiaʼs request for admission to the Union in 1850 contributed substantially to the sectional crisis that led to the Civil War. Bitter arguments over its slave or free status paralyzed the Congress and brought the Union to the brink of dissolution in 1850. The compromise that was eventually hammered out preserved the free state status that had been the desire of the majority at Californiaʼs constitutional convention in 1849. Nonetheless, pro-Southern sympathies continued to fester in southern California and made their political will felt through the state Democratic Party. In particular, Californiaʼs Tennessee-born senator William M. Gwin, through the California Fugitive Slave Act of 1851, made efforts to have fugitive slaves returned who had fled to the state before the advent of statehood.

As the sectional crisis escalated in the 1850s, Californiaʼs emerging political establishment took note, but regional issues seemed to be predominant. The anti-slavery Republican Party did well in California when local hero John C. Frémont was its standard bearer in 1856, but Abraham Lincolnʼs candidacy drew considerable opposition from a variety of the stateʼs residents and Lincoln carried the state only narrowly in the election of 1860.

The secession crisis of the winter of 1860–1861 found Californians on both sides of the issue. Newspapers such as the *Bulletin* and *Alta California* in San Francisco and the *Bee* and *Union* in Sacramento were staunch supporters of the Union. Secession sentiment found its voice in such papers as *The San Francisco Herald, Marysville Gazette*, the *Los Angeles Star*, and the *Sonora Democrat*. Politicians ranged on both sides of the issue. Still others such as Representative John C. Burch and Governor John B. Welles called for the creation of a Pacific Republic, and a flag-raising ceremony in Stockton in 1861 seemed to be the high-water mark of this impulse. The state legislature passed a resolution on 17 May 1861 (the anniversary of the convocation of the Constitutional Convention) that the "people of California are devoted to the Constitution and Union now in an hour of trial and peril." In the elections of 1861, a coalition of War Democrats and Republicans elected Californiaʼs first Republican governor, the staunchly pro-Unionist Leland Stanford. Although Stanford was careful to distance himself from support of antislavery politics, his strong support of the Union guaranteed Californiaʼs loyalty.

Much early scholarship on Civil War California suggests that the state was a hotbed of Southern sympathy and that there were serious dangers that the state would bolt the Union. The presence of future Confederate general Albert Sidney Johnston at the presidio in San Francisco, the existence of pro-Confederate societies such as the Knights of the Golden Circle and the Committee of Thirty, and "plots" to use armed schooners such as the *Chapman* as a privateer under Confederate letters of marque led many to believe that a serious possibility existed of California secessionists detaching the southland from the Union. Indeed, pockets of disloyalty existed, and concerns about a Confederate invasion of the lower part of the state appear to have flourished for a time. However, more recent scholarship has challenged this view and suggested that there never was a serious possibility that California would leave the Union. Indeed, estimates suggest that only 7 percent of Californiaʼs population came from the seceded states. Further, historians such as Ronald Woolsey have suggested that anti-Union sensibilities among southern Californians stemmed not from an affection for the Confederacy, but out of a constellation of local and regional issues related to concerns about statesʼ rights, economic issues, frustration with efforts at reform, and the intricacies of party politics.

Unionist sentiment was strong and well entrenched throughout the state. A leading apostle of Unionist sentiment and a major support for the U.S. Sanitary Commission was Unitarian minister Thomas Starr King. Kingʼs eloquence praised the Union cause and mobilized hundreds of Californians to donate to the agency. In all, California sent about 15,000 men to the Union army, including two regiments of cavalry and eight of infantry. Some of these men served in Massachusetts and Washington Territory. The California Battalion, headed by Lincolnʼs friend Edward D. Baker, saw service in other venues. The deployment of Federal troops to other locations in the East gave local California militia an opportunity to protect the Indian frontier.

California gold, about \$15 million in all, shored up the Federal treasuries during the war and helped to stabilize U.S. currency. This gift, more than the various volunteers, was Californiaʼs most important gift to the Union cause.

The Civil War had important implications for California that would help to reshape its destiny. The enactment of the Transcontinental Railroad Bill providing for the construction of a major railroad line across the country with Sacramento as its western terminus had significant implications for the state. Pro-Unionist politicians, such as Leland Stanford, and other loyal Californians, such as Collis P. Huntington, would benefit dramatically from the new line, and these bands of steel would ensure Californiaʼs linkage to the larger republic. The onset of the Civil War found California to be a remote province of a vast nation. The politics of the war left it with a new political configuration and the origins of the economic base that would provide for its future economic dominance.

—*Steven M. Avella*

See also: Baker, Edward Dickinson.
For further reading:
Gilbert, Benjamin F. "California and the Civil War, Bibliographical Essay." *California Historical Society Quarterly* (1961).

———. "The Confederate Minority in California." *California Historical Society Quarterly* (1941).

Hunt, Aurora. *The Army of the Pacific, 1860–1866* (1951).

Lewis, Oscar. *The War in the Far West: 1861–1865* (1961).

McAffee, Ward M. "California's House Divided." *Civil War History* (1987).

Posner, Russell M. "Thomas Starr King and the Mercy Million." *California Historical Society Quarterly* (1964).

Stanley, Gerald. "Civil War Politics in California." *Southern California Quarterly* (1982).

———. "Slavery and the Origins of the Republican Party in California." *Southern California Quarterly* (1978).

Woolsey, Ronald C. "Disunion or Dissent?" *Southern California Quarterly* (1984).

———. "The Politics of a Lost Cause." *California History* (1991).

CAMERON, JAMES
(1801–1861)
Union colonel

James Cameron, a younger brother of Simon Cameron (Lincoln's first secretary of war), was born in Maytown, Lancaster County, Pennsylvania. After a rudimentary education, James was apprenticed to Simon, who was then in the publishing business. By 1827, James had settled in Williamsport, where he became copublisher of the Lycoming *Gazette*. In 1829, he returned to Lancaster, where he took control of *The Political Sentinel*, which he owned while studying law in the office of James

Simon Cameron (*Library of Congress*)

Buchanan. In 1839, Cameron was appointed superintendent of motive power on the Columbia Railroad. Four years later, he was named deputy attorney general of the mayor's court in Lancaster.

When the Northern Central Railroad began construction of a line along the West Branch of the Susquehanna River, Cameron secured a management position in the company. During this time, he purchased a farm just south of Milton. Today, his mansion is owned by the Milton Historical Society.

When war erupted in 1861, Cameron, thanks to his brother Simon's influence, received a colonel's commission and was assigned to the 79th New York. As part of Colonel William T. Sherman's brigade, the 79th took part in First Bull Run on 21 July. Colonel Cameron was the inspiration of bravery to his raw recruits, personally leading a series of charges up the slope of Henry House Hill, trying to save the abandoned Union batteries in position there. During one of these attacks, Cameron was hit in the chest and instantly killed. His men carried the body to the rear, but abandoned it when the Union army began its disorganized retreat.

Cameron's body was buried on the field and remained there until Union occupation of the area in March 1862. At that time, it was identified by the peculiar buckskin shirt the colonel had worn under his uniform. The bones were disinterred, placed in a proper casket, and taken to the Cameron Family Plot in the Lewisburg, Pennsylvania, Cemetery. There, on 18 March, it was buried with full military honors, attended by a host of dignitaries. In 1874, the city of Sunbury erected its Civil War monument, surmounted by a lifesized figure of the colonel.

—*Richard A. Sauers*

See also Bull Run, First Battle of; Cameron, Simon.
For further reading:
Barto, William N. "James Cameron First Northern Colonel To Die In Civil War." *Milton Standard* (1964).

"Biographical Annals." *The Miltonian* (1889).

De Fontaine, F. G. "Death of Colonel Cameron." *Philadelphia Weekly Times* (1883).

"Obsequies of the Late Colonel Cameron." *Philadelphia Daily Evening Bulletin* (1862).

CAMERON, SIMON
(1799–1889)
U.S. secretary of war

Born in Maytown, Pennsylvania, to Charles Cameron and Martha Pfoutz Cameron, Simon Cameron was educated locally before being apprenticed to a journalist in Harrisburg, Pennsylvania. During the 1820s he worked at various newspapers in Pennsylvania and Washington, D.C., and for a time was a part owner of one. In addition to his brief journalism

career, Cameron also took an early interest in national and Pennsylvania politics. An early supporter of John C. Calhoun, Cameron supported the South Carolinian in the state convention of 1824. A staunch supporter of the protective tariff for American industry, Cameron turned against Calhoun later in the decade.

In the meantime, Cameron, in addition to his political interests, was diversifying his business activities, investing in a wide range of enterprises, including canals, railroads, and iron. He always saw his political activities as being tied to his business interests and supported candidates who he believed would advance his economic status. In 1832 he led the Pennsylvania delegation to the Democratic National Convention in Baltimore.

Until 1837, when he served as a delegate to the Pennsylvania Constitutional Convention, Cameron devoted most of his time to his business interests. By then he had become somewhat of a protégé of powerful Pennsylvania Democrat James Buchanan and, through Buchanan's efforts, in 1837 Cameron was appointed commissioner to the Winnebago Indians. Accused of using his position to cheat the Indians out of part of their treaty payments, Cameron was replaced shortly after assuming the position. The charges were never substantiated, but the incident damaged his chances for political office for a time.

In the mid-1840s, Cameron began courting the Whig Party in Pennsylvania in the hopes of gaining that minority party's support for his bid to become a U.S. senator. Such efforts succeeded in gaining him election in 1845, but it caused many of his fellow Democrats, including Buchanan, to doubt his loyalty to the party.

In the Senate, serving the unexpired term of James Buchanan, who had been appointed secretary of state, Cameron gave a glimpse of the master political manipulator he was to become. His occasional support, however, for Whig measures made him suspect in Democratic eyes, and his membership in the Democratic Party made support for him in the state legislature (in which by that time the Whigs had gained a majority) an impossibility. Therefore, in 1849 he returned home a private citizen.

After returning to Pennsylvania, Cameron worked to create a political machine to control Pennsylvania politics. He hoped to exert sufficient control to challenge the power of his old friend James Buchanan. In 1852 he worked for Lewis Cass's nomination for the presidency in opposition to Buchanan, an effort that was partially responsible for the Democratic nomination of Franklin Pierce. By the mid-1850s, aspiring Democratic candidates were seeking Cameron's support in election bids to even minor offices.

In 1855 Cameron ran again for the Senate, this time courting the support of the American Party (the "Know-Nothings"), but he once again fell short. After this failure, he aligned himself more with the American Party, which allowed him by 1856 to quickly make the transition to the new Republican Party organization in

the state. He worked hard, though unsuccessfully, for John C. Frémont's presidential candidacy in 1856 in opposition to the Democratic nominee, James Buchanan. These efforts paid off among Republicans and his old American Party allies when they combined in January 1857 to elect Cameron to the U.S. Senate. This election went a long way toward increasing Cameron's power within Pennsylvania.

One of the biggest issues Cameron championed in the Senate was the protective tariff, especially in the midst of the economic crisis that began in 1857. He also pushed for less government spending. His popularity with the rank-and-file workers of his home state because of these stands may have had some influence on his decision to seek the Republican nomination for president in 1860.

As an early move in this direction, supporters established Cameron clubs in Pennsylvania and, with less success, in other states. The biggest obstacle to his success became his lack of support outside Pennsylvania. At the Republican National Convention in Chicago, Cameron operatives ultimately made a deal with Abraham Lincoln's managers that if the Cameron people would throw their votes to Lincoln on the second ballot, Lincoln would offer Cameron a cabinet post.

Once he was elected, Lincoln was not so sure about the arrangement. He knew the stories of Cameron's political dealings and allegations of corruption, but he also knew how important it would be to have the support of Pennsylvania for his administration. On 31 December 1860, Lincoln sent a message stating that he would offer Cameron either Treasury or War. Cameron made the message public, but Lincoln quickly had second thoughts. However, the need for Pennsylvania support, especially in light of the growing secession crisis, caused Lincoln to reconsider yet again, and Cameron was formally nominated secretary of the War Department on 5 March 1861.

Cameron assumed control of an antiquated War Department that did not have a fraction of the bureaucracy needed to manage the coming conflict. Despite his previous business experience, Cameron approached his monumental undertaking tentatively. When Secretary of State William Henry Seward stepped in to try to bring some order, Cameron became angry.

To complicate Cameron's ever-mounting difficulties, he also had to deal with thousands of office seekers. As a thoroughgoing practitioner of the spoils system, he should have been prepared, and he did become quite famous for rewarding his friends with lucrative jobs.

On military situations, beginning with the Fort Sumter crisis, Cameron showed little if any leadership. During the cabinet discussions regarding whether or not Fort Sumter should be resupplied, Cameron tended to support Seward's and General Winfield Scott's position that the fort should be evacuated. Other than expressing that view, he took little interest in the matter.

Once the war began and states began answering their quotas for the 75,000 volunteers Lincoln had called for, Cameron's office found it impossible to keep up with the paperwork of processing the volunteers. When it came to putting these soldiers in the field, Cameron showed little interest in military strategy and had difficulties dealing with the egos of his generals. He seemed to be at a loss to handle the legal difficulties posed by the actions of generals like Benjamin Butler and John C. Frémont when these officers tried to confiscate or free the slaves in their districts.

Cameron's War Department is most famous for the corruption that ran rampant as a result of the proliferation of government contracts. Undoubtedly the primary reason for the mismanagement of these contracts was that Cameron and his staff were too overwhelmed with the amount of paperwork involved to oversee properly the administration of government contracts. As a result, many soldiers were issued inferior weapons, inadequate clothing, and bad food, often at terribly inflated prices.

Although many of these problems did not become nationally known until after Cameron left the cabinet, the president was aware of many of the complaints. Then, to compound Lincoln's growing disappointment with his secretary, Cameron in his annual report of December 1861 advocated the use of former slaves as soldiers, a complete diversion from Lincoln's stated policy on the matter. Putting such a statement in his report without consulting Lincoln was bad enough, but then Cameron made the report public before Lincoln had even seen it. The president forced Cameron to change the report, omitting the recommendation regarding arming former slaves, and then pushed the secretary into accepting the nomination to the recently vacated ministership to Russia. To salve Cameron's political dignity, Lincoln did it in such a way as to make it appear that Cameron had wanted to leave the cabinet.

During the previous few months, Cameron had been associated more and more with the ranks of the Radical Republicans, a circumstance that eased his confirmation as minister to Russia. In the meantime, however, his political enemies were working steadily at investigating his administration of the War Department. The results of the investigation brought about his censure by the House of Representatives before he left for Russia.

Even though he was publicly defended by the president, Cameron left for Russia in May 1862 under a cloud. Almost as soon as he arrived in Russia he began asking for a furlough. Part of his reason for wanting to come home so soon was his wife's poor health, but he also undoubtedly wanted to be in Pennsylvania for the elections of 1862. When he received permission to return home, he did so immediately and, while still holding his diplomatic post, stood as a candidate for the U.S. Senate. Even after losing his bid, he showed no

desire to return to Russia. President Lincoln finally extracted a resignation from him in February 1863. To add insult to injury, shortly after his resignation Cameron was accused of bribery in the late Senate race, and the state lower house concluded that the charges were true. He was never prosecuted in the case.

Although he no longer held a political position, Cameron still remained active in Pennsylvania politics. He worked behind the scenes for his candidates, and, beginning at the end of 1863, he started efforts on behalf of Lincoln's renomination. These efforts, along with his exertions for Lincoln's reelection, brought him back into the president's good graces and increased his ability to mete out patronage positions in Pennsylvania.

For the next few years, including the first two after the end of the war, Cameron concerned himself primarily with strengthening his Pennsylvania political machine. Initially he supported the efforts of Lincoln's successor, Andrew Johnson, but he broke with the president as Johnson's popularity declined. In early 1867, Cameron reentered the national political arena when he was elected from Pennsylvania to the U.S. Senate.

In the Senate, Cameron again joined the ranks of the Radicals, strongly supporting the impeachment and unsuccessful effort to remove Andrew Johnson from office. He also worked for the nomination and election of Ulysses S. Grant as president in the election of 1868. Throughout Grant's eight years in office, Cameron's biggest challenge was to retain control of the Pennsylvania machine he had created and to squelch the growing reform movement in the state. One of the ways he sought to perpetuate his legacy was to gradually move his son, J. Donald Cameron, into his position of leadership. He achieved part of that goal in May 1876, when his son was named secretary of war. In early 1877, Cameron resigned his Senate seat and arranged for his son to win the special election to fill the seat.

In retirement Cameron traveled, worked on his country estate, and remained interested in Pennsylvania politics. He died on his estate, "Donegal," outside Maytown, Pennsylvania, on 26 June 1889.

—*David S. Heidler and Jeanne T. Heidler*

See also Lincoln, Abraham; Pennsylvania; Seward, William Henry.

For further reading:

Bradley, Erwin Stanley. *Simon Cameron; Lincoln's Secretary of War, A Political Biography* (1966).

CAMP CHASE
Union prison

After the fall of Fort Sumter, thousands of Northerners responded to President Abraham Lincoln's call for volunteers. Columbus, located near the geographic center of Ohio, was a logical

rendezvous point for the state's soldiers and in short order became overcrowded with raw recruits. Responding to the crisis, Governor William Dennison leased a 165-acre tract located four miles west of the city. The camp of instruction—soon turned over to the War Department—was originally styled Camp Jackson, but on 20 June 1861 it was renamed in honor of one of Ohio's most notable public figures, Treasury Secretary Salmon P. Chase.

Camp Chase performed a multitude of roles during the Civil War. As a point of muster and instructional camp, it harbored such notables as James Garfield, Rutherford B. Hayes, and William McKinley. It also saw service from 1861 to 1863 as a detention site where paroled Federal soldiers awaited exchange before returning to active service. In addition, it was a mustering-out post for soldiers whose enlistment terms had expired. But its lasting image is that of a stockade for Confederate military and political prisoners, a purpose for which it was not officially designed.

The first prisoners, twenty-three in number, arrived at Camp Chase on 5 July 1861, but were soon returned to their homes in Virginia's Kanawha Valley. More and more captives arrived in the following months, until by November nearly 300 were held within the camp's wooden ramparts. By April 1862 the number swelled into the thousands after the Confederate surrenders of Fort Donelson and Island Number 10. To meet the growing numbers, three separate stockades were constructed, each adjoining one another at the camp's southeastern edge on fewer than thirteen acres of land.

Discipline in the prison's early months, however, could not be characterized as severe. Captured Confederate officers were permitted to wear their swords and sidearms, retained the services of their African-American body servants, and were often seen wandering the streets of Columbus in full uniform. Such transgressions resulted in the transfer of most officers to the Johnson's Island prison facility on Lake Erie and a necessary tightening of rules within the camp itself.

By 1863 conditions in Camp Chase had deteriorated substantially. Nearly 8,000 prisoners and approximately 4,000 Federal soldiers awaiting parole jammed the 130-acre facility. Poor drainage turned camp streets into muddy quagmires. Sanitation was typically substandard, with typhoid fever and dysentery common. Smallpox also swept through the stockade, killing nearly 500 prisoners in one month alone.

In mid-1863 Federal authorities suspended the parole system, or cartel, in response to the Confederate refusal to exchange captured black soldiers and alleged Rebel parole violations. Public opinion too came to demand harsh treatment for Confederate prisoners, especially as reports of wretched conditions at Southern stockades reached Northern domiciles. By 1864 food, clothing, and blankets were withheld from the captives, and purchases from camp sutlers were prohibited. Under these trying conditions, several escape attempts occurred—some successful—and a conspiracy to free the camp's prisoners was foiled.

As the war drew to a close, the number of prisoners at Camp Chase plummeted from a wartime high of nearly 9,000 to 3,400 by the end of May 1865. By July all remaining captives were finally released. After the war, the camp was destroyed, leaving only a cemetery containing the graves of 2,260 Confederate prisoners. In all, some 25,000 Confederate captives passed through Camp Chase's gates, as well as over 150,000 Federal soldiers.

—*Christopher S. Stowe*

See also Johnson's Island; Prisons, U.S.A.

For further reading:

Hesseltine, William Best. *Civil War Prisons: A Study in War Psychology* (1930).

King, John H. *Three Hundred Days in a Yankee Prison; Reminiscences of War Life, Captivity, Imprisonment at Camp Chase* (1904).

Knauss, William H. *The Story of Camp Chase, A History of the Prison and Its Cemetery, Together with Other Cemeteries Where Confederate Prisoners Are Buried, Etc* (1906).

McCormick, Robert W. "About Six Acres of Land: Camp Chase, Civil War Prison." *Timeline* (1994).

Shriver, Philip R. *Ohio's Military Prisons in the Civil War* (1964).

CAMP DOUGLAS, ILLINOIS
Union prison

Built in southeastern Chicago in the early fall of 1861 as a training depot for Union soldiers, Camp Douglas (named for Stephen A. Douglas, who had died in June 1861) was converted to a Union prison in 1862. Surrounded by a six-foot-high stockade fence, the barracks of very flimsy construction were originally intended for the new recruits to occupy for only a short time. Located on low, swampy ground, the camp was not a particularly healthy place even for the Union soldiers who originally occupied it. Because of the topography, sewage disposal was never adequate, and water quality was very poor.

Since the camp was not built as a prison, security there was rather poor when the first prisoners from the surrender of Fort Donelson began arriving in late February 1862. The citizens of Chicago were alarmed at the few guards provided and the resulting large number of escapes. There is no evidence, however, that any of the escapees ever harmed any local citizens.

When those first prisoners arrived, the camp still housed recruits preparing for active duty. As a result, when the prison population ballooned to 4,372 Confederate privates and noncommissioned officers at the end of February 1862, the commander of the camp, Colonel James Mulligan, was at somewhat of a loss as to how to handle the overflow. To compound these difficulties, Chicago in winter is cold in the best of circumstances, but Camp Douglas was in a particularly exposed position, and the camp's one water pump frequently froze. As a result of these conditions, about 13 percent of the original Fort Donelson prisoners died.

Relief and philanthropic organizations in Chicago and surrounding areas learned of the plight of the prisoners and began taking up collections of money and goods to ease the men's suffering. These efforts, however, caused much grumbling among the Union soldiers at the camp, who often took the relief supplies for themselves.

By the end of spring 1862, the camp housed 8,962 prisoners. The stables had to be used to handle the overflow, and escapes increased. Some of the men were aided by Southern sympathizers in Chicago. As a result of the escapes and the conditions at the camp, it quickly gained a very bad reputation not only among the prisoners but also to U.S. Commissary General of Prisoners Colonel William Hoffman and to the U.S. Sanitary Commission.

Mulligan, no doubt a bad administrator, was nevertheless hampered by a very poor budget that did not allow him to improve the drainage situation at the camp. His successor, Colonel Joseph H. Tucker, who assumed command in June 1862, was an equally poor administrator, but like Mulligan pleaded for the funds to improve the sewers and to build more barracks.

Tucker became so frustrated with the number of escapes during the summer of 1862, and the obvious help the escapees were receiving from people in the community, that he declared martial law in the area around the camp. Twenty-five prisoners escaped on 23 July, and although most were eventually recaptured, Tucker responded by arresting some of the local citizens he suspected of being involved.

Because of the prisoner cartel negotiated in the summer of 1862, Tucker's problems seemed to be over. He began to prepare to release his prisoners at the end of August and to transport them to the parole point of Cairo, Illinois. If the prisoners took an oath of allegiance they could be released immediately. Almost 1,000 did so, and more than 200 of those men were recruited into the Union army. The remainder, with the exception of those too ill to travel, were shipped out in September.

In the fall of 1862, Camp Douglas returned to the function of a training camp for recruits. Very soon, however, it took on a new role as a camp for Federal troops paroled after their capture by Thomas J. "Stonewall" Jackson at Harper's Ferry. About 8,000 of these Union soldiers had to remain at Camp Douglas until they were officially exchanged. These men, serving under the command of Brigadier General Daniel Tyler, had to endure the same bad conditions that the Confederate prisoners had lived through the previous winter, spring, and summer and as a result became mutinous. Tyler had to bring in regular

Federal troops to quell the riots. Luckily for everyone, exchanges were completed, and the parolees left the camp by the end of November 1862.

On 6 January 1863, Brigadier General Jacob Ammen assumed command of Camp Douglas. Shortly thereafter, he began receiving Confederate prisoners from the battle of Stones River. There were about 1,500 in the first batch to arrive. Soon another large group arrived from the surrender of Fort Hindman. Conditions at the camp were no better than before. Ammen was better at administration and security than his predecessors, but without additional funds, he could do little about the sanitation and overcrowding. As a result, smallpox and other diseases were rampant. Fortunately for the prisoners, another exchange was arranged, and all but the sick were gone by 3 April. Not so fortunately for the civilian population along their route to the exchange point at City Point, Virginia, the prisoners took smallpox with them, and it spread to several Northern cities through which the prisoners passed.

Since the Union intended to resume using the camp for new recruits, efforts were made in the spring and summer to improve the sewage system at the camp. By August, with the improvements not yet complete, Union victories throughout the summer forced the Union government to begin using the camp for a prison once again. The new commander for the camp was Colonel Charles V. De Land. Unfortunately for the hapless De Land, not only were conditions still very poor, but some of his new prisoners included members of John Hunt Morgan's infamous raiders. These men proved especially adept at finding ways out of the camp, and under De Land's command there were more than 150 escapes from Camp Douglas.

Partly due to De Land's problems, General William W. Orme assumed command of Camp Douglas on 23 December 1863. Orme tried to bring order to the prison ration and clothing allotment system and to improve security. Barracks were moved away from the stockade and were elevated off the ground to prevent tunneling. These efforts were somewhat successful, and escapes decreased.

In May 1864, Colonel Benjamin J. Sweet assumed command of a more orderly and cleaner Camp Douglas. Sweet was a very strict disciplinarian who increased punishments and cut rations. As a result, escape attempts increased. Throughout the end of 1864, rumors abounded of various conspiracies to free the prisoners. Some of the rumors had Confederate raiders coming out of Canada; others centered around Copperhead groups in the Midwest planning an attack on the camp. Sweet used the rumors as an excuse to round up Southern sympathizers in the Chicago area and imprison them at Camp Douglas. No attack was ever made.

With the war over, orders were received on 8 May

1865 to administer the oath of allegiance to the prisoners and to make arrangements for them to receive transportation to their homes. It took several weeks to process the prisoners, and by the end of July 1865 one of the most infamous Northern prisons was closed.

—*David S. Heidler and Jeanne T. Heidler*

See also Ammen, Jacob; Prisoners of War; Prisons, C. S. A.

For further reading:

Levy, George. *To Die in Chicago: Confederate Prisoners at Camp Douglas, 1862–1865* (1994).

CAMP JACKSON MASSACRE
(10 May 1861)

Missouri governor Claiborne Fox Jackson not only refused to provide the state's quota of four infantry regiments toward Lincoln's call for 75,000 volunteers, but also designed to break his state out of the Union. The state convention did not follow him, but secessionist "Minute Men" started arming all over the state. Unionists also took matters into their own hands. Politician Francis Preston Blair and Captain Nathaniel Lyon, the recently appointed commander of the St. Louis Arsenal, were in the forefront of the Unionist response, and the large group of veteran revolutionaries from Europe, notably those of the German Turner and Schuetzen-Vereine, were also involved. In 1848 and 1849, these revolutionaries had overthrown local and state authorities to advance grand national aspirations and democratic ideas in their native lands. In 1861, they were prepared to do so again in their adoptive country. Franz Sigel, Henry Boernstein, Dr. Adam Hammer, and Peter Osterhaus were pivotal characters among these revolutionists.

After forming the required Union regiments (including a battery of artillery that was attached to the 3d Regiment, "Lyon's Fahnenwacht") and five more regiments of Reserves (later referred to as Home Guards), the pro-Union forces in St. Louis proved much stronger than the secessionist element. Almost 80 percent of their number were German, with the balance drawn from the Anglo-American, French, Czech, and Hungarian population in St. Louis and adjacent counties.

Early in May, Governor Jackson called the militia into camp. This was his right, but many pro-Union officers had already left the ranks, and the secessionist leanings of the rest were well known, so Unionists in St. Louis feared an attempt to seize the local arsenal. The Missouri Volunteer Militia assembled in Camp Jackson on the fringe of St. Louis under the command of Brigadier General Daniel M. Frost. While most of the arms in the arsenal had been shipped to Illinois for safekeeping, other weapons arrived at Camp Jackson. Some came out of the arsenal in Liberty, Missouri, that had been seized by secessionists. A particular shipment, supposedly of heavy arms,

was used by Lyon to justify a move against Camp Jackson on 10 May 1861. Apparently stories about Nathaniel Lyon in woman's clothing conducting a reconnaissance of the camp before making this decision are not true.

On the morning of the 10th, many of the Union men still marched in shirtsleeves because no regulation uniforms had been issued. There was also a dearth of cartridge boxes, and most belts were condemned material from the Mexican-American War. Still, the Union regiments far outnumbered the state militia, and they were definitely better armed. Frost's militia—numbering between 800 and 1,200, according to varying sources—were divided into two regiments commanded by John Knapp and John S. Bowen.

About 3 P.M., the Unionists surrounded Camp Jackson, and Lyon sent a note to Frost demanding his surrender. Frost complied, his men were disarmed, and preparations were made to march them away from the camp. Several companies from Sigel's 3d Missouri occupied the camp. Meanwhile, a crowd (including William T. Sherman, still a civilian) had gathered, mostly out of curiosity. Some members of the crowd, however, were armed and meant to disrupt the capture of the camp. Before the column got under way, an altercation between Union soldiers and the mob, joined by some militia who had escaped from the camp, flared into violence.

It remains uncertain what precisely happened in the ensuing Camp Jackson massacre. Some soldiers, unnerved by verbal abuse and pelted with debris, started firing. Boernstein's 2d Missouri appears to have done most of the shooting, yet one of the first victims struck by a bullet was Captain Constantin Blandovski of Sigel's regiment. According to local newspapers, twenty-eight civilians were killed, including a woman and a 14-year-old girl. At least two soldiers were also killed. After the shooting had ceased, the captured militia were marched to the arsenal and incarcerated there. Soon they were allowed to take the oath of allegiance and go home, but many went to join the secessionist forces being assembled by Governor Jackson instead.

The Camp Jackson incident forcibly consolidated the Union position in St. Louis and subdued the secessionist element, but its overall effect was negative. The reaction of pro-Southern newspapers was predictable, but even the Union press exaggerated the scale of the violence, probably out of anti-German feelings. The result was to drive many wavering advocates of compromise such as Sterling Price into the secessionist camp. The murder of several German and Unionist citizens in St. Louis and the massacre of a Home Guard company in Cole County can also be attributed to feelings aroused by the incident.

Some evidence suggests that Camp Jackson was on the verge of being dismantled at the time of Lyon's attack. Ordnance captured from the camp certainly indicates that the assembled "Minute Men" were no immediate threat to the Union cause. The operation may have been unnecessary, and its bloodshed was even more tragic for this reason.

—*Wolfgang Hochbruck*

See also Jackson, Claiborne Fox; Lyon, Nathaniel; Missouri; Osterhaus, Peter; Price, Sterling; Sigel, Franz.

For further reading:

Boernstein, Henry. *Memoirs of a Nobody* (1997).

Rombauer, Robert J. *The Union Cause in St. Louis in 1861* (1909).

Rowan, Steven. "The Second Baden Revolution: Missouri 1861." In *1848/49 and the United States* (in press).

Winter, William. *The Civil War in St. Louis* (1995).

CAMP MORTON
Union prison

After President Abraham Lincoln's call for volunteers on 15 April 1861, Governor Oliver P. Morton of Indiana set aside the Indiana State Fairgrounds, which had been erected at Indianapolis in 1852, to serve as a recruitment and training camp for Indiana's volunteers. At that time the fairgrounds were informally given the name Camp Morton, a designation that would become official when the camp was later converted to a prisoner-of-war camp. The camp remained a training facility until the end of the year.

In early 1862 Camp Morton was converted into a prison for captured Confederates. The conversion consisted of placing a fence around the exhibition buildings that would be used to house the prisoners. Because most of these halls had been used as livestock exhibit buildings in the days when the grounds housed the fair, they contained no floors and thin walls. The poor living conditions in the barracks, however, were belied by the pleasant appearance of the fairground buildings at the entrance to the camp. When the first prisoners arrived from the engagements at Forts Henry and Donelson at the end of February, nothing had been done to make these buildings more fit for human habitation. Throughout Camp Morton's existence as a prisoner-of-war camp, it would have the reputation as one of the more uncomfortable and unhealthy of the Union prisons. Even as late at the end of 1863, some of the barracks still had no stoves for heat and none of the buildings had floors. In late 1864 new hospital buildings were erected, but this came too late for many of the sick and wounded prisoners.

The first commandant at Camp Morton, Colonel Richard Owen, did what he could to alleviate the suffering of the prisoners there, but the poor facilities and the bad drainage at the site still caused a great deal of illness at the camp. Because of the poor conditions, bad water, and cold barracks, the prison suffered about 20 percent fatalities from disease. Those conditions also led to numerous escape attempts and about 150 successful escapes. The most common means of escape at Camp Morton was through tunneling, a practice facilitated by the lack of floors in the buildings. Commandants relied on informers among the Confederate prisoners to alert them to such plans. The largest escape attempt occurred on the night of 14 July 1862 when over fifty men tried to escape through a tunnel. Most were either killed or captured.

By the fall of 1862 the prisoners at Camp Morton had been exchanged, and the camp reverted to a training facility. With the breakdown of the exchange agreement, however, the camp was reconverted into a prison in early 1863. It remained open until the end of the war. Over the last two years of its use as a prison it was commanded successively by Colonel James Biddle and then by Colonel Ambrose A. Stevens.

When Camp Morton was reopened in 1863, it was originally to be used as a camp for wounded Confederate prisoners. The demand for space soon brought thousands more prisoners there than the camp was equipped for. Over the winters of 1863–1864 and 1864–1865, overcrowding and extremely cold weather caused the deaths of many prisoners.

Winter was not the only tense time at Camp Morton, however. In the summer of 1864 there were several threats of prisoner revolts. In June the rations were cut, including the complete elimination of coffee from the ration list. Extra artillery was sent to the camp and trained on the barracks and exercise yards to prevent a concentration of prisoners.

The bad conditions at Camp Morton probably facilitated the efforts of Major General John Pope in early 1865 to recruit Confederate prisoners for federal service on the frontier. Those who refused to join Pope in the West remained, though many were released in May 1865 to make their way home. Most of the remaining prisoners were those too sick or wounded to travel, and in June 1865 they were transferred to other facilities so that Camp Morton could close.

—*David S. Heidler and Jeanne T. Heidler*

See also Prisoners of War; Prisons, C.S.A.

For further reading:

Little, Robert Henry. *A Year of Starvation Amid Plenty, or, How a Confederate Soldier Suffered from Hunger and Cruelty in a Prison of War During the Awful Days of the Sixties* (1966).

Speer, Lonnie R. *Portals to Hell: Military Prisons of the Civil War* (1997).

Winslow, Hattie Lou. *Camp Morton, 1861–1865: Indianapolis Prison Camp* (1995).

CAMP NELSON, KENTUCKY

A Federal supply depot and major recruitment center for African-American troops in Jessamine County, Kentucky, Camp Nelson was established by order of Major General Ambrose Burnside in June

1863 to serve as a supply depot for the Army of the Ohio to support its campaign in eastern Tennessee to capture Knoxville. Later in the war, the camp supported Union troops and operations in eastern and central Kentucky and southwestern Virginia.

Lieutenant Colonel J. H. Simpson was placed in charge of selecting the site and beginning construction. He located the camp on the Lexington-Danville Turnpike approximately five miles south of the county seat town of Nicholasville in an area protected by the steep palisades of the Kentucky River. Located north of the Kentucky River and thus able to use the palisade as a natural defensive barrier, the new camp replaced Camp Dick Robinson, which was south of the river. The camp was named for Major General William Nelson, who had established Camp Dick Robinson, the first Union recruiting camp in the state.

In addition to serving as a quartermaster depot, the camp also housed a military hospital, a prison, repair shops, and a bakery. Large-scale workshops built wagons and ambulances, as well as harness. There were also repair facilities. At its peak the camp covered 4,000 acres and had approximately 300 buildings. The camp was served by an elaborate water system that pumped water from the river into a half-million-gallon reservoir and then distributed the water throughout the camp through pipes. There were extensive defensive works, including Fort Bramlette, eight named earthen fortifications connected by trenches and breastworks. On three sides, however, Camp Nelson was protected by the 4,000-foot palisades that rose from the Kentucky River and Hickman Creek; the earthworks were only on its north.

Several Kentucky and Tennessee regiments were organized and trained at Camp Nelson. The number of troops garrisoned there varied between 3,000 and 8,000 and the number of civilian employees exceeded 2,000. Soon after Camp Nelson was established, it attracted large numbers of African-Americans. More than 10,000 enlisted in the Union army and formed all or part of eight regiments. Three other regiments of U.S. Colored Troops, as the African-American soldiers were designated, trained at Camp Nelson. Many of these men escaped slavery with their families, who followed them to Camp Nelson. A refugee camp was established near the present community of Hall. Its population exceeded 3,000 at times. Not all commanders of the camp were sympathetic to the freedmen and conditions at the camp were often hard. In November 1864, 102 refugees died of disease and exposure after Brigadier General Speed S. Fry ordered all of the refugees expelled from the camp.

Fry's action caused tremendous controversy and led directly to Congress's granting freedom to the families of African-American soldiers. A refugee home, with ninety-seven cottages, more than fifty tents, and a number of other buildings, including a school, was estab-lished. The home was administered jointly by the U.S. Army and the American Missionary Association. The American Missionary Association sent Reverend John G. Fee to serve as minister and administrator. Fee estab-lished a church and a school and organized the refugee camp into the community of Hall. When Camp Nelson was closed and abandoned by the army in June 1866, the Freedmen's Bureau took over responsibility for the refugee camp. Ariel Academy was established and oper-ated into the twentieth century. After the war, Fee founded Berea College to provide racially integrated higher education in Kentucky.

When the camp was abandoned, nearly all of the buildings, except those in Hall and at the camp ceme-tery, were sold for their lumber and taken down. The camp's cemetery, established the year that Camp Nelson was organized, was designated as a national cemetery in 1868. In addition to some 1,600 soldiers from Camp Nelson, including 600 African-Americans, more than 2,200 other Union casualties from Perryville, Richmond, and Covington were reburied there when military ceme-teries were consolidated.

—*William H. Mulligan, Jr.*

See also Fry, Speed S.; United States Colored Troops.
For further reading:

Lucas, Marion B. "Camp Nelson, Kentucky during the Civil War: Cradle of Liberty or Refugee Death Camp." *The Filson Club History Quarterly* (1989).
———. *From Slavery to Segregation. A History of Blacks in Kentucky*, vol. 1 (1992).
McBride, W. Stephen. "Civil War Material Culture and Camp Life in Central Kentucky: Archeological Investigations at Camp Nelson." In *Look to the Earth: Historical Archeology and the American Civil War* (1994).
Sears, Richard D. "*A Practical Recognition of the Brotherhood of Man*"; *John G. Fee and the Camp Nelson Experience* (1986).
Smith, John David. "The Recruitment of Negro Soldiers in Kentucky, 1863–1865." *Register of the Kentucky Historical Society* (1974).

CAMPBELL, JOHN ARCHIBALD
(1811–1889)

U.S. Supreme Court associate justice; Confederate assistant secretary of war

John Archibald Campbell was born in Washington, Georgia. In 1837 he moved to Mobile, Alabama, where he opened a law practice specializing in land dispute cases. Campbell was an especially gifted attorney, and his arguments in court led to wide acclaim as Alabama's preeminent advocate. His opinions on issues of the day were often solicited by such prominent people as John C. Calhoun, who was becoming acutely protec-tive of states' rights. Campbell was likewise a staunch defender of states' rights, yet his perception of the Union was far less radical than Calhoun's, and he generally understood the Union as representing a governmental system of shared powers between federal and state authority. Campbell believed that a proper balance between the relative powers of the federal and the state governments must be recognized and always observed. Yet he and many others were perplexed about where that line should be drawn. In any event, he believed that purely local concerns were beyond the reach of the national government. Believing that slavery was a "purely local concern," he thus was of the opinion that it could never be abolished by federal authority. This did not mean, however, that Campbell was an especially enthusiastic defender of slavery. Actually, his views on the South's "peculiar institution" were moderate and in some respects revolutionary: though he despised radical abolitionists, whom he felt would rid the South of slavery without the least concern for Southern rights, Campbell believed that slavery was an outmoded and inefficient system that was economically detrimental. He proposed that slaveowners recognize the need to replace slavery with free labor and that states enact a number of reforms to facilitate slavery's demise. Campbell recognized that his views differed significantly from slavery's mainstream defenders, but he felt that abolition was inevitable and that Southerners needed to prepare the slaves to become productive, law-abiding citizens upon gaining their freedom. Any attempt, however, by the Federal government to abolish slavery was, to Campbell, a gross violation of states' rights philosophy and the Constitution.

Campbell was one of eight delegates to represent Alabama at a convention in Nashville in 1850. The purpose of this Nashville Convention was to protest the impending Compromise of 1850, but Campbell sought a moderate response instead of a radical ultimatum that threatened to destroy the Union. In 1853 President Franklin Pierce nominated Campbell to fill a vacancy on the U.S. Supreme Court. Although Campbell had never served as a judge, he had often proved his mastery of the law while arguing cases before the Supreme Court.

Campbell's jurisprudence well complemented a Court that largely sought a structure of shared power between the federal and state governments. Yet, the Taney Court has best been remembered for its fateful decision in the Dred Scott case of 1857. Due largely to the gravity of the case, Campbell issued a separate, but concurring opinion. Despite charges of radicalism hurled by antislavery elements, his ruling fundamentally was an exegesis on the relative constitutional powers of the state and Federal governments and not an attempt to protect Southern institutions in the territories. Campbell recognized that Congress had previously established several precedents in which the Federal government had assumed the authority to legislate concerning the status of slavery in U.S. territories. But these actions, he argued, had been predicated on a fundamental misinterpretation of the Constitution that established far too much power for the Federal government. As a Supreme Court justice, Campbell was determined that the Court firmly establish that the Federal government had absolutely no jurisdiction over slavery, either in the states or in Federal territories. Slavery was purely a local concern, and Congress could neither facilitate its expansion nor abrogate its existence, in Campbell's view.

With Lincoln's election to the presidency prompting the secession crisis, Campbell advised his fellow Southerners to move slowly and not take precipitous acts. However, one by one the states of the Deep South seceded, and Campbell blamed radicals in both sections of the nation for bringing about the Union's destruction. He hoped that moderates would see the danger and seize an opportunity to restore the Union and repair the ill feelings between the sections, and he was genuinely alarmed when hostilities threatened to erupt over the possession of Federal properties, particularly Fort Sumter in Charleston harbor.

Consequently, Campbell began holding secret communications with Secretary of State William Seward, who informed the justice that Lincoln would soon withdraw all Federal forces from Sumter. Campbell then relayed this information to the Montgomery government, always believing that Seward had been telling the truth. Weeks passed, however, and the Federal troops at Sumter showed no signs of leaving. After several more exchanges between Campbell and Seward, the former was again convinced that Sumter would be evacuated. But, as it unfolded, the Sumter crisis was not being controlled by Seward, and his promises to Campbell that Lincoln intended to abandon the fort were groundless. Campbell was soon convinced that the secretary of state had duped him, and he greeted the opening of hostilities when Confederates bombarded the fort in April 1861 with dismay. Campbell remained in Washington until late May, when he resigned his seat on the Supreme Court and returned to Alabama. In the fall of 1862 Campbell moved to Richmond, and the recently appointed Confederate secretary of war, George Randolph, invited him to become the War Department's assistant secretary.

Campbell was hardly enthusiastic about his new post, and he accepted the position solely, as he explained, to be of some use in bringing about a negotiated end to the struggle. His duties at the Confederate War Department involved promoting the efficient operation and communication among the nine bureaus that made up the department. His primary task was to advise the secretary on a number of important legal matters that concerned conscription, exemptions, confiscations, and passports to cross enemy lines. Campbell's rather thankless role as assistant secretary was mundane, routine, and completely devoid of authority over troop movement, supplies, or military strategy. He ordered no one into battle, requisitioned

no supplies, and moved no troops. He was, in so many respects, a mere functionary, albeit a rather important one.

Campbell had always opposed the war, and he sought ways in which the two governments could end hostilities. Yet neither side was willing to enter into discussions until late in the war, when the Confederacy's chances for survival were especially bleak. Many Southerners were suggesting that the South seek an honorable end to the war, and this peace movement was growing steadily with each successive loss on the battlefield. Confederate president Jefferson Davis finally agreed to peace talks between representatives of both governments, and Campbell, along with R. M. T. Hunter and Alexander Stephens, was selected to meet with Lincoln and Seward at Hampton Roads, Virginia, for a conference in which the ending of hostilities could be discussed. However, this meeting was destined to be unproductive. Lincoln asserted that discussions could be held to reunite the nation, but Davis preconditioned such talks singularly on the South's peaceful departure from the Union. Campbell, Hunter, and Stephens—all peace advocates—were thus hamstrung in their efforts at making the conference successful. Campbell had earlier concluded that the South's military losses had so weakened its position that any hope of independence had long since faded. His main purpose in attending the conference was determining what type of Reconstruction Lincoln had in store for the defeated South. Nevertheless, as the meeting had been predicated on diametrically opposing objectives, it was productive of little else except cordial talks by the attendees.

Campbell returned to Richmond after the Hampton Roads conference dejected at its failure to end the war. Yet he was determined to convince as many high-level Confederate government officials as possible that the South should seek to end the fighting and reenter the Union quickly. In March 1865, after querying the heads of the Confederate War Department's nine bureaus, Campbell drafted a lengthy report to Secretary John Breckinridge, detailing the South's bleak situation. The message from Campbell's report was painfully clear: it was time for the South to end the fighting in any way possible. Campbell's report was indeed persuasive, but it failed to convince President Davis that the South was defeated. Instead, the Confederate president tried to rally Southerners to continue the fight. Davis's efforts were of little avail; Richmond was evacuated on 2 April and Lee surrendered just one week later. Campbell, though saddened by the South's defeat, was nonetheless relieved that the nation's horrifying nightmare had finally ended. His focus thus shifted to Reconstruction, hoping that the process of rebuilding the nation would not mean that the Southern people would needlessly suffer at the hands of vengeful Northern generals and politicians.

When the Confederate government evacuated Richmond on 2 April 1865, Campbell effectively resigned his post that day and decided that he would not leave with the government. Instead, he chose to surrender himself to Federal troops in the hope of speaking with Lincoln about Reconstruction. Lincoln visited Richmond on the fourth, and when he learned that Campbell wanted to meet, arranged an interview for the following morning aboard the *River Queen* docked at City Point. Lincoln's thoughts on Reconstruction were by no means clear, yet he asked Campbell to summon a meeting of the Virginia legislature so that Lee's army could be dismissed and Virginia returned to the Union. Lincoln's suggestion to Campbell was astonishing in its implications: the president had inadvertently recognized the validity of secession by requesting that Virginia legislators—many of whom had voted to secede in 1861—restore their state to the Union. Evidently, with his strong desire to avoid yet another bloody battle between Lee and Grant, Lincoln failed to realize that if Virginia legislators could vote to restore their relationship to the Union, by implication they likewise retained the option to destroy that relationship again.

Campbell began arrangements for the legislature to meet, but soon he received an order from Lincoln contravening his earlier permission. Upon the president's return to Washington, Secretary of War Edwin Stanton apparently convinced Lincoln that his permission for the legislature to meet had been a serious error. Campbell remained in Richmond, hopeful that Lincoln's promises of leniency would be kept, but he soon learned the dreadful news that the president had been assassinated.

On 22 May 1865, five weeks after the Lincoln assassination, Campbell was arrested at his home in Richmond. The reasons for his arrest are unclear, but at the time there was some indication that he may have been involved in a Confederate conspiracy to kill the president. A young lieutenant from Alabama had written Jefferson Davis in December 1864 offering to assassinate Lincoln, and the letter was forwarded to the Confederate War Department. Campbell endorsed the letter—as he did with all written communications—and forwarded it to the attorney general's office. This routine endorsement seemed to indicate complicity in the offer, and federal officials who believed the assassination was planned in Richmond were quick to arrest anyone who was remotely associated with Lincoln's death. Campbell remained imprisoned at Fort Pulaski, Georgia, until October 1865, when he was finally paroled by President Johnson.

Impoverished and virtually without property, Campbell eventually moved to New Orleans, where he established a new law practice. He was readmitted to argue cases before the U.S. Supreme Court in 1867, and within a few years had rebuilt his reputation and wealth. He was involved in several significant cases of the late nineteenth century, including the *Slaughterhouse Cases*,

in which the Supreme Court was asked for the first time for an interpretation of the Fourteenth Amendment. Campbell continued to practice law until his retirement in 1885. He died in Baltimore, Maryland, in 1889.

—*Robert Saunders, Jr.*

See also *Dred Scott* Case; Fort Sumter; Hampton Roads Peace Conference; Lincoln Assassination; Secession.

For further reading:
Connor, Henry Groves. *John Archibald Campbell, Associate Justice of the United States Supreme Court, 1853–1861* (1920).
Mann, Justine Staib. "The Political and Constitutional Thought of John Archibald Campbell" (Ph.D. dissertation, 1966).
Saunders, Robert, Jr. *John Archibald Campbell: Southern Moderate, 1811–1889* (1997).

CAMPBELL'S STATION, TENNESSEE, BATTLE OF
(16 November 1863)

The battle of Campbell's Station, Tennessee, was the first major engagement of the 1863 Knoxville campaign. On 4 November, General James Longstreet left Chattanooga with approximately 15,000 men, including two divisions, two artillery battalions, and General Joseph Wheeler's cavalry, to crush the Union forces under General Ambrose Burnside's command. Before crossing the Tennessee River near Loudon on 14 November, Longstreet dispatched Wheeler's cavalry for operations near Knoxville south of the Holston River. Easily outnumbered, as his forces in the area, including IX Corps and the 2d Division of XXIII Corps, totaled 5,000, General Burnside decided to allow Longstreet to cross the Tennessee River unopposed. Burnside's strategy was to maintain contact with the opposing force without entering a serious engagement, while withdrawing toward his defenses in Knoxville and luring the Confederate troops away from Chattanooga.

Early on the morning of 15 November with the Confederate forces to his west and separated by a bend in the Tennessee River, Burnside began to evacuate his forces to Knoxville. The Federal forces moved along the East Tennessee & Georgia Railroad, while the Southern troops traveled along a parallel route, the Kingston Road. Both armies stopped near Lenoir, where they were separated by only one and a half miles. Burnside realized that, if he continued along the railroad and Longstreet followed the Kingston Road toward Knoxville, he would slowly be squeezed into a trap with the Confederates on one side and the river on his other. To escape, Burnside had to get ahead of Longstreet by reaching the strategic road junction at Campbell's Station first. To prevent Burnside's escape, Longstreet split his force, sending one division commanded by General Micah Jenkins on his right to pursue Burnside, while General Lafayette McLaws's division would march ahead on his left to capture the junction at Campbell's Station.

Early in the morning of 16 November, Burnside began the almost ten-mile march from Lenoir to Campbell's Station. Heavy rains and mud slowed the march. Eventually, General Burnside ordered his extra wagons to be abandoned and destroyed, using his horses to pull what few artillery pieces he had. Although this move gave Burnside more mobility, it also benefited the Confederates, who found many of the wagons still intact and gained much needed supplies.

While his main forces were delayed in the mud, Burnside ordered Colonel John F. Hartranft's IX Corp to run ahead of the column and secure the road junction at Campbell's Station. Hartranft's mounted troops arrived at the strategic crossroads first, beating the advancing Confederate forces under General McLaws by less than an hour. Once Hartranft's forces reached the crossroads, he marched down the Kingston Road to give the Union troops and wagon trains plenty of room to maneuver through the junction toward Knoxville. McLaws's approaching troops tried to prevent passage of the Union forces and wagon trains through the road junction, but they were too few. As Burnside's troops moved through the junction, they occupied defensive positions, with the 1st Division, IX Corps, on the Union right; the 2d Division, IX Corps, on the Union left; and XXIII Corps in reserve. Burnside planned to fight a delaying action to buy time for Captain Orlando Poe of the Corps of Engineers to strengthen the defenses of Knoxville.

As the Confederates reached the crossroads in force, General Longstreet ordered McLaws to send a cavalry diversion to the north around the Union right. At the same time, Longstreet dispatched General Evander M. Law from Jenkins's division with two brigades around the Federal left to attack in their rear. Law's attack, however, did not come off as planned. He delayed. When he did move, he attacked the front, rather than the rear, of the Union left. Some officers charged that Law, who was jealous of Jenkins's command of John Bell Hood's division, had deliberately delayed the attack to prevent Jenkins from receiving the credit. Burnside's troops repulsed attacks from both Law on their left and McLaws on their right before withdrawing under cover of artillery. The ensuing darkness prevented the Confederates from mounting a counteroffensive, and the battle ended as night fell.

As night fell, Burnside continued his withdraw to the defenses of Knoxville. The battle for the strategic crossroads had cost the Union 318 killed and wounded, while the Confederates had lost 174 men. The battle had spared Burnside's forces an early defeat and bought the Federal forces occupying Knoxville time to prepare for the upcoming siege. For General Longstreet, the battle was a disappointment. If Wheeler's cavalry had been present or McLaws had reached the crossroad minutes earlier,

Longstreet would have won his campaign at the start. The discord that manifested itself in the Law-Jenkins feud did not bode well, as it foreshadowed problems in command that would plague Longstreet's campaign.

—*William Hartley*

See also Knoxville Campaign.

For further reading:

Fink, Harold S. "The East Tennessee Campaign and the Battle of Knoxville in 1863." *East Tennessee Historical Society's Publications* (1957).

Longstreet, James. *From Manassas to Appomattox: Memoirs of the Civil War in America* (1896; reprint, 1960).

Seymour, Digby Gordon. *Divided Loyalties: Fort Sanders and the Civil War in East Tennessee* (1982).

Wert, Jeffry D. *General James Longstreet: The Confederacy's Most Controversial Soldier—A Biography* (1993).

CANBY, EDWARD RICHARD SPRIGG
(1817–1873)
Union general

Edward R. S. Canby (*Library of Congress*)

Although Edward R. S. Canby's failed to attain the notoriety of such Union generals as William Tecumseh Sherman or Ulysses S. Grant, his Civil War career was nearly as noteworthy and arguably as successful. He was born in 1817 at Piatt's Landing, Kentucky, but moved to Crawfordsville, Indiana, with his family the following year. While studying at Wabash College in 1835, Canby was appointed to West Point, where he graduated thirtieth in a class of thirty-one in 1839. Shortly after graduation, Canby was assigned to a regiment assisting in the removal of the last bands of Cherokee Indians from Georgia to the Oklahoma Indian Territory. Canby then saw action in Florida during the Second Seminole War, but it was during the Mexican War that his star truly began to rise. He participated in most of the major engagements of that conflict, from the siege of Veracruz to the fighting in and around Mexico City, and was breveted twice during the war for meritorious conduct. Following the cessation of hostilities with Mexico, Canby continued to serve in the army, occupying a number of positions, ranging from frontier garrison duty to service in the so-called Mormon War. He eventually earned a promotion to major and was assigned to various posts in the New Mexico Territory.

The outbreak of the Civil War found Canby in command of Fort Defiance, New Mexico, where he was assigned the task of keeping a close watch on hostile bands of Navajo Indians in the region. A proven frontier commander, Canby was immediately promoted to colonel and placed in command of the entire Department of New Mexico, with explicit orders to defend the territory against a suspected invasion by a Confederate army under the command of Henry Hopkins Sibley. Despite being defeated by Sibley at the battle of Val Verde on 21 February 1862, Canby's troops managed to hold nearby Fort Craig, which contributed to the Confederate leader's decision to turn his attention towards the Colorado gold fields rather than Sante Fe. Canby regrouped his beleaguered troops and gave pursuit, eventually catching and defeating the Confederates at Glorieta Pass, New Mexico, on 28 March and again at Peralta, New Mexico, on 15 April. Although Canby's forces inflicted heavy casualties on Sibley's army during the two battles, Canby was unable to capture his adversary, and Sibley's ravaged command eventually managed to escape the territory.

Although some detractors criticized Canby for failing to capture Sibley's command, he was breveted a brigadier general in the regular army for his service in defending the New Mexico Territory. Canby was then transferred to the eastern department, where he served as an assistant adjutant general in Washington for a year and later participated in the suppression of draft riots in New York City during the summer of 1863. Canby returned to the field in May 1864 as a newly promoted major general in command of the Military Division of Western Mississippi, which was in severe disarray in the wake of the disastrous Red River campaign. Canby reorganized the division, and also was instrumental in planning and implementing the Union assault on Mobile, Alabama, in April 1865, which led to the fall of the city on 12 April and also the capture of Montgomery on 27 April. Following Mobile, Canby was again promoted, this time to the command of the Departments of the Gulf and Arkansas, although his successes in Alabama did not garner the public praise they might have, had they not come on the heels of Robert E. Lee's surrender at Appomattox Court House on 9 April. Despite the overshadowing of his accomplishments, as well as his being severely wounded by Confederate guerrilla forces during the Mobile campaign, Canby continued at his post for the remainder of 1865, and eventually accepted the surrender of the last remaining Confederate field armies under Generals Edmund Kirby Smith and Richard Taylor.

Following the war, Canby continued his military career with the permanent rank of brigadier general in the regular service. He served on an advisory staff in Washington and on Reconstruction duty in the South before returning to the west in 1870. Canby finished out his career in the Pacific Northwest as commander of the Department of the Columbia and later the Division of the Pacific. It was while serving in this capacity that Canby was attacked and killed by a group of Modoc Indians under the leadership of the northern California war chief Captain Jack during a meeting to renew peace negotiations on 11 April 1873.

—*Daniel P. Barr*

For further reading:
Frazier, Donald S. *Blood and Treasure: Confederate Empire in the Southwest* (1995).
Hall, Martin H. *Sibley's New Mexico Campaign* (1960).
Heyman, Max L. *Prudent Soldier: A Biography of Major General E. R. S. Canby, 1817–1873* (1959).
Josephy, Alvin M. *The Civil War in the American West* (1991).

CANE HILL, BATTLE OF
(28 November 1862)

In the fall of 1862, Union brigadier general James G. Blunt's division of the Army of the Frontier was camped near Maysville in the extreme northwestern corner of Arkansas. Seventy miles to the south at Fort Smith on the Arkansas River was Confederate major general Thomas C. Hindman and a sizable army. Hindman ordered Brigadier General John S. Marmaduke to take his cavalry division over the Boston Mountains and harass Blunt. If Marmaduke succeeded in fixing Blunt in place, Hindman intended to move north with the remainder of his army and attack Blunt's isolated division. The nearest Union reinforcements were seventy miles away near Springfield, Missouri.

Blunt refused to cooperate by remaining inert. When he learned that a Confederate force was slowly winding through the mountains in his direction, he advanced thirty-five miles in two days and struck the vanguard of Marmaduke's column near the village of Boonsboro, later known as Cane Hill. Surprised and outnumbered about 5,000 to 2,000, Marmaduke retreated. Brigadier General Joseph O. Shelby's cavalry brigade formed the rear guard and fought a series of delaying actions that allowed the rest of the division and its train to withdraw into the Boston Mountains. The battle was actually a nine-hour running fight that swirled steadily southward across twelve miles of rolling terrain. The fighting ended when the Confederates reached the safety of the narrow mountain passes. As was generally the case in mounted engagements, losses were comparatively light for the numbers involved: there were at least forty-one Union and forty-five Confederate casualties.

The next day Marmaduke rejoined Hindman on the Arkansas River. Blunt returned to Cane Hill and remained there, despite being more than one hundred miles south of the nearest supporting force and only thirty miles north of Hindman's army. Shrugging off Marmaduke's tactical defeat at Cane Hill, Hindman believed that Blunt had played into his hands by moving deeper into Arkansas. He set in motion a second operation to destroy Blunt that resulted in the battle of Prairie Grove on 7 December 1862.

—*William L. Shea*

See also Blunt, James G.; Hindman, Thomas C.; Shelby, Joseph O.

For further reading:
Banasik, Michael E. *Embattled Arkansas: The Prairie Grove Campaign of 1862* (1996).
Scott, Kim Allen, and Stephen Burgess. "Pursuing an Elusive Quarry: The Battle of Cane Hill, Arkansas." *Arkansas Historical Quarterly* (1997).

CANNON, WILLIAM
(1809–1865)

Unionist, Delaware governor

Born in Bridgeville, Delaware, to Josiah and Nancy Cannon on 15 March 1809, William Cannon received an elementary-school education but never attended high school. Cannon entered into a career in business and demonstrated considerable ability for commercial ventures. Cannon became wealthy as a merchant and landowner and maintained a special interest in the production of fruit. Within a few years, he married Margaret N. B. Laws.

As part of a family devoted to the Democratic Party, Cannon retained an keen interest in politics. Cannon was active in promoting the welfare of his native Sussex County, and he encouraged the construction of the Delaware Railroad into the area.

As a Democrat, he was won sequential elections to the Delaware house of representatives in 1844 and 1846 and served as state treasurer in 1851. Within a decade, Cannon had established himself as a prominent politician in Delaware. In 1861, he was selected as one of his state's five delegates to the Peace Conference in Washington. He supported the Crittenden Compromise as well as other measures to ameliorate tensions between regions. When all measures dedicated to preserving the Union appeared to fail, Cannon began to support the Republican Party. It is possible that in addition to his defense of union, he was also disappointed with the Democratic Party's inability to facilitate his ambition to become governor.

In November 1862, he was the Union Party's candidate for governor. While the Democrats won a majority in the state legislature, Cannon was elected by a small majority and was inaugurated in January 1863. His opponent protested the presence of Federal troops at polling booths during the election and suggested the Lincoln administration's decree to send troops was an attempt to help Cannon. Upon taking office, Cannon appointed Nathaniel B. Smithers as secretary of state. Smithers was a confidant who would have a great influence on Cannon and perhaps serve as his chief political advisor and speech writer during the remainder of his life. From the earliest moments of his governorship, Cannon was an ardent supporter of preserving the federal union. In his inaugural address he urged more federal control and proclaimed his steadfast support for the union.

Throughout his governorship, Cannon was at odds with the legislature, which was under the control of the Democratic Party. At one point, the legislature passed a law intended to outlaw federal arrests within the confines of Delaware. Cannon responded by failing to recognize the act. He suggested that following the order would weaken the state's devotion to the union. On 1 March 1865, Cannon died in office, having served just over two years. He was succeeded by Gove Saulsbury, the presiding officer of the Delaware Senate and a Democratic stalwart.

—*Lee Cheek*

For further reading:
Hancock, Harold Bell. *Delaware During the Civil War* (1961).
Journal of the House of Representatives of the State of Delaware (1863–1865).
Munroe, John A. *History of Delaware* (1993).

CAREY, HENRY CHARLES
(1793–1879)

Publisher, writer, and political economist

Henry C. Carey emerged as the leading advocate of the American free laborer in the years immediately preceding the Civil War. Through his texts on political economy, numerous pamphlets, and newspaper articles, Carey promoted the policies of high tariffs and an abundant money supply as the means for "elevating and equalizing the condition of man throughout the world." The oldest son of Irish political refugee and protectionist Mathew Carey, Carey inherited his father's deep disdain for the British rigid class system and free trade policies.

Born and raised in Philadelphia, Carey began working in his father's publishing house at the age of nine. He eschewed formal education, preferring to read and work. By the age of twenty-four he became a partner in Carey, Lea & Carey, one of the leading publishing houses in the country. In 1835, he wrote his first treatise, *Essay on the Rate of Wages,* in which he celebrated U.S. exceptionalism and advocated free trade.

After his first book, Carey left the publishing business and became a full-time political economist. He published his three-volume *Principles of Political Economy* in 1837. He countered the primary theses of the two pillars of economic theory of this period, David Ricardo and Thomas R. Malthus. Carey rejected Ricardo's belief that land lost value and productive capacity over time; instead, Carey posited that the labor expended to make land arable and fecund increased its value and, ultimately, the wealth of the nation. Similarly, Carey countered Malthus's dark predictions that population increases led to a decrease in the quality of life. Instead, Carey believed that the economy of the United States was boundless and would continue to grow. Carey's optimism for continued U.S. prosperity was based on his faith in democratic government, the guaranteed right of private ownership of property, low taxes, and the high U.S. wages, contrasted with those in Europe.

The economic downturn of 1837 forced Carey to reappraise many of his tenets. Over the next several years he examined the tariff history of the United States and concluded that high tariffs correlated with periods of prosperity. In 1848, he published his revised views on tariffs in *Past, Present, and Future,* and renounced his free trade stance. He collaborated with *New York Tribune* editor Horace Greeley, writing a plethora of articles and editorials on the virtues of protective tariffs. Carey proclaimed high tariffs as the best means for protecting the wages of U.S. employees by decreasing the competition that they faced from goods produced abroad by lower paid workers. Carey revealed his distrust for merchants and financiers, instead extolling the virtues of producers, including farmers, laborers, and manufacturers. He believed that producers, working together "in harmony" in small towns throughout the country, formed the basis for future prosperity.

Carey's conversion to protectionism came at an inopportune moment. The positive effects of the Walker Tariff of 1846, the discovery of gold deposits in California, and the beginnings of the industrial boom combined to create a decade of prosperity. Carey continued writing and speaking, but his ideas did not generate popular support until the economic downturn of 1857. The displacement of workers caused by this recession, coming on the heels of the passage of the low tariff of 1857, suddenly made Carey's message seem prophetic.

Carey's ideas were embraced by the Whig element of the new Republican Party. The Republicans took Carey's theme that protecting and encouraging agriculture, industry, and regional commerce could ensure the nation's prosperity and incorporated these ideas into their successful 1860 campaign. Carey's protectionist message resonated most successfully in Pennsylvania, a traditionally Democratic state whose iron industry had been convulsed by the 1857 downturn. Lincoln won in Pennsylvania, one of the few states where the tariff represented the main issue in the campaign.

However, Carey's influence on the new administration was tempered. He approved of the higher tariffs, eight-hour workday for government employees, and open immigration policies adopted by the Republican administration, but vehemently disapproved of the internal taxation legislation initiated during the Civil War and the postbellum contraction of the currency. Carey declared his support for the Greenback Party in the 1872 election.

Carey's antipathy for the British, high taxes, and the increasing influence of financiers on government officials increased his disillusionment with the Republicans throughout the 1870s. After his death, many of his ideas were discounted as superficial, but during his lifetime Carey's influence was tangible.

—Jane Flaherty

See also Greeley, Horace.

For further reading:

Carey, Henry C. *The Harmony of Interests: Agriculture, Manufactures, and Commercial* (1851; reprint, 1976).

Conkin, Paul K. *Prophets of Prosperity: America's First Political Economists* (1980).

Huston, James L. "A Political Response to Industrialism: The Republican Embrace of Protectionist Labor Doctrines." *Journal of American History* (1983).

Smith, George W. *Henry C. Carey and the American Sectional Conflict* (1951).

CARLIN, WILLIAM PASSMORE
(1829–1903)
Union general

William Passmore Carlin was born on 24 November 1829 in Richwoods near Carrollton, Illinois. Carlin's father was the county clerk for Greene County, and his uncle was governor of Illinois in 1838. Carlin received his appointment to the U.S. Military Academy through a competitive examination. In 1850, he graduated twentieth in a class of forty-three. Carlin entered the 6th U.S. Infantry, where he became a brevet lieutenant. He participated with his unit in campaigns against the Cheyenne and the Sioux and in the Mormon expedition of 1858. By 1860, Carlin had attained the rank of captain.

With the coming of the Civil War, Carlin was appointed colonel of the 38th Illinois Volunteers in August 1861. Colonel Carlin and his regiment were sent to Missouri and Arkansas and operated against guerrillas. By mid-1862, Carlin received command of a brigade and was assigned to Major General Don Carlos Buell's Union army during the Confederate invasion of Kentucky. Carlin distinguished himself in the battle of Perryville, Kentucky, and received a promotion to brigadier general.

Later in 1862, Carlin and his brigade were assigned to Brigadier General Jefferson C. Davis's division in the right wing of the Army of the Cumberland. This marked the beginning of the rocky relationship between General Carlin and General Davis that haunted Carlin's career throughout the war. Carlin and his men were engaged in the fierce fighting at Stones River, Tennessee, on 31 December 1862. In the summer of 1863, Carlin participated with Davis's division in the Tullahoma campaign. During the battle of Chickamauga, Georgia, in September 1863, Carlin's brigade was nearly destroyed during the retreat of Davis's division. Carlin accused Davis of directing artillery fire on his troops. The feud became so destructive that Major General George Thomas sought to separate the officers by assigning them to two different divisions during the reorganization of the Army of the Cumberland in late 1863.

Now with the 1st Division, XIV Army Corps, General Carlin's brigade served through the Chattanooga campaign of November 1863. In 1864, illness, business dealings, and the strain of campaigning forced Carlin to request several furloughs. He served with his brigade through the Atlanta campaign in 1864 and eventually rose to command of the 1st Division by August 1864. By that time, Davis was in command of XIV Corps. Throughout the Savannah campaign and during the first stages of the Carolinas campaign, there was a underlying tension in the relationship between the two generals. During the final march to Goldsboro, North Carolina, problems again started to rise between the two officers. On 17 March 1865, General Carlin was not able to effect a rapid crossing of the Black River and held up the army's advance for a day. His division was finally assigned the head of the column on 19 March 1865, and Carlin's division stumbled into prepared Confederate positions along the Goldsboro Road. After several unsuccessful probes, General Carlin's three brigades were assaulted by elements of General Joseph E. Johnston's Confederate army. Carlin's men were routed off the field, and for a time Carlin was separated from his men. When he and his division were reunited, they were

assigned a reserve role for the remainder of the fighting. Upon arriving in Goldsboro, North Carolina, Carlin applied for a leave of absence due to exhaustion and sickness. Carlin left his division so that he could travel north, and his division was assigned to another officer.

General Carlin returned to the army on 1 May 1865. He was assigned to command a division in the Department of West Virginia until August 1865, when he was mustered out of volunteer service. Afterward, he remained with the regular army, where he was reduced to the rank of major. He served with the 16th Infantry and spent several months in the Freeman's Bureau for Tennessee from 1866 to 1872. In July 1872, Carlin was promoted to lieutenant colonel and was assigned to the 17th Infantry. In April 1882, Carlin received a promotion to colonel and was given command of the 4th Infantry. Through the efforts of several individuals, Carlin received a final promotion to brigadier general on 17 May 1893. On 24 November 1893, the day that he retired from active service in the U.S. Army, General Carlin was awarded the Medal of Honor for his actions in the battle of Bentonville, North Carolina. Carlin moved back to Carrollton, Illinois, and became active in the local chapter of the Grand Army of the Republic. While traveling back from Spokane, Washington, Carlin died in his sleep on 4 October 1903. His body was taken back to Carrollton for burial.

—*William H. Brown*

See also Bentonville, Battle of; Chickamauga, Battle of; Davis, Jefferson Columbus.

For further reading:
Faust, Patricia. *Historical Times Illustrated Encyclopedia of the Civil War* (1986).

Girardi, Robert I., and Nathaniel C. Hughes, Jr., eds. *The Memoirs of Brigadier General William Passmore Carlin USA* (1999).

Heitman, Francis B. *Historical Register and Dictionary of the United States Army* (1903).

U.S. War Department. *The War of the Rebellion: A Compilation of the Official Records of the Union and Confederate Armies* (1880–1901).

Warner, Ezra J. *Generals in Blue* (1964).

CARLISLE, PENNSYLVANIA

Settled by Scots-Irish and German settlers in the 1700s, Carlisle, Pennsylvania, was a well-established legal, farming, and merchants' community by the middle nineteenth century. The county seat of Cumberland County, the town was home to Dickinson College and host to the Carlisle Barracks, the first officer's training college of the army established by George Washington. The presence of the barracks created a more cosmopolitan atmosphere in the town than in other southern Pennsylvania communities. Army officers from the South and New England settled there with their families while studying at the college.

The town and county were traditionally Democratic and, because of economic ties to Maryland and Virginia as well as to other Pennsylvania towns, viewed the rise of the Republican Party with suspicion. By 1860, however, the sectional crisis had split Carlisle residents according to their political allegiance. Abraham Lincoln received 425 votes to Breckinridge's 406, and the county handed the victory to the Republicans with only a 386-vote majority (3,593 to 3,207). During the secession crisis, Carlisle newspapers maintained a general tone of noncoercion toward the Southern states.

The attack on Fort Sumter erased all thoughts of peaceful secession or compromise. Carlisle residents responded enthusiastically to Lincoln's call for 75,000 volunteers and later contributed to numerous three-year regiments. The 11th, 36th, 78th, and 87th Pennsylvania Infantry regiments all contained large numbers of Carlisle men and fought with the Army of the Potomac in nearly all of its major campaigns.

Alarmed by Robert E. Lee's first invasion of the North, which was stopped at Antietam Creek in September 1862, Carlisle again felt the threat of enemy occupation in June 1863. Situated at the crossroads of several important highways, and home to the Army Barracks, the town was certain to be a target of Lee's second invasion. In the early evening of 27 June, elements of Fitzhugh Lee's cavalry approached Carlisle from the direction of York and occupied the Barracks, which was systematically burned to the ground in the next few days. Surprised by the sudden appearance of Confederate cavalry, citizens went into a panic and were calmed only by the presence of several companies of the 37th New York Infantry, who refused to vacate the town. Seeing no other alternative, the Confederate Horse Artillery opened fire and shelled the town from hills west of the community. Under a flag of truce, the Confederates ceased the bombardment and demanded an unconditional surrender of the town. When leading citizens refused, the shelling resumed and continued for several hours. Mrs. R. K. Hitner wrote, "the shelling commenced, not allowing us five minutes to reach a place of safety, though word was sent that our end of town must be vacated. Up town we ran amid the firing, seeing and hearing shells bursting and whizzing all around and about us—such horrors we never experienced. The old and sick, carried from their beds through the fiery shower, little children snatched from their slumbers—it was a terrible sight."

The bombardment ended only when the Confederate cavalry ran out of ammunition and departed, vowing to return and "finish the job." Despite the long period of shelling, not one Carlisle resident was killed, and the town sustained only minor damage. Most citizens either fled to the countryside after the bombardment or hunkered down in their basements. Two men from the

37th New York were wounded, one mortally. The regiment evacuated the town late on 27 June and was replaced by Confederate infantry of General Robert E. Rodes's division the next day. Carlisle residents offered no further resistance to the Confederates, who occupied the town, demanded 1,500 rations, burned the barracks, and then departed on 1 July to join the bulk of the Army of Northern Virginia concentrating at Gettysburg.

—*Christian B. Keller*

See also Gettysburg, Battle of; Pennsylvania.

For further reading:
Coddington, Edwin B. *The Gettysburg Campaign: A Study in Command* (1968).
Hitner, Mrs. R.K., to Mrs. David Hastings. Letter, Carlisle Barracks Collection (1863).
Landis, Merkel. "Civil War Times in Carlisle." Address delivered at the Hamilton Library, Carlisle, Pennsylvania (1931).

CARNEGIE, ANDREW
(1835–1919)
Industrialist

Andrew Carnegie was born in Dunfermline, Scotland, on 25 November 1835. He was the eldest of the two sons of Margaret (Morrison) and William Carnegie, a linen weaver and a Chartist supporter. At age eight, young Andrew attended the one-room school of Mr. Robert Martin. His four years at Martin's school constituted his only formal education. When the introduction of mechanized looms led to a great decline in the handloom business of his father, the Carnegies in 1848 left Scotland for America.

Living with his family in Allegheny, across the river from Pittsburgh, Carnegie held several jobs and began to learn the ways of the business and industrial world. In 1852 Thomas Scott, who was the superintendent of the western division of the Pennsylvania Railroad offered Carnegie $35 a month to serve as his telegrapher and personal secretary. During the 1850s the perceptive Carnegie became associated with the managerial revolution that affected the operations of U.S. railroads. Under Scott, he contributed in numerous ways to the leadership of the Pennsylvania Railroad and was named in 1859 to succeed Scott as head of its western division.

During the Civil War, Carnegie supported the cause of the Union. Similar to his father, who died in 1855, he was a proponent of social equality. Carnegie in fact became an abolitionist and in 1856 wrote several antislavery editorials for Horace Greeley's *New York Tribune*. Moreover, as a result of his admiration for, and sympathy with, its principles, Carnegie in 1856 joined the Republican Party. After the Civil War broke out, Thomas Scott was named assistant secretary of war in charge of military transportation and wisely brought Carnegie to Washington, where he was to supervise tele-

graphic communications for Union troops in the Washington area. Heading a railroad crew in late April 1861, Carnegie went to Annapolis Junction to repair telegraph lines; he then directed a train that carried General Benjamin Butler's troops and wounded to Washington. Prior to its arrival, Carnegie received a gash to his face while trying to fix wires that had been cut by the Rebels. Upon his arrival in the nation's capital, he was praised for his gallant feats.

Carnegie in other ways was active during the Civil War. In early May 1861 he brought David Strouse and other competent telegraph operators to Washington to promote the cause of the Union. By recruiting Strouse and other operators, Carnegie helped to establish the United States Military Telegraphers Corps. During the battle of Bull Run in July 1861, he tried to keep open telegraph stations between Alexandria and Fairfax, but met with only partial success. After the Union defeat at Bull Run, Carnegie, who had provided assistance to wounded soldiers, suffered sunstroke. In autumn 1861 he went back to Pittsburgh to perform his duties with the Pennsylvania Railroad.

Carnegie prospered in his business activities during the remaining years of the war. With William Coleman in 1861 Carnegie assisted in the formation of the Columbia Oil Company; he invested $11,000 in this company and ultimately made from his investment over $1 million. In 1862 he organized the Keystone Bridge Company, a firm that built the first iron bridges in the nation. Two years later he established the Cyclops Iron Company. Carnegie in 1865 purchased the Kloman Company and formed the Union Mills, a firm that dominated the production of iron products for the railroads. That same year, he ended his employment with the Pennsylvania Railroad and devoted his full attention to the building of his business empire.

After the Civil War, the industrial and humanitarian achievements of Carnegie were especially impressive. During the early 1870s he built the Edgar Thomson Works, the most efficiently operated steel plant in the world and one that embodied the effectively functioning Bessemer converter. By the 1880s, Carnegie acquired 50 percent interest in the Frick Coke Company and purchased the Duquesne Steelworks and Hartman Steel. Consisting of such carefully selected partners as Henry C. Frick and Charles M. Schwab, Carnegie Steel functioned as a private partnership, rather than as a public corporation. This firm greatly expanded because Carnegie insisted that profits be plowed back into it. By adhering to tenets of cost reduction, of consolidation, and of verticality, Carnegie amassed a fortune in the steel business.

However, Carnegie did encounter severe problems with labor during the 1892 Homestead Strike. Unable to negotiate a contract with the members of the

Amalgamated Association of Iron and Steel Workers in late June of that year, Frick became involved in a violent strike at this plant; he employed Pinkerton detectives to protect nonunion workers and was himself nearly assassinated. Following settlement of the Homestead Strike, Carnegie distanced himself from Frick, but was viewed both by his workers and the public as a perfidious industrialist. Consequently, Carnegie, who had published the "Gospel of Wealth" three years before the eruption of the Homestead Strike and who thought that capitalists should perceive themselves as the trustees of wealth and act to return it, wanted by the late 1890s to spend more time with charitable causes and less time with his business interests.

After J. P. Morgan bought him out in March 1901 and established the United States Steel Corporation, Carnegie devoted his energy to philanthropic projects. He funded, among other things, public libraries, the Carnegie Institute of Technology in Pittsburgh, and the Carnegie Corporation of New York. His career, consequently, revealed the conflict between his father's egalitarianism and his mother's realism. Carnegie, who had married Louise Whitfield in April 1887, died on 11 August 1919 in Lenox, Massachusetts, and was buried in Tarrytown, New York.

—William Weisberger

For further reading:
Carnegie, Andrew. *The Autobiography of Andrew Carnegie* (1920).
Hendrick, Burton J. *The Life of Andrew Carnegie* (1932).
Josephson, Matthew. *The Robber Barons* (1962).
Livesay, Harold C. *Andrew Carnegie and the Rise of Big Business* (1975).
Thomas, Benjamin P., and Harold M. Hyman. *Stanton: The Life and Times of Lincoln's Secretary of War* (1962).
Wall, Joseph Frazier. *Andrew Carnegie* (1970).

CARNIFEX FERRY, BATTLE OF
(10 September 1861)

The battle of Carnifex Ferry was small but significant. The last in a series of battles in mountainous western Virginia during the summer of 1861, Carnifex Ferry pitted Union troops commanded by Brigadier General William S. Rosecrans against Confederate forces led by Brigadier General John B. Floyd.

The battle was staged near the Gauley River in Nicholas County, Virginia (now West Virginia). Federal strategy throughout the western Virginia campaign of 1861 aimed at controlling the Baltimore & Ohio Railroad and river transportation within the region, but the battle also was pivotal due to the pending 24 October vote for statehood for western Virginia. The vote was a critical event for control of the area including access to the Ohio River.

Preceding the clash at Carnifex Ferry and after the Union victory at the battle of Rich Mountain on 10 July,

the two armies had a series of minor skirmishes. Several occurred near Hawks Nest, where Union troops under Brigadier General Jacob Dolson Cox repeatedly clashed with Confederates led by Brigadier General Henry Alexander Wise. The mutual personal antagonism of Floyd and Wise, both ex-governors of Virginia, kept the Confederates from a united effort.

The battle of Cross Lanes near Carnifex Ferry on 26 August resulted in a rout of the Federals commanded by Colonel E. B. Tyler of the 7th Ohio Volunteer Infantry. Floyd established his command on the bluffs overlooking Carnifex Ferry, one of the few places where large numbers could cross the river, and named it Camp Gauley. He protected his position by the construction of entrenchments. At the end of August, Floyd had about 2,000 troops at Camp Gauley with approximately 6,000 more in the area. Wise received orders to bring his troops up from the Gauley River area, but due to transportation difficulties and his own obstinacy, only a portion of his troops arrived in time for the battle on 10 September.

Beginning 31 August, Union forces advanced south from Clarksburgh with plans to attack the Confederate force. More than 6,000 troops with Colonel William H. Lytle and the 10th Ohio of Brigadier General Henry W. Benham's brigade in advance marched toward Camp Gauley. Starting in the early hours of the morning of 10 September, they made their final march from Summersville, south to the heavily wooded area around Carnifex Ferry. Scouts reported that breastworks near a clearing close to the road and the Patteson house indicated the presence of Confederate forces. General Benham, ignoring the intelligence, ordered Lytle and his men to push forward. As Benham with the 1st Brigade and the 10th Ohio approached, Floyd's forces fired. Having blundered into Floyd's entire army, Benham sent word back to Rosecrans asking for help. Fighting began about 3:00 P.M. and lasted the remainder of the day. By nightfall, the Union forces had 158 casualties, whereas the Confederates counted 20. Colonel John W. Lowe (12th Ohio) became the first field grade officer from Ohio killed during the war. Colonel Lytle received a serious leg wound that took him out of action for four months. At nightfall the Confederates still held their position on top of the bluff.

During the night of 10 September, General Floyd decided to abandon Camp Gauley to the larger Union force. He ordered his troops to retreat down the steep road to the ferry and escaped south to Greenbrier County, where General Robert E. Lee waited for them.

Both Rosecrans and Floyd claimed victory. Although not decisive in outcome, Carnifex Ferry holds significance because the Union forces retained firm control of the Kanawha Valley and most of western Virginia. Shortly afterward, the residents of western Virginia voted in favor of separation from Virginia and becoming a new state.

Although a minor battle, Carnifex Ferry is interesting for the large number of present or future general officers who participated (fifteen Union and five Confederate) and for the presence in the 23d Ohio of two future presidents of the United States (Rutherford B. Hayes and William McKinley).

—*Ruth C. Carter*

See also Floyd, John Buchanan; Rich Mountain, Battle of; Rosecrans, William Starke; Wise, Henry Alexander.

For further reading:

Carter, Ruth C. *For Honor, Glory and Union: The Mexican and Civil War Letters of Brigadier General William Haines Lytle* (1999).

Cohen, Stan B. *The Civil War in West Virginia: A Pictorial History* (1976).

Lamers, William M. *The Edge of Glory: A Biography of General William S. Rosecrans, U.S.A.* (1999).

Lowry, Terry. *September Blood: The Battle of Carnifex Ferry* (1985).

CAROLINAS CAMPAIGN
(1 February–23 March 1865)

Having completed his March to the Sea and rested briefly, Union general William T. Sherman marched out of Savannah on 1 February, 1865, his army of 60,000 accustomed to destructive war by its systematic depredations in Georgia. His proximate goal was to devastate Confederate resources in his path and punish South Carolina for its leadership in secession; his ultimate goal was to advance through North Carolina into Virginia and direct his forces at the rear of Lee's army, serving as an anvil to Grant's hammer. At first, his opponents were hopeful that the terrain would frustrate his purposes. In the wettest season the region had experienced in years, he had to negotiate flooded swamps by the score and cross nine swollen rivers with all their tributaries. In the face of harassing fire from the Southern troops, his engineers, commanding hastily improvised "pioneer" battalions composed of soldiers and freedpersons, accomplished daily projects of draining water, clearing brush, and building bridges, roads, and causeways. Despite the obstacles of enemy and environment, his armies made a pace of about ten miles a day, all the while achieving in their ravages a level of ferocity and thoroughness never approached in Georgia. Like their commander, the Union troops sincerely felt South Carolina must be taught an unforgettable lesson and gave full rein to their fury, leaving little in their trail but ashes. The civilian population of South Carolina suffered horribly.

At the outset, Sherman had disposed his infantry in

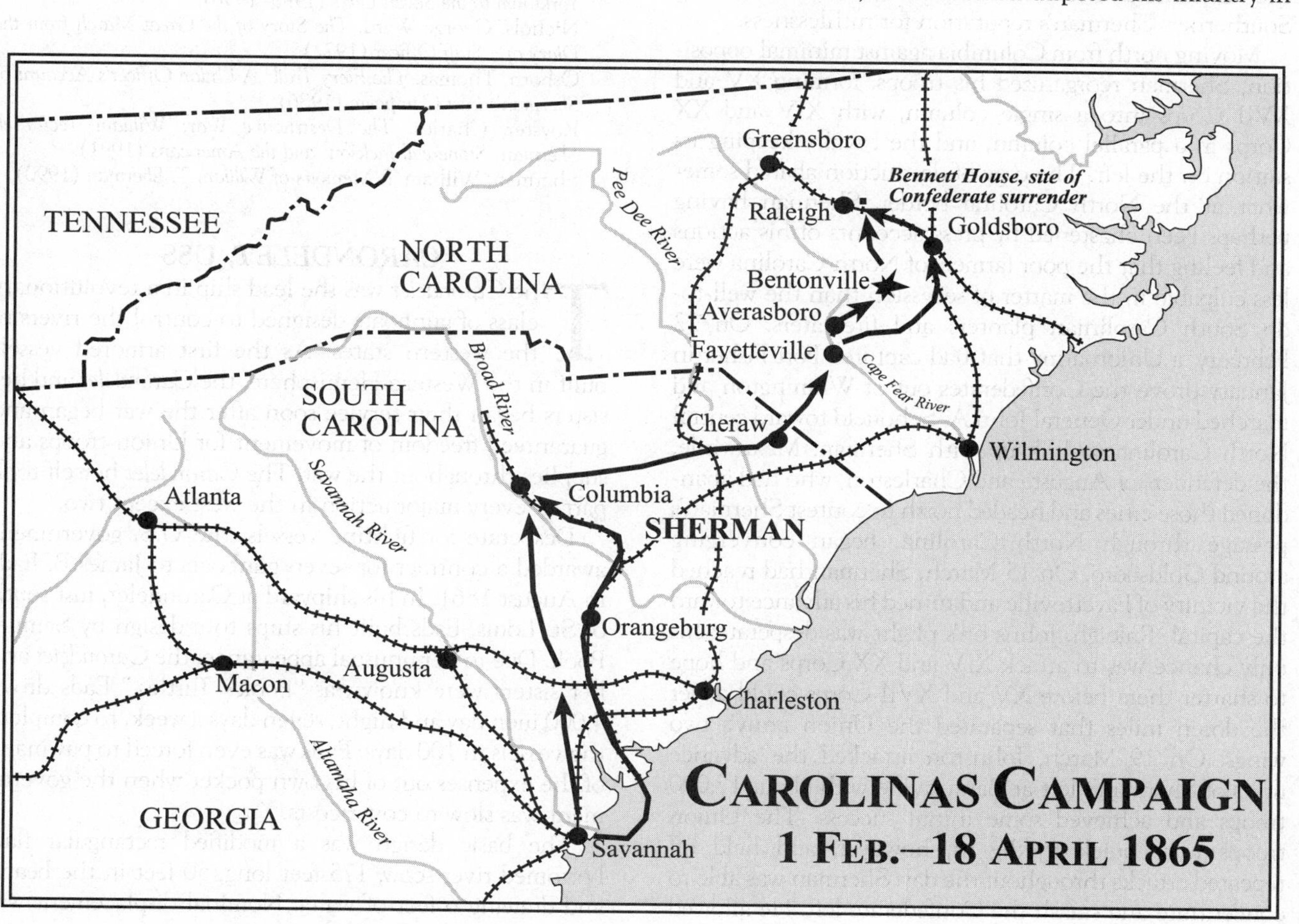

CAROLINAS CAMPAIGN
1 FEB.—18 APRIL 1865

four parallel corps marching in column and spread over a front of thirty miles with the cavalry a separate column on the left. His enemies, under the overall command of General Joseph E. Johnston, had severely limited forces at their disposal and could only guess at his intentions. The two easternmost columns, XV and XVII Corps, seemed bound for Charleston to avenge Fort Sumter; the two westernmost columns, XIV and XX Corps, for Augusta and its munitions factories. Each of those cities had been garrisoned with about 10,000 troops scraped together with some difficulty. A small rebel cavalry force under General Joseph Wheeler could do little more than observe his progress. At the Edisto River, it became evident that Sherman intended for his columns to converge on Columbia, South Carolina's capital, which had been left almost undefended and could muster only token resistance before falling on 17 February. In the confusion of the city's capture, a fire started from bales of cotton being burned by the defenders and, with the assistance of some of Sherman's troops and a gale-force wind, burned about a third of the city. Though an investigation seven years after the war established that Sherman did not intend or order the burning of the city and acted to bring the conflagration to an end as quickly as possible, the Columbia firestorm forever cemented among Southerners Sherman's reputation for ruthlessness.

Moving north from Columbia against minimal opposition, Sherman reorganized his troops, forming XV and XVII Corps into a single column, with XIV and XX Corps in a parallel column, and the cavalry keeping its station on the left. The orgy of destruction abated somewhat at the North Carolina border, Sherman having perhaps been chastened by press accounts of his actions and feeling that the poor farmers of North Carolina were less culpable in the matter of secession than the well-to-do South Carolinian planters and fire-eaters. On 22 February, a Union army that had captured Fort Fisher in January drove the Confederates out of Wilmington and marched under General John A. Schofield toward central North Carolina to link up with Sherman. Meanwhile, the defenders of Augusta and Charleston, who had abandoned those cities and headed north to contest Sherman's passage through North Carolina, began converging around Goldsboro. On 15 March, Sherman had reached the vicinity of Fayetteville and turned his advance toward the capital, Raleigh. Johnston's plight was desperate; his only chance was to attack XIV and XX Corps and hope to shatter them before XV and XVII Corps could cover the dozen miles that separated the Union army's two wings. On 19 March, Johnston attacked the advance units of Sherman's left at Bentonville with about 17,000 troops and achieved some initial success. The Union troops were quick to dig in, however, and held off repeated attacks throughout the day. Sherman was able to concentrate and smash the Confederate left. He allowed

Johnston to retreat rather than press his advantage, and on 23 March he reached Goldsboro and was joined by Schofield. His army was resting and refitting for the invasion of Virginia when news of Lee's surrender reached it. General Johnston surrendered all Confederate forces in the vicinity to Sherman on 26 April.

—*Joseph M. McCarthy*

See also Bentonville, Battle of; Columbia, South Carolina; North Carolina; South Carolina.

For further reading:
Angley, Wilson, et al. *Sherman's March through North Carolina: A Chronology* (1996).
Barnard, George N. *Photographic Views of Sherman's Campaign* (1977).
Barrett, John G. *Sherman's March through the Carolinas* (1956; reprint, 1996).
Davis, Burke. *Sherman's March: The First Full-Length Narration of General William T. Sherman's Devastating March through Georgia and the Carolinas* (1988).
Glatthaar, Joseph T. *The March to the Sea and Beyond: Sherman's Troops in the Savannah and Carolinas Campaigns* (1985).
Hitchcock, Henry. *Marching with Sherman: Passages from the Letters and Campaign Diaries of Henry Hitchcock, Major and Assistant Adjutant General of Volunteers. November 1864–May 1865* (1995).
Lucas, Marion B. *Sherman and the Burning of Columbia* (1976).
Miller, William J., ed. *The Peninsula Campaign of 1862: From Yorktown to the Seven Days* (1993–1996).
Nichols, George Ward. *The Story of the Great March from the Diary of a Staff Officer* (1972).
Osborn, Thomas. *The Fiery Trail: A Union Officer's Account of Sherman's Last Campaign* (1986).
Royster, Charles. *The Destructive War: William Tecumseh Sherman, Stonewall Jackson, and the Americans* (1991).
Sherman, William T. *Memoirs of William T. Sherman* (1990).

CARONDELET, USS

The *Carondelet* was the lead ship in a revolutionary class of gunboats designed to control the rivers of the western states. As the first armored vessels built in the Western Hemisphere, the *Carondelet* and her sisters began their service soon after the war began and guaranteed freedom of movement for Union troops and supplies throughout the war. The *Carondelet* herself took part in every major action in the west except two.

Desperate for fighting vessels, the U.S. government awarded a contract for seven gunboats to James B. Eads in August 1861. In his shipyard at Carondelet, just south of St. Louis, Eads built his ships to a design by Samuel Pook. Due to her unusual appearance, the *Carondelet* and her sisters were known as "Pook's Turtles." Eads drove 4,000 men day and night, seven days a week, to complete the vessels in 100 days. Eads was even forced to pay many of the expenses out of his own pocket when the government was slow to cover costs.

The basic design was a modified rectangular flat-bottomed river scow, 175 feet long, 50 feet in the beam, and drawing 6 feet of water. Nominal displacement was

512 tons. The gun deck was covered by a pyramidal casemate, with sloping sides to deflect shot. The front of the casemate was armored with 2.5 inches of iron plate, backed with 24 inches of oak planking. Similar plates extended 32 feet back on either side to protect the engines and boilers. The sides and stern of the casemate consisted of only 5 inches of oak, as it was intended that only the front would be turned toward the enemy. A paddle wheel was located at the stern in a deep swallowtail and was covered to protect it from Confederate shot. The *Carondelet* carried thirteen guns of varying sizes, changing throughout the war as newer weapons became available.

The *Carondelet* was commissioned on 10 January 1862, under the command of Henry Walke. Walke was a senior naval officer who viewed his assignment to the river forces as a demotion. A man with something to prove, Walke soon displayed his initiative and willingness to take chances. The *Carondelet* bombarded Fort Henry on 6 February, and, after the fort's surrender, traveled up the Tennessee River to destroy railroad bridges leading to Memphis. On 13 February, Walke and the *Carondelet* began a bombardment of Fort Donelson on the Cumberland River in support of General Ulysses S. Grant. The following day was nearly a disaster for the *Carondelet*. Defensive fire from Fort Donelson disabled her sister ships *Louisville*, *Pittsburgh*, and *St. Louis*. The *Carondelet* herself suffered severe casualties, partly from the explosion of one of her own guns. Walke still refused to break off the action until warned that several hits below the waterline had started leaks threatening the ship. Grant was forced to capture Fort Donelson by a more conventional siege.

Following repairs, the *Carondelet* returned to the Mississippi River to support General John Pope in his siege of Island No. 10. Batteries on the island prevented Union vessels from moving downriver, but Pope could not cross the Mississippi and capture Island No. 10 until gunboats could support him. Only Walke believed that it was possible to run an ironclad past the island. Following careful preparation and taking advantage of a storm, Walke attempted to run down the river on 4 April. The *Carondelet* was halfway through the danger zone when she was discovered by the Rebels. At least sixty guns fired at her, but no hits were scored. Three days later, her sister ship, the *Pittsburgh*, joined the *Carondelet* at New Madrid downriver from Island No. 10. Together, the two ironclads chased off the Confederate gunboats and ensured a safe crossing by Pope's troops. Seven thousand Confederate soldiers and 100 cannon were quickly captured.

The *Carondelet* continued to support Union army operations. In June 1862 she was among the fleet that destroyed a squadron of Confederate gunboats at Memphis. By July the fleet of river gunboats and ironclads were just above Vicksburg, where they were joined by Admiral David G. Farragut's fleet, conquerors of New Orleans. On 15 July, the *Carondelet* and two other vessels were sent up the Yazoo River to investigate rumors that the Confederate ironclad *Arkansas* was coming down to the Mississippi. Contact was made, and in a running fight the *Carondelet* was badly damaged and forced ashore. The *Arkansas* was also damaged, particularly in the funnel, and forced to take shelter at Vicksburg. The *Arkansas* later was blown up by her own crew when her engines failed.

After being repaired, the *Carondelet* and the other ironclads were busy seeking dry land for Grant's army to launch an assault on Vicksburg. In April 1863 Grant took his army down the west bank of the Mississippi. The *Carondelet* with other gunboats ran down the river past the batteries of Vicksburg. They protected the army's crossing of the Mississippi south of Vicksburg, and kept up the blockade while Grant's army laid siege to the city. When Vicksburg fell on 4 July, the Mississippi was free of Confederate forces.

The *Carondelet* spent most of the rest of the war patrolling the Mississippi's tributaries, looking for Rebel raiders. Her participation in the Red River expedition of early 1864 was undistinguished, but she supported Thomas's forces in the battle of Bell's Mill in December 1864. She was decommissioned in June 1865, and sold to a civilian buyer before the end of the year. The *Carondelet* was not the most powerful ironclad in the western states during the Civil War, but she was in the right place at the right time to help ensure a Union victory.

—*Tim J. Watts*

For further reading:
Branch, Mary Emerson. "A Story behind the Story of the *Arkansas* and the *Carondelet*." *Missouri Historical Review* (1985).
Gosnell, H. A. *Guns on the Western Waters: The Story of the River Gunboats in the Civil War* (1949).
Huffstot, Robert D. "The *Carondelet*." *Civil War Times Illustrated* (1967).
Melville, Phillips. "The *Carondelet* Runs the Gauntlet." *American Heritage* (1959).
Smith, Myron J., Jr., and Thomas Addison. "Notes on the fate of USS *Carondelet*." *Nautical Research Journal* (1974).

CARR, EUGENE ASA
(1830–1910)
Union general

Carr was a prominent figure in the Trans-Mississippi during the Civil War and a veteran of the Wilson's Creek, Pea Ridge, and the Vicksburg campaigns. He is better known for his long years fighting Indians in the West, where he earned the respectful sobriquet "War Eagle" from his Native American opponents.

Carr was born in 1830 in Boston Corner, Erie County, New York, into a family with deep roots in the New

World. His ancestors crossed the Atlantic shortly after the *Mayflower* and played a prominent role in the settling of Rhode Island. Carr graduated from West Point in 1850, the start of a distinguished forty-three–year career in the U.S. Army. Commissioned a brevet second lieutenant in the regiment of 3d Mounted Rifles (later the 3d Cavalry), Carr received the first of many wounds while fighting Indians in Texas in 1854. He received a promotion to captain in the 1st Cavalry in 1858, and was stationed at Fort Washita in Indian Territory on the eve of the Civil War.

Carr was transferred to the 4th U.S. Cavalry in August 1861, and fought with this unit at Wilson's Creek, Missouri, on 10 August. Shortly after Wilson's Creek, Carr accepted a commission as colonel of the 3d Illinois Cavalry. In command of the 4th Division of the Army of the Southwest under Brigadier General Samuel R. Curtis, Carr played a significant role in the crucial battle of Pea Ridge, Arkansas, on 7–8 March 1862. Major General Earl Van Dorn's Confederate Army of the West attempted to outflank Curtis and cut the Federals from their lines of communication. Carr's division, outnumbered by Confederate forces around Elkhorn Tavern, stubbornly held its ground and in the process gained valuable time for the remainder of the army to turn and face the Confederates. During the fighting around Elkhorn Tavern on 7 March, Carr was wounded three times. For his brave and skillful leadership in the battle, Carr received the Medal of Honor. He was promoted to brigadier general of U.S. volunteers on 7 March 1862.

Upon Curtis's promotion to head the District of the Missouri, Carr was made commander of the Army of Southwestern Missouri in October 1862. Carr became ill (probably suffering from malaria) and was transferred to command of the District of St. Louis and then the 2d Division of the Army of Southeast Missouri from February to March 1863. He was then transferred to the 14th Division of XIII Corps, Army of the Tennessee, with which he saw action at Port Gibson, Louisiana; Champion's Hill and Big Black River, Mississippi; and the siege of Vicksburg. After the fall of Vicksburg on 4 July 1863, Carr led the left wing of XVI Corps of the Army of the Tennessee before he returned to the Trans-Mississippi to command a cavalry division in the Camden expedition, the Arkansas portion of the ill-fated Red River campaign of 1864.

In his final act of the Civil War, Carr commanded the 3d Division of XVI Corps in an attack led by Major General Edward R. S. Canby on Mobile, Alabama. Carr mustered out of the U.S. volunteers on 15 January 1866. Although he held the rank of brevet major general in both the U.S. Army and the U.S. volunteers, he reverted to his prewar rank of major of the 5th U.S. Cavalry. After the war, Carr saw much action against Indians in the West, moving up through the ranks until he was appointed brigadier general in 1893. Carr retired in 1893 more famous for his exploits as an Indian fighter than for his heroics in the Civil War. He died on 2 December 1910 and was buried at West Point, New York.

Carr was an aggressive and talented leader who deserved a higher rank during the Civil War. His stubborn delaying action on the first day at Pea Ridge highlighted an impressive Civil War record. Greatly respected by his men, Carr was impatient with what he believed were incompetent superiors, and he did not hesitate to say so. This placed him in hot water with his superiors at times, but his demonstrated abilities kept his career on track. Carr's legacy has been diminished by his service in the low-profile Trans-Mississippi and western theaters, but that should in no way diminish his reputation.

—*Terry L. Beckenbaugh*

See also Mobile Campaign; Pea Ridge, Battle of; Vicksburg Campaign; Wilson's Creek, Missouri.

For further reading:

Josephy, Alvin M. *The Civil War in the American West* (1991).
King, James T. *War Eagle: A Life of General Eugene A. Carr* (1963).
Shea, William L., and Earl J. Hess. *Pea Ridge: Civil War Campaign in the West* (1992).

CARRICK'S FORD
(13 July 1861)

Confederate colonel John Pegram's surrender to George B. McClellan after the battle of Rich Mountain compelled General Robert S. Garnett to abandon his positions on Laurel Hill and retreat toward the Cheat River and northwestern Virginia. Brigadier General Thomas A. Morris mounted a Federal pursuit composed of three infantry regiments and artillery with Captain H. W. Benham in overall command. They hoped to cut off Garnett's flight.

Such was no small task. Torrential rain and the Confederate's felling of trees in Benham's path had made the daunting terrain of deep valleys and steep mountains all but impassable. Nonetheless, both blue and gray troops, unseasoned as they were, gamely slogged on. It began to rain again at dawn on 13 July and by midmorning the drizzle had become a lashing downpour that would continue into the afternoon. The Confederates managed to cross the Cheat River except for the 1st Georgia and 23d Virginia Infantry regiments, along with a section of artillery and some cavalry. Garnett's wagon train also lagged behind, especially slowed by the rain-choked roads. Near Kaler's Ford, Benham found this rear guard, drove in its pickets, and unlimbered his artillery. The inexperienced Georgians and Virginians commenced as skillful a retrograde as they could manage, falling back in good order some three and a half miles toward Carrick's Ford before taking a

The battle of Carrick's Ford, 13 July 1861 (*Library of Congress*)

stand, doing so there more or less because they had to. The problem was the river, swollen deep at Carrick's, and the wagons, several of which were lost in the crossing. Colonel William B. Taliaferro commanding the 23d Virginia got across and gained high ground on the right bank, though. After offering up a cheer for Jefferson Davis—it was early enough in the war for such gestures—they opened fire on Benham's skirmishers appearing on the other side.

The Federals soon were replying with a heavy fire of their own, but their artillery could not find the range of the enemy. Three Confederate guns and musketry held off the bluecoats for more than an hour. With his ammunition nearly exhausted, Taliaferro again had the 23d retreat, this time in enough confusion to leave wounded on the field. Soon the regiment met Garnett, who placed ten sharpshooters pulled from its ranks at a bend in the road. He sent the remainder of the men toward the main column, while he remained with the detachment to discourage too close a Federal pursuit. When Benham's advance pressed in close, Garnett was giving the order to retire when a bullet struck down the man next to him. Just that quickly, another killed Garnett. He was the war's first general officer to fall in combat.

Exhaustion and the weather prevented a continued Federal pursuit of the fleeing Confederates. The 23d Virginia had left only about thirty of their number dead

at the engagement around Carrick's Ford, but the episode made for a grim conclusion to a sobering campaign. It all had been a significant strategic setback and a profound psychological blow for the new Confederacy, the one because it dimmed the political fortunes in the region and the other because Garnett's death gave pause to those who had blustered about a gloriously short and bloodless war.

For his part, McClellan was exultant over the general success of his first campaign. Neither he nor the nation that would soon lionize him could know that it was to be the zenith of his military exploits. Moreover, the failure to smash anything other than Garnett's rear guard at Carrick's Ford contributed in part to McClellan's growing fixation with minute detail and a tendency to avoid delegating authority. The pitfalls of such an attitude would not become apparent right away, and for the time being, the man the newspapers soon dubbed an American Napoleon could bask in his success and pass judgment on his enemies. Contemplating the dead Garnett, McClellan curtly observed, "Such is the fate of traitors."

—*David S. Heidler and Jeanne T. Heidler*

See also Garnett, Robert S.; McClellan, George B.; Rich Mountain, Battle of; Taliaferro, William Booth; West Virginia.
For further reading:
McClellan, George B. *McClellan's Own Story: The War for the*

Union, the Soldiers Who Fought It, the Civilians Who Directed It, and His Relations to It and to Them (1887).

Newell, Clayton R. *Lee vs. McClellan: The First Campaigns* (1996).

Thomas, Joseph W. "The Campaigns of Generals McClellan and Rosecrans in Western Virginia, 1861–62." *West Virginia History* (1944).

CARRINGTON, HENRY BEEBE
(1824–1912)
Union general

Born in 1824, Henry Beebe Carrington was a Connecticut Yankee transplanted to Ohio. While a young man, he heard John Brown speak and became an ardent abolitionist. After attending Yale University, Carrington taught school and was practicing law in Ohio when he assisted in organizing the Republican Party there. A close friend of Ohio governor Salmon P. Chase, he organized the Ohio state militia in 1857. He accomplished this task so well that Ohio sent nine militia companies across the Ohio River to protect the western counties of Virginia so volunteers there could be organized.

In May 1861 Carrington was named colonel of the Ohio 18th U.S. Infantry. He was later made adjutant general of Ohio and placed in charge of the regular army camp in that state. In August of 1862, Indiana governor Oliver Morton requested his services in Indiana, and he was made chief mustering officer and post commander in Indianapolis. He was promoted to brigadier general of United States Volunteers in November 1862, and made commander of the District of Indiana, Department of the Ohio, in March 1863.

While in Indiana, Carrington caused controversy by investigating and putting on trial members of the Sons of Liberty and other allegedly disloyal groups. When he arrived in Indiana, political warfare between the adherents of the Lincoln administration and their opponents was beginning in earnest. The Republican Party's favorite political target, the elusive Knights of the Golden Circle, was blamed for every military and political reversal, and Carrington endorsed the view wholeheartedly. He blamed appalling desertion rates on treasonable secret societies, and in his long report of March 1863, he declared that the situation in Indiana bordered on open revolt. Yet he grossly exaggerated membership in these secret societies for political purposes, seizing upon minor and irrelevant incidents to accuse Democrats of treasonous activities.

Carrington's motives seem to have been a dread of active field service and a desire for promotion. By attributing the danger in Indiana solely to secret organizations that only he understood, he could keep his safe and comfortable position in Indianapolis and still obtain promotions often denied desk-bound warriors.

Carrington frequently clashed with Indiana civil authorities over his arbitrary arrests, Draconian displays of military force, and deprivations of civil rights. His imprudence and rashness in dealing with Indiana's heated political situation eventually got him relieved of command in April 1863. He was so unpopular in the state by this time, especially among Democrats, that he was known derisively as the "Hero of the Home Brigade." Though Democrats labeled him a coward, he served Governor Morton ably in the field of political warfare, for which he was well suited. The Supreme Court would later overturn many of Carrington's actions in Indiana, but at the time Lincoln upheld him and he enjoyed considerable support from Indiana Republicans. He was also credited with energetic leadership in stimulating enlistments in the state.

Carrington was hardly a warrior, though. When given a force to chase Confederate raider John Hunt Morgan out of the state in July 1863, Carrington fortified his courage with so much liquor that he fell off his horse. Meanwhile, he could not shake his fixation with the supposed enemy in his midst. From July 1863 until May 1864, Carrington was on detached duty in Indiana and hired a corps of detectives to infiltrate the Sons of Liberty and other suspected disloyal organizations. These spies worked with an evident determination to discover the treason they were being paid to find. Their reports, however, consisted of unfounded rumors circulating in the Union press and offered no evidence of illegal or treasonous conduct by the groups. Thus knowing every move the secret societies made, Carrington and Morton had no reason to fear them as a menace to domestic peace. Yet Morton held up the societies as strawmen and made great political capital out of exposing alleged plots and trying putative traitors. Finally, such behavior became too much even for Carrington. As the fall 1864 elections approached, Morton was eager to start the military trials of arrested Copperhead "conspirators." To Carrington's credit, he denied the legality of military trials while the civil courts were open and functioning freely. Morton broke with Carrington over the issue and had him replaced.

Mustered out of the Volunteers in August 1865, Carrington was sent west, where he built Fort Kearny. He fought in the Red Cloud War in which he was severely wounded, but he later established friendly relations with important Indian chiefs. He taught military science at Wabash College before retiring in 1870.

Carrington pursued a literary career and wrote *The Battles of the American Revolution* in 1876. He also wrote many other works on international, military, and Indian affairs. He died in 1912.

—*Ron Hamilton*

See also Copperheads; Morton, Oliver Perry; Order of American Knights; Sons of Liberty.

For further reading:

Fesler, Mayo. "Secret Political Societies in the North during the Civil War." *Indiana Magazine of History* (1918).

Stampp, Kenneth. *Indiana Politics during the Civil War* (1949).
Terrell, W. H. H. *Indiana in the War of the Rebellion: Report of the Adjutant General of Indiana*, vol. 1 (1960).
Tredway, G. R. *Democratic Opposition to the Lincoln Administration in Indiana* (1973).

CARROLL, ANNA ELLA
(1815–1894)
Pamphleteer

Anna Ella Carroll, daughter of Maryland governor Thomas King Carroll, political pamphleteer for the American (Know-Nothing) Party, and paid lobbyist for various interests in 1850s Washington, is better known for her claim to have devised the so-called Tennessee Plan for the Union army than for her pamphlets that laid out the presidential rationale for using the army to enforce Federal laws within the Southern states.

Little is known of Carroll's life prior to midcentury. Never married, she made her living as a lobbyist for various interests and politicians, using her connections with Maryland, New York, and Washington politicians to promise patronage positions to all who would hire her to write on their behalf. (Her enemies declared her to be a confidence woman as well, who "borrowed" money and never repaid it.) One of a number of women active in partisan politics rather than social reform movements and acquainted with innumerable politicians who enjoyed the attention of a bright, flatteringly attentive female listener, Carroll wrote campaign literature for Millard Fillmore's 1856 presidential campaign as the Know-Nothing candidate, and promoted the candidacies of William Henry Seward, John Minor Botts, and Thurlow Weed. The outbreak of war found her writing in support of Maryland governor Thomas Hicks's attempts to prevent any meeting of Maryland legislators to stave off a vote for secession.

Living in Washington throughout most of the war, Carroll approached the War Department in 1861 after a trip to St. Louis, where she visited a riverboat captain, Charles Scott, and discussed the apparent difficulty the Union was having invading the South. According to a letter Carroll wrote to the Washington, D.C., *National Intelligencer* shortly after the Confederate surrender in 1865, Scott pointed out the strategic value of using the Tennessee and Cumberland rivers, which flowed north, instead of the Mississippi River, to invade the Confederacy via Tennessee. Gunboats damaged by Confederate fire would float northward, back into Union territory, and the Tennessee was navigable clear to Alabama, providing excellent ingress to the heart of the Confederacy. Neither river was strongly fortified and control of them would relieve Union loyalists, particularly those in eastern Tennessee.

Carroll took Scott's information, drew up a map, and presented it to the War Department's assistant secretary,

Thomas Scott, in November 1861. She was no doubt gratified to see the Union invade Tennessee up the rivers she had suggested the following February, with victorious battles at Forts Henry and Donelson. Carroll did not realize that her plan duplicated one published in the *New York Times* earlier in November 1861. It also resembled the overall strategy undertaken by the Union army commanded by Generals Henry Halleck and Ulysses Grant, the latter of whom had captured Smithville and Paducah at the mouths of the rivers that fall and was waiting for Union gunboats before venturing farther inland.

Carroll depended upon her writing to make her living, and shortly after the war, she began petitioning Congress for money and recognition of her efforts at writing military strategy. Carroll had made a verbal agreement with Assistant Secretary Scott to write for the War Department in the summer of 1861. The agreement stemmed from Carroll's pamphlets supporting Lincoln's actions in the early days of the war. The most important of these, *Reply to Breckinridge* (1861), detailed arguments by Lincoln and Attorney General Edward Bates that, as commander in chief, Lincoln could use the armed forces to perform his duties as chief enforcement officer of the United States. In other words, he could call for volunteers, suspend the writ of habeas corpus, institute a naval blockade, and use the army to put down a domestic rebellion, a legal fiction he employed throughout the war.

Carroll's pamphlets were so clearly written and so accessible that Secretary of State William Henry Seward, who knew Carroll from the early 1850s, when she promoted his presidential candidacy for the Whig Party, ordered them printed up and laid on every desk in Congress. The legal rationale Carroll described was later delineated by notable lawyer Horace Binney and published more widely, but Carroll did provide the earliest explication of Lincoln's actions in the critical first months of the war.

Later pamphlets Carroll wrote criticized the president's actions, particularly regarding the Union's confiscation of slaves as contraband of war. She also promoted colonization efforts by Aaron Columbus Burr, illegitimate son of Aaron Burr, and suggested in a letter to the *New York Times* that, as peaceful coexistence between blacks and whites seemed unlikely, colonization in a friendly Central American colony might be the best answer to preserve the black community of ex-slaves. Such suggestions came to naught, and Carroll returned to petitioning the president, Thomas Scott, and finally Congress for payment for the creation of the Tennessee Plan as a task more likely to be compensated.

Carroll's claim was alive for years. From 1865 until her death in 1894, Carroll filed petitions, wrote pamphlets, and begged for letters of confirmation from men such as Grant, Cassius Clay, Benjamin Wade, and

Secretary of War Edwin Stanton. Her cause was adopted by the suffragists Susan B. Anthony, Sarah Ellen Blackwell, and Elizabeth Cady Stanton, and they held subscription drives to raise money for her as she aged and grew infirm. She became a symbol of the military's disregard for both civilians and women when it came to the work of the war, and her invention of evidence to support her claim was disregarded by readers who took her evidence at face value. Her role as a symbol continues to the present with continual appearances of Carroll in Civil War historiography as an unsung female hero or a romanticized player in the politics of the period. Her legal acumen, widely respected by politicians, including Lincoln, holds less appeal than her legendary status as military strategist.

Carroll lived her last years in Washington, D.C., entertaining occasional visitors curious about her declared status by supporters as the "Woman who saved the Union." She was cared for by her sister Mary and lived mostly on money from subscriptions provided by suffragists. Carroll died of kidney failure in Washington on 19 February 1894. Ironically, her gravestone is as inaccurate as much of the rest that is known about her, and is misdated 1893.

—*Janet L. Coryell*

See also American Party; Anthony, Susan B.; Stanton, Elizabeth Cady; Women.

For further reading:
Carroll, Anna Ella. *Reply to the Speech of Hon. J. C. Breckinridge* (1861).
———. *The War Powers of the General Government* (1861).
Coryell, Janet L. *Neither Heroine nor Fool: Anna Ella Carroll of Maryland* (1990).
Greenbie, Sydney, and Marjorie Greenbie. *Anna Ella Carroll and Abraham Lincoln: A Biography* (1952).
Williams, Kenneth P. "The Tennessee River Campaign and Anna Ella Carroll." *Indiana Magazine of History* (1950).

CARROLL, SAMUEL SPRIGG
(1832–1893)
Union general

The son of William Thomas Carroll, clerk of the Supreme Court, and a member of the famous Carroll family of Maryland, Samuel Sprigg Carroll was born in Washington, D.C. He was educated locally before receiving an appointment to the U.S. Military Academy. He graduated forty-fourth of forty-nine in the class of 1856. Carroll served at various frontier posts before returning for duty at West Point in 1860. He left the academy in November 1861 and a month later was named colonel of the 8th Ohio. Carroll served with his regiment in western Virginia until the following summer.

Carroll and the 8th Ohio fought in the Shenandoah Valley campaign against Thomas J. "Stonewall" Jackson in the spring of 1862. He commanded a brigade under James Shields for most of that campaign, particularly at Kernstown and Port Republic. Carroll continued to command the brigade under James B. Ricketts in the Army of Virginia at Cedar Mountain but was wounded a few days later in a skirmish on the Rapidan River. He was unable to rejoin his command until after the battle of Antietam.

In the battle of Fredericksburg, Carroll commanded a brigade of III Corps. In the spring he moved to the command of a brigade in Darius Couch's II Corps and commanded that brigade at Chancellorsville and Gettysburg. He was commended by his division commander, Brigadier General Alexander Hays, for his actions at Gettysburg on 2 July. Carroll continued to command his brigade during the Bristoe Station and Mine Run campaigns in the fall of 1863 through the early spring of 1864.

It would be during the early phases of Ulysses S. Grant's campaign against Robert E. Lee in May 1864 that Carroll gained the serious attention of higher-ranking officers. Commanding his brigade in the division of Brigadier General John Gibbon, Carroll fought in the late afternoon of 5 May in the battle of the Wilderness. The following day, Carroll received a serious wound in the arm but refused to leave the field and continued to lead his men later in the day when his brigade was placed in reserve. Four days later at Spotsylvania Court House, leading a frontal assault on Confederate works, Carroll was again wounded in the right arm and suffered severe casualties to his brigade. While temporarily in command of Gibbon's division three days later on 13 May in another charge, Carroll was shot again, this time in the left arm, and the wound shattered much of the bone in the arm. He had to be carried from the field. For Carroll's actions during these battles, George Gordon Meade, commander of the Army of the Potomac, recommended Carroll for promotion to brigadier general. When the promotion occurred, Carroll's date of rank was 12 May 1864.

Carroll's wounds required a long recuperation. Although he was able to serve on light duty such as courts-martial during the fall, he was unable to accept a field command until December 1864. Given command of the 2d Division, Department of West Virginia, under Winfield Scott Hancock, Carroll operated primarily in the Shenandoah Valley against independent Confederate cavalry commands like that of John Singleton Mosby. In April 1865 he was given command of the 4th Provisional Division, Army of the Shenandoah.

After the war, Carroll chose to remain in the army, although he found it increasingly difficult, given his wartime wounds, to hold an active command. He retired in 1869 at the rank of major general, the rank accorded him due to the wounds he had suffered during the war. Unable to lead a very active life in retirement, Carroll lived quietly in Washington and at one of the family homes in Maryland on the city's outskirts. He died on 28 January 1893 in Montgomery County, Maryland.

—*David S. Heidler and Jeanne T. Heidler*

See also Spotsylvania, Battle of; Wilderness, Battle of the.
For further reading:
Matter, William D. If It Takes All Summer; the Battle of Spotsylvania (1988).
Rhea, Gordon C. The Battle of the Wilderness, May 5–6, 1864 (1994).
Rhea, Gordon C. The Battles for Spotsylvania Court House and the Road to Yellow Tavern May 7–12, 1864 (1997).

CARSON, CHRISTOPHER HOUSTON "KIT"

(1809–1868)

Union general; federal Indian agent

Arguably the greatest frontier legend in U.S. history, Christopher H. "Kit" Carson was born on Christmas Eve, 1809, in Madison County, Kentucky, but spent the majority of his childhood years in the Boone's Lick district of western Missouri. He was apprenticed to a saddle and harness maker at age fourteen, but quickly traded in an artisan's life for the open trail, taking passage on a wagon train and eventually reaching New Mexico Territory in 1826. By his twentieth birthday, Carson had established himself in Sante Fe as an able fur trapper and scout, whose travels took him throughout the Far West from the Rocky Mountains to the Pacific Ocean. Like many mountain men of the era, Carson came into close contact with the Indians of the region, but unlike many of his contemporaries, Carson enjoyed a relatively amicable relationship with the native inhabitants of the region. He was reported to be self-restrained and temperate toward the local Indians, and he eventually married into both the Arapaho and Cheyenne tribes.

Carson's national reputation was launched in 1842, when he met John C. Frémont while on a trip to Missouri and was hired as a guide and scout for Frémont's western explorations. It was Carson who was largely responsible for leading Frémont's expeditions throughout the expanses of the Great Basin and the mountains of the West. Frémont's highly publicized and widely read reports of his travels portrayed Carson as the epitome of a heroic frontiersman, earning the young guide national notoriety and instant fame.

Carson enhanced his reputation during the Mexican-American War, when he successfully guided General Stephen Kearny's expedition from New Mexico Territory to California and helped Kearny repress a local challenge to U.S. authority in the region. Carson spent the last year of the war as a personal courier of President James K. Polk, carrying messages to and from Polk to his commanders in the Far West.

After the war, Carson returned to New Mexico Territory, where he began a successful career as a rancher and where he was appointed Federal Indian agent for northern New Mexico Territory in 1853. Carson was still serving as Indian agent when the Civil War broke out, and, like the majority of New Mexico Territory residents, Carson could not escape military entanglement in the burgeoning conflict between the North and the South. In 1861, he resigned his commission as Indian agent in order to help organize the 1st New Mexico Volunteer Infantry, to which he was appointed as a lieutenant colonel. Carson's volunteers saw action in 1862 at the battle of Val Verde, New Mexico, and again at Glorieta Pass, New Mexico, which were important steps in preventing Confederate occupation of the New Mexico Territory.

However, the majority of Carson's military efforts during the Civil War were directed at the Indians of the territory, including the Mescaleros and Kiowas, although his most notable campaigns took place against the Navajo. Although Carson, who preferred discussion and moderation to compulsion, had garnered a reputation for being a sympathetic and reasonable Indian agent in the years preceding the Civil War, his policies toward the Navajo occupying the New Mexico Territory were decidedly harsh. When bands of Navajo refused to be confined to government reservations in 1863, Carson engaged in a brutal economic war in which he led troops on punitive raids into Navajo territory, burning crops and villages and capturing or slaughtering livestock and horses. Without adequate shelter or provisions, the Navajo were left at the mercy of regional Indian rivals, including the Utes, Puebloes, and Hopis, who joined Carson's marauding units to take full advantage of the Navajo's weakened condition and wreak vengeance on their traditional enemy. In 1864 the vast majority of the Navajo in the New Mexico Territory surrendered to Carson. He then forced some 8,000 ravaged Navajo men, women, and children to endure a 300-mile forced march—what became known as "the long walk"—from their homes in present-day Arizona to the government reservation at Fort Sumner, New Mexico.

Despite being breveted a brigadier general in 1865 for his successful prosecution of the Navajo campaign and cited for meritorious service in conducting Indian affairs in the region, Carson was reduced to his original rank of lieutenant colonel shortly thereafter when his regiment was downsized. Two years later, he was mustered out of the service with his volunteer unit and resumed his career as a rancher. In 1868 Carson moved his family to Boggsville, Colorado, in the hopes of expanding his ranching interests, but died shortly thereafter at nearby Fort Lyon on 23 May 1868.

—Daniel P. Barr

See also Frémont, John Charles; Glorieta Pass, Battle of; Val Verde, New Mexico, Battle of.
For further reading:
Carson, Christopher H. Kit Carson's Autobiography (1935).
Carter, Harvey Lewis. Dear Old Kit: The Historical Christopher Carson (1968).

Gordon-McCutchan, R.C., ed. *Kit Carson: Indian Fighter or Indian Killer?* (1996).

Guild, Thelma S. *Kit Carson: A Pattern for Heroes* (1984).

Trafzer, Clifford E. *The Kit Carson Campaign: The Last Great Navajo War* (1982).

CARTHAGE, BATTLE OF
(5 July 1861)

Carthage, a small city in southwestern Missouri, can claim the sad honor of having been the site of the first large-scale land battle of the Civil War, more than two weeks before First Bull Run. Far from the capitals and big cities, with no reporters from the big newspapers at hand, it pitted a motley crowd of some 6,000 pro-Confederate Missouri State Guardsmen, one third purportedly without firearms, against an equally motley array of Union volunteers, who were predominantly German. Federal forces consisted of nine companies of the 3d Missouri Infantry and six of the 5th Missouri Infantry, plus an artillery battalion, divided into two four-gun batteries. Most of the Missouri State Guard volunteers had only some militia experience, and some had no military training at all. Several of the German officers were veterans of the European revolutions of 1848–1849, and their troops had received some training in St. Louis. The overall commander of the Union forces was Colonel Franz Sigel, the commanding officers of the infantry regiments were Anselm Albert and Friedrich Salomon, and the chief of artillery was Franz Backhoff, as well as a number of company and battery officers could be included in this group.

Following their defeat at Boonville, Missouri, in June 1861, prosecessionist forces commanded by Missouri governor Claiborne Jackson and Confederate general Sterling Price withdrew into the southwestern corner of the state to link up with each other and join with forces from Texas and Arkansas. They also could protect important lead mines in the region.

At the same time, Colonel Sigel's column of the Union expedition into southwestern Missouri, which had been organized by Brigadier General Thomas Sweeny, moved overland from the railhead at Rolla to occupy Springfield on 23 June and Neosho on 1 July, with the object of heading off the State Guard. On 5 July the opposing forces met several miles north of Carthage. After an initial exchange of fire, Sigel realized his dangerous situation. The Missouri State Guard, many of whom were mounted, outnumbered the Federals, who were already exhausted from long marches. Their grey "Forty-eighter"-style uniforms were in rags, and no cavalry was available to support them or to guard their flanks. As the pro-Confederate State Guard threatened to flank and surround Sigel's approximately 1,000 men, a battle ensued in which the Union forces kept moving back in the direction of Carthage, repeatedly repulsing charges by the State Guard. Backhoff's cannoneers outgunned those of Hiram Bledsoe and Henry Guibor on the other side, and apart from some bitter fighting at Dry Fork Creek, the State Guard apparently did not press its numerical advantage. Some reports stated that Sigel's column marched in a moving, open-square formation of infantry and wagons, with gun sections "leap-frogging" to guard front, sides, and rear simultaneously.

There was no fighting for awhile as the State Guard stayed out of reach. Some troops tried to execute an intelligent pincer movement into Sigel's back at Buck Branch. There was, however, a lack of generalship among the State Guard in decisive moments, even though several generals—John B. Clark, Monroe M. Parsons, James S. Rains, and William Y. Slack—were present, with Governor Jackson nominally having the overall command. Thus Union lieutenant colonel Franz Hassendeubel's 3d Missouri Battalion scattered the guardsmen blocking their path at Buck Branch. Sigel's column withdrew through the town of Carthage and by nightfall had managed to extract itself from danger.

In the end neither side won, although each claimed it had, and with some justification. Sigel's outnumbered command inflicted higher casualties than it suffered and, after a day of hard fighting, managed an orderly withdrawal. The badly equipped and badly led Missouri State Guard drove their adversaries from the field, proving an ability to fight under adverse conditions. Psychologically, the advantage was on the secessionist side: with reinforcements arriving from Arkansas (capturing a company Sigel had left in Neosho on the day of the battle), the pro-Confederate forces were able to consolidate and train their commands while using the lead mines. Meanwhile, Union forces held Springfield and waited for General Nathaniel Lyon's column to come up, and it was more than a month before forces clashed again at Wilson's Creek.

—*Wolfgang Hochbruck*

For further reading:

Hinze David C., and Karen Farnham. *The Battle of Carthage. Border War in Southwest Missouri* (1998).

Snead, Thomas L. "The First Year of the War in Missouri." In *Battles and Leaders of the Civil War*, vol. 1. (1956).

Steele, Phillip W., and Steve Cottrell. *Civil War in the Ozarks* (1993).

CARUTHERS, ROBERT LOONEY
(1800–1882)

Confederate governor of Tennessee; U.S. representative

Robert Looney Caruthers was born in Smith County, Tennessee, near Carthage on 31 July 1800. Caruthers escaped his impoverished upbringing, completing studies at Washington College in his home state. After his admittance to the bar, he practiced law and served as the clerk of Tennessee's House of Representatives (1823–1824) and labored as the clerk of Smith County's Chancery Court.

In 1826, Caruthers's move to Lebanon, Tennessee, proved a fortuitous one in terms of his political career. The young lawyer caught the eye of Governor Sam Houston, who tapped Caruthers as the attorney general of the 6th Judicial District, which he served from 1827 to 1832. After he resigned this position, Caruthers campaigned and won election to a seat in the state's House of Representatives. Caruthers's association with national politics proved short-lived. Elected as a Whig in 1841, Caruthers served in the House of Representatives until 1843, declining reelection.

When Caruthers returned to Lebanon, he focused his energies on the establishment of Cumberland University. He held the office of president of the Board of Trustees from 1842 to his death in 1882. In 1847, Caruthers helped create the department of law, making Cumberland the first university-affiliated law school in the state. This was quite an innovation and addition to the school, as only fifteen university law schools were operating in the United States at this time. Caruthers's knowledge of law and his reputation as an articulate, skilled attorney won him an appointment to fill a vacancy on the Tennessee Supreme Court in 1852. Two years later, Caruthers won election to the court and served until the outbreak of the Civil War.

As Southern states seceded and linked their futures to the Confederacy, the states of the upper South attempted to resolve the crisis. In January 1861, Tennessee's General Assembly elected Caruthers as a delegate from the 5th Congressional District to the Peace Convention at Washington, D.C. Caruthers opposed secession, but did not believe the federal government had the right to interfere with slavery.

The convention failed to reconcile the North and the South, and this (coupled with the firing on Fort Sumter and President Abraham Lincoln's summons for troops to quell the rebellion) propelled Tennessee voters to secede from the Union. Caruthers brought his leadership experience to the Provisional Congress of the Confederate States.

By early 1862, the Union army occupied the western and middle sections of the Volunteer State, and Governor Isham Harris and the state's Confederate government had fled Nashville. President Lincoln selected Senator Andrew Johnson as military governor of Union-occupied Tennessee. Still, Harris maintained a façade of power, and in 1863 called for a convention and a subsequent election for the offices of governor and Confederate congressmen. In a convention and an election that were irregular and specious, Caruthers was elected governor and Confederate congressmen were selected. Although the congressmen took office in Richmond, Caruthers never assumed the office.

After the war, Caruthers continued his law practice, and in 1868 accepted the position of professor of law at Cumberland University. His devotion to the school was evident in his donation of land and financing of a law building that was named in his honor. The law school produced two U.S. Supreme Court justices, Howell Jackson and Horace Lurton, and Secretary of State Cordell Hull. The law school remained there from 1878 to 1962 until declining enrollment and financial concerns prompted its move to the campus of Howard College (now Samford University) in Birmingham, Alabama.

After a long career in law, politics, and education, Judge Caruthers died on 2 October 1882.

—Kathleen R. Zebley

See also Tennessee.
For further reading:
Burns, Frank. *Wilson County* (1983).
Caldwell, Joshua W. *Sketches of the Bench and Bar of Tennessee* (1898).
Longum, David J., and Howard P. Walthall. *From Maverick to Mainstream: Cumberland School of Law, 1847–1997* (1997).
McBride, Robert M., and Dan M. Robinson. *Biographical Directory of the Tennessee General Assembly* (1975).

CASEY, SILAS
(1807–1882)
Union general

Born in East Greenwich, Rhode Island, Silas Casey received an appointment to the U.S. Military Academy at age fifteen. He graduated thirty-ninth of forty-one in the class of 1826. After receiving his commission, Casey served along the Great Lakes until the outbreak of the Second Seminole War brought his transfer to Florida. By the end of that conflict, Casey had reached the rank of captain. During the Mexican-American War, Casey served in Winfield Scott's Mexico City campaign, in which he earned two brevet promotions and was wounded twice. After the war, Casey was transferred to the Pacific Northwest, where he would spend most of the years before the outbreak of the Civil War. In 1855 he became the lieutenant colonel of the newly created 9th Infantry and its colonel in early 1861. In the same year, *System of Infantry Tactics*, for which he was primarily responsible, was published. It became more popularly known as "Casey's Tactics" and was adopted as the standard infantry manual by the U.S. Army in 1862.

At the outbreak of the Civil War, Casey commanded Fort Steilacoom in the Washington Territory. He was recalled from the northwest and was made brigadier general of volunteers in August 1861. Casey initially commanded a brigade in the Army of the Potomac, but his considerable experience led him to be tapped for extra duties in the fall of 1861. For example, he managed the military details of the Washington funeral of

Silas Casey (*Library of Congress*)

President Abraham Lincoln's friend Colonel Edward Baker.

In the spring of 1862, Casey was given command of a division in Erasmus Keyes's IV Corps for the upcoming Peninsula campaign. He commanded his division in the siege of Yorktown, the battle of Williamsburg, and the preliminary skirmishes before Seven Pines. On 31 May at Seven Pines, Casey's division was the first to be struck when Joseph Johnston attacked south of the Chickahominy River. Casey fought bravely but was pushed back by the Confederate onslaught. He was later quietly criticized by the commander of the Army of the Potomac, George B. McClellan, for being caught unawares, which greatly angered Casey. Despite his defeat, Casey was promoted to major general of volunteers for his actions at Seven Pines. Casey also led his division in the Seven Days'.

When McClellan's army was recalled from the peninsula in August 1862, Casey was transferred to Washington to supervise the training procedures for new recruits. At the end of the year he was placed in command of the provisional division of the Department of Washington. During the next few months, his primary duty was trying to combat the various Confederate raids against the Federal outposts south of the city. Since he

was in the Washington area, Casey was also tapped for various other duties, particularly courts-martial. From late 1862 to early 1863, he served as a member of the court-martial of Fitz John Porter.

In May 1863, Casey received appointment to the board that would occupy him for much of the remainder of the war. He became the president of the board that examined officers for fitness to command African-American troops. Casey took a strong interest in this new task and even published *Infantry Tactics for Colored Troops* to aid the new officers in their task. He remained president of the examination board until July 1865.

Casey stayed in the army after the war, reverting to the rank of colonel of the 9th Infantry. Physical infirmities led him to request retirement in 1868. He lived most of his retirement years in Brooklyn, New York, where he died on 22 January 1882. His remains were interred near his family's home in Rhode Island.

—*David S. Heidler and Jeanne T. Heidler*

See also Fair Oaks/Seven Pines; United States Colored Troops; Washington, D.C.

For further reading:

Cornish, Dudley Taylor. *The Sable Arm: Negro Troops in the Union Army, 1861–1865* (1966).

West Pointers and Early Washington: The Contributions of U.S. Military Academy Graduates to the Development of the Washington Territory, From the Oregon Trail to the Civil War, 1834–1862 (1992).

CASS, LEWIS
(1782–1866)

Antebellum Democratic politician

Lewis Cass, the "Father of Popular Sovereignty," was born in Exeter, New Hampshire. He attended Phillips Exeter Academy (one of his schoolmates was Daniel Webster) and moved with his family to Ohio, where his father, a Revolutionary War veteran, had received bounty lands. Lewis studied law under Return Jonathan Meigs and won a seat in the legislature in 1806. A staunch supporter of President Thomas Jefferson during the Aaron Burr conspiracy, Cass was appointed federal marshal for Ohio. He also served as a brigadier general in the militia at the outbreak of the War of 1812. Cass was included in General William Hull's ignominious surrender of Fort Detroit to the British and, after his release on parole, joined General William Henry Harrison at the battle of the Thames. With the Northwest thus secure for the remainder of the war, Harrison appointed Cass governor of Michigan Territory. Cass held that post for eighteen years, as Michigan grew to the threshold of statehood. Governor Cass was a true Democrat, believing in the ability and right of the people to govern themselves; and he was a champion of spread-eagle expansionism, convinced it was U.S. destiny to extend the blessing of liberty throughout the continent.

Lewis Cass (*Library of Congress*)

In 1831, Cass succeeded John H. Eaton as Andrew Jackson's secretary of war. The ethnocentrism and paternalism of the antebellum era were reflected in Cass's support of Indian removal to west of the Mississippi River as a humanitarian relocation. Cass also reinforced the Charleston harbor fortifications during the nullification crisis, a harbinger of the sectional conflict that led to the Civil War. After serving as minister to France, and quarreling with the provisions of the Webster-Ashburton Treaty pertaining to the African slave trade, Cass was elected to the U.S. Senate from Michigan. He became James K. Polk's administration's most strident congressional proponent for an aggressive prosecution of the Mexican-American War and rejoiced at the vast land cession that ended the conflict. He remained a senator until replaced by Zachariah Chandler in 1857, resigning briefly after his nomination for the presidency in 1848.

To ensure the preservation of the Union in the face of increasing sectional tensions, Cass worked assiduously for political compromise. His letter to Alfred O. P. Nicholson, dated 24 December 1847, was a nationally recognized effort to use the ideal of self-government to repudiate the Wilmot Proviso. As the Father of Popular Sovereignty, Cass denied that Congress had the authority to regulate slavery in the territories. Cass opposed slavery, in the abstract, yet blithely accepted black bondage as a condition of maintaining the republic. He objected to being labeled a "doughface" (a Northern man with Southern principles), but Cass was an accommodating constitutionalist who evolved into a Northern apologist for the "peculiar institution." Slavery was a political question to him, not a moral one; and Popular Sovereignty was an attempt to remove the explosive issue of slavery expansion from the halls of Congress.

Cass joined chairman Henry Clay on the Committee of Thirteen, which drafted the legislation that emerged as the Compromise of 1850. That landmark settlement implicitly adopted Popular Sovereignty regarding slavery and the territories, but within half a dozen years the doctrine was repudiated. Cass personally regretted the introduction of Stephen A. Douglas's Kansas-Nebraska Bill, because it reopened the sectional debate, but he eventually supported it as a Democratic Party measure. Cass despaired when the inflamed political atmosphere was stoked by "Bleeding Kansas" and the *Dred Scot* case, which he endorsed.

Cass served as James Buchanan's secretary of state, and repudiated the Popular Sovereignty principle during the debate over the admission of Kansas to the Union. The Buchanan administration endorsed the proslavery Lecompton Constitution, despite the demonstrated free-state majority in Kansas and Douglas's defiance. The Cass creed no longer functioned as a viable ideological bridge between Democrats.

Cass concurred with most of Buchanan's positions regarding the secession crisis, but he resigned from the cabinet in December 1860, after the president decided not to reinforce military posts in the South. The attack on Fort Sumter galvanized the old warrior. The discarded symbol of antebellum nationalism and political moderation, Cass enthusiastically addressed several Union recruitment rallies and contributed to the equipping of volunteer regiments. He also supported Abraham Lincoln's administration during the *Trent* Affair. He cabled Secretary of State William Henry Seward, recommending he take the opportunity to commit Great Britain to the American position on the right-of-search issue by releasing the Confederate agents seized from the British ship.

As the Civil War dragged on, Cass's health deteriorated. Although he lamented the "fatal error" made by the North in raising "that abominable Negro question," he contended that Southerners bore the "major responsibility for their insane attempt to break up the government." His heart remained "set upon the integrity of the Union, and…the restoration of the Seceding States to the Supremacy of the Constitution." He ended a lifetime of public service as he commenced it: defending the

United States against foreign and domestic assault. It is fitting that Lewis Cass survived the Civil War he labored so futilely to prevent.

—*Willard Carl Klunder*

See also Buchanan, James; Popular Sovereignty.

For further reading:
Dunbar, Willis Frederick. *Lewis Cass* (1970).
Klunder, Willard Carl. *Lewis Cass and the Politics of Moderation* (1996).
Smith, William L.G. *The Life and Times of Lewis Cass* (1856).
Woodford, Frank B. *Lewis Cass: The Last Jeffersonian* (1950).

Young, William T. *Sketch of the Life and Public Services of General Lewis Cass* (1852).

CASTLE THUNDER
Confederate prison

Although also the name of a prisoner-of-war facility in Petersburg, Virginia, Castle Thunder in Richmond was by far the more infamous of the two prisons bearing the same name. During the summer

Castle Thunder from Cary Street, 1865 (*Library of Congress*)

of 1862 the Confederate government acquired the Gleanor's Tobacco Factory, Palmer's Factory, and Whitlock's Warehouse, all on the same block, to convert into a prison for deserters and political prisoners. A high fence and watchtowers connected the three buildings before the prison was opened in August 1862.

The original capacity for the buildings was set at 1,400, but like most Civil War prisons, that number was quickly exceeded. Also, because of the Peninsula campaign during the earlier part of the summer, the use of the prison for only political prisoners and deserters was abandoned. Confederate deserters and male political prisoners were housed in one building, women and African-American prisoners in another, and Federal deserters and prisoners of war in the third. A brick wall in the back of the compound was used for executions, these consisting mainly of the Confederate deserters who were convicted by court-martial. Many times these men were sentenced to lashings instead, and these punishments were usually carried out in the back of the compound as well. There were reports that guards would occasionally deliver unauthorized lashings, especially of deserters, before their trials.

Captain George W. Alexander was selected the prison's commandant and remained in that position throughout the war. Alexander quickly gained a reputation for brutality, often using his large dog, Nero, to intimidate the inmates. His and his guards' alleged mistreatment of prisoners led in the spring of 1863 to an investigation by the Confederate Congress. After testimony from both sides, Alexander was exonerated, though there continued to be evidence until the end of the war that prisoners were mistreated.

Part of the problem that arose in Castle Thunder was endemic to Civil War prisons. Unexpected overcrowding, food and medicine shortages in the Confederacy, and the filth and diseases that usually accompanied such circumstances, made for a miserable experience for all prisoners. Dysentery was prevalent, and epidemics of such diseases as small pox only added to the horrors of prison life. By January 1863 Castle Thunder was at twice its expected capacity, at 3,000 prisoners.

Occasionally, the prisoners' distress was alleviated by supplies sent in by the United States government, but such packages became fewer as the war dragged on. Some of the overcrowding was eliminated when Federal deserters were transferred to other prisons later in the war. Their spaces were quickly filled, however, when it was determined to place Confederate soldiers accused of crimes such as theft or murder in Castle Thunder. Complaints arose during the summer of 1864 that such a policy not only removed those men from the front where they were desperately needed, but also effectively removed other men who were needed to guard them.

As one of the few facilities in the Confederacy with a specific area set aside for women prisoners, Castle Thunder also gained a certain notoriety. Most of the women were political prisoners, but there were a few who had been captured while disguising themselves as men in the Union army. The most famous woman prisoner was the Union physician, Dr. Mary Walker, who was captured in north Georgia in April 1864 and transferred to Castle Thunder because of the paucity of facilities for women prisoners in the Confederacy. She was kept there until August 1864, when she was exchanged after spending her months in prison writing letters to newspapers complaining about the conditions and the rations at the prison.

As it became apparent in March 1865 that the Union capture of Richmond was likely, Alexander began making arrangements to move the prisoners out of the city. On 3 April 1865 the prisoners were evacuated to Danville, Virginia. During the destruction of much of Richmond that ensued, Castle Thunder remained standing, and as a consequence was used as a prison by the Federal occupation forces. It was returned to its original owners after the occupation, but was destroyed by fire in 1879.

—David S. Heidler and Jeanne T. Heidler

See also Prisoners of War; Prisons, C.S.A.

For further reading:
Fischer, Ronald W. "A Comparative Study of Two Civil War Prisons: Old Capitol Prison and Castle Thunder Prison" (M.A. thesis, 1994).
Speer, Lonnie R. Portals to Hell: Military Prisons of the Civil War (1997).

CASUALTIES

A casualty is defined as a loss of a man due to injury, sickness, death, captivity, or desertion. During the Civil War, a total of 2.9 million men served the Union, but this number is deceptive, because many of these men enlisted for only three months or were called up only briefly for emergency circumstances. Approximately, 1.5 million men actually enlisted to serve for "three years or the duration," but even this number can be misleading, as the Union never had that many men under arms at any one time. Of these men 630,000 became casualties during the war, and 360,000 were killed in action or died of disease. The Confederate total of men is even more difficult to determine because they did not keep as complete records. It appears that 1.2 million men served the Confederacy during the war, but as in the case of the Union, this number is deceptive and represents all the men who served the Confederacy, no matter how short their term of service. Approximately 800,000 of these men actually enlisted for the "three years or the duration" of the war. Of these men, 340,000 became casualties during the war, and 250,000 were killed in action or died of disease.

In the Union army during the Civil War, only four regiments suffered more than 70 percent casualties in a single battle. The highest of these losses was the 1st Minnesota Infantry Regiment, which suffered 82 percent casualties out of 262 men engaged at the battle of Gettysburg. The highest number of total casualties (rather than percentage of casualties) suffered by a Union regiment during a single battle was the 1st Maine Heavy Artillery Regiment at the battle of Petersburg. The 1st Maine suffered 67 percent casualties out of 950 men engaged.

In the Confederate army during the Civil War, the highest percentage of casualties suffered by one regiment in a single battle was the 1st Texas Infantry Regiment, which suffered 82 percent casualties out of 226 men engaged at the battle of Antietam. The highest number of total casualties (rather than percentage of casualties) suffered by a Confederate regiment during a single battle was the 26th North Carolina Infantry Regiment at the battle of Gettysburg. The 26th North Carolina suffered 72 percent casualties out of 820 men engaged.

The costliest battle of the Civil War for both sides appears to have been the battle of Gettysburg. During that battle, the Union suffered 23,000 casualties with 3,000 men killed (the greatest loss for the Union in a single battle during the war). During the same battle, the Confederacy suffered 20,000 casualties with 2,500 men killed. Though Gettysburg was a very costly battle for the Confederacy, the worst casualties suffered by the Confederacy in a single battle occurred during the Seven Days' battles. During the Seven Days', the Confederacy lost 20,500 men as casualties with 3,500 men killed. The costliest single day of the Civil War for both sides was the battle of Antietam (17 September 1862). During the battle of Antietam, the Union suffered 12,000 casualties with 2,100 killed, while the Confederacy suffered 14,000 casualties with 2,700 killed.

—*Alexander M. Bielakowski*

See also Disease.

For further reading:
Fox, William F. *Regimental Losses in the American Civil War, 1861–1865* (1889).
Livermore, Thomas L. *Numbers and Losses in the Civil War in America, 1861–1865* (1996).
Phisterer, Frederick. *Statistical Record: A Treasury of Information about the U.S. Civil War* (1996).

CATHOLICS

While the Civil War divided a number of denominations as well as the nation, the Roman Catholic Church sought to maintain neutrality by sacrificing political unity to achieve religious unity.

By 1860 Catholics were the majority religion of the North. Southern Catholics were a minority in a culture dominated by evangelical orthodoxy. Southern Catholics tended to concentrate in the cities as well as in southern Maryland and the Kentucky bluegrass region. In addition, there were approximately 100,000 Catholic slaves in the South, with Louisiana accounting for 62,000 alone. Catholics represented a variety of ethnic groups, notably the Irish, but also French Louisianans and German farmers.

Before the outbreak of war, the Church avoided the impending crisis as much as possible. In the decrees and pastoral letters issued from the First Plenary Council at Baltimore in 1852, there was no mention of slavery, abolition, or sectional differences. Even sixteen days after the surrender of Fort Sumter, the Third Provincial Council of Cincinnati issued a pastoral letter that noted concern over the country's welfare but underscored the bishops' reluctance to enter the political arena.

Southern Catholics mirrored the society in which they lived and upheld slavery as a necessary evil. Bishop John England of Charleston said he personally was opposed to slavery but recognized it as being compatible with man's law and divine will. Shortly before becoming bishop of Savannah, Augustin Verot assailed the evils of the slave trade, but reiterated the paternalistic view of slavery as being both a duty and a burden through which heathen Africans might be brought to salvation. Nonetheless, in 1858 Bishop William Henry Elder of Natchez noted that few slaves of Catholic masters received special spiritual instruction.

Catholic laity, orders, and clergy all owned slaves. Some, such as Chief Justice Roger B. Taney, provided for the manumission of theirs. Brother Joseph Mobberly of the Society of Jesus helped run a Jesuit plantation in Maryland and did much to see to the slaves' spiritual welfare, but he was relieved of his duties because of his harsh treatment of the slaves. The Jesuit order sold all their slaves in 1836.

Catholics remained aloof from the abolitionist movement. Even though Pope Gregory XVI condemned the slave trade in 1839, no official doctrine condemned slavery as such. Northern Catholics also saw abolitionism as a New England Protestant movement aligned with nativism and other anti-Catholic movements and chose not to involve themselves.

With the outbreak of hostilities, Catholics tended to side with the local majority. On both sides, Catholic bishops blessed battle flags and prayed for victory. Exceptions did occur, such as when German Catholics in Texas opposed secession. What was important for the Church was that Catholic soldiers fight bravely and honor their faith, regardless which side they were on. Such comportment would serve as the basis of judgment on the Church. One hundred forty-five thousand Irish Catholics served in the Union army and were the most visible Catholic group. Indeed, as the war wore on, the Union actively recruited Irish immigrants to join the army.

Catholics did more than fight. Some priests became

chaplains or "Holy Joes." Most served for only a short time, as bishops would recall men to meet the needs of the local parish. Also, many Protestant officers refused to accept Catholics as chaplains. Still, Catholic chaplains sought to hold religious services, administer sacraments, and hear confessions. Priests and Catholic sisters working in hospitals sought to sustain Catholic identity and interest, especially among the dying. In particular, nearly 500 sisters of twenty or more orders served as nurses, earning the gratitude and praise of those they helped.

In the South, Catholics took on unique roles. Father John Bannon, the "fighting chaplain" of a Missouri Irish company, went to Rome as an emissary to try to persuade the papacy to extend recognition to the Confederacy. He reported to President Davis that he believed his mission to be successful, but later events proved him wrong. The Confederacy was acutely aware of Union efforts to recruit the Irish. To counter this effort, the Confederates sent Lieutenant James L. Capston and later Bannon to Ireland to dissuade Irish from going to the United States and enlisting, but many Irishmen found the $500 cash inducements too difficult to resist. Bishop Patrick Lynch of Charleston traveled to Rome to request that the Pope oppose recruitment of the Irish to fight for the Union.

The fate of the freed slaves was an issue for Catholics in a number of ways. In the North, Irish Catholics rioted against blacks in New York City in 1863, underscoring a fear that they would lose their jobs to freedmen. In the South, Bishop William Elder of Natchez sought to attend to the spiritual needs of the emancipated slaves, but he avoided supplying their material needs as he feared alienating planters and being labeled a secret abolitionist. Elder later sought to counter the Protestant influence of New England teachers educating the emancipated slaves by trying to secure the services of the black nuns of the Oblate Sisters of Providence, but he was unable to do so. At the same time Bishop Verot called for education of freedmen and their inclusion in the Catholic Church. At the Second Plenary Council in Baltimore in 1866, however, Church leaders from both North and South talked of cooperation to rebuild the Church in the South, but none offered a missionary plan for ex-slaves. Greater unity was achieved in rebuilding Catholic property destroyed during the war. However the Church turned its attention from Reconstruction to meeting the needs of the new wave of immigrants entering the country.

—*Daniel Liestman*

See also Chaplains; Churches; Jews; Religion; Sister Nurses.
For further reading:
Blied, Benjamin J. *Catholics and the Civil War: Essays* (1945; reprint, 1992).
Hausfeld, Eric Edward. "Catholic Involvement in Civil War Diplomacy" (M.A. thesis, 1965).
Holland, Timothy J. "The Catholic Church and the Negro in the United States prior to the Civil War" (Ph.D. dissertation, 1950).
Murphy, Robert Joseph. "The Catholic Church in the United States during the Civil War Period: 1852–1866." *Records of the American Catholic Historical Society* (1928).

CATLETT'S STATION, BATTLE OF
(14 October 1863)

Also known as Auburn, Auburn Ford, and Auburn Mills, Virginia, Catlett's Station was the stage for a battle in the Bristoe campaign, which has generally been viewed as one of military maneuverings. In an attempt to advance on Washington D.C., General Robert E. Lee took advantage of the relative inactivity of the days after the Gettysburg campaign. As Lee advanced, Major General George G. Meade and the Army of the Potomac withdrew. As only skirmishes resulted, Lee attempted to outflank the Union forces, sending Major Lieutenant Ambrose P. Hill to the west and Lieutenant General Richard S. Ewell to follow the Federal withdrawal north along the Orange & Alexandria Railroad.

Fronting the advancing Confederate infantry, Major General J. E. B. Stuart, riding with Captain William McGregor, commander of the horse artillery, found himself to the side of the Union forces who were making their way to Manassas. On the night of 13 October 1863, moving along the railroad line, the Union troops stopped at Auburn, near Catlett's Station. It was here that Stuart decided to make a reconnaissance of the Union forces. Within a safe distance, Stuart leisurely inspected the Federal forces who had stopped their march. What he did not expect was that a similar mass of troops was approaching within a few hundred yards of Stuart's rear. Realizing that his cavalry was surrounded by two corps of Federal infantry, he found his situation extremely critical.

Quickly he concealed his men in the nearby woods, close enough to the Union troops that their conversations could actually be heard. The Confederate cavalry remained silent and still throughout the night with only a few brave men dashing out among Federal forces and through their lines in order to inform Lee of the possibly disastrous situation of the cavalry. At dawn on 14 October, a dense fog descended on the area, further concealing Stuart's location in the woods. To Stuart's rear, one brigade of Union infantry stopped to camp on a nearby hill, within a quarter mile, just opposite the Confederate cavalry. When firing was heard in the distance off of the Warrenton Road, Stuart ordered McGregor's troops to charge out and open fire upon the encamped Union soldiers, muskets at rest and coffee pots in hand. After the initial confusion of the Confederate firing, the Union troops, under the command of Brigadier General Joshua Owen and Colonel Thomas Smyth, gathered their weapons to receive the charge of

Brigadier General James Gordon's cavalry. Gordon's charge was repulsed, after which, however, the Union forces, still unorganized, scattered and retreated. Stuart initially found himself outnumbered and disadvantaged; however, Lee, updated on Stuart's position throughout the night, sent a brigade of infantry to reinforce the cavalry. By this time, though, the Union forces had gathered themselves in retreat to join together with the main body of the Army of the Potomac.

It was Stuart's resourcefulness and ability to command and influence his troops that allowed him to escape near disaster. The encounter was not completely void of tragedy, however; the Confederates lost Colonel Thomas Ruffin of the 1st North Carolina cavalry. Taking twenty-eight prisoners, the Federals lost eleven men with forty-two others wounded. Although a minor skirmish, both forces met later in the day further down the road at Bristoe Station, a major and particularly bloody battle of the Bristoe campaign, which cost the South 1,300 lives and put an end to this military offensive.

—*Andrew Paul Bielakowski*

See also Bristoe Station, Battle of; Stuart, James Ewell Brown.

For further reading:

Blackford, W.W. *War Years with Jeb Stuart* (1945; reprint, 1993).

Garnett, T.S. *Riding with Stuart: Reminiscences of an Aide-de-Camp* (1994).

Hill, D.H., Jr. *North Carolina.* Vol. 4 of *Confederate Military History* (1899).

CATRON, JOHN
(ca. 1780s–1865)

U.S. Supreme Court associate justice

John Catron was born Pennsylvania, with some sources listing 1781 and others 1786 as his year of birth. He became an associate justice and chief justice of the Tennessee Court of Errors and Appeals and an associate justice of the United States Supreme Court. The scion of an immigrant German-Swiss family, Catron grew up in poor circumstances on a Virginia farm, then migrated to Tennessee.

After a campaign under General Andrew Jackson, Catron, who apparently was self-taught, commenced a career at the bar. Wartime popularity brought an appointment as state's attorney for his region of Tennessee. In 1818, Catron moved to Nashville, where he benefitted from the Panic of 1819. He mastered the complicated situation of Tennessee land titles; because he favored longtime possessors over actual title holders, the legislature named him to a spot on the state's highest court in 1824. There, Catron helped establish the view of state police powers that endured until the constitutional revolution of 1937: Laws must apply to all members of society alike, Catron wrote, not favor some chosen few.

Marrying a relative of James K. Polk, Catron became one of the leading Tennessee Jacksonians. Catron's 1829 newspaper series against the Bank of the United States won Jacksonians' plaudits. In 1832 he drew up nationalist resolutions supportive of Jackson's Nullification Proclamation to be adopted at a public meeting chaired by Governor William Carroll. The meeting unanimously adopted the resolutions, which denied the rights of nullification and secession. Catron privately hinted to Jackson that he would endorse the use of force to support Jackson's principles.

With Jackson's popularity in Tennessee waning, a constitutional convention abolished Catron's court. Returning to private practice, Catron spent the bulk of his time running the Jacksonian *Nashville Union*. Catron's support for the 1836 presidential campaign of Martin Van Buren earned him a nomination to the United States Supreme Court. His appointment, one of the last matters to which Jackson attended as president, won confirmation on 8 March 1837, at the start of Van Buren's term, by a Senate vote of twenty-eight to fifteen. Catron remained in correspondence with Jackson until Old Hickory's death, as well as serving as an advisor to Presidents Polk and James Buchanan.

Catron's most notorious judicial endeavor came in connection with the epochal case of *Scott v. Sanford* (U.S. 1857), best known as the *Dred Scott* case. Entering into correspondence with the president-elect shortly before inauguration day, Catron requested Buchanan's assistance in persuading Buchanan's fellow Pennsylvanian, Justice Robert C. Grier, to join the anti-Scott majority. Buchanan's intervention succeeded.

Catron concurred separately in Chief Justice Roger B. Taney's majority opinion. He held that Taney's decision to review the plea in abatement was mistaken, and he believed that Taney's discussion of the question of African-American citizenship was entirely dictum. In other words, Catron believed, though he did not publicly say, that Taney's attempt to rule Federal citizenship for blacks unconstitutional itself violated the provision of Article III that the Federal courts have jurisdiction only over "cases and controversies" properly brought before them.

Catron also maintained that domiciling a slave in a free state freed him, sojourning there temporarily did not, and returning him to slave territory negated whatever claim to freedom he might have had as a result of his journey. Catron further disagreed with Taney's insistence that Congress had no jurisdiction over the territories, but he agreed that slavery was legal in the territories under the state land cessions. The Northwest Ordinance made slavery illegal in Virginia's old lands north of the Ohio, and Congress could not undo that, so Congress could not outlaw slavery in North Carolina's and Georgia's cessions to Ohio's south. Besides, the Louisiana Purchase treaty included a guarantee that Frenchmen and Spaniards

would continue in the "enjoyment of their liberty, property, and the religion which they profess." For Catron, this provision meant that slavery, legal under the pre-1803 dispensation, could not be banned in the former Louisiana Territory.

His last argument for the Missouri Compromise's invalidity was John Calhoun's old argument about the states' common stake in the territories: the states owned the territories in common, so whatever was property in any of the states could be taken into the territories. This classically Jacksonian attention to the rights of states in the Federal system had figured in other aspects of Catron's performance as a Supreme Court justice. For example, in *Cooley v. Board of Wardens* (U.S. 1852), Catron joined the majority in holding that states had authority to regulate local aspects of interstate commerce insofar as they were not governed by congressional legislation.

When secession came, Catron remained at his post. He rode circuit in those parts of his circuit that were not behind Confederate lines, and he cooperated in the Union military effort by way of his stingy stewardship of the writ of habeas corpus. He lived to see the Union victorious, then died in Nashville on 30 May 1865, leaving no children.

—*Constantine Gutzman*

See also Dred Scott Case; Supreme Court, U.S.

For further reading:
Fehrenbacher, Don E. *The Dred Scott Case: Its Significance in American Law and Politics* (1978).
Gilman, Howard. *The Constitution Besieged: The Rise and Demise of Lochner Era Police Powers Jurisprudence* (1993).

CAVALRY, C.S.A.

One of the most romantic aspects of the American Civil War in general and the Confederacy in particular was the cavalry. Ranging in assessment from effective for screening, scouting, and raiding to foolish for supposedly being unwilling to endure combat, the Confederate cavalry produced some of the most colorful characters in the war. At least for the first half of the war, these Southern horsemen also uniformly outperformed their opponents.

Yet the dramatic images of charging horsemen and flashing sabers were rare. It became common for cavalrymen to use the animals to reach a battlefield, and then fight dismounted. Every fourth man would hold the horses while the others advanced on foot. The horseholders remained in the rear, usually the safest part of the battlefield. Should the need arise, the horses could be brought up or the men fall back to them, mount, and ride off.

As any good cavalryman would attest, care and maintenance of his horse was paramount. This was particularly true of Confederate troopers, who had to supply their own mounts. They were entitled to receive the value of the horse at the time they were mustered into the service if the animal was killed in combat. Worn-out mounts had to be replaced as well, particularly after a raid deep behind Union lines, or other arduous service. However, remounts for most of the Southern troopers became more difficult to obtain as the war progressed, and loss of a horse might mean a transfer from the cavalry.

Despite the later difficulties, several factors account for the initial advantage the Confederate cavalry arm enjoyed over its Union counterpart. One was the exposure most Southerners had to horses, as well as the quality of the animals themselves. A second factor was the organization of the Southern cavalry as independent units. At full strength a cavalry regiment would consist of ten companies of between sixty and eighty men. These regiments could cooperate with other elements of the army or operate independently. Third was the capability of its leadership. James Ewell Brown "Jeb" Stuart, Nathan Bedford Forrest, and others demonstrated the highest aptitude for mounted service.

Jeb Stuart won a reputation as a daring cavalier by literally riding rings around his opponents. Twice he rode around Union general George B. McClellan's army. In the first instance, he found the Federal flank near Richmond "in the air" or unsupported. His report of that fact to Robert E. Lee caused the Confederate general to plan a strike against that exposed flank, launching the Seven Days' campaign. In the second instance, Stuart circled McClellan's force on a raid in October 1862 that took him as far north as Chambersburg, Pennsylvania.

Forrest launched similarly spectacular cavalry operations and produced significant results in the Western theater of the war. His raid on the Union garrison at Murfreesboro, Tennessee, netted him approximately 1,200 prisoners in July 1862, while an expedition against the Union supply center at Johnsonville, Tennessee, resulted in the destruction of millions of dollars worth of supplies in November 1864. In defensive operations, Forrest proved just as effective as he had been in conducting raids. In April and May 1863 he pursued and captured Abel Streight's raiders, while throughout the summer of 1864 he thwarted repeated Union expeditions into the heart of Mississippi, highlighted by the brilliant tactical victory at Brice's Cross Roads on 10 June.

John Hunt Morgan inflicted significant damage, and garnered his share of headlines, on raids into Kentucky in 1862 and 1863, although it was a raid beyond that state into Indiana and Ohio in July 1863 that led to his capture and incarceration in the Ohio State Penitentiary. Even so, Morgan delighted Southerners by escaping from the prison and returning to the South. His daring escape added to his earlier fame as "The Francis Marion of the War."

Indeed, from the earliest days of the war, the Confederate cavalry generated attention and respect from friends and foes alike. At First Manassas or Bull Run, fear of

the "Black Horse" cavalry encouraged a rout of panicky Union troops at the end of that battle. But for all of the cavalry service's glamour, the fighting at Brandy Station, Virginia, on 9 June 1863 was the closest the Civil War came to having a classic cavalry confrontation. By no coincidence, it was also the largest cavalry battle of the war. Repeated charges and countercharges on that bloody field marked a fight in which some 17,000 mounted troopers on both sides clashed with each other. Although Stuart claimed the victory, the Federals emerged from the fight with renewed confidence in their own developing capabilities.

By the time Jeb Stuart met his end at Yellow Tavern, north of Richmond, on 11 May 1864, the Confederate cavalry's best days were past. Wade Hampton's "Beefsteak Raid" in September 1864 was one of the cavalry's last great exploits in the east.

In the Western theater, Confederate cavalry commanders like Forrest, John Hunt Morgan, Earl Van Dorn, and Joseph Wheeler launched cavalry raids that were often as destructive of Union supply lines as they were daring. They could be strategically effective as well. In December 1862, Forrest and Van Dorn so thoroughly destroyed the rail lines in western Tennessee and the forward Union depot at Holly Springs in northeastern Mississippi that their actions halted Ulysses S. Grant's initial overland advance against Vicksburg. But the Confederates failed to accomplish a similar result against William T. Sherman in 1864. Even so, Sherman worried that Southern cavalry raiders would smash his extended supply lines while he closed in on Atlanta, Georgia. However, when Forrest finally turned on those lines, it was too late; Atlanta had already fallen.

Even in the midst of a war, debates raged over the relative significance of given cavalry leaders or of the cavalry commands in the respective theaters of war. Stationed briefly with Braxton Bragg's army, Lieutenant General James Longstreet wrote to tell Stuart that his experiences in both arenas led him to consider the eastern cavalry superior to the western cavalry. And Confederate lieutenant general Daniel Harvey Hill, who had made himself unpopular in Virginia by saying that he "had not seen a dead man with spurs on," revised his thinking after watching Forrest's dismounted troopers advance on foot into combat at Chickamauga, Georgia.

Confederate cavalry functioned effectively in the Trans-Mississippi as well. Not strapped by the shortages in horseflesh that plagued the rest of the Confederacy, they launched raids, fought dismounted in major actions like Pea Ridge, scouted enemy movements, and screened friendly forces. Although the leaders generally proved less capable or popular than some of the Confederate cavalry leaders in the other theaters, they performed quite well. John Marmaduke and Joseph Shelby led or participated in several cavalry raids in Arkansas and Missouri.

Despite its romance and valor, at no point was it really likely for the Confederate cavalry alone to alter the course of the Civil War. Nevertheless, the cavalry arm proved remarkably successful at conducting raids, scouting expeditions, and screening operations that certainly helped to extend the war. In the end, it was a lack of numbers and resources, and the improvement in their opponent's organization and skills, that prevented the Confederate cavalry from being as effective a force as it had been for most of the conflict. Nevertheless, while the cavalry forces that surrendered at the end of the war were but shadows of themselves, the fact and the fiction of the exploits of the Southern horsemen were just beginning to grow.

—*Brian S. Wills*

See also Brandy Station, Battle of; Forrest, Nathan Bedford; Morgan, John Hunt; Stuart, James Ewell Brown.

For further reading:

Oates, Stephen B. *Confederate Cavalry West of the River* (1961).
Ramage, James A. *Rebel Raider: The Life of John Hunt Morgan* (1986).
Thomas, Emory M. *Bold Dragoon: The Life of J.E.B. Stuart* (1988).
Wills, Brian Steel. *A Battle from the Start: The Life of Nathan Bedford Forrest* (1992).

CAVALRY, U.S.A.

Between 1861 and 1865 the Union cavalry developed from a dispersed and ill-used force into a united and immensely powerful combat arm that significantly assisted the Northern victory. Lincoln's original 1861 call for volunteers did not include cavalry. Belief in a short war, coupled with the vast expense of equipping cavalry and the correlating lack of immediate combat readiness, supported the decision. The regular army's five mounted regiments, with the addition of a sixth in May 1861, were expected to be sufficient.

Defeat at Bull Run in July 1861 ended official opposition to volunteer cavalry, and despite initial hesitation, the Union fielded 258 regiments and 170 companies of mounted soldiers of varied enlistment terms. A standard Union cavalry regiment on paper numbered 1,200 officers and troopers, composed of five squadrons of two troops each with 100 men per troop led by a captain, a first lieutenant, and two second lieutenants. Each regiment was commanded by a colonel, a lieutenant colonel, and three majors, in addition to two surgeons, an adjutant, a quartermaster, and a commissary. The noncommissioned staff consisted of a sergeant-major, quartermaster, and commissary sergeants, as well as a saddler and chief farrier or blacksmith.

In 1863 the troop organization was given elastic strength varying from 82 to 100 men, and the supernumerary second lieutenant was discarded. A regimental veterinary sergeant was authorized, although few such positions were filled by competent individuals. The

Dismounted parade of the 7th New York Cavalry in camp, 1862 (*National Archives*)

squadron organization was also dropped and four troop battalions were implemented when units were on detached service. Although the cavalry suffered proportionally fewer casualties than the infantry, it was engaged more frequently in combat; 10,596 Union troopers were killed and 26,490 were wounded throughout the war.

Troopers were equipped with saddles designed by George B. McClellan that were fashioned to be comfortable on horses' backs and withers. The saddle had attachment eyes to strap on necessary accouterments and was padded by indigo blue woolen saddle blankets. Some officers, however, preferred nonregulation French or English flat saddles with iron stirrups. Troopers were provided single-reined bridles with curb bits. Officers usually had double-reined bridles. Regulars eschewed the use of martingales (straps that led from the harness through the forelegs to prevent rearing), although volunteers often employed them. Union cavalrymen were armed with Colt revolvers, sabers, and, originally, single-shot carbines, which were later exchanged for Henry or Spencer repeating weapons. Fully caparisoned, the cavalry horse's load, exclusive of the rider, hovered near 110 pounds; with the trooper and his weapons, the total burden ranged between 255 and 270 pounds.

Union cavalry skill and power developed slowly during the first two years of war. Throughout 1862, while Confederates operated in a body under daring commanders, Union cavalrymen suffered from organiza-

tional handicaps. Regiments were parceled out to infantry commands for use as vedettes, couriers, orderlies, and escorts. Such duty prevented concerted action and continually diminished cavalry strength. Lack of a centralized command structure further debilitated cavalry field effectiveness and subjected Union troopers to conflicting orders and purposes. These problems were only corrected in stages as successive Federal army commanders learned to mass their cavalry and employ it effectively.

In the East, Union cavalrymen endured repeated humiliations by J. E. B. Stuart's Rebel cavalry, although promising commanders such as George Bayard and John Buford emerged. When Major General Joseph Hooker took command of the Army of the Potomac in early 1863, reformation of his forty cavalry regiments became a priority. Hooker created a unified cavalry corps commanded by Major General George H. Stoneman organized into divisions and brigades with attached batteries of horse artillery. The corps had its first real test in a massive raid behind Lee's lines during the Chancellorsville campaign. The expedition's barren results and politics in the high command resulted in Stoneman's replacement by Alfred Pleasonton.

On 9 June 1863 Pleasonton hurled 9,000 cavalrymen against a like number of Confederates at Brandy Station. The battle was the war's largest cavalry engagement, and although Stuart retained possession of the battlefield, the audacity, determination, and skill exhibited by

A Union cavalry charge near Culpeper, Virginia, 14 September 1863 (*Library of Congress*)

Union troopers swelled Federal confidence, while giving Confederate pride a significant jolt. Additional cavalry probing actions at Middleburg, Aldie, and Upperville further displayed the rising skill, professionalism, and élan of the Union cavalry corps. On 1 July, at Gettysburg, Buford's two brigades delayed Confederate infantry long enough for Union infantry to concentrate on the scene. On 3 July opposing cavalries clashed fiercely east of the main battlefield. The Union cavalry corps firmly repulsed all Rebel attacks and spearheaded the pursuit of Lee's beaten army after the battle.

In the west Union cavalry suffered from similar organizational and leadership problems. Each western military department had its own cavalry division, and some mounted units were shared among several armies, further complicating concentrated action. Failure to employ cavalry efficiently meant Union armies in the west with extended supply lines were open to attack by intrepid Confederate cavalry raiders such as John H. Morgan, Nathan B. Forrest, and Joseph Wheeler.

By 1863 western cavalry forces had improved in effectiveness. General Ulysses S. Grant used cavalry to assist his Vicksburg campaign by sending Brigadier General Benjamin H. Grierson and 1,700 troopers on a diversionary raid through Mississippi. The raiders reached Baton Rouge, Louisiana, on 2 May after sixteen days of spreading alarm and confusion behind Confederate lines. A similar disruptive raid through Alabama and Georgia attempted by General Abel D. Streight from William S. Rosecrans's army in Tennessee ended in disaster and capture. The following year, however, William T. Sherman used his combined armies' cavalry forces as an important component in his Georgia campaign, despite difficult terrain. Not until December 1864 was a concerted western cavalry corps formed, consisting of seven divisions led by Brigadier General James Harrison Wilson. When John Bell Hood's Confederates suffered a staggering winter defeat at Nashville, Wilson's horsemen turned their retreat into an unmitigated rout.

The Union cavalry displayed tremendous advances in strength and military effectiveness during the war's final year and was greatly assisted by Northern industrial and agricultural resources. In horses alone, a conservative estimate would have the loyal states supplying 451,180 cavalry mounts, exclusive of those captured. The formation of a Cavalry Bureau in July 1863 was designed to improve the cavalry's field organization and efficiency. In addition, the bureau administered several nationwide remount and horse-recruiting depots to restore broken-down army animals. Giesboro Point, the largest of these facilities, situated on the Potomac River near Washington, could accommodate over 30,000 animals; however, an insurmountable shortage of competent veterinarians limited the number of horses that could be successfully tended.

In the east during 1864 the cavalry reached a new

level of success under the energetic leadership of Philip H. Sheridan and aggressive subordinate commanders like Wesley Merritt, George A. Custer, and David M. Gregg. In combat Union horsemen used mounted charges, dismounted attacks, and combinations of both to attack and defend against the Confederates. During dismounted combat, every fourth trooper held the horses in the rear of the firing line. Employment of such tactics, coupled with repeating carbines, allowed Union troopers to best Rebel cavalry repeatedly and prevail against Confederate infantry.

Sheridan used the Army of the Potomac's cavalry corps of three divisions containing 12,424 men plus twelve batteries of horse artillery to strike vigorously at the enemy's industrial and agricultural resources. In May and June 1864 Sheridan conducted two massive raids, resulting in severe engagements at Yellow Tavern, Trevilian's Station, and Meadow Bridge. In August, the 1st and 3d Cavalry Divisions were transferred to help secure the Shenandoah Valley, and Union cavalrymen played a skillful and decisive role in attaining victories at Opequon, Cedar Creek, Waynesboro, and Tom's Brook.

The war's final months witnessed several campaigns that amply illustrated Union cavalry dominance. In the west the cavalry corps of the Division of the Mississippi under James H. Wilson swept through Alabama, torching Rebel property and capturing the fortified cites of Selma, Montgomery, and Columbus. George Stoneman twice struck from eastern Tennessee, raiding into southwestern Virginia and North Carolina and wrecking railroads, as well as destroying lead and salt manufactories—movements intended to coincide with and assist Sherman's northward advance.

In Virginia the Union cavalry's stellar fighting abilities and tireless activity prevented prolongation of the war by smashing Lee's flank at Five Forks, harrying retreating Rebel columns, and finally blocking Lee's escape routes to compel him to surrender at Appomattox Court House. War's end found Union horseman to be the finest battle-hardened cavalry in the world, and in recognition of excellent service assisting the Union victory, the cavalry corps led the final review of armies in Washington in May 1865.

—*David J. Gerleman*

See also Averell's Raids; Cavalry, C.S.A.; Chambersburg Raid; Forrest, Nathan Bedford; Forrest's Raids; Pleasonton, Alfred; Stoneman, George; Stoneman's Raid (April–May 1863); Stoneman's Raid (July 1864); Stoneman's Raid (December 1864–January 1865); Stoneman's Raid (March–April 1865); Stuart, J. E. B.; Stuart's Dumfries Raid; Stuart's First Ride Around McClellan; Wheeler, Joseph; Wheeler's Raid (August–September 1864); Wheeler's Raid (October 1863); Wilson, James H.; Wilson's Selma Raid.

For further reading:
Davis, Sidney Morris. *Common Soldier—Uncommon War: Life as a Cavalryman in the Civil War* (1994).

Evans, David. *Sherman's Horsemen: Union Cavalry Operations in the Atlanta Campaign* (1996).

Keenan, Jerry. *Wilson's Cavalry Corps; Union Campaigns in the Western Theatre, October 1864 through Spring 1865* (1998).

Longacre, Edward G. *Lincoln's Cavalrymen: A History of the Mounted Forces of the Army of the Potomac* (1999).

Starr, Stephen Z. *The Union Cavalry in the Civil War* (1979–1985).

CEDAR CREEK, BATTLE OF
(19 October 1864)

Brigadier General Philip Sheridan's campaign in the Shenandoah Valley had by October 1864 handed Jubal Early's Valley Army two stinging defeats at Winchester and Fisher's Hill and had routed his cavalry at Tom's Brook. Sheridan also laid waste to the potential harvest in the valley to deprive Robert E. Lee of valuable sustenance. Confident that he had destroyed both the valley's bounty and Early's spirit, Sheridan planned to quit the Shenandoah and join Ulysses S. Grant's lines at Petersburg. He even began detaching elements of VI Corps, sending them toward Ashby's Gap, while he departed for a strategy conference in Washington. Sheridan was so sure that nothing would happen in the valley that he dismissed as a ruse intelligence that Longstreet was moving to Early's assistance. He did, however, recall the detachments.

Sheridan was right about the burnt-up valley and Longstreet, but he had missed the mark on Early completely. True, Early's Valley Army was bedraggled, but it was made up of hardened veterans unused to defeat. Also Sheridan's devastation had been so thorough that Early had a problem feeding his people. He could move down the valley toward the retiring Union army or toward supplies at Staunton. Before the disaster at Tom's Brook, his diminished force had been reinforced, not by Longstreet but by Thomas Rosser's cavalry and the return of Joseph Kershaw's infantry division. All this considered, Early elected to close on the Federal position.

Sheridan's Army of the Shenandoah sat along Cedar Creek, a meandering stream that stretched westward from the north branch of the Shenandoah River and away from hulking Massanutten Mountain. The position was not a good one, but Brigadier General Horatio Wright, whom Sheridan had left in charge, was mainly worried about the most vulnerable point of the Federal configuration on the right flank. There Wright's three divisions sat behind Cedar Creek with level, open ground inviting an attack from the west. Cavalry under George A. Custer and Wesley Merritt covered this approach, but the position remained a cause for concern. To Wright's left sat William Emory's two divisions, and to his left, across the Valley Pike, rested George Crook's two divisions, anchored by the Shenandoah, here a

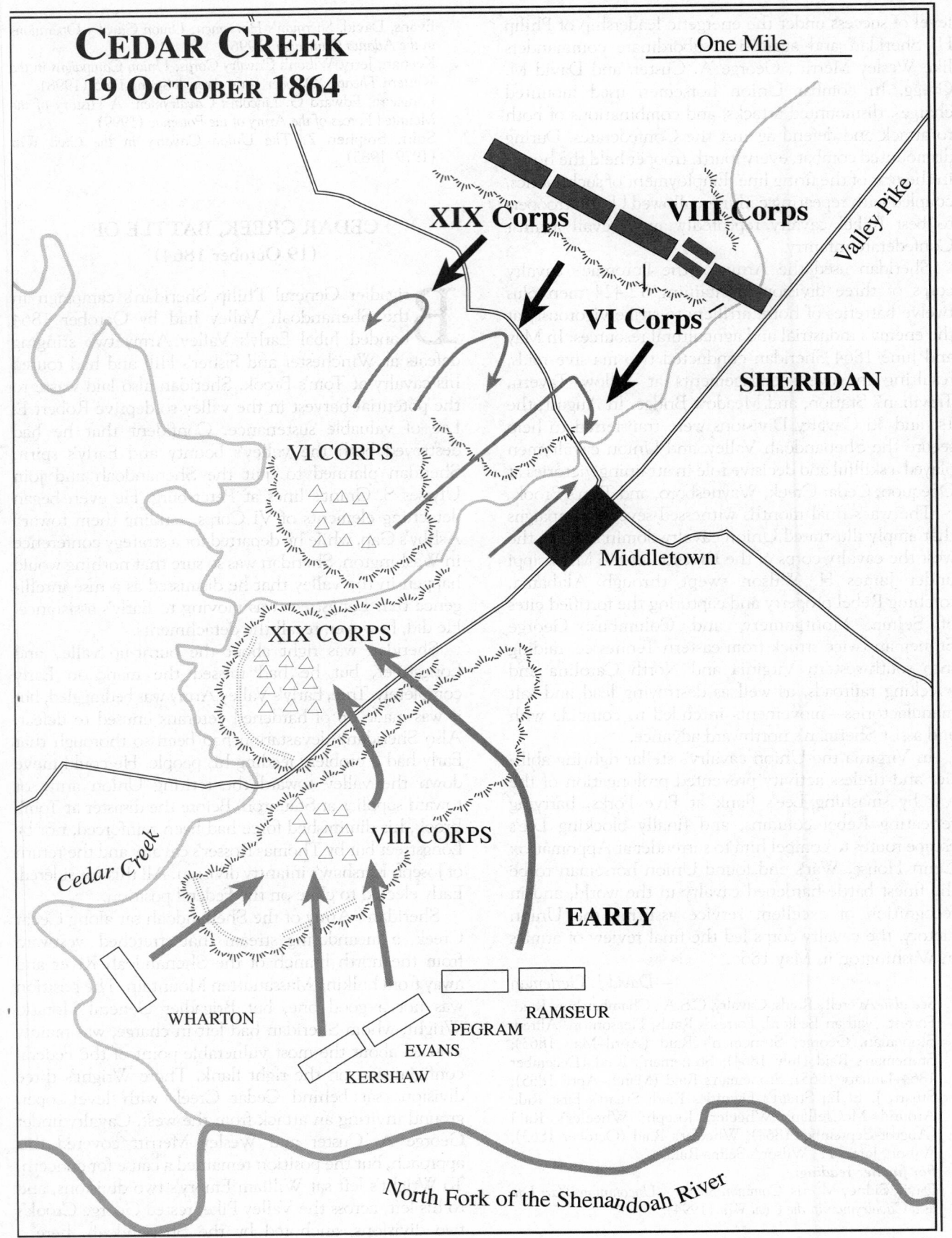

CEDAR CREEK
19 OCTOBER 1864

One Mile

XIX Corps

VIII Corps

Valley Pike

VI Corps

SHERIDAN

VI CORPS

XIX CORPS

Middletown

Cedar Creek

VIII CORPS

EARLY

WHARTON

RAMSEUR

PEGRAM

EVANS

KERSHAW

North Fork of the Shenandoah River

The battle of Cedar Creek, 19 October 1864 (*Library of Congress*)

wider stream than Cedar Creek. Crook was actually the weakest part of the line, but he could feel secure in the shadow of Massanutten Mountain's sheer face. In any event, Wright did not expect any trouble, even after it became apparent that Early was in his front.

After probing about a bit—a sharp skirmish at Hupp's Hill on 18 October produced about 200 casualties on each side—Early had his cartographer Jedediah Hotchkiss and John B. Gordon scale Massanutten Mountain to survey the Federal deployment. They returned with a plan to exploit the Union position in an unexpected way. Gordon would move three divisions across the Shenandoah River to traverse the north face of Massanutten Mountain above Cedar Creek. He would then recross the river and assail Crook on the Federal left. Meanwhile, Kershaw would cross Cedar Creek farther upstream, while Wharton advanced on the Valley Pike. After Crook was destroyed, the remainder of the bluecoats could be cut up in detail. Early agreed and just that quickly everything was set in motion.

The plan was an emulation of the sweeping flanking maneuver that Stonewall Jackson had employed so brilliantly at Chancellorsville in May 1863. At that battle,

Lee had frozen Joseph Hooker into place while Jackson had swung around to Hooker's unprotected right flank and had nearly hammered the Union army to pieces. Chancellorsville had taken too long to develop, however, and darkness had helped prevent Hooker's complete annihilation. At Cedar Creek the terrain was more daunting than the distance, but Early had everybody moving shortly after midnight. He would have the entire next day to annihilate Phil Sheridan. Early even planned to send cavalry to capture Sheridan, who was thought to be at his headquarters in Belle Grove.

The weather helped at first. A moon just past full guided the Confederates along their way. Also, a local inhabitant's guidance on a route across the north face of Massanutten sped the deployment. At dawn, everyone was in place, and as simultaneously as anything happened in this war, Gordon and Kershaw plunged across the creek, just as John Wharton's horse artillery opened on the Union center. In a half hour, Crook's VIII Corps on the Union left had collapsed, fled, or fallen prisoner. Confederate success was so complete and rapid, in fact, that unit cohesion broke down as regiments jumbled up and got out of order with others. Many also paused to plunder the Union camps, so any urgency of pursuit to press their initial advantage was lost.

Visibility became a problem as well. A lowering fog made it impossible to see more than a few yards, so the general flight of the Union army remained unexploited. Stephen Ramseur and John Pegram had folded up VIII Corps and shooed it back toward Middletown, but the commingling of their divisions and the fog gave them pause. So they sat for an hour, which gave Federal officers time to gather their wits and their panicked men, putting both in order. A small knot of resistance formed by elements of Brigadier General George Getty's division of VI Corps eventually anchored itself on the hill at Middletown's village cemetery. In the fog these men did a good job of persuading Early, Pegram, Ramseur, and Wharton—who actually tried to dislodge Getty— that they were the entire VI Corps. The bulk of VI Corps actually was rearward, establishing with elements of the shattered XIX Corps a line to resist the next Confederate onslaught.

That onslaught never came, for even after the sun burned off the fog, Jubal Early hesitated. Gordon would later intimate that Early had shown unsettling signs of lethargy for several days, and possibly the ugly failures of the previous weeks had undone him. In any case, by 10:30 A.M. Early was acting as though the battle was done and victory was his. When Gordon urged him to press forward, Early told the crestfallen Gordon that the Yankees were beaten and would retire soon enough.

General Philip Sheridan at the battle of Cedar Creek
(*Library of Congress*)

Gordon reminded Early that VI Corps of the Army of the Shenandoah was the most hard-bitten of a hardened lot and that it would have to be driven from the field. Yet Early insisted that the bluecoats in the distance were whipped and soon would be moving on. "My heart went into my boots," Gordon said later, for he believed that this lost opportunity would rank as one of the most colossal mistakes of the war. The fight at Cedar Creek would not be another Chancellorsville; it would be the first day at Gettysburg.

Just after the battle, Jubal Early bluntly declared, "The Yankees got whipped and we got scared." But that observation was only partly right and, as far as the Yankees were concerned, wholly temporary. Sheridan had returned from Washington, but he had not yet rejoined the army when the guns began to sound at Cedar Creek. Riding toward the battle from Winchester, he met stragglers, whom he successfully exhorted to join him, and then set forth with urgency on a pounding twelve-mile gallop that would later fall into the lore as "Sheridan's Ride." By the time he arrived at the hastily constructed line gathered around VI Corps, Wright had matters well enough in hand to have Sheridan thinking on the offense. When he learned what he already suspected—that Longstreet had not joined Early—he was committed to reversing this reverse. Rather than going away, as Early had predicted, Sheridan began carefully preparing a counterattack.

He took his time, so an eerie silence fell over the now sunny field as the two armies shifted here and there. Some Confederate maneuvers were unfortunate, for they stretched their lines thin and created a gap at Gordon's position. Suddenly, at 4:00 P.M. Sheridan struck, hurling XIX Corps into that gap and following it with George A. Custer's cavalry. It collapsed Gordon's division and soon had Kershaw in full retreat as well. At the center, Ramseur's people stood against VI Corps for an hour and a half. As Ramseur was mounting his third horse to resume rallying his men, a bullet tore through his lungs. The wound would kill him.

When it became clear that cavalry were gaining their rear, Wharton and Pegram also broke with little order. Everybody was streaming toward Fisher's Hill, when a bridge blocked by an abandoned wagon stalled the retreat and added to the panic. For a while, it was a headlong race in which the only advantage lay in outrunning the blue infantry.

Early briefly contemplated making a stand at Fisher's Hill, but soon abandoned that idea and the position. On 20 October he continued a general withdrawal toward New Market, his army having suffered a third major defeat and leaving the Shenandoah Valley completely in the hands of the Federals. Sheridan had lost more than 5,500 of his nearly 31,000-man army, but he had finally won the day and would enjoy a steadily increasing celebrity. Early's Valley Army was devastated by this last disaster, suffering

almost 3,000 casualties and losing virtually all of its artillery in the headlong flight from the field. Early himself was roundly criticized from nearly all quarters for the mishandling of the campaign in general, and especially for the defeat that capped its conclusion. Cedar Creek provided telling omens for the collapsing Confederacy, for it was not only a tale of missed opportunity; it was also a sign of a formerly aggressive commander's ebbing resolve upon the most crucial occasion.

—*David S. Heidler and Jeanne T. Heidler*

See also Early, Jubal; Fishers Hill, Battle of; Gordon, John B.; Pegram, John; Ramseur, Stephen; Shenandoah Valley Campaign (August 1864–March 1865); Sheridan, Philip H.; Tom's Brook, Virginia.

For further reading:
Collier, Mark C. *The Night Attack and Exploitation Portion of the Battle of Cedar Creek (Or Belle Grove), Oct. 19, 1864* (1997).
Gordon, John B. *Reminiscences of the Civil War* (1903).
Mahr, Theodore C. *The Battle of Cedar Creek: Showdown in the Shenandoah, October 1–30, 1864: Early's Valley Campaign* (1992).

CEDAR MOUNTAIN, BATTLE OF
(9 August 1862)

Mismanaged on both sides, the battle of Cedar Mountain (the location also known as Slaughter Mountain, Cedar Run, Cedar Run Mountain, and Southwest Mountain), Virginia, caused the Confederate army nearly to suffer a humiliating defeat from a Union army half its size.

Early in 1862, Brigadier General John Pope received recognition for Union military victories in the west. For such successes, he was called east and given command of the newly created Union Army of Virginia on 26 June 1862. The fragmented Army of Virginia was reorganized to consist of the Mountain Department, Department of the Shenandoah, and the Department of the Rappahannock. Positioned around Culpeper, Virginia, Pope's mission was to protect Washington, D.C., guard the Shenandoah Valley, and move east to Charlottesville to pose a threat to General Robert E. Lee in order to draw Lee's attention away from Major General George McClellan's advancing armies.

In mid-July, Lee sent Major General Stonewall Jackson northwest to protect the rail junction at Gordonsville and to watch the movements of the Union army. On 7 August, informed of the cavalry and infantry, unknown in number, Lee sent Jackson and his three divisions north to Orange Court House, taking advantage of McClellan's inactivity. Meanwhile, Pope planned an advance south to the Rapidan River, east of the Blue Ridge Mountains. Upon hearing of the Confederate advance, Pope deployed his troops in an effort to cover a wide expanse from Madison Court House to Culpeper. To the south of Culpeper, however, north of the Rapidan River, Jackson's large army of 24,000 men, doubling that of Pope's, lay in wait, intending to strike quickly and destroy the first Union corps to arrive.

Jackson's plan was to subdue the first corps, placing his forces in perfect position to defeat the other two, one at a time, as they approached. Brigadier General Nathaniel Banks's division of Pope's Union forces, fronted by cavalry, struck first, however. By midmorning on 9 August 1862 at Cedar Run, eight miles south of Culpeper, the Confederates encountered Pope's cavalry. Jackson took most of the afternoon to deploy his troops. The Confederate forces met the Union troops at 4:00 P.M., allowing enough time for the Union forces to arrive, following three miles behind Banks. Experiencing gaps in formation, the two Confederate divisions under Major General Richard S. Ewell and Brigadier General Charles S. Winder still moved forward experiencing little opposition initially, though Winder, commanding the left, was mortally wounded by a Union shell. Soon

The battle of Cedar Mountain, 9 August 1862 (*Library of Congress*)

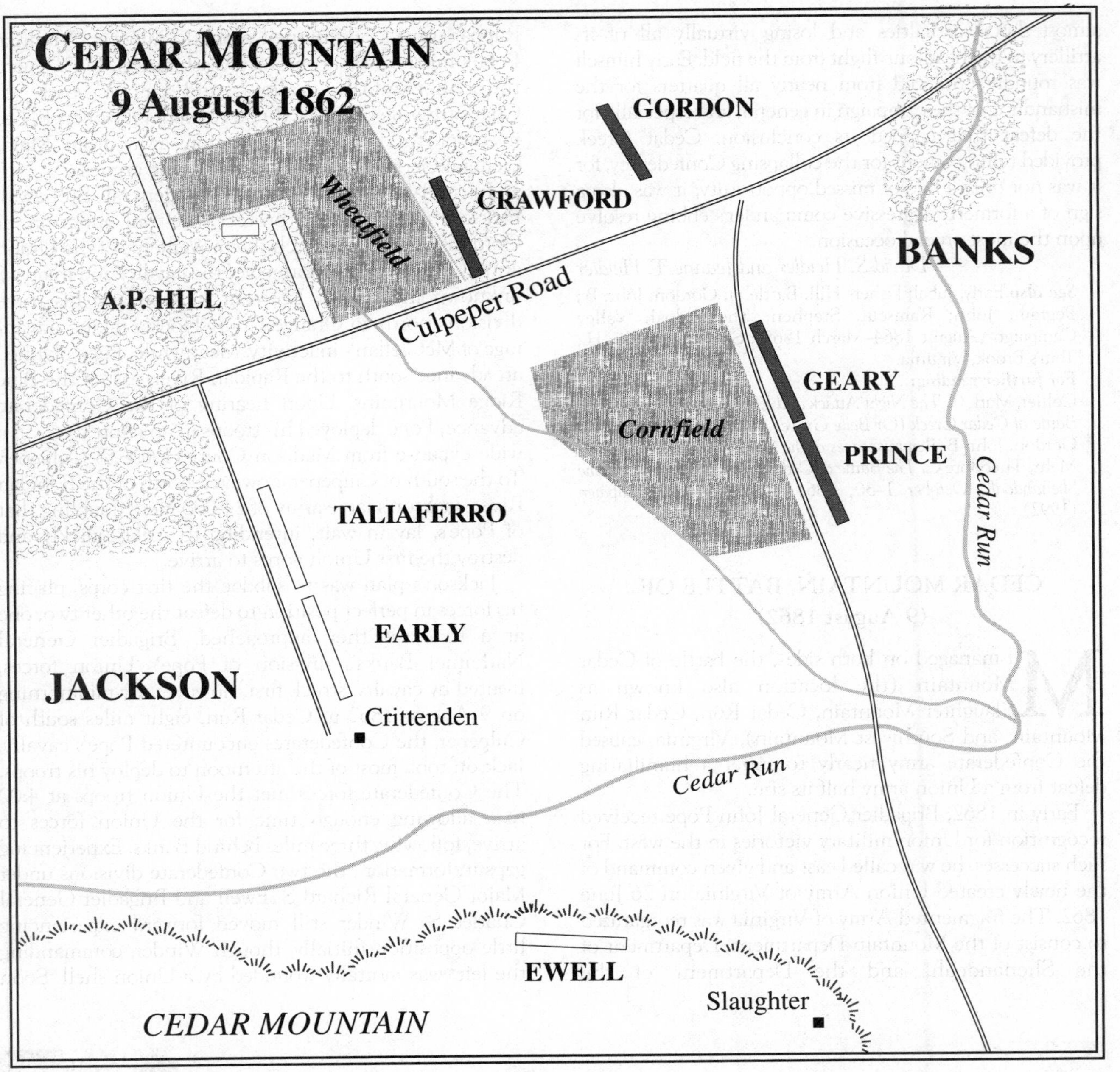

CEDAR MOUNTAIN
9 August 1862

GORDON

CRAWFORD

Wheatfield

BANKS

Culpeper Road

A.P. HILL

GEARY

Cornfield

PRINCE

TALIAFERRO

Cedar Run

EARLY

JACKSON

■ Crittenden

Cedar Run

EWELL

Slaughter ■

CEDAR MOUNTAIN

after the Confederate advance, however, Banks's troops furiously drove on to Winder's exposed left. This tremendous assault caused the Confederate army's left side to give way, devastated by the Union charge.

Alarmed at seeing his left side collapse, Jackson immediately rode into the nearby forest to rally his troops and lead them into battle. Although Banks used almost all of his 9,000 troops in the initial assault, Ewell's right side was pushed back but held its ground. In the early evening, the Union advance was stopped as the third Confederate division arrived under the command of Major General Ambrose P. Hill. The gaps caused by the Union assault were eventually mended by Hill's

12,000 men and allowed for a Confederate counterattack. Although Union reinforcements were on their way from Culpeper, they arrived much too late to allow the Federals to continue on. Still fighting hard, the outnumbered Union forces stubbornly withdrew from the field at around 6:30 P.M. Although Jackson ordered Hill to follow, artillery fire, exhaustion, and darkness put an end to the Confederate pursuit. Federal reinforcements under Brigadier General James B. Ricketts arrived in the night to halt the Confederate advance, seven miles south of Culpeper. Sometime after 11:00 P.M., Jackson, unwilling to risk any more lives in his advance, ordered his men to halt and set up camp for the night.

The Cedar Mountain battlefield, August 1862 (Photograph by Timothy O'Sullivan / *Library of Congress*)

The battle cost the Federals 314 killed, 1,445 wounded, and 622 missing, totaling 2,381 men of the 8,000 engaged. The Confederates, employing 16,800 men, suffered 1,341 casualties, not to mention the loss of Winder, greatly diminishing the value of this Confederate victory. Although Jackson claimed a victory, driving Pope from the field, he had grossly miscalculated. His drawn-out and calculated march allowed for Pope to position the rest of his men, behind Banks's initial charge. Banks, outnumbered, could have quite possibly overcome the staggering odds; however, he erred in not leaving a reserve when attacking and not requesting reinforcements from Pope.

—*Andrew Paul Bielakowski*

See also Army of Virginia; Banks, Nathaniel Prentiss; Hill, Ambrose Powell; Jackson, Thomas Jonathan; Pope, John; Winder, Charles S.

For further reading:

Krick, Robert K. *Stonewall Jackson at Cedar Mountain* (1990).
Stackpole, Edward J. *From Cedar Mountain to Antietam* (1993).

CENTRALIA MASSACRE
(27 September 1864)

In September 1864, guerrilla activity in Missouri markedly increased as a result of excitement over Confederate general Sterling Price's expected invasion of the state. Confederate officers roamed the state to fill the ranks of Price's army. Many bushwhackers, however, cared little about the larger war effort and just perpetuated the violence that had enveloped Missouri for several years. On the night of 26 September, more than 200 veteran guerrillas assembled about four miles south of Centralia, a small town in the north central part of the state. John Thrailkill, Dave Poole, George Todd, and the notoriously violent William "Bloody Bill" Anderson led the combined bands. The next morning, Anderson and thirty of his men left the camp and rode into Centralia to find news of Price and check the stocks of the local stores. The tiny town, which consisted of only two hotels, two stores, a schoolhouse, and a few homes, had been alerted to the guerrillas' presence only minutes before.

Anderson's men began terrorizing the citizenry, demanding anything that caught their eye. A whiskey barrel was found and soon emptied, adding drunken enthusiasm to the atmosphere. When a stagecoach from nearby Columbia arrived, its luckless occupants were quickly robbed of their valuables. Among the passengers was William S. Rollins, a well-known Unionist congressman, who escaped certain death by lying about his identity and then hiding out in a hotel. About an hour and a half after the destruction had begun, a northbound train from St. Louis appeared. The engineer spotted the bushwhackers and attempted to run by the station at full steam but the unknowing brakeman brought it to a squealing halt, thus delivering 125 civilian passengers and 23 unarmed Union soldiers into the guerrillas' grasp.

After robbing the civilian passengers, the guerrillas turned their attention to the Union soldiers, who were separated from the rest and stripped of their uniforms. On Anderson's order, the guerrillas began firing into the crowd of pleading men, executing them in plain sight of the horrified onlookers. Within a few minutes, all the soldiers had been killed except Sergeant Thomas M. Goodman, who Anderson hoped to exchange for a recently captured member of his company. After the train was set afire and headed down the track under steam, Anderson and his mob departed, leaving twenty-two soldiers and a civilian (an unfortunate German immigrant dressed in blue that day) dead at the railroad station.

Major A. V. E. Johnston and three companies of the green 39th Missouri had been in the field since 10:00 P.M. the previous night following rumors of the guerrillas' whereabouts. The regiment had been organized only two weeks before and consisted primarily of inexperienced farm boys armed with Enfield muskets and mounted on plow horses and mules. Johnston's troops entered Centralia around 3 P.M. on the afternoon of the 27th, having seen smoke rising from a distance. After hearing of the morning's violence, Johnston left 35 men in Centralia and followed the guerrilla's trail south with about 120 troopers. They followed the bushwhackers' pickets into an open field near Young's Creek, south of town.

The guerrilla chieftains were ready for the Federals' arrival and lured them toward a horseshoe-shaped trap outlining the field into which they rode. Upon seeing the guerrillas arrayed in a line across the opposite end of the field, Johnston dismounted his troops and sent the horses to the rear with every fifth man. The militia fixed bayonets and prepared to receive the mounted charge on foot. On Anderson's signal, the trap closed and the bushwhackers attacked the panicking young troopers from three sides. The first rush by Anderson's men from the base of the "horseshoe" galloped through Johnston's horrified line and continued toward the horseholders who broke and fled in terror.

The fighting lasted only a few minutes and ended in the complete annihilation of Johnston and his little command. The guerrillas then moved among the fallen bodies, mutilating many and even scalping some. They chased down the fleeing horseholders and slaughtered them, following one all the way into Centralia. There some of the troops left behind by Johnston were killed as well. That night, the guerrillas broke into smaller groups and returned to the brush to avoid Federal retribution. The day's toll of death and destruction marked one of the most brutal events in Missouri's Civil War. One month later, Union troops shot and killed Anderson outside Albany, Missouri, when he attempted an attack similar to the one made on Johnston and his men.

—*Ronald G. Machoian*

See also Anderson, William "Bloody Bill"; Guerrilla Warfare; Missouri; Todd, George.

For further reading:
Barton, O.S. *Three Years with Quantrill: A True Story Told by His Scout John McCorkle* (1992).
Brownlee, Richard S. *Gray Ghosts of the Confederacy: Guerilla Warfare in the West, 1861–1865* (1958).
Castel, Albert E., and Thomas Goodrich. *Bloody Bill Anderson: The Short, Savage Life of a Civil War Guerrilla* (1998).
Goodrich, Thomas. *Black Flag: Guerrilla Warfare on the Western Border, 1861–1865* (1995).
Rodermyre, Edgar T. *History of Centralia, Missouri* (1936).
War of the Rebellion: A Compilation of the Official Records of the Union and Confederate Armies (1893).

CHALMERS, JAMES RONALD
(1831–1898)
Confederate general

Born in Halifax County, Virginia, to Joseph Williams Chalmers and Fannie Henderson Chalmers, the younger Chalmers moved to Tennessee and then Mississippi as a child with his family. He graduated from South Carolina College in 1851 and after studying law began his practice in Mississippi. In 1858 he became state district attorney for the 7th District. A strong Democrat, Chalmers advocated secession in 1860 and was elected to the Mississippi Secession

Convention. He was selected the chairman of the Military Affairs Committee of that body.

At the formation of the Confederate States of America, Chalmers received a captain's commission in March 1861 and was appointed the colonel of the 9th Mississippi Regiment in April 1861. Stationed initially at Pensacola, Chalmers participated in the night raid on Santa Rosa Island on 8–9 October 1861. Chalmers was promoted to brigadier general on 13 February 1862, at which point he and his brigade, known as the "Pensacola Brigade," moved north to join Confederate forces in northern Mississippi.

Moving between Iuka and Corinth in an effort to determine Federal movements before the commencement of the Shiloh campaign, Chalmers's brigade scouted Union flanks at Pittsburg Landing during the first few days of April. During the battle of Shiloh, Chalmers commanded his brigade as part of Major General Jones Withers's division and was commended for his bravery during the two-day battle.

After Shiloh, Chalmers temporarily moved to the cavalry, but at his request returned to his brigade in July 1862. In that capacity, he moved north as part of Braxton Bragg's Kentucky campaign in the late summer of 1862. He led the attack that resulted in the successful Confederate siege of Munfordville, Kentucky. In what would become the Perryville campaign, he briefly earned the wrath of his commander, Bragg, by engaging in an unauthorized attack on a Federal position. He redeemed himself in the upcoming campaigns in the fall and winter of 1862, distinguishing himself as a brigade commander under Leonidas Polk at Stones River where Chalmers was wounded.

After that battle, Chalmers transferred permanently to the Confederate cavalry. In April 1863 he became the commander of the Military District of Mississippi serving under Nathan Bedford Forrest. During the Vicksburg campaign, Chalmers operated in northern and eastern Mississippi in attempt to harass Northern movements. After the fall of Vicksburg, Chalmers destroyed rail lines and foraged for the remaining Confederate troops in the state.

By 1864 Chalmers commanded one of Forrest's divisions, though he did not always get along with his temperamental commander. Chalmers commanded the lead elements of Forrest's attack on Fort Pillow and was present during the controversial attack on and killing of much of the African-American garrison. He continued under Forrest at the battle of Tupelo, 14–15 July 1864, after which Chalmers led his division in John Bell Hood's Tennessee campaign of the fall of 1864. By early 1865, Chalmers commanded all Confederate cavalry in Mississippi. He surrendered in May 1865.

After the war, Chalmers returned to his law practice and to Mississippi politics. He served in the state senate and three terms as a U.S. congressman. He retired from politics in 1888 and began practicing law in Memphis, Tennessee, where he died.

—*David S. Heidler and Jeanne T. Heidler*

See also Fort Pillow; Santa Rosa Island, Battle of; Tupelo, Battle of.

CHAMBERLAIN, JOSHUA LAWRENCE
(1828–1914)
Union general

Joshua Lawrence Chamberlain left his college professorship in 1862 to become lieutenant colonel in the 20th Maine, Army of the Potomac. He became a hero at Gettysburg when he helped save Little Round Top for the Union, suffered a near-fatal wound at Petersburg, and after the war served four terms as governor of Maine. His remarkable bravery and fearless battlefield conduct earned him lasting distinction.

When the war began Chamberlain was a professor of rhetoric at Bowdoin College in Brunswick, Maine. In 1861, the college's administration offered the charismatic and highly respected Chamberlain the chair of modern European languages. The position came with lifetime tenure and a two-year sabbatical for study in Europe, the college to continue his salary and pay his expenses. Chamberlain gave up the trip, but he did use his leave to accept a commission as lieutenant colonel of the 20th Maine.

The 20th Maine joined the Army of the Potomac in September 1862. It arrived just in time for the battle of Antietam, although the green regiment, newly trained, was held in reserve behind Union lines. Chamberlain and his men received their baptism of fire at Fredericksburg in December. They were involved in one of the many futile attacks launched against the Confederates entrenched on Marye's Heights. Chamberlain spent the night pinned down by Confederate fire, using dead Union soldiers for cover.

While quarantined because of an outbreak of smallpox, the regiment missed the next major engagement at Chancellorsville. Chamberlain, however, was promoted to colonel and commander of the regiment in May 1863, and his exploits at Gettysburg would make him famous. The 20th Maine, part of Colonel Strong Vincent's brigade, was held in reserve below Little Round Top. Only a few Federal signalmen occupied the small peak at the southern end of the Union line, but they spotted Confederates advancing up the hill. An urgent order from Gouverneur K. Warren brought Chamberlain and his men to the summit of Little Round Top. Vincent's four brigades reached the summit just ahead of the Confederates with Chamberlain's unit holding the left side of the makeshift Union line. William Oates's 15th Alabama assailed Chamberlain's regiment and nearly turned the Union flank, but the Maine men held. Chamberlain suffered several minor wounds, and the unit took heavy losses in close fighting, but his bold counterattack secured the critical Federal position. Chamberlain's bravery at Gettysburg later earned him the Medal of Honor.

He was also given command of a brigade, although with no promotion in rank. From 1863 to the summer of 1864 he alternated between commanding a regiment and a brigade. A stint on court-martial duty in the spring of 1864 kept Chamberlain out of the massive engagements in Virginia. He returned to his comrades in time for the battle of Cold Harbor, but the 20th Maine played no part in the disastrous Union assault at that place. After the defeat at Cold Harbor, the Army of the Potomac swung farther south and attempted to capture the rail center at Petersburg, and it was near there that Chamberlain led his brigade against a Confederate breastwork called Rives's Salient. He suffered a severe pelvic wound that caused so much internal damage that doctors at a field hospital pronounced the wound mortal. When the news reached Chamberlain's division commander G. K. Warren, he recommended that as a tribute Chamberlain be promoted before he died. U. S. Grant, recalling other times when Chamberlain had been passed over for promotion, immediately signed the order. Two weeks after being wounded—a time during which he barely clung to life—Chamberlain signed his acceptance of the commission that made him a brigadier general.

Incredibly, he began to recover. He spent the rest of 1864 convalescing in Annapolis, Maryland, and his home in Brunswick. He never completely recovered, however, and would suffer pain from his wounds for the rest of his life. Nevertheless, Chamberlain chose to return to the Army of the Potomac in February 1865, as the army began its final campaign against Robert E. Lee and the Army of Northern Virginia. His brigade played a key role in the battles of White Oak Road and Five Forks during Lee's desperate attempt to escape Petersburg. Chamberlain was wounded again, but he achieved distinction when he single-handedly reversed a Union retreat. He was able to remain in the field and was present at Appomattox Court-House. Grant, aware of Chamberlain's reputation as a brave and inspiring battlefield commander, selected him to conduct the formal infantry surrender ceremonies. Just before mustering out of the service, Chamberlain was breveted to major general.

Chamberlain returned to Maine a decorated hero, wounded six times. In 1866 he became the governor of Maine by the largest margin in that state's history, and he was reelected for three more one-year terms. When he left politics in 1870 he was the unanimous choice to become president of Bowdoin College, the institution that only reluctantly had let him go to war. At Bowdoin he instituted a drill system and military science program for all students, feeling that military training was a bene-

ficial augmentation of academic study and that future wars were inevitable. Within a year, a major uprising of students forced Chamberlain to threaten expulsion for anyone who refused to drill. Although he broke this student strike, the college first made the program voluntary and then abolished it within a decade.

After stepping down as Bowdoin's president in 1883, Chamberlain spent his remaining years in various business ventures and participating in veteran's organizations. In his final days he attended the fiftieth anniversary of Gettysburg and penned a book, published posthumously as *The Passing of the Armies*. This memoir is an account of the war's closing months and is considered one of the best personal narratives of the war. He died on 24 February 1914 from an infection in the hip wound suffered at Petersburg.

—*Richard D. Loosbrock*

See also Appomattox Court House; Gettysburg, Battle of; Petersburg Campaign.

For further reading:

Linderman, Gerald F. *Embattled Courage: The Experience of Combat in the Civil War* (1987).

Nesbitt, Mark. *Through Blood and Fire: Selected Civil War Papers of Major General Joshua Lawrence Chamberlain* (1996).

Trulock, Alice Rains. *In the Hands of Providence: Joshua L. Chamberlain and the American Civil War* (1992).

CHAMBERSBURG, BURNING OF
(July 1864)

Chambersburg, Pennsylvania, gained national notoriety when Confederate raiders under the command of General John McCausland torched it on 30 July 1864. Home to some 5,200 residents, the town lay about twenty miles north of the Mason-Dixon Line. In October 1862, Jeb Stuart's Cavalry had briefly occupied the town, which surrendered without resistance. Between 15 June and 2 July 1863, residents had faced a more substantial Confederate presence while General Robert E. Lee used Chambersburg as a concentration point for the Confederate army. Residents were largely spared full-scale looting and destruction by Lee's General Orders No. 72 and 73, which forbade injury to private property. A year later, Chambersburg was the military headquarters for the Union Department of the Susquehanna, with thousands of Northern soldiers stationed near town.

The Chambersburg raid was most directly inspired by General David Hunter's unprovoked burning of homes of three prominent Southern sympathizers in West Virginia. In return, Confederates would burn Northern homes. On 28 July, General Jubal Early put Brigadier General John McCausland in charge of a cavalry detachment that was to occupy Chambersburg and demanded $500,000 in greenbacks or $100,000 in gold as compensation for the houses that Hunter had ordered destroyed. Early and McCausland had used this strategy a few weeks earlier, raising $200,000 from Frederick, Maryland, residents. Reaching Franklin County on 29 June, McCausland found his progress slowed by a small regiment of Union cavalry, buying time for trains to leave Chambersburg with supplies, equipment, and most of the borough's cash reserves. The first Confederates arrived at Chambersburg at dawn on June 30 and swiftly occupied the town.

Chambersburg's citizens were summoned to the town center, presented with Early's demands, and given a deadline of three to six hours (depending on account) in which to produce the cash, or the town would be "laid in ashes." When the citizens refused and the deadline expired, McCausland ordered his men to fire the town. Accounts of the burning vary widely. Chambersburg residents described violent, drunken Confederates and mass looting, while Confederates tended to report a more orderly operation, although marred by a few soldiers bent on revenge or spurred on by liquor. At least one colonel refused to carry out the order to burn and was arrested, but charges were dropped the next day. No one died in the fire, but more than 550 structures were destroyed, leaving 3,000 people homeless. A state commission, set up after the war to handle property claims, estimated total damage to real and personal property at $1,628,431.

Until their deaths, McCausland and Early defended the burning as a necessary act. McCausland's raid, however, did little more than provide Confederates with a modicum of revenge while doing nothing to advance Confederate strategic and military aims. It actually hurt the Confederacy, causing Ulysses S. Grant to bring Union forces in the valley under the unified command of General Philip Sheridan. Sheridan took decisive control of the area by the end of 1864, and Chambersburg was prospering again within two years of the raid.

—Anne Sarah Rubin

See also Chambersburg Raid; Early, Jubal A.; Early's Washington Raid; Hunter, David; McCausland, John; Pennsylvania;

For further reading:

Alexander, Ted, et al. *Southern Revenge! Civil War History of Chambersburg, Pennsylvania* (1989).

Hoke, Jacob. *Historical Reminiscences of the War or Incidents which Transpired in and about Chambersburg during the War of the Rebellion* (1884).

Schenck, Reverend B. S. *The Burning of Chambersburg, Pennsylvania* (1864).

Smith, Everard H. "Chambersburg: Anatomy of a Confederate Reprisal." *The American Historical Review* (1991).

CHAMBERSBURG RAID
(9–12 October 1862)

One of Major General J. E. B. Stuart's most famous raids, the Chambersburg Raid became known as his "second ride around McClellan." Stuart handpicked 600 men each from the brigades of W. H. F. Lee, Wade Hampton, and W. E. "Grumble" Jones, and a four-gun detachment under Major John Pelham. Their objectives were to learn what they could of McClellan's army in Maryland; destroy the Cumberland Valley Railroad bridge over Conococheague Creek near Chambersburg, Pennsylvania; capture government officials to exchange for Southern prisoners; and capture horses and mules.

Crossing the Potomac at McCoy's Ford at dawn on 10 October, they narrowly missed six regiments of Federal infantry under Major General Jacob Cox. Rain hampered Union army signal stations, and when the raiders reached Chambersburg around 7:00 P.M., some prominent citizens surrendered the town. Stuart left Chambersburg early the next morning. A detail left behind under Colonel M. C. Butler destroyed 5,000 muskets and other weapons and burned the railroad depots, machine shops, and much rolling stock, although they could not burn the iron railroad bridge.

Believing that Cox's regiments would be waiting for him if he returned the way he had come, Stuart decided to ride east, then south, again taking his men around McClellan's army. The route would be twice as long but would surprise the enemy. At Cashtown, Stuart turned south and entered Maryland near Emmitsburg, where Southern sympathizers greeted him. Local troopers guided Stuart along back roads to avoid detection, and the men rode day and night, sometimes dozing in the saddle. After midnight, Stuart and a small party took a side-trip to visit a young woman he had met during the Antietam campaign, rejoining the column about 7:00 A.M.

Stuart had reports that Brigadier General George Stoneman and several thousand men were ahead of them, guarding the Potomac fords. A local officer recommended that Stuart use White's Ford, three miles below the mouth of the Monocacy. W. H. F. Lee's brigade was in the advance as the Rebels neared the ford, where 200 Union infantrymen blocked their way. Lee bluffed, demanding their surrender, and the Union soldiers abandoned their position as Lee began to attack. Pelham's guns kept them back while Stuart's men forded the river. Helped by the Union commanders' slow reactions, Stuart's force had safely slipped through a region guarded by more than 100,000 of McClellan's men.

Lee considered the raid "eminently successful." Stuart had brought the war to Northern territory and embarrassed the Union army. The raid contributed to Lincoln's dissatisfaction with McClellan and hastened the president's replacement of him as commander of the Army of the Potomac.

—David A. Norris

See also Stuart, J. E. B.; Stuart's Dumfries Raid; Stuart's First Ride around McClellan.

For further reading:

Blackford, W. W. *War Years With Jeb Stuart* (1945; reprint, 1993).

Freeman, Douglas Southall. *Lee's Lieutenants: A Study in Command* (1942–1944).

McClellan, Henry B. *The Life and Campaigns of Major General J. E. B. Stuart, Commander of the Cavalry of the Army of Northern Virginia* (1885).

Thomas, Emory. *Bold Dragoon: The Life of J. E. B. Stuart* (1988).

CHAMPION'S HILL, BATTLE OF
(16 May 1863)

General Ulysses S. Grant, commanding the Federal Army of the Tennessee, had accomplished the dangerous feat of running his army past the Confederate fortress at Vicksburg on the Mississippi River in April 1863. Grant was now in a position to move upon the rebel bastion. However, he knew that Confederate General Joseph E. Johnston was organizing an army at Jackson, the capital of Mississippi. If Grant moved immediately on Vicksburg, he might find himself trapped between two enemy armies. Therefore, the Federals marched toward Jackson to eliminate that threat while also preventing the two Confederate armies from uniting.

On 14 May, two of Grant's three corps, commanded by Generals William T. Sherman and James B. McPherson, attacked and defeated Johnston's Confederates at Jackson. While Sherman's XV Corps remained in Jackson, McPherson's XVII Corps joined General John A. McClernand's XIII Corps and headed west. On 16 May the decisive battle of the entire Vicksburg campaign was fought at a place about halfway between Jackson and Vicksburg.

The Confederates, commanded by General John C. Pemberton, occupied a height that was variously called Midway Hill or Champion's Hill. The name Midway Hill was used because it was about halfway between Jackson and Vicksburg. Champion's Hill was the more common name and was derived from the owner's name. The hill was about 60 to 70 feet high and the Vicksburg and Clinton Road ran over its crest. To the south of the hill (or left from the position of the approaching Federal army), the terrain was severely broken, cut up with ravines, hills, and tangled woods. This land was virtually impassable for an invading army. On the north side of the hill, the terrain was more accessible to an attacking force. Open and undulating fields dominated this terrain, which was the primary site of the engagement.

The Federal forces, numbering approximately 30,000 men, advanced on Champion's Hill in three columns. On the left was General Andrew J. Smith's division of McClernand's XIII Corps. Because of the nature of the terrain, Smith's men played only a minor role in the battle. In the center was General Peter Osterhaus's division of McClernand's corps. These men also had virtually no role in the battle because of the terrain. The battle would be fought almost entirely on the right of the Federal line. On the right were General Alvin P. Hovey's division of McClernand's corps and Generals John A. Logan and Marcellus M. Crocker's divisions of McPherson's XVII Corps. Also on the right were Generals Grant and McPherson.

Opposing this formidable array of blue-clad troopers were approximately 20,000 Confederates under General Pemberton. Confronting the left and center of the Federal line were the divisions of Generals John S. Bowen and William W. Loring, while General Carter L. Stevenson's division bore the brunt of the attack from the Union right.

The battle on the right commenced at about 10:30 A.M. when General Hovey threw out skirmishers. Logan's division was positioned on Hovey's right and Crocker constituted the reserve. By 11:00 A.M. the fighting started in earnest. The Federal line advanced up the slope of Champion's Hill against a withering Confederate fire. For several hours the combatants clashed and the crossroads on the hill changed hands three times. At approximately 2:30 P.M. General Hovey brought out his artillery, placing his heavy guns between his troops and Logan's men. This bombardment succeeded and Logan's division followed with a bayonet charge. By 3:00 P.M. the battle was over.

The Confederates, who suffered some 3,800 casualties, beat a hasty retreat toward Vicksburg. The Federals suffered about 2,400 casualties and followed closely behind the withdrawing enemy. The battle of Champion's Hill was a significant engagement, the most important of the entire Vicksburg campaign. It prevented a junction between Generals Johnston and Pemberton and opened the way to Vicksburg.

—*Christopher C. Meyers*

See also Jackson, Mississippi; Pemberton, John C.
For further reading:
Bearss, Edwin C. *The Campaign for Vicksburg* (1985–1986).
Miers, Earl Schenck. *The Web of Victory: Grant at Vicksburg* (1955; reprint, 1983).

CHANCELLORSVILLE, BATTLE OF
(2–3 May 1863)

A brick tavern and family residence at the intersection of the Orange Turnpike and Orange Plank Road, Chancellorsville lent its name to one of the most important battles of the Civil War. Situated at the strategic intersection of five roads in the heavily wooded region north of Fredericksburg, Virginia, Chancellorsville evolved as one of Robert E. Lee and Lieutenant General Thomas J. "Stonewall" Jackson's greatest triumphs.

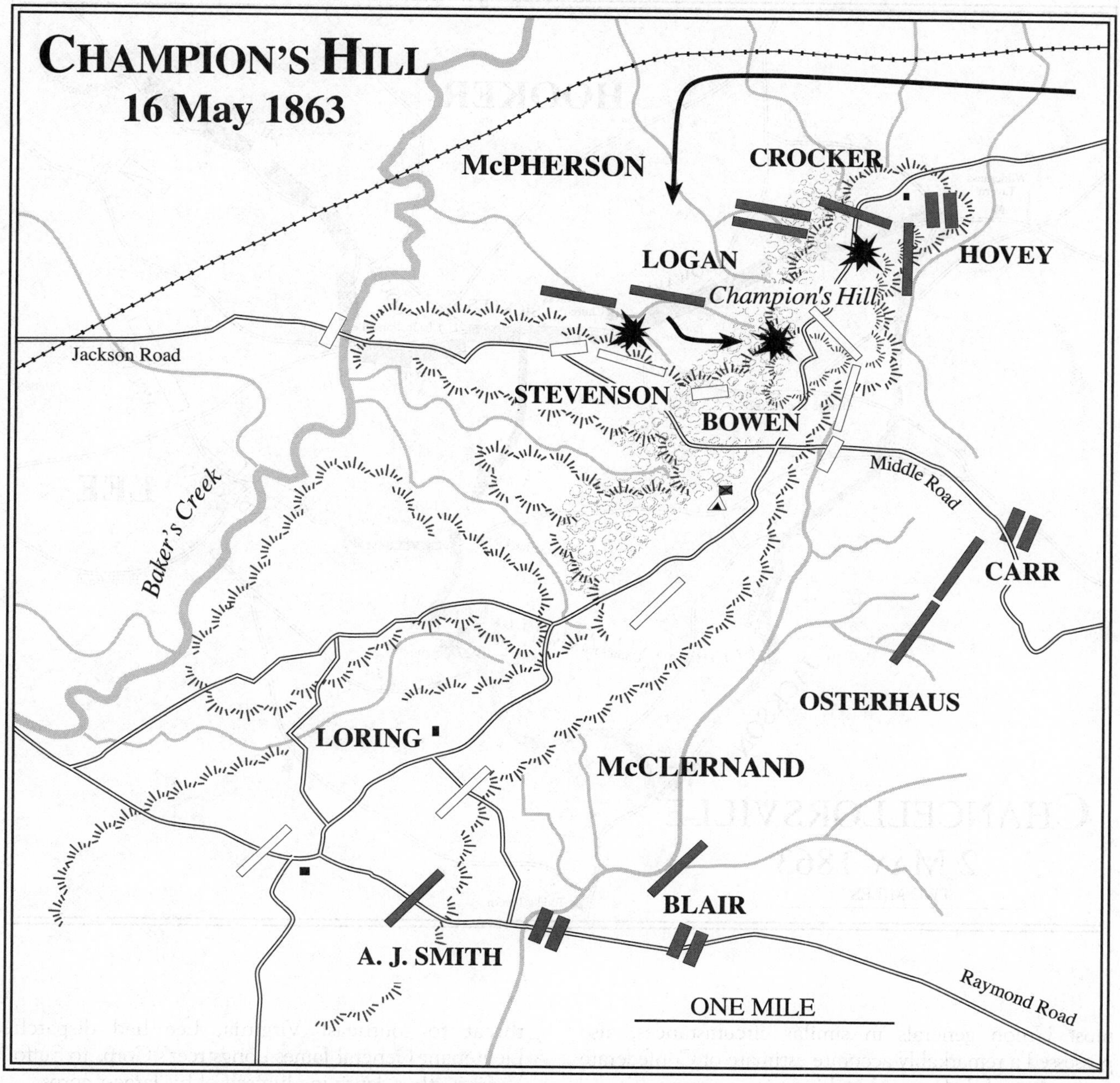

CHAMPION'S HILL
16 May 1863

McPHERSON

CROCKER

LOGAN

HOVEY

Champion's Hill

Jackson Road

STEVENSON

BOWEN

Baker's Creek

Middle Road

CARR

OSTERHAUS

LORING

McCLERNAND

BLAIR

A. J. SMITH

ONE MILE

Raymond Road

Since assuming command of the Army of the Potomac in January 1863, Union major general Joseph "Fighting Joe" Hooker focused his efforts on rebuilding his army after the previous December's debacle at Fredericksburg. His army of 130,000 shouldered the finest weapons, wore the best uniforms, and ate the highest quality rations the United States could supply. His army included over 11,000 cavalry in a newly organized corps and 496 modern, rifled artillery pieces. With new equipment and daily drilling, Hooker considered the Army of the Potomac the finest army in the world. He also created an efficient intelligence service and integrated a tactical

cover and deception operation into his plans to dislodge Lee from the trenches at Fredericksburg.

Through an adroit use of spies, line crossers, Confederate deserters, Union sympathizers, and intercepted Confederate semaphore messages, Hooker learned of the Confederate weakness around Fredericksburg. He received numerous reports of how thin Lee's line was along the Rappahannock River. Frequent updates from the Confederate side of the river allowed Hooker to formulate a plan that initially deceived Lee and allowed the Union general to steal a march around the Confederate left flank. Hooker, unlike

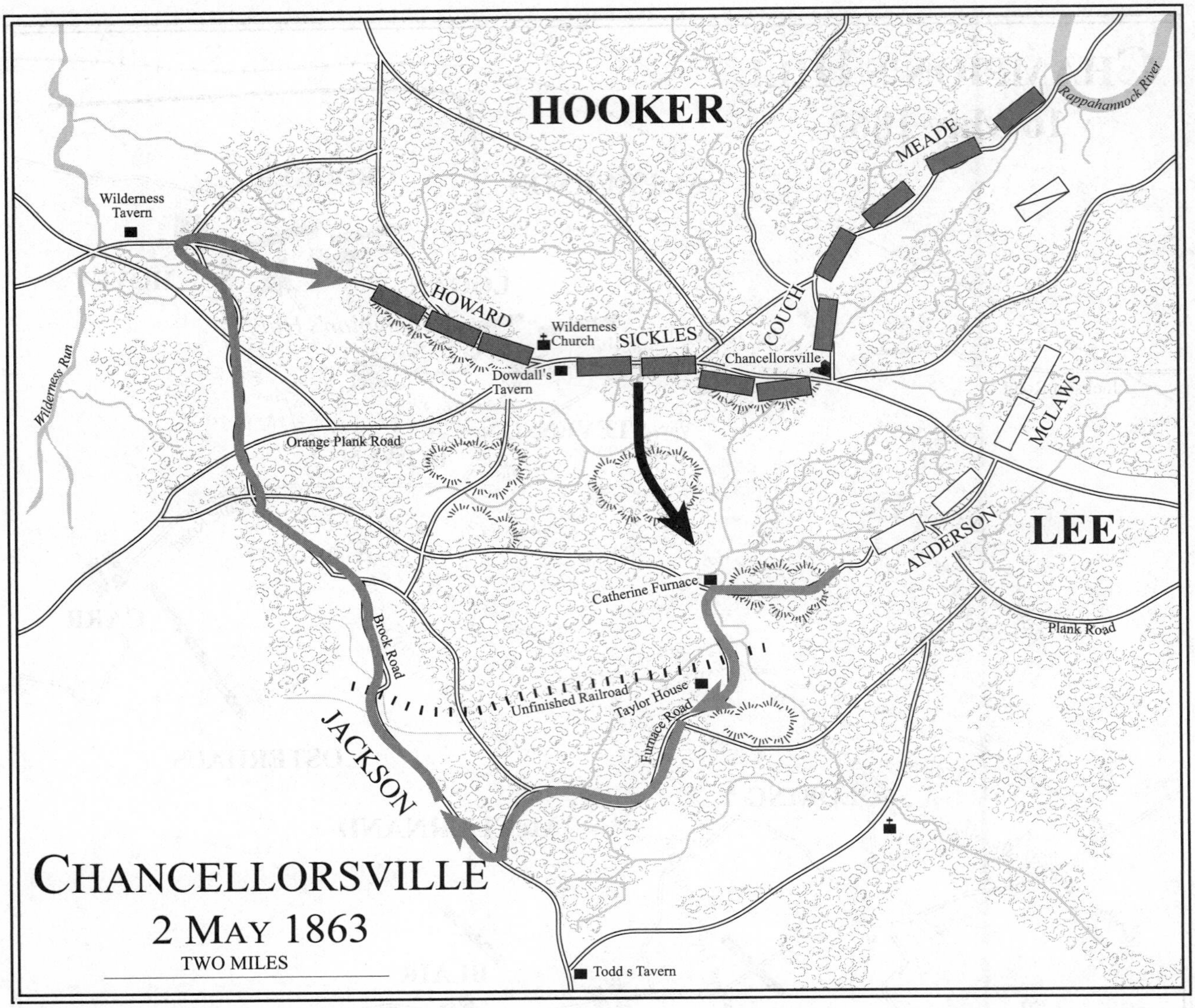

HOOKER

MEADE

Rappahannock River

Wilderness Tavern

HOWARD

Wilderness Church

SICKLES

COUCH

Chancellorsville

Dowdall's Tavern

MCLAWS

Orange Plank Road

ANDERSON

LEE

Catherine Furnace

Plank Road

Brock Road

Unfinished Railroad

Taylor House

Furnace Road

JACKSON

CHANCELLORSVILLE

2 MAY 1863

TWO MILES

Todd s Tavern

most Union generals in similar circumstances, also possessed a remarkably accurate estimate of Confederate troop strength before undertaking the campaign.

Across the Rappahannock, spread along the river's edge for almost twenty-five miles, Lee's Army of Northern Virginia numbered about 60,000 effectives. Just off a hard winter, Lee's men resembled scarecrows more than soldiers. Tattered remnants of uniforms covered their malnourished frames and many lacked adequate footgear. They subsisted on a few ounces of cornmeal and bacon a day, the bacon rancid as often as not.

The gaunt Confederate horses and mules suffered from lack of fodder as well. A single rail line ran to the rear of the Confederate line at Fredericksburg and proved insufficient to supply Lee's army. As a result he sent over 400 artillery horses to winter pasture farther south. Due to supply shortages and to counter a Federal

threat to southeast Virginia, Lee had dispatched Lieutenant General James Longstreet's Corps to Suffolk, Virginia, thus depriving himself of his largest corps.

Hooker's well-conceived strategy consisted of three major maneuvers. First, he would send his cavalry, commanded by Major General George Stoneman, far upriver with the double mission of drawing Lee's cavalry screen away from the Confederate left flank and then raiding deep into Virginia to disrupt Lee's supply line from Richmond. Second, he directed Major General John Sedgwick, with I and VI Corps, to deploy across from Fredericksburg and by strong demonstrations to divert Lee's attention from the main Union attack. If Lee weakened his line, Sedgwick was to cross the Rappahannock below Fredericksburg to become the left wing of a double envelopment, crushing Lee's retreating army. Major General Daniel Sickles's III Corps would

Union artillery before Chancellorsville, 1863 (*Library of Congress*)

remain on Stafford Heights across from Fredericksburg to command the city with its long-range artillery. Third, Hooker planned to march upriver with Major Generals George G. Meade's V, Oliver O. Howard's XI, and Henry W. Slocum's XII Corps. This force would rapidly cross the Rappahannock and crash down on Lee's unprotected left flank. Hooker believed that whether Lee chose to remain and fight or retreat toward Richmond, Hooker could destroy the Army of Northern Virginia with his superior force.

During mid-April Hooker set his plan in motion. He directed both cavalry and infantry demonstrations at all the major crossing sites in the vicinity of Fredericksburg. Lee believed that Hooker's main thrust would come from the north. Yet with all the Union activity, he could not afford to redeploy his troops until he was sure of the main point of attack. Hooker had further convoluted the situation with false messages indicating Stoneman's ultimate objective was the Shenandoah Valley. In all, his deceptions allowed Hooker to steal a march on Lee, something seldom, if ever, accomplished by Union generals. In fact, Hooker's turning movement on Lee is arguably the greatest intelligence coup of the Civil War.

On 28 April Stoneman's cavalry, hampered by inclement weather and muddy roads, finally initiated the campaign by crossing the Rappahannock and riding behind Lee's lines. Hooker's plan, however, began to unravel when Major General J. E. B. Stuart countered Stoneman's raid with a small detachment of Confederate cavalry. Discerning that Stoneman's purported thrust

toward the valley was a ruse, Stuart rapidly realigned his horsemen along the river to screen Lee's left flank. Stoneman's harried command would ride through the Virginia woods for a week without accomplishing either the diversion of Confederate cavalry or the disruption of Lee's railroad to the south.

On 29 April, Hooker pushed through Stuart's cavalry screen at Kelly's Ford north of Fredericksburg and then moved across the Rapidan River at Germanna and Ely's Fords. While Hooker's troops fought their way through Stuart's small but slashing cavalry attacks and the almost impenetrable wilderness around Chancellorsville, Sedgwick threw two pontoon bridges across the Rappahannock River in front of Jackson's positions south of Fredericksburg. Both Lee and Jackson wanted to destroy one of the Union wings, but they disagreed about which one to attack. Lee decided to wait for the situation to develop further before committing himself to a pitched battle. He did, nonetheless, order Major General Richard Anderson to move his division toward Chancellorsville to confront any Yankee advance toward Fredericksburg.

On 30 April, when Hooker unaccountably halted his advance and consolidated his position, he lost the initiative and allowed Lee time to maneuver against him. In part, Hooker's hesitation and his fading confidence resulted from his advance elements meeting stronger resistance than he had expected. Actually, he could have easily broken the thin Confederate line and advanced on both the Orange Turnpike and Plank Road. Historians still debate whether Hooker was drunk during

Confederates killed in Sedgwick's assault on Marye's Heights at Fredericksburg, 3 May 1863, during the Chancellorsville campaign (Photograph by Andrew J. Russell / *National Archives*)

the campaign. Known for his high consumption of alcohol, Hooker supposedly swore off liquor for the campaign, but some contemporary evidence indicated that he returned to his bottle for liquid courage when confronted by the determined Confederates.

When Stuart's patrols and prisoners confirmed the large Federal force advancing from the north, Lee realized that the main attack was at Chancellorsville and Sedgwick's river crossing was only a diversion. Lee immediately ordered Major General Jubal Early, with less than 10,000 effectives, to defend Fredericksburg from the trenches along Marye's Heights. Lee would shift most of his army to meet Hooker's advance. From Early's left, Lee immediately sent two brigades from Major General Lafayette McLaws's division to support Anderson near Zion Church Ridge east of Chancellorsville. Lee then directed Jackson to withdraw his men from their defensive line and move toward Chancellorsville. He also ordered Stuart to ascertain the size and locations of the Union force struggling through the underbrush around Chancellorsville.

Early on the morning of 1 May, Jackson donned a new uniform and led his corps to engage the Yankees east of Chancellorsville. When he arrived at the Confederate lines about 8 A.M., he promptly organized an attack with its axis of advance westward along both the Orange Turnpike and Plank Road. About 11:30 A.M. the Confederate skirmishers encountered the Union advance guard plodding east on the same roads. Without adequate cavalry support, the surprised Federal brigades grudgingly gave way to the advancing Rebel infantrymen. Lee soon arrived on the battlefield and assumed command from Jackson.

Utilizing an unfinished railroad bed graded through the thickets, Lee's infantry turned the Union right and forced Hooker to bend his southern flank almost 90 degrees to meet the threat. By sundown, stiffening Federal resistance halted Lee's advance through the darkening woods. Even though Sickles's and Darius Couch's corps had crossed the Rappahannock to reinforce him, Hooker unaccountably—and against his corps commanders' advice—ordered his men to return to their positions of the previous night.

Seeking an opening for a morning attack, Lee

dispatched several of his staff officers to evaluate the Federal line, while he and Jackson sat at a campfire awaiting a report from Stuart. Upon their return, members of Lee's staff adjudged the Union defenses too formidable for a frontal assault. Stuart and a local Confederate sympathizer, Charles C. Welford, on the other hand, arrived with much more decisive intelligence. Fitzhugh Lee's cavalry had discovered Hooker's unprotected right flank dangling in the wilderness, and Welford offered to lead the Confederates around Catherine's Furnace and westward along little-known forest trails to exploit the situation. Lee had discovered Hooker's weakness.

With this information Jackson, with Lee's concurrence, formulated a plan that ignored most of the basic principles of war. His audacious plan called for Lee to hold Hooker in place with only 15,000 troops, while Jackson looped to the west with approximately 30,000 soldiers to attack the unprotected Union flank.

At 4 A.M. on 2 May, Lee held a final conference with Jackson and then ordered the day's operations to commence. Jackson led the divisions of Robert Rodes, R. E. Colston, A. P. Hill, J. J. Archer, E. L. Thomas, and finally his artillery on a twelve-mile circuitous march through the heat of the day. To cover Jackson's movements, Lee committed both Anderson's and McLaws's divisions in lines of skirmishers to make Hooker think it was a major assault. When one of Sickles's divisions, situated on the high ground of Hazel Grove about one mile south of Chancellorsville, reported Confederate troops moving south near Catherine's Furnace, Hooker thought it was evidence of Lee retreating. Oliver O. Howard, deployed on the Union right, reported that he had also seen this maneuver, but he was preparing for an attack from the west. Howard was counting on the tangled wilderness and only 700 men to defend his right flank. Unconcerned, Hooker turned his attention to Lee's bothersome attacks east of the Chancellorsville crossroads. To put more pressure on what he mistakenly thought to be a retreating army, he ordered Sedgwick to attack the Confederate positions at Fredericksburg.

Jackson's advance units did not arrive on a high wooded ridge west of Howard's XI Corps until midafternoon. Jackson's assault was delayed by his desire to gain the best position on the Federal right flank. As his brigades arrived Jackson arrayed them in an attack formation almost two miles long. In the fading daylight

Wounded soldiers being tended in the field after the battle of Chancellorsville, 2 May 1863 (*National Archives*)

Jackson quietly ordered his division commanders to commence their attacks.

As Howard's men prepared their supper, a hoard of screaming Confederate infantrymen burst from the woods and routed the astonished Yankees. Jackson's men irresistibly surged forward for over two miles before gathering darkness, loss of unit cohesion in the woods, and increasing Federal resistance finally halted their advance. When Jackson returned from a personal reconnaissance ahead of his disjointed units about 9 P.M., troops from the 18th North Carolina Infantry mistook his party in the darkness for Union cavalry and fired on it. Several of his staff fell wounded, and Jackson was hit in three places. Early the next day surgeons amputated his shattered left arm. He began a normal recovery but developed pneumonia and died on 10 May. Lee and the Confederacy lost one of their most aggressive generals, a loss that would be sorely felt at Gettysburg two months later.

Stuart assumed temporary command of Jackson's corps after Jackson and his senior infantry officers fell wounded. During the night, Stuart prepared to resume the attack and drive on Chancellorsville. Confederate artillery officers identified the high ground at Hazel Grove as key to the battle, and Stuart planned to seize it at dawn. Hooker abandoned this decisive terrain before Stuart ordered his men forward, however, and Rebel artillerymen rushed to occupy the commanding terrain. Desperate fighting in the woods between Hazel Grove and Chancellorsville exacted more casualties on 3 May than had Jackson's flank attack.

Concentrated Confederate cannon fire from Hazel Grove added to Union casualties and disorder. A shell struck the column on which Hooker was leaning at Chancellor's Tavern and further addled the already disconcerted general. After a shot of brandy, Hooker ordered a general withdrawal to the north. With his separated command linked together, Lee rode triumphantly to Chancellorsville Cross Roads among his cheering men.

The situation at Fredericksburg, however, demanded Lee's immediate attention. Sedgwick, after three bloody assaults, had broken through Early's positions at Marye's Heights and the Federals were advancing on Lee's rear. The Confederate commander quickly disengaged McLaws's Division and ordered him east to meet Sedgwick. McLaws failed to react with alacrity, but General Willcox's men halted the Union troops at Salem Church, four miles west of Fredericksburg. Lee arrived on the morning of 4 May to coordinate an attack that regained Marye's Heights and forced Sedgwick to retire across the Rappahannock that night.

On 5–6 May Hooker, against most of his subordinates' advice, abandoned his line north of Chancellorsville and retreated across the Rappahannock. At any point during the campaign either of Hooker's wings outnumbered their opponents and could have achieved his primary goal of driving Lee back toward Richmond if Hooker had followed his original plan. Yet Hooker's vaunted intelligence operation broke down at the crucial moment. The absence of Stoneman's cavalry meant that Hooker was deprived of intelligence about Confederate strength and positions; with such information he may well have won the battle.

Lee suffered about 13,000 casualties to Hooker's 18,000. Yet the most portentous casualty was Stonewall Jackson, whose death on 10 May required that Lee reorganize the Army of Northern Virginia. While the spectacular victory at Chancellorsville presented Lee with an opportunity to invade the North, it would not be the same army that did so. He and his men would carry an effusive confidence into battle at Gettysburg. There awaited the grim discovery that they were not invincible.

—*Stanley S. McGowen*

See also Fredericksburg, Second Battle of; Hooker, Joseph; Howard, Oliver O.; Jackson, Thomas J.; Lee, Robert E.; Mud March; Salem Church, Battle of; Stoneman, George.

For further reading:

Fishel, Edwin, C. *The Secret War for the Union* (1996).
Furgurson, Ernest B. *Chancellorsville, 1863: The Souls of the Brave* (1992).
Gallagher, Gary W., ed. *Chancellorsville: The Battle and Its Aftermath* (1996).
Robertson, James I., Jr. *Stonewall Jackson: The Man, the Soldier, the Legend* (1997).
Sears, Stephen W. *Chancellorsville* (1996).

CHANDLER, ZACHARIAH
(1813–1879)
U.S. senator and cabinet officer

Zachariah Chandler was born in Bedford, New Hampshire, on 10 September 1813. The son of Samuel Chandler and Margaret Orr, Chandler came from a long line of Puritan stock, descending from a William Chandler, who emigrated to New England during the Great Migration of the late 1630s. Chandler was educated in Bedford schools until he was 15. He then attended academies in nearby Pembroke and Derry, graduating when he was 16 years old. After graduation, he taught school for one year in the Piscataquog or "Squog" district. In 1833 Chandler began working as a clerk for the firm of Kendrick and Foster in nearby Nashua. Later that year, he decided to move to Michigan territory with brother-in-law, Franklin Moore. Using $1,000 that Chandler had received from his father, Chandler and Moore began a dry goods business in the small town of Detroit.

Chandler quickly rose to prominence in Detroit. An energetic and ambitious businessman, Chandler dissolved his partnership with Moore in 1836 and struck out on his own. Supplying farmers who came to Detroit for market, Chandler quickly accelerated his business operations, eventually expanding into wholesale dry goods, which he supplied throughout the interior of Michigan. Chandler invested profits from his business into real estate, toll roads, and railroads. At the time of his death, he had a personal estate of $2 million. At age 31, Chandler married Letitia Grace Douglass, a wealthy New Yorker. The Chandlers had one daughter, Minnie, who was born in 1848.

Chandler took an interest in local politics shortly after arriving in Detroit; however, he did not run for office until 1850. In that year, he was elected as a Whig delegate to the Michigan Constitutional Convention. In 1851, he was nominated as the Whig mayoral candidate for the city of Detroit and defeated Democratic candidate John R. Williams. In 1852, Chandler was the Whig candidate for governor of Michigan, but was defeated by Democrat Robert McClelland. In the aftermath of the Kansas-Nebraska Act, Chandler was one of the leading Michigan Whigs favoring fusion with disgruntled Democrats and Free Soilers. He played an active role in the July 1854 Republican Convention at Jackson, Michigan, and in 1856 was elected as a delegate to the Republican National Convention in Philadelphia. Although as the first Republican gubernatorial nominee he was overlooked in favor of Kinsley S. Bingham, Chandler was regarded as a strong senatorial candidate to contest the seat of Lewis Cass in 1857. As a result of Republican electoral victory in Michigan in 1856, the Michigan legislature chose Chandler as its U.S. senator in March 1857.

Chandler was elected to three successive terms in the U.S. Senate. His skillful use of patronage allowed him to dominate Michigan politics for almost twenty years. As a U.S. senator, Chandler applied the same vigor and ambition that had characterized his business career. Throughout his senatorial career, he advocated protective tariffs, internal improvements, and other measures generally supportive of business, principles that were in accordance with his Whig background. In foreign policy, Chandler was a persistent Anglophobe who spoke frequently of annexing Canada. Consistent with his Republican principles, Chandler supported antislavery measures and spoke out frequently against slavery and the South.

During the secession crisis, Chandler was outspoken in his demand that newly elected President Abraham Lincoln make no compromises with any of the seceded states. "Without a little blood-letting," Chandler wrote Michigan governor Austin Blair, "this Union will not...be worth a rush." Throughout the war, Chandler advocated harsh, rigorous measures, including emancipation, the arming of black troops, and confiscation of rebel property. As a member of the powerful Committee on the Conduct of the War, Chandler was a persistent critic of Democratic generals that the Committee deemed too cautious and timid. Perhaps his most controversial act as a member of the committee was a highly charged and partisan speech delivered in the Senate in July 1862 criticizing then commander of the Army of the Potomac, George B. McClellan. Although Chandler and other Radical Republicans disagreed with Lincoln on the pivotal issue of Reconstruction, Chandler played an important role in unifying the Republican Party in the 1864 presidential election. While a number of party radicals were tempted to support the third-party candidacy of John C. Frémont, Chandler help arrange a deal whereby Frémont withdrew his candidacy in exchange for the resignation of Postmaster General Montgomery Blair. Because Blair was a conservative Republican who was hated by many radicals, his removal from the cabinet helped convince many Radical Republicans to support Lincoln in the presidential election.

After the war, Chandler became a forceful advocate of Radical Reconstruction and a bitter opponent of his former Senate colleague, President Andrew Johnson. A proponent of impeachment, Chandler was outspoken in his denunciation of Johnson and his Republican colleagues who voted to acquit Johnson. While some Republicans became disillusioned with the administration of Ulysses Grant and tired of Radical Reconstruction, Chandler became a loyal supporter of Grant, who continued to favor Radical Reconstruction. When disillusioned Republicans united with Democrats to nominate Horace Greeley to oppose Grant's reelection in 1872, Chandler had nothing but contempt for his former colleagues.

In 1875 Chandler was defeated in his quest for a fourth successive Senate term. He was appointed as Secretary of the Interior in the last days of the Grant administration and was also appointed national chair of the 1876 Republican presidential campaign. Despite his lack of enthusiasm for presidential nominee Rutherford B. Hayes, Chandler applied his usual energy to the campaign, even contributing personal funds. Denied an appointment to Hayes's cabinet, Chandler finally retired to his farm near Lansing, Michigan. In 1879, however, Chandler came out of retirement when Senator Isaac Christiancy resigned his Senate seat, and Chandler was chosen to complete the term. It would prove to be a brief return. While campaigning for the Republican Party in October 1879, Chandler suffered a stroke in his hotel room in Chicago and died on 31 October 1879. In a political career that spanned over twenty years, Chandler began as a Whig, turned into a Radical Republican reformer, and ended his career as a Republican stalwart.

—*Bruce Tap*

See also Johnson, Andrew; Radical Republicans; Republican Party.

For further reading:
The Detroit Post and Tribune. *Zachariah Chandler: An Outline of His Life and Public Service* (1880).

George, Sister Mary Karl. *Zachariah Chandler: A Political Biography* (1969).
Harris, Wilmer C. *Public Life of Zachariah Chandler, 1851–1875* (1917).

CHANTILLY, BATTLE OF
(1 September 1862)

Robert E. Lee was not a completely satisfied man on the morning of 31 August 1862. Although Lee had just won a spectacular victory at the Second Bull Run, John Pope's army still retained its organization and a great deal of fighting spirit as it regrouped in a strong defensive position at Centreville. However, Lee still had room to maneuver before he ran up against the powerful defenses of Washington and was determined to make the most of it. He ordered Thomas J. "Stonewall" Jackson to take his command north along the Gum Springs Road to the Little River Turnpike. From there, he was to march eastward just past the tiny hamlet of Germantown where the turnpike intersected Pope's line of communications along the Warrenton Turnpike. James Longstreet's command would maneuver in front of Centreville to hold Pope there and then follow Jackson.

Shortly after noon on 31 August, Jackson's men, screened by J. E. B. Stuart's cavalry, began their march. After a ten-mile hike through heavy rain, they reached Pleasant Valley Church on the Little River Turnpike several miles west of Germantown and bivouacked there for the night. Stuart's cavalry, however, reached Germantown by the early evening and could see Federal wagons moving along the Warrenton Turnpike. Stuart decided to have a little fun and ordered his two cannon to fire on them, causing "commotion, up-setting, collisions, and smash-ups," before heading back down the Little River Turnpike to make camp north of where it intersected the Ox Road at Ox Hill.

As this was going on, Pope was sticking to General-in-Chief Henry Halleck's instructions not to abandon Centreville. On the morning of 1 September, however, evidence of the Confederate flanking march arrived. Pope responded by ordering Joseph Hooker to take a division to Germantown and block the Confederate line of march to Fairfax. Hooker reached Germantown at around 2:30 P.M. and posted his men on high ground east of where the Little River Turnpike crossed Difficult Run. By that time, Pope had finally decided to abandon Centreville and was retreating east along the Warrenton Turnpike with Jesse Reno's IX Corps leading the way.

Jackson reached Ox Hill at about the same time Hooker arrived at Germantown. He then pushed Stuart, supported by infantry and artillery, east along Little River Turnpike toward Fairfax. Stuart encountered Hooker's line and reported to Jackson that it was too strong to be attacked successfully with the force on hand. So Jackson decided to halt operations at around 4 P.M. and wait for Longstreet to arrive before determining what to do next.

Just then, Isaac I. Stevens, commander of the lead division of Reno's corps, rode up to a knoll north of the Warrenton Turnpike and caught a glimpse of the skirmish line Jackson had pushed south to watch Pope's line of retreat. As storm clouds rolled in from the southwest, Stevens then ordered his division into line and led it north toward Ox Hill.

At approximately 5:00 P.M. the battle of Chantilly, or Ox Hill, began—as did what one participant would describe as "one of the wildest rainstorms I ever witnessed." As lightning and thunder crashed, the wind howled, and a torrential downpour drenched the combatants, Stevens's division smashed into the Confederate line north of the Reid house and caused a Louisiana brigade to break and run. Then, however, a bullet struck Stevens in the head, killing him instantly. Devastated by the loss of their leader, the Federals became dispirited and before long were falling back. A brigade from Philip Kearny's division of Samuel Heintzelman's corps arrived on the battlefield and pushed forward into a cornfield north of the Reid house where a desperate hand-to-hand struggle ensued. Learning of a possible gap in the Federal line, Kearny rode forward into the cornfield for a personal reconnaissance. There he encountered an unidentified force that turned out to be Confederate and demanded his surrender. Kearny refused and attempted to escape, but he was cut down by a Confederate bullet.

Shortly after Kearny fell, the battle wound down as officers and men on both sides recognized the futility of continuing the fight in the darkness and rain. By 6:30 the battle was over. Jackson had lost approximately 500 of the 15,000 men he had on hand; about 700 of the 6,000 Federals engaged became casualties. Later that night Pope's army began arriving at Fairfax Court House. Lee had run out of room to maneuver in Virginia. His next move would take the war across the Potomac into Maryland.

—*Ethan S. Rafuse*

See also Kearny, Philip.
For further reading:
Harsh, Joseph L. *Confederate Tide Rising: Robert E. Lee and the Making of Southern Strategy, 1861–1862* (1998).
Hennessy, John J. *Return to Bull Run: The Campaign and Battle of Second Manassas* (1993).
Smith, Robert Ross. "Ox Hill: The Most Neglected Battle of the Civil War, 1 September 1862." In *Fairfax County and the War Between the States* (1961).
U.S. War Department. *The War of the Rebellion: A Compilation of the Official Records of the Union and Confederate Armies* (1880–1901).

General Kearny's charge at Chantilly, 1 September 1862 (*Library of Congress*)

CHAPLAINS

At the outbreak of the Civil War, neither side had an official policy regarding chaplains. In May 1861 the U.S. War Department issued General Orders 15 and 16, which provided for the appointment of "regularly ordained" ministers of a "Christian denomination" to become chaplains by vote of the regimental officers. Union chaplains received little guidance. Congress and the War Department left responsibilities to the chaplain and the denomination. Army regulations only required reporting on the moral and religious state of the troops and making suggestions for improving social conditions. It was not until 1864 that holding regular services was required. In the absence of specific duties, Union chaplains relied on *The Army Chaplain, His Office, Duties, and Responsibilities, and the Means of Aiding Him* by the Reverend William Young Brown. It outlined some of the most necessary traits for chaplains, foremost of which was "ardent piety." In addition, Brown said that they needed to have proficiency as teachers, as well as resolution, energy, good health, and courage. U.S. Army chaplains received $100 a month. Approximately 2,300 served the Union army as chaplains.

Chaplains from all major denominations served the Confederate army. Although the Confederate Congress passed Bill 102 authorizing the president to appoint chaplains, Jefferson Davis deferred to his commanders. As a result, units such as Thomas "Stonewall" Jackson's II Corps were especially well served. Still, the common practice was that most were elected by troops or selected by officers. In the Confederacy an estimated 640 men served as chaplains. Confederate chaplains started out earning $85 a month, but this was soon cut to $50. In 1862 the amount was raised to $80. Some Confederate units and denominations increased their chaplains' salary by subscription. Confederate army regulations made little mention of the duties of chaplains, and like their Union brethren, Confederate chaplains received little direction. Most relied on James O. Andrew's *Letter to the Chaplains in the Army.* The thin missive by the retired Methodist bishop urged the chaplains to work faithfully and not be discouraged. Chaplains' associations formed to discuss matters of mutual concern and to petition the Confederate Congress to prohibit parades, inspections, and other activities on the Sabbath. In addition to the military chaplaincy, the Confederate army recognized

Chaplains of the 9th Corps at Petersburg, Virginia, October 1864 (*Library of Congress*)

other religious workers. Although they had no military standing, army missionaries, army evangelists, and colporteurs often served as chaplains. Whatever their background, Confederate chaplains were largely credited with the revivals that swept army camps during the war.

Chaplains in both armies shared similar activities. They worked alone or with local clergy to hold religious service. They also held prayer meetings, conducted baptisms, distributed tracts, and oversaw moral order and temperance. Sermons focused on loyalty, courage, and the righteousness of their respective cause. Chaplains also wrote letters on behalf of sick, wounded, or illiterate soldiers and also tended camp libraries. In battle they went to the front lines to offer encouragement to stragglers, aid for the wounded, and last rites for the dying. Two Union chaplains received the Medal of Honor for single-handedly rescuing wounded soldiers under fire. After battle, chaplains served the field hospitals and also wrote letters to families of the recently deceased. If captured, they served as ordinary prisoners, though they often led religious services in the prisoner camps.

Chaplains on both sides sought to keep morale high, though as the war wore on for the Confederacy, increasing numbers of troops ignored the chaplains exhortations to fight bravely. Many chaplains began to adopt the theme of the lost cause and a God who deserted the Confederacy—all of which did nothing to improve morale. In the Union army, chaplains also worked to assist and teach former slaves. They also looked after freedmen serving in the army, some even serving as chaplains of the black regiments.

Although the chaplaincy was predominantly Protestant, Roman Catholics and Jews also had chaplains. As Protestants tended to view the army as a strong opportunity for evangelism, Catholics feared that they would "steal souls" from the Catholic ranks. In that light, Catholics began having priests become chaplains in the North and to a lesser degree in the South. Still, the Federal army had only forty priests, commonly called "Holy Joes," who served an estimated 200,000 Catholics in uniform, the majority Irish. Most priests served only short times because their bishops commonly recalled them to meet local diocese needs. Further inhibiting the influence of Catholics was the reluctance and often refusal of Protestant officers to accept priests as chaplains. As a consequence, Catholic chaplains served predominantly Catholic regiments. Even here, ethnicity was an issue; it was difficult to find and place qualified Irish priests with Irish units and German-speaking priests with German units. Still Catholic chaplains made their presence known, taking confessions before battle and working to improve the general moral order of the army camps.

Jewish chaplains also participated. In July 1861 as Clement Vallandigham's bill to allow ordained rabbis to become chaplains was going down to defeat, the 5th Pennsylvania Cavalry elected one of their own, Michael Allen, a Philadelphia Hebrew teacher, to be regimental chaplain where his messages were accepted by both Jew and gentile. When a Young Men's Christian Association worker challenged Allen's appointment, Allen resigned. Rabbi Amold Fischel, an ordained rabbi, was then appointed, but Secretary of War Edwin Stanton denied the nomination and Fischel, an experienced lobbyist, spent the next year on Capitol Hill pushing his cause. In July 1862, Congress changed the law to read "religious denominations" rather than "Christian denomination." The first Jewish regimental chaplain was Ferdinand Leopold Samer, a German, who served the mostly German-speaking 54th New York Volunteers. Samer was also the first Jewish chaplain to be wounded as well as the first Jewish chaplain to be absent without leave. After being severely wounded at Gettysburg, he left the hospital for home before the arrival of his discharge papers. Although Jews were allowed to serve in the Confederate chaplaincy, none is known to have done so, even though some 3,000 Jews fought for the Confederacy.

Others served too. The Confederacy had the first African-American chaplain. A Tennessee regiment called on a pious slave known as "Uncle Lewis" to conduct religious services. He was a source of pride to the unit and was credited for leading three revivals. In addition, Unaguskie, served as chaplain of a Confederate Cherokee battalion.

The chaplaincy on both sides was exclusively male although the 1st Wisconsin Heavy Artillery unanimously elected Ella E. Gibson chaplain. She was an ordained minister of the Religio-Philosophical Society of St. Charles, Illinois. Lincoln passed the appointment to Stanton with the notation, "This lady would be appointed Chaplain…, only that she is a woman. The president has not legally anything to do with such a question, but has no objection to her appointment." Stanton, not wanting to set a precedent, however, declined to recognize the appointment.

In the postwar literature, works such as *A Narrative of the Great Revival Which Prevailed in the Southern Armies during the Late Civil War between the States of the Federal Union* and *Christ in the Camp* did much to promote the concept of muscular Christianity so much in vogue in the late nineteenth century. Images of strong and masculine Protestant chaplains were created to offset a growing popular mind set of religion seeming to be feminine. Especially in the South, many were portrayed as "fighting chaplains" who excelled in fighting both Satan and Yankees. Only more recently has scholarship turned to examining other aspects of this topic, notably diversity.

—*Daniel Liestman*

See also Chaplains, African-American; Religion.
For further reading:
Armstrong, Warren B. *For Courageous Fighting and Confident Dying: Union Chaplains in the Civil War* (1998).
Bennett, William W. *A Narrative of the Great Revival Which Prevailed in the Southern Armies during the Late Civil War between the States of the Federal Union* (1877).
Brown, William Young. *The Army Chaplain, His Office, Duties, and Responsibilities, and the Means of Aiding Him* (1863).
Faust, Drew Gilpin. "Christian Soldiers: The Meaning of Revivalism in the Confederate Army." *Journal of Southern History* (1987).
Jones, J. William. *Christ in the Camp* (1887).
Miller, Randall M., Harry S. Stout, and Charles Reagan Wilson, eds. *Religion and the American Civil War* (1998).
Pitts, Charles F. *Chaplains in Gray* (1957).
Robinson-Durso, Pamela. "Chaplains in the Confederate Army." *Journal of Church and State* (1991).
Slomovitz, Albert I. *The Fighting Rabbis: Jewish Military Chaplains and American History* (1999).
Wiley, Bell Irwin. "'Holy Joes' of the Sixties: A Study of Civil War Chaplains." *Huntington Library Quarterly* (1953).

CHAPLAINS, AFRICAN-AMERICAN

When the Civil War began the United States Army had only twenty-six chaplains on duty. These clergymen, who were all white, served as post chaplains and were not attached to any particular regiment. The outbreak of hostilities led to a tremendous increase in the size of the chaplaincy to match the increased number of regular and volunteer Union army forces. The army also began to assign chaplains to serve in individual regiments. Unfortunately, those changes led to a great deal of confusion over commissioning, uniforms, and pay. They also resulted in the admission of many totally unfit men, who hurt the reputation of the chaplaincy. Congressional legislation passed in July 1862, followed by Army General Order 91, successfully rid the army of undesirables and helped to form a thoroughly professionalized chaplaincy by the end of 1862.

Black chaplains did not enter service with the Union army until after the Emancipation Proclamation in 1863. The delay proved fortunate, for by then the professionalization of the chaplaincy had occurred. African-American chaplains were consequently spared the problems of the war's early years. The higher standards required of the chaplaincy meant that fewer black clergymen qualified, but they ensured that the men who did so were the best in the African-American community.

Henry McNeal Turner was the first African-American to serve as an army chaplain in Federal service. Turner was born free in South Carolina and became an African Methodist Episcopal (A.M.E.) Church minister in 1853. By the start of the Civil War, he was pastor of the Israel A.M.E. Church in Washington, D.C., which provided him the opportunity to meet influential Republican politicians. Turner impressed these leaders early on in the war when he helped organize African-American civilians into construction brigades to strengthen Washington's defenses. He also helped to recruit large numbers of African-American troops after Congress authorized their enlistment. Thanks to his powerful political friends, Turner was made chaplain of the 1st United States Colored Troops (U.S.C.T.) on 10 September 1863. Chaplain Turner immediately faced discrimination from whites, however. While on board the steamer *Manhattan*, a white steward refused to permit Turner to enter the dining facility through the front entrance, even threatening him with a knife. The steward was arrested and brought up on charges, but that was not the end of the challenges that faced the new chaplain. Although Congress had authorized chaplains' salaries set at $1,200 per year, army paymasters defiantly interpreted the regulations to mean that black chaplains should be paid the same rate as black common laborers. The matter finally made its way up to President Abraham Lincoln, who referred the matter to his attorney general. He ruled that black chaplains should be paid the same as white ones.

Other black ministers, such as Chaplain William Hunter of the 4th U.S.C.T. soon followed Turner into service. Hunter fought to get fair treatment for the men in his unit who had been promised at their enlistment the same pay as white troops but instead were paid less. He wrote letters and pushed the issue until Congress finally rectified the pay difference in 1864. The Reverend William J. Hodges enlisted in the 36th U.S.C.T. with the hope of becoming that regiment's chaplain. Instead, the officers named David Stevens chaplain, and Hodges rose to the rank of sergeant major. Francis Boyd thought he, too, could become chaplain of the 109th U.S.C.T. by first enlisting in that unit. When no opportunity came, Boyd skipped the chain of command and wrote directly to General Benjamin Butler. Successfully convincing Butler of his qualifications, Boyd was appointed chaplain. His victory was short-lived, however, for the 109th's commander was highly irritated that Boyd had gone over his head and worked against the new chaplain at every turn. After three months, he succeeded in having Boyd stripped of his commission and returned to the rank of private.

Garland White was more successful. A former slave of Georgia senator Robert Toombs, he had escaped to Canada where he became an A.M.E. pastor. Once the Civil War began, he commenced an intensive letter-writing campaign to the secretary of war, urging that he be appointed a chaplain. When that tactic did not work, he moved his family to Ohio and began recruitment duty. Eventually he enlisted in the 28th U.S.C.T. and served as the regiment's unofficial chaplain. The unit's commander recommended that White's role be made official, but the request was refused because regulations required that no chaplain's position could be filled until the regiment reached full strength. White's patient persistence finally paid off and on 25 October 1864 he was commissioned as the 28th's chaplain. He was part of the lead element that entered Richmond in 1865 when an elderly black lady approached troops of the 28th asking to see if a man named Garland White was among them. When the woman was brought to Chaplain White, he discovered that she was his mother; he had not seen her since being sold to Robert Toombs as a small boy.

Being an army chaplain also had its dangers. Turner contracted smallpox and later was hospitalized after being thrown from his horse in a skirmish. Samuel Harrison of the 54th Massachusetts contracted malaria shortly after his arrival in South Carolina and was discharged after only four months on duty. Some duties were simply unpleasant. Jeremiah Asher of the 6th U.S.C.T. was appalled at the sight of five hundred wounded troops at a Portsmouth, Virginia hospital, many without arms and legs. Nevertheless, he provided ministry to the men as best he could. George LeVere of the 20th U.S.C.T. had the unenviable task of spending three hours providing comfort to a condemned soldier who was then executed by firing squad. LeVere remarked that it was the saddest spectacle he had ever witnessed.

Some duties were more rewarding. African-American chaplains served as recruiters, and the black troops they enlisted obviously took pride in serving their country and helping to free their people. Many black chaplains also served as educators to their illiterate troops. The chaplain of the 62d U.S.C.T. proudly noted that more than 200 troopers had learned to read by the end of their enlistments. Another chaplain wrote that he hoped every soldier in his regiment would become literate by the end of the war.

For all chaplains, white or black, the primary mission was to proclaim the Christian gospel, and in this role the uniqueness of the black chaplains truly stands out. White chaplains who served in all-black units—such as George N. Carruthers—often had difficulty relating to the men. Carruthers criticized his black troops' custom of worship, noting that it consisted "more in emotional exercises than a conscientious performance of duty and trust in God." Another white chaplain, Thomas Stevenson of the 114th U.S.C.T., also complained, stating that black worship was "narrow and superficial...and often preposterously absurd." These men did not know that black troops' religion was a blend of their African heritage, slave experience, and evangelical Protestant Christianity that had merged to create something very different from white practices. African-American Christianity had been forged by slaves meeting secretly at night in places they called hush harbors. There they created what scholars have called the Invisible Institution. Services possessed the same external forms of the white masters' evangelical faith, but they were inherently different because of a strong and persistent element of black folk religion. Blacks shouted during worship services, sang a new type of song called the spiritual, believed in spirit possession, and were generally much more vocal and lively. Black funerals were different, too. Just as they had in Africa, blacks broke up the possessions of the dead and placed them on top of the grave to help release the spirit of the deceased.

Most white army chaplains failed to understand the faith of these black troops. But it was African-American Christianity that helped blacks deal with everyday life in a brutal form of slavery that was degrading, based on race, and permanent. Slavery severely damaged the African religious and cultural heritage of the slaves, but African-American Christianity helped blacks survive by developing a new, coherent worldview. The message black chaplains preached was one of hope, salvation, and dignity, all of which served to boost the morale of the troops.

The Union army utilized the services of 2,300 chaplains during the Civil War. One hundred thirty-three of these men served in the all-black regiments. Of these 133 clergymen, 14 were African-American. That number may seem small, but the impact the black chaplains made was significant far beyond their numbers through their work as recruiters, teachers, role models, and proclaimers of the message of African-American Christianity.

—Alan K. Lamm

See also African-American Soldiers; Chaplains; Religion.
For further reading:
Angell, Stephen Ward. *Bishop Henry McNeal Turner and Afro-American Religion in the South* (1992).
Honeywell, Roy J. *Chaplains of the United States Army* (1958).
McPherson, James. *The Negro's Civil War: How American Blacks Felt and Acted during the War for the Union* (1965).
Norton, Herman A. *Struggling for Recognition: The United States Army Chaplaincy, 1791–1865* (1977).
Raboteau, Albert J. *Slave Religion: The "Invisible Institution" in the Antebellum South* (1978).

CHARLESTON (ILLINOIS) RIOT
(28 March 1864)

Resentments centered on opposition to Lincoln administration war policies and verbal and physical abuse directed against Democrats in central Illinois exploded in a spasm of violence on 28 March 1864. When it ended, nine men lay dead or dying and twelve were wounded on the courthouse square in Charleston, Illinois. Located about 120 miles southeast of the state capital at Springfield, Charleston, the Coles County seat, was a community atop the cultural fault line that stretched across the center of the state. Along this uneven border, residents with Southern antecedents confronted those with New England or mid-Atlantic state backgrounds in cultural, political, and social conflict. The confrontational atmosphere that evolved on the Civil War Northern home front only heightened these tensions. Democrats, often termed Copperheads by Republicans, increasingly spoke out against what they perceived as suppression of free speech and conversion of the war from one to preserve the Union to a crusade to free the slaves. Large numbers of Democrats from the area served in the Union army, however, as the level of voluntary enlistments negated any need to impose conscription in Charleston or elsewhere in Coles County.

Tensions had been building in Coles and Edgar, a neighboring county to the East, for at least a year before the bloody confrontation in Charleston. Both counties were in the Seventh Congressional District, which in November 1862 sent a Democratic opponent of the Lincoln administration, John Rice Eden of Sullivan, to Washington. A supporter of appropriations for troops and equipment, Eden, like other downstate Illinois Democrats, was outspoken against perceived violations of free speech and press by Union supporters. Two months after Eden's election, an attempt by Coles County critics of the war's direction to hold a peace meeting was disrupted by Republicans. A few weeks later, they successfully staged a meeting, passing resolutions calling for an armistice, opposition to unconditional emancipation, and declaring that habeas corpus "must and shall be maintained." Democratic passions were further inflamed when an area judge was arrested by Indiana troops who crossed state lines after the jurist refused to allow four army deserters to be returned to the Hoosier state. Only a last-minute release order from a Federal judge kept the Democratic jurist from being transported to and tried in Indiana.

In Mattoon, Coles County's most populous community and, according to the Democratic *Chicago Times*, the "most fanatical, intolerant, mobocratic hole of abolitionism in this part of the State," Democrats staged a rally for free speech and peace on 1 August 1863, attracting a crowd estimated between 3,000 and 12,000. A number of speakers, including Eden, urged Democrats to maintain their rights and continue opposition to Lincoln's war aims at the ballot box, in the courts, and, if necessary, Eden proclaimed, "in another way." The next month, Eden's congressional colleague, James C. Robinson, who represented the district south of Charleston, told a rally that a government conspiracy

Clashes between soldiers and civilians erupted in several Northern cities, including Charleston, Illinois, during the course of the Civil War. (*Corbis*)

was afoot to keep Democrats from voting. As citizens it was their duty, Robinson said, to go to the polls, even if they had to "wade through blood knee deep to the ballot box." Days later, a Democratic newspaper in Shelbyville, seat of Shelby County directly west of Coles, said that if all other alternatives failed, Democrats retained the "inalienable right of revolution." Historian Jean Baker has linked such language with an antebellum Democratic tradition of republicanism, which triggered powerful fundamental associations and ideals among party members.

Further dry tinder was added when, in January 1864, members of the 54th Illinois Infantry began an extended leave in Mattoon. Idle soldiers occupied themselves by drinking and attacking Democrats in the streets of the city. Among their victims were a prominent local physician and the judge who had been arrested by Indiana troops. On 30 January 1864, members of the 54th fatally shot a Democrat who attempted to flee rather than take

the "loyalty oath" they administered. On 16 February 1864 a street altercation between Democrats and soldiers in the Edgar county seat of Paris resulted in severe wounds for one Democrat. Six days later, another confrontation in Paris left one Democrat dead and two soldiers wounded. In March soldiers attacked Democrats on the streets of Charleston in two separate incidents, one involving members of the O'Hair family prominent in Democratic politics in Coles and Edgar counties.

On 28 March Charleston's square filled with soldiers and Democrats, many of the latter farmers who were in town for a party rally to be addressed by Eden. As tensions mounted and whiskey flowed during the day, the rally was canceled and Eden moved about the square urging Democrats to return home peacefully. Hopes for peace were shattered when David Nelson Wells, a young Democrat from Edgar County, became involved in a dispute with Oliver Sallee, a soldier, outside the courthouse. Shots were exchanged and both men fell mortally wounded. Suddenly, firing became general as Democrats retrieved weapons from wagons and under their coats, directing their fire at the soldiers, many of whom were unarmed. Leading the Democrats was Coles County Sheriff John O'Hair, a Democrat elected in 1862. After about one minute, the firing ceased and O'Hair led the Democrats out of the city. Moments later, a suspected rioter was captured by the soldiers and fatally shot as he attempted to flee. The same bullet also took the life of a Republican bystander. The final toll was six Union soldiers, a Republican bystander, and two Democrats killed, and twelve men wounded. With the exception of the New York City Draft Riots, Charleston's affray resulted in the bloodiest toll for a civil disturbance on the Northern home front, surpassing casualties in Chicago and Boston.

Most of the leading Democrats, including Sheriff O'Hair, were not captured. In the panic that followed the riot more than fifty Democrats were arrested. Twenty-nine were held by the military and transported to Springfield, where thirteen were released. Those remaining were transferred to a Federal prison at Fort Delaware, where they were held without trial until released on Lincoln's orders seven months later. Although a local grand jury indicted Sheriff O'Hair, who eventually returned to Coles County, and fourteen others, only two men, both minor figures, stood trial. The trial was moved to Effingham, about forty miles southwest of Charleston, and in November 1864 both defendants were acquitted.

—*Robert D. Sampson*

See also Copperheads; New York City Draft Riots; Peace Democrats; Riots, C.S.A.; Riots, U.S.A.

For further reading:
Coleman, Charles Hubert, and Paul B. Spence. "The Charleston Riot, March 28, 1864." *Journal of the Illinois State Historical Society* (1940).
Sampson, Robert D. "'Pretty Damned Warm Times': The 1864 Charleston Riot and 'The Inalienable Right of Revolution.'" *Illinois Historical Journal* (1996).

CHARLESTON MERCURY

As the most passionate supporter first of slavery and then of the formation of the Confederacy (a position it first advocated nearly three decades before the Civil War began), it was altogether appropriate that the Charleston *Mercury* would publish the first official notice of the initial act of secession: a broadside extra published immediately following the South Carolina legislature's passage of the secession resolution, proclaiming "The Union Is Dissolved!"

Founded in 1822, the *Mercury* quickly became the most extreme opponent of abolition and a fierce advocate of nullification. Yet despite its political zealotry, it was widely respected in the North and looked to as the

most authoritative voice of the secession movement. Its wartime editor, Robert Barnwell Rhett Jr., was the son of John C. Calhoun's eventual successor in the U.S. Senate. Indeed, the elder Rhett, who for most of the previous decade had advocated a Southern Confederacy, vied with Jefferson Davis for the Confederate presidency. Passed over by the Confederate Congress even for a cabinet appointment, Rhett—although a strong proponent of civil war as a means of guaranteeing the disintegration of the Union—became a fierce critic of Davis's administration, and the *Mercury*, under his son's editorship, was recognized as Rhett's mouthpiece.

The Harvard-educated younger Rhett assumed editorial control in 1857. By time the war began, the paper's circulation had quadrupled, mostly because of the vituperative editorials that Rhett and his brother Edmund composed and that were widely credited as instrumental in pushing South Carolina towards secession. Nineteenth-century journalism historian Frederic Hudson wrote that the *Mercury* was "a paper of remarkable ability and not surpassed by any other southern paper in the support of its peculiar political views." Abraham Lincoln recognized its importance and subscribed to it long before he was elected president. Others in the North, however, tried to belittle Rhett's influence. A *New York Tribune* correspondent dismissed him as "a well-known wealthy agitator" whose slogan was "I'd rather rule in Hell than serve in Heaven" and insisted that the *Mercury*'s circulation was no more than 550 daily, half of which were exchanges with other papers.

Yet there was no denying that Rhett's *Mercury*, more than any other paper, incited the South to fever pitch. During the secession crisis of 1860, when Charles Dana, then with the *New York Tribune*, sent correspondent Charles Brigham to Charleston as a secret correspondent, the *Mercury* called for his lynching. Brigham, in turn, took to taunting Rhett in print: "If the *Mercury* is really curious as to my whereabouts," he wrote, "let him look into one of the big guns of Fort Sumter. He may find me there." Following Lincoln's election, the *Mercury* declared that the only remedy "for the crisis which is at hand (is) disunion—the separation of South Carolina, whether alone or with others, from the Union which can only be a badge of infamy to her!"

In January 1861 the paper tried to undermine Lincoln's support in the North by printing what it said was an exchange of correspondence during the previous month in which "the abolition president" declared that John Brown did not deserve to be executed, having committed at worst "a gross misdemeanor" at Harper's Ferry, and adding that he did not consider the Supreme Court's *Dred Scott* decision binding because "it is hostile to the advancement of Republican principles." The *Illinois Daily State Journal* promptly denounced the letter as "a gross forgery," but not until it had been reprinted widely.

Despite their devotion to the Southern cause, Rhett and the *Mercury* relentlessly denounced Confederate president Jefferson Davis's "imbecility" and the arbitrary nature of his administration, including "star chamber" meetings of its Congress and suspension of the right of habeas corpus. Rhett also criticized what he regarded as the gross incompetence of most of the South's generals. In this respect, the *Mercury* was a counterpoint to its rival, the pro-Davis *Charleston Daily Courier*.

A contemporary account contrasted the two papers: "The *Courier* is practical and the *Mercury* speculative. The *Courier* deals with the present and the past, and the *Mercury* more with the future. The *Courier* is content to meet events as they occur, and the *Mercury* anticipates them. There is more diffusion in the *Courier*, and more compactness in the *Mercury*. The *Courier* is pleased to hold on the even tenor of its way; the *Mercury* is bold, dashing, presumptive, and prophetic"

During the siege of Charleston, the *Mercury* continued to publish on schedule, although it was quickly reduced to a single-page edition. On the 589th day of the siege, the *Mercury's* pages were filled with an account of the burning of Charleston by fleeing Confederate troops.

For all its criticism of the South's military performance, the *Mercury* was responsible for coining the legend of one notable general. It was to Leonidas W. Sprat, the paper's correspondent at the battle of First Bull Run, that an aide to General Barnard Bee told how the mortally wounded commander had observed his colleague, Thomas J. Jackson, and declared, "There is Jackson standing like a stone wall. Let us determine to die here, and we will conquer."

Following the Union occupation of Charleston, the *Mercury* was shut down. Rhett had hoped to shift publication to Augusta, Georgia, but his press and equipment were destroyed at Charlotte Junction and he took refuge in Alabama. The *Mercury's* presses remained silent until November 1866, when publication resumed under editor Rhett. But despite seeming financial success, the paper closed for good two years later. In his farewell editorial, the younger Rhett, defiant to the end, vowed to "take my place among [the South's] ruined children—better so than to be the proudest and most honored of her successful enemies—and to wait, hoping, praying, expecting the bright coming of her final deliverance, the independence and prosperity of the South."

—*Eric Fettmann*

See also Newspapers; Rhett, Robert Barnwell.

For further reading:
Andrews, J. Cutler. *The South Reports the Civil War* (1970).
Britton, James C. "Images of the Future in the *Charleston Mercury*, 1848–1860" (M.A. thesis, 1980).
Davis, Lee Wright. "Robert Barnwell Rhett, Jr., and the *Charleston Mercury*, 1861–1865" (Honors thesis, 1977).
Harper, Robert S. *Lincoln and the Press* (1951).
Hudson, Frederic. *Journalism in the United States from 1690 to 1872* (1873; reprint, 1968).
Segars, Ernest B. "A Study of the *Charleston* (S.C.) *Mercury* during Robert Barnwell Rhett, Senior's, Tenure as an Editorial Writer, 1861–1863" (M. A. thesis, 1974).
Starr, Louis M. *Bohemian Brigade: Civil War Newsmen in Action* (1954; reprint, 1987).

CHARLESTON, SOUTH CAROLINA
See Carolinas Campaign;
Fort Sumter, Bombardment of ; Secessionville,
Battle of; South Carolina

CHASE, SALMON PORTLAND
(1808–1873)
Secretary of the treasury; chief justice of
the U.S. Supreme Court

Salmon Portland Chase came to the office of secretary of the treasury primarily because his Republican Party denied him the office he wanted most—the presidency. Chase's career was one that combined antislavery principle and political ambition. In appointing him to the treasury position, Abraham Lincoln knew that Chase would be a capable cabinet officer, but he also knew that Chase's desire to be chief executive would be unceasing, and as a member of the administration the president could more easily keep tabs on his political intrigues. Lincoln would be correct on all of these assumptions, and in 1864, in accepting Chase's fourth effort to resign, the president again realized that Chase was too reliable and principled a leader to lose. Thus, once safely reelected, Lincoln appointed Chase to be chief justice of the United States, effectively removing him from politics and hopefully ensuring the constitutional changes that had come with the Civil War.

Chase's early rise in politics began as a Cincinnati attorney. Born in New Hampshire, he had lived briefly in Ohio as a boy under the stern and watchful eye of his uncle, Episcopal Bishop Philander Chase. After teaching school briefly and reading law under former attorney general William Wirt in Washington, D.C., Chase settled in Cincinnati in 1830 at the age of twenty-two. There, as an elitist Whig, he became interested in reform and, through his brother-in-law William Colby, abolitionism. He soon attained local prominence in his unsuccessful defense of fugitive slaves. Chase used the argument that residence in free territory made the fugitive a free person, but only rarely was he able to persuade the courts to accept his reasoning. He nevertheless gained notoriety in Cincinnati as the "Attorney General for Runaway Negroes." Abandoning the conservative Whig Party, he joined with the newly formed Liberty

Salmon P. Chase (*Library of Congress*)

Party in 1841 as a supporter of presidential candidate James G. Birney. His conversion to antislavery politics and principle had been a remarkably swift one, yet was genuine, for he rejected the refusal of the two-party system to embrace reform and resolved to work toward the goal of eliminating or at least containing slavery.

By 1844, Chase sought to broaden the third-party's appeal with a more prominent candidate than Birney, and in 1848, Chase led Liberty supporters into a coalition with the more moderate antislavery Free Soil Party. The following year, Free Soilers in the Ohio legislature engineered Chase's election to the U.S. Senate along with a partial repeal of Ohio's racist black laws, but it was a victory that revealed that Chase appeared willing to go to extreme lengths to secure his own election at the expense of the third-party's independence. In the Senate, Chase opposed the expansion of slavery and the proslavery components of the Compromise of 1850. He also revealed his growing political ambition and assumed a prominent role among those promoting the new Republican Party.

In 1856, Chase mounted his first challenge for a presidential nomination. Elected in 1855 and 1857 to be governor of Ohio, he saw that office as a stepping stone to the presidency. His best opportunity came in 1860, but poor management by his political lieutenants and a

reputation for antislavery radicalism and political intrigue eliminated him. In addition, his cold and aloof manner kept people at arm's length as did his morally righteous attitude. His role in politics before 1860 had left too many enemies. Yet he loyally campaigned for Lincoln who then rewarded him by naming him treasury secretary. It was a position of unprecedented difficulty, given the expense and duration of the war.

Chase has received mixed reviews for his role in the Treasury, but the consensus of historians views his achievements as significant. Chase, as well as most Union leaders, initially assumed it would be a war of a few months that could be financed through traditional methods of borrowing and higher tariffs and taxes. As the prospect of a quick Confederate surrender faded, bolder and more imaginative financial tactics emerged. Chase reluctantly accepted greenbacks as legal tender to help raise needed revenue and in 1863 and 1864 championed a national banking system with the aid of Ohio senator John Sherman. Under the new system, nationally supervised banking associations issued bank notes guaranteed by the federal government. The result was a more secure currency in a time of economic volatility.

The sale of bonds was an added element that meant heavy government borrowing and brought great controversy. Chase made Philadelphia banker Jay Cooke a special treasury agent, a position that gave Cooke a commission for the sale of government bonds. Cooke's efforts realized more than $500 million of desperately needed revenue for the war effort, a result that meant stability for the government and charges of favoritism against both Chase and his friend Cooke. Yet Cooke produced the desired results and managed the loans well. The Union war debt, while enormous, compared favorably with later wars and especially with that of the beleaguered Confederacy.

Equally controversial were Chase's efforts to control and regulate trade, especially in Union-held areas of the South. Speculators sought to profit from trade in cotton and other products scarce in the North. Treasury agents were understaffed and subject to bribery as bureaucratic regulations expanded. Chase appointed political allies who could use their positions to advance his candidacy for 1864, but who also did a creditable job in controlling illegal trade. Overall, the results reflected credit on the economic integrity of the secretary but exposed him to charges of political manipulation.

Chase made little effort to confine his attention to financial issues, using his position in the cabinet to try to persuade the cautious president to a more advanced policy on slavery and civil rights. He complained bitterly when Lincoln rescinded the orders of Generals John C. Frémont and David Hunter freeing slaves within their commands, and he urged General Benjamin F. Butler to do the same within his New Orleans command. Chase rarely appreciated or understood the pressures that Lincoln faced from the many conservative forces, which compelled him to move slowly. Chase rejoiced when Lincoln finally responded with his preliminary proclamation of emancipation in September 1862. Clearly the pressure of Chase and Republican senators such as Charles Sumner of Massachusetts was a factor in the president's change. Chase and Sumner also urged the use of black troops in Union armies, and again the president responded with a policy that encouraged former slaves to aid the Union cause militarily. Chase's efforts on behalf of black suffrage brought more limited immediate acceptance, but again Lincoln appeared to be moving in Chase's direction. Despite his often contentious relationship with Lincoln, Chase could feel justly proud that he had helped to advance the cause of racial equality.

The president was less receptive to Chase's efforts to advise him on military and political matters, including the appointment of high officers and the movement of Union armies. In December 1862, when Chase tried to force Lincoln's hand and secure the removal of Secretary of State William H. Seward from office, the president skillfully outmaneuvered him and exposed his amateurish efforts at a meeting with cabinet and Senate leaders. Chase appeared oblivious to the fact that he could not compete with a master politician of Lincoln's ability. Still feeling himself uniquely qualified for the presidency, Chase urged supporters within and outside the Treasury to forward his candidacy. Always denying such an interest, Chase convinced few of his loyalty to the administration.

As 1864 approached, congressional supporters clumsily tried to mount a Chase movement, but they served only to point further suspicion on the secretary himself. Clearly Republican leaders and voters preferred Lincoln's steady course of moderation to the uncertainties of a Chase presidency. Again, the skillful Lincoln outmaneuvered his secretary and easily won renomination. Lincoln now felt secure enough to accept Chase's resignation over a patronage dispute involving the New York collectorship. Still the party loyalist and opportunist, the former treasury secretary campaigned vigorously for Lincoln's reelection knowing that the imminent death of Chief Justice Roger Taney could give him a new role of influence. Lincoln reluctantly agreed, realizing that the constitutional changes regarding finances and racial policy of the war years might be solidified by a Court under Chase's leadership even though Chase would continue to seek political advantage.

Indeed Chase continued to reveal both political ambition and commitment to racial equality after the war during his years as chief justice. Not always in agreement with Republican leaders in Congress, he nonetheless avoided an open confrontation between the Supreme Court and Congress. Although he opposed efforts to establish military rule in the defeated states of the Confederacy, he endorsed legislation that granted civil and political rights to African-Americans. He clashed over Senate efforts to deny him a prominent role in the impeachment trial of Andrew Johnson in 1868, and, when Republicans chose Ulysses S. Grant as their candidate for president, Chase sought a Democratic nomination instead. His efforts, in part engineered by his ambitious daughter Kate Chase Sprague, failed partly because Democrats rejected his policies of racial equality. Yet he could rejoice in the ratification in 1870 of the Fifteenth Amendment, which granted suffrage to black men.

If ability and desire were the sole criteria in choosing a president, Salmon P. Chase was more qualified than many who have occupied the White House. Yet his ambition was not matched by political savvy. Try as he might, he could never convince enough politicians of either party that his advanced racial views or his controversial ambition could win the voters' approval. His arrogant, stuffy, and pompous nature further alienated party leaders and voters alike. When Lincoln considered Chase for chief justice, Ohio senator Benjamin Wade caustically commented: "Chase is a good man, but his theology is unsound. He thinks there is a fourth person in the Trinity." Yet, if denied what he sought most, Chase is also remembered for his stern commitment to racial justice and equality. His moral courage was at least as great as his unending ambition to be president. His Civil War record was thus one of controversy, frustration, and achievement.

—*Frederick J. Blue*

See also Cooke, Jay; Financing, U.S.A.; Lincoln, Abraham; Republican Party.

For further reading:
Blue, Frederick J. *Salmon P. Chase: A Life in Politics* (1987).
Burlingame, Michael, and John R. Turner Ettlinger, eds. *Inside Lincoln's White House: The Complete Civil Diary of John Hay* (1997).
Donald, David Herbert, ed. *Inside Lincoln's Cabinet: The Civil War Diaries of Salmon P. Chase* (1954).
Niven, John. *Salmon P. Chase: A Biography* (1995).
———, ed. *The Salmon P. Chase Papers* (1993–1998).

CHATTAHOOCHEE RIVER, GEORGIA, OPERATIONS AROUND
(5–17 July 1864)

In early May 1864, Major General William T. Sherman began the Atlanta campaign by putting the Armies of the Cumberland, Tennessee, and Ohio in motion with the hope of eventually campaigning across the state of Georgia. By early July, the three armies neared the Chattahoochee River. Less than two weeks later, they had pushed the Confederate forces to a position south of the river and only a few miles from Atlanta. When the Confederate troops abandoned their defenses along the north side of the river, Sherman's army achieved one of the major goals of the campaign, namely, the taking of the territory from the Tennessee to the Chattahoochee rivers.

On 4 July, Union forces staged demonstrations in and around Nickajack Creek and Turner's Ferry. In general, they pushed back the Confederate defenders, although units of the Georgia Militia offered stiff resistance around Turner's Ferry. That night, however, the Confederate forces, commanded by General Joseph E. Johnston, withdrew to positions just on the north side of the Chattahoochee to avoid being flanked by Sherman's troops. Once their retreat had been discovered, the Union soldiers pursued the Confederates all the way to the river.

The Confederates had heavily fortified their defenses around the bridges and roads traversing the Chattahoochee. Specifically, Johnston had ordered the construction of a system surrounding the railroad bridge, pontoon bridges, and roads associated with Pace's, Montgomery's, and Turner's ferries and composed of redoubts connected by infantry and artillery parapets. According to Captain Orlando M. Poe, Sherman's chief engineer, the defenses around the railroad bridge were "by far the strongest we had yet encountered." The Union leadership doubted if these defenses could be successfully assaulted. Even if possible, they believed that many would die in the effort. So, they decided to take the position by flanking it. This would necessitate the crossing of the Chattahoochee.

All day on the 5th, heavy skirmishing occurred between the two armies. This only strengthened Sherman's resolve to cross the river before the Confederates could strengthen their defenses. He, therefore, ordered Major General John M. Schofield's Army of the Ohio to cross the river on the eastern end, while the remainder of the army created a diversion to the west. At daylight on the 8th, Schofield managed to get his army across the river at the mouth of Soap Creek without the rebels' knowledge. By that evening, Union engineers had laid a bridge. A few miles to the south of Soap Creek, Major General Oliver O. Howard's IV Corps of the Army of the Tennessee, built a bridge at Power's Ferry. Still further to the south, Union troops saved a pontoon bridge set ablaze by retreating Confederates at Pace's Ferry. Thus, by the 9th, Sherman's troops had secured three crossings over the Chattahoochee.

Johnston's retreat to the north side of the Chattahoochee greatly concerned Confederate president Jefferson Davis. He feared that Johnston had boxed himself in by placing the river at his back. Crossing the river, in Davis's opinion, was not a good option since it would allow Sherman to cut communications with Alabama and capture points important to the Confederacy. Nonetheless, in light of the Union crossing, Johnston abandoned his position and retreated across the river during the night of the 9th. By the next morning, Sherman could claim that the Union forces were the "undisputed masters north and west of the Chattahoochee."

At this point began what Sherman called "the real game for Atlanta." For the next several days, Sherman strengthened his positions along the Chattahoochee, gathered supplies, and allowed the soldiers to rest. On 17 July, however, the entire army advanced and crossed the river between Roswell and Power's Ferry; Atlanta lay only eight miles away from the Union forces.

Johnston, in the meantime, had adopted a defensive strategy due to his being outnumbered. He planned to wait for an opportunity to attack. While planning the defense of Atlanta late on the night of the 17th, he received a telegram relieving him of command. The secretary of war cited Johnston's inability to stop the Union advance, as well as the general's lack of confidence in his ability to ever do so; Johnston later disputed these charges. Command was given to Lieutenant General John Bell Hood, one of Johnston's corps commanders. His former commander told Hood that his plans had been to attack the Federal army as it was crossing Peachtree Creek. Two days later, on 20 July, Hood attacked Sherman in the battle of Peachtree Creek.

—*Scott M. Langston*

See also Atlanta Campaign; Peachtree Creek, Battle of.

For further reading:

Castel, Albert E. *Decision in the West: The Atlanta Campaign of 1864* (1992).

Hedley, F.Y. *Marching through Georgia: Pen-Pictures of Everyday Life* (1884).

Johnson, Robert Underwood, and Clarence Clough Buel, eds. *Battles and Leaders of the Civil War: Being for the Most Part Contributions by Union and Confederate Officers* (1887–1888).

Kerkiss, Sydney C., comp. *The Atlanta Papers* (1980).

The War of the Rebellion: A Compilation of the Official Records of the Union and Confederate Armies (1880–1901).

CHATTANOOGA CAMPAIGN
(November 1863)

After the stunning 20 September 1863 defeat of his Army of the Cumberland in the valley south of Chattanooga, Tennessee, along Chickamauga Creek, Union general William Rosecrans personified the collective mood of his forces: He was despondent. After craftily maneuvering the Confederates out of Chattanooga in August, Rosecrans was now a defeated man. Routed and (except for the dogged performance of General George Thomas on Snodgrass Hill during the battle) almost completely defeated by the Confederate force of General Braxton Bragg, Rosecrans's army straggled back to Chattanooga, hunkered down as best they could, and awaited their fate. Without ever realizing that time would eventually prove to be more on the Union's side than on his, Bragg, having allowed his defeated enemy to vacate the field at Chickamauga, dispersed his army into siege formation around the city of Chattanooga and attempted to starve the Union army into submission. The Confederates' primary defensive position was maintained atop Missionary Ridge, east of Chattanooga.

At the time, it would have been hard to say which commander was in the better position. Although Bragg seemed to have the upper hand, having dramatically defeated Union forces on the field and now in the possession of the high ground around his enemy, he did not have enough troops to completely circumvent the city, so the Union soldiers were never entirely cut off from some reinforcements. The newly formed Cracker Line kept the Union modestly supplied. And as time would later tell, Bragg never deployed his troops as efficiently as he could have. For his part, Rosecrans, in shock over his shattering defeat, would not have the opportunity to recover his reputation and the morale of his army: he was relieved of command by General Ulysses S. Grant, who had been given command of all forces in the Western theater of operations. Grant replaced Rosecrans with the "Rock of Chickamauga," General Thomas. In his

memoirs, Grant described the abject situation he found the Army of Cumberland in when he first visited Chattanooga soon after assuming overall command:

> We crossed to the north side of the river, and, moving to the north of detached spurs of hills, reached the Tennessee at Brown's Ferry, some three miles below Lookout Mountain, unobserved by the enemy. Here we left our horses back from the river and approached by foot. There was a picket station of the enemy on the opposite side, of about twenty men, in full view, and we were within easy range. They did not fire upon us nor seem to be disturbed by our presence. They must have seen that we were all commissioned officers. But, I suppose, they looked upon the garrison of Chattanooga as prisoners of war, feeding or starving themselves, and thought it would be inhuman to kill any of them except in self-defen[s]e.

His army utterly demoralized, Grant quickly set about regaining the fighting spirit of his soldiers. Chattanooga was a vital rail and river transportation center, a strategic embarkation point for any offensive operations into

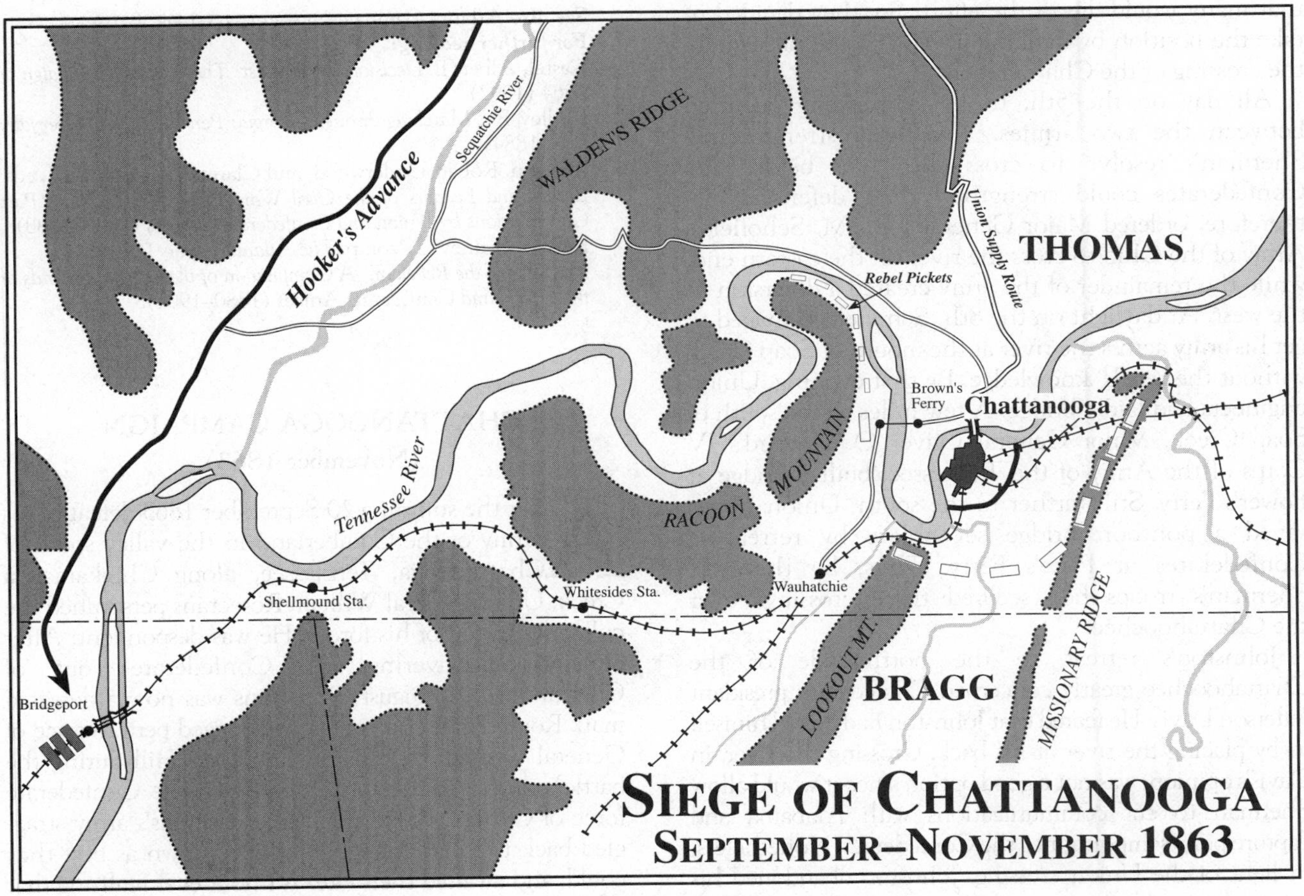

SIEGE OF CHATTANOOGA
SEPTEMBER–NOVEMBER 1863

General Sherman's headquarters at Chattanooga (*Library of Congress*)

Georgia and other Deep South territories. The complete loss of this city would have been a serious setback for Union forces.

Whereas Lincoln and Grant acted decisively in restoring effective leadership among their forces, Davis and Bragg did just the opposite. Bragg's most important subordinates, Nathan Bedford Forrest and James Longstreet, were allowed to leave Bragg's immediate command because they had openly questioned Bragg's abilities. Although he remained with Bragg, another of the Confederacy's finest officers, General Patrick Cleburne, had also alienated himself from the acerbic Bragg. On a visit to Bragg's command in October, Davis attempted to restore order in the ranks by objurgating the subordinates rather than firing Bragg, which would have been the wisest course of action. Thus, by scattering Bragg's angry, proud (and more competent) subordinates, Davis not only diluted Bragg's troop strength, he drained the Army of Tennessee of its most talented leaders as well. In the end it would prove a fateful decision.

By 15 November, when Grant finally had General William T. Sherman at his side, the Union forces were ready to fight their way out of the siege. With the Confederates spread out all over Missionary Ridge, Grant's basic strategy was to have Sherman's forces attack the northern flank and for General Joseph

Hooker's troops to clear the Confederate forces around Lookout Mountain in the south and then move toward the Rossville Gap, which was on the southern end of Missionary Ridge. Grant also devised that, to keep Bragg from freely reinforcing his flanks, he would have General George Thomas first capture Orchard Knob and then feign an attack at the center of Missionary Ridge, a position that was considered impregnable. As simple as this plan seemed at the time, in reality it would prove far more complicated to implement.

Sherman's forces, which started on the opposite side of the Tennessee River from the other Union forces, had difficulty against stubborn Confederate resistance led by General Cleburne. Anything that could have gone wrong did go wrong for Sherman, including missing the boat that was to take him back to his army from a conference with Grant. Rain and poor logistical planning delayed Sherman's expected attack from 20 November to the 23d, and when his forces did attack, they lacked their usual ferocity. According to Thomas B. Buell,

Sherman delayed. He seemed lethargic, with no sense of urgency. His lead divisions remained idle while the remaining two crossed during the remainder of the finest division, Cleburne's, to the right wing. Sherman could have used his first two divisions at daybreak to capture the objective, a rail-

Confederate prisoners at the Chattanooga depot, 1864 (*Library of Congress*)

road tunnel about a mile down the ridge, because it was undefended. When Sherman finally got underway at one o'clock, Cleburne was already there, entrenching and prepared to fight.

With Cleburne burrowing in at Tunnel Hill, Sherman seemed to be stumbling around, seemingly unaware even of the terrain ahead of him. He soon became defensive-minded when he was supposed to be responsible for the bulk of the offensive.

Grant did not seem to have a clue about the goings-on with his favorite soldier and was not completely aware of the activities of Hooker as well. He ordered that both Sherman and Thomas attack at dawn on the 25th, with the latter either taking the rifle pits at the base of Missionary Ridge or moving left to help Sherman. Grant never intended Thomas's men to attack the center of the Confederate line directly ahead because the thinking was that they would be slaughtered trying to capture the high ground. Sherman found the fighting at Tunnel Hill no more successful than the day before, and his advance was once again stalled. However, the fierceness of the

conflict forced Bragg to drain reserves from his center to relieve the pressure on Cleburne.

Grant and Thomas were waiting at Orchard Knob, hoping to hear that Hooker had been successful on Lookout Mountain and was on his way to help dislodge the Confederates from their perch on Missionary Ridge. Although Hooker had experienced an easy victory on Lookout Mountain, his troops were severely delayed in returning because retreating Confederate general Carter L. Stevenson had burned the bridge over Chattanooga Creek. Hooker's victory in the "Battle above the Clouds" had been much easier than he had ever imagined, so much so that he actually made it more difficult than it needed to be. Although he was victorious, Hooker's overcautious behavior added more delay and confusion to the overall campaign. Seemingly stalled on all fronts and frustrated by delay after delay, Grant was uncharacteristically indecisive until he ordered his troops to take only the rifle pits at the foot of Missionary Ridge, although such an action would place the Union soldiers in a precarious position from Confederate guns above. When Thomas's men took the rifle pits, overrunning the severely outnumbered Confederates, they indeed found life hellish and so spontaneously attacked up the steep ridge as a matter of survival.

Their own assault took the Union high command by complete surprise; Grant muttered that there would be hell to pay if the advance ended in disaster, but of course it did not. The attack moved forward unevenly as the Union troops ran up the slope with the Confederate defenders' guns seemingly stunned into silence. As the blue line streamed up the hill, the gray one fled in desperation and fear. Bragg could only watch in disbelief as the center of his line broke. With his headquarters on the top of the ridge threatened, Bragg hurriedly had to escape to the rear of his army in Dalton. The troops of Confederate generals William J. Hardee and John C. Breckinridge had been soundly defeated, so Cleburne's forces, the only ones on the gray side to have stopped the enemy during the engagement, then had to fight a rear-guard retreat in order to save the Confederate army from complete demolition.

On the 26th, Cleburne moved his division through the city of Ringgold, organized a defense-in-depth position between the White Oak Mountains and Taylor Ridge, and waited for Hooker to advance. Surprised by Cleburne's concealed position, the Union forces were soon pinned down and stopped in their tracks. When Grant arrived on the scene, he immediately called off Hooker's movement through Ringgold Gap because he was far more concerned about activities with General Ambrose Burnside's Union forces in Nashville that were being threatened by Confederate general Longstreet's offensive. Longstreet's campaign had been planned as a way to relieve the shaky command situation Davis had found when he visited Bragg before the battle of Chattanooga; it turned out to be a political decision that backfired. It is clear that Longstreet's leadership during the battle would have helped immensely.

Although the Confederates were soundly defeated, largely due to their misalignment but also due to their being utterly demoralized by Bragg's incompetence, they managed not to disintegrate. They eventually were able to reorganize among the hills around Dalton, situated on the rail line that ran into their main supply base in Atlanta. Bragg, whose nerves on a good day seemed to have been bad, now faced the profound defeat of an army that just several months before had celebrated a remarkable victory at Chickamauga and the siege of Chattanooga. To his credit, he immediately requested his dismissal as commander of Confederate forces in Georgia, and Davis obviously had no other choice but to accept. Acting on advice from Lee, the Confederate president brought General Joseph Johnston out of retirement and sent him to reorganize and prepare the Confederate forces for the inevitable defense of Atlanta.

The relief of the Chattanooga siege would prove to be one of the decisive events of the later stages of the war. Sherman, who soon became commander of an army when Grant was promoted to greater responsibility and sent to the eastern front, would use it as his supply base on his march to Atlanta and eventually the sea. Johnston, for his part, spent the winter of 1864 devising defensive strategies to stop the determined Sherman. The casualties for this Chattanooga campaign were approximately 5,400 for the Union and 6,900 for the Confederates.

—*James H. Meredith*

See also Bragg, Braxton; Chattanooga, Tennessee; Cleburne, Patrick Ronayne; Lookout Mountain, Battle of; Missionary Ridge, Battle of; Sherman, William Tecumseh; Thomas, George Henry.

For further reading:

Bowers, John. *Chickamauga and Chattanooga: The Battles That Doomed the Confederacy* (1994).

Buell, Thomas B. *The Warrior Generals: Combat Leadership in the Civil War* (1997).

Cozzens, Peter. *The Shipwreck of Their Hopes: The Battles for Chattanooga* (1994).

Grant, Ulysses S. *Personal Memoirs of U. S. Grant* (1885).

McDonough, James L. *Chattanooga—A Death Grip on the Confederacy* (1984).

Roland, Charles P. "Chattanooga-Ringgold Campaign: November 1863." *The Civil War Battlefield Guide* (1998).

Sword, Wiley. *Mountains Touched with Fire: Chattanooga Besieged, 1863* (1995).

CHATTANOOGA, TENNESSEE

As the Tennessee River winds through the southern Appalachian Mountains, it makes a large horseshoe bend. The town of Chattanooga sits inside this bend and between two ridges that form the Chattanooga Valley. Lookout Mountain, rising almost 1,800 feet above the river, overlooks the town's southwestern edge. Supposedly, the name "Chattanooga" derives from the Creek phrase for "rock that comes to a point," which aptly describes the narrowing of the mountain as it nears the city. To the southeast stands another formidable natural barrier, Missionary Ridge. About one-third as high as Lookout Mountain, Missionary Ridge runs fifteen miles south from just above Chattanooga to Rossville, Georgia.

Before 1850, the town's 2,500 inhabitants made their living largely from the river. Unfortunately, gorges and water hazards just below Chattanooga make large-scale riverborne commerce from Middle and West Tennessee upstream to Knoxville nearly impossible. Incorporated in 1839, Chattanooga remained a relatively small port during most of the antebellum period. However, Tennesseans rapidly accelerated railroad construction in the 1850s, and Chattanooga's unique geographical location among the mountains and on the river proved ideal for business. In less than a decade, Chattanooga became a major Southern transportation hub. Four railroad lines

A U.S. military train at the Chattanooga depot, 1864 (*Library of Congress*)

eventually passed through Chattanooga: one line connecting the Midwest to the lower South via Nashville, a second linking the Mississippi at Memphis with Charleston, a third running to Atlanta, and a fourth uniting Richmond with the Deep South via Knoxville.

The surrounding area benefited immensely from the railroads, and Chattanooga's population just before the war swelled to about 5,000 residents. When compared with other Tennessee urban areas such as Nashville, which held 40,000 people, Chattanooga curiously remained a relatively small town. Several large deposits

of iron, lead, coal, and copper were also mined within proximity, adding to its economic attractiveness. The availability of easily accessible transportation routes and abundant natural resources spawned industrial growth in northern Alabama and Georgia throughout the 1850s. By 1860, Chattanooga itself boasted two major iron works, making Tennessee the nation's third highest iron-producing region behind Pennsylvania and New York.

As Tennessee flirted with secession, Chattanooga's residents became deeply divided. A few days after leaving the U.S. Senate in January 1861, Jefferson Davis stayed in

Federal engineers constructing a temporary bridge across the Tennessee River at Chattanooga, March 1864 (*National Archives*)

Chattanooga for one night while en route back to Mississippi. Local citizens, mostly former Whigs who still hoped a compromise could be reached, gathered outside Davis's hotel, the Crutchfield House. They prodded Davis into giving an oration on current events to the assembled crowd. Despite the future Confederate president's rather moderate tone, one of the hotel's proprietors and a staunch Unionist, William Crutchfield, addressed the same crowd after the weary Davis had retired, denouncing him as a traitor. Informed of Crutchfield's charges, Davis returned, challenging his accuser to a duel. Thomas Crutchfield, William's brother and a Southern sympathizer, intervened and forcibly removed his sibling from the lobby to defuse the situation. Reports of this incident spread quickly across the South and served to polarize further the opposing factions.

Hamilton County, like most of East Tennessee, voted against secession in the Tennessee special elections of 1861, but the results reflected a peculiar pattern. The majority of the secessionist support had come from the urban districts, which had been recently settled by Georgians and Alabamians. Unionist support came from the rural districts that had been established by Northern settlers in the early 1800s. During the war, each side in the county took turns persecuting and confiscating the property of the other, control depending upon which army currently held the town. The destruction and near starvation inflicted by the war's shifting tides only worsened the suffering and deepened the animosities.

Initially, residents thought that their isolated mountain location would shield them from the ravages of war, but it was precisely Chattanooga's location that made the town a primary target. The residents failed to realize that Chattanooga's new railroads now made it the gateway to the South, and any army that occupied the city would hold a decided advantage over its enemy. For the Union, capturing Chattanooga would divide the Confederacy geographically and deprive the Army of Northern Virginia of vital foodstuffs and war materials produced in the lower South. Furthermore, Chattanooga's railroads gave Union forces the ability to leave the rivers and rely principally upon trains for supply as they pushed south toward Atlanta. The importance of Chattanooga to the Confederate war effort then ensured that the city would not be surrendered without a fight.

In August 1863, the Army of Tennessee retreated from Tullahoma to Chattanooga, but left the city when the Army of the Cumberland appeared on the Chickamauga Creek southwest of the city. The two armies clashed at Chickamauga in September 1862, and Federal forces, routed by the Confederates, retreated into Chattanooga to regroup. For two months, the Confederates laid siege to the city, preventing any supplies from entering. During the siege, Union troops

destroyed buildings for firewood and confiscated animals, including horses, for food. Ulysses S. Grant eventually broke the siege in late November 1863 by launching daring assaults on Confederate-held Lookout Mountain and Missionary Ridge. General William T. Sherman subsequently used Chattanooga as a logistical base during the Atlanta campaign and infamous March to the Sea.

As the Union army advanced southward, thousands of freed slaves began streaming into Chattanooga. Their presence placed an additional burden upon a white population already struggling to recover from the havoc wrought by battle and the Federal occupation. Violence between blacks and whites erupted throughout Chattanooga, and Union authorities were barely able to maintain any semblance of order. The Freedmen's Bureau finally arrived in 1865 and restored a measure of stability to the city.

Ironically, Chattanooga's wartime experience stimulated rather than hindered its economic growth. Many Union soldiers returned to the area after the war and brought large amounts of Northern capital to rebuild the city's damaged infrastructure. New iron factories and several additional trunk lines were built. Freedmen and returning Confederate soldiers provided the newly constructed factories and mines with an abundant supply of cheap labor. By 1877, Chattanooga had become a major Southern manufacturing center.

—*Derek W. Frisby*

See also Chattanooga Campaign.
For further reading:
Cozzens, Peter. *The Shipwreck of Their Hopes: The Battles for Chattanooga* (1994).
Goven, Gilbert E., and James W. Livingood. *The Chattanooga Country, 1540–1962: From Tomahawk to TVA* (1963).
McDonough, James Lee. *Chattanooga—A Death Grip on the Confederacy* (1984).
Wilson, John. *Chattanooga's Story* (1980).
Woodworth, Steven E. *Six Armies in Tennessee: The Chickamauga and Chattanooga Campaigns* (1998).

CHEAT MOUNTAIN, VIRGINIA
(10–14 September 1861)

Confederate fortunes in the mountainous western counties of Virginia had turned decidedly dark during the summer of 1861. The defeat at Rich Mountain, followed by General Robert Garnett's death at Carrick's Ford, had so alarmed Richmond that on 28 July Robert E. Lee departed the capital to supervise a campaign seeking to reverse the gains Major General George McClellan had made in the region. McClellan's successes had won him the foremost Union command. Conversely, Lee's record in those same mountains, starting with the abortive affair at Cheat Mountain, would only diminish his reputation.

Some things Lee could not control. The weather was inordinately wet—it had rained every day in August—and it had dampened the soldiers' spirits almost as much as the military setbacks had. It had also made them sickly. They perhaps felt—and rightly so—that their commanders were only marginally competent, and when those commanders were experienced, they could be querulous. Lee had replaced the fallen Garnett as commander of the Army of the Northwest with William Wing Loring, an officer who had outranked Lee in the United States Army before secession and who apparently now resented the arrival of his nominal superior. Lee took pains to preserve Loring's good will, even to the point of establishing a separate headquarters at Valley Mountain and framing his orders in the form of suggestions. Whether authorities in Richmond endorsed this deference or not, Lee was habituated to it and characteristically sought to preserve amiability with courtesy. The result was an odd command structure that had Lee acting more in the role of brotherly counselor than dominant general. It was a bad arrangement for several reasons. For one, although he wielded at best a modified authority, Lee would bear all the blame when things went wrong.

Officially Loring was in command, but Lee found him reluctant to mount any sort of campaign. Weighing the Confederate situation against Union strength, there was some wisdom in that caution, but Lee knew that morale both in the mountains and elsewhere could not endure prolonged inaction. Consequently, he urged Loring to make a concerted move on a Federal fortification atop the crest of Cheat Mountain. Loring instead devised a plan to attack Federal troops near Huttonsville, thus to isolate the Cheat Mountain garrison, which he apparently believed to be very formidable.

Actually, Colonel Nathan Kimball had only about 300 men of the 14th Indiana Infantry on Cheat Mountain. The real strength of Brigadier General Joseph J. Reynolds's 1st Brigade was along the Staunton-Parkersburg pike and westward near Elkwater. Lee agreed to Loring's plan, although he continued to scout for ways to fall upon the fort atop Cheat. When Colonel Albert Rust, commanding the 3d Arkansas Infantry, reported he had found just such a route, Lee and Loring revised the plan. Added now to Loring's march down the Tygart River Valley toward Huttonsville was a surprise attack on Cheat Mountain by Rust's 1,600 Arkansans. Another column would cut off Kimball's line of retreat and H. R. Jackson's brigade would poise on Cheat's first summit to occupy the ridge, once Rust had reduced the Federal fort. Loring made the orders formal on 8 September, and the following day Lee issued what was styled a special order, but actually and admittedly was an exhortation. "The eyes of the country are upon you," he proclaimed.

Curiously, no Federal eyes were. Confederate forces began moving into position on 11 September and

continued their maneuvers undetected. Lee followed the column marching down the Tygart Valley as rain again began to fall and the air took on a noticeable chill. Yet operations appeared on schedule and slated for success. Everything hinged on Rust surprising Kimball's Cheat Mountain garrison, for the sound of his guns would signal everyone else to attack. On the cold, wet dawn of 12 September, however, no sound of combat carried from Cheat Mountain. Rust had made the arduous march and had arrived on the perimeter of Cheat's fort on time—in spite of the rain, he noted—but then he captured a few Union pickets who blithely informed him that Kimball's garrison numbered between 4,000 to 5,000 men. Rust conducted a personal reconnaissance and had neither the experience nor anyone who did to expose this for the lie it was. His prisoners cheerfully began to relate how Confederate plans were common knowledge and that the telegraph was summoning Federal reinforcements for a crushing blow in the Tygart Valley. Already fearful of slaughtering his regiment with an attack on the Cheat Mountain fort, Rust now presumed the entire campaign was a doomed enterprise. Without firing a shot, he withdrew. By then, Reynolds was sending reinforcements to Kimball. Never having heard Rust's guns, the main column sat idle in the valley. Finally judging all surprise lost, it too fell back. The battle never happened, though skirmishes resulted in a few casualties and prisoners for each side.

The main casualty for the time being was Lee's reputation. On 14 September, he described the campaign as a "forced reconnaissance" and promised that it had revealed enemy weaknesses that would be exploited "at such time and in such manner as General Loring shall direct." Yet nothing could put a good face on the miscarriage. Rust more bluntly observed, "The expedition against Cheat Mountain failed." When news reached Lee that his aide Colonel John A. Washington had been killed by a sniper's bullet while conducting a reconnaissance, his desolation was nearly complete.

—*David S. Heidler and Jeanne T. Heidler*

See also Carrick's Ford; Kimball, Nathan; Lee, Robert E.; Loring, William Wing; Reynolds, Joseph Jones; Rich Mountain, Battle of; West Virginia.
For further reading:
Zinn, Jack. *R. E. Lee's Cheat Mountain Campaign* (1974).

CHEATHAM, BENJAMIN FRANKLIN
(1820–1886)
Confederate general

Benjamin Franklin Cheatham achieved fame as a leader in the Confederate Army of Tennessee. His term as commander in the Western theater included many of the area's most important battles. The quality of Cheatham's leadership during the Civil War remains unclear, but his importance is unquestioned.

Born at Nashville, Tennessee, on 20 October 1820, Cheatham came from a distinguished political family. Several of his father's relatives held political offices at the state level. His maternal ties included James Robertson, the patriarch of one of Tennessee's "first families" and an important member of the first political movements in the state. Several of Cheatham's relatives also had served in the military, including his father, Leonard, who fought with Andrew Jackson in the War of 1812.

Military service became important to Cheatham as a young man. In the early 1840s, he joined a local militia company, the Nashville Blues, and received promotion to first lieutenant before resigning his commission after five years of service. His experience with the Nashville militia proved important when the United States declared war on Mexico in 1846. Cheatham returned to his old militia company as a captain. He served with distinction at the head of Tennessee's "Bloody First" Regiment at the battle of Monterrey. After returning to Nashville for a rest, the members of the newly organized 3d Tennessee Regiment selected Cheatham as their colonel. He hoped that further service would elevate him to brigadier general, but the war ended without his realizing that goal.

Between 1849 and 1853, Cheatham spent his time in California supplying the gold-seekers with merchandise from his store and food and lodging from his hotel-restaurant. His return to Tennessee brought not only a resumption of farming activities, but involvement in political life. He was appointed a major general in the Tennessee militia. President James Buchanan considered him for the posts of governor of the Utah Territory and consul to Aspinwall (now Colón), Panama, but Cheatham was never offered the first and turned down the second. He also ran unsuccessfully for mayor of Nashville.

When Tennessee seceded from the Union in 1861, Governor Isham G. Harris appointed Cheatham to the position of brigadier general in the new Provisional Army of Tennessee. In July, Cheatham retained the same position when the Army of Tennessee joined the Confederacy. He participated in the battle of Belmont in late 1861. In April 1862, Cheatham, now a major general, led the 2d Division during the fighting at Shiloh. He was subsequently involved in the major battles that took place in Tennessee.

In the fall and winter of 1862, Cheatham led divisions at the battles of Perryville in Kentucky and Stones River in middle Tennessee. He faced controversy after Stones River when several reports alleged that he appeared intoxicated. The issue of Cheatham's alleged inebriation disappeared, however, as the Confederate

Benjamin F. Cheatham (*Library of Congress*)

army moved toward Tullahoma and then Chickamauga. Cheatham's soldiers performed admirably in defensive maneuvers at Chickamauga. Yet contention among Confederate commander Braxton Bragg and several Confederate leaders, including Leonidas Polk, Cheatham's superior and mentor, led Cheatham to resign his command. He eventually changed his mind about his resignation, but not before the Confederate forces lost Lookout Mountain. Cheatham rejoined the army in time to witness the loss of Missionary Ridge.

After the Atlanta campaign and the battle of Kennesaw Mountain, Cheatham received a promotion to corps commander when William J. Hardee left the army as a result of conflicts with Bragg. The new corps commander moved with John Bell Hood's army into middle Tennessee. Cheatham experienced his lowest point of the war when Hood accused him of failing to attack Federal troops at Spring Hill in late November 1864. The Federal soldiers escaped and helped bolster the Union defense at the battle of Franklin, which resulted in a Confederate defeat. Historians have debated whether Cheatham erred in allowing the Federal troops to escape. The blame likely lies with Hood, Cheatham, and at least one subordinate officer, John C. Brown. Cheatham's reputation never recovered from this accusation.

After the battle of Nashville, Cheatham served the rest of the war as a division commander in North Carolina under Joseph E. Johnston. After the war, he ran unsuccessfully for a congressional seat in 1872, losing to Horace Maynard. In 1874, Cheatham accepted the post of superintendent of state prisons in Tennessee, and in 1885 he became the postmaster in Nashville. He died the next year on 4 September, a man who had defended his military reputation to the end.

—*Mark R. Cheatham*

See also Franklin, Battle of; Nashville, Battle of.

For further reading:
Connelly, Thomas L. *Army of the Heartland: The Army of Tennessee, 1861–1862* (1967).
———. *Autumn of Glory: The Army of Tennessee, 1863–1865* (1971).
Losson, Christopher. *Tennessee's Forgotten Warriors: Frank Cheatham and His Confederate Division* (1989).

CHEROKEE INDIANS

At the outbreak of the American Civil War, the approximately 17,000 members of the Cherokee Nation lived in the northeastern section of Indian Territory, north of the Arkansas River. As was true for most nations living within the boundaries of Indian Territory, the Cherokees split over the issue of allegiances. The division of the Cherokees, however, had deep roots stemming from the factionalism created by the differences of opinion over the wisdom of standing up to the U.S. government and its removal policies of the 1830s. The split was also linked to the differing attitudes toward slavery and slaveholding among native people, some of whom were full-bloods who retained their traditional customs, while other mixed-bloods were more culturally akin to Southern whites. For example, before their removal, many Cherokees living in northern Georgia and Alabama adopted the institution of slavery. As removal became a reality, Cherokee slaveholders took their slaves with them and established laws similar to the slave codes in existence throughout much of the South. The retention of slaves (used primarily in Indian Territory for stock herding and salt making, as well as the more typical agricultural purposes) allowed the elites in Cherokee society to preserve their preeminence. Many mixed-bloods became affluent planters living like white planters elsewhere in the South. During the 1850s, however, non-slaveholding Cherokees grew more vocal in their opposition to the institution and found support among Protestant missionaries, who often had direct ties to the abolitionist movement in the northeast.

On 17 May 1861, Principal Chief John Ross issued a proclamation reminding the Cherokees of their obligations arising under the treaties with the United States. Foremost among Ross's concerns was fear that any course other than neutrality would provide a pretext for Federal military operations in Cherokee country. Ross also declared to the Cherokee National Council that he personally preferred that their treaties with the United States remain in effect because they provided for annuities on which the Cherokees depended for the operation of their schools, press, and government. In opposition to Ross, Stand Watie, a Georgian by birth and the lone survivor of the Cherokee leaders who formally supported removal, organized the Knights of the Golden Circle in Indian Territory. The Knights were generally a secret organization of supporters of Southern rights and the expansion of slavery. Watie and his followers actively worked to bring the Cherokees into the Confederate fold. Another secret society called the Keetowahs (or Pins) opposed the efforts of the Knights and endorsed maintaining the established treaties with the United States. Violence broke out between the two groups at Webbers Falls in the summer of 1861 over the raising of a Confederate flag.

Eager to formally bring the Cherokees into the Confederacy, Special Commissioner Albert Pike of the Confederate Bureau of Indian Affairs met with Ross at his stately mansion at Park Hill near Tahlequah. There Ross officially informed Pike of his plans to honor the treaties with the United States but to remain neutral in the impending war. More than likely, Ross was nevertheless well aware of the growing support for Stand Watie and feared that he might lose his place as principal chief at the hands of Confederate authorities eager to see Watie assume the position. On the other hand, if Ross chose to listen to Pike and break the treaties with the United States, the Cherokees stood to lose millions of dollars held in trust in Washington and to alienate all the full-blood Keetowahs who kept Ross in office.

The immense pressure manifesting itself upon the shoulders of the principal chief throughout the late summer of 1861 persuaded Ross to support a formal treaty of recognition and association with the Confederacy. The other major Indian nations in the territory had signed treaties. Stand Watie was gaining power as he organized his regiment of mixed-bloods and headed toward the northeastern border with Kansas to guard against a possible Federal invasion. There was also a rumor that Watie was going to establish a separate Cherokee government and ally with the Confederacy if Ross continued on his path of neutrality. Ross was also well aware of recent Confederate victories at Manassas and Wilson's Creek, which could be signals of imminent victory for the South.

Consequently, at a 21 August assembly at Tahlequah, John Ross won approval from the council to open negotiations with the Confederate Bureau of Indian Affairs through its special agent, Pike. For his part, Pike offered the Cherokees a treaty that included protection from invasion, the continuation of annuity payments, respect for Cherokee titles to their lands, the purchase of Cherokee neutral lands on the Kansas border at the price

they wanted, the right to maintain the institution of slavery, and representation in the Confederate Congress. Ross signed the treaty of alliance on 7 October and offered Pike the services of a regiment of home guards composed mostly of Keetowahs and commanded by Colonel John Drew, a Ross devotee.

Although Article 41 of their treaty with the Confederate States called for the Cherokees to furnish a regiment of ten companies of mounted men, with two reserve companies to serve in the armies of the Confederacy for twelve months, the only units of substance to be organized were in fact established before the alliance: Stand Watie's company of mixed-bloods and Colonel Drew's regiment of Keetowahs. Watie's command participated in the battle of Pea Ridge on 7 March 1862 and served as a home guard unit operating against bands of Indians from various nations who remained loyal to the Union.

In the summer of 1862, Union troops marched on Tahlequah and captured John Ross. The principal chief went to Washington, where he argued that he had had no choice but to sign a treaty with Pike. Ross then issued a proclamation of Cherokee loyalty to the Union and watched as three of his sons enlisted into the Union military.

With Ross in Washington, Stand Watie used the opportunity to declare himself the new principal chief of the Cherokee Nation and proceeded to consolidate his power. Thus the division of the Cherokees in Indian Territory was complete. For the remainder of the war, supporters of each faction still living in the territory staged hit-and-run campaigns against the other. Families were murdered, homes vandalized, crops burned, and livestock butchered.

The bitter, partisan experience of the Cherokee Nation in Indian Territory, however, was not shared by the Eastern Band Cherokees living in the Smoky Mountains of western North Carolina and eastern Tennessee. Although these Cherokees were not particularly swayed to the Confederate cause, their agent, William H. Thomas, was very much a Southern sympathizer. Thomas put together a regiment of 400 Cherokees who were to be used primarily as a home guard. Thomas's legion, as the group came to be called, also served as enforcers of Confederate conscription, as watchmen for possible Union invasion, and as counterespionage agents. As the war progressed, two companies of the legion were transferred to Virginia in 1864, and a few Eastern Band Cherokees were on hand at the evacuation of Richmond. Thomas and approximately 600 of his men surrendered on 9 May 1865 in Waynesville, North Carolina. They were the last sizable Confederate force to surrender east of the Mississippi River.

—*Alan C. Downs*

See also Pea Ridge, Battle of; Pike, Albert; Ross, John; Thomas, William Holland; Watie, Stand.
For further reading:
Gaines, W. Craig. *The Confederate Cherokees: John Drew's Regiment of Mounted Rifles* (1989).
Hauptman, Laurence M. *Between Two Fires: American Indians in the Civil War* (1995).
Josephy, Alvin M. *The Civil War in the American West* (1991).

CHESAPEAKE AFFAIR

Hijackers disguised as passengers seized the SS *Chesapeake*, bound from New York City for Portland, Maine, in the dark hours of 8 December 1863 off Cape Cod. John Braine, a Kentuckian vengeful from wrongful imprisonment by Union authorities, wanted to man a privateer. Once in control, Braine and his men entered New Brunswick waters and at Grand Manaan Island, picked up coal and their commander, Vernon Locke, of Shelburne County, Nova Scotia. Most of the passengers and crew were put off in a small boat. They rowed for Saint John and raised the alarm. Telegraph messages from the local American consul alerted the Washington government, and a hue and cry erupted the next day.

Meanwhile, Locke sold cargo at Shelburne, New Dublin, and Mahone Bay, Nova Scotia, to raise money. He renamed the *Chesapeake* the *Retribution* to fit an old letter of marque he carried from the Confederate government. On 14 December, he anchored at Petite Riviere and Braine fled to avoid arrest by authorities at Liverpool. Locke hid the *Chesapeake* in the Le Harve River as a Union gunboat entered Lunenburg harbor. Later, Locke steamed for Sambro, near Halifax, to rendezvous with a coaler Braine had contracted, but Union warships blockaded both ships, and on 16 December Union boarding parties took control of them. Some of the crew fled, but several, including Nova Scotians, were captured. The senior Union officer present ordered the capture legalized in Halifax to satisfy the demands of neutrality.

When the *Chesapeake* entered Halifax under a prize crew, and Union warships followed with prisoners in irons, the affair entered a critical phase for Anglo-American relations, with the potential to reprise the near disaster of the *Trent* crisis of 1862. Colonial authorities issued warrants to arrest Braine and Locke. They also accused the United States of violating British neutrality. Many Haligonians had strong anti-Union sympathies, which actually were more anti-Yankee and pro-British than pro-Confederate. When U.S. officers, under instructions by Secretary of the Navy Gideon Welles, brought their prisoners to the Queen's Wharf for transfer, a pro-Confederate crowd tussled with British authorities, and the raiders escaped.

Overall, the British and American governments were determined to avoid a clash. William Henry Seward officially disavowed and apologized for the seizures at Sambro and promised to censure those responsible. Lord Lyons, the British minister to Washington, pointedly accepted these reassurances. Public opinion as expressed in Northern and Provincial newspapers remained calm, colonial authorities moved to apply the letter of the law, and the *Chesapeake* affair slumbered in a slow legal aftermath that ran from late December 1863 to March 1864.

The trials of the hijackers in Saint John, and the later disposition of the *Chesapeake* herself, were well covered by the maritime and Northern press. New Brunswick's courts found against the hijackers tried there, but an appeal got them released in March 1864 under a writ of habeas corpus. They promptly decamped to escape rearrest under new warrants. Lincoln's government was relieved because these men had been mostly British subjects. If they had been extradited and tried in the North, diplomatic tension would have been revived. At Halifax, Judge Alexander Stewart of the Vice Admiralty Court impounded and returned the *Chesapeake*'s goods, and declared the ship herself a victim of pirates. On 19 March 1864 the vessel steamed under Union naval escort for Portland and its owners. Haligonians accused of abetting the escapees, however, received only reprimands and fines.

The *Chesapeake* issue thus ended as British and American officials had hoped. Confederate secretary of war Judah P. Benjamin sent University of Virginia law professor J. P. Holcombe to Halifax in an effort to turn events to the South's advantage, but it was all over when he arrived. Even so, the affair had echoes. Rumors swirled of further plots and Union authorities took steps to defend against future hijackings of coastal steamers. Seward ordered that anyone bound to the British provinces would need a passport and warships were stationed to check passengers' credentials at sea. The governor of Maine demanded federal protection and rumors and alarms excited the borderland towns of Calais and St. Stephen from time to time.

Overall, the *Chesapeake* affair revealed how deeply the maritime British colonies had become intertwined with the Civil War by late 1863. Many Haligonians welcomed and feted Confederates, whether they were passing through or were sojourners. The mercantile community profited from the demands for supplies and carriers even as the local population freely ventilated anti-Yankee prejudices and debated the motives and justice of the Union and Confederate causes. Those differences became academic after Appomattox, but both Confederate and Union veterans lie buried in the city, mute testimony to Halifax's status as a maritime nexus for one part of the American Civil War.

—*Reginald C. Stuart*

See also Diplomacy, C.S.A.; Diplomacy, U.S.A.; Great Britain; Holcombe, James; Privateers.

For further reading:

Cox, George. "Sidelights on the *Chesapeake* Affair, 1863–64." *Royal Nova Scotia Historical Society, Collections* (1951).

Jones, Francis I. "Treason and Piracy in Civil War Halifax: The Second *Chesapeake* Affair Revisited." *Dalhousie Review* (1991–1992).

Marquis, Greg. *In Armageddon's Shadow: The Civil War and Canada's Maritime Provinces* (1998).

McDonald, Ronald H. "Second *Chesapeake* Affair." *Dalhousie Review* (1974–1975).

Smith, Philip Mason. *Confederates Down East: Confederate Operations in and around Maine* (1985).

CHESNUT, JAMES
(1815–1885)

Confederate congressman and general

Born to James Chesnut and Mary Cox Chesnut in Camden, South Carolina, the younger Chesnut was educated at Princeton University and studied law upon his return to South Carolina. After opening a practice in Camden, Chesnut became involved in South Carolina politics. Between 1840 and 1858, he served terms in both houses of the South Carolina legislature. He also represented the state in 1850 at the Nashville Convention. In 1858, he was selected to fill the unexpired term of the late Josiah J. Evans in the U.S. Senate. Chesnut remained in that body until the election of Abraham Lincoln as president in November 1860.

An ardent secessionist, Chesnut believed that an early exit from the national legislature might start a stampede of states out of the Union. At home he worked feverishly to bring about the secession of his own state, serving as a member of the secession convention and one of the authors of the ordinance of secession. After other gulf states followed South Carolina out of the union in early 1861, Chesnut was selected to represent his state to the Provisional Confederate Congress in Montgomery, Alabama. He traveled there with his wife, Mary Boykin Chesnut, the future author of *A Diary from Dixie*.

In Montgomery, Chesnut pushed for unity within the Southern Confederacy and believed that one of the best ways to achieve such unity was to discourage South Carolina dominance of the proceedings and encourage a distribution of offices among citizens of all member states. As a result, he opposed the selection of any South Carolinian for president or vice president of the Confederacy. Some of his most important work was on the committee that drafted the Confederate Constitution.

As the crisis over Fort Sumter worsened in the spring of 1861, Chesnut returned home and offered his services as a voluntary aide to the Confederate commander in Charleston, P. G. T. Beauregard. Chesnut was one of a group of Beauregard aides who negotiated with Major Robert Anderson before the bombardment began on Fort Sumter. Privately Chesnut expressed sympathy for Anderson's predicament. Chesnut sent the note to Anderson at 3:20 A.M. on 12 April warning him that the firing would commence in approximately one hour.

After the surrender of Fort Sumter, Beauregard was sent to Virginia. In June 1861, Chesnut made arrangements to join him, leaving his home in early June and arriving in Richmond on 12 June. During the first part of the summer, Chesnut, because of his legal training, served as judge advocate on Beauregard's staff at the rank of colonel. On 13 July Beauregard sent Chesnut to Richmond with a suggestion for President Jefferson Davis that Beauregard's and Joseph Johnston's armies join at Manassas Junction to meet the potential Union attack there. During the ensuing battle of Bull Run on 21 July, Chesnut served as Beauregard's aide.

In August, Chesnut was back in the Confederate Congress, but longed for the military life. Because he was a friend of President Davis from their days in the U.S. Senate together, he was pestered for jobs. Chesnut also found himself in the middle of a growing feud between the president and Beauregard, the one his friend and president, the other his former military commander. He tried to use his influence over both to mediate the dispute, but was increasingly frustrated in his efforts. In January 1862 he received appointment as the chief of the Military Department of the Executive Council of South Carolina. He held that position for most of the remainder of 1862. One of his primary duties was to review requests for exemptions from military service, a task not at all to his liking. In the late fall of 1862, he resigned this post to accept a position as a military adviser to President Davis, again with the rank of colonel.

Serving directly under Davis for the next eighteen months, Chesnut conducted inspections of military forces as far away as the western Confederate armies. He also traveled to Chattanooga in August 1863 to meet with Braxton Bragg on Davis's behalf (and perhaps to determine if the mounting criticism of Bragg was justified). In the fall campaigns of 1863, Chesnut served as Bragg's aide. Still it was not the active command he desired, and in April 1864 he accepted the command of all reserve forces in South Carolina at the rank of brigadier general.

Headquartered at Columbia, Chesnut watched and waited with growing dread as William T. Sherman began his campaign in neighboring Georgia. There was little he could do, however, but wait. When Sherman brought his army into South Carolina in early 1865, Chesnut placed his reserves under the command of Joseph E. Johnston. Chesnut remained behind with the militia when Johnston and Sherman moved into North Carolina and remained in command in South Carolina until the end of the war.

After the war, Chesnut returned to his law practice but never regained the fortune he had accumulated before the war. He remained active in South Carolina Democratic politics, though his citizenship was not restored until the end of Reconstruction. He died at his home near Camden on 1 February 1885.

—*David S. Heidler and Jeanne T. Heidler*

See also Chesnut, Mary Boykin; Davis, Jefferson; South Carolina.

For further reading:

Chesnut, James. *James Chesnut, Jr., Papers, 1779–1872, Camden, Kershaw District, South Carolina* (1986).

Woodward, C. Vann, ed. *Mary Chesnut's Civil War* (1981).

CHESNUT, MARY BOYKIN
(1823–1886)
Southern diarist

Mary Boykin Chesnut began her diary, "I do not allow myself vain regrets or sad foreboding. This southern confederacy must be supported now by calm determination—and cool brains. We have risked all, and we must play our best for the stake is life or death." This opening set the tone for the life of one of the best personal representations of the Confederacy during the Civil War. Blessed with an amazing wit and intelligence, Chesnut was both politically and socially astute, and therefore quite capable to offer commentary on the events she saw around her.

Born on 31 March 1823 into an aristocratic family in Statesburg, South Carolina, Chesnut received all the benefits her family background afforded her. She was educated at an exclusive boarding school in Charleston, yet she was also well groomed in the domestic arts. Married at seventeen to James Chesnut, she left her childhood behind to move in with her husband's parents at his family plantation, Mulberry, near Camden, South Carolina. However, she was given little to do; her mother-in-law retained control over the household. Further complicating her situation was her inability to bear children, and the first twenty years of her marriage offered few outlets for her frustration.

Chesnut's fortunes changed in 1858 with the election of her husband to the U.S. Senate. The couple moved to Washington, D.C., where she became acquainted with many of the prominent politicians of the day including Jefferson and Varina Davis. Chesnut began to keep her diary in 1861, after James resigned his seat in the Senate in protest over the election of Abraham Lincoln as president. However, the commentary in her diary reflects both her centrality and her marginality as a Southern woman. She operated within the structure of Southern society, staunchly supporting the war, and enjoying the privilege of a slave society, yet she also criticized social conventions. Although she harbored an aversion to slavery, her allegiance to her class and social standing were much stronger. She was hardly an abolitionist, and her antislavery opinions were, as she termed it, "narrowly self-interested." Her quarrel with the slave system was that it "threatened and degraded her position as a woman." In fact, she criticized Harriet Beecher Stowe's *Uncle Tom's Cabin* for taking "an extraordinary freak of nature and presenting it as a specimen of a class—a common type." She argued that Southern women of her class "hate[d] slavery worse than Mrs. Stowe."

Chesnut used her diary to criticize both slavery and Yankee "interference" and also to record personal information. In 1862, James received a commission as an aide to President of the Confederacy Jefferson Davis, and the Chesnuts moved to Richmond, Virginia. During these years, Chesnut's diary was filled with comments in praise of General Robert E. Lee and her distress concerning the long casualty lists. She noted, "Think of all these young lives sacrificed!" The war, however, took its toll on James, and the couple moved back to South Carolina in April 1864. Chesnut noted, "We are at sea. Our boat has sprung a leak." Nevertheless, as it became apparent that the South was fighting a losing battle, Chesnut was forced to retreat once again, this time to Lincolntown, North Carolina. She wrote, "We had as much right to fight to get out as they had a right to fight to keep us in. If they try to play the masters—anywhere upon the habitable globe I will go, never to see a Yankee. And if I die on the way, so much the better." For Mary Chesnut, the war resulted in the resumption of Northern patriarchy, and upon return to Camden, South Carolina, discovery of the destruction of Mulberry by Union forces. Deeply in debt, the Chesnuts faced new challenges in the postbellum era, complications they had never had to face as members of the elite.

Mary Boykin Chesnut's diary provides not only a glimpse into the life and experiences of a privileged Southern woman, but also a look at one who defied the Southern stereotype. Her diary, however, underwent numerous revisions. At her death in 1886, she left behind many versions of the diary; entire sections between 1862 and 1864 are completely missing and may have been destroyed during the war. Chesnut had begun to revise her diary after the war, but she was forced to stop in the mid-1870s, only to resume in 1881. She continued this task until 1885 and the death of both her husband and her mother, and she never returned to the project. She died in 1886.

Historians need to remember that, as Chesnut worked on her revisions, she was aware of the South's postbellum attitudes toward slavery, and this may explain some of her ambivalence on the subject of slavery.

—*Jennifer Harrison*

See also Chesnut, James; Women.

For further reading:
DeCredico, Mary A. *Mary Boykin Chesnut: A Confederate Woman's Life* (1996).
McDonald, Kendra Lynne. "The Creation of History and Myth in Mary Boykin Miller Chesnut's Civil War Narrative" (Ph.D. dissertation, 1996).
Muhlenfeld, Elisabeth. *Mary Boykin Chesnut: A Biography* (1981).
Williams, Ben Ames, ed. *Mary Boykin Chesnut: A Diary from Dixie* (1949).
Woodward, C. Vann, and Elisabeth Muhlenfeld. *The Private Mary Chesnut: The Unpublished Civil War Diaries* (1984).

CHEYENNE INDIANS

With the coming of the Civil War, factions among the Cheyenne pursued multiple strategies to preserve their homeland. In particular, strategies for both accommodation and resistance matured during the turbulent 1850s, intensified throughout the Civil War years, and culminated under Reconstruction politics. Even though they avoided direct involvement in the sectional battles that divided the Union, the Cheyenne nation faced a war of another kind.

The Cheyenne migrated to the midlatitude grasslands during the eighteenth century, developing small-scale agriculture in the river valleys of the region. They also began to expand their political economy by exploiting the buffalo herds and the trading corridors between the Missouri River and the Rocky Mountains. Although the Northern and Southern Cheyenne were geographically split by the Platte River and the Oregon Trail, they shared a linguistic and cultural system. They also concluded an alliance with the Arapaho to drive out common enemies. By the 1860s the Cheyenne numbered approximately 3,500 in population. They were recognized among their neighbors not only for their power in war but also by their prosperity in peace.

Meanwhile, the character of the region began to change. The eventual depletion of the buffalo herds and the recurring epidemics of disease exacted a heavy toll in Cheyenne country. Although the Fort Laramie Treaty of 1851 recognized extensive territorial claims, the Cheyenne were unable to arrest the colonization of Kansas and Nebraska after 1854 and the Colorado gold rush of 1859. With the order of things collapsing, the United States Indian Bureau demanded new treaties and a greater presence for the Federal army as peace keepers—a role the bluecoats were ill prepared to fulfill. Accommodating the Federal government's demands, pacifist leaders Black Kettle, Left Hand, and Lean Bear signed the Treaty of Fort Wise in 1861. They relinquished all the hunting grounds assigned by the Fort Laramie Treaty for a reservation along the upper Arkansas River, where they were promised land allotments, annuities, and security.

Militant war parties called dog soldiers repudiated the peace accord. Originally a military society, they eschewed trade and farming but continued hunting buffalo. Carrying war medicines into battle, they traditionally fought in intertribal conflicts and adapted a fierce lifestyle to fight new enemies. Young men who joined the resistance movement lived off the booty captured from overland trails, trading posts, and frontier settlements. By 1864 the Cheyenne and Arapaho warriors were joined by cohorts from the Lakota, Comanche, and Kiowa. Together, the bands terrorized settler parties, plundered freighters, and raided ranches. Of course, their actions undermined the strategies for accommodation that were being advocated by Cheyenne peace factions.

The violence escalated into the Cheyenne-Arapaho war of 1864–1865. Among the Federal forces called to fight, the 1st Colorado Cavalry fell upon a number of Cheyenne camps, recovering some livestock but also attacking innocent village people and killing pacifist leaders. Among those killed was Lean Bear, who was shot while riding forward from his camp with papers he had received during a visit to Washington, D.C. The cavalry attacks culminated on 29 November 1864, when volunteers sworn into Federal service were led by John Chivington against the camp of Black Kettle along Sand Creek in Colorado. At least 163 men, women, and children were massacred during the attack, although Black Kettle escaped with his life.

Thereafter, Plains Indians from the Canadian border to the Red River followed a warpath for revenge. Indeed, Tall Bull became one of the most prominent dog soldiers committed to resistance. Roman Nose, a militant from the Elk Scrapper society of the Cheyenne, also refused to meet with Federal agents whom he blamed for the atrocities against his people. In January 1865, 1,000 Cheyenne and Sioux warriors attacked Julesburg, Colorado, where they pillaged the store, plundered the warehouses, and defeated a company from the 7th Iowa Cavalry.

With the Treaty of the Little Arkansas on 14 October 1865, the war ended for most Cheyenne south of the Platte River. Signed with war-weary bands, the Treaty of Medicine Lodge in 1867 assigned them to a 5-million-acre reservation between the Cimarron and Arkansas rivers in Indian Territory. Some of the most militant dog soldiers, nonetheless, joined with their kinsmen among the Sioux bands and refused to submit. In the northern plains they fought in the Powder River war from 1865 to 1866. During 1868, 700 warriors clashed with Federal patrols at the battle of Beecher Island in Colorado. Following a nine-day siege wherein Roman Nose died, black troops of the 10th U.S. Cavalry rescued the Federal command there.

The end of the Civil War enabled William T. Sherman and Philip Sheridan to expand Federal military control over the Cheyenne and their confederates. When George A. Custer led the 7th U.S. Cavalry in a winter campaign in 1868, Black Kettle was killed at the Washita River, where he had been promised a reservation. In 1869 President Ulysses S. Grant declared that the reservations were part and parcel of a Federal peace policy to move the Indians toward "civilization and ultimate citizenship." As the U.S. government began a long and difficult process for reconstructing the Union, the Cheyenne nation continued its struggle for self-determination.

—*Brad D. Lookingbill*

See also Chivington, John M.; Sand Creek Massacre.

For further reading:

Carlson, Paul H. *The Plains Indians* (1998).
Grinnell, George Bird. *The Fighting Cheyennes* (1915; reprint, 1955).
Josephy, Alvin M. *The Civil War in the American West* (1991).
Moore, John H. *The Cheyenne* (1996).
Stands in Timber, John, and Margot Liberty. *Cheyenne Memories* (1967).

CHICAGO TRIBUNE

Still a relatively young newspaper and voice in the rapidly growing Midwest, the *Chicago Tribune* was the first metropolitan newspaper to endorse Abraham Lincoln for president and was largely responsible for Lincoln's early political popularity. It provided extensive coverage of the Civil War, fielding as many as twenty-seven battlefield correspondents and suffering the first wartime correspondent casualty in U.S. history. It also took on the near monopoly of the New York press on American public opinion during the war. Capitalizing on its connections with President Lincoln and the Republican Party, the *Tribune* emerged from the war as the most influential newspaper in the Midwest but not the most popular in its own hometown of Chicago.

The *Chicago Tribune* began as a weekly literary supplement called *Gem of the Prairie* in 1847, but it became more visible in a crowded field of competitors in Chicago in September 1855 when attorney and newspaperman Joseph Medill, political activist Charles Ray, and three other partners bought and merged it with several other newspapers. Medill was a leading advocate of the newly founded Republican Party and was said to have suggested the name of the new political organization. He was an abolitionist and deeply impressed by the antislavery views and imposing physical appearance of Abraham Lincoln. Medill and other *Tribune* reporters followed the future president, reporting and transcribing all the speeches during Lincoln's unsuccessful senatorial bid in 1858 except for one, delivered on 29 May 1858. That speech so mesmerized Medill and other reporters present that they failed to write it down, and it has since been known as Lincoln's "Lost Speech." The *Tribune* did provide extensive coverage and a full text of Lincoln's

famous "House Divided" speech two weeks later. Medill became so friendly with Lincoln in the late 1850s that he later claimed to have snapped "Dammit, Abe, get your feet off my desk!" when Lincoln made a visit to the *Tribune* editorial room. Lincoln reportedly flared briefly at Medill and then removed his boots.

In the face of strident opposition from almost every other newspaper in the country, the *Tribune* championed Lincoln for president at the Republican Party's second national convention, held in Chicago in May 1860. That the convention was even held in Chicago was a minor miracle, the result of tireless boosterism by the *Tribune* and other newspapers for the young, upstart city. The *Tribune* published a special convention edition that included a political biography of Lincoln written by co-owner John Scripps and provided extensive convention coverage, encouraging local Lincoln supporters to yell whenever their candidate's name was mentioned. "Without attempting, therefore, to convey an idea of the delirious cheers, the Babel of joy and excitement, we may mention that strong men wept like children, that two candidates for gubernatorial chairs of their respective states, who looked to the nomination of Honest Old Abe to carry the Republican cause at home through the storm, sank down in excess of joy," the *Tribune* reported after Lincoln's nomination on 19 May 1860. Recognizing the threats for succession being made by the South in the wake of Lincoln's victory, the *Tribune* reiterated an opposition to disunion that had earned it a radical reputation before the war.

The Civil War, along with the purchase of the competing *Chicago Democrat* in 1861, made the *Tribune* one of Chicago's most popular papers. The newspaper published 36,000 copies of its report on the battle of First Bull Run, the largest run in its history up to that time, and it averaged about 40,000 copies daily at the height of the war in 1864. The paper specialized in western war coverage, calling for military action in the West as early as 1861. When it criticized General John C. Frémont's decision to free slaves and declare martial law in the West a year before Lincoln's Emancipation Proclamation, other Chicago and antislavery newspapers including the *New York Tribune* attacked it. Medill and Ray responded on 3 October 1861 that a newspaper was still a "watchman on the walls" even during wartime and that military men should not be exempt from editorial criticism. Albert Holmes Bodman was probably the paper's best war correspondent. As adept at poker and cotton running as he was at obtaining battlefield information, the irrepressible Bodman returned to Chicago with a nest egg of $22,000 after covering the war for only five months at a weekly salary of $16. Another *Tribune* correspondent, Irving Carson, crossed Confederate lines on scouting missions for Illinois resident General Ulysses S. Grant, until he was decapitated by a six-pound cannonball on 6 April 1862 as he stood within six feet of Grant while covering the battle of Shiloh. Carson was the first U.S. newspaper war correspondent to be killed in battle.

Even with its connections to Lincoln, the *Chicago Tribune* never equaled the influence of the *New York Tribune* and other New York newspapers during the war, but it provided the first significant Midwestern contribution to national political discourse. The Northern victory cemented the *Tribune's* reputation as a newspaper of influence and prestige in the nation at large, but it took much for it to become the most popular in Chicago. In the immediate years after the Civil War, Chicagoans were evenly split in their reading loyalties between the *Tribune* and Wilbur F. Storey's fiery *Chicago Times*, and both had about the same circulation.

—Richard Digby-Junger

See also Election of 1860; Medill, Joseph; Newspapers; War Correspondents.
For further reading:
Andreas, Alfred T. *History of Chicago from the Earliest Period to the Present Time* (1884).
Kinsley, Philip. The Chicago Tribune: *Its First Hundred Years* (1943).
Strevey, Tracy E. "Joseph Medill and the *Chicago Tribune* in the Nomination and Election of Lincoln." *Papers in Illinois History and Transactions for the Year 1938* (1939).
Wendt, Lloyd. Chicago Tribune: *The Rise of a Great American Newspaper* (1979).

CHICKAMAUGA, BATTLE OF
(19–20 September 1863)

The battle of Chickamauga was the culmination of a month-long game of cat and mouse between Major General William S. Rosecrans's Federal Army of the Cumberland and General Braxton Bragg's Confederate Army of Tennessee. Played out in the sparsely settled, heavily timbered valleys of north Georgia, Rosecrans tried to duplicate his success of late June 1863, when with spectacular maneuver he had pried Bragg out of his positions around Tullahoma, Tennessee, with virtually no losses and no major battle.

This campaign would be different. Bragg's loss of a considerable chunk of Tennessee without a fight had dismayed the government in Richmond, even though to some extent the Tullahoma disaster had been of Richmond's own making: Bragg's army was diminished by two infantry and one cavalry division in May and early June 1863 when President Jefferson Davis ordered troops sent to Mississippi to save Vicksburg. That effort proved in vain, and Bragg's weakened army was forced to retreat before an active opponent in his front. Richmond now sent troops back to Bragg as best it could. Not only were the original detachments returned from Mississippi, they brought additional men with them. A corps was moved down from east Tennessee, and on 9 September, two divisions of James Longstreet's I Corps of the Army of

Northern Virginia began boarding trains in Virginia for the trip west. That Davis was sending veterans from General Robert E. Lee's vaunted army was proof that Richmond viewed Bragg's situation as a serious emergency.

Rosecrans's Federals had crossed the Tennessee River downstream from Chattanooga on 2 September. The crossings were largely undetected and hence went unopposed because Confederates had been deceived into thinking Rosecrans would come across the river north of the town. Bragg now found Union troops south of him in force, and to avoid being trapped in the city he again retreated. This time, however, he was determined not to go without a fight. Once Rosecrans was over the Tennessee River, the mountainous terrain forced him to spread out widely, so his army was moving in three isolated columns. Clearly, these widely scattered Federal forces offered Bragg an opportunity to destroy his opponent in detail, but Rosecrans, acting on misinformation from Confederate deserters, persisted in the belief that Bragg's army was demoralized and in full retreat.

Bragg's first significant attempt to trap and crush one of the Federal columns was aimed at General James S. Negley's division on 9 September. Negley had pushed into an isolated mountain valley called McLemore's Cove that morning, and Bragg quickly concentrated troops under Confederate Generals Thomas C. Hindman and D. H. Hill to attack Negley from two directions, trapping him there.

Unfortunately for him, Bragg lacked the respect of his subordinates by September 1863 and a casual disregard for his orders had become commonplace. Much of this festering situation was Bragg's fault—he had alienated subordinates by recriminating them after the battles of Perryville and Murfreesboro. Yet it hardly reflects well on his officers that virtually none of them felt compelled to obey his direct orders. Neither Hindman nor Hill (who as a recent arrival did not even have the excuse of prior service with Bragg) chose to attack on the morning of 10 September, and Bragg waited in vain to hear the opening guns. Negley escaped the next day.

On 13 September, Bragg tried again. General Thomas L. Crittenden's 21st Corps, which Rosecrans had ordered out of Chattanooga to pursue Bragg, was alone at Lee and Gordon's Mill on West Chickamauga Creek about a dozen miles south of Chattanooga. Bragg ordered a strong force under General Leonidas Polk to attack. Polk ignored the order, however, and demanded more troops, insisting that it was he who was about to be attacked. Time again slipped away, time that Rosecrans used to collect his scattered forces.

The morning of 18 September found the two armies facing each other across West Chickamauga Creek near Lee and Gordon's Mill. Bragg now conceived a third plan: he would shift troops northward, interpose them between Rosecrans and Chattanooga, and attack southward to drive the Federals back into the mountains and destruc-

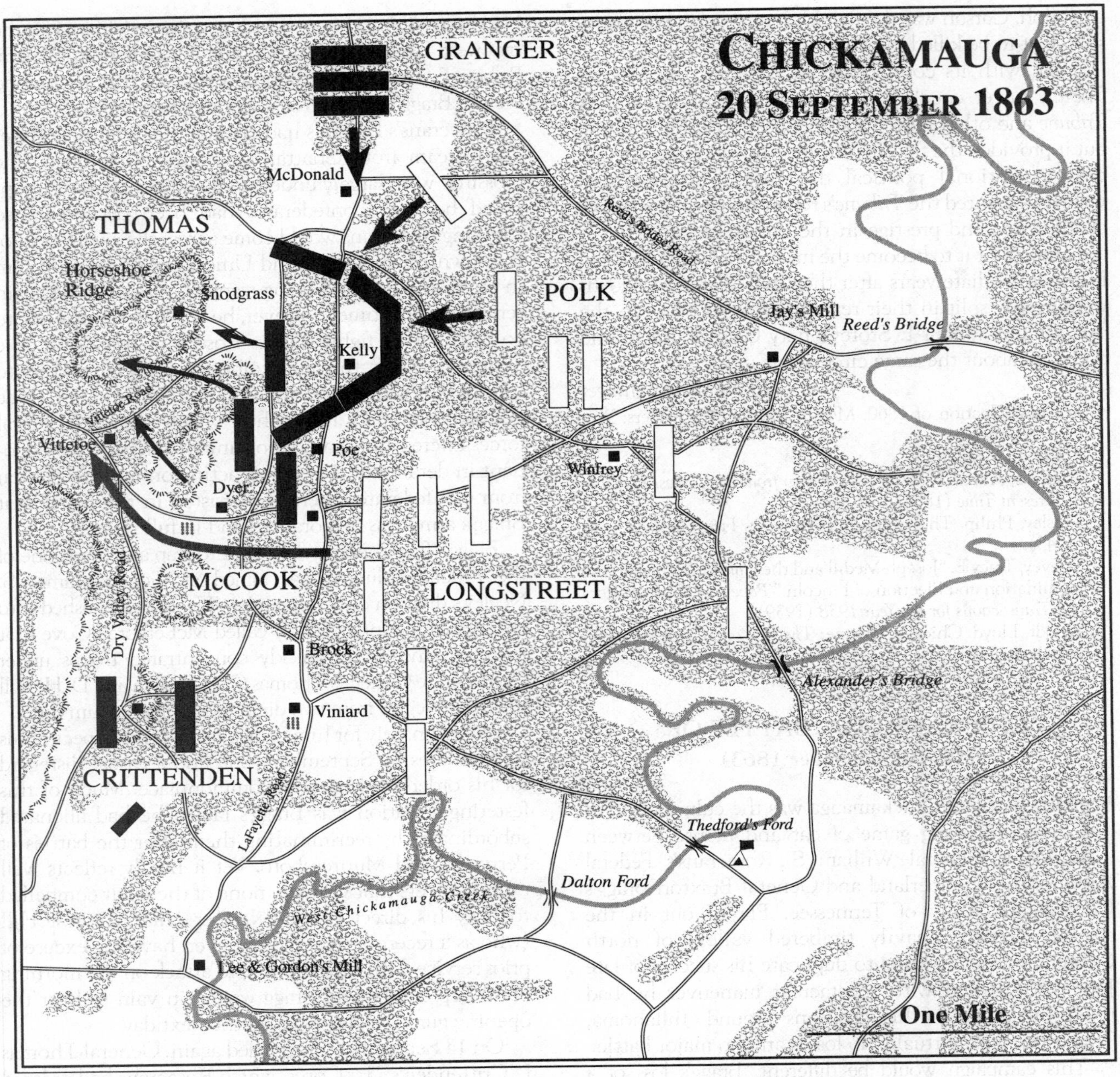

CHICKAMAUGA
20 SEPTEMBER 1863

GRANGER

McDonald

THOMAS

Horseshoe Ridge

Snodgrass

POLK

Jay's Mill

Reed's Bridge

Reed's Bridge Road

Kelly

Vittetoe Road

Vittetoe

Poe

Dyer

Winfrey

McCOOK

LONGSTREET

Alexander's Bridge

Dry Valley Road

Brock

Viniard

CRITTENDEN

LaFayette Road

Thedford's Ford

Dalton Ford

West Chickamauga Creek

Lee & Gordon's Mill

One Mile

tion. Meanwhile, the two armies sparred on the afternoon of 18 September. Union cavalry opposed Confederate crossings at Reed's and Alexander's bridges in skirmishes that greatly slowed the rebel advance and thus delayed Bragg's plan until the next morning. Rosecrans, now aware that Bragg was trying to flank him to the north, moved General George H. Thomas's XIV Corps in a difficult night march to counter the rebel move.

The next morning, Thomas started the battle of Chickamauga when he sent a division forward to strike at what he thought was an isolated Confederate brigade west of the creek. The division ran into Confederate

dismounted cavalry under Nathan B. Forrest, and a sharp engagement resulted. This brush with Federal forces alarmed Bragg, who thought he was well north of Rosecrans. He canceled an advance by three corps and instead committed reinforcements piecemeal to Forrest. As the men of Major General W. H. T. Walker's Confederate Reserve Corps escalated the battle, Thomas in turn put another Union division into the fight.

The pattern of piecemeal escalation continued throughout the day, spreading the fighting from north to south as both armies steadily hurled troops into action. Had Bragg stuck to his original plan and sent the three

The battle of Chickamauga, from a battlefield sketch (*Library of Congress*)

corps forward first thing in the morning, he might have shattered Rosecrans' army by exploiting the mile-wide gap between Thomas's corps and the rest of the Union army to the south around Lee and Gordon's Mill. However, as the day wore on, Rosecrans shifted division after division northward, closing the gap. The last gasp of the day's fighting came after nightfall, when Patrick Cleburne's Confederate division attacked, causing much sound and fury but little real damage to the Federal position.

That afternoon, Longstreet had finally arrived at Catoosa Station from Virginia after an arduous nine-day train trip. Lacking a guide to take him to the battlefield, he did not arrive at Bragg's headquarters until 11:00 P.M. Bragg immediately took the risky step of completely reorganizing his army into two wings, giving Longstreet one of them, containing more than half the Confederate force. The task confronting Longstreet was daunting, for he was unfamiliar with the setting and did not know the disposition of his command in it. Two-thirds of these men he had never commanded before.

With unhappy consequences for the rebels, Bragg made Leonidas Polk the commander of the other wing. Bragg ordered Polk's wing, including D. H. Hill's corps, to open the battle at dawn by attacking Thomas on the Union left. Longstreet's attack to the south would support this effort once Polk's men were fully engaged. The delay at least would give Longstreet a little time to get his people sorted out and in position. Yet, in what would become an infamous controversy after the war, Polk never sent proper attack orders to Hill. For his part, Hill did little to seek out either of his superior officers. The result was that at dawn on 20 September, when Bragg expected to hear the roar of battle, all was quiet.

Bragg sought out both Hill and Polk, and when they could not provide explanations for the delay, he finally ordered every available divisional commander into action at once. By then, it was 9:00 A.M., and the result was another round of piecemeal attacks similar to the previous day's fighting. A brief crisis on the Federal north flank occurred when rebel forces nearly gained the

Federal rear and possession of the critical Lafayette Road. But the Union line there under Thomas repulsed the Confederates and then held firm. By midday, the contest had produced nothing except longer casualty lists.

Fate and James Longstreet were about to change that, however. Rosecrans had become obsessed with Thomas's defensive efforts to the point of neglecting the rest of his line. At about 10:30, a Union staff officer brought word that one Union division was out of place, leaving a gap in the line. Actually, no gap existed, but Rosecrans had lost track of where everybody was. Reacting impetuously, he ordered General Thomas J. Wood to move his division at once. Any other division commander might have waited to question the order, but only recently Rosecrans had publicly admonished Wood for failing to obey an order promptly. When Wood received this one, he carried it out at once, well knowing it would create a gap rather than close an imaginary one.

At that instant and at that place, Longstreet launched his attack on the Federal right. Arrayed in a dense column six brigades deep, Longstreet's troops moved directly toward the newly created gap and smashed through the Union line with ease. Almost instantly, the right side of the Union line dissolved into chaos. Despite several determined stands, within an hour much of Rosecrans's army was in full retreat toward Chattanooga with Rosecrans

himself caught up in the withdrawal, leaving Thomas as the ranking commander. In fact, George H. Thomas's beleaguered corps, now alone on the battlefield, was about to be enveloped by Longstreet's unimpeded advance.

Two things saved Thomas from destruction. First, Colonel John T. Wilder's mounted infantry brigade launched a daring attack on Longstreet's flank and temporarily halted the Rebel onslaught. Second, a combination of fragmented Federal forces rallied on Snodgrass Hill to the right and rear of Thomas's bending line. Soon they were reinforced by the timely arrival of General Gordon Granger's Reserve Corps. By 1:00 P.M., these men had built a scratch Federal line to protect Thomas's right flank. Longstreet spent the rest of the day trying to break that line, but it managed to hold until evening, thus gaining George H. Thomas the enduring nickname "The Rock of Chickamauga." Thomas's stubborn resistance allowed the remainder of the Union army to withdraw successfully. That night, Thomas himself pulled back to Rossville, and by the next day the entire Union force had retreated to Chattanooga.

Chickamauga was one of the bloodier battles of the war with each side losing about 28 percent of their number. Approximately 58,000 Federals suffered 16,179 casualties. Confederate casualties are less precise, but accounted for approximately 18,500 of the 68,000 troops involved.

Battle of Chickamauga as depicted by Currier & Ives (*Library of Congress*)

Lee & Gordon's Mills on the Chickamauga battlefield, 1863 (*National Archives*)

Bragg's subordinates were unhappy that he did not order an aggressive pursuit, and ultimately Chickamauga proved in D. H. Hill's words a "barren victory." The rebels besieged the Union army in Chattanooga for a month, a siege ultimately broken with the arrival of Ulysses S. Grant and fresh troops. The Army of Tennessee then fell back into the north Georgia mountains to await the next Federal move—the drive toward Atlanta.

—*Dave Powell*

See also Army of Kentucky; Bragg, Braxton; Chattanooga Campaign; Chattanooga, Tennessee; Granger, Gordon; Rosecrans, William S.; Thomas, George H.

For further reading:
Cozzens, Peter. *This Terrible Sound: The Battle of Chickamauga* (1992).
Tucker, Glenn. *Chickamauga: Bloody Battle in the West* (1961; reprint, 1981).
Woodworth, Steven E. *A Deep Steady Thunder* (1998).

CHICKASAW BLUFFS, BATTLE OF
(27–29 December 1862)

This engagement, also known as the battle of Chickasaw Bayou or the battle of Walnut Hills, proved to be a Confederate victory. The battle prevented Union general William T. Sherman's Yazoo expedition from capturing Vicksburg and brought about

an end to General Ulysses S. Grant's first attempt to capture the Confederate river stronghold.

After the battle of Corinth in October 1862, Grant continued to move southward toward Vicksburg. Grant proceeded down the Mississippi Central Railroad from his forward supply base at Holly Springs. Grant's plan involved his force of 40,000 engaging the Confederate forces responsible for defending Vicksburg, while Sherman's surprise movement down the Mississippi River would easily defeat the skeleton force left to defend Vicksburg.

Grant encountered some problems during his movement into the heart of Mississippi. Cavalry leaders Generals Nathan Bedford Forrest and Earl Van Dorn caused trouble in Cavalry rear. Forrest with 2,000 men tore up nearly fifty miles of railroad track and telegraph lines, while inflicting 2,000 casualties on the Union forces and capturing or destroying a large quantity of supplies and equipment. Van Dorn inflicted an even greater loss, when his force of 3,500 swung behind Grant's army to capture the weakly defended Union forward supply base at Holly Springs.

The Holly Springs fiasco happened the same day that Sherman's Yazoo expedition left Memphis. Grant, realizing the vulnerability of his position with a force of 20,000 Confederates in front of him and his supply line compromised, called off his advance on Vicksburg. He attempted to get word to Sherman that he had to cancel his advance, but the disabled telegraph wires prevented the message from getting through. This support in which Sherman needed to keep the Confederate defenders around Vicksburg at a minimum did not materialize, and with Grant's retreat, Confederates headed back to run the Vicksburg defenses.

Sherman's Yazoo expedition left Memphis on 20 December 1862 and the following day arrived at Helena, Arkansas, to pick up the remaining troops that would complete his invasion force. The Yazoo expedition, around 32,000 strong, was divided into four divisions: Andrew J. Smith commanded the 1st Division, Morgan L. Smith led the 2d Division, George W. Morgan commanded the 3d Division, and Frederick Steele led the 4th Division. On 26 December, the Yazoo expedition and the accompanying U.S. Navy vessels turned up the Yazoo River and three of the four divisions disembarked on the left bank of the Yazoo about ten miles upstream, or about six miles north of Vicksburg.

Sherman's advance on the city became even more difficult. The Chickasaw Bluffs, offering an excellent defensive position, were between Sherman's force and Vicksburg. This location was made more defensible because the land between the bluffs and the Yazoo River was largely bottomland, comprised mostly of swamps and quagmires, made worse by continuing rainfall. Only a few roads or causeways could be used to transport the troops effectively, and these acted as focal points for the Confederate artillery, adding to the difficulty in approaching the Chickasaw Bluffs.

The Confederate forces were mainly spread between a forward line of rifle pits at the base of the Chickasaw Bluffs. The Confederates anchored the nearly four-mile-long line in a way that it could not be turned. The eastern terminus, or right end, of the rebel forward position ended at the broad Chickasaw Bayou; the western end abutted the left bank of the Mississippi River. Behind this forward line was the main Confederate position, becoming increasingly well entrenched and running along the crest of the bluffs. From this position, the rebel artillery could cover the open ground below. All of the routes through the bottomland led to the Confederate defensive positions around Chickasaw Bluffs. The terrain through which the Union army had to advance and fight had a decisive impact on battle.

Over the next two days, 27 and 28 December, as the Union forces were advancing slowly southward toward the Chickasaw Bluffs and skirmishing with Confederate picket forces, the rebels acquired more and more reinforcements, raising their numbers from 6,000 to well over 12,000. On 28 December, the forces under Sherman, notably Steele's 4th Division, came under such heavy fire that they were unable to advance on Walnut Hills to the east and later reembarked and returned to the center to support Morgan's 3d Division. On the same day, Morgan's forces drove the Confederates back in front of them, but were stopped by artillery fire.

However, the major fighting took place on 29 December. Sherman's plan of attack was relatively simple. He was determined to break through the Confederate center, and to do so required diversionary fire from Admiral David D. Porter's gunboats as well as feints against the enemy's flanks. The main part of the attack focused on the center. The attack got under way around noon after Morgan's troops completed the needed preparations for the attack. Morgan's and Steele's 3d and 4th Divisions were in the center on the move on the Chickasaw Bluffs. The only success, limited as it was, came from Frank Blair's brigade of Steele's division. They advanced on the Confederate rifle pits and chased the Rebels up the bluffs. The Confederate's heavy fire from their main line forced Blair's men to retreat back to the Confederate forward rifle pits. There they came under devastating fire from above. The fire was so intense that Blair's brigade was not able to leave until under the cover of darkness. The rest of the brigades of Morgan's and Steele's divisions were decimated when being caught in the open by heavy fire. By nightfall, Sherman's forces had made no significant progress in removing the Confederate's from the bluffs.

Although Sherman wanted to renew the attack, he thought better of it. The strength of the enemy position, coupled with the deteriorating weather conditions, forced him to call off all the attacks on Vicksburg and return to Milliken's Bend, Louisiana. The Union lost a total of 1,776 men, while the Confederates sustained 207 casualties. Sherman failed in his first independent command and his assault should never have been attempted, even if he had received word of Grant's cancellation of his advance. A frontal assault over open ground against entrenched troops proved to be suicidal; unfortunately Sherman would not be the last to learn this important lesson. The end result of the failed Vicksburg campaign was that Grant no longer attempted an overland route to Vicksburg in which his supply line would be vulnerable. Instead, he relied on the Mississippi River as a base of operations against the Confederate stronghold and incorporated lessons learned from his previous campaign into his strategy.

—James L. Isemann

See also Sherman, William Tecumseh; Steele, Frederick; Yazoo Expedition.

For further reading:

Arnold, James R. *Grant Wins the War: Decision at Vicksburg* (1997).

Miers, Earl Schenck. *The Web of Victory: Grant at Vicksburg* (1955; reprint, 1983).

Welcher, Frank J. *The Union Army, 1861–1865: Organization and Operations.* (1989).

CHICKASAW INDIANS

Removed from their Mississippi homeland in the 1830s, most Chickasaw Indians lived in the south-central portion of Indian Territory (later Oklahoma) on the eve of the Civil War. The other major southeastern Indian groups resided around the Chickasaws: the Choctaws to the east, the Creeks and Seminoles bordering them to the north, and the Cherokees located still farther north. The firestorm of secession and the Civil War struck the Indian Territory as harshly as anywhere else in the country.

As soon as the Confederacy came into being, efforts began to recruit the Chickasaws and other groups in Indian Territory into an alliance with it. Confederate officials, especially those from Texas and Arkansas, coveted the Indian Territory as an important source of livestock and food and as a strategically important location from which to launch attacks to the north and west. The Chickasaws and their Choctaw neighbors overwhelmingly supported the Confederacy throughout the war, with the Chickasaws adopting a resolution calling for independence from the United States and alliance with the Confederate States on 25 May 1861. They signed a formal treaty with the Confederates on 12 July.

The reasons the Chickasaws championed the Confederate cause were varied. Out of a total population of less than 5,000, about 200 Chickasaw slaveholders owned approximately 1,000 slaves, and many of these slaveholders held prominent positions in the Chickasaw National Government. Many Chickasaw slaveholders raised cotton and were connected to the greater "King Cotton" economy throughout the South. Federal Indian agents among the Chickasaws held strong Southern sympathies—the Choctaw-Chickasaw agent in 1861 was Mississippian Douglas H. Cooper. Furthermore, the Chickasaws, and other Indians removed from the southeast earlier in the century, retained animosity towards the government that had forced them to abandon their ancestral homes. Depredations committed by whites and corruption among U.S. officials responsible for managing Chickasaw funds also contributed to ill feelings toward the United States.

In late July 1861 Douglas Cooper began organizing a fighting force made up of Chickasaw and Choctaw volunteers, with Choctaw leader Tandy Walker as his second-in-command. Chickasaw men enthusiastically joined Cooper's First Regiment of Mounted Rifles, and several other cavalry and infantry regiments were formed in Indian Territory as well. Chronically short of supplies, the Chickasaw mission in the war was largely defensive. Chickasaws saw their first action in November 1861 against Creeks and Seminoles who were attempting to remain neutral. Except for a brief foray into southwest Missouri in 1862 (where at the battle of Newtonia Chickasaw soldiers were credited with winning the skirmish) and an interception of Union forces in western Arkansas during April 1864, Chickasaws fought mostly along the Arkansas River-Canadian River defensive line within Indian Territory. By 1863 Union armies occupied Indian Territory north of this line.

Little fighting took place within the Chickasaw Nation itself, but after 1863 a severe refugee problem arose there. Thousands of pro-Confederate Cherokees, Creeks, Seminoles, and their families fled southward away from Union armies. These newcomers seriously strained food resources and other rations. This refugee crisis resulted in deprivation for everyone in Chickasaw country, a situation that was not relieved until the end of the war.

The Civil War disrupted and permanently changed many aspects of Chickasaw life. Schools, courts, and government buildings became hospitals and barracks during the war, and the Chickasaw National Government met only irregularly. Much of the land was ruined by troop encampments and abandonment. Nearly all of the moveable property, crops, and livestock had been consumed, and marauding parties of armed men confiscated much that was left. Diseases, especially smallpox, devastated Chickasaws and other Indian peoples who had little immunity. Nevertheless, the Chickasaws held out until the very end; Chickasaw governor Winchester Colbert did not formally surrender until 14 July 1865, three months after Lee's surrender to Grant.

The postwar world looked dramatically different. Nearly 200 Chickasaw soldiers died in the war, about 4 percent of the population. Chickasaw slaves gained their freedom and the cotton economy they had supported fell apart. The United States required the Chickasaws to grant their ex-slaves forty acres of land each or $100 if they wanted to move out of Chickasaw territory. Finally, the United States ordered the Chickasaws to pay reparations to the small number of pro-Union Chickasaws who had fled during the war.

Chickasaws supported the Confederacy from principles and experiences that told them it was the best course to take, but the decision brought tremendous hardship when it became clear that the United States would win the war.

—*Greg O'Brien*

See also Cherokee Indians; Choctaw Indians; Creek Indians; Seminole Indians.

For further reading:

Abel, Annie Heloise. *The American Indian as Participant in the Civil War* (1970).

Gibson, Arrell. *The Chickasaws* (1971).

Hauptman, Laurence M. *Between Two Fires: American Indians in the Civil War* (1995).

Littlefield, Daniel F., Jr. *The Chickasaw Freedmen: A People without a Country* (1980).

CHINESE-AMERICAN SOLDIERS

In 1860, according to a U.S. Census Bureau report, all the 34,933 Chinese in the United States lived in California. It seemed that no Chinese participated in the American Civil War. However, recent research has revealed at least three Chinese volunteers in the Union army and one Chinese in the Union navy.

Hong Neok Woo, who came to the United States on board a U.S. warship, lived in Lancaster, Pennsylvania, for nine years and became a citizen on 22 September 1860. On 29 June 1863, he joined the 50th Infantry of the Pennsylvania Volunteers. After the battle of Gettysburg, Woo was honorably discharged along with his company on 15 August 1863. Woo later returned to China and worked for U.S. missionaries in Shanghai.

Joseph Pierce at age ten was bought by a captain Peck in Canton, China, and brought to Kensington, Connecticut. The Peck family named him "Pierce" after then President Franklin Pierce. In August 1862, at age twenty, Pierce joined the 14th Infantry of the Connecticut Volunteers. The 14th Infantry took part in thirty-four battles and suffered heavy casualties (234 survived to be discharged in 1865, as opposed to the 1,015 who formed the unit in 1862). Pierce received a promotion from private to corporal on 1 November 1863, and he was honorably discharged on 31 May 1865 in Alexandria, Virginia. After the war, he married Martha Morgan and lived in Meridan, Connecticut, until his death on 3 January 1916.

Antonio Dardell as a boy was bought by a sea captain and brought to Connecticut. He joined the 27th Infantry of the Connecticut Volunteers at New Haven in October 1862. The 27th Infantry suffered heavy casualties in the three battles it fought. On 27 July 1863, Dardell was honorably discharged in New Haven along with the 27th Infantry. After the war, he married Mary Payne and lived in New Haven. On 17 March 1882, he became a naturalized citizen. He died on 18 January 1933, and was buried in Madison, Connecticut.

Tsui Kuo Ying, Chinese minister to the United States, wrote in his diary in 1891 that there was a Chinese named Ah Mei in Chicago. Ah Mei studied in a military school for several years and served in the U.S. Navy during the Civil War. After the war, he became a U.S. citizen and was permitted to vote in important elections. The name and story have not been confirmed. However, in 1865 there was a Chinese in Chicago who sent letters to relatives in China. The census also shows that there was a Chinese in Chicago in 1870.

The stories of Hong Neok Woo, Joseph Pierce, Antonio Dardell, and Ah Mei demonstrate the patriotism of these Chinese-Americans who contributed to the war against slavery and helped save the Union.

—*Qingsong Zhang*

For further reading:
Zhang, Qingsong. *Mei guo Bai Nian Pal Hua Nei Mu.* [*A History of Chinese Exclusion in the United States*] (1998).

CHIVINGTON, JOHN MILTON
(1821–1894)
Union officer

Born in Warren County, Ohio, on 21 February 1821, John Chivington had public school education before entering the family lumber business at age eighteen. Chivington reached a turning point in his life in October 1842. Converted at a Methodist meeting, he soon became a minister.

As it did to many of his contemporaries, the West beckoned him. Chivington served Methodist congregations in Illinois, Missouri, and, finally, the Kansas-Nebraska Conference. Standing six feet four and a half inches, with a strong voice and "commanding presence," Chivington preached his pro-Union, antislavery beliefs wherever he preached. Described as a man of "energy, ability, and force of character," Chivington thrived under the pressures of work in the West. In 1860, he became presiding elder for the new Rocky Mountain Conference, an outgrowth of the 1859 gold rush. Chivington proved an ideal choice. He knew frontier folk and western conditions, relished hard work and travel, and had long displayed strong leadership abilities. He needed all these traits in his far-flung district. His success was graphically shown by the fact that within one year the Conference jumped from one preacher and twenty-seven members to seventeen preachers and 348 members. Colorado's only newspaper, the *Rocky Mountain News*, hailed his efforts because churches, a positive sign of civilization, had arrived.

Meanwhile, the nation was pulling apart. Initially, the region benefited because not until Southerners left Congress would Colorado be organized as a free territory. For Chivington, the outbreak of the Civil War proved agonizing because he was torn between his church and his country. The latter won, and Chivington ended his active role in the Methodist church.

Like an Old Testament prophet/warrior, Chivington enthusiastically answered his country's call. He helped recruit, organize, and train the 1st Regiment of Colorado volunteers. That needed to be done quickly because Coloradans were apprehensive about their present and future. They saw themselves isolated, with unfriendly neighbors, and separated by a month's travel from the pro-Union states. Washington neither would nor could be of much help.

Colorado was threatened in the winter of 1861–1862 by Confederate forces under General Henry Hopkins Sibley marching northward up the Rio Grande from Texas. Colorado gold could aid the South. Union forces

under General Edward R. S. Canby skirmished and withdrew to Fort Union, New Mexico, where Canby ordered the 1st Colorado to join him. These volunteers proved their worth, marching 400 miles in thirteen days.

The two small armies fought at Apache Canyon and Glorieta Pass on 26–28 March. The struggle was undecided until Chivington led troops that swept around the Confederate rear and captured and destroyed Sibley's wagon train. The "fighting parson's" bold move ended the Confederate hope of conquering the Southwest. Chivington came back to Colorado a hero.

After the New Mexico campaign, Colonel Chivington in 1862 was appointed military commander of Colorado Territory. Hampered by insufficient troops, lack of supplies, and continuing rumors of threats to outlying ranches and stage stations, Chivington worked hard to defend settlements and keep the essential and vulnerable overland trails open.

The Sioux outbreak in Minnesota in 1862, driving many of those angry Indians out on the plains, made the situation even worse. In the spring of 1863, warfare broke out, closing the trails. Travel stopped, mail arrived via San Francisco, stage stations were destroyed, and outlying farms and ranches were attacked. Because of all this, Colorado's cost of living rose alarmingly and Coloradans blamed the Indians. Neither Chivington nor Washington had the ability to stop the warfare. Patrols and a few small garrisons did not stem the attacks. Coloradans' anger and frustration mounted. That magnified the racism, misunderstanding, and fears that they had brought with them about their plains and mountain neighbors. With the coming of winter, the plains warriors withdrew, and the trails reopened. Colorado's mining had declined, however, and people already were leaving for the new promised land of Montana. It was either grow or die in nineteenth-century America. Matters worsened.

The relief from raiding and warfare proved only temporary; in the spring of 1864, it started again. The plains people's grievances had not been answered either. Their land and way of life were disappearing under the onslaught of white settlement. All the feelings of Coloradans from the previous year were intensified. Such warfare could not continue or Colorado faced a bleak future. Chivington and Governor John Evans responded, raising the 3d Colorado. The territory and Chivington had started down the road to Sand Creek.

The attack on the Cheyenne and Arapaho village by the 3d Colorado on 29 November 1864, and its aftermath, marked the end of Chivington's military career. Under mounting criticism over the attack, Chivington resigned. The Sand Creek controversy followed him throughout the rest of his life.

Chivington resigned from the army in 1865 and moved away from Colorado. He eventually returned in the 1880s and found Coloradans' attitude sympathetic toward his actions at Sand Creek. He spent his remaining years in the state and died in Denver on 4 October 1894.

—*Duane A. Smith*

See also Glorieta Pass, Battle of; Sand Creek Massacre.

For further reading:

Craig, Reginald S. *The Fighting Parson* (1959).
Josephy, Alvin, M. *The Civil War in the American West* (1991).
Roberts, Gary L. "Sand Creek: Tragedy and Symbol" (Ph.D. dissertation, 1984).
Smith, Duane A. *The Birth of Colorado: A Civil War Perspective* (1989).

CHOCTAW INDIANS

During the Civil War, most Choctaws lived in the Western Choctaw Nation in what is now southeastern Oklahoma. A few who had not been relocated by the federal government in the 1830s remained in their traditional Mississippi homeland.

Before the outbreak of war, the slaveholding Western Choctaws leaned heavily toward the Southern cause. Douglas H. Cooper, the tribe's government agent, was an active Southern sympathizer and influenced many Choctaws. He also threatened that, if they did not go with the South, they risked having property confiscated. In the same vein, white supporters of slavery from Arkansas and Texas mounted an effective, if not intimidating, propaganda campaign to persuade the Choctaws to side with them. Finally, as Union troops withdrew from Fort Washita in May 1861, many Choctaws believed that the U.S. government had abandoned them. Not all shared these sentiments, however. Peter Pitchlynn, a tribal leader, remained convinced that the tribe must remain loyal to the Union. Not a strong supporter of slavery personally, Pitchlynn argued that the tribe would lose its annuities if it broke with the United States. He also advocated neutrality as a possibility.

Nonetheless, the Choctaws held a secessionist meeting at their capital of Doakesville on 1 June 1861. At the urging of Robert M. Jones, a Choctaw with large slaveholdings, Principal Chief George Hudson appointed a committee to meet with the Confederacy to plan for the raising of a Choctaw regiment for the Confederate army. On 14 June, the Choctaw National Council declared the Choctaw Nation "free and independent of the United States." On 12 July, the Choctaw Nation signed a treaty of alliance with the Confederate States of America. The agreement guaranteed the nation a degree of independence greater than it had with the United States. The Confederacy also assumed all financial obligations of the federal government. Promised representation in the Confederate Congress, the Choctaws and other Indian tribes were seated but limited to one nonvoting delegate per tribe.

The first Indian regiment put into Confederate service was the 1st Choctaw and Chickasaw Regiment under the command of Douglas H. Cooper, by then a

Confederate colonel. Eventually the Western Choctaw formed five additional units. Most of their service was as home guards, but they did participate in several significant engagements. In November and December 1861, Choctaws fought in battles that forced neutral Indians into Kansas. In March 1862, Choctaws covered the Confederate retreat from Pea Ridge, and in July and August 1863, they unsuccessfully opposed the Federal march on Fort Smith and were later defeated at the battles of Honey Springs and Perryville.

Taking the measure of the Choctaws' weakened condition, Federal troops in late 1863 launched an invasion of the tribe's nation. In February 1864, Colonel William A. Phillips stopped his Union column near Fort Washita and sent a message to the Choctaws inviting them to surrender in return for amnesty or face destruction. Phillips, however, did not attack. Instead he turned his column south to Texas. Although Western Choctaw troops continued to engage in a number of raids, their military power was all but broken.

Initially the war had little impact on the Mississippi Choctaw. As the conflict progressed, however, the Confederacy began organizing them. The 1st Mississippi Choctaw Infantry was formed in late 1862. Commanded by Major J. W. Pearce, the entire unit was captured in March 1863 at Camp Moore Louisiana. The 1st Battalion of Choctaws for the Confederacy was then organized in February 1863 under General Arnold Spann. Other than being involved in a battle near Ponchatoula, Louisiana, and rescuing twenty-three survivors of a Confederate troop train, which plunged into the Chunky River, it saw little action.

The war affected the Choctaws in nonmilitary ways. Although the Confederacy promised to maintain federal annuities, it only did so in depreciated currency. The tribe thus found it difficult to finance its own government and was forced to close several schools. Compounding the problem was the widespread rustling of Choctaw herds. Cattle thieves commonly sold the stolen livestock to Union army contractors. This and a serious drought resulted in food shortages. By 1862, the Choctaws were also supporting 6,000 Confederate Indian refugees. Initially, the Choctaws were able to utilize a food distribution system to support the influx, but as the problem became more acute, the tribe began restricting corn to its own people. Even with such measures in place, food shortages continued. Refugees also formed gangs that stole food and property.

Given their deteriorating situation, the Choctaws elected Peter Pitchlynn principal chief in the hope that his connections with the government in Washington would serve the tribe well. Although he continued a pretense of loyalty to the Confederacy, he was instrumental in securing favorable surrender terms. After Appomattox, the Choctaw and other tribes met at Camp Napoleon on the Washita River to consider the future. Although some thought the war could be continued west of the Mississippi, the predominant sentiment was that further resistance was futile. This set the stage for the formal surrender of the Choctaw on 19 June 1865.

Unlike other tribes, Choctaw troops were allowed to return home rather than being paroled. In addition, they were given the protection of the United States. Pitchlynn called for a grand council of tribes formerly allied with the Confederacy to meet on 1 September 1865 at Armstrong Academy where a federal commission would meet with them to write a final and permanent peace. When the conference failed to occur, all sides agreed to meet again at Fort Smith. Choctaws arrived late to the peace talks and balked at a federal demand that they cede their land for resettlement of Kansas tribes. Unable to reach an agreement, the Choctaws sent a five-member delegation to Washington, D.C. The result of the visit was a treaty signed on 28 April 1866 that was more favorable than most accorded to other "rebel" tribes.

The agreement encouraged, but did not require, Choctaws to adopt former slaves and included $300,000 to facilitate their adoption or relocation. The accord also provided for limited settlement of Kansas tribes. In addition, the Choctaws agreed to railroad rights-of-way, the creation of local U.S. courts, and adjudication of loyal Indian claims. In return for these concessions, the United States agreed to resume annuities and restore pre-1861 trust funds. The Choctaws ratified the treaty on 21 December 1866.

Although the Choctaws sided overwhelming with the Confederacy, eleven tribal members joined the Union army, notably Captain Nathaniel Krebbs, who fought the 1st Choctaw and Chickasaw Mounted Rifles Regiment on several occasions.

—*Daniel Liestman*

See also Chickasaw Indians; Kansas.

For further reading:

Abel, Annie Heloise. *The American Indian in the Civil War, 1862–1865* (1992).

Baird, W. David. *Peter Pitchlynn: Chief of the Choctaws* (1972).

Bonnifield, Paul. "The Choctaw Nation on the Eve of the Civil War." *Journal of the West* (1973).

Fischer, LeRoy H. *The Civil War in Indian Territory* (1974).

Holcomb, Raymond L. *The Civil War in the Choctaw Nation* (1997).

CHURCHES

In 1865 more than 25 percent of Americans held church membership, and perhaps half of the population regularly attended worship services. These churches both shaped and reflected popular beliefs and attitudes, providing a vocabulary for believers to comprehend life's events. Churches helped to create the moral climate for fratricide and molded the zeal with which the Civil War was fought. They interpreted its occurrence as

a divine manifestation of, at least initially, uncertain direction. Until the outcome was clear, they labored to convert the soldiers at the front and to continue their programs of worship and watch care on the home front.

Large Protestant denominations had served as one major bulwark of the growing republic in the antebellum period. As moral institutions, churches found themselves mired in debates about the rectitude of slavery, specifically on questions of appointing slaveholders to ecclesiastical and missionary offices. Beginning in 1837 and continuing to early 1861, these national organizations divided over these questions along sectional lines, with Northern Christians holding that the sin of slaveholding disqualified a person from ministerial office and, in some cases, from church membership. Southern churches strongly disagreed, holding that the Bible specifically recognized the master-slave relationship.

Churches crafted powerful moral apologies for their anti- and proslavery positions, which linked the cadences of the Bible and theories of scriptural interpretation into compelling arguments affirming either the abolition or the continuation of slavery. Increasingly, these justifications embraced all aspects of moral economy, and Northerners and Southerners came to view the institutions and attitudes of their respective sections as having Jehovah's sanction and likewise perceived the structures and beliefs in the other sections as infidelity. Antebellum churches helped cloak the sectional debate and the outbreak of civil war in a moral language of theological certainty that made compromise increasingly unacceptable.

When the Civil War erupted in 1861, churches that had not already done so severed their remaining intersectional ecclesiastical bonds, with the Roman Catholics and the Old School Presbyterians each declaring their sectional loyalties. Denominations passed resolutions affirming their support for their section's armies and governments, and, despite the large numbers of church members who joined the armies, marshalled large numbers of individuals who went to the front as evangelists and colporteurs. In the North, the Roman Catholic Sisters of Charity sent scores of well-trained nurses to work in army hospitals, while other churches raised money for, and supported the efforts of, the United States Sanitary Commission. Northern and Southern churches provided chaplains for the various armies and conducted large-scale missionary and revival meetings among the troops. Churches supported Bible societies that labored to provide each soldier with a prayer book, a testament, or a Bible. They operated religious presses that produced special religious newspapers for the troops. Although the presence of camp followers, dice, playing cards, and alcohol among the soldiers indicated that the evangelistic efforts by churches did not eradicate vice in the army, these ecclesiastical efforts did do much to soften

Log church built by the 50th New York Engineers at Poplar Grove, Virginia, March 1865 (Photograph by Timothy O'Sullivan / *Library of Congress*)

some of the immoral tendencies of young male behavior. And abundant testimony exists that soldiers took quite seriously the teachings of Christianity, especially on the eve of battle, an event that promised for many a quick trip to the Judgment Seat.

Churches underwent significant transformations themselves during the war. In the antebellum era, denominations had defined themselves in strict doctrinal terms and often had little to do with groups who adhered to different creeds. The denominations themselves were often divided into conservative and reform wings that were estranged from one another. In both North and South during the Civil War, these groups came together within and across denominational lines to support ecumenical efforts among the soldiers and out of a belief that God Almighty was deciding the sectional questions that had divided the nation. In the North especially, the Civil War bridged the chasm between abolitionist and conservative Christians, who found in the Emancipation Proclamation and in the need for industrial power to crush secession a vital link connecting elements of practical and ideal conduct. This bridge led to conservative funding for the American Missionary Association, which had been founded by abolitionists in 1846. It began in 1862 establishing schools and conducting church services for former slaves who were in areas of the South now controlled by Union armies. The war years provided the experiential foundation and new theological assumptions that led many

Northern churches to embrace the social gospel by the close of the nineteenth century.

Southern churches, especially their denominational leadership, supported the Confederate war effort. Defeats, however, led many ministers to express a belief that God was chastening the South for failing to discharge its full duty to Southern slaves. Laws restricting slave literacy— meaning slaves could not legally learn to read the Bible— and the lack of legal recognition for slave marriages were two salient features in Southern society that church leaders targeted for structural reform. Methodist bishop George Foster Pierce told the Georgia legislature that it would be preferable to end slavery than operate it in a manner that jeopardized the souls of slaves.

Historians still debate whether the concerns of Southern churches hastened the Confederate defeat or prolonged resistance. Likely, one may find evidence to argue both sides of the question, but clearly the activities of evangelical missionary societies in the Army of Northern Virginia seemed to have boosted morale in the trenches around Petersburg in 1864 and 1865, suggesting that the doings of churches may have had different effects behind the lines than at the front.

On the whole, churches provided moral succor to their respective societies. They comforted the bereaved and reminded them that their love ones had died in a just cause. They exhorted their congregations on the home front to show courage in crisis, because God, they believed, was working directly in human history through the Civil War. They rallied the troops to bravery in battle and to moral conduct in the army camps. And they affirmed to their respective societies that the Civil War was a holy contest in which divine will would be revealed. At war's end, Northern churches affirmed that the United States, having been baptized in blood and purged of slavery, enjoyed Jehovah's special blessing. Unbowed, Southern churches still affirmed Southern righteousness and interpreted the Confederate defeat as God's peculiar way of disciplining his chosen people.

—*Edward R. Crowther*

See also Catholics; Chaplains; Chaplains, African-American; Jews; Sister Nurses; United States Sanitary Commission.

For further reading:

Miller, Randall M., Harry S. Stout, and Charles Reagan Wilson, eds. *Religion and the American Civil War* (1998).

Moorhead, James H. *American Apocalypse: Yankee Protestants and the Civil War, 1860–1869* (1978).

Silver, James. *Confederate Morale and Church Propaganda* (1957).

CINCINNATI, SIEGE OF
(September 1862)

The siege of Cincinnati never took place, but the threat of an invasion frightened residents and resulted in military assignments and construction during August and early September 1862. General Edmund Kirby Smith moved his forces into north-central Kentucky's bluegrass region during August with the hope of inducing local residents to take up arms for the Confederate cause. Few responded despite the enthusiastic reception that greeted Smith's arrival at Lexington and also that of John Hunt Morgan who arrived via Glasgow and Danville. At the same time, Confederate general Braxton Bragg was moving into Kentucky while General Don Carlos Buell and his Union forces were still in Nashville. The presence of so many Rebel forces with few Federal troops seemingly gave the Confederates a real opportunity to threaten Cincinnati and the Kentucky towns of Newport and Covington along the Ohio River.

Cincinnati, the nation's fifth largest city in 1860 with a population of 161,044 and known as the Queen City of the West, was a key communication center for points south and west. In the antebellum era, much of Cincinnati's commerce depended on the South. Confederates reasoned that, if they could reach Cincinnati, it would mean a tremendous psychological as well as tangible victory. Little in the way of military obstacles stood in their paths except a few siege guns near Covington and the Ohio River.

Alert to the movement of the Confederates closer to their city, the members of the Cincinnati City Council considered how best to defend the city. The council pledged to meet any expenses that the military might require during the emergency. Ohio's governor David Tod ordered all loyal men in the surrounding counties to arm themselves, form companies, and proceed to Cincinnati. At the same time, Major General Lewis Wallace, an Indiana native, received orders to assume command of the defense of Cincinnati and its Kentucky suburbs. After consulting with the mayors of Newport, Covington, and Cincinnati, Wallace declared martial law on 2 September. The proclamation of martial law appeared in the next morning's newspapers, two days before the beginning of the Confederate advance.

Cincinnati's residents obeyed the martial law order enthusiastically. While schools and businesses closed and streetcars stopped running, all able-bodied men reported for labor or military service. Thousands of citizen soldiers drilled in hastily organized companies organized by wards. Families buried their valuables or shipped them out of town. Fortifications behind Newport and Covington were strengthened, and overnight the construction of a pontoon bridge from coal barges across the Ohio enabled the transport of troops, artillery, and lumber for barracks. Mount Adams, Price Hill, and other strategic points within Cincinnati were fortified as secondary defenses.

Surrounding rural districts heeded the governor's call and hastened to support Cincinnati with large numbers of men, soon known as the Squirrel Hunters because of their long rifles. They ate at the Fifth Street market house and slept in warehouses, halls, and other available large buildings. Kirby Smith's delay at Lexington for a day or two eliminated his chance of invading Cincinnati. Just days after the proclamation of martial law, the city and its patriotic men along with the Squirrel Hunters had ensured the safety of the city. Later the citizens wondered if the situation really had warranted such severe measures.

Two days after martial law began, it ended with the exceptions that businesses had to close at 4:00 P.M. and drilling would continue in the evenings. Yet both black and white citizens continued their services; a black brigade provided labor on the fortifications while white citizens, 3,000 per day, continued their work with the spade. Militia organizations and reserve regiments continued drilling while the women of the town supplied a steady stream of provisions including coffee, ice water, sandwiches, and peaches. Some households even kept food tables outside on their porches for the home guard and citizens on guard duty or drilling. The need to join in Cincinnati's defense had brought its citizens together.

From 3 to 10 September, the trenches were staffed every night and some scouting of the front took place. Engineers had given shape to hasty fortifications, now remembered, in part, through the names of the northern Kentucky communities of Fort Wright, Fort Mitchel, and Fort Thomas. When Kirby Smith's force moved toward Cincinnati, Governor Tod responded to Major General Wright's request for help by asking the military committees of northern Ohio to send immediately all available armed men to Cincinnati. A few skirmishes occurred and again business was suspended. Events went no further. Governor Tod acted to check his call for volunteers, so many had responded.

Due to Buell's advance into Kentucky along with Smith's awareness of Cincinnati's defense preparations, General Bragg ordered Smith away from the northern advance toward Cincinnati to provide support for his army. By 12 September, General Wallace learned that Smith had retreated. Citizens rejoiced. Governor Tod announced the safety of Cincinnati and offered congratulations. The Squirrel Hunters received official commendation from the Ohio Senate and House of Representatives, and General Wallace on leaving the city paid tribute to its spirited citizens with an elegant and graceful farewell address.

Although Cincinnati was never invaded, the threat was real. Citizens, black and white, men and women, rallied in support despite the disruption brought by the curtailment of normal daily activities. Men throughout Ohio and nearby joined in the effort to defend Cincinnati, the region's dominant community. Except for raids, the threatened siege of Cincinnati, was the closest that a major Northern city in the West came to invasion during the Civil War.

—*Ruth C. Carter*

See also Smith, Edmund Kirby; Tod, David.

For further reading:
Reid, Whitelaw. "Siege of Cincinnati." In *Ohio in the War: Her Statesmen, Her Generals, and Soldiers* (1868).
Smith, David M. "The Defense of Cincinnati: The Battle That Never Was" (Website, 1999).
Tucker, Louis L. "The Siege of Cincinnati by a Pearl Street Rifle." *Historical and Philosophical Society of Ohio Bulletin* (1962).
Wallace, Lew. *Lew Wallace: An Autobiography* (1906).

CITY POINT, VIRGINIA

Located on a peninsula of the south bank of the James River where the Appomattox River comes into the James, City Point was the terminus for the City Point Railroad that connected Petersburg, Virginia, to the James River. As early as 1 April 1864, Union major general Benjamin Butler recognized the location's possible importance in supplying an army operating against Richmond from the south. Lieutenant General Ulysses S. Grant gave Butler instructions to seize it and begin operations against Richmond so as to divide Robert E. Lee's army in preparation for Grant's campaign from the north.

Because of the buildup of Federal troops at Fort Monroe and the reported visit of Grant to Butler there in early April, Lee anticipated a move on City Pont during the second week of April 1864. As a result, he instructed that defenses south of Richmond and at Petersburg be strengthened.

Butler started up the James with the Army of the James at about dawn on 5 May 1864. The first action of his men occurred when Brigadier General Edward Wild and his African-American brigade took possession of Wilson's Wharf on the north bank of the James because the high ground overlooking the wharf commanded the channel. They faced no resistance. The remainder of the army continued upriver aboard their transports.

A brigade of Brigadier General Edward Hincks's African-American division commanded by Colonel Samuel Duncan was assigned the job of being the first to land at City Point. At the wharf, the men saw a soldier exchange ship unloading recently exchanged Confederate prisoners. They also saw Confederate signalers on a bluff overlooking the wharf sending messages to another signal station in the direction of Petersburg. As a result, the troops landed quickly and hurried up the bluff, where they captured the signalmen at approximately 4:00 P.M. The Federal troops immediately lowered the Confederate flag and raised the U.S. flag. They then signaled the remainder of the army still in the river that City Point had been secured.

Wharves at City Point after the explosion of ordnance barges, 4 August 1864 (*Library of Congress*)

City Point was a very small town with virtually no businesses and few homes. Hincks took the largest house for his headquarters and began securing the defenses of the town toward Petersburg, with Federal gunboats protecting him on the river side. The remainder of the army moved up the river to unload at Bermuda Hundred Landing a few miles up the James River.

In addition to Bermuda Hundred, City Point became over the next few weeks another threatened point of invasion into the interior toward Petersburg. Major General George Pickett, the Confederate commander south of Richmond, knew that he did not have the resources to deal with threats from both positions. On 9 May he had to try when Hincks moved out of City Point along the Appomattox River to divide Confederate attention in the midst of Butler's advance from Bermuda Hundred. Hincks withdrew back to City Point at the end of the day.

During the next two weeks, City Point became the base for cavalry raids against the railroads around Petersburg. However, the failure of Butler's Bermuda Hundred campaign caused Grant at the end of May to order that troops be withdrawn down the James and that City Point be the farthest point on the river held by Federal troops.

In June 1864, City Point became the main supply base for Grant's entire army during what would become the siege of Petersburg. Supplying an army of over 100,000, the expanded wharves of the once sleepy little tobacco port became one of the busiest ports in the country. Throughout the campaign, City Point also remained the primary communication point between Grant and the rest of the nation, particularly Washington. It was also the arrival and embarkation point for President Abraham Lincoln when he visited Grant during the next year.

—*David S. Heidler and Jeanne T. Heidler*

See also Bermuda Hundred Campaign; Butler, Benjamin Franklin; Hinks, Edward; Pickett, George.

For further reading:
Robertson, William Glenn. *Back Door to Richmond; The Bermuda Hundred Campaign, April–June 1864* (1987).

CIVIL LIBERTIES, C.S.A.

The Confederate Constitution held the same guarantees for personal liberties as the amended U.S. Constitution. At his inauguration as president of the Confederacy in February 1861, Jefferson Davis stressed that point. He knew that backing for secession had not been solid, especially among plain folk. Many remained strongly pro-Union. Even after Lincoln's call for an invasion of the South, signs of disloyalty to the Confederacy persisted. In May, an Alabama friend warned Davis that there were many small farmers insisting that they would "fight for no rich man's slaves." Davis was well aware of his precarious position. He needed to maintain what support there was for the new government, and he intended to tread lightly where civil liberties were concerned.

Nevertheless, by early 1862, largely from fear of internal dissent, Congress and the Davis administration were imposing restrictions on civil liberties. In January, Congress made it unlawful for the press to publish news of military operations. But Davis was reluctant to enforce the act because it might alienate newspaper editors. In the North, many editors, aligned as they were with one political party or the other, usually remained silent when the government shut down rival newspapers. The Confederacy's lack of a party system meant that Southern editors tended to support each other on freedom of the press issues. Confederate authorities closed only one paper, the ardently pro-Union *Knoxville Whig*, edited by William G. Brownlow. Davis was not always so restrained.

In February, Congress authorized Davis to declare martial law and suspend habeas corpus. Soon after, it allowed generals in the field on their own authority to impose martial law. Civilians could now be arrested and held without charge. Even when they were charged, they could be tried in military courts. Richmond was one of the first cities that Davis placed under martial law. Its military governor, General John H. Winder, was soon rounding up civilians he considered dangerous. Among them was the Reverend Alden Bosserman, who had publicly prayed for Confederate defeat. Another was John Minor Botts, a former U.S. congressional representative. His crime had been openly declaring neutrality. Arrests of civilians became so frequent that the second floor of Richmond's Castle Thunder military prison was reserved for them.

In April, Davis asked for military conscription and Congress enacted the law for it. For non-slaveholding whites, it meant that they would be forced to fight for the "rich man's slaves" whether they wanted to or not. Even more galling was that men of wealth could avoid the draft by hiring a substitute or paying the government an exemption fee. And there was the infamous twenty-slave law, which virtually excused planters from the draft outright. From that point on, for an ever-increasing number of Southerners the conflict was a rich man's war. That seemed especially evident in the newspapers. One advertisement for a substitute offered "a good price" payable "in cash, land, or negro property." Another read: "WIFE WANTED—by a young man of good habits, plenty of money, good looking and legally exempt from Confederate service."

Reaction to conscription in general and the twenty-slave law in particular was swift and direct. When several draft evaders in Randolph County, Alabama, were arrested, an angry mob attacked the jail and set the prisoners free. Near Buena Vista, Georgia, a band of draft dodgers armed themselves and swore that they would die before being forced into Confederate service. Even Vice President Alexander H. Stephens called conscription, martial law, and habeas corpus restrictions dangerous violations of the Confederate Constitution that did little more than undermine public support. Governor Joseph E. Brown of Georgia, claiming states' rights, also opposed the Confederate draft, but declared one himself for the state militia. Planters easily avoided Brown's draft by bribing state enrolling officers or using their influence in local courts to have themselves declared exempt. One way or another, men of wealth had little trouble avoiding military duty, state or Confederate. That fact reinforced the sentiment among the general Southern population of its being a rich man's war.

Like conscription, the Confederacy's confiscation of private property, or impressment, turned many Southerners against the government. Not only did many Southerners have an aversion to the government's taking what it wanted at will, but they knew that impressment agents frequently sold goods on the open market and pocketed the proceeds. James Bush headed a committee of citizens in Early County, Georgia, who warned that corruption among impressment officials was so widespread that it would "ultimately alienate the affections of the people from the government." Sometimes the abuse did not end with simple corruption. Letters poured into government offices complaining of impressment gangs who shot up livestock and tore down fences. One victim remarked that they did more harm than the Yankees.

Though no member of any class held impressment in high regard, and many argued that it was unconstitutional, the common people were concerned that the wealthy did not contribute their fair share. With planters devoting much of their acreage to cotton, impressment fell heaviest on the general population. They were mostly subsistence farmers who tended to grow more produce, which was what the army needed. It seemed that only when their farms were stripped bare did impressment agents turn to the plantations. Even then, planters were reluctant to part with their surplus. Some used political connections to avoid impressment. Others simply hid their supplies. One soldier recalled how planters "would hide their wagons under straw piles, and carry off their horses....Some of these men [are] rich—worth fifty thousand dollars."

As reluctant as planters were to hand over produce and livestock, they were even more unwilling to part with their slaves. The government confiscated slaves for work on entrenchments and other fortifications, but paid slaveholders for their services. And if a slave died under impressment, the owner was paid $2,500. Widows and orphans of deceased soldiers enjoyed nowhere near that compensation for their loss. Still, planters complained vigorously. If they had some political influence, they could often avoid having their slaves taken at all. Alabama planter John Horry Dent went through the state's governor to have his slaves excused from work on fortifications at Mobile. When the city fell to Union forces in August 1864, however, Dent condemned its defenders for lacking resolution and courage.

Planters' unwillingness to materially support the war only reinforced the attitude of its being a rich man's war. Though there were questions about impressment's constitutionality, the issue for most Southerners was much larger. A cause that sustained corruption and planter profits at the expense of the lives and liberties of the general population could hardly sustain widespread support. And it did not. In the end, desertion and disaffection among Southerners contributed decisively to Confederate defeat.

—David Williams

See also Brownlow, William G.; Castle Thunder; Class Conflict, C.S.A.; Conscription, C.S.A.; Constitution, C.S.A.; Desertion; Impressment.

For further reading:

Escott, Paul D. *After Secession: Jefferson Davis and the Failure of Confederate Nationalism* (1977).

Mathis, Robert Neil. "Freedom of the Press in the Confederacy: A Reality." *Historian* (1975).

Moore, Albert B. *Conscription and Conflict in the Confederacy, Southern Classics Series* (1924; reprint, 1996).

Neely, Mark E., Jr. *Southern Rights: Political Prisoners and the Myth of Confederate Constitutionalism* (1999).

Robbins, John B. "The Confederacy and the Writ of Habeas Corpus." *Georgia Historical Quarterly* (1971).

Robinson, William M., Jr. *Justice in Gray: A History of the Judicial System of the Confederate States of America* (1941).

Tatum, Georgia Lee. *Disloyalty in the Confederacy* (1934; reprint, 1970).

Williams, David. *Rich Man's War: Class, Caste, and Confederate Defeat in the Lower Chattahoochee Valley* (1998).

CIVIL LIBERTIES, U.S.A.

The Lincoln administration's first violations of civil liberties came shortly after the war began. In several regions, mainly the border states, Lincoln suspended the writ of habeas corpus, which had been a constitutional protection of citizens against imprisonment without charge or trial. A number of pro-Confederate Marylanders, including Baltimore's mayor and the archsecessionist John Merryman, were thrown in jail without a warrant only weeks after the firing on Fort Sumter. Supreme Court Chief Justice Roger Taney, responding to the arrests with *Ex parte Merryman*, insisted that Lincoln had no constitutional authority to suspend the writ. Lincoln ignored the decision but made arrests sparingly, hoping that the mere threat of arbitrary imprisonment would be enough to keep dissenters at bay.

Such threats proved less effective as the war became increasingly unpopular. Deserters became a problem for the army and it was increasingly difficult to find recruits to take their places. By September 1862, Lincoln felt compelled to announced his preliminary Emancipation Proclamation and accept the services of black troops. It was not a position most white Northerners were eager to support, and opposition to the war rose dramatically. Even less popular than emancipation was military conscription, which went into effect early the next year. Northerners, especially those of the working class, already feared an influx of blacks from the South if slavery were to be abolished. For them, it would certainly mean greater job competition and perhaps lower wages. Now many would be forced to fight for slavery's end against their will. Even those who supported emancipation saw deep contradictions in holding a military draft during a war that was, at least in part, for liberty.

Opponents of Lincoln's policies became increasingly vocal in the wake of emancipation and the draft. Lincoln responded with more than words. Anticipating the firestorm of hostility, Lincoln suspended the writ of habeas corpus throughout the North just days after he announced emancipation. He defined treason very loosely as overt or implied, and in some areas, often far from the battle lines, allowed civilians to be tried by military courts. Even silence was no protection for dissenters. Said Lincoln, "The man who stands by and says nothing when the peril of his government is discussed cannot be misunderstood. If not hindered he is sure to help the enemy." Freedom of speech was trampled underfoot as Lincoln moved against dissenters. A number of newspapers critical to his administration, such as the *New York World* and the *Philadelphia Evening Journal*, were forced to suspend operations. Others, like the German-language antiwar paper *National Zeitung*, were denied use of the postal service. Thousands upon thousands of Lincoln's critics were arrested without warrant. Persons suspected of treason were sometimes tortured, a violation of the Constitution's protection against cruel and unusual punishment. Some were handcuffed and suspended by their wrists. Others were hosed down with painful jets of water. One man was subjected to this water torture for two hours until it finally broke his skin. Secretary of State William H. Seward, and probably Lincoln himself, knew of the torture. But no directives against such treatment ever came from the administration.

In trying to suppress dissent, Lincoln and other Republicans were often motivated more by politics than by patriotism. They tended to paint their opponents with a broad brush of treason, and people sometimes suffered arrest and worse for no other crime than being a Democrat. The antiwar or Peace Democrats were special Republican targets. As a sign of protest against Lincoln's suppression of civil liberties, Peace Democrats wore pennies with the head of "Liberty" emblazoned on them. This practice gave rise to the term "Copperheads," though Republicans equated them with the poisonous snake of that name. Most outspoken of the Copperheads was Clement L. Vallandigham of Ohio. A congressman at the war's beginning, he opposed every war measure Lincoln pursued and was especially critical of Lincoln's record on civil liberties. Vallandigham was on a collision course with the administration.

The inevitable clash came in 1863 when General Ambrose Burnside issued General Order No. 38. Burnside commanded a military district covering the states of Ohio, Indiana, Illinois, Michigan, and that part of Kentucky east of the Tennessee River. Though the region encompassed no battlefront, his order made clear that anyone who so much as implied treasonable sentiments would be tried not in a civil court but before a military commission. Vallandigham, running for his party's nomination to the governor's seat, decided to challenge Burnside's order directly. On 1 May he delivered an antiwar speech at Mt. Vernon, Ohio, in violation of General Order No. 38, calling the order itself unconstitutional. Vallandigham was arrested a few days later and put on trial for treason. Even prosecution witnesses said Vallandigham had denounced violent resistance to the law, saying that voters should use the ballot box to affect change. He was nevertheless convicted of treason and banished to the Confederacy. Vallandigham quickly moved to Canada and continued his antiwar efforts from exile.

Reaction to the Vallandigham case was more critical than most Republicans had expected. In some cases it was violent. The day after Vallandigham's arrest, a mob of outraged Democrats in Dayton, Ohio, attacked the Republican newspaper office and burned it to the ground. There were even Republicans who thought that arresting Vallandigham went too far. Horace Greeley, while supporting some limits on freedom of speech and the press, saw more loyal dissent than treason in Vallandigham. George William Curtis, a strong supporter of Lincoln's policies from the beginning, also opposed the arrest. And Joel Parker, the Harvard law professor who had written a strong defense of Lincoln in the *Merryman* case, now called his administration a military despotism.

Stung by the Vallandigham backlash and rising anti-administration sentiment, Lincoln and the Republicans toned down their partisan rhetoric. Civil liberties still suffered, but now victims were selected more carefully. And, afraid of losing power altogether in the 1864 elections, Republicans sought an alliance with Democrats who supported the war. Together they formed the Union Party, nominating Lincoln for a second term and Democrat Andrew Johnson of Tennessee as his running mate. Even with backing from the War Democrats, Lincoln carried the November election by only 10 percent of the popular vote.

Trials by military commission continued in the months after Appomattox, mostly in the South. Finally, in the spring of 1866, the Supreme Court declared such trials unconstitutional where civil courts were in operation. Chastising Lincoln's wartime policies, the court ruled that neither civil courts nor the writ of habeas corpus could be suspended in areas not under martial law and that martial law could be declared only in an area of actual combat.

—*David Williams*

See also Conscription, U.S.A.; Copperheads; *Ex parte Merryman; Ex parte Milligan*; Habeas Corpus, Writ of (U.S.A.); Supreme Court, U.S.; Taney, Roger B.; Vallandigham, Clement L.

For further reading:

Hyman, Harold M. "A More Perfect Union": The Impact of the Civil War and Reconstruction on the Constitution (1973).

Klement, Frank. The Limits of Dissent: Clement Vallandigham and the Civil War (1970).

———. Dark Lanterns: Secret Political Societies, Conspiracies, and Treason Trials in the Civil War (1984).

Neely, Mark E., Jr. The Fate of Liberty: Abraham Lincoln and Civil Liberties (1991).

Paludan, Phillip S. A Covenant with Death: The Constitution, Law and Equality in the Civil War Era (1975).

———. A People's Contest: The Union and the Civil War, 1861–1865 (1988).

Randall, James G. Constitutional Problems under Lincoln (1951).

CLARK, CHARLES
(1811–1877)
Confederate general; governor of Mississippi

Born outside Cincinnati, Ohio, and educated in Kentucky, Clark, as a young man, moved to Mississippi, where he taught school and read law. After admission to the bar, he practiced law and became active in Mississippi Whig politics. From 1838 until 1844 he served in the state legislature. Upon the outbreak of the Mexican-American War, he raised a state regiment, but apparently never saw combat. After the war, Clark returned to state politics and, during the sectional controversies that resulted in the Compromise of 1850, remained true to his Whig affiliation and supported the compromise measures put forth by Henry Clay.

As the sectional crisis heated up again in the late 1850s, however, Clark began to rethink his Unionist sentiments, switched to the Democratic Party, and became an advocate for secession. From 1856 to 1861 he again served in the state legislature and in 1860 served as a state delegate to the Democratic National Convention in Charleston, South Carolina. Clark was defeated by a moderate in his bid to attend the state secession convention, but upon Mississippi's withdrawal, he was chosen as one of the four brigadier generals of state forces. He quickly rose to the rank of major general of state troops. On 22 May 1861, Clark accepted a commission as a brigadier general in the Confederate army and was mustered into service in Pensacola, Florida. Sent to Virginia, he had no more than arrived before receiving orders to report to Kentucky.

On 1 November 1861, Clark took command of the Mississippi brigade under Albert Sidney Johnston in Kentucky. On his way to Kentucky, Clark stopped briefly in east Tennessee to aid in the suppression of a revolt of Unionists there. After Clark had arrived in Kentucky, his brigade was placed in William J. Hardee's Central Army of Kentucky as part of John B. Floyd's division. By March, however, Clark had assumed command of the 1st Division within Leonidas Polk's corps.

Clark commanded the 1st Division at Shiloh, where he received a wound in the hip. After his recovery, he and his division served in John C. Breckinridge's corps and participated in the Confederate offensive against Baton Rouge on 5 August 1862. Clark commanded the right in the failed attack and was so severely wounded that his men could not move him from the field when they retreated. As a result, Union forces captured and sent him to New Orleans for medical treatment. His commander, Breckinridge, tried to have money and clothing sent to him behind Union lines to make his captivity more comfortable, and his wife came to New Orleans to nurse him. Nevertheless, he failed to regain the full use of his legs and had to use crutches for the rest of his life.

Released from federal confinement in February 1863, Clark returned to Mississippi. As a result of his lack of mobility and bad health, he resigned his commission in October 1863 and was elected governor of Mississippi. He remained in that position until the end of the war.

As governor, Clark was active in communicating with Confederate military officials regarding the defense of the state. He protested the impressment of slaves into Confederate service, but he enthusiastically provided state troops whenever called for by Confederate officers. When Clark heard that Confederate forces in Mississippi had surrendered to the Union in May 1865, he called the legislature into special session to deal with the crisis. In this brief session, Clark delivered to the legislature an address in which he expressed horror and regret at the assassination of Abraham Lincoln. Shortly after this address, Union military forces arrested and sent him to Fort Pulaski, Georgia, where he remained imprisoned until October 1865.

Clark returned to his plantation and law practice in Mississippi. Toward the end of and immediately after Reconstruction, he again became active in Mississippi politics. He died in December 1877.

—*David S. Heidler and Jeanne T. Heidler*

See also Baton Rouge, Battle of; Mississippi.

CLARK, HENRY TOOLE
(1808–1874)

Confederate governor of North Carolina

Henry Toole Clark was born in Edgecombe County, North Carolina, in 1808. His father, James West Clark, was a former congressman. Young Clark entered the University of North Carolina at the age of fourteen and graduated in 1826. Clark read law in Raleigh and was admitted to the bar, although he rarely practiced. He spent several years running his family's plantation and business affairs.

In 1850, Clark entered public life as colonel of the 21st Regiment of North Carolina Militia. In the same year, he was elected to the state senate as a Democrat. He remained in the senate until the outbreak of the Civil War, and he was elected speaker of the senate in 1858 and in 1860.

Clark's post as speaker led him to the governor's office. By June 1861, Governor John Ellis was in such poor health that Clark was serving as acting governor before he officially took office upon Ellis's death on 7 July 1861. North Carolina had no lieutenant governor then, and the speaker of the senate was next in line of succession to the governor. Clark's term as governor lasted until his original term as senator was up, at the time of the elections in August 1862. Clark continued to preside as speaker of the senate while he was governor.

Clark was blamed by many when Union forces captured Hatteras Inlet, New Bern, and other strategic sites in eastern North Carolina in late 1861 and early 1862. The disasters were largely beyond his control, because nearly all of North Carolina's soldiers were being sent to Virginia, leaving few troops besides raw recruits and militia. His appeals to Richmond for more troops never yielded enough help.

Clark generally cooperated with the Davis administration. He tried to remain above politics and to avoid controversy if possible. While he was not a dynamic leader, nearly everyone acknowledged his honesty and good character. His greatest talents were not as a political leader, but as an administrator. He worked diligently and efficiently to recruit and supply his state's Confederate troops. North Carolina's soldiers were generally the best uniformed and equipped in the Confederacy, and much of the credit is due to the work of Clark and Brigadier General James G. Martin, the state's adjutant general. Clark's actions included encouraging state contracts with firms to manufacture gunpowder and arms; soliciting civilian donations of clothing, food, and medical supplies; and dispatching an agent to buy arms in Europe in the fall of 1861. One of Clark's innovations was an agreement with the Confederate quartermaster department that North Carolina would clothe its own troops and receive commutation money from the Confederate government in exchange.

Clark could not avoid becoming embroiled in political controversy; the opposition Conservatives (mainly former Whigs) identified him with the recent military defeats in the state and the increasingly unpopular policies of the Davis administration. Clark's own faction, the Confederate Party (mainly former Democrats), did not nominate him to run for governor at the end of his term.

Clark returned to his home near Tarboro after leaving office. On 20 July 1863, he was nearly captured during a Union cavalry raid on Tarboro. Clark was just about to take his daily horseback ride when the enemy troops came into sight. They pursued, but were unable to catch him, though Union soldiers did plunder and vandalize his house. The *State Journal* of Raleigh reported on 12 August 1863 that Clark's house was "shamefully abused. [The raiders] ransacked the house from top to bottom, breaking open trunks, chests, and drawers." Later that day, the Union soldiers set fire to the town bridge as they withdrew. Clark was reportedly one of the first volunteers to begin fighting the fire.

Clark was elected to the state senate for a final term in 1866, but thereafter he played little role in state politics. He spent much of his later life studying North Carolina history and sharing his knowledge with other historians. Clark died on 17 April 1874.

Clark's plantation just outside Tarboro was called Hilma, a name created by joining the first letters of his children's names. Clark's home was sold after his death and, in 1899, his plantation became one of the first golf courses in North Carolina.

—*David A. Norris*

See also North Carolina.

For further reading:

Barrett, John G. *The Civil War in North Carolina* (1963).
Mercer, Garry Carnell. "The Administration of Governor Henry Toole Clark, 1861–1862" (M.A. thesis, 1965).
Powell, William S., ed. *Dictionary of North Carolina Biography* (1979–1994).
"Tarboro" *Southerner* (27 February 1908).

CLASS CONFLICT, C.S.A.

Class animosities that surfaced in the Confederacy had been building for some time. Wealth was largely synonymous with slaveholding in the antebellum South, and three-fourths of Southern whites owned no slaves. By the 1850s, despite their racist fears, resentment among nonslaveholders toward the slave system was on the rise. That resentment was most forcefully expressed by Hinton Rowan Helper, son of a slaveless North Carolina farmer. Helper argued in *The Impending Crisis of the South*, published in 1857, that slavery kept most white Southerners locked in poverty. Such class-based discontent was beginning to spread panic among slaveholders. One planter asked nervously, "If the poor whites realized that slavery kept them poor, would they not vote it down?" When Lincoln was elected in 1860, promising only to restrict slavery's expansion, slaveholders thought that his position could encourage the development of a Southern antislavery movement. A slavery defender warned that, with Lincoln in the White House, poor farmers might one day soon have an "Abolition party" in the South. Driven largely by that fear, slaveholders and their political allies forced their way out of the Union state by state. Most Southerners had, in fact, opposed immediate secession. A leading South Carolina secessionist admitted that popular support for leaving the Union was weak. "But whoever waited for the common people when a great move was to be made—We must make the move and force them to follow."

Though there was some initial enthusiasm for the Richmond government after Lincoln's call for invasion, it was not enough to sustain a war effort. As early as the fall of 1861 it was difficult to get volunteers for the army, and desertion was already becoming a problem. The Confederacy's response served only to highlight class disparities. In April 1862, it enacted a military draft that wealthy men could avoid by hiring a substitute or paying an exemption fee. Even worse, slaveholders with twenty or more slaves were automatically exempt from the draft. Said Private Sam Watkins of this twenty-slave law: "It gave us the blues…and there was raised the howl of 'rich man's war, poor man's fight.'" What the planters wanted, said one Alabama farmer, was "to git you pupt up and go to fight for their infurnal negroes and after you do there fighting you may kiss there hine parts for o they care."

Cotton overproduction was another source of class resentment. Though cotton growing declined during the war, planters never devoted enough land to food production. When citizens in Cuthbert, Georgia, criticized Robert Toombs for raising too much cotton, he publicly insisted that he would grow as much as he pleased. An indignant local newspaper editor shot back: "We believe Toombs, because he is rich, does pretty much what he wants…if he were a poor man he would be hanged."

Confederate class conflict as parodied in *Frank Leslie's Illustrated Newspaper* (*Library of Congress*)

Toombs was far from alone. With prices on the rise, many cotton producers and dealers were getting richer than ever. Some openly bragged that the longer the war went on the more money they made.

The inevitable result of cotton overproduction was a severe food shortage that hit women especially hard. Planters had promised to keep soldiers' families fed, but they never grew enough food to meet the need. Much of what food they did produce was sold to speculators, who priced it far beyond the reach of most of the general population. While poor families with absent fathers and husbands faced hunger, wealthy Southerners enjoyed a lifestyle hardly touched by the war. As late as March 1865, one woman described a meal at the Cook House in Columbus, Georgia, where the table was so heavy with food that it actually groaned. Such class disparities were clearly reflected in the wartime illustration shown here, and they were the major source of Southern disunity.

Desperate to avoid starvation, many women turned to theft and violence. As early as 1862, food riots began breaking out all over the South. Major urban centers such as Richmond and Mobile saw the biggest riots. In Georgia alone there were food riots in all the larger cities—Atlanta, Columbus, Macon, Augusta, and Savannah. Even small towns, such as Georgia's Thomasville and Marietta, and North Carolina's High Point and Salisbury, saw food riots. Congress responded in February 1864 by reducing the twenty-slave exemption to fifteen and mandating that exempt slaveholders

provide food at reduced prices to soldiers' families. The act helped ease food shortages and class tensions in Virginia but had little impact in the Deep South. There, planters ignored the ill-enforced law and kept growing too much cotton. The result was continued hunger and rioting through the rest of the war. In Valdosta, Georgia, a band of armed women raided the government depot and made off with a wagonload of bacon. In neighboring Miller County, a mob of fifty soldiers' wives stole a hundred sacks of corn from Colquitt's depot.

It seemed increasingly obvious to husbands that their wives were fighting a rich man's war, which made the desertion problem even worse. One Confederate officer wrote home to his wife: "I can see that discontent is growing rapidley [sic] in the ranks and I fear that unless something is done...we will have no army. The laws that have been passed generally protect the rich, and the poor begin to say it is the rich man's war and the poor man's fight, and they will not stand it." Desertion became so serious by the summer of 1863 that Jefferson Davis was begging absentees to return. If only they would, he insisted, the Confederacy could match Union armies man for man. But they did not return. A year later, Davis publicly admitted that two-thirds of Confederate soldiers were absent—most of them without leave. Many deserters joined with draft dodgers and other anti-Confederates to form guerrilla bands, sometimes called "tory" or "layout" gangs. They attacked government supply trains, burned bridges, raided local plantations, and harassed impressment agents and conscript officers. So violent did this internal civil war become that on 24 November 1863, the *Confederate Union* of Milledgeville, Georgia, wrote: "We are fighting each other harder than we ever fought the enemy." Tory gangs were most numerous in the southern hill country and pine barrens, where they all but eliminated Confederate control by 1864. The Red River Valley of Texas and Louisiana served as a haven for those resisting the Confederacy, as did the Okefenokee Swamp in south Georgia.

On 5 April 1865, only days before the Confederacy's collapse, an editorial appeared in Georgia's *Early County News* that read in part, "This has been a rich man's war and a poor man's fight. It is true there a few wealthy men in the army, but nine tenths of them hold positions, always get out of the way when they think a fight is coming on, and treat the privates like dogs....there seems to be no chance to get this class to carry muskets." Such attitudes had long since undermined support for the Richmond government, and they had a decisive impact on Confederate defeat.

—David Williams

See also Conscription, C.S.A.; Desertion; Impressment; Riots, C.S.A.; Tax-in-Kind.
For further reading:
Bailey, Fred A. *Class and Tennessee's Confederate Generation* (1987).
Baker, Robin E. "Class Conflict and Political Upheaval: The Transformation of North Carolina Politics during the Civil War." *North Carolina Historical Review* (1992).
Barney, William. *The Secessionist Impulse* (1974).
Blair, William. *Virginia's Private War: Feeding Body and Soul in the Confederacy, 1861–1865* (1998).
Durrill, Wayne K. *War of Another Kind: A Southern Community in the Great Rebellion* (1990).
Escott, Paul D. *Many Excellent People: Power and Privilege in North Carolina, 1850–1900* (1985).
Moneyhon, Carl H. "Disloyalty and Class Consciousness in Southwestern Arkansas, 1852–1865." *Arkansas Historical Quarterly* (1993).
Neely, Mark E., Jr. *Southern Rights: Political Prisoners and the Myth of Confederate Constitutionalism* (1999).
Williams, David. *Rich Man's War: Class, Caste, and Confederate Defeat in the Lower Chattahoochee Valley* (1998).
Williams, Teresa C. "'The Women Rising': Class and Gender in Civil War Georgia" (M.A. thesis, 1999).

CLASS CONFLICT, U.S.A.

Expressions of Northern class conflict during the Civil War, like those in the South, reflected not only the immediate inequities that the lower class population endured but also deep-seated animosities that had been there for years. The workers' struggle in the industrial North for decent living and working conditions was decades old. Strikes were common. So was violent repression, often at the hands of government forces. Workers tried to strengthen their position by coming together in unions. Some went further and formed their own political parties. During the Lynn, Massachusetts, strike of 1860, the largest before the Civil War, disaffected laborers founded a Workingmen's Party that carried the city elections that year.

During the first months of the secession crisis, support for or opposition to war broke down mainly along class lines. Most Northerners, especially those of the lower classes, seemed willing to let secession stand rather than resort to arms. It was primarily business elites having economic ties to the South who pressured Lincoln for war. He came under intense lobbying from financial backers and other industrialists to keep the cotton states in the Union. How else could they guarantee continued access to Southern markets and cheap cotton? Reflecting those fears, the *Boston Herald* warned on 12 November 1861 that an independent Confederacy would "impose a heavy tax upon the manufactures of the North, and an export tax upon the cotton used by northern manufacturers. In this way she would seek to cripple the North."

Such arguments carried little weight with the working class. Most of them had nothing against slavery in the South, just its extension. They certainly had no desire to put their lives in danger trying to keep the cotton states in the Union by force. One newspaper in Rochester, New York, reported on the difficulty that officers had getting recruits, despite the availability of unemployed, able-bodied men by the thousands. "We hear a great deal of talk," said the editors of the *Rochester Union*, "among the ardent platform Republicans about coercing the secessionists of the south by means of Northern soldiers, but the indications are that the fighting is to be done mostly with the tongue."

Only after the Confederacy's bombardment of Fort Sumter fired enough nationalistic fervor was Lincoln able to get the volunteers he needed to combat secession. But that fervor quickly died down after the Union defeat at Bull Run. The flow of recruits slowed to a trickle, and desertion was a constant drain on the army's personnel. By late 1862, Lincoln found it necessary to do what he had resisted for more than a year—announce an Emancipation Proclamation and accept the services of black volunteers. Most white Northerners were similarly resistant, even hostile, to emancipation. Though racism was a motivation, it was strongly bolstered by economic concerns. The working classes feared a wave of black migration from the South, which might mean greater job competition and lower wages.

Anxiety among the common people rose to a fever pitch in 1863 when Congress enacted military conscription. Now they would be forced to fight in a war many did not want for an objective they did not support. Even worse, men of wealth could avoid the draft by hiring a substitute or paying a $300 commutation fee. For many

The Albany Contracters who have "influence" at Washington, and   Their Victim.

Union class conflict, from an 1861 *Harper's Weekly* cartoon (*Library of Congress*)

workers, $300 was a year's wage. One labor leader demanded the commutation fee be repealed so wealthy men could fight their own war. But they did not. Contemporary and future captains of industry had no desire to captain troops in the field. John D. Rockefeller, Andrew Carnegie, J. P. Morgan, Philip Armour, Jay Gould, and James Mellon all bought their way out of military service. Mellon's father told him he could be a patriot without risking his own life. There were, he said, plenty of other lives worth much less.

In the summer of 1863, draft protesters in New York and other cities distributed "Song of the Conscripts," a parody of the patriotic recruiting song "We Are Coming Father Abraham." One verse went:

We're coming, Father Abraham, three hundred thousand more,
We leave our homes and firesides with bleeding hearts and sore,
Since poverty has been our crime, we bow to thy decree,
We are the poor and have no wealth to purchase liberty.

The cry of "rich man's war" swept the North that summer, and the country faced the worst riots in its history. Mobs of working class New Yorkers, men and women, roamed the streets shouting, "kill the niggers,"

and went after well-dressed gentlemen too, calling them "$300 men." They torched the draft office, razed pro-Lincoln newspapers, looted and destroyed the homes of prominent Republicans and abolitionists (including the composer of "We Are Coming Father Abraham"), burned an orphan's home for black children, and lynched at least a dozen blacks. In all, more than 100 people lost their lives during the furious rampage. Federal troops straight from the battle of Gettysburg rushed in to stop the carnage. There were similar antidraft riots in Boston, Newark, Toledo, Chicago, St. Paul, Milwaukee, and numerous other towns.

Working people also resented that the war was making rich men richer, often through graft and corruption. Military contracts frequently went to suppliers who cut costs by producing poor quality goods. Inferior wool, called "shoddy," that fell apart soon after delivery was so common that the term soon came to describe any defective equipment. The wartime illustration shown here reflects the indignation that was so widespread. Even more galling to working people was that corporate profits were soaring and prices with them, but wages lagged far behind. Labor strikes were often their result. Railroad workers in New York, riggers in Boston, and coal miners in Pennsylvania were among the laboring multitudes who fought for economic justice. Capitalists struck back hard, with government forces on their side. Lincoln's army beat down striking workers in, among other places,

Rutland, Vermont; St. Louis, Missouri; Cold Springs, New York; and Tioga County, Pennsylvania.

There was widespread resentment of such heavy-handed methods. But unlike the South, the North had a well-financed party system that channeled most lower class anger into the electoral process. Strange political bedfellows developed as Democrats and Republicans alike used the rhetoric of labor and patriotism to denigrate their opponents and garner support. In Lynn, where the Workingman's Party had been so strong, the Republicans were in control by 1863. At the national level, Republicans and War Democrats joined forces in 1864 to form the Union Party, nominating Lincoln for president and Democrat Andrew Johnson of Tennessee as his running mate. Resistance by the lower class hampered the North's war effort to some degree, but a combination of political manipulation and brute force kept class conflict from having a decisive impact.

—David Williams

See also Conscription, U.S.A.; Election of 1864; New York City Draft Riots; Riots, U.S.A.
For further reading:
Bernstein, Iver. The New York City Draft Riots: Their Significance for American Society and Politics in the Age of the Civil War (1990).
Dawley, Alan. Class and Community: The Industrial Revolution in Lynn (1976).
Fite, Emerson. Social and Industrial Conditions in the North during the Civil War (1910).
Palladino, Grace. Another Civil War: Labor, Capital, and the State in the Anthracite Regions of Pennsylvania, 1840–68 (1990).
Paludan, Phillip S. "A People's Contest": The Union and Civil War, 1861–65 (1988).
Sharkey, Robert P. Money, Class and Party: An Economic Study of Civil War and Reconstruction (1959).

CLAY, CASSIUS MARCELLUS
(1810–1903)
Emancipationist, diplomat

Cassius Marcellus Clay, one of Kentucky's most colorful personalities, was born in Madison County on 19 October 1810. His father, General Green Clay, was a wealthy landholder and slaveholder and a powerful politician. His mother, Sallie Lewis Clay, came from a prominent Virginia family. Clay attended local schools, the Madison Seminary, and St. Joseph's College in Bardstown. He entered Transylvania University in 1828 but transferred to Yale College in 1831. There he became acquainted with several New England notables, and he became concerned with the slavery question. In December 1831 he wrote his brother Brutus that "all the slave holding states must soon be free!" A William Lloyd Garrison speech influenced his thinking, but Cassius Clay never accepted abolitionism, and he defended slavery as being constitutional.

After returning to the White Hall estate in 1832, Clay completed a law degree at Transylvania. He was elected to the state house in 1835, lost in 1836, and won again in 1837 as a Whig. That was his last elective office because his mild antislavery views attracted opposition. Later he freed the slaves belonging to him, but kept those belonging to the estate; Clay was attacked by both antislavery and proslavery advocates. Six feet or more tall and of powerful physique, Clay became noted for violent encounters with opponents. A bowie knife was his favorite weapon. In 1833 he married Mary Anne Warfield, daughter of a prominent family, and they had ten children, two of whom died as infants.

In opposing slavery, Clay stressed its adverse economic effect upon individuals and the state. Although he considered slavery evil, he refused to stress anything more than gradual emancipation. When some local editors refused to print his frequent epistles, Clay began editing The True American in Lexington in 1845. Anticipating adverse reaction, he armed the building for defense but, while he was ill with typhoid fever, a Committee of Sixty shipped his press to Cincinnati.

Clay regained some popularity by going to the Mexican-American War as captain of a cavalry company, although he had opposed Texas annexation because it would allow slavery to expand. Back in Kentucky, he was severely wounded on 15 June 1849 when attacked by several men, but he managed to kill Cyrus Turner with his knife. Despite Clay's efforts, no antislavery man was elected to the 1849 constitutional convention, and the institution remained firmly fixed in Kentucky's constitution. Clay ran for governor in 1851 for an Emancipation Party. Although badly beaten, he was convinced that he had helped destroy the state Whig Party. Clay turned to the Republican Party as it emerged in the 1850s. A slaveholder who opposed slavery and an effective public speaker, Clay was an exotic figure who attracted considerable attention in the North. One of his listeners at Springfield, Illinois, on 10 July 1854 was Abraham Lincoln. With characteristic modesty, Clay claimed to have influenced Lincoln's views on slavery.

Initially, Clay supported abolitionist John G. Fee and his associates in building an antislavery community at Berea. Clay and Fee were the odd couple of the state antislavery movement. The moderate emancipationist was noted for his violent encounters; the determined abolitionist was a pacifist who prayed for mobs who dragged him from his pulpit. But Clay did not protect the Bereans when they were forced to leave in December 1859.

Clay supported John C. Frémont for president in 1856, served on the Republican National Committee, and backed Lincoln in 1860. Clay received 101 votes for vice president, but factional and sectional reasons doomed him to defeat. Clay expected to be rewarded for his efforts, possibly as secretary of war, but after being passed over for top positions he accepted the ministry to Russia. When he arrived in defenseless Washington in mid-April 1861, Clay organized Clay's battalion to help secure the city until troops arrived.

A popular figure in Russia, Clay returned to the United States in 1862 to make room for Simon Cameron. Commissioned a major general, Clay was unable to secure what he thought was a suitable command. When Lincoln sent him to Kentucky to report on the situation there, Clay assured the president that loyalists were in firm control of the state, but he reported erroneously that Kentucky would accept compensated emancipation. Back in Russia during 1863–1869, Clay claimed credit for expediting the purchase of Alaska. After his return home, Clay received an "adopted" son from Russia. Active in the Liberal Republican movement, Clay's dislike of the Radical Republicans drove him into the Democratic Party. Clay favored black voting, but rejected a social revolution for the new freemen.

After a long separation, Clay divorced his wife in 1878. He continued to be outspoken in his declining years, but eccentric behavior, such as marrying a fifteen-year-old farm girl in 1894 and refusing to pay taxes, tarnished his reputation. This legendary Kentuckian died at White Hall on 22 July 1903 during a violent storm. He was buried in Richmond, Kentucky.

—Lowell H. Harrison

See also Diplomacy, U.S.A.; Kentucky.

For further reading:

Clay, Cassius Marcellus. *Life of Cassius Marcellus Clay: Memoirs, Writings and Speeches* (1886).

Richardson, H. Edward. *Cassius Marcellus Clay: Firebrand for Freedom* (1976).

Robertson, James Rood. *A Kentuckian at the Court of the Tsars: The Ministry of Cassius Marcellus Clay to Russia* (1935).

Smiley, David L. *Lion of White Hall: The Life of Cassius Marcellus Clay* (1962).

CLAY, CLEMENT CLAIBORNE, JR.
(1816–1882)

U.S. senator; Confederate senator

Clement Claiborne Clay, Jr., was born 13 December 1816 to Clement Comer and Susanna Claiborne Withers Clay in Huntsville, Alabama. He graduated from the University of Alabama in 1835, studied law at the University of Virginia, and was admitted to the bar in 1839. In 1843, he married Virginia Caroline Tunstall and the couple made their home with the Clays in Huntsville. Politically a Jacksonian Democrat and disciple of John C. Calhoun's states' rights doctrine, Clay gained modest success in state politics, elected to successive terms in the legislature in 1842 and

1844. He also practiced law and was a judge in Madison County from 1846 to 1848. In 1853, Clay was elected to the U.S. Senate, where he opposed government land acts, veterans' pensions, and federal expenditures on internal improvements. During the debate over Kansas's admission to the Union, the Alabama senator supported the proslavery Lecompton Constitution and saw the incident as proof of the South's waning influence in Congress. In the years that followed, Clay pursued sectional interests, opposing both Douglas Democrats and Republicans. In the presidential election of 1860, Clay supported John C. Breckenridge and upon Alabama's secession he resigned his seat in the Senate.

The secession crisis took a toll on Clay's precarious health, and he spent 1861 seeking relief for his asthma, hiring out his slaves, and tending to his unstable finances. When the Alabama legislature met in November, he was elected to the Confederate Senate on the tenth ballot. Arriving in Richmond the following February 1862, Clay continued to support fiscally conservative legislation as he had throughout his career and closely allied himself with Jefferson Davis and his administration. But when Clay opposed a bill to increase soldiers' pay, both his conservatism and ties to the administration raised criticism among his constituents. From April to September of 1862, northern Alabama had been occupied by the Union army, and when the Confederacy regained the area, disaffection festered over conscription, deteriorating economic conditions, and the government's ineffectiveness. Vulnerable to these criticisms as the political climate in his home stated shifted, Clay lost his bid for reelection. But his steadfast support for Davis earned him an appointment as secret envoy to Canada in April 1864.

From his post at St. Catherines, Ontario, Clay worked with other agents and Clement L. Vallandigham to encourage Peace Democrats during the presidential campaign of 1864. He met with Horace Greeley at Niagara Falls to discuss conditions for peace, but Clay lacked the authority to negotiate. Clay also orchestrated the Confederate raid on St. Albans, Vermont. But when the raiders were later captured and tried, Clay's participation was exposed and he was forced to leave Canada for violation of neutrality laws. Returning to the Confederacy, he joined his wife as a refugee and arrived in Richmond as the Confederate government was retreating. Clay then started west, intending to flee to Mexico, but when Andrew Johnson ordered his arrest for conspiracy in the assassination of Abraham Lincoln, the former senator and agent surrendered to Federal forces. For the next year, Clay was imprisoned with Jefferson Davis at Fort Monroe, during which time Virginia Clay worked tirelessly among federal officeholders to secure her husband's release. After numerous interviews with Andrew Johnson and letters of support from Ulysses S.

Grant and Thaddeus Stevens, her efforts succeeded in obtaining Clay's release in April 1866.

When Clement and Virginia Clay returned to Alabama, they found that occupation, emancipation, and unsettled debts had destroyed their family's wealth. Their difficulties were compounded because Clement had never been financially independent from his family and his father's estate was encumbered by debts. As a result, the former senator settled in a modest farmhouse on his land outside Huntsville, where he struggled unsuccessfully with free labor and declining cotton prices and liquidated family lands and railroad stock to meet debts. He also failed in an attempt to sell insurance. With his finances and health destroyed by war, and struggling at times with alcohol, Clay withdrew from public affairs, declining to enter politics after his pardon in 1880. During the same period, Virginia Clay spent more time away from her husband and their reduced circumstances, participating in society through the charity of friends and seeking loans to relieve the couple's troubled finances. On 3 January 1882, Clement Claiborne Clay died at his farmhouse, ending a life in which a once-powerful and honored scion of an elite Southern family was broken by the revolutionary forces of the Civil War.

—*Christine Dee*

See also Clay-Clopton, Virginia Caroline Tunstall.

For further reading:

Alexander, Thomas Benjamin, and Richard E. Beringer. *The Anatomy of the Confederate Congress; A Study of the Influences of Member Characteristics on Legislative Voting Behavior, 1861–1865* (1972).

Bleser, Carol K., and Frederick M. Heath. "The Clays of Alabama; The Impact of the Civil War on a Southern Marriage." In *In Joy and Sorrow: Women, Family and Marriage in the Victorian South, 1830–1900* (1991).

Clay Family Papers. In *Records of Antebellum Southern Plantations* at Duke University Library.

Clay-Clopton, Virginia Tunstall. *A Belle of the Fifties: Memoirs of Mrs. Clay of Alabama, Covering Social and Political Life in Washington and the South, 1853–66; Put into Narrative Form by Ada Sterling* (1905; reprint, 1999).

Nuermberger, Ruth K. *The Clays of Alabama: A Planter-Lawyer-Politician Family* (1958).

Thornton, J. Mills III. *Politics and Power in a Slave Society: Alabama, 1800–1860* (1978).

Tidwell, William A. *April '65: Confederate Covert Action in the American Civil War* (1995).

CLAY, HENRY
(1777–1852)
American statesman

Born in Hanover County, Virginia, on 12 April 1777, Henry Clay moved to Lexington, Kentucky, in 1798. He had been admitted to the Virginia bar the previous year, and soon he was enjoying a prosperous legal career as a trial lawyer specializing in criminal cases. He entered politics as a Democratic-Republican in 1803, serving three years in the Kentucky legislature, after which he was appointed to fill vacated U.S. Senate seats in 1806 and again in 1810. When the second Senate term expired in 1811, he won election in his own right to the United States House of Representatives. Attesting both to his popularity and to the high rate of turnover in House membership, he was elected Speaker in his freshman term.

Although Clay nurtured presidential ambitions, it was in the national legislature that he won his greatest laurels and made his most effective contributions to the growing republic. He occupied the Speaker's chair in the House off and on for the next fifteen years, thus to hold the record for the longest service in that office during the nineteenth century. The power of the speakership was due to Clay's personality and innovations, and it could be said that he was the creator of the position as it functions to the present day. Clay, however, was hardly a martinet. Instead, his penchant for tact and conciliation made him an effective political negotiator and influential power broker even when he did not wield the appointive power of the speakership. His talents, well applied during several national crises involving slavery and sectionalism, would earn him the appellation "The Great Compromiser."

During Clay's initial service in the House, he headed the War Hawks, a faction of the Republican Party that urged war with Great Britain to protect United States neutral rights during the Napoleonic Wars. Named a commissioner on the peace delegation that negotiated the Treaty of Ghent ending the War of 1812, he returned to Congress in 1815 and again became Speaker of the House. He wanted in 1817 to become President James Monroe's secretary of state, the position many saw as the anteroom to the presidency, but John Quincy Adams received the appointment. Clay was embittered by the slight and unattractively sought to embarrass the Monroe administration at every opportunity. He even abandoned his expansionism to criticize Andrew Jackson's 1818 invasion of Spanish Florida.

Clay, however, helped to resolve the potentially dangerous national crisis that loomed in 1819 when the Missouri Territory applied for statehood. The entrance into the Union of a slave state would have upset the sectional balance between the free North and the slave South. When Northerners tried to place restrictions on slavery in Missouri as a condition of its admission, Southerners caviled. An ugly debate ensued that paralyzed Congress and foreshadowed how divisive the slavery issue would become. Clay was instrumental in securing the passage of the Missouri Compromise in 1820 that arranged for Maine's admission as a free state to balance that of Missouri. The compromise also established the parallel of 36 degrees 30 minutes of latitude as slavery's northernmost boundary in the area of the

Louisiana Purchase. This uneasy arrangement quieted the sectional controversy for the time, but its real and ongoing importance was the attempt to restrict slavery with the Missouri Compromise Line, thus to prevent the need for acrimonious debate in the future.

Although Clay owned slaves, he did not approve of slavery as an institution because he thought it at variance with American ideals of liberty. Yet he also believed that debates about slavery distracted the country from its real destiny of territorial expansion, economic growth, and internal improvements. As a nationalist who favored promoting American business through protective tariffs and encouraging economic stability through the functions of a national bank, Clay's broad interpretation of federal authority ran counter to the growing popularity of Jacksonian Democracy. Advocating limited government, supporters of Andrew Jackson were disappointed in their attempt to elect Jackson president in 1824. When Jackson achieved only a plurality over a field of three other candidates, Clay included, the contest was thrown into the House of Representatives. There Clay's enormous influence proved pivotal in electing John Quincy Adams. Adams named Clay secretary of state, prompting Jacksonians to denounce Clay's support for Adams as first bought and now paid for with a "Corrupt Bargain." The charge was incessantly repeated and helped to frustrate the Adams administration, including Clay's state department, from achieving anything significant. Jackson was overwhelmingly elected in 1828, and Clay seemed repudiated as a national leader.

In 1831 Kentucky sent him to the Senate, however, and from that vantage he would be a key player in ending another sectional crisis when the nullification movement flared in 1832. Many Southerners believed high tariffs were contrived to benefit Northern industries at the expense of Southern agriculture. South Carolina "nullifiers" finally responded by announcing that no tariffs would be collected in their ports after 1 March 1833. Jackson's promise to enforce the law, with force if necessary, had the potential of setting off civil war. Clay worked with fellow senators, including John C. Calhoun, to arrange a compromise tariff reduction that allowed Jackson and South Carolina to back away from the crisis with everyone claiming victory.

Clay's political disappointments continued, though. Jackson soundly defeated him in the 1832 presidential election. As leader of the Whig Party, he became a tenacious contender for the presidency in the 1840s, but gained the party's nomination only in 1844. The Democrat James K. Polk won the election that year. Clay's personal life was tragically affected by his son's death in the Mexican-American War, a conflict that he and other Whigs, such as freshman congressman Abraham Lincoln, opposed. Nearly destroyed with grief,

he retired to Lexington, but returned to the Senate in 1849 to help avert yet another sectional crisis.

Clay was indispensable in resolving the controversies that broke over the Union in 1850. This latest and most serious assault on national harmony was a direct result of the acquisition of western territory from Mexico. California's desire to be admitted to the Union as a free state enraged Southerners as much as the Southern demand for a more stringent fugitive slave law alarmed Northerners. Added to these troublesome questions was a move to abolish the slave trade in the District of Columbia, a border dispute between slave state Texas and the territory of New Mexico, and the question of whether the remainder of the Mexican cession (New Mexico and Utah) would be organized as free or slave territory. Clay dubbed these "the five bleeding wounds" and predicted that if they were not mended, the Union would die. In helping to design the Omnibus Bill that as the Compromise of 1850 would try to resolve all five controversies at once, he adhered to the nationalist principles that had guided him from the outset of his career. The preservation of the Union was foremost, so he had no qualms about including a fugitive slave law in the package as an incentive to Southerners to accept the essentially pro-Northern balance of the bargain.

Clay's age and health worked against him in 1850 as much as Congress and President Zachary Taylor's resistance to compromise did. Having set the wheels of conciliation in motion in such way as to garner Daniel Webster's invaluable support, Clay succumbed to exhaustion and left the realization of this last meaningful compromise to others.

He died two years later, two years after John C. Calhoun and only a few months before Daniel Webster. The three were venerated as the Great Triumvirate, and their passing marked the end of an era in American politics. With them died the foremost living memories of the Constitution as a process of concessions and temporary settlements. The new generation of politicians coming to power would ultimately find concessions impossible and would demand that settlements be permanent. Clay had predicted that the Compromise of 1850 would, like the Missouri Compromise, quell the slavery debate for another thirty years. When he died on 29 June 1852, the Union had less than a decade before slavery would provoke the secession crisis that led to the Civil War. One of the reasons was that Clay and men like him were no more.

—*David S. Heidler and Jeanne T. Heidler*

See also Calhoun, John Caldwell; Fugitive Slave Act; Webster, Daniel

For further reading:

Eaton, Clement. *Henry Clay and the Art of American Politics* (1962).

Mayo, Bernard. *Henry Clay* (1937).

Poage, George R. *Henry Clay and the Whig Party* (1965).

Remini, Robert V. *Henry Clay: Statesman for the Union* (1991).
Van Deusen, Glyndon G. *The Life of Henry Clay* (1979).

CLAY-CLOPTON, VIRGINIA CAROLINE TUNSTALL
(1825–1915)
Author and suffragist

Virginia Caroline Tunstall was born in North Carolina on 16 January 1825, the daughter of Peyton Randolph Tunstall and Ann Arrington Tunstall, and was raised by maternal relatives in Tuscaloosa, Alabama. She graduated in 1840 from the Female Academy in Nashville and returned to Tuscaloosa, where her vivacity, along with her family's status, made her popular and attracted the attention of Clement Claiborne Clay, Jr. After a brief courtship, the couple married in 1843, and Virginia Clay accompanied her husband to his family's home in Huntsville, Alabama, where she resided for the next decade.

During the ensuing years, Clay only briefly occupied a home of her own, as her husband failed to profit from his law practice and her property was insufficient for their support. But when her husband was elected to the U.S. Senate in 1853, Clay achieved independence from her in-laws, accompanying her husband to Washington, D.C. Shortly after her arrival in the capital, she gave birth to a stillborn daughter. Thereafter childless, Clay played a leading role in society that would have been impossible for most women with families. Her circle included President Franklin Pierce, Jefferson Davis and Varina Davis, and James and Mary Chesnut. During this time, Clay also served as surrogate mother for numerous female relatives, orchestrating their entrance into the elite society she presided over.

As sectional tensions mounted, Clay continued to lead Washington society, but in 1860, political tensions had damaged her husband's precarious health, forcing the Clays to leave Washington. The couple returned to Huntsville, summering in the mountains and traveling to Louisiana to relieve Clement's asthma. By January 1861, the Clays returned to Washington as Alabama seceded from the Union. As a staunch advocate of states' rights and immediate secession, Clement Clay resigned his Senate seat, and the couple returned to Huntsville. When her husband was elected to the Confederate Senate in 1861, Clay accompanied him to Richmond in February 1862. This marked the beginning of her life as a war refugee, for Huntsville was occupied by Federal forces in April 1862. For most of the war, Clay lived among friends and relatives in Georgia and South Carolina, at times visiting her husband in Richmond and participating in society at the Confederate capital. Elitist and extravagant, Virginia Clay neither participated in wartime charities nor economized, but instead devoted her time to socializing and maintaining family relationships. After Lincoln's assassination, her husband was imprisoned for alleged conspiracy, and Clay traveled between Huntsville and Washington, intervening with President Andrew Johnson and other leading politicians on her husband's behalf. In May 1866, her efforts succeeded and her husband was released.

Returning to their home, the Clays found the family's wealth destroyed and their political influence reduced. In the years that followed, Clay adapted better to postwar changes than did her husband. While her husband struggled to secure a living from their modest farm, she maintained relationships, participated in society through the charity of friends, and secured loans to improve their finances. While her penchant for society remained intact, her self-reliance increased after the war, and she became the stronger spouse while her husband collapsed financially and emotionally. Capitalizing on her husband's past influence, she participated in Democratic politics. She also preferred her own apartment in Huntsville to the isolation of the farm where her husband resided. But despite these changes, the Clays marriage remained intimate and committed and when Clement died in 1882, Virginia eulogized him lovingly. In 1887, she married Alabama Supreme Court justice David Clopton, a former colleague of Clement C. Clay, Jr. and moved to Montgomery until her second husband's death 1892.

Virginia Clay-Clopton, as she referred to herself, returned to the farm outside Huntsville and remained involved in politics. Convinced of women's talents for politics and the necessity of women's achieving economic independence, she joined the campaign for women's suffrage, serving as president of the Alabama Equal Suffrage Association from 1896 through 1900. She was equally committed to preserving the antebellum and Confederate memories and began writing her memoirs in 1900. *A Belle of the Fifties*, edited by New York journalist Ada Sterling, was published in 1904 and joined a growing genre of Southern women's wartime memoirs. But sales proved disappointing, largely because *Belle* was quickly eclipsed by Mary Boykin Chesnut's *Diary from Dixie*. Although it has taken almost a century, *Belle* has become valued for its insight into both the antebellum lives of elite Southerners and one woman's attempt to memorialize that world in the postwar decades. Virginia Clay-Clopton died in 1915, yet her life and memoirs testify to the war's impact on women's lives and how women's voices have transformed our understanding of the Civil War.

—Christine Dee

See also Chesnut, Mary Boykin; Clay, Clement Claiborne, Jr.
For further reading:
Bleser, Carol K., and Frederick M. Heath. "The Clays of

Alabama; The Impact of the Civil War on a Southern Marriage." In *In Joy and Sorrow: Women, Family and Marriage in the Victorian South, 1830–1900* (1991).

Clay Family Papers. In *Records of Antebellum Southern Plantations at Duke University Library.*

Clay-Clopton, Virginia. *A Belle of the Fifties: Memoirs of Mrs. Clay of Alabama, Covering Social and Political Life in Washington and the South, 1853–66; Put into Narrative Form by Ada Sterling* (1905).

Nuermberger, Ruth K. *The Clays of Alabama: A Planter-Lawyer-Politician Family* (1958).

Wiley, Bell Irvin. *Confederate Women.* No. 38 of *Contributions in American History* (1975).

CLAYTON, HENRY DELAMAR
(1827–1889)
Confederate general

Born in Pulaski County, Georgia, the son of Nelson Clayton and Sara Carruthers Clayton, the younger Clayton graduated from Emory and Henry College in Virginia and began the study of law in Alabama. He began the practice of law in Clayton, Alabama, in 1849 and became involved in Alabama Democratic politics. As a member of the Alabama legislature, he was a strong proponent of states' rights.

At the formation of the Confederate States of America, Clayton enlisted in the Confederate army as a private and was sent to Pensacola, Florida. He did not remain a private for long. At the end of March 1861, Clayton was made the colonel of the 1st Alabama Regiment. The following year, Clayton raised and assumed command of the 39th Alabama Infantry and moved his regiment north to join Braxton Bragg in Kentucky.

Not arriving in time to participate at Perryville, Clayton commanded his regiment at Stones River, where he was seriously wounded. After a lengthy recuperation, Clayton was promoted to brigadier general in April 1863 and took command of the unit known as the Alabama brigade. He commanded this unit at Chickamauga in September 1863 as part of Alexander P. Stewart's division.

Upon Stewart's promotion to lieutenant general the following year and his assumption of the command of Leonidas Polk's corps, Clay assumed command of Stewart's division. In July 1864 he received a promotion to major general. Having already fought in the early phases of the Atlanta campaign, Clayton distinguished himself in the latter stages in the battles around that city.

After the fall of Atlanta, Clayton and his division moved north with General John Bell Hood into Tennessee. Though his division did not take part in the battle of Franklin, Clayton and his men were conspicuous in their bravery at Nashville in December 1864. Clayton and his division were commended for their devotion to duty in guarding the retreat from Nashville. In early 1865, Clayton joined Joseph E. Johnston in

the Carolinas and surrendered with Johnston's army in April 1865.

After the war, Clayton returned to Alabama, where he returned to his life as a planter and attorney. Beginning in 1866, he served for almost twenty years as an Alabama circuit judge before retiring to accept the position as the president of the University of Alabama. He died in that position at Tuscaloosa.

—*David S. Heidler and Jeanne T. Heidler*

See also Nashville, Battle of.
For further reading:
Williams, Margaret. "Henry D. Clayton: His Congressional Career" (M.A. thesis, 1942).

CLAYTON, POWELL
(1833–1914)
Union cavalry commander

Powell Clayton was born in Bethel County, Pennsylvania, in August 1833. He was educated at the Partridge Military Academy in Bristol, Pennsylvania, and later studied civil engineering in Wilmington, Delaware. In 1855 Clayton moved to Leavenworth, Kansas, and, four years later, he was elected city engineer and surveyor.

Politically, Clayton was a pro-Union Democrat who voted for Stephen A. Douglas for president in 1860. One biographer, writing of Clayton in 1861, noted that his "weather-beaten face, receding hairline, and unkempt mustache and goatee made him appear older than his twenty-seven years."

At the outbreak of the Civil War, Clayton joined the Union army and was made captain of Company E of the 1st Kansas Infantry. His company took part in the battle of Wilson's Creek near Springfield, Missouri, on 10 August 1861. Clayton fought bravely but failed to hear a crucial command to retreat and continued to advance his company while the rest of the regiment was retiring. He literally had to fight his way off the battlefield, and his company suffered more casualties than any other unit involved in the battle. Despite this stumbling start, Clayton soon developed a reputation for courage and coolness under fire. The *Leavenworth Daily Times* referred to him as "one of the bravest, most energetic and dashing officers in the service."

After Wilson's Creek, Clayton was promoted to lieutenant colonel and given command of the 5th Kansas Cavalry. The 5th Kansas moved into Arkansas as part of the Union force that occupied Helena in July 1862. When Confederate forces attacked Helena in July 1863, Clayton's command completely thwarted the northernmost wing of the three-pronged Confederate advance and contributed to the decisive Union victory. In the late summer of 1863, the 5th Kansas participated in the campaign to capture the

Arkansas state capital at Little Rock. The city fell to Union forces on 10 September 1863.

That month, Clayton and about 550 men from the 5th Kansas and the 1st Indiana Cavalry were ordered to Pine Bluff, Arkansas, to protect the town and its cotton from Rebel raiders and to pacify the surrounding countryside. Clayton made a favorable impression on many of the local citizens. One resident with a pronounced dislike for Federal soldiers nonetheless wrote to her son, "He [Clayton] is a very gentlemanly man and by his humane and obliging manner has quite won the people." Along with defending the town, Clayton had to provide for large numbers of former slaves who flooded into Pine Bluff after the Federal occupation.

In late October, 2,000 Confederates under Brigadier General John S. Marmaduke attacked Pine Bluff. Alerted to the Rebel advance, Clayton put about 300 of the former slaves to work barricading the courthouse square with cotton bales from a nearby warehouse and posted sharpshooters in adjacent houses and buildings to cover all avenues of approach. The Confederate attack began around 9:00 A.M. but, despite repeated attempts, the Rebels were unable to penetrate the Union defenses. Around 2:00 P.M. Marmaduke ordered a retreat. "The Federals," he wrote in his official report, "fought like devils." A Federal soldier at Pine Bluff noted, "Colonel Clayton rode master-spirit of the storm; his commanding figure and conspicuous uniform were seen whenever danger threatened, calmly issuing orders, and encouraging his men; he remained in the saddle throughout this action, and it is one of the strange anomalies of war that he was not killed."

The battle of Pine Bluff was the last major Civil War action for Clayton. Apart from occasional skirmishes and operations against guerrillas, he spent the rest of the war in Pine Bluff, preparing for another Confederate attack that never came. A few months before the war ended, President Lincoln promoted him to brigadier general.

While he was still the Federal commander at Pine Bluff, Clayton purchased a cotton plantation near the town, and in December 1865 he married Adaline McGraw, the daughter of a steamboat captain who had served as an officer in the Confederate army. In 1867, Clayton helped found the Arkansas Republican Party, and the following year, with many former Confederates disfranchised, he was elected governor. His tenure as governor (July 1868–March 1871) was one of the most turbulent and controversial in the state's history.

Clayton later served as U.S. senator from Arkansas and U.S. ambassador to Mexico, and he was a Republican National Committee representative from Arkansas for forty years. Powell Clayton died in Washington, D.C., on 25 August 1914.

—*Thomas A. DeBlack*

See also Arkansas.

For further reading:
Brown, A. D. "The Battle of Pine Bluff: The Yankee View." *Jefferson County (Arkansas) Historical Quarterly* (1989).
Burnside, William H. *The Honorable Powell Clayton* (1991).
Christ, Mark K., ed. *Rugged and Sublime: The Civil War in Arkansas* (1994).
Leslie, James W., ed. "Arabella Lanktree Wilson's Civil War Letter." *Arkansas Historical Quarterly* (1988).

CLEBURNE, PATRICK RONAYNE
(1828–1864)
Confederate general

One of the more interesting and tragic figures of the Civil War, Pat Cleburne earned a fame that derived from four circumstances: his Irish birth, his remarkable effectiveness as a division commander in the Army of Tennessee, his proposal in January 1864 that the South free its slaves and incorporate them into the Confederate army, and his dramatic death in the ill-fated charge at Franklin, Tennessee, on 30 November 1864.

Cleburne was born on 16 March 1828 near Ballincollig in County Cork, Ireland. His father was a Protestant country physician and his mother was the daughter of a prominent Irish Protestant family. His mother died when he was only 19 months old, but not long afterward his tutor became his stepmother and the woman he called "Mamma" all his life. From age twelve to fifteen, Cleburne attended the private Greenfield School, but after his father died in 1843, the family could no longer afford the school fees and he took a job as an apothecary's assistant in Mallow. Later he traveled to Dublin to seek admission to the Apothecaries College. Rejected, he joined the British army.

Cleburne spent two and one-half years in Her Majesty's 41st Regiment. It was an unhappy duty. Instead of journeying to exotic far away places, the regiment was assigned to constabulary duty to keep the peace in an Ireland ravaged by the potato famine. At age twenty-one, Cleburne inherited a small legacy from his father's estate and he used it to buy his way out of the army. He and his siblings then took passage to the United States and arrived in New Orleans on Christmas Day 1849.

The Cleburne siblings scattered to various parts of America. After a brief sojourn in Cincinnati, Cleburne settled in Helena, Arkansas, where he managed a drug store and later became a lawyer. When Arkansas seceded and war appeared imminent, Cleburne joined the local militia company and was elected its captain. When, after the outbreak of war, that company was amalgamated with nine others to form a regiment, Cleburne was elected its colonel, and when that regiment was brigaded together with three others under the overall command of the professional soldier William J. Hardee, that officer recommended Cleburne for command of the brigade.

Cleburne saw his first important action in the battle

of Shiloh on 6–7 April 1862. His brigade was in the front rank during the surprise morning attack on 6 April. Despite horrific casualties, he pressed his command forward until nightfall, when his remaining troops bivouacked on the battlefield. The next morning, Ulysses S. Grant's counterattack forced Cleburne's brigade back along with the rest of the army to its starting point. Of the 2,750 men in his six regiments, 1,043 were killed, wounded, or missing—losses of 38 percent. Cleburne's leadership in this, his first battle, was marked more by enthusiasm than judgment, but he absorbed several valuable lessons that he subsequently applied in other battles. In particular, these included using artillery with the advance and developing a specialized group of sharpshooters.

During the Confederate invasion of Kentucky in late summer, Cleburne commanded a small division consisting of his own brigade plus that of Preston Smith. His division led the advance northward from Knoxville, Tennessee, to Richmond, Kentucky, where Cleburne's small division played the central role in defeating and pursuing a disorganized Federal division on 29–30 August 1862. While preparing the attack, Cleburne was wounded in the face. A minié ball pierced his left cheek, smashed several teeth, and exited through his mouth. He recovered in time to participate on 8 October 1862 in the battle of Perryville, where again his command broke the enemy line, though this time the Federals did not abandon the battlefield. In both of these fights, Cleburne demonstrated his ability to apply practical lessons of combat by making effective use of both artillery and sharpshooters.

Promoted to major general and the permanent command of a division in November, Cleburne embarked on a series of remarkable battlefield performances. In the battle of Stones River (or Murfreesboro) on 31 December 1862–2 January 1863, his division routed the Union right wing and drove it four miles back onto the Nashville Pike. In the battle of Chickamauga on 19–20 September 1863, his division assailed with such ferocity an entrenched force significantly stronger than his own that the Federal commander, William S. Rosecrans, pulled forces from other parts of the field to reinforce the position on Cleburne's front. That opened the way for the successful Confederate counterattack that won the day.

Cleburne's military prowess was most evident in the battles for Chattanooga. On the north end of Missionary Ridge on 25 November 1863, Cleburne's single reinforced division hurled back repeated attacks by William T. Sherman's four divisions in what was supposed to be the major Federal effort that day. Failing to move Cleburne off Tunnel Hill, Sherman asked Grant for support, and Grant authorized a feint by George Thomas's corps in what became the charge up Missionary Ridge. After the rest of the Confederate army broke, Cleburne was assigned the task of defending the rear guard,

Patrick Cleburne (*Library of Congress*)

including the army's wagon trains. In that role, Cleburne's division beat off a concerted attack by Joseph Hooker's Corps at Ringgold Gap on 27 November 1863. Twice in three days, therefore, Cleburne's division saved the Army of Tennessee from destruction.

Though Cleburne's own prestige was at an all time high in the winter of 1863–1864, the Confederacy itself faced a bleak future. In an effort to solve the Confederacy's desperate problem of personnel shortages, Cleburne in January 1864 asked for a meeting of the army's senior officers. At that meeting he formally proposed that the Confederacy abolish slavery and recruit black troops for the Confederate army. He argued that, along with generating a potential half million new soldiers, such a step would pave the way for recognition by Britain and France and strip the Lincoln administration of a moral issue. The horrified reaction of most of those present showed him that this was an issue whose time had not yet come, and all present were ordered to keep the proposal a secret.

Cleburne remained an active and effective division commander in the campaign for Atlanta during May–July 1864, winning important tactical victories at Kennesaw Mountain on 27 June and the battle of Atlanta (or Bald Hill) on 22 July. In the battle of Jonesboro on 31 August–1 September 1864, he commanded a corps in battle for the only time in the war. None of those battles was a clear Confederate victory, however, and on 1 September 1864 John Bell Hood was forced to evacuate Atlanta.

Cleburne's division took the lead again during Hood's desperate invasion of Tennessee in the fall of 1864. Hood held him partly responsible for the "escape" of the enemy at Spring Hill on 29 November 1864, and both Hood and Cleburne may have conceived of the charge at Franklin the next day to be an opportunity for Cleburne to atone. In that attack, Cleburne's division held the position of dubious honor in the center of the Confederate line as it swept forward across two and one-half miles of open ground against well-prepared entrenchments. About fifty yards from the Federal line, Cleburne fell with a bullet in his chest, one of six Confederate generals to die in that assault.

—*Craig L. Symonds*

See also Atlanta Campaign; Chattanooga Campaign; Chickamauga, Battle of; Franklin, Battle of; Jonesboro, Battle of; Kennesaw Mountain, Battle of; Richmond, Kentucky, Battle of; Shiloh, Battle of; Stones River, Battle of.
For further reading:
Symonds, Craig L. *Stonewall of the West: Patrick Cleburne and the Civil War* (1997).

CLINGMAN, THOMAS LANIER
(1812–1897)
Confederate general

Thomas L. Clingman, one of North Carolina's leading public figures of the nineteenth century, was born in Huntsville, North Carolina. Because his father died when Clingman was only four years old, his mother and his father's brother raised him. Clingman excelled at the University of North Carolina, graduating first in his class in 1832. Afterward he studied law under the direction of William A. Graham, one of the state's leading Whig politicians, who encouraged the younger man's boundless political ambition.

Clingman served a term in the state house of commons in the 1830s and won election to the state senate in 1840. He warmly advocated the Whig program of internal improvements, particularly turnpikes and railroads. These were popular measures among the small farmers of western North Carolina who desired superior access to eastern markets. Clingman established himself as a leading proponent of the interests of the western part of North Carolina partly by emphasizing that, as he saw it, eastern interests took precedence in the minds of other party leaders. In 1843 he capitalized on his newfound stature by defeating a popular Whig incumbent for election to the U.S. House of Representatives. For the next two decades, as he was elected repeatedly to Congress, Clingman became firmly established as one of the state's most influential political leaders.

Clingman won a reputation in Washington for his fiery speeches and his considerable skill at both crafting legislation and guiding it to passage. He also made considerable waves by breaking ranks with every other Southern congressman and voting against the "gag rule" prohibiting debate on the issue of slavery. Clingman argued that this rule played into the hands of abolitionists by making them appear to be persecuted. Clingman's characteristically iconoclastic stance, which Whigs applauded in both his home state and the North, outraged Southern Democrats. He further enraged Democrats with his bitterly partisan speeches denouncing them.

William L. Yancey of Alabama responded to one of Clingman's verbal attacks with a congressional speech in which he personally insulted Clingman, causing the North Carolinian to challenge him to a duel. Because Yancey was an expert shot and Clingman had never fired a pistol, the odds seemed to favor the Alabama congressman overwhelmingly. The duel that followed resulted in plenty of publicity, although both men missed their targets.

Despite his position of influence in the Whig Party, Clingman became increasingly unhappy with the party's failure to gratify his desire for a seat in the Senate. In 1848, he cooperated with Democrats in an unsuccessful effort to replace Whig senator George E. Badger. Thereafter, Clingman gradually began moving toward the Democratic Party, bringing many of his western supporters with him. Clingman's defection clearly played a leading role in the collapse of the state's Whig Party organization soon after, although historians continue to debate whether it was the decisive factor.

During the 1850s, in response to the intensifying sectional crisis, Clingman became a vociferous supporter of Southern rights. During the presidential campaign of 1856, he issued a public letter in which he advocated secession in the event of the election of Republican John C. Frémont. Clingman also gained much attention in the 1850s as a result of engaging in a controversy with his old University of North Carolina professor Elisha Mitchell. The argument concerned the question of which man had first identified and climbed the highest mountain east of the Mississippi, now officially designated as Mount Mitchell. This complicated disagreement eventually led to Mitchell's accidentally plummeting to his death, a tragedy that many Whigs blamed on Clingman.

In 1858, North Carolina Democrats finally gratified Clingman's long-standing ambition and elevated him to the U.S. Senate to complete the term of Asa Biggs, who had recently resigned. In 1860, Clingman won election to a full six-year term; however, North Carolina's secession cut his term short in April 1861. Clingman, a strong supporter of secession, immediately resigned when North Carolina seceded.

Deciding that his staunch public advocacy of Southern independence made it necessary for him to fight for the cause personally, Clingman joined the Confederate army. He was elected colonel of the 25th North Carolina Infantry Regiment in August 1861 and received a promotion to brigadier general the next May. His appointment and promotion were purely political, for he had no military experience. His brigade saw its first action at a skirmish near Goldsboro in December 1862, when Clingman particularly distinguished himself by his personal courage. Early in 1863, however, while stationed in South Carolina, the brigade earned a reputation for low morale, high desertion rates, and general unreliability. Nevertheless, Clingman and his men performed well after being summoned to reinforce Robert E. Lee's Army of Northern Virginia in 1864. Clingman's brigade participated in the Confederate victories at Drewry's Bluff, Cold Harbor, Petersburg, and Weldon Railroad. Clingman was wounded in the leg during the latter battle, effectively ending his active service. Although he displayed no exceptional strategic or tactical abilities, his wartime service was not undistinguished.

Clingman did not return to political prominence after the war. Former Whigs in North Carolina continued to detest him, and his willingness to break ranks with Democratic leaders proved unacceptable during the bitter Reconstruction period. On one occasion, a conflict with a Democratic editor left Clingman severely beaten in the face with his own cane. Clingman did make a mark in the postwar years by his efforts to prove the feasibility of the use of zircon as an electric conductor and to promote the use of tobacco for medicinal purposes. He squandered much of his personal fortune pursuing these largely illusory goals.

Clingman increasingly regretted his failure to marry, although his belated efforts to court several wealthy widows suggest financial as much as romantic motives. He never adjusted successfully to his fall from public prominence and continued to live in Washington while Congress was in session long after he ceased to have any influence there, eventually drawing increasing ridicule from unfriendly reporters. Always eccentric—he had a lifelong habit of talking to himself and was egocentric even by the standards of antebellum Southern statesmen—Clingman's mental health entered a sharp state of decline in the last few years of his life. He died in Morganton, North Carolina.

—*Michael Thomas Smith*

See also North Carolina.

For further reading:

Inscoe, John C. "Thomas Clingman, Mountain Whiggery, and the Southern Cause." *Civil War History* (1987).

Jeffrey, Thomas E. *Thomas Lanier Clingman: Fire Eater from the Carolina Mountains* (1998).

Kruman, Marc W. "Thomas L. Clingman and the Whig Party: A Reconsideration." *North Carolina Historical Review* (1987).

CLOYD'S MOUNTAIN, BATTLE OF
(9 May 1864)

As Lieutenant General Ulysses S. Grant mounted his overland campaign against Robert E. Lee in the spring of 1864, he intended to deprive Lee of the support and sustenance that customarily flowed to the Army of Northern Virginia from east Tennessee and the Shenandoah Valley. As part of this design Brigadier General George R. Crook had the task of destroying the Virginia & Tennessee Railroad's bridge over the New River near Dublin. The railroad's bridges had been a target of several raids in the latter part of 1863, but this Federal assault on this bridge was to be the most coordinated and menacing so far. Major General Franz Sigel's advance up the Shenandoah Valley coincided with Crook's move toward Dublin, for instance, to cause the diversion of the meager Confederate defenses of the area away from the railroad bridge to the Shenandoah breadbasket.

Nonetheless, Crook had a formidable task. Daunting terrain and worse weather made his progress out of the Kanawha Valley a logistical ordeal. Setting forth from Gauley Bridge with 6,500 men and twelve artillery pieces on 2 May, he was to be followed out of Logan's Court House three days later by Brigadier General William W. Averell's 2,000-man cavalry brigade. By moving on Saltville, Averell would form yet another distraction from both Crook's column and its real purpose. Crook labored over the cragged country, marching along the Kanawha River before heading south toward Rocky Gap. By 8 May, he was near Shannon's Bridge, less than ten miles from his objective, when he discovered a Confederate force, the first real resistance he had encountered, in his front.

The multiple Union movements in the region had worked to draw away and scatter Confederate resources. Lawyer-turned-cavalry-commander Brigadier General Alfred G. Jenkins had just been placed in command of forces in southwestern Virginia when the elaborate ballet of Federal offensives was put into motion. Suddenly aware of Crook's approach, Jenkins began a desperate effort to cobble together some defenses. He barely recalled a brigade on its way to fight Sigel in the Shenandoah Valley. Jenkins's best efforts could muster less than 2,500 men, mostly home guards, and a few field pieces. Yet he was doubtless encouraged by the high ground he could occupy, and even at the last minute a few extra men were trickling into place.

The ground was near Cloyd's Mountain, extending into James Cloyd's nearby farm. Here heavily forested hills framed a wide meadow, part of the course of Back Creek. The Confederate position, enhanced by hastily constructed earthworks and log fortifications, was strong enough to give Crook pause when he looked it over on the morning of 9 May, but it was only a pause. "They may whip us," Crook commented, "but I guess not." The artillery traded shots for most of the morning before Crook directed his assault against the Confederate right. After making considerable progress, the Union advance composed of West Virginia and Ohio troops stalled just in front of the gray line and became vulnerable targets for Confederate muskets.

Meanwhile, Jenkins responded to the pressure on his right by reinforcing it from other parts of his line. A charge into the right center section of that line jarred the Confederates until they stiffened and a vicious melee ensued. The fighting nearly caused the Federals to falter, when Colonel Rutherford B. Hayes led his 1st Brigade of Ohioans into the fray and broke the Virginians. When Crook committed reinforcements the day was his. Bluecoats overran Confederate batteries, and Jenkins himself fell wounded, his left arm mutilated. Command then devolved on Brigadier General John McCausland, who put up a spirited resistance until extracting his spent forces before they, like the wounded they left behind them, fell to capture. Jenkins was among that number. Union surgeons tried to save his life by cutting off his shattered arm, but in less than two weeks he was dead. He was thirty-three.

Cloyd's Mountain was the war's fiercest contest fought in that region. Although it lasted only about an hour, the combat claimed 688 Union casualties and more than 538 Confederates. After the battle, only five miles of undefended country stood between George Crook and Dublin, and by evening the next day the Virginia & Tennessee Railroad's New River Bridge was a smoldering ruin.

—*David S. Heidler and Jeanne T. Heidler*

See also Averell's Raids; Crook, George; Hayes, Rutherford B.; Jenkins, Albert G.; McCausland, John; West Virginia.

For further reading:

Broun, Thomas L. "Cloyd's Mountain Battle." *Southern Historical Society Papers* (1909).

Cook, Roy Bird. "Albert Gallatin Jenkins—A Confederate Portrait." *West Virginia Review* (1934).

Duncan, Richard R. *Lee's Endangered Left: The Civil War in Western Virginia, Spring of 1864* (1998).

Johnson, Flora Smith. "The War Record of Albert Gallatin Jenkins, C.S.A." *West Virginia History* (1947).

Johnson, Freddie L., III. "Mountain Warrior: The Political and Military Career of Albert Gallatin Jenkins" Master's thesis, Kent State University, (1993).

McManus, Howard Rollins. *The Battle of Cloyd's Mountain: The Virginia and Tennessee Railroad Raid* (1989).

Schmitt, Martin F., ed. *General George Crook: His Autobiography* (1960).

COBB, HOWELL
(1815–1868)

Confederate general, congressman

Born at the family plantation, Cherry Hill, in Jefferson County, Georgia, to John Addison Cobb and Sara Rootes Cobb, Howell Cobb moved with his family to Athens, Georgia, when he was a child. He was educated at what would become the University of Georgia, and, after graduating at the age of nineteen, he studied law. Cobb began his practice in 1836 and in 1837 was appointed solicitor general for Georgia's Western Circuit. In addition to the law, Cobb also took a strong interest in state Democratic politics and in 1842 was elected to the U.S. House of Representatives. In Congress, Cobb quickly gained a reputation as a moderate, and it was his ability to deal with all sides that earned him election as speaker of the House in 1849.

Cobb was a strong supporter of the Compromise of 1850. He knew, however, that strong states' rights sentiment within the Georgia Democratic Party led many in the state to oppose it. Therefore, after the passage of the separate bills of the compromise package in September 1850, Cobb returned to Georgia to campaign for the people's support of the measure. Governor George Towns had called a convention to consider Georgia's response to the compromise, and Cobb and fellow unionists Alexander Stephens and Robert Toombs succeeded in persuading enough Georgians to accept the compromise that the elected convention had no desire to take drastic action.

The regular Democratic Party in Georgia, dominated by a states' rights element, turned against Cobb, causing him to briefly become affiliated with the new Union Party in the state. Cobb was elected governor in 1851 but found he could accomplish little without regular Democratic support. As a result, in 1853 he returned to the Democratic Party. Cobb now found himself not trusted by either group, and he failed in his attempt to be elected to the Senate. In 1855, Cobb returned to the House of Representatives.

During the 1856 presidential election, Cobb campaigned enthusiastically for his old friend James Buchanan. He was rewarded with an appointment as secretary of the treasury. By 1859 he was very interested in gaining the nomination to the presidency in 1860. His supporters in the Georgia legislature called for a convention to select delegates to the Democratic National Convention to be held in Charleston, South Carolina, in the spring of 1860. They called for the Georgia convention to meet on 8 December, not giving most areas of the state time to arrange for the selection of delegates. As a result, the convention was dominated by Cobb people who agreed to put his name in nomination in Charleston. Other Democrats were outraged and insisted that another convention be held in March 1860. When this one met, it refused to endorse Cobb's candidacy for the presidency.

After the breakup of the Democratic Party at Charleston and subsequently at Baltimore, Cobb campaigned for John C. Breckinridge for president. The former unionist Cobb also urged Georgia's secession should the Republican Abraham Lincoln be elected. After the election, Cobb wrote a lengthy address to the people of Georgia that was printed in pamphlet form, urging the state to immediate secession. On 8 December 1860, he submitted his letter of resignation to Buchanan and returned to Georgia.

Upon returning home, Cobb went on a speaking tour trying to influence the election of the delegates to the upcoming Georgia secession convention. He was battling strong unionist feeling in the state, and even after the delegates were selected, Cobb worked with strong secessionists to try to secure enough votes for immediate secession. The Georgia convention voted for immediate secession and then selected ten delegates to the convention that had been called to meet in Montgomery, Alabama, to form the Confederate States of America. Cobb and his brother Thomas R. R. Cobb were selected as delegates.

Once this provisional congress convened in February 1861, Howell Cobb was unanimously selected its president. While he was mentioned frequently as a possible candidate for provisional president of the Confederacy, especially by his brother, Cobb was still not trusted by a lot of Southern Democrats. The honor of course went to Jefferson Davis, and against the opposition of Cobb, former unionists and fellow Georgian Alexander Stephens was selected provisional vice president.

Cobb remained in the Provisional Congress, where he urged military preparation and a strong show of force against the Federal forts in Confederate territory. During his brief period in Congress, he showed himself to be a strong supporter of a central government and a defender of the policies of Jefferson Davis.

Cobb decided even before Congress adjourned from special session on 21 May 1861 that he would raise a regiment of Georgians and offer his military services to the Confederacy. Two of his sons were already in the Confederate army, and a third would join before the end of the year. In June, President Davis gave Cobb permission to raise his regiment, and Cobb began recruiting in Georgia. He canvassed the state for enlistees for several weeks, but the Provisional Congress was due to convene on 20 July and he had to leave the last of the recruiting to his officers. The regiment arrived in Richmond in August, and Cobb divided his time between the new military life and his congressional duties. By the end of the month, the regiment was mustered into service as the 16th Georgia Infantry.

After the adjournment of Congress, Cobb was sent with his regiment to Yorktown, Virginia, in October 1861 to become part of the command of John Bankhead Magruder's Army of the Peninsula. Cobb and his regiment spent most of their time working on the defenses of the York Peninsula. In November, Cobb had to leave his regiment periodically to attend the last session of the Provisional Congress. One of the main topics of discussion was the seizure of James Mason and John Slidell

from the H.M.S. *Trent*. Cobb hoped that this violation of British neutrality might bring Great Britain into the war on the side of the Confederacy. Other than speculate, however, all Cobb could do was hope and make arrangements to prepare his men to spend the winter on the York Peninsula.

During the winter of 1861–1862, Cobb fulfilled his final duties as president of the Provisional Congress and turned his gavel over to the incoming speaker of the regular Confederate Congress in February 1862. During the previous few months he had despaired that it would not be the short war he had expected, and he was determined to serve the Confederacy in the military rather than through politics for the duration of the conflict.

Also in February 1862, Cobb was promoted to brigadier general and was given command of Magruder's 2d Brigade. In March, Cobb was charged with manning the defenses of Suffolk, Virginia, and was then sent to North Carolina to protect the railroad approaches out of that state into Virginia. The beginning of the Union landings presaging George McClellan's Peninsula campaign quickly brought about Cobb's recall to Yorktown to help with Magruder's defense of the lower peninsula. Magruder commended Cobb for his actions during the siege of Yorktown.

Cobb and his brigade were withdrawn back toward Richmond beginning on 4 May. Cobb's 2d Brigade did not participate in the battle of Seven Pines on 31 May. At the end of June, however, Cobb and his men were heavily involved in the latter phases of the Seven Days', particularly the disastrous charges at Malvern Hill. The 2d suffered almost 33 percent casualties at that engagement on 1 July.

In the meantime, Cobb's health had begun to fail. He tried to remain with his brigade, but his efforts were hampered by his assignment by Lee to handle negotiations with the Union army for a prisoner exchange. He finally had to abandon the effort and take a leave for health reasons. He returned to Georgia to rest.

Upon Cobb's return to Virginia in August 1862, his brigade was watching what was left of McClellan's army at Harrison's Landing. Shortly Cobb received orders to move his men north to join with the remainder of the Army of Northern Virginia. Cobb and his men did not arrive soon enough to participate in the battle of Second Bull Run, but they did join the army at Frederick, Maryland, in the early phase of Lee's first invasion of the North.

As part of Major General Lafayette McLaws's division, Cobb's brigade was sent from Frederick to participate in the taking of Harper's Ferry. On 14 September, sent by McLaws to defend Crampton's Gap at South Mountain against the Federal attempt to relieve Harper's Ferry, Cobb's brigade was part of the force that was overwhelmed by an attacking Union corps and forced back into Pleasant Valley. Though much reduced in strength, Cobb's brigade then fought under McLaws at Antietam on the Confederate left.

Sharp words were exchanged between Cobb and McLaws over the behavior of Cobb's brigade at Crampton's Gap, and while the rift was eventually smoothed over, Cobb's poor health caused him to request another leave in October 1862. He returned home, from where he requested a transfer to an area closer to home. He request was granted, and he was assigned to the command of General P. G. T. Beauregard at Charleston, South Carolina.

Beauregard gave him command of the District of Middle Florida, headquartered at Quincy. Cobb left for his new assignment in December 1862. Cobb worked hard, especially to strengthen the defenses of the Apalachicola River, but his efforts were hampered by the citizens of the area, who openly collaborated with Union forces in the Gulf of Mexico. Cobb's experience in Florida was very frustrating. He could never secure requested reinforcements to man more than 100 miles of coastline, and he received very little cooperation from the local population. Luckily, no Union offensive occurred during Cobb's time in command there. Cobb's frustrations in Florida were only exacerbated by news in December 1862 that his brother Thomas had been killed at Fredericksburg.

In September 1863, Cobb was transferred to Atlanta, Georgia, to supervise recruiting of Georgia troops. What should have been a welcome assignment that would put him closer to home and family proved very unpleasant because of Cobb's dislike for Georgia governor Joseph Brown. Cobb's support for the Davis administration and Brown's antipathy toward it, however, made Cobb's presence in Georgia important to secure the release of Georgia troops to Confederate service. Cobb was also charged with organizing troops for Georgia's defense. Officially Cobb held the title of commander of the Georgia Guard. By giving Cobb this authority, the Confederate War Department hoped to wrest control of Georgia troops from Brown.

Concerned primarily with Georgia's defense, Cobb worked diligently to arm and equip the Georgia Guard. He also diplomatically avoided as many altercations with Brown as possible. In the fall of 1863 he was promoted to major general. Shortly thereafter, following his defeat at Chattanooga, General Braxton Bragg fell back into north Georgia. Since Cobb's Georgia Guard technically fell under Bragg's command, when Cobb learned that Bragg was to be replaced, Cobb went to Richmond to advise President Davis regarding the new commander. Cobb enthusiastically supported Davis's decision to replace Bragg with General Joseph E. Johnston.

In February 1864, the enlistments of the Georgia Guard expired, temporarily leaving Cobb without a command. He spent the next two months traveling around the state making speeches trying to stir up support for the Confederate government and encourage enlistments. In March he was made commander of the Georgia Reserve Force.

Cobb began organizing his new command in Macon in April 1864. The unit was to consist of able-bodied men between seventeen and eighteen years and between forty-five and fifty years old. Once organized, the men were to return home to be prepared to be called out on a moment's notice.

From the very beginning, Cobb had to do battle with Confederate military authorities, who wanted to get their hands on his new command, and with Governor Brown, who tried to exempt large numbers of men from serving in the Reserve. He surmounted these obstacles and commanded his troops in protection of middle Georgia against Federal raiders during the Atlanta campaign in the summer of 1864. He repulsed an attack by Brigadier General George Stoneman in a skirmish called East Macon on 30 July 1864.

With the fall of Atlanta in early September, the threat of raids increased, and Cobb responded as best he could. When Union general William T. Sherman started on his March to the Sea in November, the Reserve was fully activated. There was little these units could do to stop Sherman's march, and, after the fall of Savannah, Cobb had to concern himself with maintaining order in the state. In early 1865, he moved his headquarters to Augusta and waited.

As the Confederacy's military situation began its collapse in early spring, Cobb began receiving conflicting orders about where to send his few troops. The biggest threat he saw to Georgia, however, was the movement of Federal troops east through Alabama toward Georgia. As a result, he moved what men he had toward Columbus, Georgia. Arriving too late to mount an effective defense, he evacuated to Macon on 17 April and a few days later surrendered to Brigadier General James Wilson.

Cobb was paroled but was arrested about a month later for his part in the secession of Georgia and the formation of the Confederacy. President Andrew Johnson pardoned Cobb, however, before he was imprisoned.

After his release from arrest, Cobb settled in Macon, where he resumed the practice of law. While he did not hold political office after the war, he did speak out against the increasing restrictions of Reconstruction. In the fall of 1868 he took a vacation with his family to New York and died suddenly in New York City on 9 October 1868.

—*David S. Heidler and Jeanne T. Heidler*

See also Cobb, Thomas Reade Rootes; Congress, C.S.A.; Crampton's Gap; Georgia.

For further reading:
Montgomery, Horace. *Howell Cobb's Confederate Career* (1959).
Reid, Randy L. "Howell Cobb of Georgia: A Biography" (Ph.D. dissertation, 1995).

COBB, THOMAS READE ROOTES
(1823–1862)
Confederate congressman and general

Born to Joseph Addison Cobb and Sarah Robinson Rootes Cobb, Thomas R. R. Cobb was the brother of Howell Cobb. Thomas Cobb graduated from the University of Georgia and studied law before opening a practice in Athens, Georgia. Over the years he became a recognized authority in Georgia on constitutional law. Before the Civil War, Cobb worked for both the state legislature, where he codified the state's laws, and for the state supreme court. He also wrote extensively, particularly on the legality of slavery. His two most famous works were *Inquiry into the Law of Negro Slavery* and *A Historical Sketch of Slavery from the Earliest Periods*.

A strong advocate of states' rights, Cobb was prompted by Abraham Lincoln's election in November 1860 to advocate the immediate secession of Georgia by the legislature. When the legislature called for a convention instead, Cobb was elected to that body. In the convention Cobb was a strong advocate of secession. Alexander Stephens later wrote that Cobb was one of the major figures responsible for Georgia leaving the union. After secession, he was the driving force behind the revision of the state Constitution. That task accomplished, Cobb and his brother Howell were sent as delegates to the Provisional Confederate Congress in Montgomery, Alabama.

In Montgomery, Cobb's most important activity was his service on the committee to draft a permanent Confederate constitution. He also worked behind the scenes to try to secure the election of his brother Howell as provisional president.

Impatient with the political activity in Congress by the summer of 1861, Cobb resigned his seat to raise a cavalry legion that would bear his name as Cobb's Legion. Commissioned colonel, Cobb commanded the legion at the siege of Yorktown in the opening phases of the Peninsula campaign as part of his brother Howell's brigade. He fought under James E. B. Stuart during the Seven Days' battles. Continuing with the Army of Northern Virginia throughout the summer campaigns at Second Bull Run and Antietam, Cobb was recommended for promotion by Robert E. Lee on 27 October 1862. The promotion to brigadier general became effective 1 November 1862.

At Fredericksburg, Cobb and his brigade were placed on Marye's Heights in front of the Marye House. Defending his position against repeated assaults on 13 December, during one of the later attacks Cobb was struck by an enemy bullet in the thigh and bled to death before he could receive medical attention.

Certainly not a brilliant general, Cobb exhibited an unquestioned bravery that inspired his troops. In Georgia politics, he had never enjoyed prominence before the secession crisis, but he skillfully used obvious oratorical and legal abilities to influence the actions of his state.

—David S. Heidler and Jeanne T. Heidler

See also Congress, C.S.A.; Constitution, C.S.A.; Fredericksburg, First Battle of; Georgia.

For further reading:
McCash, William B. *Thomas R. R. Cobb; The Making of a Southern Nationalist* (1983).

COBURN, ABNER
(1803–1885)
Governor of Maine

Born to Eleazar Coburn and Mary Weston Coburn in Canaan, Maine, Abner Coburn was educated locally. As a young man he taught school briefly before entering the timber business with his father and brother. By the time of his father's death, the company had become one of the richest in the state and owned more timberland than any other. Coburn's wealth led him by the 1850s to invest in a variety of other enterprises including railroads. By mid-decade he had become the president of the Maine Central Railroad.

While engaging in his various business pursuits, Coburn also took an active interest in Maine politics. Beginning his political career as a Whig, Coburn served in the state legislature. With the demise of the Whig Party, Coburn was a driving force in organizing the new Republican Party in Maine. He would maintain a leadership position within the state's party for the remainder of his life.

In 1860 Coburn was seen as a strong possibility to be the Republicans' candidate for governor. He failed to gain the nomination, but used his influence for the first two years of the war to urge support for the war effort. In 1862 he received the party's nomination and won the election. He took office in early 1863 when Union forces, especially in the Eastern theater, were not faring well. The war in many Northern states, including Maine, was becoming less popular and recruiting more difficult.

While Coburn spent much of his early months in office trying to fill Federal recruiting quotas, he faced considerable opposition in some parts of the state. When Congress enacted Federal conscription in the spring of 1863, Coburn faced the task of convincing his state's citizens of the wisdom of this new policy. Those areas of the state that had already supplied a large number of

recruits to the Union army did not believe it was fair that their percentage of draftees would be the same as those areas that had not supplied as many men. Throughout the summer of 1863 Coburn tried to fill the Federal draft quota, while also keeping an already unhappy population calm. He repeatedly requested of conscription officials that they work more closely with him and keep him informed about policies and quotas quickly so that he could prevent rumors from starting among the general population.

In addition to his almost ceaseless work on filling conscription and recruiting quotas, Coburn was asked during the summer of 1863 to provide temporary 100-day troops to meet the emergency of Robert E. Lee's invasion of Pennsylvania and to recruit state troops to guard prisoners placed at Fort Preble. By fall he was nearly at his wit's end. It was then that he learned that most of the recruits and draftees were not being placed in veteran Maine regiments that had been depleted by combat but instead were being formed into new units. He argued that state pride was at stake and that many people had been following the exploits of these older units with tremendous pride in the accomplishments of their fellow citizens. To allow those units to disappear for want of replacements was a big mistake if the government wanted to continued to gain volunteers from Maine.

By the end of his one-year term, Coburn was tired and discouraged in his dealings with the Federal government. One of his last official acts was to request an extension on fulfilling the state's recruiting quota because it was almost filled. He had not even received the Republican Party's nomination for a second term, partly because he had antagonized the leadership in Washington and partly as the result of an effort by Republicans to court the War Democrats in the state. Consequently there had been a fusion in the ticket. Coburn left office in early 1864 and returned to his business activities.

Coburn continued to support the war effort and the Republican Party. After the war, while remaining active in party affairs, he devoted much of his time to civic pursuits and philanthropy. He was especially interested in improving educational opportunities in Maine and donated large sums of money to higher educational institutions in the state. In 1884 at the age of eighty-one, Coburn was selected one of the state's Republican electors. He died on 4 January 1885 as a result of a stroke suffered at one of the meetings of this group. In his will he left much of his considerable fortune to charitable groups.

—*David S. Heidler and Jeanne T. Heidler*

See also Conscription, U. S. A.

For further reading:
Fogg, Clara Newhall. *Abner Coburn* (1924).
Williams, Charles Evarts. *The Life of Abner Coburn: A Review of the Public and Private Career of the Late Ex-Governor of Maine* (1885).

COLD HARBOR, BATTLE OF
(3 June 1864)

In 1864 as the armies of Ulysses S. Grant and Robert E. Lee collided violently in Grant's drive toward Richmond, Grant made the biggest mistake of his military career when he ordered a frontal assault on entrenched Confederates at Cold Harbor, Virginia. The results were staggering casualties for the Union and a significant turning point in the war. The battle was the starkest example of how battlefield tactics and military thinking could tragically miss the measure of the war's weaponry.

Cold Harbor was only one awful battle in a horrifying campaign. In the spring of 1864, the Army of the Potomac embarked on yet another attempt to defeat Lee and take Richmond. It had become a sickening pattern for the North. Nearly a half-dozen times in the previous three years the Army of the Potomac entered Virginia to fight and conquer Lee, and each time it had failed. When the army limped away from these defeats, Abraham Lincoln usually replaced its commanding general. The army would then rest and retool before launching another attempt.

The 1864 campaign would be different. Grant, now commander of all Union forces, would accompany the Army of the Potomac while George G. Meade remained its official commander. Grant understood that his objective was not so much Richmond as it was Lee's army. In the opening battle of this epic campaign, Lee defeated Grant in the battle of the Wilderness on 5–7 May, but Grant, unlike his predecessors, did not retreat. Instead, he slid his army to Lee's right, and the two armies clashed again at Spotsylvania Court House on 10–12 May. As Grant again tried to turn Lee's flank to envelop the Confederates and reach Richmond, the campaign became a race.

From Spotsylvania, Grant continued to wheel south around Lee's right flank. Since the Confederates had the advantage of interior lines, the Federals could not outmarch them. On 30 May, a Confederate attack at Bethesda Church failed to slow down the Union advance. The following day, part of Union general Philip Sheridan's command arrived at Cold Harbor, a small tavern less than ten miles from Richmond. Finding Confederate troops under Fitzhugh Lee already in possession of the strategic crossroads, Sheridan's forces ejected the Confederates in a light action that left the crossroads in Federal hands. On 1 June, Lee failed to retake the intersection, but more troops from each side were gathering, with Federal forces outnumbering the Confederates. To exploit the advantage, Meade suggested an attack, and Grant agreed. Late on the afternoon of 1 June, Union troops assaulted the Confederate line to score some modest gains before the Confederates

Firing mortars at Cold Harbor, from a battlefield sketch by Alfred R. Waud (*Library of Congress*)

finally held. The Union lost 2,200 troops. It was an ominous indication of things to come.

Grant prepared a major attack for 2 June that would comprise a frontal assault all along the Confederate line but most heavily against its flanks. The Confederate right would be the focus because these men had fought on the previous day, and Grant was speculating that they had not had time to fortify their line. Grant also knew that Lee's right was being reinforced at the expense of his left, so there would have to be a weakness somewhere. A complete frontal assault would find it, break Lee's line, and give him no room to regroup. Yet the planned dawn attack never happened because Winfield Scott Hancock's corps was late after getting lost the previous evening and marching several extra miles to get into position. Grant rescheduled the attack for the morning of 3 June.

The delay proved tragic for Federal forces. The Confederates now had an extra day to dig trenches and construct fortifications. Just how dramatically warfare had changed would be amply illustrated by this campaign and especially this battle. The powerful and accurate Springfield rifle had made close-order linear assaults across open fields impossible. Trenches offered huge advantages for defending infantry. With proper artillery support, entrenched troops could not be dislodged. Previous battles had offered commanders a chance to learn this lesson. At

Fredericksburg, Confederates in shallow trenches and behind a stone wall thwarted numerous Union charges. At Gettysburg, Union troops entrenched on Culp's Hill easily repulsed repeated Confederate attacks. And at Spotsylvania, just three weeks before Cold Harbor, Union attacks in fog and rain had scored only moderate successes against Confederate trenches.

These lessons did not help the Union at Cold Harbor. Just why Grant chose to attack, especially after Lee's men had been given a full day to dig in, is puzzling. Between Spotsylvania and Cold Harbor, Grant had probed entrenched Confederate positions along the North Anna River and had decided against an attack. By early June, however, he apparently believed that, if his army could break through to pin the Confederates against the Chickahominy River, he would have a chance to destroy Lee. Perhaps after weeks of flanking and inconclusive fighting, Grant had decided the time had come for a decisive battle.

The Union army spent 2 June wearing itself out by shifting men back and forth, while the Confederates built a masterful system of entrenchments. Mistakes multiplied throughout the Union chain of command. Grant left many details of the assault to his corps commanders, and no one at any level conducted a proper study of the terrain to assess its disadvantages. That evening, a sense of fatalism settled in over the Army of the Potomac. Veterans knew what a frontal assault against the Confederate breastworks would mean. Horace Porter, one of Grant's staff, noticed men calmly pinning their names and addresses on their coats so their bodies could be identified.

At dawn on the morning of 3 June, Hancock's, Horatio Wright's, and W. F. Smith's corps began to move forward. They moved at the same time but terrain and lack of coordination made their line so ragged that the coming battle would actually resemble dozens of small attacks, with brigades and even regiments operating alone. In one part of the line, a division broke to avoid a thick swamp, an obstacle a proper survey by Federal officers would have revealed. As wave after wave of Union troops charged straight into withering Confederate fire, most Federals fell in the open fields, never coming close to the entrenchments. Union general Francis Barlow's division did break the Confederate line at one point, but the zigzag pattern of the trenches allowed Confederates to enfilade the spot with artillery, and the Federal penetration quickly recoiled under savage fire.

The attacks could not continue under such a murderous barrage. Within a half hour, Union troops were heading back to their lines while some of Barlow's shattered command remained cowering in holes hastily dug in the open area before the breastworks. First reports of the engagement were misleading enough to encourage Grant to continue the assault, but the order to do so found commanders so stunned by the carnage that no other attacks occurred. The toll was indeed staggering and sobered the most battle-hardened veterans. The Union lost some 7,000 men, while the Confederates suffered a relatively light 1,500 casualties. Grant would later say that this and his 22 May 1863 assault at Vicksburg were his most regretted decisions of the war.

Firing continued throughout the day, and for several more days the two sides continued sniping at each other. Meanwhile, Lee and Grant's attempts for a truce to collect their wounded fell into confusion about precise terms, stalling an agreement until 7 June. By then, most of the wounded Union soldiers in front of the Confederate breastworks had either died or been rescued by comrades. On 12 June, the Army of the Potomac began another march, this time toward the rail center of Petersburg south of Richmond. The waltz of the two

The battle of Cold Harbor, by Alfred R. Waud (*Library of Congress*)

Collecting the remains of soldiers killed in battle at Cold Harbor, 1864 (Photograph by John Reekie / *Library of Congress*)

great armies had taken them all the way around the Confederate capital.

Grant and other Union officers came under bitter criticism for the attack at Cold Harbor specifically and for the bloody campaign in general. Grant's aggressive campaign against Lee produced almost 50,000 casualties in slightly more than a month and had only reached the same spot that George McClellan occupied two years before. If in doing so, Grant was applying pressure that Lee could not long withstand, the question remained if Grant's own army could persist in that pressure. Cold Harbor changed the Army of the Potomac, making it wary of future assaults on entrenched troops, infecting it with what amounted to "Cold Harbor Syndrome." At Petersburg few such attacks were made. Instead, each army settled into the trenches it would occupy for nine months. The Civil War had become a very different type of war. The ghost of Cold Harbor became the siege of Petersburg.

—*Richard D. Loosbrock*

See also Grant, Ulysses Simpson; Hancock, Winfield Scott; Lee, Fitzhugh; Lee, Robert Edward; Meade, George Gordon; Smith, William Farrar; Wright, Horatio Gouverneur.
For further reading:
Catton, Bruce. *Grant Takes Command* (1968).
———. *A Stillness at Appomattox* (1953).
Trudeau, Noah Andre. *Bloody Roads South: The Wilderness to Cold Harbor, May–June 1864* (1989).

COLFAX, SCHUYLER
(1823–1885)
Speaker of the U.S. House of Representatives

A fierce abolitionist journalist and politician before the war, "Smiler" Colfax was a Radical Republican and Speaker of the U.S. House during the impeachment of President Andrew Johnson in 1868 and was forced out of office after one term as

Ulysses S. Grant's vice president when his name surfaced in the Crédit Mobilier scandal.

Colfax was born in New York City on 23 March 1823, six months after his Wall Street banker father died of tuberculosis. He, his mother, and his stepfather moved to Indiana in 1836, where his stepfather became involved in local politics. Young Schuyler was encouraged to study law, but he began contributing to Horace Greeley's *New York Tribune* in 1839 and showed inclinations both as a journalist and politician. At the age of twenty-two in 1845, Colfax borrowed money to buy half-interest in a struggling South Bend weekly, which was renamed the *St. Joseph Valley Register*. The paper became one of the leading Whig voices in Indiana. Colfax edited the *Register*, largely in absentia, for nineteen years, advocating local development, banking reform, railroad construction, and abolitionism. He argued that the motto of the North should be "Not another inch of slave territory!"

Colfax was elected to Congress in 1854 as a Whig, but aligned himself with the new Republican Party. He denounced Stephen A. Douglas's plan to permit slavery in Kansas, delivering a stirring speech in the House on 21 June 1856. The Republican Party circulated more than a million copies of the speech in brochure form. At the same time, Colfax opposed reforms that would have protected the property rights of married women, widows, and orphans.

Abraham Lincoln received only lukewarm support from Colfax in Lincoln's 1858 Illinois senatorial campaign, and Colfax did not attend the Republican Party National Convention in Chicago in 1860. Upon Lincoln's nomination, however, Colfax campaigned enthusiastically for the Illinois attorney in Illinois, Iowa, Missouri, and Michigan. When the Civil War began in 1861, Colfax joined others in predicting that the war would not last for long. He helped prepare Indiana to send its men to battle, but did not volunteer for the Union army, a fact used against him in future political campaigns. His first wife, whom he had married in 1844, was often ill and died in 1863.

Colfax was elected Speaker of the House on 5 December 1863, resigning as editor of his newspaper, and remained in the powerful position until he assumed the vice presidency in 1869. He was a political ally of Radical Republican Thaddeus Stevens, and he acted as a publicist for Stevens, introducing many of Stevens's ideas in congressional speeches. Capitol correspondents nicknamed him "Smiler" for his suave, always smiling personality, which became biting whenever politics were involved. Colfax considered 1 February 1865, the day he signed the House resolution for the Thirteenth Amendment, outlawing slavery, the happiest day of his life. He was also a friend of President Lincoln. He was with Lincoln in January 1863, not long after the public

release of the Emancipation Proclamation, when Lincoln and his wife were surrounded in their carriage by an angry mob outside a Washington theater. Declining an invitation to join the president at Ford's Theater, Colfax was also the last public figure to shake Lincoln's hand the night Lincoln was assassinated in April 1865.

Colfax worked with Stevens and other Radical Republicans to develop plans for reconstruction. He tried to avoid a public split with President Andrew Johnson, but he voted against Johnson when the House impeached the president in February 1868 and was surprised when the Senate failed to convict him. The popular Colfax campaigned for the nomination to be Ulysses S. Grant's vice president, and the pair was elected on 3 November 1868 on the strength of some 700,000 popular votes from the newly enfranchised African-American population. The *New York Tribune* noted that the new federal government had a record number of journalists, including Colfax and new Speaker James G. Blaine.

Colfax knew that being vice president would mark the end of his active political career. He presided over the Senate but never became part of the Republican leadership. The highlight of his term was a speech he made on 10 May 1869 at Promontory, Utah, when the first transcontinental railroad was completed. Colfax was interested in a second term in 1872, but he was accused of accepting a bribe from Crédit Mobilier, a construction company secretly owned by the directors of the Union Pacific Railroad. There was evidence that a check for $500 had been deposited in his bank account at the time the bribe was said to have been made. Colfax was not renominated and he returned to South Bend, Indiana, in 1873 at the age of 50.

Remarried in 1868, Colfax spent his final years as a public orator, earning more than his vice presidential salary. He spoke about his travels, his memories of Abraham Lincoln, and temperance. A lifelong teetotaler, no alcoholic beverages were ever served at Colfax's parties or receptions. On 13 January 1885, Colfax was changing trains at Mankato, Minnesota, when to reach another station he had to walk nearly a mile in a temperature thirty degrees below zero. He collapsed and died of a heart attack. He was identified by papers he carried.

—*Richard Digby-Junger*

See also Congress, U.S.A.; Radical Republicans.

For further reading:
Furlong, Patrick J., and Ann Leonard. "Schuyler Colfax, 1823–1885." In *The Vice Presidents: A Biographical Dictionary* (1998).
Hollister, O.J. *Life of Schuyler Colfax* (1886).
Smith, Willard H. *Schuyler Colfax: The Changing Fortunes of a Political Idol* (1952).

COLQUITT, ALFRED HOLT
(1824–1894)
Confederate general

Alfred Holt Colquitt, member of a prominent Georgia political family, had a varied Civil War career in which he rose in rank from captain to brigadier general. While in command of a brigade in the Army of Northern Virginia during 1862–1863, he generally performed well, with the notable exception of the battle of Chancellorsville. Transferred to South Carolina and later to Florida, he would earn redemption at the February 1864 battle of Olustee, where he took field command of a small force that won a decisive Confederate victory. Colquitt would earn his greatest fame, however, in the postwar years, serving two terms as governor of Georgia followed by two terms in the U.S. Senate.

Alfred Colquitt was born in Monroe, Georgia on 20 April 1824. His father, Walter T. Colquitt, had served as U.S. Senator and member of the House of Representatives. After graduating from Princeton in 1844, Colquitt studied law and two years later he earned admission to the Georgia bar. During the Mexican War he served as a staff officer with the rank of major. After that war Colquitt turned to politics, winning election to the U.S. House of Representatives in 1852. Because of concerns over the health of his wife, the former Dorothy Tarver, he did not seek reelection. Following Dorothy's death in 1855, Colquitt married her sister, Sarah. He returned to politics in 1859 and won a seat in the Georgia Senate. An ardent secessionist, Colquitt served as presidential elector for John C. Breckinridge and was a member of the Georgia Secession Convention in 1861.

Upon the outbreak of hostilities, Colquitt was commissioned a captain in the 6th Georgia Infantry. In May 1861 he was elected colonel of the regiment, and he shortly thereafter rose to command a brigade on the Virginia Peninsula. Colquitt participated in the defense of Richmond in the spring of 1862, and on 1 September of that year he received a commission to the grade of brigadier general. Over the next eight months Colquitt led his brigade of Georgians and Alabamians through the Antietam, Fredericksburg, and Chancellorsville campaigns.

Before Chancellorsville, Colquitt's performance had been solid, if not spectacular. His most distinguished service took place at Turner's Gap and Antietam. In the latter action his brigade suffered terrific casualties while defending the Cornfield and Bloody Lane. The 6th Georgia, for example, lost more than 200 men in the fighting, with only twenty-four soldiers escaping unscathed. At Chancellorsville, however, Colquitt's hesitation during Thomas "Stonewall" Jackson's 2 May attack, in the mistaken belief that Union troops were massing on his flank, slowed the Confederate onslaught and led to criticism of his abilities. Douglas Southall

Freeman wrote that Colquitt showed "doubtful achievement" at Chancellorsville and, "concerning him, the question fundamentally was one of judgment." After Chancellorsville, Colquitt and his depleted brigade of Georgians were transferred first to North Carolina, and then to Charleston. Colquitt participated in the defenses of that city during the summer and fall of 1863.

In early 1864, Colquitt received orders to move his brigade to Florida, to help repulse a Federal invasion of that state. Forced to march overland through parts of south Georgia and north Florida, Colquitt's veterans arrived in Lake City only days before they would face a Union advance from Jacksonville. On 20 February 1864, Colquitt's brigade was entrenched near Olustee Station, about thirteen miles east of Lake City. It was part of a small army of about 5,000–5,500 men under the command of Brigadier General Joseph Finegan that faced a similar-sized force of Federals led by Brigadier General Truman Seymour. After skirmishing developed east of the Confederate defenses, Finegan ordered Colquitt to advance with part of his brigade and join the fighting. The Georgian remained in tactical command for most of the engagement, with Finegan remaining at the main Confederate defense line until late in the battle. "I in common with the entire command," Colquitt would later write, "understand that Genl Finegan was not on the field of Olustee at all." The Southern forces won a decisive victory at Olustee, driving the Federals back to their Jacksonville defenses and inflicting casualties that approached 40 percent of the Union force.

Colquitt and his brigade subsequently returned to Virginia, where they participated in defending against Grant's Overland campaign and the opening portion of the siege of Petersburg. Transferred again to North Carolina, Colquitt was ordered to Fort Fisher, but the fort capitulated before he could assume command. He remained in North Carolina until the surrender.

After the war, Colquitt returned to Georgia where he practiced law and reentered politics. The Bourbon Democrat was elected governor in 1876 and 1880, and later served two terms in the United States Senate. Colquitt, along with Joseph Brown and John Gordon, composed part of the great triumvirate of Georgia postwar politics. The "Hero of Olustee" died on 26 March 1894 and was buried in Macon.

—*David J. Coles*

See also Olustee, Battle of
For further reading:
Coleman, Kenneth. "The Administration of Alfred H. Colquitt as Governor of Georgia" (M. A. thesis, 1940).
Davis, William C., ed. *The Confederate General* (1991).
Evans, Clement A., ed. *Confederate Military History: A Library of Confederate States History* (1899; reprint, 1987).
Freeman, Douglas Southall. *Lee's Lieutenants: A Study in Command* (1942–1944).

COLT, SAMUEL
(1814–1862)
Inventor

Samuel Colt, who was born on 19 July 1814 in Hartford Connecticut, is best known as the inventor of the most popular and widely used revolvers (in both the Union and Confederate armed forces) during the Civil War. From a young age, Colt displayed a talent for invention. His first major successful experiment was a demonstration of an explosive mine, which unfortunately showered spectators with mud and debris. After this incident Colt was sent to Amherst Academy, but was forced to leave after another of his experiments caused a fire on school property.

After leaving Amherst, Colt became apprenticed as a sailor. On a voyage to India in 1830, Colt conceived of the idea that would eventually become his revolver design, and he carved a wooden model of the design on the return trip. Colt perfected his famous revolver by 1835 and had obtained United States, British, and European patents on it by the following year. Without any great demand for a rapid-fire weapon during peacetime, however, Colt's company went bankrupt in 1842. The Mexican War changed his circumstances quickly and, by the outbreak of the Civil War, the Colt Patent Arms Manufacturing Company dominated the revolver market. His manufacturing plant, which had opened in Hartford in 1855, became the largest privately owned armory in the world. Colt was innovative in both his use of advanced manufacturing methods, such as the use of interchangeable parts and a production line, and his progressive treatment of his assembly-line employees.

Undoubtedly, the most famous of Colt's many revolver designs were the 0.36-caliber Colt Navy and the 0.44-caliber Colt Army. These two revolvers were essentially an identical design that was chambered in two different calibers. The 6-shot Colt revolver could be loaded with paper or linen prepackaged cartridges or simply with loose gunpowder and a lead ball. The cartridges or powder and balls were loaded into the front chambers of the revolver's cylinder, while the rear of each chamber had to be capped with a percussion cap to fire the weapon. While this system may seem horribly awkward by modern standards, it was the height of technology during the Civil War. About 200,000 Colt revolvers were produced during the Civil War era. The U.S. government purchased approximately 127,000 of these, while the remainder were probably purchased privately by many soldiers.

Along with his successful revolvers, Colt also produced the Colt-Root Model 1855 repeating rifle. The Colt repeating rifle, the design of which was based on Colt's revolver, was produced in a wide range of styles and calibers (0.40 through 0.64). During the war approximately 4,700 Colt repeating rifles were delivered to the U.S. government. The apparent reason for the relatively small number of rifles ordered relates directly to the greatest problem of the rifle itself—a dangerous tendency for more than one of the rifle's rounds to discharge at one time. This problem cost numerous soldiers a hand, an arm, or even in a few cases, their lives. As a result, the 1st U.S. Sharpshooter Regiment, which had originally been issued Colt repeating rifles, was resupplied with Sharps' rifles. The Colt repeating rifles that were issued during the Civil War were generally issued to Michigan and Ohio regiments. In fact, the 21st Ohio Infantry Regiment, which was instrumental in stopping Confederate lieutenant general James Longstreet's I Corps' breakthrough at Chickamauga did so with Colt repeating rifles.

In 1850 Connecticut governor Thomas H. Seymour had Colt commissioned a lieutenant colonel in the Connecticut State Militia. Thus, it was no surprise that Colt was authorized to form the 1st Connecticut Revolving Rifles Regiment at the outbreak of the Civil War. Due to administrative problems, however, the regiment never saw active service. Unfortunately, as the Civil War approached, the workaholic Colt's health began to deteriorate and he finally succumbed to rheumatic fever on 10 January 1862.

—*Alexander M. Bielakowski*

See also Rifles.
For further reading:

Hosley, William. *Colt: The Making of an American Legend* (1996).

Rohan, Jack. *Yankee Arms Maker: The Incredible Career of Samuel Colt* (1935).

Wilson, R. L. *Colt: An American Legend* (1986).

COLUMBIA, SOUTH CAROLINA, BURNING OF
(17 February 1865)

On 14 February 1865, William Tecumseh Sherman's army left Orangeburg, South Carolina, headed for the state capital of Columbia. The army stopped south of the city on 15 February. While waiting to proceed, many of the officers and men probably reflected on the especial distaste they felt for the state of South Carolina, which they viewed as the instigator of the war. Sherman's marchers had already been more destructive in South Carolina than they had been in Georgia, burning many of the towns in their path to Columbia. Many of the soldiers bragged that they would burn Columbia too when they entered that city.

During the night of 15 February, Confederate soldiers shelled the Union encampments, which further infuriated Sherman and his men. The following morning the

army moved forward to the Congaree River, from where they could see Columbia and Lieutenant General Wade Hampton's Confederate cavalry patrolling the streets. All the bridges across the Congaree had been destroyed, so Sherman sent XV Corps under Major General Oliver O. Howard north to move on the town from that direction. Sherman ordered Howard before the latter departed to destroy any public property, railroad property, and manufacturing concerns in the city but not to destroy private property. On the night of 16 February, Howard's engineers built a pontoon bridge across the Broad River and prepared to enter the city the following morning.

Columbia was full of people who had fled ahead of Sherman's army. Now many of these people were trying to get out of town any way they could. By the night of the 16th they knew that there was no Confederate force large enough to do them any good close enough to defend the town. The chaos of the fleeing people also made it relatively easy on the nights of 15 and 16 February for Southern looters to start to work on the abandoned houses and businesses. To add to the chaos, on the 16th Confederate gunpowder at the railroad depot accidentally ignited and exploded during the morning.

Hampton knew that there was nothing he could do, so he told Mayor T. J. Goodwin that the military was pulling out on the morning of 17 February and that Goodwin should surrender. Lieutenant General P. G. T. Beauregard was in town as well, and that night he and Hampton conferred. One of the biggest topics of discussion was the presence of many bales of cotton in the streets of the town. Hampton had planned to have it removed outside the city for burning, but now there was no time. Both he and Beauregard agreed that it would be too dangerous to the town to burn it in the streets because of the danger of fire spreading to buildings, so they decided to leave it.

On the morning of 17 February, Hampton sent the mayor and his entourage north out of the city to surrender and began pulling his men out. Howard's corps was already crossing the Broad River. The mayor found the lead elements of this corps and offered his surrender. Word was sent back to Sherman, who had ridden to the Broad, and he authorized the acceptance of the surrender. He instructed Howard to proceed with the occupation of the city.

As the first Union troops entered Columbia, they discovered that the town contained a great deal of alcohol and immediately began consuming it. Barrels of whiskey and wine were brought out into the streets, and each group of soldiers who entered the city had its pick of some of the best alcohol Columbia had to offer. A situation quickly developed in which the few sober soldiers could not control the drunk ones.

During the late morning, Sherman entered the city

General Sherman's entry into Columbia, 17 February 1865
(*Library of Congress*)

with the remainder of XV Corps. By that time it was noticed that some of the cotton the Confederates had left in the streets was on fire. Sherman later contended that the retreating Confederate soldiers had set the fires, and some witnesses confirmed that at least some of the early fires were set by Confederates, but when the wind fanned the flames and they started spreading to nearby buildings, many of the Union soldiers tried to prevent people from extinguishing the flames. There were also witnesses who saw some of the drunken soldiers set fires to cotton and to buildings. Some of those who did not go so far as to set fires cut fire hoses and impeded fire engines trying to reach the fires.

At the same time, some of the Federal soldiers tried to help put out fires, and later that afternoon Sherman promised the mayor additional help and assured him that the Union army would not destroy the town. While this promise was being made, the flames spread through the town. Under cover of darkness, some soldiers began setting new fires in different parts of the city. Many of the buildings of South Carolina College were set on fire, including a Confederate military hospital with many disabled soldiers inside. Those fires were extinguished. The Washington Street Methodist Church was then set ablaze because soldiers thought that it was the Baptist church that had housed the first meeting of the South Carolina Secession Convention before it moved to Charleston. Many private homes were looted and then burned.

While this devastation continued, some soldiers and officers still tried to prevent any further destruction and

The burning of Columbia (*Library of Congress*)

worked very hard to protect civilians from harm. A fresh, sober division was brought into town during the early morning hours of 18 February to restore order and to fight fires. Sherman even left his headquarters to help fight some of the fires. Dawn brought an end to arson but also a clear view of the tremendous destruction. At least one-third of the town had been completely destroyed and many other parts seriously damaged. After destroying some of the public property that had survived the fires, the Union army left the city on 20 February. Sherman left behind some food for the destitute people of the city.

After the war, some of the property owners of Columbia unsuccessfully tried to sue for damages to their property. In 1873 a commission investigated the fires and exonerated the officers on both sides. No real blame was assigned.

—*David S. Heidler and Jeanne T. Heidler*

See also Carolinas Campaign; Sherman, William Tecumseh.
For further reading:
Barrett, John G. *Sherman's March Through the Carolinas* (1956; reprint 1996).
Glatthaar, Joseph T. *The March to the Sea and Beyond: Sherman's Troops in the Savannah and Carolinas Campaigns* (1985).

COLUMBUS, KENTUCKY

Columbus, Kentucky, was a strategic point on the Mississippi River for both the Union and the Confederacy. In 1861 Columbus, Kentucky, was the northern terminus of the Mobile & Ohio Railroad and an important transshipment point for rail and river traffic. Steamboats called regularly to connect with the railhead. In addition, ferries carried trains between Columbus and Cairo, Illinois. The community was, therefore, a key link in movement of goods and passengers on the Mississippi. In addition, Columbus was the site of the first high bluffs along the river downstream from Cairo.

At the beginning of September 1861, Confederate general Leonidas Polk broke the stalemate over Kentucky's self-proclaimed neutrality in the national crisis that followed secession and the first battle of Manassas (Bull Run) by occupying Columbus and Hickman, Kentucky, another river port nearer the Tennessee border. Polk focused the largest part of his force at Columbus, and it became the western anchor of the Confederate defense line that spread across southern Kentucky, through Bowling Green, to the Cumberland Gap. The high bluffs made Columbus a logical point to try to control the Mississippi, and its rail and water transportation links allowed it to be supplied easily. Within two months the garrison grew to some 13,000 troops and more than 10,000 slaves who constructed extensive earth works. Fort DeRussy, as the Confederate fortification was named, had more than 140 cannon and presented a formidable obstacle to Union movement on the river. There were earthworks with cannon atop the bluff and water-level river batteries. In addition, an anchor was strung across the river, supported on pontoons and protected by torpedoes set to explode on contact. "The Gibraltar of the West" as it was known, was one of the most heavily fortified places on the continent. Polk and his troops were also rallying points for the pro-Confederate citizens in the Jackson Purchase region of Kentucky, and several Confederate regiments were raised in the area.

After Polk occupied Columbus, Federal general U. S. Grant, who was at Fort Defiance outside Cairo, moved quickly to occupy Paducah and Smithland, Kentucky. Paducah was the major city in far western Kentucky and controlled the confluence of the Tennessee and Ohio rivers. Smithland controlled the confluence of the Tennessee and Cumberland rivers. Grant observed Polk's activities closely and periodically sent gunboats down the river and troops on demonstrations to test the strength of the Confederate fortifications. In November, when Polk established a camp on the Missouri side of the Mississippi at Belmont and appeared to be extending a defensive line across southern Missouri, Grant moved quickly to stop this expansion by moving against the Confederate camp at Belmont.

Grant's troops overran the Confederate camp at Belmont, forcing a rapid withdrawal, but the cannon from Columbus quickly forced the Federal troops to withdraw in extreme disorder and Grant nearly saw his victory turn into disaster. The battle of Belmont was Grant's first action as a combat commander and it ended with the Confederates in control of the river and confident of the strength of their position.

While Grant continued to probe the defenses of Columbus by land and river, his attention quickly shifted to the Cumberland and Tennessee rivers. In February of 1862 his troops and the gunboats of Navy Flag Officer Andrew Foote captured Forts Henry and Donelson, establishing Union control of those two rivers. The capture of Forts Henry and Donelson, combined with the decimation, due to disease, of the Confederate garrison at Camp Beauregard in western Graves County, Kentucky, left Columbus exposed to attack overland from the east. Rather than wait for that attack, Polk withdrew his forces during the last days of February and the first of March, leaving nearly all the cannon and large caches of supplies. When the first attacking Union troops arrived on 2 March 1862, they rode right into the fort and seized it without opposition.

Union troops occupied Columbus for the remainder of the war. Fort DeRussy was renamed Fort Halleck. Columbus also served as a district headquarters for the Union army and was an important staging area for the Vicksburg campaign. Troops from Illinois, Ohio, and the upper Midwest transferred from riverboats to rail at Columbus. The commissary corps, quartermaster corps, and transportation corps all had district headquarters at Columbus in addition to the overall district headquarters and Fort Halleck. Although it is almost impossible to estimate the number of troops at Columbus at any one time because of their constant movement, it can be said that it was a large and active center of Federal activity. Units from Columbus patrolled the Jackson Purchase and established garrisons in other communities to protect railroad bridges, crossroads, and other strategic locations. Although Columbus was never directly attacked, the Purchase remained staunchly pro-Confederate, perhaps even becoming more so as the war continued. Confederate guerrillas and Nathan Bedford Forrest's cavalry frequently attacked patrols, supply trains, and railroad bridges. Federal officers and troops thought of themselves as being in enemy territory and at some peril, even though Kentucky never seceded and remained a Union state. They frequently delayed sending troops south to the Vicksburg campaign to provide additional resources to use against Forrest and the guerrillas. This was a source of considerable annoyance to U. S. Grant, who sent many strongly worded telegrams to Columbus to get troops moving south and frequently changed district commanders.

Early in the Federal occupation, slaves began coming to Columbus, both from the Purchase and from surrounding states, seeking freedom and the protection of the Federal army. The lack of a clear policy on how to treat escaped slaves caused a great deal of confusion at Columbus. Once the policy decision was made that they not be returned to their masters, commanders at Columbus had to provide for them. A colony of some 1,000 contrabands, as the former slaves were known at the time, was established on Island No. 10, some miles down river from Columbus after the Confederates abandoned it. Other former slaves were used as casual labor on the fortifications at Columbus and in loading and unloading riverboats and trains. Some were sent to Cairo and as far away as St. Louis in response to requests for labor from Federal commanders. By 1863 African-Americans were being enlisted into the Union army at Columbus and throughout the Jackson Purchase, although due to opposition to black military service by Kentucky's political leaders they were often credited to the District of Memphis or another Tennessee location until 1864. The 4th U.S. Heavy Artillery Colored was largely raised in the Columbus area and was headquartered there for most of the war. Units from the 4th served all over the Jackson Purchase guarding railroad bridges, crossroads, and courthouses, as well as at Columbus.

As the war in the western theater wound down, activity at Columbus slowed, although pickets were still posted daily through July 1865. The Freedmen's Bureau had a district office in Columbus that was active in helping establish schools and churches for the freed people, as well as locating African-American veterans who were due back pay and other benefits. Fort Halleck was deactivated, and the ordnance and other materiel left behind was removed by the Quartermaster General Corps in 1867–1868. The military cemetery was relocated to Mound City, Illinois, in the 1870s. In 1934 the largest part of the fortifications became Columbus-Belmont State Park.

—*William H. Mulligan, Jr.*

See also Kentucky.

For further reading:

Hughes, Nathaniel Cheairs, Jr. *The Battle of the Belmont: Grant Strikes South* (1991).

Mullen, Jay Carlton. "The Turning of Columbus." *Register of the Kentucky Historical Society* (1966).

U.S. War Department. *The War of the Rebellion: A Compilation of the Official Records of the Union and Confederate Armies* (1880–1901).

Whitesell, Hunter B. "Military Operations in the Jackson Purchase Area of Kentucky, 1862–1865." *Register of the Kentucky Historical Society* (1965).

Whitesell, Robert D. "Military and Naval Activity between Cairo and Columbus." *Register of the Kentucky Historical Society* (1963).

COMMISSARY

The term *commissary* is the shortened version of "commissary of subsistence," which referred to the staff officer or staff function that had the responsibility to procure, store, and issue food to the troops. The ultimate responsibility of this logistical mission fell to the Union or Confederate subsistence departments, each headed by a "commissary general of subsistence."

Organized in 1818, the U.S. Army Subsistence Department had an authorized strength of only twelve officers when the Civil War began. Secession brought the immediate resignation of four officers, a loss of one-third of the department. Congress remedied the situation by passing legislation in August 1861 that added twelve more officer positions, for a total of twenty-four. This was still too small a corps to oversee the procurement and issuance of food for hundreds of thousands of men, so a year and a half later the department again was modestly enlarged to twenty-nine officers. When Fort Sumter fell, the head of the Subsistence Department was Colonel George Gibson, an old man who had been an invalid for many years. Running the day-to-day operations of the department was Lieutenant Colonel Joseph P. Taylor (brother of Zachary Taylor and uncle of Confederate general Richard Taylor), who became the commissary general of subsistence when Gibson died in September 1861.

The Confederate Subsistence Department was created by act of the Confederate Congress that was signed into law on 26 February 1861. Appointed initially as the acting commissary general of subsistence, Lucius B. Northrop eventually received the full appointment and remained the commissary general of the Confederacy until February 1865. His department, like its Union counterpart, was undermanned for such a herculean task. The legislation creating the Confederate Subsistence Department authorized a commissary general with the rank of colonel, six to eight staff officers ranging in rank from lieutenant colonel to captain, and a few clerks. Northrop's abrasive personality only made a difficult situation even worse.

Unlike European wars, in which troops were generally expected to live off of the land in wartime, most food for the Union forces was purchased in the major metropolitan areas of the North and then packed and shipped to field depots. From there, the foodstuffs were issued to the commissary officers of the field armies and then transported to the troops. The exception to this procedure was the procurement of flour and beef, both commodities usually being purchased in the areas were the armies were operating. Much of the fresh beef was transported with the armies in herds and then slaughtered as needed.

The Confederates also tried stockpiling commissary supplies in centralized locations, such as Richmond. Since the Confederate armies normally were operating in their own territory, however, it did not always make sense to ship commodities to a distant warehouse only to have those same commodities shipped back to the areas of operation. Complicating matters for the Confederate commissary of subsistence was rising inflation, civilian hoarding, breakdowns in the transportation system, lack of salt and other preservatives, packaging shortages (kegs, sacks, cans, etc.), and Union victories in (or occupation of) important flour- and meat-producing regions. As the war progressed, these problems intensified, making it more and more difficult for Confederate commissary officers to provide an adequate ration of food for their soldiers.

For most of the war, the daily food allowance for Union soldiers was, by regulation, "twelve ounces of pork or bacon, or, one pound of salt or fresh beef; one pound and six ounces of soft bread or flour, or one pound and four ounces of corn meal; and to every one hundred rations, fifteen pounds of beans or peas, and ten pounds of rice or hominy; ten pounds of coffee, or, eight pounds of roasted (or roasted and ground) coffee, or, one pound and eight ounces of tea; fifteen pounds of sugar; four quarts of vinegar;…three pounds and twelve ounces of salt; four ounces of pepper; thirty pounds of potatoes, when practicable, and one quart of molasses." These rations were issued in camp; while on the march a

Commissary Department, Army of the Potomac, at Brandy Station, Virginia, February 1864
(Photograph by Timothy O'Sullivan / *National Archives*)

soldier's daily issue was one pound of hard bread, three-fourths of a pound of salt pork or one and a quarter pounds of fresh meat, and sugar, salt, and coffee. To prevent scurvy, commissary offices issued small quantities of dried fruit, potatoes, or kraut whenever possible. When periods of prolonged hunger did occur in the Union armies, it usually was not due to actual food shortages but because the armies had outdistanced their supply lines, or because of bureaucratic foul-ups.

The Confederate Subsistence Department at the beginning of the conflict used the exact same ration allocation—at least on paper—as its Union counterpart, but procurement and distribution problems forced Commissary General Northrop to curtail the daily ration. In reality, cornmeal became the staple of the Confederate soldier's diet, supplemented by whatever other foodstuffs were issued by the commissary department or appropriated by the soldiers themselves. At the end of the war, Northrop admitted that, from 1863 on, it had been "impossible to provide the ration set up by army regulations, and that the issue had been steadily declining."

Field armies of the Union and the Confederacy usually had one field-grade officer as their chief commissary of subsistence. These men were assisted by officers and enlisted men filling similar staff positions all the way from corps down to regimental level. The staff officers in the echelons below army level—normally "acting commissaries,"—consolidated requests from their subordinate units, ensured the paperwork was filled out properly, and forwarded the requests to the next higher command. When the requests were filled, these men ensured that the correct amounts of rations were picked up, transported, and issued to their subordinate commands. For example, the chief commissary of subsistence for the 1st Division, V Corps, Union Army of the Potomac, would have provided staff supervision for the requisitioning, transportation, and issue of food for the three brigades assigned to his division. The brigade chief commissaries had similar responsibilities and provided staff supervision of the regimental quartermasters (who, in most instances, also served as the commissary officer) and who were assisted by their commissary sergeants. At the company level of organization, infantry companies were authorized one commissary sergeant. Company quartermaster sergeants usually fulfilled the commissary duties in cavalry troops and artillery batteries.

—*Mark Snell*

See also Northrop, Lucius Bellinger.
For further reading:
Creveld, Martin Van. *Supplying War: Logistics from Wallenstein to Patton* (1977).
Goff, Richard D. *Confederate Supply* (1969).
Risch, Erna. *Quartermaster Support of the Army: A History of the corps, 1775–1939* (1989).

Wiley, Bell. *The Life of Billy Yank: The Common Soldier of the Union* (1952; reprint, 1993).

———. *The Life of Johnny Reb: The Common Soldier of the Confederacy* (1943; reprint, 1978).

COMSTOCK, CYRUS BALLOU
(1831–1910)
Union general

Born in Massachusetts, Cyrus Ballou Comstock received an appointment to the U.S. Military Academy in 1851. He graduated first of thirty-four in the class of 1855. After receiving his commission in the Corps of Engineers, Comstock served on a variety of engineering projects before returning to West Point as an instructor. At the outbreak of the Civil War he was called to Washington, D.C., to aid the chief engineer in preparing the capital's defenses. With the creation of the Army of the Potomac, Comstock was appointed to the position of assistant to the chief engineer, Army of the Potomac, working directly under John Gross Barnard.

Comstock traveled with the Army of the Potomac to the York Peninsula in the spring of 1862 and served as first lieutenant of engineers and Barnard's assistant during the early engagements of the Peninsula campaign. In early June after the battle of Seven Pines, Comstock was named the chief engineer of Edwin Sumner's II Corps. He served in that capacity for the remainder of the Peninsula campaign through the Seven Days.

During the Maryland campaign, Comstock commanded, still at the rank of first lieutenant, a battalion of engineers. He and his men operated both at South Mountain and the battle of Antietam. In November, after the change of command of the Army of the Potomac from George B. McClellan to Ambrose Burnside, Comstock was named chief engineer of the Army of the Potomac. His biggest challenge in this new position of responsibility was to supervise the movement of the pontoon bridges ordered by Burnside to span the Rappahannock River at Fredericksburg. The constant delays out of Washington and then the transport of the pontoons to Fredericksburg made Comstock's task a complicated one.

In the spring of 1863, Comstock was finally promoted to captain, but with Joseph Hooker's reorganization of the Army of the Potomac was reduced to commanding an engineering battalion in the Chancellorsville campaign. In that campaign he supervised the movement to and erection of pontoon bridges at Kelly's Ford in the flanking maneuver of Robert E. Lee's Army of Northern Virginia. During the Army of the Potomac's retreat he accomplished the same task at United States Ford. After the end of the campaign, Comstock was transferred to the Army of the Tennessee to aid with the siege of Vicksburg, Mississippi.

Arriving outside Vicksburg in June 1863, Comstock brought his considerable wartime experience to bear on the erection of siege works outside the city. On 1 July he had so impressed Ulysses S. Grant that the commanding general made him chief engineer of the Army of the Tennessee. Comstock held that position through the capitulation of Vicksburg and most of the fall of 1863. In November he was promoted to lieutenant colonel and became assistant inspector general of the Division of the Mississippi, headquartered at St. Louis.

In the early months of 1864, Comstock held the same position as a member of Grant's staff and traveled around the theater with the commanding general. In March, when Grant went east to assume command of all U.S. forces, Comstock became his senior aide-de-camp. Comstock served in this position for the remainder of the war with the exception of several special missions that he conducted for Grant away from the Virginia theater.

As Grant's aide-de-camp, Comstock performed a variety of duties, including passing on the general in chief's orders to corps commanders, acting as courier during battles, and acting a chief engineer for specific offensives. He was especially active during the Wilderness campaign, moving between different corps directing the commanders to the positions desired by Grant. His chief commended him for his gallantry during that campaign.

During the Federal attack on Fort Harrison outside Richmond in September 1864, Comstock was assigned by Grant to direct many of the Union preparations and was again commended by Grant for his actions in the battle. At the end of 1864, after the first attempt on Fort Fisher, North Carolina, directed by Benjamin F. Butler, failed, Grant assigned Comstock as chief engineer for the second attempt to be made in January 1865. Again, after the successful campaign against this Confederate stronghold, Grant praised Comstock's skill and dedication. Alfred Terry, commander of the expedition, also commended Comstock for his role in the campaign.

Returning to Virginia and Grant's staff, Comstock remained through much of the final phases of the siege of Petersburg. In March, however, Grant sent his trusted aide to Mobile, Alabama, to assist Edward R. S. Canby in the campaign against Mobile. As a result, Comstock was not present at Lee's surrender in April 1865. He returned at the end of April and remained Grant's aide until 1866. On 6 June 1865, Grant wrote to the War Department recommending Comstock for brevet promotions in the regular army to major for his actions in the siege of Vicksburg, to lieutenant colonel for his bravery during the battle of the Wilderness, to colonel for the attack on Fort Harrison, and to brigadier general for the Fort Fisher campaign. All of these recommendations were acted upon, with the addition of a brevet promotion to major general for his role in the Mobile campaign.

After the war, after leaving Grant's staff, Comstock returned to the Corps of Engineers. He remained in the army, serving in a variety of places as an engineering officer until being forced to retire because of age in 1895 at the rank of colonel.

—*David S. Heidler and Jeanne T. Heidler*

See also Fort Fisher; Fredericksburg, Battle of.

For further reading:
Comstock, Cyrus Ballou. *The Diary of Cyrus B. Comstock* (1987).

CONFEDERATE DIASPORA

To the farthest place from the United States, if it takes me to the middle of China." With these words, Judah P. Benjamin, Confederate secretary of state, described a journey taken by numerous Southerners in 1865. Nearly 8,000 men, women, and children entered a diaspora that required residence in Mexico, Brazil, Venezuela, Peru, Jamaica, Canada, England, and even Egypt.

Several factors motivated these self-exiles. Some, like Benjamin, feared persecution by vindictive "Yankees." He warned other prominent politicians to "risk death" in their escape efforts rather than accept "the savage cruelty" of Northern retribution. Federal law allowed the death penalty for treason, and though few expected large-scale executions, confusion and uncertainty persuaded some to leave the country.

Others could not stand to live under the U.S. flag, which Henry Derrick called "that hated emblem of cursed tyranny." "Any other country would be better than this," agreed David McCorkle. Then there was Jo Shelby, who not only refused to live in the Union but even considered a continuation of the Civil War from Mexico. Samuel H. Lockett expressed a more common reason to seek fortune elsewhere. Like all former Confederate officers, he was barred from duty with the U.S. military, while civilian jobs for men with such talents were rare. As Lockett put it, "It is awful to be poor." For most Confederate exiles, new opportunity, rather than fear of punishment, was the motivation for their exodus.

The vast majority moved to several nations in Latin America. For some, like Benjamin, or John C. Breckinridge, places such as Cuba were simply a stopover on the way to Canada or England. Many more Southerners saw Mexico or Brazil as a new home. The former refuge quickly turned sour, while the latter became the only successful Confederate "colony."

Mexico, which attracted the largest contingent of Southerners, was in the midst of a vicious war. On one side was the empire of Maximilian, a puppet government backed by France. President Benito Juárez led a powerful opposition supported by Washington. Thus it is not surprising that Southern refugees sided with Maximilian.

They even named their principal colony Carlota, after the emperor's wife. Many indicated their allegiance with offers to join the Imperial Army. In August 1865, Jo Shelby and several hundred troopers rode into Mexico City with the hope of forming a complete unit of ex-Confederates.

With nearly 3,000 ex-Union veterans serving in Republican forces, the stage seemed set for a small-scale continuation of the Civil War. Maximilian wisely figured this could result in direct U.S. intervention and refused to accept Shelby's command. Individuals, such as General John Magruder, did join the Imperial forces, but by 1867 the war ended with a complete victory for Juárez. As allies of the despised Imperialists, most Southerners now returned home.

A different story unfolded in Brazil, where a stable government invited ex-Confederates to establish colonies. In places such as New Texas, small communities attempted to transplant cotton, watermelon, and other Southern crops. The largest colony formed at Vila Santa Bárbara, in São Paulo State. The city later became Americana, while its residents were dubbed "Os Confederados." Between 1866 and 1868, numerous families moved there. Although many went home after a few years, about 500 stayed. Descendants of the original settlers maintain Southern traditions to this day, even including a Sons of Confederate Veterans Camp.

While the largest number of émigrés went to Brazil and Mexico, some famous personalities traveled much farther. Benjamin ended up in England, where he reentered the legal profession, but died in Paris in 1884, never having returned to the United States. John R. Tucker became an admiral in the Peruvian navy and gained additional fame as an Amazonian explorer. Even more exotic was the postwar career of William Wing Loring. Hired as a mercenary by the khedive of Egypt, Loring won the aristocratic title of pasha, fought a gun battle with the nephew of Benjamin Butler, and participated as second-in-command for the ill-fated Gura campaign in 1876. Like most émigrés though, he finally returned home, probably sharing the feelings of the Lockett family, who were "…very happy at being back again among white people…where there are no nasty Arabs, and fleas, and flies, and lice, and bed bugs, and dirt."

—*John P. Dunn*

See also Benjamin, Judah Philip; Breckinridge, John Cabell; Mexico; Shelby, Joseph Orville.

For further reading:
Hanna, Alfred J., and Kathryn Abby Hanna. *Confederate Exiles in Venezuela* (1960).
Hesseltine, William B., and Hazel C. Wolf. *The Blue and Grey on the Nile* (1961).
Rolle, Andrew F. *The Lost Cause: The Confederate Exodus to Mexico* (1965).
Sutherland, David. "Exiles, Emigrants, and Sojourners. The Post Civil War Confederate Exodus in Perspective." *Civil War History* (1985).

Werlich, David P. *Admiral of the Amazon: John Randolph Tucker, His Confederate Colleagues, and Peru* (1990).

CONFISCATION ACTS
(6 August 1861 and 17 July 1862)

The Confiscation Acts were proposed by Senator Lyman Trumbull (Republican, Illinois) and passed by Congress to confiscate property used to aid the rebellion and property of those who supported the Confederacy. However, neither President Abraham Lincoln nor Attorney General Edward Bates vigorously implemented either law. The acts did represent the wish of many in the North to attack slavery and pushed Lincoln to embrace emancipation but failed to have a major impact on Reconstruction.

Congress passed the first act after General Ben Butler's admission, in May 1861, of fugitive slaves into Union lines as contrabands. It authorized the president to seize any property used to aid the insurrection and terminated the claims of masters over those persons (slaves) employed to assist the Confederate military. The act, however, failed to define the status of slaves whose owners forfeited their claims to them. The proceedings were to be adjudicated in district and circuit courts with pertinent jurisdiction, that is, where the property prevailed or had been seized. This meant, in August 1861, that most property subject to confiscation was inside the Confederacy. Discussion in Congress over the first act was brief. Only Democrats and border-state Republicans in the House opposed the bill, while only one Republican voted with Senate Democrats against it.

General John C. Frémont offered a more direct attack upon those who supported the rebellion. In September 1861 he proclaimed rebel property seized and slaves freed in Missouri. When Frémont declined to change the proclamation to conform to the first act, Lincoln revoked it, in part to prevent Kentucky and other border states from joining the Confederacy. Many in the North protested the president's action and urged Congress to legislate against the rebels' property and slavery. Most Union generals, however, were reluctant to enforce the first act or encourage fugitive slaves to enter their lines. Nonetheless, slaves continued to arrive, and some were put to work on behalf of the Union.

Lincoln's 3 December message to Congress noted the pressure for more vigorous measures against the South but urged that the war not degenerate "into a violent and remorseless struggle." Trumbull introduced his second act on 5 December. It called for the "absolute and complete forfeiture forever" of all property that belonged to those who supported the rebellion. Over the next seven months, Congress debated a variety of confiscation proposals at considerable length. Supporters of sweeping confiscation argued that forfeiture could extend beyond the life of the offender because the property itself was made guilty by the rebel's support of the rebellion. Confiscation was therefore not a bill of attainder and not unconstitutional. The use of *in rem* proceedings would allow forfeiture of property without the owner's presence, and confiscation could be accomplished more expeditiously. Most Republicans were for moderate confiscation, to be executed by the president only for military purposes and only for the life of the rebel. They argued that property could not be guilty and that the *in rem* proceedings were unconstitutional. Confiscation could not extend beyond the offender's life and therefore could not be the basis for Reconstruction. Most Republicans agreed that slaves could be emancipated through confiscation, although almost no one expressed interest in their status after slavery other than to provide for their colonization outside the United States.

Moderates prevailed in the final confiscation bill. It provided confiscation and punishment for six classes of rebels, broad executive authority (including the power to pardon), the opportunity for rebels to swear allegiance and avoid confiscation, the liberation of slaves in Union controlled areas, and the colonization of willing freed slaves. The bill did not explicitly allow for forfeiture beyond the offender's life. The act also did not free slaves unless courts found their owners to be rebels, and the military had no power to adjudicate the matter of ownership. Nor did the act affect slaves of nonrebels or those who swore allegiance to the North. Only two Republicans in the House and two in the Senate joined Democrats to oppose the second act.

Lincoln had indicated that he favored less severe measures against the South. In March 1862 he had urged gradual emancipation upon the border states and reiterated this plea when Congress passed the second act. He had also revoked General David Hunter's April proclamation that freed the slaves in Georgia, Florida, and South Carolina. Moderates dispatched Senator William Pitt Fessenden of Maine to ask the president how to avoid a veto of the second act. The result was a joint resolution, subsequently passed by Congress, that guaranteed that confiscation of rebels' slaves would only be prospective and that no forfeiture of real property would extend beyond the life of the offender. This weakened an already drastically modified version of Trumbull's original bill and guaranteed that no land would be available for freed slaves or Northern soldiers and that Reconstruction would be limited. Like the first, the Second Confiscation Act was not very well crafted. Nor did Congress provide any funds for its implementation, thereby deterring local officials from enforcing it vigorously.

Lincoln signed the law on 17 July, but also sent his veto message to Congress. Although the president supported confiscation for military purposes, he worried that "a justly discriminating application of it, would be very difficult," if not impossible. His chief concern was that confiscation should not extend beyond the life of the offender. Yet Lincoln realized the importance of attacking slavery, which was a central part of confiscation. Within two weeks, he presented his preliminary Emancipation Proclamation to the cabinet and issued another proclamation, invoking the sixth section of the second act, warning all persons "to cease participating in, aiding, countenancing, or abetting the existing rebellion." He also authorized the recruitment of "free Negroes" and slaves into the military and the seizure of any property for military purposes.

Administration of the First Confiscation Act by Virginia-born Attorney General Bates, a moderate from Missouri, was strict but limited, reflecting Lincoln's concerns. Not until January 1863 did the president actually authorize the attorney general to enforce the first act. Nor did Bates produce a policy on how to implement the act; instead he urged local officials to read the act themselves and carefully pursue only that property that had been used to assist the Confederacy. The small amounts of property confiscated under the first act reflected both the conservative influence of Bates and the difficulty of finding such property in the North.

Bates's enforcement of the second act was no more vigorous. This again followed the president's example. In late August 1962, Horace Greeley, New York *Tribune* editor, had expressed disappointment at the lax enforcement of the second act. Lincoln replied that he would "save" the Union "in the shortest way under the Constitution." Lincoln said, "[I would do] *less* whenever I shall believe what I am doing hurts the cause, and I shall do *more* whenever I shall believe" it will help restore the Union. For Bates, this meant never urging vigorous enforcement of the second act. Instead, he asked district attorneys to take few risks, keep expenses down, prevent injustice to property owners, and limit embarrassment to the government.

On 13 November 1862 Lincoln charged Bates with direction to seize, prosecute, and condemn property under the second act. But he omitted any reference to slaves, thereby leaving the emancipation provisions to the military, which generally ignored them. Lincoln's orders also allowed Bates to control confiscation and deny local officials any latitude in the execution of the second act. Bates expected them to execute the law vigilantly, but with care to "avoid hasty and improvident seizures." District attorneys also proved reluctant to prosecute cases unless they were guaranteed expenses, which Bates rarely granted. Bates's greatest contribution to the confiscation effort was passing along information about property liable to seizure. Although his administration of the second act was honest and careful, it lacked any conviction that the law was just or good.

Military officers, the first to encounter property of any sort in the South, were the best potential enforcers of the Confiscation Acts. Several commanders suggested that they would be vigorous in the prosecution of the second act, but not much confiscation occurred by the military. General Benjamin Butler in New Orleans, for example, threatened confiscation and thereby persuaded a majority in New Orleans to pledge allegiance to the Union. In 1864, General Lew Wallace issued two orders for the confiscation of property in Maryland, but Bates objected because they interfered with his authority. Ultimately nothing was confiscated. In the end, few commanders showed much interest in confiscation, despite some prodding by Secretary of War Edwin Stanton, and that suited Bates, who wished to control administration of the acts.

Treasury Department officials, who followed in the military's path, also could have been effective agents of confiscation. They saw confiscable property before marshals or district attorneys appeared in most areas and could have prevented property title transfers, which often protected it from confiscation. But their responsibilities lay in collecting captured and abandoned property. Moreover, the three treasury secretaries during the war encouraged officials to cooperate with the attorney general. The inability to profit from handling confiscable property also deterred the treasury officials from expanding their opportunities. As a result, except in New Orleans, little confiscation took place in concert with treasury officers.

New Orleans realized the second largest amount of money from confiscated property, largely because it remained in Union control for such a long period and was the wealthiest city in the South. Even so, only $60,000 from the sale of confiscated property was collected there, which was almost one-fifth of the final total. Virginia proved to be the most vulnerable area for confiscation, but most of this occurred after the war.

On 8 December 1863, Lincoln offered a pardon to most participants in the rebellion, and this exercise seriously undercut confiscation for the remainder of the war. Proponents of confiscation failed to object to the pardoning process provided for in the second act, but by early 1864 some moved to repeal the joint resolution to allow confiscation beyond the life of the offender. It was even argued that Lincoln, having read the views of William Whiting, legal adviser to the War Department, now believed that forfeiture could extend beyond the life of the guilty party because confiscation did not rest upon treasonous behavior. But the various efforts over the following year to revoke the resolution failed.

By January 1865, Lincoln favored confiscation for only the most prominent rebels. According to Alexander Stephens, Lincoln even assured the South he would be lenient in his use of confiscation. President Johnson also wanted to spare the South a harsh Reconstruction based on widespread confiscation. But, unlike Lincoln, Johnson used confiscation to punish more classes of rebels, as his May 1865 pardon proclamation indicated. He focused particularly on those with property valued at over $20,000, many of whom were in Virginia. Those excluded from pardons had to request them personally from the president. In the end, most rebels were able to escape confiscation, but not before Attorney General Joshua Speed had four months in which to implement the second act with some vigor. By September, however, Johnson directed the Freedmen's Bureau to return property that was to have been rented to freedmen and suspended enforcement of the second act. The irony is that the second act was well executed only after the war ended and only for four months. Oliver Otis Howard, director of the Freedmen's Bureau, tried to circumvent Johnson's wish to restore land to former rebels, but he failed.

Contrary to predictions from both opponents and supporters of confiscation, the courts liberally interpreted both the first and second act. They granted Congress the benefit of the doubt on most procedural questions and accepted the constitutional argument for confiscation.

—*John Syrett*

See also Bates, Edward; Butler, Benjamin F.; Congress, U.S.A.; Frémont, John C.; Howard, Oliver O.; Hunter, David; Speed, Joshua; Trumbull, Lyman.

For further reading:

Basler, Roy P., ed. *The Collected Works of Abraham Lincoln* (1953–1955).

Belz, Herman. *Abraham Lincoln, Constitutionalism, and Equal Rights in the Civil War Era* (1998).

Curry, Leonard P. *Blueprint for America: Nonmilitary Legislation of First Civil War Congress* (1968).

Randall, James G. *Constitutional Problems under Lincoln* (1951).

CONGRESS, C.S.A.

Shortly after the first seven Confederate states had seceded, their state legislatures sent delegates to Montgomery, Alabama, to lay the foundations for a new nation. The delegates wanted to establish a government as quickly as possible, while secessionist sentiment was still high, and so they adopted a provisional constitution with only one day's discussion. Upon adoption of the provisional constitution, the convention became the provisional Confederate Congress. When Arkansas, Tennessee, North Carolina, and Virginia seceded after the conflict at Fort Sumter, their representatives to the provisional Congress were also chosen by the state legislatures. As such, the provisional Confederate Congress had no members chosen by popular vote.

The Provisional Congress remained in office until 17 February 1862. The task of organizing the new Confederate government took most of their attention for their first months in office. They spent their first month writing a permanent constitution, which essen-

tially mirrored the U.S. Constitution except that it explicitly protected slavery and affirmed the sovereignty of the states. Once the permanent constitution had been adopted, the provisional Congress acquired a legal code by adopting all U.S. laws consistent with the Confederate Constitution. They elected Jefferson Davis as provisional president and Alexander Stephens as provisional vice-president and then established a bureaucracy, including a postal system and judiciary, that mirrored that of the United States. The Congress arranged to have its laws published both in book form and in the largest newspaper in each Confederate state. Most rules of legislative procedure were carried over from the U.S. Congress.

Once the government had been established, the Confederate Congress had to turn to the task of preparing the new nation for a war. They initially hoped to finance the war with a low tariff, and to field a relatively small army numbering only 100,000 men, but the firing on Fort Sumter changed their plans. On 16 May 1861, the Confederate Congress authorized the issue of $20 million in Treasury notes and $50 million in bonds. They also gave the president the power to accept as many volunteers as presented themselves for duty, and placed all telegraph operations under his control. They also established a fairly high 15 percent tariff that stayed in place for the duration of the war. These measures set the Confederacy on a course that would eventually undermine their economy, essentially leaving the government unable to meet its financial obligations by the end of the war.

The first elections in the Confederacy were held in November 1861. Each state had the same representation as under the U.S. government, and the same election procedures were used. There was very little campaigning; while a few districts had heated debates over local issues, there was little discussion of national policy. Candidates usually announced themselves in newspapers and did little else. Voters tended to support the same men they had before the war, and the membership of the first elected Confederate Congress was essentially the same as that of the provisional Congress.

When the First Confederate Congress met on 18 February16 1862, the primary issue they had to be concerned with was maintaining the Confederate army. Most soldiers had enlisted for one year, which was almost up. It was clear that many soldiers were tired of war and wished to return home. Faced with the possibility of losing half of his army, President Jefferson Davis asked the Confederate Congress to approve conscription of all able-bodied men between the ages of eighteen and thirty-five. The Congress complied, though they granted exemptions to a long list of occupations that were deemed more important to the home front than the army. As the war wore on, the Congress was compelled to extend the

The Confederate Capitol at Richmond, Virginia, 1865 (*Library of Congress*)

conscription age to forty-five and then fifty, and to reduce the number of exempt professions dramatically.

Financial issues were a recurring item on the Confederate Congress's agenda. Early in their first session, Treasury Secretary Christopher Memminger asked for an issue of both treasury notes and bonds, and the Congress agreed to the request. However, the Confederate government proved unable to sell as many bonds as were issued, and so late in 1862 Congress enacted a law that forced people to buy bonds by slowly reducing the value of currency. In April 1863, the Congress levied its first taxes on citizens. Property, income, licenses, business, and agricultural products were among the taxed items.

Supplying the Confederate army was also an ongoing concern for the Confederate Congress. Early in the war, it became a matter of practice for army agents to do whatever was needed to acquire what the army needed, including taking things by force. In March 1863 the Confederate Congress essentially legalized this practice by passing the Impressment Act, which permitted material supplies and agricultural products to be seized, as long as a "fair" price was paid, to be determined by a system of arbitration. In February of the next year, the Congress enacted even stricter rules, ordering that no staple crops could be exported and that no luxury goods could be imported.

In many instances, then, the Confederate Congress found itself in the position of having to violate the principles of state sovereignty and a weak federal government upon which the Confederacy had been founded. Most of the time, at least for the first several years of the war, Confederate congressmen and the citizens of the Confederacy were willing to accept the Congress's actions on these occasions as necessary compromises to allow them to keep up the war effort. The debate became heated, however, in February 1864, when Congress considered whether to suspend the writ of habeas corpus. Suspending the writ allowed prisoners to be held indefinitely in prison without being charged with a crime, and was essentially geared toward silencing internal opposition to the war. The Confederate Congress actually suspended the writ three times, with the first instance occurring in February 1862, but their discussions in February 1864 were the most difficult and vitriolic. President Jefferson Davis was being roundly attacked in the press and by the electorate, and he felt that it was imperative that he continue to have the power to imprison people at will. His entire annual message to Congress on 4 February 1864 was a long plea for a renewal of his authority to suspend the writ. After much acrimony, the Congress consented, but it would prove to be the last time. When the bill came up for renewal in August of that year, it was defeated.

If the debate over the writ reflected some of the chinks in the Confederate armor, so did developments within the Congress. When forming the Confederate Constitution, Congress had hoped to have no political parties. However, 90 percent of those men who served in the Confederate government had been officeholders at some point in the United States government, and old habits often died hard. By 1864, the first clear developments had appeared within the legislature, between members from "exterior" and "interior" districts. Exterior districts were those occupied by U.S. troops, and sole legislation passed by the Confederate Congress had little impact there. Congressmen from those districts tended to vote in favor of legislation that could help their states escape Union control. Interior districts were still under the control of the Confederate government, and congressmen from those districts tended to focus on local concerns and on legislation designed to sustain the national government.

By November 1863, the Confederacy had a full party system. Past politics became openly important for the first time in three years, and voting was much more issue-driven. The primary concerns for a congressman were his former party, his position on whether the war should be ended, and his position on Jefferson Davis's performance. When the second Congress finally met in May 1864, party sentiment was so strong that it was difficult to enact meaningful legislation. Most Congressmen focused on attacking the president, or arguing over whether the Confederate government should try to reach a peace settlement with the enemy.

The second session of 1864 would be the Confederate Congress's last. Once again, the legislature was essentially stalemated, at a time when the Confederate economy and the armies in the field were in dire straits. Many Congressmen became so frustrated that they left Richmond and went home. By March 1865, shortly before the end of the session, desperation had set in. On 13 March, less than a month before the end of the war, the remaining congressmen passed a bill allowing the conscription of slaves into the Confederate army. For many Confederate citizens, it was the culmination of four years of Congress violating the principles upon which the nation had been founded.

—Christopher Bates

See also Conscription, C.S.A.; Davis, Jefferson.

For further reading:
Alexander, Thomas B., and Richard E. Beringer. *The Anatomy of the Confederate Congress; A Study of the Influences of Member Characteristics on Legislative Voting Behavior, 1861–1865.* (1972).
Yearns, W. Buck. *The Confederate Congress* (1960).

CONGRESS, U.S.A.

By the time the founders of the United States gathered to write a constitution to replace the Articles of Confederation, the North and South had already developed into distinctly different places. The rocky soil and harsh climate that was typical of many Northern states meant that agriculture was not especially profitable, and so the North had begun to develop a commercial economy based on trade and industrial production. The South, of course, had a slave-based economy that had a profound impact on other aspects of Southern life—social structure, culture, value system, and so forth.

The sectional differences that developed between the North and the South had origins in the Constitutional Convention. To count the South's slaves toward its population for purposes of determining apportionment in the House of Representatives led to the adoption of the three-fifths rule, a measure that would prove increasingly annoying to the North. The goal of the founders, however, was to mute the sectional issue as much as possible by creating a balance in the Congress between the North and the South. From the beginning, however, there were indications that the effort was probably futile. In 1793, less than six years after the adoption of the Constitution, Congress was compelled to address Southern complaints that escaped slaves were able to move freely throughout the North without fear of capture. After much debate, Congress passed the Fugitive Slave Act, which empowered federal marshals and magistrates to return runaway slaves to their owners. Many Northern states passed laws almost immediately trying to block enforcement of the act. Less than a decade had elapsed since the adoption of the Constitution, and already Congress was having difficulty addressing sectional issues in a way that was satisfactory to both sides.

A few decades later, mediating sectional difficulties returned to the top of Congress's agenda. Thomas Jefferson's decision to negotiate the purchase of Louisiana added a substantial amount of territory to the young nation, and both Northerners and Southerners wanted to claim it as part of their region. In 1819, Missouri petitioned for entry into the Union as a slave state, which threatened to upset the balance of power between slave and nonslave states in the Senate. Representative James Tallmadge offered a bill that would have allowed Missouri into the Union with the stipulation that slavery be restricted there. Not surprisingly, the bill passed the Northern-controlled House but not the Senate. Finally, a compromise temporarily postponed the issue. The Missouri Compromise of 1820 admitted Missouri as a slave state and Maine as a free state, and stipulated that no slavery would be permitted in the Louisiana purchase north of 36° 30' latitude.

The Missouri Compromise was the first of several sectional sectional compromises, but as time passed, keeping harmony became a much more complicated and difficult thing to do. Debates over the tariff, Texas's request to be admitted as a state, the acquisition of additional land in the Mexican-American War, and the rapid growth of the state of California after gold was discovered there all inspired lengthy and acrimonious sectional debate in the halls of Congress. In 1850, Henry Clay put together his final and most difficult compromise agreement. The Compromise of 1850 admitted California as a free state, while New Mexico and Utah were organized as territories with the fate of slavery there to be decided by the voters, a system known as popular sovereignty. In addition, the slave trade in Washington, D.C., was ended and a new, stronger Fugitive Slave Law replaced the old one of 1793. Neither the North nor the South was really satisfied with the agreement, and as it happened the Compromise of 1850 was only a temporary truce.

As Clay and the leaders of his generation passed from the scene, the magnetic and forceful Stephen A. Douglas, the "Little Giant," succeeded them. Douglas was a strong advocate of popular sovereignty, and he wanted to extend it to all territories, not just New Mexico and Utah. The Kansas-Nebraska Act of 1854 extended popular sovereignty to those two territories. It essentially repeated the Missouri Compromise, opening the possibility that slavery could exist in every state in the Union. Many congressional leaders were violently angry, and some of them joined together to publish an article in *The National Era* entitled "An Appeal to the Independent Democrats," in which they condemned Douglas and the Kansas-Nebraska Act. Congress's power to keep peace between the sections was quickly fading.

The situation quickly began to deteriorate. In 1855, there was open, armed conflict in Kansas and Missouri. Congress proved unable to take action to stop the fighting in "Bleeding Kansas." In 1856, Senator Charles Sumner made a vitriolic antislavery speech in the Senate, and shortly thereafter he was beaten with a cane by South Carolina representative Preston Brooks. With the election of Abraham Lincoln as president in 1860, the seven states of the lower South seceded. The Senate, led by John Crittenden of Kentucky, made a last-ditch attempt to save the Union, but by then there was no middle ground upon which North and South could agree. The congressmen from the states that had seceded resigned.

While Southerners were organizing the Confederate Congress, Northern congressmen were organizing rallies to stir war fever, to show support for the president, and to call for aggressive military action against the South. After the outbreak of hsotilities, and at Lincoln's request, Congress met in special session beginning on 4 July 1861. The president asked for and received congressional approval of several war measures he had already taken, most notably calling for volunteers. This pattern would repeat itself many times throughout the war as Lincoln, who interpreted his powers broadly, would take action and then get retroactive congressional approval.

The 37th Congress met for its regular session at the end of 1861. The special session in July had been brief and was called strictly to deal with war matters. The regular session, however, provided an opportunity to the Republicans that they were ready to seize. Most of the Democrats in the Congress had been from Southern states, and all of the Southern Democrats from seceded states except for Andrew Johnson had resigned, leaving the Republicans with an overwhelming majority. They quickly passed several bills that had been a part of the 1860 platform: the Homestead Act granted 160 acres of public land to any settler after five years' improvement; the Morrill Act gave land to states to establish colleges and universities; and the Pacific Railroad Act provided funds for a transcontinental railroad. Of course, the 37th

Congress also had to be concerned with matters relating to the war, and in that area it passed several groundbreaking measures, including the nation's first income tax and approving the issue of "Greenback" currency.

Relations between Lincoln and the Congress had been cordial early in the war, but they were increasingly at odds as the war wore on. The remaining Democrats in Congress had been fairly silent for the first year, but they eventually organized into two very vocal factions. The War Democrats were concerned only with reunion and did not support any measures aimed at ending slavery or aiding the freed slaves, while the Peace Democrats pushed for peace at any cost, including disunion. The Republicans also divided into factions. The moderate Republicans tended to support the president, but the increasingly prominent Radical Republicans were very critical of the president, focusing especially on his caution in emancipating the slaves and his Reconstruction plans. The Radicals were also the driving force behind the Committee on the Conduct of the War, which investigated whatever the Radicals wanted to investigate, and in the balance did more harm than good.

The Committee on the Conduct of the War was a way for congressional Republicans to vent their frustrations with the president's conduct of the war. However, as time passed, their focus was increasingly on his Reconstruction plans. At about the same time that Lincoln issued the Emancipation Proclamation, the occupation of Southern lands made it necessary for the administration to begin formulating some sort of reconstruction policy, a clear process by which states would be removed from the control of the Confederate government and be put under the control of the federal government. Congress began to debate the issue in 1862 but had reached no agreements by the end of 1863, by which time there were large amounts of Southern territory under federal control. So Lincoln decided to take action, and in December of 1863 he issued a general proclamation of amnesty and reconstruction. Lincoln's Reconstruction plan came to be known as the Ten Percent Plan. It required that Southerners wishing to rejoin the Union swear an oath of future allegiance to the United States. When 10 percent of the number of people who had voted in the elections of 1860 had done so, they would constitute an electorate that would create a new state government.

Many members of Congress, especially the Radicals, did not like Lincoln's nondoctrinaire approach. The Wade-Davis Bill, passed in July 1864, was much more stringent than Lincoln's plan. It required that 50 percent take the oath of future loyalty for the state to be readmitted. Further, once the state was readmitted, the only people who could vote were those who took an ironclad oath, guaranteeing future loyalty and swearing that they had not assisted the Confederacy in any way. Since almost everyone had assisted the Confederacy, this provision would have essentially excluded everybody. The bill also ruled out any role for the president and the military in Reconstruction. Finally, the bill restricted the vote to whites. Lincoln pocket-vetoed the bill, and Wade and Davis issued an angry manifesto attacking the president and his policies.

Congress also spent considerable time bickering about the problem of what to do about the slaves who were freed. Most Republicans felt that the government would have to take an active role in helping the South make the transition away from a slave-based economy. In March 1865, after nearly two years of debate, Congress established the Freedmen's Bureau. This marked the first time in American history that the federal government assumed responsibility for the social welfare of individuals.

The Freedmen's Bureau would enjoy many successes and would play an important role in the years after the war, but at the time the Civil War ended it was by no means clear what its role would be or how much it would achieve. And beyond the vaguely defined act creating the bureau, Congress had made no decisions as to how Reconstruction would proceed by the time it adjourned in March 1865, not to reconvene until December. Meanwhile, President Lincoln's plan for Reconstruction had been only mildly successful and had come under a great deal of criticism. As such, when Lincoln was assassinated in April 1865, there were no successfully reconstructed states and there was no clear Reconstruction policy. The task of finding a balance between the practicality of Lincoln and the consistency sought by Congress fell to Lincoln's successor, Andrew Johnson.

Andrew Johnson's Reconstruction plan proved to be a failure. The difficult task of rebuilding the Union would have brought the executive and legislature into serious conflict regardless of who was president. Congress was already wary of the extraordinary powers that Lincoln had wielded during the war and was on record as resistant to the idea of his wielding such broad authority during the rigors of reunion. Lincoln's astute political instincts had allowed him to avoid catastrophic confrontations with Congress, but Johnson lacked such talent. The inevitable result was a costly battle between the president and legislature over control of Reconstruction that was marked by Johnson's increasing political impotence and ultimately his impeachment.

During the increasing sectional tensions that preceded secession and war, Congress had labored to solve problems through the traditional methods of compromise and accommodation. Yet it failed finally to avert the crisis for the same reasons that all other national institutions failed to avoid rapture. When the war broke out, the country faced a national emergency of the first order that required a decisive and praid action, so the role of Congress was necessarily diminished by its tendency to deliberate over questions and delay in resolving them. Congressional frustration over the legislature's marginalization by a talented and popular president took on several forms, most notably the formation of the Committee on the Conduction of the War. Yet for all such frustrations, the legislative branch forged a productive partnership with the Lincoln administration that only occasionally broke into quarrels and in the main was a contributing factor in Northern victory.

—*Christopher Bates*

See also Brooks, Preston Smith; Joint Committe on the Conduct of the War; Douglas, Stephen Arnold; Kansas-Nebraska Act; Peace Democrats; Radical Republicans; Sumner, Charles; Wade-Davis Bill; War Democrats.

For further reading:
Bogue, Allan G. *The Congressman's War* (1989).
Boykin, Edward. *Congress and the Civil War* (1955).
Hyman, Harold. *The Radical Republicans and Reconstruction, 1861–1870* (1967).
Stampp, Kenneth. *The Era of Reconstruction* (1965).
Williams, T. Harry. *Lincoln and the Radicals* (1941).

CONKLING, ROSCOE
(1829–1888)
United States congressman

Born in Albany, New York, Roscoe Conkling was the son of Eliza Cockburn and Alfred Conkling, a prominent Whig congressman, diplomat, and lawyer. Conkling decided to become a lawyer, like his father, and in 1850 he moved to Utica, where he began his political and legal careers at the same time, accepting an appointment as district attorney. In 1854, he helped to found the Republican Party in New York, and the next year he married Julia Seymour, sister of New York's Democratic governor, Horatio Seymour. In 1858 he was elected to the House of Representatives, where he would serve for most of the next decade before being elected to the Senate in 1867.

In large part, Conkling owed his quick rise up the political ladder to his magnetic personality. He was handsome, and in good physical shape, and he possessed tremendous self-confidence. Conkling certainly did not build his career around his legislative accomplishments. He occasionally took a strong stand on some issues, opposing the issuance of Greenback currency and speaking out against Radical Reconstruction, but he rarely took the lead and throughout his career he was never associated with a major piece of legislation. His efforts were instead geared toward maintaining party machinery and solidifying his power base. Senate colleague John Sherman noted that "he never interests himself in anything but personal antagonisms."

As Conkling's career progressed, his grip on New York politics became increasingly tight. Many political bosses of the era based their power on patronage and personal alliances, but Conkling, who was somewhat aloof and had few close personal friends, preferred instead to focus on making trouble for those who dared cross him. Senator James A. Garfield, one of Conkling's main targets, described him as "a great fighter, inspired more by his hates than his loves." When James G. Blaine publicly made fun of Conkling's "turkey-gobbler strut," Conkling refused to speak to Blaine ever again, and the two became bitter enemies. Conkling also maintained ongoing feuds with most of the other leading political figures of his day, including Carl Schurz, Horace Greeley, George William Curtis, James A. Garfield, and Rutherford B. Hayes. Conkling even had difficulty maintaining cordial relations with his family. His relationship with his wife became strained and remote, and she rarely accompanied him to Washington. This eventually led to a highly publicized love affair with Kate Chase Sprague that caused Conkling some amount of embarrassment. Conkling also cut his daughter and only child, Bessie, off after she married a man he did not like.

The only person with whom Conkling seems to have had a close personal and professional relationship was Ulysses S. Grant. The two men had a great deal of respect and affection for one another. When Grant became president, he allowed Conkling to take responsibility for all government appointments made in the state of New York, cementing the Senator's power over the Republican Party there. At this point, Conkling was at the height of his power. When Chief Justice Salmon P. Chase died, Grant offered the job to Conkling, who refused, believing that he would succeed Grant as president.

The 1876 Republican convention proved to be the great disappointment of Conkling's political life. The convention was split between his followers and those of Blaine. To break the deadlock, the convention turned to a third candidate, Rutherford B. Hayes. After Hayes's nomination and election, Conkling had to satisfy himself with leading the antiadministration faction in Congress, known as the "Stalwarts." Conkling did everything he could to frustrate the president's agenda and to otherwise create legislative gridlock. In one highly publicized event, Conkling caused several of Hayes's nominees for patronage positions in New York to be rejected by the Senate.

At the Republican convention of 1880, Conkling led the movement to renominate Ulysses S. Grant for a third term. While he did not succeed in that, he did manage to get New Yorker Chester Arthur nominated for the vice-presidency and to keep his rivals James G. Blaine and John Sherman from securing the presidential nomination. The eventual presidential nominee, Ohioan James A. Garfield, was not entirely acceptable to

Conkling, but he eventually gave his support, believing that Garfield would give him control over New York patronage.

After being elected, however, Garfield gave the post of secretary of state to his fellow Ohioan Blaine. Several other appointments made it increasingly clear to Conkling that he was an outsider as far as the president was concerned. Outraged, he broke with Garfield and became an outspoken critic of the administration. In May of 1881, Garfield named William H. Robertson as his choice for collector of the Port of New York, the most lucrative patronage position in the country. As he had done to Hayes's first nominee for the position, Conkling tried to have Robertson rejected. Garfield refused to back down, insisting that the right to make appointments without undue Senate interference was an important presidential prerogative. Some senators were unwilling to alienate the new president, others were aware that the public largely agreed with Garfield's position, and many had tired of Conkling's constant troublemaking. Whatever the case, Conkling was defeated, and on 14 May 1881 he resigned from the Senate. He hoped to be vindicated by being reelected, but he had lost control of New York politics, and he was defeated. Conkling spent his final years in private law practice, dying in New York City in 1888.

—*Christopher Bates*

See also Blaine, James Gillespie.

For further reading:

Burlingame, Sara Lee. "The Making of a Spoilsman: The Life and Career of Roscoe Conkling from 1829 to 1873" (Ph.D. dissertation, 1974).

Conkling, Alfred R. *The Life and Letters of Roscoe Conkling, Orator, Statesman, Advocate* (1889).

CONNOR, PATRICK EDWARD
(1820–1891)
Union general

Patrick E. Connor, originally born in County Kerry, Ireland, emigrated with his family to New York City at the age of twelve. Connor's pre–Civil War career was split between military service and civilian business pursuits. He enlisted for a five-year term with a dragoon company of the U.S. Army in 1838, during which time he saw action in Florida during the Second Seminole War and served garrison duty in the Iowa Territory. After the expiration of his enlistment, Connor briefly returned to New York City to pursue business interests, but a failed mercantile enterprise prompted his move to Texas in 1846. Upon his arrival, tense relations with Mexico prompted Connor to enlist in the Texas Volunteers, with whom he eventually earned the rank of captain. During the Mexican-American War, he distinguished himself in numerous engagements along the Texas-Mexico border, including Palo Alto and Resaca de Palma, before being wounded in the fighting at Buena Vista.

His injuries forced Connor to resign his commission in 1847 and return to his civilian pursuits, which shortly thereafter swept him westward with the burgeoning tide of the California Gold Rush. In California, Connor was active in mining, construction, and other mercantile pursuits, and also joined a militant vigilante group known as the California Rangers. Their primary purpose was to hunt down outlaws, bandits, and cattle thieves. Connor won local distinction with this group in 1853 when he captured and executed the notorious bandit Joaquin Murieta. He parlayed his fame into a successful business and political career in the city of Stockton, becoming one the town's most prominent leaders and wealthiest residents.

The outbreak of the Civil War provided Connor with an opportunity to renew his military career, although his hopes for a prominent command in the East were never realized. He joined the Union army in 1861 and was appointed colonel of the 3d California Volunteer Infantry. Connor's command was instructed to move into the Utah territory to secure the lines of communication with the East and also to protect the overland trails from Indian and Confederate aggression. While serving in Utah, Connor became a staunch opponent of the Mormon church and, in particular, Brigham Young, whom he considered a traitor and secessionist in his own right. In 1862, Connor established Camp Douglas on a bluff to the east of Salt Lake City, with an eye toward keeping a tight rein on the Mormons as well as guarding the overland passage to California.

Despite his distrust of the Mormons and strong personal dislike for Brigham Young, Connor was vigilant in his pursuit of Indian groups that threatened the western travel routes. In January 1863 he led 300 men in a victorious attack against a mixed force of 250 northwestern Shoshone and Bannock Indians in the battle of Bear Creek (present-day Franklin, Idaho). As a reward for subduing this group of Indians, Connor was commissioned a brigadier general in the U.S. Volunteers. In 1865 he was placed in charge of the Powder River expedition, a largely futile campaign intended to pursue and punish hostile bands of the Sioux, Arapaho, and Northern Cheyenne inhabiting the region of present-day Wyoming. The expedition produced few tangible results, although Connor did engage and defeat a small contingent of Arapaho along the Tongue River in August 1865.

Although relations with the Indian tribes of the region remained mostly amicable for the duration of the Civil War, tensions with the local Mormons continued to run high during Connor's tenure in Utah. This was partly due to Connor's efforts to diminish Mormon influence in Utah by offering favorable terms for any non-Mormon emigrants to the region, especially

miners. After his appointment as commander of the District of the Plains in 1865, Connor increased his pressure on the Mormons by establishing an army-run newspaper, the *Union Vidette*, which actively criticized Brigham Young and opposed the Mormon-controlled *Deseret News*.

The aftermath of the Civil War saw the end of Connor's military career, as he was mustered out of service at the rank of brevet major general on 30 April 1866. After his discharge, Connor remained in the region, where he began a successful career as a miner and real estate developer in Utah and Nevada. He also founded a specifically non-Mormon political party in Utah, the Liberal Party, and ran repeatedly for high political offices. However, his continued opposition to the Mormon government of Utah and failed political campaigns reversed his early financial successes and resulted in foreclosure on the majority of his mining and real estate holdings. Despite a long and active civil and military career, Connor died in 1891 a relatively poor and obscure man.

—*Daniel P. Barr*

See also California; Young, Brigham.

For further reading:

Colton, Ray Charles. *The Civil War in the Western Territories: Arizona, Colorado, New Mexico, and Utah* (1959).

Long, E. B. *Saints and the Union: Utah Territory during the Civil War* (1981).

Madsen, Brigham D. *Glory Hunter: A Biography of Patrick Edward Connor* (1990).

Rogers, Fred B. *Soldiers of the Overland* (1938).

Varley, James F. *Brigham and the Brigadier: General Patrick Connor and His California Volunteers in Utah and along the Overland Trail* (1989).

CONSCRIPTION, C.S.A.

By the spring of 1862, the twelve-month voluntary enlistments of Confederate soldiers made at the outset of the war were beginning to expire. Disillusionment with military life and news of hardships on the home front led many of these soldiers not to reenlist, and Confederate leaders quickly realized that a continued reliance on voluntary enlistment would not keep the army adequately staffed. In response, the Congress of the Confederate States of America passed the first of three conscription acts on 16 April 1862 and began the first national military draft in U.S. history.

The first Conscription Act extended the enlistments of all twelve-month volunteers still in service for three years or until the end of the war and required all white males between the ages of eighteen and thirty-five to serve for a similar term. Numerous exemptions based on occupation were a feature of the act. Someone not otherwise exempted could hire a substitute to take his place. As an incentive, the act allowed all men who volunteered for duty before 15 May 1862 to organize their own regiments or reorganize existing ones and elect their own officers.

They would also receive a $50 bounty. Failure to volunteer by the deadline would result in a forfeiture of the bounty, loss of the right to enlist in a regiment of one's own choosing, and loss of the right to choose one's officers.

President Jefferson Davis emphasized conscription as the only fair method of consolidating control of Southern troops, distributing the burden of military service equally among the Southern states, and developing a unified system of military discipline. Many criticized the policy, however, as a usurpation of states' rights. Governors Joseph E. Brown of Georgia and Zebulon Vance of North Carolina were vocal critics, but following key decisions in the supreme courts of several Southern states, chiefly Virginia, North Carolina, and Georgia, upholding conscription as a constitutionally held power of the Confederate government, most states reluctantly recognized the act. Ideological differences, however, over control of conscription efforts, definitions of procedure, and primacy of Confederate over state conscription efforts continued throughout the war.

The Confederate Congress passed a second conscription act on 11 October 1862 that expanded the eligible ages to include white males between thirty-five and forty-five. It continued the use of substitutes and statutory exemptions, although the latter were in an amended form that expanded the list of exempted positions and tightened eligibility requirements. A third conscription act, passed on 17 February 1864, expanded the age limits to include men as young as seventeen and as old as fifty.

Built into the acts were exemption clauses that only added to the controversial nature of conscription. While this policy naturally exempted the mentally or physically disabled from military duty, it reserved most exemptions for those deemed essential to the social, political, and economic stability of the South: state and Confederate employees, politicians, contractors, overseers, shoemakers, tanners, blacksmiths, wagon makers, millers, mill engineers, millwrights, and employees of wool and cotton factories and paper mills. In the Second Conscription Act, planters with twenty or more slaves were automatically exempted under the infamous "Twenty-Negro Law." Also, the cost of a substitute was always high and ultimately enormous. Ranging from $300 in the beginning of the war to several thousand dollars by the end of it, the hiring of a substitute was beyond all but the wealthiest class of citizens.

The existence of multiple organizations charged with overseeing enlistment also added to the confusing hodgepodge of eligibilities and exemptions. West of the Mississippi River, the head of the Trans-Mississippi Department controlled enlistment efforts and answered directly to the War Department. East of the Mississippi River, the newly formed Bureau of Conscription in the Office of the Adjutant General directed recruitment. But not long after the bureau's creation, the Confederate inspector general attempted to consolidate conscription efforts under army command and directed each field commander to assign recruitment officers to draft new soldiers from the surrounding countryside. General Braxton Bragg initiated one such enlistment drive in northern Alabama under the command of Brigadier General Gideon J. Pillow that openly competed with the more timid civilian efforts in the region.

Conscription never enjoyed popular support in the Confederacy. Poor whites, angered by the socioeconomic bias built into the three acts, used conscription as a reason for desertion or failing to appear for service. Armed bands of deserters and layouts (men who refused to be enlisted) seized control of whole counties and actively fought conscription efforts by assassinating conscription agents and waging guerrilla warfare against both Confederate and state troops sent to arrest them. The largest of these deserter counties existed along the Appalachian Mountains in north Georgia, western North and South Carolina, and eastern Tennessee.

The three conscription acts point to the great disparity in war expectations between the wealthy planter and yeoman farmer. Only those white Southern males with the socioeconomic power to gain the exempted government positions, pay the required exemption fees, or hire substitutes at exorbitant prices could avoid military service. Exemption policies only accentuated those differences and led to a burgeoning black market. Enlistment agents profited from the sale of forged exemption documents. Competition for government offices increased, and new, extraneous offices offered shelter from military service to the sons of the planter elite.

While conscription did help consolidate military power under Confederate control, it did little to ensure popular support for the war effort. Corruption among enlistment officials, coupled with a rapid increase in public opposition, violent uprisings, and Confederate military defeats led to a breakdown in conscription efforts in the last six months of the war. Attempts to arrest deserter gangs and reluctant conscripts ceased in many areas, and Confederate officials had to consider the efficacy of enlisting the one remaining captive source of soldiers, the Southern slave population.

—*David Carlson*

See also Brown, Joseph E.; Conscription, U.S.A; Vance, Zebulon.

For further reading:
Moore, Albert B., ed. *Conscription and Conflict in the Confederacy, Southern Classics Series* (1924; reprint, 1996).

CONSCRIPTION, U.S.A.

The first national draft in U.S. history was authorized by President Abraham Lincoln when he signed the Enrollment Act on 3 March 1863. Before this legislation, the Federal Militia Act of 1862 had given the pres-
ident authority to draft 300,000 men, but widespread opposition and increased volunteering provoked by the measure suspended its implementation. Governors made every effort to induce volunteer enlistments after Lincoln issued two new calls for troops from the states in the summer of 1862, going as far as to offer outstanding bounties to get a sufficiency of men under arms.

By the end of 1862, however, the number of volunteers in the North had sharply declined. Military service entailed significant personal sacrifices if one had a family, ran a farm, or had a business. At the same time, wartime industries attracted many workers with wages substantially higher than a soldier's meager pay. Furthermore, there was a growing agitation against the war throughout the country, led by the Peace Democrats and other antiadministration forces. All of these forces combined greatly discouraged volunteering in the latter part of 1862.

With the decline in volunteering, governors were not very successful in meeting federal requisitions for using state militias, and a new method had to be employed to meet the personnel needs for the Union armies. Congress's answer to this problem was to pass a national conscription law known as "An Act for Enrolling and Calling Out the National Forces, and For Other Purposes," otherwise known as the Enrollment Act. In final form, the Enrollment Act consisted of thirty-eight sections. Upon the request of the president, males twenty to forty-five were to be drafted first, followed by all married men between the ages of thirty-six to forty-six. Males seventeen to twenty could serve with the permission of a parent or guardian. The need for men was first apportioned to each individual congressional district. Names were then procured through a laborious house-to-house enrollment conducted by government agents. Finally, a lottery in each congressional district determined who would go to war. If the proper number of men had volunteered in a given district, the draft would not apply there. Thus, it was in the interest of government authorities in the counties and cities to recruit men as vigorously as they could to keep the draft from affecting people in their area. The draft stirred recruiting drives all over the country and resulted in a great many men going into the army who probably would not have enlisted if left to their own devices.

The following drafts were held:

15 June 1863: 100,000 (6 months)
17 October 1863: 500,000 (3 years)
14 March 1864: 200,000 (3 years)
23 April 1864: 85,000 (100 days)
18 July 1864: 500,000 (1, 2, and 3 years)
19 December 1864: 300,000 (1, 2, and 3 years)

This legislation also created the bureaucracy neces-

sary to implement the Federal draft. Administering the draft became the responsibility of the Provost Marshal General's Office of the War Department. The country was divided into 185 congressional districts, with each congressional district becoming a draft district headed by a provost marshal whose responsibility was registering and calling up draftees. His broad authority also included the right to arrest and detain all persons resisting the draft or discouraging enlistments. To further implement this authority, the Enrollment Act also established military commissions and invested these bodies with the power to try civilians suspected of spying and, where appropriate, to impose the death penalty.

The most controversial aspect of the Enrollment Act was its provision for various exemptions, however. All men called to service could legally avoid it by obtaining one of a number of exemptions, the most common involving physical or mental disability. Also, any son responsible for taking care of aged or infirm parents, a brother whose siblings were orphaned under the age of twelve, and a father of motherless children who were less than twelve years old were all exempt from the draft.

Whether able to secure an exemption or not, however, all drafted men were guaranteed two other means of legally avoiding military service—substitution and commutation. A conscript who possessed the means could either pay a $300 exemption fee or provide a substitute. Congress deliberately inserted these provisions to soften the impact of a potentially unpopular law on a war-weary public. These exemptions nonetheless gave rise to a charge that the Civil War was "a rich man's war and a poor man's fight."

With some modifications, including the repeal of commutation in March 1864, the Enrollment Act remained in effect until the close of the war, but not without encountering major dispute along the way. All across the country, insurgent citizens protested against the federal draft. In Columbia County, Pennsylvania, enrollment officers encountered severe problems in trying to register men. One soldier sent in to round up deserters was killed, resulting in the arrest of more than forty men who were later imprisoned at Fort Mifflin. Likewise, in the town of Berkeley, in Luzerne County, Pennsylvania, citizens rioted in protest against the military draft and subsided only after the militia had fired upon them, with four or five of the insurgents left dead in the streets. Nor was this spirit of dissent confined entirely to Pennsylvania. For five days in New York City, mobs roamed throughout the city in protest of the draft. Those riots resulted in more than a thousand deaths. Likewise, similar riots took place in the West, most notably in the town of Port Washington, Wisconsin.

All in all, the conscription act was radical in that it allowed the Federal government to replace the states as the primary agency for personnel mobilization. Likewise, although the implementation of the draft itself was largely a failure in many states, with only 6 percent of Union troops being draftees, it did manage to stimulate volunteering for the remainder of the war.

—*Samantha Jane Gaul*

For further reading:

Earnhart, Hugh G. "Commutation; Democratic or Undemocratic?" *Civil War History* (1966).

Geary, James W. "Civil War Conscription in the North: A Historiographical Review." *Civil War History* (1986).

———. *We Need Men: The Union Draft and the Civil War* (1991).

Itter, William August. "Conscription in Pennsylvania during the Civil War" (Ph.D. dissertation, 1941).

Leach, Jack Franklin. *Conscription in the United States: Historical Background* (1960).

Levine, Peter. "Draft Evasion in the North during the Civil War, 1863–1865." *Journal of American History* (1981).

Murdock, Eugene C. *One Million Men: The Civil War Draft in the North* (1971).

———. *Patriotism Limited, 1862–1865: The Civil War Draft and the Bounty System* (1967).

Paludan, Phillip S. *"A People's Contest": The Union and the Civil War, 1861–1865* (1988).

Sterling, Robert E. "Civil War Draft Resistance in the Middle West" (Ph.D. dissertation, 1974).

CONSTITUTION, C.S.A.

The controversies that led to the secession crisis of 1860–1861 gained momentum from the widely held Southern presumption that the primary and explicitly stated reason for having enacted the U.S. Constitution—to form a more perfect union—was being perverted by the political aggressions of the North. Discontented Southerners had no quarrel with the Constitution itself; indeed, they were in the habit of brandishing its principles like a talisman. Countless declamations reverently hailed the Constitution while condemning what the Union had become. In 1861, having decided that they could no longer live within the Union created by the U.S. Constitution, these Southerners sought to form a more perfect union of their own, but they did so by framing a document very much like the one from which they had fled.

After the secession of the seven Deep South states (South Carolina, Georgia, Florida, Alabama, Mississippi, Louisiana, and Texas), a convention met in Montgomery, Alabama, to establish a Southern government. Convening on 4 February 1861 and calling itself the Provisional Congress of the Confederate States of America, it consisted of representatives from South Carolina, Georgia, Alabama, Mississippi, Florida, and Louisiana, which amounted to only six of the fifteen slave states and did not include the recently seceded Texas. The states represented had selected delegates in varied ways, but each had been consistent in limiting its delega-

tion to match the number of its former U.S. congressional delegation. On the matter of the Constitution, each state would have a single vote. In four days, the Congress unanimously adopted a Provisional Constitution that almost exactly replicated that of the United States. The Provisional Congress then put a twelve-man committee, headed by Robert Barnwell Rhett, to work on conceiving a permanent document.

Montgomery was considerably animated by this drama unfolding in what was actually a sleepy southern town. Office-seekers as well as delegates crowded the hotels and eateries, and entertainments filled the nights. In this atmosphere, for the next five weeks, the Montgomery convention would frame a constitution, going about it in a curiously deliberate and thorough way, as though the peace following secession was a permanent fixture and no urgency required any preparations for war.

What the convention did regard as urgent was the need to write a permanent instrument of government, establish an executive, and provide the provisional legislature with authority until regular congressional elections could be held. The appointment of provisional executive officers—Jefferson Davis as president and Alexander H. Stephens as vice president—was managed with some facility, and some delegates believed that writing the Constitution would prove just as easy, especially because framing the new document would require little originality. Georgia and Alabama delegates, for instance, had been instructed to move for the adoption of the U.S. Constitution without alteration. Although that did not happen, and the business of writing the document would be more complicated and contentious than anyone had thought, the permanent Constitution that emerged from committee on 28 February and was adopted on 11 March did closely resemble the U.S. Constitution, even in its wording. The principal differences were its emphasis on states' rights, protecting slavery, and correcting what were regarded as defects in the processes of government.

A paramount concern with states' rights was reflected throughout the document, beginning with the preamble. Rather than forming a "more perfect union," the states were acting in their "sovereign and independent" capacities to create "a permanent federal government." Officers of the Confederate government could be impeached by a state legislature. Yet the supremacy of the states was not absolute in the new document. State officers had to take an oath to uphold the Confederate Constitution, and the national government's laws and treaties were to take precedence over state constitutions and statutes. Likewise, the limitations on states in the U.S. Constitution were copied into the Confederate Constitution. No state could independently ally or confederate with another state or power. States could not coin money or pass any bill of attainder or ex post facto law. They could not impair the obligation of contracts, grant any title of nobility, keep troops or warships in time of peace, or engage in war except in case of invasion or imminent danger. Although the Confederate Constitution did not mention the right of secession, it can be inferred that the delegates believed that each state retained such a right. They were, after all, recently on record asserting that the absence of a specific right of secession in the U.S. Constitution did not impair the Southern states' power to secede from the Union.

States' rights also accounted for the main differences between Article III of the Confederate Constitution that created the judiciary and the provisions for a judiciary in Article III of the U.S. Constitution. The jurisdiction of Confederate courts did not include cases arising from diversity of citizenship, nor did the Confederate Constitution draw a distinction between cases of law and equity. The Confederate Constitution allowed for the establishment of a Supreme Court, yet the Confederacy never actually formed one.

The maintenance of slavery was specifically addressed in several places in the Confederate Constitution. For instance, it stated that no national law impinging on "the right of property in negro slaves" could be adopted. Recalling the considerable problems that slave questions had created in the Union's western territories, the delegates insisted that slavery be acknowledged and preserved by the Confederate Congress and by territorial governments in any such areas acquired by the Confederacy. The *Dred Scott* decision was institutionalized in the document as well, with the stipulation that citizens of states could take their slaves into such territories. Also reciprocal citizenship guarantees among the states assured the property rights of slaveholders in any and all states, regardless of a state's position on slavery. Advocates of reviving a legalized foreign slave trade, however, were rebuffed.

The Confederate Constitution sought to correct problems with government procedures that practice had revealed in the workings of the U.S. government. The more conspicuous of these changes included the modification of the amending process to provide for the proposal of amendments by a convention of the states. Congress had no authority to propose amendments, and ratification would be accomplished by either two-thirds of the state legislatures or by a similar number of state conventions. To cure the ills of patronage and to stop special interests from raiding the treasury and wrecking budgets, Congress could not appropriate money except by a two-thirds vote of both houses. Exceptions were clearly defined. Each appropriation bill had to register its amount and describe its intention. The president was given the authority to veto individual items in an appropriation bill, thus introducing the concept of a line-item veto. To prevent dubious initiatives from hiding in complicated legislation, each bill could address only one subject that had to be clearly indicated in the bill's title. Cabinet officers in the executive branch could take seats in either house of Congress with the pertinent body's permission. The president was to serve a six-year term and could not succeed himself, thus eliminating both the powers derived from extended incumbency and the weaknesses caused by lame duck status.

With the adoption of the permanent Constitution on 11 March 1861, the Confederate government emerged as a full-grown entity, at least in its form if not its substance. The accomplishment occasioned complaints from only a few quarters. The *Charleston Mercury* grumbled that the Confederacy's version of the U.S. Constitution merely planted the same sectional seeds that had blossomed in the American republic, but that was the voice of Rhett's disappointment regarding the exclusion of an African slave trade and the refusal to exclude free states preemptively from the Confederacy. George Fitzhugh described the Federal Constitution as "the most absurd and contradictory paper ever penned by practical men," yet it was a grumble from someone many viewed as a chronic malcontent. The Gulf states had removed themselves from the Union, but the majority of those states' citizens had not removed themselves from the American political tradition, as they understood it. "They will find it easier," muttered South Carolina planter David Gavin, "to destroy a government than to make one." But Southern secessionists had not really destroyed a government so much as they were in the process of transferring national authority from Washington (where they felt it had been corrupted) to Montgomery (where it presumably would remain incorruptible).

The similarity of the Confederate Constitution to that of the Union did not reveal a lack of imagination on the part of the delegates at Montgomery. The necessity of maintaining order in a potentially revolutionary setting made the virtually wholesale adoption of the U.S. Constitution a certainty. The delegates in Montgomery had the task of hastily satisfying the normal sentimental, cultural, and political memory of Americans who happened to be Southerners. The Confederacy would keep much of the American status quo: the Confederate seal would memorialize George Washington, just as the Confederate Constitution would emulate the government over which he had presided.

Ironically, the very things that made the South less devoted to the Union created the need for some binding tie within the new Southern one. The Southerner had a legal conception of national identity, so the Union for most Southerners had always appeared in tandem with its Constitution. The necessity for a national identity of some kind made the South embrace not just the U.S. Constitution but also the concept of constitutionalism as the natural order of things.

—*David S. Heidler and Jeanne T. Heidler*

See also Courts, C.S.A.
For further reading:
Davis, William C. *"A Government of Our Own:" The Making of the Confederacy* (1994).
Fehrenbacher, Don E. *Constitutions and Constitutionalism in the Slaveholding South* (1989).
Lee, Charles. *The Confederate Constitution* (1963).
Nieman, Donald. "Republicanism, the Confederate Constitution, and the American Constitutional Tradition." In *An Uncertain Tradition: Constitutionalism and the History of the South* (1989).

CONSTITUTIONAL UNION PARTY
(1860)

The Constitutional Union Party originated in the late 1850s as a response to the increasing sectionalism that pervaded the United States' two major political parties, the Republicans and the Democrats. Supporters emphasized the need for unconditional support for the Constitution and the preservation of the Union, regardless of ideological inclinations on other issues, particularly that of slavery. Although short-lived, the existence of the party demonstrated that there were still Americans who sought a political solution to the acrimonious divisiveness present in the country.

The late 1840s and 1850s witnessed the introduction of several new political parties. Each party highlighted a concern of Americans. The Know-Nothings put forth an "America First" slogan with its anti-immigrant, anti-Catholic platform. Others, like the Republican and the Free-Soil parties, viewed slavery as the greatest threat to American unity. As each new party appeared, however, it increasingly included members who argued for their positions without considering compromise.

This lack of compromise spawned a reaction towards moderation for some Americans. When President James Buchanan unwisely accepted the illegal proslavery Lecompton Constitution for Kansas in 1858, members of all the major parties of the 1850s—Republicans, Know-Nothings, Northern Democrats, former Whigs—called for the president to disavow the proslavery constitution that the state had drawn up under questionable circumstances.

Buchanan's failure to respond favorably presented an opportunity for a new political party to emerge. Some dissatisfied members of the Democrats and the former members of the Whig and Know-Nothing Parties organized a Unionist Party at the state level. As tensions heightened between the North and South, the Unionist leaders at the state level organized a national campaign for the presidency and named themselves the Constitutional Union Party.

On 9 May, Constitutional Union delegates from twenty-one of the thirty-three states met in Baltimore, Maryland, to select their presidential and vice-presidential candidates for the 1860 election. According to one scholar, most of the attendees "were or appeared to be venerable gentlemen representing a generation of almost forgotten politicians; most of them had retired from public life involuntarily rather than by choice." The rhetoric of the speeches reinforces this characterization of an alienated generation. Patriotic statements poured forth from the podium, all hearkening back to a more glorious past when citizens placed the nation above party or sectional interests.

When it came time to make a choice for leadership, the names of the most prominent candidates—John J. Crittenden of Kentucky, Sam Houston of Texas, and John Bell of Tennessee, among others—reflected moderation. Crittenden was the logical choice to lead the party, but he declined to submit his name. Houston's supporters pressed hard for his nomination, but his association with the Democratic Party doomed any chance of receiving the votes of the numerous former Whigs. When the votes were cast on the second ballot, Bell received the nomination. His running mate was lifetime politician Edward Everett of Massachusetts, a devoted compromiser.

Bell appeared a strong compromise candidate. Originally a Jacksonian Democrat in the late 1820s, Bell chose to enter the Whig Party in the 1830s. In the 1840s and 1850s, he served as United States senator throughout the period of sectional discord following the Mexican War. Although a slaveowner, Bell opposed his region when he voted against the Kansas-Nebraska Act of 1854 and the admission of Kansas as a slave state in 1858.

The Constitutional Union Party's platform stated that political parties normally used the platform to "mislead and deceive the people"; therefore, its members promised simply to "recognize no political principle other than the Constitution of the Country, the Union of the States, and the Enforcement of the Laws." While this statement provided the core of the platform, the rest of the document echoed the patriotic fervor of the convention.

The 1860 contest, however, was not such an election. From the opening days, it became obvious that moderation would not win the presidency. In reality, two elections took place. The first was in the Northern states, where Republican nominee Abraham Lincoln opposed Northern Democrat Stephen A. Douglas. In the Southern states, Bell and Southern Democrat John C. Breckinridge contested for votes. The result was expected: Lincoln won the presidency by a majority of the electoral and a plurality of the popular votes. Bell accumulated thirty-nine electoral and 588,879 popular votes. Kentucky, Tennessee, and Virginia—all border states—supported the Constitutional Union Party with their electoral votes.

The Constitutional Union Party fell apart after the election. Although some supporters continued the crusade, the Civil War came, and moderation disappeared by military force.

—*Mark R. Cheathem*

See also Bell, John; Election of 1860; Everett, Edward.
For further reading:
Morison, Elting. Election of 1860. In *History of American Presidential Elections, 1789–1968*. Edited by Arthur M. Schlesinger, Jr. (1971).
Nash, Howard P. *Third Parties in American Politics* (1959).
Parks, Joseph H. *John Bell of Tennessee* (1950).
Stabler, John Burgess. "A History of the Constitutional Union Party: A Tragic Failure" (Ph.D. dissertation, 1954).

CONTRABANDS

Warriors throughout history have considered all goods and property seized during a conflict to be contraband, if such items can aid and abet the enemy's ability to continue to make war. The Civil War is a unique conflict because the assets that were considered contraband often included human beings. As Southern plantations were liberated by advancing Union forces, many slaves sought self-emancipation by rushing toward the advancing Union lines. The question of what to do with these individuals, ostensibly the chattel property of Confederate sympathizers, and also the status of these liberated persons were perplexing issues that often faced Union commanders in the field. The mixed signals and miscues between the Lincoln administration and the U.S. Army suggest that no clear policy regarding former slaves as contraband had been developed at the onset of the Civil War and that the formulation of such policy was a work in progress during the first months of the conflict.

Abraham Lincoln did not issue the Emancipation Proclamation until 22 September 1862. Before then, a carefully crafted veil of discomfiture shrouded the question of emancipation. Faced with the dilemma of keeping the proslavery border states of Missouri, Kentucky, Maryland, and Delaware in the Union, the Lincoln administration believed that any rash action toward wholesale emancipation might drive these states toward secession, thus augmenting the Confederacy and extending its ability and resources to make war. In this world of high stakes politics all decisions regarding the status of slaves as contraband of war were viewed as profound decisions that could affect the conduct of the war.

On 24 May 1861, only six weeks after the opening shots were fired at Fort Sumter, Union general Benjamin F. Butler reported to authorities in the War Department that he had put a group of fugitive slaves to work at Fortress Monroe, Virginia. In his dispatch, Butler described the fugitives as "contraband of war," and stated that some were employed on construction projects while others picked cotton. Although the fugitive slaves were not considered to be legally emancipated, they were effectively free, and they did receive a small wage (usually twenty-five cents per day plus rations) from the Federal Treasury for the labor that they performed for the Union

Escaped slaves camped near Culpeper, Virginia, November 1863 (Photograph by Timothy O'Sullivan / *Library of Congress*)

forces. Nevertheless, among Northern abolitionists the catch phrase "contraband of war" became almost synonymous with emancipation. Slaves liberated in this fashion were often referred to simply as contrabands. This practice became increasingly common after Congress passed the first Confiscation Act on 6 August 1861. This measure authorized the freeing of slaves in areas that were already under Union army control and who had previously been employed to aid the Confederate cause.

Even with these policies in place, President Lincoln still proceeded very cautiously on the issue of emancipation. In September 1861, Lincoln ordered General John C. Frémont to revise a proclamation of martial law that he had issued. Frémont's initial proclamation had freed the slaves of all disloyal slaveholders in Missouri. In December 1861, Lincoln convinced Secretary of War

Simon Cameron to delete several controversial passages in his annual report to Congress. It was Cameron's wish to urge emancipation as a wartime necessity and to advocate the use of former slaves as military laborers and as soldiers. Shortly after Cameron submitted the revised report, Lincoln removed him from the War Department by naming him minister to Russia.

For many former slaves, their role as "contraband of war" was a part of the transition from slavery to freedom. The role of emancipation and contrabands was always closely linked, and when freedom finally came to the slaves in the South, Union lines swelled as tens of thousands of the newly free joined the camps and eventually the ranks of their liberators. Coping with the demands of vast contraband camps that were teeming with displaced persons was a taxing obligation to the War Department and represents one of the first social welfare efforts sponsored by the U.S. government. The provision of basic supplies of food, shelter, and clothing; the furnishing of rudimentary health services; and the establishment of schools were not skills traditionally associated with the military, but as the war progressed the efforts to assist the wards of the government in the contraband camps became more systematic. Not surprisingly, when Congress created the Bureau of Refugees, Freedmen, and Abandoned Lands in March 1865, the agency was placed under the auspices of the War Department and General Oliver O. Howard was appointed its first director.

—*Junius P. Rodriguez*

See also Border States; Butler, Benjamin F.; Emancipation Proclamation; Frémont, John C.; Howard, Oliver O.

For further reading:

Buker, George E. *Blockaders, Refugees, and Contrabands: Civil War on Florida's Gulf Coast, 1861–1865* (1993).

Eaton, John. *Grant, Lincoln, and the Freedmen: Reminiscences of the Civil War, with Special Reference to the Work for the Contrabands and Freedmen of the Mississippi Valley* (1907).

Swint, Henry L., ed. *Dear Ones at Home: Letters from Contraband Camps* (1966).

COOK, PHILIP
(1817–1894)
Confederate general

Born to Philip Cook and Martha Wooten Cook in Twiggs County, Georgia, the younger Philip Cook was educated at Oglethorpe University and the Law School of the University of Virginia. Before going away to law school, however, Cook fought briefly as part of a Georgia volunteer unit in the Second Seminole War. After receiving his law degree, Cook settled in Oglethorpe, Georgia, where he practiced law. Upon the outbreak of the Civil War, Cook enlisted as a private in a company of volunteers organized in Macon County. He and the company traveled to Virginia, where they were incorporated into the 4th Georgia Regiment.

The 4th Georgia was headquartered at Portsmouth, Virginia. After the officers of the regiment learned of Cook's education, he was made the adjutant for the entire regiment and was promoted to lieutenant. He remained in that position through the Peninsula campaign of the spring and early summer of 1862. In the Seven Days' during that campaign, he was wounded in the Confederate assault on Malvern Hill. After the Peninsula campaign, Cook was promoted to lieutenant colonel in the 4th Georgia. He held that rank through the battle of Second Bull Run and the Maryland campaign. At Antietam, Cook and his men fought in some of the bloodiest fighting of the war as part of the force that tried to defend Bloody Lane. After the battle of Antietam, when the regiment's commander George

Pierce Doles, was elevated to the command of the Georgia brigade, Cook became the commander of the 4th Georgia.

As part of the rear elements of Thomas J. "Stonewall" Jackson's corps on the Confederate right at Fredericksburg in December 1862, Cook and his regiment did not see heavy action. Chancellorsville in May 1863 would be another matter. In Jackson's attack on Joseph Hooker's flank, Cook was hit by a Union bullet that broke his leg. He was out of action for several months and returned home to Georgia to recover. During his convalescence, Cook was elected and served briefly as a state senator.

Back in command of the 4th Georgia in the late fall of 1863, Cook commanded the regiment in the Mine Run campaign at the end of the year. In the spring of 1864, Cook commanded his regiment during the opening phases of Union general Ulysses S. Grant's campaign against Robert E. Lee. In the early stages of the battle of Cold Harbor in early June, George Doles was killed at Bethesda Church, and Cook succeeded to the command of the Georgia Brigade. In August 1864 he was promoted to brigadier general and was sent with his brigade to become a part of Jubal Early's army in the Shenandoah Valley.

Cook led his Georgia Brigade in all the major battles of Early's campaign against Philip Sheridan and particularly distinguished himself at Cedar Creek. He returned with his brigade to the Army of Northern Virginia in the trenches of Petersburg in early 1865. In the Confederate assault on Fort Stedman on 25 March 1865, Cook was again seriously wounded. He was taken to one of the Confederate hospitals in Petersburg, where he was recovering when Union forces captured the town on 3 April. He was made a Federal prisoner of war.

After the war, Cook returned to Georgia, where he opened a law practice in Americus. He remained an active attorney there until 1880, but in the meantime he had also become active in Georgia state politics, an interest that he had not demonstrated before the war. He served in the state constitutional convention in 1865, and he served five terms in the U.S. House of Representatives. After his time in Congress, he retired briefly from public life but was prevailed upon to become the state's secretary of state in 1890. He died in that office on 20 May 1894.

—*David S. Heidler and Jeanne T. Heidler*

See also Antietam, Battle of; Fort Stedman; Petersburg Campaign; Shenandoah Valley Campaign.

For further reading:

Stackpole, Edward J. *Sheridan in the Shenandoah: Jubal Early's Nemesis* (1992).

Thomas, Henry W. *History of the Doles-Cook Brigade Army of Northern Virginia, C.S.A.* (1903; reprint, 1988).

Trudeau, Noah Andre. *The Last Citadel: Petersburg, Virginia, June 1864–April 1865* (1991).

COOKE, JAY
(1821–1905)
Union financier

The second son of Eleutheros Cooke, a lawyer and congressman, and his wife, Martha, Jay Cooke was born on 10 August 1821 and reared in Sandusky, Ohio. An ambitious person, Cooke left school at age fourteen to work in the Sandusky dry goods and hardware store of Hubbard and Leiter. In 1836 he went to St. Louis to work for a wholesale firm. After the Panic of 1837 brought an end to this business, Cooke found employment the next year with the Washington Packet & Transportation Company, and in 1839 ended up in Philadelphia. That year he was hired by E. W. Clarke & Company, a prominent investment firm in the Quaker City. The self-confident Cooke sold discounted bank notes and marketed with great success stocks and bonds of local companies. In 1843 he became a partner in this firm and the next year married Dorothea Elizabeth Allen. Between 1846 and 1848, Cooke sold Mexican War bonds for the Clarke firm. As a result of effective advertising in Philadelphia newspapers and of the complex operations of the Treasury's depository system, Cooke, along with other members of his firm, derived great profits from the sale of these government obligations. After the Clarke Company folded during the Panic of 1857, Cooke, who had made a small fortune with this firm, went into temporary retirement and waited for a favorable moment to establish his own investment company.

In January 1861 he opened in Philadelphia the investment firm of Jay Cooke & Company, and became the leading financier to support the cause of the Union. His firm offered stocks, bills of exchange, commercial paper, and government notes and bonds. In 1861 Cooke helped to sell for Pennsylvania $3 million of state bonds. Cooke emphasized to potential buyers the importance of patriotism, and met with great success in marketing both small and large denominations of this issue.

Cooke also attracted the attention of individuals in Washington, D.C. The close ties between his younger brother, Henry David Cooke, and Salmon Chase, the former governor and senator of Ohio who had been appointed in 1861 as Lincoln's secretary of the Treasury, greatly enhanced the opportunities of Cooke's firm to engage in business with the federal government.

After opening an office in Washington in February 1862, Cooke was named in October of that year as a Treasury agent to assist in the distribution of $500 million worth of Treasury bonds—the largest offering of bonds in American history up to that point. Cooke proved to be quite capable in offering the so-called 5-20 bond. This was a bond with a 6 percent coupon that could be paid in five years, but was required to be paid in twenty. Cooke developed a viable marketing strategy to sell these bonds; he advertised the 5-20s in newspapers and on billboards and also used bankers and insurance agents in small towns to sell them. By January 1864 Cooke had succeeded in selling the entire amount of this government bond issue, amounting to about $360 million, from which he received a small commission of about $200,000.

Before the end of the Civil War, Cooke assisted in the distribution of another Treasury issue. William P. Fessenden, who replaced Chase as Treasury secretary in June 1864, named Cooke in late January 1865 as the Treasury's fiscal agent for the offering of the 7-30 bond. These were three-year notes that paid 7.3 percent interest. Cooke also effectively marketed this issue. He especially relied upon working-men's savings banks to sell $600 million worth of this Treasury obligation within less than six months.

After the war, Cooke engaged in the Treasury's refunding activities but also encountered severe financial difficulties of his own during the early 1870s. To expand his business, Cooke had established a branch bank in New York in 1866 and one in London in 1870. George S. Boutwell, who served as secretary of the Treasury under President Ulysses S. Grant, authorized Jay Cooke & Company in 1871 to head American and European syndicates for the selling of ten-year Treasury bonds with a coupon of 5 percent. With support especially from J. & W. Seligman & Company, the syndicates of Cooke quickly sold about $133 million of this issue between June and August of that year. However, Cooke's efforts during the early 1870s to sell securities for the Northern Pacific Railroad were not marked by success. As a result of depositors withdrawing funds from his bank in August 1873, Cooke on 18 September 1873 was forced to close the doors of his firm, and thus brought about the Panic of 1873.

The career of Cooke proved important to the outcome of the Civil War and to American financial history. He is best remembered for his patriotic service to the Union's cause and for his effectiveness as a financial marketer. Cooke, who lived in a mansion in Chelten Hills, Pennsylvania, was a religious and a charitable man; he was active in the American Sunday School Union and made donations to Dartmouth, Princeton, and Kenyon Colleges. Cooke died on 16 February 1905 in Ogontz, Pennsylvania.

—*William Weisberger*

See also Chase, Salmon P.; Fessenden, William Pitt.
For further reading:
Carosso, Vincent P. *The Morgans: Private International Bankers, 1854–1913* (1987).
Geisst, Charles R. *Wall Street: A History* (1997).
Larson, Henrietta M. *Jay Cooke: Private Banker* (1936).
Niven, John. *Salmon P. Chase: A Biography* (1995).
Oberholtzer, Ellis P. *Jay Cooke: Financier of the Civil War* (1907).

Sobel, Robert. *Panic on Wall Street: A History of America's Financial Disasters* (1968).

COOKE, JOHN ESTEN
(1830–1886)
Southern novelist

Born into an old Virginian family on 30 November 1830, John Esten Cooke oscillated for years between a career in the law and the avocation of writing. His talent pointed him toward writing, and ultimately he felt most at home with that calling. His achievement in placing stories in the *Southern Literary Messenger* and *Harper's* and the success of several books he published before the Civil War settled him finally upon a career as an author. *The Virginia Comedians* (1854) was a set of stories set in the late colonial period. With his richly detailed descriptions, Cooke here anticipated the postwar local color school of fiction.

In his early writing career, Cooke was remarkably critical of the "aristocracy" and silent about slavery. His Democratic posture and his belief in progress cast him as an antebellum Southern liberal, yet Cooke became an ardent secessionist and joined Confederate forces after Virginia's secession. Throughout the war, he served as a staff officer in the Army of Northern Virginia, coming into close contact with Robert E. Lee, Thomas J. "Stonewall" Jackson, William N. Pendleton, J. E. B. Stuart, and Turner Ashby. These last two he notably depicted in his novels as the epitome of Southern and particularly Virginian chivalry.

His 1863 *Life of Stonewall Jackson* was a resounding success. The volume was pirated by a New York publishing company and republished in London. In the United States, until it was banned, it was a bestseller. Republished in 1866 in New York as *Stonewall Jackson: A Military Biography*, it appears responsible for at least some of persistent myths about Jackson. Portions of the work appeared with some editing in Cooke's novel *Surry of Eagle's Nest* (1866). For the next decade, Cooke would rework and reincorporate historical and fictional characters from the Jackson biography and *Surry* in such works as *Wearing of the Gray* (1867), *Hilt to Hilt* (1869), *Hammer and Rapier* (1870), and a sequel to the events in *Surry* entitled *Mohun: The Last Days of Lee and His Paladins* (1869). After producing a 600-page *Life of General Robert E. Lee* the year after Lee's death in 1870, Cooke reverted to romance writing.

Apart from some slurs against foreigners in the Union armies, Cooke's portrayal of Yankees was typical in that the Union armies and their leaders are described as plodding and unimaginative. The depiction, however, is largely devoid of hatred. One of Surry's brothers even fights for the Union. Essentially wicked characters such as Fenwick (also in *Surry*) exhibit no sectional or personal loyalties, and gentlemanly bearing and courage such as that of Turner Ashby are depicted as ideal qualities that transcend defeat and death.

In *The Wearing of the Gray*, a volume of romanticized but ostensibly historical personal portraits, Cooke opined that the war was not so much an "official transaction" as it was a dramatic set of events. When he was accused of perpetuating "Confederate lies," Cooke noted in a letter to G. W. Bagby in 1879 that the so-called lies were both popular and financially rewarding. The charge that he wrote lies was unfair in any case: Cooke related legends and myths, sometimes drawing on material already in a Southern oral tradition. In some respects, his works were the descendants of the historical fiction of Sir Walter Scott, but his descriptions of Southern heroes as knightly figures met the emotional needs of readers North and South after the experience of a completely unsentimental and brutal modern war.

Cooke in his later years acknowledged that the school of realism evinced by William Dean Howells had brought sentimental fiction into disfavor, though he declined to complain, conceding "that fiction should faithfully reflect life, and…[I] am now too old to learn my trade anew." Cooke died on 27 September 1886, but evidence of his influence can be detected in the work of John Fox, Mary Johnston, and in such celebrated Southern classics as William Faulkner's *Sartoris*.

—*Wolfgang Hochbruck*

See also *Southern Literary Messenger*.
For further reading:
Bratton, Mary Jo. "John Esten Cooke and His 'Confederate Lies.'" *Southern Literary Journal* (1981).
Brumm, Ursula. "Definitions of Southern Identity in the Civil War Novels of John Esten Cooke" In *Rewriting the South* (1993).
Cooke, John Esten. *Surry of Eagle's Nest* (1866).
Davidson, James Wood. *The Living Writers of the South* (1869).
Moses, Montrose. *The Literature of the South* (1910).

COOKE, PHILIP ST. GEORGE
(1809–1895)
Union general

The youngest of three sons, Philip St. George Cooke was born at Leesburg, Virginia, to Dr. Stephen and Catherine Esten Cooke. He gained appointment as a plebe to West Point under the name of Philip St. George through a clerical error made when he entered the academy. Graduating in 1827, Cooke was commissioned second lieutenant in the 6th Infantry Regiment in Missouri. He served the next six years at various western stations and on expeditions into Indian country.

Cooke served in the Black Hawk War of 1832 and the

following year was commissioned first lieutenant of the newly organized 1st Dragoons. On 31 May 1835 while stationed at Fort Leavenworth he was promoted to captain. It was from this frontier post that Cook made many inroads into the West, including one in 1845, when his command reached the South Pass of the Rocky Mountains, covering a record distance of 2,200 miles in ninety-nine days.

During the Mexican-American War, while under the command of General Stephen Watts Kearny's Army of the West, Cooke participated in the conquest of New Mexico and California, an operation achieved by hard marching rather than by fighting. At Bent's Fort (Colorado) on the Arkansas River, Cooke was ordered to advance ahead of the main force on to Santa Fe, with the intention of negotiating its surrender. With only an escort, his action resulted in the collapse of Mexican resistance before any real negotiation. It is important to note that, although initially his escort consisted of only twelve men, reinforcements from the main force, including a battalion of mostly Mormon enlistments, had been proceeding forward to join him. Cooke was placed in command of this battalion, and with the field commission of lieutenant colonel he was sent forward into California. Although his initial impression of these troops was not favorable, when he was reassigned nine months later there was no doubt that his efforts had turned them into an efficient organization.

In the years before the Civil War, Cooke was again on the frontier with escort duty or duties that placed him in the occasional skirmish with Apache and Sioux Indians. Promotions in the regular army were to major of the 2d Dragoons in 1847, lieutenant colonel in 1853, and colonel in 1858. In 1857 to 1858 Cooke took part in the Utah expedition. He also wrote a treatise for a new system of cavalry tactics for the army that would serve as the foundation for training the Union cavalry during the war. His final duty before the war was that of an army observer of the Italian war from 1859 to 1860.

At the outbreak of the Civil War in 1861, Cooke's family was divided over the competing loyalties of state and Union. Two daughters and his only son John R. Cooke followed Virginia into the war, as did his son-in-law, James Ewell Brown "Jeb" Stuart, with both becoming general officers in the Confederate army. This breach in the family was to last for many years after the war, as it left only a daughter, her husband, and Cooke's wife, Rachel Hertzog Cooke, in adherence to the Union. As for Cooke, the military commands on both sides believed that he too would follow Virginia into the Confederacy, but his loyalty to the Union was unshakable, and when a letter from a Confederate general was secretly delivered to him in Washington, he promptly handed it over to the War Department.

Because of his prewar rank of colonel, Cooke was appointed a brigadier general in the regular army on 12 November 1861. However, despite his record and experience in an army that was short of officers at the start of the war, he was placed in the rear. Commanding a cavalry brigade within Washington, D.C., and a cavalry reserve division with the Army of the Potomac during the Peninsula campaign of 1862 was his only actual field service during the war. It can only be surmised that the considerations of his origins and the divided loyalties of his family took precedence over his abilities as an officer or the needs of the Union army. For the rest of the war, Cooke commanded the district of Baton Rouge for a time, was employed on court-martial duties, and later was general superintendent of recruiting for the regular army.

After the close of hostilities in 1865, Cooke was breveted major general in the regular army. Besides his duties on boards of promotion, retirement, and tactics, he commanded successively the departments of the Platte, the Cumberland, and the Lakes. After fifty-six years of service to the army, Cooke retired from active service in 1873. He died in Detroit, Michigan, on 20 March 1895 and was buried in Elmwood Cemetery.

Cooke, a person with a good sense of humor and a stern disciplinarian with a high sense of honor and sincere religious feeling, authored other books besides his *Cavalry Tactics*. He published *Scenes and Adventures in the Army* and *The Conquest of New Mexico and California*. The former is his autobiography, which provides a picture of the West from 1827, the period of his first commission, to 1845. The book is interspersed with reflections on subjects of every conceivable nature. The second work is considered the more important of the two because it is strictly a historical narrative largely made up of extracts from the diary he kept at the time. Philip St. George Cooke was the uncle of the novelist John Esten Cooke.

—*Frank E. Deserino*

See also Cavalry, U.S.A.; Cooke, John Esten; Mormons; Stuart, James E. B.; Stuart's Ride around McClellan.
For further reading:
Cooke, Philip St. George. *Cavalry Tactics: or, Regulations for the Instruction, Formations, and Movements of the Cavalry of the Army and Volunteers of the United States* (1862).
———. *The Conquest of New Mexico and California: An Historical and Personal Narrative* (1878).
———. *Scenes and Adventures in the Army; or, Romance of Military Life* (ca. 1857).
———. *William Henry Chase Whiting, and François Xavier Aubry. Exploring Southwestern Trails, 1846–1854* (1974).
Cullum, George W. *Biographical Register of the Officers and Graduates of the U.S. Military Academy at West Point, New York, from Its Establishment, in 1802, to 1890; With the Early History of the United States Military Academy* (1891; reprint, 1940).
Tyler, Daniel. *A Concise History of the Mormon Battalion in the Mexican War, 1846–1847* (1964).
U.S. War Department. *The War of the Rebellion: A Compilation of the Official Records of the Union and Confederate Armies* (1880–1901).

COOPER, SAMUEL
(1798–1876)
Adjutant general, U.S. Army and C.S. Army

Samuel Cooper was born in upstate New York, the younger son of Mary Horton Cooper and Samuel Cooper, a Revolutionary War officer. At age fourteen he followed his brother to the United States Military Academy and was graduated as a second lieutenant, light artillery, in 1815. He was posted to various garrisons in New England, Florida, Virginia, and New York, including a tour as aide to the general in chief, Alexander Macomb, from 1828 to 1836. Also in 1836, Cooper authored *A Concise System of Instructions and Regulations for the Militia and Volunteers of the United States.* During the next twenty-five years he was exclusively a staff officer, seeing field action only once, with William J. Worth in the Second Seminole Wars. For meritorious conduct in helping to conduct the Mexican-American War Cooper was breveted colonel. In July 1852 he was named adjutant general, remaining at that post until March 1861, when he resigned to offer his services to the Confederacy.

Although a Northerner by birth, Cooper was married in 1827 to Sarah Maria Mason, descendant of a prominent Virginia family and the sister of United States Senator and Confederate diplomat James M. Mason. (Another Mason sibling was married to Robert E. Lee's brother Sidney S. Lee.) By marriage, therefore, Cooper had acquired considerable property in Fairfax County, Virginia. Additionally, he had worked closely with, and had become an ally and confidant of, Jefferson Davis, secretary of war in the Franklin Pierce administration (1853–1857). As president of the Confederate States in 1861, Davis immediately named Cooper adjutant and inspector general, describing his old friend as "a man as pure in heart as he was sound in judgment." Davis certainly valued Cooper's counsel and experience, as well as his "high literary culture." In 1877 the ex-president testified that "I never, in four years of constant consultation, saw Cooper manifest prejudice, or knew him to seek favors for a friend, or to withhold what was just from one to whom he bore reverse relations. This rare virtue—this supremacy of judgment over feeling—impressed me as being so exceptional, that I have often mentioned it."

In June 1861 Cooper was confirmed at the rank of senior general in Confederate service. His was the controlling hand in the administration of the fledgling army and his vast knowledge of military protocol, procedures, and personnel was invaluable. Prized by his superiors, the secretaries of war, Cooper was sometimes criticized for his legalistic rulings and slowness in rendering decisions, but all admired his uniform dignity and courtesy. Although he did not wield much influence in formulating strategy, he remained the Confederacy's consummate bureaucrat, even after the government was forced to flee Richmond in April 1865. He took his duties seriously to the end, turning over the vast archives of the Confederate War Department to Union authorities, thereby saving them for future generations. At the age of sixty-seven, having rendered five decades of distinguished military service, he retired to his ruined estate, dying there impoverished and all but forgotten.

—*Lynda Lasswell Crist*

See also Army Organization C.S.A.; Davis, Jefferson; Strategy, C.S.A.

For further reading:
Davis, Jefferson. *Rise and Fall of the Confederate Government* (1881).
Gow, June I. "Theory and Practice in Confederate Military Administration." *Military Affairs* (1975).
Jones, Archer. *Confederate Strategy from Shiloh to Vicksburg* (1961).
Jones, J. B. *A Rebel War Clerk's Diary at the Confederate States Captial* (1866).
Lee, Fitzhugh. "Sketch of the Late General S. Cooper." *Southern Historical Society Papers* (1877).
Younger, Edward, ed. *Inside the Confederate Government: The Diary of Robert Garlick Hill Kean* (1957; reprint, 1974).

COOPERATIONISTS

In the winter of 1860–1861, cooperationist was the label applied to Southerners who opposed immediate secession from the Union. Cooperationists favored coordinated action between the Southern states, calling for a Southern convention to resolve the issue of secession in the aftermath of Lincoln's election. The cooperationists were a complex and shifting coalition of politicians who sometimes differed on fundamental goals. While some leaders of the cooperation movement viewed it as the best way to achieve a South unified behind secession, others used the idea of cooperationism as a tactic to slow, or perhaps end, the secession movement in the South. During the secession winter of 1860–1861, cooperationists were generally stronger in the upcountry than in the plantation districts, and cooperationist leaders were more likely to be Whigs than Democrats.

In the lower Southern states, a significant minority of whites wished for some sort of cooperative action preceding secession to ensure unity among at least the Deep-South states. Of the seven Deep-South states that led secession before Fort Sumter, only South Carolina lacked a significant cooperationist opposition to immediate state secession. But the cooperationists disagreed among themselves. Some supported cooperative secession and argued that a united South could present a stronger united front if it acted in concert, rather than as individual states. For them, the disagreement with immediate secessionists was over tactics, not on the ultimate goal of Southern independence.

Other, more moderate cooperationists wished to

present some sort of ultimatum to the North. They demanded a convention of Southern states to draw up a list of demands to present to the incoming Lincoln administration, including protection of slavery in the territories, enforcement of the Fugitive Slave Law, and guarantee for slavery in the District of Columbia. If the Republicans rejected these demands, then a unified South could secede. Since Lincoln seemed unlikely to agree to these concessions and most Southerners did not trust him in any case, this position commanded little support in the secession conventions in the winter of 1860–1861.

The most conservative group of cooperationists could be described as conditional Unionists. They asked Southerners to give Lincoln a chance to prove that his intentions were moderate. Only if the president committed an "overt act" against slavery should the South resort to secession. While the ranks of the conditional Unionists included prominent men such as Georgia's Alexander Stephens, the future vice president of the Confederacy, they were disorganized in their efforts to stop immediate secession and failed to check the passions unleashed by the election of Lincoln. Cooperationists such as Stephens and the Alabama leader Jeremiah Clemens believed that secession would produce a long and bloody war. A small number of these cooperationists, including Clemens, voiced doubts about whether secession was constitutional.

Cooperationists exhibited considerable strength in all of the initial Confederate states except South Carolina and Texas, polling at least 40 percent in the election of delegates to secession conventions in Georgia, Alabama, Florida, Louisiana, and Mississippi. Nevertheless, when immediate secessionists carried the secession conventions, dissension was muted. A few cooperationists demanded popular referenda on secession, but, of the original seven Confederate states, only Texas held such an election. With very few exceptions, cooperationist leaders pledged their loyalty to the new Confederacy.

The election of delegates to the secession conventions seemed to confirm the fear held by some secessionists that non-slaveholding whites had little stake in a contest for the freedom of planters to own slaves. In many states, particularly Alabama, a split emerged between upcountry districts, which supported cooperationist delegates, and plantation-belt counties, which elected immediate secessionists. While cooperationism did not necessarily mean outright Unionism, the fact that districts that held few slaves supported cooperationists worried leaders who favored immediate secession. These men consciously worked to bring non-slaveholders into the secessionist fold, and in 1861 they experienced a remarkable degree of success in using the issues of protecting state sovereignty and constitutional liberties to win over non-slaveholders.

—*Wallace Hettle*

See also Stephens, Alexander Hamilton; Unionists.
For further reading:
Barney, William. *The Secessionist Impulse* (1974).
Freehling, William, and Craig Simpson, eds. *Secession Debated: Georgia's Showdown in 1860* (1992).
Johnson, Michael P. *Toward a Patriarchal Republic: The Secession of Georgia* (1977).
McPherson, James M. *Battle Cry of Freedom: The Civil War Era* (1988).
Potter, David M. *The Impending Crisis, 1848–1861* (1976).
Thornton, J. Mills, III. *Politics and Power in a Slave Society: Alabama, 1800–1860* (1978).

COPPERHEADS

The term Copperhead was used in a pejorative sense during the Civil War to discredit Democratic opponents of the Lincoln administration and the war. Republicans charged that Democratic dissenters with their attacks on the Union war effort were like venomous copperhead snakes. To gain partisan advantage at the polls, Republicans claimed that the Democratic Party constituted a disloyal opposition whose antiwar policies constituted a "civil war within a civil war." Throughout the war, administration officials, Union army officers, and congressional Republicans linked leading opposition Democrats to alleged secret societies formed in the North to aid the Confederacy and disrupt the Union war effort. These secret societies included the Knights of the Golden Circle, the Order of American Knights, and the Sons of Liberty. Complete with accounts of elaborate rituals, the existence of secret societies was largely the creation of Republican politicians to gain partisan advantage at the polls. The stereotype of Democratic disloyalty during the war allowed many Republican politicians to "wave the bloody shirt" on the campaign trail after the war.

Although secret societies did exist and some prominent Democratic political figures did have connections with them, most historians dismiss the notion of the Democratic Party as a disloyal opposition as exaggerated and misleading. Copperheads, in most cases, were simply Democrats who had serious questions about the way the war was being waged and the impact that the war was having on Northern society. Steeped in Jacksonian ideology that stressed states' rights, limited government, and antimonopolistic ideas, Copperheads were conservative, negrophobic, and fiercely independent.

While the firing on Fort Sumter temporarily united Democrats and Republicans in putting down secession, as the war dragged on, the action of Lincoln and the Republican-dominated Congress convinced many Democrats that their way of life was being threatened. In the lower Midwest, the closing of the Mississippi River forced numerous farmers to rely on railroad transportation to get their products to market. A rapid increase in railroad rates led to the charge that eastern capitalists were using the war to exploit the agrarian interests of the Northwest. Lincoln's conscription, the arrest and imprisonment of Democratic critics, and suspension of the writ of habeas corpus led to the charge that the war was superseding and circumventing the Constitution. Democratic critics charged that President Lincoln was a tyrant who trampled the Constitution in his effort to subdue the South.

Probably the greatest single issue prompting the rise of Copperheadism was the Republican policy on slavery, culminating in Lincoln's preliminary Emancipation Proclamation of 23 September 1862. Fiercely antiblack, many Democrats charged that their support for the war was compromised by fighting to abolish the institution of slavery. Claiming that emancipation was unconstitutional, Copperheads argued that it would have pernicious effects on Northern society. Charging that miscegenation would result, Copperheads played upon racial prejudices in numerous Civil War elections, sometimes very skillfully. Spurning Republican measures on race as too "radical," Copperheads coined the phrase "The Constitution as it is, the Union as it was, and the niggers where they are" to qualify their support for the war.

Copperheadism was also strong among certain ethnic groups such as German-Americans and Irish-Americans. Distrusting the Republican Party because of its previous connections with the Know-Nothings, many of these groups were wary of a Republican-dominated national government, associating Republican rule with New England puritan fanaticism. Ethnic opposition to the war expressed itself in antidraft violence, most prominently in the New York City draft riots of July 1863.

Although Copperheads emerged in every Northern state, there were several figures who provided key leadership. The most prominent Northern Copperhead was undoubtedly Ohio congressman Clement L. Vallandigham, who was arrested in 1863 for denouncing administration policies and banished to the Confederacy. Returning to Ohio in the summer of 1863, Vallandigham waged an unsuccessful campaign for governor of Ohio. Other prominent Copperhead political leaders included William A. Richardson of Illinois, Edward G. Ryan of Wisconsin, Samuel S. Cox and Alexander Long of Ohio, Daniel W. Voorhees of Indiana, Fernando Wood of New York, and George Woodward of Pennsylvania. A number of journalists, too, played important roles in fostering Democratic dissent against Republican war policies. Prominent Copperhead newspaper editors included Charles H. Lanphier, editor of the *Illinois State Register* (Springfield), Marcus Mills "Brick" Pomeroy, editor of the Lacrosse (Wisconsin) *Democratic*, Samuel Medary, editor of the *Crisis* (Columbus, Ohio), and Dennis Mahoney, the feisty editor of the Dubuque (Iowa) *Herald* whose criticism of the administration led to his arrest and imprisonment in Washington for a time.

The appeal of Northern Copperheadism was closely tied to Union war fortunes. Copperheadism gained widespread support in the aftermath of the preliminary Emancipation Proclamation, leading to substantial Democratic gains in the election of 1862. The disastrous defeats of the Army of Potomac at Fredericksburg in December 1862 and at Chancellorsville in May 1863 led to the so-called high tide of Copperheadism in the summer of 1863. Conversely, Union victories at Gettysburg and Vicksburg in July 1863 quelled the rise of Copperhead support and led to the eventual defeat of Copperhead gubernatorial candidates Clement Vallandigham in Ohio and George Woodward in Pennsylvania. The Union military situation in the summer of 1864 led to a temporary revitalization of Northern Copperheadism. Peace advocates within the Democratic Party dominated the committee that drafted the party's platform, adopting a plank that denounced the war as a failure. However, two prominent factors conspired to defeat the Copperheads. First, Democratic presidential candidate General George B. McClellan repudiated the peace plank. Second, the improving Union military situation—particularly with the fall of Atlanta—made Union military fortunes seem much more promising. The triumph of the Republican Party in the 1864 elections and the victory of Union arms in April 1865 also signified the triumph of Republican ideas on government, economics, and race over the conservative, individualistic, agrarian ideology of the Copperheads.

—*Bruce Tap*

See also American Party; Cox, Samuel S.; Knights of the Golden Circle; New York City Draft Riots; Order of American Knights; Sons of Liberty; Vallandigham, Clement L.; Wood, Fernando; Woodward, George W.

For further reading:

Curry, Richard O. "Copperheadism and Continuity: The Anatomy of a Stereotype." *Journal of Negro History* (1972).

Klement, Frank L. *The Copperheads in the Middle West* (1972).

———. *Dark Lanterns: Secret Political Societies, Conspiracies, and Treason Trials in the Civil War* (1984).

Silbey, Joel H. "A Respectable Minority": The Democratic Party in the Civil War Era, 1860–1868 (1977).

CORINTH, BATTLE OF
(3–4 October 1862)

In late summer of 1862, Corinth, Mississippi, with its rail crossing of the Memphis & Charleston and Mobile & Ohio lines, remained the focal point for both Federal and Confederate forces in the Western theater. Shortly after the battle of Iuka, Mississippi, on 19 September 1862, Confederate generals Earl Van Dorn and Sterling Price met to discuss a joint attack upon Corinth. The two generals decided to combine their forces, with Van Dorn being the senior commander;

march their 22,000 men northward to Pocahontas, Tennessee; and make Federal general William S. Rosecrans believe they were going to attack Bolivar, Tennessee. They wanted to make a surprise attack on Corinth before Rosecrans could assemble troops from outlying areas.

Meanwhile, Federal general Ulysses S. Grant had moved his headquarters from Corinth to Jackson, Tennessee, leaving Rosecrans in total control of the railroad town. Rosecrans continued building the city's inner defenses. He posted troops in outlying areas, but close enough for their recall in case of necessity. Receiving contradictory intelligence, Rosecrans was not sure whether the Confederates would attack Bolivar or Corinth. He was confident in the formidability of his defensive works around Corinth and doubted that the enemy would attack troops securely placed behind these lines. Rosecrans believed that if the enemy forces did not strike the other cities, they would attempt to force the Federals away from the works at Corinth to draw the battle into the "open country" around the city. Rosecrans prepared to defend Corinth. He positioned three of his divisions: General Thomas McKean's on the right; General Thomas Davies in the center; and General Charles Hamilton on the right midway between the inner fortifications and the old Beauregard line, breastworks Beauregard had built in the spring during the seige of the city. A fourth division, commanded by General David Stanley, was held in reserve.

On the morning of 3 October 1862, after marching ten miles from Chewalla to Corinth, Van Dorn positioned his three divisions for the attack on Rosecrans and his 23,000 men in Corinth. General Mansfield Lovell's division was on the right; Price's Army of the West, on the left. They had to traverse felled timber and the Beauregard line located about two miles from Corinth. Lovell's division advanced upon a ridge outside the city near the Memphis & Charleston railroad line. Once the Confederates reached the summit, the Federal soldiers, under the leadership of General John McArthur from McKean's division, fled down the east side of the hill to Battery F, leaving a 24-pound Parrot gun, the "Lady Richardson."

About the same time this action was taking place, Brigadier Generals Dabney H. Maury and Louis Hébert, under a hail of rifle and cannon fire, slowly advanced through the fallen timber and reached the open ground inside the Beauregard line. The outnumbered Federals retreated slowly. After midday, Price called a break, because of the intense heat and the soldiers' lack of water.

Around 3:00 P.M., the Federals, under Davies, made a stand on the "White House" ridge about a mile from the railroad intersection. The Confederates took the ridge and were poised to capture the city, and the Federals retreated behind Batteries Robinett and Williams. Although Van Dorn wanted to pursue, Price, realizing that his men were exhausted, insisted that they wait until the morning. During the night, both commanders repositioned their forces.

The next morning, Maury's artillery began shelling the city at around 4:00 A.M. Most rounds passed over the heads of the waiting Federals. At dawn Batteries Robinett, Williams, and Phillips bombarded the Confederates, who ceased firing.

Hébert, who should have begun his advance after Maury's bombardment, reported sick. Price assigned the Confederate left to General Martin Green, who was confused about what action he should take. An hour later, two of Green's brigades charged Battery Powell and began fighting their way to the railroad. They engaged the Federals in hand-to-hand, house-to-house combat within the city. The heaviest fighting took place near the Tishomingo Hotel.

Simultaneously, Maury's men became engaged in fierce battle at Battery Robinett. Despite grape and canister raining down upon them, Confederate troops led by Colonel William P. Rogers made three assaults on the battery. Rogers, whose horse had been shot from under him, grabbed his regimental flag from the fallen color bearer and climbed to the top of the parapet. He was shot and fell backward into the ditch. The Confederates could only retreat.

At the crossroads, the Federals pushed the scattered and exhausted Confederates out of the city. Meanwhile, Lovell, on the Confederate right, did not advance. Without his support, the Confederate attack could not be successful. The second day of battle was over by 1:00 P.M. Rosecrans reported Federal losses at 315 killed, 1,812 wounded, and 232 taken prisoner or missing. Confederate losses were 1,423 killed, 5,692 wounded, and 2,268 taken prisoner.

—*Kristy Armstrong White*

See also Corinth, Mississippi; Corinth, Siege of; Lovell, Mansfield; Maury, Dabney Herndon; Price, Sterling; Rosecrans, William S.; Van Dorn, Earl.

For further reading:

Cockrell, Monroe F., ed. *The Lost Account of the Battle of Corinth and the Court Martial of General Earl Van Dorn* (1955).
Cozzens, Peter. *The Darkest Days of the War: The Battles of Iuka and Corinth* (1997).
Rogers, Margaret G. *Civil War Corinth, 1861–1865* (1989).
Rosecrans, William. "The Battle of Corinth." In *Battles and Leaders of the Civil War* (1887).

CORINTH, MISSISSIPPI

Corinth, located in the northeast portion of Mississippi, was a young town when the Civil War entered its confines. In 1854 the leaders of Tishomingo County made a momentous decision. They invited the Mobile & Ohio and Memphis & Charleston rail companies to run lines through the county. The next year, when surveys were completed, it was determined that the lines would cross at a right angle on a section of property belonging to William Lasley. A town quickly emerged and was named Cross City. Only a few months later, the editor of the local newspaper decided that "Cross City" did not befit the emerging city. The name was changed to Corinth.

Corinth flourished throughout the remainder of the 1850s, but with the election of Abraham Lincoln and Mississippi's secession, war was close at hand. Many men from Tishomingo County served in the Confederacy and, as early as 1861, Corinth served as an assembly point for Confederate soldiers traveling by rail to various points in Florida, Alabama, Kentucky, and Virginia.

In the spring of 1862, Corinth became the focal point in the Civil War's Western theater. Both Northern and Southern leaders recognized the necessity of holding the city because of its valuable rail crossings. Corinth was also in proximity to ports on the Tennessee River, including Hamburg, Eastport, and Pittsburg Landing. Whoever controlled Corinth held an important logistical key to the entire lower Mississippi Valley.

The fall of Forts Henry and Donelson in February 1862 began a series of events leading to the Federal and Confederate advances on Corinth. The Confederates, under the leadership of General Albert S. Johnston, saw their trans-Appalachian defense line broken with the capture of these forts by Union general Ulysses S. Grant. They fell back on Corinth as the new anchor of their defense of the Lower South.

Federal general Henry W. Halleck set his sights on the same target. Early April 1862, the Federal army under Ulysses S. Grant camped at Pittsburg Landing, Tennessee, twenty-two miles northeast of Corinth. Johnston decided to take the offensive to prevent the massing of Federal forces, and he made a surprise attack upon the encamped Federal soldiers on the banks of the Tennessee River. Although the Confederates made a strong showing on the first day of the battle of Shiloh, they experienced a terrible loss when Johnston was killed. Taking his place as commander, General P. G. T. Beauregard immediately halted the attack late in the first day. Meanwhile, Grant received reinforcements, and on the second day of battle, the massed Federal troops pushed Beauregard off the battlefield. The Confederate army fell back toward Corinth.

While the Confederates were caring for their sick and wounded and improving the system of fortifications in Corinth, Halleck arrived at Shiloh, called for reinforcements, and began a march on the city. Because it entrenched every day, the Federal army took more than a month to travel the twenty-two miles from Shiloh to Corinth. Meanwhile, Beauregard knew that the Federal army was closing in on Corinth. He devised a plan to evacuate the city. By 30 May, as the Confederates were making their way southward on the Mobile & Ohio rail-road, the Federals marched into an empty city, thus beginning the occupation of Corinth.

The Confederate army, after the evacuation of Corinth, underwent significant change. They set up headquarters in Tupelo, where Beauregard suddenly absented himself because of illness. However, he failed to ask permission from his superiors to leave, and General Braxton Bragg was named to succeed him in command. By the middle of June, Bragg decided to move the bulk of his army toward Chattanooga for an invasion of Tennessee and Kentucky. The remaining Confederate forces in Mississippi were left under the commands of Generals Earl Van Dorn and Sterling Price.

It would not be until the fall of 1862 that the area again experienced fierce battles. In late September, Rosecrans engaged Price at Iuka, a small town on the Memphis & Charleston line twenty miles east of Corinth. Rosecrans was able to drive Price to the southwest of Iuka, where he joined forces with Van Dorn to make a combined attack on Corinth on 3 October. The Confederates made a two-day attack against the strongly fortified city, but could not take possession. They had no choice but to retreat.

The closely fought battles of Iuka and Corinth significantly affected both the Federal and Confederate armies. They were the last major Confederate offensive in north Mississippi. Likewise, victories in these battles enabled Grant to turn his attention toward Vicksburg. Because of the Confederate failure to take control in the Western theater of the war (and Lee's failure at the battle of Antietam), Confederate politicians lost all hope of receiving diplomatic recognition as an independent country from European leaders. Moreover, these battles seriously affected the careers of several officers. Van Dorn's failure at Corinth ruined his chances of ever leading an army again. On the contrary, Rosecrans gained much from his victories. He received higher rank and replaced General Don Carlos Buell as commander of the Army of the Cumberland.

Military activity in Corinth, however, did not end in 1862. Although the Federal army remained strongly ensconced in the area, many skirmishes took place between them and the Confederates throughout 1863. When the Federal army marched to Mobile, Alabama, in January 1864, the Confederate infantry and its artillery also evacuated the state, leaving its defenses in the hands of Confederate cavalry and bands of guerrillas. Confederate general Nathan Bedford Forrest, commander of the cavalry in northeast Mississippi, began repairing the Mobile & Ohio and Memphis & Charleston Railroads to strengthen Confederate communications and supply lines.

During early 1865, much skirmishing occurred in the area because many Federals spent the winter camped at Eastport along the Tennessee River. Finally, on 4 May 1865, the Civil War in Mississippi ended when

The battle of Corinth, 4 October 1862, from a Currier & Ives lithograph (*Library of Congess*)

Confederate general Richard Taylor surrendered to Federal general Edward S. Canby.

—*Kristy Armstrong White*

See also Corinth, Battle of; Corinth, Siege of; Mississippi.
For further reading:
Alcorn County Historical Association. *The History of Alcorn County Mississippi* (1983).
Cozzens, Peter. *The Darkest Days of the War: The Battles of Iuka and Corinth* (1997).
Rogers, Margaret G. *Civil War Corinth, 1861–1865* (1989).

CORINTH, SIEGE OF
(30 April–30 May 1862)

The Confederate army, commanded by General P. G. T. Beauregard after the death of General Albert Sidney Johnston at the battle of Shiloh, returned to Corinth, Mississippi. More than ever, Confederate leaders realized the significance of holding Corinth and its rail crossing, which afforded the army with reinforcements and supplies. Beauregard said that if he lost the city, he would lose the entire cause. Anticipating Federal pursuit, Beauregard ordered the construction of breastworks on the east and north sides of Corinth. Rifle pits were built to guard the roads from Shiloh that crossed the breastworks. Beauregard sent brigades to scout outlying areas.

Meanwhile, Federal general Henry W. Halleck, commander of the Western Department, arrived at Shiloh on 11 April 1862 and appointed General Ulysses S. Grant his second-in-command and gave leadership of the Army of the Tennessee to General George H. Thomas. Grant, though stripped of his army, was still the commander of the District of West Tennessee. With the Army of the Tennessee, General Don Carlos Buell's Army of the Ohio waited at Shiloh until the Army of the Mississippi under General John Pope could join them. On 30 April 1862, Halleck with three armies consisting of 120,000 men, the largest military force ever assembled in the United States, began the twenty-two–mile trek southward to Corinth. Despite the size of his force, Halleck worried about another surprise attack and kept his army compact, entrenched daily, and ordered his commanders to avoid general engagements. However, almost thirty skirmishes occurred during the advance, the most notable of these being at Farmington, the Russell house, and the Serratt house—all located within five miles of the Beauregard line.

On 25 May 1862, Beauregard conferred with his generals. Knowing that the Federal army was closing in on Corinth, he pointed out their lack of siege guns. Although General Earl Van Dorn's Army of the Trans-Mississippi with its seasoned troops had reinforced Beauregard, the army reported only 53,000 effectives. Moreover, the men remained weak from losses at Shiloh and from illnesses caused by poor food and inadequate sources of clean water in the Corinth area. Outnumbered two-to-one, Beauregard made the decision to save the Confederate army by evacuating the city as quickly and stealthily as possible because he feared that, if the Confederates waited any longer, they would either have to surrender or retreat under more inopportune circumstances.

Beauregard then executed a clever plan. A few days before 30 May 1862, soldiers replaced light artillery with "Quaker guns," logs painted black to give the appearance of real artillery. Trains moving southward took the sick, the wounded, and supplies toward safety. When the empty cars returned, Beauregard had the soldiers cheer as though they were welcoming reinforcements. He even had the men cook three days' rations as if they were preparing for battle. It was not until 29 May 1862 that many soldiers realized they were actually leaving town, not marching off to a new fight. Early on the morning of 30 May 1862, a detail burned or destroyed army stores and provisions that they had been unable to take with them. The Confederates hastily completed the evacuation.

Later that day, Halleck's armies marched into a deserted town. He ordered only a limited pursuit of the Confederate army. Halleck's purpose was to hold Corinth rather than bring on a full-fledged battle. Like many of his West Point counterparts, Halleck, a student of Swiss military strategist Antoine Henri Jomini, used the common-sense principles of Jominian theory to guide his actions. He believed that the capture of geographic location was more important that destroying the enemy. Within weeks, Halleck dispersed his armies throughout west Tennessee and north Mississippi, leaving only four divisions around Corinth to guard the railroad.

—*Kristy Armstrong White*

See also Corinth, Battle of; Corinth, Mississippi; Halleck, Henry W.; Mississippi.

For further reading:

Bettersworth, John K. *Mississippi: A History* (1959).

Cozzens, Peter. *The Darkest Days of the War: The Battles of Iuka and Corinth* (1997).

Force, Manning Ferguson. *From Fort Henry to Corinth* (1881; reprint, 1992).

Rogers, Margaret G. *Civil War Corinth, 1861–1865* (1989).

CORSE, JOHN MURRAY
(1835–1893)
Union general

Born at Pittsburgh, Pennsylvania, on 27 April 1835, John Murray Corse was the son of John Lockwood and Sarah Murray Corse. In 1842, the Corse family moved to Burlington, the capital of Iowa Territory, where John L. Corse owned a book and stationery store and served as mayor for six terms. John Murray Corse attended West Point from 1853 to 1855, quitting to become his father's business partner and read law. After he was admitted to the bar, Corse immersed himself in politics and was the Democratic nominee for Iowa secretary of state in 1860, losing the election.

On 13 July 1861, he was appointed major of the 6th Iowa Infantry. Corse served as inspector general on Brigadier General John Pope's staff at New Madrid and Island No. 10. By 21 May 1862, Corse advanced to the rank of lieutenant colonel of the 6th Iowa, commanding his regiment and being recognized for bravery at Corinth in October 1862. He was promoted to colonel on 29 March 1863, commanding his regiment in Mississippi. Because of his leadership at Vicksburg, Corse was named brigadier general of volunteers on 11 August 1863. He gained the confidence of the highest officers and the respect of the men under his command. Known for his moral lectures to his troops, Corse also had the reputation of being consistent and dependable in action. During the last week of August, he commanded the 4th Brigade, 4th Division, XV Corps of the Army of the Tennessee. He then commanded the division in the battles around Chattanooga. Wounded at Missionary Ridge on 25 November 1863, he returned to Burlington to recover.

By February 1864, Corse was ready to return to action. He rejoined the army for the Atlanta campaign, acting as General William T. Sherman's inspector general until 26 July 1864, when he replaced Brigadier General Thomas W. Sweeny, who was arrested after hitting General Grenville Dodge. Corse led the 14th Division, XV Corps, during the battles for Atlanta. By early October, Sherman planned to place Union troops between Confederate forces under General John B. Hood and crucial railroads. From Kennesaw Mountain, he signaled Corse, who was at Rome, Georgia, to move troops to Allatoona Pass to protect supplies there. Corse loaded 2,000 troops aboard rail cars, and they reached Allatoona shortly after midnight on 5 October, joining 890 troops under the command of Lieutenant Colonel John Tourtellotte. Corse and Tourtellotte ordered their men into position in trenches and two redoubts along a ridge above the railroad. Corse prepared for combat in a redoubt west of the railroad, and Tourtellotte stayed in a fort that was east of the tracks.

Confederate major general Samuel Gibbs French's division attacked at 7:30 that morning. The Confederate troops outnumbered the Union forces three to two and quickly cut communications lines. As Confederate troops surrounded the fort that morning, French demanded an unconditional surrender within five minutes "to avoid a needless effusion of blood" and promised that the Federals would be treated well as prisoners of war. Corse responded that "we are prepared for the 'needless effusion of blood' whenever it is agreeable to you."

During the ensuing assault, Corse lost a third of his command, but resisted the enemy attack. At 1:00 P.M., a minié ball struck Corse's ear, stunning him. Half an hour later, French suddenly withdrew his forces because he acquired incorrect intelligence stating that Union relief forces would arrive soon. From Kennesaw Mountain, Sherman watched the battle smoke and signaled, "Hold on to Allatoona to the last. I will help you." He told subordinates, "If Corse is there, he will hold out; I know the man." One of his staff officers saw a signal flag message: "We hold out. Corse here." Corse maintained his command, signaling, "I am short of a cheekbone, and one ear, but am able to whip all hell yet." Actually, Corse, who was often overly dramatic, suffered only a scratch but wore a bandage to call attention to his wound.

Regimental reports printed tributes to Corse's leadership. Sherman later praised Corse and his "handsome defense" in a general order, stressing that the preservation of Allatoona was crucial for the success of the March to the Sea, and Corse was brevetted major general. Inspired by Corse's bravery, Reverend Philip P. Bliss wrote the hymn "Hold the Fort" that included the stanza, "Faith is strong in their Commander/Gallant General Corse." The popularity of this hymn in the North caused the defense of the Allatoona supply depots to become more famous than other significant battles.

Corse joined Sherman during the advance to Savannah and led his division in the Carolinas campaign. After the war, he commanded the District of Minnesota, but disliked frontier tasks of guarding settlers from Sioux attacks. Mustered out of service on 30 April 1866, Corse served as a collector of internal revenue in Chicago, Illinois, then was employed by railroad and bridge construction firms. He settled in Massachusetts, where he was active in politics as the chairman of the state Democratic Committee. During President Grover Cleveland's first administration, Corse was Boston's postmaster. Corse married twice: in 1856 to Ellen Edwards Prince and in 1882 to Frances McNeil, niece of Franklin Pierce. Corse accompanied Sherman's remains to St. Louis in 1891. Corse died on 27 April 1893, at Winchester, Massachusetts, and was buried in an elaborate brick chapel in Burlington's Aspen Grove Cemetery. A statue of Corse stands in that city's Crapo Park.

—*Elizabeth D. Schafer*

See also Georgia, Battle of; Atlanta Campaign.

For further reading:
Castel, Albert. *Decision in the West: The Atlanta Campaign of 1864* (1992).
Salter, William. "Major-General John M. Corse." *Annals of Iowa* (1895).
Sherman, William T. *Memoirs of General William T. Sherman* (1990).
Swisher, Jacob A. *Iowa in Times of War* (1943).
Wright, Henry H. *A History of the Sixth Iowa Infantry* (1923).

COTTON

In the decades before the Civil War, the development of the cotton industry fueled the economic growth and westward expansion of the American South and played a major role in the rapid growth of the American economy overall.

Until the 1790s, the South grew and exported a relatively small amount of cotton. Rice, tobacco, and sugar cane were the most lucrative crops raised in the American South. The growth of the British textile industry, however, fueled the demand for cotton. Southern planters grew high-quality Sea Islands cotton, a long-staple cotton, along the coasts of South Carolina and Georgia. The fiber of this long-staple cotton could be separated from the seeds with relative ease, but because the warmer interior climate was not conducive to the growth of Sea Islands cotton, this variety of cotton could only be grown within forty miles of the coast. As a result, the production of Sea Islands cotton was limited.

American planters also grew Uplands cotton, a short-staple variety. Although inferior in quality to the long-staple Sea Islands cotton, Uplands cotton could be grown successfully in the South's warm interior. Until the nineteenth century, however, planters raised very little short-staple cotton. The task of separating the fiber from the seeds was time consuming. A full day's labor from a skilled field hand yielded only a single pound of seed-free fiber. The amount of labor required to process Uplands cotton did not make its cultivation a profitable venture.

In 1792 the United States exported 140,000 pounds of cotton. By 1811, however, that number soared to 64 million pounds. This dramatic growth is attributed to the invention of the cotton gin by Northerner Eli Whitney in 1793. A relatively simple machine, the cotton gin allowed field hands to separate the fiber of short-staple cotton from its seeds quickly and easily. The cotton gin immediately increased output fifty times, and later models further improved on this. Short-staple cotton could be profitably grown throughout the South and growers could meet the British demand for cotton.

By 1840 the South produced 60 percent of the world's cotton. By the time the Civil War broke out, cotton comprised half of all American exports. European nations imported a great deal of Southern cotton, but Great Britain was the South's top consumer, purchasing half of all it produced to sustain its booming textile industry. In fact, 80 percent of England's supply of cotton came from the American South.

As it became apparent that secession from the Union lay on the South's horizon, Southerners realized the benefits that might be had from England's dependence on their cotton. Southerners believed that if the cotton trade were interrupted, textile manufacturers and indeed, Great Britain itself, would face economic hardship. In 1858 Senator James Hammond of South Carolina speculated that if Britain's supply of cotton were cut off, "Old England would topple headlong and carry the whole civilized world with her." Others held similar ideas and speculated that if sectional tensions led to civil war, England would intervene on the South's behalf rather than risk suffering the catastrophic economic loss that could result from the interruption of trade. As secession grew near, this concept of "King Cotton" diplomacy gave Southerners confidence that they would gain England's economic and military support if civil war erupted.

In 1861 after the Civil War began, the Confederacy, to facilitate recognition and support from England, placed an informal embargo on cotton exported to Europe. Later, Southern planters cut cotton production in order to cultivate more food crops. By 1863, desperate for cash to help finance the war, Southerners ended their embargo and attempted to resume cotton sales to Europe. By then, however, those Southern ports that had not been seized by Union forces were subject to Union naval blockades, which effectively prevented the South from exporting goods.

The South overestimated the power of King Cotton. Britain suffered little from the interruption of trade. The 1860 cotton crop had been especially bountiful, and when the Civil War began in 1861, British warehouses were overstocked with cotton purchased in the years before the war erupted. By late 1862 when stocks did dwindle, the British textile industry felt the pinch of the cotton shortage, but the growth of other industries helped offset the ill effects. Furthermore, England now turned increasingly to Egypt and India for supplies of cotton. The South had placed too much faith in King Cotton and England never intervened in the Civil War on the side of the Confederate States.

—*Alicia E. Rodriquez*

See also Diplomacy, C.S.A.; Financing, C.S.A.
For further reading:
Bruchey, Stuart. *Cotton and the Growth of the American Economy: 1790–1860* (1967).
Hummel, Jeffrey Rogers. *Emancipating Slaves, Enslaving Men: A History of the American Civil War* (1996).
McPherson, James. *Ordeal By Fire: The Civil War and Reconstruction* (1992).
Owsley, Frank L. *King Cotton Diplomacy: Foreign Relations of the Confederate States of America* (1959).

COUCH, DARIUS NASH
(1822–1897)
Union general

Born in Putnam County, New York, the son of Jonathan Couch, Darius Couch was educated locally before receiving an appointment to the U.S. Military Academy. He graduated thirteenth of fifty-nine from the distinguished class of 1846. He went to

Mexico with most of his classmates and served under Zachary Taylor in northern Mexico, earning commendation for his conduct at the battle of Buena Vista in February 1847.

After the Mexican-American War, Couch served at a variety of posts and took a year's leave from 1853 to 1854 to conduct a scientific mission for the Smithsonian in northern Mexico. He returned to duty for one year before resigning his commission to work for his wife's family in Taunton, Massachusetts.

At the outbreak of the Civil War, Couch raised a regiment of Massachusetts troops and became the colonel of the 7th Massachusetts. Couch and his regiment arrived in Washington just before the battle of First Bull Run, but took no part in the battle. In August 1861, Couch was promoted to brigadier general of volunteers. The promotion may have come because of the intercession of his West Point classmate, George McClellan, now commander of the Army of the Potomac.

During the Peninsula campaign of the following spring, Couch commanded the 1st Division of Erasmus Keyes's IV Corps. Couch fought with distinction at Williamsburg, Seven Pines, and Malvern Hill. After the end of the campaign in early July 1862, his health began to fail. He believed that he had contracted tropical diseases while in Mexico years before and that these illnesses had permanently weakened his system. He submitted his resignation to McClellan, but rather than accept the resignation, McClellan had his old friend promoted to major general.

Couch did not see action again until the Antietam campaign of September 1862. As part of VI Corps, Couch and his division were sent to Harper's Ferry to attempt the relief of the garrison there. On this expedition, Couch fought at Crampton's Gap in an attempt to reach Harper's Ferry. After the battle of Antietam, Couch took command of II Corps and was sent by McClellan to reoccupy Harper's Ferry.

After the dismissal of McClellan, Couch remained in command of II Corps, and he led the corps at Fredericksburg in December 1862. After the debacle at Fredericksburg, Couch opposed the appointment of Joseph Hooker to replace Ambrose Burnside. In the spring of 1863, as Hooker's plan unfolded for the coming campaign, Couch argued against it. The Union defeat at Chancellorsville confirmed Couch in his opinion of Hooker, and he asked to be relieved from command of II Corps and from association with the Army of the Potomac. He was immediately transferred to command of the Department of the Susquehanna, which consisted primarily of the Pennsylvania militia.

During the Gettysburg campaign, Couch cooperated with Governor Andrew Curtin and the new commander of the Army of the Potomac, George Gordon Meade, in mobilizing the Pennsylvania militia to guard railroad

Darius Couch (*Library of Congress*)

bridges and scout Confederate positions. After the battle, Couch worked diligently to round up Confederate stragglers. Meade commended him for his cooperation during the campaign.

During the fall of 1863, Couch used the militia to keep order in the wake of the unpopular draft levy for the state, and the following spring and summer he kept watch on the lower Shenandoah Valley in an attempt to prevent Confederate raids into Pennsylvania.

On 23 November 1864, Couch was transferred to the Army of the Cumberland. He commanded the 2d Division of the XXIII Corps under Major General John Schofield and fought at the battle of Nashville, where he escaped serious injury when his horse was shot from under him. In January 1865, he took temporary command of the corps when Schofield went to Louisville, Kentucky, to arrange transportation for the corps to Annapolis, Maryland.

In February 1865, Couch was given command of the 2d and 3d Divisions of the corps in preparation for a landing on the North Carolina coast. The expedition was planned to cooperate with William T. Sherman as he moved up through the Carolinas. From March through April 1865, XXIII Corps operated in the coastal area of

North Carolina, using New Bern as a base. The entire campaign took its toll on Couch's health, and again citing that as his reason, he submitted his resignation on 8 May 1865. It was accepted on 26 May.

Returning to Massachusetts, Couch's Democratic affiliation cost him the governor's election in 1866. After several business ventures in Massachusetts and Virginia, Couch settled in Norwalk, Connecticut. He held several positions in the state militia and died in Norwalk on 12 February 1897. He was taken back to Taunton, Massachusetts, for burial.

—*David S. Heidler and Jeanne T. Heidler*

See also Gettysburg, Battle of; Hooker, Joseph; McClellan, George.

For further reading:
Kennedy, Edward F. *Lieutenant Darius Nash Couch in the Mexican War* (1977).
Smith, William Farrus. *In Memorium of General Darius Nash Couch: Read Before the Association of the Graduates of the United States Military Academy, June 10, 1897* (1897).

COURTS, C.S.A.

Article III of the Confederate Constitution established the nation's judicial system, which, like that of the United States, would function within a prescribed jurisdiction along with extant state courts. The Confederacy's court system was manifested at the district level, with each state constituting one or more districts. The district courts were given jurisdiction embracing the equivalent of both U.S. district and circuit courts, an innovation that eliminated jurisdictional ambiguities caused by the redundancy of U.S. district and circuit court levels. The Confederacy also operated an admiralty court in Key West as well as territorial courts in Arizona and what was designated as Indian Country, the southern regions of present-day Oklahoma.

Texas, Virginia, Tennessee, and Arkansas were deemed either too large or their terrain too daunting to compose a single district, so, under an amendment of 21 May 1861, Congress was allowed to create more than one district in those states. The districts were subdivided into divisions. As finally formed, the system consisted of eighteen districts: Eastern Virginia, Western Virginia, North Carolina, South Carolina, Georgia, Florida, Alabama, Eastern Tennessee, Middle Tennessee, Western Tennessee, Mississippi, Missouri, Kentucky (unorganized), Louisiana, Eastern Arkansas, Western Arkansas, Eastern Texas, and Western Texas. District judges were appointed by the president and approved by Congress.

It is frequently asserted that the Confederacy never established a Supreme Court, yet the distinction should be made between the establishment of a high court and the actual physical formation of one. In fact, a Confederate Supreme Court was authorized by both the provisional and permanent Constitutions and was established by Congress in the Judiciary Act of 16 March 1861. Under this legislation, the Supreme Court was to hold an annual session in the capital, and its bench would consist of all district court judges, a majority of whom in assembly would form a quorum. The peculiarity of district judges acting as members of the Supreme Court was a contrivance of the Provisional Constitution that persisted in the Judiciary Act of 1861. Presumably such a practice would impart regularity and uniformity to the body of Confederate jurisprudence. By the summer of 1861, however, the vast expanse of the Confederacy stretching from Virginia to west Texas made the composition of the Supreme Court bench implausible from a geographical standpoint. District judges attending Supreme Court sessions would have left their regions unattended for lengthy periods as they traveled to and from Richmond and conducted the Court's business in between. For this reason, President Jefferson Davis signed a bill on 31 July 1861 to suspend the January 1862 session of the Supreme Court until Congress could reconstitute it under the permanent Constitution's more liberal instructions about its membership. The Court technically did not cease to exist under this legislation—its opening session was merely postponed—yet actually the Court had never physically existed at all, a fact that made its reorganization the subject of subsequent legislative initiatives to "establish" the Court.

The First Congress of the Confederacy did not address reconstituting the Court until March and April of 1862. The House bill died in the Judiciary Committee, and the Senate bill, which would have established an office of chief justice and three associate justices, was tabled. Again in September the Senate took up the matter and again tabled it. The 1863 debates on this matter saw opposition emerge from those unwilling to erect a central legal authority that might impinge on the states' legal sovereignty. Apprehension about who Jefferson Davis would appoint to its bench also undermined support for a Supreme Court. And finally, the personal hostility between the bill's sponsor, Judiciary Committee Chairman Benjamin H. Hill, and its principal opponent, William Lowndes Yancey, doomed the initiative in that session. Congress took up the matter again in 1864 and finally tabled it for the last time in March 1865. The plan was to take it up again in November 1865, but by then, the Confederacy had ceased to be. The establishment of a Confederate Supreme Court, like much else in the Southern republic, had foundered on political and personal conflicts within Congress.

The opinions of the district courts were never officially reported, a practice that continued the one established by the U.S. district courts before the war. Confederate district court decisions were infrequently published as pamphlets, but usually they appeared in the newspapers, where partial or inaccurate information went uncorrected.

The courts ruled on a wide range of matters as authorized under the Judiciary Act, including the sequestration of enemy alien property, criminal cases, petitions from conscripts either to release them from service or remand them to the military, prize cases, and cases pertinent to the constitutionality of law. In matters of sequestration, copyright, and patents, the district courts held exclusive jurisdiction, but they were mutual in jurisdiction with the state courts concerning the deportation or naturalization of aliens and cases of law and equity where the dispute equaled or exceeded $5,000 in potential judgment. In the absence of a Supreme Court, the district courts also served appellate functions, including those on writs of error and alleged violations of civil liberties, such as the denial of habeas corpus privileges.

State courts continued to function as they had before the war, with the only difference being that they acknowledged the Confederate States of America as the sovereign authority. When they were formally reported, state court opinions appeared in the official reports of the states, a record of normal civil proceedings mixed with actions initiated by Confederate authorities trying to enforce conscription and taxation.

When the war ended with Confederate defeat, this entire Southern judicial system became just another manifestation of rebellion and thus was regarded as illegitimate in the eyes of the U.S. government. As the Supreme Court would remark in the 1869 case of *Hickman v. Jones,* "they were as if they were not." Yet in an 1873 ruling in *Horn v. Lockhart,* the Court would declare that there was no reason to dispute the authoritative nature of either judicial or legislative decisions in the former Confederacy "where they were not hostile in their purpose or mode of enforcement to the authority of the National government." Accordingly, rulings by Confederate courts were given the same weight and authority as the customary acts of civil government insofar as they did not promote insurrection or abet war. The U.S. government, out of practical necessity, decided that although the Confederate courts had not officially existed, the substance and consequences of their rulings did.

—*David S. Heidler and Jeanne T. Heidler*

See also Benjamin, Judah P.; Civil Liberties, C.S.A.; Conscription, C.S.A.; Constitution, C.S.A.; Impressment.

For further reading:
Neely, Mark E., Jr. *Southern Rights: Political Prisoners and the Myth of Confederate Constitutionalism* (1999).
Robinson, William M., Jr. *Justice in Gray: A History of the Judicial System of the Confederate States of America* (1941).

COURTS, U.S.A.

Under Article III of the U.S. Constitution, a federal court system was established with the creation of the Supreme Court and the sanction for Congress to establish lower courts. The Judiciary Act

of 1789 set the number of justices for the Supreme Court and three levels of a federal judicial structure. Each state would have a district court. Circuit courts would consist of a district judge and two justices of the Supreme Court, the latter of whom would act as itinerants traveling the circuit. Supreme Court justices complained about the rigors and distractions of circuit riding, but with the exception of a brief period after passage of the Judiciary Act of 1801, the regimen officially remained in place throughout the remainder of the 19th century. Thus, it was not until after the Civil War when the Judiciary Act of 1869 established a separate judicial cadre for the circuit courts that the justices enjoyed some relief from this chore, and they continued to ride the circuit off and on until 1891 with the passage of the Circuit Court of Appeals Act. Even so, Congress did not formally abolish the circuit chores of the justices until 1911.

The activities of federal courts during the Civil War were of peripheral importance, exceptions being a few prominent decisions at the Supreme Court level. Part of the reason for that lay in the extraordinary burdens the crisis of war placed on constitutional processes—burdens that were most expeditiously addressed by the political system and the military. Yet in the setting of the lower federal courts, the marginality of the judiciary resulted from procedural limitations as well. Those restrictions were long-standing, having been set by Congress at the birth of the republic. At the time of the Civil War, state courts still had the task of deciding contentious questions between state and federal law, and appeals arising from such decisions were made directly to the Supreme Court. The consequence was a general diminution of federal judicial presence and activity during the war, especially when Congress authorized the Lincoln administration to suspend the privilege of the writ of habeas corpus and establish military commissions. Such protections the judicial system was able to offer citizens detained and tried under these extraordinary conditions were rare and mostly ineffectual. In any event, the lower court referrals either to the president (as in the case of John Merryman) or to the high court (as in the case of Lambdin P. Milligan) point to the impotence of the lower courts during the exceptional crisis of the Civil War.

—*David S. Heidler and Jeanne T. Heidler*

See also *Ex parte Merryman; Ex parte Milligan; Supreme Court, U.S.*

COVERT ACTION, CONFEDERATE

Although the term covert action had not yet been invented, the Confederacy spent about $1.5 million in gold on projects that today could be characterized in those words. Basically, an action is covert whenever its perpetrator or inspiration is hidden, although the action itself, and its consequences, may not be concealed. To the Confederates, such activities were covered by the term secret service.

The use of gold for secret service purposes of all kinds was carefully controlled by Confederate president Jefferson Davis and his secretary of state, Judah Benjamin. Each project was personally approved by Davis, and Benjamin monitored its execution.

Attacked and blockaded by an enemy with vastly superior resources, the Confederates searched for new ways to frustrate that enemy and achieve their independence. Initially, their clandestine efforts were directed primarily at the collection of information, but they rapidly learned that diplomacy alone could not achieve their objectives abroad.

A major effort was undertaken to buy weapons, ships, and other equipment abroad. To facilitate this effort, the export firm of Fraser, Trenholm, and Company of Liverpool, England, was appointed as the financial agent of the Confederacy. Although much of the procurement work had to be done in a clandestine manner, and James D. Bulloch, the Confederate in charge of ship procurement in Britain, regarded it.as secret service, it was hardly covert action in the modern sense. Part of the Confederate effort in Britain, however, was devoted to propaganda, and a newspaper, the *Index*, was established as a Confederate mouthpiece in England. These activities would fit the modern definition of covert action.

Another covert action project involved the appointment of Father John B. Bannon as Confederate agent in Ireland, charged with the mission of frustrating the Union campaign to recruit Irish men for the Union army. The Irish-born Father Bannon, a chaplain of Missouri troops in the Confederate army, was persuaded to undertake the mission in September 1863. Although he worked hard at his mission, he was not successful in stopping the flow of recruits to the North.

The development of the concept of covert action was stimulated by the writings of Bernard Janin Sage, a Louisiana planter, who had served on a merchant ship in his youth. Sage was interested in the promotion of privateering at sea, and from that beginning he progressed to the promotion of irregular warfare on land as well as sea. He has received little recognition for his efforts, but he gave an important impetus to thinking about covert action, as well as other kinds of irregular warfare.

The largest true Confederate covert action project began in June 1863, when General Robert E. Lee persuaded Confederate president Jefferson Davis that the will to fight of the Northern people was the true target of the Confederacy. Lee also pointed out that, in view of the disparity in resources, the North could not be defeated by action on the battlefield alone. The people of the North needed to be persuaded that victory on the battlefield was not worth the effort.

Davis decided that it would be necessary to launch a new and drastic campaign of action to influence the population of the North, and chose as the main target the defeat of Abraham Lincoln in the election of 1864. He persuaded the Confederate Congress to pass legislation authorizing this new campaign and to appropriate money to finance it. This was finally achieved on 15 February 1864, when the Confederate Congress appropriated $5 million for secret service involving sabotage and attacks on targets behind enemy lines, as well as efforts to support antiwar politicians at the ballot box.

After some delay in finding a suitable chief for the operation, Jacob Thompson of Mississippi, a former secretary of the interior during the administration of U.S. president Buchanan, was chosen. He was given $1 million in secret service gold and sent to Canada as Confederate commissioner in April 1864. He was accompanied by Clement C. Clay, who also held the title of commissioner and represented the Confederate War Department. As Thompson had the money, it was clear that he was the senior of the two.

Thompson set up his quarters in Toronto and proceeded to establish contact with a number of antiwar politicians in the North. Clay set up operations in St. Catharines, near Niagara, a central point from which one could move west to Windsor for access to Detroit and east to Montreal for access to New York and New England. Together these operatives created a staff made up of diverse elements, including Confederate personnel already in secret service such as P. C. Martin in Montreal and Larry MacDonald in Toronto, Confederate soldiers who had escaped from Union prison camps, and a number of pro-Confederate civilians, particularly from Kentucky. These provided a pool of talent from which to recruit needed personnel. A few additional military personnel, such as Captain Thomas C. Hines of General John Hunt Morgan's cavalry, were provided by the Confederacy as the need arose.

Another member of the Confederate team was George Nicholas Sanders of Kentucky and New York. He had been active in Democratic Party politics for years, and was friendly to the Radical Republican element in a number of the European monarchies. Sanders was particularly fond of the chaos theory, which held that the removal of a few key officials by capture or assassination would disrupt normal government and provide an opportunity for antigovernment groups to seize power.

The Confederate operation in Canada tried to induce pro-Confederate Copperheads in the North to revolt, first at the time of the Democratic Party's convention in Chicago in August, and then at the time of the election. They also sponsored raids and sabotage to prove to the people of the North that the Lincoln administration was incapable of protecting them. The most notable of these raids took place in October 1864 at St. Albans, Vermont, where the Confederates seized over $200,000 in U.S. currency.

The Confederate efforts, however, were not enough to overcome the effect of Northern victories on the battlefield, and Lincoln easily won reelection in November 1864.

In 1864 the Confederates launched a parallel operation to capture President Abraham Lincoln as a hostage. John Wilkes Booth was recruited to play a leading role in this effort, and in October 1864 he spent several days in Canada in consultation with Sanders. This operation, like the broader campaign, ended in failure, and Booth unilaterally resorted to assassination.

One Confederate operation never took place, but is notable for the amount of money involved. Early in the summer of 1864 dissident Poles, suffering under the rule of the Russian Tsar, offered to raise a brigade of Polish troops to fight for the Confederacy. Jefferson Davis approved the idea and $250,000 in secret service gold was earmarked for this purpose. The money was sent to Colin J. McCrae, Confederate financial agent in Europe, but Confederate fortunes on the battlefield turned for the worse with the fall of Atlanta to General William T. Sherman, and the Poles apparently cooled to the idea. McCrae reported in December 1864 that he had not been approached by the Poles, and that the money was still under his control. Presumably it was still unspent when the war ended in 1865.

After the war Judah Benjamin wrote to all Confederate agents abroad and requested that they turn in to him any secret service funds that they might have left over. How much was turned in is not known, but there were reports of Confederate money being available to defend Confederates tried for wartime activities.

The Confederate covert action effort suffered from a lack of uniform understanding of its objectives by the diverse personnel employed, and from their lack of experience in clandestine operations, paltry training, and loose organization and discipline. In spite of these difficulties, the efforts of the Confederates involved in covert action had a major effect on public opinion in the North. If Confederate fortunes on the battlefield had remained favorable, covert action might have helped the Confederacy achieve independence.

—*William A. Tidwell*

See also Benjamin, Judah P.; Bulloch, James D.; Clay, Clement C.; Hines, Thomas H.; St. Albans, Vermont, Raid; Thompson, Jacob.

For further reading:

Bakeless, John. *Spies of the Confederacy* (1970).

Kinchen, Oscar A. *Confederate Operations in Canada and the North* (1970).

Tidwell, William A. *April '65: Confederate Covert Action in the American Civil War* (1995).

Tidwell, William A., James O. Hall, and David Winfred Gaddy. *Come Retribution: The Confederate Secret Service and the Assassination of Abraham Lincoln* (1988).

COVERT OPERATIONS, U.S.A.

During the Civil War, the Lincoln administration employed covert operations to frustrate Confederate activities in Europe, influence domestic and foreign public opinion, and, in at least one instance, possibly meddle in crucial New England elections. Such activities can be distinguished from espionage or covert activity that served to advance military missions, such as the work of Andrews's Raiders or the Kilpatrick-Dahlgren Raid on Richmond in 1864. The ostensible instrument of secret government endeavors, the U.S. Secret Service, was established on 23 July 1860, under the authority of the Treasury Department, but its only defined duties were then as now protecting the president and protecting the integrity of the currency by tracking down counterfeiters. It would not have a designated chief until after the war. Detective Allan Pinkerton worked for the army, especially for George McClellan, and he is sometimes mistakenly considered to have been the representative of a more solidly established government agency than he actually was. Lafayette C. Baker operated under Edwin M. Stanton's War Department as the chief of detectives, and he conducted operations that were secretly authorized by the president and the secretary.

Truly covert operations, however, were beyond the scrutiny of Congress. They were always funded in irregular or private ways and that, along with their purpose, always required that the administration maintain a way to exercise plausible deniability. In this regard, such covert operations were distinguishable from those conducted by the Secret Service, although the degree to which they were distinguishable remains a source of debate. The very nature of clandestine activity continues to veil its details for historians as much as it did for contemporaries. Not until the end of the 1950s, with Edwin C. Fishel's accidental discovery of the operational files of the Army of the Potomac's Bureau of Military Information, could an authoritative account of Union military intelligence be assembled.

It is known that Secretary of State William H. Seward directed secret enterprises throughout the war. He arranged to have them funded by nondescript government appropriations or frequently by private sources. They were carried out in both foreign and domestic settings and involved a makeshift, but relatively sophisticated, network of agents and informants. In Europe, Henry Shelton Sanford directed covert efforts to sway popular sentiment away from the Confederacy and toward the Union by bribing journalists and subsidizing newspapers. In addition to such ideological projects, Sanford also tried to obstruct Confederate efforts to procure ships, arms, and financial assistance from private firms.

Seward's State Department provided Sanford with his cover by appointing him U.S. minister to Belgium, and under that designation he arrived in Paris in 1861. Soon, however, he was ranging the continent, eventually establishing contacts as far away as Spain, Italy, and Prussia. In London, he worked to counter the activities of Confederate purchasing agent James D. Bulloch, a man Sanford considered so menacing that he proposed contriving a way to have the resourceful Confederate arrested. Through a helpful contact at Scotland Yard, Sanford fashioned a web of agents all over England. These operatives reported on cargoes moving out of British ports and infiltrated factories to advise Sanford of manufacturing arrangements that might be tied to the Confederacy. His secret payroll included business officials who revealed the terms of Confederate contracts, British postal workers who provided him with regular reports about correspondence to Confederate agents, and telegraph operators who shunted Confederate messages to him.

It was expensive work, especially when Sanford aggressively moved to thwart Southern manufacturing contracts by outbidding Confederate emissaries. Money was either inconsistently available or in short supply, and although Seward placed a secret fund of a million dollars at Sanford's disposal, the diplomat-agent spent about $15,000 of his own money secretly advancing the cause of the Union. Subsidizing European newspapers and bribing individual journalists was such an expensive proposition that Seward occasionally balked at the price. Instead, he enlisted prominent Americans to travel abroad and use what influence they could to accomplish the propaganda war more frugally. In Paris, U.S. Consul General John Bigelow was one such operative. Bigelow's experience as editor of the *New York Evening Post* made him all the more effective in dealing with newsmen. New York Republican Thurlow Weed performed similar service in persuading British newspapers to support the Union cause, especially when helped by Sanford's slush fund. Seward also recruited clerics to the cause, dispatching Archbishop John Hughes and covering his $5,000 in expenses to perform a wide range of sensitive tasks. Hughes reportedly met privately with Napoleon III in addition to encouraging Irish immigration to replenish the ranks of the Union army. Episcopal bishop Charles McIlvaine performed comparable work among British Anglicans. Meanwhile, impromptu mass meetings that emphasized the detestable immorality of slavery were spurred among the British working class by a host of nondescript operatives whose specialty was staging spontaneity.

Propaganda efforts marked the bulk of domestic operations conducted by Seward and his agents. In addition to waging a campaign of disinformation by planting false stories with a friendly press, the administration used direct payment through bribes and the more subtle compensation of patronage to control unfriendly newspapers and contrary journalists. Thurlow Weed successfully convinced James Gordon Bennett to alter the antagonistic stance of his *New York Herald*, a mission apparently accomplished by the administration's offer to make Bennett's son a revenue agent. There was at least one plan seriously considered by Seward and Lincoln to suborn Confederate newspapers, and in the propaganda war within the Confederacy, the clergy was again enlisted. Methodist minister James F. Jaquess, who was also a colonel in the Union army, was apparently put into contact with the administration through his superior officer, Brigadier General James A. Garfield, with the view of having Jaquess use his contacts within the Southern branch of the church. It is not clear what Lincoln expected Jaquess to accomplish as he traveled throughout the South in 1863. Possibly he was to seek out peace sentiments within his Southern brethren, but he might have been attempting to sow discontent among Southern clergy. In any event, Lincoln several times remarked that the government could have no connection with the traveling minister and that Jaquess was placing himself in some peril in undertaking his journey, observations that suggest that some people in Washington deemed him a spy.

The Lincoln administration undertook some covert activity within the Union beyond that necessary to infiltrate Copperhead groups and foil subversive conspiracies, certainly a legitimate enterprise of the state. One instance possibly involved attempts to influence the important 1863 congressional elections in New Hampshire and Connecticut, where Peace Democrats mounted a stiff campaign playing on antiadministration sentiments. The actual operation is still shrouded in shadows, but it is evident that Thurlow Weed was commissioned by Seward to make sure that Republicans won these contests. Weed accordingly raised at least $15,000 from private sources in the New York business community. How he used the money is unclear, but the Peace Democrats were narrowly defeated in the February elections.

The Civil War is often described as straddling the line that separates the last of the old wars and the first of the modern ones. Yet, in the use of covert operations, the Lincoln administration did not break new ground so much as it followed a tradition established by the founders during the American Revolution. Lincoln, the canny westerner, and Seward, the wily New Yorker, certainly understood the compelling need of extralegal activity in the face of high national peril. In the extraordinary crisis of the Union, it was part of a guiding attitude that Lincoln described as necessary to disenthrall the government from the routines of ordinary functions. Then, he said, they would save their country.

—*David S. Heidler and Jeanne T. Heidler*

See also Baker, La Fayette Curry; Copperheads; Covert Action, Confederate; Espionage; Peace Democrats.

For further reading:
Fishel, Edwin C. *The Secret War for the Union* (1996).
Klement, Frank L. *Dark Lanterns: Secret Political Societies, Conspiracies, and Treason Trials in the Civil War* (1984).
Mogelever, Jacob. *Death to Traitors; the Story of General Lafayette C. Baker, Lincoln's Forgotten Secret Service Chief* (1960).
O'Toole, G. J. A. *Honorable Treachery: The History of U. S. Intelligence, Espionage, and Covert Action from the American Revolution to the CIA* (1991).
Richardson, Albert D. *The Secret Service, the Field, the Dungeon and the Escape* (1865).

COX, JACOB DOLSON
(1828–1900)
Union general, lawyer, politician, and educator

Jacob Dolson Cox was born on 27 October 1828 in Montreal, Canada, the son of Thedia Kenyon and Jacob Dolson Cox, Sr., a builder who was working in the United States at the time. The family, of German extraction, returned to New York City, where young Jacob was raised. He apprenticed himself to read law in 1842 but moved to Ohio in 1846 to prepare for a college degree and graduated from Oberlin College in 1851. In 1849 he married Helen Finney, the daughter of the Reverend Charles G. Finney, Oberlin's president; the couple raised eight children. Cox moved the family to Warren, Ohio, to work as a high school principal and superintendent, resumed his law studies part-time, and passed the Ohio bar examination in 1853.

Cox was surrounded by abolitionist sentiment in the Western Reserve, among his wife's family, and at Oberlin College. He supported the antislavery Whigs and Free Soil Party and in 1855 served as a delegate from Warren to the first Ohio Republican Party Convention in Columbus. He was elected to the Ohio Senate in 1859 and joined Senators James A. Garfield and James Monroe to form the "Radical Triumvirate" and worked with outgoing Governor Salmon P. Chase and new Governor William Dennison to promote legislation friendly to the Union. Cox and Garfield began the study of military science, especially the works of Jomini, and secured commissions as brigadier generals of the Ohio militia.

With the outbreak of war in April 1861, Cox became a brigadier general of Ohio Volunteers and served under George McClellan in a force that moved into what is now West Virginia through the route of the Kanawha River. In July 1861 Cox advanced his army first to Charleston, then to Gauley Bridge and fought Virginia troops under Henry Wise at Scary Creek. Throughout the winter of 1861–1862, Cox held the Kanawha Valley against repeated Confederate skirmishes. In the spring of 1862, Cox joined a Union advance into Virginia under General John C. Frémont, but Union reverses in the Shenandoah Valley stopped the offensive and forced Cox to retreat to fortified positions near Princeton in western Virginia.

Cox's troops, known as the Kanawha Division, trav-

eled back to the Ohio River and from Parkersburg rushed to Washington, D.C., in August 1862 to take up defensive positions in forts around the capital. In September Cox's troops joined the Army of the Potomac's movement to South Mountain and fought at Monocacy Bridge. His troops fought at Antietam on the Union left at the stone bridge.

After Antietam, Cox returned to western Virginia to clear out remaining rebel positions and in the spring of 1863 joined Ambrose Burnside's campaign in East Tennessee. Cox commanded the 3d Division of the XXIII Corps in battles throughout the spring and summer of 1864 in north Georgia including Rocky Face, Resaca, New Hope Church, Kennesaw Mountain, Chattahoochee, Atlanta, Jonesboro, and Lovejoy.

Cox returned to Tennessee in November of 1864 to meet the threat of John Bell Hood's invasion. Cox's men protected the Union retreat from Pulaski, skirmished at Spring Hill, and were at the center of the furious fighting near the Carter House at the battle of Franklin. Cox and his division also saw action at the battle of Nashville in December. These engagements finally won him promotion to major general.

Cox spent the last months of the war fighting in North Carolina. His forces captured Fort Anderson, fought at Town Creek, and helped force Confederate forces out of Wilmington.

Cox moved up the coast to New Bern and set out to rebuild the railroad to Kingston so William Tecumseh Sherman's forces could be supplied when they reached Goldsboro. Cox's troops fought Bragg's forces near Kingston and occupied the town and then took Goldsboro and moved on Raleigh. Cox was in charge of western North Carolina after the surrender of Johnston and then was given command of the District of the Ohio to muster out and discharge the army.

Cox was nominated and elected governor of Ohio on the Republican ticket in 1865. But during the campaign the issue of black suffrage surfaced to split his party and undermine his effectiveness as governor. Cox had come to believe that the nation was not yet ready for equality of black and white, based on his observations during the Civil War. Cox believed in setting up a district for the freed people encompassing parts of several southeastern states. These views outraged his former Radical and abolitionist friends and supporters. He also tried to mediate between Andrew Johnson and his Radical critics, though Cox's sympathies clearly lay with Johnson. The suffrage question for African-Americans living in Ohio was also contentious during Cox's administration. Legislative gridlock caused by these divisions rendered his administration ineffective, and he lacked the support necessary for renomination in 1867.

Cox moved to Cincinnati to practice law after his term expired and then served as secretary of the interior in the cabinet of President Ulysses S. Grant in 1869. Disgust at the corrupt practices of his party and administration led to Cox's resignation in 1870 and to his joining the Liberal Republicans in 1872. He moved to Toledo to assume the presidency of the Toledo, Wabash & Western Railroad in 1873 and was elected to Congress in 1876 as a reformer. When he chose not to run again in 1878, his political career was finished. He returned to Cincinnati as a lawyer and became dean of the Cincinnati Law School and president of the University of Cincinnati. He also served as a trustee of Oberlin College, where he retired in 1897 to write his memoirs. He died on 4 August 1900.

—*Gregory R. Zieren*

See also Atlanta Campaign; Franklin, Battle of.
For further reading:
Cox, Jacob Dolson. *Military Reminiscences of the Civil War* (1900).
Phillip, Hazel Spencer. *The Governors of Ohio* (1954).
Reid, Whitelaw. *Ohio in the War: Her Statesmen, Generals and Soldiers* (1868).
Roseboom, Eugene H. "The Civil War Era: 1850–1873." Vol. 4 of *The History of the State of Ohio* (1944).

COX, SAMUEL SULLIVAN
(1824–1889)
U.S. congressman

Born the son of Ezekiel Taylor Cox in Zanesville, Ohio, Samuel Sullivan Cox was educated at Ohio University and Brown University, from which he graduated in 1846. Cox, who had excelled in school, had a literary bent as well as a love of travel. He wrote a book about his travels to Europe entitled *A Buckeye Abroad*, which was very popular. Shortly afterward in the early 1850s he followed his father into the newspaper business as the editor of the Ohio Statesman and gained the nickname "Sunset" Cox by using somewhat flowery language to describe a sunset. At the same time he became interested in Ohio Democratic politics, and his actions on behalf of the Franklin Pierce presidential campaign in 1854 earned Cox an appointment as a member of the U.S. legation in Peru. He was forced by ill health to resign the position before actually arriving in Peru.

In 1856 Cox accepted the Democratic nomination for Congress from his district and won the election. Taking his seat in 1857, Cox began a thirty-year congressional career, interrupted only by a four-year stint during the first years of Reconstruction and a short period as U.S. minister to Turkey. Cox came into Congress during the turbulent debates over Kansas and the Lecompton Constitution. He opposed the admission of Kansas under that document.

While in Congress over the next few years, Cox advocated what he considered any reasonable accommodation of Southern demands and worked hard to reach a compromise during the secession crisis of the winter of 1860–1861. At the same time, however, the prospect of war between the sections had him doing what he could to prepare his own state for hostilities. As early as December 1860, he wrote to the War Department requesting that Ohio be sent arms and ammunition from the federal government under the provisions of the Militia Act of 1808. The department informed him that under that law the state could be supplied with arms but that it would have to provide its own ammunition.

During the war, Cox was associated with the so-called Peace Democrats, who advocated a negotiated end to the war. He, however, never failed to vote in favor of any military appropriations that would help the troops in the field. His advocacy of peace and negotiations with the Confederacy could not help but make him suspect in Republican eyes and his friendship with notorious Copperhead Clement Vallandigham encouraged those suspicions. In 1863 Cox testified for Vallandigham, asserting that he did not believe Vallandigham to be disloyal and that he did not believe that Vallandigham had ever encouraged others to be so. Cox believed that Vallandigham had never done anything but encourage citizens to express their displeasure with the conduct of the war through their votes. Cox also stated that he himself had actually made some of the statements that were attributed to Vallandigham and interpreted as being disloyal.

In spite of some people's suspicions of Cox's loyalty, he remained active in Congress throughout most of the war, serving as a senior member of the House Committee on Foreign Affairs among others. On that committee he worked tirelessly at the end of 1861 to avert war with Great Britain over the *Trent* Affair. He also consulted with President Abraham Lincoln on a variety of issues that he hoped would ease tensions between the United States and the Confederacy. Of particular interest to him were prisoner-of-war status for captured Confederate sailors and protection of private property in occupied portions of the Confederacy.

Still, in spite of his best efforts to work with the Republican administration, Cox's activism within the Democratic Party and association with the opposition made such cooperation difficult. In 1864 he was accused of trying to persuade home-guard units in Ohio from going to the front, an accusation that was never substantiated. During the election of that year, he served as an Ohio delegate to the Democratic National Convention and offered a seconding speech for the nomination of George B. McClellan. He, along with McClellan, was defeated in November.

After leaving Congress in early 1865, Cox moved to New York City, from where he would later again serve in Congress. He returned to Congress in 1869 and became a voice for reform for the next two decades. He strongly supported civil service reform and the development and

admission of western states. After a brief stint as minister to Turkey from 1885 to 1886, he returned to Congress and died in office on 10 September 1889. During his life, he had been known as an honorable though somewhat independent congressman. He wrote extensively about his experiences in Congress and his travel abroad, publishing over half a dozen books in his lifetime.

—*David S. Heidler and Jeanne T. Heidler*

See also Congress, U.S.A.; Peace Democrats.
For further reading:
Cox, William Van Zandt. *Life of Samuel Sullivan Cox* (1899).
Lindsey, David. *"Sunset" Cox, Irrepressible Democrat* (1959).

CRAMPTON'S GAP, BATTLE OF
(14 September 1862)

The battle of Crampton's Gap (or Crampton's Pass) near Burkittsville, Maryland, was fought on 14 September 1862 between a small force of Confederate defenders, from the division of Lafayette McLaws, and the two divisions of the Army of the Potomac's VI Army Corps, commanded by Major General William B. Franklin. It was part of the larger offensive known collectively as the battles of South Mountain, during the Maryland campaign of 1862.

When the discovery of the Army of Northern Virginia's Special Orders No. 191 on 13 September gave Major General George McClellan the exact intentions and whereabouts of the divided Confederate army, he sent orders to General Franklin to take Crampton's Gap in South Mountain and then go to the defense of the Union garrison at Harper's Ferry, which at that time was under siege by Thomas J. "Stonewall" Jackson's command. McClellan's overall intent was to move swiftly against Lee's divided force and defeat each element before the Confederates could regroup. While Franklin's men attacked Crampton's Gap, the other elements of the Army of the Potomac would storm Turner's Gap and Fox's Gap, located about eight miles to the north of Crampton's Gap in the same mountain range.

McClellan organized the Army of the Potomac into three wings for the operation: the right, center, and left wings. The right wing would attack at Turner's Gap and Fox's Gap. The center wing would be held in reserve. Franklin commanded the left wing, composed of his own two divisions (commanded by Major Generals Henry Slocum and William F. "Baldy" Smith) and Major General Darius Couch's division from IV Corps. The left wing had the most important assignment. Franklin was ordered to seize Crampton's Gap, then move across the mountain into Pleasant Valley and cut off or destroy McLaws's command. Most of McLaws's force occupied Maryland Heights, overlooking the town of Harper's Ferry across the Potomac River. His command formed part of Stonewall Jackson's three-pronged attack on Harper's Ferry.

The VI Corps marched at first light on 14 September, passing over Catoctin Mountain and halting on the other side at the outskirts of the village of Jefferson to wait for Couch's division. After determining that Couch would not arrive for at least several more hours, around 10:00 A.M., Franklin decided to push VI Corps forward to Burkittsville, ten miles to the northwest of Jefferson. The head of VI Corps' column arrived at a point about two miles in front of Burkittsville around noon.

The Confederate defenders waiting for Franklin included Colonel Thomas Munford's understrength cavalry brigade—two regiments and a horse artillery battery—and the diminished infantry brigade of Colonel William Mahone, also much reduced in manpower and under the temporary command of Colonel William Parham. Attached to Parham's command was the 10th Georgia Infantry Regiment from Brigadier General Paul Semmes's brigade. On the other side of South Mountain at the far southwest edge of Pleasant Valley lay Brigadier General Howell Cobb's infantry brigade, ready to come to Munford's aid. All told, the Confederate force that initially would battle Franklin's corps—Munford, Parham, and the 10th Georgia—came to a total of no more than 1,000 men.

Even though the Confederates were vastly outnumbered—Franklin had approximately 12,800 soldiers in his two divisions—Munford and Parham took advantage of the man-made and natural obstacles confronting their antagonists. Parham's infantrymen were stretched out along a road that skirted the base of the mountain, and his men took cover behind a stone wall. Munford dismounted his cavalry regiments and posted one of them, the 2d Virginia, behind a single stone wall to the south of the road that led up to Crampton's Gap. He placed his other regiment, the 12th Virginia Cavalry, to the far left of the line, separate from the main force, to guard against a flank attack. The infantry regiments were positioned to the left of the 2d Cavalry. The 10th Georgia Infantry occupied the extreme left of the main Confederate defensive line. Halfway up Crampton's Gap, Munford sited a battery of horse artillery and a section of field artillery. About three quarters of a mile south of Crampton's Gap, a narrow road ascended South Mountain at a place called Brownsville Pass. There McLaws had instructed Brigadier General Paul Semmes to see to its defense. Semmes sent one infantry regiment and one battery of artillery.

From the outskirts of Burkittsville, Franklin surveyed the terrain and the dispositions of the enemy. He concluded that the position could be carried only by infantry attack, and directed General Slocum to advance through the village of Burkittsville and attack the Confederate right. Slocum picked the brigade of Colonel Joseph Bartlett to lead the assault. Sometime between 2:30 and 4:00 P.M., Bartlett deployed his skirmishers and began the attack. (The exact time that the attack commenced is vague. Bartlett stated that the offensive started at 4:00, two of his regimental commanders reported that it began at 3:30, while yet another claimed it started at 2:30.)

It seems apparent that neither Franklin nor his subordinate commanders initially realized the paucity of the force opposing them, given the excellent cover and concealment that the stone walls, heavy woods, and rock outcroppings provided the defenders, who also took advantage of the rapid and steep ascent of South Mountain to improve their chances of success against the Union force. As Bartlett sent his skirmishers forward, General Smith was ordered to move two of his brigades through town to protect Slocum's flank. Smith retained his other brigade as a reserve.

Once the battle started up the mountain and into the woods, Franklin could no longer see its progress. The fighting continued for several hours against a determined foe who had been ordered to hold to the last man. Just as Parham and Munford's line was collapsing, Howell Cobb's 1,300-man brigade streamed down the mountain to bolster the defenses. Now, with the added punch of Cobb's brigade, the fighting rapidly intensified to a crescendo. As Slocum's men were pushing the Confederates up the steep and rugged slopes toward Crampton's Gap, Smith's soldiers succeeded in getting around the Southerners' already crumbling right flank and took many prisoners. By this point in the battle, all but one of the VI Corps' brigades had been engaged in the fighting. Couch still had not arrived and would not show up for several more hours.

As the sun was setting, Slocum's men clawed their way up South Mountain, virtually annihilating Cobb's brigade along the way. Cobb tried to organize a hasty defense at the top of the pass, but superior numbers and the irresistible momentum of the Union advance sent the last remnants of the Confederate force fleeing down the other side of South Mountain. The battle of Crampton's Gap ended just before dusk. Union casualties came to 533, while the Confederates lost approximately 800 men.

Although Franklin had completed the first part of the mission, he failed to follow up his success. When Crampton's Gap finally fell, there was not enough daylight remaining to continue into Pleasant Valley, so the push to Harper's Ferry would have to wait until 15 September. Around 10 P.M. on 14 September, Couch and his division finally arrived, giving Franklin a fresh division of more than 7,000 men that he could use for the next day's operation. Smith's division, of which only two brigades had been employed during the fighting at Crampton's Gap, also was ready for action. It was imperative that Franklin bring as much force to bear as he could muster, and do it as early as possible, so that once the battle commenced the Union commander at Harper's Ferry would hear the fighting, signaling that friendly forces were coming to his relief.

Franklin made two critical errors in judgment on 15 September. First, he did not have his command in position to attack McLaws at first light. Second, he overestimated the size of the Confederate force facing him. Even though his own command greatly outnumbered McLaws's force, Franklin believed otherwise. Instead of attacking he requested reinforcements from McClellan. His decision was an unfortunate mistake, not only for the Harper's Ferry garrison, but one that Franklin would regret for the rest of his life, even though he would never admit it outright. Franklin's poor generalship on the morning of 15 September 1862 negated the Crampton's Gap victory and contributed to the fall of Harper's Ferry, which surrendered at 7:15 A.M. Two days later, the bloody battle of Antietam was fought near Sharpsburg, Maryland, but Franklin and VI Corps played a very small role.

—*Mark Snell*

See also Antietam, Battle of; Cobb, Howell; Franklin, William Buel; McLaws, Lafayette; South Mountain, Battle of.
For further reading:
Reese, Timothy. *Sealed with Their Lives: The Battle for Crampton's Gap* (1998).
Sears, Stephen. *Landscape Turned Red: The Battle of Antietam* (1983).
Snell, Mark A. *William B. Franklin: A Biography* (in press).

CRATER, BATTLE OF THE
(30 July 1864)

The battle of the Crater, also called the battle of the Mine, was an effort initiated by the Federal troops at Petersburg to overcome the city's Confederate defenses. Because Petersburg was an important transportation hub, with five railroads connecting it to rivers and seaports, the city played a strategic role in getting supplies to Lee's army in the South, particularly after the fall of Vicksburg. Grant's strategy was to capture Petersburg to cut off Confederate supply lines, weaken the defenses around the Confederate capital, and capture Richmond, which was just seventy miles away.

The initial unsuccessful Federal assault on Petersburg, from 15 to 18 June 1864, resulted in a prolonged siege that lasted nearly ten months. The stalemate that ensued after 18 June led to suggestions on how to end it. Former coal miners of the 48th Pennsylvania Infantry and their commander, Lieutenant Colonel Henry Pleasants, who was a mining engineer before the war, suggested that a tunnel be constructed under Confederate trenches and that explosives be placed in strategic locations to blow up Confederate fortifications above the ground. General Robert Potter, commander of the 2d Division, IX Army Corps, Army of the Potomac, took the idea to the corps commander, General Ambrose Burnside, in a formal proposal on 24 June. Burnside was receptive to the idea and General George G. Meade, Commander of the Army of the Potomac, initially approved it.

The 48th Pennsylvania's position in the trenches was in proximity to Elliott's Salient, a Confederate redoubt that was just 400 feet from the Union's outposts. Tunneling began on 25 June and was completed on 23 July. Four days later, the placing of the powder charge was finished. The main shaft of the tunnel ran 511 feet to a point twenty feet under the Confederate battery in the salient. Two lateral galleries with a total length of seventy-five feet were run under the enemy trenches. The tunnel averaged five feet in height. It was four and a half feet wide at the bottom and about two feet at the top. It was ventilated by a system whereby fire in a chimney near the entrance drew stale air out of the tunnel while fresh air was brought in through a wooden tube along the tunnel floor. The tube entered from under an airtight door at the entrance and ran to the end of the tunnel where the men were digging. The powder charge consisted of 320 kegs of gunpowder, totaling 8,000 pounds. A thirty-eight-foot section of the main tunnel was then filled with dirt and a fuse was improvised. All of this was done with few supplies from headquarters.

The plan of attack after the tunnel, or "mine," explosion occurred perhaps posed the biggest challenge. This part of the operation involved the black troops of the 4th Division, IX Corps, Army of the Potomac. The division was composed of the 19th, 23d, 27th, 28th, 29th, 30th, 31st, 39th, and 43d U.S. Colored Troops (USCT). The black 4th Division, commanded by Brigadier General Edward Ferrero, numbered 4,300 men assigned to two brigades led by Colonel Joshua Sigfried and Colonel Henry Goddard Thomas.

According to a report by Colonel Thomas, commander of the 2d Brigade, Burnside had decided that Ferrero's black troops would lead the assault because they were new, enthusiastic, filled with hope, and "not yet rendered doubtful by reverses or chilled by defeat." Moreover, the black troops were eager to prove themselves in battle. According to the official reports of various high-ranking commanders, the black troops drilled and practiced maneuvers for weeks in preparation for leading the attack after the explosion. Yet there are contrary published letters by the soldiers of the 4th Division. Writing from camp on 26 July 1864, Sergeant Major McCoslin of the 29th Infantry USCT, 4th Division informed readers of *The Christian Recorder*: "Our regiment is not in good fighting trim at present, on account of an insufficiency of officers. In other respects

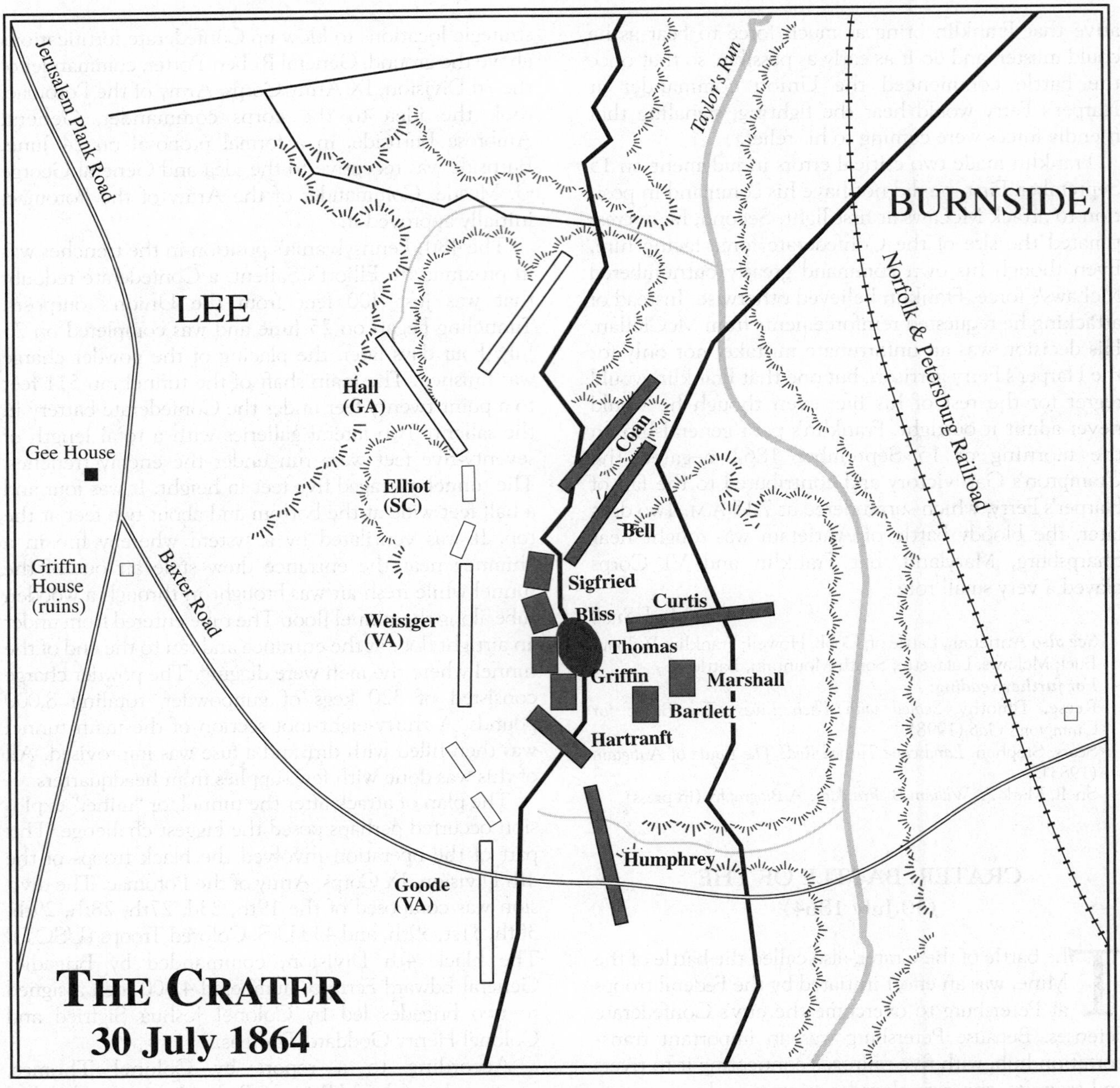

THE CRATER
30 July 1864

Map labels:
Jerusalem Plank Road · Taylor's Run · BURNSIDE · Norfolk & Petersburg Railroad · LEE · Hall (GA) · Coan · Gee House · Bell · Elliot (SC) · Sigfried · Curtis · Griffin House (ruins) · Baxter Road · Bliss · Thomas · Weisiger (VA) · Griffin · Marshall · Bartlett · Hartranft · Goode (VA) · Humphrey

they are all right. We are expecting every day to be sent to the front; but it is ordered otherwise, probably for the best. Our regiment has built two forts and about three miles of breastworks, which shows that we are not idle, and that we are learning to make fortifications, whether we learn to fight or not."

McCoslin's report on the military training of the black soldiers was corroborated in later years by Captain R. K. Beecham, who after leaving his regiment (2d Wisconsin) joined the 23d USCT in Petersburg, where he claimed to have served every day from 22 June 1864 until after the battle of the Crater. He wrote in a 20 August 1902 letter that appeared in The National Tribune: "I am prepared to

say from actual knowledge derived from personal experience with the Fourth Division that the only duty assigned to the said division for more than a month before the battle of the Mine was work upon our trenches and fortifications. The Fourth Division during all that time was drilled especially in the use of pick and shovel, and in no other manner. Of this fact I do not complain. My complaint is, that while the Fourth Division worked ceaselessly, heroically, day and night, on the trenches to the neglect of every soldierly preparation for the battle, it has been falsely and persistently reported to have received special preparation for a particular battle."

Just a few hours before the explosion was to take place,

Burnside informed the black troops and their commanders that they would not lead the attack. General Meade reportedly changed his mind about the use of the black division because "they were a new division and had never been under fire, while this was an operation requiring the very best troops." Meade also argued that, if the attack failed, the Union would be criticized for sacrificing black troops to the cannons of the enemy. Mainly for the latter reason, General Ulysses S. Grant agreed to Meade's decision. However, Burnside relentlessly attempted to persuade Meade to permit the black troops to lead the assault. Meade would not be moved. Finally, Burnside chose one of the white divisions by lot to lead the assault. Brigadier General James H. Ledlie commanded the 1st Division; Brigadier General Robert Potter commanded the 2d Division; and Brigadier General Orlando B. Willcox commanded the 3d Division. Straws were put into a hat from which each commander drew. The luck of the draw fell to Ledlie, who was considered the least able to do the job successfully.

At about 3:00 A.M. on 30 July, Pleasants entered the mine or tunnel and lit the fuse, which was expected to burn thirty minutes. However, when the explosion did not occur, around 4:15 A.M. Pleasants sent two men into the tunnel to investigate. The fuse had gone out. It was relit. At about 4:44 A.M., the four tons of gunpowder went off. The explosion made a crater from 150 to 200 feet long, sixty feet wide, and thirty feet deep. A Confederate battery and most of a regiment were blown up by the explosion. Ledlie's division entered the crater, but failed to advance promptly to the ridge (Cemetery Hill) beyond the crater. "Had they done this," reported Grant, "I have every reason to believe that Petersburg would have fallen." Grant further stated in his report on the battle that "other troops were immediately pushed forward but the time consumed in getting them up enabled the enemy to rally from his surprise (which had been complete) and get forces to this point for its defense. The captured line thus held being untenable, and of no advantage to us, the troops were withdrawn, but not without heavy loss. Thus terminated in disaster what promised to be the most successful assault of the campaign." In a hearing before the Committee on the Conduct of the War, Grant testified that "General Burnside wanted to put his colored division in front, and I believe if he had done so it would have been a success. Still I agreed with General Meade as to his objections to that plan…it would then be said…that we were shoving these people ahead to get killed because we did not care anything about them."

The official report put the Union dead at 504. In addition, 1,881 were wounded, and 1,413 were reported missing. On the Confederate side, it is estimated that at least 361 were killed, 727 wounded, and 403 missing.

Blame for the Union's failure to win the battle and capture Petersburg fell on Burnside, Ledlie, Ferrero, Bliss, and Willcox; but the Official Court of Inquiry placed most of the blame on Burnside and Ledlie. Shortly after the battle, both men were given leaves that ended with their resignations. The Joint Congressional Committee on the Conduct of the War later found that Meade was responsible for the loss of the battle because it was he who reversed Burnside's plan to use the fresh black soldiers to lead the attack. The only fault found in Burnside by the committee was the method that he used to select an alternative division to take the lead after Meade decided not to use the black division.

—*Dorothy L. Drinkard*

See also Burnside Ambrose E.; Petersburg Campaign.

For further reading:

Cavanaugh, Michael A., and William Marvel. *The Petersburg Campaign: The Battle of the Crater, "The Horrid Pit," June 25–August 6, 1864* (1989).

Drinkard, Dorothy L. *Illinois Freedom Fighters: A Civil War Saga of the 29th Infantry United States Colored Troops* (1998).

Trudeau, Noah Andre. *The Last Citadel: Petersburg, Virginia, June 1864–April 1865* (1991).

CRAWFORD, SAMUEL J.
(1835–1913)
Union officer; governor of Kansas

Samuel J. Crawford was a tough frontier soldier whose courageous battlefield exploits propelled him to two terms as governor of Kansas. While commanding the 2d Kansas Colored Infantry Regiment, he replied in kind after Confederate troops murdered black prisoners of war. He followed a similar course as governor when Indian raids devastated western Kansas.

Crawford was born near Bedford, Indiana, on 10 April 1835. Intent on a legal career, in 1857 he enrolled in the law school of Cincinnati College, where he graduated the following year. Crawford moved to Kansas in early 1859, entering local politics as a Republican. His neighbors elected him to the state legislature on 6 December 1859, but he did not take his seat until Kansas formally entered the Union in 1861.

Soon after the start of the Civil War, Crawford left the legislature and became a captain in the 2d Kansas Volunteer Infantry, a ninety-day regiment. The 2d Kansas fought at Wilson's Creek on 10 August 1861 and mustered out on 31 October, but Crawford was not ready to quit soldiering.

Seeking a new regiment, Crawford helped form the 2d Kansas Cavalry and was mustered in as a captain on 15 April 1862. While campaigning in northwest Arkansas later that year, Crawford attracted the notice of Brigadier General James G. Blunt, another Kansan. Captain Crawford's military credo was: "When in trouble, charge!" He won citations for the bravery and

tactical initiative he displayed between 22 October and 7 December at Old Fort Wayne, Cane Hill, and Prairie Grove. Impressed by Crawford's performance, the other company officers of the 2d Kansas Cavalry petitioned to have him named their colonel, but Governor Charles Robinson refused.

Unable to gain promotion any other way, Crawford accepted Blunt's offer to command the 2d Kansas Colored Infantry (later the 83d U.S. Colored Infantry), a new regiment that assembled at Fort Scott, Kansas, in the summer and fall of 1863. Colonel Crawford exerted every effort to prepare the 2d Kansas Colored for front-line service. After the regiment relocated to Fort Smith in late October, he purged his ranks of 200 physically unfit enlisted men and subjected the remainder to a strict regimen of training and discipline. He also closely screened soldiers from white commands who applied for commissions in the 2d Kansas Colored.

In March 1864, the 2d Kansas Colored joined the 14,000-man army that Major General Frederick Steele drew from the Union garrisons at Little Rock and Fort Smith to invade southwest Arkansas. While at Camden on 18 April, Crawford learned that Confederate troops had refused to spare any black personnel captured from the 1st Kansas Colored Infantry in a fight at Poison Spring, about eleven miles away. Crawford conferred with his officers, and they resolved "that in future the regiment would take no prisoners so long as the Rebels continued to murder our men." The 2d Kansas Colored kept that pledge at the battle of Jenkins' Ferry, 30 April, when it charged two enemy cannon. The enraged black soldiers bayoneted every gray gunner within reach except for an officer and five men.

In September 1864, delegates from Kansas regiments stationed at Fort Smith attended the Republican State Convention at Topeka and successfully promoted Crawford's nomination for governor. Crawford returned home to campaign, but interrupted politics for eleven days in October to serve as a volunteer aide when Major General Sterling Price and Confederate cavalry raided through Missouri and threatened eastern Kansas. Crawford's exploits at Westport and Mine Creek enhanced his political appeal, and he carried the election on 8 November. Two years later, Kansans elected him to a second term.

Governor Crawford wrestled with daunting problems stemming from the war, Reconstruction, economic development, and frontier expansion. Incensed by bloody Indian raids on Kansas homesteads, he resigned his office on 4 November 1868 to take command of the 19th Kansas Cavalry, a volunteer regiment that cooperated with the regular army in operations against the Southern Plains tribes.

Crawford aspired to a seat in the U.S. Congress, but that prize eluded him. He harmed his political fortunes by joining the Liberal Republicans in 1872, and he fared no better when he ran for the House of Representatives as a Greenbacker in 1876 and 1878.

Crawford tasted success again as a claims agent in Washington, D.C., from 1877 to 1891. He also practiced law in Washington, tested new agricultural methods on a farm in Kansas, and published his memoirs. The independent soldier/politician died in Topeka on 21 October 1913.

—*Gregory J. W. Urwin*

See also Kansas; United States Colored Troops; Westport, Battle of.

For further reading:
Cornish, Dudley Taylor. "Kansas Negro Regiments in the Civil War." *Kansas Historical Quarterly* (May 1953).
Crawford, Samuel J. *Kansas in the Sixties* (1911).
Hoig, Stan. *The Battle of the Washita* (1976).
Plummer, Mark A. *Frontier Governor: Samuel J. Crawford of Kansas* (1971).
Urwin, Gregory J.W. "'We Cannot Treat Negroes…as Prisoners of War': Racial Atrocities and Reprisals in Civil War Arkansas." *Civil War History* (1996).

CREEK INDIANS

Inhabiting the area between the Arkansas and Canadian rivers in eastern Indian Territory, the people of the Creek Nation viewed the onset of the American Civil War with mixed emotions. Factions existed within the Creek Nation, but these divisions had endured since the mid-eighteenth century when English and Scottish fur traders established ties with the Lower Creeks in Georgia and Alabama. Intermarriage led to an increase of mixed-bloods among the Lower Creeks and the appearance of Creek leaders with names such as McGillivray and McIntosh. The Lower Creeks voluntarily complied with the United States' removal policy of the 1830s endorsed by their mixed-blood leaders, while the Upper Creeks had to be forcibly removed from their traditional homelands. These two Creek factions remained separated in Indian Territory, but they were able to put their animosity aside long enough to establish a seat of government, devise a phonetic written language, draft a slave code, and build schools (with the aid of missionaries) in the 1840s and 1850s.

On 10 July 1861, Principal Chief Motey Kinnard and Daniel N. and Chilly McIntosh (sons of William McIntosh—former principal chief of the Lower Creeks) met with Special Commissioner Albert Pike of the Confederate Bureau of Indian Affairs and together signed a treaty of alliance with the Confederacy. The McIntoshes also promised to raise a regiment of Creeks, provided they would only have to fight within the borders of Indian Territory. However, in the fall of 1861 thousands of loyal and neutral Upper Creeks refused to recognize the treaty of alliance with the Confederacy signed by the Lower Creeks, and prepared to march with their leader, Opothleyahola, to Kansas and safety. A force of Lower Creeks under the McIntosh brothers opposed them. In November, sporadic violence between the two factions began and quickly intensified. Pike ordered Colonel Douglas H. Cooper to take charge of the situation and restore tranquility among the Creeks while the special commissioner departed for the Confederate capital. Cooper called on other Indian home guard units to aid in his efforts to end the hostilities and prevent the Upper Creeks from leaving Indian Territory. In doing so, Cooper began what amounted to a civil war within the borders of the territory.

When Cooper arrived near the Canadian River, he discovered almost 4,000 Upper Creek men, women, and children as well as Indians from assorted other nations crowded into encampments along with their livestock, wagons, and worldly possessions. About one-third of these Indians were armed. After failing to dissuade the Upper Creeks from their mission, Cooper chose to use force. Considering these Indians to be a threat to Confederate authority in Indian territory, Cooper assembled a body of 1,400 mounted soldiers composed of six companies of his Choctaw and Chickasaw regiment, Daniel McIntosh's Lower Creek regiment, Chilly McIntosh and John Jumper's battalion of Creeks and Seminoles, and 500 whites of the 9th Texas Cavalry. On 5 November 1861, the ever-growing group of loyal Creeks and refugees left their encampments and moved north toward Kansas. Two weeks later, Cooper attacked the slow-moving caravan at Round Mountain, near the junction of the Cimarron and Arkansas rivers. The loyal Creeks fought back, managing to escape at dusk after setting a prairie fire to impede Cooper's progress.

Slowed but undaunted, Cooper resumed the chase, now reinforced by John Drew's Cherokee regiment, which was ordered by Cooper to aid in the operation. On 9 December, Cooper found Opothleyahola and the loyal Creeks waiting for him at Chusto-Talasah, or Caving Banks, on Bird Creek near present-day Tulsa. Cooper engaged the Upper Creeks for four hours before Opothleyahola finally withdrew his band. All told, Cooper lost fifteen men killed and thirty-seven wounded, and failed once again to cut off the fleeing loyalists.

Although claiming a victory, Cooper nevertheless withdrew to Fort Gibson near Tahlequah and waited for reinforcements from Texas and Arkansas. With the arrival of 1,380 Confederate troopers under Colonel James McIntosh, Cooper had the luxury to plan a combined attack against Opothleyahola's band utilizing the converging columns of his own and McIntosh's troops. The Confederates once again took to the field, but unfortunately were unable to synchronize their convergence on the Creek camp at Chustenahlah. Rather than wait for Cooper's badly delayed troops,

McIntosh chose to engage Opothleyahola's numerically superior forces on 26 December. Weakened by exhaustion, cold weather, and lack of adequate food, the loyal Creeks could not withstand the Confederate onslaught. Warriors mixed with men, women, and children fled the field in panic pursued by white Confederate cavalrymen and the recently arrived mixed-blood Cherokee regiment under Stand Watie. Watie's 300 men killed or captured many of the stragglers who were too weak to flee. Those who did escape finally made their way to Kansas and safety. There they fared little better, owing to a lack of adequate food, clothing, and shelter for the winter. U.S. Indian agents in Kansas were unable to aid the refugees, whose numbers eventually swelled to over 10,000. Eventually hunger and disease took their toll.

In the spring of 1862, Brigadier General James G. Blunt, commander of the Union Department of Kansas, decided to return the loyal Indian refugees to their home in Indian Territory. The resulting operation resulted in frequent skirmishes with Confederate forces as the refugee column and its Federal escort entered Cherokee country north of the Arkansas River. The return of this contingent of loyal Creeks to Indian Territory fanned the flames of factionalism within the Creek Nation. While Creek soldiers participated in conventional military operations such as those that led to the battle of Honey Springs on 17 July 1863, the real fateful combat for the two factions of the Creek Nation came in the form of guerrilla raids upon each other that sowed the seeds for continued strife well after the war's end.

—*Alan C. Downs*

See also Cherokee Indians; Honey Springs, Battle of; Indian Territory; Pike, Albert; Watie, Stand.

For further reading:
Hauptman, Laurence M. *Between Two Fires: American Indians in the Civil War* (1995).
Josephy, Alvin M. *The Civil War in the American West* (1991).

CRIMPING

The American Civil War spilled over U.S. boundaries to affect the British North American provinces in a variety of ways. Historians estimate that perhaps 40,000 provincials fought in Civil War armies and navies as volunteers (more for the Union than the Confederacy because of proximity and colonial sympathies). They were often led to service by so-called crimps, who were free-lance recruiters working on commission. Despite the severe manpower demands of the war, the American government denounced crimping. However, state and local officials needed men to fill their quotas and often ignored Federal policy. Inside the United States, crimps worked immigrant communities and boarding houses, using local gamblers, idlers, and even the police in Boston, Portland (Maine), and New York City to find potential recruits. Methods ranged from press-gang tactics, to bribes and trickery, to honest appeals.

Crimps mostly lured colonials from Canada into Union regiments and the navy. They roamed borderland towns and waterfronts from Nova Scotia to the Detroit River. Using such devices as newspaper advertisements, they cajoled not only the idle and the young, but also mature men with military experience. At Fredericton, New Brunswick, in spring 1861 they led thirty 62d Regiment redcoats south. Many British tars headed for American service rather that suffer Royal Navy pay and discipline. In 1861 crimpers prowled Montreal and Toronto disguised as hiring agents for railroads and cotton mills. They recruited from black refugee communities in Canada West for black regiments such as the 54th Massachusetts.

Crimpers offered free drink, money, clothing, and free transport to a border state, where the official recruiting took place. They got what they could from their victims, although bounties, at first $15 to $25 for each recruit, provided most of their income. State and local governments offered bounties that could reach $300 per head. Massachusetts paid out $13 million in such bounties throughout the war. The Conscription Acts of 1862 and 1863 created another source of income for crimps because draftees could now legally pay for substitutes. Some offered as much as $1,000 to avoid military service.

Britain's 1819 and 1854 Foreign Enlistment Acts and the proclamation of Neutrality in the Civil War on 14 May 1861 made crimping illegal on British soil. Secretary of State William Henry Seward became cautious about infringement on British neutrality and deflected British North Americans who offered to raise troops or asked for military commissions. Official proclamations did nothing, however, to stop crimping in Canada. The reward for turning in a crimp was $50, but "victims" often refused to testify against the accused. In any case, penalties were light. Abuses increased in number and extent, and in 1864 John A. Macdonald issued a circular to all county attorneys in Canada West to search out crimps. He recruited a body of detectives to aid them. These men patrolled border towns under cover and used soldiers from local garrisons in entrapment schemes. The reward for catching a crimp rose to $200 and any American convicted was fined $160 and handed six months of hard labor. But rising profits counterbalanced the low risk of discovery and prosecution, so crimping ended only with the Civil War itself.

—*Reginald C. Stuart*

See also Conscription, U.S.A.

For further reading:
Geary, James W. "Civil War Conscription in the North: A Historiographical Review." *Civil War History* (1986).
Hamer, Marguerite B. "Luring Canadian Soldiers into Union Lines during the War Between the States." *Canadian Historical Review* (1946).
Marquis, Greg. "Mercenaries or Killer Angels? Nova Scotians in the American Civil War." *Collections of the Royal Nova Scotia Historical Society* (1996).
Rany, William F. "Recruiting and Crimping in Canada for the Northern Forces, 1861–1865." *Mississippi Valley Historical Review* (1923).

CRITTENDEN COMPROMISE
(1860–1861)

The lame-duck session of the Thirty-sixth U.S. Congress convened in December 1860 with the Lower South boiling with secessionist zeal in the aftermath of Abraham Lincoln's election as president. Congressional leaders responded by creating two special committees whose sole purpose was to find a formula that would prevent the South from leaving the Union: a "Committee of Thirty-Three" in the House and a "Committee of Thirteen" in the Senate. Public hopes for a peaceful settlement to the looming crisis especially focused on a member of the latter body, John J. Crittenden of Kentucky, a man whose political career had been largely defined by his association with Henry Clay, the man who had forged Union-saving compromises in 1820, 1833, and 1850. The seventy-three-year-old Crittenden rose to the occasion. On 18 December he presented a package of six amendments to the Senate designed to provide both a comprehensive and permanent solution to the slavery issue.

The first of Crittenden's proposed amendments denied the federal government the ability to abolish slavery or its property in slave states; the second stated that Congress had no power to interfere with the transportation of slaves across state or territorial lines; the third mandated that the federal government would compensate slave owners who were unable to recover fugitive slaves as a result of mob action and authorized the attorney general to sue counties where the recovery of fugitives was thwarted; the fourth prohibited the abolition of slavery in the District of Columbia without the consent of the inhabitants or the previous abolition of slavery in Maryland and Virginia; and the fifth resolved the territorial issue by prohibiting slavery north of the Missouri Compromise line of 36°30′ while slavery was recognized and guaranteed throughout the territorial stage in all land south of the line "now held, or hereafter acquired." The final amendment Crittenden proposed was designed to ensure the permanence of the compromise. It exempted the first five from the process of amendment and prohibited any future amendment that gave the federal government the ability to interfere with slavery in any state, constrained the slave owner's constitutional right to recover fugitive slaves, or altered the three-fifths clause of the Constitution. Crittenden also called upon Congress to adopt resolutions that asserted the constitutionality of the Fugitive Slave Law and commit the government to its rigid enforcement, declared state laws that conflicted with that law null and void and advocated their repeal, deleted clauses in the law that offended Northern sensibilities, and committed Congress to strengthening and rigorously executing laws prohibiting the foreign slave trade.

This was not a true compromise. Crittenden's plan conceded everything to the South that it could possibly want, while offering little to the North. Nonetheless, Northern Democrats led by Stephen A. Douglas and the New York business community joined border state Unionists in stepping forward to throw their support behind Crittenden and his plan. Even some Republicans, most prominently Thurlow Weed and William H. Seward, flirted with the idea of accepting the compromise, even though it asked them to disavow the commitment to keeping slavery out of the territories that held their party together.

The most important Republican, Abraham Lincoln, was not willing to do this. Although not unalterably opposed to compromise, when the outlines of Crittenden's plan became clear, the president-elect took up his pen and instructed his fellow Republicans to "entertain no proposition for a compromise in regard to the *extension* of slavery....There is no possible compromise upon it....On that point hold firm, as with a chain of steel."

Lincoln's actions effectively killed whatever chance there was for passage of Crittenden's plan by bolstering Republican resistance to surrendering their platform, which steeled the opposition of their Lower South counterparts to compromise. The Committee of Thirteen rejected the omnibus of compromise measures by a vote of seven to six on 22 December, two days after South Carolina adopted its ordinance of secession, with Republican members voting unanimously against it.

Crittenden did not give up, however. On 3 January 1861, he brought the compromise to the Senate floor and called for a national referendum to determine its fate. Again Lincoln responded by urging his fellow Republicans to remain firm. At stake, he told them, was no less than the nation's claim to possess a government of, by, and for the people. "We have just carried an election on principles fairly presented to the people," he wrote on 11 January. "Now we are told...the government will be broken up, unless we surrender to those we have beaten....[I]f we surrender, it is the end of us, and of the government."

On 16 January the Senate dealt the final blow to compromise efforts by voting twenty-five to twenty-three to reject Crittenden's call for a national referendum, even though Horace Greeley would later concede that had such a plebiscite occurred the compromise would probably have commanded a popular majority. Henceforth, hopes that the Union could be restored without war would rest upon the silent majority of Southern Unionists who Lincoln believed did not need concessions on slavery to rise up and overthrow the secession movement in the South.

—Ethan S. Rafuse

See also Crittenden, John J.; Republican Party; Thirteenth Amendment.

For further reading:
Basler, Roy P., ed. *The Collected Works of Abraham Lincoln* (1953–1955).
Kirwan, Albert D. *John J. Crittenden: The Struggle for the Union* (1962).
Potter, David M. *Lincoln and His Party in the Secession Crisis* (1942).
Stampp, Kenneth M. *And the War Came: The North and the Secession Crisis, 1860–1861* (1950).

CRITTENDEN, GEORGE BIBB
(1812–1880)
Confederate general

George Bibb Crittenden was born into a prominent political family in Russellville, Kentucky, on 20 March 1812. His father, John Jordan Crittenden, was a longstanding Kentucky statesman who attempted a final compromise to keep the Union together. As the eldest son in his family, George Bibb later attended West Point to receive a military education. He graduated in 1832, finishing twenty-sixth in his class of forty-five.

After graduation, Crittenden stayed in the army because he enjoyed its excitement. He was a brevet second lieutenant in the Black Hawk War (1832), and after that conflict was stationed at various locations across the South. With no war to feed his sense of adventure, Crittenden resigned his commission to study law at Transylvania University in Lexington, Kentucky. When his studies became cumbersome, he headed southwest in 1842 to fight with the Texans. He participated in the 1843 Meir expedition in pursuit of Mexican raiders, during which he was taken captive in Mexico. Crittenden and his fellow prisoners were forced to draw lots to see who would be executed. He drew a white bean, signifying that he would survive, but gave it to a fellow Kentuckian because the man was married and had children. Crittenden drew again, picked another white bean, and this time kept it. Crittenden's political connections helped to free him from prison, and he returned to Kentucky. He returned to the southwest to fight during the Mexican-American War (1846–1848), and afterward remained in the army.

In June 1861 Crittenden resigned his post in the New Mexico Territory and returned to Kentucky. He found his father trying to stop Southern secession by effecting a compromise that was acceptable to both sides. To the chagrin of his father, George had Southern sympathies. George joined the Confederate army and was made brigadier general. At the same time, George's younger brother, Thomas Leonidas, joined the Union as a brigadier general. The Crittendens thus exemplified the divided nation, fighting a war that pitted brother against brother.

Just two days after he was commissioned major general on 9 November 1861, George Crittenden was assigned command of the Cumberland Mountain region, where he defended an area from southeastern Kentucky to eastern Tennessee. Crittenden's only major Civil War battle experience occurred two months later in southeastern Kentucky.

Crittenden was commanding with General Felix Zollicoffer in January 1862, when the two officers met at Mill Springs on the south bank of the Cumberland River. Zollicoffer decided to take his troops to Beech Grove on the opposite bank, which angered Crittenden because of its poor defensive location. Meanwhile, Union forces were advancing in the rain under General George H. Thomas. Crittenden knew that much of his army would perish if it stayed at Beech Grove, so he decided to take the initiative and planned an attack. Crittenden's surprise attack was aimed at catching the Union armies off guard while they were separated by the rain-swollen Fishing Creek.

The battle—variously known as Mill Springs, Logan's Cross Roads, and Fishing Creek—occurred on 19–20 January 1862. The separated Union forces were able to cross Fishing Creek and join the previously engaged forces, thus giving them a decided advantage. Also, Zollicoffer's death during the battle demoralized the Southern troops. Crittenden led the Confederate retreat to Tennessee, abandoning his horses, wagons, and artillery. Crittenden's miscalculation of the river level and the size of the opposing Union army had crushed his troops.

The defeat caused Confederate officials to look for a scapegoat, and they decided on George Crittenden. He was accused of drunkenness during battle and of having Union sympathies because of his family connections. A court of inquiry found Crittenden innocent of treason, but guilty of intoxication.

Crittenden was given a chance for redemption by commanding a reserve corps that Confederate general Albert Sidney Johnston was building in northern Mississippi. But on 1 April 1862, in Iuka, Mississippi, Major General William J. Hardee found Crittenden drunk and his soldiers in disarray. Crittenden was arrested and court-martialed. His disappointing Civil War career ended on 23 October 1862, when he resigned from the Confederate army.

After the Civil War, Crittenden returned to Frankfort, where his bravery and loyalty were recognized by the state of Kentucky. He later became a state librarian from 1867 to 1871. George Bibb Crittenden died 27 November 1880, in Danville, Kentucky, and was buried with his family in Frankfort.

—*Nathan R. Meyer*

See also Crittenden, John J.; Crittenden, Thomas L.; Logan's Cross Roads, Battle of; Zollicoffer, Felix K.
For further reading:
Coleman, Ann Mary. *The Life of John J. Crittenden, with Selections from His Correspondence and Speeches.* (1871).

CRITTENDEN, JOHN JORDAN
(1786–1863)
U.S. senator, congressman, attorney general

John Jordan Crittenden, best known for his eleventh-hour attempts to forestall secession by compromise in the winter of 1860–1861, played a key role in U.S. politics from James Monroe's administration through the first two years of the Civil War. Crittenden served in the cabinet of three different presidents, was elected to the U.S. Senate on five occasions, and was offered a position on the Supreme Court by both John Quincy Adams and Abraham Lincoln. After spending much of his career as Henry Clay's top political lieutenant, Crittenden inherited Clay's mantle of compromise during the secession crisis. Despite Crittenden's failure to prevent war, Unionists in central Kentucky sent him in 1861 to Congress, where he became a spokesman for the old Union and against weakening slavery. Crittenden declined renomination in 1863 for health reasons and died that summer.

Crittenden began his political career in the Kentucky House of Representatives in 1811. After serving as a general's aide during the Thames River campaign in the War of 1812, Crittenden returned to Kentucky, spent three terms as speaker of the state House and won election to the U.S. Senate in 1817. He played an important, albeit minor, role in the development of the second party system. After Henry Clay engineered the House of Representatives' selection of John Quincy Adams as president in 1825, Crittenden advised Clay to accept Adams's offer of the State Department. Clay's agreement, partly resulting from Crittenden's guidance, led to charges of a corrupt bargain by partisans of defeated candidate Andrew Jackson, who then worked to organize the Democratic Party. Crittenden joined the opposition to President Jackson and became a key figure in the Whig Party. After the election of the first Whig president, William Henry Harrison, Crittenden entered the cabinet as attorney general. In 1842, after John Tyler's repeated rejection of a national bank, Crittenden resigned his post and replaced Clay in the U.S. Senate.

Crittenden perhaps deserved most of the credit for Zachary Taylor's election to the presidency in 1848. Although he had loyally stood by Clay for decades, Crittenden became an early supporter of General Taylor. Asserting that three-time loser Clay could not win, Crittenden turned to the popular general, who was soon "identified as his candidate." Crittenden's efforts gave political cover to many pro-Taylor Whigs in Kentucky. Once it became clear that Clay could not command the support of his own state, Whigs chose Taylor rather than their venerable champion. However, Crittenden refused his share of the spoils; rather than become Taylor's secretary of state, he opted to remain governor of Kentucky, a position he had accepted only to strengthen Whig prospects in the state. After Taylor's death in 1850, Crittenden agreed to become Millard Fillmore's attorney general, helping the president assist the Compromise of 1850.

Once Henry Clay died in 1852, Crittenden became Kentucky's most famous politician. He returned to the U.S. Senate in 1855, spending his term as a moderate against the extremes of both sections, such as the admission of Kansas under the Lecompton Constitution and the dangerous new Republican Party. In 1860, Crittenden became one of the leading figures in the new Constitutional Union Party, seeking a middle ground between proslavery Democrats and antislavery Republicans. After Lincoln's election, Crittenden became the Senate's chief advocate of compromise to prevent secession and civil war. Crittenden proposed a series of constitutional amendments to guarantee the rights of Southerners and preserve sectional peace. His compromise included dividing all territory along the old Missouri Compromise line into free and slave areas, prohibiting Congress from interfering with the interstate slave trade, compensating owners for fugitive slaves liberated by mobs in the North, and preventing certain clauses of the Constitution from being amended. Although the Crittenden Compromise seemed to have widespread popular support in the winter of 1860–1861, his appeal to sacrifice in the name of Union fell on deaf ears. Republicans refused to yield; Deep South states continued to secede. Only part of Crittenden's proposal received approval. An amendment forbidding federal interference with slavery in the states passed Congress with the necessary majorities and went to the states before war intervened. In March 1861, at the end of his term, Crittenden returned home to Kentucky.

Once war broke out in April 1861, Crittenden used his considerable influence to prevent the secession of Kentucky. Like the state, however, his family was divided by the conflict as his two sons, George B. Crittenden and Thomas L. Crittenden, parted ways to serve in the Confederate and Union armies, respectively. Meanwhile, Crittenden was part of an extralegal committee that originated Kentucky's policy of neutrality in the early months of the conflict. While the state remained aloof from battle, Crittenden and other Unionists worked hard to solidify support for the Federal war effort. To aid the Union cause, Crittenden consented to run for Congress in the May elections.

Although secessionists tried mightily to embarrass Unionists by defeating the legendary Crittenden, he prevailed. In the House, Crittenden quickly worked to confirm the conservative purposes of the war and to reassure Kentucky Unionists. His resolutions on Federal war aims, which passed Congress with little opposition, blamed the war on Southern disunionists and declared that the government sought only the restoration of the Union. Despite this initial success, Crittenden spent most of his term in the minority. He opposed any attempts to confiscate Rebels' land or slaves as grossly unconstitutional, argued against creating the Committee on the Conduct of the War, denounced the Emancipation Proclamation, protested the use of black soldiers, and fought the creation of West Virginia. Crittenden also resisted conscription, asserting that the government's lack of personnel proved that the war had become more radical than the American people would support. Although his views placed him in a minority in Congress, Crittenden echoed the concerns of many Kentuckians who had loyally backed the Union only to feel betrayed when the government changed the purpose of the war. Crittenden could have won another term in Congress, but his distaste for the government's conduct, along with his rapidly failing health, led him to retire. He died on 26 July 1863.

—*Christopher M. Paine*

See also Crittenden Compromise; Crittenden, George B.; Crittenden, Thomas L.; Kentucky.

For further reading:

Coleman, Ann Mary. *The Life of John J. Crittenden, with Selections from His Correspondence and Speeches* (1871).

Kelly, Jack. "John J. Crittenden and the Constitutional Union Party." *Filson Club History Quarterly* (1974).

Kirwan, Albert D. *John J. Crittenden: The Struggle for the Union* (1962).

Zacharias, Donald W. "John J. Crittenden Crusades for the Union and Neutrality in Kentucky." *Filson Club History Quarterly* (1964).

CRITTENDEN, THOMAS LEONIDAS
(1819–1893)
Union general

Thomas Leonidas Crittenden was born in Russellville, Kentucky, on 15 May 1819, the second son of a powerful political family. Crittenden's father was John Jordan Crittenden, the eminent Kentucky statesman who attempted a final compromise in 1861 in an effort to save the Union.

Thomas Crittenden spent much of his youth being educated by his father, who taught his son law. Crittenden passed the bar in 1840 and soon afterward began his legal career in Frankfort, Kentucky. His tenure as a lawyer was short-lived because of the Mexican War (1846–1848). The war began Crittenden's military

Thomas L. Crittenden (*Library of Congress*)

career: he recruited Kentucky soldiers and was made a lieutenant colonel in the United States Army. When the war ended, he returned to his legal career, but soon thereafter became a businessman. Because of their relationship established in the Mexican War, President Zachary Taylor appointed Crittenden consul to Liverpool.

The secession crisis threw the Crittenden household into turmoil. Senator John Crittenden tried to fashion a compromise to preserve the Union, but Thomas's older brother, George Bibb, sympathized with the South and eventually became a general in the Confederacy. For his part, Thomas opposed slavery and secession. When the war began, he volunteered for the Union army and was commissioned a brigadier general of volunteers on 17 July 1861. The Crittenden family exemplified a divided nation and a war that pitted brother against brother.

Crittenden's commission as a general angered many within the Union army. He had little military experience, had never attended military school, and had obviously benefitted from the political influence of his powerful father. Crittenden's unpopularity also could

have been due to his arrogance and his drinking, which usually caused him to use profane language. One observer described Crittenden as having a "thin, staring face, and hair hanging to his coat collar—a very wild appearing major general, but quite a kindly man in conversation."

Despite Crittenden's lack of experience, the war began well for him and his command. Crittenden took command of the 5th Division of the Army of the Ohio under General Don Carlos Buell before the battle of Shiloh in April 1862. At Shiloh, Crittenden rendered gallant and notable service and was promoted to major general of volunteers on 17 July 1862.

On 8 October 1862 Crittenden participated in the battle of Perryville, Kentucky. He made a critical mistake when a small number of Confederate horsemen, about one-tenth the size of his army, bluffed him into withdrawing his troops from the battle, a blunder that may have saved the Confederate forces from a crushing defeat.

On 24 October 1862 Crittenden was transferred to the Army of the Cumberland under General William Rosecrans. His first important experience with the Army of the Cumberland came on 31 December 1863 at the battle of Stones River in Tennessee. Crittenden appeared to have rebounded from Perryville and performed admirably. His behavior at Stones River quickly earned the respect and trust of Rosecrans, and he was breveted for gallantry.

As fall approached in 1863 Crittenden and the Army of the Cumberland continued the fight toward Chattanooga, Tennessee. That September, General Crittenden was commanding the 21st Corps of the Army of the Cumberland during the battle of Chickamauga, when he was driven back after weakening his forces to reinforce General George Thomas. Later, rumors circulated that his troops had deserted him. In any event, Crittenden's corps was routed, and his actions were investigated. He was relieved of command and sent to Indianapolis for an inquiry.

Crittenden's fellow Kentuckians were outraged by what they regarded as an inquisition, so on 14 December 1863 the Kentucky legislature forwarded a demand to President Lincoln for a rehearing. The following February a court in Louisville, Kentucky, honorably acquitted him, but the whole affair damaged Crittenden's military reputation.

Crittenden spent the rest of the war with the Army of the Potomac during the Virginia campaign. His resignation on 13 December 1864 ended his Civil War service.

Thomas Crittenden rejoined the army after the Civil War in July 1866. He served until May 1881, when advancing age forced his retirement. Crittenden died at Staten Island, New York, on 23 October 1893. He is buried with his family in Frankfort, Kentucky.

—*Nathan R. Meyer*

See also Chickamauga, Battle of; Crittenden Compromise; Crittenden, George B.; Crittenden, John J.; Perryville, Battle of.
For further reading:
Bowers, John. *Chickamauga and Chattanooga: The Battles that Doomed the South* (1994).
Cozzens, Peter. *This Terrible Sound: The Battle of Chickamauga* (1992).
Foote, Shelby. *The Civil War: A Narrative* (1958–1974).
McDonough, James L. *Stones River–Bloody Winter in Tennessee* (1980).
U. S. War Department. *The War of the Rebellion: A Compilation of the Official Records of the Union and Confederate Armies* (1880–1901).

CROCKER, MARCELLUS MONROE
(1830–1865)
Union general

Marcellus M. Crocker was born in Indiana but moved with his family to Illinois in 1830, and then, a few years later, to Jefferson County, Iowa. He was able to secure an appointment to the military academy at West Point when he was sixteen. He attended West Point for more than two years, but health problems and family hardship prevented him from graduating.

In 1849, at age nineteen, Crocker began to study law in Fairfield, Iowa, and was admitted to the Iowa bar in 1851. His first law practice was in Keokuk County, Iowa, where he earned a reputation as a successful lawyer. When he was twenty-five he moved to Des Moines, the state capital, where he worked in two law offices and was active in the Democratic Party. In 1858 he ran and was defeated for the position of district judge.

In April 1861, news reached Des Moines that Fort Sumter had been fired on and that war had begun. The result of this news was an explosion of war fever across the state. Des Moines, like most Iowa communities, was the scene of mass rallies and public displays of patriotism. Crocker was a Democrat, but he was also a strong defender of the Union. He attended the largest of the city's war rallies and took the stage to make an impassioned speech in defense of the old flag. In that speech, he called for 100 volunteers, enough men to fill a military company, to follow him into Dixie. Within a few minutes he had more than he requested.

Crocker was elected captain of the new company, and on 4 May 1861 he and his volunteers left for the mustering center at Keokuk to be enlisted in the Union army as Company D, 2d Iowa Volunteer Infantry. Crocker was made major of the regiment, and four months later was commissioned lieutenant colonel. The regiment participated in campaigns in Missouri throughout the summer and fall of 1861, and Crocker earned a reputation as an efficient leader and firm disciplinarian and drillmaster.

Crocker was transferred from the 2d Iowa in October 1861, promoted to full colonel, and placed in command of the newly formed 13th Iowa Volunteer Infantry. Crocker led the 13th Iowa at the battle of Shiloh in April 1862, where he was acknowledged by his commanding officer for his coolness and bravery and his ability to inspire his men to stand by their colors while under severe fire.

After Shiloh the 11th, 13th, 15th, and 16th Iowa infantry regiments were organized as the Iowa Brigade and placed under Crocker's command. He led the new brigade at the battle of Corinth and so impressed his superiors that he was promoted to brigadier general in November 1862. He commanded the Iowa Brigade until April 1863, when he was placed in command of the 7th Division of XVII Corps of the Army of the Tennessee. He led the division in the battles of Jackson and Champion's Hill during the Vicksburg campaign in the summer of 1863 and served, briefly, on General Ulysses S. Grant's staff in May 1863.

Crocker's health was nearly broken by consumption during the Vicksburg campaign, and under General Grant's personal advice he went home on sick leave in June 1863. Republican leaders in Des Moines ignored Crocker's history as a Democrat and actively sought to make him the party's candidate for governor. Crocker declined the honor, saying, "If a soldier is worth anything he cannot be spared from the field; if he is worthless, he will not make a good governor."

Crocker returned to service in less than a month and was given command of the 4th Division of XIII Corps of the Army of the Tennessee, which he commanded for the rest of the summer. From the fall of 1863 to May 1864 he was back with XVII Corps serving under General William T. Sherman in the Meridian and Atlanta campaigns.

Crocker's health worsened throughout the winter, and in May 1864 he submitted his resignation. Rather than accept the offered resignation, General Sherman arranged for him to be transferred to New Mexico in the hopes that the climate there would help him recover his health. He remained in New Mexico throughout the summer and fall, but in December he requested active duty and was sent to the Army of the Cumberland in Tennessee. After less than three months in his new position, his health finally failed him, and he was then transferred to Washington, D.C.

Crocker died in Washington on 26 August 1865. He was thirty-five years old. His wife traveled to Washington and escorted his body back to Des Moines, where he was buried with full military honors.

—*Kenneth L. Lyftogt*

See also Meridian Campaign; Vicksburg Campaign.
For further reading:
Brigham, Johnson. *Iowa: Its History and Its Foremost Citizens* (1916).

Gue, Benjamin F. *A History of Iowa* (1903).

Iowa General Assembly. *Roster and Record of Iowa Soldiers in the War of the Rebellion: Together with Historical Sketches of Volunteer Organizations, 1861–1866* (1908–1911).

Stuart, A.A. *17th Iowa Infantry. Iowa Colonels and Regiments: Being a History of Iowa Regiments in the War of the Rebellion* (1891).

Throne, Mildred. "Iowans and the Civil War." *Palimpsest* (1969).

CROOK, GEORGE
(1828–1890)
Union general

George Crook was born on 8 September 1828 near Taylorsville, Ohio, the ninth of ten children in a relatively prosperous farming family. His father's status as a locally prominent Whig drew Crook an appointment to the U.S. Military Academy, and after first preparing at nearby Dayton Academy, he entered West Point with the class of 1852.

After a mediocre cadet career, Crook was posted to the 4th Infantry and spent his antebellum years on the Pacific Coast. There he saw action in the Rogue River War, gaining experience in guerrilla-style warfare and carefully observing frontier administration and diplomacy. Returning east upon the outbreak of the Civil War, he received command of the 36th Ohio Volunteer Infantry and took the field in western Virginia. On 23 May 1862, Crook defeated a larger Confederate force at Lewisburg, an action for which he was brevetted a major in the regular army. After promotion to brigadier general of volunteers, he led a brigade of the Kanawha Division at South Mountain and Antietam, where he helped force the hotly contested crossing at "Burnside's bridge" on the Confederate right.

Crook then briefly returned to western Virginia before joining General William S. Rosecrans's Army of the Cumberland for the Tullahoma campaign in the summer of 1863. Later that fall, he led the 2d Cavalry Division into battle at Chickamauga and helped cover the routed Union army's retreat to Chattanooga. Reassignment back to West Virginia gave the young general an opportunity to exercise independent command at Cloyd's Mountain, where he won a complete victory and earned his men's lasting respect. Crook took part in David Hunter's Valley campaign and was also prominent at Cedar Creek—a victory for which Crook bitterly believed Philip Sheridan ungraciously accepted largely undeserved credit.

While in command of the Department of West Virginia, Crook gained the peculiar and unfortunate wartime distinction of being captured in his own bed. In February 1865, Captain Jesse McNeill's Confederate guerrillas snatched the sleeping general from a hotel bed in Cumberland, Maryland, and held him captive until exchanged a short time later. Humiliated, Crook returned to West Virginia to find his department assigned to Winfield Scott Hancock. General Ulysses S. Grant restored Crook's honor by giving him command of the Army of the Potomac's cavalry, which Crook led during the war's last days around Petersburg, at Dinwiddie Court House, Sayler's Creek, and Appomattox.

After the war, on 22 August 1865, Crook married Mary Dailey, daughter of the hotel owner where he had been captured. The marriage never assumed a prominent role in Crook's life, and Mary usually remained in Maryland during the general's frontier service, venturing west only for short visits. In November 1866, after several months of Reconstruction duty in North Carolina, Crook returned west in command of the 23d Infantry to the Idaho Territory.

Crook's frontier operations were innovative and often departed from conventional military wisdom. He employed "friendly" Indians against their hostile tribe members, a practice that he stubbornly defended against popular and professional criticism. In 1871, he was given command of the troubled Department of Arizona after achieving striking success in the Northwest. In Arizona, he again fielded Indian auxiliaries and employed pack mules instead of supply wagons to gain mobility in pursuit of hostile Apaches. Crook's techniques proved effective, and by the spring of 1873 the Arizona Territory enjoyed temporary peace.

The same tactics were applied less successfully on the plains, where, as commander of the Department of the Platte, Crook participated in the Sioux War of 1876. His reputation suffered from controversial actions taken at Rosebud Creek in June 1876. His failure to continue northward after the battle led to speculation that his decision contributed to Custer's massacre at the Little Big Horn. It was also during this period that his humanitarian views on federal Indian policy became more public. Paternalistic attempts to acculturate Indians made him a sort of hero among eastern reformers and provided a basis for his "tough but fair" administrative doctrine. Upon returning to Arizona in 1882, he attempted to permanently settle the Apaches into an agricultural lifestyle. This solution was dealt a severe blow when Geronimo and several others broke from the reservation and raided along the border.

After the subsequent campaign ended in broken promises by both Geronimo and the government, Crook felt discredited and requested reassignment, believing that external interference would never allow his methods to achieve enduring success. He ended his career as commander of the Division of the Missouri and remained an active campaigner for Indian rights. On 21 March 1890, Crook died of a heart attack in Chicago, Illinois, and was buried in Oakland, Maryland.

—*Ronald G. Machoian*

See also Cedar Creek, Battle of; Cloyd's Mountain, Battle of; McNeill, John and Jesse.
For further reading:
Bourke, John G. *On the Border with Crook* (1891; reprint, 1971).
Greene, Jerome A. "George Crook." In *Soldiers West: Biographies from the Military Frontier* (1987).
King, James T. "George Crook: Indian Fighter and Humanitarian." *Arizona and the West* (1967).
Schmitt, Martin F., ed. *General George Crook: His Autobiography* (1960).
Utley, Robert M. *Frontier Regulars: The United States Army and the Indian, 1866–1891* (1973).

CROSS KEYS, BATTLE OF
(8 June 1862)

The battle of Cross Keys was the fifth battle of Lieutenant General Thomas J. "Stonewall" Jackson's Shenandoah Valley campaign and was fought the day before the larger battle of Port Republic. The battle occurred near the small village of Cross Keys, six miles southeast of Harrisonburg and seven miles northwest of Port Republic.

At Cross Keys on 7 June, three brigades of Confederate troops, about 5,000 men commanded by Major General Richard S. Ewell, prepared to meet a Union attack by 10,500 men under Major General John C. Frémont, who had moved down the Valley Pike through Harrisonburg. Frémont, moving in from the northwest, and Brigadier General James Shields, closing from the northeast, hoped to trap Jackson's force between them.

Ewell had charge of defending Jackson's western flank. He established excellent defensive positions along a ridge facing northwest and fronted by several hundred acres of open fields with maple woods protecting both flanks. He positioned his artillery batteries in the center of the line to block the road to Port Republic. Brigadier General George Steuart's brigade held the Confederate left; Brigadier General Isaac Trimble's brigade, the right. Brigadier General Arnold Elzey's infantry brigade was in reserve.

Jackson was at Port Republic. He positioned his men there just north of that town to be able to deal with Shields's division approaching from the northeast. Jackson was thus in supporting distance of Ewell, although Ewell fought his own battle at Cross Keys against Frémont.

The battle of Cross Keys opened at about 10:00 A.M. on 8 June with a half-hearted advance by Frémont's infantry. Brigadier General Louis Blenker's division of German immigrants slowly pushed back the Confederate advance elements. The 15th Alabama Infantry of Trimble's brigade held the Union troops for about a half hour. A long-range artillery duel followed. The 44th Virginia Regiment and 1st Maryland then beat back several Union attacks.

Frémont mounted his major attack with a brigade of Blenker's Germans against Trimble's brigade on the Confederate right. Displaying excellent discipline, Trimble's men held their fire until the Union troops were close, then fired a series of volleys that repulsed the assault. Confederates located in the woods on the right flank exacted a heavy toll on the Union troops.

Trimble's men then advanced about a mile. Trimble was confident he could flank the entire Union line and asked Ewell for reinforcements. Even though the Confederates had sustained few casualties, Ewell declined. Two of his brigade commanders, Elzey and Steuart, had been slightly wounded by shell fragments, and Ewell had received reports of a Union turning movement against the Confederate left.

Meanwhile, Jackson had sent Colonel John M. Patton's brigade and Brigadier General Richard Taylor's brigade to Ewell. They arrived in the afternoon and Ewell placed them in the center of his line. Later when Frémont failed to mount an attack on the Confederate left, Ewell ordered his men forward, and by nightfall they had occupied the Union positions of that morning.

Trimble wanted a night attack, but Ewell refused, reluctant to put too much distance between himself and Jackson. Ewell gave Trimble permission to approach Jackson who told him, "Consult General Ewell and be guided by him." To give his subordinate Ewell such latitude was high praise from Jackson. Trimble then tried a second time to convince Ewell, who again refused.

The fight at Cross Keys was more a skirmish than a real battle. Ewell had lost 288 men, of whom 41 were dead. Frémont, on the other hand had lost 684, nearly half of them dead or mortally wounded. (In his report to Jackson, containing the entire Union order of battle captured during the fight, Ewell claimed 2,000 Union casualties.)

Jackson then sent orders to Ewell to leave only a holding force (Trimble's brigade) in position facing Frémont while the rest of his men marched to join him at Port Republic. Jackson hoped that once Shields had been defeated they could then both return and complete the work of destroying Frémont. Ewell's march to reinforce Jackson at Port Republic began at dawn on 9 June; the remaining Confederate troops withdrew from Cross Keys on Jackson's subsequent order later on 9 June.

—*Spencer C. Tucker*

See also Elzey, Arnold; Ewell, Richard S.; Frémont, John C.; Jackson, Thomas J.; Port Republic, Battle of; Shenandoah Valley campaign (May–June 1862); Steuart, George H.; Taylor, Richard; Trimble, Isaac.
For further reading:
Collins, Darrell L. *Jackson's Valley Campaign. The Battles of Cross Keys and Port Republic, June 8–9, 1862* (1993).
Tanner, Robert G. *Stonewall in the Valley. Thomas J. "Stonewall" Jackson's Shenandoah Valley Campaign, Spring 1862* (1976; reprint 1996).

CULLUM, GEORGE WASHINGTON
(1809–1892)
Union general

Born to Arthur Cullum and Harriet Sturges Cullum in New York City, George Cullum moved with his parents to Pennsylvania while he was still a child. He was educated locally before receiving an appointment to the U.S. Military Academy. He graduated third of forty-three from the class of 1833. Commissioned into the Corps of Engineers, Cullum worked on a variety of projects including coastal fortifications, the expansion of the buildings at West Point, and harbor improvements during the pre–Civil War years.

As the Civil War approached, Cullum had reached the rank of major and was serving in Newport, Rhode Island. With the secession crisis becoming more serious in early 1861, he tried to bring the town to some defensive readiness but could not persuade the civilian authorities in the town that a crisis was at hand. Beginning in April 1861 he served as aide-de-camp to General Winfield Scott. Cullum held this position until August 1861, at which point he was promoted to colonel. In the fall of that year he transferred west. On 1 November 1861, Cullum became brigadier general of volunteers and chief of staff to General Henry Halleck. During his first months with Halleck, he also served as the general's chief engineer.

Halleck gave Cullum a great deal of leeway in carrying out the general's orders. Cullum traveled throughout the theater reporting back to Halleck the condition of troops and the quality of officer performance. He also did not hesitate to urge commanders to be more aggressive if necessary. Halleck also relied on Cullum, given his extensive engineering background, to inspect fortifications throughout the theater, and when short-handed would send Cullum to command those fortifications until a suitable officer could be found.

In July 1862, Halleck was summoned to Washington to serve as commanding general of Union armies. Cullum accompanied his commander to act as chief of staff in Washington. Cullum was to find his duties in Washington far more bureaucratic than serving a general in the field. He handled much of Halleck's communication with generals scattered throughout the country, but did not travel to the scene of action as he had done in the West. Cullum also served on several boards during his time in Washington. In December 1862, Secretary of War Edwin Stanton appointed Cullum to a commission to study the defenses of Washington, D.C. The following year Cullum served on a board to look at the defense of the Potomac Aqueduct and another looking again at Washington's defenses.

In March 1864, Halleck's position was considerably reduced when Ulysses S. Grant became commanding general. In fact, Halleck became Grant's chief of staff, thus reducing Cullum's role substantially. Cullum remained for several months on Halleck's staff, but in September 1864 accepted appointment as superintendent of the U.S. Military Academy. He remained in that position for two years.

Upon leaving West Point in 1866, Cullum was promoted to colonel in the regular army and served as an engineer until his retirement in 1874. He married for the first time the following year Elizabeth Hamilton Halleck, General Halleck's widow. For the remainder of his life, Cullum indulged a variety of interests including active membership in the National Geographical Society and efforts as a founder of the Association of Graduates of the U.S. Military Academy. He also wrote history and compiled and wrote much of the *Biographical Register of the Officers and Graduates of the United States Military Academy*, one of the most useful reference works on the officer corps of the nineteenth century. Cullum died in New York City on 28 February 1892, leaving a large fortune to his various causes.

—*David S. Heidler and Jeanne T. Heidler*

See also Halleck, Henry Wager.
For further reading:
Livermore, William Roscoe. "Biographical Notice of George Washington Cullum." *Proceedings of the Academy of Arts and Sciences.*

CUMMING, KATE
(ca. 1828–1909)
Confederate nurse

Kate Cumming is credited with writing the most detailed and poignant narrative of Confederate hospital life. A matron in the Confederate Army of Tennessee, Cumming traveled to Okolona and Corinth, Mississippi, after the battle of Shiloh in April 1862 and worked continuously until the spring of 1865. Having assessed the tremendous need for helping hands early in the war, she advocated hospital work and criticized those who discouraged elite women from volunteering. She kept a journal throughout her tour of duty, which records early Confederate jubilation, strong religious faith, anti-Union sentiments, frustrations with hospital staff, and increasing despondency at the prospect of food shortages and Confederate loss.

Cumming was born in Leith, Scotland, around 1828. Her father, David, who worked in commerce, moved his large family to Montreal while Kate was still a child (there were eventually ten children). There Kate received her only formal education, but her letters indicate a highly engaged intellect and an eloquent style. An intermediate move to New York and a final one to Mobile, Alabama, probably in the 1840s, resulted in Kate's strong association with the South. By the time of the Civil War, her views on slavery and states' rights made Cumming seem more Southern than many born in Dixie.

Cumming first became involved in hospital work when a neighboring clergyman conducted a band of churchwomen to Confederate hospitals established in Okolona and Corinth after Shiloh. The conditions at Tishomingo Hotel, where Confederate wounded were laid out all over the floors, were so foul that only Cumming and one other woman remained beyond the first week. With inadequate space, supplies, and staff, Cumming was so busy that she could not change her bloodstained dress for ten days and was compelled to sleep, when she could steal a few hours, on boxes. She was halfway through washing a soldier's face before she realized that he had died with no one near him. "These are terrible things," she wrote, "and what is more heart-rending, no one seems to mind them."

She returned home in June, but by early fall was bound for Chattanooga, where she served at Newsom Hospital (named for Ella King Newsom) until Braxton Bragg's forces withdrew from the city in the summer of 1863. Letters to her father from Chattanooga suggest that she was responsible for locating and managing laundresses, a job she disliked intensely. She also delivered food and medicine, kept clothing and bedding fresh, wrote letters, and even cooked when slaves were not available. From 1863 to the end of the war, Cumming was constantly on the move with Surgeon Samuel Stout's medical corps in the Army of Tennessee. Known for developing a system of "flying hospitals," the precursor to twentieth-century mobile surgical units, Stout's corps was plagued by frequent and sudden mobilizations as Sherman's army invaded Georgia and the Carolinas. Cumming complained that it was bad luck whenever a new hospital kitchen was completed because the army would inevitably be called to retreat the next day.

Before the war was over, she would travel to the Georgia cities of Dalton, Ringgold, Kingston, Cherokee Springs, Newnan, Americus, and Griffin, sometimes working in field hospitals. On duty during the siege of Vicksburg and the battles of Chickamauga and Lookout Mountain, Cumming despaired at the "moral leprosy eating at the very vitals of the Confederacy," or the graft that resulted from severe food shortages by 1864. By the autumn of 1864, she went for six weeks without writing in her journal because she had no paper.

Cumming left Newnan to travel the 385 miles to Mobile in May 1865. The trip took several weeks because of broken rail lines and lack of funds. Taking command of her father's household, Kate immersed herself in readying her journal for publication. In 1866, she paid a Louisville publisher to print the book with borrowed funds, but could not repay the loan for several years—a fact that caused her considerable anguish. Working as a governess and Sunday-school teacher, she

scraped together income to help with family expenses. The Cummings moved to Birmingham in 1874, where Kate settled into a round of teaching and participated in Confederate memorial activities. Always single, she adopted a nephew in the 1870s and produced a series of novels, none of which was ever published. In 1890 she republished a sanitized version of her journal called *Gleanings from Southland*, which was more successful in a market hungry for "the romance of reunion," a term coined by historian Nina Silber to denote North-South reconciliation. When Cumming died in 1909, she was better off financially than were nurses who had donated their substantial fortunes to the Lost Cause.

—*Jane E. Schultz*

See also Nurses.
For further reading:
Cumming, Kate. *A Journal of Hospital Life in the Confederate Army of Tennessee* (1866).
Faust, Drew Gilpin. *Mothers of Invention: Women of the Slaveholding South in the American Civil War* (1996).
Harwell, Richard B., ed. *Kate: The Journal of a Confederate Nurse* (1959).
Schultz, Jane E. *Women at the Front: Female Hospital Workers in Civil War America* (2000).

CURRENCY, C.S.A.

The Confederate government could not enact more than a shade of taxation for fear of causing immediate economic and political dislocations. The Davis administration was especially concerned that taxation would arouse suspicion of central authority at a time when the war effort required the unqualified support of the people. The Confederacy consequently tried to rely on disappointing loans from domestic bond issues and foreign creditors as well as nominal tariffs and taxes. The result was an insoluble financial dilemma wherein the inadequacy of Confederate finance became apparent in the opening days of the new government's existence. Within weeks of taking the post, Secretary of the Treasury Christopher Memminger tried to pay for the exploding costs of the Civil War with treasury notes.

These treasury notes were the legendary currency whose inflationary proliferation still stuns the imagination. To his credit, Memminger never succumbed to the easy delusion that currency is money. Too many Southerners, however, at least for a time slipped into the error because currency can act just as money does in the right circumstances. Yet currency and money fundamentally differ in that money has an intrinsic value apart from any form it takes. Gold has value even if it is not minted into coin. Yet currency, in the form of treasury notes for instance, has no value other than that artificially imparted to it. Currency can act as money only when markets are confident that its value derives from a stable source, such as a proportionate amount of specie or a healthy and responsible government. In fact, in the absence of any other support, such as specie, a robust government and calm political environment become paramount. The Confederacy had neither. As the government's effectiveness diminished under the fracturing burdens of war and internal discord, it was inevitable that the viability of Confederate currency would collapse as well and destroy the Southern economy.

Shortages of almost everything, including specie, plagued the Confederacy in 1861. Even the special paper used to print currency and the engraving expertise necessary to design it were hard for the government to procure. When the government resorted to issuing treasury notes that would have been redeemable in specie two years after the war, it inaugurated a long slide of depreciation that by 1863 had attained a staggering rate of acceleration. Paper currency in all denominations, even as low as fifty cents, spewed from printing presses as costs mounted. At the end of 1861, the Confederate dollar was worth approximately eighty cents in gold. In the first two months of 1862, it lost twenty cents of that value, and a year later the dollar reached a low of 20 cents. Value plummeted like a stone after that as military misfortunes occurred, placing the dollar's value at eight cents in the summer of 1863. When Lee surrendered at Appomattox, the Confederate dollar had a value of approximately 1.5 cents in gold.

The main cause for this rapid decline was rampant inflation. Using the standard axiom that high value is a result of scarcity and low value of overabundance, the astronomical numbers of treasury notes in circulation simply gutted their value. Yet other factors also contributed to the fiscal disaster. Localities ranging from the state to the county level added to the problem by circulating their own paper currency, and the variety and crudity of notes encouraged counterfeiting. The decision not to designate the treasury notes as legal tender was designed to inspire faith in their value, but it also did not require anybody to accept them as payment for goods and services. When their declining value became their most obvious feature, the currency in some instances simply became worthless. Prices rose about 300 percent in 1862, and by 1865 an ordinary suit of clothes in Richmond could cost as much $2,500. By then, the ocean of paper had become just another aspect of Confederate disintegration and collapse.

—*David S. Heidler and Jeanne T. Heidler*

See also Financing, C.S.A.

For further reading:

Lerner, Eugene M. "The Monetary and Fiscal Programs of the Confederate Government, 1861–1865." *Journal of Political Economy* (1954).

Schwab, John C. *The Confederate States of America, 1861–1865; A Financial and Industrial History of the South during the Civil War* (1901; reprint, 1968).

Todd, Richard Cecil. *Confederate Finance* (1954).

CURTIN, ANDREW GREGG
(1817–1894)
Northern politician and statesman

Born 22 April 1817, in Bellefonte, Pennsylvania, a son of Roland and Jane Curtin, Andrew G. Curtin was educated at the Harrisburg and Milton academies and at Dickinson School of Law. Curtin was a prosperous attorney before the war and served as secretary of the commonwealth and head of public education under Governor James Pollock from 1855 to 1857. Elected in 1860 by a 32,000-vote majority over Democrat Henry Foster, Curtin served as governor of Pennsylvania from 1861 to 1865 and was the first Republican to hold that office. While often overshadowed by such luminaries as John Andrew of Massachusetts and Horatio Seymour of New York, Andrew Curtin was an astute politician and a tireless defender of the Union and of the Lincoln administration.

Curtin was seemingly the only Northern politician (Lincoln included) who comprehended the gravity of the situation in 1861. It had been one of his first acts as governor to send agents into the Confederacy to ascertain the true state of affairs there. Hence, while most Northerners dismissed Southern threats as being mere bombast, Curtin never doubted that Southerners were in earnest. He quietly began to prepare his state for war. Pennsylvania under Curtin was one of the first states to answer the president's call for volunteers after Fort Sumter. The state provided more troops than the government could handle and many had to be turned away. Rather than send them home, as the War Department recommended, Curtin instead formed them into a semi-independent state command known as the Pennsylvania Reserves. Curtin's foresight in retaining these troops was soon born out after the Union disaster at First Bull Run in July 1861, when a frantic War Department, panicked by the prospect of an attack on the capital, urgently wired Curtin to send the reserves at once.

Among his contributions to the Union war effort were his tireless efforts to improve the lot of ordinary soldiers. Governor Curtin was the driving force behind the establishment of the National Cemetery at Gettysburg, organized a state commission to minister to sick and wounded soldiers, and worked especially hard to ensure that Pennsylvania's war dead be brought home for burial. Curtin was also responsible for the establishment of a state school for war orphans. It was because of these and countless other humanitarian endeavors that Curtin became known affectionately as "the Soldiers' Friend."

Perhaps Curtin's most significant contribution to Union victory was the 1862 Altoona Governors' Conference, which Curtin not only hosted but, together with Governor Andrew of Massachusetts, also drafted its concluding resolutions calling upon Lincoln to make another request for 300,000 men for the war. This statement, coming as it did in the wake of the Union defeats at the Seven Days' and Bull Run battles and the bloodletting at Antietam, not only relieved Lincoln of the politically onerous task of issuing another such call for troops, but was instrumental in rallying support from the Northern governors at what must have seemed the darkest hours for the Union cause.

So instrumental was Curtin in rallying support for the Union cause within Pennsylvania that many deemed it essential that he seek a second term in 1863 despite poor health and Lincoln's offer of a foreign ambassadorship. His decision to accept the Republican nomination would subject Curtin to one of the bitterest campaigns in the state's history. Despite the bitter and personal nature of the opposition's attacks, Curtin easily won reelection over his Democratic opponent George Woodward, an avowed Copperhead and ally of Ohio congressional representative Clement Vallandigham. Curtin's victory not only served to discourage antiwar Democrats, but would also prove to be a bellwether for Democratic fortunes in 1864, when Lincoln would handily defeat former Commander of the Army of the Potomac general George B. McClellan.

After the war, Curtin continued as governor until 1866 and later was appointed by President Grant as minister to Russia. There was a great deal of talk within the Republican Party of Curtin being nominated for vice president or even president. The manipulations of his chief political rival, former Secretary of War Simon Cameron, denied Curtin these opportunities, however. The feud with Cameron would not only deny Curtin a chance at higher office, but would eventually cause him to switch to the Democrats in 1878. It was as a member of that party that Curtin won election to Congress in 1880, 1882, and 1884. He served as chairman of the House Foreign Affairs Committee. After leaving Congress in 1885, Curtin retired to his home in Bellefonte, where he died on 7 October 1894. To the end of his days, he remained a staunch promoter of harmony and reconciliation between North and South.

—*Ken A. Dietreich*

See also Cameron, Simon; Pennsylvania; Woodward, George W.

For further reading:
Armor, William C. *Lives of the Governors of Pennsylvania with the Incidental History of the State, from 1609 to 1872* (1877).
Curtin, Andrew G. *Annual Message of the Governor of Pennsylvania, Andrew G. Curtin, to the Legislature of Pennsylvania, at Harrisburg, 7 January 1864* (1864).
Egle, William H., ed. *Life and Times of Andrew Gregg Curtin* (1895).
Goas, Thomas Stewart. *The Contribution of Andrew Gregg Curtin to the Union: Honors to Andrew Gregg Curtin* (1869).

CURTIS, BENJAMIN ROBBINS
(1809–1874)
U.S. Supreme Court justice

The son of Benjamin Curtis III, a merchant marine officer who lost his life at sea, and Lois Robbins, Curtis grew up in Watertown, Massachusetts. He received an A.B. from Harvard in 1829 and then entered Harvard's law school. After a brief career as a country lawyer in the rural Massachusetts town of Northfield, Curtis accepted a position in a Boston law firm owned by his relative Charles Pelham Curtis. Benjamin Robbins Curtis thrived in the new firm, and he soon represented some of the more affluent merchants in the city. He likewise became prominent in Boston's Whig Party, and he served two terms as a state representative.

There was little in Curtis's professional or political background that would suggest anything other than a moderate political philosophy—particularly on the two most divisive issues of his day: slavery and states' rights. In one case, for instance, Curtis argued that Southerners had rights to bind their slaves as property even while visiting Northern states in which slavery was outlawed. Curtis was likewise one of Daniel Webster's leading advisors in drafting a defense of the Fugitive Slave Law of 1850 that created such furor among Northern abolitionists. Thus, as he had been true to moderate Whig principles, and having distinguished himself as an exceptionally gifted attorney, Curtis was appointed by President Millard Fillmore—on the advice of Daniel Webster—to the high court in 1851 to fill the vacancy created by the death of Justice Levi Woodbury.

During his short tenure on the bench, Curtis's legal positions tended to side more often than not with the majority, dominated by Southern Democrats, and he strove to maintain the dual federalism that characterized most of the Taney court's legal opinions. The two most famous cases in which Curtis is most often noted involved his majority opinion in *Cooley v. Board of Wardens* (1852) and his dissenting opinion in *Scott v. Sandford* (1857), the former establishing the doctrine that the commerce clause did not give the federal government exclusive power of regulation, while the latter rendered the Missouri Compromise unconstitutional.

Often viewed as the classic example of dual federalism jurisprudence, Curtis's opinion in *Cooley* established what some legal scholars refer to as the doctrine of selective exclusiveness. Curtis wrote that when a uniform national rule with respect to objects of commerce is necessary, the federal government has exclusive right to regulate such commercial activity. However, his opinion likewise asserted that when no such rule is necessary, states are free to regulate at their discretion. Clearly then a moderate on states' rights and the respective powers of the federal and state governments, Curtis was well respected by his co-justices, who regarded his legal opinions highly.

Yet, in 1857, when the famous *Dred Scott* case was argued before the Supreme Court, Curtis broke with the court and rendered one of the most memorable dissents in American legal history. The majority opinion, prepared by Chief Justice Taney, asserted that a slave was not automatically freed by spending time in free territory. The opinion likewise stated that slaves could not be citizens of the United States; that they had no rights to sue in federal courts; and, as the most controversial aspect of the ruling, that Congress had had no constitutional authority to establish the Missouri Compromise line in 1820.

Curtis's dissent thoroughly repudiated the majority opinion from several angles. First, Curtis showed that African-Americans had been citizens of at least five states at the time of the ratification of the Constitution, and, he argued, as that had been true, federal citizenship automatically conferred to them in 1789. Therefore, he asserted, a person of African descent could indeed be a citizen of the United States, an assertion in direct contrast to Taney's racially based argument. Second, with respect to Congressional authority to regulate slavery in the territories—an action Taney asserted was unconstitutional—Curtis described fourteen precedents when Congress had in fact lawfully regulated slavery. Therefore, he argued, the Missouri Compromise line was constitutional and Congress had had full authority to disallow the expansion of slavery north of 36° 30'.

It has been argued that Curtis's dissent, in which he so forcefully argued the constitutionality of the Missouri Compromise, literally forced the majority to expand their decision beyond what was necessary to settle the case. In other words, had Curtis not broached the subject, the majority would not have felt compelled to render such a controversial opinion. Such an indictment of Curtis lacks credibility, and in all likelihood Curtis wrote his dissent in response to the majority opinion once he realized the full implications of its pro-Southern position. Curtis had never been a firebrand on the slavery issue, yet he clearly could not follow a decision that would destroy the Missouri Compromise line and Congress's power to regulate slavery in the territories.

Due to the furor over the *Dred Scott* decision and the deep resentment among the justices raised by that ruling, Curtis lost all confidence in the Court and its ability to rule impartially. Thus, in September 1857, after only six terms as an associate justice, Curtis resigned from the bench and returned to Boston and to private practice. The breach among the justices and Curtis's resignation over the *Dred Scott* decision were but the first in a long series of schismatic events that culminated in the secession winter of 1860–1861.

—*Robert Saunders, Jr.*

See also Dred Scott Case; Supreme Court U.S.

For further reading:
Curtis, Benjamin R., ed. *The Life and Writings of Benjamin Robbins Curtis* (1879).
Fehrenbacher, Don E. *The Dred Scott Case: Its Significance in American Law and Politics* (1978).
Leach, Richard H. "Benjamin R. Curtis: Case Study of a Supreme Court Justice" (Ph.D.dissertation, 1951).

CURTIS, NEWTON MARTIN
(1835–1910)
Union general

Born in De Peyster, New York, to Jonathan Curtis and Phebe Rising Curtis, Newton Martin Curtis received his education locally and at Gouverneur Wesleyan Seminary. Before the outbreak of the Civil War, he taught school, served as the De Peyster postmaster, studied law, and farmed.

Abraham Lincoln's call for volunteers caused Curtis to raise a local company that became a part of the 16th New York. Curtis was commissioned a captain in the regiment and went with the unit to Washington. He fought at First Bull Run. In the Peninsula campaign the following year, Curtis was wounded on 7 May at West Point, Virginia. He was unable to return to duty for some months, and when he did in the fall he was promoted to lieutenant colonel in the 142d New York. He became the regiment's colonel in January 1863. Still not fully recovered from his wounds, Curtis did not see significant action until the following year, though he served briefly at the end of 1863 in the Department of the South, headquartered at Hilton Head, South Carolina.

Curtis returned to the Army of the Potomac in the spring of 1864 and fought at Cold Harbor. In June 1864 he was given command of a brigade. In October 1864 Curtis was recommended for promotion to brigadier general for his actions at New Market Heights at the end of September.

At the end of the year, Curtis became part of the Army of the James under Benjamin F. Butler and was assigned to the Fort Fisher, North Carolina, expedition. He was a part of the aborted December assault and the successful one on 15 January 1865. In the latter engagement, Curtis commanded the attack on the northwest corner of the fort and was credited with being the first man into the fort. He was hit in the head by Confederate canister and lost his left eye. On 28 May 1891, Curtis was awarded the Medal of Honor for his actions at Fort Fisher. He was promoted shortly after the battle to brigadier general dating from 15 January.

Because of the seriousness of his injury, Curtis was unable to return to duty until 15 April. On 24 April he became the chief of staff for the Army of Virginia. The

Newton Martin Curtis (*Library of Congress*)

Story of the Sixteenth New York Infantry Together with Personal Reminiscences (1906).

CURTIS, SAMUEL RYAN
(1805–1866)
Union general

Born on 3 February 1805 near Champlain, New York, Samuel R. Curtis grew up in central Ohio. He attended the U.S. Military Academy at West Point and graduated twenty-seventh in a class of thirty-three in 1831.

After only one year of service, Curtis resigned his commission and returned to Ohio to begin a successful engineering career. He worked on the National Road and later designed plans to make the Muskingum River in Ohio and the Des Moines River in Iowa navigable. He spent three distinguished years as the city engineer for St. Louis. During the Mexican-American War, Curtis mustered Ohio troops into service and then commanded the 3d Ohio Infantry. Returning to Iowa in 1853, Curtis surveyed and advocated several routes for a transcontinental railroad. In early 1856 he was elected mayor of Keokuk, and in the fall he surprisingly won a seat in Congress as a Republican. Narrowly reelected in 1858 and 1860, Curtis said his championship of the Pacific railway caused his success.

After Fort Sumter, Curtis equipped and mustered Iowa's first volunteer regiments, and the 2d Iowa Infantry unanimously elected him colonel. He resigned from Congress in August 1861 to accept a promotion to brigadier general. Assigned to John C. Frémont's command in St. Louis, Curtis brought calm and order to the city. When Henry Halleck succeeded Frémont, he ordered Curtis in December 1861 to remove organized Confederate resistance in southwest Missouri. On 7–8 March 1862, General Earl Van Dorn's 16,000 Confederates attacked Curtis's army of 10,500 entrenched near Pea Ridge, Arkansas. Although surprised by two aggressive flanking attacks, Curtis quickly reversed his front while maintaining his composure and interior lines of communication. After several desperate assaults at Elkhorn Tavern, the exhausted Confederate army disintegrated. The victory saved Missouri for the Union and earned Curtis a promotion to major general. His subsequent two-month campaign to capture Little Rock failed, but the Confederacy also lost northern Arkansas.

After Halleck's promotion to general-in-chief, Curtis became commander of the Department of the Missouri in September 1862. Military and political difficulties immediately plagued him. The acceleration of Grant's campaign to capture Vicksburg drained troops from Curtis's department. Southern Missouri experienced

following month, he served on a board to examine the qualifications for advancement for colonels. In June 1865 he was recommended for promotion to major general of volunteers. At the end of the year, he commanded the District of Southwest Virginia. Curtis left the army in early 1866 with the mustering out of the volunteers and returned home to New York.

After the war, Curtis held the position of customs collector and U.S. Treasury special agent in his home county. In the 1880s he became involved in politics, serving in the New York state legislature before being elected to the U.S. House of Representatives in 1890. He served three terms in that body. Curtis's other interests included agricultural experimentation as well as several reform movements. He worked diligently to achieve more humane treatment for the mentally ill and to abolish capital punishment. In his retirement he wrote extensively, including a memoir of the Civil War. Curtis died on 8 January 1910 in New York City.

—*David S. Heidler and Jeanne T. Heidler*

See also Fort Fisher.
For further reading:
Curtis, Newton Martin. *From Bull Run to Chancellorsville, the*

increased guerrilla activity, and Curtis's relationship with General John M. Schofield, his senior general in the field, was characterized by mutual pettiness. Curtis also clashed with conservative Missouri politicians. Governor Hamilton R. Gamble, in particular, accused Curtis of being a Radical Republican interested in substituting martial law for civil authority. Curtis's zealous crackdown on guerrilla activity and the continuation of assessments, a levy placed upon suspected Southern sympathizers, aggravated matters. Eventually Lincoln intervened, ending the assessment policy and, in May 1863, replacing Curtis with Schofield.

Upon Kansas senator James H. Lane's insistence, Lincoln assigned Curtis to command the newly created Department of Kansas in January 1864. Curtis negotiated this politically charged environment more carefully. He faced few military threats until October 1864, when Confederate general Sterling Price's invasion of central Missouri turned toward Kansas and the supply depot at Fort Leavenworth. With only 4,000 regular troops and 10,000 unreliable militia, Curtis tried unsuccessfully to stop Price's 9,000 veterans at the Big Blue River on 21 October. Forced back to Westport, Curtis's army offered stiff resistance on 23 October until General Alfred Pleasonton's cavalry threatened Price from the rear. Price beat a hasty retreat to the south with Curtis in aggressive pursuit. Curtis decimated the Confederate rear guard before Price crossed the Arkansas River to safety.

Unenthusiastic about an impending Indian war in midwinter, Curtis requested reassignment in January 1865. After the war, he helped negotiate a treaty with the Sioux and became a commissioner for the transcontinental railroad. Curtis died suddenly on 26 December 1866 at Council Bluffs, Iowa. He is buried in Keokuk.

Curtis's methodical nature and an engineer's concern for detail characterize his wartime performance. He could be "slow and unimaginative, but at the same time steady and tenacious." Advancing age and political turmoil perhaps made Curtis a marginal figure after 1863, but his success in the field secured the trans-Mississippi for the Union.

—M. *Philip Lucas*

See also Gamble, Hamilton; Kansas; Missouri; Pea Ridge, Battle of; Price's Missouri Raid; Schofield, John M.

For further reading:
Castel, Albert. "A New View of the Battle of Pea Ridge." *Missouri Historical Review* (1968).
Colton, Kenneth E., ed. "With Fremont in Missouri in 1861: Letters of Samuel Ryan Curtis." *Annals of Iowa* (1942).
Gallaher, Ruth A. "Samuel Ryan Curtis." *Iowa Journal of History and Politics* (1927).
Parrish, William E. *Turbulent Partnership: Missouri and the Union, 1861–1865* (1963).
Shea, William L., and Earl J. Hess. *Pea Ridge: Civil War Campaign in the West* (1992).

CUSHING, ALONZO HERSFORD
(1841–1863)
Union officer

Alonzo Cushing came from a family that distinguished itself during the Civil War. His brother, William B. Cushing, was one of the U.S. Navy's great heroes, specializing in commando-type raids. Another brother, Howard B. Cushing, served as a private in various artillery units in 1862 and 1863. After Gettysburg, Howard Cushing was commissioned into the U.S. 4th Artillery, his late brother's regiment. Howard Cushing remained in the U.S. Army following the war, transferred to the cavalry, and died in action in 1871 fighting the Apaches in Arizona.

Alonzo Cushing was born in Waukesha City, Wisconsin on 19 January 1841. In 1857 he was appointed to West Point from the state of New York. George Armstrong Custer was one of his classmates. Cushing graduated twelfth in his class on 24 June 1861. That day he received both his commission as a second lieutenant and a simultaneous promotion to first lieutenant in the regular army. It was the only substantive promotion he would ever receive. Immediately following graduation, Cushing reported to the 4th Artillery. He would remain in that unit for the rest of his short life.

Cushing fought in many of the major battles of the Civil War, including First Bull Run, Fair Oaks, Second Bull Run, Antietam, and Fredericksburg. He received a brevet promotion to captain for his actions at Fredericksburg on 13 December 1862. In February 1863, Cushing assumed command of Battery A, 4th Artillery and led that unit at Chancellorsville. In the subsequent Union retreat, his battery was the last unit to cross the Rappahannock River. Cushing received a brevet promotion to major for his actions at Chancellorsville on 2 May 1863.

On 1 July 1863, the first day of the battle of Gettysburg, the Union troops were forced back upon Cemetery Ridge about the same time Major General Winfield Scott Hancock arrived on the field to take command. One of his first acts was to press Cushing into temporary duty as his aide. For twelve hours Cushing moved about the battlefield, conveying orders and guiding newly arriving units to their assigned positions. All the while he was exposed to heavy Confederate fire.

Returning to Battery A, Cushing and his cannoneers remained in position on Cemetery Ridge and saw relatively little action on 2 July. Battery A's position in the Union line was just to the north of the Copse of Trees that became the orienting point of the Confederate attack on 3 July. Cushing's six 3-inch ordnance rifles were less than ten yards away from the Angle in the stone fence that fronted the Federal position. Preparatory to the charge of Pickett's and Pettigrew's

Alonzo Cushing (*Library of Congress*)

Divisions, Confederate guns pounded the Union lines for almost three hours. During the cannonade Cushing's battery returned fire, but took heavy casualties in the process. By the time the shelling lifted, Battery A had lost four of its six guns, and Cushing himself was severely wounded in the right shoulder and groin.

Refusing to relinquish his command or submit to medical attention, Cushing continued to fight at his battery. When the Confederate artillery fire ceased, the Union troops knew that the ground attack would follow shortly. Cushing moved his two surviving guns forward to the edge of the stone wall and prepared to resist the Southern onslaught. He ordered all of his battery's remaining canister rounds consolidated at the two pieces. He also ordered his cannoneers to arm themselves with trail spikes and rammer staffs in anticipation of hand-to-hand combat with the Confederate infantry.

When the attack came, Cushing's guns fired spherical case and solid shot until the Confederates came within canister range. As the leading Southern troops closed to within fifty yards of his position, Cushing's men commenced firing double canister. Shortly after that, Cushing was hit in the face by a bullet and died at his Number 4 gun. Although he had been bleeding heavily and in severe pain, Cushing remained at his post and in command for more than one and a half hours after first being wounded. He was only 22 when he died.

Immediately after Cushing fell, his German-born first sergeant, Frederick Fuger, assumed command of what was left of Battery A and fired triple canister until Pickett's troops overran their position. The Union cannoneers then engaged the Confederate infantrymen in hand-to-hand combat until a counterattack by the 72d Pennsylvania Infantry broke the Southern momentum. The attack faltered and then failed. Brigadier General Lewis Armistead died immediately to the left of Battery A's Number 4 gun, only a few yards from where Cushing fell. At the end of the battle, more than 600 dead Confederate soldiers lay directly in front of Battery A's position.

While most of the soldiers killed at Gettysburg were buried close to where they fell, Cushing's body was guarded by his loyal first sergeant until Cushing's brother could arrive to claim it. The Cushing family had the body buried in the West Point cemetery, where Cushing lies today next to Major General John Buford. Curiously enough, Cushing received a posthumous brevet promotion to lieutenant colonel for his actions as Hancock's aide on 1 July, but no formal recognition of his heroism on 3 July.

The gallant First Sergeant Fuger received a battlefield commission for his actions on 3 July, and later in the Civil War he received two more brevet promotions. In 1896 Fuger also received the Medal of Honor for his heroism at Gettysburg. He retired from the U.S. Army in 1900 as a colonel.

—*David T. Zabecki*

See also Cushing, William B.
For further reading:

Brown, Kent Masterson. *Cushing of Gettysburg: The Story of a Union Artillery Commander* (1993).
Downey, Fairfax. *The Guns at Gettysburg* (1958).
Naisawald, L. Van Loan. *Grape and Canister: The Story of the Field Artillery of the Army of the Potomac* (1983).

CUSHING, WILLIAM BARKER
(1842–1874)
U.S. Navy commando

No U.S. Navy officer emerged from the Civil War better known or more respected than William Barker Cushing. By 1865 Cushing was a living legend in the navy and, although he never obtained wartime rank above that of lieutenant commander, was more popular among Northerners than the U.S. Navy's highest ranking officers, with the exception of Admiral David G. Farragut. One of Cushing's many admirers observed that, "As Farragut was its glory and its hero…Cushing [was] the darling of the American navy." A determined and intrepid young seaman, Cushing's

daring commando-like raids behind enemy lines outwitted and bedeviled Confederate forces. Rear Admiral David D. Porter described Cushing as a "'free-lance,' who was always ready to perform any act of daring...and whether fortunate or not in his undertakings, he was sure to create a sensation."

Cushing created a sensation from the days of his boyhood. Born on 4 November 1842, he was the fourth son of Milton and Mary Barker Cushing, who made their home at the time near the present-day town of Delafield, Wisconsin. (William's well-known older brother Alonzo would die while commanding a battery of the 4th U.S. Artillery in defense of Cemetery Ridge at Gettysburg on 3 July 1863.) After her husband's untimely death in 1847, Mary Cushing moved her children to Fredonia, New York. There young Will grew up a rambunctious, fearless, and prideful young man fond of pranks who never backed down from a fight.

Cushing's undisciplined nature haunted him at the U.S. Naval Academy in Annapolis, Maryland, where, at the age of fourteen, he was appointed to the class of 1861. Although intelligent and bright, Cushing acquired numerous demerits for skylarking instead of studying. Disappointed by Cushing's bad conduct and poor work habits, the academy's superintendent forced the young midshipman's resignation on 23 March 1861, just ten weeks before graduation. The official reason for Cushing's dismissal was a "deficiency in Spanish."

The outbreak of war in April 1861 heightened the need for sailors to serve in Lincoln's navy. Cushing was given a chance to redeem himself when, with the assistance of his friend Lieutenant Charles W. Flusser, Cushing was appointed a midshipman in the U.S. Navy. Encouraged by the renewed faith shown in him, Cushing vowed to make a name for himself in the war or die trying.

For the first year of the conflict, Cushing served meritoriously on board blockading vessels off the coast of the Carolinas. During June and July 1861, Cushing was with the USS Wabash on the blockade at Charleston, South Carolina. In August 1861, he fought with the USS Minnesota at the capture of Forts Hatteras and Clark on the Outer Banks of North Carolina. As a crewman on board the USS Cambridge from the autumn of 1861 to the spring of 1862, Cushing made a name for himself as a dependable and brave volunteer on "cutting-out" expeditions against Confederate positions in tidewater Virginia.

Impressed by the courageous young seaman, the U.S. Navy appointed Cushing lieutenant on 16 July 1862. Only nineteen years old, Cushing jumped the two commissioned grades of master and ensign with his promotion. The following month Lieutenant Cushing became executive officer of the gunboat Commodore Perry, commanded by his old friend Lieutenant Commander Charles Flusser.

Cushing quickly increased his reputation for bravery.

On the Blackwater River in Virginia on 3 October 1862, he helped serve a boat howitzer in the repulse of an enemy assault, thus saving the Commodore Perry from capture. Rear Admiral S. Phillips Lee, head of the North Atlantic Blockading Squadron, awarded Cushing with command of the USS Ellis, a captured Confederate steamer, on 13 October 1862. Less than a week after assuming his new command, Cushing captured and burned his first enemy vessel, the laden schooner Adelaide, at New Topsail Inlet, North Carolina.

In late November 1862, Cushing boldly steamed the Ellis up the New River to raze salt works, and to capture boats and the little town of Jacksonville, North Carolina. After some measured success, the Ellis ran aground trying to exit the river and was destroyed in a crossfire from Confederate shore batteries. Nevertheless, Cushing managed to escape with his crew in a captured schooner and was subsequently commended by Admiral Lee for his "coolness, courage and conduct."

Between December 1862 and January 1863, Cushing made three attempts to enter the Cape Fear River in the schooner Home and kidnap pilots at Wilmington, North Carolina. Calm winds spoiled each endeavor, so Cushing shifted his efforts to Little River, South Carolina, fifty miles south of Wilmington. On 5 January, Cushing staged a bold raid up Little River, overrunning a blockhouse, driving off its Confederate defenders, and capturing provisions.

Most of 1863 found Cushing on assignment again in southeastern Virginia, where he received the thanks of the Navy Department for his good fighting on the Nansemond River and at Chuckatuck in the battle for Suffolk. Cushing returned to the Cape Fear, where he spent the longest stint of his wartime service, when he was placed in command of the gunboat Shokokon on 9 August 1863. By then Wilmington was the Confederacy's premier blockade running seaport.

Shortly after reporting for duty with the Wilmington blockading squadron, Cushing commanded the Shokokon in battle for possession of the derelict blockade runner Hebe near New Inlet, the northern-most entrance into the Cape Fear River, on 18 August 1863. Aroused by the excitement of the Hebe skirmish, Cushing steamed the Shokokon up to New Topsail Inlet, where he discovered and destroyed the Northern blockade running schooner Alexander Cooper on 22 August. In a letter to Secretary of the Navy Gideon Welles, Admiral Lee called Lieutenant Cushing a "zealous and able young officer." The 20-year-old Fredonian and Naval Academy dropout had been with the Wilmington squadron less than three weeks and was already earning high praise from the navy high command.

Consequently, when Cushing's ship, the Shokokon, proved unseaworthy, the department quickly provided him with the sturdier Monticello on 5 September 1863. Commanding the Monticello, Cushing kept a vigilant watch for blockade runners operating in and out of Wilmington.

On the night of 29 February 1864, Cushing initiated a daring raid through Old Inlet, the southern entrance into the Cape Fear River, to kidnap Confederate brigadier general Louis Hébert, commander of the Lower Cape Fear defenses and headquartered at the town of Smithville, two miles inside the bar. Though he missed General Hébert who happened to be in Wilmington upriver that night, Cushing and his men managed to capture Captain Patrick Kelly, Hébert's chief engineer. Cushing may have failed to bag his main quarry, but his "gallantry and success" again earned him the compliments of the U.S. Navy Department.

When the *Monticello* ran into and sank the USS *Peterhoff* on blockade duty at the Cape Fear on 6 March 1864, the Navy Department overlooked Cushing's responsibilty in the accident. The Navy could ill afford to lose Cushing, a daring commando who would be harder to replace than the *Peterhoff*.

On 23 June 1864, Cushing and a small group of sailors from the *Monticello* again entered the Cape Fear River, this time hoping to find and destroy the ironclad CSS *Raleigh*, which had recently tried to break the Federal blockade at New Inlet. Unaware that the *Raleigh* had run aground and sunk in the river, Cushing and his men spent three days reconnoitering the area, kidnapping passers-by and committing acts of sabotage. Again the Navy Department extended its gratitude to Cushing for his boldness. U.S. rear admiral David D. Porter later wrote that "There was not a more daring adventure than this during the course of the war."

During the summer of 1864 Admiral S. Phillips Lee selected Cushing to lead an expedition to destroy the Confederate ironclad ram *Albemarle* near Plymouth, North Carolina. Cushing set out immediately for New York to select the small boats he would use in the attempt to place a torpedo against the *Albemarle*'s hull.

Cushing selected two thirty-foot steam-powered launches. One, however, was destroyed in a storm coming down to North Carolina. Therefore he set out with thirteen other men aboard the one boat on the night of 27 October 1864 to destroy the *Albemarle*. He and his men entered the Roanoke River and were quickly spotted as they neared their target. They were fired upon but managed to draw close to the *Albemarle* only to discover that the ship was surrounded by logs chained together to prevent someone from placing a torpedo against the hull. The men managed to get their boat over the logs but knew they would not have the momentum to recross the barrier once they had placed the torpedo. As Cushing maneuvered the torpedo at the end of a long pole against the hull of the ship, several bullets tore through his clothes. He remained calm while going about his work and once he had succeeded, the resulting explosion swamped his small craft. He instructed the men to swim for shore, though most were captured before they could make an attempt. The *Albemarle* began to sink.

Cushing made it into the river and over the next several hours struggled against a strong current finally to make it to the riverbank. The next day he trudged through a swamp and stole a rowboat from a Confederate work party. He rowed for ten hours out to the Federal fleet. Once he arrived, he was treated as a hero and sent to Hampton Roads to make his report. As a result of his efforts the Federals were able to take Plymouth, North Carolina. The mission also earned Cushing a navy promotion to lieutenant commander, the thanks of the U.S. Congress, and everlasting fame as "Albemarle Cushing."

When the Federals attacked Fort Fisher, the Confederacy's largest and strongest seacoast fortification and main guardian of Wilmington, at Christmas 1864, Cushing commanded Admiral David D. Porter's flagship USS *Malvern*. Cushing also led a boat expedition to take soundings of New Inlet while under heavy cannon fire from Fort Fisher.

At Second Fort Fisher, 13–15 January 1865, Cushing and forty of his men from the *Monticello*, which he again commanded, volunteered to fight onshore with a column of more than 2,000 seamen in conjunction with the army's ground assault against Fort Fisher. Despite the failure of the navy's shore arm in the attack, Fort Fisher fell to Union forces, thus closing the harbor to blockade running and severing the Confederacy's lifeline.

Three days after the capture of Fort Fisher, Cushing took possession of abandoned Confederate fortifications on Oak Island at Old Inlet and accepted the surrender of Smithville from the town's mayor. He also declared himself governor of the province. Cushing then concocted a scheme to lure unsuspecting blockade runners into the Cape Fear estuary, now in Union hands. This led to Cushing's capture of the blockade runner *Charlotte* out of Bermuda on the night of 20 January 1865.

While the Federal high command made plans to advance on Wilmington, Cushing led several expeditions upriver to reconnoiter Confederate defenses and waterway obstructions. On the night of 11 February 1865, Cushing stole ashore at Fort Anderson, the strongest interior fortification protecting Wilmington, to witness a Confederate pep rally. He barely escaped with his life.

During the battle of Fort Anderson on 18 February 1865, Cushing employed a Quaker monitor of his own design against the Confederates in an effort to get them to explode their torpedoes in the river. The effort failed but did not dissuade Cushing from boasting to President Abraham Lincoln that his sham monitor, dubbed *Old*

Bogey and *Albemarle No. 2*, had caused the Confederates to abandon Fort Anderson. Wilmington fell on 22 February 1865, and the Confederacy collapsed soon thereafter.

Five times during the war the Navy Department rendered William B. Cushing thanks for his gallant feats and daring deeds. He also received the thanks of the U.S. Congress and high praise from President Lincoln himself. Cushing "would undertake the most desperate adventures, where it seemed impossible for him to escape death or capture," observed Admiral David D. Porter, "yet he always managed to get off with credit to himself and loss to the enemy."

Cushing's critics, who considered him vain, arrogant and foolish, believed his hazardous undertakings behind enemy lines gained little and risked or cost the lives of good seamen. Yet, as one Cushing admirer later remarked, "there was more method in [Cushing's missions] than appeared on the surface and important information was sometimes obtained, to say nothing of the brilliant example of courage and enterprise...."

Cushing remained in the navy after the war, serving in the Pacific Squadron, cruising for Chinese pirates and performing administrative duties at both the Boston and Washington Navy Yards. In Fredonia, New York, on 22 February 1870, he married Katherie Louisa Forbes. They had two daughters.

For some time after the war, Cushing's friends and family noticed symptoms of a "diseased brain." They believed the disease was brought on by "exposure and high excitement" of his wartime duties. By early December 1874, Cushing had become so violent and uncontrollable that he was confined to the Government Hospital for the Insane in Washington, D.C. He died on 17 December. The official cause of death listed on his pension papers was "acute mania."

Ironically, "Albemarle Cushing" was buried with full military honors in the cemetery on Bluff Point at the U.S. Naval Academy, the school that had ejected him only thirteen years before. Midshipmen at the Naval Academy still study the life and exploits of William B. Cushing. An admirer wrote that the young commando's life was a "fascinating story of glorious achievement and dauntless courage" that placed him "among the veritable heroes of the age."

—*Chris E. Fonvielle, Jr.*

See also Albemarle, CSS; Fort Fisher.

For further reading:
Cushing, William B. *The Journal of Lieutenant Comdr. William B. Cushing, 1861–1865* (1976).
Edwards, E.M.H. *Commander William Barker Cushing of the United States Navy* (1896).
Fonvielle, Chris E., Jr. "William B. Cushing: Commando at the Cape Fear." *Blue & Gray Magazine* (1997).
Roske, Ralph J. and Charles Van Doren. *Lincoln's Commando: The Biography of Commander William B. Cushing, U.S. Navy* (1957; reprint ed., 1995).

CUSHMAN, PAULINE
(1833–1893)
Union spy

Described by her 1865 biographer as a woman of "entrancing form," "flashing eye," and "most wondrous beauty," Pauline Cushman was a professional actress at the time the Civil War began. Born in the New Orleans, Louisiana, she was raised on the Michigan frontier where she developed a taste for adventure and equestrian skills that would serve her effectively during the Civil War.

In 1863 Cushman found herself at Wood's Theater in politically divided Louisville, Kentucky, where she had come with her acting troupe to perform a play. On her own initiative, Cushman turned the occasion into an opportunity to embark on a stint as a Union spy, courier, and scout. When some Confederate officers dared her to interrupt one of her performances to offer a toast to Confederate president Jefferson Davis, Cushman consulted with the Union army's local provost marshal, suggesting that she might offer the toast to Davis, but only as a means of misleading her audience about her political loyalties and thereby to establish a cover for herself as an intelligence agent for the Union. The provost marshal agreed to her plan, and subsequently "banished" her to Union-held Nashville, where she sought out Colonel William Truesdail, the Union army's chief of police for the Army of the Cumberland, for further instructions.

The precise nature of the instructions Truesdail gave to Cushman are not on record, but over the next several months Cushman served as a Federal courier, riding through Kentucky, Tennessee, northern Georgia, Alabama, and Mississippi. In the course of her travels, Cushman assumed a variety of disguises, including a soldier's uniform, in order to gather information on Confederate fortifications and troop movements. She strove at the same time to identify for Union officials the names of dangerous Confederate spies and activists across the region.

At some point during her service Cushman received an honorary military commission from either General William S. Rosecrans or General James A. Garfield in recognition of her daring and loyal service. Not long after she set out on her chosen mission for the Union, however, Cushman's activities began to provoke suspicion, and late in the spring of 1863 none other than Confederate general John Hunt Morgan arrested her near Shelbyville, Tennessee. Morgan turned Cushman over to General Nathan Bedford Forrest, who interrogated her at length and, convinced of her duplicity, sentenced her to death by hanging. Whether Forrest actually would have carried out the sentence is unclear. Fortunately for Cushman, Union troops arriving in

Shelbyville drove Forrest and his men away and effected Cushman's release.

Cushman continued to serve the Union to the best of her ability after this, but because of her remarkable beauty and the attention that she received as a result of her capture by Morgan, her spying days were cut short.

When Cushman visited New York City in 1864, her presence was noted in the local papers, which described her as a dedicated scout and spy for the Union. To the end of her life she would be remembered by many in this way, although her postwar years were hardly glorious. After the war Cushman resumed her stage career, often presenting monologues related to her wartime espionage activities and sometimes dressing in the uniform of a soldier. As time passed, however, popular interest in her adventures declined, and Cushman—who took up sewing to earn an income—fell victim to alcohol and possibly drug abuse, perhaps to cope with a physical disability related to her wartime exploits. Cushman married twice (she had also been married before the war to a man who soon left her a widow) and bore two children, who died in infancy. She died in 1893 in San Francisco. When the members of a local veterans group learned of her death, they claimed her body from the morgue and buried it in full military style, with an honor guard and a gun salute.

—*Elizabeth D. Leonard*

See also Espionage; Women.
For further reading:
Brockett, Linus P. *The Camp, the Battlefield and the Hospital; or, Light and Shadows of the Great Rebellion* (1866).
Kane, Harnett T. *Spies for the Blue and Gray* (1954).
Leonard, Elizabeth D. *All the Daring of the Soldier: Women of the Civil War Armies* (1999).
Sarmiento, F. L. *Life of Pauline Cushman: The Celebrated Union Spy and Scout* (1865).
Young, Agatha. *The Women and the Crisis: Women of the North in the Civil War* (1959).

CUSTER, GEORGE ARMSTRONG
(1839–1876)
Union general

George Armstrong Custer entered the Civil War fresh out of West Point and emerged as the most famous member of a generation of so-called boy generals noted for their dash and aggressiveness. Born in New Rumley, Ohio, on 5 December 1839, Custer entered the U.S. Military Academy in 1857. He scored low in academics and conduct, but displayed leadership ability in the boisterous pranks so dear to his fellow cadets and the young officers who instructed them. Thanks to the indulgence of the latter, Custer managed to graduate last in the class of June 1861.

Early on 21 July 1861, 2d Lieutenant Custer reported to Company G, 2d U.S. Cavalry, and rode into the battle of the First Bull Run a few hours later. During the organization of the Army of the Potomac in the months after Bull Run, Custer served briefly on the staff of Brigadier General Philip Kearny, whose imperious command style deeply impressed the young aide.

The opening of the Peninsula campaign in March 1862 found Custer on loan to the Topographical Engineers. A daring reconnaissance earned him an appointment as a temporary captain and aide-de-camp to Major General George Brinton McClellan, the charismatic commander of the Army of the Potomac. McClellan's dismissal in November 1862 left Custer a first lieutenant in the regular army, but he soon joined the staff of Brigadier General Alfred Pleasonton. Pleasonton's subsequent elevation to major general and command of the Army of the Potomac's Cavalry Corps brought Custer increased responsibilities and opportunities.

On 28 June 1863, Major General George Gordon Meade granted Pleasonton's request and named Custer a brigadier general of U.S. Volunteers. The elated twenty-three year old, then the youngest general in the Union army, took charge of the Michigan Cavalry Brigade in Brigadier General H. Judson Kilpatrick's 3d Cavalry Division.

Custer and his "Wolverines" proved themselves a potent combat team. On 3 July 1863, they bore the brunt of the fight that stopped Major General J. E. B. Stuart and his Confederate cavalry from turning the Union right at Gettysburg. Custer closed the action by leading a single regiment in a headlong charge that helped halt two rebel brigades. Custer continued to grow as a general in the many mounted skirmishes that filled the summer and fall of 1863. Although Custer gloried in thundering saber charges, he developed a talent for employing troopers armed with repeating rifles and carbines as mounted infantry. His most striking trait was his willingness to lead every charge himself, which caused his men to idolize him. As one Wolverine wrote: "For all that this Brigade has accomplished all praise is due to General Custer. So brave a man I never saw and as competent as brave. Under him a man is ashamed to be cowardly. Under *him* our men can achieve wonders."

Major General Philip H. Sheridan replaced Pleasonton as commander of the Cavalry Corps in March 1864, but Custer quickly won the confidence of his new chief. At Yellow Tavern on 11 May 1864, Custer ensured the success of Sheridan's Richmond Raid with a charge that culminated in the fatal wounding of Jeb Stuart. When Sheridan assumed command of the Army of the Shenandoah in August, Custer accompanied him. For turning Lieutenant General Jubal A. Early's left flank at the third battle of Winchester on 19 September,

George A. Custer, ca. 1864 (*Library of Congress*)

Custer received command of the 3d Cavalry Division. He proceeded to mold that unit into the hardest-hitting Union horsemen in the Eastern theater, winning new laurels at Tom's Brook, Cedar Creek, and Waynesboro. By the close of Sheridan's Valley campaign, Custer wore the stars of a major general, and his division was setting records in capturing Confederate cannon.

Custer excelled himself as a soldier during the Appomattox campaign. His division's timely arrival steadied Sheridan's wavering line at the battle of

Dinwiddie Court House, 31 March 1865. The next day at Five Forks, Custer swamped the enemy's right flank as Sheridan destroyed a major portion of General Robert E. Lee's Army of Northern Virginia. Lee reacted to Five Forks by abandoning Richmond and fleeing west, but Custer pursued him with a zeal that outshone the efforts of Sheridan's other cavalry commanders. Custer's troopers delivered telling blows against their prey at Namozine Church and Sayler's Creek, and they blocked Lee's retreat route at Appomattox Station on the evening of 8 April. On the basis of the nine hectic days that doomed Lee's army, some historians rank Custer second only to Sheridan as the best cavalry commander ever produced by the Union army.

With the return of peace, Custer reverted to the rank of lieutenant colonel in the regular army. He reported to the Kansas frontier in late 1866 as the acting commander of the newly formed 7th U.S. Cavalry Regiment. His career as an Indian fighter began badly in 1867. Indian tactics baffled him, and he ended up getting suspended from rank and pay for a year for shooting deserters without trial and abandoning his own command. After Sheridan had him return to duty before the expiration of his sentence, the humbled cavalier redeemed himself by destroying a small Cheyenne village in a surprise attack along the Washita River in Indian Territory on 27 November 1868. Custer followed that controversial triumph with successful operations against the Southern Plains tribes in the winter of 1868–1869, skirmishes with the Sioux along the Yellowstone River in 1873, and a much-publicized reconnaissance of the Black Hills in 1874.

On 25 June 1876, Custer located a large village of Sioux and Cheyenne in the Little Bighorn Valley in Montana Territory. Sure his foes were about to flee, Custer divided the 7th Cavalry into three battalions and attempted to head them off. By the time Custer realized that the Indians intended to stand and fight, it was too late to reunite his regiment, which was defeated in detail. Custer and the 210 troopers under his immediate command were wiped out. This disaster ensured Custer's lasting immortality in history and legend, but it eclipsed his many Civil War victories.

—*Gregory J. W. Urwin*

See also Cavalry, U.S.A.; Kilpatrick, Hugh Judson; Shenandoah Valley Campaign (1864–1865); Sheridan, Philip H.; Yellow Tavern, Battle of.

For further reading:

Hutton, Paul A., ed. *The Custer Reader* (1992).

Longacre, Edward G. *Custer and His Wolverines: The Michigan Cavalry Brigade, 1861–1865* (1997).

Urwin, Gregory J.W. *Custer Victorious: The Civil War Battles of General George Armstrong Custer* (1990).

Utley, Robert M. *Cavalier in Buckskin: George Armstrong Custer and the Western Military Frontier* (1988).

Wert, Jeffry D. *Custer: The Controversial Life of George Armstrong Custer* (1996).

CYCLORAMA

After the Civil War, artists were commissioned to paint large murals commemorating battle scenes. Called cycloramas, derived from the Greek words kyklos (circular) and horama (a view), they were large, 360-degree paintings that surrounded the viewing area and were housed in round buildings. Some credit an Irish prisoner with inventing the concept in 1788.

Cycloramas were created to earn profits as well as educate and entertain. Individuals invested in cyclorama stock and thus served as patrons to artists. Paintings usually depicted a dramatic historic incident such as a battle or Biblical story, with scenes displayed chronologically. Many cycloramas featured elaborately detailed landscapes and used vast areas of canvas to portray characters and items both in life size and in varying scales for uncanny visual effects. These artistic techniques made paintings extraordinarily realistic.

After the Civil War, several hundred cycloramas were painted and shown in Europe and North America. Their viewing became a popular social and cultural activity, encouraging interest in the war and its veterans. Designed to appeal to all spectators, the paintings depicted the heroism of both Union and Confederate forces. Some cycloramas promoted political candidates by portraying their Civil War valor. By the twentieth century, most of these murals had been damaged or lost, and few cycloramas depicting Civil War events have survived.

Perhaps the best-known Civil War cyclorama is *The Battle of Atlanta*. Considered the world's largest painting at 50 feet high and 400 feet in circumference, the Atlanta Cyclorama depicts the events of 22 July 1864. During the war, *Harper's Weekly* had secured General William T. Sherman's permission for artist Theodore Davis to record the battle. Davis observed the fighting at its intensity on the afternoon of 22 July. Twenty-one years later, the American Panorama Company in Milwaukee, Wisconsin, used Davis's sketches to create the Atlanta Cyclorama. The company's manager, William Wehner, examined European cycloramas and recruited German artists who had painted cycloramas featuring the Franco-Prussian War. Each artist specialized in some aspect of cyclorama painting, such as landscapes, people, or animals. This team first completed another cyclorama, entitled *The Battle of Missionary Ridge*, before focusing on the Atlanta mural. Davis served as technical adviser for both projects. According to tradition, the Atlanta Cyclorama was originally planned to promote former Civil War general John A. Logan's 1884 vice presidential bid, but if so, it was not ready in time.

During the summer of 1885, the American Panorama Company artists traveled to Atlanta for several months to study the battlefield site. Davis shared his 22 July 1864 sketches with the artists, who also interviewed veterans and civilian witnesses about their recollections of that day. A forty-foot wooden tower was built at the intersection of Moreland Avenue and the Georgia Railroad so the artists could locate landmarks mentioned in official reports and shown on military maps. They prepared oil sketches to record topographical details such as the red dirt roads, tree lines, and gullies. Returning to Milwaukee, the artists used scaffolding to paint sections of the massive mural. Because of their careful analysis of the site, they achieved high accuracy in placing specific components of the battle.

The completed cyclorama began its tour in Detroit, Michigan, on 26 February 1887, and then traveled to Minneapolis, Minnesota. When the cyclorama arrived in Indianapolis, Indiana, legal problems concerning Wehner's stock company forced him give the painting to property owners where it was displayed. In 1890, the Atlanta Cyclorama's new owners sold it to Paul Atkinson of Madison, Georgia.

Atkinson also owned the Missionary Ridge cyclorama and had exhibited it in Chattanooga until he purchased the Atlanta painting. The Missionary Ridge cyclorama was moved to Atlanta and then to Nashville, where it was damaged by a tornado. The Atlanta Cyclorama was relocated to a "drum-like structure" on Edgewood Avenue in Atlanta and was opened for display on 22 February 1892. Charles W. Hubner, former telegraph corps chief for Confederate generals Joseph E. Johnston and John B. Hood, presented lectures to audiences. The *Atlanta Constitution* described how viewers stood on a platform surrounded by the canvas. The newspaper claimed the cyclorama was so realistic that birds flying above the building tried to land in painted trees and that General Logan's wife fainted when she saw his artistic image.

Veterans enjoyed pointing out people and events, and descendants visited to see where their ancestors had fought. Although some inaccuracies had found their way into the painting (such as the presence of the 8th Wisconsin's mascot, an eagle named Old Abe), the artists also included precise details such as hair colors, clothing, and wounds. The cyclorama included scenes of railroad destruction, hand-to-hand combat, ambulances transporting casualties, and an abandoned drum lying on the field. From one perspective, troops appeared to be marching toward the viewer. The painting consisted of five sections sequentially illuminated during the lecture explaining the battle.

By January 1893, attendance had decreased. Then a snowstorm caved in the building's roof, damaging the painting. To satisfy debts, the Fulton County sheriff sold the cyclorama at public auction on 1 August 1893. George V. Gress and Charles Northen bought the cyclorama to preserve it as a memorial to wartime Atlanta. Gress, who had given the animals to establish the city's zoo in Grant Park, suggested that the city provide adjacent park space for the cyclorama and charge a maximum of ten cents for admission, the proceeds to be donated to charity. He gave the cyclorama to Atlanta upon the stipulation that the city repair the painting and build a structure to house it. The Atlanta Cyclorama reopened for the 1898 reunion of Confederate veterans, who reacted emotionally to the artistic rendering of vividly recalled combat. In 1921, a fireproof building became the permanent home of the cyclorama as well as the *Texas,* the locomotive that had pursued Andrews's Raiders. A diorama that skillfully blends three-dimensional figures into scenes on the canvas was added in the 1930s, and an extensive restoration has rescued the painting from the ravages of time and exposure. Other recent improvements to the facility include a rotating platform with amphitheater seating that synchronizes viewing of the battle scenes with dramatic lighting, sound effects, narration, and music. The Atlanta Cyclorama and Civil War Museum commemorated its centennial in 1992 and is visited annually by thousands of Civil War enthusiasts.

The Gettysburg Cyclorama portrays Pickett's Charge. Paul Philippoteaux, a professional cyclorama artist from France, surveyed the battlefield in 1879 and interviewed veterans and witnesses. He sketched the terrain and hired a photographer to shoot a panoramic photograph of the battle site before creating the painting with oil-based pigments on canvas. The resulting cyclorama measured 360 feet long and 26 feet high and weighed almost three tons. First displayed in Chicago in 1882, the Gettysburg Cyclorama was so successful that Philippoteaux agreed to paint an identical cyclorama for display in Boston. The latter painting was featured at the 1913 anniversary of the battle and remained at Gettysburg afterward. The National Park Service eventually bought the painting to display in the National Park Service Cyclorama Center accompanied by a twenty-minute sound and light show. Two additional copies of this cyclorama were produced. What happened to one of these is unknown; the other was cut up to be used as tents on an Indian reservation. The original Gettysburg Cyclorama was sold to a private collector.

Other cycloramas include a painting by Philippoteaux, entitled *Cyclorama of the Second Battle of Manassas,* that was displayed in Washington, D.C., in 1887. A veteran wrote to General James Longstreet to criticize this cyclorama's inaccuracies in representing troop placements and battle conditions. Philippoteaux also prepared a 400-foot-long, 50-foot-wide canvas showing Niagara Falls that toured Europe. In 1888, a special cyclorama building in Buffalo, New York, exhibited Karl Frosch's *Jerusalem on the Day of the Crucifixion.* Circa 1890, the Buffalo cyclorama building displayed Philippoteaux's *Gettysburg.* Yet by the turn of the century, cycloramas no longer enjoyed wide popular appeal, and museums increasingly turned to dioramas to depict battle scenes in smaller spaces.

—*Elizabeth D. Schafer*

See also Art; Photography.

For further reading:
Carroll, John M. *Cyclorama of General Custer's Last Fight: A Reproduction of the Original Document Complete in All Respects, and with an Introduction* (1988).

Cecchini, Bridget Theresa. "The Battle of Atlanta Cyclorama (1885–1886) As Narrative Indicator of a National Perspective on the Civil War" (M.A. thesis, 1998).

Historical Conservation Project, Inc. "Cyclorama: The Restoration of *The Battle of Atlanta*" (videotape, 1982).

Kurtz, Wilbur G. *The Atlanta Cyclorama: The Story of the Famed Battle of Atlanta* (1954).

McGinnis, Karen Hertel. "Moving Right Along: Nineteenth Century Panorama Painting in the United States" (Ph.D. dissertation, 1983).

D

DABNEY, ROBERT LEWIS
(1820–1898)
Southern theologian

Robert Lewis Dabney was one of the most prominent Southern theologians of the nineteenth century. Born on 5 March 1820 in Virginia's Louisa County, Dabney was educated at Hampden-Sidney College and then at the University of Virginia. In 1844 he entered Union Theological Seminary in Richmond to study for the ministry and went on to graduate first in his class. He would spend thirty years as a professor at Union. So accomplished was he, and so respected by Presbyterians, that he was sought out in great earnest in 1860 by Princeton Theological Seminary to replace the late Joseph Addison Alexander. Despite Princeton's immense prestige, especially in comparison to the obscure Union, Dabney, a Southern supporter to the last, declined the offer.

Unlike his colleague James Henley Thornwell, an ardent secessionist from the beginning, Dabney looked at such a prospect with dread, at least while the safeguarding of Southern rights within the Union still seemed possible. South Carolina he described as an "impudent vixen" that was "as great a pest as the abolitionists." In the months leading up to secession and war, he pleaded with his compatriots in the name of Christianity to proceed with prudence and moderation, and he urged Southerners to recall the fruits of union. As soon as Lincoln moved to use force against the seceding states, however, Dabney's sympathy to the Union gave way to the cause of Southern independence.

During the war, Dabney spent five months as adjutant-general to Stonewall Jackson, who was a great admirer of the Virginian's preaching. Poor health led Dabney to resign his post in September 1862, but so earnest was his affection for Jackson that when the general died from the wounds he received at Chancellorsville, Dabney set to work on what would become a 740-page biography of the fallen Southern hero—who to Dabney represented all that was good, pious, and noble in the Southern tradition.

His work of most lasting significance, and certainly of greatest interest to the student of the Civil War, is his *Defense of Virginia and through Her of the South*. Richard Weaver described it as "at once the bitterest and the most eloquent of the major apologias." The lack of any serious intellectual and theological defense of the Southern position struck Dabney as one of the Confederacy's most debilitating weaknesses, a shortcoming he sought to rectify in his *Defense*. "Our failure to meet the Abolition charges squarely," he later wrote, "was viewed as a confession of our own guilt" Dabney had originally intended the book to be published in Europe during the war, followed shortly afterward by publication in the United States. It was not to be—at least not while the Confederacy survived. The *Defense* was never published in London, and only in 1867, a full two years after the war had ended, did it reach an American audience.

The *Defense of Virginia* amounted in fact to a defense of slavery, an institution that Dabney claimed was sanctioned by both the Old and New Testaments as well as by sound political economy and natural ethics. The institution of slavery was open to grave abuse, to be sure, and Dabney was not slow to condemn such abuses, but to claim that slavery was per se sinful he rejected as flatly unbiblical. He held abolitionist theologians in contempt, convinced that abolitionism was but a species of the unbelief—of man standing in judgment of God's Word—that had been spreading throughout the Western world since the French Revolution.

Indeed Dabney was one of many Southern observers to compare abolition with Jacobinism and the American Civil War with the French Revolution. In both the theology and the social thought of the abolitionists he found a corrosive individualism whose principles he deemed fatal to civil society. The principal tenet of the thought he was criticizing was that the individual may be bound only by those restraints to which he has explicitly, or at least implicitly, consented. The problem with such a theory, according to Dabney, apart from the obvious difficulty of deriving civic obligation from a social contract whose own theorists admitted was a historical fiction, was that by placing the locus of authority in the individual it tended to undermine all authority. In particular he worried that abolitionist arguments against subjection to authority could be extended to the very cell of society, the family, in which also reside the relations of authority and subordination. Thus Dabney

545

could conclude his *Defense* by assuring his aggrieved compatriots that they "will be avenged through the same disorganizing heresies under which they now suffer, and through the anarchy and woes which they will bring upon the North."

Dabney continued his intense regimen of writing and speaking long after the war ended, producing major works of theology and writing articles on subjects ranging from the theory of evolution to the moral and economic aspects of labor unionism. In 1883 he accepted the chair of mental and moral philosophy at the University of Texas at Austin. A creeping blindness finally overtook him in 1889, but the university refused to accept his resignation and he continued teaching until 1894. He died in 1898.

—*Thomas E. Woods, Jr.*

See also Jackson, Thomas Jonathan; Religion; Thornwell, James Henley.

For further reading:

Dabney, Robert Lewis. *A Defense of Virginia and through Her of the South* (1867).
Holifield, E. Brooks. *The Gentlemen Theologians: American Theology in Southern Culture, 1795–1860* (1978).
Johnson, Thomas Cary. *The Life and Letters of Robert Lewis Dabney* (1903).
Weaver, Richard M. *The Southern Tradition at Bay: A History of Postbellum Thought* (1968).

DABNEY'S MILLS/HATCHER'S RUN (VIRGINIA), BATTLE OF
(5–7 February 1865)

In early February 1865, Ulysses S. Grant wanted to stop supplies coming from Hicksford, Virginia, moving by wagons along the Boydton Plank Road via Dinwiddie Court House and then into Petersburg. He ordered George Gordon Meade on 4 February to destroy the next wagon train. Meade gave this task to Brigadier General David McMurtrie Gregg's cavalry to be supported by part of Major General Andrew Humphreys's II Corps and Major General Gouverneur Warren's V Corps.

Gregg started out on 5 February and traveled through Ream's Station to Dinwiddie Court House. At the same time, Warren crossed Hatcher's Run near Vaughan Road to cut any Confederate retreat west along Stage Road at Monks Neck. Humphreys took two of his divisions in support of Warren at Vaughan Road.

Gregg arrived at Dinwiddie Court House about mid-morning on 5 February, but found only a few wagons, which he destroyed. After scouting around the area, he came to the conclusion that Confederates did not much use the Boydton Plank Road. He retraced his steps and camped at the Malone Bridge at Hatcher's Run that night.

Warren had been on the move much of 5 February as well, and when he reached the point where Hatcher's Run and Gravelly Run came together, he was attacked. He was able to push his outnumbered assailants aside and crossed Hatcher's Run. He then moved toward Dinwiddie Court House, stopping at the Quaker and Stage Roads in the late afternoon. Humphreys had moved forward to Vaughan Road, where he too was attacked initially by a small number of Confederates who were reinforced and attacked Humphreys's left with some force in the late afternoon. Humphreys repelled the attack and was reinforced during the night. These men arrived just in time because Humphreys by evening was being pressed by elements of both A. P. Hill's and John B. Gordon's corps.

During the night, Warren received instructions to linkup with Humphreys, and Gregg was ordered to join with Warren. About 4:00 A.M. on 6 February, Gregg met Warren along the Vaughan Road. By that time Humphreys had decided that, if the Confederates were still in front of him at daylight, he would attack. Warren was informed and made ready to support Humphreys's offensive. When the first light revealed the area in front of Humphreys's lines, there were no Confederates to be seen. Gregg in the meantime skirmished with a few Confederate cavalry on the Vaughan Road in the early afternoon.

Meade, in the meantime, sent word to Warren to determine Confederate positions southwest of Hatcher's Run. Warren, in the early afternoon of 6 February, sent a force toward Dabney's Mill Road and then along that road toward Dabney's Mills. When it became apparent that a fairly large force of Confederates were in front of them, Warren sent Samuel Wylie Crawford's division down Dabney's Mill Road supported by Romeyn Beck Ayres's division. Gregg was to support the left of both divisions from the Vaughan Road, but he was tied up for much of the day by an attack from Brigadier General John Pegram. Gregg finally repulsed the attack with some difficulty, and Pegram was killed in the engagement.

Crawford had by then encountered Confederate pickets on Dabney's Mill Road and pushed them back to Dabney's Mills. At that point the Confederates were reinforced by Brigadier General Clement A. Evans's division. The Confederates then counterattacked on Crawford's left and pushed the Federals back until Ayres was able to bring up part of his division on Crawford's left. Once again it was the Confederates' turn to be pushed back, and it seemed that they would be overrun when in the late afternoon Major General William Mahone brought his division in support of the beleaguered Confederates. As evening approached, the fighting became very intense, and just as the sun was setting, the Confederates staged a major attack that put part of the Federal army in retreat. During the night, however, the Union forces regrouped and attacked again the next morning, regaining all of the ground around Dabney's Mills. As a result of the actions taken on the morning of 7 February, Meade was able to extend his lines to where the Vaughan Road crossed Hatcher's Run.

— *David S. Heidler and Jeanne T. Heidler*

See also Ayres, Romeyn Beck; Evans, Clement Anselm; Gregg, David McMurtrie; Humphreys, Andrew Atkinson; Mahone, William; Pegram, John; Warren, Gouverneur Kemble.

For further reading:

Trudeau, Noah Andre. *The Last Citadel: Petersburg, Virginia, June 1864–April 1865* (1991).

DAHLGREN GUNS

Name given to a system of guns developed by U.S. Navy Commander John A. Dahlgren and used extensively throughout the Civil War by both sides. Dahlgren first arrived at the Washington Navy Yard in 1844 to conduct ordnance ranging experiments. Soon he was designing new locks for guns and had developed a new system of naval ordnance.

In 1849 Dahlgren produced a new howitzer for the Navy. Cast of bronze, these appeared as 12-pounders (light, 660 pounds, and heavy, 750 pounds) and 24-pounder smoothbores (1,300 pounds). There were also 3.4-inch (12-pounder, 870 pounds) and 4-inch (20-pounder, 1,350 pounds) rifles. Dahlgren boat howitzers

were the finest guns of their time in the world and remained in service with the U.S. Navy until the 1880s. Other navies also copied them.

But Dahlgren is chiefly remembered for the system of heavy smoothbore, muzzle-loading ordnance that bears his name. In January 1850 Dahlgren submitted a draft for a 9-inch gun to the chief of ordnance. The first prototype Dahlgren gun was cast at Fort Pitt Foundry and delivered to the Washington Navy Yard in May 1850. The original 9-inch Dahlgren had a more angular form and only one vent. Later the design was modified in favor of a curved shape and double vent, and in 1856 the side vents were restored. The purpose of the second vent was to extend the life of the gun. Repeated firings enlarged the vent opening; and when this occurred the second vent, which had been filled with zinc, was opened and the original vent itself sealed with zinc.

Dahlgren guns, with their smooth exterior, curved lines, and weight of metal at the breech, the point of greatest strain, resembled soda water bottles, and were sometimes so called. Dahlgren designed them to place the greatest weight of metal at the point of greatest strain at the breech. The 9-inch remained the most common broadside, carriage-mounted gun in the U.S. Navy in the Civil War; the 11-inch, the prototype of which was cast

The crew of a Dahlgren gun at drill aboard the U.S. gunboat *Mendota*, 1864 (*National Archives*)

in 1851, was the most widely used pivot-mounted gun. The 11-inch shell could pierce 4.5 inches of plate iron backed by 20 inches of solid oak.

Dahlgren guns appeared in a variety of sizes: 32-pounder (3,300 and 4,500 pounds), 8-inch (6,500 pounds), 9-inch (12,280 pounds), 10-inch (12,500 pounds for shell and 16,500 pounds for shot), 11-inch (16,000 pounds), 13-inch (34,000 pounds), and 15-inch (42,000 pounds). There was even a gun of 20-inch bore (97,300 pounds), which, however, did not see service aboard ship during the war. Fifteen-inch guns were used aboard Union monitors.

Dahlgrens also appeared as rifled guns, somewhat similar in shape to the smoothbores. Some of these had separate bronze trunnion and breech straps. Dahlgren rifles appeared in these sizes: 4.4-inch 30-pounder (3,200 pounds), 5.1-inch 50-pounder (5,100 pounds), 6-inch 80-pounder (8,000 pounds), 7.5-inch 150-pounder (16,700 pounds), and 12-inch (45,520 pounds, only three of which were cast). The Dahlgren rifles were not as successful as his smoothbores, and in February 1862 most were withdrawn from service.

Apart from the rifles, Dahlgren guns were extraordinarily reliable. U.S. Navy captain James Alden said that the 9-inch Dahlgrens were "the best … ever made," and he noted that their crews handled them "with as much confidence as they drink their grog."

—*Spencer C. Tucker*

See also Dahlgren, John A.; Naval Ordnance.
For further reading:
Dahlgren, John A. *Shells and Shell Guns* (1856).
Dahlgren, Madeleine Vinton. *Memoir of John A. Dahlgren, Rear-Admiral United States Navy* (1882).
Olmstead, Edwin, Wayne Stark, and Spencer Tucker. *The Big Guns. Civil War Siege, Seacoast and Naval Cannon* (1997).

DAHLGREN, JOHN ADOLPH BERNARD
(1809–1870)
U.S. Navy admiral

Born 13 November 1809 in Philadelphia, John Dahlgren was the son of the Swedish consul in that city. Dahlgren's father died suddenly in 1824, placing his family in dire financial straits. In the winter of 1824–1825 Dahlgren applied to become a midshipman, but the Navy rejected his application. Dahlgren then shipped as a merchant seaman to gain experience. This and letters from influential connections helped him secure appointment as an acting midshipman in February 1826. After cruises on the *Macedonian* and *Ontario*, Dahlgren took the exam for midshipman in April 1832 and was successful.

Assigned in 1834 to the Coast Survey, Dahlgren immediately showed his great interest in math and science. He spent three years there, achieving the rank of lieutenant in March 1837. However, this duty caused

serious eye problems for Dahlgren and led to two years ashore detached from duty.

Returned to active duty, Dahlgren during 1843 through 1844 was on the *Cumberland* in the Mediterranean, where he became close friends with Lieutenant Andrew H. Foote. On his return to the United States, Dahlgren was assigned to direct ordnance activities at the Washington Navy Yard. Here he found his true calling. Dahlgren designed a new lock for firing guns, an improved primer, and sights graduated in yards. In 1848 he tested 32-pounders and 8-inch guns and reported on his work, making ranging data available on these guns for the first time.

In 1849 Dahlgren produced a new howitzer for the navy. These appeared as 12- and 24-pounder smoothbores. There was also a 4-inch (20-pounder) rifle. Dahlgren's boat howitzers were the finest boat guns in the world for their time and remained in service with the U.S. Navy until the 1880s.

Dahlgren is chiefly remembered for the system of heavy smoothbore, muzzle-loading ordnance that bore his name. These new guns, with their smooth exteriors, curved lines, and preponderant weight at the breach, resembled soda water bottles, and were sometimes so called. These appeared in a variety of sizes: 32-pounder, 8, 9, 10, 11, 13, 15 and even—after the Civil War—20-inch bore. The 9-inch was the most common broadside carriage-mounted gun in the Union navy in the war and the 9-inch was the most widely used pivot-mounted gun. Fifteen-inchers were used aboard Union monitors.

Dahlgren also designed rifled guns in 4.4-, 5.1-, 6-, 7.5-, 8-, and 12-inch sizes. These were not as successful as his smoothbores, and in 1862 most were withdrawn from service.

Dahlgren became a commander in September 1855. When the commandant of the Washington Navy Yard, Captain Franklin Buchanan, joined the Confederacy early in 1861, Dahlgren replaced him. Promoted captain in July 1862, he was named a rear admiral in February 1863.

Dahlgren very much wanted the glory of command at sea. Never popular with his fellow officers because of his relentless pursuit of recognition and self-promotion, he used his influence with President Abraham Lincoln to advantage. When Secretary of the Navy Gideon Welles replaced Admiral Samuel Du Pont as commander of the South Atlantic Blockading Squadron, Dahlgren sought that command; but Welles, who disliked Dahlgren, gave it to Admiral Foote instead. A tentative arrangement was worked out whereby Dahlgren would go to the squadron with Foote, although Dahlgren insisted he have separate command of vessels for the attack on Charleston. All this was moot when Foote suddenly became ill on his way to take up his command and died in New York City in June 1863. Lincoln then prevailed on Welles to appoint Dahlgren in his place.

John Adolph Dahlgren and a Dahlgren gun (*Library of Congress*)

Most of Dahlgren's time with the South Atlantic Blockading Squadron was spent at sea off Charleston trying to blockade that harbor while protecting his squadron. Dahlgren personally led monitor attacks on the Confederate forts, but as with Du Pont before him, he was unable to take Charleston. Like Du Pont, he was unwilling to run risks and rejected an attempt to force the inner harbor. A boat attack on Fort Sumter on the night of 8 September 1863 was a dismal failure.

Dahlgren's lack of success partly resulted from the lack of coordination between army and navy. Dahlgren did assist Union land forces in taking Savannah and ultimately Charleston. He also directed an expedition up the St. John's River in Florida.

After the war, Dahlgren commanded the South Pacific Squadron for two years. He then returned to command the Bureau of Ordnance. During his naval career, Dahlgren was a prolific author on ordnance subjects. At the time of his death on 12 July 1870, he commanded the Washington Navy Yard.

—*Spencer C. Tucker*

See also Du Pont, Samuel; Dahlgren Guns; Foote, Andrew H.; Ordnance, Naval; Welles, Gideon.

For further reading:
Dahlgren, John A. *Shells and Shell Guns* (1856).
Dahlgren, Madeleine Vinton. *Memoir of John A. Dahlgren, Rear-Admiral United States Navy* (1882).
Olmstead, Edwin, Wayne Stark, and Spencer Tucker. *The Big Guns. Civil War Siege, Seacoast and Naval Cannon* (1997).
Schneller, Robert J., Jr. *A Quest for Glory. A Biography of Rear Admiral John A. Dahlgren* (1996).

DAKOTA INDIANS
See *Sioux Indians*

DALLAS, GEORGIA, BATTLE OF
(25–28 May 1864)

The sharp engagements around the small town of Dallas, Georgia, southwest of Chattanooga, Tennessee, were really nothing more than one episode in the long-running drama during Union general William T. Sherman's spring 1864 offensive to capture Atlanta. After the Confederates' disastrous defeat on the slope of Missionary Ridge on 25 November 1863, the cautious, canny General Joseph Johnston, a sound defensive strategist, replaced General Braxton Bragg as commander of the Confederate Army of Tennessee.

By early May 1864, General Sherman, by that time commander of the military Division of the Mississippi, was ready to begin his push to Atlanta as part of the overall spring offensive on all fronts that General Ulysses S. Grant had devised. On 7 May, Sherman's forces attacked across the railroad line crossing the Rocky Face Mountains at Snake Creek Gap. Intense pressure from Sherman's large army all along the Rocky Face Mountains finally forced Johnston to retreat to Resaca to keep from being completely outflanked by Sherman. If Sherman had forced his way into Resaca, Johnston would have been completely blocked from Atlanta by a vastly superior force.

Taking advantage of a delay among the Union forces to exploit their initial advantage at Resaca, Johnston rushed his forces to the endangered position. Sherman arrived in full force on 14 May and found the Confederates well positioned. He attacked during the day and drove the Confederates back to their defensive works, where they did damage to the Union offensive. On the 15th, Sherman decided to move on after another direct attack failed. Johnston crossed to the Oostanaula River and prepared his defenses for another advance by Sherman. Thus the pattern had been set: Johnston would defend and Sherman would outflank.

After pushing Johnston backwards through the rugged northwest Georgia mountains, Sherman cut loose from his railroad supply line and sent a large force, with George Thomas's largest army in the center, toward New Hope, south of the heavily defended Allatoona Mountains, once again threatening to outflank Johnston's forces. Sherman also sent George M. Schofield's forces north of Thomas's to a spot near Pickett's Mill and James B. McPherson's troops south of both of these positions, near the town of Dallas, Sherman's primary objective. Because McPherson had the most circuitous route to follow, he was behind the rest of the Union army in arriving at his objective. The reason Sherman avoided the Allatoona Pass was because he had remembered from his travels in the area twenty years before, when he was stationed in Marietta, that the rugged area greatly favored the defensive. So, having altered the path of his army, he had chosen ground that he thought would, if not necessarily favor the offensive, at least pull Johnston out of his advantageous defensive position as a consequence.

Having avoided an earlier confrontation around Cassville, Johnston was being heavily criticized for conceding territory without a fight, so he responded to this unexpected advance by moving William J. Hardee's corps to Dallas, John Bell Hood's to New Hope Church about four miles northeast, with Leonidas Polk's corps sandwiched in between. Johnston was now determined to fight.

Fighting on the 25th began when Union general Joseph Hooker advanced across Pumpkinvine Creek and met Hood's troops, who were just arriving at the New Hope Methodist Church. A much superior force effectively repulsed Hooker's initial attack; Hooker did not realize at the time that he was facing the entire right wing of Johnston's army and not merely an advance party. Undaunted, Hooker then massed two divisions together and sent them into a much-outnumbered group of Hood's men, led by General Alexander Stewart. Stewart's troops responded heroically, defending their position determinedly despite sustained pressure for two to three hours. Hooker could not budge the Confederate position. By the end of the day, Schofield, who temporarily had to relinquish command due to an injury he sustained falling from his horse, had reached Pickett's Mill, and McPherson had arrived around Dallas only to find the Confederates ready and waiting for him.

Although on the next day Sherman deliberately scrutinized the Confederate line for a soft spot, he could not find one to exploit. He decided on the 27th to attack Johnston's right flank, which was anchored around Pickett's Mill. General Oliver O. Howard, whose corps had ignominiously fled at Chancellorsville, was given the task of turning Johnston's right flank. Johnston, anticipating such a move by Sherman, had maneuvered his toughest divisional commander, General Patrick R. Cleburne, from Hardee's left wing position and placed him in what was to be the center of Howard's advance. Cleburne's men destroyed the blue advance in quick order.

Johnston, now satisfied that he had at least delayed Sherman's advance, decided to take the initiative himself and ordered Hardee to move against McPherson, and General William B. Bate's division got the assignment. His attack on the 28th was as stunningly repulsed, as had been both Hooker's and Howard's during the previous three days. Although the attack had been planned, supposedly, Bate's attack began spontaneously and therefore was never fully supported by Hardee's entire force. Interestingly, had the attack been somewhat later, the Union troops would have been gone; McPherson had previously been ordered to join up with Thomas's army around New Hope and then swing around Johnston's right flank to wedge in between the Confederates and the railroad. That night Hood argued for a flanking attack around Howard's position, but when he discovered the next morning that the Union had anticipated such an aggressive move, he halted his advance.

With all the segments of the opposing forces seemingly satisfied with having seen action, the main fighting around Dallas came to a halt. After a month of wrestling through the tangled Georgia hill country, both armies had been devising new tactics and means of survival, such as reinforcing their earthworks with sharpened sticks to repulse attackers. The results were to increase the efficiency of destruction. On 1 June, Sherman maneuvered left to link back up with the railroad, now at least having danced his way around the Allatoona Mountains. Johnston, having fought Sherman to a draw, moved back once again to block his opponent from direct access to Marietta and Atlanta. With Johnston's army settling in and around Lost Mountain, Sherman looked for yet another way to out-maneuver the Confederates and capture Atlanta.

— *James H. Meredith*

See also Atlanta Campaign; Johnston, Joseph Eggleston; Resaca, Battle of; Sherman, William Tecumseh.

For further reading:
Luvaas, Jay. "New Hope Church, Georgia, Paulding County, May 25–26, 1864; Pickett's Mill, Georgia, Paulding County, May 27, 1864; and Dallas, Georgia, Paulding County, May 28, 1864." *The Civil War Battlefield Guide* (1998).
Sherman, William T. *Memoirs of William T. Sherman* (1990).

DALTON, GEORGIA, FIRST BATTLE OF
(24–25 February 1864)

During the late winter of 1864, after his miraculous November 1863 victory at Missionary Ridge, which broke the Confederate siege of Chattanooga, General Ulysses S. Grant established General William T. Sherman in charge of an independent command and dispatched him to Meridian,

Mississippi, a supply depot for the Confederate forces in the south. To counter this aggressive move, Confederate president Jefferson Davis sent a large force of troops from General Joseph E. Johnston's command in northwest Georgia to reinforce General Leonidas Polk's forces defending the Confederate supply center. The ever offensive-minded Grant then sent General George H. Thomas against Johnston, whose troops were held up in Dalton, Georgia, recuperating from their resounding November defeat.

During the winter, Johnston had been reinforcing his defensive position, which stretched across Rocky Face Ridge, furthering the odds for his army. Besides checking Johnston from sending reinforcements wholesale to Polk, Thomas's primary mission against Johnston's position was to test the enemy for areas of weakness. On 22 February, Thomas's troops marched across Taylor Ridge at the Ringgold Gap and maneuvered themselves into the valley across from Mill Creek Gap, where it slices through Rocky Face Ridge, west of Dalton, the main encampment of Johnston's army. At the beginning of the advance, Thomas's forces outnumbered the weakened Confederate forces opposing them. Seasonal rains slowed Thomas's army as they slogged through the difficult terrain along the East Chickamauga Creek, east of Dick Ridge.

Finally in place north and south across from Dalton, Thomas advanced his troops against the opposition on 24 February and soon discovered what he had always suspected—that the wily Johnston had situated and built up his defensive forces well in that area. Despite the Confederate's defensive advantage, the Union forces on the 25th found limited success north of Dalton, where the mountains taper down to a more manageable level. *The Civil War Battlefield Guide* notes that "[t]hat same day US Colonel Thomas J. Harrison's 29th Indiana Mounted Infantry stormed Dug Gap, south of mill Creek Gap. The next day CS Brigadier General Hiram B. Granbury's Brigade drove them out."

Meanwhile Polk's situation had improved (he had evacuated Meridian before Sherman could reach the city), and the reinforcements Johnston had sent were returned. Now outnumbered and satisfied that Johnston's position was too difficult to conquer under present circumstances, Thomas on the 27th began withdrawing his troops back to their home base near Chattanooga. Thus ended the first of several engagements against Confederate forces in and around the city of Dalton. The Union lost an estimated 289 casualties with the Confederates losing 140. Although, as these comparatively few casualties indicate, the various engagements never amounted to any serious battle or threat to the Confederates dug in around Dalton, Thomas's activities did eventually assist Sherman in his advance to Atlanta.

Before Sherman, who was soon organizing his new

command, developed his master strategy to dislodge Johnston from his strong defensive position and take the prize of the southern Confederacy, Atlanta, he further needed to test his enemy's strength. Thomas's February advance not only warned Sherman that another more serious offensive against the gaps directly across from Dalton would be extremely risky, it also identified other gaps south of Dalton as better opportunities to exploit Johnson's defensive line. In his Civil War narrative, Shelby Foote sums up the later situation: "George Thomas, who had felt out the gray defenses back in February, as a diversion intended to discourage Johnston from sending reinforcements to Polk while Sherman marched on Meridian, came up with the suggestion that, while McPherson and Schofield took over the position he now held in front of Ringgold, confronting the Rocky Face entrenchments, he take his four-corps Army of the Cumberland down the west side of the ridge to its far end, then press on eastward through unguarded Snake Creek Gap for a descent on the railroad near Resaca, fifteen miles in Johnston's rear." Although it would be McPherson who would advance through the Snake Creek Gap in May of that year, it was Thomas who discovered the opening. This strategy of maneuver, one that would ultimately decide the fate of Atlanta, was therefore hatched out of the first engagement at Dalton.

—*James H. Meredith*

See also Johnston, Joseph Eggleston; Thomas, George Henry.

For further reading:
Foote, Shelby. *The Civil War: A Narrative* (1974).
Kennedy, Frances H., ed. *The Civil War Battlefield Guide* (1998).

DANA, CHARLES ANDERSON
(1819–1897)

Journalist; assistant secretary of war

Born into a New England family of modest means, Charles Dana was raised by relatives and largely self-taught. He entered Harvard University in 1839 but left after two years as a result of declining eyesight. In September 1841, Dana joined Brook Farm, the transcendentalist communal experiment in West Roxbury, Massachusetts. When the community began to collapse in 1846, Dana found work at the Boston Chronotype and then was hired by Horace Greeley of the *New York Tribune*. Eager for worldly experience, Dana persuaded Greeley to send him to Europe to cover the revolutions of 1848 firsthand. As he studied European politics and personalities, Dana developed a shrewd outlook and a crisp writing style and began to shed his youthful idealism. He met Karl Marx in Germany and later engaged him to write commentary on European events and the American Civil War for the *Tribune*.

Dana returned to the *Tribune* in March 1849 as the newspaper's managing editor. His steady work kept the paper on schedule while Greeley lectured or lobbied afield, and his combative temperament added fuel to the *Tribune*'s antislavery crusade. Dana proved more bellicose than his celebrated boss: whereas Greeley would permit Southern states to secede peacefully under certain conditions, Dana believed the Union perpetual and opposed secession as treason. He urged preparation for war and welcomed the Confederate attack on Fort Sumter. While Greeley nursed an injury at home, Dana headlined the slogan "Forward to Richmond!" over a series of editorials in June 1861. The disastrous Union defeat at Bull Run, partly attributable to the *Tribune*'s prodding, unnerved Greeley and strained relations with his managing editor, whom he forced to resign in April 1862.

In June 1862, Secretary of War Edwin Stanton appointed Dana to a commission that examined claims against the quartermaster bureau at Cairo, Illinois. After this assignment, Dana joined a partnership to engage in cotton speculation, but after arriving at Memphis he lobbied against the cotton trade with Stanton, claiming it demoralized the army. In early April 1863, Stanton, seeking to counter rumors about General Ulysses S. Grant's incompetence, sent Dana to Grant's headquarters above Vicksburg as a War Department special agent. In subsequent months, Dana reported directly to Stanton on the military situation in the West. Witnessing the Vicksburg campaign and the battles of Chickamauga and Chattanooga, Dana filed vivid telegraphic reports that played a major role in the promotion of Grant to commander of Union forces in the West, the replacement of General William S. Rosecrans in Tennessee, and the development of overall Union military strategy. In April 1864, Dana joined Grant for the Wilderness campaign in Virginia and remained there until asked to cover Jubal Early's raid on Washington. In 1865, Stanton again sent Dana to Virginia to report on the fall of Richmond.

When not on assignment at the front, Dana served at the War Department in Washington as assistant secretary, an appointment confirmed by the U.S. Senate in January 1864. His tasks included overseeing war supply contracts, processing requests regarding prisoners and passes, and supervising Union spies. He became a confidant of Stanton and President Abraham Lincoln and unofficially lobbied for them with Northern politicians.

Although his brusque manner injured feelings and his strong opinions damaged reputations, Dana contributed significantly to the Union war effort. His reports, which were usually trustworthy, steered Lincoln toward the right generals, and his efficient office work enabled Stanton to organize Union victory.

After the war, Dana returned to journalism. In 1868 he became editor of the New York *Sun*, a position he held until his death. In lively and often acerbic editorials, Dana criticized President Andrew Johnson's Reconstruction policy and supported Grant for election in 1868 before turning against him. Under Dana's direction, the *Sun* took an aggressively independent political tack that reflected its editor's personal animosities and his hatred of sham more than any consistent ideology.

Dana's wartime memoirs, compiled mainly from the *Official Records*, were ghostwritten by muckraker Ida Tarbell and published the year after Dana died.

—*Carl J. Guarneri*

See also Greeley, Horace; *New York Tribune*; War Correspondents.

For further reading:
Dana, Charles A. *Recollections of the Civil War* (1898).
Steele, Janet E. *The Sun Shines for All: Journalism and Ideology in the Life of Charles A. Dana* (1993).
Stone, Candace. *Dana and the Sun* (1938).
Wilson, James H. *The Life of Charles A. Dana* (1907).

DANA, NAPOLEON JACKSON TECUMSEH
(1822–1905)
Union general

Born to Nathaniel Giddings Dana, an army officer, and Mary Langdon Harris Dana at Fort Sullivan outside Eastport, Maine, Napoleon Jackson Tecumseh Dana came from a long line of military and political leaders. He received an appointment to the U.S. Military Academy in 1838 and graduated twenty-ninth of fifty-nine in the class of 1842. After being commissioned into the 7th Infantry, Dana served on a variety of frontier posts before being sent to Texas to serve in Zachary Taylor's army in the Mexican-American War. During that war, he fought in northern Mexico under Taylor before joining Winfield Scott's campaign against Mexico City. He was seriously wounded at the battle of Cerro Gordo and did not see any further action during the war.

After the Mexican-American War, Dana remained in the army until 1855, when, while stationed in Minnesota, he resigned his commission to become a businessman in St. Paul. Before the outbreak of the Civil War, Dana engaged primarily in banking, but he also indulged his interest in military affairs by becoming active in the Minnesota militia. When the Civil War started he was a brigadier general in the militia, and he used his influence to raise a regiment of volunteers. In the early fall of 1861 he was commissioned colonel of the 1st Minnesota.

In October 1861, Dana and the 1st Minnesota saw their first action of the war at the battle of Ball's Bluff. After the Union defeat there, Dana and his men were charged with ferrying the Federal forces back across the Potomac River. In February 1862, Dana was promoted to brigadier general of volunteers. During the Peninsula campaign that commenced shortly after his promotion,

Dana commanded the 3d Brigade, 2d Division (commanded by John Sedgwick), II Corps (commanded by Edwin Sumner). He fought at the siege of Yorktown, in the battle of Fair Oaks, and in the Seven Day'.

In the Maryland campaign, Dana continued in command of the same brigade. At the battle of Antietam, he was severely wounded. Commended for his bravery during the battle by Edwin Sumner, Dana—even though he was unable to return to active duty for several months—was promoted to major general of volunteers with a date of rank of 29 November 1862.

At the end of 1862, Dana was well enough to sit on the board investigating the conduct of Don Carlos Buell in the Kentucky campaign of the fall of that year. That duty completed, Dana was assigned to the Department of the Susquehanna. For most of his time in that department, Dana strengthened the defenses of Philadelphia and then commanded those defenses during the Gettysburg campaign. In August 1863 he was relieved of that duty and was sent to the Department of the Gulf.

In September 1863, Dana was given command of 2d Division, XIII Corps, operating in Louisiana. A month later, now in command of XIII Corps, he commanded an expedition to Brazos Santiago Pass in Texas. Once in Texas, Dana established his headquarters at Matagorda Bay. He remained there until March 1864, with his primary task preventing the smuggling of cotton into Mexico for sale there. He was relieved at his own request in March.

In April 1864, the War Department sent Dana on a tour of the Midwest with instructions to inspect recruiting facilities with an eye to improving efficiency. That duty completed by the end of summer, he was assigned to command the District of Vicksburg. In command of XVI Corps there, Dana guarded the area from Confederate raiders. At the end of the year he was given command of the Department of the Mississippi, headquartered at Memphis. He remained there until May 1865, when he was relieved after his resignation from the army.

After the war, Dana reentered the business world, working first as the agent for the American-Russian Commercial Company of Alaska. Later, he served as an executive for a number of railroad companies, including the Chicago, Burlington & Quincy Railroad. In 1895 he received a government appointment as deputy commissioner of pensions, a job he held for two years. In the meantime, an act of Congress placed him on the retired list at the rank of captain in 1894. In 1897, Dana retired to Portsmouth, New Hampshire, where he died on 15 July 1905.

—*David S. Heidler and Jeanne T. Heidler*

See also Antietam, Battle of; Texas.
For further reading:
Dana, Napoleon Jackson Tecumseh. *"Monterrey Is Ours!": The Mexican War Letters of Lieutenant Dana, 1845–1847* (1990).

DANA, RICHARD HENRY, JR.
(1815–1882)
Lawyer and author

A Massachusetts Brahmin, Dana was born on 1 August 1815. He counted among his ancestors politicians, judges, poets, writers, and a signer of the Declaration of Independence. Such upper-class credentials ensured his place at Harvard College, where he began studies in 1831. A bout with measles in 1833 so weakened his eyes that he suspended his studies to restore his sight. His father, intellectually rich but financially poor, lacked the resources to send his namesake on a rejuvenating tour of Europe, the customary prescription for a young Brahmin. After months of lingering in Cambridge, Dana made a decision that affected the rest of his life: He would sail to California as a common sailor.

On 14 August 1834, the brig *Pilgrim* slipped its moorings in Boston Harbor and began its journey to California. On 20 September 1836, Dana returned to Boston on the *Alert*, restored of eyesight, reinvigorated for studies, and destined to become America's foremost expert in maritime law. Dana matriculated back at Harvard College, from which he graduated in 1837 and entered law school. In 1840 he left Harvard, established a law practice in Boston, and published an account of his adventures as a sailor in *Two Years before the Mast*. (The title indicates that he lived in the forecastle of the ship with the common sailors and not in the stern with the officers.) The book, for which he received $250, became an immediate literary success.

From 1840 Dana's life wove into the fabric of antebellum issues rending the Republic. His *Two Years before the Mast* enticed Americans with its description of Mexico's California as a country rich in natural resources and potential. "In the hands of an enterprising people," he wrote, "what a country this might be!" By 1848 Americans possessed California, but failed to agree on Federal policies for settling such territories. Dana's views on those policies attracted him to the nascent Free Soil Party, and he played a prominent role in its Buffalo Convention of 1848.

An avowed free-soiler but not, in his words, a "technical Abolitionist," Dana's conservatism, heritage, and education inclined him to antislavery causes. By chance in 1849 Dana met the radical abolitionist John Brown. Commenting on the affair at Harper's Ferry, Dana said of Brown, "What judgment . . . may pronounce upon his expedition into Virginia, old John Brown has a grasp of the moral world." During the 1850s, as the rift between North and South widened, Dana participated in several celebrated fugitive slave cases, using them to rail against the Fugitive Slave Law. In 1851–1852 he defended those accused of aiding the escape of the fugitive slave Shadrach. He assisted the unsuccessful defense in 1852 of Thomas Sims, a fugitive slave arrested in Massachusetts and returned to bondage in Georgia. In 1854 Dana defended Anthony Burns, another fugitive slave and the last bondsman seized in Massachusetts. For all of Dana's efforts, Burns returned to slavery in Virginia (shortly gaining freedom by his sale to Boston friends) and a hired thug attacked Dana for his effronteries against the property rights of Southerners.

By 1860 Dana possessed an affinity with the Republican Party. His absence from the country that year prevented active participation in the presidential election, but through the efforts of his friends, Senator Charles Sumner and Charles Francis Adams, Sr., Lincoln appointed Dana as United States attorney for the District of Massachusetts (April 1861–September 1866). In that office Dana supported Lincoln's war effort by successfully defending (all the way to the United States Supreme Court), and aggressively enforcing, the president's policy of seizing ships at sea (called *prizes*) that carried cargo belonging to or intended for "insurrectionists." After the war Dana served as counsel to the United States in legal proceedings against Jefferson Davis.

The professional successes of Dana's early life would not be repeated in his later years. Although twice elected to the Massachusetts legislature, he never realized his aspiration for higher elective office. When President Grant nominated him as minister to England in 1876, the Senate failed to confirm him. In 1878 he retired from law and relocated to Europe with the intention of writing a book on international law. On 6 January 1882, he died in Rome and was buried in the Protestant cemetery there near the final resting places of the poets Shelley and Keats.

Besides *Two Years Before the Mast*, Dana authored *The Seaman's Friend* (1841), and *To Cuba and Back* (1859). He also edited Wheaton's *Elements of International Law* (1866).

—*Larry C. Skogen*

See also Burns, Anthony; Prize Cases.
For further reading:
Adams, Charles Francis, Jr. *Richard Henry Dana* (1983).
Dana, Richard Henry, Jr. *Two Years Before the Mast and Twenty-four Years After* (1909).
Gale, Robert L. *Richard Henry Dana, Jr.* (1969).
Shapiro, Samuel. *Richard Henry Dana, Jr., 1815–1882* (1961).

DANIEL, PETER VIVIAN
(1784–1860)
U.S. Supreme Court justice

B orn to Travers Daniel and Frances Moncure Daniel at the family plantation, Crows Nest, in Stafford County, Virginia, Peter Vivian Daniel was educated at home before being sent to the College of New Jersey (which would become Princeton University). Deciding upon a career in law, he returned to Virginia to study under former U.S. attorney general Edmund Randolph before graduating from college. Daniel began his practice in 1808 and immediately became active in Virginia politics.

After a brief stint in the Virginia legislature, Daniel was elected at the beginning of the War of 1812 to Virginia's Privy Council. He served on that body from 1812 to 1835. He served briefly as Virginia's lieutenant governor. A fervent Democrat, Daniel the following year accepted the appointment by President Andrew Jackson as the U.S. district judge for Virginia. He served on that bench until 1841 when the U.S. Senate confirmed him in President Martin Van Buren's appointment as associate justice of the U.S. Supreme Court.

During his nineteen years on the Supreme Court, Daniel gained a reputation as a careful, though certainly not brilliant justice. His strong views regarding Southern rights and his ardent support of the institution of slavery colored many of his opinions. He viewed attacks on slavery as attacks on the morality and honor of Southerners. Increasingly, as these attacks on slavery became more frequent, as with the Wilmot Proviso, he used his position and the prestige of the Supreme Court to defend Southern positions. In no more famous case did he use the bench to justify Southern culture than in the case of *Dred Scott v. Sanford*.

Considered the most zealous defender of slavery on the Court, no one had any doubt about how Daniel would rule regarding the legal status of Dred Scott. Perhaps the closest in agreement with Chief Justice Roger B. Taney, Daniel's final opinion in the case was that African-Americans could not be citizens of the United States; that the Missouri Compromise, because it had been a congressional limitation on slavery in the territories, was unconstitutional; and that, because Scott resided in Missouri, though he had lived for a time in Illinois, Missouri law governed his legal status and, as a result, he was a slave.

Although Daniel apparently came to these decisions rather easily, the Court did not. The case was delayed for what seemed an inordinate amount of time, and when in early 1857 it appeared that the Court would make its ruling, Daniel inadvertently caused another delay. In January 1857 Daniel's wife accidentally brushed her dress against an open flame and caught fire. She died of the burns, and Daniel, in mourning, could not return to the Court for several months. When the Court finally made its ruling shortly after James Buchanan's inauguration as the new president, Daniel's opinion probably received some of the least serious consideration because of his strong advocacy for the institution of slavery.

As the sectional crisis intensified partly because of the ruling in the case of Dred Scott, Daniel remained on the Court over the next few years. While respected and even revered in his native state of Virginia and throughout much of the South, he came under increasing attack in the Northern press for his views on slavery in the territories. He died in Richmond, Virginia, on 31 May 1860 while still serving on the Supreme Court and before seeing the worst manifestations of the sectionalism to which he unwittingly contributed.

—*David S. Heidler and Jeanne T. Heidler*

See also Dred Scott Case; Supreme Court, U.S.

For further reading:

Frank, John Paul. *Justice Daniel Dissenting: A Biography of Peter V. Daniel, 1784–1860* (1964).

Siegel, Martin. *The United States Supreme Court: Volume 3, The Taney Court, 1836–1864* (1995).

DAUGHTERS OF THE REGIMENT

As was true for the European armies of the early modern period and for George Washington's Continental army as well, the armies of the North and the South during the Civil War included significant numbers of female support staff. An 1802 act of the U.S. Congress is quite telling in its attempt to limit the number of women who traveled with the nation's armies (to no more than four per company of 100 soldiers) and to define more clearly army women's roles and responsibilities. How carefully the regiments of the Union and the Confederacy ultimately adhered to these 1802 guidelines is hard to determine.

Army women who mustered in formally with the blue and the gray as nurses, matrons, laundresses, and cooks were joined by countless other women, ranging from working-class sutlers and provisioners (or vivandières) to officers' wives. Their presence among the troops was less formally sanctioned, and their commitment to military life may have often been of limited duration, but their contributions to the welfare and the material and spiritual needs of the soldiers were as important as those made by the women whose status was more official. Not only were there numbers of women who traveled with the armies of the Union and the Confederacy; there were also among these Civil War army women some who distinguished themselves and thereby earned the honorific title "daughter of the regiment."

Some regiments went to war with a daughter of the regiment already designated, and in this case, the "daughter" usually served as a sort of regimental mascot, along with being expected to fulfill the other often wide-ranging support activities considered suitable for women at war. In some cases, however, army women were elevated to the status of daughter of the regiment in recognition of their particularly meritorious service on the battlefield, in the hospital, or in the work of rallying the troops to fight. Probably the most famous of all these "daughters" during the Civil War was Michigander Annie Etheridge, whose four years with the Union army left her a veteran of some of the war's most brutal battles and campaigns. During her service, Etheridge's face and her reputation for courage, endurance, determination, and humility in the care and support of the Union soldiers became common knowledge even to the men beyond the 5th Michigan Infantry with whom she officially traveled.

Although most army women did not engage in combat, some—such as Molly Pitcher in the Revolutionary War—were nevertheless known to bear arms when conditions required that they do so. Indeed, some army women and daughters of the regiment, including Kady Brownell of the 5th Rhode Island Infantry and Susie King Taylor of the 33d U.S. Colored Troops, trained with weapons in preparation for such exigencies, and those who did typically described their training as exhilarating and just plain fun.

The clothes that army women and daughters of the regiment wore during their terms of service were not standardized in any way. Some women wore simplified versions of standard female dress, others wore shortened dresses with long trousers and boots underneath, and still others—such as Brownell—wore modified military uniforms, with their weapons and the other tools necessary for their many tasks (bandages, canteens, medicines, and other supplies) strapped to their belts or stored in their haversacks. Soldiers' recollections of Civil War army women and daughters of the regiment routinely describe these women as cheerfully enduring the same sacrifices as the men with whom they served. They, too, typically ate hardtack, drank bitter coffee, and wrapped themselves in thin blankets to sleep on the ground with the rest of the troops in the field.

— *Elizabeth D. Leonard*

See also Etheridge, Annie; Taylor, Susie King; Women.

For further reading:
Hacker, Barton C. "Women and Military Institutions in Early Modern Europe: A Reconnaissance." *Signs* (1981).
Leonard, Elizabeth D. *All the Daring of the Soldier: Women of the Civil War Armies* (1999).
Massey, Mary Elizabeth. *Bonnet Brigades* (1966).
Mills, H. Sinclair. *The Vivandière: History, Tradition, Uniform and Service* (1988).
Young, Agatha. *The Women and the Crisis: Women of the North in the Civil War* (1959).

DAVIDS

When the Confederate States Navy was formed, it lacked both capital ships and the industrial facilities to produce them. Accordingly, Southern inventors conceived innovative weapons to challenge the Union fleet, particularly after the proliferation of Union ironclads in Southern waters in 1862. As the war progressed, the Confederacy needed inexpensive, yet effective weapons to thwart the Union warships that blockaded Southern ports and attacked riverine and coastal defenses.

While the North led the way in the development of sophisticated ironclads and heavy ordnance, the South was preeminent in the expansion of submarine warfare. By late 1862, the Confederate Torpedo Service had sown hundreds of defensive torpedo mines in Southern waters to covertly destroy Union ships. The defensive nature of submarine mines was expanded to an offensive role when offensive torpedoes and torpedo boats were developed.

The Confederacy's first torpedo boats were simple oar-rowed or steam-powered launches equipped with spar-mounted torpedoes. Unlike modern torpedo boats, armed with self-propelled torpedoes, these early torpedo boats were more fittingly called "torpedo rams;" the boat itself was the fixed torpedo's propulsion. Captain Francis D. Lee of the Confederate Torpedo Service at Charleston perfected the spar torpedo in 1862. The Lee torpedo was a cylindrical copper case that was fitted with percussion fuzes around the nose. The devices were made to attach to long wooden or metal spars. The fuzes detonated the explosive charge when the torpedo was forcefully rammed into a target.

The first torpedo boats were rather crude affairs, skiffs and launches adapted for use by the Torpedo Service. The first purposefully designed torpedo boat was envisioned and built at private expense near Charleston, South Carolina, in 1863. As this tiny craft was intended to attack "Goliaths" in the form of Union ironclads, the prototype torpedo boat was named after the Biblical character David. The generic term *David* was used throughout the war to describe boats of similar design that were laid down at Charleston, Savannah, Wilmington, and Mobile.

Dr. St. Julian Ravenel, reportedly borrowing from an earlier Ross Winan conception, designed the *David* with the assistance of David C. Ebaugh. There is some dispute over who actually designed the *David*. In a series of postwar letters, Mr. Ebaugh claimed that he was solely responsible for both the concept and the final design of the David-class torpedo boats. Although Mr. Ebaugh undoubtedly influenced the final configuration of the craft, several surviving sketches and other wartime documents indicate that Dr. Ravenel was responsible for the initial design.

Theodore D. Stoney and several prominent Charleston businessmen founded the Southern Torpedo Company and financed the *David*'s construction, specifically as a counterblockade weapon for Charleston harbor. When nearly complete, the *David* was loaned to the Confederate naval squadron at Charleston, where navy mechanics finished fitting the propulsion machinery and painted the boat "blockade runner gray." Captain Lee then fitted the boat with one of his torpedoes.

The particular construction details of subsequent David-class boats did not survive the war, but descriptions of the *David* provide general characteristics of the

The *David* aground at Charleston, South Carolina (Photograph by Selmar Rush Seibert / *National Archives*)

type. Davids were cigar-shaped vessels, cylindrical in profile and conical at the bow and stern. The unarmored hull was built of oak in the plank-on-frame manner of construction. Although hull dimensions varied between the later boats, the *David* was 54 feet long and 5.5 feet in diameter. Propulsion was provided by a steam engine through a two-blade screw. The boiler was mounted inside the hull near the bow, while the reciprocating engine was mounted near the stern. Rudder steerage was accomplished through a wheel mounted in the open, below-deck cockpit. The helmsman sat on the edge of the cockpit coaming, while the fireman and engineer worked the engine below. The commander directed operations from the cockpit.

Davids were technically semisubmersible boats. The draft of the boat was controlled through the addition or removal of iron ballast. In attack configuration, the *David* rode low in the water with only eighteen to twenty-four inches of cockpit coaming, two small funnels, and a thin smokestack visible above the waterline. While the Davids presented small targets that were difficult to spot at night, the extremely low freeboard made the vessels dangerous to operate in moderate or heavy seas.

The *David*'s torpedo was mounted on a 14-foot iron tube attached at the bow. The trunnion-mounted spar was fitted with tricing lines and tackle that allowed the crew to raise or lower the spar to control the torpedo depth. The vessel's steam plant propelled the *David* and the torpedo at a cruising speed of five knots and a top speed of ten knots.

On the night of 5 October 1863, the *David* was used to attack the ironclad USS *New Ironsides* off Charleston harbor. The torpedo exploded when the *David*'s commander, Lieutenant William Glassel, rammed the *New Ironsides,* but the charge failed to breach the hull. The explosive force cascaded water over the *David*, and its boiler fires were smothered. With his vessel disabled and musket fire from the *New Ironsides*' marines rattling down, Glassel ordered his crew to scuttle and abandon the *David*. Glassel and the boat's fireman were later captured, but the engineer, James Toombs, and the pilot reboarded the stricken torpedo boat and restarted the engine. Under a hail of bullets, the *David* limped safely away in the darkness.

Lessons learned from the *New Ironsides* attack led the *David*'s designers to incorporate armor plating around the cockpit area. Water deflectors were affixed to the

The C.S.S. *Manassas*, an armored ram (*National Archives*)

funnels, and the torpedo spar mount was redesigned to allow a more precise degree of depth control. Although many more forays against the Union fleet at Charleston were planned or attempted, the *David* made only two more recorded attacks during the war.

In the spring of 1864, Lieutenant James Toombs and his crew attempted separate attacks on the USS *Memphis* and the USS *Wabash*, but both actions were failures. Toombs twice struck the *Memphis*, but the torpedo fuzes were defective and the charge failed to detonate. In the case of the *Wabash*, heavy swells thwarted the attempt as the *David* was nearly swamped.

Although the *David* was operated by the navy, its sister boats at Charleston were deployed by the army's Torpedo Service. Several army Davids participated in the *Wabash* encounter, and three army Davids were dispatched to torpedo Union warships at Port Royal in May 1864. In both instances, mechanical problems forced the crews back to Charleston without making their attack runs. The Torpedo Service later used the stealthy craft to lay defensive torpedoes at night.

When Charleston fell, nine scuttled Davids were recovered by the Union navy. Two torpedo boats, reportedly Davids, were launched at Wilmington, North Carolina. These boats apparently never saw action and were later scuttled. Other David-like boats, allegedly laid down in Georgia and Virginia, were apparently never completed. At Mobile, the *David* CSS *St. Patrick* was used to attack the USS *Octorara* in January 1865. The

helmsman attempted to torpedo the gunboat, but failed to stay on course; the *St. Patrick* simply scraped alongside the Union warship as it steamed away. While a number of Confederate torpedo boats encountered by the Union navy were thought to be Davids, this was not always the case. The CSS *Squib*, which operated on the James River in Virginia was actually a narrow-beam, high-speed, open steam launch that was built as a torpedo boat. Union naval records referred to the *Squib* and other such boats as Davids, but these vessels were misidentified.

The Davids were operationally limited in many respects, especially when compared with later torpedo boats, with launchable torpedoes, developed in the 1870s. However, Admiral David Porter concluded that the *David* was certainly "an ingenious torpedo-boat—for the day." The efforts of the Confederacy to build Davids and other weapons of submarine warfare are particularly illustrative of the predicament faced by Confederate strategists. With comparatively few operational ironclads, the Confederate navy was increasingly forced to rely on covert weapons to defeat a significantly better-equipped naval opponent after 1862.

As was the case with Germany in World Wars I and II, the Confederacy developed torpedo boats and submarines to stealthily attack and defeat blockade ships that could not otherwise be successfully engaged in outright surface combat. Confederate submarine warfare was born out of desperation, but no matter how theoretically effective, the Davids were produced in too small

numbers and were deployed too infrequently to alter the outcome of the naval war. Despite continual problems with mechanical failures and the limited effectiveness of offensive torpedoes during the Civil War, the utility of torpedo boat warfare was readily apparent. By the end of the nineteenth century, self-propelled torpedoes and swift torpedo boats were prominently employed in all the world's major navies.

—*Charles L. Heath, Jr.*

For further reading:
Beauregard, Pierre G.T. "Torpedo Service in the Harbor and Water Defenses at Charleston." *Southern Historical Society Papers* (1878).
Glassel, William T. "Reminiscences of Torpedo Service in Charleston Harbor." *Southern Historical Society Papers* (1877).
Johnson, John. *The Defense of Charleston Harbor including Fort Sumter and Adjacent Islands, 1863–1865* (1889).
Perry, Milton F. *Infernal Machines: The Story of Confederate Submarine and Mine Warfare* (1965).
Porter, David D. *The Naval History of the Civil War* (1886; reprint, 1984).
Solomon, Robert S. *The C.S.S. David: The Story of the First Successful Torpedo Boat* (1970; Reprint, 1976).

DAVIS BEND, MISSISSIPPI
Freedmen's colony

Located approximately thirty miles below Vicksburg, Mississippi, in a bend of the Mississippi River, Davis Bend contained plantations belonging to several prominent antebellum Mississippians, including Hurricane, owned by Joseph Davis, and Brierfield, owned by Davis's younger brother, Jefferson Davis. The older Davis read extensively on political and social theory of the first half of the nineteenth century, including the works of utopian socialist Robert Owen. During Owen's trip across the country to establish his model community at New Harmony, Indiana, Davis met the Scottish thinker and had a chance to converse on Owen's controversial theories. After his retirement from the practice of law in 1827, Davis decided to implement his own version of a model community at his plantation at Davis Bend.

At Hurricane and Brierfield, which he had given to his younger brother in the 1830s but still managed during his brother's frequent absences, Joseph Davis established a community of slaves to whom he gave extensive freedoms and training in the belief that through self-sufficiency and self-governance he could receive maximum productivity. Davis's slaves lived in much larger houses than those of the neighboring planters' slaves, received more varied food and clothes, better and more regular medical care than most slaves, and were punished only after being convicted in a plantation court by a jury of fellow slaves.

Davis's motivation for his efforts seems to have been one of social experimentation. While he viewed slavery with some amount of disgust, he apparently was not preparing his slaves for a life of freedom with his lenient treatment and efforts toward self-governance. He merely thought that greater freedom would lead to greater productivity, and the prosperity of his plantation on the eve of the Civil War gives some credence to his beliefs. At the outbreak of the war, Davis was one of the wealthiest planters in the state, with extensive estates and almost 350 slaves.

For the first year of the war little changed at Davis Bend, but the fall of New Orleans in April 1862 caused Joseph Davis to move his family to a safer area of the state. He left Hurricane and Brierfield in the hands of overseers and a very trusted slave, Benjamin Montgomery. Floods soon caused most of the slaves to flee the plantations. At the end of June 1862 many of the buildings, including the Davis home, were destroyed by Union troops. With the return of drier weather, most of the remaining slaves spent the remainder of the year working under the direction of Montgomery with no white supervision.

In early 1863 things changed dramatically at Davis Bend. Admiral David Dixon Porter arrived and determined to make an example of the self-sufficiency of the Davis slaves. He encouraged the now former slaves to work the plantations for themselves and armed them so that they could defend themselves against Confederate raiders. Porter also took an interest in the educated and skilled Montgomery family and sponsored the family's move to Ohio.

The former slaves at Davis Bend enjoyed only a brief period of independence. During the Vicksburg campaign of the spring and early summer 1863, the commander of Union troops, Ulysses S. Grant, decided that Davis Bend would be the ideal location for the thousands of refugee former slaves around Vicksburg and began sending them there. In December 1863 Colonel Samuel Thomas of the 64th United States Colored Infantry was sent to take charge at the Bend.

Thomas proved an able and dedicated organizer, but the sheer number of refugees came close to overwhelming his efforts. Teachers were brought in and schools organized, but many of these devoted reformers found the climate unhealthy and often quarreled over methods of instruction. While dealing with these problems, Thomas also struggled with providing proper shelter for the refugees, bureaucratic wrangling over jurisdiction over his efforts, and the challenges of making the plantations economically viable. He solved the latter problem by leasing the land to the former slaves, who in turn were expected to pay their rent through their profits. Most were able to do so.

In early 1865 Thomas was given a freer hand in organizing the plantations and managing the refugee

former slaves, only a fraction of whom were former Davis slaves. He organized the adult former slaves into small groups and allotted a piece of land to each group. Each group then elected a leader who organized its labors. Each group was given rations, farm animals, and farm equipment to be paid for from the profits of the enterprise. When he was finished, Thomas had formed 181 such groups. To handle social control on the plantations, Thomas created courts, very much along Joseph Davis's model, with the former slaves acting as jurors but also electing their own judges.

With the establishment of the Freedmen's Bureau after the war, Thomas was appointed the assistant commissioner for Mississippi, overseeing Bureau activities for the entire state. He saw Davis Bend as a model for Bureau actions in Mississippi and lobbied against the return of the plantations there to their former owners.

As Thomas tried to organize his bureaucracy in the state during the summer of 1865, Benjamin Montgomery returned with his family to Davis Bend. Montgomery, a respected leader among the former Davis slaves, used that core of support to try to engineer more self-governance and economic freedom for the freedmen. He was resisted by the Freedmen's Bureau and as a result turned to his former owner, Joseph Davis, for legal assistance. Davis, who hoped to regain his lost lands and wanted his former slaves to provide a work force, agreed to help and formed a loose partnership with Montgomery. In a government hearing on the issue, however, both Montgomery and Davis were rebuffed in their efforts to gain control of Davis Bend. Thomas too suffered from the controversy and was removed from his position in May 1866.

In the meantime, Montgomery had become increasingly prosperous as a store owner at Davis Bend. He hoped to use his growing wealth to wrest control of Davis Bend from the Freedmen's Bureau and create a model of freedmen self-sufficiency with no government control. That opportunity came at the end of 1866 when, after applying for and receiving a pardon, Joseph Davis was again given title to his Davis Bend plantations. Quite elderly and too tired to resume his own experiment, Davis agreed to sell his holdings to Montgomery for $300,000, to be paid for in ten years. During those ten years, Montgomery had only to pay the interest on the selling price.

Montgomery and his family had a rough start to their enterprise when weather and insects threatened their first two years' crops. These first two years were followed by several years of prosperity, but the deaths first of Joseph Davis and his very lenient payment policies and then Benjamin Montgomery soon brought an end to the noble experiment. Montgomery's sons, unable to pay the principal on the mortgage, saw the properties foreclosed on and auctioned off in 1881, thus bringing an end to African-American ownership of Davis Bend.

—*David S. Heidler and Jeanne T. Heidler*

See also Freedmen's Bureau.
For further reading:
Hermann, Janet Sharp. *The Pursuit of a Dream* (1981).

DAVIS, CHARLES HENRY
(1807–1877)
Union admiral

Born to Daniel Davis and Lois Freeman Davis in Boston, Massachusetts, Charles Henry Davis was educated at Boston Latin School before attending Harvard. After two years at Harvard, Davis determined upon a naval career and accepted appointment as a midshipman in 1824. He saw his first service aboard the USS *United States* in the Pacific and then aboard the USS *Dolphin* in the South Pacific. Promoted to lieutenant in 1827, Davis served in the Mediterranean and off the coast of Brazil. When at home, he took courses at Harvard and in 1841 graduated.

Between 1841 and the outbreak of the Civil War, Davis was occupied with various harbor surveys and tidal studies, as well as one Pacific voyage. He wrote articles for scientific works detailing his findings and was the major force behind the compilation of the *American Ephemeris and Nautical Almanac*. The work was updated and published almost annually from 1849 until 1862, providing scientific data to mariners.

In 1854 Davis was promoted to commander, and two years later he went to sea again as commander of the *St. Mary's* for a three-year Pacific voyage. The most notable event of the voyage was the rescue of William Walker after one of his failed revolutions in Nicaragua. Upon his return to the United States in 1859, Davis returned to Washington, where he served on a variety of boards until the outbreak of the Civil War.

With the start of the war, Davis's knowledge of the various harbors of the nation and his acquaintance with most of the senior officers made his advice on naval matters quite valuable. He became a member of the Bureau of Detail, which chose and assigned naval officers. He also became the secretary for the Naval Department's Strategy Board, which looked at the best approach for the blockade and possible expeditions to establish beachheads on the Southern coast.

In the fall of 1861, when Admiral Samuel Francis Du Pont was given command of the Port Royal Expedition, he named Davis his chief of staff. After the fleet's arrival off of its objective, Davis on 4 November 1861 moved ahead aboard the USS *Vixen* to sound the channel and make preliminary plans for the assault on the Confederate fortifications. A few days later, Davis formulated the final plan used by the Federal ships to reduce those forts.

In December 1861, Du Pont put Davis in command

of the expedition to sink the so-called Stone Fleet, old whaling ships filled with granite, in the Charleston, South Carolina, shipping channels. This task accomplished, Davis returned to Washington, where he had already been appointed to serve on the Ironclad Board. He had already expressed doubt as to the success of John Ericsson's plan that would become the USS *Monitor*, but he did not try to block the construction of the prototype.

Because of the illness of Admiral Andrew Hull Foote, Davis was sent in early May 1862 to take command of the Western Gunboat Flotilla on the Mississippi River near Fort Pillow. He arrived on 9 May and assumed command from his old friend Foote that day. The following day he fought an unsuccessful engagement against Confederate gunboats off of Fort Pillow. When Fort Pillow was evacuated a few weeks later because of the Confederate abandonment of Corinth, Mississippi, Davis took his flotilla down to Memphis, Tennessee. On 6 June, his boats, with the help of Charles Ellet's rams, won a naval engagement off Memphis and as a result secured that city for the Union.

On 1 July 1862, Davis led his flotilla to join with David Glasgow Farragut, who had run by the batteries of Vicksburg and was north of the city. Although Davis and Farragut held differing opinions regarding how they should attempt to destroy the CSS *Arkansas* operating around Vicksburg—Davis preferring a more cautious approach—the two men cooperated in their efforts until Davis was recalled to Washington. He was replaced by acting rear admiral David Dixon Porter in September 1862.

In Washington, Davis became the head of the Bureau of Navigation. His duties included supervision of the activities that had been carried out by the Bureau of Detail. In addition, he oversaw all research and development activities within the Naval Department. For his services in combat and within the naval bureaucracy he was promoted to rear admiral in February 1863. He continued in that post until the end of the war, when he was appointed superintendent of the Naval Observatory.

In 1867 Davis returned to sea for two years in the Atlantic off Brazil. Upon returning to dry land in 1869 he commanded the Norfolk Navy Yard and then returned to the Naval Observatory. Davis died while serving at this last post on 18 February 1877.

— *David S. Heidler and Jeanne T. Heidler*

See also Du Pont, Samuel Francis; Ellet, Charles; Farragut, David Glasgow; Foote, Andrew Hull; Memphis; Port Royal Sound.

For further reading:

Davis, Charles H., II. *Life of Charles Henry Davis, Rear Admiral, 1807–1877* (1899).

Musicant, Ivan. *Divided Waters. The Naval History of the Civil War* (1995).

DAVIS, DAVID
(1815–1886)
Lincoln ally, U.S. Supreme Court justice

Born in Cecil County, Maryland, Davis attended Kenyon College in Gambier, Ohio, and read law in the office of Henry W. Bishop in Lenox, Massachusetts. He finished his education at New Haven Law School—then loosely allied with Yale—in 1835. Upon completing his studies, he migrated to Illinois with his first wife to establish a law practice. He was elected judge of the Eighth Judicial Circuit of Illinois in 1848.

For the next fourteen years Davis "rode the circuit" with the state's top lawyers, including Abraham Lincoln. Davis and Lincoln made an odd pair in their travels. The portly, dignified, but blunt Davis, and the lanky, rough-edged, but gregarious Lincoln became close friends nevertheless. Most important in the early days of their association was the practical, yet respectful, approach each took to the law. This affinity was apparent when Davis was unable to preside over a case and often had Lincoln substitute for him.

Politically, Davis and Lincoln were conservative, old-line Whigs, until the sectional crisis over the extension of slavery radicalized both men. By 1856 they were members of the newly formed Republican Party. With each man cognizant of the other's complementary talents and ambitions, Davis became one of Lincoln's most trusted advisors as Lincoln's fame grew, particularly after the celebrated Lincoln-Douglas debates of 1858.

One of the talents Davis brought to Lincoln's campaign for the presidency in 1860 was much-needed managerial skill. Before Lincoln was nominated, Davis helped keep various Illinois personalities in tow, particularly when Davis minded Lincoln's interests as a delegate to the state Republican convention in Decatur a week before the national convention was to meet in Chicago. Finding the campaign in disarray and lacking even a central location, he then rented the hotel rooms that served as the campaign's headquarters during the national meeting.

On the floor of the national convention, his managerial skill was put to the test as he strove to maintain Lincoln's balance between availability and deference, thereby allowing his candidate to be a dark horse and everyone's second choice at the same time. Once Lincoln received the nomination, Davis worked for him by raising funds, giving speeches, and meeting with party regulars, such as Senator Simon Cameron of Pennsylvania. In the election's aftermath, Davis counseled Lincoln to take a firm course toward secession and offered advice on appointments.

Differences over appointments caused a strain in the Lincoln-Davis relationship between 1860 and 1862. Part of the tension seems attributable to role reversal: It was now up to Lincoln to judge the merits of applicants, while Davis served as a loyal advocate for his friends and favorites. Davis also nursed a grudge over not being appointed to a prominent place in the administration. Prior to fall 1862, his only official service was as a member of the Holt Commission, which investigated alleged financial improprieties in John C. Frémont's Department of the West. Finding evidence of corruption that justified the general's removal in the face of strong support for his controversial emancipation decree, Davis grew even more upset with Lincoln when he appointed Frémont to another command (the Mountain Department). Good relations between Lincoln and Davis resumed after Lincoln unexpectedly appointed Davis to the Supreme Court in 1862 as an associate justice.

Although he did not differ with Lincoln as often over appointments as the war progressed, Davis did begin to differ with Lincoln over policy matters. Davis opposed Lincoln's suspension of the writ of habeas corpus; this opposition would later manifest itself in the *Ex parte Milligan* case, the decision of which Davis wrote in 1866. Davis also opposed emancipation. Disenchanted with the president's increasing comfort with party radicals, Davis, in essence, was returning to his conservative roots. Nevertheless, he did advise Lincoln during the president's reelection bid in 1864. He also served as the executor of Lincoln's estate after Lincoln was assassinated in 1865. Davis later summed up his friendship with Lincoln in a statement to biographer William Herndon: "He never asked my advice on any question. Sometimes I would talk to him & advise him & he would listen. . . . He asked no man's advice—took no man's advice— [instead he] listened patient[ly] to all that had an idea." Davis resigned from the Supreme Court in 1877. After serving a term in the Senate as a Democrat, he married for a second time in 1883. He died on 26 June 1886.

—*Robert W. Burg*

See also *Ex parte Milligan*; Habeas Corpus, Writ of (USA); Lincoln, Abraham; Republican Party.
For further reading:
Donald, David Herbert. *Lincoln* (1995).
King, Willard L. *Lincoln's Manager, David Davis* (1960).
Tap, Bruce. *Over Lincoln's Shoulder: The Committee on the Conduct of the War* (1998).

DAVIS, GEORGE
(1820–1896)

Confederate congressman and attorney general

Born to Thomas Frederick Davis and Sarah Isabella Eagles Davis at the family plantation in New Hanover County in the Cape Fear District of North Carolina, George Davis was educated at the University of North Carolina before studying law and opening a practice in Wilmington, North Carolina. He quickly gained a reputation as one of the best lawyers in the state and gained some prominence as an outspoken Whig.

At the approach of the Civil War, Davis opposed the secession of North Carolina. In February 1861 he was sent as one of the state's delegates to the Washington Peace Conference. Davis, however, disapproved of the recommendations of that body as being unfair to the South, and upon his return to North Carolina urged the secession of the state.

The secession of North Carolina brought about Davis's selection to represent the state in the Provisional Confederate Congress. In the fall elections of 1861, Davis was elected one of North Carolina's Confederate senators. He remained in the Confederate Senate from 1862 until early 1864. During those two years, he developed the reputation as a constitutional expert on many of the questions before the senate. He also generally supported the Jefferson Davis administration, although he was somewhat critical of defensive measures being taken in the Cape Fear District of his home state.

Davis's support of the president probably cost him his bid for reelection in the fall of 1863. President Davis, however, saw an opportunity to bring Davis's legal expertise into the administration and appointed him Confederate attorney general on 4 January 1864. He held that position until the dissolution of the Confederacy in April 1865.

Davis advised the president and cabinet on various legal issues, adopting fairly strong views in favor of national over state power. As a result he engaged in disputes with the governor of his home state, Zebulon Vance. One issue on which he attempted to mediate between Vance and the president was over the commissioning of state officers.

After the Confederate government fled Richmond, Davis attempted to escape federal authorities. Ultimately attempting to leave the country by sea from Key West, Florida, he was captured and imprisoned at Fort Hamilton. After his release, he returned to Wilmington and resumed his law practice. In addition he frequently delivered public lectures on the history of the Wilmington area and other cultural topics. He died in Wilmington on 23 February 1896.

—*David S. Heidler and Jeanne T. Heidler*

See also North Carolina; Washington Peace Conference.
For further reading:
Ashe, Samuel A'Court. *George Davis, Attorney-General of the Confederate States* (1916).
Connor, Henry G. *George Davis* (1911).

DAVIS, HENRY WINTER
(1817–1865)

Union congressman

Henry Winter Davis, who did more to ensure Maryland's loyalty to the Union during the Civil War than any other individual, was born in Annapolis, Maryland. His father was a minister, educator, and slave owner. His aunt supervised his early education, after which Davis attended Kenyon College in Ohio. After graduating in 1837, he studied law at the University of Virginia. He established himself at an early age as an extremely successful trial lawyer and Whig Party speaker in Alexandria, Virginia. After the death in 1849 of his first wife, Constance Gardner, Davis moved to Baltimore. There he met and in 1857 married his second wife, Nancy Morris, with whom he had two children.

Davis quickly established himself as one of the leading figures in the Maryland Whig Party. His numerous well-received 1852 stump speeches in favor of General Winfield Scott's presidential campaign nearly resulted in his receiving the party's gubernatorial nomination the next year. Davis himself withdrew his name from consideration, however, when he realized that the state constitution required the governor to have resided in the state for five continuous years, a stipulation he did not quite meet. The Whig Party in Maryland, as in the rest of the country, was soon to disappear; in July 1855 Davis formally joined the newly formed American, or Know-Nothing, Party.

Like other Know-Nothings, Davis was greatly troubled by the growing numbers of European immigrants arriving in the United States, many of whom were Catholic and most of whom allied themselves with the Democratic Party. Davis advocated barring Catholics and those born outside the country from holding office. Along with lending his oratorical skills to the new nativist party in a number of speeches, in 1855 Davis also published a pamphlet, *The Origins, Principles and Purposes of the American Party*. Like many former Whigs, Davis joined the party partly because of his skepticism about the nation's ability to assimilate large numbers of immigrants unfamiliar with the U.S. political tradition, but even more importantly because it seemed to offer an effective means of opposition to the despised Democrats. The Know-Nothings quickly emerged as a power in Maryland politics, and Davis won election to the House of Representatives as the party's candidate in the state's Fourth District in 1855, 1857, and 1859.

Davis earned a national reputation as a result of his congressional service. His eloquent speeches and combative debating style served him well in the midst of the tumultuous congressional battles of the 1850s. Davis offended die-hard Southerners, however, with both his consistent refusal to recognize the right of secession and his willingness to cooperate with the antislavery Republican Party. In February 1860, Davis cast the deciding vote in favor of a compromise candidate, William Pennington, to end the long deadlock over the election of a new Speaker of the House. This action, coming just a few months after John Brown's raid on Harper's Ferry, resulted in an outpouring of bitterness against Davis by many Southerners, who viewed him as

a traitor. The Maryland House of Delegates censured him by a vote of 62 to 1, although Republican newspapers throughout the North sang his praises.

Davis generally managed to avoid addressing the issue of slavery in the antebellum years, fearing its potential sectionally divisive consequences, particularly since the border state of Maryland would clearly be caught in the middle of any such conflict. He did not fear the supposed Republican threat to the South's "peculiar institution," however, believing that the party would not interfere with slavery in the states where it already existed, and seeing the party as a useful ally against the Democrats, whom he continued to despise.

In the 1860 presidential campaign, Davis, like many former Whigs from the border states, supported John Bell of Tennessee. Although the Republican Convention in Chicago had considered him as a possible vice presidential candidate, Davis realized that the Northern-based antislavery party as yet had no chance of electoral success in Maryland. Privately, however, he informed friends that he approved of Abraham Lincoln's candidacy. After Lincoln's election, many Republicans, including the editors of New York's three major newspapers and incoming Secretary of State William H. Seward, pressed for the inclusion of Davis in the cabinet. Newspapers variously mentioned him as a potential attorney general, secretary of the navy, and postmaster general. Lincoln instead chose Montgomery Blair of Maryland as his postmaster general because Davis's association with nativism would likely have offended foreign-born Republicans, Maryland Republicans resented his failure to support their party actively in the recent campaign, and former Democrats in the party supported Blair.

Despite being left out of the cabinet, Davis found plenty to occupy himself in the early months of the Civil War. He played a leading role in encouraging popular resistance to the secession fever that had recently swept the states south of Maryland out of the Union and offered useful advice to the administration about how to sustain the state's Unionists. Lincoln's resort to the suspension of habeas corpus and the arbitrary arrest of thousands of Marylanders suspected of disloyalty, however, deeply upset Davis. He lost his reelection campaign in 1861 largely as a result of a conservative backlash against these measures. He was again elected in 1863, however, this time as a Republican candidate. Appointed to a powerful position chairing the House Committee on Foreign Affairs, Davis now became a leader of the Radical Republicans' opposition to President Lincoln's policies.

A number of factors account for Davis's opposition to the president. Like many educated easterners, he regarded the rough-mannered Illinois "Rail Splitter" as incapable of living up to his responsibilities. Being snubbed in the selection of the cabinet, having his advice regarding arbitrary arrests disregarded, and having to share Maryland's patronage with his bitter rival Montgomery Blair also rankled Davis. He saw the 1863 removal of his good friend Rear Admiral Samuel F. Du Pont from command of the naval forces operating against Charleston as unjust and politically motivated, further lowering the administration in his estimation. Taking advantage of a shift in Maryland's political climate, Davis now advocated both emancipating and arming African-Americans, and even opposed the administration's abortive plan to provide compensation to loyal slave owners in exchange for freeing their slaves.

Davis particularly clashed with the president over the issue of the eventual political restoration of the defeated Southern states to the Union. Davis, along with many other Republicans, viewed this issue as one that Congress should properly supervise. Lincoln disagreed and proceeded with his plan to restore the political rights of Louisiana and other partly reconquered states as quickly as possible. Davis, along with Senator Benjamin F. Wade of Ohio, sponsored a bill that would instead require that a majority of the voters in a rebellious state, rather than one-tenth as the president favored, would have to take a loyalty oath before the state could return to the Union. When Lincoln pocket vetoed the Wade-Davis bill, Davis became outraged. He crafted a paper denouncing the president for failing adequately to ensure the future loyalty of the Confederate states and thwarting the will of Congress. Davis persuaded Wade to sign the document as well, although no other congressional Republican was willing to do so. Their reluctance was understandable, for public reaction to the Wade-Davis Manifesto, as it became known after its August 1864 publication in the *New York Tribune*, was extremely unfavorable. Maryland Republicans in fact replaced Davis with another candidate in the 1864 congressional elections, held a year early as a result of the state's adoption of a new constitution prohibiting slavery. Davis had vigorously supported the new constitution.

Davis died in December of the next year in Baltimore, struck down by pneumonia at the age of forty-eight. Radical Republicans mourned his passing, for he seemed likely to emerge as a leader of the impending fight against Andrew Johnson's Reconstruction policy. The House of Representatives held an unprecedented memorial service in honor of Davis, who was no longer a member of that body at the time of his death. Charles Sumner proclaimed his death "a national calamity," while George W. Julian stated that he "wept like a child" when considering "the loss of one so young, & so gifted."

Secretary of the Navy Gideon Welles, a Conservative Republican who had supported the Reconstruction policies of both Lincoln and Johnson and who had drawn Davis's fire for his administration of the navy depart-

ment, felt quite differently. Welles wrote in his diary that Davis was "an uneasy spirit, an unsafe and undesirable man, without useful talents for his country or mankind." Few of his contemporaries drew such fervent praise or such bitter criticism, making it difficult even today to evaluate the career of one of the Civil War era's most talented and controversial political leaders.

—*Michael Thomas Smith*

See also Congress, U.S.A.; Lincoln's Reconstruction Plan; Wade-Davis Bill.

For further reading:
Baker, Jean H. *The Politics of Continuity: Maryland Political Parties from 1858 to 1870* (1973).
Henig, Gerald S. *Henry Winter Davis: Antebellum and Civil War Congressman from Maryland* (1973).
Luthin, Reinhard H. "A Discordant Chapter in Lincoln's Administration: The Davis-Blair Controversy." *Maryland Historical Magazine* (1944).

DAVIS, JEFFERSON
(1808–1889)
U.S. senator; president of the Confederate States of America

Jefferson Davis was the fifth son of Jane Cook, a native of South Carolina, and Samuel Emory Davis, a Georgian and Revolutionary War veteran who had served in Georgia and South Carolina. When Jefferson, the youngest of ten, was born, his father was proprietor of a wayside inn in Christian County, Kentucky (now the village of Fairview in Todd County). The family lived briefly in Louisiana before settling about 1810 on a small plantation, later named Rosemont (still extant), in what became Wilkinson County, Mississippi. For most of his life, Samuel Davis was a farmer who owned slaves and worked the land with them. All the surviving Davis children (one died in childhood) settled in Louisiana and Mississippi. Three sons served in the War of 1812.

During his early life, Jefferson Davis used 1807 as his birth year, reflecting what he remembered as "controversy about the year of my birth among the older members of my family." He adopted 1808 "because it was just as good, and no better than another." He entered West Point in 1824 as "J. F. Davis"; his middle name is unknown, and even the initial disappeared in the 1830s.

Jefferson Davis received an excellent education. As he recalled in an autobiographical account, he attended "the usual log-cabin school-house" before going in 1816 to St. Thomas College, a Catholic boarding school near Bardstown, Kentucky, and en route he was the houseguest of Andrew Jackson, who made a lasting impression. In 1818 Davis returned home, traveling on one of the first steamboats on the Mississippi River. For the next few years he attended Jefferson College in nearby Washington, Mississippi, and the newly established

Jefferson Davis (*Library of Congress*)

Wilkinson County Academy. In the autumn of 1823 he entered the junior class at Transylvania University in Lexington, Kentucky, a well-respected school with a distinguished faculty. The next summer Samuel Davis died, about the same time that Jefferson Davis learned from Joseph E. Davis—his eldest brother and "beau ideal"—that he had been appointed a cadet at West Point, at Joseph's instigation.

Davis attended the U.S. Military Academy from 1824 to 1828, graduating twenty-third in a class of thirty-three. In 1825 Davis was court-martialed for being off limits and was arrested and confined to quarters during the Christmas 1826 "eggnog riot." By 1828 he had compiled quite a list of demerits, but also had formed a steady devotion to the army and lifelong friendships, notably with Albert Sidney Johnston and Leonidas Polk.

Davis was a brevet second lieutenant of infantry on graduation and his first assignment was to the school of practice at Jefferson Barracks near St. Louis. For the next four years he was posted to forts in Wisconsin Territory and Illinois, occasionally on commissary and quarter-master duty. He was promoted to second lieutenant in 1831, the same year he mediated troubles between settlers and miners at Dubuque Mines. On furlough during most of the Black Hawk War, he had returned to duty in time to take custody of Black Hawk and other prisoners, transporting them to Jefferson Barracks in September 1832. The next year, Davis joined the new regiment of Dragoons, served as adjutant a few months, and in 1834 was promoted to first lieutenant. He accompanied the Dragoon expedition to present-day Oklahoma and then was stationed at Fort Gibson in that territory. Court-martialed in February 1835 for defying orders of his commanding officer, Davis was acquitted, but during a subsequent furlough decided to resign his commission.

On 17 June 1835, Davis married Sarah Knox Taylor, daughter of his commanding officer at Fort Crawford in Wisconsin Territory. Zachary Taylor opposed his daughters' plans to marry army officers because he knew the difficulties of military life; additionally, Davis and Taylor had been on opposite sides of a disagreement over army regulations. Neither Taylor parent attended the wedding, held at the home of Sarah Taylor's aunt near Louisville, Kentucky.

The young couple immediately went to Mississippi to establish a home at Brierfield plantation. Considered to be Jefferson's patrimony, Brierfield bordered the Mississippi River and adjoined Joseph Davis's much larger estate, Hurricane. While on their wedding trip to meet the Davis family, both fell desperately ill, probably from malaria. Sarah died on 15 September and was buried in the family graveyard of Locust Grove at Davis's sister's home in West Feliciana Parish, Louisiana. Devastated by the loss, Davis nevertheless remained in close contact with the Taylor family. He became a particular confidant of his former father-in-law in the Mexican-American War and during Taylor's presidency, in spite of political differences. Sarah's younger brother Richard was an able and trusted general during the Civil War; various nephews served the Confederacy and remained lifetime friends.

After Davis recovered, he traveled to Havana for a rest and then to Washington, where he investigated the possibility of reentering the army. Instead, he became a cotton grower like his brother, living with Joseph Davis and his family while clearing and planting his own property. Like his father, Davis worked alongside his slaves and until 1852 had a slave overseer, an older man treated as a friend. Both Davis brothers were known as beneficent slave owners: many of their slaves were literate, some had their own businesses, they were permitted their own system of self-government, their housing was above standard, quality medical care was provided, and overseers were strictly supervised and frequently dismissed for mistreating their charges. A Union admiral noted in 1863 that on Joseph Davis's plantation, slavery "was only nominal."

Still, it was slavery. At the time that Joseph Davis fled before advancing Federal forces in 1862, the two plantations were home to nearly 500 African-Americans. Before the Civil War, Jefferson Davis said and wrote that he thought slavery preferable to Northern wage labor and feared that the "people," while educable, had been so long dependent on whites that they were incapable of living on their own and would be susceptible to those with venal motives. He quoted biblical defenses of slavery; blasted those "hostile to that species of property on which our commercial prosperity depends, and the disturbance of which would involve us in total ruin"; believed the institution was useful to all whites, elevating them above the most menial tasks; and in 1857 declared that "if measured by the standard of the practicable and real, African Slavery, as it exists in the United States, was a moral, a social and a political blessing." Even after emancipation, he professed confidence in "the truth and faithfulness of these humble friends" and their "lifelong common interest." Later, in the 1870s and 1880s, he confessed that he did not share his brother's expectation about even their own former slaves' ability to run plantations and lamented that the condition of blacks had "deteriorated from the time when they were left to govern themselves."

While learning to be a planter in the 1840s, Davis was at the same time cultivating a political career, serving as a delegate to state conventions and running unsuccessfully for the legislature in 1843. His choice of a public role was an ironic one, considering his feelings in 1829, when he wrote that he was thinking of studying law or remaining in the army rather than face "the maledictions which so often hang around the closing scene of the politician whose struggles begun in folly are closed in disgrace." A presidential elector in 1844, he traveled the state, giving speeches on behalf of the Democratic ticket. The next year he was elected to the U.S. House of Representatives.

Davis arrived in Washington with not only a new career, but also a new bride. Joseph Davis had engineered the meeting of his beloved younger brother and the daughter of a friend in 1843. Eighteen years Jefferson's junior, Varina Banks Howell (1826–1906) was brought up in a Whig household. Her father, William Burr Howell, a New Jersey native, was an early associate of Joseph Davis's in Natchez, Mississippi; her mother, Margaret Kempe, was Virginia-born and the heir to substantial properties in Louisiana. Varina attended a girls' school in Philadelphia and was tutored at home by a local judge; she was striking, bright, articulate, and opinionated, a strong personality. On 26 February 1845, they were married in Natchez.

When the couple took up residence at Brierfield, it was in a small house that Davis had built with his slaves, working from his own design. A new home was erected in 1848–1849, a one-story, U-shaped frame building with a deep gallery and large windows, not extravagant, but rambling and comfortable. Its completion coincided with the blossoming of Davis's political fortunes, thus the couple spent relatively little time there, the longest period being from October 1851 to March 1853. Management of the place fell to Joseph Davis, friends, and overseers during the Davises' long absences.

Davis's freshman term in Congress proved to be a short one, lasting only seven months, but long enough to gain Davis some recognition. He spoke out against the American Party (Know–Nothings), on issues concerning Oregon Territory, Texas, and increasing the army, and he served on committees to establish the Smithsonian Institution and to investigate corruption charges against Daniel Webster. With the Mexican-American War brewing in 1846, Davis signaled his willingness to lead a volunteer unit. On 18 June he was elected colonel of the 1st Mississippi Regiment, usually called the Mississippi Rifles because of the Whitney percussion arms he secured.

Under Zachary Taylor's overall command, Davis and his regiment during their twelve months of service saw action in the battles of Monterrey and Buena Vista. At Monterrey, Davis served as one of the commissioners to negotiate the surrender of the city. On 23 February 1847, the Mississippi Rifles won fame at Buena Vista for their disciplined fighting and for the "V" formation used to repel an attack from a large force of mounted Mexican lancers. Early in the day, Davis was severely wounded in the foot, an injury that resulted in the use of crutches for months afterward and caused pain for the rest of his life. Another legacy of the war was his close relationship with many army officers and the men of his own unit and his admiration of Taylor's leadership style and character, qualities he would seek in Confederate commanders.

In October 1846, Joseph Davis had forwarded his brother's letter of resignation from Congress. In May 1847, President James K. Polk offered the wounded hero a commission as brigadier general of volunteers, which Davis declined because volunteers were militia and therefore subject to state control. In August the governor of Mississippi, a political rival, yielded to popular pressure and appointed Davis to a vacant Senate seat; Davis was elected by the legislature to that position in January 1848.

This time, Davis traveled to Washington alone. He had been furloughed home for two months in October 1846, apparently to mediate a serious family dispute between Varina and Joseph and his wife Eliza about the construction of the new house at Brierfield and the provisions of Jefferson Davis's will. Varina's correspondence is missing for this critical period, but Davis wrote some telling letters to her. One was posted on his arrival in Texas, saying he hoped that "the season of our absence may be a season of reflection," and alluding to "ingratitude" and faithlessness. He wrote again in December as he made his way back to Mexico, confessing his own "weaknesses which belong to a morbid sensibility," yet clearly indicating that she had fallen short of his expectations. In January 1848 he stated frankly that she had

not accompanied him to Washington because he could not bear "constant harassment, occasional reproach, and subsequently misrepresentation." A few months later, he alluded to painful memories of her "injurious" treatment: "the dread of constant strife was so great, as not to be overcome by a threat of exposure to the public, of the real cause of my going alone from home…I need not say that (because I love you) it would always make me happier to be with you, if kind and peaceful." He returned home for two months in autumn 1848 and again in the summer of 1849; Varina accompanied him to Washington in December of that year.

Along with bearing up under personal crises, Davis became a senator during the crucial years surrounding the Compromise of 1850, and his own temper was made evident. He and Mississippi senator Henry S. Foote had come to blows in a Washington boarding house in December 1847 and a duel between them was narrowly averted in July 1848. In February 1850, Davis again came near to dueling, the offender an Illinois congressman who made disparaging remarks about the Mississippi Rifles at Buena Vista. During the volatile debates of 1850–1851, no less than Henry Clay accused Davis of lecturing the Senate.

A passionate Democrat, Davis frequently and consistently opposed the "enormity & unconstitutionality" of the Compromise measures, particularly the admission of California as a free state, "deemed a *fraud* upon the South." He was willing to discuss the possibility of secession but did not advocate it, foreseeing bloodshed and fearing the breakup of the Union. His attempts to be a "national Democrat" while defending slavery proved increasingly difficult as the decade progressed. As he wrote in 1852, he believed "secession was the last alternative, the final remedy, and should not be resorted to" in the face of the Compromise measures.

Included in his Senate duties were chairmanships of the Military Affairs and Library Committees. He was an active member of the Smithsonian Board of Regents and served on the building committee. Along with many hours spent on constituents' business, he debated a variety of topics, remained close friends with President Taylor and his family, helped handle arrangements when Taylor died in July 1850, and accompanied John C. Calhoun's body home to South Carolina for burial.

After the First Session of the Thirty-first Congress adjourned in 1850, having deliberated for ten stress-filled months, Davis set out on an arduous speaking tour to explain his position on the Compromise measures, spending only a few days at home before resuming his seat. In 1851 he again spoke throughout the state for the State Rights Democrats, the Mississippi party having divided into State Rights and Union factions. When the State Rights gubernatorial candidate withdrew from the race, the ill and exhausted Davis reluctantly took up the

banner against his old enemy, Henry S. Foote, who won by 999 votes.

Suddenly without a political job, Davis returned home to Brierfield, yet continued his involvement in Mississippi public affairs. He received scattered votes for vice president at the 1852 Democratic Convention and spoke for the slate during the summer. In fact, he was absent on a speaking engagement when his first child was born, a son named for his father. Joy was tempered by Davis's physical afflictions. He had suffered for sometime from eye disease, likely a herpes infection, which forced him to wear tinted goggles while canvassing the state in 1851. He eventually underwent surgery in 1860 and lost sight in his left eye. Aggravating his frail health from recurrent neuralgia, dyspepsia, and malaria was a long estrangement from his brother that led him to consider selling Brierfield. The root of the quarrel is unknown but it continued until 1855. As Varina Davis wrote at the time, "Brother Joe's alienation preys upon his mind."

Late in 1852 the president-elect, a Mexican-American War officer whom Davis had met fifteen years before in Washington, offered Davis a new challenge. Franklin Pierce first asked Davis's advice about the make-up of the cabinet, intimating he would offer the Mississippian a spot and sure "that whether our views coincide or not, from you I shall receive a friend's free and useful suggestions." Agreeing to meet with Pierce, Davis initially declined appointment as secretary of war for "private and personal reasons," but "was induced by public considerations to reconsider." As the cabinet's voice of the South and a close political and personal adviser of the president, Davis was influential in policy and patronage decisions far beyond the War Department. For example, he was instrumental in brokering passage of the Kansas-Nebraska Act in 1854. He maintained close tabs on the state Democrats—still roiling in disharmony—and kept the lines open for his return to the Senate. Traveling widely and speaking on national issues such as Kansas, slavery, and the acquisition of Cuba, he aimed to consolidate his position as a nationalist and an expansionist while acting as an advocate for the South.

Despite his reluctance to accept the office, Davis was exceptionally well qualified and proved an effective, even distinguished, secretary of war. His goals of reform and efficiency led to clashes with the entrenched departmental bureaucrats, particularly the bureau chiefs, most of whom were allied with the vainglorious general-in-chief, Winfield Scott, who happened to have been Pierce's opponent in the 1852 presidential campaign. Scott moved army headquarters to New York City when Davis took office and was openly contemptuous of him. Their personal animosity culminated in a public dispute over what amounted to trivial differences of opinion; each matched the other in unseemly exhibitions of invective. Another Mexican-American War general, John E. Wool, took on the secretary of war in a similar, well-publicized argument that harshly spotlighted both of them.

Although Davis claimed his position was "neither pleasant nor remunerative," he considered "my services here may be more beneficial to the South than those I could render elsewhere." He remained in office until the end of Pierce's term; on their parting in 1857 Pierce stated that Davis had been "strength and solace to me for four anxious years and never failed me." Davis's achievements as secretary were impressive: the first official U.S. military observers sent to a war zone—the Crimea; adoption of advanced military technology in the forms of rifled muskets, the minié ball, a new primer on tactics, and experimental breech-loading artillery, rifled cannon, and repeating weapons; for the army, four new regiments and a pay increase; revamp of the West Point curriculum and extension of it to five years; expansion of the "chain of forts" in the West to advance settlement and quell Indian raids; exploration and mapping of four routes to the Pacific for a transcontinental railroad; the Mexican boundary survey; numerous river and harbor improvements throughout the country; the use of camels for military transportation; enlargement of the Capitol, including final approval of the statue for the dome; and construction of the Washington Aqueduct and extensions of the Post Office and Patent Office Buildings.

Davis's personal life improved markedly during the 1850s. He and Varina lived in a luxurious Washington mansion while he was secretary of war and moved in the highest social circles. An easy and accomplished host, Varina continued to be an excellent helpmate to her often-unhealthy spouse. Grief-stricken when their child died in 1854, they rejoiced in the birth of a daughter in 1855 and sons in 1857 and 1859. The Davises were communicants and pew-holders at the downtown Church of the Epiphany, where Varina was confirmed and the boys were baptized in the Episcopal faith; President James Buchanan, a particular favorite of Varina's, was godfather for one of them. Davis himself would be baptized and confirmed as an Episcopalian in May 1862, and the Davises remained active members of Episcopal parishes for the rest of their lives.

During the heat of Washington summers, the family decamped to more comfortable quarters—in the Maryland mountains, at the Soldiers' Asylum, and, most importantly, to New England in 1858. In delivering a few speeches at nonpolitical meetings, Davis shone in his role as a national Democrat, surprising his audiences with his calm, measured views and personally attractive style. The addresses proved so popular that they were issued in book form, the first collection of his papers. On the other hand, his identification with national topics made him anathema in some Mississippi venues, targeted by the press and many of his constituents as less-than-loyal to the South. He was at pains to explain his posi-

tion in a November 1858 speech, proclaiming his ardent devotion to the Union, but also warning against "false security" and advising "immediate preparations for our defence, so that in the event an Abolition President should be elected in 1860, he should never be permitted to take his seat….In that contingency [Davis] would consider our Constitutional Union dissolved, and would be in favor of holding the city of Washington…and maintaining our rights and honor, even though blood should flow in torrents throughout the land."

Blood was already flowing in Kansas and in little more than two years would flow in the South. To Davis, reelected to the Senate in 1856 and taking his seat immediately after he left the War Department, the outcome of the North-South struggle in the late 1850s was not certain. Even so, the portents were alarming. By March 1857, Republicans had eclipsed Whigs and the once-mighty Democrats were riven into sectional blocs. Assuming the role of Calhoun on the national stage, Davis proved more conciliatory, but he did not apologize for slavery or for his dedication to states' rights. He objected to Republican positions on abolition, while at the same time refuting Democrat Stephen A. Douglas's doctrine of Popular Sovereignty as disingenuous and unconstitutional, with the ultimate result of stripping slaveholders of their property and of conveying the rights of states to territories. In 1864 Davis told two Northern visitors to Richmond that he had "tried all in my power to avert this war. I saw it coming, and for twelve years I worked night and day to prevent it, but I could not. The North was mad and blind; it would not let us govern ourselves."

Looking toward the presidential contest, Davis submitted resolutions to the Senate in February 1860, calling on Congress to enact legislation to protect all citizens from "unfriendly legislation." The same month he stated his conviction that "the Constitution can only be safe in the hands of a national party" and that government controlled by "a party based on sectional conflict…could scarcely fail to engender collisions between the State and federal authorities." His fears realized with Lincoln's election, he agreed to serve on the Committee of Thirteen, which strove in vain to avert disunion. Only a week earlier, on 14 December, he had added his name to a public pronouncement: "all hope of relief in the Union…is extinguished….We are satisfied the honor, safety, and independence of the Southern people require the organization of a Southern confederacy."

Davis was the last of the Mississippi delegation to leave Washington. Low in spirits, drained, ailing, he confessed to Pierce his deep sorrow in departing the Union that he and his father and brothers had proudly served: "Civil war has only horror for me, but whatever circumstances demand shall be met as a duty." The next day, 21 January 1861, he delivered a farewell address to a packed Senate chamber. "Graceful, grave, and deliberate," he spoke of the right of secession, his unalienable ties to Mississippi, and his wish "for peaceful relations with you, though we must part....The reverse may bring disaster on every portion of the country." He concluded with "my apology for any pain which, in heat of discussion, I have inflicted. I go hence unencumbered of the remembrance of any injury received."

Having never attended a national convention, Davis did not join the meeting of delegates from six Southern states in Montgomery on 4 February. He suspected that he might be considered for president, telling one of the delegates: "I have no confidence in my ability to meet its requirements. I think I could perform the function of genl." On the 9th he was informed of his election, receiving the telegram with evident distress, but accepting nevertheless. He was duly appreciative of the reception he received—and soberly realistic: "upon my weary heart was showered smiles, plaudits and flowers, but beyond them I saw troubles and thorns innumerable. We are without machinery, without means and threatened by powerful opposition but I do not despond and will not shrink from the task before me." And he did not. For the next four years all his education, experience, ability, and strength were required to marshal and lead meager forces in war. With the pattern of the United States before them, Confederates soon established a government and organized an army. But as Davis had pointed out, the vast resources of the North in personnel, machinery, money, and national prestige could never be equaled.

He forecasted in his inaugural address: "You will see many errors to forgive, many deficiencies to tolerate, but you shall not find in me either a want of zeal or fidelity to the cause." In the next four years, Davis manifested the personality traits, abilities, and flaws apparent in his previous public jobs: a penchant for micromanagement; loyalty to friends and political allies (often to a fault); attention to detail; a quick but controlled temper; masterful military knowledge; less successful "people skills"; personal courage and honesty; gentlemanly conduct; inflexible convictions and an unwillingness to compromise principle; willpower in the face of debilitating illness; faith in the army and a corresponding neglect of the navy; weakness in formulating financial policy; statesmanlike but legalistic public messages; a national vision; a strong religious faith; and an unwavering, absolute devotion to duty.

From the start his appointments were criticized. For the cabinet he chose a representative from each state, most of them men he had not known well before the war. Only two stayed at their posts for the duration, although a Davis confidant, Judah P. Benjamin served in several positions. Once war began in April 1861, the War Department was the vital nerve center of the Confederacy, employing some 80 percent of the civil service and consuming the lion's share of the national budget; six men served as secretary during four years. Longest in office (twenty-six months) was James A. Seddon, a prewar congressman with a personality and work ethic so similar to the president's that only rarely did Davis override his decisions. The same was true of Samuel Cooper, the senior Confederate general who was named adjutant and inspector general, the same position he had held in the "old army." Davis admired his "supremacy of judgment over feeling," trusted him, and upheld him in the face of criticism that the veteran officer was slow, too old, and excessively dependent on rules and regulations. Another longtime associate was the commissary general, Lucius B. Northrop, a West Point and army comrade and a personal friend. Northrop's job—to secure food for the army and prisoners—was increasingly difficult as the war continued and the South Carolinian's personality repelled many, including congressmen who continually demanded his removal. In military appointments, Davis favored those with experience, particularly U.S. Military Academy graduates. Politicians naturally requested appointees from their own states and a corresponding say in strategy and tactics.

In fact, the principle of state's rights, cornerstone of Davis's own political philosophy, was a stumbling block in nation building. A strong central government was essential in carrying out the administration's financial, political, and military policies, with the goal of winning the war and independence. Toward that end, the Confederacy enacted conscription in April 1862, a novel idea adopted by the Union early in 1863. A vast tax structure was implemented, along with unprecedented authority to impress supplies and slave labor, impose martial law, and suspend the writ of habeas corpus; Davis used the latter two powers sparingly, befitting his reputation as a strict constructionist. To supply the army, the Davis administration negotiated a huge foreign loan and suppressed state trade.

In two important areas Davis did not seize control where government authority would have maximized the war effort: railroads and the press. He was unwilling to trench on the rights of private companies in the former case, although the government directed rail traffic and provided funds to spur construction of militarily useful lines. In 1859 he had enunciated his feelings about the press: "In my political career I have had less than is usual to do with newspapers, not that I have held them in lower consideration than others, but the rather because I have felt we had separate walks which best could be trodden when we kept apart." Neither did the Confederacy establish a supreme court, an issue complicated by the nation's states' rights foundation, nor a central bank, resulting in a monetary supply derived from Richmond, the states, and private firms. The resulting financial chaos eventually bankrupted the country.

In general, a factious Congress enacted Davis's

proposals. Lacking organized political parties, the solons formed changeable alliances, approving or critical of Davis's proposals, the lines shifting among them dependent on the issue at hand. Less cooperative were some governors, who used Davis's own state sovereignty arguments against him, refusing the enlistment of state forces, protesting their use outside the state, blocking conscription, fighting impressment policies, seeking to negotiate trade routes to benefit their troops alone, trying to influence appointments, and provoking "no confidence" votes in the legislature. Chief among the recalcitrant was Georgia's Joseph E. Brown, an ally of Vice President Alexander H. Stephens.

Politics and policy-making, however, were secondary. The war itself was paramount. "A *General* in the full acceptation of the word is a rare product," Davis told his brother, and "scarcely more than one can be expected in a generation but in this mighty war in which we are engaged there is need for half a dozen." Fortunately for the South, Robert E. Lee was selected as commander for the Army of Northern Virginia after Joseph E. Johnston was wounded in 1862. Lee and Davis had a long and virtually flawless relationship that was not duplicated elsewhere. By contrast, the Army of Tennessee, serving in arguably the most important theater, was bedeviled by command troubles. Davis's top choice in the West, Albert Sidney Johnston, was killed in 1862, and another favorite, Leonidas Polk, was appointed far beyond his martial prowess. P. G. T. Beauregard fell into disfavor when, as Davis saw it, he abandoned the army after Shiloh. Davis liked and was confident in the abilities of Beauregard's successor, the crusty Braxton Bragg, as brilliant an administrator as he was unfortunate in tactical skills.

Joseph E. Johnston, morbidly jealous of Lee and so similar to Davis in disposition, never recovered from his ranking as fourth of the five full generals appointed in 1861 and always longed to return to command in his native Virginia. Although Davis admired his intellect and "great personal courage" and gave him numerous chances to shine as a commanding general, Johnston revealed "defects which unfit him for the conduct of a campaign," specifically in the Vicksburg and Atlanta campaigns. Accused by Johnston's friends, many of whom were powerful congressmen, of having personalized their differences, Davis insisted he was not "unfriendly" to the general and "would as soon trust an army to his management as almost any one when *once engaged in battle*," but that Johnston's habits of secrecy about his plans and slowness to attack had destroyed the president's confidence in him.

Problems of communicating with the West aside, Davis was preoccupied with battles in Virginia, a theater he could at least visit on occasion. He did try to keep tabs on the other armies, going several times on extended inspection/confidence-boosting tours and attempting to

settle in person ongoing strife among Army of Tennessee generals. Threats farther away assumed epic proportions before the government could meet them, resulting in the early loss of New Orleans and subsequent failure to control the Mississippi River. Davis's own plantation was overrun in 1862, and his aged brother and family were forced to flee to central Mississippi and then Alabama. Losing Vicksburg and not winning at Gettysburg in July 1863 were critical to the Confederate future. Territory continued to shrink, along with revenues and other resources. Even the South's vaunted cotton supplies did not prove to be bedrock as the blockade tightened. The demand for "King Cotton" in European markets did not induce foreign intervention; in addition, because the Confederates could not secure key victories and because of the continuation of slavery, European powers refused recognition and overt aid. Not until the final months of the conflict, with almost nothing left to lose, did Davis and Congress face the issue of enlisting slaves to augment the rapidly diminishing armies.

Often viewed as a meddler in military matters large and small, Davis in fact gave his generals generous jurisdiction, from Virginia to the Trans-Mississippi. He was determined not to be an executive who "cripple[d generals] in [their] operations by acts of commission or omission": "I rely on your special knowledge and high ability"; "it is my wish to leave you with the fullest powers to exercise your judgement"; "However desirable a movement may be, it is never safe to do more than suggest it to a Comdg. Genl."; "You can best judge of your situation & must use your discretion"; "At this distance from the field of operation…I can but suggest. For the rest, I rely upon your judgment." Not conservative in his own strategic views, Davis urged bold strokes, experimented with theater command, and in some exasperation declared in 1864, "We are not waging an offensive war, except so far as it is offensive-defensive….Let us alone and peace will come at once." To win by not losing was the key.

Of course, the Confederacy's ultimate portion was annihilation. The nation essentially ceased to exist on 2 April 1865, when Federal troops occupied the capital. Davis and other functionaries fled and attempted to keep the machinery in operation, but on 10 May, he and his party were captured by Union cavalrymen near Irwinville, Georgia. Believed by some to have conspired in the Lincoln assassination plot, Davis was charged with treason and "buried alive" at Fort Monroe, Virginia. Harshly treated at first, even shackled briefly, he was forbidden visitors, mail, and reading material and was watched constantly and deprived of sleep. Added to the isolation and degradation of prison were humiliating stories widely circulated in the Northern press that Davis had been captured in women's clothing. Hundreds of cartoons showed the disgraced ex-president in petticoats, despite many captors' testimony that he had only a shawl

(then a garment commonly used by both sexes) over his head and had mistakenly taken his wife's raglan rather than his own in a vain attempt to escape.

Davis keenly felt all his losses and suffered greatly during the initial period of incarceration. Fearing his martyrdom as his mental and physical condition deteriorated, the authorities relented. In 1866 he was allowed better quarters, more exercise, and the company of his wife and youngest child, Varina Anne, who was born in 1864. The other Davis children—daughter Margaret and sons Jefferson, Jr., and William (born in 1861)—were in school in Canada. Five-year-old Joseph had perished in April 1864 after falling from a porch at the Confederate White House.

War passions eventually subsided and the prisoner's complicity in Lincoln's death was disbelieved for want of evidence. Nevertheless, Davis had been indicted for treason, and vigorous efforts for his defense proceeded apace. Postwar politics and the realities of reconstructing the Union dictated that there would be no trial, even though the accused eagerly anticipated the chance to speak for himself, believing that "fidelity has been treated as a crime, and true faith punished as treason." Convinced of the justice of his position, he refused, then and always, to seek a pardon: "repentance must precede the right of pardon, and I have not repented." On 13 May 1867, Davis was remanded to civil custody. Officially released on bond posted by public figures North and South, he was in limbo until December 1868, when the indictment was quashed, allowing him to reclaim his life.

He was homeless and unemployed at age sixty-two. With a young family to support and educate and his plantation in ruins—and no longer his, having been sold to former Davis slaves while he was in prison to save it from confiscation—Davis traveled extensively in the late 1860s. He rejoined his family in Canada, visited Mississippi and Louisiana, went to Europe for the first time, and investigated various ideas to secure a livelihood and derive income from investments, all of which came to naught. In 1869 he accepted the presidency of the Carolina Life Insurance Company in Memphis, joining the ranks of many ex-Confederate generals and officials who became figurehead executives in the postwar business world.

In 1870 he returned to England to bring Varina and the children home. The same year he lost two mainstays of his life: Robert E. Lee and Joseph E. Davis. In 1872 young Billy Davis succumbed to diphtheria. In 1873 Davis's favorite sister died, and Davis resigned from the failing insurance company. "I am much depressed and see no light ahead," he wrote to Varina. Distraught and in poor health, he was advised to take a sea voyage and again went to Europe. The next opportunity for employment came in 1875 from the Mississippi Valley Society, an Anglo-American concern hoping to encourage emigration to the South and develop trade. Another trip to England followed, but again the project folded. Simultaneously, Davis was involved in bitter litigation with his brother's heirs over ownership of their two plantations, stemming from Joseph's never having officially conveyed title to Brierfield to Jefferson, neither before the war nor afterward when he repossessed the plantations. The first court found against him, but in 1881, twenty years after leaving it, Brierfield was again his. By then it was all but uninhabitable because the river had sliced through a peninsula in 1867, turning Davis Bend into Davis Island.

In the 1870s, Davis yielded to the pleas of family and others to write his memoirs, hoping book sales' profits would cushion his retirement and provide security for his family. He leased a cottage at Beauvoir, a modest Mississippi Gulf Coast estate belonging to Sarah Ellis Dorsey, a longtime admirer from Natchez. In 1877 work began, with the assistance of an ex-Confederate officer and Dorsey, herself a novelist and biographer. In 1878, after a year of separation aggravated by health woes and her jealousy about Dorsey's role, Varina also moved to Beauvoir to help. The Davises happiness together was short-lived: in October yellow fever claimed Davis's namesake, last of their four sons. The following March, Davis agreed to buy Beauvoir from Dorsey, only to learn after her death in July that she had willed all of her property to him. The bequest provided a comfortable income and, at last, a permanent home.

The Rise and Fall of the Confederate Government was published in two fat volumes in 1881. Far from being a rich, anecdotal autobiography, the book was legalistic, wordy, and digressive, including long constitutional arguments, speeches, and documents, while omitting much Confederate history. Davis concluded it by saying that, although he was convinced of the right of secession, "it has not been my wish to incite to its exercise: I recognize the fact that the war showed it to be impracticable, but this did not prove it to be wrong." Or, as he put it more succinctly in a letter: "Force may prevail over right, but cannot destroy truth." Sales were disappointing and even the author admitted, "My book was cumbrous." Criticism from other Confederates—specifically Joseph E. Johnston—ensued, but, following a pattern set years before, Davis did not respond, having decided to bear "unjust criticism in silence and [allow] vain men to shift the responsibilities of their grievous failures upon me." Furthermore, "A long experience has somewhat blunted my sensibility to undeserved censure."

After the tribulations of the 1850s, war, and its aftermath, Davis found a measure of peace and redemption during the 1870s and 1880s. He basked in the admiration of Confederate veterans and relished the role of elder statesman, but turned back all blandishments to reenter politics, which he could not do without being pardoned—not that he was apolitical. He wrote frequently on issues of the times, adopting his own counsel: "in a land the institutions of which are based on the theory of self-government by the people, no one has a right to wholly withdraw himself from connection with public affairs." Davis lived out his years at Beauvoir with his wife and younger daughter, eagerly anticipated the visits of grandchildren (elder daughter Margaret had married in 1876), and appreciated the quiet routine of an isolated retreat. In 1881, consoling another ex-Confederate official, he spoke for himself as well: "I dare say if we had had more electioneering talent, or had tried to conciliate the selfish, rather than rigidly to perform our duty we might have gained approval where we met criticism, but now when old and broken in fortune, we should have been without that which…is worth more than all else. The consciousness of rectitude."

Jefferson Davis died in New Orleans on 6 December 1889, having contracted bronchitis after visiting Brierfield. After a spectacular funeral procession, said to have been the largest ever in the South, he was buried at Metairie Cemetery in a suit of Confederate gray. In 1893 he was reinterred in Richmond.

In a speech delivered in 1878 he had said, "Without desire for a political future, only anxious for the supremacy of the truths on which the Union was founded, and which I believe to be essential to the prosperity and the liberties of the people, it is little to assume that I shall die, as I have lived, firm in the State rights faith." His life proved what he had often proclaimed, that "his first and his last allegiance was for the South and Mississippi."

—*Lynda Lasswell Crist*

See also Congress, C.S.A.; Constitution, C.S.A.; Courts, C.S.A.; Davis Bend, Mississippi; Davis, Varina Howell; Democratic Party; Habeas Corpus, Writ of (C.S.A.); Mississippi; Riots, C.S.A.

For further reading:
Cooper, William J., Jr. *Jefferson Davis* (2000).
Davis, Jefferson. *Jefferson Davis, Constitutionalist: His Letters, Papers and Speeches* (1923).
———. *Rise and Fall of the Confederate Government* (1881).
Davis, Varina. *Jefferson Davis, Ex-President of the Confederate States of America, A Memoir* (1890).
Davis, William C. *Jefferson Davis, The Man & His Hour* (1991).

DAVIS, JEFFERSON COLUMBUS
(1828–1879)
Union general

Jefferson C. Davis was born on 2 March 1828 in Clark County, Indiana, the son of William Davis and Mary Drummond Davis. At the age of eighteen, he enlisted in the 3d Indiana Infantry Regiment under the command of Colonel James Lane and participated in the Mexican-American War at the battle of Buena Vista. For

his gallantry at Buena Vista, Davis received a second lieutenant's commission in the regular army in 1848. During the next thirteen years he was promoted to first lieutenant, a rank he held when serving as a member of the Federal garrison at Fort Sumter, South Carolina, at the outbreak of the Civil War. A month later, Davis received a promotion to captain in the regular army.

During August 1861 Indiana governor Oliver P. Morton approached Davis and appointed him colonel of the 22d Indiana Infantry. Serving in the Western theater of operations for the Union, he commanded a brigade of the Army of the Southwest at Wilson's Creek in Missouri. Later, forces under his command played a crucial role in the Union victory at the battle of Pea Ridge (Arkansas) in March 1862. Following this service, he headed the 4th Division in the Army of the Mississippi at Booneville and Corinth. In August 1862, Davis was reassigned to the command of General William Nelson, a giant of a man weighing over three hundred pounds, who had recently been defeated by Confederate general Edmund Kirby Smith at the battle of Richmond, Kentucky. Reporting to Nelson in Louisville, Kentucky, Davis took offense at a reprimand issued by his commanding officer. During the early hours of 29 September 1862, in company with Indiana governor Oliver P. Morton, Davis headed for Nelson's headquarters in the Galt House Hotel. Davis found Nelson in the lobby, where he demanded an apology. Nelson responded with another abrupt comment, whereupon Davis wadded a playing card and tossed it into Nelson's face. Nelson reacted with a slap to Davis's face and a retreat up the hotel staircase. The irate Davis found a revolver and mortally wounded General Nelson. Placed under military arrest, Davis never came to trial for the assassination of General Nelson. Scholars believe the influence of Governor Morton prevented his court-martial. Though spared a trial, Davis's career was irrevocably harmed.

Following the incident, he returned to his division, commanding with distinction at the battles of Stones River, Chickamauga, and Chattanooga during 1862 and 1863. In 1864, under William T. Sherman's command, he led his division throughout the Atlanta campaign and the March to the Sea. For his meritorious service, he gained the brevet rank of major general. Later, in the early months of 1865, he was involved in Sherman's campaign through the Carolinas. Recommended by both William Rosecrans and Ulysses Grant for promotion, Davis met with no success, a situation that deeply embittered him.

After the war, he returned to the regular army, commanding the 23d Infantry Regiment with the rank of colonel. Stationed in the west, Davis and his regiment saw service in California and the newly purchased Alaska Territory. In 1873 he commanded troops during the Modoc campaign in Oregon and northern California. These immediate postwar assignments were followed by humdrum military activities in the late 1870s. Davis died on 30 November 1879, in Chicago, Illinois, and was buried in Indianapolis.

—*Frank R. Levstik*

See also Fort Sumter; Pea Ridge, Battle of.
For further reading:
Jones, James Pickett. "Jefferson Davis in Blue: The Military Career, 1846–1866, of General Jefferson C. Davis, U.S.A." (M.A thesis, 1954).
Peckham, Howard H. "I Have Been Basely Murdered." *American Heritage* (1963).

DAVIS, VARINA HOWELL
(1826–1906)

Second wife of Jefferson Davis;
First Lady of the Confederacy

Varina Howell Davis was born on 7 May 1826 in the Mississippi River delta, the daughter of William Howell, a slaveowning merchant, and Margaret Kempe Howell. Varina Howell received an excellent education for a white woman of her era, attending an elite female academy in Philadelphia and studying at home in Mississippi with a private tutor. By the time she met her future husband, Jefferson Davis, at a Christmas party in 1843, she was an articulate, well-read, spirited young woman, hardly the stereotypical Southern belle.

Jefferson Davis was seventeen years her senior, very handsome, and very rich. He owned many slaves and a large plantation in Mississippi, and young Miss Howell found him attractive, despite what she called his arrogant demeanor. He seems to have been drawn to her youth, beauty, and wit; he was a lonely widower and ready to marry again. The couple fell in love, but had a stormy courtship. After several misunderstandings, they nonetheless became engaged and married in Natchez in February 1845.

The early years of the Davis marriage were not tranquil. The couple lived near Jefferson's brother, Joseph Emory Davis, who still controlled the disposition of most of the family's fortune, including Jefferson's property. Soon after her wedding, Varina Davis discovered that her brother-in-law had composed a will that prevented her from inheriting her husband's estate. When she protested this grievous inequity, her husband told her simply to accept the situation. She was wounded by his reaction, and almost as hurt when he left to fight in the Mexican-American War without informing her in advance. When Jefferson Davis came home in 1847, he was appointed to the United States Senate, but he was so angry with his wife that he left her in Mississippi for almost a year. He was a very traditional, conventional man, and he expected his wife to do as she was told.

Somehow the couple managed to make peace, and Varina Davis moved to Washington, D.C., where she lived for most of the next twelve years. She enjoyed life in the capital immensely and made many friends from both regions, including Mary Chesnut, the now-famous Civil War diarist whose husband was a senator from South Carolina. The Davis marriage became somewhat more harmonious. After years of childlessness, Varina Davis bore her first living child in 1852, and she later gave birth to five more children. She and her husband continued to differ over such household matters as travel and finances, and she had not forgiven Joseph Davis for cutting her out of the family fortune.

The secession crisis of 1860–1861 very much alarmed Varina Davis, for she did not want to leave Washington. Moreover, she confided to friends and family members that she did not believe that the South had the resources to fight and win a war. But when her husband became the Confederate president, she did her duty and went to Richmond with him. There she became a controversial figure, as some whites began to suspect she was not an enthusiastic Confederate patriot, and her witty, learned manner put off members of local society. In fact, her intelligence so alarmed some of her contemporaries that they claimed she secretly manipulated Jefferson Davis. The truth was she had little influence over her husband, who made his own political and military decisions, and she was relieved when the war ended, telling a woman friend that the last four years had been the worst years of her life.

Her troubles were far from over, however, for her husband was charged with treason and spent two years incarcerated at Fort Monroe, Virginia. When he was released in 1867, the family was at the brink of destitution. Jefferson Davis tried and failed to make a living with business ventures in England and the United States. He lost his only paying job, the presidency of an insurance company in Memphis, after it went bankrupt in 1873. The family lived off the quiet charitable donations of friends, plus Varina Davis's part-time work as a seamstress. As her husband aged, she gradually took over much of the management of the family's affairs. In the late 1870s, Jefferson Davis moved to a house on the Gulf Coast, Beauvoir, which had been given to him by a family friend. After he died in 1889, Varina Davis wrote a monumental and reverential memoir of her husband, much of which blatantly contradicted the reality of her married life.

The Confederate First Lady then astonished her contemporaries by moving to Manhattan, where she lived for the rest of her life. She tried with some success to build a literary career and placed some articles in the *New York World* and other publications. Just as she had in Washington, she made friends from all parts of the country, including the widowed Julia Dent Grant. When she died on 16 October 1906, Frederick Grant, son of the famous Civil War general, organized a memorial service in her honor in New York. She was buried in Hollywood Cemetery in Richmond beside her husband, having outlived five of her six children.

—*Joan E. Cashin*

See also Davis, Jefferson.

For further reading:
Cashin, Joan E. "Varina Howell Davis." In *Portraits of American Women: From Settlement to the Present*, G. J. Barker-Benfield and Catherine Clinton, eds. (1991).

DE BOW, JAMES DUNWOODY BROWNSON
(1820–1867)
Editor

James D. B. De Bow was born in Charleston, South Carolina, on 10 July 1820. His father, Garret De Bow, was a successful merchant in New York City before he relocated to South Carolina in the early 1800s. When Garret De Bow died in 1826, he left little to his wife and their four children. Young James had to help support his family from an early age. Hard work and good fortune led him to a job as a clerk in a wholesale grocery store. The position enabled De Bow to both save the required money and read the necessary books to attend the Cokesbury Institute, Abbeville District, South Carolina. A year later he enrolled in the College of Charleston, where he graduated in 1843 at the head of his class. While in college, De Bow first showed an interest in writing and publishing as he attempted to organize a campus periodical.

Upon graduation De Bow, like many ambitious Southern men of modest means, studied law. He read for a year and passed his bar examination, but found the actual practice of law to be a dreary affair. De Bow countered the tedium of his professional life by publishing several articles on economics, politics, and philosophy in the *Southern Quarterly Review*. The warm reception to his work and his own interest in the *Quarterly Review* led its editor, Daniel K. Whitaker, to enlist De Bow as a junior editor for the journal. By 1845 the now retired lawyer made a name for himself in the Charleston, South Carolina, business community by soliciting and writing essays on Southern commerce for the *Quarterly Review*. That year, De Bow became the logical choice to represent the city at the Southern commercial convention that was held at Memphis, Tennessee.

The Memphis convention was one of many such commercial meetings held in the antebellum South. At these meetings, business leaders discussed economic issues, particularly the tariff, slavery, and federal aid for internal improvements. Preparing for this convention and his subsequent experience in Memphis changed the course of De Bow's life. The heated, and often unin-formed, debates that he read and heard during the convention and elsewhere convinced the junior editor that his native South needed a regional magazine that would examine social and business issues. Friends and associates supported De Bow's new project, and in a matter of months the South Carolinian moved to New Orleans, the South's largest city, where he published the first number of the *Commercial Review of the South and Southwest* in January 1846. The magazine's title was soon condensed to *De Bow's Review*.

De Bow modeled the *Review* after *Hunt's Merchant's Magazine*, a commercial journal published in New York. The monthly magazine included articles on trade, commerce, and agriculture, with only an occasional essay on literary or philosophical subjects. The articles that De Bow wrote and solicited for publication in the *Review* highlighted the South's commercial strength and untapped potential. The South could overthrow the commercial domination of the North and Europe, according to De Bow, if it developed a mixed economy where regional manufacturing and banking could balance agricultural profits. An initial dearth of subscribers and the constant threat of bankruptcy made his task difficult, but the *Review* survived and soon De Bow became known for his professional ability and his fervent sectionalism. When not compiling statistics to bolster his economic arguments (in 1848 he was made head of the new Louisiana Bureau of Statistics), De Bow was busy defending Southern slavery against what he characterized as "crack-brained" abolitionism from the North. He ultimately concluded that the North threatened to stifle the Southern economy as well destroy its social order by limiting the expansion of African slavery. Indeed, like many white Southerners, he maintained that slavery suited the natural abilities of Africans and that the "peculiar institution" would be the vehicle by which the South would build an independent and fluid economy in the South. Interestingly, at the same time that De Bow began to earn a reputation as a fire-eating defender of slavery and Southern rights, he was appointed superintendent of the 1850 U.S. Census. Under his leadership, the census provided more detail than ever and solidified De Bow's growing reputation as one of the nation's leading statisticians.

De Bow continued to publish his *Review* and attend Southern commercial conventions throughout the 1850s. He also found time to organize a course of economic and commercial instruction to be included in the curriculum at the University of Louisiana at New Orleans. Over the course of the decade, his calls for Southern secession grew in frequency and intensity. After Abraham Lincoln's election, the quick secession of his adopted state, Louisiana, on 26 January 1861, met with his hearty approval.

Once the Civil War erupted, De Bow obtained a position in the new Confederate government as its chief agent for the purchase and sale of cotton. Like many Southerners, De Bow expected that the world demand for cotton would break the Northern blockade and guarantee Southern independence. When foreign intervention was not forthcoming and his adopted hometown of New Orleans fell to Union forces in 1862, a crushed De Bow removed his wife and children to Winnsboro, South Carolina, where they found refuge with family. By August 1862, wartime conditions forced De Bow to suspend publication of his *Review*, which had been printed intermittently since 1860. In 1864 he did issue one last edition of *De Bow's Review* in which he attempted to rally Southerners behind the embattled Confederacy, but De Bow's powerful rhetoric and desperate support to the beleaguered Confederacy could not prevent Union victory.

De Bow and his family remained in the South after the war. De Bow obtained a pardon from President Andrew Johnson for his wartime activities and in 1866 revived the publication of the *Review* from his new home in Nashville, Tennessee. The magazine continued to promote the spread of industrial development, increased trade, and modern agricultural techniques across the South. At the same time, De Bow continued to effect Southern commercial development as president of the Tennessee Pacific Railroad Company.

Before he could help shape the face of the New South, he died of pleurisy in Elizabeth, New Jersey, while visiting his brother. He had married Caroline Poe, of Georgetown, District of Columbia, in 1854. After her death, De Bow married Martha E. Johns in 1860 and she and three children survived him.

—*Frank J. Byrne*

See also *De Bow's Review*.
For further reading:

Hall, Mark "The Proslavery Thought of J. D. B. De Bow: A Practical Man's Guide to Economics." *Southern Studies* (1982).
McMillen, James Adelbert, ed. *The Works of James D. B. De Bow* (1940).
Paskoff, Paul F., and Daniel J. Wilson, eds. *The Cause of the South: Selections from De Bow's Review, 1846–1867* (1982).
Skipper, Ottis Clark. *J. D. B. De Bow: Magazinist of the Old South* (1958).
Walther, Eric H. *The Fire-Eaters* (1992).

DE BOW'S REVIEW
(January 1846–July 1879)

De Bow's Review was a monthly Southern journal published in New Orleans, Louisiana, and owned and edited by the Southern nationalist James D. B. De Bow (1820–1867). The journal went by a variety of names during its lifetime but the economic, social, and political views found in the *Review* and espoused by its editor remained relatively constant. De Bow employed the *Review* to defend both the South and its controversial institution, slavery, against Northern criticism and, more fundamentally, to encourage Southerners to embrace greater commercial and industrial development.

Despite the growing sectional tone of the *Review* during the late antebellum period, De Bow retained a measure of economic nationalism. Articles he wrote and solicited from others typically supported a protective tariff for U.S. industry and federal aid for internal improvements. De Bow also encouraged farmers, particularly Southerners, to adopt the latest innovations in agricultural science. An innovative statistician, he employed data to show that the South had a vibrant economy that could, if properly developed, out-produce the North. Like many defenders of the South's "peculiar institution," De Bow believed that a slave society could compete with any in an industrial age.

De Bow's Review quickly achieved a national reputation in the antebellum United States. Many Southerners embraced the journal's defense of their region while Northern business leaders acknowledged De Bow's professionalism and the strength of his statistic-laden essays. Despite the growing influence of the *Review*, De Bow occasionally struggled to keep the journal solvent. The reading public for economic journals, particularly in the South, remained small. The secession crisis and the outbreak of the Civil War interrupted De Bow's work on the *Review* and eventually forced him to suspend its publication in 1864 for the remainder of the war. After the war, De Bow revived the *Review* with a new headquarters in Nashville, Tennessee. The resurrected journal continued to promote commerce, manufacturing, and modern agricultural techniques, albeit from a national rather than sectional perspective.

Before the *Review* could begin to shape the New South, De Bow died on 27 February 1867. His spouse and associates continued to publish the *Review*, but the journal struggled to keep an identity and attract subscribers without the intellect and passion of its founder. De Bow's family sold the *Review* in March 1868, and its new owners soon suspended publication in 1870. Under yet another owner, the journal finally died in 1879.

—*Frank J. Byrne*

See also De Bow, James Dunwoody Brownson.
For further reading:

Hall, Mark "The Proslavery Thought of J. D. B. De Bow: A Practical Man's Guide to Economics." *Southern Studies* (1982).
McMillen, James Adelbert, ed. *The Works of James D .B. De Bow* (1940).
Paskoff, Paul F., and Daniel J. Wilson, eds. *The Cause of the South: Selections from De Bow's Review, 1846–1867* (1982).
Skipper, Ottis Clark. *J. D. B. De Bow: Magazinist of the Old South* (1958).
Walther, Eric H. *The Fire-Eaters* (1992).

DE BRAY, XAVIER BLANCHARD
(1818–1897)
Confederate cavalry commander and staff officer

Xavier Blanchard, the son of an Imperial préfet, was born in the city of Epinal in Eastern France in 1818. Little is known of his early years. Some sources mention that he was a graduate of Saint Cyr and a French diplomat, but no evidence of this can be found. He seem to have emigrated to America in 1848, possibly in the aftermath of the Revolution, which toppled the last French monarch. He settled in San Antonio, Texas, where, under the name of De Bray, one common in the Normandy region of France, he published the Spanish-language newspaper El Bajanero. In 1855, he moved to Austin to interpret on behalf of the Texas General Land Office, and a year later opened a school in the same town. It was to last until 1861.

At the outbreak of the war, De Bray espoused enthusiastically the Confederate cause, first joining the 4th Texas Infantry and then the 2d Texas Infantry. He also briefly served as aide-de-camp to Texas governor Francis R. Lubbock, and then he joined the 26th Texas Cavalry regiment, whose colonelcy he received in December 1861. The regiment, characterized by its French-inspired uniform, became known as De Bray's Mounted Riflemen (and less officially as the "Menagerie").

In July 1862, De Bray was appointed commander of the Eastern District of Texas headquartered in Houston. In his capacity as staff officer, he efficiently seconded General John Magruder during the recapture of Galveston on 1 January 1863. De Bray continued active service as a cavalry officer during Nathaniel Banks's invasion of the Red River area of Louisiana in the spring of 1864. He participated in the battles of Mansfield and Pleasant Hill, where he crossed paths with another French-born Confederate, Camille de Polignac. For his courage under fire, De Bray was appointed brigadier general by Edmund Kirby Smith in April 1864, but it appears that the nomination was never confirmed by the Confederate administration. De Bray's brigade was credited for maintaining order in Houston at war's end.

Discharged on 24 May 1865, De Bray settled in Houston where he worked as accountant, journalist, and translator. He was naturalized in 1867, and he returned to the General Land Office and Austin in 1875. De Bray died of old age in 1897, one of the most respected citizens of the city.

—*Laurent Ditmann*

See also Magruder, John Bankhead; Red River Campaign.
For further reading:
Franklin, Robert Morris. *Battle of Galveston, January 1, 1863* (1975).
Henderson, Harry McCorry. *Texas in the Confederacy* (1967).
Lonn, Ella. *Foreigners in the Confederacy* (1965).

DE FOREST, JOHN WILLIAM
(1826–1906)
Northern novelist

Born in Humphreysville, Connecticut, in 1826, William De Forest was a widely traveled man with years of experience in Europe and the Middle East. When the Civil War broke out, he had published books on travel, history (*History of the Indians in Connecticut*, 1851), and novels (*Witching Times*, 1856, and *Seacliff*, 1859). De Forest was in Charleston, South Carolina, with his wife and son on the eve of the war but left for the North before the outbreak of hostilities. Shocked by the Union defeat at Bull Run, he started to raise a company, but it filled slowly and he was mustered into Federal service as captain of Company I, 12th Connecticut Volunteer Infantry, on 1 January 1862. His regiment saw service in Louisiana (1862–1864), including the siege of Port Hudson, and in the Eastern theater of the war in the campaign against Jubal Early in 1864, including the battle of Cedar Creek. De Forest was discharged 2 December 1864 but was recommissioned in the Veteran Corps in February 1865, although he appears to have considered applying for a position in a United States Colored Troops regiment. Brevetted to major, he served with the Freedmen's Bureau in South Carolina until January 1868.

Already during his time in Louisiana, De Forest had started taking notes for several pieces of prose and a novel. The first of the prose tales, entitled "The First Time Under Fire," appeared in *Harpers New Monthly Magazine*. Others followed, and in 1867 De Forest published what was to become his most important contribution to American literature, the novel *Miss Ravenel's Conversion from Secession to Loyalty*. Originally the story was designed for newspaper serialization, but the publishers decided on very short notice to present it as a book. The hasty decision meant that nobody corrected the printer's proofs, so printing errors riddle the original edition. Though reviewers greeted the novel warmly, the public did not embrace it, and it was not reprinted until 1939. The novel's failure was partly due to lack of enthusiasm even in 1867 for Civil War novels with a Union viewpoint, but possibly De Forest's modern style also struck readers as eccentric. Having been under fire in several engagements, he strove for ways to translate his experiences into his writing. He claimed never to have written the complete reality of what he had seen, but his portrayal of battlefield death as senseless was uncommon for an age that glorified heroism in war. In some scenes, he describes battle in burlesque form.

Such a mixture of conventional and experimental methods makes *Miss Ravenel's Conversion* an uneven work. De Forest's characters more resemble Thackeray's than those usually associated with literary realism, and they serve symbolic and didactic purposes beyond their functions in the story. Colonel Carter and Mrs. Larue symbolize the romantic, yet decadent and ultimately moribund Old South. Dr. Ravenel represents the small group of pro-Union southern intellectuals. Major Gazaway is the typical political appointee who was inept and cowardly yet enjoyed influential connections. Such people existed on both sides, but they became a literary type only in the North in the novels of Mumford, De Forest, and others. The main character, Captain Edward Colburne, whose experiences echo those of the author, is the typical Yankee—stubborn, upright, yet not very colorful and definitely unsentimental. Lillie Ravenel symbolizes the redeemable New South that has to go through the war and the pain of loss to be reconciled with the Yankee.

The topic of reunion continued to dominate De Forest's later fiction, but the optimistic view evinced in the metaphor of Colburne and Lillie Ravenel's union required the war as a driving force. Hence, the connection between experience and moral progress that is the center of *Miss Ravenel's Conversion* is an awkward artifice in the later political novels, such as *Kate Beaumont* (1871), *Honest John Vane* (1875), and *The Bloody Chasm* (1881). Two collections related to the Civil War and Reconstruction (*A Volunteer's Adventures* and *A Union Officer in the Reconstruction*) were edited for publication only after World War II. Until then, De Forest's literary reputation rested largely on William Dean Howells's statement that De Forest wrote "realism" before the term *realism* had been coined. He died in New Haven, Connecticut, in 1906.

— *Wolfgang Hochbruck*

For further reading:
De Forest, John W. *Miss Ravenel's Conversion from Secession to Loyalty* (1956).
———. *A Union Officer in the Reconstruction*, J. Croushore, ed. (1948; reprint, 1997).
———.*A Volunteer's Adventures*, J. Croushore, ed. (1946).
Fick, Thomas H. "Genre Wars and the Rhetoric of Manhood in *Miss Ravenel's Conversion from Secession to Loyalty*." *Nineteenth Century Literature* (1991).
Fluck, Winfried. *Inszenierte Wirklichkeit. Der Amerikanische Realismus 1865–1900* (1992).
Gargano, James W. *Critical Essays on John William De Forest* (1981).
Light, James F. *John William De Forest* (1965).

DE LEON, EDWIN
(1818–1891)
Confederate diplomat

Born to Mardici Heimrich De Leon and Rebecca Lopez-y-Nuñez De Leon in Columbia, South Carolina, Edwin De Leon was educated at South Carolina College and upon graduation studied law.

Preferring journalism to the law, however, beginning in 1841, De Leon began a long newspaper career. Over the next thirteen years he served stints as the editor of the Savannah *Republican*, the Columbia *Telegraph*, and the Washington, D.C.–based *Southern Press*. During that time De Leon was also active in southern Democratic politics and became an active supporter of southern rights.

In 1854, De Leon left the country, accepting the post of U.S. consul general to Egypt. He remained in Egypt until the secession of South Carolina. He returned home to offer his diplomatic experience to the C.S.A. In the spring of 1862 he received an appointment as a Confederate agent to Europe and ran the blockade to the Bahamas and then to Great Britain.

Arriving in England at the end of June 1862, De Leon immediately arranged a private meeting with British prime minister Lord Palmerston. At that time, not knowing the outcome of the Peninsula campaign, Palmerston seemed convinced that the Confederacy was near military collapse. De Leon tried to convince him that the Confederate Army was on the verge of significant military victories. De Leon reported to the Confederate government that Palmerston asked many questions but, because of the recent federal capture of New Orleans and the blockade of southern coasts, he seemed strongly disinclined to recognize the Confederacy. De Leon believed that decisive Confederate victories could change Palmerston's mind, but he doubted that the British would ever be much help and that Palmerston would probably try to persuade the French not to become involved either. For that reason, De Leon decided to quietly travel to France to begin talks with that government before Palmerston could act. Before he left Great Britain, however, De Leon planted stories in the British press lauding the southern cause and exaggerating Confederate military successes.

In France, De Leon initially settled in Vichy before eventually making his headquarters in Paris. He worked diligently through the summer of 1862 making contacts at the French court, hoping to gain an audience and eventual influence in the French government. He believed that the Confederacy had a much better chance of gaining substantial aid from France and advised the government that the appearance of financial solvency would help the cause. For that reason he suggested that large amounts of cotton be sent to Europe to establish the credit of the new nation so that its agents could better negotiate the purchase of war materiel for shipment home. By the fall, however, he had to recognize that the slavery issue was a serious impediment to French recognition.

For the next two years he continued work toward not only official British and French aid for the Confederacy, using diplomacy and propaganda carefully placed in British and French newspapers, but also used his own money on occasion to purchase and arrange shipment of supplies and war materiel for the Confederacy. Often he would escort the supplies himself through the blockade and then return to Europe after conferring with government officials, especially his friend Jefferson Davis.

In Europe, De Leon often clashed with other Confederate diplomats, particularly John Slidell in France, over the best possible course to obtaining foreign aid. He also became increasingly frustrated with the French government and what he viewed as its subservient position to the British. This frustration apparently led him to rashly criticize the French government in early 1864, ending any official contact for the remainder of the war. He remained in France, however, and traveled throughout Europe obtaining what supplies he could until the war ended.

After the war, De Leon remained in Europe and also lived for a while in Egypt. He wrote extensively about his travels, publishing several books about his adventures. He returned to the United States briefly in 1879 but, restless for his former life, returned to Egypt for a visit two years later. Returning to the United States, he spent his final days in New York City, where he died on 1 December 1891.

—*David S. Heidler and Jeanne T. Heidler*

See also Diplomacy, C.S.A.
For further reading:
Cullop, Charles P. "Edwin De Leon, Jefferson Davis' Propagandist." *Civil War History* (1962).

DE TROBRIAND, REGIS
(1816–1897)
Union general

Philippe Regis Denis Keredern de Trobriand, born near Tours, France, was the son and nephew of two French generals. As the son of a baron-general, the young Regis had among his playmates the Duc de Bordeaux, later Charles X, the king of France. Privately tutored during his early years, De Trobriand eventually graduated from the College of Tours (part of the Universite of Orleans) in 1834 with a bachelor bel lettres. Seven years later, based on a dare from a close friend, he boarded a sailing ship to America in search of "adventure and travel." While in New York he began writing for a French-American newspaper and later met Mary Jones, whose father Isaac was president of the Chemical Bank and whose mother was a leading socialite. They married in Paris in January 1843, where both the minister of war, the Duke of Chermon de Tonnere, and his deputy, the Marquis de la Rochejacqeln attended.

After several years abroad, the couple returned to New York, where de Trobriand became the editor of a French-American newspaper and continued his writing and painting. It was during this period that de Trobriand made numerous political contacts that later proved instrumental in obtaining command of a New York regiment and his promotions to brevet brigadier and major general in the latter part of the Civil War.

In spring 1861, now determined to make America his homeland, de Trobriand filed for citizenship. In August the governor offered him the colonelcy of the 55th New York Regiment—the Lafayette Guards appropriately composed mainly of French émigrés. De Trobriand engaged his first enemy action in the Peninsula campaign. After Fredericksburg, the 55th New York consolidated with the 38th New York under the command of de Trobriand and fought at Chancellorsville. The 38th participated in a night counterattack that slowed down Stonewall Jackson's famous flank attack. At Gettysburg, de Trobriand served as the 3d Brigade commander (1st Division, III Corps) and on 2 July 1863 held a wooded hill against heavy Confederate attack with two of his regiments (the 5th Michigan and 110th Pennsylvania). Following this action, de Trobriand joined the 17th Maine at the wheatfield left of the hill and drove the Confederates back to a nearby stone wall. His brigade lost over one-third of its strength on that day alone.

In 1864, de Trobriand served as the commander of New York City's defenses and then was given command of the 1st Brigade (3d Division, II Corps). By April 1865, he had been breveted to the ranks of brigadier and major general (U.S. Volunteers), and given command of the 3d division of II Corps of the Army of the Potomac. Besides de Trobriand, the only other Frenchman to obtain the rank of major general in the U.S. Army was the American Revolutionary war hero, the Marquis De Lafayette.

A year after the war, de Trobriand interviewed for a regular officer position, and then returned to France to write his memoirs of the wars. The book, *Quatre Ans de Campagnes a l'Armee of the Potomac*, published in 1866, was one of the first works written by a ranking general about the war. It was translated into English in 1867 and received praise from the likes of Ulysses S. Grant, William T. Sherman, and Phillip Sheridan—although given Sheridan's dislike of books, it is unlikely that he ever read it. While writing the work, de Trobriand received a letter from the War Department tendering him a regular commission and a colonelcy in the 31st Infantry. Later appointed as the regimental commander of the 13th Infantry, he served in Montana and the Dakotas performing Indian pacification duty, and in Utah and New Orleans during Reconstruction. He retired in 1874 from the U.S. Army. He died on 13 July 1897 at Bayport, Long Island, New York.

—*Mark R. Grandstaff*

For further reading:
Grandstaff, Mark R. "General Regis De Trobriand, The Mormons, and the U.S. Army at Camp Douglas, 1870–1871." *Utah Historical Quarterly* (1996).
Post, Marie Caroline de Trobriand. *The Life and Mémoirs of Comte Régis De Trobriand, Major-General in the Army of the United States* (1910).
Trobriand, Régis de. *Four Years with the Army of the Potomac.* Translated by George K. Douchy (1889).
Trobriand, Régis de. *Army Life in Dakota, Selections From the Journal of Philippe Régis Denis De Keredern De Trobriand.* Edited by Milo Milton Quaife, and translated by George F. Will (1941).

DECORATIONS

At the start of the Civil War, neither the Union nor the Confederate armies had any provision for rewarding battlefield valor with individual decorations. Enlisted men might be mentioned in dispatches or otherwise personally commended by their commanding officers, and officers might additionally be given brevet promotions, but there was no structured system for rewarding personal courage. The reason for the lack of this type of reward was that many officers, including the U.S. Army general-in-chief Lieutenant General Winfield Scott, believed that the awarding of decorations ran contrary to the spirit of a democratic army. Those sentiments were not universally accepted, especially by foreign-born officers who had served in armies in which the awarding of decorations was quite commonplace.

During the war, the Confederacy took steps to award decorations for bravery. Since the Confederacy lacked the resources to produce such decorations, however, they were never awarded. Instead, the Confederate Congress passed a law calling for the publication of a "Roll of Honor" following each battle that would list the names of individuals who were cited for personal valor. In addition, Confederate soldiers could be voted the "Thanks of the Confederate Congress" for personal distinction.

The Union also awarded the "Thanks of Congress" for extraordinary military achievement, but, as in the Confederacy, this was usually an honor reserved for generals and admirals. The lack of any reward for enlisted men was remedied when Senator James Grimes of Iowa introduced a bill in the U.S. Senate to help promote naval efficiency. When the bill was signed into law by President Abraham Lincoln on 21 December 1861, it established a "medal of honor" that was to be awarded to U.S. Navy and Marine Corps enlisted men for "… gallantry in action or other seamanlike qualities during the present war." On 17 February 1862, the award of the Medal of Honor was extended to army enlisted men, and this was followed by army officers on 3 March 1863. Interestingly, navy and marine officers did not become eligible for the Medal of Honor until 3 March 1915. The

Medal of Honor would remain the only national award for valor during the Civil War, although several states minted their own decorations for valor. After the war, many of the states minted and awarded campaign medals as a reward for service with that state's volunteer or militia forces. In addition, numerous veterans' organizations, both Union and Confederate, issued medals to veterans for their service. The first national campaign medals to be issued for service in the Civil War, however, were not made available until 1907 for army veterans and 1908 for navy and marine veterans.

—*Alexander M. Bielakowski*

See also Medal of Honor.
For further reading:
Borthick, David, and Jack Britton. *Medals, Military and Civilian, of the United States* (1984).
Foster, Colonel Frank C., and Lawrence H. Borts. *U.S. Military Medals, 1939–1994* (1994).
Kerrigan, Evans. *American Medals and Decorations* (1990).

DEEP BOTTOM RUN/STRAWBERRY PLAINS, VIRGINIA, SECOND BATTLE OF
(13–20 August 1864)

Between 8 and 11 August 1864, General Ulysses S. Grant, the commander of all Union forces arrayed against the South, concluded that the Confederate Army of Northern Virginia was transferring a number of infantry divisions and at least one cavalry division from the front at Petersburg, Virginia, to the Shenandoah Valley. Once there, they would link with Jubal Early's Valley Army, which had since June of that year been rampaging up and down the valley in Virginia, defeating a number of Federal forces in that area, raiding into Pennsylvania, and even threatening the Union capital at Washington, D.C. Grant was determined to prevent this new concentration of rebel force.

Acting on false and exaggerated reports that the detachment going to the valley had left Robert E. Lee's defenses north of the James River, in the vicinity of Deep Bottom Run (about ten miles southeast of Richmond) thinly manned with only 5,000 Confederates, Grant ordered his X and II Infantry Corps—under Generals David B. Birney and Winfield S. Hancock, respectively—to attack the supposedly weakened Southern position. The 2d Cavalry Division under Brigadier General David M. Gregg would also take part in the assault. Major General Hancock was put in charge of the operation. The move across the river was to start on the evening of 13 August.

First, all the Federal troops designated for the attack had to be transported from below the James River to its north shore to the area of Strawberry Plains and Bailey's Creek. This was accomplished by having Hancock's infantry travel by water transport first to City Point and then to

Deep Bottom Run. In the meantime, Birney's command, along with the II Corps' artillery and Gregg's horsemen crossed over the James on two pontoon bridges, the former above Deep Bottom Run, the latter below. Due to straggling by the troops crossing over the bridges and problems offloading the men from the steamers, the Federals of X Corps did not get to the north bank of the James until early on the morning of the 14th, with the II Corps troops not arriving until close to 8:00 A.M. on that day.

Once over the James, Hancock planned to drive the enemy from their strong defenses behind Bailey's Creek by turning the graybacks' left. X Corps would operate to the west of Deep Bottom Run, while II Corps would press north and to the right along Bailey's Creek. Cavalryman Gregg was ordered to move to the Union far right and seek an opening for a dash to the Weldon Railroad or to Richmond. Hancock's plan immediately fell apart.

Unfortunately for the Federals, none of the Confederates had left the area north of the James River and southeast of Richmond. Seven thousand members of the Army of Northern Virginia (in seven brigades) were in place, occupying good entrenched positions covering the four-mile stretch of land that was the Union forces' objective. Confederate cavalry screened their left. As a result, Hancock's piecemeal attacks throughout the 14th failed to dent the Confederate lines. By the day's end, the Union force of over 10,000 had sustained 500 casualties, while the rebels lost about half that number.

For the 15th, Hancock planned to run Birney's corps to the north (the Confederate left) and attack that flank; or, if he could not find their flank, find a suitable place to strike them. Birney's maneuvering on the 15th resulted in some skirmishing on the Charles City Road, but no large-scale strike against the Confederate lines was attempted before nightfall. Frustrated by the day's events, or lack thereof, Hancock determined to assault the enemy between the Charles City Road and Darbytown Road with X Corps the next day.

By noon on 16 August, Birney's command had broken through the Confederate position near Fussell's Mill along the Darbytown Road, but lack of troops to exploit this success allowed the Southerners to counterattack and restore their broken line. The Union lost 2,000 men, including 500 taken prisoner; the South lost about 1,000, including 300 captured.

No fighting occurred on the 17th, and not until near dark on the 18th was combat resumed. At that time, the Confederates hit Hancock's right with the intention of using their cavalry to drive the enemy from the Charles City Road, and then throwing in their infantry to roll up the entire Federal line. The end of the day found the Confederate cavalry mostly stalled in their efforts to push the Union forces back. Their supporting infantry found the enemy positions too formidable to storm, and they withdrew back to their camps after a brief firefight.

There was no fighting north of the James on 19 and 20 August. On the night of the latter, pursuant to Grant's orders, Hancock withdrew his command across the river, with II Corps and the cavalry going to Petersburg, and X Corps to Bermuda Hundred. The second battle of Deep Bottom Run had ended.

The seven-day contest north of the James River during mid-August 1864 cost the North 2,901 killed and wounded, including 721 taken prisoner. The opposing side lost 1,500 men, 400 of these having been captured.

The battle had not delivered Richmond to the Federals or broken the Weldon rail line, but it did prevent the reinforcement of the Valley Army with Field's infantry and Buffer's cavalry divisions, as well as diverting other Confederate units from the Petersburg and Howlett lines to Deep Bottom Run.

—Arnold D. Blumberg

See also Gregg, David McMurtrie; Hancock, Winfield Scott.
For further reading:

Beale, George W. *A Lieutenant of Cavalry in Lee's Army* (1918).
Horn, John. *The Destruction of the Weldon Railroad: Deep Bottom, Globe Tavern, and Reams Station* (1991).
———. *The Petersburg Campaign, June 1864–April 1865.* (1993).
Molar, James C., ed. *The Cormany Diaries: A Northern Family in the Civil War* (1982).
Trudeau, Noah Andre. *The Last Citadel: Petersburg, Virginia, June 1864–April 1865* (1991).

DEMOCRATIC PARTY

Democrats were the opposition party during the Civil War and the principal channel through which resistance to the Lincoln administration's wartime policies flowed.

The sectional crisis and controversy over immigration (which had led to the formation of an American Party) had weakened the once-powerful Democratic Party in the North in the decade before the Civil War. Even combining the votes of its two sectional presidential candidates in 1860, John C. Breckinridge and Stephen A. Douglas, the Democrats won only 46.6 percent of the electorate in the nonseceding states. They were especially weak in the upper North—the New England states and areas of New England settlement. Elsewhere they were competitive only under favorable circumstances. Strong partisanship among the electorate ensured that the Democrats would neither depart from their minority status during the war nor crumble under persistent Republican accusations of treason.

Northern Democrats had consistently celebrated their party's nationalism. Their devotion to states' rights and strict construction of the Constitution, they felt, offered the firmest basis for a perpetual Union in a diverse country. They viewed Republicans as sectional particularists, devoted to special interest groups such as manufacturers or abolitionists rather than the nation as a whole. Instead of listening to the people (understood by Democrats to include only white males), Republicans preferred to impose their radical ideas (which Democrats insisted included abolition, liquor control, and women's rights) on others through an activist government. Democrats believed the secession of the southern states to be unconstitutional but caused by legitimate fears of Republicans. Thus, they favored compromise and reassurances to the South, rather than coercion, as a means to handle the secession crisis.

The Confederate firing on Fort Sumter, however, seemed to most northern Democrats an open rejection of compromise that justified a resort to force. Led by Stephen A. Douglas, they enthusiastically supported Lincoln's call to arms. Eight Democratic congressmen and innumerable lesser party leaders were in the field by the summer of 1861. Democrats enlisted much more readily than had Federalists in the War of 1812 or Whigs in the Mexican-American War. As a unifying gesture, Republicans called for a period of no-partyism. Lincoln appointed prominent Democrats, such as Edwin Stanton as secretary of war, to posts in his administration. In some states, Republicans and Democrats ran joint "union" tickets for state offices in the fall elections of 1861.

Even when bipartisanship was at its height, however, many Democrats felt it important to retain their separate identity. They distinguished between their support for the government and for the Republicans who administered it. They feared that Republicans left unopposed might extend war aims beyond restoration of the Union or use unconstitutional means to carry on the conflict. Early moves to retain "contraband" slaves and arrest border state citizens on suspicion of treason confirmed such fears.

Some Democrats, however, such as former party stalwarts Daniel S. Dickinson, John A. Dix, and David Tod, who believed the only way to support the nation was to support its current leaders fully, became War Democrats. Separating completely from the Democratic Party organization and supporting all Republican policies, they in effect became Republicans. Most held prominent positions during the war, denounced their former allies, and never resumed their Democratic loyalties.

Most Democrats, however, as their initial enthusiasm waned, preferred to consider themselves a loyal opposition. In the 37th Congress (where northern Democrats held only 44 of 178 House and 14 of 48 Senate seats), they supported raising and funding the army and navy but held firmly to ideas of limited warfare. For them, victory and the restoration of the Union depended on defeating the Confederate armies, not destroying the South's social system. Indeed, they felt that trying to do so would only increase Confederate resistance, prolong the conflict, and create such bitterness that a shared future with the South would be impossible. They suspected Republicans of taking this risk to justify their own extension of power over their political opponents. Democrats saw the suspension of the writ of habeas corpus, seizing of newspapers, and military arrests of civilians as particularly alarming and believed that the Republicans—with their insistence on emancipation, African-American soldiers, and conscription of white men—were intent on revolutionizing the country and its institutions. They stubbornly expected the electorate to rally against such policies, restore the Democrats to power, and set the stage for war-weary Confederates to return to a no-longer-threatening federal union.

The Democrats' strongest bid to return to power came in 1862. In the aftermath of Lincoln's release of the preliminary Emancipation Proclamation, the party gained 35 seats in Congress, won the governorships of New York and New Jersey as well as the legislatures of Illinois and Indiana, and in general won races or showed greater strength across the lower North. Reflecting their constituents' anger at Republican policies, some Democratic legislators introduced bills that if passed would have withdrawn state troops from the war or halted taxes and bond issues needed to supply volunteers. The New Jersey legislature passed resolutions in March 1863 suggesting the futility of the war and calling for the appointment of peace commissioners. The strongest voice for peace through negotiation was that of former congressman Clement L. Vallandigham of Ohio, who was also a resolute critic of Republican war measures, especially conscription. Exploiting racial hostilities, Vallandigham never failed to contrast the willingness of Republicans to arrest white men or force them into the army and their horror at enslavement of African-Americans.

Ironically, the peace movement encouraged Confederates, strengthened the Republican Party, and divided Democrats. Confederate newspapers enthusiastically reported any hopeful sign of northern defeatism. Intending to foment sabotage and arson as well as organize prisoner-of-war escapes, Confederate agents in Canada secretly distributed several hundred thousand dollars to Midwestern Democrats. But Confederate-sponsored plots to free Confederate prisoners at Camp Douglas and Johnson's Island came to naught, and no Democrats rushed to help John Hunt Morgan's raiders as they crossed southern Ohio in 1863. Most Democrats, even when spending Confederate gold, saw themselves as militant defenders of the U.S. Constitution, not as agents for its overthrow. Even in wartime they intended to fight with ballots, not bullets.

Nevertheless, the existence of a peace movement enabled Republicans to make Democratic actions rather than their own the focus of controversy. Republicans blamed New York City's bloody draft riots in July 1863 on the state's allegedly pro-Confederate Democratic

governor, who had addressed the mob with the words, "my friends." Using paid informers, Republicans exposed alleged pro-Confederate plots by secret organizations whom they linked to the Democratic Party. Shadowy political groups such as the Knights of the Golden Circle, the Order of American Knights, and the Sons of Liberty (headed by Vallandigham and resembling its rival the Republican Union Leagues) did exist, but they were far weaker and less significant than Republicans claimed. Most true Confederate sympathizers had family or economic ties that linked them to the South; they were rarely motivated by Democratic partisanship.

For Republicans, treasonous plotting could simultaneously explain the slow progress of the war and the need for measures such as arbitrary arrests and conscription (to counteract Democratic-induced desertions). The arrest of Clement L. Vallandigham by military authorities and his subsequent exile to the Confederacy visibly linked active dissent and Confederate leanings. Claiming they could not cooperate with treasonous legislatures, Republican governors Richard Yates of Illinois and Oliver P. Morton of Indiana managed their states without them. Republicans also exploited apparent Democratic defeatism to curry favor with soldiers, working to pass state laws permitting voting in the field for the 1864 presidential election. In that election, 78 percent of the soldiers cast Republican ballots, compared to 53 percent of the population at large. Believing their critics were traitors undoubtedly strengthened Republican resolve to support such controversial measures as emancipation and confiscation.

As Republicans bitterly accused the Democrats of treason to the nation, the Democratic Party factionalized. As a minority party the Democrats needed to draw support from constitutional conservatives in the Republican Party or from former Whigs, now Unionists, in the border states to win. Charges of treason, however, immobilized potential converts. Overly optimistic after their improved showing in 1862, several state parties nominated Peace Democrats for major offices in 1863, including Clement Vallandigham, who ran for Ohio governor while living in Canada after his political exile. Demonstrating the disastrous possibilities of the loyalty issue, Vallandigham was crushingly defeated; Democrats won no statewide races anywhere in the North in 1863.

Certain that the party needed to neutralize the treason charges to win in 1864, a faction led principally by such New York Democrats as Samuel J. Tilden and August Belmont promoted the choice of a presidential nominee in 1864 whose patriotism could not be questioned. The convention in Chicago nominated the former commander of the Army of the Potomac, George B. McClellan, on the first ballot. To ensure party harmony, however, the platform contained concessions to the peace faction. Traditional Democratic issues relating to territorial expansion and economic policy

were ignored to focus on the Republicans' alleged constitutional usurpations. A peace plank, written by Vallandigham, called for a convention with the Confederacy to establish peace on the basis of a restoration of the union. The ambiguity of this plank—whether or not Democrats intended to stop fighting while they negotiated—played into Republican hands throughout the campaign. Democrats tried to counter by emphasizing racial fears aroused by emancipation, but in the end, McClellan won only three states and 45 percent of the vote. The party lost 38 seats in the House.

While Democrats remained a minority throughout the war, they did not lose ground as they had in the 1850s and they did force Republicans to defend their wartime policies. If Republicans could not satisfy their Democratic critics, the presence of a large, hostile Democratic bloc required them to please conservatives in their own ranks who might otherwise have acted with the Democrats. Thus, the Democrats indirectly had influence. As the war ended, they looked forward to the likelihood of returning to power when the southern states were again represented in Washington and hence favored a generous peace and quick return of home rule. Indeed, it was just this scenario that Republicans feared. The bitter partisanship of the war was destined to continue into Reconstruction, and themes related to the war would continue to echo in partisan rhetoric for the next generation.

—*Phyllis F. Field*

See also American Party; Dickinson, Daniel S.; Dix, John Adams; Douglas, Stephen A.; Knights of the Golden Circle; Order of American Knights; Peace Democrats; Peace Movements; Sons of Liberty; Tilden, Samuel J.; Tod, David; Vallandigham, Clement L.; War Democrats.

For further reading:

Baker, Jean H. *Affairs of Party: The Political Culture of Northern Democrats in the Mid-Nineteenth Century* (1983).

Curry, Leonard P. "Congressional Democrats: 1861–1863." *Civil War History* (1966).

Klement, Frank L. *Dark Lanterns: Secret Political Societies, Conspiracies, and Treason Trials in the Civil War* (1984).

Silbey, Joel H. "A Respectable Minority": *The Democratic Party in the Civil War Era, 1860–1868* (1977).

DENNISON, WILLIAM
(1815–1882)
Governor of Ohio; U.S. postmaster general

Born to William Dennison and Mary Carter Dennison in Cincinnati, Ohio, the younger William Dennison was educated at Miami University. After graduation he studied law and began a practice in Cincinnati. Along with the law, Dennison became interested in Ohio Whig politics. Early in his political career, Dennison strongly opposed the extension of slavery in the United States, making his first public pronouncement on the issue regarding the annex-

ation of Texas in 1844. In 1848 he was elected to the Ohio state senate. Dennison became a Republican shortly after that party was formed and served as a delegate to the party's national convention in 1856.

In 1859 Dennison received the state Republican Party nomination for governor and won the election. He began his two-year term in early 1860. In a state with a large Democratic population and a fairly large number of Southern sympathizers, Dennison began his term during the most serious and final phase of the sectional crisis.

At the outbreak of the Civil War, Dennison enthusiastically prepared his state for war. He worked tirelessly to raise the state's quota of volunteers and to anticipate the requirements that would be made of the state's transportation system. He also used state funds and those sent to the state by the federal government without consulting the state legislature. Dennison's rapid efforts to place Ohio on a war footing, as well as what some viewed as his highhanded methods regarding the funding of his preparations, gained him many critics. Opponents of the war naturally found his methods objectionable, but even moderates would have preferred a more systematic and democratic approach, especially to the issue of funding.

Criticism did not slow Dennison's labors, however. He feared that Ohio's proximity to slaveholding states across the Ohio River made the state more vulnerable to invasion than were most Northern states. Therefore, he believed that rapid mobilization, even if some sensibilities were offended, was necessary for Ohio. To facilitate this mobilization, he assumed control of those resources that were necessary for the war effort, and on his own authority he sent Ohio troops under the command of George B. McClellan into Virginia to occupy the western parts of that state to guard Ohio's security. He also sought to prevent communication across the state's borders, especially into Virginia and Kentucky, to prevent Confederate sympathizers in those states from learning the extent of Ohio's war preparations. Along with raising more men than requested by the government, throughout the summer of 1861 Dennison was urged by military commanders to recruit additional emergency volunteers to send into neighboring states. He also had to provide men to guard the growing number of prisoner-of-war camps being placed in Ohio.

Dennison's use of state monies and his control of transportation and communication lines made him unpopular among a cross section of the state's population. As a result, the state Republican Party believed that, if it was to retain any semblance of power in the state, it had no choice but to reject Dennison's nomination in 1861. Dennison left office in early 1862 with the inauguration of David Tod.

So great was Dennison's dedication to the war effort, however, that he offered his services to Governor Tod and became an unofficial advisor to the new governor over the next two years. Dennison's advice was also sought by military commanders in the area because of his demonstrated expertise in mobilization. In September 1862, Dennison surveyed the military situation at his hometown of Cincinnati and reported to Tod the advisability of raising ninety-day volunteers to protect the vulnerable river crossing points nearby.

Dennison's loyalty and dedication did not go unrewarded. He remained active in the Republican Party and was named chairman of the Republican National Convention in 1864. After the election, President Abraham Lincoln appointed Dennison postmaster general, and he remained in that position through the first year of Andrew Johnson's presidential term. Dennison returned to Ohio upon his resignation and remained active in that state's politics.

Besides his political activities, Dennison remained a successful Ohio business executive. His many business interests included a stage coach enterprise, banking, iron, and the railroad industry. It was only after the war that some of his critics realized that his business savvy and honorable dealings with business acquaintances had provided him with the skills necessary to be an excellent war governor. He died in Columbus, Ohio, on 15 June 1882 a wealthy and respected member of his community.

—*David S. Heidler and Jeanne T. Heidler*

See also Tod, David.

For further reading:
Mulligan, Thomas C. "Lest the Rebels Come to Power: The Life of William Dennison, 1815–1882" (Ph.D. dissertation, 1994).

DEPARTMENTS, MILITARY, C.S.A.

The Confederacy's military organization was embodied in numerous territorial departments that were created, discontinued, combined, and reformed according to the war's changing circumstances. Confederate records listing departmental command and areas are not nearly as complete as their Union counterparts. The following are descriptions of the main Confederate military departments.

The Department of Alabama and West Florida was created on 14 October 1861 to include Pascagoula Bay, the part of Mississippi that lay east of the Pascagoula River, and Pensacola. It was under the command of Major General Braxton Bragg until 28 February 1862, when Major General Samuel Jones succeeded him. Although the *Official Records* notes Bragg as announcing his resumption of command on 4 March 1862, he apparently never did so. Instead, Major General John H. Forney assumed command of the department on 28 April 1862 and remained until its discontinuance on 29 June 1862.

The Department of Alabama, Mississippi, and East Louisiana was designated on 28 January 1864 to replace the Department of Mississippi and East Louisiana. It was placed under the command of Lieutenant General Leonidas Polk. On 6 February 1864, the part of Alabama north of the 32d parallel was constituted into the Northern District of Alabama and placed under the command of Major General Jones M. Withers. The department was distinguished from the Department of Tennessee to the east by a line from Gunter's Landing on the Tennessee River to Gadsden on the Coosa River and from there down the Coosa to its junction with the Tallapoosa River; the line continued to the intersection of the northern boundary of Florida with the Chattahoochee River and from there down the Chattahoochee to the Gulf. The department's forces were surrendered to Major General Edward R. S. Canby on 4 May 1865. Its commanders were:

Lieutenant General Leonidas Polk (28 January 1864–9 May 1864)
Major General Stephen D. Lee (9 May 1864–26 July 1864)
Major General Dabney H. Maury (26 July 1864–15 August 1864)
Lieutenant General Richard Taylor (15 August 1864–4 May 1865)

Originally designated as the "Alexandria Line," with its forces under General Milledge L. Bonham, the Department of Alexandria was variously called the Potomac Department or the Army of the Potomac (C.S.A.). On 2 June 1861, it was placed under the command of Brigadier General P. G. T. Beauregard and constituted the Provisional Confederate Army holding positions in northern Virginia.

At the outset of the war, Department No. 1 was placed under the command of Major General David E. Twiggs, with headquarters at New Orleans. It ultimately comprised the state of Louisiana and extended southeast to the Pascagoula River. The capture of New Orleans effectively ended the department's existence, and those parts of it not under Federal occupation were incorporated into Bragg's Department No. 2 to the east and the Trans-Mississippi Department to the west. Its commanders were:

Major General David E. Twiggs (2 June 1861–18 October 1861)
Major General Mansfield Lovell (18 October 1861–25 May 1862)

Department No. 2 was placed under Lieutenant General Leonidas Polk on 13 July 1861. Originally it included the Mississippi Valley from the 31st parallel, Arkansas east of the White River, and Tennessee west of the Tennessee River. Additions during the year brought the rest of Arkansas and Tennessee into it, as well as the part of Mississippi that lay west of the Mississippi Central Railroad. By 26 May 1862, the department had been extended to embrace Mississippi south of the 33d parallel and west of the Pascagoula and Chickasawha rivers, as well as Louisiana east of the Mississippi. On 25 June, the department absorbed the eastern portions of Department No. 1, and on 18 July it was extended to embrace all of Mississippi, East Louisiana, and West Florida. The organization was sometimes referred to as the Western Department. It was discontinued upon the creation of the Department of Tennessee. Its commanders were:

Major General Leonidas Polk (13 July 1861–15 September 1861)
General Albert Sidney Johnston (15 September 1861–6 April 1862)
General P. G. T. Beauregard (6 April 1862–17 June 1862)
General Braxton Bragg (17 June 1862–24 October 1862)
Lieutenant General Leonidas Polk (24 October 1862–3 November 1862)
General Braxton Bragg (3 November 1862–25 July 1863)

The Department of East Tennessee was formed on 25 February 1862 and was placed under the command of Major General Edmund Kirby Smith on 9 March 1862. As of 3 June 1862, it included North Carolina west of the Blue Ridge and extended from Knoxville in a radius of about 150 miles, including Chattanooga. That city was subsequently removed from the department. On 25 July 1863, the department was merged into the new Department of Tennessee under Bragg. Its commanders were

Major General Edmund Kirby Smith (9 March 1862–1 September 1962)
Major General Samuel P. McCown (1 September 1862–1 November 1862)
General Braxton Bragg (1 November 1862–23 December 1862)
Lieutenant General Edmund Kirby Smith (23 November 1862–14 January 1863)
Brigadier General Henry Heth (14 January 1863–17 January 1863)
Brigadier General Daniel S. Donelson (17 January 1863–25 April 1863)
Major General Dabney H. Maury (25 April 1863–12 May 1863)
Major General Simon Bolivar Buckner (12 May 1863–25 July 1863)

The Department of Fredericksburg comprised the military forces in the vicinity of Fredericksburg, Virginia. Provisional Army forces were first under the command of Colonel Daniel Ruggles and then Brigadier General Theophilus Holmes. Returns of 31 August 1861 listed the department's strength at 8,678 encamped at and around Brooke's Station. A month later that number had increased to 9,407.

The Department of Georgia was created on 26 October 1861 and was placed under the command of Brigadier General Alexander Lawton. His headquarters were in Savannah, where from 17 April he had been in command of the District of Savannah. It embraced the state of Georgia. Its strength was about 5,500 men scattered in garrisons along the coast. It would be incorporated into the Department of South Carolina and Georgia on 5 November 1861.

The Department of Henrico embraced the Confederate capital of Richmond, Virginia, and its county (Henrico) as well as Petersburg and its environs (by its expansion on 27 March 1862). It was to encompass a radius of ten miles outside Richmond and was under the command of Brigadier General John H. Winder. While preparing to meet Union general George McClellan's offensive on the peninsula, Joseph E. Johnston wanted the department placed in his command, but President Davis demurred. Winder thus remained in command of the department, whose main activities were the maintenance of Richmond's city guards and military prisons. Returns for the department cease after May 1864, but Union general Ulysses S. Grant referred to a Department of Henrico on 18 February 1865 as being under the command of Richard S. Ewell.

The Department of Middle and Eastern Florida was designated on 21 August 1861 under the command of Brigadier General John B. Grayson, who died at headquarters in Tallahassee on 21 October 1861. Brigadier General James H. Trapier succeeded him. On 19 March 1862, the department was placed under the command of W. S. Dilworth, but it was nominally shifted to the Department of South Carolina and Georgia on 7 April 1862. Nonetheless, according to the *Official Records*, Brigadier General Joseph Finegan was assigned to its command on 8 April 1862. On 6 October, Finegan was assigned to command East Florida, and on the following day, the Department of Middle and East Florida was finally and actually moved to the Department of South Carolina and Georgia, in which it was designated a district.

The Department of Mississippi and East Louisiana was formed on 1 October 1862 and was placed under Major General John C. Pemberton. Forces in the department were reorganized on 7 December to rename Major Generals Earl Van Dorn's and Sterling Price's armies I and II Corps, Army of the Mississippi. Lieutenant General Leonidas Polk assumed command of the department on 22 December 1863, and on 23 December it was designated as the Department of the Southwest. On 28 February 1864, Polk's forces were named the Department of Alabama, Mississippi, and East Louisiana (see above).

The Department of North Carolina was originally under Brigadier General Richard C. Gatlin with headquarters at Goldsboro. On 19 March 1862, Brigadier General Joseph R. Anderson superseded Gatlin in command. Major General Theophilus Holmes briefly commanded the department during the summer, during which it was diminished by the shifting of that part west of the Blue Ridge to the Department of East Tennessee. It also expanded northward to the south bank of the James River. On 17 July, Major General D. H. Hill was assigned to its command. The newly constituted Department of North Carolina and Southern Virginia under Major General Gustavus Woodson Smith replaced it on 19 September 1862.

The Department of Northern Virginia was constituted on 22 October 1861 under the command of General Joseph E. Johnston. Within its broad expanse, P. G. T. Beauregard was to command the Potomac District, Theophilus Holmes the Aquia District, and Thomas J. Jackson the Valley District. Its military force was generally known as the Army of the Potomac until Robert E. Lee took command during the Peninsula campaign, at which point it was named the Army of Northern Virginia.

The Department of Richmond was formed on 1 April 1863 by reorganizing Lieutenant General James Longstreet's command, part of which became this department under the command of Major General Arnold Elzey. On 1 July 1863, D. H. Hill was assigned to temporary command until Major General Robert Ransom took over on 25 April 1864. On 13 July 1864, Lieutenant General Richard S. Ewell was placed in command, and Ransom was ordered to the Department of Western Virginia.

The Department of South Carolina, Georgia, and Florida was formed on 5 November 1861 under the command of General Robert E. Lee from the extant Department of Georgia (see above) and the Department of South Carolina under Brigadier General Roswell Ripley. Lee took command of the new organization on 8 November. Major General John Pemberton succeeded him on 4 March 1862, although, according to the *Official Records*, the assignment was not official until ten days later. On 24 September 1862, P. G. T. Beauregard superseded Pemberton in command of the department, and Samuel Jones in turn superseded Beauregard on 20 April 1864. On 5 October 1864, Lieutenant General William J. Hardee took command. Finally, as Union general William T. Sherman began his 1865 Carolinas campaign, Joseph E. Johnston took command of the department on 22 February and assumed command of all the troops in it three days later.

The Department of Southern Virginia was created out of the reorganization of Lieutenant General James Longstreet's command on 1 April 1863. Major General Samuel G. French was placed in command. It consisted of Virginia south of the James River and east of Powhatan County. On 28 May 1863, it was incorporated into the Department of North Carolina, and French was relieved of command to report to Joseph E. Johnston in Mississippi.

The Department of Southwestern Virginia was constituted on 8 May 1862 under William Wing Loring, who was succeeded on 16 October by John Echols, who was succeeded by John S. Williams on 10 November. On 25 November 1862, the department was designated as the Trans-Alleghany or Western Department of Virginia, with Samuel Jones commanding. Its area extended west to the eastern boundary of Kentucky and as far west into Kentucky as Confederate control could reach. John C. Breckinridge commanded the department from 5 March to 22 June 1864, when John Hunt Morgan took charge. Breckinridge resumed command when Morgan was killed. On 27 September 1864, the department's authority was extended over "the reserve forces of East Tennessee." Lieutenant General Jubal Early's Department of Western Virginia and East Tennessee took over the area on 20 February 1865. Echols was its last commander, succeeding Early on 30 March 1865.

The Department of Tennessee was created on 25 July 1863 by incorporating the Department of East Tennessee into Braxton Bragg's command, the Army of Tennessee. It included a large area of central Tennessee, northern Alabama, and northern Georgia extending to Augusta. It also embraced the western portions of the Carolinas and Virginia and extended north to Kentucky. On 16 December 1863, Joseph E. Johnston was assigned command of the department, although Leonidas Polk was temporarily in command at the end of the month until assuming command of the Department of the Southwest. Johnston officially took over on 27 December. The department would eventually embrace the eastern part of Alabama and some of western Florida. Meanwhile, some of northeastern Georgia was removed from its jurisdiction. The organization was essentially replaced by the Department of Tennessee and Georgia that was formed on 17 October 1864 under John Bell Hood in the wake of the disastrous Atlanta campaign.

The Department of Texas was created on 21 April 1861 and was transferred by Brigadier General Earl Van Dorn to Colonel Hugh McCulloch on 4 September 1861. On 18 September Brigadier General Paul O. Hébert took command of the department. On 26 May 1862, it was incorporated into the Trans-Mississippi Department, which also included Arkansas, Missouri, West Louisiana, and Indian Territory. Thomas C. Hindman was the first commander of this larger organization. On 30 July 1862, Theophilus Holmes succeeded

Hindman. On 9 February 1863, Edmund Kirby Smith took charge of all troops west of the Mississippi and thus incorporated the department into his command.

The Department of the West was formed on 24 November 1862 with Joseph E. Johnston in command to bring order to the occasionally conflicting commands of Braxton Bragg's Department No. 2, Edmund Kirby Smith's Department of East Tennessee, and John C. Pemberton's Department of Mississippi and East Louisiana. Inasmuch as it embraced these three departments, the organization is more appropriately characterized as division; that is, the administrative arrangement of two or more departments. Upon Johnston's assuming command of the Army of Tennessee on 27 December 1863, the Department of the West was discontinued. A Division of the West would exist in the closing months of the war. Created on 17 October 1864, it included the Department of Tennessee and Georgia and the Department of Alabama, Mississippi, and East Louisiana. The military division was under the command of P. G. T. Beauregard.

The Department of Western Kentucky was created on 6 September 1864 under the command of Brigadier General Adam R. Johnson. The department consisted of an area commencing at the mouth of the Salt River and extending through Elizabethtown, Glasgow, and Tompkinsville, Kentucky, to Carthage, Tennessee, and along the Cumberland River to Nashville. It included the Northwestern Railroad to the Tennessee River and extended west to Hickman, Kentucky, and north along the Mississippi River to the mouth of the Ohio River and along that river back to the mouth of the SaLieutenant After Johnson was captured, Brigadier General Hylan B. Lyon took command on 27 October 1864. Richard Taylor desired to have the Department of Western Kentucky incorporated into his Department of Mississippi, Alabama, and East Louisiana, but the War Department maintained the organization. On 4 May 1865, Colonel J. Q. Chenowith surrendered the department to U.S. forces under Colonel John A. Hottenstein.

—David S. Heidler and Jeanne T. Heidler

See also Army of Kentucky; Army of Middle Tennessee; Army of Mississippi; Army of Northern Virginia; Army of Tennessee; Army of the Shenandoah C.S.A.; Army of the West; Army of West Tennessee; Army Organization, C.S.A.

DEPARTMENTS, MILITARY, U.S.A.

The military department was the basis of army organization in a geographical area. Department names were usually applied to the military forces within their domains. For example, the Union Department of the Tennessee was the organizational embodiment of the force called the Army of the Tennessee, and both were first placed under the command of Ulysses S. Grant. The following is a description of the Union's military departments accompanied by lists of their commanders as they were formed and reformed during the war.

At the outset of the war, there were four main Federal military departments in existence. They were the Department of the East, the Department of the West, the Department of Florida, and the Department of the Pacific.

The extant Department of the West was merged into the Western Department on 3 July 1861. It was first commanded by Brigadier General William S. Harney (from 17 November 1860 to 31 May 1861) and then by Brigadier General Nathaniel Lyon from 31 May 1861 to 3 July 1861.

The extant Department of the East was abolished on 17 August 1861 and then revived on 3 January 1863. It was originally commanded by Major General John E. Wool, who resumed command upon its recreation and remained in that place until 18 July 1863. Major General John A. Dix commanded from 18 July 1863 to 27 June 1865.

The extant Department of Florida was merged into the Department of the South on 15 March 1861. Brevet Colonel Harvey Brown was in command from 13 April 1861 to 22 February 1862. Brigadier General L. G. Arnold, who remained in command to 15 March 1862, succeeded him.

The extant Department of the Pacific was under Brigadier General Edwin V. Sumner from 25 April 1861 to 20 October 1861. Colonel George Wright commanded from 20 October 1861 to 1 July 1864, when Major General Irvin McDowell took command to remain until 27 June 1865.

The outbreak of the war caused a significant enlargement and reorganization of this rudimentary departmental structure. The Department of Washington was created on 9 April 1861 to consist of the District of Columbia's original boundaries and Maryland as far as Bladensburg. After being merged into the Military Division of the Potomac on 25 July 1861, it was subsequently recreated on 2 February 1863. Its commanders were:

Lieutenant Colonel C. F. Smith (10 April 1861–28 April 1861)

Colonel Joseph K. F. Mansfield (28 April 1861–15 March 1862)

Major General Samuel P. Heintzelman (7 February 1863–14 October 1863)

Major General Christopher C. Augur (14 October 1863–27 June 1865)

The Department of Annapolis was created on 27 April 1861 and embraced the counties for 20 miles on either side of the railroad from Annapolis to Washington, D.C., as far as Bladensburg. Its name was changed to the Department of Maryland on 19 July 1861, and finally it was merged into the Department of Pennsylvania on 25 July 1861. Its commanders were:

Brigadier General Benjamin F. Butler (27 April 1861–15 May 1861)

Major General George Cadwalader (15 May 1861–11 June 1861)

Major General Nathaniel P. Banks (11 June 1861–19 July 1861)

Major General John A. Dix (19 July 1861–25 July 1861)

The Department of Pennsylvania was created on 27 April 1861 and embraced Pennsylvania, Delaware, and that part of Maryland not within the Departments of Annapolis and Washington. It was incorporated into the Department of the Potomac on 24 August 1861, but was subsequently recreated on 1 December 1864. Its commanders were:

Major General Robert Patterson (29 April 1861–25 July 1861)

Major General John A. Dix (25 July 1861–24 August 1861)

Major General George Cadwalader (1 December 1864–27 June 1865)

The Department of the Ohio was created on 3 May 1861 to embrace Ohio, Indiana, and Illinois. It was subsequently expanded to include West Virginia and the part of Pennsylvania north of the Great Kanawha River and north and west of the Greenbrier River. Missouri was placed into the department on 6 June 1861, while Illinois was removed to the Western Department on 3 July 1861.

The Department of the Ohio underwent another change on 19 September 1861. After that date it included Ohio, Indiana, and the portion of Kentucky within fifteen miles of Cincinnati, Ohio. Michigan and the part of Kentucky east of the Cumberland River came into the department on 9 November 1861.

On 11 March 1862, its area was split between the Mountain Department and the Department of Mississippi, but another Department of the Ohio was created on 19 August 1862 to embrace Ohio, Michigan, Indiana, Illinois, Wisconsin, and the part of Kentucky east of Tennessee River, including the Cumberland Gap. On 17 January 1865, it was added to the Department of the Cumberland. Its commanders were:

Major General George B. McClellan (13 May 1861–23 July 1861)

Brigadier General William S. Rosecrans (23 July 1861–21 September 1861)

Brigadier General Ormsby M. Mitchell (21 September 1861–15 November 1861)

Brigadier General Don Carlos Buell (15 November 1861–11 March 1862)

Major General Horatio G. Wright (25 August 1862–25 March 1863)

Major General Ambrose E. Burnside (25 March 1863–11 December 1863)

Major General J. G. Foster (11 December 1863–9 February 1864)

Major General J. M. Schofield (9 February 1864–17 November 1864)

Major General George Stoneman (17 November 1864–17 January 1865)

The Department of Virginia was formed on 22 May 1861 and was incorporated into the Department of Virginia and North Carolina on 15 July 1863. On 31 January 1865 it was revived, although it is usually more familiarly referred to as the Army of the James. Its commanders were:

Major General B. F. Butler (22 May 1861–17 August 1861)

Major General John E. Wool (17 August 1861–17 June 1862)

Major General John A. Dix (17 June 1862–15 July 1863)

Major General E. O. C. Ord (31 January 1865–May 1865)

Major General Alfred H. Terry (May 1865–27 June 1865)

The Department of Northeast Virginia was created on 27 May 1861 and included Virginia east of the Allegheny Mountains and north of the James River, excluding Fort Monroe and an area sixty miles around that fort. On 25 July 1861, it was placed in the Department of the Potomac. Major General Irvin McDowell was its sole commander.

The Department of Kentucky was created on 28 May 1861 to embrace the part of Kentucky within a hundred miles of the Ohio River. It was placed into the Department of the Cumberland on 15 August 1861 but was subsequently revived on 10 February 1865. Its commanders were

Colonel Robert Anderson (28 May 1861–15 August 1861)

Major General John M. Palmer (18 February 1865–27 June 1865)

The Western Department was created on 3 July 1861. It embraced Illinois and all states and territories west of the Mississippi and east of the Rocky Mountains as well as New Mexico. It was placed in the Department of Missouri and Kansas on 9 November 1861. Its commanders were:

Major General John C. Frémont (25 July 1861–2 November 1861)

Major General David Hunter (2 November 1861–9 November 1861)

The Department of the Shenandoah was created on 19 July 1861. It included the Shenandoah Valley of Virginia; Washington and Alleghany Counties in Maryland; and as much of Virginia as would come under Federal occupation. It was placed into the Department of the Potomac on 17 August 1861, but was subsequently revived on 4 April 1862. It was finally put under the Army of Virginia on 26 June 1862. Its only commander in both its incarnations was Major General Nathaniel P. Banks.

The Department of the Cumberland was created on 15 August 1861. It included Kentucky and Tennessee. The department was merged into the Departments of Missouri and Ohio on 9 November 1861, but was subsequently revived on 24 October 1862. This second Department of the Cumberland embraced the part of Tennessee east of the Tennessee River and the portions of Alabama and Georgia under Federal occupation. Its commanders were:

Brigadier General Robert Anderson (24 September 1861–8 October 1861)

Brigadier General William T. Sherman (8 October 1861–9 November 1861)

Major General William S. Rosecrans (30 October 1862–20 October 1863)

Major General George H. Thomas (20 October 1863–27 June 1865)

The Department of New England was created on 1 October 1861 and embraced the six states in New England. It was discontinued on 20 February 1862. Its sole commander was Major General Benjamin F. Butler.

The Department of Western Virginia was created on 11 October 1861 from the original Department of the Ohio. This new organization was merged into the Mountain Department on 11 March 1862. Its sole commander was William S. Rosecrans, then a brigadier general

The Department of New York was created in October 1861 and was placed into the Department of the East on 3 January 1863. Its commander was Major General E. D. Morgan.

The Department of New Mexico was created on 9 November 1861 to include the New Mexico Territory. Colonel William W. Loring, who resigned his commission to join the Confederate Army, had been in charge of the area before its organization as a department from 23 March 1861 to 16 June 1861. Brevet Lieutenant Colonel Edward R. S. Canby succeeded him from 16

June 1861 to 22 June 1861. Finally, Brigadier General James H. Carleton was in command from 18 September 1862 to 27 June 1865.

The Department of Kansas was created on 9 November 1861 to include Kansas, the Indian Territory west of Arkansas, and the Nebraska, Colorado, and Dakota Territories. It was merged into the Department of Mississippi on 11 March 1862 but was revived on 2 May 1862, only to be merged into the Department of Missouri on 19 September 1862. Another Department of Kansas existed from 1 January 1864 to 3 January 1865 when it was finally merged into the Department of Missouri. Its commanders were:

Major General David Hunter (20 November 1861–11 March 1862)

Brigadier General James G. Blunt (5 May 1862–19 September 1862)

Major General Samuel R. Curtis (16 January 1864–3 January 1865)

The Department of Missouri was created on 9 November 1861 to include Missouri, Iowa, Minnesota, Wisconsin, Arkansas, and Kentucky west of the Cumberland River. It was merged into the Department of Mississippi on 11 March 1862, but was revived on 19 September 1862. The second Department of Missouri consisted of Missouri, Arkansas, Kansas, and Indian Territory. The Colorado and Nebraska Territories were added to the department on 11 October 1862. Its commanders were:

Major General Henry W. Halleck (19 November 1861–11 March 1862)

Major General Samuel R. Curtis (24 September 1862–24 May 1863)

Major General John M. Schofield (24 May 1863–30 January 1864)

Major General William S. Rosecrans (30 January 1864–9 December 1864)

Major General Grenville M. Dodge (9 December 1864–27 June 1865)

The Department of North Carolina was created on 7 January 1862 to embrace North Carolina. It was merged into the new Department of Virginia and North Carolina on 15 July 1863 but was recreated on 31 January 1865. Its commanders were:

Brigadier General Ambrose E. Burnside (13 January 1862–10 July 1862)

Major General John G. Foster (10 July 1862–15 July 1863)

Major General John M. Schofield (31 January 1865–27 June 1865)

The Department of Key West was created in February 1862 and became part of the Department of the South on 15 March 1862. Its commander was Brigadier General John M. Brannan.

The Department of the Gulf was created on 23 February 1862 to embrace the Gulf Coast west of Pensacola harbor and those parts of the Gulf states occupied by Federal forces. West Florida was added to the department on 8 August 1862. Its commanders were:

Major General Benjamin F. Butler (20 March 1862–17 December 1862)

Major General Nathaniel P. Banks (17 December 1862–23 September 1864)

Major General Stephen A. Hurlbut (23 September 1864–22 April 1865)

Major General Nathaniel P. Banks (22 April 1865–3 June 1865)

Major General Edward R. S. Canby (3 June 1865–27 June 1865)

The Mountain Department was created on 11 March 1862 from the Department of Western Virginia. On 26 June 1862 it was merged into the Army of Virginia. Its commanders were:

Brigadier General William S. Rosecrans (14 March 1862–29 March 1862)

Major General John C. Frémont (29 March 1862–26 June 1862)

The Department of Mississippi was created on 15 March 1862 by combining the Departments of Missouri, Ohio, and Kansas. It was merged into the Department of Missouri on 19 September 1862 but was revived on 28 November 1864. Its commanders were:

Major General Henry W. Halleck (13 March 1862–19 September 1862)

Major General Napoleon Jackson Tecumseh Dana (8 December 1864–14 May 1865)

Major General Gouverneur K. Warren (14 May 1865–24 June 1865)

Major General Henry W. Slocum (24 June 1865–27 June 1865)

The Department of the South was created on 15 March 1862. It included South Carolina, Georgia, and Florida. The Department of Key West was placed into it on 15 March 1862. West Florida was removed from the department on 8 August 1862 and was placed into the Department of the Gulf. Its commanders were:

Major General David Hunter (21 March 1862–5 September 1862)

Brigadier General John M. Brannan (5 September 1862–17 September 1862)

Major General Ormsby M. Mitchell (17 September 1862–27 October 1862)

Brigadier General John M. Brannan (27 October 1862–20 January 1863)

Major General David Hunter (20 January 1863–12 June 1863)

Brigadier General Quincy A. Gillmore (12 June 1863–1 May 1864)

Brigadier General John P. Hatch (1 May 1864–26 May 1864)

Major General John G. Foster (26 May 1864–9 February 1865)

Major General Quincy A. Gillmore (9 February 1865–28 June 1865)

The Middle Department was created on 22 March 1862 to include New Jersey, Pennsylvania, Delaware, and Maryland and Virginia's Eastern Shore. It also embraced Cecil, Harford, Baltimore, and Anne Arundel Counties in Maryland. Its commanders were:

Major General John A. Dix (22 March 1862–9 June 1862)

Major General John E. Wool (9 June 1862–22 December 1862)

Major General Robert C. Schenck (22 December 1862–10 August 1863)

Brevet Brigadier General William W. Morris (10 August 1863–31 August 1863)

Major General Robert C. Schenck (31 August 1863–28 September 1863)

Brigadier General Erastus B. Tyler (28 September 1863–10 October 1863)

Major General Robert C. Schenck (10 October 1863–5 December 1863)

Brigadier General Henry H. Lockwood (5 December 1863–22 March 1864)

Major General Lewis Wallace (22 March 1864–1 February 1865)

Brevet Brigadier General William W. Morris (1 February 1865–19 April 1865)

Major General Lewis Wallace (19 April 1865–27 June 1865)

The Department of the Rappahannock was created on 4 April 1862 to include Virginia east of the Blue Ridge and west of the Potomac River. It also included the Fredericksburg & Richmond Railroad, the District of Columbia, and the region between the Potomac and the Patuxent rivers. It was merged into the Army of Virginia on 26 June 1862. It was commanded by Major General Irvin McDowell.

The Department of the Northwest was created on 6 September 1862 to include Wisconsin, Iowa, Minnesota, and the Nebraska and Dakota Territories. Its commanders were

Major General John Pope (16 September 1862–28 November 1862)

Brigadier General Washington L. Elliott (28 November 1862–18 February 1863)

Major General John Pope (13 February 1863–18 February 1865)

Major General Samuel R. Curtis (13 February 1865–27 June 1865)

The Department and Army of the Tennessee was created on 16 October 1862 to embrace Cairo, Forts Henry and Donelson, northern Mississippi, and Kentucky and Tennessee west of the Tennessee River. Its commanders were:

Major General Ulysses S. Grant (25 October 1862–24 October 1863)

Major General William T. Sherman (24 October 1863–26 March 1864)

Major General James B. McPherson (26 March 1864–22 July 1864)

Major General John A. Logan (22 July 1864–27 July 1864)

Major General Oliver O. Howard (27 July 1864–19 May 1865)

Major General John A. Logan (19 May 1865–1 August 1865)

The Department of the Monongahela was created on 9 June 1863 to embrace Pennsylvania west of Johnstown and the Laurel Hill range of mountains. It included Hancock, Brooke, and Ohio Counties in western Virginia (later West Virginia), and Columbiana, Jefferson, and Belmont Counties in Ohio. It was placed into the Department of the Susquehanna on 6 April 1864. It was commanded by Major General William T. H. Brooks (11 June 1863 to 6 April 1864).

The Department of West Virginia was created in June 1863 to embrace that state. Its commanders were:

Brigadier General Benjamin F. Kelly (28 June 1863–10 March 1864)

Major General Franz Sigel (10 March 1864–21 May 1864)

Major General David Hunter (21 May 1864–9 August 1864)

Major General George Crook (9 August 1864–22 February 1865)

Brigadier General John D. Stevenson (22 February 1865–28 February 1865)

Major General Winfield Scott Hancock (28 February 1865–1 March 1865)

Brevet Major General Samuel S. Carroll (1 March 1865–7 March 1865)

Major General Winfield Scott Hancock (7 March 1865–20 March 1865)

Major General George Crook (20 March 1865–22 March 1865)

Major General Winfield Scott Hancock (22 March 1865–27 June 1865)

The Department of the Susquehanna was created on 9 June 1863 to include Pennsylvania east of Johnstown and the Laurel Hill Range of mountains. Its designation was changed to the Department of Pennsylvania on 1 December 1864. It was under the command of Major General Darius N. Couch.

The Department of Virginia and North Carolina was created on 15 July 1863 by combining the separate Department of Virginia and Department of North Carolina. It was placed into the Army of the James in April 1864, but on 31 January 1865 it was recreated again as the Department of Virginia and Department of North Carolina. Its commanders were:

Major General John G. Foster (18 July 1863–11 November 1863)

Major General Benjamin F. Butler (11 November 1863–27 August 1864)

Major General Edward O. C. Ord (27 August 1864–7 September 1864)

Major General Benjamin F. Butler (7 September 1864–14 December 1864)

Major General Edward O. C. Ord (14 December 1864–24 December 1864)

Major General Benjamin F. Butler (24 December 1864–8 January 1865)

Major General Edward O. C. Ord (8 January 1865–31 January 1865)

The Northern Department was created on 12 January 1864 to include Michigan, Ohio, Indiana, and Illinois. Its commanders were:

Major General Samuel P. Heintzelman (20 January 1864–1 October 1864)

Major General Joseph Hooker (1 October 1864–27 June 1865)

The Department of Arkansas was created on 6 January 1864 and included all of Arkansas except Fort Smith. On 17 April 1864, Fort Smith and the Indian Territory were added to the department. It was placed into the Military Division of West Mississippi on 7 May 1864. Its commanders were:

Major General Frederick Steele (30 January 1864–22 December 1864)

Major General John J. Reynolds (22 December 1864–August 1865)

Military divisions were formed by the combination of two or more military departments. The Military Division of the Mississippi was created on 18 October 1863. It comprised the Department of the Ohio, the Department of the Tennessee, the Department of the Cumberland, and the Department of Arkansas. On 7 Mary 1864, the Department of Arkansas was transferred to the Military Division of West Mississippi. Its commanders were:

Major General Ulysses S. Grant (18 October 1863–18 March 1864)

Major General William T. Sherman (18 March 1864–27 June 1865)

The Military Division of West Mississippi was created on 7 May 1864 and comprised the Department of Arkansas and the Department of the Gulf. The Department of Arkansas was transferred to the Military Division of Missouri on 21 March 1865, and the Division of West Mississippi was discontinued in May 1865. It was under Major General Edward R. S. Canby from 11 May 1864 to its discontinuance.

The Middle Military Division was created on 6 August 1864 and was commanded by Major General Philip Sheridan (from 6 August 1864 to 27 February 1865) and by Major General Winfield Scott Hancock (from 27 February 1864 to 27 June 1865).

The Military Division of the James was created on 19 April 1865 and comprised the Department of Virginia and the portions of North Carolina not occupied by the William T. Sherman's forces. It was under the command of Major General Henry W. Halleck to its discontinuance on 27 June 1865.

Finally, there were also military districts and "army" organizations that engaged in field operations. The most famous of these was the forerunner of the Army of the Potomac, which was the Military District of the Potomac. It was created on 25 July 1861 by combining the Department of Washington and the Department of Northeast Virginia. Commanded by Joseph B. McClellan, its designation was subsequently changed to the Department or Army of the Potomac on 15 August 1861 and continued under McClellan until Lincoln relieved him on 9 November 1862. It was the principal field army for operations in the Eastern theater, where it opposed the Confederate Army of Northern Virginia. From McClellan's departure, its commanders were:

Major General Ambrose E. Burnside (9 November 1862–26 January 1863)

Major General Joseph Hooker (26 January 1863–28 June 1863)

Major General George G. Meade (28 June 1863–30 December 1864)

Major General John G. Parke (30 December 1864–11 January 1865)

Major General George G. Meade (11 January 1865–27 June 1865)

After the failure of McClellan's Peninsula campaign, the Army of Virginia was created on 26 June 1862 by combining the forces under Major General John C. Frémont in the Mountain Department with those of Major General Nathaniel Banks in Department of the Shenandoah and Major General Irvin McDowell in the Department of the Rappahannock. The Army of Virginia also included Brigadier General Samuel D. Sturgis's command at Washington, D.C. Major General John Pope was placed in command. After the army was soundly defeated at the battle of Second Bull Run, it was merged into Army of the Potomac on 2 September 1862.

The Army of Georgia was created on 28 March 1865 and comprised XIV and XX Army Corps that had participated in Sherman's March to the Sea. It was under the command of Major General Henry W. Slocum until its discontinuance on 1 June 1865.

At the close of the war, General Order 118 reorganized all existing military departments on 27 June 1865. Under these arrangements, eighteen new military departments and five new divisions were established. The departments were arranged and their headquarters situated as follows:

The Department of the East, under Major General Joseph Hooker at New York City, included the New England states, New York, and New Jersey.

The Middle Department, under Major General Winfield Scott Hancock at Baltimore, included West Virginia; Maryland (except Anne Arundel, Prince George's, Calvert, Charles, and St. Mary's Counties); and the Baltimore & Ohio Railroad in Virginia, Delaware, and Pennsylvania.

The Department of Washington, under Major General Christopher C. Augur at the nation's capital, included the District of Columbia; Anne Arundel, Prince George's, Calvert, Charles, and St. Mary's Counties in Maryland; and Fairfax County in Virginia.

The Department of the Ohio, under Major General E. O. C. Ord at Detroit, included Ohio, Indiana, Illinois, and Michigan.

The Department of the Tennessee, under Major General George Stoneman at Knoxville.

The Department of Kentucky, under Major General John M. Palmer at Louisville.

The Department of the Missouri, under Major General John Pope at Fort Leavenworth, included Wisconsin, Minnesota, Iowa, Missouri, and Kansas, and the Nebraska, Dakota, and Montana Territories.

The Department of Virginia, under Major General Alfred H. Terry at Richmond, included Virginia, except Fairfax County and the Baltimore & Ohio Railroad.

The Department of North Carolina, under Major General John M. Schofield at Raleigh.

The Department of South Carolina, under Major General Quincy A. Gillmore at Hilton Head.

The Department of Georgia, under Major General James B. Steedman at Augusta.

The Department of Florida, under Major General John G. Foster at Tallahassee.

The Department of Mississippi, under Major General Henry W. Slocum at Vicksburg.

The Department of Alabama, under Major General Charles R. Woods at Mobile.

The Department of Louisiana and Texas, under Major General Edward R. S. Canby at New Orleans, included those states.

The Department of Arkansas, under Major General John J. Reynolds at Little Rock, included Arkansas and the Indian Territory.

The Department of the Columbia, under Brigadier General George Wright at Fort Vancouver, included Oregon and the Washington and Idaho Territories.

The Department of California, under Major General Irvin McDowell at San Francisco, included California and Nevada and the Utah, New Mexico, and Colorado Territories.

These departments were placed into divisions as follows:

The Military Division of the Atlantic, under Major General George G. Meade at Philadelphia, included the Department of the East, Middle Department, Department of Virginia, Department of North Carolina, and Department of South Carolina.

The Military Division of the Mississippi, under Major General William T. Sherman at St. Louis, included the Department of the Ohio, Department of the Missouri, and Department of Arkansas.

The Military Division of the Gulf, under Major General Philip H. Sheridan at New Orleans, included the Department of Mississippi, Department of Louisiana and Texas, and Department of Florida.

The Military Division of the Tennessee, under Major General George H. Thomas at Nashville, included the Department of the Tennessee, Department of Kentucky, Department of Georgia, and Department of Alabama.

The Military Division of the Pacific, under Major General Henry W. Halleck at San Francisco, included the Department of the Columbia and Department of California.

—*David S. Heidler and Jeanne T. Heidler*

See also Army of Kansas; Army of Kentucky; Army of Missouri; Army of New Mexico; Army of the Cumberland; Army of the Gulf; Army of the James; Army of Mississippi; Army of the Northwest; Army of the Ohio; Army of the Peninsula; Army of the Potomac; Army of the Shenandoah U.S.A.; Army of the Tennessee; Army of the West; Army of Virginia; Army Organization, U.S.A.

DESERTION

Desertion is a barometer of an army's morale. The desertion rate of any military force reflects the level of its fighting spirit. Almost 2,000 years ago, the Roman historian Vegitius stated that the desertion of an enemy's soldiers had a greater effect on its army than battlefield casualties. Desertion both depletes an army's numbers and severely undermines its resolve. Men falling gloriously in battle serve as an example for those who survive. Deserters not only take themselves out of the contest, they cause those who remain to question the wisdom of their continued service.

The armies of the American Civil War proved uniquely susceptible to desertion, and the problem plagued both sides throughout the war. In 1862, Robert E. Lee complained that desertion so depleted his army that the government's policy of leniency that prevented him from executing deserters would only compound the problem. Available estimates place Union desertion at 200,000 and Confederate desertion at 104,000. Desertion records, however, reflect only estimates based on those present for duty or otherwise unaccounted for as dead, wounded, captured, or hospitalized. The numbers therefore are only an estimate at best. Union desertion figures may reflect the repeated desertion of a particular soldier, a practice common among men who joined for bounties. Bounty jumpers deserted only to reenlist under another name, collect a new bounty, and desert again. By strict definition, desertion was leaving the military with no intent to return. However, as the war progressed, a broad variety of conduct was interpreted as evasion of duty. Straggling, skulking, fighting in the wrong unit, or temporary absence fell under an ever-widening definition of desertion.

Many motives traditionally associated with desertion existed during the Civil War. Poor food, boredom, unhealthy camp conditions, fear of death, and homesickness caused desertion on both sides. Soldiers close to their homes were especially sensitive to conditions there, and bad news consequently contributed to desertion, particularly among Confederate soldiers. When the promise of food, clothing, and shelter for the families of southern soldiers went unfulfilled, it weakened those soldiers' commitment to the army.

After conscription in the South began in 1862 and in the North in 1863, men unwilling to fight but now compelled to do so took advantage of any opportunity to desert. Loopholes that enabled wealthy slaveholders in the South to avoid the draft and the affluent in both regions to purchase substitutes also undermined morale and contributed to desertion. The South's increasing economic instability meant that many families could not cope in the absence of sons, husbands, fathers, and brothers. The gradual elimination of furloughs and the Confederacy's policy that all enlistments bound men for the duration of the war made desertion more appealing as the war dragged into its third year.

One unique aspect of the Civil War was that each side used desertion to deplete the other's army. To induce Union soldiers to desert, the Confederacy offered sanctuary in the South, civilian jobs, and in some cases land. The North excelled in the inducement of Confederate desertion. By August 1863, the Union had developed a policy that allowed Confederate deserters coming into Union lines to swear an oath of allegiance and return home. As the war progressed, this program also provided transportation into Union-occupied areas and payment at fair market value for any equipment Confederate deserters brought with them. These Confederate deserters became the earliest Galvanized Yankees (reconstructed rebels). If their homes lay within Confederate-controlled areas or if they were unwilling to return home, deserters could remain in the North or enter the U.S. Army for service on the western frontier.

Not only did desertion drain the strength of both armies, it also affected civilians. Certain regions became "deserter country" for both northern and southern runaways who sought refuge in isolated areas. The mountains of Tennessee, Georgia, Alabama, and Kentucky, as well as areas of southeast Georgia provided safe havens for deserter bands. These irregular groups preyed on the civilian population and caused Union and Confederate military commanders severe security problems for most of the war.

—*Mark A. Weitz*

See also Conscription, C.S.A.; Conscription, U.S.A.; Galvanized Yankees.
For further reading:
Lonn, Ella. *Desertion during the Civil War* (1928; reprint, 1998).
Martin, Bessie. *Desertion Among Alabama Troops during the Civil War* (1966).
Weitz, Mark A. *A Higher Duty: Desertion Among Georgia Troops during the Civil War* (2000).

DEVENS, CHARLES, JR.
(1820–1891)
Union general

Born to Charles Devens and Mary Lithgow Devens in Charlestown, Massachusetts, Charles Devens, Jr. was educated at Boston Latin School and Harvard before embarking on a legal career by studying at Harvard Law School. He began his private practice at age twenty in Northfield, Massachusetts. Along with his successful legal practice, Devens also became interested in Massachusetts state and national politics, serving a term in the state senate and in 1849 accepting the federal position for Massachusetts as U.S. marshal. The unpleasant duty in this position of returning a fugitive slave to his owner under the provisions of the Fugitive Slave Act of 1850 made Devens a strong opponent of slavery, and after the Civil War he secured a job for that now-freed slave.

In 1854, Devens moved to Worcester, Massachusetts, and returned to private practice. Because of his growing reputation as an attorney he also worked as the city of Worcester's solicitor. Besides his busy legal career, Devens also was active in the state militia, and at the outbreak of the Civil War was a brigadier general in the state forces.

Devens volunteered for Federal service immediately after Lincoln's call for volunteers and was made major of the 3d Massachusetts Rifle Battalion, a ninety-day unit. During their service the 3d Battalion made up part of the garrison of Fort McHenry in Baltimore harbor. At the expiration of his unit's term, he was commissioned colonel of volunteers and was given command of the 15th Massachusetts. He commanded that regiment along the Potomac in the fall of 1861 and fought at Ball's Bluff in October. During that engagement, Devens was struck in the chest by a Confederate bullet, but the ball glanced off a button on his uniform, leaving him bruised but otherwise uninjured.

The following spring, Devens and the 15th were sent to the York Peninsula as part of the Army of the Potomac's Peninsula campaign. In April, Devens was promoted to brigadier general of volunteers and was given command of the 1st Brigade, 1st Division, IV Corps under Erasmus Keyes. He commanded that brigade during the siege of Yorktown and the battle of Williamsburg on 5 May. In the battle of Seven Pines on 31 May, Devens was seriously wounded late in the day trying to rally his forces. He refused to leave the field despite the severity of his injury. He was unable to participate in the remaining battles of the Peninsula campaign.

Returning to duty in time for the Maryland campaign, Devens commanded his brigade at Antietam. After that battle he transferred to command 2d Brigade, 3d Division, VI Corps. He led that brigade in the battle of Fredericksburg, where it made up the advance guard for the division and the rear guard during the retreat. Devens was commended by the division commander, Brigadier General John Newton, for his conduct during the battle.

In Joseph Hooker's reorganization of the Army of the Potomac during the spring of 1863, Devens was given command of 1st Division of XI Corps, which was commanded by Oliver O. Howard. It was this corps that felt the brunt of Thomas J. "Stonewall" Jackson's flanking maneuver at Chancellorsville in May 1863. In his attempt to rally his men and prevent a complete rout of his division, Devens was seriously wounded in the foot. Even after receiving the wound, Devens remained on the field for over an hour trying to save his decimated division.

The wound he received at Chancellorsville was very slow to heal, and it was about one year before Devens could return to field service. In the meantime, during the summer of 1863 he was given command of the draft depot at Springfield, Massachusetts. Later in 1863 he moved to Boston harbor, where he also commanded the draft depot until April 1864.

Devens returned to active duty in command of the 3d Division, XVIII Corps, Army of the James, in the spring of 1864. He was not fully recovered from his earlier wound, and at times during the campaign against the Army of Northern Virginia, he had to be carried on a stretcher while directing his troops in battle. Such an arrangement was necessary when his division fought at Cold Harbor in early June 1864. Devens's disability again forced him to relinquish field command until the fall of 1864.

In October he assumed command of the 1st Division, XVIII Corps, which he held until December, when he became the commander of the 3d Division, XXIV Corps. He held this command until the end of the war. During the latter phases of the campaign against Petersburg and Richmond, Devens commanded his division on the outskirts of Richmond and led the way into the city when it was evacuated by Confederate forces. In the same month, Ulysses S. Grant wrote to the War Department recommending Devens for a brevet promotion to major general and urged haste because he did not believe that Devens's physical problems would allow him to remain in the army much longer. The promotion was expedited, with a date of rank of April 1865.

As it happened, Grant was wrong. Devens remained in the army for another year, serving first as the commander of U.S. troops in Richmond and then as the commander of the District of Northeastern Virginia, headquartered in Fredericksburg. At the end of July 1865, Devens was sent to the Department of South Carolina. He was mustered out of the volunteer service in June 1866.

Devens returned briefly to private practice before being appointed to the bench as a justice of the

Massachusetts superior court. He remained in that position until he was appointed to the state supreme court in 1873. He left the bench temporarily to accept an appointment from President Rutherford B. Hayes as U.S. attorney general, returning to the Massachusetts supreme court at the end of Hayes's term. He died while serving in that capacity on 7 January 1891.

—*David S. Heidler and Jeanne T. Heidler*

See also Cold Harbor; Fair Oaks; Fredericksburg.

For further reading:

Devens, Charles. *Charles Devens. Orations and Addresses on Various Occasions, Civil and Military* (1891).

DEVILS

In response to the rapid evolution of submarine mine warfare in Southern waters, the Union navy was forced to develop minesweeping capabilities. Initially, sailors in small boats scoured waters with grapnels and probes in advance of warships and transports for mines. When encountered, torpedo mines were carefully raised and manually disarmed. Crude minesweeping rigs were devised by early 1862, but the devices were field expedient affairs, assembled ad hoc, attached to riverine gunboats in the Western theater.

As the threat of Confederate mines and underwater obstructions expanded, John Ericsson was asked to design a submarine weapon destroyer for the Union navy. By early 1863, Ericsson had devised a minesweeping raft that could be attached to Monitor-class ironclads. Officially designated the Ericsson Obstruction Remover, Union sailors dubbed the device the "bootjack," while Confederate engineers at Charleston called it the "devil."

Ericsson may have borrowed the basic concept for the devil from Colonel Charles Ellet. Ellet had previously constructed a bow-mounted minesweeping apparatus, referred to as a "torpedo rake," for use by Union gunboats on the Yazoo River. As conceived by Ericsson, the Obstruction Remover employed a powerful torpedo to destroy mines and other underwater obstructions. His prototype was successfully tested in New York, and several minesweepers were built for the Union blockade fleet at Charleston.

The devil was a stoutly built wooden platform, 38 feet long and 20 feet wide, with a V-shaped opening in the stern. The stern opening conformed to the bow configuration of the Monitors, and heavy chains were used to fasten the craft to a parent vessel. Ericsson's torpedo and detonating mechanism attached to the bow of the raft. In early 1863, three devils were completed and delivered to Charleston. Shortly thereafter, one raft was fitted to the USS *Weehawken* to lead Admiral Samuel Du Pont's 7 April attack on Fort Sumter.

The *Weehawken*'s commander feared that the devil's torpedo might damage his ship when it was detonated, and he ordered the torpedo removed. The torpedo was replaced by grapnels, suspended on chains below the platform. Du Pont hoped that a safe passage could be cleared for the fleet as the devil's grappling irons detonated Confederate torpedoes before they could damage the *Weehawken*.

As the action commenced, heavy swells caused the devil to batter against the ironclad's bow, and several armor plates were wrenched loose. Matters became further complicated when a grapnel hook fouled the *Weehawken*'s anchor chain. As he feared irreparable damage, the *Weehawken*'s commander ordered the devil cast adrift. Confederate forces later recovered the raft on Morris Island.

Before the ironclad captains at Charleston would deploy the devil with the torpedo attachment, further tests were required. In November 1863, the USS *Patapsco* was fitted with a devil and a torpedo was detonated. Although the explosion generated a spectacular water column, the *Patapsco* suffered no apparent damage. The *Patapsco*'s commander considered the devil to be fully functional but much too cumbersome for practical use. He noted that the raft greatly reduced the ironclad's operational speed and maneuverability.

While the trial indicated that Ericsson's device was serviceable, there were simply too many complications associated with its operation. These factors led Union commanders to abandon the minesweepers. While the basic concept was novel, it failed in execution. After the devil's apparent failure, the Union fleet was forced to rely on the cruder minesweeping methods developed earlier in the war. Union sailors tasked with such hazardous duty no doubt wished for a fleet of Ericsson's Obstruction Removers, but truly effective minesweepers were not developed until many decades later.

—*Charles L. Heath Jr.*

See also Ericsson, John.

For further reading:

Barnes, J. S. *Submarine Warfare, Offensive and Defensive* (1869).

Musicant, Ivan. *Divided Waters: The Naval History of the Civil War* (1995).

Perry, Milton F. *Infernal Machines: The Story of Confederate Submarine and Mine Warfare* (1965).

DEVIN, THOMAS CASIMER
(1822–1878)
Union general

Born in New York City, Thomas Casimer Devin received little formal education and upon reaching adulthood became a house painter. He also had a strong interest in things military and became active in the state militia. At the outbreak of the Civil

War he had reached the rank of lieutenant colonel. Using his influence over the men of his regiment, he was able to raise a three-month company of cavalry during the early summer of 1861. He was commissioned captain, and he and his men were incorporated into the 1st New York Cavalry.

Devin and his men served as part of the defenses of Washington before being mustered out of service. Devin returned home to New York, where he raised a regiment of long-term recruits. This regiment was mustered into Federal service in November 1861 as the 6th New York Cavalry, and Devin was commissioned its colonel. The unit would also later be referred to as the 2d Ira Harris Guards.

Devin and the 6th saw no real action for almost a year. They served at a variety of posts in Pennsylvania and in the spring of 1862 were part of the defenses in the District of Washington. During the campaign that resulted in the battle of First Bull Run, Devin and the 6th New York served as scouts south of Washington, patrolling between the Rapidan and Rappahannock rivers. At the beginning of the Maryland campaign, Devin and the 6th became a part of the Army of the Potomac. They served at South Mountain and at Antietam, where they fought in the opening stages of the battle.

Devin was a part of the Army of the Potomac for the remainder of the war. After fighting in the battle of Fredericksburg, he was given command of the 2d Cavalry Brigade, 1st Cavalry Division. He commanded that brigade in the battle of Chancellorsville and was commended and recommended for promotion by Alfred Pleasonton for his actions in the battle.

During the early stages of the Gettysburg campaign, Devin was part of the cavalry probes that fought J. E. B. Stuart through the first half of June. As part of John Buford's division, Devin and his men rode into Gettysburg on 30 June. The following day they held the high ground west of town against overwhelming Confederate forces until the lead elements of I Corps came to their aid. These actions ensured that the climactic battle between the Army of the Potomac and the Army of Northern Virginia would be fought at Gettysburg. After the battle, Devin's brigade participated in the pursuit of Robert E. Lee's army.

In the late summer of 1863, Devin operated around Kelly's Ford on the Rappahannock River. Late in the year, he led his brigade in the Mine Run campaign. At the end of February 1864, Devin's brigade participated in the raid on Richmond commanded by Judson Kilpatrick. In April, Devin conducted a reconnaissance mission to Madison Courthouse, Virginia, and then in May 1864 participated in Philip Sheridan's Richmond raid.

In August, having been breveted brigadier general, Devin was sent with his brigade to join Sheridan in the campaign against Jubal Early in the Shenandoah Valley.

Devin was wounded early in the campaign, but he was out of action for less than a month. He fought in all the major engagements of the campaign from Winchester to Cedar Creek. When he was finally promoted to brigadier general of volunteers in March 1865, his date of rank was 19 October 1864, the date of the battle of Cedar Creek.

In early 1865, Devin was given command of one of Sheridan's cavalry divisions, and with it beginning in late February 1865, he participated in Sheridan's raid from the Shenandoah toward Petersburg. From Charlottesville in early March, Devin was sent toward the James River with orders to destroy the James River Canal as he went. After arriving outside Petersburg at the end of March, Devin and his division participated in the final phases of the campaign against Lee's army. He fought at Five Forks and Sayler's Creek (for which he was breveted brigadier general in the regular army) and in the final pursuit of Lee's army that resulted in the surrender at Appomattox Court House.

After the war, Devin was breveted major general of volunteers; when he was mustered out of the volunteer service, he accepted a regular commission as lieutenant colonel of the 8th Cavalry. He remained in that position for eleven years, after which he was promoted to colonel and given command of the 3d Cavalry in 1877. Already in bad health, Devin took a medical leave in 1878 and returned to New York City. He died there on 4 April 1878.

—*David S. Heidler and Jeanne T. Heidler*

See also Cedar Creek, Battle of; Gettysburg, Battle of; Sayler's Creek, Battle of.

For further reading:

Devin, Thomas Casimer. *Record of Military Service. From March 4, 1861, to January 15, 1866, of Thomas C. Devin, Brigadier and Brev. Major General U. S. Vols., Late Colonel 3d United States Cavalry* (1878).

DICKINSON, ANNA ELIZABETH
(1842–1932)
Orator

During the Civil War, when public oratory was a vital source of both entertainment and information, Anna Elizabeth Dickinson was one of the nation's most popular public speakers. At a time when the leading abolitionists and women's rights advocates had been fighting the good fight for decades, Dickinson rose to prominence by her early twenties. And when few women spoke before mixed audiences, and almost none engaged in partisan political oratory, Dickinson was one of the most celebrated Republican stump speakers. Although largely forgotten by history, Dickinson was arguably one of the most important women in the United States.

Dickinson was born on 28 October 1842. When only thirteen years old, the young Philadelphia Quaker published an antislavery article in William Lloyd Garrison's *The Liberator*. Five years later, she attended a forum on women's rights and rose from the audience to disagree with a conservative speaker. Before long, the precocious teenager was receiving invitations to speak on "The Rights and Wrongs of Women." In February 1861, leading abolitionist and feminist Lucretia Mott introduced Dickinson to a large audience at Philadelphia's Concert Hall. Her career as an orator was under way.

With the outbreak of war, Dickinson took a job at the U.S. Mint, but even then she was clearly drawn to the platform. In October 1861, shortly after the disastrous battle of Ball's Bluff, Dickinson spoke at the annual meetings of the Pennsylvania Anti-Slavery Society, where she unleashed a vigorous attack on General George McClellan. The speech pleased her audience—including the famed abolitionist Garrison—but it probably also cost her the job at the mint. That spring Garrison helped arrange a series of paid engagements in New England and New York. Dickinson also spent some time visiting soldiers in Northern hospitals, eventually delivering a series of lectures on "Hospital Life."

In early 1863, just as opportunities for paid speaking engagements were on the wane, Dickinson was approached by the New Hampshire Republican State Committee to campaign in the upcoming elections. She rapidly made the transition to political partisan, delivering a series of successful lectures across the Granite State, following immediately by similar engagements in Maine. As her reputation as a stump speaker rose, the lucrative political offers poured in. Dickinson spent several busy weeks speaking for the Republicans in Connecticut, culminating her tour with a heavily publicized election eve address in Hartford's Allyn Hall. Later that year the Republicans from her home state signed her for a speaking tour of the western Pennsylvania coal country.

This flurry of political activity brought Dickinson increased fame and even larger audiences in cities and towns throughout the East. In May 1863 she earned an astonishing $1,000 fee for a lecture at Philadelphia's Academy of Music. In July she shared a stage with Frederick Douglass at a rally encouraging black enlistment. That November she became the object of controversy when she accepted a large honorarium to deliver two lectures at Chicago's Northwest Sanitary Fair. Dickinson insisted that her fees were far less than those she would have earned back East, and thus she was in fact contributing to the cause.

The highlight of Dickinson's wartime career—and powerful testimony to her contemporary importance—came in January 1864 when she accepted an invitation signed by 100 senators and congressmen to address them in the hall of the House of Representatives. The lecture had Dickinson's characteristic fire, including harsh criticisms of Abraham Lincoln's administration for its conciliatory attitude toward the South. But with the president and Mrs. Lincoln seated in the audience, the young orator opted to endorse his renomination. That April, Dickinson had a private meeting with the president where she apparently aired her grievances against his moderate stance. In the election season to come, she continued to heap criticism on the president while attacking the Democrats and nominally supporting the Republican ticket.

After the Civil War, Anna Dickinson remained in the public eye for a generation, first as one of the nation's most active lyceum speakers and later as a less successful playwright and actor. She also published several books, including a novel defending interracial marriage. In 1891, poverty stricken and increasingly irrational and irascible, Anna Dickinson was committed to an asylum for the insane by her sister Susan. The once famous orator took her case to court and eventually won her freedom and then won small settlements from several newspapers that had trumpeted her insanity. She spent the final four decades of her life in quiet obscurity, eventually dying in Goshen, New York, a week before her ninetieth birthday.

—*J. Matthew Gallman*

See also Abolitionist Movement; Mott, Lucretia; Quakers; Women.

For further reading:

Gallman, J. Matthew. "Anna Dickinson's Civil War." In *The Human Tradition in the Civil War and Reconstruction* (2000).
Giraud, Chester. *Embattled Maiden: The Life of Anna Dickinson* (1951).
Young, James Harvey. "Anna Elizabeth Dickinson and the Civil War" (Ph.D dissertation, 1941).
———. "Anna Elizabeth Dickinson and the Civil War: For and Against Lincoln." *Mississippi Valley Historical Review* (1944).

DILGER, HUBERT
(1836–?)
Union officer

Hubert Dilger was probably the best artillery battery commander of the Civil War—although the South's John Pelham also would be a serious contender for that distinction. Born in the Grand Duchy of Baden (Germany) on 5 March 1836, Dilger was a lieutenant in the Baden Horse Artillery when he resigned his commission and offered his services to the Union. He was given command of Battery I, 1st Ohio Light Artillery, a unit made up largely of German immigrants from the Cincinnati area. The battery was part of the division commanded by Carl Schurz.

Dilger commanded Battery I for almost the entire war, and it was widely regarded as the best firing unit in XI Corps. Dilger was legendary for his coolness under fire, but he also was a shrewd artillery commander who knew how to attack the most profitable targets. He concentrated on counterbattery fire in the offensive, and in the defensive he focused on attacking the enemy infantry. Dilger also was an experienced horseman who refused to wear the regulation-issue cloth uniform trousers that wore through after just a few days in the saddle. Instead, he substituted his own doeskin trousers, which earned him the nickname of "Leather Britches" from both his troops and his superiors.

Dilger and his battery fought in many of the major battles of the Civil War, including Cross Keys, Second Bull Run, Chancellorsville, Missionary Ridge, Lookout Mountain, Gettysburg, Chattanooga, and in Sherman's Georgia campaign. His most significant action came at Chancellorsville, where his battery fought one of the most impressive rearguard actions ever conducted by an American artillery unit in any war.

While conducting a routine reconnaissance on 2 May 1863, Dilger spotted Stonewall Jackson's troops advancing on the right flank of the Union positions. Narrowly escaping capture, Dilger reached XI Corps headquarters with the information. At corps, however, staff officers refused to believe that Jackson could be where Dilger said he was. They laughed at him and reprimanded him for "spreading rumors."

With a clear understanding of what the tactical situation required, Dilger immediately returned to his guns and repositioned them to engage Jackson's lead elements. By that point a Confederate force of 25,000 was bearing down along the turnpike straight for the Union flank. Dilger opened fire on the leading elements at a range of half a mile. Two other batteries joined the fight, but one was quickly knocked out of action and the other ran out of ammunition, leaving Battery I alone. When the Confederate forces were almost on top of his position, Dilger ordered all but one of his Napoleon 12-pounders to withdraw. With his remaining gun, Dilger held his ground for more than thirty minutes until his horse was shot and fell over on him. With his leg severely injured and no alternative but to retreat, Dilger started to limp away. Just as the Southern troops were about to capture him, his young orderly, a Private Ackley, rode back and rescued him.

Dilger was not through fighting. Returning to his battery, he joined a hasty defensive position formed by Union infantry units. Dilger fired his remaining guns with double canister. When that line started to collapse, he employed a leapfrogging withdrawal, leaving one gun in place, sending his other guns 100 yards to the rear, and then pulling the forward gun back under the covering fire of the rearward guns. Dilger himself always remained with the forward gun. Dilger delayed Jackson's attacking infantry all the way back to Fairview Heights, where four Union regiments supported by a large artillery force had established a strong line of resistance. There Dilger reformed his battery and continued to provide fire support throughout a night of desperate fighting.

Dilger and Battery I survived Chancellorsville to fight through two more years of war. At Gettysburg they engaged in several fierce artillery duels on the first day of the battle. By the end of the day, when Battery I reconsolidated on Cemetery Hill, it had suffered a loss of fourteen men, twenty-four horses, and one gun. In exchange, it had knocked out at least five Confederate guns.

Despite Dilger's splendid leadership and his impressive tactical skills, he remained a captain for the entire war. He was recommended repeatedly for promotion and twice he was recommended for brevets, but no action was ever taken. Even when brevet promotions were handed out on an almost wholesale basis at the end of the war, Dilger remained a captain.

It is difficult to comprehend the Union's shabby treatment of its best battery commander. Dilger was foreign-born, and there was a definite resentment in the Union army against such officers. There was as well a general prejudice against XI Corps, because it had been routed several times, although certainly through no fault of Dilger's. Thus, Hubert Dilger had to wait almost thirty years for the recognition he so justly deserved. In 1893 at the insistence of XI Corps historian, Colonel Augustus C. Hamlin, Dilger finally was awarded the Medal of Honor for his actions at Chancellorsville.

—David T. Zabecki

For further reading:
Downey, Fairfax. *The Sound of the Guns: The Story of the American Artillery* (1955).
Naisawald, L. Van Loan. *Grape and Canister: The Story of the Field Artillery of the Army of the Potomac* (1983).
Wise, Jennings. "Field Artillery in Rearguard Actions: The Historical Incident of Dilger's Battery." *Field Artillery Journal* (1932).
Zabecki, David T. *American Artillery and the Medal of Honor* (1995).

DIPLOMACY, C.S.A.

Southern leaders made the decision to secede from the Union based in part on what they confidently believed to be political realities. In the realm of diplomacy, they believed that, in the event of war between the new Confederacy and the Union, Britain and France would intervene or mediate on behalf of the South because of the dependence of their textile industries on Southern cotton.

There can be no doubt that Anglo-French intervention would have affected the outcome of the war in the United States and might well have been decisive. The Anglo-French navies could have broken the Northern blockade of the Confederacy, and the shipment of European military supplies to Southern armies might well have enabled the South to follow up its numerous early victories with a decisive thrust into the Northern states. Even Anglo-French mediation would have favored the South, because any mediation efforts would have involved recognizing the independence of the Confederacy. Thus the focus of Confederate diplomacy during the Civil War was to secure foreign mediation or active intervention.

Britain seemed to have compelling reasons for intervening on behalf of the Confederacy. An independent South would weaken a dangerous commercial and naval rival and establish a balance of power in North America that London could manipulate to its advantage. A Confederate state that owed its independence to Britain might also be expected to be favorably disposed toward the expansion of British political and economic interests in the Western Hemisphere.

The official and private papers of British prime minister Lord Henry John Temple Palmerston leave little doubt that he clearly saw the potential advantages of an independent Confederacy. But the experience of the costly and inconclusive Crimean War had made Palmerston and his foreign secretary, Lord John Russell, far more conscious of the risks involved in bold diplomatic initiatives. "King Cotton" also did not sway the British, who had stockpiled cotton in 1860 and, by 1863, had developed alternative sources for cotton in India and Egypt. Although the French emperor, Napoleon III, was more prone to often foolish diplomatic adventures than the cautious Palmerston, he was convinced that he needed Britain's approval and cooperation to make intervention effective and to support his other diplomatic schemes in Europe.

On 16 March 1861, the Confederate government sent three representatives on a diplomatic mission to Britain, France, Russia, and Belgium to negotiate treaties of friendship, commerce, and navigation. As an inducement to effectively recognize the Confederacy by entering into such treaties, the European powers were offered almost tariff-free trade with the Confederacy. The envoys received a less than enthusiastic reception in the European capitals. On 23 September 1861, the Confederate government, disappointed by the ineffectiveness of the three commissioners, decided to send two "special commissioners" to London and Paris to carry on the diplomatic effort.

The new commissioners were James M. Mason of Virginia, a former chairman of the Senate Foreign Relations Committee, and John Slidell, a prominent New Orleans lawyer. The Confederate government considered the Mason-Slidell mission so important that it chartered a special light and fast steamer to run the Union blockade to Havana, where the two were to take passage to Europe on the vessel of a neutral country.

On the night of 12 October, Mason and Slidell boarded their special steamer at Charleston. It successfully evaded the blockade, and in Havana they transferred to the British mail steamer *Trent*. On 8 November the *Trent* was stopped by the Union warship *San Jacinto*, under Captain Charles Wilkes. Wilkes seized the two Southern envoys as "contraband of war" and returned them under arrest to the United States.

At a hastily convened cabinet meeting in Compiègne on 28 November, Napoleon and his ministers resolved to back the British in any protests they might make and let them know that France was prepared to recognize the Confederacy if the British government took the lead in doing so. Despite the anger the incident inspired in Russell and Palmerston, when the British cabinet met on 29 and 30 November, it decided to do no more for the present than demand the release of the prisoners and an official apology for the seizure of persons traveling under the British flag. On 26 December the U.S. secretary of state, William Henry Seward, defused the *Trent* Affair by agreeing to release Mason and Slidell and conceding that Wilkes had erred in arresting the envoys.

With the arrival of Mason and Slidell in London and Paris in January 1862, the mission of the Confederate commissioners sent to Europe the previous March automatically came to an end. The new envoys now attempted to do what their predecessors had failed to accomplish, namely, persuade the British and French governments to grant official recognition of the Confederacy and break the Union blockade.

In Paris, Slidell heard the familiar story that Napoleon was prepared to recognize the Confederacy, but because of the overall situation in Europe he could not act unless Britain took the lead. In talking with Baron Edouard Antoine Thouvenel, Napoleon's foreign minister, Slidell argued that France need not respect the Union blockade because it was ineffective and therefore did not meet the conditions of international law. Thouvenel, who was far more cautious in foreign affairs than his sovereign, replied by posing the awkward question as to why, if the Union blockade was so ineffective, so little cotton had been shipped from Southern ports to Europe. As Slidell knew, the principle reason for this lack of cotton was that the South itself had held back shipments to cause a cotton famine that would compel European intervention, a policy that was now backfiring because it made the blockade seem more effective than it really was. Slidell was unwilling to admit Southern duplicity, and thus his argument against the legality of the Union blockade collapsed.

In London, Russell agreed to see Mason unofficially, but the foreign secretary's attitude was so discouraging that Mason did not even press the question of recognition. Mason's arguments regarding the legality of the Union blockade were so ineffective that, shortly after seeing the envoy, Russell sent a dispatch to the embassy in Washington reaffirming the British resolve to respect the blockade.

Because Mason and Slidell seemed to be getting nowhere, Judah P. Benjamin, the new Confederate secretary of state, decided that more attractive incentives were required to encourage European intervention. At his instigation the Confederate senate on 18 April authorized President Jefferson Davis to arrange treaties with Britain, France, and Spain, offering special trade privileges and other inducements to break the Union blockade. Believing that Napoleon was most amenable to such offers, Benjamin instructed Slidell to approach the French government with an offer that amounted to bribery. Slidell was to inform the emperor that the Confederacy would allow France to introduce its goods into the South duty free. Furthermore, the South would make available approximately 100,000 bales of cotton to French vessels with a subsidy equal to 12.5 million dollars—a sum sufficient to pay the costs of a French naval force to open the Confederate Atlantic and Gulf ports to French commerce. The French were to be bribed into shooting their way into Southern ports to break the blockade, win trade concessions, and obtain cheap cotton.

Slidell met with the French ruler in Vichy on 16 July and presented the emperor with Benjamin's bribe offer. With the consent of the emperor, Slidell on 24 July submitted a formal request for recognition to the French government. But the French continued to take the position that Britain must act first, and when Mason presented the British government with a similar formal request, Russell turned it aside by simply refusing to see him. Neither Russell nor Palmerston would even entertain recognition of the South absent decisive Confederate military victories. But with the Union victory in the battle of Antietam on 17 September, the Confederate drive into Maryland was stopped and prospects for an early recognition of the South dimmed.

In January 1863, one month after the Union defeat in the battle of Fredericksburg, Napoleon launched a mediation proposal to end the war. In making this new proposal, he appeared to have the additional motive of currying favor with French public opinion, as his new foreign minister, Drouyn de Lhuys, leaked the news of this latest imperial mediation effort to the press before it reached Washington. It was a typically grandiose Napoleonic scheme to resolve the Civil War by establishing a confederation of American states consisting of four roughly equal parts—the North, South, West, and Mexico. Creating such a balance of power in North America would curb U.S. expansionism and allow for the growth of a French-controlled Mexico to include Texas and at least part of the former French colony of Louisiana.

Seward flatly rejected Napoleon's proposal, and with that there was nothing France could do to further the mediation plan short of joining forces with the

Confederacy, as Slidell now advocated. Napoleon, however, still refused to intervene unless Britain led the way. Late in May 1863, John Arthur Roebuck, a British member of Parliament, tried to force Britain to do just that when he gave notice that he intended to introduce a motion in the House of Commons to accord official recognition to the Confederacy. But Russell was successful in squashing the Roebuck motion in a debate in the House of Commons on 30 June. On 4 July 1863, the South suffered defeats at both Gettysburg and Vicksburg, ending all possibility that it might score the decisive military victory that all along had been the key condition for Anglo-French intervention.

Soon afterward, the Confederate government acknowledged that the diplomatic game was lost. In early August 1863, Benjamin, the Confederate secretary of state, recalled Mason from London. In October the Confederacy severed all relations with Britain when Benjamin expelled on Confederate territory the British consuls, who had never ceased being accredited to Washington, for challenging the authority of the Confederate government, in particular the right of the Confederacy to conscript British subjects. After October 1863, the already unlikely prospects for European intervention disappeared entirely, and the success of the Confederate bid for independence came to rest exclusively on the fortunes of war.

—*Todd Anthony Rosa*

See also Benjamin, Judah Philip; Great Britain; Mason, James Murray; Napoleon III; Russell, Lord John; Slidell, John; *Trent Affair.*

For further reading:

Chamberlain, Muriel E. *British Foreign Policy in the Age of Palmerston* (1980).

Crook, D. P. *The North, the South, and the Powers, 1861–1865* (1974).

Echard, William E. *Napoleon III and the Concert of Europe* (1980).

Evans, Eli N. *Judah P. Benjamin, The Jewish Confederate* (1988).

Owsley, Frank L. *King Cotton Diplomacy: Foreign Relations of the Confederate States of America* (1959).

Willson, Beckles. *John Slidell and the Confederates in Paris, 1862–1865* (1970).

DIPLOMACY, U.S.A.

William Henry Seward was the American statesman primarily responsible for the conduct of Union diplomacy during the Civil War. Trained as a lawyer, he had been governor of New York and a U.S. senator, and he was a founder of the Republican Party. Seward was a shrewd and tough politician, and he was to prove an equally shrewd and tough diplomat. His policies often seemed dangerous and reckless, but this was part of the game of gamble and bluff he believed he must play to compensate for the relatively

Diplomats gathered at an unidentified waterfall in New York State, August 1863 (*National Archives*)

weak diplomatic position of the United States at the onset of the Civil War.

Seward was painfully aware of how vulnerable the United States was to European intervention, and he understood clearly the significance and danger of British warnings regarding trade. Instead of adopting a conciliatory stance, however, he responded to British diplomatic pressure by adopting a firm and even threatening posture of his own. He informed the British that the European governments had no legitimate right to intervene in the dispute in North America, and any move on their part to receive the representatives of the Confederacy would risk the severance of diplomatic relations with the United States.

During the secession crisis, Seward did not give up hopes for a peaceful resolution between the North and the South. He conceived a daring plan to regain Southern loyalty by a foreign adventure that would drown domestic differences in a flood of patriotic fever. Seward's plan, submitted to President Abraham Lincoln on 1 April 1861, proposed that Fort Sumter be abandoned so as to avoid military hostilities. He further suggested that the administration change the question before the public

from slavery to that of union or disunion. In order to fire the imaginations of Southerners in favor of union, Seward proposed diverting public attention from quarrels at home by playing up danger from abroad. On 31 March, Spain invaded its former colony of Santo Domingo. Seward advised that the U.S. government rally both halves of the nation by demanding that Spain withdraw its military forces from the Western Hemisphere or face war with the United States.

Seward's proposals were neither so foolhardy nor so desperate as they appear at first glance. He knew that many Southerners had long coveted Spanish Cuba, and he therefore saw reason to hope that the South could be lured back into the Union by the prospect of a war with Spain. A war with Spain in the Western Hemisphere could be considered a relatively safe affair and a risk worth taking if it led to a restoration of the Union. Lincoln, however, did not act on Seward's bold plan. Instead, he authorized the shipment of supplies to Fort Sumter, a move that provoked Southern leaders to take the fateful step that made war inevitable.

One of Lincoln's first acts in response to the South's attack on Fort Sumter was the proclamation of a blockade of Southern ports. Thus Seward's most immediate problem in the field of foreign affairs was to deal with the objections of British and other governments and to prevent attempts by foreign powers to break the blockade or otherwise intervene in the war.

An international agreement on rules governing wartime blockades had been negotiated at the 1856 Paris Peace Conference that had ended the Crimean War. This Declaration of Paris had been signed by all the powers represented at the conference, and all other states had been invited to accede. The declaration abolished privateering. It provided that all enemy as well as neutral goods transported under a neutral flag were not liable to capture by belligerents unless they were contraband of war. The agreement further required that a naval blockade, in order to be respected by neutral powers, must be effective and maintained by a force sufficient to prevent access to the coast of the enemy.

The United States had refused to accede to this agreement because it did not wish to relinquish the right of privateering, but on 24 April 1861, Seward announced that Washington would become a signatory to the declaration. Privateering, which had been so profitable to Americans in the past could now only benefit the Confederacy. Seward also hoped to gain international recognition of the Union blockade. But there was a fundamental flaw in Seward's position. At the same time that he sought recognition of the Union blockade, he did not wish other powers to accord the Confederacy with the status of a belligerent, which could be interpreted as a form of recognition.

This was an untenable position, and Seward was unable to defend it. When news of Lincoln's declaration of the blockade reached London, the British cabinet on 13 May agreed to adopt a policy of neutrality and to recognize the Confederacy as a belligerent. Seward feared that this might be a prelude to a direct recognition of Confederate independence, and his apprehensions on this score were reinforced by news that the Confederate government had dispatched commissioners to Europe to negotiate treaties of friendship and commerce with European governments.

In a dispatch of 21 May, Seward instructed Charles Francis Adams, the U.S. minister to London, to inform the British government that intercourse of any kind with the Confederate envoys could be construed as recognition of the Confederacy. If British foreign secretary Lord John Russell insisted on seeing them, Adams was to break off all diplomatic relations. Adams was also told to inform Russell that formal British recognition of the Confederacy would be construed by Washington as an attempt to overthrow the United States and would result in war with the United States. When Adams met with Russell on 12 June, the British foreign secretary responded to Seward's threats in a conciliatory tone, announcing that he had no expectation of seeing the Confederate envoys in the future.

Besides the threat to the Union of European intervention or mediation, the most serious diplomatic problem of the American Civil War developed as a result of efforts by Confederate agents to arrange for the purchase or construction of warships in France and England. Since the Crimean War, when ironclad warships were first used, Britain and France had developed screw-propelled ironclads that were much faster, more heavily armed, and with greater firepower than either the Union's ironclad, the *Monitor*, or the Confederate ironclad, the *Virgina*. Because the Union navy at the outset of the war consisted entirely of wooden ships, Confederate leaders saw in the European ironclads an ideal instrument to counter the Union's overwhelming numerical advantage. Stephen M. Mallory, the Confederate secretary of the navy, believed the possession of an ironclad to be a matter of the first necessity, and shortly after the attack on Fort Sumter he sent agents to Britain and France to purchase such ships.

Fortunately for the Union, the Confederacy found it impossible to purchase European ironclads that were already built and ready for active duty. The British and French had placed legal restrictions on their sale, and the governments of these two countries wanted to retain them for their own navies. Union diplomatic pressure on Britain and France also influenced those governments' decision not to risk a major breach with Washington while the outcome of the Civil War was still in doubt.

While not providing ironclads, the British did sell ships to the Confederacy, despite Union diplomatic pressure. In June and August 1861, the Confederacy contracted for the construction of two wooden screw-driven steamers in Liverpool. They managed to slip out of British waters the following year, thus evading British law forbidding the outfitting on British territory of any vessel intended for use by belligerents against a state with which Britain was at peace. One of these vessels, the *Alabama*, was to terrorize Union shipping over the next two years until it was sunk off Cherbourg by a Union warship in June 1864. The exploits of the *Alabama* set off an ugly Anglo-American diplomatic and legal dispute that was to continue for another ten years, when U.S. claims for damages caused by the Confederate raider were at last settled by international arbitration, which awarded the United States fifteen million dollars in compensation.

Seward may have walked his most dangerous tightrope in dealing with the French emperor's designs on Mexico. Mexico had long fascinated Napoleon III as a source of raw materials and immense economic opportunity, which needed only his brand of liberal monarchy to reach its potential. He was also interested in building a cross-isthmian canal in Mexico, similar to the one that was currently under construction by the French at Suez.

The American Civil War had the potential to immobilize the U.S. capacity to defend the Monroe Doctrine and oppose European involvement in the Western Hemisphere.

Mexico had been in turmoil since 1857, when a civil war had developed between Mexican conservatives and the reform government of Benito Juarez. As the conflict forced the Juarez regime into bankruptcy, the Mexican government on 17 July 1861 suspended payment on all foreign debts. Napoleon used this as a pretext to secure British and Spanish support for European intervention in Mexico, formally agreed to by the three powers in the Convention of London of 31 October 1861. Seward responded to the upheaval in Mexico by sending a new minister to Mexico, Thomas Corwin, with instructions to block every Confederate or foreign plot there. In a diplomatic note of 4 December 1861, the Lincoln administration refused to accede to the Convention of London for the collection of Mexican debts.

In December 1861 and January 1862, Spanish, British, and French troops landed at the Mexican port of Veracruz. The Juarez government refused to negotiate the debt problem under the gun, and by early April 1862 the Spanish and British troops began to leave Mexico. However, Napoleon had no intention of leaving Mexico, and instead he ordered French troops to march on Mexico City. French military blunders and stiff Mexican resistance delayed the conquest of the Mexican capital until 10 June 1863. In early 1864 Napoleon installed Austrian archduke Ferdinand Maximilian of the House of Habsburg as Mexican emperor.

Seward realized that, if the French were determined to maintain a satellite regime in Mexico, their best means of doing so would be to join forces with the Confederacy to secure a stalemate in the American Civil War. Seward therefore played an extremely careful diplomatic game with Napoleon, allowing him to believe that, if France and Maximilian continued to observe a policy of strict neutrality in the American Civil War, the United States would remain neutral regarding the situation in Mexico. Seward's policy was successful, and Napoleon refused Maximilian's numerous pleas to recognize the Confederacy. It was only after victory in the Civil War that Seward in 1866 insisted that the French end their intervention in the Western Hemisphere. It was a demand that resulted in the toppling of Maximilian's regime by local insurrection.

—*Todd Anthony Rosa*

See also Adams, Charles Francis; *Alabama* Claims; Blockade of C.S.A.; Great Britain; Mexico; Napoleon III; Seward, William Henry.

For further reading:
Case, Lynn M., and Wareen F. Spencer. *The United States and France: Civil War Diplomacy* (1970).
Crook, D.P. *The North, the South, and the Powers, 1861–1865* (1974).
Ferris, Norman B. *Desperate Diplomacy: William H. Seward's Foreign Policy, 1861* (1976).
Hanna, Alfred J., and Kathryn Abby Hanna. *Napoleon III and Mexico* (1971).
Paolino, Ernest N. *The Foundations of the American Empire: William Henry Seward and U.S. Foreign Policy* (1973).

DISEASE

Along with wounds, disease contributed to the massive casualty statistics of the Civil War. On average, diseases were far more deadly than bullets. Disease could diminish the effectiveness of an army in the field, even devastating it, so medical departments played a vital role by trying to keep soldiers healthy. Sanitation also became increasingly important, and promoting healthy living conditions was a material goal of both Confederate and Union medical services. Medical knowledge about the connection between sanitation and general health was sketchy, however, so camps and even hospitals were often unclean and correspondingly unhealthy. Physicians, only beginning to understand the nature of disease, performed amputations with instruments washed in water bloody from previous operations.

Germ theory and bacteriology would attain credence in the years following the war, and only then would medical science begin making strides against disease. It was unfortunately too late to help the Civil War soldier. Not until the end of the nineteenth century would the proportion of soldiers killed by disease fall below that killed by enemy fire. During the Civil War, three of every five Union soldiers who died did so from disease. For the Confederacy two of every three deaths resulted from disease. Roughly 224,000 Union officers and soldiers died of disease, while such ailments claimed about 164,000 Confederates. Yet, such figures are somewhat misleading because they count both nonwounded and wounded soldiers who fell ill. Establishing a distinction between healthy soldiers who fell ill and those who became ill after suffering wounds would be a better gauge of the severity of particular diseases.

Soldiers from isolated rural areas lacked the exposure to sickness necessary to build up immunities. Consequently, many diseases achieved almost epidemic levels during the war's early years. Infectious diseases were so commonplace that Surgeon General William Hammond was prompted to write in an annual report for 1861–1862 that there were no serious epidemics afflicting the army. Nonetheless, typhoid, diarrhea, dysentery, scurvy, gonorrhea, and syphilis afflicted both Union and Confederate forces. In regard to venereal diseases, many physicians thought that they were moral afflictions rather than medical ones and hence did not afford them serious treatment. Nutrition was also a problem and related maladies such as scurvy became widespread.

As the war progressed, the incidence of disease decreased in some areas. Contributing to this decline was the increased number of seasoned veterans who had never been vulnerable to disease or who had survived its onset to become immune to it. Yet disease rates could vary markedly from region to region or from army to army. As an example, though both units reported their camps as clean, the 12th Massachusetts Infantry had a disease rate of 4 per 1,000 in 1862 compared to the 5th Vermont Infantry's 271 per 1,000. Also, a region and its climate greatly influenced the occurrence of sickness. Union soldiers who campaigned in the South suffered an alarming increase in mortality rates because malaria and dysentery thrived in the hot and humid climate.

It is probably impossible to measure accurately the real impact of disease in the Civil War. Aside from affecting the performance of armies by striking down ordinary soldiers, it could debilitate officers, sometimes at the highest levels, to fog judgment and influence crucial decisions. And even after the shooting had stopped, disease carried on its grim work when soldiers returned home with illnesses alien to different regions, thus to infect countless civilians. The medical profession would learn invaluable lessons from the war, but the cost of that education was exceedingly high.

—Matthew Pacer

See also Medicine.
For further reading:
Adams, George W. *Doctors in Blue* (1961).
Ashburn, P.M. *A History of the Medical Department of the United Stated Army* (1929).
Cunningham, Horace H. *Doctors in Gray* (1970).
Steiner, Paul E. *Disease in the Civil War* (1968).

DIVERS, BRIDGET
(ca. 1840–?)
Union army daughter of the regiment

Very little is known about the prewar life of Bridget Divers excpet that she was a working-class Irish immigrant to the United States and was probably in her early twenties when she signed up at the start of the war for military service with the 1st Michigan Cavalry. Although perhaps as many as 1,000 women disguised themselves as men and served the Union and Confederate armies as soldiers, Divers provides a noteworthy example of those who joined the volunteer regiments of the North and the South as army women or female support staff, serving as nurses, cooks, laundresses, sutlers, and the like. The lines between these roles often blurred in the actual context of war. Often particularly dedicated and courageous army women—some of whom even assumed paramilitary roles on the battlefield—

earned the designation "daughter of the regiment." Divers was one such heroine. An army woman who was also named the 1st Michigan Cavalry's daughter of the regiment, Divers's complete devotion to the cause of her adopted country and the welfare of the soldiers with whom she served became legendary.

Bridget Divers's Irish background must have been unmistakable, for she was frequently identified as "Irish Biddy" by those who spoke or wrote of her exploits. Divers accompanied the 1st Michigan Cavalry for the duration of the war, extending her basic service as a regimental nurse and caretaker for the sick and wounded to include remarkable demonstrations of valor and commitment. On one occasion late in the war she rode her horse fifteen miles into Rebel territory in order to reclaim—and bring back for proper shipment home to Michigan—the body of a captain in the 1st who had been killed in battle.

Divers made a name for herself not only as an uncommonly brave, modest, and robust field nurse, but also as a source of battlefield inspiration, rallying "her boys" to fight whenever their courage was flagging. Moreover, she came to be known during the war for her exceptional powers of memory. According to a field agent for the United States Christian Commission, inquiries about men in the 1st Michigan Cavalry (and even about men in the division to which the 1st Michigan belonged) were often directed to Divers first, as she had repeatedly proven herself to be the best resource for determining where individual soldiers might be found at any given time and what their particular needs might be. According to agent J. R. Miller, Divers's love for the men in blue, her concern for their health, and her regard for their spiritual welfare were at all times unsurpassed. Several women nurses whom Divers met in the course of her travels—including several who came to the war from far more elevated social backgrounds than she—also spoke of Divers with great respect and enthusiasm, even a touch of envy. Bridget Divers, wrote Charlotte E. McKay, probably "saw more of the danger and hardship than any other woman during the war."

Unfortunately, we know even less about what became of Divers after the war than we know about the details of her early life. The best information available suggests that this expert equestrian, who loved the outdoors and the military, traveled west after Appomattox to serve with a regiment that had been assigned to frontier duty.

—Elizabeth D. Leonard

See also Women.
For further reading:
Brockett, Linus P., and Mary C. Vaughan. *Woman's Work in the Civil War* (1867).
Conklin, Eileen. *Women at Gettysburg, 1863* (1993).
Leonard, Elizabeth D. *All the Daring of the Soldier: Women of the Civil War Armies* (1999).
Moore, Frank. *Women of the War: Their Heroism and Self-Sacrifice* (1866).

DIX, DOROTHEA LYNDE
(1802–1887)
Superintendent of U.S. Army nurses

Dorothea Dix did not want to be remembered for her war work, which she referred to as an "episode" in an otherwise distinguished career. It is not that Dix brought shame on her position as Superintendent in the Office of U.S. Army Nurses, but that from her selection by Secretary of War Simon Cameron in June 1861 to the publication in October 1863 of War Department Order No. 351, which severely curtailed her authority, she was caught in a web of controversy concerning who would appoint providers of medical relief. When she left the service in 1865, she had logged thousands of hours looking after female personnel in military hospitals all over the Eastern theater, but had not succeeded in gilding the reputation she had already established before 1861.

Fifty-nine when the war began, Dix had compiled an impressive résumé when she offered her services in April, having experienced mob violence against Massachusetts soldiers as she passed through Baltimore on her way to Washington. This daughter of New England was born to wealth and privilege, but after the untimely death of her physician father, she went to work as a teacher and opened a finishing school in Boston. Her interest in working with the elite, however, waned rapidly. In 1834 Dix traveled to Europe to observe prisons and asylums for the mentally ill in the hope of upgrading these institutions in the United States. For the next twenty years, Dix immersed herself in reforms to benefit the mentally ill and indigent poor. After years of lobbying legislators and publicizing the plight of the sick and the poor, Dix managed to persuade Congress in the 1850s to endow millions of acres of public lands for the construction of more humane facilities. She returned to Europe in 1858 in an attempt to consult with Florence Nightingale, England's chief relief worker and nurse in the Crimea. Though Nightingale's absence in Scutari prevented their meeting, Dix absorbed everything she could about the physical layout and management of military hospitals, which served her well in the eyes of the U.S. War Department after the fall of Fort Sumter.

Elizabeth Blackwell, the nation's first female physician, was also a contender for the job of nursing superintendent. Dix's offer was so timely and her influence on Capitol Hill so significant from years of intimacy with politicians that Blackwell, who had earned little civility and even less respect from male physicians, stood little chance of preempting the mild-mannered Dix, despite her superior professional credentials. In Dix, War Department surgeons believed they were hiring an obedient hospital administrator and not a medical competitor. Blackwell went on to train about 100 nurses under the auspices of the Women's Central Relief Association in New York, but she and the Sanitary Commissioners who later superseded that organization never cooperated with Dix. One well-placed officer referred to Dix contemptuously as "that philanthropic lunatic."

Aside from the lack of clarity concerning who had the authority to appoint female nurses and the maneuvering of the U.S. Sanitary Commission to gather all Northern relief efforts under its umbrella, Dix won few friends with what many perceived to be overly stringent eligibility standards. In a now-famous circular of the War Department, Dix advertised for women between the ages of thirty-five and fifty, plain of mien, and unhooped. The many young women who had already volunteered to nurse were put off when they realized that Dix was looking for more matronly helpers; indeed the superintendent was aware that young women would be sexually vulnerable in hospitals full of men, and thus tried to head off criticism in that arena. When Georgeanna Woolsey, a blue-blooded New Yorker, encountered Dix in 1861, Dix asked her to leave her post immediately—she was only in her twenties—but sister Jane Woolsey advised her, "Outflank the Dix by any and every means in your power, remembering that…hospital visitors and people who really desire to do good have taken no notice of obstacles except to vanquish them." Many of those rejected because of their youth (among them New Jersey's Cornelia Hancock and New Hampshire's Esther Hill Hawks) found another way to the front and became trusted nurses. By the same token, some of those whom Dix had appointed left the service in disgrace when they realized the Spartan nature of the accommodations.

In October 1863, Surgeon General William Alexander Hammond truncated Dix's power with Order No. 351, which gave surgeons the authority to appoint their own hospital employees and to bypass "Dragon Dix" altogether. Dix's insistence on a certain protocol with her nurses irked surgeons, who preferred to hire nuns or younger, livelier attendants. When Dix discovered surgeons who had lovers or opposed the employment of women in hospitals, she would warn her nurses in the hope of shielding them from humiliation. But her wish to serve as mother-protector was not efficacious, and corrupt physicians could ostracize her and her appointees with impunity. In spite of her lack of popularity among medical practitioners, many of the more than 3,000 nurses whom Dix appointed appreciated her difficulties and admired her. New York's Sophronia Bucklin, who saw four years of hard service, was impressed that Dix gave her pocket money when she arrived in Washington. Official papers show that, long after Order No. 351 made Dix a superintendent in name only, she ordered transportation to women who were called home for emergencies or needed to leave on account of illness. If she could not get funding from the

War Department, she paid for the trips herself rather than leave workers stranded. Iowa's Annie Turner Wittenmyer, originator of special diet kitchens, called Dix "the stateliest woman I ever saw" after the two spent the night on the floor of a storeroom at City Point in the spring of 1865, when the wards were brimming with the slaughter of the previous summer's campaigns.

Like other reform-minded women of the period, Dix hoped to bring others into her orbit, but she was unable. She was unwilling to delegate authority to others who could advance her work, and she was not interested in joining the male-headed Sanitary Commission team. Dix attempted to befriend Mary Ann Bickerdyke and Clara Barton, perhaps to offset their growing influence, but was not successful in getting the support of either one. Still, Dix's labor on behalf of women in nursing was lauded after the war, when she settled back into asylum work in Trenton, New Jersey. For fifteen more years, she worked tirelessly to upgrade conditions for the disadvantaged, retiring seven years before her death in 1887.

—*Jane E. Schultz*

See also Hammond, William Alexander; Nurses.

For further reading:
Brockett, Linus P., and Mary Vaughan. *Woman's Work in the Civil War* (1867).
Brown, Thomas J. *Dorothea Dix, New England Reformer* (1998).
Dix, Dorothea. Papers. Record Group 94. National Archives and Records Administration, Washington, D.C.
Gollaher, David. *Voice for the Mad: The Life of Dorothea Dix* (1995).
Wilson, Dorothy Clarke. *Stranger and Traveler: The Story of Dorothea Dix, American Reformer* (1975).

John Adams Dix (*Library of Congress*)

DIX, JOHN ADAMS
(1798–1879)
Union general

John Adams Dix's life spanned from the early years of the Republic through the Reconstruction Era. He served his country as a soldier in two wars and held a host of state and federal elective and appointive offices. In the private sector he managed real estate, practiced law, and ran railroads when the nation's prosperity and growth traveled on rails. He counted as acquaintances, casual or intimate, such figures as Thomas Jefferson, James Madison, John Randolph, Henry Clay, John C. Calhoun, James Buchanan, William Wirt (under whom he studied law), and a host of other similarly recognizable Americans. Dix possessed an uncommon intimacy with the very course of U.S. nineteenth-century history.

Born in New Hampshire on 24 July 1798, Dix was a descendant of Puritans and patriots. His early life was dedicated to education, a passion of his father, Timothy Dix, Jr. To avoid the parochialism of a U.S. education, in 1811 his father sent him to the College of Montreal to immerse him in French language and culture. It was at the college that Dix contended "the real foundations of [his] classical education were laid." Between a rigorous self-study program and formal studies in the United States and Canada, Dix learned French, Spanish, Greek, Latin, mathematics, and elocution. By the age of fourteen, he was translating into English the orations of Cicero.

As the clouds of war gathered in 1812, the elder Dix summoned him home. For a time he resided with a distant relative in Boston, where his studies continued. Patriotic fervor overtook his enthusiasm for studying, however, and he persuaded his father to allow him to follow his footsteps into military service. In December 1812 he was commissioned a cadet with an admonishment from his father that he must continue his private studies. In March 1813, still only fourteen, he was promoted to ensign. Henceforth father and son campaigned together on the Canadian frontier. That year Dix entered what he called "the most trying period of [his] life" when his father died.

After the war, Dix remained in the military while returning to his studies. By the mid-1820s he reached the rank of major, studied law in Washington, D.C., and married. In 1828 he resigned his army commission and settled in Cooperstown, New York, as managing agent for his father-in-law's property.

Dix began his political life as a member of Cooperstown's Democratic Party. Beginning in 1830 he held a number of political offices. He "was called to almost every office which a citizen can hold," wrote his son Morgan. Among these offices were New York State adjutant general (1831–1833); member, state house of representatives (1842); U.S. senator (1845–1849); assistant treasurer of the United States at New York City (1853); postmaster of New York City (1860–1861); U.S. secretary of the treasury (1861); U.S. minister to France (1866–1869); and governor of New York (1873–1875).

Throughout the antebellum period, Dix, a Free Soil Democrat, consistently supported measures to limit the expansion of slavery. "He was no abolitionist in the technical sense in which the word came to be used," wrote his son, "but he cordially disliked slavery, and desired its extinction; yet not by measures which would have invaded the rights of our Southern brethren under the compact of the Federal Constitution."

As Southern states seceded, however, Treasury Secretary Dix embodied Northern resolve. On 29 January 1861, he instructed a treasury official in New Orleans to assume command of a revenue cutter. To punctuate his determination to enforce federal authority, he concluded his message, "If anyone attempts to haul down the American flag, shoot him on the spot." After war erupted, Dix accepted an appointment as a major general with the New York State volunteers and, later, from Lincoln at the same rank in the Union army. He was initially offered command of the Department of Alexandria and Arlington, but his age (sixty-two) convinced many in the administration that he was too old for such an important command. Instead he was given less threatened departments, ending the war in command of the Department of the East in New York. His Civil War military service was steady but unremarkable.

After the war, Dix served in a variety of public offices until age seventy-six. His contribution as an elder statesman to those offices was that he possessed "passive dignity." In 1876 he ran unsuccessfully for the office of mayor of New York City. For the remaining three years of his life he lived in that city, active, according to his son, "up to within forty-eight hours of his death." He died on 21 April 1879.

—*Larry C. Skogen*

For further reading:
Dix, Morgan, comp. *Memoirs of John Adams Dix* (1883).

"DIXIE"

This popular minstrel song of the late 1850s became, because of its close association with Confederate reunions in the nineteenth century, the unofficial anthem of the Confederacy and later an emotional link with the Lost Cause. When and how the term *Dixie* came to represent the South remains obscure, as does the origin of the tune's melody itself. One thing, however, remains certain. The song "I Wish I Was in Dixie's Land" had its formal debut, paradoxically, in the North, at Mechanics Hall, New York City, 4 April 1859. This song's composer was Daniel Decatur Emmett (1815–1904), who produced the song as a "walk-around," a choreographed finale for Dan Bryant's minstrel adaptation of John Brougham's popular comedy, *Pocahontas*.

A native of Knox County, Ohio, Emmett had long been associated with popular music. The founder of one of the first minstrel groups in 1842, the Virginia Minstrels of New York City, he may well have been introduced to the actual tune—as argued by Howard and Judith Sacks—by two African-American musicians, Ben and Lou Snowden, also of Knox County. The evidence remains circumstantial, as does the notion that the tune had even longer roots as a melody familiar to African-American stevedores working along the Mississippi River. Emmett later recalled that the phrase "I wish I was in Dixie" constantly came to mind when working on the finale due to his wife's complaints about Northern winters. His reflection may support one version of how the term *Dixie* itself originated: with the slaves of a Mr. Dix of Manhattan, New York, who coined the term to describe a warm, African-American paradise. The term may also have originated, of course, by allusion to Jeremiah Dixon, 1733–1779, the English surveyor who, together with Charles Mason, drew the boundary between Maryland and Pennsylvania, the Mason-Dixon Line, traditionally regarded as the line separating the North and the South. Equally plausible is the notion that the term originated in New Orleans when the Citizens Bank and Trust Company issued in the 1850s a $10 currency note that bore the word *dix*, the French word for "ten," hence a *dixes*.

If the original link of the term with the Crescent City remains tenuous, it is known that Brougham himself directed the first Southern production of his burlesque *Pocahontas*, or *The New Orleans Varieties*, in the fall of 1860. The stage show was extremely popular, and Bryant staged another production, in Montgomery, Alabama, later that year. According to some accounts, the first musical transcription of the tune was created in Montgomery. In any event, "I wish I was in Dixie's Land" created such a stir that it was played at Jefferson Davis's inauguration in that city, 18 February 1861. Although the song was popular in both North and South, this event alone firmly linked it with the South, which by 1861 had claimed the song for itself. As the North came to adopt "The Battle Hymn of the Republic" as its own battle hymn, "Dixie," by now in various music sheet forms, had little to do with the South's fight for independence. Consequently, Confederate general Albert Pike (1809–1891), perhaps the strangest of all Southern generals, composed new verses to accompany the older thirty-two musical measures. His version was, at least, peculiar to the South:

Southrons, hear your country call!
Up, lest worse than death befall you!
To arms! . . . Advance the flag of Dixie!
Hurrah! Hurrah!
For Dixie's land we take our stand,
And live or die for Dixie.

As a gesture of conciliation, Abraham Lincoln, upon being informed of General Lee's surrender at Appomattox, asked a resident military band in Washington, D.C., to strike up "Dixie." It was, and again perhaps paradoxically, one of his favorite tunes.

"Dixie" remains popular today, yet its association with the Lost Cause, together with the waving of the Confederacy's battle flag, has remained so emotive that its airing can be controversial. Just as the song's fortune remained checkered, its Northern composer, Daniel Emmett, died in reduced financial circumstances in Mount Vernon, Ohio, in 1904.

—*Rory T. Cornish*

See also "Battle Hymn of the Republic"; Music.
For further reading:
Harwell, Richard B. *Confederate Music* (1950).
Jackson, Richard. *Popular Songs of Nineteenth Century America* (1976).
Lair, John. *Songs Lincoln Loved* (1954).
Nathan, Hans. *Dan Emmett and the Rise of Early Negro Minstrelsy* (1962).
Sacks, Howard L., and Judith Rose Sacks. *Way up North in Dixie: A Black Family's Claim to the Confederate Anthem* (1993).
Tilton, Robert S. *Pocahontas: The Evolution of an American Narrative* (1994).

DODGE, GRENVILLE MELLEN
(1831–1916)
Union general

I would rather have had your experiences in the Civil War and have seen what you have seen and done," Theodore Roosevelt confided to Grenville Mellen Dodge, "than to be President of the United States." Civil War general, Indian fighter, politician, and railroad trailblazer were all hallmarks of Dodge's remarkable career, each worthy of Roosevelt's admiration. Born in Danvers, Massachusetts, on 12 April 1831, "Gren"

Grenville M. Dodge (*Library of Congress*)

Dodge had an early interest in military matters. He attended Norwich University, founded by a former commandant of West Point, and graduated in 1851 with a degree in civil and military engineering. He then ventured to Illinois, Iowa, and Nebraska as an engineer and surveyor with the Mississippi & Missouri Railroad. Dodge settled in Council Bluffs, Iowa, became captain of the Council Bluffs Guards in 1856, and supported Republican efforts to build a transcontinental railroad.

When war came in 1861, Dodge was commissioned colonel of the 4th Iowa Infantry and, after brief service in Missouri, earned command of a brigade in Samuel R. Curtis's Army of the Southwest. His performance at the battle of Pea Ridge (7–8 March 1862) won him a brigadier general's star. Assigned to the Army of the Tennessee in northern Mississippi in June 1862, he oversaw the rebuilding of the Mobile & Ohio Railroad. Harassed by Confederate cavalry and guerrillas who destroyed vital railroad trestles, Dodge installed two-story log blockhouses to protect the bridges. The success of the blockhouses led to their proliferation along other railroads in the region. On 30 October 1862, he was assigned to command the Second Division, Army of the Tennessee.

While the rest of the army moved on Vicksburg, Ulysses S. Grant placed Dodge in charge of the District of Corinth with orders to watch for Confederate reinforcements coming from Tennessee. To procure this information, Dodge assembled a corps of scouts and spies using men from his ranks and northern Alabama Unionists. Between November 1862 and July 1863, this organization became the largest and most far-reaching intelligence network of the war. He also created the 1st Alabama Cavalry, composed of Southern Unionists, and the 1st Alabama Infantry, a black regiment. From Corinth, Dodge launched several successful raids against Southern supply lines, including one in the Tuscumbia Valley in April 1863 that destroyed a large amount of supplies headed to Southern forces in Tennessee.

That same year he played a leading role in one of the war's most famous military executions. At Pulaski, Tennessee, he captured Confederate spy Sam Davis, who, despite a promise of clemency, refused to identify other Southern agents in the region. Although deeply touched by the young man's courage and loyalty, Dodge had him executed. (In 1909, Dodge would contribute money to the citizens of Pulaski to help build a statue commemorating Davis's bravery and sacrifice.)

In 1864, Dodge commanded the 16th Corps, Army of the Tennessee, and, with Grant's support, became a major general on 7 June 1864. Seriously wounded while leading his corps during the Atlanta campaign, Dodge returned in December 1864 to command of the Department of the Missouri, where he spent the remainder of the war chasing Indians and guerrillas. He would be forever associated with the Old West when one of the most legendary cowboy towns took the name Dodge City.

After resigning his commission in 1866, Dodge became the Union Pacific Railroad's chief engineer, served a term in the U.S. House of Representatives (1867–1869), and in 1873 helped railroad magnate Jay Gould lay thousands of miles of track. In 1898 the Spanish-American War again vaulted Dodge onto the national scene, this time at the head of a presidential commission investigating the U.S. Army's chaotic mobilization. The 1899 Dodge Commission report revealed basic flaws in army organization and administration and was a step toward future reform within the nation's military organization.

After laying his last mile of track in 1902, Dodge, by then a millionaire, retired but remained active, spending much of his time writing short books and articles about his experiences. Though he longed for someone to write his biography, he did not live to see it. He died in Council Bluffs on 3 January 1916 at age eighty-four.

—*William B. Feis*

See also Corinth, Mississippi; Pea Ridge, Battle of; Railroads, Union.

For further reading:

Hirshson, Stanley P. *Grenville M. Dodge: Soldier, Politician, Railroad Pioneer* (1967).

Perkins, J.R. *Trails, Rails, and War: The Life of General G. M. Dodge* (1929).

DONELSON, ANDREW JACKSON
(1799–1871)
American Party vice-presidential candidate

Historians recognize Andrew Jackson Donelson today as a minor political figure of the Jacksonian and antebellum periods. In reality, this Tennessee political fixture followed the policies of his uncle, Andrew Jackson, in preserving the Union and extending its institutions.

Born on 25 August 1799, Donelson became a protegé of Jackson at a young age. Jackson viewed Donelson's future with great political expectations. To prepare him for this career, Jackson ensured that his young nephew attend the best schools in the nation. Donelson was a student at Cumberland College in Nashville, Tennessee, until 1816. From there, he became a cadet at West Point. Donelson graduated second in his class in 1820, at which time Jackson requested that his nephew receive a commission under his command in Florida. When Jackson resigned his military command and became governor of the newly acquired territory of Florida, Donelson served as Jackson's aide-de-camp during his uncle's short term as governor. In late 1821, Donelson resigned his commission in the army and attended Transylvania University in Lexington, Kentucky, where he studied law. He concluded his studies in 1823, and Donelson became his uncle's confidential secretary upon returning to the Hermitage, Jackson's home. Donelson also practiced law with Thomas A. Duncan in downtown Nashville for a short time.

But his uncle's campaign for the presidency and Jackson's insistence that Donelson take care of his private affairs while he was away in Washington shortened what was a promising start in the law profession. By the time of Jackson's election as president in 1828, Donelson had become his uncle's chief political and personal correspondent. Jackson showed confidence in Donelson by selecting him as his private secretary for the majority of his two administrations.

Donelson experienced turbulence during the Jackson administrations, but proved successful overall. Donelson sided against his uncle during the Eaton affair, which caused the president to exile his nephew and his nephew's wife, Emily, to Tennessee on several occasions. However, Donelson and Emily eventually returned to assume their original positions as private secretary and White House hostess in Washington. During Jackson's two administrations, Donelson was an active participant in both formulating and preparing the final versions of official messages, papers, and correspondence related to Jackson's political philosophy, as well as exerting his influence on state elections.

Upon the election of Martin Van Buren in 1836, the president-elect considered Donelson for a cabinet post,

but the Tennessean declined, assisting the Democratic Party in other areas. From 1837 to 1844, Donelson worked tirelessly to attain favorable election results for Democratic candidates in Tennessee and across the nation. His efforts culminated in the nomination and eventual election to the presidency of his Tennessee colleague, James Knox Polk, in 1844. Based largely upon Donelson's ties to Jackson and Texas president Sam Houston, President John Tyler appointed him chargé d'affaires to Texas. The new American chargé used his influence and political skills to bring about the United States' offer of annexation to Texas in 1845 and did much to ensure its successful acceptance.

Upon his return to the United States, Donelson discovered that President Polk was considering him for a cabinet post. Both men believed that Donelson would better serve the country in another capacity, so instead, Donelson accepted the post of minister to Prussia and the lesser German states in 1846. During his time in Europe, the American minister witnessed the turmoil brought to the continent by the Revolutions of 1848.

The election of Whig presidential nominee Zachary Taylor in 1848 brought an end to Donelson's term as minister. Taylor relieved him of his post in 1849, and Donelson returned to an uncertain future. Almost immediately upon his return to the United States, he became involved in the Nashville Convention, a meeting called by Southerners to consider the divisive sectional issues that were dominating American politics. Donelson attended the convention as one of his state's delegates. Opposing many of the other members, Donelson voiced his support for the compromise measures that Congress was debating during the summer of 1850. The convention's first session ended with a wait-and-see attitude. After the passage of the Compromise of 1850, the convention members met a second time. The delegates took no decisive action, but compromise men like Donelson were fewer in number.

In 1851 Donelson assumed the editorship of the Democratic newspaper in Washington, the *Washington Union*. His tenure there lasted only fourteen months. His support of the Constitution and the Union over Southern radicalism quickly lost favor with the increasingly more sectionalist Democratic Party. The next few years witnessed Donelson shedding the party of his youth and becoming the vice-presidential nominee of the Know-Nothing Party in the 1856 election. Joining with another Constitution and Union politician, presidential nominee Millard Fillmore, Donelson and his new party attempted to present compromise to the American populace. Their efforts proved unsuccessful, and Donelson returned to Tennessee.

Donelson moved to Memphis in 1857 to attend more adequately to his plantations in Mississippi. The rise of the Constitutional Union Party in 1859–1860 gave him one more chance to achieve compromise. He served as chairman of the Tennessee delegation to the party's convention in Baltimore. Much like the Democratic convention held in Baltimore in 1844, Donelson saw his preference for a presidential nominee achieved at the 1860 convention in its selection of John Bell. His hopes for compromise faltered with the election of Lincoln. After the commencement of the Civil War, Donelson attempted to convince both Confederate and United States leaders that they were wrong in turning to military action instead of compromise; however, these actions only led to his detainment and arrest by both sides. With little support for compromise in a divided Tennessee, Donelson lived the rest of the war years in forced silence. He died on 26 June 1871 in Memphis, having spent the early years of Reconstruction attempting to salvage his financial situation.

—*Mark R. Cheathem*

See also American Party; Election of 1856.

For further reading:
Bryan, Charles Faulkner, Jr. "The Prodigal Nephew: Andrew Jackson Donelson and the Eaton Affair." *East Tennessee Historical Society Publications* (1978).
Owsley, Harriet Chappell. "Andrew Jackson and His Ward, Andrew Jackson Donelson." *Tennessee Historical Quarterly* (1982).
Satterfield, Robert B. "Andrew Jackson Donelson: A Moderate Nationalist Jacksonian" (Ph.D. dissertation, 1961).
Walters, Frederick Ray. "The Donelson Mission to the German Federal Government, 1848–1849" (M.A. thesis, 1964).

DOOLITTLE, JAMES ROOD
(1815–1897)
Chairman, Senate Committee on Indian Affairs

Born in Washington County, New York, Doolittle graduated from Geneva (now Hobart Smith) College in 1834. He passed the bar three years later, after marrying in Rochester. Settling in Wyoming County in 1841, the well-spoken six-footer became involved in politics. He was elected county district attorney shortly thereafter.

Though he considered moving to Texas after his term expired, Doolittle resettled his family in Racine, Wisconsin, in 1851. His devotion to the antislavery cause, which he first proclaimed as a "barn burner" delegate to the Democratic Party convention in Baltimore in 1848 (but buried for a time when he supported Franklin Pierce for president in 1852), soon took root in Wisconsin's radical environment. So too did his anti-Negro positions, which flowered after he was sent to the Senate as a Republican in 1857.

Doolittle opposed the extension of slavery, but he dreaded the competition freed blacks would bring western whites as much, if not more. He feared that blacks would be exterminated in a race war if they remained where they were—and that the "purity" of the "Anglo-Saxon" race would be threatened if widespread emigration to the frontier followed emancipation. Consequently, Doolittle favored colonization, or the removal of the freedmen to the Caribbean or Africa. In espousing this policy, he sided with other converts to the party who sought to preserve the Union and counter charges of abolitionism. Doolittle framed his concerns best before a New York crowd in 1859 when he stated that "the only question which could imperil the Union was the Negro question—a question which lay deeper even than the Slavery question."

Once Congress began to consider the role slaves played in the Confederate war effort after Bull Run, Doolittle's enthusiasm for emancipation, unsurprisingly, depended on whether a proposal included colonization or not. Though he voted for the Confiscation Act of 6 August 1861, he was more devoted to a plan that would have encouraged nonslaveholding Southern whites to support emancipation and colonization in return for homesteads on the lands of treasonous plantation owners. Likewise, he strongly supported a bill to emancipate slaves in the District of Columbia on 3 April 1862, but only after the measure was amended so that $100,000 was set aside for colonization.

Because President Lincoln supported colonization during the first year of the war, Doolittle was labeled an administration spokesman by conservative Republicans and hometown boosters. Doolittle certainly was a friend and admirer of the president—he campaigned vigorously for Lincoln in 1864—but Lincoln's known reluctance to take advice, talk strategy, or potentially alienate prospective supporters suggests such claims were exaggerated.

Lincoln's announcement of the Emancipation Proclamation after the battle at Antietam in 1862 ended debate over colonization, though Doolittle had another chance to depoliticize race relations through Federal Indian policy. The corruption that led to the Santee Sioux uprising in Minnesota during the fall of 1862 and the resulting deaths of hundreds of settlers and thirty-eight Indians executed en masse by local authorities had little impact on Doolittle's mindset. In his view, the brutal suppression only confirmed Indian inferiority; Doolittle's committee, likewise, was more interested in preventing Indians who took part in the uprising from receiving treaty payments than it was in taking steps to prevent future corruption.

This outlook would change, however, after Colonel John M. Chivington massacred approximately 200 Cheyenne women and children at Sand Creek, Colorado Territory, on 29 November 1864. Assigned to head a joint congressional committee in the aftermath of the slaughter, Doolittle began a two-year investigation that sent him traveling across the west. Besides

condemning Chivington, his committee called for the formation of civilian boards to oversee the government's handling of Indian affairs. Though this was a significant reform proposal, one that anticipated President Ulysses S. Grant's "Peace Policy," it was only a first step. Grant's more comprehensive program, unfortunately, was far more successful in removing tribes to reservations in present-day South Dakota and Oklahoma, purportedly to prevent their extinction through assimilation, than it was in stopping corruption. Nevertheless, though Doolittle's efforts to colonize the freedmen and depoliticize the "Negro question" were unsuccessful, his post–Sand Creek effort to depoliticize the "Indian problem" by laying the groundwork for Grant's policies, was more influential in the long run.

Doolittle signaled his eventual return to the Democratic Party in 1866, when he openly supported President Andrew Johnson. Doolittle opened a legal firm and lectured as a professor in Chicago after his Senate career ended in 1869. He died on 27 July 1897.

—*Robert W. Burg*

See also Chivington, John M.; Confiscation Acts; Emancipation Proclamation; Sand Creek Massacre; Sioux Indians.

For further reading:

Beard, William David. "James Rood Doolittle, A Public Life: From Democrat to Demagogue" (Master's thesis, 1979).
Chaput, Donald. "Generals, Indian Agents, Politicians: The Doolittle Survey of 1865." *Western Historical Quarterly* (1972).
Marone, Biagino M. "Senator James Rood Doolittle and the Struggle Against Radicalism, 1857–1866" (Master's thesis, 1955).

DOUBLEDAY, ABNER
(1819–1893)
Union general

Abner Doubleday is popularly known as the inventor of the game of baseball, but contemporaries knew him as the man who aimed the first Union shot of the war from Fort Sumter in 1861 and who played a key role in the Federal victory at Gettysburg, Pennsylvania, in July 1863. His career in the U.S. Army spanned over thirty years, yet Gettysburg proved to be the scene of Doubleday's greatest achievement as well as his most bitter disappointment. Despite his more than capable performance at Gettysburg, Brigadier General George G. Meade showed no faith in Doubleday and, perhaps reacting to an erroneous report, replaced him with a junior officer. Doubleday was subsequently transferred to Washington, D.C., where he remained for the rest of the conflict.

Doubleday was born on 26 June 1819 in Ballston Spa, New York. His father was a two-term congressman from New York; his grandfather, a Revolutionary War veteran. Doubleday attended West Point and received a

Abner Doubleday (*seated, third from right*) and a group of Union officers (*Library of Congress*)

commission in the artillery after graduating in 1842. He served in coastal garrisons; was a lieutenant during the Mexican-American War from 1846 to 1848; and participated in various Indian campaigns, most notably that from 1856 to 1858 against the Seminoles. Doubleday's next assignment was at Fort Moultrie in Charleston harbor in 1858, but he had become second-in-command at Fort Sumter by 12 April 1861 when the first shots of the Civil War were fired. Doubleday claims to have returned the first Union shot in response to the Confederate attack on that fateful day.

Transferred to the Shenandoah Valley the following May, Doubleday rapidly rose through the ranks. He first commanded a regiment and then led a brigade at the battle of Groveton, Virginia, on 28 August 1862, before receiving promotion to brevet brigadier general of U.S. volunteers. During the battle of Second Bull Run on 29 August 1862, he commanded a brigade in Major General Irvin McDowell's III Corps. At the battle of South Mountain, Maryland, on 14 September 1862, Doubleday's superior, Brigadier General John P. Hatch was wounded. Doubleday assumed command of the division and led it in action at the battle of Antietam on 17 September 1862. On 29 November 1862, Doubleday was promoted to major general of U.S. volunteers and his division participated in the battle of Fredericksburg, Virginia, on 13 December 1862. Although he commanded the 3d Division, I Corps, Army of the Potomac, at the battle of Chancellorsville, Virginia, in early May 1863, his men remained in reserve.

On 1 July 1863, I Corps, led by Major General John F. Reynolds, hurried to Gettysburg to relieve hard-pressed Union cavalry. Shortly after arriving, Reynolds was killed and command on the field devolved to Doubleday. His men put up a stout resistance before falling back in the face of overwhelming numbers through Gettysburg

to Cemetery Hill. There, the remnants of the I and XI Corps regrouped under the direction of Major General Oliver O. Howard and Major General Winfield Scott Hancock. On the basis of an unfounded report by Howard, who charged that Doubleday's command had been broken in its withdrawal to Cemetery Hill, Meade placed Brigadier General John Newton, an officer who was Doubleday's junior, in command of I Corps. Mortified, Doubleday protested to Meade but returned to command his division and served ably throughout the rest of the battle. After Gettysburg, Doubleday's request to be restored command of I Corps was denied by Meade. Doubleday asked for and received a transfer to administrative duty in Washington, D.C. With the exception of directing a portion of the Washington defenses against Brigadier General Jubal A. Early's raid in 1864, Doubleday saw no further combat.

While in Washington, Doubleday appeared before the Joint Committee on the Conduct of the War to criticize Meade harshly for his performance at Gettysburg. On 24 August 1865, Doubleday mustered out of the U.S. volunteers. He had been promoted to lieutenant colonel in the regular army on 20 September 1863 and received an upgrade to colonel, commanding the 35th Infantry, on 15 September 1867. Stationed in San Francisco from 1869 through 1871, Doubleday took out a patent for a cable railway before his retirement from the army on 11 December 1873. He spent the rest of his years in Mendham, New Jersey, where he died on 26 January 1893.

Doubleday was a solid, if unspectacular, commander who did not deserve censure for his actions at Gettysburg on 1 July 1863. His nickname of "Forty-eight Hours" reflected his methodical and cautious nature. Doubleday's reputation was damaged by the bitterness he held against Meade and Howard for the rest of his life. He wrote several books after the war, most notably *Reminiscences of Forts Sumter and Moultrie in 1860–'61* and *Chancellorsville and Gettysburg*, the latter work being harshly critical of Howard and Meade.

Doubleday's niche in U.S. history is due mainly to his association with baseball. Although he never claimed to have invented the game, many people have labeled him the founder of the great American pastime.

—*Terry L. Beckenbaugh*

See also Fort Sumter; Gettysburg, Battle of.

For further reading:

Chance, Joseph E., ed. *My Life in the Old Army: The Reminiscences of Abner Doubleday from the Collections of the New-York Historical Society* (1998).

Coddington, Edwin B. *The Gettysburg Campaign: A Study in Command* (1968).

Doubleday, Abner. *Chancellorsville and Gettysburg* (1882; reprint, 1994).

———. *Reminiscences of Forts Sumter and Moultrie in 1860–'61* (1876; reprint, 1998).

Gallagher, Gary W. *The First Day at Gettysburg: Essays on Confederate and Union Leadership* (1992).

Hassler, Warren W. *Crisis at the Crossroads: The First Day at Gettysburg* (1970).

Martin, David G. *Gettysburg, July 1* (1995).

Pfanz, Harry W. *Gettysburg: Culp's Hill & Cemetery Hill* (1993).

DOUGLAS, STEPHEN ARNOLD
(1813–1861)
U.S. senator

Stephen A. Douglas was born in Brandon, Vermont, where, he later recalled, he "first learned to love liberty." As a youth, he was captivated by the figure of Andrew Jackson, under whose spell he had fallen in the 1828 election, and a lifelong attachment to the Old Hero's politics had begun. "From this moment," he noted, "*my* politics became fixed." In 1830, Douglas moved with his family to upstate New York, where he completed his education and studied law for a brief time. Three years later, impatient with his legal study, he left New York for the "western country," where opportunities for professional advancement seemed brighter. In November 1833, he landed in the town of Jacksonville, in west-central Illinois. Almost immediately, he became involved in the rough-and-tumble politics of the frontier as a zealous partisan of Jackson and Jacksonian democracy. "*I* have become a *Western* man, [and] have imbibed Western feelings[,] principles and interests."

Douglas focused his attention on the organization of the Jacksonian Democratic Party, employing innovative techniques he had brought with him from the East. Democracy and the Union became the twin pillars in his political creed. The party was literally the party of democracy, the agent of national progress, and the instrument for the achievement of America's providential mission. Douglas's rise in state politics was nothing short of meteoric. In his first decade in Illinois, he served as state's attorney, member of the state legislature, register of the federal land office, secretary of state, and, at the age of 27, justice on the state supreme court.

In 1843, Douglas was elected to Congress, and for the next eighteen years his life and career were irrevocably linked with the issues of what was one of the most turbulent and critical periods in the history of the United States. He became the personification of young America, the spokesman of the popular democracy and manifest destiny that characterized the spirit of his time. His vision for America's future was without limits. The nation's democratic mission, he believed, rested on an indestructible Union. "To me, our country, and all its parts, are one and indivisible."

After two terms in the House of Representatives, where he strongly supported the annexation of Texas, the acquisition of Oregon, and the extension of the nation's boundaries after the war with Mexico, he was elected to the U.S. Senate in 1847, and he quickly became one of its most powerful members. Bold, impetuous, and at times unscrupulous, Douglas loved furor and never dodged conflict. His physical appearance belied his power and the sweep of his vision for the nation's future. Standing only five feet four inches, he soon became known as the "Little Giant."

After the war with Mexico, Douglas's devotion to the Union came under serious challenge, when the slavery issue, in its relation to territorial expansion, once again became a divisive force in national politics. To Douglas, the only course that could meet the challenge and maintain the national mission was an appeal to popular democracy. Only the voice of the people—what came to be called Popular Sovereignty—could settle the issue through the right of the people of an organized territory to govern themselves with respect to their own internal policy and domestic affairs without the intervention of the national government.

Douglas's view of slavery reflected his impatience with any issue that held within it the seeds of disunion.

Stephen A. Douglas (*National Archives*)

"I deal with slavery," he remarked, "as a political question involving questions of public policy." His attitude was pragmatic, rather than moral (although he was not proslavery), and was always conditioned by the Constitution and the Union. The institution, he insisted, could not be destroyed without risking the destruction of the Union. Popular Sovereignty formed the basis for the territorial provisions of the Compromise of 1850 and of the 1854 Kansas-Nebraska Act, both of which were written by Douglas. He intended the latter as a compromise measure that would allow both Northerners and Southerners an equal voice in determining the fate of slavery in the territories, but it had just the opposite effect. Northern abolitionists and Southern slavery expansionists denounced it. The Republican Party was born, demanding the restriction of slavery by government fiat, and the Democratic Party was weakened as a national party as Southern Democrats demanded federal protection of slavery in the territories. As the sectional conflict deepened, Douglas's commitment to Popular Sovereignty as the only just and fair course to follow became more rigid. His fear for the Union became outright alarm when his reelection to the Senate was challenged by Abraham Lincoln. Lincoln's "House Divided Speech," Douglas thought, was tantamount to a call for disunion and a sectional war. Lincoln lost that election, but in losing he won enough stature in the North to gain him the Republican presidential nomination in 1860.

Douglas was one of two Democratic candidates in that contest and campaigned vigorously in the slaveholding South, where he argued that Lincoln's election was not a sufficient cause for the breakup of the Union. Southerners turned a deaf ear. After the election, as the Southern states were leaving the Union, Douglas appealed to Lincoln to put aside political party interests and to save the country. Lincoln too turned a deaf ear. Douglas turned to his Senate colleagues and, with mounting desperation, urged them to set aside their differences and find a compromise. "Are we prepared in our hearts for war with our own brethren and kindred?" His words had little effect.

After the surrender of Fort Sumter, Douglas returned to his constituents in Illinois. Exhausted, depressed, and filled with gloom, he announced that "it is with a sad heart—with a grief that I have never before experienced, that I have to contemplate this fearful struggle." At the same time, it was the first duty of every person to stand against this "crime against constitutional freedom, and the hopes of the friends of freedom throughout the wide world." There were only two sides to the question, he emphasized. "Every man must be for the United States or against it. There can be no neutrals in this war, *only patriots—or traitors*."

The pressures of the secession winter took their toll

on the Little Giant. Worn out physically and broken in spirit, Stephen A. Douglas died in Chicago on 3 June 1861, surrounded by family and friends. He was a victim of the Civil War as surely as if he had fallen on the field of battle.

—*Robert W. Johannsen*

See also Democratic Party; Election of 1858; Election of 1860; Kansas-Nebraska Act; Lincoln, Abraham; Popular Sovereignty; Republican Party.

For further reading:

Jaffa, Harry V., and Robert W. Johannsen, eds. *In the Name of the People: Speeches and Writings of Lincoln and Douglas in the Ohio Campaign of 1859* (1959).

Johannsen, Robert W. *The Frontier, the Union and Stephen A. Douglas* (1989).

———. *Stephen A. Douglas* (1973; reprint, 1997).

———, ed. *The Letters of Stephen A. Douglas* (1961).

———, ed. *The Lincoln-Douglas Debates of 1858* (1965).

DOUGLASS, FREDERICK
(1817–1895)
African-American writer and abolitionist

Frederick Douglass was born into slavery as Frederick Augustus Washington Bailey on 7 February 1817 in Tuckahoe, Maryland. His mother, Harriet Bailey, was an African-American, but the only thing known about his father was that he was white. Douglass was soon parted from his mother and grew up with his grandmother on a nearby plantation. When Douglass was about eight years of age, his owner sent him to Baltimore to work as a servant in the house of Hugh Auld, whose wife taught Douglass to read and write against her husband's objections and in defiance of statutes against slave literacy. Much of his education, however, was sustained furtively because of fears that knowledge would make him unfit for slavery. After eight years' residence in the Auld household, Douglass was returned to the Maryland plantation as a field hand. After he tried but failed to escape to freedom, he was sent back to Baltimore to work in the shipyards as a caulker. Still resolved to flee slavery, in 1838 he contrived a ruse to pose as a free African-American sailor and managed to carry the ploy off with borrowed papers and steely nerves. In the North he began his new life by adopting the last name of Douglass, in part because an alias would help him foil slave hunters. He also married Anna Murray, the free African-American woman he had met during his captivity in Baltimore. They moved to New Bedford, Massachusetts, where Douglass hoped to work as a ship caulker, but bigotry in the shipyards excluded him from the trade. The best he could do was to become a common laborer.

In 1841, Douglass spoke at an abolitionist meeting held in Nantucket, Massachusetts, and the event changed his life. William Lloyd Garrison heard Douglass

Frederick Douglass during the Civil War period (*left*) and ca. 1879 (*right*) (*Library of Congress*)

that evening and asked him to become an emissary for the Massachusetts Anti-Slavery Society. Soon one of the movement's most celebrated advocates, Douglass traveled throughout the North addressing large audiences on slavery and abolition. His delivery and demeanor made some doubt that Douglass had been a slave, but he put such rumors to rest by publishing in 1845 a vivid memoir entitled *Narrative of the Life of Frederick Douglass.* The book would form the foundation for a series that included *My Bondage and My Freedom* in 1855 and *The Life and Times of Frederick Douglass* in 1881, works that are ranked among the best slave accounts as well as timeless self-portrayals. Publishing his original narrative carried some risk, however, because it chanced his abduction and return to slavery. Fleeing such peril partly motivated his journey to Great Britain for a speaking tour, a tour that would continue for almost two years.

Douglass returned to the United States in 1847. Friends not only collected money to purchase his freedom, they also furnished the means for him to launch an abolitionist newspaper, the *North Star.* Published in Rochester, New York, the *North Star* for the next seventeen years became a leading voice in the abolitionist movement. Douglass used the paper to promote vocational training for African-Americans and to emphasize moral dictates.

Douglass did not limit his efforts to improving only the lot of fellow African-Americans. He attended the 1848 Seneca Falls meeting that began the women's rights movement and continued to advocate women's right to vote for the rest of his life. He embraced temperance and addressed the New York State Temperance convention in 1852. Yet the abolition of slavery remained his highest priority. Marking his growing independence from William Lloyd Garrison's eschewal of compromise-laden politics, Douglass supported the Free Soil Party and in the late 1850s the Republican Party as a responsible way to effect political action toward abolition. In keeping with a rational assessment of means and ends in abolitionism, Douglass finally refused to support John Brown's raid on Harper's Ferry, Virginia, in 1859. He concluded that its consequences would be direr than any advantages. When the raid's failure ended with Brown's arrest, Douglass was concerned that he might also be arrested because of his foreknowledge of Brown's plan and his early activities to help fund it. He retreated to Canada for several months.

Despite its early focus on preserving the Union, the Civil War was a crusade for freedom from the start for Frederick Douglass. He became a persistent proponent for emancipation as a logical military stratagem and urged the Lincoln administration to enlist African-Americans in the Union army for combat. Once that policy was adopted, Douglass helped to recruit two

African-American regiments in Massachusetts, enlisting his two oldest sons in the process.

After the war, Douglass continued his advocacy of African-American equality. In his campaign for freedpeople's civil rights and suffrage, he moved to Washington, D.C., in the 1870s to edit the weekly *New National Era*. His activity for the improvement of emancipated slaves, however, also included a lamentable illustration of Douglass's innocence when he agreed to serve as president of the Freedmen's Bank. Lending his credibility and reputation to this hapless venture proved ill-starred, for when the bank failed, Douglass's defense of it revealed a sad vanity in himself and an ignorance of the unscrupulous inclinations of others.

He served in 1871 as assistant secretary of the Santo Domingo Commission, and in 1877, President Rutherford B. Hayes rewarded Douglass for his support of the Republican Party by designating him marshal of the District of Columbia. It was a minor sinecure, but Douglass was the first African-American to hold the office, and he rightly considered his appointment a step forward for black equality. When President James Garfield made Douglass recorder of deeds for the District of Columbia in 1881, he could mark his holding the post as another advance for African-Americans.

The advent of segregation, disenfranchisement, and an alarming incidence of lynching in the post-Reconstruction South, however, countervailed such advances. Douglass nonetheless persisted in his conviction that African-American equality would eventually occur in American culture. After his first wife died in 1882, Douglass married Helen Pitts, a white woman, observing that he himself had been the creation of a mixed union, if not of a marriage.

Douglass remained active, serving from 1889 to 1891 as minister-resident and consul general to Haiti, a post he held for two years. His sudden death on 20 February 1895 occurred after his attendance at a woman's suffrage convention in Washington, D.C. His life had spanned the momentous nineteenth-century American experience, a life marked, just as that experience had been, by the wretched condition of slavery and the titanic struggle that had won emancipation, if not equality. When he died at seventy-eight, he knew there was still much to be done.

—*David S. Heidler and Jeanne T. Heidler*

See also Abolitionist Movement; Abolitionists; Garrison, William Lloyd; Slaves.

For further reading:

Blight, David W. *Frederick Douglass' Civil War: Keeping Faith in Jubilee* (1989).

Douglass, Frederick. *Frederick Douglass Papers* (1979).

———. *The Life and Writings of Frederick Douglass* (1950).

Lampe, Gregory P. *Frederick Douglass: Freedom's Voice, 1818–1845* (1998).

McFeely, William S. *Frederick Douglass* (1991).

Sundquist, Eric J., ed. *Frederick Douglass: New Literary and Historical Essays* (1990).

DOW, NEAL
(1804–1897)
Union general

Born on 20 March 1804 in Portland, Maine, Neil Dow was educated at the Friends' Academy in New Bedford, Massachusetts, and subsequently became wealthy as a result of managing his father's tannery. The overarching feature of Dow's life, however, was his devout Quaker upbringing and the corresponding impulse for reform and improvement. The temperance movement became his special passion, and by 1838 he had transformed into a thorough prohibitionist who believed in complete abstinence from alcohol. He helped to make Maine the first state to adopt a statewide law in 1846 that banned the sale of liquor by the drink. Five years later, he won the Portland mayoral election and successfully lobbied for the "Maine Law of 1851" that prohibited the sale and manufacture of alcohol except for medical use. The law inspired a legislative flurry of prohibition statutes from New England through the Midwest and made Dow a national celebrity. In his second term as mayor, he sought to strengthen the prohibition law, but a riot over the harshness of enforcement, in which police killed an agitator, persuaded the legislature to repeal prohibition. The trend of prohibition repeal in other states emulated that of its earlier acceptance in the wake of these events.

Upon the outbreak of the Civil War, Dow's adherence to the Quaker tenet of pacifism was overshadowed by his abolitionism. He became colonel of the 13th Regiment of Maine Volunteers on 23 November 1861. In command of the Union Department of the Gulf from October 1863 to January 1863, he was promoted to brigadier general, and as part of XIX Corps he participated in the campaign against Port Hudson in the spring of 1863. Twice wounded in the campaign, Dow was captured by Confederate troops and was confined in Richmond's infamous Libby Prison for more than a year. His release was most notable in that he was the officer exchanged for W. H. F. Lee in March 1864. The time in Libby had severely affected his health, however, and he resigned from the army at the end of the following November.

Dow's service in the war led to his expulsion from the Society of Friends, but he resumed his prohibitionist activities with renewed zeal. His wide-ranging influence in the revived movement enhanced his renown as a political leader, and in 1880 he was the Prohibition Party's presidential nominee. He died in Portland on 2 October 1897.

—*David S. Heidler and Jeanne T. Heidler*

See also Lee, William Henry Fitzhugh; Libby Prison; Port Hudson Campaign.

For further reading:

Byrne, Frank L. *Prophet of Prohibition: Neal Dow and His Crusade* (1961).

Chalfant, Harry Malcolm. *These Agitators and Their Idea* (1931).

Dow, Neal. *The Reminiscences of Neal Dow: Recollections of Eighty Years* (1898).

DRANESVILLE, BATTLE OF
(20 December 1861)

On the evening of 19 December 1861, Brigadier General George A. McCall, commanding the division of Pennsylvania Reserves attached to the Army of the Potomac, ordered Brigadier General Edward O. C. Ord to take his 3d Brigade from Camp Pierpont and march up the Leesburg Pike to Dranesville, a small village halfway between Alexandria and Leesburg. McCall had received word that Confederate pickets had moved through the area, driving back their blueclad counterparts and arresting several Union civilians nearby. McCall instructed Ord to expel any Rebel pickets and to take along a wagon train to collect forage.

Ord started his troops on the morning of 20 December. His brigade—the 6th, 9th, 10th, and 12th Pennsylvania Reserves—was reinforced by Lieutenant Colonel Thomas L. Kane and his Pennsylvania Bucktails (13th Reserves), a squadron of the 1st Pennsylvania Cavalry, and Battery A, 1st Pennsylvania Light Artillery, commanded by Captain Hezekiah Easton.

The Pennsylvania advance guard entered Dranesville sometime between eleven o'clock and noon, scattering some enemy cavalrymen. Ord posted Kane's regiment to the south as the rest of his brigade marched along the pike to Dranesville. Soon, Kane spotted an approaching enemy force to the south, coming north on the Centreville Road. This was a Southern force of some 1,800 men commanded by Brigadier General J. E. B. Stuart. This force, four infantry regiments (11th Virginia, 6th South Carolina, 1st Kentucky, 10th Alabama), Captain A. S. Cutts's four-gun battery, and detachments of two cavalry regiments, was covering a major foraging expedition that involved most of the wagons attached to the Confederate army defending Manassas. Stuart intended to collect hay in the area west of Dranesville, and expected to occupy the village while the foragers did their work.

Stuart's cavalry found Ord's men already in the village, so Stuart decided to attack this force of unknown size while he sent orders for the wagons to head back to Centreville. Stuart deployed two regiments on each side of the Centreville Road, positioned his artillery on the road, and ordered an attack. The advancing Southerners pushed back Yankee skirmishers as Ord deployed the remainder of his brigade. Easton's battery unlimbered at the intersection of the Leesburg Pike with the Centreville Road and opened an effective fire on Cutts's artillery, which was soon silenced.

Stuart's infantry pushed forward through wooded terrain and incurred some losses as part of the 10th Pennsylvania Reserves opened fire on his right while the 9th Reserves engaged his left. Believing that he had delayed the enemy long enough for the wagons to escape safely, Stuart withdrew his troops. The action had lasted perhaps an hour and a half from the time the initial shots were fired. Stuart reported his loss as 43 killed, 143 wounded, and 8 missing, for a total of 194. Ord's casualties totaled 68 (7 killed and 61 wounded). Following the Confederate retreat, Ord withdrew to his camp. The next day, Stuart returned to the battlefield and removed his dead and wounded before marching back to Centreville.

—*Richard A. Sauers*

See also Kane, Thomas Leiper; Ord, Edward Otho Cresap.
For further reading:

Owen, Henry T. "Stuart in 1861." *Philadelphia Weekly Times* (1885).

Sharpe, A. B. "Drainsville." *Philadelphia Weekly Times* (1886).

Sypher, Josiah R. *History of the Pennsylvania Reserve Corps* (1865).

Taliaferro, W. F. "Drainsville." *Philadelphia Weekly Times* (1885).

DRED SCOTT CASE (SCOTT V. SAN[D]FORD, 60 U.S. 393 (1857))

Scott v. San[d]ford, better known as the *Dred Scott Case*, was one of the most important and controversial cases in American constitutional history. It played a key role in precipitating the American Civil War, provided a basis for far-reaching interpretations of substantive due process, and stirred up deep-seated emotions in the realm of American race relations.

The *Dred Scott* Case began unobtrusively in 1846 in the lower state courts of Missouri. Dred Scott was a slave, formerly the property of a Dr. Emerson, a surgeon in the United States Army. In 1834 Emerson took Scott to the free state of Illinois, and then in 1836 to Fort Snelling, in what was then the Wisconsin Territory (free soil under the Missouri Compromise and the act of 1836 organizing Wisconsin's territorial government). Eventually, Emerson returned to Missouri, taking Scott with him. The surgeon died shortly thereafter, leaving Scott as part of his estate in trust for his daughter, with his widow as executrix. It was against Mrs. Emerson in that capacity that, in 1846, Scott brought suit in the Missouri state courts to gain his freedom. At the time, this action apparently had no political significance. Though Scott won a favorable decision in the lower courts, the Missouri Supreme Court eventually rejected his plea, on the grounds that the laws of Illinois and of free territory did not have extraterritorial validity in Missouri and could not affect his status as a slave after his return.

When the superintendence of Scott passed to John F.

A. Sanford, a citizen of New York, Scott's attorney began in 1854 a new suit against Sanford in the United States Circuit Court for Missouri. The case now had a political character, and both sides pressed a decision to obtain a judicial opinion upon the status of slavery in the territories.

Scott's right to sue Sanford in a federal court rested upon his contention that Scott was a citizen of the state of Missouri, and that the case thus involved a suit between citizens of different states. Sanford's attorneys replied to Scott's suit with a plea of abatement—that is, they demanded that the court dismiss the case for want of jurisdiction, on the grounds that because Scott was an African-American, he was not a citizen of Missouri. The circuit court ruled that it did have jurisdiction over the case (thereby implying that Scott might be a citizen), but it then returned a verdict in favor of Sanford. Scott then appealed his case to the Supreme Court of the United States.

The Supreme Court first heard arguments on the *Dred Scott* Case in February 1856. Opinions were divided on the question of jurisdiction, however, and this division, combined with a reluctance to take up politically controversial issues in an election year, led the justices to order the case reargued in their next term, December 1857. In contrast to its first appearance, the case now aroused enormous interest, and many hoped for a judicial resolution of the slavery issue. However, the Supreme Court initially dismissed the case for want of jurisdiction.

A clear and recent precedent for such a course did exist. In 1850 in *Strader v. Graham*, the Supreme Court unanimously refused to consider the argument that a slave automatically became free through residence in a free state, and held instead that the decision of the state courts was final in determining the slave status of an African-American. A majority of seven of the current justices believed in this precedent and in accordance with their wishes, Justice Samuel Nelson prepared an opinion for the Court based on the *Strader* decision. The Court would avoid all discussions of slavery in the territories.

But outside forces—events in "Bleeding Kansas," for example—forced the Court to decide what the United States government should do about slavery. Justice James M. Wayne of Georgia proposed that a new Court opinion should be prepared to deal with the issues that the Court had side-stepped. Though Wayne made the request, responsibility for the decision to involve the Court also fell on Chief Justice Roger B. Taney and Associate Justices John McLean, Benjamin R. Curtis, and Peter V. Daniel. In conference a bare majority of five justices, all from slave states, approved the Wayne proposal, and Taney wrote a new opinion for the Court. Delivered on 6 March 1857, it became famous, or infamous, as the *Scott* decision.

Each of the nine justices filed a separate opinion, except for Justice Nelson who concurred with Chief Justice Taney. By different lines of reasoning, the seven justices concluded that Scott was not a U.S. citizen and still a slave. The aging Taney, whose opinion served as the opinion for the entire court, declared that Scott was still a slave for the following reasons. First, although African-Americans could be citizens of a given state, they were not citizens of the United States and thus did not have the right to sue in federal court. Scott's case was therefore dismissed because the Court lacked jurisdiction. Second, aside from not having the right to sue, Scott was still a slave because he had never been free in the first place. Congress exceeded its authority when it forbade or abolished slavery in territories because no such power could be inferred from the Constitution. Furthermore, slaves were property protected by the Constitution. The Missouri Compromise was accordingly declared invalid. Finally, whatever the status of a slave might have been in a free state or territory, if the slave voluntarily returned to a slave state, his or her status there depended upon the law of that state as interpreted by its own courts. Because Missouri's high court had declared Scott to be a slave, that was the law that the U.S. Supreme Court would recognize.

Six of the justices agreed with Taney that Scott was not a U.S. citizen, but disagreed over whether a freed slave could become a citizen. Justice Nelson concurred in the ruling but not in its reasoning, and Justices McLean and Curtis offered eloquent dissenting opinions.

The reactions to the *Dred Scott* Case were numerous. Republicans attacked the decision because they saw it as an attempt to destroy their party, and the Democratic Party divided over the case. Stephen A. Douglas opposed it as counter to his doctrine of popular sovereignty. President James Buchanan's supporters considered it a final answer to the sectional question, although they were unaware that Buchanan had influenced Justice Grier to join the Southern majority so that it would look less like a sectional decision.

For years, the *Dred Scott* Case remained the subject of many heated constitutional and historical debates. It widened sectional animosities so much that the case, together with other factors, such as the election of Abraham Lincoln in 1860, precipitated the Civil War in the spring of 1861.

—*Michael S. Davis*

See also Buchanan, James; Curtis, Benjamin R.; Daniel, Peter; *Strader v. Graham*; Taney, Roger B.

For further reading:

Ehrlich, Walter. *They Have No Rights: Dred Scott's Struggle for Freedom* (1979).
Fehrenbacher, Don E. *The Dred Scott Case: Its Significance in American Law and Politics* (1978).
Finkelman, Paul. *An Imperfect Union: Slavery, Federalism, and Comity* (1981).
Hyman, Harold M., and William M. Wiecek. *Equal Justice under Law: Constitutional Development, 1835–1875* (1982).

Wiecek, William M. *The Sources of Antislavery Constitutionalism in America, 1760–1848* (1977).

DREWRY'S BLUFF, VIRGINIA, BATTLE OF
(16 May 1864)

In early May 1864, Union general Ulysses S. Grant planned to exert pressure on Robert E. Lee by moving south with the Army of the Potomac toward Richmond and having Major General Benjamin Butler with X Corps under Major General Quincy Adams Gillmore and XVIII Corps under Major General William Farrar Smith move up the James River, landing south of Richmond. Butler was to move from south of the James River and threaten the Confederate capital from that direction. Securing some of the high ground along the river en route and establishing a supply base at City Point, Virginia, Butler landed most of his army on the Bermuda Hundred peninsula on 5 May. From that location he could threaten either Richmond or Petersburg or both.

Confederate general P. G. T. Beauregard commanded the defenses of both cities when Butler landed. During the next week, the small number of Confederates in the defenses of Petersburg repelled Federal probes in their direction. In addition, Federal cavalry seriously damaged the Weldon Railroad connecting Petersburg to points south.

Luckily for Beauregard, Butler's moves toward Petersburg were tentative. This allowed the Confederate commander to strengthen the defenses at Drewry's Bluff protecting the southern approach to Richmond. On 12 May 1864, Butler started from his defenses at Bermuda Hundred, approaching the outer defenses of Drewry's Bluff on the morning of 13 May. Smith's XVIII Corps was on the right and Gillmore's X Corps on Butler's left.

The Confederates in their outerworks withdrew to the stronger main defenses, and Butler spent the next two days strengthening the defenses of his flanks, allowing Beauregard time to bring in reinforcements to Drewry's Bluff. On 14 May, Beauregard came in person to the bluff to take personal command. Once he arrived and surveyed the situation, he determined to trap Butler's entire army.

Beauregard organized his ten brigades at Drewry's Bluff into two divisions of four brigades each, commanded by Brigadier General Robert Ransom and Major General Robert Frederick Hoke, leaving two brigades as a reserve force. He intended to strike Butler's right flank and center, turning the right flank and then attacking the left flank. While this was taking place, Beauregard had sent instructions to Major General William Henry Chase Whiting, recently arrived from Wilmington, North Carolina, and now commanding at Petersburg, to bring two brigades and some cavalry from the south and strike Butler's rear. This attack should occur while the two Union flanks were collapsing in on themselves.

At a little after 2:00 A.M. on 16 May, Ransom moved his division out of Drewry's Bluff's defenses. At about 4:45 A.M. his four brigades, arrayed two brigades deep, attacked in a thick fog the extreme right of Smith's XVIII Corps. The Confederate brigade commanded by Brigadier General Archibald Gracie on the Confederate left, after very heavy fighting, overwhelmed part of the Union brigade of Brigadier General Charles Adam Heckman, capturing Heckman and about 400 of his men. The proximity of Richmond allowed the Confederate authorities to process Heckman into Libby Prison by midmorning.

Because of the fog and the heavy casualties Gracie had suffered, Ransom was unable to completely turn the Union right flank. At the same time an attack by the right of Ransom's division failed to penetrate the Union center held by Brigadier General Godfrey Weitzel and Brigadier General William Thomas Harbaugh Brooks.

While all of this was happening, the Confederate division of Major General Hoke was supposed to be attacking the Union left. When he heard Ransom begin his attack, Hoke had begun artillery fire on the Union left, but the heavy fog prevented him from seeing Ransom's position and hence the point at which the two divisions were to abut their forces. Therefore he delayed sending in his infantry.

In the meantime, Butler, once he realized he was under heavy attack, sought to draw Confederate forces away from his right by ordering Gillmore to attack to the Confederate right at about 6:00 A.M. Gillmore, however, not sure of what was in front of him because of the fog, delayed. At about that time, Hoke decided that it was light enough to send in his two left brigades under Brigadier General Johnson Hagood on the extreme left and Brigadier General Bushrod Johnson next to Hagood. They were followed shortly by the two other brigades, commanded by Brigadier General Thomas Lanier Clingman and Brigadier General Montgomery Corse, intending to turn the Union left flank.

When Hagood attacked near the Union center, Ransom was not there, and the Confederates found themselves attacking fresh Union troops. By then it was light enough and the fog had lifted enough for Ransom to see what was happening, and he managed to close the gap between his and Hoke's divisions somewhat. In the meantime, however, Johnson was in trouble on his right flank, because the two other Confederate brigades attacking on the Union left had outrun his brigade. When it appeared that Johnson's right might be enveloped by a Union counterattack, Hoke was forced

Federal transports on the James River at Drewry's Bluff, April 1865 (*Library of Congress*)

to abandon the hope of moving around the Union left and recalled Corse and Clingman. This move effectively ended the Confederate offensive. Unbeknownst to Beauregard, Whiting had been delayed by a Union force at Walthall Junction and never made it to the battlefield.

The Union forces, however, did not realize that the Confederates would be unable to launch another major offensive. Smith was convinced that the Confederates were simply reorganizing for another major attack on his right flank. As a result, he began to withdraw. When he realized that his flank was not in much danger, he tried to rescind the order, causing much confusion in his lines. Ransom briefly tried to take advantage of that confusion but was not organized enough to turn the flank.

On the Union left, confusion also reigned. Gillmore had delayed following Butler's order to attack until a little after 8:30 A.M., and when he finally ordered the attack, it was carried out piecemeal. Then, around 9:30 A.M., Gillmore began receiving confused reports that there were Confederates to his rear and began planning his own retreat. For the remainder of the morning into the early afternoon, there was confused fighting on both sides of the battlefield, until Butler finally ordered his

Interior of Confederate Fort Darling at Drewry's Bluff, 1865 (*Library of Congress*)

army back to its defenses at Bermuda Hundred. Of the approximately 18,000 Confederates engaged, there were about 2,000 casualties. Of Butler's 15,000 engaged, he suffered about 4,000 casualties.

During the next few days, Beauregard established a siege line across the western end of the peninsula, effectively hemming Butler in to Bermuda Hundred and neutralizing his entire army.

—*David S. Heidler and Jeanne T. Heidler*

See also Beauregard, Pierre Gustave Toutant; Bermuda Hundred Campaign; Butler, Benjamin Franklin; Gillmore, Quincy Adams; Hoke, Robert Frederick; Ransom, Robert; Smith, William Farrar; Whiting, William Henry Chase.

For further reading:
McCartney, Martha. *The Battle of Drewry's Bluff in Chesterfield County, Virginia: The Historical Background* (1988).
Robertson, William Glenn. *Back Door to Richmond: the Bermuda Hundred Campaign, April–June 1864* (1987).

DU PONT, SAMUEL FRANCIS
(1803–1865)
Union naval officer

Born in Bayonne, New Jersey, Samuel Du Pont was appointed a midshipman in 1815. His active career began two years later and consisted mainly of routine assignments, frequently with the Mediterranean Squadron, before the Mexican-American War. In that conflict, as commander of the *Cyane*, he landed troops at San Diego and was officially commended for his role in subsequent actions. In 1855 he served on the Naval Efficiency Board, which retired hundreds of officers and helped determine the navy's first retirement policy. He married his first cousin, Sophie Madeleine Du Pont, daughter of the founder of Du Pont Powder Company.

As a captain commanding the Philadelphia Navy Yard in 1861, Du Pont was one of the navy's most experienced officers, a fact reflected in his appointment as senior member of the Strategy Board formed in June. This body helped determine the navy's overall strategic role as well as its initial operations. Meeting several times over the summer, the Strategy Board recommended the prompt capture of Southern ports to provide coaling stations for the blockading fleet, which otherwise would have to return north to provision. Additionally, it suggested means of administering the blockade in the most efficient manner possible. Most of the board's recommendations were put into effect over the course of the war, some by Du Pont himself.

In September 1861, Du Pont became commander of the newly created South Atlantic Blockading Squadron. After considerable delay, in November he led the naval component of a combined assault on Port Royal, South Carolina, in the first attempt to seize a major Southern port. After weathering a hurricane off Cape Hatteras that cost the expedition four ships, Du Pont's force arrived off Port Royal on 7 November. As a result of small boat losses related to the storm, Du Pont could not land the army forces of Brigadier General Thomas West Sherman. However, the naval forces present were sufficient to force the Confederates to abandon the harbor defenses and the operation proved successful. The capture of the port boosted morale after a generally unsuccessful summer for Union forces in the East and garnered for Du Pont a vote of thanks from Congress. Unfortunately for the Federals, however, neither Du Pont nor Sherman realized how lightly defended the region was. Before they could fully exploit their success, Brigadier General Robert E. Lee organized improved Confederate coastal defenses in the region.

Du Pont remained in command of the squadron for another two years, receiving promotion to rear admiral in July 1862. The squadron's duties consisted of maintaining the blockade against South Carolina, Georgia, and Florida and attempting to capture additional ports, primarily Charleston, but also including Fernandina, Florida, an early target of the Strategy Board. Fernandina fell without a fight in March 1862. Charleston, however, proved much more difficult. Du Pont supported the army's operations against this city with sea-based assaults on key positions throughout 1862 and into 1863.

While many Navy Department officers and officials saw ironclads as the perfect tool to aid in the capture of Southern positions, Du Pont remained skeptical of this new technology's usefulness against fortified shore facilities. He was particularly concerned with their slow rate of fire and lack of maneuverability and that most carried only two guns. His doubts were not assuaged when the new ironclad monitor *Montauk*, under Commodore John Worden, failed to capture or destroy Fort McAllister,

near Savannah, Georgia, in a pair of bombardments in early 1863. A subsequent attack by ironclads *Nahant*, *Patapsco*, and *Passaic* in early March obtained similarly unsuccessful results. Nonetheless, under pressure from Navy Secretary Gideon Welles and Assistant Secretary Gustavus Fox, Du Pont planned a full-scale assault on Charleston for 7 April 1863. As Du Pont anticipated, the attack, which continued into the 8th, proved spectacularly unsuccessful and resulted in the loss of the brand new experimental ironclad steamer *Keokuk* and in heavy damage to other ships, including the *Montauk*, *Nahant*, and *Passaic*, with little visible signs of damage to Confederate positions.

Although the commanders of Du Pont's ironclads supported the admiral's appraisal of their ships' shortcomings, the Navy Department would not admit its mistaken confidence in the new vessels. Although the department regularly released commanders' reports to the public, it refused to do so with Du Pont's account of the ironclads' failure at Charleston. Instead, it determined that the assault failed as a result of a lack of determination on the part of Du Pont and his officers. Made a scapegoat for this unsuccessful effort, Du Pont was relieved of his command in July 1863, in part because he did not support a renewed assault on Charleston. His successor, Rear Admiral John Dahlgren, who had long desired to replace Du Pont, fared little better in attempting to capture the port. Du Pont remained unemployed for nearly two years before serving on the Naval Promotion Board in March 1865. He died in Philadelphia in June 1865 and is buried near Wilmington, Delaware.

—*Stephen C. Svonavec*

See also Blockade of C.S.A.; Dahlgren, John Aldoph; Ironclads; Navy, U.S.A.

For further reading:
Anderson, Bern. *By Sea and by River: The Naval History of the Civil War* (1962).
Fowler, William M., Jr. *Under Two Flags: The American Navy in the Civil War* (1990).
Hayes, John D., ed. *Samuel Francis Du Pont: A Selection from His Civil War Letters* (1969).
Merrill, James M. *Du Pont, the Making of an Admiral: A Biography of Samuel Francis Du Pont* (1986).

DUDLEY, THOMAS HAINES
(1819–1893)
U.S. consul in Liverpool, England

Thomas Haines Dudley was a New Jersey political figure who went on to become the U.S. consul in Liverpool, England, from 1861 to 1872. Consul Dudley worked hard to build support for the North in Britain and to stop the construction of Confederate raiders in British shipyards.

According to the historian William Potts, Dudley was born in Burlington County, New Jersey, on 9 September 1819 and grew up helping his widowed mother with the chores on their Burlington farm. A local Camden attorney taught him law and he completed his examinations in 1845. After becoming a lawyer, his antislavery views soon became evident. Dudley agreed to help local Quakers rescue a black woman and her children from kidnappers who were taking them South into slavery. He dressed up as a slave trader (complete with whip and broad-brimmed hat) and talked the kidnappers into selling him the woman and her children.

New Jersey Republicans selected Dudley as a delegate to the Chicago Republican Convention of 1860. Dudley supported Abraham Lincoln's nomination and was instrumental in swinging a significant number of delegates over to him. Dudley's support for Lincoln enabled him to secure the position of U.S. consul in Liverpool, which, as it turned out, was a hotbed of Confederate sympathizers because of its close connections with the cotton trade. "Hostility towards our country," Dudley remarked, was severe and "pervaded all classes." Despite the hostile environment, Dudley was conscientious in his duties. As a result, Lincoln rewarded him with supervisory authority over every American consulate in Britain (except London) and allowed him to manage more than 100 spies. Dudley's main task was to help the U.S. minister to Britain, Charles Francis Adams, uncover and counteract Confederate shipbuilding activity in Liverpool.

After the Civil War broke out, relates the historian Frank Merli, Confederate navy secretary Stephen Mallory sent James Dunwody Bulloch, a man with an extensive seafaring background, to Britain for the purpose of procuring ships for the South's navy. Bulloch immediately became Dudley's formidable archenemy. "It is doubtful," writes the historian Philip Van Doren Stern, "whether anyone in the entire Western Hemisphere was as well fitted for his special task as Bulloch was." Dudley hired Liverpool detective Matthew Maguire (and a host of other rather unsavory characters) to check up on Bulloch's operations. Dudley's goal was to convince British legal officials that Confederate shipbuilding activity violated Britain's neutrality laws. Bulloch's lawyer, however, concluded that Bulloch could have ships built in Britain as long as they were not outfitted in Britain for military purposes. Accordingly, Bulloch decided to slip the unarmed ships out of Liverpool and equip them for battle outside of British jurisdiction.

Dudley worked persistently to prevent Bulloch from getting his ships out of Britain. He was particularly concerned about the *Oreto*, which was supposedly being built for an Italian owner. Minister Adams and Dudley informed British foreign secretary Lord Russell about the suspicious nature of the ship but the British did not detain it. Unfortunately for the Union navy, the *Oreto* slipped out of Liverpool in March 1862, and the Confederates eventually converted it into the commerce raider *Florida*. Dudley then tried to stop the escape of another one of Bulloch's ships, the dangerous raider *Alabama*. Dudley and Adams convinced the British to detain the *Alabama*, but foot-dragging port officials allowed the wily Bulloch to get the ship out of Liverpool in July 1862. The *Alabama* promptly embarked on a campaign that ravaged Union shipping all over the world.

Dudley's fortunes, however, began to improve in the spring of 1863 when he went after the Laird rams, two ironclads that Bulloch had secretly hired the Laird shipyard of Liverpool to construct for the Confederate navy. Bulloch attempted to conceal the true nature of the ships, but the British, prodded by the protests of Adams and Dudley, seized the Laird rams in October 1863. Dudley had triumphed over Bulloch and made his greatest contribution to the Union victory in the Civil War.

After the Civil War, Dudley assisted the U.S. government in settling the *Alabama* damage claims controversy with Britain. In 1872 Dudley resigned as Liverpool consul and returned to Camden, New Jersey. He later served as president of the Pittsburgh, Titusville & Buffalo Railroad and also as president of the Camden Bar Association. Thomas Dudley died on 15 April 1893.

—*David A. Proctor*

See also Adams, Charles Francis; *Alabama* Claims; Bulloch, James Dunwoody.
For further reading:
Bulloch, James. *The Secret Service of the Confederate States in Europe, or, How the Confederate Cruisers were Equipped* (1883).
Merli, Frank. *Great Britain and the Confederate Navy, 1861–1865* (1970).
Potts, William. "Biographical Sketch of the Honorable Thomas H. Dudley of Camden, New Jersey." *Proceedings of the American Philosophical Society* (1895).

DUFFIÉ, ALFRED NAPOLÉON ALEXANDRE
(1833–1880)
Union general

Although a minor Federal cavalry general, Alfred Napoléon Duffié belonged to a class of officers, many of them foreign born (Lord Percy Wyndham, Luigi di Cesnola), who reorganized and reenergized the Northern mounted arm in the months preceding the Gettysburg campaign.

Born in Paris, France, on 18 May 1833, Alfred Napoléon Alexandre Duffié descended from Irish soldiers of fortune. While well off, his father was a Parisian bourgeois with land in the Seine-et-Marne area, and by no means a count, as Duffié argued. Further,

Duffié never graduated from the Ecole Spéciale Militaire, St-Cyr, never fought in the French 1859 campaign against the Austrians, and never earned the Légion d'Honneur, which he is seen wearing on several extant photographs including one taken at Mathew Brady's Washington studio. His military training, however, was not negligible. He enrolled in the Imperial cavalry in 1852, being assigned to the 6th Dragoon regiment, and served with this unit in the Crimea, where he saw action at Balaklava, Chernaia, and Koungit. A naturally skilled noncommissioned officer, he rose through the ranks and finally earned a sub-lieutenant commission with the 3d Hussar regiment in 1859. For obscure reason, he resigned his commission and left for the United States with an unknown woman. Because he did not wait for acceptance of his resignation, he was found a deserter and sentenced to a ten-year prison sentence in absentia.

Duffié was in New York at the onset of the Civil War, having married into the prominent Pelton family of Staten Island. He joined the 2d New York Cavalry (Harris Light Cavalry) in August of 1862, quickly receiving the rank of captain. He seemed to have been well considered by General Irvin McDowell, but also spent time under arrest for confrontations with other officers. He participated in the Virginia operations in the spring 1862, apparently running afoul of General George McClellan's protégé Fitz John Porter, whom Duffié challenged to a duel. At a time when the Federal cavalry was being ridiculed by Southern troopers, Duffié's reputation as a pugnacious officer, with his dashing manner and sartorial eccentricities (hence his nickname of "Nattie"), somehow attracted the attention of Rhode Island governor William Sprague. In July 1862, the latter granted Duffié the colonelcy of the 1st Rhode Island Cavalry regiment, also known as 2d New England Cavalry after aggregation of a New Hampshire battalion.

First confronted with a quasi-mutiny of officers refusing to serve under a foreign-born officer (one also known for his quirky use of English), Duffié rapidly earned the trust of these Rhode Island blue-bloods. He masterfully reorganized the regiment into a fine fighting unit and led them with a degree of success in the desultory fighting around Cedar Mountain in August 1862. This period was crucial in the development, under experienced officers such as William Averell, of cavalry units holding their ground against veteran Confederate squadrons. Commanding a brigade, Duffié was indeed to have his moment of glory on 17 March 1863 at Kelly's Ford in a charge in which J. E. B. Stuart's troopers were checked, if not beaten. Yet Duffié, placed in command of a division in Alfred Pleasonton's newly created cavalry corps, was unable to confirm this success, doing very little to facilitate Pleasonton's extrication during the battle of Brandy Station on 9 June 1863.

Unfortunately for his regiment, Duffié had obviously reached his level of incompetence in the days preceding the battle of Gettysburg. This was to be made manifest a few days after Brandy Station in the course of an ill-fated mission initially destined to reconnoiter the area going from Manassas Junction to Middleburg and from there to Nolan's Ferry. Unbeknown to Duffié, J. E. B. Stuart's troopers had severed his communication line to the rest of the cavalry corps, intercepting him near Middleburg on 17 June. Duffié's command was virtually annihilated, Duffié himself escaping with four officers and twenty-seven men. He relinquished command of his beloved regiment and returned to Washington.

Waiting to be recalled to active duty, he first enjoyed a promotion to brigadier general on 23 June 1863. Yet his wish for command was to be fulfilled only in the fall when he was sent to West Virginia and charged with the raising and training of sizable cavalry units. His division, composed mostly of West Virginia volunteers, saw limited action against Jubal Early's men around Lewisburg in December 1863 and in April 1864 under General David Hunter around Lynchburg. More importantly, it was with such units that, under order from General Philip Sheridan, Duffié participated in operations in the Shenandoah Valley against John S. Mosby's Rangers, promising to capture the Gray Ghost and return him to Washington "in a iron cage." On 20 October 1864, Duffié's luck ran out and he was captured by Mosby's men, much to Sheridan's ire. Sent to prison camp, where he earned a reputation as an uppity officer, Duffié was paroled on 22 February 1865. He was then ordered to proceed to Texas to participate in operations against Edmund Kirby Smith, but these ended before Duffié had time to reach his destination. The Frenchman was thus mustered out of service on 24 August.

Upon his discharge, Duffié returned to Staten Island to nurse his compromised health in the midst of his family. Naturalized in 1867, he was appointed in 1869 U.S. consul to Cadiz, Spain, at the time an important naval facility. He died there from tuberculosis on 8 November 1880.

In 1876, Duffié had visited Rhode Island and reacquainted himself with some of his former officers. Upon his death, these men established a subscription that allowed for a monument to Duffié to be erected in Providence. It bears the emblem of Légion d'Honneur, which Duffié sported without due permission.

—*Laurent Ditmann*

See also Kelly's Ford.
For further reading:

Denison, Frederic. *Sabres and Spurs: The First Regiment Rhode Island Cavalry in the Civil War, 1861–1865* (1876).
Longacre, Edward G. *The Cavalry at Gettysburg: A Tactical Study of Mounted Operations during the Civil War's Pivotal Campaign, 9 June–14 July 1863* (1986).
Lonn, Ella. *Foreigners in the Union Army and Navy* (1951).

DUKE, BASIL WILSON
(1838–1916)
Confederate officer, lawyer

Basil Wilson Duke was born near Georgetown, Kentucky, on 28 May 1838, the only child of navy Captain Nathaniel Wilson Duke and Mary Pickett Currie Duke. After attending private schools in the Bluegrass Region, the youth went to Centre College, Georgetown College, and Transylvania University, where he studied law. After graduating in 1858, Duke moved to St. Louis, away from the crowded Kentucky bar. Strongly pro-Southern, Duke helped organize Confederate forces in Missouri and secure artillery for their use from the Confederate government. When the Unionists gained control of Missouri, Duke was indicted for treason and arson.

He returned to Kentucky, where on 18 June 1861 he married Henrietta Hunt Morgan, a sister of John Hunt Morgan. Duke then served in Missouri and Arkansas until General William J. Hardee suggested that he raise his own company in Kentucky. That attempt failed, Duke said, because all the Kentuckians wanted to start as captains. He enlisted as a private in John Hunt Morgan's elite Lexington Rifles but was soon elected second lieutenant. After Kentucky's unique neutrality ended in early September 1861, they joined the Confederate army in southern Kentucky.

The 23-year-old Duke, several inches under six feet and weighing 130 pounds, displayed skill in training troops as they skirmished along the Green River until the Confederates withdrew from the state in mid-February 1862.

Duke was severely wounded in both shoulders at Shiloh. Recovered, he was promoted to lieutenant colonel of the 2d Kentucky Cavalry Regiment. Duke trained Morgan's men to fight as mounted infantry with flexible tactics that enhanced their efficiency. He was an invaluable subordinate on the raids into Kentucky that became a Morgan trademark and in the Tennessee encounters that hampered the Union advance. He won praise for fights at Gallatin and Edgefield Junction; he was less successful at Augusta, Kentucky, on 27 September 1862. Duke was bitterly critical of Braxton Bragg for not fighting a decisive battle during the 1862 Kentucky invasion. He was convinced that "with the failure to hold Kentucky, our best and last chance to win the war was thrown away."

Duke was promoted to colonel before the Christmas raid of 1862. The massive railroad trestles were destroyed near Elizabethtown, but Duke was wounded by shrapnel in a rear-guard action on the Rolling Fork of the Salt River. In his report, Union colonel John M. Harlan wrote that Duke "is believed to be the life and soul of all the movements" of Morgan's command. Duke recovered in time to participate in Morgan's forbidden Indiana-Ohio raid in July 1863. During that exhausting chase, admiring Duke's men called him "The Little Whalebone."

Captured on 19 July, Duke was a prisoner of war until he was exchanged in August 1864. After Morgan's death, Duke became commander of the brigade and was promoted to brigadier general. He rebuilt the command and was active in campaigns in western Virginia and eastern Tennessee. After learning of Lee's surrender at Appomattox, he led his men to join Jefferson Davis and what remained of the Confederate government. He assisted Davis in his futile effort to escape, then held the last brigade formation on 8 May 1865; "for us the long agony was over."

In 1867, Duke published his *History of Morgan's Cavalry*, then opened a Louisville law office in 1868. Elected to the Kentucky House as a Democrat in 1869, he resigned in 1870. He was commonwealth attorney for the 5th Judicial District from 1875 to 1880, and for over twenty years he was chief counsel and lobbyist for the L&N Railroad that he had damaged so often during the war. Duke was a founder of The Filson Club and a popular public figure, always ready with a graceful toast or appropriate speech. He wrote *A History of the Bank of Kentucky, 1792–1895* (1895) and the *Reminiscences of General Basil W. Duke, CSA* (1911), along with a number of Civil War articles. He died in New York on 16 September 1916 and was buried in the Lexington Public Cemetery.

— *Lowell H. Harrison*

See also Kentucky; Morgan, John Hunt.
For further reading:

Duke, Basil W. *History of Morgan's Cavalry* (1867).
———. *Reminiscences of General Basil W. Duke, CSA* (1911).
Harrison, Lowell H. "General Basil W. Duke, CSA," *Filson Club History Quarterly* (1980).
Ramage, James A. *Rebel Raider: The Life of John Hunt Morgan* (1986).

DURANT, THOMAS JEFFERSON
(1817–1882)
Louisiana Unionist

Born 8 August 1817, Thomas Jefferson Durant of New Orleans illustrates the potential of the wartime and postwar Southern efforts to assist in the federal reconstruction of their own society. He had a good education in his native Pennsylvania before heading off on his own to Louisiana at about age seventeen.

By age twenty, Durant coedited the *Southerner and People's Friend*, a militantly Jacksonian paper that responded to the financial panic of 1837 by denouncing banking and the commercial standards. By 1840, he addressed a rally of local "workingmen" in the land reform rhetoric familiar to Northern labor, with radical agrarian leaders like George Henry Evans. After serving on the Democratic state central committee in 1844, he received an appointment as a federal attorney in 1846. By then, however, Durant embraced the social critique of Charles Fourier, the French socialist theorist, and began corresponding with Northern cothinkers. After winning election to the state senate in 1846, he proposed "mutual insurance" and other reforms to introduce Fourierism piecemeal, but Durant generally drew a strict line between practical politics and his utopian aspirations.

Durant clung to the regular Democratic Party in 1860, supporting Stephen A. Douglas and discounting talk of secession. Although serving as a private in Louisiana's militia, he saw the Confederacy as an attempt "to make a new government, radically different from the great republic; to adopt a new theory, in which the liberty of the working classes should be destroyed, and from all participation in which they should be excluded; a government in which labor should belong to capital, without regard to color. It was a question of independence, but of the extinction of liberty, whether of African or Caucasian descent."

Union seizure of the city in April 1862 opened the possibility for transforming the state. Petitioning for military assistance to the city's poor of both races, Durant gained the attention and respect of Federal general Benjamin F. Butler. Visiting the east in the late summer and fall of 1862, Durant returned convinced of the possibility for making his egalitarian principles practical. That fall, he returned with a sense that the Union government might cooperate in the overthrow of the planter aristocracy and support a new Louisiana that acknowledged human equality before the law and assured black suffrage. Appointed attorney general, he set about registering voters and building for such a radical new government. Butler's December replacement seriously moderated its prospects.

Butler's replacement, General Nathaniel P. Banks, was a politician interested in supplying cotton mills back in Massachusetts. Eager to accommodate the plantation system, Banks used the army to institute a labor system that kept many Louisiana African-Americans involuntarily on plantations for which a mere paper government would suffice. Banks grossly misrepresented Durant's

opposition to Banks' policies in Washington. By 1863, Durant led a significant faction of New Orleans Unionists, white and black, eager to remake the state in opposition to the conservative military structure. Early in 1864, Banks's plans for a Red River campaign (actually aimed at expanding the Federal cotton supply) appealed to an already misinformed Lincoln administration, itself eager for any sort of loyal government. Unable to obtain a hearing, Durant resigned as attorney general, yielding power to various figures who were willing to accommodate the convenience of the military structure and who were less rooted in Louisiana politics. As these offered repeated concessions to the old order, Durant watched the prospects of Southern radicalism fade until the 1866 New Orleans riot against even the most moderate Unionists.

Durant left the city for New York, where he reestablished his law practice, handling many of the large number of Southern suits entering the federal court system in Washington. He declined the 1867 offer of Philip Sheridan to appoint him governor of Louisiana. Two years later, he was also mentioned for vacancies on the U.S. Supreme Court, which lacked Southerners. In 1881, he was appointed U.S. counsel before the Spanish and American Claims Commission. Throughout his life, Durant remained a radical advocate of social change from the people themselves and, in his last national election, actively helped to manage the presidential bid of third-party candidate James B. Weaver. Durant died on 2 February 1882.

Linking antebellum social reform, wartime Unionism, and postwar insurgency, Durant's career demonstrated the originality and breadth of opinion permissible in the power structure of the period and the potential of the Civil War.

—*Mark A. Lause*

See also Banks, Nathaniel Prentiss; Butler, Benjamin Franklin; Douglas, Stephen Arnold; Evans, George Henry; Labor; Red River Campaign; Sheridan, Philip; Weaver, James Baird.
For further reading:
Guarneri, Carl J. *The Utopian Alternative: Fourierism in Nineteenth-Century America* (1991).
Tregle, Joseph G., Jr. "Thomas J. Durant, Utopian Socialism, and the Failure of Presidential Reconstruction in Louisiana." *Journal of Southern History* (1979).

EADS, JAMES BUCHANAN
(1820–1887)
Engineer and inventor

Born on 23 May 1820 in Lawrenceburg, Indiana, James Buchanan Eads taught himself engineering skills and used his ingenuity to strengthen the Union navy. The son of Thomas C. and Ann Buchanan Eads, James Eads was the second cousin of President James Buchanan. Thomas Eads was a merchant who moved his family to Cincinnati, Ohio, and Louisville, Kentucky, in search of economic opportunity. In 1833, the family landed at St. Louis in a steamboat that caught on fire, destroying all of their belongings. Eads's mother operated a boardinghouse, and James quit school to sell apples and clerk at a dry goods store. Mechanically adept, Eads experimented with machinery, building a model steamboat with working engines and boilers. In his spare time, Eads read engineering books.

At age eighteen, Eads accepted a job as purser on the steamboat *Knickerbocker*. He hoped to improve his health by being outdoors and performing vigorous work. For three years, Eads studied the Mississippi River between St. Louis and New Orleans. He noted how the river changed in different seasons from flooding torrents to ice-choked channels. He saw wrecks caused by currents or obstructions, and after his own steamboat was snagged and sank, he was inspired to develop ways to salvage ship parts and cargoes. In 1842, he patented a diving bell and a vessel to salvage ships. The bell was watertight with an open bottom and room for two people. Eads's salvaging boat, the *Submarine*, had a double hull, derricks, and pumps to provide oxygen to the diving bell. The boat's powerful devices could lift entire steamboats out of the river. Anchoring the salvage boat above the wreck, Eads or his employees would sit inside the bell as it was lowered into the water. Hoses pumped air into the bell to prevent water from entering the bell as the salvagers hooked lines to cargoes, which were then winched to the surface. Eads's business was immediately successful, but after three years he sold it at the insistence of his future father-in-law.

Eads established the first glass factory in St. Louis, but that business had failed by 1848. Returning to his salvaging work, Eads paid off his debts and earned a fortune within a decade. He became an expert on hydrodynamics, and in 1856 he proposed to Congress a plan to remove snags and wrecks from several Midwestern rivers to keep their channels clear, but the bill died in the Senate.

In April 1861, President Abraham Lincoln emphasized the crucial role of the Mississippi River in the coming Civil War. Union control of the Mississippi would prevent the Confederacy from using it to move troops and supplies. Because the Confederates had fortified outposts on the Mississippi and its tributaries, General Winfield Scott suggested that Union gunboats could secure the river from Cairo, Illinois, to New Orleans. As the country's foremost Mississippi River expert, Eads was charged with evaluating this Federal strategy using his knowledge of the Mississippi's navigability. He proposed building shallow-draft, steam-powered ironclad gunboats.

On 7 August 1861, the Federal government contracted Eads to prepare seven gunboats by 10 October. Eads designed the 600-ton boats with exact engineering specifications, and within two weeks he had collected resources and arranged for 4,000 workers in eight states to begin work on the project, doing so in the face of severe manpower shortages. He used the telegraph to arrange for supplies to be shipped by railroad and barge; workers harvested timber for hulls, rolled iron for 2.5-inch plating, and cast and assembled parts for engines, deck guns, and equipment. The *St. Louis*, launched on 12 October 1861, was the first ironclad to sail on American waters. Eads finished six more ironclads for the Union navy before building an eighth boat by equipping a renovated salvage vessel with steam-powered gun turrets. In the years following, Eads continued to innovate naval equipment and ordnance for new ironclads. He also devised and constructed armored troop transports and heavy mortar boats. The fleet that Eads built was used to control the Mississippi as well as to open up western rivers. These boats enabled the capture of Forts Henry and Donelson, Vicksburg, and Mobile Bay, and thus were crucial for Union dominance of the Mississippi Valley.

After the war, Eads continued his important engineering work. He designed the Eads Bridge that spanned the Mississippi River at St. Louis and helped improve waterways in the United States and abroad. He spent his final years in Washington, D.C., promoting his idea for a ship railway across Mexico. Traveling to the Bahamas in an effort to improve his health, he died at Nassau on 8 March 1887. He was buried in St. Louis's Bellefontaine Cemetery.

—*Elizabeth D. Schafer*

See also Pook's Turtles.

For further reading:

Dorsey, Florence L. *Road to the Sea: The Story of James B. Eads and the Mississippi River* (1947).

How, Louis. *James B. Eads* (1900).

McHenry, Estill, ed. *Addresses and Papers of James B. Eads, together with a Biographical Sketch* (1884).

Scott, Quinta, and Howard S. Miller. *The Eads Bridge* (1979).

EARLY, JUBAL ANDERSON
(1816–1894)
Confederate general

Jubal Anderson Early was born in Franklin County, Virginia, on 3 November 1816, into a slaveholding family. Privately educated, he was admitted to West Point in 1833 and four years later graduated a respectable eighteenth in a class of fifty. In 1837 he was commissioned a second lieutenant in the 3d U. S. Artillery and, following a brief stint of garrison duty at Fort Monroe, Virginia, Early shipped south for a year to fight in Florida's Second Seminole War. Despite lackluster performance as an officer, Early rose to first lieutenant in 1838. However, he harbored doubts about continuing in the military and resigned his commission that same year to pursue law in Virginia.

In 1841 Early gained election to the state house of delegates as a staunchly Whig conservative and he also served as commonwealth attorney from Franklin County. When war with Mexico erupted in 1846, he suspended politics to become colonel of the 1st Virginia Volunteers and part of General Zachary Taylor's army. No fighting occurred, but while performing garrison duty he contracted a severe rheumatism which rendered his already gangly figure stooped and aged beyond its years. Nonetheless, Early mustered out in 1848 and resumed political activities after the war. In April, 1861, he was elected to the state secession convention as a pro-Union delegate. He argued stridently against secession, but when Virginia voted to secede on 17 April, Early tendered his services to the Confederacy.

In July 1861, Early served as colonel of the 24th Virginia Infantry, and fought in the Southern victory at Bull Run. His determined counterattack against the Union right flank carried the day for the Confederates and gained him promotion to brigadier general. He was badly wounded leading another desperate charge at Williamsburg in May, 1862, but Early had established himself as one of the best brigade and divisional commanders in the Army of Northern Virginia. He was especially singled out for praise by General Robert E. Lee. Early next fought under Joseph E. Johnston and Thomas J. Jackson throughout 1862, and distinguished himself in hard fighting at the Peninsula, Second Manassas, Antietam, and Fredericksburg. In virtually every encounter, his trademark, savage counterthrust saved the Confederate army from destruction. Unfortunately, his reputation as a fighter notwithstanding, Early was saddled with a rude, caustic personality which alienated superiors and subordinates alike. Tall, gaunt, and much given to liquor and women, "Old Jube" became celebrated as one of the most eccentric characters to rise to high command. Lee nonetheless valued his tenacity and fortitude as a scrapper, tolerated his continual disrespect for authority, and referred to him affectionately as "my bad old man."

Early rose to major general in 1863, and he bore an important part in the Chancellorsville campaign when, vastly outnumbered, he temporarily guarded the Confederate rear at Fredericksburg. He was next closely engaged in the first day of Gettysburg, 1 July 1863, where his troops proved instrumental in driving Union forces of General O. O. Howard out of the town. But Early shares, along with General Richard S. Ewell, his superior, responsibility for failing to press the attack against Cemetery Hill. Retention of this position may materially altered the outcome of the battle in favor of the South. Nevertheless, he claimed with some validity that his troops were exhausted, disorganized, and ill-prepared to assault dug-in Union troops on the heights before him. Many historians now believe that Early's circumspection was correct. His subsequent attacks on the second day were hard-pressed and well-delivered, but repulsed with heavy loss. After Lee's retreat, Early bungled a stout fight at Rappahannock Bridge in November 1863, but substantially redeemed his reputation during the subsequent Mine Run campaign.

During the Wilderness campaign in the spring of 1864, Early temporarily succeeded Ambrose P. Hill as III Corps commander and fought commendably. The following month, at Spotsylvania, he assumed control of Ewell's corps when that officer was wounded, and turned in another fine performance. Consequently, in May, 1864, Lee arranged Early's promotion to lieutenant general and assigned him to take charge of II Corps, an independent command.

Early's responsibility was to defend the Shenandoah Valley of western Virginia, a valuable granary, against Union occupation. At that time, the vital city of Lynchburg was being threatened by a large force under General David S. Hunter. Accordingly, Early led 14,000 men against Hunter, who was so nonplused that he retreated before the enemy. With the valley firmly in Southern hands, Early next sought to provide a strategic diversion for Lee, then grappling with Ulysses S. Grant outside of Richmond. Pushing north towards Washington, D. C., he rapidly crossed the Potomac River and extorted $220,000 in levies from the towns of Hagerstown and Frederick, Maryland. Moreover, Early defeated a scratch force assembled by General Lew Wallace at Monocacy, Maryland, on 9 July 1864. This action greatly alarmed the Union capital, and defenses were hastily made to repel the intruders. Moreover, Grant was forced to divert two complete corps to the defense of the capital when they were badly needed in Virginia. Fortunately for the North, by the time Early's force arrived outside the city's defenses, he viewed them as too strong to attack with any confidence of success. He therefore withdrew his grey-clad columns back into the valley, pursued by a large cavalry force under General George Crook. On 24 July 1864, Early suddenly and typically turned and pounced on his antagonists, stampeding them at the battle of Second Winchester.

Throughout the late summer and into the fall, Early's Army of the Valley ranged freely throughout the Shenandoah region, and at one point his cavalry raided and burned Chambersburg, Pennsylvania. He ordered this act in retaliation for Union depredations in the valley and elsewhere. To end the impasse, Grant unleashed General Philip H. Sheridan with 40,000 men to evict him and devastate the region. The aggressive Sheridan quickly confronted and defeated Early at the battles of Third Winchester and Fisher's Hill that September, driving him deeper into the valley. However, Early perceived an opportunity and suddenly counterattacked Union forces at Cedar Creek in October, routing two of three corps. The battle was only saved at the last minute by Sheridan's famous ride, which rallied his troops and routed the Confederates in turn. Driven from the valley, Early attempted to make a last stand with 1,000 men at Waynesboro, but in March 1865, his men were crushed by General George A. Custer's cavalry. Early had, in retrospect, conducted a fine campaign, and succeeded as well as any other leader might have under the circumstances. Lee maintained his high opinion of his beleaguered subordinate, but public opinion blamed him loss of the valley. Early therefore suffered the final indignity of being relieved shortly before the Confederate surrender.

After the war ended, Early fled to Mexico and Canada to compose his memoirs, but he returned to Virginia in 1867 under a general amnesty. The former pro-Union delegate was by now deeply embittered and unable to reconcile himself to Confederate defeat. After resuming his legal practice, in 1877 he relocated to Louisiana to serve as commissioner of the state lottery. Early also functioned as founder and president of the Southern Historical Society, whose writings espoused a distinctly Confederate perspective of men and events. A foremost article of faith was the unimpeachable leadership of Robert E. Lee, whom Early constantly extolled. He also conducted a longstanding vendetta against General James Longstreet, who in postwar years criticized Lee and joined the Republican Party. Until their dying days, Early and Longstreet publicly squabbled as to who lost Gettysburg–and the war.

In this same capacity, Early clearly reveled in his role as an architect for the cult of the "Lost Cause." He pursued it with such vitriol that historian Robert Stiles commented that as long as he lived, "no man ever took up his pen to write a line about the great conflict without the fear of Jubal Early before his eyes." Irascible and defiant to the end, "Old Jube" never sought to have his citizenship restored. He died at Lynchburg, Virginia, on 2 March 1894, an "unreconstructed Confederate" to the end.

—*John C. Fredriksen*

See also Early's Washington Raid; Sheridan, Philip Henry.
For further reading:
Early, Jubal A. *Autobiographical Sketch and Narrative of the War Between the States* (1989)
Gallagher, Gary W. *Jubal A. Early, the Lost Cause, and Confederate History: A Persistent Legacy* (1995).
Osborne, Charles C. *Jubal: The Life and Times of General Jubal A. Early, C.S.A.* (1992).

EARLY'S WASHINGTON RAID
(14 June–7 August 1864)

On 12 June 1864 Robert E. Lee ordered Jubal Early and his corps to march to Lynchburg, Virginia, to aid John C. Breckinridge in the defense of that town against Major General David Hunter. If Early succeeded in defeating Hunter, he was to move down the Shenandoah Valley and threaten invasion of Maryland and, if possible, even threaten Washington. Lee hoped that these movements would force Grant to send at least part of his army back to the District of Columbia and thus relieve some of the pressure on the Army of Northern Virginia. Early and Breckinridge defeated Hunter at Lynchburg on 18 June. Hunter retreated westward with Early in pursuit, though the Union forces moved so quickly and so far west (to the Ohio River), that Early gave up the chase and began moving down the Valley.

Early and his roughly 10,000 infantry and 4,000-man cavalry division arrived at Staunton on 27 June and moved north from there. They arrived at Winchester on 2 July. The only serious opposition to Early's movements in the Valley was from Franz Sigel's 5,000 men at Martinsburg, West Virginia. In the face of Early's movements, Sigel withdrew his men to Harper's Ferry and then crossed over the Potomac to Maryland Heights. Rather than attack this strong position, Early moved instead up to Shepherdstown, West Virginia, and then crossed the Potomac near Sharpsburg, Maryland.

After crossing into Maryland, Early sent John McCausland's cavalry brigade north to Hagerstown and moved with the bulk of the army to Frederick. Early instructed McCausland to ask for $200,000 in repara-

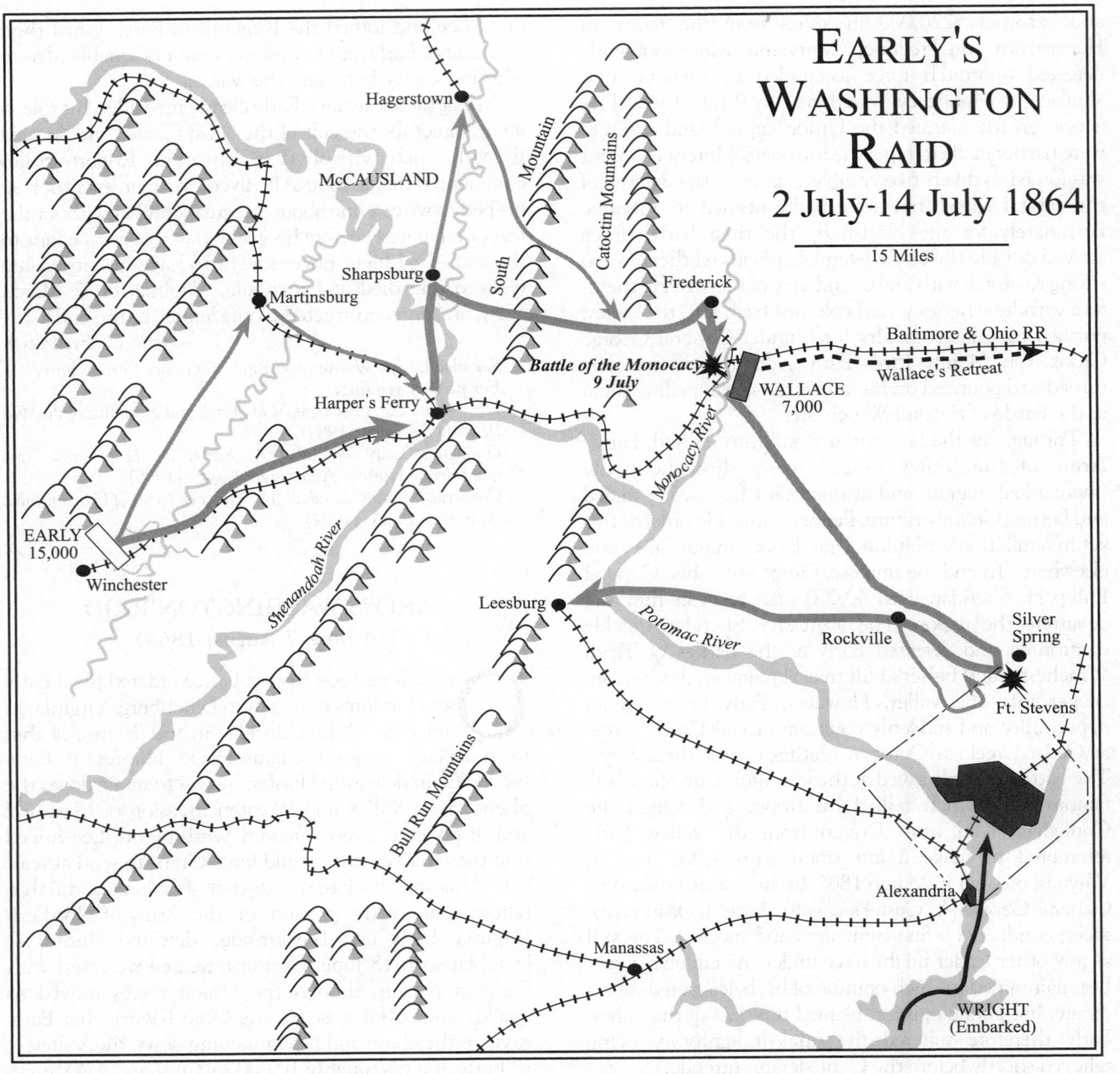

EARLY'S WASHINGTON RAID
2 July–14 July 1864

15 Miles

Hagerstown

McCAUSLAND

South Mountain

Catoctin Mountains

Sharpsburg

Martinsburg

Frederick

Battle of the Monocacy
9 July

Baltimore & Ohio RR

WALLACE
7,000

Wallace's Retreat

Harper's Ferry

Monocacy River

EARLY
15,000

Winchester

Shenandoah River

Leesburg

Potomac River

Rockville

Silver Spring

Ft. Stevens

Bull Run Mountains

Alexandria

Manassas

WRIGHT
(Embarked)

tions for the damage done by Hunter in the Shenandoah Valley. Whether he misunderstood the order or, as some have suggested, he thought the amount too large, McCausland asked for only $20,000 and received it. In the meantime Early, once he arrived at Frederick, Maryland, on 9 July demanded and received $200,000 for not destroying the town.

By that time the Federals were somewhat agitated at Early's movements. On 6 July, Ulysses S. Grant had sent James Brewerton Ricketts's division of Horatio Gouverneur Wright's VI Corps to Baltimore and 3,000 dismounted cavalry to Washington. Ricketts arrived in Baltimore on 7 July and moved out of the city to rendezvous with a cavalry and infantry brigade under

Lew Wallace near Frederick on the Monocacy River. When Early moved out of Frederick on 9 July, he encountered this force. He sent McCausland's cavalry brigade against the Federal left followed by John B. Gordon's infantry division. These two attacks succeeded in turning the Union left and subsequent attacks by Robert Emmett Rodes's division and Stephen Dodson Ramseur's division brought about a Union withdrawal back toward Baltimore. Early sent one of his cavalry brigades toward Baltimore to prevent a movement by Wallace toward Washington and then put the remainder of his army in motion toward the District of Columbia.

Early's victory at Monocacy caused Grant to send the remainder of VI Corps to Washington. In the meantime,

sending the rest of his cavalry in probes along the northwestern fringes of the District, Early took his infantry east and then started due south at what is now Silver Spring, Maryland, along the Seventh Street Road. He approached the outlying defenses about midday on 11 July and pushed the Federal pickets back toward Fort Stevens. Early's men were exhausted from having marched two days on dusty roads in 95-degree heat and from the battle at Monocacy. Therefore, he satisfied himself with letting his sharpshooters and skirmishers harass the Federal defenders of Fort Stevens.

When Early first arrived in the District he did not realize that Fort Stevens had scarcely 200 defenders and that the other forts in the arc of earthworks north of the city hardly more. Even though Fort Stevens and Forts De Russy and Slocum to the left and right of it were heavily armed with artillery, the gunners were very inexperienced. Early, of course, had no way of knowing all of this information, and only an immediate attack probably would have been successful. In early afternoon Wright's VI Corps began disembarking at Washington's wharves and marching north toward Fort Stevens. By late afternoon reinforcements were pouring into the forts. In addition a division of XIX Corps was on the way from Fort Monroe.

Also in the late afternoon, President Abraham Lincoln rode out to Fort Stevens. For the first of several times over the next two days the president was asked to remove himself from danger when he walked along Fort Stevens' parapets in full view of the Confederate sharpshooters.

Early made his headquarters at Silver Spring, the country estate of Francis Preston Blair located near the home of his son, Postmaster General Montgomery Blair. That night Early held a council of war at Silver Spring where he decided to launch a major offensive against the Federal defenses the next morning. Later that evening, he heard that those defenses were being reinforced by two Union corps (really only one corps, VI Corps, and one division of XIX Corps) and called off the attack. Instead he instructed his division commanders to continue the sharpshooter harassment and to prepare to withdraw the night of 12 July. His belief that Grant had diverted two corps from the siege of Petersburg meant that Early had fulfilled the primary goal of his mission by relieving pressure on Lee.

At dusk on 12 July, Federal forces launched an attack on Early's positions opposite Fort Stevens, which hastened the withdrawal of the Confederates. Again President Lincoln witnessed the fighting from Fort Stevens and was unceremoniously asked to descend the parapets when sharpshooter fire injured a man standing nearby. During the retreat, Montgomery Blair's house was destroyed by fire, though some Confederates later claimed that it had been done by Federal artillery.

On 14 July, Early crossed the Potomac into Virginia at Leesburg. The Confederates remained there until 16 July before going into Berryville, Virginia. Wright, with two of his divisions, slowly pursued.

From Berryville, Early went to Strasburg, leaving Ramseur behind to screen his movements. On 20 July at Winchester, a mixed cavalry/infantry force under William Averell attacked Ramseur. Ramseur was defeated and rushed with his now depleted division to join with Early. Following Ramseur's defeat, Early pulled back to Fisher's Hill to reassess his situation. Wright assumed Early was moving south to join Lee so he took his VI Corps back to Washington. George Crook, leading a part of Hunter's force east, joined with Averell at Winchester on 22 July. They learned that Early had moved back to Strasburg and in fact clashed with part of Early's cavalry on that day.

On 22 and 23 July the Confederate and Union cavalries skirmished, while Crook took most of his infantry to Kernstown. On 24 July Breckinridge, commanding Gordon's and Brigadier General Gabriel Wharton's divisions, attacked the center of Crook's lines at Kernstown. Ramseur followed with an attack on the Federal right and then Rodes on the Federal left, putting Crook's force in retreat toward Winchester and ultimately to Bunker Hill.

Following the victory at Kernstown, Early moved north, sending two cavalry brigades into Pennsylvania to demand $100,000 in gold or $500,000 in paper money from Chambersburg, Pennsylvania. When the town on 30 July did not meet the demand in the required amount of time, it was burned. Early's cavalry continued to operate in Maryland and West Virginia for the next week until McCausland was surprised and defeated by Averell at Moorefield, West Virginia, on 7 August 1864.

On the same day as McCausland's defeat, at the urging of Grant, Philip Sheridan was given command of the Middle Military Division, beginning Sheridan's campaign against Early in the Shenandoah Valley that ultimately would result in the destruction of the Valley and end Early's effectiveness as a distraction.

—David S. Heidler and Jeanne T. Heidler

See also Chambersburg, Burning of; Early, Jubal; Fort Stevens; Kernstown, Second Battle of; Lynchburg Campaign; Monocacy, Battle of; Moorefield, West Virginia, Battle of; Sheridan, Philip Henry; Wright, Horatio Gouverneur.

For further reading:
Cooling, Benjamin Franklin. *Jubal Early's Raid on Washington, 1864* (1989).

EDMONDS, SARAH EMMA
(1841–1898)
Union soldier

Born in 1841, Sarah Emma Edmonds was raised on a farm in New Brunswick, Canada. At the age of nineteen, primarily because of her desire for financial and personal independence from her family,

Edmonds disguised herself as a man, assumed the alias "Franklin Thompson," and headed across the border into the United States, where she took a job as a publisher's agent selling bibles. She was living in Flint, Michigan, when the Civil War began and had apparently either lost her job or squandered her earnings (or both), when the call came for volunteers to save the Union. She eagerly enlisted, under the same alias, in the 2d Michigan Infantry Regiment. Edmonds mustered in as a three-year recruit at Detroit on 25 May 1861.

By the middle of June, the 2d Michigan had traveled to Washington, D.C., where it participated in the defense of the capital. During her first months with the army, Edmonds was on duty at the regimental hospital, performing the work of a nurse, as did many young soldiers prior to the large-scale influx of women from the home front to military hospitals following Antietam. Subsequently, Edmonds became her regiment's postmaster and mail carrier, in which position she confronted the predictable hazards of regularly riding long distances, often at night, through contested territory. While in camp, Edmonds also adhered to standard military routines, drilling and parading with her mates, and fulfilling the various responsibilities and training of a common soldier. Through it all—including her regiment's combat service at First Bull Run, Williamsburg, Fair Oaks, the Seven Days' battles, and Fredericksburg— Edmonds raised few, if any, suspicions about her true sex. Though some in the regiment later claimed that they had considered Edmonds to be even more effeminate than many of the other teenaged boys who joined the army, at the time none openly expressed any concerns that she might in fact be a woman.

Although the evidence indicates that no one who served with her was able independently to discern that Edmonds was a woman, she revealed her sex to at least one fellow soldier, a medical steward and assistant surgeon for the 2d Michigan named Jerome John Robbins, who wrote about the event with considerable distress in his unpublished wartime diary. Beginning in October 1861, Robbins had been writing enthusiastically about his new friend Frank, and about their many conversations on the subject of religion and other topics. In the middle of November, however, Robbins's tone changed when he noted that Frank had identified himself as a woman. Obviously perturbed by this development, Robbins noted that he had immediately informed Frank of his own betrothal to a woman back home, which suggests that Edmonds's confession of her sex had been inspired by her growing affection for Robbins. From subsequent entries it is clear that Edmonds and Robbins struggled without much success in the next weeks and months to adjust to this wrinkle in their relationship. It is also clear, however, that regardless of what he personally thought about either Edmonds or

her decision to masquerade as a man and serve in the Union army, Robbins chose not to betray her trust. He glued together the pages of his diary in which he had written of her disclosure to him, and then continued to write about Edmonds only as Frank.

Gradually Edmonds and Robbins regained a bit of their earlier intimacy, but not enough to convince Edmonds to forewarn Robbins when she decided, in the spring of 1863, to desert. Although her nearly two years of service to the regiment and to the Union had been above reproach, by late April of that year Edmonds had lost her capacity to continue. When asked later why she left the army so abruptly, Edmonds claimed that she had fallen ill and, having been refused a leave of absence and having grown fearful that she would end up in a hospital and thus be discovered, she had imagined that there was no alternative. As it turns out, while there is evidence to support this explanation, other evidence suggests that Edmonds had fallen in love with another soldier, Assistant Adjutant General James Reid of the 79th New York, and had left the army because she could not bear to go through with him what she had already suffered with Robbins. In any case, Edmonds did desert on 20 April 1863, while the regiment was stationed in Kentucky. Some weeks later, she resurfaced in Ohio, took up the work of a female hospital nurse for the United States Christian Commission, and wrote a curious, popular, and much fictionalized memoir, entitled *Nurse and Spy in the Union Army*.

After the war ended, Edmonds returned to New Brunswick and married a carpenter. With her husband, Linus H. Seelye, and their adopted children, Edmonds moved many times before settling for the last years of her life in LaPorte, Texas. Having kept her military career secret except from a few trusted friends, when it became clear in 1884 that as "Franklin Thompson" she might be eligible for a veteran's pension, Edmonds began to gather the necessary materials for her application, and her story became more and more widely known. The strong and persuasive letters that many of her former comrades-in-arms wrote in connection with her application that praised "Thompson" for "his" valiant service to the Union army, were instrumental in gaining Edmonds the pension she sought and the restoration of her stature as a soldier of honor. The charge of desertion was removed from her record.

Edmonds was the only woman soldier during the Civil War to apply for a veteran's pension under her own name. She died in Texas in 1898, and was buried with full military honors at Houston's Washington Cemetery.

—*Elizabeth D. Leonard*

See also Women.

For further reading:
Dannett, Sylvia G. L. *She Rode with the Generals* (1960).
De Grave. *Swindler, Spy, Rebel: The Confidence Woman in Nineteenth Century America* (1995).

Edmonds, Sarah Emma. *Nurse and Spy in the Union Army: Comprising the Adventures and Experiences of a Woman in Hospitals, Camps, Battle-Fields.* (1865).

Leonard, Elizabeth D. *"All the Daring of the Soldier": Women of the Civil War Armies* (1999).

Wheelwright, Julie. *Amazons and Military Maids: Women Who Dressed as Men in the Pursuit of Life, Liberty and Happiness* (1989).

EDMONDSON, ISABELLA "BELLE" (1840–1873)

Confederate spy, smuggler, and courier

Isabella "Belle" Edmondson was born in Pontotoc, Mississippi. As a child, the tomboyish Edmondson freely exhibited a fondness for adventure that her parents, despite various attempts (which included sending her to finishing school), were unable to squelch. When the Civil War broke out, the unmarried and fiercely pro-Southern twenty-one-year-old Edmondson, then living with her family just outside Memphis, Tennessee, first volunteered her time as a nurse to the soldiers hospitalized in the area. These at one point included many of the wounded from the battle of Shiloh. About a year and a half into the war, however, Edmondson determined that nursing was far too tedious an occupation to engage her any longer, and she decided instead to express her political loyalties through the dangerous work of spying and serving as a smuggler and courier for the Confederacy.

By early June 1862 Memphis had fallen to the Union, a victory for the North that was crucial in the protracted campaign for control of the Mississippi River, but that nevertheless—and not surprisingly—failed to pacify Confederate sentiment or undermine subversive activity in the region. In this disputatious context, by early 1863 Belle Edmondson was proving herself an adept player, not least of all as a smuggler. Her good looks and charming manner seem to have made it particularly easy to persuade Union pickets to pass her through the lines. Like so many other women spies, smugglers, and couriers during the war, Edmondson was aided as well by mid-nineteenth-century middle-class women's fashions: hoop skirts, voluminous petticoats, elaborate hairdos, and an assortment of accessories that could easily be used to hide and transport small items of contraband. Her 16 March 1864, diary entry describes a remarkably heavy and complicated delivery: "We made a balmoral [petticoat]," she wrote, "of the Gray cloth for uniforms, pin'd the Hats to the inside of my hoops, tied the boots with a strong list, letting them fall directly in front, the cloth having monopolized the back & the Hats the side. All my buttons, brass buttons, Money &c in my bosom."

Edmondson thoroughly enjoyed her work as a spy and smuggler, noting in her diary at the end of 1863 that the year had been her happiest ever. At the same time, she frequently experienced waves of anxiety and even depression, in part because of the stresses naturally associated with her labors on behalf of the Confederacy. She underwent a series of brief arrests, for example, and by spring 1864 it appeared that Union officials' suspicions had been sufficiently aroused to make further espionage virtually impossible. Edmondson's emotional struggles derived as well from upheavals in her personal life, and indeed, the two spheres were entangled. Some have suggested that Edmondson's boldness in this work—which represented a striking challenge to conventional notions of proper female behavior—was at least partially responsible for her fiancé in 1863 deciding to call off their engagement. In June 1864, Edmondson fled south into Mississippi, having learned of yet another Yankee warrant for her arrest. She seems to have spent the rest of the war essentially in exile, near Tupelo.

Belle Edmondson never married. After the war she returned to the Memphis area, but beyond this little is known of her activities, as she seems to have stopped keeping written records of her own in November 1864, after her spying career came to an end. Edmondson died suddenly and mysteriously in 1873. Some evidence suggests that she died despondent, by her own hand.

—*Elizabeth D. Leonard*

See also Espionage; Women.

For further reading:

Galbraith, William, and Loretta Galbraith, eds. *A Lost Heroine of the Confederacy: The Diaries and Letters of Belle Edmondson* (1990).

Leonard, Elizabeth D. *All the Daring of the Soldier: Women of the Civil War Armies* (1999).

EGYPT

Geography placed Egypt far from the Civil War, yet this conflict had a significant impact on the land of the Nile. Between 1861 and 1865, Egypt figured in diplomatic initiatives by both North and South, offered weapons to the Union, and ran up against the Monroe Doctrine. Egypt also witnessed the capture of accused Lincoln conspirator, John H. Surratt, Jr., who was finally arrested in 1867 after a hunt that stretched from Maryland to Italy and Cairo. Above all, the Federal blockade pushed up the price of Egyptian cotton, fueling a three-year economic boom.

Egypt technically formed part of the Ottoman Empire. Real power, however, rested with the *wali*, or viceroy, a position held by the Muhammad Ali family since 1805. In 1861, Said ruled Egypt, and quickly demonstrated a pro-Union stance with his offer to sell the United States 40,000 rifles. Relations warmed further when Said agreed to halt any sales to the Confederacy and closed Egyptian ports to Southern privateers or commerce raiders.

Federal diplomats considered these important victories, especially since the former doyen of Egypt's Consular Corps, Edwin De Leon, now held a key position in the Confederate Department of State. Despite such beliefs, relations between Cairo and Washington were not always friendly. Here the issue was not the Civil War, but intervention in Mexico.

Said, consistently Francophile in his foreign policy, provided a battalion of Sudanese infantry to serve with the French occupation of Mexico. Although numbering only 446 soldiers, this was a valuable contribution in support of the new "Mexican Empire." Recruited from Egypt's tropical provinces, these men were more resistant to yellow fever than their European counterparts. This allowed their successful deployment about the disease-ridden lowlands surrounding the strategic port of Veracruz.

Outraged by this violation of the Monroe Doctrine, Washington pushed hard, in both Cairo and Constantinople, for the withdrawal of the unit. Egypt's new ruler, Ismail, agreed to stop reinforcements and halt deployment of an additional battalion. One reason for the policy change was Ismail's realization that France could not triumph. Another was his desire to center Egyptian resources in northeast Africa.

Sometimes dubbed, "the Magnificent," Ismail wanted to convert Egypt into a western-style nation quickly. Hiring foreign advisors, buying technology, and above all, building infrastructure were priorities. The vast sums of money needed came from loans, and these were fueled by another aspect of the American Civil War—the Federal blockade. Although disastrous for the South, what hurt the Confederacy helped Egypt, as cotton represented a major export in both nations. Europe's hungry mills devoured all that Egypt could produce. As a result, cash from cotton sales, which totaled 1.43 million pounds in 1861, jumped to 15 million in 1865. Although this economic boom ended a year later, Ismail continued spending for another decade, building massive debts with high rates of interest.

Even here, there is a connection between Egypt and the war. Army modernization was one of Ismail's many projects, and who better to help than officers with experience from the world's most recent struggle? Between 1869 and 1879, upward of fifty ex-Confederate and ex-Union officers hired on to create an Egyptian General Staff. Led by Charles P. Stone, this contingent of Civil War veterans represented a range of abilities. Yet, if they were not "the best money could buy," they did get along well because, as one put it, "There is no North or South here." Another Civil War outgrowth was Ismail's decision to purchase million's of dollars worth of weapons. U.S. manufacturers eagerly sought new markets and benefited from the Egyptian perception that Civil War needs created the best designs. Thus Remington rifles, Gatling guns, arms factories, and ammunition all figured in lucrative contracts to U.S. companies.

At best an ephemeral connection, this flurry of activity ended in the late 1870s. Mounting debts led to default on the arms contracts, layoffs for American mercenaries, and Ismail's 1879 abdication. Three years later, England began a fifty-four-year occupation, while Stone, the last of the Civil War contingent, packed his trunks and returned to the United States.

—*John P. Dunn*

See also Cotton; De Leon, Edwin; Stone, Charles Pomeroy; Surratt, John Harrison, Jr.

For further reading:
Hesseltine, William B., and Hazel C. Wolf. *The Blue and Grey on the Nile* (1961).
Hill, Richard, and Peter Hogg. *A Black Corps d'Elite* (1995).
U.S. Department of State. *Despatches from United States Consuls in Alexandria, 1835–1873.*
———. *Diplomatic Instructions of the Department of State to Egypt* (n.d.).
Wright, L. C. *United States Policy Towards Egypt 1820–1914* (1969).

ELECTION OF 1856

The presidential election of 1856 marked an important transition period in United States political history. Although the ruling Democratic Party retained its hold on the presidency, new political forces staked their claim to define the future of America.

Democrat Franklin Pierce had won the presidential election of 1852 and looked optimistically toward continuing the prosperity of the United States. His outlook changed with the passage of the Kansas-Nebraska Act, a piece of legislation that ended the quietude surrounding the slavery issue brought about by the Compromise of 1850.

Several consequences from the passage of the Kansas-Nebraska Act contributed to the political atmosphere of the 1856 election. The already weak Whigs split along regional lines and disintegrated as a party. A civil war broke out in Kansas, splintering the Democratic Party and dooming Pierce's hopes for a second term. Two new parties, the Know-Nothings and the Republicans, emerged to fill the void left by the Whigs. Most importantly, slavery again became the central point of political contention.

By the beginning of 1855, the political landscape had altered substantially. One new party that hoped to take over as the major rival to the Democrats was the American, or Know-Nothing, Party. This political movement actually began as a social organization in New York during the late 1840s, but by the early 1850s, it had grown increasingly political in its scope and expanded into other states, both North and South. In 1854, the National Council of the Know-Nothings established a national constitution and organized the group into a hierarchy. This move allowed the nativist organization to become an efficient political machine by which to campaign for and elect politicians who agreed with and supported their anti-immigrant and anti-Catholic beliefs. A large number of the Know-Nothing adherents were former Whigs

The Republican Party also sought to take advantage of the Whigs' demise. Made up largely of castoffs from other political parties, the Republicans focused on one central issue to maintain its disparate body of members: opposition to slavery extension. This stance contrasted sharply with the largely proslavery Democrats and the Know-Nothings, who determined to avoid mentioning slavery altogether.

In 1856, the three political parties met in their respective conventions to nominate candidates for the presidential election that fall. The Know-Nothings met first in February. The attending delegates disagreed vehemently over the slavery issue, inducing members of the Northern state delegations to walk out. (They would later nominate Nathaniel P. Banks of Massachusetts for the presidency.) The remaining Know-Nothings, mostly Southerners, selected former president Millard Fillmore of New York, a known "Constitution and Union" man, and Andrew Jackson Donelson of Tennessee, also a compromiser, as their ticket. The platform contained an "America first" theme and promised to eschew "all sectional problems…uniting upon those purely national."

The Democrats met in early June. Pierce and Stephen A. Douglas, who was closely identified with the Kansas-Nebraska bill, attempted to work together to keep Pennsylvanian James Buchanan, another Democratic hopeful, from obtaining the nomination. Their efforts failed, due largely to Pierce's unpopularity and the inability of Douglas to sway Northern votes. Buchanan received the presidential nomination; John C. Breckinridge of Kentucky accepted the vice-presidential designation. The party platform emphasized traditional Jacksonian views on government. As for slavery, popular sovereignty received the endorsement of the delegates as the correct course of action.

The Republican Party also convened in June. They selected their candidate, John C. Frémont of California, on the first ballot. Frémont had no political experience and thus had no liability, unlike other prominent Republicans, such as William H. Seward and Salmon P. Chase. (William Dayton was the Republican choice for vice president.) More important than the presidential candidate, however, was the Republican platform: the document exhibited Whiggish overtones on internal improvements, adamantly denounced slavery, and advocated a free-soil doctrine.

The election of 1856 became two separate encounters. Buchanan was virtually assured of the South's electoral votes unless Fillmore could persuade Southerners to suppress their emotional support of slavery and concentrate on national concerns such as internal improvements and the Catholic threat to American Protestantism. Frémont had little chance of obtaining votes in the slave South, so the Republicans submitted tickets only in the upper South.

In the North, Frémont held a decided advantage over Buchanan, but, again, the Know-Nothing candidate played an important role. While observers knew that Fillmore possessed little chance of winning more than a handful of states, the other two parties feared that the electoral count would prove insufficient for a clear victory, and the House of Representatives would have to decide the election. This possible result caused anxiety, since the 1824 election had shown that anything could happen in that situation.

The election hinged on the questions of black equality, disunion, and abolitionism. Democrats cried out for Americans to support Buchanan in opposition to the "Black Republicans" who were willing to abolish slavery, grant equality to the black race, and dismember the Union to accomplish their goals. Republicans struck back with the charge of a "slavocracy" out to destroy the country by its promulgation of slave dependency. The Know-Nothings, of course, preferred to stay out of these arguments.

The outcome of the presidential contest said much about the American voter's mind. Buchanan won with 174 electoral votes to Frémont's 114 and Fillmore's 8. The popular count ended with Buchanan gaining 1,832,955, Frémont winning 1,399,932, and Fillmore obtaining 871,731. The Know-Nothing ticket did not affect the outcome as some had dreaded. Buchanan won with the support of Northern Democrats and Southern moderates, who endorsed the Democratic platform of popular sovereignty for the territories.

The Democrats retained the presidency for four more years, but the lines of sectionalism were drawn. The Republicans established themselves in the North as the party against slavery, while the Democrats in the South adhered to the institution. Compromise parties and candidates no longer had a place for the majority of Americans. This consequence of the 1856 campaign came to fruition in the next presidential election.

—*Mark R. Cheatham*

See also American Party; Buchanan, James; Douglas, Stephen Arnold; Fillmore, Millard; Frémont, John Charles; Kansas-Nebraska Act; Popular Sovereignty.

For further reading:
Anbinder, Tyler G. *Nativism and Slavery: The Northern Know Nothings and the Politics of Slavery* 1992.
Gienapp, William. *The Origins of the Republican Party, 1852–1856* (1987).
Nichols, Roy F., and Philip S. Klein. "Election of 1856." In Arthur M. Schlesinger, Jr., ed., *History of American Presidential Elections, 1789–1968* (1971).

ELECTION OF 1858

The election of 1856 marked the first time that the Republican Party fielded candidates. The Republicans brought together members of the recently folded Whig Party, disaffected antislavery Democrats, and political abolitionists. The new party faced some significant obstacles in their first election: they were young and imperfectly organized, they had the onus of being labeled the party of disunion by both Northerners and Southerners, and they were vulnerable to charges of "Black Republicanism." Despite these problems, the Republicans performed creditably, capturing more that 60 percent of Northern votes. Republican leaders were pleased with what they had achieved, and they looked toward the election of 1858 as an opportunity to consolidate their gains.

In the two years between elections, the Republicans were increasingly vocal in warning Americans of a conspiracy that threatened the very foundations of the democracy. They charged that the Southern slave power, assisted by Northern "doughface" allies such as President James Buchanan, was attempting to convert the republic into a slave empire ruled by "a pampered and powerful oligarchy of some 350,000 slaveholders." They offered as evidence of this "slave conspiracy" the Mexican-American War, the annexation of Texas as a slave state, the repeal of the Missouri Compromise, the struggles in "Bleeding Kansas," and the *Dred Scott* decision of 1857.

In the election of 1858, then, voters were being asked to do more than simply vote for a person. They were being asked to evaluate the Republicans' interpretation of the events that had kept the United States reeling for the previous decade. The Democrats, of course, had their own message. They blamed the turmoil on a handful of agitators, and they continued to insist that the Republican agenda would tear the country apart and would lead to absolute equality for African-Americans.

As the year wore on, national attention came increasingly to focus on one contest, the race for Illinois's open Senate seat, described as the "most important battleground in the Union" by the *New York Times*. Abraham Lincoln, a former Whig, who was an important leader of Illinois Republicans, represented the Republicans, but he was essentially unknown in the rest of the country. The Democratic candidate was Stephen Douglas, the main spokesman for Popular Sovereignty and a major force on the national political scene for the previous decade.

The highlight of the Lincoln-Douglas contest was a series of seven debates held in various parts of the state. The sole topic of the Lincoln-Douglas debates was slavery. Lincoln's main thrust was his accusation that Douglas had departed from the position of the founders of the nation, while the Republicans were upholding that position. Lincoln argued that, like the founders, the Republicans saw slavery as wrong and believed that everything legally possible should be done to keep it from growing. He argued that the continued existence of slavery was a threat to the republic. In his most famous speech of the campaign, Lincoln stated his position metaphorically. "A house divided against itself cannot stand," he said, quoting Jesus. "I believe that this government cannot endure, permanently half slave and half free."

Douglas's counterattack focused on Lincoln's house divided metaphor. He wondered why the country could not continue to exist half slave and half free, and said that any party or individual trying to force Lincoln's vision on the South would be responsible for the dissolution of the Union. Douglas also exploited the race issue. "Are you in favor of conferring upon the negro the rights and privileges of citizenship?" shouted Douglas. "If you desire to allow them to come into the State and settle with the white man, if you desire them to vote … then support Mr. Lincoln and the Black Republican party, who are in favor of the citizenship of the negro."

Lincoln lost the Senate seat to Douglas, but the debates nonetheless had a major impact on the Republican Party. They received national coverage and served to clarify the issues between Republicans and Northern Democrats. Equally significant, Lincoln emerged from the debates as a Republican of national stature, allowing him to capture the Republican nomination for president two years later. Nationally, the Republicans posted impressive gains, adding seats in both houses of Congress and positioning themselves to take the presidency two years later.

—*Christopher Bates*

See also Democratic Party; Douglas, Stephen Arnold; Lincoln, Abraham; Republican Party.

For further reading:
Foner, Eric. *Free Soil, Free Labor, Free Men: The Ideology of the Republican Party before the Civil War* (1970).
Heckman, Richard Allen. *Lincoln vs. Douglass: The Great Debates Campaign* (1967).
Stampp, Kenneth M. *America in 1857: A Nation on the Brink* (1990).

ELECTION OF 1860

The victory of Republican Abraham Lincoln in the presidential race of 1860 was the immediate cause for secession and led directly to the outbreak of Civil War. Republican victory would, in any circumstances, have likely transformed American politics.

From the ascendancy of Andrew Jackson in the 1820s, American politics entailed a conflict between his Democratic Party and the Whigs. With this alignment, the Democratic Party generally enjoyed the support of most voters and lost the presidency only when the party split, as in 1840 and 1848. Within the majority party, the interests of the coherent Southern caucus generally

prevailed. Although issues like internal improvements and tariffs continued to divide them, a bipartisan consensus gradually emerged around both the idea of national expansion in the name of "Manifest Destiny" and the legitimacy of slavery and its claims to those areas so acquired.

However, a succession of third parties challenged these coalitions, and dissenting "Conscience Whigs" and "Free Soil Democrats" gained a growing importance, particularly after the acquisition of vast new territory in the 1848 Treaty of Guadalupe Hidalgo at the close of the Mexican-American War. After the defeat of the Wilmot Proviso, proposing to bar slavery from those acquisitions, tensions within the Democratic Party erupted in an 1848 Free Soil Party that briefly threatened the hegemony of the two-party system, as did the subsequent emergence of the anti-immigrant "Know-Nothing" American Party. Although this mass disaffection seemed to dissipate by 1852, former Whigs and others did build relatively successful local Nativist coalitions.

The federal passage of the Kansas-Nebraska Act of 1854 resurrected the threat to the two-party system by sparking the emergence of the Republican Party. Northern "anti-Nebraska" coalitions generally moved toward the establishment of a new party quickly in the Midwest. In the east, however, the New York coalition balked and merged with remnants of the Whigs, while Pennsylvania's People's Party and New Jersey's Opposition Party dallied with the Nativists. The two-year-old Republican Party failed to elect John C. Frémont in 1856, but it carried much of the North.

Conditions became increasingly favorable for the Republicans as political issues sectionalized the country. The plebeian base of the Democratic Party in the North also began to dissipate with the party's consistent opposition to the Homestead Bill to grant land to the landless and its support for the proslavery "bogus" territorial government in Kansas. This perception deepened with the *Dred Scott* decision, which seemed to nationalize the legality of slaveholding. Then, too, persistent Democratic adventurism in foreign policy, typified by the Ostend Manifesto and "filibustering" expeditions in Latin America resurrected concern about U.S. pursuit of "the Caribbean empire for slavery" envisaged by John C. Calhoun. Economic collapse in the Panic of 1857 gave some urgency to Republican appeals, as they clashed with the dominant Southern wing of the Democratic Party over tariffs, plans for agricultural and technical colleges, and federal subsidies of the trans-Atlantic cable, the postal system, harbor improvements, and the construction of railroads and telegraphs.

Senator Stephen A. Douglas of Illinois, the Democratic front-runner for the presidential nomination, had secured his reelection to the Senate by clinging to the doctrine of Popular Sovereignty, which allowed residents of the western territories to determine their own course on slavery. To secure party unity, Northern Democrats agreed to hold the national convention in Charleston, South Carolina. Both defensive and militant, Southern officeholders believed this to be an insufficient assurance of the future of their "peculiar institution," and a Southern Rights convention at Montgomery, Alabama, evolved into a strong and uncompromising caucus going into the national convention. In addition, many officials in the James Buchanan administration hostile to Douglas chose to cooperate with the Southern caucus.

That convention, which began its deliberations on 23 April, saw the strong Douglas organization secure the seating of contested delegations from Illinois and New York, but the environment could scarcely have been more conducive to the Southern Rights faction. The majority of the platform committee proposed replacing Popular Sovereignty with an innovative blanket assurance of federal protection for slavery everywhere under U.S. jurisdiction. The convention rejected the innovation 165 to 138. Although fifty of the latter walked out at that point, enough Southern Rights men remained to stall the nomination of Douglas for fifty-seven ballots. The flustered Democratic convention adjourned on 1 May to reassemble in six weeks a unified party at Baltimore.

The interval hardly secured party unity. Some prominent and responsible Southern leaders urged others to set aside the slave code provision, and all but one of the state delegations that walked out at Charleston returned to the convention sessions at Baltimore. However, when they reconvened on 18 June, the Democrats faced not only the same problems they had failed to resolve in Charleston but also the conflict between rival delegations of Douglas Democrats contesting the seats of the Southern Rights faction that had bolted. This issue led to another Southern walkout. The remainder nominated Douglas for president and Herschel V. Johnson Georgia for vice president.

The Southern Rights bolters organized their own impromptu convention on 23 June in Baltimore. They nominated Vice President John C. Breckinridge of Kentucky and Joseph Lane of Oregon. The dominant national party had split.

On 9 May, the largest remnant of the Whig Party, together with errant elements of the American Party, assembled in Baltimore as the Constitutional Union Party. Sometimes referred to as "the Old Gentlemen's Party," they sought to set aside the crises over slavery and nominated John Bell of Tennessee and Edward Everett of Massachusetts. Their purpose was to deny all candidates a majority of electoral votes and throw the decision on the presidency into the House of Representatives, where the sectional issues might again be compromised.

Republican hopes were very clear as their convention

opened on 16 May in Chicago. The new party had done well in the previous elections through many of the nonslaveholding states. They could afford to lose California, Oregon, and even New Jersey, but they had to win Pennsylvania, Indiana, and Illinois, which they had lost four years earlier.

The party nominated Abraham Lincoln of Illinois. In addition to various "favorite sons," several strong contenders jockeyed for their nomination. The front-runner going into the convention, William H. Seward of New York, had boldly articulated an allegiance to an antislavery "higher law" doctrine and had defied the anti-immigrant drift of many old Whigs toward the Nativists; however, these positions made the party's front-runner unpalatable, particularly in those critical states. A former Democrat, Salmon P. Chase of Ohio, suffered from a similarly radical reputation. At the other end of the spectrum, Edward Bates of Missouri had been a slaveholder, a Know-Nothing, and a recent convert to Republicanism who could carry neither his own state nor the traditional Republican constituencies. Having bounced from Democrat to Know-Nothing and attained a reputation as a ruthless spoilsman, Simon Cameron of Pennsylvania left a long trail of critics. Denied victory on the first ballot, Seward's forces receded, and delegates began turning toward Lincoln, who carried the convention on the third ballot. For vice president, the convention added Hannibal Hamlin of Maine, a former Democrat, a New Englander, and a friend of Seward.

The eager and united Republicans, with their campaign workers known as "Wide Awakes" and strong organization, clearly became the dominant power in what was emerging as the dominant section. While the candidates retained the customary silence themselves, spokesmen stumped the country on their behalf. Republicans used their broad platform with varying emphasis, though their call for the government to promote "internal improvements" was popular everywhere. The party's commitment to higher tariffs made it popular in the crowded and depression-burdened east. Midwesterners and Westerners responded to plans for the Pacific Railroad. Its call for a homestead act appealed not only in the Midwest and the West, but also to the labor groups in the larger cities. Despite the involvement of former Know-Nothings, the party's immigrant spokesmen also made great inroads among the traditionally Democratic ethnic voters. The June publication of a Senate report on financial corruption and political kickbacks in the Buchanan administration also damaged the Democrats.

However, the issue of race haunted the campaign. Facing the prospect of becoming a minority in the leadership of the nation, the Southern Rights Democrats rejected the traditional federal authority over the territories on slavery and the Popular Sovereignty compromise.

Interference with the prospect of slavery in the west entailed action against slavery where it existed. Citing Republican support for African-American suffrage in parts of the North, they raised the specter of race equality and "amalgamation." Both the Douglas Democrats and the Constitutional Unionists also sought to use racism to weaken the Republican cause. Republican spokesmen responded inconsistently, depending on the spokesman and the location.

More than this, the Southern Rights Democrats waged the only major national presidential campaign in U.S. history while asserting their right to negate the results of the election. Their leaders openly discussed seceding from the nation as readily as they had bolted from the Democratic national convention. However, such talk had episodically surfaced for a generation since the nullification crisis, and Northerners had come to regard it as a mere bluff. National Democratic leaders like Buchanan ignored the open talk of treason in the Breckinridge camp to focus their ire on Douglas.

The rhetoric of sectional resistance became the language of Southern politics. Any who publicly questioned the beleaguered condition of the section were silenced, while many who were uninterested in secession were willing to use the rhetoric of resistance, either to gain office or because the employment of such rhetoric had gained concessions in the past. While this allowed the Southern Rights men a virtual control of affairs, it also precluded the kind of checks and balances requiring discourse and deliberations.

The campaign reflected the sectionalization of the nation's politics. Neither the Douglas Democrats nor the Republicans (absent from the ballot in ten Southern states) had little prospect for success in the South against both Bell and Breckinridge. Conversely, neither Bell nor Breckinridge could expect much in the North. In short, the presidential campaign in the South generally pit the Southern Rights Democrats against the Constitutional Unionists, while, in the North, it became a contest between Lincoln and Douglas. However, victory required 152 of the 303 electoral votes: neither Bell nor Douglas could mobilize both of the contending sections, and Breckinridge could not win even if he swept the South.

Understanding the seriousness of the secessionist rhetoric and the prospect of Republican victory, Jefferson Davis of Mississippi briefly explored the prospect of forging a unified anti-Republican coalition. He secured the agreements of Breckinridge and Bell to withdraw should Douglas do so, but the "Little Giant" would not cooperate, warning that, with his name not on the ballot, many Northern Democrats would likely vote Republican. More substantively, Douglas began taking the threats seriously enough to anticipate a *coup d'etat* should Lincoln win.

The Republican sweep of Indiana and Pennsylvania

in October presaged the final results, which were as follows:

Candidate	Popular vote	Electoral vote
Lincoln	1,866,452	180
Douglas	1,376,957	12
Breckinridge	849,781	72
Bell	588,879	39

Douglas suffered most in the translation of popular support to electoral votes. He tended to run second against Lincoln in the North, against Bell in the border states, and, in some localities, against Breckinridge in the South.

Secession and the formation of the Confederacy resulted directly from the election of Lincoln.

—*Mark A. Lause*

See also American Party; Bell, John; Breckinridge, John Cabell; Buchanan, James; Constitutional Union Party; Douglas, Stephen Arnold; Election of 1858; Lincoln, Abraham.

For further reading:

Baum, Dale. *The Civil War Party System: The Case of Massachusetts, 1848–1876* (1984).

Fite, Emerson D. *The Presidential Campaign of 1860* (1911).

Hesseltine, William B., ed. *Three Against Lincoln: Murat Halsted Reports the Caucuses of 1860* (1960).

Holt, Michael F. *The Political Crisis of the 1850s* (1978).

Johannsen, Robert W. *Stephen A. Douglas* (1973).

Luebke, Frederick C., ed. *Ethnic Voters and the Election of Lincoln* (1971).

Luthin, Reinhard H. *The First Lincoln Campaign* (1944).

Nevins, Allan. *The Emergence of Lincoln* (1950).

ELECTION OF 1862

The election of 1862 was significant in several respects. It was the first national congressional election to take place during the Civil War. Since the results of the election eroded Republican control of both the national government and several state governments, the election is often interpreted as a setback to the Republican Party and as a threat to President Abraham Lincoln's ability to wage war.

The election of 1862 resulted in several important shifts in power. Nationally, Democrats gained thirty-four seats in the House of Representatives. In New York, Democrat Horatio Seymour defeated Republican James W. Wadsworth in an important gubernatorial contest. In New Jersey, Democrats gained control of the state legislature, while Democratic gubernatorial candidate Joel Parker was also elected. The state legislatures of Indiana and Illinois, key states in the Republican victory in 1860, reverted to Democratic control. As a result, in each of these states, the Democrats would gain a senator in 1863. In Illinois, William A. Richardson replaced Republican Orville Browning, while in Indiana, David Turpie

replaced Joseph A. Wright, a former Democrat who was seen as being too supportive of Republican policies.

Several important issues played a role in the election of 1862. If the firing on Fort Sumter had temporarily suspended normal partisan politics, by early 1862 partisanship had once again emerged. There were various key ingredients in the reemergence of political partisanship. One important component was the closing of the Mississippi River, and the disruption of normal trade relations between the South and the Northwest. Northwestern farmers were now forced to transport their products via railroads to the Great Lakes instead of down the Mississippi. With expanded demand, railroad rates increased rapidly. Combined with other measures such as the Morrill Tariff of 1861, Democratic politicians of the Northwest charged that the interests of their region were being sacrificed to the commercials powers of the East. Suspicious of the Whiggish antecedents of the Republican Party, Democrats abandoned calls to set aside partisanship in the 1862 elections.

The civil liberties issue also played a role in reviving Democratic opposition. Before the election of 1862, hundreds of suspected rebel sympathizers had been arrested and held without trial. While the majority of those arrested were from the volatile border states where the administration had acted decisively to keep states in the Union, there were a number of prominent Democrats jailed. Among them were Illinois congressman William "Josh" Allen and Dennis Mahoney, editor of the Dubuque (Iowa) *Herald*. Even more upsetting to many Democrats was Lincoln's suspension of the writ of habeas corpus on 25 September 1862. Suspicious that wartime emergencies were creating unhealthy precedents for unwarranted assumptions of power, Democrats feared that Lincoln's actions expanded central authority at the expense of state and local power.

Perhaps the most fundamental reason for Democratic resurgence in the election of 1862 was Republican policy on slavery. From the beginning of the war, many Republicans wanted to attack the institution that they believed was the principal cause of the rebellion. Fear of eroding bipartisan support for the war initially kept congressional Republicans and the president from attacking slavery. As the war dragged on, however, both congressional Republicans and President Lincoln began to attack the institution. The summer of 1862 saw a couple of key provisions passed that alienated many Democrats. The second Confiscation Act promised freedom to all slaves who belonged to owners who were in rebellion against U.S. authority, while the Militia Act of 1862 provided for the use of black soldiers in noncombat roles in U.S. armies. The major blow came with the preliminary Emancipation Proclamation, issued after the battle of Antietam on 22 September 1862.

Many Democrats felt this provision profoundly altered the character of the war. Bitterly negrophobic, many Democrats feared that emancipation would deluge the North with hordes of ex-slaves who would degrade white laborers by dramatically driving down the price of labor. Particularly in the Northwest, Democratic newspaper editors exploited the race issue, claiming that Republican policies on slavery would "Africanize" the North.

Finally, the election of 1862 was an expression of war weariness and frustration with the administration's conduct of the war. While several important victories had been achieved in the West, the Eastern theater was viewed as most pivotal, and here the performance of Union armies was notably undistinguished. Even the recent victory at Antietam in September was hollow, as Army of the Potomac commander George McClellan failed to follow through to destroy the retreating army of Robert E. Lee. Democratic resurgence in the fall elections became a referendum on the incompetent handling of the war thus far.

While the election of 1862 represented a Democratic resurgence, it is easy to exaggerate its significance. Republicans still had firm control of both houses of Congress as well as the presidency and a majority of state governments. Although some Democrats hoped the results of the election would force Lincoln to suspend the Emancipation Proclamation and return to a war waged solely for the preservation of the Union and the Constitution, the president refused to suspend the proclamation.

If the elections taught the Republican administration anything, it was the importance of procuring and managing the soldiers' vote. Many states did not provide for the voting of soldiers in the field. By 1864, a number of states had adopted measures to remedy this situation. In the states that did not allow soldiers to vote by absentee ballot, Republican governors made liberal provisions to furlough soldiers so they could return home to vote. These Republican officials were rewarded with overwhelming support for Lincoln's reelection.

Given the context of Civil War, perhaps the most notable feature of the 1862 elections is that they took place at all. They were a remarkable testament to the deep reverence for democratic institutions in the young republic.

—*Bruce Tap*

See also Browning, Orville Hickman; Democratic Party; Emancipation Proclamation; Republican Party.

For further reading:
Klement, Frank L. *The Copperheads in the Middle West* (1972).
McPherson, James M. *Battle Cry of Freedom: The Civil War Era* (1988).
Paludan, Phillip S. *"A People's Contest": The Union and the Civil War, 1861–1865* (1988).
Rawley, James. *Turning Points of the Civil War* (1966).
Silbey, Joel H. *"A Respectable Minority": The Democratic Party in the Civil War Era, 1860–1868* (1977).

Tap, Bruce. "Race, Rhetoric, and Emancipation: The Election of 1862 in Illinois." *Civil War History* (1993).

ELECTION OF 1864

The election of 1864 demonstrated that the war would not disrupt normal democratic processes, continued Abraham Lincoln and the Union coalition in office, and reminded Confederates that the North still supported the war.

The generation that participated in the Civil War was a highly politicized one, guaranteeing that the issues of the conflict would be thoroughly debated even as the war progressed. Although both parties in the North wished to see the Union restored, Democrats differed with Republicans on the measures that would bring this about. Democrats blamed Republicans for the sectional conflict and feared that a war that destroyed Southern property and threatened slavery would increase Confederate resistance, making the war impossible to win; Republicans saw no alternative to such policies and indeed doubted the loyalty of those who questioned them.

Despite Republican control of Congress and the White House at the war's outset, states remaining in the Union were closely divided politically. In the 1860 election, these states had cast 47.2 percent of their votes for Lincoln, 46.6 percent for the two Democratic candidates, and 6.1 percent for John Bell, the Constitutional Union nominee. Republicans had won overwhelmingly in the upper northern states (New England and areas where New Englanders had migrated). The lower North had a much narrower Republican majority, while the border slave states in 1860 had largely divided their votes between Democratic and Unionist candidates. The Republicans were quite weak there.

Although stable partisan identity was the rule during the nineteenth century—a situation that led to much continuity in the vote between successive elections—wartime events did bring some important changes, especially in the border region. Thousands of their residents left to fight for the Confederacy, and state legislatures enacted loyalty oaths to prevent others from voting. While many continued to identify themselves as "Unionists," the Republican Party grew substantially from its small 1860 beginnings.

Nevertheless, the region remained conservative. Wartime stresses and strains—emancipation, taxation, and apparent threats to individual liberties—bolstered Democrats in the border states as well as the lower North in 1862. In the 1863 state elections, however, accusations of defeatism and pro-Confederate attitudes hurt Democrats; they won no statewide contests. By 1864, the lower North, with its close political division and large number of electoral votes, was the key to whether Republicans would continue to control the White House and House of Representatives.

A campaign banner for 1864 Republican presidential candidate Abraham Lincoln and running mate Andrew Johnson (*Library of Congress*)

Political parties in the nineteenth century counted on winning elections in closely contested states less by converting their political enemies than by getting a higher proportion of their followers to the polls. In 1864, this translated into a Republican need for full, enthusiastic participation by all factions of their party, some additional support from Unionists and War Democrats, and a way for absent Republicans in the army to vote. By the election, eighteen states had arranged for absentee voting by soldiers; soldiers from the remaining states earned furloughs to return home to vote. In states where the soldiers' vote was separately tabulated, Republicans won nearly 80 percent of the total, enough in some cases to swing states to the Republicans.

Factionalism was the Republicans' greatest challenge. The importance of the lower Northern states for victory dictated a strategy of reaching out to Unionists and War Democrats, emphasizing restoring the Union as the war's goal and projecting a limited reconstruction of the South (as suggested in Lincoln's Proclamation for Reconstruction in December 1863). Such a strategy was sure to alarm party

radicals who wanted not only emancipation but equal rights for all citizens to be their party's objective.

Disappointed by the direction in which Lincoln was moving on Reconstruction, radicals looked to other nominees in 1864. There was ample precedent for this. No president since Andrew Jackson had won a second term. Secretary of the Treasury Salmon P. Chase was eager to run, as was 1856 Republican nominee John C. Frémont. Frémont's supporters demonstrated their willingness to bolt the party by nominating him on a Radical Democratic ticket the week before the Republican convention. Trying to demonstrate that it was not necessary to have a conservative platform to attract additional supporters and win the lower North, the Radical Democratic Party endorsed such reforms as a one-term presidency, abolition of the electoral college, and economy and integrity in government. The party also called for a constitutional amendment abolishing slavery, equality before the law regardless of race or sex, and confiscation of Confederate land. Leading radicals at the convention, such as Wendell Phillips and Frederick Douglass, endorsed Frémont.

Anticipating a stalemate, General Benjamin F. Butler, a former Democrat with current links to the radicals, also hinted at his availability. Lincoln, however, used his control of party machinery to dominate the Republican convention, which met in June in Baltimore. Appealing to the crucial conservatives, the party billed itself as a National Union (not Republican) convention. To symbolize its unionism, Andrew Johnson of Tennessee, a Democrat, was nominated for vice president to replace Hannibal Hamlin of Maine, a strong radical. The convention seated representatives from Lincoln's reconstructed governments in Louisiana, Arkansas, and Tennessee. But the party also acknowledged radicals in its platform, blaming slavery for causing the war, praising the Emancipation Proclamation as well as African-American soldiers, and pledging itself to a constitutional amendment completing the abolition of slavery. An attempt to condemn conservatives in Lincoln's cabinet was transformed into a call for party harmony. Looking beyond the war, the convention praised immigration, homesteads, and Pacific railroad subsidies and condemned France's interference in Mexico.

Discontent among radicals continued, however, throughout the summer. Secretary of the Treasury Chase remained hostile, and in late June Lincoln accepted his resignation from the cabinet. Fearing that Lincoln might be defeated and reconstruction come under the supervision of a Democratic president, radicals in Congress promoted the Wade-Davis bill, which asserted Congress's authority to reconstruct the South. Lincoln pocket vetoed the bill, while suggesting his differences with radicals over reconstruction were not significant. The sponsors of the failed legislation, Senator Benjamin F. Wade of Ohio and Representative Henry Winter

Davis of Maryland, replied with a manifesto accusing Lincoln of dictatorial usurpation. They insisted their loyalty was to a cause, not to a particular politician. Some radicals now pushed for a second convention to replace Lincoln, possibly with General Ulysses S. Grant.

A poll of governors, however, demonstrated continued strong support for Lincoln. Even most radicals favored Lincoln and disapproved of factional infighting during an important campaign. When the Democrats met and nominated George B. McClellan on what many perceived as a peace platform in late August, most radicals were willing to reconsider. Lincoln removed the conservative Montgomery Blair from his cabinet in September to balance the absence of the radical Chase, and Frémont withdrew his candidacy the following day.

Republican unity was related to fear of McClellan's possible victory. Democrats were also seeking to overcome factionalism. They too needed to reach beyond their core supporters to win in the contested states of the lower North. A conservative peace faction, especially strong in the lower Midwest, aimed its appeal to those frightened by wartime extensions of power over civilians and their property. They suggested the war had hopelessly divided the country; they would stop the bloodshed, hoping that negotiations among the states might eventually promote reunion of some or all the states. Another faction, centered among party leaders in New York, believed that Unionists would find such a position too defeatist and would never cooperate with a party not fully committed to the war. At their convention in Chicago in late August, the factions reached a compromise by nominating former general George B. McClellan, who clearly favored the war, and, for vice president, George Pendleton, a congressman who favored peace. The platform declared the war a failure and called for an armistice followed by a peace convention, which it asserted (but of course could not prove) would lead to reunion. McClellan in his letter of acceptance stated his opinion that peace could not be permanent without reunion. Some Democrats regarded this as a repudiation of the platform, and Republicans were quick to exploit the party's indecision. As the war faction had feared, Republicans also rushed to portray the Democrats as treasonous.

The actual military situation affected the credibility of partisan assessments of the war. In the summer of 1864 when both political conventions occurred, the overall military outlook was promising (helping the Republicans) but not without disappointments. Grant and William T. Sherman were on the offensive in Virginia and Georgia, respectively, but neither had defeated his opponent and Grant's casualty list was growing ever longer. General Nathaniel P. Banks's Red River campaign had ended ingloriously in Louisiana. In July, General Jubal Early mounted a raid into Maryland, threatening Washington, D.C.

Confederate politicians understood the importance of the Northern elections but disagreed on strategy. Vice President Alexander H. Stephens published a letter suggesting Confederates might be willing to negotiate with the North, a ploy designed to help the Democrats. In July, agents at Niagara Falls dangled apparent peace feelers before New York *Tribune* editor Horace Greeley. Abraham Lincoln had authorized Greeley to meet with them. Hinting at peace short of independence, however, was sure to disappoint Confederates who had sacrificed everything for that cause. Jefferson Davis preferred to promote northern defeatism through Confederate battlefield success (Early's raid) or using Confederate agents from Canada to organize violent disruptions of the elections. Such measures, however, risked confirming Republican claims of a conspiracy of Democrats working with Confederates to destroy the Union.

By early September, battlefield momentum moved decisively in favor of the North. Atlanta fell on 2 September, and Mobile quickly followed. Shortly thereafter, General Philip H. Sheridan began his successful campaign against Early in the Shenandoah Valley of Virginia.

By fall, with the Republican Party working together, the Democrats vulnerable because of the peace issue, and the military situation favoring the Republicans, the election fell into a predictable pattern. Democrats stressed constitutional excesses and the danger of inciting a race war, while Republicans talked of treason and commitment to the Union. Lincoln himself participated little in the campaign. Instead, his united and confident followers rallied on his behalf. The first returns came in September and showed Lincoln doing well in all but the border states. By the completion of voting in November, Lincoln had won all but three states (New Jersey, Kentucky, and Delaware) and 55 percent of the popular vote. The 39th Congress would have 149 Republicans to 42 Democrats, and the Senate, 42 Republicans to 10 Democrats.

While the Republicans had done well, especially in comparison to 1860, the election also highlighted the coming importance of Reconstruction. Partisan rivalries remained firm and deep. The best chance for Democrats to return to power would be through political cooperation with Southern Democrats, which would be all the easier as slavery and secession receded as issues.

—*Phyllis F. Field*

See also Butler, Benjamin F.; Cameron, Simon; Chase, Salmon P.; Davis, Henry Winter; Democratic Party; Election of 1860; Election of 1862; Frémont, John C.; Hamlin, Hannibal; Johnson, Andrew; Peace Democrats; Peace Movements; Radical Republicans; Republican Party; Wade, Benjamin; Wade-Davis Bill; War Democrats.

For further reading:

Long, David E. *The Jewel of Liberty: Abraham Lincoln's Re-Election and the End of Slavery* (1994).

Nelson, Larry E. *Bullets, Ballots, and Rhetoric: Confederate Policy for the United States Presidential Contest of 1864* (1980).

Waugh, John C. *Reelecting Lincoln: The Battle for the 1864 Presidency* (1997).

Zornow, William Frank. *Lincoln & the Party Divided* (1954).

ELECTIONS OF 1863, C.S.A.

From May to November 1863, gubernatorial and congressional elections were held throughout the Confederate States of America. Coming at this critical stage of the war, these elections might have revealed for history the true sentiments of Confederate citizens regarding the paramount issues of disunion and the continuation of the war. The elections might have also disclosed Southern attitudes about the growth of government power, especially regarding perceived infringements of civil liberties and the alleged despotism of Jefferson Davis's presidency. Yet, the elections did not consistently register popular feeling about any of these crucial questions.

Instead, the 1863 elections revealed an electorate paradoxically shocked into apathy, fatalism, and stern resolve. Obviously, the course of the war, which in 1863 appeared to be reaching a point of crucial determination, distracted the Confederate population. The intense interest in war news meant that newspapers either scantily reported or altogether ignored politics in runs made rarer by paper shortages. Also by 1863, many districts that were scheduled to hold elections were under Federal occupation and required special voting procedures to accommodate their fugitive and resident populations. And finally, the stretching of the elections over the better part of six months diluted interest that might have been more coherent if a single set of elections had been conducted in a shorter amount of time. Instead, contests were often highly local in character, and the popularity or disrepute of personalities frequently supplanted national issues. In such instances, elections were less a gauge of wide popular sentiment and more an indication of provincial eccentricities.

In any event, almost nobody voted. This indifference in part derived from the habit of Confederate politics to condemn partisanship. The habit of equating party loyalty to self-interest had been a persistent refrain in the antebellum South and had helped bring on the destruction of the national Democratic Party in 1860. The trauma of secession and the rigors of war only enhanced a general distrust of politicians as being self-absorbed and, worse for the political class, irrelevant. The possibility of political animals herding into parties was unlikely, and the old labels that had classified Whigs or Democrats or Know-Nothings had by 1863 become pointless. Politics as public service rather than party advancement was a recollection of the early republic and perhaps revealed nostalgia for a time before the sectional disputes over slavery had turned everything sour. Candidates universally tried to appeal to this predilection. Yet, the absence of parties meant fragmentation in the Confederate legislature, and the absence of partisanship logically deprived the election process of partisan passions. The result contributed to voter apathy, especially when many candidates ran unopposed.

Just as the elections did not serve as a bellwether for the Davis administration, neither did their results undermine it. The governors' races were illustrative in this regard. In Alabama, Governor John Gill Shorter's loss to Thomas Hill Watts reflected dissatisfaction with Shorter's support for Richmond's intrusive war policies such as confiscation and impressment. Watts was at the time the Confederate attorney general and should have been closely identified with those policies as well, but his main support came from disaffected northern counties, where he had been mistakenly perceived as an advocate of peace. Nonetheless, Watts turned out to be as loyal to the Confederate war effort as Shorter had been.

In Mississippi, Governor John J. Pettus, like Shorter in Alabama, was the victim of intrusive policies to advance the war effort, but his circumstance was doubly unfortunate because in Mississippi those policies apparently had not worked. In 1863, the state would come completely under Federal occupation with the fall of Vicksburg. In this unsettled and transient atmosphere, a dozen candidates vied for the governor's chair. The victor was the moderate Charles Clark, whose opponents had included the radical Reuben Davis, a violent critic of Jefferson Davis now apparently repudiated. The trend in Mississippi, however, was reflective of one evident elsewhere in areas under Federal occupation, where citizens in flight or remaining in place were likely to be more supportive of the war than were those in areas removed from its immediate impact.

Except for its coastal regions, South Carolina was one of the latter areas. Milledge L. Bonham took the governor's chair in 1863, but the Palmetto State persisted in having its legislature choose the executive, so the contest was institutionally removed from popular influence. Virginia, the main seat of war in the east and the home of the national government, held one of the earliest elections in 1863 by conducting it in May. Moderation again was the main victor in the Old Dominion State, when William Smith was elected. Known by his odd nickname "Extra Billy" for having milked additional U.S. government subsidies from a mail service he had owned in his youth, Smith was really a compromise candidate for those divided camps smarting from the secession debates of 1861. And on the far western end of the Confederacy, moderation also triumphed when Pendleton Murrah was elected governor in Texas, although he was elected by precious few Texans in an almost ignored contest. Murrah certainly was more preferable to the Davis administration than the possible alternatives, one of whom might have been the acrimonious Sam Houston, who was too ill to run in 1863.

After playing coy, Georgia governor Joe Brown sought another term in 1863. With his insistence on Georgia's political and military autonomy, Brown was a manifest opponent of the national government, but he also knew shrewd politicians were never absolutely inflexible. He defeated Unionist Joshua Hill and planter Timothy Furlow by shifting ground to align himself with the Richmond government. Those who might have noted the inconsistency and rebelled against it likely stayed home, for Georgia, like all the other states, had an extremely low turnout in the election.

The congressional elections of 1863 ousted a large number of representatives—nine of ten Georgia representatives were defeated, for instance—but this was not necessarily a referendum on the war and the way the Confederate government was waging it. The lack of national coherence in the elections simply made them an unreliable measure of popular support for or opposition to Jefferson Davis's administration. The secessionist faction of 1861 was soundly defeated but probably by a resurgent conservatism that wanted to repudiate radicalism and not necessarily disunion. North Carolina and Alabama, especially the northern counties of the latter state, were most vocal in their peace sentiments and complaints about Confederate "tyranny." Yet the rest of the South remained either resolutely moderate or openly supportive of the war. Consequently, while it would be too much to say that the elections were a resounding vote of confidence for the Davis government, they at least produced no organized opposition to it in Congress.

On the other hand, such a result, given the deteriorating military situation, amounted to a significant victory. A burst of patriotism that curiously followed the dismal defeats at Vicksburg and Gettysburg sustained the administration, with the places that had suffered the most proving most adamant that the cause be carried through. In that respect, the elections of 1863, underattended and largely incoherent, revealed one of modern war's most mysterious aspects. Whether among the gutted homes of siege-torn Vicksburg or in the smoldering ruins of beleaguered London or Dresden, the hard hand of war can steel resolve as often as break it.

—*David S. Heidler and Jeanne T. Heidler*

See also Alabama; Bonham, Milledge Luke; Brown, Joseph Emerson; Clark, Charles; Congress, C.S.A.; Davis, Jefferson; Georgia; Murrah, Pendleton; North Carolina; Shorter, John Gill; South Carolina; Stephens, Alexander Hamilton; Texas; Virginia; Watts, Thomas Hill.

For further reading:

Rable, George C. *The Confederate Republic: A Revolution against Politics* (1994).

ELLET, CHARLES, JR.
(1810–1862)
Union engineer

Born to Charles Ellet and Mary Israel Ellet in Bucks County, Pennsylvania, Charles Ellet determined upon a career in engineering at a young age. He left home to work first as a surveyor and then as an assistant on the Chesapeake and Ohio Canal. In the latter job, he received enough training as an engineer that he was able to enroll at age twenty in the École Polytechnique in France. Upon his return he worked on a variety of engineering projects, particularly in the areas of bridge, canal, and railroad construction. Suspension bridges became a specialty of his, and his skills were in much demand throughout the Northeast in the years preceding the Civil War. He also did a number of surveys of rivers in the West and made recommendations for their navigational improvement.

From 1848 to 1853, Ellet worked as a railroad engineer in Wheeling, Virginia, during which time he developed a strong affection for the state, which he referred to as his adopted home state. In the latter year he accepted the position as chief engineer on the Virginia Central Railroad. From 1854 to 1855, he and his family traveled to Europe ostensibly to study the railroad construction there and to buy rolling stock. While there, however, he had an opportunity to observe the steam rams being used for harbor defense during the Crimean War. He wrote to the secretary of the navy, urging the construction of such vessels for the harbors and rivers of the United States. While his suggestions were ignored at the time, Ellet continued to be interested in the construction of rams for the United States and would renew his suggestions at the outbreak of the Civil War.

Upon returning to the United States, Ellet returned to his business activities though he continued to urge the construction of a ram fleet for the United States. He spent much of his time on a small farm that he had purchased for his family outside Georgetown, District of Columbia. The threat of war at the end of 1860 caused him to suspend his private business enterprises and to devote himself to planning for the nation's defense.

In early 1861, Ellet wrote to James Buchanan's War Department, offering his services as an engineer. His letter was ignored. On 30 March 1861, he wrote to Abraham Lincoln's War Department, outlining a plan, which he offered to execute, of supplying Fort Sumter without the use of military force. Again, he was ignored. After Fort Sumter surrendered, he again offered his engineering skills for the war effort and wrote to Gideon Welles, secretary of the navy, suggesting the construction of steam rams. Both letters were ignored.

Though discouraged by these rebuffs, Ellet was determined to participate in the war. Late in the summer, he wrote to the commander of the Army of the Potomac, George B. McClellan, offering his skills as an engineer to that army. Again he was ignored, but he took it upon himself to review the military situation around Washington and to observe the limited operations of the Army of the Potomac in the early fall of 1861. From these observations he determined that McClellan was not making good use of his resources, and he wrote these

observations in a pamphlet entitled "The Army of the Potomac and Its Mismanagement." Over the next six months, this pamphlet gained a wide circulation and no doubt influenced many people regarding the inactivity of George McClellan. Still, it did not gain Ellet a position with the government.

In March 1862 everything changed. The battle between the CSS *Virginia* and the USS *Monitor* on 9 March at Hampton Roads convinced the government that perhaps Ellet had had a point about armored rams. Five days after the battle, he was summoned to the War Department by Secretary of War Edwin Stanton and consulted on the issue. At the end of the meeting, he was asked to travel to Fort Monroe to assess the situation concerning the *Virginia*. After consulting with the naval commanders at Hampton Roads, Ellet wrote back to the War Department that the officers there very much wanted construction on armored rams to proceed.

Although the government had made a complete about-face on this issue by March 1862, the War Department believed that such vessels could be of the most use on the western rivers. Therefore, at the end of March 1862 Ellet was sent west to convert small river steamers on the western rivers to armored rams. He left immediately and established acquisition and construction sites at several western river ports including Pittsburgh and Cincinnati. After about one month of conversion construction, he had nine vessels ready to go into combat. These boats would become known as the Ellet Rams.

Ellet left for Fort Pillow in command of his nine rams in May 1862. Before his departure, he had engaged in a correspondence with Stanton regarding rank. Ellet did not want a military rank, but Stanton insisted that for him to have adequate authority in any military activity he should be commissioned colonel and attached officially to Stanton's staff. For that reason, Ellet is listed on the army roles in the spring of 1862 as a colonel.

When Ellet and his boats approached Fort Pillow at the end of the month, he quickly entered a dispute with the naval commander on the scene, Commodore Charles H. Davis. Davis proved to be very uncooperative regarding coordination between his gunboats and Ellet's rams. He also proved more hesitant than Ellet liked about attacking the Confederate boats guarding the fort, so on 1 June Ellet announced to Davis that—with or without the gunboats—he was going to attack. The Confederates evacuated the fort before he had a chance to make good his threat.

The next target for the gunboats and the rams was Memphis, so they immediately set out for that destination. Davis still proved an uncooperative partner in this enterprise, and when the naval battle occurred on 6 June, Ellet operated more or less independently. His rams proved quite effective against the Confederate

defenders, though Davis gave him little credit in the official report of the battle.

In the midst of the engagement, Ellet moved out on the deck of one of the boats to observe the fighting and was hit in the leg by a pistol shot. Over the next two weeks the wound worsened, and he died on 21 June while his boat was approaching Cairo, Illinois. He was given a hero's funeral in Philadelphia. His wife died two weeks later of grief. His brother Alfred Washington Ellet assumed command of the rams.

—*David S. Heidler and Jeanne T. Heidler*

See also Navy, U.S.A.; Riverine Warfare.

For further reading:
Ellet, Charles, Jr. *The Army of the Potomac and Its Mismanagement* (1861).
Lewis, Gene D. *Charles Ellet, Jr.; The Engineer As Individualist* (1968).

ELLIOTT, WASHINGTON LAFAYETTE
(1825–1888)
Union general

Born in Carlisle, Pennsylvania, to Jesse Duncan Elliott, a renowned naval officer of the War of 1812 and afterwards, and Frances Vaughn Elliott, Washington Lafayette Elliott, while a child, made several naval voyages with his father, one aboard the U.S.S. *Constitution*. Elliott was educated at Dickinson College before accepting an appointment to the U.S. Military Academy in 1841. He remained at West Point until his second class year, when he resigned to study medicine. Financial reverses of his family following the death of his father prevented him completing his studies and forced him to accept a commission as a second lieutenant of mounted rifles at the commencement of the Mexican-American War. He participated in the siege of Vera Cruz but was forced to return to the United States because of illness rather than fight in the subsequent Mexico City campaign.

After the war, Elliott served at a variety of frontier posts. At the outbreak of the Civil War, Elliott was sent to New York on recruiting duty, after which, at the end of summer 1861, he was made a captain in the 3d U.S. Cavalry and was transferred to Missouri. He commanded his company at the battle of Wilson's Creek before being promoted to colonel in September 1861 and given command of the 2d Iowa Cavalry.

In early 1862, Elliott and his regiment were made part of the Army of the Mississippi under John Pope. Elliott commanded his regiment during the operations against New Madrid and Island No. 10. During the subsequent advance on Corinth in May 1862, Elliott commanded a brigade in the cavalry division of the Army of the Mississippi. In June he was promoted to brigadier general of volunteers and became chief of staff to William S.

Rosecrans at Corinth. He remained in that position until early August 1862, when on Pope's request he was transferred to Pope's new command, the Army of Virginia. Elliott served as Pope's chief of cavalry and was wounded in the battle of Second Bull Run.

After a long convalescence, Elliott, still unable to return to a field command, was sent at the end of November 1862 to command the Department of the Northwest, headquartered in Madison, Wisconsin. In January 1863 he was placed on recruiting duty in Baltimore, Maryland. Finally, in February 1863 he was fit enough to resume field service and was given command of the 1st Brigade, 2d Division, VIII Corps, Army of the Potomac. Despite the fact that William Rosecrans requested his transfer to the Army of the Cumberland, Elliott remained in command of his brigade through the Gettysburg campaign.

Elliott's division, commanded by Robert H. Milroy, was headquartered at Winchester, Virginia, during the advance of Robert E. Lee toward Pennsylvania. Before Lee threatened the position, Elliott's primary activity was conducting reconnaissance missions in the vicinity of Winchester. In June, however, Elliott had to lead his men in Milroy's precipitous retreat in the face of overwhelming Confederate numbers. At the end of June 1863, Elliott was given command of the 3d Division, III Corps, Army of the Potomac.

In October 1863, Elliott was transferred to the Army of the Cumberland, where he was given command of the 1st Cavalry Division of the army's cavalry corps before being given command of the entire cavalry corps in November 1863. A month later he led a part of his corps to Knoxville in relief of Ambrose Burnside there.

During the early months of 1864, Elliott commanded his cavalry in numerous skirmishes with Confederate cavalry in Tennessee. He continued to command the Army of the Cumberland's cavalry corps during the Atlanta campaign of the late spring and summer of 1864 and, after the fall of Atlanta, led his men in pursuit of John Bell Hood's army. At the end of the year, before the defense of Nashville, Elliott was given command of the 2d Division, IV Corps, Army of the Cumberland. He commanded that division in the defense of Nashville against Hood later in the month and again in the subsequent pursuit of Hood. He continued in command of that division until after the end of the war, occupying Huntsville, Alabama, in the last months. In May 1865, George Thomas, commander of the Army of the Cumberland, recommended Elliott for a brevet promotion to brigadier general in the regular army. After the war he received a brevet promotion to major general in the U.S. Army.

In July 1865, Elliott was sent at the request of his former commander John Pope to the Department of the Missouri and was given command of the District of Kansas. Elliott remained in the army after the mustering out of the volunteers, reverting back to lieutenant colonel of the 1st U.S. Cavalry. He was promoted in 1878 to colonel of the 3d Cavalry and retired the following year. In retirement, Elliott went into the banking industry in California, making his home in San Francisco. He died in that city on 29 June 1888.

—David S. Heidler and Jeanne T. Heidler

See also Island No. 10.

For further reading:

Castel, Albert E. *Decision in the West: The Atlanta Campaign of 1864* (1992).

Sword, Wiley. *Embrace an Angry Wind: The Confederacy's Last Hurrah—Spring Hill, Franklin, and Nashville* (1992).

ELLIS, JOHN WILLIS
(1820–1861)
Governor of North Carolina

Born in Rowan County, North Carolina, the son of Anderson Ellis and Judith Bailey Ellis, John Willis Ellis was educated at Randolph-Macon College and the University of North Carolina. Upon graduation from the latter institution in 1841, Ellis began the study of law and on admission to the bar, opened a practice in Salisbury, North Carolina. Along with his practice, he became active in state Democratic politics, serving several terms in the state legislature in the 1840s. Between 1848 and 1858 Ellis served as a judge on the state superior court. In 1858 he was elected to the first to two terms as governor of North Carolina.

Ellis, a strong supporter of states' rights, increasingly came to believe that Southern interests would eventually bring disunion. As the sectional crisis mounted in the fall of 1860, the governor became very angry with the U.S. War Department for sending extra troops to the Fayetteville Arsenal and strongly urged Secretary of War John B. Floyd to remove the troops before their presence provoked a crisis. Upon the election of Abraham Lincoln to the presidency in November 1860, Ellis urged the calling of a state convention to consider secession. Given the strong Unionist sentiment in the state, however, the majority of the legislature was not yet willing to take such a step. The governor abided by the legislature's decision, though he worked at the same time to strengthen the state's defenses and to acquire as many arms as possible for the state.

Ellis strongly believed that the democratic will of the people should prevail, and for that reason, in spite of his strong secessionist beliefs, he issued orders in January 1861 that no federal property was to be seized by the state or private citizens. When a group of secessionist zealots took federal Forts Johnston and Caswell, Ellis had them restored.

Lincoln's call for volunteers after the taking of Fort Sumter proved too much for Governor Ellis to bear. He refused to supply the two-regiment quota asked for by the War Department and immediately ordered Forts Johnston and Caswell seized. He called for 30,000 state volunteers to defend against federal invasion and called the legislature into session.

While the legislature called a convention to deliberate on the issue of secession, Ellis began cooperating with Virginia, which seceded first, regarding the defense of both states from federal coercion. Once the convention passed an ordinance of secession on 20 May 1861, Ellis began turning over military resources to the Confederacy. He corresponded feverishly with Confederate officials and worked constantly to put the state on a sound war footing. The hectic pace he set for himself was blamed for his untimely death on 7 July 1861. For the remainder of the war, North Carolina would never cooperate so fully with the Confederate government.

—*David S. Heidler and Jeanne T. Heidler*

See also North Carolina.
For further reading:
Ellis, John Willis. *The Papers of John Willis Ellis* (1964).

ELLSWORTH, ELMER EPHRAIM
(1837–1861)
Union officer

Elmer Ellsworth was born on 11 April 1837 to Ephraim D. and Phoebe Denton Ellsworth in Malta, New York. Reared and educated in nearby Mechanicsville, he hoped to gain admission to West Point and become a professional soldier. With only a small-town public education and without the financial support required for private tutelage, Ellsworth left his dreams of West Point behind and moved first to New York City and shortly thereafter to Chicago. Once in Chicago, Ellsworth found work as a law clerk, began to study law, and became involved in a patent soliciting business. Although his dreams of West Point remained unattainable, his interest in the military never abated.

In 1859, Ellsworth happened upon a volunteer military company of cadets and introduced them to the Zouave drill. Zouave units, which at the time were fighting in the Crimean War, were well known for their brightly colored uniform consisting of a short jacket, baggy pants or leggings, and a tasseled cap or turban. The appeal to Ellsworth was their distinctive march, consisting of a sharp step and precise timing.

Ellsworth trained the cadet company in the Zouave drill and soon the National Guard Cadets of Chicago became one of the city's main attractions. Membership was selective, with members swearing off strong drinks, tobacco, profanity, and all excesses. With its reputation growing, the U.S. Zouave Cadets, as they were now known, toured the East performing for large crowds. Upon his return to Illinois in 1860, Ellsworth entered into the study of law at the offices of Abraham Lincoln and William Herndon in Springfield, Illinois. He quickly immersed himself in Lincoln's political career and became fast friends with the future president.

Upon Lincoln's election to the presidency, Ellsworth became an official advisor, traveling with Lincoln to Washington. Once in the White House, Lincoln attempted to create a Bureau of Militia within the War Department and place Ellsworth at its head but, lacking congressional approval, the plan fell through. Upon the outbreak of hostilities, Ellsworth traveled to New York, where he recruited volunteer fire fighters to fill the ranks of his new Zouave regiment. This new regiment was intended to do more than drill, and upon its arrival in Washington, it was mustered into Federal service.

On 24 May 1861, the day after Virginia's secession was ratified, Union forces moved across the Potomac River into Alexandria. Their objective was to occupy the city and establish a buffer zone for the nearby capital. Elmer Ellsworth's 44th New York Zouaves were among the units directed to occupy Alexandria. On his way through the streets of Alexandria, Ellsworth spotted a large Confederate-styled flag flying over the Marshall House, a building easily within Lincoln's view at the Executive Mansion. Followed by his men, Ellsworth entered the hotel and made his way to the roof, where he hauled down the flag. On his way down the stairs from the roof, Ellsworth met hotel manager and rabid secessionist James William Jackson. Jackson leveled his shotgun on Ellsworth and fired, killing the young officer. Jackson was immediately shot and killed by one of Ellsworth's men.

News of the two deaths traveled quickly and both men were memorialized by their respective supporters. Ellsworth's body lay in state in the East Room of the White House, where the grief-stricken President Lincoln attended his funeral after writing Ellsworth's parents to notify them of their son's death. A train then took Ellsworth's body via New York City and Albany to his hometown of Mechanicsville, where he was buried.

Ellsworth's death served as an early catalyst for the Union war effort. Poems and songs were written about the incident at the Marshall House, turning Ellsworth into a popular figure. Hailing him as "the first to fall," Northern newspapers quickly turned Elmer Ellsworth into the "First Martyr of the Civil War."

—*Brian D. McKnight*

See also Zouaves.
For further reading:
Ingraham, Charles A. *Elmer E. Ellsworth and the Zouaves of '61* (1925).

ELMIRA PRISON

Elmira Prison occupied 40 acres along the Chemung River in south-central New York State and served as a Union prison camp during the final year of the Civil War. The prison was located one mile from Elmira, New York, and originally served as a training and marshaling center for Federal soldiers. In July 1864, the old barracks were expanded, tents were pitched, and timber walls enclosed the camp to hold Confederate prisoners of war. The prisoners who survived the deplorable conditions called the place "Hellmira."

Elmira Prison was conceived on 15 May 1864, when Adjutant General E. D. Townsend reported several empty barracks that could be used to house recently captured Confederate soldiers. As the camp was transformed into a prison, the Union built a sixteen-foot-high fence with a parapet walkway for the guards. Ironically, the first troops to serve as guards were recruited ex-slaves who were organized into regiments to guard their former owners. Union soldiers then completed thirty-five two-story barracks, with unsealed roofs and floors to hold 5,000 Confederates, and a camp bakery to feed 5,000 people as well. On 6 July, the first 400 prisoners arrived by train, and by the end of August, 10,000 men were confined at Elmira, with half of them sleeping in the open or in tents without blankets. Union guards and officers dubbed the new prisoners "Fresh Fish," and townspeople built two platforms overlooking the walls where spectators, mostly well-dressed women, could observe the prisoners for fifteen cents. To further decrease Confederate morale, unusually strict and swift punishment by the Union minimized escape attempts and other camp infractions. Common punishments were hanging by the thumbs and marching in a barrel shirt.

Soon after Elmira opened, an Erie Railroad train crowded with prisoners collided with a freight train on 15 July 1864. Forty-eight prisoners and seventeen guards died, and 100 prisoners and guards were injured. Confederate reports suggested that injured prisoners were dumped in the compound and left untreated, causing many to die within days.

On 18 August 1864, in retaliation for Southern prison camps, Colonel William Hoffman, U.S. commissary-general of prisoners, ordered rations restricted to bread and water. Broiled rat soon became a delicacy and any dog that wandered into camp was quickly consumed, even though to do so was a punishable offense. By 11 September, 1,870 cases of scurvy were reported. October brought onions and potatoes to the prison diet, but such rations were stopped later that month, and the prisoners received no meat until December. Confederates were by then dying of starvation at the rate of twenty-five a day. Soon after scurvy made its appearance, outbreaks of diarrhea and pneumonia began to occur, and by December 1864, smallpox struck 140 men at Elmira. The dreaded disease remained in the camp for the remainder of the camp's operation.

Despite a functional hospital, the medical treatment of prisoners was bad from the outset and grew even worse over time. Requisitions to Washington for badly needed medical supplies were regularly ignored or denied, and at one point, Sanitary Commission inspectors were barred from the prison. By December 1864, the hospital had seventy men lying on dirt floors because there were no more beds, and thousands were still sleeping out in the elements. A bitter New York winter increased the large death toll of the already weak prisoners fighting disease and starvation.

March rain caused the Chemung River to flood and brought more calamity to Elmira. Federals and Confederates alike built makeshift rafts to evacuate patients from the Smallpox Hospital, and prisoners crammed into second-floor barracks to escape the icy waters.

With the Confederate's surrender at Appomattox in April 1865, the prisoners received better treatment and were not guarded as closely. Prisoners were paroled in late May, and the camp became vacant on 27 September 1865, when the last imprisoned soldier left Elmira.

A rare tale of virtue in Elmira Prison was that of John W. Jones, an ex-slave who escaped via the underground from Virginia. Jones moved to Elmira and received employment at the prison burying the dead. He even buried a man from the household in which he had lived as a slave. Jones meticulously kept records and painted each Confederate's wooden headboard with the deceased's name, company, regiment, and state. John Jones buried 2,917 Confederates on the plot of two and a half acres, and his wooden grave markers lasted until 1877, when the government replaced them with headstones and named the land "Woodlawn Cemetery."

Many of the problems associated with Elmira Prison can be associated with its location. The Elmira campsite was originally believed to be healthy. The ground was level and of sandy soil with gravel below to allow drainage, and two wells and a river supplied the water. A one-acre lagoon, Foster's Pond, was a backwash for the Chemung River and stood within the camp, but overpopulation and poor prison management allowed the lagoon to serve as a latrine and garbage dump. The lagoon turned green and soon became a major reason for sickness, disease, and death within the camp.

Union corruption and profiteering allowed conditions at Elmira to grow worse. Clothing and supplies sent from the South were warehoused by Colonel Hoffman and not distributed unless they were gray. Food donated by local churches was sold to the prisoners by corrupt Union officers. Elmira's chief surgeon, D. L. Sanger, who later resigned to avoid being court-martialed, was once overheard saying that he had killed more rebels than any man at the front.

Of the more than 12,000 Confederate troops imprisoned, nearly 3,000 died of disease, malnutrition, exposure, and other associated causes. Elmira Prison's death rate of 24 percent is as high as any Civil War prison. The only remaining parts of Elmira Prison are Woodlawn Cemetery and Foster's Pond.

—*Nathan R. Meyer*

See also Prisons, U.S.A.
For further reading:
Gray, Michael P. "Elmira, A City on a Prison-Camp Contract." *Civil War History* (1999).
Hesseltine, William B., ed. *Civil War Prisons* (1972; reprint, 1992).
Holmes, Clayton W. *The Elmira Prison Camp, A History of the Military Prison at Elmira, N.Y.* (1912).

ELZEY, ARNOLD
(1816–1871)
Confederate general

Born to Arnold Elzey Jones and Anne Wilson Jackson in Somerset County, Maryland, Arnold Elzey received an appointment to the U.S. Military Academy in 1833. He graduated thirty-third of fifty in the class of 1837, and upon graduation he decided to drop his surname and adopt his paternal grandmother's name of Elzey as his surname. Commissioned into the artillery, Elzey was sent to Florida, where he fought in the Second Seminole War. After that conflict, he served on the southern frontier and was sent to Texas in 1845 in the opening phases of what would become the Mexican-American War.

During the Mexican-American War, Elzey was stationed initially at Fort Brown (now Brownsville, Texas), where he fired the first artillery shot at the attacking Mexican force. He fought in northern Mexico under Zachary Taylor before being transferred to Winfield Scott's command for the Mexico City campaign. He received two brevet promotions for his part in that campaign.

After the war, Elzey returned to frontier duty. In 1860, as a captain of the 2d Artillery, Elzey was transferred to the command of Augusta Arsenal in Georgia. He was there as the secession crisis loomed in Georgia and wrote to Washington in early January asking for instructions about what he should do should the surrender of the arsenal be demanded by state authorities. When the arsenal was reinforced on 10 January by troops from Charleston, South Carolina, he wrote the War Department again cautioning against any provocative actions that might upset the surrounding population. On 23 January 1861, Governor Joseph Brown demanded the surrender of the arsenal. Elzey again telegraphed Washington for instructions and, after receiving none, surrendered the arsenal on 24 January.

Elzey, a strong Southern sympathizer, traveled from Georgia to Washington, where he watched the situation in his home state of Maryland with great interest. He was given command at Old Point Comfort, and when Maryland failed to secede after the firing on Fort Sumter, he resigned his commission at the end of April 1861. He offered his services to the Confederate army and was commissioned lieutenant colonel of the 1st Maryland Confederate volunteers. At the end of June 1861 he was promoted to colonel and commanded his regiment under Joseph Johnston in the Shenandoah Valley.

In July 1861, Elzey traveled with the bulk of Johnston's force to Manassas Junction, where on 21 July he fought in the battle of First Bull Run. He succeeded to command of his brigade during the battle when its commander, E. Kirby Smith, was wounded. Elzey was commended for the offensive he mounted in the afternoon. Part of the Union retreat was attributed to that charge, and as a result Elzey was promoted to brigadier general that day. After Bull Run, Elzey returned to the Shenandoah Valley, where by the end of the year he was commanding his brigade under Thomas J. "Stonewall" Jackson.

Elzey fought under Jackson during the latter's Shenandoah Valley campaign in the spring of 1862, during which he received a minor injury when his horse was shot out from under him at Port Republic on 9 June. Later in the month, he traveled with Jackson's force to participate in the defense of Richmond. He fought in the Seven Days', until being wounded at the battle of Gaines' Mill on 27 June 1862.

After a lengthy convalescence, on 12 December 1862 Elzey was given command of the defenses of Richmond. He had been promoted to major general the week before. He remained in that command until March 1864 despite his requests to be allowed to return to a field command or be given command of an artillery unit. In Richmond, however, he was not bored. During the Chancellorsville campaign in the spring of 1863, Elzey had to deal with the threat posed by George Stoneman's cavalry raid toward the city. During the summer, he coped with Federal gunboats moving up the James River depositing Federal infantry along its banks. He repulsed these attempts on the city's defenses with the very limited resources at his disposal. Relying primarily on the city and national government workers, Elzey organized these men into efficient militia units who were prepared to respond to threats at a moment's notice. Along with the minor threats, Elzey also contended with more serious ones, particularly the Kilpatrick-Dahlgren Raid of February–March 1864.

In March 1864, Elzey was finally given his wish for a more active field assignment when he was charged with organizing and commanding what was termed the

Maryland Line, which was supposed to be composed of Confederate units from Maryland. However, the force never became a reality because of conflicting claims of authority and the refusal of some commanders to place their units under Elzey's command. In July he was relieved of command of this shadow unit.

In September 1864, another of Elzey's wishes was fulfilled when he was transferred to John Bell Hood's Army of Tennessee, where he became the army's chief of artillery. Elzey joined Hood's army as it was fleeing William T. Sherman's pursuit after the Atlanta campaign. He remained in this position through the disastrous battles at Franklin and Nashville and was relieved in February 1865 when there was no longer much of the Army of Tennessee left.

In March, Elzey, having come full circle since the war commenced, took command of some of the home guard defenses at Augusta, Georgia. He remained there until the end of the war, when, after surrendering to Federal authorities, he was paroled and allowed to go to Maryland. For the remainder of his life, Elzey lived quietly on a farm in Anne Arundel County, Maryland. He died in Baltimore on 21 February 1871.

—*David S. Heidler and Jeanne T. Heidler*

See also Bull Run, First Battle of; Gaines' Mill, Battle of; Richmond, Virginia.

For further reading:

Davis, William C. *Battle at Bull Run: A History of the First Major Campaign of the Civil War* (1977).

Furgurson, Ernest B. *Ashes of Glory: Richmond at War* (1996).

Thomas, Emory M. *The Confederate State of Richmond; A Biography of the Capital* (1971).

EMANCIPATION PROCLAMATION
(1 January 1863)

On 1 January 1863, after nearly two years of armed rebellion by eleven slaveholding states, President Abraham Lincoln proclaimed that the slaves in eight of those states and in large portions of two others were freed forever and that their freedom would be recognized and protected by the U.S. government and its armed forces. Apart from the Declaration of Independence, this proclamation may be the single most significant statement of policy issued by a governing authority in the history of the United States. It marked the end of governmental support for slavery, reversing a pattern of the national government to treat slavery as a domestic practice of individual states, the operation of which existed outside the scope of Federal power. It gave legal standing to the freedom already claimed by African-Americans who were throwing off the shackles of bondage and moving to Union lines. And it shifted the moral tenor of the Civil War from a quest to restore the Union and its governing authority to an armed

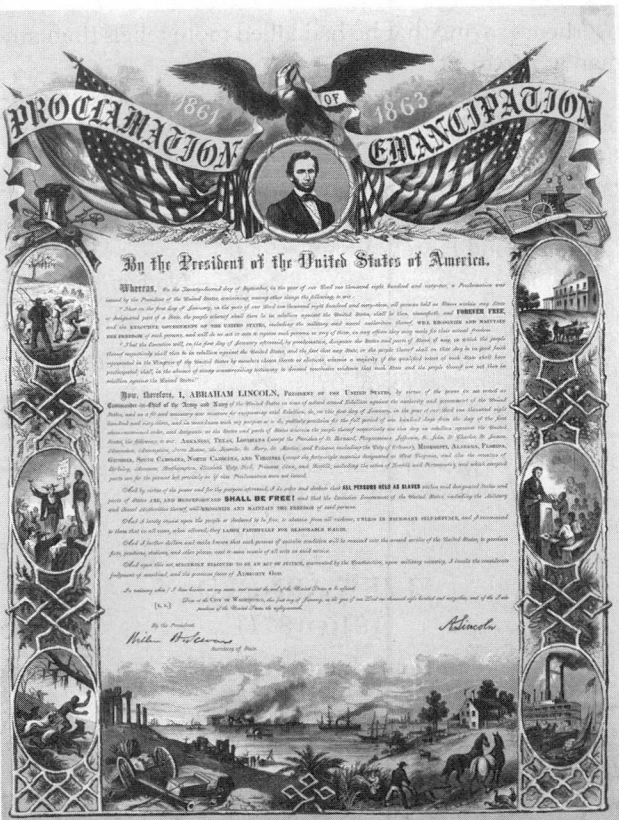

The Emancipation Proclamation, published as an engraving by R. A. Dimmick in 1864 (*Library of Congress*)

struggle for union that would also result in freedom for slaves. Despite its moral significance, the actual proclamation reads like a cargo listing. Yet therein one finds much of the meaning and purpose of the Emancipation Proclamation.

At the war's outbreak, the Union government adopted a policy to put down the rebellion, and the Lincoln administration both out of conviction and legal interest defined the rebellion as the work of a minority of Southern insurrectionists. The Union would achieve success by restoring control of the eleven seceded state governments to people loyal to the Union. In such a scenario, slaves and slavery did not play a part. Loyal Southerners had a right to their property, and Lincoln feared driving them into the ranks of the secessionists if his government appeared to use the incident of rebellion to emancipate slaves. Further, if Lincoln's government moved against slavery, the four slaveholding border states might be induced to secede as well. For this reason, Lincoln himself refused to endorse efforts by Generals John C. Frémont and David Hunter to free slaves in sectors under their command early in the war.

This reluctance angered both black and white abolitionists, who pointed out that the white Southerner's resolve to uphold slavery had caused the Civil War and that slave labor made Confederate resistance more formidable by freeing more white Southerners to serve in the military. Further, as Confederate resistance continued, the insurrection by an armed minority looked more and more like a war. Because the Lincoln government determined to treat captured Confederate soldiers according to the laws of war, it seemed to follow that the laws of war could be extended to justify the seizure of enemy property.

Slaves themselves made this extension of the laws of war a practical reality. In May 1861 three slaves fled to Fort Monroe and General Benjamin Butler refused to return them to their owner. Instead, he treated them as contraband of war, items liable to seizure. On 6 August 1861 Lincoln gave structure to Butler's action and to slave flight by signing the First Confiscation Act. It held that the United States would take possession of property used in furthering the rebellion, including slaves.

In 1862 radical Republicans, as part of their vision for perfecting the American Republic, began legislative activity designed to attack slavery. Not only did they end slavery in Washington, D.C., through compensated emancipation; they forbade military officers from returning runaway slaves to their owners. They crafted a Second Confiscation Act that permitted the seizure of property of rebelling Southerners and specifically freed forever any slaves who came into Union lines. Rules of law, however, complicated this measure. At some point, the government would have to prove that a Southerner was actually in rebellion, so the measure was not so radical as it might first seem.

By the time this legislation had appeared, the more moderate Abraham Lincoln had concluded that restoration of the pre-1861 Union was likely impossible. A long war of conquest seemed the only available route to reunion, and that road had to pass through emancipation because slavery made Southern resistance to Union arms more effective. The radical Republicans were not aware of his change of mind and continued to consider him unacceptably hesitant on slavery. Yet on 13 July 1862, four days before the Second Confiscation Act passed Congress, Lincoln told two members of his cabinet that he was prepared to use his war power under the Constitution to abolish slavery and had been working on a draft of his emancipation policy for several days.

Lincoln did not act immediately for two interconnected reasons. First, many Northerners (mostly Democrats) opposed emancipation, and their backlash might well be felt in the 1862 congressional elections. Democrats believed that the United States belonged to whites only and linked emancipation to racial mixing. Some Democrats asserted that abolitionist sanctimony had forced Southerners to secede. These folk would hardly support a war for emancipation. Second, the Union war effort had not met with much success, espe-

cially in the east, where the failures of General George B. McClellan's Peninsula campaign had disappointed a North eager for victories. Secretary of State William Henry Seward believed an emancipation policy announced without military victories would have the look of desperation, costing Lincoln both credibility and votes in the fall elections. It turned out to be good advice, because John Pope's Army of Virginia was soon trounced at Second Bull Run.

From July until September 1862, Lincoln had to juggle a variety of realities. He could not announce an emancipation policy prematurely, because doing so would alienate conservative Northerners. He could not repudiate emancipation, because he had come to believe in it, and such an announcement would estrange radical Republicans. His letter to Horace Greeley of 22 August revealed Lincoln to be a man who could tell a complex truth. Lincoln informed the bewhiskered editor that restoring the Union remained the primary goal of the United States government, and the fate of slavery was subordinate to that goal. If that was the price of union, he did note that he would indeed free all of the slaves.

Battlefield victory of a sort did come, although Lincoln had hoped for a more decisive one. McClellan's Army of the Potomac turned back General Robert E. Lee at Antietam Creek on 17 September. Five days later, Lincoln issued his Preliminary Emancipation Proclamation. Its authority lay in Lincoln's Constitutional power as commander in chief, which gave him broad latitude over property in military emergencies. The Preliminary Emancipation Proclamation declared that all slaves in areas still in rebellion on 1 January 1863 would be free. Rebelling states presumably had three months to cease behaving in an insurrectionary manner and could return to the Union with slavery intact. By stating his emancipation policy in this manner, Lincoln hoped to appeal to the broadest possible segment of Northern society and, given the growing number of Union casualties, he wanted to use every opportunity to bring the war to a speedy close and to reestablish Union as best he could. The Confederate States did not respond to the overture of reunion, but Lincoln's policy did impress Northern voters. In the 1862 elections his party experienced the smallest electoral losses that had been recorded in such off-year elections in more than twenty years.

Lincoln continued to look for ways to end the war and to effect his new emancipation policy. In December he proposed a constitutional amendment that would permit compensated emancipation over the course of the next thirty-five years for slaveholding states. Many observers missed the point and assumed that he was replacing his Emancipation Proclamation with a new policy. In fact, he intended nothing of the kind. He hoped the proposed amendment would entice the slaveholding border states to abandon slavery, because his war powers did not extend there. Although he might have traded compensated emancipation for a cessation of Confederate rebellion, the timing of his compensation proposal came too late to have been aimed at the Confederacy.

On 1 January 1863, Lincoln signed the permanent Emancipation Proclamation. It freed all slaves in the Confederate States, except those in Tennessee, whose eastern portions were considered loyal while the remainder of the state was in Federal hands. It also left unaffected those slaves in portions of Louisiana and Virginia, areas that were likewise considered loyal or were under Union control. Of course, Lincoln's proclamation depended on slaves getting to Union lines in the interim and upon the conquest of slaveholding territory in the long run. Its legal authority was rooted in Lincoln's war powers and likely subject to termination once peace was restored, which made seeking a constitutional amendment outlawing slavery a priority.

Critics immediately grasped at the apparent contradictions in the Emancipation Proclamation. It did not free slaves in lands Lincoln controlled, but declared those in areas not under his power forever free. Such critiques missed the point. First, the Emancipation Proclamation solved the problem of contraband slaves. The First and Second Confiscation Acts effectively freed slaves of rebelling masters, pursuant to proving those masters Rebels. The Emancipation Proclamation freed slaves in areas in rebellion under Lincoln's right to seize enemy property. It was not necessary to prove that an individual master was a Rebel. The status of over 100,000 slaves was thus clarified.

Second, the Emancipation Proclamation shifted the focus of the Union war aim. That aim remained the restoration of the Union, but the Emancipation Proclamation meant that it would be a transformed Union, one without slavery. The moral imperative of emancipation soon bore fruit. While there was an initial backlash among certain elements in the Northern armies, many Northern soldiers took inspiration in fighting to destroy the institution that had made the war necessary the first place. And the Emancipation Proclamation also influenced attitudes abroad. Once the Union was pledged to eradicating slavery, it became much less likely that Great Britain would extend diplomatic recognition to the Confederacy

Finally, the Emancipation Proclamation served as a fulcrum for important, if sometimes slow, changes regarding race relations. Because Lincoln carefully applied the Emancipation Proclamation only to areas that he could constitutionally affect with his war powers, he firmly linked the rule of law and the Constitution to his policy. This conservative and narrow approach removed lines of appeal and counterargument about the legality of the measure and it allowed Lincoln to continue his push for a constitutional amendment to end slavery in the border states and in the postwar South. Persons in the United States might be of different races, but the war and the policy it compelled meant that no longer would be there be the legal distinctions of master and slave.

—Edward R. Crowther

See also Confiscation Acts; Contrabands; Freedmen's Bureau; Lincoln, Abraham; Radical Republicans; Thirteenth Amendment.

For further reading:
Franklin, John Hope. *The Emancipation Proclamation* (1965).
McPherson, James. *The Struggle for Equality: Abolitionists and the Negro in the Civil War and Reconstruction* (1964).
Paludan, Phillip S. *The Presidency of Abraham Lincoln* (1994).

EMERSON, RALPH WALDO
(1803–1882)
Essayist, poet, and philosopher

Ralph Waldo Emerson's beliefs of self-reliance and individualism were transformed by the events leading up to the Civil War into a belief in the value of social institutions and collective action. Born in Boston, Emerson studied theology at Harvard and was ordained a Unitarian minister in 1829. Plagued by spiritual doubts, he resigned from the ministry in 1832, traveled abroad, and was influenced by European romantic thought. He settled in Concord, Massachusetts, in 1834. After the publication of his short treatise "Nature" in 1836, Emerson became the central figure of the transcendentalist movement in the United States and a guiding intellect for numerous American writers including Henry David Thoreau and Walt Whitman.

Although Emerson resided near the geographic and social center of abolitionism, he initially resisted an open alliance with its more militant leaders. Emerson was suspicious of organizations and viewed himself as a detached scholar rather than as a political agitator. Much as he hoped for the abolition of slavery, he thought this could best be achieved by reforming the individual rather than through collective action. Morality had to come from the consonance of individual hearts, each independently perceiving the same ideal truths.

Nevertheless, Emerson's journals show that he was concerned with the evil of slavery from his youth forward, and he even dreamed that he might somehow deliver slaves from bondage. But it was not until 1837 that Emerson was provoked by the murder of an abolitionist publisher, Elijah P. Lovejoy, into delivering a moderate antislavery address. Over the next seven years, Emerson read more deeply into the horrors of slavery, his fears concerning its expansion grew, and he acquired an admiration for the abolitionist movement.

Emerson shared the outrage of abolitionists at the Compromise of 1850 and the Fugitive Slave Law; he finally advocated open resistance to civil government. Emerson accepted that conventional political means were incapable of redressing an immoral law; the "higher law" of the individual conscience was more important than a flawed Constitution. Emerson's outrage escalated in 1854 when Massachusetts chief justice Lemuel Shaw returned the fugitive slave Anthony Burns to bondage and Congress passed the Kansas-Nebraska Act. It was shortly after these events that Emerson wrote his influential "Lecture on Slavery," which he first delivered in Boston on 25 January 1855 before the Massachusetts Anti-Slavery Society.

Rather than emphasizing individual reflection, Emerson's "Lecture on Slavery" endorses activism: "I do not cripple but exalt the social action," he wrote. He asserted unequivocally that slavery is a moral evil, a violation of America's sacred mission, and a threat to the integrity of the entire nation. The Fugitive Slave Law is unjust, he argued, and honest men are not obliged to uphold it. Most specifically, Emerson proposed that a negotiated settlement should be reached with the slaveholders, offering them compensation for emancipating their slaves without acknowledging their right to ownership. Although Emerson continued to resist the inflexibility of the Garrisonians, the crisis of the mid-1850s provoked him out of his intellectual malaise into a specific—if moderate—plan to end the "peculiar institution."

Like many intellectuals, Emerson regarded the opening of the Civil War with a sense of relief. American society, he believed, was built on a fundamental contradiction between morality and immorality, between freedom and slavery. The war would decide which would prevail. Though he did not serve in the military, Emerson's journals show that he viewed the war as beneficial to the health of the state and akin to a religious revival, a rite of national purification. Once suspicious of the federal government, Emerson embraced nationalism, and, in "American Civilization" (1862), he called upon the state to assume "the absolute powers of a Dictator." He was committed to a Union victory at all costs; Southerners, he wrote, should be "pounded instead of negociated [sic] into a peace."

In 1863 Emerson accepted an appointment as an official visitor to West Point, which shocked many of his friends. The war brought Emerson out of his reclusive life of thought and into the public arena. In the same year he joined the Union League Club of Boston and proposed the creation of a National Academy of Literature and Art, in effect, establishing a national set of cultural standards. Emerson's years as a major intellectual figure were behind him, but he remained a respected commentator and the "Sage of Concord" for the remainder of his life.

—*William A. Pannapacker*

See also Abolitionist Movement; Abolitionists; Burns,

Anthony; Hawthorne, Nathaniel; Longfellow, Henry Wadsworth; Thoreau, Henry David; Whitman, Walt; Whittier, John Greenleaf.

For further reading:

Aaron, Daniel. *The Unwritten War: American Writers and the Civil War* (1973).

Emerson, Ralph Waldo. *Collected Works* (1971).

———. *The Journals and Miscellaneous Notebooks of Ralph Waldo Emerson* (1960–1982).

Frederickson, George M. *The Inner Civil War: Northern Intellectuals and the Crisis of the Union* (1965).

Gougeon, Len. *Virtue's Hero: Emerson, Anti-Slavery, and Reform* (1990).

EMORY, WILLIAM HEMSLEY
(1811–1887)
Union general

Born to Thomas Emory and Anna Maria Hemsley Emory in Queen Anne's County, Maryland, William Hemsley Emory received an appointment to the U.S. Military Academy in 1827. He graduated fourteenth of thirty-three in 1831. Commissioned into the 4th U.S. Artillery, Emory resigned his commission after only five years in the army. He returned two years later to accept a first lieutenant's commission in the Topographical Engineers. At the outbreak of the Mexican-American War, he left his assignment on the Northeastern Boundary Survey to become the chief engineer for the Army of the West. He won two brevet promotions during that army's campaign in the Southwest.

After the Mexican-American War, Emory served on the boundary survey to determine the new border between the United States and Mexico. His primary duty in that regard was handling the astronomical aspects of the survey. He performed similar duties for the commission surveying the Gadsden Purchase. Some of his written accounts of his travels during these surveys were published in the 1850s.

In 1855, Emory was promoted to major in the 2d U.S. Cavalry. In that capacity he served in Kansas during the unsettled times there and on Albert Sidney Johnston's Utah expedition. In early 1861, having been recently promoted to lieutenant colonel, 1st U.S. Cavalry, Emory was in Washington, D.C. In April he was sent to the Indian Territory to assume command of Federal posts there. By the end of the month, however, he was forced to abandon the forts in the face of overwhelming numbers of Confederate sympathizers and a state of lawlessness in the territory. He marched his men to Fort Leavenworth without the loss of a single man. Emory then went east, where he became lieutenant colonel of the 6th U.S. Cavalry, while the men he had brought out of Indian Territory were sent to Missouri to deal with Confederate forces there.

During the winter and early spring of 1862, Emory commanded cavalry forces in the defenses of Washington, D.C. In March he was promoted to brigadier general of volunteers. During the Peninsula campaign he commanded a brigade of the Army of the Potomac's Cavalry Reserve Division. He distinguished himself in the battles of Williamsburg and Hanover Court House. In the latter battle on 27 May, Emory commanded a mixed unit of cavalry and light artillery that succeeded in dividing a part of the Confederate defenders precipitating their retreat. He was commended by the Union commander in the field, Fitz John Porter. On 6 July 1862 he was relieved of his cavalry duties and assigned command of a brigade of Erasmus Keyes's IV Corps. He remained in that command at Harrison's Landing for the remainder of the summer. In October he was detailed to Baltimore to serve in the defenses there under John Wool. George B. McClellan requested his return to the Army of the Potomac at the end of the month, but instead he was transferred to the command of Nathaniel P. Banks for that general's upcoming campaign to the Gulf of Mexico.

Beginning in January 1863, Emory commanded the 3d Division, XIX Corps, Department of the Gulf. He fought in the early stages of the Port Hudson campaign before being given command of the defenses of New Orleans in May 1863. He held that position until August 1863, when he assumed command of a division of XIX Corps operating in Louisiana for the remainder of the year.

In March 1864, in command of the 1st Division, XIX Corps, Emory led his men forward in Banks's Red River campaign. After the battle of Sabine Crossroads on 8 April, Emory's division established the defensive line that guarded the Federal retreat and held against the Confederate attack the next day in the battle of Pleasant Hill. After the campaign, beginning in May 1864, Emory was given command of XIX Corps. He continued to operate in Louisiana, headquartered at Morganza, until being called east with the corps in July 1864.

Emory arrived at Fort Monroe with the lead elements of his corps in early July and was immediately sent to the defenses of Washington to help meet the threat posed by Jubal Early's raid. In early August 1864, Emory was sent with this corps to combat Early's movements in the Shenandoah Valley. Later in the month, he and his men were incorporated into Philip Sheridan's Army of the Shenandoah.

Emory and the XIX Corps fought in all the major battles of Sheridan's Shenandoah Valley campaign. He received two brevet promotions for his actions during the campaign, one for Fisher's Hill and the other for Cedar Creek. In December, both Sheridan and Ulysses S. Grant recommended Emory for promotion to major general of volunteers. He remained in the valley until a reorganization of the army brought about the abolition of

XIX Corps in March 1865. He continued to operate in West Virginia with a remnant of his former force until the end of the war. On 22 April 1865 he was given command of the Department of West Virginia with headquarters at Cumberland, Maryland. While in that command he was finally promoted to major general of volunteers in September 1865.

Emory was mustered out of volunteer service in January 1866 and reverted to his regular rank of colonel. He held a variety of commands in the postwar army, including the Department of Washington and the Department of the Gulf. He retired in July 1876 at the rank of brigadier general. He lived quietly in retirement in Washington, D.C., where he died on 1 December 1887.

—*David S. Heidler and Jeanne T. Heidler*

See also Cedar Creek, Battle of; Fisher's Hill, Battle of; Hanover Court House, Battle of; Pleasant Hill; Red River Campaign.

For further reading:
Norris, L. David. *William H. Emory: Soldier-Scientist* (1998).

ENCHANTRESS AFFAIR
(July 1861–February 1862)

On 6 July 1861, the Confederate privateer *Jeff Davis*, out of Charleston, South Carolina, captured the merchant schooner *Enchantress* from Newburyport, Massachusetts, off the coast of Delaware. A five-man prize crew under Walter W. Smith, a former river pilot from Savannah, Georgia, was put on board the schooner to bring her in. On 22 July, the USS *Albatross* off Hatteras, North Carolina, recaptured the *Enchantress*, and the Confederate prize crew was taken to Philadelphia in irons.

The Federal government leveled charges of piracy against the privateers, and they were brought to trial in U.S. district court on 22 October. Smith and three others were found guilty and were sentenced to hang. One crew member was found not guilty and was released. Besides the prize crew of the *Enchantress*, the crew of the captured privateer *Petrel* was also condemned. The prisoners, fourteen in all, were confined in a civil prison in Philadelphia to await execution.

The prejudice of the court against the accused was apparent. When the defense attorney, Nathaniel Harrison, attempted to introduce documents showing that the Confederacy was a legitimate government that had issued letters of marque and reprisal to the privateers, the judge responded, "These papers are not received as evidence of any fact except the fact of their own existence."

The case caused great outrage in the South. Harrison believed international law had been violated and called on Jefferson Davis to intervene in defense of the prisoners. Instead, on 9 November Confederate secretary of war

Judah P. Benjamin directed Brigadier General John H. Winder, provost marshal in Richmond, to select by lot fourteen officers from the senior Union prisoners of war to stand hostage for the condemned privateers. By Benjamin's order, the first officer selected was to be confined in a cell appropriate for a convicted felon and to be treated as if he were such. The other thirteen were to be confined in cells reserved for prisoners accused of infamous crimes.

Winder went to Libby Prison on 10 November. The names of the six colonels in captivity were placed in a can and a prison official drew out the first one, Colonel Michael Corcoran of the 69th New York, then held at Charleston. Because there were only ten other captured field officers available, all of their names went on the list. Then the names of all captains were placed in the can and three were drawn to make up the total.

In addition to Corcoran, the names drawn were Colonel Alfred M. Wood, 14th New York; Colonel Orlando B. Willcox, 1st Michigan; Colonel William L. Lee, 20th Massachusetts; Colonel Milton Cogswell, 42d New York; Colonel William E. Woodruff, 2d Kentucky; Lieutenant Colonel George W. Neff, 2d Kentucky; Lieutenant Colonel Samuel Bowman, 8th Pennsylvania; Major Paul Joseph Revere, grandson of the patriot, 20th Massachusetts; Major James D. Potter, 38th New York; Major Israel Vogdes, 1st U.S. Artillery; Captain James B. Ricketts, 1st U.S. Artillery; Captain George W. Rockwood, 15th Massachusetts; and Captain Hugh McQuaide, 38th New York. Captains Ricketts and McQuaide having been wounded, another drawing was made to replace them. Captain Henry Bowman, 15th Massachusetts, and Captain Francis J. Keffer, 71st Pennsylvania, were selected. Winder reported the results to Benjamin on 11 November.

The U.S. government's legal case was weak. Privateering and the issuance of letters of marque and reprisal had been accepted practices for hundreds of years. At an international conference in 1856, the United States had declined to sign a protocol declaring privateering to be piracy, although most European powers had signed. On review, the government changed its position. The sentences were voided and the convicted men were reclassified as prisoners of war on 15 February 1862. They had already been sent to a military prison at Fort Lafayette in the New York Narrows near Brooklyn. One died in prison, but the rest were later released or exchanged. All the Federal officers were eventually exchanged, except McQuaide who died of his wounds.

Although the immediate focus of this affair was on the conviction of Walter Smith and the other privateers on charges of piracy, and the subsequent selection of the Union hostages, the case was really about the Confederate government's authority to wage war. The U.S. government's acceptance of the legitimacy of the privateers was a tacit recognition of the existence of the South as a belligerent state, a fact already recognized by the Congress's declaration the previous spring that a state of war existed. The *Enchantress* affair was a small but significant diplomatic and political victory for the government in Richmond.

A complete transcript of the trial of Walter Smith (referred to in the Official Record as William Smith) and correspondence relating to the selection of the officer hostages is in the OR, Ser. II, Vol. 3: 58-121, 738-39.

—*Russell K. Brown*

See also Privateers.
For further reading:
Robinson, William M., Jr. *The Confederate Privateers* (1928; reprint, 1990).

ENROLLED MISSOURI MILITIA

The Enrolled Missouri Militia (EMM), the largest single military organization west of the Mississippi River, provided the mechanism through which tens of thousands of Missourians saw service for the Union over and above the nearly 110,000 Federal volunteers credited to the state. As it is rarely discussed (it is generally grouped with other organizations and described as "the militia") the EMM remains the truly forgotten citizen-soldiers of the Civil War.

While war transformed militias everywhere, it likely created no greater chaos than in Missouri. Initially, the official Missouri State Guard represented the prosecessionist state government and confronted not only Federal forces but also extralegal Home Guards of Missouri Unionists determined to overthrow that government. When Unionists established a Unionist provisional government, it established a three-month, then a six-month militia. To maintain order while allowing the reassignment of volunteers to duty elsewhere, the government authorized a new Missouri state militia in the spring of 1862. The heavy toll of the war, however, soon drew the Missouri State Militia into a primary role as Federal garrison troops in constant service often far from their homes.

In July 1862, the provisional government began enrolling loyal citizens for a genuine militia. The EMM would be funded by the state and be subject to the call of the governor but would receive orders from the regular Federal military. While units of the EMM may have often been new, their ranks usually included discharged veterans and others who had often seen action. Enrollees pursued their civilian lives and contributed service when needed. Units were supplied irregularly through frequently confused jurisdictions. Their officers rarely filed reports to any Federal authority. In most parts of Missouri, the organization was largely a self-sustaining local operation, the activities of which likely depended

on the needs and whims of the local Union garrisons. An individual's total time in service was generally equivalent to that of a six-month or one-year regiment of volunteers.

Organized by locality, units did not represent standard sizes, but the organization numbered its regiments to a staggering eighty-nine with literally uncounted dozens of provisional battalions and companies serving on a rotating basis. Only a fraction needed to be in service at any given time to constitute a small army that freed tens of thousands of Federal volunteers from garrison duties; without them, major Union initiatives west of the Appalachians would have been smaller, later, and less likely to succeed.

Politically, the very process of mobilizing the EMM reflected the complexities of public opinion. The so-called Paw-Paw units of western and central Missouri often enrolled under protest, promising only to fight guerrillas and not Confederate regulars; sometimes headed by local Copperhead Democrats, they disarmed Unionists and were even suspected of collaborating with the guerrillas. However, the 28th EMM had an entire "Reb company," Osage County veterans of Missouri State Guard or Confederate service, who nonetheless served the Union well against regular Confederates. In the militarily secure area around St. Louis, the EMM frequently extended Lincoln's Emancipation Proclamation to Missouri and helped recruit black soldiers for the army.

The very flexibility of the EMM allowed for great innovations. Intended primarily to guard supply depots, public buildings, military outposts, railroad bridges, and other key installations, the EMM also pioneered small-scale counterinsurgency warfare. The nature of the organization allowed for the abandonment of traditional regimental structure for the formation of provisional EMM battalions and companies. Several units, reorganized as the 6th and 7th Provisional EMM, again reorganized as volunteer regiments, the 16th and 15th Missouri Cavalry.

The EMM, like the Union volunteer forces, held its own against Confederate volunteers. Members of the 26th, 72d, and 73d EMM participated in the January 1863 fighting around Springfield, and the 74th EMM participated in operations nearby to challenge the Confederate drive elsewhere. The spring 1863 raid into the southeastern Missouri began with a clash at Chalk Bluff with the 56th EMM. The fall Confederate raid into west-central Missouri met the 1st Provisional EMM and the 43d EMM. With few exceptions, Federal efforts to thwart Price's Missouri Raid in the fall of 1864 were almost exclusively left to the EMM.

—*Mark A. Lause*

See also Copperheads; Price's Missouri Raid.
For further reading:
Canan, Howard V. "Missouri Paw Paw Militia of 1863–1864." *Missouri Historical Review* (1968).
Parrish, William E. A *History of Missouri, Volume III. 1860 to 1875* (1971).
———. *Turbulent Partnership: Missouri and the Union, 1861–1865* (1963).

ERICSSON, JOHN
(1803–1889)
Naval architect

John Ericsson was born in Långbanshyttan, Sweden, and as a youth he displayed a great proclivity for tinkering. Accordingly, he joined the Swedish Corps of Cadets at age fourteen and within three years was commissioned a lieutenant of topographical engineers. By 1827, Ericsson had patented several ingenious devices, and he moved to England to market them. Two years later he demonstrated his mechanical mastery by designing and constructing the Novelty, an experimental locomotive that reached unprecedented speeds of 30 miles an hour. Ericsson also took great interest in naval warfare, which at that time was in transition from a centuries-old reliance upon wind and sails for propulsion to steam technology. In 1836 he designed a viable screw propellor for warships that was successfully tested, but a conservatively minded British admiralty showed no interest. Fortunately, Ericsson's endeavors came to the attention of U.S. Navy captain Robert Field Stockton, who prevailed upon him to emigrate to America.

Once in the United States, Stockton used his political influence to have Ericsson design the navy's first steam frigate, the USS *Princeton*. In 1844 it became the world's first propeller-driven warship and also incorporated such novel features as having the vital machinery below the waterline for protection. However, during trials held on 28 February 1844, a 12-inch cannon designed by Stockton exploded, killing the secretary of state, the secretary of the navy, and several dignitaries. Ericsson was officially cleared of any blame, but the incident cast a pall on his relations with the navy. He relocated back to New York and spent the next fifteen years successfully designing commercial steam vessels.

It was not until the advent of Civil War in April 1861 that the Navy Department would deal with Ericsson again. That summer, the government learned that the Confederate navy had raised the USS *Merrimack*, which had earlier been scuttled at Norfolk, Virginia, and was converting it into an ironclad ram. The Navy Department countered by soliciting bids for a similar warship, and Ericsson submitted a "floating battery" design so radical that it was initially rejected. This vessel, christened the *Monitor*, possessed a low-lying hull, was fully armored with iron plates, and sported a dual-gun, rotating turret amidships. Though initially derided as a "cheese box on a raft," Ericsson's steam-powered, propeller-driven contraption was the world's first modern

John Ericsson (*Library of Congress*)

Union victory. Thereafter, "monitors" became a standard type of warship. In a patriotic gesture, Ericsson also turned over his unpatented plans to other engineers to facilitate the production of new vessels. Within a few years, ships like the *Monitor* were being constructed for navies around the world. They persevered well into the early twentieth century.

After the war, Ericsson returned to New York, where he continued to dabble in steam technology, solar energy, and torpedo warfare. None of his creations enjoyed the success or celebrity of the *Monitor*, but his advice and technical expertise were widely sought after. At the time of his death, he was universally hailed as one of the most influential naval architects of the nineteenth century. Ericsson's remains were then returned to Sweden, by his own request, in the hold of an American monitor vessel.

—*John C. Fredriksen*

See also Monitor.

For further reading:

De Kay, James T. *Monitor: The Story of the Legendary Civil War Ironclad and the Man Whose Invention Changed the Course of History* (1997).

White, Ruth. *Yankee From Sweden: The Dream and the Reality in the Days of John Ericsson* (1960).

ERLANGER, EMILE
See Financing, C.S.A.

ESPIONAGE

Both Union and Confederate forces used scouts, balloonists, signalmen, and intercepted letters, as well as espionage, to acquire military intelligence. Nevertheless, espionage has the potential to produce the most useful information during war because if agents are intelligent and intrepid, they can gather information far superior to that yielded by any other source. Strictly defined, espionage entails the clandestine gathering of military intelligence. Once collected, information must be processed and analyzed, often the most difficult aspect of the process, especially when using inexperienced operatives. Typically in the Civil War, espionage was not as useful as was scouting, which brought in a greater volume of information.

Robert E. Lee lamented that Confederate forces had poor espionage abilities, and it was true that Federal forces were far more successful with espionage than were Confederates, particularly by gathering information in camps and on the march. One illustrative example of a successful Union espionage operation was that performed by Sharpe's bureau. This Union force made forays into Confederate territory and successfully obtained information because they typically dressed in civilian clothes or enemy uniforms.

Probably the most important figure in espionage

warship. Incensed by the department's rejection, he deliberately visited Washington, D.C., to plead with the government and convinced the board to reverse itself. The USS *Monitor* was then speedily built and launched at New York's Greenpoint shipyard in slightly over 100 days, and was hastily pressed into service. That such a technologically advanced prototype could be built so quickly affords ample proof of Ericsson's superb organizational abilities. Under the command of Lieutenant John L. Worden, the new ship sailed directly for Hampton Roads, Virginia, where on 9 March 1862 it confronted the formidable CSS *Virginia* (formerly the *Merrimack*). The climactic battle proved an inconclusive draw, but the blockade of Norfolk was maintained, ensuring its eventual capture by Union forces.

Worden's success—and Ericsson's—ushered in a new age of naval warfare: armored warships became the focus of American ship construction for the rest of the war. The Navy Department subsequently authorized Ericsson to design and build four additional classes of ironclads, and these made indelible contributions to the eventual during the Civil War was Allan Pinkerton. Pinkerton's bureau engaged in positive intelligence gathering for Union forces; that is, acquiring information on an adversary through espionage or interrogation. The bureau could not fully complete its mission because it did not use other methods such as scouting to acquire positive intelligence. Another organization, coexisting with Pinkerton's and directed by La Fayette Baker, was also not complete because it only utilized counterintelligence and military police. A lack of consistency and unity causes numerous problems in acquiring intelligence. In the Pinkerton organization, Timothy Webster was the most capable spy; however, he represented only a small aspect of Pinkerton's bureau. The bureau focused its efforts on Richmond, Virginia, the capital of the Confederacy.

One interesting example of the Union's use of espionage was at the battle of Second Bull Run. The spy who marched with the Confederate forces was Thomas O. Harter, of the 1st Indiana Cavalry. His presence was more detrimental than the missing infantry brigade. His commanding officer, General Franz Sigel, assigned him to espionage duty. Harter obtained civilian clothes and money. As a disguise, Harter was to portray himself as a refugee from Terre Haute, Indiana, seeking employment with the railroads. The espionage work that Harter engaged in was pure luck. Confederate authorities arrested him on the way to Staunton, Virginia, but he was able to secure an interview with the superintendent of the Virginia Central Railroad. The superintendent was familiar with Terre Haute and with his former employer. Having gained the confidence of the superintendent, Harter was sent to Richmond and was introduced to the superintendent of the Richmond and Danville railroads. Harter went to work on the Virginia Central, the railroad Lee's army was tasking on its way to Gordonsville. Amid all of the confusion, Harter managed to get to Gordonsville and eventually made it back to Union forces by 18 August 1862.

After Harter successfully made it to the Union lines, he immediately searched for the nearest headquarters to report his findings. His mission completed, Harter received hazard pay of $500 and an honorable discharge from the Union army. Later, he became a detective in Baltimore for Provost Marshal James L. McPhail. In 1863 he scouted the Confederate retreat after the battle of Gettysburg. He was also on the payroll of the intelligence bureau of the Army of the Potomac.

Some of the first espionage attempts by the Union Army resulted in failure. The "Pinkertons" were the ones involved, but Alan Pinkerton had no military experience and was not able to process the information acquired by his employees. This led to misrepresented information being reported to General George B. McClellan.

The practice of espionage during the Civil War was not totally beneficial for either Union or Confederate forces. As a process, espionage was an inexact science. Pinkerton's employees, along with others, simply played it by ear, hoping that they would uncover some vital information. Besides the difficulty of acquiring the information, the communication lines of both armies were not advanced enough to permit an ample flow of information.

— *Matthew Pacer*

See also Baker, La Fayette Curry; Pinkerton, Allan; Secret Service, C.S.A.; Secret Service, U.S.A.

For further reading:
Finnegan, John P., and Romana Danysh. *Military Intelligence* (1998).
Fishel, Edwin C. *The Secret War for the Union* (1996).
Manning, Michael L. *Senseless Secrets* (1996).

ETHERIDGE, ANNIE
(1840–1913)
Daughter of the regiment

Born Lorinda Anna Blair in Detroit, Michigan, the woman who came to be known as "Gentle Annie" followed her first husband, James Etheridge, into the Union army in 1861. When he deserted, she remained, first serving with the 3d and then with the 5th Michigan Infantry as daughter of the regiment, a role that required her to perform a wide range of tasks, from nursing, to riding at the head of the troops, to standing with the regimental colors, and providing inspiration for the fight to the men in the ranks. Etheridge generally traveled armed with a pair of pistols, though it is not clear that she ever used them. She carried with her as well all the equipment necessary for tending the wounded—lint, bandages, and medicines, and a blanket for her own use at night. Soldiers who remembered Etheridge noted that she typically slept on the ground just as they did, and never asked for special favors.

Over the course of her four years of service to the Union army, Etheridge participated in many of the Eastern theater's major engagements and campaigns. She was present at First Bull Run, where she reportedly was among the first to greet the Union soldiers as they fled the field. She was also at Williamsburg, Second Bull Run, Antietam, Fredericksburg, Chancellorsville, Gettysburg, and Spotsylvania. Through it all, Etheridge maintained her reputation for extraordinary bravery, endurance, enthusiasm, and tenderness. The many soldiers who mentioned her in their letters home and in their personal diaries universally described her as unflappable in the face of shot and shell, and they added that her clothes were often riddled with bullet holes, of which she took no notice herself. Soldiers also agreed that Etheridge never complained about the harsh camp and battlefield conditions that she shared with them, and that she was always the first to find her way, with her medical supplies, into the thick of the wounded on the field, even when the bullets were still flying. Indeed, in May 1863, in recognition of her great courage, Etheridge was one of two women (with daughter of the regiment Marie Tepe, of the 114th Pennsylvania Infantry) to receive the Kearny Cross for bravery, normally reserved for noncommissioned officers and privates who held to the late Philip Kearny's own high standards for courage as a soldier.

Etheridge served on the field with her regiments. In the winter of 1861–1862 and again in 1864, Etheridge spent some time as a hospital nurse and as a nurse on board a Federal hospital transport ship in response to orders from senior officers designed to move army women away from the fields of battle and relocate them in presumably less hazardous circumstances. In these positions, which she accepted only reluctantly as they took her away from the heart of the war and from her regiment in the field, Etheridge encountered other Civil War nurses who, like the soldiers she served, described her as noble, patient, caring, hearty, and fearless.

When the 5th Michigan mustered out of service in July 1865, Etheridge was there with them. "Noble Anna is with us to the last," wrote a soldier in the regiment who had known Etheridge throughout the war and who spoke of her only in words of the deepest reverence. Etheridge had hoped, upon mustering out, to write a personal account of her wartime experiences. Instead she spent the early years after the war working as a clerk in the United States Pension office. In 1870 she married Charles E. Hooks, a veteran of the 7th Connecticut Infantry. In 1886, the U.S. Congress passed a bill granting her a pension of $25 per month for her services to the army during the Civil War. Annie Etheridge died in 1913, having lived her final years in poverty. She was buried at Arlington National Cemetery.

—*Elizabeth D. Leonard*

See also Women.

For further reading:

Brockett, Linus P., and Mary C. Vaughan. *Woman's Work in the Civil War* (1867).

Crotty, Daniel G. *Four Years Campaigning in the Army of the Potomac* (1874).

Leonard, Elizabeth D. *All the Daring of the Soldier: Women of the Civil War Armies* (1999).

Moore, Frank. *Women of the War: Their Heroism and Self-Sacrifice* (1866).

Young, Agatha. *The Women and the Crisis: Women of the North in the Civil War* (1959).

EVANS, AUGUSTA JANE
(1835–1909)

Southern author and propagandist

Born on 8 May 1835 in Columbus, Georgia, Augusta Jane Evans was the daughter of Matthew Ryan Evans and Sarah Howard Evans. She enjoyed a luxurious lifestyle until her father's mercantile company went bankrupt when she was four years old. The family then moved to their country house across the Chattahoochee River in Russell County, Alabama. Suffering illnesses, Evans read voraciously in her home's library. In 1845, Matthew Evans's insurance company also failed, and he abandoned his efforts at cotton farming to relocate in Texas. While living in San Antonio, Evans became fascinated by the Alamo and historical research.

Fearful of Comanche attacks, Sarah Evans convinced her husband to return to Alabama, and the family settled in Mobile in 1849, where Matthew worked as a cotton broker and gained financial security. Augusta Evans was too ill to attend school, so she studied at home, acquiring intellectual insights into classic literature that she later incorporated into her fiction. Recurring themes of sick heroines sacrificing their art to support family or to nurse dying relatives also appear in Evans's work. In her sentimental, domestic stories, virtuous characters are rewarded and bad ones are punished unless they are redeemed by the heroines.

At age fifteen, Evans wrote a novel about the Alamo to earn money for her family. *Inez, A Tale of the Alamo* was published anonymously by Harper & Row in 1855. With a Jesuit priest cast as the villain, Evans's book was dismissed by Catholics and did not sell well. (Evans later worked with Catholic nuns during yellow fever epidemics in Mobile, and their expertise and kindness altered her negative opinions of Catholics.)

Evans traveled to New York City in 1859 to talk with J. C. Derby, a book publisher, who agreed to print Evans's second book, *Beulah* (1859). Selling more than 20,000 copies in one year, *Beulah* discussed religious faith versus intellectual reason. Evans based the book on her own religious crisis and imparted her belief that fiction should didactically reinforce morality. Now a successful novelist, she bought her family a house and elaborately landscaped the grounds. She also welcomed the attentions of New York journalist and book reviewer James Reed Spaulding but ultimately ended their romance because of sectional and ideological differences. During her New York trip, Evans had become acutely aware of varying attitudes concerning slavery. She penned unsigned essays for the *Mobile Daily Advertiser*, comparing Northern and Southern literature and declaring the latter superior. These editorials initiated Evans's reputation as a Southern propagandist.

When the Civil War began, Evans traveled in February 1861 to Montgomery, Alabama, where Henry W. Hilliard hosted a tea in her honor. Evans also corresponded with such Confederate leaders as Confederate congressman J. L. M. Curry and General P. G. T. Beauregard, who asked for her opinions and provided battle details for her fiction. She openly criticized the Confederacy for not utilizing women enough. Evans's

father and brothers enlisted and served briefly at Fort Morgan, and she organized women to sew 9,000 sandbags for embankments. Evans funded a soldiers' hospital near Mobile—soldiers named it Camp Beulah in honor of her book—and volunteered as a nurse. She visited camps such as General Braxton Bragg's post at Lookout Mountain, where she sang Confederate marching songs to soldiers.

Perhaps Evans's most significant contribution to the Civil War was her propagandistic novel *Macaria; or, Altars of Sacrifice* (1863). Evans wrote the book on wrapping paper while nursing soldiers at Fort Morgan and Camp Beulah, and she hoped to inspire women to volunteer for war duties. First printed by Richmond publishers West and Johnson, who used wallpaper for binding because of shortages, *Macaria* was smuggled through the blockade to Derby, who arranged for its distribution to the public and troops. Dedicated "To the Brave Soldiers of the Southern Army," the book presented virtuous, dignified characters who justified the Confederacy and warned about the dangers of emancipation. Defending the antebellum South as an idealized society, Evans penned sentimental scenes about men leaving for the front, women sewing clothes for troops, and slaves declaring their loyalty to their masters. Even as she glorified the Southern lifestyle, Evans suggested improvements to strengthen the Confederacy.

Combined with tributes to Confederate generals and leaders, Evans's prose proved to be effective propaganda. Considered a counter to Harriet Beecher Stowe's *Uncle Tom's Cabin*, Evans's book convinced many Northerners to become more empathetic toward the South. Union general George H. Thomas declared that Evans's book was dangerous contraband and banned it from his camp, ordering copies burned. *Macaria* became the most popular novel in the Confederacy, selling thousands of copies. A popular Confederate legend credited *Macaria* for stopping the bullet that would have killed a Southern soldier who carried a copy over his heart.

Evans continued to write propaganda for local periodicals. In "The Mutilation of the Hermae," she compared the North's devastation of the South to the destruction of sacred Athenian art. She criticized Southern writers who did not publicly support secession. Beauregard gave Evans his diamond-studded pen and a commendation for her Civil War service.

After the war, Evans raised money to reinter Mobile Civil War casualties in that city's Magnolia Cemetery. She wrote *St. Elmo* (1867), which sold a million copies within four months and gained her international acclaim. The first American woman to earn more than $100,000 from her writing, only *Ben-Hur* and *Uncle Tom's Cabin* outsold her in the nineteenth century. *St. Elmo* inspired namesakes ranging from towns, children, punch, cigars, and dogs. The story would be put on film and spoofed by a parody.

Evans married Lorenzo Madison Wilson in 1868 and completed a novel almost every decade: *Vashti; or, Until Death Us Do Part* (1869); *Infelice* (1875); *At the Mercy of Tiberius* (1887); *A Speckled Bird* (1902); and *Devota* (1907). Literary critics complained that Evans's novels relied on convoluted structures, unwieldy vocabularies, and stereotyped characters, but her work was significant for raising issues such as religion, marriage, and women's rights. An opponent of female suffrage, Evans believed women should develop their talents within the home. She died on 9 May 1909 and was buried in Mobile's Magnolia Cemetery. Her novels have been reprinted and are the subject of scholarly work about women writers and the Civil War.

—*Elizabeth D. Schafer*

See also Women.
For further reading:
Evans, Augusta J. *Beulah* (1992).
———. *Macaria; or, Altars of Sacrifice* (1992).
Fidler, William P. *Augusta Evans Wilson, 1835–1909: A Biography* (1951).
Sterkx, H.E. *Partners in Rebellion: Alabama Women in the Civil War* (1970).
Yelverton, Mildred. *They Also Served: Twenty-five Remarkable Alabama Women* (1993).

EVANS, CLEMENT ANSELM
(1833–1911)
Confederate general

Born in Stewart County, Georgia, the son of Anselm Lynch Evans and Sarah Hinton Bryan Evans, the younger Evans studied law in Augusta, Georgia, and was admitted to the Georgia bar in 1852, just shy of his nineteenth birthday. He immediately opened a practice in Lumpkin, Georgia, and became active in local Democratic politics.

Evans served as a county judge from 1854 to 1855 and was elected to the state Senate in 1859. In 1860 he was chosen a presidential elector for John Breckinridge.

Upon the secession of Georgia, Evans became interested in the military defense of the state. On 19 November 1861, he received a commission as major in the 31st Georgia Regiment of the Confederate Army. In April of the following year, he became the regiment's colonel in time to lead it in the Peninsular campaign. From its inception during that campaign through the surrender at Appomattox Court House, Evans served in the Army of Northern Virginia.

Evans temporarily gained a brigade command at Fredericksburg when Evan's brigade commander, Colonel E. N. Atkinson received a serious wound at the beginning of the battle, but was back in command of the 31st when the Army of Northern Virginia invaded Pennsylvania in June 1863. The 31st was a part of Brigadier General John B. Gordon's brigade in Jubal

Early's division of Richard Ewell's Corps. Upon Gordon's elevation to division commander, Evans assumed command of the brigade in May 1864 and was promoted to brigadier general the same month.

As a new brigadier general, Evans led his men north in the summer of 1864 as part of Jubal Early's Washington raid. He suffered a wound while leading his men in an attack on the Union left in the battle of Monocacy on 9 July, but returned to his command within two days to be a part of Early's move toward Washington.

Evans continued under Early in the latter's Shenandoah campaign in the fall of 1864, but returned east to Petersburg to assume command of Gordon's division upon Gordon's elevation to corps commander. Evans remained in command of the division until the end of the war and surrendered it at Appomattox.

Following the war, Evans entered the Methodist ministry, explaining that he had been inspired by the suffering he had seen in the war. He worked as a minister for 25 years before retiring in Atlanta in 1892. After retirement he spent much of his time writing military history and editing a twelve-volume work entitled *Confederate Military History*. He was also active in the United Confederate Veterans and died as that organization's commander in chief in Atlanta.

—*David S. Heidler and Jeanne T. Heidler*

See also Early's Washington Raid; Monocacy, Battle of; Shenandoah Valley Campaign (1864–1865).

For further reading:
Evans, Clement Anselm. *Intrepid Warrior: Clement Anselm Evans, Confederate General from Georgia; Life, Letters, and Diaries of the War Years* (1992).

EVANS, GEORGE HENRY
(1805–1856)
Labor activist

George Henry Evans was the most persistent leader of antebellum labor. Legions of workers followed his general course from what had been the new Jacksonian and Democratic politics of the 1820s to the new insurgency of the 1850s. Born in Herefordshire, England, on 24 March 1805, Evans went to upstate New York in 1820 with his widower father. With his brother (later Shaker Elder) Frederick William, George Henry learned printing at Ithaca and, in 1824, launched the iconoclastic *Museum and Independent Corrector*. At the behest of New York City "freethinkers"—critics of organized religion—he moved to the city to publish their *Correspondent*. The following year, disputes within the building trades drew Evans into a massive and united labor movement in the city.

During the 1820s, the elimination of the property requirement for voting in many states created not only an increasingly machine-based Democratic organization in the cities, but the first independent labor parties anywhere in the world. As editor of the *Workingman's Advocate* and the *Daily Sentinel,* Evans supported New York's Workingmen's Party from 1829 into 1832, but most of its constituency and leadership could not resist the Democratic rhetorical antimonopolist embrace of "the common man." From 1834 into 1837, local antimonopolists, often in conjunction with the General Trades' Union, constituted a coherent faction of the city's Democratic Party or as "Locofocos" in an independent Equal Rights Party. For part of this, Evans issued the *Man*, but sickness and business reversals forced him by 1835 to move to a farm along the Waycake Creek in Monmouth County, New Jersey. After the movement's collapse in the Panic of 1837, he continued to plan its resurrection, issuing a new periodical from his farm by 1841, *The Radical: Devoted to the Abolition of the Land Monopoly and Other Democratic Reforms.* By then, Evans's persistence, honesty, and strategic sense had made him once of the movement's most respected and admired spokesmen. While seemingly unoriginal, his "Agrarianism" understood that the values of home, family, personal autonomy, and economic security not only fostered competitive industry but structured a society that frustrated such aspirations for the majority and would inspire solutions aimed at benefiting all.

Evans returned to New York in 1844 to build the National Reform Association (NRA). He resurrected the *Workingman's Advocate* (which he later renamed *Young America*) and helped launch the *People's Rights.* The NRA initially demanded exemption of family farms from foreclosure for nonpayment of debt, a federal homestead act, and a legal limitation on individual land ownership. Partly in hopes of building a broad reform movement, the NRA quickly added the call for a ten-hour day and cooperatives, largely assimilating preexisting communitarian socialist currents. It also began addressing women's rights, slavery, urban poverty, and a broad range of social ills. By 1846, local coalitions with abolitionists appeared under the "Free Soil" rubric subsequently adopted by a broader national third-party movement; in 1847–1848, Evans and other leaders entered national politics in conjunction with the more intransigently abolitionist Liberty League. Health and money problems drove Evans back to his New Jersey farm in 1849, but he continued to urge a coalition politics in the interests of "free labor" until his death on 2 February 1856.

The influence of Evans's NRA on the sectional conflict was extensive, if subtle. Of its national officers, Alvan E. Bovay named the Republican Party and presided over its early meetings at Ripon. "Workie," Locofoco, and NRA leader John Commerford took the insurgent message into the Lower East Side of New York in an 1860 congressional campaign (and he later became one of the first Americans to correspond with Karl

Marx). Another, Benjamin F. Price, was killed in 1863 at the head of a New York volunteer company he had raised. Conversely, the wartime embrace of the Homestead Act, Greenbacks, Emancipation, and other reforms reflected the strength, scope, and complexity of the Unionist coalitions.

—*Mark A. Lause*

See also Free Soil Party; Greenbacks; Homestead Act; Labor; Republican Party.

For further reading:
Bradshaw, James S. "George Henry Evans." In *American Newspaper Journalists, 1690–1872* (1985).
Bronstein, Jamie. *Land Reform and Working-class Experience in Britain and the United States, 1800–1862* (1999).
Hugins, Walter. *Jacksonian Democracy and the Working Class* (1960).
Pessen, Edward. *Most Uncommon Jacksonians* (1970).
Wilentz, Sean. *Chants Democratic!: New York City and the Rise of the American Working Class, 1788–1850* (1984).
Zahler, Helene. *Eastern Workingmen and National Land Policy* (1941)

EVANS, NATHAN GEORGE
(1824–1868)
Confederate general

Born to Thomas Evans and Jane Beverly Daniel Evans in Marion, South Carolina, Nathan George Evans was educated at Randolph-Macon College before receiving an appointment in 1844 to the U.S. Military Academy. He graduated thirty-sixth of thirty-eight in the class of 1848. Probably while he was at West Point he received his lifelong nickname of "Shanks" because of his long, thin legs.

After graduation, Evans was commissioned into the 1st Dragoons. He later served in the 2d Dragoons and then the 2d Cavalry. He fought in a number of Indian conflicts on the frontier in the 1850s, primarily against the Comanches in Texas and the Indian Territory. He did not immediately resign his commission upon South Carolina's secession in December 1860 but did so in February 1861 to accept a major's commission in the Army of South Carolina and the position of adjutant general for that army.

In April 1861, Evans participated in the reduction of Fort Sumter before accepting a captain's commission in the Confederate cavalry. In July 1861 he was promoted to lieutenant colonel and commanded a brigade under P. G. T. Beauregard at Manassas Junction. In the battle of First Bull Run on 21 July, Evans and his brigade were positioned at the stone bridge, from where he discerned the Union movement around the Confederate flank. He met this maneuver, giving the Confederates time to shift enough forces to meet and ultimately repulse the Union attack. Shortly after the battle, Evans was promoted to colonel.

In the fall of 1861, he and his brigade were stationed at Leesburg, Virginia. From there on 21 October 1861 he met the Union attack at Ball's Bluff, forcing the Federal retreat. For his actions there he received the thanks of the Confederate Congress and a gold medal from South Carolina. Shortly thereafter, he was promoted to brigadier general with a date of rank of 21 October 1861.

After Ball's Bluff, Evans's brigade became an independent one that was frequently moved around to meet various military needs throughout the Confederacy. It soon became known as the "tramp brigade." Initially sent to South Carolina in December 1861, Evans was given command of the 3d Military District of South Carolina (later known as the 2d Military District). In April 1862 he skirmished with and repulsed Union forces at White Point, and then in May he led an expedition to John's Island. On 16 June 1862 he repulsed the Union attack on his defenses at Secessionville.

He remained in his command in South Carolina until July 1862, when he and his brigade were sent to the York peninsula in Pennsylvania to watch Union general George McClellan at Harrison's Landing while the Army of Northern Virginia moved north. He and his men skirmished with McClellan's forces in early August around Malvern Hill. Shortly afterward he moved north, and his brigade became a part of James Kemper's brigade in James Longstreet's corps in the battle of Second Bull Run.

In the Maryland campaign, Evans was placed in temporary command of a division and fought at South Mountain and Antietam. In November 1862, back in command of his independent brigade, Evans was sent to Weldon, North Carolina, to guard the railroad line there, and on 13 December he repulsed an attack by John Gray Foster at Kinston, North Carolina, but later was forced to retreat against Foster's superior force. After his retreat to Wilmington, North Carolina, Evans was accused of being intoxicated while on duty. He was acquitted of the charge and a later one of disobedience of orders, but he had lost the confidence of his commander, P. G. T. Beauregard.

Evans was on James Island, South Carolina, in June 1863 when he was sent to Mississippi, where his brigade was placed in the division of Major General William Wing Loring in Joseph E. Johnston's Department of the West. In July 1863 he participated in the unsuccessful defense of Jackson, Mississippi. In August, Evans and his brigade were sent back to the Southeast, where he assumed temporary command at Savannah, Georgia.

Beauregard still did not trust Evans in a field command and not until Beauregard moved to southern Virginia was Evans given any responsibility. In the spring of 1864, Evans received command of the 1st Military District of South Carolina, headquartered at Mount Pleasant. Unfortunately for Evans, he suffered a serious injury in a riding accident shortly after taking his new command and was forced to go on an extended leave. He was unable to return to command until the following spring, shortly before the capture of Jefferson Davis as the ex-Confederate president fled through Georgia. Evans had traveled with the Davis party during its flight through South Carolina.

After the war, Evans moved to Alabama, where he accepted a principal's job in a Bullock County high school. He remained in that position until his death in Midway, Alabama, on 30 November 1868.

—*David S. Heidler and Jeanne T. Heidler*

See also Ball's Bluff, Battle of; Bull Run, First Battle of; Secessionville.

For further reading:
Evans, Beverly Daniel IV. "Nathan George Evans, Brigadier-General, C.S.A" (Thesis, 1941).

EVERETT, EDWARD
(1794–1865)
Union statesman and orator

One of the most famous political rhetoricians in the first half of the nineteenth century, Edward Everett was an ordained minister as well as a Harvard University professor and an editor of the *North American Review* before he was elected to Congress in 1824. From this time on, Everett used the rhetorical skills and the profound knowledge he had developed and accumulated at Harvard and Goettingen, Germany, to become one of the foremost political orators of his day. As a congressman (1825–1835), governor of Massachusetts (1835–1839), U.S. minister to Britain (1841–1845), president of Harvard University (to 1849), and briefly as secretary of state in Millard Fillmore's administration, he always favored a traditional form of unionism, which he saw threatened by nullification as well as by abolitionism. Elected to the Senate in 1852 to counterbalance the radical abolitionist Charles Sumner, he resigned in 1854 over the Kansas-Nebraska Act. In the 1860 presidential election, the Constitutional Union Party ticket included Everett as John Bell's running mate. The Constitutional Union Party stood for a return to the politics of compromise. This third-party candidacy carried only Virginia, Kentucky, and Tennessee. When Abraham Lincoln was elected, the ensuing tumult ushered in the secession winter of 1860–1861.

On the whole, Everett's prewar oratory is best described as a somewhat quixotic effort to transfer the axiomatic principles of unionism into common knowledge or, rather, into a common credo. Well aware of the impact political oratory could have on the masses, Everett did not rely on arousing sentiment. His method appears to have been to achieve a cumulative effect through repetition, and with this to make the principle

Edward Everett (*Library of Congress*)

of union part of the mental history of the American public. As late as 1860, Everett gave an oration with the programmatic title "Success of Our Republic," stressing the advantages of the Federal Union and, in the true tradition of the American Jeremiad, praising the glorious past, deploring the sad state of affairs at the time of the oration, yet foreordaining a return to glory if only the principles that had governed the past were more stringently adhered to.

If Everett's oratory up to 1861 had been predominantly epideictic and celebratory, with particular focus on the Fourth of July "to strengthen the sentiment of attachment to the Union," he took a different stand when the Union was not only threatened but actually breaking apart. In the summer of 1861, even Everett saw that the time for conciliatory rhetoric was over. Ironically, the one Fourth-of-July oration that he devoted to "The Questions of the Day" was also his most effective and successful. Now that the war proved his efforts at reconciliation futile, Everett showed that his oratory could be persuasive and argumentative. "The Questions of the Day" speech was given in New York, and its very title signals the methodological shift. This is not to imply that he deviated from the one principle to which he had devoted his life, that of preserving the Union. Using historical data as evidence, Everett argued that, contrary to Southern claims, secession was unconstitutional and the eleven seceded Southern states were therefore in a state of rebellion.

This was indeed the question of the day. The North wanted to avoid a situation in which the rebelling Confederate states could characterize themselves in a manner similar to the thirteen colonies that broke away from the British colonial empire in the American Revolution. If they could portray themselves in the role of an oppressed people overthrowing an unjust regime, the North would be forced into the role of the British king as depicted in the Declaration of Independence. The effect on public opinion could be disastrous. Some Southern orators tried to employ just this tactic in their Fourth-of-July orations.

As it was, Everett's rhetoric proved convincing and successful. His New York oration was repeated and distributed in pamphlet form throughout the Union and the border states, especially in Missouri. Even though the oration itself (his longest on a Fourth of July, totalling forty-two pages) offers no spectacular vision but a rather dull legal argument as to why secession was unconstitutional and illegal, some undecided politicians and wavering anti-Lincoln Unionists may in fact have joined the Union cause due to the convincing power of Everett's argumentation.

If this part of Edward Everett's pro-Union struggle usually receives little attention in popular historiography, he is at least remembered in connection with Abraham Lincoln's "Gettysburg Address." On the occasion of the dedication of the Gettysburg National Cemetery on 19 November 1863, Everett was the featured speaker. His official oration lasted for two hours. It was followed by Lincoln's very brief address. The famous orator from Massachusetts immediately grasped the greatness of Lincoln's masterful speech, and he congratulated the president on it. Lincoln's "Gettysburg Address" signalled a development in political rhetoric away from the elaborate, metaphorical, and sometimes flowery style, ornamental and full of digressions, that had characterized the first half of the nineteenth century, and much of Edward Everett's career as a public orator.

Everett's last public speech was a regular stump oration on behalf of Lincoln during the election campaign of 1864. It was his only oration of this kind outside his own campaigns, and it shows the mark of the new, lean, and more aggressive style of political rhetoric that was about to develop. "The Duty of Supporting the Government" was again published as a pamphlet and widely distributed. Everett lived to see Lincoln reelected and the Union well on the way to winning the Civil War, but he died on 15 January 1865 shortly before the cessation of hostilities.

—Wolfgang Hochbruck

For further reading:
Everett, Edward. *Orations and Speeches on Various Occasions* (1868).
Frothingham, Paul Revere. *Edward Everett* (1925).
Hochbruck, Wofgang. "Edward Everett's Union Rhetoric." In *The Fourth of July. Political Oratory and Literary Reactions 1776–1876*. Edited by Paul Goetsch and Gerd Hurm (1992).
Reid, Ronald. "Edward Everett." In *American Orators before 1900*. Edited by Bernard K. Duffy and Halford R. Ryan (1986).
———. "Edward Everett: Rhetorician of Nationalism, 1824–1855." *Quarterly Journal of Speech* (1956).

EWELL, RICHARD STODDERT
(1817–1872)
Confederate general

Richard Stoddert Ewell was born in Washington, D.C., on 6 February 1817, and was raised in Prince William County, Virginia. His grandfather was Benjamin Stoddert, the first secretary of the navy under President John Adams. Ewell gained admittance to West Point in 1836 and four years later he graduated thirteenth out of forty-two cadets. Commissioned a second lieutenant in the 1st U. S. Dragoons, his career became closely associated with this famous unit over the next two decades.

In time, Ewell gained the reputation of a fine combat officer whose skills were honed in the course of wide-ranging frontier service. In 1843–1845 he conducted escort duty along the Santa Fe and Oregon trails under the aegis of veteran explorers Philip St. George Cooke and Stephen Watts Kearny, winning their commendation. Ewell also performed well during the War with Mexico 1846–1848, and landed at Vera Cruz as part of General Winfield Scott's army. In August 1847, he was conspicuously engaged in the battles of Contreras and Churabusco, receiving brevet promotion to captain. He also conducted a nighttime reconnaissance of the Pedregal with Captain Robert E. Lee of the engineers, and came off favorably impressed with this little-known engineering officer.

After the war, Ewell resumed his frontier activities, and between 1855 and 1857 he further distinguished himself by battling the Apache under Cochise. He also found time to explore the newly acquired Gadsen Purchase with Colonel Benjamin Bonneville, and he was wounded in a skirmish in 1857. Ewell had assumed command of Fort Buchanan, Arizona, in 1860, when illness forced him back to Virginia to recuperate. Though Unionist in outlook, he resigned his commission when his home state seceded in April 1861, and gained appointment as colonel in the Confederate army.

Ewell initially served with troops stationed along the Virginia border, and in June 1861 he became one of the first command-grade Southern officers to be wounded in a skirmish at Fairfax Court House. Shortly after, he was

elevated to brigadier general in the army of General Pierre G. T. Beauregard. Ewell was present at Bull Run in July 1861, but conflicting orders issued by Beauregard kept him out of combat. Nonetheless, his reputation as a fine officer held him in good stead when promotion to major general arrived in February 1862.

A turning point in Ewell's military fortunes occurred that spring when he was assigned to the Shenandoah Valley under General Thomas J. "Stonewall" Jackson. The two men made a curious contrast in styles. Both were regarded as somewhat quixotic in their personal behavior: Ewell was witty and infamously profane, while Jackson was stern and pious. Their leadership qualities also seemed at cross purposes. Whereas Jackson was flexible and brilliantly intuitive on the battlefield, Ewell, though brave and effective, required precise instructions to function effectively. However, this seemingly incongruous pair made an unbeatable combination throughout the ensuing Shenandoah campaign.

In May 1862, Jackson and Ewell advanced down the Shenandoah Valley, winning battles at Front Royal and Winchester against General Nathaniel Banks. Clever maneuvering by both men then evaded larger forces under General John Charles Frémont and James Shields. On 8 June 1862, the Confederates brought Frémont to battle at Cross Keys and thrashed him soundly. The following day at Port Republic, Ewell was closely engaged by sighting a field piece and participating in the final, victorious charge. Through dint of all these successful actions he established himself as one of the key Confederate divisional leaders of the Eastern theater.

Having secured the valley, Jackson next hastily repaired to the peninsula, where Lee dueled with George B. McClellan for possession of Richmond. Ewell again fought conspicuously in actions at Gaines' Mill and Malvern Hill and, the following July, he defeated Banks again at Cedar Mountain on 9 August 1862. However, during the Second Bull Run campaign, Ewell was wounded at Groveton and lost his right leg below the knee. After several months of recuperation and adjustment to a wooden leg, he rejoined the army as the Chancellorsville campaign concluded.

In May 1863, the Army of Northern Virginia under General Robert E. Lee scored its biggest tactical victory by partly routing a larger Union force under General Joseph Hooker. However, after Jackson was mortally wounded by his own men, he suggested Ewell to replace him. Promoted lieutenant general, he took command of the legendary II Corps in preparation for offensive operations in Pennsylvania. Ewell then returned to the valley and scored brilliantly at Winchester in June 1863, capturing a Union garrison of 4,000 men and twenty-three cannon. As events unfolded, unfortunately, Ewell displayed difficulty maneuvering larger numbers of men,

a liability manifesting fatal results at Gettysburg. In all fairness, Ewell proved himself a brave and worthy successor to Jackson but, in terms of decisive results, "Old Bald Head" was no "Stonewall."

Ewell was preparing to attack Harrisburg when an urgent dispatch from Lee directed him to the vicinity of Gettysburg. Ewell pushed his men hard and arrived on 1 July 1863, to assist the hard-pressed troops of General Ambrose P. Hill. The Confederate tide surged around the defenders, took the town, and chased O. O. Howard's Union forces up the nearby heights. However, at this critical juncture, Ewell's usually sound military judgment deserted him. Granted discretionary powers by Lee to attack as he saw fit, Ewell declined to assail the rapidly consolidating Union positions on Cemetery Hill to his front. He cited troop fatigue, disorganization, and the lateness of the day as grounds for not attacking. In this decision he was seconded by Jubal A. Early, his talented and aggressive subordinate. The majority of historians have also since concurred that Ewell's reasoning was sound. This hesitancy proved singularly unfortunate, for Cemetery Hill and nearby Cemetery Ridge were essential to Union defense positions over the next two days of combat. Had they been in Confederate possession, the battle may have been materially alerted in favor of the South. As events turned out, all of Ewell's subsequent attacks on 2–3 July, were bloodily repulsed and he fell back in good order with the rest of the army.

In May 1864, Ewell reverted back to usual form by rendering sterling service at the battle of the Wilderness. Soon after he commanded the Muleshoe Salient at Spotsylvania and initially repulsed several determined Union attacks. But Lee, anticipating that General Ulysses S. Grant would side-step Confederate positions again, ordered most of Ewell's artillery support withdrawn. Hours later, Grant surprised the defenders by attacking in even greater force on 12 May 1864, and succeeded in capturing most of Ewell's position and almost half his division. Ewell was badly injured by a fall from his horse and required several weeks of recuperation. Upon returning, he lobbied for his old command, which had since reverted to Jubal A. Early. Lee, cognizant of Ewell's poor health, subsequently entrusted him with the defense of Richmond. This he commanded effectively, thwarting several Union attempts at capture. However, when Lee abandoned the Confederate capital in April 1865, Ewell tried marching west to join him at Appomattox. Prompt action by General Philip H. Sheridan quickly snared Ewell's entire command at Sayler's Creek and he surrendered there on 6 April 1865.

After the war, Ewell was briefly interned at Fort Sewall, Massachusetts, before being released. He settled on his wife's plantation in Tennessee and lived quietly as a country gentleman for the remainder of his life. Both

Ewell and his wife died of pneumonia within hours of each other in January 1872.

—*John C. Fredriksen*

See also Gettysburg, Battle of; Groveton, Battle of; Sayler's Creek, Battle of; Shenandoah Valley Campaign; Winchester, Second Battle of.

For further reading:
Gallagher, Gary W., ed. *The First Day at Gettysburg: Essays in Confederate and Union Leadership* (1992).
Martin, Samuel J. *The Road to Glory: Confederate General Richard S. Ewell* (1991).
Pfanz, Donald C. *Richard S. Ewell: A Soldier's Life* (1998).

EWING, HUGH BOYLE
(1826–1905)
Union general

Born to Thomas Ewing and Maria Wills Boyle Ewing in Lancaster, Ohio, Hugh Boyle Ewing was educated locally before receiving an appointment to the U.S. Military Academy in 1844. He failed to graduate because of difficulties with his engineering courses, leaving the academy just before his class graduated in 1848. Shortly after leaving West Point, Ewing went to California in search of his fortune in the gold fields there. He failed to get rich, but he remained in California for several years, returning east in 1852. Upon his return, he studied law and began a practice in St. Louis and then in Kansas. He worked with his brother, Thomas Ewing, Jr., and his brother-in-law, William Tecumseh Sherman, who had been raised as Ewing's foster brother after the death of Sherman's father. In 1858, Ewing moved back to Ohio, where he later accepted, at the outbreak of the Civil War, a position as an assistant to Governor William Denison.

The governor made Ewing an inspector of state volunteers, but Ewing remained in the position only a short time before moving to the staff of General George B. McClellan. During the summer of 1861, Ewing served under McClellan in western Virginia and then, when McClellan was called east, under William S. Rosecrans. In August, Ewing was named colonel of the 30th Ohio volunteers. He commanded his regiment at Carnifex Ferry on 10 September 1861.

The following summer, Ewing and the 30th became a part of the Army of the Potomac. He saw his first action with that force at South Mountain and was commended by his brigade commander, Colonel Eliakim P. Scammon, for his actions in the assault on the highest point of the Confederate defenses. That evening he was given command of a brigade in Ambrose Burnside's IX Corps. In the battle of Antietam, Ewing and his brigade occupied the left of the corps and hence of the Army of the Potomac. After the battle he was lauded by Burnside for his adept handling of his brigade late in the day in preventing the Confederates from bringing about the collapse of the Union flank.

In recognition for his actions at South Mountain and Antietam, Ewing was promoted to brigadier general in November 1862. Shortly thereafter he was transferred to the command of Ulysses S. Grant in Memphis. Upon arrival he was given command of a brigade in his brother-in-law Sherman's XV Corps. He commanded his brigade during the Steele's Bayou Expedition in March 1863 as part of the Vicksburg campaign, and then in early May he garrisoned Milliken's Bend. He was in the thick of action during the final assaults against Vicksburg, after which he was given command of a division on 20 July 1863.

During the siege of Vicksburg Ewing had gained a reputation as a no-nonsense commander who would neither tolerate breaches in discipline nor the presence of the riffraff that flocked to the army camps during the siege. He cleaned up his camp and banned civilian merchants. After the siege, he attempted to maintain these restrictions in all of his future commands.

In command of XV Corps' 4th Division during the Chattanooga campaign, Ewing took the lead with his division in Sherman's attack on Missionary Ridge in November 1863. After the success of Union actions in defense of Chattanooga, Ewing and his division were charged with protecting the railroad between Scottsboro and Stevenson, Alabama. He remained in northern Alabama until being given the command of Louisville, Kentucky, at the end of February 1864.

In Kentucky, Ewing was charged with protecting the vital railroads of the state from the likes of John Hunt Morgan and other Confederate raiders. As a result, he shifted his command frequently from place to place, maintaining headquarters at Louisville and Munfordville. He remained in command there until February 1865, when he was sent to North Carolina to once again serve under the command of Sherman. At the very end of the war, he was about to participate in an expedition along the Roanoke River when Confederate general Joseph E. Johnston surrendered his entire army.

At the end of the war, Ewing received a brevet promotion to major general of volunteers. He remained in the army until he was mustered out with the volunteers in 1866. Immediately after leaving the army he was appointed U.S. minister to the Netherlands, a position he held until 1870. In 1870 he opened a law practice in Washington, D.C., before retiring to a farm in Ohio in 1874. He wrote extensively in retirement and died on his farm on 30 June 1905.

—*David S. Heidler and Jeanne T. Heidler*

See also Chattanooga Campaign; Vicksburg Campaign.
For further reading:
Arnold, James R. *Grant Wins the War: Decision at Vicksburg* (1997).
Marszalek, John F. *Sherman: A Soldier's Passion for Order* (1994).

EWING, THOMAS, JR.
(1829–1896)
Union general

Born to Thomas Ewing and Maria Wills Boyle Ewing in Lancaster, Ohio, Thomas Ewing, Jr. was educated locally along with his brothers Charles and Hugh and his foster brother William Tecumseh Sherman, all future Union generals. While his father served as secretary of the interior under Zachary Taylor, Thomas Ewing, Jr., was brought to Washington to serve as a secretary to the president. After leaving government service, Ewing attended Brown University and then studied law in Ohio. After practicing for a while in Cincinnati, Ewing moved to Kansas, where he entered a firm with his brother Hugh Boyle Ewing and Sherman, who by that time had become his brother-in-law.

In Kansas in the late 1850s, Ewing became very active in the political efforts to make Kansas a free state. He fought against the implementation of the Lecompton Constitution. When Kansas was admitted to the Union as a free state in 1861, Ewing became the new state supreme court's chief justice at the age of thirty-two. He remained on the bench only one year, however, resigning in 1862 to raise a regiment for Federal service. In September 1862 he was commissioned the colonel of the 11th Kansas volunteers.

On 28 November 1862, Ewing and his regiment in Francis Jay Herron's division of the Army of the Frontier saw their first major action at Cane Hill, Arkansas, when they participated in the defeat of the Confederate forces there. A little over a week later, on 7 December, Ewing led his men at the battle of Prairie Grove, Arkansas. For his actions in these engagements, Ewing was promoted to brigadier general of volunteers in March 1863. Given command of a division of the Army of the Frontier, Ewing operated out of Fort Scott, Kansas, against the various guerrilla and outlaw bands in the area. In June he was placed in command of the District of the Border, with headquarters in Kansas City.

In his new command, Ewing had the unenviable task of distinguishing between friend and foe in the very unsettled area of western Missouri and eastern Kansas. After fighting a guerrilla band at Sibley, Missouri, on 23 June and afterwards destroying the town to prevent it from being used as a refuge for other bands, Ewing attempted to be more systematic in dealing with the various guerrilla bands. He had relatively little luck, however, against the likes of William Quantrill during the outlaw's raid into Kansas in August 1863. In response to Quantrill's sacking of Lawrence, Kansas, and the murder of dozens of citizens there, Ewing issued Order No. 11 ordering the evacuation of all inhabitants from Jackson, Cass, Vernon, and Bates Counties, Missouri. It was believed that many of Quantrill's men lived in those counties, and Ewing was attempting to remove any possible refuge the outlaws might have among family and friends.

In September and October 1863, Ewing attempted to deal with a raid conducted by more regular forces commanded by Joseph Shelby. For the most part, however, he was occupied with the numerous irregular forces for the remainder of the year and during the early weeks of 1864. In March 1864, Ewing was given command of the District of St. Louis. One of his tasks through the summer of 1864 was to recruit African-American soldiers from Missouri for the Union's western armies.

Although the irregular forces in that part of the state were less numerous, Ewing found himself faced with a far more dangerous threat in September 1864 when Sterling Price invaded the state. Ewing took a considerable force out from St. Louis to prevent Price from threatening the city. At Pilot Knob the two forces met on 27 September. Initially, Ewing was in the very defensible work known as Fort Davidson. However, very soon Price was able to place his artillery on ground overlooking the fort, forcing Ewing to evacuate and retreat. With Price's superior force in pursuit, Ewing pushed his men to their limits until he found another defensible piece of ground near Harrison, Missouri. He was able to hold out there until being reinforced by Alfred Pleasonton. St. Louis had been saved, and Price turned to the western part of the state.

Ewing remained in command at St. Louis until November 1864, when he was given command of the District of Rolla, Missouri. He remained there until the end of the year, when he returned to St. Louis. In January 1865 he requested and was granted a leave of absence to visit Washington, D.C. While there, on 23 February, he resigned his commission. Shortly after his resignation, Ewing received a brevet promotion to major general of volunteers.

Ewing remained in Washington for several years, engaging in private law practice. During the next two years, at the height of President Andrew Johnson's difficulties with Congress, the president offered and Ewing declined the cabinet posts of secretary of war and attorney general. In 1870 he decided to return to Ohio, where he became quite active in state Democratic politics, associating himself especially with the Greenbackers in the party. He was elected to Congress on that issue in 1876 and served two terms, declining to run for a third. In his later years, Ewing practiced law in New York City, where he died on 21 January 1896.

—David S. Heidler and Jeanne T. Heidler

See also Kansas; Missouri; Pilot Knob; Price's Missouri Raid.
For further reading:
Marszalek, John F. *Sherman: A Soldier's Passion for Order* (1994).
Parrish, William E. *Turbulent Partnership: Missouri and the Union, 1861–1865* (1963).

EX PARTE MERRYMAN
(17 F. CAS. 144) (NO. 9487)
(1861)

Concern about secessionist activity around the nation's capital prompted President Abraham Lincoln to suspend the writ of habeas corpus on 27 April 1861. The area to which this initial suspension applied was limited to the region between Washington, D.C., and Philadelphia. Under the terms of this unprecedented suspension, arbitrary military arrests were authorized and detention without indictment or judicial process of arraignment could be indefinite.

On 25 May 1861 military authorities arrested a vocal secessionist named John Merryman in Cockeysville, Maryland. Merryman had compounded suspicion about his loyalty to the Union by serving as an officer in a pro-secessionist militia company. Jailed in Fort McHenry, he quickly sought release with a petition for a writ of habeas corpus directed to the Federal circuit court. The judge happened to be Chief Justice Roger Taney, who was riding his circuit, and from that coincidence the *Merryman* case attracted considerable attention. Coming at the outset of the rebellion, the *Merryman* case also had the potential to resolve at a crucial time the dominance of civil over military authority during a national crisis. Such a result was one of the reasons the Lincoln administration handled the matter as it did.

Sympathetic to Merryman's entreaty, Taney accordingly issued the writ, demanding that Merryman either be placed under terms of judicial due process or released from custody. The commanding officer of the department, General George Cadwalader, refused to honor the writ, although his reply to the chief justice was far from dismissive. In a respectful response, Cadwalader explained the circumstances of and reasons for Merryman's arrest, concluding with the information that the president's authority in suspending the writ justified the military's actions. Taney retorted by ordering Cadwalader to appear before the federal court, but the U.S. marshal dispatched to serve the order was barred from Fort McHenry.

Frustrated by such recalcitrance and aware of the significant constitutional issue the controversy portended, Taney resorted to the only device remaining to him. He wrote a blistering opinion under the auspices of the circuit court that directed the record of the entire affair be sent to Lincoln and instructed the president to "take care that the laws be faithfully executed." Taney denounced Merryman's arrest and continued detention because he insisted that charges of treason were a matter for the civil courts. Only Congress, said the chief justice, could suspend the writ of habeas corpus.

Because Taney happened to be the chief justice, confusion has surrounded this opinion, depicting it as a pronouncement of the Supreme Court. Yet officially Taney only had the opportunity to act on the matter because he was the justice designated to ride the circuit for this particular federal district. Taney issued his statement, however, from his position as a Supreme Court justice, and thus its substance indicated a possible direction the high court would take in ruling on arbitrary arrests. In the Merryman matter, Lincoln essentially ignored Taney's instructions, and he never communicated a direct response to the chief justice's conclusions. The president did use his annual message to Congress to address obliquely the issue of who could suspend the writ of habeas corpus. Lincoln insisted that common sense required that special powers be given to the executive branch in times of special emergencies. Otherwise, he observed, the inviolability of one law could allow the subversion of all other laws. It was not a very compelling explanation, and evidence suggests that Lincoln himself was not altogether comfortable with its implications.

The military soon remanded Merryman to the civil authorities, but his indictment for treason at their hands was more a display than a serious prosecution, and charges against him were eventually dropped two years after the war had ended. During the Civil War, however, the issue of civil and military authority remained a source of considerable concern because the *Merryman* case had resolved nothing. As late as 1863, the administration was worried that the Supreme Court would declare arbitrary arrests illegal, a decision that some in the cabinet believed would so hobble the executive that it would rival the consequences of the worst military defeat.

—*David S. Heidler and Jeanne T. Heidler*

See also Ex parte Milligan; Habeas Corpus, Writ of (U.S.A.); Merryman, John; Supreme Court, U.S.; Taney, Roger Brooke.

For further reading:
Anderson, Eric Paul. "The Body of John Merryman: *Ex Parte Merryman*, A Case of Executive-Judicial Conflict Over the Suspension of Habeas Corpus" (Master's thesis, 1979).
Lewis, Walker. *Without Fear or Favor: A Biography of Chief Justice Roger Brooke Taney* (1965).
Lively, Donald E. *Foreshadows of the Law: Supreme Court Dissents and Constitutional Development* (1992).
Neely, Mark E., Jr. *The Fate of Liberty: Abraham Lincoln and Civil Liberties* (1991).
Randall, James G. *Constitutional Problems under Lincoln* (1951).
Siegel, Martin. *The United States Supreme Court: Volume 3, The Taney Court, 1836–1864* (1995).
Swisher, Carl B. *History of the Supreme Court of the United States: The Taney Period, 1836–1864* (1974).

EX PARTE MILLIGAN
(4 WALL. 2, 18 L. ED. 281)
(1866)

Congress authorized the president to suspend the writ of habeas corpus by the law of 3 March 1861, but that statute had also instructed that federal courts would release any prisoner who had not been

indicted by a duly empaneled grand jury. It was under this provision that the case of Lambdin P. Milligan came to the attention of first the Federal Circuit Court for the District of Indiana and subsequently, in 1866, the United States Supreme Court.

Milligan was a prosperous attorney in Indiana, who had been admitted in 1835 to the Ohio bar in Belmont County, ironically with Edwin M. Stanton. Though plagued with chronic illness—some sources claim it was meningitis—Milligan ran a successful law practice representing minor railroad lines in Indiana. An ardent Democrat, by the outbreak of the Civil War, he had become a Southern zealot and consequently was justifiably branded a Copperhead by watchful Federal authorities.

Because he vocally opposed the prowar stance of Governor Oliver P. Morton and frequently spoke out against the Lincoln administration, Federal agents kept him under surveillance. By late 1863, they were convinced that Milligan was involved in an extensive conspiracy spreading throughout the Northwest. In October, Milligan met covertly with other Indiana Copperheads, including William A. Bowles, Andrew Humphreys, and Stephen Horsey, allegedly to revive the secret society known as the Knights of the Golden Circle. Federal agents thought the extensive plan's seriousness was indicated by the involvement of Copperheads from Kentucky and Missouri. A May 1864 meeting of these people in Indianapolis revealed this shadowy but tangible conspiracy as far advanced, for Milligan and Bowles soon were in communication with Confederate operatives, advising them of plans and asking for assistance.

On 5 October 1864, General Alvin P. Hovey had Milligan arrested and by 21 October a military commission in Indianapolis had found him and two other Copperheads guilty of treason. They were sentenced to death, and Milligan's hanging was scheduled for 19 May 1865 as a matter of military necessity. Clearly, the speed of the tribunal and the harshness of its sentence were born of fears about the extent of the so-called Northwestern Conspiracy, but that did not preclude that a grand jury was called after Milligan was sentenced and adjourned without indicting him. Accordingly, Milligan petitioned the Federal Circuit Court for Indiana, asking for his release from what he described, with some legal accuracy, as unlawful incarceration.

By then the war had ended, and President Andrew Johnson changed Milligan's sentence to life imprisonment, so the issues of the Copperhead's case would not be made irrelevant by his execution. The circuit court could not reach a determination on the matter, so the court referred it to the United States Supreme Court, which heard arguments in March 1866. The contention was one of procedure, for there was no doubt of Milligan's guilt. Instead, the question was whether the government could authorize arbitrary arrests and deny due process in an area where civil courts were operating.

A talented team of lawyers consisting of James A. Garfield, Jeremiah S. Black, Joseph E. McDonald, and David Dudley Field represented Milligan. The government's advocates were James Speed, Henry Stanbery, and Benjamin F. Butler. Milligan's attorneys made lengthy presentations that illustrated how the military commission had conducted proceedings when no Confederate threat was present in Indiana. Furthermore, Milligan's execution, allegedly justified by military necessity, was scheduled for a day when any military necessity had clearly evaporated because of the war's end. Garfield also bolstered Milligan's case with precedents from eighteenth-century English jurisprudence. These included an unsuccessful challenge of civil authority by the Royal Navy and the execution of a royal governor for ordering without due process the killing of an army private suspected of inciting to mutiny.

Ultimately, the Court was persuaded. David Davis delivered the unanimous opinion that Milligan had been illegally tried by the military because the army had no jurisdiction in an area where the civil courts were functioning. "It is difficult to see how the safety of the country required martial law in Indiana," noted Davis. "If any of her citizens were plotting treason, the power of arrest could secure them, until the government was prepared for their trial, when the courts were open and ready to try them." Furthermore, Davis drew a sharp distinction between the suspension of the privilege of the writ of habeas corpus and the constancy of the writ itself as an inviolable legal sanction. In the latter, only the courts could decide if an individual had no right to petition under the writ's protections.

Chief Justice Salmon P. Chase joined Noah H. Swayne, Samuel F. Miller, and James M. Wayne to issue a concurring decision that demurred from the assertion that the military commission in Indiana not only was unauthorized by Congress, but also that Congress had no authority to empower such a commission in any case. Chase noted that such a doctrine could lead to the conclusion that Congress also had no power to protect officers serving on such commissions from litigation in the civil courts. (When Milligan was released after the Supreme Court ruling, he sued Hovey for damages and won a nominal judgment.) These justices also concluded that, while Congress had the power to accredit such commissions, it had not authorized the one that had tried and convicted Lambdin Milligan.

While the court's decision in the Milligan case has been hailed as a significant buttress of civil liberties, political partisans at the time either lauded or deplored it. The decision came as the advocates for Congressional Reconstruction began girding for the attack

against Andrew Johnson's executive preemption of Reconstruction policy. As the enforcement of Congressional Reconstruction relied heavily on the military, the implications of the *Milligan* decision seemed a potentially crippling blow. Yet Congress's ascendancy and the resolve of Republicans in that body to protect the rights of the freedmen persuaded the Court to retreat from the forthright insistence on civil liberties in subsequent decisions during the period. Some scholars have insisted that such a circumstance does not detract from the momentousness of the decision. They argue that it plainly answered a question that had remained unresolved during the crisis of the Civil War by demonstrating for future generations that, except in the most desperate emergencies that menace domestic safety, civil courts operating under a system of due process will protect civil liberties. Others are not so certain, however, and point to evidence that whenever domestic security has clashed with civil liberty, the government has consistently promoted the former at the expense of the latter, with the blessing of the judicial branch. In that sense, the pertinence of the *Milligan* decision is considerably diminished to make it more a symbolic ideal than an applied rule dictating governmental restraint.

—*David S. Heidler and Jeanne T. Heidler*

See also Civil Liberties, U.S.A.; Copperheads; Habeas Corpus, Writ of (U.S.A.); Knights of the Golden Circle; Milligan, Lambdin P.; Order of American Knights; Supreme Court, U.S.

For further reading:

Klaus, Samuel, ed. *The Milligan Case* (1929; reprint, 1970).
Klement, Frank L. *Dark Lanterns: Secret Political Societies, Conspiracies, and Treason Trials in the Civil War* (1984).
———. *Lincoln's Critics: The Copperheads of the North* (1999).
Neely, Mark E., Jr. *The Fate of Liberty: Abraham Lincoln and Civil Liberties* (1991).
Randall, James G. *Constitutional Problems under Lincoln* (1951).
Siegel, Martin. *The United States Supreme Court: Volume 3, The Taney Court, 1836–1864* (1995).
Swisher, Carl B. *History of the Supreme Court of the United States: The Taney Period, 1836–1864* (1974).

EZRA CHURCH, BATTLE OF
(28 July 1864)

Ezra Church, a Methodist meeting house located at a road junction about three miles west of Atlanta, was the site of the third and final Confederate offensive thrust during the battle for Atlanta.

On 18 July 1864, Confederate general John Bell Hood assumed command of the Army of Tennessee; he replaced General Joseph E. Johnston. Hood immediately attempted to crush the Union forces under the command of Major General William T. Sherman at the battles of Peachtree Creek on 20 July and later Bald Hill (also called the battle of Atlanta) on 22 July. These attempts, however, ended in Confederate defeats.

In an effort to cut Atlanta's rail supply lines from Alabama, Sherman ordered his command to shift from positions east of Atlanta to an area west and slightly south of the city. A few miles southwest of Atlanta, the Macon & Western Railroad joined the Atlanta & West Point Railroad at a small town called East Point, Georgia. These were the only rail lines supplying the needs of the besieged Atlanta. Between 25 and 27 July, the Union Army of the Tennessee, commanded by Major General Oliver O. Howard, marched from the Union left flank to the Union right. Upon reaching the right flank of the Union position on 28 July, Howard turned due south toward the railroad junction at East Point. To check this move General Hood ordered his old corps, now commanded by Lieutenant General Stephen D. Lee, to march west and occupy a position from which to block Howard's extension of the Union right. Another Confederate corps, under the command of Lieutenant General Alexander P. Stewart, followed a mile behind Stephen Lee's corps. Hood planned to stop the Union advance with Lee's corps and circle the head of the stalled Federal column and strike Howard's unguarded outer flank with Stewart's corps.

On the afternoon of 28 July, Stephen Lee's corps attacked Howard near Ezra Church. From the start, things did not go according to Confederate plans. Instead of hitting the Union forces on their exposed flank, the rebels ran up against the front of Major General John A. Logan's XV Corps of Howard's Army of the Tennessee, which, in anticipation of the Confederate attack, formed a barricaded line at a right angle to the rest of Howard's forces.

Without informing Hood of the change in the situation, nor waiting until Stewart's men were in place on his left, or his own corps fully in place, Stephen Lee attacked the Union lines one division at a time. The Federals quickly fortified their lines with fence rails, logs, and pews taken out of the Ezra Church meeting house. The Federal line lay along a slightly elevated ridge that aided the defenders. Around 11:30 A.M., the first Confederate wave charged out of the thick brush. The Union line buckled under the pressure of the initial assault, but the rebel forces were beaten back. Logan's corps, composed of three divisions, poured volley after volley into the rank of Stephen Lee's men, inflicting heavy casualties upon the Confederate attackers. By 1 P.M., Lee charged again, absorbed heavy casualties, retreated, and moved forward a third time. Most of the Rebel pressure came against the Union center and right, positions held by the divisions of Generals William Harrow and Morgan Smith. After the third failed Confederate assault, and unable to get around the Union right flank, Stephen Lee ordered up portions of Stewart's corps to reinforce Southern forces attacking the Federal right. Throughout the afternoon, the Confederates launched three more charges against the Union positions; each turned back with heavy losses. By late afternoon, the Southern soldiers refused to attack and they slowly retreated back into the defensive works surrounding the city.

For the third time in eight days, Confederate losses were heavy. Stephen Lee's troops suffered 3,000 casualties to Howard's 632. In addition, only a misleading map prevented forces reinforcing Howard from falling on the left flank of the Confederates and totally destroying Stephen Lee's command and opening the way for a quick capture of Atlanta. Hood's foray at Ezra Church did stop Sherman from cutting Atlanta's supply line, but the heavy losses suffered by the Confederates in this and the previous sorties of Peachtree Creek and Bald Hill destroyed the offensive power and spirit of the Army of Tennessee. Hood remained on the defensive from this point on in the Atlanta campaign.

—*Franklin Forts*

See also Atlanta Campaign; Howard, Oliver Otis; Lee, Stephen Dill; Logan, John Alexander.

For further reading:

Castel, Albert E. *Decision in the West: The Atlanta Campaign, 1864* (1992).

Connelly, Thomas L. *Autumn of Glory: The Army of Tennessee, 1862–1865* (1971).

McDonough, James Lee, and James Pickett Jones. *War So Terrible: Sherman and Atlanta* (1987).

McMurry, Richard M. *John Bell Hood and the War for Southern Independence* (1982).

Savas, Theodore P., and David A. Woodbury, eds. *The Campaign for Atlanta and Sherman's March to the Sea: Essays on the American Civil War in Georgia, 1864* (1994).

FAGAN, JAMES FLEMING
(1828–1893)
Confederate general

Born in Louisville, Kentucky, the son of Steven Fagan and Catherine Stevens Fagan, the younger Fagan moved with his family to Arkansas when he was ten. Upon reaching adulthood, Fagan became a planter and was active in Arkansas Whig politics. He served one term in the Arkansas legislature and served as a lieutenant in one of Arkansas's volunteer regiments during the Mexican-American War. Upon Arkansas's secession, he was given the colonel's commission for the 1st Arkansas Regiment on 6 May 1861.

Fagan led his regiment at Shiloh in April 1862 and was commended for bravery by 1st Brigade commander Colonel Randall L. Gibson for leading a regimental charge on the second day. A month latter on 9 May 1862 Fagan commanded the 4th Brigade at Farmington outside of Corinth, Mississippi. On 12 September 1862 he received a formal promotion to brigadier general.

Following his promotion, Fagan was transferred to the trans-Mississippi west where he served for the remainder of the war. At the end of the year he fought at Prairie Grove, Arkansas, before assuming a leading role in recruitment in Arkansas for the first months of 1863. By summer he was back in command of a cavalry brigade under Sterling Price. Fagan served under Price in what was intended to be the diversionary attack at Helena, Arkansas, on 4 July 1863 and assumed command of Price's division on 23 July 1863 when Price became the commander of the District of Arkansas. Fagan quickly made the division his own and it was shortly known as Fagan's Cavalry Division.

Fagan commanded his division under Price the following year in April 1864 at Camden and Marks' Mill, where he led his brigade in a stunning defeat of Union forces and the capture of much-needed supplies. On 25 April 1864, he finally received the promotion to major general that befitted his responsibilities. Fagan led his men in September through October 1864 in Price's invasion of Missouri, and then in the last months of the war assumed command of the District of Arkansas.

While in this last position Fagan received a letter in April 1865 from U.S. Army major general Joseph J. Reynolds detailing the surrender of Lee at Appomattox and offering Fagan the same terms Grant had given Lee. Fagan refused to capitulate until all forces around his command had done so, formally tendering his surrender on 14 June 1865.

Following the war Fagan returned to his plantation and Arkansas politics. He joined the Republican Party during Reconstruction, which gained him federal appointments as a U.S. Marshal in western Arkansas and then as a land office receiver in Little Rock. His Republican affiliation, however, probably cost him a chance at elective office after the end of Reconstruction. He died in Little Rock in 1893.

—*David S. Heidler and Jeanne T. Heidler*

See also Arkansas; Marks' Mills, Battle of; Price, Sterling; Price's Missouri Raid.
For further reading:
Luker, Elizabeth Watson. *Mature Life of General James Fleming Fagan* (1987).

FAIR OAKS / SEVEN PINES
(31 May –1 June 1862)

In the aftermath of Confederate general Joseph E. Johnston's evacuation of Yorktown and his army's retirement up the Virginia peninsula toward Richmond, the Army of the Potomac under George B. McClellan began a slow but steady pursuit. Although tempered by a defeat of federal gunboats below Drewry's Bluff, the movement up the peninsula to the outskirts of the city created fear and consternation in Richmond. The situation appeared to be going from bad to worse as word came into Richmond that Irwin McDowell's First Corps, now essentially an army numbering more than 30,000, was preparing to move toward Fredericksburg 50 miles north of the Confederate capital. The unified commands of McDowell and McClellan would number approximately 135,000—double Johnston's strength. Responding to orders, the commander of the Army of the Potomac positioned his troops in such a way as to maintain pressure on the Confederate capital from the east while at the same time facilitating a juncture with the First Corps as it moved southward from Fredericksburg. This meant that the Federal army would

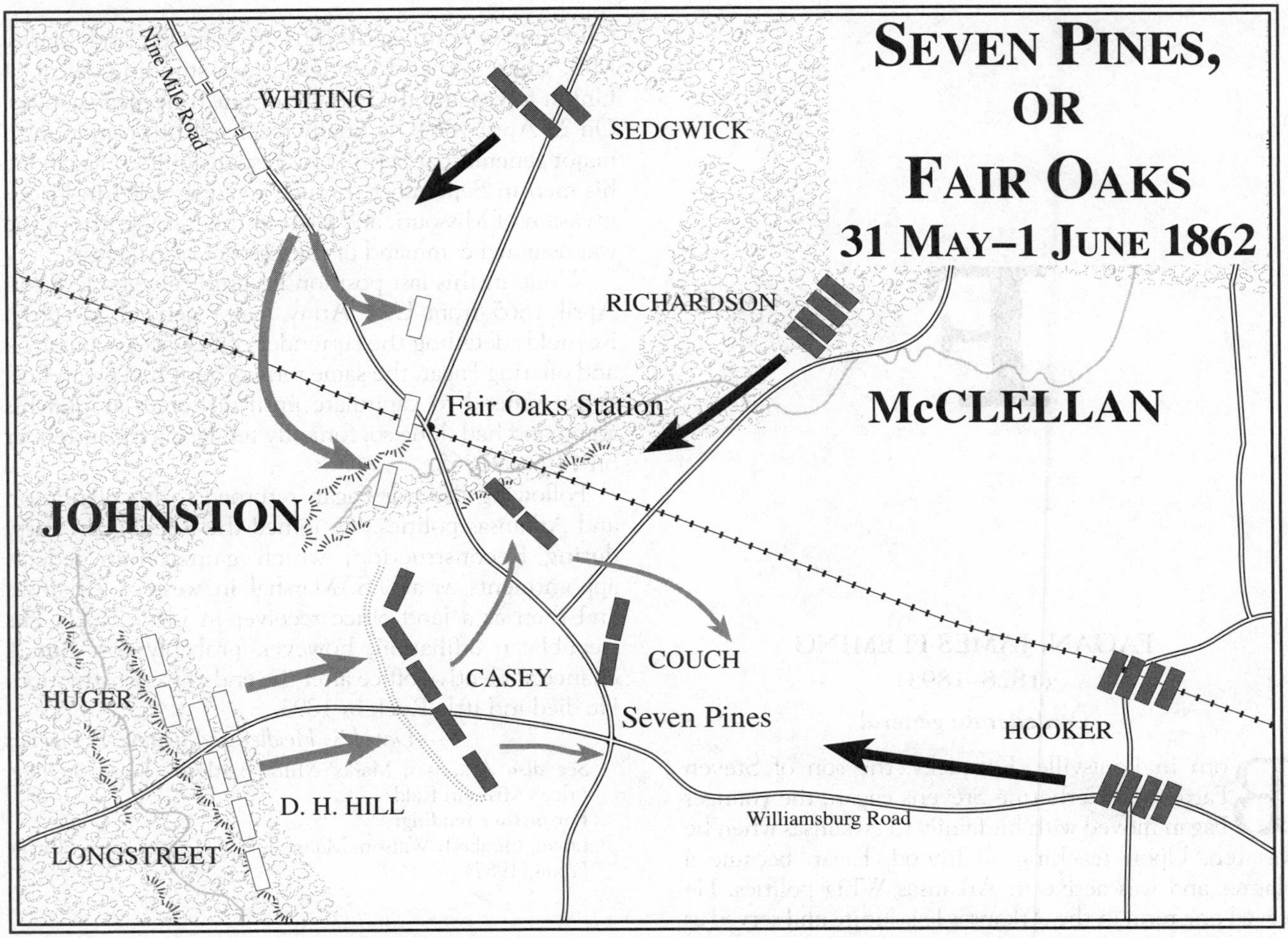

SEVEN PINES, OR FAIR OAKS
31 MAY–1 JUNE 1862

WHITING

Nine Mile Road

SEDGWICK

RICHARDSON

Fair Oaks Station

McCLELLAN

JOHNSTON

HUGER

CASEY

COUCH

Seven Pines

HOOKER

D. H. HILL

Williamsburg Road

LONGSTREET

be forced to straddle the Chickahominy River—a waterway originating north of Richmond and flowing southeastward to the James.

The proximity of the Army of the Potomac to Richmond led President Davis and Robert E. Lee, who essentially served as Davis's military advisor, to meet with Johnston to discuss the general's plans for defeating McClellan. While remaining secure behind Richmond's defenses, Johnston advocated flexibility to react quickly to any mistake or opportunity presented by his federal counterpart. In an effort to keep his options open and to limit risks, Johnston avoided making a commitment to a fixed plan.

The opportunity Johnston was waiting for materialized at the end of the month. After rebuilding Bottom's Bridge (one of the bridges across the Chickahominy destroyed by retreating Confederates), two federal corps commanded by Generals Erasmus D. Keyes and Samuel P. Heintzelman moved south across the river. Remaining to the north were three corps commanded by Generals Edwin Sumner, William Franklin, and Fitz John Porter. Efforts were underway to construct or rebuild eleven bridges between Bottom's Bridge and Mechanicsville to facilitate a speedy reunion of the army when necessary.

Thus, by 25 May the Chickahominy physically divided the Army of the Potomac into two "wings."

Johnston, recognizing the opportunity to strike McClellan while his army was divided, determined to attack one or both of the wings. Johnston began to develop his plan after further consolidating his forces by moving Major General Benjamin Huger from Petersburg to Drewry's Bluff and advising Brigadier Generals Lawrence O'Bryan Branch at Gordonsville and Joseph Reid Anderson near Fredericksburg to shift their troops closer to Richmond. He now had 75,000 men available, the largest army ever assembled in the Confederacy to that date. His initial concept was for an assault against the extreme right of the federal army north of the Chickahominy in conjunction with a strike against the right flank of the two corps south of the river. His decision to move against the federal right was based on the urgency created by the belief that McDowell was on his way to link up with McClellan. This presumption was enhanced on 27 May by an engagement fifteen miles north of Richmond at Hanover Court House in which Fitz John Porter's Fifth Corps defeated 4,000 Confederates under Branch. This action appeared to be in preparation for the arrival of McDowell. A federal

Horatio G. Gibson's C and G Batteries near Fair Oaks, June 1862 (Photograph by James F. Gibson / *Library of Congress*)

defeat along the Chickahominy would prevent such a union by driving McClellan back away from Richmond and freeing Johnston to turn on McDowell.

Johnston planned to attack on 29 May, but information coming from Confederate Cavalry under Brigadier General J.E.B. Stuart the previous evening indicated a change in the federal plans. McDowell was no longer heading south—the First Corps was being withdrawn to support federal operations against "Stonewall" Jackson in the Shenandoah Valley. Now, with an entirely different situation confronting him, the Confederate commander no longer needed to attack to forestall the unification of federal forces. Yet, circumstances were still favorable for a tactical offensive. Johnston saw an opportunity to eliminate the weaker of McClellan's two wings and then turn on the three corps north of the river.

The 31,500 men south of the river under Keyes and Heintzelman had advanced west of their river crossing and were dispersed in four lines. One division of Keyes's corps was in line one mile west of Seven Pines, a road junction six miles east of Richmond on the Williamsburg Road. Keyes's other division stretched from Seven Pines north to Fair Oaks Station on the Richmond & York River Railroad. Heintzelman's two divisions were located to the rear of Keyes, one at Savage Station, two miles east of Fair Oaks Station, and one near Bottom's Bridge. McClellan did not anticipate a Confederate offensive.

Johnston's battle plan for 31 May directed the divisions of Generals James Longstreet and Daniel Harvey Hill to assault Keyes's right and center while Huger's division, moving from the southwest, turned the enemy's left flank. General Gustavus W. Smith was ordered first to engage troops that might attempt to cross the Chickahominy to aid Keyes and Heintzelman, and then (if no federal reinforcement arrived) to support Longstreet's attack on the federal right. All troops were to advance toward the enemy using the existing road network which conveniently converged at Keyes's position. In the early morning attack, the latter division would be smashed first, then Heintzelman, moving up to support Keyes, would meet the same fate. These instructions were given orally to Longstreet who was given tactical command of the operation based on his performance at Williamsburg and his seniority in rank to Hill and Huger.

While Johnston's plan was tactically sound, he erred

in issuing his orders orally and by not informing all his division commanders that Longstreet was in tactical command. The result was confusion and delay. In addition, the weather added its own impedance. The day before the battle rain turned the roads into quagmires.

The 31 May battle at Seven Pines did not go well at all for Johnston. Longstreet did not take his assigned route to the attack. Instead he moved his 14,000-man division farther south to the Williamsburg Road currently occupied by D. H. Hill's division. This shift ultimately weakened the Confederate assault against the Federal right and created a nightmare in coordination when Huger's men prepared to enter this same road to reach their assigned point of attack. Huger, initially unaware that Longstreet was in tactical command, lost the argument that he should have priority over the road.

Johnston became increasingly concerned when the expected sounds of battle did not reach his headquarters during the early morning. His anxiety grew when Brigadier General William Henry Chase Whiting, in command of Smith's division, could not locate Longstreet's which his was to follow into position. After a delay of over six hours, the assault finally commenced at a little after 2:00. Only six of the intended thirteen brigades were in position when the battle began. Huger's three brigades and three brigades from Longstreet's division were mired in White Oak Swamp south of Seven Pines. One brigade was held back to protect the Confederate left. The assault, although bearing little resemblance to Johnston's original plan, was nevertheless gallant and determined. Longstreet sent a message to Johnston notifying his commander that the battle had been underway for several hours and requesting support for his left flank in the form of an attack upon the Federal right and rear. Longstreet anticipated that such a blow could terminate the battle before nightfall.

Johnston ordered General Smith's division to advance toward Seven Pines to aid Longstreet. The commanding general then left his headquarters and rode to the front to oversee the assault. However, instead of striking a blow against a weakened Keyes near Seven Pines, Johnston found himself facing fresh troops at Fair Oaks. Fire coming from this newly arrived Federal force struck the left flank of Smith's division as it moved past Fair Oaks. Caught by surprise, the Confederates were brought into a general engagement north of Seven Pines and were unable to aid Longstreet in his efforts against Keyes.

By 6:30, Johnston was convinced that the contest would have to be renewed the following day. He rode forward toward his frontline positions, issued orders for a cease-fire, and instructed his men to sleep on their arms. The commanding general was exposed to sporadic enemy fire during this process and around 7:00 was shot in the right shoulder. Immediately following this wound, Johnston was hit in the breast by a shell fragment which

knocked him, unconscious, off his horse. The general was carried to a less exposed position and awaited an ambulance to remove him from the field.

President Davis and General Lee, who had been at Johnston's headquarters earlier in the day, rode up on what must have been a shocking scene. The command responsibility fell briefly to General Smith. On 1 June, Smith renewed the attack with a series of poorly orchestrated assaults. By late morning the Confederates recognized the folly of continuing the battle and began a general withdrawal from the field. That same day, President Davis issued orders for Robert E. Lee to assume command of the Confederate army outside Richmond. Confederate losses for the two-day battle were 6,134 men killed, wounded, or missing, while the Army of the Potomac suffered 5,031 total casualties.

—Alan C. Downs

For further reading:
Newton, Steven H. *Joseph E. Johnston and the Defense of Richmond* (1998).
Sears, Stephen W. *To the Gates of Richmond, The Peninsula Campaign* (1992).

FAIR OAKS, SECOND BATTLE OF
(27 October 1864)

At the end of October 1864 Ulysses S. Grant began a campaign that became known as Hatcher's Run. The purpose of the campaign was to cut the South-side Railroad. He hoped to divert attention from this offensive by having General Benjamin Butler move north of the James River to launch an attack on Richmond via the York Peninsula. The Confederates had five lines of defenses extending out from Richmond onto the peninsula, some remainders of the defenses that had been placed there during George McClellan's Peninsula campaign in the spring and summer of 1862. These were quite formidable works, and as a result any move against them was viewed as simply a diversion.

Butler's offensive consisted of two parts, a small movement by Alfred Terry and part of X Corps to move along the southern part of the peninsula against Charles City, and a larger offensive along the Williamsburg Road toward Richmond led by Godfrey Weitzel and part of his XVIII Corps. Weitzel began his march on the morning of 27 October toward Fair Oaks. Colonel Samuel Perkins Spear's cavalry brigade led the advance of this offensive. At the same time, four brigades of XVIII Corps moved directly along the Williamsburg Road, while Brigadier General John Holman's African-American brigade tried to move around the Confederate left flank.

James Longstreet, temporarily in command of Richmond's defenses, sent out scouts to discern Butler's intentions and realized early on the twenty-seventh that the more serious threat to Richmond came from Weitzel. As a result, he dispatched two divisions commanded by Charles William Field and Robert Frederick Hoke to counter Weitzel's move. Hoke repulsed a Federal attack around 3:30 P.M., but Holman continued to move around the Confederate flank. Brigadier General Martin Witherspoon Gary's dismounted cavalry brigade finally challenged Holman's troops. Holman, however, enjoyed initial success against Gary's troopers, but was then pushed back in the late afternoon by a counterattack.

Weitzel assumed that the purpose of his march had been accomplished, and when Holman failed to get around the Confederate left, called off the offensive. The next morning, 28 October, Weitzel withdrew from his positions around Fair Oaks. The Union casualties in the diversion had been 1,103 and the Confederate casualties 451.

—*David S. Heidler and Jeanne T. Heidler*

See also Butler, Benjamin Franklin; Hatcher's Run; Weitzel, Godfrey
For further reading:
Trudeau, Noah Andre. *The Last Citadel: Petersburg, Virginia, June 1864–April 1865* (1991).

FAIRBANKS, ERASTUS
(1792–1864)

Businessman, reformer, and governor of Vermont

Under the direction of Erastus Fairbanks, Vermont rapidly exceeded the initial enlistment quota requested of it by the federal government. Fairbanks was born in Brimfield, Massachusetts, and moved to St. Johnsbury, Vermont, in 1812. After operating country stores in the St. Johnsbury area for a number of years, Fairbanks and his brother Thaddeus established a partnership manufacturing farm equipment and stoves. In 1830, Thaddeus received a patent for the platform scale. The brothers soon chose to concentrate on manufacturing scales and founded the E. & T. Fairbanks & Company in 1834. Erastus managed the business side of the company, and under his aggressive leadership it grew into one of the world's premier scale manufacturers, doubling its production every three years between 1842 and 1857. Among his other business ventures, Fairbanks organized the Connecticut & Passumpsic Rivers Railroad Company in 1846 and for a number of years served as its president.

As the Fairbanks family came to dominate the public life of St. Johnsbury, Erastus's attention turned increasingly to reform and politics. He was president of the Vermont Temperance Society in the 1830s and later was president of the Vermont Domestic Missionary Society. From 1836 to 1839, Fairbanks served three terms as St. Johnsbury's representative to the state legislature, and in both 1844 and 1848 he was a delegate to the Whig Party's

National Convention. In 1852, after receiving the Whig nomination for the office, Fairbanks was elected governor. This was achieved only in the state legislature; the majority in the general election demanded by the state constitution was denied him by defections to the Liberty Party. Fairbanks's first one-year term as governor was distinguished by his advocacy of a statewide prohibition bill. The bill passed, but a sizable negative reaction to prohibition contributed to Fairbanks's defeat for reelection. Such fractious politics were typical for Vermont in the decades that preceded prohibition, but were not to persist; Fairbanks's opponent was the last Democrat elected governor in Vermont for more than a century.

The religious enthusiasm that shook Vermont in the 1830s and 1840s aroused significant, but not yet consuming, abolitionist agitation. Temperance having been resolved, slavery replaced it as the foremost question of the day for a great many Vermonters, Fairbanks included. He served in the 1850s as the vice president of the Vermont chapter of the National Society for Emancipation and was a delegate to the Republican Party's first national convention in 1856. Four years later, as the Republican Party's nominee for governor, he received three times as many votes as his Democratic opponent.

The first official act of Fairbanks's second term as governor was to designate 4 January 1861 a day of fasting and prayer for the continued unity of the nation. Simultaneously, however, Fairbanks began to prepare his state for war. Later in January, the governor directed local militia officers to gather and drill their companies. Enacted three months before the first shot of the Civil War was fired, the act was necessitated by the egregious state of disorganization into which Vermont's local militias had fallen. With that act, Vermont began to mobilize for war.

On 15 April, the day after the fall of Fort Sumter, the federal government requested from Vermont one regiment of troops for immediate service. Memorably pledging to President Abraham Lincoln that Vermont would "do its full duty," Fairbanks convened a special session of the state legislature eight days later. After a stirring speech from the governor, the legislature enthusiastically appropriated $1 million for the war effort, twice most expectations. The legislature further committed the state to raising seven regiments under the governor's direction, despite Fairbanks's doubts that the total could be achieved. While coordinating recruitment, Fairbanks sought to energize patriotism with such gestures as declining his salary as governor for the duration of the war.

On 2 May, Vermont's first regiment was mustered in Rutland. The soldiers' encampment, located on the fairground south of the village, was designated "Camp Fairbanks" in honor of the governor. Two additional regiments of volunteers were raised by the end of May, and in July the first of these distinguished itself in the battle of First Bull Run. By the time Fairbanks's term

ended in October 1861, the 6th Vermont Regiment had been organized, completing the 1st Vermont Brigade.

As the war's years passed, new Vermont recruits continued to join those early recruits who survived and frequently reenlisted. In all, more than 34,000 Vermonters, more than a tenth of the state's total population, served in the Union army. Statistics compiled by the federal adjutant general's office soon after the war calculated that the death rate for Vermont troops in battle exceeded that of all other Union states except Michigan. Only one other Union brigade suffered as many men killed or wounded as the 1st Vermont Brigade, and the 2d Vermont Brigade played an important role in repulsing Pickett's charge at Gettysburg. Vermont soldiers saw action in most of the major battles in the war's Eastern theater and the lower Mississippi Valley, including Antietam, the Wilderness, Fredericksburg, and Cold Harbor. As the war drew to its conclusion in April 1865, soldiers in the 9th Vermont Infantry claimed to have been the first Union soldiers to enter Richmond.

Erastus Fairbanks did not live to see the war come to that end. He declined the offer to run for a third term as governor in 1861 and retired to St. Johnsbury. He died there in 1864, an enduring symbol of Vermont's enthusiastic response to the commencement of the Civil War.

—*Paul Searls*

See also Vermont Brigade.
For further reading:
Benedict, George Grenville. *Vermont in the Civil War* (1889).
Coffin, Howard. *Full Duty: Vermonters in the Civil War* (1993).
Hemenway, Abby Maria. *The Vermont Historical Gazetteer* (1868).
Newton, Earle W. *The Vermont Story: A History of the People of the Green Mountain State, 1749–1949* (1949).

FAIRFAX COURT HOUSE
(27 June 1863)

As Lee began his invasion of Northern territory in June 1863, Confederate general J. E. B. Stuart took part of his cavalry corps east of Joseph Hooker's army to conduct raids on Federal supply lines and to discern Union movements. Following this activity he was to move north and rendezvous with Richard Ewell's corps at York, Pennsylvania.

On 25 June, as Stuart moved around Hooker's right flank while it moved north near Haymarket, he and his men encountered Winfield Scott Hancock's corps. While shielding his troopers in the woods nearby, he had his artillery fire several rounds into Hancock's infantry. When Hancock, however, appeared ready to fight, Stuart withdrew.

After this encounter Stuart realized he would need to swing south and farther out east to avoid the main part of Hooker's army. He went through Bristoe Station and

Brentsville on 26 June and that night made camp on the Occoquan River at Wolf Run Shoals. The next morning he started out early for Fairfax Court House, where he had heard that Hooker's army had left supplies behind at the rail station.

While Stuart moved forward with most of his troopers and with Wade Hampton taking the lead, he sent Fitzhugh Lee east to Burke's Station to destroy the railroad tracks there. As the main body neared the depot at Fairfax, scouts rode up about 8:30 A.M. and informed Stuart that the depot was only lightly defended. Stuart excitedly rode forward and outdistanced Hampton's men to Fairfax where he almost rode into the midst of Major S. P. Remmington's two companies of the 11th New York Cavalry, eighty-six men in all. The men had come to Fairfax from Washington the day before with instructions to guard the supplies Hooker had left behind at Fairfax Station. Stuart turned around quickly and rejoined Hampton before the New Yorkers had time to react.

Within a few minutes the Union troopers saw the approach of Colonel Laurence S. Baker's 1st North Carolina Cavalry and attacked. The New Yorkers were grossly outnumbered and quickly overwhelmed by Baker's regiment. In this brief skirmish the Union forces suffered twenty-six casualties, which caused the remainder to flee in panic, leaving the supplies to the Confederate horsemen.

Stuart and his men feasted through the morning and took stock of the things they would be able to take with them, particularly the fresh, new hats and gloves that had been left behind by Hooker. The food and drink were also welcome changes from their mundane diet. Wine washed down lobster salad and other delicacies. After resting the horses and allowing them to graze, Stuart made a fateful decision. In spite of his delay at Fairfax, he would not retrace his steps and rejoin Lee as the Army of Northern Virginia marched into Pennsylvania. Instead, he would continue moving east around Hooker's army and join with Ewell as originally planned at York. He started out the next day with Hampton in the lead and crossed the Potomac River into Maryland.

—*David S. Heidler and Jeanne T. Heidler*

See also Gettysburg; Battle of; Hampton, Wade; Stuart, James Ewell Brown.
For further reading:
Longacre, Edward G. *The Cavalry at Gettysburg: A Tactical Study of Mounted Operations During the Civil War's Pivotal Campaign, 9 June–14 July 1863* (1986).

FALLING WATERS, BATTLE OF
(14 July 1863)

The unexpectedly fierce fight at Falling Waters, Maryland, wrote an anticlimactic close to the Gettysburg campaign. Despite the recklessness of one Union cavalry general, his brother officers managed

The charge of the 6th Michigan Cavalry at the battle of Falling Waters, 14 July 1863 (*Library of Congress*)

to cut off and capture 700 infantrymen from the Army of Northern Virginia's rear guard.

After the Confederate defeat at Gettysburg, General Robert E. Lee and his Army of Northern Virginia retreated toward the Potomac River, seeking safety in Virginia. Heavy rains had turned the Potomac into an unfordable torrent, however, stranding the rebels within easy reach of the Union Army of the Potomac. Lee met the crisis with characteristic resourcefulness, having his divisions dig a line of earthworks stretching from Williamsport, Maryland, to Downsville, ten miles to the southeast. Sheltering behind their fortifications, the rebels waited for the Potomac to fall. By 13 July, the Potomac's water level had subsided sufficiently for Lee's infantry to ford the river at Williamsport. Confederate engineers had also placed a pontoon bridge at Falling Waters, about four miles downstream. Soon after sunset, Lee's troops began crossing the Potomac at both locations.

As luck would have it, Major General George Gordon Meade, the commander of the Union Army of the Potomac, chose the evening of the 13th to authorize a strong reconnaissance in force along Lee's lines commencing the next day at 7:00 A.M. Four hours before the scheduled foray, Brigadier General H. Judson Kilpatrick, commanding the 3d Division in the Army of the Potomac's Cavalry Corps, learned that enemy pickets had disappeared from his front. Suspecting a Confederate evacuation, Kilpatrick hurled his division toward the Potomac. At 6:00 A.M., Kilpatrick's vanguard, Brigadier General George A. Custer's Michigan Cavalry Brigade, topped the hills overlooking Williamsport and spotted the rear of Lieutenant General Richard S. Ewell's II Corps crossing the Potomac. Custer's 5th Michigan Cavalry Regiment charged into Williamsport, captured some stragglers, and swept others

into the water. Local residents informed Kilpatrick that many other rebels had marched to Falling Waters, and he told Custer to pursue them.

By 7:00 A.M., Brigadier General John Buford, the commander of the Army of the Potomac's 1st Cavalry Division, discovered that the Confederates had abandoned their trenches around Downsville. Buford immediately sent Kilpatrick a dispatch stating that he intended to thrust the 1st Cavalry Division between Lee's rear guard and the Potomac.

Custer and his lead elements reached a patch of woods within sight of Falling Waters by 7:30 A.M. Two Confederate infantry brigades under Brigadier General J. Johnston Pettigrew manned half a dozen crescent-shaped earthworks on a hill near the crossing. To buy time until the rest of the Michigan Brigade arrived, Custer instructed Major Peter A. Weber to dismount Companies B and F of the 6th Michigan Cavalry, form a skirmish line, and have the men engage the rebels with their seven-shot Spencer rifles. Impatient for a glorious victory, the impetuous Kilpatrick countermanded Custer's order and sent Weber's fifty-seven men forward in a suicidal mounted charge.

Mistaking the approaching horsemen for their own cavalry, the Confederates held their fire until the Michiganders rode among them, sabers slashing and revolvers popping. General Pettigrew fell mortally wounded, but his men made short work of their opponents. A bullet smashed through Weber's skull, and thirty-five of the fifty-seven Union troopers were killed or wounded.

Dismounting the rest of the 6th Michigan, Custer continued the attack in a more sensible fashion, feeding two other regiments into the fray as they reached the scene. Shortly thereafter, Buford swept in behind the beleaguered Confederates. Lee's engineers cut the Maryland end of the pontoon bridge, leaving 700 of

their comrades in Federal hands. Custer's "Wolverines" also captured three battle flags and two cannon. Custer was conspicuous in the melee that extinguished the final knot of Confederate resistance. As one Michigander wrote his wife: "General Koster…commanded in person and I saw him plunge his saber into the belly of a rebel who was trying to kill him. You can guess how bravely soldiers fight for such a general."

While the Federals could boast of scorching Lee's tail, Falling Waters represented a squandered opportunity. Had Kilpatrick restrained himself until Buford got into position, the damage to the Confederates would have been far heavier. By charging two brigades with only two companies, Kilpatrick revealed Union intentions and accelerated his prey's movement across the Potomac. He tried to conceal his blunder by reporting that his division nabbed more than 1,500 prisoners, a claim that drew a heated denial from General Lee.

—*Gregory J. W. Urwin*

See also Custer, George Armstrong; Kilpatrick, Hugh Judson; Pettigrew, James Johnston.

For further reading:

Coddington, Edwin B. *The Gettysburg Campaign: A Study in Command* (1968).

Longacre, Edward G. *The Cavalry at Gettysburg: A Tactical Study of Mounted Operations during the Civil War's Pivotal Campaign, 9 June–14 July 1863* (1986; reprint, 1993).

Starr, Stephen Z. *The Union Cavalry in the Civil War* (1979–1985).

Urwin, Gregory J. W. *Custer Victorious: The Civil War Battles of General George Armstrong Custer* (1990).

Wert, Jeffry D. *Custer: The Controversial Life of George Armstrong Custer* (1996).

FARMVILLE/HIGH BRIDGE, BATTLE OF
(6–7 April 1865)

The action in and around the town of Farmville, Virginia, on 6–7 April 1865 capped the middle segment of the retreat of the Army of Northern Virginia from Petersburg and led to the final march to Appomattox Court House. Besides the battle of Sayler's Creek, the fighting included two engagements at High Bridge (a railroad bridge across the Appomattox River) and a pitched battle three miles north of Farmville at Cumberland Church. It was during the brief stop for supplies at Farmville that Confederate general Robert E. Lee, pressed hard by Union forces under Generals Andrew A. Humphreys and George Crook, abandoned his immediate plan to turn south for Danville in favor of continuing the retreat farther west to Lynchburg.

On the rainy morning of 6 April, Major General Edward O. C. Ord, commander of the Federal Army of the James, received orders to destroy any bridges over the Appomattox River that could be used by the Confederates, then in flight from Amelia Court house to Farmville. He detached three infantry regiments and three companies of cavalry to capture and burn the High Bridge, a span four miles south of Farmville belonging to the South-side Railroad. Built in 1852, High Bridge was a marvel of nineteenth-century engineering, as it crossed the entire river valley, a length of almost a half-mile. With a height of 125 feet at the river's edge, the bridge was defended by Confederate infantry stationed in earthen redoubts.

Confederate scouts detected Ord's detachment, and General James Longstreet quickly dispatched two divisions of cavalry in pursuit. Led by Generals Thomas L. Munford and Thomas L. Rosser, the Confederates overtook the enemy troops and pinned them against the fortifications at the southeast end of the bridge. The ensuing battle involved fierce hand-to-hand combat, and a number of officers were killed, including the commander of the Union troops, brevet Brigadier General Theodore Read. Outmaneuvered, the Federals were soon forced to surrender. The Southerners captured almost 800 infantrymen, six flags, and a brass band. Most importantly, the bridge was saved for use by Lee's retreating army.

After the disaster at Sayler's Creek in the afternoon of 6 April, the Confederate army marched through the night to Farmville, where seven supply trains awaited. Following a wagon road, Longstreet's corps reached the town in the early morning and crossed the bridge there to the north bank of the Appomattox River. His corps was soon met by the leading elements of General John B. Gordon's corps, which had crossed at High Bridge and marched west along the railroad.

Gordon's troops were pursued closely by the Federal II Corps, under General Humphreys. Approaching High Bridge at about 7:00 A.M., the Federals rushed to capture the span just as the fleeing Confederates blew up one of the redoubts and put fire to a smaller wagon bridge below. Although fire did render High Bridge unusable, the Federals managed to extinguish the blaze on the wagon bridge. The first units to cross came under heavy fire from a Confederate rear guard sent by General William Mahone. Mahone's men attempted to retake the bridge and initially drove the Union troops back, but Federal artillery and infantry reinforcements prevailed, and by midmorning the entire II Corps had crossed the river.

Robert E. Lee rode into Farmville with Longstreet's column. While Longstreet's men received rations of bread and meal, Lee conferred with Secretary of War John Breckinridge. Daunted by the strong Federal pressure from the east and south, Lee discarded earlier plans to march south from Farmville and decided instead to continue trying to outdistance the pursuit by retreating to the west. The immediate goal would now be Appomattox Court House, a march of thirty-eight miles by the roads north of the river.

As the hungry Confederate soldiers began to eat, the sound of approaching skirmish fire was heard from the

The High Bridge of the Southside Railroad near Farmville, April 1865
(Photograph by Timothy O'Sullivan / *Library of Congress*)

direction of High Bridge. Suddenly, a brigade of Federal cavalry under General Crook appeared on the main street of the town. Alarmed, the Southerners broke from their meal, burned the town bridges, and hastily dispatched the unpacked supply trains. Lee's beleaguered army was forced to take up the march again.

The Confederates turned to the west a few miles north of Farmville, near Cumberland Church. Here they were met by the Federal II Corps, which had marched from High Bridge to intercept them. The Southerners dug entrenchments in a hook-shaped line and prepared for battle. Units under Mahone and Brigadier General G. T. "Tige" Anderson successfully fended off a series of late-afternoon attacks, and Confederate cavalry under Munford broke up an attempt to overtake a wagon train, capturing Federal general J. Irvin Gregg in the process.

Frustrated over his failure to separate his army from its pursuers, Lee realized that General Ulysses S. Grant, then with the Federal VI Corps under General Horatio G. Wright, had occupied Farmville and would soon reinforce Humphreys. Again Lee was compelled to withdraw his troops under cover of darkness and begin a night march, his last as commander of the Army of Northern Virginia.

—*Charles E. Kinzer*

See also Amelia Court House /Jetersville; Appomattox Court House; Sayler's Creek/Harper's Farm, Battle of.
For further reading:
Calkins, Chris M. *The Appomattox Campaign: March 29–April 9, 1865* (1997).
Davis, Burke. *To Appomattox: Nine April Days* (1959).
Korn, Jerry. *Pursuit to Appomattox: The Last Battles. The Civil War* (1987).

FARNSWORTH, ELON JOHN
(1837–1863)
Union general

Born to James Patten Farnsworth and Achsah Hudson Farnsworth in Green Oak, Michigan, Elon John Farnsworth moved with his parents to Rockton, Illinois, when he was a teenager. Farnsworth returned to Michigan in 1855 to enter the University of Michigan but left school in 1857 to participate in Albert Sidney Johnston's Utah expedition. He remained in the West until the outbreak of the Civil War. When he learned that the war had begun, he returned east and was commissioned a first lieutenant in the 8th Illinois Cavalry, which was commanded by his uncle, John Franklin Farnsworth. The young Farnsworth was quickly

named the regiment's adjutant. In December 1861 he was promoted to captain.

As part of the Army of the Potomac, Farnsworth fought with his regiment in the Peninsula campaign, most notably at the siege of Yorktown and during the Seven Days'. During the Maryland campaign, Farnsworth fought at Antietam as part of Alfred Pleasonton's cavalry corps. After the battle, Farnsworth led his company in reconnaissance actions from Sharpsburg to Shepherdstown and Martinsburg, Virginia. He was commended by Pleasonton for the manner in which he conducted these missions.

Farnsworth saw some action at Fredericksburg in December 1862, after which he returned to reconnaissance duty through the early months of 1863. After being promoted to lieutenant colonel and serving a brief stint as chief quartermaster of IV Corps in the early spring of 1863, Farnsworth returned to the cavalry. He led his company in George Stoneman's raid toward Richmond during the Chancellorsville campaign. On the return trip, Farnsworth volunteered his services as well as those of his men to help transport the ammunition for the horse artillery across the swollen Virginia rivers in their path.

After the battle of Chancellorsville, Farnsworth became Pleasonton's aide-de-camp. Pleasonton had been very impressed with Farnsworth's fighting ability and initiative in battle as well as in staff duties and had grown quite fond of the twenty-five-year-old officer. During the next month and a half, Farnsworth would further impress his commander. At the end of June, on Pleasonton's recommendation, Farnsworth was promoted to brigadier general of volunteers.

At the time of Farnsworth's promotion, the campaign that would result in the battle of Gettysburg was well under way, and Farnsworth was given command of the 1st Brigade in Hugh Judson Kilpatrick's cavalry division in pursuit of J. E. B. Stuart's Confederate cavalry. On 30 June, while in Hanover, Pennsylvania, Farnsworth and his brigade were attacked by Stuart. Although they were initially pushed back through the streets of the town, Farnsworth was able to rally his men and repulsed the attacking Confederates, almost capturing Stuart. Farnsworth fought Stuart again the next day at Hunterstown, Pennsylvania.

On 3 July, Kilpatrick's division was within the Union lines at Gettysburg. After the failure of Pickett's Charge in the afternoon, Kilpatrick believed that the right flank of the Confederate line could be turned with a cavalry charge and ordered Farnsworth to lead the attack. After surveying the point of attack and determining that the Confederate position was too strong and of unsuitable terrain for a cavalry attack, Farnsworth informed Kilpatrick, who nonetheless ordered the attack to move forward. Farnsworth prepared his men for the assault and led them

out from the Union lines. Union soldiers watched with awe as the cavalrymen charged into the heavily armed and fortified Confederates. Hit five times by Confederate fire, Farnsworth died on the field. His uncle later arranged for his body to be disinterred from its resting place on the battlefield and taken to Illinois for burial.

—David S. Heidler and Jeanne T. Heidler

See also Gettysburg, Battle of.

For further reading:
Jenkins, James H. *Elon J. Farnsworth: The Story of His Life* (1904).

FARRAGUT, DAVID GLASGOW
(1801–1870)
Union naval officer

David Glasgow Farragut has gone down in U.S. naval history as the man who issued one of its most famous orders: "Damn the torpedoes. Full steam ahead." His years of devoted service to the U.S. Navy culminated in his command of the Federal fleet in the U.S. Civil War.

George Farragut, David Farragut's biological father, was born at Ciudadela, the chief town of Minorca, one of the Balearic Islands off the eastern coast of Spain, in 1755. He was of distinguished lineage, being a descen-

David Farragut (*Library of Congress*)

dant of a Don Pedro who had played a prominent role in expelling the Moors from Minorca and from Spain. For a while the elder Farragut served in the Russian navy in the war with Turkey. In 1776 he journeyed to Charleston, South Carolina, to offer his services to the colonies in their revolt against Great Britain. He became a first lieutenant in South Carolina's navy and took part in land operations, fighting as a volunteer under the "Swamp Fox," General Francis Marion. He also saw action at Cowpens and in the campaign against Cornwallis. In 1807 President Thomas Jefferson appointed him a sailing master in the navy. This soldier of fortune, who had fought in so many battles on land and sea, finished his military career fighting against the British under Andrew Jackson at New Orleans. In 1795, while serving as a major in the Tennessee militia, he had married Elizabeth Shine, of Scotch-Irish ancestry, and took up residence at Campbell's Station, not far from Knoxville. It was there that the future first admiral of the U.S. Navy, James (later David) Glasgow Farragut, was born on 5 July 1801.

Shortly after James was born, George Farragut took his family to New Orleans. At about the same time, Commodore David Porter, father of David Dixon Porter, was posted to New Orleans as the senior naval officer. With the commodore was his father, the venerable David Porter, who had been appointed a sailing master in the U.S. Navy by George Washington. The elderly Porter, eighty-four years of age, enjoyed fishing. One day while fishing on Lake Pontchartrain, he collapsed from sunstroke. George Farragut happened to find him lying in the boat. He took him home, but the old man was so weak that he could not be moved. The elder Farragut and his wife cared for Porter until he died. Soon after, Mrs. Farragut died of yellow fever. As both families grieved their losses, Commodore Porter wanted to repay the kindness of the Farraguts and offered to become the guardian of George's son James. George Farragut agreed, and James went to live with the commodore and his family. Young James spent fewer than three years with the Porter family, for in 1810, Commodore Porter obtained for James, who was only nine years old, an appointment as a midshipman in the U.S. Navy.

In the War of 1812 James served with his adopted father on the *Essex*, the first naval vessel to display the American colors in the Pacific. James was only thirteen when the *Essex*, driven by a storm into the harbor of Valparaiso, was blockaded by two British ships, the *Cherub* and the *Phoebe*. Attempting to run the blockade, the *Essex* was attacked by the British ships in neutral waters. The ensuing battle was the longest and most bloody of all the battles in which Farragut participated— before the *Essex* surrendered she lost 155 of her crew of 225. In the midst of the battle it was reported to Commodore Porter that a gunner had deserted his post.

Porter found his adoptive son and told him to do his duty. Farragut immediately seized a pistol and went after the gunner, but he never found him.

It was in this engagement that Farragut received his first and only wound in all his years in the U.S. Navy. During the battle, a gunner was struck in the face by a cannon ball and was hurled on top of Farragut, causing both of them to fall down an open hatch. Farragut struck his head when the gunner landed on top of him, but he was virtually unscathed. Porter commended his adoptive son's actions during the battle, and in honor of his adoptive father, young James took the name David.

Like all midshipmen of the nineteenth-century U.S. Navy, David Glasgow Farragut served his apprenticeship as an officer in cruises in the Mediterranean, where he made the acquaintances of the noted captains and commodores of the day. One of the favorite stops of the navy was the harbor of Mahon, at the island of Minorca where Farragut's father had been born. Farragut had no interest in the fact that his father had come from Minorca, but after the American Civil War, when the European squadron that he commanded stopped there, he paid a visit to the Ciudadela, his father's birthplace, and received a hero's welcome. On one of these particular Mediterranean cruises, Farragut came under the influence of his chief schoolmaster, Chaplain Charles Folsom, who was not only his teacher, but also instructed him in the highest principles of morality. Folsom eventually was appointed American consul to Tunis, and he invited young Farragut to accompany him. Farragut spent almost a year there, and in that brief period he learned literature, mathematics, Italian, French, Spanish, and Arabic. After eight years of routine sea duty, Farragut rejoined Porter to fight West Indian piracy in the Gulf of Mexico, ultimately commanding his first naval vessel, the *Ferret*.

In 1823 Farragut settled in Norfolk, Virginia, and served several tours of duty on ship and ashore from Norfolk for more than thirty years. Commissioned lieutenant in 1825, he served aboard the *Brandywine*, escorting the Marquis de Lafayette on his return journey to France, then did a tour of duty aboard the *Vandalia* in 1829–1830. In the Nullification Crisis of 1832–1833, Farragut was executive officer of the sloop *Nachez* and showed the U.S. flag at rebellious Charleston.

In 1838, while commanding the sloop *Erie* off Veracruz, Mexico, Farragut witnessed the French bombardment and capture of the Mexican castle of San Juan de Uloa. He then sought shore duty to care for his ailing first wife, who died in 1840. After serving as executive officer of the *Delaware* in 1841, he was promoted to commander and given the command of the sloop *Decatur*.

At the outbreak of the Mexican War in 1846, Farragut, because of his past service in Gulf waters, his familiarity with the fortifications at Veracruz, and his

knowledge of Spanish, sought active duty. He did not, however, receive a significant assignment until January 1847, when he was given command of the sloop of war *Saratoga*. He quickly sailed to Veracruz, only to find that the castle had already surrendered to the U.S. Army under Winfield Scott. Assigned to blockade duty, he had no chance to distinguish himself or reveal his talents.

In subsequent years, Farragut was assigned primarily to shore duty. While on ordnance duty, he rewrote the navy's ordnance regulations and experimented with naval gun improvements. In 1854 he was sent to California to establish the Mare Island Navy Yard (San Francisco), where he was commissioned captain, the highest rank in the navy. After four years at Mare Island, he returned east and took command of the *Brooklyn* in 1859.

The tumultuous winter of 1860–1861 found Farragut at Norfolk, Virginia, awaiting orders. Farragut hoped that he would not have to raise his sword against the South, especially Virginia. He had close ties in Virginia because of his first and second wives. On 17 April Virginia seceded from the Union and Farragut had to make a very important choice: to fight for the North or the South. Farragut openly declared that President Lincoln was justified in taking military measures to recover the national forts that had been seized by the seceding states. When informed by a friend that a man who entertained such pro-Union sentiments would find life difficult in Norfolk, Farragut decided to move. He left Norfolk and took his family north, where he established them in a cottage in New York at Hastings-on-Hudson. But his Southern heritage followed him wherever he went. His Southern ties aroused enough suspicions to keep him on land duty. (There were rumors that he was one of a group of Southern sympathizers who were planning to wreck the Croton Dam Aqueduct, then New York City's main source of fresh water.) So late 1861 found the U.S. Navy's future first admiral sitting on a board examining officers for retirement. But that was soon to change, for in December 1861, largely on the recommendations of Assistant Secretary of the Navy Gustavus Vasa Fox and Farragut's foster brother, Commander David Dixon Porter, David Glasgow Farragut was chosen to command the West Gulf Blockading Squadron, which primarily operated in the Gulf of Mexico.

In spring 1862 Farragut was ordered to sail his fleet up the Mississippi River to meet a second Union naval group sailing south from New Madrid. Together, the two fleets would stop river traffic and subsequently cut the Confederate States of America in two. The fleet that Farragut assembled for the operation consisted of eight steam ships, nine gunboats, twenty mortar-carrying vessels, and a great number of miscellaneous craft. He was also given a large military force to support him.

On 24 April 1862 Farragut made the first move in his campaign by attacking New Orleans, the largest Confederate port on the mouth of the Mississippi. A Confederate squadron of eleven ships trying to intercept the Federal force was engaged, and in a short fight nine of the eleven Confederate ships were destroyed. Confederate troops abandoned New Orleans and the city subsequently surrendered. Farragut converted New Orleans into a Federal naval base from which he could resume his attacks up the Mississippi River and on the city of Vicksburg. Though his first attempt failed, he regrouped his vessels, bringing his mortar boats close in to provide covering fire as the squadron ran the gauntlet of Vicksburg's batteries.

Once he passed the guns, Farragut sailed upriver to link up with the other Union fleet as originally planned. His ships ran the gauntlet of Vicksburg's batteries again in order to attack the Confederate ship *Arkansas*, which had fought its way through the Union fleet to reach the safety of Vicksburg.

For his services, Farragut was promoted to rear admiral, and in March 1863 he set out to attack Vicksburg again. This time yielded different results. After a prolonged siege, Union efforts were successful. The navy's initial goals were finally achieved: Confederate shipping was swept from the Mississippi and the Confederacy was divided in two. Yet, the situation at sea was less satisfactory: many Southern ports were still open to blockade runners. The newly appointed vice admiral was determined to put an end to this. Farragut's first target was Mobile.

Mobile was situated within a bay, the narrow entrance to which was guarded by Fort Morgan. Farragut's attacking squadron would consist of four ironclad monitors and fourteen wooden ships. On August 14 Farragut set out. Running the gauntlet of Fort Morgan's guns, Farragut sailed his ships into Mobile Bay and deployed them in battle formation. He could see that his chief opponent would be the Confederate ironclad *Tennessee*. But what he did not see were the mines—known in those days as torpedoes—that the Confederates had laid in the approaches to the inner harbor.

It did not take long for Farragut's advance to run into difficulties. The *Tecumseh*, the leading monitor in Farragut's first line, ran into a mine and sank within minutes. The other leading ships made desperate maneuvers to avoid the mines and the vessels following them. All was in disarray. In a bold maneuver, Farragut turned his flagship, the *Hartford*, directly into the minefield, ordered himself tied to the Hartford's rigging, and issued his famous order, "Damn the torpedoes. Full steam ahead."

Farragut guessed that many of the mines would be ineffective because of their long immersion in sea water. Fortunately, he was correct and in the ensuing battle the *Tennessee* and the two small forts protecting the harbor surrendered. On 23 December, for his heroism at the battle of Mobile Bay, Farragut was promoted to the rank of vice admiral.

The secretary of the navy, Gideon Welles, next asked Farragut to take command of the North Atlantic Squadron in the contemplated attack on Fort Fisher at Wilmington, the last important port available to blockade runners. But Farragut refused to accept Secretary Welles's offer and asked to be excused from duty because his health was failing. The countless days of boring blockade duty and the fierce battles that Farragut had fought over his career had finally taken their toll on his sixty-three-year-old body. He returned to New York where he was granted $50,000 for a new home. Farragut was also one of the first to enter Richmond upon its fall in 1865.

In the years after the Civil War, the United States thanked Farragut for his fifty-plus years of service in its navy. On 26 July 1866, David Glasgow Farragut became the first man to hold the rank of full admiral in the U.S. Navy. Following his promotion to the rank of admiral, Farragut made a goodwill tour of Europe as commander of the Mediterranean Squadron. But this was the last sea duty that the beloved admiral would ever see. On 14 August 1870, while on an inspection tour of the naval yard at Portsmouth, New Hampshire, Farragut had a heart attack and died.

—*Michael S. Davis*

See also Mobile Bay; Navy, U.S.A.; New Orleans, Capture of; Porter, David Dixon.

For further reading:

Hearn, Chester G. *Admiral Glasgow Farragut: The Civil War Years* (1997).

Hill, Jim Dan. *Sea Dogs of the Sixties: Farragut and Seven Contemporaries* (1935).

Lewis, Charles Lee. *David Glasgow Farragut* (1941–1943).

Mahan, Alfred Thayer. *Admiral Farragut: First Admiral of the United States Navy* (1879).

Still, William N., Jr. "David Glasgow Farragut: The Union's Nelson." In *Captains of the Old Steam Navy*, edited by James C. Bradford (1986).

FAYETTEVILLE ARSENAL

The arsenal at Fayetteville, North Carolina, was the largest federal arsenal constructed in the South during the antebellum period. Construction of the sprawling complex, designed by the Scottish-American architect William Bell, began in 1838. A 40-acre walled compound was eventually erected over a twenty-year period on the 104-acre arsenal park. The building complex, composed of imposing sandstone-trimmed brick structures, was surrounded by brick walls topped with wrought iron railings and punctuated with stout iron gates. The compound was dominated by four masonry and sandstone towers situated at each corner of the quadrangle. The enclosure contained quarters for officers and enlisted men, an armory, a commissary, magazines, gun carriage and caisson shops, and a number of machine shops. The arsenal's impressive architecture and well-manicured grounds led many antebellum visitors to consider the Fayetteville Arsenal grounds to be one of the finest urban parks in the South.

On 22 April 1861, four weeks before North Carolina seceded from the Union, North Carolina state troops zealously seized the Fayetteville Arsenal. In view of the impending war, North Carolina's governor, John Ellis, ordered the seizure of the arsenal and all Federal fortifications in the state. Unlike the armory commander at Harper's Ferry, Virginia, Fayetteville's commander, a secession sympathizer, did not attempt to destroy the arsenal and its weapons stocks. Along with the arsenal facilities, the jubilant state troops captured 37,000 stand of arms, a field artillery battery, ammunition, and other military stores. The captured firearms (primarily smoothbore muskets) and other stores were later distributed to Confederate volunteer units in North Carolina and Virginia. In early June 1861, North Carolina transferred control of the facility to the Confederate States government.

Before the Civil War, the Federal Arsenal at Fayetteville was originally intended to be the principal small-arms depot and maintenance facility for the southeastern states. As such, machinery and structures necessary for weapons production were not incorporated into the original complex. However, the arsenal, was well equipped with tools and machinery needed to convert obsolete flintlock muskets to the newer percussion ignition system. In 1861, the Fayetteville Arsenal was the only Confederate government arsenal, other than the Richmond Arsenal, with steam power capabilities sufficient to operate rifle production machinery. The Confederate chief of ordnance, Josiah Gorgas, later wrote, "No arsenal, except that at Fayetteville, N.C., had a single machine above a foot lathe" in 1861; the Fayetteville Arsenal was the best equipped public arsenal in the Confederacy at the time of secession.

By August 1861, more than eighty machinists and workmen labored to upgrade older muskets and produce small-arms ammunition in the Fayetteville shops. In the fall of 1861, part of the rifle machinery salvaged from the Harper's Ferry Arsenal was shipped to Fayetteville. A number of machinists and skilled laborers from Harper's Ferry moved along with the equipment to work in Fayetteville. Additional buildings were hastily constructed of wood and production lines were set up to manufacture modified copies of the .58-caliber Model 1855 "Harper's Ferry" rifle (M1855).

M1855 rifles and rifle-muskets originally incorporated the notoriously undependable Maynard tape priming system. Many of the prewar production pieces were later altered in both Union and Confederate armories to use the more reliable percussion cap ignition system. In the Fayetteville productions lines, the Harper's Ferry dies were retooled to produce lock plates patterned after the improved Springfield Model 1861 percussion lock. The

modified weapons manufactured or assembled at Fayetteville are now generally referred to as M1855/61 Fayetteville rifles.

As the war progressed, the arsenal's labor force swelled to some 200 workers, who generally produced between 350 and 500 of the distinctive, brass-banded Fayetteville rifles per month from 1862 through the winter of 1865. The Fayetteville plant was capable of producing some 2,500 weapons per month, but the chronic shortage of skilled machinists and weapons-grade steel greatly hampered production throughout the war. Although manufacturing operations focused on production of new rifles, flintlock muskets scoured from the countryside were reworked, and thousands of Northern weapons captured on the battlefield were refurbished or repaired as needed at the facility.

Whites, free blacks, and enslaved blacks all worked in the sprawling complex to manufacture small arms, gun carriages and caissons, small arms cartridges, and knapsacks. A limited quantity of artillery projectiles and fuzes were apparently produced as well. Interestingly, the Confederate government regarded the Fayetteville rifle production line as a temporary operation. A central armory for small arms production was planned for Macon, Georgia. When completed, the Macon facility was to inherit Fayetteville's rifle machinery, but the Macon plant was not completed by war's end.

When Union major general William T. Sherman entered North Carolina in 1865, he was particularly keen on the destruction of the Fayetteville Arsenal. As Sherman's advance units threatened Fayetteville in early March, Confederate troops abandoned the facility. They removed arsenal stores and as much of the machinery as possible. Some machinery and the bulk of the stores, along with a number of the skilled machinists, were moved by rail and wagon to Greensboro, North Carolina. A portion of the machinery was rail shipped and hidden in abandoned coal mines in Chatham County, North Carolina. Soon after Union troops occupied Fayetteville, Sherman ordered the complete destruction of the arsenal. On 11 March 1865, all arsenal buildings and the remaining machinery, except for two small houses, were razed and burned by the 1st Regiment, Michigan Engineers. In 1881, the federal government sold the old arsenal property to private interests.

Rifle production at Fayetteville rarely exceeded 400 units per month, and on several occasions production was completely stalled from the lack of steel. The majority of the small arms machinery salvaged from Harper's Ferry was sent to the Richmond Arsenal, where the famous M1855/1861, "Dixie" or "Richmond" rifle-muskets and other arms were produced. The Richmond Arsenal received much greater material and labor support from the Confederate Ordnance Bureau, and as a result, it greatly eclipsed Fayetteville's weapons production and regularly manufactured 1,000 to 1,500 units per month throughout

the war. Despite the Fayetteville Arsenal's subordinate status, it contributed significantly to the Confederate war effort by consistently producing rifles and other stores with a reputation for quality and dependability.

—*Charles L. Heath, Jr.*

See also Armories, Arsenals, Founderies; Ordnance, Naval; Rifles; Small Arms; Springfield Armory.

For further reading:

Barrett, John G. *The Civil War in North Carolina* (1963).

Edwards, William B. *Civil War Guns: The Complete Story of Federal and Confederate Small Arms: Design, Manufacture, Identification, Procurement, Issue, Employment, Effectiveness, and Postwar Disposal* (1962; reprint, 1997).

Gorgas, Josiah. "Notes on the Ordnance Department of the Confederate Government." *Southern Historical Society Papers* (1884).

Taylor, M. P. "Sixth Battalion (Armory Guards)." *Histories of the Several Regiments and Battalions from North Carolina in the Great War, 1861–'65* (1901; reprint, 1999).

Vandiver, Frank E. *Ploughshares into Swords: Josiah Gorgas and Confederate Ordnance* (1952; reprint 1994).

FENTON, REUBEN EATON
(1819–1885)
New York governor and representative

Reuben Fenton was born on 4 July 1819, during the spirited nationalism of the so-called Era of Good Feelings. Besides holding locally elected office, he also served terms in both houses of Congress and as governor of New York.

Raised in a financially comfortable family in upstate Chautauqua County, New York, he attended local schools and academies. He intended to become a lawyer. That all changed in the Panic of 1837—at that time the United States' worst economic depression—when his father's business went bankrupt. Instead of law school, Fenton went into the lumber business and from the outset became quite successful. He became active in local politics and at age twenty-three was elected town supervisor. Ever ambitious, he was elected to Congress in 1852 as a Democrat. After the passage of the Kansas-Nebraska Act of 1854, the political landscape changed, and many Northern Democrats left the increasingly Southern-oriented party. Fenton joined the brand-new Republican Party, and later that year he helped found the new party in New York State and presided at its first state convention. Although he was defeated in 1854 by the powerful though short-lived "Know-Nothing" (American) Party, he was elected handily in 1856 and served in the House of Representatives for eight years. Fenton adhered completely to party ideology. He called for the repeal of the Fugitive Slave Act; he fought the expansion of slavery westward, and he condemned the Supreme Court's *Dred Scott* decision. He believed firmly that the U.S. government was controlled by a "slave power conspiracy." In 1864 he defeated incumbent Democrat Horatio Seymour in his bid for the governership of the Empire State. Seymour ran a corrupt campaign and had been somewhat sympathetic to the draft rioters the year before. Fenton, who had been a strong supporter of Lincoln throughout the war, won by a margin of less than 1 percent.

As governor he was a reformer, advocating change in education and improvements in state mental hospitals. In 1866 he lost to Schuyler Colfax, "The Smiler" of Indiana. However, the following year he was elected to the U.S. Senate. He became increasingly disenchanted with the Grant administration, which led him to join the Liberal Republican movement that supported Horace Greeley, an old New York ally of Fenton's, for president in 1872. However, Fenton's power had been waning in New York, as Roscoe Conkling had gained ascendancy in Republican Party circles.

Fenton retired in 1875 after one term in the Senate. President Hayes appointed him chairman of the U.S. Commission to the International Monetary Conference in 1878. In his final years he returned home to Jamestown, where he was a successful banker. Married twice (his first wife had died two years after they were married), he had three children with his second wife. He died suddenly in 1885 of an apparent heart attack.

—*Stephen G. Weisner*

See also New York Draft Riots.
For further reading:
McMahon, Helen Grace. "Reuben Eaton Fenton" (M.A. thesis, 1939).

FERRERO, EDWARD
(1831–1899)
Union general

Edward Ferrero was born on 18 January 1831 in Grenada, Spain, to Italian parents who relocated to New York City while he was an infant. His father, a dancer, established a successful school of dance in New York City. As a young man, Ferrero taught at his father's school and at the U.S. Military Academy at West Point. In 1859, his book, *The Art of Dancing, Historically Illustrated*, was published, making him one of the best-known experts in his field.

After gaining the rank of lieutenant colonel in the local militia, Ferrero was mustered into the Union army as colonel of the 51st New York—the Shepard Rifles—in October 1861. His infantry unit saw action throughout North Carolina during the winter of 1861–1862; in northern Virginia at Second Bull Run, Fredericksburg, and Chantilly; and at Antietam, where

on the battlefield he received his appointment to brigadier general.

The army's IX Corps, to which Ferrero's brigade was attached, was sent west to fight in Grant's army in June 1863. While with Grant, the 51st fought in the last days of the Vicksburg campaign, and in late 1863, Ferrero commanded a division in the defense of Knoxville. With the war in the West winding down, IX Corps was sent back East and reattached to the Army of the Potomac in spring 1864.

Ferrero displayed great leadership while in command of a regiment or smaller unit, but commanding a division at Knoxville, he was less effective. His men defended the city gallantly, but it has been noted that the defense was not on his orders. Yet the defense of Knoxville appeared to be his successful trial by fire, so at Petersburg, Virginia, he was put in command of IX Corps' 4th Division, which consisting of 4,300 black troops. During the siege at Petersburg, Ferrero volunteered his division to lead the charge at what would become the battle of the Crater. After receiving approval from Generals Ambrose Burnside and George Meade, Ferrero spent the following weeks readying his men for their task. Shortly before midnight on 29 July, only hours before the explosives were to be detonated, Meade changed his mind to insist that a more experienced division lead the attack. At 4:15 A.M. on 30 July 1864, the explosion devastated Confederate lines, but Ferrero and his men watched the carnage and confusion from a safe distance. They were finally allowed into the fray about 7:30 A.M.

Although instigated by one of the most daring exploits of the war, the battle of the Crater was marked by a poorly executed Federal attack. After the explosion, men charged toward the newly created chasm and, completely unprepared for the slaughter the blast had caused, they stopped. As Confederate guns behind nearby earthworks began pouring fire upon them, the Federals squandered much of the advantage of surprise by pausing to pull Confederate soldiers out of the hole. Worse for Ferrero, by the time his men made it to the Crater, he had taken shelter with General James H. Ledlie in a bombproof, where they allegedly drank rum while the fight raged. Confederate lines had been reformed, and by the end of the battle Union troops had suffered nearly two and a half times the casualties as the Confederates had. Ferrero was sternly criticized for his dereliction during the fiasco, although he continued to hold divisional commands in IX Corps of the Army of the Potomac until leaving the army in August 1865.

Ferrero was a much better businessman than soldier, and after his departure from the army, he returned to New York City. Once back at home, he leased a series of popular ballrooms until shortly before his death on 11 December 1899. One of his ballrooms was Tammany

Hall but, although he joined the Tammany Society, his interest was dancing, not politics.

—Brian D. McKnight

See also Crater, Battle of the.
For further reading:
Bradford, Ned, ed. Battles and Leaders of the Civil War (1957).
Cavanaugh, Michael A., and William Marvel. The Petersburg Campaign: The Battle of the Crater, "The Horrid Pit," June 25–August 6, 1864 (1989).
Drinkard, Dorothy L. Illinois Freedom Fighters: A Civil War Saga of the 29th Infantry, United States Colored Troops (1998).
Miller, Edward A., Jr. The Black Civil War Soldiers of Illinois: The Story of the Twenty-ninth U.S. Colored Infantry (1998).
Trudeau, Noah Andre. The Last Citadel: Petersburg, Virginia, June 1864–April 1865 (1991).

FESSENDEN, FRANCIS
(1839–1906)
Union general

Born to William Pitt and Ellen Deering Fessenden in Portland, Maine, Francis Fessenden was educated locally before attending and graduating from Bowdoin College in 1858 at the age of nineteen. Shortly after graduation Fessenden enrolled in Harvard Law School from where he graduated before the Civil War. When the Civil War erupted in 1861 Fessenden was on an extended trip to Minnesota, but he returned East where Secretary of War Simon Cameron gave him a regular captain's commission.

As commander of a company in the 19th United States Infantry Fessenden served primarily in garrison duty around Washington for much of the first year of the war. Sent to the west to serve under Don Carlos Buell in March 1862, he was seriously wounded in the arm at the campaign Shiloh after which he returned to Washington. Sufficiently recovered to resume field service by early fall, Fessenden was promoted to colonel and given command of the 25th Maine, a short-term regiment stationed in the defenses of Washington, D.C. For a time in the fall of 1862 Fessenden commanded a brigade at Camp Seward, Virginia. Upon the expiration of the 25th's term, Fessenden performed administrative duties in Washington before being given command of the 30th Maine in January 1864.

The 30th though a new regiment was composed of veteran soldiers from other units that had been disbanded because of high casualties. Therefore they were all acquainted with heavy combat duty. As soon as the regiment was organized it was sent to the Department of the Gulf to be used in the upcoming Red River campaign as part of XIX Corps. In February Fessenden assumed command of 3d brigade, 1st division, XIX Corps. He commanded that brigade at Sabine Crossroads, Pleasant Hill. On 23 April during the retreat at Monett's Bluff, Fessenden led a charge against the Confederate army that allowed the retreat to continue. However, in the charge Fessenden received a severe wound in the right leg. After several days of trying to save the limb, the surgeons were finally forced to amputate. Back east, where Fessenden's father was a prominent senator and soon to be named secretary of the treasury, rumors circulated that Fessenden had fallen into the hands of the Confederates, and the highest echelons of the War Department were mobilized to learn his fate. When it was determined that he was not a prisoner and that he would survive his wound, he was made a brigadier general of volunteers.

After recuperating through the summer of 1864, Fessenden was sufficiently recovered to travel to Washington where he served in several administrative posts for the remainder of the year. He felt sufficiently recovered by the spring of 1865, when the war had nearly reached its conclusion to request a field command. In March Winfield Scott Hancock requested that Fessenden be assigned to his command, but not until May, after Robert E. Lee's surrender, was the transfer accomplished. At that time Fessenden assumed command of a brigade under Hancock in West Virginia.

At the end of the summer of 1865, Fessenden returned to administrative duties. He was placed on the board of officers who heard the case of Henry Wirz, the former commandant of the Confederate Andersonville prison. Wirz was convicted by this board and executed for war crimes. In November 1865 Fessenden received a brevet promotion to major general of volunteers. Mustered out of the volunteer service in 1866, he was offered a regular infantry command at the rank of lieutenant colonel but believed that the wounds he had suffered during the war would prevent him from fully doing his duty. He requested instead to be retired from the regular service. His request was granted, and he retired at the rank of brigadier general.

Upon retirement, Fessenden returned to Portland, Maine where he practiced law with his brother, James Deering Fessenden, also a Civil War Union general. Fessenden, however, showed little interest in the politics that had so consumed his father's life though he did pay tribute to the elder Fessenden by collecting his important writings and letters for publication. In his later years the younger Fessenden wrote a biography of his father to accompany the publication of his father's papers. The volume was not published until after Francis Fessenden's death, which occurred in Portland on 2 January 1906.

—David S. Heidler and Jeanne T. Heidler

See also Fessenden, William Pitt; Red River Campaign.
For further reading:
Jellison, Charles A. Fessenden of Maine, A Civil War Senator (1962).
Johnson, Ludwell H. Red River Campaign: Politics and Cotton in the Civil War (1958).

FESSENDEN, JAMES DEERING
(1833–1882)
Union general

Born to William Pitt and Ellen Deering Fessenden in Westbrook, Maine, James Deering Fessenden was educated locally before graduating from Bowdoin College. After graduation he studied law and then entered his father's firm. During the five years that he practiced law before the Civil War, Fessenden demonstrated great talent for the legal profession. At the outbreak of the war, however, he resigned his position to join the army.

He spent the summer of 1861 recruiting a company of riflemen who subsequently formed a part of the 2d Regiment of U.S. Sharpshooters. Fessenden was commissioned captain of the company in November 1861 and immediately left for Washington, D.C. Fessenden served with the regiment in the defenses of Washington through the winter of 1861–1862 and into the spring of 1862, seeing no action during that time.

In the spring, however, his father's position as U.S. senator from Maine gained him promotion to lieutenant colonel and transfer to the staff of David Hunter on the coast of South Carolina. While serving as Hunter's aide-de-camp in the summer of 1862, Fessenden organized what was reported to be the first African-American regiment for the U.S. Army. The War Department refused to accept these soldiers, and the Lincoln administration rebuked Hunter for taking such action. At the end of 1862, Fessenden was promoted to colonel and continued on Hunter's staff through the early operations against Charleston, South Carolina, in the spring of 1863. A riding accident, however, prevented him from being present during the major actions against the city's defenses in the summer of 1863. Instead, Fessenden did light administrative duty during his recovery in Washington and then recruiting duty before he was physically able to return to field service.

In the fall of 1863, Fessenden was placed under the command of Joseph Hooker as the latter transferred XI and XII Corps from the Army of the Potomac to Chattanooga. During the upcoming campaign to save Chattanooga for the Union, Fessenden served as Hooker's aide-de-camp. Hooker commended him for his behavior at Missionary Ridge and recommended his promotion to brigadier general of volunteers.

Fessenden continued to serve as Hooker's aide-de-camp during the Atlanta campaign in the spring and summer of 1864. During the campaign, Fessenden acted primarily as Hooker's messenger to his field-grade officers, directing troop movements in Hooker's name during the battles. He was commended for his actions at Resaca, Kennesaw Mountain, and Peachtree Creek. Again recommended by Hooker for promotion, Fessenden was made brigadier general of volunteers in August 1864.

By then Hooker had already left the army that was besieging Atlanta, and Fessenden, without a command, returned on leave to his home in Portland, Maine. While there, he learned that he had been given a brigade in Philip Sheridan's Army of the Shenandoah combating Confederate general Jubal Early in the Shenandoah Valley. The order directing Fessenden to Virginia, however, was revoked when it was learned that the officials who had directed it had mistaken him for his brother, fellow Union general Francis Fessenden. However, at that time, Francis Fessenden was recovering from losing his leg during the Red River campaign and was unable to assume any command. Therefore, despite the mistake, James Fessenden was ordered to Virginia in his brother's place.

Given the command of a brigade in William Emory's XIX Corps, Fessenden arrived in the Shenandoah Valley in time to fight at Cedar Creek on 19 October. After that battle, Fessenden conducted routine reconnaissance duty in the valley before being put in command of the garrison at Winchester in January 1865. He remained in command there until after Robert E. Lee's surrender at Appomattox Court House. During the Grand Review in Washington in May 1865, Fessenden led a brigade in the parade. In July 1865 he was placed in command of a brigade in the Middle Department under Winfield Scott Hancock. Shortly thereafter he was transferred to South Carolina, where he served until being mustered out of volunteer service in 1866. Before leaving the army, however, he was given a brevet promotion to major general of volunteers for his service during the war.

Fessenden returned to Portland, Maine. He practiced law in partnership with his brother Francis and became involved in Maine politics. In addition to occupying a federal appointment as register of bankruptcy, he also served three terms in the Maine state legislature. He remained an active attorney in Portland until his death there on 18 November 1882.

—*David S. Heidler and Jeanne T. Heidler*

See also Atlanta Campaign; Chattanooga Campaign.
For further reading:
Jellison, Charles A. *Fessenden of Maine, A Civil War Senator* (1962).

FESSENDEN, WILLIAM PITT
(1806–1869)
Secretary of the treasury

William Pitt Fessenden emerged as the leader of the Republican majority in the U.S. Senate during the Civil War. His intellect, unmatched debating skills, and integrity gave him great clout in crafting Civil War legislation.

Born out of wedlock and separated permanently from his mother a few days after his birth, Fessenden grew into a precocious youth. His father, Samuel Fessenden, was renowned as one of the best lawyers in Maine, an early supporter of the abolitionist movement, and an active member of the Federalist Party. At the age of thirteen, Fessenden enrolled at Bowdoin College. After a moderate start, he buckled down, improved his grades, and earned a degree by the time he turned seventeen. The college withheld his diploma initially as a result of a wild evening of "irregularity of eating and drinking at Wardsworth Tavern…." His father cajoled the administrators into granting the degree.

In 1827 Fessenden was admitted to the bar. He settled in Portland and established a law practice that lasted for twenty years. He rose quickly through the ranks of Maine's lawyers, often appearing in court against his father. He became an active member of the Whig Party; he brought his bride to the Young Men's Whig Convention in 1832 for their honeymoon.

Fessenden served in the Maine legislature intermittently from 1831 to 1840, at which time he agreed to run for an available seat in the U.S. Congress. During his tenure in the Twenty-sixth Congress, he supported John Quincy Adams's efforts to revoke the "gag rule" that blocked discussion of slavery on the House floor. Fessenden left Congress after one term, "enraged with the subserviency of Northern Democrats to Southern political dictation and with increased antipathy to slavery."

In 1854 Fessenden was elected to represent Maine in the Senate. He established his reputation immediately, giving a greatly admired speech against the Kansas-Nebraska Bill just after taking his seat. In 1857 he was appointed to the Finance Committee; when Southern senators withdrew after the secession of their states, Fessenden became the committee's chair. He opposed the introduction of greenbacks and vigorously pushed for the broad tax programs inaugurated during the Civil War. Fessenden endorsed a progressive income tax well before his peers. Continually he extolled his colleagues to pay for the war as it was prosecuted, rather than resorting to an inflationary paper currency or burdening later generations with debt. He favored high tariffs as a revenue necessity.

Fessenden was appointed secretary of the treasury in July 1864 after Salmon P. Chase tendered his resignation. Many in Congress welcomed Fessenden's appointment, hoping he would reverse the policies established by Secretary Chase, but once in office, Fessenden found that his options were limited. When bond sales stalled, he rehired Jay Cooke, whose high commission fees rankled many in Congress. Fessenden continued the cotton trade with Southern planters though he found the practice morally distasteful. Fessenden's term at the Treasury lasted only one year. Plagued by the mysterious "National Hotel illness" and weary of the thankless demands of the position, Fessenden resigned and returned to the Senate.

In December 1865 he reluctantly assumed the chairmanship of the Joint Committee on Reconstruction, fearing that if he turned down the appointment the more radical Senator Charles Sumner would take the position. Fessenden pushed to have the seceded states reincorporated but wanted the Confederate leaders to lose their political privileges. He also believed that the government was obligated to protect the freedmen and that their best means for protection lay in granting them suffrage.

Fessenden's health declined and his effectiveness waned. He scorned his colleagues as they mounted their drive for President Andrew Johnson's impeachment. Fessenden harbored great contempt for the president, but he never believed Johnson committed an impeachable offense. Fessenden's consistent objections to the entire procedure, culminating in his "not guilty" vote, undoubtedly saved Johnson from an inglorious fate. Though Fessenden was maligned immediately after the vote, once tempers cooled, he was congratulated by many for standing by his principles.

When Fessenden left Washington in April 1869, he found that much of his support in Maine had eroded. He died 7 September before testing his strength in an election. His colleague and friend, Senator James Grimes, eulogized Fessenden as "the highest-toned man he had ever known, the purest man he had ever known in public life, and the ablest man of his day."

—*Jane Flaherty*

See also Chase, Salmon P.; Cooke, Jay; Financing, U.S.A.
For further reading:
Cook, Robert. "The Grave of All My Comforts: William Pitt Fessenden as Secretary of the Treasury, 1864–1865." *Civil War History* (1995).
Fessenden, Francis. *The Life and Public Services of William Pitt Fessenden* (1907).
Jellison, Charles A. *Fessenden of Maine: Civil War Senator* (1962).

FIELD, CHARLES WILLIAM
(1828–1892)
Confederate general

The son of Willis Field and Isabella Miriam Buck Field, Charles William Field was born in Woodford County, Kentucky. In 1849, he graduated from the U.S. Military Academy twenty-seventh in his class of forty-three and received a dragoon commission. He served in a variety of frontier posts before returning to West Point in 1856 as an instructor of cavalry. By the outbreak of the Civil War, he had attained the rank of captain.

Field resigned his commission on 30 May 1861 and soon accepted a Confederate commission as the colonel of the 6th Virginia Cavalry, placed that fall in Brigadier General J. E. B. Stuart's brigade. On 9 March 1862, he received a promotion to brigadier general and switched to the Confederate infantry.

During the opening months of the Peninsula campaign, Field and his brigade were stationed north of Richmond to ward off an attack from the north by Irvin McDowell. Field's brigade was involved in skirmishing with McDowell's army around Fredericksburg in April 1862. As the planning commenced for what would become known as the Seven Days' battle, however, Field was placed in A. P. Hill's division and led his brigade in the first line of attack across the Chickahominy River at the battle of Mechanicsville on 26 June 1862.

On 9 August 1862, Field led his brigade to the battle of Cedar Mountain though he did not arrive on the field until late in the fighting. He continued to command his brigade under Hill at Second Bull Run, where he was seriously wounded in the hip. This wound put him out of action for most of the next year. During that time, he served in a staff position in Richmond as the superintendent of the Conscription Bureau.

Promoted to major general on 12 February 1864, Field was given command of John Bell Hood's old division of the Army of Northern Virginia in time to command it at the battle of the Wilderness in early May 1864. He protected the right wing of Robert E. Lee's army there. A few days later, this division repulsed a major assault of Ulysses S. Grant's army at Spotsylvania. As Grant moved across the James River in June 1864, Field was sent with his brigade on 16 June to resecure the Bermuda Hundred defensive line that had been abandoned when P. G. T. Beauregard pulled back toward Petersburg. Field continued to command his division through the long siege of Petersburg and withdrew from those lines in April as part of Lee's evacuation. He surrendered his division of 4,953 (one of the largest of Lee's remaining divisions) at Appomattox.

After the war, Field engaged in various business activities until 1875, when he accepted a colonel's commission in the Egyptian army. He remained in Egypt until 1878. Upon his return to the United States, he served as the doorkeeper for the U.S. House of Representatives before accepting a position with the U.S. government as a civil engineer and then as a superintendent of an Indian reservation in Arkansas.

Field returned to Washington shortly before his death in 1892. He was buried in Baltimore.

—*David S. Heidler and Jeanne T. Heidler*

See also Bermuda Hundred; Mechanicsville, Battle of; Wilderness, Battle of the.

For further reading:
Matter, William D. *If It Takes All Summer: The Battle of Spotsylvania* (1988).

Rhea, Gordon C. *The Battle of the Wilderness, May 5–6, 1864* (1994).

FILLMORE, MILLARD
(1800–1874)
Fourteenth president of the United States

Born desperately poor on a Cayuga County, New York, farm, but encouraged and assisted by his future wife, Abigail Powers, Millard Fillmore educated himself and became a highly successful Buffalo lawyer. After promoting numerous civic and educational causes, he was elected to the state assembly in 1828. There he led successful efforts to abolish imprisonment for debt and the religious oath for courtroom witnesses. Elected to the U.S. Congress (1833–1835 and 1837–1843), he was runner-up in the vote for Speaker of the House and won high praise as chairman of the Ways and Means Committee. Elected New York state comptroller in 1847, he enlarged the Erie Canal basin, established a new banking code, and designed a state currency system that was later copied by the National Banking Act of 1861. In 1848 he was nominated for vice president by delegates hoping to balance Zachary Taylor's ownership of 140 slaves with Fillmore's previous opposition to the Mexican War and support for the Wilmot Proviso, which sought to limit the extension of slavery.

In 1850 Southern senators combined Henry Clay's compromise proposals into a single Omnibus Bill. President Taylor opposed this linkage of California with the Texas claim to New Mexico as a plot to give most of free New Mexico to the slave state of Texas. Taylor hoped to stop the sectional conflict by having California and New Mexico become states as soon as possible. Presiding over the Senate, Fillmore agreed with Taylor, but was ready to support the Omnibus if the final amended version should leave New Mexico intact.

On 9 July 1850 Taylor died, and Fillmore became president. He immediately sent additional troops to New Mexico and with Senator James A. Pearce of Maryland planned a strategy by which a series of amendments broke up the Omnibus. Within a few weeks its provisions were passed as separate amended bills. The Texas settlement preserved New Mexico and came only after Fillmore warned that he would resist any invasion of New Mexico by Texas.

Fillmore accepted the compromise provisions, but agonized over signing and enforcing the new Fugitive Slave Act. It violated his conscience, but it was the only concession made to the South. Adherence to the compromise was necessary to help the Southern Unionists defeat the secessionists in the elections of 1850–1852.

Fillmore therefore signed the bill and gave the law

nominal support, although in most cases the slave or slaves had escaped before he acted. Meanwhile, he also strengthened the Charleston forts and sent additional troops to North and South Carolina.

In foreign policy, Fillmore successfully upheld American rights against Britain in Nicaragua and kept the French from establishing a protectorate over Hawaii. He also launched Commodore Matthew Perry's expedition that opened Japan to the outside world. When Mexico nullified a treaty authorizing an American company to dig a canal across the Tehuantepec Peninsula, Senator Judah P. Benjamin threatened to send 500 men against Mexico, but Fillmore announced that he would arrest anyone who got involved.

Fillmore tried to prevent Southern filibustering efforts to take Cuba, but Narciso Lopez sailed from New Orleans with 400 young Americans. Defeated and captured in Cuba, Lopez and 50 Americans were executed and 160 were taken to Spain for servitude in the mines. Americans everywhere were furious and a New Orleans mob sacked the Spanish consulate and a Spanish newspaper. Fillmore, however, apologized to Spain and skillfully negotiated the release of the prisoners.

By 1851 Fillmore was immensely popular and could have ensured his nomination for another term, but he informed various supporters that he wished to retire and hoped that Secretary of State Daniel Webster could be elected. Meanwhile, Senator William H. Seward, bitterly hated throughout the South, was mustering delegates for General Winfield Scott. Finally recognizing the danger to the Whig Party if Scott should be nominated, Fillmore became a candidate too late. At the convention he led for several ballots and Webster's small number of delegates could have given him the necessary two-thirds majority. Webster, however stayed in the contest until his confused delegates shifted to Scott. Southern Whigs voted overwhelmingly for the Democrat Franklin Pierce, and Scott's crushing defeat destroyed the Whig Party.

Abigail died shortly after Fillmore left office, and his daughter died a year later. Seeking diversion, the distraught Fillmore joined the American or "Know-Nothing" Party, which attracted a great many Northern Whigs who disliked both the radical Republicans and the Southern-dominated Democrats.

Nominated for president by the Know-Nothings in 1856, Fillmore ignored the party's anti-Catholic, antiforeigner platform and made twenty-seven speeches warning that the election of the entirely Northern Republican, John C. Frémont, would cause a civil war. He received 28.6 percent of the vote and may have prevented the election of Frémont.

Abandoning politics, Fillmore married a wealthy widow and became Buffalo's most distinguished senior citizen, ready to donate both time and money to numerous worthy causes and institutions. He supported the Northern war effort fully. He died on 8 March 1874. His Know-Nothing candidacy should not negate the fact that he overcame dire poverty to become an outstanding public servant who handled every responsibility with ability and dedication.

—*Elbert B. Smith*

See also American Party; Election of 1856; Frémont, John C.; Pierce, Franklin.
For further reading:
Grayson, Benson L. *The Unknown President: The Administration of Millard Fillmore* (1981).
Hamilton, Holman. *Prologue to Conflict: The Crisis and Compromise of 1850* (1964).
Rayback, Robert. *Millard Fillmore: Biography of a President* (1959).
Smith, Elbert B. *The Presidencies of Zachary Taylor and Millard Fillmore* (1988).

FINANCING, C.S.A.

During the American Civil War, the Confederate States of America's government and its individual states spent approximately $2.1 billion on the war effort. However, the Confederacy possessed neither the fiscal policies nor the financial system capable of sustaining such an expanded wartime economy. Poor financial leadership in the national government dealt with fiscal problems in an ad hoc manner, rather than planning for the necessary economic expansion and preparing for fiscal contingencies.

In April 1861 the cash-poor Confederacy possessed only $27 million in specie, the "hard" currency that was itself a precious metal or redeemable in a certain quantity of a precious metal. Most of the region's real value was tied up in land, slaves, and agricultural produce. Of these, only agricultural produce could be readily converted into liquid assets. The Southern staple crop of cotton represented a potentially important financial, as well as political, asset. Other staple crops included sugar, tobacco, and rice. The agricultural production of these four made up about two-fifths of the Confederacy's gross national product; cotton alone was the largest single export in antebellum America.

In a move designed to appeal to the elite of South Carolina, President Jefferson Davis appointed Christopher G. Memminger as the Confederacy's first secretary of the treasury. An honest and diligent native-born German, Memminger had risen from poverty to become an influential attorney and large slaveholder in Charleston. Before the war he had long championed the use of a metal-backed currency as part of solid and reliable economic policy. During the war, however, economic circumstances and the Confederate Congress forced him into the opposite economic policy of printing Treasury notes—"soft" currency that is paper money often unbacked by specie. More than $1.5 billion worth of Treasury notes were printed over the four years of the conflict. This figure amounted to approximately 60 percent of the Confederacy's revenue.

The Confederacy generated almost 25 percent of its revenue through loans. In the domestic Produce Loan of 1861, the Confederate national government issued Treasury notes in exchange for pledges of proceeds from cash-crop sales. This program brought in revenue of only $34 million, much of it coming too late in the conflict to have any great effect. In the domestic Bankers Loan, also of 1861, the national government sold interest-bearing bonds worth $150 million. The Confederacy also sought credit from international sources like the Erlanger Loan of March 1863. Originally borrowing $15 million from the French banking house of Emile Erlanger in March 1863, this loan in fact only yielded $8.5 million.

As the war dragged on, the Confederate government even resorted to confiscation of supplies, the value of which accounted for slightly more than 15 percent of the South's wartime revenue. Confiscation further undermined trust in the central government by disrupting the everyday lives and finances of Southerners. As a result, this also stirred up resentment towards the Confederate military.

Under Christopher Memminger's direction, the Confederate Treasury possessed several options for generating government revenue, such as exchanging imports with cash-crop exports, establishing taxes on property, and exploiting trade through blockade running. The self-imposed, voluntary embargo on cotton shipments to Europe made the possibility of exchanging cash crops for war supplies a moot point. With better financial understanding and management, the staple crops might have been used to make in-kind payments to foreign countries for war supplies. Instead, the Confederacy stopped cotton export to other countries in hopes of driving prices higher and, more importantly, securing foreign intervention in the Civil War. Taxation on income and property generated only tiny amounts of revenue because of an inefficient collection mechanism and relatively easy evasion of those taxes assessed. Prioritizing war supplies as the major cargo for Confederate blockade running may also have helped Confederate finances in particular and the war effort in general. However, none of these viable alternatives were utilized on a scale large enough to put the Confederacy on a solid financial foundation. They represented short-term, small-scale solutions that actually exacerbated problems facing the Confederate financial system in the long term.

By the summer of 1863, the Confederate government's fiscal troubles had filtered down to the common people. Severe inflation and material shortages wracked the South because of military defeats and financial trou-

bles. Within three months of the defeats at Gettysburg and Vicksburg, prices rose 58 percent alone. By the winter of 1864, a barrel of flour cost $250, and prices of other goods increased at a similar rate of inflation. In terms of the consumer's buying power, Southerners' real wages declined by more than 65 percent in four years of the conflict. During the conflict, Southerners suffered financially from 6,000 percent inflation.

In 1864 Treasury Secretary Memminger and the Confederate Congress cooperated in an ill-fated endeavor to curb inflation by authorizing the Compulsory Funding Measure. An act of desperation, this de facto loan to the government required Confederate citizens either to convert Treasury notes to low-interest bonds or to exchange already circulated Treasury notes for deflated newly issued notes. Any unconverted or unexchanged Treasury notes were devalued retroactively. Although it stabilized the Southern economy for a few months, the Compulsory Funding Measure failed in the long term, in part because Southerners lost faith in the their country's financial stability.

With ever-mounting fiscal problems, Treasury Secretary Memminger resigned his post in June 1864. President Davis replaced him with George A. Trenholm, another wealthy merchant from Charleston, South Carolina. Trenholm attempted to raise revenue for the government through increasing taxes and selling bonds, but too little hard currency and too few liquid assets remained in the South in late 1864. Instead, the Confederate Treasury fed its hunger for revenue by printing more Treasury notes and thus further increasing inflation. In the final months before Appomattox in April 1865, Secretary Trenholm called for charitable donations from Confederate citizens and even contributed $200,000 of his own fortune. Such patriotic sacrifices had little effect on the South's hopeless economic situation.

Because the reasons for the failure of Confederate finances were numerous, blame cannot be placed on any single person or factor. Instead, multiple causes combined to bring about financial decline and collapse. Southerners deluded themselves regarding the economic and political power of so-called King Cotton in Europe. Jealously guarded states' rights handicapped the Confederacy's fiscal policies by limiting the national government's power of taxation and enforcement of taxation. Selfish and short-sighted individuals misunderstood or undermined the economic needs of the nation as a whole. As much as anything else, the Confederacy suffered from a lack of financial and economic leadership. Lastly, the conservative and arrogant Southern mentality retarded any creative impulses that might have solved its fiscal problems.

—David J. Ulbrich

See also Impressment; Memminger, Christopher; Tax–in–Kind; Trenholm, George.

For further reading:

Ball, Douglas B. *Financial Failure and the Confederate Defeat* (1991).

Koistinen, Paul A. C. *Beating Plowshares into Swords: The Political Economy of American Warfare, 1606–1865* (1996).

Roark, James L. "Behind the Lines: Confederate Economy and Society." In *Writing the Civil War: The Quest to Understand.* Edited by James M. McPherson and William J. Cooper Jr. (1998).

Schwab, John C. *The Confederate States of America, 1861–1865: A Financial and Industrial History of the South during the Civil War* (1901; reprint, 1968).

Schweikart, Larry. *Banking the American South from the Age of Jackson to Reconstruction* (1987).

Todd, Richard Cecil. *Confederate Finance* (1954).

FINANCING, U.S.A.

The government of the North financed its war effort with a combination of war bonds, taxation, and legal-tender notes. Most important was the sale of war bonds, which covered approximately two-thirds of the war's total cost; taxes covered about 21 percent.

The Union's greatest financial difficulties came early in the war. Even before fighting had begun, the national debt reached its highest level in decades, due to a decline in revenues that started in 1857. After secession of the Confederate states, specie left the nation as the North's credit rating dropped. The Treasury, under the leadership of Salmon P. Chase, relied on loans because Congress would not meet again until July 1861. Using authority granted by laws passed before secession, Chase issued $14.4 million in bonds and Treasury notes.

When Congress convened, the Treasury, members of Congress, and most other people underestimated the war's length and cost. On 5 July, Congress received Chase's proposals for the next fiscal year. At that time he believed that $320 million would be sufficient, with approximately one-fourth provided by taxation. Congress soon granted Chase authority to issue securities up to $250 million. He negotiated with banks in Boston, New York, and Philadelphia to acquire a total of $150 million in specie, which they paid in three installments from August through November. The banks basically became underwriters of the loan while the securities were being sold to the public. This system worked well while the banking community had confidence in the government's finances. That collapsed in December 1861 due to the *Trent* Affair (which threatened war with Britain) and to Chase's annual report (which showed that revenues were below projected levels while expenses were higher, causing a shortfall of about $40 million). Those events led to hoarding of specie and declines in the market value of government securities, which in turn forced a suspension of specie payments on 30 December.

Because state banks no longer had to redeem their currency notes, bankers could have profitably issued additional millions of currency without risk. Instead of permitting inflation by such a means, the government chose to issue its own legal-tender currency. Congressman Elbridge G. Spaulding prepared a bill, enacted in February 1862, called the Legal Tender Act. It permitted the Treasury to issue $150 million of notes that would be legal tender for all public or private debts, except for customs duties and interest on government bonds. Subsequently Congress passed two more acts, raising the authorized total to $450 million. The Treasury actually issued only $431.5 million.

The legal-tender notes (commonly called greenbacks) permitted the government to continue financing the war at a time before it had arranged for adequate taxes or for efficient marketing of large amounts of government bonds. Even before Congress passed the Legal Tender Act, however, it had begun considering other means of raising money.

In July 1861, when Secretary Chase proposed that 25 percent of the government's needs come from taxes, he believed (mistakenly) that 75 percent of necessary taxes could come from land sales and a few changes in the tariff. That would leave $20 million to be collected by some other form of taxation, which Chase left to the determination of Congress. After working more than a month, Congress enacted a measure that raised tariffs on some items, created an income tax of 3 percent on annual incomes over $800 (the first ever in U.S. history), and laid a direct tax on the states of $20 million.

When Congress reconvened in December and received Chase's negative financial report, the Treasury was aware that significantly more revenue would be needed. However, Chase had no substantial recommendations on taxation, suggesting only adjustments in tariff rates, raising the direct tax on states, and imposing excise taxes.

It was clear to most members of Congress that more would be needed. At the very least, they wanted to be sure that adequate money would be available to pay interest on government securities. During this session, Congress enacted two tariff measures that raised rates considerably. More importantly, a subsequent measure, known as the Internal Revenue Act, passed. It included excise taxes on liquor, playing cards, tobacco, and luxury items; stamp taxes; ad valorem taxes on manufactured goods and processed meats; inheritance taxes; gross receipts taxes on corporations, banks, and insurance companies (and a tax on interest or dividends paid to investors); license taxes on almost every service or profession (except clergy); and an income tax of 3 percent on incomes of $600–10,000 and of 5 percent on those above $10,000. The law also created the Internal Revenue Bureau within the Treasury. As a result, nearly every free Union resident now had to pay some form of

tax to the federal government. Enactment of substantial internal revenue measures assured that the Treasury could market war bonds successfully.

In his December 1861 report, Chase suggested a system of national banks authorized to issue notes secured by government bonds. That would serve the dual purpose of providing loans to the government and a uniform currency for the nation. During the 1862 congressional session, his proposal got lost due to the press of other business and opposition of state bankers, but Chase remained committed to it.

In the meantime, Chase concentrated on the sale of government bonds. In 1862 Congress authorized sale of $500 million having 6 percent interest, callable in five years and maturing in twenty. Because sales were slow, Chase turned to Jay Cooke to undertake high-pressure sales to small investors, a process Cooke had been suggesting for a year. In October 1862, Cooke became the Treasury's special agent. He used patriotic advertising combined with information about potential profits to sell bonds in denominations as small as $50 to be paid in monthly installments. In 1865 he became the government's agent for sale of three-year notes at 7.3 percent. Of those two securities, he marketed a total of $1.2 billion, earning a net profit of around $700,000. Total gross debt of the Union government rose to $2.7 billion in 1865.

Late in 1862, Cooke also began active support for Chase's national banking proposal. That, combined with a vigorous endorsement from President Abraham Lincoln and a renewed recommendation from Chase, revived the issue in Congress. All three emphasized the economic benefits of a permanent circulating medium that would be acceptable nationwide. Chase added, however, that at the war's end the Treasury would still require a much larger investment market than had ever previously been available.

The administration's bank bill encountered significant opposition in the House; however, in the Senate it gained the support of John Sherman. He forcefully connected those who argued for the rights of state banks to those making similar claims for slavery and secession. To cap his argument, he quoted former President Thomas Jefferson as saying in 1814 that the state banks should be destroyed and their notes replaced by Treasury notes. Sherman made minor modifications in the bill, which helped to convince key House opponents to accept it after the Senate approved it. The National Banking Act became law on 25 February 1863.

Sherman's victory had little impact on financing the war. National bank notes did not supplant existing state bank notes and greenbacks, nor did inflation cease. However, the law did continue an on-going shift in the relative powers of states and the federal government. Both the Legal Tender Act and the Internal Revenue

Act had increased federal powers. The banking act more directly infringed on a power states had exercised since the American Revolution. Its opponents were advocates (in a small way) of states' rights, which explains why the National Banking Act passed. The same nationalism also explains the enactment in 1865 of a 10 percent tax on state bank notes that halted their issue. Even though state banks continued to exist, the long-term economic growth of the nation was probably helped by the availability of a uniform currency (although other aspects of the law contributed to periodic panics in the money market before 1914).

The U.S. government financed its wartime requirements (about $4 billion) in a fairly efficient way. The fumbling approach in 1861 led to an unnecessary crisis in the winter of 1861–1862. To some extent that may be blamed on Chase's inexperience and his prejudice against selling government bonds below par. However, the greater problem was that no one grasped the duration and size of the war effort in its early months. At no time after the passage of the first Legal Tender Act was the government's ability to meet its obligations threatened. The Union did experience inflation, but the 80 percent rate for 1861–1865 was less than that of World War I (84 percent). If the Treasury had undertaken a stringent taxation policy and an efficient method of selling bonds in 1861, the suspension of specie payments might not have occurred and the circulation of greenbacks might not have been necessary. But, given the general expectations for a short war, Chase and Congress did a reasonably good job.

—*Sue C. Patrick*

See also Chase, Salmon Portland; Cooke, Jay; Financing, C.S.A.; Greenbacks; Legal Tender Acts; Spaulding, Elbridge Gerry.

For further reading:

Curry, Leonard P. *Blueprint for Modern America: Nonmilitary Legislation of the First Civil War Congress* (1968).

Hammond, Bray. *Sovereignty and an Empty Purse: Banks and Politics in the Civil War* (1970).

Larson, Henrietta M. *Jay Cooke: Private Banker* (1936).

Sharkey, Robert P. *Money, Class, and Party: An Economic Study of Civil War and Reconstruction* (1959).

FINEGAN, JOSEPH
(ca. 1810–1885)
Confederate general

One of six Irish-born generals in the Confederate army, Joseph Finegan was a native of Clones, County Monaghan. His date of birth is usually listed as 17 November 1814, but statements made in later life by Finegan, as well as his military records, indicate that he was born in 1810 or 1811. Little is known of either his early years in Ireland or exactly when he arrived in the United States. Finegan was in America, however, at least as early as August 1832, for in that month he enlisted in the U.S. Army at New York. Finegan served for the next five years in Company G of the 3d Artillery, rising to the rank of first sergeant and acting sergeant major. He participated in the Second Seminole War before being discharged in 1837 at Fort Harlee, Florida.

Finegan evidently remained in Florida after leaving the army. He eventually settled in Fernandina, where in the years before the Civil War he worked as a lawyer and became prominent in the lumber and railroad industries. He became a partner with David Levy Yulee in the construction and operation of the Florida Railroad, which linked Fernandina on the Atlantic coast with Cedar Keys on the Gulf of Mexico.

Elected to attend the Florida Secession Convention, which met in Tallahassee in early 1861, Finegan voted with the 62 to 7 majority to withdraw Florida from the Union. Upon the outbreak of the war, Finegan helped raise and was elected captain of a company known as the Fernandina Volunteers, which was stationed at Fort Clinch on Amelia Island during early 1861. Finegan also served as commander of the post of Fernandina. By mid-May, he had been promoted to lieutenant colonel in the Florida State Troops and was acting as military aide to Florida governor Madison Starke Perry. In this capacity Finegan would eventually earn promotion to colonel.

In April 1862, almost certainly because of his political connections, Finegan earned promotion to brigadier general and assumed command of the District of Middle and East Florida. In November of that year the district was divided, with Finegan exercising authority control over the portion of Florida east of the Suwannee River. His district included the coastal towns of Jacksonville, Fernandina, and St. Augustine. Federal forces had occupied the latter two locations in early 1862, and Jacksonville would suffer through four separate occupations between 1862 and 1864. Finegan had only a handful of units, largely untried, with which to defend such a large area.

During 1862–1863 his troops skirmished several times with Federal forces near Jacksonville. In 1862, elements of his command occupied St. Johns Bluff on the St. Johns River below Jacksonville. That October, a Union expedition of about 1,500 men marched against the rebel position, which was abandoned without a fight. In the aftermath, Finegan quarreled with the fort's commander, Lieutenant Colonel Charles Hopkins, over responsibility for the incident. In March 1863, Finegan's men skirmished once more with a Northern force that had again occupied Jacksonville.

Early in February 1864, Federal forces mounted their largest invasion of Florida. Led by Brigadier General Truman Seymour, a force of about 7,000 men occupied Jacksonville and mounted raids into the interior.

Finegan, meanwhile, scrambled to consolidate his scattered troops, while calling frantically for reinforcements from South Carolina and Georgia. By 19 February he had assembled a force of between 5,000 and 5,500 men and had constructed entrenchments near Olustee Station east of Lake City. On the morning of 20 February, Seymour's advanced forces approached the Confederate defenses, and what began as skirmishing soon developed into a heated engagement several miles to the east of the main rebel lines. Finegan remained behind at Olustee Station for most of the battle, sending reinforcements as needed to Brigadier General Alfred H. Colquitt, who directed most of the actual fighting. Finegan reached the field during the latter stages of the battle, accompanied by his son, who served as his aide. When a Union artillery round exploded close by, the elder Finegan implored to his son: "Go to the rear, Finnegan me B'ye, go to the rear! me B'ye! Ye know ye are ye mither's darlin."

Olustee proved a signal victory, with the Federal forces retreating hastily back to their defenses at Jacksonville and suffering nearly 1,900 casualties. Despite a bungled Confederate pursuit that enabled the Yankees to escape complete destruction, the Confederate Congress would pass a resolution honoring Finegan and his command for their actions.

In May 1864, General Robert E. Lee requested that a brigade of troops be sent from Florida to reinforce his battered army. Finegan gathered together various units from his command that would eventually be organized into the 9th, 10th, and 11th Infantry Regiments. He accompanied this force to Virginia, taking command of the Army of Northern Virginia's Florida Brigade, which consisted of the new regiments along with the deleted 2d, 5th, and 8th Florida Regiments. At Cold Harbor on 3 June, the Floridians counterattacked when Federal troops broke through a thinly held portion of the Confederate lines. They repulsed the attack, though with heavy casualties. Finegan remained in command of the brigade through the long siege of Petersburg, and, during the absence of William Mahone, he served as acting division commander on several occasions. His troops performed well at Globe Tavern in June 1864, and, during the engagement at Hatcher's Run in early 1865, while wearing a "citizen coat, Beaver hat and [with] a walking stick," he led Mahone's Division into battle. Shouting "'On ye go brave lads,'" he exhorted his troops.

At the age of fifty-four, Finegan was exhausted by the constant campaigning during the winter of 1864–1865. Florida's congressional delegation urged his return to the state, and in January 1865 he wrote to support the request, asking for a transfer "to a climate more congenial to my health and age." In March, shortly before the final collapse of the Confederacy, he sent a

letter of resignation to Secretary of War John C. Breckinridge and returned to his adopted state.

Shortly after the war, Finegan spent one term in the Florida legislature, and then he moved to Savannah. He was a cotton broker, and he practiced law and fought to regain property confiscated during the war. He eventually settled in Rutledge, Florida, where he died on 29 October 1885. Although Finegan's military performance during the war was mixed, he had performed well in the Olustee campaign and during the long siege of Petersburg, for which he deserves greater recognition.

—David J. Coles

See also Colquitt, Alfred H.; Florida; Jacksonville, Florida; Olustee, Battle of; Perry, Madison Starke; Yulee, David Levy.

For further reading:
Burdett, Susan. "The Military Career of Brigadier-General Joseph Finegan of Florida" (M.A. thesis, 1930).
Gleeson, Ed. *Erin Go Gray! An Irish Rebel Trilogy* (1997).
Lonn, Ella. *Foreigners in the Confederacy* (1940).
Trudeau, Noah Andre. *The Last Citadel: Petersburg, Virginia, June 1864–April 1865* (1991).

FINLEY, CLEMENT ALEXANDER
(1797–1879)
Union surgeon general

Born to Samuel Finley and Mary Brown Finley in Newville, Pennsylvania, Clement Alexander Finley was educated at Dickinson College and the University of Pennsylvania Medical School. Upon graduation from the latter in 1818, he entered the army as a surgeon's mate in the 1st Infantry. In 1821 he became an assistant surgeon and became surgeon in 1832 at the rank of major. He served in the Black Hawk War and the Second Seminole War and at a variety of frontier posts before going to Mexico during the Mexican-American War.

By the outbreak of the Civil War, Finley had risen to the rank of lieutenant colonel and was the second ranking medical officer in the army behind Surgeon General Thomas Lawson. On 15 May 1861 Lawson died, and as a result, Finley was named the new surgeon general because of his senior position within the medical department. His new position also brought about his promotion to the rank of colonel.

Finley had a tremendous job ahead of him in organizing a medical department to meet the needs of a rapidly growing war effort, and for that reason alone, the selection of this relatively old, unaccomplished man was criticized before he even had a chance to begin his new job. In addition to organizing facilities and personnel to care for wounded and ill soldiers, Finley's office was responsible for the shipment of medical supplies and equipment to all armies in the field and to the scene of any battles fought by those armies. Because armies were seldom static entities, the logistics of constantly moving the supplies and equipment with the army sorely taxed a very understaffed and underfunded medical department.

In addition to this activity, Finley also had to concern himself with the growing hygiene problem of the camps of thousands of soldiers gathering around Washington, D.C. This issue became even more critical as summer heat exacerbated the odors and the potential for disease from these camps. While Finley was certainly concerned about the issue, he had neither the personnel nor the energy to do much about it other than issue directives to officers to clean up the camps.

Once the fighting began in earnest during the summer of 1861, Finley had other concerns. He soon learned that he did not have enough surgeons or orderlies to minister to the wounded or even to remove the men from the battlefield. In addition, he had the burden of tending to captured wounded Confederate soldiers as well as providing physicians for prison camps. To handle the battlefield problems, it was proposed to Finley during the summer of 1861 that an ambulance corps be organized. Finley directed that a study of the feasibility of such a corps be conducted, but he resisted the actual organization of such a group, citing recruitment and organization difficulties. Not only was Finley severely criticized for this decision, but during the summer, when he had the opportunity significantly to increase the numbers of surgeons and orderlies in his department, he requested only a fraction of the number he probably could have obtained.

While Finley was widely criticized for his relative inactivity in preparing the medical department for the war, such criticism found little focus or organization until he came up against the supporters of the creation of the U.S. Sanitary Commission. From the beginning of the talk concerning this group, Finley strongly opposed its creation. He advised President Abraham Lincoln against the Sanitary Commission and argued strenuously against tying it to his organization. When he ultimately lost the argument, he proved uncooperative with the officials of the commission. He insisted that commission workers not be allowed to minister to regular soldiers and that their activities be confined strictly to the volunteers.

Finley's lack of cooperation quickly gained him the hostility of the commission's executive secretary, Frederick Law Olmstead, and the other politically connected people in the upper echelons of the organization. It did not help Finley that many of the generals in the army soon came to see the work of the commission as being useful to the health and well-being of their troops. With the generals and increasingly the politicians in strong support of the commission, Finley quickly found himself very much in the minority. In September 1861, the directors of the Sanitary Commission voted to recommend Finley's replacement as surgeon general. Strong supporters of the commission in Congress began

working on a medical department reorganization bill that would legislate Finley out of the service.

In the meantime, Finley made another political blunder at the end of the year that managed to turn the powerful New York *Tribune* against him. When Brigadier General Thomas West Sherman, in command of the Port Royal expedition at the end of the year, ordered the creation of a hospital for his soldiers on the coast of South Carolina, Finley overruled the order, saying that because of the mild climate of South Carolina such a facility was unnecessary. The *Tribune* launched a campaign against Finley that exposed his early attempts to block increased efficiency and gave a great deal of ammunition to those in Congress who were working on the bill that would remove Finley.

In the spring of 1862, Congress passed a reorganization bill that, in addition to increasing the size of the department, called for a brigadier general to head it. Because Finley had no chance of being confirmed as a brigadier general, he was essentially legislated out of his position and forced to retire. He was replaced by one of his assistant surgeons, William Alexander Hammond, who had the confidence of the Sanitary Commission directors.

Finley left the service quietly and for his cooperation was brevetted for earlier service a brigadier general at the end of the war. He died on 8 September 1879 in Philadelphia, Pennsylvania.

—*David S. Heidler and Jeanne T. Heidler*

See also Medicine; United States Sanitary Commission.
For further reading:
Adams, George W. *Doctors in Blue* (1961).
Denney, Robert E. *Civil War Medicine: Care and Comfort of the Wounded* (1994).

FINLEY, JESSE JOHNSON
(1812–1904)
Confederate general

Jesse Finley commanded the 6th Florida Infantry during the early stages of the Civil War and eventually rose to command the small brigade of Floridians that served in the Army of Tennessee. He was an unspectacular, yet competent, commander who distinguished himself on several battlefields during the war and who enjoyed a long, prominent postwar career in law and politics.

Finley was born in Wilson County, Tennessee, on 18 November 1812. He received his early education in Lebanon, and he later studied law and was admitted to the bar. The future general saw his first military service during the Second Seminole War, in which he commanded a company of cavalry. Around 1840 Finley moved to Arkansas, where he served in the state senate. He then settled in Memphis, Tennessee, and in 1845 was elected mayor. The next year he moved to Florida and settled in Marianna. He served in the Florida senate during the early 1850s and as a circuit judge from 1853 until 1861. In the latter capacity, Finley dealt with widespread Regulator violence in the years before the Civil War. He was also a presidential elector for the Whig Party in 1852.

Upon the outbreak of war, Finley continued his judicial service, this time as a Confederate district judge. Despite his advanced age, in March 1862 Finley enlisted into Confederate service. He evidently served briefly as a private before being elected captain of what would become Company D of the 6th Florida Infantry Regiment. The following month the regiment was formally organized and mustered into Confederate service, and Finley was elected colonel. Shortly thereafter, the 6th Florida was ordered to Knoxville, Tennessee, and placed in a brigade commanded by William G. M. Davis. Finley led the regiment during the 1862 Kentucky campaign, where it comprised part of Edmund Kirby Smith's command. In the aftermath of that failed campaign, the 6th Florida was positioned first at Cumberland Gap before being ordered back to Knoxville for the winter of 1862–1863.

The regiment remained in Knoxville and its vicinity for the first half of 1863, while Finley spent most of his time on court-martial duty. The first serious fighting for the colonel and his command came at Chickamauga in September 1863. The 6th Regiment formed part of a brigade commanded by Colonel Robert Triggs, and on both September 19 and 20 it participated in attacks on the Union lines. The Floridians suffered heavy casualties, but earned praise from their superiors.

After Chickamauga, Finley received a promotion to the grade of brigadier general, replacing William Davis, who had resigned. Finley was placed in command of a newly consolidated Florida Brigade, consisting of the 1st, 3d, 4th, 6th, and 7th Infantry Regiments and the 1st Florida Cavalry. Finley's command was small, and combat losses eventually forced the merger of the 1st and 3d Infantry and the 1st Cavalry and 4th Infantry Regiments. Yet over the next year the Floridians would perform well under his leadership. At Chattanooga in November 1863, part of Finley's brigade was placed in exposed rifle pits at the foot of Missionary Ridge. The Federal attack of 25 November pierced the Confederate lines, but Finley gathered together the remnants of his command and assisted in a rear-guard action to cover the Southern retreat.

In the spring and summer of 1864, the Florida Brigade was heavily engaged during the campaign for Atlanta. Finley fell wounded at Resaca and had to leave his command for a period of recuperation. He returned for the battles around Atlanta and was wounded again at Jonesboro. The latter injury ended his active campaigning.

In early 1865, after recovering, Finley was unable to

rejoin his command because of the advance of Sherman's forces through the Carolinas. Instead, he reported to Columbus, Georgia, where he served under Howell Cobb until near the close of the war. Finley then returned to Florida and formally surrendered at Quincy on 11 May 1865.

The former general enjoyed a long postwar career. He lived in Lake City for a decade after the war, before moving to Jacksonville. In the 1870s, Finley won a seat in the U.S. Congress. He served two terms, but his third election in 1879 was contested, and Finley lost his seat. In 1887, Governor Edward Perry appointed Finley to complete a term in the U.S. Senate, but legal wrangling led to his seat being denied. He also served for many years as a U.S. circuit judge. Finley died in Lake City on 6 November 1904.

—*David J. Coles*

For further reading:
Compiled Service Records for Jesse J. Finley. National Archives, Washington, D.C.
Davis, William C., ed. *The Confederate General* (1991).
Robertson, Fred L. *Soldiers of Florida in the Seminole Indian, Civil and Spanish-American Wars* (1903).

FIRE-EATERS

Defined as a combative person always eager for a fight, a "fire-eater" was a radical Southern secessionist in the years before the Civil War. Alabama's William Lowndes Yancey and South Carolina's Robert Barnwell Rhett were the most prominent fire-eaters, and Rhett's work for his state's secession from the Union was the chief occupation of his life. Yancey is best remembered as the sponsor of the Alabama Platform that helped to fracture the Democratic Party in 1860 by insisting that the presidential nominee endorse a territorial slave code. Other Southern states also had similarly focused and rhetorically violent men. Albert Gallatin Brown of Mississippi, Henry L. Benning of Georgia, Beverley Tucker and Edmund Ruffin of Virginia, and Louis Wigfall of Texas would number among them.

The fire-eaters resembled moderate Southerners in trying to use the political process to protect the South from what they perceived as Northern political aggression. Yet they were unique in consistently promoting secession as a permanent solution to what moderates and conservatives regarded as the temporary problem of sectional discord. Fortunately for national unity, the fire-eaters were remarkably inept as politicians. Before sectionalism grew into a towering problem, their warnings about Northern perfidy seemed foolish, especially during the national expansion and prosperity of the Jacksonian period. Furthermore, labeling individual radicals as fire-eaters creates the illusion of them as conspirators who worked in close concert to bring about

secession and form the Confederacy. They were not conspirators, however. Their inflexible attitudes often made them personally difficult and politically obtuse, and they were consistently unable to forge meaningful coalitions even among themselves, let alone ally with the many shades of moderate opinion throughout the South. Robert Barnwell Rhett routinely urged the doctrine of separate state action, meaning that South Carolina alone should secede regardless of the plans of the other Southern states. It was a quixotic posture that before 1860 was as unrealistic in the face of federal authority as it was unpopular with sober opinion.

The fire-eaters routinely shunned compromise as corrupt and insisted on an unqualified defense of states' rights. Before 1860, their most ambitious bid for power occurred during the turmoil of 1850–1851. Appearing to act as a group because their message and motives were similar, they played on Southern discontent over several points of sectional contention, especially the admission of California as a free state. Realizing that they remained a minority because of their political technique as well as their political philosophy, some fire-eaters, such as Beverley Tucker and Rhett, attempted to establish a connection to the Southern majority by muting their rhetoric and abandoning the doctrine of separate state action. They even participated in a Southern rights convention in Nashville, Tennessee, in June 1850. Yet their evocation of Southern nationalism sounded hollow. Moderates rightly suspected the fire-eaters' real project was not Southern rights but disunion. Their extreme states' rights doctrine contradicted allegiance to anything other than localism, and sometimes not even that, as Yancey and Rhett showed by occasionally baring shameless self-interest. After the Compromise of 1850 calmed sectional anger in the fall of that year, secessionist candidates for state offices were soundly defeated across the South. In the wake of these disastrous elections, secessionists who did not publicly moderate their views ceased to be public figures of any consequence.

For the rest of the decade, unabashed secessionists were usually marked as dangerous zealots. Even the revival of sectional tensions upon the passage of the Kansas-Nebraska Act in 1854 did not revive their political fortunes. Yet it was during this time of political exile that unrepentant fire-eaters emphasized their role as guardians of the traditional Southern culture rooted in slavery. It was a role that allowed them to take rank with a Southern majority that felt itself increasingly isolated and demeaned by Northern antislavery advocates. The fire-eaters gave voice to apprehensions about societal changes that Southerners little understood and liked even less. Industrialism, socialism, and modernism as well as abolitionism were denounced as "isms" and depicted as cancers growing rampant in Northern society. The fire-eater found common cause with moderates in favorably contrasting Southern slavery to the odious "wage slavery" of Northern factories. They joined political moderates in condemning the mercenary commercialization of the Northern marketplace and the unprincipled demagoguery of the Northern politician. They exalted pastoral Southern society as virtuous and nurtured the belief that the South was the last citadel of civilization in a world gone mad with chaotic change. The Northern assault on slavery was condemned as a subversion of private property and an attempt to erode the foundation of agrarian virtue. When many Southerners came to believe that these cultural differences had become political issues, as they did during the election of 1860, the fire-eaters were able to assume the mantel of prophets and adopt the role of unsullied leaders.

But it was frantic alarm, not the persuasiveness of the fire-eaters, that made secession a plausible remedy in 1860, even if heightening turmoil in the late 1850s did set the stage for a brief resurgence of radicalism. Yancey's renewed influence in the Alabama Democratic Party allowed him to dominate the state's delegation to the party's national convention in Charleston, where he would participate in the Southern withdrawal from the convention and the beginning of the irreparable division of the party. When Abraham Lincoln was elected president in 1860, the fire-eaters might have believed that their past warnings were vindicated and their future influence was ensured. Yet many Southerners already believed that the radicals' destruction of the Democratic Party was a self-interested ploy to advance their own political fortunes and provoke secession with a Republican victory. Even in South Carolina's compulsive act of secession, Robert Barnwell Rhett was regarded with suspicion and disdain. And the dissolution of the Union by the rest of the South was for all its apparent haste a halting and fitful process in which moderates and conservatives first contemplated and then accepted the dreadful consequences of secession and possible war.

Despite the presence of Yancey, Rhett, and a few others, fire-eaters were only passably represented at Montgomery when the Confederacy was created, and only the Alabama fire-eater Leroy Pope Walker would land a cabinet post in the new Confederate administration. As the Confederacy began its struggle for survival, the fire-eaters soon began caviling at the excessive authority of the government and the corruption of the political process. Unable to get along with each other or anyone else, they were again demoted in popular esteem to the rank of unreasonable men with dangerous opinions.

—*David S. Heidler and Jeanne T. Heidler*

See also Benning, Henry Lewis; Cobb, Thomas R. R.; Colquitt, Alfred; Democratic Party; Election of 1860; Keitt, Lawrence; Miles, William Porcher; Rhett, Robert Barnwell; Ruffin, Edmund; Walker, Leroy P.; Wigfall, Louis; Yancey, William Lowndes.

For further reading:
Heidler, David S. *Pulling the Temple Down: The Fire-eaters and the Destruction of the Union* (1994).
Walther, Eric H. *The Fire-Eaters* (1992).

FIRST MANASSAS, BATTLE OF
See Bull Run, First Battle of

FISHER'S HILL, BATTLE OF
(21–22 September 1864)

Trying to contain Philip Sheridan's destructive raid on the Shenandoah Valley, Jubal A. Early was forced to withdraw after the Winchester campaign and move up the Valley Pike south to Strasburg to a defensible position at Fisher's Hill, deep in the heart of the valley, on 21 September 1864. The hill was a natural stronghold with the Shenandoah River to the east and dense woods to the west. Early's soldiers added earthworks and abatis to complement the natural impediment formed by the hill's steep grade, making the position a seemingly impregnable citadel. The only likely way to take the position was to flank it and hope to surprise its defenders, possibly by gaining their rear.

Union general Philip Sheridan, after several weeks of hard combat against a resilient Confederate force, had grown impatient with the protracted campaign. Enjoying numbers superior to those of the Confederates, Sheridan planned an attack that would shatter Confederate resistance in the Shenandoah Valley once and for all. Forming his ranks along the base of Fisher's Hill, Sheridan hoped to distract Early's infantry with a demonstration while cavalry under Alfred Torbert moved up the Luray Valley, parallel to the Shenandoah and hidden from Fisher's Hill. The Federal cavalry could cut off Early should he try to retreat. Once this operation was set in motion, Sheridan began the next phase of the attack.

Sheridan's infantry at the foot of Fisher's Hill concealed General George H. Crook's corps situated well behind the front line of the Union forces and thus out of sight. Sheridan relates the reasoning behind such a decision:

"I resolved to move Crook, unperceived if possible, over to the eastern face of Little North Mountain [to the immediate Confederate left], whence he could strike the left and rear of the Confederate line, and as he broke it up, I could support him by a left half-wheel of my whole line of battle. The execution of this plan would require perfect secrecy, however, for the enemy from his signal-station on Three Top [a hill near Fisher's Hill] could plainly see every movement of our troops in daylight."

During the night of 21 September, Crook's force moved to the right of the Union forces and toward the Confederate left flank using the cover of woods, darkness, and mountains. The following morning, as directed by Sheridan, General William Woods Averell feinted an attack on the Confederate left, pressing in as close as possible with dismounted cavalry to occupy the Confederate forces while Crook's men maneuvered into place. A similar feint was made on the Confederate right and was followed shortly thereafter by the engagement of the entire front along Fisher's Hill. Then came the most significant moment of the battle, as Sheridan's carefully laid trap was sprung. General Crook's men assaulted the enemy's extreme left, catching the Confederates completely by surprise. As he watched the Federals leap over his works, scattering and rolling up his left flank, Early realized his whole army was in immediate danger of being destroyed. Union forces along the front, seeing their comrades shatter the Confederate left, began to push forward with such vigor that Early's entire army began to flee in disarray with Federals in pursuit for seven miles up the valley. Although plans had called for the cutting off of such a withdrawal, the retreat was protected by Confederate cavalry that had impeded Torbert in the Luray Valley, and his troopers were therefore unable to stop Early's retreat south.

Jubal Early managed to withdraw to the town of Woodstock about twenty-five miles south of Fisher's Hill. There he took a defensive position on Mount Jackson to await the pursuing Union forces the following day. Yet the damage had been done. Though Early remained a force to be reckoned with, his army had suffered two mauling defeats and its morale was sagging. Early would report more than 1,200 losses (Sheridan's losses were about 520), although the Confederate killed and wounded likely numbered less than 250. Among those mortally wounded was Alexander "Sandie" Pendleton, who would die in Federal hands, widowing a young bride who carried their child.

—*Chad Reisig*

See also Shenandoah Valley Campaign (August 1864–March 1865); Winchester, Third Battle of (Opequon).

For further reading:

Amato, Nicholas J., and Edward Eckert, eds. *Ten Years in the Saddle: The Memoir of William Woods Averell: 1851-1862* (1978).

Early, Jubal A. *Lieutenant General Jubal Anderson Early, C.S.A.: Autobiographical Sketch and Narrative of the War Between the States. With Notes by R. H. Early* (1912).

Pond, George E. *The Shenandoah Valley in 1864* (1883).

Sheridan, Philip. *Personal Memoirs of Philip Henry Sheridan, General of the U.S. Army. New and Enl. Ed., with an Account of his Life from 1871 to His Death, in 1888, by Brigadier-General Michael V. Sheridan* (1904).

Wert, Jeffry D. *From Winchester to Cedar Creek: The Shenandoah Campaign of 1864* (1987).

FISK, CLINTON BOWEN
(1828–1890)
Union general

Clinton Bowen Fisk fought for a socially reconstructed Union. Born 8 December 1828 to an old Yankee family transplanted to western New York, he grew up in the country town of Coldwater in what was still the Michigan Territory when his family arrived. He was an early supporter of the Liberty and Free Soil Parties, although, as a merchant and banker, he shared the town's prosperity with the arrival of the railroad. However, the Panic of 1857 left him destitute. The outbreak of the war found Fisk an insurance broker in St. Louis.

Fisk reportedly participated in the Unionist seizure of Camp Jackson in May 1861, but he formally entered the war only as a colonel commanding the 33d Missouri in September 1862. An ardent Methodist, he did not drink, and he asked his regiment to allow him to do all the swearing for them. (When he later recalled this to a teamster who had engaged in loud profanity, the man excused himself on the grounds that Fisk had not been around to address a situation that had called for swearing.) Liked by his men and superiors despite these peculiarities, he rose to a brigadier generalship in November and commanded a division in the Union Army of the Tennessee by January 1863. His evenhandedness and generosity of spirit in dealing with other Unionists allowed him to thrive even after his transfer to the faction-ridden Department of Missouri.

Fisk's record in Missouri included command of military districts in southeastern Missouri (July–November 1863), St. Louis (November 1863–March 1864), and northern Missouri (June 1864–May 1865), in which capacity he served during Price's Missouri Raid (September–October 1864). At that time, the garrison troops from southwestern, central, and northern Missouri concentrated in defense of the state capital at Jefferson City, where Fisk, as the senior brigadier, assumed command. Having built strong inner defenses, Fisk bluffed the much larger Confederate force with heavy skirmishing along the Osage and Moreau rivers. Although Price's army got within two miles of the capital, Fisk's impressive-looking, but only partly manned defenses saved Jefferson City.

Fisk's postwar career in the Freedmen's Bureau had an even greater impact. In 1865, he took charge of refugees, freedpeople, and abandoned lands for Kentucky and Tennessee. As in his Missouri days, he retained the confidence of both the Radical Republicans and their critics. Andrew Johnson, supposedly said "Fisk ain't a fool, he won't hang everybody." Imposing what amounted to martial law, he seized an abandoned barracks at Nashville, which became a school for the freedpeople in 1866 and, a year later, gained a charter as Fisk University. By then, it enjoyed the active support of Fisk himself, who had resumed his banking career.

The administration of Ulysses S. Grant subsequently appointed Fisk to the Board of Indian Commissioners in 1874. He assumed its presidency in 1881 and served until his death.

Fisk became interested in extending the government's role in society through abolishing the slavery of alcohol. He became interested in prohibition but remained an ardent Republican until 1884. In that year, Kansas governor John P. St. John polled some 150,000 votes and a wave of temperance activities swept the country. Two years later, the Prohibitionist Party in New Jersey nominated Fisk for governor. In 1888, eastern Prohibitionists determined to make him their presidential candidate. He won almost 250,000 votes, the largest number any Prohibitionist had yet won for the office. Fisk died two years later on 9 July 1890.

—*Mark A. Lause*

See also Army of the Tennessee; Camp Jackson; Freedmen's Bureau; Free Soil Party; Grant, Ulysses Simpson; Johnson, Andrew; Price's Missouri Raid.

For further reading:
Hopkins, Alphonso A. *The Life of Clinton Bowen Fisk* (1888).

FITZHUGH, GEORGE
(1806–1881)
Southern author

Known by contemporaries as a polemical defender of slavery who published a series of articles in *De Bow's Review* throughout the late 1850s, George Fitzhugh consistently attacked the North's free labor system as exploitative and considerably more demeaning than the South's "peculiar institution." A native of Prince William County, Virginia, Fitzhugh claimed—questionably as it turns out—direct lineage to one of Virginia's aristocratic families. Inadequately educated in what were then termed "field schools," Fitzhugh read for a legal career and subsequently opened a law practice in Port Royal, Virginia. He married Mary Brockenbrough in 1829, and had nine children, three of whom died in infancy.

Though never receiving much formal education, Fitzhugh was nevertheless quite familiar with the writings of the leading political philosophers of his day. Harboring contempt for Adam Smith's free-market philosophy, Fitzhugh became increasingly critical of capitalism, which he believed allowed those privileged few who owned the means of production to become wealthy and powerful by exploiting the labor of others. Though it is clear that he was influenced by Karl Marx and by the writings of French Utopian Socialists such as

Charles Fourier and Henri Saint Simon, Fitzhugh never accepted socialism—either scientific or utopian—as a proper remedy for society's economic inequalities.

Aside from socialist literature, Fitzhugh was most profoundly influenced by a generation of southern proslavery writers such as Thomas Dew, William Gilmore Simms, William Grayson, and Nathaniel Beverly Tucker, who provided the generally accepted political, economic, and religious justifications for slavery. In 1854, with the appearance of *Sociology for the South; or, the Failure of a Free Society*, Fitzhugh joined the proslavery argument by offering a theory of society that in many respects combined Marxian attacks on capitalism with Dew's defense of slavery. The thrust of *Sociology for the South* was not merely an exegesis of the inherent evils of the Industrial Revolution, but rather one that maintained the harmful effects of industrial growth coupled with a free labor system. According to Fitzhugh, Northern workers who depended entirely on the owners of capital for their livelihood were subjected to abuse and exploitation by employers who cared little for their well-being, who dehumanized laborers by forcing them to become little other than machine appendages, and who demeaned them by paying wages so low that most lived in abject poverty. These unfortunate people were, according to Fitzhugh, "wage slaves." He suggested that the principal cause of social, political, and economic inequality was a chronic lack of value placed on labor. The result of one's labor having little or no merit was that Northern laborers were relegated to political insignificance, while their employers operated solely for personal enrichment without concern for their employees' well-being.

Fitzhugh's criticisms of capitalism were hardly novel in the 1850s, yet this Virginian advanced his arguments further by stating that Southern slaves in reality enjoyed more freedom than did Northern free laborers. He asserted that because Southern slave owners were ultimately responsible for the well-being of their slaves, and also because the master-slave relationship was not predicated on wages, slaves were in essence healthier and happier than the average Northern factory worker. Such arguments—while ringing hollow in modern ears—clearly established Fitzhugh as one of the South's most provocative defenders of slavery.

One influential moment in Fitzhugh's life occurred during a trip to Boston he made in 1856 to visit relatives, among whom was the abolitionist Gerrit Smith. Fitzhugh was introduced to Harriet Beecher Stowe by Smith, and he attended several abolitionist society meetings. He examined their presses, attended their rallies, listened to their speeches, and yet returned to Virginia as convinced as ever about the righteousness of Southern slavery and the injustices inherent in Northern society. Evidently believing himself better informed about the many differences between North and South, Fitzhugh's brief sojourn to Boston thereby prompted him to enhance his theories concerning slave and free labor systems.

In 1856 Fitzhugh's work most often discussed by historians appeared under the title *Cannibals All!, or, Slaves Without Masters*. Admitting that in his earlier work he had succeeded only in "vindicating slavery in the abstract," Fitzhugh explained that *Cannibals All!* was intended to add substance to his argument that slavery was a much preferred labor system than one based on wage laborers. Here, as in his earlier book, Fitzhugh defended slavery by attacking free labor. Fitzhugh, convinced that capitalism bred class division and ultimately social and political revolution, claimed that such a revolution was imminent in the United States. He suggested that because the Southern states were devoid of such class antagonisms and because slavery could be credited for producing such harmony, Northern states would be well advised likewise to adopt slave labor as the basis of their factory system.

The absurdity of Fitzhugh's ideas did not escape his contemporaries, and it certainly has not been overlooked by historians. To begin with, Fitzhugh seems to have operated under the delusion that Southern society was without class-based tension. That was hardly the case. Secondly, Fitzhugh asserted that American slavery should in no manner be predicated solely on racial considerations. Without race as the determining factor behind American slavery, Fitzhugh argued, the masses of free, white laborers in both the North and the South could be enslaved. Because of its obvious flaws and chimerical advocacy of slavery, Fitzhugh's work was certainly not taken seriously, though it did achieve a contemporary popularity due largely to its novelty. In the final analysis, his sociological theories were exceedingly impractical, and Fitzhugh's contemporaries never viewed him as a mainstream defender of slavery. He should not, therefore, be considered as such by modern historians.

From 1858 until 1866, Fitzhugh published a series of articles in *De Bow's Review*. He had met James D. B. De Bow in 1857, and their relationship afforded Fitzhugh a well-circulated journal in which to print his ideas. Most of these articles promoted Southern manufacturing to enable Southern states to achieve economic parity with the North. Fitzhugh opposed secession in 1860, but he eventually accepted the South's withdrawal as necessary for survival. He attempted to maintain his family and law practice in Port Royal, but once Federal troops assumed command of the area, Fitzhugh moved to Richmond. Soon after his arrival in the Confederate capital, he accepted a relatively insignificant post as a clerk in the Confederate Department of the Treasury. He continued to publish in any outlet that would grant him an audience, yet with De Bow's death in 1866, Fitzhugh

ceased publishing. He returned to Port Royal after the war and eventually moved to Texas, where he died in relative obscurity in 1881.

—*Robert Saunders, Jr.*

See also De Bow, James; *De Bow's Review*.

For further reading:

Fitzhugh, George. *Cannibals All! or, Slaves Without Masters* (1960).

———. *Sociology for the South, or, The Failure of Free Society* (Reprint, n.d.).

Wish, Harvey. *George Fitzhugh, Conservative of the Old South* (1938).

———. *George Fitzhugh, Propagandist of the Old South* (1943).

FIVE FORKS, BATTLE OF
(1 April 1865)

The battle of Five Forks, often called "The Waterloo of the Confederacy," concluded Ulysses S. Grant's operations against Robert E. Lee's right flank and ended the siege of Petersburg to open the final days of the war in northern Virginia. White Oak Road (running east and west), Scott's Road to the southwest, Ford's (or Church) Road to the North, and the Dinwiddie Court House Road to the southeast intersected to form the place called Five Forks. Essential in covering General Robert E. Lee's last supply line along the South-side Railroad, this rural area boasted a few large plantations and farmhouses. An old house in ruins was called "the chimneys," and there was the Gravelly Run Methodist Episcopal Church, a small white frame structure. Ravines, swamps, and open spaces occasionally interrupted the tangled underbrush and pine thickets that mostly characterized the area. Large granite formations also marked the fields and woods.

Beginning on 29 March, Major General Philip Sheridan's cavalry and elements of Major General Gouverneur K. Warren's V Corps had pushed Confederate forces back toward the White Oak Road to take possession of Boydton Plank Road. On 31 March 1865, Sheridan ran into Major General George E. Pickett's infantry of 6,400 men northwest of Dinwiddie Court House. Sheridan was soon in trouble. Pickett's force and Fitz Lee's 4,200 cavalry along Chamberlain's Bed, a creek branch of Stony Creek, moved out of their positions at Five Forks to attack Sheridan's left flank and drive the Federal troopers back toward Dinwiddie. By nightfall Sheridan had managed to entrench a mile north of the village, but Pickett was between him and Five Forks and had essentially halted the Federal cavalry commander.

Meanwhile, General Robert E. Lee, who was riding along the front, personally directed three different Confederate forces to fall upon two unsuspecting divisions of V Corps resting south of the White Oak Road. Attacking Confederates pushed Warren's men all the

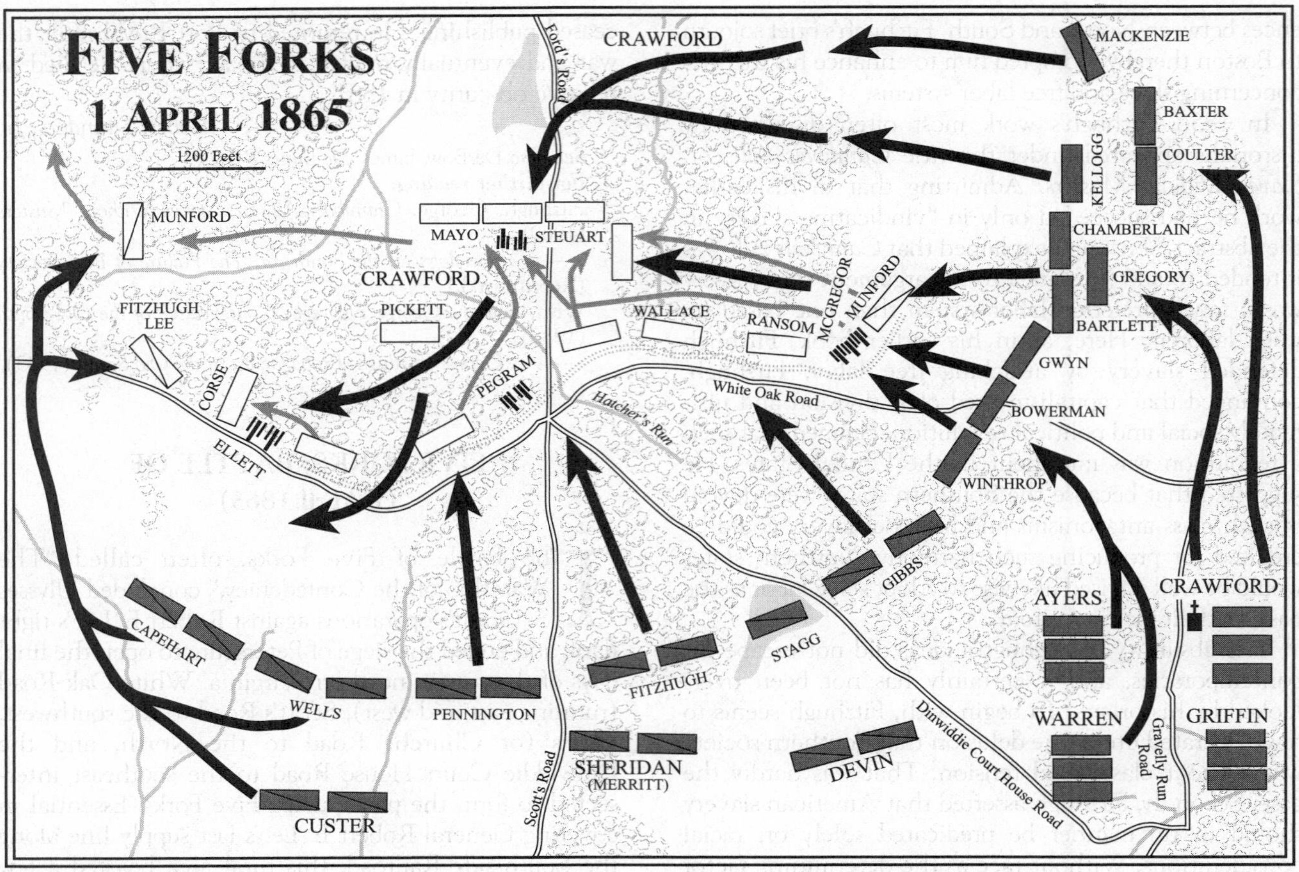

FIVE FORKS
1 APRIL 1865

1200 Feet

CRAWFORD

MACKENZIE

BAXTER

COULTER

KELLOGG

CHAMBERLAIN

GREGORY

BARTLETT

GWYN

BOWERMAN

WINTHROP

CRAWFORD

AYERS

WARREN

GRIFFIN

Gravelly Run Road

MUNFORD

MAYO

STEUART

CRAWFORD

PICKETT

FITZHUGH LEE

WALLACE

RANSOM

McGREGOR

MUNFORD

CORSE

ELLETT

PEGRAM

White Oak Road

Hatcher's Run

GIBBS

STAGG

FITZHUGH

Dinwiddie Court House Road

Ford's Road

CAPEHART

WELLS

PENNINGTON

SHERIDAN
(MERRITT)

DEVIN

Scott's Road

CUSTER

way to a branch of rain–swollen Gravelly Run before the Federals were able to hold their ground. After receiving reinforcements, Warren was able to drive the Confederates back into their works along the Claiborne Road, a maneuver that cut off the White Oak Road to the west. The battle of White Oak Road (or Gravelly Run) had the effect of confining Lieutenant General Richard H. Anderson's small number of men in their lines along White Oak Road. More importantly, they were cut off from Pickett four miles westward.

To assail Pickett, Sheridan wanted VI Corps to reinforce him, but Grant elected to use the closer V Corps instead. At 10:30 P.M., Grant ordered Warren to support the cavalry, but Romeyn B. Ayres's division, moving on Boydton Plank Road, was delayed while the Gravelly Run bridge was rebuilt. Warren's other two divisions under Charles Griffin and Samuel W. Crawford did not head for Dinwiddie Court House until the next morning. After gaining a hold on the White Oak Road, Warren placed a brigade behind Pickett's left flank, a move that forced Pickett to withdraw to Five Forks early on the morning of 1 April. Soon the vanguard of V Corps appeared on the Dinwiddie Court House Road and joined Sheridan's troopers in pressing Pickett at the strategic crossroads.

At Five Forks, Pickett dug in along a line extending one and three-quarter miles. Its left flank was anchored by a "return" (an angle) about 150 yards long and protected by four artillery pieces. From the left Brigadier General Matthew W. Ransom's North Carolinians and Brigadier General William H. Wallace's South Carolinians were linked to Brigadier General George H. Steuart's Virginians. Colonel William J. Pegram's Battalion of three artillery pieces covered the forks. Brigadier General William R. Terry's Virginians stretched westward (under Colonel Joseph Mayo), then Brigadier General Montgomery D. Corse's Virginians. General William Henry Fitzhugh Lee's cavalry joined with other troopers and three additional field pieces protected the Confederate right flank. Lee had communicated with Pickett in the bluntest terms: "Hold Five Forks at all hazards. Protect road to Ford's Depot and prevent Union forces from striking the Southside Railroad. Regret exceedingly your forced withdrawal, and your inability to hold the advantage you had gained [at Dinwiddie Court House]."

Impatiently waiting for the remainder of Warren's forces, Sheridan also received word from Grant via a courier. "General Grant directs me to say to you, that if in your judgment the Fifth Corps would do better under

The last stand of Pickett's men, sketched by Alfred R. Waud at the Battle of Five Forks, 1 April 1865 (*Library of Congress*)

one of the division commanders, you are authorized to relieve General Warren, and order him to report to General Grant, at headquarters." Gouverneur K. Warren's fate as an army commander was suddenly placed in Sheridan's hands.

By 4 P.M. Warren finally had his 12,000 men arrayed for the attack along a bottom south of Gravelly Run Church. He directed his three division commanders—Ayres on the left, Samuel J. Crawford on the right, and Charles Griffin massed in the rear—to move forward *en echelon* until they traversed the White Oak Road. Then, according to a sketch provided by Sheridan, they were to turn left and assail the Confederate flank at the return. Sheridan's troopers, numbering about 9,000 to 10,000 (not all would be engaged), would move on the Southern line along its entire front.

An erroneous scouting report and an incorrect map created the mistaken impression that Pickett's left flank stretched to the intersection of the road V Corps was on (Gravelly Run Church Road) and the White Oak Road. Consequently when the advancing columns reached the point for their wheeling maneuver, they were still three quarters of a mile east of the return. Although the error caused them to diverge from their intended alignment, the columns easily crushed the Confederate angle and commenced to roll up Pickett's line. Crawford's division, now buttressed on the right by Brigadier General Ranald S. Mackenzie's cavalry, swung north of the Confederates

to gain Pickett's rear at the forks along Ford's Road. On the Confederate right, General W. H. F. Lee's cavalry fought Brevet Major General George Armstrong Custer's troopers, desperately trying to hold the ground behind the Gilliam plantation. As Brigadier General Thomas C. Devin's dismounted troopers tried to drive between Custer and Warren, Crawford's men, led by Warren, attacked down the White Oak Road and across the Gilliam field. The assault broke the final stand of the Confederate army on the right.

The Confederates, now knotted in little groups, tried to put up resistance along the line, but it was no use. Worse, Pickett and two officers, Tom Rosser and Fitz Lee, had spent most of the afternoon at a shad bake two miles in the rear. The heavily forested region, damp with recent rains, muted the sounds of battle, so Pickett did not arrive on the field until the day was lost. Those Confederates who eluded capture scattered into the woods as dusk ended the fighting. Campfires soon dotted the area around the crossroads, now in Federal hands and giving Grant the key to the South-side Railroad.

That night Sheridan relieved Warren of command and replaced him with Charles Griffin. Asked by Warren to reconsider the decision, Sheridan bluntly replied, "Reconsider? Hell! I don't reconsider my determination." (An 1882 Court of Inquiry would clear Warren of all charges of misconduct.)

The next day V Corps and cavalry rested while Grant

made his final assaults on the Confederates around Petersburg. As his western defenses crumbled and Federals began encircling the town, Lee evacuated his army from both Richmond and Petersburg. Before the end of the day, a division of II Corps under Brigadier General Nelson A. Miles moved up the Claiborne Road to Sutherland Station on the Southside Railroad. Three assaults on the Confederate force defending the railroad gave the Federals control of the line. Lee's final supply route was closed, and seven days later the war in northern Virginia ended at Appomattox Court House.

—*Chris M. Calkins*

See also Appomattox Court House.
For further reading:
Calkins, Chris M. *The Appomattox Campaign, March 29–April 9, 1865* (1997).
———. *Thirty-Six Hours before Appomattox* (1980).

FLAGS

Made of silk, wool bunting, or occasionally some other fabric, flags played an important part in the Civil War. From the battle-scarred relics prized by veterans both blue and gray, to the national flags displayed by patriotic citizens across the war-torn country, flags were a symbol of bravery, patriotism, and a cause worth fighting for.

In the North, the U.S. flag continued to be the most common banner. The Stars and Stripes of 1861 contained thirty-four stars, with each new state contributing an additional star thereafter. Kansas in 1861 and Nevada in 1864, respectively, provided the thirty-fifth and thirty-sixth stars to the flags. These stars could appear in any pattern (rows and ovals were most common) within the blue canton, which itself could vary in size.

Infantry regiments were authorized to carry two flags, or "colors," as they were known. Measuring 72 by 78 inches, the flags included a national color and a regimental color—the latter a blue flag with the national eagle emblazoned in the center. Each of these silk flags usually included the painted or embroidered name and number of the regiment and was edged with yellow fringe. The government generally supplied flags upon requisition by the regimental quartermaster. Some regiments did not bother to carry a regulation regimental color and instead used a flag presented by local citizens or businesses. These presented colors differed widely in appearance but generally followed regulation size. A few states, such as Pennsylvania and New Jersey, issued national flags that included the state coat of arms in the blue canton, surrounded by the requisite number of stars.

The infantry flags were affixed to staffs 9 feet 10 inches in height, which included a brass finial, and were accompanied by blue and white cords and tassels. A color bearer (usually a sergeant) and assigned guards carried the flag into battle, where the flag's large size made it conspicuous on the field. Easy to rally around and use as guides, the flags also were targets for enemy rifles and artillery; hence the mortality rate of color bearers was high.

Cavalry regiments were each assigned a 27-inch by 29-inch standard, a flag with a blue field containing the national coat of arms (eagle) beneath which was a scroll painted with the regimental name and number. Each cavalry company was authorized to carry a swallowtail guidon, the top half red and the bottom half white. The company letter appeared on this guidon, as did the letters "U.S." None of the cavalry flags included cords and tassels. Later in the war, the regulations were changed, and the swallowtail guidon design became the national flag.

Artillery regiments carried both national and regimental colors, both the same size as the corresponding infantry flags. However, the regimental color for artillery was a yellow field with crossed cannon in the center. Individual batteries carried guidons, usually modeled after the swallowtail versions borne by the mounted units.

In all these flags described by army regulations, individual preference of the regimental commander also played a part. Most units adhered to regulations, but others did not. A few infantry regiments carried three colors (two regulation and a presented color), while many used only a national flag. Smaller flags called camp colors and general guide (or flank) markers were also prescribed by regulations, but not always followed in practice.

To differentiate the numerous brigades, divisions, and corps, the Union army adopted a complicated series of "designating flags." These wool bunting flags were carried by the appropriate headquarters for the larger commands and were meant to provide quick identification during the confusion of battle. Designating flags used a series of stripes and numbers to provide such identification. Later, the Army of the Potomac adopted a series of headquarters flags easily recognizable by their shapes—swallowtail for corps, rectangular for divisions, and triangular for brigades. Other Union armies generally followed this system by war's end.

The Union navy sported a variety of national flags on its ships. Each naval vessel flew a large Stars and Stripes, called an ensign, which could be hoisted at different positions depending on the occasion; nine sizes of ensigns corresponded to a ship's class. A vessel's launches (boats) flew smaller flags, while commissioning pennants, signal flags, designating flags, and jacks also featured in the array of naval banners.

Within the first month of its existence, the Confederate Congress adopted an official flag, known as the Stars and Bars. This flag consisted of three wide horizontal stripes in the order of red, white, and red. In the upper left was a blue canton with seven white stars, arranged in a circle, to represent each state in the Confederacy. The stars eventually numbered thirteen.

A second flag, called the "stainless banner," replaced the Stars and Bars on 1 May 1863. This rectangular flag contained a white field, with a red canton displaying a white-bordered blue cross that contained thirteen white stars. This flag remained as the Confederacy's flag until 4 March 1865, when it was replaced by a shorter flag almost identical to the stainless banner except that it contained a vertical red stripe along the fly edge.

Confederate armies used a wide variety of battle flags. In the East, most units carried what became known as the Southern Cross, a square flag, made of silk at first and then, when this material became unobtainable, wool bunting, as the general rule. These battle flags consisted of a red field upon which appeared a blue cross, bordered in white, containing the requisite number of stars. Unlike Union colors, the Southern Cross flags were not edged in fringe; early issues were trimmed in white, while those issued in 1863 to the Army of Northern Virginia had an orange border.

Most Southern units carried only one of these battle flags. Infantry regiments carried a model that was 48 inches square, artillery batteries displayed flags 36 inches square, and cavalry units used flags 30 inches square. Many units also used presented flags, while both Virginia and North Carolina issued state flags to several of their regiments. A color bearer and his guards marched into battle proudly bearing these banners, which also contained the regimental number and often were painted with the names of the battles in which they were used.

West of the Allegheny Mountains, Southern armies carried flags less uniform than in the East. Different corps within the Army of Tennessee each adopted different flags. Units serving under General William J. Hardee carried a blue flag edged in white with a central white disk. General Leonidas Polk's men used a rectangular flag that had a white-edged red cross of Saint George on a blue field. Other units carried variations on the eastern Southern Cross battle flag, generally varying in size and shape from the more official square version.

Warships and merchant vessels of the Confederate states flew the national flag and sometimes hoisted a larger flag to ensure proper identification during military actions. Most ships also carried smaller storm flags, jacks (flown from either the bow or mast while in port for identification), and boat flags (used on the sterns of small boats).

—*Richard A. Sauers*

For further reading:
Cannon, Devereaux D., Jr. *The Flags of the Confederacy: An Illustrated History* (1988).
———. *The Flags of the Union: An Illustrated History* (1993).
———. "Rebel Flags Afloat: A Survey of the Surviving Flags of the Confederate State Navy, Revenue Service, and Merchant Marine." *Flag Bulletin* (1986).

Sauers, Richard A. *Advance the Colors! Pennsylvania Civil War Battleflags* (1987–1991).

FLANAGIN, HARRIS
(1817–1874)
Governor of Arkansas

Born to James Flanagin and Mary Flanagin in Roadstown, New Jersey, Harris Flanagin was educated in New Jersey and taught school for a while in Pennsylvania before moving to Illinois. There he also taught school and studied law on the side before moving to Clark County, Arkansas, in 1837. Eventually settling in Arkadelphia, Flanagin developed a lucrative legal practice and briefly became involved in politics when he was elected to the state legislature in 1842.

In 1861, he was elected as a unionist delegate to the Arkansas secession convention. He opposed putting the matter of secession to the voters. The Fort Sumter crisis and Abraham Lincoln's call for volunteers caused Flanagin to change his mind and support secession.

After Arkansas' secession, Flanagin received a commission in the Confederate Army as a captain in the 2d Arkansas Regiment of Mounted Rifles. Before leaving the army in 1862, he rose to the rank of colonel.

A faction of Arkansas politics led by R. H. Johnson became dissatisfied with the leadership of Governor Henry Rector in 1862 and put forward Flanagin's name in the election of 1862. According to Flanagin, who was stationed in Knoxville, Tennessee, during the election, the first he heard of his candidacy was when he was notified that he had won the election. He immediately traveled home, where he was inaugurated in November 1862.

Flanagin served as he Confederate governor of Arkansas for the remainder of the war, even after a rival unionist government was established under Isaac Murphy in 1864. During his years as governor, he worked diligently to provide for the defense of the state but also felt a strong responsibility to the people left indigent by the war. He encouraged the legislature to provide for the civilian poor while also meeting the military needs of the state.

In spite of his close relationship with some of the officers defending the state (he even accompanied General Theophilus Holmes as a voluntary aide on the Helena campaign of July 1863), Flanagin developed a growing resentment of the Confederate military's tendency to take troops out of the state to defend other locations. When officers and even President Jefferson Davis explained that many times using these forces outside the state provided the best defense for Arkansas, Flanagin continued to protest. Still, he did what he could to augment the state's dwindling resources by calling for all able-bodied men to defend the state.

As the Confederacy collapsed in the spring of 1865, Flanagin worked with other western Confederate governors to negotiate the best possible peace for their states. He traveled to Marshall, Texas, to meet with those governors to arrive at a plan of surrender. When he returned home he offered a deal to Union general J. J. Reynolds to convene the Arkansas legislature to repeal all legislation related to secession. After Flanagin had signed the repeals he would resign as governor. Reynolds refused any negotiated settlement, although he did unofficially promise Flanagin his freedom if he simply disbanded his government. Flanagin did so and returned to Arkadelphia.

After the war, Flanagin again practiced a law. He died in Arkadelphia on 23 October 1874.

—*David S. Heidler and Jeanne T. Heidler*

See also Arkansas.
For further reading:
Flanagin, Harris. *Papers of Harris Flanagin, 1862–1874* (1965).

FLORIDA

Florida followed the lead of South Carolina and Mississippi by seceding from the Union on 10 January 1861. Though only a state since 1845, delegates voted 62 to 7 in a state secession convention to sever all ties with the United States and cast its lot with the new Confederacy. This fateful step became reality with the approval of many secessionist-minded Floridians who believed this to be the only true option after Abraham Lincoln's election.

Florida men flocked to enlist in the defense of their new country after the firing on Fort Sumter, with over 15,000 joining the Confederate army out of a population of only 140,000. Many of these saw active service in both the Army of Northern Virginia and the Army of Tennessee. Floridians like Edmund Kirby Smith and William W. Loring contributed their talents as general officers to the Southern cause, and Stephen R. Mallory of Key West proved to be a very able Confederate secretary of the navy.

Governor John Milton labored to place his peninsula state on a wartime footing and aid the greater Confederate war effort. He firmly believed in cooperating with the Richmond government and was willing to defer to it for the national good. Milton faced many difficult challenges in his office, one of which was how the large state of Florida could be defended from the Unionists. Federals already retained control of Fort Pickens at the mouth of Pensacola harbor, along with Forts Taylor and Jefferson far to the south in the Florida Keys. By mid-1862 Union troops held Fernandina, Saint Augustine, and Key West and began a series of occupations of Jacksonville. Union blockading warships also effectively sealed off Apalachicola and Tampa on the Gulf coast.

In the spring of 1862 the rebel government decided to pull troops out of Florida and move them to bolster more threatened fronts. For the duration the state received relatively little military support from Richmond and often had to fend for itself in terms of defense. Local units such as the "Cow Cavalry" battalion and irregulars led by the colorful John J. Dickison operated from the interior and struck Federal columns when the opportunity arose. These activities grew increasingly important by 1863 when Florida became a major source of supplies for the Southern armies.

Florida's most important contribution to the rebel war effort was in the form of vital saline extracted from boiling salt water. The heaviest concentration of salt works extended from Saint Marks to Saint Andrews Bay on the northern Gulf shore. These elaborate salt plants represented an investment of over $10 million by the end of the war. Saltwater boiled day and night despite Union sailors landing along the coast to smash the precious boilers. Tons of salt from these plants made their way into Georgia and Alabama, where they preserved meat for army rations and help tan leather. Florida remained a primary salt supplier for the lower South well into 1865.

The state's major food contribution to the Confederacy was in the form of beef cattle. After 1863 herds in south Florida were tapped for at least 75,000 head to feed hungry soldiers from north Georgia to Charleston. However Richmond authorities held unrealistic expectations of what the peninsula could do in terms of beef supplies. They very often failed to take into account the long distances involved and Florida's lack of a direct railroad connection to Georgia. Floridians did manage to construct a functioning supply collection system that forwarded agricultural products to Confederate commissaries till war's end. Early 1865 found government warehouses in north Florida full of food supplies with no one to send them too.

Florida citizens on the home front worked to meet such wartime demands and sustain themselves under increasingly difficult conditions. Many staple items grew rare then disappeared from store shelves altogether. Even the occasional blockade-runner failed to keep up with civilian requirements. Women often struggled to manage farms and businesses alone since the war had taken so many military age men out of the state. Rumors flew of attacks on isolated settler by Unionists, Confederate deserters, and even possibly Seminoles. The real hardships of civil war, combined with Confederate conscription and impressment policies, caused many to defect to the Union side. By 1865 two regiments of Florida Union Cavalry had been organized and set to breaking the Confederate will to resist in the region.

In 1864 the Lincoln administration concluded that Florida was ready to return to the Union under the president's "10 percent" reconstruction plan. To make this a reality in time for the 1864 presidential election John Hay ventured to Florida to sign up as many loyal voters as possible. His efforts realized few positive results, but did inspire Union military leaders to plan a campaign that would separate the peninsula from the rest of the South, cut rebel supply lines, and produce new recruits from Florida's slave population.

In February, 1864 General Truman Seymour led over 5,000 blueclad troops westward from Jacksonville in the direction of Lake City to accomplish the above-mentioned goals and possibly seize the state capital at Tallahassee. Confederates moved energetically to block this move by rushing additional men from Georgia to reinforce Rebel general Joseph Finegan's command then in Seymour's path. Both forces clashed in the 20 February 1864 battle of Olustee, which after a long day of combat ended with a clear but costly Confederate victory and a Federal retreat. Olustee, with its over 2,800 casualties, proved to be the largest Civil War battle fought on Florida soil.

One last Union advance in Florida took place in March 1865 when a Federal force invaded the Gulf shore near Saint Marks and moved on Tallahassee from the south. They ran into a scratch home defense force that managed to halt Union troops in the 5 March 1865 fight at Natural Bridge. Tallahassee would remain the only Confederate state capital east of the Mississippi not to fall to Northern forces during the war. This was cold comfort to Governor Milton, who took his own life in April rather than face Southern defeat. Union soldiers ultimately occupied Tallahassee and rebel Floridians laid down their arms and headed homeward.

Florida's Civil War was over, but the contest to find a way for ex-rebels, Unionists, and the over 60,000 newly freed slaves to live together in peace was only beginning.

—*Robert A. Taylor*

See also Jacksonville, Florida; Milton, John; Natural Bridge, Battle of; Olustee, Battle of; Pensacola.

For further reading:

Davis, William W. *The Civil War and Reconstruction in Florida* (1913).

Dickison, John J. "Florida." In *Confederate Military History.* Clement A. Evans, ed. (1899).

Johns, John E. *Florida During the Civil War* (1963).

Nulty, William H. *Confederate Florida: The Road to Olustee* (1990).

Taylor, Robert A. *Rebel Storehouse: Florida in the Confederate Economy* (1995).

FLORIDA, CSS

Unable to match the U.S. Navy with firepower, the Confederacy turned to the classic tactics of a weaker naval power, the *guerre-de-course*, or "war against commerce." The strategy called for the *Florida* to avoid combat with Union ships and instead prey upon vulnerable merchant shipping. In strategic terms, the tactics of the *Florida* and her sister ship the CSS *Alabama* prefigured the submarine warfare of the two world wars.

The CSS *Florida* was the first cruiser built for the Confederacy in Liverpool, England. The firm of W. C. Miller & Sons was the general contractor. Confederate naval agent James Dunwody Bulloch supervised her construction, begun in June 1861. The ship's maiden voyage was in March 1862. The *Florida* was a two-screw, wood-hulled steamer of 700 tons displacement. Average speed was approximately 9.5 knots. The *Florida* was built on the plans of a Royal Navy dispatch gunboat. Because of the need for deception, the *Florida* began life as the *Oreto*, ostensibly built for service in the Italian navy. During the ship's construction the British government acknowledged the obvious fact that the *Oreto* was designed as a warship. The lack of weapons or ammunition on board, however, provided no legal reason for seizure, as U.S. minister Charles Francis Adams demanded.

On 22 March 1862 the *Oreto* ostensibly set sail for Palermo, Italy. But once in international waters the *Oreto* instead sailed to Nassau, Bahamas, where she arrived in April 1862. Confederate naval captain John Newland Maffitt took command and oversaw the recruiting of a crew and the bringing on of armaments surreptitiously. The U.S. naval consul surveyed the ship and pressed the British government to seize it. The American consul's legal efforts prevented the transfer of arms on board the newly named CSS *Florida* until August. The British Admiralty had seized the *Florida* in May but released her in June.

Other incidents plagued the *Florida*, most notably a yellow fever epidemic among the crew and the theft of instruments. An oversight during the weapons transfer left the *Florida* without the necessary equipment to load, aim, or fire its main guns.

The *Florida* left the Bahamas for Cuba to elude Federal warships lurking nearby. Captain Maffitt sailed for Mobile Bay to obtain a crew and materiel. He arrived on 4 September 1862 flying a British flag and with only a handful of crewmembers fit for duty. While approaching the bay, the *Florida* clashed with the USS *Oneida* and was damaged. The USS *Winona* and *Rachel Seaman* pursued and poured heavy fire into the *Florida*. Speed enabled Maffitt to elude a devastating confrontation and anchor in the bay.

In October the fever epidemic passed and needed repairs and replenishments were commenced while a new crew assembled. On 16 January 1863 the *Florida* finally made for the open seas and began her commerce-raiding career. This first cruise resulted in the capture of twenty-four ships. Two ships captured by the *Florida* were outfitted as raiders and themselves captured twenty-one additional ships.

In August Captain Maffitt made port at Brest, France. Due to poor health, he was relieved by Commander

Joseph N. Barney, who was soon relieved by Lieutenant Charles Manigult Morris. In February 1864 the *Florida* began her second cruise, capturing thirteen ships before putting into port on 4 October at Bahia, Brazil.

The *Florida* shared the port with the USS *Wachusett*. Assuming safety under international rules of naval warfare, Morris gave shore leave to the crew. The gesture proved to be a serious mistake. In port on 7 October the *Wachusett* rammed the *Florida*, which had only a small crew on board, capturing and sailing her out to sea.

The Brazilian government protested this violation of its neutrality, and the U.S. government agreed to return the *Florida* and its crew. On 19 November 1864 a Federal army transport ship collided with the *Florida* in a putative accident at Hampton Roads, Virginia. The raider began taking on water, which was initially contained, but went to the bottom on 28 November. The U.S. government officially repudiated the capture of the *Florida* and apologized to the Brazilian government with a cannon salute to the Brazilian flag in Bahia.

The *Florida's* short career and inglorious end belies the disproportionate effect she and other Confederate raiders had on the U.S. naval effort. The *Florida*, along with other Confederate raiders, contributed to a decline in U.S. merchant shipping by driving up shipping rates and sending American ships to the protection of foreign flags. The commerce raiders also forced the U.S. Navy to disperse its ships in numerous cruises to track them down.

—*James V. Holton*

See also Blockade of C.S.A.; Maffitt, John Newland.

For further reading:
Luraghi, Raimondo. *A History of the Confederate Navy* (1996).
Owsley, Frank Lawrence, Jr. *The C.S.S. Florida: Her Building and Operations* (1965).

FLOYD, JOHN BUCHANAN
(1806–1863)
Confederate general

Born 1 June 1806 at the family estate, Smithfield, in Montgomery County, Virginia, John B. Floyd graduated in 1829 from South Carolina College, where he studied under Thomas Cooper, a strong proponent of Southern nationalism. Going into planting and law, he was soon prominent in state politics and won the governorship of Virginia in 1848 on a states' rights platform.

For his efforts in stemming the nativist tide in his state in the 1856 campaign, Floyd was appointed secretary of war by James Buchanan. Floyd's record in this office was marred by charges of favoritism toward friends and relatives and of improper dealings in Indian trust funds. By the end of 1860, even Southern members of the cabinet called for his resignation.

Floyd also attracted criticism in his handling of the more purely military duties of his office. His foes, including Jefferson Davis, accused him of nepotism in his 1860 selection of Joseph E. Johnston, his cousin by marriage, as quartermaster general of the army over more senior candidates such as Robert E. Lee and Albert S. Johnston. This quarrel regarding precedence and rank order would carry over into the Confederacy.

Of even greater controversy was Floyd's transfer of 125,000 small arms to Southern arsenals. His defenders claimed that he was making space for the new rifled muskets coming into the army's inventory. His opponents charged that he was putting a treasure trove of ordnance within reach of secessionists. In February 1861, a special committee of the House of Representatives investigating these accusations returned no verdict; its Ohio chairman privately exonerated Floyd.

By that point, Floyd was out of the cabinet, partly due to the allegations of peculation relating to the Indian funds, but more immediately to differences with Buchanan over South Carolina's secession. When Major Robert Anderson shifted his garrison from Fort Moultrie to the safer haven of Fort Sumter, Floyd pressed Buchanan to order Anderson back to Moultrie. Failing, Floyd resigned on 29 December.

After the secession of Virginia, Floyd entered the Confederate army on 23 May with the rank of brigadier general. On 11 August, he took command of the Army of the Kanawha with about 3,500 men and the mission of protecting the lower Virginia Alleghany front. Floyd led troops for the first time in the small and inconclusive actions in western Virginia at Cross Lanes and Carnifex Ferry.

Late in the year, his command was transferred to Albert Sydney Johnston's army defending the Confederate heartland. Arriving in Bowling Green, Kentucky, Floyd received surprising latitude from Johnston, who told Floyd on 8 February to "distribute your forces as you think proper."

As Brigadier General Ulysses S. Grant struck against the Confederate defenses on the Cumberland River, Floyd and his brigade arrived at Fort Donelson at daybreak on 13 February. Floyd immediately assumed command from Gideon Pillow. After an inspection tour, Floyd concluded that the site was "illy chosen," but nonetheless elected to fight for the position, perhaps encouraged in this course by his bombastic subordinate, Pillow.

Floyd's irresolution during the subsequent battle is well illustrated by his telegram to Johnston as the Confederate heavy guns repulsed the Union gunboats on 14 February: "The fort cannot hold out twenty minutes. Our river batteries working admirably." Worse, during the Confederate breakout attempt the next day, Floyd took little part in planning or leading the assault, nor did he intervene when Pillow inexplicably ordered the successful Confederate troops back into their trenches.

During the fateful command conference on the following night, Floyd initially counseled another escape attempt, but then fell prey to the pessimism of his third-in-command, Brigadier General Simon B. Buckner. Passing responsibility to his subordinates for the surrender of the fort, Floyd led his Virginians to the river, commandeered two steamboats, and made his escape to Nashville.

Despite this inept performance, Johnston placed Floyd in charge of the evacuation of Nashville. Floyd soon fell back to Chattanooga and then to Knoxville, where on 11 March he learned that President Jefferson Davis, without court of inquiry, had relieved him of his command.

Floyd's subsequent military duty was as major general of Virginia state forces, a rank granted him by the legislature on 17 May and a measure of his political, not military, prominence. For the next year, he guarded the salt works and rail lines of southwestern Virginia against Union raids. His health plummeted with his reputation. Floyd died 26 August 1863 in Abingdon at his daughter's home.

—Malcolm Muir, Jr.

See also Army of the Kanawha; Carnifex Ferry, Battle of; Fort Donelson, Battle of; Fort Sumter, Bombardment of.

For further reading:

Connelly, Thomas L., and Archer Jones. *The Politics of Command: Factions and Ideas in Confederate Strategy* (1973).

Cooling, Benjamin Franklin. *Forts Henry and Donelson: The Key to the Confederate Heartland* (1987).

McPherson, James M. *Battle Cry of Freedom: The Civil War Era* (1988).

FOGG, GEORGE GILMAN
(1813–1881)

U.S. minister to Switzerland

Born to David Fogg and Hannah Gilman Vickery Fogg in Meredith Center, New Hampshire, George Gilman Fogg was educated at New Hampton Academy and Dartmouth College. Upon graduation from the latter in 1839, Fogg enrolled in Harvard Law School. He began his law practice in 1842 near home, but within a few years moved to Concord, New Hampshire. Besides his legal practice, Fogg was active in New Hampshire politics. In the years before the Civil War, he occupied only one significant public office, a one-year term as New Hampshire's secretary of state. In the 1840s, he was a member of the Free Soil Party and, upon its founding in the mid-1850s, the Republican Party. Rather than through political office, Fogg preferred to convey his political opinions of the day through writing, and to that end he founded in 1846 a Concord newspaper called the *Independent Democrat*. He ran the paper until 1861 and returned to it after the war.

In the years before the Civil War, Fogg used the *Independent Democrat* as a forum for his views in opposition to the expansion of slavery into the territories and to advocate Republican candidates and policies throughout New England. These efforts in an increasingly Republican-dominated state gained him the state government printing contract at the end of the 1850s.

In 1860 Fogg was selected one of his state's delegates to the Republican National Convention in Chicago. There he strongly supported the nomination of Abraham Lincoln by the party and after the nomination used his paper vigorously to campaign for Lincoln's election. This support earned Fogg the gratitude of the new president and appointment after the inauguration as U.S. minister to Switzerland. He served in that position until the fall of 1865.

The Swiss government in Bern and the vast majority of the Swiss people strongly opposed the institution of slavery and, when they followed the war at all, strongly supported a Union victory. As a result, Fogg conducted primarily routine diplomatic activities in Switzerland and did not have to concern himself, as diplomats in many other countries did, with offsetting Confederate negotiations in the country in which he served. He was credited with being a capable, efficient diplomat, but he probably hardly felt the effect of the war during his years in Switzerland.

Perhaps out of boredom or to influence the momentous events taking place in the United States, Fogg tried to become involved in the negotiations surrounding the *Trent* Affair in the fall of 1861. He wrote to the U.S. minister to Great Britain, Charles Francis Adams, as that diplomat worked tirelessly to prevent an irrevocable breach between Great Britain and the United States, that the United States should ask Napoleon III of France to arbitrate the dispute. Adams apparently thought little of the suggestion but nevertheless passed it on to Secretary of State William Henry Seward. It was never acted upon. Beyond that little foray into Civil War diplomacy, Fogg did little else during the war except to maintain friendly relations between the United States and Switzerland.

Fogg resigned his post at the end of the war and returned to the United States in October 1865. He resumed his career in journalism, but his long absence from the United States and the growing power of the Radical Republicans in his absence left him with less influence than he had before he left. In 1866 he was appointed to serve out one year of an unexpired term in the U.S. Senate, but apparently made little impact on congressional policy during that time.

Returning to Concord in 1867, Fogg never regained the importance in New Hampshire political circles that he had enjoyed before the war. While he continued to edit his newspaper, he devoted increasingly more of his time to philanthropic pursuits. In his later years he retired from public life due to poor health. He died in Concord on 5 October 1881.

—*David S. Heidler and Jeanne T. Heidler*

See also Diplomacy, U.S.A.; *Trent* Affair.
For further reading:
A Memorial of George Gilman Fogg (1882).

FOGG, ISABELLA MORRISON
(ca. 1823–1873)
Union relief worker and nurse

A native of New Brunswick, Canada, Isabella was the sixth child in a family of Scottish immigrants. In 1837, she married William Fogg of Calais, Maine. The couple had three children, but only the second, Hugh Morrison, appears to have survived. The fate of her marriage is unclear. According to the 1860 U.S. Census, she lived alone in a boarding house in Calais, supporting herself as a "tailoress."

At the outbreak of the Civil War, her son Hugh enlisted as a private in Company D of the 6th Maine Volunteers. When the Regiment journeyed south to join the Army of the Potomac, Fogg soon followed. Like Clara Barton, she responded to the appalling conditions of inadequate supplies, disease, and battle casualties. She volunteered to nurse in the contagious wards of the U.S. Army hospital in Annapolis when spotted fever broke out in the fall of 1861. During the Peninsula campaign in 1862, she first worked on hospital ships organized by the U.S. Sanitary Commission, then helped establish and run the main field hospital at Savage Station, Virginia. A model of its kind, the facility had to be abandoned on 29 June, before being overrun by Confederate forces. Fogg was evacuated with the last wagonload of patients, but 2,500 more sick and wounded had to be left behind.

In the fall of 1862, Fogg returned to the front after a brief visit to Maine to solicit support and collect relief supplies. Traveling with her was the widow of a prominent minister from Portland, Harriet Eaton, representing the Ladies Committee, later known as the Maine Camp Hospital Association. They arrived in Washington, D.C., organized supplies, then journeyed by wagon to the camps of the Maine regiments in the aftermath of Antietam. These two women of different classes and temperaments were forced to live and work together under extraordinary circumstances. Each resented the other's presence and had her own ideas of how the relief efforts should be carried out. Always outspoken, Fogg did not shrink from criticizing the quartermaster of the 20th Maine for mistreating sick soldiers, asserting "a more wicked, profane, cruel, unprincipled man I think could not be found in the State of Maine."

After Chancellorsville, in May 1863, Eaton returned to Portland, while Fogg remained at the front. She followed the Army of the Potomac on its march to Gettysburg, arriving with supplies and mail the day after the battle. While her efforts were appreciated by ordinary soldiers and most officers, some military authorities had more negative views of women's relief work. A colonel in the 1st New York Artillery described her in his journal as "a meddling pest, doing ten times the harm that she does good."

Back in Maine, directors of the Maine Camp Hospital Association reviewed Eaton's accounts of her work with Fogg in the field. In November 1863, they voted to dismiss Mrs. Fogg as their agent and appointed a replacement. She responded vigorously with letters of recommendation from officers of Maine regiments, including Joshua Chamberlain, attesting to her service and character, and continued her work at the front. In May 1864, she accompanied Dorothea Dix to inspect the relief efforts after Fredericksburg and labored tirelessly in the Sanitary Commission hospitals there and at City Point.

In September 1864, the U.S. Christian Commission in Bangor, Maine, appointed her an agent. She had just returned to the field, when she was called to Martinsburg, Virginia, to nurse her son Hugh, whose left leg had been amputated on 19 October at the battle of Cedar Creek. In January 1865, she resumed her nursing duties, serving on the hospital ship *Jacob Strader* in Louisville, Kentucky. One night, while caring for patients on deck, she fell through an open hatchway, seriously injuring her back, thus ending her relief work.

Confined to bed, Fogg spent the next two years in hospitals as a ward of the public. By 1867, she had returned to Washington and worked as a copyist in the Pension Office. This income, combined with a government disability pension for wartime service, enabled her to support herself until chronic intestinal disease, most likely contracted during the war, caused her death in December 1873.

Isabella Fogg is buried in Forest City Cemetery in South Portland, Maine. Until recently, her grave was in ruins and untended, but the efforts of local Civil War historians have had it repaired. In 1994, a bronze plaque was erected to honor the courageous, voluntary service of this working-class woman from Maine.

—*Judith Bielecki*

See also Dix, Dorothea; Nurses; United States Christian Commission; Women.
For further reading:
Brockett, Linus P., and Mary C. Vaughan. *Woman's Work in the Civil War: A Record of Heroism and Self-Sacrifice* (1867).
Desjardin, Thomas J. *Stand Firm Ye Boys From Maine: The 20th Maine and the Gettysburg Campaign* (1995).
Maine Sunday Telegram, 14 August 1994.
Moore, Frank. *Women of the War: Their Heroism and Self-Sacrifice* (1866).
Nevins, Allan, ed. *A Diary of Battle: The Personal Journals of Colonel Charles S. Wainwright, 1861–1865* (1962).

FOOTE, ANDREW HULL
(1806–1863)
U.S. Navy admiral

Born in New Haven, Connecticut, on 20 June 1806, Andrew Hull Foote was the son of a future U.S. representative, later senator, Samuel A. Foot (Foote departed from family tradition by adding the "e" to his name). Foote briefly attended the U.S. Military Academy at West Point during June through December 1822. He resigned to accept an appointment as an acting midshipman in the U.S. Navy.

Foote served first in the West Indies, then spent three years in the Pacific. His religious conversion in 1827, during another Caribbean cruise, led to a lifelong interest in furthering Christianity and in reform. Following cruises in the Mediterranean and around the world during 1837 through 1841, he spent three years ashore as the executive officer at the Philadelphia Naval Asylum. In 1843, he became first lieutenant of the *Cumberland* and succeeded in making her the first temperance ship in the U.S. Navy. Foote was undoubtedly the key advocate in the navy for the abolition of the spirit ration, which was done in 1862.

From 1849 through 1851, Foote commanded the brig *Perry* off the southwest coast of Africa, protecting U.S. trade and cruising against the slave trade. In the process, the *Perry* took two slavers. After his return to the United States, Foote published a book about his experiences; *Africa and the American Flag* was both a plea for enhanced American action against the slave trade and for support of the African colonization movement in Liberia.

After five years ashore, where he remained active in naval reform, including service on the 1855 efficiency board that cut "dead wood" from the Navy, Foote returned to sea as commander of the sloop *Portsmouth* in the Asia Squadron. In November 1856, he personally led a force ashore to destroy four Chinese forts guarding the river approach to Canton in retaliation for the Chinese firing on U.S. vessels.

At the outbreak of the Civil War, Foote commanded the Brooklyn Navy Yard. In August 1861 Secretary of the Navy Gideon Welles sent him to command the Union flotilla in the West, replacing Captain John Rodgers who had run afoul of General John C. Frémont. Foote made only minor changes in the gunboats already contracted for and undergoing conversion; his chief accomplishment was to bring the warships to completion; oversee their manning, equipment, and training; and lead them in battle. Foote had already proven a capable administrator, and these tasks well suited him.

Foote got along well with his army counterpart, Brigadier General Ulysses S. Grant. An aggressive commander, Foote pushed for an attack on Fort Henry, and his flotilla took the leading role in the 6 February 1862 Union attack on that fort and actually secured its surrender before Grant's troops arrived. Foote then sent Lieutenant Seth L. Phelps on a raid up the Tennessee River. In the subsequent Union attack on Fort Donelson on the Cumberland River, Foote's ironclads were rebuffed and he himself was slightly wounded, although Donelson did ultimately fall to Grant. Foote claimed afterward that he had been forced to fight at Donelson before he was ready.

In many ways the affair at Fort Donelson changed Foote. He became much more cautious and, working to strengthen his gunboats, he delayed their participation in attacks against New Madrid and Island No. 10. Foote now preferred to use 13-inch mortars mounted on his newly ready mortar boats to reduce the Confederate forts. To those who called for his ships to assault the Confederate positions, Foote pointed out that substantial Confederate land batteries could disable his gunboats; in contrast to the situation at Donelson and Henry, helpless Union gunboats would then drift downriver into Confederate hands.

Finally, after repeated pleas from Union general John Pope, Foote did send two ironclads past the Confederate forts to cut off Island No. 10 and operate in conjunction with Pope's Army of the Mississippi. The Confederates then surrendered Island No. 10.

Foote and Union troops then moved farther down the Mississippi to Fort Pillow. By now Foote was virtually immobile, his leg wound having failed to heal. Furthermore, his exertions had left him mentally exhausted. On 9 May 1862 Captain Charles H. Davis took over the flotilla and Foote went on a leave of absence. He remained in nominal command of the squadron until June.

In July 1862 Foote returned to active duty to head the bureau of equipment and recruiting in Washington, D.C. One of the first Union naval officers promoted to the new rank of admiral, he was unhappy ashore. He did not seek the position, but when Welles relieved Admiral Samuel Du Pont as commander of the South Atlantic Blockading Squadron, Foote agreed to take that post. He was preparing to go to Charleston, with Admiral John Dahlgren as his second-in-command, when he was suddenly struck down by Bright's disease. After a short illness, Foote died in New York City on 26 June 1863. Much respected, even beloved, by his men, Andrew Foote was a capable administrator and a brave and tenacious commander.

—*Spencer C. Tucker*

See also Belmont, Battle of; Dahlgren, John Adolph Bernard; Du Pont, Samuel; Fort Donelson, Henry, Battle of; Fort Battle of; Fort Pillow; Frémont, John C.; Island No. 10; Grant, Ulysses S.; Phelps's Raid; Welles, Gideon.

For further reading:

Hoppin, James M. *The Life of Andrew Hull Foote, Rear Admiral, United States Navy* (1874).
Milligan, John D. "Andrew Foote: Zealous Reformer,

Administrator, Warrior." In *Captains of the Old Steam Navy. Makers of the American Naval Tradition, 1840–1880.* Edited by James C. Bradford (1986).

Tucker, Spencer C. *Admiral Andrew H. Foote* (1999).

FOOTE, HENRY STUART
(1804–1880)

U.S. senator, governor of Mississippi, and Confederate congressman

Henry Stuart Foote's longwinded bravado and general irascibility made him one of the most controversial political figures in the United States during the middle decades of the nineteenth century. An attorney by trade, Foote served in the U.S. Senate, as governor of Mississippi, and in the Confederate Congress. After the Civil War, he wrote prolifically to keep both his name and his often severe political insights before the public. Although an intelligent man, he once counseled a friend that "ignorance and impudence will succeed far better than intellect and modesty." On the stump he was relentless, unpredictable, rude, and effective, and his enemies hated him accordingly.

Foote was born in Fauquier County, Virginia, on 28 February 1804. Schooled at home by tutors, he briefly attended Washington College and studied law in a private office in Warrenton, Virginia. He was admitted to the bar in 1823, and two years later he relocated to Tuscumbia, Alabama. There he established a law practice and edited a small weekly newspaper. He quickly made political enemies through his sometimes scathing newspaper editorials and in 1827 fought a duel against future Alabama governor John A. Winston. Neither man was seriously injured, but because Foote instigated the duel he was barred from practicing law in Alabama for three years. He subsequently moved to Mississippi, settling first in Vicksburg and then in Jackson, where he built up one of the state's most lucrative law practices. He was a vocal supporter of Andrew Jackson and by the 1840s had established himself as an influential member of Mississippi's political community.

In 1844 Foote traveled Mississippi with future congressman Jefferson Davis in support of the national Democratic ticket. During the canvas, differences of opinion and temperament caused a falling out between the two men that marked the beginning of a life-long personal feud. In 1847 the Mississippi legislature sent Foote to the U.S. Senate as a reward for his service to the Democratic Party. That same year, Mississippi governor Albert Gallatin Brown appointed Davis to serve out the term of recently deceased U.S. Senator Jesse Speights. The hard feelings between Foote and Davis surfaced on Christmas Day in 1847, when they came to blows in the parlor of a Washington, D.C., rooming house during a discussion of sectional issues.

As a senator, Foote was a staunch Unionist and actively supported the passage of the Compromise of 1850. At one point during a heated debate over the legislation, he pulled a loaded pistol on Thomas Hart Benton of Missouri. After the Mississippi legislature censured him for his support of the Compromise, Foote left Washington and returned home to plead his case before the people. He organized the Union Democratic Party in Mississippi and entered the state's 1851 gubernatorial race as the new party's candidate. By a narrow margin he defeated Davis, who had resigned his senate seat to represent mainstream Democrats. Foote's election was a victory for Mississippi Unionists, but by 1854 the states' rights wing of the Democratic Party had established firm control of state politics. Foote resigned as governor that year and moved to California, where he mounted an unsuccessful campaign for the Senate.

Still urging support for the Union, Foote returned to Mississippi for a time during the late 1850s and then relocated to Nashville, Tennessee. In 1860 he supported Stephen Douglas for president. Foote eventually backed secession once it became inevitable and won a seat in the Confederate Congress, representing Tennessee's Fifth Congressional District. As a Confederate lawmaker, he continued to be a thorn in Davis's side by consistently criticizing the president's leadership.

As the Confederacy crumbled in early 1865, Foote traveled north in an attempt to open peace negotiations independently. Confederate authorities detained him, but in a second attempt he successfully reached Union lines. Secretary of State William Henry Seward rebuffed Foote's advances and ordered him to either return to Richmond or leave the country. Foote left the United States for Europe, but returned six weeks later and was arrested by Federal authorities. Again ordered to leave the country, he went to Canada, where he remained until after Abraham Lincoln's assassination.

Foote eventually returned to Nashville and in the years after the war wrote numerous books and articles on antebellum politics, many of which were highly critical of Davis. He retained a law office in Washington and in 1876 supported Republican presidential nominee Rutherford B. Hayes. Two years later, Foote secured an appointment as superintendent of the mint in New Orleans, a position he held at the time of his death on 20 May 1880.

—*Ben Wynne*

See also Brown, Albert Gallatin; Davis, Jefferson; Democratic Party; Mississippi.

For further reading:

Foote, Henry Stuart. *Casket of Reminiscences* (1874).

———. *War of Rebellion; or, Scylla and Charybdis, Consisting of Observations upon the Causes, Course, and Consequences of the Late Civil War in the United States* (1866).

Gonzales, John Edmond. "Henry Stuart Foote in Exile—1865." *Journal of Mississippi History* (1953).

———. "Henry Stuart Foote: A Forgotten Unionist of the Fifties." *Southern Quarterly* (1963).

FORCE, MANNING FERGUSON
(1824–1899)
Union general

Born to the historian Peter Force and Hannah Evans Force in Washington, D.C., Manning Ferguson Force received his undergraduate education at Harvard, and then he graduated from Harvard Law School. After graduation he moved to Cincinnati, Ohio, where he began practicing law in 1850. At the outbreak of the Civil War, he left his law practice to accept a major's commission in the 20th Ohio Volunteers. In September 1861, he became lieutenant colonel of the regiment.

Force and his regiment saw their first serious action at Fort Donelson in February 1862. Shortly after the capitulation of the fort, Force assumed command of the 20th and commanded it in Major General Lew Wallace's division at Shiloh. After the battle of Shiloh, Force was promoted to colonel of volunteers. During the summer and fall of 1862, Force and the 20th Ohio operated in southwestern Tennessee, primarily along the Mississippi Central Railroad. He was commended by his brigade commander, Mortimer Leggett, for his bravery during a skirmish at Bolivar, Tennessee. In September he fought at Iuka; the following month, in defense of Corinth.

In early 1863 during the Vicksburg campaign, Force performed railroad patrol in an effort to protect some of the supply lines to the forces operating against that city. He and the 20th joined the main campaign in early May 1863 when they participated in the battle of Port Gibson on 1 May. Almost two weeks later on 12 May, Force led the regiment in the fight at Raymond, Mississippi. Two days later during William T. Sherman's advance on Jackson, Mississippi, Force again guarded the rail lines between there and Clinton. On 4 June 1863 during the siege of Vicksburg, Force was given command of his brigade. After the surrender of the city, Force was one of the officers awarded a gold medal for his actions over the previous year. He was promoted to brigadier general of volunteers in the fall with a date of rank of 11 August 1863.

During the fall of 1863, Force operated along the Big Black River, skirmishing frequently with small Confederate forces there. He remained there through January 1864, when he and his brigade participated in Sherman's Meridian campaign. After the conclusion of that expedition, he returned to the Big Black River.

In May 1864, Force took his brigade to Clifton, Tennessee, to prepare for the upcoming Atlanta campaign. For a brief time in late May and early June he commanded the division, though for the actual campaign he commanded 1st Brigade, 3d Division, XVII Corps. He led his brigade in all the early battles of the Atlanta campaign. In the battle of Atlanta on 22 July 1864, in defense of a hill that the Federals had taken the day before, Force was struck in the face with a Confederate ball. He was carried from the field unconscious, and the doctors reported that his wound was mortal. However, over the next few weeks he began making a miraculous recovery, and in October, though terribly disfigured, he reported for duty.

Force was placed back in command of his old brigade, which he led during Sherman's March to the Sea. In December 1864, he was recommended by his division commander Leggett for a brevet promotion to major general of volunteers with Leggett describing him in the recommendation as one of the finest officers in the army.

Force continued to command his brigade in the subsequent Carolina campaign, during which he and his men were primarily occupied in January and February with destroying Confederate rail communications. In March he received a brevet promotion to major general for his conduct during the Atlanta campaign. In the latter part of the campaign, Force was given command of 3d Division, XVII Corps, a command that he held until Joseph E. Johnston's surrender.

After the war, Force was sent to the Department of Mississippi. Once he arrived in August 1865, he assumed command of the Western District of Mississippi. He remained there until mustered out of volunteer service in early 1866.

After leaving the army, Force returned to his law practice, though shortly after returning home he was elected to the court of common pleas. Ten years later he was elected to the superior court. He served on the bench for eleven more years before retiring. In 1892 he was awarded the Medal of Honor for his performance at the battle of Atlanta. Before and after retirement, Force also wrote extensively on legal matters, history, and his wartime experiences. Many of these works were published. He remained an active author until his death in Cincinnati on 8 May 1899.

—*David S. Heidler and Jeanne T. Heidler*

See also Atlanta Campaign; Meridian Campaign; Port Gibson; Vicksburg Campaign.
For further reading:
Memorial of Manning F. Force (1899).
Force, Manning Ferguson. *From Fort Henry to Corinth* (1881; reprint, 1992).
———. *General Sherman* (1899).
———. *Manning Ferguson Force Papers, 1835–1885* (1965).
———. *Personal Recollections of the Vicksburg Campaign* (1888).

FORD, ANTONIA
(1838–1871)
Confederate spy

Antonia Ford—the daughter of a wealthy merchant, twenty-three years old, daring, independent, and widely considered beautiful and charming at the time the war broke out—took no time in choosing sides and dedicating herself completely to the support of the South. Already by the fall of 1861, Confederate military officials in the area had begun to reward Ford for her patriotism and loyalty, and presumably for the steady supply of information that she was gathering and faithfully transmitting from a range of sources, including the many young soldiers in blue who competed for her attention and a host of unsuspecting guests in her plush family home. Indeed, on 7 October 1861 Confederate cavalry commander General J. E. B. Stuart honored Ford with a document declaring her an unofficial member of his staff. Although one witness to the ceremony in which Ford received her "commission" from Stuart later insisted that the action was taken only in good-natured jest, the document Ford received from Stuart that day later proved to have great significance in the federal government's judgment regarding her actions as a Confederate spy.

Ford's name has been linked persuasively to espionage activities in connection with the first and the second battles of Bull Run, but her fame arises more directly from her involvement in Southern guerrilla fighter John Singleton Mosby's embarrassing March 1863 capture of Union general Edwin H. Stoughton, along with some forty of his men, more than fifty horses, and a substantial cache of Federal weapons. Early in 1863 Union troops had begun to gather in Fairfax Court House under Stoughton's command, and initially Mosby was content simply to harass the intruders with regular raids and assaults. Soon, however, Mosby decided to take more conclusive action against his enemy, and made the Ford family home the base of his operations. There he colluded with Ford in determining more precisely his target's movements and habits. One soldier under Stoughton's command openly complained about Stoughton's lack of judgment in spending so much time riding about the countryside socializing with Ford, and warned in a letter, later reprinted in the *New York Times*, that "If Stoughton gets picked up some night, he may thank her for it." The soldier's warning was prescient. On 8 March 1863, Mosby and more than two dozen of his raiders made their move on the sleeping—and possibly drunk—Stoughton at his headquarters.

Almost immediately following Stoughton's capture, the United States Secret Service, under the leadership of La Fayette C. Baker, began to investigate and exact retribution for the humiliating affair. Baker later insisted that

he knew right away that Ford was to blame. Still, rather than arrest Ford at once, Baker sent a woman agent to the Ford family home disguised as a Confederate sympathizer to pump Ford for information. Carelessly, Ford let down her guard and began to boast of her familiarity with the location and the movements of the Federal troops in the area, and in a moment of misguided camaraderie also proudly showed her "commission" from General Stuart to her visitor. In so doing, Ford sealed her own fate. On 16 March she was arrested and searched, and two days later was remanded to the Old Capitol Prison in Washington, D.C., where she remained for several months.

During her imprisonment, Ford had at least one strong advocate, a young major in the Union army named Joseph C. Willard, who first encountered Ford while she was undergoing a preliminary investigation prior to being sent to the Old Capitol. Willard apparently fell in love with Ford on sight and spent the next months agitating for her release (even as she reciprocated by agitating for his resignation from Union army service). It is not entirely clear that Willard's efforts on her behalf greatly influenced officials to release Ford when they did, but by the fall of 1863 she was free. The following March she married Willard, who had finally acceded to her request that he leave army life behind, presumably in return for her promise not only to become his wife but also to give up her spy work on the Confederacy's behalf.

The Willards' happy life together ended in 1871 with Antonia's premature death, possibly related to the delivery of her third child. Tradition has it that the heartbroken widower kept Antonia's room as she left it. He never married again.

—*Elizabeth D. Leonard*

See also Baker, La Fayette Charles; Mosby, John Singleton.
For further reading:
Baker, Lafayette Curry. *History of the United States Secret Service* (1867).

Eskew, Garnett Laidlaw. *Willard's of Washington: The Epic of a Capital Caravansary* (1954).

Kane, Harnett T. *Spies for the Blue and Gray* (1954).

Kinthen, Oscar. *Women Who Spied for the Blue and Gray* (1972).

Leonard, Elizabeth D. *All the Daring of the Soldier: Women of the Civil War Armies* (1999).

FOREIGN VISITORS

The American Civil War, the largest conflict anywhere in the world during the second half of the nineteenth century, attracted considerable attention in Europe. In an era of international tension and nation formation, England, Prussia, and France all sent observers to find out what they could about the latest innovations in battle strategies and the technology

A group of foreign observers with Major General George Stoneman at Falmouth, Virginia, 1863 *(National Archives)*

of war. In an unofficial capacity, many European journalists and private individuals also observed the Civil War. Taken together, the official and unofficial observances of Europeans provide an international vantage on the events and strategies of the Civil War.

There are surprisingly few secondary studies of foreign observers of the Civil War. No major study has been published since Jay Luvaas's *The Military Legacy of the Civil War* (1959). But this book provides rich primary source documentation for the interested scholar to pursue.

Military intelligence was an ill-perfected art in the 1860s. There was little effort to engage in secret surveillance, and neither the Union nor the Confederate army was reluctant to receive foreign observers and candidly share strategic plans and technical information. In general, foreign observers were well received by both sides, and this was especially true in the South, where officials were keen to gain recognition in Europe. But the American Civil War was an alien affair to most European observers. In contrast to the professional armies of Europe, American troops seemed amateurish and poorly led. Moreover, the battlefield strategies of American commanders—in particular the willingness to devolve stewardship of a campaign once the battle was under way

and a reluctance to deploy cavalry as an offensive force—struck many Europeans as odd. As a consequence, Europeans failed to realize all the military lessons to be learned from the Civil War, although their often bewildered reports on the particularities of the conflict point the historian to the distinctive elements of the war.

British observers provided the broadest commentary of any European country. Official military observers came mainly from garrisons in Canada and belonged either to the Royal Artillery or the Corps of Royal Engineers. Charged with getting detailed answers to specific questions from British military officials on fortifications, artillery, and transportation, British military observers rarely saw action. Their observances were published contemporaneously in professional periodicals such as *Army and Navy Gazette,* the Royal Engineers' *Professional Papers,* and the *Journal of the Royal United Service Institutions.*

Although most diplomats and official military observers remained in the North, many British officers sympathized with the Confederacy and on their own initiative traveled in the South. Perhaps the most famous was Sir Garnet Wolseley, who was serving at the time as assistant quartermaster general in Canada. Wolseley, who would eventually serve as commander in chief of the

British army, took two months' leave and sojourned with Generals Robert E. Lee and Thomas J. Jackson in Virginia. He viewed Civil War troops as amateurish but admired Lee greatly, and, as British commander after 1895, he revived the study of the American Civil War in British military academies. Another freelance British observer was Lieutenant Colonel Henry Charles Fletcher of the Scots Fusilier Guards, who published the three-volume *History of the American War* (1864–1865) before the fighting was actually over. Despite being written by a man who traveled with the Union army during the Peninsula campaign and visited both armies in the west, Fletcher's *History* is surprisingly bereft of first-hand observances and relies mainly on secondary sources.

The most notable observer from within the Confederate lines was Lieutenant Colonel James Fremantle of the Coldstream Guards. With the exception of Florida, Fremantle visited every Confederate state east of the Mississippi and visited with Generals Joseph E. Johnston, Leonidas Polk, and P. G. T. Beauregard. Fremantle viewed the battle of Gettysburg from Lee's headquarters and before sailing for England witnessed the New York City draft riots. Fremantle's published account of his three-month excursion, *Three Months in the Southern States*, provides a vivid and engaging portrait of conditions in the Confederacy. At Gettysburg, Fremantle observed that the battle quickly escalated beyond the stewardship of military commanders. He proclaimed astonishment that Lee "during the whole time the firing continued … only sent one message and only received one report." Although Fremantle admired the bravery of infantry troops at Gettysburg, like many European observers he had a low regard for Civil War cavalry, mainly because of its focus on reconnaissance and reluctance to engage in offensive assault. Cavalry fights, Fremantle observed, were "miserable affairs" and even J. E. B. Stuart's corps could "hardly be called cavalry in the European sense of the word."

Beginning with Sir William Howard Russell of the London *Times*, a number of British newspaper correspondents provided a distinct commentary on the war. Russell, a seasoned and celebrated war correspondent, spent the first two months of the war behind Confederate lines. He then angered Northerners with a tactlessly honest account of Union deficiencies at Bull Run, which provoked Secretary of War Edwin Stanton to refuse Russell permission to travel with George McClellan's army in the Peninsula campaign. Russell sailed for England and later published an account of his experiences in *My Diary North and South* (1863). Francis C. Lawley, a former private secretary to William E. Gladstone and future editor of the London *Telegraph*, wrote strongly pro-Confederate articles for the *Telegraph* from Richmond. Other notable correspondents for British newspapers included Frank Vizetelly, correspon-

dent and artist for the *Illustrated London News*, and S. Phillips Day of the London *Herald*, who published his experiences and view of the war in *Down South* (1862).

The Civil War stimulated much less official attention in Prussia and Austria than in either England or France. Most German states gave their sympathies to the Union but were too absorbed in the conflicts of Central Europe to think that they had much to learn from the American war. However, many German natives (an estimated 200,000) served in the Union army. Otto Heusinger's *Amerikanische Kreigsbilder* (1869) is an outstanding first-hand account of the war. Serving with the largely German immigrant 41st New York, Heusinger was both perceptive and well informed. Another famous German veteran, Heros von Borcke, served the Confederacy as a member of J. E. B. Stuart's staff from May 1862 until he was wounded in June 1863. Von Borcke's *Memoirs of the Confederate War for Independence* provides insights into Stuart's cavalry tactics and became hugely influential on the organizers of modern German cavalry.

In 1863, the Prussian general staff commissioned Captain Justus Scheibert to observe the American war and report on the effects of rifled artillery. Scheibert was originally to accompany the Union army, but his sympathies were with the Confederacy, and he successfully petitioned his superiors to let him visit the Confederate army in an unofficial capacity. In time, Scheibert became an eyewitness of fourteen battles (including Gettysburg, which he observed from the same tree as Fremantle). In later publications, Scheibert commented on Confederate military operations (including his conversations with Lee, Jackson, and Stuart) and on general conditions in the Confederacy. Unfortunately, however, none of his writings are available in English. This is not the case with an associate of Scheibert's, the Austrian soldier of fortune Fitzgerald Ross, whose *Visit to the Cities and Camps of the Confederate States* was published in London in 1863.

In the early 1860s, France continued to bask in the glow of its Napoleonic tradition and thus saw less need than Britain to closely observe the events of the American Civil War. The most prominent French observer, the Prince de Joinville, traveled with McClellan's staff during the Peninsula campaign. In 1862, Joinville published *The Army of the Potomac: Its Organization, Its Commander, and Its Campaign*. Joinville identified weaknesses in the general staff structure, an inadequate replacement system, and an unwieldy supply service. But in general he believed that the volunteer system was the real fault with the Union army. "Amateur soldiers" were "costly and capricious," but Joinville believed that American leaders did not want to acknowledge the comparative value of regular troops. To do so, he argued, "would involve a renunciation of the general and deeply rooted creed, that every American, when he wishes to do a thing, may find within himself, without any apprenticeship, the power to do it." In tactical matters, Joinville observed McClellan's defensive tendencies and expressed limited admiration for the new rifled gun. Even in the thickly wooden terrain of North America, Joinville preferred the familiar smoothbore rifle. Accompanying Joinville in the Peninsula campaign was his nephew, the exiled Orleans prince the Comte de Paris. He had enlisted in the Union army as a captain and would subsequently publish a massive eight-volume history of the war, which was published in the United States as *History of the Civil War in America* (1875–1888). Because his own participation in the war so brief, the Comte de Paris's history is essentially a secondary work and in scope resembles Fletcher's *History*.

The first official military mission from France was sent in 1864. Colonel François de Chanal and Captain Pierre Guzman, both of the French Artillery Corps, were charged with studying American military technique. They inspected arsenals, hospitals, and military installations in New York, Philadelphia, and Washington before joining the staff of General George G. Meade, commander of the Army of the Potomac. Before returning to France in January 1865, Guzman submitted six detailed reports on munitions manufacturing and after the war became an intelligence expert on the American military. Chanal later wrote a book-length study, *The American Army in the War of Secession*, which was published in the United States in 1894. Chanal admired the work of the army engineers and the "admirable sanitary condition" of the Union army. His study lacks an analysis of tactics but contains much statistical information about the organization, equipment, and regulations of the Union army. Chanal concluded that Americans generally made good soldiers. On this point he contradicted most other European observers. Outward appearances, he noted, could be misleading, and "an observer who merely passes through …may thus be deceived."

—*Edward John Harcourt*

See also Great Britain; Russell, William Howard.

For further reading:

Lord, Walter, ed. *The Fremantle Diary: Being the Journal of Lieutenant Colonel James Arthur Lyon Fremantle, Coldstream Guards, on His Three Months in the Southern States* (1954).

Luvaas, Jay, and Wilbur S. Nye. *The Military Legacy of the Civil War: The European Inheritance* (1959; reprint 1988).

Russell, William Howard. *My Diary North and South* (1988).

Von Borcke, Heros. *Memoirs of the Confederate War for Independence* (1938; reprint 1985).

FORREST, NATHAN BEDFORD
(1821–1877)
Confederate general

Nathan Bedford Forrest, the eldest of eleven children, was born in middle Tennessee and moved with his family to northern Mississippi in 1834.

His father's death three years later left young Forrest with the enormous responsibility of supporting the large family. Like most frontier children, Forrest lacked a formal education and gained much of his knowledge from experience. Violence and personal hardships shaped Forrest's character during these formative years. By age twenty-one, he had become the embodiment of Southern honor, self-reliant and family-oriented, but possessing a quick temper if crossed.

Forrest accepted an uncle's invitation to join in a business partnership at Hernando, Mississippi, twenty miles south of Memphis, Tennessee, in 1842. While accumulating a modest degree of wealth in Hernando, Forrest also gained local prominence through several highly publicized disputes. One such incident in 1845 left Forrest wounded, his uncle killed, and two of their four opponents dead in the town square. Despite the death of his uncle, Forrest continued to operate their store and dabble in other business ventures.

By 1851, Forrest had married, started his own family, and moved to Memphis. At Memphis, he concentrated on building a slave trading business and became the region's largest and most reputable slave trader in less than a decade. In 1860, Forrest was one of the South's wealthiest men and served as a Memphis alderman.

Forrest built his fortune on slavery, and each crisis of the 1850s threatened to destroy all he had achieved. He nervously watched the presidential election of 1860 hoping another compromise could be reached, but all attempts failed. Although Mississippi had seceded a few months earlier, Forrest deferred his decision to choose a side until his native state, Tennessee, voted on the issue.

In June 1861, Tennessee and Forrest cast their lot with the Confederacy. Forrest, a skilled equestrian, enlisted as a private in a local cavalry regiment, but the people of Memphis soon petitioned Tennessee's secessionist governor, Isham Harris, to commission Forrest as an officer. Using his own money, Lieutenant Colonel Forrest personally raised and equipped his regiment.

After several minor engagements, Forrest's regiment received its first taste of battle and victory at Sacramento, Kentucky, in December 1861. Employing tactics that would later become his trademarks, Forrest fixed the Union position in place with a small frontal assault while using the speed and mobility of his mounted infantry to attack the flanks simultaneously. At times outdistancing his own men, Forrest personally led the charges, engaging in hand-to-hand combat on many occasions. This type of personal warfare seemed well suited to a man who had matured along the often-violent Southern frontier. After the war, Forrest calculated that he had killed thirty men, "one more enemy soldier than the twenty-nine horses shot out from underneath him."

Forrest's men joined in the defense of Fort Donelson

in February 1862, but the decision to surrender outraged their commander. Forrest, by nature never comfortable with playing a subordinate's role, chastised his superiors for choosing to capitulate rather than fight. Using the darkness and snowy weather to mask his movement through enemy lines, he led his men and any who would follow out of Fort Donelson before the surrender took place. They arrived at panic-stricken Nashville a few days later. The local commander in Nashville employed Forrest to stop the rampant looting of Confederate supplies and to provide a rear guard for the army's retreat. Forrest managed to bring some order to the evacuation and save a substantial amount of supplies from falling into the enemy's hands.

After a brief pause to rest and refit his men at Huntsville, Alabama, Colonel Forrest proceeded to join Albert Sidney Johnston's Army of Tennessee. As the Confederates retreated from Shiloh in April 1862, Forrest charged the pursuing Union forces alone, firing his pistol and slashing enemies with his sword. The impetuous Forrest soon found himself surrounded by Union troopers, all aiming their muskets toward him. One musket pressed deep into his side and fired at point blank range, lifting the more than six-foot tall, well-framed Forrest up in the saddle. Though severely wounded, he wheeled his horse around, hoisted a hapless Union soldier onto the back of the animal to act as shield, and raced for the safety of his lines. This gallant action halted the Union pursuit of the Army of Tennessee's withdrawal to Corinth, Mississippi, and bought precious time for both the army and Forrest to recover from their wounds.

Forrest recovered fairly quickly and was given a new regiment in the summer of 1862. On 13 July 1862, he led a daring raid on Federal encampments at Murfreesboro, Tennessee. During this operation, Forrest introduced a ruse that with several variations he used frequently during in the war. Having already captured a large portion of the Union garrison, he arranged a truce to negotiate the surrender of the remaining Union garrison. With only a small force, Forrest conspicuously lined his men along the streets and escorted the Union officers through town. As the procession passed, Forrest's men circled around buildings ahead of the group and reformed to make their numbers seem larger. Unaware that they were seeing the same men repeatedly, the Union officers promptly surrendered, believing themselves heavily outnumbered. The Murfreesboro raid's success brought Forrest increased recognition from senior Confederate officers. He was promoted to brigadier general and conducted raids on General Ulysses S. Grant's supply lines in western Tennessee and northern Mississippi for almost a year.

Forrest narrowly escaped defeat and capture at Parker's Crossroads, Tennessee, in late 1862 when an unexpected Union force appeared in his rear while he was attacking a force to his front. After reporting their the situation, Forrest's junior officers anxiously awaited further orders. The general's response: "Charge them both ways!" Despite heavy losses, Forrest and his command survived. These raids, in conjunction with those of General Earl Van Dorn, wrecked Grant's supply lines and forced the abandonment of his first drive toward Vicksburg.

Forrest regrouped after Parker's Crossroads and was soon ordered to General Braxton Bragg's Shelbyville headquarters for reassignment to General Joseph Wheeler's cavalry. Wheeler had gathered some intelligence of a suspected weak Union position at Dover, Tennessee, near Fort Donelson and planned an attack. During the assault, Forrest mistakenly believed the enemy was in retreat and moved quickly to capture the position. Union troops, however, stood their ground and inflicted heavy casualties on their attackers, forcing Forrest into a rare retreat. Stunned by the repulse and angered at Wheeler's negative assessment of his performance, Forrest requested a transfer from Wheeler's command.

For nearly a month, Forrest remained idle. Finally, General Van Dorn asked Forrest to accompany him on a raid against Franklin, Tennessee. At Thompson's Station and Brentwood, Forrest's men redeemed their unit's pride by handily defeating the enemy and capturing nearly 2,000 Union soldiers. In the spring of 1863, Forrest again used his techniques of deception to compel the surrender of Union colonel Abel Streight's raiders before they could interdict the Western & Atlantic Railroad supplying Bragg at Tullahoma.

Command of the Army of Tennessee's left wing passed to Forrest after General Van Dorn's death in May 1863. By June, however, Bragg was in full retreat from middle Tennessee. Forrest had always disliked Bragg's propensity to retreat and his favoritism shown toward more agreeable or formally educated officers. After Bragg's refusal to pursue and destroy the routed Union forces after Chickamauga, Forrest angrily confronted Bragg, even threatening to kill him. Confederate president Jefferson Davis, already concerned about Bragg's leadership, granted Forrest's requests for a transfer and an independent command in west Tennessee.

The new assignment rated Forrest a promotion to major general, but it prevented all but a small number of the seasoned veterans to travel with him. Upon arriving in west Tennessee, Forrest faced the difficult task of recruiting a new force from an area that had been largely under Union occupation since 1862. Undeterred, Forrest enlisted a sizable force and filled the ranks with highly competent officers, including his youngest brother, Jeffery. Jeffery, born four months after his father's death, was especially important to the elder Forrest, who had raised him as a son. Wasting little time, Forrest began roaming through northern Mississippi and western Tennessee attacking the widely dispersed Federal garrisons left to protect the waterways and railroads. He also used the raid to conscript available men to augment his force.

Dissatisfied with the lack of initiative among his commanders, Union general William T. Sherman launched an offensive in early 1864 toward Meridian, Mississippi. His intent was to destroy a large portion of the Confederacy's crops before the harvest and any industry that could aid the Rebel war effort. The Confederacy immediately dispatched Forrest to harass their movement. The speed and size of Sherman's columns made it impossible for Forrest to intercept the main body before it reached Meridian. Instead, Forrest staged a series of hit-and-run attacks upon a slower supporting column led by General William "Sooy" Smith. Slowed by swamps, large numbers of freedmen, and confiscated property, Smith was unable to rendezvous with Sherman at Meridian and began his return to Memphis. During an attack on Smith's column near Okolona, Mississippi, Jeffery Forrest was mortally wounded. A devastated Forrest raced to where his brother's body lay on the field and grieved quietly for a few moments. He then returned to the battle, determined to avenge his brother's death. Led by a wrathful Forrest, the Confederates renewed their attacks with such ferocity that Smith's retreat was almost constantly under fire until it reached the security of Memphis.

Returning to Tennessee in February 1864, Forrest's men surveyed the damage inflicted to their homes during the Union occupation and saw their families living in a state of fear. Most of the men clamored for retaliation, especially after it was charged that the perpetrators were Tennessee Unionists and freedmen serving in the Union army. Forrest agreed to the troops' demands for a short leave to arrange adequate shelter for their loved ones, and he promised to exact revenge on the traitors who committed these outrages upon their return. During this time, Forrest outlined a new plan to interdict Sherman's supply routes running through the area toward Chattanooga, the primary staging area for the Atlanta campaign.

In late March, the men reassembled at Jackson, Tennessee. Forrest then initiated assaults on Union positions at Union City, Tennessee, as well as, Paducah, Kentucky. At Union City, the Tennessee Unionist force under Isaac Hawkins surrendered after succumbing to a ruse that caused him to overestimate the size of the force opposing him. This marked Hawkins's second surrender to Forrest during the war, and Hawkins's men, after discovering that they had been tricked, ridiculed their commander as a coward.

The attack on Paducah was more difficult. Black troops holding the town's fortifications maintained their ground but allowed Forrest to loot and burn the town. A demonstration against Memphis also netted Forrest the infamous Tennessee Unionist Fielding Hurst. Hurst was allegedly responsible for extorting money from the town of Jackson, Tennessee, and destroying substantial amounts of private property. Only one Federal garrison remained, a combined force of Tennessee Unionists and U.S. Colored Troops stationed on the Mississippi at Fort Pillow, an old Confederate fortification.

The battle of Fort Pillow remains the most controversial of Forrest's career. Forrest surprised the disorganized and poorly fortified garrison on 12 April 1864. The Confederate assault, despite outnumbering the Federal troops three-to-one, stalled after the defenders retreated into a six-foot redoubt along a bluff in the river. Confederate sharpshooters had plunged the fort into disarray by killing the ranking officer earlier in the day. Command of the defense then devolved upon an inexperienced Tennessee Unionist, William Bradford, who rebuffed three surrender offers, signing his dead superior's name each time. Bradford even refused the assistance of passing steamers loaded with fresh Union troops as they passed along the river. Unaware of the confusion inside the fort, Forrest ordered a final charge to take the fort late in the afternoon. Infuriated by the presence of white Tennesseans serving with former slaves, the attacking Confederates poured into the fort, killing more than half the garrison.

The survivors charged that Forrest personally ordered the murder of black soldiers, even after they had surrendered. A congressional committee composed of Radical Republicans rushed to document their accounts for maximum propaganda effect. Historians have debated the merits of these allegations ever since. Although clearly some Confederate soldiers did commit murders, the question of whether Forrest gave specific orders to execute these men has been questioned. Bradford's culpability for the inadequate defense of the fort has been left unexplored, especially during the final assault, when black troops were left to conduct a fighting retreat from the works, while whites waited to counterattack below the bluff. During the confusion, it is possible that many black soldiers died from friendly fire as the Unionists began firing prematurely before they passed through the line. Nevertheless, most modern biographers have assigned blame for the massacre to Forrest for failing to control his men. These accusations have remained a permanent scar upon Forrest's otherwise extraordinary record.

In the summer of 1864, Forrest achieved spectacular victories at Brice's Crossroads and Tupelo, Mississippi. He then proceeded to wreak further havoc upon Union rear areas in Tennessee. At the Johnsonville supply depot on the Tennessee River, Forrest almost succeeded in an elaborate plan to capture gunboats and create his

own river fleet. These exploits earned both Sherman's admiration and disdain. Sherman once referred to his adversary as "that devil Forrest."

With the fall of Atlanta, Confederate fortunes were growing increasingly dim by November. Forrest suspended his campaigning in western Tennessee to join the newly appointed commander of the Army of Tennessee, General John Bell Hood, on the disastrous Franklin and Nashville expeditions. Again, Forrest conducted a brilliant rear-guard action at Nashville that managed to protect what remained of Hood's force from destruction. Although promoted to lieutenant general in 1865, Forrest was left with little to command. Finally, Forrest accepted the Confederacy's demise and surrendered at Gainesville, Alabama, in May 1865.

Forrest attempted to rebuild his fortune after the war by investing heavily in the Reconstruction railroad boom. This investment and several others eventually failed. He did, however, dabble in postwar politics, seeking to restore conservative Democratic rule to the South. Frustrated by the imposition of Radical Republican rule and unable to see blacks as equals, Forrest assumed the leadership of the Ku Klux Klan (KKK), a secret organization committed to white supremacy. His suspected affiliation with the KKK brought him before a congressional investigation in 1871 into the organization and violence against blacks. As expected, Forrest denied any connection. Forrest died on 28 October 1877 in Memphis.

—*Derek W. Frisby*

See also Brentwood, Tennessee; Brice's Crossroads, Battle of; Cavalry, C.S.A.; Forrest's Raids; Fort Donelson; Fort Pillow Massacre; Meridian Campaign; Parker's Cross Roads, Battle of; Thompson's Station (Spring Hill), Battle of; Tupelo, Battle of.

For further reading:
Hurst, Jack. *Nathan Bedford Forrest: A Biography* (1993).
Jordan, Thomas, and J. .P. Pryor. *The Campaigns of Lieutenant General Nathan Bedford Forrest, and of Forrest's Cavalry* (1868; reprint 1988).
Maness, Lonnie. *An Untutored Genius: The Military Career of General Nathan Bedford Forrest* (1990).
Wills, Brian Steel. *A Battle from the Start: The Life of Nathan Bedford Forrest* (1992).
Wyeth, John Allen. *Life of General Nathan Bedford Forrest* (1899; reprint, 1989).

FORREST'S RAIDS
(December 1862–October 1864)

A proven leader of cavalry at every major battle in the western theater from Shiloh to Franklin, Nathan Bedford Forrest earned much of his fame from a series of spectacular raids in northern Mississippi, northern Alabama, and middle and western Tennessee. The fast-moving and hard-fighting style that Forrest favored on these raids foreshadowed the tactical innovation of mechanized infantry in the twentieth century

while his grasp of the basic elements of mobile warfare earned him the praise of renowned military scholars such as Viscount Wolseley and B. H. Lidell Hart.

After the battle of Shiloh in April 1862, P. G. T. Beauregard charged Forrest with gathering and training the tiny and irregular cavalry regiments in southeastern Tennessee. In the summer of 1862, Forrest had the opportunity to transform these somewhat unruly units of Tennesseans, Kentuckians, and Texans into an effective fighting force when he was ordered to disrupt Union general Don Carlos Buell's snail-like advance on Chattanooga. Choosing a strike against Murfreesboro, Tennessee, garrisoned by a Federal force of similar size with his own, Forrest set out with his green horsemen on 9 July.

Forrest struck the Federal camp east of Murfreesboro on 13 June at 4:30 A.M., his Texans capturing about eighty men of the 7th Pennsylvania and then charging into a Michigan infantry regiment whose troops, though surprised from sleep, formed a sturdy line of defense. Meanwhile, the rest of Forrest's command swept into town, breaking open the jail (which a fleeing Federal officer had set ablaze) and freeing the imprisoned Confederate sympathizers.

West of town, Forrest personally led a charge against an infantry regiment of Minnesotans encamped separately from their Michigan compatriots because of intramural wrangling among the general officers. Finding the 3d Minnesota holding a strong position flanked by artillery, Forrest turned his attention back toward the south of town. Urged by his lieutenants to retreat before the arrival of Union reinforcements, Forrest demurred. Surrounding and capturing what remained of the Michigan regiment, he verbally bullied the 3d Minnesota into surrender. Forrest not only bagged the entire Union garrison and freed the secessionist sympathizers (several of whom faced execution at cockcrow), but he also captured a Union battery that later became the nucleus of his artillery.

Forrest followed this success up with a raid into Nashville, the state capital that had fallen into Union hands after the disastrous outcome of Fort Donelson. In this audacious strike, Forrest and his troopers broke a railway that functioned as a major artery of Buell's supply line. This success further slowed Buell's ponderous advance and tied up thousands of Federal troops called out of northern Alabama to meet the threat. The combined effect allowed Braxton Bragg's Army of the Mississippi to make their way to Chattanooga, checking Federal hopes of rapidly securing that important railroad junction.

In December 1862, General Braxton Bragg, now commanding the Army of Tennessee, sent Forrest to western Tennessee with orders to harry Ulysses S. Grant's supply line and slow down his advance on Vicksburg. Crossing the icy Tennessee River on 16 December, Forrest detached a small force to demonstrate against the large Federal concentration at the Tennessee town of Jackson while the bulk of his troops swung north and broke the railroad as far as Union City on the Tennessee and Kentucky line. Garrisons from all over west Tennessee moved against Forrest, one Federal column striking his reunited forces at Parker's Cross Roads. Surprised and almost surrounded, only the quick thinking and hard fighting of the 8th Tennessee Cavalry under George C. Dibrell saved Forrest's forces from destruction.

After the battle of Chickamauga in September 1863, and a violent quarrel with Braxton Bragg, Forrest received the assignment of organizing the partisan units of western Tennessee and northern Mississippi. After a successful defensive action against Union general William Sooy Smith, Forrest organized his command and set out in March 1864 from his base at Columbus, Mississippi, for west Tennessee. This raid took Forrest as far as Paducah, Kentucky, and became the least successful and most controversial of his forays. The hastily assembled command managed to hold Paducah for much of 25 March, though an attack on nearby Fort Anderson met with a bloody repulse. Forrest later claimed that he would have held the town longer had it not been for an outbreak of smallpox among the civilian population. However, the shelling of the town from Fort Anderson and Federal gunboats on the Ohio River likely had more to do with the decision to abandon the unfruitful occupation. Forrest returned to northern Mississippi with his band of 2,000 troopers being chased by as many as 20,000 Federal troops assembled from west Tennessee garrisons. A stop on his flight southward at Fort Pillow, just north of Memphis, ignited a controversy still lingering over whether Forrest ordered a massacre of black Union troops who garrisoned the strongpoint.

A series of raids at the end of 1864 firmly established Forrest as a Confederate legend. The first grew out of Federal general A. J. Smith's invasion of north Mississippi with some 14,000 troops. Unable to meet this overwhelming threat head-on, Forrest left a small detachment under General James Chalmers near the north Mississippi town of Oxford while the bulk of his force moved northwest toward Smith's own base at Memphis. Forrest intended by this move both to force Smith out of Mississippi and to capture the west Tennessee department commander, Major General Cadwallader Washburn, and perhaps two other Union general officers, Brigadier General R. P. Buckland and Major General Stephen Hurlbut.

The Memphis expedition succeeded in turning back the pawns but not in seizing any kings. Forrest's move on Memphis ended A. J. Smith's motivation for entering north Mississippi. However, a comedy of errors led to the failure of the attempted kidnappings. Faced with a strong line of infantry south of town, the Confederates headed south, the 6th Illinois cavalry snapping at their heels.

The beginning of September 1864 saw Forrest on the move again, this time into Alabama and middle Tennessee, leading a force of cavalry 4,500 strong. Lieutenant General Richard Taylor had sent Forrest into this region with the hope that a strike at William T. Sherman's supply lines would aid John Bell Hood's embattled troops west of Atlanta. To that end, Forrest struck at Athens, Alabama, a point that held the only major Federal fortification on the Decatur and Nashville line. The main column of Confederates seized two blockhouses while a detachment fought off and captured a small Union relief column. Forrest then turned his forces east in hopes of cutting the railroad at the major artery of Tullahoma. Finding Tullahoma too strongly held, Forrest's command turned south toward a Tennessee River swollen by a summer of unusually heavy rain. The difficult crossing forced almost 1,000 of Forrest's troops to swim their horses to safety while 15,000 Federal troops moved against them from all points on the map.

Still hoping to break Sherman's tenuous but sturdy supply line, Taylor ordered Forrest and his saddle-weary command to return to western Tennessee in October. Forrest crossed the Tennessee River with his main force near Eastport, Mississippi, leaving young John Morton's artillery and a detachment of troopers under Abraham Buford to set an ambush for unwary Federal supply ships. On 29 October, Morton's guns disabled the supply ship *Mazeppa*, a prize the Confederates quickly had to burn due to the approach of Federal gunboats. The following day, a transport convoy accompanied by the gunboat *Undine* fell into Buford and Morton's trap with both the *Undine* and the transport *Venus* falling into the hands of Forrest's troops. Forrest sent both ships upriver toward the Union supply depot at Johnsonville while his ground force followed along the riverbank.

Forrest's career as a naval commander proved short-lived. Around a bend in the river just below Johnsonville, the Federal gunboats *Tawah* and *Key West* struck the *Undine* and *Venus*, sinking *Venus* and forcing the amateur crew of the *Undine* to seek refuge by hugging the bank beneath Morton's artillery. This setback did little to hinder Forrest's larger purpose. Later in the afternoon, Forrest's meticulously placed artillery opened on Johnsonville's wharves, the eleven Federal supply ships docked there, eighteen fully stocked barges, and a number of supply warehouses. After two hours of steady bombardment, the Federal supply depot at Johnsonville had been reduced to a smoking ruin. Federal estimates of the damage went as high as 2.2 million dollars.

The destruction of the Federal stores at Johnsonville became both Forrest's final raid and his final triumph of the war. In December, he and his troops accompanied Hood on his ill-starred Tennessee campaign. After that debacle, Forrest's dwindling forces attempted the defense

of northern Mississippi and Alabama from the large Federal raiding parties now moving at will across the interior South. He disbanded what remained of his command on 9 May 1865.

Nathan Bedford Forrest's forays raised Confederate morale and left Union commanders storming with frustration. Many of Forrest's admirers speculate that the Confederate effort might have turned out differently had he been granted a larger sphere of command, but it should be remembered that he had little experience with leading large-scale operations. Forrest's tactics remain, however, a preeminent example of warfare's evolution from heavy columns and clashing armies to speed, stealth, and subterfuge.

—W. Scott Poole

See also Cavalry, C.S.A.; Fort Anderson; Fort Pillow Massacre; Parker Cross Roads, Battle of; Wilson's Selma Raid.

For further reading:
Henry, Robert Selph. *"First with the Most" Forrest* (1944).
Hurst, Jack. *Nathan Bedford Forrest: A Biography* (1993).

FORSTER, WILLIAM EDWARD
(1818–1886)
Member of Parliament

Although a newcomer to the House of Commons, William Edward Forster played a prominent role in squelching the attempts of pro-Confederate legislators to influence the British government's policy during the American Civil War. At the same time, he mobilized public opposition to British intervention in the American conflict. These efforts earned the respect of Charles Francis Adams, the American minister to Britain, who praised Forster as the most valuable British supporter of the Union.

Born on 11 July 1818 at Bradpole, Dorsetshire, England, Forster was the son of William Forster, a prominent Quaker minister. His mother, Anna Buxton, was also a Quaker preacher whose brother, Thomas Fowell Buxton, played a prominent role in Britain's abolitionist movement. A studious youth, Forster attended Quaker schools in Bristol and Tottenham between 1831 and 1835. Although Forster wished to study law, his father placed him as a clerk in a wool-weaving factory run by relatives in Norwich. Two years later, in 1838, Forster moved on to Darlington where he worked in a woolen mill.

During his stay at Darlington, Forster began to show a serious interest in politics. His uncle, Thomas Fowell Buxton, had launched a campaign to end the slave trade in Africa through a combination of force and trade. Buxton believed that an increased British naval presence off the West Coast of Africa, coupled with the introduction of education and modern agriculture would end slavery in the region. This policy culminated in the Niger Expedition of 1841 that attempted, but failed, to found a model agricultural colony on the Niger River. Forster energetically supported his uncle's efforts in the face of criticism from many in the abolitionist movement who sought to end slavery through moral suasion alone.

In 1839 Forster moved to London, where he worked in a counting house. Around 1841 he moved to the industrial town of Bradford, where he and a partner, William Fison, set themselves up in worsted manufacturing. The business eventually proved a great success and provided Forster with a steady income, allowing him to embark upon a political career.

In 1850 Forster married Jane Arnold, daughter of Thomas Arnold, the famous headmaster at Rugby, and sister of Matthew Arnold, who later became a prominent poet and social critic. The Society of Friends "disowned" Forster—that is, expelled him—for marrying a non-Quaker. By this point, however, Forster had already become somewhat alienated from the Society of Friends. His marriage proved a happy one.

Throughout the 1840s and 1850s Forster became prominent in local politics as a public speaker and organizer of charities. Unlike many of his fellow Liberal factory owners, Forster believed that the government had a role in resolving social problems. He supported the government's attempt to limit working hours in factories, backed the repeal of the Corn Laws, expressed some sympathy for the democratic Chartist movement, and sought to reform the franchise. As a former Dissenter, he also wished to abolish church rates, remove university religious tests, and expel Anglican bishops from the House of Lords.

Forster grew restive with the limited scope of his political activities and sought to enter the House of Commons. After several abortive attempts, he got his name on the ballot for Bradford in 1859, but failed to win a seat by twenty-two votes. In 1861, however, after one of Bradford's sitting members resigned, Forster obtained the seat without a contest. He would represent Bradford until his death in 1886.

Forster quickly made a name for himself in the House of Commons with his vociferous and effective support of the North during the American Civil War. A long-time opponent of slavery by virtue of his Quaker background, he saw the conflict exclusively in moral terms. A Northern victory, he firmly believed, would culminate in the destruction of slavery in North America, whereas a Confederate triumph would deal a great blow to the world's moral progress. At the same time, as a radical or "advanced Liberal," his sympathies also lay with what he saw as the more democratic North.

Above all else, Forster sought to prevent the British government from intervening in the conflict on behalf of the Confederacy. To this end, he made a number of important public speeches outside the House of Commons in an attempt to educate and sway British public opinion. After John Bright, Forster was the leading champion of the Northern cause in Britain. Within the House of Commons, Forster opposed the machinations of members who sympathized with the South and who sought to take steps that would lead to recognition of the Confederacy. He developed a close working relationship with Charles Francis Adams, the American minister to Britain. The two shared information and coordinated opposition to pro-Confederate sympathizers.

Forster fought against William H. Gregory's motion to recognize the Confederacy in June 1861. Like most Britons during the *Trent* Affair, he believed the United States was in the wrong. Unlike his countrymen, however, he hoped that if the United States rejected the British demand for reparation, Britain would subject the dispute to international arbitration instead of declaring war. In March 1862 Forster challenged another motion by Gregory that questioned the legality of the Federal naval blockade. Gregory charged the Federals with conducting an ineffective "paper blockade" that violated international law. In a well-received speech, Forster demolished the arguments of his opponent and won the respect of the House.

In 1862 the British government allowed a Liverpool firm to build the CSS *Alabama*, despite clear evidence that the vessel would become a Confederate commerce-raider. After the cruiser had embarked upon an epic course of destruction, Forster chastised the government for its delinquency in the hopes that he could prevent the recurrence of such an incident. Indeed, he played a crucial role in the government's confiscation of two more Confederate commerce-raiders under construction in Liverpool.

In June 1863 Forster helped defeat John Roebuck's motion in the House of Commons that sought recognition of the Confederacy. Appealing to British self-interest, Forster pointed out the risks inherent in such a course. Moreover, he castigated Roebuck's connection to Napoleon III and charged that the emperor sought to manipulate British foreign policy to suit French ends. Thus ended Confederate sympathizers' last attempt to obtain British recognition of the South in the Commons.

Forster's activities during the American Civil War brought him national prominence. If the North had benefitted from his activities, so had his political career. Forster went on to become one of the leading figures of the Liberal Party. In 1865, he became undersecretary of the colonies. He played a significant role in the debates over extension of the franchise that took place in 1866 and 1867. In 1869 he became vice president of the council, charged mainly with reforming British education. A year later, he became a member of the cabinet as lord president

of the council. While in office, Forster proved responsible for passing the Education Act of 1870 and subsequent legislation that overhauled public funding and administration of education. During this period, he also helped convince the cabinet to settle the *Alabama* claims by international arbitration. In 1875 he sought the Liberal Party's leadership and failed by a narrow margin. He later served as chief secretary of Ireland from 1880 to 1882 and remained a leading figure in the Liberal Party until he died on 5 April 1886 in London.

—*Hubert F. Dubrulle*

See also Adams, Charles Francis; *Alabama* Claims; *Alabama,* CSS; Diplomacy, U.S.A.; Great Britain; Lyons, Lord Richard; Palmerston, Viscount; Roebuck, John; *Trent* Affair.
For further reading:
Jackson, Patrick. *Education Act Forster: A Political Biography of W. E. Forster, 1818–1886* (1997).
Reid, T. Wemyss. *Life of the Right Honourable William Edward Forster* (1888).

FORT ANDERSON

Fort Anderson was the strongest interior fortification guarding Wilmington, North Carolina, the Confederacy's principal blockade-running seaport. Situated on the west bank of the Cape Fear River eleven miles north of Old Inlet, the main entrance into the harbor, Fort Anderson defended the river and the city's western land approaches. It also served as a quarantine station for incoming blockade runners, which were detained for inspection for contagious diseases and illegal cargoes.

Construction on the earthwork defenses that became Fort Anderson began in late March 1862. Brigadier General Samuel G. French, then commanding the District of the Cape Fear, assigned Lieutenant Thomas Rowland to erect an artillery battery and a line of entrenchments at Brunswick Point, a low bluff overlooking the river channel where the colonial town of Brunswick once stood. Until the American Revolution, Brunswick was Great Britain's main port of entry in North Carolina and the major supplier of naval stores.

Built by slaves and free black laborers in tandem with Tar Heel soldiers, Rowland's works comprised a gun battery near the riverfront adjoined by a broad, six-foot-high wall of dirt that ran westward from the river for a mile to Orton Pond. Initially the defenses were called Fort St. Philip, in commemoration of St. Philip's Anglican Church, the only standing colonial ruin at Brunswick.

Major John J. Hedrick of the 36th North Carolina Regiment commanded the Brunswick fort in 1863. Under his direction, the defenses nearest the riverfront were strengthened and expanded into two massive 24-foot-high bastions. Nine 6.4-inch, 32-pounder seacoast guns mounted en barbette constituted the armament of

the L-shaped work. Torpedoes (mines) and obstructions in the river bolstered the adjacent land defenses.

Fort St. Philip underwent another change during Hedrick's tenure. On 1 July 1863, the fort was renamed Fort Anderson, in honor of Brigadier General George Burgwyn Anderson of North Carolina, who died of complications from a wound he received in the battle of Sharpsburg.

With the fall of Fort Fisher in mid-January 1865, Federal forces quickly gained control of the Cape Fear estuary and turned their sights on Wilmington. General Ulysses S. Grant traveled from Virginia to the Cape Fear on January 28, 1865, to help plan the attack on the "city by the sea." He wanted Wilmington's railroads and the Cape Fear River for sending reinforcements and supplies to General William T. Sherman, whose army at Savannah, Georgia, was set to invade the Carolinas. Grant agreed with the advice of his subordinates to advance on Wilmington by way of Fort Anderson, the last major obstacle between the Federals and the city fifteen miles upstream.

On 17–18 February 1865, Rear Admiral David D. Porter's flotilla of fifteen light-draft gunboats and the monitor *Montauk* on the Cape Fear River bombarded Fort Anderson. The warships unleashed about 3,000 rounds of shot and shell during the two-day battle, while 6,000 blue-clad troops of Major General Jacob D. Cox's 3d Division, XXIII Army Corps, moved against the fort. Major General John M. Schofield, the XXIII Corps' leader, was in overall command of U.S. Army operations against Wilmington.

Fort Anderson's 2,300 defenders, led by Brigadier General Johnson Hagood, comprised Hagood's brigade of South Carolina infantry and Tar Heel artillerists from Cape Fear forts and batteries abandoned after the fall of Fort Fisher. Hagood's 32-pounder cannon were no match for the U.S. Navy's heavy artillery. Strongly entrenched behind their earthen defenses, however, the Confederate infantry and light artillery discouraged Jacob Cox from launching a headlong frontal assault.

Instead, while two Union brigades demonstrated south of Fort Anderson, Cox led two brigades around Orton Pond and the fort's far west flank. By nightfall on 18 February, Federal infantrymen were poised to strike Fort Anderson from behind.

Late that same night, Lieutenant Commodore William B. Cushing of the U.S. Navy deployed a sham monitor (dubbed "Old Bogey") against Fort Anderson, in hopes that the Confederates would mistake it for the *Montauk* and detonate their torpedoes in the Cape Fear River in an effort to sink it. In a meeting with President Abraham Lincoln shortly after the incident, Cushing claimed that his Quaker ironclad caused the Confederates to "skedaddle" from Fort Anderson.

In reality, Anderson's garrison paid little attention to Cushing's bogus monitor. But with his rear now threatened by Cox's ground force, General Hagood believed he had little choice but to evacuate Fort Anderson. The Southerners made a hasty withdrawal before dawn on 19 February.

Having heard the sounds of evacuation during the night from their entrenched position just south of Fort Anderson, Union soldiers stormed the works at first light. They entered in time to capture part of the Confederate rear guard and the garrison flag, which was found rolled up and lying on the ground.

Shortly after sunrise on 19 February, Porter's warships renewed the bombardment, only to discover that the Union army now occupied Fort Anderson. Admiral Porter went ashore to claim possession of the Brunswick bastion in the name of the U.S. Navy. The sailors boasted that they captured the Confederate fort from the U.S. Army, perhaps the only such incident of the war.

Union forces marched victoriously into Wilmington only three days after the battle of Fort Anderson. The capture of the important city helped guarantee the success of Sherman's Carolinas campaign. The remarkably well-preserved Confederate fort is now part of the Brunswick Town State Historic Site.

—*Chris Fonvielle*

See also Fort Fisher; Wilmington, North Carolina.
For further reading:
Fonvielle, Chris E. Jr. *The Wilmington Campaign: Last Rays of Departing Hope* (1997).
Gragg, Rod. *Confederate Goliath: The Battle of Fort Fisher* (1991).

FORT BLAKELY
(March–April 1865)
See Blakely, Alabama, Battle of

FORT CRAIG, BATTLE OF
(February 1862)

Situated twenty-five miles south of Socorro, New Mexico, and just west of the Rio Grande, Fort Craig was established in 1854 and was named after Captain Louis Craig of the 3d U.S. Infantry. Consisting of several adobe buildings surrounded by a wall measuring 1,050 by 600 feet and encircled by a large ditch, the fort was one of a few U.S. strongholds along the Rio Grande when the Civil War erupted.

Colonel Edward Richard Sprigg Canby, who commanded the U.S. forces and loyal militia in the New Mexico Territory, intended to block the anticipated Confederate invasion of New Mexico by volunteers from Texas under the command of Henry Hopkins Sibley by strengthening Fort Craig's defenses. He moved some

3,800 troops, including 1,200 regulars, to the vicinity of Fort Craig by early January 1862.

Canby's decision was sound. A sizeable Confederate invasion force had to follow the Rio Grande if its horses, cattle, and soldiers were to subsist off the land. The dry winds and sparse forage in the Jornado del Muerto and the small stream flow in the Pecos River made these other invasion routes unlikely. An unassailable post along the river might well deter the Confederates. Indeed, when Sibley's army reached Fort Craig on 16 February 1862, its commander concluded that the fort could not be taken and decided to bypass it. Sibley hoped to lure its defenders into a battle on the flood plain of the river, which was open terrain to the north.

Sibley ordered his troops to cross to the east bank of the Rio Grande and move north of the fort beginning on 19 February. He preferred not to move toward Albuquerque with a large Union force astride his lines of communication and retreat. For his part, Canby was reluctant to permit a Confederate force to isolate Fort Craig's supply lines to the north and so on 20 February, he dispatched about 2,800 of his troops to contest Sibley's movements.

After some preliminary skirmishing, the armies came together on 21 February. The battle was joined about 7:30 A.M. along two fords and a dry riverbed of the Rio Grande at Val Verde. The Confederates fought aggressively, especially because so many were armed with shotguns and had to engage the Union troops at close range. Several of the Confederate cavalry units had equipped themselves with nine-foot-long lances, a weapon rendered obsolete by rifle and artillery fire. Throughout much of the day, the bold conduct of the Confederates simply lengthened casualty lists, but at 4:00 P.M., this élan led the 750 troops under Tom Green to charge and carry McRae's battery, which anchored the Union line.

The collapse of the center created a chain reaction among Canby's troops, who withdrew across the Rio Grande and returned to Fort Craig. This episode produced most of the controversy about the battle. Green's charge exposed his flank to enfilading fire and the possibility of being turned if Canby had ordered Major Thomas Duncan, holding the Union right, to attack. The order never came. Second, the members of the 3d New Mexico Volunteers who were helping to secure the flanks of McRae's battery fled the scene under fire, leading to charges of cowardice against the mostly Hispanic troops and countercharges of racism against those who had made the allegations.

The engagement was bloody, with the Confederates suffering 230 causalities and the Union 475, and its outcome unsatisfying. Sibley continued the march that would end in his defeat at Glorieta Pass, but already his troops had come to loathe him as a drunkard and, perhaps, a coward. He spent most of the afternoon of the battle of Val Verde in his ambulance recovering from a "colic" that he treated with whiskey. On the other side, Canby's officers considered him a coward for breaking off the battle after the collapse of McRae's battery. They asserted that he had not fought harder because Sibley was his brother-in-law.

Canby's decision to return to the fort proved to be sound enough. From its adobe walls, he could interdict any Confederate forces coming from the south to reinforce Sibley. He also believed that terrain, distance from a friendly base, and an uncertain reception by the people of northern New Mexico might well undo Sibley's plans. When Sibley's forces met defeat in March, the presence of a powerful Union force at Fort Craig led him to abandon any thought of holding Santa Fe and Albuquerque and sending for reinforcements.

As the Civil War in the West deteriorated into a war of extermination against Indians, Fort Craig was used primarily as a staging area for incursions against Apaches, before it was permanently deactivated in 1884.

—*Edward R. Crowther*

See also Canby, Edward R. S.; New Mexico; Sibley, Henry Hopkins; Val Verde, New Mexico, Battle of.

For further reading:

Frazier, Donald S. *Blood and Treasure: Confederate Empire in the Southwest* (1995).

Grinstead, Marion C. *Life and Death of a Frontier Fort: Fort Craig, New Mexico, 1854–1884* (1973).

Taylor, John. *Bloody Valverde: A Civil War Battle on the Rio Grande, February 21, 1862* (1995).

FORT DELAWARE PRISON, DELAWARE

Located downriver from Wilmington, Fort Delaware was the third fort since 1813 to occupy marshy, 178-acre Pea Patch Island. Although it was completed by 1859, the fort was left ungarrisoned until February 1861, by which time seven states had already seceded from the Union. Although the five-sided bastion could accommodate up to 2,000 soldiers, the force sent to guard its 32-foot-high walls consisted of a captain and twenty men. After the surrender of Fort Sumter in April, 130 reinforcements landed, but it was May before the first artillery pieces were mounted.

During the early summer, war seemed far away as excursion boats brought curious residents down the Delaware River from Philadelphia and Wilmington to view what appeared to be an impregnable granite stronghold. These pleasure cruises were curtailed after soldiers discovered some cannon had been spiked, probably by Southern sympathizers. In July 1861, eight Confederates captured when General Joseph E. Johnston retreated from Harper's Ferry were confined in the fort's guardhouse, but they were soon exchanged.

Just about the time fear of a possible naval attack by the C.S.S. *Virginia* faded in April 1862, news reached the fort that 258 Confederates captured at the battle of Kernstown were on their way to Pea Patch Island. While the fort's commandant, Captain Augustus Gibson, protested that he could not find room for such a large number, word came from Baltimore that he could expect 400 more prisoners.

Carpenters from Philadelphia quickly erected temporary shanties on the fort's two-acre parade ground. Then in late April, Quartermaster General Montgomery Meigs ordered the construction of additional wooden barracks large enough to accommodate 2,000 more prisoners of war north of the fort. In June, Colonel William Hoffman, commissary general of prisoners, visited the site and recommended the prison be enlarged to hold 5,000 men.

Captain Gibson insisted he needed more guards for such a large number of the enemy. His pleas went unanswered until 200 prisoners escaped on the night of 19 July 1862. A boat was immediately dispatched from New York and directed to patrol the waters surrounding Fort Delaware while additional troops rushed to bolster the garrison. Gibson, who had been accused of having Southern sympathies, was succeeded by Major Henry Burton. During the latter's tenure, the first civilian prisoners arrived at the fort. Burton angered Secretary of War Edwin Stanton over his release of a political prisoner and was removed from command in December. Burton's replacement, Lieutenant Colonel Delevan Perkins, was himself superseded in early 1863 by Colonel Robert Buchanan, who lasted only until April 1863.

When Brigadier General Albin F. Schoepf took over from Colonel Buchanan, approximately 8,000 prisoners were held on the island, ranging from Brigadier General James Johnston Pettigrew of North Carolina, captured at the battle of Seven Pines in May 1862, to Madison Y. Johnson of Galena, Illinois, a personal friend of Lincoln but an advocate of peace. The officers and political prisoners occupied quarters located inside the fort itself, while noncommissioned officers and privates lived in the barracks standing outside the walls.

After the battle of Gettysburg, over 12,500 men strained the prison's overcrowded facilities. Summers were muggy on the mosquito-infested island, and winters brought bone-chilling temperatures to the poorly clad and undernourished inmates. As could be expected, dysentery, scurvy, and smallpox devastated the captives' ranks. Of the approximately 32,300 men held at one time or another on the island, at least 2,400 were ferried across the Delaware and buried at Finn's Point, New Jersey—thus earning Fort Delaware the sobriquet "Andersonville of the North." Others were interred on the island, and some were sent South for burial.

After the surrender of General Lee in April 1865, only about 1,000 of the remaining 8,000 men agreed to take an oath of allegiance that would secure their freedom. Finally, on 27 June, General Grant ordered the release of all detainees still held at the fort.

As the former prisoners sailed from Pea Patch, a new cadre of captives arrived. Headed by Confederate Lieutenant General Joseph S. Wheeler, the group included Burton S. Harrison, private secretary to President Jefferson Davis. Throughout the summer and fall, all but Harrison were repatriated. Finally, in January 1866, Harrison was able to return to Richmond.

Fort Delaware, already obsolete, was upgraded and garrisoned through World War II, but it would never again serve any actual role in the nation's defense. In 1951, the fort became one of Delaware's first state parks. Tourists can board a ferry at Delaware City from April through September to visit the island and the fort.

—*Dave Page*

See also Hoffman, William; Prisons, U.S.A.
For further reading:
Keen, Nancy. *Confederate Prisoners of War at Fort Delaware* (n.d.).
Wilson, W. Emerson. *Fort Delaware* (1957).

FORT DONELSON, BATTLE OF
(13–16 February 1862)

Located on the west bank of the Cumberland River two miles north of Dover, Tennessee, Fort Donelson was on a steep bluff overlooking a straight stretch of several miles of river. The fort itself was only about 15 acres, but its outer works extended over 100 acres. Four hundred log cabins within the fort served as barracks.

Fort Donelson had two river batteries cut into the slope of the ridge facing downriver. The lower battery contained a 10-inch Columbiad and nine 32-pounders. The upper battery had a 10-inch Columbiad rifled as a 32-pounder and two 32-pounder carronades. The fort itself had eight additional guns. On 7 February, the day after the fall of nearby Fort Henry, Fort Donelson's garrison numbered only about 6,000 men, including two brigades of infantry from Fort Henry.

Confederate Western theater commander General Albert S. Johnston now blundered. Although he decided to extract his garrisons in Kentucky and at Columbus, he reinforced Fort Donelson with 12,000 men to hold Brigadier General Ulysses S. Grant's troops until he could withdraw most of his eastern forces to Nashville. Johnston could have concentrated some 30,000 men at Fort Donelson, outnumbering Grant there two to one.

Johnston appointed Brigadier General John B. Floyd to command Fort Donelson. Floyd was at best incompetent; his second in command, Brigadier General Gideon J. Pillow, was both ambitious and incompetent. Brigadier General Simon Bolivar Buckner was the one capable senior Confederate officer at Fort Donelson.

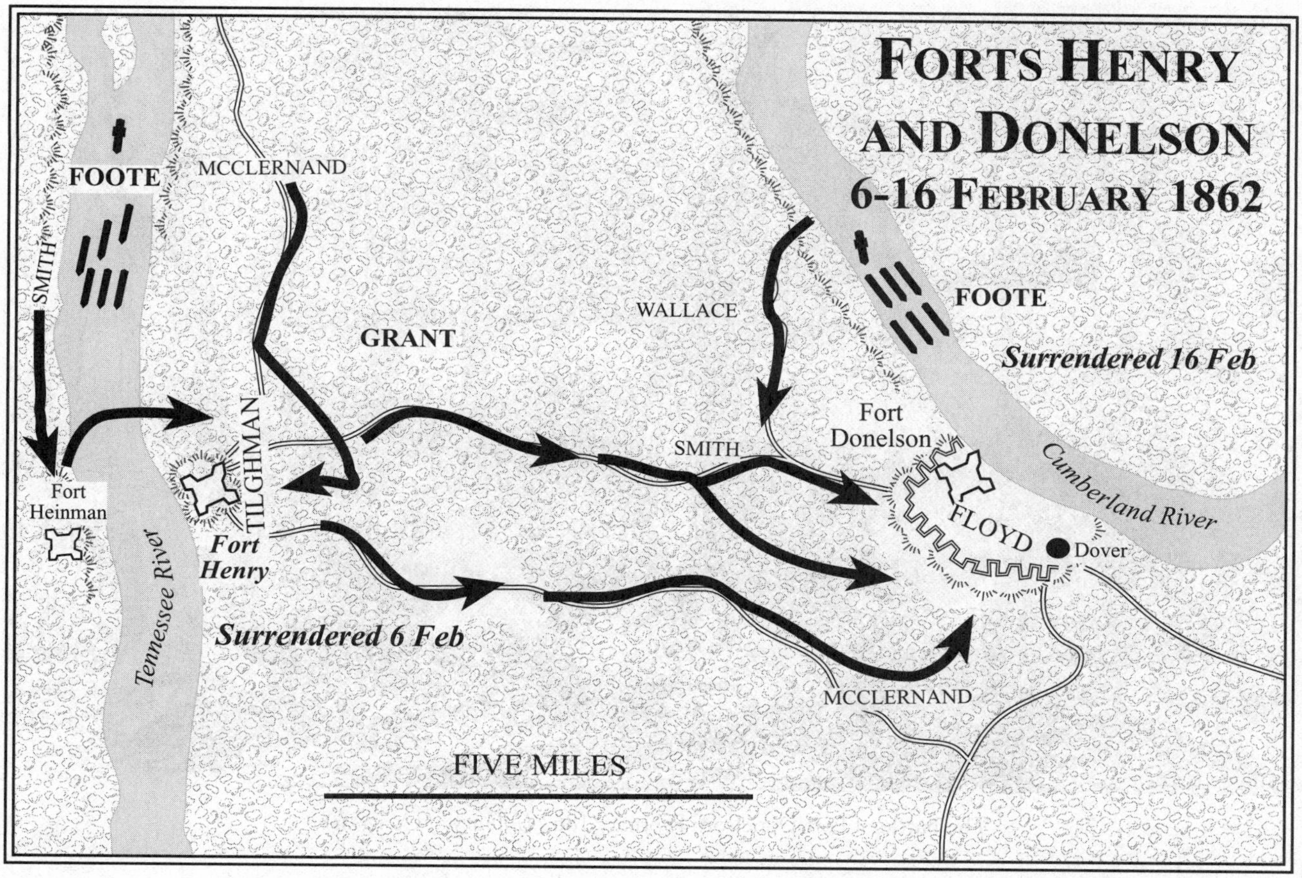

FORTS HENRY AND DONELSON 6–16 FEBRUARY 1862

Surrendered 16 Feb

Surrendered 6 Feb

FIVE MILES

Bad weather imposed a delay, but on 12 February Grant moved from Fort Henry to Fort Donelson. At the same time, Union flag officer Andrew H. Foote sailed with his gunboats and Union troop transports, arriving near Fort Donelson on the night of the 13th. That day 15,000 unentrenched Union troops confronted 21,000 entrenched Confederates; but fortunately for Grant, Floyd made no effort to attack. In fact, Union troops initiated what little fighting occurred.

Shortly after noon on the 13th, despite Grant's order not to bring on a general engagement, Brigadier General John A. McClernand ordered his men to capture a battery in the center of the Confederate line, but repeated Union assaults failed. Grant was displeased, but the action did serve to mask Union inferiority in numbers. That afternoon the weather changed dramatically from near summer to winter conditions; driving wind brought sleet and snow and suffering to both sides.

By the 14th the Confederates were completely invested, except along the Cumberland River above Dover, where the river had flooded the land. As Grant strengthened and extended his lines, the Confederate commanders decided to attempt to break out, but on the 14th Floyd countermanded the order on the insistence of Pillow, who thought it too late that day.

Grant planned to hold the Confederates within the fort from the land while the Union flotilla destroyed the water batteries. Shortly before 3:00 P.M. on the 14th, the Union flotilla attacked with four ironclads; two vulnerable timberclads formed a second division astern, beyond the range of Fort Donelson's guns.

The Union ships closed to within 400 yards. The plunging fire hit the sloping Union armor at right angles, and in the exchange three of the four ironclads were disabled and drifted downstream. The other vessels then withdrew. In the 90-minute engagement the flotilla had eleven men killed and forty-three wounded (including Foote). Although none of the gunboats were fatally damaged, from this point on the navy contributed little to the battle. In contrast, the fort was little damaged in the attack.

Union troop reinforcements continued to arrive. Before dawn on the 15th, Grant left his headquarters to meet with Foote at the latter's request. Before leaving, Grant instructed his commanders not to initiate an engagement unless he ordered it. Grant assumed that he would be the one to begin any new fighting. The Confederate commanders knew their position was untenable, however. On the night of the 14th they agreed to attempt to break out along the west bank of the

The battle of Fort Donelson, February 1862 (*Library of Congress*)

Cumberland River. Pillow was to open an escape route by rolling up the Union right while Buckner sortied and struck the center. When the Union right flank had been pushed back, Pillow would lead the retreat to Charlotte and Buckner would serve as the rear guard.

The Confederate attack at 6:00 on the morning of the 15th caught Union troops completely by surprise. In a hard-fought close action the Confederates drove the Union troops back, although in good order. Buckner then sent men forward. Union troops soon used up their ammunition and were forced to retreat.

With the road to Charlotte open, Pillow now threw away the chance to escape. Imagining that he was in position to defeat Grant, he continued the attack. With the situation desperate, Union brigadier general Lew Wallace ordered his men forward, driving the Confederates back.

Grant now arrived on the scene and ordered the lost ground retaken. He also assumed that to break through, the Confederates must have weakened their lines elsewhere, and he ordered Brigadier General Charles F. Smith to mount an immediate attack on the Confederate right. Grant told an aide that the first side to attack would be victorious.

Smith then attacked, and his men soon breached Fort Donelson's breastworks. Although Buckner finally halted the Union advance, he could not force the invaders out of the works, and the entire Confederate position was now in jeopardy. General Wallace's division was also successful, retaking ground lost earlier.

Additional Federal infantry regiments reached the Fort Donelson area by river transport that evening, bringing Union strength to 27,000 men. It was now no longer possible for the bulk of the Confederates to escape. During the night of 16–17 February, Generals Floyd, Pillow, and Buckner again met. With the situation hopeless, Pillow and Floyd decided to escape across the Cumberland. Buckner announced he would share the fate of the garrison and assumed command. Colonel Nathan Bedford Forrest also got away with some 500 men on horseback; they forded the creek between the Union right flank and the river. In all, perhaps 5,000 Confederates escaped.

Early on the 16th, Buckner asked for an armistice and surrender terms. On General Smith's urging Grant replied, "No terms except unconditional and immediate surrender can be accepted. I propose to move immediately upon your works." Buckner then capitulated.

Some 15,000 Confederates surrendered at Fort Donelson. Union troops also secured a considerable number of small arms, 57 light and heavy guns, and equipment and rations. Estimates of Confederate killed and wounded vary from 1,500 to 3,500. Union losses were 2,832: 500 killed, 2,108 wounded, and 221 captured or missing.

The fall of Fort Donelson led directly to the Union capture of Nashville, the first Confederate state capital taken. The loss of Fort Donelson's garrison also affected, perhaps decisively, the subsequent battle of Shiloh.

—Spencer C. Tucker

See also Buckner, Simon Bolivar; Floyd, John B.; Foote, Andrew H.; Forrest, Nathan Bedford; Fort Henry, Battle of; Grant, Ulysses S.; Johnston, Albert Sidney; McClernand, John A.; Pillow, Gideon; Tennessee; Wallace, Lewis.

For further reading:

Ambrose, Stephen E. *The Campaigns for Fort Donelson: A Review* (1983).

Cooling, Benjamin Franklin. *Forts Henry and Donelson: The Key to the Confederate Heartland* (1987).

Force, Manning Ferguson. *From Fort Henry to Corinth* (1881; reprint, 1992).

Tucker, Spencer C. *Andrew Hull Foote* (1999).

FORT FISHER

Fort Fisher was the largest and strongest seacoast fortification in the Confederacy and the main guardian of Wilmington, North Carolina, the South's most important blockade-running seaport. Union and Confederate observers alike deemed Fort Fisher virtually impregnable and referred to it as the "Gibraltar of the South." Two Federal attacks against the imposing work in 1864 and 1865 constituted the largest army-navy operations of the Civil War, and the fort's ultimate fall closed the Confederacy's last major seaport to trade with the outside world.

In late April 1861, engineers began constructing artillery batteries near New Inlet, the northernmost of two inlets into the Cape Fear River and Wilmington's harbor. Authorities were determined to protect North Carolina's maritime trade from President Abraham Lincoln's recently proclaimed naval blockade of the Southern states. Built almost entirely of beach sand, the defenses were located on Federal Point (called Confederate Point by Southerners during the war), a narrow peninsula bounded by the Cape Fear River on the west and the Atlantic Ocean on the east. The sand spit tapered to a point at New Inlet, about one mile south of the batteries under construction.

The first battery on Federal Point was named Battery Bolles after its architect, Major Charles Pattison Bolles. Subsequent engineers added to the works along the ocean shoreline and riverfront. On 13 September 1861, Colonel Seawell L. Fremont, then director of military and engineering projects in southeastern North Carolina, named the principal battery on Federal Point

The Army of the Potomac receives news of the capture of Fort Fisher. (Engraving from *Harper's Weekly* / *Library of Congress*)

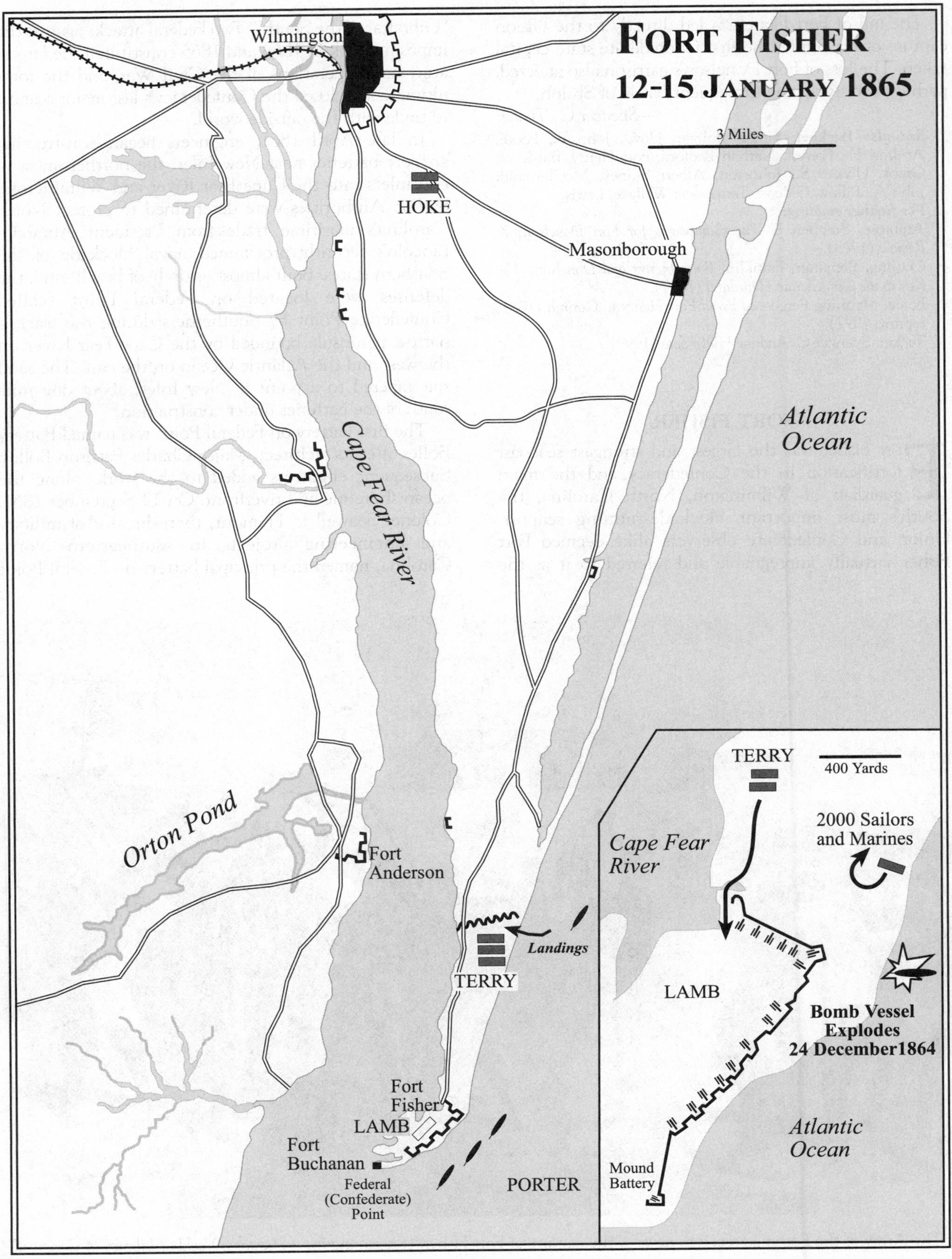

FORT FISHER
12-15 JANUARY 1865

3 Miles

Wilmington

HOKE

Masonborough

Atlantic Ocean

Cape Fear River

Orton Pond

Fort Anderson

Landings

TERRY

Fort Fisher

LAMB

Fort Buchanan

Fort Federal (Confederate) Point

PORTER

Inset map

TERRY

400 Yards

2000 Sailors and Marines

Cape Fear River

LAMB

Bomb Vessel Explodes 24 December 1864

Atlantic Ocean

Mound Battery

"The Pulpit" at Fort Fisher, January 1865 (Photograph by Timothy O'Sullivan / *Library of Congress*)

Fort Fisher, in honor of Colonel Charles F. Fisher of the 6th North Carolina Infantry, who was killed in the battle of First Manassas on 21 July 1861. The auxiliary works were soon incorporated into the larger Fort Fisher.

Despite the flurry of military construction on Federal Point, the batteries were scattered and weak when Colonel William Lamb, newly appointed commander of the 36th North Carolina Regiment, assumed command of them on 4 July 1862. Lamb determined at once to build a fortification of such size and strength that it could withstand the fury of the U.S. Navy's heaviest cannon. Lamb's redesign of Fort Fisher was based on his own plans, though influenced by fortifications like the Malakoff, a Russian earthwork stronghold that had protected the city of Sevastopol during the Crimean War.

Under the watchful eye of his superior officers, especially Major General W. H. C. Whiting, who commanded the District of the Cape Fear after 8 November 1862, Colonel Lamb spent two and a half years modifying, expanding, and strengthening Fort Fisher.

Lamb built a series of elevated gun batteries connected by a broad sand rampart on two fronts, one facing northward and the other facing the ocean. From a bird's-eye view, the fort looked like a giant numeral 7. The land front ran from the edge of the Cape Fear River

for 500 yards toward the sea, and it guarded against a ground assault from north of the fort. The land face rampart, twenty-three feet high and twenty-four feet thick at the base, was pocked with sixteen gun chambers emplaced with twenty-two big seacoast guns—mostly 8-inch and 10-inch Columbiads and 6.4-inch 32-pounders—mounted en barbette. Each artillery compartment was separated by a traverse, a large mound of sand nine to twelve feet higher than the parapet. Inside these traverses were hollowed-out bunkers containing either an ordnance and powder magazine or a bombproof, where soldiers could seek refuge during a bombardment. A minefield and a nine-foot-high palisade of sharpened pine logs loopholed for musketry were situated in front of the land face.

The land and sea faces intersected at a full bastion 100 yards from the ocean's high water mark. This huge thirty-two-foot-high battery in the northeast corner of the fort (called the Northeast Bastion) boasted an 8-inch Columbiad and an 8-inch Blakely rifle. From the Northeast Bastion the sea face defenses turned southward, running parallel to the shoreline for approximately 1,300 yards. The self-contained batteries mounted twenty-two pieces of heavy artillery—Columbiads and Brooke rifles—and were connected by an immense sand

Interior view of Fort Fisher, showing a gun destroyed by heavy bombardment, January 1865
(Photograph by Timothy O'Sullivan / *Library of Congress*)

curtain. The pride of Fort Fisher's ordnance collection was a British-manufactured 8-inch, 150-pounder Armstrong rifle, imported through the blockade in 1864 as a gift for the Confederacy from Sir W. G. Armstrong & Co. of London. It came mounted on a mahogany and rosewood carriage with brass furniture. Captured in 1865, Fort Fisher's Armstrong rifle is now the centerpiece of the ordnance collection at the U.S. Military Academy at West Point, New York.

On the southernmost point of Fisher's sea face towered a forty-three-foot-high conical gun emplacement formally named Battery Lamb, but dubbed "the Mound." Mounted with two seacoast guns, the Mound was also fitted with a signal light to help guide approaching blockade runners into New Inlet's intricate channel. Fort Fisher protected hundreds of blockade runners that imported supplies vital to the Confederacy's war effort. Blockade-running captains referred to Colonel Lamb, his garrison, and the guns of Fort Fisher as their guardian angels.

Union efforts to close Wilmington to blockade running did not materialize until the last year of the war. Until then, the U.S. War Department and the Lincoln administration devoted their resources and energies to the capture of higher-priority targets—especially Richmond—over the protestations of Secretary of the Navy Gideon Wells and the North Atlantic Blockading Squadron commander, acting Rear Admiral S. Phillips Lee.

The government's attitude toward Wilmington finally changed when Rear Admiral David G. Farragut sealed Mobile Bay, Alabama, to blockade running in August 1864. That Union naval triumph left Wilmington as the only major Confederate seaport open to overseas trade. Hoping a quick victory at the Carolina seaport would not only sever the Confederacy's lifeline but also invigorate his reelection bid in the upcoming presidential race, President Lincoln endorsed Gideon Welles's renewed request for an attack on Wilmington. At the same time, the chief executive deferred final approval to the army commander, General Ulysses S. Grant.

Grant hesitantly promised to provide an expeditionary force to join the navy for the Wilmington expedition as soon as possible. Welles, meanwhile, devised several plans for closing Wilmington to blockade running, but concluded to attack Fort Fisher, which protected the blockade runners' favorite entrance into the harbor. A decisive campaign against the Confederacy's strongest fortification, which the navy would lead, might also increase awareness of the U.S. Navy's valuable contributions to the war effort, which Welles believed had gone largely unappreciated, especially by the War Department. A continuous naval bombardment on 13–15 January 1865 preceded an assault mounted by 9,600 soldiers of XXIV and XXV Army Corps acting as Brigadier General Alfred H. Terry's Provisional Corps. This force captured Fort Fisher. Among those Confederates captured were Colonel William Lamb, Fort Fisher's commander, and Major General W.H.C. Whiting. Having closed the harbor to blockade running, Union forces then prepared for the assault on Wilmington.

—*Chris Fonvielle*

See also Wilmington, North Carolina.

For further reading:
Fonvielle, Chris E., Jr. *The Wilmington Campaign: Last Rays of Departing Hope* (1997).
Gragg, Rod. *Confederate Goliath: The Battle of Fort Fisher* (1991).

FORT HENRY, BATTLE OF
(6 February 1862)

Fort Henry was a Confederate garrison on the Tennessee River, the capture of which was the first significant Union victory of the Civil War.

Because of its food production, mineral resources, labor supply, and railroads, Tennessee was the key to the West. While the Confederates enjoyed unity of command in the Western theater under General Albert Sidney Johnston, Union forces there were divided between the Department of the Missouri, commanded by Major General Henry W. Halleck, and the Department of the Ohio under Brigadier General Don Carlos Buell. Despite their twofold superiority in manpower, the two Union commanders disagreed on strategy and claimed insufficient resources and logistical problems.

Halleck's subordinates, Brigadier General Ulysses S. Grant, who commanded the Cairo Military District with 20,000 men, and Flag Officer Andrew H. Foote, who commanded the Western Flotilla, both wanted to attack Fort Henry on the Tennessee and Fort Donelson on the Cumberland River. This would flank the powerful Confederate fortress at Columbus on the upper Mississippi and Confederate defenders at Bowling Green, Kentucky.

Halleck saw the need to offset successes by Buell in Kentucky, and President Lincoln was also applying pressure. But what finally prompted him to act was an erroneous report that Richmond was sending reinforcements west. On 30 January, Halleck ordered Grant to take and hold Fort Henry. The Union expedition set out on 2 February.

Fort Henry covered three acres of ground in a solidly built five-sided earthwork parapet. Rifle pits extended to the river and two miles east toward Fort Donelson. Although it lay in a bend of the Tennessee River, commanding a straight stretch of water three miles long, Fort Henry was on low ground washed by the river and had higher terrain on both sides. Work to fortify the heights on the west bank, known as Fort Heiman after Fort Henry's second in command, was incomplete when the Federals arrived. Brigadier General Lloyd Tilghman commanded both Forts Henry and Donelson.

Fort Henry mounted seventeen heavy guns: twelve faced the river and five guarded the land approaches. The fort had eight 32-pounders, two 42-pounders, one 128-pounder Columbiad rifled gun, five long 18-pounder siege guns, and a 6-inch rifled gun.

In early February 1862 the Tennessee was in flood and some of the land within the fort's perimeter was two feet under water. The Confederates also had no ammunition for their 42-pounders, leaving only nine guns able to counter a water approach. Tilghman also had only 2,610 men in two brigades under Colonels Adolphus Heiman and Joseph Drake. Many were raw recruits who had only shotguns and hunting rifles; some had only flintlocks.

On 2 February the Union flotilla left Cairo. Four ironclads led: the *Cincinnati* (flagship), *Carondelet*, *Essex*, and *St. Louis*. The transports followed, and a division of timberclads brought up the rear: the *Conestoga*, *Lexington*, and *Tyler*. Two lifts were necessary to transport all of Grant's 17,000 men.

Early on the 4th the Confederates learned of the Union advance. Tilghman then left Fort Donelson to take up direction of Fort Henry's defense. Although Tilghman telegraphed General Leonidas Polk at Columbus for reinforcements, none were sent.

Grant debarked his troops three miles from the fort and just beyond the range of its guns. He then returned to Paducah with the empty transports to hurry the second lift of Brigadier General Charles F. Smith's division.

Late on the 5th three of the Union gunboats approached Fort Henry and opened a "vigorous and well-directed fire," which killed one defender and wounded three others. The Confederates replied with six shots and the gunboats then withdrew.

All Union troops were not ashore until the night of the 5th, when it rained heavily. Although he did not yet

have all his men in place, Grant believed that prompt action was imperative to prevent the Confederates from reinforcing. Hopeful all his men would have arrived in time, Grant ordered the advance to begin at 11:00 A.M. on the 6th.

Grant planned a simultaneous land and water attack. During the night of the 5th he sent Smith with two of his brigades along the west bank of the river to prevent any reinforcement from that direction, to cut off a Confederate escape, and to seize Fort Heiman for possible artillery emplacement. Smith's men discovered that the Confederates had already evacuated Heiman. Brigadier General John A. McClernand's division with a brigade from Smith mounted the main Union land effort on the east bank.

On the night of the 5th, Tilghman called together his officers. All were pessimistic, believing they could not withstand an attack by a force they estimated at 25,000 men. At 10:00 A.M. on the 6th Tilghman ordered all defenders except for the artillery company manning the batteries to withdraw to Fort Donelson. This left only about a hundred men, including those too sick to move. Tilghman intended to delay the attackers long enough for the rest of his command to escape.

At 10:50 the Union flotilla got under way, the iron-clads forming in line abreast: the *Essex* on the right, then the *Cincinnati*, *Carondelet*, and *St. Louis*. Because of the narrowness of the river, the last two gunboats were lashed together and remained so during the battle. A half mile behind them came Lieutenant Seth L. Phelps's division of timberclads. As the flotilla neared Fort Henry there was no sign of the Union troops, and Foote decided to begin the battle alone. At 11:45, from about 1,700 yards' range, the *Cincinnati* fired a shot, the signal for the other gunboats to open fire. At about a mile's range Taylor ordered the water battery to respond, and firing then became general. Phelps's division remained at long range, lobbing shells into the fort.

Confederate fire was both lively and accurate. Although Fort Henry had only nine guns that could respond, the rebel gunners succeeded in hitting all gunboats many times (fifty-nine hits in all) but most of the damage was slight, except to the *Essex*, when a Confederate shell tore into its middle boiler. The blast and steam killed or wounded thirty-two men, including Commodore William D. Porter, who was seriously scalded. The gunboat drifted out of control downriver but was towed to safety by a tug. A seaman was also killed and nine others wounded on board the *Cincinnati*. A musket ball killed another man aboard the *Essex*.

From the beginning Union fire was quite accurate, and the crews could see shell explosions throwing up earth around the rebel guns. Then the 6-inch rifled gun blew up, killing or wounding all its crew, and a priming wire stuck in the vent of the 10-inch Columbiad, spiking

it. Two 32-pounders were then struck at almost the same time.

With only four of his guns able to return fire and the Union gunboats sweeping the fort with their fire, at 2:00 P.M. Tilghman surrendered. He had saved the bulk of the garrison. Only ninety-four men, including Tilghman and sixteen aboard a Confederate hospital boat, surrendered at Fort Henry. Confederate losses were only five dead, eleven wounded, and five missing. The victors did capture Fort Henry's guns as well as supplies and equipment abandoned by the garrison, which had retreated to Fort Donelson on foot without wagons.

The roads were mired in mud, and the Union land force arrived at Fort Henry only after the battle. McClernand had learned that the Confederates might be evacuating Fort Henry and sent cavalry ahead to verify it. It pursued the retreating Confederates, who were slowed by muddy roads, and captured six guns and thirty-eight stragglers. But the first Union troops did not arrive at Fort Henry until an hour after its surrender.

Immediately after the capture of Fort Henry, Grant called together his officers to discuss the possibility of taking Fort Donelson. All declared themselves in favor of moving against Fort Donelson as soon as possible.

—*Spencer C. Tucker*

See also Buell, Don Carlos; Foote, Andrew H.; Fort Donelson; Grant, Ulysses S.; Halleck, Henry W.; Johnston, Albert Sidney; McClernand, John A.; Porter, William David; Tennessee; Tilghman, Lloyd.

For further reading:
Cooling, Benjamin Franklin. *Forts Henry and Donelson: The Key to the Confederate Heartland* (1987).
Milligan, John D. *Gunboats Down the Mississippi* (1965).
Tucker, Spencer C. *Andrew Hull Foote* (1999).

FORT HUGER/HILL'S POINT
(April 1863)

Fort Huger was one of a number of such earthworks that Confederate and Virginia state engineers designed and developed or renovated to defend the Nansemond River. Navigable to the town of Suffolk, the Nansemond represented an avenue of approach for Union forces wishing to sever the railroad connections between the interior of the state and the port city of Norfolk. These railroads, the Norfolk & Petersburg and the Seaboard & Roanoke, served as the chief lifeline for transportation and communication over land for Portsmouth and Norfolk.

An earlier incarnation of Fort Huger stood on the western bank of the river to guard against the advance of British naval forces during the War of 1812. The outbreak of the Civil War encouraged the renovation of the position. These defenses became moot with the evacuation in May 1862 of Norfolk and Suffolk by the

Confederates. Southern forces retired beyond the Blackwater River, leaving the Nansemond unaffected except for small raiding or scouting expeditions for the next year.

In the spring of 1863, Confederate forces under General James Longstreet approached the now heavily fortified town of Suffolk. Elements of these troops under the command of Major General John Bell Hood reoccupied the western bank of the Nansemond and restored the old fort to fighting trim. The Confederates placed batteries in various points along the river, including Fort Huger, to interdict Union river traffic and encourage the Union garrison under Brigadier General John James Peck to surrender or evacuate the town.

Although Hood had command of this sector of the lines, Longstreet had placed the artillery under the authority of Major General Samuel French. The New Jersey–born Confederate was disgruntled that Lee's "Old War Horse" had appropriated his infantry command before moving against Suffolk. Although Longstreet named him commander/advisor of all artillery, French was still quite angry and less attentive to his duties than he might ordinarily have been.

Nevertheless, the Confederate artillery positions proved devastating to the Federal vessels in the narrow channel of the Upper Nansemond during the first few days of the Suffolk campaign. Union acting rear admiral Samuel P. Lee considered removing the vulnerable ships rather than risk their destruction or capture. However, Union brigadier general George W. Getty's actions in targeting the Southern battery at Norfleet's House that had severely damaged the Union flotilla in one confrontation gave the naval forces a momentary respite.

During this period, General Getty and naval lieutenants Roswell H. Lamson and William B. Cushing devised a daring plan for the capture of Fort Huger. This plan called for a joint military operation with the embarkation of Union infantry on one of the gunboats. These men were to be carried near the Confederate fort and landed and were to assault the fort with the gunboat's support.

As it turned out, the plan almost worked as it had been drawn. At 5:30 P.M. on 19 April, 270 men from the 8th Connecticut and the 89th New York boarded the gunboat *Stepping Stones*. They situated themselves behind a canvas covering to hide their presence. The gunboat gave the appearance of running past the Confederate battery, which remained silent in anticipation. When only 300 yards away, Lamson headed the vessel for the bank. The men scrambled from their positions into the water and raced across a spit of land into the rear of the earthwork, sealing the garrison's fate.

The Southerners had barely enough time to produce even a feeble show of resistance before the Federal assault overwhelmed them. The daring operation netted the

Federals 7 officers, 130 men, and 5 field pieces from Captain Robert M. Stribling's Fauquier Artillery. Indeed, the attack had been so swift and so instantly successful that supporting infantry units heard the Union cheers, went to investigate, and found the position solidly in enemy hands, the prisoners already hustled away for safekeeping.

Although the Federals would soon abandon Fort Huger, deeming it untenable for them to hold, the loss of the fort and its battery was a particular embarrassment for Longstreet and his commanders, the infantry units that were supposed to support the battery, and the Southern press. Many critics hastily blamed Northern-born General French for the disaster. Officers from the 55th North Carolina and the 44th Alabama engaged in two duels over the matter. Fortunately, these ended without producing more than a damaged hat and a grazed neck to go with the antagonists' wounded pride.

The loss of Fort Huger and Stribling's battery took much of the life out of the Confederates at Suffolk. They ceased to be aggressive on the Nansemond River, although the Union evacuation of the position prompted Admiral Lee to pull his gunboats into the Lower Nansemond anyway. Lieutenants Lamson and Cushing received special praise for their participation, while an officer on Getty's staff, Captain Hazard Stevens, was awarded the Medal of Honor for leading the assault.

—*Brian S. Wills*

See also French, Samuel Gibbs; Suffolk, Siege of.
For further reading:
Cormier, Steven A. *The Siege of Suffolk* (1989).
Oates, William C. *The War Between the Union and the Confederacy* (1905).
U.S. Naval War Records Department. *Official Records of the Union and Confederate Navies in the War of the Rebellion* (1894–1922).
U.S. War Department. *War of the Rebellion: A Compilation of the Official Records of the Union and Confederate Armies* (1880–1901).

FORT JEFFERSON AND FORT TAYLOR

During the rapid construction of the coastal defense system, begun as a response to the exposed areas along the Gulf of Mexico and the Atlantic coast of Florida, two fortifications came into existence. One, Fort Jefferson, was constructed in the isolated stretch of islands known as the Dry Tortugas. The other, Fort Taylor, came into being on the island of Key West. The object of these two was to protect the Gulf and the Florida Straits. They were to be the Scylla and Charybdis for any foreign fleet threatening the United States from the Caribbean Sea. Their importance in the defense scheme of the Gulf was early recognized by Union officialdom: "Florida keys and reefs: This portion of the coast, which commands the great outlet of

the Gulf of Mexico by the course of the Gulf Stream, begins at Virginia Key...and extends to the Tortugas....Fort Jefferson, at the Tortugas, and Fort Taylor, at Key West, with certain supplementary works, will easily hold this part of the coast against any but a first-rate naval power."

Colonel Joseph G. Totten, later chief of engineers, was the person most responsible for the design and construction of these fortifications. Totten pushed for the construction of the duo in his 1836 recommendation to Congress. Although the Dry Tortugas was secured in the early 1830s, the site for the construction of Fort Taylor was not selected until 1844. In December of that year, Captain J. G. Bernard selected the southwest point of the island as the most appropriate location. Construction began in June 1845 under the direction of Captain George Dutton. Dutton used a large force of immigrant labor and several slaves hired out under contracts to their masters, including Mrs. Stephen R. Mallory, whose husband would later become Confederate secretary of the navy. The multi-tiered fortification was actually constructed out into the water with three seaward walls (curtains). The material, after much debate, was concrete with hard-burned brick and granite facing. Two tiers of casements mounted the majority of the armament with additional weaponry stretched along the terreplein of each curtain. Each fortification was constructed to allow each salient angle where the curtains joined to have a bastion containing flank casements where the fire could sweep along the walls. The landward wall was accessible only by crossing a "temporary pier" with a moat between the land and the actual fort. Fort Jefferson had no need of these latter features.

The construction of both fortifications suffered delays because of hurricanes and yellow fever. However, on the eve of the Civil War, only Fort Jefferson was near completion. Fort Taylor had not been completed, but the quarters were finished "sufficiently for occupancy." As the storm clouds of war approached, it became necessary to ready Fort Taylor for possible surprise attack from the land. This had not been contemplated in the initial planning, and rapid deployment of the available labor force quickly closed off the gorge front and made embrasures for the mounting of 8-inch Columbiads facing shoreward. Lieutenant Edward B. Hunt, in charge of a small work force for the construction since 1857, effectively employed his men and ensured their loyalty. Yet, even with Hunt's best efforts, there was doubt as to the security of the fort should the rebellion begin too soon.

In addition to the delayed construction of Fort Taylor, the troops stationed at Key West, under the capable command of Captain John M. Brannan, were living in the barracks, across town from the fort. Brannan had forty-four men in the barracks to hold the town should trouble begin. Key West, at the time, was the state's second largest city, numbering more than 2,800 inhabitants, most of whom were sympathetic to the Southern cause. Key West's primary industries were salt making and "wrecking," from the numerous disasters along the Florida reef. The population was extremely mixed with Hispanics, slaves, and large numbers from New England, the Bahamas, and Southern ports. This population, whose leadership was heavily Southern in sympathy, was the force that Brannan's small garrison had to control or risk losing what the Charleston *Mercury* called the most important fortresses along the Southern coast.

The mood of Key West at the time of secession was hostile to anyone favoring the Union. Judge William Marvin, who served before and during the war, called the interval between the secession convention and the outbreak of war, "a period in the history of my life of great mental anxiety and suffering." Unionists were liable to local persecution and social isolation. Marvin and the few others found solace among the troops, especially Hunt and Brannan. With such tension in the air, Brannan made a bold move, one that secured the island for the Union. The captain had no direct orders under which to act, Key West receiving mail only irregularly, but, in consultation with Hunt and others, he decided to occupy Fort Taylor on 21 January 1861. He made his move under the cover of darkness and kept everyone quietly in their place by attending church services the next morning. Before anyone could realize what had happened, Key West had been secured.

Within two days of Brannan's bold action, naval vessels and supply ships had begun arriving at Fort Jefferson and Key West. On 6 February 1861, Brannan informed the War Department that, "it is very doubtful now if any attempt will be made on this fort." In this prediction he was correct because neither Fort Taylor nor Fort Jefferson was ever attacked during the war. Although a number of Key Westers did flee the island and join the Confederate forces, Key West maintained a relative calm throughout the war. It became the home base for the East Gulf Coast Blockading Squadron and its numerous raids on the important salt works of Florida. As the linchpin between the Gulf and Atlantic, the fortifications served as the main support bases for the increasingly effective Union blockade of the South. Their closeness to Cuba and the Bahamas made the forts important for cutting off the trade between these points and the Confederacy. Brannan's action, Hunt's support, and the relatively rapid deployment of troops and ships to these "Keys to the Gulf" effectively assisted the Union effort in the defeat of the Confederacy.

—*Joe Knetsch*

See also Blockade of C.S.A.; Brannan, John Milton; Totten, Joseph Gilbert.

For further reading:

Camp, Vaughn, Jr. "Captain Brannan's Dilemma: Key West, 1861." *Tequesta* (1960).

Johns, John E. *Florida during the Civil War* (1963).

Kearney, Kevin E., ed. "Autobiography of William Marvin." *Florida Historical Quarterly* (1958).

Roth, Clayton D., Jr. "150 Years of Defense Activity at Key West, 1820–1970." *Tequesta* (1970).

Williams, Ames W. "Stronghold of the Straits: A Short History of Fort Zachary Taylor." *Tequesta* (1954).

FORT MACON

Built between 1826 and 1834, Fort Macon, North Carolina, was a pentagonal casemated fortification on the eastern end of Bogue Banks commanding the channel to Beaufort and Morehead City, North Carolina. The masonry fortification stood near the site of earlier wooden fortifications dating back to 1756. By 1861, the fort was in a bad state of repair and housed fewer than its assigned complement of guns. Many of the cannons that were in the fort had decaying or damaged carriages.

Inspired by the dramatic events occurring farther south at Fort Sumter in Charleston harbor, Josiah S. Pender and his small band of Beaufort Harbor Guards captured Fort Macon and its lone defenders—fifty-year-old Sergeant William Alexander and his wife. Although North Carolina had not yet seceded from the Union, Pender held the fort until Governor John Ellis officially authorized the seizure of Federal property on 16 April 1861. After North Carolina's secession from the Union and subsequent admittance into the Confederacy, Ellis moved to enhance the state's coastal defenses by repairing damaged structures and acquiring more artillery from Richmond, Charleston, and the Norfolk Navy Yard. Consequently, by the end of the year, Fort Macon was patched up and housed over fifty heavy-caliber cannons, including at least five rifled guns.

In January 1862, Brigadier General Ambrose E. Burnside launched a major Federal expedition, including 15,000 troops and a fleet of eighty ships, to the Outer Banks of North Carolina with the intention of capturing Roanoke Island and the coastal towns and counties bordering Albemarle and Pamlico sounds. By 14 March, Burnside had accomplished his goal and began an occupation of New Bern, the state's old colonial capital.

After Burnside's successful operation, the newly promoted major general next moved to occupy the port cities of Beaufort and Morehead City—the latter linked by rail to New Bern. On 17 March he detached Brigadier General John G. Parke to accomplish this task, with the added responsibility of seizing Fort Macon, now serving not only to protect the entrance to Beaufort's harbor, but also to provide covering fire for approaching blockade runners. Parke's brigade had little trouble capturing Morehead City, but Colonel Moses White and his garrison at Fort Macon refused to capitulate. Parke considered a general assault against the fort, but the open fields of fire available to its defenders and the fort's deep (albeit dry) moat precluded such a scheme. Consequently, Parke chose the only other option available to him: a siege.

On 24 April, after almost five weeks of an unproductive investment of the fort, Burnside personally tried to convince Colonel White to surrender when he met with the young West Pointer across the bay at Shackleford Banks. Polite but obstinate, White refused, and at 5:40 A.M. on 25 April the Federals began a general bombardment of the fort. Fort Macon's masonry walls were unable to withstand the accurate and piercing fire of Parke's 30-pound rifled cannons, compelling White to raise a flag of truce after only eleven hours. The bombardment cost Burnside ten men killed and wounded, while White suffered 480 casualties, of whom all but twenty-four were captured.

For the military strategist, the fall of Fort Macon demonstrated the weakness of masonry fortifications when tested by heavy-caliber rifled artillery fire. For Burnside and the Federal war effort, the fort's capitulation meant that Morehead City could be developed into a port of entry for U.S. military supplies and a coaling station for the North Atlantic Blockading Squadron. Finally, Burnside's success in eastern North Carolina in 1862 closed much of this shoreline to Confederate navigation, leaving Wilmington on the Cape Fear River as the state's only remaining port of entry for British goods.

—*Alan C. Downs*

See also Burnside, Ambrose Everett.
For further reading:
Barrett, John G. *The Civil War in North Carolina* (1963).
Marvel, William. *Burnside* (1991).

FORT MCALLISTER, REDUCTION OF
(13 December 1864)

Located on Genesis Point along the banks of the Great Ogeechee River, Fort McAllister guarded the southern approach to Savannah, Georgia. The fort was an earthen bastion begun in 1861 as a four-gun battery and grew by the fall of 1864 into a sizable fort with a dry moat, bombproofs, glacis, and strong armament of heavy 32-pound guns, Columbiads, and a variety of smaller field pieces. Although most famous for its role in the culmination of Sherman's March to the Sea, Fort McAllister withstood some of the most intense naval bombardments of any fortification during the Civil War. Ironclads USS *Montauk*, *Passaic*, *Patapsco*, and *Nahant* all tested their mettle against the imposing earthwork. Additionally, the Confederate raider CSS *Nashville* was destroyed by the monitor USS *Montauk* on 28 February 1863, just upriver from Fort McAllister's guns where the trapped raider had sought security from the probing Federal navy. Ultimately the fort withstood every

Signal station at Fort McAllister, December 1864 (*Library of Congress*)

attempt of the Federal navy to dislodge the Confederate garrison. It was up to a land attack to reduce the fort.

On 12 December 1864, Major General O. O. Howard's troops of General William T. Sherman's army arrived in the environs of Fort McAllister. William B. Hazen, and his 2d Division, XV Corps, was ordered to take the fort by storm. Awaiting the overwhelming force confronting them was the fort's garrison of some 200 defenders. Major George Anderson, the fort's commanding officer, ordered several land "torpedoes" buried along the approaches to the fort and awaited the attack he knew was forming. By

the afternoon of 13 December 1864, Hazen's assaulting division was in place, having marched through marsh and other natural barriers to arrive at the rear of the fort. Around 4:45 P.M., Hazen's men, formed in line of battle, stepped off to the attack. Confederate fire was not strong enough to stem the rush of Federal troops, although the land torpedoes worked to strong effect and inflicted a number of casualties among the attackers. The Federal troops crested the fort's walls and engaged in hand-to-hand fighting with the fort's defenders. Captain Nicholas Clinch, a Confederate artillery officer, was wounded nine times, including a gunshot wound to the arm and seven saber wounds. Clinch, amazingly, survived and recovered while a prisoner of war. The remaining members of the garrison were overwhelmed and captured in an action lasting fifteen to twenty minutes. The Federals lost twenty-four killed and 110 wounded, while the Confederates lost seventeen killed and thirty-one wounded. The Federals captured twenty-four pieces of artillery and sixty tons of ammunition.

The fort's fall allowed Sherman to open his line of communication with the Federal navy operating in nearby Ossabow Sound. Operations against Savannah now opened in earnest with his Southern flank secure. General William Hardee, Confederate commander in Savannah, evacuated the town on 20 December 1864, and Savannah was occupied the following day. Fort McAllister's vast armament and defenses were dismantled by the victorious Federal troops, and the now impotent earthworks were abandoned to time.

The fort has been restored by the state of Georgia and is now a state historic park. The earthworks are open to the public and a museum dedicated to the fort's history is located nearby.

—*G. Judson Smith, Jr.*

See also Savannah, Siege of; Sherman's March to the Sea.
For further reading:
Scaife, William R. *The March to the Sea* (1993).
Christman, William E. *Undaunted: The History of Fort McAllister* (1996).

FORT MONROE

Named after President James Monroe, Fort Monroe was garrisoned in 1823, and construction was completed in 1834. During the War of 1812, the British had demonstrated how vulnerable Washington, D.C., was to an attack by sea via Chesapeake Bay. Constructed under the guidance of French military engineer Brigadier General Simon Bernard, the fort was designed to serve as part of a series of coastal defenses. The fort was designed to hold 200 guns that would command the channel from Chesapeake Bay into Hampton Roads, the roadstead into which flows the James, Elizabeth, and Nansemond rivers. The guns also commanded the passage between Hampton Roads and the mouth of the York River. The current moated, irregular, hexagon-shaped fortress is the largest in the United States and remained in Union hands throughout the Civil War.

Captain of the port's office and the Hygeia Dining Saloon, Fort Monroe, ca. 1864 (*Library of Congress*)

The post band, Fort Monroe, ca. 1864 (*Library of Congress*)

Among those stationed at Fort Monroe before the war were poet Edgar Allan Poe, and future generals Joseph Eggleston Johnston and Benjamin Huger. Robert E. Lee reported for duty as a young lieutenant on 7 May 1831. Lee spent most of his time working on the outworks and moat. In the three decades leading up to the Civil War, the majority of artillery soldiers in the U.S. Army saw service there, in part because it was the host to the Army's Artillery School of Practice.

Fort Monroe's position seventy-five miles southeast of Richmond made it the ideal staging area for General McClellan's Peninsula campaign in 1862. Union troops disembarked from steamers on 24 March and advanced towards Richmond on 4 April. The strategic position of Fort Monroe kept Confederate president Jefferson Davis and Generals Lee and Johnston in the dark as to McClellan's intentions. McClellan could plan to attack from Fort Monroe up the stretch of land between the York and James rivers and capture Richmond. However, Confederate high command could not be sure that this move was not a diversion to draw Confederate reserves away from a projected advance from Manassas or Aquia Creek, located north of Richmond. Once it became clear that Fort Monroe was the disembarking point for McClellan's campaign, General Johnston began consolidating his forces up the peninsula and closer to

Richmond. The result of this movement gave McClellan the opportunity to push further up the peninsula.

President Lincoln's diminishing confidence in McClellan's ability to carry out an effective offensive led him to travel to Fort Monroe to review the Peninsula campaign on 7 May 1862. He stayed in Quarters No. 1, just inside the fort's East Gate. Johnston's consolidation near Richmond had nevertheless left a small contingent of Confederates to defend the coastal town of Norfolk, Virginia. President Lincoln wanted McClellan to challenge the defenders to secure the James River. With McClellan apparently indifferent to the matter, the president decided to take matters into his own hands. After conducting a reconnaissance with Treasury Secretary Salmon Chase, Lincoln remained at Fort Monroe while Chase led Union forces across the river and easily defeated Norfolk's defenders under General Benjamin Huger.

The loss of Norfolk set the stage for the end of Confederate naval opposition in the James. The CSS *Virginia* (formerly the *Merrimack*) had already dueled with a contingent of Union warships, including the *Monitor*, but with the loss of Norfolk, the *Virginia* was without a port. Because Fort Monroe blocked the entrance to the James River, Flag Officer Josiah was forced to run his vessel aground near the mouth of the Elizabeth River and set her afire.

General Benjamin F. Butler used Fort Monroe as a launching point against Richmond as part of Lieutenant General Grant's Overland campaign of 1864. According to plans, Butler's Army of the James would advance up the James River and land south of Richmond to cut off the Confederate capital from points south and perhaps threaten the city itself. Although the scheme foundered, Butler's presence at Fort Monroe forced Lee to divert men and resources from the crucial area opposite Grant's position along the Rapidan and Rappahannock rivers.

Jefferson Davis was imprisoned at Fort Monroe on 22 May 1865, after being captured in Irwinville, Georgia, on 10 May. He was kept in an improvised cell in Casemate No. 2 and forcibly shackled with ankle irons until a public outcry forced his removal to more commodious quarters. After four and a half months, Davis was moved to Carrol Hall, a brick building that no longer exists, and after two years he was released on a bail bond for $100,000. In June 1951, Jefferson Hayes-Davis, the grandson of the Confederate president, participated in the formal dedication of the Jefferson Davis Casemate Museum.

—*Kevin M. Levin*

See also Army of the James; Bermuda Hundred Campaign; Davis, Jefferson; Peninsula Campaign.

For further reading:

Hattaway, Herman, and Archer Jones. *How the North Won* (1983).

Sears, Stephen. *To the Gates of Richmond* (1992).

Weinert, Richard P. *Defender of the Chesapeake: The Story of Fort Monroe* (1990).

FORT MYERS, BATTLE OF
(20 February 1865)

As one of the last engagements of the Civil War, the battle of Fort Myers proved significant as possibly the southernmost land battle of the war and the southernmost land duty of the U.S. Colored Troops (USCT). Located in the heart of Confederate territory in the southern peninsula, the old Seminole Wars post on 20 February 1865 provided the subtropical scene for a battle that dramatically reflected the Union's control of the deep, southern reaches of Florida. Although not remembered as a major conflict of the Civil War, the battle of Fort Myers remains significant to any understanding of the Union and Confederate strategies and strengths in the lower peninsula and of the actions of African-American soldiers in that land theater.

Union commander General Daniel P. Woodbury ordered reoccupation of Fort Myers on 6 January 1864. At that time, Captain Richard A. Graeffe of the 47th Pennsylvania Volunteers took control of the abandoned Seminole Wars post. Fort Myers thus became the Union's only active post on mainland south Florida.

Woodbury ordered the occupation of this frontier site both to embarrass and to disrupt the local Confederates and to capture cattle from the numerous local herds of "scrub cows" to help fill the Union larder.

The Union's sudden reoccupation of Fort Myers in early 1864 dramatically altered the events of the war in this southernmost theater. The new Union presence not only roiled local Confederate sympathizers, but it also attracted area Confederate draft dodgers, deserters, and refugees. Confederate officials so despised the Union operations out of Fort Myers that they sent light cavalry commander John J. Dickison to destroy the fort. Dickison was, however, peremptorily called back to assist in a more critical Confederate action in north Florida. Though only a threat, Dickison's fleeting presence in south Florida convinced the Union command that Fort Myers needed fresh troops to repel any similar dangers. That the North chose to reinforce the post largely with USCT further aggravated the local Confederates.

In April 1864, Companies D and I of the 2d USCT redeployed from Key West to Fort Myers, where they joined elements of the 110th New York Infantry and the 2d Florida (Union) Cavalry. The USCT thereafter led the Union forces in a number of actions, some ranging as far north as Tampa. Local partisans so despised the black troops that they created a home-guard battalion to protect both their slaves and their cattle. The rebel unit officially was named the 1st Battalion, Florida Special Cavalry, but it was generally known in Florida as the Cattle Guard or Cow Cavalry. The Cow Cavalry quickly assumed the lead in Confederate resistance to the troops out of Fort Myers, and the unit's eventual attempt to destroy the fort itself proved the major engagement of the war in south Florida.

In January 1865, Cow Cavalry commander Colonel Charles J. Munnerlyn ordered three companies under the command of Major William Footman to attack and destroy the Union redoubt at Fort Myers. Footman's Cow Cavalry units departed Fort Meade, near Tampa Bay, in February for the 200-mile march along palmetto-choked Indian wars trails to Fort Myers. Footman placed his force at 275 men, but the Union commander at Fort Myers, Captain James Doyle of the 110th New York Infantry, and an eyewitness newspaper reporter later estimated that Footman attacked the garrison with a body of up to 500 rebels. Footman's assault force possibly swelled on the march with the addition of local "volunteers" and the temporary impressment of local farmers and fisher folk.

Footman attempted a frontal attack on the fort on 20 February 1865, but all did not go well for the Confederates. Alerted by their approach, the Union troops at the fort, mostly light-duty soldiers of the 2d USCT, Companies A and B of the 2d Florida (Union) Cavalry, and detachments from the 110th New York Infantry, quickly engaged the enemy in what would

become a day-long battle. The ensuing conflict involved heavy small arms fire and a running dual between the Confederate 12-pounder artillery piece and its Union counterpart, two Federal cannon operated by the men of the 2d USCT. As evening approached, Footman withdrew his dispirited troops and began the long march back to the Tampa region. Union scouts later found the Confederate retreat trail littered with bandages and splints and even recovered the rebels' discarded brass artillery piece. Memoirs and military and personal records indicate that the remote battle of Fort Myers resulted in forty Confederates wounded and four Union losses and three Union missing in action (all members of the 2d USCT). In the heated exchange, former slave John Wallace received a slight wound to the head, a wound he would tout as a badge of honor during Florida's Reconstruction period, when he served as a Radical Republican legislator and gained acclaim as the author of *Carpetbag Rule in Florida.*

Even though not recorded as a major conflict of the Civil War, the battle of Fort Myers demonstrated the Union's ability to hold its advantage in perhaps the southernmost land battle of conflict. Moreover, the engagement also marked the southernmost land duty of black troops in the American Civil War. Sadly, racism prevented the proper recognition from being bestowed upon these brave soldiers. Even though denied their military honors, the committed soldiers of the 2d USCT received singular acclaim of another form in the *New York Times.* A reporter visiting Fort Myers at the time of the battle published this account in the *New York Times:* "The colored soldiers [at Fort Myers] were in the thickest of the fight. Their impetuosity could hardly be restrained; they seemed totally unconscious of danger, or regardless of it and their constant cry was to 'get at them.'"

—*Irvin D. Solomon*

See also Florida; United States Colored Troops.

For further reading:
"Attack upon Fort Myers." *New York Times* (1865).
Boggess, Francis C.M. *A Veteran of Four Wars* (1900).
Buker, George E. *Blockaders, Refugees, & Contrabands: Civil War on Florida's Gulf Coast, 1861–1865* (1993).
Solomon, Irvin D., and Grace Erhart. "The Peculiar War: Civil War Naval Operations at Charlotte Harbor, Florida, 1861–1865." *Gulf Coast Historical Review* (1995).
———. "Race and Civil War in South Florida." *Florida Historical Quarterly* (1999).

FORT PICKENS

Fort Pickens was a coastal defense fortification built on Santa Rosa Island at the entrance to Florida's Pensacola Bay. During the secession crisis of early 1861, U.S. troops refused to surrender the fort to Confederate authorities, and for a time it appeared likely that hostilities might erupt either at Fort Pickens or at Fort Sumter, where similar circumstances prevailed.

Ultimately an informal truce was implemented at Pensacola and the crisis there faded, while Fort Sumter earned notoriety as the location where the Civil War began.

Built between 1829 and 1834, Fort Pickens was a five-sided brick fortification with walls more than forty feet thick and twelve feet high. If fully manned and equipped, it could mount more than 250 artillery pieces. Along with Fort McRee, which was on Foster's Island on the opposite side of the main ship channel, and Fort Barrancas, which was on the mainland, Fort Pickens guarded the entrance to Pensacola Bay as well as the valuable Pensacola Navy Yard.

At the time of Florida's secession in January 1861, Lieutenant Adam Slemmer evacuated his small force of army regulars from Fort Barrancas and occupied Fort Pickens. While theoretically more defensible, the fort had been essentially abandoned for a number of years and had fallen into disrepair. Slemmer's meager force, complemented only by a few sailors and two naval vessels, would be hard pressed to defend the vulnerable fortification.

Meanwhile, on 12 January, a force of Alabama and Florida troops seized the Pensacola Navy Yard from the ineffectual Commodore James Armstrong. That same evening a Southern delegation visited Fort Pickens and demanded its surrender, but Slemmer refused to do so without orders from Washington. On 15 January, the Federal officer met with Major William Chase, who had been appointed the commander of Confederate forces at Pensacola by Florida governor Madison Starke Perry. After consulting with the commander of one of the U.S. Navy ships that supported him, Slemmer refused the demand.

After this exchange, a group of Southern senators, including Florida's Stephen A. Mallory, met with President James Buchanan and Secretary of the Navy Isaac Toucey to discuss the situation. Buchanan and Toucey convinced the Southern delegation that a commencement of hostilities would only benefit the incoming Lincoln administration. The navy secretary then sent word to Slemmer that he was to maintain his garrison at Fort Pickens but was not to allow Federal vessels to land reinforcements on Santa Rosa Island. Several telegraph messages were also sent to both Governor Perry and Major Chase to convince them not to order an attack on the fort. Pickens, it was argued, "is not worth one drop of blood to us."

In late January, Buchanan seemingly reversed himself and ordered the USS *Brooklyn* to land an artillery company for the reinforcement of Fort Pickens. After Mallory threatened that this provocation could mean "instant war, " the president ordered that the troops remain aboard ship unless the fort was directly threatened. By the end of January 1861 an uneasy truce had settled over Pensacola Bay. While the Federals were prevented from landing reinforcements for Fort Pickens, however, additional Southern troops arrived at Pensacola until their strength reached 5,000. In early March, Major General Braxton Bragg took command of this force and began strengthening Forts McRee and Barrancas and constructing additional batteries aimed across the bay.

After his inauguration in early March, President Lincoln made plans to reinforce both Fort Pickens and Fort Sumter. On 12 March, orders were sent to Captain Israel Vodges to land his artillery company, which was still aboard the *Brooklyn,* as soon as possible. Naval captain Henry Adams, under the impression that the provisions of the earlier truce were still in effect, refused to cooperate with Vodges. Lincoln learned of the stalemate in early April. An expedition to relieve Fort Sumter was preparing to sail, and the president feared that Confederate forces might seize the more vulnerable Fort Pickens in retaliation. Lincoln hurriedly ordered navy lieutenant John Worden to travel by land to Pensacola with orders that Adams was to cooperate with the landing of reinforcements. Worden reached Pensacola on 11 April, received permission from an unsuspecting Bragg to visit the fleet, and by the evening of 12 April, the same day that the attack on Fort Sumter commenced, Union reinforcements had been landed on Santa Rosa Island.

Secretary of State William Seward then convinced Lincoln that more troops were needed at Fort Pickens, and a larger expedition was sent, which arrived later in April. When Colonel Harvey Brown arrived with these additional troops, he took command of Fort Pickens and the Department of Florida.

Throughout the summer of 1861, both sides strengthened their positions on Pensacola Bay. No major military operations occurred, although in September the Federals did mount raids that destroyed a dry dock and burned a Confederate ship. On the night of 8–9 October 1861, about 1,200 Confederate soldiers were ferried across Pensacola Bay and landed on Santa Rosa Island about four miles east of Fort Pickens. The rebels overran the camp of the 6th New York Infantry but were driven off by regulars from the fort's garrison. Casualties for both sides totaled about 150. In retaliation for the raid, Colonel Brown ordered a massive bombardment against Confederate positions that began on 22 November and lasted for two days. Although casualties on both sides were low, Fort McRee was seriously damaged. On New Year's Day 1862, another bombardment erupted between Fort Pickens and the Confederate forts, with neither side suffering serious damage.

In the months that followed, Pensacola's Confederate forces were transferred to other theaters of the war, while Federal forces would occupy the abandoned Fort Barrancas on the mainland. Fort Pickens, where the Civil War might possibly have begun, played only a minor role in the remainder of the conflict.

—*David J. Coles*

See also Bragg, Braxton; Florida; Pensacola; Perry, Madison Starke; Slemmer, Adam Jacoby.

For further reading:

Current, Richard N. *Lincoln and the First Shot* (1963).
Davis, William W. *The Civil War and Reconstruction in Florida* (1913).
Dibble, Ernest F. "War Averters: Seward, Mallory, and Fort Pickens." *Florida Historical Quarterly* (1971).
Johns, John E. *Florida during the Civil War* (1963).
Roberts, Robert B. *Encyclopedia of Historic Forts: The Military, Pioneer and Trading Posts of the United States* (1988).

FORT PILLOW
(April–June 1862)

The Union capture of this Confederate fort on the Mississippi River in June 1862 allowed an attack on Memphis. Located 60 miles to the south of Island No. 10 and just north of Fulton on the Tennessee shore, Fort Pillow guarded the northern approach to the vital Confederate railhead of Memphis 40 miles downriver.

Originally Fort Pillow was seen as a backup position to Columbus and Island No. 10, although its commander, Captain Montgomery Lynch, did what he could to make it capable of withstanding a siege. After the loss of Forts Henry and Donelson, Major General Leonidas Polk had reinforced Fort Pillow by sending a detachment there under Brigadier General John B. Villepigue. After the loss of New Madrid, General P. G. T. Beauregard had ordered its garrison there. After the Union capture of Island No. 10 and the Confederate defeat at Shiloh, Beauregard ordered a thousand slaves to Fort Pillow to improve its entrenchments.

Fort Pillow was made into a strong defensive position with batteries located on the high, nearly vertical Chickasaw Bluffs and in their face at the water's edge. When completed it mounted forty heavy guns, including 10-inch Columbiads. Most were in the lower batteries. Some 6,000 men manned its extensive earthworks.

On 14 April the Union Western Flotilla of ironclads, mortar boats, towboats, transports, supply ships, and tugs reached a point just above Fort Pillow. At 2:00 that afternoon Union mortar boats along the Arkansas side of the river fired the first shells at Fort Pillow. The mortar bombardment continued for the next seven weeks.

The original Union plan of attack developed by Flag Officer Andrew H. Foote and Brigadier General John Pope called for the mortar boats, protected by the gunboats, to bombard the land batteries while Pope's Army of the Mississippi went ashore upriver and outflanked the fort from the rear and Foote's gunboats

assaulted it from the front. But Pope quickly determined that he could not reach the rear of Fort Pillow from any point of the river above it, and he decided to repeat the plan of Island No. 10 by digging a six-mile long canal on the Arkansas side of the river across Craigshead Point to get Federal gunboats below the Confederate position. In the meantime, both sides engaged in harassing fire. It seemed that Fort Pillow would be taken only in a lengthy operation.

When Halleck withdrew Pope's troops for his snail-like campaign against Corinth, he dashed any possibility of a quick strike at Fort Pillow. Foote and Pope learned of this decision the evening of 16 April. The bulk of the Union land force departed upriver the next day in twenty transports, taking with them tools for cutting through the swamps and leaving behind only Colonel Graham N. Fitch and 1,200 infantry to garrison Fort Pillow should the Confederates decide to evacuate it.

The Union naval bombardment of Fort Pillow continued, but it was principally harassing fire. On 8 May, three Confederate rams of the River Defense Fleet came out, but they soon retired on discovering the presence of three Union ironclads. The next day Foote left the flotilla for health reasons, replaced by Flag Officer Charles H. Davis. On 10 May, the battle of Plum Point Bend occurred, the war's first real engagement between naval squadrons. Although suffering much higher personnel losses, Southern rams temporarily disabled two of the more powerful Union gunboats.

For three weeks Davis continued a slow bombardment of the Confederate positions. By 25 May all seven of Colonel Charles Ellet's steamers of the Army Mississippi Ram Fleet were with the flotilla. These converted Ohio River steamers, conceived solely as rams with no ordnance, were the Union answer to the Confederate rams.

Ellet wanted an immediate blow against Fort Pillow, which Davis resisted, but the Confederates took the decision out of Union hands. On 29–30 May, General Beauregard, deciding to save his 50,000 men, evacuated Corinth to General Henry W. Halleck's 120,000-man army and retired to a new line along the Tuscumbia River in Alabama. This left Fort Pillow outflanked and untenable, and on 4 June, the Confederates blew up their guns and burned what provisions and stores they could not carry away.

On 5 June, Davis's flotilla and Ellet's rams moved past Fort Pillow to take Memphis. The next day in the battle of Memphis, Union gunboats and rams destroyed all but one of the eight Confederate vessels. Memphis then surrendered.

—*Spencer C. Tucker*

See also Davis, Charles Henry; Ellet, Charles; Foote, Andrew H.; Island No. 10; Memphis; Plum Point Bend; Pope, John.

For further reading:
Milligan, John D. *Gunboats Down the Mississippi* (1965).

FORT PILLOW MASSACRE
(12 April 1864)

Fort Pillow was located on the east bank of the Mississippi River, 40 miles north of Memphis, Tennessee. Constructed by Confederate general Gideon Pillow in 1861, it overlooked the river, and its principal function was to control river traffic on the Mississippi. On 12 April 1864, the fort became the site of one of the most controversial events of the American Civil War: the Fort Pillow massacre.

The fort consisted of a dirt parapet, approximately 6 to 8 feet high and forming a 125-foot semicircle. Built on a steep bluff that descended rapidly to the Mississippi, the fort faced east. To the north, a small stream, Coal Creek, entered the river. To the south, a small town consisting of storage buildings and bunkhouses sat in a ravine below the fort.

The fort was protected by three semicircular lines of defense. The outer line spanned about two miles and ran from the small town to the south of the fortress to Coal Creek on the other side of the fort. The second line was approximately 600 yards inside the outer lines. The final line was the fort itself. The terrain around the fort was hilly with numerous ravines. The fort was manned by 580 Union soldiers; 285 belonged to the 13th Tennessee Cavalry, while 292 were African-American soldiers who were part of either the 6th U.S. Heavy Artillery or the 6th U.S. Colored Light Artillery. Major Lionel F. Booth commanded the fort, with Major William F. Bradford second in command.

On the morning of 12 April, Confederate troops under General Nathan Bedford Forrest, who had been conducting raids throughout western Kentucky and Tennessee, surrounded the garrison on three sides. The Confederates had quickly seized the small town south of the fort and a ravine north of it. After waiting for his ammunition to be replenished, Forrest sent out a flag of truce at 3:30 that afternoon and demanded the garrison's immediate surrender. He told the Federals that if they surrendered, they would be treated as prisoners of war, but, if they refused, they would be shown no quarter. Major Booth had been killed by sniper fire, so the decision fell to Major Bradford, who asked Forrest for 1 hour to deliberate. Suspecting that the Federals were stalling to procure the assistance of a Union gunboat (the *New Era*) on the Mississippi, Forrest gave Bradford 20 minutes to decide.

When Union forces refused to surrender, Forrest launched a vigorous assault on the fort. With good position and superior numbers, the Confederates quickly

Rebel massacre of black Union soldiers after the surrender of Fort Pillow, 12 April 1862 (*Library of Congress*)

overwhelmed Union forces. What made the assault on Fort Pillow infamous, however, was the manner in which it was conducted. As Confederate soldiers gained the parapet, panic seized Union soldiers, who hastily retreated down the bluff. Many Union soldiers jumped into the Mississippi River, hoping to swim to the *New Era*. Other Union soldiers laid down their weapons and attempted to surrender. Confederate troops, however, did not acknowledge surrender and subjected the garrison to a merciless fire of bullets. Many Union soldiers were gunned down after they had thrown away their weapons. Black soldiers were the especial target of Confederate wrath. Not only did the Confederate government refuse to recognize African-Americans as bona fide soldiers, the average Confederate soldier was particularly threatened by the sight of former slaves wearing Union blue. Cries of "No quarter" and "kill the damned niggers" punctuated the confusion. Countless accounts told of black soldiers gunned down or bayoneted in the most brutal fashion.

When Forrest finally gained control of the situation

and ordered his forces to cease firing, close to 50 percent of the Federal troops had perished. The death rate for black troops, however, was significantly higher than for white soldiers (64 percent compared with 31 percent). In addition to high casualties, stories of all sorts of atrocities quickly spread throughout the North. These included such gruesome acts as live burials, the killing of women and children who were in the town south of the fort, and wounded soldiers being set on fire.

Northern public opinion was outraged, and in a public speech shortly after the massacre, President Lincoln threatened retaliation if the allegations were proved true. In Congress, the Joint Committee on the Conduct of the War was directed to investigate the Fort Pillow massacre. After interviewing dozens of witnesses, the committee published a report in early May that charged that the Confederates were indeed guilty of many of the reported atrocities.

While the Lincoln administration threatened retaliation and discussed various options in cabinet meetings, nothing came of such threats. In the end, the administration realized that Richmond authorities would never recognize African-American soldiers as legitimate, and to avenge Fort Pillow would result in a cycle of meaningless reprisals.

Although reports of the massacre were not without exaggeration, particularly the accounts of live burials and the slaughter of women and children, most historians believe that soldiers, particularly African-Americans, were needlessly butchered. While historians sympathetic to Forrest argue that there was no "official" surrender of the garrison, there can be little doubt that many soldiers tried to surrender and were killed after they had thrown down their weapons. While Forrest may not have explicitly ordered the massacre, given the well-known attitude of Confederate soldiers toward African-American soldiers, Forrest understood what the outcome of an attack would be. Indeed, for numerous African-American soldiers, Fort Pillow being came a rallying cry. There are numerous accounts of black troops going into battle crying "Fort Pillow." Instead of unnerving black soldiers, as the Confederates had intended, the massacre at Fort Pillow had the opposite result.

—*Bruce Tap*

See also African-American Soldiers U.S.A.; Forrest, Nathan Bedford; Fort Pillow Massacre.

For further reading:
Castel, Albert E. "The Fort Pillow Massacre: A Fresh Examination of the Evidence." *Civil War History* (1958).
Cimprich, John, and Robert Mainfort, Jr. "The Fort Pillow Massacre: A Statistical Note." *Journal of American History* (1989).
Fuchs, Richard L. *An Unerring Fire: The Massacre at Fort Pillow* (1994).
Hurst, Jack. *Nathan Bedford Forrest: A Biography* (1993).
Tap, Bruce. *Over Lincoln's Shoulder: The Committee on the Conduct of the War* (1998).

FORT PULASKI, REDUCTION OF
(10–11 April 1862)

Perhaps the most formidable of all American coastal forts before the Civil War, Fort Pulaski guarded the river entrance to Savannah, Georgia, during the first year of the conflict. Pulaski represented the very best that American engineers produced in terms of permanent works, yet it surrendered just thirty hours after Union forces began their attack. The destruction of Pulaski provided the first solid evidence that even the strongest of masonry forts was obsolete due to the routine use of rifled artillery.

Bombardment of Fort Pulaski, 10–11 April 1862 (*Library of Congress*)

Pulaski is located at the mouth of the Savannah River on the mile-long island of Cockspur. Despite surrounding marshes, the island was an ideal location for a fort because of its command of the river and its protection from Atlantic storms. Pulaski's location on an island prevented a land attack, traditionally the weakest point in a seacoast work's defense. The nearest land capable of accommodating siege guns, Tybee Island, was beyond the effective range of smoothbore weaponry at approximately 1,700 yards distance. The surrounding river banks, also marshland, made siege warfare almost impossible. The fort itself had pentagon-shaped brick walls 7.5 feet thick, encircled by a wet moat. Pulaski's emplacements could house 140 weapons, although the Confederates only had forty-eight artillery pieces of various calibers mounted during the siege and reduction.

The United States Corps of Engineers had completed Pulaski in 1847 after eighteen years and a cost of $1 million dollars. The fort was part of the Totten system of coastal defense, a program designed by the Board of Engineers of 1816 and supervised by Brevet Lieutenant Colonel Joseph G. Totten. American military engineers considered Pulaski one of the strongest forts in America's coastal defense, with a life expectancy of decades. The fort's name honored Polish Count Casimir Pulaski who had died while defending Savannah against a British attack during the American Revolution.

Georgia's governor, Joseph E. Brown, ordered the fort seized on 2 January 1861, even though the state had not yet seceded from the Union. The new commanding officer, Colonel Charles H. Olmstead, immediately strengthened the fort's position by adding weapons and obstructing the river channel. During the fall of 1861 General Robert E. Lee, commander of the Confederate Atlantic seacoast defenses, inspected the area during his tour of the southeast coast. He pointed to Tybee Island 1,700 yards away and remarked, "Colonel, they will make it very warm for you with shells from that point, but they cannot breach at that distance." This comment showed that even an engineer as experienced as Lee did not fully recognize the obsolescence of masonry works brought about by the widespread use of rifled artillery.

Union brigadier general Quincy A. Gillmore arrived in the area in February 1862 and preceded to "go by the book" in reducing Pulaski. Gillmore required two months to prepare for the attack, spending most of his time installing smoothbore columbiads, the standard breaching weapon of the day. Gillmore divided his armament into eleven batteries for a total of thirty-six pieces, ten of which were rifled. The batteries ranged between 1,650 and 3,400 yards from Pulaski. Ironically, the weapons that Gillmore and Olmstead both credited with destroying the fort were the lighter, rifled guns, which took only a week to put in place. Gillmore found the smoothbore guns practically worthless during the engagement.

Interior view of the front parapet, Fort Pulaski, April 1862 (Photograph by Timothy O'Sullivan / *Library of Congress*)

At 8:15 A.M. on 10 April 1862, Federal batteries commenced a fierce barrage that lasted throughout the day and continued into the night. The performance of the rifled guns impressed Gillmore, who noted that the areas hit were "deep and effective," particularly on the fort's southeast wall. By the end of the day Gillmore assessed that his troops would breach the wall within a day or two. That evening Olmstead also inspected the southeast wall. His findings yielded the same results: the fort would fall within two days. Olmstead realized that continued resistance had no benefits and would only lead to unnecessary loss of life. Shortly after 2:00 P.M. on the following day when rounds started striking the powder magazine, Olmstead signaled for surrender.

Fort Pulaski fell due to the devastating effects of rifled fire. Its walls were inflexible; instead of absorbing or deflecting artillery rounds as would other construction material, the brick simply crumbled. Prior to the attack, Olmstead believed the fort to be virtually impregnable, as did Lee. Gillmore calculated the reduction of Pulaski as extremely difficult, perhaps even impossible, and spent almost three months preparing. The quickness of Pulaski's demise proved all three men wrong.

Although the lessons provided by Pulaski did not change the immediate future of coastal defenses, they did have an impact later in the nineteenth century. Under the Endicott system of fortifications (1880s), United States engineers constructed new coastal forts as one-tier works with dispersed batteries. Earth and reinforced concrete became the new building blocks for seacoast defenses. By the turn of the century the United

States had abandoned the impressive forts of the Totten system in favor of the Endicott forts.

—*David P. Eldridge*

See also Fortifications; Gillmore, Quincy; Totten, Joseph Gilbert.

For further reading:
Gillmore, Quincy A. *Siege and Reduction of Fort Pulaski, Georgia* (1862; reprint, 1988).
Hawes, Lilla Mills, ed. *Collections of the Georgia Historical Society: The Memoirs of Charles H. Olmstead* (1964).
Lewis, Emmanuel. *Seacoast Fortifications of the United States: An Introductory History* (1970).
Olmstead, Charles H. *Fort Pulaski* (1917).

FORT SANDERS, BATTLE OF
(29 November 1863)

The battle of Fort Sanders was the major engagement during the 1863 siege of Knoxville. After the defeat of the Confederate forces on 16 November at the battle of Campbell's Station, the Union forces commanded by General Ambrose Burnside continued their retreat toward the defenses of Knoxville. To buy time to strengthen the city's defenses further, General Burnside ordered his cavalry commander, General William P. Sanders, to delay the Confederate advance. On 19 November, as the Confederate forces under General James Longstreet approached Knoxville, one mile west of the city Sanders and a dismounted brigade of 700 men held off the Confederates throughout the afternoon. Although his men retired into Knoxville that evening, General Sanders was mortally wounded during the skirmish. Burnside honored Sanders's gallantry by renaming the extreme western military work at the edge of the city's defenses Fort Sanders.

As the Confederates laid siege to the city of Knoxville, the Federal forces continued to build up their defenses. The natural topography of Knoxville helped protect the city, with the Holston River running along the south and a ridge approximately 150 feet high and 1,300 yards wide extending along Knoxville's north side. Along this ridge, the Union forces under Captain Orlando Poe of the Army Corps of Engineers constructed a series of fortifications. At the extreme northwestern end of the defense line stood Fort Sanders. Fort Sanders was constructed as an irregular quadrilateral, with salients at the northwest and southwest corners, leaving the eastern side open for troops to move in and out of the fort. The sides of the fort

Generals Grant, Sherman, Sheridan, Hooker, Harney, Dodge, Gibbon, and Porter at Fort Sanders (*Library of Congress*)

The rebel assault on Fort Sanders (*Library of Congress*)

were protected by an earthen wall that was thirteen feet high and surrounded by a ditch averaging twelve feet in width and six to eight feet in depth. The approaches to the fort were defended by a line of rifle pits surrounded by a field of tree stumps around which old telegraph wire had been fastened.

As the siege of Knoxville continued, Longstreet began to plan how best to attack the city's defense. After a failed attempt to place artillery on the south side of the Holston River, he considered an attack along the eastern defenses of the city, but ruled this out because of the open terrain in the area. Instead, Longstreet decided to attack the western edge of the city at Fort Sanders. Here his troops would be able to approach under cover until they were about eighty yards from the fort. After watching a Federal soldier cross the ditch in front of the fort while walking along a plank, Longstreet incorrectly assumed that the ditch was about three feet deep and only five or six feet wide.

Confident in his intelligence and bolstered by two cavalry brigades commanded by General Bushrod Johnson from southwest Virginia and additional reinforcements from General Braxton Bragg, Longstreet prepared to attack. Heavy fog on the morning of 28 November forced him to delay his attack until the

daylight of the next day. Longstreet also changed his original plan of attack by ordering his sharpshooters to advance the evening before the attack to be in position to cover the bayonet charge the following morning. As the Confederates assumed their positions, the Union troops were alerted, and Longstreet had lost his advantage of surprise. Also, the night before the attack, Longstreet's division commanders, Generals Micah Jenkins and Evander McLaws expressed their misgivings at the plan of attack. They suggested that Longstreet await news of the rumored engagement at Chattanooga before proceeding.

Despite these misgivings, the attack commenced at daybreak on 29 November. As they screamed the rebel yell, the Confederate troops rushed toward the parapet with their bayonets fixed. When they reached the ditch outside the fort, however, they realized they had entered a death trap. The ditch was wider and deeper than expected and the embankment in front of them was steep, muddy, icy, and devoid of any foothold. Without ladders, the Confederate soldiers were easy targets for the Union artillery and riflemen. Despite the treacherous conditions, about fifty Confederate soldiers were able to reach the top of the parapet, only to be killed or captured. After about twenty minutes the fighting ceased. Longstreet considered a second attack, but, considering the nature of the terrain and the weariness and low morale of his men, he decided against it.

Although the battle was short, the costs for the Confederates were high. They lost 129 men killed, with another 458 wounded and 226 missing, whereas the Union troops lost 5 killed and 8 wounded. Shortly after the battle, Longstreet learned of General Bragg's defeat at Chattanooga. Although Longstreet remained in Knoxville for six more days, after the battle there were no major engagements and the Union troops knew that reinforcements would shortly arrive from Chattanooga. The siege of Knoxville was effectively over.

—*William Hartley*

See also Campbell's Station, Battle of; Knoxville Campaign.

For further reading:
Davidson, James F. "Michigan and the Defense of Knoxville, Tennessee, 1863." *East Tennessee Historical Society's Publications* (1963).
Fink, Harold S. "The East Tennessee Campaign and the Battle of Knoxville in 1863." *East Tennessee Historical Society's Publications* (1957).
Seymour, Digby Gordon. *Divided Loyalties: Fort Sanders and the Civil War in East Tennessee* (1982).

FORT SMITH, ARKANSAS

Chosen in 1817 as the site for the first military post in the Southwest, Fort Smith's location at the juncture of the Poteau and Arkansas rivers served notice to warring Native Americans that law and order had arrived at this remote corner of the United States. In 1824, the first log and stone stockade was abandoned, but nearby residents pleaded for renewed occupation of the income-producing installation. Succumbing to pressure, the War Department ordered the construction of a masonry fort near the original ruins.

With no obvious military threat, work proceeded slowly until it was halted in 1841. Additional lobbying persuaded the army to turn the incomplete fort into a supply depot.

When sectional conflict erupted two decades later, secessionists fully expected their river defenses to blunt federal naval thrusts down the Mississippi. Any Union advance on the Trans-Mississippi, they concluded, would be forced to sweep west into Indian Territory and then strike the Confederacy's rear via the Arkansas and Red rivers. Fort Smith appeared to be in an ideal position not only to protect the back door to Arkansas, Louisiana, and Texas but also to exert control over the Five Civilized Tribes and their beef, horses, grain, salt, lead, and potential manpower.

Even before Arkansas officially seceded, therefore, Governor Henry Rector called for volunteers to seize Fort Smith. When news reached Union captain Samuel Sturgis that Arkansas state forces were steaming up the Arkansas River, he abandoned Fort Smith on 23 April 1861 and headed southwest toward Fort Washita.

Eventually placed in charge of a frontier army gathering in northwest Arkansas, Confederate general Ben McCulloch marched from Fort Smith at the end of June to link up with General Sterling Price in southern Missouri. The two commanders defeated Union forces on 10 August at Wilson's Creek.

The new year found Union brigadier general James Blunt ordering an invasion of the Cherokee Nation, which had allied itself with the Confederacy, from Kansas while General Samuel Curtis pushed south from Missouri. Union victories in the spring and summer of 1862—most notably at Pea Ridge—convinced newly appointed Confederate district commander General Earl Van Dorn to withdraw all but a few of Fort Smith's garrison. When Blunt's soldiers mutinied and Curtis headed east toward Helena, however, the post remained under Confederate control.

In the fall of 1862, Thomas Hindman took his turn trying to reorganize Confederate forces at Fort Smith. Twice General Hindman headed north to face Yankees under General John Schofield, and twice the rebels were mauled, the second time at Prairie Grove. By the end of the year, Schofield was encamped on the Arkansas River, cutting Hindman's river supply line and causing him to evacuate Fort Smith. Cold weather forced Union troops back to Missouri before they could reoccupy the depot.

In January 1863, Confederate general William Steele was given the task of defending northwest Arkansas. Despite a lack of food and ammunition, Steele assumed the offensive after he heard that Union forces under Colonel William Phillips had struck south from Kansas to burn Fort Davis and capture Fort Gibson, located upriver from Fort Smith. Hoping to destroy Fort Gibson before it could be reinforced, Steele sallied from Fort Smith to Honey Springs in Indian Territory. On 17 July, Federals under Blunt and Phillips were able to drive the Confederates from the field before Steele could join his forces with troops approaching from Texas. Forced to split his defeated command to meet a separate threat from southern Missouri, Steele sent Brigadier General William Cabell back to Fort Smith. Blunt pushed Steele deep into the Choctaw Nation and then turned north. On 1 September 1863, he crossed the Poteau River and entered Fort Smith on the heels of the retreating Cabell.

To hamper any Confederate reoccupation plans, the Federals erected extensive earthworks around the depot. Although Union soldiers garrisoned Fort Smith for the remainder of the war, Confederate partisans and Cherokee and Creek regiments almost forced its abandonment because of their raids on supply lines. In July and August 1864, Confederate forces under the combined command of General Richard Gano and General Stand Watie made a series of unsuccessful attacks on the fort's defenses.

In September 1865, Fort Smith played one final role in the Civil War. Emissaries from the federal government came there to inform belligerent tribes that all rights guaranteed under previous treaties had been forfeited because of their support for the Confederacy. The Indians were also required to cede roughly half their lands for relocation of the various Plains tribes. "As harsh as Reconstruction was for the rest of the South," wrote journalist Randy Krehbiel, "it was nothing like this; no one suggested Georgia surrender half its land for settlement by Ohio farmers."

In 1871, the army abandoned the depot for good, although it was utilized until 1917 as a federal prison. The site became a unit of the National Park Service in 1961.

—Dave Page (Tom Wing, contributing)

See also Arkansas; Cherokee Indians; Creek Indians; Hindman, Thomas C.; Rector, Henry M.

For further reading:

Bearss, Edwin C., and Arrell M. Gibson. *Fort Smith: Little Gibraltar on the Arkansas* (1988).

Hart, Herbert M. *Old Forts of the Southwest* (1956).

Krehbiel, Randy. "Indians in Blue and Gray." *America's Civil War* (1991).

FORT STEDMAN, BATTLE OF
(25 March 1865)

The Army of Northern Virginia's last tactical offensive in the war occurred east of Petersburg, Virginia, at the battle of Fort Stedman on 25 March 1865. Desiring to relieve the nine-month siege of Petersburg, General Robert E. Lee sought to attack a weak point in the Union defensive position, puncture it with a decisive stroke, and force General Ulysses S. Grant to retract his lines around Petersburg. Lee could then dispatch a portion of his army to unite with General Joseph E. Johnston in North Carolina and defeat General William T. Sherman's army. Upon Sherman's defeat, these troops, in conjunction with Johnston's army, could return to Virginia to deal with Grant.

Lee instructed his youngest corps commander, General John B. Gordon, to locate a weak point in the Union defenses and lead the assault. After a careful reconnaissance, Gordon selected an area where the opposing lines were only 150 yards apart—between a section of Confederate defenses known as Colquitt's Salient and the Union's Fort Stedman. Union troops had named the fort after Colonel Griffin Stedman, 11th Connecticut Infantry, who had been mortally wounded near the site in August 1864. Fort Stedman was an earthen redoubt with a four-foot deep moat and walls nine feet high protected by an abatis and sharp-pointed sticks known as a fraise. To the north of the fort were Batteries IX and X, while Batteries XI and XII and Fort Haskell lay to the south. The Federal IX Corps under General John G. Parke defended this line of entrenchments. Gordon would use his entire corps in the attack and could call on troops from Generals James Longstreet and A. P. Hill. Once his attack was successful, Gordon could call on a cavalry division to wreak havoc in the Federal rear.

At about 4:00 A.M. in the predawn darkness, Gordon began his attack. Approximately 11,500 troops from Gordon's corps and General Bushrod Johnson's division moved in three columns across the land from Colquitt's Salient to Fort Stedman. In a sudden and vigorous attack, the Confederates broke through the Union lines and captured cannon, mortars, and hundreds of prisoners, including General Napoleon B. McLaughlin, who, while trying to rally his troops, had accidentally ridden into Confederate lines after they had captured Fort Stedman. Gordon's initial assault quickly seized 1,000 yards of entrenchments, including Fort Stedman and Batteries X, XI, and XII. While the attackers pressed the assault north to Battery IX, and to Fort Haskell, 600 yards to the south, three special-mission groups probed eastward, seeking to overrun redoubts located in the rear of the Federal army.

However, the Confederate attack soon lost its momentum. The forts to the east could not be found, and a strong defense of Battery IX and Fort Haskell turned back numerous attacks. By 7:00 A.M., the Rebel troops had been forced into a defensive posture, as reorganized Union troops tightened the ring around the Confederates. Reinforcements from the Union 3d Division under General John F. Hartranft prepared for a counterattack. At 7:45 A.M. Hartranft ordered a charge of 4,000 men against the tenuous Confederate position around Fort Stedman. The Union assault succeeded and forced Gordon to order a withdrawal from the Union lines. Many Confederate casualties occurred as they fled back to the safety of Colquitt's Salient.

The Union IX Corps suffered 1,044 casualties (72 killed, 450 wounded, 522 missing or captured) in the four-hour fight. Confederate casualties, though never officially reported, were probably between 2,500 and 3,500, including no less than 1,500 captured as prisoners.

The failed attack presaged the end of the once indomitable Army of Northern Virginia. Lee wrote President Jefferson Davis after the battle, "I fear now it will be impossible to prevent a junction between Grant and Sherman, nor do I deem it prudent that this army should maintain its position until the latter shall approach too near." Indeed Lee's position would soon be proven untenable. Grant ordered his final offensive movement to begin on 29 March, and Petersburg fell on 3 April. On 9 April, just two weeks after the battle of Fort Stedman, Lee surrendered his army at Appomattox.

—Judkin Browning

See also Petersburg Campaign.

For further reading:
Gordon, John B. *Reminiscences of the Civil War* (1903).
Hartranft, John F. "The Recapture of Fort Stedman." In *Battles and Leaders of the Civil War* (1888; reprint, 1982).
Kilmer, George L. "Gordon's Attack at Fort Stedman." In *Battles and Leaders of the Civil War* (1888; reprint, 1982).
Power, J. Tracy. *Lee's Miserables: Life in the Army of Northern Virginia from the Wilderness to Appomattox* (1998).
Trudeau, Noah Andre. *The Last Citadel: Petersburg, Virginia, June 1864–April 1865* (1991).

FORT STEVENS, DISTRICT OF COLUMBIA
(11–12 July 1864)

One of a series of forts in the northern part of the District of Columbia near Silver Spring, Maryland, Fort Stevens was the focus of two days of fighting during Jubal Early's raid on Washington in July 1864. After the heavy fighting at the battle of Monocacy on 9 July, Early and his roughly 10,000 men moved toward Washington.

Out of what is now Silver Spring, Maryland, Early took the road south (known as Union Road in Maryland and the Seventh Street Road in the District of Columbia), moving directly toward Fort Stevens. The fort, part of a string of primarily earthworks, was located on high ground overlooking the Seventh Street Road. It was heavily armed with ten 24-pounders, two howitzers, and five 30-pound Parrott guns. While it contained plenty of artillery, the fort was not heavily manned (209 men upon Early's approach) and those men in the fort were not very experienced artillerists.

Early, however, also had his problems. His men had been exhausted by the heavy fighting at Monocacy and had been on the march for much of the time since. The temperature during the two days since the battle had averaged in the mid-90s during the day, and the roads were extremely dusty.

As Early's army trudged south, Robert Emmett Rodes's division led the way, followed by Stephen Dodson Ramseur's division, and then John Brown Gordon's. On the morning of 11 July, Major General Alexander McCook commanded all the Federal forces in the north of Washington. They were on alert about a possible Confederate move in their direction and were not surprised when, in the early morning hours, the Federal pickets outside of the fort were attacked by the lead elements of Rodes's division. The pickets were pushed back to the outlying earthworks of Fort Stevens.

During the early morning Major General Christopher Augur, commander of the Department of Washington, had come to the fort as part of an inspection tour of the Northern defenses. When the pickets were attacked, he summoned reinforcements and called

Detachment of Company K, 3d Massachusetts Heavy Artillery, at Fort Stevens, 1865
(Photograph by William Morris Smith / *Library of Congress*)

Fort Stevens in 1861, when it was known as Fort Massachusetts (*National Archives*)

for the activation of the city's militia, composed primarily of government employees.

In the meantime, the Confederate forces continued to move south past U.S. postmaster general Montgomery Blair's country home and the famous country estate of his father, Francis Preston Blair, known as Silver Spring. Early established his headquarters at the latter. By about 1 P.M. Early's exhausted men had pushed back the Federal defenders outside the fort to within about 100 yards of the walls. About that time, however, militia reinforcements were coming into the fort, as well as about 500 to 600 dismounted Federal cavalry. At the same time, artillery from Fort Slocum, about one mile southeast of Fort Stevens was being brought to bear on the attacking Confederates. In response to this firing, Gordon had one of his batteries brought forward to return fire.

At about 1:30 P.M. the Federal reinforcements counterattacked and pushed Rodes's division back about 1,000 yards. For the remainder of the afternoon, because of the heat and fatigue, the Confederates were satisfied with letting their sharpshooters and a few skirmishers use the houses and outbuildings nearby as shelter while picking off the Federal pickets one by one. The Federal artillery continued to fire throughout the afternoon to little effect.

During the late afternoon Major General Horatio Gouverneur Wright's VI Corps sent by Ulysses S. Grant from the siege of Petersburg began disembarking at the city's wharves. President Abraham Lincoln came down to the docks to meet them and then took his carriage out to Fort Stevens. Some have speculated that if Early had attacked with everything he had before the arrival of VI Corps, he could have carried the works and marched into Washington. Whether from fatigue or concern with the strength of the Federal works, he did not attack.

About 5 P.M. the Federal skirmish line started to weaken in the face of Confederate pressure from their sharpshooters and skirmishers. More Federal reinforcements were brought up and during the early evening hours continued to strengthen the two-mile-long line in front of Fort Stevens. Lincoln arrived in time to witness some of these preparations and, for the first of several times over the next two days, was unceremoniously instructed to stay down when walking along the fort's parapets. During the night more reinforcements arrived and spread out along the line. Quartermaster General Montgomery Meigs was placed in command of the area in front of the fort.

The Confederates were also busy during the night of 11 July. Early held a council of war at Silver Spring in which he initially determined to launch a major attack the next morning. After coming to this decision, however, he received word about the arrival of two of Grant's corps in Washington and called off the attack. He decided instead to spend the day of the twelfth letting the sharpshooters and skirmishers continue their activities of the previous day and then withdraw during the night.

During the early part of the day on 12 July more of VI Corps arrived, along with Major General Wright at Fort Stevens. In the afternoon Lincoln also returned and climbed on to the parapets to watch the action. A Confederate sharpshooter shot one of the men standing next to Lincoln, and the president was entreated—by some accounts, ordered—to remove himself from danger.

With a large part of VI Corps in place, as well as other reinforcements, the Federal commanders at Fort Stevens determined to wait until dusk and then make an effort to clear the area in front of the fort of the sharpshooters and skirmishers. As the sun began to go down, the attack commenced with an artillery assault that destroyed many of the buildings sheltering the sharpshooters. That goal accomplished, one brigade of VI Corps moved out with another in reserve to engage the now exposed Confederates. As the Southerners were pushed back, Rodes brought his division forward in support, but it was too late to stop the retreating sharpshooters. The Confederates were driven back, though not routed, and both sides suffered heavy casualties.

This early evening engagement effectively ended the battle of Fort Stevens and Early's threat to the Federal capital. During the night he withdrew his army. At some point in the retreat Montgomery Blair's home was destroyed. Some Confederates later claimed it had been done by Federal artillery, while the Union forces said that it was burned by Early's troops. On 14 July, Early and his men crossed the Potomac into Virginia at Leesburg.

—*David S. Heidler and Jeanne T. Heidler*

See also Early's Washington Raid; Monocacy, Battle of.
For further reading:
Cooling, Benjamin Franklin. *Jubal Early's Raid on Washington, 1864* (1989).

FORT SUMTER, BOMBARDMENT OF
(12–14 April 1861)

A five-sided fort situated on a manmade island guarding the main ship channel into Charleston Harbor, Fort Sumter had been under construction off and on for over thirty years when it became the site for the beginning of the Civil War. Troops occupying the forts protecting Charleston harbor at the end of 1860 were commanded by Kentuckian Major Robert Anderson. During the secession crisis following the election of Abraham Lincoln in November 1860, numerous threats were made against Anderson and his men, most of whom occupied Fort Moultrie on Sullivan's Island. As soon as Lincoln was elected, Anderson began asking for reinforcements from the War Department. He also began contemplating moving his men from Fort Moultrie, which was almost indefensible from land, to the more secure Castle Pinckney on an island closer to Charleston or to the unfinished Fort Sumter near the entrance to the harbor.

Despite assurance from South Carolina political leaders that no effort would be made to secure Federal posts in the Charleston area until after secession, Anderson was nervous. It was apparent to him and his men that militiamen in the area were arming and that such activity could be for only one purpose.

South Carolina seceded on 20 December 1860, and pressure was exerted immediately on Governor Francis Pickens to do something about Anderson and his men. Pickens believed he had an unwritten agreement with the James Buchanan administration that Anderson would remain at Fort Moultrie. There was concern among some South Carolinians that Anderson might not abide by that agreement and move his men to Fort Sumter. Unbeknownst to them and even to Buchanan, Anderson had been authorized to do just that when Buchanan endorsed without thoroughly reading a recommendation to that effect. Even before secession occurred, Anderson was preparing to move.

Still, Pickens hoped to secure the forts through negotiation rather than by military force. On 24 December he sent Robert W. Barnwell, James H. Adams, and James L. Orr to Washington to negotiate with the federal government. Anderson, in the meantime, was making his final preparations to move and kept his plans secret from everyone but his officers. On the night of 26 December, all of the men at Fort Moultrie were assembled without notice, loaded onto boats, and rowed to Fort Sumter. Upon arrival they surprised the construction workers there who, along with the soldiers, set about to make the fort more defensible.

The following morning, Charleston awoke to an occupied Fort Sumter, news the people learned from some of the Southern workmen at the fort who refused to continue their labors and returned to Charleston. Pickens, who had moved his seat of government to Charleston in the midst of the crisis, was very upset by this turn of events. He was immediately attacked in the press for not anticipating the move. The governor responded by sending his military aide, Colonel J. Johnston Pettigrew, to confer with Anderson and to request that he return to Fort Moultrie. Anderson refused.

Pickens later that day sent Pettigrew with some militiamen to seize Castle Pinckney. The only people there were Lieutenant R. K. Meade, a private, and some workmen. Meade, of course, had no choice but to surrender. Later that day, Carolina troops also occupied empty Fort Moultrie.

Interior view of Fort Sumter, 1861 (*Library of Congress*)

On 27 December, the South Carolina commissioners in Washington heard about the events in Charleston. They accused the administration of bad faith, an accusation that must have surprised Buchanan, since he had no idea that Anderson had planned such a move. The cabinet met to discuss the matter, and after much deliberation in which Buchanan considered ordering Anderson back to Fort Moultrie, the president was persuaded to leave Anderson where he was.

One of the reasons for the division within the cabinet was the presence of Virginian John Floyd as secretary of war. Floyd resigned during this crisis, however, and was replaced by Postmaster General Joseph Holt, who favored holding Fort Sumter. Once it had been decided that Anderson should stay at Fort Sumter, the question of the reinforcements requested by Anderson arose. On 2 January, Buchanan decided to reinforce Anderson but to send the men aboard an unarmed merchant vessel, the *Star of the West*, so as not to be overly provocative to the South Carolina authorities. The vessel was chartered by the government and was loaded with 200 relatively new recruits dressed as civilians so as to maintain the secrecy of the ship's mission. However, shortly after the ship left New York City on 5 January 1861, word leaked as to its mission and destination.

In the meantime, Pickens had begun to erect batteries on Morris Island. He also temporarily cut Fort Sumter's communications with the outside world, including mail. Still the garrison's infrequent contact with Charleston allowed the rumors about the *Star of the West* to reach them.

The ship arrived off of Charleston on the night of 8 January. On the morning of 9 January, prominently flying the U.S. flag, it began moving past the batteries of Morris Island. The newly erected guns opened up on the unarmed ship. The firing caused the garrison of Fort Sumter to ascend the ramparts to watch the show. The ship made it past Morris Island but had to come within range of the guns from Fort Moultrie to reach Fort Sumter. When the guns of that fort opened up on the merchantman, some of Anderson's officers wanted to return fire, but Anderson, under orders from Washington to remain on the defensive, refused. *Star of the West* could not make it past the guns of Fort Moultrie and had to turn back.

Anderson sent a note of protest to Pickens asking him to disavow the firing on the U.S. flag. If Pickens refused, Anderson asserted he would not allow any vessel to come within range of Fort Sumter's guns. Pickens refused to disavow the action.

Instead the governor began to increase measures to add more artillery coverage of Fort Sumter. Once the fort was thoroughly covered by land batteries, he sent a note on 11 January 1861 asking Anderson to surrender the fort. Anderson refused.

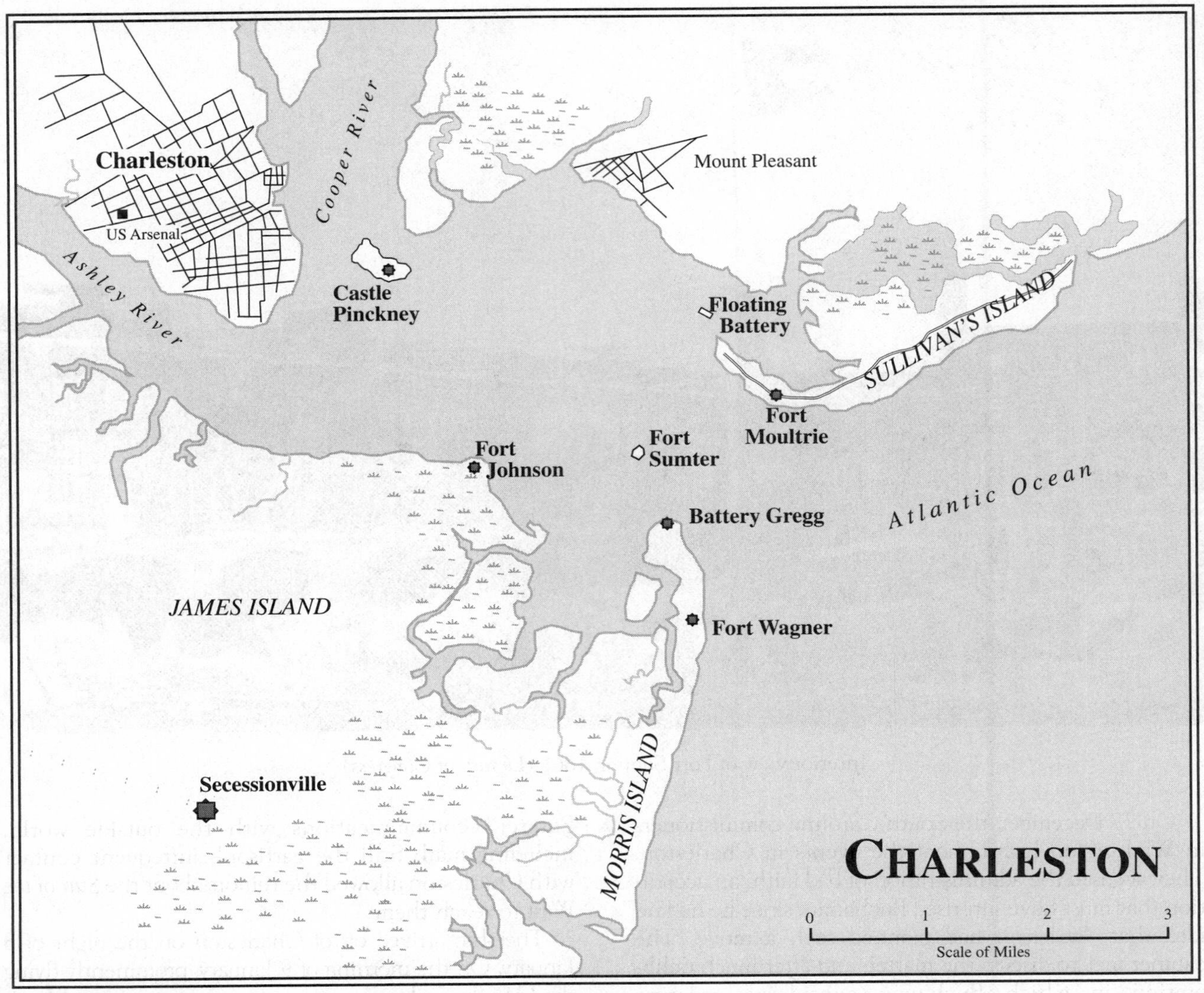

Charleston map:

Charleston

US Arsenal

Cooper River

Ashley River

Castle Pinckney

Mount Pleasant

Floating Battery

SULLIVAN'S ISLAND

Fort Moultrie

Fort Johnson

Fort Sumter

Battery Gregg

Atlantic Ocean

JAMES ISLAND

Fort Wagner

MORRIS ISLAND

Secessionville

CHARLESTON

0   1   2   3
Scale of Miles

Pickens also sent another emissary, Isaac W. Hayne, to Washington to insist on the evacuation of Fort Sumter. The governor used the time taken during these unofficial negotiations to give South Carolina more time to build up Charleston's harbor defenses. The negotiations ended in early February, and Hayne returned home.

While these negotiations were going on, Fort Sumter was running low on supplies. The news that the men at the fort were low on food put Pickens in a bad light among moderates, and as a result he sent some food to the fort on 20 January. Anderson sent the provisions back with a message that the men would do without until the garrison was allowed to purchase what it needed as it always had. To ease the food crisis Anderson received permission from Pickens to send forty-five women and children to New York. Pickens also allowed mail to come and go from the fort once again.

Pickens was under a great deal of pressure from radicals to do something and from moderates to do nothing.

President Buchanan, while also under pressure, was determined to leave the situation to his successor, Abraham Lincoln. Lincoln's future secretary of state, William Henry Seward, thinking he was far more qualified to solve this problem than Lincoln, was already working on what he believed would be a peaceful solution. At the same time in Washington, the Peace Convention tried to work out a compromise that would restore the Union. While the convention deliberated, the Confederate States of America was being formed in Montgomery, Alabama.

There things stood, with Anderson sitting and waiting for instructions, when on 1 March 1861, new Confederate brigadier general P. G. T. Beauregard arrived in Charleston, sent from new Confederate president Jefferson Davis to take command of the military situation in Charleston. Ironically, Beauregard had been one of Anderson's artillery students at West Point.

On 4 March 1861, Abraham Lincoln was inaugurated

President of the United States. Shortly after his inauguration, Lincoln received a report from Anderson that he was low on supplies and that he would need reinforcements and naval support to hold his position. Major General Winfield Scott, commanding general of the U.S. Army, recommended evacuation of the fort. Seward agreed, as did most of the cabinet, with the exception of Postmaster General Montgomery Blair.

In the meantime, the Confederate government had sent Martin J. Crawford, John Forsyth, and A. B. Roman as commissioners to Washington to negotiate the evacuation of the remaining forts in Confederate territory. Although he could not meet with these emissaries lest it be interpreted as official recognition, Seward began dealing with them through intermediaries. He gave the decided impression that at least Fort Sumter and possibly all of the forts would be evacuated. Seward made this implication while Lincoln was still mulling the question and under increasing pressure from Blair to reinforce Fort Sumter.

While all of these machinations were taking place in Washington, Beauregard continued the work of strengthening the defenses of the harbor entrance and the gun emplacements facing Fort Sumter. The garrison had briefly been allowed to buy food in Charleston, but by early March was no longer permitted to do so. The men were still receiving mail but had not heard anything from Lincoln's War Department. The unofficial reports that they were to be evacuated did reach the fort.

The Lincoln administration wanted to learn the condition of the fort and its occupants before reaching a decision, and so, during March 1861, it sent several unofficial emissaries to Charleston to determine the situation. Former naval officer Gustavus V. Fox, who had already proposed a reinforcement plan to the administration, came and was allowed to visit the fort. He learned after talking briefly with Anderson that the garrison would be out of food by about 15 April. Lincoln's friend Ward Lamon also came and gained a good deal of information by claiming to be there to arrange the fort's evacuation.

Since the evacuation seemed imminent, Beauregard and Anderson began exchanging notes on how it would be handled, but, much to everyone's chagrin, no official instructions arrived from Washington. Anderson wrote anxiously to Washington on 3 April that the men were dangerously low on food, but still no instructions arrived.

Seward had been working almost nonstop in trying to persuade the president to remove the garrison from the fort. He argued that holding Fort Pickens at Pensacola would be enough of a symbolic gesture and that that fort should be reinforced. Instead of taking Seward's advice, however, the president decided to send relief expeditions to both forts. The Fort Sumter expedition was to be prepared under the direction of Fox.

On 6 April, State Department clerk Robert L. Chew was sent to South Carolina to inform Pickens that a supply expedition was being sent to Fort Sumter, leaving it up to Confederate authorities as to whether there would be war. Chew arrived on the night of 8 April and immediately met with Pickens. Anderson also received a letter from Secretary of War Simon Cameron, his first, informing him of the relief expedition. Shortly afterward, mail was stopped to and from Fort Sumter.

Fox departed from New York on 10 April, unaware that his best warship, the USS *Powhatan*, due to the machinations of Seward, had been diverted to the Fort Pickens expedition.

Everything was happening very fast now. President Davis had been informed immediately regarding Lincoln's message to Pickens. After cabinet deliberations, Confederate secretary of war Leroy Pope Walker sent a telegram to Beauregard instructing him to demand the fort's surrender and to reduce it if the surrender request was refused. Before doing so, however, Beauregard began moving men and equipment around in preparation for the artillery assault on Fort Sumter and to prevent landings by the relief expedition.

Finally, on the afternoon of 11 April, Beauregard sent James Chesnut, Captain Stephen D. Lee, and A. R. Chisolm to Fort Sumter to demand its surrender. After polling his officers, who unanimously opposed surrender, Anderson wrote out a refusal. Anderson then went with the emissaries to their boat and told them that the garrison was nearly out of food and would have to surrender soon anyway. When Beauregard learned of this, he telegraphed the news to Walker, who wanted to know exactly how long it would be before Anderson surrendered. As a result, the original commissioners were sent back to the fort a little after midnight on 12 April to ask how long the food could last. After lengthy discussions with his officers, Anderson, hoping that the relief expedition would arrive soon, said that he would surrender at noon on 15 April. Chesnut replied that that was not soon enough and that firing would commence in about one hour, 4:30 A.M. The commissioners then left. After a signal gun was fired at 4:30 alerting all of the batteries, elderly Virginia fire-eater Edmund Ruffin was given the honor of firing the first gun at Fort Sumter.

Anderson had made the decision that only the guns from his lower casemates would be used in returning fire so as to minimize casualties. He had only nine officers, sixty-eight noncommissioned officers and privates, eight musicians, and forty-three construction workers in the fort. He could not afford to lose any of them if he was to defend the fort. He also needed to conserve ammunition. Therefore, the guns from Fort Sumter did not begin to return fire until a little before 7:00 A.M. on 12 April. Captain Abner Doubleday fired the first return shot.

Later in the morning, the barracks caught fire and

many of the men had to be used as a fire crew, but the end of the ordeal seemed in sight when in the afternoon the garrison spotted three ships flying the U.S. flag off the harbor bar. They believed that they would be reinforced and supplied during the night. Fox, out in the Atlantic watching the spectacular show in the harbor, did not realize that the *Powhatan* was not coming but did know that the ships he had could not make it past the harbor entrance batteries, so he waited.

During the night Anderson ceased firing, and the Confederates reduced their fire but resumed a full bombardment the next morning. Despite the fact that it was a rainy day, the barracks caught fire again and the flames threatened to spread to the magazine. The fire made life miserable for the men in the fort. At about 1:00 P.M. the flagstaff was shot away. The flag was retrieved and put up on the ramparts on a makeshift staff.

When he saw the flag shot away, Texas fire-eater and former U.S. senator Louis Wigfall, who had volunteered to serve as an aide to Beauregard, decided without consulting anyone to row out to Fort Sumter to determine if Anderson was trying to surrender. When he arrived, Wigfall was told that the fort was not surrendering, so he suggested to Anderson that he could surrender on the same terms as originally suggested. Such terms would allow the men to take their guns and property and to fire a salute to the U.S. flag. Anderson decided that further resistance was futile and that the fires were still a danger, so he agreed. Wigfall then left. At about 1:30 P.M. the U.S. flag was replaced with a white sheet. Meanwhile, Beauregard, who knew nothing of Wigfall's mission, sent Stephen D. Lee, Roger Pryor, and William Porcher Miles to the fort. When they found out about Wigfall's mission they told Anderson that Wigfall was not authorized to grant any terms. Anderson then said that he would not surrender under any other terms and that the fighting would continue. After some deliberation, the three commissioners agreed to the original terms and set the time for the surrender to occur the following day, 14 April.

The people of Charleston, who had watched the bombardment from the city's battery and rooftops, now came out in boats on 14 April to watch the evacuation of the fort and the firing of the final salute. Halfway through what was to be a 100-gun salute, one of the cartridges exploded prematurely, killing Private Daniel Hough and mortally wounding Private Edward Galloway. After burying Hough at the fort, the remaining men marched out to the band playing "Yankee Doodle." They were then taken by boat out to the relief ships they had been watching with such hope and disappointment.

On 15 April 1861, President Abraham Lincoln called for 75,000 volunteers to suppress the rebellion.

—*David S. Heidler and Jeanne T. Heidler*

See also Anderson, Robert; Beauregard, Pierre Gustave Toutant; Ruffin, Edmund; Seward, William Henry.
For further reading:
Klein, Maury. *Days of Defiance: Sumter, Secession, and the Coming of the Civil War* (1997).
Swanberg, W. A. *First Blood: The Story of Fort Sumter* (1957).

FORT WAGNER, BATTLE OF
18 July 1863

The storming of Fort Wagner typified the poorly planned frontal assaults launched by so many Civil War commanders. It ended in a bloody repulse for the Union attackers. The only consolation the Northern public found in the disaster was the self-sacrificing bravery displayed by the 54th Massachusetts Volunteer Infantry Regiment, which was cited as proof that black soldiers could fight and die as well as whites.

In the summer of 1863, Brigadier General Quincy A. Gillmore, the commander of the Union Department of the South, assembled 11,000 infantry, 350 artillery, and 400 engineers to besiege Charleston, South Carolina. Gillmore intended to seize Morris Island, a 400-acre barrier island on the southern side of Charleston harbor. Cummings Point, the northern tip of Morris Island, sat just 1,390 yards from Fort Sumter, the Confederate stronghold controlling entry to Charleston harbor. Gillmore expected he could easily neutralize Fort Sumter with heavy rifled artillery placed on Cummings Point. That would permit Union warships under Rear Admiral John A. Dahlgren to approach Charleston and compel its surrender.

On the morning of 10 July 1863, Union infantry landed on lower Morris Island. Supported by batteries on nearby Folly Island and naval gunfire, the Federals quickly secured most of their objective. All that stood between them and full possession of Morris Island was Fort Wagner, a massive earthwork located 1,200 yards south of Cummings Point.

Fort Wagner stretched 630 feet from east to west, and 275 feet from north to south. Its walls consisted of sand piled 30 feet high and held in place by turf, sandbags, and palmetto logs. Two bastions projected from the south wall, which was shielded by a moat 50 feet wide and 5 feet deep. A sturdy bombproof shelter inside the southeast bastion could hold 900 men. Ten heavy guns and one seacoast mortar looked over Fort Wagner's ramparts, eight of them pointing south.

The only way for Gillmore's troops to approach Fort Wagner was along a beach no more than 100 yards wide. Bordered on the east by the Atlantic Ocean and on the west by marshy Vincent's Creek, this narrow corridor offered the Federals no cover or room to maneuver.

Underestimating Fort Wagner's strength, Gillmore tried to take the place with a simple surprise attack. Three Federal regiments rushed Fort Wagner at first light

The storming of Fort Wagner (*Library of Congress*)

on 11 July, but vigilant Confederate defenders blasted their assailants to a standstill, inflicting 339 casualties.

Gillmore decided to storm Fort Wagner again, but only after thorough artillery preparation. Between 12 and 16 July, his engineers erected four batteries containing forty-one guns and siege mortars at ranges of 1,330 to 1,920 yards from the rebel works. In the meantime, the Confederates relieved Fort Wagner's garrison with fresh troops and increased the post's armament to eleven guns and one mortar aiming south, two guns facing seaward, and two field pieces covering the beach.

At 9:00 A.M. on 18 July, Gillmore's batteries started pounding Fort Wagner. Admiral Dahlgren joined in with five monitors, one ironclad frigate, and five wooden gunboats. The Federals subjected Fort Wagner to the most intensive bombardment of the war, but the 9,000 projectiles hurled at the fort did minimal damage. The 1,620-man garrison lost only eight killed and twenty wounded under that terrible iron storm.

To capture Fort Wagner, Gillmore chose Brigadier General Truman Seymour's infantry division, fourteen regiments mustering 6,000 effectives. At the head of Seymour's assault column stood the 54th Massachusetts,

the Union army's model black regiment. The rest of Seymour's division stretched a mile down the beach.

At 7:45 P.M., the 54th Massachusetts received the signal to commence the assault, and the black soldiers marched resolutely toward Fort Wagner, 1,200 yards away. Confident that Gillmore's bombardment had either killed the fort's defenders or driven them toward Cummings Point, Seymour committed his division piecemeal, a brigade at a time. The attacking regiments were shot to pieces as they neared Fort Wagner. Portions of the 54th Massachusetts and other Northern units penetrated the fort at two points, but they lacked the numbers to overrun the hard-fighting garrison. After Seymour's first two brigades shattered themselves against Fort Wagner, Gillmore refused to let the third go forward and called an end to the slaughter.

This embarrassing failure cost Gillmore 1,515 casualties, including the lives of two brigade commanders. Seymour himself was wounded by a shell fragment. The 54th Massachusetts suffered 272 killed, wounded, and missing, the greatest losses among any of the attacking regiments, but its performance vindicated the Union army's decision to recruit black soldiers. Wagner's defenders suffered only 222 casualties. Gillmore would have to resort to a formal siege before the fort fell into his hands two months later.

—Gregory J. W. Urwin

See also African-American Soldiers U.S.A.; Gillmore, Quincy; Shaw, Robert Gould; South Carolina.

For further reading:
Adams, Virginia M., ed. On the Altar of Freedom: A Black Soldier's Civil War Letters from the Front (1991).
Duncan, Russell, ed. Blue-Eyed Child of Fortune: The Civil War Letters of Colonel Robert Gould Shaw (1992).
Emilio, Luis. A Brave Black Regiment: The History of the Fifty-fourth Regiment of Massachusetts Volunteer Infantry, 1863–1865 (1995).
Wise, Stephen R. Gate of Hell: Campaign for Charleston Harbor, 1863 (1994).
Yacovone, Donald, ed. A Voice of Thunder: The Civil War Letters of George E. Stephens (1997).

FORT WARREN, MASSACHUSETTS

Work on Fort Warren began in 1833 and lasted until the beginning of the Civil War. Named after Major General Joseph Warren, killed at the battle of Bunker Hill, the star-shaped fort with ten-foot-thick granite walls protected the channel to Boston harbor from Georges Island, seven miles southeast of the city. Once the Civil War began, it served as a training center for a number of Massachusetts regiments. The song "John Brown's Body" ("The Battle Hymn of the Republic" was later written by Julia Ward Howe to be sung to the same tune) was composed at the fort and was first sung by troops stationed there during the war.

As the summer of 1861 progressed, Union victories along the Atlantic coast added to pressure to find prison space. That fall, Fort Warren was selected as a detention site, and Colonel Justin Dimick was put in command. Told to expect 100 prisoners, he arrived at the island's dock to find 155 political prisoners and 600 prisoners of war. Lack of bedding and food became immediate problems, but Dimick strove to treat his charges humanely, even seeking help from Boston's citizens.

His efforts were successful, and conditions significantly improved. During Christmas 1861, one prisoner even singled out Dimick for a toast, saying he was a "very kind gentleman" who "appears anxious to do all he can to make our time pass off pleasantly." This level of comfort became a local election issue, as some Bostonians felt "the traitors at Fort Warren" were being treated too well.

The two most famous men held at Fort Warren during this period were James Mason and John Slidell, Confederate commissioners to Great Britain. Following threats of war from Great Britain, they and their secretaries were sent on New Year's Day 1862 to Provincetown, Massachusetts, to board a British warship and continue their journey to London.

Less than two months later, after the surrender of Fort Donelson, Tennessee, Confederate Generals Simon Buckner and Floyd Tilghman along with their field officers landed at Fort Warren. Orders from Washington, D.C., forbade the two generals from having contact with other prisoners; otherwise, they were provided with adequate shelter and food. At least one of their subordinates, in fact, felt the fare at Fort Warren was better than what he received in Confederate service.

By the end of the summer of 1862, all military prisoners had been exchanged. That fall, even the few remaining political prisoners who had refused to take the oath of allegiance were released. There would be no prisoners on Georges Island again until after the battle of Gettysburg.

Colonel Dimick transferred for health reasons late in 1863. His departure coincided with changes in federal policies regarding prisoners. First, the virtual elimination of prisoner exchanges led to overcrowding in all prisons, North and South. When prisoners at Fort Warren complained, Major Stephen Cabot, the new commander, asserted that Union prisoners suffered much greater privations.

Next, prisoners with money were prohibited from purchasing extra rations. At the close of summer of 1864, even packages sent by acquaintances were not allowed on the island.

Nonetheless, relations between the captives and their guards remained cordial, except for the cool reception given to Major Harvey Allen, the prison commandant when the war ended. Though a North Carolinian, Allen had remained loyal to the Union, so Confederate prisoners refused to acknowledge his presence.

Once hostilities ceased, prisoners continued to trickle onto the island, including Confederate vice president Alexander Stephens and Postmaster General John Reagan. By this time, however, most of the harsher rules were relaxed. Lieutenant General Richard Ewell, captured near the end of the war at Sayler's Creek, Virginia, wrote his sister from Fort Warren to say that she could again send him food to supplement his rations.

Although 5,000 prisoners were held at Fort Warren during the Civil War, a mere dozen died in captivity, a remarkable record. According to legend, at least one of the war's victims continues to walk the fort's corridors. As the story goes, a prisoner by the name of Samuel Lanier managed to inform his new bride about his exact location. She made her way to Hull, Massachusetts, and from there rowed to the island. Caught trying to free Lanier, she aimed a pistol at Colonel Dimick. The weapon exploded, killing her husband instead. For her crimes, she was hanged in a black gown used in a play at the fort.

Before the Spanish-American War, the island's armaments were upgraded, and in both world wars it served as a control center for mine-laying operations. Georges

Island was sold as surplus in 1957. It now serves as the entranceway to Boston Harbor Islands State Park.

—*Dave Page*

See also Prisons, U.S.A.

For further reading:

Finnerty, Cheryl, et al. *'96 Guide to Boston's Harbor Islands* (1996).

McLain, Minor H. "The Military Prison at Fort Warren." In *Civil War Prisons*, edited by W. B. Hesseltine (1992).

Roberts, Robert B. *Encyclopedia of Historic Forts* (1988).

FORTIFICATIONS

Fortifications were temporary works that protected defenders and impeded the advance of attackers. Different from extant forts such as Fort Monroe or Fort Sumter that were elaborately designed and often took years to construct, works like the forts that defended Washington, D.C., were built on a standard scheme closely emulating that of field fortifications. There were always some variations in design from fort to

Entrance to the mine in Fort Mahone, intended to undermine Fort Sedgwick (*Library of Congress*)

Fortifications at Yorktown, Virginia, May 1862: 13-inch seacoast mortars of Federal Battery No. 4 with officers of the 1st Connecticut Heavy Artillery (Photograph by James F. Gibson / *Library of Congress*)

fort. Generally, earthworks were fashioned into steep banks (called ramparts) at least twelve feet thick. Artillery situated along the tops of the ramparts (the parapets) was mounted on platforms to cover a broad angle of approach. The exterior formed a precipitous incline to a dry trench, beyond which abatises (timber fashioned into sharp stakes with points outward) were arranged to encircle the entire structure. Any thickets or trees that might serve as cover for an approaching enemy would be cleared, sometimes at a distance of two miles.

The main entrance to the structure was called the sally port. The fort's powder magazine contained ammunition and gunpowder kegs, so it was the most sensitive and vulnerable part of the works. It was usually circular and consisted of heavy beams on which

was piled at least ten feet of compacted dirt. Shelter for soldiers consisted of a structure called a bombproof. This also was an arrangement of dirt on a timber frame especially contrived to protect soldiers while they fired on an advancing enemy. A source of potable water, usually from a spring but from a well if necessary, was a necessity.

Field fortifications of both the major and minor type were temporary because they were fashioned to hold positions for campaigning armies that shifted according to circumstance. Major works were built both to protect defenders and impede attackers, while minor works were essentially meant to provide protection. Field fortifications usually consisted of some combination of major and minor works.

Major fieldworks resembled semipermanent works in many respects. They usually featured the dry moat at the base of ramparts, for instance. Depending on the ground, major works could consist of a series of redans, ramparts shaped like Vs with their points facing the attacker and connected by walls or trenches. Lunettes also faced their salient angles toward the enemy. These configurations had the advantage of creating overlapping or crossing fields of fire. Redoubts were breastworks (low barricades to shield riflemen) that were used in both permanent and temporary fortifications as part of a parapet. Depending on how transitory the field fortifications were, redoubts could be hastily fashioned breastworks placed to protect the flanks of trenches.

Siege or field guns formed an important part of major field fortifications. Artillery was usually arranged to fire above the parapet from a platform called a barbette or from an embrasure, which was an aperture in the parapet. Both types of mountings had advantages and disadvantages. The barbette gun could cover a broad area, but its exposed position was dangerous to its crew. The embrasure gun was shielded, but it covered only a limited angle of the field, and the embrasures could offer a determined enemy a means of accessing the parapet. Whether mounted as a barbette or at an embrasure, cannon always required a platform to prevent their becoming mired and consequently impossible to handle.

Cleared ground in front of fortifications and the moat at the base of the rampart were usually strewn with objects to hinder attackers as they advanced on the works. A series of obstacles cleverly placed could thoroughly jumble an otherwise orderly advance and subject it to merciless fire. Abatises were such an obstruction, but a variety of others were also used. Pointed stakes bristling from the ramparts (fraises) or sunk in the ground to form a fence (palisades) were typical. Chevaux-de-frise (long timbers with spikes jutting from them) were especially effective against cavalry, and wire entanglements (first used in 1863) could stall an infantry attack for the slaughtering. Barbed wire had not yet been invented and hence was never used in the Civil War.

Minor fieldworks usually consisted of rifle pits (that era's version of the foxhole) and blockhouses or stockades. Such minor fortifications could shield a soldier from enemy fire, but they were not intended to fortify against attack.

The extent of fortifications was determined by how much manpower and artillery were available and the actual situation of the works in relation to their surroundings, especially if they were to be incorporated into a larger scheme of fortification. It was the job of military engineers to fashion works from a standard set of configurations—such as redans, lunettes, and redoubts—but talented engineers could quickly adapt standard fortifica-

tions to any peculiarities of the ground or the strengths or weaknesses of the army's men and equipment.

—*David S. Heidler and Jeanne T. Heidler*

See also Artillery; Tactics.

For further reading:

Aman, Christopher Alan. "The Use of Field Fortifications during the American Civil War" (M.A. thesis, 1986).

Johnson, Wait Chatterton, and Edwin S. Hartshorn. "The Development of Field Fortifications in the Civil War." In *Professional Memoirs, Corps of Engineers, U. S. Army, and Engineer Department-At-Large* (1915).

Wright, David Russell. "Civil War Field Fortifications: An Analysis of Theory and Practical Application" (M.A. thesis, 1982).

FOSTER, ROBERT SANFORD
(1834–1903)
Union general

Born to Riley Foster and Sarah Wallace Foster in Vernon, Indiana, Robert Sanford Foster was educated locally before moving to Indianapolis to make his fortune. He apprenticed with a tinner there before deciding that that trade did not suit him. He then became a clerk in his uncle's dry goods store.

At the outbreak of the Civil War, Foster helped raise a local company and was elected its captain. The company was incorporated into Colonel Lew Wallace's ninety-day 11th Indiana Infantry. Foster and his men saw their first action in June 1861 at Romney, Virginia. Shortly thereafter, Foster transferred to a long-term regiment, the 13th Indiana, in which he was given the rank of major. Placed in the brigade of Brigadier General William S. Rosecrans, Foster and the 13th fought at Rich Mountain, Virginia, on 11 July 1861.

Foster continued to serve in western Virginia through the fall of 1861, and in October of that year he became the lieutenant colonel of the 13th Indiana. Serving in James Shields's division of Nathaniel P. Banks's V Corps during the Shenandoah Valley campaign of the spring of 1862, Foster was promoted to colonel of his regiment in April 1862 and commanded it through the campaign. In early July 1863, Foster and his regiment were ordered to remove to the York Peninsula, where they participated in the final phases of the retreat of the Army of the Potomac to Harrison's Landing.

Foster and the 13th remained at Harrison's Landing until the end of the year when Foster was made commander of the 1st Provisional Brigade as part of the defenses of Suffolk, Virginia. He commanded his brigade through the siege of the city conducted by James Longstreet from 11 April through 4 May 1863 and was commended by his commander, Major General John J. Peck, for his actions during the siege.

For the next two months, Foster commanded his

brigade out of Fort Monroe up the York Peninsula as part of the Union efforts to divert Confederate military strength back toward Richmond. In August he and his brigade were sent to South Carolina, where they were stationed on Folly Island during the operations against Charleston. Before leaving Virginia, Foster was promoted to brigadier general with a date of rank of 12 June 1863.

Foster remained on Folly Island until January 1864. During his time there, he came to the attention of the commander of the Department of the South, Quincy Adams Gillmore. Gillmore was so impressed with young Foster that he placed him in command of a portion of the north end of Folly Island. With the defenses of northeast Florida in a precarious state in early 1864, Foster and his brigade were sent to Jacksonville in January. Foster's primary job was to aid in strengthening the defenses of the city and clearing the surrounding area of Confederate forces. His task accomplished, Foster and his men were summoned back to South Carolina in April 1864.

After a short stay on Hilton Head, the entire X Corps, of which Foster's brigade was a part and Gillmore the commander, was ordered to report to Benjamin F. Butler and the Army of the James at Bermuda Hundred, Virginia. Upon arrival, Gillmore made Foster the chief of staff for X Corps for the upcoming campaign against Richmond.

Preferring combat duty to staff work, Foster's request for return to brigade command was granted in June 1864. Shortly after receiving the command, he and his men established a Federal base at Deep Bottom near Richmond. From that point through the summer of 1864, Foster operated the Confederate defenses of Richmond in cooperation with larger Federal forces, most notably during the major Union offensive from 13 to 20 August.

In September Foster and his brigade moved to the trenches of Petersburg where they remained until the final weeks of the war. Foster's abilities were recognized in October 1864, when he was given command of his division. At the end of the year, X Corps was abolished and its units became a part of the XXIV Corps. Foster served briefly as chief of staff of the new corps and then commander of the corps' 1st Division. In the waning days of the campaign against Petersburg, on 2 April 1865 Foster led his division in the attack against Fort Gregg. He was cited for gallantry by both Edward Ord and John Gibbon for this offensive.

After the surrender of Robert E. Lee, Foster commanded his division in Richmond briefly before being ordered to Washington, D.C. During the summer, he was one of the board of officers who heard the evidence and returned the conviction against the Lincoln conspirators. Foster remained in the army for two months after the executions, but resigned his volunteer commission in September 1865 to return to Indianapolis.

When the army was reorganized in 1866, Foster was offered a regular commission but declined. He spent the remainder of his life in Indianapolis serving in a variety of city government jobs and a brief stint as a U.S. marshal. He was also active in the Grand Army of the Republic. He died in Indianapolis on 3 March 1903.

—*David S. Heidler and Jeanne T. Heidler*

See also Deep Bottom; Lincoln Assassination; Suffolk.

For further reading:
Smith, Charles W. *Life and Military Services of Brevet-Major General Robert S. Foster* (1915).

FOSTER, STEPHEN COLLINS
(1826–1864)
Composer and poet

When Stephen Collins Foster died at the early age of thirty-seven, he supposedly had nothing in his pockets but 38 cents and a note saying "Dear friends and gentle hearts," possibly the starting line for yet another typical Foster-style sentimental song. In another version of his end, the papers he had on himself were the manuscript of "Beautiful Dreamer," which came out on 10 March 1864, two months after his death. It is one of his songs that continues to be popular to this day. In 1864, however, the names of Henry Clay Work, George Frederick Root, and Daniel Emmett certainly superseded Foster's in the public mind. Few of Foster's many songs and arrangements had been published under his own name, and millions of people apparently sang or hummed "The Camptown Races" or "My Old Kentucky Home" with no idea of who had written the tunes or the words.

Foster's songs and tunes have been divided into three categories: comical, sentimental, and pathetic (that is, drawing on pathos as the main sentimental component). Foster scored popular successes in all three categories, mostly in the decade preceding the war. About three of every four of his songs fall into the sentimental category, the most popular of which was probably "Old Folks at Home" (also known as "Swanee Ribber"), which German-exile writer Ottilie Assing heard "cranked out by a thousand hurdy-gurdies" in New York in 1853 and described as being as popular as "Yankee Doodle."

"Old Folks at Home" may actually refer to the expulsion of the Seminoles, including the numerous African-Seminoles, from Florida and notably the Suwannee River area after the Seminole Wars, when many of them were transferred to the Indian Territory. This immediate reference to the loss of home and family was never acknowledged in the popular reaction to the song. Instead, "Old Folks at Home" was understood in a context determined by Harriet Beecher Stowe's *Uncle Tom's Cabin* and the numerous "Tom" and "Anti-Tom" novels, dramatic adaptations, poems, and songs that appeared throughout the

1850s. In fact, it was seen as using the approach to slavery delineated in antebellum literature by authors such as William Gilmore Simms. Foster himself used the same approach in "Ring de Banjo": "Once I was so lucky/My massa set me free/I went to old Kentucky/to see what I could see/I could not go no farder/I turn to massa's door/I lub him all the harder/I'll go away no more." According to this literary myth, slaves did not want to be free because they lacked the ability to live and prosper under the conditions of freedom. The rhetorical construction of the myth cleverly puts it into the "darkie's" own mouth in fabricated "oral" form. In view of Foster's clearly Unionist leanings during the sectional conflict, it is ironic that he, however unwittingly, contributed to the longevity of one of the more insidious myths that grew out of slavery and the Civil War. Because of their popularity, his "comic" songs in particular were supposed to draw on "genuine" African-American examples. As a matter of musicological fact, they, like his sentimental songs, are more closely related to European and Euro-American conventions.

With his successes from the 1840s and 1850s, such as "Oh! Susannah" and "Jeanie," Foster set the musical scene for the Civil War period. During the last years of his life, Foster was writing and composing at a fast rate, but even though he worked in partnership with another poet, George Cooper, few of their products matched the popularity of Foster's earlier songs. Still, one may assume that these songs and their parodies ("Hard Tack Come Again No More") were sung more often in soldiers' camps than many of the verses expressly written and published for the armies on behalf of one side or the other.

—Wolfgang Hochbruck

See also Music.

For further reading:

Assing, Ottilie. "The Tombs—The Washington Exhibition—The Minstrels." In *Radical Passion: O. Assing's Reports on America and Letters to F. Douglass* (1999).

Austin, William W. "Susanna," "Jeanie," and "The Old Folks at Home." In *The Songs of Stephen C. Foster from His Time to Ours* (1975).

Elliker, Calvin. *Stephen Collins Foster: A Guide to Research* (1988).

Saunders, Steven. *The Music of Stephen Collins Foster: A Critical Edition* (1990).

FOX, GUSTAVUS VASA
(1821–1883)
Union naval officer

Gustavus Fox was born in Saugus, Essex County, Massachusetts. His father was a country doctor of moderate means. At the age of sixteen, young Fox was appointed midshipman in the navy, where he remained for eighteen years and had a varied career. He served in the Mediterranean, East Indian, Pacific, Brazil, and African squadrons, participated in the naval operations of the Mexican War, and for a time assisted in the work of the Coastal Survey. In 1852 Fox won a promotion to lieutenant and for the next four years he commanded a mail steamer, which traveled between New York and the Isthmus of Panama. In July 1856 he resigned from the navy and accepted the position of agent of the Bay State Woolen Mills (textiles), at Lawrence, Massachusetts.

Early in 1861 when South Carolina demanded the surrender of Fort Sumter in Charleston harbor, Fox presented a sound relief plan to General Winfield Scott, commanding general of the U.S. Army. Fox so impressed General Scott that he introduced the bald, goateed, heavily mustached Fox to Secretary of War Joseph Holt, who in turn laid Fox's plan before President James Buchanan.

Fox's plan was based on the simple idea that, given the factors of surprise, speed, low visibility, or any combination of these, the Confederate batteries watching Fort Sumter could be run with acceptable risks. Depending on the circumstances, he would use either fast, heavily armed, shallow-draft tugs or iron whale boats. A small fleet of warships would lend support just outside the waters that surrounded the narrow ship channel leading into Charleston. Once within the harbor, the small boats would be covered by Sumter's guns. If feasible, elements of the supporting fleet might even enter the channel and join in the bombardment of Charleston's defenses or deal with any hostile vessels. Fox requested to be placed in charge of everything except the actual command of the warships.

But President Buchanan had other things on his mind. On 8 February at Montgomery, Alabama, the Provisional Congress of the Confederate States of America voted to accept the constitution for their new "nation," and elected Jefferson Davis president. In regard to the Fort Sumter plan, President Buchanan had decided to make no further efforts to relieve the fort.

On 4 March 1861 Abraham Lincoln became the sixteenth president of the United States. Following his inauguration, Lincoln received word from Sumter's commander, Major Robert Anderson, that the garrison had only a month's provisions left—maybe forty days if they conserved food. Lincoln convened his cabinet and asked if it would be prudent to provision Sumter. The cabinet consulted with General Scott, Gustavus Fox, and other high-ranking naval officers.

Most of Lincoln's cabinet thought that resupplying Sumter would not be a good idea. Secretary of State William Seward hesitated because he was still negotiating with Southern commissioners in Washington through intermediaries for the peaceful evacuation of the fort. Secretary of the Navy Welles, because of the resignations of Southern naval officers, the weakened

status of the U.S. Navy, and the fact that he thought that the relief expedition would result in a civil war, advised against Fox's plan. The only member of Lincoln's cabinet to agree that it was the right time to provision Fort Sumter was Postmaster General Montgomery Blair, Fox's brother-in-law. Blair felt that provisioning Sumter would "vindicate the hardy courage of the North, and the determination of the people and their President to maintain the authority of the Government."

On 12 March, Blair ushered Fox into Lincoln's office. After explaining his plan to the president, Fox suggested that he should take a trip to Charleston to assess the situation himself. When he got there he found Major Anderson in a dejected mood. Anderson believed that the navy could do nothing to alleviate the situation and that nothing short of 10,000 men could force the issue ashore. Fox thought otherwise, but after investigating the harbor defenses, he saw that Anderson was right. Unless actions were taken soon, Sumter would surely fall within the next three weeks. On his return late in the month, Fox convinced the president that his plan was feasible. On 29 March Lincoln reached the decision to relieve Fort Sumter.

Secretary of the Navy Welles promptly ordered the commandants at the Brooklyn, Washington, and Norfolk navy yards to make ready the *Pawnee*, *Harriet Lane*, and the powerful steam sloop *Powhatan*. The *Powhatan* had returned to New York from Vera Cruz on 14 March and on 28 March Welles had ordered her placed out of commission. Now, after the decision to resupply Sumter came, he ordered the *Powhatan* to be prepared for sea service. Welles felt that the powerful *Powhatan* would provide added insurance for Fox's plan. Fox himself chartered the steamer *Baltic* and three tugs, one of which, the *Yankee*, he equipped with a weapon to shoot hot water. All was ready.

Fox sailed from New York on 10 April with transports carrying 200 troops, provisions, and supplies. But along the way, the relief force ran into a bad storm, delaying its arrival. It finally arrived off Charleston early on the twelfth, where Fox expected to join the assigned naval vessels. Two of them were already there, but the *Powhatan* failed to appear. Unbeknownst to Fox and everyone else associated with the Sumter relief expedition, the *Powhatan* had been secretly reassigned to an expedition against Fort Pickens in Pensacola, Florida. As it happened, however, the confusion did not matter because by the time it was discovered, Sumter's hour had already come.

Confederate commissioners in Washington sent frantic messages to their government about the relief expedition and its final destination. The latter was clarified on 8 April; a special emissary from Lincoln arrived in Charleston to inform General P. G. T. Beauregard, commander of Confederate forces in Charleston, and Governor Pickens of South Carolina that Fort Sumter was shortly to be reprovisioned peaceably, but by force if necessary.

When Jefferson Davis learned this, with his cabinet's approval he authorized Beauregard to demand the surrender of the fort at his discretion. The surrender demand was made on 10 April, but Major Anderson rejected it. A bombardment of the fort commenced on 12 April, the day Fox arrived off the harbor, and Major Anderson was forced to surrender late the next day. The bombardment signaled the beginning of the American Civil War. Gustavus Fox was not done however. He was given the "honor" of transporting Major Anderson and his troops north from Sumter instead of reinforcing them.

The energy, tact, and initiative that Fox showed in the Sumter expedition, plus his family connections—his father-in-law Francis P. Blair was one of the leaders at the National Republican convention of 1860 and his brother-in-law Montgomery Blair was Lincoln's postmaster general—gave him a great deal of political capital. Consequently, on 9 May 1861 Fox was appointed chief clerk of the Navy Department. After a short stint as chief clerk, he was promoted to assistant secretary of the navy, a newly created position, which he held from August 1861 to May 1866.

At first, Secretary of the Navy Gideon Welles was skeptical of his new assistant, but he soon found Fox to be energetic, resourceful, and loyal. Fox supplied the operational and technical expertise that Welles lacked, and though some of Welles's critics jeered that he was a "puppet" in Fox's hands, the two men complemented each other perfectly. Fox provided new ideas, ranging from the brilliant to the impractical, while Welles steered their direction. Together, the inflexible Welles and his ebullient aide located the funds, built the ships, and recruited the officers and men in sufficient numbers to transform the United States Navy into one of the most powerful forces in the world.

In addition to serving as an invaluable aid to Secretary Welles, Fox promoted the construction and deployment of vessels of the monitor class and applied his extensive knowledge of naval affairs in highly productive ways. It was Fox who planned the expedition against New Orleans in 1862, suggested David G. Farragut as its commander, and planned the opening of the Mississippi River.

Fox resigned his position as assistant secretary of the navy in 1866. In that same year, to show his confidence in the seaworthiness of armored vessels, Fox went with an impressive naval escort that included the *Miantonomoh*, the first monitor to cross the Atlantic, on a diplomatic mission to Russia. While there he negotiated informally for the purchase of Alaska for the United States. He then returned to the United States and devoted the rest of his life to the woolens business. He died in New York City on 29 October 1883.

—*Michael S. Davis*

See also Anderson, Robert; Fort Sumter; *Monitor*, USS; Navy, U.S.A.; Welles, Gideon.

For further reading:

Hayes, John D. "Captain Fox—He Is the Navy Department." *United States Naval Institute Proceedings* (1965).

Macartney, Clarence Edward. *Mr. Lincoln's Admirals* (1956).

Musicant, Ivan. *Divided Waters: The Naval History of the Civil War* (1995).

Niven, John. *Gideon Welles: Lincoln's Secretary of the Navy* (1973).

Thompson, Robert M., and Richard Wainwright, eds. *Confidential Correspondence of Gustavus Vasa Fox, Assistant Secretary of the Navy,* 1861–1865 (1918).

FRANCE
See Mercier, Henri; Napoleon III

FRANK LESLIE'S ILLUSTRATED NEWSPAPER

The first issue of the weekly journal, *Frank Leslie's Illustrated Newspaper* (FLIN) was published in December of 1855. *FLIN* was not unique, nor even a new idea. Its editor and publisher, "Frank Leslie" drew on his experience as an illustrator for the *Illustrated London News*, but expanded and marketed that model in ways that made *FLIN* the first truly mass-market illustrated news purveyor, the *Life* magazine of its time. *FLIN* was a major news source for thousands of U.S. and European readers hungry for information on the Civil War.

Henry Carter, the creator and publisher of *FLIN*, was born on 29 March 1821 in Suffolk, England. In 1838 Carter moved to London, where, using the name "Frank Leslie," he began submitting drawings and woodcuts to journals and publishers. By 1842 he had abandoned any use of his birth name, and it was as Frank Leslie that he joined the staff of the *Illustrated London News*, the leading mass-market journal in London at the time. Leslie stayed with the *News* until 1848, eventually becoming the head of the engraving department. At the *Illustrated London News*, Leslie learned both the technical skills needed to support newspaper illustration and how to run a successful newspaper.

In 1848, Leslie emigrated to the United States and opened his own engraving office. One of his first customers was P. T. Barnum, for whom he illustrated the programs used for Jenny Lind's 1850–1851 U.S. tour. Leslie continued to work with Barnum, as well as with several U.S. publishing firms, for the next few years, while planning his own publishing enterprise. His first efforts were *Frank Leslie's Ladies Gazette of Fashion* and *Frank Leslie's New York Journal of Romance*, both of which were begun in 1854 and both of which immediately became profitable. With the profits from these enterprises, Leslie was ready to launch a national general interest journal, which he named, as was his pattern,

Frank Leslie's Illustrated Newspaper. Throughout the firm's long life, *FLIN* was the flagship and most important—if not always the most profitable—of Leslie's journals.

A typical issue of *FLIN* included something for everyone. News from across the nation and the world was always included, as were columns on sports, travel, and the arts, including music. Book reviews, fiction, and poetry were regularly included, as were "gossip" items. Illustrated jokes, resembling single-panel cartoons, also appeared.

Many contemporary observers criticized the paper for its focus on the sensational, saying that Leslie was willing to print anything that would help sell papers. *FLIN* did eagerly cover society murders and other notable crimes and scandals of every sort. The newspaper also published many serial stories and shorter one-issue pieces of fiction that were often full of romance and mayhem and often illustrated with images of high fashion or high drama. Extended coverage was given to any dramatic event. For example, *FLIN* was happy to give ample space to recounting the exploits of American adventurers such as General William Walker and his filibusters in Nicaragua. At times, the firm was not above "creating" news, as it did with a series of investigative reports and illustrations on what they called the New York City "milk swill" scandal. But in response to his critics, Leslie argued that, far from being merely sensationalist, *FLIN* was giving the public information it wanted and needed. He was especially proud of the effects of *FLIN's* "milk swill" effort, which is today recognized as an early example of investigative reporting that ultimately helped to change the laws in New York and provide safer milk for everyone in the city.

In the years between 1855 and the start of the Civil War, *FLIN* could be described as politically neutral, though leaning toward the Democratic Party and favoring compromise on the slavery issue. But despite his political views, Leslie almost always recognized and went after the "good story." One of the most dramatic and popular of *FLIN's* early pictorial stories was its coverage of John Brown's raid on Harper's Ferry. The paper's coverage was more complete and immediate than that of any other journal of the day, and the issues that included news of the Harper's Ferry raid and its aftermath sold out.

Frank Leslie's personal distaste for the Republican Party's politics did affect the paper's approach to the 1860 presidential campaign. Most Republican events were ignored. Nevertheless, Leslie was keenly aware of the news value of the coming conflict, and in January of 1861 he announced that he had an artist (William Waud) stationed in Charleston. Throughout the early months of the year, *FLIN* readers were provided with images of Fort Sumter and the troops on both sides. Then, in April, Eugene Benson, another *FLIN* artist, was also sent to the area. Benson sent back sketches of the April bombardment that were immediately transformed by the engravers working for Leslie and published in an issue that had a huge sale.

By the start of the Civil War, *Frank Leslie's Illustrated Newspaper* boasted on its masthead a circulation of 140,000 or more with readers "in every city, town and village in the United States and Canada…." Although its circulation claims may have been slightly exaggerated, readership was certainly extremely high, and each issue was probably seen by more than 100,000 U.S. residents. From its first days, *FLIN* had drawn readership from every strata of society. Group discounts on the regular 10 cents/issue price and various other kinds of promotions enabled even readers with little extra cash to follow the news in the pages of *FLIN* and to use it as a primary news source throughout the conflict. The lavish use of full-page illustrations allowed even the illiterate to learn not only about every aspect of the war but also about the celebrities and sensations of the conflict.

At least sixteen different artists worked in the field for *FLIN* during the war and produced more than 1,300 drawings. Leslie sometimes called them his "bohemian brigade," and often gave a by-line to the artist who was responsible for the original sketch on which the newspaper's illustration was based.

Joshua Brown has described the process of the production of a *FLIN* illustration from the artist's vision to finished page: The field artist sent back drawings that were evaluated by the "art superintendent." Then, a staff artist would draw a new version of the image on paper. This was in turn "rubbed down" in reverse on the whitewashed surface of a block of Turkish boxwood. The block was composed of many smaller blocks, held together with a system of nuts and bolts. After various draughtsmen had applied further details—with each taking responsibility for a specialty, figures, or architecture, or landscape, and so on—the composite block was sent to the engraving department. After the engravers, also working on the illustration piecemeal, by area of expertise, had done their work, the block would be rebolted for a review by the supervising engraver. The finished block was sent to the composing room to be locked into a page of type, and then the whole page was electrotyped onto a copper plate.

Leslie's use of multiple engravers to create large pictures more quickly (up to seven times faster than a single engraver) was an innovation that, along with his financial resources that permitted him to send reporters and artists to every major battle, helped to keep *FLIN* a leading journal throughout the war, despite unrelenting competition from the Harper Brothers' *Harper's Weekly*.

Double-page images were a common feature of *FLIN*, and sometimes more than one would appear in a single sixteen-page issue. On the occasion of *FLIN*'s first images of Gettysburg (in the 18 July 1863 issue), a four-page foldout was produced, an expensive choice, but one that was extremely popular. (The writers and artists working for Leslie immediately understood the importance of Gettysburg, not only as a battle but in the larger story of the war. In the 1 August issue, a small note about the continuing images of the battle that were being published begins, "In future years the traveller [sic] will, with a fieldbook of the civil war, visit few spots with greater respect and interest than the quiet cemetery overlooking the town of Gettysburg.")

Although Leslie's system enabled sketches to be transformed into press illustrations in about two weeks from the date of the event (a speed not matched by any competitor before the end of the war), the paper almost always had written reports of major Civil War events before pictures were ready. In some cases, the home office artists might provide a generic scene as illustration. At other times, the paper received multiple perspectives, as different artists all produced pictures of the same event. Sometimes these were used in different issues. At other times, pieces of the various pictures would be combined by the home office artists into a single illustration. Or, if a version of an event arrived too long after the event itself to have any currency, the editors might ask the New York artists to revise the image to make it more applicable to current news. *FLIN* did not advertise such editing and did not even want to admit to it. The editors instead made every effort to assure readers that the illustrations were "true" and "authentic" renderings of the war's progress.

Early in 1864, the New York Historical Society questioned the value of newspaper illustrations (both those of *FLIN* and those appearing in *Harper's Weekly* and other venues) by saying "when they are not taken from photographs [they] are not always reliable." Taking space in the first columns of the 21 May issue, Leslie responded to the criticism, arguing, "Our Artists are with every important army…and the sketches will be too numerous and valuable to give us even a temptation to invent." But any reader who pages through the volumes of the war years will begin to question whether inventions were not sometimes at work. In the very next week after Leslie's defense, the front cover illustration showed Generals Grant and Meade in "consultation" during the battle of the Wilderness—a highly stylized scene that is difficult to accept as taken from life.

Generals, battle and camp scenes, and maps of the conflict were not the only ways that *FLIN* illustrated the war. A particularly horrific cover (14 June 1864) illustrated the skeletal condition of Union prisoners of war who had been exchanged. Other illustrations were more benign, such as those showing combatants exchanging goods and greetings during a truce. There were also many scenes of the ways in which civilians were affected by the conflict. Leslie sent artists to record the various "sanitary fairs" and published floor plans of the larger fairs as well as scenes of the sales. Readers across the country were provided with images of the New York City Draft Riots and scenes of captured Southern cities, including images such as the "Recruiting Office for Contrabands" showing former slaves looking for work with the Union army in Wilmington, North Carolina (1 April 1865 issue). Having begun his coverage of the battlefields with images of Fort Sumter, Leslie sent artists to record the fort again in 1865, featuring a full two-page spread of "The Ruins of Fort Sumter" in the 25 March issue.

Recognizing the popularity of the Civil War illustrations published in *FLIN*, Leslie recycled the material in several ways. In 1861 and 1862, four special publications were created to chronicle the war: *Frank Leslie's Pictorial History of the War of 1861*; *Frank Leslie's Pictorial History of the American Civil War*; *Incidents of the Civil War in America*; and *Frank Leslie's Pictorials of Union Victories*. These compilations were, as the titles suggest, intended for export and sale to Canadian, British, and European readers as well as those in the United States. In 1865, Leslie published another compilation, *Frank Leslie's Pictorial Life of Abraham Lincoln*.

Frank Leslie died in 1880, but the firm continued under the leadership of his wife, Miriam (to whom in his will Frank Leslie left "the sole right to use the name 'Frank Leslie'"). At the end of the nineteenth century, she published three more compilations of the war materials: *Frank Leslie's Scenes and Portraits of the Civil War* (1894); *Frank Leslie's Illustrated History of the Civil War* (1895); and *Frank Leslie's Illustrated Famous Leaders and Battle Scenes of the Civil War* (1896).

The images of the Civil War published in *Frank Leslie's Illustrated Newspaper* remain striking and evocative representations of a conflict that we, like the original readers far from the battlefields, can only begin to imagine. The images also provide a way for us to begin to understand how the war appeared to contemporary readers and to see the beginnings of the images and motifs that still represent the war for us.

—JoAnn E. Castagna

See also Newspapers.
For further reading:
Brown, Joshua. "*Frank Leslie's Illustrated Newspaper*: The Pictorial Press and the Representations of America, 1855–1889" (Ph.D. dissertation, 1993).
———. "Reconstructing Representation—Social Types, Readers, and the Pictorial Press, 1865–1877." *Radical History Review* (1996).
Gambee, Budd Leslie, Jr. *Frank Leslie and His Illustrated Newspaper, 1855–1860* (1964).
Pearson, Andrea G. "*Frank Leslie's Illustrated Newspaper* and *Harper's Weekly*: Innovation and Imitation in Nineteenth-Century American Pictorial Reporting." *Journal of Popular Culture* (1990).
Stern, Madeleine Bettina. *Purple Passage, the Life of Mrs. Frank Leslie* (1953).

FRANKLIN, BATTLE OF
(30 November 1864)

General John Bell Hood stood on the high slope of Winstead Hill, just south of Franklin, Tennessee, on the afternoon of 30 November 1864. Hood appeared older than his thirty-three years, as he leaned on a crutch supporting the stump of an amputated leg, while a useless arm hung by his side, the results of wounds at Chickamauga and Gettysburg, respectively. He stood on the approximate site of the present-day battlefield map, holding a pair of field glasses to his eyes as he surveyed the Federal line on the southern edge of the little town. Immediately to the front and below Hood, two corps of the Confederate Army of Tennessee were assembled. The general was deciding whether to attack the Union position, where artillery bristled through strong earthworks fronted by abatis. Cavalry commander Nathan Bedford Forrest, infantry corps commander General Benjamin F. Cheatham, and probably others, had advised him not to make a frontal assault. But the young general did not accept their advice. Returning the field glasses to a leather case, Hood announced something to the effect that the army would make the fight.

Shortly after 4:00 P.M., on that Indian summer day, the Confederates moved forward, bands playing and regimental flags waving, as they marched across the bluegrass fields toward Franklin, where the Yankee troops waited in their formidable entrenchments. For the attackers the battle would be a terrible defeat—in some ways the worst fight in which the Army of Tennessee was ever engaged. Of a total force of about 23,000, there were 1,750 Southern troops killed. Another 5,500 men were wounded or captured. Six generals were killed, five wounded and one captured. Of 100 Confederate regimental commanders, more than 60 were killed or wounded. The Federals, with more than 15,000 engaged, suffered approximately 2,500 casualties, with about 200 of those killed. Clearly, General Hood had made an awful mistake in launching a frontal assault at Franklin.

The background for the Franklin battle began with the conclusion of the Atlanta campaign. After the Confederate evacuation of Atlanta, Hood hoped to draw General William T. Sherman away from that city by attacking his railroad supply line in north Georgia. Sherman sent some forces to give chase, briefly, but then stopped, complaining that Hood could twist and turn until his army would be worn out in pursuit. Besides, Sherman had something else in mind. He "would infinitely prefer to…move through Georgia, smashing things to the sea." For such a march, Sherman did not need a railroad, nor a base. His men would take what they needed from the countryside. In his own words: "I can make the march and make Georgia howl!"

Meanwhile, General Hood moved into north Alabama. He planned to march his army into middle Tennessee, capture Nashville, and continue north into Kentucky, maybe even Ohio, or turn east to join forces with Robert E. Lee. Hood believed that Sherman would be compelled to come after him. It was not to be. By mid-November, Sherman was moving toward Savannah and Hood toward Nashville. Sherman, ironically, thought that Hood would probably follow him. If not, General George H. Thomas must shoulder the responsibility of dealing with Hood and the Army of Tennessee.

Thomas was then at Nashville in command of the Department of the Cumberland. While he was in overall charge of the Federal troops that would be massing in Tennessee's capital to stop Hood, the actual field commander of forces deployed south of Nashville to delay Hood's advance was John M. Schofield. Schofield had been a classmate of Hood's at West Point. He had been detached by Sherman to help Thomas defend against Hood, and he commanded the IV and XXIII Army Corps, along with a small contingent of cavalry.

A Confederate flanking march almost cut Schofield off at the Duck River. Hood came even closer at Spring Hill on the afternoon of 29 November, but somehow failed—a failure never fully explained—to block the road north to Franklin. Thus Schofield's forces marched through the little town during the night. By the morning of 30 November, the Federals were in Franklin, where they occupied and strengthened the earthworks that had been prepared more than a year before. By noon the Union position was formidable.

Hood was enraged when he learned that the Federals had marched by him during the night. Proceeding to blame nearly everyone except himself, he then put the Confederates in motion toward Franklin. Somehow, by afternoon, Hood had convinced himself that for purposes of discipline and restoration of élan what the army needed was to make a frontal assault. Yet he did not do the things that might have enabled a frontal assault to succeed.

When Hood gave the signal for the advance, most of Stephen D. Lee's corps was not present, but still on the march south of Franklin. Also, most of the army's artillery was not up, but in the process of being brought forward with Lee's Corps. Thus Hood would assail the Franklin works with only two of his three corps, and artillery support would be virtually nonexistent. Worst of all, Hood did not position his troops properly for a successful attack. His hope for smashing the Federal center along the Columbia-Franklin Pike depended upon two divisions, one advancing on each side of the pike. Together, the two divisions possessed only seven brigades of the total of eighteen infantry brigades that Hood had on the field. His forces were not properly massed to achieve their objective.

The Confederate attack was in near perfect alignment, an unforgettable martial display, according to numerous witnesses. It was the last grand charge of the war. The rebel leading units overwhelmed the Federals who were stationed about a third of a mile in front of their main line and chased them into the works along the Columbia-Franklin Pike. The Confederates charged through the yard of the Carter House (still extant) only to be met by the countercharging brigade of Colonel Emerson Opdycke. Other Federals quickly rallied to drive back the Confederates and close the penetration in fierce hand-to-hand fighting. The Southerners hung on at the outer ditch of the main earthworks, only to find, some of them, that they were subjected to enfilading fire. The rebels at different points along the line made numerous separate charges usually with heavy casualties. The fighting lasted until about 10 P.M., when the sounds of guns gradually died away.

In the outer ditch, Confederate dead and dying laid five or six deep in some places. Wounded soldiers of both sides suffered further as the temperature dropped through the night. During the night, General Schofield, as he had intended all along, pulled his army out and headed for Nashville. The Confederates advanced to Nashville the next day, but the Army of Tennessee never recovered from the battle of Franklin.

—*James L. McDonough*

See also Hood, John Bell; Nashville, Battle of; Schofield, John M.; Thomas, George H.

For further reading:
McDonough, James Lee, and Thomas L. Connelly. *Five Tragic Hours: The Battle of Franklin* (1983).
Sword, Wiley. *Embrace an Angry Wind: The Confederacy's Last Hurrah—Spring Hill, Franklin, and Nashville* (1992).

FRANKLIN, WILLIAM BUEL
(1823–1903)
Union general

William Buel Franklin was a key figure in the American Civil War and an important contributor to the internal expansion of the United States before and after the nation's bloodiest conflict. Franklin is remembered primarily as the scapegoat for the disastrous Union defeat at the battle of Fredericksburg in December 1862. Yet he played significant roles in all of the early campaigns in the Eastern theater, including First Bull Run, the Peninsula, the Seven Days', Second Bull Run, and the Maryland campaign, and he was second-in-command to Nathaniel Banks during the 1864 Red River campaign in Louisiana.

Franklin was born on 27 February 1823 in York, Pennsylvania, the son of Walter and Sarah Buel Franklin. Walter was a Democrat, and by virtue of his position as clerk of the U.S. House of Representatives he had many connections with his party's leadership. Those contacts were instrumental in securing for young William in 1839 an appointment to the U.S. Military Academy.

After his graduation from West Point in 1843—he graduated first in the class; Ulysses S. Grant finished twenty-third the same year—Franklin spent most of the next eighteen years supervising various civil engineering projects as a member of the U.S. Army's Corps of Topographical Engineers. In addition to hydrographic surveys, mapping expeditions, and the construction of lighthouses and Treasury Department structures, Franklin also served as secretary of the Light House Board and just before the Civil War oversaw the construction of the dome and extension of the U.S. Capitol. By virtue of these assignments, his antebellum career essentially was that of a mid-level public administrator. Franklin, however, was destined for high-level command, and, except for brief service during the Mexican-American War on the staff of General Zachary Taylor, his military career had not prepared him for such a position.

Once the Civil War began, Franklin rose quickly in rank. He commanded a brigade in the Army of Northeastern Virginia at the battle of First Manassas, a division during the first two months of the Peninsula campaign, and the XI Corps of the Army of the Potomac from May through November 1862, a period that included the Seven Days' battles, Second Manassas, and the Maryland campaign. Franklin's ascendancy through corps-level command mainly was a result of his close friendship to the Army of the Potomac's commander, Major General George B. McClellan, also an engineer and Democrat. Franklin's career under McClellan's command was spotty, at best. During the Seven Days', Franklin performed capably, most notably at the battles of Savage's Station and White Oak Swamp Bridge. During the Second Manassas campaign, he was charged by General John Pope with failure to obey orders (later dropped), although Franklin was under the direct command of McClellan the entire time. At the battle of Crampton's Gap during the Maryland campaign, Franklin oversaw a smashing Union victory, but then failed to relieve the Union garrison at Harper's Ferry before it surrendered. The battle of Antietam was fought three days later, but only one of Franklin's brigades was committed, even though Franklin personally urged McClellan to allow him to attack the Confederate left flank.

McClellan's relief from command in the autumn of 1862 was the beginning of a chain of events that culminated in the early winter of 1863 when Franklin likewise was relieved. When Ambrose Burnside took command of the Army of the Potomac, he promoted Franklin to command the newly constituted Left Grand Division for the upcoming campaign to take Fredericksburg, Virginia. Believing that his own command was going to make the main attack on 13 December, Franklin was astounded when orders seemingly to the contrary arrived just moments before he was supposed to launch his assault. Rather than indicate that the Left Grand Division would attack in force, Burnside told Franklin to attack "with a division at least." By this point in the war, Franklin already had demonstrated that he was not an aggressive commander, and so he interpreted his orders to mean that he was not making the main attack, which in fact Burnside had intended. Franklin initially attacked with three divisions, actually exceeding his orders, and he temporarily cracked the Confederate position. A Confederate counterattack foiled this breakthrough, however, and Franklin did not follow up his early success. Franklin's attack ended in total repulse, just like the rest of attacking corps at other parts of the Union line.

In the wake of this defeat, Franklin went over Burnside's head and proposed another campaign plan directly to President Abraham Lincoln. Then two of Franklin's generals traveled to Washington and complained to Lincoln about Burnside's present plan and the poor morale in the Army of the Potomac. Franklin later claimed that he did not know his generals' reason for going to Washington, and there is no evidence to the contrary. When Burnside discovered what had happened, he drafted an order removing several generals from command, Franklin included. Although Lincoln did not allow the order to stand, he did remove Burnside and Franklin of their commands. In the ensuing months, Franklin was called to testify before the Joint Congressional Committee on the Conduct of the War, which was dominated by Radical Republicans. Looking for a scapegoat, they quickly and unfairly pinned the blame for the Fredericksburg disaster on Franklin, a conservative Democrat and well-known friend of General McClellan.

General Franklin spent five months waiting for orders, and subsequently was banished to Louisiana, where he was given command of the XIX Corps, Army of the Gulf. He commanded the army element during an army/navy operation to take Sabine Pass, Texas. The operation was botched terribly by the navy, but, as the ranking officer, Franklin shouldered the blame for this defeat, which further diminished his already tarnished career.

Franklin was wounded at the battle of Mansfield during the ill-fated Red River campaign in April 1864, ending his stint as a field commander for the remainder of the war. During the Union retreat down the Red River, the naval force under Admiral David Porter was faced with losing its ships due to low water. Franklin's chief engineer, Lieutenant Colonel Joseph Bailey, suggested the idea of building a dam at Alexandria to get the ships over the rapids there. Although both General Banks and Admiral Porter initially rejected Bailey's idea,

they changed their mind when Franklin, who was held in high regard for his engineering expertise, supported the ultimately successful plan

General Ulysses S. Grant attempted to resurrect Franklin in the summer of 1864 and give him a command in the East, but Secretary of War Edwin Stanton would not approve the idea. During his return from discussions with Grant at Petersburg in July, Franklin was taken prisoner when the train on which he was traveling was captured by Confederate partisan rangers. Even though he still suffered from his leg wound, Franklin escaped when his guard fell asleep. Franklin finished the war as president of an officers' retirement board.

In 1866 Franklin resigned from the army and became vice president of Colt's Patent Firearms Manufacturing Company in Hartford, Connecticut. His management of the company saved it from certain ruin. During the postbellum period, he also served on several federal advisory boards and was a Democratic elector during the disputed Tilden/Hayes presidential election of 1876. He also held many important civil positions in Hartford, including chief engineer for construction of a new state capitol building. Franklin was appointed president of the Board of Managers of the National Home for Disabled Volunteer Soldiers (the forerunner of the Veterans Administration), serving from 1880 through 1902. He died in Hartford on 8 March 1903 and is buried in his hometown of York, Pennsylvania. Franklin was predeceased by his wife, the former Anna Clark, with whom he had been married since 1852 and who died in 1900.

If Franklin's life is measured only by his Civil War career, he would be remembered as an average to mediocre general who allowed to slip through his fingers several golden opportunities during which he might have achieved everlasting military fame. Like his friend and mentor, George McClellan, Franklin was a conservative in politics, social values, and military strategy. Unlike McClellan, he was not very good at promoting himself. Although Franklin believed in a vigorous prosecution of the war, he was strongly opposed to emancipation, nor did he embrace the concept of total war. He was a victim of his own failings, his loyalty to McClellan, and the vindictiveness of the Radical Republicans.

Yet the Civil War filled only four years of William Franklin's eight decades. He also must be remembered for the important government projects that he supervised in the years before the war when the country was expanding its boundaries, economy, and infrastructure. The war over, he became a respected business leader who continued to serve his country, state, and community. It was only during the war that he did not rise to the heights that were expected of him.

—*Mark A. Snell*

See also Crampton's Gap, Battle of; Fredericksburg, First Battle of; Mansfield, Battle of; Red River Campaign.

For further reading:
Snell, Mark A. *Major General William B. Franklin: A Biography* (2000).

FREDERICKSBURG, FIRST BATTLE OF
(13 December 1862)

The first battle of Fredericksburg was a key battle between Robert E. Lee's Army of Northern Virginia and General Ambrose E. Burnside's Army of the Potomac. Northerners, shocked by Lee's escape following the battle of Antietam on 17 September 1862, were further upset by General George B. McClellan's procrastination in pursuing Lee and by General J. E. B. "Jeb" Stuart's daring cavalry raid into Pennsylvania around Gettysburg (10–12 October 1862).

On 7 November 1862 President Abraham Lincoln replaced McClellan as commander of the Army of the Potomac with Major General Ambrose E. Burnside. The new commander wanted to shift his entire force forty miles east to Fredericksburg and advance from there on the Confederate capital of Richmond, Virginia. Fredericksburg, a city of about 5,000 people, was on the Rappahannock River, midway between Washington and Richmond where the river turned suddenly south.

Lincoln favored this so-called covering approach to attacking Richmond because it protected Washington. But he and Union general-in-chief General Henry W. Halleck were concerned that Burnside's plan had as its principal goal the capture of the Confederate capital rather than the destruction of Lee's army. Burnside persuaded them to accept his strategy, and on 14 November, Lincoln approved the plan, provided that Burnside moved quickly. Lincoln believed that the plan was doomed unless it could be executed swiftly.

On the day he received Lincoln's approval, Burnside, a capable administrator, regrouped his seven corps (three divisions in each) into Right, Center, and Left "Grand Divisions" of two corps each, commanded respectively by Major Generals Edwin V. Sumner, Joseph Hooker, and William B. Franklin. The 7th Corps, under Franz Sigel, became an independent reserve.

The next day, the Army of the Potomac began the march down the north bank of the Rappahannock to Falmouth. Burnside arrived there on the nineteenth, just ahead of the army's rear guard. Sumner's two corps were in position across the Rappahannock opposite Fredericksburg, and Burnside reported to Washington, "The enemy do not seem to be in force."

Lincoln had wanted speed and Burnside had given it. But now his army simply sat in place. Burnside had cabled Washington, "As soon as the pontoon trains arrive, the bridge will be built and the command moves over." But Burnside had assigned securing the pontoon

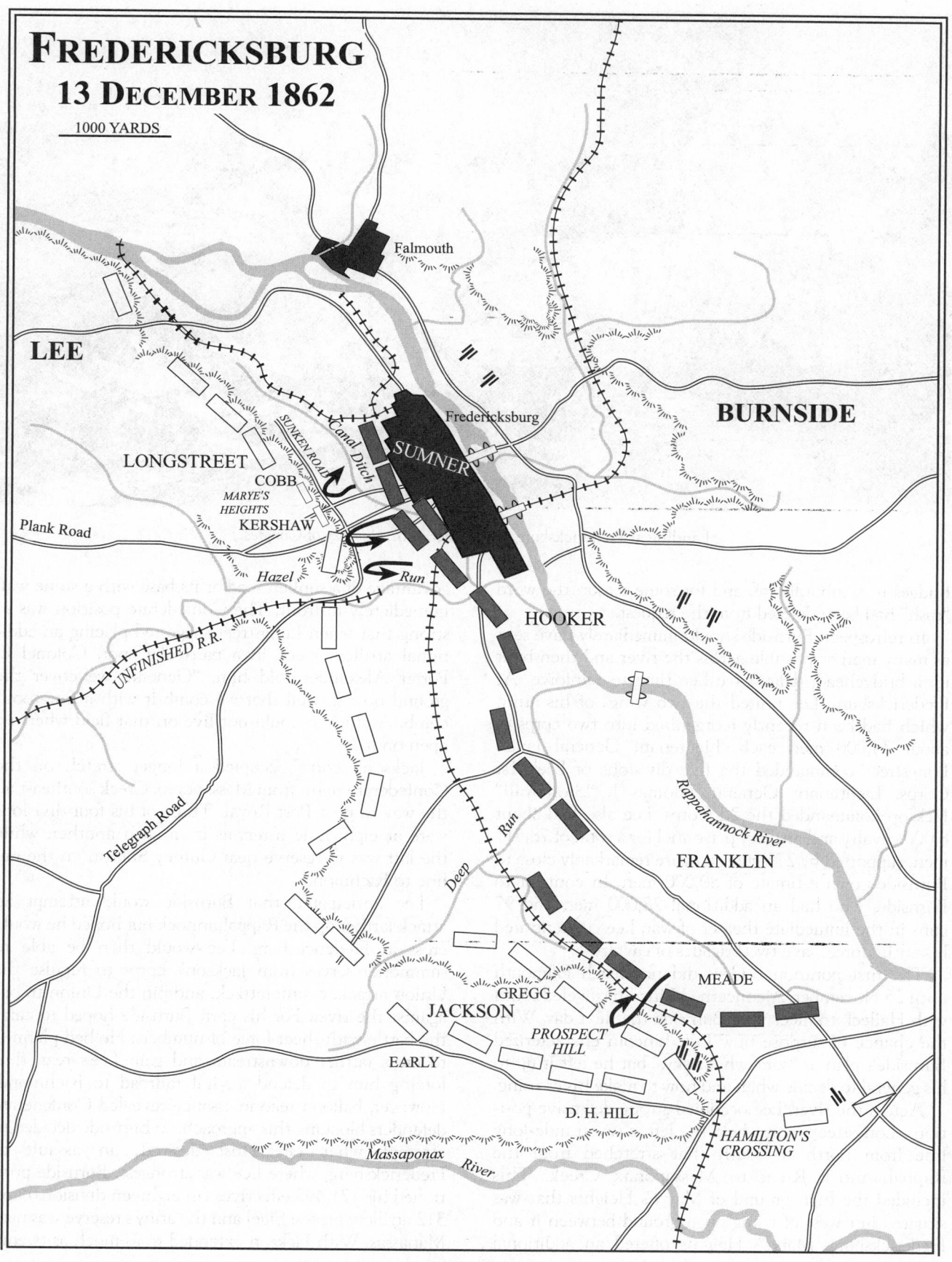

FREDERICKSBURG
13 DECEMBER 1862

1000 YARDS

Falmouth

LEE

Fredericksburg

BURNSIDE

SUMNER

LONGSTREET

COBB

Canal Ditch

Sunken Road

MARYE'S HEIGHTS

KERSHAW

Plank Road

Hazel

Run

HOOKER

UNFINISHED R.R.

Telegraph Road

Deep Run

Rappahannock River

FRANKLIN

MEADE

GREGG

JACKSON

PROSPECT HILL

EARLY

D. H. HILL

HAMILTON'S CROSSING

Massaponax River

Landing at Fredericksburg, December 1862 (*Library of Congress*)

bridges to a subordinate, and for some reason the word "rush" had been deleted from the request.

In retrospect, Burnside should immediately have sent as many men as possible across the river and then built up a bridgehead; delay gave Lee time to reinforce. At Fredericksburg, Lee united the two wings of his army, which had been recently reorganized into two corps of about 35,000 men each. Lieutenant General James Longstreet commanded the five divisions of Lee's 1st Corps. Lieutenant General Thomas J. "Stonewall" Jackson commanded the 2d Corps. Lee also had about 8,000 cavalry and artillery personnel for a total of 78,511 men, supported by 275 guns, a figure remarkably close to Burnside's own estimate of 80,000 men. In contrast to Burnside, who had an additional 28,000 men and 97 guns in the immediate theater of war, Lee concentrated his entire force, save two brigades of cavalry.

The first pontoon bridges did not reach Falmouth until 25 November. A concerned Lincoln traveled south with Halleck to meet with Burnside the next day. With the chance of surprise now lost, Lincoln characterized Burnside's plan as "somewhat risky," but he left it up to his general to decide when and how to make his crossing.

Across the river, Lee occupied strong defensive positions. Longstreet's corps held the left, a seven-mile-long line from north to south that stretched from the Rappahannock River to Massaponax Creek. This included the high ground of Marye's Heights that was situated just west of rising open ground between it and Fredericksburg. Marye's Heights offered an additional advantage of a sunken road at its base with a stone wall immediately in front. The Confederate position was so strong that when Longstreet suggested placing an additional artillery piece in a particular spot, Colonel E. Porter Alexander told him, "General, we cover the ground now so well that we comb it with a fine-tooth comb. A chicken could not live on that field when we open on it."

Jackson's corps occupied a longer stretch on the Confederate right, from Massaponax Creek southeast all the way to near Port Royal. Three of his four divisions were at eight-mile intervals from each another, while the last was in reserve near Guiney Station on the rail line to Richmond.

Lee anticipated that Burnside would attempt an attack farther up the Rappahannock but hoped he would cross at Fredericksburg. Lee would then be able to summon reserves from Jackson's corps to repulse the Union attack, counterattack, and pin the Union troops against the river. For his part, Burnside hoped to carry the battle with sheer force of numbers. He had planned to cross farther downstream and gain Lee's rear, thus forcing him to defend a vital railroad to Richmond. However, balloon reconnaissance revealed Confederate defenders blocking this approach, so Burnside decided to attempt what Lee most desired, an assault at Fredericksburg, where Lee was strongest. Burnside positioned his 121,492 effectives (in eighteen divisions) and 312 artillery pieces; Sigel and the army's reserve was near Manassas. With Jackson extended to as much as twenty miles away, Burnside hoped that speed and numbers would enable him to carry the day before Confederate reinforcements could arrive.

The Union attack would have two prongs, consisting of the Left and Right Grand Divisions commanded by Franklin and Sumner, respectively. Hooker detached divisions from the Center Grand Division, two to Franklin and the other four to Sumner, so that Left and Right would each have about 60,000 men, including artillery and cavalry. On the left, Franklin's job was to take the lower end of the ridge and then sweep northward along it toward Marye's Heights while Sumner attacked out of Fredericksburg to hold the Confederates in position.

The Union crossing began before dawn on 11 December when engineers sought to construct six pontoon bridges across the Rappahannock for infantry and cavalry. When the engineers had spanned about half of the Rappahannock's 400-foot-width, Confederate brigadier general William Barksdale's 1,600-man Mississippi Brigade opened up from the west bank,

halting the work on the bridges. With his plans well behind schedule and fearing that Jackson's men were probably on the march, Burnside ordered the 147 heavy guns posted on Stafford Heights to open up on Fredericksburg. For an hour the ground shook as each of the guns fired a round every two minutes. But the bombardment did not diminish the ardor or effectiveness of the Mississippians. In fact, they were better able to take cover behind the rubble while picking off Union troops working on the bridges.

Not until that afternoon did the Federals get across the river by using the pontoons as makeshift assault boats. A Michigan regiment was the first to cross; as it cleared out the snipers, six bridges were finally put in place. Not until 7 P.M. were the last Union troops across.

Choosing to remain in his defensive positions, Lee did not contest the Federal crossing. Burnside was also cheered by balloon reports indicating that Jackson's men were still in place. With nothing seemingly lost by the delay, and while his troops looted Fredericksburg,

The sacking of Fredericksburg, December 1862 (*Library of Congress*)

Battle of Fredericksburg (*Library of Congress*)

Burnside spent all of 12 December positioning his forces and planning the assault.

When fog lifted at noon that day, Lee could see that this was the major Union effort, and he immediately ordered Jackson's farthest divisions to begin their long march toward him. Lee guessed the Union attack would occur the next day. "I shall try to do them all the damage in our power when they move forward," he said.

On the morning of 13 December, thick fog again shrouded Fredericksburg. Jackson asked permission to attack, which Lee denied. About 10 A.M., the fog began to dissipate. First the Union and then the Confederate guns opened up, although Lee ordered most not to return fire until Union troops came within range.

Sumner's assault on the Union right fell on the heart of Lee's defenses on Mayre's Heights directly behind the town of Fredericksburg. Here Confederate infantry two ranks deep defended the 400-yard-long four-foot-high stone wall. They had deepened the sunken road behind the wall, throwing the spill on the townward side to create additional protection. Six hundred yards of open field stretched between this position and the town, now teeming with Union soldiers.

Union forces began their assault on Marye's Heights at noon and concealed Confederate guns soon opened

up, cutting the attackers to pieces. Other Union attempts followed, supported by artillery beyond the river on Stafford Heights. Their commanding elevation and heavier weight of metal enabled the Union guns to rake the Confederate line at will.

Franklin's assault on Jackson's front achieved temporary success at Prospect Hill, when Major General George G. Meade's division of 4,500 Pennsylvanians briefly penetrated Confederate lines, threatening to get astride the lower ridge and roll up the defenders; however, Confederate reinforcements drove Meade back to his original positions. Meanwhile, Lee had reinforced the defenders in front of Marye's Heights to four ranks deep behind the stone wall. From there they proceeded to scour the field in front of them with a rapid and continuous storm of lead.

Throughout the afternoon, Burnside sent wave after wave of his infantry to the slaughter. Nightfall brought an end to this, but not before seven Union divisions had dashed themselves against the wall in fourteen different charges. No Union soldier ever reached the wall; few got within fifty yards. Observing the carnage, Lee remarked to Longstreet: "It is well that war is so horrible, or else we should grow too fond of it."

Expecting the Union assault to be resumed the next

Part of the 6th Maine Infantry on parade after the Battle of Fredericksburg
(Photograph by Mathew Brady Studio / *Library of Congress*)

day, Lee had his army dig and improve entrenchments. Burnside had indeed planned to continue the attack, but the usually aggressive Sumner convinced him it would only lead to further slaughter. On 15 December, Burnside requested a truce to retrieve Union dead and those wounded who had managed to survive two days and nights of exposure without treatment. Lee obliged. That night, under cover of a darkness and amid a heavy thunderstorm, the Army of the Potomac recrossed the Rappahannock. In the morning, the embarrassed Confederates discovered they were gone.

The Fredericksburg campaign was Lee's most one-sided victory of the war. The Union side suffered 12,653 casualties, as opposed to only 4,201 for the smaller Confederate force. The Confederates also recovered 11,000 Union firearms. On 25 January 1863, Lincoln replaced Burnside as commander of the Army of the Potomac with General Joseph Hooker.

—*Spencer C. Tucker*

See also Alexander, E. Porter; Barksdale, William; Burnside, Ambrose; Franklin, William B.; Hooker, Joseph; Jackson, Thomas J.; Lee, Robert E.; Longstreet, James; Meade, George Gordon; Sigel, Franz; Sumner, Edwin.

Houses near Fredericksburg damaged by the shelling of 13 December 1862
(Photograph by James Gardner / *Library of Congress*)

1st Connecticut Artillery on drill at Fredericksburg (Photograph by Mathew Brady Studio / *Library of Congress*)

For further reading:
Gallagher, Gary W., ed. *The Fredericksburg Campaign. Decision on the Rappahannock* (1995).
Stackpole, Edward J. *Drama on the Rappahannock: The Fredericksburg Campaign* (1957).
Whan, Vorin E., Jr. *Fiasco at Fredericksburg* (1961).

FREDERICKSBURG, SECOND BATTLE OF
(3 May 1863)

The second battle of Fredericksburg was part of a larger campaign that was centered west of the city around Chancellorsville. Joseph Hooker, commander of the Union Army of the Potomac and known for his aggressive style on and off the battlefield, adopted an ambitious plan in April 1863 to reverse Confederate momentum in the Virginia theater. He ordered a 15,000-man cavalry force to threaten the Confederate capital and sever supply lines for Robert E. Lee's Army of Northern Virginia. His plan also included leading his 75,000 men north and west of Confederate-occupied Fredericksburg, crossing the Rapidan and Rappahannock rivers and threatening the enemy from the rear. To keep Federal forces in place, Hooker left VI Corps at Fredericksburg under Major General John Sedgwick.

By the end of April, Hooker reached Chancellorsville and prepared to crush the Army of Northern Virginia between the two wings of his army. Lee, however, was not fooled by diversionary Union demonstrations opposite Fredericksburg. On 1 May, he marched the majority of his troops to meet Hooker's threat, while Major General Jubal A. Early's division remained to stave off a possible Union advance. Lee marched 42,000 men west toward Chancellorsville, attacked, and by the end of 2 May threatened to rout the larger Union army. To stem the Confederate tide, Hooker called upon Sedgwick and his 27,000 troops at Fredericksburg to advance.

As the fighting at Chancellorsville unfolded, Hooker informed Sedgwick that Fredericksburg was lightly defended and therefore urged him at midday on 2 May to push through the enemy lines and help crush Lee between the two converging Union forces. Poor communications and a lack of initiative prevented a successful outcome. Hooker's telegrams and dispatches were often delayed and unclear, and Sedgwick advanced too slowly against Fredericksburg. Historians generally agree that "Uncle John" Sedgwick, who graduated from West Point in the same class as both Hooker and Jubal Early, was an able and much-beloved officer but also a cautious and deliberate one who refused to commit his men frivolously to battle. Wounded once at the Seven Days' battle and three times at Antietam the previous year, his movements were as guarded as ever. Sedgwick disagreed with Hooker's assertion that Fredericksburg was virtually unguarded and therefore failed to attack.

At approximately the same time that Sedgwick was prodded by Hooker to advance, Jubal Early received word from Lee to pull back from Fredericksburg and reinforce Confederate troops to the west. Lee's order had actually been a discretionary one, but chief of staff Robert Chilton miscommunicated it as a directive. Early protested, realizing that his 12,000 men tied down a disproportionately large number of Union soldiers, but he eventually relented. Leaving only 3,000 troops to hold Confederate defenses, the bulk of Early's force headed for Chancellorsville. Union soldiers detected this movement on 2 May, as well as that by Thomas J. "Stonewall" Jackson's corps nearly ten miles to the west, and mistakenly reported a general retreat. Then at about 5:00 P.M., as Union prospects seemed to improve, the Federals' right wing sustained a crushing blow by Jackson. Hooker this time demanded that Sedgwick immediately join him for a counterattack.

In the predawn hours of 3 May, Sedgwick moved his corps in place for an assault on Fredericksburg, although more confusion over Hooker's communications slowed the process and gave Confederate forces additional time to regroup. Lee by this time had corrected Chilton's error, and Early's troops reoccupied the Fredericksburg defenses in time to meet the Union advance. Sedgwick focused initially on the Confederate flanks, trying to avoid the costly frontal assaults that Ambrose Burnside had ordered five months before at the first battle of Fredericksburg. Brigadier General John Gibbon's brigades attempted to turn Early's left flank and then Brigadier General Albion P. Howe's troops advanced against the right. Neither succeeded, and so Sedgwick called for the attack on the Confederate center that he had sought to avert. Early predicted that his former classmate would avoid Burnside's earlier blunder and consequently left his defenses on Marye's Heights sparsely manned. As a result, Sedgwick's reluctant order to attack found the weak spot in the Confederate line. Union forces advanced with bayonets mounted, received a withering fire from William Barksdale's Mississippi brigade, and within minutes breached the stone wall before Marye's Heights.

Early's division withdrew from Fredericksburg, having lost the high ground and suffering 475 casualties to the Federals' 1,100. Sedgwick then pushed his VI Corps west to combine with Hooker's main army. Lee, however, intercepted him at the battle of Salem Church.

—*J. Mark Thompson*

See also Chancellorsville, Battle of; Early, Jubal Anderson; Hooker, Joseph; Sedgwick, John.

For further reading:
Sears, Stephen. *Chancellorsville* (1996).
Furgurson, Ernest B. *Chancellorsville, 1863: The Souls of the Brave* (1992).

FREE SOIL PARTY
1840s and 1850s
Third-party movement

The Free Soil movement flourished primarily in New England, New York, and in certain areas near the Great Lakes. Its supporters were a loose coalition of radical Democrats (often called "Barnburners" or "Conscience" Whigs), and carryovers from the short-lived Liberty Party.

Free Soil proceeded from a complex interaction between general Northern unease over the spread of slavery and internal stresses that afflicted the second American party system of Whigs and Democrats. These mainstream political parties were intersectional alliances focused on economic issues such as currency and tariffs; they scrupulously avoided moral issues such as slavery in the interests of party unity. But during the 1830s and 1840s slavery steadily intruded itself into the national political consciousness. As the Cotton Kingdom surged westward, Northern fears of a "slave power" hostile to the interests of free, white labor mounted.

These fears intensified when the Republic of Texas applied for admission to the United States during the late 1830s and early 1840s. Although American expansionism was an article of faith in all sections, Texas was perceived as a threat among substantial portions of the Northern electorate. It lay outside the boundaries the Louisiana Purchase of and was thus not subject to the limitations of the Missouri Compromise; it was large enough to be divided into several slave states; and its admission promised certain war with Mexico, which had never acknowledged its independence. Democratic president Martin Van Buren (1837–1841) treated annexation as the political bombshell it was, but between 1841 and 1845 Texas was the first priority of John Tyler's presidential agenda. Tyler's stubborn insistence made Texas the uninvited focus of the campaign of 1844. In that campaign, both Van Buren and the Whig candidate, Henry Clay, attempted to sidestep the issue by arguing that annexation would bring on an unneeded war. Van Buren lost his party's nomination to James K. Polk, an outspoken annexationist, who in turn beat Clay. Ironically, Tyler succeeded in annexing Texas after the election was over. By 1846 the United States and Mexico were at war.

Annexation and the ensuing war with Mexico exposed serious stresses within the major parties. Few in either party were abolitionists, yet the events of 1844 through 1846 helped persuade many that a slave power existed that ultimately threatened Northern institutions. Van Buren's radical Democrats, the Barnburners, blamed Southerners for depriving their hero of the 1844 nomination. That, plus increasing factionalization within their own state organization in New York, pushed them toward a hard-line stance on the extension of slavery. Barnburners accepted the annexation of Texas as a fait accompli, but calculated that the Democratic Party could not survive indefinitely unless the demands of its Southern, proslavery wing were brought under control. Sentiment among Northern Whigs was similar and somewhat sharper, especially in New England and those areas of the Old Northwest populated by New Englanders. These "Conscience" Whigs were growing disgusted with their party's compromises with Southern Whigs and increasingly were convinced that traditional economic issues were secondary in importance to moral ones. The situation within the Liberty Party was different. By 1846 it was leaderless, adrift, and split between those who favored a harder, more uncompromisingly abolitionist stance and those—notably Salmon P. Chase of Ohio—who advocated a broader coalition.

These factions came together after August 1846, when a one-term congressman from Pennsylvania, David Wilmot, offered a proviso to an army appropriations bill that would have barred slavery from any lands or territories gained from Mexico as a result of the war. This remarkable proviso (which never passed both houses) focused the slavery issue into a single, but encompassing goal—keeping the territories free from slavery. It was a powerful stance. The Wilmot Proviso proposed only to contain slavery, not abolish it where it stood. It thus appealed to many Northerners who would otherwise have shunned an "abolitionist" posture. More subtly, keeping slavery out of the territories meant keeping those same territories white; hence the proviso tapped an insidious racism among Northern voters. Abolitionists publicly dismissed the measure as inadequate, but pragmatists in all parties saw it as an effective litmus test on the slavery question.

Naturally, the major parties failed the test. Both Whigs and Democrats needed unity in all sections, and a proviso that condemned slavery, however vaguely and for whatever reason, was anathema in the South. In the campaign of 1848 the Democrat, Lewis Cass of Michigan, put forward the idea of "popular sovereignty,"

a compromise that would have organized the territories without reference to slavery and let the settlers decide the matter. Cass's appeal did not satisfy the Barnburners, and they bolted. The Whig candidate, Mexican War hero General Zachary Taylor, dodged the question entirely, and Conscience Whigs bolted. The two factions met with representatives of the Liberty Party in Buffalo in August 1848, and nominated Van Buren for president and a Conscience Whig, Charles Francis Adams, as his running mate. They proclaimed themselves the party of "Free Soil, Free Labor, and Free Men" with the Wilmot Proviso as the core of the platform. In the election they polled about 14 percent of the Northern vote, with their heaviest turnout in Massachusetts, rural New York, the Western Reserve of Ohio, and along the Great Lakes north of Chicago. Democrats were hit hard by the new party (without New York they could not win), and Taylor was elected.

Between 1848 and 1852 Free Soilers faced severe challenges. The discovery of gold in California accelerated westward expansion and made some sort of national policy regarding the territories mandatory. A year of heated controversy ultimately produced the Compromise of 1850, a series of acts that, among other things, admitted California as a free state while organizing the New Mexico and Utah Territories without restrictions on slavery. The Compromise eased tensions over slavery somewhat and thus marginalized much of the Free Soil Party's ideological appeal. Free Soilers turned their attention to state and local politics, with widely varying intents and results. In New York, Barnburner Free Soilers used their disruptive power to force concessions from the state Democrats and then hurried back into their old organization. In Ohio Free Soilers were successful in forming coalitions that overturned that state's restrictive Black Laws and elected Chase to the Senate, but by 1852 the old party loyalties had so undercut Free Soil unity that the party was in shambles. In Massachusetts a combination of Democrats and Free Soilers won a seat in the Senate for Charles Sumner, yet the demands of fusing Conscience Whigs with Democrats were so taxing that the party fell into vicious infighting. The situation in other states was similar. By 1852 pragmatists in the party found themselves isolated as hard-liners from the old Liberty Party assumed greater prominence. In the election of 1852 the party nominated John P. Hale of New Hampshire on a platform that was more openly abolitionist, and thus more radical, than the Free Soil document of 1848. Hale garnered only about half Van Buren's total, and the party faded quickly.

Yet Free Soil was one of the most important failures of its time. It introduced key leaders into Northern politics who would go on to form the backbone of the radical wing of the Republican Party. (Chase, for example, was Lincoln's secretary of the Treasury and later chief justice

of the Supreme Court; Sumner remained a senator until his death in 1874 and was a close adviser to Lincoln.) More important, by challenging the major parties' focus on economic topics and arguing that slavery was the crucial issue confronting Americans, the Free Soil Party helped redefine the ideological basis of partisan politics during the 1850s. The Whig Party was unable to survive this challenge, and thus the second American party system collapsed. Moreover, when Stephen A. Douglas introduced the Kansas-Nebraska Act in 1854—an act predicated on popular sovereignty—his opposition was able to crystallize around the antiextensionist ideology of the Free Soilers. By 1856 a new and more lasting coalition, the Republican Party, had taken form.

—*John Mayfield*

See also Chase, Salmon; Sumner, Charles.

For further reading:
Berwanger, Eugene. *The Frontier Against Slavery: Western Anti-Negro Prejudice and the Slavery Extension Controversy* (1967).
Blue, Frederick J. *The Free Soilers: Third Party Politics, 1848–1854* (1973).
———. *Salmon P. Chase: A Life in Politics* (1987).
Brauer, Kinley J. *Cotton versus Conscience: Massachusetts Whig Politics and Southwestern Expansion, 1843–1848* (1967).
Foner, Eric. *Free Soil, Free Labor, Free Men: The Ideology of the Republican Party before the Civil War* (1970).
Gienapp, William. *The Origins of the Republican Party, 1852–1856* (1987).
Mayfield, John. *Rehearsal for Republicanism: Free Soil and the Politics of Antislavery* (1980).
Rayback, Joseph G. *Free Soil: The Election of 1848* (1971).
Sewell, Richard H. *Ballots for Freedom: Antislavery Politics in the United States, 1837–1860* (1976).

FREEDMEN'S BUREAU
(1865–1872)

Formally known as the Bureau of Refugees, Freedmen, and Abandoned Lands, the Freedmen's Bureau was a federal agency within the War Department that was charged with supervising the transition from slavery to freedom in the erstwhile Confederacy. During the Civil War, and especially after President Abraham Lincoln had issued the Emancipation Proclamation on 1 January 1863, abolitionists and many Republicans argued that the federal government had a responsibility to assist the former slaves of the South in adjusting to their new status. Abandoning a strict laissez-faire approach, the government accepted the need to establish a temporary and limited guardianship over the ex-slaves. Consequently, on 3 March 1865, Lincoln signed into law congressional legislation creating the Freedmen's Bureau. On 12 May, Major General Oliver Otis Howard assumed command of the bureau as its commissioner and would continue to serve in that position until the agency's demise. Shortly

thereafter, Howard appointed subordinates known as assistant commissioners; they were army officers who supervised the agency in one or more states. State bureau organizations varied, but they extended the agency's reach down to the county and local level through subassistant commissioners, agents, special agents for relief, surgeons, and education officials.

During the years immediately after the war, the South's economy was recovering from wartime destruction in the face of bad harvests. Bureau men brought relief in the form of food and clothing to hard-pressed white and black Southerners. This type of assistance, however, was always considered an emergency measure, necessary only until the new free-labor system could bear fruit. Freedmen's Bureau officers and agents instructed both the freedpeople and their ex-masters in their obligations and rights within the new system. The reliance on written contracts, as Howard later explained, was the best way to gain the confidence of all involved parties. Bureau men tried to prevent fraud against the freedpeople and to make sure they received just compensation, in their minds a cornerstone for building a successful new system. Many officers and agents assumed that slavery had retarded the freedpeople's intellectual and moral development, but they also believed that the position of the ex-slaves within a free-labor society was a dynamic one. The freedpeople's fairly paid hard work and thrift would allow them to move beyond their status as laborers to that of independent landowners, just as education would allow them to leave behind the ignorance imposed on them by their ex-masters. To assist the freedpeople in the latter area, the Bureau coordinated the efforts of the ex-slaves and Northern benevolent societies, such as the American Missionary Association, in establishing a network of schools.

The bureau oversaw abandoned and confiscated property, initially with the expectation of leasing and then selling land to the freedpeople. Because of decisions made in Washington, D.C., however, the bureau eventually supervised the restoration of most property to former white owners. During 1866 and 1867, this restoration was especially tragic in the Sherman Reservation, a swath of land along the coast of South Carolina, Georgia, and Florida where ex-slaves had been settling since General William Tecumseh Sherman had set aside the area for their use in January 1865. The restoration of land to white Southerners earned the bureau the freedpeople's animosity, but the efforts of the agency in other areas, such as contract enforcement and education, convinced freedpeople that, as imperfect as it was, the bureau was there to assist them. Bureau men risked their lives trying to protect the freedpeople's claim to civil and, eventually, political rights. Often, the only medical assistance a freedperson could expect was from a bureau-supported clinic, while

destitute, elderly freedpeople found some relief in bureau hospitals. The bureau also helped black veterans obtain their bounties from the government. Such work made the bureau the federal government's first wide-ranging welfare and regulatory agency, touching the lives of a large number of individuals black and white who had never before been in such intimate contact with the federal government.

The bureau was by law a temporary agency performing duties that all but the most radical Republicans believed should be terminated as soon as possible, a belief that limited the bureau's strength from the outset. The first bureau law refrained from giving the agency direct funding, expecting that it would make ends meet by selling confiscated and abandoned property. But beginning in 1866, legislation provided the bureau with a budget. Initially unable to pay salaries for agents, the bureau failed to establish a strong presence throughout the South during the critical early years of Reconstruction. Even after the bureau could hire paid agents it never grew to a size that would justify depicting it as a significant arm of federal power in the South. At the bureau's peak in staff at the end of 1868, the agency had a total of 901 men on its rolls, but 348 of them were clerks. Overwhelmed by the freedpeople's needs, hindered by President Andrew Johnson's lenient Reconstruction policies, and stymied by the lack of cooperation and the outright resistance of white Southerners, the bureau was at a serious disadvantage in implementing its program. Furthermore, Howard, bureau men, and most Republican politicians always worried about breaking the initiative of the newly freed slaves by giving them too much assistance for too long a period of time. Thus, almost from its inception the bureau began to shrink its programs because of ideological limitations that prevented policy makers from acknowledging the need for a long-term federal police or mediatory presence in the South. The agency's activities waxed and waned until it restricted its work to education and bounty collecting in January 1869. It terminated its work with education in June 1870 and its involvement in helping black veterans collect bounties in June 1872.

In the end, the agency failed to accomplish all that its supporters expected of it. Still, the unhappy outcome of Reconstruction was not what Howard and his subordinates had planned to leave behind. The bureau, never an uncritical advocate of the freedpeople nor the pawn of white planters, expected that equal justice and an impartial free-labor system would allow the freedpeople to improve their own condition while encouraging the South to become more like the North.

—*Paul A. Cimbala*

See also Douglass, Frederick; Emancipation Proclamation; Howard, Oliver O.; Radical Republicans; Slaves; Thirteenth Amendment.

For further reading:
Belz, Herman. *A New Birth of Freedom: The Republican Party and Freedmen's Rights, 1861–1866* (1976).
Bentley, George R. *A History of the Freedmen's Bureau* (1955; reprint, 1974).
Cimbala, Paul A. *Under the Guardianship of the Nation: The Freedmen's Bureau and the Reconstruction of Georgia, 1865–1870* (1997).
Cimbala, Paul A., and Randall M. Miller, eds. *The Freedmen's Bureau and Reconstruction: Reconsiderations* (1999).
Crouch, Barry A. *The Freedmen's Bureau and Black Texans* (1992).
Finley, Randy. *From Slavery to Uncertain Freedom: The Freedmen's Bureau in Arkansas, 1865–1869* (1996).
Nieman, Donald G. *To Set the Law in Motion: The Freedmen's Bureau and the Legal Rights of Blacks, 1865–1868* (1979).
Schmidt, James D. *Free to Work: Labor Law, Emancipation, and Reconstruction, 1815–1880* (1998).

FREEPORT DOCTRINE
(1858)

As the 1858 Illinois Senate campaign saw Republican Abraham Lincoln challenging the incumbent Democrat Stephen A. Douglas, the Lincoln-Douglas debates focused on a number of sectional issues that had driven a wedge between the North and the South in the 1850s. One of those issues was the question of slavery expansion into new territories. At Freeport, Illinois, on 27 August 1858, Lincoln asked Douglas to clarify his views regarding popular sovereignty's viability in the wake of the *Dred Scott* decision. "Can the people of a United States Territory," he asked, "in any lawful way, against the wish of any citizen of the United States, exclude slavery from its limits prior to the formation of a State Constitution?"

Lincoln already knew how the senator would respond. In a speech at Springfield on 12 June 1857 wherein he had responded to the recent *Dred Scott* decision's guarantee that slave owners could take slaves into a territory, Douglas had already announced his position. According to Douglas this right under *Dred Scott* was "barren and worthless" if slavery were not protected by local regulations. According to Douglas, "These regulations...must necessarily depend entirely upon the will and wishes of the people of the territory, as they can only be prescribed by the local legislatures." At Freeport, Douglas merely restated his views in what became known, somewhat exaggeratedly, as the Freeport Doctrine: "Slavery cannot exist a day in the midst of an unfriendly people with unfriendly laws."

As a result of this stance, Douglas found himself in a precarious position that jeopardized both his chances of winning reelection to the Senate in 1858 and gaining his party's nomination for the presidential election of 1860. In short, he alienated Southern Democrats who were

pushing for a territorial slave code and annoyed Northern Democrats who were opposed to slavery on moral grounds.

Lincoln was careful not to spend an inordinate amount of time on the Freeport question and did not pursue the issue in the five debates that followed. He feared that some Republicans would arrive at the same answer as Douglas for different reasons. Instead, he wanted to show antislavery voters that Douglas's position differed from their own. Republicans supported the exclusion of slavery from the territories on moral grounds while Douglas insisted that slavery expansion was a local issue to be decided by indigenous populations. Lincoln thus chose to focus on the broader issue that pitted opponents of slavery who wanted it barred from the territories and eventually abolished—a goal he believed the Founding Fathers had originally intended—against those who wanted slavery constitutionally protected.

Douglas's position proved untenable, and by 1859 he abandoned the Freeport Doctrine altogether. Hoping to pacify Southern voters during his quest for the presidency, Douglas published an article in *Harper's Magazine* that advanced the principle of nonintervention. He explained his shift in position with an argument that concluded the founding fathers originally intended to refrain from interfering in the issue of slavery expansion. Yet, Douglas's Freeport position had resulted in a growing sense of apprehension in Southerners who felt increasingly beleaguered regarding slavery. Southerners demanded that slavery be put on a firm foundation that would ensure its survival, and many viewed Douglas's stance as departing from this goal.

Southerners continued to push hard for a Federal slave code, ignoring Douglas's attempt to stake out a middle position. At the opening of Congress in 1859, President James Buchanan, in his annual message to Congress, interpreted the Dred Scott decision as the final word on the issue of slavery in territories and "to have it protected there under the Federal Constitution." Mississippi senator Jefferson Davis immediately responded with a series of resolutions introduced in the Senate demanding a Federal slave code. Douglas's so-called Freeport Doctrine had proved ineffective in quelling the issue Lincoln had adroitly raised and in fact had the effect of only heightening concerns in both the North and South.

—*Kevin M. Levin*

See also Democratic Party; Douglas, Stephen Arnold; Election of 1858.

For further reading:
Holzer, Harold, ed., *The Lincoln-Douglas Debates* (1993).
Johannsen, Robert W. *Stephen A. Douglas* (1973).
Zarefsky, David. *Lincoln, Douglas and Slavery: In the Crucible of Public Debate* (1990).

FRÉMONT, JESSIE BENTON
(1824–1902)
Political activist

The daughter of Senator Thomas Hart Benton, Jesse Benton Frémont is best known for her influence on the controversial career of her husband, John Charles Frémont. She converted the information amassed by Frémont's expeditions into highly readable prose that inspired and assisted a generation of westward emigrants and made Frémont a national hero. Her later memoirs and articles shed much light on America's nineteenth-century history.

In 1841 at the age of seventeen, Jessie defied her father's objections and was secretly married to Frémont by a Catholic priest after several Protestant clergy were unwilling to alienate her father. The elder Benton soon forgave them, however, and provided powerful support for Frémont's subsequent career. In 1843 Jessie destroyed War Department orders canceling Frémont's second major expedition and sent him a message to "trust and start at once." Benton later accepted responsibility for her action and the eighteen-month expedition was highly successful.

In 1845, after Commodore Robert Stockton and Frémont had conquered California, Stockton insisted that Frémont continue as governor even after General Stephen Kearny had arrived with authority to form a government. Because Frémont obeyed Stockton and disobeyed Kearny, he was court-martialed and dismissed from the army, although President Polk canceled the penalty. Frémont resigned, however, and assumed the role of persecuted hero in the eyes of the general public.

For the next few years the Frémonts settled in California amid serious dangers and hardships and became rich from a gold strike. In 1849 Frémont was elected senator for a two-year term, but was defeated for reelection in 1851 by the proslavery party, even though California had become a free state.

In 1856, urged on by Jessie, Frémont accepted the presidential nomination of the new free-soil Republican Party. Women could not vote, but they could organize meetings and influence their husbands, and campaign manager Francis P. Blair made Jessie a vital part of the effort. "Our Jessie" was featured in campaign pamphlets and songs, and she became America's best-known woman. She also wrote a biographical sketch of Frémont that editor John Bigelow turned into a best seller. Accused of Catholicism because a priest had married them, the Frémonts refused to deny it. To Jessie's dismay, Benton helped defeat Frémont by delivering twenty speeches warning that the election of a Northern free-soil president would lead to civil war. Frémont carried most of the Northern states, and Jessie's performance helped strengthen both the Republican Party and the incipient movement for women's rights.

When the Civil War began in April 1861, the Blairs persuaded Lincoln to appoint Frémont major general in command of the western department, with headquarters in St. Louis. While the inexperienced Frémont struggled to recruit, train, equip, and organize several thousand volunteers in a city overrun by Confederate sympathizers, Jessie organized a Western Sanitary Commission to provide for the sick and wounded and worked tirelessly to recruit and train nurses. Frémont was criticized harshly for reasons both just and unjust, including the influence of "General Jessie." Ultimately, Colonel Frank Blair reported to Lincoln through his brother, Postmaster General Montgomery Blair, that Frémont was in danger of losing Missouri.

On 30 August 1861 Frémont declared martial law and proclaimed freedom for the slaves of all Rebels in his area. Lincoln, struggling to keep Kentucky from seceding, asked him to revoke the emancipation decree, but Frémont refused until publicly ordered to do so by Lincoln in September 1861. Meanwhile, Jessie immediately entrained for Washington to plead Frémont's case. Arriving travel weary at night she was directed by Lincoln to come for an immediate interview. Each later remembered that the other was rude and demanding. Lincoln insisted that Frémont should have ignored the slavery question, and was not pleased by Jessie's arguments to the contrary. He also remembered later that she even hinted at the possibility of a military rebellion. On the following day, the elder Francis P. Blair scolded Jessie and remembered later that when he accused her of trying to be Catherine the Great, she had answered, "Not Catherine, Josephine." Jessie returned to St. Louis filled with hatred for the Blairs, and at her suggestion, Frémont arrested Frank Blair for insubordination. Jessie's advice and actions strengthened Frémont's popularity with the antislavery radicals, but Lincoln was president, and Frémont was relieved.

To appease the radicals, Lincoln gave Frémont a new command in West Virginia in March 1862, where he was matched unsuccessfully against Stonewall Jackson. When his command was merged into a larger unit, Frémont angrily resigned. Jessie, meanwhile, worked tirelessly to raise large sums of money for military hospitals and sanitary commissions.

In 1864 the radical Republicans nominated Frémont for president, but Jessie realized that his candidacy would only elect the Democrat George B. McClellan. She persuaded Frémont to withdraw, after Senator Zachariah Chandler promised him another military command and the resignation of Montgomery Blair.

For several years after the war, the Frémonts lived happily on a Hudson River estate. Jessie gave generously to charities and colleges, and helped various protégés, including Bret Harte. Their son John Charles, Jr., became

a naval commander, and their son Frank Preston, named after Blair, enjoyed a successful army career. Then, however, their mine was lost through faulty titles, and Frémont invested in a railroad scheme with corrupt partners who left him charged with fraud and overwhelmed by debt. Suddenly bankrupt, they settled in New York, where Jessie supported them by writing stories and articles. Relief finally came in 1878, when Frémont was appointed governor of Arizona Territory. There Jessie organized cultural activities, lectured at the school, helped found a hospital, and defended the rights of the Indians. In 1883 the Frémonts returned to New York, where they wrote John Charles's two-volume memoirs, and then moved back to California. Frémont died in 1890, while Jessie lived in Los Angeles until her death in 1902. She wrote her own memoirs, as well as numerous articles defending Frémont. In all she wrote four books and coauthored another, in addition to more than sixty-four magazine articles, and her published letters are an important historical source.

Jessie Benton Frémont was a brilliant and generous woman whose errors on the side of love and loyalty were well balanced by her humanitarian achievements and her literary role in promoting America's westward expansion.

—Elbert B. Smith

See also Frémont, John C.
For further reading:
Herr, Pamela. *Jessie Benton Frémont: A Biography* (1987).
Herr, Pamela, and Mary Lee Spence, eds. *The Letters of Jessie Benton Frémont* (1993).
Laas, Virginia J., ed. *Wartime Washington: The Civil War Letters of Elizabeth Blair Lee* (1991).
Phillips, Catherine Coffin. *Jessie Benton Frémont: A Woman Who Made History* (1995).
Smith, Elbert B. *Magnificent Missourian: The Life of Thomas Hart Benton* (1958).
Stone, Irving. *Immortal Wife* (1944).

FRÉMONT, JOHN CHARLES
(1813–1890)
Union general, politician

Born in Savannah, Georgia, John Charles Frémont was reared in Charleston, South Carolina, after his father, a French émigré, died in 1819. After a brilliant academic career, despite irregular attendance at the College of Charleston, he served from 1833 to 1836 as a mathematics professor aboard the naval sloop *Natchez* on a South American cruise. In 1838 he joined the army as a second lieutenant of topographical engineers, and for three years he helped Jean Nicholas Nicollet map the area between the upper Mississippi and Missouri rivers. In 1841 he led an expedition to explore the Des Moines River.

In 1841, defying her father's objections, Frémont secretly married Jessie Benton, the 17-year-old daughter of Senator

Thomas Hart Benton, chairman of the Committee on Military Affairs and a strong supporter of western explorations. A Catholic priest married them because the Protestant ministers they knew would not incur Benton's wrath, but the angry senator soon forgave them and provided a great deal of support for Frémont's career.

Frémont spent the next few years exploring and mapping much of the area between the Mississippi River and the Pacific Ocean. In 1843, his most successful expedition violated army orders, which his teen-aged bride conveniently destroyed before sending a messenger to his camp urging him to depart without delay. This expedition, with Kit Carson as guide, took him to Oregon and California, and, aided by Jessie's literary talents he published a detailed report that gave him a national reputation and provided much encouragement and valuable information for settlers eager to move west.

In spring of 1845, Frémont led sixty-two well-armed men on a "scientific" expedition back to California, where he helped promote the "Bear Flag" revolt of dissident U.S. citizens against Mexico and joined Com. Robert Stockton's naval force in conquering the area. Appointed governor and encouraged by Stockton, Frémont foolishly refused to surrender the office to General Stephen W. Kearny, who arrived with official orders to establish a government. For this he was court-martialed and dismissed from the army for insubordination. Benton served as his attorney and argued that Frémont's only real sin was not being a West Point graduate. President Polk approved the verdict but remanded the sentence.

Despite widespread public support, the angry Frémont resigned and spent the next few years laboring tirelessly in California, where he struck gold and became a millionaire. Unfortunately, however, he ultimately lost his property after a long and expensive litigation because of a faulty title. Meanwhile, in 1849 he was elected senator, but had to stand for reelection in 1851 and was defeated by the proslavery party even though the state constitution barred slavery.

In 1853–1854 Frémont led a highly publicized expedition into central Utah and was very available when the new free-soil Republican Party was looking for a popular presidential candidate opposed to slavery but untainted by earlier political conflicts. He was defeated for president in 1856 in an exciting campaign, but he carried most of the Northern states. He and Jessie greatly enhanced the popularity of the new party and help pave the way for Abraham Lincoln's victory in 1860. To his credit, he refused to respond to attacks by anti-Catholics because of his marriage by a Catholic priest. Fearing that a Republican victory would bring a civil war, Benton made twenty-one speeches in opposition to his favorite son-in-law.

When the Civil War began, Lincoln, on the advice of Postmaster General Montgomery Blair and the Blair family, made Frémont a major general in command of the western department based in St. Louis. Recruiting, organizing, arming, and effectively commanding a large untrained and ill-equipped army surrounded by Confederate sympathizers was a Herculean task beyond Frémont's experience and ability. The Blairs and others blamed him for inaction and for the Union defeat at the battle of Wilson's Creek, in which General Nathaniel Lyon and a Blair cousin were killed. Frémont answered the criticisms by ordering the emancipation of the slaves and the confiscation of the property of all Rebels in Missouri. Still trying to keep the border slave states in the Union, Lincoln asked Frémont to rescind the order, but Frémont defended his action and insisted that he would comply with Lincoln's request only if publicly ordered to do so. Returning to Washington to plead his case, Jessie, according to Lincoln, by implication threatened him with a military rebellion, and during a heated argument with her long-time friend Francis P. Blair, she suggested that she might become another "Josephine." As Frémont continued to founder, Lincoln relieved him of command, but to assuage the anger of congressional antislavery radicals, he gave Frémont command of another army centered in Virginia. Pitted against Thomas J. "Stonewall" Jackson, Frémont performed without distinction, and when his army was merged with another under the command of his long-time enemy, John Pope, he resigned.

Frémont was nominated for president again in 1864 by a convention of Radical Republicans impatient with Lincoln's delaying tactics toward slavery, and his candidacy might have threatened the president's majority in several states. He was persuaded to withdraw, however, and was promised that Lincoln would discharge Montgomery Blair. For the next several years he was involved without financial success in various western railroad projects, and he was ultimately bankrupted by a railroad swindle in which he was innocent but held liable. He served without controversy as governor of Arizona Territory from 1878 to 1883, and died in New York City in 1890.

Frémont's daring, physical toughness, and skill in coping with the wilderness won the respect of Kit Carson and other westerners, but his political and military judgments were often unwise. His ambitious wife, whom he adored, often pushed him into opportunities for spectacular achievement that made him equally vulnerable to harsh judgments when he failed, and his Benton connections helped him cultivate arrogant attitudes toward superior authority. His greatest contribution was the mapping and describing of much of the American West, which made immigration and settlement faster and easier. Also, his popularity and his position as a leader of those demanding the immediate abolition of slavery may have speeded up the process.

—*Elbert B. Smith*

See also Election of 1856; Election of 1864; Frémont, Jesse Benton; Missouri.

For further reading:

Bartlett, Ruhl J. *John C. Frémont and the Republican Party* (1970).

Dellenbaugh, Frederic S. *Frémont and '49* (1914).

Egan, Ferol. *Frémont, Explorer for a Restless Nation* (1977).

Frémont, Jessie Benton. *Souvenirs of My Time* (1887).

Nevins, Allan. *Frémont: Pathmarker of the West* (1955).

Preuss, Charles. *Exploring with Frémont: The Private Diaries of Charles Preuss, Cartographer for John C. Frémont* (1958).

Smith, Elbert B. *Francis Preston Blair* (1980).

FRENCH, SAMUEL GIBBS
(1818–1910)
Confederate general

Born in Gloucester County, New Jersey, Samuel Gibbs French received an appointment to the U.S. Military Academy in 1839. He graduated fourteenth of thirty-nine in the class of 1843. Commissioned into the artillery, French served with distinction in the Mexican-American War, serving under Zachary Taylor in northern Mexico. He received two brevet promotions and was wounded at the battle of Buena Vista in February 1847. Upon returning the United States, French entered the quartermaster's department and served there until resigning his commission in 1856. Through his marriage to a Southern woman, French owned a plantation near Vicksburg, Mississippi, to which he then devoted his full energies.

In Mississippi French became the chief of ordnance for the state militia. He continued in that role until the spring of 1861, when he accepted a commission as major of artillery in the Confederate army. In early October he was under the command of General Albert Sidney Johnston and stationed at Jackson, Mississippi. Shortly thereafter, on 23 October 1861, he was promoted to brigadier general and was called east to help with the defenses of the lower Potomac River.

French remained on the lower Potomac at Evansport, Virginia, until March 1862, when he was given command of the District of Pamlico in North Carolina. French had the difficulty of coping with an already successful Union campaign along the northern North Carolina coast at Roanoke and New Bern. In June he moved down to the southern coastline to strengthen the defenses of Wilmington at Fort Fisher.

In July, French became the commander of the Department of Southern Virginia and North Carolina and went to strengthen the defenses at Petersburg, Virginia, against a possible move by Major General George McClellan off the York Peninsula in that direction. In the fall of 1862, French was promoted to major general with a date of rank of 31 August 1862. During the next nine months French divided his time between southern Virginia and North Carolina. While there was little French could do about the Federal positions in coastal North Carolina, he did formally protest to Major General John Gray Foster the treatment of civilians and private property in the New Bern area.

In March 1863, with the situation at Vicksburg, Mississippi, potentially becoming more dire, Confederate secretary of war James Seddon consulted French because of his familiarity with the area, regarding the best way to prevent transports from operating on the Mississippi River. French wrote a detailed report on the best use of the levees to the Confederates' advantage and the best places to put defensive forces.

In April 1863, French took his division to aid General James Longstreet in his siege of Suffolk, Virginia. Shortly after Longstreet abandoned the siege in early May 1863, French was relieved of his command and ordered to report to Lieutenant General Joseph E. Johnston in Mississippi. There was still hope in Richmond that Vicksburg might still be saved, and President Jefferson Davis thought that perhaps French's knowledge of the Vicksburg area could be of some assistance.

By the time French arrived in Mississippi there was little hope for Vicksburg, and all he could do was participate in Johnston's retreat from Jackson, Mississippi. He continued to serve under Johnston until early August 1863, when he was granted a sick leave because of recurrent fever.

French returned to duty in Mississippi in the fall of 1863 and remained there until the spring of 1864, when he was summoned to join Joseph Johnston in north Georgia. French commanded a division in the Atlanta campaign, distinguishing himself at Cassville early in the campaign.

After the fall of Atlanta, French led his division in General John Bell Hood's attempt to draw Major General William T. Sherman north. On 5 October 1864, French attacked the Federal supply depot at Allatoona, Georgia. After demanding the garrison's surrender, French attempted to take the position by storm. That failing, he withdrew before Federal reinforcements arrived from Sherman.

French continued north as part of Hood's invasion of Tennessee and fought at the battle of Franklin. Shortly after that battle, French suffered a debilitating illness that nearly cost him his eyesight. As a result, he did not participate in the battle of Nashville.

Once French was able to return to duty, he was transferred to Mobile, Alabama, where he fought in the defense of the city in the spring of 1865. He surrendered near Mobile in April 1865.

After the war, French returned to Mississippi, where he worked to rebuild his plantation. He also wrote extensively, and he is most famous for his memoir of his military career. In old age he moved to Florida, where he lived quietly in retirement. He died in Florala, Florida, on 20 April 1910.

—*David S. Heidler and Jeanne T. Heidler*

See also Allatoona; Atlanta Campaign; Suffolk, Siege of.

For further reading:
French, Samuel Gibbs. *Two Wars: An Autobiography of General Samuel G. French* (1999).

FRENCH, WILLIAM HENRY
(1815–1881)
Union general

Born in Maryland, William H. French graduated from West Point in 1837, twenty-second in a class of fifty. Commissioned second lieutenant in the artillery, French served for a decade in the Second Seminole War, in the Cherokee removals, and on the Canadian border. During the Mexican-American War, French was aide-de-camp to Brigadier General (later President) Franklin Pierce, and won brevets to major for the battles of Cerro Gordo, Contreras, and Churubusco. Promoted to captain in 1848, French spent the years prior to the Civil War at frontier posts, campaigning in Florida during the Third Seminole War, and as a member of a three-officer board reworking the army's light artillery manual.

French was at Fort Duncan, Texas, with a battalion of the First Artillery when Texas seceded in February 1861. As federal authority in Texas evaporated, French daringly led a combined battalion of artillery and infantry to Fort Taylor (Key West, Florida) in March 1861. This exploit, along with his efficient curtailment of anti-Union activities in Key West in May 1861, won accolades from the army.

Commissioned brigadier general of volunteers in September 1861, French took command of the Third Brigade, Sumner's Division, Army of the Potomac in November. French's skillful performance at Fair Oaks and the Seven Days' battles during McClellan's Peninsula campaign of March and June 1862 brought command of the Third Division, II Corps at Antietam in September. In four hours of brutal fighting near Roulette's Farm and "Bloody Lane," French's division suffered 1,700 casualties but helped restore the Federal line at a crucial moment and earned praise for "gallantry" from McClellan.

Newly promoted to major general of volunteers, French led his division in the first attacks on Marye's Heights at Fredericksburg in December 1862, and at Chancellorsville in May 1863. French's rising star reached its zenith in the Gettysburg campaign of June–July, 1863. Commanding troops around Harper's Ferry, Virginia, French demonstrated initiative in saving Federal supplies while destroying pontoon bridges the Confederates would need for their retreat after the Union triumph.

As recognition of his success, French received command on 7 July 1863 of III Corps, Army of the Potomac. French's first months as a corps commander passed uneventfully, but in early November 1863, General George Meade led the Army of the Potomac into the Rappahannock/Mine Run (Virginia) campaign. Meade hoped to surprise Lee and crush his army in detail with well-timed and well-executed movements in a heavily wooded area with few good roads.

On 7 November, French's adroit handling of I, II, and III Corps in crossing the Rappahannock at Kelly's Ford contributed markedly to Union success there, but he completely bungled the Mine Run operation. On 26 November, III Corps began its movement several hours late and impeded the other Union corps. After French finally got most of his men across the Rapidan River, he promptly got lost on 27 November. As III Corps again halted, a Confederate division seized a position that blocked both III and VI Corps. Despite increasingly strident communiqués from Meade, French did not advance. Lee then had time to overcome his initial surprise to erect formidable fieldworks. Facing the prospect of another bloody fiasco like Fredericksburg, the disappointed Meade retreated into winter quarters.

Blame for the failure fell on French, and although no concrete evidence exists, many contemporaries claimed he had been intoxicated. French denied all personal responsibility for the campaign's failure and blamed bad luck and incompetent subordinates, but most historians place responsibility for the debacle on French. Not surprisingly, when Meade reorganized the Army of the Potomac in March 1864, III Corps was disbanded and French reverted to his regular army rank of lieutenant colonel. He awaited orders in Philadelphia.

Other than brief, inconsequential service during Early's Washington raid in July 1864, French saw no more action, despite a March 1865 brevet to major general. After the war, French continued in routine duties until being promoted to colonel of the Fourth Artillery on 2 July 1877. That same month, French led federal forces in crushing the Great Railroad Strike of 1877 in portions of West Virginia, Maryland, and Virginia.

Retiring in July 1880, French died of a stroke the following May. French's Civil War service, checkered with notable success and glaring failure, paralleled that of many others during the war. While a capable brigade and division commander, French resembled his Confederate counterpart A. P. Hill, who proved to be "promoted beyond his talents" while leading a corps.

—Broeck N. Oder

See also Mine Run Campaign.
For further reading:
Coddington, Edwin B. *The Gettysburg Campaign: A Study in Command* (1968).
Heitman, Francis B. *Historical Register and Dictionary of the United States Army* (1903).
Johnson, Robert Underwood, and Clarence Clough Buel, eds. *Battles and Leaders of the Civil War* (1887–1888).

Luvaas, Jay, and Wilbur S. Nye. "The Campaign That History Forgot." *Civil War Times Illustrated* (1969).

FRIETSCHIE, BARBARA
(1766–1862)
Inspiration for poem by John Greenleaf Whittier

Barbara Frietschie, of Frederick, Maryland, is immortalized by John Greenleaf Whittier's patriotic and controversial poem "Barbara Frietchie," first published in *The Atlantic* in 1863. (Whittier misspelled her name.) Frietschie was a woman of ninety-five in 1862 when the Confederate army, in their invasion of Maryland, passed through Frederick. She had lived her entire life without notoriety, as a wife, mother, and homemaker until it was reported to Whittier that she had defied the rebels as they shot at the U.S. flag. In Whittier's apocryphal poem, Frietschie is mythologized for her bravery as a defenseless elderly woman patriotically and courageously defending the Union flag against the invading Confederates led by General Stonewall Jackson. Whittier has Frietschie utter the immortal lines, "Shoot if you must this old gray head, but spare your country's flag." Jackson, shamed by the inspired appeal, replies, "'Who touches a hair of yon gray head Dies like a dog! March on!'" Immediately after publication there was a great public reaction throughout both the North and South. Northerners were inspired by the poem's patriotism and began to flock to Frietschie's home in Maryland. Southerners had a vastly different reaction. They challenged the accuracy of the incident, and they especially did not like the way in which General Jackson was portrayed.

Whittier, as a Quaker, was an ardent abolitionist. When friend Emma Southworth, a popular novelist, wrote to him an account of the flag incident, Whittier wielded the only weapon available to him as a pacifist, effectively using his pen and poetic talent to inspire Union support. He did not investigate the story further, accepting its accuracy as related to him by Southworth. It was a simple story that was at once melodramatic, extravagant, and told with the rhythm of marching boots. "Barbara Frietchie" is a powerful poem of thirty couplets that brilliantly captured the imagination of a nation desperate for heroes. The poem was reprinted in a collected volume, *In War Time*, and was also set to music and performed publicly innumerable times.

Eventually the mythology surrounding Frietschie's life took on the characteristics of a metaphor for the young country. Tradition developed that as a girl she had once served Washington supper and was later a pallbearer in an honorary funeral procession. Both stories are probably not true. She then lived out her long life as a homemaker until in her ninety-fifth year, when she supposedly defended the flag against the Confederates. Frietschie died several weeks later, reportedly from the excitement.

The main challenges to the accuracy of the facts were that Frietschie was bedridden at the time of the invasion, General Jackson did not ride by her house, and certainly there was no shooting aimed at her flag. In the 1870s, relatives of another woman, a Mrs. Quantrell, claimed that she was the real flag waver. Most of the evidence is fragmented and anecdotal, but local newspapers at the time of the invasion recounted several incidents concerning flags, none of which alluded to Frietschie. However, her obituary stated that she waved a flag at Union troops in an earlier incident. The heated emotional debate over the accuracy of Whittier's poem raged throughout the late nineteenth century, generally with Northerners accepting the poem as a true account and Southerners hotly disputing the account. The incident as told by Whittier almost certainly did not happen.

Modern scholars now agree that "Barbara Frietchie" may not be historically accurate, but that does not render it historically insignificant. Indeed, the poem inspired a warring nation desperately in need of unifying symbols. Despite being derided by critics, the Northern public embraced and loved the poem because it spoke so directly to their love of country. "Barbara Frietchie" is no longer considered a historically accurate account of a true incident but rather an important cultural phenomenon that captured the patriotic sentiment of the Northern people.

—Minoa Uffelman

See also Whittier, John Greenleaf.
For further reading:
Bennett, Whitman. *Whittier: Bard of Freedom* (1972).
Pickard, John B., ed. *The Letters of John Greenleaf Whittier* (1975).
Quynn, Dorothy Mackay, and William Rogers Quynn. *Barbara Frietschie* (1942).
Warren, Robert Penn. *John Greenleaf Whittier's Poetry: An Appraisal and a Selection* (1971).

FRONT ROYAL, BATTLE OF
(23 May 1862)

The battle of Front Royal was a Confederate victory and an important part of the successful Shenandoah Valley campaign of 1862 that propelled Thomas J. "Stonewall" Jackson to fame.

In early 1862, the Confederacy was menaced by several Union threats in Virginia: George B. McClellan's Army of the Potomac advanced up the peninsula between the York and James rivers; Major General Irvin McDowell commanded a large force south of the U.S. capital; and Major Generals Nathaniel P. Banks and John C. Frémont each led much smaller but still significant armies in the Shenandoah Valley and the Alleghenies, respectively. Robert E. Lee feared that

McClellan's massive force would be reinforced by McDowell's and together they would converge upon the Confederate capital. Lee consequently sought to divert Union attention and troops away from Richmond and toward the Shenandoah Valley. To execute that plan, he turned to Thomas Jonathan Jackson.

"Stonewall" Jackson had distinguished himself the previous summer in the battle of First Bull Run. Thereafter, he proved to be an ambitious, aggressive, hard-driving commander and one of Lee's most trusted generals. His devout Christianity and eccentricities, such as his supposed fondness for lemon and quirky ideas about human health and anatomy, added to his enormous public appeal. In mid-1862, Lee sent Jackson with fewer than 18,000 troops to harass and engage scattered Federal forces numbering 60,000.

Moving by foot and by rail, Jackson drove his Army of the Valley at an impressive speed that left poorly coordinated and dispersed Union forces confused about his whereabouts and strength. Confederate troops struck at Kernstown on 23 March to engage Federal troops in the valley and keep them from being withdrawn to support McClellan's Peninsula campaign. Brigadier General James Shields repulsed the Confederate attack, but Jackson's attempt nevertheless convinced U.S. officials to deny McClellan his reinforcements.

Jackson subsequently pushed his army up the Shenandoah Valley in time to defeat Union troops in the battle of McDowell on 8 May. From there, the Confederate general led his men first east, then down the valley toward Banks and his 8,000 regulars at Strasburg. To hide his intentions, Jackson slipped through a pass in the Massanutten Mountains on 21 May and used Turner Ashby's cavalry and the mountains themselves to screen his movement. Moving steadily northward, Jackson's force was in a position on 23 May to strike an isolated detachment of 1,000 Federals guarding the rail line at Front Royal.

The assault on Front Royal began with Confederate cavalry destroying Federal communication links between the Union garrison in Front Royal and Banks's larger force to the west at Strasburg. With Front Royal now isolated, Jackson proceeded to attack. The 1st Maryland received the order to lead the advance, but, unbeknownst to Jackson, the regiment was embroiled in internal bickering over transfers and enlistments that resulted in half the regiment placing the other half under arrest. Adding to this unusual circumstance was the fact that the regiment the 1st Maryland had been ordered to attack was from their home state—the U.S. Army's 1st Maryland. Marylanders were pitted against Marylanders both within Jackson's command and also between the two opposing forces.

Motivated by the opportunity to strike at their pro-Union kinsmen, the members of the Confederate 1st Maryland put aside their differences and drove quickly into town. They, along with Brigadier General Richard Taylor's Louisiana brigade, spearheaded the assault on Front Royal. By early afternoon, the Valley Army poured into Front Royal and drove the enemy out the other side of the town. Confederate artillery was unprepared to engage, and the fleeing Federals made their way across a nearby bridge over the North Fork of the Shenandoah River before setting it ablaze. Jackson's infantry raced across the burning bridge in pursuit, but ultimately it was the 6th Virginia Cavalry that overtook the retreating Union forces three miles north of town near Cedarville.

Of the 1,000 Federal troops at Front Royal, 90 percent were killed, wounded, or captured. Jackson's casualties probably totaled less than 100. The defeat prompted Banks to retreat to Winchester, while Jackson pursued with the bulk of his forces. A small detachment of Confederate troops left behind to guard Front Royal were surprised on 30 May by Federals from Shields's division, who subsequently regained control of the town.

—*J. Mark Thompson*

See also Jackson, Thomas Jonathan; Shenandoah Valley Campaign (1862).

For further reading:
Robertson, James I. *Stonewall Jackson: The Man, the Soldier, the Legend* (1997).
Tanner, Robert G. *Stonewall in the Valley: Thomas J. "Stonewall" Jackson's Shenandoah Valley Campaign, Spring 1862* (1976; reprint, 1996).

FRY, JAMES BARNETT
(1827–1894)
Union general

Born to Jacob Fry and Emily Turney Fry in Carrollton, Illinois, James Barnett Fry was educated locally before being admitted to the U.S. Military Academy in 1843. He graduated fourteenth of thirty-eight in the class of 1847. Commissioned as an artillery officer, Fry was sent upon graduation to serve in the latter phases of the Mexican-American War and then returned as an instructor to West Point. Until the outbreak of the Civil War he served on staff and instructional duty in the East.

A few weeks before the start of the Civil War, Fry received a brevet promotion to captain and was attached to the adjutant general's office. He served in that capacity through much of the spring of 1861. In June he joined the staff of Brigadier General Irvin McDowell and served as McDowell's adjutant through the First Bull Run campaign. It was a busy time for Fry, who assisted McDowell and the remainder of the staff in organizing the army, directed officers and their men throughout northern Virginia, and issued numerous instructions regarding the behavior of troops once the campaign commenced. One of the things that McDowell insisted on throughout the campaign was that the soldiers respect private property and that any damage done to such property be paid for. Enforcing this requirement was especially difficult for Fry. During the battle itself, Fry issued most of the orders from McDowell directing the various movements of the army. McDowell commended him for his actions during the battle.

In the fall, Fry was transferred to the Army of the Ohio to serve as Don Carlos Buell's adjutant and chief of staff. During his year in that position, Fry developed a close rapport with Buell that led him to defend the general's conduct for years to come. In the spring, Fry worked closely with Buell as the latter directed his army toward Pittsburg Landing, Tennessee, to reinforce Ulysses S. Grant. Fry arrived with Buell during the night of 6 April 1862 and helped direct Buell's army the next day during the second day of the battle of Shiloh. Buell strongly commended Fry for his actions that day, and Fry returned the favor years later by asserting that it had been Buell's efforts that had ultimately won the battle on the seventh. Shortly after the battle, Fry directed a raid of Union forces that attacked Confederate communication lines between Chattanooga, Tennessee, and Marietta, Georgia.

Fry remained Buell's adjutant and chief of staff through the advance on Corinth in the late spring of 1862. He was again commended for that duty and then returned with Buell to Kentucky later in the summer. Fry served in the same capacity during Braxton Bragg's invasion of Kentucky and helped direct the Union troops during the battle of Perryville. With Buell's removal shortly thereafter, Fry was recalled to Washington, where he served for a few months in the adjutant general's office.

With the passage of the first Conscription Act in March 1863, Congress also created the Bureau of the Provost-Marshal-General. The function of this office was not only to organize the procedures for conscription in the states but also to interpret the exemptions provided by Congress and to curtail the desertion rate. While there were several candidates for the new position, a number of officers, including Ulysses S. Grant, saw Fry's organizational abilities as ideal for the job. Fry, who had been promoted to lieutenant colonel the previous December, received the appointment at the rank of colonel on 17 March 1863. He held the position until the abolition of the bureau in 1866.

For his first few months in office, Fry worked tirelessly to organize his bureau and all the provost marshals around the country who served as his conscription agents. Given the newness of such procedures, Fry was largely credited with doing an admirable job. He advocated taking a hard line with those individuals who sought to evade the draft or to impede its enforcement, stands that would make him unpopular in many states. He was unable to monitor the activities of every local

agent, and as a result many abuses and some corruption in the system occurred. He became especially unpopular in New York City when he urged Secretary of War Edwin Stanton to use troops to suppress the draft riots there in the summer of 1863.

Besides his other duties, Fry also was charged with revamping the entire Federal recruiting system and directing the apprehension of subversives and Confederate agents in the United States. He performed these activities with tremendous efficiency, earning promotion to brigadier general of volunteers in the spring of 1864. At the end of the war, his office aided in the capture of Confederate officials and he was brevetted major general for his actions during the war.

Through the early months of 1866, a rancorous debate consumed much of the activity of Congress regarding not only the reorganization of the army but also a proposal made by James G. Blaine of Maine that the Provost-Marshal-General's office be made a permanent part of the army. The act that had created the bureau back in March 1863 was due to expire in August 1866. Roscoe Conkling of New York, still angry with Fry for the way conscription had been enforced in his state, argued strenuously against such a move and attacked Fry's running of the bureau in the process. The bureau was allowed to expire, and Fry reverted to the rank of lieutenant colonel in the adjutant general's office. He was promoted to colonel in 1875 and served for the next six years at various posts throughout the country.

Fry retired in 1881 to devote his life to writing. Already prolific in his writings on the war and other topics, Fry spent the remaining years of his life writing on a variety of subjects in book form and for various periodicals. He died on 11 July 1894 in Newport, Rhode Island.

—*David S. Heidler and Jeanne T. Heidler*

See also Buell, Don Carlos; Conscription, U.S.A.; Desertion.
For further reading:
Fry, James B. *McDowell and Tyler in the Campaign of Bull Run, 1861* (1884).
———. *Operations of the Army under Buell from June 10th to October 30th, 1862, and the "Buell Commission"* (1884).
U.S. Congress. *Hon. Roscoe Conkling and Provost Marshal General Fry* (1866).

FRY, SPEED SMITH
(1817–1892)
Union general

Speed Smith Fry was born on 9 September 1817 on a farm known as Spring House outside Danville, Kentucky. He studied law but succeeded at being a merchant in Danville until he organized a company for the 2d Kentucky Regiment, which fought most famously in the battle of Buena Vista during the Mexican-American War. On 7 November 1847, Fry married Mildred T. Smith of

Jefferson County, Kentucky, but she died in June 1849 after giving birth to their daughter, Mildred. Speed married Cynthia Hope in 1851, the same year he ran for and was elected to the position of county judge. They had three sons: Frank W., Thomas J., and Speed S.

When the Civil War broke out, Fry espoused his Unionism and immediately organized a militia. In April 1861, he enrolled 100 young men and gathered the famous "Lincoln Guns" to arm these home guards. When President Lincoln called for troops from Kentucky, General William Nelson gave Fry the authority to raise a regiment. On 6 August 1861, Fry and a few recruits established Camp Dick Robinson in Garrard County; on 9 October 1861, General George H. Thomas mustered into service his regiment, the 4th Kentucky Volunteer Infantry.

In mid-January 1862, Colonel Fry was a key figure in the battle of Logan's Cross Roads (or Mill Springs). It was Fry who shot and killed Confederate general Felix K. Zollicoffer as he wandered into the Union lines. On 26 May 1863, Fry was made commander of the Eastern Division of Kentucky and established his headquarters at Camp Nelson.

In 1863 Camp Nelson was established south of Nicholasville in Jessamine County and on the Kentucky River. Though the federal government began recruiting Northern blacks that summer, white Kentuckians protested and President Lincoln backed away from the controversy. Finally on 10 March 1864, Governor Thomas E. Bramlette agreed to the recruitment of Kentucky blacks, but only to fill the state's quota deficits left over from whites. U.S. recruiting of Kentuckian African-Americans had already begun months earlier by agents for Northern states and by the Military Department of Tennessee in Kentucky west of the Cumberland River.

The draft of Kentucky's African-Americans began on 10 March, and Camp Nelson was the most important recruiting station and training camp for the many regiments of U.S. Colored Troops there, including the 5th and 6th U.S. Colored Cavalry regiments and the 114th and 116th U.S. Colored Heavy Artillery regiments. Because President Lincoln's Emancipation Proclamation did not apply to Kentucky, slave owners received up to $300 bounty for each slave recruited in the army until July, when it was decided that the enlistee should receive the money. More significantly, Camp Nelson was not a legal refuge for the dependents of those recruits who had been slaves, but this did not deter the flood of camp followers who set up shanty towns in the area.

During the summer and fall of 1864, Brigadier General Fry refused to feed or shelter the relatives of central Kentucky recruits. He ordered all those who were unfit for military service, that is, women, children, the elderly, and the sick, to return to their slave owners. According to the *National Anti-Slavery Standard* of 18 June 1864, he threat-

ened to whip any refugee found at Camp Nelson. *The Liberator* of 24 June 1864 reported that Fry had bound three women and whipped them as an example for all. Reports abounded of men, women, and children either tied together and guarded by Union soldiers until the slave owners claimed them or hunted by squads of soldiers through the camp. Fry's Order No. 19, issued on 23 August, ordered that all officers who had "negro women in their employment" to let the patrol take the women to headquarters and threatened to arrest any officer who refused. No matter how many women and children were expelled from the camp, new refugees arrived every day, and many of those who were sent away returned.

The shortage of basic necessities and health care at Camp Nelson made it a case study of horrific proportions often noted by the U.S. Sanitary Commission workers. Nevertheless, the black troops and refugees found the time and energy to educate themselves. By the late fall, thirteen volunteer missionaries, including the abolitionist minister John G. Fee, taught classes at Camp Nelson, but countless numbers of soldiers taught reading, writing, and vocal music to the refugees.

On 23 November 1864, the temperature was below freezing. Under orders from General Fry, the provost guard swept through the poor makeshift shacks and pushed out 400 women and children into the snow-filled road. Some went to Ohio, but most made it to Nicholasville, where missionaries tried to feed and shelter them.

Once the tragedy was exposed in the Northern press, the U.S. Army felt compelled to change its policy. Advised by his adjutant, J. B. Dickson, General Steven G. Burbridge countermanded Fry's order and ordered Fry to assist abolitionist Captain T. E. Hall in erecting dwellings for the soldiers' families. Fry placed Hall under arrest. Dickson eventually arranged to have Fry removed from command, and by 1 December 1864, 200–300 women and children returned to Camp Nelson. Groups of two to twenty refugees continued to arrive daily.

On 15 December 1864, General Lorenzo Thomas announced that shelter and rations would be provided for families of recruits in all rendezvous camps. He explained carefully that better attention to the needs of their dependents could result in more successful recruitment of African-Americans into the Union army. Despite the new barracks, a pneumonic epidemic broke out and more than half of the refugee population was critically ill. Of the 250 refugees who made it back to camp after their expulsion in November, 102 eventually died in the new shelters. That spring, Fee convinced the superintendent for refugees, Captain Hall, to build duplex cottages, thirty-two by sixteen feet; each sixteen-foot-square apartment was supposed to house ten to twelve refugees. Twenty-nine cottages were completed by the end of the war.

Not all of those who found refuge at Camp Nelson were from the local area. In the spring of 1865, General

John Palmer gave the order for freed slaves to have free railroad tickets called "Palmer passes." Elijah P. Marrs from Shelby County, third duty sergeant of Company L, 12th U.S. Colored Heavy Artillery Regiment, led 750 refugees from Bowling Green to Nicholasville on the train. When they stopped in Louisville and Lexington, African-American women's aid societies gave them the food and health care they desperately needed. Then the refugees, ranging in age from six months to eighty years, walked the eight miles to Camp Nelson. The U.S. Army had provided only one ration for each refugee during the whole expedition.

In early March 1865, federal law freed the wives and children of black soldiers, and Camp Nelson was the chief center issuing emancipation papers to the dependents of Kentucky's U.S. Colored Troops. By March 1865, it was estimated that 71 percent, or all but about 65,000 of enslaved Kentuckians, were legally freed. Slavery in Kentucky did not officially end until December 1865 when the Thirteenth Amendment was ratified—without the support of the Kentucky legislature. Of the 3,060 refugees who were registered at Camp Nelson, 1,300 died. Yet no other posts where African-American soldiers were stationed gave refugees even the rudimentary protection and security they received at Camp Nelson. The legend of the camp as a "City of Refuge" continues today.

In 1866 Fry ran as a Republican for Congress, and his policy of harassment of refugees did not hinder his success. He also worked to collect claims against the government. In April 1869, he was appointed supervisor of internal revenue for his district. His wife, Cynthia, died on 31 August 1884, and he died eight years later on 1 August 1892 at age 75.

—*Randolph Hollingsworth*

See also Kentucky; Logan's Cross Roads, Battle of; Palmer, John McCauley; Thomas, Lorenzo; United States Colored Troops; United States Sanitary Commission; Zollicoffer, Felix K.

For further reading:
Harrison, Lowell H. *The Civil War in Kentucky* (1975).
Howard, Victor B. *Black Liberation in Kentucky: Emancipation and Freedom, 1862–1884* (1983).
Lucas, Marion B. *A History of Blacks in Kentucky, Vol. 1: From Slavery to Segregation, 1760–1891* (1992).
Sears, Richard. "*A Practical Recognition of the Brotherhood of Man,*" John G. Fee and the Camp Nelson Experience (1986).

FUGITIVE SLAVE ACT OF 1850

Certainly the antebellum era's most controversial legislative measure, the Fugitive Slave Act of 1850 polarized the already strained relationship between the antislavery North and the proslavery South. Many Southerners viewed the measure as a natural affirmation of their constitutional right to recapture all fugitives from labor who sought to escape from the chattel slavery that defined Southern institutional life. For the slaveholders and the slave catchers whom they employed, the right to recapture fugitive slaves was an obvious extension of common law property rights long considered essential to free market capitalism. For many Northerners, the Fugitive Slave Act was an assault upon the integrity of freedom, an appalling contradiction for a society with cherished origins as a land of liberty. Abolitionists and their supporters decried the measure upon moral grounds and mounted sustained efforts to render it useless by encouraging acts of civil disobedience.

When the states ratified the U.S. Constitution in 1789 they instituted a document that included a fugitive slave clause (Article IV, Section 2), which stipulated the return of criminal fugitives and fugitives from labor. However, the clause neither stated who was responsible for conducting this action, nor did it describe the process of recovering fugitives. Congress enacted the Fugitive Slave Act of 1793 to clarify the vague provisions of how this constitutional guarantee should function, but many Northerners remained dissatisfied with specific internal weaknesses of this measure. Many believed that the 1793 Act did not do enough to protect the civil liberties of free blacks who might be falsely accused of being fugitive slaves. Others balked at the act's recognition of the right of recaption, the common law provision that Southern slaveowners maintained gave them the right to recapture their property without the burden of using the court system. Between 1780 and 1850, fourteen states enacted so-called personal liberty laws to protect the rights of free blacks within their jurisdictions by imposing a judicial hearing before a suspected fugitive could be removed from the state.

The internal weaknesses of the Fugitive Slave Act of 1793 were recognized by the courts, and the measure's effectiveness plummeted with time. In the case of *Prigg v. Pennsylvania*, 41 U.S. 539 (1842), the U.S. Supreme Court struck down an 1826 Pennsylvania personal liberty law that had added additional hindrances to the process of recaption that were in violation of the Fugitive Slave Act of 1793. The Pennsylvania law had required that slave catchers obtain a "certificate of removal" from a local magistrate before removing a suspected fugitive from the state. The Supreme Court's ruling was a rather hollow victory for proslavery forces in that it asserted the constitutional right of recaption, but also stated that while local and state officials should enforce the Fugitive Slave Act, the national government could not mandate such compliance. In the wake of the *Prigg* decision, local and state officials began to refuse to cooperate with slave catchers and this systematic noncompliance marked the effectual demise of the Fugitive Slave Act of 1793.

Southern political leaders demanded a new and stronger Fugitive Slave Act to force compliance upon Northern magistrates whose efforts had made recaption more difficult. The push for such legislation became the

Fugitive slaves fording the Rappahannock River, Virginia, August 1862
(Photograph by Timothy H. O'Sullivan / *Library of Congress*)

chief agenda item of the South's congressional caucus, and many feared that if Congress failed to act upon such a measure, some proslavery states might consider seceding from the Union. Hoping to defuse the growing sectional crisis through effective compromise, Kentucky senator Henry Clay included such a fugitive slave measure in his Omnibus Bill, but that legislative package failed to win Senate approval in 1850. Illinois senator Stephen A. Douglas was able to repackage the provisions of Clay's measure into five separate bills that each won approval as shifting coalitions consolidated in the so-called Compromise of 1850.

The Fugitive Slave Act of 1850 was harsher than the 1793 measure, as it specifically forbade states from interfering with recaption. It also authorized federal marshals and specially appointed commissioners to sign warrants for arrest and certificates for removal of suspected fugitives. Although the new act made it easier for recaption to occur, most Northern states maintained their personal liberty laws and urged noncompliance with what they perceived as an unjust federal law.

A wave of outrage and righteous indignation swept the North upon the passage of the Fugitive Slave Act and fanned the flames of antislavery sentiment.

Massachusetts citizens deemed Senator Daniel Webster a traitor for having supported the measure, and, adding his own vitriol, abolitionist poet John Greenleaf Whittier immortalized Webster's fall from grace in the poem "Ichabod." In 1851 Harriet Beecher Stowe began publishing portions of *Uncle Tom's Cabin* in serial form, and when the entire book was released in 1852, it galvanized Northern opposition to slavery and its apologists. Antislavery sentiment and opposition to the Fugitive Slave Act grew so strong in the North that in 1854 the U.S. government had to spend $100,000 to cover the costs associated with returning the fugitive slave Anthony Burns from Boston to the South. It required hundreds of Massachusetts militia and 2,000 federal troops to escort Burns from his jail cell to the dock where he boarded the vessel that carried him back to Virginia.

In 1855 Wisconsin's supreme court declared the federal Fugitive Slave Act to be unconstitutional in the case of *In re Booth and Rycraft*, 3 Wis. 157 (1855), but the U.S. Supreme Court later ruled in *Ableman v. Booth*, 62 U.S. 506 (1859), that state courts could not subvert federal law. The U.S. Supreme Court decision also upheld the constitutionality of the Fugitive Slave Act of 1850.

Although the Fugitive Slave Act of 1850 made life

more difficult for those slaves who attempted to escape from bondage, the measure truly had little effective consequence in stemming instances of escape or in raising aggregate rates of recaption. While the passage of the measure may have salved the consciences of Southerners who demanded affirmation of the proslavery position, the act's affective consequences did much more to galvanize the antislavery position of the abolitionists and their supporters.

—*Junius P. Rodriguez*

See also Burns, Anthony; Personal Liberty Laws; *Prigg v. Pennsylvania*; Stowe, Harriet Beecher; *Uncle Tom's Cabin*; Whittier, John Greenleaf.

For further reading:

Campbell, Stanley W. *The Slave Catchers: Enforcement of the Fugitive Slave Law, 1850–1860* (1968).

Gara, Larry. *The Liberty Line: The Legend of the Underground Railroad* (1967).

Nye, Russell B. *Fettered Freedom: Civil Liberties and the Slave Controversy, 1830–1860* (1963).

Pease, Jane H., and William H. Pease. *The Fugitive Slave Law and Anthony Burns: A Problem in Law Enforcement* (1975).

FURMAN, JAMES CLEMENT
(1809–1891)
South Carolina Baptist leader

James Clement Furman participated in the Secession Convention in South Carolina and then ardently supported the Confederate cause through his efforts on the home front. The son of Richard Furman, an eminent South Carolina Baptist pastor and educator during the Revolutionary and Early Republic eras, and Dorothea Maria Burn, Furman worked as a Baptist pastor and educator in South Carolina. He graduated from the College of Charleston in 1826, and originally planned to pursue the medical profession. He, however, was converted during the preaching of Dr. Basil Manly, Sr., and began ministerial pursuits, preaching his first sermon and being licensed all in 1828. After studying for a time at the Furman Institution, he was ordained in 1832. The following year, he married Harriet E. Davis and began pastoring the Welsh Neck Church at Society Hill, South Carolina. When the Southern Baptist Convention was formed in May 1845, Furman participated in the inaugural convention.

His career as an educator began in December 1844, when he resigned his church to became the senior professor of the Furman Theological Institution (formerly the Furman Institution), an office that placed the leadership of the school upon him. When the institution became Furman University in 1852, he became chairman of the faculty. He also served as professor of intellectual philosophy and professor of sacred rhetoric and pastoral duties. In 1859, he accepted the position of president of the university, serving until his resignation in 1879. During the Civil War, the university closed, and Furman served as president and professor at the Greenville Baptist Female College. After his departure from Furman University, he remained active as a preacher and as the associate editor of the *Baptist Courier* until his death.

With the coming of the Civil War, Furman never hesitated regarding his support of secession. On 22 November 1860 at the courthouse in Greenville, South Carolina, he participated in a meeting designed to elect five candidates from the Greenville district to attend the state's Secession Convention. This district was one of the few in the state where a significant portion of anti-secessionist citizens resided. Many speeches were given that day arguing the merits of both sides, but in the end, the people elected five secessionist candidates, including Furman, to represent them in the convention to be held beginning on 17 December.

In his speech, Furman argued that the principles of the Constitution of the United States had been violated and unfulfilled by the Northern states. The government, for example, had trampled upon the principle of justice by failing to secure the property rights of the South and robbing Southerners of thousands of dollars. He cited the protective tariff system and the fugitive slave laws as examples. Abolitionist characterizations of slavery as a crime and the efforts to exclude slaveholders from the territories insulted the dignity of the Southern states, he said. Furthermore, the government had failed to uphold domestic tranquility by allowing the dictatorial North to monopolize the oppressed South. He asserted that, "Domestic tranquility for Southern members of Congress is to play the part of a hen-pecked wight forever annoyed by a noisy vixen." Southerners could relieve their representatives by sending them to the Congress of the Southern Confederacy. Finally, Northerners had caused slaves to despise their masters, thereby creating perpetual turmoil. The election of Abraham Lincoln as president signaled continued hostility toward the South.

Furman maintained these sentiments even after Confederate losses during 1862–1863. During that time, he continued to question Northern motives for maintaining the Union, charging that the one master passion of the North was the love of money. This love was the only reason why the North desired any association with the South. Yet, they hypocritically cloaked such desires in the love of the flag. Years later, Furman remained convinced that the North had violated the rights of the South, as well as the principles of the Constitution. At a Memorial Day address in 1880, he continued to argue that the denial of the right of secession was tantamount to the denial of self-government. He hoped that in years to come, those who had been seen as the enemies of the "best" government in the world would be heralded as the truest friends of liberty.

Furman had a great impact on Baptist life and on education in South Carolina. His primary contribution to the Civil War effort came from his leadership in bringing about secession and his attempts to maintain popular confidence in it. In the difficult years after the war, his efforts greatly aided Furman University's ability to remain open.

—Scott M. Langston

See also Churches.
For further reading:
Cook, Harvey Toliver. *The Life Work of James Clement Furman* (1926).
Dictionary of American Biography (1943).
Encyclopedia of Southern Baptists (1958).
McGlothlin, W.J. *Baptist Beginnings in Education: A History of Furman University* (1926).
Special Collections. James B. Duke Library, Furman University.

Chickahominy or Cold Harbor. It took place on some of the same ground as the 1864 battle of Cold Harbor. After repelling the attacks of Hill's Division at the battle of Mechanicsville (26 June 1862), Fitz John Porter's V Corps remained strongly entrenched in their position overlooking Beaver Dam Creek. McClellan was concerned about a flank attack by Jackson's troops just arrived from the Shenandoah Valley, and he was erroneously convinced that he was greatly outnumbered. He sent orders to Porter to withdraw from Beaver Dam Creek and fall back about four miles to Boatswain's Creek, a stream that emptied into the Chickahominy. Porter's new position on the eastern bank of Boatswain's Creek was similar to his of the day before at Mechanicsville; he held a stretch of high ground overlooking a barrier of creek and marshes. The Federals had only a few hours to dig in, in contrast to having a few days to work on the Beaver Dam Creek fortifications, yet they presented a formidable obstacle to Lee's army.

On 27 June Lee sent Jackson and D. H. Hill to Old Cold Harbor, which would place them in position to strike Porter's right flank. Longstreet was sent in support of A. P. Hill, who was pursuing Porter's rear guard. The first real fighting of the day began about noon, when General Maxcy Gregg's brigade of Hill's command drove

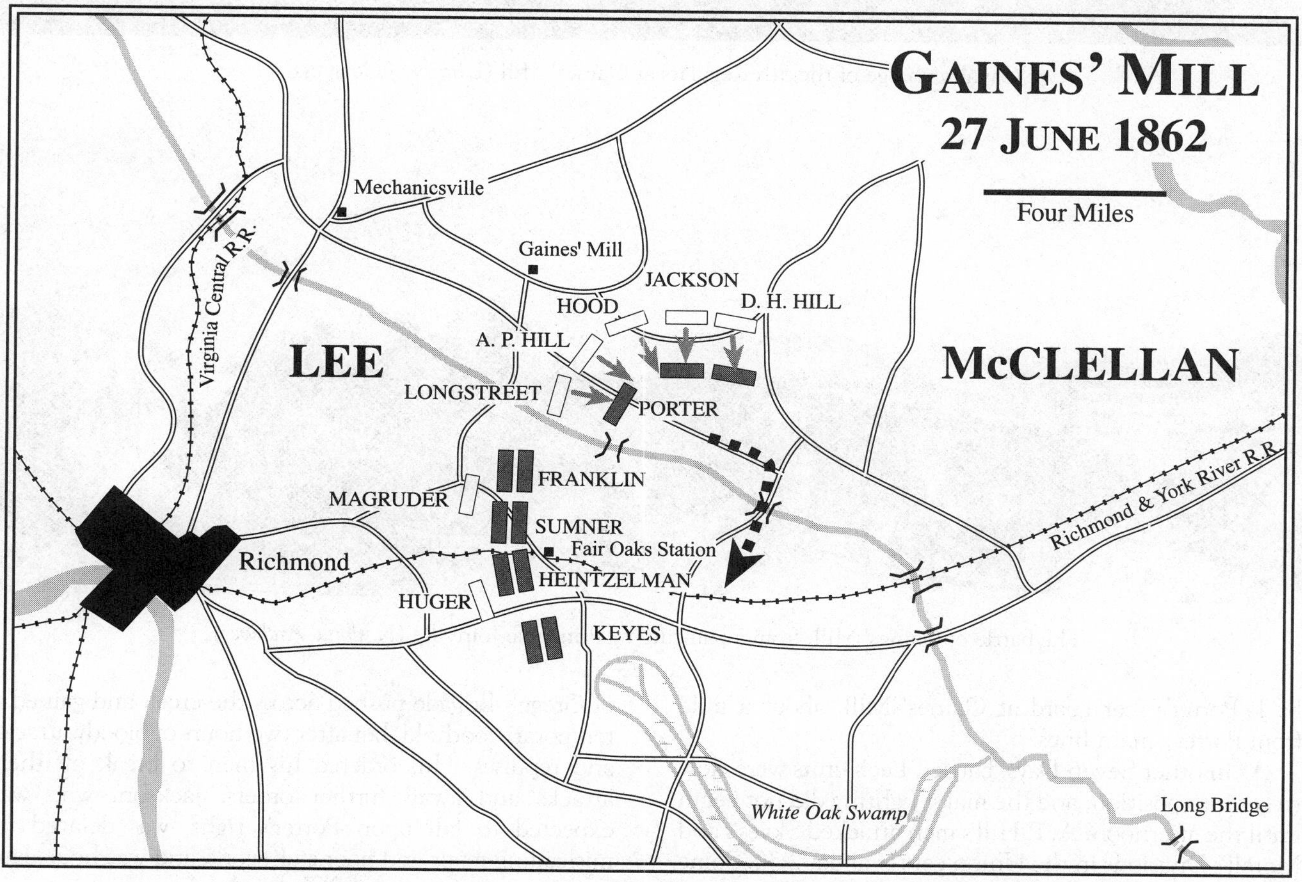

GAINES' MILL, BATTLE OF
(27 June 1862)

The battle of Gaines' Mill was the second, and the bloodiest, of the Seven Days' battles. The engagement is also known as the battle of

799

Cavalry charge of the 5th Regulars at Gaines' Mill (*Library of Congress*)

The battle of Gaines' Mill, from a painting by Prince de Joinville (*National Archives*)

back Porter's rear guard at Gaines' Mill, about a mile from Porter's main lines.

As in other Seven Days' battles, Lee's units were slow to get into position, and the major fighting did not begin until the afternoon. A. P. Hill's men attacked Skyes's and Morell's Divisions in the Union center about 2:30. Some of Gregg's Brigade pushed across the creek and gained a temporary foothold, but after two hours of bloody attacks and repulses, Hill ordered his men to break off their attacks and await further orders. Jackson, who was expected to fall upon Porter's right, was delayed by misleading maps and poor staff work, and was hours late

Unburied dead on the battlefield at Gaines' Mill, 1862 (*Library of Congress*)

reaching the battlefield. As at Mechanicsville, the usually swift and aggressive Jackson was uncharacteristically slow and indecisive at Gaines' Mill.

At about 4:30 some of Jackson's troops under D. H. Hill and Richard Ewell arrived and were committed to the battle. D. H. Hill attacked the Union right and Ewell's Division joined A. P. Hill in another attack on the Union center. Longstreet sent four brigades against the Union left. All of these Rebel attacks, conducted across stretches of open ground that led down to the woods, brush, and swamps along the creek, were bloodily repulsed. Much of the burden of Porter's defense was borne by George Sykes's division of U.S. regulars. Sykes had been D. H. Hill's roommate at West Point.

Lee had so far been unable to make a general attack all along his line mainly because of Jackson's lateness in reaching the field. Jackson joined Lee late in the afternoon. The firing quieted about 6 P.M. as Lee's commanders readied themselves for a final attempt to overrun Porter before dark.

Porter, bracing for an all-out attack on his lines, urgently requested reinforcements, but McClellan sent only two brigades of infantry from his 60,000 available men. It would prove to be too little, too late.

About 7 P.M. the Confederates attacked all along Porter's lines. Hood's Brigade, holding their fire until ten yards from the enemy, unleashed a volley that crumbled Brigadier General George Taylor's brigade. Hood's men poured through the gap, pushing steadily toward the artillery positions behind the lines. After shattering a desperate charge by the 5th U.S. Cavalry, they reached the batteries and took fourteen guns. Nearly

Ruins of Gaines' Mill, photographed in 1865 (Photograph by John Reekie / *Library of Congress*)

simultaneous breakthroughs, by D. H. Hill near the Union right and by Longstreet on the enemy left, forced Porter's men into headlong retreat after withstanding two days of determined attacks. The gathering darkness, the steadiness of Sykes's regulars, and the arrival of Meagher's and French's Brigades as reinforcements helped to cover their retreat.

McClellan told his commanders at 11 P.M. that they were going to abandon their positions in front of Richmond and withdraw to the James River. There, sheltered by navy gunboats, they would await reinforcements. Although McClellan called this move a "change of base," it was plainly seen as a retreat to the disappointed North. Lee continued his pursuit, and the next battle was fought at Savage's Station on 29 June.

Southern hopes were revived by Lee's victory at Gaines' Mill, although the cost was sobering. Union losses, totaling 6,837 casualties, were surpassed by Southern losses of about 8,750. Many veterans would remember Gaines' Mill as one of the fiercest clashes of the war.

—*David A. Norris*

For further reading:
Davis, William C., ed. The Guns of '62. In *The Image of War 1861–1865* (1982).
Freeman, Douglas Southall. *Lee's Lieutenants: A Study in Command* (1942).
Hill, Daniel H. "Lee's Attacks North of the Chickahominy." In *Battles and Leaders of the Civil War* Vol. 2.
Official Records. Series I, Vol. 11, pt. 2.
Porter, Fitz John. "Hanover Court House and Gaines' Mill." In

Battles and Leaders of the Civil War Vol. 2.
Robertson, James I., Jr. *A. P. Hill: The Story of a Confederate Warrior* (1987).
Sears, Stephen W. *To the Gates of Richmond* (1992).

GALVANIZED YANKEES

Galvanized Yankees" was the name given to captured Confederate soldiers who agreed to enlist in the Union army in exchange for release from prison camp. Six regiments, designated as the 1st through the 6th U.S. Volunteer Infantry, were composed of these former Confederate soldiers.

These men enlisted in the Union army for various reasons: some wanted to escape from the disease or boredom of imprisonment; some were disillusioned with the Confederate cause; and perhaps some intended to desert and return to the Confederacy. Whatever their reasons, almost 6,000 Confederate prisoners from prison camps in the Midwest enlisted with the understanding that they would not be forced to fight their former comrades. These regiments spent the entirety of their service on the Great Plains fighting Indians. Besides the six regiments made up entirely of Galvanized Yankees, others contained former Confederates who enlisted as individuals or in small groups.

Many who became Galvanized Yankees were foreign born. For them, the Civil War evoked little of the emotion that it stirred among native southerners. Many Irish or German prisoners enlisted in ethnic Union regiments, including 228 Irish prisoners from Camp Douglas (Chicago) who served in several Illinois regiments during a two-month period in the spring of 1862. The most famous of these foreign-born Galvanized Yankees was Henry Morton Stanley, an Englishman by birth, who would become a newspaper correspondent and an African explorer.

The decision to enlist these prisoners in the Union army was not taken lightly by the federal government. Both President Abraham Lincoln and Secretary of War Edwin M. Stanton resisted the idea until 1864, when the need for manpower in the face of draft riots in Eastern cities made the decision credible. Even after the men were mustered into service, many Union officers remained highly suspicious of the former Confederates. Most changed their minds, however, when they saw the Galvanized Yankees in battle. Many veteran Union officers came to believe that the U.S. Volunteers were among the best troops they had ever seen. Whatever their reason for enlisting, the former Confederate soldiers who made up 1st through 6th U.S. Volunteer Infantry Regiments served the Union well during their two years of existence.

Part of the reason for the excellent service record of the U.S. Volunteers was the quality of their officers.

They tended to be Union veterans (many had served as noncommissioned officers in state regiments) who were young and energetic. Of the six regimental commanders, Colonel C. A. R. Dimon, 1st U.S. Volunteers, had begun the war as a private in the 7th Massachusetts Infantry Regiment; Colonel Andrew P. Caraher, 2d U.S. Volunteers, was an Irish-born veteran of Fredericksburg and Gettysburg; Colonel Christopher McNally, 3d U.S. Volunteers, was an English-born veteran of fighting in the Southwest; Colonel Charles Thornton, 4th U.S. Volunteers, had served as an officer in the 12th Maine; Colonel Henry E. Maynadier, 5th U.S. Volunteers, was a West Point graduate (class of 1851); and Colonel Carroll H. Potter, 6th U.S. Volunteers, had attended West Point before being expelled in 1860 for academic deficiency. In addition, the Galvanized Yankees themselves had the opportunity to earn commissions, and several made it to the rank of captain.

Between September 1864 and November 1866, the 1st through 6th U.S. Volunteer Infantry Regiments served on the western frontier from Minnesota to the Oregon Territory in the North and from New Mexico to California in the South. Serving in desolate posts throughout the frontier, many died in combat or from disease. Some became victims of the harsh weather of the Great Plains. Yet their desertion rate was only slightly higher than that of state volunteer regiments and was markedly lower than that of regular regiments serving on the frontier after the Civil War.

Union prisoners also volunteered to serve in the Confederate Army during the war, but these men, known as Galvanized Confederates, very seldom took up arms against their country. Instead, most frequently surrendered to Union forces when the first opportunity arose.

—*Alexander M. Bielakowski*

See also Desertion.
For further reading:
Brown, D. Alexander. *Galvanized Yankees* (1963).
Jones, Robert H. *Civil War in the Northwest* (1960).

GALVESTON, TEXAS

A thriving town of more than 7,000 in 1860, Galveston was the second-largest city in Texas, a major processor and exporter of cotton (200,000 bales in 1860) and sugar, and an industrial center with two iron foundries and numerous manufacturers of sails and other maritime products. As a major port for the western Confederacy and potential anchor for the Union blockading fleet, the island city of Galveston was considered vital by Texas, Confederate, and Union authorities alike.

In February 1861, even before Texas officially seceded from the Union, men from Galveston, under the command of John "Rip" Ford, a well-known Texas Ranger, sailed to the U.S. Army post at Fort Brown and

Attack on the Union gunboat flotilla at Galveston, 1 January 1863 (*Library of Congress*)

confiscated federal armaments and supplies. In the meantime, the state's Committee on Public Safety met in Galveston and set about collecting arms and building up the city's defenses. Despite their efforts, however, a lack of resources and more serious manpower and material needs in the Eastern theater caused authorities in Richmond to ignore the defense of the long and practically unguarded Texas coast. By late 1861, Galveston was "defended" by a battery of "Quaker" guns and city militiamen.

The first blockading vessel arrived off Galveston in July 1861, and throughout the next year and a half, federal ships occasionally shelled the city and seized a number of alleged blockade runners. In October 1862, Galveston remained virtually undefended, and a small U.S. Navy flotilla of gunboats and makeshift mortar boats captured the city. By the end of the year, 300 men from the 42d Massachusetts had arrived to defend the abandoned city against counterattack.

That attack came in a stunning New Year's surprise by Confederate troops under the command of Major General John Magruder, who had reached Texas as commander of the Confederate District of Texas, New Mexico, and Arizona a few weeks after Galveston fell. Leading a rag-tag army of Confederate soldiers, Texan volunteers, and "cottonclad" gunboats, Magruder

launched a night attack against the island from land and from sea. Outnumbered and plagued by the same lack of fortifications and artillery that had made Galveston so easy to capture three months before, the Yankees surrendered after a sharp battle. In one of the fight's most dramatic moments, Confederate volunteer Albert Lea boarded the USS. *Harriet Lane* only to find his mortally wounded son, U.S. Navy lieutenant Edward Lea, lying on the deck. A few days after the battle, the famous raider CSS *Alabama* made a surprise appearance just in time to drive off a Union squadron preparing to attack the city.

The following months saw the frantic construction of a series of forts and batteries on the island. Yet as the immediate threat to the port eased, the garrison was stripped for campaigning in Louisiana and Arkansas, and the hastily built forts were defended by undermanned and barely armed units. Shortages of water and firewood plagued the army and returning civilians alike, while the drunkenness and lack of discipline among the troops, combined with poor rations, led to a brief and bloodless mutiny by members of the 3d Texas in August 1863. Soldiers protested again in March 1864, when hundreds of hungry, disgruntled men assembled outside a ball being given in Magruder's honor. Finally, a yellow fever outbreak in the fall of 1864 further demoralized the inhabitants and defenders of Galveston. To end the year on a sour note, a cutter launched from a Union blockader managed to sneak into Galveston harbor and capture a blockade runner loaded with cotton.

Despite the grim conditions, Galveston remained an important haven for Confederate blockade runners. As many as nine or ten ships were in port at any given time, with arrivals and departures taking place every night. Thousands of tons of cotton left the Confederacy via Galveston, with more tons of military supplies and luxuries coming into the South through one of the few Confederate ports to remain open until the end of the war. On those occasions when a ship successfully put in to Galveston, the stores would open for a few days for the benefit of the residents.

By 14 May 1865, with the war over in Virginia and conditions continuing to deteriorate in Texas, hundreds of weary Confederates vainly attempted to desert en masse. A few weeks later, General E. Kirby Smith formally surrendered what was left of the Army of the Trans-Mississippi on a Union vessel anchored off Galveston. Union troops entered the city on 5 June, and it was there, on 19 June—known forever after as "Juneteenth"—that General Gordon Granger issued the order emancipating slaves in Texas.

—*James Marten*

See also Blockade of C.S.A.; Texas.
For further reading:
Cotham, Edward T., Jr. *Battle on the Bay: The Civil War Struggle for Galveston* (1998).
Kerby, Robert L. *Kirby Smith's Confederacy: The Trans-Mississippi South, 1863–1865* (1972).

GAMBLE, HAMILTON ROWAN
(1798–1864)
Governor of Missouri

Born in Winchester, Virginia, on 29 November 1798, Hamilton Gamble studied law before moving to St. Louis in 1818. He served as deputy clerk of the St. Louis circuit court, then later as Missouri's secretary of state under Governor Frederick Bates. Gamble also served one term in the Missouri legislature. Elected to the Missouri supreme court in 1851, he became presiding judge and participated in some celebrated cases, including the *Dred Scott* case. Resigning from the court in 1854 due to ill health, Gamble entered semiretirement in 1858, moving to Pennsylvania.

The secession crisis brought Gamble back to Missouri in January 1861. He was elected to the Missouri state convention, which was called to discuss secession. Meeting in March 1861, the convention chose a select committee to deliberate on Missouri's future. Appointed as chairman of this committee, Gamble dominated it by force of personality. He penned the committee report, which proposed that Missouri's interests lay with the Union and that sufficient reasons for secession did not exist. The convention adopted the report and adjourned on 22 March 1861.

After the firing on Fort Sumter, Missouri governor Claiborne Jackson and other Southern sympathizers failed to come to an understanding with Federal authorities. In June 1861, hostilities broke out between the two sides. Jackson, along with the lieutenant governor and portions of the state legislature, abandoned the capital. They retreated into Arkansas as Federal forces pursued them.

The state offices stood vacant for a month before the state convention reconvened on 22 July. Another committee was appointed to address the situation. Arriving on 26 July, Gamble was added to the committee, which he again dominated, rewriting the committee's report. It suggested declaring the offices of governor, lieutenant governor, and secretary of state and the general assembly abandoned. The convention adopted the report and on 31 July appointed a provisional government with Gamble as governor. The convention planned an election in November 1861; however, the elections were repeatedly postponed until 1864. The actual authority of the state convention to declare the state offices vacant and appoint a provisional government was questioned. However, Abraham Lincoln's administration quickly recognized the provisional government, giving it legitimacy.

Once in office, Gamble worked to restore order in Missouri. To undermine Confederate support, Gamble offered amnesty to those who had joined the Confederate cause early in the war but who quickly wished to return home. The government suppressed Southern support by confiscating property and imposing fines on Southern supporters to compensate for damages inflicted on Missouri by Confederates. The government also issued a loyalty oath designed to suppress the voice of Confederate sympathizers. At first, the oath was administered only to state officials; however, it was later extended to the public sectors and was finally made a requirement for voter qualification.

While Gamble worked closely with Federal authorities throughout the war, he also struggled to maintain state authority. Gamble had to work in conjunction with the departmental commanders who also had military jurisdiction over Missouri. This dual control sometimes caused conflicts. The first major conflict concerned John C. Frémont's 1861 emancipation proclamation. In addition, Gamble was concerned with the tensions caused by Federal troops policing the state. He worked to reorganize the Missouri militia to replace those Federal troops with state forces. The inability of both state and Federal officials to stop guerrillas such as William

Quantrill only added to the tensions. Frequently, President Lincoln was required to mediate these disputes, and Gamble often traveled to Washington to consult on state matters. Additionally, Gamble was forced to rely on Federal funding, since Governor Jackson had emptied the state treasury when he retreated.

The slavery issue also caused Gamble concern. When he was appointed governor, Gamble chose not to interfere with slavery, fearing that such action would cause slave owners to side with the Confederacy. By 1862, however, emancipation had become a major issue, and Gamble called the state convention back into session to address it. In early 1863 they adopted a plan of gradual emancipation. While it was largely accepted, the Radical Republicans, who had begun to disapprove of Gamble's conservative policies, resented the gradual nature of the plan. They increasingly challenged Gamble's wing of the party in local elections.

The strain of office took its toll on Gamble. For most of his term, he had suffered frequent bouts of illness, and he died on 31 January 1864. Lieutenant Governor William Hall served out the remainder of his term. Gamble had served two and a half years as provisional governor. His conservative and moderate leadership guided Missouri through the storm of the Civil War.

—*James G. Downhour*

See also Dred Scott Case; Frémont, John Charles; Missouri; Quantrill, William Clarke; Thompson, Meriwether Jeff.

For further reading:
March, David D. *The History of Missouri* (1967).
Parrish, William E. *Turbulent Partnership: Missouri and the Union, 1861–1865* (1963).
Potter, Marguerite. "Hamilton R. Gamble, Missouri's War Governor." *Missouri Historical Review* (1940).

GARDNER, ALEXANDER
(1821–1882)
Photographer

The first child of James and Jean Glenn Gardner, Alexander Gardner was born in Paisley, Scotland, on 17 October 1821. Shortly after Alexander's birth, the Gardners moved to Glasgow, where twins Agnes and Catherine (1826) and a brother James (1829) were born and completed the family.

Encouraged to pursue academic studies, Gardner excelled in the subjects of astronomy, botany, and chemistry. At fourteen he became an apprentice to a Glasgow jeweler. In 1847, Gardner became manager of the Clydesdale Discount and Loan Company and became a member of the Glasgow Athenaeum. The Athenaeum membership enabled Gardner to develop friendships with notable thinkers throughout the Scottish city as well as gave him the privilege of using the club's reading rooms and reference library.

Influenced by the writings of reformer Robert Owen, Gardner embarked on his own experiment in utopian communities. In 1848, he formed the Clydesdale Joint Stock Agricultural and Commercial Company. By 1850, nine Scots—including Gardner's brother James, and their future brother-in-law, Robertson Sinclair—embarked on the long journey to the United States. The Clydesdale Company was established in Clayton County, Iowa, five miles west of the Mississippi River and was based on a shares and dividend system. Though he did not make the trip himself, Gardner oversaw the company from Scotland.

In 1851, Gardner bought the *Glasgow Sentinel* newspaper, in which he regularly wrote editorials supporting the rights of the working class. The same year he attended the Crystal Palace Exhibition at which he may have met photographer Mathew Brady. In 1852, however, Gardner changed course again, becoming less involved in the *Sentinel*, possibly due to the failure of his utopian experiment in Iowa. His brother James returned home from the United States in 1853. During this time, Gardner became interested in the medium of photography, though it is unclear where the first impetus struck him. He first offered his photographic services in 1855.

Perhaps due to unfavorable business or perhaps to try his luck in a new land, Gardner decided to emigrate to America. The spring of 1856 found Gardner, his mother, his wife Margaret, his brother James, son Lawrence, and daughter Eliza aboard a ship bound for the United States.

Upon arriving in the United States, Gardner discovered the remnants of his utopian experiment nearly in ruins. Thus, instead of traveling to Iowa to settle, he remained in New York, where he came into contact with Mathew Brady. Working the Brady Studio, Gardner not only honed his photographic skills but also worked on trying to right Brady's muddled finances. Brady recognized Gardner's varied abilities and sent him to Washington, D.C., in 1858 to administer his studio there.

In Washington, Gardner introduced to the Brady establishment the carte de visite, a 2- by 4-inch calling card–sized photograph. Though Brady found the artistic merits of the format lacking, economically the affordable, mass-produced photograph was a shrewd business investment.

The onset of the Civil War brought new photographic opportunities for both photographers. Brady and Gardner were equally eager to go to the field and record the great conflict. Brady received permission from President Abraham Lincoln to accompany and photograph the army, and Gardner used his connection with Scotsman Allan Pinkerton to gain access to the troops. Gardner was permitted complete access to the Army of the Potomac. He and photographers under his employ recorded scenes from the Peninsula campaign to Culpeper, Second Manassas to Antietam, and their

Alexander Gardner and his photographic wagon at Fort Riley, Kansas, 1867 (*Library of Congress*)

photographs brought the horrors of war to the Northern populace.

A couple of months after Antietam, Gardner severed relations with Brady to embark on his own photographic endeavors. In 1863, he and his staff photographed military scenes from Aquia Creek, Falmouth, and Fredericksburg. In July of the same year, Gardner was prepared to photograph the impending battle at Gettysburg, Pennsylvania. Traveling to Pennsylvania he had missed the three-day's action, but upon arriving at Emmitsburg, Maryland, just south of the state line, on 5 July he was promptly captured by retreating Confederate

soldiers under the command of General J. E. B. Stuart. Gardner was detained only briefly and by the next day was on the Gettysburg battlefield with his camera recording the aftermath of the decisive battle.

In September 1863, Gardner published the *Catalogue of Photographic Incidents of the War*. In the catalog, his war photographs were offered for sale in a variety of sizes and prices. Meanwhile, Gardner's staff remained in the field with the armies, photographing scenes at Belle Plain, Cold Harbor, Petersburg, and Appomattox. After the surrender at Appomattox, Gardner decided to publish a compendium of war photos in book form. *Gardner's*

Photographic SketchBook of the War appeared in two volumes and cost $150 in 1865. The next year, Gardner issued a second edition of his work. Approximately 200 sets of the book were produced, of which only one-tenth survive intact.

Gardner was present and photographed the trial and hanging of the Lincoln assassination conspirators. After that, he set his sights to the west, where he undertook a project to record the life and faces of the native peoples of the Plains and far west. In 1872 Gardner was named the official photographer for the Office of Indian Affairs.

Retiring from photography in 1879, Gardner turned to philanthropy in an effort to aid the poor. He was elected president of the Masonic Mutual Relief Association in 1882, the same year he was elected president of the Equitable Co-Operative Building Association, an organization that helped individuals buy their own homes.

In December of 1882 Gardner fell ill and his condition progressively grew worse. On 10 December 1882, Alexander Gardner died at the age of sixty-one.

—*Heidi Campbell-Shoaf*

See also Brady, Mathew; Photography.

For further reading:
Katz, D. Mark. *Witness to an Era: The Life and Photographs of Alexander Gardner: The Civil War, Lincoln, and the West* (1991).

GARDNER, FRANKLIN
(1823–1873)
Confederate general

Son of army officer Charles K. Gardner and Ann Eliza McLean Gardner, Franklin Gardner was born in New York City. Gardner graduated seventeenth of thirty-nine in the U.S. Military Academy class of 1843. Upon graduation, Gardner served in a variety of frontier posts and in Florida before fighting in the Mexican-American War. He was in most major engagements of that conflict, winning two brevets. After the war, Gardner returned to frontier duty and rode with Albert Sidney Johnston in the Utah expedition. Before the Civil War, Gardner married a Louisiana woman and bought a plantation in that state.

Upon the formation of the Confederate States of America, Gardner accepted a commission as a lieutenant colonel in the Confederate army. He never officially resigned, however, from the U.S. Army and was dismissed from that service on 7 May for deserting his command. His brother fought for the Union during the war, and his father served as a civilian in the federal government in Washington. Early in the war, Gardner served in the Western theater as an infantry officer before transferring to the cavalry. He commanded a cavalry brigade at Shiloh in April 1862 and received a promotion to brigadier general on 11 April for his service there. Soon General P.

G. T. Beauregard gave him command of all cavalry in the Army of Mississippi. He led his brigade in Bragg's Kentucky invasion in the fall of 1862.

On 13 December 1862, he was promoted to major general and given command of Port Hudson, Louisiana. He spent the first few months of his command using his considerable engineering experience to strengthen the defenses of Port Hudson and to accumulate sufficient supplies for his men. During Grant's Vicksburg campaign in the spring of 1863 and the subsequent siege, Gardner held out with 7,500 men against 30,000 Union troops commanded by Major General Nathaniel P. Banks. On 27 May, Banks unsuccessfully attempted to take Gardner's fortifications by storm. On 13 June, Banks staged a major bombardment of Gardner's works and then tried another attack on 14 June. This assault failed to carry the works as well. Banks then settled in for a lengthy siege. Gardner repeatedly refused calls for his surrender. However, after receiving word of Vicksburg's capitulation on 4 July, Gardner began considering terms. On 9 July 1863, he surrendered Port Hudson. In his attempt to protect Port Hudson he had suffered more than 1,000 casualties while inflicting over 10,000 on the Union attackers.

During his imprisonment, Gardner was held at Fort Lafayette and was exchanged in August 1864. After his release, he commanded the District of the Gulf at Mobile briefly before being given command of the District of Mississippi and East Louisiana with headquarters at Jackson, Mississippi. One of his main tasks in that command was combating the raids orchestrated by Brigadier General Benjamin H. Grierson in late 1864 and early 1865.

After the war, Gardner returned to his Louisiana plantation, where he died in obscurity.

—*David S. Heidler and Jeanne T. Heidler*

See also Grierson's Raid; Port Hudson Campaign.

For further reading:
Cunningham, Edward. *The Port Hudson Campaign, 1862–1863* (1963).
Hewitt, Lawrence. *Port Hudson, Confederate Bastion on the Mississippi* (1987).

GARDNER, JAMES
(1813–1874)
Newspaper publisher

A powerful and articulate voice in state politics for twenty-five years, James Gardner was born in Augusta, Georgia, 28 January 1813, the son of James Gardner, a Scottish immigrant, and Elizabeth McKinne. Confederate brigadier general William Montgomery Gardner (1824–1901) was his younger brother. The younger James graduated from Union College in Schenectady, New York, was admitted to the

Georgia bar in 1834, and formed a law partnership in Augusta with future governor George W. Crawford. In November 1840 Gardner was elected solicitor general of the middle circuit of Georgia superior court, a position he held for four years.

Gardner bought the *Augusta Constitutionalist*, a Democratic newspaper, in 1845. He was an advocate of the Southern rights branch of the party, although he was considered a moderate among that group. At the party state convention in 1847, the year he married Martha Jordan of Milledgeville, with whom he had six children, Gardner spoke critically of the secessionist policies of John C. Calhoun. Even after the Compromise of 1850, when the militant Southern rightists gained the ascendancy in Georgia, Gardner still asked for recognition of Howell Cobb of the Constitutional Union Party as leader of Georgia Democrats. In 1853, in the "newspaper nomination," Gardner editorialized for Cobb for reelection to the U.S. Senate and, in a personal call at the White House, lobbied President Franklin Pierce to support his candidate.

In 1857 Gardner was a candidate for the Democratic nomination for governor and led in balloting at the state convention for three days, but, failing to attain a two-thirds majority, he withdrew in favor of Joseph E. Brown, who won the governorship that year and again in 1859. Gardner opposed Brown for reelection in 1861 because he thought an unprecedented third term was unwise, but supported him in the gubernatorial campaign of 1863. Gardner's editorials emphasized the governor's administrative skills and pointed out the dangers of making a change during the wartime crisis.

Gardner launched the periodical *Southern Field and Fireside* in 1859. It was a journal for literature, agriculture, and horticulture and served as an outlet for Southern literary talent. Writers such as Augustus Baldwin Longstreet and William Wilberforce Turner were published in its pages. The magazine was a popular success and had a circulation of 13,000 at its peak. Gardner sold it in 1864 and it soon went into decline.

Out of a sense of national unity, Gardner supported the Northern candidate Stephen Douglas and his running mate, Senator Herschel V. Johnson of Georgia, for the Democratic nominations in the presidential campaign of 1860. After the failed national convention at Charleston, Gardner spoke against the need for congressional guarantees for slavery in the territories. He believed that the combination of the *Dred Scott* decision and the party policy of popular sovereignty were sufficient protection, even though he personally believed that Popular Sovereignty was wrong. During the ensuing campaign, Gardner voiced the opinion that immediate Southern resistance to a Republican victory would be a violation of the Constitution. Possibly through Gardner's influence, Douglas carried Richmond County, Georgia, by a plurality. After Lincoln's election the *Constitutionalist* came out for unhindered independence from the Union for those states that wished to secede and took up a call for the South to arm at once in its own defense.

With some reservations, Gardner and his newspaper backed the Southern war effort and Jefferson Davis's administration. Gardner's editorials in November 1864 supported Davis's call to arm the slaves as a means of saving the Confederacy, although Gardner believed that emancipation of the blacks would be unwise. In 1863, however, when it was proposed that the Southern states, because of their superior credit rating abroad, guarantee Confederate bonds, the *Constitutionalist* was opposed.

Although personally friendly with Governor Brown and Confederate vice president Alexander Stephens, Gardner did not support their 1864 peace movement. When his editor, Henry W. Cleveland, backed Brown and wrote in favor of his initiative in June 1864, Gardner first restricted Cleveland's editorials and then directed him to criticize the questionable activities of the movement. Brown and Stephens offered to buy the newspaper to make it their own organ, but Gardner refused to sell and soon dismissed Cleveland.

After the war, with his finances in ruins, Gardner moved to New York City and went into business. In 1867 he became a partner in the Gold Exchange Bank and prospered until "Black Friday," 24 September 1869, when speculators caused a panic in the gold market. Gardner's bank went into receivership and he returned to Augusta. He resumed the editorship of the *Constitutionalist* and opened a law practice. In the summer of 1873, he retired from public life.

Despite their wartime differences, Gardner and Brown remained close during the Reconstruction period. In 1871 Gardner received a one-fourth share of ownership in the Western & Atlantic Railroad, a Brown project, in return for a friendly press for Brown against charges of bribery concerning leases for the rail line. In 1872, after Robert Toombs made accusations that Brown had defrauded the state on land claims in Atlanta, Gardner was Brown's adviser and agreed to act as his second when the latter called Toombs out; the duel was never fought. That year, when Horace Greeley was the Democratic and Liberal Republican nominee for president, Gardner supported him in hopes of ending Radical Republican rule and the military occupation of the South.

James Gardner died of typhoid at his home near Augusta on 7 October 1874 and was buried in Magnolia Cemetery.

—*Russell K. Brown*

See also Brown, Joseph E.; Election of 1860; Georgia.
For further reading:
Bryan, T. Conn. *Confederate Georgia* (1953).
Candler, Allen D., and Clement A. Evans, eds. *Cyclopedia of*

Georgia (1906).

Dillard, Philip D. "The Confederate Debate over Arming Slaves: Views from Macon and Augusta Newspapers." *Georgia Historical Quarterly* (1995).

Greene, Helen Ilone. "Politics in Georgia, 1853–54: The Ordeal of Howell Cobb." *Georgia Historical Quarterly* (1946).

Hill, Louise Biles. *Joseph E. Brown and the Confederacy* (1939).

Parks, Joseph H. *Joseph E. Brown of Georgia* (1977).

Porter, David L. "Attitudes of the Georgia Press in the Presidential Election of 1860." *Georgia Historical Quarterly* (1975).

Talmadge, John E. "Peace-Movement Activities in Civil War Georgia." *Georgia Review* (1953).

GARFIELD, JAMES ABRAM
(1831–1881)

Union brigadier general, U.S. congressman, twentieth president of the United States

James A. Garfield was the son of Abram Garfield and Eliza Ballou. In 1820 the elder Garfield emigrated with his new bride, Eliza, to the Western Reserve region of northern Ohio to settle into a life of subsistence farming. Thus raised in a wildly frontier environment that civilization had barely touched, Garfield receved a meager early education. Yet, he showed intellectual promise early in life, and he was always an avid reader and enthusiastic learner.

During his late teen years, Garfield was highly influenced by the Campbellite religious crusade—named for its founder Alexander Campbell—and within a short period he was an enthusiastic convert to one of the few organized faiths in the reserve. Campbellites were most commonly referred to as the Disciples of Christ, and as Garfield's devotion to his faith increased, his standing within this tightly knit brotherhood mounted. Garfield possessed natural speaking ability, a clear and powerful intellect, and a strong sense of right and wrong. He similarly developed an appreciation of hard work while working breifly as a canal boy, a period in his life that would later be greatly romanticized for political gain.

Garfield's first formal education was at a Baptist-owned academy in northern Ohio. But once he converted to the Disciples of Christ, Garfield transferred to the Disciple's Western Reserve Eclectic Institute in Hiram. And it was at the Eclectic that his religious faith blossomed and his speaking talents matured to the point that he regularly ranked top among the students in forensics. In 1854 he entered Williams College in Massachusetts, where he earned an A.B. in 1856. He then returned to Hiram and accepted a post as professor of ancient languages. He quickly rose to become president of the school, but he was drawn to politics. In 1859, Garfield was elected as a Republican to the state legislature, and in 1860 with Lincoln's election and the subsequent secession crisis, Garfield's antislavery rhetoric was widely applauded throughout the state.

With the outbreak of hostilities in 1861, Garfield immediately offered his services to the state. Yet, due to the disorganized nature of mobilization, Garfield was not summoned for service for several months. During that time he returned to Hiram and raised a company of Eclectic volunteers. Finally, in mid-August 1861, Garfield was sworn in as lieutenant colonel of the 42nd Ohio Volunteer Infantry, Company A, which was filled primarily with his students.

Dispatched to Camp Chase for training and drill instruction, the 42nd was hardly prepared for full combat when Garfield was ordered to move his regiment toward its first assignment in eastern Kentucky to confront a Confederate invasion of that part of the state being led Brigadier General Humphrey Marshall, reported to be commanding nearly 7,000 troops. Though not an overly serious threat to Union strategy for holding Kentucky, Marshall's invasion could not be ignored. Thus, General Don Carlos Buell ordered Garfield to reverse Marshall's moves in eastern Kentucky. Buell also placed Garfield in overall command of the newly created 18th Brigade, made up of the 42d Ohio, the 40th Ohio, and the 14th Kentucky, and he dispatched these troops for the Sandy Valley Campaign to stop General Marshall's advance.

Actually, the Confederate "invasion" of eastern Kentucky was far less spectacular than Union officials had feared, and the hapless Confederates suffered from no real supply line out of western Virginia and from a feeble and overly cautious commander. After both forces spent an especially miserable and muddy winter planning the others' demise, the two forces met in a mild skirmish at Middle Creek on 10 January 1862. This small engagement, however, was sufficient to convince Marshall that he was seriously outgunned. Thus, the Confederate commander ordered eastern Kentucky evacuated and effectively left the entire half of the state in Garfield's hands. And to victory-starved Northerners, Garfield's heroics in eastern Kentucky brought him considerable praise in Ohio and recognition from the Union high command with promotion to brigadier general.

By the spring of 1862, Garfield's brigade had been ordered to bivouac with Buell's army at Louisville for a rapid procession into Tennessee, where the Union and Confederate armies were building toward a showdown at Pittsburg Landing. Upon meeting up with Buell, Garfield was given command of the 20th Brigade of the Army of the Ohio, a force of green troops comprised largely of the 64th and 65th Ohio Regiments. Garfield's troops and the rest of the Army of the Ohio were stretched out for several miles along rivers in Tennessee while the first shots at Shiloh opened on Ulysses Grant's unsuspecting army. Buell finally got his army on the move, and after a frantic fifteen hour march throughout the early morning hours of 7 April 1862, Garfield's brigade arrived at the battle scene and were hurried to the front five miles away. Though Garfield's men experienced some enemy fire at Shiloh, their arrival at the front coincided almost precisely with the final withdrawal of the Confederates, who had spent a murderous morning losing the bloodied ground that had been gained the previous day. In sum, Garfield's brigade arrived at Shiloh just as the battle had ended, and that battle for his men was more burial detail than fighting.

Garfield spent the next several months in Washington awaiting his next assignment, a prolonged period during which he agonized over his inactivity. Though once a supreme pacifist based on his profoundly deep religious convictions, by 1862 Garfield had accepted the brutal nature of warfare and the necessity of destroying the South's "peculiar institution," which he believed to be a stain on the entire nation. While in Washington he and Secretary of the Treasury Salmon P. Chase became close friends and confidants, and it was through this personal connection that Garfield received orders to join the Army of the Cumberland, which was commanded by General William S. Rosecrans.

Garfield and Rosecrans soon developed a close friendship despite their religious differences. Rosecrans was a devout Catholic, whereas Garfield possessed deep animosity against Popery, that deepest of all Protestant enemies. Their friendship, however, became so strong that in February 1863 Rosecrans elevated Garfield to his chief of staff. And it was in that position that Garfield assumed the duties associated with the everyday management of an army, a thankless role and one that hardly would bring the battlefield glories that Garfield evidently harbored.

Nevertheless, he performed his duties faithfully—at least for the first several months in his new post. However, by summer 1863 Garfield had grown impatient with Rosecrans's increasingly apparent timidity while his entire staff urged an aggressive attack on the Confederates at Chattanooga. With surprising audacity—some might suggest blatant insubordination—Garfield even took the liberty of writing the War Department asking for orders to move against the Confederates and requesting additional troops and supplies. By the end of 1863, Rosecrans was finally convinced that an assault against the Confederates was necessary and could prove decisive in ending the war. Garfield was ecstatic that his general had finally decided to attack, and he diligently poured over maps and made preparations for what would ultimately become the battle of Chickamauga, one of the bloodiest and hardest-fought engagements of the Civil War.

Instead of providing the crushing blow against General Braxton Bragg's Confederate troops, however, Chickamauga ended in a near disaster for Rosecrans's army. After receiving faulty intelligence, Rosecrans ordered one division to abandon its position to reinforce

James Garfield (*National Archives*)

what was believed to be a gaping hole in the Union line. This maneuver, however, created a gap almost at the same time that General James Longstreet ordered a frontal assault. Rosecrans and Garfield could do little other than flee for safety as a veritable sea of Union troops rushed toward them in retreat. Rosecrans was so despondent over this monumental disaster that he was largely oblivious that his right flank, protected by Union General George H. Thomas, was fending off Longstreet's advance. Garfield, realizing that the main battle had shifted toward the Union right, immediately rode to Thomas's assistance. By the time of his arrival, however, the battle was all but over as the Confederates ceased fighting for the night. Rosecrans then ordered his entire army to pull back into Chattanooga to salvage what left of his army and his ruined career.

After an assessment of the Army of the Cumberland's situation in Chattanooga, Garfield was dismayed, for he quickly realized that the Army of the Cumberland was surrounded on three sides by Confederate forces and was positioned with the river to its back. In sum, Rosecrans's army was trapped at Chattanooga. However, due largely to the efforts of Secretary of War Edwin Stanton, the Army of the Cumberland was quickly resupplied and reinforced and was thus able to fight its way out of what could have proved to be a deadly situation. By then, however, Garfield had been ordered to return to Washington. Although he would forever think highly of William Rosecrans as a friend, Garfield had lost all faith in him as a general. He was genuinely relieved to have been ordered back to the nation's capital.

Garfield had previously been elected to Congress by his constituents in Ohio, and though he would have preferred another military assignment, President Lincoln convinced him to resign from the army and stand as the president's ally in Congress. He spent the next seventeen years in Congress, and his oratorical skills and staunch Republican allegiance brought him considerable respect among his fellow politicians. In the election of 1880 Garfield was nominated as the dark-horse candidate by a deadlocked Republican convention, and he successfully won the campaign of 1880. However, four months after his inauguration, Garfield was mortally wounded by a disgruntled and insane office seeker named Charles Guiteau. After lingering near death for two months, President James Garfield died of his wounds on 19 September 1881.

—*Robert Saunders, Jr.*

See also Army of the Cumberland; Chickamauga, Battle of; Rosecrans, William S.

For further reading:

Doenecke, Justus D. *The Presidencies of James A. Garfield and Chester A. Arthur* (1981).

Leach, Margaret, and Harry J. Brown. *The Garfield Orbit* (1978).

Peskin, Allan. *Garfield: A Biography* (1978).

GARNETT, RICHARD BROOKE
(1817–1863)
Confederate general

A member of the Tidewater aristocracy, Richard Brooke Garnett was born at Rose Hill plantation in Essex County, Virginia, on 21 November 1817. He attended the United States Military Academy with his cousin, Robert Selden Garnett, and graduated twenty-ninth of fifty-two in his class in 1841. Immediately after graduation he served in the Florida War of 1841–1842. Unlike many other future Civil War officers, Garnett did not see action in the Mexican-American War, but instead served in frontier garrisons in Texas, the Dakotas, and California, where he earned a reputation as a well-regarded Indian fighter. After twenty years of service in the U.S. Army, the likable Virginian resigned as captain in the 6th U.S. Infantry in May 1861 and offered his services to the Confederacy.

Initially commissioned a major of artillery in the regular Confederate army, Garnett became brigadier general in the Provisional army on 14 November 1861. He was given his first field command on 7 December 1861, when he was named commander of the famed Stonewall Brigade after General Thomas J. "Stonewall" Jackson became leader of the Shenandoah Valley department. Garnett, a blue-eyed, wavy-haired, handsome man, soon earned the respect and admiration of the soldiers in his brigade. His method of leadership was a welcome change from Jackson's stern approach. Though he firmly ruled his men, Garnett was not as strict a disciplinarian as Jackson, and unlike the gruff "Old Jack," he displayed a willingness to listen to his soldiers' grievances.

However, Garnett's leadership received a stinging rebuke soon after the battle of Kernstown in western Virginia on 23 March 1862. In the battle, Garnett's brigade held the Confederate center against a larger contingent of Federal troops for several hours. Late in the day, many of his men had exhausted their ammunition, and Union attacks pressed the center and both flanks, threatening to overrun his position. Deeming it suicidal to remain, Garnett ordered a withdrawal without consulting his commander. Jackson, incensed at this unauthorized retreat, relieved Garnett from command on 1 April and sent him to Harrisonburg under arrest for neglect of duty. Outraged at the treatment of their beloved brigadier, the Stonewall Brigade gave Jackson icy receptions immediately following their brigadier's dismissal and was openly hostile to Garnett's replacement, General Charles S. Winder.

The humiliated Garnett immediately sought a court-martial to clear his name. After four months of wrangling, he finally had one convened. However, pressing war matters caused an adjournment at its beginning, and Garnett was never again granted a similar audience. In August 1862, General Robert E. Lee transferred Garnett to General George Pickett's division, where he commanded a brigade. Disgraced by the reproach upon his honor, Garnett never let an opportunity pass to demonstrate his courage. An officer in Pickett's division commented soon after Garnett's arrival: "He was thereafter anxious to expose himself, even unnecessarily, and to wipe out effectually by some great distinction in action, what he felt to be an unmerited slur upon his military reputation."

Garnett served capably and effectively at the battles of South Mountain and Antietam in September 1862, but his most conspicuous service came on 3 July 1863 at the battle of Gettysburg. Injured by a recent kick from a horse, and so extremely ill that he wore a heavy overcoat over his uniform on the oppressively hot afternoon, Garnett rode at the head of his brigade, which was in the front rank of Pickett's Charge. The mounted general expertly led his five Virginia regiments to within twenty yards of the Union lines, when he and his horse were hit by Union fire and crumpled to the ground together. His horse bolted up and returned to Seminary Ridge grievously wounded, but Garnett's body was never recovered.

It is probable that Union soldiers removed his pistols, sword, and insignia after the battle, and he was then buried in a mass grave with his soldiers. Years after the war, his sword turned up in a Baltimore pawnshop.

— *Judkin Browning*

See also Gettysburg, Battle of; Kernstown, First Battle of.

For further reading:

Robertson, James I., Jr. *The Stonewall Brigade* (1963).
Tanner, Robert G. *Stonewall in the Valley: Thomas J. "Stonewall" Jackson's Shenandoah Valley Campaign, Spring 1862* (1976; reprint 1996).
Warner, Ezra J. *Generals in Gray: Lives of the Confederate Commanders* (1959; reprint 1987).

GARNETT, ROBERT SELDEN
(1819–1861)
Confederate general

Born to Robert Selden Garnett and Olympia Charlotte DeGouges Garnett at his family's plantation in Essex County, Virginia, the younger Garnett received an appointment to the U.S. Military Academy in 1837. He graduated twenty-seventh of fifty-two in the class of 1841, the same class as his cousin, Richard Brooke Garnett. Commissioned into the dragoons, Garnett transferred to the 4th Artillery six months later and served two years on the border between the United States and Canada before being detailed back to West Point to teach tactics. After his assignment at West Point, he occupied a staff position as aide-de-camp to General John Wool. He then went back to the artillery and was sent to Texas in 1846. After fighting in the two opening engagements of the Mexican-American War at Palo Alto and Resaca de la Palma in May 1846, Garnett was made Zachary Taylor's aide-de-camp in June. During the war Garnett received two brevet promotions for actions during Taylor's campaign in northern Mexico. He remained on Taylor's staff until the general resigned his commission in early 1849.

Beginning in 1849, Garnett served a three-year stint in the infantry. During that year, he traveled to California carrying dispatches and while there submitted the design that became California's state seal. His next special mission came in 1850 when he commanded the escort for a group of Seminole Indians from Florida to Indian Territory. That mission complete, he served two years in Texas before being transferred back to West Point in 1852 as commandant of cadets. He served in that position for three years during the superintendency of Robert E. Lee. His tour there complete in 1855, Garnett was transferred to the Pacific Northwest. From 1855 to 1858 he commanded several expeditions against the Indians there and in 1856 was charged with the construction of Fort Simcoe in Oregon. He served there until 1858 when his wife and infant son suddenly died in September of that year. He requested a leave to take

their bodies east for burial. After the interment of his family, he requested a year's leave to travel in Europe. He left in October 1859, received an extension while abroad, and did not start back until 31 March 1861. Upon his return, he requested another leave until he could determine the course that Virginia would take in the sectional conflict. Upon the secession of that state, he submitted his resignation on 30 April 1861.

Garnett immediately accepted the position of adjutant general of all Virginia forces at the rank of colonel. Serving directly under Major General Robert E. Lee, commander of state troops, Garnett had as his primary duty to organize Virginia soldiers into some semblance of an army. He worked diligently for two months and was rewarded for his efforts in early June when he was promoted to brigadier general and given command of Virginia troops in the northwestern part of the state (the area that would become West Virginia in 1863).

From the time Garnett took over his new command on 14 June 1861, he faced great difficulties. Federal forces under George B. McClellan were making considerable inroads in the area, and the sympathies of the local population were generally with the Union. At best, Garnett could hope for neutrality from the locals. Still he persisted, establishing bases at several points and making his own headquarters at Laurel Hill. However, in spite of Lee's best efforts to procure supplies, weapons, and ammunition for state forces, Garnett's men in western Virginia seemed to be of low priority when it came to distributing what little the state had. Chronically short of everything he needed to prevent Federal occupation of the entire area, Garnett persevered with what he had until the second week of July 1861.

He divided his force between Laurel Hill and Rich Mountain, with the latter contingent under John Pegram. William S. Rosecrans attacked Pegram on 11 July and over the next twenty-four hours was able to cut off his retreat back to Laurel Hill. When Garnett heard about Pegram's retreat (what would soon be Pegram's surrender), he realized that his position was untenable and also began to retreat. He was slowed by his efforts to save his few supplies and ammunition and forced to fight at Carrick's Ford on 13 July. After successfully extricating most of his men, Garnett remained in the rear of the army personally directing the actions of the rear guard. In the midst of this activity, immediately after giving the order for his skirmishers to retreat, he was struck by a Federal bullet in the back and killed instantly. His body was left behind by his fleeing troops and fell into the hands of the advancing Federals. McClellan saw to it that Garnett's body was not buried with the other Confederate dead and arranged for its transfer to Washington several days later. Garnett was temporarily interred by relatives in Baltimore until the war ended, at which time he was moved to rest beside his wife and son.

—*David S. Heidler and Jeanne T. Heidler*

See also Carrick's Ford; Rich Mountain, Battle of.

For further reading:

Burton, Matthew Wade. "The River of Blood and the Valley of Death: The Lives of Two Cousins for the Cause, Robert Selden Garnett and Richard Brooke Garnett, C.S.A" (M.A. thesis, 1996).

Guie, Heister Dean. *Bugles in the Valley: Garnett's Fort Simcoe* (1977).

GARRARD, KENNER
(1828–1879)
Union general

Born to Jeptha Dudley Garrard and Sarah Bella Ludlow Garrard in Bourbon County, Kentucky, at his mother's ancestral home, Kenner Garrard grew up in Cincinnati, Ohio. Garrard attended Harvard University before accepting an appointment to the U.S. Military Academy. He graduated eighth of forty-two in the class of 1851. Initially commissioned an artillery officer, Garrard moved to the cavalry and served on a variety of frontier posts before the Civil War.

He was serving in Texas at the outbreak of the war as part of the 2d Cavalry. Though most of the Federal troops in that state had been evacuated shortly after the surrender of Federal forces there in February 1861, some remained to supervise the evacuation. Garrard was one of the unlucky ones, and when word reached the state of the firing on Fort Sumter, Confederate sympathizers captured him. Shortly afterward, he was paroled and served the next months before his official exchange working for the commissary service. He also served duty at West Point as a cavalry instructor and briefly as commandant of cadets. During that time he read and wrote on cavalry tactics. He was exchanged in August 1862 and given command at the rank of colonel of the 146th New York and immediately sent to join the Army of the Potomac.

Garrard first saw action in the war at the battle of Fredericksburg as part of Daniel Butterfield's V Corps. He commanded the regiment in the attack on Marye's Heights, the following spring at Chancellorsville, and then at the battle of Gettysburg. At the latter engagement, Garrard assumed command of his brigade when its commander, Brigadier General Stephen H. Weed, was killed on Little Round Top on the second day. George Gordon Meade, commander of the Army of the Potomac, commended Garrard for his actions during the battle and recommended him for promotion to brigadier general of volunteers. Garrard was promoted to that rank on 23 July 1863.

Garrard commanded his brigade at Bristoe Station and then, on 7–8 November 1863, commanded the skirmishers of V Corps at the action at Rappahannock Station. He returned to his brigade for the Mine Run campaign, but on 15 December 1863 he was relieved of duty with the Army of the Potomac and sent to head the Cavalry Bureau in Washington. He did not care for the staff position, so in February 1864 he transferred to the Army of the Cumberland.

Given command of the 2d Cavalry Division of the Army of the Cumberland headquartered at Huntsville, Alabama, Garrard assumed command of his division on 10 February 1864. Garrard commanded his unit during the Atlanta campaign in the summer of 1864, and by the end of July as Sherman closed in on Atlanta, Garrard commanded the main cavalry force in the army. One of his most valuable services during this period of the campaign was a daring raid conducted on the town of Covington, Georgia.

After the fall of Atlanta, Garrard operated against John Bell Hood's army as it tried to lead Sherman north out of Georgia. Garrard was relieved in November 1864 from command of the 2d Cavalry Division and transferred to the Army of the Tennessee, where he commanded the 2d Division of XVI Corps. He remained in this command for the remainder of the war. For his services with the Army of the Cumberland, Garrard was recommended by its commander, George Thomas, for a brevet promotion to major general of volunteers.

Garrard took his new command just in time to fight in the Nashville campaign and won praise for his actions there. In the spring he led his division in the Mobile campaign and, following the fall of the city, took command of the District of Mobile. He held that command until August 1865. For the remainder of his military career he served in Missouri, resigning from the army in November 1866.

After leaving the army, Garrard returned to his home in Cincinnati, where he devoted his time to various civic pursuits. He encouraged the arts in his home city and spent much of his efforts promoting the preservation of the history of the town. He died in Cincinnati on 15 May 1879.

—*David S. Heidler and Jeanne T. Heidler*

See also Atlanta Campaign; Gettysburg, Battle of; Nashville, Battle of.

For further reading:

Garrard, Kenner. *Nolan's System for Training Cavalry Horses* (1862).

GARRETT, ROBERT & SONS

Robert Garrett (1783–1857) was born in Lisburn, County Down, in Northern Ireland on 2 May 1783. He was the youngest of the six children of John and Margaret (MacMechen) Garrett, a Presbyterian family that immigrated to the United States in 1790. After her husband died during the crossing to

America, Margaret Garrett purchased a farm in Cumberland County, Pennsylvania, sold it eight years later, and then bought another one in 1798 in Middletown, a village in Washington County, Pennsylvania. Having spent three years on the Middletown farm, Robert, at age eighteen, went to Baltimore in 1801 and learned much in working in the produce and commission house of Patrick Dinsmore for three years. Young Garrett in 1804 became a partner in the firm of Wallace and Garrett, a business that sold western farm produce in Baltimore and that marketed eastern finished goods in western Maryland and Pennsylvania. After his marriage to Martha Hanna of Baltimore in 1811 and after her sudden death that year, Garrett in 1812 dissolved his partnership and returned to Middletown to operate a retail store. However, he frequently made business trips to Baltimore, met Elizabeth Stouffer during one of his visits, and married her in 1817. Two years later, Garrett sold his store and, with financial backing from his father-in-law, the merchant Henry Stouffer, went to Baltimore to pursue a new business opportunity.

In 1819, Robert Garrett & Company opened as wholesale commission house selling and buying from country storekeepers Garrett had known in western Maryland and Pennsylvania. Garrett accrued great profits from the western trade, and in 1840 he brought his two sons, John and Henry, into the business to establish the partnership of Robert Garrett & Sons. The firm especially began to engage in investment activities, buying and selling at considerable profit commercial paper and state bonds. In 1846, the Garretts not only provided food to American troops in Texas during the Mexican-American War, they also later offered Treasury bonds with a 6 percent coupon to help finance the war.

By the 1850s, Robert Garrett & Sons had become involved in railroad financing marketing investments for such varied lines as the Baltimore & Ohio Railroad, the Central Ohio Line, and the Northern Virginia Railroad. Both John and Henry Garrett were elected to the Baltimore & Ohio's board of directors. After the death of Robert Garrett on 4 February 1857, John assumed leadership of the family's prospering business. The following year he was appointed as the president of the Baltimore and Ohio.

Upon the outbreak of the Civil War, the firm strengthened already established ties with George Peabody & Company, receiving from the London firm bond coupon payments and engaging with it in foreign exchange transactions. The Garretts also did business with Pierpont Morgan & Company. Despite the disruptive effects of the war, the Garretts between 1861 and 1862 financed through this New York firm corn and flour exports to England and Europe. The war also led to disputes between the Garrett brothers: Henry supported

the Confederate cause and was arrested for treason in Baltimore in September 1861. After his release that year, Henry continued to suffer from health problems and died on 10 October 1867. Unlike his brother, John supported the Union; the younger Garrett believed that the Baltimore & Ohio had to be protected from the Confederacy and correctly felt that the Union, with superior military strength, would win the war. Moreover, he established cordial relations with Salmon P. Chase, Edwin M. Stanton, and other prominent Union leaders. On 3 October 1862, Garrett provided President Lincoln with a special train to visit Antietam and accompanied him there. The next year, Garrett significantly contributed to the Union's cause, transporting by rail more than 20,000 men from the Potomac River to Chattanooga and thus demonstrating the importance of his railroad to the conduct of the war. After the conclusion of the war, Garrett, until his death on 26 September 1884, continued to reorganize and to expand the Baltimore & Ohio.

The firm of Robert Garrett & Sons significantly contributed to nineteenth-century America. The Garrets were major contributors to American merchant and finance capitalism. Before the Civil War, the three Garretts shared a common vision. Through mercantile, investment, and railroad activities, they tried to transform Baltimore into one of the nation's leading cities. Well after the war, their vision, in many respects, became a reality.

—*William Weisberger*

See also Financing, U.S.A.

For further reading:

Carosso, Vincent P. *The Morgans: Private International Bankers, 1854–1913* (1987).

Chandler, Alfred D., Jr. *The Visible Hand: The Managerial Revolution in American Business* (1977).

Garrett Papers. Library of Congress, Washington, D.C..

Hungerford, Edward. *Story of the Baltimore and Ohio Railroad, 1827–1927* (1928).

Parker, Franklin. *George Peabody: A Biography* (1995).

Williams, Harold A. *Robert Garrett & Sons Incorporated: Origin and Development, 1840–1865* (1965).

GARRISON, WILLIAM LLOYD
(1805–1879)
Abolitionist

William Lloyd Garrison was born in 1805 in Newburyport, Massachusetts. In 1808, his father, Abijah, abandoned the family, and Garrison was forced to do small jobs to help his mother earn a living. These childhood difficulties left Garrison with a compassionate attitude toward the poor and a desire to fight social injustice. In 1818, he began his career as journalist for the local newspaper *The Herald*, where he worked as both writer and editor. After 1820,

with slavery becoming an issue of national resonance, Garrison felt increasingly attracted toward it and became a member of the prominent antislavery organization the American Colonization Society. In March 1828, he met Quaker editor Benjamin Lundy, who convinced him of the need of radical action against slavery and asked him to help him edit his Baltimore-based paper, *The Genius of Universal Emancipation*. Between 1829 and 1830, under the influence of Lundy, Garrison developed the idea that the problem of slavery could be resolved only with the immediate emancipation of the slaves.

In the summer of 1830, after spending forty-nine days in jail for libeling a slave trader, Garrison dissolved his friendship with Lundy and moved back to Boston, where he started planning the publication of his own paper. In the first issue of *The Liberator* on 1 January 1831, Garrison clarified the radical implications of his position about slavery with the famous words "I will be as harsh as truth, and as uncompromising as justice … AND I WILL BE HEARD." The use of such direct language in an antislavery publication was new and was aimed at making readers aware that the problem of slavery could no longer be ignored by the nation. Garrison contended that slavery was a violation of the principles of the Declaration of Independence, and therefore he demanded immediate action for its abolition. For the next thirty-four years, *The Liberator* retained its status as the preeminent antislavery publication and served as the main vehicle of expression for Garrison's often unorthodox ideas. Through *The Liberator*, Garrison managed both to attract national attention over the issue of slavery and to establish contacts with radical antislavery advocates based in other Northern states.

Between 1831 and 1833, Garrison refined his doctrine of abolitionism, always focusing on the necessity of immediate emancipation of the slaves. As a convinced Baptist, Garrison believed that slavery was first and foremost a sin in the eyes of God, while slaveholders were sinners who inflicted pain upon innocent victims. Moreover, Garrison thought that all Northerners carried a share of guilt because they allowed slavery to continue without taking action against it. Therefore, the fight against slavery needed to focus on persuading Americans, North and South, that slavery was wrong. To this end, with a few friends Garrison established the New England Anti-Slavery Society in 1832 and took a prominent part in the following year, together with abolitionists from New York and Ohio, in the foundation of the American Anti-Slavery Society. In the latter's "Declaration of Sentiments," Garrison characteristically mixed the religious argument against slavery with the doctrine of human rights, echoing both the Bible and the Declaration of Independence. Moreover, he emphasized the idea of implementing a tactic of "moral suasion" through the foundation of other antislavery organizations and the spread of antislavery literature throughout the country.

Until 1835, Garrison presided over the activities of the American Anti-Slavery Society as its unchallenged leader. Following his position on "immediatism" and "moral suasion," the organization achieved national prominence and attracted the hostility of both Southerners and conservative Northerners, who organized mobs with the aim of attacking and threatening abolitionist activists. After the launch of the 1835 postal campaign, aimed at flooding the post offices of the North and South with abolitionist pamphlets, one such mob attacked Garrison in Boston with the intention of lynching him. The city mayor and the police, who fended off the mob, rescued him. By 1835, Garrison had acquired a reputation of being "harsh and uncompromising" not just about the condemnation of slavery, but also about a general indictment of American society. To Garrison, the fight against slavery was just one of several battles against the sins of social inequality and moral depravity that pervaded America. He therefore sought to collaborate with several other reform movements.

The next five years saw increasing ideological differences between Garrison's supporters and opponents within the American Anti-Slavery Society. Garrison welcomed women in the society and actively supported the agitation for women's rights; he thought that the women's cause and the slaves' cause were tightly linked and equally important. Similarly, Garrison tried to fight inequality related to racial prejudice and supported actions aimed at securing equal rights for African-Americans. His radicalism on issues of social reform was married to an attitude of nonviolent resistance and rejection of governmental politics; rather than involvement with the kind of corruption that derived from politics, he stressed "perfectionism." In 1840, anti-Garrisonian abolitionists, who did not endorse Garrison's program of moral reform and wanted to use political means to achieve the abolitionist ends, formed the American and Foreign Anti-Slavery Society, based in New York rather than Boston.

In the 1840s and 1850s, Garrison's radical opinions grew even stronger, as he was relegated to the fringes of American politics, where there was a place for his uncompromising attitude against slavery. Still very active, Garrison continued to support women's rights and racial equality, and he watched with disdain as several abolitionists transformed into political advocates of the containment of slavery, first attached to the Liberty Party, then to the Free Soil Party, and finally to the Republican Party. While in the 1840s he denounced the American Union as a failed experiment of freedom that allowed the existence of slavery, in the 1850s he became convinced that the "slave power" dominated Congress. On 4 July 1854, after fugitive slave Anthony Burns was returned to his owner under provisions set forth in the 1850 Fugitive Slave Law, and after passage of the Kansas-Nebraska Act allowed the spread of slavery into the western territories, Garrison staged a public burning of the Constitution, which he despised as a proslavery document, calling it "a covenant with death."

In 1859, Garrison admired John Brown for his attack on Harper's Ferry and called him a "martyr" for the cause of the slave. At the same time, he acknowledged the pitfalls of his doctrine of nonviolent resistance by maintaining that "resistance to tyrants—in whatever form—is obedience to God." Although he had no sympathy for Lincoln's mild antislavery politics, at the outbreak of the Civil War Garrison supported the Union and continued to demand that the federal government emancipate the slaves. In 1863, Garrison rejoiced at the issuance of the Emancipation Proclamation, which he took as the recognition of slavery as the real cause of the war and which he saw as permanently relating the war for the Union to the abolition of slavery in the South. After the victory of the Union in 1865, Garrison believed his mission was finished. Therefore, in May 1865 he abandoned the American Anti-Slavery Society, and in December of the same year he closed down *The Liberator*. He spent the following years supporting the Radical Republican plans for Reconstruction in the South and writing in the New York–based paper *The Independent* in support of the Fourteenth and Fifteenth Amendments, which guaranteed civil rights to African-Americans.

—*Enrico Dal Lago*

See also Abolitionist Movement; Abolitionists; Burns, Anthony.

For further reading:

Cain, William E., ed. *William Lloyd Garrison and the Fight against Slavery: Selections from* The Liberator (1995).

Kraditor, Aileen S. *Means and Ends in American Abolitionism: Garrison and His Critics on Strategy and Tactics, 1834–1850* (1969).

Stewart, James B. *William Lloyd Garrison and the Challenge of Emancipation* (1992).

Thomas, John L. *The Liberator: William Lloyd Garrison, A Biography* (1963).

GATLING GUN

The Gatling gun, one of the most recognizable pieces of weaponry produced in America, saw only limited use during the Civil War. Both the U.S. Army and U.S. Navy used later forms of the weapon, and descendants of the original design are still in use. Unfortunately, the initial 1862-model Gatling gun suffered from design flaws and an unsympathetic Army Ordnance Department that refused to purchase the weapon from its designer.

Richard Jordan Gatling (1818–1903), already a well-established inventor living in Indianapolis, Indiana, had patented several inventions, including a rice-planting machine in 1839, a steam plow in 1857, and five farm-related inventions in 1860. After the declaration of war, the inventor turned his attention to providing a weapon of increased firepower to the Union army. His idea may have emerged from a discussion Gatling had with his friend and future president, Benjamin Harrison, who in 1861 commanded a regiment of Indiana volunteers. Encouraged by these conversations and the Northern press, which urged inventors to produce a war-winning machine, Gatling worked diligently on his invention and finished the prototype late in 1861. He demonstrated the weapon to prominent Indiana officials and military officers early in 1862, and by November of that year had received patent number 36,836 for "Improvement in Revolving Battery-Guns."

The design of the weapon was revolutionary, but simple. The 1862 model consisted of six rifled barrels revolving around a central axis, turned by a hand crank. This assembly was then mounted on a modified artillery-type carriage. Initially, the weapon used a preloaded chamber with percussion caps and paper cartridges firing a 0.58 caliber projectile. This design had several inherent flaws that limited its reliability, including gas leakage between the preloaded chambers and the barrels that reduced muzzle velocity and caused excessive fouling. The weapon fired on average 200 rounds per minute.

To correct some of the design flaws, Gatling developed a second model in 1862 that utilized copper-cased rimfire cartridges. These new all-metal cartridges solved the gas leakage and fouling problems, but the weapon's action made it difficult to maintain alignment between barrel and chamber. Faulty alignment resulted in the shaving off of a portion of the bullet as it entered the barrel, and once in flight the bullet tumbled, reducing its range and accuracy.

Gatling continued to try to market his weapon to the U.S. Army, but in late 1862 Federal agents reported that Gatling had joined the Knights of the Golden Circle, a secret organization with Southern sympathies. Military officials, suspecting Gatling to be a Copperhead, were concerned that Gatling might try to sell his invention to the South. In fact, however, Gatling's only marketing attempt made outside of the Union was to France, and it was unsuccessful. Gatling was eventually proved innocent of Copperhead affiliations, and he continued his quest to have his weapon accepted.

Entrance into service for any weapon required approval from the U.S. Army Ordnance Department and its chief, Colonel James W. Ripley. Ripley took an inflexible stand on introducing new weapons into the Union army and adopted a strict policy of relying on weapons at hand instead of new models produced by inventors. Ripley refused to consider the weapon before

his retirement in September 1863, mainly because of the meticulous loading and cleaning procedures the Gatling gun required.

With official channels closed to him, Gatling had the good fortune of meeting with Major General Benjamin F. Butler, who was interested in a demonstration of the weapon. After seeing the gun in action, Butler purchased twelve weapons and carriages and 12,000 rounds of ammunition for $12,000. Whether Butler actually used the weapons in combat is unclear. He failed to mention the guns in his autobiographical *Butler's Book*, but several eyewitness accounts insist that the weapons were deployed and used in Butler's retreat to the Bermuda Hundreds after his defeat at Drewry's Bluff in May 1864.

While the army refused any official trials, the U.S. Navy agreed to a demonstration, and in summer 1863 the weapon was tested at the Washington Navy Yard. After a favorable performance, Rear Admiral John A. Dahlgren allowed his commanders to order the weapons, but few were requisitioned due to Gatling's failure to have a significant number manufactured. Admiral David Dixon Porter obtained one of the weapons for his Mississippi Squadron but never used it in battle.

The 1862-model Gatling gun, plagued with mechanical problems and unsympathetic official channels, failed to make any significant impact on the Civil War. Only later models met with acceptance from the military.

—Eric L. Bobo

See also Ordnance, Naval; Rifles.

For further reading:
Berk, Joseph. *The Gatling Gun: 19th Century Machine Gun to 21st Century Vulcan* (1991).
Johnson, F. Roy. *The Gatling Gun and Flying Machine of Richard and Henry Gatling* (1979).
Stern, Philip Van Doren. "Doctor Gatling and His Gun." *American Heritage* (1957).
Wahl, Paul. *The Gatling Gun* (1965).

GEARY, JOHN WHITE
(1819–1873)
Union general

Born 30 December 1819, at Mount Pleasant, Pennsylvania, to Richard and Margaret White Geary, John Geary was educated at Jefferson College, Canonsburg, Pennsylvania. His father's death forced young Geary to leave school for a time and seek work, especially because his father's failed business ventures had left the family deeply in debt. After graduating, Geary spent some time as a clerk in a Pittsburgh wholesale house and in Kentucky before going to work as assistant superintendent and engineer for the Allegheny Portage Railroad. Geary was married twice, first to Margaret Ann Logan in February 1843 and then to Mary Church Henderson in August 1857, and he had four children. Always politically ambitious, he would later be elected the first mayor of San Francisco and, after the Civil War, governor of Pennsylvania.

Although Geary compiled a solid, if undistinguished, military record during the Civil War, his most important contribution may have been as territorial governor of Kansas, a position he held from September 1856 to March 1857. In accepting his appointment as governor, Geary expressed a determination to restore order to the territory and a sense of justice to its law enforcement. He lost little time, acting quickly to disband the proslavery state militia and replace it with one loyal to himself. Then, to demonstrate that he would play no favorites, Geary arrested a band of Free Soilers who had attacked a proslavery party at Hickory Point. Geary's balanced approach seemed to work, and for a while tensions within Kansas subsided.

Despite this initial success, in the end Geary proved no more capable of dealing with the situation in Kansas than had his predecessors. His plan for reforming the territorial court system was completely thwarted by proslavery Chief Justice Samuel Lecompte. Geary tried to replace Lecompte, only to be blocked by the U.S. Senate, which refused to confirm a replacement chief justice. Geary's efforts to block the proslavery Lecompton legislature resulted in a riot in which two people were shot. Disgusted by obstructionists, threats against his life, and calls for his removal, Geary resigned as governor on 4 March 1857, citing poor health and lack of support from Washington.

Although not a West Point graduate, Geary's service with the state militia and in the Mexican-American War were enough to win him an appointment as colonel of the 28th Pennsylvania Infantry. In an army where amateur soldiers were often regarded with scorn by their West Point comrades, Geary proved more able than most, eventually rising to the rank of major general, although some attributed his success more to a talent for self-promotion than military skill.

Geary saw action in a number of engagements during the war including Cedar Mountain, Chancellorsville, Gettysburg, Lookout Mountain, Peachtree Creek, Dug Gap, and several lesser engagements. It was in one of those lesser engagements at Wauhatchie, Tennessee, that General Geary's son, Lieutenant Edward R. Geary, was killed in action on 28 October 1863. Geary himself was twice wounded and nearly killed on one occasion by an artillery shell that narrowly passed between Geary and the horse on which he was mounted. Geary's finest moment in the war probably came at Gettysburg, where, on the morning of 3 July 1863, he staged a daring counterattack that drove the Confederates from their occupied breastworks on Culp's Hill.

After the Civil War, Geary was twice elected governor of Pennsylvania, in 1866 and again in 1869, running as a Republican despite having been a lifelong Democrat. As governor, Geary worked for the reform of working conditions, especially in the mining and railroad industries, and was instrumental in calling a convention to revise the state's constitution. Soon after leaving office, John White Geary died of a heart attack on 8 February 1873.

—*Kenneth Deitreich*

See also Kansas.
For further reading:
Blair, William, ed. *A Politician Goes to War: The Civil War Letters of John White Geary* (1995).
Couch, Darius N. "Outgeneraled by Lee." In *Battles and Leaders of the Civil War* (1956).
Geary, Mary deForest. *A Giant in Those Days. A Story about the Life of John White Geary* (1980).
Hunt, Brev. Major General Henry J. "I Proceeded to Cemetery Hill." In *Battles and Leaders of the Civil War* (1956).
Tinkcom, Harry Martin. *John White Geary: Soldier-Statesman, 1819–1873* (1940).

GENERAL ORDERS, NO. 100

("Instructions for the Government of Armies of the United States in the Field")

General Orders, No. 100, also know as Lieber's Code, established a code of conduct for the Federal army toward the Confederacy's army and its civilians. Written primarily by Francis Lieber, the code would prove resilient, standing as the policy of American soldiers in the field during wartime into the twentieth century and continuing to influence similar policies in the future. In addition, several European nations subsequently adopted the code as their own. The code also had a strong influence on the Hague and Geneva conventions.

At the outbreak of the Civil War, the Federal military found the existing articles of war insufficient for dealing with the issues raised by the conflict, particularly in regard to prisoners and exchanges, guerrilla warfare, and the treatment of civilians in occupied territory. Francis Lieber, a Prussian immigrant, renowned scholar of international law, and staunch Unionist, immediately took interest in such issues and began writing essays for newspapers and delivering lectures concerning various aspects of war and international law in the context of the existing strife. His concern also had a personal side. His three sons all participated in the war, two in Federal blue and one in Confederate gray. The Confederate son died from wounds received at the battle of Williamsburg, where he fought against one of his brothers.

While visiting his third son, wounded at the attack on Fort Donelson, Lieber met the Department of Missouri commander, Henry Halleck, a scholar of international law in his own right and an admirer of the Prussian. As a result of the meeting, Halleck asked Lieber to write down his thoughts on guerrilla warfare and the appropriate measures to use in response. Upon receiving the finished document, Halleck, now serving in Washington as general-in-chief of the army, ordered that copies of "Guerrilla Parties Considered with Reference to the Laws and Usage of War" be sent to officers in the field to use as guidelines for treating guerrillas.

Lieber then turned to broader issues related to the war. He proposed to Halleck that a committee be formed to prepare "a set of rules and definitions" to guide Federal army policy "where the Articles of War are silent. Although the appointed committee consisted of five members, four generals and Lieber, the resulting code with few exceptions came from the scholar's pen. On 24 April 1863 the War Department issued General Orders, No. 100, comprising ten sections and 157 individual articles. Broadly written to apply to all armed conflict, the code became the general policy for soldiers in the field, although individual commanders of the various military departments and districts tailored the code to meet the specific circumstances of their regions.

Much of the code dealt with enemy combatants. It addressed matters related to prisoners and exchanges, flags of truce, treatment of wounded, partisans and guerrillas, and others. According to the definitions of types of armed conflicts set forth by Lieber, the present hostility represented a rebellion, "a war between the legitimate government of a country and portions or provinces of the same who seek to throw off their allegiance to it and set up a government of their own." Under these terms, Confederate soldiers could be treated as belligerents under the laws of war, but the "legitimate government" still had the right to try "leaders of the rebellion or chief rebels for high treason."

Also, the civilians of the Confederate states were still subject to Federal law. In this context the code described three categories of civilians in areas of occupation: those who remained loyal to the government, those who sympathized with but did not positively aid the rebellion, and those who "without taking up arms, give positive aid and comfort to the rebellious enemy without being bodily forced thereto." While the first group merited the full protection of the army, the latter two could be deprived of property for the benefit of the military or subjected to retaliatory acts in response to the depredations of Confederate soldiers or guerrillas. Indeed, the code's ambiguous treatment of what constituted "military necessity" and "retaliation" allowed officers in the field to follow a harsh policy toward civilians under occupation. Confederate authorities attacked the code as propaganda and argued that the latitude could lead military commanders to act with barbarity.

—*Thomas F. Curran*

See also Lieber, Francis.
For further reading:
Freidel, Frank. *Francis Lieber: Nineteenth Century Liberal* (1947).
Hartigan, Richard Shelly, ed. *Lieber's Code and the Law of War* (1983).

GEORGIA

Georgia voters, like those in other Southern states, were deeply divided over the issue of secession. In his definitive study *Toward a Patriarchal Republic: The Secession of Georgia*, Michael P. Johnson concluded that just over half the popular vote for delegates to the state convention went against immediate secession. Nevertheless, enough delegates ignored their constituents' wishes to give secessionists a 166 to 130 majority in the initial convention vote.

Despite early divisions, there was some general enthusiasm for the war after the Fort Sumter crisis and Lincoln's call for volunteers to invade the South. By May 1861, Georgia had furnished some 18,000 troops for the Confederacy, second only to Virginia. Georgia's entrepreneurs also caught war fever and rapidly built up military industrial centers at Columbus, Macon, Augusta, and Atlanta. So successful were they and other Southern industrialists that Confederate armies never lost a major battle for want of munitions. What Southern troops constantly lacked was food. Part of the problem lay with the South's inadequate rail system, but a much greater share of the blame rests with the planters.

Though cotton growing declined during the war, planters never devoted enough land to food production. In the spring of 1862, a southwest Georgia man wrote to Governor Joseph E. Brown about planters growing too much cotton and warned him to "stop those internal enemies of the country, for they will whip up sooner than all Lincolndom combined could do it." Brown supported state legislation limiting planters to three acres of cotton per hand, but enforcement was lax and most planters ignored the law. When citizens in Cuthbert criticized Robert Toombs for raising more cotton than the law allowed, he replied that he would continue to grow as much as he pleased. Many planters and merchants defied the Confederacy's cotton export restrictions and smuggled it out by the ton. Some Georgia planters openly bragged that the longer the war went on the more money they made.

The inevitable result of cotton overproduction was a severe food shortage that hit Georgia women especially hard. With so many of their husbands in the army, it was difficult for many women to feed themselves and their children. Planters had promised to keep soldiers' families fed, but they never grew enough food to meet the need. Much of what food they did produce was sold to speculators, who priced it far beyond the reach of most plain

"Sherman's March through Georgia, the 'Rear Guard'" by Thomas Nast (*Library of Congress*)

folk. Desperate to avoid starvation, many women turned to theft and violence. In early 1863, food riots began breaking out all over the state. In Columbus, a mob of about sixty-five women, brandishing pistols and knives, marched down Broad Street, looting stores as they went. Atlanta, Augusta, Macon, and Milledgeville saw women rioting that spring as well. In April 1864, a band of Savannah women numbering perhaps a hundred raided stores on Whitaker Street. Such riots were not restricted to the larger urban centers. Women staged riots in and around smaller towns like Marietta, Thomasville, Forsyth, Cartersville, Blackshear, Hartwell, Stockton, Colquitt, and Valdosta. So many women wrote of their plight in letters to absent husbands that thousands of Georgia soldiers abandoned the army and went home.

Desertion had been a problem in the Confederacy from near the war's beginning. Once the early war fever died down, soldiers began drifting from the ranks, and there were few recruits to replace them. As early as October 1861, Captain Edward Croft of Columbus reported that it was almost impossible to get new volunteers. Congress responded by imposing a military draft in 1862, but the act angered common people by exempting those who owned twenty or more slaves. Governor Brown, claiming state rights, led opposition to the Confederate draft, but imposed one himself for the state militia. Planters avoided Brown's draft by bribing state enrolling officers or using their influence in local courts to have themselves declared exempt. Judge Richard Henry Clark of Georgia's southwestern judicial district granted exemptions to planters on a regular basis, and Colonel Carey Styles, commanding southeast Georgia's fifth military district, offered exemptions for $1,000 to anyone who could afford to pay. One way or another, men of means who desired to do so had little difficulty evading military service. It became increasingly obvious to plain folk that this was a rich man's war, which made the problem of desertion even worse.

Some deserters joined "tory" or "layout" gangs that were especially active in the north Georgia mountains and south Georgia pine barrens. They raided government depots, fought off conscript companies, and generally resisted Confederate authority wherever they found it. Some went further than that. One gang of Georgia tories led by Alonzo Rogers and Porter Southworth formed a battalion and called it the Volunteer Force of the United States Army from Georgia. So violent did Georgia's internal civil war become that on 24 November 1863, the editor of Milledgeville's *Confederate Union* wrote, "We are fighting each other harder than we have ever fought the enemy."

Georgia blacks, too, struck out against the authorities. Sometimes they cooperated with whites to do it. In the spring of 1862, three white citizens of Calhoun County

An unidentified battery at drill, Ringgold, Georgia (*National Archives*)

were arrested for supplying area slaves with firearms in preparation for a rebellion. Two years later, slaves in Brooks County conspired with a local white man, John Vickery, to take control of the region. Most resisted enslavement by more subtle means, expanding their personal liberties as the opportunity arose. Many fled to the Union-held Sea Islands, and thousands more followed William T. Sherman's army during its devastating March to the Sea.

By the time of Sherman's march in late 1864, social and economic disparities among Georgians had long since undermined what support there had been for the Confederacy. Even most of those who stuck with the cause to its painful end did so with little enthusiasm. William Andrews of Clay County had joined the army in February 1861 and remained through the entire war. Still, in May 1865 he wrote: "While it is a bitter pill to have to come back into the Union, don't think there is much regret for the loss of the Confederacy. The treatment the soldiers have received from the government in various ways put them against it." That was just as true of the civilian population, not only in Georgia but throughout the South. Such attitudes contributed significantly, perhaps decisively, to the Confederate defeat.

—*David Williams*

See also Atlanta Campaign; Atlanta, Georgia; Hood's Second Sortie; Sherman's March to the Sea; Savannah, Georgia; Savannah, Siege of; Southern Unionism; Stoneman's Raid.

For further reading:

Bryan, T. Conn. *Confederate Georgia* (1953).

Carlson, David. "'The Distemper of the Time': Conscription, the Courts, and Planter Privilege in Civil War South Georgia." *The Journal of Southwest Georgia History* (1999).

DeCredico, Mary A. *Patriotism for Profit: Georgia's Urban Entrepreneurs and the Confederate War Effort* (1990).

Dyer, Thomas G. *Secret Yankees: The Union Circle in Confederate Atlanta* (1999).

Formwalt, Lee W. "Planters and Cotton Production as a Cause of Confederate Defeat: Evidence from Southwest Georgia." *Georgia Historical Quarterly* (1990).

Johnson, Michael P. *Toward a Patriarchal Republic: The Secession of Georgia* (1977).

Mohr, Clarence L. *On the Threshold of Freedom: Masters and Slaves in Civil War Georgia* (1986).

Weitz, Mark A. *A Higher Duty: Desertion Among Georgia Troops during the Civil War* (2000).

Williams, David. *Rich Man's War: Class, Caste, and Confederate Defeat in the Lower Chattahoochee Valley* (1998).

Williams, Teresa C. "'The Women Rising': Class and Gender in Civil War Georgia" (M.A. thesis, 1999).

GERMAN-AMERICANS

The American Civil War was a major catalyst in bringing about the assimilation of and preserving the ethnic identity of German communities in America. Germans more than any other ethnic group taught Americans how to live with ethnic difference in the nineteenth century. Moreover, German participation in the Civil War displayed a patriotism that contradicted nativist doubts about the loyalty of Germans citizens. German-Americans who mustered into volunteer units, particularly into all- or nearly all-German units, attracted national attention to them as an ethnic presence when German identity appeared to be diminishing. Though the bulk of Germans who fought for the Confederacy or the Union served in units in which Americans greatly outnumbered them, significant influences such as language, camaraderie, community pressure, location, and above all, the persuasion of ethnic political leaders, encouraged some Germans to enlist in German-only units. In many ways, the ethnic struggles of the German soldiers and German regiments reflected the ethnic political battles in the larger societal context. Whatever the level of their involvement, their participation in the war gave German-Americans considerable visibility in American society.

In 1860 the ethnic German population of the entire United States was 1,301,136. In the states comprising the Union side in the conflict there were 1,229,174. Of this population it has been estimated that between 180,000 and 216,000 (or roughly 15 percent) of those served in the Union army, and at least 18,000 of these soldiers served in all-German units under German commanders, although high estimates put this number at roughly 36,000. A strict definition of an ethnic German regiment, however, would likely make the lower figure more accurate. Still, whatever the exact figure, the overwhelming number of German-Americans served in nonethnic units under American officers. The numbers also do not reflect the thousands of Swiss, Austrians, Poles, Hungarians, and Czechs who spoke German. Moreover, as the war entered its latter phases, the German ranks thinned to include more Americans. Thus, it is difficult to estimate an exact number of Germans who fought in either army.

Union Army — At least 145 units (militia, regiments, batteries, cavalry, companies, etc.) in the Union army are estimated to have comprised all or nearly all German soldiers. Units that have been identified include those from the following states: New York (twenty-four units), Massachusetts (two units), Connecticut (three units), Pennsylvania (six units), New Jersey (three units), Ohio (fifteen units), Indiana (six units), Illinois (eighteen units), Missouri (eighteen units), Wisconsin (thirteen units), Iowa (three units), Maryland (two units), Nebraska (one unit), Minnesota (four units), Kansas (two units), West Virginia (one unit), Kentucky (four units), and Texas (one unit).

Some of the more prominent German units that fought for the Union included the 24th Illinois Infantry, known as the Hecker Jaeger Regiment for Friedrich Hecker, and the 82d Illinois Infantry, also commanded for a time by Hecker. Both of these regiments were drawn primarily from the Chicago metropolitan area. The 43d Illinois Infantry, known as the Koerner Regiment in honor of Gustave Koerner, was drawn from downstate Illinois in the Belleville-East St. Louis area. Although over half of Indiana's immigrants were German, and the largest concentration was in and around Indianapolis, the state mustered in only six German units. Among the most distinguished of all German regiments in the war was the 32d Indiana Infantry, commanded for a time by August Willich, who led the regiment at the battle of Shiloh.

With its large German population, New York fielded more German regiments than any state in the North or the South. Among the more interesting, though hardly distinguished, was the 8th New York Infantry (First German Rifles) led by Louis (Ludwig) Blenker, which stood in great contrast to the heroics of the 32d Indiana. Another prominent unit was the 46th New York Infantry, the Frémont Rifles, led by Rudolph von Rosa.

Germans in Ohio created between six and twelve all-German regiments. Some of the more prominent included the 9th, 28th, 37th, 106th, 107th, and 108th Ohio Infantries. The first German regiment created in Ohio was the 9th Ohio, which comprised Germans from Cincinnati and was led by Scots-Irishman Robert McCook and later by August Willich. Pennsylvania's 74th Infantry, led by Alexander von Schimmelfennig, was drawn largely from Pittsburgh. Other prominent regiments from Pennsylvania included the 27th, 73d, 75th, and 98th Infantries, all of which comprised a number of Germans from the Philadelphia metropolitan area. Missouri's most prominent German-American regiments included the 3d, 12th, and 15th Infantries. The 3d Infantry was led by Franz Sigel, who eventually rose to the rank of brigadier general and whose admirers sang, "I fights mit Sigel." The 15th Infantry, known as the Swiss Rifles, was composed of Germans and German-speaking Swiss soldiers from St. Louis. Of all the Missouri regiments, Peter J. Osterhaus's 12th Infantry was perhaps the most distinguished. The regiment included Henry Kircher, whose surviving letters written in both English and German provide a valuable picture of rank-and-file life in a German regiment. The 4th Missouri Cavalry was among the few German cavalry regiments created during the war.

Wisconsin contributed several regiments, including the 26th Infantry drawn from the Milwaukee area. It was known as the "Sigel Regiment" in honor of Franz Sigel. The 26th Wisconsin fought in the 11th Corps of the Army of the Potomac, which added to the corps reputation as the "foreign contingent" or the "German Corps" because of the large number of ethnically mixed soldiers. Two of the corps' three divisions (Carl Schurz and Adolf von Steinwehr), four of its six brigades (Leopold von Gilsa, Alexander von Schimmelfennig, Adolphus Buschbeck, and Wladimir Krzyzanowski), twelve of its twenty-six regiments, and six of its eight artillery units were commanded by foreign-born officers. Brigadier General Oliver Otis Howard, commander of the corps, reported at the battle of Chancellorsville that 8,345 officers and men, more than two-thirds of the 11th Corps troops available for duty, were in eleven exclusively German and four "mixed nationality" regiments. The defeat of the Union army at the battle of Chancellorsville cast a negative light on the entire corps for its performance and earned the soldiers, whether German or not, the epithet "the Flying Dutchmen."

Confederate Army — It has been estimated that between 71,000 and 73,500 Germans lived in Confederate states in 1861. Germans were the second-largest ethnic group in the Confederacy behind the Irish. The bulk of the German population (some 53,000–55,000) in the Confederacy resided in Texas, Louisiana, and Virginia. The remaining 20,000 were scattered throughout the other states. Of that population, between 3,500 and 7,000 fought for the Confederacy. A majority of the German regiments came from the cities where they were most numerous, such as New Orleans, Charleston, Richmond, and Memphis. In the officer rank from brigadier general to captain there were more than seventy Germans. Like their Northern counterparts, Germans in the Confederacy fought in regiments that were predominately American. There were at least forty regiments that included Germans, but not one Confederate unit was entirely German. Units that have been identified include those from Alabama (four units), Georgia (four units), Louisiana (two units), North Carolina (one unit), South Carolina (five units), Tennessee (one unit), Texas (twenty-one units), and Virginia (four units).

Forty-eighters — Of the estimated 180,000 to 216,000 Germans who participated in the Civil War for the Union, nearly 5,000 had previously fought in the revolutionary armies and insurrections in Baden, the Palatinate, Hungary, the Rhineland, Poland, Bohemia, Berlin, or Saxony in 1848–1849. These German "Forty-eighters," as they came to be known, fought to establish a democratic and unified Germany. Many also participated in insurrections in other European countries. At least eighteen Forty-eighter colonels commanded German regiments at one time or another, and six or seven commanded non-German regiments. Some of the more prominent Forty-eighters include: Alexander Asboth, Franz Backhoff, Fritz Anneke, Peter Osterhaus, Franz Sigel, Friedrich Solomon, Alexander Schimmelfennig, Max Weber, August Willich, Friedrich

Hecker, Gustave Struve, Ludwig Blenker, Henry Boernstein, Adolf Engelmann, and Julius Stahel-Szamwald.

German-American sports clubs, known as *Turnvereine*, actively recruited and organized German units. Besides their physical training and youth, recruits from these organizations (called "Turners") had the social formation and political character to make them well suited to military training and operations. In fact, Turners and former Turners supplied several thousand troops, and in some cases formed whole Turner units in Ohio, New York, Illinois, Pennsylvania, Louisiana, Texas, and Virginia. Turners who enlisted in predominately German units generally came from the urban areas where their numbers were greatest, such as Cincinnati, New Orleans, Philadelphia, New York, Pittsburgh, Chicago, St. Louis, Charleston, Richmond, Milwaukee, and San Antonio. There were at least four Turner infantry regiments that served in the Union army: 20th New York Infantry (United Turner Regiment), 17th Missouri Infantry (Western Turner Rifles), 9th Ohio (Ohio Turners), and the 32d Indiana Infantry. Turners also formed a number of batteries.

The German-American military performance elicited a mixed evaluation, particularly in the North. Some Northern critics came to believe that the Germans were too mechanical, drank too much, and were slow to the offensive. They branded them the "Damned Dutch," "Bloody Dutch," or "Dutch Devils." Nativists, for example, blamed German soldiers of the 11th Corps for the Union defeat at Chancellorsville. Still, Confederates who fought against them considered the German-Americans to be some of the best soldiers in the Union. Germans of Cincinnati's 9th Ohio Regiment helped secure Union victories in Kentucky at Rowlett's Station, Mill Springs, and Perryville. The New York press credited German soldiers with preventing a complete rout at Second Bull Run by standing and fighting in the midst of a chaotic retreat. At the battle of Shiloh, the 32d Indiana played a critical role on the second day in helping to turn the tide in favor of the Union. William T. Sherman praised the Germans of this regiment highly for their efforts during the battle.

Because Germans participated in large numbers in Union outfits, the North's German-American communities closely monitored their operations in the field. Newspaper dispatches and soldiers' letters to relatives, friends, and newspapers kept the home front informed about life in the Union army. Though these accounts chronicled their military activities, they also detailed incidents of nativism that followed immigrants into military life. German soldiers sometimes accused American military authorities of keeping them out of action, mistreating them, passing them over for promotion, and denying them access to food and adequate supplies. The home front generally responded by reinforcing its support for the German troops by forming local committees to press the claims of individual German officers (such as Franz Sigel) or to raise money to purchase clothing, medical supplies, and food for immigrant units neglected by others. Germans at home personalized the affairs of German soldiers and used the German press and political leaders to gain recognition for their cause both on and off the battlefield.

—Stephen D. Engle

See also Asboth, Alexander; Howard, Oliver O.; Immigrants; Immigration; Kryzanowski, Wladimir; McCooks of Ohio; Osterhaus, Peter; Schurz, Carl; Sigel, Franz; Von Steinwehr, Adolph W.A.F.; Willich, August; .
For further reading:
Burton, William L. *Melting Pot Soldiers: The Union's Ethnic Regiments* (1988; reprint 1998).
Kaufmann, Wilhelm. *Die Deutschen in Amerikanischen Burgerkrieg* (1911).
Lonn, Ella. *Foreigners in the Confederacy* (1940).
———. *Foreigners in the Union Army and Navy* (1951).
Rosegarten, Joseph. *The German Soldier in the Wars of the United States* (1886).

GETTY, GEORGE WASHINGTON
(1819–1901)
Union general

Born in Georgetown in Washington, D.C., on 2 October 1819, George Washington Getty received an appointment to the U.S. Military Academy at West Point at age sixteen. Graduating in 1840 ranked fifteenth in a class of forty-two, he obtained a commission as a second lieutenant. During the Mexican-American War, Getty served as an artillery officer under Winfield Scott. He participated in the battles of Contreras, Molino del Rey, Chapultepec, and Mexico City. For his gallantry under fire, he earned a brevet promotion to captain. Getty also fought against the Seminole Indians in Florida from 1849 to 1850 and again in 1856 and 1857. Between these conflicts he obtained promotion to captain. Getty was stationed in the Dakota Territory at Fort Randall when the Civil War opened.

The war offered him, as it did every officer in the old army, the chance for rapid advancement if he sought a field command. Consequently, Getty secured an appointment as a lieutenant colonel on 28 September 1861. He distinguished himself in George B. McClellan's Peninsula campaign by commanding four batteries, seeing action at Gaines' Mill and Malvern Hill. After McClellan's withdrawal from the York peninsula, the colonel fought in the Antietam campaign during Confederate general Robert E. Lee's first invasion of the North. For this service, Getty received a commission as brigadier general in September 1862.

Getty commanded the 3d Division of the IX Corps at Fredericksburg. Although his command remained in the reserve for much of that engagement, they went against the Confederate lines late in the day. Despite the odds against them, Getty followed his orders dutifully and led his men into the Southern cauldron of fire. By dusk, the badly mauled survivors pulled back to the relative safety of the town, having enjoyed no more success against the Confederate defenses than their predecessors on that bloody day.

In March 1863, Getty's division was transferred to Suffolk, Virginia. His performance in this relatively remote post was exceptional. His vigilance and cool-headedness led to the successful defense of the fortified post against the battle-hardened veterans of James Longstreet's command. During this campaign, he was responsible for securing the army's vulnerable right flank anchored on the Nansemond River. He helped to mastermind and execute a combined operation that led to the capture of a powerful Confederate battery named Fort Huger on 19 April 1863.

Getty remained in Virginia during the Gettysburg campaign, leading the VII Corps for a brief period in the summer of 1863. His most notable duty at this time was leading a raid against Confederate lines in the area of the South Anna River. For the remainder of the year he served as commander of the Federal forces protecting Portsmouth and Norfolk. Then, in early 1864, Getty became the acting inspector general of the Army of the Potomac. Assigned to the 2d Division in the VI Corps, Getty acquitted himself well in the fighting in the Wilderness. In that battle, he and a small entourage of staff held a critical intersection under severe fire while waiting for the main portion of the command to come up. In subsequent fighting on 6 May, Getty suffered a severe wound in the shoulder.

After his recovery from his Wilderness wound, Getty returned to participate in the fighting at Petersburg. Then, when Confederates under Jubal A. Early crossed the Potomac and threatened to march on Washington, Getty's corps was one of two that General Grant sent in response. After Early's retreat, Getty joined General Philip Sheridan's Army of the Shenandoah. During Sheridan's subsequent campaign in the Shenandoah Valley, Getty once again performed admirably. At Cedar Creek, his stubborn defense allowed the Federals the time to rally and turn an almost certain defeat into victory.

Getty became a major general in March 1865 and led the division when it made the initial penetration of the Confederate lines at Petersburg on 2 April. The stalwart Union general next participated in the Appomattox campaign, fighting at Sayler's Creek. He was also with the Army of the Potomac when General Lee finally surrendered his command on 9 April.

After the war, Getty mustered out of the volunteer service but continued in the regular army with the rank of colonel. He remained in the infantry until 1871, when he transferred to the branch of the service he had entered when he left West Point. Getty commanded the artillery school at Fort Monroe for six years, from 1871 to 1877, finally retiring from the service in 1883. He settled on his farm at Forest Glen, Maryland, and died there on 1 October 1901.

As a general, George Getty demonstrated tenacity on the battlefield, tempered by practicality and common sense. His character can perhaps best be found in a set of remarks he once made concerning duty: "I always obey an order," Getty explained. "If I was ordered to march my division across the Atlantic Ocean, I'd do it." But, he added, "I would march them up to their necks in the sea, and then withdraw and report that it was impractical to carry out the order."

—*Brian S. Wills*

See also Cedar Creek, Battle of; Fort Huger; Suffolk, Virginia, Siege of.

For further reading:
Cormier, Steven A. *The Siege of Suffolk* (1989).
Lewis, Thomas A. *The Guns of Cedar Creek* (1988).
Rhea, Gordon C. *The Battle of the Wilderness, May 5–6, 1864* (1994).
Warner, Ezra J. *Generals in Blue, Lives of Confederate Generals* (1964).
Wert, Jeffry D. *From Winchester to Cedar Creek: The Shenandoah Campaign of 1864* (1987; reprint 1997).
Woodworth, Steven E. "George Washington Getty." In *American National Biography* (1999).

GETTYSBURG ADDRESS
(19 November 1863)

By the fall of 1863, President Abraham Lincoln had decided that the time had come for a public statement that would articulate the meaning and significance of a civil war that had just entered its third bloody year. On 2 November the opportunity to make that statement arrived in the form of an invitation to contribute "a few appropriate remarks" to a ceremony scheduled for Thursday, 19 November 1863, dedicating seventeen acres of the Gettysburg battlefield for a cemetery where Union soldiers who had fallen in the July battle would be properly interred. Lincoln accepted, and a little over two weeks later delivered one of the great speeches of American history. Contrary to popular myth, he did not write the speech on the back of an envelope on the train ride north to Gettysburg, but evidently began composing it on White House stationery in the weeks before his departure from Washington on 18 November.

The trip to Gettysburg involved no small hardship for Lincoln personally. His son Tad was seriously ill, and the thought of the president leaving Washington drove

The crowd at the dedication of the Gettysburg battlefield cemetery, 19 November 1863, reputedly showing Abraham Lincoln (in top hat, *top row center*). (*Library of Congress*)

his wife, who had lost another son to illness a little more than a year before, to hysterics. Fortunately, upon his arrival at Gettysburg at around 5:00 P.M. on the 18th, a note arrived informing Lincoln, "your son is better this evening." Greatly relieved, the president completed his speech that night at the home of David Wills, the man who had conceived the Gettysburg cemetery project and who was the main organizer of the 19 November ceremony.

At ten the following morning, clad in a new black suit, Lincoln mounted a horse and headed to the cemetery. The audience first heard a moving and eloquent two-hour speech by the main speaker for the event, Edward Everett, and a brief hymn. Ward Lamon then introduced the president to the crowd.

Lincoln stepped forward and began his Gettysburg address by articulating his vision of the founding of the United States:

Four score and seven years ago our fathers brought forth, upon this continent, a new nation, conceived in liberty, and dedicated to the proposition that all men are created equal."

After a brief interruption by applause, he then addressed the nation's current situation:

Now we are engaged in a great civil war, testing whether that nation, or any nation so conceived and so dedicated, can long endure. We are met on a great battle-field of that war. We have come to dedicate a portion of that field, as a final resting place for those who here gave their lives that that nation might live. It is altogether fitting and proper that we should do this. But in a larger sense we can not dedicate—we can not consecrate—we can not hallow—this ground. The brave men, living and dead, who struggled here, have consecrated it, far above our poor power to add or detract.

After again being interrupted by applause, Lincoln looked to the future and the task that remained before the nation:

The world will little note, nor long remember what we say here, but it can never forget what they did here. It is for us the living, rather, to be dedicated here to the unfinished work which they who fought here have thus far so nobly advanced. It is rather for us to be here dedicated to the great task remaining before us—that from these honored dead we take increased devotion—that we here highly resolve that these dead shall not have died in vain—that this nation, under God, shall have a new birth of freedom—and that government of the people, by the people, for the people, shall not perish from the earth.

The address was only two minutes long, and its brevity surprised the 15,000 people in attendance. Consequently, a myth arose that the speech was poorly received by the audience and by the general public at first—a myth to which Lamon contributed by later writing that Lincoln lamented "that speech won't scour" when he was done. This was not the case. Everett immediately recognized that Lincoln had delivered an oratorical masterpiece and a statement of profound significance, and told the president as much in a letter the following day. It also became evident rather quickly that the general public's response to the speech was highly favorable and that Lincoln had achieved what he set out to do, although the speech's transcendent greatness was not widely acknowledged until after his death.

The Gettysburg Address has justly earned a hallowed place in American literature because in just 272 words Lincoln articulated for millions of Americans the higher ideals to which they wanted their nation and the Union cause dedicated. The North, Lincoln stated, fought for more than simply the restoration of a political union and the enforcement of the laws under the Constitution. Rather, it fought to preserve a noble experiment in republican government and a single nation whose bedrock principle was stated in the Declaration of Independence—that all men are created equal. It was this noble idea, Lincoln told the people, and the prospect that the war would produce "a new birth of freedom" that made the Union cause worth fighting for and had been advanced by the men in blue who made the ultimate sacrifice at Gettysburg.

—*Ethan S. Rafuse*

For further reading:
Barton, William E. *Lincoln at Gettysburg: What He Intended to Say; What He Said; What He Was Reported to Have Said; What He Wished He Had Said* (1930).
Basler, Roy P., ed. *The Collected Works of Abraham Lincoln* (1953–1955).
Donald, David Herbert. *Lincoln* (1995).
Warren, Louis A. *Lincoln's Gettysburg Dedication: "A New Birth of Freedom"* (1964).
Wills, Garry. *Lincoln at Gettysburg: The Words that Remade America* (1992).

GETTYSBURG, BATTLE OF
(1–3 July 1863)

Considered by many historians to be the turning point of the Civil War, the Gettysburg campaign began on 3 June 1863 when elements of General Robert E. Lee's Army of Northern Virginia began leaving their positions near Fredericksburg and heading for the Shenandoah Valley. Lee planned a raid into Pennsylvania to relieve the strained Virginia countryside, disrupt Union economic security east of the Susquehanna River, and bring foreign recognition to the Confederacy.

After Stonewall Jackson's death in May 1863, Lee reorganized his 80,000-man army into three infantry corps, each consisting of three divisions commanded by a lieutenant general. James Longstreet led I Corps; Richard S. Ewell, II Corps; and Ambrose P. Hill, III Corps. Both Ewell and Hill were new to their positions. Major General James E. B. Stuart led the cavalry of the army. Each division included an artillery battalion, and each corps had two more artillery battalions in reserve. Southern artillery numbered 274 pieces.

Union cavalry led by Major General Alfred Pleasonton battled Jeb Stuart's cavalry on 9 June in a day-long series of engagements known as Brandy Station. Cavalry of both armies sparred with each other as the Confederate infantry began moving north, the Army of the Potomac under Major General Joseph Hooker moving more slowly while trying to ascertain enemy intentions.

Hooker's army had contained more than 120,000 men at Chancellorsville, but the mustering out of two-year and nine-month regiments during late May and June reduced its strength to fewer than 100,000. Hooker's army consisted of seven infantry corps and Pleasonton's three divisions of cavalry. Each corps was led by a major general, and consisted of either two or three divisions plus an artillery brigade. The corps were led by John F. Reynolds (I), Winfield S. Hancock (II), Daniel E. Sickles (III), George G. Meade (V), John Sedgwick (VI), Oliver O. Howard (XI), and Henry W. Slocum (XII). Brigadier General Robert O. Tyler commanded the five brigades of the Artillery Reserve, which contained 114 cannon of the army's total of 372 guns.

Troops of Ewell's II Corps defeated and drove off the Union garrison of Winchester and then swept north,

The Battle of Gettysburg, from a battlefield sketch (*Library of Congress*)

crossed the Potomac River, and entered Maryland and southern Pennsylvania. By late June, Ewell's men were approaching Harrisburg, Pennsylvania, skirmishing with Union militia west of the Susquehanna. One of Jubal Early's brigades narrowly missed seizing a bridge over the river at Wrightsville before it was burned by retreating militia. Lee was hampered by the absence of most of his cavalry. Stuart, acting under discretionary orders from Lee, found himself separated from the main army by Union troops and had to circle around behind the northward-moving Yankees before rejoining Lee on 2 July.

Hooker's troops, meanwhile, crossed the Potomac and headed north to stay between Lee and Washington. Hooker, unhappy with the controls placed on him by the War Department, asked to be relieved of command. His offer was accepted, and on the morning of 28 June, Major General George G. Meade, commander of V Army Corps, was placed in command of the army. Meade took stock of the situation and developed a plan to fight a defensive battle behind Pipe Creek, Maryland.

Lee finally learned from scouts the whereabouts of the Army of the Potomac, canceled his drive on Harrisburg, and ordered a concentration of the army in the mountains between Chambersburg and Gettysburg, the latter a Pennsylvania town of some 2,500 people in Adams County. Union cavalry under Brigadier General John Buford entered Gettysburg on 30 June and sighted rebel infantry to the west.

Buford sent word of his discovery to General Reynolds, leader of I Army Corps and commander of Meade's left wing. Buford decided to hold Gettysburg, and on the morning of 1 July his two brigades, fighting dismounted, fended off Major General Henry Heth's Division of Hill's III Corps for several hours until infantry of Reynolds's corps arrived on Seminary Ridge west of Gettysburg. The Union infantry drove back Heth's men, but Reynolds was killed during the action and command of the field devolved upon General Howard, commander of XI Army Corps.

As the troops of I Army Corps, now led by Major General Abner Doubleday, deployed along McPherson's Ridge, two of Howard's divisions moved north through town and deployed in the fields to guard against Confederates of Jubal Early's division, heading south toward Gettysburg. Further Confederate reinforcements from Robert Rodes's division of Ewell's corps and William D. Pender's of Hill's gave Lee, who had arrived on the field, a significant numerical advantage over Howard's divisions.

A concentrated attack by Lee's men late in the afternoon swamped the Union defenders. Early's attack

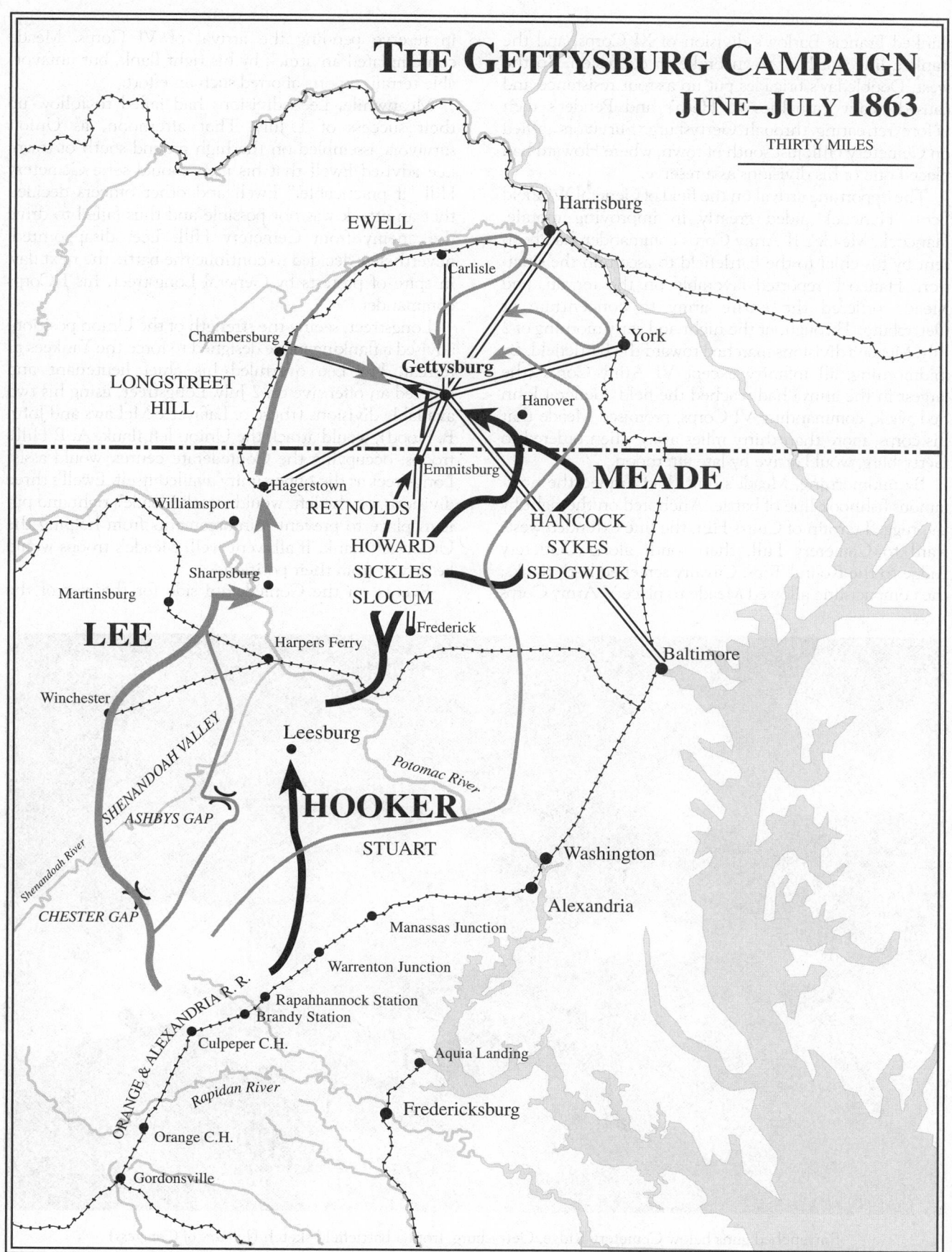

THE GETTYSBURG CAMPAIGN
JUNE–JULY 1863

THIRTY MILES

Harrisburg

EWELL

Carlisle

Chambersburg

York

LONGSTREET
HILL

Gettysburg

Hanover

Hagerstown

Emmitsburg

MEADE

Williamsport

REYNOLDS

HOWARD

HANCOCK

SICKLES

SYKES

Sharpsburg

SLOCUM

SEDGWICK

Martinsburg

Harpers Ferry

Frederick

LEE

Winchester

Baltimore

SHENANDOAH VALLEY

Leesburg

Potomac River

ASHBYS GAP

Shenandoah River

HOOKER

CHESTER GAP

STUART

Washington

Alexandria

Manassas Junction

Warrenton Junction

ORANGE & ALEXANDRIA R.R.

Rapahhannock Station

Brandy Station

Culpeper C.H.

Aquia Landing

Rapidan River

Fredericksburg

Orange C.H.

Gordonsville

flanked Francis Barlow's division of XI Corps, and the Yankee line north of town broke in confusion. To the west, Doubleday's brigades put up a stout resistance and caused heavy casualties to Heth's and Pender's men before retreating through Gettysburg. Survivors rallied on Cemetery Hill, just south of town, where Howard had placed one of his divisions as a reserve.

The opportune arrival on the field of General Winfield Scott Hancock aided greatly in improving morale. Hancock, Meade's II Army Corps commander, had been sent by his chief to the battlefield to ascertain the situation. Hancock reported favorably on the terrain, and Meade ordered the entire army to concentrate at Gettysburg. Throughout the night and early morning of 2 July, Meade's divisions marched toward the battlefield. By midmorning, all infantry except VI Army Corps (the largest in the army) had reached the field. General John Sedgwick, commanding VI Corps, promised Meade that his corps, more than thirty miles away when ordered to Gettysburg, would arrive by late afternoon.

By midmorning, Meade's units had formed the now-famous fishhook line of battle. Anchored on the right by the rugged terrain of Culp's Hill, the line extended westward to Cemetery Hill, then south along Cemetery Ridge to the Round Tops. Cavalry screened both flanks; the compact line allowed Meade to place V Army Corps in reserve pending the arrival of VI Corps. Meade contemplated an attack by his right flank, but unfavorable terrain reports aborted such an effort.

Meanwhile, Lee's divisions had failed to follow up their success of 1 July. That afternoon, as Union survivors assembled on the high ground south of town, Lee advised Ewell that his men should seize Cemetery Hill "if practicable." Ewell and other officers decided that an attack was not possible and thus failed to drive the enemy from Cemetery Hill. Lee, disappointed, nevertheless decided to continue the battle the next day, in spite of protests by General Longstreet, his I Corps commander.

Longstreet, seeing the strength of the Union position, advised a flanking move designed to force the Yankees to retreat, but Lee overruled his chief lieutenant and ordered an offensive on 2 July. Longstreet, using his two available divisions (those of Lafayette McLaws and John B. Hood), would attack the Union left flank. A. P. Hill's troops, occupying the Confederate center, would assist Longstreet as the opportunity availed itself. Ewell's three divisions, on the left, would attack Meade's right and pin it in place to prevent reinforcements from helping the Union left flank. If all went well, Meade's troops would be driven from their positions.

Events on the Confederate side for the rest of the

Entrenched guns below Cemetery Ridge, Gettysburg, from a battlefield sketch (*Library of Congress*)

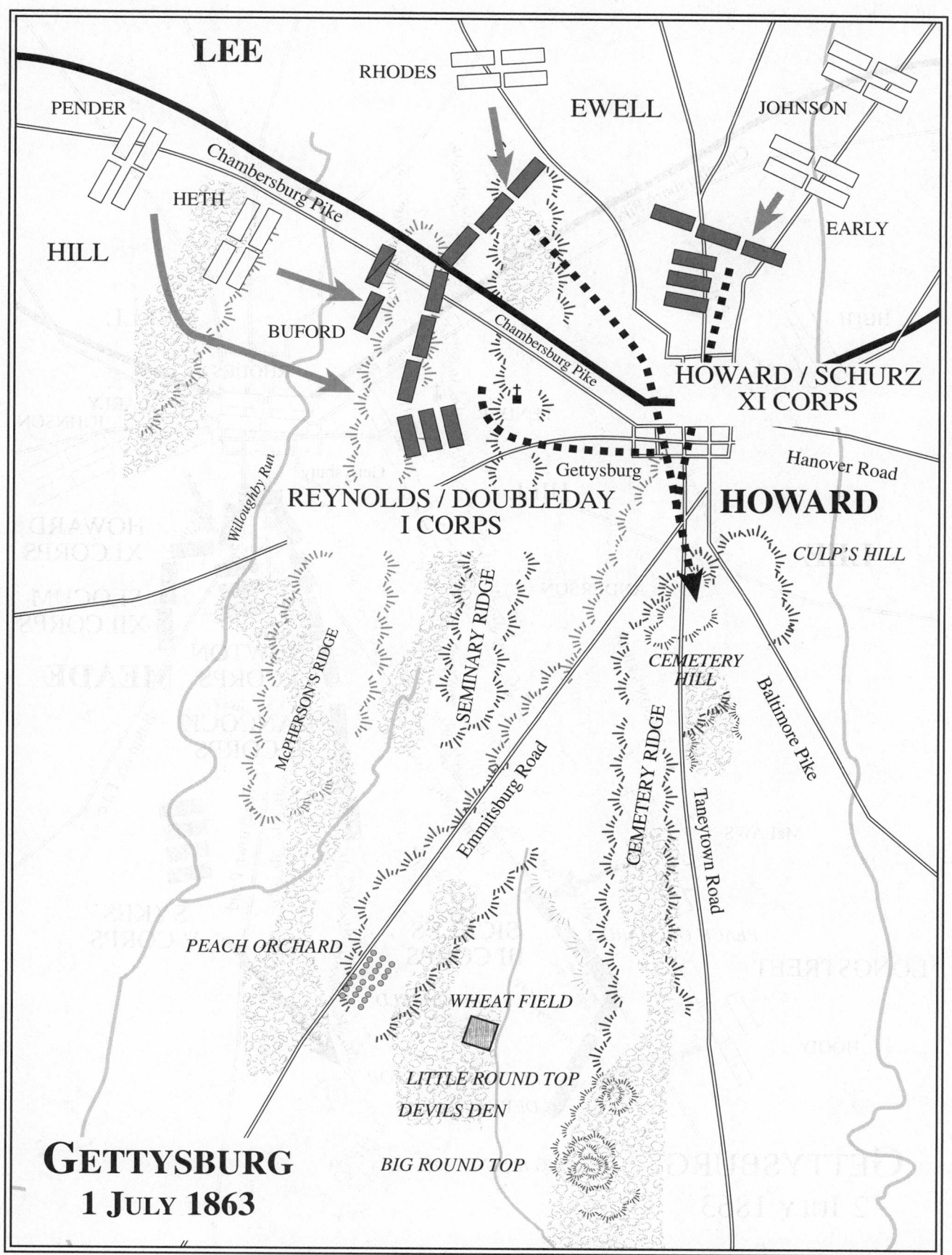

LEE

RHODES

PENDER

EWELL

JOHNSON

HETH

HILL

EARLY

Chambersburg Pike

BUFORD

Chambersburg Pike

HOWARD / SCHURZ
XI CORPS

†

Hanover Road

Gettysburg

HOWARD

REYNOLDS / DOUBLEDAY
I CORPS

CULP'S HILL

Willoughby Run

CEMETERY
HILL

Baltimore Pike

McPHERSON'S RIDGE

SEMINARY RIDGE

CEMETERY RIDGE

Taneytown Road

Emmitsburg Road

PEACH ORCHARD

WHEAT FIELD

LITTLE ROUND TOP

DEVILS DEN

GETTYSBURG
1 July 1863

BIG ROUND TOP

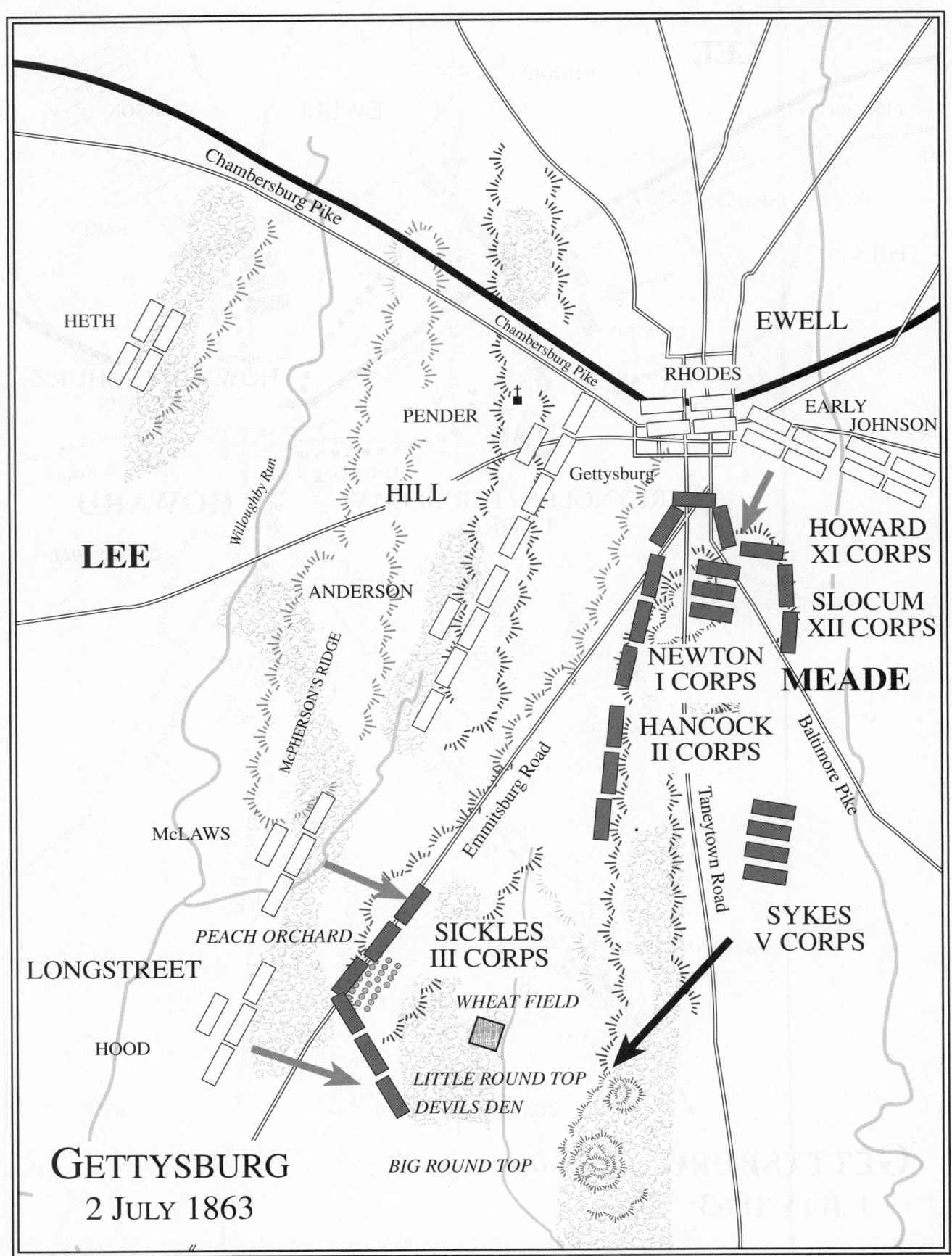

HETH

Chambersburg Pike

Chambersburg Pike

EWELL

RHODES

EARLY
JOHNSON

PENDER

HILL

Gettysburg

HOWARD
XI CORPS

LEE

Willoughby Run

ANDERSON

SLOCUM
XII CORPS

NEWTON
I CORPS

MEADE

McPHERSON'S RIDGE

HANCOCK
II CORPS

Emmitsburg Road

McLAWS

Baltimore Pike

PEACH ORCHARD

SICKLES
III CORPS

Taneytown Road

SYKES
V CORPS

LONGSTREET

WHEAT FIELD

HOOD

LITTLE ROUND TOP

DEVILS DEN

GETTYSBURG
2 JULY 1863

BIG ROUND TOP

Barlows' Knoll, Gettysburg, after the first day's fighting (Photograph by James Pierce / *Library of Congress*)

morning and afternoon are controversial to the extreme. Longstreet waited for an Alabama brigade to arrive before beginning his march to the Union left flank. Proponents of Lee argued later that Longstreet's delay was unnecessary and resulted in a lost opportunity to destroy Meade's army that morning before it could entirely assemble on the field.

Controversy also erupted on Cemetery Ridge. General Daniel Sickles, the political general in charge of III Army Corps, stationed on the army's left, was unhappy with the terrain north of Little Round Top and sought permission to change his deployment. Meade ordered his testy subordinate to remain in line and deploy according to general instructions received earlier in the morning. Sickles sent Colonel Hiram Berdan's sharpshooters out to Seminary Ridge to reconnoiter. The green-clad sharpshooters encountered Richard H. Anderson's Division of Hill's III Corps maneuvering into position to await Longstreet's arrival on its right flank. Sickles, uneasy over learning about the enemy, took it upon himself to advance his two divisions to occupy higher ground to his front along the Emmitsburg Road. The V-shaped salient that Sickles occupied isolated his corps from Hancock's. Meade did not learn about

Sickles's disobedience of orders until late in the afternoon, when he called his corps commanders together for a conference, just as VI Army Corps was sighted on the Baltimore Pike.

Meade inspected Sickles's faulty position and ordered a withdrawal, but it was too late. Longstreet's two divisions had finally moved into position on Anderson's left, and at 4:00 P.M. the Confederate artillery opened fire on Sickles's line, just as Meade was ordering Sickles to return to Cemetery Ridge. Meade quickly countermanded the retreat order and instead went about finding reinforcements for Sickles.

Longstreet's attack began on the right, with Hood's division, which swept forward over rough terrain and almost seized Little Round Top, left unguarded by Sickles's movement. Luckily, Brigadier General Gouverneur K. Warren, Meade's chief engineer, had climbed the hill and noticed the beginning of the Southern advance. He called for reinforcements and personally commandeered a brigade from the advancing V Army Corps and ordered it to occupy Little Round Top. Colonel Strong Vincent's four regiments deployed on the southern end of Little Round Top just in time to meet elements of Hood's division. After a fierce struggle,

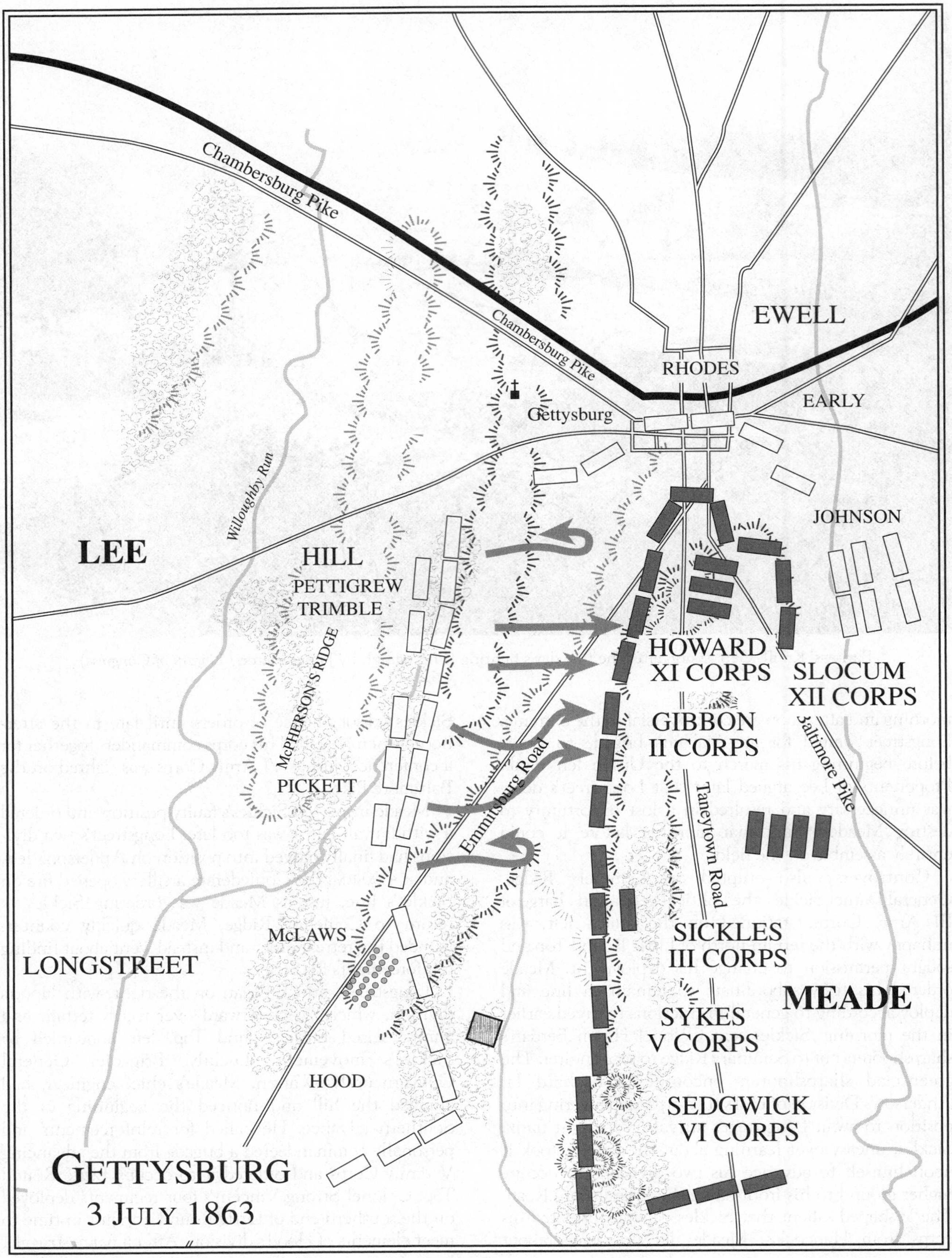

CHAMBERSBURG PIKE

Chambersburg Pike

EWELL

RHODES

EARLY

Gettysburg

JOHNSON

LEE

HILL

PETTIGREW
TRIMBLE

McPHERSON'S RIDGE

Willoughby Run

HOWARD
XI CORPS

SLOCUM
XII CORPS

GIBBON
II CORPS

Baltimore Pike

PICKETT

Emmitsburg Road

Taneytown Road

SICKLES
III CORPS

MEADE

McLAWS

LONGSTREET

SYKES
V CORPS

HOOD

SEDGWICK
VI CORPS

GETTYSBURG
3 JULY 1863

climaxed by the epic stand of the 20th Maine, and arrival of further reinforcements, Little Round Top remained firmly in Union hands.

Longstreet's divisions crashed into Sickles's men and made famous a field of wheat (now known as the Wheatfield), an outcrop of granite boulders (Devil's Den), and a large peach grove (now known as the Peach Orchard). Reinforcements from Hancock's II Army Corps, Doubleday's I, Sedgwick's VI, and even from Slocum's XII Army Corps, ordered away from their entrenchments on Culp's Hill, finally stemmed the Confederate assault. By nightfall, Sickles's corps had been pushed back to Cemetery Ridge, with Sickles himself wounded in a leg, which was amputated that night.

On the Union right, Edward Johnson's division of Ewell's corps moved forward in the coming darkness and occupied a section of abandoned Union earthworks on the eastern side of Culp's Hill. A lone brigade of New Yorkers led by Brigadier General George S. Greene held the crest of the hill, and, aided by reinforcements, fended off Johnson's attacks. Two brigades of Early's division stormed up the steep slopes of Cemetery Hill, drove off some XI Corps infantry, and fought hand-to-hand with Yankee gunners defending their batteries, but had to retreat when reinforcements assisted in driving them back.

Having been repulsed on both Union flanks, General Lee decided to attack the Union center on 3 July. That morning, a terrific battle erupted on the Union right as troops from VI and XII Army Corps dueled with Ewell's men for possession of the works on Culp's Hill. By late morning, the weight of Union infantry and artillery drove back the rebels and solidified the Federal position.

Colonel Edward P. Alexander, acting under Lee's instructions, assembled more than 100 artillery pieces to bear on the Union center. The rebel artillery opened fire shortly after 1:00 P.M. and was answered by more than eighty Federal cannon. The artillery duel continued for more than an hour, after which an infantry force variously estimated at between 10,500 and 15,000 soldiers moved forward to attack Hancock's II Army Corps at the

A dead Confederate soldier in Devil's Den, Gettysburg (Photograph by Alexander Gardner / *Library of Congress*)

The John Burns house, Gettysburg, with Burns seated in rocker, 1863 (*Library of Congress*)

Federal center. Composed of Major General George Pickett's three Virginia brigades, supported by brigades from Heth's and Pender's divisions, Longstreet's assault, popularly known as Pickett's Charge, moved against the Union center across a mile of open fields.

Union artillery blasted the attackers, and by the time the spearhead reached the Union line, the assault had been largely broken up and disorganized. Several hundred Virginians led by Brigadier General Lewis A. Armistead seized some Union cannons at the Bloody Angle, but were driven off or captured by the Union defenders. The failed charge ended the major action at Gettysburg, although some V Army Corps troops on Meade's left charged across the Wheatfield and mauled one of Longstreet's Georgia brigades.

Meanwhile, cavalry actions took place on both flanks. Jeb Stuart, with several brigades of cavalry, moved toward the right rear of the Union army but was met by Yankee cavalry, including the Michigan brigade led by George A. Custer. After a furious action involving both mounted and dismounted troopers, Stuart admitted defeat and withdrew.

On the Confederate right, two brigades of Yankee cavalry moved to attack but were repulsed, with

Brigadier General Elon J. Farnsworth losing his life during a confused charge over rough terrain in front of Big Round Top. The 6th U.S. Cavalry was detached to intercept a rebel forage train said to be operating near Fairfield (southwest of Gettysburg), but was met by a brigade of rebels and largely destroyed.

Both armies remained in position on 4 July, which was a day of rain. Lee's army of 75,000 effectives had suffered 28,000 casualties and thus the general decided to retreat to Virginia. The retreat began in the rain of 4 July as a wagon train estimated at nineteen miles long carried thousands of wounded men south toward the Potomac.

Meade's army suffered casualties of 3,149 killed, 14,501 wounded, and 5,157 captured or missing, for a total of 22,807. Of the seven infantry corps commanders, one (Reynolds) was killed and two (Hancock and Sickles) wounded. Two division commanders and eleven brigade leaders were also *hors de combat*, the combination of which severely disabled the Army of the Potomac. As a result, Meade directed a cautious pursuit, which was highlighted by a series of cavalry actions as Yankee cavalry attempted to interdict Lee's wagon trains.

Lee's army halted at Williamsport, Maryland, and entrenched. The Potomac River, swollen by the rains,

The town of Gettysburg in 1863 (Photograph by Mathew Brady Studio / *Library of Congress*)

The pursuit of Lee's army following the Battle of Gettysburg (*Library of Congress*)

prevented an easy crossing, made all the more serious after Union cavalry operating from Harper's Ferry destroyed a pontoon bridge erected during the march north. Meade's army deployed to face the enemy and probed the strong defenses. A council of war voted not to attack, but Meade overruled his subordinates and ordered the assault. However, Lee's army slipped across the river via a new bridge and the Yankee attack merely netted some stragglers and the rear guard on 14 July. The Army of the Potomac crossed into Virginia soon thereafter and the campaign ended officially on 1 August, when both armies came to a halt in the Loudoun Valley.

— *Richard A. Sauers*

See also Aldie, Virginia, Battle of; Brandy Station, Battle of; Hancock, Winfield Scott; Lee, Robert E.; Longstreet, James; Meade, George Gordon; Pickett, George E.; Reynolds, John; Winchester, Second Battle of.

For further reading:
Coddington, Edwin B. *The Gettysburg Campaign: A Study in Command* (1968).
Frassanito, William A. *Early Photography at Gettysburg* (1995).
Sauers, Richard A. *The Gettysburg Campaign, June 3–August 1, 1863: A Comprehensive, Selectively Annotated Bibliography* (1982).
Vanderslice, John M. *Gettysburg Then and Now. The Field of American Valor. Where and How the Regiments Fought and the Troops They Encountered. An Account of the Battle Giving Movements, Positions, and Losses of the Commands Engaged* (1899).

GIBBON, JOHN
(1827–1896)
Union general

John Gibbon was born at Holmesburg, Pennsylvania, a suburb of Philadelphia. His father, John H. Gibbon, was a physician, and his mother, Catherine Lardner Gibbon, was a member of a prominent Philadelphia family. In 1837 Dr. Gibbon took up an appointment at the U.S. Mint in Charlotte, North Carolina, and the entire family moved there. His father obtained, through political connections, an appointment for Gibbon at West Point, which he entered in 1842. Academic and disciplinary problems forced him to repeat his plebe year, and he narrowly escaped dismissal. The experience turned Gibbon into a cold and strict disciplinarian, devoted to the rulebook and demanding of both subordinates and superiors alike.

He graduated from West Point in 1847, became a second lieutenant of artillery in that year, and saw uneventful service in Mexico, Florida, and Texas. In 1850 he received promotion to first lieutenant, and in 1854 was assigned to West Point as instructor of artillery tactics. While there, he married Francis Moale of Baltimore. In 1860 he was promoted to captain and assigned to command of Battery B, 4th U.S. Artillery, stationed at Camp Floyd, Utah Territory. After the election of Abraham Lincoln, increased tensions at Camp

Floyd and Gibbon's Southern connections made his loyalty suspect. A somewhat farcical series of accusations followed, ending with a court of inquiry. The result was that Gibbon adhered to his oath and remained in the U.S. Army when North Carolina seceded.

As an experienced officer, Gibbon obtained employment training the incoming recruits for the Army of the Potomac. He became chief of artillery to Irvin McDowell's 1st Division, as well as retaining his battery command. On 2 May 1862 he was promoted to brigadier general of Volunteers and given command of a brigade of infantry. Gibbon rapidly became one of the Army of the Potomac's premier combat leaders and an excellent trainer of troops. He did not display the mingled sense of contempt and condescension toward volunteer soldiers that characterized many of his brother West Pointers. Although demanding that they pay attention to regulations, drill, and disciplinary requirements, he found ways to respect their individuality and sense of local identity and pride. He also made their initiative and intelligence work for him and the brigade. This unit of four (later five) Wisconsin, Michigan, and Indiana regiments, on his order, wore distinctive uniforms. Their outfit of dark blue frock coat, white leggings and the full black dress hat caused them to be called the "Black Hat Brigade."

Gibbon's first exposure to combat took place during the Second Bull Run campaign, when his brigade was ambushed along the Warrenton-Alexandria Turnpike on 28 August 1862 by part of Stonewall Jackson's corps. The firefight was only halted by darkness. Some of Gibbon's regiments suffered 40 percent casualties. Jackson declined to pursue, and the brigade continued its retreat toward Manassas and Centreville, where it took part in the last day's fighting of Second Bull Run.

At the beginning of September, with Major General George B. McClellan again in command, Gibbon and his brigade began to move into western Maryland, as the Army of the Potomac maneuvered to counter Lee's invasion of the North. Gibbon led his brigade in an attack on Turner's Gap through South Mountain, where he succeeded in dislodging the Confederates blocking the road. It was here that Joseph Hooker gave the men their most famous nickname, the "Iron Brigade."

After Antietam, where half of the brigade fell, Gibbon continued a Civil War career that included hard fighting at Fredericksburg, where he first functioned as a divisional commander, and at Chancellorsville. At Gettysburg, Gibbon both commanded a division of II Corps under Winfield S. Hancock and acted as II Corps' commander in his friend's absence. It was at Gettysburg that Gibbon received his second wound, a minié ball through the left shoulder. His division occupied the stone wall section of the Union center, and played a major role in repulsing Pickett's Charge.

The years 1864 and 1865 were times of increasing disillusion and bitterness for Gibbon. He did not agree with the radical path the war had taken, lamented the dismissal of McClellan, and hoped for promotion that did not come. His mood was not improved by a growing feud with Hancock and the disintegration of their friendship. Although turning in his usual solid performances at the battles of the Wilderness, Spotsylvania Court House, and Cold Harbor, the growing animosity between the two officers made his departure from II Corps inevitable. Promoted to major general of Volunteers in June 1864, Gibbon left II Corps that fall and received command of XXIV Corps, Army of the James, at the end of the year. As its commander, he participated in the siege of Petersburg and the Appomattox campaign, serving as one of the surrender commissioners when the Army of Northern Virginia stacked arms.

Although Gibbon's postwar service lasted until 1891, when he retired as a brigadier general in the regular army, only two events ranked in his estimation to the Civil War years. Those were his participation in the Little Big Horn campaign of 1876, when his column found the dead and survivors of the Custer fight, and in 1877, when his command was defeated while attempting to halt Chief Joseph and the Nez Perce in their movement to Canada. Promoted to brigadier general in 1885, Gibbon retired from the U.S. Army while commander of the Military District of the Pacific. During his brief retirement, he served as commander of the Military Order of the Loyal Legion until his death from pneumonia on 6 February 1896. He was buried at Arlington National Cemetery, where in 1911 the Iron Brigade Association erected a large granite monument over his grave.

—*Dennis S. Lavery*

See also Bull Run, Second Battle of; Gettysburg, Battle of; Iron Brigade; South Mountain, Battle of.

For further reading:

Gibbon, John. *Personal Recollections of the Civil War* (1928).

Lavery, Dennis S., and Mark H. Jordan. *Iron Brigade General: John Gibbon, a Rebel in Blue* (1993).

Nolan, Alan T. *The Iron Brigade: A Military History* (1961; reprint, 1994).

GIDDINGS, JOSHUA REED
(1795–1864)
Ohio congressman

Joshua Reed Giddings was one of the venerable old "Conscience Whigs" who led the antislavery faction of the Whig Party into the series of third-party efforts that resulted in the election of Abraham Lincoln to the presidency. The descendant of an old New England family that had moved west, Giddings was born on 6 October 1795 in Bradford County, Pennsylvania, and grew up in Canandaigua, New York, and Ashtabula County, Ohio. Although long hours of work at the frontiers of white settlement left little time for his education, Giddings taught school and served in the War of 1812 before entering the study of law in an office at Canfield. After admission to the bar in 1821, he built a solid practice at Jefferson and became active in Whig politics, serving a term in the Ohio legislature in 1826 and in 1838 winning election to the U.S. House of Representatives as a Whig.

In Congress, Giddings quickly joined John Quincy Adams in an effort to maintain the body's right to receive antislavery petitions. He also vigorously attacked the use of federal authority and funds to support slavery. On that basis, he opposed the annexation of Texas, the removal of the Seminole Nation, and the Mexican-American War as efforts to place the national government at the disposal of the slaveholders and to expand the power of slavery within the government. When Giddings took positions that seemed to undercut the U.S. position in Anglo-American negotiations over the *Creole*, the body censured him by 125 to 69, after which he resigned in order to place the question before his constituents, who reelected and vindicated him.

Giddings's career had considerable influence on the course of national politics. He was messmate in Washington with newly elected representative Abraham Lincoln. His congressional work established a strong antislavery current in the "Old Northwest" that, increasingly, transcended party lines. Giddings himself broke with the Whigs in 1848 to support the new Free Soil Party. Upon the 1854 passage of the Kansas-Nebraska Act, he turned to the Republican Party and became a powerful figure in its first national convention, which nominated John Charles Frémont. In 1860, Lincoln's reputation as a moderate cost him some support among eastern abolitionists, but Giddings also brought many Midwestern abolitionists into the coalition on behalf of Lincoln .

When his health failed him in April 1858, Giddings chose not to run for reelection. However, he was quite active in the 1860 Republican campaign. He also wrote *The Exiles of Florida* (1858) and *The History of the Rebellion* (1864). Appointed consul general in Canada, Giddings served until his death on 27 May 1864 in Montreal.

—*Mark A. Lause*

See also Adams, John Quincy; Free Soil Party; Frémont, John Charles; Kansas-Nebraska Act; Lincoln, Abraham; Republican Party; Texas.

For further reading:

Buell, Walter. *Joshua R. Giddings: a Sketch* (1882).

Julian, George W. *The Life of Joshua R. Giddings* (1892).

Stewart, James B. *Joshua R. Giddings and the Tactics of Radical Politics* (1970).

GILLMORE, QUINCY ADAMS
(1825–1888)
Union general

Quincy Adams Gillmore was a Union military engineer who developed a successful plan for reducing Fort Pulaski, a masonry fort that guarded the approaches to the port of Savannah, Georgia. His use of rifled cannon revolutionized the art of siege warfare.

Gillmore was born on 28 February 1825 in an area that later became Lorain, Ohio. He graduated from West Point at the top of his class in 1849, and by 1853 he had become a second lieutenant in the U.S. Army Corps of Engineers. Gillmore served as a West Point engineering instructor and he also worked on New York City's defenses. He became a first lieutenant in July 1856 and a captain after the outbreak of the Civil War.

Gillmore, explains historian Stephen Wise, served as chief engineer during the November 1861 seizure of the Port Royal Sound forts in South Carolina. This victory enabled Union forces to establish the Department of the South, which consisted of the states of South Carolina, Georgia, and Florida, and was headquartered at Hilton Head Island. Gillmore then turned his attention to Fort Pulaski, which guarded the entrance to Savannah, Georgia. Fort Pulaski was a masonry fort that the Confederacy considered invincible. Gillmore, however, established a battery of siege guns on neighboring Tybee Island that included rifled cannon known as James rifles and Parrot guns. Gillmore's battery devastated the walls of Fort Pulaski during the April 1862 Union siege and forced the Confederate garrison to surrender. Union commanders quickly promoted Gillmore to brevet lieutenant colonel for "gallant and meritorious services." Most importantly, Gillmore's reduction of Fort Pulaski with rifled cannon rendered masonry forts obsolete.

Gillmore's next promotion raised him to the rank of brigadier general in the volunteer army and took him to Kentucky. He commanded Union forces at the 30 March 1863 battle of Somerset and he was again cited for gallantry. Gillmore, however, remained interested in the use of rifled cannon in the seacoast areas of the Department of the South.

Major General Henry Halleck, the overall Union commander, was planning an attack on Charleston, South Carolina, and Gillmore expressed interest in the planned campaign to Brigadier General George Cullum, Halleck's chief of staff. Halleck proceeded to promote Gillmore to the rank of major in the Corps of Engineers in June 1863 and then put him in charge of the Department of the South. Gillmore immediately set to work preparing for the defeat of Fort Sumter, which guarded Charleston harbor.

Gillmore, however, first had to restore discipline to the Union garrison on nearby Folly Island. The soldiers were fishing, swimming, and trading tobacco with the Confederates. Gillmore disciplined the men and began preparing Folly Island for use as a base from which to attack Morris Island, which Gillmore believed would be a good base from which to bombard Fort Sumter. The nurse Clara Barton, who had come to the Department of the South, noticed the new activity and described Gillmore as a general who "acts more than he talks."

Gillmore, Wise relates, ordered an attack on Morris Island that began on 10 July 1863. The Union forces were able to take part of the island, but the Confederates doggedly held on to Fort Wagner, their main position. Gillmore unleashed a ferocious bombardment of the fort on 18 July by Union navy monitors and his own artillery batteries. He thought that the fort had been heavily damaged, but its sand walls were actually absorbing much of the bombardment and protecting the Confederate garrison. Wagner, of course, was not a masonry fort, and Gillmore, with much overconfidence, directed the Union forces to begin an infantry assault on the fort. The Confederate garrison was still strong, and the Union attack, led by the 54th Massachusetts, was a disaster. Gillmore was forced to revise his plans for the capture of Charleston.

Gillmore then resumed the bombardment of Fort Wagner and Fort Sumter. "Like a giant factory that continuously turned out shot and shell," writes Wise, "Gillmore and his men seemed to personify the efficient, mechanical, north." Gillmore's use of powerful artillery and trenches against the two Confederate forts, along with his shelling of Charleston with an 8-inch Parrot gun, known as the "Swamp Angel," presaged the arrival of modern warfare. The Confederates evacuated Fort Wagner on 7 September 1863 and Gillmore's bombardment reduced Fort Sumter's masonry walls to rubble. The Union army promoted Gillmore to the rank of major general of U.S. Volunteers after the Confederate evacuation of Fort Wagner. Gillmore, who commanded the X Army Corps, was then transferred to the operations on the James River, near the Bermuda Hundred area of Virginia, where he participated in the battle of Drewry's Bluff on 6 May 1864.

After the Civil War, Gillmore resigned his volunteer commission and served as superintending engineer of Surveys of Rivers and Harbors in North and South Carolina, Georgia, and East Florida. He was promoted to lieutenant colonel in June 1874 and then to colonel in the Corps of Engineers in February 1883. He authored a number of military engineering treatises, including *Siege and Reduction of Ft. Pulaski, Georgia*, and was granted the Ph.D. degree from Rutgers College in 1878. Quincy Adams Gillmore died on 7 April 1888 in New York.

— *David A. Proctor*

See also Fort Pulaski; Fort Wagner.

For further reading:
Cullum, George. *Biographical Register of the Officers and Graduates of the U.S. Military Academy at West Point, New York, from its Establishment, in 1802, to 1890; With the Early History of the United States Military Academy* (1891).
Warner, Ezra J. *Generals in Blue: The Lives of Union Commanders* (1964).
Wise, Stephen R. *Gate of Hell: Campaign for Charleston Harbor, 1863* (1994).

GILMER, JEREMY FRANCIS
(1818–1883)
Confederate general

Born in Guilford County, North Carolina, the son of Robert Shaw Gilmer, an army officer, and Anna Forbis Gilmer, Jeremy Gilmer graduated fourth of thirty-one from the United States Military Academy in 1839. His brother, John Adams Gilmer, served as a Confederate congressman during the Civil War.

Upon graduation from West Point, Gilmer taught for a year at the Academy before assuming frontier duty with the Corps of Engineers, primarily engaged in the construction of posts. During the Mexican-American War Gilmer served as the chief engineer for the Army of the West. Following the war he served for a while in the South before being transferred to California in 1858. While in California, Gilmer heard of the secession of North Carolina, and on 29 June 1861 he resigned his commission.

In September 1861 Gilmer accepted a lieutenant colonel's commission in the Confederate States Army. His considerable engineering experience earned him the position as General Albert Sidney Johnston's chief engineer in the Western theater. In this capacity in the early months of 1862 he inspected the fortifications at Fort Henry and Fort Donelson. He was present at the latter when Ulysses Grant laid siege to it and he fled with Brigadier General Gideon Pillow before the surrender of the fort. Gilmer was later criticized for not doing enough to strengthen Forts Henry and Donelson. A few months later Gilmer fought at and was wounded in the battle of Shiloh.

After recovering from his wound, Gilmer transferred to the east in August 1862, where he became chief engineer of the Department of Northern Virginia. Two months later he was attached to the Confederate War Department as the chief of the Engineering Bureau and promoted to brigadier general. The following year in August he was promoted to major general, and while still chief engineer was given the position as second-in-command of the Department of South Carolina, Georgia, and Florida under General P. G. T. Beauregard headquartered in Charleston, South Carolina. In 1864 his engineering skills were once again brought to bear when he was called on to help strengthen the defenses of Atlanta. He was recalled to Virginia, however, before

Sherman arrived outside that city. He spent the remainder of the war engaged in the futile defense of Richmond.

Following the war, Gilmer worked as an engineer in Savannah, Georgia, where he died in 1883.

—*David S. Heidler and Jeanne T. Heidler*

See also Fort Donelson, Battle of; Fort Henry, Battle of.

For further reading:
Rhodes, Steven B. "Jeremy Gilmer and the Confederate Engineers" (Master's thesis, 1983).

GILMER, JOHN ADAMS
(1805–1868)
U.S. and Confederate congressman

John Adams Gilmer, the oldest of twelve children, was born in Guilford County, North Carolina. Gilmer's father, a farmer and Revolutionary War veteran, named his son after the Federalist second president of the United States, an indication of his opposition to the Democratic Party and the current president, Thomas Jefferson. Following in his father's footsteps, John Gilmer would ally himself with the Whig Party and its successors, and would consistently oppose the measures of the Democrats. After spending his early years working on his father's farm and attending a local school for a few months each winter, at the age of nineteen Gilmer entered a Greensboro school run by Eli W. Caruthers. After two years of study, Gilmer spent three years as a schoolteacher in South Carolina. He returned to Greensboro in 1829 and began studying law under the supervision of Archibald D. Murphey, the state's leading exponent of educational reforms and internal improvements, measures that Gilmer would also staunchly advocate throughout his subsequent career.

Gilmer gained admission to the bar in 1832, the same year in which he married Juliana Paisley, with whom he would have six children. Gilmer became one of the state's leading attorneys and embarked on a successful political career. A man of great personal charm and attractiveness, Gilmer developed into one of the most popular public figures on the state, and later national, scene. After serving in important town and county offices, Gilmer won election to the state senate in 1846. He supported Dorothea Dix's proposal for the creation of a state insane asylum, as well as bills for the development of railroads, other internal improvements, and better-funded public schools—all measures consistent with his adherence to the principles of the Whig Party. With the collapse of that party's national organization in the 1850s, however, Gilmer joined the newly formed nativist American Party, which nominated him for governor in 1856. Democratic candidate Thomas Bragg soundly defeated him in the gubernatorial election, but Gilmer thereafter won election to the U.S. Congress in 1857 and was reelected two years later.

In Congress, Gilmer earned a reputation for moderation and willingness to rise above party lines and narrow sectional considerations. He broke with most Southern representatives by voting against the acceptance of the fraudulent Lecompton Constitution legalizing slavery in Kansas. His stance earned him the scorn of proslavery Southern Democrats. This stand did not, however, prevent Gilmer from becoming one of the most respected members of the Southern Whig/American Party congressional delegation in Washington. In 1859 this group nominated Gilmer for the position of Speaker of the House, but the failure of Southern Democrats to support his candidacy led to the election of a compromise candidate, William Pennington. To promote cooperation between Republicans and Southern Unionists, Pennington in 1860 appointed Gilmer chairman of the influential Committee on Elections.

After the election of Abraham Lincoln as president in 1860 and the secession of the states of the lower South, Gilmer desperately attempted to turn back the secessionist tide in North Carolina and the other doubtful states of the upper South. On the floor of the House of Representatives in January 1861, he delivered a moving, widely admired speech in favor of sectional compromise and subsequently paid for the distribution of thousands of copies of it in North Carolina. Gilmer also privately wrote to President-elect Lincoln, imploring him to reassure Southerners that he did not intend to interfere with slavery in the states and asking him to reconsider his opposition to slavery expansion. Although Lincoln refused to make a conciliatory public statement or consider such a compromise, he did ask Gilmer to come to Springfield, Illinois, for a personal interview. At the urging of Thurlow Weed, Lincoln intended to offer Gilmer, who owned more than fifty slaves, a cabinet position. Lincoln hoped that this appointment would help to retain the loyalty of the wavering Southern states. Despite the urging of Weed, William H. Seward, and several of his constituents and fellow congressmen, Gilmer declined both the proposed interview and the proffered position. Gilmer believed that his acceptance of a place in the Lincoln administration would have effectively ended his influence in North Carolina, and perhaps even made him an outcast in his home state. After the outbreak of fighting at Fort Sumter, Gilmer reluctantly gave his consent to the state's secession.

During the Civil War, Gilmer supported the gubernatorial administration of another former Whig, Zebulon B. Vance. Elected to the Confederate Congress in the fall of 1863, Gilmer became a leader of the strong congressional faction opposing Jefferson Davis's administration. Gilmer was also named chairman of the Committee on Elections, as he had been in the U.S. Congress. Gilmer

refused, however, to support the growing movement in North Carolina and elsewhere in the Confederacy in favor of a negotiated peace. In early 1865 he did propose the creation of an "American diet," in which the Confederacy and the United States would remain separate and independent but would each send delegates to a coordinating body. This proposal did not find much support, and Gilmer thereafter remained committed to the continuation of the military struggle for independence. Gilmer's once-robust health declined greatly after the close of the war he had struggled to avoid, and he died in Greensboro at the age of sixty-two.

— *Michael Thomas Smith*

See also American Party; Congress, C.S.A.; North Carolina.
For further reading:
Caldwell, Bettie D., ed. *Founders and Builders of Greensboro, 1808–1908* (1925).
Crofts, Daniel W. *Reluctant Confederates: Upper South Unionists in the Secession Crisis* (1989).
Kruman, Marc W. *Parties and Politics in North Carolina, 1836–1865* (1983).

GILMORE, JAMES ROBERTS
(1822–1903)
Writer, abolitionist

James Roberts Gilmore, one of the informal circle of *New York Tribune* writers and thinkers, also played an important informal role for the federal authorities during the Civil War. Born 22 September 1822 in Boston and destined for college, he instead entered business. By age twenty-five, he headed a New York City firm that grew large and lucrative dealing in Southern cotton.

Earning enough to retire by 1857, Gilmore entered antislavery ranks with an intimate knowledge of Southern conditions. His first publication was the *Continental Monthly*, which agitated for abolition until the 1862 promulgation of the Emancipation Proclamation. His books, such as *Among the Pines* (1862) or *On the Border* (1867), offered more lackluster looks inside the South. However, his shorter pieces in the *New York Tribune* reflected an alliance of sorts with Horace Greeley.

As an emissary of Greeley in 1863, Gilmore visited the headquarters of General William S. Rosecrans, who Greeley hoped might be an acceptable political alternative to Abraham Lincoln. While Rosecrans proved to be a rather conservative figure, he enlisted Gilmore's support for a scheme by the militant Methodist colonel James F. Jacquess, who believed he could persuade the Confederate government to accept a peaceful restoration of the Union. On their behalf, Gilmore visited Lincoln who, in the process, won the writer's admiration and support. Although nothing came of Jacquess's 1863 visit, the increasing turn in the fortunes of the war and an upcoming presidential election increased pressures to attempt some sort of settlement in the following year.

In April 1864, Gilmore persuaded Lincoln to permit another effort. The immediate restoration of the Union could not be compromised, nor slavery restored, but Lincoln proposed amnesty for all rebels, the immediate restoration of their states to the Union, and $500 million in compensation for slaveholders. In likelihood, Lincoln, Gilmore, Greeley, and others hoped that the Confederate rejection of the plan would convince Unionists disgusted by the war's human cost to stay the course in the upcoming presidential election.

In early July, Gilmore and Jacquess passed through the lines to Richmond. Their lack of a formal mandate from Washington delayed until the evening of 17 July their meeting with Jefferson Davis, who located the gathering at the Custom House. Davis insisted that there would be no peace terms without Southern independence and the Federal evacuation of all territory claimed as Confederate. Gilmore reported to Lincoln on 21 July and, the following day, as "Edmund Kirk," he placed the highlights of the interview before the readers of the *Boston Transcript*. In addition to longer accounts published in the September and December issues of the *Atlantic Monthly*, he joined Jacquess to visit some Northern governors and give campaign speeches.

After the war, Gilmore married Laura Edmonds, daughter of Judge John W. Edmonds of New York, and he reentered business in 1873. He published a campaign *Life of James A. Garfield* (1880) and edited with Lyman Abbott *The Gospel History* (1881), turning more closely to local history after his second retirement in 1883. Gilmore died 16 November 1903 at Glens Falls, New York.

—*Mark A. Lause*

See also Greeley, Horace; Lincoln, Abraham; Rosecrans, William Starke.

For further reading:

Gilmore, James R. *Personal Recollections of Abraham Lincoln and the Civil War* (1898).

Long, David E. *The Jewell of Liberty: Abraham Lincoln's Re-Election and the End of Slavery* (1994).

GIST, STATES RIGHTS
(1831–1864)
Confederate general

Scion of a wealthy family with roots in colonial Maryland, State Rights Gist was born in the Union District of South Carolina on 3 September 1831. He owed his name to his father Nathaniel's nullification politics. After an early education in local schools, the young Gist graduated from South Carolina College in Columbia (1852) and attended Harvard Law School for a year. He was admitted to the South Carolina bar in 1853 and opened a law practice in his home district.

Gist entered the militia as captain of a volunteer company soon after his return to Carolina. He was quickly advanced to aide-de-camp to the governor in 1854 and elected to brigadier general in 1856 at the age of twenty-four. His career blossomed during the term (1858–1860) of his older cousin, Governor William Henry Gist. The governor appointed States Rights his "especial" aide-de-camp and brought him to Columbia to live in the governor's household. In April 1860 Gist resigned from the militia to become full-time adviser to his cousin. In October 1860 Governor Gist sent his aptly named cousin on a mission to six other Southern governors to elicit support for a planned secession convention in the likelihood of a Republican president's election.

Governor Gist left office in December 1860, but the new governor, Francis Pickens, appointed States R. Gist to be state adjutant and inspector general in January 1861. Gist was faced with the twin tasks of mobilizing South Carolina's military resources while overseeing support of active operations in Charleston. He was relieved of the latter burden when the Confederate government assumed responsibility for Fort Sumter at the end of February. On 14 April 1861 Gist accompanied Governor Pickens and General P. G.T. Beauregard to Sumter for the raising of the Confederate and state flags over the fort.

Continuing with his function to raise troops for Confederate service, in July 1861 Gist went to Richmond on business and while there received an introduction from President Jefferson Davis to General Joseph E. Johnston, then at Winchester. Johnston sent Gist to be volunteer aide-de-camp to General Barnard E. Bee, and Gist accompanied Bee's brigade to Bull Run on 20 July. After the deaths of Bee and Colonel Jones of the 4th Alabama, Beauregard assigned Gist to lead that regiment for the remainder of the battle. Gist was slightly wounded at Bull Run. Returning to Columbia, he prepared state forces to defend against the Federal invasion at Port Royal in the fall of 1861 and readied them for entry into Confederate service in the winter of 1862.

On 20 March 1862, through the influence of Senator James Chesnut of South Carolina, Gist was commissioned as a brigadier general in the provisional Confederate army and assumed command of a district and a brigade in the Carolina coastal defenses from May 1862 to May 1863. He was third in command of the Confederate forces at the battle of Secessionville in June 1862; commanded troops sent to repel a landing at Pocataligo, South Carolina, in October 1862; led a small division sent as reinforcements into North Carolina from December 1862 through January 1863, and was present at the Union naval attack on Charleston on 7 April 1863. During none of these events was he personally involved in combat operations.

In May 1863 Gist and Brigadier General William H. T. Walker of Georgia were selected to lead two brigades from South Carolina to bolster Confederate forces under

Joseph E. Johnston in Mississippi. Gist was the senior officer and was placed in charge of the expedition, but soon after arriving in Mississippi, Walker was promoted to major general and Gist's brigade was made part of Walker's division. While in Mississippi, Gist and his brigade participated in the Vicksburg campaign and the battle of Jackson (9–16 July 1863).

At the end of August 1863 Walker's division was sent to Chattanooga to join Braxton Bragg's Army of Tennessee. Gist's brigade was stationed first at Rome, Georgia. On 17 September, in preparation for the battle at Chickamauga, Gist was summoned to return to the main army. With a brigade of only 980 effective infantry and no artillery, he took a train from Rome to Catoosa and then marched to the battlefield, arriving at sunrise on 20 September. Here he found that he was acting commander of Walker's division, Walker having been advanced to temporary corps commander. Gist's brigade was thrown immediately into line to plug a hole in Breckinridge's division and lost more than 170 men in forty-five minutes. The brigade withdrew until the general advance later that day.

Gist commanded the division again in November 1863 while Walker was on leave and led it through the battle of Chattanooga. The division served as rear guard for Breckinridge's corps during the retreat from Missionary Ridge and Gist was commended in Bragg's report following the battle.

During the political turmoil that beset the Army of Tennessee in the fall of 1863 pitting Bragg against some of his principal subordinates, both Walker and Gist supported Bragg. When Bragg was relieved and transferred to Richmond, Walker and Gist maintained a correspondence with him. Following Patrick Cleburne's proposal to arm slaves for Confederate service in January 1864, it was Walker who notified President Davis of the affair, and it was to Gist that Bragg wrote inquiring for details of the "treason." Part of Gist's interest was based on his desire for promotion to major general, but he also demonstrated a genuine loyalty to Bragg.

Gist remained with Walker's division in the Army of Tennessee during the Atlanta campaign of 1864. At the battle of Atlanta on 22 July 1864 Walker was killed and Gist was wounded in the hand, putting him out of action for several days. On 24 July Walker's division was broken up and Gist's brigade was assigned to the division of Benjamin F. Cheatham. Gist accompanied the army on John Bell Hood's Tennessee invasion. He was killed at the battle of Franklin on 30 November 1864 while leading his brigade on foot after his horse had been shot. He was buried near the battlefield, but in 1866 his remains were reinterred in Columbia, South Carolina.

Though not professionally trained, Gist was an unusually competent soldier, both in camp and on the field. Frequently trusted with command higher than his nominal rank entitled him to, he always was equal to the occasion. Personally brave, his conduct on the battlefield was always commendable and at Chattanooga distinguished. He was a strict disciplinarian and his brigade was deemed by superiors and peers to be one of the finest in the Army of Tennessee in appearance as well as in conduct. States Rights Gist was the model of a civilian gentleman turned soldier.

Gist married Jane Margaret Adams, daughter of a former governor of South Carolina, on 6 May 1863. There were no children from the marriage.

—*Russell K. Brown*

See also Franklin, Battle of; Walker, W. H. T.
For further reading:
Brown, Russell K. *To The Manner Born: The Life of General William H. T. Walker* (1994).
Cisco, Walter Brian. *States Rights Gist: A South Carolina General of the Civil War* (1991).

GLADSTONE, WILLIAM EWART
(1809–1898)
British statesman

One of the most powerful men in the British cabinet, William Gladstone proved to be the most enthusiastic proponent of ending the American Civil War through the mediation of the European great powers. As the British government considered the policy of intervention, Gladstone sought to influence the cabinet's decision by delivering a widely publicized speech at Newcastle in October 1862. His oration convinced many that the British government had decided to recognize the Confederacy and brought the question of intervention to the forefront of British politics. Nevertheless, Gladstone could not persuade the cabinet to abandon its policy of strict neutrality.

Born in Liverpool on 29 December 1809, William Ewart Gladstone was the fourth son of John Gladstone, a prominent merchant, and Anne Robertson. After attending Eton between 1821 and 1827, he went to Christ Church College at Oxford University in 1828. At Oxford, he earned a reputation for hard work, religiosity, and brilliant oratory.

In December 1832, Gladstone won a seat in the House of Commons as a Conservative representing Newark. For the first fifteen years of his political career, he loyally followed Sir Robert Peel, leader of the Conservative Party and prime minister from 1834 to 1835 and again from 1841 to 1846. While serving at the Board of Trade (first as vice president and later as president), Gladstone enthusiastically supported Peel's drive toward free trade, administrative efficiency, and financial responsibility. When the Conservatives split over the issue of free trade in 1846, Gladstone joined the "Peelites," those followers of Peel who still supported free trade.

When a coalition of Whigs and Peelites held office from 1852 to 1855, Gladstone served as chancellor of the exchequer and became a political figure of the first rank due to his efforts to overhaul British finances. In 1859, under Lord Palmerston's leadership, Whigs, Radicals, and Peelites formed a coalition that eventually developed into the Liberal party. Gladstone joined this administration as chancellor of the exchequer. Although Palmerston and his colleagues did not like Gladstone, they believed him indispensable. Indeed, Gladstone provided the government with the bulk of its domestic policy. In this age, however, when ministers did not devote themselves exclusively to their departments, cabinets often met to decide important national questions. In his capacity as the cabinet's second most important minister (after Palmerston), Gladstone also exerted an influence on Britain's foreign policy. During the American Civil War, this influence would almost succeed in prompting British intervention in the conflict.

Unlike many other British statesmen, Gladstone did not bear any hostility toward the United States. Indeed, he felt that the Union had served British interests far better than a divided North and South ever could. During the *Trent* Affair, he had assumed a moderate position, suggesting to the cabinet that instead of sending a demand for reparations, it merely ask the American government for an explanation. Nevertheless, quite early in the war, certainly by the end of 1861, Gladstone concluded the North could not reconstruct the Union. Force might defeat Confederate forces, he believed, but it could not instill Southerners with the good will necessary to participate in a democratic, federal union. As the war dragged on into 1862, Gladstone came to see it as foolish and vain. He told his Northern acquaintants that the federal government had undertaken the impossible by attempting to coerce the South back into the Union.

The Confederacy's victories during the Seven Days' battles and at the second battle of Bull Run prompted the British cabinet to take a closer look at intervening in the conflict. To many, such victories indicated the Confederacy had achieved the status of a de facto state. Gladstone believed that Britain had a moral duty to intervene in the conflict. First, it seemed clear to him that the Confederacy had already won its independence and further fighting would serve no useful end—indeed, it would only perpetuate misery for Americans on both sides. Second, the Federal blockade would soon produce an acute cotton shortage in Britain, leading to widespread unemployment and suffering among British cotton operatives. Third, the longer the war lasted, the greater the likelihood that it would spark a collision between the European great powers. The three most important men in the British cabinet—Palmerston, Gladstone, and Lord John Russell (foreign secretary)—all began leaning toward mediating the conflict.

In the eyes of these British statesmen, the Emancipation Proclamation, issued soon after the battle of Antietam, only threatened to make the war far more destructive and would in no way lead to Federal victory. So far from seeing the document as indicative of a great moral stance, the British conceived of it as the Federals' last desperate gamble. Under these circumstances, the cabinet prepared to act. Before it could meet, however, Gladstone made his position public at a banquet at Newcastle on 7 October 1862. Probably hoping he could push the cabinet toward intervention, Gladstone observed: "We may have our own opinions about slavery; we may be for or against the South; but there is no doubt that Jefferson Davis and other leaders of the South have made an army; they are making, it appears, a navy; and they have made what is more than either, they have made a nation." Many took this speech to mean that the cabinet had already decided to recognize the Confederacy. Although both Palmerston and Russell probably agreed with Gladstone in sentiment, they scolded him for making such a statement before the cabinet had reached a decision on the issue.

For the next several weeks, the cabinet exchanged memoranda on the issue of intervention. Russell advised that Britain, France, and Russia should propose mediation. If the North refused their good offices, they would proceed to recognize the Confederacy. Napoleon III endorsed the plan. Sir George Cornewall Lewis, the secretary of state for war, however, mobilized opposition within the cabinet against Russell's proposed move. On 11 November 1862, the cabinet finally met to decide the issue. Although Gladstone enthusiastically backed Russell's proposal, Palmerston only gave it half-hearted support. The rest of the cabinet, led by Lewis, strenuously objected, and Russell's plan came to nothing. Gladstone's attempts to influence the cabinet had availed Russell nothing.

Well into 1864, Gladstone believed the North had little chance of conquering the South, let alone reconstructing the Union on a democratic basis. Nevertheless, when Federal forces did prove victorious, Gladstone appeared to greet the news with optimism for the future. Interestingly enough, during the *Alabama* arbitration, the American delegation introduced Gladstone's comments at Newcastle as proof of the British government's hostility to the United States.

Gladstone served as chancellor of the exchequer until 1866 and would go on to serve as prime minister four times: 1868–1874, 1880–1885, 1886, and 1892–1894. Soon after he retired from politics, Gladstone described his speech at Newcastle as one of the greatest errors of his political career, a mistake of "incredible grossness" that pained him all the more since "I have for the last five-and-twenty years received from the government and people of America tokens of goodwill which could not fail to arouse my undying gratitude." Gladstone died of cancer on his estate at Hawarden on 19 May 1898.

—*Hubert F. Dubrulle*

See also Adams, Charles Francis; Diplomacy, U.S.A.; Great Britain; Lyons, Lord Richard; Palmerston, Viscount; Roebuck, John; *Trent Affair.*

For further reading:
Feuchtwanger, E.J., *Gladstone* (1975).
Matthew, H. C. G., *Gladstone, 1809–1898* (1997).
Morley, John, *The Life of William Ewart Gladstone* (1903).

GLASGOW, MISSOURI, BATTLE OF
(15 October 1864)

As Confederate general Sterling Price's Missouri Raid moved northwest of Jefferson City into the bend of the Missouri River, the Confederates captured boats, and, for the first time, had the option of crossing the Missouri River to the North, where before it had only guerrillas, scouts, and recruiters. On 14 October, about 2,500 Confederates, including new recruits, crossed the river at Arrow Rock under John B. Clark to attack about 750 Federals under Colonel Chester Harding sixteen miles upriver at Glasgow, which was reported to have a cache of several thousand small arms. Only a few days earlier, Harding, with several newly raised companies on their way downriver to reinforce Jefferson City, had heard that the Confederates had bypassed Jefferson City and were advancing on Glasgow. At that time, the garrison at Glasgow was manned by single companies of the Enrolled Missouri Militia, the Missouri State Militia, and some Citizens Guards, supplemented by a handful of cavalrymen and some men home on sick leave. Harding took charge of preparing the rifle pits and breastworks on the high ground of the courthouse square.

In recognition of this, another Confederate force moved opposite the town on the other bank of the river. This artillery began the battle at sunrise on 15 October, lobbing its shells from the west. Confederate infantry turned up south of the town at 9 A.M. For two hours, the Confederates pressed the mixed force of Unionists while extending their own line east and north, eventually to encircle the town. Federal sharpshooters in the brick buildings northeast of town had such a commanding position as to permit Harding to turn back demands for surrender at 11 A.M. However, by noon, the Confederates took those same buildings, and within half an hour, the defenders had been driven back to their fortifications on the square. As three rebel guns moved into position, Clark also threatened to unleash guerrillas on the town if it did not immediately surrender.

With little ammunition and no hope for reinforcement, Harding surrendered. The terms included his safe passage to Union lines, parole for the men and officers,

and respect for civilians and their property. Nevertheless, the guerrillas among the victors detained a few civilians and shot some prisoners, including a local militia officer and an officer of a black regiment who had been back on sick leave. These added to the 11 killed and 32 wounded among the Federals, while the unreported casualties of the Confederate attackers ran far more than 100.

The capture of Glasgow, coinciding with the surrender of smaller garrisons at Paris and Ridgely, marked the appearance of Price's army north of the Missouri River. This more directly severed the already politically strained communications between the Union forces gathering under Generals William S. Rosecrans in St. Louis and Samuel R. Curtis in Kansas, the coordination of which would be essential to the capture of Price's army.

—*Mark A. Lause*

See also Price's Missouri Raid.
For further reading:
Hinton, Richard J. *Rebel Invasion of Missouri and Kansas, and the Campaign of the Army of the Border against General Sterling Price, in October and November 1864* (1865).
Monaghan, Jay. *Civil War on the Western Border, 1854–1865* (1955).

GLENDALE (WHITE OAK SWAMP), BATTLE OF
(30 June 1862)

Sometimes referred to as the battle of White Oak Swamp, the battle of Glendale on 30 June 1862 presented General Robert E. Lee perhaps his greatest opportunity during the Seven Days' battles to destroy a significant part of General George B. McClellan's Army of the Potomac. Much of the fighting took place across the fields of a 200-acre farm that once belonged to the Frayser family, and the engagement was often referred to as the battle of Frayser's farm. Lee had opened his first offensive as commander of the Confederate army on 26 June, and in a series of bloody, confused, and mismanaged battles, Confederates had driven the Union army nearly 15 miles from the Chickahominy River. Lee now sought to crush McClellan's army before it reached the safety of Union gunboats and a new supply base on the James River.

On 30 June, after a bloody fight at Savage's Station the day before, Lee ordered Major Generals James Longstreet, A. P. Hill, John Magruder, Benjamin Huger, and Thomas J. "Stonewall" Jackson to attack the Union army near Glendale. By attacking the front, flank, and rear simultaneously, Lee hoped to overwhelm the jammed Union forces at the junction of the Charles City Road, Long Bridge Road, and Quaker Road (also referred to as the Willis Church Road). McClellan's retreat had bottlenecked at the crossroads as his wagons and equipment slowed the movement to the James. Nearly half of McClellan's army was trapped on three sides by

Kearny's division fighting in the woods at White Oak Swamp (*Library of Congress*)

Confederate forces, with the Quaker Road as the only avenue of escape. If Lee's attackers could reach the crossroads or the Quaker Road before it was cleared of wagons, then great destruction could be wrought on the Army of the Potomac. McClellan himself spent the afternoon removed from the field of battle, frantically telegraphing despairing messages to the War Department regarding the salvation of the army. The "Young Napoleon," who had been clearly rattled by Lee's offensive, left the tactical battle to his generals on the field.

As had happened at each previous battle of the campaign however, Lee's ambitious plans misfired. Magruder spent the day marching and countermarching in the rear of Confederate lines and never participated in the attack. Benjamin Huger, whose forces were to initiate the attack from the Charles City Road, wasted much of the day cutting a lane through wilderness instead of clearing the road of logs that Union engineers had placed in a desperate delaying tactic. Huger's troops never became involved in the battle.

In the most inexplicable performance of the day, Jackson remained north of White Oak Swamp, content to engage in a harmless artillery duel with two divisions of General William B. Franklin's VI Corps. Union troops defended the bridge that crossed the swamp, and Jackson dallied instead of forcing a crossing. Even when some of his officers located suitable fords to cross the swamp, Jackson still remained strangely inert while fighting raged within earshot. Though Jackson had won acclaim the previous month as the brilliantly aggressive commander in the Shenandoah Valley, lethargy and complacency characterized his performances at Glendale and throughout the Seven Days'. While Jackson remained inactive, Union troops in his front were able to move to the threatened sector of battle and provide much needed reinforcements to beleaguered Federals along the battlefield at Frayser's farm.

At 4:00 P.M., after a personal reconnaissance revealed that the bulk of the Union army was on the point of slipping away from his three attacking columns, Lee

Fighting at the White Oak Swamp bridge (*Library of Congress*)

View of White Oak Swamp, ca. 1862 (*Library of Congress*)

ordered Longstreet and Hill, whose troops had already born the brunt of much of the fighting in the campaign, to attack the Union lines. Lee sent the troops in without support, anticipating that Huger and Jackson would join the battle once it was in progress.

Longstreet and Hill's initial attacks breached the lines of General George McCall's division, even capturing McCall himself. However, Union troops under Generals Joseph Hooker, Phil Kearny, and John Sedgwick checked the advance. In severe fighting that was hand-to-hand in many places, the two armies clashed until darkness fell. Unsupported by either Huger or Jackson, the attacking divisions of Longstreet and Hill failed to gain the threatened crossroads, and the window of opportunity to trap a substantial portion of the Federal army closed. Union forces escaped to a strong defensive position two miles away at Malvern Hill.

Confederates suffered 3,673 casualties, while the battle cost McClellan's army 3,797 men, 1,800 of whom were reported missing. Though the Army of Northern Virginia had nearly 55,000 troops within striking distance of the Union contingent of approximately equal strength, it sent only 18,000 men into the fight. The battle was a victory for Lee in only the most technical sense. This most recent failure to entrap and crush the Union army was fresh on the Southern commander's mind the next morning. When an officer commented that McClellan might escape, Lee snapped in uncharacteristic anger, "Yes, he will get away because I cannot have my orders carried out!" Though Lee failed in his attempt to destroy McClellan's army at Glendale, he succeeded in driving the Federal forces even farther from the gates of the Confederacy's capital.

— *Judkin Browning*

See also Malvern Hill, Battle of; Peninsula Campaign; Savage's

Station, Battle of; Seven Days', Battles.

For further reading:

Dowdey, Clifford. *The Seven Days: The Emergence of Lee* (1964).

Freeman, Douglas Southall. *Lee's Lieutenants: A Study in Command* (1942–1944).

Longstreet, James. "The Seven Days, Including Frayser's Farm." In *Battles and Leaders of the Civil War* (1888; reprint, 1982).

Sears, Stephen W. *To the Gates of Richmond: The Peninsula Campaign* (1992).

GLOBE TAVERN, VIRGINIA
(18–21 August 1864)

In mid-August 1864, during the siege of Petersburg, Union major general Gouverneur Kemble Warren was charged with taking his V Corps from its position facing Petersburg to the area around Globe Tavern and from there destroy as much of the Weldon Railroad south of that point as possible. The purpose of this move was to attempt to extend the Union trenches out to Globe Tavern and to lengthen the number of miles Robert E. Lee's army would have to transport supplies by wagon rather than by rail.

Warren, who was also given control of a cavalry brigade under Brigadier General Samuel Perkins Spear, departed with his corps at about 4:00 A.M. on 18 August 1864 in a hot, steamy rain shower. Initially V Corps moved very slowly because of the mud. The men were slowed even more when the wagons and artillery pieces sank in the boggy ground. After skirmishing with a Confederate cavalry brigade under Brigadier General James Dearing, Warren's corps arrived at Globe Tavern about 9:00 A.M. on 18 August.

After establishing his headquarters at the tavern, Warren put his 10,000 men to work. Brigadier General Charles Griffin's division was assigned the task of destroying track, while Brigadier General Romeyn Beck Ayres and Major General Samuel Wylie Crawford moved their divisions north along the track to guard the approach to the laboring men of Griffin's division. Ayres's men were positioned on the Union left and Crawford on the right. Maneuverability was limited on either side of the tracks because of heavy forests on both sides. The presence of the thick trees and undergrowth inhibited not only movement but also visibility. Warren kept Brigadier General Lysander Cutler's division back at Globe Tavern in reserve.

General P. G. T. Beauregard, in command of Confederate forces in Petersburg, learned of Warren's

The Globe Tavern, near Petersburg, Virginia (*Library of Congress*)

movement from Dearing's cavalry. He immediately sent Major General Henry Heth, of Lieutenant General A. P. Hill's corps, with most of his division to try to dislodge the Union forces before too much damage was done to the railroad. At about 2:00 P.M. coming out of the dense woods, Heth attacked the extreme left flank of Ayres's division. Two of Ayres's brigades were sent running, and the Union general suffered heavy losses trying to shift his left to meet further assaults. Receiving reinforcements from Crawford and Cutler, Ayres was finally in a position to deliver a brief counterattack. While he was able to regain the ground he had lost, Ayres suffered about 900 casualties in this opening engagement at Globe Tavern. There was no more fighting that day.

During the night, Warren was reinforced by Brigadier General Gershom Mott's division of II Corps. Early the next day on 19 August, three divisions of IX Corps were sent to Warren's lines. On the Confederate side, A. P. Hill began extricating six of his brigades from the trenches at Petersburg and moving them toward Globe Tavern. As his reinforcements came in, Warren began extending his lines out into the woods on either side of the tracks. Because of the thickness of the trees, some of Warren's units lost contact with one another, and as a result, some points in his lines were quite thin.

At about 4:15 P.M. on 19 August, Warren's right flank was attacked by the division of Major General William Mahone. The Federal right threatened to collapse, and matters were only worsened when Federal artillery tried to repulse the Southerners by firing into the melee, hitting as many Union soldiers as Confederates. In fact, the artillery fire seemed to panic the Union forces even more. Crawford tried to calm his men but almost got himself captured in the process.

While chaos reigned on the Union right, Heth was attacking on the left and near the Union center. Ayres's men did a better job of holding their position. While Ayres held on, Warren used some of the incoming reinforcements from XI Corps to reestablish his right and then ordered a counterattack. Mahone retreated back into the woods, taking several hundred Union prisoners. Night fell with Warren in possession of his original lines. Crawford had lost about 1,800 men captured by the attack on his flank.

During the night, Warren pulled back to more open ground so as to better guard against flanking attacks. There was little fighting on 20 August, but during the night Robert E. Lee sent in more reinforcements from the defenses of Richmond. Hill directed the attack the following day, 21 August. The Confederates quickly found that the Union forces, who had spent the 20th digging in, were in too strong a position. Lee arrived later in the day to assess the situation and decided not to commit any additional troops. In the four days of fighting, the Union had suffered about 4,400 casualties

of more than 20,000 engaged, and the Confederates had suffered about 1,600 casualties of 15,000 engaged. The results of the fighting were that Ulysses S. Grant now could extend his siege lines around Globe Tavern, thus cutting off Confederate use of the Weldon Railroad to that point.

—*David S. Heidler and Jeanne T. Heidler*

See also Ayres, Romeyn Beck; Crawford, Samuel Wylie; Heth, Henry; Mahone, William; Petersburg Campaign; Warren, Gouverneur Kemble.
For further reading:
Trudeau, Noah Andre. *The Last Citadel: Petersburg, Virginia, June 1864–April 1865* (1991).

GLORIETA PASS, BATTLE OF
(28 March 1862)

The engagement at Glorieta Pass, New Mexico Territory, fought on 28 March 1862, marked the end of Confederate expansion in the Southwest and the turning point in Brigadier General Henry Hopkins Sibley's attempt to seize New Mexico. After defeating the main Union forces at Val Verde on 21 February and bypassing Fort Craig, Sibley planned to concentrate his 2,000 Texans near the last Federal outpost, Fort Union, in the northeast corner of the territory.

A 200-man Confederate detachment stayed at Albuquerque to watch movements by the Fort Craig garrison. A second force of about 350 men under Major Charles Pyron occupied the capital. A third column, composed chiefly of some 800 footsoldiers under Lieutenant Colonel William Scurry, took a circuitous route through the mountains, planning to rendezvous with Pyron near Glorieta Pass in the Sangre de Cristo Mountains east of Santa Fe.

On 26 March, Pyron, proceeding with the rebel plan, blundered into the vanguard of a 1,300-man army of mostly Colorado volunteers under Colonel John Slough at the west end of Glorieta Pass known as Apache Canyon. Pyron, taken by surprise, saw a third of his troops captured, while the Federals lost fewer than a dozen before withdrawing. Scurry, alerted to Pyron's danger, led his men in a freezing night march, reaching Apache Canyon the next morning.

On 28 March, after a quiet day of waiting, the 1,300-man Federal force divided, with about 450 making a flank march over a rugged mesa to strike the rebel rear while the balance marched down the pass. Scurry, unaware of the enemy plans, left a hundred-man detachment at the mouth of Apache Canyon to guard the wagons, and led the remaining 950 Texans toward Slough's command in Glorieta Pass.

The two forces met at 11 A.M. near Pigeon's Ranch. The Federals were thrown back in confusion before taking position around the adobe ranch buildings. The battle raged as a number of disjointed gun duels throughout the afternoon until Scurry ordered a three-pronged attack against the Union line around 4 P.M. The Confederates turned the Federal right, forcing the Colorado volunteers back to another line farther down the pass. The Confederates did not pursue; darkness ended the battle. Thirty-six Texans had been killed, seventy wounded, and some twenty-five captured, while the Federals counted thirty-eight killed, sixty-four wounded, and about twenty captured.

During the day, however, disaster had struck the rebel rear. The Union flank detachment under Major John Chivington routed the Texan wagon guard at midafternoon, burning some ninety wagons and killing over 800 draft animals. The destroyed supplies constituted the bulk of the Confederate commissary and crippled Sibley's campaign.

On 29 March, Scurry withdrew his force to Santa Fe, where Sibley and the rest of the army met him. After a week's delay, the Texans retreated, evacuating New Mexico Territory and Confederate Arizona forever by June.

—*Donald S. Frazier*

See also New Mexico; Sibley, Henry Hopkins.

For further reading:
Alberts, Don E. *The Battle of Glorieta: Union Victory in the West* (1998).
Frazier, Donald S. *Blood and Treasure: Confederate Empire in the Southwest* (1995).
Hall, Martin H. *Sibley's New Mexico Campaign* (1960).
Josephy, Alvin M. *The Civil War in the American West* (1991).

GOLDSBORO, NORTH CAROLINA
(March 1865)

The town of Goldsboro, North Carolina (incorporated 1847) is on the banks of the Neuse River in eastern North Carolina. This river linked Goldsboro westward to Smithfield, North Carolina, and eastward to the port of New Bern, North Carolina. In 1850s, the North Carolina Railroad Company constructed tracks eastward from Raleigh, North Carolina, to the coastal ports, thereby connecting Goldsboro to the other river towns along the Neuse River by rail. Later Goldsboro and Wilmington, North Carolina, would be connected by rail through the construction of the Wilmington & Weldon Railroad, which would link Wilmington, North Carolina, to Petersburg, Virginia. By 1861, Goldsboro would represent a major hub for rail and river traffic in eastern North Carolina and Virginia. From 1862 through 1864, Goldsboro was an objective of Union raiding parties coming out of Federal coastal bases and was also a vital link in the Confederate supply system.

Union major general William T. Sherman's Carolinas campaign in early 1865 soon incorporated Goldsboro into future Union military operations in North Carolina. In January 1865, Lieutenant General Ulysses Grant expressed concern that General Sherman's columns might be caught facing a Confederate army without a secure supply line. Wilmington soon became the focal point to land supplies, and by February 1865 the city was secured by Major General John Schofield's Army of the Ohio. After securing the port facilities, General Schofield soon discovered that Wilmington would not be able to handle the amount of traffic needed to resupply General Sherman's columns. General Schofield decided to change the focus of Federal supply operations back to the established port at New Bern. From this port, General Schofield could advance a supply line along the rail lines to Goldsboro, where he could link up with General Sherman's two armies and Major General Alfred Terry's provisional corps. He quickly formed a provisional corps and began his advance on 7 March 1865.

In February 1865, Confederate general Joseph E. Johnston was appointed by General Robert E. Lee to assemble a field army to stop Sherman's advance through the Carolinas. Smithfield, North Carolina, was chosen as a central rally point to assemble several scattered commands into a field army. Goldsboro was a vital supply depot for General Johnston's new army and was also a necessary intersection for rail traffic northward. With three Federal columns converging on the Goldsboro, time was needed to move the needed supplies westward for future military campaigns. In addition, Lee ordered a portion of these supplies to be sent to the Army of Northern Virginia to prepare that army for any future spring operations.

To deal with Schofield's advance, General Johnston agreed to detach a portion of his new army to General Braxton Bragg to defend the eastern approaches to Goldsboro. In an indecisive engagement known as the battle of Southwest Creek on 8–10 March 1865, General Schofield's forward advance came to a halt at Kinston, North Carolina. On 8 March, General Sherman's two armies arrived in Fayetteville, North Carolina, some fifty miles southeast of Goldsboro. General Johnston now had to shift his attention back to Sherman, and he replaced Bragg's force with a demi-brigade of two regiments to screen Schofield. General Johnston prepared for the evacuation of Goldsboro, while General Schofield waited for reinforcements.

Confederate forces now worked to remove all supplies and rail equipment before the arrival of the combined forces of Generals Schofield and Terry. On 19 March, General Johnston opened the battle of Bentonville, North Carolina, by attacking Sherman's left wing. At Kinston, Schofield began his advance to secure Goldsboro for Sherman. By 20 March, Schofield's column had rapidly marched to the Neuse River bridges on the eastern side of the town. After severe combat on

21 March, Johnston learned that Goldsboro had fallen that day to Schofield's forces.

With his army now facing a possibly uniting three Federal forces numbering nearly 100,000, General Johnston pulled back his army to a position where he could monitor the Union forces moving into Goldsboro. By 23 March, General Sherman's two armies united with Schofield's and Terry's men in Goldsboro. As Sherman's four corps moved into camps, Terry's provisional corps was assigned the task of guarding the lower Neuse River crossings to the city. On 24 March, Lieutenant General Wade Hampton led a Confederate cavalry force to attempt to retake those bridges from General Terry. General Hampton's strike was the last Confederate attempt to hinder the union of three Federal columns at Goldsboro and to prevent an opening of another front in North Carolina.

—*William H. Brown*

See also Carolinas Campaign; Johnston, Joseph Eggleston; Schofield, John McAllister; Terry, Alfred Howe.

For further reading:

Barrett, John G. *The Civil War in North Carolina* (1963).
———. *Sherman's March through the Carolinas* (1956; reprint 1996).
Johnston, Joseph E. *Narrative of Military Operations Directed during the Late War between the States* (1874; reprint 1959).
Lash, Jeffrey N. *Destroyer of the Iron Horse: General Joseph E. Johnston and the Confederate Rail Transport, 1861–1865* (1991).
Long, E. B. *The Civil War Day By Day: An Almanac* (1971).
Powell, William S. *The North Carolina Gazetteer: A Dictionary of Tar Heel Places* (1968).
U.S. War Department. *The War of the Rebellion: A Compilation of the Official Records of the Union and Confederate Armies* (1880–1901).

GORDON, GEORGE HENRY
(1823–1886)
Union general

George Henry Gordon was born in Charlestown, Massachusetts, to Robert Gordon and Elizabeth Carlisle Gordon. When George was a small child, his father died, and he moved with his mother to Framingham, Massachusetts. Gordon received an appointment to the U.S. Military Academy, from which he graduated forty-third of fifty-nine in the class of 1846. Commissioned a mounted rifleman, Gordon received further training at Jefferson Barracks before being sent to Mexico to participate in Winfield Scott's Mexico City campaign of the Mexican-American War. Gordon participated in virtually every stage of the campaign from Vera Cruz to Mexico City. He received praise for bravery at the battle of Cerro Gordo, where he was wounded. Two months after the fall of Mexico City, an attack by Mexican bandits again left him wounded.

After the war, Gordon served at posts in the Pacific Northwest and in Kansas. He resigned his commission in 1854 and returned to Massachusetts. After studying law at Harvard, Gordon practiced law before the outbreak of the Civil War. The beginning of that conflict saw him raise a regiment that became the 2d Massachusetts. Gordon was commissioned its colonel in May 1861.

Upon arrival in Washington, D.C., Gordon and the 2d were sent to Robert Patterson in Martinsburg, Virginia. In the early spring of 1862, Gordon led a brigade in the command of Nathaniel P. Banks in the Shenandoah Valley. In May, Gordon persuaded Banks to withdraw in the face of Stonewall Jackson's advance toward Winchester. Against Gordon's advice Banks decided to make a stand at Winchester, and with Gordon's brigade on the right of the Union position, Banks was defeated. Gordon guarded the retreat. He was promoted to brigadier general of volunteers on 9 June 1862.

In August 1862, again in command of one of Banks's brigades, Gordon fought at Cedar Mountain. After the battle of Second Bull Run, Gordon fought at Chantilly and then in the Maryland campaign. At Antietam he commanded the 3d brigade, 1st division of XII Corps and went in support of Joseph Hooker on the Union right.

Bad health kept Gordon out of action until late 1862, when he had the task of guarding the Potomac at the approaches to Washington. In April 1863 he went to Fort Monroe, from where he commanded the 2d Division, Erasmus Keyes's IV Corps, in relief of the Federal garrison at Suffolk, Virginia. In the actions of 1–4 May, Gordon commanded the reserve. Gordon remained at Suffolk until the middle of July.

In August 1863 Gordon was sent to Morris Island, South Carolina, and by the end of the war commanded the forces on Folly Island. The following spring he was placed in command of the District of Florida. Through the spring into June 1864 he conducted operations along the St. John's River out of Jacksonville. In June he transferred again, this time to E. R. S. Canby and the Military Division of Western Mississippi.

Gordon's first assignment from his new command was to travel to Memphis, Tennessee, and from there to the White River in Arkansas to guard communications in that area. The area secure, Gordon took a division to Mobile Bay in August to cooperate with the naval expedition there. After the battle of Mobile Bay, Gordon took command of Fort Morgan on 23 August. From there at the end of the month he traveled to New Orleans.

In New Orleans, Gordon received word that he had been transferred to the command of Benjamin F. Butler and the Department of Virginia. Gordon operated as Butler's chief of staff until Butler was relieved from his command in January 1865. In February 1865, Gordon became the commander of the District of Eastern Virginia, headquartered at Norfolk. He remained in command there until June 1865, when he was relieved at his own request due to bad health. He resigned from the army in August of that year.

Gordon returned to Massachusetts after the war. He practiced law in Boston but spent much of his time writing history about the war. He died in Framingham, Massachusetts, on 30 August 1886.

—*David S. Heidler and Jeanne T. Heidler*

See also Winchester, First Battle of.
For further reading:
Gordon, George Henry. *A War Diary of Events in the War of the Great Rebellion, 1863–1865* (1882).

GORDON, JOHN BROWN
(1832–1904)
Confederate general

The fourth of twelve children, John Brown Gordon was born in Upson County, Georgia on 6 February 1832 to Zachariah Gordon, a prominent minister and plantation owner, and Malinda Cox Gordon. The family moved in 1840 to Walker County, Georgia, where Gordon's father built a summer resort that soon gained favorable appeal as a result of the medicinal springs located on the property.

Gordon attended the University of Georgia but, although a fine student, he left before graduating to study law in Atlanta. After passing the bar, he married Rebecca Haralson, who was a sister-in-law of a partner in the firm where he had studied. However, the law was not profitable for him, and he became a partner with his father in the Castle Rock Coal Company. Through his participation in political campaigns, Gordon gained a reputation for his prowess as a public speaker, a talent that would serve him throughout the war as an inspiration to his men.

With the start of the war in 1861, Gordon, residing with his family in Jackson County, Alabama, won election as captain of a mountaineer company known as the "Raccoon Roughs." Upon being informed that the services of his company would not be needed in his native state, Gordon left for Montgomery, Alabama, where the company was incorporated into the 6th Alabama Infantry Regiment, of which he was named colonel.

The 6th Alabama's first taste of combat came in Virginia on 31 May 1862 at the battle of Seven Pines (Fair Oaks), where it suffered heavy casualties. During the subsequent Seven Days' battle, Gordon's character on the field was exemplary. Even though he was the recipient of several enemy bullets that tore through his uniform, he was left unscathed. However, Gordon's luck did not hold during the battle of Antietam on 17 September 1862.

Commanding a regiment in Major General Daniel Harvey Hill's division, Gordon was assigned to hold a position, a sunken road, now know as Bloody Lane, in the Confederate center. This position became the focal point of a massive Union attack. Soon outnumbered by successive enemy attacks, Gordon judged that the only hope for his men was to hold their fire until the enemy was nearly on top of them. The plan worked, as line upon subsequent line of Federals failed to take the road. Even so, Gordon's own command continued to dwindle. It was at the moment of one of the Union charges that the first ball passed through Gordon's calf, but still he continued to command. Then, another ball hit him in the same leg; a third passed through his left arm, severing a small artery; and yet a fourth bullet hit him in the shoulder. Despite these wounds, and the pleas of his men for him to retire from the field, he continued to lead them on. Gordon was finally halted by a bullet that entered through his left cheek and exited his jaw, leaving him so severely wounded that only a bullet hole in his hat prevented him from drowning in his own blood as he lay on the ground unconscious.

Gordon was appointed brigadier general on 1 November 1862 and, after his recovery and return to duty, he was placed in command of a brigade that consisted of six Georgia regiments. They saw duty at the battles of Chancellorsville and Gettysburg, where he again led his men to distinction. During the Wilderness and Spotsylvania campaigns, Gordon was promoted to

John B. Gordon (*Library of Congress*)

major general on 14 May 1864. At Spotsylvania, Gordon's performance at the Bloody Angle was essential in halting the Federal's attempt to defeat outnumbered Confederate forces. Gordon later was placed in divisional command at both the siege of Petersburg, Virginia, and Lieutenant General Jubal A. Early's Shenandoah Valley campaign. Returning to Petersburg near the end of 1864, Gordon planned and led the assault on Fort Stedman on 25 March 1865, and although his men seized the fort, Federal counterattacks forced him to retreat. On the retreat from Petersburg toward Appomattox, he was eventually in command of one-half of Lee's organized infantry. Although he was never promoted to lieutenant general, by the time Confederate forces surrendered Gordon had both the responsibilities and authority of a corps commander. He was also a participant in one of the most memorable scenes of the war. Three days after Lee's surrender at Appomattox, Gordon was leading the Confederate column to the ceremony wherein it would surrender arms when Union general Joshua Chamberlain spontaneously ordered his men to salute the bedraggled Southern troops. Touched by the gesture, Gordon returned the compliment and ordered the passing Confederates to answer with a salute as well.

As a result of the devastation wrought on north Georgia as an outcome of the war, Gordon's coal mines were in need of repair. Lacking the necessary funds caused Gordon to look elsewhere for a new occupation. After briefly owning and managing several sawmills near Brunswick, Georgia, he moved back to Atlanta, where he engaged in the insurance business and several publishing ventures.

In 1873 the Georgia general assembly elected him to represent Georgia in Washington on the promise, among other things, to restore home rule to the state. Shortly after his arrival in Washington, he obtained the promise from President Ulysses S. Grant to remove Federal officials in Georgia who had gained their office through fraud or corruption. Throughout his three terms in the Senate, 1873–1880 and 1891–1897, Gordon concentrated on economic issues and fostered national reconciliation.

However, during his political career, mistakes made by the Memphis insurance company whose Atlanta branch Gordon headed caused the company to go bankrupt. This left Gordon's financial situation unsound, a problem that dogged him for the rest of his life; it also gave rise to rumors that he exchanged political favors for money. In 1880 the people of Georgia were shocked by the announcement that Gordon had resigned from the Senate. A second announcement soon followed that Governor Alfred H. Colquitt would appoint the controversial and unelectable war-time governor Joseph E. Brown to replace Gordon. Rumors soon turned to open

accusations that the financially distressed Gordon had resigned in exchange for financial gain. Gordon's answer to these allegations was that he resigned out of concern for his family's well-being in light of his precarious personal financial situation.

A semblance of financial stability brought Gordon back into politics. In 1886 he ran and won the governorship and won reelection two years later. While governor, he continued to invest in a variety of businesses. When the United Confederate Veterans was organized in 1889, he was made president, a post he held until his death in 1904. Three months before he died, Gordon published a book, *Reminiscences of the Civil War*, which went through several printings in its first year. Gordon died on 9 January 1904, in Miami, Florida, and is buried in Oakland Cemetery in Atlanta.

—*Frank E. Deserino*

See also Antietam, Battle of; Cedar Creek, Battle of; Fort Stedman; Petersburg Campaign; Shenandoah Valley Campaign (1864–1865).

For further reading:
Eckert, Ralph Lowell. *John Brown Gordon: Soldier, Southerner, American* (1989).
Gordon, John B. *Reminiscences of the Civil War* (1903).
Tankersley, Allen P. *John B. Gordon: A Study in Gallantry* (1955).

GORGAS, JOSIAH
(1818–1883)
Confederate chief of ordnance

Josiah Gorgas was born on 1 July 1818, at Running Pumps, Pennsylvania. His parents, Joseph and Sophia (Atkinson) Gorgas, were poor, and they moved often to secure employment, interrupting their son's education. When he was eighteen, Josiah Gorgas lived with his sister Elizabeth and her husband, Daniel Chapman, in Lyons, New York, where Gorgas was an apprentice at a newspaper. He also read law in the office of Graham Chapin, a congressman who nominated Gorgas for an appointment to West Point. Gorgas graduated sixth in his class in 1841, selecting the Ordnance Corps for his service. He served at the Watervliet and Detroit Arsenals as an assistant ordnance officer before the War Department approved a European tour to study foreign ordnance from May 1845 to May 1846.

Returning to the United States, Gorgas served in the Mexican-American War. In late 1846, he readied a siege train of artillery for General Winfield Scott's expeditionary force and early the following year built army batteries and gun placements for the siege and capture of Vera Cruz. After accompanying the army to Cerro Gordo, he returned to Vera Cruz to manage ordnance storage and transportation. Assailed by yellow fever and suffering from boredom, Gorgas asked to be reassigned. Although he did not enjoy this military service, he

gained recognition for his ordnance expertise and befriended officers he would serve with in the Civil War. Independent and sometimes resentful of his superiors, Gorgas was not brevetted like other officers in the Mexican-American War because of his conflicts with Secretary of State James Buchanan and Secretary of War William L. Marcy, but his service did ultimately result in his promotion to the rank of first lieutenant in March 1847.

Gorgas served at several arsenals in New England before being assigned to Mount Vernon Arsenal north of Mobile, Alabama, in June 1853. Miserable because of the humidity and heat, Gorgas wanted to be reassigned, but a yellow fever epidemic occurred that autumn, and Amelia Gayle, sister of the arsenal's surgeon, Dr. Matt Gayle, was one of the refugees who fled to the arsenal because of its higher elevation. When Gorgas married Gayle in December 1853, he joined a politically prominent family in Alabama. Married life pleased Gorgas, who penned journals for self-discipline and to instruct his children. Professionally, he worked on the military facilities at Pensacola, Florida, and improved them enough to prevent their seizure by Confederates during the Civil War.

Gorgas was a captain and in command of the Frankford Arsenal in Philadelphia, Pennsylvania, when the Civil War began. Gorgas was torn by indecision about whether to side with his native North or his wife's South. He initially refused a major's commission in the Confederate artillery. Yet when he did not receive a position he considered worthy from the Union, he resigned from the U.S. Army on 27 March 1861. He traveled to Montgomery, Alabama, and accepted the Confederacy's proffer to become chief of ordnance on 8 April. General P. G. T. Beauregard had encouraged President Jefferson Davis to appoint Gorgas, citing his previous service as a benefit for the Confederacy.

Gorgas's immediate concern was the dearth of manufacturing in the agrarian South. Although potentially there were plentiful supplies of raw materials such as minerals, coal, and iron, few foundries existed to produce weapons and ammunition. Gorgas dispatched Major Caleb Huse to Europe to trade cotton for ordnance supplies. He also encouraged Confederate soldiers to scavenge battlefields for weapons and to procure lead pipes, church bells, and window sash weights to melt down for bullets, guns, and cannons. He formed a nitre and mining corps to obtain minerals.

Settling his family in quarters at the Virginia State Armory in Richmond, Gorgas directed the building of foundries, smelting works, rolling mills, powder mills, and arsenals to supplement private forges. He expanded and reinforced the prewar network of railroads in the South to deliver raw materials to factories and finished goods to troops. In the Deep South, Selma, Alabama,

and Columbus, Georgia, were the largest manufacturers of Confederate ordnance. At its peak, the Selma ironworks processed thirty tons of pig iron daily. Gorgas's efforts were made more difficult by the Union blockade of Confederate ports, and he organized a fleet of blockade runners to smuggle in munitions, powder, copper, tin, saltpeter, and lead. Gorgas established the Bureau of Foreign Supplies to make purchases abroad for transport by blockade runners in the Caribbean.

Gorgas's efforts made the ordnance department the best-supplied bureau within the War Department. He secured raw materials, supported research for improved weapons, established domestic production of munitions, developed international contacts for war materials, and envisioned future needs, planning for them accordingly. He chose skilled subordinates and laborers to carry out his orders. The nonindustrial South was mobilized to produce munitions for large armies, and Gorgas administratively arranged for efficient distribution. On 8 April 1864, Gorgas wrote in his journal that he had succeeded beyond even his high expectations.

Six months later, Gorgas noted the passage of legislation that made the chief of ordnance a brigadier general and remarked that he would welcome his return to the rank of lieutenant colonel and the advent of peace. Weary of his service, Gorgas had busily overseen all aspects of ordnance management throughout the war. He regularly reported to the Committee on Ordnance Stores of the Confederate House of Representatives and to President Davis about the status of the department. Sometimes things went wrong. A March 1863 accident in an ordnance laboratory killed and wounded workers. Occasionally blockade runners and their cargoes fell to capture. Also, Gorgas felt financially overwhelmed by the burden of supporting his large family, especially when he saw that manufacturers and import businesses were profiting from the war. Describing the energy he had spent establishing a war industry for the Confederacy, Gorgas was proud that the Confederacy had produced ample weapons and ammunition until the last months of the war. Yet the Confederacy's increasing military failure discouraged him, and as Union troops moved through Georgia and the Carolinas, Gorgas fretted over the destruction of Confederate munitions. In April 1865, he evacuated his family from Virginia to Alabama with members of the Confederate government.

Estranged from his Northern family, after the war Gorgas sought to earn a living in Reconstruction Alabama. By 1869, low prices had driven his attempt to manufacture iron to failure. He taught at the University of the South in Sewanee, Tennessee, and was vice chancellor by the time he resigned because of conflicts with the board of trustees. In July 1878, Gorgas accepted the presidency of the University of Alabama in Tuscaloosa. He suffered a stroke in 1879 and resigned, but university administrators appointed Gorgas the university librarian. It was mostly an honorary title, and Gorgas's wife and daughters performed his library work. He lived with his family on the school's campus until his death on 15 May 1883 and was buried in Tuscaloosa's Evergreen Cemetery. Gorgas's son William was an Army surgeon who eradicated yellow fever, enabling the completion of the Panama Canal. The University of Alabama has preserved the Gorgas home as a museum.

—*Elizabeth D. Schafer*

See also Artillery.

For further reading:

Gorgas, Josiah. "Ordnance of the Confederacy, I, II." *Southern Historical Society Papers* (1884).

Johnston, Mary Tabb. *Amelia Gayle Gorgas: A Biography* (1978).

Vandiver, Frank E., ed. *The Civil War Diary of General Josiah Gorgas* (1947).

———. *Ploughshares into Swords: Josiah Gorgas and Confederate Ordnance* (1952; reprint, 1994).

Wiggins, Sarah Woolfolk, ed. *The Journals of Josiah Gorgas 1857–1878* (1995).

———. "A Victorian Father: Josiah Gorgas and His Family." In *In Joy and In Sorrow: Women, Family, and Marriage in the Victorian Era* (1991).

GOSPORT NAVY YARD

One of the U.S. Navy's most important naval bases, Gosport Navy Yard at Norfolk, Virginia, contained a very large shipbuilding area, naval stores, and many other military supplies. At the start of the Civil War it contained about 1,200 cannon and ten ships, four of which were valuable warships. The most important ship there was the steam frigate USS *Merrimack*, armed with forty guns. The yard was manned by 800 sailors and marines commanded by Commodore Charles McCauley.

When McCauley learned on 18 April that several thousand Virginia militia, sent by former Virginia governor Henry Wise, were moving on the yard, he seemed to be at a loss about what to do. When it was suggested that the four warships be put out to sea, McCauley refused. The following day, when attack seemed imminent, McCauley finally issued orders to destroy the yard's buildings, destroy the ships, spike the cannon, and abandon the yard. None of these orders was carried out fully. When the Virginians occupied the yard the following day on 20 April, they were able to salvage most of the cannon, repair some of the construction facilities, and raise the hull of the *Merrimack*. In addition they found over 2,800 barrels of untouched gunpowder. The damaged *Merrimack* was converted to the Confederacy's first ironclad, the CSS *Virginia*.

A little over a year later, in the wake of the Confederate army's retreat up the York Peninsula in early May during Union major general George B. McClellan's Peninsula campaign, the Confederate forces at Gosport realized they could not hold their position. As a result, on 10 May they set fire to most of the yard and evacuated. The *Virginia* tried to move up the James River to safety. The same day, Union major general John Wool moved a force from Fort Monroe to occupy the yard. When the crew of the *Virginia* found the James too shallow for their ship, they blew it up to prevent it from falling into Union hands.

Gosport and Norfolk remained in Union hands for the remainder of the war.

—*David S. Heidler and Jeanne T. Heidler*

See also Navy, C.S.A.; Peninsula Campaign; *Virginia* CSS.

For further reading:

Robertson, James I., Jr. *Civil War Virginia: Battleground for a Nation* (1991).

GOVAN, DANIEL CHEVILETTE
(1829–1911)
Confederate general

Daniel Chevilette Govan was born to Andrew Robison Govan and Mary Pugh Jones Govan in Northampton County, North Carolina. His family moved to Mississippi when he was a small child. He attended the University of South Carolina before heading west in the California gold rush with his cousin Ben McCulloch. Gordon remained in California for three years, serving for a time as Sheriff McCulloch's deputy in Sacramento, California.

In 1852 Govan returned to Mississippi, where he was a planter. In 1860 he decided to take advantage of the relatively low land prices in Arkansas and moved to Phillips County in that state. Upon the secession of Arkansas in May 1861, Govan helped raise a regiment for Confederate service that became the 2d Arkansas. Govan was commissioned the regiment's lieutenant colonel, and early the following year he became the regiment's colonel. In April 1862, he commanded the regiment at Shiloh, after which he became very ill and had to leave the army temporarily. He later served in Braxton Bragg's Kentucky campaign in the late summer and fall of 1862 and fought at Perryville.

At Stones River he remained in command of the 2d Arkansas, which then was a part of St. John R. Liddell's brigade of Patrick Cleburne's division, William Hardee's Corps. Though often commended by his superiors, Govan remained a colonel through much of the following year, still commanding the 2d Arkansas during the Tullahoma campaign of June 1863.

At Chickamauga Govan commanded the brigade when Liddell advanced to division command. Govan continued in command of the brigade during the Chattanooga campaign. As part of Cleburne's division, Govan and his brigade were an important component of

Confederate rear guard at Ringgold Gap after the disaster at Missionary Ridge. The actions of these men saved much of the army's artillery and supplies, for which Cleburne commended Govan.

At the end of the year, Govan was promoted to brigadier general. The following spring he led his brigade, still as part of Cleburne's division, in the Atlanta campaign. He was commended for his actions during the battle of Atlanta on 22 July. On 1 September late in the day during the battle of Jonesboro, Govan and his brigade were cut off from the remainder of the army, and most of the men were either killed or captured. Govan found himself a Federal prisoner sent to Chattanooga for safekeeping.

Luckily for Govan, Union cavalryman, Brigadier General George Stoneman, had fallen into Confederate hands back in July, and William T. Sherman was willing to exchange one brigadier general for another. Therefore, Govan was back in command of his brigade by the end of September.

Govan and his brigade were part of John Bell Hood's force that moved north after the fall of Atlanta. After Sherman broke off pursuit to commence his March to the Sea, Hood determined to attack what he believed to be the isolated Union position in Tennessee. Govan opposed Hood's plan to attack Franklin, Tennessee, on 30 November, but the assault proceeded as planned. In the battle Cleburne was killed. Rumors were rampant that Govan had suffered the same fate, though he was not injured in the fight. He fought at the disastrous Confederate defeat at Nashville before taking what was left of his brigade to join Joseph Johnston in the attempt to block Sherman's progress up through the Carolinas in early 1865. Govan was with Johnston's army when it surrendered to Sherman.

After his parole, Govan returned to his Arkansas plantation. He lived there quietly for the next few decades, writing about his Civil War career. The 16th Iowa volunteers invited him to their reunion in September 1883 because he and his brigade had captured that regiment's colors during the Atlanta campaign. He attended the reunion and while there returned the regiment's colors that had been in his keeping since the summer of 1864. In 1894, President Grover Cleveland appointed him one of the Indian agents in Washington state. He served in that position until 1898, when he returned to Arkansas. Over the next years he lived with several of his children in the states of Mississippi and Tennessee. He died at the home of one in Memphis, Tennessee, on 12 March 1911.

—*David S. Heidler and Jeanne T. Heidler*

See also Atlanta Campaign; Chattanooga Campaign; Franklin, Battle of.
For further reading:
Bowers, John. *Chickamauga and Chattanooga: The Battles That*

Doomed the Confederacy (1994).
Castel, Albert. *Decision in the West: The Atlanta Campaign of 1864* (1992).

GRACIE, ARCHIBALD, JR.
(1832–1864)
Confederate general

Born in New York City to Archibald Gracie and Elizabeth Davidson Bethune Gracie, young Gracie attended school in Germany before receiving an appointment to the U.S. Military Academy. He graduated fourteenth in a class of forty-six in 1854. Upon graduation, Gracie was stationed at various posts in the Pacific Northwest and was serving in Idaho when he resigned his commission in 1856 to join his father's business in Mobile, Alabama.

Active in local militia affairs, Gracie attained the command of the Washington Light Infantry Company in Mobile before the war. In that capacity he received an order from Governor A. B. Moore to seize the federal arsenal at Mount Vernon, Alabama, before the state seceded. Gracie carried out the order, and upon the secession of Alabama and its incorporation into the Confederacy, he led his company as it became part of the 3d Alabama Infantry.

On 12 July 1861, Gracie transferred to the 11th Alabama as a major. By spring of 1862, however, Gracie had raised the 43d Alabama and become its colonel. He commanded this unit in the Peninsula campaign before being transferred to East Tennessee to command the 43d in Henry Heth's brigade in the corps commanded by E. Kirby Smith. While serving under Heth, Gracie commanded the expedition that took Fort Cliff from Tennessee Unionists. He then moved forward in August 1862 as part of Kirby Smith's invasion of Kentucky. After Kirby Smith's occupation of Lexington, Kentucky, in early September, Gracie became the military governor of the town. On 4 November 1862, as a result of his part in the Kentucky campaign, Gracie was promoted to brigadier general.

During the spring of 1863, Gracie commanded the Confederate forces guarding the approach through Cumberland Gap. Later in the summer he was involved in the fighting around Knoxville before being ordered south toward Chattanooga and then into north Georgia, where he participated in the battle of Chickamauga.

Commanding his brigade at Chickamauga, Gracie led one of the major Confederate attacks toward the end of the battle against George Thomas's position on Snodgrass Hill. Gracie's brigade suffered tremendous casualties in this assault and failed to dislodge Thomas.

In October 1863, when James Longstreet was detached from Bragg's army to move against Union forces occupying Knoxville, Gracie and his brigade

participated in that campaign. Gracie was wounded in the arm at Bean's Station on 15 December 1863 toward the end of the campaign.

In the spring of 1864 Gracie was transferred with his brigade to Richmond, from where he was quickly dispatched to Petersburg in the second week of May to aid in the weak defenses there. When Union general Benjamin Butler began his move on Petersburg from the south side of the James River, Gracie and his brigade were placed in the Confederate defenses at Drewry's Bluff. Gracie was commended for bravery for his actions at Drewry's Bluff, particularly for his involvement in the attack on Butler's positions on 16 May 1864.

In June 1864, Gracie's brigade was placed under the command of P. G. T. Beauregard. Gracie would remain in Petersburg as part of the defenses of that position as Grant began his siege of the city. In the fall, Gracie was recommended for promotion to major general, but was killed in the trenches of Petersburg on 2 December 1864 before his promotion could be confirmed. Some reports attribute his death to a sharpshooter's bullet, though most accounts agree that an exploding artillery shell killed him.

The remainder of Gracie's family had remained loyal to the Union during the war, and they arranged for the transfer of his body to Union lines, where it was transported to New York City for burial.

—David S. Heidler and Jeanne T. Heidler

See also Bean's Station; Drewry's Bluff; Knoxville Campaign.

GRADY, HENRY WOODFIN
(1850–1889)
Journalist

Henry Grady achieved national recognition as a renowned orator and editor of the *Atlanta Constitution* during the 1880s. Grady became the foremost spokesman and proponent of the "New South" ideology, which prophesied postwar regional regeneration through sectional reconciliation, industrialization, and Northern investment in the region. The ideas Grady espoused influenced Southern politicians and businessmen into the twentieth century.

Henry Woodfin Grady was born on 24 April 1850 in Athens, Georgia. The local and familial environment that surrounded young Henry influenced his later dedication to industrialism and economic strength. Many of Henry's relatives worked in Athens, a town bustling with commercial activity at the time, as prosperous businessmen. The Grady family also occupied an elite position in Athens society, and intended for Henry to assume a similar role. The front porch of the Grady home overlooked the University of Georgia campus, and Grady's parents stressed the importance of education to him from

a young age. Such an environment contributed to Grady's success in private schools, until the Civil War temporarily delayed Grady's educational journey.

Although Grady was too young to serve the Confederacy in battle, the war and its aftermath directly affected him. The Grady family generally favored the Union's survival, but Grady's father joined the Confederate Army and fought in Virginia under Robert E. Lee. After the war ended, Grady entered the University of Georgia in 1866. Soon thereafter, he joined a campus debating society where he developed and sharpened his oratorical skills. He entered graduate school at the University of Virginia. Although Grady entered the university with political aspirations, he abandoned such plans and left the school before graduating. In 1869 Grady returned to Athens and contemplated his future.

During the summer of 1869, Grady decided to become a journalist. He submitted editorial essays to several Southern papers. The rapidly expanding *Atlanta Constitution* took an interest in Grady, published his letters, and hired him as a reporter. In September 1869 Grady moved to Rome, Georgia, as the assistant editor of the town's *Courier*. He later purchased two newspaper companies in the city and returned to Atlanta as coowner of the city's *Herald* in 1872. The venture failed, and Grady took several writing jobs until the *Constitution* rehired him in 1876. Four years later, he bought a quarter interest in the paper.

During his early years as a reporter, Grady wrote about the economic disparity that the post-Appomattox South experienced in comparison with the North. He desperately wanted to restore Southern prestige and dedicated many editorials to his vision of regional growth. Grady also presented his ideas in national publications, such as *Harper's*, and through his status as an increasingly popular lecturer. In 1886 Grady rekindled his interest in politics and served as former Confederate General John B. Gordon's campaign advisor during his successful gubernatorial campaign. A reemergence of Southern pride accompanied Gordon's victory, as well as the congressional elections of 1886, and a concerned Grady worried how the elections would effect sectional reconciliation and Southern rejuvenation. In late 1886 Grady accepted an invitation to address the New England Society of New York City. He decided to feature his ideas at the appearance, and delivered his famous "New South" speech.

On 21 December 1886, in front of 360 distinguished guests, including William T. Sherman, J. P. Morgan, and several members of the Northern industrial elite searching for investment opportunities, Grady offered his view of the postwar South. He used glowing metaphors and positive rhetoric to proclaim that many Southern traditions died with the Confederate defeat. In their place, a "new" South emerged that wanted to resemble its Northern counterpart. Grady maintained that the reborn region harbored no resentment against the North, all Southerners welcomed sectional reconciliation, and racial peace existed in the region. Most importantly, the New South desired a new social and economic order based on industrialization. Grady argued that the region contained the resources needed to reach industrial superiority, such as land, raw materials, and efficient and virtuous workers, but needed Northern investment to reach its potential. In his "New South" speech, therefore, Henry Grady presented the South as a born-again region that was economically and socially progressive, investment-friendly, and a potential industrial power. Grady's vision and speech were overwhelming successes.

Many Northern newspapers eagerly embraced Grady's New South concept. Nearly overnight, he became the foremost spokesman and most ardent supporter of the ideology. Grady also inspired scores of other Southern editors and speakers to adopt his philosophies, and lectures extolling New South virtues proliferated at the time. The growth of the *Atlanta Constitution* reflected the promise and fervor Grady's vision inspired. By 1888 it had the largest circulation in America.

Grady gave speeches throughout the nation that reinforced New South philosophy. In a 27 October 1888 speech in Dallas, Texas, entitled "The South and Its Problems," Grady also stressed that the New South was a white South. In the speech, he reassured his audience that because of their inherent inferiority, blacks would remain farm laborers in the new social and industrial order, while whites would form the bulk of industrial workers and benefit most from Northern investment. Grady's declarations of white supremacy continued to resonate with fellow Southerners decades later. During the infamous Atlanta race riot of 1906, frenzied whites placed the lifeless bodies of three blacks in front of a monument of Grady that stood in front of the *Atlanta Constitution* offices.

Grady spent his last months lecturing Southern crowds on the importance of unity in the new order. He believed that any conflicts evident within the region presented Northern businessmen with risky investment conditions, and delivered many speeches extolling the virtues of unity to fellow Southerners. Grady urged farmers, who faced tumultuous economic conditions, to place the region's best interests first and continue voting for Democrats to maintain the image of a "solid South." In his final speeches, Grady also reassured Northern audiences that a stable Southern social order existed. During a December 1889 speaking engagement in the Northeast, an already weakened Grady contracted pneumonia. On 23 December 1889, Henry Grady died in Atlanta, before he could witness the full effect his boosterism had on his beloved region. Over a century since his death, Henry Grady continues to be an important figure for understanding the economic, social, and political development of the post–Civil War South.

—Mike Butler

For further reading:
Davis, Harold E. *Henry Grady's New South Atlanta, A Brave and Beautiful City* (1990).
Gaston, Paul Morton. "The New South Creed, 1865–1900" (Ph.D. Thesis, 1961).
Nixon, Raymond B. *Henry W. Grady, Spokesman of the New South* (1943).
Woodward, C. Vann. *Origins of the New South 1877–1913* (1951).

GRAHAM, CHARLES KINNAIRD
(1824–1889)
Union general

Born in New York City, Charles Kinnaird Graham joined the U.S. Navy as a midshipman when he was seventeen. He served for eight years, including duty in the Gulf Squadron during the Mexican-American War. He resigned in 1848 to return to New York to study law. After admission to the bar, he did not find the law to his liking and studied engineering. As a civil engineer in New York before the Civil War, he was one of the men responsible for laying out Central Park. He also worked on the construction of the Brooklyn Navy Yard.

At the outbreak of the Civil War, Graham raised a regiment consisting primarily of men from the Brooklyn Navy Yard. Eventually this regiment, with Graham as its colonel, was mustered into the U.S. volunteers as the 74th New York, part of Daniel Sickles's Excelsior Brigade. The regiment's first service was seen along the Potomac River, where it saw its first action in a skirmish at Mathias Point, Virginia, on 9 November 1861. Its first serious action would come in the Peninsula campaign the following spring.

During the Peninsula campaign, Graham led his regiment at Seven Pines and the Seven Days'. Shortly after the campaign, however, Graham's health began to fail, and he was forced to take a medical leave of absence. While back in New York, he worked hard to recruit more men for the army. He returned in time to command a brigade of Sickles's III Corps at Chancellorsville. He had been promoted to brigadier general in March 1863 dating back to November 1862.

In June 1863 Graham led his brigade north. At Gettysburg on 2 July, still commanding the same brigade in Sickles's corps, Graham, at Sickles's instructions, took his men off Cemetery Ridge into the Peach Orchard. In the heavy fighting that took place there that day, Graham was struck a glancing though incapacitating blow in the head by Confederate fire. Left on the field as his brigade withdrew, Graham was captured by the Confederates.

Graham's division commander, Major General David B. Birney, commended him for bravery at Gettysburg.

Graham was imprisoned in Richmond for the next two months. Upon his exchange to Fort Monroe on 22 September 1863, Graham immediately wrote a letter to Secretary of War Edwin Stanton telling everything he was able to determine about Confederate movements during his imprisonment. He reported that James Longstreet had moved south with most of his corps and that the remaining units were nowhere near Richmond. Because he had not completely recovered from his wound at Gettysburg, Graham took a short leave of absence on his return to Washington.

On 16 November 1863, Graham was relieved from duty with the Army of the Potomac and transferred to the Department of Virginia and North Carolina, commanded by Benjamin F. Butler. Graham's initial assignment, probably due to his naval experience, was command of the army's gunboats at Fort Monroe. With these craft he patrolled coastal waters as far south as North Carolina and up the rivers in the lower Chesapeake Bay. On 28 April 1864 Graham was officially given command of what was known as the Naval Brigade in the Army of the James.

With this crack unit of sailors and soldiers, Graham was able to penetrate deeply up the myriad riverways to scout Confederate fortifications and positions and make raids into the interior. In May 1864, he scouted Confederate positions up the Appomattox River. After Jubal Early's Washington raid that left U.S. postmaster general Montgomery Blair's house burned, Butler ordered Graham up the Rappahannock River to destroy the house of James Seddon's brother.

On 17 February 1865 Graham was relieved from duty with the Naval Brigade and given command of the Union position at Bermuda Hundred. He left the army in August 1865.

After the war Graham returned home to New York City, where over the next two decades he held a variety of posts with the Port of New York. He died on 15 April 1889 in Lakewood, New Jersey.

—*David S. Heidler and Jeanne T. Heidler*

See also Gettysburg, Battle of; Sickles, Daniel Edgar.

For further reading:

Longacre, Edward G. *Army of Amateurs: General Benjamin F. Butler and the Army of the James, 1863–1865* (1997).
Pfanz, Harry W. *Gettysburg, The Second Day* (1987).

GRAND REVIEW
(23–24 May 1865)

Before sunrise on 23 May 1865, the firemen of the District of Columbia started sweeping Pennsylvania Avenue clean and watering it down. As they worked, the first of the nearly 100,000 Union troops bivouacked in Washington and across the Potomac River in Virginia awoke to the bugler's call and prepared to march. The day promised to be mild, with just enough breeze to stir the flags and miles of bunting blooming everywhere in the capital. The black crepe for the slain president that had shrouded Washington since April had been taken down and the trial of the conspirators suspended for this, the last and greatest pageant of the war, the grand review of the armies of the republic.

Even after four years of teeming throngs, Washington staggered under the invasion of visitors intent on watching the spectacle. Crowds swelled by government employees and school children who had the day off began to line the parade route at dawn. Isaac Bassett, assistant doorkeeper of the Senate, who was watching from the Capitol, claimed that "from one extremity to the other, Pennsylvania Avenue was lined on both sides with a forest of faces." Every window, porch, balcony, and housetop along the route was occupied with spectators clutching bouquets and waving flags and handkerchiefs.

The official reviewing stands in front of the White House, festooned with flags, flowers, and evergreens and the names of the great battles of the war—Gettysburg, Donelson, Petersburg, Shiloh, South Mountain—filled with cabinet members and dignitaries. Notably absent was Secretary of State William Henry Seward, who was at home with a bandaged head and wired jaw, the victim of John Wilkes Booth's fellow conspirator, Lewis Paine. At nine o'clock, a signal gun heralded the beginning of the review. First to swing into sight was a solitary horseman, bespectacled General George Meade, at the head of the Army of the Potomac. The crowd took up the cheer of the Pennsylvanians in the stands: "Gettysburg, Gettysburg, Gettysburg!" Meade drew his sword and raised the blade in the sunlight as his troops poured down the avenue behind him.

For nearly six hours the steady, even lines of men sixty abreast, stretching from curb to curb, passed down Pennsylvania Avenue. The crowds shouted until they were hoarse, but none cheered louder than the Washingtonians among them. This was the Army of the Potomac, whose men had built the capital's fortifications, formed a living barrier across northern Virginia to protect it, and less than a year before, stopped General Jubal Early at the edge of town.

The last troop of cavalry did not clatter by until late afternoon on the first day of the Grand Review. For Marian Hooper, who would later marry Henry Adams, and who had defied her father by coming to Washington with four other young ladies to watch the review, the trip from Boston had been worth it. She wrote home to her cousin that night:

"And so it came, this glorious old army of the Potomac, for six hours marching past, eighteen or

The Grand Review, showing the reviewing stand with President Johnson (*front row in stand, fourth from left*) and Johnson's cabinet. (Photograph by Mathew Brady Studio / *Library of Congress*)

twenty miles long, their colors telling their sad history. Some regiments with nothing but a bare pole, a little bit of rag only, hanging a few inches, to show where their flag had been . . . all the rest shot away."

That night, while the Army of the Potomac caroused, nearly 100,000 troops of the Army of the Tennessee and the Army of Georgia marched into town and bedded down in the capital's streets. The next day, 24 May, "humanity of all ages, sexes and conditions" packed Pennsylvania Avenue again to get a glimpse of these strangers from beyond the Alleghenies. Though they had fought to save the Union, for most of these men this was their first glimpse of their nation's capital.

As the starting signal boomed, Generals William Tecumseh Sherman and Oliver O. Howard with his empty sleeve rode out onto the Avenue. In Sherman's honor, the bands played a jubilant new tune, "Marching through Georgia." Sherman was worried that his rough, gangling, ill-clothed westerners might compare unfavorably with the polished eastern troops that had passed by the day before. But as he topped the rise at the Treasury building and turned in his saddle for a backward glance, his fears were put to rest. The crowds declared his men magnificent. They were cheered and pelted with flowers. "Handkerchiefs," claimed one reporter, "shook like aspen leaves. . . . Roses bloomed in the muzzles of guns."

The armies of the West marched down Pennsylvania Avenue for six hours. After they disbanded, their rowdy celebrating kept the city awake long into the night. In hell raising, as in everything else, Sherman's men tried to outdo the Army of the Potomac.

—*Kathryn Allamong Jacob*

For further reading:
Leech, Margaret. *Reveille in Washington, 1860–1865* (1941).

Thoron, Ward, ed. *The Letters of Mrs. Henry Adams: 1865–1883* (1936).
Washington Star (23–25 May 1865).

GRANGER, GORDON
(1822–1876)
Union general

Born to Gaius Granger and Catherine Taylor Granger in Joy, New York, Gordon Granger was educated locally before receiving an appointment to the U.S. Military Academy. He graduated thirty-fifth of forty-one from the class of 1845. Commissioned into the infantry, Granger transferred to the mounted riflemen in 1846, and with his unit went to Mexico, where he fought in Winfield Scott's Mexico City campaign of the Mexican-American War. He received two brevet promotions during that campaign. After the war Granger served on a number of western frontier posts.

Early in the Civil War, Granger was promoted to captain of the 3d Cavalry. In August 1861 he was stationed in Missouri and fought at the battle of Wilson's Creek. He was cited for conspicuous bravery for that engagement and was named the colonel of the 2d Michigan Cavalry. From September until the end of the year Granger and his unit guarded the St. Louis Arsenal.

Early in 1862, Granger and the 2d Michigan became part of the Army of the Mississippi under John Pope. In March 1862, Granger was promoted to brigadier general of volunteers and was given command of all the cavalry in the Army of the Mississippi. Granger and his cavalry division participated in the New Madrid and Island No. 10 campaigns, and he led them in the siege of Corinth in June 1862. Throughout the summer of 1862, Granger commanded his division in operations in northern Mississippi. In the late summer he went to Lexington, Kentucky, to command the Army of Kentucky. In November he became the commander of the District of Central Kentucky as major general of volunteers dating back to 17 September.

The following spring, Granger was named commander of the Reserve Corps of the Army of the Cumberland. He led his men forward in the Tullahoma campaign in June 1863 and then into north Georgia in September 1863 in what would become the battle of Chickamauga.

At Chickamauga, Granger guarded one of the avenues of retreat for the army. When he heard that George Thomas's corps on Horseshoe Ridge was in danger of envelopment, he brought forward two brigades that drove back the Confederate attackers on the Union right. In doing so these units suffered over 40 percent casualties but saved Thomas's corps.

On 10 October 1863, Granger took command of IV Corps of the Army of the Cumberland just in time for the Chattanooga campaign. He led his men bravely in the engagements of this campaign, especially at Missionary Ridge. He continued to command IV Corps in the Knoxville campaign, and afterward reinforced retreating Federals after the engagement at Bean's Station.

On 10 April 1864, Granger was relieved as commander of IV Corps and was sent to E. R. S. Canby in the Department of the Gulf in New Orleans. The governor of Tennessee, Andrew Johnson, wrote to Abraham Lincoln in June 1864 expressing his dismay at Granger's removal from the Army of the Cumberland and requesting that such an aggressive soldier be returned to where he was needed. He was not.

In July 1864 Canby sent Granger to the Alabama Gulf coast to cooperate with the naval expedition under David Glasgow Farragut that would result in the battle of Mobile Bay. As part of that campaign Granger invested Fort Morgan on 23 August 1864.

Granger became the commander of the District of West Florida and South Alabama in September 1864. He commanded that district until February 1865 when he was made the commander of XIII Corps, Department of the Gulf. He led this corps in the Mobile campaign in the spring of 1865.

At the end of the war, Granger was stationed in New Orleans. In the early summer he was sent to occupy Galveston, Texas. While there he found it necessary to enforce the Emancipation Proclamation, freeing the slaves in Texas. As a result, he became a hero to African-Americans there for his action of 19 June 1865, the first "Juneteenth."

Mustered out with the remaining volunteers in 1866, Granger became a colonel of infantry. He served the rest of his life on the frontier, primarily in New Mexico. He died in Santa Fe, New Mexico, on 10 January 1876.

—David S. Heidler and Jeanne T. Heidler

See also Chickamauga, Battle of.
For further reading:
Bowers, John. *Chickamauga and Chattanooga: The Battles that Damned the Confederacy* (1994).
Cozzens, Peter. *This Terrible Sound: The Battle of Chickamauga* (1992).

GRANT, LEWIS ADDISON
(1829–1918)
Union general

Born to James Grant and Elizabeth Wyman Grant in Winhall, Vermont, Lewis Addison Grant was educated locally before embarking on a teaching career. After a few years teaching, Grant decided to study law and began in 1855 what would be a successful practice in Bellows Falls, Vermont.

At the outbreak of the Civil War, Grant offered his

services to the Union and on 15 August 1861 was commissioned a major in the 5th Vermont Infantry. The 5th was a part of the Vermont Brigade, which Grant would eventually command. He was promoted to lieutenant colonel in September 1861.

The first serious action for the regiment came in the Peninsula campaign in the spring and summer of 1862. At the battle of Savage Station on 29 June 1862, Grant commanded the regiment, and late in the day was part of the Federal counterattack that stopped the Confederate advance. The 5th suffered very heavy casualties in the engagement and was unable to fight in any of the remaining battles of the summer. Grant became colonel of the 5th in September 1862.

At Fredericksburg on 13 December 1862, Grant led the Vermont Brigade and was wounded. He returned to command the following spring when, as part of John Sedgwick's VI Corps, he remained opposite Fredericksburg while the remainder of the Army of the Potomac crossed the Rapidan and engaged Robert E. Lee in the battle of Chancellorsville. Sedgwick then led his men across the Rappahannock, routed the small Confederate force in Fredericksburg, and marched toward Chancellorsville. At the battle of Salem Church on 3 May, Grant led a charge that captured three Confederate battle flags. In 1893 he received the Medal of Honor for this action.

Detailed to Washington and then New York, Grant and the Vermont Brigade did not see significant action again until the spring of 1864. In April 1864 Grant was promoted to brigadier general of volunteers just in time to fight in the battles of the Wilderness and Spotsylvania Court House. In these two engagements, the Vermont Brigade again suffered heavy casualties (some units as much as 40 percent). On 9 July 1864, the brigade was sent quickly to Washington to serve as part of the defense against Jubal Early's raid. After the repulse of Early, Grant and his men went to participate in Philip Sheridan's Shenandoah Valley campaign.

As part of George W. Getty's division of VI Corps at the battle of Cedar Creek on 19 October 1864, Grant and his brigade again distinguished themselves. As part of the force that found the defensible Union position on the ridgeline that became the rallying point for the Union army, these men then could provide the nucleus for the Federal counterattack that won the battle.

Grant and the Vermont Brigade returned to the trenches of Petersburg, where they fought in the final months of the war. At Five Forks on 2 April 1865, Grant again was wounded.

After the war, Grant resigned from the army in August 1865 and declined a regular commission when offered one the following year. He returned for a time to Vermont and his law practice, but in 1867 he decided to move to the Midwest, eventually settling in Des Moines, Iowa, and then Minneapolis. In 1890 he became Benjamin Harrison's assistant secretary of war and held that position until 1893. He died in Minneapolis on 20 March 1918.

—David S. Heidler and Jeanne T. Heidler

See also Cedar Creek, Battle of; Salem Church; Shenandoah Valley Campaign; Vermont Brigade.

For further reading:
Heatwole, John L. *The Burning: Sheridan in the Shenandoah Valley* (1998).
Lewis, Thomas A. *The Guns of Cedar Creek* (1988).

GRANT, ULYSSES SIMPSON
(1822–1885)

Union general; general-in-chief of the United States Army (1864–1869); eighteenth president of the United States

Born Hiram Ulysses Grant, he unprotestingly accepted the clerical error changing his name to Ulysses Simpson Grant when he entered West Point in 1839. His new name, U.S. Grant, lent itself to his Old Army nickname, Uncle Sam Grant, or simply Sam Grant, and to his Civil War nickname, Unconditional Surrender Grant. Such names symbolize Grant: as a soldier, his loyal patriotism and relentless pursuit of victory; yet as a man, his unchallenged acceptance of a bureaucratic blunder changing his identity rather than risk his opportunity for advancement.

Advancement at first appeared unlikely for this eldest child of Jesse Root Grant and Hannah Simpson Grant. Born 27 April 1822 in Point Pleasant, Ohio, and raised in Georgetown, Ohio, he grew up in modest circumstances that hardly portended his future greatness. However, opportunity arose in 1839, when his ambitious father obtained for him appointment to the U.S. Military Academy as the best means to get a good education for free.

Grant's years at West Point proved solid but not outstanding. He excelled only in horsemanship, reflecting his lifelong love of animals, but he worked sufficiently diligently in his studies and deportment to rank midway in his class. Out of sixty-three cadets entering the Military Academy in 1839, he placed twenty-first among the 39 who actually graduated in 1843. More important than his studies or standing were his ability to master the rigors of discipline and education, his exposure to a wider world than small-town Ohio, and his friendship with classmates who became comrades during the Civil War, especially Rufus Ingalls, Isaac Quinby, and Frederick Steele. Evidence also suggests that, even when General-in-Chief, he continued according undeserved admiration to the head of his Class of 1843, William B. Franklin.

Two other cadets with whom he enjoyed not only life-

Ulysses S. Grant (*National Archives*)

long friendship but also family ties were James Longstreet, Class of 1842, his future wife's cousin; and Frederick Dent, Grant's own roommate and his future brother-in-law. Grant met Dent's sister Julia in 1843 while serving as a second lieutenant in the 4th U.S. Infantry Regiment at Jefferson Barracks, south of St. Louis. Grant soon began courting Julia, and on 22 August 1848 they married. Four children were born to their union: Frederick, 1850; Ulysses Jr., 1852; Ellen, 1855; and Jesse, 1858. Sam and Julia remained in love for the rest of their lives. She would prove an inspiration during his introduction to warfare in Mexico, a comfort during low points of his life, a reassurance during the trials of senior leadership, and a helpmeet to whom he could unburden himself openly and unreservedly.

By the time they married, Grant had experienced war. In May 1844, his regiment transferred from Missouri to Natchitoches, Louisiana, then America's southwestern frontier. After Texas joined the Union, the 4th Infantry became part of Zachary Taylor's army at Corpus Christi. Grant, who always admired Taylor's "rough and ready" ways, participated in that general's splendid victories at Palo Alto, Resaca de la Palma, and Monterrey. Transferred with most Regular regiments to the army of Winfield Scott, whom he respected but did not like, Grant fought in the great campaign from Vera Cruz to Mexico City. These operations earned him brevets as first lieutenant for Molino del Rey and as captain for Chapultepec, and he received the substantive rank of first lieutenant as of 16 September 1847, two days after the enemy capital fell.

Politically, Grant opposed war with Mexico. Militarily, however, the Mexican War proved critical to his soldierly development. It showed him that battlefields were horrid yet survivable. It demonstrated how using the tactical and strategic initiative could dominate an enemy, even deep in enemy territory. And, equally importantly, it made him appreciate the critical importance of logistics. As regimental quartermaster of the 4th Infantry from Camargo until the Americans evacuated Mexico in 1848, and again from November 1848 to August 1853, he gained experience and understanding of supplying troops in wartime and peacetime. Such understanding set him apart from so many other Civil War generals, whose grandiose concepts of grand strategy collapsed for lack of logistical undergirding.

Following the Mexican-American War and marriage, Grant served with his regiment at East Pascagoula, Mississippi; Fort Wayne, Michigan; and Madison Barracks, New York. Then in 1852 the 4th Infantry transferred to the Pacific Coast, where Grant eventually served at Fort Humboldt, California. The transfer brought promotion to captain on 5 August 1853. It also necessitated separation from his beloved Julia. Separation, isolation, and lack of prospects for further promotion weighed heavily on Grant. Like many other Regular officers, before and after the Civil War, he turned to the bottle. Drinking further depressed morale and performance. On 31 July 1854, he resigned from the Army under a cloud. To help pay his fare back to Missouri, he had to rely on the generosity of his fellow officer and friend since West Point, Simon Bolivar Buckner.

Missouri brought him reunion with Julia but not success. He merely eked out an existence farming at Hard Scrabble near the Dent plantation, White Haven, and he was denied a coveted county job. In 1860, economic straits and increasing uneasiness with secessionist St. Louis made him move to Galena, Illinois, to work as a clerk in his father's leathergoods store.

From cadet to captain to clerk, Sam Grant had risen from obscurity on the Ohio River to serve his country well from the Rio Grande to Mexico City, but now he was sinking back into oblivion on the upper Mississippi. Had he died in 1860, he would rate no more than a footnote in Mexican-American War histories and a brief paragraph in West Point alumni directories.

The Civil War rescued Grant from such anonymity and afforded him opportunity to earn the highest military and civil offices the United States can bestow. Context and circumstance created that opportunity, but it was Grant's abilities both innate and acquired, which enabled him to succeed in a war where so many officers with far more illustrious records at West Point and in the Old Army would fall short.

Some of those officers suffered the disadvantage of immediate elevation to high command in 1861. Grant, in contrast, worked upward from modest beginnings. His first service came as Galenans selected him to preside over a patriotic meeting when war erupted. He declined command of Galena's company (later Company F/12th Illinois Infantry Regiment), but he did train that outfit. He also accepted Governor Richard Yates's appeal to make his experience available to the state Adjutant General in raising and organizing Illinois' first sixteen regiments. The national government proved less interested in Grant, as both the War Department and George B. McClellan, commanding the Department of the Ohio, ignored his offers of service in May. Again, it was Yates who recognized Grant's ability. On 15 June 1861, the governor appointed him colonel of the 21st Illinois Infantry at Springfield. Grant promptly shaped up that refractory regiment. On 28 June, he and the unit were mustered into Federal service. Within days, the 21st was deemed ready to go to war. But was Grant himself ready?

In the summer of 1861, Kentucky's neutrality skewed the Western theater into borderland operations in western Virginia and Missouri. Ohio and Indiana troops covered the Appalachian sector. It fell to Illinois and Iowa to secure Missouri. Grant's regiment was ordered to Quincy on 3 July. Nine days later, it crossed into Missouri to help guard the Pacific Railroad. General Thomas A. Harris's pro-Secessionist Missouri State Guard division threatened that railroad. On 17 July, Grant advanced against Harris at Florida on the Salt River. Grant had fought in many battles in Mexico but always as a subaltern. This was his first operation as commander, and the responsibility of command weighed heavily on him.

"As we approached…Harris' camp…," Grant later remembered, "my heart kept getting higher and higher until it felt to me as though it was in my throat. I would have given anything then to have been back in Illinois, but I had not the moral courage to halt and consider what to do; I kept right on. When we reached a point from which the valley below was in full view I halted. The place where Harris had been encamped a few days before was still there…but the troops were gone. My heart resumed its place. It occurred to me at once that Harris had been as much afraid of me as I had been of him. This was a view of the question I had never taken before; but it was one I never forgot afterwards. From that event to the close of the war, I never experienced trepidation upon confronting an enemy, though I always felt more or less anxiety. I never forgot that he had as much reason to fear my forces as I had his. The lesson was valuable."

Due not so much to this victory at Salt River as to influential Congressman Elihu B. Washburne of Galena, who would prove a continuing benefactor, Grant was promoted to brigadier general of volunteers on 31 July, ranking from 17 May. He briefly commanded at Ironton, Jefferson City, and Cape Girardeau. On 1 September, he took charge of the District of Southeast Missouri, including southern Illinois, headquartered at Cairo. This new responsibility put him in position to confront the Confederate invasion of Kentucky, which ended that state's neutrality. Without awaiting authorization, Grant boldly countered by occupying Paducah on 6 September, thus forestalling Southern efforts to seize the mouth of the Tennessee River.

Such boldness recurred almost as rashness, as on 7 November, when he led five regiments down the Mississippi against the camp at Belmont, Missouri. Grant overran the camp but was lucky to escape before reinforcements from the nearby Confederate stronghold of Columbus, Kentucky, could intercept him. Despite its limited achievements, the Belmont foray shone forth amid a series of Union defeats that summer and autumn. It marked Grant as one commander who did not insist on perfection but who was willing to advance with the resources at hand.

The Belmont expedition proved only the first of Grant's many operations along navigable western rivers. In early February, he led two divisions up the Tennessee River against Fort Henry. The nearly flooded fort surrendered to the cooperating Federal navy on 6 February, before the army could engage. Grant then boldly moved overland against Fort Donelson on the Cumberland River. Although the Graycoats repulsed Union warships on 14 February and nearly rolled up Grant's right on 15 February, he contained their breakout and captured some trenches. In a cowardly collapse of will, the two senior Southern commanders fled. On 16 February, the ranking remaining officer, Simon B. Buckner—Grant's Old Army friend—asked for terms of capitulation. "No terms except an unconditional and immediate surrender can be accepted," replied Grant; "I propose to move immediately upon your works." Rather than face further assault, Buckner surrendered approximately 17,000 men.

Losing Forts Henry and Donelson broke the Confederate defense line in Kentucky, doomed Nashville, and forced the military frontier back to the Memphis-Corinth-Chattanooga line. Those victories instantly made Grant a national hero and gave him the nickname Unconditional Surrender Grant. It also brought promotion to major general of volunteers, as of 16 February. By mid-March he was the senior subordinate in the Western theater under overall commander Henry W. Halleck. Along with new rank came a new name for his command. Technically, he operated against Henry and Donelson while heading the District of

Cairo, as his expanded territory had been known since 23 December. On 17 February, however, he assumed command of the new District of West Tennessee, "limits not defined." In eventually defining its limits as the district expanded into the Department and Army of the Tennessee, Grant would create one of the great combat forces of American history.

That army and its achievements lay in the future. Grant barely survived that long, indeed barely lasted beyond his February triumphs. When Grant visited occupied Nashville, Halleck unjustly suspected that he was abandoning his command to resume drinking. General-in-Chief McClellan uncritically authorized Halleck to arrest or relieve Grant. Halleck would not go that far, but on 4 March he ordered Grant to remain at Fort Henry and to turn over to Charles F. Smith command of the field army then preparing to advance up the Tennessee River. Smith had been commandant of cadets while Grant was at West Point and had led a light battalion with great distinction in 1847. Many officers, including Grant, thought Smith worthy of army command.

Yet Grant was severely struck by such a slur so soon after his splendid successes and sought to be sent from Halleck's department. The senior soldier, however, relented and restored him to command of the field army on 11 March. By the time the Illinoisan rejoined his forces on 17 March, Smith was fatally ill and would die on 25 April. Both Grant and the Union would miss the old hero in upcoming operations.

The army had now grown from three divisions at Donelson to six. Five divisions concentrated at Pittsburg Landing on the west bank of the Tennessee, preparing to attack the key rail junction at Corinth, Mississippi. The remaining division stayed farther north. Grant's own headquarters, too, were downriver. Immediate command at Pittsburg Landing rested with William T. Sherman, who had headed the District of Cairo during Donelson and who was now beginning decades of service and friendship with Grant.

Neither Grant nor Sherman fortified the landing. They thought primarily of attacking Corinth once Don Carlos Buell's Army of the Ohio arrived from Nashville. However, Albert Sidney Johnston's Butternuts planned to strike first. He not only reconcentrated troops from Kentucky but also summoned reinforcements from the Gulf coast and Arkansas. Without awaiting the Trans-Mississippi column, Johnston attacked on 6 April. Desperate fighting drove Union troops from their camps back toward the Tennessee River. Grant arrived during the battle to help rally his men. Equally important was the arrival of Buell's vanguard. The next day, Grant led the combined armies counterattacking. The exhausted Confederates eventually withdrew to Corinth, leaving Grant holding the field.

This battle of Shiloh was the largest, bloodiest battle in American history up to then. It awoke both nations to the reality of war and to each side's commitment to its cause. Both Grant and Sherman bristled at charges of being taken by surprise. Tactically, they were not surprised. But unquestionably they were caught off guard, strategically. They so focused on their own preparations to gain yet another victory at Corinth that they did not take account of Confederate capability to concentrate and counterattack. Southern misdeployments and miscalculations, Johnston's death, Federal forces' bravery, and Grant's own determination not to flee but to fight back and to counterattack on 7 April, all cost Graycoats, but to their great gamble, and enabled Yankees to claim at least limited success. In reflecting upon the battle decades later, Grant wrote that "The Confederates fought with courage at Shiloh. . . . The troops on both sides were American, and united they need not fear any foreign foe. It is possible that the Southern man started in with a little more dash than his Northern brother; but he was correspondingly less enduring."

Halleck reached Pittsburg Landing on 11 April and assumed direct command of the "gray group" threatening Corinth (Army of the Ohio, Army of the Tennessee, and soon John Pope's Army of the Mississippi). Grant became second-in-command, an office without responsibility, and his beloved Army of the Tennessee passed to George H. Thomas—a change perhaps explaining Grant's enduring resentment of Thomas. Grant played virtually no role in Halleck's sluggish campaign that finally occupied Corinth on 30 May. That figurehead status proved so galling that Grant considered taking prolonged leave just to get away. Fortunately for the Union, Sherman and Halleck persuaded him to remain.

Grant's situation improved over the summer as Halleck and Pope went to Washington and as Buell advanced against Chattanooga, taking Thomas with him. Three of Pope's divisions joined Buell by early autumn. Pope's other two divisions under William S. Rosecrans remained with Grant, who resumed direct command of his District of West Tennessee. Grant's mission was defensive: guarding Federal conquests of the past twelve months, from Paducah and Columbus to Corinth and Memphis. When Sterling Price's Butternuts passed through the region toward Middle Tennessee, Grant struck them at Iuka, but they repulsed Rosecrans and escaped on 19 September. Two weeks later, Price and Earl Van Dorn pounced on Rosecrans at Corinth. The Yankees saved the city, but the secessionists eluded Grant's efforts to intercept their retreat.

Standing on the defensive would never conquer the Confederacy and risked losing earlier gains. In autumn, Federal armies from Virginia to Missouri resumed advancing. Grant's mission was to move southward along the Mississippi Central Railroad against Jackson,

Grant (*standing over bench, left*) examines a map held by General George Meade. Massaponax Church, Virginia, 21 May 1864. (Photograph by Timothy O'Sullivan / *Library of Congress*)

thence westward against Vicksburg. His command was designated the Department of the Tennessee on 16 October, and eight days later it was named the XIII Corps. Calling an army of ten divisions one corps was incongruous. The addition of four more divisions in December made that appellation even more inept. On 18 December, the War Department ordered the Army of the Tennessee divided into the XIII, XV, XVI, and XVII Corps. Two divisions each from Arkansas, Missouri, and Kentucky joined Grant in 1863. At the height of the Vicksburg campaign, his field army contained sixteen divisions, and six other divisions served elsewhere in his department.

Such force increases reflected the growing success of Grant's Vicksburg campaign. Those operations, however, began badly. The farther he penetrated along the Mississippi Central Railroad, the more vulnerable his supply line became. When Van Dorn's and Bedford Forrest's cavalry cut those communications in December, Grant had to abandon his overland campaign and withdraw to Memphis. In so doing, he learned to live off the land, without formal supply lines and depots. He would use that experience well in later operations against Vicksburg.

Sherman's repulse at Chickasaw Bayou, 27–29 December, and the advent of Grant's former subordi-

nate and enduring rival John A. McClernand to command the drive down the Mississippi led Grant himself to take charge of all forces on both banks of that river, including McClernand's. Grant spent early 1863 in four fruitless attempts to reach firm ground east of Vicksburg. Finally, in mid-April, the U.S. Navy, with which Grant always maintained effective cooperation, ran the Vicksburg batteries. His army then marched down the Louisiana side of the river, and on 30 April, the navy began ferrying the forces to the left bank. "When this was effected," Grant later recalled, "I felt a degree of relief scarcely ever equaled since. . . . I was on dry ground on the same side of the river with the enemy. All the campaigns, labors, hardships and exposures from the month of December previous to this time that had been made and endured, were for the accomplishment of this one object."

On dry ground at last, Grant then conducted one of the most brilliant strategic campaigns in American military history. First, he defeated local Butternut defenders at Port Gibson on 1 May. Then he turned east and dispersed Confederate reinforcements gathering near Jackson on 12–14 May. Next, he struck back westward, routing the main Southern army on 16–17 May, and drove it into Vicksburg. His two assaults failed on 19 and 22 May, but he relentlessly besieged the city, while providing Sherman sufficient force to counter Confederates reassembling at Jackson. On 4 July, Vicksburg's army of four divisions surrendered. Five days later, the last Secessionist position on the Mississippi also capitulated. As President Lincoln said, "The Father of Waters again goes unvexed to the sea." Achieving this great result, so vital to Midwesterners and so crippling to Southerners, brought Grant promotion to major general in the Regular Army, ranking from 4 July, and assured his place in American history.

Sherman then chased away the small Confederate army in Jackson. Grant wanted to attack Mobile promptly, but General-in-Chief Halleck again scattered the large army, just as after Corinth. Seven divisions were diverted to Kentucky, Arkansas, and West Louisiana, and Grant's remaining forces went on the defensive. The general himself recuperated from a severe injury while visiting New Orleans.

Grant did not long remain idle. He already ranked as the most successful Federal general of the war. Washington again turned to him after disaster struck Rosecrans's army at Chickamauga on 19–20 September. On 18 October, Grant was assigned to command the new Military Division of the Mississippi, embracing the entire Western theater from the Appalachians to the Mississippi. He promptly removed his rival Rosecrans and then concentrated on relieving besieged Chattanooga. Four divisions from his own army, now under Sherman, and four divisions from Virginia under

Joseph Hooker reinforced Thomas's beleaguered Army of the Cumberland. Hooker promptly opened better supply routes into the city. In late November, Grant broke out at Orchard Knob, Lookout Mountain, and Missionary Ridge, sending the routed Secessionists streaming into Georgia. He then dispatched Sherman to relieve the Army of the Ohio in Knoxville, saving that city, too.

Henry, Donelson, Shiloh, Corinth, Vicksburg, now Chattanooga and Knoxville—everywhere Grant had gained tactical success, usually accompanied by profound strategic success which secured federal conquests, dealt devastating blows to the Confederacy, and netted many Southern prisoners. No Butternut army or general in the West could withstand him. Only one Confederate army and general continued enjoying success. Grant had earned the right to challenge that army and that commander. On 10 March 1864, he was promoted to general-in-chief of all federal armies with the rank of lieutenant general (dating from 2 March), the first American officer holding that grade since George Washington in 1798–1799. Unlike Halleck, Grant would not make this a desk job. Unlike Sherman, Grant would not insist on remaining in the West. The Illinoisan understood his place and his mission: the Eastern theater with his "headquarters, armies in the field," fighting to the death with General Robert E. Lee and the Army of Northern Virginia.

To attack Lee and the Confederate power center, Virginia, Grant developed a dual approach. Grand strategically, he concerted all Union armies to strike simultaneously. "There were...seventeen distinct [Yankee] commanders," Grant later wrote. "Before this time these various armies had acted separately and independently of each other, giving the enemy an opportunity often of depleting one command, not pressed, to reinforce another more actively engaged. I determined to stop this. To this end I regarded the Army of the Potomac as the centre, and all west to Memphis...the right wing; the Army of the James...as the left wing, and all the troops south, as a force in rear of the enemy.... My general plan now was to concentrate all the force possible against the Confederate armies in the field. . . . Accordingly, I arranged for a simultaneous movement all along the line [in early May]."

His keen perception of all federal forces as one concerted grand army finally allowed the North to bring its manpower and materiel superiority to bear. This approach, moreover, threatened all Graycoat armies east of the Mississippi, thus allowing none to reinforce another more endangered. Most significantly as events actually developed, Grant's grand strategy undercut the Virginia powerbase by devouring the rest of the Confederacy, on which the Old Dominion depended for manpower and supplies.

Yet Grant also determined to defeat Lee directly. The

Illinoisan became an "army group" commander in central Virginia, initially coordinating George G. Meade's Army of the Potomac and Ambrose E. Burnside's IX Corps and after mid-June Meade's army and Benjamin F. Butler's Army of the James (later Edward Ord's). Grant left grand tactics and minor tactics to his army and corps commanders. The lieutenant general concentrated on theater and front strategy. Whether to strike, when to attack, where to advance, who to command, how to allocate forces among sectors and fronts and theaters, and which reinforcements to obtain—these were the elements of strategic leadership which he exercised.

Right away, his deep understanding of logistics, founded in Mexico and forged in Mississippi, led him to abandon the vulnerable Orange & Alexandria Railroad, along which Pope and Meade had suffered setbacks. He instead advanced by his strategic left flank so as to draw supplies along Virginia's tidal rivers, from the Potomac to the James, invulnerable supply lines which the Secessionists could never sever.

To use such lines of communications, Grant risked entering the tangled Wilderness of Spotsylvania. He hoped to hurry through there and battle Lee in more open country farther south. Grant felt confident of battering the Butternuts badly enough that they could not keep the field but would have to retreat into Richmond, where he hoped to capture them as he had bagged two other armies in Donelson and Vicksburg.

Now as always, however, Lee fought back. The great Virginian struck the Yankees in the Wilderness, where terrain offset manpower and artillery preponderance. Massive attacks and counterattacks, 5–6 May, proved bloody but inconclusive. Clearly, the opening battle did not bring Grant the expected victory. After such a mauling, all his predecessors against Lee withdrew and rested for months. The Illinoisan paused only one day. Then he moved—not rearward but forward more deeply into Virginia. Stymied tactically, he retained the initiative strategically. He never relinquished it (save for three weeks in July) until he finally destroyed the Army of Northern Virginia.

Heavy fighting erupted again at Spotsylvania during 8–19 May; the North Anna, 23–24 May; and throughout Hanover County, 27 May–3 June. On every field, Grant was checked, tactically. From every field, Grant advanced, strategically. In one month, he carried the war from central Virginia to Richmond's outskirts He thereby nullified Lee's proven strategy of protecting Richmond from afar and forced upon the Virginian the constricting imperative of his capital's close and immediate defense.

These bloody battles, from 5 May to 3 June, cost Grant perhaps 53,000 casualties. Ever since, critics called him a "butcher," heedlessly slaughtering his own men to inflict irreplaceable losses on the South. The

final futile assault at Cold Harbor on 3 June supposedly epitomizes Grant's mindless "war of attrition." In truth, Cold Harbor no more characterizes Grant than Malvern Hill typifies Lee. Both officers were far superior generals than those two battles would suggest. Grant, after all, had seen the tactical offensive succeed splendidly from Belmont to Missionary Ridge. Understandably, then, when he first came East, he applied the approach which served him so well in the West. But the East was not the West; the Army of Northern Virginia was not the Donelson garrison; and Robert E. Lee was not John B. Floyd, John C. Pemberton, or Braxton Bragg. These terrible truths Grant learned from spring's sanguinary struggles. One of his greatest strengths, not only against Vicksburg but throughout the Civil War, was his ability to perceive and apply the lessons of experience.

After 18 June, Grant never assaulted frontally a fortified position thought to be strongly defended until the final grand onslaught of 2 April 1865. Throughout the summer and autumn, his orders to Meade and Butler brimmed with explicit prohibitions against frontal attacks. The general-in-chief was far too protective of his soldiers' lives to risk them in further onslaughts.

Grant's war of attrition was never waged tactically. Rather was his war of attrition fought and won in the strategic arena. Grant deprived Lee of the strategic initiative; pinned him in place strategically; ate away at his communications and attenuated his army; and relied on Federal armies elsewhere—principally the Shenandoah Valley, Middle Tennessee, Georgia, and the Carolinas—to consume the Confederacy while he fixed Lee in Virginia. "My own opinion," Grant informed Sherman on 18 December 1864, "is that Lee is averse to going out of Virginia and if the cause of the South is lost, he wants Richmond to be the last place surrendered. If he has such views it may be well to indulge him until we get everything else in our hands."

Long before the Illinoisan so summarized his grand strategy, he shifted from above Richmond to below the James River. After resting eight days around Cold Harbor, he daringly struck across the peninsula and over the James against Petersburg, rail center for Richmond. His vanguard overran outer fortifications on 15 June, but the defenders retained Petersburg itself and its three most important railroads, repulsing the great attack of 18 June—the futile assault that persuaded Grant to prohibit further such onslaughts. The defeat of his latest effort to extend his left around the Graycoat right, on 22–23 June, moreover, made him pause to rest his weary armies.

With this pause, the mobile warfare of spring stagnated into the siege of summer. Like all of Grant's Virginia operations, the siege of Petersburg was not tactical but strategic. From his great entrenched camp east of the city and on nearby Bermuda Hundred, he launched intermittent offensives into lightly defended

and often unfortified country north of the James River and south of Petersburg. Highlights were his Fourth Offensive, 14–25 August, cutting the Weldon Railroad; his Fifth Offensive, 29 September–13 October, nearly netting Richmond; and his Seventh Offensive, 5–7 February, extending his left flank southwestward to Hatcher's Run. From July's Third Offensive to October's Sixth Offensive, the timing of his two-pronged strikes north and south of the James evolved from sequential to simultaneous blows. The Sixth Offensive's total failure, 27–28 October, taught Grant a more fundamental lesson. He thereafter relied on massive first strikes with his left wing: the strategy that carried him to Hatcher's Run in February and to total victory in April.

Throughout these operations against Lee, Grant continued performing his responsibilities as general-in-chief. He diverted some of his own forces to the Shenandoah Valley, first to contain and then to crush that granary's defenders. He coordinated with his friend Sherman in capturing Atlanta, marching to the sea, and driving northward through the Carolinas to threaten Lee's rear. He fumed at subordinates' tardiness in invading Alabama. And he begrudged great victories to his rivals Rosecrans and Thomas, who helped destroy the last invasions of Missouri and Tennessee late in 1864.

By spring 1865, most of Philip Sheridan's victorious valley veterans had rejoined Grant. Other Federal armies threatened Virginia from the northwest, west, and south. Grant unleashed his final offensive, 29 March. Skillful and determined as always, Lee fought back and stopped one Union drive after another. But the Northerners kept coming. Sheridan crushed Lee's last mobile reserve at Five Forks on 1 April. Even more decisively, Meade stormed outer Confederate defenses at Boisseau's House and severed the last outside railroad into Petersburg, 2 April. Overnight on 2–3 April, Lee abandoned Petersburg, James River, and Richmond itself, and desperately dashed toward North Carolina.

Grant, whose sound strategy placed many Federal forces including cavalry south of the Secessionists, blocked Lee at Jetersville. Too weak to break through, the Butternuts fled westward. Grant ripped their rear at Sayler's Creek on 6 April. First Sheridan and then Ord headed them off at Appomattox Station and Court House during 8–9 April. With Ord in his front and Meade threatening his rear, Lee was trapped. The great Confederate soldier met with Grant, 9 April 1865, and surrendered the once mighty Army of Northern Virginia. Relentless in war, Grant proved reconciling in victory and accorded the Graycoats honorable terms of surrender.

Appomattox doomed the Confederacy. Within weeks all other Southern armies surrendered or disbanded. Conscious of the war's great cost, financial as well as human, Grant promptly returned to Washington to begin downsizing the Union army. His presence in the North almost proved fatal when he was singled out as a target in the assassination plot against President Lincoln. Grant's assassin, however, lost his nerve, and the Victor of Vicksburg lived for another twenty years.

Grant's great contributions in winning the Civil War earned him promotion to full general on 25 July 1866, the first American officer to achieve four-star rank. Both political parties also sought him as presidential candidate. His increasing alienation from Andrew Johnson over Reconstruction made him more comfortable with Republicans. He was elected eighteenth president of the United States on 3 November 1868. On assuming that office on 4 March 1869, he vacated the generalcy-in-chief.

Grant was reelected on 5 November 1872, and he even considered running in 1880. During his two terms, Colorado joined the Union, and the last four "unreconstructed" ex-Confederate states—Virginia, Georgia, Texas, and Mississippi—reentered Congress. The Fifteenth Amendment became part of the Constitution. On the other turbulent frontier, the West, major victories were won over Indians (despite Little Big Horn), and the policy of putting tribes on reservations began. Internationally, the *Alabama* Claims, concerning commerce raiding in the Civil War, were arbitrated in America's favor. Yet his administration was rocked with scandals. His Reconstruction policies, moreover, proved alternately repressive or conciliatory but ultimately ineffective. And the Panic of 1873 caused a major financial downturn throughout his second term. On balance, Grant is not regarded as a great or even successful president.

His subsequent career as financier proved disastrous because of dishonesty by those he trusted. His one final success came in writing *The Personal Memoirs of U.S. Grant*, one of the great autobiographies in American history, made all the more memorable because he wrote it with death imminent. Ulysses S. Grant died of cancer at Mount McGregor, New York, 23 July 1885. He is buried in Grant's Tomb in New York City. The magnificence of the mausoleum and the memorability of the memoir continue to attract attention—not, however, because of Grant the president but because of Grant the general.

U. S. Grant was the quintessential U.S. general of the nineteenth century. Neither soldier-king nor military genius, he was fundamentally a citizen of the republic who, with millions of other Americans, offered to serve his country in time of crisis. In 1861, he emerged from the obscurity of a small mining town. During the next four years, he led Federal forces to victory. Had he, like Lincoln, been assassinated on 14 April 1865, history would forever honor the greatness and lament the loss of further accomplishments of those two citizens from Illinois.

What elevated Grant above the millions of other

soldiers and enabled him to achieve so much was only partially his military background. Unquestionably, his Mexican War experience on the battlefield and as supply officer benefited him in the Civil War. His West Point education cannot have hurt, but that undergraduate institution marked the extent of his schooling. In the mid-nineteenth century, the American military profession was still maturing and had yet to develop the advanced officer education system which highlighted the armed forces from the 1880s onward. Nor did Grant observe foreign wars, visit foreign armies, or even devote personal study to the profession of arms the way many brother officers who also became Civil War generals did.

Rather did Grant the professional soldier succeed in the sixties because of the innate qualities of Grant the man. In wartime (far more than in peacetime) he understood himself and was comfortable with himself and with exercising command. Because he knew that he was not a luminary of the Old Army, he realized that he had to apply himself all the more diligently during the Civil War in order to succeed. Far from relying on reputation or professional education—let alone, genius—Grant benefited from his especial aptitude for learning from wartime experience, particularly his own. He could perceive and apply approaches that worked and could modify or discard approaches that did not.

Searching for effective approaches, then applying or adapting them, made him responsive to new realities. His flexibility of process, moreover, excellently complemented his fixity of purpose. His unshakable resolve to press on to victory was legendary—highlighted in his campaign against Vicksburg, epitomized in his summation at Spotsylvania: "I . . . propose to fight it out on this line if it takes all summer." This resolve, like so much of Grant's generalship, operated in the strategic realm, not the tactical. The mindless massacre of Burnside's brigades at Marye's Heights was diametrically opposite to Grant's approach to warfare.

In pursuing whatever approach would produce the ultimate victory which he felt sure lay ahead, Grant did not dwell on setbacks, linger over battles at hand, or dread possible dangers. The man who never turned back never looked back but always faced forward in search of future opportunity to win battles, campaigns, the war itself. Indeed, so confident was he of eventual victory that even potential disasters (for example, Monocacy) which many Unionists regarded as calamities Grant perceived as opportunities to attack the attacking Southerners.

Such certainty of success strengthened Grant in adversity and inspired him to victory. Hooker's hollow boasting or Sheridan's appalling arrogance had no counterpart in Grant's character. Rather was his certainty grounded in calm, quiet, self-assured confidence that he could do the job. "Our work progresses here slowly, and I feel will progress securely until Richmond finally falls," he wrote Julia as the Petersburg siege began; "the task is a big one and has to be performed by some one." Month after month, the siege continued. That Christmas eve, he wrote her, "I know how much there is dependent on me and will prove myself equal to the task. I believe determination can do a great deal to sustain one, and I have that quality certainly to its fullest extent!"

Grant's self-assurance, willingness to look forward, and moral courage in combining flexibility of method with fixity of purpose understandably manifested themselves in onward movement. Grand strategically, strategically, grand tactically, and tactically, he carried the conflict to the Confederates. Maintaining the initiative offensively enabled him to control the course of operations, dominate the strategic and tactical domains, and compel the Secessionists to react to him. This approach he summarized in recounting his first (overland) drive against Vicksburg: "My entire command was no more than was necessary to hold these [extended supply] lines, and hardly that if kept on the defensive. By moving against the enemy and into his unsubdued, or not yet captured, territory, driving their army before us, these lines would nearly hold themselves; thus affording a large [Federal] force for field operations."

His broadening responsibilities, moreover, enabled him to bring increased force to bear against the Confederacy. His grasp of grand strategy caused him to concert the armed might of the Union. His understanding of logistics led him to keep his forces well supplied. Throughout the Civil War, the North enjoyed vast preponderance of manpower and materiel. One of Grant's greatest strengths, which elevated him above other Yankee generals, was his ability to convert these potential advantages into positive achievements.

He was, furthermore, permitted to apply his strengths, approaches, and self-confidence because he understood that his national enemy was centered in Richmond, not Washington. Like Lee and unlike McClellan, Rosecrans, P. G. T. Beauregard, Joseph E. Johnston, and other talented generals on both sides, Grant recognized that in a wartime republic, the president is never a meddler. The president has the right to involve himself in national strategy and the conduct of war. Great generals like Grant and Lee worked with their respective presidents instead of fighting them. Grant earned Lincoln's trust while first serving in the West; he kept that confidence after coming east. By making clear he welcomed the president's involvement, Grant was actually accorded greater latitude to apply his abilities than were generals whose resistance provoked their presidents to rein them in. Indeed, the effective working relationship between Lincoln and Grant (and the comparable relationship between Jefferson Davis and Lee) exemplifies how a constitutional commander-in-chief and a uniformed general-in-chief should work together in wartime.

Grant's command relations with his brother officers were more mixed. Here his great sense of loyalty and his fixity of determination sometimes served him and the Union well but not always. In some cases, he recognized able officers and advanced them to increasingly more responsible positions, such as Sherman, Sheridan, Ord, Steele, James B. McPherson, James H. Wilson, George Crook, and Chief of Staff John A. Rawlins. He also shunted aside more marginal generals: McClernand, Stephen A. Hurlbut, and Charles S. Hamilton. Less laudably, however, Grant sidetracked some sound soldiers who crossed him or apparently rivaled him: Rosecrans, Thomas, and Gordon Granger. Only Lew Wallace managed to fall from Grant's grace and then restore himself during the war. Then, too, Grant continued according undeserved admiration to such officers as David Hunter and Franklin long after their wartime record made clear they were not living up to prewar reputations. Even for generals whom he respected, such as Meade, he sometimes showed unintentional insensitivity that bruised that highly competent but high-strung commander. This decidedly mixed record with subordinates and staff presaged the poor personnel selections scarring his presidency.

Nor was Grant a great leader of men. Qualities which bonded other commanders to their soldiers—Lee's awe-inspiring nobility, McClellan's captivating magnetism, Sheridan's rousing electricity—were lacking in the general from Galena. Grant never inspired his soldiers to love him, and only on great occasions did they cheer him, certainly not every time he passed marching columns. But neither did they hate him as they hated Buell, Charles Gilbert, or Irvin McDowell. And in his own quiet way he loved them: not in the hot, effusive, shouting love of parades and rallying cries but in a calm, dedicated determination to provide for them, to care for them, to uphold their rights when captured even after military necessity made him cancel prisoner exchanges, to use them in battle when necessary but never to squander their lives needlessly. "Grant the Butcher" was far too devoted to his soldiers ever to risk their lives without good cause.

Yet his war of attrition unquestionably took its toll. Although he waged that war strategically against the Army of Northern Virginia and the Confederacy, the severe fighting, 5 May–18 June 1864, inflicted heavy losses on both sides tactically. Such casualties were not just quantitative but qualitative, often claiming the best officers and the bravest soldiers. Some returned to duty; all too many were killed, captured, or wounded out. Those losses dulled the fighting edge of his forces and impeded his ability to shorten the war.

His willingness to incur such casualties in order to help produce victory was both a weakness and a strength in his generalship. His aforementioned mixed record in dealing with fellow officers also dimmed the luster of his leadership. Grant would readily acknowledge that he was not a perfect general, any more than that he was a perfect person. Yet, on balance, his many strengths as a commander, which derived largely from his many strengths of character, accomplished great results that were central to Federal victory. These achievements mark Ulysses S. Grant as the greatest general of the Northern army and one of the great generals of American military history.

—*Richard J. Sommers*

See also Appomattox Court House; Belmont; Chattanooga Campaign; Fort Donelson, Battle of; Fort Henry, Battle of; Lincoln, Abraham; Meade, George Gordon; Petersburg Campaign; Rawlins, John Aaron; Richmond Campaign; Sherman, William Tecumseh; Shiloh, Battle of; Vicksburg Campaign.

For further reading:
Catton, Bruce. *Grant Moves South* (1960).
———. *Grant Takes Command* (1968).
Grant, Ulysses S. *The Papers of Ulysses S. Grant* (1967–2000).
———. *Personal Memoirs of U.S. Grant* (1885).
Perret, Geoffrey. *Ulysses S. Grant: Soldier & President* (1997).
Simpson, Brooks D. *Ulysses S. Grant: Triumph over Adversity, 1822–1865* (2000).

GRATIOT STREET AND MYRTLE STREET FEDERAL MILITARY PRISONS (ST. LOUIS)

Missouri's divided loyalties and its proximity to areas of active military engagement demanded the creation of prison facilities in St. Louis within the early months of the war. At first Union authorities confined prisoners in the Federal arsenal in the city. The growing demand for prison space necessitated the opening of St. Louis' first structure designated specifically as a military prison in September 1861, on Myrtle and Fifth Streets. A slave auction house before the war, the Myrtle Street Prison quickly proved insufficient for its new function as its population swelled to 150 (50 percent above its expected capacity).

In December 1861 Union authorities converted a prewar medical college a few blocks away on Gratiot Street into a prison to hold up to 500 additional captives. The Gratiot Street Prison also suffered overcrowding, holding 1,800 prisoners at one point. In 1863 authorities devised a plan to maintain an average of 140 prisoners in the Myrtle Street Prison and 650 in the Gratiot Street Prison. Both held captured soldiers and political prisoners, including some women. In addition to these two facilities, several other smaller structures in St. Louis served temporarily as prisons during the war.

—*Thomas F. Curran*

See also Alton Federal Military Prison; Andersonville; Belle Isle; Camp Chase; Camp Douglas, Illinois; Camp Morton;

Elmira Prison; Fort Delaware; Fort Warren, Massachusetts; Johnson's Island; Libby Prison; Old Capitol Prison; Prisoner Exchanges; Prisoner Paroles; Prisoners of War; Prisons, Confederate; Prisons, Union; Rock Island Prison; Salisbury Prison.

For further reading

Frost, Griffin. *Camp and Prison Journal* (1994).

Hesseltine, William B.. ed. *Civil War Prisons: A Study in War Psychology* (1930; reprint, 1998).

———. "Military Prisons of St. Louis, 1861–1865." *Missouri Historical Review* (1929).

Speer, Lonnie R. *Portals to Hell: Military Prisons of the Civil War* (1997).

GRAY, HENRY
(1816–1892)
Confederate general

Henry Gray was born on 19 January 1816 in Laurens District, South Carolina. In 1834 he graduated from South Carolina College and began a career in law. In 1840 Gray moved to Winston County, Mississippi, where he worked as district attorney. He served one term in the state legislature and in 1848 lost an election bid for Congress. In 1851 Gray moved to Bienville Parish, Louisiana, where he established a reputation as an outstanding criminal attorney. He served in the Louisiana legislature and in 1856 was an elector for presidential nominee James Buchanan. Gray espoused strong secessionist views and in the 1859 senatorial race suffered a narrow defeat in an attempt to unseat Judah Benjamin.

Before the outbreak of war, Gray enlisted as a private in a Mississippi unit. Jefferson Davis, Gray's friend from his earlier years in Mississippi, made a personal appeal for him to raise a regiment in Louisiana. Gray returned to organize the 28th Louisiana Infantry, and on 17 May 1862 the regiment elected him colonel. Designated as Gray's 28th, they saw action exclusively in the Trans-Mississippi theater and became one of General Richard Taylor's most reliable regiments. Gray first saw action in spring 1863 during the Bayou Teche campaign. After the battle of Irish Bend (14 April), during which Gray suffered a minor wound, Taylor reported that the regiment fought like seasoned veterans and placed Gray in command of the Louisiana brigade.

During the Red River campaign of 1864, the Louisiana brigade served in Jean Jacques Alfred Mouton's division and played a crucial role at the battle of Mansfield on 8 April. Gray's brigade sustained the battle's heaviest losses with the Consolidated Crescent regiment losing 200 men. After the battle of Pleasant Hill on 9 April, Taylor recommended Gray for promotion to brigadier. Edmund Kirby Smith, however, refused to promote Gray, noting in his official report that Gray's "habits are not good." Smith may have been concerned about Gray's dislike of military trappings. A Louisianan

noted that the only thing Gray hated more than a Yankee was a new uniform. More likely, however, Smith resented Gray's criticism of his strategy and may have suspected that Gray played a role in bringing on a battle at Mansfield against orders. Smith later reversed himself, however, and approved Gray's promotion. In October 1864, Gray was nominated to run in a special election called by Louisiana's governor to fill a vacant congressional seat. The election also served as a public referendum on Smith's policies in Louisiana. Gray won a lopsided victory over the pro-Smith candidate.

During his term in the Confederate Congress, Gray addressed complaints of graft leveled against Smith's department. He supported a commission to investigate charges against Smith and was instrumental in the passage of a law designed to curb Smith's authority. Gray was also critical of peace negotiations and opposed extensions of presidential powers.

After the war, Gray served briefly in the Louisiana senate before retiring from public service. He reportedly sank into a deep depression after the death of his son and his wife. Gray lived his remaining years as a recluse. He died on 11 December 1892 at his daughter's home in Coushatta, Louisiana, and was buried at the Springville Cemetery.

—*Jeffery S. Prushankin*

See also Congress, C.S.A.; Irish Bend; Mansfield, Battle of; Pleasant Hill, Battle of; Red River Campaign.
For further reading:

Bergeron, Arthur W. Jr., ed. *Reminiscences of Uncle Silas: A History of the Eighteenth Louisiana Infantry Regiment* (1981).

Jones, Terry L. "The 28th Louisiana Volunteers in the Civil War." *North Louisiana Historical Association Journal* (1978).

Warner, Ezra J., and W. Buck Yearns. *Biographical Register of the Confederate Congress* (1975).

GREAT BRITAIN

The secession of the Southern states and the ensuing war took the British by surprise. Both the British government and the general public had become accustomed to the bickering that took place between the North and the South during the 1850s. Indeed, the press referred to it as the "American difficulty." Throughout the war, the tide of British public opinion was determined more by events in America than by innate support for one side or the other. This wavering occurred because many Britons saw no great principles at stake in the American fighting. Those Britons long active in the abolition movement remained suspicious of Northern propaganda that the war would bring an end to slavery, even after the issuance of the Emancipation Proclamation.

Among the working classes was genuine favoritism for the Confederacy. The Irish especially supported the South because of Northern efforts to recruit Irishmen to

serve in the Union army. In England many working men regarded Southerners as a subjugated people attempting to break the yoke of their oppression. These pro-Southern attitudes were shaped both by labor leaders and by labor newspapers. T. J. Dunning, secretary of the Bookbinder's Union, and George Patton, manager of the London *Bee-Hive*, openly announced their sympathy for the South. The *Bee-Hive* expressed little regard for the slave and expounded on the inferior status of blacks in general. Other labor newspapers that made no secret of their pro-Confederate sympathy included the *Reynolds News*, controlled by the Board of Workingmen; the *British Miner*; the Manchester *Weekly Budget*; and in Scotland, the *Glasgow Gazette*.

British upper classes tended to be pro-Southern because of their disdain for democracy. While many upper-class Britons were active in the nineteenth-century abolition movement, they appeared to have little concern that a Southern victory might prolong slavery and retain a Southern aristocracy in power. Some of the leading abolitionists (for example, Samuel Wilberforce, bishop of Oxford and son of the well-known abolitionist William Wilberforce), believed that slavery was doomed even if the South won its independence. They regarded the war as a Southern struggle for self-determination instead of a fight to retain slavery.

Support for the North was strong among the leading members of the Conservative Party, which was out of power and did not control the government during the war. Nevertheless, Conservative leaders advocated a policy of neutrality and opposed any attempt to offer mediation, claiming that it would be an insult to the North and only prolong the war. Among these leaders were Lord Derby, Lord Stanley, Benjamin Disraeli, and Lord Malmesbury. They voiced their approval of the British proclamation of belligerency early in the war and acted to restrain party members Seymour Fitzgerald and Lord Salisbury when they urged mediation.

For members of the British cabinet events in Europe were of more immediate concern then the American Civil War. From the beginning of the fighting, Prime Minister Henry Palmerston urged a policy of neutrality out of fear about Napoleon III's European aspirations and Bismarck's activities in Germany, and because of his own dislike of slavery. Within the cabinet the most consistent supporter of the South was William Gladstone, chancellor of the exchequer. He even delivered an address at Newcastle in October 1862 that implied that the cabinet was on the verge of extending diplomatic recognition to the Confederacy. Foreign Minister John Russell's sentiments wavered between the North and South, but he did support the idea of mediation in 1862. It was the opposition of George C. Lewis, secretary of war, that helped persuade the cabinet to postpone such an offer. Lewis opposed becoming involved in the conflict out of concern for its impact on future British-American relations and fear that the war could spread beyond its American limits.

British responses to issues arising from the war were dictated by that nation's own past policies and national interests. Despite pressure from pro-Confederate Britons and Confederate agents to break the Union blockade, the British government failed to act even in the early stages of the war when the blockade was ineffective. This failure stemmed partly from the desire to remain neutral but also from the fact that Britain had long insisted that neutrals observe her blockades, whether enforced or not. During the years preceding the War of 1812, American shippers had refused to observe Britain's "paper" blockades of Napoleonic Europe and the issue became a major point of contention between the two nations. If Britain now broke the Union blockade, ineffective as it might be, she would, in effect, be sustaining the earlier American position.

Britain also had a longstanding policy of noninterference in the internal affairs of other nations. Indeed, concern about becoming involved in the internal affairs of European nations caused the British government to withdraw from the Quadruple Alliance of 1815, an agreement signed after the Napoleonic wars by which the signatories agreed to suppress uprisings wherever they might occur. While Britain willingly entered European wars that threatened the balance of continental power, the government had little interest in involving itself in strictly internal affairs of European countries. Aware of this fact, American secretary of state William Seward stressed again and again the internal nature of the American Civil War.

The *Trent* Affair was the first major Civil War crisis that the British confronted. In November 1861, Captain Charles Wilkes of the USS *San Jacinto* intercepted the British mail carrier *Trent* in the West Indies and removed James Mason and John Slidell who were travelling to Europe as the newly appointed Confederate agents to Britain and France. The British government immediately protested because Wilkes's action was a violation of international law. Under its terms persons could be regarded as contraband of war, but such decisions were to be made by prize courts and not by individual commanders. When news of the incident arrived in England, the government immediately demanded that the United States release Mason and Slidell and apologize for removing the Confederates. In anticipation of a refusal, it also ordered the Admiralty to rush preparations for war, dispatched 8,000 troops for the defense of Canada, and temporarily prohibited the further export of arms and ammunition. While members of the cabinet seemed inclined to take a hard line, other political leaders called for caution. Benjamin Disraeli urged the cabinet to assume a "generous interpretation" of Wilkes's action, while Prince Albert's rewording of the diplomatic dispatch to American officials allowed them to accede to British demands with good grace. Faced with the rightness of the British position, the Lincoln government agreed to release Mason and Slidell, despite the public approval of Wilkes's actions. About two months after their capture, Mason and Slidell were quietly transferred from an American to a British warship off the New England coast.

If Britain's position was correct in the *Trent* Affair, it was less defensible in her actions regarding Confederate Raiders and Laird Rams. Confederate agents contracted for the building of the raiders, ostensibly as merchant ships, from British shipbuilders. Upon completion, the ships were taken to the Azores or the West Indies and outfitted with Confederate crews and armaments. They then sailed the high seas attacking American merchant vessels and wreaking havoc on American shipping. Among the better known raiders were the *Alabama*, the *Florida*, and the *Shenandoah*. Although the British government was not responsible for the building or launching of the raiders, it was slow to act when Charles Francis Adams, the American minister, protested. As a result, Confederate agents next placed an order for a gunboat, the *Alexandra*. This time the government seized the ship but was forced to release it when the courts ruled that as long as the ship was not equipped in British waters there was no law that prevented British citizens from building and selling warships to belligerents.

The situation became more acute when Confederate agents contracted with the Laird shipyard to build several ironclad rams. The design of the ships left little doubt that they were destined to become blockade breakers. In addition to their speed and iron plating, each ship was to have a seven-foot iron prong added to the bow to enable it to ram Union blockaders. Despite Adams's protest, Lord Russell maintained that the court decision in the *Alexandra* case prevented it from seizing the ships. Worried, however, that its decision might lead to war with the United States and also set a precedent for future enemies to order warships from neutrals that could then be used against Britain, the cabinet decided to retain the rams and later in October 1863 seized them. In 1871 Great Britain paid the United States $15,500,000 for damages done by Confederate raiders.

An ongoing problem with both the Union and Confederate governments involved intervening on behalf of British citizens affected by the conflict. In the early months of the war, this group included Britons in the United States whose activities aroused suspicion or ships' captains who sailed into Southern ports despite Lincoln's declaration of 19 April 1861 blockading the entire Confederate coast. Such individuals were usually sent either to Fort Warren in Boston or Fort Lafayette in New York. From there they appealed to the British consuls in those cities or to the British embassy in Washington, D.C. Secretary Seward, whose office was in charge of dealing with these cases, developed a lenient policy to avoid conflict with the British government. Depending upon the severity of the charges, most British prisoners were released within three days to five months on the promise that they would refrain from further activities that might benefit the Confederacy.

When Great Britain declared its neutrality in the early months of the war, it also invoked the Foreign Enlistment Act of 1819, which forbade its citizens from taking part in wars between other nations. British citizens living in the Union states used this act to claim exemption from military service. Their refusal to serve caused extreme tension in a number of states west of Ohio because these states allowed foreigners to vote if they had lived in the state for one year and had declared their intention to become American citizens. Officials in those states argued that individuals given the rights of citizenship should be willing to undertake its obligations. In London, Foreign Secretary Russell voiced his disapproval of this interpretation and insisted that British citizens in the United States should not be required to violate British law. Lincoln solved the problem in May 1863 by issuing a proclamation requiring all foreigners who had declared their intention to become American citizens, but then refused to serve in the military to leave the country in sixty-five days or face the possibility of military service. Harsh as the proclamation may seem, it satisfied Russell who claimed, "the period of sixty-five days is a reasonable period."

The problem of foreign enlistments continued in the North because of the activities of "bounty brokers." Using liquor or unscrupulous devices, bounty brokers encouraged men to enlist and took all or the greater part of their bounty. They especially preyed upon immigrants in eastern port cities because the bounties were higher in those states. Following the passage of the Contract Labor Law in 1864, which allowed the importation of immigrants as laborers, a few plots were hatched to bring large numbers of Irishmen to America by offering jobs, but really to force them to enlist once they arrived in the country and also to take their bounty. Complaints from both the British embassy and the Foreign Office finally caused Congress to pass an act declaring that any individual who forcibly or fraudulently enlisted another person in the military service could, if found guilty, be fined $1,000 and imprisoned for two years.

Impressment problems were also widespread in the Confederacy. Because the British government did not have formal diplomatic relations with the Confederate government, most impressment problems were handled by British consuls located in Richmond, Charleston,

Savannah, and Mobile. The smaller number of men of military age in the South also exacerbated the problem. British citizens complained of physical punishment, mental intimidation, and attempts at starvation when they refused to enlist in the Confederate army. Although the Confederate government declared that military service could not be required of immigrants, enrolling officers who had to meet quotas took little notice of this restriction. Following the defeats at Vicksburg and Gettysburg in 1863, pressure on foreigners to enlist became more intense and complaints from the consuls more numerous. Exasperated by quarrels between Southern governors, who demanded the right to enlist foreigners, and the consuls, who insisted that such enlistments violated a man's rights, Confederate secretary of state Judah P. Benjamin in October 1863 expelled the British consuls and ordered them to leave the country. Subsequent efforts by the British Foreign Office to deal with the impressment issue were spurned by the Southern government, with the result that when the Confederacy made a last ditch effort to secure diplomatic recognition from Great Britain in 1865, the Foreign Office refused to consider the offer.

—*Eugene H. Berwanger*

See also Adams, Charles Francis; *Alabama*, CSS; Albert, Prince; Blockade of the C.S.A.; *Florida*, CSS; Mason, James M.; *Shenandoah*, CSS; Slidell, John; *Trent* Affair; Wilkes, Charles.

For further reading:
Bauer, Kinley. "Slavery in Diplomacy of the American Civil War." *Pacific Historical Review* (1977).
Beloff, Max. "Great Britain and the American Civil War." *History* (1952).
Berwanger, Eugene H. *The British Foreign Service and the American Civil War* (1994).
Crook, D. P. *The North, the South, and the Powers, 1861–1865* (1974).
Gwin, Stanford. "The Campaign of John Bright Against English Recognition of the Confederacy." *Southwestern Speech Communications Journal* (1984).
Harrison, Royden. "British Labor and the Confederacy." *International Review of Social History* (1957).
Hermon, Joseph. "British Sympathies in the American Civil War." *Journal of Southern History* (1967).
Jones, Wilbur. "British Conservatives and the American Civil War." *American Historical Review* (1953).
Larimer, Douglas. "The Role of Anti-Slavery Sentiment in British Reaction to the Civil War." *Historical Journal* (1976).
Merli, Frank. "The British Cabinet and the Confederacy." *Maryland Historical Magazine* (1970).
Neely, Mark. *The Fate of Liberty: Abraham Lincoln and Civil Liberties* (1991).
Pelzer, John. "Liverpool and the American Civil War." *History Today* (1990).
Reid, Robert. "Gladstone's Insincere Neutrality during the American Civil War." *Civil War History* (1969).
Whitridge, Arnold. "British Liberals and the American Civil War." *History Today* (1962).
Zorn, Roman. "John Bright and British Attitudes to the American Civil War." *Mid-America* (1956).

GREELEY, HORACE
(1811–1872)
Newspaper editor

Born into an impoverished New Hampshire farm family, Horace Greeley ended his formal schooling at age fourteen. In 1826 he was apprenticed to a newspaper printer in a small Vermont village. Five years later, he arrived in New York City with rustic ways, a few dollars, and enough journalistic skill to land a series of printing jobs. In 1838 Greeley joined forces with the leaders of New York's Whig Party, Thurlow Weed and William Seward, who financed a weekly newspaper endorsing the party's candidates and causes. The three formed a political alliance that lasted until 1854, when it became clear to Greeley that his partners would not support his political ambitions.

In April 1841, Greeley launched the New York *Tribune* as the first Whig daily newspaper in New York City. In the next decade, Greeley developed the paper into an influential shaper of Northern opinion. His stellar staff included former Brook Farm members Charles A. Dana and George Ripley as well as literary lights Margaret Fuller and Bayard Taylor. Despite the diverse talents of its staff, the *Tribune* was unmistakably stamped with Greeley's personality, and its pages reflected his interests and causes. Over the years, Greeley crusaded against slavery, land monopoly, alcohol abuse, and capital punishment while supporting westward expansion, the labor movement, Fourierist socialism, women's rights, and vegetarianism. The disheveled, white-haired editor, moralizing in a whiny voice, became a revered figure to reform-minded members of the North's working and middle classes, for whom the *Tribune* served as a political Bible. In the 1850s Greeley was a popular lyceum lecturer, and the *Tribune* became the most widely read newspaper in the United States.

Under Greeley's leadership the *Tribune* took a consistently strong antislavery stand, supporting the Wilmot Proviso and admission of California as a free state and opposing the Fugitive Slave Law, the Kansas-Nebraska Act, and the *Dred Scott* decision. When the Whig Party dissolved in 1854, Greeley helped to organize the Republican coalition. The *Tribune's* editor worked hard to transfer the Whig economic program of high tariffs, internal improvements, and sound currency onto the Republican platform. The Homestead Act of 1862, based on a bill that Greeley had introduced during a brief stint in Congress in 1848–1849, exemplified his faith in opportunity for the common citizen as well as his long-held antislavery principles.

When the sectional struggle headed toward civil war, Greeley proved less steady. Greeley irritated Republican leaders by vowing that the South could secede peacefully if it used democratic means, but he held fast against

Horace Greely (*National Archives*)

compromise on slavery and endorsed Lincoln's decision to hold Fort Sumter. The *Tribune* pushed the Union army to move "Forward to Richmond!," but when General Irvin McDowell's forces panicked at Bull Run, Greeley wrote in despair to the president, promising editorial support for an armistice or whatever course Lincoln favored. As the war dragged on, Greeley vacillated between advising the Union army to attack boldly and calling for a negotiated peace, his personal mood and editorial policy swinging with the pendulum of Union fortunes. In July 1864, Greeley took part in an abortive peace meeting with Confederate agents in Niagara Falls, Canada. He opposed Lincoln's renomination until September 1864, but supported the president as the war progressed toward Confederate surrender.

Greeley's campaign to end slavery was more consistent and courageous. In "The Prayer of Twenty Millions," a famous editorial of August 1862, he pressed Lincoln to have Union commanders liberate the slaves of Confederate slave owners. Greeley hailed the Emancipation Proclamation when Lincoln issued it in January 1863 and he praised the valor of African-American soldiers who fought for the Union.

During Reconstruction, Greeley took a characteristically warm-hearted and inconsistent position, combining leniency toward former Confederates with support for African-American civil rights and office-holding. When white Southerners' resistance to black equality made this stance untenable, Greeley's ardor for transforming Southern race relations cooled. Toward the end of Grant's first term, Greeley split with the Union hero over charges of corruption in his administration and vindictiveness toward former Confederates. In 1872 both Liberal Republican dissidents and the Democratic Party nominated Greeley for the presidency. This awkward coalition, together with his conciliation of the

South, brought Greeley ridicule in the Republican press, most mercilessly in the vivid cartoons of Thomas Nast. Greeley's wife died a few days before the election, in which Greeley carried only six states and 44 percent of the popular vote. The double loss broke Greeley's spirit and he died a few weeks later.

—*Carl J. Guarneri*

See also Dana, Charles Anderson; Nast, Thomas; New York *Tribune*.
For further reading:
Greeley, Horace. *Recollections of a Busy Life* (1868).
Horner, Harlan Hoyt. *Lincoln and Greeley* (1953).
Isely, Jeter Allen. *Horace Greeley and the Republican Party, 1853–1861* (1947).
Van Deusen, Glyndon G. *Horace Greeley: Nineteenth-Century Crusader* (1953).

GREEN, TOM
(1814–1864)
Confederate general

Born in southwestern Virginia, Tom Green moved at a young age with his family to middle Tennessee. Like many Southerners of his generation, Green traveled to Texas to participate in its revolution against Mexico in 1835–1836. He participated as a private of artillery in the decisive battle of San Jacinto on 21 April 1836. Green relocated permanently to Texas in 1837, settling in LaGrange. He briefly entered elected politics in 1839, but soon showed greater talent and inclination for his appointments as engrossing clerk for the Texas house of representatives and secretary of the senate. His longest held position was that of clerk of the Texas Supreme Court, a position he assumed in 1841. By all accounts, the well-read and intellectual Green was extremely popular in all these positions.

In the frequent recesses during court and legislative sessions, Green participated in many of the campaigns of the Republic of Texas. As a volunteer ranger, he rode on two successful expeditions against the Penateka Comanches. As a volunteer officer in the army of the republic, he raised mounted companies and served as a staff officer in campaigns against Mexican incursions. During the Mexican-American War, Green served as a company commander in Colonel John Coffee Hays's 1st Texas Mounted Rifles, where he served with distinction in the Monterrey campaign.

When that regiment disbanded in October 1846, Green returned to Texas and domestic pursuits. He married Mary Chalmers, the oldest daughter of a prominent Austin editor, in January 1847. Within months of the wedding, both of her parents died, prompting the couple to adopt her six siblings and raise them as well as six children of their own. Green, now responsible for a sizable family, put his energy into his twenty-year career as clerk of the supreme court, where he became a protégé of Justice John Hemphill, an outspoken advocate of states' rights.

When secession occurred in 1861, Green sprang to the call. He received appointment as a general in charge of a militia district, but left that post to assume command of the 5th Texas Mounted Volunteers in late summer 1861. Green's first campaign was with Brigadier General Henry Hopkins Sibley in New Mexico. Green earned the victory at the battle of Val Verde on 21 February 1861, but showed mediocre leadership during the rest of the campaign, and rumors began circulating that he was a boon companion of the notoriously drunk General Sibley. At the battle of Peralta on 15 April, Federal troops surprised Green's command in the midst of a fandango at a captured estate, shaking the Texans badly. By the time the 5th Texas returned to Texas at the end of the disastrous campaign, Green's reputation had clearly suffered.

Passed over for promotion, and eager to salvage his good name, Green fought the rest of the war with a vengeance. At the battle of Galveston on 1 January 1863, he made sure that his command, now designated the 5th Texas Cavalry, played a prominent role, and he received many of the laurels for the stunning victory. After reinforcing General Richard Taylor's army in Southwestern Louisiana in March 1863, Green earned a reputation as a tenacious fighter. In the Bayou Teche campaign in April, Green's rear-guard tactics led Taylor to recommend him for promotion, which the Confederate Congress confirmed.

Placed at the head of the disgraced Sibley's old brigade, Green led the 4th, 5th, and 7th Texas Cavalries in a number of ferocious battles in the summer of 1863. Most of the time, Green was the de facto commander of a small cavalry division that including the brigade of his brother-in-law, Colonel James P. Major. On 23 June, as Taylor attempted to relieve pressure on the besieged garrison of Port Hudson across the Mississippi, Green proved instrumental in the capture of Federal general Nathaniel P. Banks's depot at Brashear City, Louisiana. The Texan led a poorly coordinated assault on Fort Butler at Donaldsonville on 28 June, resulting in heavy casualties among his command. Afterward, Confederates bypassed the fort, and field artillery and sharpshooters harassed shipping on the Mississippi, temporarily interrupting Banks's communications with New Orleans. After the fall of Port Hudson on 8 July, U.S. troops moved to contain Taylor. Green soundly drubbed them at the battle of Cox's Plantation on 13 July, allowing Taylor to abandon the Bayou Lafourche country in good order with his important captures intact.

Green earned two more battlefield successes in 1863 and emerged as Taylor's most reliable—and aggressive—subordinate. On 12 September, he led his brigade, Major's brigade, and a brigade of Texas infantry under

Colonel Joseph Spaight in a well-executed ambush of a Union brigade-sized outpost at Sterling's plantation on Bayou Fordoche. When General Banks launched an offensive toward Alexandria that same month, Green's troops harassed the advance. When the Federals withdrew in November, Tom Green's Texans jumped a Union brigade at Bayou Borbeau on 2 November, leading to its destruction. After a year of active campaigning, Taylor ordered Green's command to protect the Texas coast for the winter.

Early in 1864, Green received greater responsibilities while leading his men in the decisive campaign for Louisiana. Confederate authorities promoted Green to major general, and Taylor appointed him to lead all of the cavalry in his department. In March, General Banks launched his land and riverine Red River campaign toward Shreveport, Louisiana, prompting Taylor's superior, Lieutenant General Edmund Kirby Smith, to summon all available troops to the state to aid it in the defense. Green, his old command, and an additional small division of Texas cavalry responded. The Confederates under Green skirmished actively with Union troops before joining Taylor's main body of troops just south of Mansfield. On 8 April, the Confederates turned on Banks's army and routed it. The following day, at Pleasant Hill, Louisiana, Confederate assaults against the battered Federal troops achieved nothing, but did convince Banks to retreat to safer ground. Green immediately ordered a pursuit by his mounted troops.

Green led a large part of his mounted command to the banks of the Red River, hoping to capture Union transports passing back down toward Natchitoches. While Green was coordinating an attack on the Union navy at Blair's Landing on 12 April 1864, sailors aboard the USS *Osage* fired a round of grapeshot at a conspicuous Confederate officer within easy range of their guns. One of the projectiles hit Green in the upper forehead, killing him instantly.

—*Donald S. Frazier*

See also Galveston, Texas; Red River Campaign; Sibley, Henry Hopkins; Texas; Val Verde, Battle of.
For further reading:
Faulk, Odie B. *General Tom Green: Fightin' Texan* (1963).
Frazier, Donald S. *Blood and Treasure: Confederate Empire in the Southwest* (1995).
———. *Cottonclads!: The Battle of Galveston and the Defense of the Texas Coast* (1996).

GREENBACKS

Greenbacks were federal paper currency, the printing of which largely underwrote the costs of the Civil War. The Panic of 1857, the prior reduction of federal tariffs, and the stock market panic that followed the election of 1860 left the incoming administration of Abraham Lincoln facing particularly

grim fiscal circumstances, which the administration resolved through the pragmatic approach characteristic of its government. After the first season of the fighting disabused all hopes for a speedy resolution of the conflict, the tariff revenues, even with the increase proposed by the Republicans, fell far short of what was needed to pay for the war's continuance.

Most importantly, Secretary of the Treasury Salmon P. Chase, in conjunction with the banking firm of Jay Cooke, arranged for the sale of government bonds at fixed rates of interest to the general public as well as to financial concerns. These provided $1.2 billion for the cost of the war. Some funding later came from a pioneering but only marginally implemented graduated income tax, begun in July 1862.

Although these bonds provided about two-thirds of the revenues required to prosecute the war, most of the balance came from the federal printing of paper money. In February and July 1862, the administration secured passage of Legal Tender Acts that authorized issuance of about $300 million in paper currency. Wartime greenbacks were not redeemable for "hard specie," precious metals like gold. Defined as money only by federal law, greenbacks were discussed and later denounced as "fiat money." The policy also led to the National Banking Act of 1863, which established some mechanism for the federal management of the money supply.

As with other policies of the Lincoln administration, it had both pragmatic justifications and radical implications. Governments under similarly extraordinary pressures, like the revolutionary governments in eighteenth-century America and France, had resorted to simply printing paper money. However, antebellum social theorists like Edward Kellogg and Josiah Warren had urged the sufficiency of paper notes unsupported by reserves of precious metals; they argued that money represented wealth in a broader sense, could viably represent units of confidence in the economy's future, and, most importantly in their thinking, would free the monetary supply from the banking and private interests that had controlled it.

While paper currency failed to remake society, its economic impact seems undeniable. The extent of industrial development specially fostered by the war is still hotly debated. Citing overall national indices and other sources, some scholars argue that the war only deepened a trend evident earlier. However, much of antebellum industry relied on access to cotton; while access to this commodity clearly dwindled, maintaining economic growth required really significant expansion in other industries. The availability and fluidity provided by paper currency permitted this kind of redeployment of capital.

The social impact of the policy was more mixed. For landless workers in cities, small towns, and rural areas,

wages never kept pace with the escalating cost of living. However, greenbacks also fueled a wave of wartime prosperity among farmers who, with a larger money supply, tended to find some reprieve from the seasonal debt cycle. The availability of capital freed large numbers of farmers from the cycle of debt. Wartime inflation, then, both contributed to and mediated the polarization of wealth and property ownership.

The Legal Tender Acts, along with the Emancipation Proclamation, the Homestead Act, and other measures left a powerful but somewhat contradictory legacy that seemed both to promote greater egalitarian justice and to spur development. As the latter emerged as the central concern of postwar Republican leaders, the former persisted to contest those priorities. The Grant administration later sought to stabilize banking and finance through the Resumption Act, which scheduled the 1879 replacement of greenbacks, driving Midwestern farmers—a key component of the white rural Protestant constituency of the Republicans—to launch what became the "Greenback" movement. Claiming the mantel of the wartime Republicans, they sought to repeat the success of the earlier insurgents under leaders like James B. Weaver. The Greenback parties achieved some local successes, established periodic alliances with labor, and launched a generation of political conflict culminating in the People's or Populist Party of the 1890s. The meaning of Union victory remained contested for a generation after the war.

—*Mark A. Lause*

See also Chase, Salmon Portland; Cooke, Jay; Financing, U.S.A.; Homestead Act; Labor; Legal Tender Acts; Spaulding, Elbridge Gerry; Weaver, James Baird.
For further reading:
Ritter, Gretchen. *Goldbugs and Greenbacks: The Antimonopoly Tradition and the Politics of Finance in America* (1997).
Sharkey, Robert P. *Money, Class, and Party: An Economic Study of Civil War and Reconstruction* (1959).

GREENBRIER RIVER, VIRGINIA, BATTLE OF
(3 October 1861)

In mid-September 1861, after their ill-fated Cheat Mountain expedition, the Confederate Army of the Northwest withdrew eastward to Camp Bartow on the Greenbrier River in Pocahontas County, Virginia (now West Virginia). There, on the Confederate Monterey or Alleghany Line, Brigadier General Henry Rootes Jackson and his 1,800-man garrison prepared to settle into winter quarters.

Possibly motivated by the improved weather conditions and the fact that a large portion of the Confederate army had left the region to reinforce the Army of the Kanawha, the Federal commander at Cheat Mountain,

Brigadier General Joseph J. Reynolds, determined to strike Southern forces at Camp Bartow.

The position that the 1,800 Confederates occupied at Camp Bartow was not a strong one. The Southern line extended for approximately 1 mile. The earthworks were only partially completed, with the right flank and rear particularly vulnerable. Posted on the extreme right was a cavalry detachment and units under the command of Colonel Edward Johnson. Colonel William B. Taliaferro commanded the center of the line and Colonel Albert Rust the left. Two field pieces supported the left, and five guns were ready to support the center or right flank.

At dawn on the morning of 3 October 1861, the Federal forces, numbering approximately 5,000 in all, drove in Jackson's picket outposts near the eastern foot of Cheat Mountain and pursued them toward the Confederate encampment. At about 7:00 A.M., the Union forces ran into Edward Johnson's advance guard about 1 mile west of Camp Bartow. Johnson was commanding in person, and for the next hour his small unit held the Federal column in check, stalling the advance and causing Reynolds to deploy a large portion of his force. Johnson then withdrew, regaining his own lines with little loss to his command.

At 8:00 A.M., the Federals opened their attack with a heavy and rapid artillery shelling that lasted without intermission for nearly 4 hours. The Southern guns responded, making for an artillery duel "rendered peculiarly interesting by the character of the field and its mountain surroundings." At 9:30, the Confederate left beat back a determined attack. At the same time, a Federal force ascended the wooded hill across the Greenbrier River opposite Johnson's units on the right, making contact with the Southerner's advanced positions and challenging his right flank. As soon as Jackson realized Federal intentions, he reinforced Johnson's position. "Distinctly could their officers be heard," wrote Jackson of his Union counterparts, "with words of mingled command, remonstrance, and entreaty, attempting to rally their battalions into line and to bring them to the charge; but they could not be induced to reform their broken ranks nor emerge from the cover of the woods in the direction of our fire. Rapidly and in disorder they returned into the turnpike, and soon thereafter the entire force of the enemy—artillery, infantry, and cavalry—retreated in confusion along the road and adjacent fields, leaving behind them at different points numbers of their killed, guns, knapsacks, canteens, &c."

By 2:30 P.M. the battle was over. Confederate losses were six killed, thirty-three wounded, and thirteen missing. The Federals lost eight dead and thirty-five wounded.

Afterward, October and November 1861 were relatively inactive. The difficulties encountered in western Virginia were so great, with the chances of success so doubtful, that the Confederate leadership began to place less and less emphasis on the recovery of its lost territory. Temporarily at least, the Monterey Line remained the northwestern border of the Confederacy.

—*Eddie Woodward*

See also Johnson, Edward; Reynolds, Joseph Jones; Taliaferro, William Booth.
For further reading:
Hotchkiss, Jed. "Virginia." In Clement A. Evans, ed. *Confederate Military History* (1899; reprint, 1987).
Stutler, Boyd Blynn. *West Virginia in the Civil War* (1966).
White, Robert. "West Virginia." In Clement A. Evans, ed. *Confederate Military History* (1899; reprint, 1987).

GREENE, GEORGE SEARS
(1801–1899)
Union general

A grandson of Revolutionary War general Nathanael Greene, George Sears Greene was born on 6 May 1801 in Apponaug, Rhode Island. After graduating second of thirty-five from the U.S. Military Academy in 1823, Greene was commissioned a second lieutenant in the 3d Artillery and was appointed to the West Point faculty. He taught mathematics for three years and engineering for one year before joining his regiment as an ordnance officer. On 31 May 1829, Greene was promoted to first lieutenant.

Greene married Elizabeth Vinton on 14 July 1828. Their marriage was tragically short-lived. By 22 February 1833, Greene's wife and their three children had died within a space of eight months. Four years later, on 21 February 1837, Greene began a forty-six-year marriage with Martha Barrett Dana. They had six children, of which four boys and the one girl lived to maturity. After being a lieutenant for twelve years, Greene took a one-year leave in 1835, and then resigned his commission to work as a civil engineer.

Twenty-five years later, when the Civil War began, Greene was the chief engineer and commissioner of the Croton Aqueduct Department of New York City. He offered his services to the governor of New York, and on 18 January 1862, he received an appointment as colonel of the 60th Infantry Regiment, New York Volunteers, stationed outside Washington, D.C. The sixty-year-old colonel earned a reputation as a gruff, no-nonsense drillmaster. On 28 April 1862, "Pap" Greene was promoted to brigadier general, U.S. Volunteers, a rank he held until 13 March 1865, when he was brevetted to major general for gallant and meritorious services, principally at the battles of Cedar Mountain, Antietam, Chancellorsville, and Gettysburg.

At Cedar Mountain, on 9 August 1862, Greene commanded the 3d Brigade, 2d Division of Major General Nathaniel P. Banks's II Corps of the Army of

Virginia. The 3d Brigade anchored the Union's extreme left. When A. P. Hill's Division stopped and reversed the Union attack, Greene's artillery stubbornly held its position and blunted the Confederate pursuit, allowing the retreating II Corps time to recover its composure and conduct an orderly retrograde movement.

At Antietam on 17 September 1862, Greene commanded the 2d Division of the XII Corps. When the I Corps' opening assault was turned back, XII Corps attacked at 7:30 A.M. As the right wing's advance stalled, Greene wheeled two of his brigades out of the East Woods. They surged through the cornfield and pushed the Confederates past the Dunker church into the West Woods, marking the Union's farthest advance in that first phase of the battle. Unable to secure flank support and receive timely resupply, Greene had to fall back in the face of repeated Confederate counterattacks. His brigade retired in good order and remained on the field until the end of the battle.

When the Army of the Potomac faced the Army of Northern Virginia at Chancellorsville in May 1863, the XII Corps was placed in the center of the line. Greene commanded the 3d Brigade of the 2d (White Star) Division. When the Union right collapsed, Greene's brigade came under enfilade artillery fire and then an infantry assault. Greene ordered a counterattack that turned back the Confederates and, as at Cedar Mountain, stiffened the wavering Union line and avoided disaster. When the Army of the Potomac retired across the Rappahannock River, it passed safely through defensive positions built by the XII Corps under Greene's supervision.

Two months later, XII Corps occupied Culp's Hill, the extreme right of the Union position at Gettysburg. On the morning of 2 July, Greene ordered his brigade to prepare defense works by cutting trees and stacking boulders. At 7:00 P.M. XII Corps was ordered to reinforce the sagging Union center and left. Only Greene's brigade of 1,350 men remained to defend a half mile of defense works. At 8:00 P.M. the 4,000 men of Johnson's division of Richard S. Ewell's II Corps assaulted Culp's Hill. After an hour of stiff resistance, Greene's line was flanked on its right, and Steuart's brigade occupied some of the XII Corps rifle pits. Greene's men retreated behind a traverse wall built earlier that day. After two more hours of fighting, the returning XII Corps reinforced Greene's lone brigade. The tenacious resistance of the 3d Brigade had stopped the Confederate advance 400 yards from the Baltimore Pike and half a mile from George G. Meade's headquarters.

In the fall of 1863, XII Corps joined the Army of the Cumberland to help break the siege of Chattanooga. While encamped near Wauhatchie Junction in Lookout Valley, Tennessee, the 2d Division was attacked just before midnight on 28 October 1863. During the battle,

George Sears Greene (*National Archives*)

Greene was shot through the mouth and jaw. After a six-week medical leave, Greene was assigned court-martial duty until January 1865, when he joined William T. Sherman's army in North Carolina. He participated in the battle of Kinston, the capture of Raleigh, and the pursuit to the surrender of General Joseph E. Johnston's army. After riding with XIV Corps in the Grand Review down Pennsylvania Avenue in May 1865, Greene returned to court-martial duty. He was mustered out of service on 30 April 1866 and returned to the engineering profession.

By 1892, Greene was the oldest surviving Union general and the oldest living graduate of West Point. In that same year, Greene petitioned Congress for a commission as captain in the regular army to make his family eligible for pension benefits at his death. Congress declined to promote him, but restored him to his highest rank while in Federal service. On 18 August 1894, at age ninety-three, George Sears Greene took the oath of office as a first lieutenant of artillery. For forty-eight hours Greene was the oldest lieutenant in the U.S. Army, and perhaps the oldest lieutenant in the history of the army. Greene's companions in the Military Order of the Loyal Legion of the United States proudly proclaimed him the oldest lieutenant in world history.

Greene died on 28 January 1899, four months before

his ninety-eighth birthday. He was buried near his birth-place in Apponaug, Rhode Island. On his grave the family placed a stone from Culp's Hill and a bronze plaque explaining its significance.

—*Paul E. Kuhl*

See also Antietam, Battle of; Cedar Mountain, Battle of; Wauhatchie, Battle at.

For further reading:

Collins, George K. *Memoirs of the 149th Regt. N.Y. Vol. Inf., 3d Brigadier, 2d Div., 12th and 20th A.C.* (1891; reprint, 1995).

Cubbison, Douglas R. "Midnight Engagement: John Geary's White Star Division at Wauhatchie." *Civil War Regiments: A Journal Of the American Civil War* (1993).

Krick, Robert K. *Stonewall Jackson at Cedar Mountain* (1990).

Pfanz, Harry W. *Gettysburg—Culp's Hill and Cemetery Hill* (1993).

Sears, Stephen W. *Landscape Turned Red: The Battle of Antietam* (1993).

GREENHOW, ROSE O'NEAL
(1817–1864)
Confederate spy

Maryland native Rose O'Neal Greenhow was a widowed mother of four daughters living in Washington, D.C., when the Civil War broke out. Having been married to a man of substantial wealth and social position, Greenhow had established powerful connections to various members of the Washington social and political elite that were to serve her effectively during the war. In 1861 Greenhow was widely reputed to be a beautiful, compelling, and brilliant woman, whose refined manners were complemented by her ability to obtain favors for her friends and influence members of Congress. Among her closer friends and associates was the powerful senator from Massachusetts, Henry Wilson, a man of unqualified devotion to the Union, but of questionable judgment in his choice of confidants.

Even before Fort Sumter was fired upon, Greenhow had revealed her "pronounced rebel proclivities" to all who cared to notice, and once the war was underway she wasted no time in making known her desire to make use of her personal connections to help the Southern cause. A former U.S. Army quartermaster, Lieutenant Colonel Thomas Jordan (alias Thomas John Rayford), readily accepted Greenhow's offer to help establish an elaborate Confederate spy network in the Federal capital. Using a simple cipher and other devices developed with Jordan, Greenhow began her work as a bold and effective informer for the Confederacy.

It was not long before Greenhow had occasion to demonstrate her usefulness to the Confederate army. An 1863 letter written by Confederate general P. G. T. Beauregard makes clear that prior to the first battle of Bull Run in July 1861, a female spy sent by Greenhow

conveyed an important message to Beauregard at his Fairfax Court House headquarters in Virginia, informing him of Union general Irwin McDowell's intention to advance on the Confederacy on 16 July. Some days later Greenhow sent Beauregard a second message, reiterating the contents of the first and providing additional detail. According to Beauregard, Greenhow's messages played a key role in provoking him to request that Confederate president Jefferson Davis order General Joseph E. Johnston, the Confederate army's ranking officer who was stationed some fifty miles away, to bring his troops to Bull Run as reinforcements for Beauregard's men. This move ultimately resulted in the embarrassing defeat at Bull Run of the Federal troops and their commander, who had assumed that their own movements had remained undiscovered. On 22 July, Greenhow received a written statement of appreciation from Davis for her loyal service on the South's behalf.

The humiliation of the Union's inexperienced soldiers at Bull Run, combined with Greenhow's espionage activities right in the heart of the Federal capital, contributed significantly to the relative speed with which U.S. officials closed in on her operations. After a few weeks of observing the comings and goings around her house, on 23 August 1861 Allan Pinkerton, the head of the Federal government's new secret service organization, personally placed Greenhow under house arrest. As she recalled in her memoir, *My Imprisonment*, Greenhow chafed angrily at this rude intrusion on her home and her work. Her home, which was nicknamed "Fort Greenhow," soon housed several other women similarly accused of spying for the Confederacy. But despite Federal officials' determined efforts to the isolate her, Greenhow continued to funnel important information, some of which was carelessly supplied by her good friend Henry Wilson, to the South. In January 1862, tired of trying to secure her home against leaks of information, Federal officials transferred Greenhow and her youngest daughter, "Little Rose," to the Old Capitol Prison, where they held her for about five months. Early in June 1862 she was released and exiled to the South, where her supporters greeted her with enthusiasm.

Not long thereafter, Greenhow traveled to England and France with Little Rose, hoping to generate support for the Confederacy among the European nations. In England she wrote her memoir, then realized that she missed her native land and yearned to return and serve the Confederacy more directly. In September 1864, just four months after Belle Boyd's capture aboard the blockade runner the *Greyhound*, Greenhow boarded a similar ship, the *Condor*, in England and headed home. Greenhow was carrying a substantial amount of money in gold on her person, and when the ship was run aground by a Union gunboat off the North Carolina coast, her insistence that she be allowed to try to reach the shore safely in one of the *Condor's* lifeboats was Greenhow's undoing. The lifeboat overturned in the rough waters and she drowned. Her body washed up on the beach the following day, and was subsequently laid in state in a hospital chapel wrapped in the flag of the country in the service of which she had given her life.

—*Elizabeth D. Leonard*

See also Pinkerton, Allan; Wilson, Henry.

For further reading:

Burger, Nash K. *Confederate Spy: Rose O'Neal Greenhow* (1967).

Greenhow, Rose O'Neal. *My Imprisonment, and the First Year of Abolition Rule at Washington* (1863).

Leonard, Elizabeth D. *"All the Daring of the Soldier": Women of the Civil War Armies* (1999).

Pinkerton, Allan. *The Spy of the Rebellion: Being a True History of the Spy System of the United States Army during the Late Rebellion* (1883).

Ross, Ishbel. *Rebel Rose: Life of Rose O'Neal Greenhow, Confederate Spy* (1954).

GREGG, DAVID MCMURTRIE
(1833–1916)
Union general

Born to Matthew Duncan Gregg and Ellen McMurtrie Gregg in Huntingdon, Pennsylvania, David McMurtrie Gregg was first cousin to Pennsylvania's Civil War governor, Andrew Gregg Curtin. Gregg was educated locally before attending what is now Bucknell University. While there he received an appointment to the U.S. Military Academy. He graduated eighth of thirty-four in the class of 1855. Sent west to various frontier posts, Gregg was serving at the Warm Springs Indian Reservation in Oregon as a second lieutenant at the outbreak of the Civil War. Promoted to first lieutenant and then captain, Gregg was ordered east, where he joined the defensive force around Washington after the battle of First Bull Run.

In early 1862, Gregg received promotion to colonel and was given command of the 8th Pennsylvania Cavalry. He commanded his regiment in the Peninsula campaign, where it screened McClellan's retreat in the latter part of the campaign and fought in the Maryland campaign. Gregg was promoted to brigadier general in November 1862. He commanded a brigade at Fredericksburg but missed the action at Chancellorsville because he had been detached to take part in George Stoneman's raid toward Richmond. Early in the year, Gregg had become commander of the 3d Division of the Army of the Potomac's Cavalry Corps. While Stoneman's raid succeeded in destroying railroad track and bridges and generally disrupted communications,

because it started too late in the campaign, it had no impact on the battle of Chancellorsville.

In the latter part of May 1863, Gregg was headquartered with his division at Warrenton Junction. His primary activity during that time was patrolling in search of John Singleton Mosby's elusive raiders. In June the division became more active as it became apparent that Robert E. Lee was on the move.

At Brandy Station on 9 June, Gregg commanded the attack at Kelly's Ford and then moved north, now as the commander of the corps' 2d Division, with the remaining units of the corps engaging in various actions with J. E. B. Stuart's cavalry as it tried to screen Lee's movements. While part of Gregg's division fought at Aldie on 17 June, Gregg led the bulk of the division at Middleburg two days later.

At the battle of Gettysburg on the third day, Gregg was placed with approximately 5,000 men north of the Union line to protect the Baltimore Pike and to prevent any Confederate movement around the Union right flank. His position was attacked by approximately 7,000 troopers under Stuart on 3 July. In a hard-fought, sometimes hand-to-hand or sabre-to-sabre battle, Gregg held the Union flank and repulsed Stuart. During Lee's retreat from Gettysburg, Gregg aggressively followed the Confederate army, skirmishing numerous times with its rear guard and cavalry, most notably at Charles Town, West Virginia, on 15 July and at Shepherdstown, West Virginia, on 16 July. He continued to skirmish with Confederates for the remainder of the summer into the early fall of 1863.

Gregg commanded the 2d Division during the Bristoe Station and Mine Run campaigns. At the end of the year, from 8 to 25 December, he led his men in a raid on the Virginia & Tennessee Railroad. In the early months of 1864, Gregg held temporary command of the Cavalry Corps and spent much of his time skirmishing with Mosby. In the spring he prepared his men for the upcoming campaign against Lee. He fought at the Wilderness and then in Philip Sheridan's raid toward Richmond from 9 to 24 May. Once Lee dug into his trenches at Petersburg, Gregg led his division in a number of attacks on Lee's communication lines, including the failed attempt at Reams' Station on 25 August 1864.

For the remainder of 1864 into early 1865, Gregg engaged in similar activities and then suddenly resigned his commission on 3 February 1865. He remained with the army for several more weeks until a suitable replacement could be named. Gregg never gave an explanation for his resignation.

After leaving the army, Gregg lived in Reading, Pennsylvania. After serving briefly in 1874 as Grant's consul to Prague, he retired to Reading, where he was active in civic affairs. In his later years he wrote and published an account of the Gettysburg campaign. He died in Reading on 7 August 1916.

—*David S. Heidler and Jeanne T. Heidler*

See also Aldie, Virginia, Battle of; Gettysburg, Battle of; Stoneman's Raid (April–May 1863).

For further reading:

Burgess, Milton V. *David Gregg; Pennsylvania Cavalryman* (1984).

Gray, Elmer W. "Major General David McMurtrie Gregg, Unsung Hero of Gettysburg." *Historical Review of Berks County* (1962).

Longacre, Edward G. *The Cavalry at Gettysburg: A Tactical Study of Mounted Operations during the Civil War's Pivotal Campaign, 9 June–14 July 1863* (1993).

———. *Lincoln's Cavalrymen: A History of the Mounted Forces of the Army of the Potomac* (1999).

GREGG, MAXCY
(1814–1862)
Confederate general

Born in Columbia, South Carolina, Maxcy Gregg followed his father's footsteps and attended law school, graduating first in his class. In 1846, he was commissioned a major in the 12th U.S. Infantry Regiment, but did not see action during the Mexican-American War. After resigning from the army, Gregg resumed his law practice. He also found time to study Greek drama, botany, ornithology, and astronomy. He even had his own observatory in Columbia.

An outgoing proponent of states' rights and an avowed advocate of resuming the slave trade, Gregg was a member of the South Carolina convention of 1860 that voted for secession from the Union. On 17 January 1861, Gregg was commissioned a colonel of the 1st South Carolina Infantry, a unit that he helped organize on terms of a six-month enlistment. The regiment, which included some of Columbia's most prominent businessmen, attorneys, and physicians, was stationed at Sullivan's and Morris islands in Charleston harbor for training. After the fall of Fort Sumter, the 1st South Carolina moved to Richmond and, as one of the first Confederate regiments, entered the city to grand celebration.

The regiment was then ordered to Centreville and eventually Fairfax Court House as part of the defenses of Northern Virginia. Its first engagement occurred at Vienna, Virginia, on 17 June 1861, when Gregg led the unit on a reconnaissance toward the Potomac River and ambushed a trainload of Ohio soldiers who were using the Alexandria, Loudon & Hampshire Railroad to conduct reconnaissance. The 1st South Carolina, along with a battery of artillery and a company of cavalry, managed to destroy six rail cars and inflict twelve casualties. The remainder of the Union troops scattered to flee toward Washington before Gregg's men could inflict any more damage. With the enlistment period of Gregg's

volunteers scheduled to end on 1 July, he disappointedly marched his men back to Richmond for disbanding. Although most of the men in the regiment returned to their homes in Columbia, many did reenlist and the unit was at full strength in six weeks.

In December 1861, Gregg was promoted to brigadier general and ordered to South Carolina to take command of a brigade that included elements of his old unit. During the Seven Days' campaign as part of A. P. Hill's famed "Light Division," Gregg's South Carolina brigade led an attack at the very center of the Union line during the initial assault at Gaines' Mill, Virginia, on 27 June. At Frayser's farm he led a charge and captured a Union battery. Gregg's presence on the battlefield earned him the respect of his men. Later that summer at Second Bull Run, Gregg was cited for heroism when his brigade held the Confederate left against a series of desperate Union charges. Despite heavy losses, Gregg bravely galloped through the line to encourage his men to stand firm, shouting "Let us die here my men, Let us die here."

During the battle of Antietam, Gregg and his brigade were instrumental in thwarting Burnside's main advance as part of Hill's division when it arrived late in the day's fighting. A bullet knocked Gregg from his horse, but the wound proved to be only a bruise, and he immediately returned to the battle. Despite his success as an officer in Stonewall Jackson's command, Gregg and the strict disciplinarian were at odds on a number of occasions. In one instance, members of Gregg's brigade disobeyed Jackson's firm order of not disturbing private property. While camped near a farmhouse, the South Carolinians dismantled the owner's fence to use as firewood. As a result, Jackson had all of Gregg's regimental commanders arrested.

At Fredericksburg—which was Gregg's final campaign—his brigade took a position in a wooded area about 500 yards behind Jackson's line. During the afternoon of 13 December, Union troops opened a gap in the line, allowing them to break through and charge toward Gregg's men. Confusion ensued. Gregg rode along the position and, mistaking the advancing Union troops for the men of Archer's brigade, he ordered his brigade not to fire. During the melee, the Federals fired a volley that hit Gregg and knocked him from his horse. The wounds were serious. He was discovered during a successful Confederate counterattack and carried to the Yerby house, not far from Hamilton's Crossings. He held on until 15 December, finally dying of wounds to the spine. General Stonewall Jackson eulogized the South Carolinian in an official report as "a brave and accomplished officer, full of heroic sentiment and chivalrous honor." He was returned to Columbia for burial.

—*Mitchell Yockelson*

For further reading:

Krick, Robert K. *Maxcy Gregg: Political Extremist and Confederate General* (1973).

GREGG, WILLIAM
(1800–1867)
Confederate businessman

Born to William Gregg and Elizabeth Webb Gregg in Carmichaels, Virginia, the younger Gregg was reared a Quaker, first by his parents and then by his uncle, Jacob Gregg. With his uncle he moved to Georgia as a young boy, where he helped Jacob Gregg establish a cotton mill. He was later apprenticed in the crafts of watchmaking and silversmithing, first in Kentucky and then in Virginia. In 1824 he opened his own business in Columbia, South Carolina. In the 1840s he moved to Edgefield, where he assumed control of a failing cotton mill.

William Gregg had come to believe after his long residence in South Carolina that the state was suffering economically from its dependence on staple agriculture. For that reason, he intended not only to capitalize on the abundant supply of cotton to increase his own fortune but also to encourage other entrepreneurs to do the same. He wrote articles for the *Charleston Courier* that became his *Essays on Domestic Industry*, a pamphlet that advocated Southern economic independence from Northern and foreign manufactured goods.

In spite of Southern suspicions of large industry, Gregg persuaded the South Carolina legislature to give him a charter of incorporation for the Graniteville Manufacturing Company. In the years before the Civil War, this company not only became a model for other Southern manufacturing concerns but also earned healthy dividends for its investors. By carefully recruiting and ministering to the material needs of a work force of Southern poor whites, Gregg gradually built a thriving cotton manufacturing concern in the interior of South Carolina. His success gave him hope that the South could truly become economically independent, and as a delegate to the South Carolina legislature in 1856 and 1857, he advocated more emphasis on economic development.

As the country moved toward civil war in 1860, Gregg published several essays in *De Bow's Review* carrying his argument one step further by advocating an economic war footing for the South. After the election of Abraham Lincoln, Gregg was selected to serve in the South Carolina secession convention, where he supported South Carolina's exit from the Union.

During the war, Gregg worked diligently to keep his factory open and producing. Despite the labor shortage due to enlistments and conscription, the factory continued to operate throughout the war. He argued strongly against the South's dependence on blockade running throughout the war, pleading for an increase in domestic manufacturing as the solution to the South's supply problems.

After the war, Gregg traveled north and to Europe to acquire more modern equipment. His untimely death on 13 September 1867 resulted from an illness he contracted repairing machinery while standing in water from a broken milldam.

—*David S. Heidler and Jeanne T. Heidler*

See also Cotton; South Carolina.
For further reading:
Gregg, William. *Essays on Domestic Industry, An Inquiry into the Expediency of Establishing Cotton Manufactures in South Carolina* (1941).
Mitchell, Broadus. *William Gregg: Factory Master of the Old South* (1928).

GRESHAM, WALTER QUINTIN
(1832–1895)
Union general

Walter Quintin Gresham was born near Lanesville, Indiana, to William Gresham and Sarah Davis Gresham. William Gresham was murdered when Walter was two years old. Gresham was educated locally and worked on the family farm until he became a clerk for the county auditor when he was seventeen. He saved the money he earned from this and other employments, and as a result was able to attend college for two years before beginning the study of law. He began to practice law in 1854.

In addition to his law practice, Gresham became active in Indiana politics. Initially a moderate Whig who hoped for a gradual end to slavery, the passage of the Kansas-Nebraska Act and the growing troubles in Kansas led him eventually into the Republican Party. He campaigned actively for the Republican ticket in 1856. In 1860 he won election to the Indiana state legislature. With the outbreak of war, Gresham worked in the legislature to strengthen the state militia and make it a more efficient military organization. Some of his efforts put him at odds with the governor, Oliver P. Morton. As a result, Gresham was refused a state military commission when he sought one during the summer of 1861.

Gresham was determined to offer his military service to the Union, and, after his failure to gain a commission, he returned home to raise troops for the army. The company he raised elected him captain, although by the end of the summer he was promoted to lieutenant colonel of the 38th Indiana Volunteers. At the end of the year he was promoted to colonel and was made the commander of the 53d Indiana.

In early 1862, Gresham and the 53d Indiana were placed under the command of Ulysses S. Grant. During the Shiloh campaign, Gresham and the 53d were instructed to protect the Union supply lines and so were not present at Pittsburg Landing. Serving in the division of Brigadier General Stephen Hurlbut in the spring of

1862, Gresham and his regiment participated in the advance on Corinth. During the Vicksburg campaign, Gresham and his regiment were very active; after the fall of Vicksburg they participated in the campaign against General Joseph Johnston at Jackson, Mississippi.

In August 1863, Gresham was promoted to brigadier general and was given command of a brigade and placed in command of the District of Natchez. In early September he led his brigade into Louisiana but was back in Natchez by the end of the month. He remained in Natchez through the end of the year. His primary activity during that time was to prevent the smuggling of Southern cotton out of the country. As a result, he and his men spent a great deal of their time patrolling the countryside confiscating cotton hidden throughout the area.

In February and March 1864, Gresham led his brigade in the Meridian campaign, after which he was given command of a division for William T. Sherman's upcoming Atlanta campaign. In preparation for the campaign, Gresham traveled to Cairo, Illinois, where his division, as part of Francis Preston Blair Jr.'s XVII Corps, was being trained and outfitted. At the end of the month he and his men set out to join Sherman in Tennessee.

Gresham led his men in all of the early engagements of the Atlanta campaign and was especially conspicuous at the battle of Kennesaw Mountain. As Sherman's army closed in around Atlanta on 20 July, Gresham and his men occupied a position at Leggett's Hill. On that day a Confederate sharpshooter chose Gresham as one of his targets, hitting the general in the knee. He was carried from the field and, because of the crippling nature of the injury, was unable to return to active field service for the remainder of the war.

Despite his injury, Gresham chose to remain in the volunteer service, sitting on boards and courts-martial until being mustered out of the service in 1866. He had been given a brevet promotion to major general in March 1865 for his efforts in the Atlanta campaign.

After leaving the army, Gresham returned to Indiana and his law practice. He also resumed his interest in Republican politics but was perennially unsuccessful in his bids for elective office. He did serve briefly as a U.S. district judge for Indiana on an appointment from his former commander, President Ulysses S. Grant. In 1883 he began an eighteen-month stint as postmaster general, appointed by President Chester Arthur. He also served briefly as secretary of the treasury before leaving the cabinet to accept another district judge appointment. Through the remainder of the 1880s, Gresham was frequently mentioned as a Republican presidential candidate but never received the nomination. By the early 1890s he had broken with the party over his opposition to a protective tariff. He campaigned for Democrat Grover Cleveland in 1892 and, after Cleveland's victory,

was appointed secretary of state. During his two years in office he was very active in averting several foreign crises. He died in office in Washington, D.C., on 28 May 1895.

—*David S. Heidler and Jeanne T. Heidler*

See also Atlanta Campaign.

For further reading:
Calhoun, Charles W. *Gilded Age Cato: The Life of Walter Q. Gresham* (1988).
Gresham, Matilda. *Life of Walter Quintin Gresham, 1832–1895* (1919).

GRIER, ROBERT COOPER
(1794–1870)
Supreme Court justice

Born to Isaac Grier and Elizabeth Cooper Grier in Cumberland County, Pennsylvania, Robert Cooper Grier was educated by his father, a teacher, before enrolling in Dickinson College. Upon his father's death, Grier took over the management of the local college that his father had founded and studied law. Upon entering into the practice of law, Grier's talent in that area quickly gained him a wide reputation and a prosperous practice. Politically, in his youth Grier had been a Federalist but, as he became more active in the political affairs of the state, he switched to the Democratic Party.

Grier's growing prominence through his legal practice and an important marriage brought about his appointment in 1833 as a state district judge in Allegheny County. He served on that bench until 1846, when President James K. Polk nominated him as an associate justice to the U.S. Supreme Court. Grier sat on the Supreme Court from 1846 until his retirement soon before his death in 1870.

As an associate justice, Grier quickly gained a reputation as a moderate on most issues including slavery, the issue that would dominate U.S. politics for almost the next two decades. He inclined personally toward neither the proslavery nor antislavery viewpoint. He did, however, have a rather negative view of abolitionists, especially regarding what he viewed as their contempt for fugitive slave legislation.

Much of Grier's judicial career, however, has been overshadowed by the fact that he was one of the two Northern justices who ruled with the Southern majority in the *Dred Scott* case in 1857. In the months preceding the case, no one was sure how Grier would rule. Southerners were fairly certain that the five Southern justices would rule against Scott in his bid to gain his freedom, and they hoped that the Court would also take the opportunity to rule on the legality of slavery in the territories. Yet they hoped that the ruling would not be along purely sectional lines. Having one or more of the Northern justices rule with the majority would give more legitimacy to any pro-Southern ruling. Grier seemed a likely possibility. He had close ties to Southern friends, had expressed his dislike for abolitionists, and was a distant cousin of prominent Georgia congressman Alexander Stephens. Further, in a misguided hope that such a ruling would settle the issue conclusively, incoming president and fellow Pennsylvanian James Buchanan wanted the ruling to remove congressional authority from slavery in the territories. Buchanan was not above using subtle and not so subtle pressure to gain such a ruling, and he personally urged Grier to side with the majority. Grier was persuaded and returned the favor by tipping off Buchanan in February 1857 what the ruling would be.

One way or another, every justice issued his own opinion in the case. Grier gave as his opinion that the Missouri Compromise was unconstitutional and that Missouri law was applicable regarding Scott's status, and hence Scott was still a slave.

This decision seriously damaged Grier's legal reputation among many Northerners, and he was dismissed by many as being either a tool of the South or the president or both. When the Civil War began, however, Grier quickly demonstrated himself to be a strong supporter of the Union and opponent to secession. All of his rulings during the war demonstrate this support and his concurrence with the president regarding broad war-making powers. After the war, these sentiments continued to come through in his rulings, particularly in his views that Southerners should have to demonstrate marked loyalty before enjoying full rights within the Union.

In 1867 Grier suffered a partially paralyzing stroke. He never fully recovered and he found it increasingly difficult over the next few years to keep up with his caseload. The other justices finally persuaded him in February 1870 to retire from the bench. Grier died a few months later on 25 September 1870 in Philadelphia, Pennsylvania.

—*David S. Heidler and Jeanne T. Heidler*

See also Dred Scott Case; Supreme Court, U.S.

For further reading:

Fehrenbacher, Don E. *The Dred Scott Case: Its Significance in American Law and Politics* (1978).

Siegel, Martin. *The United States Supreme Court: Volume 3, The Taney Court, 1836–1864* (1995).

GRIERSON, BENJAMIN HENRY
(1826–1911)
Union general

An exceptionally able Union cavalry commander who had a long career in the postwar U.S. Army on the frontier, Benjamin Grierson was born in Pittsburgh, Pennsylvania. His family moved to Ohio in 1829, and from there moved to Jacksonville, Illinois, in 1849. From early childhood, Grierson had remarkable musical ability, and he became an accomplished musician, music teacher, and composer. At the age of eight, he was seriously injured by a runaway horse. The accident gave him a lifelong distrust of horses, a strange attribute for a future cavalry commander.

After his marriage to Alice Kirk in 1854, Grierson became a merchant in Meredosia, Illinois. He was involved in the Republican Party in its earliest days in that state. Abraham Lincoln stayed in the Grierson home when he spoke in Meredosia at the time of the Lincoln-Douglas debates. Grierson's business failed, partially due to the Panic of 1857, and he and his family were living with Grierson's parents when the Civil War began.

Grierson joined the army in May 1861 as an unpaid volunteer aide-de-camp to Brigadier General Benjamin M. Prentiss. Although he had never had any military training beyond a stint as a bugler in the Ohio militia, he showed notable military ability in a number of early clashes with rebels in Missouri. Grierson was appointed a major in the 6th Illinois Cavalry in October 1861. He worked hard to procure decent uniforms and food for his ill-clad and poorly managed regiment and instituted regular drills and strict discipline. Although he was an efficient and sometimes demanding officer, he was popular with his men, who found him to be fair and concerned for their welfare. In April 1862, he was promoted to colonel. He and his regiment performed well during the rest of the year in Tennessee and Mississippi. He was given command of a brigade in December 1862. Grierson's most famous action was the famous cavalry expedition known as Grierson's Raid. To divert Confederate efforts away from Grant's attacks on Vicksburg, Grierson's 1,700-man brigade, consisting of the 6th and 7th Illinois Cavalry and the 2d Iowa Cavalry, left La Grange, Tennessee, on 17 April 1863 on what would be one of the greatest cavalry exploits of the war. Grierson's men rode 600 miles over the length of Mississippi, fought numerous skirmishes, wrecked large portions of two railroads, and destroyed vast amounts of supplies. During the devastating raid, Grierson's men halted their work in the towns of Hazelhurst and Brookhaven to douse fires that threatened to spread from burning railroad facilities to civilian homes. They safely reached Baton Rouge, Louisiana, on 2 May, and they were immediately hailed as heroes by the army and the Northern press. His small force had tied up thousands of enemy troops and badly damaged rebel communication and supply lines during the Vicksburg campaign. For this raid, Grierson was promoted to brigadier general to rank from 3 June 1863.

After the raid, Grierson was given command of a larger brigade and took part in the fighting around Port Hudson, until its fall on 8 July 1863. After some unlucky campaigning under lackluster commanders, Grierson

again commanded a spectacularly successful cavalry raid. Leaving La Grange, Tennessee, on 21 December 1864, Grierson led 3,500 men on a 450-mile raid through Mississippi, reaching Vicksburg on 5 January 1865. He later participated in the campaign against Mobile. He remained in the army during the early days of Reconstruction and left the service on 30 April 1866 after being promoted to major general of volunteers.

Grierson did not stay out of the army for long. He rejoined as a colonel in July 1866 and was given command of one of the new black regular army regiments, the 10th U.S. Colored Cavalry. Grierson commanded the regiment for the next 22 years, and spent most of his time on duty in the Southwest. He gained a reputation for treating his men, and the Indians, with respect and fairness. It was through his insistence that the designation "colored" was dropped from his regiment, and it became officially known as the 10th U.S. Cavalry. Partly because of his sympathy for the Indians, he was not promoted to brigadier general until three months before his retirement in July 1890. He died at his summer home in Omena, Michigan, on 1 September 1911.

—*David A. Norris*

See also Grierson's Raid; Prentiss, Benjamin M.; Vicksburg Campaign.

For further reading:
Brown, D. Alexander. *Grierson's Raid* (1962).
Leckie, Shirley Anne, ed. *The Colonel's Lady on the Western Frontier: The Correspondence of Alice Kirk Grierson* (1989).
Leckie, William H., and Shirley A. Leckie. *Unlikely Warriors: General Benjamin H. Grierson and His Family* (1984).

GRIERSON'S RAID
(17 April–2 May 1863)

As General Ulysses S. Grant's Army of the Tennessee marched south from Milliken's Bend in search of a way to cross the Mississippi River and attack Vicksburg in April 1863, he needed a diversion. The cavalry provided the diversion and carried out one of the most spectacular cavalry adventures of the war. Borrowing heavily from Confederate cavalry tactics, Grant ordered Colonel Benjamin H. Grierson into the heart of Mississippi to destroy supplies and tear up railroad track and telegraph lines. Grant also hoped this raid would deflect Confederate attention away from his army as it crossed the Mississippi and moved closer to Vicksburg.

The leader of this cavalry expedition was Colonel Benjamin H. Grierson, a music teacher from Illinois who disliked horses ever since one kicked him in the head as a youth. Grierson's command in this raid numbered roughly 1,700 men from the 6th and 7th Illinois and 2d Iowa Cavalry Regiments. His orders were vague and discretionary. He was to destroy enemy supplies, communications, railroads, and generally cause as much

mischief as possible. He was specifically ordered to destroy the Southern Mississippi Railroad, an extremely important rail line.

Grierson and his men left La Grange, Tennessee, on 17 April 1863 bent on causing havoc in Mississippi. In a span of just over two weeks these raiders swept through the entire state, combining speed, shrewd tactics, and boldness. Confederate cavalry forces were dispatched to chase the Yankee troopers, but the blue-clad horsemen were never where the rebels expected them to be. This was part of Grierson's brilliance. When Confederates got close, he detached some of his men to threaten different locations. Therefore the Confederates never really knew where Grierson was.

Four days into the raid, Grierson, hard-pressed by pursuing cavalrymen, dispatched the 2d Iowa under Colonel Edward Hatch to threaten the Mobile & Ohio Railroad. After this diversion Hatch and his men returned to La Grange. Confederates followed Hatch, giving Grierson the freedom to ride virtually unopposed. The next day, 22 April, Grierson duplicated the deed as he sent Company B of the 7th Illinois to cut telegraph lines in Macon. Grierson then moved to Newton Station, some 100 miles directly east of Vicksburg, and

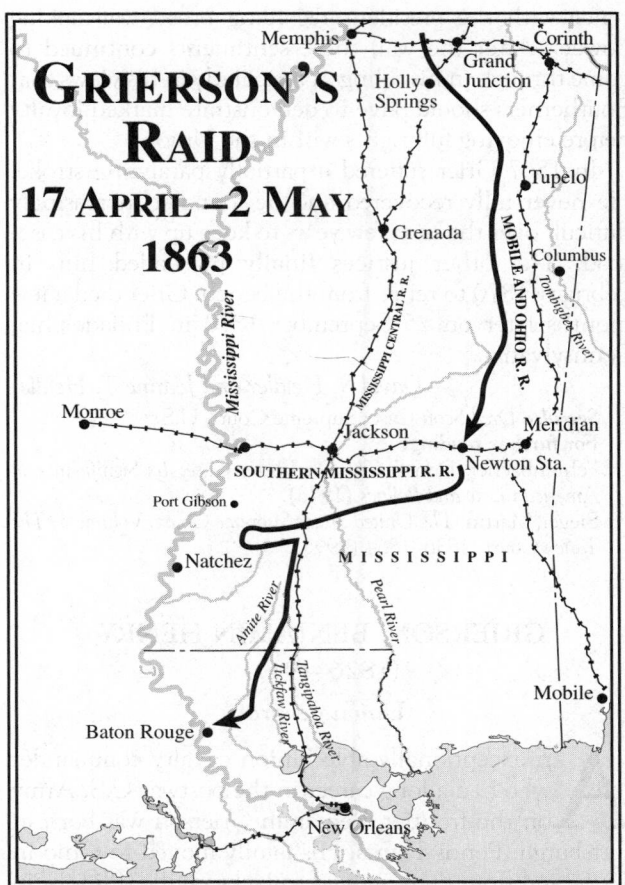

GRIERSON'S RAID
17 APRIL –2 MAY 1863

on 24 April tore up the Southern Mississippi Railroad. Destroying the railroad was an important objective, as it ran from Vicksburg through Jackson and eastward, connecting the eastern and western halves of the Confederacy. Serendipity greeted the Yankee raiders when they reached Newton Station, as two trains were pulling in, and both were loaded with ammunition. The munitions were promptly destroyed.

When General John C. Pemberton, Confederate commander at Vicksburg, received the news of the destruction at Newton Station, he sent out more men to chase Grierson. He dispatched two infantry regiments and a battery of artillery from Jackson to try to block Grierson from the west. He ordered cavalry from Port Hudson into the field to prevent an escape in that direction.

By the end of April, Grierson decided against returning to La Grange and instead ride forward to support General Grant's Mississippi River crossing, expected to be near Grand Gulf. However, as he approached the vicinity he saw no indications of a successful crossing, so Grierson decided he and his troopers must escape. On 2 May the Yankee horsemen rode into Union lines at Baton Rouge, Louisiana, ending one of the most daring cavalry raids of the Civil War.

After his foray through Mississippi, Grierson reported that his raiders had killed about 100 Confederates, taken 500 prisoners, wrecked 50 to 60 miles of railroad and telegraph lines, and destroyed massive amounts of supplies, weapons, and ammunition. Grierson's men rode some 600 miles through enemy territory and fought numerous engagements in 16 days. All this at a loss of 3 killed, 7 wounded, 9 missing, and 5 sick left behind. In addition, Grierson was promoted to brigadier general for his accomplishments. More importantly, however, Grierson's raid confused Confederate officials and distracted them while General Grant's army crossed the Mississippi River.

—*Christopher C. Meyers*

See also Grierson, Benjamin; Hatch, Edward; Vicksburg Campaign.

For further reading:
Bearss, Edwin C. *The Campaign for Vicksburg* (1985–1986).
Brown, D. Alexander. *Grierson's Raid* (1962).
Leckie, William H., and Shirley A. Leckie. *Unlikely Warriors: General Benjamin H. Grierson and His Family* (1984).
Miers, Earl Schenck. *The Web of Victory: Grant at Vicksburg* (1955; reprint, 1983).

GRIFFIN, CHARLES
(1825–1867)
Union general

Born the son of Apollos Griffin in Granville, Ohio, Charles Griffin was educated locally and at Kenyon College before accepting an appointment to the U.S. Military Academy. He graduated twenty-third of thirty-eight in the class of 1847. On being commissioned into the artillery, Griffin was sent to fight in the Mexican-American War but arrived after most of the fighting had ended. After the war he served on a variety of frontier posts before being detailed to West Point as an instructor in 1860.

In January 1861, Griffin was charged with organizing a battery from the artillerymen stationed at West Point and taking it to Washington. This became known as the West Point battery, and it became a part of the 5th Artillery with Griffin as its captain. Griffin's battery was a part of Irvin McDowell's army that marched on the Confederate position at Manassas Junction. In the battle of First Bull Run, Griffin and his men distinguished themselves by holding their ground under very heavy Confederate fire. The battery suffered over 50 percent casualties and lost five of its six guns.

During the late summer and fall of 1861, Griffin was involved in reconnaissance activities in northern Virginia. In the spring he took his battery to the York peninsula to participate in George McClellan's campaign against Richmond. Griffin earned praise for the handling of his artillery at the siege of Yorktown from the commander of the siege, Fitz John Porter. Again at Hanover Court House on 27 May, Porter complimented Griffin for the part he played in the battle. Two weeks later, on 9 June 1862, Griffin was promoted to brigadier general of volunteers, and during the Seven Days' he commanded a brigade in Porter's V Corps.

Griffin had a reputation as an outspoken officer, and the habit caused him considerable trouble in the campaign that culminated at the battle of Second Bull Run. Neither Porter nor Griffin approved of the creation of the Army of Virginia and the seeming supplanting of their commander George McClellan by John Pope. When V Corps was sent back to Washington from the peninsula and attached to Pope's army for the upcoming campaign against Richmond, both officers made no secret of their distaste for the new assignment. During the battle of Second Bull Run, Porter failed to carry out orders to Pope's satisfaction and Griffin was heard during the midst of battle loudly questioning Pope's qualifications for command. As a result, Pope later accused both men of disrespect for their commanding officer. During Porter's eventual court-martial, Griffin strongly defended his commander, but Porter was convicted and cashiered. Griffin never stood trial and retained his command. The experience neither chastened nor ended Griffin's habit of speaking his mind, however.

Before Porter's trial began in December 1862, Griffin commanded his brigade in Porter's V Corps during the Maryland campaign. Held in reserve, Griffin did not fight at Antietam, though his brigade harried Lee's

retreat at Blackford's Ford on the evening of 19 September to the morning of 20 September.

Later in the fall, Griffin took command of the 1st division of V Corps to lead it at the battle of Fredericksburg. He and his division made one of the ill-fated attacks on Marye's Heights, suffering serious casualties. With the permanent removal of Porter from command in early 1863, Griffin temporarily commanded the entire corps from 26 January 1863 until 1 February. Reverting to the command of 1st Division, Griffin commanded this unit at Chancellorsville.

Shortly after Chancellorsville, Griffin became seriously ill and therefore missed most of the Gettysburg campaign. He returned to duty on the last day of the battle but saw no action. The following spring he led the 1st Division in every major battle of Ulysses S. Grant's campaign against Robert E. Lee. Beginning in June 1864, Griffin and his division would participate in the siege of Petersburg and many of the engagements over the next nine months that stretched Lee's lines to their limit. In July 1864, the commander of V Corps, Gouverneur K. Warren, recommended Griffin's promotion to major general of volunteers. The recommendation would not be acted on until the following year and, ironically, under circumstances at Warren's expense. In the meantime, Griffin persisted in his criticisms, often directing them at the handling of the siege. According to one story, after he had made one such statement within earshot of General Grant, Grant recommended to the Army of the Potomac's commander George Gordon Meade that Griffin be arrested. Meade dismissed the remark, however, and told Grant that it was just Griffin's way.

On 1 April 1865, at the battle of Five Forks, Griffin became the commander of V Corps when Philip Sheridan suddenly removed Warren from command. The following day, in keeping with his new status, Griffin was promoted to major general of volunteers. Seven days later, at the surrender of Lee's army at Appomattox, Griffin was one of the commissioners appointed to carry out the surrender terms.

After the war with the mustering out of the volunteers, Griffin became colonel of the 35th Infantry. Stationed in Galveston, Texas, he contracted yellow fever during an epidemic in the late summer of 1867 and died on 15 September 1867.

—*David S. Heidler and Jeanne T. Heidler*

See also Blackford's Ford; Bull Run, Second Battle of; Five Forks, Battle of; Porter, Fitz John.
For further reading:
Hendrickson, Robert. *The Road to Appomattox* (1998).
Hennessy, John J. *Return to Bull Run: The Campaign and Battle of Second Manassas* (1993).
Trudeau, Noah Andre. *Bloody Roads South: The Wilderness to Cold Harbor, May–June 1864* (1989).

GRIFFING, JOSEPHINE SOPHIA WHITE
(1814–1872)
Abolitionist, suffragist, and Freedmen's Aid reformer

The daughter of Joseph White and Sophia Waldo, Josephine White married Charles Stockman Spooner Griffing in 1835. The Griffings moved to Litchfield, Ohio, shortly thereafter, as they appear there in the 1840 census. The couple had three surviving daughters, Josephine Emma, Helen, and Cora.

Griffing and her husband became involved in the antislavery movement as members of the Western Anti-Slavery Society. In 1850, Abby Kelley Foster encouraged Josephine to become an antislavery lecturer, and she subsequently toured throughout the West with Giles B. Stebbins, Parker Pillsbury, and other prominent agents of the American Anti-Slavery Society. She became active in the women's rights movement at the same time, attending and organizing Ohio women's rights conventions during the 1850s.

Griffing's most significant efforts for social reform, however, were made during and after the Civil War, on behalf of former slaves. Griffing joined the Loyal League, an organization started by Elizabeth Cady Stanton and Susan B. Anthony, and helped petition Congress to free the slaves. In 1864, she began her own petition campaign to Congress, asking that Northern and Western women be allowed "to share more fully in the responsibility and labor, so remarkably laid upon the government and the men of the North, in the care and education of these Freedmen." Later that year, Griffing and her daughters moved permanently to Washington, D.C., leaving Charles in Ohio. Griffing's activism alienated her from her husband, and it is possible that they divorced.

Griffing joined the National Freedmen's Relief Association of the District of Columbia and advocated the establishment of the Freedmen's Bureau. One biography reported that it was only through Griffing's "brave and unwearied efforts" that the Freedmen's Bureau bill was passed in March 1865. As thanks for her labor on behalf of the bill, Charles Sumner, George Julian, and other Radical Republicans persuaded General Oliver Otis Howard, Commissioner of the Freedmen's Bureau, to appoint her Assistant to the Assistant Commissioner for the District of Columbia. As part of her duties for the Freedmen's Relief Association and the Freedmen's Bureau, Griffing ran an employment agency and an industrial sewing school for freedwomen and distributed relief to destitute freedpeople.

Another aspect of Griffing's efforts, which grew out of her career as an antislavery lecturer, was to raise awareness in the North of freedpeople's situation in Washington, D.C. Griffing published an appeal in Northern newspapers that described the increased population of African-Americans. She stated that the previous

winter she had found 900 families without fuel and that very few among the "twenty thousand" lived in decent condition. Although this appeal gained material and financial donations to freedmen's aid societies, it also had unintended consequences. In November 1865, Griffing was fired from her duties at the Freedmen's Bureau, and Lieutenant S. N. Clark publicly disassociated the bureau from Griffing's appeals to the North. Bureau agents and other freedmen's aid reformers worried that the North would perceive freedpeople as "dependents" upon the government and white benevolence.

After the Freedmen's Bureau relieved Griffing of her official duties, she remained an agent of the National Freedmen's Relief Association and continued to work closely with the bureau in her efforts as an employment agent. Though the bureau denied that a large number of impoverished freedpeople were suffering in Washington, bureau agents viewed it as expedient to find employment for freedpeople outside of Washington, either in the South or in the North. Griffing assisted approximately 7,000 freedpeople to migrate to Northern jobs and homes.

Although Griffing's work for freedmen's aid took up most of her time and energy, she also found time to participate in the post–Civil War women's rights movement. Griffing was an important member of the National Woman Suffrage Association, founded by Elizabeth Cady Stanton and Susan B. Anthony, and hosted several of the association's conventions in Washington, D.C. In addition, she lectured on behalf of women's rights throughout the mid-Atlantic. Griffing saw women's suffrage and participation in freedmen's aid as necessary to the reconstruction of the nation. When Griffing died in February 1872, she was remembered for her faithful labor on behalf of women and freedpeople.

—*Carol Faulkner*

See also Abolitionist Movement; Abolitionists; Anthony, Susan B.; Freedmen's Bureau; Howard, Oliver O.; Stanton, Elizabeth Cady; Women.
For further reading:
Griffing, Josephine. Letters. Columbia University.
———. Letters, Records of the Bureau of Refugees, Freedmen, and Abandoned Lands. Record Group 105, National Archives.
McPherson, James. *The Struggle for Equality: Abolitionists and the Negro in the Civil War and Reconstruction* (1964).
Melder, Keith. "Angel of Mercy in Washington: Josephine Griffing and the Freedmen, 1864–1872." *Records of the Columbia Historical Society of Washington, D.C.* (1863–1865).
Stanton, Elizabeth Cady, et al. *History of Woman Suffrage* (1970).

GRIMES, BRYAN
(1828–1880)
Confederate general

Born in Pitt County, North Carolina, to Bryan Grimes and Nancy Grist Grimes, the younger Grimes was educated at the University of North Carolina at Chapel Hill. After graduation Grimes became a planter and dabbled in North Carolina Whig politics, although he never held an elective office. He did serve, however, in the North Carolina secession convention, where he voted in favor of secession in May 1861.

Upon the secession of North Carolina, Grimes enlisted in the Confederate army and was made a major in the 4th North Carolina Regiment. At the battle of Seven Pines in May 1862, the regiment suffered 90 percent casualties, and the command (due to the wounds of his superior officers) devolved upon Grimes. He was promoted to lieutenant colonel shortly after the battle and then to colonel on 19 June 1862. Grimes continued to command the unit through the Seven Days' battle, but contracted typhoid fever shortly thereafter and was not available for duty until after the battle of Antietam.

At Fredericksburg, Grimes temporarily commanded a brigade, but most reports have him back in command of the 4th at the battle of Chancellorsville. Remaining in command of the 4th as the Army of Northern Virginia moved into Pennsylvania, Grimes and his regiment made up the vanguard of Richard Ewell's corps as it moved into Gettysburg on 1 July 1863. For the remainder of the battle Grimes and the 4th stayed in the northern part of the battlefield operating against Cemetery Hill.

Grimes remained with the Army of Northern Virginia during its retreat back to Virginia. On 19 May 1864, Grimes received a promotion to brigadier general, after which he led his brigade beginning in June 1864 in Jubal Early's Shenandoah Valley campaign and Early's Raid on Washington. In the fall Grimes briefly commanded a division of John B. Gordon's Corps in the valley before returning to fight the rest of the war in the trenches of Petersburg.

On 15 February 1865 Grimes was promoted to major general. When the remnant of the Army of Northern Virginia made a run from the trenches of Petersburg in early April 1865, Grimes led his division forth. Grimes continued to fight the pursuing Federals to the last, leading his men in one final assault against Union positions on 9 April at Appomattox, the day Lee finally surrendered.

Following the war, Grimes returned to his plantation in North Carolina. He retired from public life, but apparently became involved in a local feud between longtime residents of his counties and recent immigrants. He was killed on his plantation by one of the immigrants in 1880.

—*David S. Heidler and Jeanne T. Heidler*

See also Early's Washington Raid; Shenandoah Valley Campaign (August 1864–March 1865)
For further reading:
Allen, T. Harrell. *Lee's Last Major General: Bryan Grimes of North Carolina* (1999).
Daniels, James Douglas. "The Civil War Career of Major-General Bryan Grimes" (M. A. thesis, 1961).
Grimes, Bryan. *Extracts of Letters of Major-General Bryan*

Grimes, to His Wife: Written While in Active Service in the Army of Northern Virginia, Together with Some Personal Recollections of the War (1986).

GRIMKÉ, ANGELINA EMILY
(1805–1879)
Abolitionist, feminist

Born on 20 February 1805, at Charleston, South Carolina, Angelina Emily Grimké was the daughter of John Faucheraud and Mary Smith Grimké. The Grimké family owned plantations, and both the Grimkés and Smiths were powerful in South Carolina society and politics. Siblings and cousins were influential judges, attorneys, politicians, and editors, publicly voicing proslavery sentiments. Angelina Grimké's older sister, Sarah Moore Grimké, was her godmother, vowing by the baptismal font to nurture and raise the infant. Thirteen years younger, Angelina Grimké referred to her sister as "Mother." Educated by tutors and at the Charleston Seminary, Angelina Grimké also learned from her sister's humanitarian tendencies. They both resented their father's patriarchal attitudes toward his daughters and recognized the cruelties of slavery. According to tradition, Grimké fainted at

Angelina Grimké (*National Archives*)

school when she observed a slave boy's bloodied, scabby back injured by whipping. Influenced by her sister, Grimké began questioning her society, especially how the Episcopalian Church could condone slavery. She began attending Presbyterian services instead.

After her sister traveled to Philadelphia with their dying father in 1819, Grimké listened to her tales of contacts with Quaker abolitionists. Two years later, Sarah Grimké moved from South Carolina permanently to devote herself to abolition work. In her diary, Angelina Grimké confessed her feelings of remorse when family slaves were punished. She questioned her mother about why the family perpetuated slavery and its cruel injustices but was rebuffed. Feeling alienated from her family and disgusted by her community, in the autumn of 1829 Angelina Grimké joined Sarah in Philadelphia, immersing herself in the Quaker culture. More extroverted and self-confident than her older sister, Angelina Grimké was also more vocal in her protests against slavery. The Grimkés in South Carolina were bewildered by their daughter's behavior, asking her to return home. Family ties were strained, and the Grimké sisters stayed in contact but did not live in the South again.

As a member of the Society of Friends, Angelina Grimké performed charity work. She was frustrated that the Quakers did not do more to abolish slavery and were too politically conservative. For example, her suitor, Edward Bettle, the son of a Quaker elder, disapproved of Grimké's desire to study at Catharine Beecher's Hartford school. Bettle died of cholera in 1832, and Grimké embraced her independence to devote herself to abolition. She began attending antislavery meetings, read abolitionist newspapers, and joined the Philadelphia Female Anti-Slavery Society after hearing the British abolitionist George Thompson lecture.

Aware of the dangers posed by mob violence directed against abolitionists in New York and Philadelphia, she wrote a letter to William Lloyd Garrison in which she declared, "The ground upon which you stand is holy ground: never—never surrender it" because "this is a cause worth dying for." In September 1835, Garrison printed Grimké's letter in the *Liberator,* and it was reprinted in other periodicals. As a result, the Grimké surname became publicly identified with abolition.

Angelina Grimké eagerly embarked upon her public life as an abolitionist. Joined by her more reluctant sister, Grimké traveled to New York to learn how to promote the antislavery movement. Together they attended an indoctrination course for abolitionist workers taught by noted orator Theodore Dwight Weld. Inspired by this workshop, Grimké wrote *An Appeal to the Christian Women of the South* (1836), beseeching women to demand the cessation of slavery. Grimké's words convinced many Northerners to support abolition, but Southerners burned her pamphlet and warned her not to return to South Carolina. The pamphlet was of interest to many people because it was written by a member of a prominent Southern family. "I ask you now, for the sake of former confidence, and former friendship, to read the following pages in the spirit of calm investigation and fervent prayer," Grimké began. "It is because you have known me, that I write thus unto you." Writing from "conviction and duty," Grimké hoped to convey "unwelcome truths" about slavery and convince readers to follow the examples of courageous women in the Bible. Explaining that it was their religious duty, she urged women to help slaves gain freedom from "the wicked laws that require woman to enslave, to degrade and to brutalize woman." She asked women to speak to their legislators and wrote a second pamphlet, *Appeal to the Women of the Nominally Free States* (1837).

The American Anti-Slavery Society, which had published the pamphlet, asked Grimké to speak at meetings of women in New York City. She and her sister were the first women to join that organization. In 1837 and 1838, they lectured throughout the Northeast—the first women to do this—sometimes speaking to mixed groups of men and women. The crowds were often hostile and angry, and Weld taught them how to cope with audiences as well as hone their arguments. Speaking to a total of approximately 40,000 people in sixty towns, Grimké skillfully debated dubious listeners, using her personal knowledge of slavery to win arguments. Criticized by ministers, the sisters defended their right to speak publicly to male audiences and became pioneers in the women's rights movement. "We have given great offense on account of our womanhood, which seems to be as objectionable as our abolitionism," Grimké declared. "I believe it is woman's right to have a voice in all the laws and regulations by which she is governed." On 21 February 1838, the Grimké sisters were the first women to present antislavery petitions to the Committee of the Legislature of the State of Massachusetts, testifying over three days. Grimké's *Letters to Catherine Beecher, in Reply to an Essay on Slavery and Abolitionism, Addressed to A. E. Grimké* (1838) responded to Beecher's criticism of women joining abolition societies.

Grimké married Theodore Weld on 14 May 1838, with Garrison delivering the vows and freed slaves sitting among the guests. As a result, she was asked to leave the Quaker church. Two days later, Grimké spoke at the Philadelphia antislavery convention, and an angry mob burned the hall afterwards. She decided to stop lecturing.

Sarah Grimké lived with the couple, and they moved to New Jersey. The trio wrote *American Slavery As It Is: Testimony of a Thousand Witnesses* (1839), a collection of Southern newspaper accounts of slavery. This book was considered the most factual account of slavery published

before *Uncle Tom's Cabin* and was used by Harriet Beecher Stowe as a source. Grimké continued to support abolition and the women's rights movements. She was a pioneer in coeducation, teaching history in schools with her husband and sister. Grimké's health declined, however, and she retired to a farm with her husband, children, and sister.

During the Civil War, Grimké supported pacifism and was critical of President Abraham Lincoln for not being more committed to ending slavery. She supported the Union, however, realizing the war might achieve emancipation. Grimké contacted her family in Charleston to find out how conditions were from them. She moved to Hyde Park, Massachusetts, where in 1870, the Grimké sisters led a group of local women who attempted to vote in an election. Learning her brother Henry Grimké had fathered two sons with a slave, Angelina Grimké acknowledged and aided her nephews in their legal and theological studies. Suffering a stroke that partially paralyzed her for six years, Grimké died on 26 October 1879, at Hyde Park, and was buried in Boston's Mount Hope Cemetery.

—*Elizabeth D. Schafer*

See also Abolitionist Movement; Abolitionists; Garrison, William Lloyd; Grimké, Sarah Moore; Quakers; Weld, Theodore Dwight.

For further reading:

Barnes, Gilbert H., and Dwight L. Dumond, eds. *Letters of Theodore Dwight Weld, Angelina Grimké Weld and Sarah Grimké, 1822–1844* (1934; reprint, 1970).

Birney, Catherine H. *Sarah and Angelina Grimké: The First American Women Advocates of Abolition and Woman's Rights* (1885; reprint, 1970).

Ceplair, Larry, ed. *The Public Years of Sarah and Angelina Grimké: Selected Writings 1835–1839* (1989).

Grimké, Angelina. *An Appeal to the Christian Women of the South* (1836).

Lerner, Gerda. *The Grimké Sisters from South Carolina: Rebels Against Slavery* (1967).

Lumpkin, Katharine Du Pre. *The Emancipation of Angelina Grimké* (1974).

Weld, Theodore D. *In Memory: Angelina Grimké Weld* (1880).

GRIMKÉ, SARAH MOORE
(1792–1873)
Abolitionist, suffragist

Sarah Moore Grimké was born on 26 November 1792 at Charleston, South Carolina. The daughter of John Faucheraud and Mary Smith Grimké, Sarah Grimké grew up in a privileged environment. Her father was a wealthy judge who owned vast amounts of property. When she was four, Grimké saw a slave woman being whipped at the family's plantation. Grimké's nurse later found Sarah on the wharves, begging a captain to take her someplace where slavery did not exist. She prayed for the family's slaves not to be punished and was especially close to one slave girl who was her playmate.

Sarah Moore Grimké (*National Archives*)

Grimké treated the slave as an equal, mourning her when she died. She later wrote, "Slavery was a millstone around my neck, and marred my comforts from the time I can remember myself." As a child, Grimké developed a close relationship with her older brother Thomas Grimké and was frustrated when her patriarchal father and aloof mother forbade her to participate in educational opportunities that her brothers enjoyed. Grimké studied her brothers' lessons in mathematics, science, and classical languages. Her father admitted that he appreciated her mind and permitted his daughter to join in debates with her brothers as they prepared to practice law. John Grimké said that his daughter would have been a great jurist if she had been born male. Sarah Grimké endured societal expectations that she participate in etiquette lessons, learning how to be a lady. She took care of the family home during her mother's absences, mending clothes and cleaning rooms as directed by her often critical father. Grimké frequently sought comfort in her black nurse, Mauma, whom she was shocked to discover was a slave and vulnerable to the injustices of being sold or punished.

Lonely when Thomas enrolled at Yale University, twelve-year-old Sarah Grimké was discontented, feeling stifled by her restrictive environment. Deeply religious, she wanted to teach the family's slaves to read the Bible,

but her father forbade her to do so, explaining that South Carolina law prohibited slave literacy. At night, when her maid was supposed to be brushing her hair, Grimké taught her to read.

Feeling helpless, Grimké agreed to embrace the roles expected of women in the early nineteenth century. She supported her brothers in achieving their intellectual goals that she had hoped also to attain. When her younger sister, Angelina, was born, she accepted the responsibility of being her godmother and was called "Mother" by the child. Although outwardly she seemed to have conformed to rigid antebellum expectations, Grimké seethed with rebellion. In 1819 she accompanied her ailing father to Philadelphia and New Jersey, seeking a cure for his illness. He died, but the trip reinforced Grimké's independence. She met Quakers who impressed her with their simple, pious lifestyles and antislavery attitudes. Returning home, she angrily criticized her family and friends for perpetuating slavery. She quit the Episcopalian Church that she considered hypocritical because of its endorsement of slavery to become a member of the Society of Friends, moving to Philadelphia in 1821.

Grimké gradually became disenchanted with the Quakers. Her speaking style was not fluid enough to please Quaker audiences. A widowed Quaker merchant, Israel Morris, proposed marriage, but Grimké refused. She disliked how Quakers discriminated against blacks in meetings despite their abolitionist rhetoric. While attempting to speak at a meeting, she was publicly silenced by a disapproving Quaker leader, Pope Jonathan Evans. Her sister Angelina had moved north to focus on abolition work, and the more conservative Sarah, believing her Quaker connections were irreparably dissolved, went to New York to join the antislavery movement with Angelina. They learned abolitionist tactics from Theodore Dwight Weld, a noted orator. Sarah Grimké became a public figure when her sister's proabolition letter was published in the *Liberator* in 1835. Northerners were interested in why these southern women had rejected their family's prestige and luxuries. In *Epistle to the Clergy of the Southern States* (1836), Sarah Grimké disputed Biblical justifications for slavery. The publication of Angelina Grimké's 1836 pamphlet, *An Appeal to the Christian Women of the South*, resulted in warnings that the sisters should not return to South Carolina.

The first women to join the American Anti-Slavery Society, the Grimké sisters lectured to mixed audiences of men and women during a tour of New England in 1837 and 1838, concluding with a lecture series in Boston's Odeon Hall. Curious though often hostile crowds thronged to hear the first white Southern female abolitionists. While in Massachusetts, the Grimkés presented an antislavery petition to a committee of the Massachusetts legislature. They were the first American women to testify to such a body. Criticized by clergy for overstepping gender boundaries, the Grimké sisters spoke in favor of women's rights despite some worries that it might detract from abolitionist successes. The Grimkés were the first American women to argue in writing for women's legal rights, using scriptural references to support their arguments. They inspired other suffragists to campaign for gender and racial equity. Sarah Grimké published *Letters on the Equality of the Sexes* (1838), addressing issues confronting both women and blacks. "I ask no favors for my sex," she declared. "All I ask of our brethren is that they will take their feet from off our necks, and permit us to stand upright on that ground which God designed us to occupy."

When Angelina Grimké married Weld in 1838, Sarah Grimké lived with the couple. Deciding not to speak publicly, the trio focused on preparing *American Slavery As It Is: Testimony of a Thousand Witnesses* (1839), which documented the conditions of slavery. Living in New Jersey and Massachusetts, Sarah Grimké taught in several schools with her sister and brother-in-law. She busily took care of her ill sister's children and managed the house. Interested in universal suffrage and educational reform, the Grimké sisters resumed their passion for abolition during the Civil War. Although a pacifist, Sarah Grimké supported the war, hoping it would result in emancipation for slaves. She criticized President Abraham Lincoln for not pursuing abolition more diligently. "The government, with Lincoln at its head, has not a heartthrob for the slave," she lamented. "I want the South to do her own work of emancipation. She would do it only from dire necessity, but the North will do it from no higher motive, and the South will feel less exasperation if she does it herself."

She contacted her family in South Carolina to learn how the war affected them and how she could help comfort them. Moving to Hyde Park, Massachusetts, with the Welds, she taught, wrote newspaper articles, and translated French. The Grimké sisters participated in an effort by Hyde Park women to vote in a local election. Sarah Grimké discovered that two mulatto college students named Grimké were her brother Henry's sons, and she publicly recognized them as her nephews, supporting their advanced studies in law and religion. Suffering laryngitis in her later years, Grimké died on 23 December 1873 at Hyde Park and was buried at Mount Hope Cemetery in Boston.

—*Elizabeth D. Schafer*

See also Abolitionist Movement; Abolitionists; Grimké, Angelina; Quakers; Weld, Theodore Dwight.
For further reading:
Barnes, Gilbert H., and Dwight L. Dumond, eds. *Letters of Theodore Dwight Weld, Angelina Grimké Weld and Sarah Grimké, 1822–1844* (1934; reprint, 1970).
Bartlett, Elizabeth Ann. *Letters on the Equality of the Sexes and Other Essays. By Sarah Grimké* (1988).
Birney, Catherine H. *Sarah and Angelina Grimké: The First American Women Advocates of Abolition and Woman's Rights* (1885; reprint, 1970).
Ceplair, Larry, ed. *The Public Years of Sarah and Angelina Grimké: Selected Writings 1835–1839* (1989).
Lerner, Gerda. *The Grimké Sisters from South Carolina: Rebels against Slavery* (1967).

GRINNELL, JOSIAH BUSHNELL
(1822–1891)
Iowa abolitionist, Republican congressman

Josiah B. Grinnell was born in New Haven, Vermont, in 1822 to a hardworking, religious farming family in which one had to memorize and recite Bible verses in order to get Sunday supper. He received little formal education in his youth, but by age sixteen he was engaged as a schoolteacher. He later attended Castleton Academy in Vermont and Oneida College in New York. As a student, Grinnell came under the influence of abolitionists such as Henry Ward Beecher, and the abolition of slavery became one of the most important causes of his life. He studied theology at Auburn, New York, and became a Congregational minister, preaching in upstate New York and in New York City. In 1851 he took a church in Washington, D.C.

Health problems, combined with the unpopularity of his abolitionist oratory, caused Grinnell to leave Washington and return to New York City. While in New York he became close friends with newspaper editor Horace Greeley and worked as a teacher among the poor workers of the city. His health problems continued, affecting his throat and voice, and he reluctantly surrendered his teaching and speaking responsibilities. His friend Greeley, Grinnell always insisted, then gave him for the first time the famous advice to "Go West, young man, go West."

Grinnell had previously visited the Midwest and had been impressed by both the land and the people, and in 1853 he proposed to establish a community in Iowa, which was a free state. He selected several thousand acres in Powesheik County and took the lead in establishing the town of Grinnell. He helped organize its first Congregational church and served as its first minister. He later helped establish Iowa College, of which he was a trustee for thirty years. He also helped the town earn a reputation as one of Iowa's way stations of the Underground Railroad, helping escaped slaves to freedom.

Grinnell entered politics in 1856 and was one of the principal organizers of the new Republican Party in Iowa and was elected state senator, serving for four years. His political campaign emphasized the three leading principles of his life: abolition, temperance, and support for education.

The focus of the antislavery movement in Iowa in the late 1850s was directed toward "Bleeding Kansas," a territory then in a condition of virtual civil war over the expansion of slavery. The militant abolitionist John Brown used Iowa as a staging ground for strikes into Kansas and as an escape route from Kansas. In March 1859 Brown, at the head of a wagon train of family members, abolitionist followers, escaped slaves, and stolen horses, unexpectedly knocked at Grinnell's door and asked for shelter. Grinnell took the party in, gave them a place to rest for two days, allowed Brown to address the sabbath meeting, and helped raise funds for the rest of their journey. Grinnell received much criticism for this support of Brown, but he never regretted or apologized for his actions.

In 1860 Grinnell was a delegate to the Republican national convention in Chicago. He was an early supporter of William Seward, the strongest antislavery candidate, but was finally persuaded to cast his ballot for Abraham Lincoln. In 1862 and 1864 he was elected to Congress from Iowa's Fourth District and earned a reputation as a Republican radical during the Civil War. He would accept no compromise with the South and was one of many members of Congress who urged President Lincoln to use his authority to issue the Emancipation Proclamation and to enlist African-Americans into the Union army.

After the assassination of Lincoln, his vice president, Andrew Johnson, succeeded him and was soon at odds with Republican radicals in Congress over the issue of the future rights of the freed slaves. This conflict was exemplified by a clash between Grinnell and Lovell H. Rousseau, a Democrat member of Congress and veteran officer in the Union army. The two engaged in a spirited debate on the floor of Congress over the issue of "Negro equality." The debate became fiercely personal and insulting on both sides, and several days later Rousseau confronted Grinnell on the capital steps and demanded an apology. Grinnell refused to apologize and Rousseau attacked him, striking him repeatedly with his cane until the stick shattered, and then laying into him with his fists. Grinnell refused to walk away but also refused to strike back.

Many praised Grinnell for not degrading himself by participating in a public brawl, but others criticized him for not being manly enough to defend himself when attacked. Some historians came to take the position that the Rousseau incident destroyed Grinnell's political career, but the truth was that weeks before the attack the 1866 Iowa Republican Party had already rejected Grinnell in favor of another nominee.

Grinnell returned to Iowa, where he remained active in local and national politics, giving his support to Horace Greeley's failed 1872 campaign for the presidency, but he was never again elected to state or federal office.

—*Kenneth L. Lyftogt*

See also Republican Party.
For further reading:
Grinnell, Josiah B. *Men and Events of Forty Years: Autobiographical Reminiscences of an Active Career from 1850 to 1890* (1891).
Gue, Benjamin F. *A History of Iowa* (1903).
Payne, Charles E. *Josiah Bushnell Grinnell* (1938).
Sage, Leland L. *A History of Iowa* (1974).

GRISWOLDVILLE, GEORGIA, BATTLE OF
(22 November 1864)

The battle of Griswoldville occurred about a week after Major General William Tecumseh Sherman's army marched from Atlanta toward their ultimate destination of Savannah. The Army of the Tennessee, composed of the XV and XVII Corps and commanded by Major General Oliver O. Howard, departed on 14 November 1864. The XV Corps, under the command of Major General Peter J. Osterhaus, formed the right column and proceeded through Rough and Ready, Georgia, until on 20 November it approached Macon. The next day, a large force of Confederates were reported at Griswoldville, near Osterhaus's outer column. Brigadier General Charles R. Woods's 1st Division was then ordered to take up a strong defensive position on the Irwinton Road and move toward Macon. As a part of this move, Brigadier General Charles C. Walcutt's 2d Brigade was sent toward Macon in search of the enemy.

The Confederate troops that Walcutt's brigade was moving toward were composed primarily of the Georgia Militia, along with the two regiments of the Georgia State Line, two local defense battalions from Athens and Augusta, and a battery of light artillery. In anticipation of the Union forces moving toward Augusta, the 1st Brigade of Major General Gustavus W. Smith's Georgia Militia had been sent by railroad on 21 November from Macon to Augusta. That afternoon, his remaining forces were ordered to Augusta, and on 22 November, they began marching toward Griswoldville, located about ten miles northeast of Macon. The 2d Brigade of the Georgia Militia left Macon around 8 A.M. and arrived about one mile from Griswoldville some time between noon and 1:00 P.M. At 12:20 P.M., General Smith, still in Macon, dispatched an order to Brigadier General Pleasant J. Phillips, the 2d Brigade's commander, to avoid a fight with a superior force.

Some skirmishing had been going on in the area for a few days. The Confederate cavalry commander, Major General Joseph Wheeler, reported that on 19 November a large Union force was moving toward Griswoldville. On the 20th and 21st, he skirmished with Union cavalry in and around the town. On the 21st, portions of the Union 3d Cavalry Division under the command of Brigadier General Judson Kilpatrick destroyed four miles of the Macon & Savannah Railroad around

Griswoldville, along with railroad cars and equipment. In addition, they destroyed several of the city's factories, a foundry, wagons, carts, carpenter's tools, and 400 boxes of soap. As Phillips approached, some of Wheeler's cavalry told him that the Union forces numbered between 800 and 1,200.

During the morning of the 22d, Confederate and Union cavalry continued to skirmish until the Confederates were driven from the field by reinforcements from Walcutt's brigade. Walcutt's troops then were withdrawn to a defensive position near the Duncan farm. Stationed in the edge of some woods, the Union troops overlooked an open field, with a swamp located on their flanks. Approximately 1,500 Union soldiers from Ohio, Indiana, Iowa, Illinois, and Michigan waited in the cold for the Confederates.

Around 2 P.M., the battle began, with more than 4,000 Georgia troops forming a battle line. The 3d Brigade of the Georgia Militia attacked the Union right, while the Athens and Augusta Battalions attacked the left. The Militia's 4th Brigade and the Georgia State Line attacked the center, while the 2d Militia Brigade waited in reserve. Captain Ruel Anderson's Light Artillery Battery offered support.

The Confederates made three assaults on the Union position. The first line of soldiers, composed of the Georgia State Line, the local defense battalions, and Brigadier General Charles D. Anderson's 3d Brigade, Georgia Militia, advanced. The remaining two lines soon followed, as Ruel Anderson's battery shelled the Union position. When the first line approached within about 250 yards of the Union rifles, it encountered a fierce response. As it drew nearer, the Confederate reserves entered the action. In spite of the devastating Union fire, the Confederates continued to regroup and advance. The greatest threat to the Union lines came from General Anderson's troops as they attempted to turn the Union's right flank. Anderson's men made seven charges on the Union line, but without success. As night approached, the Confederates retreated, having suffered more than 600 casualties compared with fewer than 100 endured by the Federals. The Confederates could hardly afford the loss of more than a quarter of their effective muskets, and the battle of Griswoldville did little to slow down Sherman's army. Some of these same Georgia troops, however, would be in combat again about a week later at the battle of Honey Hill.

—*Scott M. Langston*

See also Honey Hill, South Carolina, Battle of; Sherman's March to the Sea; Wheeler, Joseph.

For further reading:
Livingston, Gary. *Fields of Gray: The Battle of Griswoldville* (1996).
McInvale, Morton R. "'All That Devils Could Wish For': The Griswoldville Campaign, November, 1864." *Georgia Historical Quarterly* (1976).

Smith, Gustavus W. "The Georgia Militia during Sherman's March to the Sea." In *Battles and Leaders of the Civil War* (1956).
U. S. War Department. *The War of the Rebellion: A Compilation of the Official Records of the Union and Confederate Armies* (1880–1901).

GROSE, WILLIAM
(1812–1900)
Union general

Born to William Grose and Mary Hubbell Grose outside Dayton, Ohio, William Grose moved with his family to Indiana while he was still a child. He received a rudimentary local education, and after reaching adulthood he made his living as a day laborer. He began the study of law in his late twenties and, after admission to the bar, began practicing in Newcastle, Indiana. He also showed an interest in politics. Initially a Democrat, Grose switched to the Republican Party in the mid-1850s and was elected to the state legislature as a Republican in 1856. In 1860 he became a judge.

At the outbreak of the Civil War, Governor Oliver P. Morton of Indiana offered Grose the colonelcy of the 36th Indiana Infantry. Grose accepted the commission. Taken into federal service in October 1861, Grose and the 36th did not see significant action until the battle of Shiloh in April 1862. As part Don Carlos Buell's command, Grose and the 36th went ahead of the rest of the army to join with Ulysses S. Grant at Pittsburg Landing. As a result, Grose's regiment was the only unit of Buell's army to see action on both days of Shiloh. After the battle, Grose was given command of a brigade and commanded it in the Corinth campaign.

During the summer of 1862 Grose operated out of Murfreesboro, Tennessee. On 27 August 1862 he fought a sharp skirmish with Nathan Bedford Forrest when the audacious Confederate cavalry commander attacked the rear of Grose's column near Round Mountain. Grose was able to repulse the attack.

Grose continued to command his brigade in the division of Thomas L. Crittenden at Stones River at the end of 1862. Still headquartered at Murfreesboro, Grose operated nearby in early 1863 fighting a skirmish at Woodbury, Tennessee, on 24 January 1863. Grose commanded his brigade in the Tullahoma campaign in June 1863 and then at Chickamauga in September. For the latter engagement, he was commended for his actions by Crittenden and recommended by Rosecrans for promotion to brigadier general.

Grose continued to command his brigade as a colonel in the Chattanooga campaign, most notably at Missionary Ridge. From 22 to 27 February 1864, Grose led his brigade in a demonstration against the Confederate position at Dalton, Georgia, and in the spring joined the upcoming

Atlanta expedition. Grose participated in every important battle of that campaign through the summer of 1864. Division commander David Stanley praised Grose for his actions at Kennesaw Mountain, and he finally received the long overdue promotion to brigadier general on 30 July 1864. Grose earned notice for his bravery in the latter part of the Atlanta campaign.

In the fall of 1864, Grose's brigade was assigned to George H. Thomas's Army of the Cumberland and went north with Thomas to fight John Bell Hood. Grose was conspicuous in his actions at both the battles of Franklin and Nashville. Grose remained in Nashville under Thomas until the end of the war. On 9 June 1865 he was relieved from command of his brigade to serve on a court-martial at Thomas's request. He remained at that duty for the remainder of the year. Before leaving the army in January 1866, he received a brevet promotion to major general.

After the war, Grose return to civilian life. From 1866 to 1874 he served as the collector of internal revenue in his district. He also engaged in a number of civic pursuits, including sitting on a commission that founded mental hospitals in Indiana. He also served in the state senate and wrote a history of the exploits of the 36th Indiana. He died in New Castle, Indiana on 30 July 1900.

—*David S. Heidler and Jeanne T. Heidler*

See also Atlanta Campaign.
For further reading:
Castel, Albert E. *Decision in the West: The Atlanta Campaign of 1864* (1992).
Sword, Wiley. *Embrace an Angry Wind: The Confederacy's Last Hurrah—Spring Hill, Franklin, and Nashville* (1992).

GROVER, CUVIER
(1828–1885)
Union general

Born in Bethel, Maine, the son of John Grover and Fanny Lary Grover and brother of future Oregon governor and senator La Fayette Grover, Cuvier Grover was educated locally before accepting an appointment to the U.S. Military Academy. He graduated fourth of forty-four in the class of 1850. Grover served at frontier posts and in 1853 was assigned to an exploratory mission through the Rocky Mountains to determine the feasibility of a northern route for a transcontinental railroad. During the winter of 1854, Grover's party of five crossed the Rockies, demonstrating the possibility of a northern railroad. Later in the decade, Grover served in the Mormon expedition.

When the Civil War began in 1861, Grover commanded Fort Union in New Mexico. Confederate sympathizers in the territory demanded that he surrender the fort. Instead, he destroyed anything of military value that his men could not carry and marched his men to the Missouri River. Once he had traveled back east, in the spring of 1862 Grover was promoted to brigadier general of volunteers.

Given command of a brigade in Joseph Hooker's division of Samuel Heintzelman's corps, Grover commanded his men during the Peninsula campaign. Grover fought at the siege of Yorktown and the battles of Williamsburg and the Seven Days'. Transferred with his brigade to the Army of Virginia, he fought in the battle of Second Bull Run. During the fall of 1862, Grover commanded an independent brigade on the upper Potomac guarding the crossings there.

In December 1862 Grover transferred to the Army of the Gulf, where he was given command of a division. He participated in the reoccupation of Baton Rouge on 17 December 1862, and in early 1863 he operated in western Louisiana before participating in the siege of Port Hudson.

The following year he fought in the Red River campaign and the fighting around Alexandria during the withdrawal. On 3 July 1864, however, Grover received orders that he was to bring his division to Fort Monroe for service in Virginia. Upon arrival he was immediately sent to become part of the Department of Washington.

In August 1864, Grover joined Philip Sheridan's Shenandoah Valley campaign. He fought at Winchester and Fisher's Hill but especially distinguished himself at the battle of Cedar Creek, where he was seriously wounded. For his actions there, Grover received a brevet to major general of volunteers to date from the day of the battle (19 October 1864).

When Grover was sufficiently recovered from his wounds, he was sent south to assume command of the District of Savannah (Georgia). He arrived on 20 January 1865 and assumed command the following day. He remained in this position until the end of the war.

After the war, Grover remained in the army, eventually reaching the rank of colonel of the 1st Cavalry. Never in good health because of his injury and illnesses contracted during the war, in 1885 Grover traveled to Atlantic City, New Jersey while on leave, hoping the sea air would improve his health. He died there on 6 June 1885.

—*David S. Heidler and Jeanne T. Heidler*

See also Cedar Creek; Port Hudson.
For further reading:
Hennessy, John J. *Return to Bull Run: The Campaign and Battle of Second Manassas* (1993).
Lewis, Thomas A. *The Guns of Cedar Creek* (1988).

GROVETON, VIRGINIA, BATTLE OF
(28 August 1862)

After feasting on Union stores at Manassas Junction on 27 August 1862, Thomas J. "Stonewall" Jackson's 24,000-man command took up a position near the old Bull Run battlefield behind an unfinished railroad cut north of the Warrenton Turnpike. Late in the afternoon of 28 August, Jackson spotted a Union force marching east along the turnpike. It was the division of Irvin McDowell's corps commanded by Rufus King. A report had reached the headquarters of John Pope, commander of the Army of Virginia, of which McDowell's corps was a part, that Jackson's force was at Centreville. At 6:00 P.M., Jackson corrected this misperception by ordering his artillery to open fire on King's column.

When Jackson attacked, King's brigades were spread out along the turnpike with John P. Hatch's lead brigade at the crossroads hamlet of Groveton. John Gibbon's all-western brigade, clad in their distinctive black hats, followed Hatch and had just emerged from a thirty-acre thicket of trees known as Brawner's Woods with Abner Doubleday's brigade just behind them. Marsena Patrick's brigade brought up the rear and was at the intersection of the turnpike and Pageland Lane, where King was enjoying a picnic dinner, when Jackson opened fire. At that moment, King suffered an epileptic seizure that would incapacitate him for several hours.

Upon hearing the sound of Jackson's guns, Gibbon rode up to a small rise north of the turnpike to determine what was going on. From what he could see and had been told about the whereabouts of Jackson, he deduced that the source of the trouble was some isolated units of J. E. B. Stuart's horse artillery. After a brief consultation with Doubleday, he decided to attack them. Gibbon then called up the only one of his regiments that had seen combat, the Second Wisconsin, and led it 500 yards up the gentle rise north of the turnpike under the cover of Brawner's Woods.

When they emerged from the woods, Gibbon and his men were stunned to see lines of rebel infantry marching toward them. It was the famed Stonewall Brigade, worn down to only eight hundred muskets by over a year of hard and distinguished service. Eager to redeem their poor performance at First Bull Run, the 450 Federals did not flinch at the appearance of Jackson's battle-hardened veterans but immediately began pouring a steady fire into the rebel lines.

Gibbon then ordered up the rest of his command along with two regiments from Doubleday's brigade. Hatch's men were pinned down around Groveton by artillery fire and were not going anywhere, while Patrick refused to go to the aid of Gibbon, his junior in rank, without explicit orders from King. One half hour after the first shots of the battle had been fired, both sides had about eight hundred men engaged. Jackson then began bringing up his reinforcements. By 7:00 Gibbon's entire brigade, plus Doubleday's two regiments, 2,500 men in all, were battling Jackson's 3,600 Confederates, with John Brawner's home marking the western flank of both forces. Why Jackson did not commit more of the 24,000 men he had at his disposal remains a mystery.

The battle at the Brawner farm was a stand-up fight of unmitigated ferocity in which both sides maintained almost perfectly dressed lines less than a hundred yards apart as they poured shot after shot into each other. At 7:30 Jackson, frustrated by what had become a stalemated fight, ordered a series of frontal assaults. When these were bloodily repulsed, Jackson decided to flank Gibbon's position to the west using three regiments from A. G. Taliaferro's brigade and two guns from John Pelham's battery. Solomon Meredith's 19th Indiana, which held the Federal left, responded to this threat by falling back to a rail fence. There the Indianans managed to hold on until darkness put an end to fighting all along the line. Gibbon then pulled back to the turnpike. Later that evening, a still shaky King decided to withdraw his division to Manassas Junction.

In just two hours of fighting, 1,150 Federals and 1,250 Confederates were either killed or wounded in the opening engagement of the battle of Second Bull Run. Among the wounded Confederates were two division commanders, William B. Taliaferro and Richard Ewell, whose services would be dearly missed. For Gibbon's men, the fight at the Brawner Farm was the first in a series of superb performances that would win them renown as the "Iron Brigade."

—*Ethan S. Rafuse*

See also Bull Run, Second Battle of; Iron Brigade.
For further reading:
Gaff, Alan D. *Brave Men's Tears: The Iron Brigade at Brawner Farm* (1985).
———. *Return to Bull Run: The Campaign and Battle of Second Manassas* (1993).
Hennessy, John J. *Second Manassas Battlefield Map Study* (1990).

GROW, GALUSHA AARON
(1822–1907)
U.S. congressman

Born to Joseph Grow and Elizabeth Robbins Grow in Windham County, Connecticut, Galusha Aaron Grow moved with his widowed mother to Voluntown, Connecticut, when he was four years old. When he was twelve his mother moved the family again, this time to Glenwood, Pennsylvania, where she bought a farm. In addition to farming, the family also became involved in the lumber business. Grow was educated locally and at the age of eighteen gained admission to Amherst College, from which he graduated in 1844. After leaving college, Grow began the study of law and became involved in Pennsylvania Democratic politics. This interest was fed when he entered legal practice with David Wilmot in Towanda, Pennsylvania.

Wilmot's growing association with the more anti-slavery wing of the Democratic Party caused his rejection by conservative members of the party in Pennsylvania when he sought reelection to the U.S. House of Representatives in 1850. Grow was proposed and accepted as a compromise candidate and won election. What the conservative elements perhaps did not realize was that Grow described himself as a free-soil Democrat and was every bit as opposed to the expansion of slavery as was Wilmot. He quickly endeared himself to his constituents as a friend of the small farmer and won reelection to his seat five successive times.

Grow's first speech in Congress, "Man's Right to the Soil," was a preview of what would become his primary mission while in Congress. He believed that the federal government was stingy with its public lands and that those lands should be made available to the citizens of the country. As a result, after he was reelected in 1852 he introduced for the first time a homestead bill that would have made available public lands at no charge to people who were willing to farm the land. Although his measure was defeated, he would reintroduce the measure in every successive Congress until it finally passed in 1862.

In 1854, Grow strongly opposed the passage of the Kansas-Nebraska bill because of its potential to allow the spread of slavery. He had grown increasingly disenchanted with those Northern Democrats who apparently had no qualms about slavery in the territories, and after the passage of the Kansas-Nebraska Act, he left the Democratic Party and became a founding member of the Pennsylvania Republicans.

As the chairman of the House Committee on Territories and the House Committee on Agriculture in 1856, Grow was in the midst of the controversy surrounding the settlement of and violence in Kansas. He never hesitated to speak his mind on the expansion of slavery and what he feared it would do to the small farmers of the country. As a result, he became increasingly unpopular with Southern congressmen. At 2:00 A.M. on 6 February 1856, during a long, exhausting debate on the Kansas question, he became involved in a verbal exchange with South Carolina fire-eater congressman Lawrence Keitt. Keitt decided to escalate the conflict by grabbing Grow around the throat. Several other congressmen became involved in what turned into a brief brawl. Keitt later apologized to the House but not to Grow.

When Congress convened in 1859, Grow was the leading Republican candidate for speaker of the House, but when the House deadlocked during the balloting, Grow withdrew his name in the interest of harmony. Two years later, however, when Abraham Lincoln called Congress into special session after the reduction of Fort Sumter, Grow was elected speaker in July 1861.

With most Southern Democrats gone from Congress,

Grow had hope that his homestead legislation would pass. Upon being reelected speaker in 1862, he was able to secure the passage of the Homestead Act. Unfortunately for Grow, the election districts in Pennsylvania had been realigned, and he was defeated for reelection in the fall of 1862. While he continued to be active in the state Republican Party, Grow's refusal to ally himself with the Republican machine of Simon Cameron in the state made it impossible for him to return to national politics for many years.

He devoted much of the next few decades to business pursuits and served in minor positions within the party leadership in Pennsylvania. Finally, with most of his political enemies dead, he was elected to the U.S. House of Representatives in 1893 to fill the unexpired term of a congressman who had died in office. He retired in 1903 at age eighty. He died four years later, on 31 March 1907, in Glenwood, Pennsylvania.

—*David S. Heidler and Jeanne T. Heidler*

See also Congress, U.S.A.; Homestead Act; Wilmot, David.
For further reading:
DuBois, James T. *Galusha A. Grow: Father of the Homestead Law* (1917).
Ilisevich, Robert D. *Galusha A. Grow: The People's Candidate* (1988).

GUERRILLA WARFARE

Irregular, or guerrilla, operations played a prominent role in several theaters of the Civil War. Although they were most conspicuous in Missouri and Kansas, guerrillas operated in virtually every Southern state, from the mountains of East Tennessee and western North Carolina to the swamps of Florida and Louisiana. The number of Union and Confederate guerrillas and quasi-guerrillas reached perhaps as high as 25,000. In retrospect, their actions had little effect on the campaigns of the regular armies, but they certainly contributed to a brutalization of the war—devastating as they did portions of the South and bringing terror and misery to large numbers of noncombatants.

Two of the principal areas of guerrilla operations were the Missouri-Kansas region and Virginia. Guerrilla activities in the former region were an extension of the violence that had erupted there in the 1850s, when Missouri Border Ruffians and Kansas Jayhawkers terrorized the region. At the outbreak of the Civil War, Missouri governor Claiborne Jackson advocated secession and the attachment of his state to the infant Confederacy. These actions prompted Kansas Jayhawkers to invade Missouri to protect their state's eastern border. Senator James Lane, along with other Border War veterans such as Charles Jennison and James Montgomery, led Jayhawker bands that roamed throughout western Missouri, committing depredations against both secessionists and neutral civilians alike.

These actions certainly contributed to the vicious guerrilla fighting that would plague Missouri and Kansas in the following years, eventually reaching "a scale and ferocity unequalled anywhere else." By the end of 1861, Union general Henry Halleck had issued an order declaring as outlaws all Confederate guerrillas and authorizing their immediate execution. The guerrillas quickly adopted a no-quarter policy in return.

Confederate guerrilla leaders included Colonel M. Jeff Thompson, who operated in southeastern Missouri and became well known for his raids on Union outposts. In the summer of 1862, Major General Thomas Hindman also sent a number of Confederate officers into Missouri with orders to organize partisan ranger battalions. They conducted raids and ambushes on Federal outposts and columns and led to a mobilization of Union militia that eventually drove the Confederates out of the northern portion of the state. Most notorious, however, were the Confederate guerrillas who operated in western Missouri. They resisted the Jayhawker incursions and mounted retaliatory raids into Kansas. William Clarke Quantrill, an Ohio native, led a band of guerrillas that sacked Aubry, Kansas, in March 1862. Among the most savage of the Southern guerrillas, Quantrill attracted men such as George Todd, Dave Poole, Coleman and Robert Younger, Jesse and Frank James, Arch Clements, and William "Bloody Bill" Anderson to his command. In August 1863, Quantrill's band raided Lawrence, Kansas, burning much of the town and killing some 150 civilians. That same month, a jail in Kansas City, which held a number of relatives of Quantrill's men, collapsed, killing several of the prisoners. Union general Thomas Ewing, Jr., also issued a series of controversial general orders, which freed the slaves of disloyal Missourians, began the deportation of guerrilla families, and eventually called for the wholesale evacuation of a number of border counties. These events only increased the ferocity of the western guerrilla war.

As the war progressed, Quantrill became less prominent, with William Anderson and George Todd forming their own bushwhacker bands. At Centralia in September 1864, Anderson committed one of the worst atrocities of the war. After robbing a passenger train, the guerrillas murdered a group of unarmed Union soldiers and then decimated a force of militia sent to capture them. Anderson's men scalped and otherwise mutilated many of the Union casualties. Todd and Anderson would shortly thereafter be killed by Union troops, while Quantrill was mortally wounded in Kentucky in 1865. By the spring of 1865, guerrilla warfare in the west had decreased, but its earlier ferocity would leave a bitter legacy in the war's aftermath.

Confederate guerrilla and partisan leaders also rose to prominence in the region east of the Mississippi River.

Perhaps the best known was John Singleton Mosby, who operated from 1863 to 1865 in Union-occupied northern Virginia in the area between the Blue Ridge and the Bull Run mountains. An enlisted man and one-time adjutant of the 1st Virginia Cavalry, Mosby's abilities as a scout and raider attracted the attention of Major General J. E. B. Stuart. After Stuart's Dumfries Raid of December 1862, Mosby received permission to maintain a small force behind enemy lines near Middleburg. In two nights he captured several Union outposts and earned Stuart's admiration as a practitioner of irregular warfare. Mosby won national attention in March 1863 when he captured the sleeping Union brigadier general Edwin Stoughton at Fairfax. In the aftermath of these victories, Mosby was commissioned a captain and was authorized to organize his small band of guerrillas into the 43d Virginia Partisan Ranger Battalion.

According to a biographer, Mosby "danced on the nerves of opponents where they were most vulnerable." His Rangers mounted small raids and ambushes throughout north central Virginia, focusing much of their attention on the Union-controlled railroads of the region. During their campaigns of 1863 to 1865, Mosby's men burned bridges and cut telegraph lines in such profusion that they forced Union officials to detail significant numbers of troops to guard their lines of supply and communication. Among Mosby's more prominent successes were those of July 1863, when he captured twenty-eight loaded sutler wagons at Fairfax Court House in what became known as the Ice Cream Raid; and August 1864, when he captured or destroyed a large Union supply train near Berryville. In October of the same year, he first raided the Manassas Gap Railroad and shortly thereafter robbed a Federal payroll train near Harper's Ferry in the Greenback Raid and took $170,000.00 in U.S. currency.

In December 1864, Federal troops seriously wounded the guerrilla chieftain, but he survived and continued his operations until 21 April 1865, when he disbanded his battalion. Federal officials initially considered him an outlaw and refused to accept his surrender until 17 June, when he was paroled at Lynchburg. Mosby was perhaps the most successful Confederate guerrilla commander. He had risen to the rank of colonel by the end of the war and had earned the respect of Robert E. Lee. He also generally conducted his operations in an honorable fashion, without the atrocities committed by guerrillas in other theaters. Consequently, when the Confederate government repealed the Partisan Ranger Act in early 1864, Mosby's battalion was one of two exceptions allowed to remain in existence (the other being the company led by Captain John McNeill).

Kentucky was another area of bitter guerrilla warfare, and the flamboyant John Hunt Morgan became the state's most famous partisan leader. Morgan was certainly more of a legitimate military figure than Quantrill, Anderson, or other western guerrillas, but his favorite type of warfare was guerrilla-style raids behind enemy lines. Serving first as colonel of the 2d Kentucky Cavalry and later as brigadier general, Morgan led a series of raids into Kentucky during 1862 and 1863, the most prominent of which was his Ohio Raid of July 1863. Captured at the end of this raid, he was imprisoned in the Ohio Penitentiary for a time but later escaped. Federal troops killed Morgan in September 1864. Late in the war, in response to the Emancipation Proclamation, Union military rule, and the recruitment of African-American troops, Confederate guerrilla activity increased in Kentucky, and Union officials responded with severe countermeasures. As a result, by 1864–1865, "the situation in Kentucky verged on anarchy."

Some level of guerrilla activity occurred in virtually every Confederate state. In Florida, pro-Union or anti-Confederate guerrillas operated in the southern part of the peninsula, in the western panhandle, and in along the north central gulf coast, where Confederate control was weak. The East Gulf Blockading Squadron provided supplies and weapons for these small bands. Federal officials ultimately raised two regiments of cavalry from among these guerrilla bands, although other groups preferred to "lay out" in remote areas, avoiding both Union and Confederate service. Confederate deserter William Strickland was perhaps Florida's most notorious Union guerrilla. After serving early in the war in the Confederate cavalry, Strickland deserted and organized a band of friends and relatives named the Independent Union Rangers that operated in Taylor and LaFayette counties. Confederate efforts to capture Strickland failed, although the families of the guerrillas were imprisoned for a time near Tallahassee. Strickland eventually joined the 2d Florida Union Cavalry, but during the March 1865 St. Marks Expedition, Confederate troops captured and executed him.

From 1863 until 1865, Captain John J. Dickison of the 2d Florida Confederate Cavalry engaged in operations comparable to those of John Mosby, though on a smaller scale. In command of a single regular company, often reinforced with a few militia, Dickison defended the interior of Florida against Federal incursions while also mounting a number of small-scale raids into Union-held portions of the state. He earned the sobriquet of Florida's Civil War Swamp Fox.

Other guerrilla activity took place in northern Georgia and Alabama, as well as in western North Carolina and eastern Tennessee, where sizable Unionist minorities organized themselves into quasi-military organizations to protect their families and homes. Louisiana was beset with both pro-Union and pro-Confederate guerrillas, as was Arkansas to the north. In north Texas, Unionists formed armed bands to resist conscription, forcing Confederate officials to mount retaliatory raids against them.

While Confederate guerrillas won a number of minor yet spectacular victories, they did little to affect the course of the war. They did force the North to maintain larger numbers of troops in rear areas prone to guerrilla activity, and their attacks on railroads and wagon trains did lead to temporary logistical problems for Union armies. In addition, the colorful exploits of Mosby, Morgan, and others increased Southern morale and engendered a great deal of concern in the North. Conversely, Unionist guerrillas weakened Southern morale and forced the Confederate military to spend considerable time and effort in curtailing their activities. Consequently, the main legacy of Civil War guerrillas, both Union and Confederate, is that of devastation, misery, and bloodshed, and of contributing to a lasting bitterness that remained in some areas of the South for years after the war.

—*David J. Coles*

See also Centralia Massacre; Kansas; Lawrence, Kansas; Missouri; Morgan, John Hunt; Mosby, John Singleton; Quantrill, William Clarke.

For further reading:

Brownlee, Richard S. *Gray Ghosts of the Confederacy: Guerrilla Warfare in the West, 1861–1865* (1958).

Castel, Albert. "The Guerrilla War, 1861–1865." *Civil War Times Illustrated* (1974).

Fellman, Michael. *Inside War: The Guerrilla Conflict in Missouri during the American Civil War* (1989).

Jones, Virgil Carrington. *Gray Ghosts and Rebel Raiders* (1956).

Neely, Mark E., Jr. "'Unbeknownst' to Lincoln: A Note on Radical Pacification in Missouri during the Civil War." *Civil War History* (1998).

Ramage, James A. *Gray Ghost: The Life of John Singleton Mosby* (1999).

GUROWSKI, COUNT ADAM
(1805–1866)
Northern diarist

Count Adam Gurowski was born near Kalisz, Poland, on 10 September 1805. Descended from a noble Polish family that could trace an ancestor back to the Crusades, Gurowski's father, Count Wladyslaw, was the Chamberlain of the Prussian Royal Court until the partitions of Poland began. Wladyslaw Gurowski thereafter fought alongside Tadeusz Kosciuszko against the Prussian and Russian invaders of Poland and, later, alongside Prince Jozef Poniatowski's Polish Corps in Napoleon Bonaparte's Grand Army. As a result of his efforts, however, Wladyslaw Gurowski found himself stripped of his honors, titles, and most of his land.

Adam Gurowski, therefore, grew up in a comfortable, though not a wealthy household that was vehemently Polish. Expelled from school by the Imperial Russian government for expressing his Polish patriotism, he was forced to travel to Berlin, where he became a pupil of the philosopher Georg Hegel. After his involvement in the Polish Uprising of 1830 against Russian rule and in a plot to kidnap Czar Nicholas I and his family on their state visit to Warsaw, Gurowski was sentenced to death in absentia. In 1834, however, Gurowski became an ardent advocate of Pan-Slavism and was pardoned by the same czar that he had earlier tried to kidnap. After his pardon, he traveled to St. Petersburg and received a junior position in the Ministry of Public Information and Education. For the next ten years, Gurowski worked for the ideal of a Pan-Slavic Russian Empire. Unfortunately, he discovered that the Czar's claims of interest in Pan-Slavism were only further attempts to increase Russia's power at the expense of the Prussian and Austrian Empires. Disillusioned, Gurowski left Russia and spent the next five years wandering Europe and writing about his travels and his political ideas. Finally in 1849, he abandoned Europe for the hope of a brighter future in America.

Once in America, Gurowski hoped to teach at Harvard University but failed to impress its faculty. Almost penniless, he was forced to find employment on the editorial staff of Horace Greeley's *New York Tribune*. For more than a decade, Gurowski wrote articles and pamphlets about domestic and international politics. An ardent opponent of slavery, he had freed the serfs on his family's lands in Poland long before the institution of serfdom had been abolished throughout the Russian Empire. As a result of his ardent opinions on the issue of slavery, Gurowski become a leading abolitionist and an early member of the Republican Party.

Soon after secession began, Gurowski traveled to Washington, D.C., in the hope of securing a major position in the new Republican administration. For almost two years, instead of having a major policymaking role, he worked as a minor clerk in the State Department. After the publication of his *Diary*, he was fired. In his *Diary*, Gurowski gave his opinions of many of the leading Republicans, including President Abraham Lincoln, Secretary of State William H. Seward, and Secretary of War Edwin M. Stanton. Lincoln, he believed, had a "rather slow intellect" and a "slow power of perception." Lincoln was, in Gurowski's mind, much like French King Louis XVI at the beginning of the French Revolution—both had "similar goodness, honesty, [and] good intentions; but the size of events seems too much for him." Gurowski despised Seward for his conciliatory attitude toward the South and for the way he "controlled" Lincoln's direction of the war. "To his ambition, selfishness, ignorance, and innate insincerity he has sacrificed as much of the people's honor, of the people's interests, and the people's blood as was feasible." Stanton, however, emerged a hero in Gurowski's eyes. Stanton was "the only and last true

Roman," and "the statesman so long searched for by me." From his victory at Fort Donelson in 1862 until the end of the war, General Ulysses S. Grant was another one of Gurowski's heroes. "Grant has overpowered men, soil—and [the] elements."

Gurowski was an early advocate of the employment of African-American troops in the war effort. He proposed a bold plan to create whole brigades and divisions of such troops for the purpose of "whipping" the aristocratic slaveholding first families of Virginia. He constantly pestered his hero, Secretary Stanton, for a commission as a colonel in command of a black regiment but was ultimately disappointed by the slow progress on this issue. Gurowski was also a member of the Radical Republican faction that called for President Andrew Johnson's impeachment, though the impeachment would not take place until after his death. Gurowski died of typhoid fever at the Washington, D.C., home of a close friend on 4 May 1866. During his lifetime, some considered Gurowski nothing more than eccentric, while many Radical Republicans considered him one of the greatest thinkers of the age. Regardless of their opinion of the individual, however, most would agree that Count Adam Gurowski was highly influential in both European and American politics.

—*Alexander M. Bielakowski*

See also New York Tribune.
For further reading:
Fischer, LeRoy H. *Lincoln's Gadfly: Adam Gurowski* (1964).
Wytrwal, Joseph A. *Poles in American History and Tradition* (1969).

GUTHRIE, JAMES
(1792–1869)

Compromise committee chair of the 1861 Washington Peace Conference

James Guthrie was born near Bardstown, Kentucky, to Adam and Hannah Polk Guthrie. He studied law with Judge John Rowan and was admitted to the Kentucky bar in 1817. Governor John Adair appointed him commonwealth's attorney in 1820 and Guthrie moved to Louisville. There he met Elizabeth Prather and married her in 1821 and they had three daughters. His wife died in 1836. Guthrie served in both houses of the Kentucky legislature from 1827 to 1840, and in 1849 he presided over Kentucky's third constitutional convention. President Franklin Pierce appointed him secretary of the treasury in 1853. Upon the end of Pierce's term, Guthrie returned to Louisville to serve as vice president and then president of the Louisville & Nashville (L&N) Railroad until 1868, when he supported General William T. Sherman as his successor. Guthrie's leadership in business, transportation, and politics made him one of the wealthiest men in the state.

In 1860 at the Charleston Convention he was a candidate for the presidency at age 69. In February 1861, Guthrie was one of Kentucky's six delegates sent by the legislature to the Washington Peace Conference called by Virginia. On 9 February the delegates from twenty-one states elected former President John Tyler to preside over the Conference, and Guthrie accepted the key role of chair of the Compromise Committee.

Thirteen states, five in the North, had refused to send any delegates at all. The Republican delegates organized a caucus and agreed as a bloc to pass on all proposals. Because the conference commissioners had been named on no uniform basis, they had early on agreed to vote by state even though this put the seven slave states at a disadvantage. This voting procedure checked the conservative minority in several Northern delegations and left the border state conservatives convinced that the Republican Party would not compromise for peace. The convention, conducted in secret sessions, continued despite these obstructions until inauguration eve.

Guthrie tried to revise and reintroduce the compromise plan, proposed by Kentuckian John Crittenden, that had never made it out of the congressional committee a few months before. Sure that the seceding states had begun a "revolution," Guthrie was a states' rights Democrat opposed to secession. He was sure that if the Southern states had stayed in the Union they would have controlled Congress and the judiciary, rendering the Republican president Abraham Lincoln helpless.

The Compromise Committee proposed to the Peace Conference that Congress should focus on Henry Clay's compromise of 1820. The parallel 36° 30' should again be used to divide the existing territory of the United States into free and slave, and no more territory should be annexed except with the consent of equal representation from both the North and the South. The committee described seven constitutional amendments in total. The delegates then asked Congress to call a national convention to consider this idea. The Peace Conference report issued on 27 February was rejected.

After sending a personal appeal to President Lincoln, Guthrie returned to Kentucky. In May 1861 he joined the Border State Convention assembled in Frankfort, where he advocated Kentucky neutrality. This gathering also failed to avert the crisis.

Guthrie returned to his business as president of the L&N Railroad. Though only 286 miles long, the L&N was the only road beginning in Northern territory and ending in Southern territory. The history of the Civil War in Kentucky revolved around the military strategy of the L&N. In 1861 its trains had transported food and supplies into Confederate Tennessee, but after 1862 it was used almost exclusively for transporting the Federal armies advancing into the South. The tracks, bridges, and stations were frequent targets for guerrilla raids; however, work crews of impressed black labor under military guard quickly restored service. Despite millions of dollars of damage, the L&N was liberally supported by the federal government and was paid higher rates for troop transportation than any railroad in the North. Though pressured to give up all management to the military, Guthrie kept control of his lucrative government business. Over one-half of the road's total earnings came from passenger rates. By the end of the war, the road was in better condition than at the beginning, and the board subscribed heavily to building projects such as the bridge over the Ohio River.

Guthrie opposed the Freedmen's Bureau, the Civil Rights Bill, and the Fourteenth Amendment, and he often publicly defended the decisions of President Andrew Johnson. In January 1865 the Kentucky legislature narrowly elected the elderly and conservative Democrat Guthrie to the U.S. Senate over the Lincolnite Radical, general Lovell H. Rousseau, also of Louisville. Guthrie served until 7 February 1868, when he resigned because of his poor health. He died a year later and was buried in Cave Hill Cemetery in Louisville.

—*Randolph Hollingsworth*

See also Kentucky; Railroads, Union; Washington Peace Conference.

For further reading:
Baber, George. "James Guthrie: Lawyer, Financier, and Statesman." *Register of the Kentucky Historical Society* (1912).
Chittenden, L. E. *Report of the Peace Convention in 1861* (1864; reprint 1971).
Cotterill, Robert Spencer. "James Guthrie—Kentuckian, 1792–1869." *Register of the Kentucky Historical Society* (1922).
Harrison, Lowell H. *The Civil War in Kentucky* (1975).
History of the Ohio Falls Cities and their Counties (1882).

H

HABEAS CORPUS, WRIT OF (C.S.A.)

A court-ordered inquiry about the circumstances of an individual's confinement, the writ of habeas corpus—or simply the "writ" or the "plea," as it became known—held serious implications for the Confederate states as a new nation founded on the principle of individual and states' rights.

Unlike Abraham Lincoln, President Jefferson Davis never attempted to suspend the writ without congressional permission. Concern that such powers at the presidential level might encourage military leaders to violate civil liberties made Congress cautious about granting the power of suspension to anyone. Some Confederate leaders, including Vice President Alexander H. Stephens, argued that giving such authority to a central government might infringe on states' rights. They justified their opposition by citing the potential for abuse rather than questioning the integrity of the president or the subordination of the Confederate military to civilian government. Others, however, feared the consequences of not having the power of suspension, citing the growing instances of Unionist meetings, open disloyalty, and espionage as adequate proof that martial law was essential to national security.

Increasingly violent Unionist activities in North Carolina, eastern Tennessee, and Richmond persuaded the 1862 Confederate Congress to grant Davis limited power to suspend the writ of habeas corpus. Congress restricted such suspensions to areas where martial law would aid in local defense and limited the suspensions to a specific length of time, usually thirty to forty-five days. Under these stipulations, Confederate officials could arrest and hold, without due process of law, any suspicious person if that person's detention was deemed essential to the public good.

Popular support for the measure was short-lived. Confederate attorney general Thomas Watts advocated the power of suspension but also warned that average citizens would take little note of subtle restrictions on what they regarded as an oppressive law. Soon the overzealous application of martial law, the suspension of the writ by local military commanders, and the aggressive tactics of Confederate conscription officers forced many Southerners to question any suspension of civilian judicial power.

While civil courts had neither original nor appellate jurisdiction over military cases dealing with conscription or desertion, they did have the right of review under the writ of habeas corpus. Because there was no Confederate Supreme Court and presidential authority was so restricted, voids existed between spheres of Confederate, military, and state influence. Local magistrates and county judges frequently used the writ to gain the release of conscripts, as well as deserters, planters, and political cronies, from the custody of enrollment officers.

The ease of obtaining such writs angered Confederate military leaders from the beginning of conscription efforts. John A. Campbell, assistant secretary of war, wrote that "in every State some local judges seem to have bestirred themselves to withdraw from the service all who by any subtlety could be released." Abolitionists had exercised the writ on numerous occasions to free fugitive slaves arrested in the North and now "some judges, apparently catching the distemper of the time to relieve from the burden of the military service that class of men who above all others are interested in carrying through a revolution commenced for the security of their rights and interests" were exerting "a pernicious influence upon the organization of the Army and the measures of the Confederate government for filling its diminished numbers to a proper standard."

Judicial interference with conscription finally became so prevalent in some areas that the War Department investigated the situation. Because most locally issued writs exploited jurisdictional conflicts between Confederate and state authorities, Attorney General Watts tried to limit local courts' power to issue writs by declaring the supremacy of Confederate law. Thus state courts could exercise no jurisdiction over any matter that Confederate laws touched, and any county or circuit court judge who acted on any writ involving a Confederate soldier or official was exceeding his authority. Subsequent congressional action in February 1864 made it illegal for judges to issue writs affecting men held by Confederate military authorities.

Neither Watts's nor Congress' efforts had any real impact. Many civilian judges ignored Confederate mandates. They continued to issue writs, even in areas under martial law, and did not hesitate to order the arrest of any military official who violated their decisions. And despite the writ's "pernicious influence" in shielding the planter class from military service, it also proved successful in releasing young boys, old men, and the mentally or physically disabled who had been swept up by indiscriminate conscription efforts.

The Confederate government and individual judges never resolved their ideological differences. And even though Congress couched its debate about suspension in states' rights rhetoric, it correctly focused on the potential for despotic government. Moreover, by granting even a restricted power of suspension, Congress took a significant step toward centralizing political and military power in Richmond. Ultimately the subordination of state governments to the national government was deemed necessary for the national war effort.

—*David Carlson*

See also Civil Liberties, C.S.A.; Constitution, C.S.A.; Courts, C.S.A.; Habeas Corpus, Writ of (U.S.A.).

For further reading:

De Roulhac Hamilton, J.G. "The State Courts and the Confederate Constitution." *Journal of Southern History* (1938).
Mitchell, Memory F. *Legal Aspects of Conscription and Exemption in North Carolina, 1861–1865* (1965).
Moore, Albert B., ed. *Conscription and Conflict in the Confederacy* (1924; reprint, 1996).
Robbins, John B. "The Confederacy and the Writ of Habeas Corpus." *Georgia Historical Quarterly* (1971).

HABEAS CORPUS, WRIT OF (U.S.A.)

The so-called great writ of liberty—literally "right of the body"—is an order, given by any judge, that requires authorities to bring prisoners to court and specify the crimes for which they are being held. It is specifically addressed in Article I of the Constitution, where it is written that, "The privilege of the writ of habeas corpus shall not be suspended, unless when in cases of rebellion or invasion the public safety may require it." Prior to the Civil War, the government's right to suspend the writ, and thus imprison people indefinitely without cause, had rarely been exercised. The last time had been in 1815, when General Andrew Jackson suspended it after the battle of New Orleans. During the Civil War, however, suspension of the writ would be a fairly common occurrence.

President Lincoln first suspended the writ on 27 April 1861 "at any point or in the vicinity of the military line…between the City of Philadelphia and the City of Washington." He allowed General-in-Chief Winfield Scott to make arrests at his discretion to prevent unfriendly Marylanders from interfering with communications between Washington, D.C. and the rest of the North. Several sensational arrests resulted, including Baltimore's chief of police and mayor. Several members of the Maryland legislature were also arrested to keep them from voting to secede from the Union. The arrest that would prove most significant occurred on 25 May,

when a Southern sympathizer named John Merryman was imprisoned. Merryman sued, and Chief Justice Roger Taney ruled in *Ex parte Merryman* that the suspension of the writ was illegal. Lincoln ignored Taney's ruling, and in a speech on 4 July 1861, he wondered whether it was wise to allow "the government itself to go to pieces" for the sake of one law.

The exchange between Lincoln and Taney did not end the debate, however. Doubt over the issue stemmed from the vague wording of the Constitution, which allowed for the writ to be suspended but did not specify which branch of government had the power to do so. Before Lincoln suspended the writ, it was generally assumed that the power was vested in the Congress. The president's position, however, was supported by his attorney general, Edward Bates, who wrote an opinion on the matter that argued that the government's three branches were "co-ordinate and coequal" and that therefore "the judgment of one of them is not binding upon the other two." Lincoln was also defended in a widely circulated pamphlet entitled *The Privilege of the Writ of Habeas Corpus under the Constitution*, written by a Philadelphia lawyer named Horace Binney.

As the debate raged, American citizens continued to be arbitrarily arrested. On 24 September 1862 and again on 15 September 1863, the president suspended the writ "throughout the United States." A few of those arrested really were enemy collaborators, but the majority of them were arrested for political crimes, namely opposing the policies of the administration. There is some debate as to exactly how many citizens were arrested. A number as high as 40,000 has been suggested, while the commissary general published an official figure of 13,535. Given the spotty nature of Civil War era bookkeeping, this number is probably a little low, and the real number is likely somewhere near the middle of the two extremes. Arrests were initially carried out under the auspices of the State Department, but the authority was transferred to the War Department shortly after Edwin Stanton took control.

Over the course of the war, Democrats repeatedly charged Lincoln with being a tyrant for allowing arbitrary arrests. It is certainly true that he suspended the writ and that he used the power freely and without compunction when he felt it was necessary. Lincoln believed that dissent in the North helped the Southern cause, and he was correct, at least to an extent. The president defended himself in a well-publicized letter to Erastus Corning in June 1862, noting that he was "thoroughly imbued with a reverence for the guaranteed rights of individuals" and that he was "slow to adopt the strong measures, which by degrees I have been forced to regard as being within the exceptions of the constitution, and indispensable to the public safety." Lincoln never used the power for personal gain, and in the balance it seems that Democratic charges that he was a tyrant were essentially political rhetoric. However, it was political rhetoric that worked, as the habeas corpus issue hurt Republicans and Lincoln in the 1862 and 1864 elections.

In March 1863, Congress passed the Habeas Corpus Indemnity Act that authorized the President to suspend the writ. This action was, in part, an attempt by Congress to assert itself and to affirm that the right to suspend the writ belonged to them. The act was also an attempt to regularize and control the arbitrary arrest of citizens, by requiring that lists of prisoners be submitted to federal judges within 20 days of their arrest.

The suspension of the writ in some ways set the stage for Congressional Reconstruction, as politicians began to take a pragmatic, rather than an idealistic, view of civil rights and the government's right to grant or deny them. Certainly the civil rights of both African-Americans and former Confederates were among the main issues of Reconstruction, and the military control of defeated Southern states mirrored the treatment of Northern dissenters during the war.

—*Christopher Bates*

See also Ex parte Merryman; Habeas Corpus, Writ of (C.S.A.).
For further reading:
Anderson, Eric Paul. "The Body of John Merryman: *Ex Parte Merryman*, a Case of Executive-Judicial Conflict over the Suspension of Habeas Corpus" (M.A. thesis, 1979).

HAHN, GEORG MICHAEL DECKER
(1830–1886)

Governor of Louisiana and U.S. congressman

Georg Michael Decker Hahn (known throughout his life in the United States as Michael Hahn) was born in Klingemünster, Bavaria. He came to the United States with his widowed mother when he was a small child and for a time lived in New York City. When Hahn was ten years old, his mother moved with the family to New Orleans, Louisiana. He was educated locally before embarking on the study of law at the University of Louisiana. He graduated in 1851 and began practicing in New Orleans.

In the years before the Civil War, Hahn became a prominent citizen of the community and was active in Democratic politics. He strongly opposed secession (and slavery) and worked for the election of Stephen Douglas in the state. With secession and the outbreak of the Civil War, he remained in New Orleans, quietly practicing law. The Federal capture and occupation of New Orleans in 1862, however, allowed him to express his true feelings.

Hahn was one of the first citizens of New Orleans to swear an oath of loyalty to the United States. His views regarding the Union before the war were well known,

and as a result he quickly had the trust of the military occupiers of the city. When elections were held in the late fall of 1862 to fill the occupied area's seats in Congress, Hahn was elected as a Republican to represent one of the districts. Irregularities in the voting procedures and perhaps Hahn's previous affiliation with the Democratic Party caused a delay in his taking his seat. He served only one month, from February to 4 March 1863, before his term expired. During that short time, however, he demonstrated himself to be a loyal Republican. He returned home to help organize the civilian government in the increasingly large Union-occupied parts of Louisiana.

Upon Hahn's return to New Orleans, the military government appointed Hahn as prize collector for the port. Over the next few months, he urged through the newspaper he had purchased, the *Daily True Delta*, the establishment of a civilian government, and when elections were held in early 1864, he was elected the first Union governor of the state. He held the position for a little over one year, during which time he maintained close ties with the military in Louisiana, becoming a good friend of General Nathaniel P. Banks.

One of Hahn's first acts as governor was to call a state constitutional convention to produce a new constitution to replace the one that had been in effect under the Confederacy. Hahn also worked over the next year to implement President Abraham Lincoln's plan for reconstruction, attempting to make Louisiana a model for other occupied areas. In the occupied areas, Hahn's efforts to rebuild the economy of the state made him popular even in some areas that had been strongly pro-secession before the war. When elections for the U.S. Senate were held in the fall of 1864, Hahn was elected to one of Louisiana's seats. He resigned the governorship in early 1865 to go to Washington to assume his new position. Again irregularities in the election procedures caused a delay in his taking his seat, and after the assassination of President Lincoln, the efforts on the part of Congress and the new president, Andrew Johnson, to start over with regard to the reconstruction of Louisiana caused Hahn to leave the capital in disgust. He never assumed his Senate seat.

Hahn returned to New Orleans, where he returned to journalism, the pursuit that would occupy him for much of the remainder of his life. In 1866 he was wounded in one of New Orleans's periodic street brawls and never fully recovered his health. In 1867, when he was able to resume some work, he founded the New Orleans *Daily Republican*. He edited the paper for four years, but then his health forced him to retire to his plantation in St. Charles Parish. Not able to remain inactive for long, however, the following year he founded a newspaper in the parish and laid out a new town for workers in the area that became known as Hahnville. In the same year,

he was elected to the state legislature from his new district and served two terms.

Hahn remained active in state Republican politics even after the end of Reconstruction, and because of his reputation as an honest, civic-minded man, he won election to Congress in the fall of 1884. He served one year of his two-year term. He died in his sleep in Washington at the beginning of his second year in Congress on 15 March 1886.

—*David S. Heidler and Jeanne T. Heidler*

See also Louisiana.
For further reading:
U.S. Congress. *Memorial Addresses on the Life and Character of Michael Hahn (A Representative of Louisiana) Delivered in the House of Representatives and in the Senate, Forty-ninth Congress, First Session* (1886).
Winters, John D. *The Civil War in Louisiana* (1963).

HALL, MARIA M. C.
(?–1912)
Union relief worker

Born in Washington, D.C., to an elite family, Maria M. C. Hall worked in general and field hospitals in the Eastern theater during all four years of the war. Like one of hundreds of women initially turned down by Union army Nursing Superintendent Dorothea Dix because they were in their twenties, Hall circumvented the application process and found regular work as her nursing skill and dedication became known. Before conflict ensued in 1861, Hall cared for sick soldiers in her parents' home. After the battle of First Bull Run, she and a sister sought the help of Almira Fales, a nurse already established in Washington, to find them places at the Patent Office Hospital. After a year of service, Hall joined the crew of the *Daniel Webster* during George B. McClellan's inauspicious Peninsula campaign of 1862. From White House Landing on the Pamunkey River and later from Harrison's Landing on the James River, Hall washed, fed, and tried to sustain the lives of hundreds of soldiers wounded at Fair Oaks and during the Seven Days' battles as they were transported back to Washington. Many of the 11,000 casualties from these two battles had received no food, water, or medical attention for three days, and died on board.

Hall is best known for her work at Smoketown Hospital established in the field two weeks after the battle of Antietam in September 1862. Situated in a grove of oak and walnut trees, by October this tent hospital had 527 patients who were recovering from amputations and gunshot wounds. Working with nurses Eliza Harris and Mary Morris Husband of Philadelphia, Hall remained at Smoketown until it closed in May 1863, for months the only woman on site and the only woman to have been photographed there. Surgeon Bernard A. Vanderkieft,

the ranking medical officer at Smoketown, asked Hall to join him at the naval hospital in Annapolis as wounded poured in from Gettysburg in July 1863; later she would nurse Union prisoners exchanged from the Confederacy's Libby, Andersonville, Florence, and Salisbury prisons. She remained in Annapolis through the summer of 1865, succeeding Adaline Tyler as superintendent in the spring of 1864. Little is known about Hall's life after the war; she wrote no memoir or narrative as did several other relief workers included in this encyclopedia. She ultimately married a man named Richards and received a monthly pension of $12 after Congress passed the Army Nurses Pension Act in 1892.

—*Jane E. Schultz*

See also Nurses; Women.
For further reading:
Brockett, Linus P., and Mary Vaughan. *Woman's Work in the Civil War* (1867).
Moore, Frank. *Women of the War: Their Heroism and Self-Sacrifice* (1866).
Scott, Kate M. *In Honor of the National Association of Army Nurses* (1910).

HALLECK, HENRY WAGER
(1815–1872)
Union general

Henry Wager Halleck was born at Westernville, New York, seemingly destined for a life on the farm. Detesting agriculture, he ran away from home at an early age and was raised by an uncle. Young Halleck showed promise as a scholar, and in 1837 he gained admittance to the U.S. Military Academy. He quickly became a favorite of theorist Dennis H. Mahan and was allowed to teach classes while still a cadet. In 1839, Halleck graduated third in his class, and he functioned as a second lieutenant in the Corps of Engineers. After spending several years improving the defenses of New York harbor, he was chosen to conduct a lengthy inspection of European fortifications. Rising to first lieutenant in 1845, Halleck returned home and gained additional renown by delivering a series of lectures on warfare in Boston. These were subsequently published as *Elements of Military Art & Science* (1846) and are now recognized as one of the first expressions of American military professionalism.

When the Mexican-American War erupted in 1846, Halleck volunteered for duty and sailed to the West Coast as aide-de-camp to Commodore John T. Shubrick. He spent the six-month transit rendering the first English-language edition of Henri Jomini's *Vie politique et militaire de Napoleon*, which further enhanced his reputation for scholarship. Lower California at that time was something of a military backwater, so Halleck spent several months with little else to do than construct fortifications. His first exposure to combat occurred with the 11 November 1847 capture of the port of Mazatlan, after which he efficiently served as lieutenant governor of the city. Brevetted captain in May 1847, he transferred north under General Bennet Riley, then governor general of the newly annexed California Territory. Halleck favorably impressed Riley with his administrative acumen, and he gained appointment as secretary of state. In this capacity, Halleck demonstrated a flair for politics and assisted in drawing up the California state constitution. He also found time to establish a law firm in San Francisco, whose very success prompted his resignation from the army in 1854. The following year he married Elizabeth Hamilton, granddaughter of Alexander Hamilton.

During the next six years, Halleck made a fortune through legal activities and land speculation. His talent for administration subsequently led to an appointment as president of the Atlantic & Pacific Railroad, and he also functioned as a major general of militia. In 1861, Halleck further displayed his mastery of legal matters when he published a treatise entitled *International Law,* which was widely read and went through several editions.

Halleck was nominally a Democrat and was sympathetic to the South. However, he evinced strong Unionist sympathies, and when the Civil War commenced in April 1861, he tendered his services to the War Department. Largely because of his pristine reputation and the advice of General Winfield Scott, President Abraham Lincoln made him one of only a handful of full major generals. In November 1861, he transferred to St. Louis as head of the Department of the Missouri and was ordered to clean up the mess left behind by his predecessor, John C. Frémont. Regional Union forces at that time were totally disorganized and demoralized, while the lower reaches of the state were firmly in the hands of the former governor, Confederate general Sterling Price. However, Halleck proved fully equal to the task of overhauling the department's creaking bureaucracy. Within months, his troops were systematically paid, equipped, and trained, and Missouri was kept firmly in the Union fold. The Union victory at Pea Ridge on 7 January 1862 was in fair measure the outgrowth of his administrative endeavors. In recognition of this success, Halleck's command was enlarged and reconstituted as the Department of the Mississippi. He also gained the moniker of "Old Brains" in recognition of his bureaucratic wizardry.

With his backyard in order, Halleck began to survey his theater and sensed a strategic opportunity before him. In concert with another new general, Ulysses S. Grant, he devised a successful scheme to penetrate the main Confederate line of defense and sever the critical Memphis & Charleston Railroad. In the spring of 1862, Halleck unleashed troops under Grant and naval forces

Henry W. Halleck (*Library of Congress*)

under Andrew H. Foote against Forts Henry and Donelson on the Cumberland and Tennessee rivers. Their ensuing success meant that Union forces were enabled to advance deeper into Confederate territory, and Halleck selected the strategic railroad center at Corinth, Mississippi, as his next objective. From St. Louis, he then orchestrated a concerted effort by Grant and the armies of John Pope and Don Carlos Buell in a large-scale offensive. Pope masterfully secured Island No. 10, which cleared the Mississippi River as far south as Vicksburg. Grant, however, was surprised and nearly defeated by Albert S. Johnston at Shiloh on 6–7 April 1862. This close call induced Halleck to leave St. Louis and take to the field. He ignored cries to replace Grant and, fortunately for the war effort, kept him as a subordinate.

Halleck's subsequent advance on Corinth proved overtly methodical. Moving at a snail's pace and constantly erecting defensive works, Union forces proceeded so ponderously against their objective that the outnumbered forces of General Pierre G. T. Beauregard easily escaped. Public criticism of his performance angered Halleck, and he expelled reporters

from his camp, an act that did little to endear him to national newspapers. Moreover, his uninspiring debut induced Lincoln to relieve Halleck and summon him to Washington, where his scholarly abilities were thought to be better suited. Nonetheless, and to his lasting credit, Halleck left Union prospects for success in the west infinitely better than when he arrived.

In July 1862, Halleck gained appointment as general-in-chief of all Union forces. He was so posited in an attempt to bring strategic direction and coordination to the foundering war effort. As expected, he excelled at marshaling the raw resources of war, and his efforts greatly facilitated the training, equipping, and deployment of thousands of Union troops over vast areas. Moreover, being conversant in the nuances of both military and civilian life, he was well suited to serve as a liaison between the commander in chief, the secretary of war, and their generals. Simply put, Halleck had a knack for making the concerns of either party intelligible to the other.

However, Halleck was uniformly unsuccessful in the role of grand strategist. For all his genius, he was saddled with a cold, abrasive personality which alienated subordinates and did little to promote unity of command. One observer characterized him as a "cold, calculating owl." His testy disposition and grotesque, goggle-eyed appearance also made him an easy target for the Union press corps, who savaged him at every available opportunity. But most importantly, Halleck the bureaucrat greatly overshadowed Halleck the soldier. He showed little stomach for taking risks and steadfastly refused responsibility for events or operations that went awry. Subordinates in the field seemed intuitively aware of these shortcomings, and for two years strong personalities like George B. McClellan, Pope, and Ambrose Burnside routinely brushed off or ignored his advice and instructions. Thus, American strategy was allowed to drift under the succession of differing commanders, none of whom shared Lincoln's vision of a broad advance along many fronts.

Halleck's tenure in the east was marked by an inability to get along with commanders in the field or make them adhere to his strategic prerogatives. This, coupled with a nearly manic obsession with the security of Washington, D.C., almost neutralized his performance as commanding general. McClellan, meanwhile, did a masterful job ignoring his superior's pleas for action throughout the 1862 Peninsula campaign. His subsequent refusal to come to the aid of John Pope during Second Bull Run, and the ensuing rout, exercised a debilitating effect on Halleck. Thereafter, he withdrew further and further into his administrative duties and took less interest in field operations. In January 1863, when President Lincoln ordered him to visit and consult with General Ambrose Burnside in the field, he refused and threatened to resign if forced to do so. When the

president finally relented, Halleck simply resumed his role as a superefficient bureaucrat.

However detached and politically isolated Halleck was in Washington, he took a special interest in western affairs. Throughout the crucial Vicksburg campaign, he gave useful advice and support to Grant and saw to it that he possessed the men, supplies, and wherewithal to succeed. Grant, naturally aggressive, formed a good working relationship with his superior. But, typically, Halleck had much less success in prodding lead-footed generals like William S. Rosecrans and Benjamin Butler to advance in support. He waxed ineffectually during initial phases of the decisive Gettysburg campaign and, when Robert E. Lee invaded Pennsylvania, he rejected General Joseph Hooker's plausible suggestion for a surprise attack on a thinly defended Richmond. He wielded even less influence over Hooker's successor, General George Gordon Meade, and could not convince him to vigorously pursue the retiring enemy. Thus, into the third year of the war, Halleck failed to lend much in the way of strategic leadership or coherence to the war effort. Outside the realm of men and materiel, his impact on the course of events remained minimal.

The impasse finally broke in the spring of 1864, when Lincoln appointed Grant to the position of commanding general. Halleck, weary of the post, graciously accepted a "kick upstairs" to become the army's chief of staff. This senior administrative post played to his strengths perfectly as, for once, Halleck did not have to beg his subordinate to attack. Throughout the arduous Wilderness campaign of 1864, Halleck saw to it that Grant's battered battalions were properly supplied, equipped, and reinforced on a scale that ultimately wore out the Confederates. Moreover, he drew the same conclusions as General William T. Sherman respecting the implementation of "total war" toward the Southern civilians, and authorized both the destructive March to the Sea and General Philip H. Sheridan's spoilation of the Shenandoah Valley. At length, the combination of Grant's strategic aggressiveness and Halleck's bureaucratic finesse culminated in total victory over the Confederacy. And, alongside Sherman and Sheridan, he is rightly regarded as one of the fathers of modern warfare.

After hostilities ceased, Halleck was assigned to command the Military Division of the James, headquartered at Richmond. There he quarreled with his former associate Sherman over the latter's leniency toward former Confederates; the tenor of their dispute caused an irreversible rupture between the former friends. Consequently, in August 1865 he was transferred to a less sensitive position with the Division of the Pacific. Halleck languished there in military exile until March 1869, when he was reassigned to the Division of the South, headquartered at Louisville. He died there in

January 1872, unloved, and with his genuine contributions to Union victory overlooked or derided.

—*John C. Fredriksen*

See also Corinth; Grant, Ulysses Simpson; Lincoln, Abraham; Stanton, Edwin.

For further reading:
Ambrose, Stephen E. *Halleck: Lincoln's Chief of Staff* (1962).
Green, Carl R. *Union Generals of the Civil War* (1998).
Simon, John Y. *Grant and Halleck: Contrasts in Command* (1996).

HALPINE, CHARLES GRAHAM
(1829–1868)
Writer and Union officer

Born to Nicholas John Halpine and Anne Grehan Halpine in County Meath, Ireland, Charles Graham Halpine was educated at Trinity College before embarking on a journalistic career in Dublin and then London. In 1851 he moved to the United States, where he made a living as a secretary for a time to Stephen Douglas and as a part-time writer before turning to journalism in New York. He also published some of his poetry in various periodicals.

As a journalist Halpine reported on some of the exciting events of the day, including those that contributed to the growing sectional rift between North and South. One of his most famous series in the *New York Times* covered one of William Walker's filibustering expeditions to Nicaragua. After these articles, he was advanced to Washington, D.C., correspondent for the *Times*. Before the Civil War, Halpine became the editor of the *Leader*, and he used his position to further political reform in New York City. Along with his journalism, Halpine contributed poetry and humorous pieces to a variety of publications, gaining a wide reputation throughout the United States as a writer.

At the outbreak of the Civil War, Halpine enlisted as a private in the 69th New York militia, a ninety-day unit. Before being mustered out in August 1861, he had risen to the rank of lieutenant. In September 1861 he received a major's commission and joined the staff of Brigadier General David Hunter on his way to assume command of the Western Department headquartered in St. Louis.

Halpine became Hunter's adjutant general and would serve in that capacity for much of the remaining time he was in the army. He served in the West until the following spring, dividing his time between St. Louis and Fort Leavenworth. In the spring of 1862 when Hunter was made commander of the Department of the South, Halpine left for South Carolina. He accompanied his commander on the siege of Fort Pulaski, Georgia. While there, Halpine prepared Hunter's proclamation of 12 April 1862 freeing all the slaves within Union lines and the following month's document that proclaimed the freedom of all slaves in the Department of the South. President Abraham Lincoln overruled Hunter on both counts.

Later in the summer of 1862, after the army had returned to headquarters at Hilton Head, South Carolina, Halpine prepared Hunter's orders organizing the first African-American regiment. When many Northerners, military and civilian, protested this action, Halpine wrote a poem, titled "Sambo's Right to be Kilt," which defended the action and was published in the New York *Herald*.

While in the army, Halpine also continued to write pieces for various Northern newspapers. These works took the form of both letters, written under pseudonyms and criticizing the lack of support for the war effort, and humorous articles, written by his creation, Private Miles O'Reilly. O'Reilly was an uneducated Irish immigrant who educated the Northern public about the war effort at the same time that he amused them. Halpine's articles became popular among the Northern reading public.

Halpine continued to serve along the South Carolina coast until June 1863, when Hunter was relieved from command of the department. In the meantime, Halpine had been promoted to lieutenant colonel of volunteers at the end of 1862. By the summer of 1863, however, he had learned that his eyesight was becoming progressively worse and as a result took an extended leave of absence in New York City. While there, he continued to write extensively, primarily under his various pseudonyms, in support of the war effort.

In May 1864, Hunter assumed command of the Department of Western Virginia, and he sent a summons to his former adjutant to join him there. Halpine did so, reassuming his adjutant position in this new theater. Halpine served under Hunter until the end of July, during which time he gained the enthusiastic commendation of this commander for his conduct at the battle of Piedmont on 5 June 1864. Halpine's eyes, however, had not improved, and he could not keep pace with the paperwork of this demanding position. As a result, he resigned on 31 July 1864. At the end of the war, he received a brevet promotion to brigadier general for his service during the conflict, most notably at Piedmont.

After leaving the army, Halpine continued his crusade against corruption in New York City, first as the editor of the reform paper, the *Citizen*, and then in the elected office of register of the City of New York. He also continued to write, publishing some of his Private O'Reilly pieces and other works. He died in New York on 3 August 1868 after breathing a large amount of chloroform as treatment for insomnia.

—*David S. Heidler and Jeanne T. Heidler*

See also Fort Pulaski; Hunter, David; Piedmont, Virginia, Battle of.

For further reading:
Hanchett, William. *Irish: Charles G. Halpine in Civil War America* (1970).

HALSTEAD, MURAT
(1829–1908)
Journalist

Born to Griffin Halstead and Clarissa Willets Halstead in Ross Township, Ohio, Murat Halstead was educated locally before enrolling in Cincinnati's Farmers' College. He graduated in 1851 having already determined upon a career in journalism. After two years writing for a variety of papers, Halstead went to work for the Cincinnati *Commercial*, the paper that he would be associated with for much of the rest of his life.

Halstead, who from the beginning of his career with the *Commercial* began buying interests in the paper, quickly gained the reputation of an active journalist who liked to travel to the news. His partial interest in the paper allowed him to indulge in that travel. Politics became his specialty in these early years. He attended both the Democratic National Convention and the first Republican nominating convention in 1856 and wrote extensive articles about both for the *Commercial*. In 1859, he traveled to Charlestown, Virginia, to cover the execution of John Brown. In 1860 his coverage of both of the Democratic Conventions in Charleston, South Carolina, and Baltimore, Maryland, and the Republican Convention in Chicago became classics of political reporting.

By the outbreak of the Civil War, Halstead was editing the *Commercial*, though these duties did not stop him from spending most of his time in Washington, D.C., and at the front. Halstead was one of the first journalists in the United States openly to criticize the performance of military commanders in the field, opening the door for what would become steady and unrelenting criticism from war correspondents throughout the conflict. His first foray into such criticism came when he wrote a scathing attack of the handling of Union forces at Big Bethel on the York Peninsula on 10 June 1861. Halstead considered the commander of Union forces on the Peninsula, Massachusetts Democratic politician Benjamin Butler, to be politically corruptible and militarily incompetent and did not waste time informing his readership of these opinions.

In his efforts to be first with a story, Halstead sometimes fell into the trap during the war of publishing first and substantiating later. This was particularly the case in late 1861 when he rushed to print with the story circulating throughout the West that William Tecumseh Sherman, who had been relieved from command in Kentucky at his request, was really relieved from duty because he was insane. Although Sherman had shown some effects of stress in Kentucky, never was he insane, and Halstead and the *Commercial* had trouble explaining why the paper had rushed to print with the story.

Some of Halstead's best reporting came in December 1862 and January 1863 when he traveled to the front at Fredericksburg, Virginia, and reported on the battle there. Not only did he provide vivid accounts of the carnage of the battle, but his efforts to portray the human side of the drama by writing about the normal conversations of officers and men before the battle brought the war home for his readers.

While Halstead was certainly interested in making the war more real for readers in the North, he never gave up trying to influence military matters that he believed the government ignored. In early 1863 he became incensed with what he believed were the wasteful activities of Ulysses S. Grant in his efforts to take Vicksburg, Mississippi. He believed that Grant was wasting time, money, and lives on a fruitless campaign of maneuver and Halstead wrote to his acquaintance, Secretary of the Treasury Salmon Chase, trying to have Grant removed from command. This lapse aside, through the entire war, Halstead had the reputation as one of the most talented and insightful of the country's war correspondents.

After the war Halstead continued as editor of the *Commercial*. He missed the excitement of war correspondent, however, and in 1870 traveled to Europe to cover the Franco-Prussian War. Upon his return to the United States, Halstead resumed his editorial duties with the *Commercial* and, with that, indulged his continued interest in politics. He and the paper supported the presidential candidacy of newspaper editor Horace Greeley in opposition to Grant in 1872. Halstead continued in his position until the *Commercial* merged with the Cincinnati *Daily Gazette* in the early 1880s, at which time he took over editing chores for the resulting paper, the *Commercial Gazette*.

At the end of the 1880s Halstead moved to New York, where he edited the Brooklyn *Standard-Union* for a short time. He was nominated in 1889 to serve as minister to Germany but was rejected by the Senate. He then turned his writing abilities to books. He wrote on a variety of subjects over the next decade and a half, including history and current affairs. He died on 2 July 1908, one of the country's most respected journalists and authors.

—*David S. Heidler and Jeanne T. Heidler*

See also Newspapers; War Correspondents.
For further reading:
Andrews, J. Cutler. *The North Reports the Civil War* (1955).
Curl, Donald W. *Murat Halstead and the Cincinnati Commercial* (1980).
———. "Murat Halstead, Editor and Politician" (Dissertation, 1964).

HAMBLIN, JOSEPH ELDRIDGE
(1828–1870)
Union general

Born to Benjamin Hamblin and Hannah Sears Hamblin, Joseph Eldridge Hamblin spent most of his youth in Boston, Massachusetts. He was educated in Boston but as a young man moved to New York City. There he made his living as an insurance broker and became active in the 7th New York National Guard. He moved for a time to St. Louis where he was also active in militia organizations. Hamblin returned to New York before the firing on Fort Sumter. After that event, he accepted a lieutenant's commission in the 5th New York, also known as Duryée's Zouaves. After arriving in Washington, D.C., the unit was mustered into U.S. service on 10 May 1861.

Placed under Major General Benjamin F. Butler, Hamblin and the 5th fought at Big Bethel in June 1861. In August 1861 Hamblin was promoted to captain and detailed to Baltimore, where he worked on fortifications there. In November, Hamblin received another promotion to major and moved to the 65th New York. As part of his new regiment, Hamblin fought in all the major engagements of the Peninsula campaign and earned promotion to lieutenant colonel in July 1862.

As lieutenant colonel of the 65th, Hamblin fought in the Maryland campaign and at Fredericksburg. At Chancellorsville the following May, he commanded the regiment and earned promotion to colonel by the end of the month. Hamblin led his regiment to Pennsylvania in the Gettysburg campaign, but as part of John Sedgwick's VI Corps he did not see action until the third day of the battle. Positioned to guard the left flank of the Union position, Hamblin and the rest of VI Corps experienced some of the Confederate morning attacks that were intended to divert men away from the Union center, later the object of Pickett's Charge.

Hamblin continued to command the 65th during the Bristoe Station and Mine Run campaigns in the fall of 1863 and at the end of the year temporarily commanded the brigade. By the end of January 1864, he was back in command of the 65th and began Ulysses S. Grant's campaign against Robert E. Lee at the Wilderness in May 1864 in that position. He again temporarily commanded the brigade in the middle of the month.

Once the campaign had settled into the trenches of Petersburg at the end of June 1864, Hamblin was transferred with the 65th to Major General David Hunter's Department of West Virginia. Upon Hunter's resignation, Hamblin became a participant in Phil Sheridan's Shenandoah Valley campaign. He fought at Winchester, Fisher's Hill, and Cedar Creek, where on 19 October 1864 Hamblin received his first injury of the war, a severe bullet wound to the thigh. He was commended by his brigade commander, Brigadier General Frank Wheaton, for gallantry and recommended for promotion to brigadier general of volunteers for his actions at Cedar Creek. Hamblin spent three months recuperating from his wound. Sheridan recommended Hamblin for a brevet promotion to brigadier general for the same action, and Hamblin received that promotion on 29 December 1864.

Hamblin returned to duty with the Army of the Potomac in the trenches of Petersburg in late January 1865. He commanded a brigade in the Appomattox campaign and was again commended by Phil Sheridan for his actions at Sayler's Creek on 6 April 1865. Sheridan recommended that Hamblin be promoted to brigadier general of volunteers for his actions there. He was promoted to that rank on 19 May 1865. He was brevetted major general for Sayler's Creek.

After the war Hamblin returned to New York City. He reentered the insurance business. He became an executive in the Commonwealth Fire Insurance Company and remained active in the New York National Guard. He died suddenly in New York City on 3 July 1870.

—*David S. Heidler and Jeanne T. Heidler*

See also Cedar Creek; Sayler's Creek.
For further reading:
Hamblin, Deborah. *Brevet Major-General Joseph Eldridge Hamblin, 1861–65* (1902).
Lewis, Thomas A. *The Guns of Cedar Creek* (1988).

HAMILTON, ANDREW JACKSON
(1815–1875)
Military and provisional governor of Texas

Named by his father, a militia captain under Andrew Jackson, A. J. Hamilton was, like Old Hickory, a die-hard Union Democrat. Hamilton moved from Alabama to Texas in 1846 and to Austin in 1849, where he established a law practice. After stints as acting attorney general and as a state senator, he went to Congress in 1859 as an Independent Democrat and ally of the Unionist governor of Texas, Sam Houston. Two years later, he served on the Congressional Committee of Thirty-Three, which vainly tried to find some sort of compromise solution to the impending conflict between the states. Although he refused to resign his seat in the U.S. House of Representatives when Texas seceded, Hamilton did eventually return to Austin. In 1862, with a price on his head, he fled to Mexico and then to Washington, D.C., where he received a commission as brigadier general of volunteers in the Union army.

Hamilton never commanded troops in the field, but he was lionized by the *New York Times* during a speaking tour of the North in the fall of 1862 as one "of those sturdy and irrepressible patriots who ennoble their race by devotion to their country." His conversion to abolitionism—he was a former slaveowner—and heated attacks on the "slaveocracy" won him friends in high places. Appointed military governor of Texas by President Lincoln, he went to New Orleans in 1863 to await the anticipated Union invasion of the Lone Star State. When it came in the form of the Rio Grande campaign later that same year, Hamilton set up a provisional government in Brownsville. Federal interest in Texas waned, however, and most of the troops were withdrawn in summer 1864. Hamilton went back to New Orleans to wait out the war.

It was more than a year before he finally returned to Texas. Several weeks after Federal authority in the state was reestablished in June 1865, Hamilton returned to Austin as provisional governor of Texas. Hamilton had been selected because of his steadfast Unionism and availability. As the first of the state's four Reconstruction governors, his relative moderation (he had only a limited interest in extending full civil rights to African-Americans) seemed too moderate to Radical Republicans and still too liberal to former Confederates. Like all of the provisional governors of the vanquished Confederate states, Hamilton's first order of business was to appoint state, county, and local officials of known loyalty. During his year in office, he refused to pardon large planters who had supported the Confederacy. Yet in his appointments he walked a fine line between the need to have trustworthy Union men in office and the need to have experienced administrators and judges. Not surprisingly, his administration was rarely satisfactory to members of either faction.

Hamilton delayed calling a convention to revise the state constitution until early 1866. He then asked the assembled delegates to declare the 1861 act of secession not only null and void, but also unconstitutional. He also requested them to repudiate Texas's war debts, ratify the Thirteenth Amendment to the United States Constitution, and guarantee the civil and property rights of freedmen—with the exception of the right to vote. Although the convention did repudiate the war debt, it incorporated virtually none of Hamilton's other recommendations. A few months later, former Confederate James W. Throckmorton won the gubernatorial election, and late in August 1866 President Andrew Johnson declared the insurrection at an end in Texas.

Hamilton remained an important force in Texas politics, however, along with his brother Morgan, a Radical Republican who would later become a United States senator. By late 1866, A. J. Hamilton had come out in favor of suffrage for the former slaves. He also believed that a federal military presence would be necessary to protect the freedmen. And yet A. J. Hamilton would never be identified as a radical. As a delegate to the 1868 Constitutional Convention, he successfully led the

opposition to the political disqualification of former Confederates and he was a persistent critic of Radical Republican governor Edmund Davis's administration for its high taxes and centralization of power in the state government.

Hamilton served on the Supreme Court of Texas and ran unsuccessfully for governor as a moderate Republican/Democrat fusion candidate in 1869. He died of tuberculosis at the age of sixty in 1875.

—James Marten

See also Houston, Sam; Texas.

For further reading:
Campbell, Randolph B. *Grass-Roots Reconstruction in Texas, 1865–1880* (1997).
Marten, James. *Texas Divided: Loyalty & Dissent in the Lone Star State, 1856–1874* (1990).
Waller, John L. *Colossal Hamilton of Texas: A Biography of Andrew Jackson Hamilton* (1968).

HAMILTON, SCHUYLER
(1822–1903)
Union general

Born to John Church Hamilton (the son of Alexander Hamilton) and Maria Eliza Van den Heuval in New York City, Schuyler Hamilton entered the U.S. Military Academy at age fifteen. He graduated twenty-fourth of fifty-two in the class of 1841. Hamilton served on several posts in the Midwest before returning to West Point as an instructor.

At the outbreak of the Mexican-American War, Hamilton was sent to Mexico. In the war he received two serious wounds from which he would never fully recover and was brevetted twice. At the end of the war, he became aide-de-camp to Winfield Scott, a position he would hold for seven years. Hamilton resigned his commission in 1855. He tried his fortune in California working for a mine partly owned by his brother-in-law Henry Halleck. Not caring for that line of work, he returned east, where at the outbreak of the Civil War he was a Connecticut farmer.

News of Fort Sumter immediately brought Hamilton's enlistment as a private in the 7th New York Volunteers. He went with his regiment to Washington, where when Winfield Scott heard of his former aide's arrival, he immediately made him a lieutenant colonel and Scott's military secretary. Hamilton held that position until Scott retired in the fall of 1861. During that time, Hamilton handled most of Scott's correspondence with officers in the field. He was especially active during the First Bull Run campaign, communicating Scott's views to Irvin McDowell.

At the end of 1861, Hamilton was transferred to the command of his brother-in-law Halleck in the West. Promoted to brigadier general of volunteers, Hamilton was given command of the District of St. Louis in January 1862.

On 4 March 1862, Hamilton took command of the second division of John Pope's Army of the Mississippi at New Madrid and Island No. 10. Pope credited Hamilton with the plan for digging the canal that turned the Confederate defenses at Island No. 10. Hamilton commanded the occupation forces at New Madrid after the Confederate evacuation. Later in the spring, Hamilton commanded the left wing of the Army of the Mississippi in the advance on Corinth, Mississippi. Shortly thereafter, Pope was ordered east to take command of what he would dub the Army of Virginia. He made a special request to Secretary of War Edwin Stanton that Hamilton be allowed to accompany him. Halleck protested vigorously (it is not known whether at his brother-in-law's request), and Hamilton remained behind in the West.

In November 1862 Hamilton was transferred to William Rosecrans's Army of the Cumberland. At the same time, the president named him a major general of volunteers, and his name was sent to the Senate. By this time Hamilton had contracted malaria that forced him to take an extended sick leave. As a result, he fell short of the regulation requiring an officer's fitness for duty before his confirmation in the higher rank. Rather than face rejection by the Senate, Hamilton resigned his commission. As it happened, his health would not have permitted him to take the field again.

After the war, Hamilton was unable to engage in any profession for any length of time. He worked intermittently as an engineer. He did mount a fruitless campaign to have his name placed on the army retirement list rather than have it appear as a resignation. He lived out the remainder of his life unable to travel far from his home in New York. He died there on 18 March 1903.

—*David S. Heidler and Jeanne T. Heidler*

See also Island No. 10.
For further reading:
Hamilton, Schuyler. *Petition of Major-General Schuyler Hamilton to the Congress of the United States: Amended Letter to Hon. John Sherman, United States Senate, President Pro Tem* (1886).

HAMLIN, HANNIBAL
(1809–1891)
Vice president of the United States

Hannibal Hamlin was a famous, powerful, and influential politician in the United States during the middle of the nineteenth century. Hamlin was known by many as an honest, hard-working, and conscientious statesman. He was born on 27 August 1809, in Paris Hill, Maine. In his youth, he did not attend school often or go to college, but he became a voracious reader. After trying his hand at surveying and teaching, Hamlin decided at age twenty to become a lawyer. He moved to Columbia, Maine, to study law with his oldest brother, but his father's death forced him to return to the family farm. Determined to pursue this profession, Hamlin began studying law in 1831 at the office of Samuel C. Fessenden and Thomas A. Dublois in Portland and passed the bar in 1833. Hamlin's political career began two years later when he received the nomination as state representative from Penobscot County.

Hamlin quickly impressed the assembly and received his nickname, the "Carthaginian of Maine" in a dispute over the Democratic leadership of the House. He was reelected in 1837 and served as speaker in 1837, 1839, and 1840. Hamlin won the congressional seat in 1843. In his career at both the state and congressional levels, Hamlin was a staunch Jacksonian Democrat. His opposition to a protective tariff, to federally funded internal improvements, and to the Bank of the United States, as well as his "hard-money" views, represented his partisanship. He also did not drink and was a strong advocate of temperance legislation. One issue, however, would be the focus of his legislative efforts and define his political career: slavery.

Hannibal Hamlin (*Library of Congress*)

Hamlin was not an abolitionist. He did not believe that the federal government had the power to abolish the institution where it existed, but he bitterly opposed the extension of slavery westward. In 1844 he supported legislation that would usurp the "gag" rule in Congress, and in 1847 he was instrumental in the creation and passage of the Wilmot Proviso by the House of Representatives. He also believed that the Mexican-American War sprang from a conspiracy of Southern slaveholders determined to gain new territory. In 1848 Hamlin entered the U.S. Senate and continued his antislavery position. He rejected the Clayton Compromise, which enabled the Oregon government to overturn its antislavery laws and prevented California and New Mexico from passing antislavery legislation. He also voted against a bill that extended the Missouri Compromise to the Pacific Ocean and opposed the Omnibus Bill, which he believed appeased the slave states. Hamlin's views toward slavery clearly coincided with those of the newly formed Republican Party, but his strong partisan beliefs prevented him from breaking with the Democrats. However, the Democratic platform's endorsement of the Popular Sovereignty doctrine in the Kansas-Nebraska Act forced Hamlin to resign from that party in 1856. That same year, he returned to Maine and was elected as the first Republican governor of the state. Shortly thereafter, he resigned this office and returned to the Senate in 1857. He remained in that body until 1861, when he left to begin his duties as vice president.

Hamlin's nomination as Abraham Lincoln's vice presidential candidate in 1860 was a perfect balancing of the ticket. Lincoln was from the West; Hamlin was from the East. Lincoln was a former Whig; Hamlin was a former Democrat and his strong antislavery stance complemented Lincoln's nebulous position. Not seeking the nomination, Hamlin was initially reluctant to accept, but, out of a strong sense of duty, he acquiesced. After the election, Hamlin was crucial in helping Lincoln organize the cabinet, and he advised the president to pursue strong measures toward the seceding states. During the war, Hamlin's official duties in the administration were limited to rousing support for the war effort. Although Lincoln often welcomed Hamlin's advice, he rarely acted on it. Hamlin believed that Lincoln was too slow in prosecuting the war. He also believed that the president should free the slaves and allow them and other free African-Americans, to fight for the Union. As the war progressed, Lincoln partly accepted Hamlin's view on emancipation and black troops. He even allowed Hamlin to review the Emancipation Proclamation before its presentation.

During his tenure as vice president, Hamlin became increasingly associated with the radical wing of the Republican Party. This was one reason Lincoln secretly undermined Hamlin's renomination in 1864. Another, more significant, reason was Lincoln's desire to balance the Republican ticket with a Southern Democrat. Hamlin was not disturbed by this slight because it was widely known that he did not enjoy the office. This was not the result of any mutual animosity between him and the president. Both men were friendly toward one another, but the political tradition of the time prevented Lincoln from delegating any authority to Hamlin. Also, Hamlin wanted to return to the Senate, but he could not resign from the vice presidency, thereby possibly damaging the party. For a person of his energy and experience, Hamlin found the mundane duties and responsibilities of the office tedious and frustrating. After Hamlin lost his bid for a Senate seat in 1864, Lincoln arranged for him to be appointed collector of the port of Boston.

In August 1866, Hamlin resigned his commission as collector in protest of President Andrew Johnson's reconstruction policies. Hamlin believed that Johnson's plan was too mild. Hamlin was willing to forgive ordinary soldiers, but not the high-ranking conspirators he blamed for the war. In 1869 Hamlin returned to the Senate, where he continued his work on numerous committees, especially the prestigious Foreign Relations Committee, and supported the reconstruction policies of his party. In his final terms, Hamlin continued to be a "working" politician, not just a "talking" one, and demonstrated his characteristic party loyalty. He finally retired from the Senate in 1881 and was appointed minister to Spain, a post he held for one year.

In 1882, Hamlin retired from public life to work on his farm and to fish, read, and play cards. On 4 July 1891, he suffered a heart attack and died in Bangor, Maine.

—*Peter S. Genovese*

See also Election of 1860; Election of 1864; Lincoln, Abraham.

For further reading:
Hamlin, Charles Eugene. *The Life and Times of Hannibal Hamlin* (1899).
Hunt, H. Draper. *Hannibal Hamlin of Maine: Lincoln's First Vice-President* (1969).
Lives and Speeches of Abraham Lincoln and Hannibal Hamlin (1860).
Scroggins, Mark. *Hannibal: The Life of Abraham Lincoln's First Vice President* (1994).

HAMMOND, JAMES HENRY
(1807–1864)

U.S. Senator; governor of South Carolina

James Henry Hammond was born in Newberry District, South Carolina, the son of Elisha Hammond and Catherine Fox Spann. Elisha Hammond, who struggled financially throughout his life, had heady ambitions for his first-born son, and James internalized his father's aspirations at a young age. Enrolling in South Carolina College in Columbia in 1823, Hammond mingled in the world of privilege and power in which he hoped to make his mark.

After graduation, Hammond held teaching positions in Orangeburg and Cheraw, but before long he began to prepare for a career in law. He was admitted to the bar in 1828 and began his practice in Columbia. Hammond sided with the nullification faction in the controversy that gripped the state in the late 1820s over the federal tariff. In 1830 he was tapped to edit the *Southern Times*, a newly established nullifier paper in Columbia. During his brief stewardship, Hammond developed the states' rights, strict construction philosophy that would guide his political career. His aggressive editorials attracted the attention and respect of the state's political leadership, including John C. Calhoun, the patriarch of South Carolina politics.

In 1831 Hammond married a young Charleston heir, Catherine Fitzsimons, against the wishes of her family, who rightly suspected Hammond's motives. His marriage gave Hammond control over a 10,000-acre plantation on the Savannah River and 147 slaves. Departing Columbia for his new home at Silver Bluff, Hammond devoted himself to the supervision of his new plantation. Although his attempts to mold his slaves into a disciplined and efficient labor force were resisted at every turn, his efforts to rationalize his agricultural production were far more successful. After a successful experiment with marl to improve his soil, Hammond became an enthusiastic disciple of scientific agriculture and its chief proponent, Virginian Edmund Ruffin. Hammond's meticulous management transformed Silver Bluff from a marginal enterprise into a highly profitable plantation and made Hammond one of the wealthiest men in the South.

Hammond's planter status did not distract him from his political ambitions. In 1835 he won a seat in the U.S. House of Representatives. Shortly after the start of the session, the upstart congressman sparked a crisis in the House by challenging the reception of abolition petitions. Congress eventually passed a "gag rule" in May 1836 automatically tabling antislavery petitions, a prohibition that persisted in some form for eight years. Hammond, however, had already retired from the House in April, citing a vague nervous condition. Hoping travel would improve his health, Hammond and his family embarked on a therapeutic tour of Europe.

Hammond returned home more than a year later to find South Carolina politics transformed by the Panic of 1837 and Calhoun's renewed alliance with the Democrats. Caught between two warring factions, Hammond suffered a humiliating defeat in the 1840 gubernatorial election when Calhoun supported Hammond's opponent. He regained his stature by winning the governor's chair in 1842. Despite the limited powers accorded to South Carolina governors,

Hammond was determined to be more than a ceremonial figure. He spoke out on several national and state political issues, including the 1842 tariff, the proposed annexation of Texas, the powers of the State Bank of South Carolina, and public education. His term was overshadowed, however, by news of sexual dalliances with his four nieces, which reached the ears of their powerful father, Wade Hampton II, in 1843. The scandal effectively barred Hammond from public office for thirteen years.

Exiled from politics, Hammond turned to his pen as his instrument of influence, writing extensively on agricultural and political topics. In 1845 he published a lengthy defense of slavery in the form of two letters to British abolitionist Thomas Clarkson. Hammond's philosophical and religious justification of slavery won him widespread acclaim in the South, yet he remained convinced that Southerners did not fully appreciate his contributions. Like other Southern intellectuals, Hammond felt alienated from the larger community, whose affirmation he so desperately needed.

In 1857 Hammond was elected to the U.S. Senate. Although he defended the admission of Kansas as a slave state in 1858, warning the North not to make war on "King Cotton," Hammond became increasingly suspicious of the reckless extremism of Carolina secessionists. During the presidential campaign of 1860, Hammond repeatedly urged moderation and privately rejected Abraham Lincoln's election as grounds for withdrawal from the Union. But when his senatorial colleague James Chesnut resigned his seat in November 1860, Hammond quickly followed suit.

Surprised by the popularity of secession in other Southern states, Hammond belatedly embraced it in 1861. His enthusiastic conversion, however, failed to win him any influence in the councils of the Confederacy. Once again, Hammond felt rebuffed by the region to which he had devoted his talents and energy. Throughout the war, Hammond carped at Jefferson Davis's administration's economic and military policies and denounced measures to mobilize Southern society. He balked at government requisitions for slave labor and vigorously resisted Confederate impressment of his livestock and crops. He discouraged his sons' military service and ranted at the policy of conscription, which threatened to erode class distinctions among whites. The greatest blow came when his supposedly loyal slaves cast off their pretended allegiance to Hammond with each Union victory, dispelling the myth of his benevolent paternalism. For Hammond, the experience of war had eroded the fundamental principles of the South's racial and social order.

Isolated and embittered, Hammond's health deteriorated after 1861. Long a hypochondriac, Hammond began to suffer intermittent hemorrhaging from the bowels, a condition likely caused by his copious doses of mercury-based laxatives. In 1864 he died at his plantation mansion, Redcliffe. Despite his considerable financial success, Hammond never satisfied his political aspirations. Insatiably ambitious, yet perpetually insecure, Hammond warped his closest relationships with his demand for control, and, one by one, his family members resisted his domination. His "design for mastery," in the words of his biographer, ultimately eluded him.

—Susan Wyly-Jones

See also Chestnut, James; South Carolina.

For further reading:
Bleser, Carol K., ed. *Secret and Sacred: The Diaries of James Henry Hammond, a Southern Slaveholder* (1988).
Faust, Drew Gilpin. *James Henry Hammond and the Old South: A Design for Mastery* (1982).
Selections from the Letters and Speeches of the Hon. James H. Hammond of South Carolina (1866).

HAMMOND, WILLIAM ALEXANDER
(1828–1900)
U.S. surgeon general

Born to John W. Hammond and Sarah Pinkney Hammond in Annapolis, Maryland, William Alexander Hammond was educated in Harrisburg, Pennsylvania, and received a medical degree from the University of the City of New York. After graduation in 1848, Hammond worked for a year at the Pennsylvania Hospital and practiced briefly in Maine before entering the army as an assistant surgeon. Hammond spent his ten years in the army primarily at frontier posts, but he also served a stint at the U.S. Military Academy. During his time at these various locations, he also displayed an interest in medical research, publishing an award-winning study on nutrition. He resigned from the army in 1859 to join the medical faculty of the University of Maryland in Baltimore.

The commencement of the Civil War brought Hammond back into the army again as an assistant surgeon. He spent his first months of service in Baltimore before being transferred to the command of William S. Rosecrans in western Virginia. During his time in the field, Hammond came to the attention of U.S. Sanitation Commission workers, whom he impressed with his interest in reforming medical practice and care for soldiers. Members of the commission began lobbying for Hammond to replace Colonel Clement A. Finley as U.S. surgeon general. On 28 April 1862, their efforts paid off when Hammond assumed the post at the rank of brigadier general.

Hammond as surgeon general quickly gained a reputation for efficiency and compassion. He made personal inspection tours of the various armies to write extensive reports about needed reforms. He also corresponded frequently with Secretary of War Edwin Stanton, making recommendations for the improvement of soldiers' health care and diet. One of his most important reforms was the creation of an ambulance corps to aid in the removal of wounded from battlefields. He wrote Stanton a lengthy letter in September 1862 outlining in graphic detail the need for this reform.

Even with his extensive duties as head of the army's medical department, Hammond did not lose his interest in medical research. When Hammond learned of the march of the California column from California across the desert to New Mexico in the spring and summer of 1862, he wrote to one of the surgeons in New Mexico to request details about the exploit. He specifically wanted to know the force's composition, how it had accomplished such a feat, and under what conditions. A year later Hammond completed a report to Stanton in which he provided a statistical study of how tropical diseases affected different races. He concluded that African-American soldiers would be more suited to fight in the Deep South because of their greater immunity to malaria.

In spite of Hammond's popularity in some circles and his apparent improvements in the army's medical service, he could be difficult. He thought that the logic of his proposals would warrant automatic approval from the government bureaucracy, but Hammond worked for a strong willed, opinionated man in Secretary of War Stanton. The two did not get along almost from the beginning of their relationship, and by 1864 Stanton could not stand the sight of him. The secretary sent Hammond out of the capital and appointed an acting surgeon general in his stead. On 18 August 1864, Joseph K. Barnes replaced Hammond as surgeon general.

Hammond requested a court-martial, and Stanton obliged him. The secretary had his minions comb all the records of the medical department during Hammond's tenure as the surgeon general. The best they could find were a few irregularities in some whiskey contracts and complaints that Hammond occasionally had exhibited ungentlemanly conduct. Nevertheless, Hammond was convicted and dismissed from the army.

After leaving the army, Hammond returned to private practice and his research. Practicing initially in New York City, he also taught on the faculty of several medical schools. He became a specialist in the relatively new fields of neurology and mental illness and wrote extensively on those subjects.

In spite of his growing success, the circumstances of his departure from the army still rankled him, and in 1878 he was able to gain the passage of a bill by Congress that called for the president to review the case. In 1879, President Rutherford B. Hayes overturned the findings of the court-martial and reinstated Hammond, placing him as a brigadier general on the retired list. Hammond

continued to research and practice medicine up to his death in Washington, D.C., on 5 January 1900.

—*David S. Heidler and Jeanne T. Heidler*

See also Medicine; Stanton, Edwin; United States Sanitation Commission.

For further reading:
Blustein, Bonnie Ellen. *Preserve Your Love for Science: Life of William A. Hammond, American Neurologist* (1991).

HAMPTON ROADS PEACE CONFERENCE
(3 February 1865)

The Hampton Roads Peace Conference had its genesis in the fertile mind of Horace Greeley, editor of the New York *Tribune*. Greeley had followed closely the reports of the peace movement in the South, and on 15 December 1864 he wrote to Francis Preston Blair, the seventy-three-year-old patriarch of a powerful Maryland family and advisor of presidents since the administration of Andrew Jackson. Greeley declared that the "right man," armed with sufficient authority from the Lincoln administration, could "open relations" with the people of the South and persuade them to "stop this murderous fray." That "right man," Greeley believed, was Blair, and Blair agreed completely with this assessment.

Blair immediately sought an audience with Lincoln, and in late December he received permission to journey South to confer with the president of the Confederacy. He met with Jefferson Davis on 12 January 1865, and in that conference he proposed a scheme in which the two warring sides would conclude a cease-fire and then join in the common military mission of ousting the French-supported regime of Maximilian in Mexico. Blair was certain that such a venture, undertaken after the establishment of a temporary truce that would allow passions to cool, would restore fraternal relations between the two warring sections and provide the foundation for a lasting peace. Davis agreed that such a plan might work, and he provided Blair with a letter to deliver to Lincoln. In the letter Davis wrote that he was prepared to dispatch commissioners to a conference with the objective of "securing peace to the two countries." Blair delivered the letter to Lincoln, and although the president evidenced no interest in the Mexican intervention idea, he also did not wish to abort a chance for negotiations. In an 18 January letter he authorized Blair to inform "Mr." Davis that he would indeed meet with Confederate commissioners "with the view of securing peace to the people of our one common country."

On 21 January Blair again met with Davis in Richmond. He presented the Confederate president with Lincoln's message of 18 January, and, given Lincoln's refusal to support the Mexican proposal, suggested that the two presidents authorize Generals Lee and Grant to enter into direct negotiations for the restoration of peace. Davis quickly agreed to this second proposal from Blair, but upon hearing of the plan Lincoln flatly refused to accord Grant any such authority. As Davis later recorded, Blair "subsequently informed me that the idea of a military convention was not favorably received at Washington, so it only remained for me now to act upon the letter of Mr. Lincoln."

In determining how best to act, Davis sought the counsel of his vice president, Alexander H. Stephens. Stephens tendered his whole-hearted support for a conference based on Blair's Mexican proposal. So following the advice of his cabinet, Davis selected John A. Campbell, a former justice of the U.S. Supreme Court who was then Confederate assistant secretary of war; R. M. T. Hunter, president pro tem of the Confederate senate; and Stephens as commissioners. On 28 January he assembled the three men, briefed them on his conversations with Blair, and presented them with their official commission that directed them to meet with Lincoln "for the purpose of securing peace to the two countries." As Campbell later recalled, Davis provided the commissioners with "the power (orally) to make any treaty, but one that involved reconstruction of the Federal Union."

The commissioners departed for Petersburg the following day. A dispute over whether their credentials were valid delayed their progress until, through General Ulysses S. Grant's personal intercession, they were allowed to enter Union lines. As they crossed the no man's land between the trenches, shouts of "Peace! Peace!" rose from the soldiers of both sides. The trio was escorted to Grant's headquarters at City Point and from there to Hampton Roads where they met with Lincoln and Secretary of State William H. Seward on 3 February.

The only detailed account of the conference is that penned by Campbell shortly after his return to Richmond. The meeting, as Campbell recalled, opened with an exchange of pleasantries between Stephens and Lincoln as the two recalled their days together in the Congress and their joint labors in the Whig Party. After some minutes Stephens turned the conversation to the possibility of an armistice. Lincoln responded ("with some emphasis," as Campbell remembered) that such subjects could be considered only after unconditional restoration of the Union. Stephens attempted to circumvent the president's declaration by suggesting that Blair's Mexican proposal might afford a chance for ending the fighting. The president replied that Blair possessed no official authority whatever, and that an armistice would be possible only if the commissioners could pledge that the Union would first be restored.

This, of course, they could not do, but Campbell, eager to keep the negotiations afloat, asked under what terms a restoration might be effected. Seward suggested

that Campbell's question be deferred until Stephens explained how the Mexican proposal might work. Stephens offered that the two governments would first conclude a secret treaty that would end the fighting, consolidate the troops in designated locations, and provide for the division of tariff receipts. Once these arrangements had been finalized, Union and Confederate armies would attack in concert to drive the French out of Mexico, an operation Stephens was certain would draw the two nations together.

Lincoln heard Stephens out, but then responded that such a proposal could not be entertained because Congress alone possessed the power to declare war and make treaties, and consideration of Stephens's plan would be tantamount to official recognition of the Confederacy. An armistice, Lincoln repeated, could be accomplished only after Southern troops had been disbanded and Federal authority acknowledged.

Seward reminded the commissioners that the president was on record as insisting that all congressional and executive acts in regard to emancipation also be accepted. Campbell asked for clarification as to the status of confiscated property, and Seward replied that while that was a question for the courts, he believed Congress would be liberal in its policies of restitution. Hunter asked whether West Virginia would remain independent or be reunited with Virginia, and Lincoln answered that, while he personally favored continued independence for the state, that question also would be decided by the courts.

There then arose one of the most controversial exchanges of the entire conference. In response to the question of whether the Emancipation Proclamation would remain in effect after the war, Lincoln responded that in his opinion the proclamation was a wartime measure that would be terminated once peace returned. Further, the president stated that he believed the measure applied only to those slaves who had already been freed under its provisions. The eventual status of the proclamation, Lincoln concluded, would be determined by the courts, and the courts might decide either way.

Seward then raised the subject of the Thirteenth Amendment, adopted only days before. As Campbell recalled, Seward characterized the amendment as a "war measure" that would surely be withdrawn once peace cooled the "revolutionary passions" that had led to its passage. Lincoln advised Stephens to return to Georgia, pull the state out of the war, and then vote to ratify the amendment "prospectively, so as to take effect say in five years." Hunter, who had said little to this point, offered that emancipation, whenever it occurred, would constitute a terrible hardship for the slaves. He was astonished and chagrined when Lincoln answered this concern with one of his barnyard analogies, the conclusion of which

was that once freed, former slaves, like pigs in winter, would have to "root" for themselves.

Hunter, citing the example of Charles I, then asked Lincoln if he would tender a preliminary agreement for study by any states that might consider reunion. Lincoln demurred, adding that all he knew of Charles I was that he had lost his head! Sensing that all options were swiftly being exhausted, Hunter remarked with some passion that the president had offered the Southern states little beyond unconditional surrender. Seward replied that neither he nor Lincoln had used those terms, and assured Hunter that a reunited South would be afforded all the protections and safeguards of the Constitution. Lincoln reinforced this note of conciliation, guaranteeing the commissioners that he would be very lenient in the execution of the confiscation and penal powers accorded him. The North, he told Hunter, bore as much responsibility for the blight of slavery as the South, and as president he would support compensation to slaveowners for the loss of their property.

By this time the five men had been in conference for four hours, and there was little left to be said. There followed some desultory discussion of prisoner exchanges, and Stephens once more attempted, without success, to raise the possibility of an armistice. Lincoln and Seward then rose, tendered their goodbyes, and departed the room. Late that same afternoon the president sailed for Annapolis and the commissioners departed Petersburg for Richmond. The Hampton Roads Peace Conference was at an end, and the fighting would go on.

—*Charles W. Sanders, Jr.*

See also Blair, Francis Preston; Campbell, John A.; Greeley, Horace; Hunter, Robert M. T.; Stephens, Alexander H.

For further reading:

Campbell, John A. *Reminiscences and Documents Relating to the Civil War During the Year 1865* (1887).

Davis, Jefferson. *Rise and Fall of the Confederate Government* (1881).

Escott, Paul D. *After Secession: Jefferson Davis and the Failure of Confederate Nationalism* (1977).

Kirkland, Edward Chase. *The Peacemakers of 1864* (1927).

Smith, William E. *The Francis Preston Blair Family in Politics* (1933; reprint 1969).

HAMPTON, WADE
(1818–1902)
Confederate general

Born Wade Hampton III in Charleston, South Carolina, the man who would assume J. E. B. Stuart's mantle had much to live up to even at birth. His grandfather, the first Wade Hampton, had served in the American Revolution, and both his father and grandfather had fought in the War of 1812. Along the way, the Hampton family had amassed an enormous fortune from cotton plantations in South Carolina and Mississippi and a profitable sugar plantation in Louisiana. This fortune would propel the scion of the family to a series of terms in both houses of the South Carolina legislature between 1852 and 1860.

A large slaveholder, Hampton yet evinced Unionist political sympathies throughout his political career. However, when his native Palmetto State seceded, Hampton quickly threw in his lot with the Confederacy, using his own personal fortune to raise and equip a force of infantry, cavalry, and artillery known as Hampton's Legion. A number of South Carolina's important, and colorful, brigadiers, including Martin W. Gary and Matthew C. Butler, would cut their teeth in Hampton's Legion during the early days of the war.

Shortly after receiving a colonelcy, Hampton first saw combat at the battle of First Bull Run. On 19 July, he moved his troops from the environs of Richmond to Manassas Junction, detraining in the midst of the fight. Late in the day on 21 July, Hampton suffered the first of his many war wounds, a minié ball cutting down the colonel as he led his infantry against Henry House Hill. Hampton would receive another slight wound the following June at Seven Pines.

In May 1862, Hampton was promoted to brigadier general and granted command of one of Jeb Stuart's two cavalry brigades, the other being commanded by Fitzhugh Lee. This undoubtedly suited the six-foot tall South Carolinian, who had spent much of his youth atop a horse, avidly engaged in all manner of field sports. One observer of the general's equestrian acumen noted that Hampton upon a horse looked like nothing so much as a centaur.

In June of 1863, Hampton's performance at Brandy Station provided a glimmer of his possibilities as a cavalry commander. This engagement also foreshadowed the personal tragedy that would stalk him throughout the war; one of his brother's fell in a confused exchange of fire just five miles south of the main engagement. Later that month, Hampton played an important role in Stuart's efforts to contain the increasingly professional Federal cavalry while the Confederate army moved down the Shenandoah Valley into Pennsylvania. The South Carolinian led a charge at Ashby's Gap that confirmed to many observers his personal battlefield charisma.

The battle of Gettysburg saw the genesis of a controversy with Fitzhugh Lee that would dog Hampton during the remainder of his tenure with the Army of Northern Virginia. The young Lee had ordered a calamitous charge in Hampton's absence and Hampton suffered perhaps his worst wounding of the war, at least two saber strokes to the head and a shrapnel wound in the leg, while attempting to retrieve and rally his cavalry. During Hampton's convalescence, both he and Fitz Lee received promotion to major general, a move intended to both salve hard feelings between the two cavalrymen and to transform the Confederate army's cavalry arm into a clearly defined command corps.

After the death of Stuart at Yellow Tavern in 1864, Robert E. Lee again attempted to navigate choppy waters by appointing neither his nephew nor Hampton to command the cavalry, instead ordering both to report directly to him. This state of affairs continued until after the cavalry engagement at Trevilian Station in June. Hampton's hard fighting and dexterous use of the topography in his role in checking Philip Sheridan's charge on Richmond seems to have convinced Lee to grant Hampton command of the Army of Northern Virginia's Cavalry Corps in September 1864.

The defense of Petersburg showed Hampton at his best, carrying out a series of sorties, raids, and flank actions that did much to sustain the Confederacy's tenuous morale. The most audacious of these actions came to be known as the Hampton Beef Raid. In a spectacular move worthy of the indefatigable Stuart, Hampton led three brigades in a raid around the Federal left, rustling 2,500 beeves grazing six miles to the rear of Ulysses S. Grant's City Point headquarters. In late October, Hampton brilliantly checked a probing attack on the Confederate army's south flank in the battle of Burgess Mill. The cost of this success, however, proved prohibitively high for Hampton personally, as one of his sons, Frank Preston Hampton, fell to a volley of Federal fire that also gravely wounded another son, Wade Hampton, Jr.

Hampton was transferred to Joseph Johnston's command in January 1865. Lee and Johnston hoped that the Carolinian could stir his native state to resist Sherman's advance, to that end promoting Hampton to lieutenant general in February. Little came of these hopes, and Hampton spent much of the remaining months of the war helping to orchestrate a series of often unsuccessful retreats. Hampton was not interested in surrendering with the army he had served in since the early days of the war. After both Lee's and Johnston's surrender, the one-time Unionist exchanged correspondence in April with a fugitive Jefferson Davis, correspondence in which he urged Davis to continue the fight in the Trans-Mississippi. Missing Davis's small band at Charlotte as the president of the fallen Confederacy moved South to eventual capture, Hampton seems to have realized that the cause had truly become lost.

The end of the war found the once wealthy Hampton destitute, a number of his plantations destroyed, and the family home of Millwood near Columbia burned by Sherman's troops. Though never able to recoup his financial losses, Hampton played a central role in redeeming South Carolina from its Reconstruction government and became governor in 1876. Hampton later served as a U.S. Senator, earning a reputation throughout his political career for both honest fiscal policies and racial moderation and being one of the few Bourbon Democrats to appeal for the votes of emancipated blacks. Hampton died at his Columbia home in 1902.

—*W. Scott Poole*

See also Brandy Station, Battle of; Bull Run, First Battle of; Cavalry, C.S.A.; Lee, Fitzhugh; Stuart, James E. B.; Trevilian Station, Battle of.

For further reading:
Freeman, Douglas Southall. *Lee's Lieutenants: A Study in Command* (1942–1944).
Wellman, Manly Wade. *Giant in Gray: A Biography of Wade Hampton of South Carolina* (1949).
Williams, Alfred B. *Hampton and His Redshirts* (1935).

HANCOCK, WINFIELD SCOTT
(1824–1886)
Union general

Called by his admirers "Hancock the Superb," Winfield Scott Hancock is recognized as an outstanding Union general who was key to the success of George Meade's troops at Gettysburg. Moreover, his military career saw his participation in many significant events of the nineteenth century, including the Mexican-American War, the turmoil over "Bleeding Kansas," expansion to California, confrontation with Native American tribes, Reconstruction in the South, railroad strikes, and several campaigns for the presidency of the United States. It is, however, for his contributions to the Northern cause during the Civil War that Hancock is best remembered.

Winfield and Hilary Hancock were twins, born on 14 February 1824 in Montgomery Square, Pennsylvania, to Elizabeth and Benjamin Hancock. A lawyer and patriotic Democrat, Benjamin Hancock exerted much influence on his son's life. After some hesitancy, he supported Winfield's admission to West Point. Thus at the age of fifteen, young Hancock's career was determined. In 1844, he graduated eighteenth of twenty-five and was assigned to the infantry as a brevet second lieutenant.

Three years after graduating, Hancock arrived in Mexico for the last month of fighting in the Mexican-American War. He fought well with the 6th Infantry and received a brevet promotion to first lieutenant. Eventually, he was appointed acting regimental quartermaster.

After the Mexican-American War, Hancock met Almira ("Allie") Russell in St. Louis, and they married on 24 January 1850. Allie gave birth to two children, Russell in October 1850 and Ada in February 1857. Both children died before their parents. In 1856, the army ordered Hancock to Florida for service in the Third Seminole War. He then went to Kansas and to Utah, where his 6th Infantry arrived after the so-called Mormon War had ended. Finally posted in California,

where he and his family lived until the start of the Civil War, he would form friendships with Lewis Armistead and other Southern officers.

At the start of the war, Hancock was a captain and served as chief quartermaster in California. He arrived in Washington, D.C., in late summer of 1861. Hancock was prepared for war. He had read extensively, had carefully observed generals with whom he had served, and had fought well in Mexico. He was soon promoted to brigadier general of volunteers and given command of a brigade under General William "Baldy" Smith in the Army of the Potomac.

Hancock and his brigade participated in George B. McClellan's Peninsula campaign, and four months later they were at Antietam. There, in the horrible fighting that took place at Bloody Lane, the commander of the 1st Division of II Corps fell, and Hancock was ordered to replace him. He did so, plugging holes in the line and maintaining it despite heavy casualties. In accordance with his position as a division commander, he was promoted to major general of volunteers as well as major in the regular army.

At Fredericksburg, Hancock's men participated in the disastrous assault on the stone wall at Marye's Heights. After a brief respite with Allie, he passed the winter of 1863 making some administrative changes and drilling his troops. At Chancellorsville, Hancock formed and held a line, withdrawing only after receiving orders to do so. After three days of fighting, he sustained a successful rear guard while the rest of the Army of the Potomac withdrew. Later, Hancock testified to the Joint Committee on the Conduct of the War that, had the Army of the Potomac pushed forward at Chancellorsville, it would have been successful.

When Darius Couch, commander of II Corps, asked to be transferred, Hancock was the clearly preferred replacement, so in June 1863 he was appointed commander of II Corps, thus to command at Gettysburg more men than had been in the entire peacetime army. When George Gordon Meade heard that John Reynolds had been killed during early fighting near Gettysburg, he ordered Hancock there to take command. Hancock protested that both Oliver O. Howard and Daniel Sickles, who were already there, outranked him, but Meade acted on the assumption that Hancock was the superior soldier. Upon arriving, his first view of the action was of defeated Union soldiers struggling up Cemetery Hill. He immediately reorganized them, ordering one division to surround Culp's Hill. He then established Little Round Top and Cemetery Ridge as the center of the line. Once these positions were secured, he surveyed the area and sent a dispatch to Meade informing him that it would be a good place to fight, thus selecting the strong position from which the Army of the Potomac would fight this titanic contest.

On the second day at Gettysburg, Hancock and his II Corps maintained the center and left of the line on Cemetery Ridge. Additionally, he sent two regiments to Culp's Hill to help strengthen Union positions there. James Longstreet's assault, Pickett's Charge, hit Hancock's position on the afternoon of 3 July after a morning of heavy artillery bombardment. Hancock rode his horse among the men, inspiring them and redirecting regiments to weak points as necessary. When a bullet that probably hit his saddle forced pieces of it and a tenpenny nail into his thigh, he nevertheless refused treatment until victory was ensured. Hancock's key role on the third day at Gettysburg was crucial to Northern victory.

Recovering from his wound, Hancock temporarily left active field service to concentrate on his recuperation and to raise troops for his corps. Though his wound continued to give him considerable pain, he returned to the army by March 1864 and in May participated in the battle of the Wilderness. A tactical stalemate and high casualties briefly halted the fighting, but it resumed at Spotsylvania for another ten days. Though slowed by rain, Ulysses S. Grant ordered an attack that included Hancock's II Corps on a crescent-shaped position dubbed the "Mule Shoe," where much of the Southern artillery was located. More than 20,000 Federals swarmed over the barricades not only to push back the enemy but also to capture nearly 3,000 prisoners, among them one of Hancock's old friends, General Edward Johnson.

In early June, Robert E. Lee's army was entrenched along the Chickahominy River when Grant ordered the disastrous assault at Cold Harbor. Within minutes, 3,000 men from Hancock's II Corps had fallen in an attack from which the corps never fully recovered. Despite the losses, they marched toward Petersburg, where XVIII Corps had successfully attacked the city, but had not taken it. Hancock arrived on 15 June and could have assumed command. However, Baldy Smith was already there and familiar with the territory, so when Smith counted as too great the risks of trying to take Petersburg, Hancock acceded. Had Smith or Hancock seized the initiative, the war could have ended in the summer of 1864. When II Corps moved on to Deep Bottom to provide a diversion for Ambrose Burnside's direct attack on Petersburg, Hancock was successful, but Burnside was not. Meanwhile, Hancock was promoted brigadier general in the regular army.

The II Corps, now made up of about 6,000 green cadets, was sent to destroy railway lines at Reams's Station. After a day of fighting, the corps collapsed when support failed to arrive. For the first time, Hancock watched his troops driven back while his lines and guns were taken, but in October, II Corps defeated Confederates at Hatcher's Run in the continuing siege

around Petersburg. Poor health forced Hancock to Washington, D.C., where he was to head up the newly conceived corps of veterans. His days as a Union soldier had ended. During the war, his II Corps lost about 40,000 men and captured forty-four Confederate colors before it lost one of its own.

After the war, Hancock continued to participate in significant historical events. He supervised the execution of the Lincoln conspirators; he attempted negotiations with Plains tribes; during Reconstruction he served briefly as commander of the 5th Military District, where he supported President Andrew Johnson's mild restoration policy and issued his conservative General Order No. 40; he oversaw the military involvement in several strikes; and he directed the ceremony that followed Grant's death. Significantly, Hancock made several attempts at the Democratic presidential nomination, finally securing it for the 1880 election. Due to the disunity of the Democrats in New York, he lost the presidency to James A. Garfield in a close election (by about 7,000 votes of 9 million cast).

As commander of the Division of the Atlantic, Hancock spent his remaining years on Governor's Island in New York harbor with Allie. He died on 9 February 1886, probably from diabetes and an infected carbuncle. He was buried in Montgomery Cemetery, in Norristown, Pennsylvania. An excellent soldier and gifted commander, he deserved the title he had earned early in the war: Superb.

—*Mary Lynn Cluff*

See also Antietam, Battle of; Armistead, Lewis; Chancellorsville, Battle of; Cold Harbor, Battle of; Gettysburg, Battle of; Spotsylvania, Battle of.

For further reading:
Dawson, Joseph G. III. "Army Generals and Reconstruction: Mower and Hancock As Case Studies." *Southern Studies* (1978).
Hancock, Almira Russell. *Reminiscences of Winfield Scott Hancock by His Wife* (1887).
Jordan, David M. *Winfield Scott Hancock: A Soldier's Life* (1988).
Longacre, Edward G. "The Blackest of All Days." *Civil War Times Illustrated* (1976).
Lord, Frank. "Hancock's First Veterans Corps." *Military Collector and Historian* (1974).
Tucker Glenn. *Hancock the Superb* (1980).

HANOVER COURT HOUSE, BATTLE OF
(27 May 1862)

By late May 1862, the Army of the Potomac had advanced to within 12 miles of Richmond, Virginia. Major General George B. McClellan had deployed most of his army south of the Chickahominy River but had placed two corps north of the stream, hoping to link up with Union troops advancing south from Fredericksburg before attacking the Confederate capital.

McClellan heard reports that a sizeable enemy force was

in the vicinity of Hanover Court House, a village fourteen miles north of Richmond on the Virginia Central Railroad. This rail line linked Richmond to the Shenandoah Valley, and Brigadier General Lawrence O'Bryan Branch's reinforced brigade of 4,000 men was indeed in the area to protect the line against a Federal attack.

Worrying about the safety of his right and rear, McClellan sent orders to Brigadier General Fitz John Porter, his V Corps commander, to move to Hanover Court House and disperse the Rebels there. Porter instructed his 1st Division commander, Brigadier General George W. Morell, to accomplish the task.

Morell, reinforced by a brigade from the Second Division, moved north from his camps near New Bridge early on the morning of 27 May, but a heavy rainstorm delayed the Yankee advance. By noon, the sun was out and Federal cavalry ran into the 28th North Carolina, which deployed to the south of the courthouse to counter an enemy advance. The Carolinians put up a good fight and Morell sent the 25th New York to assist the cavalry. The Tarheels held off the New Yorkers until more reinforcements arrived and forced the Southerners to withdraw northward toward Hanover Court House.

As the Yankees advanced, Morell halted some of his troops at a crossroads to protect the main column as it moved north. Union cavalry scouting westward along the Ashcake Road soon encountered Branch's main force, which followed the retreating horsemen toward the Federals guarding the crossroads. Here, Brigadier General John H. Martindale deployed the 2d Maine, 25th New York, 44th New York, and a two-gun section of the 3d Massachusetts Battery to oppose the oncoming enemy.

Branch, observing the compact Union line, decided to attack. The 37th North Carolina moved toward the enemy right, while the 12th and 33d North Carolina headed to the left, leaving the 18th North Carolina to launch a frontal assault across open fields. The colonel of the 2d Maine recorded that the 18th "appeared boldly in front, advancing in perfect order . . . the Stars and Bars defiantly flying." Although the 18th was repelled, the Carolinians flanking the Union line caused disorder in both New York regiments and silenced the Bay State artillerists.

Just as the Federal line was beginning to break, reinforcements arrived in response to Martindale's couriers. Two brigades moved up and pitched into Branch's troops, which began withdrawing under the heavy pressure. Covered by two fresh regiments, Branch's brigade began to retreat, followed by Union pursuers until darkness halted the action. Union casualties were 62 killed, 223 wounded, and 70 captured or missing, for a total of 355. Branch's command suffered a loss of 73 killed, 192 wounded, and perhaps 730 captured, an overall loss of 995.

Morell's troops remained in the area overnight, then burned railroad bridges and ripped up track before returning to New Bridge. McClellan believed that

13,000 Rebels had opposed the V Corps troops, which had thus won a "glorious victory over superior numbers."

—*Richard A. Sauers*

See also Peninsula Campaign.
For further reading:
Powell, William H. *The Fifth Army Corps (Army of the Potomac). A Record of Operations During the Civil War in the United States of America, 1861-1865* (1896).
Sears, Stephen W. *To the Gates of Richmond: The Peninsula Campaign* (1992).

HANOVER, PENNSYLVANIA, BATTLE OF
(30 June 1863)

The battle of Hanover, though small in scale, had a significant impact on the subsequent battle of Gettysburg, which began the next day and ten miles to the west. As the Army of the Potomac searched for the Army of Northern Virginia in northern Maryland and south-central Pennsylvania, the Union cavalry division of Brigadier General Judson Kilpatrick encountered Major General J. E. B. "Jeb" Stuart's Confederate cavalry at the small town of Hanover, Pennsylvania, in the extreme southwestern part of York County just above the Mason-Dixon Line.

Stuart and his troopers had lost contact with the Army of Northern Virginia's infantry columns and were desperately trying to find them when advance elements of Confederate colonel John R. Chambliss's brigade engaged a rear guard of Union brigadier general Elon Farnsworth's brigade on the outskirts of Hanover sometime after 10:00 A.M. on 30 June. The fighting quickly escalated as Stuart—who originally wanted to avoid a fight—brought his command into action. Farnsworth likewise ordered his entire brigade, which already had passed through town, back into Hanover to meet the threat. Part of another Confederate brigade, this one under Brigadier General Fitzhugh Lee, also became engaged. The early part of the battle was characterized by mounted charges, sometimes through the streets of town. Stuart himself narrowly escaped capture as the battle became more intense. Both sides by this time had brought up horse artillery.

Farnsworth—a brand-new brigadier general who had only recently taken command—eventually deployed his entire brigade, consisting of the 18th Pennsylvania, 5th New York, 1st Vermont, and 1st West Virginia, in the center of Hanover and extending south and east of the town. General Kilpatrick and his other brigade, composed of Michigan regiments under the command of another newly promoted brigadier general by the name of George Custer, soon galloped into Hanover and extended Farnsworth's line to the northwest. Union troopers barricaded Hanover's streets with boxes, hay bales, fence rails, and overturned wagons.

Stuart, meanwhile, stabilized his line on the southern edge of Hanover, placing Chambliss's brigade on the right and Fitzhugh Lee on the left. The brigade of Brigadier General Wade Hampton arrived around 2:00 P.M.—it previously had been guarding a captured Union wagon train taken outside of Washington a few days earlier—and deployed on Chambliss's right flank, extending the Confederate line to the southeast. Hampton also deployed another battery of horse artillery, which immediately opened on Farnsworth's troops in the streets of Hanover and east of town.

Fitzhugh Lee's artillery had been firing from high ground west of Hanover. Custer decided to silence these guns, ordering some 600 dismounted troopers of his 6th Michigan Cavalry to take the Confederate battery. The Michiganders were able to get within 300 yards of the Confederate guns when, undetected, they opened fire with their pistols and Spencer rifles. Lee's gunners were totally surprised, abandoning their guns and their wounded. A Confederate counterattack forced back the Union troopers, but the Michigan men rallied and tried again. Although they were unable to seize their objective, Custer's soldiers continued to threaten the Confederate left flank. Concerned with the danger to both flanks and also his rear, which was being threatened by slow-moving

Union infantry, Stuart waited until darkness and withdrew from Hanover, moving to the east, farther away from the Army of Northern Virginia. Union casualties at the battle of Hanover were fewer than 200; Confederate casualties also were slight, approximately 150.

Although the battle of Hanover soon would be eclipsed by the momentous battle at Gettysburg, the engagement nonetheless had far-reaching ramifications for the Army of Northern Virginia. As a result of the Union cavalry resistance, Stuart would be forced to take an even wider detour to link up with its infantry counterparts. Thus, Robert E. Lee would not have the services of his trusted cavalry commander for the first one and half days of the battle of Gettysburg, which many historians have cited as a major reason for the Army of Northern Virginia's lack of success during its second invasion of the North.

—*Mark Snell*

See also Custer, George Armstrong; Farnsworth, Elon John; Gettysburg, Battle of; Stuart, James Ewell Brown.
For further reading:
Longacre, Edward G. *The Cavalry at Gettysburg: A Tactical Study of Mounted Operations during the Civil War's Pivotal Campaign, 9 June–14 July 1863* (1986; reprint, 1993).

HARDEE, WILLIAM JOSEPH
(1815–1873)
Confederate general

Born the son of John Hardee and Sarah Ellis Hardee in Camden County, Georgia, William Hardee was educated at the U.S. Military Academy and graduated twenty-sixth of forty-five in the class of 1838. Upon graduation he was commissioned into the 2d Dragoons and in 1840 was sent to Europe to study cavalry tactics in Paris. Upon his return, Hardee was stationed at Fort Jesup, before traveling to Mexico as part of Winfield Scott's Mexico City campaign in 1847. He fought at the siege of Vera Cruz and the battles around Mexico City and received two brevets for his service in the war.

After the war, Hardee put to use his combat experience and European military studies to produce at the behest of the War Department *Rifle and Light Infantry Tactics*, a work that became known as *Hardee's Tactics*. In 1856 he was promoted to lieutenant colonel and transferred to West Point to serve as commandant of cadets. He remained there until September 1860, when he was transferred to the 1st Cavalry and given a five-month leave.

Hardee spent much of his leave in the South, visiting family in St. Augustine, Florida, and Georgia. In his home state, he advised Governor Joseph Brown on preparing the state's defenses in the event of secession. He also wrote to Secretary of War John Floyd in December 1860 asking the secretary's advice on weapons to be purchased by the state of Georgia.

His sympathies in the growing sectional crisis obvi-

William Hardee (*Library of Congress*)

ously inclined toward his native state, and, once Georgia seceded, Hardee resigned his commission and offered his services. He was made the colonel of the 1st Georgia Regiment and in March 1861 transferred his services to the Confederate Army. As colonel in the Confederate service, he commanded Fort Morgan at Mobile, Alabama. He remained there until June, when he was promoted to brigadier general and sent to command Confederate forces in northwest Arkansas. The brigade he created there became known as Hardee's brigade.

In September 1861, Hardee was ordered to move his troops to Kentucky. He made his headquarters at Bowling Green. In October he was promoted to major general and in December assumed command of the Army of Central Kentucky. The fall of Fort Henry in early February 1862 caused Hardee to withdraw his army to Nashville, and the fall of Fort Donelson forced another retreat with the remainder of Albert Sidney Johnston's force to Corinth, Mississippi.

After regrouping at Corinth, Johnston determined to attack the pursuing Federals under Ulysses S. Grant at Pittsburg Landing, Tennessee. Hardee commanded part of the lead elements of Johnston army as it moved north in early April 1862. Hardee skirmished with a part of Grant's force on 4 April and then led part of the attack on the first day at Shiloh on 6 April.

During the summer of 1862, Hardee fought at the siege of Corinth and was placed in temporary command of the Army of the Mississippi. In the fall he participated in Braxton Bragg's Kentucky campaign. On 7 October Hardee's troops controlled the spring at Perryville that provided most of the drinking water in the area. As a result, this position precipitated the main Union attack on 8 October that became the battle of Perryville. On 11 October 1862, Hardee was promoted to lieutenant general for his actions there.

Later in the year, Hardee commanded part of the Confederate left at Stones River. During the summer of 1863, he went temporarily to Mississippi where he commanded the Army of Mississippi and Eastern Louisiana. In the fall, however, he was back as a corps commander with the Army of Tennessee just in time for the debacle at Missionary Ridge. After Bragg's embarrassment there and subsequent relief, Hardee was placed in temporary command of the Army of Tennessee. During his time in command of the army, Hardee spent most of his time rebuilding and reorganizing for what would surely be a grueling campaign season in the spring. In December 1863, he relinquished command to Joseph E. Johnston, and over the next seven months Hardee developed a strong respect for his new commander.

In February 1864, Johnston sent Hardee to Mississippi to counter William T. Sherman's Meridian campaign, but Hardee arrived too late to have any impact on the campaign. He returned to Johnston's command in north Georgia in time for the beginning of Sherman's Atlanta campaign.

During the Atlanta campaign, Hardee fought in virtually all the major engagements. He remained loyal to his commander during this fighting retreat even though increasingly he doubted the effectiveness of Johnston's plans. In July 1864, when Johnston was relieved in favor of John Bell Hood, Hardee could not hide his disappointment. Hood was junior to Hardee, but besides this slight to his seniority, Hardee did not believe that Hood had the ability to do a better job than Johnston. Hood's performance outside Atlanta in July and August confirmed Hardee in his opinion. From August until the fall of Atlanta in September 1864, Hardee attempted to gain a transfer from the Army of Tennessee. Finally, on 28 September, his request was granted when he received instructions to take command of the Department of South Carolina, Georgia, and Florida, headquartered at Charleston.

Hardee's first task in his new command was to strengthen the defenses of Savannah, Georgia. These efforts became increasingly frantic by late November 1864, when it became apparent that Savannah was Sherman's objective. As Sherman drew near, however, and moved part of his force to the South Carolina side of the Savannah River, Hardee had no choice but to order the evacuation of his force or risk envelopment. He left the city with his army on 20 December 1864 and moved to Charleston.

Charleston's defenses became Hardee's next priority as it was assumed that Charleston would be Sherman's next objective. As Sherman moved into South Carolina, however, Hardee determined that, rather than being trapped along the coast, he should evacuate Charleston and move north. He left Charleston on 17 February and joined with Joseph Johnston, who had been returned to command, at Fayetteville, North Carolina, on 9 March.

As Johnston took most of the army north from Fayetteville, Hardee remained behind with part of the army to delay Sherman. He fought a rearguard action at Averasboro, North Carolina, on 16 March 1865 and then joined Johnston. Hardee fought at Bentonville on 19 March and then retreated with the army. He surrendered with what was left of Johnston's army in April.

After his parole, Hardee moved to Alabama, where he spent the remainder of his life running his plantation there. He also engaged in a variety of business activities including serving as president of the Selma & Meridian Railroad. He died on 6 November 1873 in Wytheville, Virginia, and was returned to Selma for burial.

—*David S. Heidler and Jeanne T. Heidler*

See also Averasboro, Battle of; Missionary Ridge, Battle of; Perryville, Battle of; Shiloh, Battle of.
For further reading:
Hughes, Nathaniel Cheairs. *General William J. Hardee: Old Reliable* (1965).

HARDIN, MARTIN DAVIS
(1837–1923)
Union general

Born the son of John J. Hardin in Jacksonville, Illinois, Martin Davis Hardin lost his father in 1847 when the elder Hardin, serving as major general of volunteers, was killed in the battle of Buena Vista in the Mexican-American War. The younger Hardin received an appointment to the U.S. Military Academy in 1855 and graduated eleventh of twenty-two in the class of 1859. Upon graduation Hardin was sent to the Pacific Northwest, where he was serving at Fort Umpqua in Oregon at the outbreak of the war.

Ordered east, Hardin arrived in time to serve as aide-de-camp to Colonel Henry J. Hunt, chief of reserve artillery during the Peninsula campaign. Hardin fought in every major engagement of that campaign, earning promotion to lieutenant colonel of the 12th Pennsylvania Reserves on 8 July 1862.

In August 1862 Hardin fought at Groveton and Second Bull Run, where he was wounded twice. He was promoted to colonel of the 12th on 1 September 1862, but was unable to participate in the Maryland campaign as a result of his wounds. Hardin tried to return to duty at the end of the year as the commander of a brigade in the I Corps in William B. Franklin's Grand Division of the Army of the Potomac, but found he was not fit for duty. As soon as he was able, Hardin served on court-martial duty until able to return to the field. This came in the Gettysburg campaign in summer of 1863. Hardin led the 12th at Gettysburg and in the pursuit of Lee into Virginia. He continued in command at Bristoe Station and in the Mine Run campaign.

Hardin was knocked out of action again in December 1863 when, while walking along his picket line at Catlett's Station, he was ambushed by Confederate guerrillas. His wound cost him his left arm. He was back in action by May 1864 just in time for Ulysses S. Grant's campaign against Robert E. Lee.

Commanding the 1st brigade of the Pennsylvania Reserves, Hardin fought at the Wilderness and Spotsylvania before being wounded again at the attempted crossing of the North Anna River. Upon recovery, Hardin was promoted to brigadier general of volunteers on 2 July 1864 and on 8 July ordered to Washington, where he was given command of defenses North of the Potomac. Commanding those defenses against Jubal Early's raid, Hardin during the two days (11–12 July) that Early really threatened the city moved from place to place, strengthening defenses and reporting back to the War Department.

After the threat of Early was gone, Hardin patrolled the Potomac River, sending back a report to the War Department outlining his recommendations for the improvement of Washington's defenses. He also combated smaller Confederate attempts to penetrate those defenses, especially by the intrepid Confederate raider, John Singleton Mosby. Hardin remained in the Washington area for the remainder of the war.

After the war, Hardin chose to stay in the army. In July 1866 he was sent to the Department of North Carolina. With the mustering out of the volunteers in 1866, Hardin became major in the 43d Infantry. Over the next four years, however, his injuries began to hamper his ability to do his duty, and in 1870 he was retired at the rank of brigadier general for injuries received during the war.

For a time after his retirement (at the age of 33), Hardin lived in Chicago, where he studied law and began a successful practice. He retired from law to St. Augustine, Florida, where he died 12 December 1923. He had been the last living member of the West Point class of 1859.

—David S. Heidler and Jeanne T. Heidler

See also Washington, D.C.

For further reading:
Cooling, Benjamin Franklin. *Jubal Early's Raid on Washington, 1864* (1989).
Stackpole, Edward J. *Sheridan in the Shenandoah; Jubal Early's Nemesis* (1961).

HARDTACK

"Sheet-iron biscuit," "worm castles," "teeth-dullers," "hard cracker," and "hard bread" are but a few of the nicknames Yankee troops gave to hardtack, a flour-and-water biscuit that was a staple of Union soldiers' rations. The product was often inedible, as the unleavened bread lived up to its name by requiring that hungry troops bash the roughly 3-inch square, half-inch thick morsels into pieces with their musket butts. The pulverized bread could then be boiled in coffee or fried in pork fat until it softened and became somewhat palatable. Insect larva also quickly made the ration their home as the boxes of crackers sat in infested warehouses and rail yards for weeks awaiting shipment, rendering the foodstuff even more noxious.

Perhaps no other item of army life came to symbolize the communal misery of soldiers more than a piece of hardtack. Federal veteran John Billings chose to title his famous story of army life *Hard Tack and Coffee*, and described in great detail the various ways his comrades cooked the item.

Despite its flaws, hardtack did offer nutrition, and in comparison to other foods of the period, kept relatively well in the rank haversacks of dusty troops. Although soldiers constantly complained about the quality of hardtack, they missed its filling qualities when denied its issue. One of the more famous examples of this occurred during the siege of Vicksburg when Ulysses S. Grant's troops chanted "hardtack!, hardtack!," to let their leader know of their displeasure with shortened rations.

Indeed, though often distasteful, wormy, and flint-hard, hardtack was, as one Wisconsin soldier put it, "the grand staff of life to the boys in blue," throughout the war.

—*Dana B. Shoaf*

See also Rations, C.S.A.; Rations, U.S.A.
For further reading:
Billings, John D. *Hardtack and Coffee, or the Unwritten Story of Army Life* (1887; reprint, 1990).
George, Philip B. *Soldier Life, Voices of the Civil War Series* (1996).
Wiley, Bell I. *The Life of Billy Yank, the Common Soldier of the Union* (1952; reprint, 1993).

HARPER'S FERRY, (WEST) VIRGINIA

The small town of Harper's Ferry, Virginia (now West Virginia), stood at the crossroads of early national history. Located at the confluence of the Shenandoah and Potomac rivers, it first gained prominence as the site of a national armory founded in 1799. In his *Notes on the State of Virginia* (1785), Thomas Jefferson described the location as follows: "The passage of the Potomac through the Blue Ridge is perhaps one of the most stupendous scenes in nature. You stand on a very high point of land. On your right comes up the Shenandoah, having ranged along the foot of the mountain an hundred miles to seek a vent. On your left approaches the Potomac, in quest of a passage also. In the moment of their junction they rush together against the mountain, rend it asunder, and pass off to the sea." The town of Harper's Ferry grew in the wedge of land that separated the two rivers, beneath the gaze of Loudoun Heights that stood across the Shenandoah, Maryland Heights across the Potomac, and Bolivar Heights to its rear.

As president, George Washington sponsored legislation in 1794 to create four federal armories to lessen the new nation's reliance on imported firearms. The first armory was established at Springfield, Massachusetts. As historian Merritt Roe Smith argues, the meager appropriation of $81,865 for this task was insufficient to build three additional armories. Faced with a choice between retooling Revolutionary War–era magazines—which could be found at Carlisle and Philadelphia, Pennsylvania, as well as West Point, New York, and New London, Virginia—or developing an entirely new site, Washington favored the creation of an entirely new armory on the Potomac, upriver from the proposed site for the national capital. Self-interest determined Washington's choice: as a shareholder in the joint-stock Potomac Company, he stood to reap personal gain from the development of the river valley, development that would surely be encouraged by the presence of a national

armory. Despite the opposition of two successive secretaries of war, Henry Knox and Thomas Pickering, a survey of the area and construction of the necessary buildings began in 1798. Opponents of the site pointed out that the area was prone to periodic flooding, distant from supplies of tools and even iron, and difficult to defend. It was this last quality that made the town famous during the Civil War.

On Monday, 17 October 1859, radical abolitionist John Brown led a band of twenty-one men across the Baltimore & Ohio Railroad bridge, took the acting superintendent, master armorer, and master machinist hostage, and awaited the slave uprising he fervently believed his actions would precipitate. Yet the slaves of the surrounding region did not rise up, and the townspeople cornered Brown and his men in a small brick enginehouse. The raiders had killed five free citizens of the town (four white and one black); the residents responded with violence and brutality more than equal to that of their attackers. Harper's Ferry residents cut the ears off the corpse of Dangerfield Newby, a biracial follower of Brown. At least two of Brown's men were executed after they were captured. Brown's raid ended after troops led by brevet Colonel Robert E. Lee and including Lieutenant J. E. B. Stuart attacked and subdued those trapped in the enginehouse. For his crimes, Brown was sent to the gallows on 2 December, but not before uttering a prophetic declaration: "I, John Brown, am now quite certain that the crimes of this guilty land will never be purged away but with Blood."

Although Brown intended this statement to foretell a massive slave insurrection, most historians have seen it as a presentiment of the impending Civil War. Earlier fears that the armory would be impossible to defend proved accurate: the town changed hands eight times between 1861 and 1865. The armory superintendent, Alfred Barbour, served as a representative to the Virginia convention that began in February 1861 to debate the question of secession. Events rapidly overtook men like Barbour, who advocated a compromise that would have kept Virginia in the Union. Former Virginia governor Henry Wise organized and led a band of irregular forces in a move to capture the Harper's Ferry armory on 17 April. Despite his initial opposition to the scheme, the current governor, John Letcher, ordered the state militia to reinforce Wise's men. That same day the Virginia convention voted 88 to 55 (with one abstention) in favor of secession.

With only fifty soldiers at his disposal, the garrison commander, Lieutenant Roger Jones, ordered his men to set fire to the armory and retreat northward. The main arsenal and some 15,000 arms were destroyed, but local residents put out the fires before they could spread to other buildings. Confederate troops then confiscated the surviving firearms and moved the factory equipment to

Wartime view of Harper's Ferry from the Maryland shore, showing ruins of the Baltimore & Ohio Railroad bridge
(Photograph by C. O. Bostwick / *Library of Congress*)

the state armory at Richmond. In June, Colonel Joseph E. Johnston's troops destroyed the Baltimore & Ohio Railroad Bridge that connected Harper's Ferry to Maryland. Federal forces regained the town in 1862 only to lose it once again in the battle of Harper's Ferry on 15 September.

After General Robert E. Lee's forces invaded Maryland on 4 September 1862, troops under Major General Thomas J. "Stonewall" Jackson, Major General Lafayette McLaws, and Brigadier General John G. Walker were dispatched from Frederick to encircle and subdue Harper's Ferry. Jackson's men marched west across South Mountain to Williamsport, where they scattered 2,500 Federal troops back toward Harper's Ferry. From there, Jackson crossed the Potomac and advanced to take up positions opposite Bolivar Heights. Walker marched south, crossed the Potomac, and then looped around behind Loudoun Heights. McLaws crossed over South Mountain and moved onto the ridge of Elk Mountain behind Maryland Heights. As historian Stephen Sears notes, McLaws faced the most demanding and tactically important fight. From Maryland Heights, "two 9-inch naval Dahlgren rifles, one 50-pounder

Parrott rifle, and four 12-pounder smoothbores" covered both southern and western approaches to Harper's Ferry.

The battle for Harper's Ferry was won and lost on Maryland Heights due to the inadequate preparations that had been made there. With no available springs, and no cisterns, the 1,600 Federal troops under the command of Colonel Thomas H. Ford of the 32d Ohio were in no position to withstand a siege. Nor were there adequate fortifications to defend the ridge from a prolonged assault. Matters never reached this stage, however, because the soldiers in the 126th New York assigned to Ford were so inexperienced (having been in the army but three weeks) that they broke formation when fighting commenced on the morning of the 13th.

Ford sent a dispatch to Colonel Dixon Miles, in command of the Harper's Ferry garrison: "I cannot hold my men. The One hundred and twenty-sixth all run, and the Thirty-second are out of ammunition. I must leave the hill unless you direct otherwise." Miles apparently interpreted his orders to hold the town of Harper's Ferry literally, and gave Ford permission to abandon his position. After destroying his own artillery pieces, Ford and his men crossed a pontoon bridge into Harper's Ferry. At the same time, Walker's men overran Loudoun Heights and Jackson drew up his forces opposite Bolivar Heights. Colonel Benjamin Franklin Davis and 1,300 cavalrymen broke out of Harper's Ferry, eluded Jackson's men, and crossed into Maryland, where they happened across a Confederate ammunition train. The capture of approximately forty wagons laden with vital supplies was the only bright spot for the Union in the disastrous Harper's Ferry conflict. Despite dire warnings, Major General George McClellan failed to hasten reinforcements to relieve the troops at Harper's Ferry. McClellan did order VI Corps under Major General William B. Franklin to dislodge McLaws from his position, but their advance was tardy. McLaws was forced off the heights on 14 September but took up positions in the valley floor. Despite a numerical and tactical advantage, Franklin did not press the attack. Six miles away, the position of the Harper's Ferry garrison had become untenable.

On the morning of 15 September, after repositioning his artillery to fire directly upon the Federal troops on the left of Bolivar Heights, Jackson's men opened fire with devastating effect. Caught in a crossfire, the men on Bolivar Heights and their commander, Colonel Miles, decided to surrender. The Union force numbering 12,419 Federal troops was captured in addition to thousands of arms and seventy artillery pieces. Miles did not live, however, to receive the public rebuke that the War Department issued over his surrender. One of the last Confederate artillery rounds fired left him with a mortal wound. The War Department also rebuked McClellan for his failure to promptly relieve Miles's command, and rebuked Colonel Ford for abandoning Maryland Heights prematurely.

The battle of Harper's Ferry was a crucial victory for Confederate forces during the 1862 Maryland campaign. At the battle of Antietam, troops rushed directly from Harper's Ferry to Sharpsburg played a decisive role in staving off defeat for Confederate forces. Harper's Ferry emerged from the war in 1865 a battle-scarred ruin of its former self. With the armory gone, the population dwindled. Eager to preserve the memory of John Brown, Baptist missionaries from New England and officials of the Freedmen's Bureau founded Storer College in vacant armory buildings in 1867. The school was endowed by Maine businessman John Storer for the education of young men and women without regard to race or color. John Brown's "fort"—the enginehouse—was moved uphill as a symbol of the struggle against slavery. The

Harper's Ferry, with ruins of the the federal armory below (*National Archives*)

college closed shortly after the *Brown v. Board of Education* decision in 1954 forced the desegregation of public schools. In 1968, National Park Service officials moved Brown's fort from the campus to its present location near the foot of the town.

—Robert S. Wolff

See also Antietam; Brown, John; Jackson, Thomas Jonathan.

For further reading:

Frye, Dennis E. "Drama between the Rivers: Harper's Ferry in the 1862 Maryland Campaign." In *Antietam: Essays on the 1862 Maryland Campaign* (1989).

Hearn, Chester G. *Six Years of Hell: Harper's Ferry during the Civil War* (1999).

Oates, Stephen B. *To Purge This Land with Blood: A Biography of John Brown* (1970).

Sears, Stephen W. *Landscape Turned Red: The Battle of Antietam* (1983).

Smith, Merritt Roe. *Harper's Ferry Armory and the New Technology: The Challenge of Change* (1977).

HARPER'S WEEKLY

For nearly six decades the most important of American pictorial magazines, *Harper's Weekly* was the most widely read journal during the Civil War, when its battlefield sketches by Albert A. Waud and evocative and emotional drawings by Thomas Nast provided a graphic and accurate record of the conflict, even as it rallied Northerners behind the Union cause.

Founded in 1857 by Fletcher Harper, for whom it "became his pet enterprise," the *Weekly* was not the first pictorial magazine—indeed, it modeled its appearance on the *Illustrated London News*—but it quickly surpassed such rivals as the *New York Illustrated News*, *Gleason's Pictorial*, *Ballou's Pictorial*, and its principal competitor, *Frank Leslie's Illustrated Newspaper*, which had been founded the previous year. Calling itself a "Journal of Civilization," it stressed political news, pictures, and literature equally and won a wide following when it began publishing the works of Charles Dickens and Willkie Collins in serial form.

Before the war, the *Weekly's* politics resembled those of its sister publication, *Harper's Monthly*. As expressed by political writer Theodore Sedgewick, a former associate editor on William Cullen Bryant's *New York Evening Post*, the editorials espoused conservative, Democratic politics, and urged compromise on the slavery question. The editors did not want *Harper's* to be seen as a regional, partisan journal. Its object, they said, "will be to unite rather than to separate the views and feelings of the different sections of our common country ... leaving the discussion of sectarian opinions in Religion, and sectional questions in Politics to their own appropriate organs." It derided John Brown's raid on Harper's Ferry as "the work of a half-crazed white" and predicted he would "cost the Republicans many thousand votes."

Front page of *Harper's Weekly* for 6 December 1862, depicting Major-General Nathaniel Banks (*Library of Congress*)

As late as Lincoln's inauguration, four months after South Carolina led the march of Southern secession, *Harper's* continued to urge compromise, predicting that holding the Union together by force "would prove futile." But following the attack on Fort Sumter, *Harper's* joined in the general Northern outrage and urged military action—although it was not until 1863 that the *Weekly* became a full-fledged and enthusiastic Lincoln supporter.

The change came about largely because of two people: George William Curtis, who took over from John Bonner as editor of the magazine in 1862, and artist Thomas Nast, who was hired by *Harper's* from the *New York Illustrated News* and who was a passionate radical Republican. Curtis mobilized a fleet of correspondents and, especially, artists, to accompany the Northern armies and sketch accurate renderings of the battles. He also recognized the importance of the wartime photography of Matthew Brady and Alexander Gardner: with competent halftone reproductions still a

THE REBEL RAID OF STEWART'S CAVALRY TOWARDS THE WHITE HOUSE.

"To give the rebel his due," it must be confessed, that one of the most dashing things the Confederates have done is the raid of Stewart's cavalry towards the White House, on the night of the 13th of June. Their course was first to Old Church, where they had a skirmish with a squadron of the 5th United States cavalry, who gallantly cut their way through the greatly superior numbers of the enemy, killing a rebel Captain. This our Artist has illustrated. The rebels then proceeded to Garlick's Landing on the Pamunky river, and only four miles from the White House. From thence to Tunstall's Station; then to Baltimore Cross Roads, near New Kent Court House, on their way to Richmond, which they reached by crossing the Chickahominy, between Bottom Bridge and James River. Our Artist, who had a narrow escape of being captured on that occasion, has sent us some sketches, illustrating an adventure which resembles more a border foray of the times of Flodden Field than the days of broadcloth and Nicholas Biddle. Doubtless undertaken for reconnoitreing objects, with true rebel malignity they resolved to flavor the ride with as much murder as they could safely

THE REBEL'S RAID—THE REBEL CAVALRY RAID TOWARDS THE WHITE HOUSE—DESPERATE SKIRMISH AT OLD CHURCH, NEAR TUNSTALL'S STATION, VA., BETWEEN A SQUADRON OF THE 5TH U. S. CAVALRY AND STEWART'S REBEL CAVALRY, JUNE 13TH—DEATH OF THE REBEL CAPTAIN JETANE.—FROM A SKETCH BY OUR SPECIAL ARTIST, MR. WM. WAUD.

Illustrated battle coverage in *Harper's Weekly*, June 1862 (*Library of Congress*)

decade from realization, Curtis had his artists copy many of Brady's photos.

But if artists such as Waud, Theodore R. Davis, and A. W. Warren delivered a pictorial history of the war, it was Nast whose grand pictorial centerfolds brought home the war's impact and bolstered the North's often flagging spirits. His passionate and emotional drawings—combined with his ruthless attacks on everything Southern—were meant to shore up support for the embattled Lincoln, and they succeeded. "Thomas Nast has been our best recruiting sergeant," the president proclaimed towards the end of the war. *Harper's* editorial columns, in turn, hailed Lincoln's "wisdom and passionless equity" and Nast's classic political cartoon, "To the Memory of Union Heroes in a Useless War" was widely reprinted by the president's 1864 reelection campaign. "Nast is a genius," proclaimed the contemporary journalism historian Frederick Hudson. "He cannot be compared to any other artist, living or dead.". Equally celebrated were Winslow Homer and his portraits of camp life. His most famous wartime works, *The Sharp-Shooter* and *Snap the Whip*, remain classics.

Throughout the war, *Harper's* outdid its rivals, especially *Leslie's*, in both the quantity and the quality of its woodcuts portraying this first war to have widespread pictorial coverage, although it trailed its major competitor in sheer liveliness. Its circulation numbers remained high: about 120,000 for the duration of the war. Its influence was felt early on, when it succeeded in making Captain Robert Anderson, the defender of Fort Sumter, into a folk hero overnight by featuring woodcuts of everything from his cot to his candlesticks. At least once, however, the magazine was a victim of its own popularity: Military censors seized every available copy of *Harper's* that contained a woodcut of the Confederate works before Yorktown and Secretary of War Edwin Stanton ordered the magazine suppressed, accusing it of having given "aid and comfort to the enemy." Fletcher Harper later not only got the decision reversed, he actually won Stanton's public thanks for the *Weekly's* service to the Union cause.

Not everyone appreciated the *Weekly's* drawings. Rival magazines accused each other of drawing most of their battle scenes in their New York offices—a claim endorsed by the New York Historical Society, but which is contradicted by the letters and papers of the artists themselves. Theodore Davis became a particular favorite of General William T. Sherman's staff during the 1864 march through Georgia; according to one account, he habitually exchanged clothes with dead Confederate soldiers "in full view of the combatants and not infrequently when under fire ... simply for the novelty of the change."

Still, *Harper's* and other pictorial weeklies were derided for the alleged inaccuracy of their pictures from the front. "Those who draw their conceptions of the appearance of the rebel soldiery from *Harper's Weekly* would hardly recognize one on sight," claimed the *Cincinnati Gazette*.

Harper's continued to prosper after the war, largely on the strength of Nast's pen. In 1871, the *Weekly's* pages were filled with Nast's classic attacks on the corrupt Tammany Hall ring headed by William "Boss" Tweed. The following year, Nast mercilessly savaged *New York Tribune* editor Horace Greeley's quixotic and disastrous presidential campaign; even *Weekly* editor Curtis thought Nast had gone overboard. It was in these years that Nast created images still used by cartoonists today: the Tammany tiger, the Democratic donkey, and the Republican elephant. But there was little criticism of Nast's savage attacks on Catholics in general and Irish immigrants in particular. Nast was an unapologetic nativist who feared a "papist plot" to destroy the American public school system.

The magazine suffered two blows during the 1880s: its endorsement of Democrat Grover Cleveland for president in 1884 alienated its largely Republican readership, and Nast's retirement in 1887 cost *Harper's* its most popular feature. But the move hurt Nast, as well: "In quitting *Harper's Weekly*," Henry Watterson wrote later, "Nast lost his forum; in losing Nast, *Harper's Weekly* lost its political influence." The *Weekly* found new quality writers in Carl Schurz and Richard Harding Davis; in Frederic Remington, it had an artist who was the equal of Homer. It also revived the quality of its serials, publishing Lafcadio Hearn, Henry James, and William Dean Howells, among others. But circulation, which had approached 500,000 in the wake of the Tweed exposés, began to fall.

Harper and Brothers publishing house collapsed in 1899, and the *Weekly* was taken over by George Harvey, who, *Life* magazine later said, "did almost everything [with it] that he should have done, except make it pay"—although he is widely credited with having spurred the movement to elect Woodrow Wilson president in 1912. The magazine was sold to *McClure's* in 1913 after two decades of unprofitability. Sold again two years later, it finally folded in 1916.

—*Eric Fettmann*

See also Nast, Thomas; Waud, Alfred.
For further reading:
Andrews, J. Cutler. *The North Reports the Civil War* (1955).
Grossbach, Barry Leonard. "*Harper's Weekly*: A Critique of the Editorial Viewpoints, 1860–1886" (M. A. thesis, 1961).
Harper, J. Henry. *The House of Harper* (1912).
Mott, Frank Luther. *A History of American Magazines* (1938).
Paine, Albert Bigelow. *Thomas Nast, His Period and His Pictures* (1904).
Starr, Louis M. *Bohemian Brigade: Civil War Newsmen in Action* (1954).

HARRIET LANE, USS/CSS

In one of the most varied careers of any Civil War naval vessel, the USS/CSS *Harriet Lane* saw service as a U.S. revenue cutter, as a warship in both the Union and Confederate navies, and as a Rebel blockade runner.

Originally built as the United States Revenue Cutter *Harriet Lane* in 1857–1858, this ship was the only steam-powered cutter in the U.S. service at the time. She was designed by Samuel Pook and built by William Webb, two well-regarded names in the business. The *Harriet Lane* was a wooden sidewheeler with a two-masted brigantine rig. She displaced just under 675 tons, measured 180 feet in length with a 30-foot beam, and drew 10 feet of water. Her original crew numbered 100, and at the beginning of the Civil War, the vessel was armed with 3 32-pounders and 4 24-pounders. The vessel was named for Harriet Lane, the niece of James Buchanan, America's only bachelor president. Lane served as an unofficial first lady during Buchanan's term.

The USRC *Harriet Lane* took part in the Navy's 1858 punitive expedition against Paraguay. Afterward, the ship was stationed at New York and was toured by the first visiting Japanese delegation to the United States and by the Prince of Wales.

In April 1861, the USRC *Harriet Lane*, under the command of Captain John Faunce of the U.S. Revenue Marine, was part of the unsuccessful naval relief expedition sent to Fort Sumter. The *Harriet Lane* and the other ships arrived off Charleston on 12 April, only to find that the Confederate batteries had opened fire on Fort Sumter, and the ships were unable to help the garrison. When she fired a warning shot across the bow of the U.S. mail steamer *Nashville*, which was attempting to enter Charleston Harbor, the *Harriet Lane* fired what some consider the first Union shot of the war.

Later in April 1861, the *Harriet Lane* and the USS *Constitution* transported the midshipmen of the Naval Academy when the school was moved from Annapolis to Newport, Rhode Island. The *Harriet Lane* also took part in the capture of the Confederate forts at Hatteras Inlet, North Carolina, on 28–29 August 1861. On 10 September 1861, the vessel was officially transferred to the Navy.

In April 1862, the *Harriet Lane*, under command of Lieutenant Jonathan M. Wainwright, served as the flagship of Commander David D. Porter's mortar flotilla on the Mississippi River. On 28 April, the Confederate officers in charge of forts Jackson and St. Philip signed surrender papers on board the *Harriet Lane*. Wainwright was about to sign the papers when he was called on deck by one of his officers, who warned that the Confederate ironclad *Louisiana* was afire and drifting toward their position. Porter later wrote that "an explosion took place that fairly shook us all out of our seats and threw the *Harriet Lane* over on her side, but we finished the terms of capitulation."

The *Harriet Lane* took part in the capture of Galveston, Texas, on 3 October 1862. On 1 January 1863, when Major General John B. Magruder took Galveston by surprise, the *Harriet Lane* bore the brunt of a Confederate naval attack by two cottonclads, the *Neptune* and the *Bayou City*. Sustaining much damage by firing from the shore and the enemy vessels, the *Harriet Lane* sank the *Neptune*, but was rammed and boarded by the *Bayou City*. Commander Wainwright was killed in the fighting before the ship surrendered.

After being attached to the Confederate army, the *Harriet Lane* was converted to a blockade runner and renamed the *Lavinia*. The *Lavinia* slipped out of Galveston on the night of 30 April 1864 and made her way to Havana. The *Lavinia* never made a return trip through the blockade. The United States recovered her after the Civil War and sold her to private interests. The former *Harriet Lane* was converted into a sailing vessel and renamed the *Elliot Richie*. She was abandoned off Pernambuco, Brazil, in 1884.

—*David A. Norris*

See also Fort Sumter; Galveston, Texas; Magruder, John B.; Navy, C.S.A.; Navy, U.S.A.; Porter, David Dixon.

For further reading:

Canney, Donald L. *U.S. Coast Guard and Revenue Cutters, 1790–1935* (1995).

Magee, Kenneth J. "Most Disgraceful Affair." *America's Civil War* (1993).

Naval History Division, Navy Department. *Civil War Naval Chronology 1861–1865* (1971).

Porter, David D. "The Opening of the Lower Mississippi." In *Battles and Leaders of the Civil War*, vol. 2.

Salta, Remo. "Guardians of the Coast." *America's Civil War* (1994).

HARRIS, ELLEN OSBORNE
(1816–1902)

Union relief worker

Ellen Osborne Harris, known affectionately as "Eliza," was one of the most eloquent relief workers the war produced. As secretary of the Philadelphia Ladies Aid Society, she spent over three years distributing supplies and nursing in general, field, and floating hospitals—activities she chronicled in poignant letters sent back home. Forty-four and a wife of twenty-four years in the spring of 1861, Harris and a band of Philadelphia society women formed an organization, not unlike the U.S. Sanitary Commission, to systematize the collection and distribution of soldiers' aid. Traveling to Washington after First Bull Run in July, Harris took stock of the medical facilities of the Army of the Potomac and determined not only to transport food to the front but to cook and deliver it to troops herself. Though of a sickly constitution, Harris managed to stay well enough to help others throughout most of the war.

Back at the Philadelphia office during the cold months of 1861, Harris prepared for McClellan's spring campaigns. In March 1862, she was at Fairfax Seminary acting as "apothecary," "physician," "nurse," and "Christian friend" to soldiers leveled by typhoid and dysentery. By May she had retreated with the army to the Virginia Peninsula and was stationed at Fortress Monroe, where she moved among Union and Confederate soldiers wounded during the siege of Yorktown. In June Harris helped evacuate wounded from the battle of Fair Oaks aboard the *Vanderbilt*, one of scores of military transports engaged to carry soldiers from the peninsula to Washington-area hospitals. After the 800 men on board were fed—some of whom had not had food in four days—Harris returned to her quarters at Fort Monroe, stripped off her bloody clothes, and "was glad to lie down, every bone aching, and head and heart throbbing, unwilling to cease work where so much was to be done, and yet wholly unable to do more. There I lay, with the sick, wounded, and dying all around, and slept from sheer exhaustion, the last sounds falling upon my ear being groans from the operating room." Harris remained until the end of the summer with the wounded and malaria-ridden men of the Chickahominy swamps. She then moved supplies to South Mountain in anticipation of the battle of Antietam in mid-September. Harris's postbattle descriptions of dead men are nothing if not ghoulish.

After several weeks at Sharpsburg, where she worked alongside Maria M. C. Hall, Harris went to Alexandria's Convalescent Camp, dubbed "Camp Misery," for six weeks. The first woman to shed public light on the horrors of the camp, Harris's pleas led veteran nurse Amy Morris Bradley of Maine to assume its management in December 1862. That month, in the wake of the siege of Fredericksburg, Harris was in the field at Falmouth, where she remained feeding, clothing, and medicating sufferers through the spring 1863 campaigns that resulted in the battle of Chancellorsville. In July she went without permission, like many others, to Gettysburg. Erroneously anticipating more bloodshed in Maryland, she left for Fredericksburg a week later and stayed through September nursing convalescents of Fredericksburg, Chancellorsville, and Gettysburg.

In October 1863, a worn-out Harris traveled west to Nashville and Chattanooga where Braxton Bragg's forces had defeated those of William Rosecrans at Chickamauga. Becoming sick herself, she pressed on, aiding the 25,000 men wounded there, until she returned east in May 1864, in time for some of the fiercest fighting yet, at the Wilderness. In the late summer, Harris took her first furlough, but ended it by September when she joined the Army of the Shenandoah near Winchester. Here she remained, with one brief interruption to nurse her dying mother, until the spring when the release of Union prisoners from Andersonville and Salisbury at Wilmington, North Carolina, commanded her attention, as it had done for Harriet Hawley.

Harris returned home to Philadelphia in the summer of 1865, but her residence in the United States was of short duration. In 1870, her husband, physician John Harris, was appointed U.S. consul to Italy. The couple moved to Venice and lived there until John's death in 1881, whereupon Eliza relocated to Florence. There she remained for twenty more years until she died in 1902.

—*Jane E. Schultz*

See also Bradley, Amy M.; Hall, Maria M. C.; Hawley, Harriett F.; Nurses.

For further reading:

Brockett, Linus P., and Mary Vaughan. *Woman's Work in the Civil War* (1867).

Conklin, Eileen. *Women of Gettysburg 1863* (1993).

Dannett, Sylvia. *Noble Women of the North* (1959).

Moore, Frank. *Women of the War: Their Heroism and Self-Sacrifice* (1866).

Semi-Annual Reports of the Ladies Aid Society of Philadelphia (1861–1865).

HARRIS, ISHAM GREEN
(1818–1897)
Governor of Tennessee

Born to Isham Green Harris and Lucy Davidson Harris in Tullahoma, Tennessee, the younger Harris attended local schools before entering the mercantile business first in Tennessee and then in Mississippi. After moving to Mississippi, Harris began the study of law and, after being admitted to the bar there, began his practice. He also became active in Democratic politics in Mississippi and was elected to the state senate in 1847. Two years later, he was elected from his district to the U.S. House of Representatives. He served two terms in the House before relocating to Memphis, Tennessee, where he hoped to establish a more lucrative law practice. He also became active in Tennessee politics once he had established his practice.

In 1857 Harris was elected governor of Tennessee on a states' rights Democratic platform; he won reelection successively in 1859 and 1861. When Abraham Lincoln was elected, Harris became a strong proponent for the secession of Tennessee. However, Unionist sentiment was strong in the state. Therefore, when with his urging the state legislature put the question of a secession convention to the voters, the measure was overwhelmingly defeated. Expecting the state to secede eventually, if he had anything to do with it, Harris wrote to President James Buchanan's Secretary of War, John Floyd, asking when the state's yearly allotment of arms would be shipped to the state.

Having failed in his direct attempt to take Tennessee out of the Union, Harris then adopted an officially neutral stance, arguing that the state was neither in nor out of the Union, but would certainly lend no support to any U.S. attempt to coerce the new Confederate States of America back into the Union. He then sought politically to isolate Unionists politicians by accusing them of ignoring what was best for the state. After the Confederate attack on Fort Sumter and President Lincoln's subsequent call for volunteers, Harris refused to supply Tennessee's quota. He then called the legislature back into session and pushed through that body a declaration of independence for the state and alliance with the Confederacy. During the term of the alliance, Harris supplied troops to the Confederate army as an allied power and then engineered another vote by the legislature formally joining the Confederate States of America.

From the very beginning of Tennessee's involvement in the Civil War, Harris was involved in the defense of the state. In the fall of 1861, he became convinced that one of the best ways to preserve the safety of Tennessee was for both sides to honor the neutrality of Kentucky. For that reason, when Confederate forces moved briefly into southern Kentucky, he wrote to the Confederate War Department and to the officers in the field that those forces should be removed immediately. By early 1862, however, he had more immediate problems to worry about.

Ulysses S. Grant's invasion of Tennessee and the subsequent fall of Forts Henry and Donelson brought about the fall of Nashville and the virtual collapse of Harris's government. While he still worked to recruit troops for the Confederacy and corresponded frequently with the Confederate government about Tennessee's military situation, he remained virtually a governor-in-exile for the remainder of his term.

Not having a functioning government to administer, Harris believed that he could best serve the defensive needs of the state with the army. Therefore he offered his services as a voluntary aide-de-camp to General Albert Sidney Johnston. Serving as Johnston's aide at Shiloh on 6 April, Harris was at the general's side when he received his mortal wound during the battle. Harris helped the general from his horse and according to witnesses was holding Johnston in his arms when the general died.

Harris then offered the same services to General P. G. T. Beauregard, Johnston's successor, and would perform similar services to General Braxton Bragg, Joseph Johnston, and John Bell Hood. In that capacity Harris was a participant in and witness to virtually every major engagement in the state of Tennessee.

When the Confederate forces surrendered, Harris fled to Mexico and from there to Great Britain. The Unionists whom he had persecuted pushed through the Tennessee legislature a $5,000 reward for his capture, thus preventing Harris's early return from England. Eventually, his political nemesis, William G. Brownlow, worked to have the price removed from his head, and Harris returned to Memphis in 1876.

Harris immediately resumed his law practice and reentered Tennessee politics. He was elected to the U.S. Senate in 1877 and remained in that position until his death in 1897. During the later part of his Senate career, Harris became involved in the Populist movement, working primarily to expand the currency. He died in Washington, D.C.

—*David S. Heidler and Jeanne T. Heidler*

See also Shiloh; Tennessee.

For further reading:
Looney, John Thomas. "Isham G. Harris of Tennessee: Bourbon Senator, 1877–1897" (M.A. thesis, 1970).
Watters, George Wayne. "Isham Green Harris, Civil War Governor and Senator from Tennessee, 1818–1897" (Ph.D. dissertation, 1977).

HARRIS, NATHANIEL HARRISON
(1834–1900)
Confederate general

Nathaniel Harrison Harris was born on 22 August 1834 in Natchez, Mississippi. After obtaining a law degree from the University of Louisiana (now Tulane), he moved to Vicksburg to practice with his brother.

After receiving news of Fort Sumter, Harris organized a volunteer company at Vicksburg known as the Warren Rifles. The unit mustered into Confederate service in late May 1861 as Company C, 19th Mississippi Infantry, with Harris as its captain.

Assigned to the Virginia theater, the 19th Mississippi's baptism of fire came on 5 May 1862 at the battle of Williamsburg. In that fight, Harris was singled out for "special praise…not only for his gallant bearing on the field, but for his unremitting attention to his command." With the death of Colonel Christopher Mott at Williamsburg and subsequent resignation of Lieutenant Colonel L. Q. C. Lamar, Harris received the appointment as major of his regiment.

As part of a demibrigade directed by General W. S. Featherston, Harris and his Magnolia Staters fought in quick succession at Seven Pines, Gaines' Mill, and Frayser's Farm. Harris served on the staff of General Cadmus Wilcox in the former battle and received a slight wound in the latter. At Second Manassas, Harris was again wounded, this time being incapacitated for three months.

On 2 April 1863, Harris received the appointment as colonel of the 19th Mississippi, to be effective from 5 May 1862. The unit was assigned to General Carnot Posey's brigade, in R. H. Anderson's division.

At Chancellorsville, Harris and his troops were tireless. On 3 May, Harris led a charge against entrenched Federals through "a murderous fire of musketry and artillery" that dislodged the enemy, and they then joined Anderson's troops at Salem Church, preventing General John Sedgwick from relieving General Joseph Hooker. Harris also advanced the 19th Mississippi to support General A. R. Wright's futile charge of 2 July at Gettysburg, but unsupported could do little to carry the Federal lines.

Harris was on sick furlough when Posey was killed at Bristoe Station. Harris stood next in line to replace Posey, but R. H. Anderson recommended Colonel Samuel Baker, of the 16th Mississippi. President Jefferson Davis, always loath to ignore seniority, overruled Anderson and named Harris brigadier of a brigade consisting of the 12th, 16th, 19th, and 48th Mississippi Infantry. In the last eleven months of the war, Harris consistently confirmed the wisdom of Davis's decision.

On 6 May 1864, at the Wilderness, an afternoon charge by Harris's Magnolia Staters prevented a possible break in the Confederate lines, but its most significant action came six days later at Spotsylvania. When a massive Federal assault overwhelmed the Confederate position in the Mule Shoe salient, Lee rushed Harris's brigade into the breach. Fighting desperately in a pouring rain, in trenches literally flowing with blood, Harris and his men battled for twenty hours, buying time with their blood while Lee patched together a new defensive line. Few episodes of the war can match the courage or importance of the furious engagement of Harris' Mississippians at the "Bloody Angle."

As part of General William Mahone's division, Harris and his brigade continued to fight with distinction during the subsequent battles of the war. They helped repulse a Federal charge along the banks of the North Anna River (24 May) and were engaged during the siege of Petersburg at Weldon Railroad (22–23 June) and at Deep Bottom (16–18 August). Three days later, a historian of the 19th Mississippi reported the "brigade was in battle on the Weldon Railroad near Yellow Tavern, charging the Federal works, from which they were repulsed with heavy loss." They also participated in engagements at Burgess' Mill (27 October) and at Hatcher's Run (5–7 February 1865).

After the Union breakthrough at Five Forks, Harris hurried his men to Forts Gregg and Whitworth while General James Longstreet formed a new defensive line. Hammered by repeated assaults by the Union XXIV Corps, Fort Gregg was finally captured, and Harris abandoned Fort Whitworth under orders and joined the retreat of Lee's army. Without any hope of victory, Harris' Magnolia Staters had bought a little time for the Army of Northern Virginia. The cost had been terrible. At Appomattox Court House, Harris surrendered only 33 officers and 339 men.

After the war, Harris practiced law at Vicksburg, served as president of a Mississippi railroad, and acted as registrar of the U. S. Land Office in South Dakota. Harris moved to San Francisco, California, in 1890. He wrote copiously about his war experiences, and died in 1900 while on a business trip to England. The year after his death, Harris' younger brother published *Movements of the Confederate Army in Virginia and the Part Taken Therein by the Nineteenth Mississippi Regiment from the Diary of General Nat H. Harris*. It is among the rarest of Civil War books.

—*Zack C. Waters*

See also Mahone, William; Spotsylvania Court House, Battle of.

For further reading:

Harris, William M. *Movements of the Confederate Army in Virginia and the Part Taken Therein by the Nineteenth Mississippi Regiment from the Diary of General Nat H. Harris* (1901).

Holt, David A. *Mississippi Rebel in the Army of Northern Virginia: The Civil War Memoirs of Private David Holt* (1995).

Krick, Robert K. "General Nat Harris' Diary: The Rarest Army of Northern Virginia Book?" *Blue & Gray* (1991).

Rietti, J. C. *Military Annals of Mississippi: Military Organizations which Entered the Service of the Confederate States of America from the State of Mississippi* (1988).

Sommers, Richard J. "Nathaniel Harrison Harris." *The Confederate General* (n.d.).

HARRISON, BENJAMIN
(1833–1901)

Union soldier, U.S. senator, and twenty-third president of the United States

An Ohio native who made his home in Indiana for most of life, Harrison had a distinguished political pedigree. His great-great grandfather was one of the signers of the Declaration of Independence; his grandfather, William Henry Harrison, was elected as the country's ninth president; and his father served as a Whig congressman.

An 1852 graduate of Miami (Ohio) University, Harrison read law in the Cincinnati office of Storer and Gwynne. Admitted to the bar in 1854, Harrison moved to Indianapolis with his wife, Caroline Lavinia Scott, whom he had married the year before, to open his own law practice. A charter member of the Republican Party in Indiana, Harrison won election as Indianapolis city attorney in 1857, served as secretary of the Republican state central committee, and captured the statewide office of reporter of the Indiana Supreme Court in 1860 and 1864.

With the outbreak of the Civil War, Harrison, with the support of Indiana governor Oliver P. Morton, raised Company A of the 70th Indiana Volunteer Infantry and won appointment as colonel. Harrison, who stood only five feet, seven inches tall, captured the respect and affection of his troops, who nicknamed their commander "Little Ben." During the war, Harrison engaged in campaigns in Kentucky, Tennessee, and Georgia, and was brevetted a general. His service included commanding the 1st Brigade in General William Tecumseh Sherman's final drive on Atlanta and halting a Confederate attack at Peachtree Creek. Although he had lost his office as court reporter in 1862, Harrison received his party's approval for the job and recaptured his position in the 1864 election. (Harrison had returned to Indiana to assist in winning the state back for the Republican Party.) Harrison participated in the Grand Review in Washington, D.C., before being discharged in June 1865. Upon his discharge, he returned to Indianapolis and resumed his job as court reporter.

In 1872, Harrison unsuccessfully sought the Republican nomination for Indiana governor. His chance for Indiana's top office came again in 1876 when he replaced the Republican Party's initial nominee, Godlove Love, who had been implicated in a financial scandal. Harrison lost that election to his Democratic challenger, James D. "Blue Jeans" Williams. Just four years later, with his party controlling the Indiana general assembly, Harrison won appointment to the U.S. Senate. During his six years in office, he gained a national reputation through his work to increase pensions for veterans and his staunch support for a high protective tariff.

In 1888 Harrison received his party's nomination for president against incumbent Democrat Grover Cleveland. The Hoosier politician benefited from Indiana's importance as a swing state in national politics. Harrison conducted a low-key campaign, preferring to remain at his palatial Indianapolis home on North Delaware Street, where he greeted the thousands of visitors who daily flocked to Indiana to see him. Although Harrison trailed in the popular vote by approximately 90,000 votes, he won the Electoral College (233 to 168 votes) and became the country's twenty-third president. The election saw charges of vote buying from both parties and contributed to the passing in Indiana of the Australian ballot system for voting. After the election, Harrison had told Senator Matt Quay of Pennsylvania,

Benjamin Harrison at the battle of Resaca, May 1864
(*Library of Congress*)

Republican national chairman, that "Providence has given us the victory." Quay, a veteran politico who considered the new president a political amateur, was unmoved by Harrison's oratory. Quay later exclaimed to a Philadelphia journalist that providence played no role in capturing the presidency and Harrison might never learn how close many men came to going to jail in order to win him his office.

During his administration, Harrison signed into law much significant legislation, including the Sherman Antitrust Act and the McKinley Tariff, and presided over the admission of six new western states into the Union in 1889 and 1890. Unpopular with his own party leaders for his often cold manner, Harrison nevertheless was renominated by the Republicans for the 1892 presidential race to face, once again, Democratic challenger and former president Cleveland. Harrison did little campaigning due to his wife's ill health. (She died a few weeks before the election.) This time, Cleveland comfortably defeated Harrison in both the popular vote and the Electoral College. After his defeat, Harrison returned to Indianapolis and resumed his lucrative law practice. In 1896 he married Mary Scott Dimmick, his deceased wife's niece. Harrison died on 13 March 1901 and is buried in Indianapolis's Crown Hill Cemetery.

—*Ray E. Boomhower*

See also Atlanta Campaign; Peachtree Creek, Battle of.
For further reading:
Calhoun, Charles W. "Benjamin Harrison." *Encyclopedia of Indianapolis* (1994).
Geib, George. "Benjamin Harrison." *Traces of Indiana and Midwestern History* (1996).
Gray, Ralph D. *Indiana's Favorite Sons, 1840–1940* (1988).
Kinzer, Donald L. "Benjamin Harrison and the Politics of Availability." In *Gentlemen from Indiana: National Party Candidates, 1836–1940* (1977).
Sievers, Harry J. *Benjamin Harrison: Hoosier President, the White House and After* (1968).
———. *Benjamin Harrison: Hoosier Statesman, from the Civil War to the White House, 1865–1888* (1959).
———. *Benjamin Harrison: Hoosier Warrior, 1833–1865* (1952).

HARRISON'S LANDING, VIRGINIA

Harrison's Landing, on the James River in Charles City County, Virginia, served as the headquarters of the Army of the Potomac after the Seven Days' battles in the summer of 1862. Controversy surrounded General George B. McClellan's decision to move his troops to Harrison's Landing, as well as his prolonged stay from early July to mid-August. Close to 100,000 men occupied the site, and many suffered from the intense heat, ravaging disease, and profound boredom.

The Harrison's Landing occupation was centered at Berkeley, one of Virginia's historic James River plantations. Benjamin Harrison V, who signed the Declaration of Independence, had lived at Berkeley, and President William Henry Harrison had been born there. At the end of June 1862, McClellan chose the site as his new base of operations, viewing it as the perfect place to give the army a rest and await reinforcements under the protection of Union gunboats. Advance troops arrived at Harrison's Landing on 30 June. Because McClellan had decided to change his headquarters, he never considered following up the army's victory at Malvern Hill on 1 July, much to the dismay of many of his officers. McClellan, however, always denied that the move to Harrison's Landing was a retreat and emphasized his successful execution of a risky flank movement. Although morale was low among the soldiers as they slogged through rain and mud on 1–2 July, many of the men shared McClellan's view that they were considerably outnumbered by General Robert E. Lee's Confederate forces.

The first few weeks at Harrison's Landing provided the army with rest and rejuvenation. The mansion house at Berkeley and its larger outbuildings were transformed into hospitals for the wounded from Malvern Hill. The Sanitary Commission arrived with nurses, tents, medical supplies, and food. Soldiers took advantage of the opportunity to bathe in the James, and they all received new uniforms. Many also foraged throughout the countryside, raiding area crops and farms. An early threat from Confederate general J. E. B. Stuart's cavalry, which fired on the camp, transports, and gunboats on the morning of 3 July, was quickly extinguished.

On 8 July, President Abraham Lincoln arrived at Harrison's Landing to confer with McClellan and review the army. Lincoln wanted McClellan to go back on the offensive as soon as possible, but McClellan believed that he needed 50,000 more troops before doing so. During their meeting, McClellan gave Lincoln a letter describing his views of the political goals of the war. Known as the Harrison's Landing Letter, McClellan's memo advised Lincoln that the aim of the war should be to restore the Union, not to interfere with civilian life in the South or free the slaves. Although Lincoln had given McClellan permission to express his views, he did not share McClellan's assessment and no doubt resented his patronizing tone. Although Lincoln did not reply directly to McClellan's letter, on 11 July he appointed Henry W. Halleck general-in-chief of the army, an obvious signal of his dissatisfaction with McClellan. McClellan later used the Harrison's Landing Letter as the basis for his 1864 presidential platform.

As the month of July progressed, the troops at Harrison's Landing became increasingly restive. General Daniel Butterfield and bugler Oliver W. Norton composed the bugle call that would become known as "Taps." Most of the soldiers were eager to depart "Mud City." Oppressive heat, bothersome flies, and unsanitary conditions began to take their toll, and several hundred men died of disease. In addition, a Confederate bombardment of the camp from the southern bank of the James during the night of 31 July–1 August killed ten Union soldiers before the Confederates backed off.

By late July, both Lincoln and Halleck had despaired of convincing McClellan to push on toward Richmond. On 3 August, Halleck ordered McClellan to move the Army of the Potomac to Fort Monroe, near Hampton, Virginia, so troops could be transferred to Northern Virginia to reinforce General John Pope. McClellan protested the order and eventually took almost two weeks to carry it out. He made extensive preparations and then, beginning on 15 August, evacuated the army en masse so as not to alert the enemy. Numerous Charles City County slaves followed the troops to Fort Monroe.

On 12 June 1864, the Army of the Potomac under General Ulysses S. Grant returned to the banks of the James, near Harrison's Landing. Under Grant, however, the Union troops did not linger but crossed the river and began to lay siege to Petersburg.

—Antoinette G. van Zelm

See also Butterfield, Daniel; Malvern Hill, Battle of; Petersburg Campaign; Seven Days', Battles.

For further reading:

Coski, John M. *The Army of the Potomac at Berkeley Plantation:* *The Harrison's Landing Occupation of 1862* (1989).

Kilmer, George L. "The Army of the Potomac at Harrison's Landing." In *Battles and Leaders of the Civil War* (1887–1888; reprint, 1956).

Sears, Stephen W., ed. *The Civil War Papers of George B. McClellan: Selected Correspondence, 1860–1865* (1989).

HARTFORD, USS

The USS *Hartford* served as Admiral David G. Farragut's flagship throughout the Civil War, from his earliest assignment with the West Gulf Blockade Squadron in 1862, to his last campaign against Mobile, Alabama, in 1864. This vessel deserves particular mention for her services in Farragut's capture of New Orleans in April 1862, her participation in the blockade of the Red River in May 1863, and her pivotal role in the defeat of Mobile's coastal defenses in August 1864.

Completed at the Boston Navy Yard in the fall of 1858, the navy launched the *Hartford* on 22 November. In today's terms she would be a cruiser. Her official class designation was screw steamer, but sailors commonly called her a sloop of war. This simply meant that, unlike one-masted commercial sloops, she had two main masts. Sloops also had various square riggings on the fore and aft portions of the ship that distinguished the different families. Her sister ships included the USS *Brooklyn*, USS *Pensacola*, and USS *Richmond*. The *Hartford* averaged 8 knots, with a maximum speed of 13.5 knots. She was a sleek-looking ship, with a length of 225 feet and a width of 44 feet. At 2,900 tons, the *Hartford* carried a draft of 17 feet 2 inches when fully loaded.

Commissioned on 27 May 1859, the *Hartford* sailed to China on her first overseas assignment, replacing the USS *Mississippi* as flagship of the East India Squadron. The *Hartford* made considerable contributions to U.S. foreign policy by displaying the American flag, and by transporting U.S. minister John Elliott Ward to Chinese ports to settle American claims and arrange favorable trade agreements. In August 1861 the navy recalled the *Hartford* to help in the restoration of the Union, and by the end of December the Philadelphia shipyard had equipped her with a powerful armament of twenty 9-inch Dahlgren smoothbores and two twenty-pounder rifled Parrotts. Her first wartime assignment was serving as Farragut's flagship for the West Gulf Blockade Squadron. On 20 January Farragut received orders from the Navy Department to take New Orleans, to secure all ports up to Vicksburg, and then to capture Mobile.

New Orleans was the largest city of the Confederacy and arguably the most important port. Two formidable forts guarded the mouth of the Mississippi River, ninety miles south of New Orleans. Fort Jackson, on the river's west bank, mounted sixty-seven weapons. Fort St. Philip, on the east bank, mounted nineteen weapons.

The USS *Hartford* (*Library of Congress*)

The *Hartford* and others passed the forts on the night of 24 April after six days of mortar bombardment. Farragut then destroyed Confederate commodore Mitchell's small river force of six gunboats, and captured New Orleans the following day without resistance. He relinquished control of the Crescent City to Brigadier General Benjamin F. Butler on 1 May and sailed past the Grand Gulf and Vicksburg batteries to rendezvous with the Mississippi Flotilla. Starting on 4 May the vessel blockaded the mouth of the Red River while Farragut returned to New Orleans. The *Hartford* played an important role in stopping supplies from reaching the Vicksburg garrison via the Red River. In August she returned to New Orleans to continue blockading the Gulf coast.

In March 1863 the *Hartford* traveled to Vicksburg to participate briefly in the siege. The following month she and six warships tried to repass the batteries at Grand Gulf, where Confederate gunners destroyed, disabled, or turned back all but two of the force. Only the *Hartford* and her companion, the USS *Albatross*, successfully passed the batteries.

Upon completion of repairs at the Brooklyn Naval Yard during the fall, the navy sent the *Hartford* back to the Gulf in January 1864 to focus her efforts against Mobile. On the morning of 5 August, Farragut launched an intense three-hour attack against the two powerful forts guarding Mobile Bay, Forts Gaines and Morgan. The formidable CSS *Tennessee* targeted the *Hartford* once she was inside Mobile Bay, and the two vessels engaged in a titanic clash. With superior numbers, Union vessels quickly disabled the *Tennessee* and forced a surrender. The Confederate forts fell 16 days later, but the city remained in Southern hands for nine more months without access to the Gulf. The *Hartford* returned to New York City in December 1864 with the ailing admiral aboard, and subsequently the navy decommissioned her for major repairs.

After the war the *Hartford* served as the flagship for the recently organized Asiatic Station Squadron (July 1865–August 1868). She patrolled again the familiar Asian waters between October 1872 and October 1875. After a major overhaul, the *Hartford* served as Captain Stephen B. Luce's flagship for the North Atlantic Station in 1882. Luce later became an important naval reformer and father of the Naval War College.

Between January 1887 and August 1926, the *Hartford's* duties alternated between sea-training for midshipmen, patrolling near Charleston Harbor, and anchoring for repairs. Permanently decommissioned in August 1926, the navy docked her at various naval yards along the Atlantic until she sank in her berth at the Norfolk Navy Yard on 20 November 1956. The yard dismantled the remains of the vessel, where relics are on display at several naval museums in the Washington, D.C., area.

—*David P. Eldridge*

See also Farragut, David Glasgow; Mobile Bay; New Orleans, Capture of; *Tennessee, CSS*

For further reading:
Duffy, James P. *Lincoln's Admiral: The Civil War Campaigns of David Farragut* (1997).
Jones, Virgil Carrington. *The Civil War at Sea: The River War* (1961).
Milligan, John D. *Gunboats Down the Mississippi* (1965).
United States Navy. *Dictionary of American Naval Fighting Ships*, Volume III (1968).

HARTRANFT, JOHN FREDERICK
(1830–1889)
Union general

Born in Montgomery County, Pennsylvania, John F. Hartranft studied at the local Treemount Seminary and then graduated from Union College in Schenectady, New York, in 1853 with a degree in civil engineering. Hartranft was a bright student; none of his final grades were below a 96. After brief employment with two eastern Pennsylvania railroads, Hartranft returned home to Norristown to assist his father in the real estate and stage line businesses. While home, Hartranft's attention drifted into law. In October 1860, he was admitted to the Montgomery County bar.

Hartranft married Sallie Douglas Sebring in 1854, and they had seven children, two of whom died in infancy and one of whom died on the day of birth. Hartranft also became a Mason, served with a local fire company, became an officer in the Norris Rifles and a lieutenant colonel in the state militia, served as a deputy sheriff for almost five years, and devoted time to other area agencies and clubs.

Upon the outbreak of war in 1861, Hartranft tendered his services and was commissioned colonel of the 4th Pennsylvania Volunteer Infantry, a three-months' regiment whose term expired on 21 July. Even as the Union army marched forth to battle, Hartranft's regiment voted to return to Washington rather than continue in service. Hartranft himself, with one of his company captains, volunteered to remain in the field. The colonel served as a volunteer aide on Colonel William B. Franklin's staff, performing heroically during the fighting. In 1886, Congress awarded him a Medal of Honor for his valiant services.

After his service in 1861, Hartranft returned home and immediately set about raising a new regiment. He was commissioned colonel of the 51st Pennsylvania Volunteer Infantry, which was assigned to the expedition being gathered by General Ambrose E. Burnside for coastal operations. In North Carolina, Hartranft led his regiment in battle at Roanoke Island on 8 February 1862 and New Bern on 14 March 1862.

When Burnside took some of his troops north as the new IX Army Corps, Hartranft accompanied his regiment and fought at Second Bull Run on 29–30 August, South Mountain on 14 September, and Antietam on 17 September. In this latter battle, the 51st gained immortality as the unit that charged across the lower stone bridge (Burnside's Bridge), suffering 120 casualties in taking the bridge. The regiment also was engaged at Fredericksburg before going into winter quarters.

When Burnside was transferred to the Department of the Ohio, the 51st Pennsylvania was part of IX Corps that went with the general. After a brief garrison stint in Kentucky, Hartranft accompanied IX Corps' detachment that went to Vicksburg and took part in the July operations that resulted in the capture of Jackson, Mississippi. After returning to Kentucky, Hartranft's unit participated in the expedition to Knoxville, Tennessee. When General James Longstreet launched his operation against the city, Hartranft, still a colonel and in command of the 2d Division, IX Corps, performed brilliantly at Campbell's Station on 16 November during the retreat to the city.

The IX Corps then returned to Virginia and accompanied the Army of the Potomac during the 1864–1865 operations against Petersburg and Lee's army. Hartranft was placed in command of a brigade and led his troops competently at the Wilderness, Spotsylvania, North Anna, and Petersburg. He was finally promoted to brigadier general to rank from 12 May 1864. When IX Corps was reorganized, Hartranft was given command of a new 3d Division, consisting of newly raised Pennsylvania regiments. His division was in reserve when Confederate troops attacked and captured Fort Stedman on 25 March 1865. Hartranft brought his untested brigades into battle and recaptured the fort, which resulted in his promotion to major general.

At war's end, Hartranft was assigned to the command of the Old Capitol Prison, which housed Abraham Lincoln's assassination conspirators. The general supervised the 7 July hangings of David Herold, George Atzerodt, Lewis Payne, and Mary Surratt. Hoping to the last to avoid hanging Surratt, Hartranft delayed as long as possible, waiting in vain for a presidential pardon.

After Hartranft's mustering out of service, he returned home and entered politics. He was state auditor general from 1865 to 1868 and served two terms as governor from 1873 to 1879. During his gubernatorial tenure, Hartranft was faced with the Molly Maguires and the 1877 steel strike in Pittsburgh. He reformed the state militia into the National Guard, and from 1879 to 1889 Hartranft served as the state guard commander. He served as postmaster of Philadelphia from 1879 to 1880 and then as collector of the port of Philadelphia from 1880 to 1889. Hartranft died in 1889 and is buried in Montgomery Cemetery, Norristown.

—*Richard A. Sauers*

See also Fort Stedman, Battle of; Lincoln Assassination; Surratt, Mary.

For further reading:
Evans, Frank B. *Pennsylvania Politics, 1872–1877: A Study in Political Leadership* (1966).
Gambone, Albert M. *Major-General John Frederick Hartranft: Citizen Soldier and Pennsylvania Statesman* (1995).
Parker, Thomas H. *History of the 51st Regiment of P.V. and V.V.* (1869; reprint, 1998).

HARTSUFF, GEORGE LUCAS
(1830–1874)
Union general

Born in Tyre, New York, George Lucas Hartsuff moved to Michigan with his family when he was a child. He was educated locally and received an appointment to the U.S. Military Academy in 1848. He graduated nineteenth of forty-two in the class of 1852. Upon graduation he served in New York and Texas. The beginning of the Third Seminole War brought his transfer to Florida. Hartsuff was seriously wounded in that conflict. Upon his recovery, he served a three-year tour as an instructor at West Point. His next post was Fort Mackinac in Michigan, where he served from 1859 to 1861. He was then sent to Key West, Florida. From Key West, Hartsuff, a brevet captain, was part of the group sent quietly to reinforce Fort Pickens in April 1861.

During the summer of 1861, Hartsuff was sent to the command of William S. Rosecrans in western Virginia. There Hartsuff became Rosecrans's assistant adjutant general and chief of staff. Hartsuff served in these positions at the engagement at Carnifex Ferry on 10 September 1861 and was commended by Rosecrans for his actions there.

Hartsuff remained in western Virginia until the spring of 1862, when he was detailed to the War Department to work as an assistant adjutant general there. He was promoted to brigadier general of volunteers in April 1862

and assumed command at the end of April of a brigade under Irvin McDowell. On 4–5 May 1862, he fought at Culpeper Court House, Virginia. Later in the summer, Hartsuff fought at Cedar Mountain, Second Bull Run, and South Mountain. At Antietam, he commanded a brigade in Joseph Hooker's Corps and was severely wounded in Hooker's offensive on the Confederate left.

Hartsuff's wound kept him out of action until the spring of 1863 though by the end of 1862 he was able to sit on a board that reviewed and proposed changes to the Articles of War. In November 1862 he had been promoted to major general of volunteers. In the first months of 1863 he sat on courts-martial. In April 1863 he was relieved of that duty and sent to serve under Ambrose Burnside in the Department of the Ohio.

On 28 May 1863, Hartsuff assumed command of the newly created XXIII Corps in Kentucky. In late summer Hartsuff joined with Burnside for the East Tennessee campaign and participated in that campaign until November, when his old injuries forced him to take an extended sick leave. He did not return to duty until July 1864, and even then he was fit only for court-martial duty.

In March 1865 Hartsuff reported himself fit for duty, and on 12 March he was sent to report to Ulysses S. Grant at City Point, Virginia. Upon Hartsuff's arrival, Grant placed him in command of the Union position at Bermuda Hundred. He remained in command there until Robert E. Lee's surrender, at which point Hartsuff was given command of the District of Petersburg. He remained there until June 1865.

For five years after the war, Hartsuff served in the adjutant general's office at various posts in the rank of lieutenant colonel. His health, however, had never recovered from the wound he received in the Third Seminole War nor the one he received at Antietam. In 1871 he was allowed to retire at the rank of major general because of these wounds. He died three years later of a lung infection that an autopsy revealed was caused by his Seminole War wound.

—*David S. Heidler and Jeanne T. Heidler*

See also Antietam, Battle of.

For further reading:
Twenty-Third Army Corps Association. *Proceedings of the Twenty-Third Army Corps Association, at Its Annual Reunion* (1865).

HARVEY, CORDELIA PERRINE
(1824–1895)
Wisconsin relief agent

Cordelia Harvey found her way into military nursing, like many other relief workers, through the death of an intimate. Harvey's loss was noteworthy because her husband was governor of Wisconsin at the time. On hand after Shiloh to distribute supplies to men who were convalescing in field hospitals, Louis P. Harvey slipped into the Tennessee River and drowned at Savannah (Tennessee) on 19 April 1862, while transferring from one boat to another. Keenly aware of her husband's commitment to the relief of Wisconsin soldiers, the governor's widow now dedicated herself to continuing his work.

Appointed a state relief agent, Harvey traveled to St. Louis in the summer of 1862 where she visited hospitals supplied by the western branch of the Sanitary Commission. By August she had moved 116 miles downriver to Cape Girardeau, Missouri, where she met up with the ailing 1st Wisconsin Cavalry, returning from assignment in Arkansas. In the next year of her service, Harvey would be an advocate for gravely ill soldiers seeking discharges and furloughs. She spent the fall, winter, and spring supplying hospital posts along the Mississippi, from Keokuk, Iowa, where Annie Turner Wittenmyer was organizing relief efforts, to Vicksburg, where Grant's soldiers were perishing from malaria and a host of infectious diseases. She herself fell ill at Young's Point, Louisiana, across the river from Vicksburg and had to return home before the Federal siege of that city began in May.

While she convalesced in Madison, Harvey laid the groundwork for opening a general hospital there, so that soldiers wounded during the summer campaigns could be transported to cooler climes for speedier recovery. Harvey went to Washington twice to argue the merits of her plan, but military officials worried that soldiers recuperating so close to their homes would be tempted to desert. Well schooled in the politics of negotiation, she knew when the situation called for an appeal to higher authority. After a visit to President Lincoln, Harvey was given the go-ahead, and by autumn 1863, traveled to Fort Pickering near Memphis, where she helped convey her first hundred patients by water and rail to Harvey Hospital. Two more convalescent facilities opened in Milwaukee and Prairie du Chien in 1864.

For the remaining nineteen months of the war, Harvey continued as a transport nurse, picking up Union soldiers as far south as New Orleans and bringing them upriver and overland to Madison—a daunting distance of more than 1,200 miles. She returned repeatedly to the garrison at Vicksburg, when the summer of 1864 proved as noxious to soldiers' health as the previous season.

Her postwar work advanced the charitable project she was embarked on when news came of her husband's death back in 1862: that of aiding families made indigent by the war. In 1865 Harvey raised funds to convert Harvey Hospital into a home for war orphans, giving her an opportunity, as superintendent, to nurture the children that she and her husband had never had.

—*Jane E. Schultz*

See also Harvey, Louis Powell; Nurses; Wittenmyer, Annie.

For further reading:
Brockett, Linus P., and Mary Vaughan. *Woman's Work in the Civil War* (1867).
Hurn, Ethel Alice. *Wisconsin Women in the War between the States* (1911).
Massey, Mary Elizabeth. *Bonnet Brigades* (1966).
Moore, Frank. *Women of the War: Their Heroism and Self-Sacrifice* (1866).

HARVEY, LOUIS POWELL
(1820–1862)
Governor of Wisconsin

Born to David Harvey and Almira Powell Harvey in East Haddam, Connecticut, Louis Powell Harvey moved with his parents to Strongsville, Ohio, when he was a child. He was educated locally before gaining admission to Western Reserve College. He was able to afford only two years of college, after which he taught school before moving to Wisconsin to found his own academy. To supplement his profits from the school in Southport, Wisconsin, Harvey edited a local Whig newspaper, the *Southport American*. Still not able to support himself in Southport, Harvey moved to Clinton, Wisconsin, in 1847 and became a dry goods merchant. In that year, he entered Wisconsin politics as a member of Wisconsin's constitutional convention. In 1850 he moved to Rock County and maintained his residence there for the remainder of his life.

In Rock County, Harvey became a moderately prosperous businessman, operating stores and a flour mill. He retained his interest in politics and was elected to the Wisconsin state senate in 1852. In 1855 he became president pro tempore of the Wisconsin senate. In 1860 he was elected secretary of state for Wisconsin and in that capacity in 1861 became acting governor on the death of the governor. He was elected in his own right later in the year.

As acting governor and governor during the early phases of the war, Harvey worked tirelessly to recruit Wisconsin's quota of soldiers for federal service. Most Wisconsin troops were sent during that first year to St. Louis to be mustered into federal service, and Harvey took it as a special responsibility that Wisconsin men were well supplied before beginning that journey. Along with his recruiting duties, Harvey also was responsible for establishing temporary facilities for the Confederate prisoners of war who were sent to Wisconsin. In the spring of 1862 alone, 2,000 to 3,000 Confederate prisoners arrived in Wisconsin.

Since most of the Wisconsin recruits were used in the Western theater of war during that first year, Harvey was able to follow their activities closely. When word reached Madison about the horrific casualties suffered at the battle of Shiloh on 6–7 April 1862, and Harvey learned that a large number of Wisconsin troops had been engaged in the battle, he determined to travel to Tennessee with hospital supplies to aid in the recovery of the Wisconsin wounded. After visiting the field hospitals and delivering his supplies, Harvey started home. At Savannah, Tennessee, on the night of 19 April 1862, while moving from a smaller boat to the steamer that would take him part of the way home, he slipped and fell into the river. The current was too strong for him to swim against, and he drowned. His body was not recovered until late the next day, about sixty-five miles downstream. His remains were returned to Madison for burial.

—*David S. Heidler and Jeanne T. Heidler*

See also Shiloh, Battle of.

For further reading:
Love, William DeLoss. *Wisconsin in the War of the Rebellion: A History of All Regiments and Batteries the State Has Sent to the Field, and Deeds of Her Citizens, Governors and Other Military Officers, and State and National Legislators to Suppress the Rebellion* (1866).

HATCH, EDWARD
(1832–1889)
Union general

Born in Bangor, Maine, on 22 December 1832, Edward Hatch spent two years at Norwich University in Northfield, Vermont, before shipping out to sea as a sixteen-year-old cabin boy. After discovering that a sailor's life was not for him, Hatch decided to head west. He subsequently settled in Iowa and entered the lumbering business, at which trade he was engaged when the Civil War broke out.

Bold, aggressive, and at times impulsive, Hatch had perhaps the ideal temperament for a horse soldier. In August 1861, he was commissioned a captain in the 2nd Iowa Volunteer Cavalry. His rise in rank thereafter was rapid, being promoted to major in September, lieutenant colonel in December, and colonel the following June.

Hatch first saw action in 1862 at Island No. 10, and later that year at Iuka and Corinth, where he commanded the 1st Cavalry Brigade, Army of Mississippi. The following spring he commanded the 2nd Iowa during General Benjamin Grierson's celebrated raid through Mississippi.

On 21 April 1863, four days after leaving LaGrange, Tennessee, Grierson sent Hatch on a diversionary mission to decoy pursuing Confederates into following him rather than Grierson. After a clash with Confederates near Columbus, Hatch retired toward Memphis.

Hatch next commanded a cavalry brigade in the XVI Corps until October 1863, at which time he was named to command a cavalry division in the District of West Tennessee, again under Grierson. In December, Hatch was severely wounded in a fight near Moscow,

Tennessee, and commanded the Union cavalry depot at St. Louis during his convalescence.

During the spring and summer of 1864, Hatch operated mainly in Tennessee and north Mississippi against Nathan Bedford Forrest. That fall, Hatch and his cavalry division were reassigned to Major Gen. James Harrison Wilson's new Cavalry Corps, Military Division of the Mississippi. During the subsequent Franklin-Nashville campaign, Hatch's 5th Division, together with the cavalry brigade of John Croxton, kept Federal authorities apprised as to the movements of General John Bell Hood's Confederate Army of Tennessee. Hatch's division played a pivotal role in the battle of Nashville, 15 and 16 December 1864. To Hatch "more than anyone else [wrote Wilson] was due the early and exact knowledge which we obtained of Hood's movements from the time he left the Tennessee [River] til he sat down in front of Nashville." After the defeat of Hood's army at Nashville, Hatch was on sick leave and spent part of that time observing Sheridan's cavalry operations in Virginia.

Because his division lacked a full complement of horses as a result of losses incurred during the Franklin-Nashville campaign, Hatch did not participate in Wilson's Selma campaign. Instead, his division remained behind to deal with rampant guerrilla activity in Middle Tennessee during the closing weeks of the war.

After the war, Hatch remained in the regular army and in July 1866, was appointed colonel of the 9th Cavalry, a black regiment, and the following year was named brevet major general in the regular army for his Civil War service.

Hatch spent the next decade in Texas, dealing mainly with race riots and unrest along the Mexican border. One incident involved lynchings at Jefferson, Texas. This affair ushered in what proved to be an ongoing feud with his second-in-command, Lieutenant Colonel Nathan Augustus Dudley.

In 1875, Hatch was named commander of the Department of New Mexico. His tour of duty there occurred during what was perhaps the most turbulent in New Mexico's history. Not only did Hatch have to contend with raiding Apaches, he had also to deal with the notorious Lincoln County War. The affair in Lincoln County found him again in conflict with Dudley.

In 1881, Hatch was transferred to Fort Robinson, Nebraska, where, in 1889, he died from complications resulting from a broken hip suffered when his buggy overturned.

Although during his tenure in New Mexico, he was often censured by the press for his failure to bring about an end to the Indian raids, Edward Hatch had proved an able and energetic soldier, who had participated in more than forty battles and skirmishes during a career that spanned nearly three decades.

—*Jerry Keenan*

See also Grierson's Raid; Nashville, Battle of; Wilson, James H.
For further reading:
Brown, D. Alexander. *Grierson's Raid* (1954).
Keenan, Jerry. *Wilson's Cavalry* (1998).
Roster and Record of Iowa Soldiers in the War of the Rebellion: Together with Historical Sketches of Volunteer Organizations, 1861–1866 (1908–1911).
Wilson, James Harrison. *Under the Old Flag* (1912).

HATCH, JOHN PORTER
(1822–1901)
Union general

Born to Moses Porter Hatch and Hannah Reed Hatch in Oswego, New York, John Porter Hatch was educated locally before receiving an appointment to the U.S. Military Academy. He graduated seventeenth of forty-one in the class of 1845. Upon graduation Hatch went to Texas, where he became part of Zachary Taylor's Army of Observation. He fought in the early engagements of the Mexican-American War before being transferred to Winfield Scott's command. Hatch fought in all the major battles of the Mexico City campaign, receiving two brevet promotions.

After the Mexican-American War, Hatch served on a variety of frontier posts. At the outbreak of the Civil War, he was serving as Commissary to the Department of New Mexico. He transferred east and achieved the rank of brigadier general of volunteers in September 1861. In December 1861 he was ordered to report to George Stoneman to command a cavalry brigade, but before he could do so, he was sent to Annapolis, Maryland, to command the Federal forces there. In March 1862 he took command of Irvin McDowell's (I Corps) cavalry but by the end of the month was given the same job under Nathaniel P. Banks.

Under Banks, Hatch fought effectively at Front Royal on 23 May and at Winchester on 25 May. Transferred to command of 1st Brigade (Infantry), 1st Division, III Corps of the Army of Virginia, Hatch fought at Groveton and then as division commander at Second Bull Run. He received a slight wound at Bull Run but did not leave the field. Back with the Army of the Potomac during the Maryland campaign, Hatch commanded the 1st Division of I Corps under Joseph Hooker. At South Mountain on 14 September during Hooker's attack on the Confederate position at Turner's Gap, Hatch received a severe, incapacitating wound.

Hatch was unable to return to duty until the summer of 1863 and then only on administrative duty. From July to October 1863 he commanded the conscription depot in Philadelphia. From there he went to St. Louis, where he commanded the cavalry bureau. Relieved from that duty in St. Louis in February 1864, Hatch was sent to the Department of the South headquartered at Hilton Head, South Carolina. His first assignment in the department was to command the District of Florida headquartered at Jacksonville.

From Jacksonville, Hatch directed raids into the interior against supply areas and railroads. In early May 1864 Hatch traveled to Hilton Head to take temporary command of the Department of the South. He remained there through the summer, returning to Jacksonville briefly in October and then to Morris Island, South Carolina, in November. From there on 30 November he commanded the operation that resulted in the battle of Honey Hill, South Carolina, where he was repulsed by Georgia militia commanded by Major General Gustavus Woodson Smith. In December 1864, Hatch was given command of the Northern District of the Department of the South and Coast Division then headquartered at Morris Island.

Hatch remained in this command for the remainder of the war. During Sherman's march through the Carolinas, Hatch was sent in February 1865 to destroy rail links into Charleston. When Confederates evacuated Charleston, Hatch made that city his headquarters. After the war, he briefly commanded the District of Charleston.

Once mustered out of the volunteers, Hatch became a major of cavalry. He served on a number of frontier posts, fought in several of the western Indian wars, and reached the rank of colonel and commander of the 2d Cavalry. He retired in 1886 to New York City. In 1893 he was awarded the Medal of Honor for his actions at South Mountain. He died in New York on 12 April 1901.

—*David S. Heidler and Jeanne T. Heidler*

See also South Mountain, Battle of.
For further reading:
Priest, John M. *Before Antietam: The Battle for South Mountain* (1992).

HATCHER'S RUN/BURGESS MILL, VIRGINIA, BATTLE OF
(27 October 1864)

During the fall of 1864, Union general Ulysses S. Grant continued his siege of Petersburg. Throughout the period from early August through mid-October, he gradually extended his encirclement of the city, trying to cut supply lines into it and find weaknesses in the Confederate defenses. By early October, Grant's entrenchments extended westward three miles beyond the Weldon Railroad, one of the major supply arteries into Petersburg and Richmond. But the Federal commander had been unable to completely cut all the vital routes into the area. As the cold, wet weather of winter approached, Grant decided to make one final effort to capture the Southside Railroad (which ran westward from Petersburg to Danville, Virginia), the last major line connecting Petersburg with the rest of the South. He placed the commander of the Army of the Potomac, General George G. Meade, in charge of the operation.

On 27 October 1864, Meade ordered his troops to advance through the rainy darkness just before dawn. He had elements of General Winfield S. Hancock's II Corps, General Gouverneur K. Warren's V Corps, and General John G. Parke's IX Corps taking part in this action. These troops would assault the Confederate forces stationed in earthworks along a creek known as Hatcher's Run, about seven miles southwest of Petersburg. Parke was to move his men two miles to the west along the north side of the creek and strike what the Federal commanders believed to be the far right of the rebel lines. If he could break through there, he was to turn north and drive toward the Southside Railroad, only four miles away. If Parke found the entrenchments to be well defended, he was to make a demonstration against the works and let Warren's troops (which were moving up on his left) make the main attack. Warren also moved up the north side of Hatcher's Run and had similar instructions as Parke—attack if he could, otherwise keep the Confederates in that area occupied. Hancock's men moved along the south side of the creek. He and his men were to advance beyond the end of the Confederate lines, then turn northward, cross Hatcher's Run, and attack the Southside Railroad. General David Gregg's cavalry division guarded Hancock's exposed left flank. In all, 40,000 Federal infantry and 3,000 cavalry would make this assault.

Parke's men quickly struck the Confederate earthworks and found them to be more heavily defended than the Federals expected. So Parke began to make a series of threatening maneuvers against his portion of the line. The troops under Warren and Hancock continued to move forward. South of Hatcher's Run, the men of II Corps found the terrain made for much easier going than north of the creek. By noon, Hancock had advanced more than a mile ahead of Warren's corps. General Meade became concerned with the gap between Hancock and Warren and he halted the former along the Boydton Plank Road while the other caught up. Warren sent General Samuel W. Crawford's division westward to link up with the II Corps. But Crawford's men found a mile of dense woods blocking their path and quickly became split up. The division commander halted his men and had them reform their lines. Since the time was getting late, Meade ordered the troops to halt and prepare to continue the advance the next day.

However, the Confederate defenders refused to let Hancock and Warren continue their advances unmolested. Part of General Wade Hampton's cavalry stepped up their attacks on Hancock's left flank. General A. P.

Hill sent two of his divisions forward to drive the Union II Corps back. General Henry Heth advanced with his division toward the center of Hancock's line. At the same time, General William Mahone's division advanced through the same woods that had blocked Crawford's Federal division only a little while earlier and came upon the right rear of Hancock's corps. The three Confederate advances struck almost simultaneously and threw II Corps into disarray. But Hancock quickly redeployed his infantry and artillery, driving the Confederate forces back and capturing large numbers of prisoners. The combat continued well past dark, with neither side able to gain an edge on the other. During the night, Hancock and the other Federal troops withdrew to their original lines.

The Union losses during the battle numbered over 1,700 men (with almost 1,200 being captured). Hancock's corps suffered the most casualties, having borne the brunt of the fighting. Total Confederate casualties are not known, but they probably numbered less than 1,000 (with most being taken prisoner).

The battle of Hatcher's Run could only be classified as a failure for the Union army. Unlike other operations around Petersburg and Richmond, this one resulted in no gain in territory for the Federals or significant weakening of Lee's army. It also threatened to be a serious public relations fiasco for President Abraham Lincoln as the 1864 elections drew near. Grant and his commanders deliberately downplayed the number of casualties suffered during the battle until after election day. Hatcher's Run turned out to be the last Federal offensive around Petersburg for the year. After the battle, Grant ordered his troops into winter quarters while he worked on new plans to dislodge Lee from his defenses around Petersburg and Richmond.

—*David McGee*

See also Hancock, Winfield Scott; Petersburg, Campaign.
For further reading:
Davis, William C. *Death in the Trenches: Grant at Petersburg* (1986).
Horn, John. *The Petersburg Campaign, June 1864–April 1865* (1993).
Trudeau, Noah Andre. *The Last Citadel: Petersburg, Virginia, June 1864–April 1865* (1991).

HATTERAS INLET, CAPTURE OF
(28–29 August 1861)

As the sole deepwater passage between the Atlantic Ocean and Pamlico Sound, Hatteras Inlet was a strategic asset to whichever side could control the region. With neither government capable of mustering many resources early in the war, the side that best used its limited resources would ultimately control North Carolina's inland sea. North Carolina's Outer Banks, a series of long narrow islands punctuated with a few shallow inlets, offered many potential routes for Confederate ships to elude the Union naval blockade. Treacherous shoals surrounded the Outer Banks preventing blockading vessels from standing close to shore. Hatteras Inlet offered easy access to North Carolina's sounds and navigable rivers, and through the Dismal Swamp and the Albemarle and Chesapeake canals, a back door route to Norfolk and the Chesapeake Bay. Confederate privateers operating out of Hatteras Inlet were a painful nuisance to the Union; one such vessel, the *Winslow*, took at least sixteen prizes during the summer of 1861. To protect Hatteras Inlet, the Confederates built Fort Hatteras overlooking the inlet by June 1861, and by the next month Fort Clark, a smaller position defending the landward approach to Fort Hatteras.

With their limited resources dedicated to the coastal blockade, the Union Navy Department developed a plan to end the privateer problem. A small naval force would eliminate any Confederate opposition, land an army detachment to seize the inlet, block the inlet with "stone ships" (merchantmen filled with rocks), and barricade Confederate privateers inside. By August 1861, the North was ready to launch a combined army-navy assault against Hatteras Inlet. The Navy vessels sent against Hatteras included the warships *Wabash*, *Minnesota*, *Harriet Lane*, *Pawnee*, and *Monticello*, and several smaller steamers and sailing ships, under the command of Commodore Silas H. Stringham. The sloop-of-war *Cumberland* was to join the expedition at sea. The army sent around 880 men aboard the *Adelaide* and *George Peabody*. Commanded by Major General Benjamin Butler, the troops were from the 9th and the 20th New York Volunteers, the "Union Coast Guard" (the 99th New York), and Company B of the 2d U.S. Artillery. The expedition left Hampton Roads on 26 August, and anchored off Cape Hatteras on the afternoon of 27 August.

The Confederate defense constituted by Fort Hatteras and Fort Clark was inadequate to the task. They were garrisoned by around 350 men of the 7th North Carolina Volunteers under the command of Colonel William F. Martin. Fort Hatteras was a square redoubt mounting 12 smoothbore guns. Five more guns, one a 10-inch Columbiad, were not mounted in time for the battle. Fort Clark mounted only five guns. The forts' ramparts were mostly sand backed by wood barricades.

Despite the limited Confederate threat, the Union attack bordered on disaster. At 6:45 A.M. on 28 August, a landing party of 318 men from Colonel Max Weber's 20th New York headed for shore. The Union Navy could not provide enough experienced crewmen to man all the landing boats, and many crafts handled by inexperienced troops were swamped in the high surf. The Union troops slogged ashore with wet powder and no supplies.

Opening at 10:00 A.M., Stringham's bombardment enjoyed greater success. The USS *Susquehanna*, which passed by while returning from the West Indies, joined in the bombardment. Having commanded the Mediterranean Squadron in the 1850s, Stringham knew of recent naval tactics developed during the Crimean War, especially the reduction of shore fortifications. Instead of the standard tactic of firing from an anchored position, Stringham ordered his ships into a firing circle that shelled the Confederate forts on the inward leg and reloaded on the outward leg. The firing circle permitted the Union ships to pound the forts constantly while presenting a moving target to enemy gunners. Confederates who frequently found their targets out of range in any case.

Concentrating on Fort Clark, the accurate gunfire forced the Confederates to flee the position, which Weber's men occupied without firing a shot. Stringham, seeing no flags on either Rebel fort, ordered the fleet to cease fire and sent the *Monticello* into the inlet. When the ship was within range of Fort Hatteras, the Confederate garrison opened fire and struck the ship several times before it was able to get away. The Navy resumed the bombardment until 6:15 P.M., some of the shells nearly hitting some of Weber's men in Fort Clark. Weber's men spent a tense night stranded ashore, but the enemy garrison did not attack them. Meanwhile, Rebel vessels brought reinforcements and Commodore Samuel Barron, who replaced Martin as commander of Fort Hatteras.

At 8:00 the next morning, the naval bombardment resumed. Fort Hatteras was so small that most of the defenders had to take shelter outside the walls, especially when Stringham employed the Crimean War tactic of high-angle fire. Instead of firing low to destroy the Confederate ramparts, Stringham's gunners fired at maximum elevation. The plunging shells dismounted several of Fort Hatteras' guns and threatened to penetrate its ammunition magazine. After about three hours with the fort's magazine in danger of fire, Barron surrendered. Confederate losses were stated as from 4 to 14 killed, with about 700 taken prisoner. No Union fatalities were reported.

Without suffering any fatalities, the Federal forces removed the privateer threat in Pamlico Sound. Moreover, the victory boosted Federal morale after the debacle at the battle of First Bull Run. Butler's orders were to destroy the forts, block the inlet with stone-laden ships, and return to Virginia. Realizing the importance of Hatteras Inlet, Butler instead decided to hold it by leaving four of the warships and most of his troops there. The War Department upheld his decision. The Union now had a foothold on the coast of North Carolina, which the Burnside Expedition would exploit in 1862.

Both sides learned lessons from Hatteras Inlet. The Union Navy recognized that aggressively handled ships could defeat Confederate shore batteries, a tactic later proven at New Orleans and Vicksburg. Also, the Union understood the value of combined army and navy operations, and cooperative ventures were common during the war. The Confederates learned the benefit of strong fortifications, and seldom again in the war would Southern coastal fortifications be so easy a target.

—David A. Norris; Steven J. Ramold contributing

See also Butler, Benjamin F.; *Harriet Lane*; Navy, U.S.A.; North Carolina; Stringham, Silas.

For further reading:

Barrett, John G. *The Civil War in North Carolina* (1963).
Browning, Robert M. *From Cape Charles to Cape Fear: The North Atlantic Blockading Squadron During the Civil War* (1993).
Jones, Virgil Carrington. *The Civil War at Sea* (1961).
Mallison, Fred M. *The Civil War on the Outer Banks* (1997).
Merrill, James M. "The Hatteras Expedition, August, 1861." *North Carolina Historical Review* (1952).
Sauers, Richard A. "A Succession of Honorable Victories": The *Burnside Expedition in North Carolina* (1996).
Stick, David. *The Outer Banks of North Carolina 1584-1958* (1958).
Trotter, William R. *The Civil War in North Carolina*. Volume 3: *Ironclads and Columbiads* (1989).
West, Richard S. *Mr. Lincoln's Navy* (1976).

HAUPT, HERMAN
(1817–1905)
Union officer

Herman Haupt was born on 26 March 1817 to Jacob and Anna Wiall Haupt. He attended private schools in Philadelphia before moving to Woodville, New Jersey. From there he entered West Point at the age of fourteen, the youngest cadet ever to attend the academy. After graduation in 1835, Haupt was commissioned a brevet second lieutenant in the 3d Infantry Regiment. He showed more of an interest in the Republic's burgeoning railway expansion than in the army, however, and he resigned his commission on 30 September 1835. He immediately accepted an appointment as the principal assistant engineer of the state of Pennsylvania. Haupt's civilian career earned him a reputation as a genius in railroad engineering, a distinction supported by his extensive publications.

When war commenced in 1861, Haupt sought the newly created position of assistant secretary of war, but was rejected. The following year, however, Secretary of War Edwin Stanton summoned Haupt to take charge of U.S. military railroading with the rank of colonel. Although he accepted the position, Haupt insisted on civilian operation of the military railroads. This stipulation was vehemently opposed by many of the Union army's field officers and quartermasters, who wished to operate their own railroads. Haupt eventually gained control of this operation when the difficulty of operating railroads during wartime became apparent to his superiors. To ensure even more independence for himself, Haupt published regulations in June 1862 aimed at abolishing interference by army officers with railroad transportation.

One of Haupt's first duties was to safeguard the rail lines in the Washington area from Confederate raiders. He accomplished this task by placing stockades around machine shops, arming and drilling his men to make them self-protective, and upgrading the telegraphic communications along the rail lines. The secret to this success was his personal supervision and detailed inspection.

Haupt's first large-scale project was repairing the rail line from Aquia Creek Station to Fredericksburg. Amazingly, he repaired its longest bridge in just nine days. An impressed President Abraham Lincoln commented that it is "the most remarkable structure that human eyes ever rested upon. That man Haupt built a bridge across Potomac Creek…over which loaded trains are running every hour and…there is nothing in it but beanpoles and cornstalks." Although built mostly from materials growing about the site, the bridge was strong enough to carry trains of ten to twenty cars in each direction and withstand severe storms.

Haupt was not shy about taking on matters outside his normal duties, such as transporting supplies and munitions and rebuilding bridges. Most significantly, Haupt developed a car ferry that saved much time and labor in supplying the army. Even more impressive is that Haupt carried out his assignment with little assistance from other army officers, who were annoyed by his lack of military discipline. There is no doubt that Haupt's strongest supporter was President Lincoln, who considered him one of the army's few assets. Often Lincoln called upon him for advice or insight into particular campaigns, such as Second Bull Run and Fredericksburg

During the three-day battle of Gettysburg, Haupt's railroad system moved 1,500 tons of supplies a day to General George Meade. Although one of the railroads leading into Gettysburg had been destroyed during the fighting, Haupt set forth to make repairs shortly after the fighting ceased. He ordered locomotives and cars sent up from Alexandria; improvised water tanks, brought in loads of fuel, and posted repair crews on the scene with fabricated bridges and culverts. By the third day of the battle of Gettysburg, Haupt had made the railroad useable again.

After Gettysburg, Haupt busied himself by reconstructing the Orange & Alexandria Railroad for use in resupplying Meade's army. Haupt spent the bulk of 1863 guarding the rail lines and experimenting with his various innovations. He also used this period to involve himself in personal matters outside the military, such as the Troy & Greenfield Railroad and the Hoosac Tunnel in Massachusetts, for which Haupt had served as chief engineer and contractor since 1856. This did not sit well with Secretary of War Stanton, who promoted Haupt to brigadier general on 5 September 1862 and pressured him to accept the commission with the condition that he relinquish his private affairs. Haupt, fearing a limitation on his freedom to conduct private business, wanted to remain a civilian. Stanton denied Haupt this option, so Haupt appealed to general-in-chief of the army Henry Halleck and hoped that President Lincoln would intervene for him. When that hope proved fruitless, Haupt left office on 12 September 1863 to resume life as a full-time civilian engineer. Appropriately, he died aboard a train in Jersey City, New Jersey, on 14 December 1905, the last living member of his West Point class.

—Mitchell Yockelson

See also Logistics; Railroads, U.S.A.
For further reading:
Lord, Francis A. *Lincoln's Railroad Man: Herman Haupt* (1969).
Ward, James A. *That Man Haupt: A Biography of Herman Haupt* (1973).

HAWES, RICHARD
(1797–1877)
Confederate governor of Kentucky

The second, and last, governor of Confederate Kentucky, Richard Hawes was born in Caroline County, Virginia, on 6 February 1797, the son of Richard and Clara Walker Hawes. The family moved to Kentucky in 1810. Young Richard may have attended Transylvania University, but most of his education was obtained at Samuel Wilson's private school. The young man read law with two prominent Bluegrass attorneys and was admitted to the bar in 1818. That year he married Hetty Morrison Nicholas, youngest of the seventeen children of George Nicholas, one of Kentucky's political leaders before his death in 1799. They had two children, neither of whom survived Hawes. After 1843, Hawes lived in Paris, Kentucky. Along with his legal practice, he invested in a rope walk and a bagging factory. Moderately prosperous, he owned thirteen slaves in 1860.

Hawes was active in Whig politics, with Henry Clay as his political idol. Hawes was elected to the state House in 1828, 1829, and 1836, and in 1837–1841 he represented Clay's "Ashland District" in Congress. When the Whig Party dissolved in the 1850s, Hawes became a Democrat who supported John C. Breckinridge in the fateful 1860 campaign. In the months preceding Kentucky's entry into the Civil War, Hawes was active in the pro-Southern group. Charging that the sectional conflict had been caused by the

Republicans and denying the right of the federal government to coerce a state, he favored recognition of the Confederacy with an equitable division of the national debt and common property. Hawes and his associates, denying that they were secessionists, would have accepted a compromise such as the one John J. Crittenden proposed.

When Kentucky's neutrality ended in early September 1861, Hawes fled south to avoid arrest. Despite his years, he secured a commission as major and was made a brigade commissary in General Humphrey Marshall's command in eastern Kentucky. Thus Hawes was not involved in the creation of the Provisional Government at Russellville, and he declined to become its auditor. Because of his political connections, Hawes frequently ignored the military chain of command and wrote directly to President Jefferson Davis and Secretary of War Judah P. Benjamin. This irked General Marshall who expressed no regrets when on 27 January 1862 he endorsed Hawes's request for resignation.

Before leaving the command, Hawes learned that the council had elected him governor after the death of George W. Johnson at Shiloh. Hawes took the oath of office at Corinth, Mississippi, on 31 May 1862. When the Confederates invaded Kentucky in the summer of 1862, the exiled government followed Braxton Bragg's army. Bragg hoped to install Hawes in Frankfort and then enforce conscription to raise troops. On 4 September 1862 Hawes was installed in Frankfort, the only Union state capital captured by the Confederates during the war. The approach of Federal troops caused a hasty cancellation of planned festivities.

Hawes and the rest of the Provisional Government left Kentucky with the Confederate armies after the battle of Perryville. During the remainder of the war, Hawes tried with little success to head a viable state government. He had little influence, and his dreams of a successful return to Kentucky never materialized. His government just dissolved at the end of the war. Hawes returned to Paris, secured a pardon, and resumed his legal practice. Elected county judge of Bourbon County in 1866, he was reelected in 1870 and 1874. In 1866 he was elected master commissioner of the circuit and common pleas courts, a position he held until his death on 25 May 1877.

—Lowell H. Harrison

See also Bragg, Braxton; Johnson, George W.; Kentucky; Marshall, Humphrey.
For further reading:
Clift, G. Glenn. *Governors of Kentucky, 1792–1942* (1942).
Coulter, E. Merton. *The Civil War and Readjustment in Kentucky* (1926).
Duke, Basil W. *History of Morgan's Cavalry* (1867).
Harrison, Lowell H. "George W. Johnson and Richard Hawes: The Governors of Confederate Kentucky." *Register of the Kentucky Historical Society* (1981).

HAWKINS, JOHN PARKER
(1830–1914)
Union general

Born in Indianapolis, Indiana, John Parker Hawkins was educated locally before accepting an appointment to the U.S. Military Academy. He graduated fortieth of forty-three in the class of 1852. Commissioned into the infantry, Hawkins served at a variety of frontier posts and in the three years before the outbreak of the Civil War acted as quartermaster for the 2d Infantry. At the commencement of the Civil War, Hawkins changed from the infantry to the Subsistence Department.

During the Bull Run campaign, Hawkins served as acting commissary of subsistence. Shortly thereafter he transferred to St. Louis, where he acted as assistant commissary for a time before becoming chief commissary of the District of Southwest Missouri. In March 1862 Hawkins was appointed inspecting commissary of the District of West Tennessee, bringing him under Ulysses S. Grant. Hawkins was present at the battle of Shiloh with Grant and was commended by the latter for the efforts he made as commissary during the campaign.

Hawkins continued in the Subsistence Department for another year, holding a variety of posts including chief commissary, Army of the Tennessee, and rising to the rank of brigadier general of volunteers. With the increase in rank, Hawkins switched to the infantry and on 16 April accepted the command of all African-American troops in the command of Ulysses S. Grant. Hawkins was unable to exercise his new duties for long. Forced to take an extended sick leave in June, he did not return to duty until 18 August 1863.

Upon his return to duty, Hawkins was given command of the District of Northeastern Louisiana. To staff his district, Hawkins relied almost exclusively on a brigade of African-American troops, men he would command for the remainder of the war. Although he considered the men perfectly acceptable soldiers, he did not believe that the army supplied him with enough men to defend the territory under his command. He also became increasingly irritated with the type and quality of the weapons supplied African-American troops. In November 1863, he complained bitterly that the Austrian weapons supplied his men were unreliable. He demanded that his men be supplied with the same Springfield rifles as other troops in the theater. Transferred to Vicksburg in February 1864, Hawkins commanded the 1st Division, U.S. Colored Troops (USCT) in the Army of the Tennessee. Later in the year, he took command of the 4th Division (USCT), XVI Corps, Army of the Tennessee. At the end of the year, he and his division were transferred to the command of Edward R. S. Canby (Hawkins's brother-in-law) in the Division of West Mississippi.

Canby sent Hawkins to the District of West Florida at Pensacola in February 1865 in preparation for the upcoming campaign against the city of Mobile. He was to command a newly organized division of African-American troops. Hawkins and his division fought in this campaign, participating in the taking of Blakely, Alabama, on 9 April and then garrisoning the town after its fall.

After the war Hawkins returned to his commissary duties at the rank of captain. He remained in the army and gradually rose in rank until promoted to brigadier general in 1892. At the same time, he was made head of the Subsistence Department and remained in that position until his retirement in 1894. He spent his last years in his hometown of Indianapolis and died there on 7 February 1914.

—*David S. Heidler and Jeanne T. Heidler*

See also Blakely, Alabama; Commissary; Mobile Campaign; United States Colored Troops.
For further reading:
Bergeron, Arthur W. *Confederate Mobile* (1991).
Glatthaar, Joseph T. *Forged in Battle: The Civil War Alliance of Black Soldiers and White Officers* (1990).

HAWLEY, HARRIET FOOTE
(1831–1886)
Union relief worker

Though she never wrote a narrative of her war work, Harriet Foote Hawley's service to Union hospitals is richly documented in her correspondence, her husband's diary, and a postwar sketch written by her Connecticut neighbor, Harriet Beecher Stowe. Hawley's war fortunes were shaped by husband Joseph Roswell Hawley, whom she married in 1855, and who initially discouraged "Hattie" from serving as nurse because of her poor health. His letters from the Sea Islands in 1861 and 1862, where he was part of the Union's besieging forces, beg his wife not to come to him. The living conditions are rough, the officers surly, and the weather steamy. Joe, who studied law and founded an abolitionist newspaper before the war, would rise in the ranks to brevet major general by war's end and would go on to a political career that included governor, representative, and senator from Connecticut. After Hattie's death in 1886, he remarried at age 61 and went on to father two children, his first marriage having produced none. Once Hattie received a commission to teach former slaves as a part of the Port Royal "experiment," she never looked back. Joining Joe in Fernandina, Florida, in January 1863, she was swept up into hospital work, which took precedence over her teaching assignment. With only one short furlough in 1864, she continued to care for Union soldiers until July 1865.

Beginning with relatively mild hospital service in Fernandina and St. Augustine, Hawley went to the Sea Islands in November 1863, where she remained until

April when Joe's brigade was transferred to Benjamin Butler's command in Virginia. Casualties from the battle of Olustee in February were light compared to those Hawley would encounter at Armory Square Hospital, whose staff she joined a day after wounded began to arrive from the battles of the Wilderness. In a letter to her cousin, Hawley notes that she has been working sixteen-hour days and that she still cannot do enough: "I thought I knew something about it before, but I didn't know anything. I know of no words to describe the amount & intensity of the suffering I see around me every moment." She tells the story of a soldier who has just died of a leg amputation, while another amputation is taking place in the ward, only twelve feet away ("You do not dream of what these men undergo.") On one June day alone, forty-eight men died of complications following amputations. After a two-month furlough in September, Hawley returned to Armory Square, where she remained until March 1865.

Heading to Wilmington, North Carolina, where Joe, now a brigadier general, had been assigned, Hawley encountered the even more horrifying spectacle of 9,000 Union prisoners, recently released from Andersonville and Florence. Half-naked and starved nearly to death, many of the prisoners had suffered permanent brain damage. Hawley was inconsolable about the "rotted" state of the men's feet, which surgeons were obliged to "cut . . . off with scissors above the ankle!" An entourage of poor white and black Southerners followed the soldiers into Wilmington, where an outbreak of typhoid killed many, including the chief surgeon and two of Hawley's four female coworkers.

Hawley continued at Wilmington until July when she and Joe left for Richmond, but a freak ambulance accident in October rendered her an invalid until her death two decades later.

—*Jane E. Schultz*

See also Nurses; Women.
For further reading:
Brockett, Linus P., and Mary Vaughan. *Woman's Work in the Civil War* (1867).
Dannett, Sylvia G. L. *Noble Women of the North* (1959).
Hawley, Joseph Roswell. Diary and Papers. Library of Congress, Washington, D.C.
Moore, Frank. *Women of the War: Their Heroism and Self-Sacrifice* (1866).

HAWLEY, JOSEPH ROSWELL
(1826–1905)
Union general

Joseph Roswell Hawley served competently as a brigade and division commander during the Civil War. He fought from First Bull Run through the Petersburg campaign and, despite his lack of formal military training, this politician and newspaper editor turned soldier earned respect for his courage and fighting abilities. During the war he also, however, feuded with several officers, particularly fellow political general Benjamin Butler.

Born in North Carolina on 31 October 1826, Hawley's mother was a Southerner, but his father was a Northern-born Baptist minister who actively opposed slavery. Consequently, Hawley and his family moved to Connecticut, his father's native state, when Joseph was eleven. He was educated at Hamilton College and trained as a lawyer. In the early 1850s, Hawley became active in the Free Soil Party and, in the middle part of the decade, he was an early leader of the state Republican Party. After supporting Republican presidential candidate John C. Frémont in 1856, Hawley took over the editorship of the *Hartford Evening Press*, the state's major Republican newspaper, the following year.

An ardent supporter of the Union war effort, Hawley helped organize the 1st Connecticut Infantry in the spring of 1861 and was commissioned a captain in the unit. He fought with the regiment at First Bull Run and after the expiration of its term of enlistment in September 1861, he was appointed lieutenant colonel of the new 7th Connecticut Infantry Regiment.

Much of Hawley's subsequent military service took place along the lower Atlantic seaboard. In late 1861 he led the 7th in the Port Royal expedition, and in April 1862 he participated in the campaign that captured Fort Pulaski, near Savannah, Georgia. Two months later Hawley received a promotion to colonel. For much of the next year he was active in the Union operations around Charleston, including the battles at Secessionville and Pocotaligo.

At the battle of Olustee, Florida, in February 1864, Hawley commanded a brigade of troops that consisted of the 7th Connecticut, the 7th New Hampshire, and the 8th United States Colored Infantry (USCI) regiments. His brigade led the Union advance and was the first unit to come under heavy Confederate fire. Hawley, while attempting to form his troops into line of battle, either gave an incorrect command, or his men misunderstood his order. As a result the 7th New Hampshire, whose ranks were filled with recently enrolled substitutes, broke and fled the field in confusion. The 8th USCI, which was completely untried, stood its ground for a time, but after suffering terrific casualties, also withdrew in confusion. The remaining two brigades managed to stabilize the Union lines for a time, but eventually the Federals were driven from the field with heavy losses. It was probably Hawley's worst performance of the war. He later criticized both the political nature of the campaign as well as the actions of Generals Quincy Gillmore, who commanded the Union army's Department of the South, and Truman Seymour, who was in command of the Florida expedition. "The campaign will not bear military

criticism," he wrote "it was in violation of the soundest, plainest military rules."

Hawley and his brigade were transferred to Virginia in the spring of 1864, as part of the newly organized Army of the James under Major General Benjamin Butler. The army was to threaten Richmond from the east, while the Army of the Potomac moved southward towards the Rebel capital. Because of his performance in this otherwise unsuccessful operation, he earned promotion to brigadier general in September 1864. That fall, Hawley commanded a division of black troops during the fighting around Richmond and Petersburg, and he temporarily commanded the division of Alfred Terry during that officer's absence. He later served as Terry's chief of staff in North Carolina and commanded a military district in that state at the close of the war.

Hawley left military service in 1866, after receiving a major general's brevet. For the rest of his long life, he was prominent in Connecticut politics. Elected governor in 1866 on the Republican ticket, he also served three terms in the U.S. House of Representatives. In 1881 Hawley was elected to the U.S. Senate, where he remained for nearly a quarter century. He died in Washington on 18 March 1905 at the age of seventy-eight and was buried in Hartford.

—*David J. Coles*

See also Bermuda Hundred Campaign; Olustee, Battle of.
For further reading:
Nicolson, John. "New England Idealism in the Civil War: The Military Career of Joseph Roswell Hawley." (Ph.D. dissertation, 1970).
Putnam, Albert D., ed. *Major General Joseph R. Hawley, Soldier and Editor (1826–1905)* (1864).

HAW'S SHOP, BATTLE OF
(28 May 1864)

Haw's Shop, Virginia, was the second all-cavalry victory credited to the Army of the Potomac's Cavalry Corps in the opening month of Lieutenant General Ulysses S. Grant's Richmond campaign. To some observers, Haw's Shop confirmed the newly won ascendancy of Major General Philip H. Sheridan and Federal mounted forces in the Eastern theater. It occurred seventeen days after Sheridan's triumph at Yellow Tavern, where the South lost its most beloved cavalier, Major General J. E. B. "Jeb" Stuart. Nevertheless, the Confederate troopers who retreated from Haw's Shop came away with the knowledge that they had found a leader to replace Stuart. Major General Wade Hampton, the senior surviving officer in the Army of Northern Virginia's Cavalry Corps, matched Stuart in personal bravery, but was more prudent and a better tactician.

After General Robert E. Lee checked Grant at Spotsylvania Court House, 10–12 May 1864, he with-

drew to a strong defensive position below the North Anna River. Realizing the futility of attacking Lee head-on, Grant decided to turn his enemy's right flank. He directed the Army of the Potomac to sidle to the southeast and cross the Pamunkey River, a stream formed by the junction of the North Anna and South Anna. While Brigadier General James H. Wilson's 3d Division of Sheridan's Cavalry Corps feinted against Lee's left flank, Brigadier General Alfred T. A. Torbert's 1st Division and Brigadier General David M. Gregg's 2d Division rode downstream to secure a suitable ford across the Pamunkey.

At first light on 27 May, Brigadier General George A. Custer's Michigan cavalry brigade from Torbert's division scattered the mounted Confederate pickets guarding Hanovertown Ford and established a Union bridgehead on the south side of the Pamunkey. Covered by Custer's "Wolverines," an engineer regiment quickly constructed a pontoon bridge. Once the engineers completed their work, the rest of Torbert's division crossed the Pamunkey, followed by Gregg's horsemen and a division of Union infantry.

On 28 May, while more Union infantry, artillery, and wagons rumbled across the pontoon bridge, Sheridan's cavalry probed west from Hanovertown, searching for Lee's army. Gregg's 2d Division led this scouting movement. Three miles from Hanovertown, Gregg's troopers passed a large blacksmith's shop called Haw's Shop. Less than a mile beyond that, Gregg ran into a large force of Confederate cavalry under Hampton.

General Lee had sent Hampton's cavalry division and that of Major General Fitzhugh Lee to Haw's Shop to discern Federal intentions. At the approach of Sheridan's cavalry, the Confederates dismounted in a wooded area behind a swamp and threw up breastworks made of logs and rails. Hampton supported this sturdy line with skillfully placed horse artillery.

Though outnumbered, Gregg tried to dislodge Hampton with a frontal assault. This decision turned Haw's Shop into one of the bloodiest cavalry fights of the war. Among Hampton's units was a brigade fresh from South Carolina. The South Carolinians carried Enfield rifles, which outranged the carbines issued to their Federal opponents. The Confederates greeted Gregg's division with a wall of fire, killing or wounding 256 officers and men. As Gregg's advance ground to a halt, Hampton's men, sensing their edge in numbers, sortied from their works and started to press back Gregg with a series of counterattacks.

Sometime around 2:00 P.M., Sheridan became aware of Gregg's predicament and summoned Custer's Michigan brigade to the front. As Custer reached the scene, Sheridan pointed toward the Rebels and commanded, "Custer, I want you to go in and give those fellows hell!" Since the ground ahead was too densely wooded for mounted maneuvers, Custer had his brigade dismount and deploy in a long, double-ranked line of battle, just like infantry. To rouse his Michiganders' fighting spirit, Custer stayed in the saddle as he led them forward, waving his hat in full view of the enemy. Forty-one of Custer's troopers died charging after him, but the rest subjected the Confederates to a hot fire from their seven-shot Spencer repeaters. A Rebel marksman killed Custer's horse, but the Michigan brigade continued to surge forward, and its impetuosity turned the tide, forcing Hampton's divisions to withdraw.

The battle of Haw's Shop lasted seven hours. The Federals held the battlefield and claimed another victory, but they paid dearly for the privilege. Hampton suffered heavy losses as well, but he accomplished his mission. The Confederates did not quit their position until they verified that Grant's infantry had crossed the Pamunkey in force. This information prompted General Lee to shift the Army of Northern Virginia to a new blocking position at Cold Harbor.

—*Gregory J. W. Urwin*

See also Custer, George Armstrong; Gregg, David McMurtrie; Hampton, Wade; Lee, Fitzhugh; Sheridan, Philip Henry; Torbert, Alfred T. A.

For further reading:
Longacre, Edward G. *Custer and His Wolverines: The Michigan Cavalry Brigade, 1861–1865* (1997).
Starr, Stephen Z. *The Union Cavalry in the Civil War* (1979–1985).
Urwin, Gregory J.W. *Custer Victorious: The Civil War Battles of General George Armstrong Custer* (1990).
Wellman, Manly Wade. *Giant in Gray: A Biography of Wade Hampton of South Carolina* (1949).
Wert, Jeffry D. *Custer: The Controversial Life of George Armstrong Custer* (1996).

HAWTHORNE, NATHANIEL
(1804–1864)

American author

Born in Salem, Massachusetts, on 4 July 1804, Nathaniel Hawthorne was brought up in the house of his mother's parents after his father, a sea captain, died at sea in 1808 and left his family with little means of support. Hawthorne was educated at local schools until his ninth year, when he seriously injured his foot. He spent more than a year at home, during which time he developed a strong interest in reading.

When Hawthorne was fourteen, the family moved to Maine and he was enrolled in a boarding school near Portland. He was sent back to Salem in 1820 to prepare for college and in the fall of 1821 entered Bowdoin College in Brunswick, Maine. While in college he became close friends with another student, Franklin Pierce. It was a friendship that would endure literally until Hawthorne's dying day.

After graduation, Hawthorne moved back to Salem, where he determined upon a literary career. For a few years he was supported in this endeavor by his family and a small inheritance. He developed at this time a strong interest in the history of New England and used tales of Puritans and characters from New England's past for his stories. By the mid-1830s, he was finding it increasingly difficult to support himself solely through writing and in early 1836 became the editor of the *American Magazine of Useful and Entertaining Knowledge* in Boston. Unfortunately, the publisher went bankrupt before the end of the year, and Hawthorne returned to Salem.

Still in need of a steady income, Hawthorne took advantage of his ties to the Democratic Party to gain an appointment in 1839 as an inspector in the Boston Customs House. He left the position in the early 1840s after he became enthralled with the idea of the utopian Brook Farm. Within a short time of taking up residence on the communal farm, he discovered that a life of farm toil was not for him, and he left. He returned to his literary pursuits while his friends, like Pierce, sought some sort of patronage job for him with the government. With the return of the Democrats to power in 1845, Hawthorne received a customs house job in Salem. He remained there until removed by the Whigs in 1849. During the year after leaving his position he wrote *The Scarlet Letter*.

With *The Scarlet Letter* published, Hawthorne moved in 1850 to Lenox in the Berkshires. There he became close friends with Herman Melville and wrote *The House of the Seven Gables*. By now Hawthorne was a well-regarded literary figure in the country, but still found it difficult to make a living as an author. Therefore in 1852 when asked by his old friend, Franklin Pierce, to write Pierce's campaign biography for the upcoming presidential campaign, Hawthorne agreed. As a great admirer of Pierce, Hawthorne had little difficulty saying nice things about his friend. He was, of course, roundly criticized by the Whigs for the biography.

After the election and Pierce's victory, Hawthorne, as a good friend of the president-elect, was much sought-after by office seekers wanting him to intercede with Pierce. During the transition period Hawthorne met with Pierce and apparently advised him on some of the presidential appointments. Pierce, of course, did not forget his old friend and appointed Hawthorne consul to Liverpool, one of the most prestigious and lucrative appointments in the State Department. Hawthorne departed with his family for Great Britain in the spring of 1853 and did not return to the United States until 1860.

During his four years as consul, Hawthorne found virtually no time for writing or seeing Europe, so that when he left office in 1857, he took his family on an extended tour. In 1859 he had a chance to renew and strengthen his friendship with Pierce when the ex-president and his wife visited Italy. They spent many hours together and became even closer friends than they had been before.

Hawthorne and his family returned in June 1860 to their home in Concord, Massachusetts. Hawthorne found that abolitionism was much stronger than when he had left and that Franklin Pierce was widely criticized and even vilified in the Northeast. While not a supporter of slavery, Hawthorne opposed the extremism of abolitionists and increasingly did not socialize with his old circle of friends, which included Ralph Waldo Emerson.

During the sectional crisis and after the war started, Hawthorne publicly and privately said that the North and South never belonged together as one country. While he supported the war, partly out a patriotic duty, and supported the abolition of slavery should the North win, and even encouraged efforts to prepare slaves for citizenship, he still thought the South should not be brought back into the Union. In 1862 he traveled to Washington where he met Lincoln, watched troops drilling, and toured fortifications. From his experience there he believed it necessary to put his feelings about the war on paper and wrote an essay for the *Atlantic Monthly* about the war. In the essay, entitled "Chiefly about War Matters," Hawthorne expressed his belief that one of the results of the war would be decades of mistreatment for African-Americans. He also expressed some sympathy for Southerners who were genuinely fighting out of loyalty to their states and said that John Brown deserved to be hanged. He closed by saying that there were worse things than the South not coming back into the Union. Hawthorne was roundly criticized throughout the North for the essay, but by that point he had apparently ceased to care. The following year he dedicated his book *Our Old Home* to Franklin Pierce, again ruffling more than a few feathers.

By the end of 1863 Hawthorne's health began to deteriorate rapidly. In the spring he took a carriage tour with Pierce, ostensibly to recover his health, though he probably realized he was dying. During the trip he died in his sleep on 18 May 1864.

—*David S. Heidler and Jeanne T. Heidler*

See also Emerson, Ralph Waldo; Melville, Herman; Pierce, Franklin.

For further reading:

Miller, Edwin Haviland. *Salem is My Dwelling Place: A Life of Nathaniel Hawthorne* (1991).

Turner, Arlin. *Nathaniel Hawthorne, A Biography* (1980).

HAY, JOHN MILTON
(1838–1905)

Presidential secretary, historian, poet, diplomat, novelist, and journalist

The career of John Milton Hay is that of a man who always made the most of his associations. Friendship and fortune were his constant companions and he was always ready to capitalize on opportunity. There seemed to be little in his youth that would commend him to fame or fortune. He was born in Salem, Indiana, and as a child was taken to Warsaw, Illinois, on the Mississippi River. His education was in public schools and then at Pittsfield Academy in Pike County. There he met student John George Nicolay, with whom he was to be associated for almost twenty-five years during and after the Civil War years. As a fourteen year old, already able to read Latin and Greek, Hay entered Illinois State University, which later became Concordia College and was more a high school than a university. Three years later, Hay was sent to Brown University, from which he graduated in 1858 with honors as class poet and a Phi Beta Kappa membership. He apparently also took an M.A., which by Ivy League tradition could be had for $25. He had cultivated a taste for the refined atmosphere of the east, but he had no employment prospects. He had a predilection for snobbery that became more enhanced as he matured.

Hay had hopes of becoming a poet, but he soon realized how impractical that was. He was sent to his uncle Milton's law office in Springfield, Illinois, as an apprentice in 1859. The office was adjacent to Abraham Lincoln's, and Lincoln's law secretary at the time was Hay's childhood friend, John Nicolay, who suggested that Hay might be useful as an assistant secretary. Because Lincoln had risen in status after his senatorial race against Stephen Douglas, the office was a center of political action.

Hay worked with Nicolay handling the correspondence and planning appointments. The groundwork for establishing Lincoln's drive for the presidency was being planned, and opportunity and fortune became Hay's companions. Lincoln's election encouraged Nicolay to ask that Hay be appointed an assistant secretary to the new president. There was budgetary provision for only one secretary, so Hay was given a job as a clerk in the pension office with assignment to the White House. He was admitted to the bar in 1861, and now at the age of twenty-two he was a confidante of the president on the eve of civil war.

The workload was huge for the two men and invaluable for Hay as they handled appointments of important visitors, dealt with correspondence, and attended the needs of the first family. There were crises every day of Lincoln's presidency, and the craving for patronage appointments and party favors was endless. First Lady Mary Todd Lincoln required special tact, and Hay was often given this special assignment. The two secretaries lived in the White House as part of the official family, a vantage point that provided Hay with an increased admiration for the man who was the embodiment of the frontier that he had come to disown. Hay gained the trust and confidence of the president, who gave him delicate assignments and often confided privately with him on virtually a daily basis. Hay spent almost five years as Nicolay's assistant.

Military rank during the war years was to become immensely important after the war. In 1864 Hay was given a commission as major and assistant adjutant general in the volunteers and elevated to colonel in 1865, though he did not serve on active duty. Hay left the White House in May 1865, a month after Lincoln's death, and retained his rank until 1867. He had grown in awe of Lincoln, whose manner with his two secretaries was always ingratiating and sociable. Conversations, correspondence, ideas, humor, and private assessments of daily matters were fodder for the three men. These were defining years of Hay's life. In his dying days he still had dreams of Lincoln.

His experiences in the White House meant that Hay could never go home again. The excitement of government had infected him. Hay secured foreign appointments as secretary to the U.S. legation in Paris for a year, an interim appointment as secretary and chargé d'affaires at Vienna for another year to 1868, and secretary at Madrid to 1870. He also found time to work on his poetry, publishing in *Harper's Weekly* and also a collection entitled *Pike County Ballads and Other Pieces* in 1871. Mark Twain admired his work and they became friends.

Hay was hired by Whitelaw Reid to write editorials for the *New York Tribune*, where he worked until 1875 and had opportunities to mix socially and professionally with the best writers in the east. He was at last comfortable economically, but in 1874 he advanced himself by marrying Clara Louise Stone, daughter of Amasa Stone, Cleveland financier and railroad entrepreneur. Hay moved to Cleveland to help manage his father-in-law's business interests and to accept an offer from his old friend Nicolay to write a definitive history of the Lincoln presidency. Nicolay had gained permission from Robert Todd Lincoln to use the masses of documents in his possession. Before beginning the writing, Hay took an appointment as assistant secretary of state in James A. Garfield's administration in 1881, but the assassination of the president brought Hay's resignation and return to Cleveland.

In 1885 Hay joined with Nicolay to begin the great historical memoir of the Lincoln presidency, a project that extended ten volumes and took ten years to complete. It was serialized in *Century* magazine from 1886 to 1890 and finally published in 1895. Hay also wrote a novel, *The Bread-winners* (1883), which, like that of his friend Henry Adams's *Democracy*, was published anonymously. The book betrayed the conservatism of Hay who held the working class in contempt for challenging their employers. The new immigrants came in for particular disdain by Hay who believed that obeisance to one's economic and social betters was imperative in an orderly society. Hay despised the Democratic Party, which had cultivated the votes of the working classes.

Hay and his wife mixed with the elite of society. Hay's close friend was Henry Adams and their special friend was the genial and adventurous Clarence King, who had become head of the geological survey. The three men were diminutive in size but large in social and intellectual significance. Clara Hay and Adams's wife, Marian, completed what became known as the Five of Hearts, an association brilliantly depicted in Patricia O'Toole's work of the same title (1990). The three men were very close and joined by understanding of each one's foibles. Hay financially supported King's secret black wife and children even after King's death. Only when Mrs. King sought her inheritance in court did Hay's widow end the subsidy. Hay, of course, had commiserated with Adams after the suicide of his wife. The two men built adjoining houses in Washington designed by the architect H. H. Richardson. Their homes later became the site of the Hay-Adams Hotel.

Both men were shameless in their sympathies toward England. Hay especially appreciated the social distinctions of the English and the notion of the white man's (Anglo-Saxon) burden. He tried to gain the ambassadorship under Benjamin Harrison's administration, but failed despite his generous contributions to the Republican Party. He finally got his wish realized by President William McKinley in 1897. Hay had written speeches for McKinley attacking the Democrats, and he had created a special fund to aid him financially. He also contrived to displace Whitelaw Reid from contention for the ambassadorship in order to gain the job himself. The joy he felt as ambassador was shared by Henry Adams who saw it as a perfect fit of man and job. Hay, in his year and a half as ambassador, was solicitous of England's interests and sought to bind U.S. policy with the British. He was vexed at the dispatch of special emissaries by McKinley to handle problems such as seal hunting in the Bering Sea, currency regulation between the two countries, and even stand-in for the president at Queen Victoria's jubilee celebration. Hay had to take a back seat.

Hay was called back to the United States to become secretary of state with the nation in crisis over the sinking of the *Maine* in Havana harbor, but he seemed oblivious to the significance of the act and was on holiday in Egypt rather than at his desk in England at the time. The war was over when he reached Washington, and his contribution was the comment about it being a "splendid little war." Hay supported the idea that peace negotiations should take the nation on an imperial path of dominance in the Caribbean and in the Pacific Ocean. Concern over European partitioning of China pushed Hay to offer a policy of open-door economic relations. Despite evidence to the contrary, Hay presumed that Europe was in concert with his policy. He also encouraged McKinley to maintain a military presence in China. Curiously, despite the contempt inherent regarding China, the idea of a U.S. military presence became popular in the United States. Hay was to oppose American opinion when he sought to align the United States with Britain in the Boer War on the eve of McKinley's reelection bid. Hay even appointed his twenty-four-year-old son Adelbert as consul in Pretoria to replace those he fired for their Boer sympathies. Adelbert, as newly appointed assistant secretary of state, became a tragic figure shortly thereafter, when he met his death in a fall from a dormitory window while attending a class reunion at Yale.

Hay's Anglo sympathies persisted in his negotiations over the Canada-Alaska boundary and when the prospect arose of building an interocean canal in Central America. Hay was thwarted in his compromise attempts by the Senate and by nationalistic enthusiasm for U.S. interests. Hay lost his patron McKinley in 1901, again by assassination. McKinley's successor, Theodore Roosevelt, had his own ideas of how to negotiate foreign policy, especially in Central America. In dealing with Roosevelt, Hay proceeded to support a revolution in Panama and to negotiate a canal treaty with the new nation. Roosevelt had come to see Hay as a "useful ornament" in the state department, but Hay's health was failing. Hay died at his summer home in New Hampshire on 1 July 1905.

—Jack J. Cardoso

See also Lincoln, Abraham; Nicolay, John George.

For further reading:
Cater, Harold Dean. *Henry Adams and His Friends* (1947).
Dennett, Tyler. *John Hay: From Poetry to Politics* (1963).
Hay, John M., and John G. Nicolay. *Abraham Lincoln: A History* (1890).
Kushner, Howard I., and Anne Hummell Sherrill. *John Hay: The Union of Poetry and Politics* (1977).
Monteiro, George. *Henry James and John Hay: The Record of a Friendship* (1965).
O'Toole, Patricia. *The Five of Hearts: An Intimate Portrait of Henry Adams and His Friends, 1880–1918* (1990).
Thayer, William Roscoe. *The Life and Letters of John Hay* (1915).
Wilkins, Thurman. *Clarence King: A Biography* (1958).

HAYES, RUTHERFORD BIRCHARD
(1822–1893)
Union general

Born and raised in Ohio, and a graduate of Harvard Law School, Hayes was practicing law in Cincinnati when the South seceded from the Union. Intensely patriotic and an ardent Republican, he volunteered, preferring to die as a soldier than to live sitting out the war. Commissioned a major, he was ulti-

mately breveted major general but considered himself "one of the good colonels in the great army." As an amateur citizen officer in a democratic army of amateur citizen soldiers, he understood his men and early recognized that he had to mediate between them and their spit-and-polish, West Point–trained superior officers. Yet Hayes, who was eager to acquire their military knowhow, read books on the art of war and discussed what he had read with his more knowledgeable superiors. Very quickly he gained the confidence of these officers and the affection of his men.

Hayes held a front-line view of the Civil War that focused on his 23d Ohio Volunteer Infantry. Leading it into battle he was energetic, fearless, and, as he freely admitted, lucky. While his battlefield purview was necessarily narrow, his vision of the war was broad and inspirational. Although he entered it to save the Union, he soon thought of it as a crusade to destroy slavery.

Serving in western Virginia, Hayes fought under William S. Rosecrans at Carnifex Ferry (10 September 1861), was judge advocate of the Army of the Ohio (19 September–2 November 1861), captured and then abandoned Giles Court House (6–10 May 1862), and participated in minor raids. Although ordered to eastern Virginia by John Pope, Hayes and the 23d missed Second Bull Run (29–30 August 1862), but participated in the Antietam campaign. At South Mountain (14 September 1862), Hayes distinguished himself before being severely wounded in the arm. Appointed a full colonel while recuperating, he soon returned to the 23d in western Virginia. He was still weak, but fortunately his regiment was ready to go into winter quarters. It was not until the summer of 1863 that Hayes—now commanding a brigade—was strong enough for strenuous raids into enemy territory. In July he played a key role in capturing General John Hunt Morgan, who with over 2,000 cavalry was raiding Ohio and trying to escape over the Ohio River. Hayes headed him off at Gallipolis (18 July 1863), at Pomeroy (19 July), and again at Buffington Island (20 July), where Morgan's force collapsed.

In spring 1864, as part of George Crook's Army of West Virginia, Hayes and the 23d participated in two strenuous expeditions through the mountains into Virginia. At Cloyd's Mountain (9 May 1864) he and Crook victoriously charged breastworks and, after wrecking rail communications, toiled with their men over muddy roads back to West Virginia. Crook's army then linked up with General David Hunter's force in the Valley of Virginia, but failed to capture Lynchburg (16–18 June 1864) and returned to West Virginia.

After a week's rest Crook's men were ordered east to the Shenandoah Valley. There, in the summer and fall, Hayes, commanding a brigade and then a division of Crook's army, was involved in constant marching and fighting. At the second battle of Kernstown (24 July

1864), Hayes experienced defeat but proudly covered with his brigade the retreat of Crook's army. In August Crook's army became a corps in Philip Sheridan's Army of the Shenandoah and fought to a draw at Berryville (3 September). Sheridan then pushed down the valley and won stunning victories at Opequon Creek (19 September), where Hayes led a crucial charge; at Fisher's Hill (22 September), where Crook's Corps flanked and surprised the Confederates; and at Cedar Creek (19 October), where Hayes and his men were badly mauled. Cedar Creek was Hayes's last battle.

On 8 June 1865, having completed four years of service, Hayes was mustered out of the army. He had experienced physical hardship, personal danger, and mental strain, and had proved himself a worthy warrior; he had been wounded five times (once badly) and had had four horses shot from under him. In combat, he was "intense and ferocious," daring, self-possessed, and efficient.

Being a warrior had been hard, but it had given Hayes the experience of a lifetime. Although he would be a radical congressman (1865–1867), a reform governor of Ohio (1868–1872 and 1876–1877), and would enhance the power of the U.S. presidency while holding that office (1877–1881), he sensed that the four most glorious years of his life were ending. Cherishing the camaraderie of camp and field, Hayes for the rest of his life participated in veteran encampments, marched with his men at funerals, and fought for pensions for the defenders of the Union.

—Ari Hoogenboom

See also Cloyd's Mountain, Battle of.

For further reading:
Hoogenboom, Ari. *Rutherford B. Hayes: Warrior and President* (1995).
Williams, T. Harry. *Hayes of the Twenty-third: The Civil War Volunteer Officer* (1965).

HAYNE, PAUL HAMILTON
(1830–1886)
Poet, journalist

Referred to in his lifetime as "poet laureate of the South," Paul Hamilton Hayne was born to a prominent Charleston, South Carolina, family on 1 January 1830. His father, of the same name, was a naval officer who died when Hayne was a child. Thereafter, the major male influence in his youthful life was his uncle, Robert Young Hayne, governor, senator, and the opponent of Daniel Webster in the famous states' rights debate of 1830.

After graduation from Charleston College in 1850, Hayne read and practiced law briefly. He had been writing and publishing verse while in school, and he soon left the bar to become editor and owner of the *Literary Gazette.* In 1857 *Russell's Magazine* was launched with Hayne as editor, but it ceased publication after three years. Meanwhile, Hayne had published three volumes of poetry, *Poems* (1855), *Sonnets and Other Poems* (1857), and *Avolio* (1860). Hayne was too frail for military service, and for four months early in the Civil War, he was on the staff of Governor Francis Pickens. He then retired to take up patriotic and martial writing. His home was burned during the bombardment of Charleston, and Union soldiers looted his belongings early in the occupation.

Looking for a means to support his family, in 1865 Hayne moved to Augusta, Georgia, where he became an editor and literary columnist with the *Augusta Constitutionalist.* For dwelling he built a cabin he called Copse Hill in the piney woods of Columbia County, near present-day Grovetown, Georgia, about fifteen miles from Augusta. He soon gave up editing but continued to send his columns and contributions to newspapers and magazines throughout the nation until his death. His poetry improved with his maturity and his work appeared in *Appleton's Journal, Scribner's Monthly, Harper's New Monthly,* the *Century Magazine,* and *Atlantic Monthly.* He published three more volumes of verse, *Legends and Lyrics* (1872), *The Mountain of the Lovers* (1875), and *Poems* (illustrated republication, 1882). He attracted the attention and admiration of renowned poets, mostly in the North and in England, and he maintained a correspondence with Henry Wadsworth Longfellow, Oliver Wendell Holmes, John Greenleaf Whittier, and Sidney Lanier in America, and Alfred Lord Tennyson, Algeron Charles Swinburne, and others in Britain. It was during this period that he earned his title of poet laureate of the South.

As his fame spread, Hayne was called upon as a regional spokesman for literature and culture. He wrote pieces to commemorate battles, centennials, inaugurations, and even college commencements. He was made an honorary member of historical and literary societies, awarded an honorary degree by Washington and Lee College, lectured at Emory and Vanderbilt, and served on a board of examiners at the University of Georgia. Despite all his praise and honors, he remained near destitution and continued to live in his cabin in the woods. He came to appreciate Georgia as his "second mother," and wrote "Aspects of the Pines" about his life in the country. Hayne died in Grovetown on 6 July 1886 and was buried in Magnolia Cemetery in Augusta. His name appears on a monument in Augusta memorializing Southern poets. His cabin in the woods gradually sank into decay and burned down in the 1950s.

Hayne and his poetry are now little remembered. He has been criticized as imitative, excessively sentimental, and too prolific, and his work as bearing the mark of little editing. At the same time, even modern readers recognize the beauty and feeling expressed in his works

about nature and his rustic environment. Tennyson praised his sonnets as the best by any American writer. Hayne's work exalted the beauty of life in the antebellum South and perhaps contributed to sectional divisiveness, but personally he was never partisan and strove for national harmony. He was a poet suited to his place and his time.

Hayne married Mary Middleton Michel of Charleston in 1852. Their son, William Hamilton Hayne (1856–1929), was a poet of distinction on nature themes in a later generation.

—*Russell K. Brown*

See also Cooke, John Esten; Simms, William Gilmore.
For further reading:
Moore, Rayburn S. *Paul Hamilton Hayne* (1972).
——, ed. *A Man of Letters in the Nineteenth Century South: Selected Letters of Paul Hamilton Hayne* (1982).

HAYS, ALEXANDER
(1819–1864)
Union general

Winfield Scott Hancock never forgot his 3d Division, II Corps commander during Pickett's Charge at Gettysburg. "Fighting Alex. Hays rode along our cheering lines, upon his foaming horse, bearing aloft in his right hand the stars and stripes and dragging under the trampling heels of his horse a rebel flag just taken from the repulsed foe. The act was significant and symbolic...."

Better known as "Sandy," Alexander Hays was born in Franklin, Venango County, Pennsylvania, 8 July 1819, the fifth child, fourth son of Agnes Broadfoot Hays and Samuel Hays. Befitting the son of an Irish immigrant who had enjoyed a successful political career, the future division commander was tutored and attended two academies away from home before enrolling in 1837 at Allegheny College, Meadville, Pennsylvania. However, shortly before graduating from there, Hays left to enroll at the U.S. Military Academy because he had almost reached the maximum age for new cadets.

Hays graduated twentieth in the class of 1844, which included future Major General Winfield Scott Hancock. Hays served in the 4th Infantry in Louisiana with Ulysses S. Grant, who had graduated in the class ahead of Hays's, and with future C.S.A. lieutenant general James Longstreet, who had graduated in the class of 1842.

During the Mexican-American War, Hays fought in the battles of Palo Alto and Resaca de la Palma. In the latter, while helping to capture a cannon, he received a severe leg wound. For his gallantry he was promoted to first lieutenant and was transferred to the 8th Infantry. While recovering from his wound, he recruited a 500-man battalion and rejoined the army at Vera Cruz.

On 19 February 1846, Hays married Annie Adams McFadden. They had four children. After the Mexican-American War, he resigned his commission. Thereafter until the fall of Fort Sumter, except for an unsuccessful quest for gold in California, he engaged in bridge engineering for the Allegheny Valley Railroad.

After Fort Sumter, Hays enlisted in the City Guard, a Pittsburgh militia company, of which he became captain, and was promoted major when the company was made part of the 12th Pennsylvania Infantry. During the summer of 1861, Hays was promoted captain of the 16th U.S. Infantry. Afterward he recruited and was elevated to colonel of the newly mustered 63d Pennsylvania, which included men from the City Guard.

His III Corps division commander, David Birney, recommended him for promotion after the battles of Williamsburg and Fair Oaks, claiming that Hays's "record is as brilliant as any officer in the service." However, Hays was not awarded the star until after Second Bull Run, where his leg was shattered by a bullet.

Though still not recovered, in mid-November 1862 Hays was assigned to command the 3d Brigade of Silas Casey's division near Washington, a brigade branded the "Cowards of Harper's Ferry" as a result of its perceived conduct there a month earlier. Yet, less than five months later Hays proudly proclaimed that "'The Harper's Ferry Boys' have turned out trumps, and when we do get a chance look out for blood."

At Gettysburg, Hays's men lived up to his expectations, routing Barksdale's brigade in the late afternoon 2 July and capturing three flags and a number of prisoners on 3 July. Yet, as Hays sadly reported, "their history is now written in blood." The brigade's conduct there may well explain why Hays could claim that thereafter it seemed that his men were always in the advance on attacks and in the rear during retreats. Clearly that was the case in the battles of Auburn and Bristoe Station on 14 October 1863, when Hays's division embarrassed Major General A. P. Hill.

With the March 1864 reorganization of the Army of the Potomac, Hays was relegated to command of the 2d Brigade, 3d Division, II Corps, which battled Hill's corps at the Wilderness. In the afternoon of 5 May 1864, Hays was killed leading his old 63d Pennsylvania Infantry. Though a magnificent statue at Gettysburg memorializes "Fighting Alex" Hays, an upright cannon more fittingly marks the spot near the intersection of the Brock and Orange Plank roads where he fell.

—*Wayne Mahood*

See also Gettysburg, Battle of; Wilderness, Battle of the.
For further reading:
Fleming, George T. *The Life and Letters of Alexander Hays* (1919).
Hays, Gilbert. *Under the Red Patch* (1908).
Jordan, David M. *Winfield Scott Hancock: A Soldier's Life* (1988).
Scott, Winfield. "Pickett's Charge." Robert L. Blake

Collection.

U.S. War Department. *The War of the Rebellion: A Compilation of the Official Records of the Union and Confederate Armies* (1880–1901).

HAZEN, WILLIAM BABCOCK
(1830–1887)
Union general

William Babcock Hazen was born in Vermont, but his family moved to Ohio, from where he received his appointment to the U.S. Military Academy. He graduated twenty-eighth of thirty-four in the class of 1855. Appointed to the infantry, Hazen served on the Oregon and Texas frontiers and received three citations for good conduct and a brevet promotion to first lieutenant. He also received a wound that contributed to death from kidney poisoning thirty years later. Hazen taught infantry tactics at West Point after recovery from his wound. His reprimand of cadet George A. Custer was only the beginning of his reputation as a strict disciplinarian.

The Union army needed a man of Hazen's military talents commanding troops in the field. Through the influence of another Ohioan James A. Garfield, Hazen received an appointment as colonel of the 41st Ohio on 29 October 1861. The regiment hailed from the northeast Ohio region and consisted of raw recruits with little military background. Through hard work, Hazen turned these volunteers into a superb regiment. In the process, Hazen lost much of his popularity with his men, but later, in battle he earned their respect as a result of his tactical competence.

Hazen served in the Western theater of the war and fought in most of the major western battles. On 3 January 1862, he received command of the 19th brigade in William "Bull" Nelson's division in the Army of the Ohio. With only modest command changes, these troops served under Hazen at Shiloh, Perryville, Stones River, and Chickamauga.

Where the fighting was the most intense, one could find Hazen. He became one of the outstanding brigade commanders in the Union army. At Shiloh he aggressively attacked Confederates on 7 April. At Perryville, as a result of poor communication in the Union high command, his forces were not engaged. At Stones River, Hazen's stand at the Round Forrest may have saved the Union army. For this, the first Union monument was dedicated to him. General William S. Rosecrans chose Hazen's brigade as part of the force he wanted to use to make a feint against the city of Chattanooga. Hazen performed superbly. At Chickamauga, Hazen fought well and participated in the heroic stand at Snodgrass Hill under George H. Thomas.

Hazen's command was reorganized after Chickamauga. He called for the removal of incompetent superiors such

William Babcock Hazen (*Library of Congress*)

as A. M. McCook and Thomas L. Crittenden. At Brown's Ferry, Hazen's men performed brilliantly and at Missionary Ridge Hazen's troops broke the Confederate lines. After the battle, Hazen and Philip Sheridan began a long acrimonious debate over who was first to the top and how many cannons each had captured. This dispute did not help Hazen's later career.

Hazen served with distinction during the Atlanta campaign. Sherman promoted him to divisional command on 17 August 1864, and he led the 2d Division of the XV Corps of the Army of the Tennessee through the rest of the war. Hazen had truly earned the promotion by his sparkling performance with the Army of the Cumberland. The general received high praise for his capture of Fort McAllister. However, the soldiers of the Army of the Tennessee always viewed Hazen as an outsider. Hazen commanded the XV Corps from 23 May until 1 August 1865.

Hazen remained in the army after the war. He served at various frontier posts from 1865 to 1870. His views about the conduct of the Indian wars bought him into conflict with some of his superiors, especially his old nemesis Sheridan. Custer, not Hazen, was the favored subordinate of Sheridan.

A golden opportunity came Hazen's way when he

served as an observer during the Franco-Prussian War and concluded that the U.S. Army needed to modernize its forces. He published *The School and the Army in Germany* in 1872 and established himself as a leading military intellectual. His peers greeted his findings with indifference and sometimes outright hostility, but U.S. military scholars of a later generation would pick up Hazen's call for modernization.

Old feuds with David Stanley and Sheridan continued to plague Hazen. Stanley spread rumors of Hazen's misconduct at the battle of Shiloh. President Rutherford Hayes dismissed the charges, but Stanley went to the press with the story. Hazen challenged this account and a spectacular joint court-martial began in 1879. Sheridan backed Stanley's version of events. Although the charges against him were dropped, Hazen believed that the public had not heard his version of events. Thus, he began to write his memoirs.

Hazen added new enemies in the 1870s. One in the person of Secretary of War William Belknap when he criticized the politician for corruption in his department. Belknap's disgrace vindicated Hazen's position. Another enemy was the railroad companies. Hazen also aroused a storm of controversy for his criticism of railroad company deceptions in the development of the Great Plains.

Luck seemed to change for Hazen in 1881 when his old friend James A. Garfield was elected president. Garfield appointed Hazen chief signal officer. However, controversy soon developed. Hazen sharply criticized the secretary of war, Robert Todd Lincoln, for his failure to send a relief party to a polar signal station. Several members of the station died because of the failure and Hazen blamed Lincoln for the deaths. Lincoln censured Hazen and Hazen went to the press with the story. A court-martial resulted, and a reprimand followed. Tired and sickly, Hazen died shortly afterward.

Hazen was a consummate professional soldier. A hard worker and a strict disciplinarian, he drove himself and his men hard. As a perfectionist, he easily found the weaknesses of others and would fearlessly expose them. Few people doubted Hazen's ability but many wondered at his absence of tact. Controversy followed the general throughout his career, and one can only wonder how much higher Hazen could have risen if he had curried favor more astutely.

—*Damon R. Eubank*

See also Chickamauga, Battle of; Fort McAllister; Missionary Ridge, Battle of; Sheridan, Philip H.; Stones River, Battle of.
For further reading:
Cozzens, Peter. *The Civil War in the West: From Stones River to Chattanooga* (1996).
Hazen, William B. *A Narrative of Military Service: The Civil War through the Eyes of a Controversial Fighting General* (1885; reprint, 1993).
Lamers, William M. *The Edge of Glory: A Biography of William S. Rosecrans* (1961).

McKinney, Francis. *Education in Violence: The Life of George H. Thomas and the History of the Army of the Cumberland* (1961).
Van Horne, Thomas B. *History of the Army of the Cumberland: Its Organization, Campaigns, and Battles, Written at the Request of Major-General George H. Thomas Chiefly from His Private Military Journal and Official and Other Documents Furnished by Him* (1875).

HÉBERT, PAUL OCTAVE
(1818–1880)
Confederate general

Born to Paul Hébert and Mary Eugenia Hamilton Hébert in Iberville Parish, Louisiana, the younger Hébert was educated in Louisiana before accepting an appointment to the U.S. Military Academy. He graduated first in his class of forty-two in 1840. He taught at West Point for several years before resigning his commission in 1845. He returned to Louisiana where he worked briefly as an engineer for the state before returning to the army during the Mexican-American War. He was commended for bravery at Molino del Rey and received a brevet promotion to colonel.

Returning to Louisiana and civilian life after the war, Hébert became involved in Louisiana politics and planting. He was elected governor of the state in 1852 and served in that office until 1856.

At the outbreak of the Civil War, Hébert was commissioned colonel of the 1st Louisiana Artillery. He was promoted to brigadier general in August 1861. Through the summer of 1861 he served under Major General David E. Twiggs, the Confederate commander at New Orleans. During that time, Hébert's primary duties were to advise Twiggs on the strengthening of the defenses of New Orleans.

In the fall of 1861, Hébert was made commander of the Department of Texas. His initial concerns were for the defense of the essential port city of Galveston and the disposition of the prisoners of war that had been detained in Texas when David Twiggs, as the former U.S. commander of the department, surrendered all the federal posts in the state to Confederate sympathizers.

As the Vicksburg campaign unfolded in early 1863, the subdistrict of North Louisiana was added to Hébert's command. In June of 1863 as part of that campaign, Hébert fought at the battle of Milliken's Bend, Louisiana, the only major battle in which he participated. After the fall of Vicksburg, Hébert continued to command in northern Louisiana, but by the end of he summer of 1863 he was forced to retreat in the face of superior Union numbers.

Hébert returned to Texas, where he served out the remainder of the war. He had the dubious distinction at the end of the war of receiving command of all Trans-Mississippi Confederate troops from John B. Magruder just in time to surrender those forces to the Union army.

After the war Hébert returned to civil engineering and state politics. He died in New Orleans of cancer.

—David S. Heidler and Jeanne T. Heidler

See also Louisiana; Milliken's Bend; Texas.

For further reading:

Winters, John D. *The Civil War in Louisiana* (1963).

HEINTZELMAN, SAMUEL PETER
(1805–1880)
Union general

Born to Peter Heintzelman and Ann Elizabeth Grubb Heintzelman in Manheim, Pennsylvania, Samuel Peter Heintzelman was educated locally before receiving an appointment to the U.S. Military Academy. He graduated seventeenth of forty-one in the class of 1826. Upon graduation, Heintzelman served at a variety of frontier posts before the Mexican-American War. In that conflict Heintzelman fought in Winfield Scott's Mexico City campaign. He received a brevet promotion for his role in that campaign.

After the Mexican-American War, Heintzelman served in the Southwest, receiving another brevet promotion in 1851 for his actions there. He remained on the southwestern frontier until early 1861, when he was summoned to Washington. Arriving 8 May 1861, Heintzelman was made acting inspector general to Brigadier General J. K. F. Mansfield. In that capacity Heintzelman commanded the forces that occupied Arlington Heights and took Alexandria, Virginia, on 24 May 1861. Heintzelman had been made colonel of the 17th Infantry on 14 May and three days later was made brigadier general of volunteers.

Given command of the 3d Division of Irvin McDowell's army as it organized to march on the Confederate position at Manassas Junction, Heintzelman led his men in the attack on Henry House Hill during the battle of First Bull Run. Heintzelman's troops had been marching all day in the hot July sun and when a party of Confederates were mistaken for Union troops and succeeded in taking one of the division's batteries and turning the guns on the Union troops, Heintzelman's men lost heart and began retreating. Heintzelman worked frantically to rally his men for an assault on the Confederates but only succeeded in getting himself seriously wounded.

After his recovery, Heintzelman spent the fall of 1861 through the early spring of 1862 in patrolling operations in northern Virginia in command of his own division of the Army of the Potomac. On 5 March 1862, he and his men skirmished with Confederates at Pohick Church, Virginia. Shortly thereafter, he was given command of III Corps of the Army of the Potomac as it prepared for the upcoming Peninsula campaign.

In the early phases of that campaign, Heintzelman and III Corps approached the position of Confederate general John Bankhead Magruder at Yorktown. After surveying the situation and scouting Magruder's defenses, Heintzelman recommended to Commanding General George B. McClellan that the position would have to be taken by siege rather than by storm. This assessment was later demonstrated to be foolish as Magruder had only a tiny fraction of the soldiers that McClellan had. Although Heintzelman's recommendation was not the only factor influencing the already cautious McClellan to employ a siege at Yorktown, it certainly contributed to the unnecessary delay of the campaign.

With the Confederate withdrawal from Yorktown on 4 May, Heintzelman was sent with III Corps and Union cavalry in pursuit. He encountered Confederate troops outside of Williamsburg, precipitating the battle of Williamsburg on 5 May 1862.

Later in the campaign, Heintzelman commanded his corps at the battle of Seven Pines. When much of the Union army began to fall back in the face of the Confederate attack, Heintzelman moved forward to rally the men, but with little effect. Although he had a wide reputation for unshakable courage, he was curiously unable to inspire it in his troops. In spite of this,

Samuel Peter Heintzelman (*Library of Congress*)

Heintzelman's III Corps began the offensive on 25 June that would quickly become the Union defensive campaign of the Seven Days', although Heintzelman did not particularly distinguish himself in this episode.

On 14 August, Heintzelman and III Corps joined the Army of Virginia under John Pope in the campaign against Robert E. Lee. Heintzelman attacked a well-positioned corps under Stonewall Jackson on 29 August in the opening day of Second Bull Run.

As the Maryland campaign got under way, Heintzelman on 9 September took command of the Washington defenses south of the Potomac. During the fall of 1862, his main job was guarding against Confederate cavalry raids that continued to pose a problem into the next year. Hampered by technically remaining a part of the Army of the Potomac and having to pass all communications through that chain of command, Heintzelman asked Secretary of War Edwin Stanton in January 1863 to make the Washington defenses a separate department.

In February 1863, the Department of Washington was created with Heintzelman given command of it and the XXII Corps. He would soon see his busiest time in the Washington defenses during the Gettysburg campaign. In June and July 1863, Heintzelman's command worked nonstop to bolster the defenses of the city and to maintain careful contact with the Army of the Potomac to determine the destination of Lee's Army of Northern Virginia.

In October 1863, Heintzelman was relieved of command in Washington and in January 1864 made commander of the Department of the North headquartered in Columbus, Ohio. Although not a combat command, the new position did not allow Heintzelman to be idle. Along with supervising recruiting and directing new soldiers to commands in the South, he also kept vigilant watch on antidraft agitators and Copperhead groups in the Midwest. Heintzelman remained in this command until October 1864, then for the remainder of the war he served court-martial duty.

After the war, Heintzelman remained in the army, reverting to colonel of the 17th Infantry after he was mustered out of the volunteers. He commanded this regiment in Texas during Reconstruction. He retired in 1869 at the rank of major general as granted by an act of Congress.

Heintzelman lived for a time in New York City after his retirement. He moved to Washington, D.C., after a few years, and there he died on 1 May 1880.
—*David S. Heidler and Jeanne T. Heidler*

See also Fair Oaks/Seven Pines; Peninsula Campaign; Seven Days', Battles; Williamsburg, Battle of; Yorktown.
For further reading:
Heintzelman, Samuel Peter. *The Papers of Samuel Peter Heintzelman* (1977).

HELENA, BATTLE OF
(4 July 1863)

The bungled Confederate assault on Helena, Arkansas, came too late to divert Union forces from the siege of Vicksburg. It also left the attackers so weakened and demoralized that the Federals were able to capture Little Rock two months later.

On 23 May 1863, Jefferson Davis's secretary of war, John A. Seddon, urged that Confederate troops in the Trans-Mississippi Department make some move to take the pressure off Lieutenant General John C. Pemberton and the 30,000-man army that Major General Ulysses S. Grant had trapped at Vicksburg. In particular, Seddon suggested the capture of Helena, which had been a source of concern since falling into Federal hands the previous July. Overlooking the Mississippi River at a point 70 miles below Memphis and 230 miles above Vicksburg, the port city served as a convenient base for Union raids into northeast Arkansas and for Grant's operations against Vicksburg. It also posed a threat to Little Rock.

The Confederate chain of command forwarded Seddon's wishes to Lieutenant General Theophilus H. Holmes, the commander of the District of Arkansas, but they did not reach him until 14 June. Despite heavy rains and other difficulties, Holmes managed to slap together a sizable field army from the various units scattered across his district. By 3 July, he was within five miles of Helena with 7,646 effectives, including 4,434 infantry organized into three brigades and three cavalry brigades containing 3,212 men.

Helena's Union garrison numbered only 4,129 officers and men, but they were well prepared for the coming storm. The Federals had surrounded Helena with an extensive network of entrenchments, especially after Major General Benjamin M. Prentiss, the hero of the "Hornet's Nest" at Shiloh, assumed command of the District of Eastern Arkansas in February 1863. Determined never again to be surprised by the enemy, Prentiss had his troops bolster their existing fortifications with additional rifle pits and breastworks. Four steep hills guarded the city's western approaches, and Prentiss crowned each one with a sturdy little earthwork known from north to south as Batteries A, B, C, and D, respectively. Behind the hilltop batteries stood Fort Curtis, the heart of Helena's defenses, which mounted nine 32-pound siege guns.

Forewarned of Holmes's advance by different intelligence sources, Prentiss announced on 28 June that henceforth his troops were to be awake and under arms each day at 2:30 A.M. He also sent out large details to fell trees for abatis and roadblocks. To augment the firepower of the Helena garrison, the Union navy dispatched the tinclad *Tyler*, which had rendered valuable support to embattled Federal troops at Shiloh.

Holmes was taken aback by Prentiss's vigilance and defensive precautions, but he decided to proceed with his plans. He directed his cavalry to dismount and strike the enemy's lines from the northeast, while his infantry stormed Batteries C and D farther south. Hoping to conceal his approach until the last possible moment, Holmes ordered the attack to begin on 4 July at daybreak, an imprecise term open to interpretation. Consequently, the rebel cavalry engaged the Federals at first light, as did the one infantry brigade assigned to take Battery D, but Holmes's other two infantry brigades did not start moving against Battery C until sunup.

The battle began shortly before 4:00 A.M., as the rebels drove in Prentiss's pickets, a clash that alerted Helena's defenders and gave them plenty of time to staff their fortifications. To the north, the Federals easily checked the half-hearted thrusts of Holmes's cavalry. At Battery D, a brigade of Arkansas infantry captured some outlying rifle pits, but it was pinned down by the defenders' brisk rifle and artillery fire. Though late in getting into the fight, the two rebel infantry brigades commanded by Major General Sterling Price managed to overrun Battery C, but they received no chance to exploit their breakthrough. From Fort Curtis and Batteries A, B, and D and other positions, Union cannoneers pounded the captured stronghold. The *Tyler* also hurled its massive shells at Price's soldiers with terrifying effect. In the meantime, Union officers rallied the defenders of Battery C and brought up new units to seal the breach with a counterattack.

Unable to make further headway or retain Battery C, Holmes ordered a retreat shortly after 11:00 A.M. The repulse cost him 1,636 casualties, 1,560 of them infantry. The rebels also suffered a severe loss of confidence in their leaders and their cause, especially after they learned that Vicksburg had surrendered on the same day as their ill-fated assault. Union casualties, in contrast, numbered only 239 killed, wounded, and missing.

—*Gregory J. W. Urwin*

See also Holmes, Theophilus; Prentiss, Benjamin M.; Price, Sterling; Vicksburg Campaign.
For further reading:
Bearss, Edwin C. "The Battle of Helena, July 4, 1863." *Arkansas Historical Quarterly* (1961).
———. *The Campaign for Vicksburg* (1985–1986).
Castel, Albert. *General Sterling Price and the Civil War in the West* (1968).
Christ, Mark K., ed. *Rugged and Sublime: The Civil War in Arkansas* (1994).
Roberts, Bobby, and Carl Moneyhon. *Portraits of Conflict: A Photographic History of Arkansas in the Civil War* (1987).

HELM, BENJAMIN HARDIN
(1830–1863)

Confederate general

The son of John Larue Helm and Lucinda Barbour Helm, Ben Helm was born in Elizabethtown, Kentucky. After a local education, he was admitted to the U.S. Military Academy, where he graduated ninth of forty-two in the class of 1851. Not caring for the military life, he resigned his commission the following year to study law. After admission to the bar, he opened a practice and became active in Kentucky politics. He married Emilie Todd, the younger half-sister of Mary Todd Lincoln. When he was elected president in 1860, Abraham Lincoln offered his wife's brother-in-law a position in the U.S. Army. Helm refused the appointment, preferring instead, once hostilities erupted, to raise a cavalry regiment for the Confederacy.

Helm served as the colonel of the 1st Kentucky Cavalry (C.S.A.) until his promotion to brigadier general in March 1862. Throughout the spring of 1862, before his promotion was confirmed, he commanded his regiment in scouting chores in north Alabama. After his promotion, Helm was given command of what would become known as the "Orphan Brigade" of Kentucky under Major General John C. Breckinridge near Vicksburg, Mississippi. Helm remained in Mississippi through the summer of 1862, but in the fall he transferred to Louisiana, where he suffered injuries in a riding accident. Helm served desk duty for the remainder of the year into 1863. In the spring of 1863, he returned to command his brigade, again under Breckinridge, in time for the Tullahoma campaign of June 1863.

Helm and his brigade remained in Breckinridge's division for the Chickamauga campaign of September 1863. On the second day of the battle (20 September), while leading a charge of the left of his brigade, Helm was mortally wounded. He died later in the day.

—*David S. Heidler and Jeanne T. Heidler*

See also Breckinridge, John C.; Chickamauga, Battle of; Lincoln, Mary Todd.
For further reading:
McMurtry, R. Gerald. *Ben Hardin Helm* (1948).

HELPER, HINTON ROWAN
(1829–1909)

Antislavery author, racist, and polemicist

Hinton Rowan Helper was born near Mocksville, Rowan County, North Carolina, one of seven children of Daniel and Sarah Brown Helper. The family lived on 200 acres of land granted them by Cannon Brown, the prosperous father of Sarah. The Helpers apparently owned a family of four slaves who were let go upon the death of Sarah's father in 1830. The land was also appropriated by Thomas Brown, eldest son of Cannon Brown. The Helper family was left as poor relations, with the eldest child but eleven years old. Care of the destitute family was in the hands of the uncle, a devout Presbyterian who exercised strict authority and provided a minimal education for the children at the Mocksville Academy, where Hinton Helper received his

only formal schooling. Unlike the Brown sons, Hinton had no opportunity for further education. While the Brown family prospered in the tobacco business and owned slaves, the Helper family foundered.

The academy catered to children of the affluent and those who had some schooling. Helper had been taught at home and was literate when he entered. He was graduated at nineteen, and there is no record of his having made any friends in his school years. He was apprenticed to another relative who owned a store in Salisbury, North Carolina. Helper served his apprenticeship satisfactorily in two years, but he had embezzled $300 and made his way to New York. Soon he was on his way to California, where news of gold had enticed many Southerners to seek a fortune. An irony lies in that he sailed on *Star of the West*, which was the ship that the Union dispatched in 1861 to supply Fort Sumter when it was under siege.

Helper spent more than two years in California with little success other than compiling a notebook on his sour view of mining, the environment, the Chinese, and the blacks. He returned to North Carolina and in 1855 published *The Land of Gold*, which sold enough to whet his appetite for writing. He also made an accomodation regarding the embezzled money, though the matter was brought up after the publication in 1857 of his second book, *The Impending Crisis of the South: How To Meet It*. The book arrived at a critical time in U.S. history, as the North and South had developed critical differences over trade, tariffs, territorial expansion, slavery, and politics. Abolitionists and antislavery reformers were coalescing in attacks on slavery as the central issue retarding national development and its place in a world that had virtually ended slavery. Helper's argument was against cash-crop culture dependent on slavery and benefiting only the owners of large landholdings and slave labor. He was reflecting certainly something of personal experience in which his family was thrust into the yeoman, nonslaveholding majority whose status was frozen by the lack of economic opportunity. Helper did a masterful study of the Census of 1850 to prove the overall weakness of the South, which he blamed on slavery.

The South was caught completely off-guard by the didactic rendition and summarization by a Southerner. The North was delighted by the prospect that within the South there were opponents to slavery who might be used in the crusade that centered on whether slavery should be allowed to expand into new territory. Southern newspapers and journals were unable to address the issues put forth by Helper. Some Northern papers tried to address the issue for fear that abolitionism would threaten an orderly society, but Helper's book prevailed. He had to have the book published in the North and then only after his guarantee that the book agent would not suffer a loss. Major publishers shied from taking the book, but it became a runner-up bestseller to Tom Brown's *School Days* with $14,000 in sales at $1.00 per copy. Helper got the lesser share, however, because he had to guarantee both printing and distribution.

Helper soon found that no place in the South was safe for him, his book, or even readers of his book. Ordinances were passed proscribing ownership of the book and postmasters were put on alert to report any suspicious packages that might contain it. Faculty in colleges were harassed and even fired over the book, and ministers such as the Reverend Daniel Worth, a Methodist, was put in prison for citing the book in sermons. The fragility of democracy in the South was never more evident as curfews were established for all blacks for fear of insurrection.

The new national Republican Party, which had kept abolitionism at arm's length previously, saw in the book an opportunity to use a Southerner as messenger while still keeping a respectable distance from the issue. The party published a compact version of the Helper book, which they distributed as a campaign vehicle in 1859. It was sold cheaply at first and then eventually given free as elections came to a head.

What Helper called "the redeeming act" of his life now thrust him into finding a place among the militant social and political reformers of the North. He was never to succeed because there was no consciousness among abolitionists that opposition to slavery could also mean opposition to the African-American. His book took on a life of its own as it became an issue in the choosing of the Speaker of the House of Representatives, and Southern slave owners joined together in fear of internal revolution by both yeoman whites and African-American people. Promoters of the book endorsed Abraham Lincoln's election, which guaranteed secession of the South. It also meant that Helper would turn to the administration for a position. Government files are filled with his petitions for an appointment, but distance from Helper was the guideword as events moved precipitously toward war. Helper was finally made consul in Buenos Aires, as remote from the conflict as could be found. There he stayed and performed his duties satisfactorily and also married Maria Louisa Rodriguez, a woman from an influential Argentine family. They had a son, but after their return to the United States in 1867, Helper was unable to find a suitable position, and his wife and child returned to Argentina.

With Andrew Johnson in the White House, Helper believed that the realization of his dreams of social evolution in the South would occur. He saw in Johnson the salvation of the yeoman and poor whites and the turning of society inside out. However, the forces of abolition had taken control of reconstruction policy, which demanded that the freedmen be guaranteed equal rights. The pursuit of such a policy was unconscionable to Helper, who proceeded to write diatribic monographs such as *Nojoque* (1867); *The Negroes in Negroland* (1868); and an autobiographical *Noonday Exigencies in America* (1871), the first two of which were virtual alliterative encyclopedias of hate for black people. Helper was shouting in a vacuum, for there were no listeners in a nation whose people had put both blood and treasure at risk to fight for a cause that they were certain was right.

It is curious that Helper had originally sought deportation of slaves, something that Lincoln himself had attempted in a disastrous venture during the war. Helper was now an unwelcome presence in both the North and the South for the same reason: apostasy to abolitionism and to Southern culture. He sought another appointment in South America, but he had used up his credit. The leaders of the Republican Party distanced themselves from him despite that his *Exigencies* book called for programs for civil service, legal and political rights for women, Americanization of immigrants, exclusion of Asians, and even the creation of a national workingmen's political party. Some of these ideas became visible in the planks of Populist and Progressive Parties.

Helper worked at selling real estate in North Carolina, Chicago, Mexico, New York, and New England and as an agent for Americans with claims against South American republics. He embarked on a railroad venture to build an intercontinental railroad from the Bering Sea to Buenos Aires. He published *Oddments of Andean Diplomacy and Other Oddments* (1879), followed by *Thirteen Papers in Support of Mr. Helper's Scheme for Constructing a Longitudinal Double-Track Steel Railway through North and South America* (1880), *The Three Americas Railway* (1881), and *Railway Communication between North and Central and South America: A Memorial of the Subject to the Congress of the United States of America* (1882), each of which found a publisher and even support from isolated sources. However, the Credit Mobilier scandal over the Union Pacific Railroad had chilled enthusiasm for use of public monies on more railroad ventures.

Helper was now an isolated crank to be avoided or, at best, tolerated. He wandered the streets of Washington, rested in hotel lobbies, avoided blacks by design, and badgered any who would listen to his ideas. He lived in a rooming house and tried his best to keep up a genteel Southern appearance with a trimmed full beard, frock coat, and string tie. He committed suicide by gas in his room on 8 March 1909.

—*Jack J. Cardoso*

See also Abolitionists.
For further reading:
Bailey, Hugh C. *Hinton Rowan Helper: Abolitionist-Racist* (1965).
Barbee, David Rankin. "Hinton Rowan Helper." *Tyler's Historical and Genealogical Magazine* (1934).
Cardoso, Joaquin Jose. "Hinton Rowan Helper: A Nineteenth Century Pilgrimage" (Ph.D. dissertation, 1967).
Gilbert, Benjamin F. "The Life and Writings of Hinton Rowan Helper." *Register of the Kentucky Historical Society* (1955).
Helper, Hinton Rowan. *The Impending Crisis of the South: How to Meet It* (1852; reprint, 1968).
Lefler, Hugh Talmadge. *Hinton Rowan Helper: Advocate of a White America* (1934).
Polk, William. "The Hated Helper." *South Atlantic Quarterly* (1931).

HENDRICKS, THOMAS ANDREWS
(1819–1885)
Democratic politician

Thomas Andrews Hendricks was born in Ohio but spent most of his life in Indiana, where his family was prominent in the Democratic Party. Hendricks was admitted to the bar in 1843, and soon thereafter became engaged in politics. In 1848 he was elected to the Indiana Assembly, and in 1850 he served as a delegate to the convention drawing up a new state constitution. The next year, he was elected to the U.S. House of Representatives, an office that he held until a coalition of Know-Nothings, Whigs, and prohibitionists organized against him in 1854.

While in Congress, Hendricks supported Senator Stephen A. Douglas of Illinois and his divisive Kansas-Nebraska Act. His aligning with Douglas in turn engendered opposition to his reelection. However, after his congressional defeat, Hendricks was appointed commissioner of the General Land Office by President Franklin Pierce. Hendricks continued in that office under President James Buchanan until 1859, when he resigned as a result of policy differences, especially those involving Buchanan's disputes with Douglas.

In 1860, Hendricks ran as the Democratic gubernatorial candidate in Indiana but lost to his Republican opponent. However, in 1862, as the Civil War gripped the nation many Indianans began to question the war effort, or at least the Republicans' leadership. Hendricks took the lead in blaming the Republican administration and Republican policies for the ongoing depression in agriculture and general hard times. He also criticized the administration for high taxes and arguably unconstitutional wartime measures. However, he recognized that while the War Democrats might make political capital on these issues, a majority of Hoosier voters still supported the war and were not Peace Democrats. Consequently, following the leadership of Hendricks, Unionist Democrats captured the state legislature, and in 1863 they elected Hendricks to the U.S. Senate.

Throughout these years, Hendricks gained a reputation not only for his political endeavors but also for his generally conservative views, especially on race. While not considering himself a defender of slavery, he had opposed allowing free African-Americans into Indiana.

During the war, he opposed emancipation and the recruitment of African-Americans into Union forces. He argued against the passage of the Thirteenth Amendment to the Constitution. He did not believe in racial equality and espoused the view that Southerners should also have a voice in determining the legal fate of slavery. At the same time, he also objected to the conscription of Union men. Vociferously taking these stands, he became a leader among the twelve Democrats in the Senate.

Although he disagreed with the actions of President Abraham Lincoln, Hendricks maintained a cordial relationship with the president, and, despite his often outspoken criticism of the Republican administration, he never advocated illegal disobedience to government authority. And when Andrew Johnson assumed the presidency after Lincoln's assassination, Hendricks supported Johnson's Reconstruction actions, which Johnson maintained were in line with Lincoln's plans. In turn, as a Democratic leader in the Senate, Hendricks fought strongly against Radical Reconstruction. In particular, he opposed the Fourteenth Amendment to the Constitution, and he led Democratic support for President Johnson during his impeachment trial.

In 1868, Hendricks ran for governor of Indiana, but he suffered defeat in a close election. That same year he also received some support for the Democratic presidential nomination. He finally succeeded in getting elected governor of Indiana in 1872. He also soon became a well- known adherent to the "greenback" or "soft money" inflationary views that were particularly popular with Midwestern and Western farmers. However, he lost the Democratic presidential nomination in 1876 to Samuel J. Tilden, the "hard money," reform-minded governor of New York. To balance the ticket, "soft money" Midwesterner Hendricks from the politically pivotal and important state of Indiana accepted the vice presidential nomination. Tilden and Hendricks won more popular votes nationally than their Republican opponents but lost the election as a result of the resolution of a dispute over electoral votes.

Hendricks had thus become an even more noted national figure in the Democratic Party. His presidential aspirations resurfaced in 1880, but he was not selected. In 1884, although weakened by two strokes, he agreed to run on the ticket with presidential nominee Grover Cleveland, another "hard money," reform-minded governor of New York. Cleveland and Hendricks won, but in November of 1885, after serving as vice president for only nine months, the sickly Hendricks died.

—*Thomas Burnell Colbert*

See also Democratic Party.
For further reading:
Hayes, Ralph D., ed. *Gentlemen from Indiana: National Party Candidates 1836–1940* (1977).

Holcombe, John W., and Hubert M. Skinner. *Life and Public Services of Thomas A. Hendricks* (1886).
Purcell, Edward L., ed. *The Vice Presidents: A Biographical Dictionary* (1998).

HERNDON, WILLIAM HENRY
(1818–1891)
Abraham Lincoln's law partner

William Henry Herndon was born in Greensburg, Kentucky. His father died when he was an infant, and his mother, Rebecca Day Johnson, remarried Archer G. Herndon. Her young son took his stepfather's name. The younger Herndon moved with his family to Illinois when he was two, and they settled in Springfield, Illinois, when he was seven. Herndon was educated in local schools and briefly attended Illinois College in Jacksonville, Illinois. His father forced him to leave the school when it became apparent that he was associating with abolitionists.

After leaving college, Herndon became increasingly active in the Illinois antislavery movement, which naturally drew him into local politics. In the meantime, however, he had to make a living and did so at a variety of tasks, including store clerking, until choosing a career in law. He read law in the office of Stephen T. Logan and his partner Abraham Lincoln. When that partnership was dissolved in 1844, Lincoln asked Herndon to become his partner.

This partnership proved a happy one. Neither man was especially organized, but Herndon was a talented researcher and Lincoln an accomplished trial lawyer. Therefore their individual skills complemented one another, and their partnership prospered. Politically, the two were also quite compatible. Both were Whigs in the early days of their association; Herndon's ties to the younger, more antislavery wing of the Illinois party and Lincoln's affiliation with the more established members of the local party furthered Lincoln's political career. Herndon was more than willing to help.

Satisfied with his own local activities and his growing reputation as a rising young attorney, in 1848 Herndon helped organize Whigs for Zachary Taylor in Springfield and was elected mayor of Springfield in 1854. He also served as a state bank examiner. Herndon aided Lincoln's political efforts when he could, working hard during the senatorial campaign of 1858 and the presidential campaign of 1860. When Lincoln was elected, he asked Herndon that their partnership not be dissolved and that his name remain on their sign so that he could return to that profession after his presidency.

Herndon continued to practice law through the Civil War and took on new partners when Lincoln was assassinated. However, his efforts proved less than lucrative. Perhaps he would have been more successful if he had not

spent so much of his time after Lincoln's death gathering abundant biographical material about the martyred president. He traveled to the various places Lincoln had lived and interviewed numerous people while gathering as many documents as he could find, all in the hope of one day writing the definitive biography of Lincoln. He did not manage to put much to paper until he was very old, but in the meantime he did supply other biographers with much of the invaluable information he had gathered.

Herndon probably exaggerated some of his own experiences and relationship with Lincoln, including his impact on Lincoln's views about slavery. He also tended to believe stories that he had heard from other sources. His interpretation of Lincoln's relationship with Ann Rutledge was perhaps an attempt to attack Mary Todd Lincoln, whom he had hated even before she and Lincoln were married. Though never entertained socially in the Lincoln home, Herndon later would assert that the marriage was unhappy and would unfairly depict Mary as a shrill termagant.

Whatever the accuracy of some of Herndon's facts and interpretations, his extensive research, particularly that part of it he conducted during the years immediately following the president's death, was to be of great use to future historians. As with many other people who came into Lincoln's orbit, Herndon's chief fame derives from his association with him. Yet we would not know as much about Lincoln as we do had it not been for the man who Lincoln fondly called "Billy."

—*David S. Heidler and Jeanne T. Heidler*

See also Lincoln, Abraham.

For further reading:
Davis, Rodney O., and Terry Wilson, eds. *Herndon's Informants: Letters, Interviews, and Statements about Abraham Lincoln* (1998).
Donald, David Herbert. *Lincoln's Herndon: A Biography* (1948).
Herndon, William Henry. *The Hidden Lincoln* (1938).
Wilson, Douglas L. *Lincoln before Washington: New Perspectives on the Illinois Years* (1997).

HERRON, FRANCIS JAY
(1837–1902)
Union general

Born and educated in Pennsylvania, Francis Jay Herron moved to Dubuque, Iowa, in 1855. There he operated a bank with his brothers. Holding an interest in military activity, in 1859 he helped organize the Governor's Grays, an independent militia company. In January 1861, facing the prospect of disunion and war, Herron and his men offered their services to the secretary of war. They were turned down but would have the distinction of being the first troops to offer their services. In April 1861, the Governor's Grays did become part of the 1st Iowa Infantry.

Captain Herron and his company fought in early small engagements in Missouri and in the battle of Wilson's Creek. However, their three-month enlistment then expired, and Herron, who lobbied Governor Samuel Kirkwood for higher rank in a new regiment, became the lieutenant colonel in the 9th Iowa Infantry. At the battle of Pea Ridge, Herron, who was wounded and captured, distinguished himself for courage. (He was awarded the Medal of Honor in 1893 for his actions at Pea Ridge.) He returned to Union forces under a prisoner exchange, and, as a result of his heroism, he gained promotion to brigadier general in 1862, bypassing the rank of colonel.

Herron commanded the 2d and 3d Divisions of the Army of the Frontier under General John M. Schofield in Missouri when, in December 1862, General James G. Blunt called for reinforcements as he confronted Confederate general Thomas C. Hindman near Fayetteville, Arkansas. Herron saved Blunt from defeat by force-marching his 6,000 men and 30 guns 150 miles in four days. Herron's tired troops were attacked by Hindman's forces, but after much hard fighting in a seeming stand-off, Hindman retreated. This Union victory in the battle of Prairie Grove opened northern Arkansas and the Arkansas River to Union control. In turn, Herron was promoted to major general of volunteers, becoming at that point in the war the youngest major general in the Union army. He also replaced Schofield as commander of the Army of the Frontier.

In June 1863, the Army of the Frontier was dismantled, and Herron led the division under his command to join General Ulysses S. Grant's Army of the Tennessee in his siege of Vicksburg, Mississippi. Herron's men held Grant's extreme left wing. When the Confederates surrendered Vickburg, Herron was one of the three generals who took possession of the town. Soon thereafter, Grant sent Herron and his forces to operations against Confederates at Yazoo City and Port Hudson. In August, he took his forces to New Orleans and assumed leadership of an expedition to the Red River. Overcome by ill health, he left his command to recuperate.

Herron returned to duty to command the XIII Corps in the Department of the Gulf in Texas, with his headquarters at Brownsville. He oversaw an army on the Rio Grande from October 1863 until August 1864. At that time, he worked under secret instructions to help President Benito Juárez of Mexico as much as was legally possible in Juárez's fight against Maximilian, the French-imposed Emperor of Mexico. (Juárez eventually even offered Herron an important command in his army.)

Herron headed next to Baton Rouge, Louisiana, and from there he was sent on an inspection tour through Arkansas and Indian Territory. He returned to command the Northern Division of Louisiana. He aided in the capture of Mobile, Alabama. When the war came to an

end in May 1865, he negotiated the surrender of the Confederate Trans-Mississippi District, the last of the four largest Confederate armies to surrender. He was then appointed to a commission charged with negotiating new Indian treaties. However, he resigned his military commission in June 1865 and thus spent little time in treaty making.

Remaining in Louisiana after the war, Herron engaged in legal business and Republican politics. He served as tax collector of New Orleans and later as U.S. marshal. Republican governor Henry C. Warmoth appointed Herron secretary of state in 1871, but they had a falling out in 1873, leading Warmoth to remove Herron based on charges of corruption while he was tax collector.

In 1873, Herron moved to New York City, where he participated in veterans organizations and reportedly engaged in different business enterprises—manufacturing, law, and banking. When he died in 1902, however, he was possibly unemployed and poor, perhaps destitute.

—*Thomas Burnell Colbert*

See also Blunt, Gilpatrick; Prairie Grove, Battle of; Schofield, John McAllister.

For further reading:

Carlson, Gretchen. "Francis Jay Herron." *Palimpsest* (1930).

Herr, Pamela, and Mary Lee Spence, eds. "Major General F. J. Herron." *Annals of Iowa* (1867).

"Military Gossip." *New York Times* (1878).

Stuart, A.A. *17th Iowa Infantry. Iowa Colonels and Regiments: Being a History of Iowa Regiments in the War of the Rebellion.* Des Moines, Mills and Company, 1891.In Throne, Mildred, ed. *The Civil War Diary of Cyrus F. Boyd: 15th Iowa Infantry, 1861–1863* (1865; reprint 1977).

HETH, HENRY
(1825–1899)
Confederate general

Born to John Heth and Margaret Pickett Heth in Chesterfield, County, Virginia, Henry Heth was educated at Georgetown College (now University) before accepting an appointment to the U.S. Military Academy at West Point. He graduated thirty-eighth of thirty-eight cadets in 1847. Upon receiving his commission, he was immediately dispatched to Mexico to make up part of the U.S. occupation force in Matamoros, Mexico. After the end of the Mexican-American War, he served in a variety of frontier posts, fought in engagements with Indians, and participated in Albert Sidney Johnston's Utah expedition. In 1858 after participating in test trials for a new rifle, he published a manual for the War Department entitled *A System of Target Practice.*

Virginia's secession from the Union brought Heth's resignation. Initially part of the state's forces, Heth commanded the Virginia Quartermaster Department in Richmond before that office was taken over by the Confederate army. Taken into Confederate service, Heth initially received a captain's commission, but quickly rose through the ranks to colonel of the 45th Virginia.

Heth's regiment was placed under the command of Brigadier General John B. Floyd in anticipation of that officer's western Virginia campaign in the late summer and fall 1861. Heth planned and organized the campaign. Heth fought at Carnifex Ferry on 10 September and ultimately used his regiment to guard Floyd's retreat from western Virginia. Heth remained with his regiment to command near Lewisburg, Virginia.

Promoted to brigadier general in January 1862, Heth continued in western Virginia into the spring of 1862, fighting engagements against John C. Frémont and George Crook before being transferred to Edmund Kirby Smith's command in East Tennessee. Heth commanded his brigade in Bragg and Kirby Smith's Kentucky campaign, after which Heth was given command of the Department of Eastern Tennessee. During January 1863, his brigade's primary duty was to suppress Unionist sentiment in the eastern part of Tennessee. In February 1863, Heth and his brigade were transferred to the Army of Northern Virginia, A. P. Hill's division, Stonewall Jackson's corps.

Heth participated in the Chancellorsville campaign of May 1863, where he was slightly wounded. He was promoted to major general shortly after the battle. With the death of Jackson and the elevation of Hill to a corps commander, Heth commanded a division in Hill's corps.

In Lee's invasion of Pennsylvania in June 1863, it was the lead elements of Heth's division that approached Gettysburg on 30 June in search of supplies and encountered John Buford's cavalry brigade. The ensuing skirmish brought both armies converging on Gettysburg the next day.

Heth's division opened the battle on 1 July with a furious attack on Buford's position west of town. In that engagement Heth's division suffered severe casualties, and Heth was wounded, removing him from the remaining two days of the battle. Command of the division devolved upon one of Heth's brigade commanders, Brigadier General James Johnston Pettigrew. Pettigrew led the remainder of the division in the attack on the Union position on 3 July that became known as Pickett's Charge. Upon his recovery, Heth returned to command the division and would remain in command for the remainder of the war.

Heth and his division fought at Bristoe Station in October 1863, where the division suffered 30 percent casualties. They fought at the Wilderness and Spotsylvania the following spring, and during the siege of Petersburg they protected the line of the Weldon Railroad. Heth surrendered with Lee at Appomattox.

After the war, Heth became a Richmond businessman

and worked as a civil engineer and in the Office of Indian Affairs for the U.S. government. He also served as one of a group of ex-Confederate officers who helped compile *The War of the Rebellion: A Compilation of the Official Records of the Union and Confederate Armies.* He died in Washington, D.C.

—*David S. Heidler and Jeanne T. Heidler*

See also Bristoe Station; Floyd, John B.; Gettysburg, Battle of; Smith, Edmund Kirby.

For further reading:

Heth, Henry. "Letter from Major-General Henry Heth." *Southern Historical Society Papers* (1877).

Morrison, James L., Jr., ed. *The Memoirs of Henry Heth* (1974).

HICKS, THOMAS HOLLIDAY
(1798–1865)
Governor of Maryland

Born and raised on a farm on the Choptank River in Dorchester County on Maryland's Eastern Shore, Hicks spent his entire adulthood in politics, first as a Democrat, then as a Whig, and then was elected governor of Maryland in 1857 as a member of the American, or Know-Nothing, Party. His popularity was due in part to his support for a movement on the Eastern Shore to secede from the state of Maryland, a movement that surfaced periodically during the antebellum decades. Hicks's stand on that issue was ironic in light of his actions during the national secession crisis of 1861.

Hicks's popularity was also a reflection of what many Marylanders believed about the growing crisis of the 1850s: that Maryland represented the middle ground between two extremes. "Maryland is devoted to the Union and all of the states" and has "never listened to the suggestions of disunion from the Southern states and has refused to join with the misguided people of the Northern states in their assaults on slavery," he stated in his inaugural address on 13 January 1858. It was an untenable position, of course, but the square-jawed, thrice-married, fifty-nine-year-old Hicks was remarkably consistent about upholding it.

Following Lincoln's election in November 1860, many people urged Governor Hicks to call a special session of Maryland's legislature to declare the state's position. Several mass meetings were held from December 1860 through March 1861 in different localities, at which participants either urged Hicks to call the legislature into session or denounced him for not doing so. Two of these meetings in Baltimore in February and in March called for an extralegal convention to meet and debate secession. In addition to reflecting this general division in public opinion, Hicks's indecision had a strategic dimension to it. Maryland was traditionally loyal to the Democratic Party, and the Know Nothing governor confronted a Democratic legislature.

Hicks explained his indecision by claiming that a plot existed to take Maryland out of the Union when the legislature met. The Southern wing of the Democratic Party, which had supported John Breckinridge's bid for the presidency, constituted the majority in the Maryland legislature. These men had even officially resolved in 1860 that "if the hour ever arrive when the Union must be dissolved" that Maryland would cast her "lot with her sister states of the South." The areas of Maryland that had supported Breckinridge were represented by many members who declared their support for secession, including the Speaker of the House of Delegates, Elbridge G. Kilbourn, from Anne Arundel County.

Matters reached a crisis in April 1861 following the firing on Fort Sumter. Lincoln called for volunteers, Virginia seceded, and the Baltimore riot on 19 April tipped the balance toward secession. It was logical for Hicks on Monday, 22 April, to call the legislature into session for Friday, 26 April, to determine the state's sentiment. Because Massachusetts militia under the command of General Benjamin F. Butler had arrived in Annapolis on that very day, the twenty-second, Hicks directed the meeting to convene in the courthouse in Frederick County, where sympathy for the Union was stronger. Ironically, the Northern press, which had generally interpreted Hicks's delaying actions as evidence of his pro-Unionism, now castigated him as a secessionist.

Events took an even stranger turn in Frederick. The state legislature could not come to a decision. Hicks said in his address that he did not want Maryland to secede and he did not want Union troops to pass through the state; even a hand-delivered note from Virginia inviting Maryland to join the Confederacy was coldly received. The state senate resolved that it had no authority to decide the question of secession; and when the House of Delegates received a petition from Prince George's County demanding immediate secession, the house said it had no authority to decide such a matter. The legislature adjourned having resolved nothing.

But events were taken out of Hicks's, and all civilian, hands by the increasing presence and widening role of the Federal military after Lincoln suspended the writ of habeas corpus on 27 April. A Department of Maryland was created within the Union army. Union troops under Butler moved from Annapolis and Anne Arundel County to Baltimore on 13 May and began the suppression of all support for secession and the Confederate cause. During the next six months, martial law replaced civilian government as the city marshall, the four members of the Police Commission, the mayor, and several members of the city council were arrested. Prosecession newspapers were closed and their editors arrested, and property vacated by Marylanders who joined the Confederacy was confiscated. Union troops continued to occupy Annapolis and fanned out along the railroad and telegraph lines, encamping at switching points. They also occupied Cumberland, Williamsport, and other points along the Chesapeake & Ohio Canal, as well as Cockeysville and Havre de Grace to protect the railroads to York and Philadelphia. Anyone who suggested peace or outright secession was arrested, no matter his office or prestige, as the detention of former Governor Thomas G. Pratt, Judge Richard Henry Alvey of Hagerstown, U.S. Congressman Henry May, twenty-six state legislators, and both clerks of the two houses of the legislature proves.

Hicks could do nothing about this and his term was ending. The gubernatorial election in November 1861 brought about a realignment of civilian to military authority when Augustus W. Bradford, the candidate of the Union Party—hastily formed in the summer—defeated Democrat Benjamin C. Howard in an election controlled by the military. Although Hicks's term officially ended on 8 January 1862, Governor Bradford appointed Hicks to the U.S. Senate to replace James Alfred Pearce, who had died in office. Hicks himself was in declining health. He played but a small role in the U.S. Senate and displayed the same indecision that he had during the secession crisis: he supported President Lincoln even as he opposed establishing the Freedmen's Bureau in Maryland. He died on the middle ground of that dilemma in 1865.

—*Gary L. Browne*

See also Baltimore Riot; Bradford, Augustus W.; Habeas Corpus, Writ of (U.S.A.); Maryland.

For further reading:

Brugger, Robert J. *Maryland, A Middle Temperament: 1634–1980* (1988).

Radcliffe, George L. *Governor Thomas Hicks of Maryland and the Civil War* (1901).

White, Frank F., Jr. *The Governors of Maryland, 1777–1970* (1970).

HIGGINSON, THOMAS WENTWORTH
(1823–1911)
Union colonel

Thomas Wentworth Higginson was a Union colonel who commanded the 1st South Carolina Volunteers, the first unit of emancipated slaves to see combat in the Civil War. In the fall of 1862, Union general Rufus Saxton, in charge of the Department of the South, requested that Colonel Higginson take command of a regiment of freed slaves assembled at the Beaufort River in the Sea Islands area of South Carolina.

Higginson was an appropriate choice to lead the 1st South Carolina Volunteers. Born in 1823 into an academic family educated at Harvard, his formative years were strongly influenced by the liberal intellectual climate of the college. Higginson graduated from Harvard in 1841 at the age seventeen and eventually became a Unitarian minister. He joined the Boston Anti-Slavery Vigilance Committee and was arrested in the attempt to free Anthony Burns, an escaped slave who had been arrested in Boston under the Fugitive Slave Law of 1850. By the eve of the Civil War, Higginson had become a radical abolitionist and a strong supporter of the antislavery crusader John Brown. He even signed an appeal advocating the separation of the free states from the South.

Higginson once wrote that war was "brutal and disgusting" and, after the Civil War broke out, he initially declined to serve in the military because he was not sure if President Abraham Lincoln would take a strong stand against slavery. Nevertheless, Higginson possessed an adventuresome nature and soon proposed to Pennsylvania governor Andrew G. Curtin that a guerrilla force of Kansas antislavery veterans attack into Virginia from Pennsylvania.

Governor John A. Andrew of Massachusetts, however, believed that the plan was too risky and Higginson abandoned the idea. Andrew instead gave Higginson permission to begin recruiting in Massachusetts, and in August 1862, at age thirty-eight, he became a captain in the Massachusetts 51st Regiment. General Rufus Saxton, knowing Higginson's abolitionist views, decided in November 1862 to offer him command of the 1st South Carolina Volunteers. Higginson, who strongly favored the arming of black troops, departed for the Union base at Beaufort, South Carolina, to determine if the army was serious about the new regiment.

General Saxton had already employed some of the volunteers in an attack on Confederate salt works, and, as Howard Meyer points out, Higginson was favorably impressed when he visited their encampment. Higginson, who later described his experiences with black troops in his book *Army Life in a Black Regiment*, decided to resign his Massachusetts commission and take command of the new black unit. Higginson set high standards for the troops, treated them with dignity, and banned the use of racial epithets. Their first expedition, in January and February 1863, involved sailing southward to the St. Mary's River on the Georgia-Florida border and launching a raid up the river. The raid succeeded, and the volunteers successfully drove off a Confederate cavalry unit and captured prisoners and lumber supplies. They came under fire from Confederates along the river bluffs as they steamed back down, and one officer, Captain Clifton, was killed.

Higginson and the volunteers faced their next major operation when General Saxton directed them to participate in the occupation of Jacksonville, Florida, in March 1863. Union forces had already taken the city twice during the war but were unable to hold it. The

volunteers landed with other Union regiments and occupied the city, sporadically engaging Confederate forces operating in the surrounding countryside. In late March, however, Union commanders decided that the situation was too precarious and evacuated the volunteers and the other units. The volunteers then returned to South Carolina to serve as pickets for Port Royal. While at Port Royal, General Quincy Gillmore directed the volunteers to join in a raid up the nearby Edisto River, where they were to forage on rice plantations and destroy a strategic railway bridge. The Union raiders came under heavy attack, however, and were forced back down the river. A cannonball grazed Colonel Higginson's side during the action, leaving him feeling paralyzed.

Higginson, weakened by his wounds, left for Massachusetts to recover. He returned to Port Royal during the winter of 1863 and the spring of 1864, but his health was still poor. Nevertheless, Meyer notes, he campaigned vigorously against the War Department's decision to pay black soldiers at a lower rate than white soldiers. Finally, his weakened condition forced him to resign from the army in October 1864. After the war, Higginson became active in the causes of public school integration and women's rights. He died on 9 May 1911.

Colonel Thomas Wentworth Higginson is best known for his commitment to arming black troops during the Civil War. Under his leadership, the 1st South Carolina Volunteers helped dispel the myth that blacks could not be effective soldiers.

—*David A. Proctor*

See also Burns, Anthony; United States Colored Troops.
For further reading:
Cornish, Dudley Taylor. *The Sable Arm: Negro Troops in the Union Army, 1861–1865* (1966).
Higginson, Thomas Wentworth. *Army Life in a Black Regiment. With Notes and Biographical Introduction by John Hope Franklin* (1962).
Meyer, Howard. *Colonel of the Black Regiment: The Life of Thomas Wentworth Higginson* (1967).

HILL, ADAMS SHERMAN
(1833–1910)
Journalist

Born in Massachusetts, Adams Sherman Hill graduated from Harvard and Harvard Law School. Not finding the law to his liking, Hill entered the field of journalism and joined the staff of the *New York Tribune* in 1858. At the start of the Civil War, he was serving in the *Tribune's* Washington, D.C., office and during the war became the head of that office.

Hill discovered early in the war, however, that he was not suited to cover the military aspects of the war and did much better reporting about the politics of the

conflict. Evidence of this became all too apparent when he, like so many other reporters, accompanied Irvin McDowell's army toward Manassas Junction, Virginia, in July 1861. At Blackburn's Ford on 18 July, in one of the first skirmishes of what would be the First Bull Run campaign, Hill got too close to the action and had a bullet travel dangerously close to his head. The experience so unnerved him that he fled the field in terror and rode his horse all the way back to Washington. Other reporters made light of his performance for the remainder of the war.

Hill was able to overcome this incident and his rather quiet, bookish ways to become one of the most successful of the Washington correspondents. He was very methodical about finding sources in every government office, bureau, and in Congress. He used these sources to investigate every possible angle for a story before reporting to the *Tribune* readers. This approach sometimes put him into conflict with the paper's powerful and opinionated editor, Horace Greeley. Greeley expected his reporters to use their stories to advocate the editorial positions of the paper, whereas Hill believed in giving every possible side of a story and allowing the readers to come to their own conclusions. Even though Hill ran one of the most productive and efficient newsrooms in Washington, his constant conflict with Greeley brought about his resignation in December 1863.

Upon resigning from the *Tribune*, Hill, along with Henry Villard and Horace White of the *Chicago Tribune*, formed the news syndicate the Independent News Room to compete with the Associated Press of New York. While all three partners worked hard to make this news group a national leader in supplying news stories to smaller, regional papers, it did not succeed financially and was closed at the end of the war.

After the war, Hill remained in journalism for seven more years, supplying stories on the national politics of the day to numerous papers across the nation. He found such a life, however, less and less satisfying. Always of a more scholarly bent than most of his fellow journalists, he decided in 1872 to enter academia. He accepted a position as a professor of rhetoric in the English department of his alma mater Harvard. Returning to his home state, Hill spent the remainder of his working life in Cambridge, rising to the position of department chair of Harvard's English department. He became a nationally known expert on the subject of rhetoric. Hill died in retirement in Massachusetts.

—*David S. Heidler and Jeanne T. Heidler*

See also Newspapers; Villard, Henry.
For further reading:
Paine, Charles. *The Resistant Writer; Rhetoric as Immunity, 1850 to the Present* (1999).
Starr, Louis M. *Bohemian Brigade: Civil War Newsmen in Action* (1954; reprint, 1987).

HILL, AMBROSE POWELL
(1825–1865)
Confederate general

Born and raised in Culpepper County, Virginia, A. P. Hill earned a reputation as a hard fighter and loyal officer. Known to his friends as "Little Powell," Hill combined a fierce battlefield persona with a deep devotion to family so strong that not even war separated him from his wife. His first love, Mary Ellen Marcy, would never be his, despite their mutual affection. Her father did not think Hill merited his daughter's hand, and she eventually married George B. McClellan. In 1858 Kitty Morgan McClung, a sister of John Hunt Morgan, became the love of his life. Affectionately called "Dolly" by Hill, she married him in 1859, and during the Civil War she traveled with him in the field whenever possible.

Although counted among the illustrious West Point class of 1846, for health reasons Hill did not graduate until 1847. Hill's military service before the Civil War included garrison duty in the Mexican-American War, engagements with the Seminoles in Florida, and a taste of Indian fighting on the frontier. In March 1861, Hill resigned his commission in the U.S. Army and accepted a commission as a colonel in the 13th Virginia Infantry. After a brief stint in western Virginia and a reserve role at the battle of First Bull Run, Hill spent the winter of 1861–1862 with what would become the Army of Northern Virginia. Promoted to general in February 1862, Hill took command of a brigade in James Longstreet's division and saw his initial Civil War action in the spring of 1862.

Hill's first taste of battle came outside Williamsburg, Virginia, as General George McClellan's slow but persistent advance up the York peninsula pushed the Confederate army back toward Richmond. Assigned to the Confederate right, Hill's brigade successfully combined with that of Camdus Wilcox to drive back the Union forces under Joseph Hooker, enabling Longstreet's division to complete its withdrawal toward Richmond. Hill's brigade fought well under its new commander and demonstrated the discipline and tenacity that became characteristic of his commands.

On 26 May 1862, Hill received his commission as a major general and took command of a division in Longstreet's corps. Hill named his new unit the Light Division, a testament to its marching ability. However, contrary to its name, the division was far from light, with six brigades and nearly 14,000 men at full strength. Within a month, Hill took his new command into combat and began a year of almost constant fighting.

The Seven Days' battles (26 June–3 July 1862) revealed three traits that defined Hill as a commander throughout the war: a fondness and talent for battle, an impatience that clouded his judgment, and a tendency to fight with his superiors. Hill's division took part in three of the five battles of the Seven Days, as the Army of Northern Virginia under Robert E. Lee drove George McClellan's army off the York Peninsula. At Mechanicsville and Gaines' Mill, Hill attacked well-entrenched positions after waiting for support that never came. The prudent move would have been to wait, but Hill forged on, suffering heavy losses and accomplishing little. At Frayser's Farm, Hill combined with Longstreet to strike the retreating Federals, and his division performed well. However, McClellan's fleeing army successfully escaped to strong positions on Malvern Hill. Throughout the campaign Hill never hesitated to get in the fray. However, he and his division might have been better served had he resisted the urge to attack. The Seven Days' campaign produced a dispute with James Longstreet that resulted in Hill's transfer to Stonewall Jackson's corps.

On 9 August 1862, Hill's division came up late in the afternoon at the battle of Cedar Mountain. With Jackson's left flank collapsing, Hill threw three of his brigades into action, not only stopping the advance of General Nathaniel Banks, but counterattacking and driving the Federals back. Hill's ability to get his men into position quickly and strike a decisive blow rescued Jackson's corps from almost certain destruction. Again, however, Hill argued with his superior, Stonewall Jackson, in a dispute over the order and timing in which Hill's division had initially moved out of its encampment. The dispute saw Hill placed under arrest and, even after Hill's being restored to command, the bad blood lingered until Jackson's death in 1863.

After Cedar Mountain, Jackson's corps moved north as part of Lee's Second Bull Run campaign, and Hill's Light Division went with it. After successfully plundering Union supplies, the Light Division took up a position on the extreme left of Jackson's corps near Manassas Junction. The battle of Second Bull Run (29–30 August 1862) demonstrated Hill's ability to fight on the defensive. The Light Division repulsed repeated assaults by Union infantry on the 29th as Jackson waited for Longstreet to come up. At one point, Hill's men hurled rocks at the advancing Federals, having exhausted their ammunition supply. On 30 August, Longstreet struck the Federal left and, as the Union army retreated, Hill launched a successful counterattack.

Lee did not hesitate to exploit his latest victory and ordered his army across the Potomac into Maryland, directing Jackson to take the Federal arsenal at Harper's Ferry. He did so with ease and left Hill behind to mop up. On the morning of 17 September 1862, Hill received an order to move toward Sharpsburg. Lee had hastily reassembled his army along Antietam Creek to brace for an assault from the numerically superior Union army under his old nemesis, George McClellan. Departing at 7:00 A.M., Hill drove his division relentlessly for 17 miles, arriving in Sharpsburg at 2:30 in the afternoon and not a moment too soon. Lee's army had held out all day, but as the afternoon wore on, his right flank began to collapse. Just as the Union IX Corps under Ambrose Burnside appeared ready to rout Lee's army, up came Hill. Within minutes, Hill put his exhausted division into action, stopping the Federal advance. Once again, Hill's diligence had saved the Confederate army.

Confederate victories at Fredericksburg in December 1862 and Chancellorsville in May 1863 saw Hill's division amid the fighting, but did not provide an opportunity for Hill to shine. At Fredericksburg, Hill actually disappeared for hours and was thought to have been killed. At Chancellorsville, his men remained in reserve and did not take an active part in the fight until the second day. By that point Jackson had been mortally wounded, and Hill had also fallen. Although not seriously injured, his wound took him out of action.

With Jackson dead, Lee reorganized his army into three corps and Hill became the commander of III Corps. Despite the promotion, Hill's best days were now behind him. Ill-suited for corps command, his performance at Gettysburg in July 1863 reflected the general confusion that pervaded the Confederate army in Pennsylvania. Hill allowed two of his divisions under the command of Henry Heth and Dorsey Pender to stray in search of shoes. They wandered into the advance elements of Meade's army at Gettysburg, and by the end of the first day both units were so shot up that they had to be rested. Hill appeared to suffer from an unknown illness that, based on his jaundiced condition, may have been some type of liver disease. Plagued with a recurring bout of venereal disease acquired in his West Point days, Hill's health never allowed him to meet the demands of his new command.

In October 1863, Hill blundered at Bristoe Station, Virginia. Striking what he believed to be the tail of the retreating Union army, he led his corps into ambush, losing more than 1,000 men. The next spring, General Ulysses S. Grant launched his summer offensive in the Wilderness, moving on to Spotsylvania Court House, the North Anna River, Cold Harbor, and ultimately Petersburg. Hill, still sick, was virtually relieved as Lee took personal command of the army in the Wilderness. On sick leave at Spotsylvania, Hill returned for the North Anna and Cold Harbor battles without distinguishing himself. In June 1864, he moved with the rest of Lee's army to defend Petersburg.

Often a lifetime of preparation finds its purpose in a series of brief, defining moments. Such was the case for A. P. Hill. From 4 May 1862, when he led his brigade into battle at Williamsburg, until 2 May 1863, when he

went to the aid of a mortally wounded Stonewall Jackson at Chancellorsville, A. P. Hill performed as well as any commander on either side during the Civil War. Hill's units fought in every major engagement of the Army of Northern Virginia. Although Hill did not stop fighting after Chancellorsville, from Gettysburg until the end of the war he was not the same man.

Loyal to the end, and as tenacious as ever, Hill fell victim to the harsh realities of command: few possess the requisite skills to command a corps or an army, and Hill was not one of them. At the head of a brigade and later a division, Hill operated with the confidence of a man who had found his calling. Although sometimes prone to hasty action, Hill's willingness to seize the moment and make decisions under fire served the Confederacy well when anything short of decisive action spelled disaster. When Hill made mistakes, they always came from his willingness to act, never from his inability to move. Regrettably, his impetuous nature sometimes meant that men died needlessly. However, when nothing but the supreme effort would do, Hill's ability to bring up his division at the exact time and position in which it was needed delivered Lee and Jackson from the very brink of defeat. In the final analysis, perhaps Robert E. Lee best defined Hill's place by how he treated him in defeat. As Little Powell walked behind Lee in the wake of the disaster at Bristoe Station in October 1863 searching for words to explain the costly blunder, Lee remarked, "bury these poor men and let us say no more about it." Lee understood that one must take the bad with the good, and over the course of the war when "A. P. Hill came up," the good had far outweighed the bad.

Like any good commander, Hill bore the weight of his decisions during the war, but fate would not force him to grapple with the South's final defeat. His war and his life ended where he had spent most of both. In the midst of the fray, on 2 April 1865 at approximately 2:30 in the afternoon, A. P. Hill fell in battle, one week before the Army of Northern Virginia surrendered. Legend has it that, as both Lee and Jackson lay dying, they called for Hill to bring up his division. Regardless of its truth, the myth itself testifies to A. P. Hill's fighting spirit and dependability.

—*Mark A. Weitz*

See also Antietam, Battle of; Army of Northern Virginia; Cedar Mountain, Battle of; Gettysburg, Battle of; Harper's Ferry, (West) Virginia; Jackson, Thomas J.; Lee, Robert E.; Petersburg Campaign; Seven Days' Battles.

For further reading:
Freeman, Douglas Southall. *Lee's Lieutenants: A Study in Command* (1942–1944).
Hassler, William W. *A. P. Hill: Lee's Forgotten General* (1957).
Robertson, James I., Jr. *A. P. Hill: The Story of a Confederate Warrior* (1987).
Schenck, Martin. *Up Came Hill: The Story of the Light Division and Its Leaders* (1958).

HILL, BENJAMIN HARVEY
(1823–1882)
Confederate congressman

Born in Jasper County, Georgia, to John Hill and Sarah Parham Hill, Benjamin H. Hill graduated from the University of Georgia before entering the study of law. After his admission to the bar, he opened a practice in Troup County and quickly became one of the most respected attorneys in the state. Also active in state Whig Party politics, Hill established a reputation as a strong supporter of the Union and an excellent orator. Very vocal in his support of the Compromise of 1850, Hill won election the following year to the Georgia legislature. He served as a Whig in that body for two years, but the disintegration of that party in the South caused him to become a member of the American (Know-Nothing) Party in 1855. He served as an elector for Millard Fillmore, the Know-Nothing presidential candidate, in 1856, and he served in the Georgia senate in 1859.

With the election of 1860, the sectional crisis became more heated. Hill, still a strong opponent of secession (though he upheld the right of secession under the right circumstances), supported the presidential candidacy of John Bell of the Constitutional Union Party. With the defeat of his candidate and the election of Abraham Lincoln, Hill urged caution on his state and urged cooperation with the new government and a wait-and-see attitude regarding the Republicans and slavery.

Selected as a delegate to the Georgia secession convention, Hill urged the same course on that body. While still believing in the right of secession, Hill believed that the South's greatest hope of success as a nation was to secede as a body. When it became apparent, however, that the secessionists had the votes to pass an ordinance of session, Hill voted with the majority to present a united front. He was then chosen to represent the state at the meeting of seceded states in Montgomery, Alabama, that would organize the Confederate States of America.

In Montgomery, Hill was an active member of the Georgia delegation in a number of areas. He strongly supported the ultimate consensus of the convention to have the Confederate Constitution mirror as closely as possible the U.S. Constitution. As a former cooperationist, he had little quarrel with the constitution, only the manner in which it had been interpreted by some Northerners.

When time came to select the provisional president of the Confederacy, Hill initially supported the election of fellow Georgian Alexander Stephens. Many people found Hill's advocacy of Stephens to be ironic at best because the two men had not spoken since 1856. A feud had developed between the two over the election in that year that nearly led to a duel. During the Montgomery convention, however, Hill had come to the conclusion that Stephens's views on governmental power more closely reconciled with his own views than any of the other potential candidates. Intermediaries arranged for a rapprochement between the two antagonists and at least through the convention they seemed to have ended their disagreement. When it became apparent that Jefferson Davis would be selected provisional president, Hill enthusiastically supported Stephens's selection as provisional vice president.

After the formation of the Confederate States of America, Hill remained a member of the Provisional Congress. He was elected to a full term to the Confederate Senate in November 1861. In the Senate, Hill became an outspoken advocate for strong measures to win the war. From this position he never wavered and, as such, became a strong supporter of President Davis. Hill supported the institution of conscription even though many Georgians, including Vice President Stephens and Governor Joseph Brown opposed the measure. Hill's advocacy of conscription and his efforts to convince the people of Georgia of its necessity gained him the lasting enmity of Brown and Stephens, a situation that at least in the case of Stephens he was used to.

In the Senate, Hill also chaired the Judiciary Committee, where he was a strong advocate in his losing battle to create a Confederate Supreme Court. Also in his capacity as chair of that committee he supported Jefferson Davis's suspension of the writ of habeas corpus. This support and his advocacy of conscription were consistent with the view that strong measures were necessary to win the war. Because of his consistent endorsement of Davis's measures, Hill became a confidant of the Confederate president.

Toward the end of the war, Davis kept Hill informed about the deteriorating state of Confederate fortunes and the efforts (of which they both disapproved) of Vice President Stephens to reach a negotiated peace with the U.S. government. Like many high-ranking officials in the Confederacy, Hill was arrested with the fall of Richmond. After a brief imprisonment in New York, he was released to return to Georgia, where he resumed his law practice.

Initially Hill took no part in Georgia politics, satisfied to rebuild his practice and his finances. However, the passage of the Reconstruction Acts in 1867 brought him back to the stump. He traveled the state, speaking out against the measures that probably did a great deal to help his future political career once Reconstruction ended.

In 1875 Hill was elected to the U.S. House and in 1877 to the U.S. Senate. He spent the remainder of his life in that body. In both houses of Congress, Hill became known as a strong advocate of Southern rights and remained until his death in Atlanta in 1882 a passionate defender of Jefferson Davis.

—David S. Heidler and Jeanne T. Heidler

See also Congress, C.S.A.; Davis, Jefferson; Georgia; Stephens, Alexander.

For further reading:

Hill, Benjamin Harvey, Jr. *Senator Benjamin Harvey Hill of Georgia: His Life, Speeches, and Writing* (1891).

Pearce, Haywood Jefferson. *Benjamin H. Hill, Secession and Reconstruction* (1928).

HILL, DANIEL HARVEY
(1821–1889)
Confederate general

Daniel Harvey Hill was born in the York District of South Carolina on 12 July 1821. The family plantation quickly became a small farm out of necessity when his father died only four years later. Hill's mother and oldest brother were left to raise a family of eleven children, and the results were an austere upbringing during which a strong Presbyterian faith was instilled in young Harvey. His sense of morality was drawn along immovable lines, and he often lacked patience with those who failed to meet his own high standards.

In 1838, Hill entered the U.S. Military Academy. While at West Point, he worked hard to overcome a poor first year, finally finishing twenty-eighth in the class of 1842. During the Mexican-American War, Hill served with the 4th Artillery, a regiment that saw its heaviest action while used as infantry. In battle, he built a reputation for courage almost to the point of rash self-disregard, winning laurels at both Contreras and Chapultepec and finishing the war as a brevet major. His service won him the gratitude of the South Carolina legislature, which presented him an ornate sword for bravery.

After returning from Mexico, Hill met and courted Isabella Morrison, daughter of a prominent Presbyterian minister. On 2 November 1848, the couple married, and Hill resigned from the army to begin a second career in education. First at Virginia's Washington College, and then at North Carolina's Davidson College, he taught mathematics with a flair for the strong discipline that had marked both his upbringing and years at West Point. At Davidson, he led a somewhat disciplinary reformation in an attempt to end the raucous behavior that characterized many antebellum colleges and universities. During this period his regional loyalties became sharply apparent, peculiarly obvious in even the written problems of a mathematics text he authored, *Elements of Algebra*. Sectional politics and the threat of civil war may have influenced his decision in 1858 to accept a position as superintendent and professor of the newly established North Carolina Military Institute. The school's growing success was cut short when the attack on Fort Sumter in April 1861 drew both faculty and cadets into state service.

Hill volunteered his services to North Carolina and was placed in charge of a training camp near Raleigh. Shortly after, he was elected colonel of the 1st North Carolina Infantry, a regiment he led to its baptism at Big Bethel on 10 June 1861. Hill fought with the same tenacity he had shown in Mexico, quickly reaffirming his reputation for bravery under fire. He was rewarded with a Confederate brigadier general's commission and given a brigade in Joseph E. Johnston's army in northern Virginia after overseeing the strengthening of North Carolina's coastal defenses. In March 1862, he was made a division commander and promoted to major general in time to play a key role in the Confederate defense of the York Peninsula.

At the battle of Seven Pines, Hill attacked the Union left and achieved marked success before being ordered to withdraw to his previous lines. During the Seven Days' battles, his division distinguished itself at Gaines' Mill and endured the bloody repulse at Malvern Hill. Hill demonstrated heroic battlefield leadership during this vital campaign, but afterward, as newly appointed commander of the North Carolina district, he disappointed Robert E. Lee with a seeming lack of independent initiative. After Lee noted this in a letter to Jefferson Davis, Hill was ordered to return to the Army of Northern Virginia to command of his old division.

Hill was a prominent figure in the 1862 Maryland campaign, not only in the field but also in the mystery surrounding the loss of Lee's Special Order No. 191. The so-called Lost Order, addressed to Hill's headquarters, made its way into enemy hands and gave George B. McClellan a clear picture of Confederate intentions. Though Hill denied responsibility and later produced his copy of the order, the episode became a topic of postwar debate and has been a source of historical speculation ever since. When Lee split his army, Hill was left to defend the mountain passes that stood between McClellan and the separated Confederate divisions. At South Mountain, Hill stubbornly held Turner's and Fox's gaps against overwhelming numbers until Longstreet arrived with reinforcements late in the day. Three days later, at Antietam, Hill held the Confederate center along the Bloody Lane, a sunken road that was the scene of some of the war's most bitter fighting. After the retreat from Maryland, Hill bitterly criticized the campaign's costly errors in an official report that typified his increasingly outspoken personality. This habit likely built resentment in Lee, who after the war complained of Hill's propensity to "croak."

In February 1863, after attempting to resign for health reasons, Hill accepted command of Confederate troops in North Carolina. This responsibility was enlarged a few months later to include the defense of Richmond during Lee's Pennsylvania campaign. A half-hearted Union threat to the Confederate capital was easily

Daniel Harvey Hill (*Library of Congress*)

repulsed. In the wake of Gettysburg and Vicksburg, Hill was promoted to lieutenant general and given a corps command in Braxton Bragg's Army of Tennessee.

At Chickamauga, Hill battled his way through stout defenses to help collapse the Union line, but he also became embroiled in a controversy that forever tarnished his record. After failing to exploit the Confederate victory, Bragg responded to widespread criticism by unfairly blaming Hill and Leonidas Polk, eventually demanding their removal from corps command. Hill exacerbated the situation by becoming loudly critical of Bragg and was one of many general officers to petition for his replacement as commander of the Army of Tennessee. After more than a month of paralyzing intrigue, Jefferson Davis sided with Bragg, a personal friend, and acquiesced in Hill's removal. Hill left the Army of Tennessee as a victim of his own critical wit as well as unjust handling by both Davis and Bragg. Subsequently, Davis refused to forward Hill's nomination as a lieutenant general for senate confirmation, and Hill thus reverted to his previous rank in early 1864.

Despite failed attempts to clear his name, Hill unselfishly returned to service as a major general, first as a volunteer aide to P. G. T. Beauregard at Petersburg and later as commander of the District of Georgia. During the war's last days, he fought at Bentonville with the same tough determination that had marked his earlier efforts. After the war, he edited *The Land We Love*, a regional periodical dedicated to Southern culture and Confederate reminiscences, and later published a similar weekly paper, *The Southern Home*. In 1877, he returned to education as president of the Arkansas Industrial University (1877–1884) and then the Middle Georgia Military and Agricultural College (1885–1889). As an educator, he exhibited visionary leadership in a frustrating attempt to rebuild the South through agricultural and industrial education. Hill died of cancer on 24 September 1889 in Charlotte, North Carolina.

—*Ronald G. Machoian*

See also Antietam, Battle of; Big Bethel, Battle of; Bragg, Braxton; Chickamauga, Battle of; South Mountain, Battle of.
For further reading:
Avery, A. C. "Memorial Address on the Life and Character of Lieutenant General D. H. Hill." *Southern Historical Society Papers* (1893).
Bridges, Hal. "D. H. Hill and Higher Education in the New South." *The Arkansas Historical Quarterly* (1956).
———. *Lee's Maverick General: Daniel Harvey Hill* (1961; reprint, 1991).
Freeman, Douglas Southall. *Lee's Lieutenants: A Study in Command* (1942–1944).
Ratchford, J.W. *Some Reminiscences of Persons and Incidents of the Civil War* (1909; reprint, 1971).

HINDMAN, THOMAS CARMICHAEL
(1828–1868)
U.S. Congressman; Confederate general

Thomas C. Hindman was born in Knoxville, Tennessee, the son of Thomas C. Hindman, Sr., and Sallie Holt. Hindman's early years were spent in Knoxville, where his father was a merchant licensed to trade with the Cherokee Indians along the Tennessee and Alabama and Georgia border. Subsequently, the family moved to Jacksonville, Alabama, and President James Monroe appointed the elder Hindman U.S. agent to the Cherokee Nation. Young Tom Hindman attended school in New York and New Jersey, graduating in 1843 from the prestigious Lawrenceville Classical Institute in Lawrenceville, New Jersey. Joining his family in Ripley, Mississippi, where his father had purchased a large cotton plantation, he read law under the tutelage of Orlando Davis, a highly acclaimed local attorney, until the Mexican-American War interrupted his studies. He enlisted in the 2d Mississippi Infantry as second lieutenant.

Returning from duty in Mexico in 1848, Hindman resumed his studies and was admitted to the bar in 1851. He joined the local Sons of Temperance and became active in Democratic Party politics in the wake of discord over the Compromise of 1850. Stumping the state on behalf of Jefferson Davis's unsuccessful gubernatorial bid in 1851, Hindman earned the reputation as "a most noisy and unscrupulous advocate of…secession." He was elected to the Mississippi state legislature in 1851 and served one term.

In 1854 Hindman moved to Helena, Arkansas, where he practiced law and again became active in Democratic politics. Bursting on the scene like a whirlwind, he soon became the pivotal figure in the state. Beginning in 1855, he successively rescued the Democratic Party from the threat of the Know-Nothings and wrought a revolution by destroying the organization that had dominated Arkansas politics since the territorial era. Elected to Congress in 1858, he joined the ranks of the Southern fire-eaters championing immediate secession if the South did not receive guarantees that slavery would be protected where it existed and be allowed to expand into territories acquired as a result of the Mexican-American War. His role in the 1859 fight to elect a Speaker of the House acceptable to states' rights Southerners and his speech on Hinton Rowan Helper's *Impending Crisis of the South* made him a national figure. In the presidential election of 1860, he stumped for John C. Breckinridge. After Abraham Lincoln's election, Hindman advocated the immediate secession of Arkansas.

When Arkansas joined the Confederacy, Hindman raised a regiment at his own expense. He rose rapidly from colonel to major general and served as commander of the Trans-Mississippi District from 31 May to 20 August 1862. As the most able Confederate commander to serve in the Trans-Mississippi, stepping into a vacuum of leadership, he transformed Arkansas from a state virtually devoid of troops, weapons, and ammunition into an armed camp capable of supplying most of its own military needs. He raised an army of 18,000 effectives where none had existed when he arrived, stimulated home manufacturing, authorized guerrillas to operate behind enemy lines, made the cavalry useful rather than ornamental, and temporarily saved the Arkansas valley from capture by Union forces.

Vowing to "drive out the invader, or perish in the attempt," Hindman swept aside any obstacles in his path, instituting martial law, rigorously enforcing conscription, and imposing price controls. These actions spawned a howl of protest and resulted in the assignment of Theophilus Holmes to supersede him.

Undaunted, Hindman convinced Holmes to continue many of his policies and to let him launch an offensive against Union troops in northwest Arkansas. A stalemate at Prairie Grove (7 December 1862) ultimately led to Hindman's transfer to a new command east of the Mississippi River. He subsequently fought at Chickamauga, where he received a serious neck wound, and in the Atlanta campaign, where he was thrown from his horse and severely injured.

When the war ended, rather than surrender, Hindman went to Mexico, where he remained until just before the collapse of Maximilian's government.

Thomas C. Hindman (*National Archives*)

Unpardoned and disfranchised, he returned to Arkansas and soon became the leader of the Young Republican Party, which, although opposed to the Republican Party, was willing to accept the First Reconstruction Act as the basis for restoration of the Union. In September 1868, although still unable to vote or hold office and under indictment for treason, Hindman seemed on the verge of forging a biracial coalition capable of competing with the Republican Party. However, on 27 September an unknown assassin shot him as he sat quietly in his living room. He died the next morning, survived by his wife Mary Biscoe Hindman and four of their five children.

—*Diane Neal*

See also Arkansas; Fire-eaters; Holmes, Theophilus; Prairie Grove, Battle of.

For further reading:
Harrell, John M. "Arkansas." In *Confederate Military History* (1899).
Hindman, Biscoe. "Thomas Carmichael Hindman." *Confederate Veteran* (1930).
Nash, Charles Edward. *Biographical Sketches of General Pat Cleburne and General T. C. Hindman Together with Humorous Anecdotes and Reminiscences of the Late Civil War* (1895; reprint, 1977).
Neal, Diane, and Thomas W. Kremm. *The Lion of the South: General Thomas C. Hindman* (1993).

HINCKS, EDWARD WINSLOW
(1830–1894)
Union general

Born in Bucksport, Maine, Edward Winslow Hincks was educated locally and took up the printing trade as a young man. At nineteen he moved to Boston, where he became interested in state Democratic politics. In 1855 the relative newcomer was elected to the state legislature, where he met the influential Benjamin F. Butler. At the outbreak of the Civil War his political connections gained him commissions in both the state forces and the regular United States Army. In August 1861 Hincks combined both by accepting a colonel's commission and command of the 19th Massachusetts Infantry.

Hincks commanded his regiment at the debacle at Ball's Bluff in October 1861. His most notable action in that regard was to write a report that accused one of the New York regiments of retreating too early, a report that would anger many people and gain him a rebuke for being too hasty in his accusations.

He continued to command the 19th in the Peninsula campaign the following spring, being seriously wounded at the battle of White Oak Swamp on 30 June. Hincks recovered in time for the Maryland campaign, where he was again severely wounded at Antietam. He was unable to return to duty until the following year and then only as a staff officer. In November 1862, however, in recognition for his earlier service, Hincks was promoted to brigadier general. In spring 1863 Hincks served on court-martial duty and during the summer of that year served as the commander of the draft depot at Concord, New Hampshire.

Returning to active duty in the early spring of 1864, Hincks was placed temporarily in command of the Point Lookout, Maryland, prisoner-of-war camp. In late April he was ordered to report to his old political mentor, Benjamin F. Butler and the Army of the James. Upon arrival Hincks was given command of Butler's United States Colored Troops Division.

Because Hincks had not been in a field command since the United States had begun using African-American combat troops, he was unaware of the disparities in treatment of these soldiers compared with their white counterparts. He was outraged that his soldiers received inferior arms and equipment and yet faced much greater dangers than white soldiers. That these soldiers were seldom taken prisoner and were often shot while trying to surrender meant to Hincks that they should receive better weapons than white soldiers, not inferior ones. In fact, he wrote that African-American soldiers should be issued repeating rifles so that they would have a better chance of survival if faced by superior numbers.

During May 1864, while Ulysses S. Grant battled Robert E. Lee down toward Richmond, Hincks, under Butler on the York Peninsula, began looking at other approaches to Richmond. On 17 May he reported to Butler that there were very small numbers of Confederate soldiers in Petersburg and that taking the city south of Richmond might be beneficial. Again on 1 June he recommended to Butler that they attempt to take Petersburg. When an attack was finally made on 9 June, Butler did not organize the attack well enough for it to succeed. Hincks and his division participated in the 15 June assault on the Petersburg defenses.

On 8 July 1864 Hincks was ordered to Washington to aid in the defense of the city against Jubal Early's raid. Later in the summer he was put on court-martial duty and then sent to New York harbor to command the recruiting and draft depot there. In February 1865 he was relieved of that duty and sent to Harrisburg, Pennsylvania, to do similar tasks. In June 1865 he resigned his volunteer commission and reverted to the regular commission he had secured at the beginning of the war.

With the reorganization of the army in 1866 Hincks became the lieutenant colonel of the 40th Infantry. He served several years in the infantry, retiring at the rank of colonel in 1870. After leaving the army, Hincks worked as the governor of disabled soldiers' homes in Virginia and Wisconsin. He retired in 1880 to Massachusetts. He died on 14 February 1894 in Cambridge, Massachusetts.

—*David S. Heidler and Jeanne T. Heidler*

See also Ball's Bluff; Petersburg Campaign.
For further reading:
Farwell, Byron. *Ball's Bluff: A Small Battle and Its Long Shadow* (1990).
Glatthaar, Joseph T. *Forged in Battle: The Civil War Alliance of Black Soldiers and White Officers* (1990).

HINES, THOMAS H.
(1838–1898)
Confederate officer

Thomas H. Hines was a somewhat shadowy Confederate cavalryman famous for his thrilling escapes from Union captivity and his involvement in the Northwestern Conspiracy. He was born in the Windswept House in Woodbury, Kentucky, in 1838. Though a small man physically, for he was only 5 feet 9 inches tall and weighed 140 pounds as an adult, he was often called "the Confederacy's most dangerous man."

Hines joined the Confederate 9th Kentucky Cavalry, later known as Morgan's Raiders, which was led by the "Thunderbolt of the Confederacy," John Hunt Morgan. With the rank of captain, Hines became one of Morgan's ablest raiders, often appearing in the misty fog of morning and attacking unsuspecting Union forces. He led successful raids in Kentucky and Tennessee to burn and loot and then ride away. He often disappeared into Union territory to make secret contacts with the underground anti-Union group whose members were known as Copperheads.

In June 1863 Hines was put in charge of a "convalescent camp" in Clinton County, Kentucky, for Morgan's spent horses. Bored with this duty, Hines petitioned Morgan for permission to scout north of the Cumberland River. With Morgan's blessing, Hines started on a raid in Kentucky that had him destroying Federal stores, robbing Federal payroll trains, and collecting plunder. Thinking he could rouse Copperheads in southern Indiana and acting on his own youthful exuberance, he and a handful of Confederates went on a horse-stealing expedition aimed at Newburg, Indiana. This foray, however, accomplished little more than to provoke the Indiana militia into an aggressive pursuit of Hines and his little band until they escaped back across the Ohio River into Kentucky.

In July 1863 Hines joined his leader, Morgan, on a raid through southern Indiana and Ohio that became famously known as Morgan's Raid. Although the band looted and plundered its way through territory thought to contain widespread Confederate sympathy, Morgan and his men found little support and were unceremoniously chased out of the area, finally falling to capture near Salinville, Ohio. Other than stealing some horses, general plundering, and destroying railroad facilities, Morgan accomplished little, aside from throwing Indiana and adjacent states into a panic and mangling his own force.

Authorities intended to confine Hines, along with Morgan and other officers, in the State Penitentiary Building in Columbus, Ohio, for the duration of the war, but Hines planned an ingenious breakout. The prisoners tunneled out of their cell block, scaled an outer wall, and escaped back to Kentucky.

After returning to Kentucky, Hines accompanied Morgan on a trip to Richmond, where he received a new assignment. Working under direct orders from Confederate secretary of state James A. Seddon, Hines was to proceed to Canada and join Confederate agent James P. Holcombe in collecting all the Confederate soldiers in Canada, most of whom were escaped prisoners, to assist their return to the South. He received bales of cotton to finance his activities. It was upon his return journey from Canada through Chicago that Hines became involved in the so-called Northwestern Conspiracy, an insurrectionary scheme allegedly proposed by Copperheads to free Southern prisoners of war and take the northwestern states out of the Union. Hines soon realized he was dealing with politicians, not revolutionaries, and the plan fell apart. By that time, however, Union spies within the Copperhead movement had identified him, and with a $100,000 price on his head, Hines elected to depart for Canada. He remained there, studying law until 1867.

After 1867 Hines moved to Bowling Green, Kentucky, to practice law. He eventually became a newspaper editor and later a county judge. He advanced to the Kentucky Court of Appeals, the state's highest court, in 1878 and became the chief justice in 1884. Hines died in Frankfort, Kentucky, in 1898, after practicing law in Frankfort for the last nine years of his life.

—Ron Hamilton

See also Copperheads; Covert Activities, C.S.A.; Morgan's Raids.

For further reading:
Duke, Basil W. *History of Morgan's Cavalry* (1867).
Fesler, Mayo. "Secret Political Societies in the North during the Civil War." *Indiana Magazine of History* (1918).
Gray, Wood. *The Hidden Civil War: The Story of the Copperheads* (1964).
Klement, Frank L. *Dark Lanterns: Secret Political Societies, Conspiracies, and Treason Trials in the Civil War* (1984).
Tredway, G. R. *Democratic Opposition to the Lincoln Administration in Indiana* (1973).

HITCHCOCK, ETHAN ALLEN
(1798–1870)
Union general

Born in Vergennes, Vermont, grandson of Revolutionary War officer Ethan Allen, Ethan Allen Hitchcock graduated from the U.S. Military Academy in the class of 1817. As an infantry officer, Hitchcock served at a variety of frontier posts and in numerous frontier conflicts. Returning to West Point from the West, Hitchcock served a stint as the commandant of cadets. He next fought in the Second Seminole War, was involved in Indian removal in the Southeast, and served in the Pacific Northwest. In the meantime Hitchcock had become one of the experts on infantry drill in the army. In the Mexican-American War, Hitchcock was inspector general of the army as it marched on Mexico City. After the war, he was stationed in California. He resigned from the army in 1855 when Secretary of War Jefferson Davis refused to extend a leave of absence even though it was for health reasons.

Before the Civil War, Hitchcock lived in St. Louis, Missouri, where he spent much of his time writing about literary subjects. He had cultivated a strong interest in literature while in the army and had found time to write commentary on some of his favorite works. Once out of the army and with more time, he published some of his commentaries on the works of Shakespeare and other authors. He also developed an interest in spiritualism and the occult.

Accounts vary of how Hitchcock returned to service in the Civil War. Some claim that he was summoned by the Lincoln administration and that he reluctantly went to the

Ethan Allen Hitchcock (*Library of Congress*)

during the Peninsula campaign that he reportedly offered (probably without Lincoln's knowledge) command of the Army of the Potomac to Hitchcock. Then sixty-four, Hitchcock realized, and everyone since has agreed, that his acceptance would have been a disaster. Stanton did send Hitchcock to Fort Monroe, Virginia, in April 1862 to report on McClellan's progress up the York Peninsula. During May 1862, Hitchcock temporarily acted as the military governor of Washington, D.C.

Though he would continue to fill various jobs for Stanton, Hitchcock's service on the War Board ended when it was supplanted in July 1862 by Henry W. Halleck's appointment as general-in-chief. In November 1862, Hitchcock found the calling that would be his primary occupation for the remainder of the war and beyond; he was appointed commissioner for the exchange of prisoners. Hitchcock handled the complicated duties of this position with skill and efficiency, traveling throughout the United States and dealing with his own agents, prisoner-of-war camps, and Confederate commissioners. Meanwhile, Stanton continued to use him for other jobs. In December 1862, Hitchcock was one of the hand-picked officers to sit on the Fitz John Porter court-martial. In the same month, he took a seat on and would eventually preside over a board to amend or modify the Articles of War. The panel completed and published its work in April 1863. Hitchcock's job concerning prisoner exchanges, however, took the lion's share of his time and continued even after the war was over. Because so many Union prisoners returned disabled or with claims against the government (such as for lost property), the bureaucracy had to expand to administer these tasks. Consequently, in November 1865 Hitchcock became the commissary general of prisoners. He held this position until October 1867, when he was finally mustered out of federal service.

In retirement Hitchcock lived first in Charleston, South Carolina, and then in Sparta, Georgia. He devoted his final years to his literary pursuits, publishing several works of literary criticism and editing his diary. He died in Sparta on 5 August 1870.

—*David S. Heidler and Jeanne T. Heidler*

See also Prisoner Exchanges; Prisoners of War.
For further reading:
Hitchcock, Ethan Allen. *Fifty Years in Camp and Field; Diary of Major-General Ethan Allen Hitchcock, U.S.A.* (1909).

capital. Others state that Hitchcock traveled uninvited to Washington to offer his military expertise to the government, and his presence posed a problem for Lincoln. Hitchcock's age, health, and eccentricities may have caused the government to hesitate. Apparently at the insistence of retired General Winfield Scott and because of requests from other officers—Henry W. Halleck in the West wanted Hitchcock made a major general of volunteers and sent to him to solve the problem of numerous brigadier generals at the same date of rank—Hitchcock was made a major general of volunteers in February 1862.

Whatever the case, when Lincoln reorganized the army in March 1862 and relieved McClellan as general-in-chief, Hitchcock became the head of the president's innovative War Board. The board consisted of the heads of the army bureaus with Hitchcock essentially as its chair. It was supposed to take the place of a general-in-chief and is occasionally described as the forerunner of the modern joint chiefs of staff. The War Board was never that well-defined, however, and Hitchcock's role on it was ambiguous. Officially he was placed on special duty under the immediate command of Secretary of War Edwin Stanton, who had already offered him the post of adjutant general and chief of the ordnance bureau. In March 1862, Stanton was so frustrated with McClellan's slow progress

HODGERS, JENNIE
(1844–1915)
Union soldier

Jennie Hodgers was born poor in Ireland in 1844, immigrating to the United States as a child and settling with family in Belvidere, Illinois. Some years before the Civil War broke out Hodgers seems to have assumed a male identity, along with the pseudonym Albert D. J. Cashier, probably in connection with a job that her uncle found for her when she first arrived in the shoe factory where he worked. By the time the Civil War erupted, Hodgers was well accustomed to masquerading as a male. Having been raised in a sheepherding family, she was hardly a stranger to the laborious outdoor life that characterized nineteenth-century military service. Apparently content with the independence and financial self-sufficiency she had cultivated since her arrival in America, in August 1862 Hodgers (as Cashier) enlisted in the 95th Illinois Infantry Volunteers, with which she served for the duration of the war.

Active in the Western theater, Hodgers's "fighting 95th" regiment saw battle repeatedly, primarily in Mississippi and Tennessee. Hodgers successfully concealed her true identity, doing her share of the fighting while drawing as little attention to herself as possible. In June 1863 Hodgers came close to being discovered when she developed chronic diarrhea and was hospitalized briefly. Somehow she persuaded the medical personnel on hand to release her, which allowed her to avoid the sort of careful scrutiny that might have revealed her sex. Instead, Hodgers recovered and resumed her place in the line, where she continued to prove herself a worthy and dependable soldier. Decades later her former comrades in arms were amazed to discover that Cashier was a woman, though they recalled being struck by her diminutive size (five feet tall, and slender) and her shyness.

After the war Hodgers returned to Illinois, to the small community of Saunemin. Unlike most women soldiers of the Civil War, Hodgers continued her life as a male, working as a handyman and general laborer, for almost half a century. In the 1890s Cashier asserted "his" status as a Civil War veteran by joining the Grand Army of the Republic and applying successfully for a Federal veteran's pension. Only in 1911 did Hodgers's true identity come to light, when she broke her leg and was forced to undergo the sort of physical examination that she had avoided for so long. Her sex was revealed, at first only to a few close friends, but gradually to a wider and wider audience of stunned community members, and finally to the Federal government and the pension bureau. Hodgers—who shortly after her accident had been placed for long-term care in the Soldiers and Sailors home in Quincy, Illinois—endured a humiliating transfer to the Hospital for the Insane in Watertown. She lived there for about eighteen months, during which time she actively rebelled against the regulation that she don dresses by pinning her skirts together between her legs to simulate trousers.

Hodgers died in October 1915 and was buried in her soldier's uniform with full military honors by members of her G. A. R. local, who now knew that she was a woman but who believed nevertheless that her courageous years of service as a common soldier of the Union had earned her such a tribute.

—*Elizabeth D. Leonard*

See also Women.
For further reading:
Clausius, Gerhard. "The Little Soldier of the 95th: Albert D. J. Cashier." *Journal of the Illinois State Historical Society* (1958).
Leonard, Elizabeth D. *All the Daring of the Soldier: Women of the Civil War Armies* (1999).
Wheelwright, Julie. *Amazons and Military Maids: Women Who Dressed as Men in the Pursuit of Life, Liberty and Happiness* (1989).

HOFFMAN, WILLIAM
(1808–1884)
Union commissary general of prisoners

William Hoffman began the Civil War as a lieutenant colonel in the 8th Infantry. He became a prisoner of war when David E. Twiggs surrendered the Union command at San Antonio, Texas, on 18 February 1861. Hoffman remained inactive until his formal exchange on 27 August 1862, receiving a promotion to colonel on 25 April 1862 while awaiting his exchange.

Born in New York, Hoffman graduated from West Point as part of Robert E. Lee's class of 1829. No stranger to combat, Hoffman served in the regular infantry for almost 30 years. He fought against the Seminoles and the Indians in the West. During the Mexican-American War, Hoffman was wounded at Churubusco and received two brevet promotions.

Despite his combat experience and infantry training William Hoffman's contribution to the war did not come from his exploits on the battlefield. It was in his administrative capacity as commissary general of prisoners that Hoffman made his mark. Appointed almost immediately after his exchange in 1862, Hoffman served as the head of the Union prisoner-of-war system for the duration of the war. Breveted a general for his war service and a major general for his supervision of prisoners, Hoffman became a central figure in the evolution of the Union's policy for the treatment of prisoners of war and deserters.

When the war began, the Union was unprepared for the administrative problems created by the large number of Confederate prisoners and deserters. Approximately 104,000 Confederate soldiers deserted with almost one-third surrendering to the Union army. The volume of prisoners of war far exceeded that number. A prisoner exchange system operated from 1862 until the fall of 1863, when it broke down for a variety of reasons. Thereafter, Hoffman faced the arduous task of providing facilities, staff, and support for a virtual archipelago of Union prisons. Despite Hoffman's best efforts, Union prisons throughout the war were plagued with over-

General William Hoffman and staff at the Commissary office, Washington, D.C., ca. 1865 (*Library of Congress*)

crowding, food shortages, and disease. Unable to release Confederates under the parole system, Hoffman helped create another avenue for releasing Confederate soldiers in Union custody. Not only did this system lessen the strain on the prison facilities, but it provided both a source of recruitment for the Union army and a method for allowing truly repentant Confederate soldiers to swear their allegiance to the Union and secure their freedom.

As the fighting increased in the spring of 1862, the numbers of prisoners grew, as did the frequency of Confederate desertion. From the outset, one of the war's primary goals was the reconstruction of the Union. Part of the this process required restoring Southerners to the status of full-fledged U.S. citizens. In 1862, Confederate prisoners of war began refusing to be exchanged, insisting that if exchanged they would not return home. Many professed a willingness to swear an oath of allegiance to the Union and either to remain North or return home if the Union controlled the areas where they lived.

Working with President Lincoln, Secretary of War Edwin Stanton, Union military commanders, and prison commandants, Hoffman helped develop a procedure allowing prisoners of war and deserters to swear allegiance to the United States and secure their release. As the war progressed, release requests from Union officials, Confederate soldiers, and Southern civilians came to Hoffman's office for review and evaluation. Hoffman came to believe that prisoners and deserters were different. Unlike deserters, prisoners had not voluntarily left the Confederate service and, if allowed to swear the oath, they might return to their units to fight again. The Union could not afford to subsidize rebellion by returning able-bodied men to the Confederate service. Deserters, however, had already renounced their military obligation and risked severe punishment by returning to their units. Hoffman believed that deserters presented an opportunity to "reconstruct" Rebel soldiers and undermine the Confederate war effort.

Eventually, prisoners of war could be released only after each case was reviewed by Hoffman's office and approved by Stanton. Deserters could be released and allowed to take the oath of allegiance if the military field commanders verified the deserter's story and confirmed that he was not a spy. Eventually the Union encouraged desertion and offered inducements, including transportation home. Prisoner-of-war releases gradually disappeared as Hoffman narrowed the conditions for allowing loyal Confederate soldiers to take the oath.

Hoffman retired from the army in 1870 as a colonel. At the time of his retirement, he was not assigned to any particular duty station. Although far from the Civil War battlefields, he played a significant role within the Union program to undermine the Confederate war effort.

—*Mark A. Weitz*

See also Desertion; Prisoner Exchanges; Prisoner Paroles; Prisoners of War; Prisons, U.S.A.; Twiggs, David E.
For further reading:
Weitz, Mark A. "Preparing for the Prodigal Son: The Development of the Union Desertion Policy during the Civil War." *Civil War History* (1999).

HOGE, JANE BLAIKIE
(1811–1890)

U.S. Sanitary Commission agent

Jane Hoge was fifty, and a veteran of thirty years of marriage and thirteen pregnancies, when she joined Mary Livermore in the relief of Union soldiers in the Western theater. The two had met in church charity work in Chicago in the 1850s and maintained a close friendship throughout the war. Even before Chicago's Northwestern Sanitary Commission opened its doors in the fall of 1861, Hoge went to work at Camp Douglas caring for the sick comrades of one of her soldier sons. As mainstays of the Chicago office, along with Eliza Chappell Porter, Livermore and Hoge initially distributed supplies donated by local aid societies to those who would see action at Forts Henry and Donelson and at Pittsburg Landing (Shiloh). Before the end of 1861, Army Nursing Superintendent Dorothea Dix, overwhelmed with appointments in the Eastern theater, authorized them to hire and place female nurses in western hospitals. By early summer 1862, they had visited hospitals in Cairo, Mound City, and St. Louis, convinced that they needed to launch a grass roots effort to organize contributors and contributions all over the northwest. Before their enterprise was finished, their office had sent over 77,000 boxes of food, clothing, and medical supplies to Federal soldiers in the west.

Tireless fundraisers, Livermore and Hoge also teamed up to plan the Commission's first Sanitary Fair in the fall of 1863. Selling everything from a contraband's homespun sheet to President Lincoln's original manuscript of the Emancipation Proclamation, the fair was so successful that it exceeded the expectations of the Commission's male officers and its projected income of $25,000 by a factor of four. The Chicago fair became the model for all subsequent wartime fundraisers and was for Hoge her most momentous wartime achievement. Fully one-third of her 1867 memoir, *The Boys in Blue*, consists of detailed descriptions of the Chicago fair and the eastern copies it spawned.

Though ensconced in war philanthropy, Hoge was seldom distant from the lives of soldiers in the field. During a mission to Vicksburg early in 1863, her ship made a side trip to observe Confederate fortifications on Arkansas' White River, where she became a de facto nurse for two weeks. After visiting Grant's waterlogged troops at Young's Point along the Mississippi, Hoge returned to Chicago intent on shipping vegetables South to discourage an outbreak of scurvy. When the siege of Vicksburg began in June, Hoge was back at the front, nursing the gravely wounded. There she survived a tornado and saved an Ohio officer's life by stanching a postoperative hemorrhage of his leg.

Part of a prewar generation of well-to-do, reform-minded women, Hoge moved seamlessly in and out of war work. In the 1870s she became an advocate for women's education, helping found a Chicago-area women's college, and volunteered her time to the Presbyterian Church's foreign mission program. Even though Hoge was from a prominent Philadelphia family and lived comfortably throughout most of her marriage to merchant Abraham Hoge, reverses in the late 1870s prompted her to seek post office work. Unsuccessful at landing a job, Hoge spent the last decade of her life supported by her children. She died in Chicago in 1890, just a few months after her husband.

—*Jane E. Schultz*

See also Livermore, Mary Ashton Rice; Nurses; United States Sanitary Commission; Women.

For further reading:
Brockett, Linus P., and Mary C. Vaughan. *Woman's Work in the Civil War* (1867).
Dannett, Sylvia G. L. *Noble Women of the North* (1959).
Hoge, Jane Blaikie. *The Boys in Blue: Or, Heroes of the "Rank and File"* (1867).
Livermore, Mary A. *My Story of the War* (1887; reprint 1995).
Moore, Frank. *Women of the War: Their Heroism and Self-Sacrifice* (1866).

HOKE, ROBERT FREDERICK
(1837–1912)
Confederate general

Robert Frederick Hoke, the youngest major general in the Confederate army, was born in Lincolnton, North Carolina, to Michael and Francis Burton Hoke. Michael Hoke, an attorney, died of malaria a few months after he lost the race for governor of North Carolina in 1844. Robert Hoke graduated from the Kentucky Military Academy in 1854 and returned home to run the family's cotton mill, iron works, and other properties.

Hoke joined the 1st North Carolina Volunteers as a second lieutenant on 22 April 1861. He saw his first action at Big Bethel on 10 June 1861. Hoke rose to the rank of major, transferred to the 33d North Carolina, and was then promoted to lieutenant colonel. At the battle of New Bern on 14 March 1862, Hoke's leadership was one of the few bright spots in a catastrophic Confederate defeat. Hoke commanded his regiment after Colonel C. M. Avery was captured and saved most of his regiment after leading a stubborn defense of the Confederate right.

Hoke commanded the 33d at Hanover Court House, the Seven Days' battles, Second Bull Run, and Antietam. When Avery returned, Hoke was sent as colonel to command the 21st North Carolina, which was part of Brigadier General Isaac R. Trimble's brigade. Because Trimble had been wounded at Second Manassas, Hoke, as ranking colonel, took temporary command of his brigade. At Fredericksburg, Hoke helped plug a dangerous gap in the Confederate right and led a decisive charge. He was promoted to brigadier general after the battle and given command of a reconstituted Trimble brigade.

Hoke was badly wounded while leading a charge on 4 May 1863 at Salem Church during the Chancellorsville campaign. Despite his shoulder's being smashed by a minié ball, he led his men from horseback until he collapsed from loss of blood. Hoke's brigade performed well at Gettysburg, but Hoke was unable to rejoin them for over three months.

Hoke was sent to North Carolina in the autumn of 1863, where he led a sweep of some of the Piedmont

counties to round up deserters and outlaws. Early in 1864, on instructions from President Jefferson Davis, Hoke drew up plans for an attack on New Bern; however, Davis felt that Hoke was too junior in rank and entrusted command to Major General George Pickett. Despite some initial success, Pickett's efforts failed and New Bern remained in enemy hands.

Hoke was not blamed for the failure of Pickett's attack; in fact, he was given command of Pickett's army when that general returned to Virginia. Hoke's next action was an attack on the Union forces at Plymouth, North Carolina, with the cooperation of the navy's ironclad ram *Albemarle*. Plymouth and its 3,000 troops surrendered to Hoke on 20 April 1864. It was the greatest Confederate victory in North Carolina. Hoke quickly moved against New Bern, but was ordered to break off his operations and join Beauregard's forces near Petersburg.

Promoted to major general just before his twenty-seventh birthday for his victory at Plymouth, Hoke commanded a division at Drewry's Bluff, Cold Harbor, and at Petersburg. Hoke's career as a division commander was less brilliant than his time as a brigadier. Some historians see him as uncooperative and too cautious. However, both Lee and Hoke's men seemed to have kept their confidence in him.

In December 1864, Hoke's division was sent to North Carolina. They fought in defense of Fort Fisher and Wilmington in January, at Southwest Creek on 8 March, and at Bentonville on 19–21 March. Hoke surrendered with Joseph E. Johnston's forces at Bennett's Farmhouse, near Durham, on 26 April 1865.

Hoke married Lydia Van Wyck, a niece of Texas rancher Samuel Maverick, on 7 January 1869. Among their children was Dr. Michael Hoke (1874–1944), founder of the Shriner's Hospitals. After the war, Hoke was held in great esteem by his home state. North Carolina named Hoke County in his honor in 1911. Always reluctant to write or talk about his wartime experiences, he also refused many opportunities to run for political office. He spent his postwar years involved in mining, railroads, and insurance and in running his Lithia Springs Hotel in Lincolnton. Late in life, his white hair and beard gave him a startling resemblance to Robert E. Lee. Hoke died in 1912 and was buried in Raleigh.

—*David A. Norris*

See also New Bern, Battle of; North Carolina; Plymouth, Battle of; Salem Church, Battle of.

For further reading:
Barefoot, Daniel W. *General Robert F. Hoke: Lee's Modest Warrior* (1996).
Barrett, John G. *The Civil War in North Carolina* (1963).
Clark, Walter, ed. *Histories of the Several Regiments and Battalions from North Carolina in the Great War, 1861–1865* (1901).

HOLCOMBE, JAMES PHILEMON
(1820–1883)
Confederate congressman and agent

Born to William James Holcombe and Ann Eliza Clayton Holcombe in Lynchburg, Virginia, James Philemon Holcombe was educated at Yale University and the University of Virginia, studying law at the latter. After briefly practicing law in Virginia, Holcombe moved to Cincinnati, Ohio. While living in Ohio, along with practicing law, Holcombe wrote extensively on legal and constitutional topics. He moved back to Virginia after a few years, accepting a faculty position at the University of Virginia Law School.

Holcombe used his position as a forum for more publications, though in Virginia he wrote more on topics such as states' rights and the legality of slavery. Holcombe's strong states' rights and pro-slavery views were somewhat ironic given that his father had some years before freed the family slaves and moved to Indiana to reside in a free state.

The younger Holcombe's views led him to seek election to the Virginia secession convention in early 1861. Once elected, he proved a tireless advocate for the state's withdrawal from the union. His goal achieved after Abraham Lincoln's call for volunteers on 15 April 1861, Holcombe served on the state commission that negotiated with Confederate vice president Alexander Stephens for Virginia's entry into the Confederacy. The Virginia secession convention ratified the agreement on 25 April 1861.

In the fall of 1861, Holcombe was elected to the Confederate House of Representatives and served one term as a member of that body. During that time, he was a member of the Judiciary Committee but otherwise does not appear to have been an especially active house member. After the end of his term in February 1864, he received an appointment from Confederate president Jefferson Davis to serve as a Confederate commissioner to Canada. His first assignment was to negotiate with the British government in Canada over the fate of a U.S. vessel, the *Chesapeake*. The *Chesapeake* had been taken by a Southern commerce raider, but apparently the Southern ship did not have the proper papers to operate as a raider. Before Holcombe arrived in Canada the *Chesapeake* had been released.

With this duty removed, Holcombe worked for the next several months with Confederate agents Clement Clay and Jacob Thompson to secure the repatriation of Confederate soldiers who had escaped to Canada from federal prisons. In addition to this task, the Confederate commissioners also were expected to gauge the extent of pro-Confederate sympathy in Canada and the degree of war weariness in the United States along the Canadian border.

The three Confederates began a correspondence with

New York newspaper editor Horace Greeley intimating to him that they had the power to open peace negotiations with the Union but apparently with the primary purpose of encouraging a peace movement in the United States. Holcombe and his compatriots also encouraged Copperhead antiwar activity in the upper Midwest.

After the war ended, Holcombe returned to Virginia, where he founded and ran a boys' boarding school for a few years before retiring to Capron Springs, West Virginia. He died there and was buried in Lynchburg.

—*David S. Heidler and Jeanne T. Heidler*

See also Clay, Clement; Copperheads; Greeley, Horace; Peace Movements; Thompson, Jacob.

For further reading:

Headley, J. W. *Confederate Operations in Canada and New York* (1906).

Kirkland, Edward Chase. *The Peacemakers of 1864* (1927).

Tidwell, William A., James O. Hall, and David Winfred Gaddy. *Come Retribution; The Confederate Secret Service and the Assassination of Lincoln* (1988).

HOLDEN, WILLIAM WOODS
(1818–1892)
Southern journalist

As editor of the Raleigh *North Carolina Standard*, Holden led the Democratic Party to dominance in the state during the 1850s. At the end of the decade, however, he lost out to Governor John W. Ellis for control of the party. When Ellis and his faction took a strong Southern rights stance in the presidential contest of 1860, Holden, who had earlier supported the theory of secession, swung toward a moderate position though supporting John C. Breckinridge for president.

After Lincoln's election, Holden used the columns of the *Standard* to proclaim a "watch and wait" policy toward the new president. To counter the drive for the state's secession after South Carolina left the Union, Holden almost single-handedly organized in early 1861 the Constitutional Union Party. In a 28 February election, Holden's party by a narrow margin defeated a call for a state convention that might have taken North Carolina out of the Union.

Holden's watch-and-wait policy ended when fighting broke out in Charleston harbor on 12 April, followed immediately by Lincoln's call for troops to suppress the insurrection in the lower South. Holden denounced Lincoln's "gross usurpation" of power and appealed to North Carolinians to unite in an armed crusade to prevent the state from being "polluted by the tread of armed men sent to make war on the Confederate States." He served as a delegate to the state convention that on 20 May unanimously took North Carolina out of the Union and into the Confederacy. Holden later wrote that his vote for dissolving North Carolina's ties with the Union "was the saddest and most reluctant act of his life."

Like other editors and political leaders, Holden called for a moratorium on party politics while the war raged. However, he soon found fault with the state Democratic administration. He criticized Governor Ellis and his successor, Henry T. Clark (Ellis died in July 1861), for their failure to prepare adequately for coastal defense and for their refusal to appoint former Unionists to state military positions. Holden organized a caucus of "conservative" delegates in the state convention, which continued to meet into 1862. The purpose of these conservatives, or old Unionists, was to oppose the secession Democrats, or "Destructives" as Holden labeled them, who controlled not only the state executive branch but also the legislature.

When Roanoke Island, New Bern, and other coastal areas fell to Federal forces in early 1862, Holden unleashed a wave of criticism against the Jefferson Davis administration in Richmond, associating it with the Destructives in the state government. He charged that President Davis in his determination to defend Virginia had done nothing to protect North Carolina from the enemy and had discriminated against the state in appointments to both military and civil positions. When the Confederate Congress passed the first Conscription Act in April 1862, Holden denounced it as an unconstitutional violation of individual rights; however, he did not advocate resistance to it.

Without admitting that he had contributed to the renewal of partisan conflict in North Carolina, Holden during the spring of 1862 organized the Conservative Party and secured the nomination of Colonel Zebulon B. Vance to oppose the secession Democratic or "Confederate" candidate for governor in August. Primarily as a result of Holden's efforts through the *Standard's* columns, the Conservatives swept to victory in the gubernatorial election and won control of the General Assembly. Ironically, a majority of the Conservatives were old Whigs, including Governor Vance, whom Holden had bitterly opposed during the antebellum period. These Conservatives never completely trusted Holden, and they were soon at odds with him. Holden's confrontational style also did not suit their moderate approach to wartime issues. His persistent attacks on old secessionists and his unrelenting criticism of Confederate policies particularly upset Vance and Senator William A. Graham. Many staunch Confederates, including General Robert E. Lee, charged, with some justification, that Holden's shrill editorials gave aid and comfort to the enemy and encouraged deserters from the army. Though Holden vehemently denied that he was disloyal to the cause, President Lincoln and other Northern leaders wishfully believed that the Raleigh editor's vilification of the Davis government was clear evidence of growing Unionism in the state.

In mid-1863 Holden called for peace rallies in the state to demand that the Confederate government initiate negotiations to end the war. He advocated a peace that would "arrest this awful evil" and "preserve the rights of the sovereign States and the institutions of the South [slavery]." Approximately 100 peace meetings were held, causing great alarm among staunch Confederates and threatening a civil war within the state. Finally, at the urging of Vance and Graham, Holden in September called off the peace rallies, a few days before Georgia troops, passing through Raleigh, sacked his newspaper office.

In 1864 Holden, on a platform advocating a state convention to launch separate peace negotiations, suffered a humiliating defeat in the gubernatorial election against Vance. After the war, President Andrew Johnson appointed Holden provisional governor. In 1867, Holden cast his lot with the Republicans in Congress and their plan of Reconstruction. For his efforts in organizing the party in North Carolina, Holden in 1868 became the state's first Republican governor, only to be impeached and removed from office in 1871 by resurgent Conservative Democrats. Except for a brief period as U.S. postmaster in Raleigh, Holden retired to private life. He died in Raleigh in 1892.

—*William C. Harris*

See also Conscription, C.S.A.; North Carolina; Peace Movements; Vance, Zebulon.

For further reading:
Harris, William C. *William Woods Holden: Firebrand of North Carolina Politics* (1987).
Kruman, Marc W. *Parties and Politics in North Carolina, 1836–1865* (1983).
North Carolina Standard (Raleigh) (1861–1865).
Raper, Horace W. "William Woods Holden and the Peace Movement in North Carolina." *North Carolina Historical Review* (1954).
Yates, Richard E. *The Confederacy and Zeb Vance* (1958).

HOLLINS, GEORGE NICHOLS
(1799–1878)
Confederate naval officer

Born to John Hollins and Janet Smith Hollins in Baltimore, Maryland, George Hollins, after being educated locally, entered the navy at the age of fifteen as a midshipman. His first ship was the USS *President*, commanded by Stephen Decatur. Hollins was captured by the British along with the rest of the crew when Decatur tried to get past the British blockaders off Long Island in January 1815. Hollins was released when the peace treaty was ratified. He continued aboard the *President* during the Algerian War. Over the next thirty years, Hollins rose in the ranks of the navy to captain by 1855, his most controversial action to that point being, while in command of the *Cyane* in 1854, his bombard-

ment of San Juan de Nicaragua because of attacks on Americans in Nicaragua.

At the outbreak of hostilities between the North and South, Hollins commanded the USS *Susquehanna* in the Mediterranean squadron. When he put into port in Naples in May 1861, he received orders to return to New York. Upon his arrival, he resigned his commission and offered his services to the Confederacy. He was commissioned a captain on 20 June 1861. Within days of receiving his commission, Hollins, in command of a hastily outfitted expedition, captured the steamer *St. Nicholas* near the mouth of the Potomac River. Using the *St. Nicholas* to augment his forces, Hollins proceeded to take three more prizes over the next few weeks. At the end of July 1861, he was sent to New Orleans to command all naval forces there and received a promotion to commodore.

Operating out of New Orleans with a small makeshift force dubbed the "Mosquito Fleet," Hollins fought a larger Federal force on 12 October, sinking one ship and capturing a supply vessel. Over the next few months he assembled more vessels and began a construction program for Confederate ironclads. Most of these vessels went with him when he received command of all Confederate naval forces in the upper Mississippi. In spite of all of his hard work, however, the superiority of Union naval forces on the Mississippi were soon brought to bear on his little fleet. In the early months of 1862, Hollins fought a losing war for control of the upper Mississippi, having his best success in the defense of Columbus, Kentucky. He was back in New Orleans by spring and requested that he be able to shift the bulk of the naval forces on the Mississippi to the defense of that city. He was refused and summoned east to sit on a court of inquiry. New Orleans fell to David Farragut on 25 April 1862. Hollins later testified in the board of inquiry called to investigate the fall of New Orleans.

For the remainder of the war, Hollins occupied a variety of clerk jobs in Richmond and was captured when the city fell in April 1865. After the war, he worked in Baltimore city government and died in that city.

—*David S. Heidler and Jeanne T. Heidler*

See also Navy, C.S.A.; New Orleans.
For further reading:
Hollins, George N. "Autobiography of Commodore G. N. Hollins." *Maryland Historical Magazine* (1939).
Luraghi, Raimondo. *A History of the Confederate Navy* (1996).

HOLLY SPRINGS RAID
(17–28 December 1862)

Maneuvering one's army to strike a weaker opponent is sound military strategy, but it can be done only if the commander has access to ample supplies of food and ammunition. A dependable, protected supply line is a necessity for any army operating in the field. Union general Ulysses S. Grant's first attempt to capture the Confederacy's last major stronghold on the Mississippi River, Vicksburg, came to naught because the enemy cut his supply line.

In late 1862, Grant devised a two-pronged attack to capture Vicksburg. His plan called for him to lead 40,000 troops southward into Mississippi, while William T. Sherman took 30,000 men down the Mississippi River to assault the bluffs north of Vicksburg. Things went smoothly at first as Grant's army easily pushed aside the outnumbered Confederates. "We can go as far as supplies can be taken," Grant said prophetically.

Meanwhile, the outnumbered Confederate army searched for ways to halt Grant and decided that Grant's only weakness was his supply line. Lieutenant Colonel John S. Griffith, a Texas cavalryman, built upon that idea when he suggested a cavalry raid to departmental commander General John C. Pemberton. With such a raid, Griffith stated, "we will penetrate the rear of the enemy, capture Holly Springs…and, perhaps force him to retreat…." Griffith even suggested someone to lead such a foray: Earl Van Dorn.

Van Dorn was a peculiar choice considering his record up to that point. He suffered military failures at Pea Ridge and Corinth, and stories of his drunkenness and visits with prostitutes ran rampant in Mississippi. Nevertheless, Pemberton liked the idea and ordered Van Dorn to move and assigned him 3,500 men.

Van Dorn's command consisted of three cavalry brigades. Griffith and his Texas brigade were joined by Tennesseans led by Colonel William A. Jackson and Colonel Robert M. McCullough's Missouri and Mississippi brigade. Van Dorn informed his subordinates of the plan to raid behind enemy lines and cautioned secrecy. Gathering rations, Van Dorn's contingent left Grenada, Mississippi, on 17 December 1862.

The force moved northward quickly. They took back roads and avoided Union patrols; they narrowly missed a large Federal detachment at Pontotoc on 18 December. By the next evening, they neared Holly Springs, Grant's prime stockpile of food, ammunition, clothing, and all other material necessary to sustain an army.

Holly Springs' destruction was Van Dorn's primary objective. After receiving word on Union developments from a spy, Van Dorn organized a three-pronged attack with each brigade given precise instructions on what to do upon entering the town. He ordered the attack to begin at dawn.

Confederate movements concerned Holly Springs' garrison commander Union colonel Robert C. Murphy. He believed his 500 troops were no match for any attack arrayed against him. Nevertheless, Van Dorn's attack surprised Murphy and his men on the 20th. The Confederates dashed into town, avoided Union pickets who failed to issue a proper warning, and captured Murphy's infantry command. Only a detachment of Illinois cavalry offered any resistance. Within a few hours, Holly Springs was completely in Van Dorn's possession.

The Confederates quickly began destroying Federal property. The town's stockpile of Union wares was soon up in smoke. Damages fell between $400,000 and $1,500,000. Their task completed, Van Dorn's men left the town quickly to avoid pursuit.

Van Dorn's men continued northward to threaten Bolivar, Tennessee. They tore up railroad track and cut telegraph wire. On two separate occasions, Federals at Davis' Mill, Mississippi, and Middleburg, Tennessee, withstood Confederate attempts to dislodge them. The lack of artillery doomed the Confederates.

Union cavalry finally forced Van Dorn to seek the safety of his own lines. On 28 December, Van Dorn's men crossed the Tallahatchie River. His men had ridden 500 miles in two weeks, destroyed valuable Union supplies, and given a much needed morale boost to the South.

More importantly, the raid threw Grant's campaign into shambles. Van Dorn's destructive foray along with Nathan Bedford Forrest's simultaneous West Tennessee Raid totally wrecked Grant's supply line. Lacking basic necessities for his army, Grant pulled his men back. Consequently, Sherman's men landed at Chickasaw Bayou, and the solo attack was repulsed on 28–29 December. Grant's first attempt to take Vicksburg ended in failure.

Van Dorn's Holly Springs Raid was the highlight of the much-maligned general's career. He was killed in May 1863 by a jealous husband at Spring Hill, Tennessee. Union colonel Murphy's career was over as well. He became Grant's scapegoat and was dismissed from service.

—*Clay Williams*

See also Grant, Ulysses S.; Van Dorn, Earl; Vicksburg Campaign.

For further reading:
Bearss, Edwin C. *The Campaign for Vicksburg* (1985).
Brown, A.F. "Van Dorn's Operations in Northern Mississippi—Recollections of a Cavalryman." In *Southern Historical Society Papers* (1878; reprint, 1977).
Deupree, J. G. "The Capture of Holly Springs, Mississippi, Dec. 20, 1862." In *Publications of the Mississippi Historical Society*. Vol. 4.
Hartje, Robert G. *Van Dorn, The Life and Times of a Confederate General* (1967).

HOLMES, OLIVER WENDELL, JR.
(1841–1935)
Union officer

Born in Boston, Massachusetts, on 8 March 1841, Holmes attended Harvard College from 1857 to 1861. With the outset of the Civil War, however, he left on 25 April of his senior year to join the 4th Battalion of the 20th Regiment of the Massachusetts

Voluntary Infantry as a private. He felt strongly that honor compelled him, as the son of a Boston Brahmin, to enlist. As a college student, he had opposed the continued existence of slavery and had shown concern about threats of disruptions of antislavery meetings. Also, believing in the constitutional principle of a permanent Union, he had been seriously affected by Southern secessionism. Ardently anticipating fighting the South but not yet given any additional orders, he returned to Harvard for the two remaining months, thus graduating.

Both his parents were supportive of his yearning for combat. Dr. Oliver Wendell Holmes, an eminent physician and poet, upheld the Union cause, which he promoted throughout the war. Amelia Lee (Jackson) Holmes was an abolitionist who believed that young men had a duty to fight in the war.

On 23 July 1861, Holmes was commissioned first lieutenant in Company A of his three-year regiment attached to the Army of the Potomac. He was wounded in the chest on 21 October 1861 in the battle of Ball's Bluff (Virginia), where casualties were heavy. (Thinking that he was dying, he rejected the Deity with finality upon his survival.) Commissioned captain in Company G on 23 March 1862, he fought in the battle of Fair Oaks (Virginia). The young soldier's toughness stemmed from his devotion to the Union, his loyalty to the Army of the Potomac, and his pride in the 20th Regiment. Writing from the field of battle to his parents on 2 June 1862 that "we licked them," he told of being struck by the indifference shown to the strewn Confederate slain (7,000 Confederate and 5,000 Union casualties).

On 17 September 1862, Holmes was seriously wounded in the neck—his closest encounter with death—at Antietam Creek. The Union losses were staggering, and by November he became convinced that the weary and mismanaged Union army could not "subjugate" the South, which he felt was a "great civilized nation." Concluding that the Confederacy had just about achieved its objective—independence—he was nearly prepared to hope for an early termination of the war. On 20 December 1862 in a letter to his father, Holmes, though never faltering in the righteousness of the cause, spoke of Southern unity and resolve to win (Dr. Holmes disagreed).

Continually expecting to be killed, the heroic Holmes was wounded in the heel on 3 May 1863, at Fredericksburg, although dysentery had kept him out of the actual battle. Incapacitated, he could not return to his regiment until 3 January 1864. He was engaged in the calamitous battles of the Wilderness for forty murderous days.

Witnessing fearful losses and doubting that a decisive contest could take place that would point to a Northern victory, Holmes, faced with thorough physical and mental exhaustion, thought himself unable to discharge his duties properly. With his enlistment period about to expire, he decided, after six months of deliberation, that he owed it to himself to pursue a scholarly career. He resigned effective 17 July 1864. He had written in his class book in July 1861 that his ambition, if he lived through the war, was to study law. He entered Harvard Law School in 1864 and graduated in 1866.

In the postbellum period, Holmes generally had little desire or interest to return to Civil War issues and effects. He remembered, however, his early enthusiasm for the war for the rest of his life and came to agree with the positive image of President Abraham Lincoln's leadership but not enthusiastically. Above all, he could not detach himself from a war that had become his teacher. Holmes assembled a scrapbook of war memorabilia that included news items of casualties, and on 30 May 1884, in his Memorial Day address before a group of Civil War veterans at Keene, New Hampshire, he sadly remembered some of his courageous fallen comrades. Among them were 1st Lieutenant James J. Lowell, commanding Company E, killed on 30 June 1862, in the Seven Days' battles, and Major Henry L. Abbott, commanding the 20th Regiment, killed on 6 May 1864 in the Wilderness campaign. (Holmes was proud that he was able to survive his decimated regiment.) He referred in the same address to the experience of battle, which had taught him that the enemy, fighting and dying for their convictions, compelled respect. Holmes thought that "as life is action and passion, it is required of a man that he should share the passion and action of his time at peril of being judged not to have lived."

In his Memorial Day address, "The Soldier's Faith," delivered on 30 May 1895 before a meeting called by the graduating class at Harvard University, Holmes observed that "War, when you are at it, is horrible and dull." Still, his earlier belief (after the brief encounter with death at Ball's Bluff)—that the right to use force, that is, the right to kill, was acceptable when two conflicting groups sought to prevail in a society—had hardened. For Holmes, who after the war took a harsh view of the South, Union military might and success legitimized Northern dominance. This realistic acknowledgment about the nature of life remained his core belief.

In 1881 Holmes published his famed book, *The Common Law,* which led to a professorship at the Harvard Law School. He achieved his goal with his appointments to the Supreme Judicial Court of Massachusetts from 1882 to 1902 and to the U.S. Supreme Court from 1902 to 1932. Holmes died in Washington on 6 March 1935.

—*Bernard Hirschhorn*

For further reading:
Holmes, Oliver Wendell. *Speeches* (1913).
Howe, Mark DeWolfe. *Justice Oliver Wendell Holmes: The*

Shaping Years, 1841–1870 (1957).

———. *Touched with Fire: Civil War Letters and Diary of Oliver Wendell Holmes, Jr., 1861–1864* (1946).

Novick, Sheldon M. *Honorable Justice: The Life of Oliver Wendell Holmes* (1989).

Wilson, Edmund. "Justice Oliver Wendell Holmes." In *Patriotic Gore: Studies in the Literature of the American Civil War* (1962).

HOLMES, THEOPHILUS HUNTER
(1804–1880)
Confederate general

Many generals who wore the gray of the Confederacy distinguished themselves through courageous actions and daring strategic maneuvers. Theophilus Hunter Holmes was not one of them. His service to the South was filled with blunder and failed opportunities.

Holmes, born on 13 November 1804, in Simpson County, North Carolina, benefited from his prominent family. Failing at plantation management, he turned to his father, a former governor and current congressman, to gain him an appointment to West Point. Holmes graduated in 1829, finishing forty-fourth among forty-six graduates. His contemporaries at West Point included Robert E. Lee and Jefferson Davis.

Like most other future Civil War generals, he spent most of his prewar career serving on frontier outposts. In the Mexican-American War, his courageous action at Monterrey, witnessed by Jefferson Davis, gained him promotion to brevet major.

After the bombardment of Fort Sumter, Holmes returned to his native North Carolina. As he helped organize troops for the South, his old friend Jefferson Davis, now president of the Confederacy, appointed him brigadier general. Assigned to General P. G. T. Beauregard, Holmes contributed little at the battle of First Bull Run. Beauregard had fashioned orders for him to attack the Federal left across Bull Run Creek, but the orders never reached him. He maintained his position until after midday, when he finally received new orders to march to the fighting. By the time his brigade arrived, the Confederacy had already claimed victory.

After doing a creditable job of strengthening defenses in North Carolina, Holmes joined the Army of Northern Virginia to help drive George McClellan and the Army of the Potomac off the York Peninsula. Unfortunately, Holmes displayed traits that would hamper him the rest of his career. As Southern troops pursued the Federals toward Malvern Hill, the Union guns produced a tremendous racket. At this crucial juncture, Holmes emerged from a house with his hand cupped to his ear and exclaimed, "I thought I heard firing." His chronic deafness had caused him to be caught totally unaware.

The following afternoon, Holmes's men provided no support for the tragic assault on Malvern Hill. Fellow general Daniel H. Hill blasted his inactivity, but Lee's own reports either placed no blame on Holmes or failed to mention him altogether.

Despite Holmes's mediocre record, Davis inexplicably made him a lieutenant general and placed him in charge of the mammoth Trans-Mississippi Department. The Confederate president apparently chose Holmes because of their friendship and the general's inconspicuous manner. Holmes tried to change Davis's mind, but Davis remained firm. According to one historian, it was "the most incomprehensible assignment he [Davis] made as president." Holmes took command 30 July 1862.

Holmes's biggest failure as commander of the Trans-Mississippi was his inability to perform his department's most important task, supporting the South's efforts east of the Mississippi River, especially the defense of Vicksburg. Holmes continuously made excuses instead of sending troops to defend the Confederacy's last major stronghold on the river.

Civilians and military personnel ridiculed Holmes's weaknesses and peculiarities. "Granny Holmes," "a very old man with memory, will, judgment all debilitated to a degree which incapacitates him for any administration," and "unfit for high command involving combat operations" were just some of the comments made against Holmes. Clearly, few people west of the Mississippi had any confidence in him. Finally accepting the obvious and much to Holmes's delight, Jefferson Davis relieved him of departmental command effective 18 March 1863.

The Confederacy would have been better served had that been the last of Theophilus Holmes, but it was not. His replacement, Kirby Smith, made Holmes head of the District of Arkansas. After debating options and using "neither common sense nor tactical perspicacity," Holmes decided to launch an attack against Union-held Helena, Arkansas. His 7,650-man force had no chance of capturing Helena, made impregnable by fortifications and Union gunboats on the river. The 4 July attack ended in absolute failure. Returning to Little Rock, Holmes temporarily relinquished command and took to a sickbed.

Holmes would play no further active role in the war. He briefly returned to his command, but the numerous requests for his removal forced him to resign his post on 28 February 1864. The remainder of the war saw him back in his native state commanding the North Carolina Reserves, mostly boys and old men. He lived the rest of his life on a farm, dying in 1880.

Although Holmes was unsuited for combat command, he continued to gain appointments that proved detrimental to the Confederacy. As a result,

whenever historians write about the Civil War, Holmes's name is either forgotten or ridiculed.

—*Clay Williams*

See also Davis, Jefferson; Helena, Battle of.
For further reading:
Castel, Albert E. "Theophilus Holmes—Pallbearer of the Confederacy." *Civil War Times Illustrated* (July 1977).
Davis, William C. *Jefferson Davis, The Man & His Hour* (1991).
Freeman, Douglas Southall. *Lee's Lieutenants, A Study in Command* (1942–1944).
Kerby, Robert L. *Kirby Smith's Confederacy, the Trans-Mississippi South, 1863–1865* (1972).
Warner, Ezra J. *Generals in Gray, Lives of Confederate Generals* (1959; reprint, 1987).

HOLT, JOSEPH
(1807–1894)
Union judge advocate general

Born to John Holt and Eleanor Stephens Holt in Breckinridge County, Kentucky, Joseph Holt was educated at Centre College before studying law and opening a practice in Elizabethtown, Kentucky. As a young man, Holt also became interested in state Democratic politics. After practicing law successfully in Mississippi for several years, Holt returned to Kentucky in 1842. He did not become politically active again until the mid-1850s. His efforts on behalf of James Buchanan's presidential candidacy in 1856 earned him several federal appointments over the next few years. After serving as commissioner of patents, in 1859 Holt accepted appointment as postmaster general. At the end of 1860, with the secession crisis looming, Buchanan's secretary of war, John B. Floyd, resigned on 29 December. Buchanan appointed Holt as Floyd's interim replacement on 31 December, and Holt remained the acting secretary until confirmed by the Senate on 18 January.

Holt became secretary of war at a time of great crisis for the nation. He had moderately supported states' rights before the secession crisis and had even given his legal opinion that a state could not be forced to remain in the Union. Yet, when secession actually occurred, he opposed it and in his new position became a staunch supporter of the Union. In the limited time that he was in office, he worked diligently to strengthen the U.S. military and to ensure the loyalty of his native Kentucky. Leaving office upon Abraham Lincoln's inauguration, Holt was not satisfied with merely preventing Kentucky's secession; he worked to persuade state leaders to join in suppressing the rebellion.

Holt's vigorous unionism brought him to the attention of the Lincoln administration. Lincoln and his cabinet, realizing what a political asset this border state Unionist could be, looked for an appropriate Federal appointment for Holt. In early 1862 he received a temporary appointment to a board auditing government

arms contracts. But in September 1862, he was given the job that he would hold for the remainder of the war and beyond. The Lincoln administration created the office of judge advocate general and appointed Holt with the rank of colonel as its first occupant.

Holt had a variety of duties that included overseeing courts-martial and military commissions and supervising all military investigations. One of his first duties was presiding over the court-martial of Fitz John Porter. President Lincoln also hoped to use the position to gain control of political prisoners from unreliable civilian courts. As the war dragged on and the threat from subversives seemed to increase, Holt in his zeal to win the war was all too willing to cooperate in this endeavor. His use of military commissions to try such cases as Lambdin P. Milligan's and Clement L. Vallandigham's brought the army into the business of handing down civil as well as military justice. Along with conducting such trials, Holt's office also investigated the members of organizations such as the Sons of Liberty and Knights of the Golden Circle. Holt proved effective enough to earn promotion to brigadier general in June 1864.

Aside from these controversial activities, much of Holt's work was mundane. He had to review numerous courts-martial held during the war with charges that ranged from serious to trivial. He oversaw boards of inquiry that potentially could result in courts-martial, and he rendered legal opinions on any laws of a military nature, most often dealing with the various exemptions available for potential draftees.

Holt's most famous and controversial cases came after the war. Using extensive powers that had been established during the crisis of the rebellion, he presided over the irregular military trial of the Lincoln conspirators. Possibly his earlier successes in dispensing quick and draconian justice had become a habit, for when he took Mary Surratt's execution to President Andrew Johnson, Holt failed to inform the president of the other commissioners' call for leniency. The president signed her death warrant, and she was hanged with George Atzerodt, Lewis Paine, and David Herold. Soon Henry Wirz, commandant at Andersonville prison, was sent to the gallows as well. In the meantime, Holt had time to oversee the trial of Captain Frederic Speed whose serious errors in judgment, according to his conviction, resulted in the *Sultana* disaster.

When the furor over Lincoln's assassination abated, criticism began to surface regarding Holt's methods. When the Supreme Court in *Ex parte Milligan* struck down the practice of trying civilians before military tribunals, the decision further eroded faith in the judge advocate general's office. The case also prevented Holt's office from trying Confederate government officials such as Jefferson Davis. Holt tried to defend himself in the press, but few were interested. He resigned his position in 1875 and spent the remainder of his life defending his methods. He died in Washington, D.C., on 1 August 1894.

—*David S. Heidler and Jeanne T. Heidler*

See also Ex parte Milligan; Lincoln Assassination; *Sultana*; Wirz, Henry.

For further reading:

Allen, Mary Bernard. "Joseph Holt, Judge Advocate General, 1862–1875" (M.A. thesis, 1927).

Bartman, Roger J. "Joseph Holt and Kentucky in the Civil War." *Filson Club Historical Quarterly* (1966).

Burnett, Henry Lawrence. *Some Incidents in the Trial of President Lincoln's Assassins. The Controversy between President Johnson and Judge Holt* (1891).

HOMER, WINSLOW
(1836–1910)
Artist

Winslow Homer, known for his realistic Civil War paintings and his illustrations for *Harper's Weekly* from 1859 to 1875, was born in Boston and apprenticed to a local lithographer, John H. Bufford, in 1855. Homer set up his own studio in Boston in 1857 and then moved to New York City in 1859 as a freelance illustrator. Largely self-taught, he had been selling his drawings to *Ballou's Pictorial* and *Harper's Weekly*, and, when the Civil War broke out, *Harper's* hired him to provide illustrations of the Peninsula campaign.

The Civil War was the making of Homer as an artist. It presented opportunities to depict scenes that would have been considered inappropriate had he pursued a more formal education in Europe. Working in the military camps near the front lines, Homer soon adopted a reporter's detachment from his subject matter. He began to move beyond romantic depictions of martial glory to become one of the most important painters of the American Civil War.

Homer's first tour as a correspondent was in mid-October 1861, when the Union army was deployed around Washington. He produced the engraving, *A Night Reconnaissance*, which appeared in *Harper's* on 26 October 1861. Homer visited the front again six months later, spending two months with the 61st New York Volunteer Infantry during the siege of Yorktown, Virginia. During this period, he acquired the experience—and an inventory of sketches and studies—that would produce most of his illustrations during 1862, his most prolific year with *Harper's*. *The War for the Union, 1862—A Cavalry Charge* (5 July 1862) and *The War for the Union, 1862—A Bayonet Charge* (12 July 1862) are based on conventions that emerged during the Napoleonic Wars. Most remarkable is his engraving *The Army of the Potomac—A Sharp-shooter on Picket Duty* (15 November 1862), which is based on an oil painting that Homer was producing from his firsthand sketches of camp life.

Homer's painting, *The Sharp-shooter on Picket Duty* (1863), marks a transformation of his style. Modern, mechanistic warfare was incompatible with the tradition of individual heroism depicted in military art. Rather than representing a heroic charge of bayonets, Homer depicts the isolated, concealed sharpshooter picking off an anonymous enemy at a great distance using a rifle with a telescopic sight. Similarly, *Defiance: Inviting a Shot Before Petersburg* (1864) presents a Confederate soldier jeering the Union line and, perhaps, about to be killed by a Union sharpshooter. Homer was emerging as one of the leading realist painters of the nineteenth century.

Most of Homer's Civil War paintings, such as *Home, Sweet Home* (1863), *The Briarwood Pipe* (1864), *Pitching Quoits* (1865), *The Bright Side* (1865), and *A Rainy Day in Camp* (1871), are depictions of ordinary life in the Union camps. All of these paintings represent quiet, almost pastoral moments of comradeship among soldiers amid the tedium of daily routine. The closest Homer ever came to a serious battle painting is *Skirmish in the Wilderness* (1864), which accurately depicts the battle of the Wilderness as a blurred confusion amid densely tangled forest. The soldiers appear as faceless savages groping through the underbrush.

Homer's paintings are psychologically complex, but they are also allegorical, pointing to larger themes in American culture. *The Veteran in the New Field* (1865), for example, shows a recently disbanded soldier scything hay instead of men. The veteran suggests the ideal of Cincinnatus, who returns to his farm after serving his country. The image also evokes Isaiah 2:4: "they shall beat their swords into plowshares, and their spears into pruning hooks." Painted shortly after Lincoln's assassination, *The Veteran in the New Field* has been interpreted as an elegy for the martyred president.

Prisoners from the Front (1866) is Homer's most celebrated Civil War painting. It depicts three Confederate prisoners being reviewed by a Union officer. Each figure is a study in regional character types: the self-satisfied New Englander in his clean, crisp uniform faces an intransigent Confederate cavalier; a cunning, grizzled old soldier in rags; and a loutish boy, who becomes the frontiersman in Homer's later paintings. *Prisoners from the Front* attempts to express in a frozen moment the irreconcilable tensions that produced the Civil War.

In 1866 Homer went to France, where he fell under the influence of Gustave Courbet and Edouard Manet. When he returned in 1867, he began to focus on beach resorts and rural life, particularly children at play. In *Snap the Whip* (1872), Homer reflects a cultural shift away from the harshness of the war. Homer remained a realist, however, and by 1881, after briefly living in England, he turned to maritime life as a source of inspiration. He set up a studio in Prout's Neck, Maine, in 1884 and dedicated the rest of his career to representing humanity's eternal conflict with the sea. Most notable, perhaps, is *The Gulf Stream* (1899), which suggests the uncertain future of African-Americans after emancipation.

—*William Pannapacker*

See also Art.
For further reading:
Cikovsky, Nicolai, Jr., and Franklin Kelly. *Winslow Homer* (1995).
Grossman, Julian. *Echo of a Distant Drum: Winslow Homer and the Civil War* (1974).
Simpson, Marc. *Winslow Homer: Paintings of the Civil War* (1988).
Wood, Peter H., and Karen C. C. Dalton. *Winslow Homer's Images of Blacks: The Civil War and Reconstruction* (1988).

HOMESTEAD ACT

The Homestead Act grew from a formative paradox of American civilization: The nation was long characterized by resources that could not be exploited due to the shortage of population and labor. The federal government and many state governments owned vast tracts of lands that remained unused and unproductive. Using sales of land to generate revenue had always brought disappointing results.

Early in the nineteenth century, figures as diverse as Albert Gallatin, secretary of the treasury under Thomas Jefferson, and William Henry Harrison of the Northwest Territory sought to cut the costs of government lands to make them more salable and accessible. By the 1830s, a Jacksonian Democrat, Senator Thomas Hart Benton of Missouri, proposed the first Homestead Bill to allow landless American citizens to claim and develop potential farmland in the public domain. The West and its representatives always favored some such mechanism to settle and develop the region.

The continued urbanization and industrialization of society in the east produced a powerful supporter of such a bill in labor. Predisposed politically to Jacksonian politics, the city "lacklanders" made an issue of Federal land policy, their efforts culminating in the 1844 formation of the National Reform Association (NRA) by George Henry Evans. Two years later, in conjunction with the abolitionist Liberty Party, they began running coalition slates for public office under the rubric of "Free Soil." The combination demonstrated sufficient strength in New York and Massachusetts to inspire former president Martin Van Buren to lead a revolt of Northern Democrats that founded the national Free-Soil Party on a much moderated program. The insurgency left a residue of sympathetic officeholders in Congress and, in 1849, the newly elected Horace Greeley introduced the NRA's Homestead Bill. From 1850 to 1852, the NRA spearheaded what was, to that point, the largest nationally coordinated petition drive in American history.

While the House of Representatives passed the measure, it was blocked in the U.S. Senate, largely through an alliance led by Southern Democrats. For the eastern workers and western promoters, this largely dissolved their Democratic allegiances. Their vision of a West, decisive of the nation's future, shaped by small landholdings clashed directly with that of Southern leaders. The subsequent passage of the Kansas-Nebraska Act in February 1854 seemed to define the conflict of those aspirations, and the subsequent conflict over "Bleeding Kansas" confirmed it. The dispute over "the land question" was vital to making a conflict over slavery and slaveholding a national issue of concern to westerners and eastern workers.

The new Republican Party readily embraced the issue, though enthusiasm varied from state to state. A homestead bill was again thwarted in 1858, but Democratic senator Andrew Johnson of eastern Tennessee secured passage with Republican support of a very modified measure to reduce land costs in 1859. Its veto by Democratic president James Buchanan provided an essential prelude to the split within the party and Republican victory in the election of 1860.

As with other reform measures of the Lincoln administration, the Homestead Act of 1862 had sweeping and radical implications but could be soundly justified on pragmatic grounds. Secessionist and, later, Confederate forebodings of potential "agrarian leveling" found some confirmation as wartime radicals began urging the confiscation of plantation lands and their redistribution to the freedpeople and other landless Southerners. The Southern Homestead Act (1864) did extend the idea to the South, but only to unoccupied and unowned lands. Federal forces moving into the South, however, encouraged African-Americans to farm what lands were available contributed to expectations of getting "forty acres and a mule" along with emancipation.

In the North and West, the innovative offering of free land to all who would work it did initially contribute to putting more land into production during the war, but self-contradictory policies thwarted its long-term impact. In particular, vast land grants of the best and most marketable lands to the railroads effectively marginalized both the areas available for free settlement by individuals and the importance of the act to the emerging markets. By 1890, the government had granted fewer than 373,000 homesteads on roughly 48,000,000 acres, less than 3.5 percent of the territory west of the Mississippi. Vast grants to states, railroads, and other large concerns arguably thwarted the impact of the Homestead Act. In effect, the measure had eased the privatization of government land.

—*Mark A. Lause*

See also Election of 1860; Evans, George Henry; Free Soil Party; Greeley, Horace; Johnson, Andrew; Kansas-Nebraska Act; Labor; Republican Party.

For further reading:
Gates, Paul W. "The Homestead Law in an Incongruous Land System." In *The Public Lands: Studies in the History of the Public Domain* (1962).
Hibbard, Benjamin H. *A History of the Public Land Policies* (1924).
Shannon, Fred A. "The Homestead Act and the Labor Surplus." In *The Public Lands: Studies in the History of the Public Domain* (1962).

HONEY HILL, SOUTH CAROLINA, BATTLE OF
(30 November 1864)

On 22 November 1864, Major General John G. Foster, Union commander of the Department of the South, reported to the chief of staff, Major General Henry W. Halleck, that the people of Charleston and Savannah were in a state of panic over the advance of Major General William Tecumseh Sherman's army. In response to this threat, Confederate commander Lieutenant General William J. Hardee left Charleston and was gathering every able man in order to meet Sherman. This move had depleted the force guarding the Savannah & Charleston Railroad. Foster believed that an opportunity to capture some point on the railroad had arisen and he, therefore, was assembling troops to do so. He had been considering such an operation for a few days, and, ironically, on the same day he sent his dispatch to Halleck, Foster had received a letter from Halleck instructing him to attack the railroad. These actions culminated in the battle of Honey Hill, South Carolina.

On the night of the 28th, Foster left Hilton Head, South Carolina, and headed toward Boyd's Creek with 5,000 infantry, cavalry, and artillery, plus 500 sailors and marines. At 2:30 A.M. on the 29th, the force set sail. A thick fog, however, impeded its progress, causing some boats to get lost and others to run aground. The first troops did not begin to land until 11:00 A.M., and the last did not come ashore until late in the afternoon. This episode was the first of a series of mishaps that cost the Union troops precious time.

Once ashore, Brigadier General John P. Hatch, commander of the Coast Division, assumed command. The naval brigade was sent ahead to occupy a crossroads, meeting and driving off a small Confederate force. Late that afternoon, an infantry brigade accompanied by cavalry was sent to capture the railroad at Grahamville, South Carolina. As a result of the use of unreliable maps and guides, the naval brigade had followed the retreating Confederates for two miles in the opposite direction of Grahamville. The infantry brigade followed, overtook

their predecessors, discovered the error, and then countermarched. Not only had they lost time, but the sailors were exhausted, having drug the artillery by hand, and were left at the crossroads for the night. The infantry continued on for another two miles to a fork in the road. Once again, they took the wrong road (on the advice of their guide) and marched four miles before discovering their error. After countermarching, they arrived back at the fork at 2 A.M. and bivouacked for the night.

While these troops had spent the day marching a total of fifteen miles, the Confederates were hurriedly sending soldiers toward Grahamville. They began arriving at 8:00 A.M. on the 30th under the command of Major General Gustavus W. Smith of the Georgia Militia. By Georgia law, the militia was not to serve outside of the state, but after seeing the seriousness of the situation, Smith and his 1st Brigade decided to temporarily cross the state line. They were joined by the Georgia State Line, the Athens and Augusta local defense battalions, the 47th Georgia Infantry, and a mixed contingent of South Carolina cavalry and artillery. The Confederates were able to field about 1,400 men in battle.

Not long after the Confederates established their position at Honey Hill, the Union troops advanced up the Grahamville Road. At first, they encountered a small force of Confederates who retreated to the Confederate lines. Before doing so, the Confederates set fire to the thick brush in the area, slowing the Union advance. The Federals, however, made it to Honey Hill around 11:00 A.M., where they faced formidable Confederate defenses. The Union troops, which included regiments composed of African-Americans, not only had to contend with a well-entrenched enemy, but also had to advance through thick underbrush and swamps. After unsuccessfully charging the Confederate position most of the day, the Federals retreated at dusk. They suffered almost 750 casualties compared with approximately 100 of the Confederates.

Luis Emilio, who participated in the battle with the 54th Massachusetts Infantry, attributed their defeat to their failure to seize the railroad before the Southern troops arrived, as well as to the strong defensive position of their opponent. Undoubtedly, the lost time due to the fog and the errant marching greatly hindered the Union effort. More importantly, the Confederates managed to keep open the railroad between Savannah and Charleston for almost two more months, which helped them evacuate their troops from Savannah during Sherman's siege.

—*Scott M. Langston*

See also Hatch, John Porter; Sherman's March to the Sea; Smith, Gustavus Woodson.
For further reading:
Abercrombie, John J. *Battle of Honey Hill, S.C.* (1911).

Emilo, Luis. *A Brave Black Regiment: The History of the Fifty-Fourth Regiment of Massachusetts Volunteer Infantry, 1863–1865* (1995).

Hudson, Leonne M. *The Odyssey of a Southerner: The Life and Times of Gustavus Woodson Smith* (1998).

Jones, C. C., Jr. "The Battle of Honey Hill." *Southern Historical Society Papers* (1885).

Trudeau, Noah Andre. *Like Men of War: Black Troops in the Civil War, 1862–1865* (1998).

U.S. War Department. *The War of the Rebellion: A Compilation of the Official Records of the Union and Confederate Armies* (1880–1901).

HONEY SPRINGS, BATTLE OF
(17 July 1863)

Honey Springs was the most important Civil War battle fought in Indian Territory. It preserved Union ownership of Fort Gibson and dealt Confederate forces a blow from which they never fully recovered. It also opened the way for the Federal capture of Fort Smith, Arkansas, and helped justify the recruitment of black regiments by the Union army.

In April 1863, Colonel William A. Phillips and a Union column out of Kansas challenged Confederate authority in Indian Territory by occupying Fort Gibson on the Arkansas River. Confederate brigadier general Douglas H. Cooper decided to retake that vital post, and he began gathering troops and supplies at Honey Springs, a Confederate depot twenty miles southwest of his objective.

By mid-July, Cooper had massed a mixed force of 6,000 Texans and Indians at Honey Springs. He also had a four-gun battery. Another 3,000 Confederate soldiers under Brigadier General William L. Cabell were en route from Fort Smith, and Cooper expected them at Honey Springs sometime around 17 July. Once these reinforcements arrived, Cooper planned to advance on Fort Gibson, whose garrison barely numbered more than 3,000 men.

Unfortunately for Confederate hopes, Major General James G. Blunt, the aggressive commander of the Union District of the Frontier, learned of Cooper's offensive preparations. Blunt realized that he had to smash the enemy at Honey Springs before Cabell arrived or forfeit Fort Gibson. Organizing a field force consisting of 3,000 men and twelve cannon, Blunt forded the Arkansas above Fort Gibson on 15–16 July and followed the Texas Road south. A rainy night march brought the Federals within six and a half miles of Honey Springs by daybreak on 17 July.

The battle of Honey Springs, 17 July 1863 (*Frank Leslie's Illustrated Newspaper / Library of Congress*)

Blunt discovered that Cooper had advanced a mile and a half from Honey Springs to meet him at Elk Creek. Cooper took advantage of the timber fringing the north bank of the creek to deploy his Texans and Indians in a sheltered line one and a half miles long, but his position was not as strong as it looked. Blunt's superiority in artillery offset the Confederates' superiority in numbers. Furthermore, nearly a quarter of Cooper's troops lacked serviceable firearms, and their gunpowder was an inferior brand imported from Mexico. An early morning rain turned much of this powder into useless paste, leaving many rebels virtually defenseless.

The battle opened at 10:00 A.M. with a one-hour artillery duel. The Confederates knocked out a Federal 12-pound Napoleon howitzer, but their opponents responded by disabling a mountain howitzer. Dismounting his cavalry units to fight on foot, Blunt sent them and his infantry to rake Cooper's line with rapidly delivered small arms fire.

In keeping with his abolitionist principles, Blunt entrusted the 1st Kansas Colored Infantry, the first black combat regiment in the Union Army, with holding the center of his line. After nearly two hours of fighting, Blunt directed the 1st Kansas to advance and capture the rebel artillery.

The black soldiers soon found themselves exchanging volleys with the dismounted 20th and 29th Texas Cavalry, posted in support of Cooper's guns. In the midst of this standoff, the Union 2d Indian Home Guard Regiment blundered into the 1st Kansas Colored's field of fire. As the Indians scampered out of the way, the Confederates mistakenly assumed that Blunt's entire line was giving way. The 29th Texas surged forward with a cheer. The 1st Kansas calmly permitted their opponents to close to twenty-five paces and then unleashed a series of destructive volleys that sent the Texans reeling to the rear without their regimental colors. A jubilant Blunt later reported: "I never saw such fighting as was done by the negro regiment. They fought like veterans, with a coolness and valor that is unsurpassed. They preserved their line perfect throughout the whole engagement and, although in the hottest of the fight, they never once faltered. Too much praise cannot be awarded for their gallantry."

With the center of the Confederate line shattered beyond repair, Cooper retreated across Elk Creek. Blunt drove the Confederates past Honey Springs and managed to save much of the depot's stocks of foodstuffs from fires hastily set by his beaten foes. The fighting ended at 2:00 P.M., two hours before Cabell arrived on the scene with his 3,000 men from Fort Smith.

At a loss of seventeen killed and sixty wounded, Blunt had saved Fort Gibson and the Union foothold in Indian Territory. Cooper admitted to 134 killed and wounded and forty-seven captured, but his army had suffered a major blow. Henceforth, Confederate forces in Indian Territory would confine themselves to hit-and-run raids against Union supply trains.

—*Gregory J. W. Urwin*

See also African-American Soldiers, U.S.A.; Blunt, James G.; Fort Smith, Arkansas.

For further reading:

Britton, Wiley. *Memoirs of the Rebellion on the Border, 1863* (1993).

Cornish, Dudley Taylor. *The Sable Arm: Negro Troops in the Union Army, 1861–1865* (1966).

Fischer, LeRoy H. *The Civil War Era in Indian Territory* (1974).

Josephy, Alvin M. *The Civil War in the American West* (1991).

Rampp, Larry C., and Donald L. Rampp. *The Civil War in Indian Territory* (1975).

HOOD, JOHN BELL
(1831–1879)
Confederate general

John Bell Hood was one of the most complex and controversial Confederate generals in the Civil War, and he was the youngest man to hold four-star rank on either side of the conflict. Hood was born in Owingsville, Bath County, Kentucky. His father, a physician, was a prosperous member of the Montgomery County community and at one time owned thirty slaves. Despite his Kentucky heritage, John Bell Hood was eventually known as a Texan because of his leadership of the Texas Brigade during the early phase of the Civil War. He adopted his Texas identity when his home state failed to secede from the Union.

A rather unremarkable graduate of the U.S. Military Academy class of 1853, Hood was originally assigned to infantry duty, until he was made a second lieutenant in the 2d U.S. Cavalry, assigned to Jefferson Barracks, outside of St. Louis, Missouri. The newly formed 2d Cavalry was then commanded by Colonel Albert Sidney Johnston; second in command was Lieutenant Colonel Robert E. Lee. Other officers in this unit included William J. Hardee, Earl Van Dorn, Edmund Kirby Smith, George H. Thomas, George Stoneman, and many other men who would hold flag rank on both sides of the Civil War. After spending only enough time organizing the new unit, the 2d Cavalry troops made their way to their new posting on the frontier of Texas, where Hood remained until civil war broke out and Texas seceded in 1861. During his service with the 2d Cavalry, Hood experienced his first combat in 1857.

Kentucky eventually failed to secede from the Union, and Hood resigned from the army in April 1861 and embraced Texas as his sponsoring state into the Confederate army. In the fall of 1861, Hood, now a colonel, assumed command of the newly formed 4th Texas Regiment, which was stationed near Richmond, Virginia. Hood, a veteran of tough frontier conflicts and

a professionally educated soldier, soon turned the raw Texans into a formidable fighting force. After minor engagements in the Seven Pines campaign, Hood gained distinction during the battle for Gaines' Mill. By this time, Hood had been appointed brigade commander of the Texas units, receiving brigadier general rank in the early spring of 1862. After Lee replaced General Joseph E. Johnston as commander of the Army of Northern Virginia, Lee proceeded to clear Union forces that were hovering around the Confederate capital. Hood and his brigade were dispatched to an area near Cold Harbor, where the forces of Generals James Longstreet and A. P. Hill were engaging the enemy, who were well entrenched on Turkey Hill, near Gaines' Mill, which would become the name of the engagement. The subsequent fight was a major victory for Hood and his men and served as a prescient example of Hood's ability to lead men into battle and his willingness to go on the offensive.

The next test of his battle leadership came during the second battle near the Bull Run River at Manassas, Virginia. On 29 August, Hood's men, the advance party of reinforcements that Lee had sent in support, were placed in the center between "Stonewall" Jackson's corps, which had formed along the sunken ground of an unfinished railroad line, and Longstreet's forces, which had just linked up with Jackson's. After John Pope furiously assaulted Jackson's forces, Hood was ordered to advance, but Longstreet, aware of Hood's aggression and fearing an improper alignment of his forces caused by one unit advancing farther than the others, summoned Hood to explain his concern. By the time Hood returned to the fight, his men had already annihilated the forces in his path, eventually pushing Union forces all the way back to the Bull Run River in their rear. In the process of mopping up the battlefield, Hood and a group of Texas scouts confiscated some Union ambulances, which were soon claimed by Confederate general Nathan Evans, whose sector of the battlefield Hood's men had spread into and who also outranked the younger Hood. Hood subsequently ignored the order and was placed under arrest until Lee needed him in support of his invasion of Maryland. Although Lee never officially dropped charges and Hood never admitted culpability, the matter was never fully pursued. Hood quickly regained his leadership of the Texas Brigade just in time to engage in the battle that would make him one of the most famous combat leaders in the war.

Extricated from his legal complications, Hood and his troops advanced along with Longstreet's corps toward Sharpsburg, Maryland, a hamlet along Antietam Creek. Bivouacked on the Hagerstown turnpike, Hood's Texans saw limited action late on 16 September. With his men exhausted and without adequate food and clothing, Hood that evening retired several brigades to the rear to cook hot meals. No sooner had his men gotten their fires

started than the roar of battle and a formal summons to arms forced Hood and his men from their cooking and rest. Hood's men rushed to their original position with such force that the Union troops, which were just about to turn the fate of the battle in their favor, were stopped in the cornfield across from the Dunker Church. The shock of Hood's men, numbering merely 2,000 against a force of many times more, as they crashed into General Joseph Hooker's line, created one of the most devastating killing fields in U.S. military history. Hood's subsequent promotion to major general and assumption to a divisional command in the I Corps was effective 10 October 1862. Richard M. McMurry writes that in "three of the war's greatest battles his role had been impressive, if not decisive. It was also his good fortune to have fought under the eyes of the most important leaders of the army—Lee at Gaines' Mill, Longstreet at Second Manassas, and Jackson at Antietam. At thirty-one, the Texan was the youngest and most distinguished of Lee's nine major generals of infantry."

Hood's supreme test would come in the same battle that would prove to be the greatest test of Lee as well, Hood's leader and hero. Gettysburg would be the battle where both men would experience their greatest defeats. Hood was severely wounded before he was even heavily engaged in combat, and his troops were severely beaten on Little Round Top during fighting on the second day. Hood's confidence in Lee's military acumen had been somewhat shaken.

Not only did Gettysburg mark the beginning of the war's end; it also marked the last direct connection Hood would have with the Army of Northern Virginia and Lee, as he would be transferred to the Army of Tennessee. Longstreet's whole I Corps was sent by rail to join Braxton Bragg's outmaneuvered troops in the thick northwest Georgia woods just south of Chattanooga. Hood, who had been recuperating from his wounding at Gettysburg, joined his division as it passed through Richmond, his residence of convalescence. On 19 September, Hood's men crossed Chickamauga Creek so that Confederate forces could establish themselves against the Union forces building there. Eventually, the Confederates developed into a formation in which Hood's troops were in the center of the fight. On the 20th, Hood, finally impatient with the lack of advance, spurred his men forward. (For the day he had been given command of five divisions.) General Bushrod Johnson's troops, who were leading Hood's forces, miraculously found an unexpected vacant spot in the Union line and exploited it into one of the greatest routs not only in the war but in U.S. Army history as well. Meanwhile, Hood, who had noticed atypical confusion in his old 4th Texas, was severely wounded in the leg as he attempted to restore order in his former regiment. His leg was subsequently amputated. His second major wounding within the year came at the time of one more major victory on the battlefield. Hood, and the Confederacy for that matter, would never find such success on the battlefield again.

Hood was promoted to lieutenant general on 1 February 1864 and assigned to the command of Joseph E. Johnston, who had replaced Bragg as commander of the Army of Tennessee after Bragg had squandered his victory at Chickamauga and had allowed Union forces once again to secure Chattanooga. The Army of Tennessee was in Dalton, Georgia, awaiting Hood's return and William T. Sherman's inevitable advance.

Hood would eventually replace Johnston as commander of the Army of Tennessee. Hood served as Johnston's key corps commander during defensive engagements at Dalton, Resaca, Adairsville, Cassville, and Kennesaw Mountain, as Johnston back stepped to Atlanta. Hood seemingly maneuvered his way to replace Johnston as army commander just in time to find Sherman at the gates of Atlanta and the Confederates with few options to pursue. Hood's early attempts at army leadership resulted in sharp engagements at Peachtree Creek, Atlanta, and finally Ezra Church, where he defended his position against probing actions by Sherman. None of these fights relieved Hood of

Sherman's pressure on Atlanta. Hood then had to face Sherman's long-distance artillery, the effect of which was to diminish the value of Atlanta by blowing everything up. Hood, realizing that he could not wait indefinitely, sent General Joseph Wheeler's cavalry to attack Sherman's supply line that extended through North Georgia. The raid failed to pull Sherman back from the city to protect his supply line. Finally, after Sherman severely punished one of Hood's corps at Jonesboro, even Hood had to realize that his continued defense of Atlanta was hopelessly untenable.

After abandoning Atlanta, Hood retreated to western Georgia and eastern Alabama and attempted to harass Sherman's communication lines. Battles at Allatoona were typical of these engagements, but Hood soon found out just how careful a commander Sherman was in preparing his army for any contingency. Hood then devised a plan that he believed would be bold enough to turn the tide of the war: take his army into middle Tennessee and dislodge the Union forces from Nashville, which would then force Sherman from Atlanta. What followed was one of the most needless wastages of life in this phase of the war.

After gathering and nominally resupplying the remnants of his army in northwestern Alabama, Hood

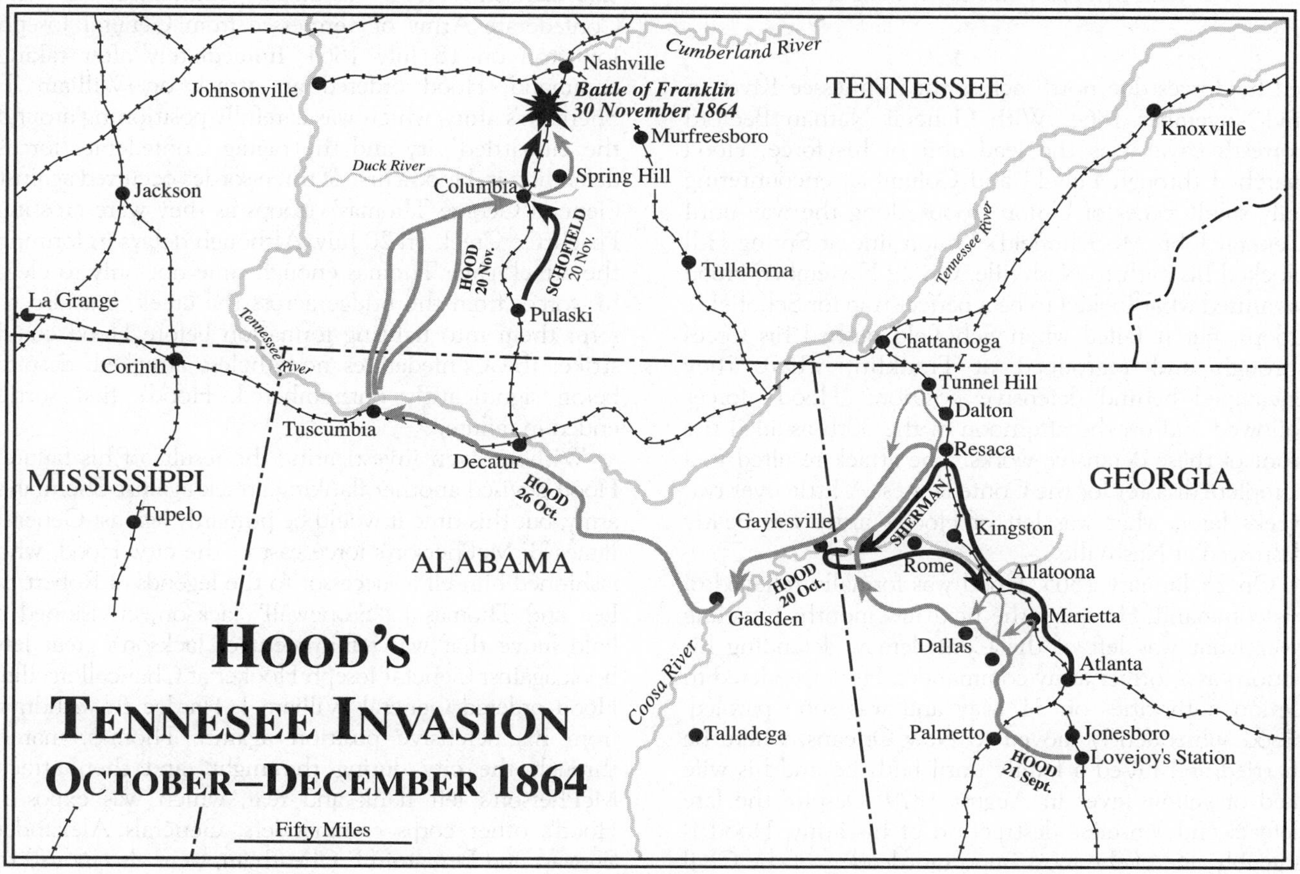

HOOD'S TENNESEE INVASION OCTOBER–DECEMBER 1864

John Bell Hood (*Library of Congress*)

War. Had it not been for his aggressive actions in the early battles, Lee would have had a much more difficult time finding victories than he did, especially at Antietam, where Lee's whole army was in danger of destruction until Hood turned the tide.

—*James Meredith*

See also Antietam, Battle of; Army of Tennessee; Atlanta Campaign; Chickamauga, Battle of; Franklin, Battle of; Nashville, Battle of.

For further reading:

Coffey, David. *John Bell Hood and the Struggle for Atlanta* (1998).

Freeman, Douglas Southall. *Lee's Lieutenants: A Study in Command* (1942–1944).

Hood, John Bell, General. *Advance and Retreat: Personal Experiences in the United States and Confederate States Armies* (1993).

McMurry, Richard M. *John Bell Hood and the War for Southern Independence* (1982).

O'Connor, Richard. *Hood: Cavalier General* (1949).

HOOD'S SECOND SORTIE (BATTLE OF ATLANTA)
(21–22 July 1864)

Hood's Second Sortie, also known as the battle of Atlanta, occurred just days after General John Bell Hood assumed command of the Confederate Army of Tennessee from General Joseph Johnston on 18 July 1864. Immediately after taking command, Hood ordered an attack on William T. Sherman's army, which was carefully positioning around the embattled city and the ragtag Confederate forces defending it. Hood's first of three sorties occurred against General George Thomas's troops as they were crossing Peachtree Creek on 20 July. Although delays in forming the attack gave Thomas enough time not only to clear his forces from the bridge across the creek, but also to form them into fighting formation before Hood could strike, the Confederates nonetheless attacked, despite being significantly outnumbered. Hood's first sortie ended in failure.

Without even investigating the results of his failure, Hood devised another flanking attack against Sherman's army, but this time it would be primarily against General James B. McPherson's force east of the city. Hood, who fashioned himself a successor to the legends of Robert E. Lee and Thomas J. "Stonewall" Jackson, envisioned a bold move that was reminiscent of Jackson's great left hook against General Joseph Hooker at Chancellorsville. Hood ordered General William J. Hardee to withdraw from his defensive position against Thomas, march through the city during the night, and then attack McPherson's left flank and rear, which was exposed. Hood's other corps commanders, Generals Alexander Stewart and Benjamin F. Cheatham, were also moved to

led his forces due north across the Tennessee River in mid-November 1864. With General Nathan Bedford Forrest's cavalry as the lead unit of his force, Hood marched through Pulaski and Columbia, encountering only small forces of Union troops along the way until General John M. Schofield's Union line at Spring Hill blocked his path to Nashville. On 29 November, Hood organized what looked to be a perfect trap for Schofield's troops, but it failed when Schofield pushed his forces through and regrouped at Franklin, where they encamped behind defensive positions. Hood's forces followed and on the afternoon of the 30th assailed the front of these defensive works. The attack resulted in a complete disaster for the Confederates. A little over two weeks later, what was left of Hood's army was nearly destroyed at Nashville.

On 23 January 1865, Hood was formally relieved of his command. He spent the next few months traveling over what was left of the Confederacy, defending his actions as a former army commander. He surrendered to Union authorities on 31 May and was soon paroled. Hood subsequently moved to New Orleans, where he married and raised a family until both he and his wife died of yellow fever in August 1879. Despite the late defeats and senseless destruction of his army, Hood is arguably one of the most important leaders of the Civil fill in where Hardee's men vacated. In addition to these movements of his infantry, Hood's cavalry was also ordered first to screen Hardee's movements and then move on to attack the Union's supply center in Decatur, which was several miles in the Union rear.

Hardee's nighttime march was not only slowed by the crowded roads, which the cavalry cleared from time to time as they tried to move out ahead, but the Confederates were still exhausted from their strenuous defeat at Peachtree Creek. By the time Hardee got his forces into battle formation, it was several hours behind schedule and McPherson, not fully aware that something was afoot, had nonetheless cautiously turned two divisions to protect his rear. McPherson, fearing that his line was too thin to defend a frontal advance, had also contracted his forces. When Hardee's lead elements did attack, McPherson's Union forces were miraculously ready to defend.

The clash did not go as Hood had initially planned. Hardee's offensive met with limited success, as one of his three division commanders was killed immediately and the other two were finding the going tough as well. While Union general Grenville Dodge's two divisions, having marched into the battle just minutes before the clamor began, were holding their own, McPherson's other positions were in more trouble. Confederate general Patrick Cleburne's troops, having attacked the Union line at an angle, had already pushed the Union opposition back and some of his men were roaming in the Union rear lines by the time McPherson got back from his early-morning visit with Sherman. Traveling only with an orderly, McPherson stumbled into a group of Confederates, who shot and killed him as he galloped away. He was the highest-ranking Union officer to die in the war. Sherman was deeply troubled by the death of his friend and fellow Ohioan, but he quickly replaced McPherson with General "Black Jack" Logan, who immediately worked to restore his line, which had been significantly disturbed by Cleburne's fierce advance. The battle raged for several more hours, with the most continuous fighting taking place at Leggett's Hill. But Logan roused the spirit of his men, particularly that of his embattled troops at Leggett's Hill, which was now being attacked by yet another Confederate division. However, despite the Confederates' spirited attack, especially by Cleburne's troops, the clash ended once again in disappointment for Hood, not much better than the fate of the first sortie, except that his men did capture a large collection of guns that had been moved forward to bombard Atlanta. Again, Hood's offensive plans ended up merely bleeding his already greatly diminished force; but despite even this pointless attack against greatly superior forces, Hood was not satisfied and immediately planned his third sortie. Casualties for the Confederates numbered around 8,500, and Union losses were about 3,650.

—*James H. Meredith*

See also Atlanta Campaign; Atlanta, Georgia; Hood, John Bell.
For further reading:
Coffey, David. *John Bell Hood and the Struggle for Atlanta* (1998).
Kennedy, Frances H., ed. *The Civil War Battlefield Guide* (1998).

HOOKER, JOSEPH
(1814–1879)
Union general

An ambitious general officer, Joseph Hooker is best known for being the victim of Confederate general Robert E. Lee when the Army of Northern Virginia humiliated the Army of the Potomac at Chancellorsville in 1863. Originally from Hadley, Massachusetts, Hooker was born on 13 November 1814 and graduated twenty-ninth in his West Point Class of 1837. He was first assigned to artillery and drew duty in the Second Seminole War. After serving back at West Point, he fought in the Mexican-American War, where he earned three promotions for distinguished service.

Before the Civil War began, Hooker reached the rank of lieutenant colonel and served duty on the West Coast. Hooker's biographer, Walter H. Hebert, notes that during this assignment he cultivated the bad habits that would taint the rest of his life and career. Hooker resigned from the U.S. Army on 21 February 1853. When the Southern states seceded from the Union, Hooker returned east to seek a prominent military command. After attempting to gain the rank that his background deserved, Hooker's efforts were repulsed by the general of the army, Winfield Scott, who held enmity against him. Hooker eventually procured his promotion to brigadier general.

Hooker was assigned to the Army of the Potomac, where he served his new commander, General George McClellan, well. Hooker organized and drilled his men hard and soon was promoted to command a division of about 10,000 combined troops. Hooker's first chance to demonstrate his leadership in serious combat came during McClellan's Peninsula campaign near Yorktown and Williamsburg, Virginia. On 5 May 1862, while Hooker was waiting for McClellan's army to fully unlimber from their boat ride out of Washington, D.C., he decided independently to attack a Confederate fortification, resulting in casualties involving 20 percent of his division. Hebert comments that although the battle was unnecessary, it was "the roughest fighting any division of the Army of the Potomac had experienced to date." News coverage of this battle gave him notoriety and the basis for his "Fighting Joe" agnomen, a reference the general seemed to chafe at throughout his life. Although his command was somewhat tested at the battle of Oak Grove, it was actually nothing more than an extended confrontation to advance picket lines. His division did capture Malvern Hill, a potentially important objective to be used against Lee, but McClellan was too busy trying to extricate his army from the Virginia Peninsula to take advantage of Hooker's determined effort. Hooker's division suffered 25 percent of the Army of the Potomac's entire casualties, although they represented less than 10 percent of the force.

While McClellan was retreating back to Washington, another Union army, led by General John Pope, was lurking in northern Virginia as a potential threat to Lee's force. Hooker's men fought almost continually during confrontations that were a prelude to the battle of Second Bull Run and took an exceptional beating during the actual battle itself, including participating in a bayonet charge and hand-to-hand combat against Thomas J. "Stonewall" Jackson's troops as well. After Pope's defeat and transfer, McClellan moved ahead to stop Lee from his impending offensive into Maryland.

Despite participating in another Union defeat at Second Bull Run, Hooker had furthered his reputation as a highly capable divisional commander.

Lee's probe into Maryland would not only dramatically test McClellan and the nerves of President Lincoln and the Army of the Potomac, it would also challenge Hooker's new responsibility as a corps commander. In charge of I Corps of the Army of the Potomac, Hooker was ordered into Maryland by his wing commander, General Ambrose Burnside. Hooker's corps confronted the Confederates and fought the battle of South Mountain, which he considered a significant achievement. During this battle, Hooker demonstrated competence in moving his large force around the battlefield. Hooker's corps advanced to Sharpsburg and stopped on 16 September just north of town. On the 17th, his men drew artillery fire early in the morning as they advanced toward the gray line awaiting them in a cornfield and woods just north of the Dunker Church. Hooker's guns

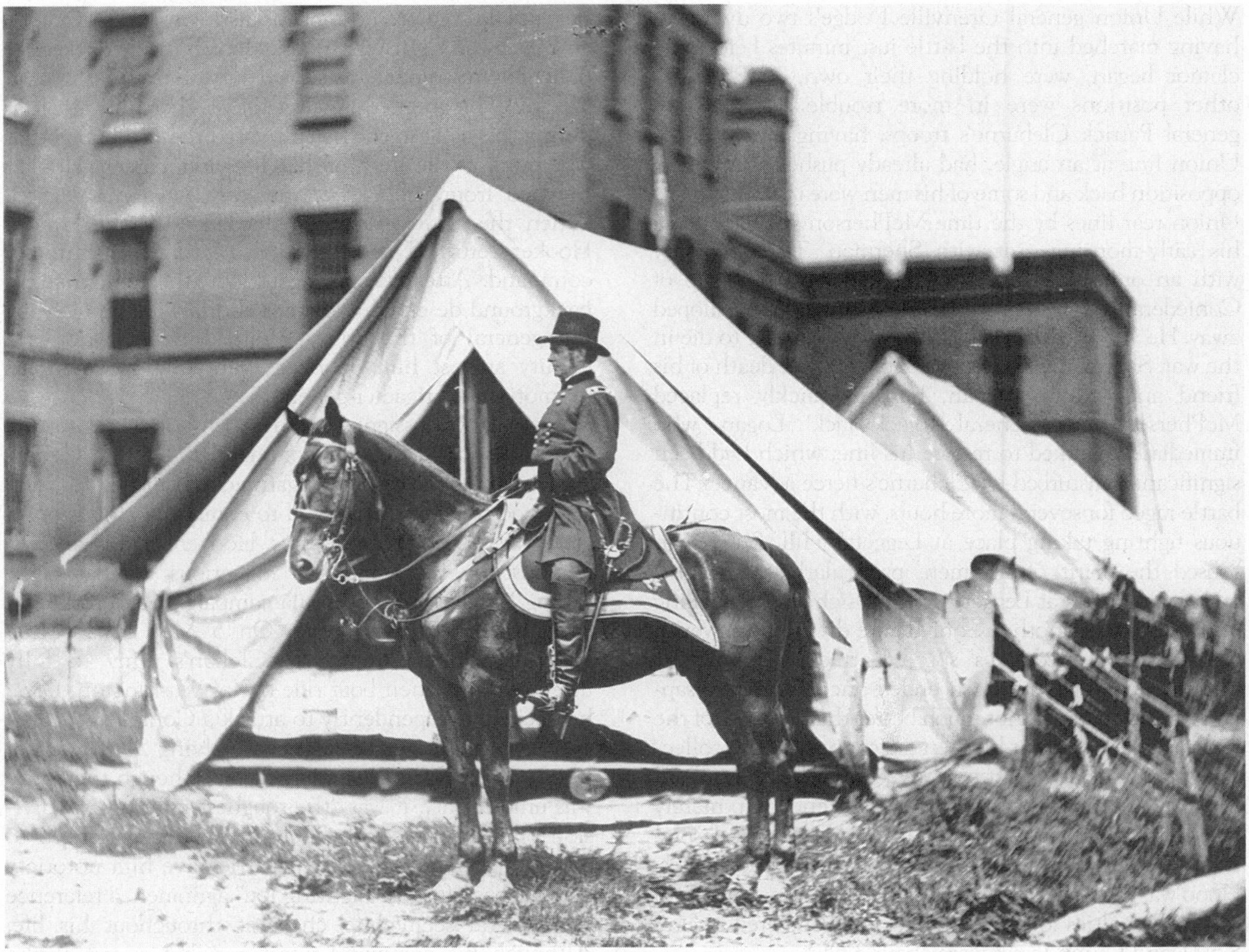

General Hooker on horseback (*Library of Congress*)

answered back and cut into the corn and the Confederates as his men pushed their way into the enemy position. The carnage on both sides was like nothing ever seen until that day. Both sides seemed determined to destroy the other and settle the fight on that day. Hooker's determined men soon ran into another group of tough fighters, led by Confederate general John Bell Hood, whose men ran into the battle from campfires in the rear, where they had been attempting to cook a quick meal. The result of this collision was one of the most horrific killing fields in history, even wounding Hooker, who had loitered too close to the battlefield. Hooker's demonstrative resolve to carry the fight to the enemy at Antietam may have been his greatest battlefield achievement of the war; his men almost demolished Jackson's opposing corps, which would have certainly imperiled Lee's whole army. Although the intense shock of Hood's charge into Hooker's men halted his advance, the punishment that he was willing to give the Confederates showed the enemy that the Union was now willing to fight to the death.

With his wounded foot making him too disabled to maintain command, Hooker convalesced in Washington, where he could keep up with the politics of the day and the advancement of his career until duty put him back in command. Burnside, his new commander, put Hooker in charge of the Center Grand Division, a combination of III and V Corps. McClellan had failed to follow up on Lee's precarious situation after the battle of Antietam and therefore had been replaced; Hooker of course was disappointed in not being named as overall commander and began a campaign to erode confidence in Burnside.

General James Longstreet's utter defeat of Burnside on Marye's Heights above Fredericksburg, Virginia, in December quickly diminished Lincoln's confidence in his new commander, but it took the great Mud March humiliation of the Army of the Potomac in January to finish off Burnside, and Hooker thus got his chance to command an army, with War Department General Order No. 20 of 25 January 1863.

Hooker quickly reorganized the army into twelve separate divisions and implemented a badge system to build unit cohesion in the different units. Because so much of the command structure had been in such disarray throughout the war, the morale of the army was dismal, so Hooker energetically set about correcting the situation. By spring of that year, however, Hooker was getting pressure to attack, and when the weather did finally cooperate, he began his much-anticipated offensive. On 27 April 1863, Hooker put into motion one of the most brilliant opening moves of the war that would lead to the battle of Chancellorsville. Maintaining a holding force opposite Fredericksburg with General John Sedgwick, his old West Point classmate, Hooker swung the preponderance of his force around the left flank of Lee's army at Kelly's Ford and then moved back toward the Union's own left wing, covering the various fords that crossed the Rapidan River as they progressed back toward Fredericksburg on the other side of the river. The objective of the movement was to come completely behind Lee and force him to leave his defensive position at Fredericksburg. Lee, initially caught off guard by the audacity of Hooker's move, ordered a counter move that proved equally audacious—he divided his already inferior army and decided to fight the greatly superior force on two fronts. Of course, Lee would eventually further divide his army again and send Jackson around the right flank of Hooker's, but that would come later.

Hooker's maneuver worked well as his army safely crossed the Rapidan, but by the last day of April his own success seemingly caught him more off guard than it did Lee, and he became inexplicably defensive. Lee used Hooker's indecision to gather his forces in front of the Union's main force; he had not taken Hooker's bluff. Hooker never realized that Lee had taken advantage of the Union's divided force to attack, and Hooker was never able to recover the initiative after he encountered Lee on 1 May. Hooker awoke the next day from his sleep in the Chancellor House confident of his position and totally unaware of Lee's operations.

Hooker ordered a contraction of his line, giving up the best ground on the field in the process. On 2 May, it would get even worse for Hooker. During the night before, Lee and Jackson had their famous conference in the Wilderness, and the next day, 2 May, Jackson made his way around Hooker's flank and attacked him late in the evening; General Oliver O. Howard's corps was completely routed, and Hooker was defeated. It would take two more days of conflict, however, for Hooker to extricate his army from the "brilliant" trap he had put them in. Not only was Hooker stunned after the battle from the nearby explosion that had temporarily incapacitated him on 3 May, but his miserable defeat, when so much success had been anticipated, put him in a funk as well. Because of deteriorating relations between himself and the national leadership, including the president, Hooker resigned and was relieved on 28 June 1863. General George G. Meade was hurriedly named the new commander because Lee had already began his invasion of the north that led to Gettysburg.

After the Union's complete defeat at Chickamauga in September 1863, which led to their ignominious siege in Chattanooga, Hooker was finally dispatched to General William Rosecrans's Army of the Cumberland, taking XI and XII Corps with him. Grant soon took charge of all operations in Chattanooga, and Hooker assisted him in breaking the siege. Hooker's troops were victorious on Lookout Mountain, in the "Battle above the Clouds." And when Sherman replaced Grant in the West,

Hooker was a reliable lieutenant in the drive through the rugged mountains of north Georgia to take Atlanta and the eventual "March to the Sea." At New Hope Church, a spot four miles from Dallas, Georgia, Hooker regained his tenacious form and stubbornly sent his troops into a highly defensible Confederate position. Although his forces were twice repulsed, and he received the far greater number of casualties in the engagement, his fire at least demonstrated that his former epic defeats, especially the unreconciled humiliation at Chancellorsville, had not completely extinguished his fighting spirit. But of course none of these later fights ever seemed to matter to Hooker, especially since Sherman would not trust him for higher command. The ultimate insult came when Sherman replaced General James McPherson, who had been killed in battle, with the same General Howard whom Hooker pointedly blamed for his defeat at Chancellorsville. Hooker resigned from Sherman's command and was subsequently sent to Chicago to command reserve troops there, where he served the rest of the war. Hooker died suddenly on 31 October 1879 and was buried in Garden City, New York.

Hooker's military career is best summarized by stating that he was successful as a divisional and corps commander, but on his one occasion in charge of an army, he was an absolute failure. However, despite his humiliation, his vicious assault at Antietam could be argued as one key turning point in the war.

—James Meredith

See also Antietam, Battle of; Atlanta Campaign; Burnside, Ambrose Everett; Chancellorsville, Battle of; Fredericksburg, Battle of; Peninsula Campaign; South Mountain, Battle of.
For further reading:
Hebert, Walter H. *Fighting Joe Hooker* (1944).

HOPKINS, JULIET OPIE
(1818–1890)
Confederate hospital official

As the daughter of wealthy Virginia planters and the wife of one of Alabama's most influential men, Juliet Opie Hopkins might have insulated herself from the horrors of bloodshed and the ensuing dreariness of hospital life. But early experience and high social position had fitted her for a life of public service. Juliet's education at a Richmond finishing school came to an abrupt end in 1834 when her mother died and the sixteen year old was called home to take charge of the household, which included 2,000 slaves. In 1837 she married a naval lieutenant who left her property at his death twelve years later. At thirty-six she was married to Arthur Hopkins, a sixty-year-old political party leader, railroad tycoon, and the chief justice of the Alabama Supreme Court. Managing her parents' slaves and Judge Hopkins's extensive property taught the mild-mannered

Juliet how to rule with an iron fist. A Mobile neighbor wrote in 1861, "If you had been a man you would have been a commanding general."

Forty-three and childless when the war began, Hopkins and her husband used their fortune to establish hospitals for Alabama soldiers in Richmond. As early as April 1861, Juliet organized relief efforts in Mobile for the sick under General William Hardee's command. When the Confederate capital moved from Montgomery to Richmond in early summer, so did the Hopkinses. Before the Confederate government appointed her superintendent of Alabama hospitals in November, Hopkins had already advertised in the *Richmond Dispatch* for nurse volunteers and opened two hospitals: one on Fifth Street between Clay and Leigh, the other at Twenty-fifth and Franklin. A third hospital was operating three blocks away from the second by the spring of 1862.

As chief executive of the Alabama hospitals, Hopkins was responsible for hiring support staff. Girls in their twenties from rural Alabama wrote inquiring about what was expected of nurses: "If a soldier should have his leg amputated or be wounded in his stomach," asked one modest applicant, "would it be expected of a young lady to dress those wounds?" Hopkins turned away nursing hopefuls if she thought that the necessary compromise of delicacy would vex an applicant's family members. Richmond's first families hired out their slaves to do cooking, cleaning, laundering, and heavy lifting in the hospitals—jobs that working-class whites were glad to get. Surgeons reported to Hopkins when workers were "noisy, troublesome and ill-bred," expecting her to produce less objectionable replacements. Along with managing personnel and maintaining a voluminous correspondence, Hopkins procured food and supplies from the medical purveyor's office. A windfall of a chicken coop and eight dozen eggs in 1861 was unheard of by midwar, when the Federal blockade of the Mississippi River and Southern ports along the Atlantic imperiled delivery.

Throughout her tenure as superintendent, Hopkins ruled with a high level of approval, an unusual accomplishment considering her considerable responsibilities and the tensions that caring for the dying inevitably excited. Men recognized her competence and deferred to her. Patients appreciated her fairness and proved their devotion in letters praising her after they returned to the field. When the Confederate government decided to centralize relief operations in the fall of 1862, administrators of state hospitals lost clout. Hopkins kept her hospitals running for another year, when the spring and summer campaigns of 1862 and 1863 produced thousands of casualties. Indeed, she believed she could do the job better than the Confederate surgeon general. But after being wounded in the leg as she directed the removal of wounded men from the field at Fair Oaks—an injury that permanently compromised her gait—Hopkins began to think about phasing out the hospitals. By November 1863 she had moved back to Alabama, where she volunteered in Montgomery hospitals and at Camp Watts near Tuskegee in 1864 and 1865.

Hopkins told Confederate nurse Kate Cumming that she and her husband had only corn bread and bacon to eat as they made their way back to Mobile after the war, an indication not only of scarcity but of their personal losses as a result of the war. When Judge Hopkins died in 1866, Juliet settled in Fort Hamilton, New York, with an adopted niece, on land it is believed she inherited from her first husband. The seventeen-year-old niece, also named Juliet, married a fifty-four-year-old army officer in 1880, she later confessed, to provide a home for her aunt. His death in 1888 further impoverished the Hopkins women. Taking in sewing to augment household income, the woman whose image had once graced Confederate bills spent her last years in relative obscurity. She died in Washington, D.C., in 1890 at the age of seventy-one.

—*Jane E. Schultz*

See also Cumming, Kate; Nurses.

For further reading:

Bridges, Edwin. "The Alabama Hospitals in Richmond." Unpublished manuscript.
Griffith, Lucille. "Mrs. Juliet Opie Hopkins and Alabama Military Hospitals." *Alabama Review* (1953).
Hopkins, Juliet Opie. Collection. Alabama Department of Archives and History, Montgomery.

HOTCHKISS, JEDEDIAH
(1828–1899)
Confederate mapmaker

"Make me a map of the valley," Stonewall Jackson ordered his topographical engineer in 1862, cementing Jedediah Hotchkiss's reputation as the Confederacy's foremost military cartographer. Hotchkiss, the topographical engineer for the 2d Corps of the Army of Northern Virginia, had a gift for both assessing terrain and making clear and comprehensible maps. Hotchkiss's maps, particularly those he made for Stonewall Jackson, made possible some of the Confederacy's greatest victories.

Jedediah Hotchkiss was born on 30 November 1828 to Stiles Hotchkiss and the former Lydia Beecher (a distant relative of the abolitionist Beechers—Lyman, Henry Ward, and Harriet Beecher Stowe) in Windsor, Broome County, New York. After graduating from Windsor Academy in 1846, Hotchkiss taught for a year in the coal country of Pennsylvania. While on a walking tour of western Virginia during the summer of 1847, Hotchkiss was offered a position as a tutor in Mossy Creek, Virginia, a small hamlet in the Shenandoah Valley county of Augusta. He accepted the job and within a few years had opened his own school, the first of two Hotchkiss would run in Augusta county during the 1850s. In his spare time Hotchkiss studied both engineering and the principles of mapmaking. He was also a devout Presbyterian who taught a popular young men's Bible class. Hotchkiss married Sarah Ann Comfort, a Pennsylvania woman, in 1853, and the couple had two daughters: Nellie and Anne.

As the sectional crisis intensified in 1860 and 1861, Hotchkiss was living quietly in Churchville, Virginia, with his young family and running the very successful Loch Willow Academy. Although his brother was a staunch Unionist, Hotchkiss tried to avoid involvement in politics until Virginia seceded in April 1861. At this point Hotchkiss had been living in Virginia for fourteen years and felt that his allegiance lay with his adopted state. Thus, in June he closed his school (which had already lost the majority of its students to the army) and joined the Confederate Army as a military topographer. Ironically, although Hotchkiss became the Confederacy's best known mapmaker, his lack of an engineering degree kept him out of the Confederate Engineering Corps, which was dominated by West Point graduates.

The Confederacy needed maps desperately, and Hotchkiss was put to work immediately. His job was to explore and report on a region, taking note of both the physical or geological features of the terrain (for example, hills, streams, forests), and the man-made additions (for example, farms, bridges, macadamized roads). He noted locations of wood for fires, forage for horses, and water for drinking. Despite being self-taught, Hotchkiss was skilled at estimating distances and elevations, and his maps were praised for their clarity and elegant style. A bout of typhoid fever sent Hotchkiss home to convalesce in August 1861, but he returned to the field in March 1862 as a member of Stonewall Jackson's staff.

Hotchkiss did some of his finest work for Jackson, who as skilled a general as he was, had difficulty in reading the lay of the land around him. Hotchkiss's maps, and particularly his careful uses of different colored pencils to distinguish features, made Jackson's work easier in the 1862 Shenandoah Valley campaign. Hotchkiss continued his mapmaking at Second Manassas and during the 1862 invasion of Maryland. He was with Jackson at Chancellorsville, and shared a tent with James Boswell, who was wounded along with Jackson on 2 May 1863. Hotchkiss felt keenly the loss of his friend and his general, and wrote his wife that he was so despondent that "I do not know whether I shall stay here or not."

Hotchkiss did stay with the army for the remainder of the war, except for a few trips home either to handle business or recover from illness. He performed recon-

naissance around Gettysburg for General Richard Ewell and after the battle mapped out the route for the retreating Army of Northern Virginia. In 1864 he again drew on his familiarity with the Shenandoah Valley to help General Early, and participated in Early's summertime raid on Washington, D.C. The end of the war found him in Lynchburg, and he received his parole in Staunton in May 1865.

Immediately after the war Hotchkiss reopened Loch Willow Academy and returned to the classroom. During the fall of 1865 he was ordered to turn over his war maps to the Union Army. He refused, and protested to Ulysses S. Grant that to do so would destroy their historical value. Grant agreed, and allowed Hotchkiss to submit copies while keeping his originals. In the years after the war, Hotchkiss was much sought after as a reference for Confederate soldiers and officers writing their memoirs, and he himself contributed the Virginia volume to Confederate Military History. He left teaching in 1867 and dedicated the rest of his life to engineering work and encouraging commercial and mining development in Virginia. During the 1880s he contributed his maps to the Official Records of the War of the Rebellion, and half of the maps in the atlas are his. He died on 17 January 1899, at home in Staunton.

—Anne Sarah Rubin

See also Cedar Creek, Battle of; Jackson, Thomas J.; Shenandoah Valley Campaign (1862); Shenandoah Valley Campaign (1864–1865).

For further reading:

LeGear, Clara E. *The Hotchkiss Map Collection: A List of Manuscript Maps* (1977).

McDonald, Archie P., ed. *Make Me a Map of the Valley: The Civil War Journal of Stonewall Jackson's Topographer Jedediah Hotchkiss* (1973).

Miller, William J. *Mapping for Stonewall: The Civil War Service of Jed Hotchkiss* (1993).

Roper, Peter W. *Jedediah Hotchkiss, Rebel Mapmaker and Virginia Businessman* (1992).

"The Valley of the Shadow: Two Communities in the American Civil War" <http://jefferson.village.virginia.edu/vshadow2> (website)

HOTZE, HENRY
(1833–1887)
Confederate agent and editor

Born in Zurich, Switzerland, to Rudolph Hotze and Sophia Esslinger Hotze, Henry Hotze came to Mobile, Alabama, as a young man. He quickly became involved in publishing and soon became one of the editors of the Mobile *Register*. He also became interested in commercial and diplomatic issues and served for one year as a secretary to the U.S. ministry in Brussels, Belgium. He returned to Mobile to accept the chief editorship of the *Register*.

At the outbreak of the Civil War, Hotze wasted no time in demonstrating his allegiance to the Confederacy. He wrote to Confederate secretary of war Leroy Pope Walker in April 1861 asking if Confederate president Jefferson Davis would mind if a group of Confederates seized the U.S. transport *Illinois*, then in port in New Orleans. Hotze also briefly served in the Confederate army before being summoned to Richmond in August 1861.

In Richmond, Hotze was asked to travel to Europe as a purchasing agent for arms and munitions and to work directly for the secretary of war. Hotze accepted the appointment and left for Canada, from where he would travel by British steamer for Europe. En route to Canada, however, he was delayed for several days when involved in a train wreck in Indiana. After finally making it to Canada, he sailed for England.

Hotze made his headquarters in England, where he made arrangements for supplies to be shipped back to the Confederacy. He lamented, however, that he and other agents would probably be more successful in their endeavors if the Confederacy would free the slaves.

This belief in the propaganda value of freeing the slaves fit well into Hotze's other primary activity in England—the editing of a Confederate propaganda newspaper called the *Index*. This paper, aimed primarily at western Europe, was designed to convince the people and governments of Europe of the correctness of the Confederate cause so that aid to that cause might be forthcoming.

After the war, Hotze chose not to return to the United States. He remained active in journalism in several European countries and died in Switzerland.

—David S. Heidler and Jeanne T. Heidler

See also Walker, Leroy Pope.

For further reading:

Cullop Charles P. *Confederate Propaganda in Europe* (1969).

HOUSATONIC

Best known for the unique manner in which it was lost, the *Housatonic* was one of the numerous vessels built during the war to enforce the Union's blockade of Southern ports. The 1,240-ton screw sloop, which carried 11 guns and a crew of 160, was launched at the Boston Navy Yard in November 1861. Commissioned in August 1862 under Commodore William R. Taylor, the *Housatonic* departed Boston for blockade duty the following month, arriving soon afterward at Charleston for duty with the South Atlantic Blockading Squadron under Rear Admiral Samuel Du Pont.

In January 1863, its boat crews help to board and refloat the blockade runner *Princess Royal*, which had gone aground carrying engines for Confederate ironclads. Later that month, the *Housatonic* helped repulse a sortie by two Confederate ironclad rams, *Chicora* and *Palmetto State*, but not before the blockader *Mercedita* was captured (it was immediately released with its crew forced to give their parole) and three other Union vessels damaged. There followed for the *Housatonic* a period of routine service, interrupted by the capture of two blockade runners, *Neptune* in April and *Secesh* in May. Along with the other wooden ships blockading Charleston, the *Housatonic* remained in reserve during the unsuccessful ironclad assault on the port's defenses in early April.

In mid-July the *Housatonic*'s howitzers fired in support of an assault on Battery Wagner as part of the Union effort to capture Charleston. The failure of this assault was followed by another seven months of blockade duty, during which time the *Housatonic* contributed boat crews for coastal bombardment and landing raiding parties. This period of activity ended in the assault by the Confederate submarine *Hunley* on 17 February 1864.

Maintaining its regular station about five and a half miles outside Charleston harbor, the *Housatonic*, now commanded by Captain C. W. Pickering, was approached by the *Hunley*, which was under orders not to submerge. A combination of calm seas and clear weather allowed the officer of the deck, Acting Master J. N. Crosby, to spot the oncoming Confederate vessel. Crosby initiated evasive maneuvers and called the crew to quarters, but within two minutes the *Hunley* had rammed its spar torpedo, armed with 90 pounds of explosive, into the *Housatonic* just forward of the mizzenmast on the starboard side. The resulting explosion settled the *Housatonic* quickly by the stern in 28 feet of water. Because most of the crew had rushed topside upon hearing Crosby's alarm, only two officers and three men were lost. Many of the crew found safety in the rigging, which remained above water even after the ship hit bottom.

The *Housatonic* thus became the first vessel ever sunk by a submarine. Its loss was not noticed by its squadron mates until morning, when its survivors were rescued. However, the *Hunley* and its crew of nine failed to return from their mission.

—*Stephen C. Svonavec*

See also Blockade of C.S.A.; Blockade Runners; Fort Wagner, Battle of; *Hunley*.

For further reading:

Anderson, Bern. *By Sea and by River: The Naval History of the Civil War* (1962).

Fowler, William M., Jr. *Under Two Flags: The American Navy in the Civil War* (1990).

Mooney, James L., ed. *Dictionary of American Naval Fighting Ships* (1976).

HOUSTON, SAM
(1793–1863)
Governor of Texas

Whether it meant dressing in Native American clothing, abandoning political office because of a failed marriage, or leading a newly formed country, Sam Houston was his own man. His life was intimately involved with the issues of Jacksonian

Sam Houston (*National Archives*)

America and the antebellum United States, and Houston attempted, ultimately unsuccessfully, to preserve his native country of the United States and his adopted country and state of Texas.

Born 2 March 1793 near Lexington, Virginia, Houston asserted his independence at an early age. Shortly after moving to Tennessee following the death of his father, Houston ran away and lived with the Cherokee in eastern Tennessee. This three-year excursion shaped his later relationships with this native group.

When the War of 1812 began, Houston enlisted as an ensign in the state militia of Tennessee. His first experience with military conflict occurred during the battle of Horseshoe Bend in March 1814. By then a third lieutenant, Houston led a charge against the Creek Indian fortification, receiving wounds in the shoulder and thigh for his efforts. General Andrew Jackson recognized Houston's amicable camaraderie with the Cherokee in the militia and in 1817 recommended that Houston become a subagent to the Cherokee. Houston's duty was to persuade his longtime friends to give up their lands in the east and move to the Arkansas Territory.

Houston resigned his commission in March 1818 and returned to Nashville, Tennessee. He was admitted to the bar and, after studying and practicing law in nearby Lebanon and then serving as district attorney of

Davidson County (Nashville), he abandoned a career in law to enter Congress in 1823. With the full support of Jackson and Tennessee governor William Carroll, Houston ran unopposed for one of Tennessee's House seats. In 1825, he won reelection. These victories encouraged him to seek the governorship in 1827, which he won. While campaigning for reelection in 1829, Houston's recent marriage to Eliza Allen fell apart, possibly because her youth had been so sheltered that she was unable to abide scars from his War of 1812 wounds. Heartbroken and probably angry, Houston resigned his office and moved to Three Forks in the Arkansas Territory to live with the Cherokee.

Houston spent the next few years interceding on behalf of the Cherokee, negotiating treaties with Indian groups in Texas at the behest of President Jackson, and speculating in land ventures. As his reputation grew among the American settlers in Texas, they looked to him when the Texas Revolution needed a military commander in 1836. Houston's leadership of the Texas army played a crucial part in the capture of the Mexican leader, General Antonio Lopez Santa Anna, at the battle of San Jacinto. Texas won its independence as a result of this victory. Its residents elected Houston as their first president in 1836. He served two years in office, during which time he unsuccessfully attempted to bring about the annexation of Texas to the United States.

After leaving office for one term because of constitutional limitations, Houston won the presidency again in 1841. By now married to his third wife, Margaret Lea (his second wife was Tiana Rogers, a Cherokee), Houston ventured again to bring about annexation of his adopted country without result. However, shortly after the end of his three-year term, he realized his hopes when the United States annexed Texas, and then made it a state in 1845. Houston became one of the first U.S. senators from the new state in 1846. For the next thirteen years, he watched his fellow Southerners slowly and decisively isolate themselves from their Northern counterparts. Houston alone of the Southern senators voted for every item contained in the legislation of 1850 that eventually passed as the Compromise of 1850. When the Know-Nothing Party arose with its emphasis on "America first," Houston supported its principles.

Houston's compromise stance and support of the Union and Constitution eventually brought unfavorable consequences to his political career. In 1857 he lost his campaign for the governorship of Texas. Two years later, he lost his Senate seat but won the gubernatorial race. He opposed the calls for secession within the state and nation, but to no avail. Texas residents voted to remove the state from the Union in February 1861. Houston refused to give up easily and tried to establish an independent Republic of Texas. His efforts failed, and he left

office in March of that year with the knowledge that Texas was part of the Confederacy.

Houston died 26 July 1863 in Huntsville, Texas. To his death, Houston regarded secession as a mistake and lamented the decision made by his fellow citizens.

—*Mark R. Cheathem*

See also Texas.
For further reading:
De Bruhl, Marshall. *Sword of San Jacinto: A Life of Sam Houston* (1993).
James, Marquis. *The Raven: A Biography of Sam Houston* (1929).
Williams, John Hoyt. *Sam Houston: A Biography of the Father of Texas* (1993).

HOVEY, ALVIN PETERSON
(1821–1891)
Union general

Alvin Peterson Hovey, the twentieth governor of Indiana, was born on 6 September 1821 in Posey County, Indiana. He was the youngest of eight children born to impoverished pioneers, Abiel and Frances Peterson Hovey, who had come west to recover lost fortunes. Orphaned at fifteen, young Hovey was very much a self-made man and received his education at common schools. Starting work as a bricklayer, Hovey later taught school, studied law, was admitted to the bar, and began a law practice in Mount Vernon in southern Indiana.

During the Mexican-American War, Hovey was commissioned first lieutenant in a company of the 2d Indiana Regiment, but this company was never called into active service. He was elected to the Indiana Constitutional Convention in 1850 and was the youngest person ever to become a circuit court judge in the Hoosier State, serving from 1850 to 1854. He sat on the state supreme court from May 1854 to December 1855 and was U.S. district attorney until 1858.

Hovey was an early supporter of the Democratic Party. But like many free-soilers, he was induced by the issue of popular sovereignty and the possible expansion of slavery into Kansas to join the new Republican Party in 1858. He ran unsuccessfully for Congress in 1858 and returned to military service when the war broke out in 1861.

Because of his military record in the Mexican-American War and his political connections, Hovey was at once commissioned colonel of the 1st Regiment, 1st Brigade, Indiana Legion. Later in the summer of 1861 he took command of the 24th Indiana Regiment. The unit first saw service in the interior of Missouri, spent the winter there, and proceeded to Kentucky, where it was organized under Ulysses S. Grant's command. Hovey and the 24th Indiana participated in Lew Wallace's famous march to the field at Shiloh in April 1862. For his performance on the second day at Shiloh, Hovey was promoted to brigadier general of volunteers for gallantry. Two years later he was promoted to major general. Grant credited him with the Union victory at Champion's Hill, Mississippi, where his brigade lost a third of its strength in killed or wounded.

In December 1863 Hovey was assigned to duty in his home state of Indiana, recruiting and serving as liaison between Grant and Indiana governor Oliver Morton. When the Atlanta campaign commenced in May 1864, Hovey returned to the field commanding a division in XXIII Corps.

In June 1864 Hovey was sent back to Indiana and directed to recruit 10,000 men. Accepting only unmarried men, the group was known as "Hovey's Babies." He was breveted for war service July 1864 and became military commander of Indiana in October of that year.

While serving as military commander in Indiana, Hovey became deeply embroiled in the controversy regarding the abridgement of Peace Democrats' constitutional rights. He used money taken from bounty jumpers to pay espionage agents to spy on supposedly disloyal Democrats. He also threatened to interfere with the fall 1864 elections to prevent a Democratic triumph at the Hoosier polls. Before the state elections were held, however, Republican prospects grew brighter with news of Northern military victories. Republicans had also succeeded in pinning the label of treason on Democrats. Hovey and other Republicans thus abandoned whatever plans they had devised to control the elections.

Nonetheless, Hovey had no qualms about ordering arbitrary arrests or conducting military trials, even when the civil courts were open and functioning freely. Although once an ardent Democrat, during the war he converted to the most militant form of Republicanism. Absence from Indiana during his service in the field seems to have clouded his perceptions about his home state, and he sincerely believed that Indiana was imminently in the throes of domestic insurrection. He even accused Democratic journalists of accepting Confederate money. His role in the Indianapolis treason trials marked him as extremely partisan and revealed him as willing to sacrifice constitutional rights for political expediency. His earnest opinions made him impervious to appeals for leniency, and he persisted in supporting the most extreme penalties for accused conspirators.

Hovey resigned from the army in October 1865 and in December was sent to Peru as U.S. minister. He remained there until 1870. Returning to his native Indiana, he again took up the practice of law in Mount Vernon. In 1872 the Indiana Republican Party offered him the nomination for governor, but he declined. He continued his law practice until 1886, when he began a term in Congress. In 1888 the Republican Party again

offered him the gubernatorial nomination, and this time he accepted and won by a narrow margin.

During his administration, Hovey was often at odds with the Democratic-controlled legislature, especially on the issue of appointive powers and public school policy. He died in office, 23 November 1891, and is buried at Bellefontaine Cemetery in Mount Vernon.

—Ron Hamilton

See also Copperheads; Morton, Oliver Perry; Peace Democrats.
For further reading:
Encyclopedia of Biography of Indiana (1895, 1899).
Merrill, Catherine. The Soldier of Indiana in the War for the Union (1866, 1869).
Stevenson, David, and Theodore T. Scribner. Indiana's Role of Honor (1864, 1866).
Tredway, G. R. Democratic Opposition to the Lincoln Administration in Indiana (1973).

HOWARD, JOSEPH, JR.
(1833–1908)
Journalist

Born the son of John T. Howard in Brooklyn, New York, Joseph Howard, Jr. was named for his grandfather and always added "Jr." to his name to distinguish himself from his namesake. Howard graduated from Troy Polytechnic Institute. Then after working at various jobs, Howard chose journalism. He went to work for the New York Times in early 1860. In that year Howard covered all the national political conventions, and in the fall the visit of the prince of Wales to the United States.

At the outbreak of the Civil War, Howard became a war correspondent for the Times. He traveled with other reporters in a carriage to First Bull Run and in the fall covered the Federal defeat at Balls Bluff. Howard's colorful writing style made his stories on the war very popular with Times readers, but his off-duty antics sometimes angered his superiors. Apparently, a jolly prankster, Howard on occasion crossed the line between good fun and bad judgment. Early in the war he held open the paper's lines and occupied them telegraphing Jesus's genealogy. In September 1862 he violated an order banning all reporters from attending the funeral of Phil Kearny by dressing in clerical robes to sneak in. This conduct ultimately became too much for his editors, and he was forced to start selling his stories to a variety of newspapers. In 1864, to have a steady income, he accepted the relatively boring position of city editor for the Brooklyn Eagle.

Almost immediately after leaving the excitement of Washington and the war, Howard began trying to obtain another war correspondent's position with one of the larger dailies. Apparently frustrated by his lack of success, bored with his desk job, and maybe wanting some measure of revenge against the papers that would not hire him, Howard in May 1864 had his worst lapse in judgment. With an acquaintance who hoped to make a profit on declining gold prices if news from the front were bad, Howard acquired the stationery and other accoutrements necessary to indicate that a story had come in on the wires to the headquarters of the Associated Press of New York, the clearing house for official wire stories coming from Washington. Once they had what they needed to make it look as though the story was coming from the War Department, Howard and his accomplice composed a forged proclamation from the president asserting that Ulysses S. Grant's campaign in Virginia was a failure and that 400,000 additional men would have to be drafted. They then had the proclamation delivered to the offices of various New York newspapers. Only two published the story, but it caused such a firestorm that the War Department closed the two papers and launched a major investigation. While a large number of people were detained, the investigation soon homed in on the two perpetrators. Howard was arrested two days after the story appeared and placed in Fort Lafayette Prison. He was released on Lincoln's personal order on 24 August 1864.

Perhaps as some sort of penance after his release, Howard served for several months working for the War Department recording military trials. After leaving that job, he served out the remainder of the war writing for several newspapers.

After the war Howard went back to the *Times* briefly and served as a correspondent for several New York papers. In 1869 he was named editor of the *New York Star*. He remained in that position for six years before moving to the *New York Herald*. Howard had rebounded completely from his unfortunate prank in 1864 and actually served one term after the war as the president of the New York Press Club. In the 1880s Howard worked primarily as an independent columnist known as "Howard" and became one of the first to be syndicated throughout the country. He traveled extensively and wrote about the social and political events of the day. Along with his popular columns, Howard also lectured during his wide travels. He died in New York City on 31 March 1908.

—*David S. Heidler and Jeanne T. Heidler*

See also Newspapers; War Correspondents.

For further reading:
Starr, Louis M. *Bohemian Brigade: Civil War Newsmen in Action* (1954; reprint, 1987).

HOWARD, OLIVER OTIS
(1830–1909)
Union general

Oliver Otis Howard was born in Leeds, Maine, on 8 November 1830, the son of Rowland Bailey Howard and Eliza Otis Howard. In 1846, Howard matriculated at Bowdoin College in Brunswick, Maine. After his graduation in 1850, he received an appointment to the U.S. Military Academy at West Point.

In 1854, Howard completed the course of study at West Point, graduating fourth in his class of forty-six. His first posting was at the Watervliet Arsenal near Troy, New York, and for six months during 1855–1856, he acted as temporary commander of the Kennebec Arsenal in Augusta, Maine. On 14 February 1855, he married Elizabeth Ann Waite and with her would have seven children. In April 1855, he was promoted from the rank of brevet second lieutenant to second lieutenant.

During 1857 he served in Florida during the campaign against the Seminoles. Howard had been religious in the past, but it was in Florida that he experienced conversion to evangelical Christianity and seriously began to consider becoming a minister. His piety later would earn him the sobriquet "the Christian general," as well as the derision of some of his more profane army compatriots.

In September 1857, Howard reported to West Point to become an instructor of mathematics. In 1858, he received his promotion to first lieutenant. Howard continued to consider entering the ministry, but with secession and the surrender of Fort Sumter, he decided to remain in the service of his country. In June 1861, Howard assumed the duties of colonel of the 3d Maine Volunteers and resigned his regular army commission.

Howard temporarily commanded a brigade at the battle of First Bull Run (21 July 1861). Despite the Union disaster and a short period back in command of his old regiment, he earned a promotion to brigadier general of volunteers dated from 3 September 1861 and the permanent command of a brigade. On 31 May, during the battle of Fair Oaks, he was wounded twice and had a horse shot out from under him before he left the field. One of his injuries required that his right arm be amputated above the elbow. He soon returned to duty with the Army of the Potomac and participated in many of the most significant campaigns of the war. In the process, he achieved the rank of major general of volunteers on 29 November 1862 and corps command in early 1863.

As commander of the XI Corps, Howard participated in the battle of Chancellorsville, where, on 2 May 1863, he suffered the brunt of Thomas "Stonewall" Jackson's surprise attack. Later, Howard commanded the XI Corps at Gettysburg on 1–3 July 1863. On the first day of the battle, he was temporarily in command of the Union army on the field after Major General John Reynolds was killed. Howard ordered the retreat through the town of Gettysburg under the pressure of superior numbers, but he had also selected some of the ground that would allow the Union army to withstand consequent Confederate assaults on its position.

After Major General William S. Rosecrans's defeat at Chickamauga in September 1863, Howard and his XI

Corps was transferred to the Western theater and the Army of the Cumberland. During the Atlanta campaign in the spring and summer of 1864, he commanded the IV Corps of the Army of the Cumberland. He achieved his highest Civil War field command when Major General William T. Sherman elevated him to commander of the Army of the Tennessee after the death of Major General James B. McPherson. Howard assumed command of that army on 27 July 1864 and led it through the remainder of the Atlanta campaign, the March to the Sea, and the campaign in the Carolinas. On 21 December 1864, Howard received an appointment as a brigadier general in the regular army.

Howard's wartime record was tainted with failure and controversy, but generally it reflected his bravery and competence. At Chancellorsville, Howard was unprepared for Jackson's attack, thus earning the reputation for being the cause of that defeat. He also earned the lasting disdain of Major General Joseph Hooker, his commander at that battle. Howard's promotion to army command further aggravated Hooker's ill will because Sherman passed over Hooker, who also was a corps commander under Sherman at that time. On the first day at Gettysburg, Howard quibbled with Major General Winfield Scott Hancock over seniority, even though Major General George Gordon Meade, the commander of the Army of the Potomac, had ordered Hancock to take command of the field. Howard's performance at Gettysburg won him the special thanks of Congress, which in turn earned him the enmity of Hancock's friends, who believed that their hero had been slighted when Congress ignored him in its vote of thanks. Instead of ignoring criticism of his Gettysburg performance raised from that quarter, Howard felt the need to defend himself in the press.

Still, Howard's wartime record provides numerous examples of his physical courage and his ability to command large bodies of men. At Fair Oaks, he commanded his brigade from the front line. At Chancellorsville, he personally rallied his troops, delayed Jackson's advance, and urged Hooker to renew contact with the enemy. At the battle of Ezra Church the day after he assumed command of the Army of the Tennessee, he proved he had learned from his failure at Chancellorsville when he prepared his men for a Confederate attack that Sherman did not expect.

As army commander, Howard lived up to Sherman's expectations. When writing his memoirs, Sherman delineated the qualities that he believed recommended Howard for such high command. "I wanted to succeed in taking Atlanta, and needed commanders who were purely and technically soldiers, men who would obey orders and execute them promptly and on time," he explained. "I knew that we would have to execute some most delicate maneuvers, requiring the utmost skill, nicety, and precision. I believed that General Howard would do all these faithfully and well, and I think the result has justified my choice." Howard, a man shaped by his experiences in battle, became a skilled corps commander. He was able to move beyond Hooker's memory of him to live up to the high standards of one of the Union army's best generals.

At the end of the war, Howard became the first and only commissioner of the Bureau of Refugees, Freedmen, and Abandoned Lands. Appointed to that position by President Andrew Johnson on 12 May 1865, Howard remained with the agency until its closing in 1872. Howard had been a moderate antislavery person before the war, but took on his new duties with the best interest of the freed people at heart. Howard's agency dealt with a wide range of Reconstruction matters but, like so many nineteenth-century reformers, Howard strongly believed in the primacy of education as an engine of uplift for the freed slaves. He used the bureau to promote and coordinate the establishment of schools throughout the South. He also was instrumental in establishing the historically black university in Washington, D.C., that still bears his name. Congress chartered Howard University on 2 March 1867 and Howard served as its president from 1869 to 1874.

As commissioner of the Freedmen's Bureau, Howard did his best to help the ex-slave within the parameters of the possible. Nevertheless, Howard did not leave the freed people much of a lasting legacy. He failed to fulfill the freed slaves' wishes to become landowners—for which he continues to receive much criticism—and the legal and physical protections that his Bureau provided the freed people were short-lived.

The general failure of Howard's agency was not the result of incompetence, dishonesty, or unconcern on Howard's part. Hindered by the lack of support of his commander (President Andrew Johnson), stymied by inadequate congressional allocations, and opposed by white Southerners who were willing to ignore the constitution, Howard and his temporary, understaffed bureau faced almost insurmountable obstacles. Furthermore, Howard and the bureau could only execute the wishes of the government; criticizing him for not protecting the land claims of the freed people ignores the real source of that failure.

After his work with the bureau, Howard became involved with Indian affairs. In March 1872, with the bureau's activities now confined to bounty collection for the freed people, he temporarily left his bureau work behind to travel to the Southwest. There he held council with various bands of Indians before returning to Washington. This physically demanding work convinced him to remain in the army. He returned to the Southwest that summer and eventually in October made a treaty with Cochise and the Chiricahua Apache.

In July 1874, Howard was given command of the Department of the Columbia, in the Pacific Northwest. During 1877, Howard embarked on the Nez Perce campaign, which led to the surrender of Chief Joseph and his band on 5 October 1877.

Howard remained in the army, serving as superintendent of West Point (1880–1882); commander of the Department of the Platte (1882–1886); and, after being promoted to the rank of major general in the regular army to date from 2 April 1886, the Military Division of the Pacific (1886–1888). Howard's last command was the Military Division of the Atlantic (1888–1894). In 1893 Howard received the Medal of Honor for his work at the battle of Fair Oaks. After retiring in 1894, he established his family residence in Burlington, Vermont.

During his postwar years in the army, Howard began to write and lecture about his experiences, activities to which he devoted much more time after retiring in 1894. Still interested in education, in 1896 he became involved in the establishment of Lincoln Memorial University, which was chartered on 13 February 1897. After serving with the Army and Navy Christian Commission during the Spanish-American War, Howard continued to raise money for the university while remaining active in the school's direction. He maintained an active lecture schedule, speaking to audiences about Gettysburg and other topics almost until the day he died. Howard succumbed to what was probably a heart attack on 26 October 1909, in Burlington, Vermont.

—*Paul A. Cimbala*

See also Atlanta Campaign; Chancellorsville, Battle of; Freedmen's Bureau; Gettysburg, Battle of; Hancock, Winfield Scott; Hooker, Joseph; Sherman, William Tecumseh.

For further reading:

Carpenter, John A. *Sword and Olive Branch: Oliver Otis Howard* (1964).

Howard, Oliver Otis. *Autobiography of Oliver Otis Howard, Major General United States Army* (1908).

McFeely, William S. *Yankee Stepfather: General O. O. Howard and the Freedmen* (1968).

Sherman, William T. *Memoirs of William T. Sherman* (1990).

HOWE, JULIA WARD
(1819–1910)

Reformer and author of "Battle Hymn of the Republic"

Born 27 May 1819 in New York City, the fourth child of Julia Rush Cutler and Samuel Ward, Jr., a Wall Street banker, Julia Ward had all the advantages of an upper middle-class upbringing. Educated by private tutors and attending several female academies, Ward was fluent in Greek, Italian, and French. As a girl she developed an interest in writing poetry and prose, an avocation inherited from her mother and encouraged by her aunt Eliza Cutler Francis, who raised the Ward children after their mother's death in 1824. Julia Ward's early years were filled with contrasting, often competing, views of life from her father's strict Episcopal/Calvinist beliefs to her aunt's love for parties and entertaining.

In 1841, two years after the death of her father, Ward met reformer Samuel Gridley Howe while she was on a trip to Boston. The forty-year-old Howe was the head of the esteemed Perkins Institute for the Blind when the couple married on 23 April 1843. From 1844 to 1859 Julia Ward Howe gave birth to six children: Julia Romana, born on their lengthy European honeymoon; Florence Marion (1845), Henry Marion (1848); Laura Elizabeth (1850); Maud (1854); and Samuel Gridley, Jr. (1859). All the Howe children survived to adulthood except Samuel, who succumbed to diphtheria at the age of three.

The Howe family lived first at the Perkins Institute and then at Green Peace a small house near the school. Though such famous reformers as Theodore Parker and Charles Sumner befriended Howe, her husband, believing that married women should not be involved in public life, barred her from participating in the burgeoning reform movements of the day. However, she aided her husband for a short time in 1853 when he was editor of the *Commonwealth*, a Free Soil periodical. The Howe's fractious marriage came twice to the brink of divorce in 1854 and again in 1857, but the couple remained together until Samuel Gridley Howe's death in 1876.

Howe continued educating herself and writing for publication. Her first full-length works, *Passion-flowers* (1854) and *Words for the Hour* (1857), as was typical for female authors of the era, were published anonymously. In addition, Howe wrote two inauspicious plays, *Leonora, or the World's Own* (1857) and *Hippolytus* (published posthumously in 1941). Rounding out her antebellum works was a travelogue written for *Atlantic Monthly* about her trip to Cuba in 1859 and that was later published in book form as *A Trip to Cuba* in 1860.

Howe added journalism to her literary pursuits, providing accounts of Newport society to the *New York Tribune* during the early years of the Civil War. Concurrently, she joined other women in the New England Sanitary Commission and worked toward the improvement of the conditions in which Union soldiers lived.

The Civil War brought Howe her most recognized contribution to American culture. During a visit to view Union troops encamped around Washington, D.C., in 1861, Howe was inspired by the marital order of the men to write a poem elucidating the Union cause. "Battle Hymn of the Republic" was published by *Atlantic Monthly* in 1862. The words caught the imagination of the Northern populace when they were later set to the tune of the well-known folk song *John Brown's Body*, and the new anthem was on the lips of many Unionists by 1864.

The popularity that the song brought its author was to remain with her to the end of her life. After the war, Howe continued to write, although with limited success. In contrast, her reform work brought her more recognition and opportunities to lecture. Howe participated in the peace movement of the late nineteenth century, but her major calling came within the suffrage and women's rights movement. In 1868 she joined noted abolitionist and women's rights crusader Lucy Stone to form the New England Woman Suffrage Association, and a year later she and Stone became leaders of the American Woman Suffrage Association. These activities were undertaken in clear disregard of her husband's wishes. Interestingly, however, after her husband's death Julia Ward Howe wrote *Memoir of Dr. Samuel G. Howe* in glowing prose despite their rocky marriage and her husband's admitted extramarital affairs.

Howe's writing turned even more to the cause of women with the publication in 1874 of *Sex and Education*, which supported coeducation; a biography of early feminist Margaret Fuller in 1883; and a popular weekly suffrage periodical, *Women's Journal*. In addition to suffrage, Howe encouraged women's presence in the increasingly industrial and money-driven Gilded Age. She espoused the formation of women's clubs throughout the country and founded the Association of the Advancement of Women (1870) and the General Federation of Women's Clubs (1890).

Howe continued to write and lecture in her later years, publishing her memoirs, *Reminiscences*, in 1900 and was the first woman to be elected to the American Academy of Arts and Letters in 1908. Invariably at each of her speaking engagements the audience sang "Battle Hymn of the Republic" in her honor, a tribute repeated after her death at the age of ninety-one in 1910, when the approximately 4,000 mourners at her memorial service lifted their voices in song.

—*Heidi Campbell-Shoaf*

See also Howe, Samuel Gridley.
For further reading:

Clifford, Deborah Pickman. *Mine Eyes Have Seen the Glory: A Biography of Julia Ward Howe* (1979).
Richards, Laura E., and Maud Howe Elliot. *Julia Ward Howe, 1819–1910* (1915).
Tharp, Louise Hall. *Three Saints and a Sinner: Julia Ward Howe, Louisa, Annie and Sam Ward* (1956).

HOWE, SAMUEL GRIDLEY
(1801–1876)
Abolitionist and social reformer

Prickly, arrogant, and determined, Samuel Gridley Howe was the sort of reformer that mid-nineteenth-century Boston made. Howe devoted his entire adult life to social justice, and yet his nearly abso-lutist sense of righteousness gave him little appreciation for democracy or compromise.

Howe was born on 10 November 1801 to Patty Gridley and Joseph Neals Howe. Howe's was a venerable and wealthy Boston family until the War of 1812 ruined the family's fortunes. The family's fortunes, in fact, sunk so low that only Samuel, of his three brothers, was able to attend college. Howe, as a young man, possessed an unremarkable intellect. He entered Brown in 1817 and graduated in the middle third of his class. After graduation in 1821, he entered Harvard Medical School, where he became more conscientious as a scholar. Still, when Howe completed his medical studies in 1824, he was no closer to a settled vocation.

Over the objections of his family and following the example of English poet Lord Byron, Howe went to Greece in 1824 to aid that country's great romantic war for national independence. Howe was one of only a handful of Americans who went to Greece, and it was there that he would spend most of the next seven years as a soldier, surgeon, and philanthropist, distributing monies raised mostly in Boston for the cause of Greek relief. During a fundraising tour of the United States in 1828, Howe wrote about his experiences in *An Historical Sketch of the Greek Revolution*.

Howe returned to Boston in April 1831. Now thirty, Howe was at something of a crossroads. Tempered by the rigors of Greek war and poverty, Howe still had never settled into an occupation. After an unsuccessful stab at journalism, college friend John Fischer hired Howe to be the director of the new New England Asylum for the Blind. The directorship gave Howe a sense of purpose and launched his career as a social reformer. The institution opened in August 1832 with seven students and three staff members including Howe. After research in Europe, Howe would eventually pioneer new methods for the education of the disabled. Not satisfied with merely institutionalization, Howe attempted to normalize the education of the blind by teaching them skills that would make them self-sufficient in the world at large. Howe and his students were an immediate and unqualified success. After touring with his pupils around the state, the Massachusetts legislature committed $6,000 a year for the institution's upkeep. In 1833, Thomas Perkins donated a Pearl Street mansion to the school, which in his honor was renamed the Perkins Institution and Massachusetts School for the Blind. Howe's work with the blind, and later the deaf-blind, embodied the values of Northern reformers. Not unlike his eventual abolitionism, Howe's philanthropy epitomized the broader culture of reform's commitment to the redemptive value of suffering; the infinite value and sacredness of all human life; the moral nature of economic independence and autonomy; the inevitability of progress; the benevolent correctability of human nature; and, most of all, the responsibility of society to develop an individual's intellectual, moral, and physical capabilities.

Howe's work with the deaf-blind eventually introduced him to Julia Ward, whom he would marry in April 1843. Still a bachelor at the age of forty, Howe had been sustained essentially by a Harvard network of internationally renowned men that included Horace Mann, Henry Wadsworth Longfellow, and Charles Sumner. Ward was a New York socialite, eighteen years his junior, who was highly educated and possessed her own literary and political ambitions. Her brother Sam was an accomplished painter, protégé of Ralph Waldo Emerson, and intimate friend of Margaret Fuller. In 1862, Ward would pen the Union war anthem, "Battle Hymn of the Republic."

Though throughout the 1840s he continued his philanthropic work, Howe was thrust to the center of political controversy by local and national events during the middle part of the decade. In 1845, Howe was transformed by the question of Texas's annexation, the event that finally and fully engaged him with the question of slavery. Howe had written "Letter on Slavery" in 1833 for the *New England Magazine*, but his arguments were conventional, Whiggish, and conservative, critical of Garrisonian abolition and sympathetic to the South. Then, Howe was cautious, viewing slavery as a barrier to Southern progress, but advocating compensated emancipation and colonization. In 1842 and 1843, Howe visited the South and was disillusioned by the effect of slavery upon Southern whites. Texas annexation, though, thoroughly radicalized Howe. With Sumner, Howe helped organize the anti-Texas movement in Massachusetts, and after the outbreak of the Mexican-American War, he abandoned the state's regular Whig Party. In 1846, Howe unsuccessfully opposed Whig standard-bearer Robert Winthrop as the candidate of independent, anti-extensionist Conscience Whigs. In 1848 Howe joined the Free-Soil Party.

Howe, like many others in his state, tolerated Southern slavery until national politics made Northern states symbolically complicit with the institution's protection and extension. Howe was particularly vexed by "slave power" efforts to compel Massachusetts to arrest and return fugitive slaves. His involvement with the issue of fugitive slaves antedated the Fugitive Slave Act of 1850. In 1846, his efforts on behalf of the anonymously known escaped slave "Joe" resulted in a public address at a Faneuil Hall protest meeting. Thereafter, Howe was elected chairman of a committee of eighty organized to defend against the return of fugitive slaves. This relatively informal organization would later cohere as the Vigilance Committee, a more determined effort to resist the enforcement of the Fugitive Slave Act.

The Vigilance Committee, which viewed the Fugitive Slave Act as a threat to traditional New England liberties, openly defied the law. Acting upon the rumor that Southern agents were already circulating in Boston with warrants, the Vigilance Committee removed the fugitive couple William and Ellen Craft to England. In February 1851, the Committee organized a successful prison rescue of a fugitive slave known only as "Shadrach." In April 1851, the committee failed to save fugitive Thomas Sims from a return to bondage, but the effort only hardened its resolve. The 1854 seizure of fugitive Anthony Burns was the culmination of Vigilance Committee efforts. Renewed Southern determination to have the Fugitive Slave Act enforced in Boston provoked an equally determined response. Thanks to Vigilance Committee agitation, Boston during Burns's trial was in a state of full-blown armed revolt. After Burns's imprisonment and trial, protest escalated until a concerted but fruitless attack upon the courthouse where Burns was held resulted in the death of one guard and the imposition of near martial law upon the city of Boston. The Burns case, along with the Kansas-Nebraska Act, which was passed the same year, radicalized Howe and abolitionist Boston. Driven to violence by slavery's intransigence, Howe and his cohort came to embrace a "higher law" that transcended constitutions or compromise.

In 1855, Howe became a director of the Kansas Emigrant Aid Company, an organization devoted to the settlement of Kansas with Free-Soil New Englanders. Financially, the company was sponsored by Amos Lawrence, once the leader of the Cotton Whigs, and no event signaled Boston's radicalization more than Lawrence's efforts for Kansas insofar as he was the heir to a textile fortune dependent upon Southern cotton. Howe, still fired by the Burns case, pushed the company in a revolutionary direction by raising money to supply settlers with ammunition, revolvers, rifles, and even canon. After the sack of Lawrence, Kansas, Howe accelerated efforts to arm Free-Soil Kansans in their violent struggle against the "slave power." When, in May 1856, friend Charles Sumner was savagely beaten on the Senate floor by South Carolina representative Preston Brooks, Howe decisively lost faith in the value of the Union.

By the late 1850s, Howe and other New England abolitionists were openly discussing secession from a Union corrupted by compromise with slavery. In 1857, Howe and other antislavery Bostonians came under the spell of John Brown. Brown and his band of Kansas guerrilla insurgents had long been funded by the Kansas Aid Committee. January 1857, though, found Brown in Boston, for the first time making the acquaintance of his New England patrons. Brown's magnetic conviction struck a chord with the Kansas Aid Committee leadership that included Howe, Theodore Parker, Franklin Sanborn, Thomas Wentworth Higginson, George Stearns, and Gerrit Smith (the only New Yorker in the group). The committee's leaders would become the "Secret Six," an informal organization that funded Brown's campaign of antislavery terror that would not end until his capture at Harper's Ferry in October 1859. Brown acted independently of the Secret Six, but there was no question what the eastern men were subsidizing. Howe himself personally gave Brown a rifle and two pistols.

The Kansas Aid Committee and other organizations had been sending weapons to Kansas for years. With Brown, though, it was unclear what they had in mind. By 1857, the violence in Kansas had largely been pacified. Although constitutional questions in Kansas were yet outstanding, and the peace imposed by the new governor, John Geary, was delicate, Brown's only real options at this point were either to wait for disorder to reemerge in Kansas or to provoke conflict himself by launching a broader offensive against slavery and its supporters. Brown chose the latter and his decision was supported by the Secret Six. When Brown outlined his plan to incite a slave rebellion east of the Appalachians, the Secret Six looked to Howe, the only member with military experience to assess the operation's possibilities. When Howe pronounced the plan feasible, the others gave their consent. After a number of delays and defections, Brown's raid went forward well-subsidized by Howe and the others. It turned into a suicide mission. Though a tactical disaster, Brown became an antislavery martyr in the North, polarizing sectional opinion and plunging the nation toward civil war.

After Brown's capture, Howe attempted to gather resources for Brown's defense and to prevent his execution. Brown insisted to his captors that he was acting alone, but on his person were diaries and letters that clearly implicated Howe and the Secret Six in his activities. When word reached Boston, Howe publicly denied foreknowledge of the raid. Soon after, he fled to Canada, where he remained for several weeks, returning to Boston only after Brown's execution. Despite incriminating evidence, Howe escaped arrest as either a witness or a defendant.

As the Civil War approached, Howe faced secession with optimism. Unlike most, he viewed the Union as artificial and compromise with slavery immoral. When the war commenced, Howe relied upon his medical background and his experience in Greece to supervise the health of Massachusetts volunteers. Later, he was one of many who lobbied for the creation of the U.S. Sanitary Commission. When the commission was instituted, Howe became a member. For the remainder of the war, he traveled between Boston and Washington, overseeing the health of Union soldiers.

During the war, Howe was also a participant and founder of the Emancipation League, which lobbied the government to make the eradication of slavery a war aim. After the Emancipation Proclamation (which he criticized as a half-measure), Howe, as a member of the American Freedmen's Inquiry Commission, monitored the condition of former slaves. In his official capacity, he urged the enlistment of former slaves, the subsidization of schools, and the integration of army regiments. As a member of the commission, Howe was in a position to influence federal race policies. With Robert Dale Owen, the utopian socialist, and James McCaye, Howe was asked by Secretary of War Edwin Stanton to author a report that would serve as the basis, in the broadest sense, of the Union's emancipation policies. Under the influence of Harvard naturalist Louis Agassiz, the three-member committee was particularly interested in the relationship between race, intelligence, and climate. Not surprisingly, these early efforts at social science proved inconclusive. The commission finally recommended complete emancipation, light civil rights protections in the upper South, and military occupation in the lower South, where they suspected that emancipation would be followed by some other form of bound servitude. In 1864, Howe published his own research on the condition of blacks in Canada, *Refugees from Slavery in Canada West*, in which he argued that, although Africans were not suited to northern climates, they did possess the character and virtue required for economic independence and full citizenship.

At the conclusion of the war, Howe "retired" to occasional public service and his work at Perkins. He died in Boston in 1876.

—*Adam-Max Tuchinsky*

See also Abolitionists; Brown, John; Howe, Julia Ward.
For further reading:

Howe, Samuel Gridley. *The Letters and Journals of Samuel Gridley Howe* (1906).
Richards, Laura E. *Samuel Gridley Howe* (1935).
Schwartz, Harold. *Samuel Gridley Howe: Social Reformer, 1801–1876* (1956).

HUDSON, FREDERIC
(1819–1875)
Journalist and editor

Although the force of James Gordon Bennett towered over the paper that he founded, the *New York Herald* was, in effect, primarily shaped in the decade before the Civil War by Frederic Hudson who was the paper's managing editor from 1846 to 1866. Born in 1819 in Quincy, Massachusetts, Hudson received only a basic education at the town school in Concord. At seventeen, he left New England for New York City, joining his brothers who had already opened a news room in the city. There, at Hudson's News Room, Hudson met James Gordon Bennett in 1836, and not long thereafter, he became one of the *Herald*'s two full-

time employees. Apart from a six-month sojourn with the *New York Daily Whig*, Hudson's fate would be tied to Bennett's for the next thirty years.

Hudson's steady and sober attention to detail was the perfect complement to Bennett's often erratic combativeness. Hudson's attention to detail was severe. Intensely serious, the thin, long-faced Hudson was known to be a living index of the paper. He would arrive at the *Herald* precisely at 9:30 in the morning, seven days a week. His day regularly lasted until late in the evening. He had few interests outside of the newspaper. Bennett, after the paper was securely established, was rarely found at the newspaper's New York office. Often traveling in Europe, Bennett once left New York for eleven months. Hudson, on the other hand, was absorbed by the daily operation of the newspaper. As his brother remembered, Hudson eschewed even the twin pillars of nineteenth-century America: politics and religion.

That Hudson was said to have never voted embodied the spirit of the paper that he directed. The *Herald*, of course, covered politics intensely but, unlike most newspapers during the period, it was not formally aligned with a political party. Bennett, like the Democrats, was militantly racist, hostile to reform, and expansionist in foreign policy, but he never officially associated his paper with the party. Bennett, who made his reputation with his coverage of the Ellen Jewett murder case, bridged the divide between regular and sensational journalism. The *Herald*'s coverage of politics and international events had few equals but, unlike most newspapers in the period, the *Herald* was without political principles or patrons. The *Herald*'s first priority was the size of its circulation. Dismissed by Victorian America's "respectable" classes, the *Herald* survived a moralist boycott in 1840 with its racy and often bigoted coverage of events that appealed especially to its New York City mass readership.

The *Herald*'s course did not deviate during the Civil War. Still antiabolitionist and sympathetic to the South, the paper remained officially independent but congenial to the aspirations of Northern Democrats. Minimally Unionist, the *Herald* supported the Crittenden resolutions, which called for new federal protections for slavery. Failing constitutional reconciliation, the *Herald* backed peaceful separation over what it termed a fanatical abolitionist total war. With the outbreak of actual hostilities at Fort Sumter, the *Herald* immediately backed the Union war effort, but throughout the conflict it pressed the administration to resist the abolitionist elements within the Republican Party.

Bennett's sensitivity to Northern public opinion forbade any open opposition to the Union war effort. To Frederic Hudson fell the daily details of war journalism. The *Herald*'s coverage of the war was elaborate. Hudson employed some sixty-three field correspondents while still maintaining the paper's extensive coverage of commerce and international events. The Civil War was good business for U.S. newspapers. News of the Fort Sumter assault sold 135,000 *Heralds*. The public's demand for news was so avid that police had to protect the *Herald*'s office from the crush of eager readers. The war's drama of blood, political gossip, and military intrigue suited the *Herald*'s taste for the sensational. Hudson exchanged the paper's political principles for intimate access by hiring Republican friend of the administration Henry Villard. Bennett lured George Townsend away from the *Philadelphia Press* to provide familiar and exclusive reports of *Herald* hero George McClellan. Many of the *Herald*'s correspondents received staff commissions in the military and the War Department that facilitated reporting from sources in the highest reaches of the army and the government. The *Herald* even became an organ of sorts for George McClellan, who even revealed future troop movements exclusively to the paper out of friendship to Bennett and Hudson.

The *Herald* did not spare any expense in its coverage of the conflict, and for its efforts the newspaper was rewarded handsomely. Its sales for 1865 were more than a million dollars. The Civil War changed the practice of journalism, and Frederic Hudson was one of the central foot soldiers in the evolution. Moreover, the total nature of the Civil War rested upon the consent of a democratic public. Much of that consent was mediated through the prism of a national press, heavily capitalized, that dictated the flow of information and opinion. The decade before the Civil War transformed the newspaper from a local, individually driven institution to a far ranging, near bureaucratic organization that required unprecedented speed and coordination. Though still headed by the signature charisma of editor celebrities, the newspaper was at the mercy of the demands of capital and technology that centralized the institution and, eventually, the flow of information. The *Herald* epitomized this new world of journalism. The singular and acerbic personality of Bennett established the *Herald* as a recognizable article in the newly national market of print; Frederic Hudson, the consummate insider, presided over a media operation of unprecedented scale and scope.

In 1866, Hudson left the *Herald*, but he remained indirectly in journalism. In his retirement, Hudson wrote the *History of Journalism in the United States from 1690 to 1872*, a work that, in effect, foretold the future of journalism. Hudson defended the *Herald*'s mode of amoral journalism—its political independence, its submission to circulation, and its sense of news as entertainment—against a journalistic style, represented by the *Herald*'s great rival, Horace Greeley's *Tribune*, that viewed the newspaper as the moral conscience of the community. Frederic Hudson died in 1875.

—*Adam-Max Tuchinsky*

See also Bennett, James Gordon; McClellan, George Brinton; Newspapers.

For further reading:

Andrews, J. Cutler. *The North Reports the Civil War* (1955).

Crouthamel, James L. *Bennett's* New York Herald *and the Rise of the Popular Press* (1989).

Fermer, Douglas. *James Gordon Bennett and the* New York Herald: *A Study of Editorial Opinion in the Civil War Era, 1854–1867* (1986).

Weisberger, Bernard A. *Reporters for the Union* (1953).

HUGER, BENJAMIN
(1805–1877)
Confederate general

Benjamin Huger (*Library of Congress*)

Born in Charleston, South Carolina, the son of Francis Kinloch Huger and Harriet Lucas Pinckney Huger, Benjamin Huger graduated eighth of thirty-seven in the U.S. Military Academy class of 1825. Upon graduation he served in a variety of posts, but primarily in the East as an ordnance officer. During the Mexican-American War, he served on Winfield Scott's staff. He received three brevet promotions during that conflict for bravery in the Mexico City campaign and was personally commended by Scott. Returning to ordnance after the war, he served at several armories including Harper's Ferry, Pikesville near Baltimore, and during the secession crisis, Charleston, South Carolina.

In November 1860, Secretary of War John Floyd and President James Buchanan sent Huger to Charleston ostensibly to take command of the arsenal there but in reality to assess the situation there and meet with the U.S. Army commander in Charleston Harbor, Major Robert Anderson. Because Charleston was Huger's hometown and he had strong family connections there, the administration assumed Huger could determine the seriousness of the military situation there without arousing too much suspicion. While there, Huger met with Anderson and South Carolina government officials and then went to Washington to report on his findings. Because Huger did not resign his commission upon the secession of South Carolina and instead waited until the fall of Fort Sumter, he was criticized by many people in South Carolina.

Upon his resignation, he accepted a colonel's commission in the Confederate army. In May 1861 he was made commander of the Department of Southern Virginia and North Carolina headquartered at Norfolk, Virginia. One of his primary occupations while in this command was handling prisoner exchanges. In June 1861 he was promoted to brigadier general and in October to major general.

He was later severely criticized by the Confederate Congress for the fall of Roanoke, North Carolina, in February 1862. In May 1862 he was forced to abandon Norfolk. Shortly thereafter, he was given command of one of Joseph Johnston's divisions in preparation for George McClellan's march up the York Peninsula to Richmond.

At Seven Pines and the subsequent Seven Days' at the end of June 1862, Huger remained in command of his division, though as the campaign progressed he came under increasing criticism for the slowness of his division's movements. After the campaign, especially when Huger failed to prevent McClellan's retreat after Malvern Hill, Huger was removed from command. His repeated requests for a court-martial to defend his conduct were refused.

After a leave, he was sent to Charleston, South Carolina, and Savannah, Georgia, to inspect the ordnance at those two places. In March 1863 he was sent to inspect ordnance in the Department of the Trans-Mississippi. Huger dutifully obeyed the order, though he consider it a banishment. He served as the chief of ordnance and inspector of artillery in the Trans-Mississippi for the remainder of the war. He surrendered in May 1865.

After the war, Huger farmed in North Carolina and

Virginia but ultimately moved back to Charleston. He died there on 7 December 1877.

—*David S. Heidler and Jeanne T. Heidler*

See also Ordnance; Seven Days' Battles; Fair Oaks Seven Pines.

For further reading:

Rhoades, Jeffrey L. *Scapegoat General: The Story of Major General Benjamin Huger* (1985).

HUMPHREYS, ANDREW ATKINSON
(1810–1883)
Union general

Andrew Atkinson Humphreys ranks among the finest soldiers of the Union Army of the Potomac. Humphreys was born on 2 November 1810 into a distinguished Philadelphia family. Both his father and grandfather were noted shipbuilders; the latter designed the frigates *Constitution*, *Constellation*, and *United States*. Humphreys graduated from the U.S. Military Academy at West Point in 1831, ranking thirteenth in a class of thirty-three.

Assigned to the 2d U.S. Artillery, the young second lieutenant saw subsequent service in the Second Seminole War. Humphreys's health sagged under the stifling Florida heat, however, and in September 1836 he was compelled to resign from the army. Returning to Philadelphia's more temperate climate, Humphreys searched for a profession worthy of his ambition and social station. He found his calling in the burgeoning field of engineering, and after two years' service as a government-appointed civil engineer, Humphreys in 1838 reentered the army as a first lieutenant in the Corps of Topographical Engineers.

Over the next two decades, Humphreys engaged himself in various federal engineering projects. A lasting scientific reputation was earned through his brilliant hydrographic studies of the Mississippi River and Delta. His *Report upon the Physics and Hydraulics of the Mississippi River*, published in 1861, won him international acclaim, was translated into several foreign languages, and gained him membership into numerous major U.S. and European engineering societies.

Humphreys spent the Civil War's early months completing the massive *Delta Report*. His work at last accomplished, in November 1861 Humphreys was assigned to Major General George B. McClellan's staff. During the 1862 Peninsula campaign, he served as the Army of the Potomac's chief topographical engineer with the rank of brigadier general of volunteers.

Although rising in the army's hierarchy, Humphreys, like many of his staff-bound colleagues, yearned to lead troops in the field. He finally received his command in September 1862 when assigned to divisional command in the Potomac Army's V Corps. Composed entirely of nine-month recruits, Humphreys's force saw little action during the subsequent Maryland campaign. But at the battle of Fredericksburg on 13 December 1862, the untried division performed heroically under Humphreys's leadership. It is said that Humphreys's men, of all those who charged that ill-fated day, came closest to piercing Confederate lines along the famed stone wall astride Marye's Heights. Indeed, the general's personal bravery on the Fredericksburg plain was without equal, winning him both the respect of his troops and esteem from his peers.

Humphreys saw limited action at the battle of Chancellorsville in May 1863. After his force was disbanded later that month, he was transferred to the command of a division in Major General Daniel E. Sickles's III Corps. On 28 June, the Army of the Potomac's new commander, Major General George G. Meade, recognized Humphreys's abilities and offered him the position of army chief of staff. Humphreys politely declined the request, preferring instead to continue field command. Humphreys's decision served the Federal cause well. On 2 July at Gettysburg, the general again fought doggedly, resisting the slashing Confederate attacks of Major Generals Lafayette McLaws and Richard H. Anderson. Humphreys's fighting retreat from the Emmitsburg Road line bought the time necessary for Meade and other officers to rush up reinforcements, thus stemming the Confederates' tide on that day.

Gettysburg confirmed Humphreys's reputation as one the army's foremost officers, and on 8 July 1863 he was promoted to major general of volunteers and brevet brigadier general, U.S. Army. That same day he finally accepted Meade's offer and assumed duties as the army's chief of staff. He served his commander faithfully and capably for the next seventeen months, helping direct operations that brought the army to the gates of Petersburg in June 1864.

Humphreys, however, yearned for a return to battle, of which he had grown quite fond, and on 25 November 1864 he was appointed to command the army's II Corps. He led the corps in the 1865 operations resulting in the capture of Petersburg, including the battles of Hatcher's Run, White Oak Road, and Sutherland Station. In the final week of the war, Humphreys again distinguished himself at Sayler's Creek, and he blocked General Robert E. Lee's northernmost escape route at Appomattox Court House.

Brevetted major general, U.S. Army, for meritorious service at Sayler's Creek, Humphreys in 1866 was named commander of the U.S. Army Corps of Engineers with the permanent rank of brigadier general. After retiring in 1879, Humphreys spent his remaining days writing on various military topics. He died in Washington, D.C., on 27 December 1883.

—*Christopher S. Stowe*

See also Gettysburg, Battle of; Peninsula Campaign; Sayler's Creek, Battle of.

For further reading:
Barry, John M. *Rising Tide: The Great Mississippi Flood of 1927 and How It Changed America* (1997).
Humphreys, Henry, A. *From Gettysburg to the Rapidan. The Army of the Potomac, July 1863 to April 1864* (1883).
———. *The Virginia Campaign of 1864 and 1865. The Army of the Potomac and the Army of the James* (1883).
Humphreys, Henry H. *Andrew Atkinson Humphreys: A Biography* (1924).
Reardon, Carol. "Brigadier General Andrew A. Humphreys's Pennsylvania Division at Fredericksburg." In *The Fredericksburg Campaign: Decision on the Rappahannock* (1995).

HUNLEY

Named for its creator, Horace Lawson Hunley, the CSS *Hunley*, sometimes more colloquially known as the "Fish Boat," was the first submarine to sink an enemy vessel in combat. The designers of the unusual craft built it in Mobile, Alabama, from a cylinder boiler. As crude as the submarine was, it benefited from earlier incarnations and its designer and creator considered it to be quite safe when operated by a knowledgeable crew.

The *Hunley* was to be operated manually with a crew of eight men cranking a propeller shaft. There were two hatchways, one fore and one aft. The vessel's commander controlled the diving planes, worked the rudder, and navigated through sightings taken through glass viewing ports in the hatch cover. The other officer opened or closed the sea valves as ordered to control the boat's ballast. All work was done in near darkness, with the only candle used by the skipper to read a depth gauge. The *Hunley* could function in depths of water but required calm seas to operate safely.

After a successful test run in Mobile, the *Hunley* won the grudging support of the veteran commander of the CSS *Virginia* and naval commander in Mobile, Admiral Franklin Buchanan. He sent an endorsement of the boat to General P. G. T. Beauregard, commanding at Charleston, South Carolina. Beauregard saw the vessel's potential for smashing the Union blockade of the port and authorized its transfer by rail. The *Hunley* arrived in Charleston on flatcars on 12 August 1863. Immediately it began to be readied for its historic task.

Unfortunately, early on the *Hunley* seems to have had a greater propensity for endangering its own crew more than the enemy. Perhaps that was why the crew of the civilian-owned craft failed to engage the enemy despite taking it out repeatedly. Finally, an exasperated General Beauregard convinced the Confederate government to assume ownership of the vessel. By late August, a naval officer had formal command of the volunteer crew.

Tragedy followed almost immediately. While commanding the boat on a trial run, Lieutenant John A. Payne got tangled in part of the *Hunley's* mechanism, causing the vessel to dive while the hatch covers were still open. Water poured through the openings as the panicked crew tried desperately to escape. Payne and two others managed to swim free. Six others went down with it. Of these, only Charles Hasker, an officer who had joined the crew for the test (the regular officer having been held up by other duty) succeeded in freeing himself once the boat reached the bottom of the harbor. Hasker became the only man ever to go down with the submarine and survive.

Undeterred, Beauregard ordered the vessel to be raised and cleaned. Although the salvage operation succeeded, there was some difficulty in finding another crew willing to risk their lives on what many were calling a death trap. Into this void stepped the intrepid inventor, Horace Hunley. He assured Beaureagard that further mishaps need not occur and that if he were given charge of the craft he could assemble a crew from Mobile.

Once more Beauregard assented. Trial runs followed as the new crew familiarized themselves with the boat's workings. Then on 15 October, only days before it was to go out to take its chances against the Union blockading fleet, the *Hunley* experienced another unexpected disaster. While making a practice dive beneath a Confederate ship, the *Hunley* failed to surface. The horrified spectators slowly realized that the craft had claimed another crew. This time, Horace Hunley and the entire boat's complement had perished.

Lieutenant George E. Dixon, a former infantryman who had suffered a severe wound at Shiloh, but was fit for command and well versed with the vessel, assumed command of the ill-fated craft. Ironically, another near accident, when the cable bearing a contact explosive became entangled in the rudder of the boat towing the *Hunley*, prompted a final improvement. Instead of dragging a line beneath a Union ship, the vessel would be equipped with a spar torpedo, which could be attached to the target while the submarine backed away to safety.

By the time the *Hunley* was ready to go out for its rendezvous with the Union fleet, information from deserters and agents led the Federals to take precautions against such an attack. These precautions, particularly by the ironclads, rendered those targets inaccessible, but the wooden vessels farther out in the harbor remained vulnerable to attack. Dixon opted to try for one of these ships.

After numerous trials, including one in which the crew remained submerged for two hours and 35 minutes, the submarine and its crew found the opportunity for which they had waited and trained. With the benefit of calm seas and favorable tides, the *Hunley* left its moorings on the night of 17 February 1864. It headed for the USS *Housatonic*, a powerful Union sloop-of-war. The

Federal commander had instructed his crew to be on the lookout for blockade runners attempting to slip by and had the vessel's fires stoked should it have to make steam on short notice.

Dixon paused the *Hunley* in its run long enough to take in fresh air through the open hatchway and check his bearings. Then he began closing in on his quarry for the final run. At 8:45 P.M., the sentries aboard the *Housatonic* spotted a strange object in the water. Some thought it to be a log or board, but as it came on they began to open fire. Bullets ricocheted off metal as the submarine rammed the barb of its torpedo into the Union ship's hull. The men inside began to reverse their propeller as fast as they could crank the shaft, still taking small arms fire. Suddenly, there was the muffled sound of an explosion and a geyser of water erupted alongside the Union ship. The *Housatonic* began to take on water. All but five of the crew scrambled into the rigging or made it into the ship's launches. Because of the shallowness of the water where it sank, the men in the rigging were rescued.

Investigations followed the sinking of the *Housatonic*, but the crew of the *Hunley* never returned to port. The details of its exact fate are not known, although divers found the submerged vessel in 1995. A 1999 television movie dramatized the attack on the *Housatonic*. On 8 August 2000, the *Hunley* was raised. After restoration, it will be exhibited at the Charleston History Museum.

—*Brian S. Wills*

See also Housatonic; Navy, C.S.A.
For further reading:
Duncan, Ruth Henley. *The Captain and Submarine* (1965).
Kloeppel, James E. *Danger Beneath the Waves* (1987).
Ragan, Mark K. *The Hunley* (1995).

HUNT, HENRY JACKSON
(1819–1889)
Union general

Hunt, whose brother was Brigadier General Lewis Cass Hunt, was born in Detroit, Michigan, on 14 September 1819. Because both his father and paternal grandfather had been regular army officers, Hunt pursued the same career. Graduating near the middle of his class from West Point in 1839, he was commissioned an artillery officer. During the Mexican-American War, Hunt, who participated in Major General Winfield Scott's campaign from Vera Cruz to Mexico City, was wounded twice and breveted both captain and major for gallantry. In 1856, Hunt, along with artillerists and future Major Generals William F. Barry and William H. French, was a member of the board organized to revise the army's system of light artillery tactics. The board's report was adopted as the standard operating procedure for light artillery on both sides during the Civil War.

On 14 May 1861, after preparing the Harper's Ferry Arsenal for "defense or destruction," Hunt, who had been a captain since the Mexican-American War, was promoted to major in the newly organized 5th U.S. Artillery Regiment. On 21 July 1861, at the battle of First Bull Run, he commanded his old unit, Battery M of the 2d U.S. Artillery Regiment, on the extreme left of the Union forces. With a mere four guns, he covered the withdrawal of the green Union army from an exposed position and was one of the few Union heroes of the battle. On 28 September 1861, as a reward for his conduct at Bull Run, Hunt was promoted to colonel of volunteers and given the position of chief of artillery of the defenses of the District of Columbia. Next, he organized the Artillery Reserve of the Army of the Potomac and commanded that unit during the Peninsula campaign. On 1 July 1862, at Malvern Hill, the final battle of the Peninsula campaign, Hunt, who during the battle had two horses shot from under him, commanded the 100 guns that devastated the charging Confederate infantry and played a major part in the Union victory.

Promoted to brigadier general of volunteers on 15 September 1862, Hunt was appointed the chief of artillery of the Army of the Potomac by the army's commander, Major General George B. McClellan. On 13 December 1862, Hunt massed 147 guns to cover the river crossing of the Army of the Potomac at the battle of Fredericksburg. Most historians agree that the Union's artillery was also the main reason that Lee did not counterattack after the Union forces were repulsed at Fredericksburg. After Burnside's removal, Major General "Fighting Joe" Hooker, the new commander of the Army of the Potomac, curtailed much of Hunt's authority. As a result of Hooker assigning Hunt primarily to administrative duties, the army's artillery performed poorly at the battle of Chancellorsville, and Hunt was restored as chief of artillery.

On 3 July 1863, the third day of the battle of Gettysburg, Hunt quarreled with Major General Winfield Scott Hancock, commander of II Corps, over the use of the artillery. Hancock wanted counterbattery fire against the Confederate guns, but Hunt rightly wished to save his ammunition for the Confederate charge. In the end, the Union artillery would tear great gaps in the Confederate infantry during Pickett's Charge and thereby ensure the Union victory. Breveted major general of volunteers on 6 July 1864, Hunt continued to serve as the chief of artillery of the Army of the Potomac under Major General George G. Meade, with whom Hunt feuded frequently. After the Overland campaign of 1864, Lieutenant General Ulysses S. Grant appointed Hunt to command all siege operations against Petersburg, Virginia.

Breveted major general in the regular army on 13 March 1865, Hunt reverted to the permanent rank of lieutenant colonel in the 3d Artillery at the war's end. In 1869, he was promoted to colonel and given command of his old regiment, the 5th Artillery. Widely recognized as the army's leading authority on the use of artillery, Hunt would write a series of articles for *Battle and Leaders of the Civil War*. Stationed in the South after the war, Hunt was widely criticized for his lenient treatment of Southerners. Upon his retirement in 1883, the animosity he had earned among Radical Republicans prevented his being retired at the rank of major general. After his retirement, Hunt was the governor of the Soldier's Home in Washington, D.C., where he died on 11 February 1889.

—*Alexander M. Bielakowski*

See also Artillery; Gettysburg, Battle of; Malvern Hill, Battle of.
For further reading:
Downey, Fairfax Davis. *The Guns at Gettysburg* (1958).
Longacre, Edward G. *The Man Behind the Guns: A Biography of General Henry Jackson Hunt, Chief of Artillery, Army of the Potomac* (1977).

HUNTER, DAVID
(1802–1886)
Union general

David Hunter was born on 21 January 1802 in Washington, D.C., the son of a Presbyterian minister. After graduating from West Point in 1822, Hunter began his controversial military career, one that almost ended as soon as it started. Known for his short temper, Hunter killed three men in duels before finally being court-martialed and sentenced to immediate removal from the service. President John Quincy Adams, however, overruled the military decision and Hunter remained in the military. Ten years later in 1836, Hunter resigned from the army to pursue a real estate career in Chicago, only to return six years later as a paymaster. He served during the Mexican-American War, but saw no action and was assigned to a post in the Northwest after the war. It was here that Hunter married Maria Kinzie from Illinois.

After Abraham Lincoln's election in 1860, Hunter began writing a series of letters to the president-elect concerning possible Southern uprisings. Lincoln must have been impressed by this officer, for he invited Hunter to accompany him on his inauguration train to Washington and appointed him head of the volunteer forces guarding the White House. Hunter's warm relationship with the president facilitated his appointment as a brigadier general by May 1861.

Hunter's first combat action came at the battle of First Bull Run, where he spearheaded Irvin McDowell's assault. During the early part of the battle, Hunter was seriously wounded and evacuated from the field before the Confederate forces managed to take the initiative. After Hunter recovered from his wound, Lincoln sent him to advise Major General John Frémont in the Western Department, where Hunter became temporary department commander in November 1861 when Frémont was relieved from command of the Western Department. Hunter believed he was on the track to higher promotion, but his hopes were dashed when reassigned to Kansas, a largely inactive department.

Hunter's new command in Kansas also included forces in Colorado, Nebraska, and South Dakota, but involved primarily Indian and not Confederate adversaries. Attempting to escape his new post, Hunter began writing to the War Department in Washington. When he received no reply, he turned to the president, hoping to utilize their previous friendship. Lincoln, however, also ignored Hunter, which caused the distraught general to send a very morbid note to the president in December 1861. Lincoln replied with a stinging letter stating that Hunter's actions were very unprofessional and would surely lead to the ruin of his military career.

Despite these setbacks, General Hunter escaped Kansas and found himself in command of the Department of the South in March 1862. Commanding federally occupied areas in South Carolina, Georgia, and Florida, Hunter provoked deep indignation in Southerners. On 7 May 1862, he issued his own emancipation edict, which theoretically freed all slaves within his area of operations. If this was not enough to enrage both governments of the North and South, Hunter next created the first black military regiment, the 1st South Carolina. Twelve days after the emancipation decree, President Lincoln repealed the act, stating that Hunter had overstepped his authority as a general. President Davis also replied by issuing his own declaration, placing a bounty for Hunter's capture, planning for his close confinement and execution if he were caught.

Hunter's controversial activities placed him in Washington performing court-martial and inspection duties. Hunter remained at this post for more than a year before he received another troop command. After Franz Sigel's decisive defeat in May 1864 at New Market, a battle that included cadets from the Virginia Military Institute, Lincoln appointed Hunter to command in the Shenandoah Valley. Although not the best choice for command, Hunter had gained the favor of the ever-growing Radical Republicans in Washington.

General Ulysses S. Grant ordered Hunter, as part of his three-part plan to strangle Richmond, to advance (south) up the Shenandoah Valley, cut its railroad links with the Confederate capital, and destroy the supply depot at Lynchburg. Hunter began by routing a small Southern force at Piedmont and continued quickly to

Lynchburg. Frustrated by constant guerrilla attacks, Hunter's men looted and burned everything in their path, eventually arriving in Lexington, Virginia, where they burned the Virginia Military Institute. General Robert E. Lee saw the problem posed by Hunter and sent General Jubal Early to stop his advance. Early prevented the link between Hunter and General Philip Sheridan by occupying Lynchburg before either of the Union generals could arrive. Hunter arrived at Lynchburg and attacked on 18 June, but he failed to take the town. He retreated into West Virginia, leaving the whole valley open to Early.

After his defeat in the Shenandoah Valley, General Hunter returned to Washington, never to command again, yet after Lincoln's assassination he accompanied the body back to Illinois. Hunter was also appointed president of the military commission to investigate and try those suspected in the assassination conspiracy. He remained in the army until 1866 and died in Washington, D.C., twenty years later, still regarded by Southerners as one of the most hated Union generals of the war.

—Brad Arnold

See also Bull Run, First Battle of; Early, Jubal; Early's Washington Raid; Frémont, John C.

For further reading:
Hubell, John T., and James W. Geary, eds. *Biographical Dictionary of the Union: Northern Leaders of the Civil War* (1995).
Walker, Gary C. *Hunter's Fiery Raid through Virginia Valleys* (1989).

HUNTER, ROBERT MERCER TALIAFERRO
(1809–1887)
Confederate cabinet member and senator

Born to James Hunter and Maria Garnett Hunter, Robert M. T. Hunter was educated on the family plantation before enrolling in the University of Virginia. After graduation he studied law under states' rights advocate Henry St. George Tucker. Hunter began his practice in 1830 and early in his career evinced an interest in politics, though he refused initially to affiliate with any organized party. From 1834 to 1837, he served in the Virginia legislature and then beginning in 1837 served the first of three consecutive terms in the U.S. House of Representatives. In 1839 he began a one-year term as Speaker of the House. During this stint in Congress, Hunter increasingly came under the influence, and became a supporter, of John C. Calhoun. After a two-year absence, Hunter returned to the House in 1845 and in 1847 was elected to the U.S. Senate. He served in that body until March of 1861.

During his fourteen years in the Senate, Hunter paradoxically earned the reputation as both an extreme supporter of states' rights and a moderate accommodationist. As a result, many people never knew what to expect from him on any issue and simply waited for him to test the winds before making up his mind. The same senator who attended the strongly pro–states' rights Nashville Convention supported the pro-Northern tariff of 1857. The support for the latter measure won him a number of supporters in the North and was one of the reasons why he was seriously considered by some Northern Democrats for the party's nomination in 1860.

Many Virginia Democrats certainly supported him as a possible compromise candidate at the Charleston Convention of the national party in 1860. Hunter apparently supported such a move himself and for that reason would not release his supporters to John C. Breckinridge (considered by many a far more viable national candidate) until it was too late to secure Breckinridge's nomination.

With Abraham Lincoln's election in November 1860, Hunter still held out hope for compromise. He accepted appointment to the Senate committee of thirteen, charged with arriving at a compromise of the sectional differences. Hunter supported the proposed compromises and conferred frequently with President James Buchanan over the growing crisis. After Lincoln's inauguration on 4 March, Hunter remained in Washington for several more weeks, still hoping for a miracle, but, finally giving up hope, he resigned on 28 March.

Robert Hunter (*Library of Congress*)

After Virginia's secession after the Sumter crisis, Hunter became a member of the Confederate Provisional Congress. He also corresponded frequently with President Jefferson Davis regarding what he believed to be the proper defense for Virginia. With the resignation of Robert A. Toombs from the position of Confederate secretary of state, Hunter was brought into the administration in that post on 25 July 1861. He served there until 17 February 1862.

As Confederate secretary of state, Hunter remained concerned about the defense of Virginia. Another of his concerns was gaining positions for friends and family in the Confederate army and government. One of his few initiatives in the cabinet was an attempt to forge an alliance between the Confederacy and Spain. He left the cabinet in February 1862 to accept election by Virginia to the Confederate Senate.

In the Confederate Senate, Hunter assumed few leadership roles. While considered a supporter of the administration, he could not be relied on for forthright statements defending administration policies. An acquaintance of Virginian general Joseph E. Johnston, Hunter became involved in the pro-Johnston clique in Congress in the fall and winter of 1863. In early 1865, his seniority and former national prominence earned him a place on the ill-fated peace commission with John A. Campbell and Confederate vice president Alexander Stephens. This effort was doomed to failure from the start, however, because the commissioners were not allowed to negotiate on the issue of Southern independence. In the last weeks of the war, Hunter opposed the arming of African-American soldiers for the Confederacy, but at the same time urged unconditional surrender.

After the evacuation of Richmond by the Confederate government, Hunter remained behind. His house was searched by Northern soldiers and the papers confiscated there carefully examined for any possible role Hunter may have played in the Lincoln assassination. On 7 May 1865, though no evidence had been found, General Ulysses S. Grant ordered Hunter's arrest and imprisonment. At the end of May, Hunter was transported to Fort Pulaski, Georgia, and was held there until November 1865.

Upon his release, Hunter returned to his family estate, which had been virtually destroyed by Union general Benjamin Butler during Hunter's imprisonment. Hunter resumed his law practice and for the remainder of his life held a variety of state and local offices. He died in Essex County, Virginia, on 18 July 1887.

—David S. Heidler and Jeanne T. Heidler

See also Congress, Confederate; Peace Movements.
For further reading:
Ambler, Charles H., ed. C.S.A. of Robert M. T. Hunter (1971).
Simms, Henry Harrison. Life of Robert M. T. Hunter; A Study in Sectionalism and Secession (1935).

HUNTON, EPPA
(1822–1908)
Confederate general

Born to Eppa Hunton and Elizabeth Marye Brent Hunton outside Warrenton, Virginia, the younger Hunton was educated locally before studying law. After admission to the Virginia bar, he opened a practice in Brentsville, Virginia. In addition to his law practice, Hunton served as commonwealth attorney for Prince William County and was active in the local militia, eventually rising to the rank of militia general.

Before the Civil War, Hunton was an avid Democrat and served as a John C. Breckinridge elector in the election of 1860. After the election of Abraham Lincoln, Hunton ran for and was elected to a seat in the Virginia secession convention, where he pushed for immediate secession. With the firing on Fort Sumter, he resigned his seat to raise the 8th Virginia Regiment. As the colonel of that regiment through the first two years of the war, he fought in virtually every major engagement in the Eastern theater.

After recruiting the regiment, he commanded the vicinity around Leesburg, Virginia. When he heard of Irvin McDowell's movement toward Manassas Junction, he moved his regiment there, arriving on 19 July 1861. Though apparently seriously ill at the time, Hunton fought well at the battle of First Bull Run especially around Henry House Hill late in the afternoon and proved valuable to his commanders because of his intimate knowledge of the area.

Though not recovered from his illness, Hunton continued to command his regiment. Too indisposed to ride a horse, in the fall he had a wagon with him in the rear pulled alongside the regiment while they fought at Balls Bluff.

During the Peninsula campaign, Hunton commanded the 8th as part of George Pickett's brigade in James Longstreet's division and temporarily took command of the brigade when Pickett was seriously injured at Gaines' Mill.

For the next year, Hunton remained in command of the 8th, fighting in Richard B. Garnett's brigade, Pickett's division at Gettysburg, where he was severely wounded in Pickett's Charge. He was promoted to brigadier general on 9 August 1863, but because of his injury and ill health was placed on recruiting duty until the spring of 1864.

Sufficiently recovered to return to the Army of Northern Virginia, Hunton led his brigade in the battles of the Wilderness, Cold Harbor, Drewry's Bluff, and the siege of Petersburg. When Lee broke out of his defenses at Petersburg, Hunton and his brigade fought at Sayler's Creek, where Hunton was captured on 6 April. He was a prisoner until July 1865.

After the war, Hunton returned to Warrenton, Virginia where he resumed the practice of law. He was also a vocal opponent of Radical Reconstruction, a stance that gained him enough notoriety to win him election to the U.S. House of Representatives in 1875. He served until 1881. While in the House, he served on the electoral commission that decided the results of the president election of 1876 between Rutherford B. Hayes and Samuel Tilden. From 1892 until 1895 he served in the U.S. Senate. He died in Richmond, Virginia.

—*David S. Heidler and Jeanne T. Heidler*

See also Bull Run, First battle of; Pickett, George.
For further reading:
Hunton, Eppa. *Autobiography of Eppa Hunton* (1933).
Maddex, Jack. *The Virginia Conservatives, 1867–1879; A Study in Reconstruction Politics* (1970).

HUNTSVILLE, ALABAMA

Located in the foothills of Monte Sano in Madison County, northeastern Alabama, Huntsville (population 3,634 in 1860) passed back and forth between Confederate and Union forces during the Civil War. The town had strategic importance as a center of northern Alabama's critical transportation routes, including the Tennessee River and railroad network. The Memphis & Charleston Railroad had its corporate offices for its eastern division and local passenger house in the Huntsville Depot, a three-story brick building built in 1860. Although no major battles took place in northern Alabama, the area changed hands many times. Each army took food and livestock, causing the civilians to suffer greatly and exacerbating the region's already divided loyalties.

On 11 April 1862, Federal troops commanded by Brigadier General Ormsby Mitchel occupied Huntsville. From 14 April until 31 August, Colonel William Haines Lytle, then commanding the 17th Brigade, 3d Division, the Army of Ohio, made his headquarters in Huntsville. Lytle described Huntsville in glowing terms and thought it one of the most beautiful towns in the United States. The elegant private residences and fine gardens that he praised survived the war, in part, due to the support given the Union by some local businessmen.

On 4 June and 2 July 1862, skirmishing took place near Huntsville as Confederates considered Mitchel and the Federal forces as a threat to Chattanooga. When Confederate guerrillas fired into trains in Huntsville, the Federal authorities ordered the arrest of ministers and leading churchmen who had supported secession and stipulated that each day one should be placed on board the trains. Despite these actions and occasional raids near the town, the Union officers and accompanying family members located in or near Huntsville found time to enjoy a Fourth of July picnic and the scenic view from the top of Monte Sano.

On 29 August, as General Braxton Bragg moved Confederate troops toward Kentucky, Lytle received orders from General Don Carlos Buell to withdraw from Huntsville due to the difficulties of sustaining communication. The orders specified that the intention to withdraw be kept secret, even from Lytle's own officers. Only the hospitals and sick were left behind, along with at least two weeks' worth of supplies. After destroying a small portion of stores and machinery, Lytle marched for Murfreesboro on 31 August with a long train and 400 head of horses and cattle.

On 13 July 1863, General William S. Rosecrans dispatched an expedition to Huntsville under the command of Major General David S. Stanley, who arrived on 22 July. Stanley's report noted that the Huntsville country could support a force of 10,000 with its abundance of corn, mutton, and beef.

Skirmishing resumed near Huntsville and throughout northeastern Alabama in October and November 1864 in conjunction with Confederate actions to try to overturn the capture of Atlanta. Northern Alabama and the southeast corner of Tennessee remained transportation centers with control of the railroads vital to both sides. Skirmishes took place in or near Huntsville on 1 October and 18 October. The final military action at Huntsville occurred in April 1865 when a Federal scouting unit went from Huntsville on 3 April to near Vienna, Alabama. On 5 April, the Federals operated a three-day scouting mission from Huntsville to New Market and Maysville, Alabama.

—*Ruth C. Carter*

See also Alabama; Lytle, William Haines; Mitchel, Ormsby Macknight.
For further reading:
Carter, Ruth C. *For Honor, Glory and Union: The Mexican and Civil War Letters of Brigadier General William Haines Lytle* (1999).
Fleming, Walter Lynwood. *Civil War and Reconstruction in Alabama* (1905).
McMillan, Malcolm C. *The Alabama Confederate Reader* (1963).

HURLBUT, STEPHEN AUGUSTUS
(1815–1882)
Union general

Born to Martin Luther Hurlbut and Lydia Bunce Hurlbut in Charleston, South Carolina, Stephen Augustus Hurlbut was educated locally before studying law and opening a practice in Charleston. He became active in the local militia and went with some of his comrades to Florida to fight in the Second Seminole War. He moved to Illinois in 1845 and opened a law practice in Belvidere, Illinois. He became active in Whig state politics, serving in the state constitutional convention in 1847 and as a presidential elector in 1848. In the mid-1850s, he became a Republican and was elected to the state legislature in 1858. He left the legislature at the outbreak of the Civil War to accept a commission as a brigadier general of volunteers.

During the summer of 1861, Hurlbut served first in Illinois and then in Missouri guarding the Hannibal & St. Joseph Railroad. Under Ulysses S. Grant in early 1862, Hurlbut fought at Fort Donelson in February. Afterward, he was given command of Grant's 4th Division. He commanded that division at Shiloh in April 1862. In August and early September 1862, Hurlbut commanded his division, operating out of Memphis until he was transferred to the District of Jackson on 5 September 1862. From there he fought in the Corinth campaign, where he led part of the pursuit of Earl Van Dorn's army. Hurlbut had been promoted to major general of volunteers on 17 September.

After Corinth, Hurlbut took command of the District of Memphis. In December 1862, as part of that command he was made commander of the XVI Corps. With the exception of a short leave of absence in January 1863, Hurlbut remained in that command until April 1864. During this rather lengthy tour by Civil War standards, Hurlbut maintained control of the supply depot and base of operations for Grant's Vicksburg campaign, a task complicated by the operations of very mobile Confederate cavalry commanded by officers such as Nathan Bedford Forrest.

After the successful conclusion of the Vicksburg campaign, Hurlbut tendered his resignation. Along with the formal resignation, he wrote a personal letter to Abraham Lincoln outlining the reasons for his decision. He stated that he believed that with the fall of Vicksburg the war was virtually over and therefore his services were no longer as important as they once were. He also told the president that his long absence from his law practice had put his personal finances in some disarray and that he needed to return to the law to salvage his career. In spite of this lengthy explanation, shortly after sending the letter to Lincoln, Hurlbut withdrew his resignation and remained in the army.

During the fall of 1863, Hurlbut continued to monitor the activities of Forrest and other Confederates near Memphis, but enjoyed little success against them. In early 1864, he took two of his divisions to participate in William T. Sherman's Meridian campaign. While there was no mention at the time of Sherman's dissatisfaction regarding Hurlbut's performance, shortly after returning to Memphis Hurlbut received a letter from Sherman relieving him of command. Sherman gave as his reason Hurlbut's timidity in pursuing Forrest. It revealed Sherman's frustration with the Confederate cavalry commander and especially the stinging defeat of Federal forces at Westpoint, Mississippi, that February. True enough, for more than a year Hurlbut had done

little to combat Forrest's elusive cavalry. Now essentially banished, Hurlbut went to command the supply depot at Cairo, Illinois.

In September 1864, Hurlbut took command of the Department of the Gulf in relief of Nathaniel P. Banks. Though the posting was technically temporary, Hurlbut remained in command there until 22 April 1865. His time in New Orleans was somewhat tumultuous though curiously not from a military standpoint. One of his first acts, for instance, was to conduct a study of his department that resulted in an extensive report to the War Department. He complimented some of the department's commanders, but he criticized others for inefficiency and occasional corruption (a charge heavy with irony since Hurlbut was known to feather his own nest). Yet most controversial was his criticism of the alleged corruption in the civilian government established by the Lincoln administration. Such accusations obviously embarrassed the administration, and Louisiana Republicans countered with charges of corruption against Hurlbut. The danger of a wholesale political scandal caused by the trial of a prominent Republican general prompted both the military and the administration to squelch the entire thing. After his relief as commander of the Department of the Gulf, Hurlbut was allowed to resign and was quietly mustered out of service in June 1865.

After the war, Hurlbut led a varied public career. He served again in the Illinois legislature and sat for two terms in the U.S. Congress. One of the founding members of the Grand Army of the Republic, he was its first commander in chief. In 1869 he went to Colombia for a three-year stint as the U.S. minister there, and in 1881 he became the U.S. minister to Peru. Hurlbut's service in Colombia was uneventful, but his brief time in Lima was troubled when he breached U.S. neutrality by siding with Peru in the War of the Pacific. Hurlbut died in Lima in the midst of the controversy on 27 March 1882.

—*David S. Heidler and Jeanne T. Heidler*

See also Corinth; Louisiana; Meridian Campaign.
For further reading:

Bearss, Margie Riddle. *Sherman's Forgotten Campaign: The Meridian Expedition* (1987).
Winters, John D. *The Civil War in Louisiana* (1963).

HUSE, CALEB
(1831–1905)
Confederate purchasing agent

Born to Ralph Cross Huse and Caroline Evans Huse in Newburyport, Massachusetts, Caleb Huse graduated seventh of forty-two in the U.S. Military Academy class of 1851. After receiving his commission, Huse reported to Key West, Florida, as an officer of the

1st Artillery Regiment. After only a year in Florida, Huse returned to West Point as an instructor from 1852 to 1859. In 1860 he took a leave of absence. After traveling to Europe he returned to accept an appointment as the commandant of cadets at the University of Alabama.

In February 1861, Huse resigned his commission in the U.S. Army and accepted a captain's commission in the Confederate army. Huse's decision to side with the South in the Civil War has been explained variously by his Southern associations at West Point, his short residence in the South, and his Southern marriage.

After a short stint in the Confederate artillery, Huse was sent to Europe in April 1861 to serve as a Confederate purchasing agent. His primary charge was to purchase as much ordnance and other military supplies as possible, but he found when he reached England in May 1861 that he was being outbid by the U.S. agents there. He was assisted in his efforts beginning at the end of May by Major Edward C. Anderson.

Both men, finding little to buy in England, began looking to other European countries for military supplies. Huse, Anderson, and Confederate navy purchaser James D. Bulloch bought large amounts of supplies from countries such as Austria and France (much on credit) and then shipped them to Great Britain. In England, Huse arranged with British shippers to transport the goods to either Nassau or Havana and from there make arrangements for the blockade to be run into the Confederacy. Huse's immediate superior, Confederate chief of ordnance Josiah Gorgas believed that Huse's efforts were essential components of many Confederate military victories.

Perhaps because some Southerners were suspicious of Huse's Northern background, compounded by his loose bookkeeping and tremendous reliance on credit, Huse was accused in 1863 of misappropriation of funds. A subsequent investigation cleared him of any malfeasance. In fact, in the same year, Huse helped to negotiate the Erlanger Loan with famed German-Parisian financier, Emile Erlanger.

Huse did not return to the United States until 1868. Having no money, he turned to teaching to support his family. He began a school at Sing Sing, New York, that he later moved to Highland Falls, New York. The primary purpose of the institution was to prepare young men for entrance to the U.S. Military Academy. He died at Highland Falls.

—*David S. Heidler and Jeanne T. Heidler*

See also Bulloch, James D.; Gorgas, Josiah.
For further reading:
Huse, Caleb. *The Supplies of the Confederate Army* (1904).
Thompson, Samuel Bernard. *Confederate Purchasing Operations Abroad* (1935).

I

IMBODEN AND JONES'S RAID
(24 April–14 May 1863)

This spectacular Confederate raid into western Virginia was primarily directed against the Baltimore & Ohio (B&O) Railroad, important for Union military operations in the region as well as for the movement of coal and timber supplies for the Union war effort. Brigadier General John D. Imboden strongly supported such a raid in a letter to General Robert E. Lee. Imboden hoped it would defeat Federal garrisons and destroy bridges and trestles on the B&O. He also saw it as a means to assist Confederate recruiting, topple the Union state government of western Virginia at Wheeling, and yield food stuffs, horses, and cattle. Confederate leaders in Richmond hoped it would draw off Federal troops from Winchester. They also hoped Imboden might hold much of western Virginia and destroy a wide swath of the railroad system west of the Alleghanies, goals beyond Imboden's means.

Richmond expanded the raid by adding forces under Brigadier General William E. "Grumble" Jones. Imboden and Jones met and, after conferring with Lee, agreed on a two-pronged attack. Imboden would lead one brigade in a single column against Beverly, Philippi, and Grafton. Jones's brigade would parallel Imboden's route to the north, advance to Moorefield, and then secure control of the Northwest Turnpike and attack the B&O at Oakland and Rowlesburg. The two would then simultaneously strike the B&O at Oakland and Grafton.

Lee thought the raid significant enough to give Imboden two veteran regiments, the 25th and 31st Virginia. After almost a month in preparation, on 20 April 1863, Imboden set his men in motion west from Shenandoah Mountain. He had 3,365 men, several hundred of whom were mounted. The weather was vile; pouring rain turned into snow, and the march over the mountains was on roads that became quagmires.

At the same time, Jones left Lacey Springs with 3,500 men. His route of march went through Brock's Gap to Moorefield, but high water at Moorefield forced Jones into a twelve-mile detour to Petersburg to cross the Potomac River. He then sent back his dismounted men and wagon trains, along with a 300-man cavalry escort. This reduced his force by 1,000 men.

Most Federal units had moved westward on the railroad to intercept Imboden, so that at Greenland Gap Jones's force encountered only a detachment of eighty-three men of the 23d Illinois. At a cost of seven killed and twenty-two men wounded, the Federals held up Jones for four hours.

Meanwhile Imboden's force ran into 1,500 Union troops south of Beverly. Imboden split his force and flanked the defenders, who after several hours then withdrew toward Philippi. Darkness halted the Confederate pursuit. Casualties on both sides were slight: sixteen Union and three Confederate. Beverly yielded some $100,000 in supplies, including badly needed ammunition.

Union area commander Brigadier General Benjamin Roberts wired Union general-in-chief Henry Halleck that the poor state of the roads prevented him from protecting the B&O. Halleck fired back a scathing reply ordering him to defend the railroad and stating that he did not understand how the roads could be impassable to Union troops "when, by your own account, they are passable enough to the enemy."

On 26 April, Imboden departed Beverly for Buckhannon. He was halfway there when he received word that a Union brigade had arrived at Philippi by rail from New Creek. With one Union force at Buckhannon and another at Philippi, Imboden then fell back on Beverly rather than risk being cut off. Roberts, meanwhile, concentrated at Buckhannon. Worried about that position and aware that Clarksburg with its military stores and railroad was vital, on 28 April he concentrated his 2,800 men there. When Imboden's scouts informed him that Federal troops were evacuating Buckhannon, he immediately resumed his advance. The Confederates found most of the Union stores destroyed, but they rounded up horses and cattle in the area.

Imboden now rested his men and awaited word from Jones. On 29 April, Jones and part of his command arrived at Buckhannon. Jones's men had destroyed nine railroad bridges; they had captured two trains, an artillery piece, 500 prisoners, 1,200–1,500 horses, and 1,000 cattle.

Jones and Imboden originally planned to attack Clarksburg, but they decided that even their combined force was too weak to take an entrenched position. Their force had been reduced from sickness and the need to

guard captured livestock. The two decided to separate again; Imboden would head south toward Summersville while Jones moved westward to attack the B&O.

Jones then captured the railroad guard at West Union and Cairo, burned five more bridges, and damaged a tunnel. His men then ravaged the Kanawha Valley petroleum fields, setting fire to 150,000 barrels of oil at Oiltown. Jones then set off to rejoin Imboden. Meanwhile, Imboden at Summersville took a 28-wagon Federal provision train pulled by 170 mules, captured a large number of livestock, and damaged the Federal depot.

Jones rejoined Imboden at Summersville on 14 May. The two Confederate generals agreed they had accomplished their aims and separated. Imboden then moved toward Lewisburg. Along the way, at Fayetteville the Confederates defeated a Union cavalry thrust to seize the Confederate supply train.

The raiders returned to the Shenandoah Valley by the end of May. They had brought off more than 5,000 cattle and 1,200 horses; and their raid had destroyed 24 bridges, damaged a tunnel, and cut telegraph lines. They had also burned large stocks of oil, captured 1,000 small arms and an artillery piece, and destroyed Union supply depots; and they had inflicted 800 Union casualties of killed, wounded, and captured. Confederate losses were slight. Politically the raid temporarily broke up the Unionist convention at Wheeling and diverted thousands of Union troops there. However, on its reconstitution, the Wheeling assembly voted to create the state of West Virginia. General Lee summed up that the raid "rendered valuable service in the collection of stores and in making the enemy uneasy for his communication with the West."

—*Spencer C. Tucker*

See also Imboden, John D.; Jones, William E.
For further reading:
Woodward, Harold R., Jr. *Defender of the Valley. Brigadier General John Daniel Imboden, C.S.A.* (1996).

IMBODEN, JOHN DANIEL
(1823–1895)
Confederate general

John Imboden was a Confederate general who proved to be a capable and aggressive cavalry commander, especially in advance guard and independent commands. Born on Christian's Creek near Fishersville, in Augusta County, Virginia, on 16 February 1823, Imboden attended Washington College (later Washington and Lee University) during 1841–1842. He then taught school and studied and practiced law in Staunton before serving two terms in the Virginia state legislature. The strongly secessionist Imboden failed, however, to win a seat in the state convention that passed the secession ordinance.

John Daniel Imboden (*Library of Congress*)

Active in the militia, he helped organize the Staunton Artillery. When Virginia joined the Confederacy, Imboden led the Staunton Artillery to Harper's Ferry and captured it. Securing a commission as a colonel, Imboden then distinguished himself at the 21 July 1861 battle of First Bull Run (Manassas), especially in defending Henry House Hill.

In 1862 Imboden organized a cavalry unit, the 1st Partisan Rangers, which fought under General Thomas J. "Stonewall" Jackson in the Shenandoah Valley campaign of that year. Imboden participated in the battles of Cross Keys (8 June 1862) and Port Republic (9 June 1862). During Lee's invasion of the North that summer, Imboden assisted in the capture of Harper's Ferry (15 September 1862).

Promoted to brigadier general on 28 January 1863, Imboden showed great ability in semi-independent command. On 20 April of that year, Imboden led a 3,300-man force into western Virginia. He was supported by another force of 2,200 cavalry under Brigadier General William E. Jones, and the two joined forces at Weston. The raid cut Baltimore & Ohio Railroad lines, captured large amounts of livestock, and ravaged the Kanawha Valley petroleum fields.

Imboden then returned to Virginia and took part in General Robert E. Lee's invasion of Pennsylvania. His forces helped screen the Army of Northern Virginia's left flank during the advance, but arrived at Gettysburg only at noon on 3 July 1863. Lee assigned Imboden the important task of covering the Confederate withdrawal. Imboden's men performed this task well, engaging in a fight at Williamsport that helped prevent Union troops from capturing the Confederate baggage trains and wounded.

In October 1863, Imboden raided into West Virginia for a second time and captured the Union garrison at Charleston. This action won him Lee's written commendation. In May 1864 Imboden's 1,500 cavalry played a key role in defeating Union major general Franz Sigel's thrust up the Shenandoah Valley. On 11 May, Imboden's force surprised and captured 464 Union troops in a cavalry regiment on outpost duty near Port Royal. Operating with Confederate general John C. Breckinridge, Imboden helped defeat Sigel in the battle of New Market on the 15th. Imboden then participated in Confederate lieutenant general Jubal A. Early's June–July Valley campaign, in which rebel forces threatened Washington. Imboden also fought unsuccessfully to stem the subsequent advance of Union forces under Major General Philip H. Sheridan down the Shenandoah Valley. In late 1864 Imboden contracted typhoid fever; returning to duty, he closed out his war service in command of a Confederate prison at Aiken, South Carolina.

After the war, Imboden resumed the practice of law for a time, but he spent the last two decades of his life in Washington County, Virginia. In 1872 he published a book, *The Coal and Iron Resource of Virginia*. He also wrote a number of articles for *Battle and Leaders of the Civil War*. He was active in promoting the development of iron and coal resources in Virginia. Imboden died at Damascus, Virginia, on 15 August 1895.

—*Spencer C. Tucker*

See also Breckinridge, John C.; Early, Jubal; Jones, William Edmondson; New Market (May 1864); Sheridan, Philip H.; Sigel, Franz.

For further reading:

Alexander, Edward Porter. *Military Memoirs of a Confederate. A Critical Narrative* (1907).

Hager, William D. "The Civilian Life and Accomplishments of John Daniel Imboden" (M.A. thesis, 1988).

Woodward, Harold R., Jr. *Defender of the Valley. Brigadier General John Daniel Imboden, C.S.A.* (1996).

IMMIGRANTS

By the outbreak of the Civil War, 4 million Americans of a total population of 31.4 million were foreign-born—more than 13 percent of the population in the North and the same portion of that in the South. In the first months of fighting, some groups enlisted for military service in a ratio often exceeding that of the native population. As volunteers and draftees, they shouldered a considerable part of the burden; as civilians, they were just as much affected by the consequences of the war as the population in general. Furthermore, immigrants not only filled the ranks of soldiers and sailors but also of others whose services were needed in the war. They served as doctors, nurses, workers for private relief agencies, engineers, sketch artists, photographers, and even spies.

The social and cultural background of the different ethnic groups varied so greatly that responses to the fight as well as to the question of slavery might have taken as many different forms. Many had come to America not only to till a piece of land that would be their own or to follow the promise of a job. Many had come to pursue their callings in peace, free from the factional conflicts raging in their home countries or simply free from the state forcing its political and military demands onto citizens. Thus it was to be expected that the experience of strife or fighting in Europe would make immigrants in the United States "[take] steps…to keep easily out of the toils of war," as one German-American father put it in his memoirs.

More recent newcomers to America were even more likely to reject the conflict as none of their business. In addition, the position of many immigrant groups, especially in Northern cities, could strengthen an inclination to keep out of the war. Some immigrant groups believed that fighting for the emancipation of the slaves would eventually lead to an onrush of workers who would compete with them for the lowest-paying jobs. A fear of African-American labor competing for jobs was particularly virulent among Irish-Americans, who had been almost completely hostile to the antislavery movement in the prewar years.

Despite all these potential obstacles to immigrant participation in the war, the response to the call for volunteers at the outbreak of war was equally enthusiastic among both native-born and foreign-born Americans. Throughout the war, the portion of foreign-born Americans within the ranks of the forces continued to be high. In some cases it was markedly higher than the ethnic group's portion of the overall population: 166,000 Irish-Americans served in Union and Confederate forces; and some 200,000 German-Americans, or roughly one-tenth of the overall number of Union soldiers, fought in Union regiments alone. In North and South, foreign-born Americans served in both ethnic and nonethnic regiments, the latter being the more common situation.

The reasons for commitment varied. Enlistment was a means to avoid unemployment or to earn more than an unskilled laborer's wage. Recruiting officers offered

bounties, that induced some immigrants in the war's later years to join the army immediately on their arrival. Political motives were another strong incentive, especially for those who had most acutely experienced injustice and oppression in their home countries. Taking up the cause of the Union could be seen as fighting another phase of the struggle between aristocracy and democracy, an extension of the long-standing conflict raging in Europe. It could be seen as fighting for freedom in the spirit of the revolutions of 1848–1849 or simply fighting for freedom and the Union, just the same as other patriotic Americans. Similarly, those who rallied to the Confederate cause wanted to defend the way of life in that part of the United States that they had chosen to be their home. Gratitude and the urge to demonstrate loyalty to their adopted country proved strong motives too. The willingness to do one's share often combined with the hope that the prestige of a particular ethnic group would be boosted and thus its integration into American society facilitated.

As it turned out, the reality was much more complicated. Although immigrants served as Union and Confederate troops in all theaters and on the frontier, they were not automatically treated as equals. That many had not readily mastered English, and hence were frequently not seen as officer material, or that they lacked military discipline or exhibited rough or brutal behavior in the field—something common among all groups—does not completely explain the prejudicial discrimination suffered by immigrant soldiers. American nativism continued to be strong, if at a lesser pitch than in the 1850s, and followed immigrants into military life.

Wages, salaries, and incidence of promotion are among the areas of discrimination that historians can analyze easily, and these areas provide a broad quantitative basis, allowing for sound conclusions. It has been shown that, in Minnesota volunteer regiments, soldiers of German and Scandinavian descent did not earn promotion at the same rate that Anglo-Saxons did, despite their military expertise. In one case, even a letter of recommendation from a state politician did not suffice to persuade the governor to appoint a German-American with extensive military experience.

On the other hand, however, immigrants could experience an improvement of status. The war brought foreign-born soldiers and civilians nearer to acceptance by, and equality in, an American society that had denied integration, sometimes violently, to some newcomers. At the same time, many immigrants wanted to retain part of their ethnic identity and thus reanimated some persistent nativist tendencies, making the process of acceptance only a limited one. In this sense, the Civil War for immigrants may well be seen both as "an ending and a new beginning."

—*Angela Schwarz*

See also Chinese-Americans; Irish-Americans; Immigration; German-Americans; Italian-Americans.
For further reading:
Jones, Maldwyn Allen. *American Immigration* (1960).
Lonn, Ella. *Foreigners in the Confederacy* (1940).
———. *Foreigners in the Union Army and Navy* (1951; reprint, 1969).
Reemelin, Karl. *Life of Charles Reemelin, a German: Carl Gustav Rümelin, from 1814–1892* (1892).
Weddle, Kevin J. "Ethnic Discrimination in Minnesota Volunteer Regiments during the Civil War." *Civil War History* (1989).

IMMIGRATION

In the decade and a half preceding the Civil War, the United States experienced its largest influx of immigrants to that point in history. Between 1845 and 1860 more than 3 million men, women, and children arrived in America, primarily from Ireland and Germany. Escaping famine, war, and political and economic upheaval, these immigrants dramatically changed the nation's ethnic makeup and provided a catalyst for political upheaval.

The largest group, 1.5 million between 1845 and 1855, came from Ireland. Beginning in 1845 the potato blight devastated the Irish potato crop, the island's primary foodstuff, forcing those who could to escape in record numbers, while leaving those too poor to depart to starve. Although better off than many of their neighbors, those immigrants who could pay their way to the United States were still the poorest ever to enter the country, and many lacked the skills to compete for anything but marginal work.

The Irish generally settled in Northern cities, taking what jobs they could. Men often ended up in coal mines or accepting the most dangerous work on railroad or canal projects, while women took employment as servants or labored in textile mills. Relatively few settled in the South, where the slave economy offered little paid labor.

Cities like New York, Boston, and Philadelphia saw their immigrant populations explode seemingly overnight. The social pressures from this ethnic demographic change brought a quick response from native-born Americans. Greeted with "no Irish need apply" signs and lumped together with another downtrodden minority, free blacks, the Irish were stereotyped as drunken criminals who filled the jails and paupers who drained the public charities. Anti-Catholicism was rampant, and approximately 90 percent of the new Irish immigrants were Catholic. Numerous nativist organizations rioted and burned Catholic churches. A series of prohibition acts, the so-called Maine laws, attempted to legislate away Irish drinking culture.

The Irish had allies, however. They soon dominated the Catholic Church, and through it ran schools and charities and helped to maintain a sense of community

in their adopted land. The Democratic Party also tendered the Irish a means of overcoming their persecution. Needing the immigrant vote, especially at the local level, party machines like Tammany Hall in New York City helped settle newcomers and find them work. In the Irish the Democrats discovered a willing partner in the protection of slavery as an institution. Fearful of competition for jobs and association with the nation's most persecuted population, the Irish actively and violently opposed abolition and the free-soil politics of Northern Republicans.

The largest group of immigrants other than the Irish came from the German states of central Europe. Fleeing from crop failures and economic dislocation, as well as the failed revolutions of 1848, more than 1.3 million Germans emigrated to the United States between 1846 and 1859. Generally better off than the Irish and with a greater percentage of skilled laborers, the Germans moved in large numbers to western states and cities like Cincinnati, Chicago, Milwaukee, and St. Louis, commonly settling together in chains of migration from German towns. Unlike the Irish, German communities were often led by former revolutionaries like Carl Schurz who spoke out against slavery. Although ordinary Germans frequently voted Democratic, like their Irish counterparts, they gained a reputation for opposition to slavery.

German immigrants, many Catholic like the Irish, were attacked by nativist organizations as well. The largest of these was the so-called Know-Nothing Party, which between 1854 and 1856 threatened to become the nation's second largest political party and campaigned to take away citizenship rights from all immigrants, especially Catholics. They advocated preventing immigrants from voting or holding office for twenty-one years after their arrival, while Catholics would never be eligible for public office. The Know-Nothings lost the 1856 election, but this political struggle, combined with the role both the Irish and Germans played in the sectional confrontation over slavery, placed the nation's newest population in the middle of the political crisis of the 1850s.

Immigration died down by 1861 because of a lessening of the crises in Ireland and Germany and the beginning of the Civil War. Even more than they had in the 1850s, German and Irish immigrants participated in the nation's struggle for survival. Prominent Germans put together all-German ethnic regiments within the Union army, while both Germans and Irish served in large numbers in regular regiments. Approximately 150,000 Irish and nearly 200,000 Germans served the Union fighting cause. Although few immigrants lived in the South, those who did often enlisted in the Confederate army as well. Not all participation in the North aided the Union war effort, however. Beginning on 11 July 1863, in reaction to emancipation and a new military draft that seemed to target the poor, Irish in New York City rioted, burning and looting for four days, and killing at least 105 people, mostly black, in the worst riot in U.S. history. Despite this, the immigrant Irish and German contribution helped win the war for the Union and in turn moved both groups closer to being considered full-fledged Americans.

—*John David Bladek*

See also German-Americans; Immigration; Irish-Americans.
For further reading:
Burton, William L. *Melting Pot Soldiers: The Union's Ethnic Regiments* (1988; reprint, 1998).
Hansen, Marcus Lee. *The Atlantic Migration, 1607–1860* (1951).
Jones, Maldwyn Allen. *American Immigration* (1960).
Levine, Bruce. *The Spirit of 1848: German Immigrants, Labor Conflict, and the Coming of the Civil War* (1992).
Miller, Kerby A. *Emigrants and Exiles: Ireland and the Irish Exodus to North America* (1985).

IMPRESSMENT

Impressment refers to the process by which the Union and Confederate governments could forcibly purchase private property for use by the military. In addition to food and goods, the Confederacy also impressed slaves. Although both governments had the right of impressment, only the Confederacy systematically resorted to it. The North could only impress during an emergency; because their economy and transportation system were more secure, the circumstance seldom arose.

As the Southern economy failed and inflation mushroomed, farmers throughout the South preferred not to sell to the army. Harvests were dismal, set prices were too low, and the currency suspect. In some cases the lack of currency necessitated the use of script, which was understandably not well received. Hunger and want, though not endemic, were consistent enough in the South to trigger demands that food stay in the local area. The situation was so difficult that by 1862 several of the states either debated or granted the right of impressment to their governors to fulfill their wartime obligations.

In October 1862 the Confederate attorney general, T. H. Watts, argued that their Constitution would allow a national use of impressment if there were just compensation. His analysis was late; the resulting Confederacy's Impressment Act of 1863 (General Order No. 37) simply put into law what was already reality. Agents for the War Department had the right to go into an area and take what the army needed. Although the Confederate government set prices that were assumed to be fair, because of the rampant inflation and variations in state and county prices, what was viewed as equitable in one area was not necessarily fair in another. Transportation difficulties added to the dilemma. President Jefferson Davis and his cabinet knew that food was plentiful in some areas, but getting supplies to those in need proved to be difficult. Yet when the Confederate government tried to take the cost of transportation into account in calculating prices, state legislatures loudly demanded equal prices across the region. Additionally, corruption among the agents—although never consistently proven—became an article of faith among the citizenry. The inequities of this act, in theory and in practice, affected more of the poor and middle class.

What concerned the upper class was the impressment of slaves. At the beginning of the war, a large number of slaves, their services donated by patriotic masters, helped to build fortifications in the South. As the war progressed, the demand for the labor of slaves increased not only back on the farms to plant and harvest crops but also by the Confederate army. As the shortage of white personnel deepened, the Confederate army resorted to impressing the slaves, but the army was supposed to follow certain procedures, pay the masters a certain amount per day, and insure that labor against injury or death.

As resentment grew against the act, individual civil disobedience, which occasionally erupted into violence, evolved into organized reaction by state governments. These usually took the form of allusion to the sacred principles of states' rights. Some state governments, particularly Georgia, Florida, and Louisiana, were more vociferous than others. For as much as Virginia devoted itself to the sacred image of Robert E. Lee, that state made it a state crime for Confederate governmental agents to illegally or incorrectly impress slaves. The result was that opposition to impressment, conscription, and gouging of local prices by unscrupulous merchants created an ambivalence to the Confederate government that undermined the increasing need for patriotism or a national identity. What remains unclear, however, is how the government could have done anything different from what it did.

—*Dorothy O. Pratt*

See also Slaves; Watts, Thomas Hill.

For further reading:
Nelson, Bernard H. "Confederate Slave Impressment Legislation, 1861–1865." *Journal of Negro History* (1946).
Reiger, John F. "Deprivation, Disaffection, and Desertion in Confederate Florida." *Florida Historical Quarterly* (1970).
Taylor, Ethel. "Discontent in Confederate Louisiana." *Louisiana History* (1961).

INDIAN BRIGADE
(1862–1865)

On 28 June 1862, Union forces invaded Indian Territory. Along with white troops from Kansas and Wisconsin were the 1st and 2d Indian Home Guard—two regiments of Native American soldiers. The invasion was initially successful but ultimately ended in an ignominious retreat.

Despite the invasion's failure, the Native American regiments remained in Indian Territory and were consolidated into the Indian Brigade. They were joined by the newly created 3d Indian Home Guard, consisting primarily of deserters from John Drew's Mounted Rifles, a Confederate Cherokee regiment. The 1st Indian Home Guard Regiment was composed of eight Creek and two Seminole companies, whereas the 2d was a more heterogeneous mix of Creek, Seminole, Choctaw, Chickasaw, Cherokee, Delaware, Kickapoo, Osage, Shawnee, and Seneca soldiers.

Both white and Indian officers commanded the new brigade. Initially Native Americans primarily commanded the 1st and 2d Indian Regiments, but by the end of 1862 whites held the majority of commissioned ranks. In the 3d Regiment, more Indians retained their commissions and more than three-quarters of the regiment's captains were Native American. Although whites dominated the Indian Brigade's command structure, evidence suggests that Native American soldiers still played a role in command decisions.

In 1861, most tribes in Indian Territory had pledged their support to the Confederacy, but bitter internal divisions drove many tribal members to flee to Union-controlled areas. In the spring of 1862, Union commanders decided to use a combination of white and Indian troops to wrest control of Indian Territory from the Confederacy and return Indian refugees to their homes. Although the invasion temporarily drove Confederate forces out of Indian Territory, it had few lasting effects. In the spring of 1863, the Indian Brigade spearheaded a second invasion that captured Fort Gibson and broke the Confederacy's hold on Indian Territory.

Despite the capture of Fort Gibson, the brigade's hold on Indian Territory remained tenuous. Their supply lines were constantly threatened, and an estimated 7,000 Native American refugees soon clustered around the fort for protection. The brigade's principal adversary was Confederate Cherokee general Stand Watie, and despite successful raids into Confederate Territory in 1864, the brigade was never able to eliminate Watie as a military threat or establish a secure zone for Indian refugees. This brutal guerilla war terrorized civilians on both sides, destroyed homes and livestock, and resulted in the deaths of up to a quarter of the Indian population.

Although Native American soldiers in the Indian Brigade fought for the North, they were not committed to the Union cause. Indian soldiers enlisted in the Union army to defend themselves against tribal members who supported the Confederacy and to ensure the survival of their nations. Indian soldiers needed the Union's support against their Confederate opponents, but they also anticipated that their service would persuade the Union of their loyalty. This hope was not realized. After the war, the United States virtually ignored the service of the

Indian Brigade and imposed harsh treaties on the tribes in Indian Territory, ostensibly because the governments of these nations had initially supported the Confederacy.

—*Trevor M. Jones*

See also Indian Territory; Watie, Stand.
For further reading:
Abel, Annie Heloise. *The American Indian As Participant in the Civil War* (1919).
Britton, Wiley. *The Union Indian Brigade in the Civil War* (1922).
Gaines, W. Craig. *The Confederate Cherokees: John Drew's Regiment of Mounted Rifles* (1989).
Hauptman, Laurence M. *Between Two Fires: American Indians in the Civil War* (1995).

INDIAN TERRITORY

The U.S. policy of removal in the early nineteenth century relocated the large Indian nations of the Southeast (the Five Civilized Tribes) into unorganized public-domain land west of Arkansas and north of the Red River—officially referred to as Indian Territory. It was not a territory in the political sense of the term, owing to the fact that it never had a territorial legislature nor territorial governor appointed by Congress.

At the beginning of the Civil War, this area (much of which is today the state of Oklahoma) was populated by approximately 55,000 native people, 3,000 whites, and 8,376 slaves. It was "home" to Cherokee, Creek, Choctaw, Chickasaw, and Seminole people who had emigrated (either voluntarily or by force) from their traditional homelands east of the Mississippi River. Also living in this area were other bands of indigenous people, including Quapaw, Wichita, Seneca, Shawnee, Delaware, Comanche, and Osage. Although the U.S. Office of Indian Affairs oversaw relations with these tribes in early 1861, most of these Indians became de facto Confederate allies as Confederate volunteers from Arkansas and northern Texas obliged the United States to withdraw its undermanned garrisons from Forts Washita, Arbuckle, and Cobb in Indian Territory and move north to Fort Leavenworth, Kansas. Texans under the command of Colonel William C. Young filled the vacated posts.

The importance that Confederate politicos placed on Indian affairs is evident in the organization of the government. The delegates to the Confederate Congress represented the eleven states of the Confederacy as well as Missouri, Kentucky, Arizona Territory, and the Indians of the Cherokee, Choctaw, Creek, Seminole, and Chickasaw Nations. Territorial and Indian delegates, however, could not vote. Matters concerning specific Indian nations were placed in the hands of the War Department by an act of the Provisional Congress on 21 February 1861. A little less than a month later (15 March 1861) and before the firing on Fort Sumter in Charleston harbor, the Bureau of Indian Affairs was officially created within the War Department by the Provisional Confederate Congress. The bureau's charge was to initiate negotiations with Indian nations adjoining the Confederacy and those located on "reserves" within the various Confederate states.

Albert Pike was given the title of special commissioner of Indian affairs and was charged with the responsibility for carrying out the desires of the government by cementing alliances with the various nations in Indian Territory—and hopefully encouraging service in the Confederate military. The new commissioner was to head the Red River Superintendency and cooperate with Brigadier General Ben McCulloch, the Confederate commander at Fort Smith, Arkansas. In a letter written to Confederate secretary of state Robert Toombs on 29 May 1861 as Pike prepared to leave Fort Smith for Tahlequah, the seat of government of the Cherokee Nation, the newly appointed special commissioner wrote, "We shall have no difficulty with the Creeks, Seminoles, Choctaws, and Chickasaws, either in effecting treaties or raising troops."

While exaggerating the potential ease of the task at hand, Pike nevertheless accurately gauged the split among many native people—indeed, among all the nations who had experienced removal from the southeast. The division had deep roots stemming from the factionalism created by the differences of opinion over the wisdom of standing up to the U.S. government and its removal policies of the 1830s. The split was also linked to the differing attitudes toward slavery and slaveholding among native people, some of whom were full-bloods who retained their traditional customs, while other mixed-bloods were more culturally akin to Southern whites. The retention of slaves (used primarily in Indian Territory for stock herding and salt making, as well as the more typical agricultural purposes) allowed the elites to retain their dominance. Many mixed-bloods became affluent planters living like white planters elsewhere in the South.

Setting out with a military escort replete with wagons bearing cases of wine and potted food, Pike headed into Indian Territory authorized to spend $100,000 for treaties of alliance with the various nations. Pike met with Cherokee principal chief John Ross at his mansion at Park Hill near Tahlequah. There, Ross officially informed the Confederate special commissioner of his plans to honor the treaties with the United States but to remain neutral in the impending war.

Choosing for the moment to accept Ross's decision for neutrality, Pike left the Cherokee Nation and headed south to meet with representatives of the Creek Nation on the Canadian River. As was true for the Cherokees, factions existed within the Creek Nation. The Lower

Creeks voluntarily complied with the removal policy of the 1830s endorsed by their mixed-blood leaders, while the Upper Creeks had to be forcibly removed from their traditional homelands. On 10 July 1861, Pike met with Principal Chief Motey Kinnard and Daniel N. and Chilly McIntosh (sons of William McIntosh, former principal chief of the Lower Creeks), who signed a treaty of alliance with the Confederacy. The McIntoshes also promised to raise a regiment of Creeks provided they would only have to fight within the borders of Indian Territory. Two days later, Pike met with members of the Chickasaw and Choctaw Nations. Even though the people of both of these nations experienced the tragedy of removal, they were not nearly as factionalized as the Cherokees and the Creeks. Almost all of the 5,000 members of the Chickasaw Nation wholeheartedly inclined toward an alliance with the Confederacy. Only 212 of the 13,666 Choctaws in Indian Territory remained loyal to the Union. Aided by the efforts of local pro-Confederate Indian agent Colonel Douglas H. Cooper, as well as by the fact that the two nations were situated near the northern border of Texas, the Chickasaws and Choctaws signed a joint treaty of alliance with Pike and likewise promised to raise military units for the war effort. For its part, the Confederacy recognized continuous Chickasaw and Choctaw title to their lands, assumed all financial commitments of the United States, and agreed to supply and pay troops.

Pike next headed into the central part of Indian Territory where the Seminoles were located. The Seminoles initially sought a path of neutrality, but the withdrawal of U.S. troops from Indian territory, combined with the nonpayment of the 1860 annuities owed to the nation, swayed the majority of the 2,600 Seminoles to be receptive to the bureau's gestures. Pike met with a five-man delegation headed by Principal Chief John Jumper on 1 August, and the latter signed the treaty of alliance with the Confederacy. The Seminole delegation also promised to raise troops for military service.

The final destination for Special Commissioner Pike was the Wichita Agency near Fort Cobb in the western portion of Indian Territory. Pike hoped to meet with representatives of various Indian nations who traditionally called the southern plains home. Accompanied by Motey Kinnard, Chilly McIntosh, John Jumper, and a mounted escort of Creek and Seminole Indians flying a Confederate flag, Pike rode to the agency and prepared for a rendezvous with the Tonkawas, Caddos, Wichitas, and several chiefs and headmen from assorted Comanche bands. The Indian representatives agreed to Pike's terms and officially signed the treaty of alliance, yet most remained detached from the Confederacy's wartime concerns and did little to support the Confederate military.

Having found success in forming alliances with the Creeks, Chickasaws, Choctaws, Seminoles, and the so-called "wild" Indians of western Indian Territory, Pike returned to his efforts to sway John Ross and the Cherokee toward a formal treaty of recognition and association. He was aided by the immense pressure already manifesting itself on the shoulders of the principal chief. The other major Indian nations in the territory had signed treaties. Stand Watie, a prominent pro-Southern Cherokee, was gaining power as he organized a regiment of mixed-bloods and headed toward the northeastern border with Kansas to guard against a possible Federal invasion. Consequently, the principal chief signed the treaty of alliance on 7 October 1861 and offered Pike the services of a regiment of Home Guards composed mostly of Keetowahs and commanded by Colonel John Drew, a Ross devotee. While at Tahlequah, Pike also signed treaties with representatives of the Osage, Quapaw, Seneca, and Shawnee Indians.

The immediate tangible result of Pike's efforts was the recruitment of Indians into the Confederate military. With the general understanding that they were to serve only within the borders of the territory, a significant number of Indians answered the call to arms. Although Article 41 of their treaty with the Confederate States called for the Cherokees to "furnish a regiment of ten companies of mounted men, with two reserve companies, ... to serve in the armies of the Confederacy for twelve months," the only units of substance to be organized were in fact established before the alliance: Stand Watie's company of mixed-bloods and Colonel Drew's regiment of Keetowahs. The Chickasaw Nation furnished four military units. The most well-known of these was the 1st Regiment Mounted Rifles (which included some Choctaw Indians as well), under the command of Colonel Tandy Walker and Choctaw-Chickasaw Indian agent Cooper. The Choctaws organized the 2d and 3d Regiments of Choctaw Cavalry, the First Choctaw Mounted Rifles, Deneale's regiment of Choctaw Warriors, and a company of Choctaw infantry. Choctaw troops served mainly in the capacity of home guards, but they did see action in eight significant battles. The Seminoles raised a battalion of 300 men organized under the leadership of Principal Chief Jumper—now holding the rank of major. Like the majority of Indian troops fighting for the Confederacy, the Seminoles for the most part served as home guards within Indian Territory.

In the fall of 1861, trouble developed within the Creek Nation. Thousands of loyal and neutral Upper Creeks refused to recognize the treaty of alliance with the Confederacy signed by the Lower Creeks and prepared to march with their leader, Opothleyahola, to Kansas and safety. They were opposed by a force of Lower Creeks under the McIntosh brothers. In November, sporadic violence between the two factions began and quickly intensified. Colonel Cooper was ordered to take charge of the situation and restore tranquility among the Creeks. Cooper called upon other Indian home guard units to aid in his efforts to end the hostilities and prevent the Upper Creeks from leaving Indian Territory. In doing so, Cooper began what amounted to a civil war within the borders of the territory. Traditional factions within the various nations started to actively reassert their differences of opinion with those who supported an alliance.

When Cooper arrived near the Canadian River, he discovered almost 4,000 Upper Creek men, women, and children as well as Indians from assorted other nations crowded into encampments along with their livestock, wagons, and worldly possessions. Considering these Indians to be a threat to Confederate authority in Indian Territory, Cooper attacked the slow-moving caravan on November 19 at Round Mountain, near the junction of the Cimarron and Arkansas rivers. The loyal Creeks fought back, managing to escape at dusk after setting a prairie fire to impede Cooper's progress.

Slowed but undaunted, Cooper resumed the chase. On 9 December he found Opothleyahola and the loyal Creeks waiting for him at Chusto-Talasah, or Caving Banks, on Bird Creek near present-day Tulsa. Cooper engaged the Upper Creeks for four hours before Opothleyahola finally withdrew his band.

Although claiming a victory, Cooper nevertheless withdrew to Fort Gibson near Tahlequah and waited for reinforcements from Texas and Arkansas. With the arrival of 1,380 Confederate troopers under Colonel James McIntosh, Cooper had the luxury to plan a combined attack against Opothleyahola's band utilizing the converging columns of his own and McIntosh's troops. The Confederates once again took to the field but unfortunately were unable to synchronize their convergence upon the Creek camp at Chustenahlah. Rather than wait for Cooper's badly delayed troops, McIntosh chose to engage Opothleyahola's numerically superior forces on 26 December. Weakened by exhaustion, cold weather, and lack of adequate food, the loyal Creeks could not withstand the Confederate onslaught. Warriors mixed with men, women, and children fled the field in panic pursued by white Confederate cavalrymen and the recently arrived mixed-blood Cherokee regiment under Stand Watie. Watie's 300 men killed or captured many of the stragglers who were too weak to flee. Those who did escape finally made their way to Kansas and safety.

Despite the general success of Confederate efforts in Indian Territory in the summer and fall of 1861, the action taken against the Upper Creeks fleeing to Kansas and the experience of Pike's command across the border in northwestern Arkansas at the battle of Pea Ridge had long-term ramifications for Confederate-Indian relations west of the Mississippi. Many disenchanted and embit-

tered Indian refugees in Kansas joined Union forces and returned to Indian Territory determined to take revenge on the Confederate Cherokees, Creeks, and their allies. In the summer of 1862, 6,000 Union troops under Colonel William Weer together with their native allies marched on Fort Gibson and Tahlequah, captured John Ross, and returned to Kansas. Ross went to Washington, where he argued that he had no choice but to sign a treaty with Pike. The exiled principal chief of the Cherokee Nation then issued a proclamation of Cherokee loyalty to the Union and watched as three of his sons enlisted into the Union military.

With Ross in Washington, Stand Watie used the opportunity to declare himself the new principal chief of the Cherokee Nation and proceeded to consolidate his power. Thus the division of the Cherokees in Indian Territory was complete. Although Watie and his regiment participated in numerous conventional battles and smaller skirmishes with Federal troops, for the remainder of the war, supporters of each faction still living in the territory staged hit-and-run campaigns against the other. Families were murdered, homes vandalized, crops burned, and livestock butchered.

By the summer of 1863, Confederate hopes for retaining control of Indian Territory vanished. Northwestern Arkansas was in the hands of Union forces after their strategic victory at Prairie Grove the previous December. A combined force of U.S. troops and loyal Indians under Major General James G. Blunt invaded Indian Territory and defeated Cooper (recently promoted to brigadier general) at Honey Springs on 17 July. The defeat forced many pro-Confederate Cherokee, Creek, and Seminole Indians to flee far south to the Red River Valley to become refugees among the Chickasaw and Choctaw Nations. The Confederate defeats at Gettysburg and Vicksburg in July dampened hopes for ultimate triumph. Even ardent Confederate Stand Watie recognized the unlikelihood of a Southern victory in the war. Nevertheless, Watie remained true to the alliance for the remainder of the conflict, motivated primarily by the desire to maintain his power within the Cherokee Nation over the supporters of John Ross. On 15 June 1864, Watie captured the Federal steamboat *J. R. Williams* on the Arkansas River with its $100,000 worth of supplies, including 150 barrels of flour and 16,000 pounds of bacon. Three months later, in what one historian has called the biggest Confederate victory in the Indian Territory, Watie and his men captured a 300-wagon Federal supply train and its $1.5 million worth of supplies in the second battle of Cabin Creek on 19 September 1864.

Much like their experiences under the control of the U.S. government, the people of Indian Territory discovered that the Confederacy could not or would not keep its promises. As the fortunes of war turned against the

Confederacy in the east as well as along the banks of the Mississippi and Tennessee rivers, the importance once attached to the maintenance of peace and stability on the frontier for the future of Southern manifest destiny all but disappeared. On 26 May 1865, Confederate general Edmund Kirby Smith surrendered his command of the Trans-Mississippi to Union major general Edward R. S. Canby, and on 23 June, Stand Watie yielded to the inevitable and surrendered at Doaksville, the Choctaw capital. The war had been costly for the indigenous people of Indian Territory, but the price they would have to pay to reestablish treaties with the United States would prove to be even more so.

—*Alan C. Downs*

See also Cherokee Indians; Chickasaw Indians; Choctaw Indians; Creek Indians; *J.R. Williams*; Pike, Albert; Ross, John; Seminole Indians; Watie, Stand.

For further reading:

Franks, Kenny. *Stand Watie and the Agony of the Cherokee Nation* (1979).

Josephy, Alvin M. *The Civil War in the American West* (1991).

INGALLS, RUFUS
(1818–1893)
Union general

Born in Denmark, Maine, Rufus Ingalls received an appointment to the U.S. Military Academy in 1839. He graduated thirty-second of thirty-nine in the class of 1843. After fighting in the Mexican-American War, for which he received one brevet, Ingalls transferred from the dragoons to the quartermaster department. In the years before the Civil War, he served as quartermaster on a variety of expeditions and frontier posts.

In the early days of the Civil War, Ingalls served as quartermaster to Colonel Harvey Brown's expedition to reinforce Fort Pickens at Pensacola, Florida. In September 1861, Ingalls was summoned to Washington, D.C., where he was promoted to lieutenant colonel and made aide-de-camp to Major General George B. McClellan, commanding general of the Army of the Potomac. During the Peninsula campaign the following spring and summer, Ingalls served as McClellan's aide but also as assistant to the chief quartermaster, Army of the Potomac. One of his primary duties during that campaign was to provide guards for supply depots, a task made doubly difficult during J. E. B. Stuart's raid in June 1862. Ingalls performed so much to McClellan's satisfaction, however, that on 10 July 1862 Ingalls was named chief quartermaster, Army of the Potomac, a position he would hold under every commander of that army.

Ingalls's first big task as the Army of the Potomac's chief quartermaster was supervising the evacuation of all the quartermaster supplies when McClellan was ordered to return to Washington, D.C. This effort, however, paled in comparison to the complications that Ingalls faced when John Pope's Army of Virginia was dismantled. Ingalls had to account for the supplies of both those units of the Army of the Potomac that had been involved in Pope's Second Bull Run campaign and those belonging to the Army of Virginia.

In late November 1862, Ingalls tried to speed delivery of pontoon bridges ordered by the new commander of the Army of the Potomac, Ambrose Burnside. The bridges were necessary for Burnside's attack across the Rappahannock River at Fredericksburg, Virginia, but Ingalls could do little to hurry their arrival opposite Fredericksburg. It was one challenge Ingalls did not meet, but all the commanders he worked for nonetheless had nothing but praise for his efforts and creativity.

The following spring, as a reward for his efforts, Ingalls was promoted to brigadier general of volunteers. During the subsequent Gettysburg campaign, along with the difficulty of moving the equipment necessary for the campaign in pursuit of Lee, Ingalls's biggest challenge was procuring replacement cavalry horses. In the early phases of the campaign, Union cavalry and Confederates under J. E. B. Stuart fought several engagements as Stuart tried to screen Lee's movements north. Ingalls had the job of replacing the large numbers of horses lost in these battles.

After the challenges of the Gettysburg campaign, Ingalls provided the equipment and supplies for those men sent to New York to quell the draft riots. Simultaneously he supervised the movement of the Army of the Potomac's equipment out of Pennsylvania. Over the next nine months until the commencement of Ulysses S. Grant's campaign against Lee in the spring of 1864, Ingalls's job, though never easy, was less stressful. Grant's campaign changed all of that.

Ingalls and his staff worked constantly to meet the supply and equipment needs of the huge Army of the Potomac. Added to this burden was the presence in the campaign by June 1864 of other forces, most notably the Army of the James under Benjamin F. Butler. To ease the complications of this situation, on 16 June 1864 Ingalls was made chief quartermaster of Armies Acting against Richmond. He held this job for the remainder of the war, through the siege of Petersburg and the Appomattox campaign.

Throughout all the battles and campaigns, Ingalls not only retained the confidence of numerous generals in the field but also his superiors in Washington, especially, Montgomery C. Meigs, quartermaster general of the U.S. Army. Ingalls wrote Meigs frequently from the field, explaining specific difficulties he had procuring certain items. Those letters were also full of Ingalls's perceptions of the campaigns, revealing a keen interest in things military and the state of the army.

After the war, Ingalls remained in the army and the Quartermaster Department. He reverted to the rank of colonel and served in various locations including the Pacific coast and New York City. He became quartermaster general of the army in 1882 and retired in 1883. In retirement he lived in New York City, where he died on 15 January 1893.

—David S. Heidler and Jeanne T. Heidler

See also Army of the Potomac; Meigs, Montgomery C.; Quartermaster.

For further reading:
East, Sherrod D. "Montgomery C. Meigs and the Quartermaster Department." *Military Affairs* (1961–1962).
Warfield, A.B. "The Quartermaster's Department, 1861–1864." *Military Affairs* (1928).
Weigley, Russell F. *Quartermaster General of the Union Army: A Biography of M. C. Meigs* (1959).

INVALID CORPS

As the Civil War progressed and casualty lists grew longer, the U.S. War Department searched for additional men to fill the depleted ranks of the Union army. Many veteran soldiers who had suffered wounds or contracted illnesses that rendered them unfit for active campaigning could still perform limited duty. In 1863, the War Department established the Invalid Corps, later called the Veteran Reserve Corps, as a means of utilizing these soldiers. More than 60,000 men eventually joined this organization. They performed guard and provost marshal duty, served in hospitals, performed in bands, garrisoned prisoner-of-war camps, and occasionally came under hostile fire. Their presence allowed thousands of able-bodied soldiers to be sent to more active theaters of the war, thus contributing to the defeat of the Confederacy.

General Orders No. 105 from the Adjutant General's Office, dated 28 April 1863, authorized the establishment of the Invalid Corps. Its companies would consist of individuals "who, from wounds received in action or disease contracted in the line of duty, are unfit for field service, but are still capable of effective garrison duty, or such other light duty as may be required of an invalid corps." Regimental commanders were to prepare rolls of officers and enlisted men who met the stated criteria and were "meritorious and deserving," and transmit them to the office of the provost marshal general. Similarly, medical officers could recommend individuals in convalescent camps or hospitals. In addition, honorably discharged veterans could, upon examination of a board of enrollment, reenlist in the new corps. The provost marshal general's office had responsibility for selecting the organization's officers.

In May 1863, the War Department divided the Invalid Corps into three battalions, with soldiers assigned to each based on their physical condition. Men serving in the 1st Battalion could still use a musket and would be used for provost and guard duty, while those in the 2d Battalion were primarily used in hospitals. A third battalion, consisting of those in the poorest physical condition, was authorized but apparently never organized. Eventually, the War Department formed the corps into 24 regiments and 188 independent companies. Regiments were composed of companies from both the first and second battalions, so they could perform a variety of duties. Many Invalid Corps' units were organized in Washington, D.C., while other mustering locations included Alexandria, Albany, Baltimore, Chicago, Detroit, Elmira, Harrisburg, Indianapolis, Louisville, New York City, Rock Island, and St. Louis. Altogether, 60,508 veterans served in these units.

The corps wore a distinctive uniform, consisting of a sky blue cavalry-style jacket with dark blue trim, along with sky blue pants. Officers wore a sky-blue frock coat and sky blue pants with a double stripe of dark blue. Troops were initially issued obsolete weapons such as .69-caliber smoothbore muskets converted to percussion and .69-caliber Austrian and Prussian rifled muskets, while some later received the more modern Springfield rifled muskets.

Although the experiment in using partially disabled soldiers proved successful, the name Invalid Corps inspired scorn, as its initials were the same as those allegedly placed on government property and animals that had been "Inspected and Condemned." Alfred Bellard, a combat veteran who served in the corps, remembered that its members were often derisively called "Condemned Yanks." Consequently, in March 1864 the name of the organization was changed to the more acceptable Veteran Reserve Corps (VRC).

In addition to their provost and hospital duties, Invalid/Veteran Reserve Corps soldiers helped suppress the New York City draft riots of July 1863, suffering a number of casualties. They also guarded Confederates at a number of Northern prisoner-of-war camps. Their most significant military service, however, took place in July of the following year, when a number of VRC units, including among others the 1st, 6th, 9th, 7th, 10th, 12th, 19th, 22d, and 24th Regiments, helped defend Washington against a raid by Confederate forces under Jubal Early. They skirmished with the enemy during the 11–12 July attack on Fort Stevens, when President Lincoln came under Confederate fire. Alfred Bellard, who had served in the Seven Days' battles and at Fredericksburg and Chancellorsville, later remembered that his VRC regiment was not heavily engaged at Fort Stevens because it lacked modern weapons. Still, "with the burning houses, the bursting of shell and the rattle of small arms, it looked and sounded very much like old times."

During the course of the war, 27 men from Invalid/Veteran Reserve Corps were killed or mortally

wounded, while 1,645 died from disease or other causes. VRC units remained on active duty until well after the end of the war, with the last unit being mustered out of service in October 1866.

While the Federal army established a large veteran reserve corps that was organized into regular units, Confederate officials formed their own Invalid Corps. This consisted of wounded or otherwise disabled men who could remain on the army payroll and perform limited duties. They might continue in this capacity for the remainder of their enlistment, or, if their condition improved they were to return to their original unit.

—*David J. Coles*

See also New York City Draft Riots.
For further reading:
Donald, David Herbert, ed. *Gone for a Soldier: The Civil War Memoirs of Private Alfred Bellard* (1975).
Todd, Frederick P. *American Military Equipage, 1851–1872* (1980).
Welcher, Frank J. *The Union Army, 1861–1865: Organization and Operations* (1989).

IRISH-AMERICANS

In the four decades before the American Civil War, approximately two million Irish immigrated to the United States. Here they joined with first-generation Irish-Americans to form a significant portion of all ethnics who served in the war. Approximately 144,000 Irish-Americans filled the ranks of the Union army and navy, and nearly 20,000 served in the Confederate forces.

Most Irish-Americans, North and South, served in nonethnic regiments. Some, however, chose to fight with those of similar cultural heritage, and the reasons for this decision vary. Many embraced the concept that the Irish were by nature the best fighters and should serve together to form superior regiments and brigades. Others were motivated by a need to demonstrate loyalty to their adopted country and hoped to earn a respected position in society through military service.

Unique to the Irish units was the motivating factor of Irish nationalism. Many Irish-American soldiers, both North and South, were involved in the Fenian movement, which supported a Free Ireland. They were motivated not only by patriotism to the United States, but by the opportunity to gain valuable military experience to support armed rebellion in Ireland.

The most popular Irish units in the Union army include the Irish Brigade and Corcoran's Legion, or the Irish Legion. The Irish Brigade was composed of the 69th New York Infantry (formerly the 69th New York state militia), the 63d New York Infantry, and the 88th New York Infantry ("Mrs. Meagher's Own") since its formation in February 1862. The 29th Massachusetts Infantry (the only non-Irish regiment in the brigade) served with the unit through the Peninsula campaign and the battle of Antietam, after which the 28th Massachusetts replaced it. At that time, the 116th Pennsylvania Infantry ("Brian Boru United Irish Legion") joined the brigade as well.

The battles of Antietam and Fredericksburg dominate the history of the Irish Brigade, where, commanded by Irish nationalist Thomas Meagher, they made heroic charges with deadly costs. At Antietam, the 63d and 69th New York suffered nearly 60 percent losses, while at Fredericksburg, the Irish Brigade lost nearly 40 percent of their force in the numerous charges against the Stone Wall on Marye's Heights. In a tragic irony, some of the Confederates opposing them at the wall were Irish in the 24th Georgia.

The Irish Legion, or Corcoran's Legion, was composed of the 155th New York Infantry Regiment, the 164th New York, the 170th New York, and the 182d New York. This brigade-sized unit was led by Colonel Michael Corcoran, former commander of the famous 69th New York Volunteer Militia, and leading Fenian promoter. Other famous Union Irish regiments that saw service during the war included the 37th New York, the 9th Massachusetts, the 28th Massachusetts, the 23d Illinois, the 19th Illinois, the 35th Indiana, and the 10th Ohio.

Irish Confederates were fewer than their Northern counterparts, but still comprised the largest of the Confederate ethnic units. The most famous Irish Confederate regiment was the 6th Louisiana Volunteers ("Louisiana Tigers"). The 6th Louisiana was composed largely of Irish from New Orleans, the city containing the largest Irish-born and first-generation Irish population in the South. As in Northern regiments, Confederate Irish were motivated by a desire to demonstrate their loyalty to their adopted country. Some Southern Irish saw parallels between the Confederate rebellion and the struggle for independence in their Irish homeland.

The 6th Louisiana suffered heavy losses at Port Republic, as well as at Antietam and Fredericksburg in the fall and winter of 1862. In 1863, the regiment saw service at Chancellorsville and Gettysburg, and in 1864 it participated in the battles of the Wilderness and Spotsylvania Court House. As a result of this difficult service, fewer than 75 of the original 1,000 members of the regiment remained in the ranks when the 6th Louisiana surrendered with Lee at Appomattox.

Other famous Irish Confederate units served throughout the South, representing eight of the eleven Confederate States. These include the 10th Tennessee Infantry, and Irish companies in the 1st Georgia Volunteers, the 1st Virginia Infantry, the 1st South Carolina Infantry, and the 8th Alabama Infantry.

The most famous Confederate Irish-born officer was Major General Patrick Ronayne Cleburne, one of only two foreign-born officers to reach that rank in the Confederate service. Cleburne is known for his heroic leadership in the Army of the Tennessee at the battles of Shiloh, Murfreesboro, Chattanooga, and finally Franklin, where he was mortally wounded on 30 November 1864.

Some historians argue that military service proved a catalyst in the assimilation of Irish into American society; others argue that Civil War service in Irish regiments fostered the retention of ethnic identity. Scholars may differ concerning the motivations of individual soldiers and the long-term cultural effects of Civil War service on Irish-Americans and the communities they formed. Few, however, question the dedication or superb combat performance of those men who went into battle "under the green" or that the contributions of Irish, both Union and Confederate, form an important and colorful chapter in the history of the war.

—*Susannah U. Bruce*

See also Cleburne, Patrick; Irish Brigade; Meagher, Thomas.

For further reading:
Burton, William L. *Melting Pot Soldiers: The Union's Ethnic Regiments* (1988; reprint, 1998).
Conyngham, David P. *The Irish Brigade and Its Campaigns* (1867; reprint, 1994).
Gannon, James P. *Irish Rebels, Confederate Tigers: A History of the 6th Louisiana Volunteers, 1861–1865* (1998).
Gleeson, David. "The Irish in the Old South: 1815–1877" (Ph.D. dissertation, 1997).
Lonn, Ella. *Foreigners in the Confederacy* (1940).
———. *Foreigners in the Union Army and Navy* (reprint, 1951).

IRISH BEND/BAYOU TECHE
(12–14 April 1863)

In the spring of 1863, Union attempts to secure control of the Mississippi River intensified. While Grant targeted Vicksburg, a secondary part of the Federal plan, directed by Major General Nathaniel P. Banks, commander of the Department of the Gulf, aimed at Port Hudson, Louisiana. To protect New Orleans, clear central Louisiana of Confederates, and cut Port Hudson's supply lines from the west, Banks dispatched a combined land and naval force totaling about 16,000 men (three divisions of XIX Corps) up Bayou Teche.

Opposing Banks was a Confederate force of about 4,000 men under Major General Richard Taylor, giving the Federals a numerical advantage that had some Union officers envisioning the capture of Taylor's entire command. Taylor recognized that danger, but he knew that offering no meaningful resistance would devastate morale, not only among civilians, but also among his troops. Desertion from his forces, already a problem, could become wholesale. Thus treading a desperately thin line, Taylor's options seemed both limited and poor.

By 10 April 1863, Banks had advanced his force to Brashear (now Morgan) City, approximately fifteen miles below Fort Bisland, a crude, hastily-erected Confederate-held earthwork fortification straddling Bayou Teche. Banks ordered the 4,500 men of Brigadier General Cuvier Grover's division to move up Grand Lake via naval transports to threaten Taylor's rear, while Banks himself moved overland against Fort Bisland. Hoping to delay Grover with a small detachment, Taylor deployed about 3,000 men behind the mile-long works of Fort Bisland, the troops equally divided on each side of the bayou, with the captured steamer *Diana* in midstream to help where possible.

Various problems delayed Grover's sailing until 12 April, and late that afternoon Banks moved against Fort Bisland, precipitating a three-hour artillery duel curtailed by darkness. Knowing Banks's proclivities well from having opposed him the previous year in the Shenandoah Valley, and having absorbed Stonewall Jackson's lessons on keeping numerous, superior enemy forces off balance with speedy maneuvers, Taylor hatched a daring plan. Correctly surmising that Banks would merely hold his position until Grover moved against the Confederate rear, Taylor ordered Brigadier General Henry Sibley's brigade to attack Banks's left flank at dawn, hoping to frighten Banks into recalling Grover.

Unfortunately, the incompetent Sibley did nothing, so on the fog-shrouded morning of 13 April, the initiative remained with Banks, but he fulfilled Taylor's expectations by doing little until hearing from Grover, who did not get ashore until the late afternoon that day. Somewhat desultory combat advanced the Federals to within 400 yards of Fort Bisland, so Banks planned a frontal assault for the morning of 14 April to crush Taylor between his two forces.

Around 9:00 P.M. on 13 April, Taylor learned that Grover had landed and was about to cut off the only route by which the Confederates could retreat. Facing imminent destruction, Taylor responded promptly, and fortune favored him as Grover, warily moving through the thick foliage, unknowingly stopped short of capturing an undefended bridge that Taylor's force needed for retreat. Leaving a rear guard to delay Banks and a small detachment to hold Grover, Taylor withdrew his troops from Fort Bisland after darkness on the night of 13–14 April, hoping to skirt northward past Grover's division.

At dawn on 14 April, Taylor audaciously attacked Grover near Irish Bend, forcing the surprised Grover to deploy his division for battle. Grover, not knowing Taylor's true strength, cautiously engaged the roughly 1,100 Confederates facing him, while Banks entered abandoned Fort Bisland. Had Banks moved resolutely, he could have brushed aside the Confederate rear guard under Colonel Thomas Green and probably overwhelmed Taylor's retreating force. As it was, Banks dawdled before advancing, and Taylor slipped out of the

trap with his men and supply train, despite further blunderings by the inebriated or ill Sibley.

The actions at Fort Bisland and Irish Bend cost Banks nearly 600 casualties; Taylor's casualties went unreported, but gunboats *Diana* and *Queen of the West* were lost. The results of the engagements proved mixed: although forced to continue retreating, Taylor outperformed Banks and salvaged morale among his soldiers and civilians alike. For his part, Banks seized central Louisiana and enormous amounts of cotton and sugar worth millions of dollars, but bungled the opportunity to destroy virtually all Confederate field forces in Louisiana and perhaps expedite the end of the war in the Trans-Mississippi Department.

—*Broeck N. Oder*

See also Banks, Nathaniel P.; Green, Thomas; Port Hudson Campaign; Sibley, Henry Hopkins; Taylor, Richard.
For further reading:
Arceneaux, William. *Acadian General: Alfred Mouton and the Civil War* (1981).
Harrington, Fred Harvey. *Fighting Politician: Major General N. P. Banks* (1948; reprint, 1970).
Josephy, Alvin M. *The Civil War in the American West* (1991).
Parrish, T. Michael. *Richard Taylor: Soldier Prince of Dixie* (1992).
Taylor, Richard. *Destruction and Reconstruction: Personal Experiences of the Late War* (1879; reprint, 1983).

IRISH BRIGADE

Raised in New York City in the autumn of 1861, the Irish Brigade was one of the finest combat units of the Army of the Potomac. Initially designated 2d Brigade, 1st Division, II Corps, it originally comprised the 63d, 69th, and 88th New York Volunteer regiments and the 2d New York Light Artillery. In the spring of 1862, it was reinforced by a non-Irish regiment, the 29th Massachusetts; and in October 1862, by the 116th Pennsylvania Regiment. The following November, the 29th Massachusetts was traded to the IX Corps for another Irish regiment, the 28th Massachusetts. Under its only brigadier general, Thomas F. Meagher, the brigade was renowned for its bravery under fire, and it suffered the third highest casualty rate of any brigade in the Union army. Of the 7,715 soldiers

The Irish Brigade fighting at the Battle of Gettysburg (*Library of Congress*)

enrolled in its ranks, 4,000 were either killed or mortally wounded. Many survivors, proud of their brigade, published their memoirs after the war.

The cornerstone of the brigade was the 69th New York Militia, which, under its Irish-born colonel, Michael Corcoran, had attracted prewar notoriety for refusing to parade before Edward Prince of Wales, during his visit to New York City. Know-Nothing demands that the regiment be disbanded were quieted by its valiant service at First Manassas in July 1861 and Corcoran's capture. Returning to New York City when its ninety-day federal enlistment was completed in September 1861, many of its men reenlisted in what became the 69th New York Volunteer Regiment. The idea for an all-Irish brigade was largely the notion of Thomas Meagher, who hoped that such a unit would counter Know-Nothing hostility toward the Irish as well as relive the glory of previous Irish brigades that had fought in the Catholic armies of both France and Spain. In effect, the Irish would fight two wars, one to display their loyalty to their adopted country and another to defeat anti-immigrant hostility evident in the prewar years. Meagher did much to recruit and organize the other units in the brigade, and, when James Shields, an Irish-born veteran of the Mexican-American War and friend of President Abraham Lincoln, refused command, Meagher, with the backing of Governor Edwin Denison Morgan of New York, was appointed its brigadier in February 1862.

The Irish Brigade first saw action in George McClellan's Peninsula campaign and won great praise for its bravery at Gaines' Mill in June 1862, at Savage's Station, and at Malvern Hill on 1 July 1862. The brigade helped cover McClellan's retreat to Harrison's Landing. While encamped there, according to Lieutenant James M. Birmingham of the 88th New York, President Lincoln on a visit to General McClellan lifted a corner of the green flag of the 69th New York, kissed it, and exclaimed "God bless the Irish flag." Although the brigade missed the battle of Second Bull Run in August 1862, its actions in the last four months of 1862 would enhance its reputation as a combat unit.

At Antietam on 17 September 1862, the brigade took part in a desperate frontal assault by the 1st Division on General D. H. Hill's Confederate position at the sunken road, later known as "Bloody Lane." As General Meagher personally formed the brigade for the attack, Father William Corby, later president of the University of Notre Dame, rode down the line administering a general act of absolution. In a doomed advance, which Meagher hoped would reenact the famous bayonet charge of the Irish Brigade in French service at Fontenoy in 1745, the command was caught in a murderous Confederate fire. The brigade, nonetheless, held its ground until it was relieved by General John Curtis Caldwell's brigade. The Irish Brigade made an even more

famous charge at Fredericksburg on 13 December 1863 against Marye's Heights. After the failed assaults by Generals William H. French and Samuel K. Zook's troops against the position, the Irish Brigade surged forward with shouts of the old Irish cheer *Faugh-a-Bellagh* (Clear the Way) and charged amid the dead and wounded into the deafening cacophony of battle. As blasts of Confederate artillery tore gaps in their formation, the Irish continued forward only to be halted by repeated Confederate infantry volleys. A correspondent of the *London Times* reported that never at Fontenoy nor even at Waterloo was the undaunted courage of the sons of Erin better displayed. Fredericksburg, however, shattered the brigade, which reported only 340 men present for duty in February 1863.

During the battle of Chancellorsville in May 1863, the undersized brigade was held in reserve at Scott's Mills, yet it played an important role in covering General Joseph Hooker's retreat, and one of its decimated regiments, the 88th New York, was one of the last Union regiments to leave the field. When General Hooker refused General Meagher's request to take the brigade out of the line to recruit in New York City, Meagher resigned his commission in protest and finally left the brigade on 19 May 1863. The regiments were consolidated into one battalion under Colonel Patrick Kelly that arrived with the rest of General Winfield Scott Hancock's division on the field of Gettysburg on 1 July 1863. Although its depleted ranks could now cover only a 150-yard front, the brigade fought valiantly in the wheatfield and at Devil's Den and on the evening of 2 July was assigned to a reserve position on Cemetery Ridge. From there it witnessed on the third day of Gettysburg the repulse of General James Longstreet's massive assault, Pickett's Charge, an action that many thought sweet revenge for the carnage of Fredericksburg.

In the winter of 1863–1864, the brigade was reinforced and placed under the command of another Irish-born colonel, Thomas A. Smyth. During General Ulysses S. Grant's Wilderness campaign in the spring of 1864, the brigade took part in General Hancock's assault on the Confederate salient, the "Mule Shoe," at Spotsylvania on 12 May 1864. In the grueling attempt to break down the Army of Northern Virginia, the brigade took part in yet another disastrous and pointless charge, at Cold Harbor on 3 June 1864. Fighting throughout the siege of Petersburg, it was present at General Philip Sheridan's victory at Five Forks during 31 March–1 April 1865. On 2 April 1865, the day the VI Corps broke General Robert E. Lee's lines, the Irish Brigade advanced to Sutherland Station and, until 9 April 1865, pursued and constantly skirmished with the retreating Confederates. Present at the surrender at Appomattox, the brigade began its long march home on 11 April 1865.

Although vastly reduced in numbers, and having been

consolidated with other New York regiments into the Consolidated Brigade, II Corps, in June 1864, the Irish Brigade survived as a command unit. Under its last commander, Colonel Robert Nugent, it took part in the Grand Review of the Army of the Potomac in Washington, D.C., on 22 May 1865. While the veterans of the 28th Massachusetts returned to Boston, Nugent paraded the 400 veterans of the New York regiments on July 1865 at Irving Hall, New York City, where they were addressed by General Meagher and mustered out of service.

The memory of the Irish Brigade is kept alive today by perhaps the most tradition-conscious unit of the U.S. Army, the 69th New York National Guard. The brigade's actions at Gettysburg are remembered by two attractive monuments, and a new monument was erected at Antietam on 25 October 1997 to commemorate the Irish Brigade's heroic charge at Bloody Lane.

—*Rory T. Cornish*

See also Antietam, Battle of; Fredericksburg, Second Battle of; Meagher, Thomas Francis.

For further reading:

Bilby, Joseph G. *The Irish Brigade in the Civil War: The 69th New York and Other Irish Regiments in the Army of the Potomac* (1998).

Burton, William L. *Melting Pot Soldiers: The Union's Ethnic Regiments* (1988; reprint, 1998).

Conyngham, David P. *The Irish Brigade and Its Campaigns* (1867; reprint 1994).

Corby, William. C.S.C. *Memoirs of Chaplain Life: Three Years in the Irish Brigade with the Army of the Potomac* (1992).

Jones, Paul. *The Irish Brigade* (1969).

Kohl, Lawrence F., and Margaret Crosse Richards, eds. *Irish Green and Union Blue: The Civil War Letters of Peter Welsh, Color Sergeant, 28th Massachusetts* (1986).

Lonn, Ella. *Foreigners in the Union Army and Navy* (1951).

O'Brien, Kevin E., ed. *My Life in the Irish Brigade: The Civil War Memoirs of Private William McCarter, 116th Pennsylvania Infantry* (1996).

Seagrave, Pia Seija, ed. *The History of the Irish Brigade: A Collection of Historical Essays* (1997).

IRON BRIGADE

Organized on 1 October 1861 in the Washington, D.C., area, this brigade was initially composed of the 19th Indiana Volunteers and the 2d, 6th, and 7th Wisconsin Volunteers. The 2d Wisconsin had fought at Bull Run in July 1861, but the other regiments were new. Battery B of the 4th U.S. Artillery, a regular army battery but composed in large part of infantry detached from the infantry regiments of the brigade, was closely associated with the Iron Brigade. Because the soldiers wore the high-crowned, regular army dress black Hardee hat, instead of the more typical blue kepi, the unit was originally nicknamed the Black Hat Brigade. After the fighting at Antietam in September 1862, sharply reduced by sickness and casualties, the brigade was reinforced by the newly raised 24th Michigan

Volunteers from the Detroit area. The brigade was the only all-western brigade in the eastern Federal armies. This regional identity played a large part in sustaining the morale of the men.

The brigade was initially commanded by General Rufus King, a West Point graduate transplanted from New York and living in Milwaukee, Wisconsin, at the war's outbreak. When King was promoted, General John Gibbon, also a West Pointer and regular army officer and commander of Battery B, took command of the brigade on 7 May 1862. Gibbon trained the men rigorously and remained in command until promoted to division command on 4 November 1862. An outstanding officer who was later to achieve corps command, Gibbon exhibited leadership and psychological insights that are generally credited with the initial excellence of the western soldiers. It was Gibbon who standardized their uniform, equipping them with the regular armies' dress garb, and he played heavily on their unique western origins to build their morale. His sensitivity to their western origins caused him to insist that a western regiment reinforce the brigade after Antietam. Gibbon's successor in command was Brigadier General Solomon Meredith, a transplanted North Carolinian and Hoosier politician who was originally a colonel of the 19th Indiana Volunteers. Meredith commanded the brigade at Gettysburg.

Coincidentally withheld from McClellan's 1862 Peninsula campaign, the brigade saw its first significant action at Brawner Farm in northern Virginia on 28 August 1862, on the eve of the battle of Second Bull Run. There it clashed with divisions of Stonewall Jackson. The green western soldiers were surprised and outnumbered along the Warrenton Turnpike by Jackson's command. In unusually vicious close combat (one-third of the Federals went down) the brigade behaved extremely well. From that time forward—at Second Bull Run, South Mountain (where the brigade acquired its proud name of Iron Brigade), Antietam, Fredericksburg, Chancellorsville, and Gettysburg—the western soldiers justified their name. Officially designated at Gettysburg as the 1st Brigade, 1st Division, I Corps, the brigade's desperate fighting on the initial day west of the town was a major contribution to I Corps's success in delaying a larger force of Confederates until the rest of the Army of Potomac arrived on the field. The Union forces then occupied the high ground south of the town—Cemetery Hill, Little Round Top, and Cemetery Ridge—from which the Confederates were soundly defeated on the second and third days of the battle. In that first day's fighting, the Iron Brigade's 1st Division came on the field as Henry Heth's Confederates were overwhelming John Buford's cavalrymen, who had put up the first Federal resistance along McPherson's Ridge. The Iron Brigade, minus the 6th Wisconsin, decisively defeated James J. Archer's Confederate brigade. Then the 6th Wisconsin and Brigade Guard overwhelmed other Confederates in the railroad cut that roughly paralleled the Chambersburg Pike. Assailed that afternoon by overwhelming Confederate numbers, the brigade was forced back. In this Gettysburg action, the brigade lost 1,712 of 1,883 officers and men. After these losses, the remnants of the western unit remained in the field but were brigaded with nonwestern units and consequently the brigade lost its all-western integrity while participating in Grant's final Virginia campaign. During Grant's Overland campaign, the much-reduced 19th Indiana was merged with the 20th Indiana. The 2d Wisconsin, which exceeded all Federal regiments in total battle fatalities and in the percentage of such fatalities, was mustered out in June 1864. The Michigan soldiers of the brigade left the field in the spring of 1865. But the 6th and 7th Wisconsin were on hand at Appomattox, remaining as symbols of the Iron Brigade.

Historians believe that a coincidence of three factors led to the unusual distinction of the brigade. First, the regiments had an unusually long period in which to be trained. They were not in significant combat from 1 October 1861 until 28 August 1862. Second, they were fortunate in their officers. Along with the superb Gibbon, the roll of volunteer regimental field officers contained unusually effective men. Finally, their regional identity was the basis of an unusual esprit de corps enlarged by their distinctive uniforms of which the men were proud. As the eminent historian T. Harry Williams has said, the Iron Brigade was "probably the best fighting brigade in the army."

At war's end, the records show that the brigade led all Union brigades in percentage of deaths in battle. Further, more men had fallen at the guns of Battery B, the brigade's artillery kinsmen, than in any other Union battery. William F. Fox, the war's premier casualty statistician, says that this record means that they faced enemy fire most often and for the longest periods of time.

—*Allan T. Nolan*

See also Bull Run, Second Battle of; Gettysburg, Battle of; Gibbon, John; Meredith, Solomon; South Mountain, Battle of.
For further reading:
Fox, William F. *Regimental Losses in the American Civil War, 1861–1865* (1889).
Herdegen, Lance J. *The Men Stood Like Iron* (1997).
Nolan, Alan T. *The Iron Brigade: A Military History* (1961; reprint, 1994).
Nolan, Alan T., and Sharon E. Vipond. *Giants in Their Tall Black Hats: Essays on the Iron Brigade* (1998).

IRONCLADS

The American Civil War was distinguished by the first large-scale employment of ironclad warships in battle. At the same time, there was an enormous technological disparity between Union and Confederate ironclad warships that reflected the two belligerents' greatly differing levels of industrial development. The Union could construct all of its ironclads, broadside or turret, completely in its own shipyards. The Confederacy basically could do little more than convert existing hulls to an ironclad configuration, or construct lubberly floating armored box batteries. Consequently, Union ironclads, particularly the monitors, were technically far superior to their Confederate counterparts.

From the war's earliest months, both sides almost simultaneously saw the need for ironclads in the looming struggle. There was nothing particularly novel about ironclads by 1861. The British and the French had actually employed ironclad gunboats in action during the Crimean War, and by 1861 both the French wooden seagoing ironclad, *La Gloire* and the Royal Navy's oceanic iron-constructed *Warrior* (still in existence and restored) were in service. Thus both the Confederate and the Union navies could learn from recent European ironclad experience.

The Union — The Union navy combined two conventional and one innovative design in its first three ironclads. One of the two orthodox designs was the giant *New Ironsides* with its broadside guns, initial full sailing rig, and patch of armor along the gun deck. The other was the small, schooner-rigged *Galena*, which was protected by a complex system of interlocked one-inch iron plates to a maximum thickness of 3.125 inches that shielded a broadside gun deck. The final ironclad of the three, John Ericsson's unprecedented USS *Monitor*, has understandably overshadowed all other armored warships of the Civil War. A single-turreted, low-lying, mastless vessel, it was unlike any previous warship. Yet its design represented a dead end in naval architecture. Here, again, North America was behind Europe. During the Crimean War, Captain Cowper Coles, RN, had mounted a single gun on a turntable, which was in turn fitted on a raft, and had thereby engaged Russian shore batteries. Furthermore, Coles had also designed and built two mastless, coastal ironclads, the *Prince Albert* and the *Royal Sovereign*, which, however, entered service well after the *Monitor*, and which had nothing like the *Monitor*'s extremely low freeboard. There can be little question that Coles's ship design and turret technology were superior to Ericsson's. While Ericsson's turret rotated on a spindle and was thus liable to jamming, Coles's rested on rollers below the waterline and always seemed to rotate freely. Further, the first monitor and its initial follow-on class had a "raft" upper body that worked water through the joint with the underwater hull, a fault that would doom the original *Monitor* during a moderate gale. There was no such equivalent design in any Royal Navy warship. Finally, and through no fault of Ericsson's, U.S. armorclads were protected by laminated

Deck of the Union ironclad *Galena*, showing its stack damaged by fire from Fort Darling. James River, Virginia, June 1862
(Photograph by James F. Gubson / *Library of Congress*)

2-inch thick plates because U.S. mills could produce nothing thicker. By contrast, at the time mills in the United Kingdom could roll plates up to six inches. (Whether Ericsson was aware or convinced of Royal Navy qualitative ironclad superiority, he put a brave face on matters: the *Monitor*'s very name was intended as a warning, or "admonition," to the British and the French, whose governments and upper classes made little secret of their pro-Confederate sympathies.)

The USS *New Ironsides*, for all her conventional technology, became one of the Union's most valued weapons, her rate of fire compensating for her smaller guns. In fact, by far the majority of Union naval officers, including Admiral David Farragut, preferred a *New Ironsides*-type of armorclad to the monitor style. The *Galena*, on the other hand, proved an abject failure, her armor easily pierced in operations along the James River. She suffered the ultimate ironclad indignity when a disgusted Navy Department actually ordered her armor removed.

The *Monitor*'s success in deflecting the CSS *Virginia* in the first ironclad-to-ironclad clash in history, the battle of Hampton Roads (March 1862), produced something of a "monitor mania" throughout the North, with even popular sheet music hymning the praises of the turreted warship. The U.S. Navy quickly contracted for an entire fleet of turreted armorclads on a modified *Monitor* plan. This class, the Passaics, numbered no less than ten vessels and were the first ironclads anywhere to be built in more than pairs to one set of plans. They were awkwardly armed with one 11-inch and one 15-inch smoothbore. With this group the U.S. Navy also began the policy of giving the monitors North American aboriginal names, something fitting for a type of warship that, for better or for worse, was unique to the New World. (The *Monitor*, *Dictator*, and *Puritan* were the only exceptions.)

The Passaics were followed by the nine of the Canonicus class, distinguishable by the removal of the objectionable upper deck overhang and by an armament

The USS *Onondaga*, James River, Virginia, 1864 (*Library of Congress*)

of matching 15-inch smoothbores. One vessel of this class, the USS *Tecumseh*, is noteworthy as the first warship sunk almost instantaneously in battle, after she exploded an underwater mine at the battle of Mobile Bay (August 1864).

Less successful turreted ironclads of this early period were the *Keokuk* and *Roanoke*. The *Keokuk* was a monitor type, but with a single gun mounted in each of two stationary armored structures. A turntable in the "turrets" lined up the ordnance with gunports arranged around the structures. The armor protection was equally unusual, consisting of a "sandwich" of iron and wood. The *Keokuk* earned the dubious distinction of being one of the very few ironclads in the nineteenth century to have been sunk as a result of having her armor pierced in battle. The *Keokuk* foundered a few days after being

badly holed during the ironclad attack on Charleston in April 1863.

The *Roanoke*, a cut-down wooden sloop from the same class that provided the *Virginia* to the Confederates, mounted three turrets, the only U.S. ironclad with more than two of these armored housings. The *Roanoke* was, in theory, the Union's most powerful monitor, but her wooden hull could not provide a strong enough platform for its three heavy, armor-plated turrets, and all of this weight topside caused the warship to roll heavily. These faults, combined with her deep draught, limited the *Roanoke* to harbor defense duties at New York. Rather more successful was the large iron-hulled, twin-turreted *Onondaga*, mounting one 15-inch smoothbore and one 150-pounder smoothbore. But it would be difficult to imagine more troubles than those that

Side view of the USS *Onondaga*, Aiken's Landing, Virginia, 1864 (*Library of Congress*)

prolonged this ironclad's construction. Labor shortages, materials difficulties, workers' strikes, and the terrible New York draft riots, which closed down its shipyard in 1863, were among the tribulations. The *Onondaga* therefore had only one year to serve before the war's end, but she did make up for lost time, acting as a powerful deterrent to Confederate ironclads on the James River. Notably she clashed with *Virginia II*, in which conflict she punched a 2-foot square hole in her enemy's plating, one of the very few occasions in this era when armor was ever punctured. The French purchased the *Onondaga* after the war, modified her protection and armament, and kept her on hand until 1905.

Later Union ironclads, the giant single-turreted *Dictator* and her near-sister ship *Puritan* of 3,000 tons, with 6 inches of armor and mounting two 15-inch Dahlgrens, were both intended as seagoing warships.

Only the *Dictator* was completed, but it saw no action. However, it could be argued that the *Dictator* somewhat lived up to its name. During the national elections of 1864, and with the New York City draft riots of the previous year much in mind, the *Dictator* stood off Manhattan's Battery, guns run out and shotted with canister to sweep the streets in case of any repetition of such disorder.

Other large Union navy monitors were the *Monadnock*, *Agamenticus*, *Miantonomah* ("My Aunt Don't Know Me," according to the sailors who served in her) and *Tonawanda*. All were single-screw, mounted two 15-inch guns in two turrets protected by 11 inches of armor on timber-built hulls (thus no watertight doors were possible). None went into battle, but the *Monadnock* steamed around Cape Horn to San Francisco, and the *Miantonomah* crossed the Atlantic to

The ironcald USS *St. Louis*, renamed the *Baron de Kalb* in 1862 (*Library of Congress*)

Russia on a diplomatic mission; both voyages were without incident.

The eminent engineer James Eads designed four whaleback, double-turreted monitors of the Milwaukee class, a hybrid design featuring one turret on the Ericsson system and the other on Eads's unique design. The Eads turrets, patterned on the Coles design, also never jammed. But Eads's design was actually even more advanced than Coles's; the guns' recoil would actually drop the entire turret floor below the waterline where the guns could be safely reloaded, then elevated and run out by steam power. Perhaps the design was too complicated, for it was never replicated on the ironclads of any other naval power.

The earliest Union navy riverine ironclad, the USS *Essex*, was a scow-like converted Mississippi wooden-paddle ferryboat hastily plated with three-quarter inch iron and useless one-inch rubber. After the battle of Fort Henry in February 1862, the *Essex* was rebuilt with more powerful armament and better protection. A similar converted river ironclad, the *Benton*, with sixteen guns, was the most powerful ironclad on the Mississippi. The next riverine ironclads were the seven city class paddle-wheel, special-built casemate warships, the first squadron of American ironclads that, with the *Essex* and *Benton*, took the brunt of Mississippi River fighting. These riverine ironclads actually predated the *Monitor*, and were, in fact, the first ironclads designed and built in the Western Hemisphere.

The *Chillicothe*, *Tuscumbia*, and *Indianola* followed the City class. These were broad-hulled, paddle-wheel vessels, with six guns mounted in a casement and protected by 3-inch iron plating and India rubber or gutta-percha, the terms apparently were used interchangeably. Apparently, this flexible protection did nothing more than to hasten the rot between the iron armor and its wood backing.

These four were followed by the monstrous paddle-wheel river ironclads, the *Lafayette*, *Choctaw*, and *Eastport*. But these giants could carry only roughly the same armament and protection (including the useless rubber/gutta-percha) as their immediate, and much smaller, predecessors. With their maximum speed a risible two knots, their main advantage was that their very bulk allowed them to absorb a great amount of shot and shell. These warships were also classified as rams, but their only success with their underwater iron snouts ("the ever-loaded weapon") was the *Choctaw*'s inadvertent impaling and sinking of the tug *Lily*—a U.S. Navy vessel!

Technologically, the most interesting of the river ironclads were two single-turreted monitors designed by Eads for work on western rivers. The *Osage* and *Neosho* were unique as the only monitors propelled by paddle wheels that were protected by armored casings. A larger version, *Ozark*, was screw driven and mounted 11-inch Dahlgren guns.

The Union Civil War ironclad program ended on a farcical note with the twenty light-draft monitor class. The original plans were drawn up by Ericsson but greatly modified by the inspector of ironclads, Alban Stimers, to Ericsson's outrage. The responsibility for these monitors'

almost complete failure is lost in a maze of administrative confusion. But there could be no arguing that all drew far more draft than designed. Five were completed without turrets, and in a face-saving gesture were classified as "torpedo vessels," worthless vessels if there ever were such. The remaining fifteen did mount turrets, all but two carrying two 11-inch guns, but any kind of seaway would nearly swamp them. Not surprisingly, there were wholesale Navy Department firings in the wake of this design fiasco.

Paradoxically perhaps, it was the much less publicized broadside ironclads that were involved in the bulk of the coastal and riverine combat that so distinguished the American Civil War. In all, the Union completed seventy-one ironclads, far more than any other naval power of the time.

The Confederacy — Historians disagree whether the South adopted an offensive or defensive naval strategy or a combination of both, or different strategies at different times throughout the war, but there can be little argument that the Confederate government was quick enough off the mark in the construction and deployment of ironclad warships. In the words of Confederate Secretary of the Navy Stephen Mallory, "Inequality of numbers may be compensated by invulnerability."

Early efforts to purchase ironclads in Europe having proved unsuccessful, Mallory determined to construct such vessels in the Confederacy. Yet the Confederacy could not produce any significant part of an ironclad except the hull. Apparently not a single shipyard in the entire South could manufacture a complete set of marine engines. Neither were there foundries that could roll armor, nor arsenals that could cast reliable heavy guns. Nevertheless, the Confederate ironclads never lacked good armament, as they used captured Union and purchased British guns. Probably wisely, the Confederates concentrated on rifled guns in contrast to the Union's preference for smoothbores.

From a technological viewpoint, Confederate ironclads are relatively uninteresting. The Confederates did plan for two double-ended casemated ironclads and actually had some plans for a monitor-type of their own. The first were not completed due to a lack of armor plate, and the last because Navy secretary Mallory actually preferred casemated ironclads to monitors. This latter decision was not so retrograde as it might seem; the major maritime powers of Europe continued to build casemated ironclads through the 1870s.

Thus, the historic *Virginia* was constructed on the hull of the sunken Union steam frigate *Merrimack*. This pioneer ironclad was armed with two 7-inch Brooke rifles, two 6.4-inch Dahlgren smoothbores, and two 12-pounder smoothbore howitzers. Its armor was rolled from railroad iron into plates and attached in two courses to a probable thickness

of 4 inches. With that ironclad, the Confederacy set the pattern for the great majority of its subsequent ironclads: a sloping, barnlike armored casemate, pierced for broadside guns, resting on a very low hull. The fate of the *Virginia* is also indicative of what awaited almost all Confederate ironclads: her own crew burned her to the waterline in the face of advancing Federals.

Because of its very limited maritime facilities, the South turned to foreign sources for some of its ironclad strength. The Confederate government was able to purchase three armorclads from private European shipyards, but could take possession of only one, the CSS *Stonewall*. The *Stonewall* was built in a French yard along traditional lines, with a high, wooden hull, but carried only five guns (one 10-inch and four 6.4-inch Armstrong muzzle-loading rifles). These rifles could have wrought considerable damage to the Union ironclads' laminated armor, but her main weapon was a giant underwater ram. The *Stonewall* made her way across the Atlantic to Cuba, only to find that the war was over. Her builders subsequently sold the warship to Japan.

The twin-masted, twin-Coles-turreted, iron-built coastal armorclads, the *Scorpion* and *Wyvern*, posed a much greater threat. In the face of their solid 4.5-inch armor and four 9-inch rifled guns, plus their great action radius, it is difficult to see how the Union could have maintained its blockade. They exemplified the fact that the Royal Navy's ironclads were about a generation advanced over those of the Union. This truth was obvious to both Confederate and Union representatives abroad. In a well-known diplomatic demarche, Charles Francis Adams, the U.S. minister to the United Kingdom, bluntly warned British foreign secretary Lord Russell that if the two ironclads fell into the hands of the Confederacy, it would be tantamount to war. Lord Russell took the point. The Royal Navy quickly seized the warships and entered them into that service.

Although the Confederate-built ironclads could not begin to break or even to challenge seriously the Union blockade, their mere presence as a "fleet in being" vastly complicated the Union navy's blockade work. Still, that the primarily agrarian Confederacy managed to construct no less than twenty-five ironclads is perhaps more impressive than their battle honors.

In sum, the Union's armorclads remained considerably superior in almost every technological point, with the important exception of ordnance, throughout the Civil War. On the other hand, even the Union's heralded monitors were technologically inferior to any contemporary Royal Navy ironclad, and it is just as well that the Lincoln administration did not press matters in the *Trent* or *Scorpion/Wyvern* diplomatic imbroglios. After Appomattox, that ironclad disparity would increase even more. The Royal Navy's chief constructor, E. J. Reed, was completing plans for three great seagoing, mastless, turreted war engines, the *Devastation, Thunderer,* and *Dreadnought,* which even individually, could have destroyed in detail the entire Union ironclad fleet. This U.S. naval inferiority was ruefully admitted by John Ericsson himself in 1870, when he wrote that the *Devastation* alone could cross the Atlantic and "dictate terms off Castle Garden [New York City]," an admission that must have stuck in the throat of the *Monitor's* anglophobic designer. When late in the century the thread of development of the mastless, oceanic turreted capital ship was again seized upon, it was the *Devastation* that the world's naval powers emulated, enlarged, and improved upon, not the *Monitor.* The U.S. Navy would not have any capital ships that could somewhat challenge those of the European naval powers until the completion of the *Maine* and *Texas* in 1895.

The first North American ironclads were the hasty and indigenous products of the particular circumstances of the American Civil War, and it is as such that they should be evaluated.

—Stanley Sandler

See also Blockade of C.S.A.; Eads, James B.; Ericsson, John; Farragut, David Glasgow; Mobile Bay; *Monitor; Monitor v. Virginia;* Navy, C.S.A.; Navy, U.S.A.; *New Ironsides;* Riverine Warfare; *Tecumseh,* USS; *Tennessee,* CSS.

For further reading:
Bennett, Frank M. *The Monitor and the Navy Under Steam* (1900).
Cracknell, William H. *Warship Profile: United States Monitors of the Civil War* (1973).
Eskew, G. L. "Our Navy's Ships and Their Builders, 1775–1883." Typescript, Bureau of Ships, U.S. Navy (1962).
Greene, Jack, and Alessandro Massignani. *Ironclads at War: The Origin and Development of the Armored Warship, 1854–1891* (1998).
Parker, Foxhall. *The Battle of Mobile Bay, and the Capture of Forts Powell, Gaines, and Morgan by the Combined Sea and Land Forces of the United States under the Command of Rear-Admiral David Glasgow Farragut, and Major-General Gordon Granger, August, 1864* (1878).
Sandler, Stanley. *The Emergence of the Modern Capital Ship* (1979).
Shapack, Arnold. "Oak to Iron—Monitors in United States Naval History" (M.A. thesis, 1973).
Tucker, Spencer C. *Handbook of Nineteenth Century Naval Warfare* (2000).
U.S. National Archives. Bureau of Construction and Repair. Plans of Ships and stations, with related records (1794–1910).
U.S. Navy Department. Naval History Division. *Monitors of the U.S. Navy, 1861–1937* (1969).
———. *Report of the Secretary of the Navy in Relation to Armored Vessels 1864* (1864).

IRWINVILLE, GEORGIA

Site of the capture of Confederate president Jefferson Davis on 10 May 1865, Irwinville was situated approximately twenty-five miles southwest of the Great Bend of the Ocmulgee River in south central Georgia. Irwinville was the third county seat of Irwin County. Although Irwin County was one of the first three counties formed in south Georgia from ceded Creek Indians lands in 1823, it was still sparsely populated at the beginning of the Civil War. Sandy soil prevented the region from developing large-scale cotton production, so slave populations remained low and white populations remained poor. This economic separation inhibited Confederate loyalty and made the lands surrounding Irwinville a haven for deserters, Unionists, and runaway slaves.

Perhaps the most notorious of Irwinville's anti-Confederates was Willis J. Bone, a man whose notoriety stemmed from the use of his farm as a refuge for deserters, runaway slaves, and escaped federal prisoners. Bone at times made them pay for their stay by clearing his land. Bone's reputation reached its peak during the winter of 1864–1865 when he, along with a large number of deserters, convened a Union meeting at Irwinville. When an infuriated enrolling officer and one other man attempted to disrupt the meeting, Bone knocked the officer to the ground with the butt of his musket, led three cheers for Abraham Lincoln, and drove the two men from town.

Irwinville is best known as the site of the capture of Confederate president Jefferson Davis. Despite advice to the contrary (his military escort pressed for an escape south to vessels waiting in the Gulf of Mexico), Davis's plan was to escape via a land route from South Carolina, through Georgia, and westward into Texas or Mexico, where he would re-form his government and renew the war effort. He did not know that his route was being blocked by the surrender of Confederate forces meant to clear his way and the increased activity of Union patrols searching for him. General James Wilson's cavalry rode east from Columbus, Georgia, while members of the 1st Wisconsin and 4th Michigan cavalries followed the Davis party south from Abbeville, South Carolina, across the Ocmulgee River and into Irwin County.

On the morning of 10 May 1865, aided by information from a freed slave and local citizens, both cavalries approached Davis's Irwinville campsite from different directions. In the predawn darkness, both units mistook each other for Confederate troops and opened fire. Davis's coachman sounded the alarm as Union cavalrymen burst from the surrounding woods. The confusion created by the Union crossfire had not allowed any of the attacking troops to identify Davis's location, and Varina Davis urged her husband to sneak out of camp and make his escape. He reluctantly agreed. His attempted escape has produced one of the most enduring, and questionable, images of the war.

Numerous versions of the story of Davis's capture exist. One claims that Davis threw on a rain cloak, but that when he turned to exit the tent, his wife threw one of her shawls over his head. Other stories claim that

Davis mistakenly grabbed his wife's shawl instead of the rain cloak and threw it over his head. One of the myths that arose from this incident was that Davis was captured wearing one of his wife's dresses.

Davis, accompanied by his wife's mulatto maid, slipped out of his tent and walked quickly toward a nearby river while Varina created a diversion. However, one horseman saw the two fleeing figures and ordered them to halt. The two changed directions but did not stop. A second cavalryman rode up and blocked Davis's path, threatening to shoot if he did not stop. Davis later claimed that he had hoped to pull the horseman from his mount, swing himself into the saddle, and ride off. Only Varina's intervention prevented him from doing so.

Davis and his family were loaded onto wagons and transported to General Wilson's headquarters at Macon. From there, Davis was moved by train to Augusta via Atlanta, then by boat to Savannah, and finally to Fort Monroe in Virginia, where he spent the next two years in prison.

—*David Carlson*

See also Davis, Jefferson; Davis, Varina Howell; Wilson, James H.

For further reading:
Ballard, Michael B. *A Long Shadow: Jefferson Davis and the Final Days of the Confederacy* (1986).
Clements, J.B. *History of Irwin County* (1989).
Davis, Varina. *Jefferson Davis, Ex-President of the Confederate States of America, A Memoir* (1890; reprint, 1990).
Davis, William C. *Jefferson Davis, The Man & His Hour* (1991).

ISLAND NO. 10, BATTLE OF
(7 April 1862)

Island No. 10 was the site of a key Confederate fort on the upper Mississippi River. After Union victories at Forts Donelson and Henry in February 1862, commander of the Department of the Missouri Major General Henry W. Halleck authorized an operation down the Mississippi. The immediate goal of the operation was to secure New Madrid, Missouri, and nearby Island No. 10.

Island No. 10 no longer exists; it is now a part of the Missouri shore. In 1862 it was about a mile long and a quarter-mile wide and lay at a long inverted S-shaped bend in the river about forty miles south of Columbus. Surrounded by cypress-entangled swamps, Reelfoot Lake, and the great river itself, the island was not easily accessible to land forces. The defenders were dependent for communications and resupply on the river and a single road on the Tennessee side through Tiptonville. If Union troops could sever these, the garrison would be trapped.

When on 3 March the Confederates evacuated Columbus, Major General Leonidas Polk ordered Brigadier General John P. McCown's division south to join 1,500 troops already in garrison at Island No. 10. At the same time, Polk ordered Commodore George N. Hollins to move his five gunboats there. Using heavy guns from Columbus, the Confederates created a formidable defensive position. The outer works consisted of field batteries along the river banks commanding the channel for ten to twelve miles north. The island held nineteen guns; the land bluffs, forty-three with batteries arranged to deliver concentrated fire. The Confederates also had a floating battery with nine heavy guns.

At Island No. 10, the Mississippi made a sharp bend and then ran northwest. The town of New Madrid, Missouri, actually farther north than Island No. 10, was six miles downriver. There the river resumed a southerly direction. To prevent the island from being attacked by land forces from the Missouri side, the Confederates fortified New Madrid with two earthen forts and a total of twenty-one guns. They also fortified the Tennessee side of the river. McCown, who took command of the Madrid Bend area on 26 February, had 7,500 men.

To take Island No. 10, Union forces would first have to capture New Madrid and cut the fort off from communication downriver. Halleck assigned this task to Brigadier General John Pope's new Army of the Mississippi. Pope's 18,000 men marched fifty miles overland and brought New Madrid under siege on 3 March. On 12 March, Union siege guns arrived, and the next day Union gunners opened a heavy bombardment. Panicking, McCown abandoned New Madrid. The evacuation on the night of the 13th was poorly executed and much equipment was simply abandoned. A heavy thunderstorm did mask the withdrawal; Union troops did not realize what had happened until the morning. The fifteen-day long campaign had seen few casualties—about fifty killed and wounded on each side—but Island No. 10 was now cut off from most river communication and means of supply.

McCown's superior, Brigadier General P. G. T. Beauregard, hoped that Island No. 10's defenders would at least buy time to strengthen Fort Pillow and enable General Albert S. Johnston to attack Grant at Pittsburg Landing. Beauregard now ordered the Madrid Bend garrison south to Fort Pillow and informed McCown that he would not be reinforced.

Union flotilla commander Foote had delayed moving to Island No. 10 to prepare his ironclads, but he was apprehensive about fighting downstream because of the strong current that would drift any disabled boat downriver under the Confederate guns. Foote finally set out on 14 March from Cairo with seven gunboats, ten mortar boats, and an assortment of other craft. At Columbus the flotilla met 1,200 Union troops in transports and convoyed them south. It reached the vicinity of Island No. 10 on the morning of the 15th.

On the 16th, Foote positioned his mortar boats with

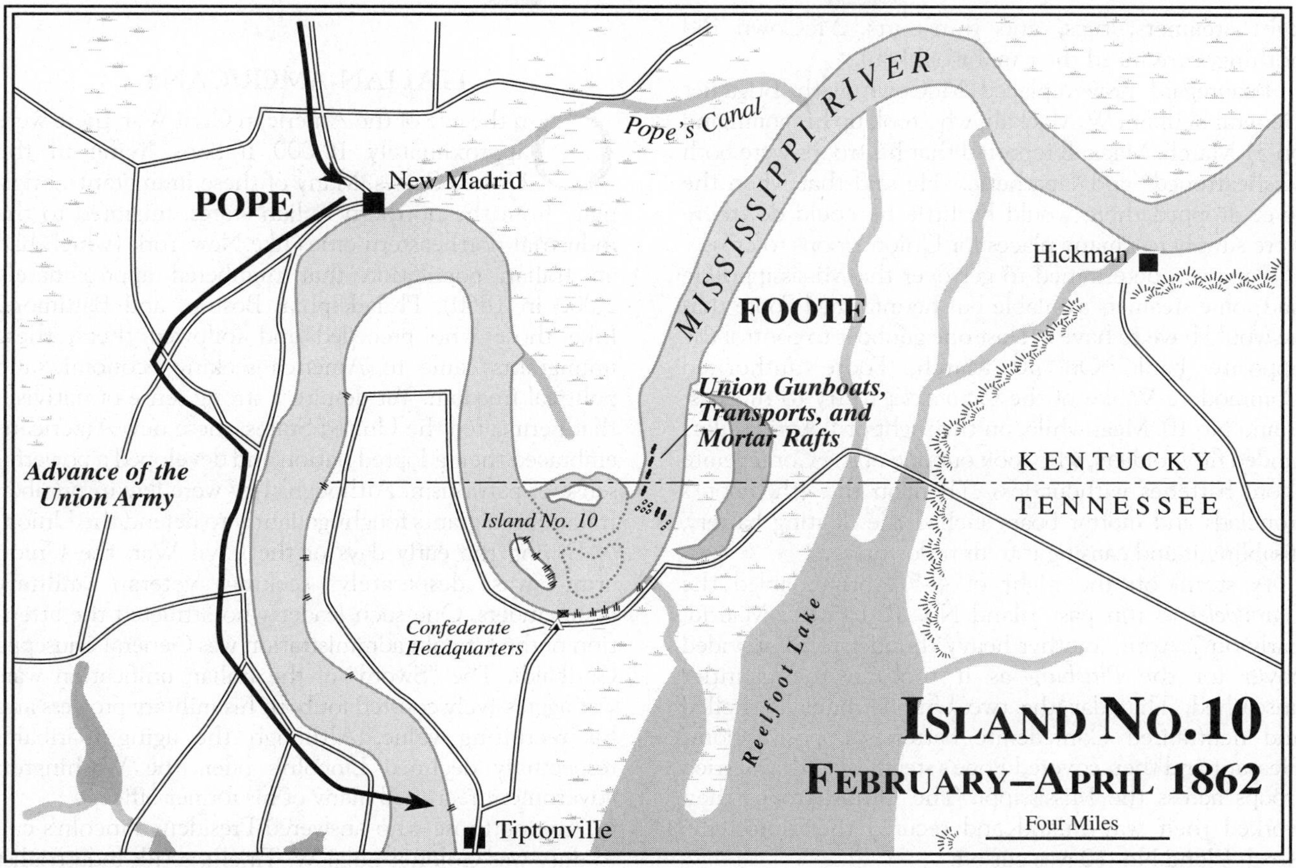

Pope's Canal

MISSISSIPPI RIVER

POPE

New Madrid

Hickman

FOOTE

*Union Gunboats,
Transports, and
Mortar Rafts*

KENTUCKY

TENNESSEE

*Advance of the
Union Army*

Island No. 10

*Confederate
Headquarters*

Reelfoot Lake

ISLAND NO. 10
FEBRUARY–APRIL 1862

Four Miles

Tiptonville

their 13-inch mortars along the shore in the hope that their fire would reduce the Confederate positions before he ran his gunboats to New Madrid. Shelling began that afternoon, but it was inaccurate and had little effect beyond driving some of the defenders from their positions.

On the morning of the 17th, Foote attempted a long-range attack on the Confederate defenses with his iron-clads, but its net effect was one gun dismounted and one man killed and seven wounded. The flotilla took some hits, but the most costly blow was self-inflicted; an old army rifled 42-pounder burst on one of the gunboats, killing and wounding fifteen officers and men. Foote now settled in for a long siege, shelling the defenses around the clock from long range. But the small, dispersed forts were difficult targets.

Meanwhile, on the other side of Island No. 10, Union troops moved a 24-pounder upriver along the shore, and on the morning of the 18th they opened fire on Confederate steamers unloading supplies across the river at Tiptonville, damaging several Confederate vessels. Hollins, unwilling to risk his vulnerable wooden vessels to heavy Union guns, withdrew below Tiptonville, taking with him many of the garrison's provisions. His squadron was no longer a factor in the battle.

Although Pope now held New Madrid, swamps

prevented his reaching the vicinity of Island No. 10 on the Missouri side. And with no transports, he had no means of crossing over to the Tennessee side to attack the Confederate rear. On 18 March, Foote rejected Pope's request that he send gunboats past Island No. 10. In a meeting of gunboat captains on the 20th, all but one declared themselves opposed to an attempt.

By 24 March, there was stalemate and little action except daily shelling by the Union mortars, which had little effect. Occasionally the gunboats would join in. On 25 March, the monotony of the siege was broken by the ascent of the *Eagle*, a Union balloon, the only use of balloon observation in the West during the war.

Meanwhile, on 23 March, work had begun on one of the more innovative engineering achievements of the war. Over a three-week period, hundreds of Union soldiers and sailors, supported by four shallow draft steamers and six coal barges, used a variety of tools and two million feet of lumber to cut a canal fifty feet wide and twelve miles long from the bend of the Mississippi near Island No. 8 across the swampy peninsula to near New Madrid. Three-fourths of a mile went through solid earth and six miles ran through timber that had to be cut off and dragged out from under water. Although not deep enough for Foote's gunboats, the canal could take

light steamers, tugs, and transports. McCown did nothing, convinced the canal would fail.

Beauregard now replaced McCown with Brigadier General William W. Mackall, who took up his command on 31 March. Mackall reported that his troops were both "disheartened" and "apathetic." He said that when the river dropped there would be little he could do; there were simply too many places for Union troops to cross.

Pope was determined to get over the Mississippi. He had some steamers available but he informed Foote that he would have to have at least one gunboat to control the opposite bank. On 30 March, Foote authorized Commodore Walke of the *Carondelet* to try to run past Island No 10. Meanwhile, on the night of 1 April, sailors landed fifty soldiers, who took out one of the Confederate shore batteries without loss. Then on the 4th, Foote's ironclads and mortar boats shelled the floating battery, disabling it and causing it to drift downriver.

A storm on the night of 4–5 April enabled the *Carondelet* to run past Island No. 10 to New Madrid. Early on 7 April, another heavy thunderstorm provided cover for the *Pittsburg* as it too ran the gauntlet unscathed. That day the two Union ironclads shelled and neutralized Confederate batteries opposite Point Pleasant and then covered Pope's steamers as they ferried troops across the Mississippi. The Union troops then worked their way inland and secured the Tiptonville Road. Island No. 10 was cut off.

Mackall, caught in a trap with a Union army-navy assault imminent and large numbers of his men deserting, now ordered a withdrawal. On the evening of 7 April, Captain W. Y. C. Hume, commanding Island No. 10, sent officers to Foote asking for terms. Foote demanded unconditional surrender, which Hume accepted early on 8 April. Only about 1,000 Confederates, principally from the upper batteries on the Tennessee side of the river, managed to escape, most through the swamps.

The loss of Island No. 10 was more grievous for the South than the carnage of Shiloh. The Union took 4,500 prisoners, 5,000 small arms, and 109 cannon and mortars. It also secured four steamers and the floating battery, as well as quantities of ammunition, supplies, and provisions. And it was a cheap victory in terms of Union casualties: seven killed, fourteen wounded, and four missing, more than half to accidental causes. Fort Pillow was the next Union objective.

—*Spencer C. Tucker*

See also Foote, Andrew H.; Fort Donelson; Fort Henry; Fort Pillow Massacre; Hollins, George N.; Pope, John.
For further reading:
Daniel, Larry J., and Lynn N. Bock. *Island No. 10: Struggle for the Mississippi Valley* (1996).
Milligan, John D. *Gunboats Down the Mississippi* (1965).

Tucker, Spencer C. *Andrew Foote: Civil War Admiral on Western Waters* (2000).

ITALIAN-AMERICANS

On the eve of the American Civil War, there were approximately 10,000 Italians living in the United States. Many of these immigrants, originally from the northern Italian states, migrated to the industrial northeastern cities like New York (which had an Italian population that numbered approximately 2,000 in 1860), Philadelphia, Boston, and Baltimore. Like those who preceded and followed them, these immigrants came to America seeking economic and political freedom. Yet despite a strong sense of nativism that permeated the United States, these new Americans embraced their adopted nation and developed a powerful sense of patriotism. Although they were few in number, Italian immigrants fought gallantly to defend the Union.

During the early days of the Civil War, the Union army was desperately seeking veteran military commanders. One such leader who attracted the attention of the Lincoln administration was General Giuseppe Garibaldi. The "Sword" of the Italian unification wars was aggressively courted for both his military prowess and his recruiting value. Although the aging Garibaldi respectfully declined Lincoln's offer, the Washington government recruited many of his former officers.

Among those who answered President Lincoln's call to duty was Colonel Luigi W. Tinelli, a silk industrialist and former American consul to Portugal. A colonel in the New York militia as early as 1843, Tinelli conceived the idea of forming an Italian regiment to defend the Union. Unfortunately, there were not enough Italian nationals to support such a regiment, and many were eventually assigned to the New York 39th Infantry—the "Garibaldi Guard." Italian-American volunteers were well represented in this flamboyant polyglot regiment that also consisted of Hungarian, German, Spanish, Swiss, and French volunteers. For example, Alexander Repetti, a Genoese Garibaldian, was appointed lieutenant colonel of the regiment, second in command behind the controversial Frederick D'Utassy. In all, Italian-Americans made up one full company of the Garibaldi Guard. Although the New York 39th Infantry experienced some early discipline problems, and its first commander was jailed for embezzlement, the regiment distinguished itself throughout the war, participating in such battles as Gettysburg, Petersburg, and other important engagements.

Not all Italian-Americans during the Civil War fought with the Garibaldi Guard. In fact, the most distinguished and decorated Italian-American soldier was a cavalry officer—Count Emmanuele Pietro Maria Luigi Palma di Cesnola. Born in 1832 in the Italian Piedmont region, di Cesnola, a Sardinian cavalry officer, distinguished himself in both the Revolution of 1848 and the

Crimean War before journeying to the United States in 1858. At the onset of the war, di Cesnola opened a private military school in New York City, where he trained some 800 officers. Anxious to see action, the former Savoyard officer joined the 11th New York Cavalry Regiment, known as "Scott's 900." Frustrated with the regiment's inactivity, di Cesnola resigned his commission. Through his political connections, however, he soon secured a field command of the New York 4th Cavalry. It was while commanding this cavalry unit that di Cesnola earned the greatest recognition that can be bestowed upon an American soldier: the coveted Medal of Honor.

In the early summer of 1863, di Cesnola's 4th New York Cavalry tangled with the Confederates in several skirmishes and battles in northern Virginia, including the battle of Aldie, one of the early engagements of the Gettysburg campaign. Despite being under arrest for insubordination, Colonel di Cesnola, without a weapon, rallied his troops against the 2d Virginia Cavalry. During the fierce exchange, the young Italian officer lay desperately wounded and pinned underneath his horse. Di Cesnola's incredible act of bravery was not without consequence; besides receiving life-threatening wounds, he was taken prisoner and shipped to the notorious Libby Prison.

Miraculously, di Cesnola survived his nine-month ordeal at Libby. Upon his release, Colonel di Cesnola rejoined his old cavalry unit, participating in a number of battles, including the savage engagement at Trevilian Station. Di Cesnola's illustrious career ended in late summer of 1864; soon afterward he was appointed by Lincoln as U.S. consul to Cyprus. He later became the first director of the Metropolitan Museum of Art in New York, serving for over twenty-five years and making it one of the most renowned museums in the world.

General Francis Spinola was another Italian-American who defended the Union against the rebel forces. Born of Italian parentage on Long Island, New York, Spinola was a well-known Brooklyn Democrat and had served in both the New York assembly and senate before the Civil War. Despite his philosophical and political differences with the Lincoln administration, Spinola rallied to the Union cause, declaring in a speech before the New York legislature, "this is my flag, which I will follow and defend." At the onset of the conflict, Spinola raised four regiments of troops known as the "Spinola Empire Brigade." He was subsequently rewarded for his loyalty by receiving a commission as a brigadier general. During the war, General Spinola participated in several campaigns in southeastern Virginia and North Carolina. While pursuing Robert E. Lee after the battle of Gettysburg, he was wounded at Manassas Gap. After his service in the Union army,

General Spinola served several terms in the U.S. House of Representatives.

Altogether, hundreds of Italian-Americans fought to preserve the Union. More than 100 served as officers, including three—Enrico Fardella, Eduardo Ferrero, and Francis Spinola—who became brigadier generals.

—*Frank Alduino*

See also Immigrants.
For further reading:
Amfitheatrof, Erik. *The Children of Columbus: An Informal History of Italians in the New World* (1973).
Bacarella, Michael. *Lincoln's Foreign Legion: The 39th New York Infantry, The Garibaldi Guard* (1996).
Burton, William L. *Melting Pot Soldiers: The Union's Ethnic Regiments* (1988; reprint, 1998).
McFadden, Elizabeth. *The Gitter and the Gold: A Spirited Account of the Metropolitan Museum of Art's First Director, the Audacious and High-Handed Luigi Palma di Cesnola* (1971).
Schiavo, Giovanni. *Four Centuries of Italian American History* (1952).

IUKA, BATTLE OF
(19 September 1862)

During September 1862, north Mississippi was a center for troop movement. General Braxton Bragg, commander of the Army of Mississippi, ordered General Sterling Price's Army of the West to prevent the Federal army headquartered in Corinth from reinforcing General Don Carlos Buell in central Tennessee. Price contacted General Earl Van Dorn, inviting him to join forces. Although Van Dorn implored Price not to leave Mississippi, he advised Price that he could not be ready for a campaign until later in the month. Unable to wait for Van Dorn, Price began moving his army toward the Tennessee border.

Meanwhile, Federal forces guarding the Memphis & Charleston Railroad were also moving. With his advance into central Tennessee, Buell requested more reinforcements, and General Henry W. Halleck ordered General Ulysses S. Grant to send troops from his command. The only way Grant could afford to send troops was to pull a division from the guard of the railroad, which Halleck authorized. Grant sent word to William S. Rosecrans in Iuka, a small town thirty miles east of Corinth and near the Tennessee River, instructing him to send a division to Buell and pull the remaining two divisions from the railroad. Because of the many sick and the large amount of commissary stores in Iuka, Rosecrans delayed. After a succession of rumors that Price and Van Dorn, who was now at Holly Springs, were joining forces to attack Corinth, Grant ordered all troops back to Corinth.

On 14 September, the last regiment of Rosecrans's army evacuated Iuka as Price's Confederates occupied the town. Price immediately notified both Bragg and

Van Dorn that Iuka had been captured and Rosecrans had fallen back toward Corinth. By 17 September, Price heard nothing from Van Dorn, but Bragg had sent a dispatch. He feared that all of Rosecrans's army was in central Tennessee and again ordered Price to hurry. However, Price knew that at least a portion of Rosecrans's men were between Iuka and Corinth. Price sent a second dispatch to Van Dorn. Considering Bragg's directions, Price could no longer stay in Iuka. On 18 September, Van Dorn finally instructed Price to rendezvous with him in Pocahontas, Tennessee. Price made preparations to leave Iuka the next day.

Grant, after hearing that Price occupied Iuka, planned a combined attack and arranged his forces in the following manner. Rosecrans with Generals Charles S. Hamilton's and David S. Stanley's divisions was to move to Iuka from the south via the Fulton and Bay Springs roads. General E. O. C. Ord with approximately 8,000 troops was to approach from the west from Burnsville, where Grant made his headquarters. On 18 September, Ord was within six miles of Iuka and had orders to attack the following day. Rosecrans, who was delayed on the march, reported that he would not be able to attack until late on the 19th. Grant instructed Ord to wait until he heard the noise of battle before he moved.

By late afternoon on 19 September, Price learned that the Federal army under Rosecrans was marching up the Bay Springs Road. Deciding that the attack was going to take place south of Iuka, Price called General Henry Little's division from Ord's front to move into that area. At around 4:30 P.M., Little's force attacked Hamilton's division on the ridges about one and a half miles south of Iuka. The Confederates quickly advanced down a ridge and across a wooded ravine. At first, the Federals were able to fight off the strong Confederate attack, but despite heavy losses, the Confederates captured Sears's 11th Ohio Battery and drove the Federals back several yards. Rosecrans sent Colonel Joseph A. Mower's brigade of Stanley's division to assist Hamilton. The reinforced Federals finally halted the Confederate attack. While the battle raged, Ord sat poised to attack, but an acoustic shadow kept him from hearing the noise of the guns. Rosecrans fought alone.

That night, Price, convinced by Generals Dabney Maury and Louis Hébert that Grant would attack in force at daybreak, decided to escape Iuka. Price moved his troops southward down the Fulton Road, which Rosecrans had neglected to guard.

On the morning of 20 September, Grant received notice of the prior day's battle. He immediately sent Ord to Iuka, but he found Rosecrans already there. The Federals gave limited pursuit through the rugged countryside but suspected that Price and Van Dorn were already planning another attack for somewhere in Grant's district.

Total Federal casualties at the battle of Iuka numbered 782; Confederate losses were around 1,516.

—*Kristy Armstrong White*

See also Maury, Dabney Herndon; Ord, Edward; Price, Sterling; Rosecrans, William S.; Stanley, David.

For further reading:

Bearss, Edwin C. *Decision in Mississippi: Mississippi's Important Role in the War between the States* (1962).

Cozzens, Peter. *The Darkest Days of the War. The Battles of Iuka and Corinth* (1997).

Kitchens, Ben E. *Rosecrans Meets Price: The Battle of Iuka, Mississippi* (1987).

Snead, Thomas. "With Price East of the Mississippi." *Battles and Leaders of the Civil War* (1887).

IVERSON, ALFRED
(1798–1873)
Antebellum U.S. senator, fire-eater

Born to Robert Iverson and Rebecca Jones Iverson in Liberty County, Georgia, Alfred Iverson was educated at Princeton, from which he graduated in 1820. Returning to Georgia, he studied law and opened a practice in Clinton, Georgia. In addition to his legal practice, Iverson took an interest in Georgia Democratic politics and served several terms as a member of the Georgia legislature at the end of the 1820s.

A strong supporter of Indian removal, Iverson moved to the newly created Muscogee County as soon as the area was vacated by the Creek Indians. In a place of conflicting land claims and new towns, the law was a very lucrative profession, and Iverson soon became a leading citizen of the new town of Columbus, Georgia. He served two years on the state superior court from his circuit and was elected to the state legislature from Muscogee County in 1843.

By the 1840s, Iverson was identified with the states' rights wing of his party, and he used the local *Columbus Times* to advocate measures he considered beneficial to the South and to Georgia. National expansion was one way that Iverson believed the South could regain some of its lost power, and for that reason he supported not only the annexation of Texas but also further territorial gains from Mexico. He was able to express these views in a national forum when he won election to the U.S. House of Representatives in 1846. He served only one term in the House, but during that time, especially during the debates over the Wilmot Proviso, Iverson became convinced that the South's way of life was threatened by Northern aggression. After leaving Congress, he increasingly supported unified Southern state action to halt that perceived aggression and strongly supported the Nashville Convention held in the summer of 1850.

After leaving Congress, Iverson once again—this time for four years—served as superior court judge. In a sharply contested election pitting moderate Democrats against those of a more radical bent like Iverson, he won election to the U.S. Senate in 1854. In the Senate Iverson initially was only one of a small number of radical supporters of Southern rights. As a result, he often found himself at odds even with fellow Georgia senator Robert Toombs. Still he did not hesitate to speak out. One of his most famous efforts came in early 1859, when he seemed to advocate secession as the only alternative left to the South. Coming before the John Brown raid of October 1859 and before the dissolution of the Democratic Party the following year, this speech seemed radical indeed, even to most Southerners. Still, Iverson, rather than backing down, in an effort to make his views more clear to Georgians, made another speech at Griffin, Georgia, on 14 July 1859 that put him even more in the camp of the fire-eaters. In that speech he defended slavery as uplifting to all white men and an institution that must be defended with blood if necessary.

During the next year, helped in his efforts by the fear instilled in Georgia hearts by John Brown's raid on Harper's Ferry, Virginia (now West Virginia), Iverson spoke and worked tirelessly to defeat the Democratic nomination of Stephen Douglas for the presidency. Even moderate Southerners, feeling the change in the prevailing winds, determined on a plank in the Democratic platform that would provide protection for slavery in the territories. Iverson and fellow fire-eaters knew that with such a platform provision, Stephen Douglas could not possibly run on the Democratic ticket. The resulting split in the Democratic Party proved to be the last major effort in Iverson's political career.

After the election of Abraham Lincoln in the fall of 1860 and the subsequent secession of Georgia in January 1861, Iverson and Toombs resigned their Senate seats. Back home in Columbus, Georgia, Iverson increasingly withdrew from public life. When it appeared that he would be elected to the Confederate Senate in the fall of 1861, he removed his name from consideration. He devoted the war years to his legal practice, and after the war's close, he retired to Macon, Georgia. He died there on 4 March 1873. Iverson's son, Alfred Iverson, Jr., served in the Confederate army during the war and rose to the rank of brigadier general.

—*David S. Heidler and Jeanne T. Heidler*

See also Fire-eaters; Iverson, Alfred, Jr.

For further reading:
Carey, Anthony Gene. *Parties, Slavery and the Union in Antebellum Georgia* (1997).
"The Irrepressible Conflict." In *Great Debates in American History* (1970).

IVERSON, ALFRED, JR.
(1829–1911)
Confederate general

Born to Alfred Iverson and Caroline Holt Iverson in Clinton, Georgia, Alfred Iverson, Jr., was educated at a military school in Tuskegee, Alabama, but decided against a military career in favor of the law. While in the midst of this study as a teenager, he learned of the outbreak of the Mexican-American War and offered his services to a Georgia volunteer unit. He rose to the rank of second lieutenant during that conflict.

Upon his return to civilian life, Iverson continued with his legal studies, but increasingly came to see the military life as more suited to his temperament. Using his father's connections as a prominent Georgia politician, he gained a commission in the regular army in 1855. Assigned to the cavalry, Iverson served at a variety of frontier posts, in Kansas, and on Albert Sidney Johnston's Utah expedition. He ranked as a first lieutenant before the outbreak of the Civil War.

Iverson resigned his commission and returned home when he learned of the secession of Georgia. After the secession of North Carolina, Iverson was commissioned a captain in a North Carolina regiment and fought along the North Carolina coast early in the war. He was promoted to colonel of the 20th North Carolina in August 1861 and commanded that regiment over the next year.

In North Carolina Iverson and the 20th North Carolina fought in the division of Theophilus Hunter Holmes and went with Holmes when he was ordered to the York Peninsula in the spring of 1862. On the peninsula, Iverson fought in the first part of the Seven Days' battles, receiving a severe wound at Gaines' Mill. Stonewall Jackson and D. H. Hill commended him for his bravery in that battle.

Upon his recovery, Iverson returned to the command of the 20th, which was placed in the brigade of Samuel Garland for the Maryland campaign. When Garland was killed at South Mountain on 14 September 1862, Iverson temporarily succeeded to command of the brigade. He led his men at Antietam, after which Robert E. Lee recommended his promotion to brigadier general and that he be given permanent command of Garland's brigade. He was promoted on 1 November 1862.

At Fredericksburg Iverson commanded his brigade as part of D. H. Hill's division, Jackson's Corps. He and his men were in the thick of the fighting on the Confederate right in this engagement. Following the battle, when Hill was sent to North Carolina, Iverson and his brigade came under the command of Robert Rodes. During the battle of Chancellorsville, Iverson and his brigade, as part of Rodes's division, remained with Robert E. Lee on the Federal left during Jackson's famous flanking maneuver.

Iverson continued in Rodes's division, now Richard Ewell's Corps, for the invasion of Pennsylvania. He saw his heaviest fighting on the first day of the battle of Gettysburg, when Ewell's corps entered the battle from north of the town. During the late afternoon, much of his brigade became cut off from the remainder of the division and suffered tremendous casualties. Iverson was able to rally the remnant of his brigade and joined the pursuit of the Union forces to Cemetery Hill. He and his men remained in that position, engaging in some of the fighting around the base of the hill over the next two days. They were withdrawn on 4 July.

Following the Gettysburg campaign, Iverson's brigade was a shadow of its former self. Placed in the division of Edward Johnson for the next few months, Iverson was sent to Rome, Georgia, at the end of 1863.

As a native Georgian, Iverson, whose brigade had all but ceased to exist, seemed the ideal candidate to organize recruits in north Georgia. He spent the first few months of 1864 engaged in this activity, after which he was placed in command of a cavalry brigade in Joseph Wheeler's cavalry corps for the Atlanta campaign. In the early summer Iverson was promoted to division commander. On 30 July, he commanded the force that captured George Stoneman and 700 Union troopers outside Macon, Georgia, at Hillsboro during Stoneman's Georgia Raid.

Iverson continued to command his division through the latter phases of the Atlanta campaign. On 18 August he was dispatched to Griffin, Georgia, to provide a rendezvous point for all the cavalry that had been scattered during the campaign. As a result, Wheeler's cavalry was fairly intact when Sherman commenced his March to the Sea later in the fall. Iverson led his division in Wheeler's shadowing of Sherman's march, harassing the Union flanks and then watching the Federals' movements once they had occupied Savannah.

During the Carolina campaign of the winter and spring of 1865, Iverson led his division in the futile attempt to harry Sherman's march through those states. The end of the war found him at Greensborough, North Carolina, attempting to rally his disintegrating command. News of the surrenders of Lee and then Joseph Johnston caused him to give up the effort and go home to Georgia.

After the war, Iverson engaged in a variety of business pursuits in Macon, Georgia. In 1877 he moved to central Florida, where for the remainder of the century he was a prominent orange grower. He retired to Atlanta early in the twentieth century and died there on 31 March 1911.

—*David S. Heidler and Jeanne T. Heidler*

See also Atlanta Campaign; Stoneman's Georgia Raid (July 1869)

For further reading:
Castel, Albert. *Decision in the West: The Atlanta Campaign of 1864* (1992)

J

JACKSON, CLAIBORNE FOX
(1806–1862)
Fifteenth governor of Missouri

Missouri's prosecessionist governor, Claiborne Fox Jackson, was born on 4 April 1806 in Fleming County, Kentucky. He moved to Missouri in 1825 and worked in banking before becoming Missouri's first state bank commissioner. He served in Missouri's House from 1836 to 1848, in Missouri's Senate from 1848 to 1852, and as chairman of Missouri's Democratic Party. Initially allied with Senator Thomas Hart Benton, Jackson later helped engineer Benton's defeat over extending slavery into the territories. In 1860 Jackson ran for governor as a Douglas Democrat, winning a narrow victory over the Constitutional Unionists.

Jackson's inaugural speech in January 1861 ended any question of his political loyalties. He declared that Missouri's destiny lay with the Southern states and warned that Missouri would secede if the North attempted coercion against the South. Jackson cautiously worked to remove Missouri from the Union, urging the legislature to call a convention to debate the matter. To his dismay, however, Conditional Unionists dominated the convention and decided that secession was not warranted. Undaunted by this setback, Jackson continued to work for Missouri's eventual withdrawal from the Union. In April 1861, he refused to furnish troops for President Abraham Lincoln's call of 75,000 volunteers to put down the rebellion. Jackson declared Lincoln's action "illegal, unconstitutional, and revolutionary."

Jackson ordered the Missouri militia into training encampments during the first week in May, hoping to use them to seize the U.S. Arsenal in St. Louis when the opportunity presented itself. He also secretly sought arms from the Confederacy for this endeavor. Four Confederate guns arrived at Camp Jackson, the militia encampment just outside of St. Louis. By then, however, Captain Nathaniel Lyon had strengthened the arsenal's defenses, neutralizing any chance the militia had of taking the facility. Nevertheless, Lyon saw the militia's continued existence as a threat and demanded its surrender. The state forces capitulated without a struggle. As they were marched toward the arsenal, however, a riot broke out among the civilians in the streets, and twenty-eight persons were killed.

Reacting to these events and rumors of Federal invasion, the state legislature approved Jackson's proposals for reorganizing and funding the state militia. Jackson appointed Sterling Price to head the reorganized Missouri State Guard. Price and General William Harney, commander of the Department of the West, achieved an agreement designed to ease the crisis in Missouri; however, it failed to satisfy extremists. In a final attempt to find a peaceful solution to the crisis, Jackson and Price met with new Brigadier General Lyon and Francis Blair in St. Louis on 11 June 1861. Lyon, however, refused to compromise with Jackson, refused to honor the Price-Harney agreement, stated he would continue using Federal troops on state property at his discretion, and ended the meeting by declaring, "This means war."

Returning to Jefferson City, the governor called for 50,000 volunteers to defend Missouri against Federal encroachment. Jackson's forces abandoned the capital, deciding it could not be defended against Lyon. Lyon occupied Jefferson City and then attacked Jackson's forces, routing the State Guard at Boonville on 17 June 1861. Jackson led his forces toward the southwestern corner of the state to regroup, defeating a Union force under Franz Sigel at Carthage along the way. Jackson traveled to Richmond, Virginia, in mid-July 1861 to consult with Jefferson Davis before returning to New Madrid, Missouri. There he learned that the old secession convention had reconvened at Jefferson City, deposed the state's top three officials and the General Assembly, and appointed a provisional government under Hamilton Gamble.

After the Confederate victories at Wilson's Creek and Lexington, Jackson called the legislature to meet at Neosho. On 28 October 1861, the assembly, some have claimed lacking a quorum, passed an ordinance of secession. Exactly one month later, the Confederate Congress formally accepted Missouri as its twelfth state.

The battle of Pea Ridge ended immediate hopes of retaking Missouri. Jackson established a temporary capital at Camden, Arkansas. In July 1862, he met with the governors from Louisiana, Texas, and Arkansas over

the situation in the Trans-Mississippi Department. Jackson established reception camps along Missouri's border for refugees fleeing the state and dealt with financial and military issues that surfaced. Throughout the exile, however, the power of the governor's office deteriorated. Jackson expended most of the government funds. He failed to keep the offices running continuously, and its records were scattered across three states.

Already suffering from tuberculosis and stomach cancer, Jackson died of pneumonia in Little Rock on 7 December 1862. Thomas Reynolds succeeded him on 14 February 1863.

—*James G. Downhour*

See also Boonville, Missouri, Battle of; Gamble, Hamilton; Lyon, Nathaniel; Missouri; Price, Sterling.

For further reading:
Kilpatrick, Arthur Roy. "Missouri's Secession Government, 1861–1865." *Missouri Historical Review* (1951).
Laughlin, Sceva B. *Missouri Politics during the Civil War* (1930).
Lyon, William H. "Claiborne Fox Jackson and the Secession Crisis in Missouri." *Missouri Historical Review* (1964).
Yearns, Buck, ed. *The Confederate Governors* (1985).

JACKSON, MISSISSIPPI, BATTLE OF
(14 May 1863)

After the Union victory at Raymond, Mississippi, on 12 May 1863, Ulysses S. Grant, commander of the Army of the Tennessee, changed his mind about the next objective in his Vicksburg campaign. The original plan called for a move north on Edwards Station, a depot town along the Vicksburg & Jackson Railroad. Instead of putting his army into a potentially dangerous position between two Confederate forces of unknown strength, one to the west around Vicksburg and the other to the east at Jackson, Mississippi, Grant chose to implement a Napoleonic strategy of preventing the unification of enemy forces and defeating each in detail. This would prevent the Confederate forces from uniting or attacking him simultaneously, which could possibly give the Rebels a numerical advantage.

The defense offered by the Confederates at Raymond concerned Grant because he realized he had no idea of the number of the growing Confederate forces arriving at Jackson. Grant did not risk his army in a piecemeal attack on Jackson. To minimize the surprise factor, and thus defeat the Confederates, Grant committed his entire army to the move on Jackson, the state capital and an important rail junction, which connected Mississippi to the rest of the seceded states to the north and east. Another benefit of such a move was that the majority of supplies reaching Vicksburg came through Jackson. Grant turned his entire army ninety degrees to the right (now the army was facing to the east), leaving forces in his rear to secure his flank, and moved in the direction of Jackson.

Grant's final plan for the move on Jackson involved a simultaneous attack on 14 May by two of his three corps. Major General James B. McPherson's XVII Corps attacked from Clinton, Mississippi, nine miles to the west, while Major General William T. Sherman's XV Corps moved on Jackson from the direction of Raymond from the southwest. The XIII Corps under Major

The Battle of Jackson, Mississippi (*Library of Congress*)

General John A. McClernand, moved north to the vicinity of Bolton Depot, eight miles to the west of Clinton, and established a strong position in case of a move east by the Vicksburg forces.

On 9 May 1863, General Joseph E. Johnston received orders from the War Department in Richmond stating that he was to take overall command of the Mississippi defenses and promising him reinforcement to help him in this endeavor. Johnston arrived in Jackson on 13 May, the day after the battle of Raymond. Realizing the deteriorating Confederate position in Mississippi due to the central position of the Army of the Tennessee between the two main Confederate forces, Johnston ordered Jackson to be evacuated. To allow the Confederates an orderly withdrawal and removal of much needed supplies, Johnston ordered Brigadier General John Gregg to cover the retreat.

Gregg had under his command about 6,000 troops to carry out the holding action. He had his troops deploy in front of the previously prepared positions across the two main roads heading into Jackson from the west. The leading force of McPherson's corps made contact with Confederate pickets around 9 A.M. on 14 May. McPherson ordered his troops to deploy into formation, but halted the attack until the heavy rain abated. He was afraid that the ammunition would be too damp to work properly, needlessly exposing his troops to higher casualties or dooming the assault to failure.

Gregg at first knew only of the federal column coming toward Jackson from the west. The delay in McPherson's advance allowed Gregg time to learn of a second Federal force heading toward Jackson from the southwest. Sherman's corps forced Gregg to redeploy his forces, spreading them even thinner in the defense of Jackson. At 10 A.M. McPherson ordered his artillery into action, although still reluctant to commit his corps. On hearing the guns, Sherman ordered his leading division to press forward. The Confederates were easily routed by an artillery bombardment and retired into the fieldworks surrounding the city. Ten artillery pieces were able to delay Sherman's advance for more than two hours.

In the meantime, the rain let up and McPherson ordered his leading division, Brigadier General Marcellus Crocker's, to advance on the Confederate position around 11:00 A.M. From the volume of fire, McPherson correctly concluded that the rebel force was relatively small. A bayonet charge was ordered. After some intense fighting, the superior number of the Federals caused the Confederates to break and to retreat into the earthworks. Sherman sent a reconnaissance force forward to check the extent of the Confederate presence and discovered that the left flank of the rebel defenses was unstaffed. The Union troops exploited this weakness and quickly captured the guns and their operators.

McPherson was reorganizing his force for an attack on the Confederate position when the skirmishers reported back that the trenches were empty. About 2:00 P.M. Johnston sent word to Gregg that the army trains had vacated the city, and Gregg ordered his troops to evacuate their positions and escape north of town. Around 4:00 P.M. Union troops entered the city. Leaving Sherman's corps behind to destroy the railroads and warmaking capacity of Jackson, Grant could now turn west and focus on the Confederate forces defending Vicksburg. In the battle, the total of killed, wounded, missing, and captured Federals was approximately 300 casualties; for the Confederates, 845 casualties.

—*James L. Isemann*

See also Johnston, Joseph Eggleston; Raymond, Battle of; Vicksburg Campaign.

For further reading:

Arnold, James R. *Grant Wins the War: Decision at Vicksburg* (1997).

Miers, Earl Schenck. *The Web of Victory: Grant at Vicksburg* (1955; reprint 1983).

Welcher, Frank J. *The Union Army, 1861–1865: Organization and Operations Volume II: The Western Theater* (1993).

JACKSON, MISSISSIPPI, CAPTURE OF
(9–16 July 1863)

Following the surrender of John C. Pemberton's army at Vicksburg on 4 July 1863, General Joseph E. Johnston, the Confederate department commander, fell back on Jackson, the state capital, with the forces he had collected to relieve the siege. Johnston felt it essential to hold that city for the Confederacy to maintain a position in Mississippi. Reaching Jackson on 7 July, his four infantry divisions took up a defensive line on the west side of town in the works prepared by Pemberton earlier in the year. From north to south, beginning where the railroad entered the city, Johnston placed the divisions of William W. Loring, William H. T. Walker, Samuel G. French, and—carried back around to where the railroad exited Jackson on the south—the division of John C. Breckinridge. William H. "Red" Jackson's cavalry division was posted to watch the fords of the Pearl River north and south of Jackson. Confederate effective strength was about 26,000 of all arms. Characteristically, Johnston described his defenses as a "very light line of rifle pits...very badly located and constructed." In his report to Grant, Sherman wrote that the works were "enlarged and much strengthened [with] well constructed embrasures of sod and cotton bales."

While still engaged at Vicksburg, Grant had alerted Sherman to be prepared to move to drive Johnston out of Mississippi and complete the destruction of the Rebel infrastructure in the state. Sherman left Vicksburg on 4 July with three army corps, 40,000 men in nine divisions. He had his own XV Corps under Major General

Fred Steele; XIII Corps, led by Major General E. O. C. Ord; and Major General John G. Parke's IX Corps. Brigadier General Jacob Lauman's division of XVI Corps was attached to Ord. The Union army arrived at Jackson on 9 July and by the following day had dug in facing the Confederate defenses, with Ord on the right, Steele in the center, and Parke on the left. Johnston expected an immediate attack, but Sherman settled down to shell and skirmish with Johnston's outnumbered but entrenched army. The Union plan was to extend their lines gradually around one flank or the other and eventually threaten Johnston's line of communication to the east, thus forcing a Confederate withdrawal.

On 12 July, a weak and unsupported attack was made on Breckinridge's front, Sherman's extreme right, by Colonel Isaac Pugh's brigade of Lauman's division, but it was easily repulsed. Ord reported to Sherman that the attack had been made by Lauman without his knowledge, without orders, without coordination, and without preparation. Lauman was relieved from duty. The attacking brigade lost almost 500 out of 880 engaged. Other skirmishes occurred along the front for the next three days.

On 14 July, learning that a large train-load of artillery ammunition had left Vicksburg enroute to Jackson, Johnston dispatched W. H. Jackson's cavalry division to intercept the train, but the attempt was unsuccessful. In anticipation of the expected bombardment and attack, Johnston felt that defense would be hopeless, and he ordered the evacuation of Jackson. This was carried out in secrecy on the night of 16 July, the army first withdrawing four miles to Brandon and then back to Morton, thirty miles east of Jackson, on 19 July. As Johnston retreated eastward, Sherman followed for a few miles before abandoning the chase.

While the siege had been going on, Sherman had been busy at the task of destroying railroads, rolling stock, and means of production. Rails were torn up and cars destroyed as far as sixty miles north or south of Jackson. After Jackson fell, a large part of the city went up in flames. Sherman reported to Grant that Jackson was "one mass of charred ruins." The Yankee soldiers referred to the city as "Chimneyville."

Johnston reported a total loss of 600 during the seven-day siege. Union losses at Jackson amounted to 1,122, the largest single cause being the botched attack on 12 July.

—*Russell K. Brown*

See also Jackson, Mississippi, Battle; Vicksburg Campaign.

For further reading:
Govan, Gilbert E, and James W. Livingood. *A Different Valor: The Story of General Joseph E. Johnston, C.S.A.* (1956).

Johnston, Joseph E. *Narrative of Military Operations Directed during the Late War between the States* (1959).

Official Records, ser. I, vol. 24, pt. 2 (Serial 37), The Jackson Campaign.

Symonds, Craig L. *Joseph E. Johnston: A Civil War Biography* (1992).

JACKSON, THOMAS JONATHAN
(1824–1863)
Confederate lieutenant general

Thomas Jonathan Jackson was known as "Stonewall," but "the Christian soldier" would have been a more appropriate title. His military experience was in artillery, yet he excelled as a commander of infantry. Soldiers adored him, despite the fact that he was a tight-lipped, stern-disciplined eccentric. Fellow generals were in awe of him because his silence concealed a fiery combativeness smoldering deep inside. Although he was in the field but two years during the Civil War, he more than any other individual became the radiant hope of the Southern cause. More astounding are the number of people—past and present—who assert that had he not died in 1863, his genius would have enabled the Confederate States to achieve their independence. Such was the mystique of Thomas J. Jackson.

His life personifies the American rags-to-riches story. It began with a childhood so sad that Jackson would not talk about it except with the women he loved.

Jackson was born near midnight on 20–21 January 1824, at the village of Clarksburg in the mountains of what was then northwestern Virginia. His father, Jonathan Jackson, was a struggling, ne'er-do-well attorney whose debts overwhelmed the obligations of caring for a young wife and three small children. Thomas was only two when his father and a sister died of typhoid fever. For four years Mrs. Julia Neale Jackson and her children were wards of the town of Clarksburg. Young Tom Jackson's clothing consisted of a torn shirt and one pair of ragged trousers.

His mother remarried, but Jackson's stepfather was financially unable to care for the children. Hence, they were sent individually to live with relatives. Jackson's mother died within a year. At an early age, the boy was an orphan too familiar with death.

He grew up at Jackson's Mill, the family estate some twenty miles south of Clarksburg. Jackson was under the care of an uncle, Cummins E. Jackson, who ran lumber and grist mills, raised crops and livestock, operated a racetrack, and pursued other businesses—all with little regard for honesty or decency. Cummins Jackson gave his nephew security; he was incapable of the familial love a lonely boy needed. Tom Jackson became accustomed to hard work. He also became a loner—shy, withdrawn, and introspective. What education he received came from a love of reading and local tutors who taught him basic rudiments from time to time.

In 1842, Jackson secured an appointment to the U.S. Military Academy. The opportunity came only because the boy who had originally been picked from his congressional district decided against a military education. Few

Thomas J. "Stonewall" Jackson following the Mexican-American War (*left*) and during the Civil War (*right*) (*Library of Congress*)

youths have ever entered West Point with less academic preparation than 18-year-old Tom Jackson. In appearance and personality, he was an awkward, almost comical mountaineer devoid of social graces. No one gave young Jackson much chance of completing the requirements at what was then America's finest engineering college. Yet no one was aware of the iron self-discipline inside the unimpressive lad.

Jackson realized that West Point probably offered him the only chance for a college education that he would ever have. If he could graduate, a respectable career as an army officer would elevate him far above his orphan background. So the proud mountain boy developed impassivity as a protection while he concentrated all of his energies on the single purpose of learning.

For four years Jackson did little else but study. He pored over his books at night by the light of the coal fire in his room until, a classmate said, he literally burned the lessons in his brain. They remained there. Jackson never forgot anything.

He made few friends, took no part in extracurricular activities, attained no cadet rank. He allowed himself solitary walks, and he was a faithful correspondent with his sister, Laura, back in Virginia. Those were the only "diversions" Jackson allowed himself to have.

Resolution, patience, and constant study overcame all the handicaps that Jackson had faced. In the graduating class of 1846, he ranked seventeenth among fifty-nine seniors. Professors and cadets alike were unanimous in their opinion that had the curriculum lasted one more year, the orphan boy from the mountains would have been number one in his class.

At West Point, Jackson began jotting down in a small notebook one-line statements of life that he encountered here and there. What became the most famous of those quotations was also a testimonial to his four years at the Academy: "You may be what ever you will resolve to be."

War with Mexico was under way when Jackson entered the U.S. Army as a lieutenant in the 3d Artillery Regiment. At a time when the average man was five feet, seven inches tall and weighed 135 pounds, Jackson stood a full six feet and carried 175 pounds. He had an extended forehead, a sharp nose, unusually large hands and feet, and a surprisingly high-pitched voice. The physical feature that attracted instant attention were pale blue eyes that stared at everything with deep intensity.

Jackson's battery was in reserve for the first six months after arriving in Mexico. The young lieutenant despaired of ever knowing the emotions of battle. Then, in March 1847, he saw his first action at Vera Cruz;

thereafter, he was in the thick of the fighting at Contreras and Chapultepec. Within seven months, Jackson gained three brevet promotions for gallantry under fire. None of his classmates achieved as much, and no American officer received more citations for valor.

For the next two years, Major Jackson performed uneventful duties at various army posts in New York. It was at the first of these assignments—Fort Hamilton—that his interest in religion emerged to the forefront. A reader of the Bible since his teenage years, Jackson now pursued a search for a religious home. He received baptism at an Episcopal church near Fort Hamilton, and he attended different services at various churches. None fulfilled his spiritual needs.

Although still an artillery officer, Jackson was also an assistant quartermaster at most of the posts to which he was sent. His most frequent duties were courts-martial. Such appointments took him to a number of military installations in New York and Pennsylvania. In his spare time, Jackson preferred reading. History was his favorite subject, Napoleon his favorite figure. Jackson also maintained a steady correspondence with his beloved sister, Laura. By then she had married and was living in Beverly in northwestern Virginia. For the next ten years, Jackson would make periodic visits to Beverly. He was very close to Laura, and he exhibited a growing affection for her small son, Thomas Jackson Arnold.

Concerns over health became a near obsession with Jackson. Stomach disorders and weak eyesight were the chief disorders, but Jackson was convinced at one time or other that every one of his organs was malfunctioning to some degree. He attributed his troubles as punishment from God for his sins. Jackson, like so many of his contemporaries, treated himself with a wide variety of medications. He also sought relief from several New York physicians.

The result of all the dosages, ministrations, and exercises was a twofold regimen that Jackson followed. To curb the pangs of dyspepsia, he ate only those things he did not like—and in small quantities. His strict diet actually brought an improvement over that ailment. To aid in combating all of his other physical problems, Jackson became an ardent devotee of hydrotherapy. He regularly visited spas in the summertime and became convinced that two or three weeks in such heavy water was quite beneficial.

In December 1850, Jackson's artillery company transferred to duty at Fort Meade in the remote interior of Florida. The isolation and the boredom of that assignment, in addition to Jackson's growing devotion to the word of God, were all instrumental in a bitter disagreement between Jackson and his superior, Major William H. French. Each soon filed formal accusations of misconduct against the other. At least one court-martial seemed imminent.

Such proceedings never occurred, because Jackson left the army. In the midst of the explosive situation, he received an offer to join the faculty of the Virginia Military Institute (VMI). Located at Lexington in the upper (southern) end of the Shenandoah Valley, the academy, barely 12 years old, was small and somewhat unproven. Yet it offered Jackson a new life, a change of scenery, and an opportunity to return to western Virginia. He arrived in Lexington in late summer 1851 and entered a new world as a college professor.

Jackson spent a fourth of his life at VMI. While his name and that of the Institute are permanently intertwined, it was not because of performance in the section room. Unfamiliar with the subject matter he was to teach (Natural and Experimental Philosophy), and equally unfamiliar with teaching young boys, Jackson struggled for years to be effective in the classroom. He was forced to study as he taught, because topics in his course such as magnetism, acoustics, astronomy, and physics were alien to him. Mastering the subject was bad enough; learning how to present it was even more difficult. Jackson, a stickler for discipline, expected the same from students. Indifferent to opinions, he also lacked warmth and humor. Poor eyesight led him to memorize his lectures the day before he delivered them. Class presentation was a high-pitched monotone. If questioned on a point by a student, he was unable to respond with a different approach. Jackson could only repeat verbatim what he had just said. Finally, he never seemed to realize that he was dealing with immature boys, not soldiers accustomed to receiving orders.

Students initially took an instant dislike to him. Cadets referred to him as "Tom Fool," "Old Blue Light," "Hell and Thunder," "crazy as damnation," "the worst teacher that God ever made," and similar derogations. They played pranks on Jackson and scoffed with frustration because he never seemed aware of anything out of the ordinary.

"The Major" brought much of this on himself because of a number of eccentricities that he regularly exhibited. Without warning, he sometimes would thrust his arm into the air and make several, violent pumping motions with it—to create better blood circulation, he explained. On occasion, Jackson would forget to eat; he was known to wear winter clothing in the summer and vice versa; he walked with exaggerated strides, never looking right or left. Always did he seem wrapped in an inner concentration which no one could pierce for any length of time. His reticence led him at times to stare at a blank wall for hours.

On the other hand, Jackson displayed a number of positive qualities. He was honest to a fault, a careful businessman, neatly dressed at all times, conscientious in everything he did, and pleasant in the confines of small, private gatherings. VMI cadets came to see good qualities in him both as a teacher and as a leader. The ridicule of freshmen evolved to respect by seniors.

Within three months after arriving in Lexington, Jackson found his religious home. He joined the Presbyterian faith and rapidly became one of the most devout Calvinists of his day. Jackson attended every service at the Lexington Presbyterian Church. (To the amusement of the congregation, he slept through every service. Yet he would sit bolt upright, his back never touching the pew. This was self-induced pain he inflicted for the sin of not being able to stay awake.)

Jackson's major contributions to the Lexington church were threefold. He organized a young men's Sunday school class that still exists; he established a Sunday afternoon Bible class for slaves of all ages in the area; and he was appointed one of three deacons in the church.

So faithfully did Jackson honor the Sabbath that he would not read or talk of secular matters on the Lord's Day. Jackson found solace in prayer, which he offered throughout his waking hours, and strength in faith, because he knew that God was always there as a friend and helper.

His favorite scripture was Romans 8:28: "And we know that all things work together for good to them that love God, to them who are the called according to *his* purpose." His favorite hymn was "Amazing Grace," but he could not explain why. He was completely tone-deaf. Most of all, Jackson bore his faith as if it were the sole staff of life. "Never have I known a holier man," his best friend remarked. "Never have I seen a human being as thoroughly governed by duty. He lived only to please God; his daily life was a daily offering up of himself."

In 1853, at age twenty-nine, Jackson fell in love for the first time in his life. Elinor Junkin was the daughter of a Presbyterian clergyman. Their marriage was joyful, faithful, and tragically short. Elinor died in childbirth fourteen months after the marriage. The son she was bearing also perished. Only Jackson's faith sustained him in the tragedy. That same faith led quickly to a second tragedy.

Jackson and "Ellie's" favorite sister Margaret gravitated to one another in their common grief. They came to enjoy one another's company with growing ardor. Friendship ripened into love. However, by the tenets of the Presbyterian Church of that era, a person's in-laws were his family. His sister-in-law, "Maggie," thus in the eyes of the Church was his sister. Marriage was impossible. Once again Jackson endured pangs of sorrow and emptiness.

Within a year, he found a second wife. Anna Morrison also was a Presbyterian minister's daughter. She and Jackson had known each other casually for several years. The VMI professor waged a courtship with all the fervor of a military operation. Thomas and Anna married in July 1857. This second marriage lasted for the remainder of Jackson's life. To Anna he opened his heart in complete trust and gentle tenderness. However, their first child, a daughter, died shortly after birth.

The Jacksons had just settled into the only home he ever owned when, in the autumn of 1859, rumblings of disunion came closer and grew louder. Abolitionist John Brown led a bloody raid on the arsenal at Harper's Ferry, Virginia. A Marine detachment from Washington quickly crushed the uprising. In December, Jackson led part of the VMI corps of cadets to Charles Town to serve as a gallows guard for the public hanging of Brown.

Basically apolitical in nature, Jackson watched the growing national crisis from two perspectives. He considered the United States as established by the Constitution of 1787 to be a gift of God; conversely, any attempts to change the nature or language of that union Jackson regarded as heresy. Second, Virginia was his birthright. A federal government in Washington, D.C., took care of "housekeeping chores" such as delivering the mail. It had no business interfering with the affairs of the Old Dominion, which had existed for 180 years before a nation came into being.

The increasing unrest worried Jackson. In January 1860, he wrote to an aunt, "I think we have great reason for alarm, but my trust is in God; and I cannot think that he will permit the madness of men to interfere so materially with the Christian labors of this country."

Jackson believed in the right of secession but not in its practice to adjust national wrongs. Yet when Virginia left the Union, he promptly did the same. On 20 April 1861, he departed Lexington with a contingent of cadets who were to serve as drillmasters for the thousands of recruits flocking to Richmond. Jackson would never see his adopted hometown again. It had been fourteen years since he had last experienced combat. Yet Jackson swept into war with a cool professionalism that reflected devotion to duty and confidence in himself.

None of that was obvious in his appearance. For the first year of the war, he wore the threadbare blue coat of a VMI faculty member, a battered kepi cap that seemed to rest on the bridge of his nose, and enormous boots that reached above his knees. While he never made mention in the war of his dyspeptic condition, weak eyesight and a hearing impairment (the result of an attack of neuralgia) were ever-present.

Faith molded Jackson the soldier. He viewed the Civil War as a test of allegiance to God. For reasons man could not know, the Almighty had ordained that America undergo a trial by fire. The war, for the faithful, was a religious crusade, because God would surely bless the side that most obeyed His word.

Jackson viewed Christian faith and the Confederate cause as one and the same. While some generals aspired to be another Napoleon or Frederick the Great, Jackson's inspirations were Joshua, Gideon, and David. To be worthy of New Testament love, Jackson believed, he must fight with Old Testament fury.

It took awhile for Jackson to put that faith into practice. After reaching Richmond in late April 1861, he

received an appointment as colonel of infantry. His first assignment was to take command of gaudily dressed militia and inexperienced recruits gathering at Harper's Ferry. The new post commander wasted no time in putting Harper's Ferry into good military trim. Units accustomed to occasional parades underwent hours of daily drill; incompetent officers were sent home; all liquor in the town was poured into the streets; furloughs were nonexistent; men lived by a schedule; their camps were orderly and clean. Those who made honest mistakes were taught the correct way of doing things. Those who violated the rules knowingly received harsh punishment. Jackson expected his soldiers to share his rigid devotion to duty. He neither took leave nor granted it. (Throughout his Civil War career, he never spent a night away from army duty.)

An officer who returned to Harper's Ferry a short time after Jackson took command exclaimed, "What a revolution three or four days had wrought! I could scarcely realize the change."

The colonel ensured that Harper's Ferry was properly fortified. With an artilleryman's eye, Jackson saw at once that the key to defending Harper's Ferry (and the Shenandoah Valley) was to place cannon atop commanding South Mountain across the Potomac River. Unfortunately, South Mountain was in Maryland, a neutral state. Jackson thought expediency more valuable than politics. The guns went into position. His action in violating neutrality for the sake of security was a factor in President Jefferson Davis's dispatching General Joseph E. Johnston to replace Jackson as post commandant.

On 3 July 1861, Jackson received appointment as a brigadier general. His command was the 1st Virginia Brigade, five regiments raised in the Shenandoah Valley region. The unit's first duty was in destroying sections of the Baltimore & Ohio Railroad. Jackson did a thorough job; yet, he wrote his wife, "If the cost of the property could only have been expended in disseminating the gospel of the Prince of Peace."

The new general and his troops acquired the most famous nickname in American military history in the Civil War's first major battle. On 21 July 1861, on high ground overlooking Bull Run near Manassas Junction, Union and Confederate forces waged an all-day fight. Jackson carefully placed his regiments behind the brow of the highest eminence and waited. Soon, shattered Confederate forces retired to the base of the hill, with Federals in close pursuit. Confederate general Barnard Bee attempted to rally his broken units by pointing to the hilltop and shouting, "Look, men! There stands Jackson like a stone wall! Rally behind the Virginians!"

Jackson stood firm a while longer, then launched an attack as Federals advanced up Henry House Hill. A late-afternoon counterattack by fresh Southern troops sent Union soldiers staggering from the field. Jackson

urged a pursuit of the Federals into Washington itself. Yet authorities were content with the day's success. The South had gained a stunning triumph and found a hero as well.

While many generals welcomed national attention, Jackson was uncomfortable in the spotlight. He did not particularly like the name "Stonewall." It certainly proved to be a misnomer, for more often he would be the hammer rather than the anvil.

In the weeks that followed, the North mobilized for full-scale war while the South languished in a victor's light. Jackson's brigade lay quietly in encampment near Centreville until early November, when Jackson was promoted to major general and given command of the Shenandoah Valley district. The general established his headquarters at Winchester, collected a small force and, on 1 January 1862, began an expedition to clear Federals from river and railroad installations to the west.

This Romney campaign bordered on a disaster. Sleet, snow, and strong winds turned the march into a nightmare. Jackson ignored the weather and pushed forward. The farther he marched, the angrier he became at the heathen in his front. He railed against "the conduct of the reprobate Federal commanders who … have not only burned valuable mill property, but also many private houses.… The number of dead animals lying along the roadside, where they had been shot by the enemy, exemplified the spirit of that part of the Northern army."

The Confederates occupied the town of Romney and removed all Federal menaces from the area. A satisfied Jackson left General William Loring's troops to occupy Romney and returned to Winchester with the rest of his command.

Loring immediately began complaining of isolation and hardships. The complaints went directly to the War Department in Richmond. Secretary of War Judah Benjamin conferred with President Davis, then ordered Jackson to recall Loring's men to Winchester. Jackson did so at once—and submitted his resignation from the army because of what he regarded as unwarranted interference with his authority. A storm of public outcry followed. Virginia governor John Letcher and other friends persuaded Jackson to remain in command. Loring was transferred elsewhere, and that was the last time Confederate authorities interfered with Jackson's responsibilities.

This incident revealed much of Jackson the general. He was a man of unbending determination and self-confidence. The principal object of life, he maintained, was the discharge of duty. While his men came to look on him with wonder and to refer to him affectionately as "Old Jack," the general's relations with his immediate subordinates was often stormy. He expected blind obedience because he gave it himself. He kept division and brigade commanders uninformed of movements because he viewed secrecy as one of the most valuable of military weapons. If friends did not know where he was going, Jackson once commented, enemies surely would not know either.

Such a policy left subordinates in the dark and created friction. Jackson ignored the unrest. He wanted his forces to be "an army of the living God," he told his wife. Fighting for the Almighty, Jackson cared little about wounding the pride of his officers.

Jackson's greatest achievement may have been the 1862 Shenandoah Valley campaign. His responsibilities were twofold: to block any Union advance southward up the Shenandoah and to prevent Federal forces in that area from joining General George B. McClellan's massive army then advancing slowly up the peninsula toward Richmond. The War Department had only to suggest an offensive. Jackson took it. One of the Confederacy's better generals later declared that Jackson "suddenly broke loose ... & not only astonished the weak minds of the enemy almost into paralysis, but dazzled the eyes of military men all over the world by an aggressive campaign which I believe to be unsurpassed in all military history for brilliancy & daring."

On 23 March, at Kernstown just south of Winchester, Jackson attacked a Federal force preparing to depart the valley. Union brigades repelled the Confederate assaults, yet Jackson's sudden activity caused Washington authorities to become uncertain of the situation in the Shenandoah.

Three Federal armies totaling 64,000 men were soon moving against Jackson from north, west, and east. With never more than 17,000 troops, Jackson unhesitatingly went after each. His principal weapons were secrecy, knowledge of the valley's terrain, hard marches, an uncanny ability to deliver heavy attacks at unexpected points, singleness of purpose with each thrust, and an abiding trust that God's will was behind his efforts.

Late in April, Jackson momentarily disappeared from Federal view. He reappeared on 8 May by blocking Union general John C. Frémont's advance at McDowell, west of the vital railroad town of Staunton. Jackson disappeared again. His "foot cavalry" (as the infantrymen proudly dubbed themselves) marched rapidly down the valley and, on 23 May, overpowered the Union garrison at Front Royal. The main Union army, under General Nathaniel P. Banks, desperately retired to Winchester. There, on 25 May, Jackson's onslaught drove the enemy not only from Winchester but all the way across the Potomac River.

Officials in Washington hastily diverted troops toward the valley, motivated partly by apprehension for the Northern capital and partly by the desire to use converging columns to trap Jackson between Winchester and Harper's Ferry. Union armies under Frémont and James Shields then sought to squeeze Jackson from east and west. The Confederate commander escaped the trap by an incredible march up the valley to a point east of Harrisonburg. Skillfully burning bridges to keep the two Union armies separated, Jackson patiently awaited their arrival. He struck Frémont on 8 June at Cross Keys and Shields on 9 June at Port Republic. Victories in both engagements cleared the valley of Union forces and ended the campaign.

The fruits of victory were many. Jackson had inflicted over 5,000 casualties and captured 9,000 small arms and tons of supplies, while losing only 3,100 troops (half of whom were captured). A dread of "Jackson in the rear" paralyzed thousands of Union soldiers who might have reinforced McClellan's army at the gates of Richmond. A New York newspaper grudgingly stated, "He handles his army like a whip, making it crack in out of the way corners where you scarcely thought the lash would reach."

The test of a good general is morale inside the ranks. Jackson instilled high spirits among his soldiers. They viewed him as a military mastermind ordained by God to gain victory in battle. His skill implanted pride, unconquerable spirit, and elitism among the men. To be a member of "Jackson's foot cavalry" set them a cut above all other soldiers.

In addition, Jackson's Valley campaign demonstrated that this strange, complex, seemingly lonely Presbyterian was one of those generals who performed best when the immediate situation was entirely in his control. While Jackson did not have to be completely in charge of everything, he wanted to be in command of the immediate task he was performing. Jackson could execute any assignment as long as he had complete control within his sphere. Ultimately self-reliant, never seeking advice (nor giving it, unless requested to do so), he earned his reputation and, in the process, created his legend.

Once asked his formula for success, Jackson looked back at his campaign in the Shenandoah and replied, "Always mystify, mislead and surprise the enemy, if possible; and when you strike and overcome him, never let up in the pursuit so long as your men have the strength to follow; for an army routed, if hotly pursued, becomes panic-stricken, and can then be destroyed by half their number. The other rule is, never fight against heavy odds, if by any possible maneuvering you can hurl your own force on only a part, and that the weakest part, of your enemy and crush it. Such tactics will win every time, and a small army may thus destroy a large one in detail, and repeated victory will make it invincible."

Jackson gave the South a much-needed hero at a critical point in the war. Yet no time existed after the Valley campaign to rest on laurels. General Robert E. Lee, the new commander of the South's principal army, had watched the valley operations with fascination and pleasure. While others saw Jackson as a strange, rough-hewn leader, Lee saw in Jackson a kindred spirit who adhered to one of his own basic axioms: namely, that the

inferior side must always be daring and willing to fight when the opportunity presented itself. Lee thereupon ordered Jackson to bring his forces to the Richmond front for a major counteroffensive against the Union Army of the Potomac.

The ensuing Seven Days' campaign was a Confederate victory that brought instant fame to Lee. Yet Jackson's performance was at least disappointing and at most controversial. The root of the problem with Jackson was utter fatigue. He had had no rest since the end of April, almost two months previously. Unfamiliarity with the terrain, poor communication with headquarters, and misunderstandings at high command were other factors present in this first major offensive by the Army of Northern Virginia.

Jackson was a day behind schedule at the start. Inexplicable delays marked his movements; his famed "foot cavalry" crawled across country that was low, wet, and alien. Jackson never reached the opening engagement on 26 June at Mechanicsville. He was tardy the following day at the battle of Gaines' Mill. On 30 June, Jackson seemed to become lethargic at White Oak Swamp. He failed to attack the high ground in his front or to lend any assistance to Confederates engaged in a severe fight a few miles away at Glendale. The brilliant tactician in the valley was glaringly absent in Lee's first campaign.

Lee made no censure of Jackson. Perhaps the army commander saw the genius inside the shy, uncommunicative, humorless officer who would become his principal lieutenant for the next eleven months. Lee learned to give Jackson plenty of latitude in movements. His confidence was well founded. After the Seven Days', Jackson won new laurels with each succeeding engagement, for, like Lee, Jackson seized the initiative, divided enemy forces, and fought to destroy rather than merely to defeat.

In mid-July, Lee dispatched Jackson's forces to central Virginia. A second Union army, under General John Pope, was advancing on Richmond from the northwest. Jackson struck the van of that army on 9 August at Cedar Mountain. In the fighting, Jackson personally rallied part of his command before Confederates sent beaten Federals reeling northward.

The Jackson of the Shenandoah Valley had replaced the Jackson of the Chickahominy. He again had become the Confederate man of the hour. A Georgia lieutenant spoke for the whole army when he wrote his wife, "O my dear, I wish you could just see him. See him before or after a battle as he passes the boys. They will run two hundred yards just to see him and yell like wildcats. He invariably, when they cheer him, uncovers his head and dashes along at a rapid pace glancing his proud eagle eye from side to side. Then you aught to see him riding along when we are on the march, always calm and thoughtful with neat standing collar and old gray cap drawn down on his braud forehead."

Pope promptly drew back to regroup. That bought time for Lee to secure Richmond against the hapless McClellan and reunite with Jackson. The full Confederate Army of Northern Virginia then advanced on Pope.

Jackson executed one of the brilliant flank marches known to Southerners and feared by Northerners. His men swung around Pope's army, marched fifty-six miles in two days, and captured the main Federal supply depot miles in the rear of the Union forces. An angry Pope wheeled and came after Jackson. Fighting exploded on 28 August near the old Manassas battlefield. Combat continued for the next two days, at which point Lee's half of the army assailed Pope's undefended flank and sent another Union force on the road of defeat to Washington.

Lee then carried the war to the North with an invasion of Maryland. Jackson's brigades overwhelmed the Union garrison at Harper's Ferry in the largest capture of American soldiers until Corregidor in World War II. At Antietam on 17 September, the two opposing armies fought the bloodiest one-day battle in American annals. Jackson's thin ranks manned Lee's left and withstood heavy Union attacks throughout the morning. This defense reaffirmed Jackson's nickname "Stonewall." Lee held off McClellan skillfully but was forced to retire to Virginia for lack of resources.

Army reorganization came in the autumn, and with it a final promotion for Jackson. Lee wished to divide the Army of Northern Virginia into two corps. Each commander would hold the rank of lieutenant general. James Longstreet, the senior division commander, was a natural choice for one of the slots. Jackson was Lee's most dependable general and the logical second recommendation. "I have only to intimate to him what I wish done," Lee said, "and he promptly obeys my wishes." Lee stated to President Davis, "He is true, honest, and brave; has a single eye to the good of the service and spares no exertion to accomplish his object." The appointments were duly made.

Lee, with Longstreet's half of the army, took a defensive position near Fredericksburg; Jackson's corps was left to guard the Shenandoah Valley.

"Old Jack" spent the next weeks polishing his corps, reshuffling officers, replenishing supplies, and personally ensuring that religious services, Bibles, and tracts were available in all encampments. A widening disagreement with General A. P. Hill, who led the largest division under Jackson, overshadowed much of this period. However, Jackson's spirits received an exhilarating boost with the news late in November that his wife had given birth to a daughter. Both mother and child were healthy. An uncharacteristic impatience then consumed Jackson. He longed to see his wife and to give love to a child of his own.

Before that could happen, the Army of the Potomac made another move toward Richmond. Lee and Jackson were waiting on high ground at Fredericksburg. The 13 December battle was Lee's easiest victory.

By then, the aura and legend of Jackson were firmly established. He was the army's aggressive general—the leader with an unquenchable fire for battle—the principal lieutenant who gained victory with unbroken regularity. His piety had become infectious enough to convince the soldiers that their cause was truly righteous. Everyone in the army talked about the time a mother hesitantly walked up to the mounted general and asked him to bless her 18-month-old son. Jackson cuddled the baby in his arms and, while soldiers stood in silence with hats removed, put his face against the child's and silently prayed.

That Jackson was also shy, private, almost reclusive, inserted a certain mysteriousness that only added to his image of invincibility.

Even his small, plain horse, "Little Sorrel," became part of the apparition. A staff officer observed that Jackson's "old sorrel is not more martial in appearance than his master, and the men say it takes a half dozen bomb shells to wake either of them up to their full capacity, but when once aroused there is no stopping either of them until the enemy has retreated."

Four months of winter inactivity followed the battle of Fredericksburg. Jackson used much of the period seeking to enkindle a deeper religious spirit among his men and in overseeing the preparation of his official battle reports. His formal summations are easily recognizable by their references to "the blessings of Almighty God" and "an all-wise Providence." Jackson took no credit for victory. "Unto His holy name be the praise," he insisted. He considered himself but God's instrument in a crusade to purify America. This is why, at the height of one of his greatest military successes, Jackson turned to an aide and exclaimed joyfully: "He who does not see the hand of God in this is blind, sir, blind!"

In late April 1863, Anna Jackson visited Jackson with their five-month-old child. Jackson was never happier than during those few days. The visit ended abruptly with news that the Union army again was on the offensive. Lee dispatched Jackson ten miles westward into the wooded jungle of the Wilderness. Jackson blunted the Federal advance near a crossroads known as Chancellorsville. Lee arrived on the scene, the two generals conferred, and Jackson embarked quickly on another flanking movement. This time he led 28,000 men on a twelve-mile march around the unprotected right flank of the Federal army.

Late in the afternoon of 2 May, Jackson struck. One Federal corps all but fell apart in the face of Jackson's onslaught; the Union line bent at ninety degrees as Jackson's men drove the Federals for almost two miles. Darkness, weariness, and the confusion of the Wilderness stopped the advance.

Jackson was not content with what had been accomplished. He saw this moment as possibly the war's climax. A night attack would surely rout the enemy and might bring the war to an end. Toward that end, Jackson rode from his lines and made a personal reconnaissance of the Union position. He was returning through the woods to his lines when one of his brigades mistook the general and his staff for Union cavalry. Confederates delivered a point-blank volley into the horsemen.

Three bullets struck Jackson. While two made flesh wounds, the third shattered the bone in his left arm below the shoulder.

Amputation of the limb followed five hours later at a field hospital. For safety reasons, Lee ordered Jackson removed to the railhead at Guiney Station. The wounded commander endured the bumpy, 27-mile wagon ride without complaint. Yet pneumonia rapidly developed. Jackson had always expressed the hope that he might be blessed to die on the Sabbath. Around 3:15 P.M. on Sunday, 10 May, he emerged from a terminal coma long enough to say: "Let us cross over the river and rest under the shade of the trees."

The gifts of a supreme military leader were united in Jackson: imagination, speed, boldness, determination. To start before dawn, to march hour after hour, to pray long and hard, to fight with the relentless fury of a crusader, to look after his soldiers with the protective air of a stern father—these were part of Jackson's makeup. He was harsh, because he hated weakness. He demanded so much of his men because he demanded so much of himself. He could insist on the impossible, for he was confident that with aggressive leadership and God's blessing, the impossible could be accomplished.

A military genius fighting for the Lord must die to be defeated. Jackson's death was the greatest personal loss suffered by the Confederate States. An estimated 25,000 people filed by his coffin in the rotunda of the Virginia State Capitol. Many Federal commanders refused for weeks to believe that Jackson was dead and not making another secret flanking movement. In contrast, the idea dawned on more than one Southerner that with Jackson's passing, God was preparing the Confederacy for defeat.

Today the general is buried beneath his statue, which is the centerpiece of the Stonewall Jackson Cemetery at Lexington, Virginia.

—*James I. Robertson, Jr.*

See also Bee, Barnard Elliott; Bull Run, First Battle of; Bull Run, Second Battle of; Chancellorsville, Battle of; Fredericksburg, First Ferry, Battle of; Harper's, (West) Virginia; Lee, Robert Edward; Shenandoah Valley Campaign (1862); Stonewall Brigade.

For further reading:

Allan, Elizabeth Preston. *The Life and Letters of Margaret Junkin Preston* (1903).

Allen, Ujanirtus. *Campaigning with "Old Stonewall"* (1998).

Blackford, Susan L., compiler. *Letters from Lee's Army* (1947).

Henderson, G. F. R. *Stonewall Jackson and the American Civil War* (1898).

Jackson, Mary Anna. *Memoirs of Stonewall Jackson, by His Widow* (1895).

Robertson, James I., Jr. *Stonewall Jackson: The Man, The Soldier, The Legend* (1997).

JACKSONVILLE, FLORIDA

The city of Jacksonville, Florida, is situated on the banks of the St. Johns River, which drains north-ward into the Atlantic Ocean at Mayport, Florida. The river has been one of the main arteries of commerce for the region since before the arrival of Europeans. Jacksonville was founded at the junction of the old King's Road and the river at a place known as the Cow Ford. Before the outbreak of the Civil War, it was a growing town of around 2,000 inhabitants and had acquired a modest reputation as a health resort. Jacksonville also had begun to exploit the vast timber resources of the river region and had no less than eight steam sawmills operating at the beginning of 1861. It possessed a fine hotel, a telegraph office, nine brick business buildings, and an intelligent and sociable population, given to dances and dinner parties. The town was becoming important within the state and region.

As a center of the burgeoning lumber industry, Jacksonville had many ties to Northern centers of commerce. Many of its leading officials had Northern roots

Signal tower at Jacksonville, Florida (*Library of Congress*)

or were married to Northern women. Unionist sentiment was strong among a significant segment of Jacksonville society. With the passage of the ordinance of secession, the position of these citizens became very precarious. Many lived under the threat of death from the more violent of the local secessionists. According to one of this group, at least one-half of Jacksonville's population would meekly submit to President Abraham Lincoln's rule.

Many of the Union sympathizers remained in Jacksonville until early March 1862. Just before then, the city of Fernandina had fallen into Union hands and many refugees fled south into Jacksonville. Some made up "irregular" units with a mind for vengeance. As the Union fleet under Admiral Samuel F. Du Pont approached the St. Johns bar, some of the irregular units began to terrorize suspected Unionists. The mayor of Jacksonville, Halstead H. Hoeg, had already publicly pleaded with the citizens not to resist Union occupation, as Jacksonville was defenseless and vulnerable. On the evening of 11 March 1862, a Confederate force, estimated between 400 and 500 strong, under the command of Major Charles Hopkins, set fire to the lumber mills, the railroad depot, a foundry, a machine shop, and numerous other buildings to deny their use to the enemy. Admiral Du Pont wrote to his wife describing this incident: "General Trapier, after ingloriously flying and discovering the gunboats could not get over the bar, sent back four hundred rebel pirates calling themselves 'guerrillas' and set fire to seven fine sawmills at Jacksonville; the hotel, the finest in the South; and a gentleman's house, Union man. When the boats arrived they were still smoldering."

After a heavy rainfall had prevented more of the city from burning, Jacksonville was occupied by Federal troops on 12 March 1862 for the first of five times. The occupation led to the widespread belief that Union forces were in Jacksonville to stay, but the Federal operation was little more than a reconnaissance in force. The Unionists of the town petitioned the government and announced the meeting for organizing a loyal state government, but nothing could change the Federal plans. Jacksonville was evacuated on 9 April 1862, and many Northerners had to leave all they had built.

The second occupation of Jacksonville came as a result of Federal concerns about a newly constructed battery of artillery at St. Johns Bluff. This battery had the potential of controlling the entrance and use of the St. Johns River. On the evening of 1 October 1862, a Union expeditionary force of more than 1,500 men arrived at Mayport Mills. Colonel Charles F. Hopkins, commanding about 500 men, led the force opposing this expedition. The next day, the Federal force was augmented by gunboats and crews of the naval squadron and began landing operations near Mt. Pleasant Creek. Hopkins, believing he could not hold the position, quietly abandoned the St. Johns Bluffs late in the evening of 2 October 1862. As one observer put it: "The enemy had got scared, as our bungling and loading and unloading so many nights had led them to believe that the whole Union army was coming." Three days later, Jacksonville was occupied for the third time, but for only four days. Captain V. Chamberlain of the 7th Connecticut Volunteers wrote of the appearance of Jacksonville, "Desolation & distress are before you....Grass & weeds grow rank & tall in the principal streets. Houses with blinds closed attest the absence of inmates. Stores with shelves but no goods."

The fourth occupation of Jacksonville took place on 10 March 1863, with the arrival of Colonel T. W. Higginson's 1st Regiment of South Carolina Volunteers, an African-American unit. Part of the reasoning for this landing was to recruit and enroll Florida's African-American population in the Union army while resecuring part of Florida for the Union. The Union troops erected two small fortifications, Jacksonville's first in this war, commanding the railroad terminus. Although it appeared at this time that the occupation would be permanent, changes in the situation elsewhere led to the withdrawal of Federal forces on 29 March. This evacuation led to another fire that destroyed about twenty-five buildings, including the St. Johns Episcopal Church and the courthouse.

The final occupation of Jacksonville was the prelude to the battle of Olustee (or Ocean Pond). As a staging area for the largest battle fought in Florida, Jacksonville had numerous advantages. Its wharf facilities were quickly put into order and the railroad and roadways were efficiently utilized. This invasion of Florida also had other objectives. It was to procure an outlet for cotton, lumber, and other products of the state, while cutting off one of the enemy's sources of commissary supplies. It also was used to obtain recruits for the "colored" regiments and inaugurate measures for the speedy restoration of Florida to the Union. General Q. A. Gillmore, commanding the Department of the South, was given this directive by John Hay, President Lincoln's personal secretary. It was thought that finally securing and retaining Jacksonville could obtain these aims. Thus, the importance of Jacksonville became political as well as military.

After the defeat at Olustee, the Federal government decided to maintain its presence in Jacksonville for the purpose of rallying Unionist sentiment and recruiting African-American soldiers from the ever-increasing number of "contrabands" arriving in the city. Although jokingly referred to as the "third annual conquest of Florida," this time the conquerors remained.

—*Joe Knetsch*

See also Florida; Gillmore, Quincy Adams; Olustee, Battle of.
For further reading:
Beecher, Herbert W. *History of the First Light Battery Connecticut Volunteers, 1861–1865* (n.d.).
Davis, T. Frederick. *History of Jacksonville, Florida and Vicinity: 1513 to 1924* (1925).

Hayes, John D., ed. *The Mission: 1860–1862*. Vol. 1 of *Samuel Francis Du Pont: A Selection from His Civil War Letters* (1969).
Johns, John E. *Florida during the Civil War* (1963).
Martin, Richard A. "Defeat in Victory: Yankee Experience in Early Civil War Jacksonville." *Florida Historical Quarterly* (1974).
Schwartz, Gerald, ed. *A Woman Doctor's Civil War: Esther Hill Hawks' Diary* (1984).

JENKINS, ALBERT GALLATIN
(1830–1864)
Confederate general

Born in Cabell County, Virginia, the son of William Jenkins and Janetta McNutt Jenkins, Albert G. Jenkins attended but did not graduate from the Virginia Military Institute. Instead he graduated from Harvard Law School at age 20 but opted for a farming career rather than the law.

Along with his farming, Jenkins became active in state Democratic politics and served as a Virginia delegate to the Democratic National Convention in 1856 and as a member of the U.S. House of Representatives from 1857 until 1861. Though not a supporter of secession, he resigned his congressional seat upon the withdrawal of Virginia from the Union in April 1861.

Jenkins immediately raised a cavalry company. In June 1861 he commanded a party that rounded up about fifty Unionists in western Virginia. This action gained him popularity in his home district and, while serving as the colonel of the 8th Virginia, he was elected in November 1861 to the first Confederate Congress. Although he served briefly in the first Congress, Jenkins believed that his greatest contributions would be in the military arena. In August 1862 he accepted a brigadier general's commission and was placed in command of a brigade in A. P. Hill's division. Shortly thereafter, Jenkins transferred to the cavalry. While Robert E. Lee staged his first invasion of the North in late summer 1862, Jenkins led a raid into western Virginia and Ohio. During the raid, he insisted that his men respect private property whenever possible and thus gained the reputation in Union territory as a true Southern gentleman. He continued to operate in western Virginia, primarily in the Shenandoah Valley, until the end of May 1863, when he was summoned to be a part of the advance for what would become the Gettysburg campaign.

In the middle of June after mishandling his part in the advance on Berryville, he led a raid into Pennsylvania with the primary goal of bringing horses and cattle back to Virginia for the invading army. When the army moved north, Jenkins's brigade was part of the lead elements that moved into Pennsylvania first, capturing Chambersburg and making it as far as Harrisburg before moving back toward Gettysburg. He was wounded outside Gettysburg.

Back in command of his brigade by fall 1863, Jenkins moved back into western Virginia, where he tried to prevent George Crook from cutting the rail lines from eastern Tennessee. Jenkins was wounded while trying to prevent the retreat of his brigade at the battle of Cloyd's Mountain on 9 May 1864. Carried behind his lines, Jenkins was left behind later in the day when the Confederates were forced to retreat. Captured and treated by Union forces, Jenkins died on 21 May after the amputation of his arm.

—*David S. Heidler and Jeanne T. Heidler*

See also Berryville, Virginia; Cloyd's Mountain, Battle of; Gettysburg, Battle of.

For further reading:

Cook, Roy Bird. "Albert Gallatin Jenkins—A Confederate Portrait." *West Virginia Review* (1934).
Duncan, Richard R. *Lee's Endangered Left: The Civil War in Western Virginia, Spring of 1864* (1998).
Johnson, Flora Smith. "The War Record of Albert Gallatin Jenkins, C.S.A." *West Virginia History* (1947).
Johnson, Freddie L., III. "Mountain Warrior: The Political and Military Career of Albert Gallatin Jenkins" (Thesis, 1993).
McManus, Howard Rollins. *The Battle of Cloyd's Mountain: The Virginia and Tennessee Railroad Raid* (1989).

JENKINS' FERRY, BATTLE OF
(30 April 1864)

At Jenkins' Ferry, General Edmund Kirby Smith, the commander of the Confederacy's Trans-Mississippi Department, missed his chance to destroy the major portion of the Union forces in Arkansas. This failure compounded Kirby Smith's earlier blunder in permitting the escape of Major General Nathaniel P. Banks and his battered Union expedition down Louisiana's Red River.

When Confederate cavalry captured enemy supply trains at Poison Spring and Marks' Mills on 18 and 25 April 1864, respectively, Major General Frederick Steele and the 12,000 Union troops occupying Camden, Arkansas, found themselves in a perilous position. Not only were 4,000 Confederate horsemen poised to cut Steele's communications with his Arkansas River posts, but Steele now faced three infantry divisions that Kirby Smith had brought up from the Red River. Steele realized that remaining in Camden would doom his army to starvation, encirclement, and capture. His one hope was to beat a hasty retreat to his main base at Little Rock.

Steele gave Kirby Smith the slip by silently evacuating Camden on the night of 26–27 April. The Federals increased their lead the following day because the Confederates had to construct a raft bridge to cross the Ouachita River. Nature, however, soon negated the Federals' head-start advantage. Steady rain began falling on Steele's column at noon on 29 April, and the rain continued for eighteen hours. When the Union vanguard reached the west bank of the Saline River at 2:00 P.M., that already swollen stream began spilling onto the two and a half miles of swampy bottomland that led to Jenkins' Ferry. There Steele placed his pontoon bridge and quickly passed his cavalry division to the east bank, but his artillery and wagons got bogged down in the ever-worsening mud. Steele was still trying to extricate his wheeled transport when Kirby Smith overtook him on the morning of 30 April. The Federals would have to fight before they could flee.

Steele chose to supervise affairs at the pontoon bridge personally, which meant that his senior infantry commander in the VII Corps, Brigadier General Friedrich Salomon, should have taken charge of the ensuing rear-guard action. Curiously, Salomon spent most of the next few hours as a passive observer, and the actual direction of the battle fell to Brigadier General Samuel Rice, commander of the 1st Brigade in Salomon's 3d Division. Rice was an Iowa politician who had developed into an excellent soldier in less than two years of service.

While Union skirmishers delayed the cavalry brigade screening Kirby Smith's advance, Rice formed several Union infantry regiments in a strong line with its right anchored on Cox Creek. Eventually, Rice responded to enemy efforts to turn his other flank by bringing up more regiments and extending his left until it rested on a steep wooded hill. Rice's front was so narrow that only 4,000 of the 8,000 Confederate infantry present could attack at one time.

From 8:00 A.M. until 12:30 P.M., Rice's line fended off a series of Confederate frontal attacks delivered in a piecemeal fashion. Brigadier General Thomas J. Churchill's Arkansas division was the first to test the Federal position. Then the Arkansans tried again with the support of Brigadier General Mosby M. Parson's Missouri division. Finally, Major General John G. Walker's larger Texas division tried its strength against the Federals and ultimately recoiled.

Because ankle- to knee-deep water covered most of the battlefield, Jenkins' Ferry was almost exclusively an infantry fight. The Rebels tried to bring six artillery pieces into play, but one had to be abandoned after it stuck fast in the mud, and two more were captured in a bold charge by the 2d Kansas Colored and 29th Iowa Infantry Regiments. Shortly thereafter, the Confederates made their last assault and General Rice was mortally wounded.

Beaten to a standstill in a merciless firefight, the Confederates stood clear while Steele, who had finished saving his movable wagons and burning the rest, removed his infantry across the Saline. Left behind to cover the Union withdrawal, the 2d Kansas Colored avenged the massacre of black soldiers at Poison Spring by murdering enemy wounded who had fallen near Rice's line.

Neither side filed complete casualty returns for Jenkins' Ferry. The best estimates place Union losses at 700 of 4,000 men engaged and Confederate losses at 1,000. Considering the numbers involved, it was one of the war's bloodiest battles.

With the Saline between his army and the enemy, Steele destroyed his pontoon bridge and continued unmolested to Little Rock. Kirby Smith held the battle-field, but the victory he claimed was a hollow one.

—*Gregory J. W. Urwin*

See also Arkansas; Smith, Edmund Kirby; Steele, Frederick.
For further reading:
Bearss, Edwin C. *Steele's Retreat from Camden and the Battle of Jenkins' Ferry* (1967).
Christ, Mark K., ed. *Rugged and Sublime: The Civil War in Arkansas* (1994).
Cornish, Dudley Taylor. *The Sable Arm: Negro Troops in the Union Army, 1861–1865* (1966).
Johnson, Ludwell H. *Red River Campaign: Politics and Cotton in the Civil War* (1958).
Urwin, Gregory J. W. "'We Cannot Treat Negroes…As Prisoners of War': Racial Atrocities and Reprisals in Civil War Arkansas." *Civil War History* (1996).

JENKINS, MICAH
(1835–1864)
Confederate general

Born to John Jenkins and Elizabeth Clark Jenkins on Edisto Island, South Carolina, Micah Jenkins graduated from the South Carolina Military Academy. Upon graduation he opened the King's Mountain Military School, which he ran until the outbreak of the Civil War.

With the advent of hostilities, Jenkins became the colonel of the 5th South Carolina regiment. He led this regiment in the battle of First Bull Run, after which he raised a new regiment that became known as Jenkins's Palmetto Sharpshooters. Jenkins commanded the Sharpshooters in the opening battles of the Peninsula campaign, where they quickly gained a reputation as one of the best regiments in the Confederate army. Because of injuries early in the campaign, however, Jenkins received a brigade to command at Seven Pines though the Sharpshooters were one of the brigade's regiments. Jenkins continued to command the brigade through the Seven Days' and received promotion to brigadier general in July 1862 because of his conduct during the campaign.

At Second Bull Run at the end of August 1862, Jenkins received a severe wound that kept him out of action until Fredericksburg in December 1862. Jenkins also fought at Gettysburg and then as part of Longstreet's corps joined Braxton Bragg at Chickamauga, where he commanded the division of the injured John Bell Hood. After Chickamauga, Jenkins fought at Chattanooga and Knoxville before returning to Virginia with Longstreet in the spring of 1864. While riding with Longstreet on the second day of the battle of the Wilderness, Jenkins was mortally wounded by Confederate forces just a short time before Longstreet too was seriously injured by friendly fire. Jenkins was seen by many, including Robert E. Lee, as one of the rising stars in the Confederate army.

—*David S. Heidler and Jeanne T. Heidler*

See also Bull Run, Second Battle of; Chickamauga, Battle of; Longstreet, James.

For further reading:

Baldwin, James J. *The Struck Eagle: A Biography of Brigadier General Micah Jenkins, and a History of the Fifth South Carolina Volunteers and the Palmetto Sharpshooters* (1996).

Jenkins, Micah. *The Future's Promise: The Civil War Correspondence of Micah Jenkins* (1996).

Swisher, James K. *Brigadier General Micah Jenkins, C.S.A.* (1996).

Thomas, John Peyre. *The Career and Character of General Micah Jenkins, C.S.A.* (1903).

JEWS

Approximately 150,000 Jews lived in the United States during the time of the Civil War, about half a percent of the entire U.S. population. At least 10,000 Jews served on both sides of the war—7,000 for the Union and 3,000 for the Confederacy. An estimated total of 600 Jewish soldiers died in the line of battle.

The Union army recruited two Jewish companies—the 82d Regiment of the Illinois Volunteers, composed mostly of recent European immigrants, and the "Perkins Rifles" from Syracuse, New York. The Confederate army had a couple of dozen Jews in the Tatnall Guards, Company C, of the Georgia Volunteer Regiment. Typical of this national war between brothers, Emanuel Kahn of Marshall, Texas, fought for the Confederacy but his brother, Lionel, joined the Union army. After the war, they both returned to their Texas hometown.

Most Jewish soldiers did not want to serve in minority units. Many companies, such as the Light Infantry Blues of Richmond and Company D of the 8th New York National Guard Regiment, contained Jews who enlisted based on their geographic location, not on the perceived need to fight alongside their coreligionists. Yet several events during—and even before—the Civil War highlighted the special problems confronting a non-Christian minority group.

Although Jews living both in the Union and Confederacy were willing to sacrifice their lives for the larger causes, they were still discriminated against and persecuted because of their religious beliefs. On 22 July 1861, Congress passed legislation requiring that all chaplains be ordained Christian ministers. But nationwide protests and petitions (in Bangor, Maine, 200 non-Jews signed a petition in a community where only three Jews lived) eventually led to the appointment of Jacob Frankel as the first American rabbi to serve as a military chaplain. In the Confederacy, however, there was no controversy about the lack of Jewish chaplains.

The age-old scourge of economic anti-Semitism manifested itself both in the North and the South. The shortage of available consumer goods in the South created an easy scapegoat—immigrant Jewish shopkeepers. In Talbot County, Georgia, a grand jury denounced Jews as profiteers. When the Jews of Thomasville, Georgia, were forced to flee, the German Jewish community of Savannah, Georgia, rallied to the defense of their coreligionists, issuing four support resolutions published in the *Savannah Republican* during September 1862. Even Judah P. Benjamin, known as the "brains of the Confederacy," was subjected to vicious anti-Jewish attacks.

In the North, meanwhile, Detroit's *Commercial Advertiser* wrote that "the people who look up to Abraham as their father…hooked-nose wretches speculate on disasters and a battle lost to our army is chuckled over by them, as it puts money in their purse."

In the most flagrant instance of anti-Jewish decrees in U.S. history, General Ulysses S. Grant issued General Order No. 11 on 17 December 1862, ordering the expulsion "within twenty-four hours" of the "Jews, as a class" from the Department of Tennessee (including Kentucky, Mississippi, and Tennessee). Ostensibly, this declaration was aimed at punishing smugglers and commercial offenders. Bertram Wallace Korn's meticulous research has shown that the number of Jewish smugglers in various Tennessee districts constituted a mere 6.03 percent of the accused. Korn concluded that "other traders and speculators, civilian and military" stood most to profit by making Jews scapegoats. President Abraham Lincoln revoked the order on 4 January 1863.

On the great issues that tore apart the nation, Jews also were divided. Michael Heilprin, a Polish-Jewish intellectual, and Baltimore rabbi David Einhorn were outspoken abolitionists, whereas Dr. Morris Raphall of New York City denied any biblical opposition to slavery. Rabbi Bernhard Felsenthal of Chicago refused to take a pulpit in Mobile, Alabama, because he could not live in a place that promoted slavery.

The religious and polemic writings of these rabbis and intellectuals soon elicited much debate throughout the country among Jews, Gentiles, lay people, and clergy. Nevertheless, national Jewish organizations such as B'nai B'rith did not take specific stands on the fierce national debates involving the questions of slavery, states' rights, and secession.

Abraham Lincoln, who was considered sympathetic to Jewish causes, had some close Jewish friends. His assassination, which occurred during the Passover holiday, occasioned enormous grief among American Jews. In New York City, 3,000 Jews, representing a wide variety of Jewish fraternal, religious, and literary organizations, marched in a mourning procession.

The war that prevented the country from breaking apart also helped to unite the American Jewish community. Confronting anti-Jewish prejudice, American Jews boldly and unapologetically asserted their rights as both Americans and Jews.

—*Donald Altschiller*

See also Catholics; Chaplains; Chaplains, African-American; Churches.

For further reading:
Diner, Hasia. *A Time for Gathering: The Second Migration, 1820–1880. Jewish People in America* (1992).
Korn, Bertram Wallace. *American Jewry and the Civil War* (1951).
Simonhoff, Harry. *Jewish Participants in the Civil War* (1963).

JOHNSON, ANDREW
(1808–1875)

U.S. senator; military governor of Tennessee; seventeenth president of the United States

Andrew Johnson was born in Raleigh, North Carolina, in 1808. Johnson's parents, Jacob and Mary Johnson, were impoverished tavern workers, and Andrew's childhood was marked by extreme deprivation, a situation exacerbated by his father's death when Johnson was four. Mary Johnson, unable to provide for her sons' education, apprenticed Andrew and his older brother William to local tailor John Selby when Johnson was fourteen. After two years, Johnson fled, ultimately settling with his mother, brother, and stepfather in Greenville, Tennessee, a small community in the mountains of the eastern portion of the state. Johnson set up shop in Greenville and soon met and married Eliza McCardle. Having some degree of formal education, Eliza Johnson used her skills to help Johnson learn to read and write, often reading to her husband as he worked. Johnson joined a local debating society to improve his speaking skills, and at the age of twenty, he was elected an alderman of Greenville. It was the first of many campaigns that would ultimately land Johnson in the White House, but despite his rapidly growing fame, Johnson never forgot his humble roots and he remained a champion of the common people until his death.

Johnson's political career advanced rapidly. In 1830, Johnson was elected mayor of Greenville, and this was followed by terms in the Tennessee State House and Senate. The voters of his district elected Johnson to what would be the first of five terms in the U.S. House in 1843. Four years in the governor's mansion followed, and the state legislature elected Johnson to the U.S. Senate in 1857. Throughout Johnson's early career, he was a strong proponent of homestead legislation and public education and, despite his Southern roots, an opponent of state's rights doctrines. Johnson supported the Southern

Andrew Johnson (*Library of Congress*)

Democrat John C. Breckinridge in the 1860 presidential contest, but fiercely denounced secessionist efforts after Abraham Lincoln's election. Johnson denounced Democratic president James Buchanan for not taking steps to stop the dissolution of the Union, declaring "...my blood, my existence I would give to save this Union." Johnson campaigned tirelessly throughout early 1861 to prevent Tennessee from leaving the Union, and when Tennessee voted to secede, Johnson became the only Southern senator to refuse to resign his seat. Forced to flee to Kentucky, Johnson quickly became a national symbol of Southern Unionism and was hailed throughout the North as one of the country's greatest patriots.

As the sole senator from any state that now styled itself a part of the Confederacy, Johnson staunchly supported the Lincoln administration and advocated a vigorous prosecution of the Union's war effort. Lincoln rewarded Johnson's loyalty in March 1862 by naming him military governor of Tennessee after that state had come under the control of Union armies. In his three years as military governor, Johnson moved resolutely to eradicate all pro-Confederate influences in the state, dismissing all officials who refused to take an oath of loyalty, closing down pro-Confederate newspapers, and arresting clergy who supported the Confederate cause. Johnson frequently displayed great personal courage; when Confederate forces threatened Nashville, he

refused to leave, declaring that he would burn the city before he would allow it to fall under Confederate control.

Johnson's unwavering commitment to the Union, combined with Lincoln's desire to create a nonpartisan, prowar ticket, persuaded the president to support Johnson for the vice presidency on the Union Party ticket in the election of 1864. Lincoln's election carried Johnson back to Washington, D.C., in early 1865. Lincoln's assassination in April propelled Johnson into the presidency in April 1865, and from there, Johnson presided over the final defeat of the Confederacy and the restoration of his beloved Union.

Reconstruction of the Union proved to be more difficult than Johnson anticipated. He advocated a quick return to the Union for the Southern states once disloyal elements had been removed from public life. Radical Republicans in Congress, however, wanted guarantees that the former slaves would receive decent treatment, a concern that Johnson did not share; his primary goal was the assumption of power by common whites in the South. Repeated, and frequently unnecessary, conflicts with Congress eventually led to Johnson's impeachment and near removal from office by exasperated congressional Republicans.

Denied nomination by either party in the 1868 presidential election, Johnson returned to Tennessee, where he remained active in Democratic politics, campaigning unsuccessfully for the Senate in 1871 and the U.S. House in 1872. The Tennessee state legislature returned Johnson to the U.S. Senate in 1875, but he died after making only one speech before the body that had come within one vote of removing him from office just seven years earlier. Johnson was buried outside Greenville, Tennessee, on 3 August 1875, with his body wrapped in a U.S. flag and his head resting on a copy of the U.S. Constitution.

—*James L. Sledge III*

See also Election of 1864; Southern Unionism; Tennessee.

For further reading:

Bergeron, Paul, ed. *The Papers of Andrew Johnson* (1967–1995).

Castel, Albert E. *The Presidency of Andrew Johnson* (1979).

McCaslin, Richard B., comp. *Andrew Johnson: A Bibliography* (1993).

McKitrick, Eric L. *Andrew Johnson and Reconstruction* (1988).

Trefousse, Hans Louis. *Andrew Johnson: A Biography* (1957; reprint, 1997).

Winston, Robert. *Andrew Johnson, Plebian and Patriot* (1928).

JOHNSON, BUSHROD RUST
(1817–1880)
Confederate general

Born to Noah Johnson and Rachel Spencer Johnson in Norwich, Ohio, Bushrod Rust Johnson was educated locally and, in spite of a Quaker upbringing, graduated twenty-third of forty-two in the

U.S. Military Academy's class of 1840. Johnson served in the latter part of the Second Seminole War, at frontier posts, and in the early phases of the Mexican-American War. While serving as a commissary officer at Vera Cruz in 1847, Johnson was accused of smuggling and forced to resign his commission.

In 1848, Johnson moved to Georgetown, Kentucky, where he accepted a position as professor of chemistry at Western Military Institute. He was promoted to superintendent in 1851 and served until 1855, during which time he also held a commission as a colonel in the Kentucky militia. In 1855, Johnson moved to Nashville, Tennessee, where he served as the superintendent of the military college of the University of Nashville. From 1855 to 1861 he also was a colonel of the Tennessee militia.

Johnson was an ardent supporter of secession and upon the secession of Tennessee he accepted a colonel's commission of Confederate engineers having served as chief of engineers of Tennessee. During the first part of the war, Johnson served under Albert Sidney Johnston, was promoted brigadier general on 24 January 1862, and was in Nashville when he received orders from Johnston on 6 February to take command of Fort Donelson. He commanded the fort from 7 February until the arrival of Gideon Pillow on 9 February. Although captured at the fort, Johnson escaped.

Johnson commanded a brigade at Shiloh but was wounded on the first day and had to be carried from the field. He recovered in time to lead his brigade in Braxton Bragg's Kentucky campaign of the fall of 1862, fighting at Perryville. At the end of the year, Johnson commanded his brigade at Stones River, doing most of his fighting on the first day. He participated in the Tullahoma campaign in June–July 1863 before succeeding the command of Simon Bolivar Buckner's division at Chickamauga. At this engagement, Johnson was positioned on the Confederate left and was credited with causing the Union right to collapse.

Johnson served under James Longstreet during the Knoxville campaign and followed Longstreet to Virginia in the spring of 1864. Initially part of the Richmond defenses in early May, Johnson rushed to reinforce the small Confederate force at Drewry's Bluff on the night of 6 May. On 21 May 1864 he was promoted to major general under the command of P. G. T. Beauregard and was part of the defensive efforts that prevented Ulysses Grant from taking Petersburg in June 1864. For the remainder of the war, Johnson and his division remained in the trenches of Petersburg. In July 1864, Johnson's division was instrumental in stopping the federal assault at what became known as the battle of the Crater. Johnson led his division in the final retreat away from Petersburg, fought at Sayler's Creek, and surrendered at Appomattox.

After the war, Johnson returned to the University of Nashville, where he taught engineering and natural philosophy. He became chancellor in 1870 and retired in

1874. He died on a farm in Brighton, Illinois, on 12 September 1880.

—David S. Heidler and Jeanne T. Heidler

See also Crater, Battle of the; Drewry's Bluff, Virginia, Battle of; Fort Donelson, Battle of.

For further reading:

Cummings, Charles M. "Forgotten Man at Fort Donelson: Bushrod Rust Johnson." *Tennessee Historical Quarterly* (1969).

———. *Yankee Quaker, Confederate General; the Curious Career of Bushrod Rust Johnson* (1971).

JOHNSON, EDWARD
(1816–1873)
Confederate general

Born on 16 April 1816 in Chesterfield County, Virginia, Edward Johnson at an early age moved with his family to Kentucky. In 1833, Johnson received an appointment to the U.S. Military Academy, where he performed so poorly that he had to repeat his third class or sophomore year. By his senior year, however, he improved somewhat, finishing thirty-second of forty-five.

After his graduation in 1838, Johnson was commissioned a second lieutenant in the 6th Infantry. He advanced to first lieutenant in a little more than a year, and then to captain in April 1851. For the first three years after his graduation, Johnson served in the Second Seminole War in Florida. Before the Mexican-American War, he was stationed on the western and southwestern frontier. In Mexico, Johnson was twice breveted and saw action at Vera Cruz, Cerro Gordo, Churubusco, Molino del Rey, and Chapultepec. After the war, he again served on the western frontier.

In 1861 Johnson was stationed at Governor's Island, New York. One newspaper account suggests that because of his strong secession sentiments, Johnson was arrested and thrown in prison. He then "contrived to make his escape and embark in disguise on board of a vessel bound for some port in Central America. Thence he contrived to reach home in July."

Johnson's first Confederate commission, that of lieutenant colonel, took rank from 16 March 1861. On 2 July 1861, Johnson took command of the 12th Georgia Infantry with the rank of full colonel, and immediately he was sent to reinforce Robert S. Garnett and his small army in the mountains of western Virginia.

The 45-year-old Johnson quickly developed a reputation as a diligent officer and oddly charismatic character. He participated in the Cheat Mountain campaign and the battle of Greenbrier River. Late in November 1861, Johnson was given command of a brigade in the Army of the Northwest and stationed on the summit of Alleghany Mountain in Pocahontas County, in western Virginia. As a result of his 13 December 1861 victory at the battle of Alleghany Mountain, he was elevated to brigadier general and won forever his nom de guerre, Edward "Alleghany" Johnson. In addition, it was in these mountains that Johnson first earned his reputation for wielding his trademark club in combat; he would carry a staff or bludgeon throughout the war.

In May 1862, after enduring an unusually severe winter in the mountains, Johnson and his small army cooperated with "Stonewall" Jackson's Army of the Valley, defeating Robert H. Milroy at the battle of McDowell. A severe ankle wound during this engagement, however, ended his military service for one year.

As a result of the reorganization of the Army of Northern Virginia after Jackson's death, Johnson was promoted to major general and given command of the Stonewall division in Richard S. Ewell's II Corps. Johnson was healthy enough to take command of his division in late May 1863 and played an active role in the Confederate army's invasion of the North. On the way to Pennsylvania, his division, along with Early's, routed Union general Robert H. Milroy's command at the second battle of Winchester. Johnson's command fought conspicuously on the Confederate left at Culp's Hill on both the second and the third days at Gettysburg. In the fighting of the following winter, Johnson's division had a major role in Lee's Mine Run campaign. Johnson's units also played a conspicuous part in the series of battles that began in the spring of 1864.

Edward Johnson was so highly regarded by Lee that, when Longstreet was seriously wounded in the fighting at the Wilderness, Lee considered Johnson temporarily to replace the fallen corps commander. A few days later, on 12 May 1864, at a point in the Confederate line known as the "Bloody Angle" or "Mule Shoe" near Spotsylvania Court House, Johnson and his entire division were captured during hand-to-hand combat in the trenches.

Johnson was incarcerated at Fort Delaware and later transferred to Morris Island as a member of the "Immortal 600." In the late summer of 1864, Johnson was exchanged and sent to Tennessee, where he commanded a division in Stephen D. Lee's Corps in the Army of Tennessee. His participation in John Bell Hood's Spring Hill, Franklin, and Nashville debacle ended with his capture at Nashville on 16 December 1864. He was again a Union prisoner of war, this time incarcerated at Johnson's Island. As the war concluded, Johnson was moved to Old Capitol Prison and held along with other Confederate leaders as a possible coconspirator in the Lincoln assassination. The accusations proved to be unfounded, and he was released.

Johnson was without vanity, had little untoward ambition, and was gruff, unpolished, and profane. By the war's end, he was highly regarded by men such as Lee and Ewell as well as the men who he led into battle and those he opposed there. He never failed to do his duty and earned a reputation as one of the Confederacy's finest division commanders.

After the war, Johnson returned to Chesterfield County and began farming. He never married. He died on 2 March 1873 in Richmond where he was mourned throughout the city as flags flew at half-mast. His body lay in state at the Capitol until moved for burial at Hollywood Cemetery on 4 March 1873.

—*Eddie Woodward*

See also Lee, Stephen D.; McDowell, Battle of; Milroy, Robert H.; Spotsylvania Courthouse, Battle of; Winchester, Second Battle of.
For further reading:
Davis, William C., ed. *The Confederate General* (1991).
Hotchkiss, Jed. *Virginia*. In *Confederate Military History* (1899; reprint, 1987).
Woodward, Edward V. "Holding the Alleghany Line: Edward Johnson, the Army of the Northwest, and the Battle of Alleghany Summit" (M.A. thesis, 1998).

JOHNSON FARM (DARBYTOWN AND NEW MARKET ROADS)
(7 October 1864)

At the end of September 1864, Federal troops succeeded in capturing New Market Heights and Fort Harrison, vital parts of the exterior defensive line guarding Richmond, Virginia. Following the loss of these positions, General Robert E. Lee determined to retake them and repair the damage done to the capital's defenses. On 7 October, he ordered the divisions of General Charles Field and General Robert Hoke to advance down the New Market and Darbytown roads, respectively. Lee planned to drive the 1,700 cavalrymen under General August V. Kautz from their position on the far right of the Union line. With the Federal cavalry out of the way, the Confederate divisions would then be able to roll up the enemy's flank and force them back toward the James River to the south.

At dawn on 7 October, the two Confederate divisions began their advance. Hoke's troops worked their way along the north side of the Darbytown Road until they were even with Kautz's right flank. As they attacked the cavalry's vulnerable side, two brigades from Field's division struck the front of the Federal line. To further add to the problems of Kautz's men, General Martin Gary's Confederate cavalry brigade struck the Union rear. This three-pronged attack utterly routed the Federal troops. They fled to the south, not stopping until they reached the protection of the earthworks held by General Alfred Terry's division from the X Corps. In their flight, the Federal horsemen left behind eight cannon, which were captured by the Rebels.

It took several hours for the Confederate infantry to make their way through dense underbrush and slashing to the right of the Federal infantry line. Terry used this time well, bringing up additional troops and artillery to defend the flank of his division. By 10:00 A.M., Lee was chafing to attack, but only the Texas Brigade of Field's division was in position. Just before noon the Confederates were in position to attack, but Terry's forces waited to repel them. Federal artillery fire broke up the attack of Hoke's division well before it reached the line of northern infantrymen. Field's division went in piecemeal—one brigade at a time—and was repulsed with heavy losses.

In the afternoon, the Confederates withdrew back to their original starting point. Federal infantry reoccupied the works that Kautz had held around Johnson Farm. The Union troops had lost over 400 men in the fighting, but had inflicted over 700 casualties (including General John Gregg, commander of the Texas Brigade) on the Confederates. Lee gave up any ideas of retaking the old defensive positions and concentrated on establishing new lines closer to Richmond.

—*David McGee*

See also Field, Charles William; Hoke, Robert Frederick; Terry, Alfred Howe.
For further reading:
Davis, William C. *Death in the Trenches: Grant at Petersburg* (1986).
Horn, John. *The Petersburg Campaign, June 1864–April 1865* (1993).
Sommers, Richard J. *Richmond Redeemed: The Siege at Petersburg* (1981).

JOHNSON, GEORGE W.
(1811–1862)
Governor of Confederate Kentucky

The first governor of Confederate Kentucky was born near Georgetown in Scott County on 27 May 1811 to William Johnson and Betsy Payne Johnson. After attending local schools, he received three degrees from Transylvania University. In 1833 he married Ann Viley, daughter of a wealthy farmer and horse breeder in Scott County. Johnson practiced law briefly, but preferred farming in Scott County and on a 1,000-acre cotton plantation in Arkansas. The Johnsons had ten children, seven of whom survived infancy. The large Johnson home was noted for lavish hospitality and extended political discussions.

Johnson was elected to the Kentucky House as a Democrat in 1838, 1839, and 1840; thereafter, he avoided political office. In 1845 he headed the Committee of Sixty that removed Cassius M. Clay's *True American* press from Lexington. Johnson revered the "Old Union," which he saw as being destroyed by such radical groups as the abolitionists; he believed that slavery was a state issue to be handled by each state. He supported John C. Breckinridge in 1860. When Johnson saw that Abraham Lincoln would probably win, he advised opposition within the Union;

soon the Republicans would not control the Senate or the Supreme Court. Johnson believed that some reasonable compromise could be found that would keep the states from exercising their right to secede. If ten Southern states did secede, Johnson believed that they would be so strong as to preclude war to bring them back into the Union. He was sure that Great Britain and France would ally with the Confederacy.

After the Confederacy was formed, Johnson urged Kentucky to secede and join it, but he also had an active role in attempting to preserve Kentucky's neutrality as an alternative to Union commitment. When neutrality ended in early September 1861, Johnson fled to avoid arrest. He soon went to Bowling Green, where he served as a volunteer aide to General Simon Bolivar Buckner. Johnson and other pro-Confederate Kentuckians were embarrassed by their state's failure to secede, and he assumed leadership in holding a Russellville convention on 29–30 October to devise a plan of action. Appealing to the revolutionary right of a people to alter their government, this body called for a sovereignty convention to convene in Russellville on 18 November. Johnson did much of the preliminary planning for the convention and was its leader. This convention denounced the Frankfort Union government as not reflecting the wishes of the people and declared Kentucky free of all connections with the federal government. They formed a Provisional Government headed by a governor and a council of ten members, one from each congressional district. Johnson was elected governor, council members were chosen, and the government moved to Bowling Green, which was General Albert Sidney Johnston's headquarters. This Kentucky government was admitted into the Confederate States of America on 10 December 1861.

Johnson and the Council labored to create a viable government, but their jurisdiction extended only as far as the Confederate army advanced, and many Kentuckians behind the Confederate lines were Unionists. When Johnston withdrew from Kentucky in mid-February 1862, the Provisional Government went into exile. Johnson's age, his position, and a disabled arm seemed to preclude active military participation, but on Sunday, 6 April, the first day of battle at Shiloh, he served as a volunteer aide to General John C. Breckinridge. Later that day, Johnson assisted Colonel Robert P. Trabue, who led the 1st Kentucky Brigade. When his horse was killed under him, Johnson fought with Company E, 4th Kentucky Infantry, and that evening he insisted on being sworn in as a private in that company.

On Monday afternoon Johnson was struck by bullets in the right thigh and abdomen. Recognized by a fellow Mason on Tuesday, Johnson was carried to the Union hospital ship *Hannibal*, where he died on 8 April. He had made a last effort to explain his motives: "I wanted personal honor and political liberty and constitutional state government, and for these I drew the sword." Friends in the Union army had his remains packed in salt and shipped to Georgetown, where he was buried.

—*Lowell H. Harrison*

See also Buckner, Simon Bolivar; Kentucky.
For further reading:
Harrison, Lowell H. "George W. Johnson and Richard Hawes: The Governors of Confederate Kentucky." *Register of the Kentucky Historical Society* (1981).
Johnson, George W. "Letters of George W. Johnson." *Register of the Kentucky Historical Society* (1942).
McDowell, Robert Emmett, ed. *Resolution of the [Confederate] Congress [in Kentucky], 1861* (1970).
Quisenberry, A. C. "The Alleged Secession of Kentucky in 1861." *Register of the Kentucky Historical Society* (1917).

JOHNSON, HERSCHEL VESPASIAN
(1812–1880)
U.S. and Confederate senator

Born to Moses Johnson and Nancy Palmer Johnson in Burke County, Georgia, Herschel Johnson was educated at the University of Georgia and studied law before opening a practice in Augusta, Georgia. Johnson also purchased a plantation and spent much of his time engaged in the business of commercial agriculture and a growing interest in Georgia Democratic politics. From 1848 to 1849 he served the remaining year of an unexpired term in the U.S. Senate.

By 1850, Johnson had become interested in the territorial question. Although he supported the Compromise of 1850 as a way to preserve the peace between the sections, he believed that the South must maintain some equilibrium within the national government if it was to retain any power. Nevertheless, he also believed that the citizens of an individual territory had the right to determine the status of slavery within the territory, and for that reason he supported the Kansas-Nebraska Act. Johnson's moderation is credited with his election to the Georgia governorship in 1852. He served two terms beginning in 1853 and ending in 1857.

As the sectional crisis became more heated in 1860 and the disintegration of the Democratic Party threatened, Johnson, believing that the only hope for the nation was the unity of the party, worked hard to prevent such a split. For that reason he accepted the position as vice presidential candidate on the ticket with Stephen A. Douglas, a move that caused states' righters in the South and especially in Georgia to condemn him. During his candidacy, he worked to fuse the two Democratic tickets.

After the election of Abraham Lincoln in the fall of 1860, Johnson argued against secession, urging a wait-and-see attitude regarding presidential policy. In January 1861, Johnson served in the Georgia secession convention, where he worked to prevent Georgia's secession, but

once the vote had carried for disunion, he publicly supported the stance of the convention. He went home to his plantation outside Louisville, Georgia, holding little hope for the ultimate success of a Southern confederacy.

In the fall of 1861, Johnson was elected to the Confederate Senate for a two-year term and was returned in the next election. He served in the Confederate Senate for the remainder of the war. In Richmond, Johnson served on a variety of committees, including Foreign Affairs, Finance, and Naval Affairs. While always respectful of the administration, Johnson did not always agree with Jefferson Davis's policies, particularly when he believed such policies violated states' rights. Johnson especially opposed conscription and the suspension of the writ of habeas corpus for that reason. From virtually the moment he entered the Confederate government, he expressed his view that the administration should be attempting to negotiate a peaceful settlement to the war on almost any terms short of the abolition of slavery.

General William T. Sherman's invasion of Georgia in the spring of 1864 caused Johnson to take an increasing interest in military affairs. As Sherman moved closer to Atlanta, Johnson criticized the strategy of Confederate general Joseph E. Johnston. When Johnston was removed in July 1864 and replaced by John Bell Hood, Johnson complained to Jefferson Davis that the move had not been made sooner.

Even as the war wound to a close, Johnson remained interested in various aspects of the war effort from the promotion of blockade running to his opposition to army commissaries distilling corn into whiskey. After the war, he returned to Georgia, where he worked to rebuild his state.

A member of the Georgia constitutional convention at the end of 1865, Johnson again entered the moderate camp. In 1866 his moderation earned him election to the U.S. Senate, but like most Southerners elected in that year, he was refused his seat. In 1873 he became a circuit court judge. He died in this position on 16 August 1880.

—*David S. Heidler and Jeanne T. Heidler*

See also Congress, C.S.A.; Georgia.

For further reading:
Flippin, Percy Scott. *Herschel V. Johnson of Georgia, State Rights Unionist* (1931).

JOHNSON, REVERDY
(1796–1876)
U.S. senator and attorney general

Reverdy Johnson, born into a distinguished Maryland family, became one of that state's leading public figures and one of the nation's most respected attorneys for more than fifty years. He graduated from St. John's College in Annapolis in 1811 and thereafter studied law under the guidance of his father,

John Johnson, a former judge and state attorney general. Reverdy Johnson opened his own law office in Baltimore in 1817, and two years later he married Mary Mackall Bowie, the granddaughter of a governor of Maryland. The Johnsons had fifteen children.

Johnson's keen memory, impressive manner, speaking ability, and careful preparation enabled him quickly to win an enviable reputation as a constitutional lawyer. Despite losing the sight in his left eye as a result of an 1833 pistol accident, Johnson remained a formidable presence in the courtroom well into his seventies. His legal skill and willingness to champion vigorously the interests of railroads and other corporations resulted in his amassing a considerable fortune, as the Baltimore & Ohio Railroad, among others, frequently retained his increasingly in-demand services.

Johnson's political career began in the 1820s, when he was twice elected to the Maryland Senate. Although he mostly devoted himself to the pursuit of his legal career in the 1830s and early 1840s, he also became associated with the emerging Whig Party. His wealth and conservatism made that party's emphasis on economic development and the preservation of the social order appealing. In 1845 the Whig-dominated Maryland legislature sent Johnson to the U.S. Senate. He quickly broke with most of the other Whigs by supporting Democratic president James K. Polk's aggressive war with Mexico, although he joined most Whigs in opposing Democratic demands for the seizure of the entire Oregon Territory from Great Britain and the acquisition of Mexican land. Like many border-state conservatives, Johnson particularly feared the annexation of additional western territory because he believed that it would lead to divisive sectional conflict over the issue of slavery expansion. Johnson had freed the slaves that he inherited from his father and believed the "peculiar institution" at best a necessary evil, but he adhered to the constitutional view that slavery was a local matter that the federal government had no business concerning itself with.

Recognizing Johnson's growing stature in the Whig Party as well as his legal talent, President Zachary Taylor appointed him U.S. attorney general in 1849. Unfortunately, Johnson soon found himself embroiled in a scandal and a resulting congressional investigation that greatly tarnished both his own reputation and that of the administration and nearly forced his ouster from the cabinet. Johnson's controversial decision dealt with the decades-old Galphin claim for reimbursement from the federal government for the seizure of land in the 1700s. The government had already decided to pay more than $43,000 to the heirs, and Johnson was asked to determine if interest should also be paid. He overruled an earlier decision and ruled that the government owed more than $191,000 in interest, a vast amount of money in 1850 dollars. Apparently unknown to Johnson, his cabinet colleague George W. Crawford represented the Galphin heirs and received a considerable portion of this payment.

The resulting outcry and investigation, although it cleared Johnson of wrongdoing, greatly embarrassed Taylor, Johnson, and Crawford. Nevertheless, Johnson remained in office until the entire cabinet resigned in the wake of Taylor's 1850 death.

After leaving the cabinet, Johnson resumed his legal practice. He played an important role in two Supreme Court cases in the 1850s involving the patent rights to the McCormick reaper, and in 1857 he successfully argued against the slave Dred Scott's claim to freedom. After the collapse of the Whig Party in the early 1850s, Johnson became affiliated with the Democrats. In 1860 he supported Stephen A. Douglas for the presidency, but after Abraham Lincoln's election he strove to keep Maryland in the Union. Johnson served as a delegate to the Washington Peace Conference in February 1861, unsuccessfully attempting to reach a compromise on the slavery expansion issue that would prove acceptable to both the North and South.

The Maryland legislature returned Johnson to the U.S. Senate in 1862, although his appointment by Lincoln to head an investigation into Benjamin F. Butler's military administration in Louisiana prevented him from taking his seat until early 1863. Once in the Senate, Johnson emerged as one of the most vigorous and eloquent leaders of the Democratic opposition to Republican policies. Johnson particularly denounced the Emancipation Proclamation, which he viewed as unconstitutional. He recognized the president's legal right to suspend the writ of habeas corpus, but criticized the administration's use of its arbitrary arrest powers to influence elections in Maryland and other border states.

Johnson briefly served as Mary Surratt's lawyer during the Lincoln assassination conspiracy trial, but some have speculated that he did so only to highlight his opposition to military tribunals. Nevertheless, during Reconstruction, Johnson enraged many Democrats by supporting Radical Republican–sponsored measures such as military rule of the defeated states and citizenship and voting rights for African-Americans. Johnson defended his position on the grounds of expediency, arguing that it was necessary to accept these measures to end the Reconstruction process.

After Johnson voted to acquit President Andrew Johnson in the Senate impeachment trial, the president showed his gratitude by appointing the Marylander minister to Great Britain in 1868. Johnson worked with the British government to negotiate a settlement for the damages done to Union shipping by British-built Confederate raiders during the war, but the Senate rejected the resulting treaty. The incoming Ulysses S. Grant administration removed Johnson from his diplomatic position in 1869, and Johnson devoted his remaining years to his still-flourishing legal practice. He died in Annapolis in 1876 as the result of an accidental fall.

—*Michael Thomas Smith*

See also Congress, U.S.A.; Lincoln Assassination; Surratt, Mary; War Democrats; Washington Peace Conference.
For further reading:
Perlman, Phillip B. "Some Maryland Lawyers in Supreme Court History." *Maryland Historical Magazine* (1948).
Steiner, Bernard C. *The Life of Reverdy Johnson* (1914; reprint, 1970).
Warren, Charles. *A History of the American Bar* (1966).

JOHNSON, RICHARD W.
(1827–1897)
Union general

Born to James L. Johnson and Jane Leeper Johnson in Livingston County, Kentucky, Richard W. Johnson (the initial did not stand for a name) was educated locally before receiving an appointment to the U.S. Military Academy. He graduated thirtieth of forty-three in the class of 1849. In the years before the Civil War, Johnson served at a variety of frontier posts in various states and territories including Minnesota, Texas, and the Indian Territory. He served in both the infantry and the 2d and 5th Cavalry before the war.

At the outbreak of the Civil War, Johnson remained loyal to the Union, though his brother John Milton Johnson became a Confederate surgeon. In August 1861, Johnson was made lieutenant colonel of the 3d Kentucky Cavalry and in October 1861 was promoted to brigadier general of volunteers after William T. Sherman wrote to Abraham Lincoln recommending him as an excellent officer.

Assigned to the Army of the Ohio commanding a brigade in Alexander McDowell McCook's division, Johnson was ill during the Shiloh campaign and unable to participate in the battle. Back in command of his brigade, he led it in the advance on Corinth and received praise for his actions during the campaign. On 21 August 1862 in a skirmish at Hartsfield, Tennessee, near Gallatin, Johnson was captured by John Hunt Morgan. After Johnson's exchange that December, he was sent to the Army of the Cumberland. At the end of the year, he commanded a division at Stone's River and again was commended for gallantry.

Early in 1863, Johnson temporarily commanded XX Corps, Army of the Cumberland. During the early months of 1863, he led foraging parties out from Murfreesborough, Tennessee, and in June he led his division in the Tullahoma campaign, again attracting notice for his actions. As a result of his performance at Chickamauga in September 1863, Johnson received special commendation for bravery from William S. Rosecrans, who also recommended him for promotion to major general of volunteers. George H. Thomas duplicated both the praise and the recommendation.

In the Chattanooga campaign, Johnson commanded

the 1st Division, XIV Corps, and led it at Missionary Ridge. He would remain in command of the division through much of the Atlanta campaign. Before the commencement of that campaign, Johnson and his division participated in the demonstration at Dalton, Georgia, 22–27 February 1864. In the Atlanta campaign, Johnson fought at Resaca before being wounded by a shell fragment at New Hope Church near Dallas, Georgia, on 28 May 1864. Over the next two weeks, he tried to stay in command, but his wound became too painful. He relinquished command of his division on 13 June and was not able to return to duty until 13 July.

Johnson fought in the remainder of the Atlanta campaign and took temporary command of XIV Corps on 7 August when Major General John M. Palmer asked to be relieved as a result of a seniority dispute with commanding general William T. Sherman. Johnson held that command until 22 August, when he was given command of the cavalry corps of the Army of the Cumberland. He commanded the 6th Cavalry Division under James H. Wilson beginning in November and continued in that command for the remainder of the war. He led his division in the Nashville campaign at the end of the year and was commended for gallantry there.

In early 1865 Johnson's division was headquartered at Pulaski, Tennessee, guarding the Tennessee & Alabama Railroad. He operated from there until the end of the war. In May 1865 George Thomas again recommended him for promotion to major general of volunteers.

After the war, Johnson continued to command a part of the occupation in central Tennessee until the fall of 1865. He retired from the army in 1867 at the rank of major general and accepted a position at the University of Missouri as a professor of military science. He later moved to the University of Minnesota, where he also taught military science and became involved in state Democratic politics. He failed in a bid for the governorship of Minnesota in 1881. Along with his teaching, Johnson wrote extensively on his wartime experiences. He died on 21 April 1897 in St. Paul, Minnesota.

—David S. Heidler and Jeanne T. Heidler

See also Atlanta Campaign; Chickamauga, Battle of; Dalton, Georgia, First Battle of; Nashville, Battle of.

For further reading:
Johnson, Richard W. *A Soldier's Reminiscences in Peace and War* (1886).

JOHNSON'S ISLAND
Union prison

Selected by Confederate commissary general of prisoners William Hoffman as one of the first sites for a prisoner-of-war camp, Johnson's Island is located approximately one mile offshore in Sandusky Bay, Lake Erie, and about three miles from the town of Sandusky, Ohio. Hoffman selected the island because of the difficulty of escape, the distance from Canada, and the proximity of Sandusky's rail connections. Unlike most prisons in the North and South, the facility at Johnson's Island was built as a prison, rather than being converted from some other type of buildings.

Work began on the prison in November 1861 and was not completed at the end of February 1862, when the first prisoners arrived from the Confederate defeats at Forts Henry and Donelson. The first commandant of the prison was William S. Pierson, the former mayor of Sandusky. Upon receiving his appointment to the position, Pierson was commissioned at the rank of major, though he was soon promoted to lieutenant colonel. The guards for the camp were a specially recruited battalion, usually referred to as the Hoffman Battalion after the commissary general.

The men at the prison were housed in barracks divided into rooms of various sizes. Originally envisioned as a camp for officers, many of the barracks had small, private rooms. The demand for more prison space, however, quickly saw the camp housing prisoners of all ranks and even a few political prisoners. The construction of additional facilities and the conversion of other sites into prisons caused Johnson's Island in June 1862 to be designated for officers again. By the end of the summer, with the exchange agreement in place, most of the prisoners had left the island.

By the end of 1862, however, the exchange agreement had broken down. Johnson's Island had over 2,000 prisoners by the beginning of 1863. By summer 1863, overcrowding brought the introduction of tents to supplement the overcrowded barracks. While this did not prove to be much of a hardship during the summer months, the following winter of 1863–1864 was one of the coldest in memory. During that time the prison housed over 2,300 prisoners, with all but fifty-nine of them being officers. To bring some civility to an otherwise unpleasant situation, the officers organized themselves into messes. In spite of the cold, it was considered then to be one of the best of the Union prisons, with good barracks and a low death rate.

The cold temperatures provided new challenges for the crowded facility. Even with the relative good conditions, procuring enough fuel for the stoves in the barracks was almost impossible. To make matters even more uncomfortable, the pumps on the island's wells also froze, which forced the commandant to allow the prisoners under guard to travel in groups to the lake shore to procure drinking water. On the other hand, winter was not without its rewards for the prisoners. While escape was impossible during the spring, summer, and fall months, during this hard winter and the one that followed, Lake Erie froze to the mainland, giving the prisoners, if they could make their way outside the stockade, some avenue of escape. During the winters of 1863–1864 and 1864–1865, the camp saw its only escape attempts and twelve prisoners were successful in their efforts. A less tangible reward that came with winter was that the Southern soldiers, many of whom had never seen much snow, enjoyed some rather intense snowball battles between different barracks.

While escape was all but impossible from Johnson's Island, rumors abounded throughout the war that efforts would be made out of Canada to rescue the prisoners on the island. The first of these rumors circulated in June 1862, but they became more prevalent in the last year of the war. As a result of these reports, security was increased at the prison.

Once the war ended in the spring of 1865, all the enlisted and noncommissioned officer prisoners were transferred from Johnson's Island, leaving about 3,000 Confederate officers. All but 150 of the officers were transferred or released by the end of June. Plans were afoot in July 1865 to transfer the remaining men as well, when the orders were issued to release all Confederate soldiers. Johnson's Island prison closed shortly thereafter.

—*David S. Heidler and Jeanne T. Heidler*

See also Prisoners of War; Prisons, U.S.A.

For further reading:
Breen, Donald J. "History of the Federal Civil War Prison on Johnson's Island, 1862–1865" (M. A. thesis, 1962).
Frohman, Charles E. *Rebels on Lake Erie; the Piracy, the Conspiracy, Prison Life* (1975).
Schultz, Charles R. "The Conditions at Johnson's Island Prison During the Civil War" (M.A. thesis, 1960).
Shepherd, Henry E. *Narrative of Prison Life at Baltimore and Johnson's Island, Ohio* (1917).
Speer, Lonnie R. *Portals to Hell: Military Prisons of the Civil War* (1997).

JOHNSONVILLE, TENNESSEE
(November 1864)

On 1 May 1864, 98,000 Federal troops in three armies under the overall command of Major General William T. Sherman left their winter quarters for a campaign that would end with the capture of Atlanta. Throughout the campaign, Georgia governor Joseph E. Brown, General Joseph E. Johnston, and others urged the Confederate government to send raiders like Major General Nathan Bedford Forrest against Sherman's extended supply lines. Repeated Union excursions from Memphis kept Forrest in Mississippi throughout the summer months. Although he won astounding tactical victories over these opponents, they succeeded in keeping him away from the Federal supply lines.

Not until September did Forrest finally free himself to move into northern Alabama and middle Tennessee, but while he devastated the Nashville & Decatur Railroad, he failed to disrupt the direct line between Nashville and Chattanooga. Even so, the expedition proved personally grueling for Forrest. Uncharacteristically, the Confederate cavalry commander sought a furlough, but the service could not spare him.

So, he prepared for another raid deep into enemy-held territory. This expedition would allow him to replenish his ranks and his mounts, but it would also be an opportunity to strike a decisive blow against the Union supply lines. A key chokepoint seemed to be the system of wharves and warehouses and the railroad line at Johnsonville on the Tennessee River.

The raid on Johnsonville began on 16 October 1864. By the 28th, a portion of his command under Brigadier General Abraham Buford had reached the river near Fort Heiman. From this point, batteries could be put into place to shut down the river traffic and thereby disrupt the flow of supplies into Johnsonville.

Buford let several empty vessels pass unmolested, but early on the 29th, when the *Mazeppa* appeared with a barge in tow, he unleashed the Southern gunners. Unwittingly, the *Mazeppa*'s master had passed into the Confederate gauntlet and the pilot could do nothing but ground the vessel on the opposite bank and let the crew abandon it. One of the more enterprising Southerners stripped down and swam across the Tennessee with a line by which the ship could be brought over. When they seized their prize, the Confederates found the vessel loaded with goods, including a jug of French brandy that General Buford requisitioned for himself. However, the appearance of Union gunboats caused the Southerners to panic and set fire to the *Mazeppa* rather than risk losing it.

The next day, another vessel, the *Anna*, came into view. Although it was empty, the Confederates decided not to let it pass. The skipper of the boat brought out a white flag, which caused a lull in the firing. But rather than submit, the Union captain used the opportunity to escape. Ironically, when the *Anna* reached Paducah and warned of the Confederate presence on the Tennessee, this action proved as effective a blockade as anything the Southerners might have attempted.

Subsequently, the Confederates succeeded in taking the Union gunboat *Undine* and the steamers *Venus* and *J. W. Cheeseman*. The latter proved too badly damaged for further use and had to be scuttled, but Forrest had the unusual opportunity to turn his horse soldiers into marines. To that end, he placed the vessels under a couple of subordinates, who wisely refused to accept responsibility until their volatile chief promised not to blame them if they lost their ships.

Forrest next turned his attention to the depot and storage facilities at Johnsonville. It was at this point that

Camp of the Tennessee Colored Battery at Johnsonville, Tennessee, 1864 (*Library of Congress*)

he suffered his first setback. Inclement weather prevented the land-based forces from being able to keep up with, and offer protection for, the captured gunboats. On 2 November, the Confederate "navy" suffered for its complacency. Union gunboats struck the lightly armed *Venus*, forcing its commander to abandon and destroy it. Two days later, it was the *Undine*'s turn to be removed from the Southern service.

Despite the loss of these vessels, Forrest spent the latter part of 3 November and the early part of 4

November helping to place artillery units opposite Johnsonville. Inexplicably, the defenders and the workers at the depot remained oblivious to the Confederate presence nearby. Perhaps one reason for this lack of concern was a strong earthwork that boasted a dozen guns and approximately 2,000 men to guard the depot and storage facilities. Additional security lay anchored in the river in the form of three Union gunboats.

At 2:00 P.M. on 4 November, the Southern gunners

unmasked their hidden batteries and unleashed a barrage upon the wharves and the warehouses of Johnsonville. Within minutes the air filled with smoke and the smells of burning rations. As one observer put it, "The wharf for nearly one mile up and down the river presented one solid sheet of flame." Union lieutenant Edward M. King compounded the chaos and confusion by ordering the Union gunboats to be destroyed rather than risk their capture.

An exuberant Forrest joined in firing one of the artillery pieces, with other officers serving as his makeshift gun crew. By the time he was done, the Confederate cavalryman appraised the damage he had inflicted as "4 gunboats, 14 transports, 20 barges, 26 pieces of artillery and $6,700,000 worth of property." Federal estimates were lower, but no one denied the effectiveness of this operation against Sherman's supply base at Johnsonville.

For his part, William T. Sherman assessed the situation concisely on 6 November in a telegram to Ulysses S. Grant. "That devil Forrest was down about Johnsonville, making havoc among the gunboats and transports." The expedition added to Forrest's reputation, but it came too late to have a larger impact on the war in the Western theater.

—*Brian S. Wills*

See also Atlanta Campaign; Buford, Abraham; Forrest, Nathan Bedford.

For further reading:

Brooksher, William R., and David K. Snider. "Devil on the River." *Civil War Times Illustrated* (1976).

Henry, Robert Selph. *"First With the Most" Forrest* (1944).

Williams, Edward F., III. "The Johnsonville Raid and Nathan Bedford Forrest State Park." *Tennessee Historical Quarterly* (1969).

Wills, Brian Steel. *A Battle From the Start* (1992).

Wyeth, John Allan. *Life of General Nathan Bedford Forrest* (1899; reprint 1989).

JOHNSTON, ALBERT SIDNEY
(1803–1862)
Confederate general

Early in the Civil War, Confederate general Albert Sidney Johnston received from the mother of a young soldier in his command a letter that defined Johnston precisely. Hoping to have her son transferred to his army, she wrote: "I wish him to be near the moulding influence of such a Texan, such a soldier, and such a gentleman."

Johnston qualified splendidly on all three counts. He was a Texan. Though born in Kentucky, he migrated to Texas early in his career and early in the history of an independent Texas. He was a soldier. He served gallantly under the colors of three republics: the United States of America, the Republic of Texas, and the Confederate States of America. He was a gentleman. Every acquaintance, including those who fought against him in the Civil War, attested to this quality within him.

Johnston was born 2 February 1803, in Washington, Kentucky. He came of New England stock; his parents had migrated to Kentucky when it was still in the frontier stage. But he grew up to become an ingrained Kentuckian and Southerner. He would give his life in defense of the South against the land of his ancestors.

Educated in private schools and at Transylvania University in Lexington, Kentucky, Johnston entered the U.S. Military Academy in 1822 at age nineteen. Though not brilliant or exceptionally articulate, he was good in mathematics and he took easily to soldiering. He served during his senior year as adjutant of the Corps of Cadets, the most coveted position in the Corps at that time, and he graduated eighth in the class of 1826. All of the cadets admired him. Two of them—Jefferson Davis and Robert E. Lee—would play conspicuous roles in his later career.

After graduating from the Military Academy, Johnston was stationed at numerous posts around the country. During the spring, summer, and fall of 1832 he served in the Black Hawk Indian War as adjutant to General Henry Atkinson, the commanding general of the U.S. force. Johnston entered this affair a garrison soldier; he emerged a field soldier. His behavior impressed all who knew him. General Atkinson wrote, "He has talents of the first order, a gallant soldier by profession and education." A comrade later said of him, "He was a cool, clearheaded man, and an excellent officer." Another said, "He acquired a very high reputation for his wise and successful conduct during the Black Hawk War."

In April 1834, at the urging of his invalid wife, Johnston resigned his army commission and cared for her until her death more than a year later. In the summer of 1836, he went to the newly independent Republic of Texas and joined its army as a private. Within the next three years, he became successively adjutant general of Texas, commanding general of the army, and secretary of war of the Republic. As a hawk in his attitude toward both the Texas Indians and Mexico, he conducted all of these jobs with outstanding ability.

He resigned from the Texas War Department in March of 1840 and for the next three years spent his time between Texas and Kentucky, where, in October 1843, he was married to Eliza Griffin, cousin to his first wife. For the next two years, the couple lived by turns in Texas and Kentucky. In March 1845, Johnston made a decision to move with his family to a plantation on Oyster Creek near Galveston. He had hardly arrived in that city when he learned that the United States was at war with Mexico, a turn of affairs that he heartily welcomed.

He at once tendered his services and was elected colonel of a Texas volunteer regiment in General Zachary Taylor's army. When the soldiers' terms of enlistment ran out, they left and the regiment disbanded; he was appointed to a division staff. He fought in one battle (Monterrey), where he distinguished himself for courage and coolness under fire and for an extraordinary quality of leadership in the turmoil of combat. When shortly his term of service expired, he honored his promise to his wife that he would not reenlist and returned home.

For more than three years he and his family lived on his Texas plantation. It failed to produce the income he had anticipated, and he was barely able to eke out a living. General Taylor, now President Taylor, rescued Johnston by appointing him paymaster of the frontier Texas forts with the rank of major. Johnston labored in this wearisome job for nearly six years.

He escaped the paymastership in 1855 through the influence of friends, including, significantly, Secretary of War Jefferson Davis, by being appointed colonel of the newly created 2d Cavalry Regiment that was ordered to protect the Texas frontier against the incursions of the Comanche Indians. Lieutenant Colonel Robert E. Lee was second-in-command, and the unit included various other officers who would soon distinguish themselves on both sides during the Civil War.

In August 1857, Johnston was appointed commander of a U.S. force that was on the march to Utah Territory to suppress a threatened rebellion by the Latter Day Saints of Jesus Christ, familiarly known as Mormons. No combat occurred in this affair; Johnston found himself for almost three years at the head of an army of occupation.

His conduct on the difficult march and in the monotonous and worrisome occupation duties earned him the high praise of his superiors and a promotion to brevet brigadier general. In February 1858, General Winfield Scott, commanding general of the army, wrote: "Colonel Johnston is more than a good officer—he is a God send to the country thro' the army....I told [the President]...he would find himself constrained, by admiration, to add a second brevet before the end of the year."

A sketch of Johnston published by *Harper's Weekly* during the Utah confrontation captured him superbly: "[He] is now in the matured vigor of manhood. He is above six feet in height, strongly and powerfully formed, with a grave, dignified, and commanding presence. His features are strongly marked, showing his Scottish lineage, and denote great resolution and composure of character. His complexion, naturally fair, is, from exposure, a deep brown. His habits are abstemious and temperate, and no excess has impaired his powerful constitution. His mind is clear, strong, and well cultivated. His manner is courteous, but rather grave and silent. He has many devoted friends, but they have been won and secured rather by the native dignity and nobility of his character than by his powers of address. He is a man of strong will and ardent temper, but his whole bearing testifies the self-control he has acquired."

He needed every ounce of his vaunted self-control for the Utah assignment. In August 1859, he wrote his daughter, calling the place an "infernal region—It is to me worse than any imagined Siberian exile." Not until the following January did he receive orders relieving him of the despised command. On 1 March 1860, he reviewed his troops for the last time, then wheeled his horse and rode away as the regimental bands played a number titled, ironically, "Come out of the Wilderness."

In November 1860, Johnston was appointed commander of the Pacific Department of the Army, with headquarters in San Francisco. Hardly had he settled into this position when the secession crisis arose. His own adoptive state of Texas seceded on 1 February 1861. Johnston was cruelly torn by this turn of events; he loved both the Union and Texas. But his strongest allegiance lay with Texas, and when he learned of the state's action he submitted his resignation from the U.S. Army.

Initially, he proposed to remain neutral in faraway California, and did so for several months. But eventually he succumbed to the urge to get into the fray. Telling his wife "It looks like fate Texas has made me a rebel twice," he joined a company of horsemen who made their way across the southwestern desert to enter the Southern forces. Early in September 1861, he arrived in Richmond, where he presented himself to his former cadet classmate and his warm friend Jefferson Davis, president of the Confederate States of America.

Davis assigned Johnston to command Confederate Department No. 2, a vast area spreading west from the Appalachians, through Kentucky, across the Mississippi River, and as far as and including Indian Territory (the present state of Oklahoma). Johnston went immediately to Nashville and from there ordered troops to Bowling Green, Kentucky, where he established his headquarters.

In February 1862, Johnston suffered a calamity in the loss of Fort Henry on the Tennessee River and Fort Donelson on the Cumberland River, both in northwestern Tennessee, to the combined army-navy force under General Ulysses S. Grant and Flag Officer Andrew H. Foote. With the Confederate line irreparably penetrated because of Union control of the rivers, thus rendering the Confederates vulnerable to entrapment north of the streams, Johnston withdrew the widely separated wings of his army and united them at the strategic rail center, Corinth, Mississippi, which lay just twenty miles outside the great bend of the Tennessee River. On 6 April, he attacked Grant's unprepared army at Pittsburg Landing on the river. The fighting began near a rural Methodist church named Shiloh, from which the battle received its familiar name.

The fight nearly destroyed Grant's force, but in the early afternoon Johnston was mortally wounded, after which the Confederate attack faltered. General P. G. T. Beauregard, second-in-command, took over, resumed the attack after a two-hour delay, halted it shortly before dark, and renewed it the following morning. During the night, Grant had received heavy reinforcements, and on the second day he counterattacked and drove the Confederates back to Corinth, turning Shiloh into a significant Union victory.

Johnston's death in the first major encounter of the war leaves unanswerable the question of his ultimate capacity as a general. He made serious mistakes in his failed defense of Kentucky, particularly by sending several thousand additional troops into Fort Donelson where they were captured, and he appeared hesitant and indecisive in contrast to the brilliant, impulsive, and voluble Beauregard.

Yet in the Shiloh campaign Johnston clearly outgeneraled Grant in concentrating his forces almost within Grant's sight and achieving a virtually unprecedented surprise in the assault. He also clearly demonstrated better judgment, stability, resolve, and insight into his opponent's mind than did Beauregard, who the day before the battle became thoroughly unnerved and urged that the attack be canceled. In what the great Prussian military theorist Clausewitz calls the "moment of truth" that precedes a battle, Johnston was compelled to overrule his shaken subordinates and order his army forward.

During the battle, Johnston made all the major Confederate tactical decisions, bringing the various corps into action and committing his reserve at the critical time and the crucial point of engagement. Though doubtless he should not have exposed himself to enemy fire as he did on the field, all participants agreed that his electric presence at the front added a potent weapon to the attack.

The consensus among historians of today is that he would not have been able to accomplish his objective of destroying the Union army at Shiloh if he had remained alive. But this is a speculative conclusion. Perhaps a fourth of the Union soldiers abandoned the line early in the day; many others continued to drift away throughout the fighting. Johnston's army was advancing when he was killed, and he was confident of victory.

Johnston's death was an incalculable loss to the Confederacy. One may fairly surmise that if he had survived Shiloh and had been given an opportunity to develop his capabilities fully, as were the other top generals of the war, he would have been a source of great strength. He alone possessed the character (in the Clausewitzian or military sense) and the stature among his subordinates and with the Richmond authorities to have provided the Confederate army in the West a quality of leadership comparable to that of Lee in the East.

— Charles. P. Roland

See also Beauregard, P. G. T.; Davis, Jefferson; Fort Donelson, Battle of; Fort Henry; Shiloh, Battle of.
For further reading:
Johnston, William Preston. *The Life of Gen. Albert Sidney Johnston* (1878).
Roland, Charles P. *Albert Sidney Johnston: Soldier of Three Republics* (1964).

JOHNSTON, JOSEPH EGGLESTON
(1807–1891)
Confederate general

One of five full generals in the Confederate army, Joe Johnston was also one of the more controversial commanders of the war. An 1829 classmate of Robert E. Lee at West Point, Johnston was the senior-ranking U.S. Army officer to resign and fight for the Confederacy. His experience and temperament made him an effective organizer and logistician, and he was well liked—even loved—by the troops he commanded. But his poor relationship with Confederate president Jefferson Davis and his track record of repeatedly declining combat led to his dismissal at a critical moment in July 1864. Controversial then, his dismissal remains so today. His defenders argue that his Fabian strategy of trading space for time was appropriate to the realities of Confederate circumstances in the Civil War, whereas his critics argue that he simply lacked the will or strength of character to commit his troops to battle.

Johnston was born in Prince George County, Virginia, near Farmville on 3 February 1807, but grew up in Abingdon in the far southwestern corner of the state. He was the seventh son of Peter Johnston, a judge of the General Court, and Mary Valentine Wood, a niece of Patrick Henry. Appointed to West Point in 1825, Johnston compiled a distinguished record as a cadet, graduating thirteenth in a class of forty-six. His record there suggests that he was competent and determined rather than brilliant, and his West Point nickname (The Colonel) hints that he was likely a meticulous and fastidious young man.

Johnston's early army career was fairly typical. He spent tours at the Artillery School at Fortress Monroe on the tip of the Virginia peninsula; he was part of an expedition sent to Illinois to settle the Black Hawk War in 1832; and he participated in the Creek wars in Alabama in 1833. He saw his first action in Florida from 1836 to 1838 during the Second Seminole War. In a skirmish near Jupiter Inlet in January of 1838, Johnston received his first wound, and won his first public commendation for bravery.

Johnston was a member of Major General Winfield Scott's staff from 1847 to 1848 during the Mexican-American War. Scott's staff was an impressive group that included Robert E. Lee, P. G. T. Beauregard, George B. McClellan, and George G. Meade. During the siege of Vera Cruz in March 1847, Scott selected Johnston to carry the official demand for surrender to the Mexican commander. In April, Johnston was badly wounded while scouting the enemy position before the battle of Cerro Gordo. After recuperating over the spring, Johnston rejoined the army at Puebla in June in time to participate in the decisive campaign for Mexico City. He participated in the attack on Contreras on 19 August, and led a battalion of voltigeurs (volunteer light infantry) in the climactic assault on Chapultepec just outside the city on 13 September.

Johnston's personal bravery in this campaign won him two brevets, or temporary promotions. Because Congress decreed that officers who won brevets during the war could keep their promotions permanently, Johnston believed that his two brevets had raised him to the rank of colonel. But the Department of the Army determined instead that Johnston was a lieutenant colonel. Johnston's protests against this decision marked the first evidence of a tendency to quarrel with superior authority over perceived slights. Not until 1859 did a friendly secretary of war, John B. Floyd, who was a distant relative of Johnston's by marriage, finally accept Johnston's interpretation and elevate him to the rank of colonel. Then, almost immediately, Floyd appointed Johnston to the vacant position of quartermaster general of the army, an administrative post that carried with it an automatic promotion to the rank of brigadier general.

Johnston opposed Virginia's secession until President Abraham Lincoln called for volunteers to suppress the South. Only then did he tearfully submit his resignation and leave for Richmond, and then for Montgomery, to offer his services to the new Confederate government. Confederate president Jefferson Davis made him a brigadier general and sent him to command the forces gathering at Harper's Ferry, Virginia.

From there, Johnston fell back to Winchester, where on 18 July 1861 he received news that Beauregard's army at Manassas Junction was under attack and that, "if practicable," he should bring his Army of the Valley to Manassas. Johnston did not hesitate. He got his army on the move that same morning and, by utilizing the Manassas Gap Railroad, he managed to get three of his four brigades to Manassas before the battle began on 21 July.

During the battle of First Bull Run, Johnston initially left the tactical decisions to Beauregard, but it was Johnston who grasped the Federal maneuver against the Confederate left and redirected the focus of the battle to Henry House Hill. There he sent his three brigades (those of Bernard Bee, Francis Bartow, and Thomas J. Jackson), and later in the day when it arrived he sent his fourth brigade (Edmund Kirby Smith's) as well. Those decisions were decisive in the outcome, but Johnston was

nettled that most of the public credit for the subsequent victory went to Beauregard or to Jackson, the latter of whose men stood like a "stone wall."

On 31 August 1861, Davis announced the names of the five full generals of the Confederate States Army in order of seniority. Johnston knew that Confederate law mandated that officers who resigned from the U.S. Army to fight for the South would keep their same relative rank in the Confederate Army. Because he was the *only* general officer who had done so, Johnston assumed that he would be ranked first. But Johnston's rank as a brigadier general was a staff rank—it derived from his position as quartermaster general. As an infantry officer, Johnston was still a colonel, and as such he was junior to Samuel Cooper, Albert Sidney Johnston, and Robert E. Lee. Davis therefore ranked him fourth. Johnston complained about it, asserting that his honor was impugned. His protest did nothing to change his relative rank, but marked the beginning of an erosion of trust between the president and the general.

This erosion of trust continued during the Peninsula campaign. As McClellan's huge Federal army debouched on the Virginia Peninsula in April 1862, Davis ordered Johnston to bring his army there and assume command. Although Johnston disapproved of fighting on the Virginia Peninsula, where the Federals could make effective use of their naval superiority, he was overruled by the president and assumed command at Yorktown in mid-April. When McClellan's siege lines appeared nearly complete, however, Johnston abandoned his Yorktown line on 3 May and fell back, first to Williamsburg and then to the outskirts of Richmond. Johnston's plan was to assemble a large army near Richmond and then counterattack once McClellan had advanced beyond the range of the Federal gunboats.

When it came, Johnston's counterattack was poorly coordinated. In the battle of Seven Pines on 31 May 1862, he attempted to converge twenty-one brigades against an isolated corps of the Federal army (that of Erasmus Keyes). Major General James Longstreet misunderstood his orders and took the wrong road. Other units were delayed. The result was a modest tactical victory rather than the decisive engagement necessary to reverse the campaign. Worse for Johnston was that, in attempting to salvage the situation, he rode to the front and was badly wounded. Carried from the battlefield on a stretcher, he had to surrender command of the army.

Johnston was hors de combat for six months. By the time he reported himself as again ready for service in November, Robert E. Lee had won victories in the Seven Days' and at Second Bull Run and had invaded Maryland in the Antietam campaign. Even Johnston knew that he was unlikely to get back his former command. Davis therefore sent him west, where his job would be to coordinate Braxton Bragg's Army of

Tennessee and John C. Pemberton's Army of Mississippi. Johnston did not like his assignment, conceiving of it as an administrative rather than an operational command. He complained that the two armies were too far apart for mutual support. As if to prove him wrong, in December Davis ordered him to send a division from Bragg to support Pemberton. Not only did that division fail to arrive in time to help Pemberton, its absence left Bragg weakened for the battle of Stones River (or Murfreesboro) on 31 December 1862 to 2 January 1863.

In May 1863, Davis (through Cooper) ordered Johnston personally to go to Mississippi to assist Pemberton in the defense of Vicksburg. Johnston arrived in Mississippi's capital at Jackson on 13 May. By then, Grant's forces were between Johnston and Vicksburg. In a telegram, Johnston notified Davis that he was "too late." After the battle of Champion's Hill, Pemberton fell back into the Vicksburg defenses, and Johnston set about trying to find some way to relieve him. Yet, the two generals never saw eye-to-eye: Johnston wanted Pemberton to fight his way out of Vicksburg, thus saving his army; Pemberton wanted Johnston to fight his way in, thus saving the city. In the end, Pemberton was forced to surrender both the city and his army, and he blamed Johnston for the disaster. More importantly, so did Davis.

Johnston held no important command from July to December 1863. Then, just before Christmas, Davis (with great reluctance) appointed him to command the Army of Tennessee, the last major Confederate field army west of the Appalachians. Almost at once Johnston began to receive suggestions from Richmond to initiate an offensive to regain Chattanooga. He argued that the army was not ready, that there was no forage for the animals in the winter, and that it was best to wait until spring. In the spring, however, it was Union general William T. Sherman who took the offensive. In early May, Sherman flanked Johnston out of his defensive position on Rocky Face Ridge near Dalton and then flanked him again at Resaca. These movements set a pattern for the campaign as Johnston gave ground, falling back into central Georgia. By the end of the month, however, Johnston decided that, despite his retrograde movements, the campaign was working out well after all. Sherman was not only losing more men by assuming the tactical offensive, he was compelled to leave men behind to guard his supply lines. Johnston calculated that, if he could inflict three casualties on the enemy for every Southern soldier lost, eventually Sherman would become vulnerable to a counterattack. Johnston was encouraged by the results of Sherman's headlong assault on 27 June 1864 at Kennesaw Mountain, where the Federals lost five times as many men as the Confederates. But in Richmond, Davis was losing patience; after Johnston retreated south of the

Chattahoochee River just north of Atlanta, Davis relieved him of command and replaced him with John Bell Hood on 17 July 1864. Johnston went into effective retirement.

In March 1865, the Confederate Congress passed an act naming Robert E. Lee as commander in chief, and Johnston's old classmate appointed him again to command an army: the remnants of Confederate units left from Hood's wrecked Army of Tennessee and other troops from the Carolinas. In that capacity Johnston fought the battle of Bentonville on 19 March 1865. Technically a tactical victory for the Confederates, it did little more than slow Sherman's advance by a day or two. Meanwhile, Lee was forced to abandon Richmond.

With Lee's surrender at Appomattox, Johnston considered the war at an end. Davis wanted to continue to fight. In a tense meeting in a railroad car in Greensboro, Johnston asked permission from Davis to open negotiations with the enemy to seek an armistice. Davis was skeptical but granted permission. Johnston met with Sherman near Durham Station, North Carolina, on 17 April 1865, and they worked out a political settlement that was rejected by a U.S. government still reeling from Lincoln's assassination three days earlier. Instead of renewing the war, Johnston surrendered his army on 26 April 1865.

After the war, Johnston wrote a self-serving memoir that was particularly critical of Davis. Like many other Confederate veterans, he served as an insurance company executive. From 1879 to 1881 he spent one term as a U.S. congressman from Virginia. When the Democrats recaptured the White House, President Grover Cleveland appointed him commissioner of railroads from 1885 to 1891.

Johnston's wife, Lydia, died in 1887. The couple had always been close, though they had no children. In February 1891, Johnston contracted a cold while serving as a pallbearer at Sherman's funeral in New York, and he died of complications from pneumonia on 21 March.

—*Craig L. Symonds*

See also Atlanta Campaign; Bentonville, Battle of; Bull Run, First Battle of; Champion's Hill, Battle of; Fair Oaks/Seven Pines; Peninsula Campaign; Rocky Face Ridge, Battle of; Stones River, Battle of; Vicksburg Campaign.

For further reading:
Davis, William C. "Jefferson Davis and His Generals." In *The Cause Lost* (1996).
Downs, Alan Craig. "Gone Past All Redemption? The Early War Years of General Joseph Eggleston Johnston" (Ph.D. dissertation, 1991).
Langley, Lee M. "The Strategy and Tactics of C.S.A. General Joseph E. Johnston against U.S. General William T. Sherman in North Georgia: Dalton to Kennesaw, May 4–July 3, 1864" (M.A. thesis, 1986).
Newton, Steven H. *Joseph E. Johnston and the Defense of Richmond* (1998).
Symonds, Craig L. *Joseph E. Johnston: A Civil War Biography* (1992).

JOINT COMMITTEE ON THE CONDUCT OF THE WAR
(1861–1865)

Created in early December 1861 by the Thirty-seventh Congress and popularly known as the War Committee, the Joint Committee on the Conduct of the War was believed necessary to counteract a rash of Union military setbacks in the summer and fall of 1861. Armed with the power of subpoena, the committee was given broad discretion to investigate any aspect of Northern military affairs, "past, present, and future."

Because the Republican Party controlled the U.S. Congress during the Civil War, Republicans also dominated the committee by a margin of five to two. Senate members included Republicans Benjamin F. Wade of Ohio (chairman) and Zachariah Chandler of Michigan, two of the most prominent radicals in the Republican Party. Andrew Johnson of Tennessee, the only senator from a seceded state, was the sole Democratic senator on the committee. When Johnson was appointed military governor of Tennessee in March 1862, he was replaced by Joseph Wright, the former governor of Indiana. House members included Republicans George W. Julian of Indiana, John Covode of Pennsylvania, and Daniel Gooch of Massachusetts. Moses Fowler Odell from Brooklyn, New York, was the sole Democratic house member.

Reappointed by the Thirty-eighth Congress, the committee's membership was the same with two exceptions. On the Senate side, Democrat Benjamin F. Harding of Oregon replaced Joseph Wright. When Harding's senate term expired in 1865, Charles R. Buckalew of Pennsylvania served briefly on the committee. In the House, Republican Benjamin F. Loan replaced John Covode, who had not sought reelection to Congress in 1862. Loan, a brigadier general in the Missouri State Militia, was the only committee member with significant military experience.

Throughout its investigative tenure, the committee delved into many subjects. These included examining allegations of rebel barbarities after the battle of First Bull Run; the administration of specific military departments (John C. Frémont's tenure as military commander of the Department of the West, for instance); contraband trade in enemy districts; government negotiation of ice contracts; the manufacture of heavy ordnance and light draught monitors; the treatment of Union prisoners of war in Confederate prisons; the controversial peace accord negotiated by William Tecumseh Sherman with Confederate general Joseph Johnston; and massacres such as those that occurred at Fort Pillow, Tennessee, and on the banks of Sand Creek in Colorado. The committee's principal focus, however, was the investigation of military battles (usually defeats), particularly

those involving the Army of the Potomac. During the thirty-seventh session of Congress, the committee conducted major investigations of the battles of First Bull Run and Ball's Bluff and the operations of the Army of the Potomac (the Peninsula campaign, the Second Bull Run and Antietam campaigns, and the battle of Fredericksburg). During the Thirty-eighth Congress, the committee again conducted a major investigation of the Army of the Potomac (the Chancellorsville and Gettysburg campaigns) as well as the Red River expedition of Nathaniel Banks and the unsuccessful siege of Fort Fisher by Benjamin F. Butler.

Lacking knowledge about warfare and military matters, the committee had simplistic criteria for evaluating military performance. Convinced that Northern superiority in personnel should produce an automatic and quick victory, committee members were often impatient with generals who did not endorse aggressive, offensive operations. Failing to understand the advantage that rifled weaponry afforded tactical defense, committee members often believed that caution on the part of the Union's West Point–educated officers was a sign of cowardice or questionable loyalty. Because the leading spirits on the committee were fervently devoted to antislavery principles, committee members also judged the performance of military leaders in terms of their own commitment to the abolition of slavery. Regardless of competence, the committee tended to support generals associated with antislavery principles and the Republican Party, while attempting to remove officers who attempted to remain neutral on the slavery issue and were identified with the Democratic Party.

For the entire war, the committee quarreled with the Lincoln administration and many of the army's top officers over control of the nation's armies, particularly the Army of the Potomac. During the Thirty-seventh Congress, the committee devoted an inordinate amount of time attempting to remove George B. McClellan from command. Convinced that McClellan's Democratic sentiments and style of warfare was counterproductive to Union victory, the leading Republicans on the committee were thoroughly convinced that McClellan and his junior officers should be purged from the Army of the Potomac. In the summer of 1862, Zachariah Chandler delivered a scathing rebuke of McClellan before the U.S. Senate, an unprecedented action, especially considering that McClellan was still in command of the Army of the Potomac at Harrison Landing, Virginia.

To replace McClellan, the committee sponsored a number of different Union generals: John C. Frémont, John Pope, Ambrose Burnside, and Joseph Hooker. All of these generals endorsed the Republican position on slavery, although not all had been Republicans before the outbreak of war. Although none of these generals were particularly successful in the commands they were

given, committee members typically explained their lack of success in conspiratorial terms: a West Point–educated professional soldiery, firmly committed to George McClellan, was responsible for hampering the work of these generals.

During the Thirty-eighth Congress, the committee members spent an inordinate amount of time attempting to remove George Gordon Meade from command. As with McClellan, committee members were again convinced that Meade was a Copperhead whose questionable loyalty hampered the effectiveness of the Army of the Potomac. As in the Thirty-seventh Congress, the committee also advanced the interest of generals it saw as "ideologically correct" for command. Joseph Hooker and Benjamin F. Butler were two such generals. Despite Hooker's obvious failings at Chancellorsville, committee members saw him as better suited to command than George Gordon Meade. In the case of Butler, his disastrous handling of the siege of Fort Fisher did not convince committee members that he was unfit for command. Focusing on his antislavery rhetoric and actions earlier in the war as military commander of New Orleans, the committee sang the praises of Butler while criticizing President Lincoln and Ulysses S. Grant for removing him from command.

The Joint Committee on the Conduct of the War was appointed as a way for the legislative branch to check and monitor executive direction of the war. There were a number of different ways in which the committee tried to control President Lincoln's direction of military affairs. In some cases, the committee supplied popular daily newspapers with secret testimony to sway public opinion in its direction. Hence, John C. Frémont's testimony was leaked to the *New York Daily Tribune*. A few weeks later, Frémont, who had earlier been relieved from the command of the Department of the West, was appointed to head the Mountain Department. Individual committee members often made speeches before the House or Senate to advance the committee's point of view. House member George W. Julian supplied some of the most hard-hitting speeches to advance the committee's causes. Finally, through the release of its official reports, the committee hoped to sway public opinion in favor of the Republican war program. In this latter regard, the committee's most notable successes were in the area of war-time propaganda, particularly with the publication of its reports on the treatment of Union prisoners of war and the Fort Pillow massacre. Intended to portray the Southern enemy as backward and benighted, these reports were important morale-building tools.

How successful was the committee in influencing Lincoln in his direction of the Union war effort? The record was mixed. In some cases the president clearly bowed to their pressure and demands. The reappoint-

ment of Frémont to a command was the most obvious case in point. The arrest and imprisonment of Charles Pomeroy Stone for alleged disloyalty after the battle of Ball's Bluff was another indication of the committee's influence. In other respects, however, the president stood firm and was not cowed by his congressional counterparts. When the president removed George McClellan, for instance, he did so on his terms and according to his schedule, not the committee's. Similarly, when the committee attempted to force the removal of Meade, Lincoln would not give in—despite the committee's threat to go public with damaging information. Fortunately for the nation, the president often held his own against the rash judgment of committee members.

The committee's overall impact on Northern military operations is mixed. In some instances, it efforts had positive results. For instance, its investigations of light draught monitors, heavy ordnance, and ice contracts did expose waste, inefficiencies, and bureaucratic red tape. Its report on Union prisoners of war and the Fort Pillow massacre gave a much needed boost to Northern morale at a critical juncture of the war. At the same time, many of its investigations, particularly where the committee was successful in forcing Lincoln's hand, had a negative impact on the war efforts. In many cases, the generals the committee endorsed were "correct" on the slavery issue, but militarily incompetent: Frémont and John Pope being two of the most obvious examples. Perhaps the biggest drawback to the committee's work was its contribution to an atmosphere of jealousy and distrust among the nation's elite officer corps—something that could only detract from waging war. Finally, in many investigations, the impact the committee had was neither positive nor negative. Hour after hour of testimony was taken, witness after witness was interviewed, yet nothing of practical value emerged. In many cases, the committee's work was a waste of time, energy, and resources—something superfluous, something that detracted from the Union's ability to wage war. Committee members were motivated by patriotic and humanitarian sentiments; however, lack of military knowledge combined with too broad of an investigative latitude conspired to limit their usefulness to the Union war effort.

—*Bruce Tap*

See also Chandler, Zachariah; Johnson, Andrew; Julian, George W.; McClellan, George B.; Stone, Charles P.; Wade, Benjamin.

For further reading:
Pierson, William Whately. "The Committee on the Conduct of the War." *American Historical Review* (1918).

Reid, Brian Holden. "Historians and the Joint Committee on the Conduct of the War." *Civil War History* (1992).

Tap, Bruce. *Over Lincoln's Shoulder: The Committee on the Conduct of the War* (1998).

Trefousse, Hans Louis. *The Radical Republicans: Lincoln's Vanguard for Racial Justice* (1969).
Williams, T. Harry. *Lincoln and the Radicals* (1941).

JONES, CATESBY AP ROGER
(1821–1877)
Confederate naval officer

Catesby ap Roger Jones was born on 15 April 1821 in Clark County, Virginia, the eldest son of Army adjutant general Roger Jones and Mary Ann Page Mason, who was a cousin of Robert E. Lee. Jones entered the U.S. Navy as a midshipman in June 1836 and briefly served in the Pacific before embarking on a four-year tour with the East India Squadron. After attending the Philadelphia Naval School in 1841, Jones became a passed midshipman and was posted to the Depot of Charts in Washington, D.C., which was commanded by Matthew F. Maury. This appointment introduced Jones to naval science and allowed him to field test the latest technical advances.

From the Depot of Charts, he moved to the Hydrographical Office, recording magnetic and meteorological measurements and acquiring scientific knowledge that cleared a path for future appointments. After another tour in the Far East, he spent the Mexican-American War aboard the ship-of-the-line *Ohio*, though without seeing much action. Immediately after the war, he served aboard the steamer *St. Mary*, conducted a thorough survey of the bay at San Francisco, and in May 1849 was promoted to lieutenant. He took a lengthy leave, prolonged by the effects of an injury he suffered in Paris in December 1851, when he was caught in the street fighting during the coup d'état in which President Louis Napoleon Bonaparte became Emperor Napoleon III.

Upon his return home in February 1853, Jones became an ordnance officer at the Washington Navy Yard, where he assisted Lieutenant John A. Dahlgren in experiments on a new type of weapon, the results of which produced the famous Dahlgren smoothbore gun. In early February 1856, at Dahlgren's request, Jones became the ordnance and watch officer aboard the USS *Merrimack*. For more than a year, he worked with Dahlgren and his guns aboard the *Merrimack* before being transferred to the ordnance steamer *Plymouth*. In 1858 Jones participated as ordnance officer aboard the *Caledonia* in the navy's Paraguayan expedition, and in 1859 he acted in the same capacity while preparing the *Pawnee* for sea duty.

The twenty-five-year officer placed his loyalty to Virginia above his loyalty to the Union and on 17 April 1861 resigned his commission in the U.S. Navy. Less than two months later, he participated in an unauthorized attack on the Union's Gosport Navy Yard at Norfolk that captured 300,000 pounds of powder and many shells. After that attack Jones was commissioned a lieutenant in the Confederate States Navy; he took command of the defenses at Jamestown Island on the James River, where he oversaw the construction of fortifications and batteries.

On 11 November 1861, Confederate Secretary of the Navy Stephen Russell Mallory appointed Jones executive and ordnance officer aboard the CSS *Virginia* (formerly the USS *Merrimack*), then being outfitted as an ironclad warship. Jones played an important role in the completion and arming of the ironclad and the recruiting and training of its crew and officers; by early March 1862 the *Virginia* was prepared for its first cruise. On 8 March 1862, the first day of the battle of Hampton Roads, the *Virginia* wreaked havoc on the Union blockading force in Chesapeake Bay; the ironclad sank two Union frigates, drove three steam frigates aground, and exchanged fire with several small armed steamers and shore batteries. As executive and ordnance officer, Jones supervised the ironclad's activities. Late that afternoon, with Captain Franklin Buchanan wounded, Jones assumed command and sank the Union frigate *Congress* before sunset.

The following morning, 9 March 1862, Jones commanded the *Virginia* in its momentous duel against the Union ironclad *Monitor*. Beginning at about 8:45 A.M., the two ships circled one another while trying to gain an advantageous position. Although the ironclads battled furiously at close range for the next four hours, they did minimal damage to each other; neither vessel could claim a clear victory.

Jones remained the *Virginia's* executive officer until it was destroyed in May 1862. Afterward he commanded the ironclad *Chattahoochee* at Columbus, Georgia, and naval works at Charlotte, North Carolina. Promoted to commander in 1863, he was transferred to the Confederate naval gun foundry and ordnance works at Selma, Alabama, where he remained until the end of the war. In fact, Jones supplied the cannon at Fort Morgan in Mobile and the guns for Franklin Buchanan's fleet at Mobile Bay in 1864. After the war, Jones worked for a short time in South America, where several nations sought his ordnance expertise. Retiring with his family to Selma, he was shot in a domestic quarrel with a neighbor on 20 June 1877.

—*Gene A. Smith*

See also Buchanan, Franklin; Navy, C.S.A.; Ordnance, Naval; *Virginia*, CSS.

For further reading:

Davis, William C. *Duel between the First Ironclads* (1975).
Jones, Catesby ap R. "Services of the *Virginia* (*Merrimack*)." *Southern Historical Society Papers* (1876).
Jones, Lewis Hampton. *Captain Roger Jones of London and Virginia* (1891).
Mabry, W. S. *Brief Sketch of the Career of Captain Catesby Ap R. Jones* (1912).
Smith, Gene A. *Iron and Heavy Guns: Duel between the Monitor and Merrimack* (1996).

JONES, CHARLES COLCOCK, JR.
(1831–1893)
Confederate officer

Charles Colcock Jones, Jr., was born in Savannah, Georgia, on 28 October 1831. Jones was a multi-talented individual who would serve his community as a lawyer, civil official, military officer, archaeologist, and historian. His many accomplishments reflect his privileged social position as the son of a prominent Georgia planter, the Reverend Charles Colcock Jones, Sr. The elder Jones owned several plantations in the Georgia Low Country and gained national recognition as a missionary and vocal advocate for evangelizing African-American slaves. Reverend Jones, a Presbyterian minister, embraced slavery as being divinely ordained and sought to elevate both the institution and African-Americans by making Christian principles their guiding focus. Thus, Charles the younger grew up in an environment where plantations, paternalistic mastery, and Gullah-speaking slaves dominated the landscape. These early experiences largely shaped his worldview and guided his endeavors throughout his life.

In keeping with his social status, Jones was well educated and received a bachelor's degree from Princeton in 1852, followed by a juris doctorate from Harvard University in 1855. After graduating from Harvard, Jones returned to Savannah, where he practiced law for six years with his partner, John Elliot Ward. Jones assumed the office of city alderman in 1859, before his election as mayor of Savannah in 1860. During his two-year tenure as mayor, Jones made clear his strong support for secession. Following the outbreak of the Civil War, he declined reelection and joined his comrades in Savannah's oldest volunteer company, the Chatham Artillery, in entering Confederate service.

Jones began the Civil War defending Georgia's coastline as senior first lieutenant of the Chatham Artillery. In 1862 Jones received promotion to the rank of lieutenant colonel and assumed the position of chief of artillery for the Military District of Georgia. He saw his most notable combat in 1864 during the siege of Savannah, when he was responsible for providing a covering barrage for Confederate troops retreating across the river into South Carolina. After the loss of Savannah, Jones served as chief of artillery for General William Hardee and ultimately surrendered with the forces commanded by General Joseph E. Johnston.

Jones has received the greatest notoriety for his activities after the Civil War. In 1866 he moved to New York City, where he resumed practicing law with his partner John Ward. Jones remained in New York until 1877, when he moved his law practice to Augusta, Georgia. Throughout his stay in New York and return to Georgia, Jones wrote prolifically about his native region and its

inhabitants. During his lifetime he wrote no fewer than eighty published works. His contemporaries thought so highly of his work that noted American historian George Bancroft dubbed Jones "the Macaulay of the South."

As a historian Jones had a tremendous interest in American Indian antiquities and published several works on the subject, including *Historical Sketch of Tomo-chi-chi, Mico of the Yamacraws* (1868), and *Antiquities of the Southern Indians* (1873). However, Jones reserved his greatest passion for commemorating the history of Georgia and the Old South. He wrote a detailed two-volume history of Georgia up to the American Revolution, as well as individual studies of Savannah and Augusta. In works such as *Historical Sketch of the Chatham Artillery* (1867), *The Siege of Savannah in December 1864* (1874), and *Negro Myths from the Georgia Coast* (1888), Jones celebrated his vision of Southern gallantry and the grandeur of the Old South. Jones lamented the passing of this bygone era and in his writings and public speeches repeatedly defended the institution of slavery, states' rights, secession, and the South's conduct during the Civil War. He openly opposed the industrial growth of the New South as he believed it made the region too much like the North and thereby dishonored Southern ancestors and the agricultural society they had created. To protect his vision of the Old South, in 1877 Jones organized and served as president of the Confederate Survivor's Association of Augusta. He would serve in this position until his death on 19 July 1893. Because he attempted to romanticize the Southern and, especially, Confederate past in his extensive postwar publications and public activities, Charles Colcock Jones, Jr., should be considered a leading architect of the mythology associated with the Old South and the Lost Cause.

—*Daniel L. Fountain*

See also Georgia; Lost Cause.
For further reading:
Jones, Charles Edgeworth. *In Memoriam Colonel Charles C. Jones, Jr., LL.D., Historian, Biographer, and Archaeologist, 1831–1893* (1893).
Myers, Robert Manson, ed. *The Children of Pride: A True Story of Georgia and the Civil War* (1972).
Stacy, James. *History of the Midway Congregational Church, Liberty County, Georgia* (1899).

JONES, JOHN BEAUCHAMP
(1810–1866)
Confederate war clerk

Born in Baltimore, Maryland, and reared in Kentucky and Missouri, John B. Jones attended local schools in the latter two states. As a young man, he made his living as a journalist. He served as the editor of the *Baltimore Saturday Visitor*, the *Madisonian*, and the *Southern Monitor*. He also wrote and published

an extensive amount of fiction and poetry, using his writing to advocate Southern issues but to discourage secession. Jones also served a brief stint during the James K. Polk administration as U.S. consul in Naples.

When hostilities erupted between the North and South, Jones traveled from Philadelphia to Montgomery, Alabama, to seek an appointment in the Confederate government. He was given a clerk's position in the Confederate War Department and worked directly for Secretary of War Leroy Pope Walker. During his time in the War Department, Jones kept a diary that would form the basis for one of the more widely used sources for activities within the Confederate government. Written with publication in mind, the diary contained as much insider information as Jones could gather. Besides his rather time-consuming duties in the War Department and keeping his detailed diary, Jones also served from 1862 through April 1863 as the captain of a Richmond artillery company.

After the war, Jones prepared his diary for publication. It was published in 1866 as *A Rebel War Clerk's Diary at the Confederate States Capital*, but Jones died in Burlington, New Jersey, before the book reached print.
—*David S. Heidler and Jeanne T. Heidler*

For further reading:
Brockman, Clark. "John Beauchamp Jones" (M.A. thesis, 1937).
Jones, J. B. *A Rebel War Clerk's Diary at the Confederate States Capital* (1866).

JONES, JOHN ROBERT
(1828–1901)
Confederate general

One of the least well-known, yet most controversial, of the generals in Robert E. Lee's Army of Northern Virginia, John Robert Jones was born 12 March 1828 in Harrisonburg, Virginia. He entered Virginia Military Institute (VMI) in 1845 and graduated seventh in his class on 4 July 1848. Upon graduation, he also stood second in tactics and had earned the highest rank and honor in the corps of cadets, first captain or battalion commander.

Because Jones attended VMI as a state cadet, which meant he relied on the commonwealth to pay his tuition, he was required to teach in Virginia for two years. He taught first at Staunton Academy, then at Rappahannock Academy in Caroline County. He later moved to Maryland and operated a military school in Urbanna. Jones was teaching at a male and female seminary in Quincy, Florida, at the outbreak of the Civil War. On 5 January 1861, under orders from the governor of Florida, Jones commanded a company that marched from Quincy to Apalachicola, seizing the U.S. arsenal there on 6 January.

Jones returned to his hometown in April and organized a unit that mustered into Confederate service on 22 June 1861, as Company I, 33d Virginia Infantry Regiment, with Jones as captain. Although the 33d was assigned to Thomas J. Jackson's brigade, soon to be immortalized as the Stonewall Brigade, Jones and his company were on detached duty guarding prisoners in Winchester, Virginia, during the battle of First Bull Run on 21 July 1861. Appointed lieutenant colonel one month later, Jones participated in Stonewall Jackson's 1862 Shenandoah Valley campaign and was cited for distinguished service at the first battle of Kernstown on 23 March 1862. In April Jackson sent Jones on an expedition to quell a militia insurrection in his native Rockingham County. Not only did Jones put down the rebellion, he also won the favor of his commanding general.

Jackson recommended Jones for appointment as a brigadier general in June 1862, a move subsequently endorsed by Lee and Confederate president Jefferson Davis. Jones received his appointment on 25 June and took command of the 2d Brigade, Jackson's Division, Army of Northern Virginia. Colonel John A. Campbell, who commanded one of the regiments in the Second Brigade, protested the appointment and resigned his commission. The Confederate Senate never confirmed Jones's promotion.

Jones led his brigade during the Seven Days' battles and was cited favorably for his performance at the battle of Gaines' Mill on 27 June. While moving the brigade into position at Malvern Hill on 1 July, Jones was wounded in the knee by a shell fragment and left the field. He returned to duty within a few days, but soon contracted typhoid fever and again relinquished command of the brigade. Jones did not rejoin the army until 6 September during Lee's campaign into Maryland.

Because he now was the senior brigadier general, Jones took command of Stonewall Jackson's old division on 7 September 1862. He participated in the capture of Harper's Ferry on 14–15 September, and was wounded by the concussion of an artillery round on the morning of 17 September at Antietam. Soon afterward, Lee sent Jones to gather stragglers in the Shenandoah Valley. Jones reassumed command of the 2d Brigade and led it on 13 December 1862 at the battle of Fredericksburg. Although the brigade was held in reserve, the new division commander, Brigadier General William B. Taliaferro, favorably cited Jones in his official report of the battle.

In February 1863 a captain in one of the regiments in Jones's brigade preferred cowardice charges against him, most likely because of Jones's early departure from the battlefield at Antietam. A court-martial board met in March to decide his fate and honorably acquitted him in April on four counts of misbehaving in front of the enemy. He commanded his brigade at the battle of Chancellorsville on 2 May 1863, helping to carry out Jackson's famed flank attack on Union general Joseph Hooker's army. Late that night, Jones left the field due to an ulcerated leg and never again commanded a unit in the Army of Northern Virginia.

Because the Confederate Senate would not confirm his promotion, and possibly because his chief supporter, Stonewall Jackson, had died, Jones resigned from the Confederate army in May 1863 and was replaced by Brigadier General John M. Jones. After returning to Harrisonburg, Jones decided to travel to Maryland in the wake of Lee's invasion of Pennsylvania to retrieve his wife's belongings in Frederick County. On 4 July 1863, Jones was captured as a civilian by Union cavalry forces attacking Lee's retreating wagon trains at Smithsburg, Maryland. Jones served time in Fort McHenry (Maryland), Johnson's Island (Ohio), and finally Fort Warren (Massachusetts), where he was released on 24 July 1865.

After the war, Jones returned to Harrisonburg and established a successful agricultural implement business and sold real estate and insurance. Jones's involvement in Confederate memorial activities was limited. He did not join the local Confederate veterans group and gave away the frock coat he wore as a Confederate general and a saber he captured at the fall of Harper's Ferry in September 1862. He served on Harrisonburg's first school board, on the town council, and as a vestryman for a local Episcopal church. He was appointed a commissioner in chancery of the Rockingham County Circuit Court in 1877 and served in this position until his death in Harrisonburg 1 April 1901. He was buried there in Woodbine Cemetery.

Jones's life during and after the Civil War proved to be controversial in the eyes of former Confederates, citizens in his hometown, and Civil War historians. His tendency to depart early from various battlefields with relatively minor wounds helped establish a reputation of cowardice among some of his contemporaries and most twentieth-century Civil War historians. Douglas Southall Freeman found Jones's battlefield conduct to be so distasteful that he hesitated mentioning him by name in his monumental work, *Lee's Lieutenants*. While he was not a stellar leader, no significant documentary evidence has been produced to substantiate a lack of bravery on his part. The testimony and evidence presented at his court-martial were not revealed.

Jones further tarnished his reputation among his neighbors by fathering at least four children with an African-American woman after the war. One of these children, Mary Rice Hayes Allen, became an early black civil rights leader, helping form NAACP branches in Lynchburg, Virginia, and Montclair, New Jersey. Jones audaciously acknowledged his illegitimate offspring

publicly, helping to ensure his name would be largely forgotten by citizens in his hometown. When one historian wrote to Harrisonburg resident and former Confederate T. L. Williamson requesting information on Jones, Williamson advised, "[Y]ou would do well to drop his name from the list of honorable men, if such is to be your roster when complete....Draw a line through his name and be sure and have it Black."

—*Dale F. Harter*

For further reading:
Freeman, Douglas Southall. *Lee's Lieutenants: A Study in Command* (1942–1944).
Harter, Dale F. "Ignored by History." *Montpelier* (1992).
McCray, Carrie Allen. *Freedom's Child: The Life of a Confederate General's Black Daughter* (1998).

JONES, JOHN WILLIAM
(1836–1909)

Baptist minister, chaplain, and promoter of the Lost Cause

John William Jones was born in Louisa County, Virginia, to Colonel Francis W. Jones and Ann Pendleton Ashby Jones. As a young adult, he underwent a conversion experience at a camp meeting. This conversion experience led Jones to pursue a career in the ministry. He first attended the University of Virginia and then the Southern Baptist Theological Seminary in Greenville, South Carolina. In 1860, Jones was ordained to the Baptist ministry and accepted the pastorate of Little River Baptist Church in Louisa County. Later that same year he married Judith Page Helm.

Jones originally hoped to serve as a missionary in China, but Virginia's secession from the Union changed those plans, and Jones enlisted in the Virginia 13th Regiment in A. P. Hill's corps. Within a year, the soldiers of his regiment elected him chaplain of the regiment, and in 1863 Jones was appointed as missionary to Hill's corps. By the end of 1863, Jones also served as a colporteur for the Evangelical Tract Society, the Confederate counterpart to the American Tract Society. In late 1864, Jones helped organize the Association of Chaplains and Missionaries, a fraternal gathering where colporteurs and chaplains could share stories of their work in the army.

Jones's wartime experience and especially his participation in the large revivals that swept through the Confederate armies stand at the center of his later ministry. After Robert E. Lee surrendered to Ulysses S. Grant at Appomattox, Jones returned to the parish ministry as pastor of the Baptist Church in Lexington, Virginia, and chaplain at nearby Washington College. During this period he developed a lasting friendship with Lee, who served as president of the college. Soon after Lee's death, Jones resigned his pastorate and went to work for the Southern Baptist Theological Seminary in

Louisville, Kentucky. He also served stints as chaplain at the University of North Carolina and the University of Virginia. Through all these appointments, Jones remained dedicated to Confederate ideals and worked diligently to preserve the Confederacy's heritage by collecting letters and reminiscences from former Confederate chaplains and soldiers and publishing several volumes, including the first memoir of Lee published after his death and numerous articles on Confederate leaders. Jones also served as secretary-treasurer for the Southern Historical Society.

Jones' frequent lectures and writings made him a visible and popular propagator of the Confederacy's past. He is best remembered for his book, *Christ in the Camp, or, Religion in Lee's Army* (1887), which sold tens of thousands of copies and remains in print to this day. The volume is largely a compilation of contemporary and postwar reminiscences about the religious life and especially the revivals in the Confederate army. *Christ in the Camp*, along with Jones's diligent effort to preserve the Confederacy's heritage, endeared Jones to many Southerners in the postwar decades and has led many to portray Jones as a principle speaker for the Lost Cause.

The traditional view has suggested that Jones, with his defense of the Lost Cause, promoted a Southern civil religion, one that fused transcendent ideals with the Confederacy's past. To be sure, Jones energetically promoted the Confederate heritage and at the same time spoke of religion. But Jones's Lost Cause was not so much a civil religion as an evangelical one. Jones did not create a new civil religion in the aftermath of defeat. Rather, he restated the message of the war for Southerners but, in light of Union triumph, ensured that the traditional gospel themes dominated his message. After all, the gospel message of Southern evangelical churches stood at the heart of their identity.

For *Christ in the Camp*, Jones culled material from religious newspapers such as *Army and Navy Messenger*, *The Soldier's Friend*, and *The Soldier's Visitor* that the Southern churches printed for the soldiers. These newspapers had carefully fused traditional evangelical conversion messages and current military news with encouraging words of hope and the promise of eventual triumph. Those writings reveal the rationale that ministers offered as a way to build morale and inspire hope. Military defeats, ministers insisted, should be understood as divine chastisement for past sins and not as harbingers of eventual doom for Southern civilization. What made that message of hope possible were the revivals within the Confederate army. And while Jones and others may have been blind to subtle transformations of that message during the war, they clearly did not loose sight of what was important: their faith in God and the belief that God had special blessings for the South. In other words, Jones's Lost Cause message was less a civil religion and more an evangelical message. Although many who heard Jones's postwar pronouncements fashioned them into a civil religion and utilized it to undergird white supremacy and discriminate against and suppress African-Americans, Jones was not similarly motivated. After the war, he modified his wartime evangelical message to account for Confederate defeat, but the thrust remained the same. He called upon individuals to experience a religious conversion, even as he continued to praise those elements of Southern society and Confederate heroes that he believed exemplified Christian virtues.

—*Kurt O. Berends*

See also Chaplains; Churches; Lost Cause.
For further reading:
Gordon, Armistead C., Jr. "John William Jones." In *Dictionary of American Biography* (1932).
Taylor, George Braxton. *Virginia Baptist Ministers* (1915).
Wilson, Charles Reagan. *Baptized in Blood: The Religion of the Lost Cause, 1865–1920* (1980).

JONES, SAMUEL
(1819–1887)
Confederate general

Born in Powhatan County, Virginia, the son of Samuel Jones and Ann Moseley Jones, the younger Jones graduated nineteenth of fifty-two in the 1841 class at the U.S. Military Academy. He served in Maine and Florida before returning to West Point in 1846 as an instructor. Between 1853 and 1858 he served in New Orleans and Texas. In 1858 he moved to Washington, D.C., to become the assistant judge advocate. When Virginia seceded in April 1861, he resigned his commission and offered his services to the Confederacy.

Receiving a colonel's commission and serving under P. G. T. Beauregard at Manassas Junction, Jones was Confederate chief of artillery at the battle of First Bull Run. He was promoted that day to brigadier general. For the remainder of the year he commanded a brigade in western Virginia.

In January 1862, Jones was transferred to Pensacola, Florida. Shortly after his arrival, he was instructed to oversee the dismantling of all Confederate military works around the town and send any ordnance and supplies to Mobile. After supervising this activity, Jones shifted his headquarters to Mobile, where he was promoted to major general in March 1862. His official title was commander of the Department of Alabama and West Florida.

In late summer 1862, Jones was transferred to the command of the Department of Middle Tennessee, headquartered at Chattanooga. In that capacity he fought at the battle of Corinth in October 1862, one of his few combat roles of the war. Shortly afterward he was transferred to the command of the Department of Western Virginia, headquartered in Dublin, Virginia. He held that command, which also included eastern Tennessee, until March 1864. During that time, he was not perceived as being very effective and, because of his lack of success in preventing Union incursions into his territory, he was transferred to Charleston, South Carolina, in April 1864.

From April until December 1864, Jones commanded the Department of South Carolina, Georgia, and Florida. His primary duty was to see to the coastal defenses of each of these states. He had to perform this duty with limited resources, particularly after William Sherman began his invasion of Georgia in the summer of 1864. With the fall of Savannah to Sherman in December 1864, Jones was transferred to command the District of Florida headquartered in Tallahassee. It was there that he surrendered on 10 May 1865. He was paroled on 12 May.

After the war Jones returned to Virginia, where he became a farmer. In 1880 he accepted a job as a War Department clerk. He died in Virginia.

—*David S. Heidler and Jeanne T. Heidler*

See also Corinth, Siege of; Florida; Georgia; South Carolina.
For further reading:
Burton, E. Milby. *The Siege of Charleston: 1861–1865* (1970).
Jones, Samuel. *The Siege of Charleston and the Operations on the South Atlantic Coast in the War among the States* (1911).

JONES, WILLIAM EDMONSON
(1824–1864)
Confederate general

Born in Washington County, Virginia, William Edmonson Jones was educated at Emory and Henry College before accepting an appointment to the U.S. Military Academy in 1844. He graduated tenth of thirty-eight in the class of 1848. Jones served at a variety of frontier posts for the next nine years. He resigned his commission in 1857 to travel to Europe and then to return to his family estate in Virginia. He concentrated on farming until Virginia seceded at the end of April 1861.

Upon Virginia's secession, Jones organized a company of mounted riflemen known as the Washington County Mounted Rifles. Shortly afterward, he was promoted to major in the state forces and charged with training cavalry. He served under J. E. B. Stuart at First Bull Run, beginning an association with that officer that would not always be a happy one, perhaps one of the reasons for Jones's nickname of "Grumble." At Bull Run, Jones's most significant action was protecting Thomas J. Jackson's right flank during the fighting on Henry House Hill.

In September 1861, Jones was promoted to colonel and given command of the 1st Virginia Cavalry. He held that command until March 1862, when he transferred to the command of the 7th Virginia Cavalry. In that month he fought under Stuart along the Orange & Alexandria Railroad. Jones and his regiment continued to protect rail lines until August 1862.

On 2 August 1862, Jones and the 7th fought a skirmish with Federal cavalry at Orange Court House before linking up with Stonewall Jackson and fighting at Cedar Mountain on 9 August. Almost three weeks later, Jones and his regiment fought with Jackson's corps again at Groveton on 28 August and then at Second Bull Run. After that engagement, Jones and the 7th were detached to guard the railroads in northern North Carolina during Robert E. Lee's invasion of Maryland.

In September 1862, Jones was promoted to brigadier general and given command of Thomas T. Munford's cavalry brigade, the one originally commanded by Turner Ashby during Stonewall Jackson's Valley campaign. Jones led that brigade during Stuart's Chambersburg Raid in October 1862. The tensions between Jones and Stuart, however, reached new heights during this raid, and after its conclusion, Stuart tried to have Jones transferred from the Army of Northern Virginia. In December, probably temporarily to separate the two tempestuous officers, Lee gave Jones command of the Confederate Valley District, and over the next six months Jones used his brigade to protect Confederate positions and to threaten the Baltimore & Ohio Railroad.

During the early months of 1863, Jones and his troops skirmished frequently with Federal forces around Winchester, Strasburg, and Woodstock. Yet even though he was seen as a serious nuisance by the Federal forces in the area—Union cavalryman George Stoneman referred to Jones and his men as "guerrillas"—Jones was never able to cut the vital Baltimore & Ohio rail link. By the end of February 1863 Confederate secretary of war James Seddon had lost patience and suggested to Lee that Jones be replaced. Lee wrote back that if ordered to do so he would remove Jones, but he argued that, given his personnel shortages and other considerations, Jones had done as well as anyone under similar circumstances.

At the end of April 1863, Jones confirmed Lee's faith in him by conducting a raid in cooperation with John Imboden on the bridges of the Baltimore & Ohio in western Maryland and Virginia. Jones's part of the raid destroyed a number of bridges and disrupted Federal communications. Shortly after completing his mission, Jones was summoned east with his brigade to join with Stuart for the upcoming invasion of the North. Rather than serving under Stuart again, Jones resigned. Lee, however, persuaded him to withdraw his resignation

Jones arrived in time to participate in the battle of Brandy Station. Stuart commended him for his actions during the engagement. Though unhappy with the

assignment, Jones fought under Stuart for the remainder of the Gettysburg campaign and afterward participated in the screening of the infantry as it retreated southward.

In the early fall, the strain between Jones and Stuart reached the breaking point when Jones publicly criticized his commander, and Stuart had him arrested. Jones was convicted by a court-martial of disrespect to a superior and reprimanded. Lee, however, realized that the two men could no longer work together and sent Jones to serve under Samuel Jones in the Department of Southwest Virginia and East Tennessee. In his request for Jones's transfer, Lee remarked that, with the exception of Jones's inability to work with Stuart, he was an excellent officer.

Jones reported to his new commander on 11 October and assumed command of a cavalry brigade. His primary job was to combat Union cavalry in the department, and in his first major action on 6 November he was quite successful. On that day he attacked a 700-man cavalry contingent at Rogersville, Tennessee, and captured most of the Federal troopers. At the end of November, Jones took two brigades from the department to participate in James Longstreet's campaign against Knoxville, Tennessee.

Jones returned to Virginia at the end of the year and on 3 January 1864 attacked 300 Union cavalry at Jonesville, Virginia, and captured them all. He found himself, however, again in the midst of a controversy, this time not of his own making. Brigadier General John S. Williams complained to Major General Samuel Jones that since Grumble Jones's arrival in the department he had been given preferential treatment and assignments even though Williams was the senior officer. Williams requested transfer as a result of what he saw as his unfair treatment. Shortly after this complaint was made, Jones was again placed temporarily under Longstreet's command in East Tennessee.

In the spring of 1864, Jones was sent to serve as second-in-command to John C. Breckinridge in West Virginia. After fighting at Cloyd's Mountain in May 1864, Jones was charged with preventing the joining of the forces of David Hunter and George Crook. He encountered Hunter near Piedmont, Virginia, on 5 June, and after a lengthy artillery duel and infantry attacks on both sides, the Confederates were forced to retreat. During the withdrawal, Jones was struck by a Federal bullet and killed. His body fell into Union hands, but it was returned to his family under a flag of truce.

—*David S. Heidler and Jeanne T. Heidler*

See also Imboden's and Jones's Raid; Piedmont, Battle of.

For further reading:

Collier, Mark C. *Engagement at Piedmont, Va., June 5th, 1864* (1997).

Lambert, Dobbie Edward. *Grumble: The W. E. Jones Brigade of 1863–1864* (1992).

McDonald, William N. *A History of the Laurel Brigade, Originally the Ashby Cavalry of the Army of Northern Virginia and Chew's Battery* (1907).

JONESBORO, BATTLE OF
(31 August–1 September 1864)

By late summer 1864, William T. Sherman's Union army stood before Atlanta. Unwilling to attack strong fortifications or conduct a lengthy siege, Sherman attempted to slip around the Confederate flanks and cut the rail lines upon which the city depended. After his cavalry failed to cut the rail lines, Sherman moved his infantry westward. On 28 July, the Confederates struck the Northern forces but failed to drive them back at Ezra Church. On 10 August, John Bell Hood sent his cavalry to raid Sherman's lines of communication. Joseph Wheeler's horsemen accomplished little and were absent during the critical battles. With Wheeler out of the picture, Sherman moved his forces on 28 August against the Macon Railroad at Jonesboro.

General William Hardee soon had his Confederate corps moving toward Jonesboro. On 30 August, the forward elements of Sherman's army (XV, XVI, and XVII Corps and Judson Kilpatrick's cavalry), commanded by Oliver O. Howard, crossed the Flint River and seized a strong position one mile from Jonesboro. They found Hardee's forces already there.

Hood determined to strike Sherman's advance forces. Stephen D. Lee's corps was ordered to reinforce Hardee and throw Howard's forces back across the Flint River. Lee was then to rejoin Hood, and together they would fall on Sherman's left flank while Hardee crossed the Flint and attacked Sherman's exposed right. Hood, however, had no hope of success because of the weakness of his forces.

Lee's movement began at 11:30 P.M. His forces did not reach the battlefield until late on 31 August, giving Howard's men time to strengthen their positions.

The Union position was a semicircle along a high piece of ground a half mile in diameter, facing east, centering on the road to Renfroe Place and backing on the Flint River. The XVII Corps covered the northern end. The right (southern) end of the Union defense was anchored on the Flint River and was held by John M. Corse's division of XVI Corps. Kilpatrick's cavalry held Anthony's Bridge, half a mile south of the Union position. Howard's forces comprised 12,000 men in line with 8,500 in close reserve.

Hardee advanced with his 20,000 troops spread over a one-and-a-half-mile front. Patrick Cleburne's corps (Hardee's) was on the Confederate left in a formation designed to provide a heavy mass of infantry for the attack at the southern end of Howard's position. Lee's corps was spread over nearly a mile of ground, with its greatest strength massed to strike the northern end.

Hardee planned a direct frontal assault over open ground against an entrenched enemy. The attack was to

The battle of Jonesboro, 1 September 1863 (*Library of Congress*)

be made *en echelon* beginning at the left of Cleburne's corps. It was after 3:00 P.M. when the attack started, and immediately things went wrong. The inexperienced Lee mistook the gunfire of skirmishers for Cleburne's main assault and launched his own unsupported forces prematurely. The effort of the exhausted troops, who had had little sleep or food for two days and who had futilely attacked entrenched positions three times in a month, was feeble.

To the left, Cleburne's attack also misfired. Hiram Granbury's Texas brigade on the extreme left was assigned to brush Kilpatrick's cavalry away from the army's flank as it swung north to attack Corse's division. Instead, the Texans followed the fleeing cavalry across the Flint River, taking themselves out of the battle. The remnant of John C. Brown's brigade quickly failed in its attack.

The losses (between 1,725 and 2,200 for the Confederates and 178 for the Union) reflect the one-sided nature of the battle and reaffirmed the difficulty of attacking entrenched positions. Hardee's flaws—a poor plan of attack, slowness in starting, and lack of control on the battlefield—were aggravated by the failures of his subordinates, Lee and Cleburne, to control their forces in the action.

During the night, Hood, expecting Sherman to attack toward Atlanta, recalled Lee's corps. Instead, Sherman,

who had cut the rail line above Jonesboro, turned to attack Hardee on 1 September with six strong corps.

Recognizing that he was holding open the escape hatch from Atlanta for Hood's entire army, Hardee prepared to defend Jonesboro. He moved Mark Lowrey's brigade to the right to cover the line vacated by Lee. George Maney's brigade stretched to the left to cover the area vacated by Lowrey. Hardee had only 12,000 men to defend a two-mile line.

Believing that Lee was with Hardee, Sherman planned to trap the Confederates at Jonesboro by using almost his entire force. He intended to feed Jefferson C. Davis's XIV Corps into the left of Howard's line, and then, as John M. Schofield's XXIII Corps and David S. Stanley's IV Corps arrived, they would outflank and overwhelm Hardee's right flank to the north. Sherman expected Hardee to be trying to retreat.

Instead, Hardee reinforced Lowrey with States Rights Gist's and Joseph H. Lewis's brigades, and they hastily threw up fortification facing north and east to await the Union assault. Both sides waited a long time for Stanley, whose forces began arriving in late afternoon.

About 4:00 P.M., Davis launched a strong attack with James D. Morgan's and William P. Carlin's divisions at the exposed northern end of the fishhook-shaped Confederate position. Swampy ground, ravines, and thick underbrush broke the attack into a series of unco-ordinated, piecemeal attacks, which were repulsed, although the Confederate positions were only weakly held. Around 5:00 P.M., Davis renewed the assault, spear-headed by George P. Estey's Indiana Brigade of Absalom Baird's division. It broke the thin Southern lines, lapping around and overrunning Daniel C. Govan's brigade, which was trapped. Farther east, Lewis's brigade and the left of Henry McCullough's brigade were rolled up by Carlin's division. Some 900 prisoners were taken.

Hardee reacted to the threat by hurriedly shifting Benjamin Cheatham's division, which was on his unen-gaged southern flank to the threatened area. Vaughn's Tennessee brigade, along with Granbury's Texas brigade and the remnants of Govan's and Lewis's brigades, launched a counterattack that stopped Davis's assault. The remainder of the division was deployed to face the belatedly arriving IV Corps. Stanley's men found the rebels digging in, so they pulled back, taking no further offensive action.

Davis and his XIV Corps were apparently satisfied with their victory and, although fresh troops were at hand, declined to renew the assault. Meanwhile, the rest of the Union forces on the field remained passive.

Hardee held his lines at dark. Sherman was confident that he had the rebels trapped, but Hardee slipped away in the darkness.

Although they had been unable to drive Sherman's army from the railroad, Hardee and his men had with-stood assaults by powerful Union forces and kept open the escape route from Atlanta. Sherman, in between the widely separated wings of the Confederate army with superior forces, failed to trap either part. The failure to drive Sherman away from the railroad forced Hood to abandon Atlanta, which assured Lincoln's reelection and the inevitable defeat of the Confederacy.

—*Walter E. Pittman*

See also Atlanta Campaign; Hardee, William Joseph; Howard, Oliver Otis; Lee, Stephen Dill.

For further reading:
Castel, Albert. *Decision In The West: The Atlanta Campaign of 1864* (1992).
Hughes, Nathaniel Cheairs, Jr. *General William J. Hardee, Old Reliable* (1965).
Sherman, William T. *Memoirs of General William T. Sherman* (1990).

J. R. WILLIAMS

The *J. R. Williams* is first mentioned in *the Official Records of the Union and Confederate Navies* as a boat suspected of running contraband goods for the Confederacy on the Mississippi during the Vicksburg campaign. Later the Federal government obtained the sternwheeler and used it as a ferry at Little Rock and Fort Smith.

On 15 June 1864 the *J. R. Williams* left Fort Smith, Arkansas, via the Arkansas River with a load of commis-sary and quartermaster stores intended Fort Gibson in Indian Territory. The purpose of the journey was twofold. First, Fort Gibson desperately needed the supplies. Second, on the return trip Fort Smith would receive a load of salt and lime, both plentiful near Fort Gibson. Brigadier General John M. Thayer detailed an escort consisting of a sergeant and twenty-four privates of the 12th Kansas Volunteer Infantry under the command of Second Lieutenant Horace Cook to protect the boat.

At about 4 P.M. on 15 June 1864, about fifty miles from Fort Smith, artillery fire from a concealed position brought the crew and escort to life. Cherokee Confederate brigadier general Stand Watie executed a well-planned ambush with approximately 400 men and three pieces of artillery. Watie had chosen his position on a south bank bluff overlooking the Arkansas River, where the boat would have to pass close to the shore. The first round fired hit the water in front of the craft, while the second round hit the smokestack. The third round hit the pilothouse. Another artillery round hit the boiler, which resulted in a dangerous release of steam. At that point, the boat ran aground about forty yards from the north bank. Lieutenant Cook ordered the men of the 12th Kansas to leave the boat and take cover under the trees on the north bank. Cook planned to reoccupy the boat after nightfall.

An interesting chain of events followed. The boat captain and Lieutenant George Huston, regimental quartermaster of the 14th Kansas Cavalry, who was in charge of the cargo, emerged from the hull and took the boat to the Confederates on the south shore. Lieutenant Cook decided to take the escort back to Fort Smith, and he and his men made their way back, arriving at 3 P.M. on 16 June. General Thayer accused Lieutenant Cook of abandoning his post, yet nothing came of the accusation.

Watie had a prize that included 16,000 pounds of bacon, 150 barrels of flour, and a quantity of tin ware. His men quickly unloaded the boat on a sandbar. Watie allowed his men to take some of the supplies to nearby homes in the Creek and Seminole Nations. Yet Watie's willingness to satisfy his men imperiled his success. The river rose quickly and washed a significant number of the supplies off the sandbar. When Watie received informa-tion that a column of troops from Fort Smith was marching in his direction, he chose to burn the *J. R. Williams* rather than risk returning it to Federal control, especially after Indian Home Guard troops arrived and fired on his position.

The 700–man column led by Colonel Samuel J. Crawford consisted of the 2d Kansas Colored Infantry, a detachment of the 11th U.S. Colored Infantry, a company of cavalry and a section of artillery. Watie sent a force of 150 men under the command of Major J. D. P.

Campbell to intercept Crawford. Campbell's orders were to hold Crawford's force at the iron bridge on the San Bois River, thirty-five miles west of Fort Smith, as long as possible. On 17 June, a sharp skirmish occurred at the Iron Bridge. The Confederates under Campbell held for a couple of hours, then broke off with Crawford's men in pursuit. Crawford pursued till dark, then headed back to Fort Smith.

In the days following the attack on the *J. R. Williams*, barrels of flour floated down the Arkansas River and were spotted by Federal soldiers at Fort Smith. While Watie did not get the full benefit of his efforts, his brilliantly executed attack served notice to Federal troops in Indian Territory and Arkansas that the war was far from over. Watie's disruption of Federal supply and communication would go on for another full year until he surrendered his command 23 June 1865.

—*Thomas A. Wing*

See also Cherokee Indians; Choctaw Indians; Crawford, Samuel J.; Indian Territory; Seminole Indians; Thayer, John M.; Watie, Stand.

For further reading:
Franks, Kenny. *Stand Watie and the Agony of the Cherokee Nation* (1979).
Josephy, Alvin M. *The Civil War in the American West* (1991).
Knight, Wilfred. *Red Fox: Stand Watie's Civil War Years in Indian Territory* (1988).

JULIAN, GEORGE WASHINGTON
(1817–1899)

U.S. congressman

Lawyer, reformer, and politician, George W. Julian was born near Centreville, Indiana. He was the son of Isaac and Rebecca Hoover Julian. Isaac Julian, a veteran of the War of 1812 and an Indiana state legislator, died when Julian was six. Julian's mother became the dominant force in his early life. From Quaker roots, Rebecca's religious convictions left a definite imprint on her son. Serious and bookish growing up, Julian at an early age became familiar with the works of Unitarian minister William Ellery Channing. Julian also was an early convert to the ranks of abolitionism. After finishing his education in the local common schools, Julian briefly became a teacher. He then decided upon a career in law, traveling to New Boston, Illinois, to commence his studies. In 1840, Julian returned to Indiana, where he began practicing law in New Castle. He moved on to Greenfield, Indiana, and eventually returned to his native Centreville.

By the mid-1840s, Julian had become attracted to politics. Joining the Whig Party, he won a seat in the state assembly in 1845, but was defeated in his attempt to win a seat in the state senate in 1847. Disillusioned by the Mexican-American War and the Whig Party's nomi-

nation of Zachary Taylor for president, Julian joined the Free Soil Party in 1848. Along with his support for the abolition of slavery, Julian was also an enthusiastic supporter of labor rights, homestead legislation, and women's rights. In 1848, Julian was elected to Congress as a Free Soil representative of his home district. He was defeated for reelection, however, chiefly through the opposition of Oliver P. Morton, who endorsed Julian's Whig opponent. Morton's opposition to Julian was the beginning of a political rivalry that would last some twenty years.

Although Julian was the 1852 vice presidential nominee of the Free Soil Party, he eventually joined the newly formed Republican Party in the mid-1850s. From the beginning of the Republican Party, Julian was one of its most radical members. He criticized severely the inclusion of Know-Nothings in the party and worked hard to ensure that antislavery principles were given their proper due. Although Julian was an enthusiastic supporter of the Republican Party's first presidential nominee, John C. Frémont, he was much more circumspect in his attitude toward Abraham Lincoln, particularly because Lincoln's antislavery credentials were not that well established.

In 1860, Julian again ran for Congress in his home Fifth District. This time he was victorious. He served five consecutive terms before being defeated in 1870. During his tenure in Congress, Julian continued to earn his reputation as a Radical Republican. As a member of the powerful Joint Committee on the Conduct of the War, Julian helped champion a vigorous prosecution of the war. His speeches before the House were well known for their bluntness and advocacy of emancipation and other Republican principles. As chair of the House Committee on Public Lands, Julian was an early advocate of confiscation of Southern landed estates. Unlike many Republicans, Julian understood that emancipated slaves in the South could be truly free only if that freedom was grounded in economic independence, particularly land ownership.

After the war, Julian was an avid supporter of Radical Reconstruction. A supporter of the state suicide theory, Julian believed that the South could be reformed only after a long, transitional state. Pivotal to the reconstruction of the South for Julian was African-American suffrage. Despite its unpopularity in many Northern states, including Indiana, Julian supported a constitutional amendment guaranteeing black suffrage. A bitter opponent of Andrew Johnson, Julian was an enthusiastic supporter of impeachment and desperately (but unsuccessfully) sought to become one of the House managers of the impeachment proceedings in the Senate.

After suffering defeat in 1870, Julian drifted into the Liberal Republican camp. Like many other Republicans, he was not only disillusioned with "Grantism," but also

endorsed a number of other causes such as civil service reform, free trade, and land reform. Ironically, in 1876, Julian would come full circle politically and join the Democratic Party. Believing that the Republican Party was too fraught with cronyism and corruption, Julian believed his decision was consistent with his political principles. Never an avid supporter of protectionism, Julian believed the interests of small, independent farmers and workers was now best represented by the Democratic Party.

Julian would never hold elective office after 1870. After his retirement from politics, he moved to the Indianapolis suburb of Irvington, where he practiced law and worked for a collection agency in Indianapolis. He returned to government service when he was appointed to the post of survey general of New Mexico from 1884 to 1889. He then returned to his home in Irvington, where he lived in retirement until his death in 1899.

In the 1896 presidential election, Julian was a gold Democrat and a supporter of Grover Cleveland. Julian was married twice, first to Anne Finch, who died in 1861, and then to Laura Giddings in 1863, the daughter of antislavery activist, Joshua Giddings. Laura Giddings Julian died in 1884. Their daughter Grace Julian Clark was Julian's constant companion in his retirement years. She wrote a biography of his life and political career.

—*Bruce Tap*

See also Abolitionists; Congress, U.S.A.; Joint Committee on the Conduct of the War; Morton, Oliver P.; Radical Republicans; Republican Party.
For further reading:
Clark, Grace Julian. *George Washington Julian* (1932).
Julian, George W. *Political Recollections, 1840–1872* (1884).
Riddleburger, Patrick W. George Washington Julian, Radical Republican: A Study in Nineteenth-Century Politics and Reform (1966).

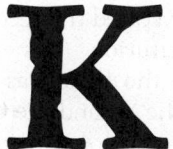

K

KANE, THOMAS LEIPER
(1822–1883)
Union general

Born to John Kintzing Kane and Jane Duval Leiper Kane in Philadelphia, Pennsylvania, Thomas Leiper Kane was educated locally before going abroad at seventeen to study in Great Britain and France. Upon returning home, he studied law. His brother was Elisha Kent Kane.

Kane's father was a U.S. district judge, and for a time Kane clerked for him before accepting a position as a U.S. commissioner in his father's district of eastern Pennsylvania. During this time, Kane increasingly embraced the antislavery cause, and in the election of 1848 he actively supported the Free Soil Party. Upon the passage of the Compromise of 1850, Kane, like all abolitionists, caviled at the inclusion of the stricter Fugitive Slave Act. His role in enforcing that act as a U.S. commissioner for the district court especially concerned him, so he tendered a letter of resignation to his father. The letter so provoked the elder Kane, who apparently did not share his son's pangs of conscience, that he had his son jailed for contempt of court. The U.S. Supreme Court overruled the arrest.

After his release, Kane moved to western Pennsylvania. He founded a town, naming it for himself, and used it as a stop on the Underground Railroad. During these years before the Civil War, he also developed sympathy for the Mormons, perhaps because of their stand against slavery. He befriended Brigham Young, and in 1858 Kane helped prevent bloodshed by mediating the dispute between the Mormons and the federal government.

At the commencement of the Civil War, Kane raised a mounted rifle regiment of western Pennsylvanians that became known as the "Bucktails." He deferred to Charles J. Biddle, a Mexican-American War veteran, as the regiment's colonel and became its lieutenant colonel on 21 June 1861.

On 22 August 1861, he commanded his men in a skirmish with J. E. B. Stuart at Catlett's Station, Virginia. Later in the year, while leading his men back to their base after a patrol from Dranesville, Virginia, he clashed with Confederates trying to cut off their return. In the ensuing battle, Kane was wounded.

During the spring and summer of 1862, Kane commanded the Bucktail Battalion as part of Brigadier General George D. Bayard's cavalry brigade in the Shenandoah Valley. On 6 June 1862 at Harrisburg, Virginia, Kane was captured. After his exchange in the late summer, he was promoted to brigadier general of volunteers and given command of the 2d Brigade, 1st Division, XII Corps of the Army of the Potomac. Because XII Corps was in reserve at Fredericksburg, Kane did not see action there, but he commanded a brigade of the same corps at Chancellorsville. Shortly thereafter he contracted pneumonia and was sent to Baltimore, where he remained in the hospital through June 1863.

In the early hours of the battle of Gettysburg, it became apparent that the Confederates had discovered one of the most important Federal ciphers. Someone had to convey this information to the commander of the Army of the Potomac, George Gordon Meade. Kane volunteered, though he had not recovered from pneumonia. Dressed in civilian clothes, he made his way through Confederate territory and even through a portion of Stuart's cavalry to Meade at Gettysburg. On 2 July he resumed command of his brigade, then occupying a position on the extreme right of the Union line—the business end of the "fishhook." At 3:30 A.M. on 3 July his position was attacked, and though he was still too weak to sit on a horse, Kane led his men in the repulse of the Confederates through the late morning. The following day Kane's health forced him to relinquish command, and he went to oversee the draft depot at Pittsburgh, Pennsylvania. The posting had the advantage of being near his home. His health never really recovered, though, and he resigned his commission in November 1863. At the end of the war, he received a brevet promotion to major general for gallantry at Gettysburg.

Once Kane had marginally recovered, he devoted much of his time to charitable work. He also wrote extensively. His old nemesis pneumonia killed him in Philadelphia on 26 December 1883.

—*David S. Heidler and Jeanne T. Heidler*

See also Dranesville, Battle of; Gettysburg, Battle of.
For further reading:
Zobell, Albert L. *Sentinel in the East: A Biography of Thomas L. Kane* (1965).

KANSAS

The territory that became Kansas, part of the area west of Missouri and Iowa and north of the line 36° 30′ north latitude, was acquired for the United States by Thomas Jefferson in the Louisiana Purchase. As a result of reports of Kansas's desolate nature, early settlers traveling to the West on the Santa Fe and Oregon trails bypassed the territory. However, some settlers reported the land's potential, and Congress made four attempts to organize a single territory for the area. All failed because of Southern opposition and because of competition between Northern and Southern advocates over a transcontinental railroad route.

The region's political status was governed by the Missouri Compromise, which forbade slave holding north of 36° 30′. Senator Stephen A. Douglas of Illinois was a proponent of the northern route for the railroad, and to win Southern support for it, he proposed dividing the region into two territories and that the principle of Popular Sovereignty be applied to both. This proposal would allow the settlers in each territory to decide for or against slavery themselves. The resulting Kansas-Nebraska Act was passed by Congress on 30 May 1854, establishing the territories of Kansas and Nebraska. The legislation had several deleterious effects on national and territorial politics. It effectively repealed the Missouri Compromise of 6 March 1820, reopening the controversy over the extension of slavery into the West. It also enraged Northern antislavery forces, who quickly coalesced into the new Anti-Nebraska Party (soon renamed the Republican Party), and it led to a rush of antislavery and proslavery settlers into Kansas. Eleven years of armed conflict from 1854 to 1865 followed, mostly characterized by guerrilla warfare between the proponents of slavery and the so-called "Free Staters" in "Bloody" or "Bleeding Kansas."

After the passage of the Kansas-Nebraska Act, the settlement of Kansas immediately became a national issue. To secure popular sentiment and a majority of votes, organizations such as the New England Emigrant Aid Company arose promoting antislavery Northern immigration. Proslavery Southerners mounted a similar effort from Missouri. These two adversarial camps established rival governments as violence erupted in the eastern part of the territory. Proslavery Southerners controlled the territorial legislature at Lecompton, by then the capital of the Kansas Territory, and acted first, drafting the Lecompton Constitution between October and November of 1857, designed to bring Kansas into the Union as a slave state. The "Free Staters" meanwhile set up a rival government at Topeka and elected as governor Charles Robinson, an Amherst-educated physician and an agent of the New England Emigrant Aid Company. James Henry Lane, the "liberator" of Kansas, commanded the free-state militia in the guerrilla war against proslavery forces that ensued.

The Lecompton Constitution was presented to the territory's voters in December 1857, but the "Free Staters" boycotted the election. President James Buchanan urged Congress to admit Kansas as a state under the Lecompton Constitution, and the Senate concurred. However, the House of Representatives rejected the Lecompton Constitution and it was resubmitted to the territory's voters. In August 1858 the proslavery forces boycotted the second election, and the Lecompton Constitution was defeated. Congress admitted Kansas to the Union as a free state in 1861 under the terms of the Wyandotte Constitution of 1859.

The Kansas-Nebraska Act had done nothing but inflame the sectional tensions between North and South as the election of 1860 approached. With the division of the Democratic Party at their national convention in Charleston and the failure at Baltimore to mend the breach, the election of the first Republican president was all but assured. The nation edged closer to a civil war that had already been raging in Kansas for almost six years.

Charles Robinson, who had been reelected governor in 1859 under the Wyandotte Constitution, assumed office in 1861 as Kansas was admitted to the Union, while James Henry Lane had become one of its U.S. senators. Robinson served as the state's first governor until 1863. During his tenure, guerrilla raids continued along the Missouri-Kansas border, as they did throughout the Civil War.

The military Department of Kansas was created on 9 November 1861, comprising the State of Kansas, the Territories of Nebraska, Colorado, and Dakota, and the Indian Territory West of Arkansas. Major General David Hunter was appointed to the command on 20 November 1861, and he remained in the position until the command was merged into the Department of the Mississippi on 11 March 1862. Active campaigning by formed bodies of Union and Confederate forces was slow to start in Kansas. However, James Lane, having secured a commission as brigadier general of volunteers, went to Fort Scott to lead the Kansas Brigade. He conducted a series of raids into western Missouri during the autumn and later raised one of the first African-American regiments in the Union army.

Guerrilla activity continued along the Missouri border in 1862. The Department of Kansas was recreated on 2 May 1862 under Brigadier General James G. Blunt, who held the command until 19 September 1862. During his tenure Union troops mounted an expedition between 8 and 23 September out of Fort Leavenworth, Kansas, through Jackson, Cass, Johnson, and LaFayette Counties, Missouri. The department was merged into the Department of Missouri on 19 September 1862 as the expedition was winding down. Between 6 and 11 November the 3d Wisconsin Cavalry mounted another expedition from Fort Scott.

In 1863 operations were conducted by Union forces against the incursions of William Quantrill and his "bushwhackers." The 5th and 9th Kansas Cavalry (Detachments), the 11th and 12th Kansas Infantry, the 1st and 4th Missouri State Militia Cavalry, and the 5th Enrolled Missouri Militia Infantry all pursued Quantrill during his raid into Kansas from 20 to 28 August. The 9th Kansas Cavalry engaged in a skirmish with some of his men on 21 August at Brooklyn and Paloa. Later that autumn, Quantrill again rode into Kansas. After James Blunt had been relieved of command of the Department of Kansas, President Lincoln assigned him to command the Army of the Frontier in Indian Territory. Blunt chose Fort Smith, Arkansas, as his new headquarters and proceeded there with a military band and about 100 cavalry reinforcements. At Baxter Springs, Kansas, the Union army grazed stock animals on the open prairie under the watchful eyes of a detachment of the 12th Kansas Infantry and Company B of the 2d Colored Infantry. On 6 October, "Dave" Pool, commander of the advance detachment of Quantrill's "regiment," attacked the guard. Quantrill arrived and, spying Blunt's wagon train approaching the post, attacked the outnumbered wagon guard, killing all the musicians and burning the wagons. Union losses were eighty killed, eighteen wounded, and five missing. Blunt escaped the debacle and limped into Fort Smith where he was soon removed from his newly appointed post. His services were then employed in recruiting African-American troops along the border, with whom he was quite popular for otherwise usually winning battles against rebel Indians and guerrilla bushwhackers.

The main fighting moved into Arkansas in 1864. However, in the autumn, Confederate general Sterling Price determined to strike deep into northern Missouri with 12,000 cavalry. His great raid threatened Kansas, and indeed his plan called for him to attack Independence and Kansas City and then withdraw afterward through Kansas to the Indian Territory. On 25 October, Union and Confederate forces fought an engagement at Mine Creek on the Little Osage River. This battle was the first time that regular troops had been employed by both sides at once on Kansas soil. It followed on the heels of the battle of Westport, Missouri, where the Union forces had not decisively beaten Price's Confederates but had driven them from Missouri. Price was now retreating in good order south through Kansas with a vast wagon train of plunder and was being pursued by the Union troops. He ordered John Marmaduke's division to establish a delaying line on the prairie near the Marias des Cygnes. A Union cavalry brigade soon drove this line back. Price then ordered Marmaduke to establish a new line north of Mine Creek while a second line was formed south of the creek by James Fagan's division. In a battle in which the next governor of Kansas, Samuel Crawford, figured prominently in spurring the tired Union troops to action,

Marmaduke's division was shattered. More than 1,000 prisoners, including Marmaduke, and ten artillery pieces were captured. Price's reserves managed to repulse the tired Union troops, and Price effected his escape from Kansas. Bickering among the Union commanders prevented them from taking the opportunity to pursue and destroy Price's worn-out command. The Union forces retired with their prisoners to Fort Scott, Kansas, and Price burned his wagons and went into Missouri.

There were no significant operations in Kansas in 1865, although a few minor actions, skirmishes, and reconnaissance took place. The last expedition was to the Powder River against hostile Indians between 20 June and 7 October by elements of the 12th Missouri Cavalry and 2d Missouri Artillery.

—*Duane C. Young*

See also Blunt, James Gilpatrick; Kansas-Nebraska Act; Lane, James Henry; Lecompton Constitution; Price's Missouri Raid; Quantrill, William Clarke.

For further reading:

Britton, Wiley. *The Civil War on the Border* (1890–1899).

Castel, Albert E. *A Frontier State At War: Kansas, 1861–1865* (1958).

Dyer, Frederick H. *A Compendium of the War of the Rebellion* (1908).

Monaghan, Jay. *Civil War on the Western Border, 1854–1865* (1955).

KANSAS-NEBRASKA ACT

The Kansas-Nebraska Act, passed by Congress on 30 May 1854, may be the most controversial law ever passed in the history of the U.S. Congress. It accelerated and expanded the national debate over slavery in the territories and set into motion a series of events that led directly to the American Civil War.

In January 1854, Senator Stephen A. Douglas of Illinois introduced into the Senate a report of the Senate Committee on Territories, which he chaired. This report recommended the creation of two new territories in the former Louisiana Purchase Territory, Kansas and Nebraska. Douglas was interested in the opening of western lands, which, he believed, would add to the vigorous growth of the new nation. This expansion, perceived by Douglas and many other early nineteenth-century politicians as part of the national "manifest destiny" to extend from the Atlantic to the Pacific, came at the expense of Native Americans, who were viewed as troublesome barriers to the growth and economic development of American civilization.

Historians continue to debate the motivations behind the actions of Senator Douglas in advancing this plan. His ambition for the advancement of his political career and his interest in a transcontinental railroad from Chicago across the western plains are often presented in discussions of his motives.

The Missouri Compromise of 1820 had specifically

outlawed the institution of slavery in the former Louisiana Territory north of the line of 36° 30´, except for Missouri. For over a decade, Douglas had attempted to move the Senate to create these same two territories without any provision that would alter the 1820 arrangement. But between 1850 and 1854, the political situation had changed dramatically, and Douglas and his political allies sought to move the debate over slavery from the halls of Congress into the hands of the people who would settle in the new territories. By a principle known as Popular Sovereignty, which had been first developed by Douglas as a part of the Compromise of 1850, the proposed law affirmed that "all questions pertaining to slavery" in the new territories and states should be "left to the people residing therein." This provision would open the door to the possibility of slavery in the former Louisiana Territory, thus canceling out the Missouri Compromise, which had been the law of the land for thirty-four years.

In the final bill, the determination on slavery was that "when admitted as a State or States, the said Territory or any portion of the same, shall be received into the Union with or without slavery, as their constitution may prescribe at the time of the admission." This, indeed, moved the issue from Congress to the people in the former free area and placed great emphasis on the election that would have to approve the proposed state constitution. It was in the final writing of the bill that Douglas provided that the former Louisiana region be divided into two separate territories, Kansas and Nebraska. Neighboring Missouri was a rapidly growing slave state and clearly remembered the 1820 compromise that provided for the admittance of one slave and one free state. If this precedent was followed, then one of these new territories would be slave, the other free.

The bill passed the Senate on a vote of 37–14 and the House of Representatives by a vote of 113–100 and was signed by President Franklin Pierce. The public response could best be called tumultuous. Proslavery and anti-slavery adherents raced to Kansas, the first of the two territories to be organized, to shape the territory and the new state constitution that would have to be written. To get to Kansas, they fought their way across Missouri, and once in the new territory they clustered in communities that reflected their views on slavery. Each side was committed to the control of the new state for their position, which became a cause.

The first elections in 1855 favored the Southern proslavery position but were influenced by Missourians who came across the border, seized polling places, and cast illegal votes. Antislavery settlers refused to accept the results of the election and conducted their own election. As a result of this action, Kansas soon had two rival governments, both claiming to be the legal government of Kansas Territory. The struggle between the two groups soon turned into a civil war that led to the area's identification as "Bleeding Kansas."

President Pierce supported the proslave forces that had won the first election. Troops were sent in to establish order and permit a new election, also won by the proslavery position, amidst charges of further corruption. Congress, which has the authority to admit new states, refused to accept the proslavery constitution, and the issue continued as an explosive and unresolved issue. Not until early 1861, when national attention had turned to even more explosive issues, was Kansas admitted to the Union as a free state. In the growing shadow of war clouds over the nation, hardly anyone noticed.

The historical significance of the Kansas-Nebraska Act was great. The idea that slavery could be extended to an area in which it had been banned since 1820 changed America. Antislavery spokespeople considered the act a moral outrage. Defenders of slavery asserted the right to carry slaves into any new territory as a right guaranteed by the Constitution and six decades of legal precedent. In historical perspective, the Kansas-Nebraska Act repealed the Missouri Compromise of 1820, nullified much of the Compromise of 1850, divided the Democratic Party, destroyed the Whig Party, and created an all-new, all-Northern, antislavery Republican Party. It made further compromise difficult if not unlikely, and thus created the political landscape that led to disunion and civil war. Few acts of Congress have had such far-reaching impact.

—*Frank Nickell*

See also Douglas, Stephen Arnold; Kansas; Pierce, Franklin.
For further reading:
Blue, Frederick J. *The Free Soilers: Third Party Politics, 1848–1854* (1973).
Cooper, William J., Jr. *The South and the Politics of Slavery, 1828–1856* (1973).
Foner, Eric. *Free Soil, Free Labor, Free Men: The Ideology of the Republican Party before the Civil War* (1970).
Freehling, William W. *The Road to Disunion: Secessionists at Bay, 1776–1854* (1990).
Gienapp, William. *The Origins of the Republican Party, 1852–1856* (1987).
Holt, Michael F. *The Political Crisis of the 1850's* (1978).
Johannsen, Robert W. *Stephen A. Douglas* (1973).
Malin, James C. *The Nebraska Question, 1852–1854* (1953).
Nichols, Roy F. "The Kansas-Nebraska Act: A Century of Historiography." *Mississippi Valley Historical Review* (1956).
Potter, David M. *The Impending Crisis, 1848–1861* (1976).
Rawley, James A. *Race and Politics: "Bleeding Kansas" and the Coming of the Civil War* (1969).

KAUTZ, AUGUST VALENTINE
(1828–1895)
Union general

Born in Ipspringen, Baden, Germany, August Valentine Kautz emigrated to the United States with his parents as a young child. Growing up on a farm near Ripley, Ohio, the young Kautz showed an early interest in the military, and when the Mexican-

American War broke out, he enlisted as a private in the 1st Ohio Volunteers. After the war, Kautz was admitted to West Point and graduated in 1852. Assigned to the Washington and Oregon Territories, he became known as a good Indian fighter, and, after returning from a two-year trip to Europe, he was appointed a captain in the newly formed U.S. Cavalry.

Kautz was one of the leaders, along with Philip Sheridan and George A. Custer, who raised both the reputation and the fighting efficiency of the Union cavalry. When Fort Sumter was fired on, Kautz immediately offered his services to the state of Ohio and became the lieutenant colonel of the 2d Ohio Cavalry under Abner Doubleday. He participated in George B. McClellan's Peninsula campaign as a captain in the U.S. 6th Cavalry, and then returned to his old volunteer regiment as its colonel after Doubleday's promotion. Kautz's talent for mounted operations remained mainly obscured by the bungling of senior officers until 1863, but he was nonetheless instrumental in the capture of Monticello, Kentucky, and the pursuit and capture of John Hunt Morgan's force of Confederate raiders in Ohio. Commanding Camp Chase from December 1862 to April 1863, he was rewarded for his competence with a brigadier generalship. Kautz became known for his lightning attacks, fast marches, and careful selection of approach routes. He pushed his troopers to the limit, but they and Kautz's superiors soon realized that he could successfully complete his missions with only a minimum number of casualties, while inflicting large losses on the enemy. Few Union cavalry leaders could boast of his record or skills in the first half of the war.

Kautz became most famous for his service in the Virginia theater in 1864 and 1865. Commanding a cavalry division in the Army of the James, Kautz repeatedly cut the railroads supplying Richmond and Petersburg, endangering Robert E. Lee's supply line and the integrity of the Confederate defenses. The Weldon Railroad was particularly hard-hit one day, as one Maine chaplain asserted in his postwar memoirs: "A thunderbolt from a clear sky could hardly have been more astounding to the enemy. Instantly he was attacked. In an incredibly short time the action was over, the enemy was whipped, the railroad was cut, the public buildings in flames." Kautz's achievements in this raid were equaled only by the logistical miracle that created it—a forced march of seventy miles. Such bold, well-conceived strokes were characteristic of Kautz's performance. He even successfully attacked Petersburg in June 1864, with a greatly outnumbered force, and was rewarded with a brevet promotion to lieutenant colonel in the regular army.

Kautz commanded the first division of XXV Corps in 1865 and helped create the sequence of events that caused the fall of Richmond. His division was composed of African-American troops, a fact that apparently failed to concern Kautz as it did some other Union officers. On 3 April 1865, he accompanied General Godfrey Weitzel with his division as it entered the Confederate capital. Kautz had a right to be proud of his accomplishments that day, as his cavalry had become a model for other Union cavalry units by the end of the war. Turning the tables on the Confederate horsemen, Kautz's troopers continually disrupted the communications and supply lines of the Army of Northern Virginia from the summer of 1864 until the surrender at Appomattox. Shortly before the fall of Richmond, Kautz was brevetted again as a major general of both U.S. and volunteer forces.

Having fought in over 100 engagements, Kautz was also active in letters. Throughout the war and during its immediate aftermath, he wrote a variety of instructional texts, such as *The Company Clerk* (1863), *Customs of the Service for Noncommissioned Officers* (1864), and *Customs of the Service for Officers of the Army* (1866). He resumed active duty in the regular army as a lieutenant colonel after 1865, serving in Florida, the western territories, and the southwest throughout the 1870s and 1880s. He was promoted to regular brigadier general in 1891 and retired in 1892 in Seattle, Washington.

—*Christian B. Keller*

See also Camp Chase; Cavalry, U.S.A.; German-Americans; Morgan, John Hunt.
For further reading:
Kaufmann, Wilhelm. *Die Deutschen im Amerikanischen Buergerkriege* (1911).
Lonn, Ella. *Foreigners in the Union Army and Navy* (1951).
Starr, Stephen Z. *The Union Cavalry in the Civil War* (1979–1985).

KEAN, ROBERT GARLICK HILL
(1828–1898)
Confederate bureaucrat

Robert G. H. Kean is best known for the diary that he kept from 1861 until the end of the war describing the inner workings of the Confederate government. Born into a prominent family of Caroline County, Virginia, Kean in 1848 entered the University of Virginia, where he earned a bachelor of arts degree in 1850 and a bachelor of laws degree in 1853. It was during this period that he met, courted, and married Jane Nicholas Randolph, Thomas Jefferson's great-granddaughter. Young Kean was undoubtedly well prepared for a professional career because of his education, and his marriage placed him among Virginia's wealthiest and most influential citizens. He opened a law practice in Lynchburg and settled into what promised to be a long and rewarding career.

Seismic events of the 1850s and the secession crisis of 1860, however, interrupted his legal career. Kean had

become increasingly alarmed by the sectional strife then tearing at the Union, and after John Brown's raid at Harper's Ferry in 1859, he joined a company of volunteers that was eventually reorganized as the 131st Virginia Militia. With the bombardment of Fort Sumter in April 1861, Kean's company marched to Richmond and was mustered into Confederate ranks as Company G of the 11th Virginia Infantry. This unit was then sent to join James Longstreet's brigade at Manassas. On 18 July, Union general Irvin McDowell sent a sizable force against Longstreet's position at Blackburn's Ford, but the Confederate defenders—Kean among them—successfully repelled this attack. Though but a prelude to the larger battle of Manassas that occurred three days later, the small engagement on the 18th was the only combat of the war in which Kean was directly involved.

After Kean unsuccessfully ran for a seat in the Confederate Congress in November 1861, he continued serving with his unit in defensive positions in northern Virginia. He had earlier been promoted to captain and was hopeful of future promotions and battle experience. Yet, in late February 1862 he received word that he had been appointed assistant to General George Wythe Randolph, then preparing Confederate defenses at Suffolk, Virginia. Kean's assignment to Randolph's staff was a result Randolph's being Jane Kean's uncle. Such family connections aside, Kean proved most useful to Randolph, whose efforts around Suffolk gained the attention of Jefferson Davis in Richmond.

With Judah Benjamin's resignation as Confederate war secretary in March 1862, Davis appointed Randolph to be his replacement. Kean accompanied his uncle-in-law to Richmond and was at once named head of the Bureau of War, one of nine subdepartments composing the War Department. Other than Randolph, Kean's immediate supervisor was the assistant secretary of war, who at that time was Albert Taylor Bledsoe. Though Kean and Bledsoe maintained cordial relations and worked together effectively, the latter grew dissatisfied with the many mundane tasks associated with his position. When Bledsoe resigned in September 1862 to accept a diplomatic appointment, Randolph asked John Archibald Campbell, a former associate justice of the U.S. Supreme Court, to serve as the new assistant secretary.

Considering Kean's lofty sounding title, "head of the Bureau of War," one might conclude that he was empowered with decision-making authority over matters of great import. Actually, Kean's position required that he function primarily as the department's office manager. His principal duty was to supervise the many clerks who painstakingly copied the voluminous correspondence. Working closely under Assistant Secretary Campbell's supervision, Kean developed an efficient routine that facilitated dispatching official orders to Confederate commanders.

Kean also served as a research assistant to the secretary, providing important information regarding troop strength, provisions, reconnaissance, and evidence for courts-martial proceedings. Campbell regularly called on Kean to help review the many applications for passports that came before the War Department. This task was by far the most laborious and time consuming because so many people wished to cross enemy lines for many different reasons. Some of the less scrupulous ones crossed the lines, bought food and other supplies, and then slipped back into the Confederacy to sell their goods for enormous profits. Each application for a passport, therefore, needed to be scrutinized so that such war profiteering could be minimized. Campbell and Kean were nearly overwhelmed by the tedium.

When Robert E. Lee abandoned his entrenched position at Petersburg and Jefferson Davis subsequently ordered the Confederate government evacuated from Richmond, Kean diligently gathered all the War Department's papers and made certain that these records were protected and preserved. He fled south with the government, but he returned to Virginia early that summer. Kean soon moved his family back to Lynchburg, where he eventually rebuilt his law practice. He successfully practiced law in Virginia, became active within that state's bar association, served on the Board of Trustees for the University of Virginia, and was a well-respected member of his community. R. G. H. Kean died in Lynchburg in 1898 at the age of sixty-nine.

Kean's greatest contribution to history was not so much his services to the Confederacy, but rather the diary that he wrote about his war-time experiences. Published as *Inside the Confederate Government* in 1957, this primary source is for the most part accurate, critical, objective, and reflective of the drama that was the Civil War. Virtually every significant character, of both the military and civilian sectors, who comprised the highest levels of the Confederate government is discussed within this diary. It remains an indispensable resource for those seeking first-hand, in-depth discussion and analysis of the Richmond government.

—*Robert Saunders, Jr.*

See also Campbell, John A.; Randolph, George Wythe.
For further reading:
Younger, Edward, ed. *Inside the Confederate Government: The Diary of Robert Garlick Hill Kean* (1957; reprint 1974).

KEARNY, PHILIP
(1814–1862)
Union general

Born to Philip Kearny and Susan Watts Kearny in New York City, Philip Kearny lived much of his young life with his mother's father, a wealthy New Yorker who had lost all of his sons when they were young. Groomed to be his grandfather's heir, Philip Kearny attended the best schools. In spite of Kearny's great

Philip Kearny (*Library of Congress*)

interest in things military, his grandfather nevertheless refused to let him attend the U.S. Military Academy. Instead Kearny graduated from Columbia University and studied law. Upon his grandfather's death in 1836—an event that left Kearny an inheritance of approximately $1 million—he could now pursue the career of his dreams. Already a superb horseman, he entered the 1st Dragoons as a second lieutenant. The regiment was commanded by his uncle Stephen Watts Kearny.

Philip Kearny served with the 1st Dragoons on the frontier for two years. In 1839 he was sent to the French Cavalry School at Saumur to study tactics, but while there traveled to Algiers with the Chassers d'Afrique. When Kearny returned to the United States, he served as aide-de-camp to the commanding general of the army, Alexander Macomb, and then to Winfield Scott upon his succession to the same position.

Early in 1846 Kearny resigned his commission, but when the Mexican-American War commenced, he requested that his resignation be rescinded. He recruited a squadron of dragoons that became the bodyguard of Winfield Scott during the Mexico City campaign. At Churubusco, Kearny led a charge that left him with a serious wound to his left arm. The limb was amputated. Captain Robert E. Lee witnessed this charge and remarked upon the gallantry of Captain Kearny.

After the war, Kearny remained in the army, serving on the frontier. He left the army again in 1851 and retired to his estate outside Newark, New Jersey. Longing for the military life, he traveled to France in 1859, where he became a staff officer in the French cavalry. He fought in Italy in 1859, for which service he received from Napoleon III the Cross of the Legion of Honor.

Kearny was still in France at the outbreak of the Civil War, but returned to offer his services to the United States. On 7 August 1861, with a date of rank of 17 May, he received a brigadier general's commission and command of a New Jersey brigade.

Kearny and his men did not see serious action until the Peninsula campaign in the spring and summer of 1862. He was temporarily given a division command on 13 March and given permanent command of 3d Division, III Corps, on 30 April 1862. He fought in the siege of Yorktown. On 5 May, he led his division in support of Joseph Hooker's division at Williamsburg and was commended for bravery by commander of the Army of the Potomac George B. McClellan for this action. At Seven Pines, Kearny led part of his division in support of Erasmus D. Keyes's IV Corps. Kearny continued to command the division during the Seven Days, particularly distinguishing himself at White Oak Swamp on 30 June. On 4 July 1862, Kearny was promoted to major general of volunteers.

Summoned back to Washington in August 1862 to participate in John Pope's campaign against Lee, Kearny fought at Groveton and Second Bull Run. Two days after the latter battle, Kearny led his division at Chantilly. While personally reconnoitering the Confederate position, he accidentally traveled behind Confederate lines. When he tried to escape, he was shot and killed. The following day, Lee had his body sent to Pope's headquarters under a flag of truce. A month later, after the Antietam campaign, Lee received a request from Kearny's widow, Diana Moore Bullitt Kearny, that Kearny's horse, saddle, and sword be returned to her. Because the horse and equipment were considered property of the Confederate Quartermaster Department, Lee convened a board of officers to determine their value. He then paid the assessed value to the quartermaster's office and returned the requested items to McClellan.

At the time of his death, Kearny was considered a rising star in the Union army. Not only was he known for conspicuous gallantry, but he had instituted several practices within his division that would be adopted by later commanders. Most notably, he had required that his division wear a red patch of cloth to identify them and encourage unit pride.

—*David S. Heidler and Jeanne T. Heidler*

See also Chantilly, Battle of; Peninsula Campaign; Bull Run, Second Battle of; Seven Pines, Battle of; Williamsburg, Battle of.

For further reading:
Kearny, Philip. *Letters from the Peninsula: The Civil War Letters of General Philip Kearny* (1988).
Kearny, Thomas. *General Philip Kearny, Battle Soldier of Five Wars, Including the Conquest of the West by General Stephen Watts Kearny* (1937).
Werstein, Irving. *Kearny the Magnificent: The Story of General Philip Kearny, 1815–1862* (1962).

KEARSARGE, USS

One of the most famous of Union vessels of the Civil War, the *Kearsarge* was victorious over the Confederate cruiser *Alabama*. Laid down at Portsmouth in May 1861 and launched on 5 October 1861, the *Kearsarge* was commissioned on 24 January 1862. This third-rate screw sloop weighed 1,550 tons and was 198 feet 6 inches in length between perpendiculars, with a beam of 33 feet 10 inches and depth of hold of 15 feet 9 inches. At 11 knots maximum speed, it was slightly faster than the *Alabama*. It had a crew of 160 men. It carried in broadside four 32-pounder (42-cubic weight) guns. It also mounted one 30-pounder rifled gun. A small 12-pounder boat howitzer, not included in its official armament, was also aboard. Its real strength rested in two 11-inch pivot-mounted smoothbore Dahlgren guns, each throwing a 135-pound shell.

Built under the 1861 emergency construction program, the *Kearsarge* was, on commissioning, attached to the European Squadron. In June 1864 it was riding at anchor off the northeast coast of France, monitoring the *Georgia* and *Rappahannock* at Calais, when Captain John A. Winslow received word that the *Alabama* had put into Cherbourg. Winslow recalled his crew and immediately got the *Kearsarge* under way.

Winslow knew Raphael Semmes, the *Alabama's* captain, well. They had served together on the *Raritan* and fought together in the Mexican-American War. Both were Southerners by birth, but Winslow had been educated in New England and married a Boston woman. He became an ardent abolitionist who believed in the moral duty of the North to eradicate slavery. Winslow and his well-trained crew had spent a year searching for the *Alabama*, and he was determined that it would not again elude him. In June 1864 the *Kearsarge* was two months' out of a Dutch dockyard and in excellent condition.

The *Kearsarge* arrived at Cherbourg on 14 June and

Captain John Winslow (*third from left*) and his officers aboard the USS *Kearsarge* following its battle with the CSS *Alabama*, 19 June 1864 (*Library of Congress*)

quickly located the *Alabama*. Winslow then positioned his ship off the breakwater to prevent the *Alabama* from escaping. Semmes, well aware that Union warships would only grow in number, elected to fight.

The engagement occurred on 19 June 1864, in the English Channel off Cherbourg. Despite Semmes's later claims that the *Kearsarge* had the advantage in size, weight of ordnance, and number of guns and crew, the two ships were actually closely matched. The *Kearsarge*'s strength was in medium- to short-range fire, whereas the *Alabama*, with its large Blakeley rifled gun, had the advantage at long range. The *Kearsarge* mounted seven guns, but could fight only five on one side. The *Alabama* also fought five guns on a side. The *Kearsarge*'s broadside weight of metal was about a quarter greater than that of its opponent (364 pounds to 274).

The deciding factor in the hour-long battle that began at about 11:00 A.M. in international waters some six to seven miles offshore was the pivot-mounted 11-inch Dahlgren guns aboard the *Kearsarge*. But the crew of the Union warship was fortunate that one shell from the large Blakeley gun on the *Alabama* failed to explode. It lodged in the *Kearsarge*'s wooden sternpost, and had it gone off it would have destroyed the ship's steering and made the *Kearsarge* unmanageable.

The *Kearsarge* also had the advantage of chain strung over the vital middle parts of the ship to protect its engines, boilers, and magazines from enemy fire; this technique had been proven in fighting along the Mississippi River and the chain had been in place on the *Kearsarge* for some time. An outward sheathing of one-inch-thick wood painted the same color as the rest of the hull concealed this from Confederate observation, but the French had informed Semmes about it. Semmes might have used chain in the *Alabama*'s lockers for the same purpose, but he elected not to do so. Later he would deny that he knew about this before the battle.

Throughout the fight, Winslow was able to dictate its range because his vessel was both faster and more maneuverable than his opponent. Shell from the 11-inch Dahlgrens tore into the *Alabama* and had a terrible effect on the ship and its crew. The raider's hull was repeatedly hit and large holes ripped in it side. The *Alabama* then went down. In the engagement only three men were wounded aboard the *Kearsarge*, one of whom later died of his wounds.

After the Civil War, the *Kearsarge* continued in service with the U.S. Navy. On 2 February 1894, it wrecked on Roncador Reef, Central America.

—*Spencer C. Tucker*

See also *Alabama*, CSS; Semmes, Raphael; Winslow, John A.
For further reading:
Silverstone, Paul H. *Warships of the Civil War Navies* (1989).
Tucker, Spencer C. *Raphael Semmes and the* Alabama (1996).

KEENE, LAURA
(1826-1873)
British actor

Laura Keene is best known as the British actor who, on 15 April 1865, appeared in *Our American Cousin*, the play that President Abraham Lincoln was attending when he was shot by John Wilkes Booth. Even before the night of the assassination, Keene was closely associated with the play, having performed the lead role of Florence Trenchard more than 1,000 times. As an actor himself, Booth was familiar with the script of *Our American Cousin* and timed his shot to coincide with an outburst of laughter from the audience. In the mayhem and confusion immediately after the shooting, Keene appealed to the audience for calm by walking to the footlights of the stage and saying, "For God's sake have the presence of mind and keep your places and all will be well." She then managed to enter the presidential box to comfort the sobbing Mary Todd Lincoln. Tradition has it that Keene held Lincoln's bleeding head in her lap, cooling his forehead with water as his blood soaked her pale gray costume.

Ironically, Keene's role the night of Lincoln's death was as dramatic as any she played on stage and has forever linked her with the assassination. Unfortunately, her association with this single event eclipses the historic significance of her contributions to the development of the modern American theater. She was an extremely talented actor and savvy businesswoman who was influential in American theatrical life of the mid-nineteenth century.

The woman known to history as Laura Keene was born in Westminster, England, in 1826. Named Mary Frances, she was the fourth child of Thomas King and Jane Moss. She received a remarkably good education in a loving and close-knit family. In 1841 her father died suddenly, and Mary Frances was forced to help support her family by waiting tables at a local pub. There she met Henry Taylor, a twenty-seven-year-old army officer, whom she wed in 1844 at age eighteen. The couple had two daughters, Emma and Clara. It appears that sometime in 1851 Taylor was transported to Australia for a felony conviction, leaving his young wife to support herself, her two small children, and her mother. Choosing acting as her new career, Mary Frances Moss Taylor also chose a stage name, Laura Keene, the name by which she would be known for the rest of her life.

Soon after her husband's departure, Keene decided to seek her fortune in the United States, where most major cities had theaters and opportunities for young actors abounded. Joined by her mother and children, the family decided to transform themselves into a more traditional one. The entire family began to use the Keene name and the daughters were taught to call their mother aunt.

Keene soon began a lifelong attachment to John Lutz, a married man permanently estranged from his wife.

Keene's stage career flourished. She found steady roles and received favorable notices. In 1852 she unsuccessfully attempted to become the first woman in the United States to manage a theater, the Charles Street Theater in Baltimore. She then toured in Australia and the United States with Edwin Booth, one of the members of the famous acting family. In 1855 Keene returned to New York, where she opened the Laura Keene's New Theatre, which she successfully managed from 1855 to 1863. The actor was instrumental in making New York a theatrical center of the United States because of her many successful productions in the "Laura Keene's Varieties." Important to the theatrical world, she developed one of the finest acting companies in the United States, giving many actors who would later become famous the opportunity to develop their talents in her productions. Keene also demonstrated great philanthropy by using her talent and popularity to aid numerous charitable causes by performing benefits.

Keene continued to tour after the assassination and spent the 1869–1870 season at her own theater in Philadelphia. During this time, she returned to Washington, where she reprised her most famous role in *Our American Cousin* at Wall's Theater. Keene was a popular lecturer and also worked with her daughters to produce a magazine titled *Fine Arts*. Her health declined and she died of consumption on 4 November 1873. Because of Keene's role in the Lincoln assassination, Keene's contribution to the theater has been overlooked. She spent three decades as a professional in the theatrical world, where she achieved great success and influence.

—*Minoa Uffelman*

See also Lincoln Assassination.
For further reading:
Bryan, Vernane. *Laura Keene: A British Actress on the American Stage, 1826–1873* (1993).
Creahan, John. *Life of Laura Keene: Actress, Artist, Manager and Scholar* (1897).
Henneke, Ben Graf. *Laura Keene: A Biography* (1990).
Theodore, Terry. "Laura Keene and Mr. Lincoln." *Lincoln Herald* (1971).

KEITT, LAWRENCE MASSILLON
(1824–1864)
Confederate congressman and officer

Born the son of George Keitt and Mary Magdelene Wannamaker Keitt in Orangeburg District, South Carolina, Lawrence Keitt was educated at South Carolina College before studying law. He opened a practice at Orangeburg Court House and as a young man became interested in South Carolina politics. In 1848 he was elected to the South Carolina House of Representatives. Already at age twenty-four a strong believer in states' rights, Keitt became one of a growing number of South Carolina fire-eaters over the next few years.

Keitt represented South Carolina in 1850 at the Nashville Convention, where he strongly urged the secession of the South. When that body refused to adopt such an extreme stand, Keitt recommended that South Carolina secede alone. In 1853 he took his crusade to Washington when he won election to the U.S. House of Representatives. He remained there with only a brief interruption until December 1860.

The interruption occurred in the summer of 1856, when Keitt tried to prevent anyone from rescuing Senator Charles Sumner from the beating being given him by South Carolina congressman Preston Brooks. The House's disapproval of Keitt's actions prompted him to resign. Constituents returned him to his seat in a special election.

Upon the election of Abraham Lincoln, Keitt refused to resume his seat though he remained in Washington into the month of December. According to some accounts, he was attending a reception given by President James Buchanan when the telegram arrived announcing the secession of South Carolina. He reportedly jumped up and down in celebration over the news.

Returning to South Carolina, Keitt was selected to represent the state to the Provisional Confederate Congress. In that body, he took an active part in the selection of a provisional president, preferring Howell Cobb to the convention's choice of Jefferson Davis. Keitt also worked on several committees, including the one that wrote the permanent constitution, the Foreign Affairs Committee, and the Indian Affairs Committee.

Deciding that his services could better be utilized in the army, Keitt did not seek a seat in the First Confederate Congress. Instead he raised the 20th South Carolina Volunteers in January 1862 and became its colonel. For the next two years, Keitt commanded the 20th near Charleston. Initially commanding Confederate forces on Sullivan's Island, Keitt managed the Confederate defense there during the major Union attack on Charleston harbor on 7 April 1863.

During the summer of 1863, Keitt moved his regiment to Battery Wagner on Morris Island. By September 1863, Keitt was holding the battery against increasingly heavy Union bombardment. On 6 September, he declared the regiment's position there as untenable and was ordered by General P. G. T. Beauregard to evacuate it. Keitt did so during the night of 6–7 September, earning praise from Beauregard for his strong defense.

In early 1864, Keitt and the 20th were headquartered at Mount Pleasant, but with the increasing pressure placed on the Army of Northern Virginia by Grant's Virginia campaign, growing numbers of South Carolina troops, including Keitt and his regiment, were called north. Through April and May, Keitt was stationed around Richmond, but on 30 May he was ordered to join Lee near Cold Harbor.

On that day Keitt took command of Kershaw's brigade. When the preliminary fighting around his position began the following day, part of the brigade broke ranks to flee the field. Keitt spurred his horse forward to rally the men, but a shot felled him. He died the following day and was taken home for burial.

—*David S. Heidler and Jeanne T. Heidler*

See also Congress, C.S.A.; Fire-eaters; South Carolina.

For further reading:
Merchant, John Holt. "Lawrence M. Keitt: South Carolina Fire-eater" (Ph.D. dissertation, 1976).

KELL, JOHN MCINTOSH
(1823–1900)
Confederate naval officer

Born in Darien, Georgia, to John Kell and Margery Baillie Kell, John Mcintosh Kell graduated in 1845 from the U.S. Military Academy. Upon graduation he received a commission in the U.S. Navy. He served first off California during the Mexican-American War and afterward on a variety of stations and with Matthew Perry on his trip to open trade with Japan.

On leave at home in Georgia during the secession crisis, Kell resigned his commission within hours of the vote on Georgia's secession and offered his services to his home state. He received a commission in the Georgia Navy on 13 February at the rank of commander. His first assignment was command of the *Savannah*, the only ship in the state's navy.

In May 1861 Kell accepted a lieutenant's commission in the Confederate Navy with orders to report to Commander Raphael Semmes in New Orleans. Upon arrival, Kell learned that he would be serving as Semmes's executive officer aboard the commerce raider *Sumter*. On 30 June 1861, the *Sumter* ran the Union blockade, eluding the USS *Brooklyn*, and headed out to sea. Though not considered a particularly able vessel, the *Sumter* took eighteen prizes in the Caribbean over the next six months. Semmes then sailed the ship to Gibraltar and abandoned it there. Semmes and Kell made their way to England, where they booked passage in the spring of 1862 first to Nassau and then on a blockade runner back to the Confederacy. Upon their arrival, the two officers learned that they were to return to Great Britain, where Semmes was to take command of a new commerce raider procured by Confederate agents.

When Semmes and Kell arrived in England, they discovered that the ship had been sent to the Azores to prevent its confiscation by the British government.

Catching up with the ship in those islands, they discovered it christened the *Alabama*. Beginning a momentous voyage in September 1862, the ship and its crew captured sixty-nine prizes before being caught in a battle with the USS *Kearsarge* off Cherbourg, France, in June 1864. The *Alabama* was sunk in the encounter. Kell, Semmes, and several crew members were rescued by a British yacht and avoided capture.

Kell returned from England to the Confederacy, avoiding Federal attempts to capture him en route. After visiting with family, Kell went to Richmond in December 1864. During his absence, he had been promoted to commander, and upon his arrival in the Confederate capital he was given command of the ironclad *Richmond*. As part of a squadron intended to harass Union shipping in the James River, the *Richmond* proved ineffective. As a result of illness in January 1865, Kell had to relinquish command and saw no action for the remainder of the war.

After the war, Kell returned to Georgia, where he spent the remainder of his life farming and writing his memoirs. He also served for fourteen years near the end of his life as the state's adjutant general. He died on 5 October 1900 in Sunnyside, Georgia.

—*David S. Heidler and Jeanne T. Heidler*

See also Alabama, CSS; *Kearsarge*; Navy, C.S.A.; Semmes, Raphael; *Sumter*, CSS.

For further reading:
Delaney, Norman C. *John McIntosh Kell of the Raider* Alabama (1973).
Kell, John McIntosh. *Recollections of a Naval Life, Including the Cruises of the Confederate States Steamers, Sumter and* Alabama (1900).

KELLEY, BENJAMIN FRANKLIN
(1807–1891)
Union general

Born in New Hampton, New Hampshire, Benjamin Franklin Kelley in 1826 moved to Wheeling, Virginia (now West Virginia), where he took a job with the Baltimore & Ohio Railroad. He remained with the company, transferring to Philadelphia later in the decade. He maintained close ties to the area, however, and at the outbreak of the Civil War returned to Wheeling, where he raised the 1st Virginia, U.S. Volunteers, becoming its colonel.

Kelley commanded his regiment on 3 June 1861 under George B. McClellan at Philippi, Virginia, where he was seriously wounded. For his actions there, he was promoted to brigadier general of volunteers to date from 17 May 1861. As soon as he had recovered from his wounds, Kelley commanded a brigade in the Army of Occupation in West Virginia and in August was given command of the District of Grafton. Most of his activi-

ties in this command were designed to guard the line of the Baltimore & Ohio Railroad, a task that would occupy Kelley's time for the remainder of the war.

In October 1861, Kelley prevented Confederate forces from taking control of Romney, a key communications link with forces along the Potomac River. In November he became the commander of the Department of Harper's Ferry and Cumberland. In early 1862, Kelley established his headquarters in Cumberland and operated from there for much of the remainder of the war. One of his primary tasks in guarding the line of the B&O was to keep the lower Shenandoah Valley free of Confederate guerrillas, a nearly impossible task given the terrain, the unknown sympathies of many of the inhabitants, and the staff allotted to Kelley for the task. Still, he persevered through the changes in commanders, the bureaucratic shakeups, and the political machinations of many civilian officials in the area and in Washington.

Throughout 1862, Kelley continued at his task. At the end of the year, he became the commander of the Railroad Division, District of West Virginia, Department of the Ohio. In the early months of 1863, he patrolled out from Harper's Ferry, alternating in the spring between that place and Cumberland, trying to cover as wide an area as possible with his limited resources. During Robert E. Lee's advance north in June 1863, Kelley remained for the most part in Harper's Ferry and on 24 June, after Robert Milroy's defeat at Winchester, was named commander of the Department of West Virginia. He remained in that command until the following March.

For the remainder of the year, headquartered primarily at Cumberland, Kelley remained busy. His command participated in the pursuit of part of Lee's forces out of Pennsylvania. In the fall, partly to pull some of the Confederate guerrilla forces away from the B&O, he ordered William W. Averell's raid against the Tennessee & Virginia Railroad that resulted in the battle of Droop Mountain. Still the Confederate raids continued, primarily because Kelley did not have enough men to stop them.

In early 1864 the civilian government of West Virginia became increasingly vocal in its criticism of the way Kelley was defending the state. He was also criticized for being too soft on Confederate sympathizers—people who were naturally suspected of aiding the guerrilla bands. In February 1864, the West Virginia legislature passed a resolution calling for Kelley's replacement by a major general. As it happened, the War Department had one it was not using. German-American Franz Sigel, while viewed by no one as a particularly able general, was extremely popular with other German-Americans, and 1864 was an election year. As a result, in March 1864 Sigel superseded Kelley as the commander of the Department of West Virginia. Upon Sigel's arrival, Kelley promised full cooperation with his new

commander and promptly took a thirty-day leave of absence. Upon his return, Kelley was given command of the line of the B&O from Wheeling, West Virginia, to Monocacy, Maryland.

From Cumberland, Kelley fought a number of engagements through the summer and fall of 1864. In August he even repelled an attack on his positions around Cumberland itself. Philip Sheridan dispersed much of the Confederate resistance in the Shenandoah in the fall of 1864, and Confederate partisans in the area became desperate and in some cases increasingly bold. On 21 February 1865, Confederate captain John H. McNeill, dressed his men in U.S. Army uniforms to conduct a raid on Cumberland itself, taking Kelley and Major General George Crook, Sigel's replacement, captive. Kelley spent several weeks as a prisoner in Richmond before being exchanged. By then, the war was almost over.

Kelley resigned his commission in June 1865 and returned to private life. For the remainder of his life, he occupied a number of federal offices, including tax collector in Wheeling and pension examiner. He retired to Oakland, Maryland, where he died 6 July 1891.

—*David S. Heidler and Jeanne T. Heidler*

See also McNeill, John; Philippi; West Virginia.

For further reading:
Duffey, Jefferson Waite. *Two Generals Kidnapped: A Complete Account of the Capture of Federal Generals George Crook and Benjamin Kelly [sic] by McNeill's Rangers, and a Roster of Those Who Participated in the Raid, February 1865* (1944).
Duncan, Richard R. *Lee's Endangered Left: The Civil War in Western Virginia Spring of 1864* (1998).

KELLY'S FORD, VIRGINIA, BATTLE OF
(17 March 1863)

The winter of 1862–1863 did not bring about a significant improvement in the battlefield fortunes of the Federal cavalry in the East in relation to their gray counterparts. In his Chambersburg, Pennsylvania, raid of 9–13 October 1862, J. E. B. Stuart circled McClellan's Army of the Potomac with 1,800 men while a befuddled force of Union cavalry, more than twice as strong as the raiders, first could not locate the intruders and then failed to prevent their exit to the south shore of the Potomac and to safety. The action at Barbee's Cross Roads, Virginia, on 5 November 1862 showed that the Union horsemen could fight, but that their leaders feared to exploit any success their men achieved on the battlefield. Finally, a Confederate ride to Hartwood Church, Virginia, between 24 and 26 February 1863, carried out by Fitzhugh Lee and 400 troopers of his brigade, not only frustrated their Federal mounted pursuers, but literally had them running around in circles looking for their enemy. This episode sent a sense of helplessness when it came to dealing with the rebel cavalry that was felt not only at army headquarters, but even by the Lincoln administration in Washington, D.C.

The recently appointed commander of the Army of the Potomac, Major General Joseph Hooker, demanded that the embarrassment caused by the latest Confederate penetration into his army's positions be avenged. He felt that the only way to stop the harassment of his lines by the enemy was by vigorous attacks on the opposing cavalry by his own mounted arm. To that end, he authorized Brigadier General William W. Averell to take his 2d Cavalry Division (3,000 soldiers strong), supported by a six-gun horse artillery battery (Martin's 6th Light New York Artillery), to "attack and rout or destroy 'the cavalry forces of the enemy reported to be in the vicinity of Culpeper Court House.'"

Averell was eager to comply with Hooker's orders, and on 16 March he assembled his command at Morrisville, about eight miles from the Rappahannock River crossing at Kelly's Ford. Culpeper Court House was a further ten miles to the west. Fearing a reported enemy force to his north in the area of Catlett's Station, the cavalry leader detached 900 of his division to guard that flank. The peeling off of so many of his men to deal with a rumored Confederate threat foreshadowed the caution that would hamper the Federals' activities at the Kelly's Ford fight.

By the time Averell's column moved toward the ford in the early hours of 17 March, the Union commander had learned that Fitzhugh Lee's cavalry brigade was encamped at Culpeper Court House; and Lee knew from his scouts that Averell was coming. Forewarned of the Federal movement, the Confederate leader strengthened his Kelly's Ford defenses: the ford was blocked by fallen trees, and the south bank of the water crossing was lined with rifle pits that were manned by sixty sharpshooters.

Arriving at the ford by about 8 A.M. on 17 March, Averell immediately dismounted 100 men to storm the abatis that was situated in the ford. Three times the Yankees charged into the water only to be repulsed. A fourth try was made by a party of 20 mounted men led by Lieutenant Brown, who succeeded in capturing the position. By noon Averell's entire command was south of the river and ready to march to Culpeper.

Once the ford was taken, the Federal crossing was carried out in an almost leisurely fashion with no sense of urgency apparent. As a result, Averell's plan to proceed to Culpeper was forestalled by the arrival of Lee and his 800 hard-riding troopers. Along with him came a two-gun section of artillery overseen by Captain James Breathed. Lee advanced to the charge immediately.

Averell's scouts had seen the advance elements of Lee's force heading toward Kelly's Ford. Reacting to this, and thus passing the tactical initiative to his opponent, the Federal leader arranged his division in line of battle ready to receive the Confederate onslaught. Colonel Duffié's brigade was stationed on the left, with Colonel McIntosh's in the center, and Captain Reno's two regiments of regulars on the right.

With his five regiments in line abreast, Lee came at the bluecoats a half mile south of the ford. Averell had seized a stone fence to his front and placed two dismounted regiments behind it. Confederate sharpshooters ran toward the Federal position, followed by the 3d Virginia Cavalry in column of four. Joined by the 5th Virginia, the two formations ran along the stone fence until they found a narrow gate. They rushed through the gate in the wall and attempted to turn the enemy line. They failed, as the carbine fire of the 16th Pennsylvania Cavalry and shelling from Martin's battery met them.

At about this time, Duffié, at the other end of the Union line, disobeyed Averell's orders to keep his station until told otherwise and initiated his own charge. The surprise thrust by the Federals, and the fact that the Union

The battle of Kelly's Ford, sketched by Alfred R. Waud (*Library of Congress*)

line overlapped his own, forced Lee to withdraw his command back through a strip of woods to a clearing just behind the wood. Here Lee determined to make a stand.

As the bluecoats neared his new position, Fitzhugh Lee ordered another charge. Again it broke down in the face of Federal artillery fire and mounted and dismounted small arms discharges coming from the Union line. The rebel retreat would have turned into a rout if Reno's brigade had charged the fleeing enemy on the flank, as they were in a perfect position to do so. But that coup de grace never occurred, due to Averell's earlier order to his subordinates to maintain a solid front and not advance unless supported on either flank.

Instead of taking advantage of the confusion in the enemy ranks and the Rebel retreat, Averell recalled his men and ordered them to recross Kelly's Ford to the north bank of the Rappahannock River. He later explained that the presence of "Jeb" Stuart on the field heralded the likelihood of Confederate cavalry reinforcements entering the battle. Furthermore, he reported the approach of railroad cars, which could only mean the imminent arrival of Confederate infantry forces. Thus ended the first cavalry brigade versus cavalry brigade combat in the east during the Civil War.

There were three major results of the battle of Kelly's Ford. First, Averell lost 78 killed, wounded, and missing from his command; Fitzhugh Lee lost 133 killed, wounded, and missing. Second, Major John Pelham, chief of the Stuart Horse Artillery Battalion, and one of the most accomplished and aggressive artillerists on either side of the war, was killed by a shell splinter while urging his compatriots on during their first charge through the stone fence's gateway. Finally, after Kelly's Ford, both Confederate and Union horsemen in the east realized that in the future the blue cavalry could and would become a force to be reckoned with.

—*Arnold D. Blumberg*

See also Averell, William Woods; Lee, Fitzhugh; Pelham, John.
For further reading:
Bigelow, John, Jr. *The Campaign of Chancellorsville: A Strategic and Tactical Study* (1910).
Milham, Charles G. *Gallant Pelham* (1959; reprint, 1987).
Nichols, James Lynn. *General Fitzhugh Lee: A Biography* (1989).
Sears, Stephen W. *Chancellorsville* (1996).
Starr, Stephen Z. *The Union Cavalry in the Civil War* (1979–1985).

KEMPER, JAMES LAWSON
(1823–1895)
Confederate general

Born in Madison County, Virginia, to William Kemper and Maria Elizabeth Allison Kemper, James Kemper was educated at Virginia Military Institute and Washington College. He began the prac-

tice of law in 1843. Suspending his practice in 1846 to captain a volunteer company in the Mexican-American War, he did not see combat in the conflict. Returning to Virginia, he resumed his practice and became active in Virginia politics. He served as a member of the Virginia House of Delegates (1848–1860) and as speaker of that body (1858–1860).

Kemper did not support secession but, upon the withdrawal of Virginia from the Union, he raised and became the colonel of the 7th Virginia Regiment. He led the 7th at First Bull Run and in the early phases of the Peninsula campaign. Commended for bravery by A. P. Hill at the battle of Williamsburg, 5 May 1862, Kemper's actions there gained him a promotion to brigadier general after the battle of Seven Pines.

During the Seven Days', Kemper commanded the 1st Brigade, James Longstreet's division. He remained in command of that brigade until Pickett's Charge at Gettysburg, though he temporarily commanded a division at Second Bull Run. After Second Bull Run, Kemper fought at South Mountain, Antietam, and Fredericksburg. Detached to North Carolina with much of Longstreet's corps after Fredericksburg, Kemper missed the battle of Chancellorsville. Back in time to move north for Lee's second invasion, Kemper and his brigade brought up the rear of the invasion force as part of George Pickett's division.

Not arriving in Gettysburg in time to participate in the first two days of fighting, Kemper and the remainder of Pickett's division comprised a large part of the attacking force for the third day. In the assault that would become known as Pickett's Charge, Kemper's brigade composed the extreme right wing of the attack. Kemper was severely wounded and captured in this disastrous offensive. Not expected to live, he was exchanged within a few months.

Kemper survived his injuries, but was unavailable for field command for the remainder of the war. He held a variety of posts including the head of he Conscript Bureau and the commander of the Virginia Reserve. In recognition for his services he was promoted to major general in September 1864. After Lee withdrew from the defenses of Richmond and Petersburg, Kemper remained in command of the home guard in Richmond and surrendered to the Union troops when they entered the city.

After the war Kemper returned to his law practice and briefly to politics. From 1874 to 1877 he served as governor of Virginia, after which he retired from public life. He died in Orange County, Virginia.

—*David S. Heidler and Jeanne T. Heidler*

See also Gettysburg, Battle of; Pickett, George.
For further reading:
Harrison, Walter. *Pickett's Men: A Fragment of War History* (1870).
Stewart, George Rippey. *Pickett's Charge: A Microhistory of the Final Attack at Gettysburg, July 3, 1863* (1959).

KENNER, DUNCAN FARRAR
(1813–1887)
Confederate congressman

Born into a wealthy Louisiana family, Duncan Kenner was a well-educated member of the New Orleans aristocracy. By the mid-1830s, he had acquired a 600-acre sugar plantation in Ascension Parish that he named Ashland in honor of Henry Clay of Kentucky.

Within a few years, Kenner had become one of Louisiana's wealthiest sugar planters and largest slaveholders. His personal views on slavery, however, were moderate; despite his large slaveholdings, for example, Kenner considered the South's labor institution supremely wasteful and of but limited benefit to the Southern economy. At the same time, though, he was dismayed by the growing free labor movement in the North that threatened to strangle Southern slavery into oblivion before Southern planters could find a suitable substitute. Like many other Southern moderates, by midcentury Kenner had become a staunch defender of Southern economic interests and political rights.

Kenner served in the Louisiana assembly as a Whig from Ascension Parish. Ideologically conservative, he opposed all attempts by Louisiana Democrats to institute Jacksonian electoral reforms. In 1854 Kenner joined the fledgling Know-Nothing Party, but his affiliation with that nativist, anti-Catholic party was short-lived, and he soon thereafter declared himself a Democrat. Lincoln's election in November 1860 proved to be the long-anticipated spark for Southern secession, and Kenner accepted the South's departure from the Union as fundamental to that region's survival. At the end of January 1861, Louisiana's secession convention named Kenner as one of seven delegates to represent Louisiana in the newly formed Confederate Congress.

Kenner's services to the Confederacy center on his years as a representative from Louisiana and on a secret diplomatic mission to Europe late in the war. Reflective of his prewar nationalism, Kenner supported Confederate versions of the protective tariff, internal improvements, property confiscation, sequestration laws, and considerably higher taxes. Yet high taxes were hardly popular, and loans to the government accounted but for roughly 40 percent of its total revenues. Much to Kenner's disgust, the Confederacy was forced to print more and more money to finance the war effort. As he had predicted, the literal flooding of the country with paper currency caused rampant inflation and economic ruin. But there was little that Kenner or anyone else could do to alleviate the South's financial woes.

After Federal admiral David Farragut's flotilla successfully captured New Orleans, Kenner hurried home to Ashland to be with his wife Nanine and their three children. In late July 1862, 300 federal troops commanded by Colonel John A. Keith of the 21st Indiana appeared on the plantation to arrest Kenner and seize all of his property. But Kenner had earlier fled the estate on one of his fastest thoroughbreds, leaving Nanine to greet their unwanted visitors. Though Colonel Keith would not allow his troops to venture upstairs at the manor house, his men enjoyed the run of the property. Once Keith's men had had their fill of Kenner's large store of liquor and food—and once anything of any value had been confiscated—the Federal troops left Ashland a plundered shell.

Kenner returned to Richmond in the fall of 1864 to a rapidly deteriorating military situation, and he resolved that the South's only possible salvation lay in gaining for the Confederate government diplomatic recognition by European powers. As a means of enticing England into recognizing the Confederacy, Kenner proposed that all Southern slaves be emancipated. His most important ally in advocating such an extreme measure was Judah P. Benjamin, another Louisianian who had served as Confederate attorney general, secretary of war, and secretary of state. As prospects for victory dimmed throughout winter 1864, Benjamin ultimately convinced Jefferson Davis that emancipation must be offered to England in return for recognition. In late December, Kenner was informed that President Davis had selected him to depart for England and France with near plenary authority to persuade those European governments to recognize the Confederacy. Though he was pleased that Davis finally had consented to trade slavery for recognition, Kenner was hardly enthusiastic about his mission, as he believed that this last-ditch effort would be simply too late.

Understanding the immediacy of his mission, Kenner opted for an exceptionally daring plan requiring that he depart out of New York harbor. This, of course, meant that he would have to cross Federal lines and travel overland without being recognized as a Confederate congressman. Using the alias "A. B. Kinglake of Philadelphia," and with the assistance of a Confederate sympathizer from Maryland, Kenner crossed the Potomac River and walked through thick snow to a safe house in Washington. From there the agent rode by carriage to Baltimore, where he boarded a northbound train. Kenner finally reached New York City on 6 February 1865 and arranged trans-Atlantic passage aboard the steamship *America*.

Upon arrival a few weeks later, Kenner quickly established contact with John Slidell and James M. Mason, the Confederacy's envoys to France and England, respectively, and informed them of his mission. Slidell arranged a conference with Napoleon III, who, despite the Confederacy's offer to emancipate all slaves, refused to grant recognition without the British government having

done so first. Kenner and Mason then went to England and arranged a conference with Prime Minister John Palmerston. An interview between Palmerston and Mason was held on 14 March, and though Kenner opted not to attend the meeting, Mason delivered Kenner's offer from the Confederate government. Palmerston listened attentively to Mason's recital, but the prime minister asserted that, though the message was interesting, he could not agree to its terms because slavery in fact had never been an obstacle to recognition. He added that the Confederacy was doomed, and though personally sympathetic to the South's struggle for independence, the Confederacy's defeat was to him a fait accompli. Obviously dejected by Palmerston's refusal to grant recognition, Kenner made plans to return home. Before his departure, however, he received word that Richmond had fallen and that Robert E. Lee had surrendered.

The Kenner mission was the final diplomatic gasp of the beaten Confederacy, and it reflects the lengths to which the Richmond government was willing to go to achieve independence. Kenner believed that, had he been sent earlier in the war, perhaps a Southern emancipation proclamation would have persuaded England to recognize the South. Kenner was able to put the war

behind him, rebuilding Ashland into an extremely profitable sugar estate. He died in New Orleans at the age of seventy-four.

—*Robert Saunders, Jr.*

See also Congress, C.S.A.; Louisiana; Palmerston, Viscount.
For further reading:
Bauer, Craig A. "The Last Effort: The Secret Mission of the Confederate Diplomat, Duncan F. Kenner." *Louisiana History* (1981).
———. *The Life and Times of Duncan Farrar Kenner* (1993).
Price, Grady Daniel. "The Secret Mission of Duncan F. Kenner, Confederate Minister Plenipotentiary to Europe in 1865" (M.A. thesis, 1929).
Yearns, W. Buck. *The Confederate Congress* (1960).

KENNESAW MOUNTAIN, BATTLE OF
(27 June 1864)

The largest engagement fought north of the Chattahoochee River during Union major general William Tecumseh Sherman's campaign for Atlanta in 1864, the battle of Kennesaw Mountain proved to be a tactical success for Confederate

The battle of Kennesaw Mountain (*Library of Congress*)

commander Joseph E. Johnston. The victory was short-lived, however, as Sherman sidestepped the impenetrable Confederate position and continued his advance toward the third largest city in Georgia.

Beginning on the first week of May 1864, Sherman and his three armies totaling nearly 100,000 men began moving south along the line of the Western & Atlantic Railroad toward Atlanta. Johnston's 60,000 troops from the Army of Tennessee and the Army of Mississippi tried to block the Federal advance by entrenching across its path and inviting an assault against their prepared defenses. For a month the two forces gradually moved deeper into Georgia as they battled each other, yet Sherman refused to totally commit his troops to an attack. Choosing instead to use his superior numbers to turn Johnston out of his well-constructed defenses, the campaign became one of maneuver as Sherman moved to get behind Johnston and the latter shifted to block him.

On the evening of 18 June, Johnston's troops began moving into newly constructed defensive works along the slopes of a ridgeline anchored by Kennesaw Mountain, just west of Marietta, having withdrawn from their previous positions at Pine Mountain, Lost Mountain, and Mud Creek. Rising to a height of 691 feet, the position was as indomitable as any the Confederates had held since the onset of Sherman's campaign. Choosing at first to avoid attacking Johnston head-on, Sherman continued his pattern of flanking movements and sent Major General John M. Schofield's Army of the Ohio and Joseph Hooker's XX Corps to maneuver around the Confederate left flank then eastward to the rail line, cutting off Johnston's line of retreat. Detecting this Federal movement, Johnston responded by swinging Lieutenant General John Bell Hood's corps from the Confederate right flank to the threatened left. There, near a farm owned by Peter Valentine Kolb, Hood massed his troops for an attack.

Having inadequately reconnoitered the area, Hood assumed that Federal troops were in a column marching eastward up the Powder Springs Road. In fact, Hooker, knowing of Hood's presence, ordered his 14,000 men and forty cannons to prepare barricades and move into a line of battle. On 22 June, the misguided Hood ordered his 11,000 men to attack. As the Confederates advanced to within 500 yards of the Federal line, Hooker's batteries opened up a lethal barrage of solid shot and

Union entrenchments near Kennesaw Mountain, 1864 (*National Archives*)

canister. Infantry volleys finished the task, driving Hood's men from the field. The battle at Kolb's farm cost Hood 1,500 men; Hooker lost 250. Johnston was furious with Hood for the unauthorized and impetuous attack. Although he continued to hold strong defensive ground, the past month's fighting had whittled Johnston's force down to 43,000 men. The last thing that he needed was a renegade subordinate.

For Sherman, the time seemed right to change his tactics. Believing Johnston's eight-mile line was stretched too thin, the Federal general ordered Schofield to feign an attack against the Confederate left flank while Major General James B. McPherson's Army of the Tennessee did the same against Johnston's right. McPherson was to follow up his successful feint with an attack against the Confederate line south and west of Kennesaw Mountain. Assuming his adversary would be forced to send reinforcements to both apparently endangered flanks, Sherman could then throw the Army of the Cumberland, under the command of Major General George H. Thomas, at the center of the Confederate line and penetrate on through. Sherman hoped to breach Johnston's line at two points, establish a "secure lodgement beyond…[and advance] toward Marietta and the railroad in case of success."

The Federal attack began as planned at 8:00 in the morning on 27 June—an artillery barrage aimed at Kennesaw Mountain signaled the assault. Soon, Sherman's plans began to go awry. The feints against the Confederate flanks did not achieve their desired effect. McPherson's main assault with 5,500 troops against Pigeon Hill, on the ridgeline south of Kennesaw Mountain, achieved initial success in driving in Confederate skirmishers, but McPherson's men were soon met and pinned down by deadly fire from Major General Samuel G. French's well-entrenched division. After two hours the attackers withdrew.

The largest assault against the Confederate line occurred two miles south of Pigeon Hill at a point defended by two divisions under Major Generals Patrick R. Cleburne and Benjamin Franklin Cheatham. Arranged in five columns, the 8,000 Federals were ordered to remove the percussion caps from their rifles and advance on the run using only fixed bayonets. Speed was the essence of this attack—no one was to pause to fire a shot until the Confederate line was broken. Beginning at 9:00, the assault soon degenerated into confusion as men in the rear caught up with those in the vanguard, who had been halted by concentrated fire from the Confederate earthworks to their front. The fighting was particularly ferocious at a salient in Cheatham's line later called the "Dead Angel." There Federal soldiers advanced to within fifteen yards of the Confederate line before falling. By noon, Thomas's men could take no more and withdrew. The battle had proved to be a disaster for Sherman. Federal casualties for the day totaled 3,000; Confederate losses were 552.

Sherman's army remained in front of Kennesaw Mountain for four more days, burying their dead and recovering from the exhausting battle. When word arrived at the commanding general's headquarters that Schofield's feint had successfully placed the Army of the Ohio in a position to threaten the Confederate rear, Sherman decided to return to his strategy of maneuver, flanking Johnston to the west and racing for the Chattahoochee River and Atlanta. On 2 July, the Confederate commander had no choice but to withdraw from his Kennesaw line and move south, hoping once again to entice Sherman into battle on ground favorable to the defense.

—*Alan C. Downs*

See also Atlanta Campaign; Hood, John Bell; Johnston, Joseph Eggleston; Sherman, William Tecumseh.
For further reading:
Castel, Albert. *Decision in the West: The Atlanta Campaign of 1864* (1992).
Symonds, Craig. *Joseph E. Johnston: A Civil War Biography* (1992).

KENTUCKY

Kentucky was relatively a larger and more important state in 1861 than at the start of the twenty-first century. Its population then was ninth in the nation; livestock ranked in fifth place; the number of farms was seventh. Even in manufacturing, Kentucky was slightly above the national average. The state's geographical location was of great strategic importance, and President Lincoln saw the state of his birth as the bellwether among the four loyal slave states. As he wrote Orville H. Browning on 22 September 1861, "I think to lose Kentucky is nearly the same as to lose the whole game."

Slavery was an obvious tie with the South, river traffic had made a strong connection with that section, the Kentucky Resolutions of 1798 and 1799 had been among the first declarations of states' rights, and Kentucky had separated from Virginia. But Henry Clay and John J. Crittenden had reflected the nationalism of many Kentuckians, the new railroads tied Kentucky more closely to the North, many Kentuckians had come from free states, and many former Kentuckians lived in the free states of the old Northwest Territory. With sentiments so divided, John Bell of the Constitutional Union Party carried Kentucky in the 1860 presidential election. Republican Abraham Lincoln received less than 1 percent of Kentucky's popular vote.

As the secession movement developed, Crittenden was a major figure in the unsuccessful efforts to find a compromise that would avert war. When fighting started at Fort Sumter, Governor Beriah Magoffin refused to supply troops to help put down the rebellion. State Unionists prevented the calling of a convention that might have adopted secession. The May declaration of Kentucky's neutrality in the struggle made sense then, although it was no more constitutional than was secession. Two summer elections proved that most Kentuckians were Unionists. Unionists captured nine of ten congressional seats as they gained more than a two-thirds majority in both houses of the General Assembly. Pro-Southern Governor Magoffin resigned in August 1862.

Neutrality ended in early September 1861 when the Confederates seized Columbus on the Mississippi River. Union troops poured into the northern part of the state while Confederates occupied the southern portion. Confederate general Albert Sidney Johnston established his headquarters in Bowling Green. Embarrassed by their state's refusal to secede, pro-Confederates met in Russellville in two conventions and, appealing to the right of the people to reject tyranny, established a Provisional Government of Kentucky that was admitted into the C.S.A. on 10 December 1861. Several minor skirmishes were fought in various parts of the state in late 1861 as the rival forces sparred for position and endeavored to construct effective fighting forces. The Union victory at Mill Springs on 19 January 1862 was the first battle of consequence and the first breach in the defense line that Johnston had tried to establish across southern Kentucky. Then in February 1862 General U. S. Grant, with the aid of Union gunboats, captured Forts Henry and Donelson in northern Tennessee, and the Confederates withdrew from Kentucky. The battle that occurred at Shiloh on 6–7 April 1862 might have been fought at Bowling Green given other circumstances. In any event, Shiloh took a heavy toll. General Johnston and Governor George W. Johnson of the Provisional Government were among the casualties there.

The other major Confederate invasion of Kentucky came in the summer of 1862 when Generals Braxton Bragg and E. Kirby Smith led poorly coordinated armies into the state. Bragg had wanted to defeat the Union army in Tennessee before invading Kentucky, but Kirby Smith forced his hand by advancing into the eastern and central areas. Smith captured Lexington and Frankfort after almost destroying a small Union army at the battle of Richmond on 29–30 August. The Frankfort government fled to Louisville to avoid seizure. Bragg delayed at Munfordville to capture more than 4,000 Federals on 17 September 1862, and Union general Don Carlos Buell declined battle there and marched into Louisville. Bragg and Smith spent some time installing Richard Hawes as the Confederate governor in Frankfort, and they failed to consolidate their forces. Kentucky's major battle was fought at Perryville on 8 October 1862 with neither commander using his full strength. Losses were heavy for both sides as the Confederates made gains against the Union left flank. However, Bragg decided to withdraw

from Kentucky to preserve his army for the defense of the lower South. He finally achieved union with Kirby Smith, and they escaped through Cumberland Gap. Disappointed by the failure of Kentuckians to volunteer in large numbers, Bragg's disparaging comments made him hated in the state.

Such leaders as John Hunt Morgan and Nathan B. Forrest led raids into the state that caused considerable economic damage and embarrassed Federal commanders who were unable to thwart them. Guerrilla activities became more numerous and more vicious as the war continued. The harsh measures adopted in efforts to control them turned many loyal Kentuckians into anti–Lincoln administration advocates. Civil rights were frequently violated and elections were interfered with. Governor Thomas E. Bramlette (1863–1867) clashed frequently with President Lincoln. In the 1864 presidential election, Kentucky was one of only three states carried by Democrat George B. McClellan.

Although the Emancipation Proclamation did not apply to Kentucky, many Kentuckians bitterly resented its interference in what they saw as a state matter. They became even more incensed with the decision to use black soldiers. Kentucky rejected all of Lincoln's efforts to get the state to accept some form of voluntary, gradual, compensated emancipation. More than 20,000 of Kentucky's some 100,000 Union soldiers were blacks, and by the war's end 71 percent of the 225,000 slaves of 1860 had become free. Estimates of Kentuckians in Confederate service range between 25,000 and 40,000. Adoption of the Thirteenth Amendment in December 1865 abolished the last remnants of slavery, although many years would pass before some of the attributes of freedom were obtained.

Kentucky had considerable economic losses during the war as much of its agriculture declined and property was seized or destroyed. Promising prewar educational advances were checked, and such social institutions as churches underwent severe strains. Many promising young men died in the service of one side or the other; others were handicapped mentally and physically by their war experiences. For decades after the war, Kentucky voted as a part of the solid Democratic South. Not until 1895 was a Republican elected governor.

—*Lowell H. Harrison*

See also Bragg, Braxton; Bramlette, Thomas E; Johnson, George W.; Johnston, Albert Sidney; Magoffin, Beriah; Morgan, John Hunt; Perryville, Battle of; Richmond, Kentucky, Battle of; Smith, Edmund Kirby.

For further reading:
Connelly, Thomas L. *Army of the Heartland: The Army of Tennessee, 1861–1862* (1967).
Coulter, E. Merton. *The Civil War and Readjustment in Kentucky* (1926).
Harrison, Lowell H. *The Civil War in Kentucky* (1975).
Lucas, Marion B. *A History of Blacks in Kentucky: From Slavery to Segregation, 1760–1891* (1992).

McDonough, James L. *War in Kentucky: From Shiloh to Perryville* (1994).

KERNSTOWN, FIRST BATTLE OF
(23 March 1862)

General Thomas J. "Stonewall" Jackson's innovative ideas of warfare helped his men win numerous victories against unfavorable odds. One tactical defeat, however, might have led to his greatest strategic victory. Jackson lost the battle of Kernstown, Virginia, in March 1862, but the defeat altered Union military strategy and launched Jackson's Shenandoah Valley campaign.

In March 1862, Confederate general Joseph E. Johnston's men, situated near Manassas, Virginia, withdrew southward in the face of Union general George B. McClellan's rapidly growing force. Johnston sent word to Jackson, whose men protected Johnston's left flank at Winchester, to do the same.

By this time, McClellan had developed a plan to sail to the Virginia Peninsula and attack Richmond from the east rather than attack Johnston's strong defensive positions in northern Virginia. McClellan wanted to use the largest force possible for this offensive, and therefore, he left behind only a small force to guard Washington. He knew, however, that Jackson's army had to be dealt with before he could implement his plan.

Jackson faced a difficult situation. He sought to prevent the 30,000 Union men under General Nathaniel Banks, located north of Winchester, from

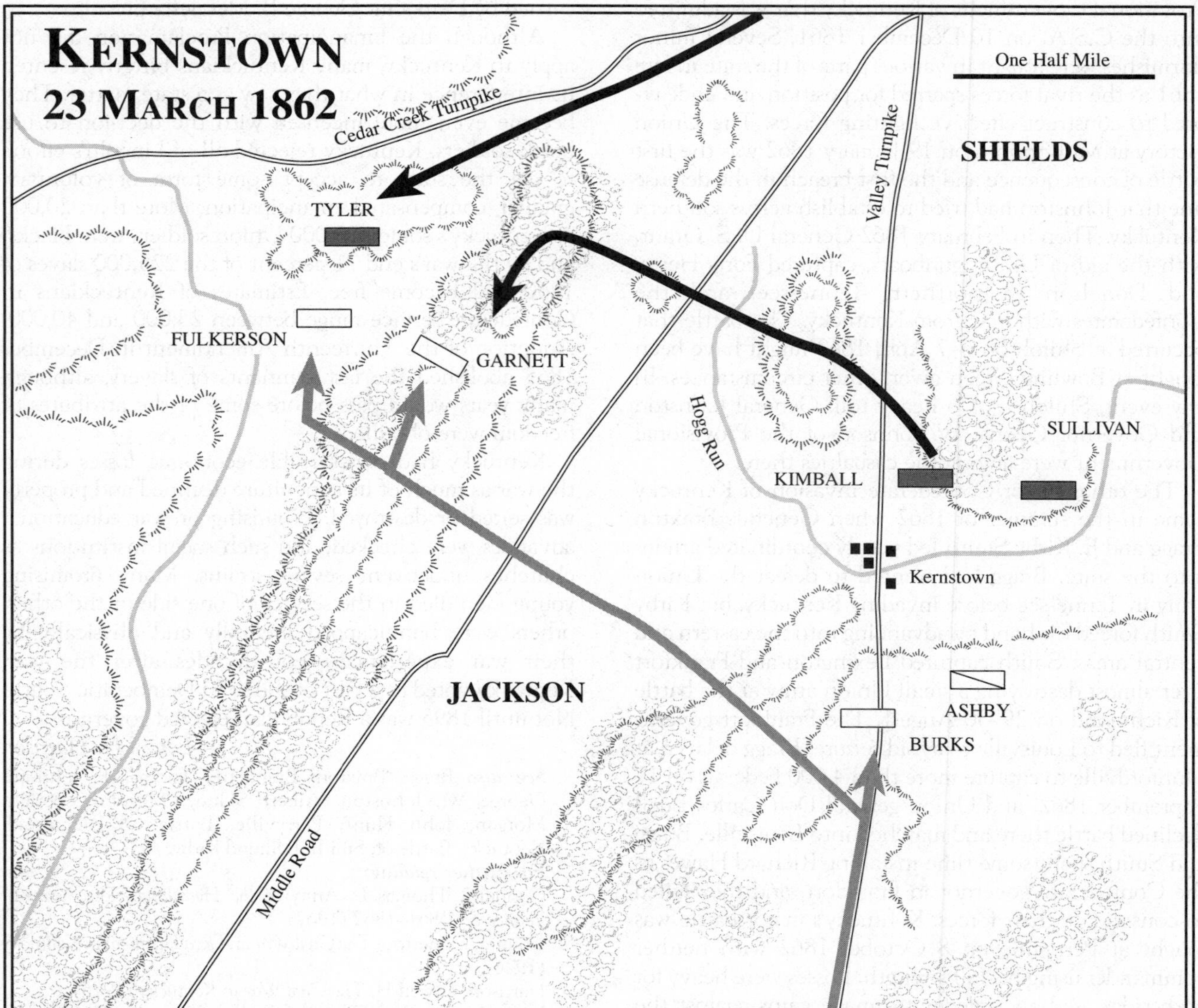

KERNSTOWN
23 MARCH 1862

One Half Mile

Cedar Creek Turnpike

Valley Turnpike

SHIELDS

TYLER

FULKERSON

GARNETT

Hogg Run

KIMBALL

SULLIVAN

Kernstown

JACKSON

ASHBY

BURKS

Middle Road

joining with McClellan to defeat Johnston. Although he had only 4,000 men, Jackson believed that striking a blow against Banks would prevent McClellan from using Banks's men in any attack. "If we cannot be successful in defeating the enemy should he advance," Jackson wrote, "a kind Providence may enable us to inflict a terrible wound and effect a safe retreat in the event of having to fall back." Unfortunately for Jackson, miscommunication among his subordinates prevented this action. Jackson's men abandoned Winchester in early March and retreated forty miles southward.

Because Jackson no longer posed a threat, Banks began shifting his troops eastward to take part in McClellan's amphibious expedition. These Union movements, however, did not go unnoticed. Jackson's cavalry commander, Turner Ashby, sent word on 21 March that Banks's men were pulling out of the valley. Jackson knew he could not allow Banks to join McClellan, so he began marching north to engage him.

On 22 March, Ashby's men struck Federal pickets south of Winchester near the hamlet of Kernstown. During the skirmish, Union commander, James Shields, kept the majority of his 9,000 available men hidden. Ashby was fooled and sent word to Jackson that only four Union regiments remained; he urged his commander to hurry forward.

Jackson's men arrived at 2:00 P.M. the next day, 23 March, after marching almost forty miles in thirty-six hours. Jackson wanted to attack immediately, but being a firm believer in keeping the Sabbath, he tried never to fight on Sunday. Unfortunately for Jackson, Union troops occupying the high ground in front of him could see his deployment, so he had no choice but to order his men forward.

Jackson launched a flank attack on the left. The Confederates pushed the Union forces aside and took a strong position by a stone fence. From there, they fired volley after volley upon the surging Federals.

The tide soon turned as increasingly more Union troops pressed forward. Nathan Kimball, now commanding the Union forces on the field as a result of Shields having been wounded the previous day, finally recognized Jackson's flank attack and shuffled the majority of his men toward that sector.

The battle remained in doubt until Richard Garnett, who led the Stonewall Brigade, ordered his men to retreat due to a lack of ammunition and overwhelming numbers of opposing troops. Garnett's withdrawal uncovered another Confederate brigade's flank. The rout was on. Not even Jackson's presence on the battlefield could stem the tide, and soon his entire army withdrew.

Confederate casualties amounted to 718 compared with Union losses of 568. Jackson was upset over this defeat, but his effort at Kernstown unnerved Abraham Lincoln and others in Washington. They believed that

Jackson would not have attacked without substantial reinforcements. Fearing for the capital's safety, Lincoln altered McClellan's troop dispositions, demanding more men to defend Washington against the threat posed by Jackson. By fighting at Kernstown, Jackson had helped lower the odds against Johnston and Richmond during the upcoming battles on the Virginia Peninsula.

The battle of Kernstown marked the beginning of Jackson's famed Shenandoah Valley campaign. Over the next several months, his men marched hundreds of miles and won numerous battles. None of those battles, however, produced more favorable results than the one defeat at Kernstown.

—*Clay Williams*

See also Ashby, Turner; Garnett, Richard Brooke; Peninsula Campaign; Shenandoah Valley Campaign (1862); Shields, James.
For further reading:
Henderson, G. F. R. *Stonewall Jackson and the American Civil War* (1898).
Jackson, Mary Anna. *Memoirs of Stonewall Jackson by His Widow* (1895).
Kimball, Nathan. "Fighting Jackson at Kernstown." In *Battles and Leaders of the Civil War* (1887–1888).
Robertson, James I., Jr. *Stonewall Jackson, the Man, the Soldier, the Legend* (1997).
Vandiver, Frank. *Mighty Stonewall* (1957; reprint 1988).

KERNSTOWN, VIRGINIA, SECOND BATTLE OF (24 July 1864)

On 13 June 1864, Confederate lieutenant general Jubal Early marched the II Corps of the Army of Northern Virginia out of the Petersburg trenches and headed north for the Shenandoah Valley of Virginia. Ordered by Robert E. Lee to rid the valley of Federal forces, "Old Jubal" did an admirable job of doing just that. Between mid-June and late July, the Confederate Valley Army, as the II Corps had begun to be called, had repulsed Union general David Hunter in front of Lynchburg (18 June), forcing him to quit the valley altogether.

Not satisfied with that feat, Early proceeded to cross over the Potomac River into Maryland. General Lee encouraged this movement in the hope that Early's appearance on the banks of the Potomac might cause the Union forces in front of Richmond and Petersburg to be weakened. Early's movement did trigger reinforcements in the form of the Army of the Potomac's VI Corps being sent north to Washington, D.C. On 9 July, the Valley Army defeated a Federal force under Lewis Wallace at the battle of Monocacy outside Frederick, Maryland. An attack on the Union seat of government seemed certain.

The Second Battle of Kernstown, sketched by Alfred R. Waud (*Library of Congress*)

But Early never attempted such a thing. After exchanging fire with the defenders of Washington, he methodically retreated on 14 July back to the lower valley. By 22 July, the Valley Army was concentrated on the south side of Cedar Creek and in front of Strasburg, Virginia. Early rested his troops there for a few days and awaited an opportunity to strike the enemy. His chance soon came.

On 23 July, Early's cavalry reported that the Union VI and XIX Infantry Corps had given up their pursuit of the rebels and had returned to Washington. This left only William W. Averell's cavalry division and General George Crook's 8,000 infantry and cavalry in the lower Shenandoah Valley. With this information in hand, Early set his 12,000-man force in motion toward Winchester, Virginia.

On the 23d a cavalry fight erupted near Kernstown, less than two miles south of Winchester, between Early's mounted command and Crook's cavalry under General Alfred N. Duffié. The action ended in a draw, but it should have warned Crook of the storm that was about to break over him.

Next day, the 24th, Early formed his line of battle before noon in front of Kernstown: Gordon's infantry division on the left and Wharton's on the right of the Valley Pike. Stephen D. Ramseur's infantry was posi-

tioned on the left in order to fall on the enemy's right flank. Two brigades of gray cavalry were set on each end of the Confederate line to move to the rear of the Federals and cut off their retreat to Winchester. The Federal line facing Early ran along the north side of Hogg Run just to the front of Kernstown.

The Confederate assault was led by General John Breckinridge, who at Early's bidding flanked the Yankees on their left, which was in the air. Wharton's men carried out the attack, and soon the bluecoats were broken and crowding the Valley Pike in their effort to retreat to Winchester. Gordon's men soon joined the charge and drove any remaining enemy from the field. The Federals retreated so quickly that Ramseur's command hardly engaged them.

Early's infantry swept toward and through Winchester, compelling the enemy to abandon every position from which they attempted to make a stand. The retreat of the Union army became a race. The Confederates, mainly Robert E. Rodes's division, followed their foe to Stephenson's Station, about five miles north of Winchester. There the pursuit ended due to exhaustion on the Rebels' part. The gray army had marched 27 miles since that morning, and they could go no farther.

Although completely defeated, the Federals were

lucky that the Confederate cavalry could not be made to better coordinate their actions during and just after the battle. Some of the rebel units rode with the infantry and did not use their speed to properly pursue the defeated Federals. Other cavalry brigades went in the wrong direction after the enemy; one brigade got to the battle too late to help cut off the Union's line of retirement.

Early's victory at Second Kernstown sowed the seeds for his eventual defeat. The battle so alarmed the Lincoln administration that they urged General Ulysses S. Grant to reorganize the Union forces in the Shenandoah Valley. This led to the appointment of Philip Sheridan as commander of that military district in early August and the sending of substantial Union reinforcements. Under its new chief, the Union army in the valley would defeat Early's command time and again between September and October 1864, and would finally deprive the South of the Shenandoah's resources.

—*Arnold D. Blumberg*

See also Early, Jubal Anderson; Early's Washington Raid; Sheridan, Philip Henry.

For further reading:

Delauter, Roger U., Jr. *Winchester in the Civil War* (1992).

Early, Jubal A. *The Memoirs of General Jubal A. Early* (1994).

Osborne, Charles C. *Jubal: The Life and Times of General Jubal A. Early, CSA* (1992).

Pond, George E. *The Shenandoah Valley in 1864* (1883).

Taylor, James E. *The James E. Taylor Sketchbook: With Sheridan Up the Shenandoah Valley in 1864* (1989).

KERSHAW, JOSEPH BREVARD

(1822–1894)

Confederate general

Born in Camden, South Carolina, to John Kershaw and Harrietta Du Bose Kershaw, Joseph Kershaw was educated locally and studied law. After practicing for a brief time in Camden, Kershaw volunteered for the Palmetto Regiment during the Mexican-American War and saw action in northern Mexico as a first lieutenant, but had to resign in early 1847 because of ill health.

Returning to South Carolina and his law practice, Kershaw became active in South Carolina politics. From 1852 to 1856 he served in the South Carolina legislature and in December 1860 was selected a delegate to the South Carolina secession convention. As soon as the war began, however, he abandoned his political aspirations and accepted the colonelcy of the 2d South Carolina Infantry. He traveled with his regiment and led it into battle at First Bull Run as part of the brigade of Milledge Luke Bonham. The following February he was promoted to the rank of brigadier general.

His brigade, which became famous as Kershaw's brigade, was placed in the division of Lafayette McLaws for the upcoming Peninsula campaign. Kershaw led his brigade through the entire campaign, fighting from Yorktown through the Seven Days'. Kershaw's brigade fought bravely at Second Bull Run and South Mountain and was commended for its actions at Antietam. At Fredericksburg in December 1862, the brigade was positioned in the sunken road at the base of Marye's Heights.

Remaining with Lee when much of Longstreet's corps was detached to North Carolina in the spring of 1863, Kershaw's brigade fought at Chancellorsville. While Jackson swung around to Hooker's rear, Kershaw and his brigade remained east of Hooker and was part of the force that Lee sent back toward Fredericksburg to check Sedgwick's advance.

With the corps reunited after Chancellorsville, Kershaw's brigade moved into Pennsylvania at the end of June 1863. During the three-day battle of Gettysburg, the brigade saw its heaviest fighting on the second day, when it fought Sickles's corps in the Peach Orchard. Kershaw's brigade suffered more than 50 percent casualties that day.

In the late summer, Kershaw and his brigade went with most of Longstreet's corps to reinforce Braxton Bragg's army in north Georgia. Kershaw took temporary command of the division during the battle of Chickamauga and was given command of the division by Longstreet after the battle of Knoxville when Longstreet relieved McLaws of command.

In the spring of 1864, Kershaw returned to Virginia with Longstreet's corps and fought at the Wilderness and Spotsylvania before being promoted to major general on 18 May 1864. He commanded a division at Cold Harbor and in the opening months of the siege of Petersburg. In the fall of 1864 he led his division in Jubal Early's Shenandoah Valley campaign and the raid on Washington before returning to the Army of Northern Virginia and the trenches of Petersburg in the early months of 1865. In the retreat from Petersburg, Kershaw was captured at Saylor's Creek. He was not paroled until July 1865.

After the war Kershaw returned to South Carolina where he practiced law and became a judge. In his spare time, he wrote about his Civil War experiences including articles for the *Battles and Leaders of the Civil War* volumes. He died in Camden.

—*David S. Heidler and Jeanne T. Heidler*

See also *Battles and Leaders of the Civil War*; Fredericksburg, Second Battle of.

For further reading:

Dickert, D. Augustus. *History of Kershaw's Brigade, with Complete Roll of Companies, Biographical Sketches, Incidents, Anecdotes, Etc.* (1899; reprint, 1973).

Johnson, Robert Underwood, and Clarence Clough Buel, eds. *Battles and Leaders of the Civil War* (1887–1888).

KEYES, ERASMUS DARWIN
(1810–1895)
Union general

Born to Justus Keyes and Elizabeth Corey Keyes in Brimfield, Massachusetts, Erasmus Darwin Keyes moved with his family to Kennebec County, Maine, when he was a child. He was educated locally before receiving an appointment to the U.S. Military Academy. He graduated tenth of forty-five in the class of 1832. Upon commissioning, Keyes served briefly at Fort Monroe in Virginia before being transferred to Charleston harbor during the nullification crisis. For the next ten years, Keyes served at several frontier posts as well as two stints as aide-de-camp to Winfield Scott.

During the Mexican-American War, Keyes was acting as an instructor at West Point, making him one of the few West Point–trained generals in the Civil War not to fight in Mexico. During the 1850s, Keyes served primarily in the Pacific Northwest, seeing combat against Indians in Washington. He returned east in late 1859 and received the appointment in January 1860 as Winfield Scott's military secretary, a position he held at the rank of lieutenant colonel until April 1861.

Keyes vexed Scott, however, when he became involved in forming plans for the relief of Fort Pickens in Florida. At the end of April 1861, when Keyes was sent by the War Department to serve as military aide to Governor Edwin Denison Morgan of New York, he was replaced as Scott's military secretary by Schuyler Hamilton, another former Scott aide. In New York, Keyes's primary job was to help the civilian government raise and organize volunteers to be sent to Washington. This duty completed, in mid-May Keyes became the colonel of the 11th U.S. Infantry.

Keyes commanded the 1st Brigade, 1st Division, during the Bull Run campaign. His brigade, like so many during that battle, did not particularly distinguish itself. Keyes's personal conduct, however, was commended, and he was promoted in August to brigadier general of volunteers with a date of rank of 17 May. For the remainder of the year, Keyes commanded his brigade and then a division in northern Virginia as part of the Army of the Potomac.

In March 1862 with the organization of the Army of the Potomac into corps in preparation for the Peninsula campaign, Keyes was given command of IV Corps. He commanded this corps on the York Peninsula, fighting in all of the major battles of the campaign. He was promoted to major general of volunteers on 5 May 1862. His most notable achievement during the campaign was his guarding of the movement of the Army of the Potomac from Malvern Hill to Harrison's Landing at the end of the Seven Days'.

After that campaign, Keyes wrote directly to President Abraham Lincoln on 10 July 1862 recommending that the Army of the Potomac be brought back to Washington. He disagreed with his commander George B. McClellan that with reinforcements the army could resume the campaign against Richmond. Keyes believed that no less than 100,000 additional men would be necessary for such a move. Ironically when the Army of the Potomac was withdrawn a month later, Keyes and IV Corps were left behind to operate the Union defenses at Yorktown as part of the Department of Virginia commanded by Major General John Adams Dix.

Keyes remained in that command until the following summer. During that time he conducted raids out from Yorktown and Fort Monroe designed to relieve the Confederates of some of their supplies on the York Peninsula and to draw Confederate forces away from northern Virginia. In none of these raids, particularly those conducted in 1863, was Keyes's corps particularly effective in diverting Confederate forces. In July 1863 he entered into a controversy with Dix over what Dix viewed as Keyes's failure to exploit an advantage in what was supposed to be a diversionary raid toward the Chickahominy River to draw Confederate forces away from the Gettysburg campaign. This campaign resulted in a skirmish at Baltimore Cross Roads in the midst of a Federal withdrawal. Keyes requested a court of inquiry but was refused. On 15 July 1863 he was relieved of command and sent to New York City to serve on a retirement board. He remained in that position until he resigned his commission in May 1864.

After his resignation, Keyes moved to California, where he became involved in the gold mining industry and winemaking in the Napa Valley. He also wrote extensively about his wartime experiences. While on a vacation trip to France, he died in Nice on 14 October 1895. His body was returned to West Point for burial.

—*David S. Heidler and Jeanne T. Heidler*

See also Dix, John Adams; Harrison's Landing, Virginia; Peninsula Campaign.
For further reading:
Keyes, Erasmus D. *Fifty Years' Observations of Men and Events, Civil and Military* (1884).

KILPATRICK-DAHLGREN RAID
(February–March 1864)

The Kilpatrick-Dahlgren Raid to Richmond evolved out of the desires of Union leaders, including President Lincoln, for the dissemination behind Confederate lines of the Proclamation of Amnesty and Reconstruction and for the release of Union prisoners of war from camps at Richmond. Major General George G. Meade approved of the plan to use a cavalry force to accomplish these tasks after he learned that, except for

militia, Richmond was practically undefended. Brigadier General Judson Kilpatrick, with whom Lincoln held a conversation on 12 February on Kilpatrick's plan for such a raid, was selected to lead the expedition. Kilpatrick was given a picked force of about 3,500 cavalrymen composed of his own 3d Division, Cavalry Corps, Army of the Potomac, and several mixed detachments from other commands of the corps. Included was a force of 500 men placed under Colonel Ulric Dahlgren, son of Rear Admiral John Dahlgren, that was to act to secure the prisoner release while Kilpatrick covered them with the main body. Dahlgren's force was drawn from the 1st Vermont, 2d New York, 5th New York, and 5th Michigan Cavalry from Kilpatrick's division, and from the 1st Maine Cavalry from 2d Division.

The raid was not planned in isolation. Major General John Sedgwick was to lead the Union VI Corps to Madison Court House as a diversion. Using Madison Court House as a springboard, Brigadier General George A. Custer was then to lead 1,500 cavalry on another raid to destroy the key Lynchburg railroad bridge over the Rivanna River, near Charlottesville, to distract the Confederates. Although Custer destroyed much Confederate property, neither he nor Sedgwick appears to have done much materially to aid Kilpatrick.

Kilpatrick's command departed his encampment at Stevensburg, Virginia, on the evening of 28 February. By 11 P.M. they had captured the Confederate cavalry picket at Ely's Ford and crossed the Rappahannock River. Dahlgren's commanded split off from the main body the next day at Spotsylvania. While Kilpatrick rode along the Virginia Central Railroad tearing up track, Dahlgren rode south intending to cross the James River, penetrate Richmond's defenses from the rear, and release the Union prisoners at Belle Isle.

Kilpatrick reached the outskirts of Richmond on 1 March. While waiting for Dahlgren to complete his task and rejoin the main column, he skirmished before the city's defenses with the few battalions of the Local Defense Brigade he encountered. However, an unreliable—or perhaps untrustworthy—black guide delayed Dahlgren. When Dahlgren discovered he had been led to an unfordable point on the James River, he hanged the man on the spot. Meanwhile, Major General Wade Hampton, whose pickets the Union cavalry had captured while crossing the Rappahannock, had ascertained Kilpatrick's objective and had followed him. With Hampton's cavalry in pursuit, Kilpatrick was forced to withdraw without waiting longer for Dahlgren. On the evening of 1 March, Hampton discovered the camp of one of Kilpatrick's brigades near Atlee's Station. Hampton dismounted 100 men and, supported by cavalry and two artillery pieces, attacked at night in a snowstorm and drove the one brigade onto the remaining two of Kilpatrick's division, after which, Hampton asserted, Kilpatrick's whole force then mounted and fled. The following day, 2 March, Hampton pursued Kilpatrick down the peninsula to Old Church. Kilpatrick's force was defeated, but found refuge with elements of Major General Benjamin F. Butler's troops of the Department of Virginia and North Carolina at New Kent Court House.

Dahlgren and his men, having been unable to penetrate Richmond's defenses, tried to escape pursuit by riding through King William and King and Queen Counties towards Gloucester Point. In the process the command was beset by small parties of Confederate

The Kilpatrick-Dahlgren Raid, sketched by Alfred R. Waud (*Library of Congress*)

General Kilpatrick and staff at Stevensburg, Virginia, March 1864 (*Library of Congress*)

cavalry and dispersed. About 11:30 P.M. on 2 March, Dahlgren and a detachment of about 100 of his men were ambushed by a detachment of furloughed men from the 5th and 9th Virginia Cavalry Regiments and some Home Guards of King and Queen County near Mantapike Hill. Dahlgren was killed and most of his men captured. The remainder of his force, led by a Captain Mitchell of the New York Cavalry, successfully rejoined Kilpatrick's division at Tunstall's Station on the York River Railroad.

Papers found on Dahlgren's body indicated that he had ordered his men, if successful in liberating the Union prisoners, to burn Richmond with the latter's aid, and kill President Jefferson Davis and his cabinet. These were published on 5 March in the *Richmond Daily Examiner* and caused a political furor. Queried by Robert E. Lee, Generals Meade and Kilpatrick, and President Lincoln, all disavowed any knowledge of the Dahlgren papers. Survivors of Dahlgren's command testified that Dahlgren had neither published the papers to the men nor

addressed them on the subject before starting out on the raid. Duane P. Schultz in *The Dahlgren Affair* argues the case that the papers were forged. Regardless of their authenticity, the papers ignited a controversy with the upshot that President Davis ordered Canadian-based secret agents to launch a terror campaign in the North.

Kilpatrick's main body inflicted considerable damage upon the Virginia Central Railroad, especially by destroying the Beaver Dam depot and its stores, and many thousands of proclamations were "scattered throughout the entire country." Kilpatrick was also heartened by the fact that out of 3,585 men engaged, he suffered only 335 killed, wounded, and missing, and he lost none of his guns or caissons. However, even Kilpatrick reckoned "the expedition failed," as the most emotional of the aims, the liberation of the Union prisoners, had not been achieved. Another Union cavalry raid had ended in a Confederate victory.

—*Duane C. Young*

See also Kilpatrick, Hugh Judson; Richmond, Virginia
For further reading:
Longacre, Edward G. *Mounted Raids of the Civil War* (1975; reprint 1994).
Schultz, Duane P. *The Dahlgren Affair: Terror and Conspiracy in the Civil War* (1998).

KILPATRICK, HUGH JUDSON
(1836–1881)
Union general

Born in Deckertown, New Jersey, on 14 January 1836, Kilpatrick grew up on the family farm. Despite a rather limited preparatory education, he obtained an appointment to the United States Military Academy in 1856. At that time, the academy's course of study lasted five years. Kilpatrick graduated in the May class of 1861, in which he ranked seventeenth out of forty-five cadets. As with many ambitious young officers of the Civil War, Kilpatrick's rapid rise in rank came through his service in the volunteer state regiments. Kilpatrick began his army service as a captain in the famous Duryea's Zouaves, of the 5th New York Infantry. While engaged with this regiment at Bethel, Virginia, Kilpatrick became the first regular army officer wounded in battle. Kilpatrick next served as lieutenant colonel and later colonel of the 2d New York Cavalry and participated in the major campaigns and battles of the Eastern theater in 1862 and 1863. All the while, he steadily drew the attention of his superior officers. Kilpatrick received his appointment to brigadier general on 13 June 1863, after which he took command of the Army of the Potomac's 3d Cavalry Division. He led this command during the Gettysburg campaign.

As a general officer, Kilpatrick immediately established the traits by which his career in the cavalry would be characterized and that quickly earned him the derisive nickname of "Kill Cavalry." General Kilpatrick combined the ability to attract advantageous personal and political associations with unsinkable self-confidence, and an instinctive aggressiveness on the battlefield, to a degree rivaled in the Federal army only by George Armstrong Custer. General Kilpatrick's penchant for aggressiveness, however, often proved reckless and frequently bordered on destructiveness.

Two well-publicized incidents aptly illustrate these negative characteristics. Following the repulse of Pickett's Charge on the third day at Gettysburg, Kilpatrick ordered a charge by the brigade of Brigadier General Elon Farnsworth. The ill-fated attack resulted in Farnsworth's death and the unnecessary mauling of his command. Criticized for this action, Kilpatrick attempted to regain his reputation by making a bold raid against Richmond in the spring of 1864. The Kilpatrick–Dahlgren Raid, as this operation is now

Hugh Judson Kilpatrick (*Library of Congress*)

known, proved a disaster. Poorly managed and controversial—its objectives remain the focus of debate—this mission resulted in the death of Colonel Ulric Dahlgren. The raid also cast further doubts over Kilpatrick's leadership. These actions demonstrate that, despite his personal courage under fire, General Kilpatrick's ambitions often outweighed his judgment on the battlefield.

In spite of Kilpatrick's growing reputation as a "Hell of a damned fool," or perhaps because of it, Major General William T. Sherman personally selected Kilpatrick to command the 3d Cavalry Division of the Army of the Cumberland during the campaign against Atlanta. During this campaign Sherman used Kilpatrick's cavalry primarily to raid behind Confederate lines, especially against rail and supply stations and lines of communication south of Atlanta. General Sherman hoped that such operations would draw John Bell Hood's forces out of the besieged city of Atlanta. On 20 August 1864, Kilpatrick led a raid against the Macon & Western Railroad. This raid, however, failed to destroy that vital supply line. Brigadier General William H. "Red" Jackson's combined force of Confederate cavalry and infantry, under the direct field command of Brigadier General Daniel Harris Reynolds, defeated Kilpatrick's raiding force at Lovejoy's Station, Georgia, to preserve Confederate control of that important rail line. Kilpatrick sustained a serious wound later in the Atlanta campaign, at the battle of Dalton, but returned to Sherman's army in time to command the heavily reduced cavalry force during the March to the Sea and the march through the Carolinas.

Kilpatrick finished the war as a major general of both regulars and volunteers, but resigned his commission shortly after the war. Following the war, President Andrew Johnson appointed Kilpatrick to the post of United States minister to Chile. He served at this post until 1868, when he returned to the United States. Kilpatrick ran for Congress in 1880, but failed to gain election. Soon thereafter, President Chester A. Arthur appointed Kilpatrick to a second term as minister to Chile, where he soon married a Chilean woman. He also wrote a largely forgotten four-act melodrama, based on the Civil War, entitled *The Blue and the Gray, or War is Hell*. He died in Santiago, Chile, at his consular post. His remains are buried in the cemetery at West Point.

—*Robert Patrick Bender*

See also Atlanta Campaign; Kilpatrick, Hugh Judson; Lovejoy, Georgia, Battle of.

For further reading:
Hitchcock, Henry. *Marching With Sherman: Passages from the Letters and Campaign Diaries of Henry Hitchcock, Major and Assistant Adjutant General of Volunteers. November 1864–May 1865* (1927).
Kilpatrick, Judson. *The Blue and the Gray, or, War is Hell* (1930).
Marszalek, John F. *Sherman: A Soldier's Passion for Order* (1994).

KIMBALL, NATHAN
(1823–1898)
Union general

Born in Fredericksburg, Indiana, to Nathaniel Kimball and Nancy Furgeson Kimball, Nathan Kimball attended Asbury College (later to become DePauw University), after which he taught school and then studied medicine. At the outbreak of the Mexican-American War, Kimball raised a company of the 2d Indiana and became its captain. He fought at Buena Vista, where he led his company forward as the remainder of the regiment fled. After the war he returned to Indiana, where he practiced medicine in Loogootee until the outbreak of the Civil War.

Upon hearing of the firing on Fort Sumter, Kimball raised a regiment for Federal service. On 7 June 1861 he was commissioned the colonel of the 14th Indiana and took his men to Virginia. In the late summer and fall of 1861, Kimball and the 14th served in western Virginia. On 12 September 1861, Kimball's command was attacked at Cheat Mountain when Robert E. Lee attempted to regain that part of western Virginia from the Federals. Kimball was able to repulse the attack. Less than a month later, on 3 October, he fought off another Confederate attack at the Greenbrier River.

The following spring Kimball commanded a brigade in the Shenandoah Valley. On 22 March 1862, he assumed command of James Shields's division when that officer was wounded in the opening engagement at Kernstown. The next day, in command of the division, Kimball repulsed Stonewall Jackson's attack.

On 15 April 1862, Kimball was promoted to brigadier general of volunteers. He continued through the spring and early summer to command his brigade in the Shenandoah Valley. In early July he was transferred to the York Peninsula, where he commanded his brigade as part of Edwin Sumner's II Corps. On 3–4 July he fought in a skirmish at Herring Creek. In August 1862 he and his brigade transferred back to Washington, though Kimball did not arrive soon enough to participate in the Second Bull Run campaign. He did, however, lead his brigade at Antietam as part of Edwin Sumner's II Corps. He fought bravely in support of Joseph Hooker's corps on the Union right. On 1 October 1862, he and his brigade were sent on a reconnaissance of the area between Harper's Ferry and Leesburg.

During the Fredericksburg campaign, Kimball's brigade was a part of Darius Couch's II Corps, Edwin Sumner's Grand Division. Kimball led his men forward in the attack on Marye's Heights on 13 December. He suffered a severe thigh wound and had to be carried from the field. Several months of recuperation removed him from active duty.

Upon his recovery, Kimball was sent west to command a brigade under Ulysses S. Grant in the Vicksburg campaign. In the spring he commanded the District of Jackson and between 26 May and 4 June 1863 commanded a division in the expedition from Haynes's Bluff to Mechanicsburg, Mississippi. After returning, he commanded his division in the remaining weeks of the siege of Vicksburg.

After the fall of Vicksburg, Kimball commanded his division under Major General Benjamin Prentiss in the District of Eastern Arkansas. In the fall of 1863, he commanded a division under Major General Frederick Steele in the Army of Arkansas in the efforts to reclaim that state for the Union. At the end of the year, Kimball was sent to Washington to report directly to Abraham Lincoln regarding the situation in Arkansas. He returned to the state in early 1864. In February he supervised the administering of loyalty oaths in the state, and the following month he assumed temporary command of the Army of Arkansas in Steele's absence. By 22 April, however, his frustrations boiled over in a letter to Steele. Asking to be relieved, he complained that dishonest and disloyal citizens pretending fealty to the Federal government were in fact undermining his position. He was transferred to the Army of the Cumberland, where he commanded a brigade in the first months of the Atlanta campaign as part of IV Corps.

Kimball was commended for his actions at Peachtree Creek and in early August was given command of 1st

Division of IV Corps. He commanded that division for the remainder of the campaign.

After the fall of Atlanta, Kimball returned to Indiana briefly to use his influence to help suppress antiwar groups such as the Knights of the Golden Circle. By November, however, he was back with the Army of the Cumberland and fought at the battle of Franklin. George H. Thomas, the commanding general of the Army of the Cumberland, commended him for gallantry and recommended his promotion to major general of volunteers. Kimball also commanded a division at Nashville at the end of the year. For his services in these campaigns, he received a brevet promotion to major general in February 1865.

For the remainder of the war, Kimball served in garrison duty in Tennessee. He left the army in August 1865 and returned to Indiana. He became active in Indiana Republican politics and commanded the state's Grand Army of the Republic. In 1873 he received an appointment as surveyor general of Utah and moved to that territory. He remained there until the end of his life, occupying various federal appointments, including postmaster. In his later years he wrote about his Civil War experiences. He died in Ogden, Utah, on 21 January 1898.

—*David S. Heidler and Jeanne T. Heidler*

See also Arkansas; Cheat Mountain, Virginia; Franklin, Battle of.

For further reading:
Pool, J. T. *Under Canvass, or, Recollections of the Fall and Summer Campaign of the 14th Regiment Indiana Volunteers, Colonel Nathan Kimball, in Western Virginia, in 1861* (1862).

KING, JOHN HASKELL
(1820–1888)
Union general

Born in Sackett's Harbor, New York, John Haskell King moved to Michigan with his parents when he was a small child. In 1837 he received a commission as a second lieutenant in the U.S. Army. He fought in the Second Seminole War and served at several frontier posts before the outbreak of the Mexican-American War. In that conflict, he fought in Winfield Scott's Mexico City campaign, though he served most of his time in the war at the port city of Vera Cruz.

At the outbreak of the Civil War, King was a major of the 15th Infantry serving in San Antonio, Texas. When U.S. forces in Texas were surrendered to Confederate sympathizers in February 1861, King refused to submit and instead marched his men to the coast, loaded them on a ship, and brought them to New York City.

Assigned to the Western theater, Major King commanded a battalion of regulars at Shiloh and was commended for his actions there. He continued to command his battalion in the Corinth campaign of June 1862. Later in the year he was seriously wounded at the battle of Stone's River and was commended for gallantry there.

In April 1863 King was promoted to brigadier general of volunteers with a date of rank at 29 November 1862. He commanded a brigade in the Tullahoma campaign in June 1863. At Chickamauga in September 1863, King served under George H. Thomas. King's regulars on the second day of the battle were partly responsible for Thomas's heroic stand on Horseshoe Ridge. King was again commended for bravery and later in the war received a brevet promotion for his actions at Chickamauga.

Commanding a brigade in the Army of the Cumberland, King fought in the Chattanooga campaign. In early 1864, he and his brigade participated in the demonstration against Dalton, Georgia. During the Atlanta campaign, King commanded his brigade during all the early engagements, including Resaca and Kennesaw Mountain, and, as the army closed in on Atlanta, at Peachtree Creek. On 26 July he was given temporary command of a division. He continued in that command through most of the siege of Atlanta.

On 1 September 1864, King received command of a brigade in Major General James Steedman's District of Etowah. In this position, he operated primarily in southern Tennessee for the remainder of 1864 into early 1865. In March 1865 he received a brevet promotion to major general.

After the war, King remained in the army, having been promoted to colonel of the 9th Infantry in the regular army in the summer of 1865. He commanded his regiment at several frontier assignments. He retired as a colonel in 1882. After leaving the army, King lived in Washington, D.C. He died in that city on 7 April 1888 and was buried at Arlington.

—*David S. Heidler and Jeanne T. Heidler*

See also Atlanta Campaign; Chickamauga.

For further reading:
Castel, Albert. *Decision in the West: The Atlanta Campaign of 1864* (1992).
Cozzens, Peter. *This Terrible Sound: The Battle of Chickamauga* (1992).

KING, RUFUS
(1814–1876)
Union general

Born in New York City in 1814, Rufus King was the grandson and namesake of the Rufus King who had been a Massachusetts delegate to the Continental Congress and had drafted the resolution prohibiting slavery and involuntary servitude in the Northwest Ordinance of 1787. He had also been a delegate to the

Constitutional Convention and a prominent Federalist appointed by President George Washington as minister to Great Britain. The younger Rufus King attended New York's Columbia College, of which his father was president. Graduating at West Point in 1833, King resigned from the Army Corps of Engineers in 1836 and thereafter edited various newspapers in the state of New York, including an Albany daily at which he was associated with Thurlow Weed. King was appointed New York's adjutant general by Governor William H. Seward, but moved to the Wisconsin Territory in 1845 and settled in Milwaukee.

In Milwaukee King was editor and, for a time, part owner of the *Milwaukee Sentinel and Gazette*. He was also active with respect to the statehood of Wisconsin and was a delegate to the 1848 Constitutional Convention in Wisconsin that resulted in the admission of Wisconsin to the Union. His other Wisconsin interests included public education, and he had been Milwaukee's superintendent of schools and a regent of the State University of Wisconsin at Madison. In 1861 President Lincoln appointed King as minister to the Papal States. He obtained a leave of absence from this appointment when Sumter was fired on and in 1861 was commissioned as a brigadier general of volunteers assigned to the command of Wisconsin regiments in the Washington area. He was the first commander of an infantry brigade composed of the 19th Indiana and three regiments from Wisconsin, the 2d, 6th, and 7th. This brigade later was known as the Iron Brigade and achieved fame under the leadership of Brigadier General John Gibbon and Brigadier General Solomon Meredith.

King was a victim of, and occasionally disabled by, epilepsy. He was ill at the time of Brawner Farm and the Second Bull Run campaign. In the former battle, he failed to send reinforcements from the division to the embattled Iron Brigade. His performance at this time was deemed unsatisfactory and the McDowell Court of Inquiry informally censured him. In spite of this, he was promoted to division command and was offered and rejected command of I Corps. Having sat on the Fitz John Porter court-martial, he was relieved shortly after his appointment to division command because of ill health.

King resigned from the army in 1863 for health reasons and undertook the Papal State's appointment. Congress later failed to appropriate funds for a U.S. representative at the Papal Court, and King resigned the ministership in 1868. Returning to the United States, he was appointed deputy collector of customs for the port of New York City, a position he resigned in 1869 for health reasons. He died in New York City in 1876.

—*Alan T. Nolan*

See also Bull Run, Second Battle of; Iron Brigade.
For further reading:
Nolan, Alan T. *The Iron Brigade: A Military History* (1961; reprint, 1994).

KIRKWOOD, SAMUEL JORDAN
(1813–1894)
Governor of Iowa

Samuel Kirkwood was born in Maryland on 20 December 1813 and spent much of his youth in Washington, D.C. Migrating west, he read law as a young man in Mansfield, Ohio. In 1843, he was admitted to the bar. The young Kirkwood was a staunch Democrat, and his political activism won him selection as the prosecuting attorney for Richland County, Ohio. In 1850 he served in a constitutional convention elected to revise Ohio's founding document.

Kirkwood remained a loyal Democrat until 1854, when he broke with the party over Senator Stephen Douglas's Kansas-Nebraska bill, which repealed long-standing sectional compromises and reopened the issue of slavery in the territories. In 1855, business prospects prompted Kirkwood to join family members near Iowa City, Iowa. He began to work as a miller and farmer, becoming quite prosperous.

Kirkwood was selected as a delegate to a convention that organized the Iowa Republican Party in 1856. In 1857, he was chosen as a member of the Republican State Central Committee, and his work in this position brought him to the attention of James Grimes, the founder of Iowa Republicanism.

An advocate of the state's expanding market economy, Kirkwood served as a director of the state bank in 1858. However, while serving as a delegate to an 1859 Iowa state railroad convention, he urged caution and economy with regard to state aid for internal improvements.

In October 1859, Kirkwood was elected governor, defeating the popular Democrat Augustus C. Dodge. Kirkwood soon garnered national attention when Virginia officials attempted to extradite Barclay Coppoc. Coppoc, a member of John Brown's 1859 abolitionist raiding party, had escaped from Virginia and returned to his home in Iowa. Kirkwood resorted to legal technicalities to forestall extradition, while the fugitive was warned that he was in danger. By the time Virginia could produce extradition papers that Kirkwood deemed valid, Coppoc had fled to safety. Democrats in the legislature demanded an investigation into the affair, but the governor remained unapologetic about his actions.

At the 1860 national Republican convention, Kirkwood and other leading Iowa Republicans helped to secure the nomination of Abraham Lincoln for president. In the early months of the Civil War, Kirkwood found volunteers in abundance but weaponry scarce, and was largely preoccupied with the logistical difficulties posed by outfitting the troops. Iowa Democrats split into War Democrat and Peace

Democrat factions in 1861, ensuring Kirkwood's reelection that fall.

During his second term, Kirkwood remained bedeviled by the task of supplying new Iowa regiments, finding that rifles were in short supply. In private communication with President Lincoln, Kirkwood urged the removal of General George McClellan. The Iowan, who had a low opinion of the Army of the Potomac, believed that the key to Union victory would be in the Mississippi Valley. By 1862, he outspokenly supported the use of black troops by the Union.

Border defense was a central concern for the Iowa governor. He feared that Missouri "border ruffians" and "bushwhackers" would encroach into Iowa's southern counties, although Missouri posed a relatively insignificant threat to the security of his state. The governor also worried that diminished federal protection could increase the potential for Indian raids in northwest Iowa. In 1862, Kirkwood responded to Sioux raids in southern Minnesota by building blockhouses and organizing the Northern Iowa Border Brigade.

During 1862 and 1863, Kirkwood worried that emancipation and conscription might provoke unrest in his state. Kirkwood approved of the military arrests of Copperheads such as Dubuque newspaper editor Dennis Mahoney. He also urged active investigation of Copperhead secret societies such as the Knights of the Golden Circle. In reality, dissent in Civil War Iowa was quite limited. Democrats fought among themselves, and the state had adequate numbers of volunteers to ensure that Kirkwood never had to enforce conscription. After leaving the governor's office in 1864, Kirkwood returned to a quiet life in Iowa City. The legislature selected him for a one-year stint as U.S. senator in 1866. In 1876, he was inaugurated for a third and less eventful term as Iowa governor. In 1877, he was elected to a full term in the Senate and focused his attention on veterans pensions, post offices, and foreign relations. In 1881, he resigned from the Senate to serve briefly as secretary of the interior. Returning to Iowa, he remained an influential figure in Republican politics, actively opposing his party's majority faction on the divisive issue of prohibition. He died on 1 September 1894.

—*Wallace Hettle*

See also Republican Party.
For further reading:
Clark, Daniel Elbert. *Samuel Jordan Kirkwood* (1917).
Dykstra, Robert. *Bright Radical Star: Black Freedom and White Supremacy on the Hawkeye Frontier* (1993).
Hake, Herbert V. "The Political Firecracker: Samuel J. Kirkwood." *Palimpsest* (1975).
Lathrop, Henry W. *The Life and Times of Samuel J. Kirkwood, Iowa's War Governor* (1893).
Wubben, Hubert H. "The Maintenance of Internal Security in Iowa, 1861–1865." *Civil War History* (1964).

KNIGHTS OF THE GOLDEN CIRCLE
(1854–1864)

The Knights of the Golden Circle was first established by Cincinnati physician George W. L. Bickley in 1854. Bickley founded the Knights as a filibustering organization dedicated to expanding the slaveholding society of the U.S. South into Mexico. The term "Golden Circle" referred to plans to restore the balance of power between free and slave states by establishing a ring of colonies around the Caribbean that would mature into new slave states.

Bickley planned a series of filibustering expeditions in 1859, but these never came to fruition. There is little evidence that the Knights attracted widespread interest. Bickley relocated to Tennessee in 1860 and involved himself in that state's secessionist movement. He transformed the Knights into a secret society dedicated to establishing Confederate rule in Kentucky. He may have succeeded in establishing temples of the Knights in a few counties, but, as in 1859, his claims far outstripped his real successes.

Northern Republicans, however, saw in the Knights a sinister, subversive menace of national scope. Sensational exposés and widespread rumors portrayed the Knights as an organization numbering more than 100,000 members and dedicated to overthrowing the Union. A series of investigations launched in Indiana and Illinois in 1862 found no evidence that the Knights existed in those states. Nevertheless, Republican politicians seeking to taint the Democratic Party with evidence of treason kept the rumors percolating. The specter of the Knights was further reinforced in the spring of 1863. In southern Indiana and Illinois, dozens of local mutual protection societies sprang up under names such as the Circle of Honor and the Mighty Host. In a series of incidents, members of these societies resisted draft enrollment officers and military detachments in search of deserters. Republicans charged that these acts of resistance were the work of disloyal Copperheads enrolled in the Knights of the Golden Circle. Republicans began to use the terms Democrats, Copperheads, and KGCs interchangeably.

There is no evidence that these mutual protection associations had any ties to Bickley or any larger, pro-Confederate organization. However, in the winter of 1864, the Order of Sons of Liberty did establish ties to some of these local groups. William A. Bowles, a major general in the Sons of Liberty, sent recruiter John W. Stone to foster ties with the associations of southern Indiana. In an odd example of life imitating art, Stone attempted to revitalize these associations by telling recruits that he was swearing them into the Knights of the Golden Circle. Thus, a handful of rural Democrats in southern Indiana would later swear that they were members of the Knights of the Golden Circle, an organ-

ization that probably never existed in that state. The final chapter in the legend of the Knights of the Golden Circle came in 1865, when prominent Republicans and Union military authorities charged that the organization was behind the assassination of President Lincoln.

—*Robert H. Churchill*

See also Bickley, George; Copperheads; Sons of Liberty.

For further reading:
Churchill, Robert H. "Liberty, Conscription, and Delusions of Grandeur: The Sons of Liberty Conspiracy of 1863–64." *Prologue Quarterly* (1998).

Klement, Frank L. *Dark Lanterns: Secret Political Societies, Conspiracies, and Treason Trials in the Civil War* (1984).

Tredway, G. R. *Democratic Opposition to the Lincoln Administration during the Civil War* (1973).

KNIPE, JOSEPH FARMER
(1823–1901)
Union general

Born in Mount Joy, Pennsylvania, Joseph Farmer Knipe was educated locally before becoming a U.S. Army private in 1842. He remained in the army for six years, including fighting in the Mexican-American War. After leaving the army, he returned to Pennsylvania, where he worked for the Pennsylvania Railroad and became active in the Pennsylvania militia. At the outbreak of the Civil War, he helped raise and became the colonel of the 46th Pennsylvania Infantry.

Knipe and his regiment's first major actions came in the spring of 1862 when they served under Nathaniel P. Banks in the Shenandoah Valley. Knipe also fought under Banks at Cedar Mountain on 9 August 1862, where Knipe was seriously wounded. He was unable to return to duty until the Maryland campaign in September 1862, at which time Knipe commanded a brigade in Joseph Mansfield's corps at Antietam.

It was soon apparent that he had returned to duty too soon for his health. Knipe had to take a medical leave until the following spring. On 28 March he was given command of 1st Brigade, 1st Division, XII Corps, Army of the Potomac, and commanded his brigade at Chancellorsville. Shortly thereafter, because of his ties to the Pennsylvania militia, Knipe was transferred to the Army of the Susquehanna, consisting primarily of militia units serving as home guard in Pennsylvania. In April he had been promoted to brigadier general of volunteers with a date of rank back to 29 November 1862. Knipe served in that capacity during the Gettysburg campaign and as a result saw no serious actions during that pivotal battle.

After the battle of Gettysburg, Knipe returned briefly to the Army of the Potomac to command a brigade of XII Corps, but in the early fall of 1863 he was transferred to Tennessee. Commanding a brigade in XX Corps of the Army of the Cumberland, throughout the fall of 1863

Knipe guarded the railroad outside his headquarters at Decherd, Tennessee.

In the spring of 1864, Knipe participated in the preparations for the Atlanta campaign. He commanded his brigade through all the early battles of that campaign and was wounded at the battle of Resaca in May 1863. He returned to duty in time for the battles around Atlanta and at the end of July assumed command of the 1st Division, XX Corps. He commanded that division until the fall of Atlanta in September 1864.

On 22 September 1864, Knipe was sent to Memphis by William T. Sherman to serve as chief of cavalry, Army of the Tennessee. Knipe's biggest problem in trying to organize his force was finding enough horses to mount a cavalry. After accomplishing this task, he took command in November of the 7th Division, Cavalry Corps, Military Division of the Mississippi. In late 1864 he ranged into north Alabama to disrupt communications and supplies to John Bell Hood's army in Tennessee. After the battle of Nashville, Knipe and his division pursued what was left of Hood's army and captured several thousand Confederates.

In early 1865 Knipe and his division went to Vicksburg and then in March fought in the Mobile campaign. On 16 April 1865, Knipe was relieved of command at Blakely, Alabama, because he had complained that his command had been reduced from a division to a brigade. The following day the order was changed to have him being relieved at his own request, and he was sent to E. R. S. Canby at New Orleans. Canby dispatched him to Baton Rouge to raise a cavalry brigade. In May, with the need for such a brigade obviously diminished by the close of hostilities, Knipe was again relieved of command and sent to George H. Thomas in Nashville. Knipe mustered out of the army in August 1865 and returned to Pennsylvania.

After the war, Knipe served for a time as postmaster of Harrisburg, Pennsylvania, before receiving appointment as the superintendent of the Fort Leavenworth federal penitentiary. He retired to Pennsylvania and died on 18 August 1901 in Harrisburg.

—*David S. Heidler and Jeanne T. Heidler*

See also Army of the Cumberland; Atlanta Campaign; Nashville, Battle of.

For further reading:
Van Horne, Thomas B. *History of the Army of the Cumberland: Its Organization, Campaigns, and Battles, Written at the Request of Major-General George H. Thomas Chiefly from His Private Military Journal and Official and Other Documents Furnished by Him* (1875).

KNOXVILLE CAMPAIGN
(November–December 1863)

During the fall of 1863, Knoxville, located along the Tennessee River in the heart of east Tennessee, was the object of an unsuccessful siege.

The bridge at Strawberry Plains near Knoxville, on Longstreet's line of retreat
(Photograph by George N. Barnard / *Library of Congress*)

Today, most historians view the campaign as a minor affair, but at the time, both the Union and Confederate leaders placed great significance on the actions in east Tennessee. East Tennessee was critical to both sides for its economic resources of grain and livestock, its political significance as a hot bed of Unionist support in the Confederacy, and its strategic value as a rail link between Virginia and Chattanooga. The campaign not only affected east Tennessee, but it had an impact on the ensuing battles for Chattanooga. It also reunited the opposing commanders of the battle of Fredericksburg.

During the investment of Chattanooga, General Braxton Bragg had requested that Confederate president Jefferson Davis order General James Longstreet to assault the Union forces in Knoxville. The Union Army of the Ohio had moved into east Tennessee in September, and Bragg feared that it might reinforce the Federal troops outside Chattanooga. Bragg also viewed the Knoxville

Strawberry Plains following Longstreet's withdrawal (Photograph by George N. Barnard / *Library of Congress*)

campaign as a means of ridding himself of Longstreet, with whom he constantly quarreled.

On 4 November, Longstreet left Chattanooga with two divisions, two battalions of artillery, and 5,000 cavalry troops for a total force of 17,000. Longstreet's journey northward was difficult and slow. Nine days after he departed, his forces had moved only sixty miles to Sweetwater, half the distance he had hoped to cover. Longstreet also expected General Bragg to provide provisions and supplies for his forces. Bragg's failure to do so

only intensified the feud and mistrust between the two generals. Although they were ragged and ill fed, Longstreet's troops continued the slow trek north.

As the Confederate troops approached the Tennessee River, Longstreet dispatched three brigades of cavalry under General Joseph Wheeler to scout the approaches to Knoxville that lay south of the Holston River. Longstreet anticipated that Wheeler's cavalry could seize the hills south of Knoxville. At the very least, the feint would divert attention away from the main body of his forces. On 14 November, Longstreet's infantry and artillery crossed the Tennessee River at Loudon. General Ambrose E. Burnside rushed from Knoxville to organize the withdrawal of the Federal IX and XXIII Corps to Knoxville. Burnside's strategy was to retire to Knoxville while maintaining contact with Longstreet's army, but not engaging it. Thus, Burnside hoped to draw Longstreet farther from his base of supplies and the unfolding operations around Chattanooga.

On 17 November, both the Union and Confederate forces moved along a parallel course toward Knoxville, separated by little over a mile. Longstreet's objective was Campbell's Station, which lay fifteen miles southwest of Knoxville. If his army could reach the crossroads there before Burnside could, he could destroy the Union forces before they could reach Knoxville. Burnside foiled Longstreet's plan as elements of his IX Corps arrived at Campbell's Station just minutes before the Confederates. During the brief engagement that followed, the Union troops temporarily stopped the advancing Confederates before retiring to the defenses of Knoxville that night. The next day, Burnside dispatched General William Sanders and 700 cavalry troopers to delay Longstreet's advance into the city. Sanders was mortally wounded, but he was able to buy time for Burnside's chief engineer, Captain Orlando Poe, to strengthen further the defenses around Knoxville.

After arriving at Knoxville, Longstreet lay siege to the town. However, uncertainty and indecision marked Confederate operations. Longstreet had hoped to take the town by force, but waited for reinforcements from Bragg before launching his attack. Confederate forces encircled the town along its north edge, although the Federal forces still controlled the hills south of the Holston River. As a result, Longstreet was able to bring pressure to bear on the Union troops, but could not completely cut them off from their supplies. Most importantly, Longstreet's wait for reinforcements and his indecision about where, how, and when to attack gave the Union soldiers time to buttress the defenses of the city, particularly Fort Sanders.

After the arrival of two brigades of reinforcements, Longstreet ordered the attack on Fort Sanders. On the morning of 29 November, the Confederate troops attacked Fort Sanders as they rushed, bayonets fixed and giving the rebel yell, across a field of stumps strewn with telegraph wire. When the troops reached the edge of the fort, they discovered that the ditch surrounding the fort was deeper and wider than expected. The earthworks around the fort were also covered in mud and made slick by ice. Many of the soldiers found themselves trapped in the ditch, although a few managed to climb the parapet, only to be taken prisoner or killed. The assault on Fort Sanders lasted only twenty minutes and cost the Confederates more than 800 casualties, with the Union suffering only minor losses.

After the failed assault, Longstreet decided not to attempt another. As he pondered his next move, he received word of Bragg's defeat at Chattanooga. Longstreet also received instructions ordering him to support Bragg. Unwilling to rejoin Bragg, Longstreet also felt such a move would be impracticable. He informed Bragg that he would retire north to Virginia, but would maintain the siege of Knoxville as long as he could to draw off Federal forces to reinforce Burnside. Longstreet's plan worked, as General Ulysses S. Grant sent General William T. Sherman with approximately 25,000 men to Knoxville to break the siege. Longstreet remained in Knoxville until the night of 4 December, as his beleaguered Confederates, many without shoes, marched away in the rain.

General Sherman arrived on 6 December to reinforce Burnside. The next day, a force of 8,000 infantry and 4,000 cavalry headed by Burnside's chief of staff, General John G. Parke left Knoxville in pursuit of Longstreet, who had marched sixty-five miles northeast of Knoxville to Rogersville. After receiving reinforcements from Virginia, Longstreet waited until Sherman returned to Georgia before reversing direction. On 14 December, Longstreet attacked elements of Parke's dispersed force at Bean's Station. After this battle, both Union and Confederate forces retired to their winter quarters, ending the Knoxville campaign.

During the campaign, the Confederates lost 1,296 killed, wounded, and missing, and the Federals lost 681. The campaign was a source of frustration and disappointment for Longstreet, while it allowed Burnside to demonstrate tactical skill and restore his reputation. Most importantly, the operations around Knoxville deprived the Confederacy of much needed reinforcements during the battles for Chattanooga.

—*William Hartley*

See also Bean's Station, Engagement at; Campbell's Station, Battle of; Chattanooga Campaign; Fort Sanders, Battle of.

For further reading:

Fink, Harold S. "The East Tennessee Campaign and the Battle of Knoxville in 1863." *East Tennessee Historical Society's Publications* (1957).

Marvel, William. *Burnside* (1991).

Seymour, Digby Gordon. *Divided Loyalties: Fort Sanders and the Civil War in East Tennessee* (1982).

Wert, Jeffry D. *General James Longstreet: The Confederacy's Most Controversial Soldier—A Biography* (1993).

KRYZANOWSKI, WLADIMIR
(1824–1887)
Union general

Wladzimierz Bonawentura Kryzanowski was born on 8 July 1824 in the Prussian-controlled Polish city of Roznowo. His father, Stanislaw, had been an officer in Prince Jozef Poniatowski's Polish

Corps in Napoleon Bonaparte's Grand Army, and his first cousin was the composer and pianist Frederic Chopin. After Kryzanowski's father died penniless and the family estates were sold for debts, Kryzanowski's uncles took part in the unsuccessful Polish Revolution of 1830. It was in this environment that the young Kryzanowski grew up and that his future character was formed.

After the unsuccessful Polish Revolution of 1848, Kryzanowski (or Kriz, as he was known to his American friends) fled Europe and settled in New York State. In the United States, he worked as a civil engineer and was an early member of the Republican Party, and in 1854 he married the daughter of an industrialist. In October 1861, Kryzanowski recruited and was commissioned colonel of the 58th New York Infantry Regiment (Polish Legion).

After performing guard duty in Washington, D.C., the 58th New York fought under Major General John C. Frémont in the Shenandoah Valley at the battle of Cross Keys on 8 June 1862. The regiment then became part of the 2d Brigade, 3d Division, XI Corps of the Army of the Potomac. During the Second Bull Run campaign, Kryzanowski commanded the 2d Brigade of Major General Carl Schurz's 3d Division. At the battle of Second Bull Run on 30 August 1862, Schurz claimed that the 2d Brigade contested every inch of ground against the heavy pressure of a greatly superior force, while Kryzanowski had a horse shot from under him and was severely wounded. On 29 November 1862, as a reward for his battlefield accomplishments, Kryzanowski was appointed brigadier general of volunteers by President Abraham Lincoln, but the U.S. Senate failed to act on the appointment and it expired on 4 March

1863. Schurz later claimed that the reason that the Senate did not vote on Kryzanowski's appointment was that none of the senators could pronounce his name.

The 2d Brigade was again heavily engaged at the battle of Chancellorsville in May 1863 and was badly mauled at the battle of Gettysburg in July 1863. In the fall of 1863, the 2d Brigade was transferred to the XII Corps and took part in the Chattanooga campaign. In February 1864, after the Chattanooga campaign and a month of reenlistment leave, the 2d Brigade was detached for guard duty in Tennessee along the Nashville & Chattanooga Railroad. Kryzanowski and the 2d Brigade served in this capacity for the remainder of the war.

Discharged on 1 October 1865 with the brevet rank of brigadier general of volunteers, Kryzanowski then worked as an official in the Treasury Department in Washington, D.C., and Alaska. In 1880, he was appointed a customs inspector in Colombia, but the unhealthy climate led to his wife's death and his resignation. Returning to New York City, Kryzanowski was appointed the director of the customs office for New York harbor, a post that he held until his death. He died on 31 January 1887 in New York City from a lung infection that he had contracted during his stay in Colombia.

—*Alexander M. Bielakowski*

See also Immigrants; Schurz, Carl.
For further reading:
Grot, Zdzislaw. *General Wladzimierz Kryzanowski* (1970).
Grzelonski, Bogdan. Poles in the United States of America, 1776–1865 (1976).

LABOR

The question of labor and its changing relationship to capital bears directly upon both the cause and result of the Civil War. From the 1820s to 1860, the Industrial Revolution increased the numbers of skilled and semiskilled adult white workingmen from around 200,000 to nearly 1.5 million. A large proportion of these—as many as 30,000 to 35,000 by the mid-1830s and more than 120,000 in the early 1850s—organized themselves.

Antebellum labor organizations remained very unstable. Insofar as society remained primarily agricultural, demand for nonagricultural work rose and fell seasonally, leaving the hundreds of members of local unions in the late summer to handfuls to rebuild from scratch the following spring. Such numbers also sustained political associations that might be mobilizing hundreds during election campaigns. Periodic hard times also exacerbated the tendency of members to scatter and punctuated the modest power of the labor movement.

Insofar as workers in different trades faced common problems, they sought to construct common organizations. Starting in the late eighteenth century, they began building city-wide associations, securely establishing such city centrals in a number of cities. In the 1830s, locals within the crafts began forming national craft unions and the city federations launched a National Trades Union, all of which collapsed with the Panic of 1837. The revived labor movement in the decade before the war organized dozens of trades at the local levels, rebuilding city-wide and national associations. At least nine national unions emerged, including an ambitious attempt to unite the building trades; only those of the printers, stone cutters, and hat finishers survived the Panic of 1857 as national unions. New national unions formed among various trades—cotton mule spinners (1858); machinists and blacksmiths, iron molders, painters, and cordwainers (1859); and coal miners (1861)—but many local unions functioned without such national affiliation and a loose regional association led a 1860 work stoppage by 17,000 New England shoemakers, the largest strike of antebellum history. Perhaps 40,000 organized unionist and 100,000 workers with trade unionist experience faced the crisis of 1861.

Labor's role in the war period, often discussed in terms of Democratic efforts to mobilize white working-class fears of emancipation and black competition, was far more complex. Labor politics had been endemic from the local Workingmen's parties of the 1820s through the worker-based National Reform Association of George Henry Evans, which agitated for the Homestead Bill. These represented a significant force in shaping workers' affinity for the new Republican Party and its "free labor" ideology.

If they were unenthusiastic about war, workers clearly had far less enthusiasm for disunion. Entire locals entered the Federal service, and organized labor provided numbers equivalent to a small army. Unions generally discouraged group enlistments, which employers fostered for obvious reasons, but general labor organizations constituted the core of several companies. Members in specific units helped elect their own to serve as officers, and a disproportionate number attained high rank if they survived; 1860 shoe strike leader A. G. Draper became a brigadier general. Of perhaps a thousand members of the printer's union, three won the Medal of Honor, including John M. Tobin and Amos J. Cummings, as well as the union's president John M. Farquhar.

Notwithstanding the devastation of enlistments, the modern labor movement actually grew as the costs of living on the home front outstripped wages. By 1863 and 1864, employers began pressing innovative legislation to successfully mobilize the power of the courts, the army, and the government against labor. Workers waged large and often desperate strikes, sometimes coordinated by city-wide trade assemblies. These in turn established the ambitiously named International Industrial Assembly, which soon became the National Labor Union, the direct forerunner of the American Federation of Labor.

—*Mark A. Lause*

See also Evans, George Henry; Homestead Bill; Republican Party.

For further reading:

Bernstein, Iver. *The New York City Draft Riots, Their Significance for American Society and Politics in the Age of the Civil War* (1990).

Foner, Philip S. *History of the Labor Movement in the United States: From Colonial Times to the Founding of the American Federation of Labor* (1972).

Grossman, Jonathon P. *William H. Sylvis, Pioneer of American*

Labor: a Study of the Labor Movement During the Era of the Civil War (1945).

Palladino, Grace. *Another Civil War: Labor, Capital, and the State in the Anthracite Regions of Pennsylvania, 1840–68* (1990).

Sumner, Helen. "Citizenship." In John R. Commons et. al., *History of Labour in the United States* (1946).

LADIES MEMORIAL ASSOCIATIONS

White women in the American South actively supported the Confederate war effort through their work in soldiers' aid societies, joining other women to roll bandages and sew flags and uniforms. Once the war was over, these groups did not dissolve. Rather, they reorganized as ladies' memorial associations (LMAs). The first LMA was organized in Columbus, Georgia, in 1866, and within a few short years women in nearly every town in the region had formed an LMA. These groups flourished in the late nineteenth century and continued to be active in the early twentieth century. Although LMAs functioned as independent organizations for numerous years, they eventually became part of a regional network in 1900 when the Confederated Southern Memorial Association was formed.

The primary goal of each LMA was to publicly honor the memory of the men who died fighting for the Confederacy. The first LMAs assumed the grisly task of overseeing the reinterment of Southern soldiers from mass graves to individual graves in newly designated Confederate cemeteries. Once this activity was completed, members raised money to erect monuments within the cemeteries—an activity with which they became identified. These same women originated Confederate Memorial Day, an annual observance held each spring that paid homage to the soldiers who had died for the Southern cause. Confederate Memorial Day was, and still is, commemorated by Southern states on either 26 April (the day of Joseph E. Johnston's surrender) or 10 May (the day Thomas "Stonewall" Jackson died).

The memorial activity of LMAs in the post–Civil War South marked the beginning of women's involvement in what is referred to as the "Lost Cause." Beginning in 1865 and continuing through the early twentieth century, the Lost Cause involved the commemoration, celebration, and memorialization of the former Confederacy. Women were vital to the success and longevity of the Lost Cause, and many of them gained local, state, and sometimes regional celebrity for their efforts.

During Reconstruction, LMA members were the primary activists of the Lost Cause and remained undaunted in their efforts to memorialize men, even in the face of federal control. Despite a depressed economy, they were successful in raising funds to build monuments. Such memorial activities were very important to Southern whites during this period of social upheaval. Moreover, it allowed them to replace the negative aspects of defeat with the more positive connotations associated with having fought a "just cause." Confederate veterans, it followed, were no less than heroes.

Women of the Old South elite were a visible element in the postwar LMAs. In fact, much of the success of the LMAs can be attributed to the elite status of its members. Their work building Confederate monuments and caring for the graves of the Confederate dead made them important public figures. Indeed, their efforts to memorialize men became an important source of their own social power. Even as Lost Cause activists invented new ways of celebrating the Confederacy by writing and publishing history, forming new Confederate organizations, and building larger and more public monuments, Southern women maintained and defined the role they played in the Confederate tradition.

After Reconstruction and as former Confederates returned to hold office in Southern state governments, the Lost Cause entered a new phase. The era of bereavement was replaced by a period of celebration of the former Confederacy, beginning in the 1880s. LMAs continued their work of caring for graves, erecting monuments, and organizing Confederate Memorial Day ceremonies. By 1890, the work of the memorial associations entered its third decade, and a new generation of Southern women joined the LMAs. Within a few years, this younger generation broadened the focus of women's memorial activities. They founded a new organization, the United Daughters of the Confederacy (UDC), who carried the message of the Lost Cause into the twentieth century, becoming one of the most influential women's organizations in the South before World War I.

The UDC sought to include longtime members of the LMAs in its organization, and some LMAs became chapters of the UDC. Yet the LMAs retained their place within Southern communities and, perhaps in response to the success of the UDC, came together in 1900 to create the Confederated Southern Memorial Association. The Confederated Southern Memorial Association never achieved the success of the UDC. Its formation in 1900 came as LMAs were in decline. Still, the history of the LMAs offers evidence of how Southern women used the Confederate tradition to assume public roles for themselves, all the while maintaining their status as bearers of tradition.

—*Karen L. Cox*

See also Lost Cause; Memorials, C.S.A.; Sons of Confederate Veterans; United Daughters of the Confederacy; Veterans' Organizations.

For further reading:

Cox, Karen Lynne. "Women, The Lost Cause and the New South: The United Daughters of the Confederacy and the Transmission of Confederate Culture, 1894–1919" (Ph.D. dissertation, 1997).

Whites, LeeAnn. *The Civil War as a Crisis in Gender: Augusta, Georgia, 1860–1890* (1995).

LAMAR, CHARLES AUGUSTUS LAFAYETTE
(1824–1865)
Entrepreneur

A member of a prominent Georgia and Texas family, Charles A. L. Lamar was born in Savannah on 1 April 1824, the son of banker Gazaway Bugg Lamar and Jane Meek Cresswell. His godfather, the Marquis de Lafayette, was visiting in the United States at the time of his birth. The family included such other luminaries as Mirabeau Bonaparte Lamar, president of the Republic of Texas, and future U.S. Supreme Court justices Lucius Q. C. Lamar and Joseph Rucker Lamar.

Charles was the only child of his father's first marriage to survive the explosion and sinking of the steamer *Pulaski* off North Carolina in 1838. By age twenty-four he was managing the family businesses in Savannah and beginning to organize his own. He took part in railroading, road building, flour milling, cotton factoring, fertilizer importing, gold mining, insurance, and steamship management. So adept and successful was he in business that the family entrusted him with hundreds of thousands of dollars for investment. Charles also took a role in the life of Savannah. He was a city alderman, a captain of militia, and an unsuccessful American Party candidate for Congress in 1855. He was an official of the Savannah Aquatic Club and president of a race track, and he raced his own horses.

On one issue, Lamar parted with the rest of his family and associates. He believed that the federal ban on the African slave trade was unconstitutional in that it interfered with the right of an individual to obtain, possess, and dispose of property. In support of his position he gave speeches, attended conventions of like-minded thinkers, and in 1858 brought a cargo of slaves from Africa to Cuba and attempted to bring them into the United States legally as émigrés or apprentices. He was refused permission to do so by Secretary of the Treasury Howell Cobb, his uncle by marriage.

Lamar next turned to illegal importation. In the summer of 1858 he dispatched the schooner *Wanderer* to the east coast of Africa for a cargo of slaves. The ship returned in November with 409 Africans who were landed at Jekyll Island, Georgia, and sold throughout the South before federal officials learned that they had arrived. The *Wanderer* was seized by the authorities, its crew was arrested and charged with piracy, and Lamar was accused of violating the slave trade law. When the ship was sold at auction, Lamar bought it back and then knocked down the sheriff, the only man who dared to bid against him.

The ensuing events were a mockery of justice. When a group of his newly imported African slaves was captured by a posse, Lamar got them back and had the posse arrested for "stealing" his two domestic slaves who were driving the wagons. Another of the *Wanderer's* "cargo" was taken from the Savannah jail by several armed men. In the trials that followed, the government was unable to prove either that the *Wanderer* was owned by a U.S. citizen or that the defendants had been members of the crew of a slave ship. One by one, the charges were dropped. Lamar was eventually fined $500 and sentenced to thirty days' confinement, which he served in his own apartment. Afterward he wrote, "I am not in jail, and the damned Government has not the power to put me and keep me there. I can whip the Government any time they make the issue, unless they raise a few additional regiments."

The *Wanderer* affair ended Howell Cobb's favorite son bid for the presidential nomination in 1860. When the Georgia Democratic Party selected delegates to the national convention in Charleston, Lamar and his associates blocked every attempt at an endorsement of Cobb. As a result, Georgia sent two opposing delegations to Charleston and Cobb's campaign died.

Lamar had been a secessionist for years before the Civil War. With the outbreak of hostilities he raised a regiment, later designated the 61st Georgia, and was elected lieutenant colonel. He commanded the defenses on Jekyll Island in late 1861, but resigned in April 1862 to return to shipping. With his father, Lamar went into blockade running for the benefit of the Georgia state government and was highly successful.

After the fall of Savannah in December 1864, Lamar returned to military service with the Georgia Reserves. Ironically, he was first assigned as aide to his old adversary, now major general, Howell Cobb. On 16 April 1865, Lamar joined in opposing Union cavalry advancing into Georgia from Alabama. He was captured near Columbus and, while being led to the rear, was shot by one of his captors, who mistakenly thought he was armed. He was buried nearby, but his body was reinterred in Savannah in 1866.

Charles Lamar epitomized the Southern class and generation to which he belonged. Vigorous and forthright, he was successful at almost everything he turned his hand to. He insisted on what he saw as his constitutional and individual rights, regardless of the law, and was willing to take whatever measures necessary to secure them. He tolerated no opposition and went to lengths to make his opponents suffer. Some of Lamar's family members believed he was destined for prison or an asylum, but his own words serve as his best epitaph: "A man of influence can do as he pleases."

—*Russell K. Brown*

See also Georgia.
For further reading:
Barber, Henry E. "Charles Augustus Lafayette Lamar." *Dictionary of Georgia Biography* (1983).

Wells, Tom Henderson. "Charles Augustus Lafayette Lamar." *Georgia Historical Quarterly* (1963).
———. *The Slave Ship Wanderer* (1967).

LAMAR, LUCIUS QUINTUS CINCINNATUS
(1825–1893)
Confederate officer and diplomat

L. Q. C. Lamar was born 17 September 1825 in Putnam County, Georgia. After his father committed suicide in 1834, Lamar and his siblings were educated and cared for by their large and wealthy family. In 1845 Lucius graduated from Emory College, where he became close to school president Augustus Baldwin Longstreet, who had played a significant role in the separation of the American Methodist Church along sectional lines over slavery. The bond was reinforced by Lamar's 1847 marriage to Longstreet's daughter.

In 1849 Lamar followed his father-in-law to Mississippi, where he found employment as a professor of mathematics at the state university and opened a law practice. Six years later, Lamar acquired on the Tallahatchie River in Mississippi a large plantation, which he named Solitude. In 1857 he won election to Congress, where he championed states' rights and was an outspoken critic of those Democrats he felt were too willing to sacrifice Southern interests to preserve party and national unity.

After winning reelection in 1859, Lamar attended the 1860 Democratic Convention in Charleston, South Carolina, as an unofficial spokesperson for his friend Jefferson Davis. Although his strong unionism led him to opposed the move initially, he participated in the walkout of Southern delegates and in a fiery speech repudiated his formerly moderate position by proclaiming the Democratic Party as split and incapable of mending. In July Lamar decided to accept a professorship at the University of Mississippi and announced he would not seek another term in Congress.

Abraham Lincoln's election ended Lamar's hopes for a peaceful resolution of the sectional crisis. When Mississippi convened a secession convention in January, Lamar was appointed chairman of a committee that was assigned the task of drafting a secession ordinance. Lamar had been working on such a document for some time before the convention, and it took the committee only a day to report out an ordinance of secession. It was adopted by the convention on 9 January, and Lamar resigned his congressional seat three days later.

Lamar and law partner C. H. Mott then organized the 19th Mississippi Regiment with Mott as colonel and Lamar as lieutenant colonel. The unit reached Richmond in June, but when it left for the front, Lamar suffered an attack of apoplexy that incapacitated him. After a convalescence in Mississippi, he returned to Richmond in November and was a conspicuous figure in the salons of the capital during the winter of 1861–1862.

In March 1862 Lamar joined his regiment in the Yorktown trenches. On 5 May Lamar saw his first combat at the battle of Williamsburg. He acquitted himself well. When Mott fell mortally wounded, Lamar assumed command of the regiment and his performance won praise from his superiors. Shortly thereafter, however, his career as an infantry officer ended when he suffered another debilitating attack of apoplexy. Lamar's health improved enough by the fall to allow him to return to the army as a staff officer. Then, on 19 November, President Davis appointed him commissioner to the Russian court.

Lamar arrived in Great Britain in March 1863 and spent several months there and in France assessing the Confederacy's prospects for assistance from those countries. He saw little to inspire hope for the Southern cause in either France or Britain and quickly deduced that traveling to Russia would be pointless, as there was little chance the czar would intervene on behalf of the Southern independence movement when he was busy crushing an insurrection in Poland. In June 1863, Lamar learned that the Confederate Senate had refused to confirm his commission. Nonetheless, he remained in Europe for several months afterward, assisting the editor of the *Index*, the South's propaganda paper in Britain, and conferring regularly with other Confederate agents.

Upon returning to Richmond in January 1864, Lamar reported to Davis and Secretary of State Judah Benjamin to discuss his experiences. He was then dispatched to Georgia to deal with rising discontent with the central government in that state. Although in poor health, Lamar gave several speeches attacking President Davis's critics and vigorously defending the administration's policies on conscription and suspension of habeas corpus. On 3 December 1864, Lamar finally returned to the army as a colonel and was appointed judge advocate in the military court of the III Corps. When Lee surrendered at Appomattox, Lamar was serving as an aide to General James Longstreet.

After his political disability was removed, Lamar, who had assumed a leading role in the effort to restore white Democratic rule in Mississippi, entered Congress in 1873. Upon reaching Washington, he shrewdly recognized that his goals would be best served if he assumed a conciliatory stance to persuade the North that the South accepted the results of the war. Lamar's most significant action in this regard occurred in March 1874, when he delivered an eloquent eulogy in honor of Massachusetts senator Charles Sumner that was enthusiastically received by a public whose interest in Reconstruction was already fading.

After Reconstruction, Lamar became one of the most powerful men in Mississippi and a close ally of the conservative northeastern wing of the Democratic Party. There was some grumbling among many of his constituents, however, over this relationship, Lamar's approach to economic development and monetary policy, and his paternalistic attitude toward African-Americans. Before this discontent could be translated into political action, Lamar left electoral politics in 1884 by accepting Grover Cleveland's offer to serve as secretary of the interior. Three years later, Cleveland nominated Lamar to the Supreme Court. Lamar took his seat on the Court in January 1888 and served until his death on 23 January 1893.

—*Ethan S. Rafuse*

See also Diplomacy, C.S.A.; Mississippi.
For further reading:
Cate, Wirt Armistead. *Lucius Q. C. Lamar: Secession and Reunion* (1935).
Halsell, Willie D. "The Friendship of L. Q. C. Lamar and Jefferson Davis." *Journal of Mississippi History* (1944).
Murphy, James B. *L. Q. C. Lamar: Pragmatic Patriot* (1973).

LAMON, WARD HILL
(1828–1893)
Friend of Abraham Lincoln

One of President Abraham Lincoln's closest friends, Ward Hill Lamon was born in the Shenandoah Valley of Virginia in 1828, the second son of a middle-class farmer who owned considerable acreage and a few slaves. Educated in local schools, Lamon taught for a few years before moving to frontier Illinois in 1847, lured by the enticing reports of cousins who had already located there. After reading law with a local practitioner in Danville, Illinois, followed by one winter in Louisville, Kentucky attending law school, Lamon opened a practice in Danville, the county seat of Vermilion County. He returned to Virginia to marry Angeline Turner, but he made Danville his home until 1857.

Lamon prospered as an attorney. During these years he met Abraham Lincoln—then a prominent lawyer practicing in nearby Springfield, Illinois—and became a Danville associate of the future president. The friendship between the two men deepened when they traveled around central Illinois trying cases as part of the Eighth Judicial Circuit. Their coterie of traveling attorneys also included Bloomington lawyer Leonard Swett and Judge David Davis. In 1856, with the assistance of his friends in the legal community, Lamon won election as prosecuting attorney for the Eighth Circuit. He moved to Bloomington the following year. Lamon was a competent attorney, though not a brilliant one.

Known as "Hill" to his friends, Lamon supported Abraham Lincoln's political ambitions, helping him

campaign for the U.S. Senate in 1858. In 1860, during the Republican Convention, when Lincoln's Illinois friends conspired to secure the Republican nomination away from front-runner William H. Seward, Lamon forged passes to the Chicago Wigwam gallery so that Lincoln supporters might pack the facility and create a thundering ovation. When Lincoln won the presidential contest, he invited his tall, brawny friend to accompany him to Washington as unofficial bodyguard. They traveled secretly, fearing a rumored plot to assassinate the president-elect. During the Fort Sumter crisis, the president sent Lamon to Charleston, along with another Illinoisan, Stephen A. Hurlbut, hoping these two native-born Southerners could learn first-hand information about public opinion there.

In April 1861, Lincoln appointed Lamon U.S. marshal for the District of Columbia, a position that allowed him a comfortable income, social position, and access to the president. Charming and extroverted, Lamon enjoyed Washington society, and he remained close to Lincoln during the presidential years. The president clearly liked having Lamon around, calling him "my particular friend." Lamon's jokes, storytelling, and singing provided the president with much-needed escape from the burdens of war. Lamon accompanied Lincoln to Gettysburg and introduced him when the president gave his momentous speech dedicating the military cemetery there. Lamon later claimed that Lincoln believed the audience lacked enthusiasm for his speech.

Lamon appears not to have been a major player in politics or policy making during the war. Nevertheless his appointment as marshal and his well-known friendship with the president brought him under suspicion with some political constituencies. Abolitionists and Radical Republicans distrusted him for his connections to Virginia and for his treatment of fugitive-slave cases. For his part, Lamon made no attempt to hide his dislike of those he regarded as extremists on the slavery question. Lamon felt increasing concern for the president's safety against rumored assassination plots and attempted to strengthen White House security. When Lincoln was assassinated in April 1865, Lamon had left the city to visit Richmond, sent there by Lincoln on an inspection tour.

After the war, Lamon's public career ended. Already viewed critically by the Radical Republicans, who quickly gained national ascendancy, Lamon was criticized further for publicly supporting President Andrew Johnson. He sealed his fate in 1872 by publishing a biography of Lincoln, ghostwritten by his law partner Chauncey F. Black and based in part on transcriptions of interviews with Lincoln friends that he had purchased from Lincoln's former law partner William H. Herndon. Lamon attempted to produce a folksy biography of Lincoln at a time when the Republican Party sought to elevate the slain president to a loftier status. The book

was a critical and financial failure, and Lamon never held public office again. From 1879 to 1886 he resided in Colorado and practiced law. Out of anger over Lamon's biographical treatment of his father, Robert Todd Lincoln blocked Lamon's nomination to become postmaster of Denver. He died in 1893, having been preceded in death by his first wife, who died in 1859, and his second wife, Sally Logan Lamon, who died in 1892. Lamon was survived by a daughter.

—*Wendy Hamand Venet*

See also Fort Sumter, Bombardment of; Lincoln, Abraham.
For further reading:
Donald, David Herbert. *Lincoln* (1995).
Hamand, Lavern. "Ward Hill Lamon: Lincoln's 'Particular Friend'" (Ph.D. dissertation, 1949).
Lamon, Ward Hill. *Recollections of Abraham Lincoln, 1847–1865* (1911; reprint, 1994).
Wilson, Douglas L., and Rodney O. Davis, eds. *Herndon's Informants: Letters, Interviews, and Statements about Abraham Lincoln* (1998).

LANE, HARRIET REBECCA
(1830–1903)
Official Executive Mansion host

As the niece of unmarried President James Buchanan, Harriet Lane presided over social functions at the Executive Mansion (informally, the White House) from 1857 to 1861 and served as her uncle's political confidante. Known for her dignity and tact, she maintained an atmosphere of cordiality within official Washington despite rising sectional tensions.

Harriet Rebecca Lane was born in Mercersburg, Pennsylvania, on 9 May 1830 to Elliot Tole Lane and Jane Buchanan Lane. Both parents died when she was a child, and Lane became the ward of her favorite uncle, James Buchanan, then a U.S. senator. Buchanan provided for her education, first at a boarding school in Charlestown, Virginia, and then at the Academy of the Visitation Convent in Georgetown, District of Columbia. Before graduating in 1849, Lane cultivated her interest in politics by listening in on Buchanan's discussions of foreign affairs while he served as President James K. Polk's secretary of state.

After completing school, Lane joined Buchanan at his country estate, Wheatland, near Lancaster, Pennsylvania. A spirited woman, Lane entertained frequently and developed her skills as a host. In 1854–1855, she further perfected the social graces when she spent a year in London while Buchanan served as minister to England. Highly praised by Queen Victoria, Lane became a favorite with London society. She promoted the U.S. position on international issues and has been credited with introducing American Indian art to England.

Returning to the United States as an accomplished unofficial diplomat and a talented social observer, Lane soon emerged as a national icon. After Buchanan's inauguration, she became the "presiding lady of the White House." She distinguished herself by organizing elegant receptions and dinners, championing the arts, and voicing concern about the plight of American Indians. Lane's name became a household word: babies, organizational clubs, streets, and types of clothing were named after her, as was a U.S. revenue cutter launched in 1857.

Under Lane's tenure, social life at the White House thrived, despite forebodings of civil war. Alabama's Virginia Clay-Clopton, whose husband served in the U.S. Senate during the Buchanan administration, later recalled that Lane "served to keep the surface of society in Washington serene and smiling, though the fires of a volcano raged in the under-political world." Jefferson Davis later commented that the Buchanan White House came close to fulfilling his ideal of a Republican court.

While the Civil War likely colored such memories, Lane did exercise a shrewd social diplomacy at the White House. Along with her cousin, James Buchanan Henry, who was the president's private secretary, Lane organized weekly dinners for federal officials and legislators. She was in charge of the delicate task of seating guests according to rank. After John Brown's raid, Lane's efforts to foster congenial relations within the political set became more challenging. She struggled to enforce her rule against political discussion at White House functions. Stephen A. Douglas's wife boycotted her receptions. The successful Washington visit of Albert Edward, Prince of Wales, in October 1860 provided a brief respite from these difficulties.

Throughout the sectional crisis, Lane supported Buchanan's policy of conciliation. Like him, she held on to the hope that moderates would prevail. After President Abraham Lincoln's inauguration in 1861, Lane returned to Wheatland with Buchanan. Ever loyal to him, she lamented the criticism that he received after the war began. Although a Union supporter, Lane did not play a prominent role in relief efforts. She led a quiet life at Wheatland, traveling occasionally to New York, Philadelphia, Washington, D.C., and Bedford Springs, Pennsylvania. Lane mourned the death of her only remaining sibling early in 1863, and later that year she joined the Episcopal Church. Both Lane and Buchanan supported George B. McClellan in the 1864 presidential election.

After the war, Lane retained her interest in politics even as she began to focus more on her private life. On 11 January 1866, she married Henry Elliott Johnston of Baltimore. The Johnstons lived in Baltimore and had two sons, James Buchanan and Henry Elliott. By mid-1884 Lane's husband and both of her sons had died. She dedicated the remainder of her life to advancing pediatric medicine, collecting art works abroad, and redeeming the public image of her uncle, who had died in 1868.

Harriet Lane Johnston died of cancer in Narragansett Pier, Rhode Island, on 3 July 1903. Her many philanthropic bequests resulted most prominently in establishment of the Harriet Lane Home for Invalid Children at Johns Hopkins Hospital in Baltimore, a National Gallery of Art (now the National Museum of American Art) at the Smithsonian Institution in Washington, and the Meridian Hill monument to President Buchanan in Washington.

—Antoinette G. van Zelm

See also Buchanan, James.

For further reading:

Clay-Clopton, Virginia. *A Belle of the Fifties: Memoirs of Mrs. Clay of Alabama, Covering Social and Political Life in Washington and the South, 1853–66; Put into Narrative Form by Ada Sterling* (1905).

Klein, Philip Shriver. *President James Buchanan: A Biography* (1962).

Moore, John Bassett, ed. *The Works of James Buchanan: Comprising His Speeches, State Papers, and Private Correspondence* (1908–1911; reprint, 1960).

Peacock, Virginia Tatnall. *Famous American Belles of the Nineteenth Century* (1901).

Pryor, Mrs. Roger A. *Reminiscences of Peace and War* (1905).

Taylor, Lloyd C., Jr. "Harriet Lane—Mirror of an Age." *Pennsylvania History* (1963).

LANE, JAMES HENRY
(1814–1866)
U.S. senator and general

James Henry Lane was born 22 June 1814 on the Ohio River either in Boone County, Kentucky or Lawrenceburg, Indiana. His father was the first speaker of the Indiana House of Representatives and later a judge and member of Congress. His mother was from a prominent New England family and was a devout Methodist whose religion, her son later claimed, had a major impact on him. Later in his life, when Lane wished to appeal politically to men of different sections, he claimed a southern birth, a western boyhood, and a maternal New England ancestry.

Lane studied law and was admitted to practice in 1840. He served in city government in Lawrenceburg, Indiana. When the war with Mexico broke out, Lane joined the army. He led Indiana troops in the battle of Buena Vista in February 1847.

Lane followed his father into Indiana politics. He served as lieutenant governor from 1849 to 1853, when he was elected a member of Congress. In Congress, Lane voted for the Kansas-Nebraska Act and then moved to Kansas Territory in April 1855.

A Democrat in party affiliation, Lane may have intended to organize the Democratic Party in Kansas, but the fraud that marked the national Democratic administration's rule in Kansas became the catalyst for the formation of a bipartisan, free-state organization called the Topeka movement. The Topeka movement was a coalition of New Englanders, led by Lane's chief nemesis Charles Robinson, and westerners, led by Lane. Like the westerners he represented, Lane was not problack, but he did resent the efforts of the proslavery party to force slavery into the territories by force and fraud. And Lane saw in the deepening controversy in Kansas the chance to promote his own political ambitions. While Robinson headed the extralegal Topeka government, Lane was its military leader. One Kansan commented that Lane always dressed in military fashion.

Lane's political scheming was legendary. An observer said that Lane could not survive twenty-four hours without intrigue. His closest coworkers in the free-state movement distrusted his duplicity, but his power as an orator and leader of westerners made him essential to their cause. He was repeatedly elected president of free-state conventions, including the one at Topeka that founded the free-state movement. In spring 1856, Lane presented a memorial from the Topeka government to the U.S. Congress asking for statehood for Kansas. The memorial was marred by interlineations and the fact that all the signatures were in the same handwriting. These flaws opened Lane up to the charge of forgery, and he came close to a duel with Senator Stephen A. Douglas over these accusations.

His visit to Washington, D.C., as emissary of the Topeka government meant that Lane was absent from the territory when fighting began in the summer of 1856. He raised a force, Lane's Army of the North, to invade Kansas Territory from Iowa and Nebraska. Lane's army, however, did not arrive until much of the fighting had ended and a new territorial governor, John W. Geary, had begun to restore order. Although U.S. Army troops failed to capture Lane, they did round up 100 of his men after an attack in September 1856 on a proslavery settlement at Hickory Point.

After Geary, with the support of U.S. Army troops, suppressed the fighting in Kansas, Lane turned to his law practice and farming. He continued active in territorial politics and served at president of yet another Kansas constitutional convention, at Leavenworth, in 1857.

In 1858, Lane killed a fellow free-state settler, Gaius Jenkins, in a dispute over their property lines. Although he was acquitted, many predicted the end of his political influence. Nonetheless, he continued to be a formidable power in Kansas politics.

In 1861, when Kansas became a state, Lane became a U.S. senator and forged an odd friendship with President Abraham Lincoln. In the first weeks of the war, when Washington, D.C., seemed isolated from the rest of the North, Lane formed a "Frontier Guard" of Kansas men to protect the White House. Lincoln, perhaps feeling a kinship with another westerner whose humble origins and rough-hewn demeanor in some respects closely modeled his own, took Lane's part in quarrels with

Kansas governor Charles Robinson. Robinson rightly resented Lane's interference, with the president's indulgence, in affairs more strictly regarded as the province of the governor, such as raising troops in Kansas. Lincoln appointed Lane a brigadier general of volunteers in 1861. Through various devious machinations, Lane managed to hold both his military appointment and his Senate seat. He led men in some small actions along the Missouri-Kansas border during the Civil War and was reelected to the Senate in 1865.

In 1864, Lane took credit for restoring Lincoln's political fortunes. Lane spoke in favor of the president's renomination during the Republican Convention. Lane's friends claimed that his speech thwarted an effort by some Republicans to dump the president in favor of another candidate, but the opposition to Lincoln's renomination had already been severely weakened before Lane's speech.

Some of Lane's biographers claim that his experiences in Kansas radically altered his views on race. He was notorious for having entered Kansas Territory declaring that he would as soon buy a black as a mule. Yet during the Civil War, he raised black troops for the army.

After Lincoln's assassination, Lane sided with the administration of Andrew Johnson and defended Johnson's veto of the 1866 Civil Rights Bill. Lane alienated the Radical Republicans and miscalculated politically. In addition, he was threatened with an investigation of war contracts from which it was rumored he had profited illegally as senator. Depressed at his political and financial woes, Lane committed suicide on 1 July 1866 by shooting himself in the mouth with a revolver while riding in the company of two friends. He died on 11 July and was buried in Lawrence, Kansas.

—*Nicole Etcheson*

See also Kansas; Kansas-Nebraska Act; Robinson, Charles.
For further reading:
Connelley, William E. *James Henry Lane: The "Grim Chieftain" of Kansas* (1899).
Organization of the Free State Government in Kansas with the Inaugural Speech and Message of Governor Robinson (1856).
Rawley, James A. *Race and Politics: "Bleeding Kansas" and the Chining of the Civil War* (1969).
Speer, John. *Life of General James H. Lane. "The Liberator of Kansas" with Corroborative Incidents of Pioneer History* (1897).
Spring, Leverett W. "The Career of a Kansas Politician." *American Historical Review* (1898).
Stephenson, Wendell Holmes. *The Political Career of General James H. Lane* (1930).

LANE, JAMES HENRY
(1833–1907)
Confederate general

The son of Walter Gardner Lane and Mary Ann Henry Barkwell Lane, James Henry Lane was born in Mathews Court House, Virginia, and educated at the Virginia Military Institute and the University of Virginia. Upon completion of his master of arts degree in science at the latter institution, he returned to teach mathematics at the former. Before the outbreak of the Civil War, he taught briefly at Florida State Seminary and North Carolina's Charlotte Military Institute. Upon the secession of North Carolina, Lane received a commission as a major in the 1st North Carolina Volunteers.

Lane traveled with his regiment to Virginia. On 10 June, Lane commanded a scouting party of the regiment that precipitated the battle of Big Bethel. The regiment would afterward be known as the Bethel Regiment. Lane was promoted to lieutenant colonel in September 1861 and shortly thereafter became the colonel of the 28th North Carolina Regiment.

In the spring and summer of 1862, Lane led his regiment in the Peninsula campaign. He fought at Hanover Court House on 27 May 1862 and was wounded twice during the Seven Days'. His brigade commander, Lawrence O'Bryan Branch, commended him for his actions during the latter series of battles. Lane fought at Cedar Mountain, Second Bull Run, Harper's Ferry, and Antietam, where he succeeded to command of the brigade on the death of Brigadier General Branch. On 1 November 1862, Lane's permanent command of the brigade was confirmed with his promotion to brigadier general. Extremely popular with his men, Lane had enjoyed the support of his officers who lobbied hard for his permanent command. The men celebrated the promotion of their "Little General."

Lane led his brigade at Fredericksburg, Chancellorsville, and as part of Lee's second invasion of the North in June 1863. As part of A. P. Hill's corps at Gettysburg on the first day, Lane attacked the Union positions on Seminary Ridge and helped Henry Heth's division drive them onto Cemetery Hill. He took little part in the fighting on the second day, and because he troops were relatively fresh, he was assigned to Isaac Trimble's division in what became known as Pickett's Charge on the third day. In this famous charge, Lane's brigade suffered approximately 30 percent casualties. On the retreat from Pennsylvania, brigade survivors guarded the Army of Northern Virginia's rear.

In the Virginia campaign of the following spring, Lane continued in command until he fell seriously wounded at Cold Harbor on 3 June 1864. He did not return to his brigade until the fall, when he joined his men in the trenches of Petersburg. In April 1865 he joined the retreat that became the Appomattox campaign and was arraying his men for battle on 9 April when he received word that the Army of Northern Virginia had surrendered.

Paroled, Lane returned to his family home in Virginia and made his living teaching. He taught for a while at what would become Virginia Polytechnic Institute. After a brief stint at the Missouri School of Mines, he accepted an appointment as professor of civil engineering at Alabama Polytechnic Institute (now Auburn University). He taught there from 1882 until his retirement in 1907. He died in Auburn, Alabama, on 21 September 1907.

—*David S. Heidler and Jeanne T. Heidler*

See also Big Bethel; Cold Harbor.

For further reading:

Phillips, Kenneth Edward. "James Henry Lane and the War for Southern Independence" (M.A. thesis, 1982).

LANE, JOSEPH
(1801–1881)
United States senator

Born to John Lane and Elizabeth Street Lane in Buncombe County, North Carolina, Joseph Lane moved with his family to Henderson County, Kentucky, when he was three years old. He was educated locally and at the age of fourteen moved to Indiana, right across the Ohio River, to accept a position as a store clerk. He saved his money from that job and from working as a flatboatman on the Ohio to buy a farm in Vanderburg County, Indiana. Along with farming, Lane also became involved in Indiana Democratic politics. He served in the Indiana legislature for much of the 1820s, 1830s, and early 1840s.

At the outbreak of the Mexican-American War, Lane received an appointment as a brigadier general of volunteers. In that conflict he became famous for his bravery in leading his entire brigade into several engagements. At the end of the war he was brevetted a major general of volunteers. Lane's wartime performance enhanced his political career, giving him a national reputation.

In 1848 President James K. Polk named Lane the territorial governor of the new Oregon Territory. Lane accepted the appointment, thus beginning his long association with Oregon. Lane traveled overland to his new position and took his oath of office on 3 March 1849. Because of the election of the Whig Zachary Taylor to the presidency, however, Lane remained in the governor's chair for little more than a year. In the summer of 1850 a Whig replaced him.

Lane's replacement angered many Oregon residents who had been especially pleased with how the Democratic governor had dealt with the Indian population of the territory. His popularity and the protests about his removal may have had some impact on Lane's decision to remain in the territory after his removal from office. He had also acquired much good timber land during his short residence there and probably wanted to remain in the territory to exploit the economic opportunities such land gave him. Whatever the case, Lane's popularity was demonstrated in 1851 when he was elected as the territory's delegate to the United States House of Representatives.

While most of Lane's activities in Congress for this term and the succeeding terms to which he would be elected concerned Oregon issues, he also took an interest in national issues and spoke on them when he deemed it appropriate. A strong supporter of states' rights and particularly Southern rights, Lane could be counted on to support territorial issues that would benefit the South. Still very active in Democratic Party circles, he was mentioned several times, especially by Indiana Democrats like Jesse Bright, as a possible presidential nominee in 1852.

Though Lane certainly would have entertained the notion of a presidential bid, he was perfectly satisfied with the party's choice of Franklin Pierce as its nominee. Lane worked hard for the Pierce candidacy and when Pierce won the election, Lane was rewarded with control of most of the presidential patronage in the Oregon Territory.

Returning to Congress after the election, Lane worked hard to have that body approve measures that would allow for the quicker, cheaper acquisition of land in Oregon. He also spoke out in favor of the United States annexing Cuba from Spain.

Meeting often with President Pierce, Lane pointed out to the new president that there was a Whig territorial governor in Oregon and as a result brought about the Taylor appointee's removal. Pierce immediately named Lane to the open post, and Lane left for home. Once he arrived, however, Lane had apparently rethought this change in position and shortly after being inaugurated, he resigned the governor's chair to run again as territorial delegate. He was overwhelmingly elected.

During the Pierce administration Lane supported the Kansas-Nebraska Act. Under Pierce's successor, James Buchanan, Lane defended the administration's advocacy of the proslavery Lecompton Constitution for Kansas. In early 1859, when Oregon was finally admitted as a state, Lane was able to make his voice heard more frequently on these issues when he was elected one of Oregon's first senators.

Increasingly identified as an advocate of Southern causes, Lane was mentioned frequently in late 1859 and early 1860 by states' rights supporters as a presidential candidate for 1860. When the Democratic Party divided—first at Charleston and then at Baltimore—in the spring and summer of 1860, Lane was nominated for vice president by the largely pro-Southern National Democratic Convention. He accepted the nomination, explaining that while he supported the constitutionality of secession, he did not believe that it was the best course for the South to take should there be a Republican victory in November.

Lane's vice presidential candidacy on the John C. Breckinridge ticket hurt him politically in Oregon. The state was becoming increasingly Republican and even the Democratic Party in the state was embarrassed by Lane's association with avowed secessionists. Even after the election, however, Lane continued to speak out in favor of the Southern right to secede and argued in his final speech before the Senate at the end of his term in March 1861 that Southern states had been driven to secede by the policies of the North. He left the Senate and returned home to Oregon.

Lane received a cool reception from his former constituents in Oregon. Many citizens of the state suspected him of disloyalty, and there was talk of arresting him or expelling him to the Confederacy. When he went quietly to live on his farm, most people forgot him, and he lived in obscurity there throughout the war. His son Lafayette Lane, however, left West Point against his father's wishes to fight for the Confederacy.

After the war, Lane continued to live on his farm, though he did regain some of his interest in the Democratic politics. He actively campaigned for state and national Democrats and regained some of his former standing in state political circles. In 1880, at the age of seventy-nine, he ran unsuccessfully for the state senate. Shortly after the election, his health began to fail and he died in Roseburg, Oregon, on 19 April 1881.

—David S. Heidler and Jeanne T. Heidler

See also Election of 1860.

For further reading:
Hendrickson, James E. *Joe Lane of Oregon: Machine Politics and the Sectional Crisis, 1849–1861* (1967).
Kelly, Margaret Jean. *The Career of Joseph Lane, Frontier Politician* (1942).

LANGSTON, JOHN MERCER
(1829–1897)
African-American statesman

Following Frederick Douglass, John Mercer Langston emerged as this nation's preeminent African-American statesman of the nineteenth century. A proponent of legal equality, Langston represented a tradition in black political thought that emphasized integration, education, and racial uplift.

Born free in 1829, Langston was the third child of Ralph Quarles, a prosperous Virginia planter, and Lucy Langston, a freedwoman of African and Indian ancestry. After both parents died in 1834, Langston left Virginia with his older brothers for Chillicothe, Ohio, where he lived with a family friend who promised to educate the child and safeguard his inheritance. An Ohio court dissolved this relationship in 1839, ruling that the guardian's impending move to the slave state of Missouri would threaten Langston's freedom. The court's decision effectively unmasked the light-skinned Langston, confronting him with a racial identity that he had so far eluded.

In 1840 Langston moved to Cincinnati, a city alive with antislavery sentiment and a vibrant black community. Langston boarded with several well-to-do black families, eventually joining the Bethel A. M. E. Church and attending school at a local Baptist church. Langston's stay was punctuated by the race riot of 1841. Sheltered from the white mob by one of his brothers, Langston recalled the resolve of black Cincinnatians, who were "learning what their rights were, and how to advocate and defend them."

Langston returned to Chillicothe in 1843, continuing his studies with two black teachers from Oberlin College. Langston entered Oberlin in 1844 and became its fifth black graduate, earning both bachelor's and master's degrees. After considering Oberlin's seminary, Langston chose a legal career. Rejected by several law schools, Langston apprenticed with an Ohio judge before passing the state's bar examination in 1854.

After attending his first national black convention in 1848, Langston rose quickly within abolitionist circles, exhibiting a penchant for organizing and leading antislavery activities. An early advocate of emigration, Langston reversed his position in 1854 as antislavery forces coalesced around the Kansas-Nebraska controversy. That year Langston addressed a stunned National Emigration Convention about America's potential for integration and racial equality. Langston's confidence grew after his 1855 election as township clerk, making him the first African-American to hold public office. Langston believed his election foreshadowed "the inevitable . . . annihilation of American prejudice."

Politics presented Langston an answer to society's racism. He spearheaded efforts to enfranchise black Ohioans, contending that "political influence" would "check and guide to our advantage the selfishness of American demagogues." To this end, Langston campaigned for free-soil and later Republican candidates. But Langston maintained his radicalism, organizing in 1858 the black-governed Ohio State Anti-Slavery Society and supporting John Brown's ill-fated raid.

During the Civil War, Langston became a national figure, coordinating western recruitment for the 54th and 55th Massachusetts Regiments and for Ohio's 5th United States Colored Troops. At the 1864 National Black Convention in Syracuse, New York, the first such gathering to regard emancipation a reality, Langston was selected president of the newly formed National Equal Rights League. The league's constitution reflected Langston's own thoughts, advocating black self-improvement and equal citizenship. Langston subsequently toured the country, announcing that the "colored man is not content when given simple emancipation. . . . he demands absolute legal equality. . . . [and] the free and untrammelled use of the ballot." Langston welcomed Radical Reconstruction, receiving from Republican friends in 1867 dual appointments as educational inspector for the Freedmen's Bureau and political organizer among Southern blacks. In 1868 Langston established Howard University's law department, and he later served as the university's acting president until 1875. Throughout these years, Langston advanced Charles Sumner's Civil Rights Bill, arguing that blacks had yet to exercise their rights as equal citizens.

Langston's hope for an integrated America faded after Reconstruction, but he retained his Republican allegiance and was appointed minister to Haiti from 1877 to 1885. Langston returned to Virginia in 1885 and became president of the Virginia Normal and Collegiate Institute. Forced to resign by Virginia Democrats, Langston broke with local Republicans and ran as an independent for Congress in 1888. Defeated, Langston challenged the results and was declared victorious, though he served just three months before losing his bid for reelection.

Langston spent his final years in Washington, D.C., practicing law, writing his autobiography, and becoming doyen for the city's African-American elite. Langston's death in 1897 came quietly. His pursuit of legal equality now seemed misplaced in a nation whose highest court had one year earlier sanctioned the doctrine of "separate but equal."

—*Bruce E. Matthews*

See also Abolitionist Movement; Abolitionists; African-American Sailors U.S.A.; African-American Suffrage; Brown, John; Douglass, Frederick; Emancipation Proclamation; Free Soil Party; Freedmen's Bureau; Kansas-Nebraska Act; Radical Republicans; Republican Party; Sumner, Charles; United States Colored Troops.

For further reading
Cheek, William, and Aimee Lee Cheek. *John Mercer Langston and the Fight for Black Freedom, 1829–1865* (1989).
———. "John Mercer Langston: principle and politics." In *Black Leaders of the Nineteenth Century* (1988).
Langston, John Mercer. *From the Virginia Plantation to the National Capitol; or, The First and Only Negro Representative in Congress from the Old Dominion* (1894).
Ripley, C. Peter et al., eds. *The Black Abolitionist Papers* (1985–1992).

LAW, EVANDER MCIVOR
(1836–1920)
Confederate general

The son of Ezekiel Augustus Law and Sarah Elizabeth McIvor Law, Evander Law was born in Darlington, South Carolina. He was educated locally and at the South Carolina Military Academy. He studied and practiced law briefly before teaching for a year at the Citadel. He moved next to a teaching job at the King's Mountain Military Academy that had been founded by another South Carolina Military Academy graduate, Micah Jenkins. Law remained at King's Mountain from 1858 until 1860, when he moved to Tuskegee, Alabama, and opened a new military school.

Upon the secession of Alabama, Law raised a company of his students who elected him captain. After the formation of the Confederacy, he led his company down to join Confederate forces at Pensacola. Shortly thereafter, he was commissioned a lieutenant colonel of the 4th Alabama. He regiment was transferred to Virginia after the firing on Fort Sumter. He fought at First Bull Run on Henry House Hill, where he was wounded. He became the colonel of the 4th Alabama in October 1861.

Law led his regiment in the Peninsula campaign, where he fought under Stonewall Jackson. During this campaign, Law temporarily commanded William Whiting's brigade, and his unit was most conspicuous at Malvern Hill. Law fought at Second Bull Run, where he again commanded Whiting's brigade, making a charge on 29 August that netted 100 Union prisoners. At Antietam his command of the brigade around the Dunker Church earned him a promotion to brigadier general in October 1862.

At Fredericksburg as part of John Bell Hood's division, Law was commended for bravery by Hood. During that battle Law had a horse shot out from under him, but he continued to direct his brigade's actions on foot. As part of Hood's division at Gettysburg, Law led his brigade in the attack on Little Round Top on 2 July 1863. He was forced to assume command of the division before the end of the day because of the severe injury to Hood. Law later criticized Robert E. Lee for the plan of attack that day. In the late summer, Law went with Longstreet to join Braxton Bragg and fought at Chickamauga and Knoxville. At Chickamauga Law again took command of Hood's division.

Returning to the Army of Northern Virginia in the spring of 1864, Law was wounded at Cold Harbor. Upon his recovery, he transferred to Joseph Johnston's army in the Carolinas in February 1865 and commanded a cavalry brigade until his promotion to major general in March 1865. He surrendered with Johnston and was paroled.

After the war, Law lived briefly in South Carolina until moving back to Tuskegee for a few years and then to Florida in 1881. He founded a military school in Bartow, Florida, which he ran until 1903. He spent the remainder of his life in Bartow working as a journalist and educator. He died in 1920, reputedly the last living Confederate major general.

—*David S. Heidler and Jeanne T. Heidler*

See also Chickamauga, Battle of; Gettysburg, Battle of; Malvern Hill, Battle of.

For further reading:
Laine, J. Gray. *Law's Alabama Brigade in the War between the Union and the Confederacy* (1996).
Pfanz, Harry W. *Gettysburg The Second Day* (1987).

LAWLER, MICHAEL KELLY
(1814–1882)
Union general

Born in County Kildaire, Ireland, Michael Kelly Lawler moved to the United States with his parents when he was two years old. The family moved from New York City to Maryland and eventually to Gallatin County, Illinois, where Lawler spent most of his childhood. Reaching adulthood, he became a prominent local farmer and was active in the Illinois militia. Lawler served as a captain in Winfield Scott's Mexico City campaign during the Mexican-American War.

At the outbreak of the Civil War, Lawler helped to raise a regiment of state troops and in June 1861 was commissioned the colonel of the 18th Illinois. For the remainder of 1861 Lawler and the 18th operated in Missouri and Illinois, headquartered mainly at Cairo, Illinois. In early 1862 Lawler served under Ulysses S. Grant in the capture of Fort Henry and during the siege and capture of Fort Donelson, where Lawler was wounded.

Because of his wounds, Lawler missed the Shiloh campaign, but in the meantime he faced a court-martial for charges brought against him because of his methods of disciplining his troops. Although popular with many of his men, Lawler dealt with those he viewed as shirkers in an unorthodox fashion. When men did not perform their duties to Lawler's expectations, he beat them up. Nonetheless, he was acquitted in his court-martial.

Recovered by May 1862, Lawler led his regiment in the advance on Corinth, Mississippi. During the late summer and early fall of 1862, he operated along the Mississippi Central Railroad, skirmishing with Confederates near Medon Station and Britton's Lane, Tennessee. By that time, though still a colonel, he commanded a brigade. Working out of Medon Station, Lawler and his brigade operated primarily against guerrilla bands in the area. In October 1862 he participated in the battle of Corinth.

In early 1863 Lawler commanded the District of Jackson, Tennessee, skirmishing with Nathan Bedford Forrest near Clifton. Then in May during the Vicksburg campaign he fought at Port Gibson, seeing action at Thompson's Mill on 1 May. Later in the month he fought at Big Black River Bridge on 17 May after which he commanded his brigade in the siege of Vicksburg. During May, Lawler was promoted to brigadier general with the rank dating from 29 November 1862. Lawler served in John Alexander McClernand's XIII Corps, and

when that self-serving officer called a meeting of his officers in early June 1863 to have them pass resolutions praising their commander, Lawler, calling such actions unprofessional, refused to attend.

After the fall of Vicksburg, Lawler operated in Louisiana for the remainder of 1863 as a commander of a division in the Department of the Gulf. He was briefly in Texas early in 1864, operating out of Pass Cavallo, but was back in Louisiana by March. In spring 1864 he led his division in the Red River campaign and then operated out of Morganza, Louisiana, in the late spring and summer of the year. During part of May 1864, Lawler served as John Alexander McClernand's chief of staff, effectively commanding XIII Corps due to McClernand's bad health. From 30 May to 1 June he led an expedition out of Morganza that destroyed a bridge and a sawmill being used by Confederates.

In November 1864 Lawler was transferred to the White River near Memphis to serve under Major General J. J. Reynolds in the Military Division of West Mississippi. He did not remain in that command long before going on a leave of absence. Upon his return in February 1865, Lawler was transferred to the Department of the Gulf. As part of that department, he was given command of the District of Baton Rouge on 23 March. He held that command until the end of May 1865 when he was sent to New Orleans.

After leaving the army in 1866, Lawler remained for a while in Louisiana, but ultimately decided to return to farming in Illinois. He died at home near Equality, Illinois, on 26 July 1882.

—*David S. Heidler and Jeanne T. Heidler*

See also Big Black River; McClernand, John Alexander.
For further reading:
Crichton, Jane Wallace. "Michael Kelly Lawler, A Southern Illinois Mexican War Captain and Civil War General" (Master's thesis, 1965).

LAWRENCE, KANSAS

For the eastern Kansas town of Lawrence, the American Civil War was a transforming force. The war had both destructive and creative effects. On the one hand, Lawrence was on the receiving end of one of the most atrocious acts of the Civil War. On the other hand, during the war, Lawrence's population boomed, citizens prospered, a free African-American community was established, and an economic future began to emerge.

The destructive force of the war struck with a vengeance on 21 August 1863. For a number of reasons Lawrence was an attractive target for William Clarke Quantrill and other pro-Confederate guerrillas. Settled in 1854, Lawrence became a center of Kansas Free-Soil activity. The town was the focus of antislavery activities. It served as a station on the Underground Railroad, and local citizens organized and conducted several raids against proslavery forces before 1861. At the outbreak of the Civil War, the town became an important recruiting center for Union volunteers and was the headquarters of antislavery leader James Henry Lane, governor of the territory Charles Robinson, and the Red Legs (a Unionist band of bushwhackers). Lane and his followers conducted raids against Confederate sympathizers in Missouri and returned to Lawrence with stolen goods, stolen horses, and liberated slaves. For Quantrill and others, these were ample justifications to target Lawrence citizens and their property.

Early in the war, citizens responded to this assumption by forming home guard units to protect the town. But with no attack, apathy was pervasive by the summer of 1863. After rumors of a planned raid circulated in the summer of 1863, patrols returned and a handful of Union troops arrived, but by mid-August this heightened state of readiness was relaxed. When Quantrill and 450 men on horseback approached Lawrence at dawn on 21 August, they had the benefit of complete surprise. With most military firearms stored in the armory, there was little armed resistance.

Mounted and well-armed, the invaders broke into small bands and quickly spread throughout the town. Among their first targets was a camp of African-American Federal recruits. While many escaped, a dozen were killed before they could return fire. During their four-hour reign of terror, the raiders shot every adult male they encountered but did not rape or kill any women. Additional damages included the robbing of banks, the looting of stores and homes, the systematic burning of homes and businesses, and the theft of whiskey, jewelry, and other property. Quantrill left behind a wake of death and destruction that can be quantified as follows: between 150 and 200 dead, 30 wounded, 200 burned buildings and homes, and $2.5 million in total damages. Lawrence Congregational minister Richard Cordley witnessed the aftermath of Quantrill's violent raid and recorded the following scene of horror: "The buildings on Massachusetts street were all burned....The fires were still glowing in the cellars. The brick and stone walls were still standing bare and blackened. The dead lay along the street, some of them so charred that they could not be recognized, and could scarcely be taken up....As [I] passed along the street, the sickening odor of burning flesh was oppressive."

Lawrence did survive Quantrill's raid and quite remarkably found its future during the war years. Federal spending for agricultural products (especially corn and wheat), livestock, and war supplies created unprecedented prosperity in this frontier town and the surrounding countryside. In 1864 the Union Pacific Railroad reached the town and connected it to eastern markets. The same year, the University of Kansas was founded. The direction of the town's economic future as an important trade and education center was thus established during the Civil War.

Wartime prosperity drew many and the population soared from 2,000 to 3,000. Attracted by Lawrence's reputation as the center of abolitionism and by abundant jobs, a significant number of African-Americans settled in Lawrence during the war. The majority were newly freed slaves from Missouri. The freedmen and freedwomen established a thriving African-American community, including a school, and gained the grudging respect of whites by enlisting in the Union army and working as laborers and craftspeople. Lawrence's experience mirrors the paradoxical consequences of the nation as a whole with both destruction and creativity existing side by side.

—*Bruce D. Mactavish*

See also Kansas; Lane, James Henry; Quantrill, William Clarke; Robinson, Charles.
For further reading:

Castel, Albert. *Civil War Kansas: Reaping the Whirlwind* (1958; reprint, 1997).
Cordley, Richard. *History of Lawrence, Kansas, from the First Settlement to the Close of the Rebellion* (1895).
Leslie, Edward E. *The Devil Knows How to Ride: The True Story of William Clarke Quantrill and His Confederate Raiders* (1996).

LAWTON, ALEXANDER ROBERT
(1818–1896)
Confederate quartermaster general

Born on 4 November 1818 to Alexander James and Martha Lawton near Robertville, South Carolina, Alexander Robert Lawton attended the Black Swamp Academy for early schooling. In 1835 he was appointed to West Point Military Academy and graduated thirteenth in a class of thirty-nine in 1839. Among his classmates was Henry W. Halleck, future general in the Union army. Lawton was commissioned first lieutenant in the U.S. Artillery and spent several months in tedious garrison duty on the U.S.–Canadian border. Disillusioned with the military, he retired his commission in 1840 and matriculated at Harvard Law School. Admitted to the bar in 1843, he opened a legal office in Savannah, Georgia.

In Savannah, he met and married Sarah Hillhouse Alexander of Washington, Georgia, sister of future Confederate artillerist Edward Porter Alexander. On 5 November 1845, they wed in her home and took up residence in Savannah. Lawton maintained his legal career there and in 1849 became president of the new Augusta & Savannah Railroad. After serving a term as alderman for the city, he was elected to the Georgia House of Representatives in 1855, as a Southern Democrat.

Lawton had already been a lieutenant in the Savannah militia when in 1852 he was promoted to colonel. He was elected to the Georgia Senate in 1860,

but he found his militia duties more compelling as secession threatened. On 3 January 1861, before the state seceded, he was ordered by Governor Joseph Brown to seize strategic Fort Pulaski; this initiated the first overt act against Federal authority and, because it came before secession, it constituted treason, as Lawton regretted. On 26 January 1861, he seized Oglethorpe Barracks, another Federal installation in Savannah. He was commissioned brigadier general in the Confederate State Provisional Army on 13 April 1861 and placed in command of Savannah, Fort Pulaski, and coastal Georgia.

On 28 May 1862, Lawton was ordered to Virginia with a brigade of six regiments. As part of "Stonewall" Jackson's force, he fought in the Peninsula campaign and at Second Bull Run. When General Richard S. Ewell was wounded at the latter battle, Lawton was given command of the division. In Maryland in September 1862, he participated in the reduction of Harper's Ferry and with Jackson's exhausted force moved to join Robert E. Lee at Sharpsburg. There on the evening of 16 September, his division relieved John Bell Hood's division in the Cornfield and East Woods. The next morning, his force was almost annihilated when Union general Joseph Hooker's corps attacked. Lawton was badly wounded.

After recovering from his injury, Lawton requested another field assignment. Instead, Confederate president Jefferson Davis appointed him quartermaster general of the Confederacy, where he served nobly in spite of dwindling resources. When Richmond fell in 1865, Lawton fled with Davis to Washington, Georgia. After the war, he resumed his law practice in Savannah. In 1887, he was appointed minister to Austria, where he stayed until retirement in 1889. He died 2 July 1896, the last survivor of his West Point graduating class.

—*G. Judson Smith, Jr.*

See also Quartermaster; Savannah, Georgia.
For further reading:
Smith, G. Judson, Jr. "The Life of Alexander Robert Lawton" (M.A. thesis, 1995).

LECOMPTON CONSTITUTION
(1857–1858)

The Lecompton Constitution was a bold attempt by a proslavery minority in Kansas Territory, with the support of President James Buchanan and Southern Democrats, to bring Kansas into the Union as a slave state. Efforts in 1857 and 1858 to force the adoption of the Lecompton Constitution not only failed to establish a slave state but they also widened the growing divide within the Democratic Party over the issue of slavery in the territories. The episode weakened support for the Democratic Party in the North, proved to many that Popular Sovereignty was unworkable, and confirmed a pattern of fraud and corruption in Kansas politics.

When Buchanan entered office in 1857, he held high hopes for moving Kansas Territory smoothly through the process of statehood. His plan called for the election of delegates to a constitutional convention, creation of a constitution, ratification by voters, and approval by Congress. From the start, the political process was plagued by partisanship, widespread fraud, and the environment of violence and intimidation that was bleeding Kansas.

In February 1857 the proslavery legislature met and scheduled for June the election of delegates for a constitutional convention to be held in September. The legislature stipulated that local officials, all of whom were proslavery, would be responsible for conducting a fair election and that the constitution would not be submitted to voters. Free-state citizens, who now outnumbered proslavery supporters two or three to one, newly appointed governor William Walker, and to a lesser degree Buchanan were angered by these and other stipulations. Actions by the proslavery minority to achieve a victory compromised the integrity of the process and led free-state supporters to boycott the June elections. Only 2,200 of 9,250 eligible voters participated and elected delegates firmly committed to the protection and expansion of slavery in Kansas Territory. The Lecompton convention began its work in September.

In October, elections for the territorial legislature were held. Although returns initially gave victories to proslavery candidates, fraud on the part of proslavery activists was uncovered. When Governor Walker threw out almost 3,000 ballots, free-state representatives gained a majority and control of the legislature. Walker's actions to correct election fraud were severely criticized by proslavery Kansans and Southerners.

Delegates completed their work in November 1857. The Lecompton Constitution was partly a conventional state constitution as well as a document that reflected the views of the proslavery minority. To protect slavery in the face of a booming free-soil population, it prohibited adding amendments for seven years. The constitution also included a twenty-year residency requirement for all governors, excluded free blacks, and guaranteed protection of the property rights of slave owners. In a bow to heavy pressure from Democrats in Congress, delegates reversed themselves and added a provision whereby an extremely narrow issue would be given to Kansas voters for their approval. In essence this referendum required voters to favor either limited slavery, which meant that only the 200 slaves in Kansas and their progeny could remain, or unlimited slavery. The proposed Lecompton Constitution outraged Kansas free staters and a growing number of Northern voters.

In late 1857 and early 1858 two competing referendums were held in Kansas Territory. The results further divided Kansas and sparked controversy in Congress. In December 1857 the proslavery referendum was submitted to voters. With Free Soilers boycotting, it was approved with unlimited slavery by a margin of 6,226 (2,720 of which were later thrown out) to 569. In January, the free-state legislature held a referendum in which proslavery voters refused to participate. In this vote, 10,226 Kansans rejected the constitution while fewer than 200 approved of it.

Despite clear evidence that a large majority in Kansas Territory were against the Lecompton Constitution, in February 1858, Buchanan sent it to Congress with his strong endorsement. Opposition was led by Democratic senator from Illinois Stephen Douglas. The battle in the Senate featured lengthy speeches and heated debate, a Senate chamber fistfight involving dozens of senators, and a Democratic Party increasingly at war with itself. Due largely to overwhelming pressure and numerous promises from the Buchanan administration, the Senate approved the Lecompton Constitution on 23 March by a thirty-three to twenty-five margin. The outcome was different in the House. On 1 April, after a fierce battle and by a 120 to 112 vote the Lecompton Constitution was rejected. Kansas entered the Union in January 1861 as a free state.

The battle over Lecompton had a significant impact on U.S. politics. President Buchanan and his administration never regained their influence. Northern Democrats joined with Republicans to wrestle control of the House of Representatives from the hands of Southerners. A unified Republican Party took advantage of the sectional split within the Democratic Party and won the presidency in 1860.

—*Bruce D. Mactavish*

See also Buchanan, James; Democratic Party; Douglas, Stephen Arnold; Kansas.

For further reading:

Johannsen, Robert W. "The Lecompton Constitutional Convention: An Analysis of Its Membership." *Kansas Historical Quarterly* (1957).
Potter, David M. *The Impending Crisis: 1848–1861* (1976).
Stampp, Kenneth M. *America in 1857: A Nation on the Brink* (1990).

LEDLIE, JAMES HEWETT
(1832–1882)
Union general

Born in Utica, New York, James Hewett Ledlie attended Union College, where he studied engineering. Before the Civil War, he worked as a construction engineer in the railroad industry. At the outbreak of the war, he helped raise a New York infantry regiment, some of which was transferred to the artillery. He received his commission as major in the 3d New York Artillery on 22 May 1861. He became the regiment's lieutenant colonel by the fall and its colonel and commander by the end of the year.

Sent to North Carolina, Ledlie and the 3d served as part of the Department of North Carolina under Ambrose Burnside in the early months of 1862. With Burnside's departure in the spring of 1862, Ledlie and his regiment remained on the coast of North Carolina, headquartered at New Bern. In December 1862, Ledlie became the commander of the department's artillery brigade and Major General John G. Foster's chief of artillery. In the same month upon receiving this command, Ledlie led his artillery brigade on an expedition from New Bern to Goldsborough, North Carolina. He was promoted to brigadier general on 24 December 1862, but the Senate did not confirm the promotion and hence it expired. He was promoted again in the fall of 1863 and this time was confirmed.

Ledlie remained in this command until the end of October 1863, when he was sent to Fort Monroe. As part of the Department of Virginia and North Carolina under the command of Benjamin F. Butler, Ledlie commanded the District of Currituck, North Carolina, until February 1864. Transferred to the Army of the Potomac, Ledlie was given command of a brigade in his old commander Ambrose Burnside's IX Corps. On 7 June 1864, Ledlie succeeded to the command of the 1st Division of IX Corps, and on 17 June, Ledlie led his division in some of the early assaults on Petersburg, Virginia.

Up to this point in Ledlie's Civil War career, he had neither been excessively praised for his battlefield leadership nor condemned. He was simply one of many average, perhaps even mediocre, generals of the war. This was soon to change, and not for the better, as far as Ledlie's military reputation was concerned.

At the end of July, Ledlie's division was designated as one of the lead elements for the attack against Confederate lines after the explosion that resulted in the Crater. His men became hopelessly bogged down in their attack because of the walls that the explosion had produced, some as high as thirty feet. As a result, all the units behind the division also could not advance. If Ledlie had been with his men, directing the attack and even calling for scaling ladders, his military reputation may have been saved even in defeat. However, he had positioned himself far to the rear in a bombproof enclosure and was rumored to be drinking heavily at the time of the debacle.

The court of inquiry that looked into the disaster at the Crater blamed many officers, most especially the commander of IX Corps, Ambrose Burnside. Ledlie, however, did not escape his share of blame. Although he was not officially punished for his behavior, Ledlie was found in neglect of duty for his conduct. From that point on, Ulysses S. Grant refused to place Ledlie in any position of responsibility. Not really having anything to do,

Ledlie obtained a medical leave of absence in August 1864. Upon his return to duty, he was still without real employment. Finally, in December he was ordered to return to his home in New York to await further orders. A follow-up note from the Army of the Potomac commander George Gordon Meade informed Ledlie that Grant had stated that he would not allow him another command in the army. As a result, Ledlie resigned his commission in January 1865.

Upon his resignation, Ledlie returned to his lucrative engineering activities. Over the next years he worked on a number of projects for the Union Pacific Railroad. He also worked for a while in Chicago designing harbor improvements. He died on Staten Island, New York, on 15 August 1882.

—David S. Heidler and Jeanne T. Heidler

See also Burnside, Ambrose Everett; Crater, Battle of the.
For further reading:
Pleasants, Henry, Jr. *The Tragedy of the Crater* (1938).
Trudeau, Noah Andre. *The Last Citadel: Petersburg, Virginia, June 1864–April 1865* (1991).

LEE, FITZHUGH
(1835–1905)
Confederate general

Born in Fairfax County, Virginia, on 19 November 1835, Fitzhugh Lee was the eldest of six sons and one daughter (the latter dying in infancy) of Sydney Smith Lee and Ann Maria Mason. The young Lee spent his early years living at Clermont, his maternal grandfather's home in Alexandria, Virginia, and attended private school in that vicinity and later the secondary school at Timothy's Hall in Catonsville, Maryland. In 1852, at age sixteen he secured an appointment to the U.S. Military Academy at West Point. Considering his family's martial tradition, it was not surprising that Lee eagerly took this route.

Fitzhugh's father, Sydney Smith Lee, had had a distinguished career in the U.S. Navy for over forty years. His active sea duty included command of a streamer at Vera Cruz during the Mexican-American War, and later, with the rank of commander, commanded Commodore Matthew C. Perry's flagship during the latter's historic visit to Japan in 1853. Before the outbreak of the Civil War, Sydney Smith Lee did a three-year tour as commandant of the Naval Academy in Annapolis, Maryland. He served another three years as the superintendent of the Philadelphia Navy Yard, and he served as chief of the Bureau of the Coast Survey at Washington, D.C. He resigned this last position to join the newly formed Southern Confederacy.

Besides his father, Fitzhugh Lee was inclined toward the military life by the example and reputation of his father's brother, Robert E. Lee, one of the rising stars in the pre–Civil War U.S. Army. Finally, the young Lee took great pride in knowing that his grandfather, General Henry "Light Horse Harry" Lee—the legendary American partisan leader of the Revolutionary War—had also been an accomplished military man.

Lee—called "Fitz" by friends and family all his life—graduated from West Point in 1856, ranked forty-fifth in a class numbering forty-nine. His class standing was based on the fact that his school work reflected his love of reading novels, which left little time for him to pursue the Academy's prescribed course of study. Furthermore, Lee indulged, for four years at West Point, in missing bed checks, laughing and dancing during drills and parades, and showing slight regard for authority and discipline. Nevertheless, his excellence in cavalry tactics and horsemanship revealed that he could be a valuable asset to that arm of the service.

From graduation to 1858, Lee was assigned as an instructor of recruits at the Cavalry School, Carlisle Barracks, in Carlisle, Pennsylvania. He was next posted to Texas with the 2d Cavalry Regiment. On 13 May 1859, the young officer was among the cavalry scouts who chased about 2,000 Comanche and Kiowa Indians in the area of the Washita River. In the fight that ensued, Lee was shot under his arm and through both lungs by an enemy arrow. Despite his severe injury, he stayed on the battlefield until the action was over. It took three months for his dangerous wound to heal. Upon his recovery, Lee was ordered to report to West Point as an instructor of cavalry. He was then a first lieutenant.

With the start of the Civil War in April 1861, Lee resigned his U.S. Army commission to join his native state and the Confederacy. His first duties found him acting as a staff officer first under General P. G. T. Beauregard and then under General Richard S. Ewell during the First Bull Run campaign. By March 1862 he was a part of J. E. B. Stuart's cavalry command and a full colonel of the 1st Virginia Cavalry Regiment. Distinguished service in scouting, in rearguard duty during the rebel retreat from Yorktown, and in Stuart's raid around the Union army in June of that year earned him promotion to brigadier general.

As leader of a mounted brigade, Lee saw action at Second Bull Run and at Antietam and led successful raids into enemy territory during the winter of 1862–1863. During the Chancellorsville campaign, he led Thomas J. "Stonewall" Jackson's flanking force on its daring move around Union general Joseph Hooker's Army of the Potomac. Missing the cavalry battle of Brandy Station on 9 June 1863 due to serious rheumatoid arthritis, he participated in the Gettysburg campaign, fighting in almost every action of that epic series of battles from mid-June to its conclusion on 14 July 1863.

Promoted to major general, to date from 3 August 1863, Lee was given command of a cavalry division of the Army of Northern Virginia and led it through all the actions of the remainder of 1863 into 1864. During the Wilderness campaign Lee prevented the Federal army from taking Spotsylvania Court House and thus flanking the Army of Northern Virginia. After Stuart's mortal wounding at Yellow Tavern on 11 May 1864, Lee shared command of the cavalry corps with Wade Hampton during the cavalry fights at Hawe's Shop and Trevilian Station.

Transferred in August 1864 to the Shenandoah Valley as General Jubal Early's chief of cavalry, he participated in the battle of Third Winchester (19 September 1864), in which he was wounded in the thigh and rendered unfit for duty for the next several months.

Placed in charge of the cavalry of the Army of Northern Virginia in January 1865, Lee's command was part of the defeated Confederate force at the battle of Five Forks. With the surrender of the Southern army under Lee's uncle, Robert E Lee, at Appomattox, the younger Lee retired to his home in Stafford County, Virginia, and later to Alexandria.

The postwar years were kind to Fitzhugh Lee. He was governor of Virginia from 1885 to 1890 and then the president of the Pittsburgh & Virginia Railroad. After Lee's defeat for a seat in the U.S. Senate, President Grover Cleveland appointed him consul general to Cuba in 1896. Made a major general of volunteers during the 1898 war with Spain, he was appointed military governor of Havana at end of those hostilities.

Fitzhugh Lee retired from the army in 1901 with the rank of brigadier general. General Lee died in Washington, D.C., on 28 April 1905 and is buried at the Hollywood Cemetery, Richmond.

—*Arnold D. Blumberg*

See also Chancellorsville, Battle of; Gettysburg, Battle of; Spotsylvania Court House, Battle of.

For further reading:

Evans, Clement, A., ed. *Confederate Military History: A Library of Confederate States History* (1899; reprint 1992).

Freeman, Douglas Southall. *Lee's Lieutenants: A Study in Command* (1942–1944).

Goode, John. *Recollections of a Lifetime* (1906).

Nichols, James Lynn. *General Fitzhugh Lee: A Biography* (1989).

LEE, GEORGE WASHINGTON CUSTIS
(1832–1913)
Confederate general

Born to Robert Edward Lee and Mary Custis Lee at Fort Monroe, Virginia, George Washington Custis Lee was educated at various boarding schools in Virginia to prepare him to follow in his father's footsteps at the United States Military Academy. As the oldest son from a marriage of two prominent Virginia families, Lee was inculcated with a high sense of duty to his parents and his state. When he was unable to gain admission to West Point at the age of sixteen, his father arranged for his educational emphases to change to more technical subjects. After his father wrote personally to the commanding general of the army, Winfield Scott, for intervention on his son's behalf, the younger Lee gained admission in 1850 at the age of seventeen.

During his first year at West Point, Custis Lee, as he was known to the family, excelled in his academic and military pursuits, but toward the end of that first year he was almost expelled when liquor was found in his room. He claimed that he had not put the liquor in the room and escaped with only a minor punishment. He continued to do well in his second year, and at the beginning of his third year, his father was appointed superintendent of the academy, thus bringing his entire family to West Point for his final two years. Custis Lee graduated first of forty-six in the class of 1854, the same class of his friend J. E. B. Stuart.

Like his father, Lee went into the Corps of Engineers and served at a variety of posts, including California, for the remainder of the decade. Stationed in Washington, D.C., during the secession and Fort Sumter crises, Lee resigned his commission on 2 May 1861, about two weeks after his father had done so, and offered his services to the state forces of Virginia commanded by his father. He served in the state forces until July 1861, when he was given a captain's commission in the Confederate army. Through the months of July and August 1861 he worked as part of the Confederate engineer corps that constructed fortifications in and around the new capital city of Richmond. At the end of August, he was offered and accepted the position of aide-de-camp to Confederate president Jefferson Davis. He was promoted to colonel of the Confederate cavalry for his new position.

Lee served as Davis's aide for more than three years and during that time became a close confidante of the Confederate president. He spent much of his time in Richmond, but because Davis relied on him for accurate and sometimes immediate reports on the military situation of the Confederate army, he was often sent on missions to determine strength and readiness and then returned to report to Davis. These missions took him to such places as Norfolk in the early fall of 1861 and then to carry reinforcements to coastal North Carolina in October 1861. Because Davis liked to maintain frequent contact with his commanders, once Robert E. Lee assumed command of the Army of Northern Virginia on 1 June 1862, Custis Lee frequently was able to visit with his father in the field. Through such visits, the elder Lee was able to maintain more constant contact with his wife and daughters, who spent most of the war in Richmond. During the Peninsula campaign in June 1862 and under his father's direction, Custis Lee was given the job of supervising the engineers who placed obstructions in the James River at Drewry's Bluff.

In spite of the importance of his position and his advancement to brigadier general in June 1863, Lee began to chafe at the relative inactivity of an aide's job. He was discouraged from taking a field command by Davis, who appreciated Lee's loyalty and quiet efficiency, but at the same time encouraged by his father who suggested he would never gain confidence as a field commander until he actually held such a position. Nevertheless Custis hesitated, apparently afraid of failure, and until the end of the war never seriously sought a real field command.

Still he had brief opportunities during the war to demonstrate his military abilities. During the Gettysburg campaign he commanded part of the cavalry force left to defend Richmond, and the following year in May 1864, with Ulysses S. Grant moving down from the north and Benjamin Butler a threat along the James River, Lee was placed in command of Richmond's local defense. Forced to rely primarily on government clerks and workers from industries in Richmond, Lee mounted such a competent defensive network that in the middle of June 1864 he was sent to take charge of the city's eastern defenses at Chaffin's Bluff. In July, his makeshift brigade was placed in the corps of Richard Ewell.

Lee remained at Chaffin's Bluff throughout most of the remaining months of the war and in October 1864 was promoted to major general and given command of a division there. On constant alert for a Union attack in that quarter, Lee remained at this position until ordered to evacuate as part of the general Confederate retreat on 2 April 1865. He participated in the fighting retreat away from Richmond and Petersburg. His division was surrounded at Sayler's Creek on 6 April, and he was forced to surrender.

After gaining his parole, Lee came to Richmond where he lived with his parents and sisters. He sought and gained a position teaching engineering at the Virginia Military Institute (VMI) and for a time lived again with his parents in Lexington, his father having been appointed president of Washington College there. Even after moving out of his parents' house, the younger Lee continued to come almost daily to visit and dine there. Lee remained at VMI and upon his father's death in 1870, at which Custis was present, assumed his father's position as president of Washington College. He remained there until retirement in 1897, and during his time in office inaugurated several funding and curricular reforms. He retired to a home in Fairfax County, not far from the former family estate of Arlington, which he had inherited from his grandfather, George Washington Parke Custis, but had never taken possession of before it was confiscated by the Federal government. He died at his home in Fairfax County on 18 February 1913.

—*David S. Heidler and Jeanne T. Heidler*

See also Davis, Jefferson; Lee, Robert Edward; Sayler's Creek,

Battle of.
For further reading:
Freeman, Douglas Southall. *R. E. Lee: A Biography* (1934).
Thomas, Emory. *Robert E. Lee: A Biography* (1995).

LEE, ROBERT EDWARD
(1807–1870)
Confederate general

Robert Edward Lee was born on 19 January 1807 at Stratford Hall, Virginia, the third son and fifth child of Henry "Light-Horse Harry" Lee and Ann Hill Carter Lee. His father had been a hero of the Revolutionary War and governor of Virginia and uncles and other relatives had signed the Declaration of Independence, served in Congress, and otherwise achieved notable reputations.

Henry Lee's fiscal irresponsibility caused the family to move to Alexandria, Virginia, in 1811. When Robert was six, his father left for the West Indies and never returned. Much of Robert's later life can be read as an attempt to avoid the personal and financial recklessness that had plagued Light Horse Harry and brought much unhappiness to his family.

Ann Carter Lee instilled in Robert a strong sense of duty and a belief that the qualities of a gentleman do not depend on monetary fortune. With few financial resources, the family settled on a career in the army for Robert. Political connections helped secure an appointment to West Point, and in June 1825 Lee set out to begin his career as a soldier.

Lee's time at West Point and during his early years in the army revealed patterns that would be evident during the remainder of his professional life. He worked hard, held himself to the most rigorous standards of performance and behavior, and won the admiration of peers and superiors. He ranked second in his class at graduation in 1829 and along with five classmates completed four years at the academy with no demerits.

Apart from his exceptional academic record and conduct, Lee also exhibited qualities of leadership at West Point. Fellow cadets referred to him as the "Marble Model"—a nickname that probably reflected some envy as well as admiration. Just under six feet tall, handsome, and with black hair and brown eyes, Lee cut a striking figure. High class ranking entitled him to enter the Engineer Corps as a second lieutenant on 1 July 1829.

More than a decade and half passed before Lee saw a battlefield. Promotions to first lieutenant on 21 September 1836, and to captain on 7 July 1838, punctuated this long stretch of peacetime service. Postings took him from Fort Pulaski, under construction on Cockspur Island near Savannah, Georgia (1829–1831), to Fort Monroe (1831–1834), to Washington, D.C. (1834–1837), to St. Louis (1837–1841), and to Fort

Hamilton in New York harbor (1841–1846; a five-year assignment interrupted by a short return to Washington in 1844).

Shortly after reaching Fort Monroe, Lee traveled to Arlington, where on 30 June 1831, he married Mary Anna Randolph Custis. The only daughter of George Washington Parke Custis, himself the grandson of Martha Washington, Mary Anna and Lee would share a thirty-nine-year marriage that produced four daughters and three sons.

Marriage gave Lee noteworthy ties to George Washington and the many Washington relics carefully preserved at Arlington. He looked to Washington as a model and sought to emulate him throughout his life. The Confederate people later would compare the two Virginians, viewing the Army of Northern Virginia and its commander as the bulwark of their struggle for independence much as the American colonists had looked to Washington and the Continental Army as theirs.

In the mid-1840s, the United States and Mexico edged toward a conflict that would bring promotions to many officers. On 13 May 1846, the United States Congress declared war. Lee watched events unfold from his post at Fort Hamilton and on 19 August received orders to report to Washington, whence he would depart for San Antonio, Texas, and assignment as assistant engineer with the American force commanded by General John E. Wool. After a relatively uneventful period with Wool in northern Mexico, Lee was instructed in mid-January 1847 to join General Winfield Scott's army then preparing to invade Mexico via Vera Cruz. Scott immediately formed a favorable impression of his new staff officer, adding Lee to his "little cabinet," a group of subordinates who advised him on tactical and engineering questions.

Two months after joining Scott, Lee went ashore at Vera Cruz with the invading Americans. Between March and September 1847, Scott conducted a brilliant campaign from Vera Cruz to Mexico City that ended with the capture of the Mexican capital. Lee performed exemplary service throughout these operations, including a daring three-hour crossing of the Pedregal—a lava bed of jagged rocks and deep fissures—to deliver a critical message to army headquarters prior to the battle of Churubusco. General Scott called Lee's trip across the Pedregal "the greatest feat of physical and moral courage performed by any individual" during the entire campaign, and Lee's exploits in Mexico brought brevets for gallantry to the ranks of major, lieutenant colonel, and colonel. More important, he impressed influential officers—none more so than Winfield Scott, who, recorded one officer, came away from Mexico with an "almost idolatrous fancy for Lee."

Scott's audacious offensive against the Mexican capital taught Lee lessons about how a smaller army can

Robert E. Lee in 1863
(Photograph by Julian Vannerson / *Library of Congress*)

overcome numerical odds, how turning movements can discomfit a foe, and how frontal assaults sometimes can succeed. Fifteen years hence, when at the helm of a much larger and more famous army, Lee would apply these lessons (though he would lose a far higher percentage of his soldiers in battle).

Lee returned from Mexico as a hero but soon resumed a familiar routine of peacetime engineering work. He labored overseeing the construction of Fort Carroll at Baltimore before assuming the superintendency of the United States Military Academy on 1 September 1852. During his tenure at the academy, Lee oversaw changes in the curriculum and the addition of a fifth year to the traditional four-year course of study.

Promotion and transfer to a line command ended Lee's time at West Point. On 3 March 1855, Congress expanded the army by four regiments, and Lee was offered the lieutenant colonelcy, to rank from that day, of the new 2d Cavalry.

Nearly six years with the 2d Cavalry yielded more low than high moments for Lee. He spent March 1856 to October 1857 and February 1860 to February 1861 with

the regiment in Texas, where he periodically pursued Comanches and was often assigned to court-martial duty.

George Washington Parke Custis's death in October 1857 saddled Lee with the task of settling a complicated estate. He returned to Arlington during a series of leaves in 1857–1860, and in late October 1859 chanced to be there when John Brown mounted his raid on Harper's Ferry. Summoned to the War Department on 17 October, Lee quickly proceeded to Harper's Ferry with a detachment of Marines. On the morning of the 18th, he orchestrated the capture of Brown and later gave testimony in an investigation of Brown's raid before traveling west to assume command of the Department of Texas. Lee monitored escalating sectional tensions in 1860–1861, reporting to Winfield Scott in Washington shortly after Texas seceded from the Union on 1 February 1861.

The national crisis deepened soon after Lee's return to Virginia. Jefferson Davis headed a new Confederate government in Montgomery, Alabama, and tensions intensified over Fort Sumter in Charleston harbor. Lee's promotion to colonel of the 1st Cavalry came on 16 March. In the meantime, the Confederacy offered him a brigadier generalcy. Lee apparently did not respond to the Confederate offer but on 30 March accepted the colonelcy.

The final storm broke in mid-April. Confederates fired on Fort Sumter on the 12th, the Federal garrison capitulated on the 14th, and Lincoln issued a call on the 15th for 75,000 volunteers to suppress the rebellion. On 18 April, Lee was offered command of the army being raised to put down the rebellion. He declined with the explanation that he opposed secession but could not take the field against the Southern states.

Powerful emotions must have pulled at Lee as he pondered his future. Word of Virginia's secession appeared in the newspapers on 19 April, and the next day Lee composed a one-sentence letter of resignation from the United States Army. He also wrote a much longer letter to Winfield Scott on the 20th, acknowledging his debt for "the kindness & consideration" the general habitually had shown him. There followed one of the most famous statements Lee ever penned: "Save in the defense of my native State, I never desire again to draw my sword."

Although this decision pained him deeply, Lee could have chosen no other course. Undoubted affection for a Union that had sprung from the efforts of George Washington and other revolutionary figures gave way to the stronger ties of family and place. As a member of the slaveholding aristocracy of Virginia and the South, Lee's sense of honor dictated that he stand with those of his blood, class, and section.

The United States War Department took five days to process Lee's resignation, which became official on 25 April. By then he had been offered command of Virginia's military forces with the rank of major general, and on 23 April he accepted his native state's call. The new major general spent a feverish six weeks organizing resources to defend Virginia's borders. By the end of May, more than forty thousand Virginians were under arms.

Political developments kept pace with military preparations. The Confederate Congress voted on 21 May to move the newly proclaimed republic's capital from Montgomery to Richmond. On 8 June, Governor John Letcher transferred to the Confederacy all the volunteers who had been mustered into Virginia's service. Shortly thereafter, Lee's service as a major general of state forces ended and his career as a Confederate officer began.

Lee embarked on a year marked more by frustration and trial than public acclaim. He was appointed a Confederate brigadier general on 14 May, and two days later Congress authorized his advancement to the rank of full general (he would not be confirmed in the latter rank until 31 August 1861, at which time he became the third ranking officer in the Confederate army behind Samuel Cooper and Albert Sidney Johnston). Lee remained in Richmond as a military adviser to the president and chafed at his relative inactivity. "My movements are very uncertain," he confessed to his wife on 24 June, "& I wish to take the field as soon as certain arrangements can be made." He watched from a distance as Confederates under P. G. T. Beauregard and Joseph E. Johnston won the battle of First Manassas on 21 July.

On 28 July, President Davis directed Lee to coordinate the defense of western Virginia. Federals had established a menacing presence west of Staunton at Cheat Mountain; farther southwest, they also stood poised to move through the Kanawha Valley. Lee formulated a plan—undoubtedly too optimistic considering the situation and the personalities involved—to push the Federals westward toward the Ohio River. Awful weather, bad roads, poor subordinate leadership, and Lee's overly complex plan contributed to ignominious failure in September and October. On 30 October, he departed from western Virginia, a majority of whose citizens had voted six days earlier to separate from Virginia and create a new state loyal to the Union.

The campaign in western Virginia seriously diminished Lee's military reputation. The best that could be said was that he had prevented further Union advances in the region and protected the railroads. Such meager accomplishment failed to satisfy fellow Confederates who yearned for decisive success on the battlefield. Influential Richmond newspaper editor Edward A. Pollard spoke for many others in terming the Lee of September and October 1861 "a general who had never fought a battle and whose extreme tenderness of blood induced him to depend exclusively upon the resources of strategy, to essay the achievement of victories without the cost of life."

Shortly after the close of the campaign in western Virginia, Davis named Lee to head a new department encompassing the coastal regions of South Carolina, Georgia, and eastern Florida. Lee spent the next four months constructing a defensive line along the coast—work that showed his engineering and administrative skills and rendered the area better able to resist northern incursions. His efforts along the South Atlantic coast convinced him that many white Southerners had not made the requisite commitment to win their independence. "It is so very hard to get anything done," he confided to Mary Lee in early February 1862, "& while all wish well & mean well, it is so difficult to get them to act energetically & promptly."

In early March 1862, Lee returned to Richmond where, under Davis's direction, he would manage "the conduct of military operations in the armies of the Confederacy." It was another desk job, this time as principal military adviser to the president, and Lee informed his wife that he saw neither "pleasure or advantage in the duties."

Although lacking real power, Lee helped mold Southern military policy over the next ten weeks. He threw his full weight behind a national conscription act, which he considered essential if the Confederacy were to make the most of its limited pool of manpower. Lee dismissed arguments that state rights should come before the central government's war-making needs. The conscription act passed by Congress on 16 April 1862, marked a crucial step toward maintaining a protracted resistance against the North.

Growing Federal threats in Virginia occupied much of Lee's attention. By mid-April, George B. McClellan had placed his 100,000-man Army of the Potomac on the peninsula below Richmond. Another 60,000 Federals spread in a great arc from Fredericksburg, across the Shenandoah Valley, and into the Alleghenies. At Lee's suggestion, Davis instructed Joseph Johnston to concentrate his strength opposite McClellan on the peninsula. Lee then formulated a strategic offensive that would deny McClellan reinforcements from Federal forces north and northwest of Richmond. He entrusted execution of this strategy to Stonewall Jackson, who responded with his famous Valley campaign of May and June 1862.

Meanwhile, McClellan's host moved inexorably closer to Richmond. On 31 May, Johnston ordered assaults against the Army of the Potomac at Seven Pines, just five miles from the capital, in a battle that continued the next day. Indecisive tactically, this fighting nevertheless ranked with the most important engagements of the war because Johnston received a disabling wound on the first day's battle. Command of the army passed on 1 June to Robert E. Lee.

Davis's choice of Lee to lead the Army of Northern Virginia provoked a mixed reaction. Some Confederates applauded the appointment, but many others took a far dimmer view. The campaign in western Virginia and service along the South Atlantic coast had created an impression that Lee lacked aggressiveness, preferred entrenching to fighting, and otherwise failed to meet popular conceptions of a strong general. A woman in North Carolina voiced a common attitude about Lee in early June: "I do not much like him," she wrote, "he 'falls back' too much. His nick name last summer was 'old-stick-in-the-mud'.... There is mud enough now in and about our lines, but pray God he may not fulfil the whole of his name."

A member of Lee's staff recalled the hostility with which many Confederates viewed Lee at this juncture. Edward Porter Alexander, who served as chief of ordnance in the Army of Northern Virginia from June through September 1862, wrote that at the time Lee took command "some of the newspapers—particularly the *Richmond Examiner*—pitched into him with extraordinary virulence, evidently trying to break him down with the troops & to force the president to remove him." The *Examiner* claimed that "henceforth our army would never be allowed to fight" but only to dig, "spades & shovels being the only implements General Lee knew anything about."

Lee spent just more than three weeks preparing to engage McClellan's army. As he would do in all of his subsequent campaigns, Lee sought to take the initiative, to force the enemy to react to his moves rather than waiting to respond to theirs. He counted on the arrival of Jackson's troops from the Valley to provide vital support and eventually set 26 June as the day he would launch his offensive. McClellan had placed his army in a vulnerable position, with approximately one-third of it under General Fitz John Porter north of the Chickahominy River and two-thirds south of that sluggish stream. Lee targeted the portion north of the Chickahominy, which he hoped to overwhelm before turning against the remainder of the Northern invaders.

The Seven Days' campaign commenced on 26 June with the battle of Mechanicsville. Jackson was late in reaching the field, and Federal defenders sharply repulsed a series of Confederate frontal attacks. The next day at Gaines' Mill, massive Southern assaults carried Porter's position but failed to prevent his withdrawal across the Chickahominy. McClellan then began to retreat southward toward the James River, opening an opportunity, believed Lee, for a telling blow. At Savage Station on 29 June and again at Frayser's Farm on the 30th, Federals fended off clumsy Confederate assaults. A series of Confederate attacks at Malvern Hill on 1 July achieved nothing beyond littering the slopes of the hill with thousands of casualties. That evening McClellan retreated to safety at Harrison's Landing on the James.

Lee had won a victory that lifted spirits across the Confederacy. Just three weeks earlier, Southern prospects had looked exceedingly grim. Unremitting defeat stalked Confederate efforts in the West, where much of Tennessee and key cities such as New Orleans, Nashville, and Memphis had fallen. In Virginia, McClellan had edged close to Richmond. Only Stonewall Jackson's little victories in the Shenandoah Valley had broken this gloomy spell. Now Southerners could glory in a spectacular offensive victory that had saved their capital and driven the enemy's largest army into a turtle-like defensive posture. Grumbling about Lee's lack of aggressiveness ceased immediately, a phenomenon that prompted comment from the *Richmond Dispatch* eight days after Malvern Hill: "The rise which this officer has suddenly taken in the public confidence is without precedent."

In strictly military terms, Lee's victory had not been a masterpiece. Working with an unwieldy collection of division commanders, he had attempted to execute overly-complicated plans with woefully inadequate staff support. His hewing to the tactical offensive also had resulted in more than 20,000 Confederate casualties to McClellan's 16,000. Yet none could dispute that Lee's first major campaign as a field commander increased Confederate prospects for independence. His congratulatory order to his soldiers did not exaggerate in observing that their "service rendered to the country in this short but eventful period can scarcely be estimated."

Lee reorganized the Army of Northern Virginia after the Seven Days' into a Right Wing consisting of five divisions under James Longstreet and a Left Wing of three divisions under Stonewall Jackson. Jeb Stuart commanded the army's three cavalry brigades. Lee also removed several weak division leaders from the army.

The revamped Army of Northern Virginia and its commander confronted a daunting strategic situation in mid-July 1862. McClellan's army remained just below Richmond at Harrison's Landing, while 50,000 Federals under General John Pope advanced in north-central Virginia toward the vital rail center at Gordonsville. Although heavily outnumbered, Lee pondered how best to strike the enemy before Pope and McClellan could concentrate against him. The result was a dazzling series of maneuvers that cleared Northern forces from most of the state.

Between mid- and late July, Lee boldly divided his army, sending Jackson's wing to confront Pope near Gordonsville while he retained Longstreet's divisions near Richmond to watch McClellan. Jackson defeated Pope's advance guard at the battle of Cedar Mountain on 9 August. Shortly thereafter, Lee reunited the wings of his army, maneuvering and skirmishing with Pope's troops along the Rappahannock River on 15–25 August. Convinced he could accomplish little along that line,

Lee sent Jackson on a strategic flanking march around the Federal right. Jackson captured Pope's supply depot at Manassas Junction on the 27th and took up a defensive position on the old Manassas battlefield. Pope hurried his army from the Rappahannock to Manassas and attacked Jackson's wing on 29–30 August. Lee and the rest of the army reached the battlefield on the 29th. On the afternoon of 30 August, Longstreet launched a powerful assault against Pope's left flank that drove the Federals from the battlefield. Hoping to inflict further damage, Lee struck again in the inconclusive battle of Chantilly on 1 September.

The action at Chantilly ended the campaign of Second Manassas. Pope's battered force withdrew into the Washington defenses, and each side tallied another depressing harvest of casualties—more than 9,000 Confederates and 16,000 Federals. Since taking command of the army, Lee had completely reoriented the war in Virginia by pushing the Confederacy's eastern military frontier back to where it had been in April 1861. For many Confederates, Lee's decisive leadership and victories had catapulted him to the top position among their military figures. The colonel of the 22d Georgia Infantry reflected this attitude, observing on 5 September 1862: "Genl Lee stands now above all Genls in Modern History. Our men will follow him to the end."

Lee's thoughts after Second Manassas focused on the war's strategic picture. "The present seems to be the most propitious time since the commencement of the war," he wrote Jefferson Davis on 3 September, "for the Confederate Army to enter Maryland." Lee conceded that the army lacked much in the way of supplies, including shoes for thousands of troops. But he argued against assuming a static defense. "Though weaker than our opponents in men and military equipments," he explained, "[we] must endeavor to harass, if we cannot destroy them." Believing the armies of McClellan and Pope to be "much weakened and demoralized" in Washington, he thought a movement across the Potomac, though risky, could prove successful.

Such a campaign would draw the Federals northward, freeing Richmond from threat and giving the farmers of northern Virginia and the Shenandoah Valley a respite from the destructive presence of armies. The Army of Northern Virginia would remain north of the Potomac through most of the autumn to collect desperately needed food and fodder. Apart from these logistical and military benefits, Lee's strategic offensive might fuel pro-Confederate sentiment in Maryland, help convince European leaders that the Confederacy deserved diplomatic recognition, and deal a blow to Lincoln and the Republicans in the autumn elections.

The Army of Northern Virginia crossed the Potomac at White's Ford on 4–7 September. A ragged assemblage, it numbered about 55,000 soldiers. On 8 September, Lee

issued a proclamation to the people of Maryland announcing that the Confederate army had come among them as liberators. The next day he issued Special Orders No. 191, which directed three columns under Jackson to sever the Baltimore & Ohio Railroad and capture Harper's Ferry (thereby securing Lee's line of supply to the lower Shenandoah Valley) while the rest of the army moved across the South Mountain range toward Hagerstown and Boonsboro.

The campaign began to unravel over the next six days. Federal soldiers found a copy of Special Orders No. 191 in the abandoned Confederate camps at Frederick on 13 September. George B. McClellan, reinstated after Pope's defeat, thus learned the positions of each component of Lee's army.

Moving more quickly than usual, "Little Mac" pushed Lee's rearguard westward out of the passes on South Mountain on the 14th. That evening Lee decided to abandon Maryland, changing his mind the next morning when word arrived that the 12,000 Federals at Harper's Ferry were to be surrendered. He ordered the concentration of his army along a series of ridges near Sharpsburg, a hamlet just across the Potomac from Shepherdstown, Virginia.

The decision to stand at Sharpsburg highlighted Lee's combative military temperament and ranked among his most questionable decisions. He knew the Army of Northern Virginia had hemorrhaged badly since leaving White's Ferry. "Our great embarrassment," he had written Jefferson Davis on 13 September, "is the reduction in our ranks by straggling. Our ranks are very much diminished, I fear from a third to a half of the original numbers." He knew as well that his soldiers would face a cruel disparity in manpower against McClellan's pursuing army. Moreover, the Confederates would fight with their backs against the Potomac and a single ford below Shepherdstown the only avenue of escape to Virginia. Perhaps most important, McClellan's seizure of the gaps in South Mountain had allowed the Federals to join Lee's army in the Cumberland Valley, thereby severely restricting Confederate room for maneuver.

By dawn on 17 September, more than 80,000 Union soldiers faced roughly 35,000 Confederates near Sharpsburg. Federal attacks began at six o'clock that morning and continued for several hours. Lee performed magnificently during a day of near catastrophes. Along with Jackson and Longstreet, he provided an active presence on the field, shifting troops to threatened sectors and pushing his army to its physical limit. Lee's best efforts would have come to naught, however, had A. P. Hill's division, summoned early that morning from Harper's Ferry, not moved onto the field late in the afternoon. Striking the attacking Federals on their left flank, Hill's brigades ended the day's last crisis and brought the battle to a close.

Northern minié balls and artillery rounds had claimed more than 10,000 victims—a ghastly third of the Confederates who fought on the 17th. At least 12,500 Federals also had fallen. Lee had achieved a tactical stalemate by the narrowest of margins. Had McClellan coordinated his attacks or used the thousands of Federal soldiers who never fired their muskets, he probably would have crushed the Confederates. Lee remained on the field throughout the 18th, a seemingly reckless decision that McClellan declined to exploit. The Army of Northern Virginia retreated toward the Potomac that night, and soon Lee and his soldiers were safely back in Virginia.

The Maryland campaign brought mixed results for Lee and the Confederates. It accomplished the goals of taking the war out of Virginia and gathering supplies in Maryland. Because McClellan chose not to pursue after Antietam, Lee maintained a presence in northern and north central Virginia for several more weeks. The soldiers who fought at Antietam added luster to their already high reputation. Lee remarked that "nothing could surpass the determined valor" his men exhibited on 17 September. More than 12,000 prisoners and dozens of cannons captured at Harper's Ferry constituted an unexpected dividend. Yet Lee had lost thousands of troops in a battle he need not have fought. In choosing to confront McClellan at Sharpsburg, suggested Edward Porter Alexander, Lee committed his "greatest military blunder." The campaign also gained nothing on the political or diplomatic fronts, and Marylanders did not flock to the Confederate colors.

The campaign can best be considered a complex finale to a three-month drama that had begun with the Seven Days'. Lee had pressed his worn army too hard in the end, finding himself at Sharpsburg with a much-diminished force. But overall he had crafted a striking Confederate success. His victories had driven major enemy forces from Virginia, raised Confederate civilian morale, sent tremors through the North, and laid the foundation for a memorable bond between himself and his soldiers.

A victory at Fredericksburg in December 1862 increased public confidence in Lee. This unusual winter campaign opened in mid-November when Ambrose E. Burnside, who had succeeded McClellan, advanced from the vicinity of Warrenton toward Fredericksburg. The first Federals reached Fredericksburg on 17 November but could not cross the Rappahannock River because they lacked pontoon boats. As days slipped by, Lee directed first Longstreet and then Jackson to concentrate opposite Burnside's 120,000 Federals.

The Confederate army that gathered at Fredericksburg scarcely resembled the one that had fought so desperately at Antietam. Lee had reorganized it into the First and Second Corps, led by Longstreet and Jackson respectively, and a cavalry division under Jeb

Stuart. Many incompetent officers also had departed or been removed by Lee since the retreat from Maryland. Overall, Lee had made excellent progress toward shaping the Army of Northern Virginia, which numbered 75,000 in early December, into the force that soon would become the Confederacy's most important national institution.

The Federals laid their pontoon bridges across the Rappahannock under fire on 11 December and crossed in great numbers the next day. By 13 December, Lee had perfected his deployment to meet them. Longstreet's soldiers held the left, part of them sheltered in a sunken road at the foot of imposing Marye's Heights, and Jackson's troops the right. Well placed artillery supported the Southern infantry. Lee set up headquarters south of Marye's Heights on an eminence (known thereafter as Lee's Hill) that afforded a grand view of the battlefield.

From that high ground, Lee took in a grand spectacle of Confederate victory on 13 December. Burnside mounted a daylong offensive that struck first at the Confederate right. His soldiers achieved a temporary breakthrough, but Jackson orchestrated a counterattack that restored the line. An admiring Lee watched Jackson's veteran infantry punish the Federals. Turning to Longstreet, he said in an even voice, "It is well this is so terrible! We should grow too fond of it!" Those two sentences did much to define Lee and his army for future generations of Americans: the brilliant commander, his combative nature aroused, quietly exulting as his army demonstrated its martial prowess.

The fighting soon shifted to the Confederate left, where waves of attackers made no headway against Longstreet's position. Thousands of Northern soldiers fell on an open killing plain. Burnside belatedly realized the futility of further assaults and ordered an end to the slaughter. The battle had claimed 12,653 Northern and 5,309 Southern casualties. Lee hoped the Federals would renew their offensive, expressing disappointment when Burnside withdrew across the Rappahannock after dark on the 15th. "They suffered heavily as far as the battle went," Lee said of the Federals, "but it did not go far enough to satisfy me. The contest will have now to be renewed, but on what field I cannot say." The following summer Lee told an officer that after Fredericksburg "our people were greatly elated—I was much depressed ... we had not gained a foot of ground, and I knew the enemy could easily replace the men he had lost."

Lee's pessimistic evaluation overlooked the battle's impact on Northern civilian morale and on his own reputation. Abraham Lincoln faced a serious crisis after news from the Rappahannock spread across the North. "If there is a worse place than Hell," the president told a friend, "I am in it." Behind the lines in the Confederacy,

Fredericksburg spread optimism and heightened faith in Lee. A Georgia woman expressed a widespread sentiment: "I have not the words to express the emotions I feel for this signal success.... What confidence [General Lee's] wisdom, integrity, and valor and undoubted piety inspire!"

The winter and early spring of 1862–1863 tested Lee. Shortages of supplies plagued his army, and Federal movements compelled him to detach half of Longstreet's corps to Southside, Virginia. Lee himself suffered poor health as the winter gave way to spring, coping with a tenacious cold and, more ominously, a weakening heart. On 10 April, a physician reported that the general "is every day getting better.... He is cheerful and we all feel hopeful and determined and expect to win more victories over our insolent and wicked foes."

Those foes in April 1863 numbered more than 130,000 under the command of Joseph Hooker, Lee's fourth opponent in less than a year. Reduced to just more than 60,000 soldiers after Longstreet's departure, Lee's army nonetheless maintained a jaunty confidence.

In late April, Hooker commenced an imaginative offensive. Leaving a strong force at Fredericksburg to hold Lee's attention, he marched the bulk of his army up the Rappahannock to get around the Confederate left flank. He hoped to catch Lee between these two pieces of the Army of the Potomac and compel him either to retreat or to attack at a disadvantage. The turning column reached Chancellorsville, a crossroads some ten miles in Lee's rear, on 30 April.

Lee declined to follow Hooker's script, reacting instead with a series of characteristically daring moves. He left Jubal A. Early with 10,000 men at Fredericksburg, while he and Stonewall Jackson hastened to confront Hooker at Chancellorsville with the rest of the army. The campaign's defining moment occurred on the morning of 1 May, when the vanguards of Hooker's and Lee's forces collided near Zoan Church on the road between Chancellorsville and Fredericksburg. Hooker immediately seemed to lose all confidence and ordered a withdrawal to Chancellorsville.

Lee and Jackson met that night to plan a bold flanking movement, which Jackson executed with considerable success the next day. Jackson's troops routed one Federal corps late on the afternoon of 2 May, but the largest part of Hooker's army still lay between the two pieces of Lee's force at Chancellorsville. Southern assaults on the morning of 3 May reunited the Confederates in Hooker's front and produced a memorable moment of triumph for Lee. As he rode into the midst of his veteran infantry near the Chancellorsville crossroads, his soldiers cheered lustily. That dramatic moment underscored the profound faith Lee and his men shared in each other.

Within minutes of this episode, Lee learned that

Federals had broken Early's lines at Fredericksburg. He divided his army a third time, leaving Jeb Stuart and 25,000 men to keep an eye on Hooker while he concentrated the rest of his strength several miles west of Fredericksburg at Salem Church. There the Confederates won an awkward victory on 3–4 May. By dawn on 6 May, the Army of the Potomac had retreated to the north bank of the Rappahannock.

Chancellorsville confirmed Lee's reputation as an unexcelled Confederate field commander. Utterly dominating Hooker psychologically, he had wrested victory from circumstances that would have undone most generals. He also lost nearly more than 12,750 men—22 percent of his army. Among the fallen was Stonewall Jackson, who died on 10 May after being wounded by some of his own men on the evening of 2 May. Lee mourned the loss of his brilliant lieutenant and found little satisfaction in repulsing Hooker's offensive. "At Chancellorsville we gained another victory," he remarked later, "our people were wild with delight—I, on the contrary, was more depressed than after Fredericksburg; our loss was severe, and again we had gained not an inch of ground and the enemy could not be pursued."

As in his assessment of Fredericksburg, Lee's comments about Chancellorsville ignored the battle's impact on the Northern and Confederate home fronts. His victory sent waves of disappointment rippling across a North already torn by dissension over the draft and other highly charged issues. "My God! my God!" said an anguished Abraham Lincoln when he realized that Hooker had failed, "What will the country say?" The Confederate people understandably welcomed news of the victory and made Lee their leading military idol. In this vein, the *Lynchburg Virginian* observed on 12 May 1863: "The central figure of this war is, beyond all question, that of Robert E. Lee."

Chancellorsville also completed the process by which the Army of Northern Virginia became almost fanatically devoted to Lee. In language echoed by countless others, a Georgian described the deep bond that had formed between Lee and his men: "Wherever he leads they will follow. Whatever he says do, can and must be done. Language is inadequate to convey the idea of the supreme confidence this army reposes in its great and good leader."

The next test for Lee would come on Northern soil. In mid-May, he met with political leaders in Richmond and spoke against weakening his army to reinforce Confederates defending Vicksburg. President Davis declined to go against Lee's advice. Often cited as evidence that Lee was unable to grasp the larger strategic picture, these discussions in fact demonstrated his excellent understanding of how best to achieve Southern independence. He knew his army had supplied the victories that sustained Confederate national morale and that most people looked to the Eastern theater to determine who was winning the war. He understandably thought it made sense to give him—the Confederacy's only successful field commander—as many resources as possible.

Lee argued for a second invasion of the North. He believed such an operation would thwart Federal offensive plans, direct the focus of action away from Richmond and Virginia's hard-pressed agricultural areas, permit the Army of Northern Virginia to forage on enemy soil, and fuel Northern political discontent. Once in Pennsylvania, he could maneuver in such a way as to force the Federals to attack him or provide an opening for a successful Confederate tactical offensive. Above all he hoped to avoid being caught in a siege in Richmond. On 8 June, Lee observed that unless Hooker's force could "be drawn out in a position to be assailed, it will take its own time to prepare and strengthen itself to renew its advance upon Richmond, and force this army back within the entrenchments of that city. This may be the result in any event, still I think it is worth a trial to prevent such a catastrophe."

The Confederate army that prepared to march northward numbered 75,000 men. Longstreet and his two divisions had returned from Suffolk, and the government had sent a few other reinforcements as well. Lee had revamped the army after Jackson's death into three corps. Longstreet retained command of the First; Richard S. Ewell succeeded Jackson at Second Corps headquarters; and A. P. Hill took the helm of the new Third Corps.

Lee's second invasion of the North began smoothly. Ewell's corps led the way toward the Potomac on 10 June, followed by Hill's and then Longstreet's. Ewell's troops captured several thousand Federals at Winchester on 15 June, began crossing the Potomac the next day, and soon marched through Maryland and into Pennsylvania. By 27 June, Ewell's leading units were approaching the Susquehanna. Lee was at Chambersburg with the bulk of Longstreet's and Hill's troops. The Confederates had gathered immense quantities of food and other supplies and triggered a frenzy of fear in Pennsylvania. But Lee conducted the last phase of his march without adequate intelligence from Jeb Stuart, who had sent no communications since the afternoon of 23 June. Given orders on that day to connect with Ewell's right flank north of the Potomac, Stuart had decided to ride around the Army of the Potomac and been caught east of Hooker's force when it began moving north. He would remain out of touch for more than a week before rejoining Lee on 2 July.

Information that indirectly led to the battle of Gettysburg arrived at Lee's headquarters about ten o'clock on the night of 28 June. A member of

Longstreet's staff reported that his chief had learned from a paid civilian scout of the Federal army's crossing the Potomac. In the absence of information from Stuart, Lee had assumed the enemy remained south of the river. An interrogation of the scout convinced Lee that the enemy indeed had marched north, revealing as well that George G. Meade had replaced Hooker as the Federal commander. Just as during the preceding autumn's Maryland campaign, Lee confronted an approaching foe with his own army scattered. He issued orders early on 29 June for his three corps to unite along the eastern slope of the South Mountain range.

The Confederate concentration remained incomplete when Henry Heth's division of Hill's corps engaged Federal cavalry west of Gettysburg on the morning of 1 July. What began as a meeting engagement escalated rapidly into full-scale fighting and eventually into the largest clash of the war.

Lee made crucial decisions on each of the battle's three days. At first hoping to avoid a general engagement prior to concentrating his army, he changed his mind when he reached the battlefield on the afternoon of 1 July and found a favorable tactical situation. He instructed Hill and Ewell to press the enemy, and the Confederates drove two Federal corps through Gettysburg and onto high ground south of town. Lee decided to continue the tactical offensive the next day with assaults against the Federal right and left by Ewell's and Longstreet's corps respectively. The attacks achieved no coordination but almost succeeded, which convinced Lee that one more effort might carry the field. He initially hoped to repeat the offensive pressure against both Northern flanks on 3 July, settling in the end for the alternative of the Pickett-Pettigrew assault against the Federal center. When that fabled effort ended in bloody repulse, Lee abandoned further aggressive tactics in Pennsylvania.

High drama and unimaginable slaughter had marked the three days of combat. More than 23,000 Federals and at least 25,000 Confederates fell. A third of Lee's generals were killed, wounded, or captured. Many critics have pointed to Gettysburg as proof that Lee's aggressiveness sometimes overcame his better judgment. Others have argued that Ewell's failure to carry Cemetery Hill on 1 July and Longstreet's questionable performance on 2 July cost Lee an opportunity to win a sweeping victory. Lee himself stated after the war that "Stuart's failure to carry out his instructions *forced the battle of Gettysburg, & the imperfect, halting way in which his corps commanders* (especially Ewell) *fought the battle, gave victory … finally to the foe.*"

In the immediate aftermath of the battle, Lee typically took full responsibility. As the soldiers of Pickett's broken division staggered back to Seminary Ridge on 3 July, he told Cadmus M. Wilcox, whose brigade had fought on Pickett's right, "Never mind General, *all this has been MY fault*—it is I that have lost this fight." In late July, Lee wrote Jefferson Davis that "No blame can be attached to the army for its failure to accomplish what was projected by me.… I am alone to blame, in perhaps expecting too much of its prowess & valour." "With my present knowledge," he added, "& could I have foreseen that the attack on the last day would have failed to drive the enemy from his position, I should certainly have tried some other course."

There is no reason to doubt Lee's own explanation about why he pursued the tactical offensive at Gettysburg. Momentum and high morale count heavily in warfare, and he knew his army had both in ample quantity following Chancellorsville. The events of 3 May 1863, when Lee saw his outnumbered infantry close in on Chancellorsville, probably influenced his decision to ask them to accomplish even more at Gettysburg. Aware in retrospect that he had erred regarding the Pickett-Pettigrew assault, and stung by criticism in some Southern newspapers, Lee offered to step down as commander of the Army of Northern Virginia. Jefferson Davis immediately assured him that isolated newspaper carping could not "detract from the achievements which will make you and your army the subject of history and object of the world's admiration for generations to come."

Most Confederate soldiers and civilians did not view Gettysburg as a military disaster equivalent to the loss of Vicksburg, and fewer still regarded it as a major blemish on Lee's record. Although losses had been heavy, Lee's army had withdrawn safely from Pennsylvania by the middle of July. Moreover, the Army of the Potomac seemed to be in no hurry to find another battleground. A diarist in South Carolina, expressed a typical reaction to Gettysburg: "Lee has recrossed the Potomac, in admirable order, and the army in splendid trim and spirits without loss.… His retreat from Gettysburg was strategic, to draw Meade's army from the high hills behind which they took refuge."

Shortly after Gettysburg, Lee told an officer that the Federals had suffered such damage at Gettysburg that "it will be seen for the next six months that *that army* will be as quiet as a sucking dove." In fact, it would not be until ten months later, when Ulysses S. Grant began his Overland campaign, that the Army of the Potomac opened another major offensive in Virginia.

Back along the Rappahannock River frontier by early August, Lee contended with a brief period of increased desertion. In early September, Federal advances against Knoxville and Chattanooga convinced Jefferson Davis that Braxton Bragg's Army of Tennessee must be reinforced. Lee grudgingly agreed to send Longstreet and two First Corps divisions to Bragg's assistance. Longstreet's veterans arrived in northern Georgia in time to help

Bragg win the battle of Chickamauga, then spent the next several months in increasingly frustrating service in eastern Tennessee.

Two brief periods of activity preceded the winter of 1863–1864. The Bristoe campaign of mid-October and the Mine Run campaign of late November and early December yielded no decisive results, leaving Lee and the Army of Northern Virginia to keep vigilant watch along the Rappahannock and Rapidan rivers during a hard winter and spring. Chronic shortages of food, fodder, medicine, and clothing plagued the Confederates. As late as 12 April 1864, Lee grimly informed Jefferson Davis: "I cannot see how we can operate with our present supplies.... There is nothing to be had in this section for man or animals."

Despite physical hardships, morale remained high in the army. Most of the men looked with unqualified trust to their army commander. "General Robt. E. Lee is regarded by his army as nearest approaching the character of the great & good Washington than any man living," wrote one brigadier in late January 1864. "He is the only man living in whom they would unreservedly trust all power for the preservation of their independence."

A new opponent took the field against Lee in the spring of 1864. Ulysses S. Grant brought to Virginia a dazzling record of success in the West. His presence with the Army of the Potomac raised hopes among Northerners that they finally had a champion who could vanquish Lee. The Confederate people and soldiers in the Army of Northern Virginia held an equally firm belief that Lee would triumph against Grant. Walter H. Taylor of Lee's staff probably reflected the dominant feeling at army headquarters when he prophesied that Grant, who had faced modestly talented Confederate generals in the West, "will find, I trust, that General Lee is a very different man to deal with."

Lee entered the campaign with doubts about his own physical capacity and an army only slightly more than half the size of Grant's. He had suffered from severe pains in his back during the autumn of 1863, and on 9 April 1864, admitted to his son Custis, "I feel a marked change in my strength since my attack last spring at Fredericksburg, and am less competent for my duty than ever." On a more positive note, he welcomed James Longstreet's two divisions back to the army at an emotional review in late April. One observer at the review noted that "a wild and prolonged cheer, fraught with a feeling that thrilled all hearts, ran along the lines and rose to the heavens." Even with Longstreet's troops, the Army of Northern Virginia mustered only about 65,000 men to face roughly 120,000 Federals.

A month of unprecedented fury opened on 4 May when the Federals crossed the Rapidan River and moved into the Wilderness, a desolate, scrub forest where the armies had grappled during the Chancellorsville campaign. Lee hoped to find an opening to strike the enemy, fearful that a protracted defensive campaign would culminate in a siege at Richmond. The 1864 Overland campaign witnessed almost constant fighting—large battles followed by skirmishing and smaller engagements and then other large battles—and set a chilling new standard for slaughter.

Lee and Grant first tested each other on 5–6 May in the battle of the Wilderness. The first day's fighting ended in a stalemate, but early the next morning Federals routed most of A. P. Hill's corps on the Confederate right. Lee rode into the swirling action at the Widow Tapp field, seeking first to rally Hill's men and then urging the Texas Brigade, just arriving on the field with the vanguard of Longstreet's corps, to counterattack. In the earliest and most famous "Lee to the Rear" episode, the Texans and their Arkansan comrades made Lee go to safety before they would advance. Later on 6 May the Confederates managed to turn both of Grant's flanks but failed to deliver a knockout blow. The two days of combat felled more than 18,000 Federals and 11,000 Confederates, among the latter James Longstreet, Lee's best corps commander.

Unlike previous Federal generals who had retreated after being roughly handled by Lee, Grant ignored his losses and pressed southward. The armies fought again during 8–21 May in the battles of Spotsylvania Court House. The heaviest combat of the Overland campaign took place on 12 May, when Federals smashed through the Mule Shoe salient in Lee's lines and almost split the Confederate army into two vulnerable pieces. Once again Lee rode to the front, rallying soldiers and directing reinforcements to the point of danger.

Stalwart fighting by several Confederate brigades stabilized the situation in the Mule Shoe and enabled the army to withdraw safely to another position. By 21 May, when the armies marched away from Spotsylvania, another 18,000 Federals and 12,000 Confederates had joined the list of casualties.

The first two weeks of campaigning had ravaged the Confederate high command. A Southern minié ball had cost Lee the invaluable services of James Longstreet; A. P. Hill had missed crucial action because of recurring ailments; and Richard S. Ewell had performed in a manner that prompted Lee to remove him from the army. The full cost of this breakdown of command stood out starkly on 24–25 May. Grant maneuvered his army into an awkward position astride the North Anna River, offering a tempting target that Lee normally would have attacked. But the Confederate commander lay prostrate in his cot with severe dysentery, unable to oversee an assault and unwilling to commit such a task to any available lieutenant. A staff officer later described a frustrated Lee as saying, "We must strike them a blow—we must never let them pass us again—we must strike them a blow!"

A week after the missed opportunity at the North Anna, the armies had shifted southeast to the vicinity of Cold Harbor. There Lee constructed a defensive line between Totopotomoy Creek and the Chickahominy River, his right flank resting near the old Gaines' Mill battlefield. On 3 June, more than 50,000 Federals struck the well-engineered Southern positions. In a battle more lopsided than Fredericksburg, Lee's soldiers inflicted 7,500 casualties while suffering no more than 1,500 of their own. Yet Lee knew the inexorable progression of the campaign had taken the armies ever closer to Richmond and a possible siege. Just after Cold Harbor, he spoke with Jubal Early about his deepest fear. "We must destroy this army of Grant's before he gets to [the] James River," said Lee, "if he gets there, it will become a siege, and then it will be a mere question of time."

On 12 June, Grant began a movement that set the stage for the scenario Lee most dreaded. Fooling Lee completely, the Federal chief disengaged from the Confederates at Cold Harbor and crossed the James. Northern units hastened toward Petersburg, where on 15–18 June they mounted a series of disjointed assaults that failed to take the city. Once certain that Grant had crossed the river, Lee shuttled troops to the Petersburg defenses in time to participate in the repulse of Federal attacks on the 16th and 17th.

The Overland campaign ended on 18 June as the armies settled into their lines around Petersburg. Since crossing the Rapidan on 4 May, the Federals had lost more than 60,000 men and their Confederate opponents more than 30,000—a roughly equal ratio of casualties to strength on each side. The two armies scarcely resembled the forces that had opened the campaign. For the rest of the conflict they would engage in a more static form of warfare, constructing a maze of works along the Richmond-Petersburg front while Grant steadily extended his lines westward and worked to cut Lee's supply lines.

The siege of Petersburg lasted more than nine months. A number of sharp actions broke the tedium of siege life during the remainder of 1864 and into 1865. Lee also ordered the last major Confederate strategic diversion in Virginia during this period, sending Jubal Early to the Shenandoah Valley. Early won a number of small victories, crossed the Potomac River and marched to the outskirts of Washington, and tied down more than 40,000 Federal troops before losing three sharp battles to Philip H. Sheridan's forces between 19 September and 19 October. The last of Early's defeats, at Cedar Creek, marked the end of a significant Confederate presence in the Shenandoah. Along with William Tecumseh Sherman's capture of Atlanta, Northern success in the valley helped ensure Abraham Lincoln's reelection.

The final period of the war offered scant good news to Lee and his army. Although many Confederates took heart at Lee's appointment as general-in-chief of all national forces on 6 February 1865, the promotion came too late to have any practical effect. In private, Lee had decided victory was impossible. He confided to one correspondent on 5 March that it was his soldierly "duty to fight it out to the last extremity as long as the contest continues," but as "a patriot and citizen" he thought the government should try to "close the war on the best terms we could."

Lee's public support for continued resistance extended to recommending that slaves be armed and placed in the army. He also suggested that slaves who served faithfully in this capacity, together with their families, should be freed. Lee's views on this volatile subject, made public in late February, promoted considerable support for arming and freeing slaves. "With the great mass of our people," noted the *Richmond Sentinel* with some hyperbole, "nothing more than this letter [from Lee] is needed to settle every doubt or silence every objection." In March 1865, the Confederate Congress passed legislation permitting the enrollment of slaves as soldiers but refused to provide any guarantee of freedom.

The siege of Petersburg neared its end during the last week of March. Lee made a desperate effort to break Grant's grip with an attack against Fort Stedman on 25 March. The assault achieved momentary success before counterattacks restored the Federal position. On 1 April, Philip Sheridan crushed George E. Pickett's defending Confederates in the battle of Five Forks, turning Lee's right and forcing the evacuation of Richmond on the night of 2–3 April.

A weeklong retreat westward from Richmond and Petersburg ensued. Lee hoped to join Joseph Johnston's army in North Carolina, but Grant's pursuit denied him an opening. Under relentless pressure, the Confederates fought at Sayler's Creek on 6 April, losing thousands of prisoners and prompting Lee, who witnessed the debacle from high ground, to exclaim, "My God! Has the army been dissolved?" Two more days took the armies to the vicinity of Appomattox Court House, where Northern cavalry blocked the front of Lee's column. On 9 April, Lee knew the end had come. Hemmed in by powerful Northern forces to the east, south, and west, he told a group of officers, "There is nothing left me to do but to go and see General Grant, and I would rather die a thousand deaths."

The war's two most famous generals met in the parlor of Wilmer McLean's home in Appomattox Court House on 9 April. Grant extended generous terms, Lee accepted them, and the two men signed the document of surrender. The Army of Northern Virginia, reduced to just 28,000 men, had shed its last blood for Robert E. Lee.

Lee took leave of his soldiers with words that applied

to him as much as to them. In General Order No. 9, dated 10 April, he told the survivors that they had logged "four years of arduous service, marked by unsurpassed courage and fortitude." Near the end of this farewell to the army, Lee affirmed that his veterans would return to their homes with "the satisfaction that proceeds from the consciousness of duty faithfully performed." From Lee, who always tried to perform his own duty as he understood it, there could have been no higher compliment.

Because Lee and his army personified their cause for so many Confederates, word of events at Appomattox prompted feelings of anguished resignation. Thousands of other Confederate soldiers remained under arms, but for most white Southerners the surrender of the Army of Northern Virginia understandably signaled the end of the war. "Everybody feels ready to give up hope," was a Georgia woman's representative response to news of Appomattox. "'It is useless to struggle longer,' seems to be the common cry," she wrote sadly, "and the poor wounded men go hobbling about the streets with despair on their faces."

Lee returned to Richmond following the surrender as a paroled prisoner of war. After nearly thirty-six years as a professional soldier, he found himself unemployed and facing an uncertain future. Arlington had been seized by the United States government and turned into a military cemetery, and he and Mrs. Lee owned no other residence. He had no immediate means of supporting his family. On 13 June 1865, he formally requested a pardon from President Andrew Johnson (the pardon would never be granted). Lee's attitude toward defeat can be summed up simply: the Confederate people had waged a bitter struggle for independence, had failed to achieve that goal, and now must abide by the rules of the victors.

Nearly four months passed between Lee's surrender and the arrival of an offer that would define the work of his last years. In early August 1865, Washington College of Lexington, Virginia, offered him its presidency. On 24 August, Lee expressed a willingness to take up the post.

He proved to be an able educator who left an indelible mark on Washington College. When he assumed control in the autumn of 1865 the school was struggling to keep its doors open. The student body consisted of only a few dozen young men. Four years of Lee's leadership worked a remarkable change. The student body increased to more than 300, the physical condition of the institution improved dramatically, and the faculty grew in size and stability. Lee also revised the curriculum, adding courses in science and engineering to the traditional offerings in classical subjects.

Whenever Lee traveled in the postwar South former Confederates demonstrated affection for their old hero. "It would not be easy, for one who had not been in the midst of it, to realize the enthusiasm that existed among the Southern people for General Lee at the conclusion of the war," wrote a neighbor in Lexington. Lee and his daughter Agnes toured several Southern states in the spring of 1870. They endured a procession of dinners, receptions, and public appearances that taxed his waning strength. At about the midpoint of this trip, Lee described his physical condition to his wife: "The warm weather has dispelled some of the rheumatic pains in my back, but I perceive no change in the stricture in my chest. If I attempt to walk beyond a very slow gait, the pain is always there."

Lee passed a final summer and watched autumn bring its colors to Lexington. On 28 September 1870, he was stricken with an unusual stroke that inflicted no paralysis but left its victim largely incapacitated. He lingered for two weeks, uttering an average of just one word a day, until he died peacefully on 12 October.

—*Gary W. Gallagher*

See also: Antietam, Battle of; Bull Run, Second Battle of; Chancellorsville, Battle of; Cheat Mountain, Virginia; Davis, Jefferson; Fredericksburg, Battle of; Gettysburg, Battle of; Jackson, Thomas Jonathan; Peninsula Campaign; Richmond Campaign; Wilderness, Battle of the.

For further reading:

Connelly, Thomas L. *The Marble Man: Robert E. Lee and His Image in American Society* (1961).
Freeman, Douglas Southall. *R. E. Lee: A Biography* (1934).
Gallagher, Gary W., ed. *Lee the Soldier* (1996).
Nolan, Alan T. *Lee Considered: General Robert E. Lee and Civil War History* (1991).
Roland, Charles P. *Reflections on Lee: A Historian's Assessment* (1995).
Thomas, Emory M. *Robert E. Lee: A Biography* (1995).

LEE, SAMUEL PHILIPS
(1812–1897)
Union naval officer

The son of Francis Lightfoot Lee and a third cousin of both Robert E. Lee and Captain Sydney Smith Lee, C.S.N., Samuel P. Lee received appointment as acting midshipman in 1825, beginning a naval career that spanned more than fifty years. His prewar service included duty with the U.S. Surveying and Exploring Expedition that circumnavigated the globe in 1838–1842. In addition, Lee served on blockade duty during the Mexican-American War and spent many years with the coast survey.

Commander Lee took command of the sloop of war *Vandalia* in November 1860 and one month later departed for his assigned station with the East India Squadron even as the nation began to fragment. On his own initiative, he returned to the United States after sailing as far as South Africa. Although a Southerner, he remained loyal to the Union, perhaps influenced by his marriage to the sister of Montgomery Blair, postmaster general of the United States in Abraham Lincoln's administration. In June 1861 he took the *Vandalia* to join the blockade off Charleston, South Carolina. He later took command of the new steamer *Oneida* for service under Captain David Farragut in the Gulf of Mexico. Lee took part in Farragut's passing of the forts at New Orleans and later operations on the Mississippi River, taking the *Oneida* and a division of gunboats as far as Vicksburg, Mississippi, where his demand for the town's surrender was promptly refused.

In July 1862 Lee was selected to command the vital North Atlantic Blockading Squadron, responsible for maintaining the blockade of Virginia and North Carolina. Promoted to captain in that month, he assumed the rank of acting rear admiral upon taking up his duties in September. With his flag flying successively on the *Philadelphia*, *Minnesota*, *Agawan*, and *Malvern*, Lee's responsibilities included not only maintaining the blockade of Virginia and North Carolina but also cooperating with the army in capturing and holding Confederate positions along the coast and rivers. His force numbered 48 ships when he assumed command, and it grew to as many as 119 ships in 1864, making his the largest of the blockading squadrons.

Lee instituted a more aggressive blockade strategy, especially off Wilmington, North Carolina, the main Southern port within his jurisdiction. Located twenty-eight miles up the Cape Fear River, Wilmington provided a formidable challenge. Nevertheless, Lee began planning a combined attack on the city with army forces under Major General John Foster. However, difficulties in finding a viable approach to the port's defenses, as well as a shift in Navy Department priorities to capturing Charleston, led to the attack being canceled early in 1863. Lee continued to call for an assault on Wilmington for the remainder of his tenure, but a lack of cooperation from the War Department limited him to tightening the blockade as much as possible, with increasingly positive results.

Although unable to capture Wilmington, Lee's forces cooperated with the army on numerous occasions, ranging from modest raiding to assisting General Benjamin Butler's James River campaign in 1864. Lee's hopes for significant action during this campaign were frustrated by Butler's unwillingness to take the offensive.

Thanks to the prize rules of the day, which gave the squadron commander a percentage of every capture, Lee amassed a sizable fortune while on blockade duty. This fact, coupled with his Southern birth and doubts as to his aggressiveness, roused resentment among some of the officers. After two years of exemplary service, he was relieved in October 1864, to be replaced by David Dixon Porter. Lee was named to command the Mississippi Squadron, an important assignment and the navy's second largest squadron. In this assignment Lee, still an

acting rear admiral, readily supported the operations of General George Thomas, himself a Southerner who remained loyal to the Union. Lee worked well with Thomas, collaborating successfully until the end of the war in repelling Confederate general John Bell Hood's advance into Tennessee as well as commanding other minor operations.

After the war, Lee reverted to captain but received promotion to commodore in 1866 and rear admiral in 1870. From 1866 to 1867, he served as head of a board examining volunteer officers for permanent commissions and in 1869 as a member of another inspecting East Coast navy yards. After serving as the navy's chief signal officer for nine months, Lee assumed command of the North Atlantic Squadron in August 1870. Unable to secure the bureau command he desired, Lee was placed on the retired list in February 1873 and died in Washington in 1897. He is buried in Arlington National Cemetery.

—Stephen C. Svonavec

See also Blockade of C.S.A.; Navy, U.S.A.
For further reading:
Anderson, Bern. *By Sea and by River: The Naval History of the Civil War* (1962).
Cornish, Dudley Taylor, and Virginia Dean Laas. *Lincoln's Lee: The Life of Samuel Phillips Lee, United States Navy, 1812–1897* (1986).
Fowler, William M., Jr. *Under Two Flags: The American Navy in the Civil War* (1990).

LEE, STEPHEN DILL
(1833–1908)
Confederate general

Promoted to lieutenant general at age thirty, Stephen Dill Lee was the youngest of the Confederacy's seventeen lieutenant generals. He also was one of the least successful.

His poor record as a lieutenant general cannot be attributed to lack of sufficient training, experience, intelligence, or zeal. A native of Charleston, South Carolina, where his father was a physician, he obtained his basic education at a North Carolina boarding school. In 1850 he entered West Point, from which he graduated four years later ranked seventeenth in a class that included J. E. B. Stuart, under whom he would serve, and Oliver Otis Howard, against whom he would fight. Assigned as a second lieutenant to an artillery regiment, during the next six years he served in Texas, Florida, Kansas, and the Dakotas, becoming a first lieutenant in 1856.

After the secession of South Carolina he resigned, in February 1861, from the U.S. Army and obtained a captain's commission in the Confederate army. As a member of Brigadier General P. G. T. Beauregard's staff, he participated in the negotiations that eventuated in the Confederate bombardment of Fort Sumter on 12 April 1861—an act he enthusiastically approved. Next, in June 1861, he became commander of the artillery battery in Hampton's Legion, South Carolina's most aristocratic military unit. His battery arrived in Virginia too late to take part with the rest of the legion in the battle of First Bull Run (21 July 1861), but it saw significant action in the Peninsula campaign (April–July 1862), during which he so favorably impressed his superiors that he was jumped to the rank of colonel and placed in charge of the artillery for a division. Then, immediately after that campaign, he headed one of Stuart's cavalry regiments, but at the outset of General Robert E. Lee's northward offensive in August 1862 he returned to his specialty as commander of an artillery battalion in Major General James Longstreet's corps. At Second Bull Run (29–30 August 1862) and then at Antietam (17 September 1862) he again performed well, especially during the second day of the first battle, when his massed cannons smashed a Union attack and thereby set the stage for a Confederate counterattack that routed the enemy.

In November 1862, having been promoted to brigadier general, he assumed command of an infantry brigade at Vicksburg, the key Confederate stronghold on the Mississippi. In that capacity he repulsed an attempt by William T. Sherman to break through Vicksburg's defenses at Chickasaw Bayou on 29 December 1862. He did as well as could be reasonably expected in the Confederate defeat at Champion's Hill on 16 May 1863, and he performed creditably during the siege of Vicksburg from 18 May to 4 July 1863. Paroled with the rest of Vicksburg's garrison after its surrender, he was soon exchanged and received a merited promotion to major general on 3 August 1863. Placed in charge of all Confederate cavalry in Mississippi and Alabama, he did what little was possible to slow Sherman's march in the fall of 1863 from Memphis to Chattanooga to reinforce the beleaguered Federal forces there, and then to oppose Sherman's Meridian Expedition in Mississippi (3–28 February 1864).

On 9 May 1864, most of Lieutenant General Leonidas Polk's Army of Mississippi having been transferred to Georgia, Lee was placed in command of the Department of Mississippi and Alabama and on 23 June 1864 was promoted to lieutenant general. Nathan Bedford Forrest's brilliant victory on 10 June 1864 at Brice's Crossroads turned back one Federal foray into Mississippi but on 14 July 1864, with Lee personally commanding, an ill-conceived and ill-executed assault on a superior and well-entrenched Union force near Tupelo, Mississippi, suffered a bloody repulse. The Federals, to be sure, retreated back to Memphis after this engagement, but they were in the process of doing so in any case.

Having been erroneously credited with a victory at Tupelo, Lee soon afterward was ordered to Atlanta,

Georgia, to take command of a corps in General John B. Hood's army, which was defending that city against Sherman's army. On 28 July 1864, Lee marched out to the west side of Atlanta with two of his divisions with orders from Hood to establish a defense line. Instead, believing he had a golden opportunity to strike the advancing Federals while in the open, he attacked. The result, in what became known as the battle of Ezra Church, was a severe defeat in which his troops and those of a division from another corps that joined in the assault at his behest suffered 3,000 casualties, compared with the enemy losses of 632. This one-sided slaughter further impaired the morale of his corps, which already was poor as a consequence of its having been badly mauled in the battle of Atlanta (22 July 1864). On 31 August 1864, at the first battle of Jonesboro, Lee again made what he angrily but accurately described as a "feeble" attack on the Federals, with most of his men either refusing to advance or if they did, taking shelter as soon as they came under fire.

The debacle at Jonesboro obliged Hood to evacuate Atlanta on the night of 1 September 1864. Then, toward the end of that month, he embarked on a counteroffensive that took him into Tennessee, where his army suffered a ruinous repulse at Franklin on 30 November 1864 and total defeat at Nashville on 15–16 December 1864. Significantly, Lee's corps took no part in the first battle and remained strictly on the defensive in the second. After the Tennessee campaign, Lee, who had been wounded at Nashville, went on sick leave. On 31 March 1865 he rejoined his corps in North Carolina, where it formed part of the small army under General Joseph Johnston that surrendered to Sherman on 20 April 1865.

After the war, Lee operated a plantation in Mississippi, was active in that state's politics, served as the first president of what is today Mississippi State University, and was a member of a federal commission to establish a national military park at Vicksburg. In 1904, by then the highest-ranking Confederate general still alive, he became commander of the United Confederate Veterans, a post he retained until his death.

Lee performed well as an artillery officer and infantry brigadier, and adequately as a cavalry leader, but as a lieutenant general in command of a department and then of a corps he was a failure. In fairness, he achieved that rank at a time when the Confederate cause was desperate, and it is unlikely that greater competence on his part would have made any major difference. Even so, his penchant for foredoomed frontal attacks made what was bad much worse. Obviously he failed to realize the fundamental tactical fact of the Civil War—that the defense dominated the offense—and his blaming his defeats on his troops did him no credit.

—*Albert Castel*

See also Ezra Church, Battle of; Jonesboro, Battle of; Meridian Campaign; Tupelo, Battle of.
For further reading:
Castel, Albert. *Decision in the West: The Atlanta Campaign of 1864* (1992).
Freeman, Douglas Southall. *Lee's Lieutenants* (1942–1944).
Hattaway, Herman. *General Stephen D. Lee* (1976).
Wyeth, John Allen. *Life of General Nathan Bedford Forrest* (1899; reprint, 1989).

LEE, WILLIAM HENRY FITZHUGH
(1837–1891)
Confederate general

William Henry Fitzhugh Lee was born on 31 March 1837 at Arlington, Virginia, the third of Robert Edward and Mary Custis Lee's seven children. Through his parents he was related to two of the foremost Revolutionary War era figures. His paternal grandfather was "Light-Horse Harry" Lee and his maternal great-grandmother was the first First Lady, Martha Washington. Although addressed by his father as "Fitzhugh," Lee was mainly known by his nickname of "Rooney."

As a child of a career military officer, Lee lived in a number of locations before he was admitted to Harvard in the fall of 1854. According to classmate Henry Adams, his performance was less than stellar, which may have prompted his decision to accept an 1857 appointment directly into the U.S. Army as a second lieutenant in the 6th Infantry. During the next two years he served in the far West, spending time in Texas, the Pacific Northwest, and Utah Territory, where he participated in Colonel Albert Sidney Johnston's campaign against the Mormons. Having served just two years, he resigned his commission in 1859 and returned to Virginia to become a farmer.

That same year he married Charlotte Wickham and moved to his estate, White House, in New Kent County, Virginia. The coming Civil War, however, soon brought an end to his life as a farmer. After Virginia seceded in April 1861, Lee joined the Confederate service as a captain in the 9th Virginia Cavalry. He served in that regiment for more than a year and was eventually promoted to its colonelcy. During that time, he saw action in the Seven Days' and Second Manassas campaigns and performed excellent service during the September Antietam campaign. All that time, the 9th Virginia had been part of cousin Fitzhugh Lee's cavalry brigade. Upon the reorganization of the Army of Northern Virginia's cavalry in November, Lee was promoted to brigadier general, to rank from 15 September, and assigned his own brigade. Like the rest of J. E. B. Stuart's troopers his command saw limited duty during the Fredericksburg campaign in December.

Lee's participation in the 1863 campaigns was limited. Again he and the cavalry performed only minor duty at Chancellorsville, but he played a prominent role at the 9 June battle of Brandy Station. Near the end of the fighting he was wounded in the leg, which incapacitated him for further service. While recuperating at the Hanover County home of one of his wife's relatives, he was taken prisoner and held for nine months, first at Fort Monroe and later at Fort Lafayette. During his internment, his wife became increasingly ill and died in December.

After his March 1864 exchange, he rejoined the Confederate cavalry, at which time he was put in charge of a division. Along with the command came a promotion to major general in April, making him the youngest officer to hold that rank. For the last year of the war, Lee led his division competently and was one of the most reliable cavalry officers in the army. In August, after his cousin Fitzhugh Lee was sent to bolster Lieutenant General Jubal Early's forces in the Shenandoah Valley, Lee remained with the main army. During the last months of the year he was active in fending off attempts by Union cavalry to break up the railroad network running into the Confederate lines around Petersburg and Richmond.

The following March at the battle of Five Forks, Lee was the senior officer on the field after Fitz Lee and Major General George Pickett left their commands to enjoy a lunch of fresh shad at Major General Thomas Rosser's command post. Unaware of this situation, he fought a vigorous, yet uncoordinated, battle against overwhelming Union forces. Despite his best efforts, the Confederates were soundly defeated, an outcome that determined the fate of the Confederate troops in the trenches. Like the cavalry in general, he performed diligently in the face of increasing odds as the army began its retreat. Unlike some of the other mounted troops, he surrendered with the main army on 9 April.

After the war, Lee returned to farming and in 1867 married Mary Bolling. The couple had two sons. Although he did not live a particularly long life, Lee was quite active until his death. Among his activities were a number of years as president of the Virginia State Agricultural Society and later one term as a state senator from 1875 to 1879. After eight years away from politics, he was elected as a Democrat to the U.S. House of Representatives in 1887 and served until the expiration of his second term in March 1891, just seven month before his death. He died at his estate, Ravensworth, on 15 October 1891.

—*James R. Jewell*

See also Brandy Station, Battle of; Five Forks, Battle of; Lee, Robert Edward.
For further reading:
Adams, Henry. *The Education of Henry Adams, Henry Adams: Novels, Mont Saint Michel, and the Education* (1983).
Freeman, Douglas Southall. *R. E. Lee: A Biography* (1934–1935).
Hotchkiss, Jed. *Virginia.* Vol. 3 of *Confederate Military History* (1899).
Warner, Ezra J. *Generals in Gray, Lives of Confederate Generals* (1959; reprint 1987).
Wayland, John. *Robert E. Lee and His Family* (1951).

LEGAL TENDER ACTS
(1862–1863)

The absolute necessity of expanding purchasing power in the North had manifested itself by December 1861, when the state banks suspended specie circulation. The only real question was whether the banks or the government would create the additional purchasing power. Secretary of the Treasury Salmon P. Chase, in his annual report to Congress, suggested a system of national banks authorized to issue notes secured by government bonds. Congressman Elbridge G. Spaulding prepared a bill, based on the Free Banking Law of New York, that became the National Banking Act of 1863. Recognizing that his proposal would take months to pass Congress, Spaulding introduced another bill to permit the Treasury to issue $150 million of notes (in denominations as low as $5) that would be legal tender for all public or private debts (except for customs duties and interest payments on government bonds). Many bankers opposed the bill, arguing that the government should acquire the needed money by marketing bonds below par. Spaulding adamantly rejected that idea because it would put the government's credit totally at the mercy of securities markets. Congressman Clement L. Vallandigham proposed an issue of noninterest-bearing Treasury notes that would not be legal tender. Discussion revealed, however, that his plan would not have worked, because people and banks would simply have refused to accept them.

The Legal Tender Act became law on 25 February 1862. Other sections authorized a bond issue of $500 million at 6 percent interest to be redeemed in five to twenty years and imposed penalties for counterfeiting. Although many had doubts about the constitutionality of legal-tender notes, the House voted ninety-five to fifty-five and the Senate thirty to seven to approve it, in large measure because Chase told Congress that "the Treasury is nearly empty."

In June 1862 and March 1863 Congress passed two more Legal Tender Acts. Each authorized an additional issue of $150 million in legal-tender notes (commonly called greenbacks). The third law also permitted the issue of $400 million of interest-bearing legal-tender notes. During the Civil War, total net issues of greenbacks were $431,500,000.

The Legal Tender Acts worked reasonably well. They gave the Treasury Department resources to pay its bills and did not destroy investor confidence in government bonds. They also stimulated some inflation and created a speculator's market in gold. However, the inflation rate of 80 percent for 1861–1865 compares well with World Wars I (84 percent) and II (70 percent), in part because the Union raised taxes significantly starting in 1862, which countered inflationary pressures. The price of gold rose (slowly in 1862 but faster afterwards), so that at its peak in 1864 it required $285 in greenbacks to purchase what had previously cost $100 in gold.

After the war ended, greenbacks became a focus of debate. The constitutionality of the Legal Tender Acts came before the U.S. Supreme Court. In *Hepburn v. Griswold* (1870), the Court ruled unconstitutional the practice of requiring the acceptance of greenbacks for debts that had been contracted before passage of the first act. However, the Court soon reconsidered; it upheld the constitutionality of all the acts for all debts, regardless of when contracted, in *Knox v. Lee* (1871).

Another debate concerned whether (and when) to redeem the greenbacks in gold. That became entangled with arguments about the proper government economic policy during the depression that began in 1872. Not until 1879 did the Treasury begin to redeem greenbacks in gold.

The Legal Tender Acts provided a convenient way to finance the war during a time when people had just realized that the fighting would continue longer and would cost much more than the Mexican-American War. The acts marked the transition between the inadequate financial policy of 1861 and the government's later large-scale tax collections and bond issues. If the government had undertaken a stringent taxation policy and an efficient method of selling bonds in 1861, greenbacks might have been unnecessary; however, it is possible that gold hoarding would still have occurred, specie payments would have been suspended, and an irredeemable currency would have been needed.

—*Sue C. Patrick*

See also Financing, U.S.A; Greenbacks; Spaulding, Elbridge G.
For further reading:
Hammond, Bray. *Sovereignty and an Empty Purse: Banks and Politics in the Civil War* (1970).
Mitchell, Wesley Clair. *A History of the Greenbacks, with Special Reference to the Economic Consequence of Their Issue, 1862–1865* (1903; reprint, 1960).
Sharkey, Robert P. *Money, Class, and Party: An Economic Study of Civil War and Reconstruction* (1959).
Spaulding, Eldridge G. *A Resource of War—The Credit of the Government Made Immediately Available.* (1869; reprint, 1971).

LEGGETT, MORTIMER DORMER
(1821–1896)
Union general

Born to Isaac Leggett and Mary Strong Leggett outside Ithaca, New York, Mortimer Dormer Leggett moved to Ohio with his family when he was a teenager. As a youth, Leggett studied to be a teacher and then changed to law. After admission to the bar, he moved to Akron, Ohio, where he maintained his strong interest in education, being instrumental in establishing public schools in that city. His success led to his

employment by other towns for similar activities. At one point, he even combined his two interests by teaching law. Leggett eventually settled in Zanesville, Ohio, where he served as school superintendent and practiced law. For a time he was a law partner to future Civil War general Jacob Cox.

During his rather peripatetic existence, Leggett had also made friends with George B. McClellan. Therefore, one of his first activities at the beginning of the Civil War was to serve as a volunteer aide to McClellan during that officer's early campaigns in western Virginia. When McClellan was named commander of the Army of the Potomac, Leggett returned to Ohio to raise a regiment for Federal service. He received his commission as lieutenant colonel of the 78th Ohio in December 1861 and became its colonel and commander in January 1862.

Sent to the command of Ulysses S. Grant, Leggett and the 78th saw their first action at Fort Donelson. After the capitulation of the fort, Grant named Leggett acting provost marshal. Leggett led his regiment as part of Lew Wallace's division at Shiloh and the advance on Corinth, Mississippi, that followed. During the summer of 1862, Leggett commanded a brigade that operated and skirmished with Confederates along the Mississippi Central Railroad. In October 1862 Grant recommended Leggett for promotion to brigadier general. Although the promotion was not forthcoming until April 1863, his date of rank was 29 November 1862.

In early 1863 Leggett and his brigade became a part of Grant's Vicksburg campaign. Leggett fought at Port Gibson on 1 May and at Champion's Hill on 16 May 1863. He then commanded his brigade in the formal siege of Vicksburg and was there at the surrender.

During the fall of 1863, Leggett and his brigade operated out of Vicksburg, helping to consolidate Federal control of the area. In the spring he commanded a division in William T. Sherman's Meridian campaign and then traveled to Tennessee with most of the Army of the Tennessee to prepare for what would become the Atlanta campaign.

During the Atlanta campaign, Leggett commanded the 3d Division, XVII Corps. In the battle of Atlanta on 22 July 1864, Leggett held a high position against repeated Southern assaults. Afterward, this place was known as Leggett's Hill. For his actions there, Leggett was recommended for promotion to major general. After a return from a medical leave of absence, he was given a brevet promotion to major general.

In the fall, Leggett led his division and sometimes the XVII Corps in Sherman's March to the Sea. After the surrender of Savannah in December 1864, Leggett moved with the army into the Carolinas but had to leave that campaign shortly after it began because he became ill. He was able to return to duty before the surrender of Joseph Johnston.

After the war Leggett was sent to the Department of Ohio. While serving there in August 1865, he was promoted to major general of volunteers. During the war, he had been known for his bravery and had received a gold medal inscribed with the names of some of the battles in which he had participated. He resigned his commission in September 1865.

For a few years after the war, Leggett practiced law in Zanesville, but in 1871 moved to Washington, D.C., when President Grant appointed him commissioner of patents. He held that position for three years, after which he used the expertise he gained in Washington to become a successful patent attorney. In his later years, he was president of Brush Electric, one of the early electricity companies. He died on 6 January 1896 in Cleveland, Ohio.

—*David S. Heidler and Jeanne T. Heidler*

See also Atlanta, Battle of; Atlanta Campaign.

For further reading:

Stow, Mary Catherine. "Civilian General" (M.A. thesis, 1956).

LEISURE

Leisure of the Civil War generation reveals much about the divergence between North and South that only war could reconcile. Indeed, leisure represented one of the key social characteristics separating the two sections. By the mid-nineteenth century, dramatic differences in the way Americans in each section pursued free-time activities reflected the distinctive economic systems evolving since the days of the early republic. Just as these economic systems shaped work, community, technology, and the family in contrasting ways, so leisure followed suit.

Northern and Southern leisure patterns began diverging in colonial times. Both sections inherited premodern leisure forms from British folk culture, which merged work and play within the agricultural cycle. Challenges of the American frontier stimulated the need for harvest festivals, work-related competition, and "blood sports" involving violence between men or animals. Old-world leisure found a receptive environment in Southern rhythms of agrarian production and customary parish festivals of the Anglican Church. Contrastingly, the influence of religious groups such as Puritans, Dutch Calvinists, and Quakers tended to restrain traditional pastimes in the North as impediments to the divine summons for steady industry and orderly community.

Industrialization in the nineteenth century accentuated differences in leisure. While the North's industrial development, fueled by free labor, spurred the growth of cities, national markets, and communication improvements, the South tied itself to plantation agriculture based on slave labor. With one section on a course of rationali-

Officers of the 114th Pennsylvania Infantry playing cards near Petersburg, Virginia, August 1864 (*Library of Congress*)

zation and urbanization, and the other remaining traditional and agrarian, the leisure gap widened.

Although in the antebellum era a majority of Northerners continued living in rural areas, industrialization enfolded both country and city folk in the sweep of its economic and cultural changes. The North's tempo amazed visitors from overseas, who marveled at the sober diligence everywhere visible. Discipline required to meet production schedules drove leisure from the work day, segmenting time into work and nonwork units for ever-increasing numbers of workers. Evangelical Christianity supported the new system by invoking familiar strictures about industry, self-improvement, frugality, sobriety, and self-control. Often revivalists went so far as to condemn all leisure, except observance of the Lord's Day, as morally suspect. In the process, they confronted commercial entertainment that emerged to satisfy the new need for play. Ranging from circuses, theater, and minstrel shows to cockfights, these entertainments reflected rationalization of the industrial era. Staged by specialists, they offered passive amusement rather than the participatory play of the premodern world.

An answer to the dilemma of leisure in a society demanding industry came from the Victorian culture that spanned the North by mid-century. Dominated by a genteel elite, this culture valued purposeful, methodical work and rejected both the lavishness of the elite and the irregular excesses of the working class. In the belief that economic and moral progress went hand in hand, however, this ethic encouraged leisure that aided human improvement. Leisure could serve as a handmaiden to progress, refreshing individuals for work, elevating character, and inculcating aesthetic sensibility. Optimistic and full of aspiration, the genteel elite believed that all Americans could be united under its moral direction.

At the center of Victorian culture rested belief in the family-centered domestic environment, where women created a morally nurturing and edifying haven from the

competitive world outside. For the decorous Victorian male, self-control and aesthetic sensibility replaced aggression as the hallmark of masculine identity. From the communal and earthy pastimes of earlier America, leisure fell back on the home. A variety of leisure activities might be defined as elevating, including reading (literary journals proliferated thanks to printing improvements), playing musical instruments and singing, gathering natural specimens, or collecting stereographs of significant places. Raucous old communal holidays such as Christmas, long condemned as a pagan bacchanal by many Protestant churches, were sanitized and transformed into treasured, even sacred, family gatherings.

By extension, Victorian culture sought to extend the nurturing influence by creating uplifting literature, architecture, graphic arts, and public spaces. New York's genteel elite, for example, created Central Park in the 1850s as a vehicle for unifying rich and poor, but also to refine and promote family life. Genteel approval of morally improving purchases helped popularize the belief that self-fulfillment could be found in consumerism. Goods such as pianos, carpets, prints, and books, or experiences such as theater, museums, and travel to scenic places could be justified for their uplifting potential. Of course, impresarios tailored their promotion to capture the market for improving leisure. Successful showmen as exemplified by P. T. Barnum spread a patina of morality over sensational amusement. Circuses with animal acts might be billed as instructive of the natural world; museums advertising educational displays masked the macabre and prurient with exhibits of mummies or artwork featuring nudes.

But the genteel agenda never completely prevailed over other forms of leisure. By no means did the North realize a uniform, mass society in the years before the Civil War. Immigrants, working poor, and single men gravitated to leisure that the genteel hoped to vanquish. Traditional forms of leisure such as drinking, gambling, visiting houses of prostitution, and attending commercialized blood-sports events continued for those who sought masculine identity in such pastimes. Newspapers and book publishers captured a working-class and rural market for sensational literature with racy, monstrous, and morbid crime stories. Premodern folk pastimes persisted in the countryside, although in a piecemeal fashion revolving around work.

From other quarters too appeared resistance to genteel reform. Some Victorians who agreed that leisure should uplift disagreed that it required repose. To them, Victorian culture seemed to smother manly nature with domestication and to breed American males too enervated for leadership roles. Genteel elites such as Oliver Wendell Holmes, Henry Ward Beecher, and Thomas Wentworth Higginson argued for a "muscular Christianity" that used physically demanding leisure to invigorate character and body. Higginson, for example, whose *Army Life in a Black Regiment* later became a classic chronicle of the war, wrote in 1858 that only strenuous exercise could prepare youth to "grasp the rudder of the age" and confront social crises. Baseball clubs that mushroomed before the war, playing an organized version of an old English children's game variously known as "townball" and "rounders," provide an example. They attempted to demonstrate that through vigorous leisure young men might avoid violence, drinking, and other vices while imbibing virtues through gentlemanly competition.

Some traditional pastimes outpaced reformers when those pastimes were somewhat cleansed and promoted in a nation connected by mass print media and telegraphy. Although most leisure remained local, some sports of ancient lineage, such as horse racing and prize fighting, captured an enormous popular following—to the genteel elite's dismay. Yet the demand for such leisure augured the emergence of mass society with its love of spectacle, presaging large-scale spectator sports later in the century. Sports reporting in the penny press and specialized sporting journals, a departure in publishing, tried to quench the public thirst for sports information. In a scenario increasingly repeated later in the century, genteel elites disagreed but could not ignore the power of this burgeoning market for unimproving leisure. In 1860, for example, *Frank Leslie's Illustrated Newspaper* railed against prizefighters as the heroes of brothels, gambling dens, and saloons, yet nevertheless dispatched reporters and artists to cover a much-anticipated bout in London the same year.

Although elements of Northern leisure existed in the South, Southern leisure in general reflected the region's precapitalist status. Agrarian life along with a homogeneous population encouraged the persistence of leisure integrated with the seasonal nature of work. With wealth gravitating upward, plain folk and slaves never reached the stage of a consumer market for commercial leisure. Instead of a genteel elite promoting leisure as a means of complementing industry, a planter elite set the tone for work as a means to enjoy free time. Leisure unified the South, but hardly in the manner envisioned by the North's genteel elite.

Travelers in the South invariably expressed shock or amusement over the indolent and improvident behavior they witnessed. One observer wrote in 1855 of Southerners: "Life to them is but a play-day, and the question of every morning is—how to kill time?" From the lowland South's cotton cycles to herd farming of the upland, customary leisure contrasted with labor-intensive industry of Northern mills and small farms. In the Southern environment, where leisure permeated the entire social order, virtues prized in the North such as industry, self-control, discipline, and thrift never took root. As in premodern Europe, time flowed from the present backward with little pensiveness about the future.

The institution of slavery provided the stoutest pillar supporting this leisure-indulgent society. Slavery blurred class differences among whites because the "mudsills" represented a servile class that bore the burden of work. Instead of dignifying labor, slavery degraded it. Work in Southern culture meant perpetual servitude and toil, the mark of Cain rather than a purposeful, organizing principle. Slavery bonded all whites because all whites shared the privilege of its opposite, leisure. Through play and not work, whites earned status in the South's patriarchal system. Status could be achieved in a number of ways harking back to premodern Europe. These included displays of strength, aggression, and skill.

Photographer Mathew Brady (*center*) and General Ambrose Burnside (*right*) relaxing in camp, probably near Cold Harbor, Virginia, 1864 (*Library of Congress*)

The English aristocracy provided planters a model for a leisurely lifestyle that cotton supported. Visitors at sumptuous mansions recorded lavish hospitality, including banquets, fox hunting, balls, and card parties. A Northerner remarked about the typical planter: "Leisure and ease are inmates of his roof....He takes no note of time." Although the planters comprised a tiny minority of Southerners, the planters' conspicuous consumption and sporting leisure earned status from those below. Mutuality that characterized the patriarchal system rested on sociability of planters toward common folk. A planter might invite neighbors to barbecues, harvest festivals, or horse races. But he also might participate in the common Southerners' more typical pastimes such as cockfights, hunting parties, fist fights, or "gander pulling" (a live gander with greased neck would be hung upside down while mounted riders competed to yank off its head). By sharing frolic and aggressive sport, white males demonstrated their status and reconfirmed their dominance over women and slaves.

Play unified white males and maintained the social hierarchy, but it also enabled planters to retain control of slaves. A planter might threaten his operation by neglecting to indulge slaves and participate in their leisurely diversions. Some planters more than others permitted slaves more leisure, allowing them to attend horse races or cockfights, fish, and own firearms for hunting. On many plantations, slaves looked forward to Saturday night dances that an eyewitness termed "one of the finest specimens of animated nature I ever gazed upon." (Ironically, but poignantly, urban audiences simultaneously paid to watch songs and dances by blackface minstrels that purported to enact plantation life.) Planters usually joined slaves in work-related festivities such as hog killing or corn shuckings. Slaves often fondly remembered such occasions that featured drinking, eating, dancing, singing, and shouting while the work went on.

Few planters dared not host annual Christmas holidays, which slaves eagerly anticipated all year. Replicating premodern Christmas, the holiday involved suspension of ordinary routine and inversion of the social hierarchy. Slaves, for example, entered the "big house" and demanded gifts. A week of convivial drinking, eating, and dancing followed, lubricated by liquor supplied by the planter. The reuniting of slave families made the holidays all the merrier. "The whole exhibited a scene which might more than compare with the bacchanal feasts and amusements of antiquity," a jarred Bostonian remembered of one Christmas scene. Like the European aristocracy, planters encouraged the Christmas revelry as a safety valve ensuring loyalty the rest of the year. In his autobiography, Frederick Douglass identified the holidays as a psychological tool that planters used not only to maintain control, but also to create greater dependency. "Their object seems to be, to disgust their slaves with freedom, by plunging them into the lowest depths of dissipation," Douglass wrote.

Leisure then acted as a thread drawn from top to bottom of Southern society. As slaves enabled Southerners to employ leisure as a kind of cultural glue, so perhaps were Southerners willing to commit themselves to war as a way to protect their leisure and hence their status. On the basis of Northern and Southern disparities in leisure, it is perhaps less surprising that such divergent societies could settle their differences only on the battlefield. One society set itself on a path of rationalized and commercial leisure based on systematic work; in the other, leisure reflected premodern play and formed an integral, not auxiliary, part of the social system.

Once under way, the war curtailed leisure for a brief time. With three million men under arms during the conflict, participation in pastimes such as yachting, baseball, rowing, and horse racing dwindled. The public initially abstained from commercial entertainments such as theater and travel. But in the North the war galvanized new forms of leisure. For example, the first exchange of New York, Brooklyn, and New Jersey baseball teams with Philadelphia teams occurred during the war years. During the war, baseball teams played to crowds of as many as 15,000. New wealth in the North opened floodgates of consumer spending and ushered in excesses of extravagance that the genteel elite found immoral. For rich and poor, the war signaled a holiday from the genteel agenda. Horse racing, prizefighting, and billiard matches ratcheted stakes upward like never before. Elite summer resorts such as Saratoga and Nahant boomed with patrons fitted out in luxurious finery. During the war, entrepreneur A. T. Stewart built his Cast Iron Palace, an eight-story retail establishment that occupied a full block in Manhattan. Illuminated with gaslights, hundreds of windows, and a glass dome, its lush shopping areas featured laces, silk gowns, and $1,000 camel-hair shawls. "There is something saddening, indeed revolting, in the high glee with which the people here look upon what ought to be, at any rate, a grievous national calamity," a *London Times* correspondent observed in a 3 November 1863 column. "The indulgence in every variety of pleasure, luxury, and extravagance is simply shocking."

Yet Southerners hardly displayed abstemious behavior either, although new money did not prompt their immoderation. In fiery sermons, Southern clergy thundered against pleasurable leisure activities that angered God against the Southern cause. These excesses were the timeless sins of drinking, gambling, sex, and merrymaking. Concert halls and theaters in Southern cities continued to do a brisk business. In 1863, residents of Richmond, a city "favored with fun," according to the *Richmond Enquirer*, could choose among burlesque, drama, concerts, and comedy in a variety of theaters.

Soldiers at rest after drill, Petersburg, Virginia, 1864 (*National Archives*)

Soldiers from both sides appear to have shown fewer differences in their leisure than did their respective regions. Soldiering was, in a sense, a form of leisure itself, for it provided a way to prove one's masculinity much like a fight, a wager, or a feat of strength. But it also provided boys with excitement, adventure, and release from the endless humdrum of labor on farms or in mines and mills. Army life presented long stretches of free time punctuated by the terror of combat. It assembled tens of thousands of men from different classes who brought their leisure practices to camp. Premodern, modern, and improving leisure forms mingled and pervaded camp life. Traditional pastimes familiar to country boys included foot races, hunting, shooting matches, gander pulling, brawling, and other folderol. Yet, as reformers pointed out, some traditional leisure threatened self-discipline, self-control, and sober habits. Many soldiers testified to the pernicious influence of army camps on morals. Removed from the restraints of home and community, soldiers on both sides gambled, drank, and visited prostitution houses. Gambling, perhaps the most common indulgence, introduced many youths not only to cards, dice, and chuck-a-luck, but also to traditional wagering events such as cockfighting and horse racing. Drinking

proved such a problem that it concerned both commanders and moralists. General George B. McClellan, for example, claimed that abstinence from liquor would mean an extra 50,000 troops to his army.

Union and Confederate recruits integrated modern leisure activities into the playful chaos of premodern pastimes. Thanks to printing improvements and the common school, soldiers on both sides read extensively, although Federals enjoyed an abundance of print unknown to Confederates. Newspapers, religious material, and pulp fiction such as Beadle's Dime Book series predominated. Music also provided a popular pastime in all camps. Soldiers sang whenever possible, formed glee clubs, and played banjos, fiddles, and guitars brought from home. Publishers capitalized on the rage for music with a flood of patriotic and sentimental song sheets printed in an accordion fold-out format. Commercial theater, minstrel shows, and circuses were emulated in camp, with organizers often charging admission. Baseball became the favorite organized sport in both Union and Confederate camps, although versions of the game differed. Because of the game's challenging diversion and orderly release of energy, officers often staged baseball matches.

As might be expected, in Union camps soldiers and outsiders tried to restrict play to improving activities. Army chaplains, U.S. Christian Commission representatives, and other reform-minded missionaries tried to discourage common camp vices, but with mixed results. Dismayed at drunkenness, gambling, obscene literature, pictures of minimally clothed or naked women, and bawdy singing, reformers tried to introduce the moral influences of domesticity into camp. Some tried to improve soldiers' use of leisure by organizing literary associations with lending libraries. Soldiers formed debating societies and mounted genteel "lyceums" that included an edifying agenda of recitations, speeches, and spelling bees.

Soldiers returned home exposed to new leisure forms and practices. The irregular pattern of army life legitimized leisure for many accustomed to continual toil, and it introduced others to both meaningful and debased ways to spend free time. In camp, recruits created the largest aggregate of Americans ever to play organized sports up to that time, aiding the postwar boom in team sports. But the conflict transformed leisure in more significant ways than promoting the spread of leisure through veterans. Appreciation of war's physical and spiritual demands brought muscular Christianity and its derivatives into the mainstream of the genteel agenda. After the war, vigorous exercise was viewed as a way to build character and avoid national decadence. Cultural leaders promoted team sports such as football to inculcate selfless action and moral toughness in youth.

More important, long-term effects from the war's expansion of capital, markets, productive capacity, and communication networks helped create a national culture. Leisure grew ever more commercial, uniform, rational, and specialized. With the triumph of free-labor industrial capitalism over slavery, the war kicked out leisure as a prop of the South's old social order and began the slow process of bringing the South into national life. New wealth produced by the conflict introduced thousands of Northerners to commercial entertainment and the purchase of luxury goods, which moved the nation closer toward its transformation into a consumer culture. By the end of the century, the genteel elite no longer could contain pressure that burst forth as mass culture in amusement parks, popular literature, department stores, and spectator sports. In its effects on leisure, the Civil War was no less revolutionary than in other areas of American life.

—*Jim Weeks*

For further reading:
Cress, Gary. *A Social History of Leisure Since 1600* (1990).
Douglass, Frederick. *Narrative of the Life of Frederick Douglass, an American Slave: Written by Himself* (1968).
Dulles, Foster Rhea. *A History of Recreation: America Learns to Play* (1965).
Fite, Emerson D. *Social and Industrial Conditions in the North during the Civil War* (1910).

Genovese, Eugene D. *Roll, Jordan, Roll: The World the Slaves Made* (1974).
Gorn, Elliot, and Warren Goldstein. *A Brief History of American Sports* (1993).
McWhiney, Grady. *Cracker Culture: Celtic Ways in the Old South* (1988).
Rader, Benjamin G. *American Sports: From the Age of Folk Games to the Age of Televised Sports* (1996).
Wiley, Bell Irvin. *The Life of Billy Yank, the Common Soldier of the Union* (1952; reprint 1993).
———. *The Life of Johnny Reb, the Common Soldier of the Confederacy* (1943; reprint 1997).

LEMMON V. PEOPLE, 20 N.Y. 562 (1860)

This decision of the New York Court of Appeals involved the rights of slave owners and of states. Juliet Lemmon of Virginia took eight slaves on a sea journey to Texas. Her transport stopped in the port of New York. On application by a black New York citizen, her slaves were seized under a writ of habeas corpus issued by a New York judge.

An 1817 New York law proclaimed, "No person held as a slave shall be imported, introduced, or brought into this State, on any pretence whatever. Every such person shall be free." While an exception was originally made for people in transit with slaves, that exception was repealed in 1841.

Lemmon's counsel, relying on the Supreme Court's opinion in the case of *Gibbons v. Ogden* (1824), held that this matter implicated the power of the federal Congress to regulate commerce among the several states. Further, Lemmon argued that Congress's power in this area was exclusive, so that New York—whatever its people's desires—could not legislate in this matter.

The state of New York argued that slavery was contrary to natural right, thus disfavored by systems of justice. Because the U.S. Constitution delegated only limited powers to the federal government, the state's lawyer reasoned, any powers not granted were reserved. By the provision of the federal Constitution requiring states to return fugitive slaves, he concluded, any requirement for states to render nonfugitive slaves was excluded. *Expressio unius, exclusio alterius.*

The New York Court of Appeals began its opinion by noting that no necessity had impelled Lemmon to take her slaves to Texas via New York. Thus, the question presented was one simply of the authority of the legislature to ban slavery in New York and to declare that all slaves entering the state became free. Responsibility for interstate comity, it continued, rested entirely with the legislature; courts would not alter legislative enactments to extend comity to other states. (The court hinted that it believed the legislature had erred in repealing the exception for travelers.)

Inclusion of the Fugitive Slave Clause in the federal Constitution, the court reasoned, showed that that document's authors had not thought that the fact of a federative union in itself necessarily entailed return even of slaves illegally fleeing their masters. How much weaker, then, the idea that such a union by its nature required the return of slaves legally taken to New York.

The court pointed to the English precedent in the case of *Somerset v. Stewart* (1772). There, the Court of King's Bench had declared that only positive law could uphold slavery, since it was contrary to the law of nature, and that since England had no laws upholding slavery, slaves entering English territory became free.

Judge Hiram Denio made short work of the argument that citizens carried the property rights of their own states with them wherever they went. Would anyone argue that the gambling, usurious, and other contracts contrary to New York law that were entered into within New York by citizens born in states where such contracts were legal must be enforced by New York courts? The right to own slaves was similar. The privileges and immunities guaranteed to citizens of one state when traveling through another were not superior to the privileges and immunities of citizens of the host state, and New Yorkers had no right to own slaves.

Judge Denio easily brushed aside *Gibbons v. Ogden*, too. The slaves freed under the New York writ were staying in a house in New York. Had they been in coastal waters, the matter might have been different. In this case, though, any question of the exclusivity of Congress's commerce power was irrelevant.

Judge William B. Wright averred that the issue here was New York's sovereignty. To New York alone, he insisted, was reserved the power to determine the status of everyone within its territory. This power was exclusive. New York had exercised its sovereign will to ban the status of slavery from its territory. Comity did not necessarily extend, he concluded, to maintenance of Virginia's laws "repugnant to her policy" within New York's territory.

By a vote of four to three, with the dissenters pointing to comity concerns in justification of their dissents, the Court of Appeals upheld the lower court's decision. In dissent Judge Thomas W. Clerke insisted that, under the *Dred Scott* ruling, slavery not only was not disfavored by the law, but slaves were recognized as property by the Federal Constitution. This decision, not the *Somerset* case, had precedential weight in the United States, according to Judge Clerke. He also asked whether it was consistent with the "purpose of a perfect union" mentioned in the Federal Constitution's preamble for a citizen travelling from state A to state C via state B to have his property seized by state B. South Carolina answered this question negatively, pointing to *Lemmon v. People* to justify its secession. Abraham Lincoln, on the other hand, claimed to see the makings of a new *Dred Scott* case (1857) decision in Lemmon's decision to appeal to the United States Supreme Court, which he expected to side with Lemmon. Before the Supreme Court could hear the appeal, the dissolution of the Union made the legal dispute irrelevant.

—*K. R. Constantine Gutzman*

See also *Dred Scott* Case; Personal Liberty Laws.

LESLIE, FRANK
See Frank Leslie's Illustrated Newspaper

LETCHER, JOHN
(1813–1884)
Governor of Virginia

Born on a farm near Lexington, Virginia, on 29 March 1813, John Letcher grew up in a middle-class Methodist home with strong Democratic leanings. He received his education in an old field school and at Washington College. As a young man he took an interest in politics and law. He contributed articles to Democratic newspapers and became editor of the Lexington *Valley Star* from 1839 to 1841.

Letcher continued to nurture his interest in obtaining political office while engaging in his law practice. By 1848, these political aspirations were beginning to reach fruition. He became a presidential elector, participated in the state constitutional convention of 1850–1851, and secured a seat in the U.S. House of Representatives in 1851. Letcher's service in Congress earned him the nickname "Honest John, Watch Dog of the Treasury." In 1859, he ran for the governorship in Virginia and won by a narrow margin.

During the next volatile year in the life of his state and the nation, Governor Letcher championed Stephen Douglas as the Democratic presidential candidate and sought a moderate course in the increasingly extreme atmosphere of the day. Despite his efforts, the Constitutional Union candidate, John Bell, carried Virginia, and the Republican candidate, Abraham Lincoln, won the general election. Lincoln's victory convinced South Carolinians to take their state out of the Union rather than submit to Republican authority.

With an impending conflict increasingly likely, Governor Letcher cautiously prepared Virginia for its own defense. He attempted to recruit officers from the U.S. Army for important state posts, although he did not always succeed, as with Southampton Countian George H. Thomas.

The Confederate bombardment of Fort Sumter and President Lincoln's subsequent call for 75,000 volunteers forced Letcher and Virginia to face the crucial decision of whether or not to fill the quota of troops demanded or secede and cast the state's lot with the Confederate

States of America. The governor chose the latter path. Letcher authorized state troops to seize critical installations and equipment at Harper's Ferry and Norfolk. Despite Federal efforts to destroy or disable these facilities, their capture ensured that Virginia's war-making capabilities would increase dramatically. Machinery from Harper's Ferry proved invaluable to small arms production, and the capture of the burned hull of the USS *Merrimack* and the dry docks of Gosport Navy Yard were as important for the future of the Confederate navy.

In these early days, Virginians rallied to the cause. Letcher appointed former West Point commandant Robert E. Lee to take charge of the state troops. But the challenges were enormous. Situated as it was, Virginia endured immediate invasion. Union columns penetrated the commonwealth with regularity, threatening or capturing the Shenandoah Valley, the port city of Norfolk, and the capital of Richmond itself by the summer of 1862. Letcher responded to the defense of his state with vigor, demanding that the people sacrifice their "rights," if necessary, in order to win the war. For instance, such efforts included the slaves he expected plantation owners to supply as laborers on the state's military defenses.

The spring of 1863 saw hardship, shortage, and inflation rock the state. Civilians became so disgruntled that bread riots broke out in Richmond. Letcher addressed the crowd and threatened to turn the state militia on them when they did not disperse. This hard-line stance proved successful but won him few supporters.

Whatever the issue, Letcher sought to place himself and Virginia on the side of obtaining Confederate victory and independence. This put him at odds with those who sought to retain state sovereignty at all costs. The governor's role in the war and his willingness to subordinate his state to the demands of his nation eventually cost him politically. He failed to win a bid for a seat in the Confederate Congress from the Shenandoah Valley. Yet, despite this personal setback, Letcher continued to support the war effort. He delivered numerous speeches designed to bolster public morale and sustained a belief in the possibility of ultimate Confederate success.

In late 1864, Union raiders visited further indignity upon the former governor by targeting his home for destruction. Forced to flee for his own security, Letcher returned and resumed his law practice. At the close of the conflict, Federal troops arrested and removed him to Washington, D.C., holding him in confinement for two months. Upon his parole and release, Letcher made his way back to his home state and took up residence once more in Lexington.

During the postwar period, Letcher remained a strong supporter of the local educational institutions of Washington College and the Virginia Military Institute,

helping to repair the latter as a member of its board. He continued to work to restore his own financial condition through his law practice, eventually working himself back into politics, winning a seat in the Virginia House of Delegates in 1875. Shortly thereafter, a debilitating stroke and the resulting temporary paralysis greatly affected him. Even so, Letcher hoped to hold onto his House of Delegates seat. His supporters obligingly renominated him, but the election went against him. Letcher retired from public life, deteriorating steadily in his health before dying on 26 January 1884.

—Brian S. Wills

See also Gosport Navy Yard; Virginia.
For further reading:
Boney, F. N. *John Letcher of Virginia* (1966).
Dabney, Virginius. *Virginia* (1971).
Thomas, Emory M. *The Confederate Nation* (1979).
———. *The Confederate State of Richmond: A Biography of the Capitol* (1971; reprint, 1998).

LEXINGTON, MISSOURI, BATTLE OF
(17 September–20 September 1861)

By September 1861, the Civil War was already a few months old. In August, the battle of Wilson's Creek in Missouri resulted in more than 2,500 casualties as Union and Confederate forces struggled for control of the state. Union forces scrambled to organize after the death of General Nathaniel Lyon and the losses sustained from the battle. Confederate forces too had taken a beating, but a force under General Sterling Price started on a northern course through Missouri intent on claiming the state. Union scouts reported Price's advance, but his main target was not entirely clear. The target for the Confederate force was Lexington, a small, wealthy town located between Kansas City and St. Louis. Union forces in Kansas under General John C. Frémont were too small to oppose Price's movement, but Frémont sent orders to other field commanders to concentrate on Lexington. Colonel James A. Mulligan, from Chicago, learned of Price's advance and led his Irish Brigade through treacherously bad roads to Lexington just days before the Confederate arrival.

A regiment of Illinois cavalry under Colonel Thomas A. Marshall and a small contingent of 350 home guards were in Lexington. Mulligan took command of the small force numbering around 2,800 men. Confederate forces consisted of more than 10,000 veterans of Wilson's Creek and new volunteers. Mulligan set about building a set of fortifications containing seventeen acres surrounding a Masonic college on a hill overlooking the Missouri River. Work had barely begun when the first Confederate forces were sighted on 11 September 1861 south of town. Small skirmishes took place for a few days, including one incident in which two German immigrants supplied homemade cannonballs that were fired into the surprised Confederate camp. The new Confederate recruits scattered in fright. Price decided to wait for the rest of his men.

By 17 September, Price's ammunition wagons had arrived. Union troops had used the precious days to dig in on the hill and watch the Confederate forces surround the camp. A Confederate line was posted at the bank of the river, cutting off the Union water supply. On 18 September, Price's artillery opened up on the besieged Union troops. For hours, artillery and musket fire were exchanged with no serious effect.

During the day, Confederate skirmishers complained of sniper fire from a brick house just over 100 yards outside the Federal trenches. The Anderson house was used as a Union hospital and had been spared by the Confederates. An attack was then ordered on the house. When the Confederate attackers overran the hospital with minor casualties, the snipers had escaped and only sick and wounded men occupied the house. As the Confederate soldiers searched the house, they looked down right into the Union trenches. It was a perfect place to pick off Union soldiers.

Enraged by the Confederate attack upon the hospital, Mulligan called upon his Montgomery Guards to take back the house. The Irishmen and a company of Peabody's Germans charged the home, taking casualties as they advanced. The Northerners burst through the back door, firing at the fleeing Rebels. Three Southern soldiers surrendered, only to be bayoneted while under guard. The Union soldiers did not hold the hospital for long. Exhausted from the attack and a lack of water, the men were driven back by a counterattack.

Nineteen September was hotter than the day before. The water shortage became a serious problem for the beleaguered Union troops. A small rain shower brought some relief, but the heat and the smell of the dead and rotting horses only added to the misery. Outside town, Union forces marching to relieve Mulligan were warned of an impending ambush and abandoned the plan. Although he did not know it, Mulligan was on his own. He struggled to hold out. Confederate cannonballs heated red hot were sent into the college to start fires. However, men with shovels worked feverishly to throw out the incoming missiles, thereby saving the structure.

During this time, Confederate forces developed an ingenious plan to end the siege. By using hemp bales as portable breastworks, Rebel troops could push their way up the hill protected from Union fire. The bales would be soaked in the river to prevent them from catching fire. The next morning, Union soldiers saw a long dark line extending on both sides of the hospital. The line began moving closer, parting for trees and closing again. Men behind the bales were laboring to push and pry the line forward, while other rebels fired shots as they approached. Mulligan's artillery fired hot shot into the bales, but the wet bales would not light. As the line closed in, some Union troops realized that the end was inevitable and a white handkerchief was raised. Mulligan had not ordered the cease-fire, but after a vote by his officers, 4 to 2, the Union forces surrendered. The Union troops relinquished the position, giving up their guns. Mulligan's Irish troops reluctantly left the trenches and ended the siege.

The battle of Lexington was not a large encounter by eastern standards. Confederate losses amounted to 25 killed and 72 wounded. Union losses were reported as 39 killed and 120 wounded. The North had sustained a painful defeat in the struggle over Missouri, but further battles were to come.

—Ian M. Spurgeon

See also Missouri; Price, Sterling; Wilson's Creek, Missouri.
For further reading:
Castel, Albert. General Sterling Price and the Civil War in the West (1968).
Monaghan, Jay. Civil War on the Western Border, 1854–1865 (1955).
Shalhope, Robert E. Sterling Price: Portrait of a Southerner (1971).

LEXINGTON, TENNESSEE, BATTLE OF
(18 December 1862)

The battle of Lexington was the first engagement of Nathan Bedford Forrest's raid into western Tennessee in December 1862. Confederate general Braxton Bragg had ordered Forrest to move into western Tennessee to cut Federal supply lines and disrupt rail transportation into northern Mississippi. Forrest departed from Columbia, Tennessee, on 11 December 1862 with about 2,500 men. When he reached the Tennessee River at Clifton, Tennessee, on 13 December, he set his men to work building flatboats to effect a crossing. After crossing the river on the fifteenth, he instructed his men to mark the spot and then sink the boats in shallow water so that they could be retrieved if the need arose for a hasty retreat back across the river.

Once the boats were disposed of, Forrest and his men headed toward Lexington, Tennessee. News of Forrest's crossing reached Brigadier General Jeremiah Sullivan at Jackson, Tennessee, and he dispatched Colonel Robert G. Ingersoll toward the Tennessee River to discern Forrest's movements. Ingersoll, with 200 men from the 11th Illinois Cavalry and one battery, left Jackson on 16 December and arrived in Lexington early on the seventeenth. At Lexington, about 470 additional men reinforced Ingersoll, but many of these men were new recruits who had never seen combat.

About noon on 17 December Ingersoll led a reconnaissance mission toward Beech Creek about five miles east of town. At the creek, he sent a scouting party

ahead to determine Forrest's whereabouts. The scouts soon returned with the news that about 1,000 Confederate troopers were moving in their direction. Ingersoll ordered his forces to pull back toward Lexington. Once in what he considered to be good defensible positions guarding the two roads (Old Stage Road and Lower Road) approaching the town, Ingersoll ordered scouts back toward the Confederate positions to try to determine the route the Southerners would take and to destroy bridges across Beech Creek.

In the meantime, Forrest had decided not to attack until the next morning, leaving Ingersoll's men to wait uneasily through the night. In the early morning hours of 18 December, Ingersoll determined that the main Confederate attack would come along the Old Stage Road. Therefore he placed the bulk of his men along that route, while sending only two companies to protect the Lower Road. Ingersoll's suspicions seemed confirmed when pickets spotted part of Forrest's force moving toward them on the Old Stage Road. The initial attacks by the Confederates were repulsed, when Ingersoll suddenly heard firing coming from the Lower Road. He rode to that position and quickly surmised that the main Confederate attack was coming from that direction. He later learned that the bridge he had ordered destroyed along that road had not been destroyed after all.

Ingersoll pulled back and had his battery moved into position to try to repel the unexpected Southern onslaught. By that time the green troops defending the Lower Road were fleeing in panic, and the battery was about the only thing standing between Forrest and Lexington. Forrest and his men charged against the Federal artillery three times before overwhelming the few Union defenders. The remainder of Ingersoll's men fled in panic back toward Jackson. Forrest captured 147 of them, including Ingersoll.

Along with the human prisoners, Forrest also captured two artillery pieces that were the beginnings of another battery that Forrest would use throughout the rest of the war, seventy horses, a large supply of Federal rifles and ammunition, and other assorted supplies. After assessing his good fortune, Forrest moved toward Jackson, but found the defenses there too strong. He continued his raid, however, deeper into Federal-held territory—destroying railroad bridges between Columbus, Kentucky, and northern Mississippi and generally disrupting communications. On his return trip toward the Tennessee River he lost a battle at Parker Cross Roads but escaped with most of his force intact.

—*David S. Heidler and Jeanne T. Heidler*

See also Forrest's Raids; Parker Cross Roads.

For further reading:

Maness, Lonnie E. "Forest and the Battle of Parker's Crossroads." *Tennessee Historical Quarterly* (1975).

Wills, Brian Steel. *A Battle from the Start: The Life of Nathan Bedford Forrest* (1992).

LIBBY PRISON

During the war, Richmond, Virginia, became virtually a prison city, housing thousands of captured Federals. One of its best-known prisons was Libby, a large three-story brick tobacco factory that consisted of three separate buildings, each measuring 110 feet by 44 feet. When John Enders, Sr., built it sometime between 1845 and 1852, the structure occupied all the western half of a block bounded by Cary and Dock Streets at 20th Street.

Enders, a founder of the Richmond tobacco industry, was killed instantly during the buildings' construction when he fell from a ladder through a hatch of the central building. He had also been a leader in developing real estate in the dock area along the James River, and with his in-laws, the Ege family, he owned much of the property. Upon his death, several of his slaves burned down all the buildings between 21st and 22d Streets when they discovered that his will did not set them free as expected.

In 1854 Captain Luther Libby leased one of the three buildings on a renewable three-year lease from the Enders family, and it was he who erected the sign reading "L. Libby & Sons, Ship Chandlers," which gave the building its memorable name. A native of Maine, Libby closed down his operation at the outbreak of war, in part because most of his business was with Northern shipping, but he continued to maintain the lease. However, within a week after the battle of First Bull Run on 21 July 1861, Richmond was bulging with so many prisoners that this structure was among several buildings commandeered for prisoner and hospital use. Brigadier General John H. Winder, appointed inspector general, readily saw Richmond as a collection point from which prisoners could be sent to locations farther from the front. Supported by accusations that Libby harbored Union sympathies, Winder gave Libby only forty-eight hours to vacate the premises. So immediate was the need for the building that during its conversion to a prison the sign remained in place, and thus the name Libby Prison came into use.

Initially a thousand Union prisoners were crowded haphazardly into Libby, but soon officers and enlisted men were separated, with the latter being sent to the tent city on Belle Isle in the James River. For most of the war, the prison's commandant was Major Thomas P. "Dick" Turner. It was Turner, along with Major James W. Pegram, who were to command the first "Negro brigades" in late March 1865. Although arrested at war's end, Turner did not suffer the same fate as the more notorious commandant of Andersonville, Major Henry Wirz.

Although many prisoners were relocated throughout the Confederacy's fledgling prison network, approximately 2,000 remained in Richmond throughout 1861. These actions did relieve the prison population somewhat, but in a city struggling to secure transport and

Side view of Libby Prison, 1865 (*Library of Congress*)

adequate supplies to feed the Confederate capital's ever growing population, the prisoners were viewed as an unnecessary burden. With the Seven Days' campaign of June 1862, the prison population of Richmond rose to dangerous levels, adding to the strain. By the winter of 1863–1864, more than 1,000 officers were crammed into Libby Prison. Combined with the overcrowded conditions, all faced starvation rations and a lack of warm clothing. However, by May 1864 the officer population at Libby Prison was significantly reduced when

these men were moved to a new prison for officers in Macon, Georgia. From then until the end of the war, the officer population in the prison did not approach its former 1863 levels, despite the continued overcrowding at Belle Isle and the siege of Richmond from July 1864 to April 1865.

Prisoners did not occupy the ground floors. The west ground floor was used as offices and guardrooms; the middle, as the prison's kitchen. The second floor was used to house the prisoners, and it was these three rooms that they referred to as "Streight's," "Milroy's," and the "Chickamauga Room." The cellars contained cells for dangerous prisoners, spies, and slaves under sentence of death, as well as a carpenter shop. Inner doors connected all three buildings, but the different buildings were given the designations of East, Middle and West.

There were quite a few escapes from Libby Prison during the war. The most noteworthy was led by Colonel Thomas E. Rose of the 77th Pennsylvania Volunteers and assisted by Major A. G. Hamilton of the 12th U.S. Kentucky. On 9 February 1864, 109 officers tunneled their way out by constructing a fifty-three-foot-long tunnel in seventeen days. The only tools that they had to use in the digging were an old pocketknife, some chisels, a piece of rope, a rubber cloth, and a wooden spittoon. Although forty-eight were recaptured, fifty-nine were able to reach Union lines, but two drowned during the escape. Rose himself was later captured by Confederate provost guards, but later was exchanged on 30 April 1864.

After the Federal occupation of Richmond on 3 April 1865, Union authorities also used Libby as a prison to house high-ranking former Confederates until 3 August 1868. After this, the West Building was sold to the Southern Fertilizing Company, and the other two structures continued as property of the Enders family, being owned by Mrs. George S. Palmer.

In 1888, a Chicago syndicate purchased the buildings for $23,000. Work commenced in December of that year to remove the structure from Richmond to Chicago, a project never before equaled in the history of building relocation. Each part of Libby Prison was numbered and lettered for ease of handling, and then the building parts were loaded on 132 freight cars.

In Chicago the enterprise was incorporated as the Libby Prison Museum Association and given the title Great Libby Prison War Museum. The structure was assembled in the area of Wabash Avenue, between 14th and 16th Streets, and housed an extensive Civil War collection. In total, the cost of dismantling and moving the building exceeded $200,000 and was completed in September 1889. During the life of the Libby Prison Museum Association, the museum was highly profitable and operated until 1899. In that year the venture was disbanded, and the structure was torn down to make room for a coliseum. Libby Prison's bricks and timbers were either sold off or discarded.

—*Frank E. Deserino*

See also Belle Isle; Prisoner Exchanges; Prisoner Paroles; Prisoners of War; Prisons, C.S.A.

For further reading:
Parker, Sandra V. *Richmond's Civil War Prisons* (1990).
Ryan, David D. *Cornbread and Maggots—Cloak and Dagger: Union Prisoners and Spies in Civil War Richmond* (1994).
Speer, Lonnie R. *Portals to Hell: The Military Prisons of the Civil War* (1997).

LIEBER, FRANCIS
(1798 or 1800–1872)
Political scientist

Francis Lieber was born on 18 March in 1798 or 1800, in Berlin, Germany. His father, Friedrich Wilhelm Lieber, was an iron maker; his mother's name is unknown. During his childhood, Lieber was influenced by the Napoleonic Wars, including Berlin's capture, and the emotional feelings of nationalistic patriotism in his community. Lieber's older brothers enlisted in 1813, and Lieber was old enough to join the Prussian army with them in 1815. He served under the command of Gebhard L. von Blücher in the Colberg militia, fighting in the Waterloo campaign. At the battle of Namur, Lieber was wounded and almost died. Returning home, Lieber sought to continue his education with Friedrich Ludwig Jahn. In 1819, the government targeted Jahn's students as liberal thinkers, and Lieber was arrested with his teacher. His first publications were liberty songs that Lieber had composed and that the government printed as its proof of his danger to authority.

During the four months he was in prison, Lieber read and studied. After his release, he was forbidden to enter any university except the school at Jena, eliminating his opportunities for advancement in his native province. He completed his doctorate at Jena in 1820 and received orders to leave the area. Lieber spent the next year studying surveying at Halle and Dresden. He joined German liberals supporting the Greek war of liberation. Enlisting in the military forces, Lieber departed from Marseilles to sail to Greece in January 1822. Quickly disillusioned by the lack of food and shelter, attacks by thieves, and incompetent Greek soldiers, Lieber decided to travel to Rome, Italy, where poverty forced him to accept a position as tutor to the son of the German ambassador. During his time in Italy, he wrote his first book, *Tagebuch Meines Aufenthaltes in Griechenland* (1823). Lieber's *Reminiscences of an Intercourse with Mr. Niebuhr the Historian* (1835) explained that this period of his life was the most crucial for his intellectual development.

Lieber returned to Berlin in the summer of 1823. In August 1824, he was arrested with a group of young men that the government believed was fomenting a liberal conspiracy. Arrested as a witness, Lieber was incarcerated at the prison in Köpenick and threatened with life imprisonment because he refused to confess or provide evidence. With the help of friends, Lieber was released and secretly emigrated in 1826 to England, where he taught languages and wrote for German periodicals.

On 20 June 1827, Lieber arrived in New York City and then traveled to Boston, Massachusetts, where he managed a gymnasium and swimming school. He befriended significant individuals who assisted him in his literary pursuits. He also envisioned and edited the

Encyclopaedia Americana, (1829–1833), a thirteen-volume series that included articles about history, politics, and science written by prominent authors. On 21 September 1829, Lieber married Mathilda Oppenheimer, whom he had tutored in England. The couple moved to Philadelphia, Pennsylvania, to advance Lieber's literary work, and he wrote a constitution and regulations for Girard College in 1834. One year later, he was chosen to chair history and political economy at South Carolina College. For twenty-one years Lieber taught there, where he was considered a good teacher but an ineffective disciplinarian. Although he owned slaves, Lieber's empathy for abolitionist principles bothered the college community. When the office of college president was vacant, Lieber was not chosen to fill it, and he resigned in 1855.

Lieber had often complained that he was in exile from his friends while in South Carolina; however, his years in South Carolina were especially productive. During that time, he wrote the two-volume *Manual of Political Ethics* (1838–1839), *Legal and Political Hermeneutics* (1839), and the two-volume *On Civil Liberty and Self-Government* (1853). These books discussed the obligations of citizens to participate in their governments, carefully create their laws, and protect liberty and suggested ways to reform state constitutions. Considered the first systematic works addressing political science in the United States, Lieber's treatises examined the philosophy of the state. He strove to offer readers intellectual foundations to interpret texts.

In 1857 Lieber accepted a professorship at Columbia College in New York City, becoming a prominent political philosopher and expert on international relations. He was considered the first officially titled political scientist in the country. Lieber was at Columbia when the Civil War began. Already well known for his legal writings, Lieber had been one of the first critics of secession, delivering a speech in South Carolina as early as 1851. He had also promoted the concept that military officers were responsible for their actions even if they were only obeying orders. Lieber continued to speak about the dangers of secession during the war and penned pro-Union writings.

General Henry W. Halleck of the War Department consulted with Lieber regarding legalities about an internal civil war and whether the Union should handle partisans and guerrillas as prisoners of war. Lieber wrote *Guerrilla Parties Considered with Reference to the Laws and Usages of War* (1862) to establish guidelines. Secretary of War Edwin M. Stanton asked Lieber to travel to Washington, D.C., and consult with him and Halleck about the legal aspects of war. President Abraham Lincoln suggested that Lieber should write a code of war, which was originally published as *A Code for the Government of Armies* (1863) and then revised as *Instructions for the Government of the Armies of the United States in the Field* (1863), which was issued as General Order No. 100 of the War Department and which Lieber referred to as the "old hundred." No similar work in any language existed when Lieber created his pioneering code that was considered the standard for compilers of military law. By 1870 Germany adopted Lieber's code, and it influenced the Hague Conferences of 1899 and 1907. In the late twentieth century, Lieber's code remained the foundation of international understanding regarding the conduct of war and treatment of prisoners.

During the Civil War, Lieber also founded and served as president of the Loyal Publication Society, writing such treatises as "No Party Now, but All for Our Country" and "The Arguments of Secessionists." Three of his sons served in the war: one fought and died for the Confederacy, and two fought for the Union. After the war, Lieber transferred to Columbia's law school as a legal professor. He also served as custodian of captured Confederate papers and arranged and classified those archives. He scrutinized the documents for evidence of potential treason by Confederate leaders. Focusing on scholarship addressing constitutional reform, nationalism, and international law, Lieber was a referee for the Mexican Claims Commission for two years. He helped create the American Social Science Association and a political science school within Columbia. Lieber devised a project for political servants to codify international law that the Institut de Droit International approved after his death on 2 October 1872 in New York City.

—*Elizabeth D. Schafer*

See also Halleck, Henry W.; Prisoners of War.

For further reading:

Brown, Bernard Edward. *American Conservatives: The Political Thought of Francis Lieber and John W. Burgess* (1951).

Farr, James. "Francis Lieber and the Interpretation of American Political Science." *Journal of Politics* (1990).

Freidel, Frank B. *Francis Lieber, Nineteenth-Century Liberal* (1947).

Harley, Lewis R. *Francis Lieber: His Life and Political Philosophy* (1970).

Hartigan, Richard Shelly, ed. *Lieber's Code and the Law of War* (1983).

Perry, Thomas S., ed. *The Life and Letters of Francis Lieber* (1882).

Phinney, Chester S. *Francis Lieber's Influence on American Thought and Some of His Unpublished Letters* (1918).

LINCOLN, ABRAHAM
(1809–1865)
Sixteenth president of the United States

Abraham Lincoln was born on 12 February 1809 in a one-room cabin near Elizabethtown in Hardin County, Kentucky. His parents, Nancy Hanks and Thomas Lincoln, were already the parents of a two-year-old daughter Sarah. Named for his paternal grandfather, Abraham represented the seventh generation of

one branch of the Lincoln family that had migrated to Massachusetts from England in the seventeenth century. His father, Thomas Lincoln, had been born in Virginia, married in Kentucky, and would die in Illinois. His mother, Nancy Hanks, whom Lincoln believed to have been born out of wedlock, came from a less well-established and documented family. Lincoln later said that his parents came from "undistinguished families." Yet on both the maternal and paternal side of his genealogy, his ancestors included hardworking yeomen husbands and wives, on the move for better land and more secure property titles.

There was nothing in Abraham Lincoln's childhood to suggest an auspicious future. On the contrary, the death of an infant brother followed by that of his mother in 1818, when he was nine years old; the constant uprooting of the family to new farms in Kentucky, Indiana, and Illinois; and the lack of any formal schooling save a few months in inferior schools might have stifled any ambition. In 1819 his father remarried, and his new wife, Sarah Bush Johnston, and her three children joined Abraham and Sarah. At the time, the Lincolns were living in Perry (now Spencer) County in southern Indiana. But even after the welcome addition of a loving stepmother to the household, Lincoln's early life remained the austere, routine existence of a farm laborer. Tall and strong, he helped his father clear forest land; he cut up wood, ploughed fields, and planted the corn and vegetables for his largely self-sufficient rural family. Lincoln's life differed little from that of other farm boys throughout the United States whose physical labor was essential to their family's well being.

Abraham Lincoln was unusual, however, in his preoccupation with reading. He often stole moments away from his work to read and memorize from the few books owned by his father and stepmother. With no more than a year of formal school, Lincoln educated himself. Soon he was so proficient that illiterate neighbors in the Pigeon Creek community in Indiana asked him to write letters for them.

In the spring of 1830, the Lincoln family moved from southern Indiana to central Illinois. Twenty-one-year-old Lincoln helped the family relocate. A year later, after a trip to New Orleans on a flatboat, he left his family's farm permanently and settled in the village of New Salem, Illinois, on the Sangamon River. He worked briefly as a clerk in Denton Offut's store until the business floundered. Without a job in the spring of 1832, Lincoln volunteered for the militia in the Fourth Illinois Regiment as it prepared to fight the Black Hawk Indians. His regiment elected him a captain. Returned to New Salem after a summer's service, he ran unsuccessfully for the Illinois state legislature in the fall of 1832.

For the next five years, Abraham Lincoln lived in New Salem. He earned his living in a variety of different ways. He was the part owner of a store. He served as the postmaster of the faltering town, and he undertook increasingly complex surveys for roads and property lines. He also turned his attention to a career in politics. In 1834, as a member of the Whig Party, he won a seat in the lower house of the Illinois legislature. In the state capital of Vandalia, where the legislature met before its move to Springfield, Abraham Lincoln supported his political party's program of state subsidies and bonds for internal improvements such as roads, canals, and railroads. Reelected to the legislature in 1836, 1838, 1840, and 1844, Lincoln emerged as a leader of the 1836 local delegation from Sangamon County, called the Long Nine because of their height.

While he lived in New Salem, often struggling to support himself, Lincoln attended to his education. He learned from discussions with customers in the store, but he learned more from his disciplined and solitary study of grammar and geometry. In his brief autobiography written in 1860, Lincoln acknowledged that at this period of his life he had "studied English grammar, imperfectly of course, but so as to speak and write as well as he now does." At some point—perhaps after his first legislative session—he decided that his future profession would be the law. In this ambition he was helped by the sponsorship of John Todd Stuart, whom he had first met in the militia and later in the legislature. Stuart, a prominent Whig lawyer, served as a political and legal mentor to Lincoln, lending him law books and offering him a partnership in his Springfield law office. But Lincoln's was never a traditional apprenticeship. Instead he worked on his own, later stating that he had studied "with nobody."

During Lincoln's second term in the legislature, he led a faction committed to transferring the Illinois capital from Vandalia to the more flourishing county seat of Springfield, where he moved in April 1837. He shared lodgings with Kentucky-born Joshua Speed, who became one of his few intimate friends. But in the growing community of the new state capital of Springfield he had many acquaintances among the leaders of the bar and politics. Many appreciated Abraham Lincoln for his storytelling and good humor.

Licensed to practice law after the clerk of the Illinois Supreme Court entered his name on the list of attorneys in March 1837, Lincoln energetically pursued his profession from Stuart's office. In 1841 he left to practice with a new partner, Stephen Logan. In 1844 Lincoln joined the best known of his associates, William Herndon, who during Lincoln's presidency remained his law partner.

At first Abraham Lincoln was involved in general practice, especially in litigation and appellate work. He attended to the mundane affairs of a growing number of clients. He drafted wills, wrote deeds, and drew up papers of incorporation. He quickly gained a reputation as a

Abraham Lincoln ca. 1846–1847 (*left*) and in 1865 (*right*)
(Photographs by Nicholas H. Shepherd (*left*) and Alexander Gardner (*right*) / *Library of Congress*)

common-sense lawyer who took criminal as well as civil cases. By the 1840s, Abraham Lincoln had developed a large practice that took him throughout central Illinois. In the small county seats of the Eighth Judicial Circuit he defended his client's interests. By the 1850s he was among a dozen of the best known lawyers in Illinois, and his standing led to lucrative work for corporations such as the Illinois Central Railroad. Accordingly, he prospered financially, earning approximately $2,000 a year at a time when day laborers earned no more than $400 a year. The 1860 Census listed his assets as $5,000 in property and a personal estate of $12,000.

Just as he had been in New Salem, in Springfield Abraham Lincoln was a civic-minded joiner. He became a member of the Young Men's Lyceum whose purposes coincided with his intention of self-improvement. He also supported the principles of the local temperance society and was a well-known speaker. In Springfield he participated as well in the city's active social life. He served as the sponsor of an evening dance, and in the late 1830's met his future wife, the well-born belle from Lexington, Kentucky—Mary Todd.

In 1842 Abraham Lincoln and Mary Todd were married and set up housekeeping, first in the Globe Tavern. Next they rented a small house near the Springfield courthouse. In 1844 Lincoln bought the only home he ever owned. It was a clapboard cottage on the corner of Eighth and Jackson streets, costing $1,200, and property worth $300. In 1856 the Lincolns enlarged this home, adding a second-floor needed to accommodate their growing family. They remained in this house until leaving for the White House in 1861.

In the summer of 1843, Robert Todd Lincoln, the first of Lincoln's four sons, was born. Three more sons followed—in 1846 Edward Dickinson, who died of tuberculosis in 1850; William Wallace, who died of typhoid fever in the White House in 1862; and Thomas (Tad), who was born in 1853. Only Robert and Tad survived their father.

Along with his interest in family and profession, Lincoln also pursued his political career. Many residents of Springfield thought that he became a lawyer in order to further his political ambitions. Certainly his contacts through his law practice introduced him to the influential public men of his state. In 1841, during his fourth term in a state legislature that met only every other year for six weeks, he sought new possibilities. By this time Abraham Lincoln was well known in the state of Illinois as a Whig leader who faithfully supported his party's principles of economic growth, a protective tariff, and

support for a national bank to provide currency and credit. It was a logical credo for a self-made man on the rise. In 1843 Lincoln hoped to win the Whig Party's congressional nomination for a congressional seat from the Seventh District in central Illinois. Despite his efforts, he was unsuccessful. In 1846 he did become the Whig candidate, easily defeating his Democratic opponent Peter Cartwright.

The only Whig in the Illinois delegation, Abraham Lincoln served in the 30th United States Congress from 1847 to 1849. In the House of Representatives he was best known for his challenge to President James Polk's war policy in Mexico. In a speech in which he demanded to know the exact spot where Mexican soldiers had "invaded" the United States, Lincoln indicted the Democratic administration for starting an unjustified war as the result of an incident that in fact occurred on Mexican soil. During his term he also introduced a resolution for the gradual compensated abolition of slavery in the District of Columbia that was not voted on.

After his term in Congress ended, Lincoln returned to Springfield. According to an arrangement with his Whig friends, the party's nomination now rotated to another aspirant. He was unsuccessful in his efforts to get a patronage appointment from the Whig president Zachary Taylor. Yet politics remained a focus of his energy. One of the most prominent Whigs in Illinois, Abraham Lincoln now watched the party he had joined in the 1830s disappear across the United States. Still anxious for public office, in 1854 he won a seat as a state assemblyman. When he discovered that newly elected legislators were ineligible for election to the United States Senate, he resigned his seat.

In 1854 Congress passed the controversial Kansas-Nebraska Act, which installed the principle of popular sovereignty in the territories, thereby overturning the Missouri Compromise. For more than thirty years the latter had prohibited slavery north of the 36°30' latitude. Lincoln believed fervently in the sanctity of that prohibition, and the possibility that slavery would become national was an abomination to him. When the Kansas-Nebraska Act became law, Lincoln confessed that he was "thunderstruck and stunned." With his interest in politics now revived, Lincoln ran for the United States Senate as an anti-Nebraska former Whig. In January 1855, during voting in the Illinois Senate, he threw his support to another candidate Lyman Trumbull so that a Democrat supporting popular sovereignty in the territories would not be elected.

In the presidential year of 1856, Lincoln played an important role in the organization of the new Republican Party which emerged from the myriad of political coalitions in this period of party realignment. He gave speeches, wrote letters to influential leaders, and articulated the cardinal faith of his new party—that

slavery must not be extended to the territories. By this time he was so prominent that at the first national convention of the Republican Party, the Illinois delegation nominated Abraham Lincoln for vice-president. He received a losing but respectable one-third of the votes.

In 1858 the Republican state convention nominated Abraham Lincoln as their candidate for the United States Senate. In his acceptance speech he asserted that "A house divided against itself cannot stand. I believe that this Government cannot endure, permanently, half-slave and half-free." His opponent was the incumbent U.S. Senator Stephen Douglas, one of the principal authors of the Kansas-Nebraska Act. In a series of appearances across Illinois, these two formidable politicians debated popular sovereignty and the recent Supreme Court decision in the *Dred Scott* case. To Lincoln and many Northerners' anger, the court had held in 1857 that blacks were so inferior and deficient that they could never be American citizens and had no rights that whites were bound to respect.

In all, Lincoln gave sixty-three political addresses during this campaign. Yet it was the seven direct confrontations between the incumbent Douglas and the Republican Lincoln known as the Lincoln-Douglas debates that mesmerized Illinoisians and reporters from all over the United States. In these debates Lincoln and Douglas laid out the differences between their two parties. Douglas accused Lincoln and the Republicans of creating a sectional, abolitionist party that would abide by neither the Fugitive Slave Law nor the *Dred Scott* decision. On his part Lincoln charged that Douglas was trying to make slavery national. For Lincoln the great issue of the campaign was "the difference between the men who think slavery a wrong and those who do not think it wrong." In the election that followed neither Douglas's nor Lincoln's name was on the ballot, because the state legislature elected United States Senators in this period. But given the majority of Democrats in the legislature, Douglas won the balloting in that body in January 1859.

Lincoln remained politically active despite his loss. He expanded his political arena beyond Illinois into other states, where he gave speeches and met the principal leaders of the Republican Party. Especially important was a well-publicized speech delivered in February 1860 at the Cooper Institute in New York. In it he argued that slavery must not be extended and that the Republican Party was not revolutionary for saying so. He attacked the position of Douglas and other Democrats that popular sovereignty had begun with the founders of the United States.

Measured across the spectrum of Republicans, Lincoln was nevertheless a moderate on the issue of slavery. He would not abolish it in the states where it already existed, but he would prevent its extension into

the territories. As his reputation grew and the time for holding presidential nominating conventions approached, Lincoln benefited from the activities of a group of dedicated friends and managers who promoted his candidacy for the Republican nomination.

In May 1860, the Republican Party nominated Abraham Lincoln for the presidency of the United States. Something of a dark horse at the beginning, he gained from the delegates' belief that his principal opponent William Henry Seward of New York was too radical on the slavery issue and too opposed to the Know-Nothing movement whose members were turning to the Republicans. Meanwhile the Democrats split into two factions, both nominating candidates. When a third-party candidate of the Constitutional Party, John Bell, joined the race, there were four candidates vying for the presidency. Lincoln, in the tradition of American presidential politics, did not campaign. He did, however, inform his supporters that he would not agree to the creation of any new slave states which was a possibility if popular sovereignty was applied in the Western territories. He wrote Lyman Trumbull, "Stand firm. The tug has to come, and better now, than any time hereafter."

In the election that followed, Lincoln received a plurality of 40 percent of the popular vote and a decisive majority of 180 electoral votes out of a total 303. Even a united Democratic Party would not have defeated him, as he carried the North and middle West, New England, and Pennsylvania, along with California and Oregon. But in the South, where he was not on the ballot in most states, Lincoln was considered an abolitionist whose election justified leaving the Union.

By March 1861 when Lincoln took office as the sixteenth president of the United States, seven Southern states had already seceded. In February these states formed the Confederate States of America and considered themselves an independent nation. Lincoln, the former Whig who believed that Congress rather than the president should be the center of power, now acceded to a position that demanded executive action during the most threatening times in the history of the republic.

In a conciliatory inaugural address directed to the Confederacy, the new president made it clear that the government would maintain its authority against the secessionists. He would "hold, occupy and possess" (not repossess) the federal forts that Southerners were intent on occupying. But he would not interfere with slavery in Southern states. He closed with a stirring appeal to the Southern people. "We are not enemies, but friends. We must not be enemies."

The day after his inauguration, Lincoln confronted the issue of Fort Sumter in Charleston Harbor and its need for provisions. He ordered two relief expeditions fitted out with supplies for Fort Sumter in South Carolina and Fort Pickens off the coast of Pensacola in Florida. Lincoln informed the governor of South Carolina of his plans. But the president of the Confederacy, Jefferson Davis, had previously encouraged local commanders to initiate military actions against these forts. When Major Robert Anderson, the Union commander at Fort Sumter, refused to surrender, in the early morning hours of 12 April 1861 batteries in Charleston began their bombardment of the fort. Anderson surrendered two days later. The Civil War that would frame Abraham Lincoln's presidency and test the nation's survival had begun.

There was no formal declaration of war. Like most Americans, including Northern Democrats, Lincoln termed Southern aggression an insurrection. Throughout the war he referred to the Confederates as rebels, and he hoped that Unionist sentiment among a majority in the South could be organized to end the sectional division. On 15 April, he called on the states to supply 75,000 militiamen to suppress this uprising, expecting the conflict to be brief. In taking this action, he noted "combinations too powerful to be suppressed by the ordinary course of judicial proceedings."

On 19 April, Lincoln instituted a naval blockade of the Southern coast. In these early months of his presidency, as Tennessee, Arkansas, North Carolina, and Virginia left the Union after the firing on Fort Sumter, the president continued to appeal to Unionists. He hoped to keep all the border slave states in the Union. "To lose Kentucky," said the president, "is nearly the same as to lose the whole game." The same could be said for Maryland and Missouri. Lincoln moved gingerly to keep these states' allegiance, indicating that he would take no aggressive action against them if they committed no hostile actions against the national government.

In May, in a series of proclamations, the president increased the size of the army—calling for forty-two thousand volunteers and additional regiments in the regular army and navy—without either previous appropriations or congressional authority. His actions were unilateral and undeniable expansions of presidential power. Such extensions of executive authority were based on Lincoln's view that his presidential office represented the will of the people and that his powers "whether strictly legal or not," were undertaken in the name of "popular demand and public necessity." Believing the United States an exceptional nation, he saw the war as a struggle to maintain "that form of government whose leading object is to elevate the condition of men-to lift the weights from all shoulders...to afford all, an unfettered start, and a fair chance, in the race of life."

For the next four years, Lincoln served as an active commander-in-chief of the army and navy under the powers given to the president in Article 2 of the

Lincoln with Allan Pinkerton (*left*) and Major General John A. McClernand (*right*) following the battle of Antietam, 3 October 1862 (Photograph by Alexander Gardner / *Library of Congress*)

Constitution. He also functioned in more traditional roles as a civilian leader, marshalling support among Northerners and residents of the border states for a long and bloody war. He directed the nation's foreign policy, successfully preventing France and Great Britain from giving any official aid to the Confederacy. He was as well the leader of the Republican Party. To all these responsibilities the president brought his intelligence, flexibility, and innate caution.

Necessarily his presidency was mostly taken up with

military matters and the war effort. In fact Abraham Lincoln was the only chief executive in American history whose entire administration took place in wartime. Lincoln did not lead troops into battle, as had George Washington. But he did make it clear to Congress in an address in July 1861 that he was in charge of the prosecution of the war and that in wartime he could exercise certain powers reserved in peacetime to the legislative branch of government.

Without any background save his summer service in the Illinois militia, Lincoln became a quick study in military matters. He investigated and encouraged certain strategic plans and even battle tactics. He read military manuals. At times he was the principal coordinator of the overall war effort between the Eastern and Western theaters. He traveled to the battlefield to consult with his commanders. He spent hours pouring over maps in the White House, sometimes spending all night in the telegraph office of the War Department waiting for news from the front.

Never did he delegate to professional military men the selection of his top generals. He understood from the beginning of the war the importance of morale on the home front, and so chose for his commanders both Republican and Democrats as well as Irish- and German-born leaders. In one famous anecdote, when he encountered the obviously German name of Alexander Schimmelfanning in a list of officers for promotion to general, sensitive to the need for all groups to support the war, the president named this man of German extraction to division command. His first choice for high command was Democrat George B. McClellan, who served briefly as both the commander of the Army of the Potomac and general-in-chief until Lincoln realized that the joint posts were beyond the capabilities of even a man who boasted that he could do it all.

Astutely, Lincoln rejected the plan promoted by the veteran General-in-Chief Winfield Scott before the latter's resignation in November 1861. In his Anaconda Plan, Scott proposed that the Navy should blockade the coast, control the Mississippi River, split the Confederacy in two, and wait for a suffocating Confederacy to return to the Union. Such a plan was too passive for Lincoln, who did, however, institute the important and somewhat successful blockade of the Southern coast. From Scott's ideas and from his own Western heritage, the president came to appreciate the critical importance of the Western theater. In the early days of the war, Lincoln also insisted that Washington as the capital of the United States must be protected by the Union army from any Confederate assault.

In the summer of 1861, the president authorized an advance into northern Virginia. Its mission was to attack the Confederates before they could be reinforced. But General Irvin McDowell's army was routed at the battle

of Bull Run on 21 July 1861. Three weeks later, Lincoln wrote one of his frequent memorandums on the war. In it he proposed not only keeping a line open from Bull Run to Washington, but also moving into Tennessee. He called for 500,000 more volunteers, and he brought General George McClellan, who had had some success against Confederate forces in western Virginia to Washington, to train the army.

With the Army of Potomac soon full of spit, polish, drill, and 275,000 men, Lincoln now clarified his military ideas. "We must fail, unless we can find some way of making our advantage [of greater numbers] an overmatch for his; and ...this can be done only by menacing *him* with superior forces at *different* points at the *same* time ...." The concept identified here was to concentrate forces during offensives that best utilized the North's advantage of manpower and minimized the South's advantage of shorter interior lines. On 27 January 1862, Lincoln issued General Order No. 1 that set George Washington's birthday as the day for "a general movement of the Land and Naval forces."

But McClellan had developed his own plan for attacking Richmond from the east by taking his troops down the Potomac River, landing on 4 April on the peninsula between the York and James rivers. In an agonizingly slow advance from Norfolk up the Virginia peninsula in the spring and early summer of 1862, the Amy of Potomac fought within miles of Richmond only to be repulsed. McClellan complained that Richmond would have fallen if Lincoln had not detached Union divisions under General McDowell to protect Washington.

The Peninsula campaign was only one example of the close attention that Lincoln paid to military tactics throughout the war. Later the president told Ulysses Grant that he never wanted to interfere in the actual ways in which campaigns should be conducted. He sometimes broke that rule in the early part of the war. The president fumed about the procrastination of commanders and public pressure to win the war quickly which sometimes forced this interference. Certainly the president was furious with General McClellan after the battle of Antietam in September 1862. In this campaign, Lee had moved into Maryland and had been forced to retreat to Virginia. But McClellan had not pursued the Confederate army. The president's distress led to a three-day visit by Lincoln with McClellan who was still at Antietam rather than, as Lincoln had hoped, across the Potomac chasing the Confederates southward.

In other instances of his close attention to military strategy, the president informed Grant that his initial plans in 1863 to surround Vicksburg were untenable. (Later, when Grant's tactics led to the siege and eventual surrender on 4 July 1863 of that important position on the Mississippi River, Lincoln acknowledged that he was

wrong.) In 1863 Lincoln also complained to General George Meade about the latter's failure to follow and destroy General Lee's army after the three-day battle of Gettysburg in July 1863.

Lincoln was an activist president not only in so far as battle plans were concerned, but also with regard to personnel. He constantly removed generals as he searched for effective commanders. In early 1862 he removed McClellan from his position as general-in-chief of all the armies, replacing him in July 1862 with the much respected but overrated General Henry Halleck. Halleck's contribution to Lincoln's thinking on the strategy of the war was his conviction that controlling the West—especially the Confederate breadbasket of Tennessee—would deprive the Confederacy of critical resources.

Lincoln also asserted his powers to remove McClellan from his command of the Army of the Potomac, first by reorganizing the Army of Potomac into corps commanded by generals chosen by the president. For as McClellan believed in slow movements, flanking operations, reconnaissance, and caution, so Lincoln believed that the Union war goals required frontal assault, unconditional surrender, and boldness. "It is indispensable to you," he wrote to McClellan in April 1862, "that you strike a blow."

In Lincoln's view, the road to the capitulation of the Confederate government lay across battlegrounds in the South where the Confederate army would be destroyed. "We have the *greater* numbers, and the enemy has the *greater* facility of concentrating forces upon points of collision; ...if he *weakens* one [point] to *strengthen* the

Lincoln at the Grand Review of the Army of the Potomac, 9 April 1863, from an eyewitness sketch by Alfred R. Waud (*Library of Congress*)

other, forbear to attack the strengthened one but seize, and hold the weakened one...." The president continued to believe that the end of the war would come in a decisive battle, not, as was to be the case, in the steady deterioration of Lee's army.

In November 1862, Lincoln dismissed the commander of the Army of the Potomac. Linclon made the especially unfortunate choices of Ambrose Burnside and then Joseph Hooker. In all these instances, Lincoln acted alone and without much discussion with Halleck.

In March 1864, Lincoln's search for a general who agreed with his strategic thinking ended when he appointed Ulysses Grant, who had been serving in the West, to the new rank of Lieutenant General in charge of all Union armies. Finally the president had discovered a commander who concurred with him not only on the importance of attacking rather than maneuvering, but also on the need to coordinate the Northern armies. Lincoln and Grant both understood that only with a concerted simultaneous action of all the Union armies could the North's superiority in numbers crush the Confederacy. As the president expressed it in one of his homely metaphors, "Those not skinning can hold a leg." And later to Grant during the costly Wilderness campaign, the president insisted, "Hold on with a bulldog grip, and chew and choke, as much as possible."

At first Lincoln did not understand the importance of General William Tecumseh Sherman's 1864 march through Georgia by way of Atlanta, which fell in September, and then on to Savannah and northwards into South Carolina. Soon, however, the president grasped the idea that only a total war against the Confederate home front and through its heartland would accomplish the Union war goal of unconditional surrender.

Throughout the war Lincoln made hard impolitic decisions not only about generals but about the need for more troops. He supported and signed the first draft in U.S. history—the Conscription Act of 1862 and its extensions. Even in the election year of 1864, when there was grumbling about the length of the war and its continuation, he issued a call for 500,000 more men for the army. In this case his proclamation required that local districts fill their quotas by September—two months before the election—or face a draft in November.

In his final message to Congress on 6 December 1864, Lincoln established his two peace conditions—the government of the Confederate States of America must surrender. There could be neither conditions nor a truce. "The war will cease on the part of the government, whenever it shall have ceased on the part of those who began it." And his second condition—that slavery must end—he had earlier ordered in the Emancipation Proclamation.

Lincoln had come more slowly than some of his fellow Republicans to the idea of an executive order ending slavery. This was not because he supported the institution. The protection of the territories from the cancer of slavery had been his bedrock position in the 1850s. But he had always insisted that slavery, as it existed in the Confederate states, was sanctioned by the United States Constitution, and that liberating the slaves could only be accomplished voluntarily by those states. During the war his efforts at ending slavery had included compensation for border slave states like Maryland and Delaware if they would free their slaves. Early in the war, he had rescinded the directives of two of his generals—General David Hunter and General John Frémont—when they had freed slaves in their military departments without consultation with him. He had also encouraged the removal of slaves to South America, and in his annual message of 1862 he had even suggested an amendment to the constitution that would end slavery gradually, voluntarily, with compensation—and only by 1900.

Ever alert to the importance of public opinion, Lincoln was restrained in his approach to emancipation because of the need to maintain the allegiance of the border states whose support he believed necessary to the winning of the war. Sanctioned by the United States Constitution, slavery was imbedded in the legal apparatus of the government. "I would save the Union…If there be those who would not *save* the Union, unless they could at the same time save slavery, I do not agree with them. If there be those who would not save the Union unless they could at the same time *destroy* slavery, I do not agree with them." Sensitive to the extent of his constitutional authority during a period of weak executive power, Lincoln hesitated.

But just as the president moved toward an understanding of the necessity of an uncompromising military effort that would shake the morale of Southern civilians, so he came to understand that as commander of the armed forces he had the constitutional power to emancipate the enemy's slaves. There were signs of this change in his attitude by 1862. The president did not veto the Second Confiscation Act, which included slaves in its provision that the Union could confiscate the property of those who supported the Confederacy. Next he discussed with his cabinet his conviction that military law and government necessity necessitated the emancipation of slaves by an executive order. On 22 July1862, Lincoln read a draft of the proclamation to his surprised cabinet. Later he agreed with Secretary of State Seward that he must wait for a military victory. "I do not want to issue a document that the whole world will see must necessarily be inoperative, like the Pope's bull against the comet! Would *my word* free the slaves, when I cannot even enforce the Constitution in the rebel States?" By fall Lincoln had his victory on the battlefield at Antietam.

The Emancipation Proclamation had two parts. On 22 September 1862, five days after the battle of Antietam, Lincoln issued the first part, a preliminary Emancipation Proclamation. It declared that the slaves in areas still in rebellion against the United States on 1 January 1863 would be free. The president also promised to recommend to Congress a program of gradual and compensated liberation of slaves for concurring states. And the military was not to enforce the fugitive slave laws that required their return.

On 1 January 1863, with fingers aching from shaking hands at a reception, Abraham Lincoln signed the final Emancipation Proclamation. It freed "henceforth and forever" slaves "within any State or designated part of a State whose people…shall then be in rebellion against the United States." It directed that the military protect the freedom of slaves and accept blacks, who were already serving in the armed service of the United States. (This latter provision was the most significant change between the preliminary and the final proclamations.) Lincoln based the authority of his proclamation on his power as the commander in chief and he specifically termed the measure "a fit and necessary war measure for suppressing [the] rebellion…"

In the Emancipation Proclamation, Lincoln specifically exempted various parts of the former Confederacy, mentioning particular states and parts of states that were already under the control of the Union army. Hence his critics said that he had in effect freed no one. Always conscientious about his power, Lincoln believed his military prerogatives did not extend into regions in the former Confederacy that were in the process of returning to the union and accordingly under the civilian authority of state and local officials. Hearing of the emancipation order through the slave grapevine, thousands of slaves even in territory still controlled by the Confederacy fled to the protection of the Union lines. Later both Lincoln and Seward believed that the Emancipation Proclamation freed at least 200,000 slaves by February 1865.

No matter how many slaves were actually freed under the auspices of Lincoln's Emancipation Proclamation, what was essential to the war was that Lincoln had made the liberation of slaves a goal of the Union government. Not only did emancipation remove the useful labor of blacks from the Confederacy, but it added their labor power to the union cause. As the Northern armies moved deeper into the Confederacy, more and more slaves were freed. The end of slavery thus became a national war goal of the United States government and for many white Northerners and all black ones, the moral justification of a brutal conflict.

The Emancipation Proclamation also encouraged the

use of blacks ("suitable persons") to "garrison forts, positions, stations, and…man vessels." Some African-Americans had already fought in battles in Louisiana, Tennessee, and Kansas. But Lincoln—who had never before called for blacks as infantry—now, as he did on many important issues, changed his mind and became a fervent advocate of black troops. The president spoke to the importance of "inducing the colored people to come bodily over from the rebel side to ours." And when they did, he noted in a letter to Governor Andrew Johnson in March 1863, they represented "the great *available* and yet *unavailed* of, force for restoring the Union. The bare sight of fifty thousand armed and drilled black soldiers on the banks of the Mississippi, would end the rebellion at once."

After 1863 Lincoln sought other ways to advance emancipation in the slaveholding border states of Maryland, Delaware, Kentucky, and Missouri, where he did not have military authority to end slavery. He insisted on a plank in the Republican platform supporting a Thirteenth Amendment to the Constitution that would abolish slavery throughout the United States. He lobbied for the amendment and in February 1865, he approved the congressional resolution submitting the Thirteenth Amendment to the states for ratification. But the president was dead before its ratification in 1865.

Throughout the war, Lincoln absorbed various judicial and congressional powers that in peacetime would have been under the jurisdiction of the courts and the legislature. From mid-April to 4 July 1861, after the war had begun and before he called Congress into special session, the president undertook a series of unilateral actions. Acting swiftly in a perilous time, he nationalized the state militias; he instituted the blockade of the Southern coast, and he suspended the writ of habeas corpus, the common law protection of individuals from the government, in certain areas along the railroad line from Washington to Philadelphia. He sent two secret agents to New York to borrow money from private sources before any official requisition had been made.

In 1864 he accepted, though grudgingly, the legitimacy of the new West Virginia government as fulfilling the constitutional mandate that existing state governments—in this case Virginia—must agree to the creation of new states within their territory. He briefly closed down newspapers; he exiled Clement Vallandigham, who had been found guilty by a military commission of discouraging enlisting. He justified these actions by pointing to the exigencies of a devastating civil war. Lincoln believed that he would have broken his oath of presidential office if he had allowed the inflexible observance of one law to stand in the way of preserving all the others. Then he would have been responsible for allowing the government to disintegrate. In time, both Congress and the courts ratified his actions. Compared

to the violation of civil liberties under Jefferson Davis, Lincoln's behavior was less drastic.

His opponents, especially the Peace wing of the Democratic Party, which sought an immediate truce and a negotiated peace with the Confederacy, complained that presidential policy was dictatorial and tyrannical. Lincoln responded by arguing that during the undeniable threat to the survival of the Union government that the Civil War represented, he could do no less.

By the summer of 1864, Lincoln's attention to, though not his concern over, military matters lessened. His efficient secretary of war, Edwin Stanton, had relieved him of some of the burden. So too had his effective commanders—Ulysses Grant and Philip Sheridan in the east and William Sherman, who was beginning his march through Georgia. With their support dwindling at home and on the battlefield, Confederate troops now faced the Union army in brutal battles in northern Virginia, Georgia, and northern Alabama.

In 1864 Lincoln confronted a different kind of campaign—a political one. He fought not only for his election, but even for his renomination. Like nearly all American presidents, this president understood himself to be the head of his party. In the early days of the war he had tried unsuccessfully to create a wartime coalition of former Democrats, Whigs, Know-Nothings, and new voters. But partisan habits remained too strong. By 1862 the Democrats had revived their organization, and they continued to win governorships and to control state legislatures for the duration of the war. During these local elections they criticized the Republicans not only for the government's so-called excesses in the area of civil liberties, but for domestic policies that Lincoln had supported.

Like all nineteenth-century presidents, Lincoln did not initiate programs. But he did support most of the policies that formed the core of a progressive Republican agenda. He signed congressional legislation setting up a free land policy for settlers by means of a Homestead Act. He signed a tariff bill that raised rates; he approved a higher education act that set aside land for state public institutions. He encouraged the national banking act drawn up by Secretary of Treasury Salmon Chase that centralized the credit functions of the American economic system.

Throughout his administration, Lincoln used the patronage to support his party, removing Democrats in a familiar partisan ritual. During the war the number of patronage jobs increased dramatically. By 1865 nearly 195,000 civilians worked for the federal government, many in newly created, war-spawned jobs. The support of some of these Republicans was important for the president's renomination in the face of opposition from Secretary of Treasury Chase, who stayed in the cabinet until July 1864, and an insurgent movement led by

Lincoln's funeral procession on Pennsylvania Avenue, Washington, D.C., 19 April 1865 (*Library of Congress*)

Radical Republicans, including Frémont. Despite the opposition, Lincoln was easily renominated at the party convention in Baltimore in June 1864, though the threat remained of a Radical Republican Frémont candidacy until September 1864.

Now unified, the Republicans faced a divided Democratic Party led by McClellan. The latter was forced to disavow a party platform that called the war a failure. Even with this advantage, Lincoln at first did not think he would win the election. He took the traditional position that it was not customary to campaign or even to write public letters to be presented at political meetings. He did not need them when the fortunes of the war turned in the Union's favor, and Atlanta fell eight weeks before the election.

In November 1864, Lincoln was reelected to the presidency with 55 percent of the popular vote and an overwhelming majority of 212 to 21 in the electoral college.

He lost only New Jersey, Kentucky, and Delaware, and he received strong support from soldiers who were allowed by their states to vote in the field. But for Lincoln the great question of this election, besides his victory and the continuation of Republican programs, was "whether any government, not *too* strong for the liberties of its people, can be strong *enough* to maintain its own existence in great emergencies." The answer—on a calm election day for which the president deserved credit—was yes.

After his election, another bloody six months elapsed before the end of the war. Lincoln had already turned his attention to the problem of how to get the Southern states back into the Union. For the parishes around New Orleans that had come under Union control, and later in Tennessee, where he appointed Andrew Johnson, the vice president in his second administration, the president had constructed a plan for bringing the South back into the Union. In his Proclamation of Amnesty and

Reconstruction of December 1863, he proposed the creation of a new state constitution and subsequently a new government when ten percent of those who voted in 1860 had taken an oath of future loyalty to the Union. Lincoln offered amnesty and restoration of property to all who took the oath of allegiance, although he excepted high Confederate officials. But in the summer of 1864 some congressional leaders challenged Lincoln's plan as too conservative.

On 11 April, in his last speech, Lincoln spoke to the issue of restoring Louisiana to the Union, this time with the votes of "intelligent" blacks and those who had served in the army. But Lincoln made clear that he was not committed to any specific plan for a problem that would trouble the nation in the coming years.

On 3 April 1865, Richmond fell to the advancing Union armies. On 5 April, Lincoln visited the capital of the Confederacy, even sitting in Jefferson Davis's chair in the Confederate White House. Two days later, General Robert E. Lee surrendered the Army of Northern Virginia. To many, the Civil War had ended. All of Washington was celebrating. On 14 April 1865, the president and Mrs. Lincoln, always devotees of the stage, went to Ford's Theater. For months the president's staff had warned him of possible assassination attempts, but he had always brushed them off, saying that he would take care of himself. That night the rabid Confederate sympathizer John Wilkes Booth shot the president in the back of the head. The next day—in the fifth week of his second term—Abraham Lincoln died. His legacy to the nation was an essential one —the preservation of the Union and the liberation of the slaves.

—*Jean Harvey Baker*

See also Booth, John Wilkes; Cameron, Simon; Civil Liberties, U.S.A; Douglas, Stephen Arnold; Election of 1858; Election of 1860; Election of 1862; Election of 1864; Emancipation Proclamation; Grant, Ulysses Simpson; Habeas Corpus, Writ of (U.S.A.); Hamlin, Hannibal; Johnson, Andrew; Lincoln Assassination; Lincoln, Mary Todd; Lincoln, Robert Todd; Lincoln's Reconstruction Policy; McClellan, George Brinton; Seward, William Henry; Stanton, Edwin McMasters; Wade-Davis Bill.

For further reading:

Basler, Roy P., ed. *Collected Works of Abraham Lincoln* (1953–1955).

Donald, David Herbert. *Lincoln* (1995).

Neely, Mark E., Jr. *The Last Best Hope of Earth: Abraham Lincoln and the Promise of America* (1993).

Paludan, Phillip S. *The Presidency of Abraham Lincoln* (1994).

LINCOLN ASSASSINATION
(14 April 1865)

President Abraham Lincoln knew that the possibility of his assassination was a constant possibility. In his desk drawer was an envelope marked "Assassination," full of threats written to him during his administration. On the evening of Good Friday, 14 April 1865, Lincoln attended a production of *Our American Cousin* starring Laura Keene at Ford's Theatre in Washington, D.C., with his wife, Mary. The Lincolns enjoyed the theater and went as often as possible. A young army officer named Henry R. Rathbone and his fiancée, Clara Harris, daughter of Senator Ira T. Harris of New York, accompanied them.

Ironically, the theater was full that evening because many expected General Ulysses S. Grant and his wife to be in attendance. While Lincoln was a familiar sight, Grant was not. The Grants canceled at the last moment to travel out of town. The performance had begun at 7:45 P.M., and the Lincolns arrived late, at 8:15. Two hours later, at approximately 10:15, as he sat in his presidential box, Lincoln was shot once in the back of the head at close range by a .44-caliber single-shot muzzle-loading derringer fired by John Wilkes Booth.

Unlike other presidential assassins, Booth was a prominent figure. One of the best-known actors of his time, he was the son of famed tragedian Junius Brutus Booth and brother of Edwin Booth, America's best-known Shakespearean actor. Booth himself had performed in front of Lincoln.

The bullet entered near the president's left ear and lodged behind his right eye. Rathbone rushed the assassin and was wounded in the left arm by a large knife brandished by Booth. Several hundred theatergoers heard Booth utter "sic semper tyrannis" ("so always to tyrants"), the motto on the state flag of Virginia, and saw him leap almost twelve feet to the stage floor below, breaking his right leg in the process. In the confusion, many in the audience thought for a moment that this was a part of the theatrical production. Despite his injury, Booth was able to escape out a rear door of the theater.

At almost the same time, coconspirator Lewis Paine (whose real name was Lewis T. Powell) was breaking into the home of Secretary of State William H. Seward, where he attacked the secretary with a knife but failed to kill him. A neck collar the bedridden secretary was wearing at the time, the result of a carriage accident he had suffered several days earlier, saved Seward's life. Paine also fled into the night.

The mortally wounded president was immediately attended to by an army surgeon, Dr. Charles Leale, and two other doctors in attendance, Dr. Charles A. Taft, also an army surgeon, and Dr. A. F. A. King, of Washington. They ordered the wounded president transported to a bedroom across the street in the Petersen house, where six soldiers carried him. The sixteenth president of the United States died at 7:22 the following morning. The Reverend Phineas D. Gurley, pastor of the New York Avenue Presbyterian Church, was in attendance and offered a prayer.

President Lincoln's box at Ford's Theater, Washington, D.C., April 1865 (*Library of Congress*)

Standing at Lincoln's bedside, Secretary of War Edwin Stanton exclaimed, "Now he belongs to the ages."

On 18 April, thousands viewed the remains of the president in the East Room of the White House. Funeral services were held there the next day. On 20 April, thousands more viewed the casket in the rotunda of the Capitol. On 21 April, Lincoln's body began the long 1,700-mile journey back home to Illinois on board a funeral train that traveled through Philadelphia, New York, Buffalo, Cleveland, and Chicago. He was laid to rest on 4 May at Oak Ridge Cemetery in Springfield, Illinois.

After the shooting, Booth rendezvoused with coconspirator David Herold, and together they traveled to the

Execution of the four conspirators, Washington, D.C., 7 July 1865 (Photograph by Alexander Gardner / *Library of Congress*)

Surratt Tavern, a gathering spot for Confederate opera-tives in Surrattsville (modern Clinton), Maryland. The tavern sat about a dozen miles from Ford's Theater and was owned by Mary Surratt. Her son John Surratt, Jr., was a known Confederate agent. Booth and Herold next traveled to the home of Dr. Samuel A. Mudd just outside Bryantown, Maryland, fifteen miles south of the Surratt Tavern. Here in the early morning hours of 15 April, Dr. Mudd set Booth's broken leg. Mudd's role in the conspiracy has been the object of much debate. Mudd claimed to have known nothing of the assassination and said that Booth wore a false beard when he set his leg. Much circumstantial evidence tends to cast doubt on Mudd's claims.

Leaving Mudd's, the pair traveled to the home of Samuel Cox near Bel Alton, Maryland, where they hid in a pine thicket for several days. They were provided a rowboat with which to cross the Potomac River into Virginia by Cox's foster brother Thomas A. Jones, a Confederate spy and blockade runner. In Virginia they hid out near Port Royal in a tobacco barn owned by Richard Garrett. It was there that Booth and Herold were cornered by Federal troops on 26 April. Herold surrendered, but Booth refused to give up, and the barn was set on fire. Booth was shot to death by soldier Boston Corbett, who fired against orders through a small opening in the barn wall.

After Booth's death, details began to emerge about

the chain of events that led up to the assassination of President Lincoln. Late in 1864 Booth had devised a plot to kidnap the president and exchange him for Confederate prisoners of war. In August 1864, General Grant had terminated prisoner exchanges, reasoning that the numerical superiority of Union troops made it unnecessary. Booth had apparently felt that extreme steps were necessary to replenish Confederate ranks.

Besides Herold, Booth's group of conspirators in the kidnapping plot included Samuel Arnold and Michael O'Laughlin, former schoolmates who had fought for the Confederacy. Lewis Paine was a Confederate deserter from Florida. George Atzerodt was a German immigrant whose role was to ferry the kidnappers across the Potomac River. John Surratt was a Confederate agent and courier. The conspirators met frequently at the boarding house of Mrs. Mary Surratt, mother of John, in the city of Washington.

After at least two failed attempts to kidnap Lincoln in January and March 1865, Booth ran out of time. Lee surrendered to Grant at Appomattox, Virginia, on 9 April signaling an end to the war in Virginia. In a rage, Booth changed his kidnapping plot to murder. He awaited his opportunity, and his chance came on 14 April when he picked up his mail at Ford's Theatre and discovered that the president and Mrs. Lincoln would be attending that evening. Quickly searching out his former group of kidnap conspirators, he found that Paine, Herold, and Atzerodt were available. Arnold and O'Laughlin had tired of Booth's schemes and left town. They quickly drafted a plan that called for Paine to murder Secretary of State Seward and Atzerodt to murder Vice President Johnson, while Booth would shoot Lincoln. The entire government would be brought down at once. As it happened, only Booth would succeed in carrying out his part of the scheme. Paine wounded Seward but did not kill him. Atzerodt got drunk and never even approached Johnson.

Hundreds of individuals were arrested and questioned, but most were eventually released. On 10 May, a military tribunal was convened to try Herold, Mary Surratt, Lewis Paine, George Atzerodt, Edman Spangler, Michael O'Laughlin, Samuel Arnold, and Samuel Mudd for their roles in the conspiracy to assassinate the president. (John Surratt would evade capture for two years and would be released when his trial ended in a hung jury.) All were convicted, and on 7 July Atzerodt, Herold, Paine, and Mary Surratt were hanged for their part in the assassination. Historians have long debated whether Mary Surratt deserved the death penalty, for her role might have been marginal. The remaining defendants all received life sentences except Spangler, who was sentenced to six years in prison for helping Booth escape from Ford's Theatre. President Johnson pardoned all in 1869 except O'Laughlin, who had died of yellow fever in prison in 1867.

In the years since the assassination, a number of theories have arisen regarding additional individuals who possibly may have been involved in the plot to kill Lincoln. The government clearly believed that Lincoln was simply the victim of a conspiracy organized by Booth, and that all participants were identified. A number of works support this theme, among them *The Great American Myth* by George S. Bryan (1940, reprinted in 1990); *The Assassination of Abraham Lincoln and its Expiation* by David M. DeWitt (1909); and *The Death of Lincoln: The Story of Booth's Plot, His Deed, and the Penalty* by Clara Laughlin (1909).

Vice-president Andrew Johnson was an early suspect. There is evidence that Booth and Johnson may have known one another, but a congressional investigation looked into the relationship and found nothing suspicious. Mary Todd Lincoln for years continued to suspect that the vice-president had a part in her husband's death.

Chemist and armchair historian Otto Eisenschiml in his 1937 work, *Why Was Lincoln Murdered*, points blame at Secretary of War Edwin Stanton. Stanton, according to Eisenschiml, did not feel that Lincoln was prepared to go far enough to punish the South in his Reconstruction policies and so sought to remove him from office by any means. According to this theory, Stanton maneuvered Grant away from Ford's Theater on the fateful evening, because Grant's presence would require military guards. He refused to allow Major Thomas T. Eckert to accompany the Lincolns to the theater, even after Lincoln had personally requested him. He refused to notify guards at the Navy Yard Bridge, which Booth used as an escape route. He tampered with Booth's diary and may have been responsible for arranging to have Booth shot before he could be brought to trial.

Later research would first support and later contradict Eisenschiml's position. *The Web of Conspiracy: The Complete Story of the Men Who Murdered Abraham Lincoln* by Theodore Roscoe (1959), and *The Lincoln Conspiracy* by David Balsinger and Charles E. Seller (1977) expanded on Eisenschiml's thesis, but William Hanchett's landmark work *The Lincoln Murder Conspiracies* (1983) demolished it. Hanchett examines the Eisenschiml thesis point by point and finds numerous errors and distortions of fact. Stephen B. Oates's *Abraham Lincoln: The Man behind the Myths* (1998) finds that many of Stanton's acts at the time have innocent explanations or were mere coincidence. Stanton is today no longer considered a suspect in the Lincoln assassination.

Several recent publications have argued that a broader Confederate conspiracy existed in the assassination of President Lincoln. The most prominent of these are *Come Retribution: The Confederate Secret Service and the Assassination of Lincoln* by William A. Tidwell, James O. Hall, and David Winfred Gaddy (1988); Tidwell's *April '65: Confederate Covert Action in the American Civil*

War (1995); and *Wilkes Booth Came to Washington* by Larry Starkey (1976). According to this theory, Lincoln was considered a war target and fair game for assassination. Papers found on the body of Ulric Dahlgren after his part in Judson Kilpatrick's failed raid on Richmond allegedly outlined a plan approved by Lincoln to murder Jefferson Davis, though there is some question as to their authenticity. Whether the Confederate government directed Booth's plans, was aware of them, or whether Booth worked alone remains unclear.

—*Steven Fisher*

See also Booth, John Wilkes; Lincoln, Abraham; Mudd, Samuel; Powell, Lewis; Stanton, Edwin; Surratt, John; Surratt, Mary.

LINCOLN, MARY TODD
(1818–1882)
Wife of Abraham Lincoln; First Lady

Born into an aristocratic slaveholding family in December 1818, Mary Todd grew up in luxury in the sophisticated surroundings of Lexington, Kentucky. Her father was a well-known Whig politician who earned his living as a banker and owner of a cotton factory. He supported the education of women and sent his daughter, who was one of seven children by his first marriage, to a female academy and later to a boarding school outside Lexington. Mary Todd's twelve years of schooling placed her among only a handful of American women with a such an extensive education.

In 1839 Mary Todd moved to Springfield, the growing capital of the frontier state of Illinois. Living in her older sister's household where the leading politicians often gathered in the parlor, she met, and in November 1842, married Abraham Lincoln, a state legislator and popular lawyer. From 1842 until her husband's election to the presidency in 1860, Mary Todd Lincoln lived a conventional domestic life, raising her three surviving sons (one died in 1850) and running her home. Besides organizing the household, Mary Lincoln contributed to Abraham Lincoln's career by teaching him the manners and etiquette of nineteenth-century middle-class Americans.

Even in this period of her life, she stood out as a woman who was ambitious for her husband's political career. During the 1850s Lincoln's efforts to become a U.S. senator were twice rejected, although he was emerging as a respected member of the newly formed Republican Party. As his most fervent supporter, his wife continued, even in these years when he held no office, to encourage his political aspirations.

In November 1860 Lincoln was elected the sixteenth president of the United States. There was no one in the country more gratified than his wife. In testament to her support, when he heard the good news, the president-elect hurried home, calling out, "Mary, Mary, We are elected." Before her husband's inauguration in March 1861, Mary Lincoln had already initiated her preparations for her role as First Lady. She traveled to New York to buy new clothes and began to consider what would be her contribution to American history—the improvement of the public rooms of the White House. She also intended to make her mark as a well-bred, congenial host, and a leader in women's fashions.

But Mary Lincoln lived in the White House during the most brutal war in U.S. history, when such ambitions seemed frivolous. Just weeks after her husband's inauguration, the Confederacy fired on the federal fort at Fort Sumter, South Carolina. And her official tenure as First Lady ended when her husband was assassinated in Ford's Theater, on 14 April just weeks after the Confederate commander Robert E. Lee surrendered the Army of Northern Virginia at Appomattox Court House to the Union commander Ulysses S. Grant. Between these epochal dates, Mary Todd Lincoln left her mark on the nation's capital.

She accomplished a significant, if untimely, redecoration of the White House. When the Lincolns took up residence, she had been shocked at the condition of the thirty-one room mansion, with its broken furniture, peeling wall paper, soiled rugs, and cheap decorations. Refusing to return to Illinois despite fears of a Confederate invasion of Washington, Mary Lincoln instead traveled to Philadelphia and New York to buy new furnishings and wallpaper for the White House. Believing that the home of the president should represent the power of the Union to foreign ambassadors and that her job was to make the White House symbolize that authority, she began her campaign of redecorating. In doing so, the First Lady reversed the customary arrangement that the commissioner of public building was responsible for any White House expenses. Instead, she led the way into the stores, making expensive choices of furniture, rugs, wallpaper, and upholstery. Soon those who attended her parties—and as many as 4,000 came to the soirees she called her "handshake days"—were marveling at the elegance and charm of both their host and the newly refurbished White House. Most of Washington sought invitations to her dinner parties, and she emerged as a celebrity.

Such notoriety came with criticism. Official Washington had always believed her a Southern sympathizer, though such an accusation was incorrect. When she overspent the appropriation for the White House, she was criticized for her extravagance. Few acknowledged her devoted attention to her family as well as to the wounded Union soldiers in Washington hospitals. Given this First Lady's interest in patronage matters, many Republicans came to see her instead as a meddler. What Mary Lincoln saw as protecting her husband from those who conspired against him, party leaders held as

Mary Todd Lincoln (*Library of Congress*)

an unnecessary female trespass onto the male preserve of politics.

Amid her public acclaim, Mary Lincoln suffered a series of private blows while the Lincoln family was living in the White House. Twelve-year old Willie died of typhoid fever in 1862; two of her half brothers, who had joined the Confederate army, died in the war. But the greatest tragedy was the assassination of her beloved husband in 1865. The seventeen remaining years of Mary Lincoln's life were filled with anguish and unhappiness, as distraught and homeless, she struggled to survive amid financial and emotional challenges.

Twice after Lincoln's assassination Mary Lincoln traveled to Europe with her youngest son Thomas ("Tad" as his father had affectionately dubbed him). But in 1871 this third son died of pleurisy in a Chicago hotel. Then in 1875 at the urging of her only surviving son Robert she was brought to public trial in Chicago, as required by Illinois law, on the grounds that she was mentally incompetent. She was sent to a private mental institution outside Chicago where she remained, in testimony to her sanity, only four months. Convinced that her son would try to send her back to a mental asylum, Mary Lincoln fled to France, where she lived until shortly before her death in 1882.

—*Jean Harvey Baker*

See also Lincoln, Abraham; Lincoln, Robert Todd.
For further reading:
Baker, Jean H. *Mary Todd Lincoln: A Biography* (1987).
Helm, Katherine. *The True Story of Mary, Wife of Lincoln* (1928).
Randall, Ruth Painter. *Mary Lincoln: Portrait of a Marriage* (1953).
Turner, Justin, and Linda Levitt. *Mary Lincoln—Her Life and Letters* (1972).

LINCOLN, ROBERT TODD
(1843–1926)
Union officer

Robert Lincoln, the eldest of Abraham and Mary Todd Lincoln's children and the only one to survive to adulthood, was born on 1 August 1843 in Springfield, Illinois. After entering Harvard University in 1859, Lincoln, at his mother's request, continued his studies even after the Civil War erupted. After graduating from Harvard in 1864, he entered Harvard Law School, but after only a few months he left school to enter the U.S. Army at his father's request. Abraham Lincoln, who was running for reelection as president, had been sharply criticized in Northern newspapers because his son, while a draft was in effect throughout the Union, had avoided doing any military service. Robert Lincoln was commissioned a captain and served on General Ulysses S. Grant's staff as the assistant adjutant general of volunteers. After the fall of Petersburg, Lincoln returned to Washington, D.C., to visit his parents and decided not to accompany them to Ford's Theater on 14 April 1865. He would never forgive himself for this decision, because he believed that he might have been able to prevent his father's assassination.

Lincoln resigned his commission on 10 June 1865 and returned with his widowed mother and one surviving brother (Tad) to Chicago to continue to study law. In 1868, he married Mary Harlan, the daughter of Senator James Harlan, and they had three children, one a son, Abraham Lincoln II (1873–1890), who was the last direct male descendent of Abraham Lincoln. After the death of her only other surviving son in 1871, Mary Todd Lincoln's increasingly erratic behavior prompted Robert Lincoln to have his mother declared insane and institutionalized. A year after being institutionalized, Mary Lincoln was declared sane, but she remained bitter over her son's "betrayal."

Lincoln served as the secretary of war during James Garfield's and Chester Arthur's administrations (1881–1885) and later as minister to the United Kingdom during Benjamin Harrison's administration (1889–1893). Lincoln's tenure in both of these offices was unremarkable, though he was able to withstand the charms of London society so well that Theodore

Robert Todd Lincoln (*National Archives*)

Roosevelt later remarked that, "all of our ministers to England [were] pro-British except Bob Lincoln."

Though he was urged to run for elected office, Lincoln refused to capitalize on his father's name. Lincoln served as president of the Pullman Company from 1897 to 1911, after which he retired from public life completely. He became a semirecluse after his retirement and died in 1926. Upon his death, Lincoln willed his father's papers to the Library of Congress, where they were to remain sealed until twenty-one years after his own death.

—*Alexander M. Bielakowski*

See also Lincoln, Abraham; Lincoln, Mary Todd.
For further reading:
Goff, John S. *Robert Todd Lincoln: A Man in His Own Right* (1969).
Randall, Ruth Painter. *Lincoln's Sons* (1955).

LINCOLN'S RECONSTRUCTION POLICY

Although Reconstruction is usually associated with the period after the Civil War, it actually began when Abraham Lincoln, in his 1861 inaugural address, announced his intention to preserve the Union. Lincoln never recognized the secession of the Southern states, and he believed that it was his supreme constitutional duty to restore legitimate, loyal governments in each state. These governments would consist of a "tangible nucleus" of Unionists whose support would expand as the armed insurrection was suppressed. Lincoln, especially during the early period of the war, had great faith in the "good sense" of the Southern people and expected them to desire peace and a return to the Union. Lincoln believed that his policy would ensure a large measure of self-reconstruction, a position that owed a great deal to the nineteenth-century United States commitment to local self-government as the cornerstone of republicanism and the nation's federal system of government. Though he admitted that Congress could deny seats to any elected members, Lincoln declared that once loyal governments had been organized (and after 1862, emancipation) the states would be restored to their "proper practical relations with the Union." Even his emancipation policy, despite his strong personal distaste for slavery, was designed primarily to secure an early reconstruction of the South to the Union. Lincoln never wavered in his limited objectives regarding reconstruction.

Soon after the war began, Lincoln recognized as the loyal government of the Old Dominion the "Restored Government of Virginia" that met first in Wheeling and later in Alexandria, although it contained only Unionists from the western part of the state. Later in the year, he encouraged a similar movement among Unionists in east Tennessee, only to be foiled by the Confederate forces in the area. When Federal troops began to penetrate central Tennessee, the Mississippi Valley, and coastal North Carolina in 1862, Lincoln dispatched military governors to launch the process of civil reconstruction. He also appointed Andrew Jackson Hamilton as military governor of Texas, but he had no territory to reorganize until late in the war. Former congressman Edward Stanly, Lincoln's proslavery military governor in eastern North Carolina, resigned in early 1863 after the issuance of the Emancipation Proclamation. He was not replaced.

Lincoln had high hopes that his appointment of Andrew Johnson as military governor of Tennessee would lead to a rapid restoration of that border state to the Union. He was soon disappointed when Johnson refused to hold statewide elections until Unionist east Tennessee had been redeemed by Federal military forces, an event that did not occur until late in the war. Lincoln was likewise displeased with the failure of Unionists in southeastern Louisiana to hold elections and restore loyal civil governments in that state after the fall of New Orleans in April 1862.

In his preliminary Emancipation Proclamation (22 September 1862), Lincoln used the threat of black freedom to urge whites in Federal-controlled districts to elect members to Congress even before their state governments had been reorganized. The president promised to exclude districts from emancipation that held congressional elections. Sham elections occurred in several occupied districts. Though Lincoln exempted these areas, including the whole state of Tennessee, from his final Emancipation Proclamation, Congress rejected most of the newly elected congressmen; a notable exception was the seating in 1863 of two representatives from Louisiana.

Disappointed with the slow pace of reconstruction, Lincoln on 8 December 1863, citing the republican guarantee clause in the Constitution as his authority, announced a new plan for the restoration of the Southern states to the Union. Issued as the Proclamation of Amnesty and Reconstruction, Lincoln's plan provided that Southerners could "resume their allegiance to the United States" by taking a simple oath of future loyalty, which also contained the promise to abide by all federal laws and presidential proclamations regarding slavery. Certain categories of Confederates, including those who had unlawfully treated black soldiers or their officers, would be denied immediate amnesty, but would have to seek presidential pardons. Having obtained amnesty, Southerners then could regain all of their rights, except the right to own slave property. When 10 percent of the 1860 electorate had taken the oath, they could "reinaugurate loyal State governments" and elect members to Congress, thereby completing the process of civil reorganization. Lincoln reaffirmed, however, that Congress was the sole judge for the admission of Southern members to seats in that body. He declared that his plan was the best that he could suggest, but "it must not be understood that no other possible mode would be acceptable." As Lincoln informed Thomas Cottman of Louisiana a few days after issuing his proclamation, he wanted "to avoid the substance and the appearance of dictation" in the reorganization of the state governments.

Prodded by Lincoln, Unionists in Louisiana, Arkansas, and Virginia held elections, called conventions, and framed free-state constitutions. Louisiana became the president's "model of reconstruction," as radical Republican and Lincoln antagonist Wendell Phillips sarcastically remarked. In that state, General Nathaniel P. Banks in partnership with moderate Unionists led by Michael Hahn defeated a radical faction and won control of the state. In a 13 March 1864 letter to Governor Hahn, Lincoln "barely suggest[ed] for your private consideration whether some

of the colored people may not be" enfranchised. Neither the state constitutional convention nor the legislature that met in the fall seriously considered the president's suggestion. When Radical Republicans criticized the Louisiana constitution for its failure to extend suffrage and other rights to blacks, Lincoln defended it, observing that it was "better for the poor black man than we have in Illinois."

On 2 July 1864, Radical Republicans in Congress put forth their own plan of reconstruction designed not only to ensure black freedom but also provide for a more stringent Union settlement in the South. Lincoln pocket-vetoed the bill, mainly because it would undercut the work of reconstruction begun by him in Louisiana, Arkansas, and Tennessee. (Congress had recognized the Restored Government of Virginia.) The president's veto brought down the wrath of the bill's sponsors, Senator Benjamin F. Wade and Representative Henry Winter Davis, and they issued a blistering attack on his reconstruction policy. Nevertheless, Lincoln's reelection in November strengthened his hand and set the stage for the final act in wartime reconstruction.

Though Congress made an effort to compromise with the president by admitting representatives from Louisiana and Arkansas in exchange for legislation requiring black rights and a harsher reorganization process for the other Southern states, Lincoln in early 1865 refused to compromise, and no congressional reconstruction bill was passed. However, in a sleight-of-hand parliamentary maneuver at the end of the congressional session, Radical Republicans, joined by conservative Democrats, secured the postponement of the issue of seating representatives from Louisiana and Arkansas. Though this action stunned Lincoln, most observers did not believe that it represented a serious blow to his control of reconstruction policy.

With the war ending, Lincoln on 11 April in his last public address defended and elaborated on his reconstruction policy. Though some historians have concluded that Lincoln in this address indicated that he planned to make major changes in his policy toward the defeated South, a close reading of what he said—and placed in the context of what had occurred since his reelection—suggests otherwise. Focusing his remarks on reconstruction in Louisiana, Lincoln declared that 12,000 voters had formed a loyal government and adopted a free-state constitution that gave the benefit of public schools to blacks as well as whites and empowered the legislature to extend the franchise to the freed people. "I would myself prefer that [suffrage] were now conferred on the very intelligent, and on those who serve our cause as soldiers," he declared, but he stopped short of indicating that he would impose a black voter requirement on Louisiana. The president announced that "what has been said of Louisiana" regarding reconstruction "will apply generally" to other Southern states. Yet, he insisted, the policy for each state must be flexible while the "important principles"—emancipation and loyalty—"may, and must, be inflexible." Lincoln maintained that the debate over whether the so-called seceded states were in or out of the Union was "good for nothing at all—a merely pernicious abstraction."

In concluding his 11 April address, Lincoln indicated that "it may be my duty to make some new announcement to the people of the South." He probably had in mind a declaration extending temporary military control to states where no loyal governments existed, a purpose that became clearer when he met with his cabinet three days later. Though Lincoln-inspired governments survived the war in Louisiana, Arkansas, Virginia, and Tennessee, his assassination unleashed a wave of vengeance in the North that meant the end of his conservative and conciliatory policy toward the South. A cottage industry in speculation has developed on what Lincoln might have done had he lived. It is reasonable to assume that he would have managed Southern affairs a great deal better than his successor, Andrew Johnson.

—*William C. Harris*

See also Banks, Nathaniel P.; Davis, Henry Winter; Emancipation Proclamation; Hahn, Michael; Hamilton, Andrew Jackson; Johnson, Andrew; Lincoln, Abraham; Wade, Benjamin; Wade-Davis Bill.

For further reading:

Basler, Roy P., ed. *The Collected Works of Abraham Lincoln* (1953–1955).

Belz, Herman. *Reconstructing the Union: Theory and Policy during the Civil War* (1969).

Harris, William C. *With Charity for All: Lincoln and the Restoration of the Union* (1997).

LINDSAY, WILLIAM SCHAW
(1816–1877)
British statesman

William Schaw Lindsay was a businessman, member of Parliament, and an advocate for British intervention during the Civil War. Born in Ayr, Scotland, and orphaned at an early age, Lindsay went to sea at the age of fifteen and by hard work and application had risen to the command of a merchantman by 1836. Wealthy enough to retire from active sea command by 1840, he relocated to London and established W. S. Lindsay and Company, one of Britain's largest ship-owning concerns. Purchasing Shepperton Manor, Middlesex, England, he was elected to Parliament in 1854 as the member for North Shields. A radical Liberal, Lindsay was the member for the English northern constituency of Sunderland when the Civil War broke out.

A respected expert and author on international maritime law, Lindsay was consulted over the terms of the Chevalier Treaty, the Anglo-French commercial agreement of 1860. It was his concern to promote free trade and his opposition to the United States's Morrill Tariff of 1861 that allied him to the Southern cause. Consequently, he opposed the Union blockade, which he considered contrary to maritime regulations established by the international 1856 Declaration of Paris. His position damaged his commercial links with the United States, as well as cost him the friendship of his fellow radical Liberal colleagues, John Bright and Richard Cobden.

By October 1861 Lindsay openly supported recognition of the Confederacy in the House of Commons. As the British cotton-manufacturing industry began to suffer, he advocated British action to break the Union blockade. Furious over the removal of the Confederate envoys to France and Britain from the British ship *Trent* in November 1861, he supported a declaration of war against the Union. On 8 March 1862, Lindsay tabled a parliamentary motion supporting British intervention in the Civil War, a motion he withdrew due to Federal military successes in the west. Frustrated by his own party's inactivity and the administration's policy of strict neutrality, Lindsay visited Paris in April 1862 to interest Napoleon III in possible joint Anglo-French intervention.

In meetings on 11 and 13 April 1862, Napoleon III assured Lindsay of his personal support and informed him of his own communications to London regarding possible intervention. Upon Lindsay's return to London, Foreign Secretary Lord John Russell denied Napoleon's claims. An additional interview with the French emperor in Paris on 18 April 1862 convinced Lindsay of Russell's duplicity and prompted him to table another motion in June 1862, proposing British intervention. Delayed to the evening of 18 July 1862, the debate began when Lindsay rose in the Commons to speak. To a House electrified by a false rumor that General George B. McClellan's army had been captured outside Richmond, Virginia, the motion nonetheless proved fruitless. A poor speaker, Lindsay alienated sympathetic members with unnecessary exaggeration, fostered suspicion regarding his contacts with Napoleon, and lost support when he advocated the destruction of the American Union for British self-interest. The furious debate was brought to an end when Prime Minister Lord Palmerston rose to attack the motion as ill timed and asked the House to leave foreign policy to the administration. Lindsay withdrew the motion without division but continued his activities supporting Southern independence.

In September 1862 Lindsay personally advanced the Confederate naval agent in Liverpool, Captain James D. Bullock, £60,000 to continue his activities until further funds arrived from Richmond. When news of the Confederate victory at Fredericksburg in December 1862 reached London, Lindsay supported further parliamentary activity in favor of the South. The movement for intervention was strengthened by the Southern victory at Chancellorsville in May 1863, and to mobilize public support for a motion of intervention tabled by his colleague, John A. Roebuck, member for Sheffield, Lindsay helped establish a committee to raise funds for a statue of the fallen Stonewall Jackson, a popular hero in England. The Roebuck motion, finally debated on 30 June 1863, was so mismanaged, however, that it collapsed into a fiasco. Withdrawn without a division, news of Confederate defeats at both Gettysburg and Vicksburg in July 1863 effectively ended the possibility of British intervention during the Civil War. Although the more aristocratic pro-Southern members of Parliament gradually became more concerned with European affairs, Lindsay continued to support what had become a lost cause.

In January 1864 he helped create and fund the Southern Independence Association. A private London gentleman's club, the Association lobbied for parliamentary action to stop the war. In June 1864 Lindsay again tried personally to interest Palmerston in supporting a petition sent to Parliament by the Society for Promoting the Cessation of Hostilities, an organization supported by Confederate finance. Palmerston refused once more, and Lindsay's last effort before he retired from public life due to ill health was to ask the government on 25 July 1864, whether it would intervene with other European powers to prevent further bloodshed in America. Again unsuccessful, he retired to Shepperton Manor but continued to use his pen to advance the cause of international free trade. Between 1874 and 1876, he published his most influential work, the four-volume *History of Merchant Shipping and Ancient Commerce.*

A man of rare ability, William Lindsay proved to be one of the Confederacy's strongest supporters in Britain. Scrupulously refusing all business offered him by the Confederate government, he was nonetheless attacked by radical Liberal newspapers as a man motivated by economic self-interest. Before he died at Shepperton Manor on 28 August 1877, he at least had the satisfaction of seeing the statue of Stonewall Jackson commissioned in 1863 delivered to Virginia. Completed by J. H. Foley, the most prominent English sculptor of his day, the statue was unveiled in a public ceremony in Richmond on 25 October 1875. The statue stands on the grounds of the Virginia state capitol.

—*Rory T. Cornish*

See also Great Britain.
For further reading:

Adams, Ephraim D. *Great Britain and the American Civil War* (1925).
Crook, D. P. *The North, the South, and the Powers 1861–1865* (1974).
Cullen, Joseph P. *Confederate Propaganda in Europe, 1861–1865* (1969).
Cullop, Charles P. "English Reaction to Stonewall Jackson's Death." *West Virginia History* (1967).
Ellison, Mary. *Support for Secession: Lancashire and the American Civil War* (1972).
Jenkins, Brian. *Britain and the War for the Union* (1974).
Jones, Howard. *Union in Peril: The Crisis over British Intervention in the Civil War* (1992).
Owsley, Frank L. *King Cotton Diplomacy: Foreign Relations of the Confederate States of America* (1959).
Vanauken, Sheldon. *The Glittering Illusion. English Sympathy for the Southern Confederacy* (1988).

LIVERMORE, MARY ASHTON RICE
(1820–1905)
U.S. Sanitary Commission official; nurse

Born in Boston to middle-class parents, Mary Livermore was educated at Miss Martha Whiting's Female Seminary in Charlestown, where she later taught French, Latin, and Italian. In 1839, she accepted a job as teacher to the children of a wealthy family in southern Virginia, remaining until 1842. The experience led her to oppose slavery, though she was never very active in organized abolition work. In 1845 she married Universalist minister Daniel Parker Livermore, whom she met while teaching school in Duxbury, Massachusetts. They had three daughters, two of whom lived to adulthood. Both Livermores supported the temperance movement, and Mary Livermore published several temperance stories and a variety of poems and short works before the Civil War.

In 1857, the Livermores moved to Chicago. Daniel Livermore wanted to settle in frontier Kansas as part of the organized effort to populate the region with opponents of slavery. Mary Livermore disliked rural life, and they compromised on Chicago. As a favor for an editor friend, she attended the Republican nominating convention at Chicago's Wigwam in 1860, proudly recalling in later years her role as the only female journalist in attendance. She remained a strong supporter of Abraham Lincoln throughout the war.

Livermore believed that the emergency of war called for unprecedented female public activism, and with her husband's support, she hired a housekeeper to care for their children so she could devote much of her time to the war effort for the next four years. She urged other women to make similar commitments. Appointed an associate and later cohead, with Jane Hoge, of the U.S. Sanitary Commission's Chicago office, she began an extraordinary career as nurse, hospital inspector, and lobbyist for common soldiers. She would write in detail about these experiences in *My Story of the War*, published in 1887, a book that detailed both her own role and the experiences of many Northern nurses and volunteers. Livermore expressed horror at the lack of adequate medical care and nutrition at the beginning of the war, recalling "There was no system, no organization, no knowledge what to do, and no means with which to work." Through her efforts and those of others in the Sanitary Commission, soldiers began to receive better care and better food. She became a tenacious advocate, once meeting with General Ulysses S. Grant to secure discharges for twenty-one dying men.

Perhaps Livermore's most notable public achievement was her organization (with Jane Hoge) of the Great Northwestern Sanitary Commission Fair, a fundraiser held in October and November 1863. She wrote to Abraham Lincoln, requesting his donation of the Emancipation Proclamation, which he readily agreed to do, while expressing some reluctance at relinquishing this prized document. Livermore and Hoge planned this fair with the help of women volunteers, for "The city of Chicago regarded it with indifference, and the gentlemen members of the Commission barely tolerated it." And yet the fair proved a great success, netting nearly $100,000 for soldiers and becoming a model for other such fairs in the North.

As part of her effort to encourage women to organize Sanitary Commission local auxiliaries, Livermore began speaking publicly throughout the Midwest. She approached this task with great trepidation, believing, along with most Americans before the war, that oratory did *not* fall within women's appropriate sphere. Because of her commitment to the war effort and her belief in women's important role in it, she overcame her timidity and began speaking to audiences of both men and women. After the war, she would parlay her wartime experiences into a successful career as a lyceum lecturer, earning thousands of dollars and traveling extensively. She was one of the first women to earn a substantial income from public speaking.

Livermore also embraced the women's rights movement, convinced by her wartime experiences that women needed and deserved the vote. She organized Chicago's first suffrage convention in 1869 and began a newspaper called *The Agitator*. In 1870, friends in Boston invited her to combine this newspaper with the new *Woman's Journal*, published by the American Woman Suffrage Association (AWSA). Livermore accepted, moved with her family to suburban Melrose, Massachusetts, served as editor of the *Woman's Journal* for several years, and later as president for the AWSA.

For the rest of her life, Livermore remained publicly active in suffrage, temperance, and club work, while spending extended periods traveling the lyceum circuit. Although her public speeches often focused on issues of women's education, health, and employment, she incorporated her Civil War experiences and published two volumes of autobiography in part as an effort to instill what she regarded as the moral lessons of her generation to future ones. By being both a patriotic woman and a

public feminist, Livermore helped gain acceptance for women's fights in the late nineteenth and early twentieth centuries.

—Wendy Hamand Venet

See also Hoge, Jane; United States Sanitary Commission.
For further reading:
——— *My Story of the War* (1887; reprint, 1995).

LOCKE, DAVID ROSS
(1833–1888)
Newspaper editor and satirist

David Ross Locke was born in Choconut, Pennsylvania, on 20 September 1833, the son of Nathaniel and Hester Ross Locke and the grandson of two Revolutionary War veterans. Nathaniel was a farmer and a tanner, affiliated with the Methodist Church and involved with the antislavery branch of the Whig Party. The third of six children in a family of modest means, David was sent at age 12 to be an apprentice printer at the Cortland, New York *Democrat*.

In 1850 Locke moved to Corning, New York, and then to Cleveland, Ohio, in 1851 to work as a journeyman printer, and then to Pittsburgh, where he also worked as a reporter. Locke, then just 20 years old, and a partner purchased a small weekly newspaper, the *Advertiser*, in the village of Plymouth, Ohio, in 1853. There he married Martha Bodine in 1855, and the couple had three children. In 1856 he purchased the Bucyrus *Journal* in neighboring Crawford County. He made the *Journal* the official Republican Party newspaper and began his lifelong involvement in the party. He used his editorial pen to ridicule the prejudices of the Ohio Senate when it revoked the privileges of an African-American reporter, and he mocked the U.S. Supreme Court in 1857 for its decision in the *Dred Scott* case. He railed against slavery, the Democratic Party, and the power of Southern planters in Congress. He demanded the rejection of the proslavery LeCompton Constitution for Kansas and elevated John Brown to martyr status after his failed raid at Harper's Ferry and execution in 1859. During his years in Plymouth and Bucyrus, he also began writing humorous letters to the editor under pseudonyms.

A backer of Abraham Lincoln for the Republican nomination for president in 1860, Locke had traveled to Illinois in 1858 to hear the last Lincoln-Douglas debate, and he met the future president then and again in 1859 in Columbus, Ohio. As a partisan Republican and Lincoln supporter, Locke naturally backed the Union war effort enthusiastically after April 1861 and continued to do so when he took over ownership of *The Jeffersonian* in the larger town of Findlay, Ohio, later that year. Findlay, in Hancock County, was in western Ohio, home of many Copperheads like Clement Vallandigham. Locke tried to counter their influence in a weekly letter to the editor signed Petroleum Vesuvius Nasby, a fictional denizen of "Confedrit X Roads," Kentucky. Nasby was a boastful, ignorant drunkard who liked to misquote the Bible in support of his prejudices against African-Americans, his approval of slavery, the Democratic Party, and the South.

The letters made up a running narrative on the issues of the day, and Nasby could be relied upon to express bigotry, demagoguery, and defeatism. In Nasby, Locke perfected a foolish lout as a foil against which Locke's own positions were crystal clear.

The Nasby letters attracted the attention of well-known Cincinnati editor Murat Halstead, who reprinted them in the *Commercial*. Within months many Northern newspapers were reprinting the Nasby letters and counting Locke, along with Josh Billings and Artemus Ward, as one of the preeminent satirists of the day. Lincoln was such an admirer of the letters that he interrupted Cabinet meetings to read them out loud and invited Locke to visit him in the White House in 1863. The letters were especially popular among Union soldiers, who found in Locke an outspoken and unequivocal advocate for their cause. It was Commissioner of Internal Revenue George S. Boutwell, and not Lincoln, who credited the Union victory to "the army, the navy, and the Nasby letters," but Lincoln himself sent Locke a telegram at the end of the war thanking him for his services for the Union.

After Appomattox, Locke became editor and later publisher of *The Blade* in Toledo, Ohio, an association he maintained until the end of his life in 1883. He also published *The Weekly Blade* for an audience of mainly Midwestern farmers and transformed both newspapers into influential publications with large circulations. Though not affiliated with the radical wing of the Republican Party, Locke finally broke with President Andrew Johnson in the summer of 1866 and later supported the attempt to impeach him. Always a supporter of equal rights for the Freedmen, Locke became one of the most successful speakers on the lecture circuit in 1868 with his speech, "Cussid be Canaan," a comic refutation of racism based on the Bible. Locke also wrote novels and plays and lived for several years in New York City, where he edited *The Mail*. Locke continued to support the Republican Party and to engage in a variety of successful business ventures until his death from tuberculosis on 15 February 1888.

—*Gregory R. Zieren*

See also Newspapers.
For further reading:
Coburn, Mark. "The Man They Loved to Hate: Petroleum V. Nasby, America's Own Rascal." *Civil War Times Illustrated* (1987).
Harrison, John M. *The Blade of Toledo: The First 150 Years* (1985).
———. *The Man Who Made Nasby, David Ross Locke* (1969).

LOGAN, JOHN ALEXANDER
(1826–1886)
Union general

John Alexander Logan, arguably Lincoln's most able and successful political general, was born in Jackson County, Illinois, on 9 February 1826. The first of Dr. John and Elizabeth Jenkins Logan's eleven children, Logan spent his formative years on the family farmstead in present-day Murphysboro, Illinois. His father, Dr. John Logan, was a successful medical practitioner and an important political figure in state and local government. The elder Logan was an ardent Democrat and served four terms in the Illinois state assembly, representing Jackson and Franklin counties. While winning elections in 1836, 1838, 1840, and 1846, Dr. Logan lost his initial bid for office in 1834, and was also defeated in 1844. The elder Logan was also a successful farmer, whose farmstead and related holdings were among the area's finest.

As a young man, John A. Logan attended school in nearby Brownsville, Illinois, until 1842, when John and his brother Tom attended Shiloh Academy in Randolph County, Illinois. The two returned home in 1845 and were subsequently instructed by a private tutor with the

John A. Logan (*Library of Congress*)

rest of the Logan children. On 9 May 1847, John Logan enlisted with Company H of the 1st Regiment of the Illinois Volunteers to fight in the Mexican-American War. After a relatively uneventful tour at Santa Fe, New Mexico, were he was named adjutant of the post, second lieutenant Logan was mustered out in October 1848 and returned home to Murphysboro. In 1850 he began his studies as a law student at Louisville University.

After his graduation from law school in February 1851, Logan won his first election as prosecuting attorney for the Third Judicial District and relocated to Benton, Illinois. After less than a year, Logan resigned the position and opted to follow his father's lead into politics as a Democrat, and won back Dr. Logan's state assembly seat in 1852. This must have greatly pleased the elder Logan, who passed away shortly thereafter in November 1853. On 27 November 1855, Logan married Mary Simmerson Cunningham. Three children were born to the couple. John Cunningham Logan, born in November 1856, died in infancy. A daughter, Dorothy Logan, was born during the autumn of 1858, and a second son, Manning Alexander Logan, was born on 24 July 1865.

Logan was elected to the U.S. Congress in November 1858 as the representative for the Illinois Ninth District, and was reelected to a second term in 1860. He was a vocal opponent of abolitionism, and earned the nickname "Dirty Work" Logan for his enthusiastic support of fugitive slave laws. Logan, while viewed as strongly pro-Southern, was ardently antisecession and worked hard to preserve the Union. After the election of Lincoln to the presidency in 1860 and the attack on Fort Sumter in April 1861, pursuing such a tenuous political position was no longer possible. In the summer of 1861, Logan decided to support the North, much to the dismay of his relatives, friends, and other associates in southern Illinois. At Bull Run on 21 July 1861, Logan followed the 2d Michigan Infantry into battle as a civilian observer for the War Department and took part in the conflict, firing on Confederate troops.

In August 1861, Logan enlisted in the U.S. Army and accepted a commission as colonel of the 31st Illinois Volunteer Regiment. As a regimental commander, Logan saw combat at Belmont, Fort Henry, and Fort Donelson. Logan was gravely wounded at Fort Donelson as the 31st Illinois caught the main thrust of General Gideon J. Pillow's attempt to break the Union siege. The volunteer regiment repelled the Confederate charge but suffered heavy casualties, and Logan was initially reported dead from his wounds. General Ulysses S. Grant took note of Logan's outstanding battlefield conduct, and on 12 April 1862, Logan assumed command of the 1st Brigade, 3d Division, XVII Army Corps.

Although a political general in origin, John Logan excelled in his new occupation and never lost an engage-

ment. After a brief term administering affairs as a post commander at Jackson, Tennessee, he became a central figure in the campaigns for Vicksburg, Atlanta, and the Carolinas. Logan continued to rise quickly through the ranks: he became commander of the 3d Division of XVII Corps at the start of the Vicksburg campaign in late 1862 and was promoted to major general on 13 March 1863. On 27 October 1863 he was placed in command of XV Corps, Army of the Tennessee. After the death of General James B. McPherson during the battle of Atlanta on 22 July 1864, Logan was placed in temporary command of the Army of the Tennessee, but the position was permanently assigned to West Point graduate O. O. Howard soon thereafter.

The reluctance of General William T. Sherman to keep Logan in command of the Army of the Tennessee led to a falling out between the two Union leaders, and this bad blood was clearly evident in Logan's postwar dealings with the professional military establishment. At the heart of the matter was the natural tension between the officers who were trained graduates of West Point and those who had a political background such as John Logan. Logan, in fact, spent the latter portion of 1864 campaigning vigorously in Illinois for Lincoln's reelection bid, after taking an extended leave of absence from the Army of the Tennessee on 21 September 1864.

After Lincoln's successful election to a second term, Logan was a general without a command. On 13 December, Grant dispatched Logan to Nashville to potentially relieve George H. Thomas of command of the Army of the Cumberland; if Thomas had not moved by the time he arrived, Logan was instructed to take over. While Logan traveled to Nashville, the Army of the Cumberland finally went on the offensive and scored a major victory against John Bell Hood in the battle of Nashville. Logan returned to Washington, and on 18 January 1865 he resumed command of XV Corps in time for the start of the Carolinas campaign. Logan and his troops were headed toward Raleigh, North Carolina, when the news of Robert E. Lee's surrender arrived. On 23 May 1865, Logan was named permanent commander of the Army of the Tennessee, and he led the Western Army in the celebratory Grand Review at Washington, D.C., on 24 May.

Logan returned to politics after the conclusion of the war and switched his party affiliation from Democrat to Radical Republican. He won a seat in the House of Representatives in 1866 and was successfully reelected in 1868. Logan was also a staunch opponent of President Andrew Johnson and took a highly visible role in the impeachment effort of 1868. On 13 January 1871, Logan was elected to the U.S. Senate by the state legislature of Illinois. He was reelected to the Senate in 1879 and 1885, after a losing effort to win the party nomination for the presidency in 1877. In 1884, Logan was the

Republican Party's nominee for vice president, with James G. Blaine as the presidential candidate. The Republican Party lost their first presidential contest since the Civil War to Grover Cleveland and Thomas Hendricks, and Logan remained in the U.S. Senate until his death on 26 December 1886.

John Logan was a founding member of the Grand Army of the Republic, and as the organization's most visible leader he helped develop the group into a highly effective political entity. Throughout this period, Logan remained true to his postwar Radical Republican roots and was a recognized champion of Union war veterans and African-American civil rights. He is also credited as being the founder of Memorial Day. Logan authored two books in his later years. The first, *The Great Conspiracy*, was published in 1886 and outlined Logan's history of the Civil War and Reconstruction. His second work, *The Volunteer Soldier of America*, was published posthumously in 1887 and reiterated his strong belief in the value of a civilian military.

Over the course of his lifetime, Logan suffered only three defeats: the loss of the command of the Army of the Tennessee in 1864, his 1877 senate reelection bid, and the campaign for vice president in 1884. After his death, Logan was laid in state in the U.S. Capitol, and his pallbearers included Roscoe Conkling, Simon Cameron, Robert Todd Lincoln, C. H. Andrews, Colonel Fred Grant, General Lucius Fairchild, General M. D. Leggett, Governor Jeremiah Rusk, General Wiliam T. Sherman, General William F. Vilas, General John C. Black, and Dr. Charles McMillan. Logan was survived by his wife, Mary, until her passing in 1923.

—*Dane Magoon*

See also Atlanta Campaign; Grand Review.

For further reading:

Cottingham, Carl D., Preston Michael Jones, and Gary W. Kent. *General John A. Logan: His Life and Times* (1989).

Jones, James Pickett. *Black Jack: John A. Logan and Southern Illinois in the Civil War Era* (1967).

———. *John A. Logan: Stalwart Republican from Illinois* (1982).

Logan, John A. *The Great Conspiracy, Its Origin and History* (1886).

———. *The Volunteer Soldier of America* (1887).

Logan, Mary S. C. *Reminisces of a Soldier's Wife* (1913).

———. *Thirty Years in Washington* (1901).

LOGAN'S CROSS ROADS/MILL SPRINGS/ BEECH GROVE, KENTUCKY, BATTLE OF
(19 January 1862)

Confederate brigadier general Felix Kirk Zollicoffer had been operating in eastern Kentucky near Cumberland Gap since September 1861. In an attempt to guard as much territory in southeastern Kentucky as possible, he moved to Mill Springs on the south bank of the Cumberland River in November 1861.

He then crossed the river immediately opposite Mill Springs to Beech Grove and fortified his position. The only real threat to his position in November 1861 was a brigade of the Army of Ohio under the command of Brigadier General Albin Schoepf of Brigadier General George Henry Thomas's 1st Division, fifteen miles away at Somerset, Kentucky.

In late November, Zollicoffer received an order from Major General George Bibb Crittenden in Knoxville, Tennessee, to withdraw back to the south bank of the Cumberland River. Concerned about the growing Federal presence in Kentucky, Crittenden went to the state in early January 1862. He arrived on 3 January 1862 to find Zollicoffer still at Beech Grove and a Federal force under George Thomas on the way. Zollicoffer had dug in fairly effectively with the Cumberland on his left flank and Fishing Creek on his right. The Cumberland was especially high, and it would have been difficult to move the approximately 4,000 men across if Beech Grove were attacked during the crossing. For that reason, Crittenden decided to stay there.

Thomas had departed from Lebanon, Kentucky, with part of his division on 1 January 1862. He made his way to Columbia, Kentucky, over almost impassable muddy roads. From Columbia he made it to Logan's Cross Roads on 17 January. He made camp, waited for the remainder of his force to slog its way in on the muddy roads, and sent word to Schoepf to send him three regiments.

Thomas's scouts almost immediately told him that Crittenden was preparing to move out of his earthworks at Beech Grove only ten miles from Logan's Cross Roads. As a result, Thomas began preparing for an attack. He planned to absorb the first blows of whatever Crittenden and Zollicoffer planned and then counterattack after he determined their weaknesses. He hoped to have the rest of his men at Logan's Cross Roads, Schoepf's men from Somerset, and a brigade he called for from London, Kentucky, before the fighting began. He placed strong guards on the roads and sent out a large patrol to warn of any Confederate probes. On the night of 17 January, that patrol repelled a strong Confederate reconnaissance of his position.

During the day of 18 January, more of Thomas's men arrived, along with word that the forces from Somerset and London were on the way. Thomas went to bed that night after sending out scouts to give plenty of warning of a Confederate march. Thomas was awakened at midnight with the news that the Confederates were on the move. He immediately dressed and conferred with his officers regarding the disposition of the troops.

The Confederate march was slowed by a steady rain and poor roads. As a result, Thomas had time to receive full scouting reports about the strength and arrangements of the Southern force. He knew that two

The battle of Logan's Cross Roads, 19 January 1862 (*Library of Congress*)

Confederate brigades under Zollicoffer and Brigadier General William Carroll, led by two cavalry companies and flanked on either side by a cavalry battalion, were moving toward his position and that they would be supported by two artillery batteries.

The two lead Confederate cavalry companies first made contact with Thomas's cavalry at about 5:30 A.M. The Federal cavalry fell back to Colonel Mahlon Dickerson Manson's brigade. Manson's defensive line was attacked by Zollicoffer's brigade. Zollicoffer spread his men out to the right of the road and tried to maneuver his men around the Union left flank. Just as it appeared that he might succeed, the troops from London, Kentucky, under Colonel Samuel Powhatan Carter, arrived. Thomas was able to place them on his left, and the flank held.

The Confederates next attacked in force against the center of Thomas's line. Unfortunately for the Union forces there, the attack came when many of them were low on ammunition. In a quick maneuver, Thomas moved up two fresh regiments, allowing those in front to go for ammunition.

While the Confederates pressed the attack on the center, Thomas was able to swing Carter's brigade slightly to the right to enfilade the attacking Confederates. During the confusion this maneuver caused, Thomas ordered his left to advance in a counterattack. About that time, Zollicoffer became confused and mistook one of the moving Federal regiments for one of his own. He approached the commander of the Union 4th Kentucky, Colonel Speed Smith Fry, and told him to quit firing. When one of Zollicoffer's officers realized that Fry was a Union officer, the Confederate fired. Fry fired back, and either intentionally or because the Confederate general was in the way, struck and killed Zollicoffer.

About that time, the Union center, taking advantage of the gains made by the left, pressed forward. The effect was infectious all along the Confederate lines, as first the front ranks, followed by the others, fell back and began moving in a rout back to their defenses at Beech Grove.

Thomas had his men regroup and resupply, and then moved in pursuit. However, because of the condition of the roads, they did not arrive until early evening. All Thomas could do, without having a better view of the Confederate defenses in daylight, was to bombard the Confederate positions with his artillery.

During the night, Crittenden decided to retreat by ferrying his men across the Cumberland. He was able to do so but had to leave most of his artillery, horses, and supplies behind. Crittenden led his men to Mill Spring and then marched southeast to Cumberland Gap. Crittenden had suffered about 400 casualties and

Thomas 246. Crittenden was severely criticized for his conduct of the campaign, and, after being censured, he resigned in the fall of 1862.

—*David S. Heidler and Jeanne T. Heidler*

See also Crittenden, George Bibb; Kentucky; Thomas, George Henry; Zollicoffer, Felix.

For further reading:

Cleaves, Freeman. *Rock of Chickamauga, the Life of General George H. Thomas* (1948; reprint, 1974).

McKinney, Francis F. *Education in Violence: The Life of George H. Thomas and the History of the Army of the Cumberland* (1961).

Reid, Richard J. *The Rock Riseth: George H. Thomas at Logan's Crossroads* (1988).

LOGISTICS

In the American Civil War, the United States of America and the Confederate States of America enlisted, trained, and supported almost three million soldiers over four years. Accomplishing these logistical feats meant that both sides struggled to harness industrial, technological, human, and natural resources. For the most part, Northerners understood and applied logistics to war making more effectively than Southerners.

Understanding the significance of logistics in the Civil War requires an inclusive definition. The process of logistics includes: (1) supply, which entails determining military requirements and then procuring, maintaining, storing, and distributing those requirements; (2) transportation, which entails the moving of troops and equipment; (3) evacuation and hospitalization, which entails moving and treating sick and wounded troops; and (4) service, which entails administration and communications. The Civil War reveals the degree to which logistics increasingly became a major feature of modern war. It can be argued that the conflict's outcome was decided as much in railroad yards or by commissary officers as it was on the battlefields or by generals.

When the Civil War started in April 1861, neither side possessed the logistical capabilities to maintain huge armies in campaigns stretching across hundreds of miles, nor did they have mobilization plans or staffs to coordinate their respective war efforts. The Union added to its significant demographic advantages by empowering a national government with centralized constitutional authority, organizing an efficient logistics system in the military, and placing competent managers within that system. Conversely, the Confederacy negated its strategic advantages by creating a national government with limited and decentralized authority, organizing an inefficient logistics system in the military, and placing often incompetent managers within that system.

In 1861 the populations of the Union and the Confederacy stood at approximately 23 million and 9 million people, respectively. Yet, the number for the Confederacy is somewhat misleading, because the Southern population included about 3.7 million slaves, who did not fight in the conflict, yet whose labor did allow much of the white male population to serve in the military. The Union also enjoyed overwhelming superiority in manufacturing capacity, possessing 110,274 industrial establishments with 1.3 million workers as compared to 18,026 industrial establishments with 110,000 workers in the South. In 1860 the Northern states produced firearms valued at $2.2 million, while the Southern states produced firearms valued at $73,000. In the final year before Fort Sumter, the North constructed an impressive 451 locomotives, while the South constructed only nineteen. In addition, the Union boasted 22,000 miles of track and 4.7 million horses and mules for more transportation capacity than could be afforded by the Confederacy's 9,000 miles of track and 2.5 million draft animals.

Confederate Logistics — The Confederate States of America may have offset its demographic disadvantages with better allocation of logistical resources to military objectives. To win, the Confederacy did not necessarily need to win on every battlefield; holding Union forces at bay until political and moral support for the war waned in the North or until political and military support increased in Europe might have brought victory. The South could counter the North's threats using interior lines of communication and transportation along established rivers and railroads.

Despite this somewhat favorable position, the Confederacy lagged behind the Union in relative logistical capabilities. More grievous than its material disadvantages, the Confederacy suffered from a constitutional system that favored autonomy at the state level. Likewise, the military's logistical infrastructure allowed for too much competition and duplication of effort. The Confederacy's Quartermaster Department was the obvious choice to supervise the logistical aspects of the war effort; but, until his dismissal in August 1863, Quartermaster General Abraham C. Myers did little more than establish a cumbersome bureaucracy that misappropriated resources. Myers's successor, Alexander R. Lawton, faced the nearly impossible task of supporting the Confederate military while also reforming military logistics. As a result, no single government agency ever supervised all logistical aspects of the war effort, whether in the military or civilian sectors.

Railroads represent the most glaring example of the South's failure to centralize its wartime administration. Establishing transportation priorities, settling disputes, balancing competing requirements, and coordinating available resources proved problematic for the Confederacy's civilian government. Delays occurred because private railroads shipped the more lucrative commercial and private freight, rather than less profitable military freight. State governments also fiercely

guarded their constitutional prerogative to regulate transportation within state boundaries. Only in February 1865 was the secretary of war empowered to compel private railroads, canal, and telegraph companies to serve the Confederate military. By then, however, the Confederate rails and locomotives had fallen into such disrepair that the Confederacy's logistical demands could not possibly be sustained. The failure to maintain, let alone expand, the railway system is another indication of the Confederacy's inability to mobilize and prolong industrial production levels.

Although the Confederates failed for the most part in the area of logistics, there were some achievements worthy of note. In the battle of First Bull Run in July 1861, Confederate Joseph Johnston used railroads to reinforce P. G. T. Beauregard's forces and turn the apparent defeat into a Southern victory. During the summer of 1862, Braxton Bragg successfully moved 25,000 soldiers by rail from Tupelo, Mississippi, to Chattanooga, Tennessee, to counter Union forces also moving eastward from Mississippi; the first element of Bragg's command traveled 776 miles in six days. In September 1863, James Longstreet shifted his 12,000 men some 900 miles by rail from Virginia to Georgia and helped defeat Union forces at the battle of Chickamauga.

These achievements notwithstanding, insufficient provisioning and inadequate transportation deprived Confederate forces of opportunities to exploit tactical victories. After his victory at First Bull Run, Beauregard could not pursue a defeated and demoralized Union army because the Subsistence Bureau did not move food forward to support any further maneuvers. In hastily moving his troops those 900 miles to Chickamauga, Longstreet left provisions and horses behind in Virginia and thus lost his strategic mobility. In February 1864, Confederate general Joseph Finegan defeated Union forces at Olustee, Florida. If a rail line between Florida and Georgia had existed, Finegan could have received reinforcements and perhaps driven Union forces from the state. Using rail lines in a Confederate-controlled Florida also could have proved a vital link for moving cattle to Georgia and then to the battlefront. In all these examples, Confederate forces failed to convert tactical victories into truly strategic successes because of poor logistics.

On a more human scale, the Confederacy's poor logistics system affected its ability to provide for soldiers' basic needs. Confederate armies suffered more and more from shortages in food, clothing, medicine, and shoes as the conflict wore on. Poor administration, miscommunication, and nonexistent transportation greatly hampered the movement of supplies from storage to the combat areas where they were desperately needed. Union forces also purposefully seized Confederate food and isolated Confederate armies from their agricultural production areas. While Lee's Army of Northern Virginia starved in Petersburg in March 1865, hundreds of thousands of bread and meat rations were available elsewhere in Virginia and North Carolina. Even when foodstuffs existed, spoilage emerged as a serious problem, in part because of insufficient amounts of salt for preservation. Unreliable transportation and inexperienced personnel also hurt Confederate medical care. Living under these poor conditions depleted the troops' morale as well as their physical ability to fight.

Although Confederate logistics may be best characterized as an inefficient system with incompetent people, a few individuals, such as Chief of Ordnance Josiah Gorgas, did make made significant contributions to the South's logistical effort. In April 1861 Gorgas faced the almost impossible assignment of generating and maintaining a manufacturing base capable for munitions production. With the exception of Tredegar Iron Works in Richmond, Virginia, no other large foundry existed in the South. Gorgas accordingly supervised the construction of facilities such as a gunpowder mill in Augusta, Georgia, a lead smelting facility at Petersburg, Virginia, and additional foundries in Macon, Columbus, and Augusta, Georgia. Gorgas also cleverly devised methods for obtaining the necessary raw materials; his subordinates in Ordnance scoured the Southern countryside for copper for percussion caps and bronze for cannon. He sent Major Caleb House to Europe to purchase weapons and ammunition. Under Gorgas's able direction, the Ordnance Bureau miraculously succeeded in giving the Confederate Army relative self-sufficiency in weapons manufacturing.

Over the four years of the Civil War, the Confederacy's ever-multiplying logistical problems seriously impaired its military effectiveness at every level. Too few Southern military or civilian leaders grasped the magnitude and complexity of logistical requirements of the Confederate war effort. The South's agrarian culture doubtlessly contributed to this basic misapprehension. To make matters worse, no centralized infrastructure existed within the Confederate military or civilian government to facilitate the support of men and material in the field.

Union Logistics — The United States of America enjoyed seemingly overwhelming advantages in human and industrial resources, and Union grand strategy called for a complete victory in the conflict. This entailed defeating the South's military forces on the battlefield, crippling the region's ability to support those forces, and destroying the Confederate soldiers' will to fight. Carrying out such an offensive strategy required manpower to fight battles and, just as significantly, to operate supply lines and consolidate conquered Southern territory. As the war progressed, these support duties depleted available officers and men for combat operations.

In the first year of the war, much competition and duplication of effort occurred among government and military organizations. However, the War Department assumed control of logistics activities for the Union army by the fall of 1862. Secretary of War Edwin M. Stanton and Quartermaster General Montgomery C. Meigs emerged as the most influential individuals in the North's logistics infrastructure. Under their supervision, significant advances occurred in standardizing baggage, food, and other essential equipment.

Along with career officers and government officials, the Union made maximum use of business leaders in manufacturing, administration, and transportation. Managing railroads represented the most complex task in mid-nineteenth-century America. Before the war, men like Herman Haupt and Thomas Alexander Scott had gained valuable experience in operating large railroad companies, which they used to create an efficient rail system. Haupt served as chief of construction and transportation of the U.S. military railroads, while Scott, as assistant secretary of war, directed a railroad expansion totaling 4,000 miles of new track, in contrast to the South's meager 200 miles of new track during the war. The North's national government also operated its own telegraphs and riverboats.

Unlike the Confederacy's fiercely independent state and local authorities, the Union possessed a centralized logistics system governing the military and civilian spheres. Abraham Lincoln's administration maintained strict control over the North's human and material resources. This bureaucracy formally or informally coordinated every stage of logistics, from production on factories and farms, transportation on riverboats and railroads through supply depots, and finally delivery to the soldiers at the battle front.

Under the direction of Quartermaster Montgomery C. Meigs and his talented subordinates, the Union army employed a three-tiered supply line. The Quartermaster Department purchased supplies at general or principal depots at St. Louis and Washington. From these central logistics bases, quartermaster units used railroads, rivers, and wagons to distribute supplies to advance depots such as Nashville, Tennessee, or City Point, Virginia. Lastly, wagon trains carried supplies to temporary depots near the front lines, where they were distributed directly to the combat units. At each tier, careful coordination was necessary to avoid bottlenecks. Besides the Quartermaster Department, the Ordnance, Subsistence, and Commissary Departments also played significant logistical roles in supplying the Union military in the field.

The Union's efficient logistics system positively affected both strategy and tactics. Even when the Union forces failed to achieve decisive strategic or tactical objectives, little blame can be placed on the Union's logistical system. The Peninsula campaign from March to August 1862 was a military failure, yet it stands as one of the North's greatest logistical triumphs. Union general George B. McClellan planned to land 105,000 men, 300 artillery pieces, and 25,000 horses and mules on the peninsula in Virginia formed by the fork between the James and York rivers to threaten Richmond, the Confederacy's capital, seventy miles away. Quartermaster General Meigs arranged for 400 boats and barges to transport the massive army. McClellan's campaign plan also required more than one million pounds of supplies daily. To achieve this level of support after the landing, Meigs's flotilla maintained a waterborne supply line; several hundred wagons transported supplies overland as McClellan's troops moved inland. The Peninsula campaign's military failure was not from the lack of logistical support. Likewise, throughout the Civil War, Union forces seldom lost battles due to the insufficient logistical support.

At the strategic level, effective logistics translated into the capability to exploit victories when possible or recover quickly from defeats when necessary. Ulysses S. Grant's capture of Vicksburg and William Tecumseh Sherman's March to the Sea served as two prime examples of how logistics could affect strategy. By carrying out these campaigns, Grant and Sherman disrupted the Confederacy's transportation routes and destroyed major sources of its supplies. Consequently, the South's war-making capabilities slowly dwindled until movement of troops and supplies became impossible. Confederate strategy thus became untenable from a logistics perspective.

The fall of Vicksburg, Mississippi, to Grant's Union forces on 4 July 1863 dealt a crushing blow to the Confederacy just one day after the defeat of Lee at Gettysburg. From a manpower standpoint, that John Pemberton surrendered his 31,000 Confederate soldiers after a siege was devastating. Losing the 172 cannon and 60,000 small arms proved still more devastating to the Confederacy. From a logistics standpoint, the Union gained free navigation of the Mississippi River and finished what had been started with the capture of New Orleans in April 1862. Capturing Vicksburg also gave Union forces control of the rail line connecting Texas, Arkansas, and western Louisiana with those states east of the Mississippi River. The Confederacy was cut into two sections; no means existed to move substantial amounts of food in the western Confederacy. Lastly, whereas the South lost a major waterborne supply route, the North gained yet another means of moving supplies and troops quickly. Later, Union forces under Grant again disrupted the Confederacy's supply routes by capturing the strategically placed rail hub at Chattanooga in November 1863.

For forty days from November through December 1864, William Tecumseh Sherman and 60,000 Union soldiers made the so-called March to the Sea, a massive raid sixty miles wide and 285 miles long from Atlanta to Savannah, Georgia. Sherman intended to destroy Confederate logistics and crush Southern morale. Consequently, it has been argued that Sherman made war in the modern and total senses in which nonmilitary parts of an enemy's war effort became legitimate targets.

After leaving Atlanta, Sherman quickly broke away from the Union supply lines and lived off the land in northern Georgia. Sherman moved so quickly because his troops foraged in the Southern countryside and utilized Confederate resources to supply themselves. What they did not consume they destroyed, accounting for more than $100 million in Confederate losses. Facing little opposition along the way, his 62,000 seasoned veterans wrecked some 200 miles of Confederate railroad track and deprived the starving Confederate soldiers in Virginia of rations. By Christmas of 1864, Sherman occupied Savannah and effectively isolated the upper South from the lower South. His massive raid had achieved its goal of demolishing Confederate logistics.

Logistics affected Southerners' morale because Sherman's March to the Sea also hurt the Confederacy's will to fight by showing the region's vulnerability. Because of the psychological effects of this campaign, Southerners came to realize that the North was not only capable of grinding them into dust, but willing to do so. Little hope was left.

On a human level, Northern soldiers benefitted from the Union's efficient logistics system, which helped ensure a relatively high quality of life in the field. Union soldiers rarely suffered in the long term from shortages of food, clothing, shelter, or ammunition. Improvements were also made in medical logistics. After reforming and restructuring its transportation and hospital organization, the Union army's medical department successfully evacuated sick and wounded from battlefields, sometimes several thousand casualties in the same day. Such consideration of their well-being had a direct and positive effect on the Union soldiers' morale, as well as their physical fighting ability.

Although an efficient system with competent people for the most part, shortcomings did exist in Northern logistics, such as when the Ordnance Department was under James W. Ripley's direction from April 1861 until September 1863. Ripley stifled attempts to introduce breech-loading and repeating rifles into the Union army. During his tenure, he only purchased some 8,200 breech-loaders out of the total of 700,000 rifles. Until George D. Ramsay replaced Ripley, the Ordnance Department remained too slow and too conservative to take advantage of technological advancement in weaponry. Ripley was, however, a notable exception among Northerners.

During the four years of the American Civil War, the Union's logistical system grew increasingly more efficient, even as the task of supporting its military also grew more challenging. Not only did many Union commanders understand the importance of keeping their own soldiers supplied, they also grasped the strategic and tactical importance of disrupting Confederate logistics. The Union army's support arms combined with the civilian government to mobilize and manage Northern resources. As a result, the North's centralized logistics infrastructure successfully maintained a total of 1.9 million men in the Union military and ultimately helped the Union win the war.

—David J. Ulbrich

See also Gorgas, Josiah; Haupt, Herman; Lawton, Alexander R.; Meigs, Montgomery; Myers, Abraham; Northrop, Lucius B.; Quartermaster; Railroads, Confederate.; Railroads, Union; Ripley, James Wolfe; Telegraph.

For further reading:

De Luc, William G. *Recollections of a Civil War Quartermaster: The Autobiography of William G. De Luc* (1963).

Duncan, Louis C. *The Medical Department of the United States Army in the Civil War* (1987).

Goff, Richard D. *Confederate Supply* (1969).

Huston, James A. *The Sinews of War: Army Logistics, 1775–1953* (1966).

Koistinen, Paul A. C. *Beating Plowshares into Swords: The Political Economy of American Warfare, 1606–1865* (1996).

Marszalek, John F. *Sherman: A Soldier's Passion for Order* (1994).

Sharpe, Henry Granville. "The Art of Supplying Armies in the Field as Exemplified during the Civil War." *Journal of the Military Service Institution of the United States* (1896).

Symonds, Henry C. *Report of a Commissary of Subsistence, 1861–1865* (1888).

Turner, George Edgar. *Victory Rode the Rails: The Strategic Place of the Railroads in the Civil War* (1953).

Vandiver, Frank E. *Ploughshares into Swords: Josiah Gorgas and Confederate Ordnance* (1952; reprint, 1994).

Weigley, Russell F. *Quartermaster General of the Union Army: A Biography of M. C. Meigs* (1959).

LOMAX, LUNSFORD LINDSAY
(1835–1913)
Confederate general

The son of Virginians Mann Page Lomax and Elizabeth Virginia Lindsay Lomax, Lunsford Lomax was born in Newport, Rhode Island. Lomax was educated in Virginia before accepting an appointment to the U.S. Military Academy. He graduated twenty-first of forty-nine in the class of 1856. Upon graduation Lomax was sent to Kansas. When Virginia seceded, he resigned his commission and accepted a captain's commission in the Virginia commonwealth forces.

Initially serving as Joseph Johnston's assistant adjutant general, Lomax remained with that officer when he entered Confederate service. Shortly thereafter, however, Lomax was transferred to the Western theater, where he served as inspector general to Brigadier General Ben McCulloch. Lomax fought at Pea Ridge, where McCulloch was killed in March 1862. After the battle Lomax served as Earl Van Dorn's inspector general at the rank of lieutenant colonel. As part of Van Dorn's staff, he saw action at Corinth in October 1862. That same month he was transferred to east Tennessee, where he also served as inspector general.

Eager for a more active combat command, Lomax worked for another transfer that was granted in the spring of 1863 with a promotion to colonel and his move to the Army of Northern Virginia with the command of the 11th Virginia Cavalry. One of his earliest actions in this command was participation in William E. Jones's raid into western Virginia at the end of April 1863. Lomax fought at Brandy Station in June 1863, and he commanded the 11th at the battle of Gettysburg. For his actions there, he gained a promotion to brigadier general at the end of July 1863, a recommendation made personally by Robert E. Lee.

Lomax commanded his new brigade in his classmate and friend, Fitzhugh Lee's division in the Bristoe Station campaign, at Culpeper, the Wilderness, Cold Harbor, and Yellow Tavern. In August 1864 he was promoted to major general. Shortly after his promotion, Lomax was sent with a division to Jubal Early in the Shenandoah Valley. Lomax was captured in September 1864 but managed to escape and return to his division.

Lomax remained in the valley through the winter of 1864–1865, primarily using his cavalry division to ward off raids out of eastern Tennessee. On 29 March 1865, he was given command of the entire Valley District. When he heard of Lee's surrender on 9 April, Lomax wrote to President Davis asking permission to move into North Carolina to form a juncture with Joseph E. Johnston. Apparently not receiving a response from the now fleeing Davis, Lomax moved south. Upon hearing of Johnston's surrender to Sherman, Lomax sent word to Sherman that he too would be interested in surrendering. He surrendered his command in May 1865.

After the war, Lomax farmed near Warrenton, Virginia, until 1885, when accepted the presidency of Blacksburg College (Virginia Polytechnic Institute). He held that position until 1899, when he became one of the compilers of the series that would become *The War of the Rebellion: A Compilation of the Official Records of the Union and Confederate Armies*. In 1905 he became the commandant of the Gettysburg National Military Park. He died in Washington.

—*David S. Heidler and Jeanne T. Heidler*

See also Jones, William E.; McCulloch, Ben; Van Dorn, Earl.
For further reading:
U.S. War Department. *The War of the Rebellion: A Compilation*

of the Official Records of the Union and Confederate Armies (1880–1901).

LONG, ARMISTEAD LINDSAY
(1825–1891)
Confederate general

Born to Armistead Long and Callista Cralle Long in Campbell County, Virginia, the younger Long was educated locally before accepting an appointment to the U.S. Military Academy. He graduated seventeenth of forty-four in the class of 1850. After graduation he was sent to Fort Moultrie, South Carolina, where he spent two years, and then from 1852 until 1860 he was stationed at a variety of frontier posts in the Indian Territory and Kansas. In 1860 he was transferred to Augusta Arsenal in Georgia.

Long resigned his commission on 10 June 1861. He accepted a lieutenant colonel's commission from the Confederacy and was sent to western Virginia to act as inspector general to General William Loring's forces there. In the fall of 1861, Long was transferred to South Carolina, where he became the military secretary to Robert E. Lee. Long also held the position of chief of ordnance and artillery for the Department of South Carolina and Georgia. He was promoted to the rank of colonel in fall 1861.

Long continued to serve as Lee's military secretary until his promotion to brigadier general in the fall of 1863. Even while serving as Lee's secretary, Long used his expertise with artillery to command artillery units at Fredericksburg, Chancellorsville, and Gettysburg, for which he was commended by Lee. With his promotion to brigadier general, Long became the chief of artillery for the II Corps of the Army of Northern Virginia. In the fall of 1863, Long commanded the artillery of II Corps at Bristoe Station and Mine Run.

In the summer of 1864 he was given command of the artillery in Jubal Early's Valley campaign and subsequent raid on Washington. Returning to Richmond in late 1864, Long was with the Army of Northern Virginia as it fled Richmond and the trenches of Petersburg. He surrendered at Appomattox.

After the war, Long worked as an engineer for the Kanawha Canal Company. He lost his sight in 1870 and was forced to retire. He spent much of the next few years dictating and writing on a slate what would become his *Memoirs of Robert E. Lee*, first published in 1886. Long died in Charlottesville, Virginia.

—*David S. Heidler and Jeanne T. Heidler*

See also Lee, Robert E.
For further reading:
Long, Armistead Lindsay. *Memoirs of Robert E. Lee; His Military and Personal History Embracing a Large Amount of Information Hitherto Unpublished* (1983).

LONGFELLOW, HENRY WADSWORTH
(1807–1882)
Poet

Although overshadowed by the popularity of his contemporaries, specifically Ralph Waldo Emerson and Walt Whitman, Henry Wadsworth Longfellow represents the American passion for breaking new ground. As the author of the first important anti-slavery poems, Longfellow established his place in American social commentary. The relationship of his poetry to history is often indirect; events often served as catalysts for his poetry rather than the actual subject matter, as in his *Poems on Slavery*.

Born in Portland, Maine, on 27 February 1807, Longfellow spent much of his early professional career as a teacher and translator. Proficient in modern languages, he was in demand as a translator in Europe, thus allowing him to make European literature available to the American reading public. After Longfellow returned to the United States, the years 1842 to 1860 were his most productive, resulting in his successful long poems *Evangeline* (1847) and *The Song of Hiawatha* (1855). A continuing source of anxiety, however, during this period was the increasing pre–Civil War tensions and his own difficulties reconciling his abhorrence of slavery with his antiwar stance. His 1842 *Poems on Slavery* represented a new strain in his work, a turn toward social concerns. He also developed a friendship with the fiery Senator Charles Sumner, a somewhat surprising relationship since Sumner was as brash as Longfellow was taciturn.

Longfellow's poetry during the antebellum era was a thinly veiled political and social commentary. In a poem entitled "The Building of a Ship," Longfellow weaves a subtle warning to the American lawmakers. Published just after the formation of the Free Soil Party in Massachusetts, and the signing of the Fugitive Slave Bill by President Millard Fillmore, this poem was Longfellow's outlet for the expression of his anxiety. With the line, "Thou, too, sail on, O Ship of State!," Longfellow makes an analogy between the construction of a ship and the political scene. After the 1856 attack on Sumner in Congress, Longfellow wrote a letter to his friend, noting, "You have torn the mask off the face of traitors; and at last the spirit of the North is aroused."

With the political world crashing down around him by 1861, Longfellow's personal life shattered as well. On 9 July 1861, his wife was killed in a tragic accident and he himself suffered scars so severe that he would never be able to shave again, thus contributing to the picture of Longfellow as a white-bearded gentleman. Yet Longfellow referenced the death of his wife in only one poem, not written until 1879, in which he described "the

seasons, changeless since the day she died." Forced to resume his writing to combat his grief, Longfellow published a series of narrative poems, beginning with *Tales of a Wayside Inn* in 1863. No sooner had it been published, however, than his eldest son ran off to join the army, so Longfellow immersed himself into a translation of Dante's *Divine Comedy*, an effort that took until 1867 to complete. His subsequent works, *Flower-de-Luce* (1867), *Three Books of Song* (1872), and *Ultima Thule* (1880), however, lacked the luster of his earlier works and perhaps reflected his own personal losses as well as that of the nation.

The central characteristics of Longfellow's poetry included his approach to humanity and his opinion that art could be seen only "through man." Longfellow, like many nineteenth-century reformers, followed William Ellery Channing's belief in the essential goodness of humanity. At his core, Longfellow believed, that humans were fundamentally good and endowed with reasoning capabilities and a religious ideal. Longfellow's poetry is an expression of that end, concentrating on the conflict between good and evil. The conflict is often described, avoiding an explicit resolution. His poems are primarily meditative, and the inspiration for his symbols, such as bells, walled forts, castles, or music, are usually drawn from nature. The archetypes of the darkness of night, implying the cold and damp grave, and the sun, representing vitality and warmth, express the circadian-like rhythm of his poems. His poems, particularly those of the mid-nineteenth century, often communicate some type of warning. One is aptly entitled "The Warning."

Emblematic of an era, Longfellow never achieved national acclaim during his lifetime. In his later years, he acted as a cultural bridge between Europe and America, translating some of the works by European masters into English, but his subtle references to the political scene were often overlooked in favor of works by his contemporaries. He received honorary degrees from the universities of Oxford and Cambridge, but after the death of his wife in 1861, he never again found complete solace in his work. His death on 24 March 1882, although observed in Europe, went largely unnoticed in the United States. It would not be until well within the twentieth century that his work would be taken seriously by American scholars.

—*Jennifer Harrison*

See also Sumner, Charles.
For further reading:
Fletcher, Angus. "Whitman and Longfellow: Two Types of the American Poet." *Raritan* (1991).
Gorman, Herbert S. *A Victorian American: Henry Wadsworth Longfellow* (1926).
Hirsh, Edward L. *Henry Wadsworth Longfellow* (1964).

LONGSTREET, JAMES
(1821–1904)
Confederate general

James Longstreet was born on his paternal grandfather's plantation near Edgefield, South Carolina, on 8 January 1821 and then taken to his parents' home near Gainesville, Georgia. His father, James, impressed by his young son's rocklike character, informally called him "Peter," and Longstreet was thus later often known as "Old Pete."

In 1830 the boy went to live with his uncle, Augustus Baldwin Longstreet (1790–1870), a newspaper editor, educator, and Methodist minister, near Augusta, Georgia. He remained with his uncle after his father died in 1833 and his mother, the former Mary Anne Dent, moved to Somerville, Alabama.

Although largely identified with Georgia, Longstreet was appointed to the U.S. Military Academy in 1838 through Alabama's U.S. representative, his kinsman, Ruben Chapman. At West Point Longstreet befriended the shy Ulysses S. Grant, later serving as best man at Grant's wedding to Longstreet's fourth cousin, Julia Dent, on 22 August 1848.

Graduating fifty-fourth in a class of sixty-two in 1842, Longstreet was assigned to the 4th Infantry (the regiment Grant joined one year later), posted at Jefferson Barracks outside St. Louis. There in 1844 he met Maria Louisa Garland, his post commander's daughter. Married on 8 March 1848 in Lynchburg, Virginia, they had ten children; two died in infancy and three others died of scarlet fever within one week in January 1862.

Longstreet fought in the Mexican-American War in the battles of Palo Alto, Resaca de la Palma, Monterrey, Vera Cruz, Cerro Gordo, San Antonio, Churubusco, and Molino del Rey, winning brevets to captain and major. Wounded at Chapultepec (12 September 1847) while charging up a hill with the 8th Infantry's colors, he handed the flag to his lifelong friend, George E. Pickett. After his recovery, he fought in several Indian wars and was promoted to captain in 1852 and then major and paymaster in 1858.

Upon the outbreak of the Civil War, Longstreet resigned effective 1 June 1861, after almost twenty years' active military service. Writing to Alabama's governor from Albuquerque (15 February 1861), he offered his services as the most senior Alabama officer in the army. With the rank of brigadier general, he reported to Pierre Gustave Toutant Beauregard at Manassas in July.

At this time G. Moxley Sorrel, one of Longstreet's staff officers, said that Longstreet brought "a high reputation as an energetic, capable, and experienced soldier," and described "a most striking figure, about forty years of age, a soldier every inch, and very handsome, tall and well proportioned, strong and active, a superb horseman and with an unsurpassed soldierly bearing, his features and expression fairly matched; eyes, glint steel blue, deep and piercing; a full brown beard, head well shaped and poised."

Another of Longstreet's young officers, Thomas J. Goree, in a letter to his family (17 August 1861), called him "one of the kindest, best hearted men I have ever known. Those not well acquainted with him think him short and crabbed," but his gruff manner could become as proper as that of the typical Southern gentleman if the occasion required.

William B. Pettit, an enlisted artillerist, gave this description in a letter to his wife (16 December 1862): "He is about six feet 2 inches high, of strong round frame, portly and fleshy but not corpulent or too fat. His hair is dark auburn and long, his whiskers and moustache of same color and thick and heavy. His forehead is broad and full, his brows heavy. His nose, straight and rather fleshy, and his eyes, which set in close to his nose, are dark and steady in their movements and gaze. The lids come quite close together. He is about medium size and height and weighs, I suppose, 190 pounds." The young gunner added: "Next to Lee I should prefer entrusting the chief command of our armies to him."

Longstreet was present at the Civil War's first major battle on 21 July 1861, when Joseph E. Johnston and Beauregard routed Irvin McDowell's overconfident

James Longstreet (*Library of Congress*)

Union forces at the battle of First Bull Run. On 18 July 1861 his 4th Brigade, composed of the 1st, 11th, and 17th Regiments of Virginia volunteers, saw preliminary action at Blackburn's Ford on the right flank of the Confederate line, where the attack was expected. When the main Union attack came on the left in the actual battle, Longstreet's brigade, although under artillery fire for nine hours, played a relatively minor role. After Beauregard sent orders not to pursue the retreating enemy, Sorrel found Longstreet in a rage. "He dashed his hat furiously on the ground, stamped, and bitter words escaped him."

Promoted to major general on 7 October 1861 Longstreet was responsible for about 14,000 men in what eventually became I Corps of the Army of Northern Virginia. It consisted of six brigades led by Pickett, A. P. Hill, R. H. Anderson, C. M. Wilcox, R. E. Colston, and Roger A. Pryor. Longstreet distinguished himself during the Peninsula campaign (April to July 1862) as rear guard commander at Yorktown and at Williamsburg (5 May 1862). He reported (16 May 1862) that Williamsburg was "a very handsome affair," modestly claiming that his "part in the battle was comparatively simple and easy, that of placing the troops in proper positions at proper times." By contrast, Sorrel found that battle "a stubborn, all-day fight, with serious losses on both sides, but the enemy was beaten off and we resumed the march that night, the Federals having enough of it. . . . General Johnston was present on the field all day, but seeing Longstreet, the rearguard commander, carrying things very handsomely, generously forbore any interference and left the battle to his handling." Longstreet did less well during the engagement at Fair Oaks/Seven Pines (31 May–1 June 1862) near Richmond. Muddy roads and almost impassable streams swelled by a storm the previous night delayed the right wing's movement. Although Longstreet never fully accepted blame, he did misunderstand his orders and marched his men in the wrong direction down the wrong road, causing confusion when they ran into Benjamin Huger's soldiers. Because Johnston's orders were imprecise, Longstreet argued with Huger for some time about who was in charge. Eventually Longstreet prevailed and compounded the already deteriorating situation by sending Huger's command to where it could take only a small part in the ensuing battle. Longstreet's report on 10 June 1862 implied that Huger was to blame for the South's losses.

Fair Oaks had halted George B. McClellan's move to take Richmond. After J. E. B. Stuart's cavalry raid encircled McClellan's forces near Richmond, Robert E. Lee drove McClellan back in the Seven Days' battles, ending with Malvern Hill on 1 July 1862. Longstreet's command now consisted of his division's six brigades under Winfield Scott Featherston, James L. Kemper, Anderson, Pickett, Wilcox, and Pryor, and nine brigades from Hill's

and T. T. Holmes's divisions. On 17 June 1862, immediately before the Seven Days' battles, Longstreet told soldiers under his command: "If ever men were called upon to defend the beloved daughters of their country, that now is our duty. Let such thoughts nerve you up to the most dreadful shock of battle; for were it certain death, death would be better than the fate that defeat would entail upon us all." After Longstreet's many quick maneuvers in this series of battles, Lee called him the staff in his right hand.

Union general Henry W. Halleck then ordered McClellan to unite with the forces of John Pope, Longstreet's West Point classmate; but, before McClellan arrived, Longstreet and Thomas J. ("Stonewall") Jackson routed Pope's Army of Virginia in the battle of Second Bull Run on 28–30 August 1862. When Pope advanced, Jackson pretended to retreat but remained in place until Lee and Longstreet reinforced him. Longstreet's right wing consisted of five divisions led by John Bell Hood, D. R. Jones, Anderson, Wilcox, and Kemper. After some delay, Longstreet's forces joined with the rest of the Confederate army to deliver a crushing counterattack, forcing a Union retreat back to Washington.

The unflappable Longstreet had proved himself Lee's capable subordinate. This great Confederate victory was due largely to his effective tactics. Sorrel wrote that his "consummate ability in managing troops was well displayed that day and his large bodies of men were moved with great skill and without the least confusion."

When Lee invaded Maryland, McClellan, who had succeeded Pope, met him along Antietam Creek at Sharpsburg. While McClellan hesitated for a whole day, Jackson's three divisions joined Longstreet's command, consisting of divisions led by Lafayette McLaws, John George Walker, Anderson, Jones, and Hood. When McClellan finally attacked on 17 September 1862, he met Lee's reunited forces. The arrival late that afternoon of another of Jackson's divisions, under A. P. Hill, denied McClellan a decisive victory. When Lee retreated into Virginia, McClellan made no attempt to follow him.

Before Antietam, Longstreet's boot had chafed his heel and, because it refused to heal, he had to wear a slipper. According to Sorrel at Antietam he "was in no good humor at such footwear and the need of occasionally walking in it. In fact, a wobbly carpet slipper was not a good-looking thing for a commander in the field."

Longstreet commended (10 October 1862) his officers and men for their actions at this time: "In one month these troops had marched over 200 miles, upon little more than half rations, and fought nine battles and skirmishes killed, wounded, and captured nearly as many men as we had in our ranks, besides taking arms and other munitions of war in large quantities."

After Antietam Lee recommended on 2 October 1862 that Jefferson Davis promote Longstreet and

Jackson to the newly created rank of lieutenant general. Longstreet's promotion on 9 October 1862 was dated one day before Jackson's and made him superior in rank to all other lieutenant generals. Lee made little comment on Longstreet's qualifications because his exemplary service required no explanation. From now on he was known as Lee's old war horse.

Longstreet's command was reorganized on 6 November 1862 as I Corps with divisions under Robert Ransom Jr., McLaws, Anderson, Pickett, and Hood. Lee moved about 78,000 men to Fredericksburg, where the Union suffered a costly defeat on 13 December 1862. About 120,000 men under Ambrose E. Burnside made six unsuccessful assaults against strongly entrenched Confederates, losing 12,653 men to the defenders' 5,309. Setting up ample artillery support, the confident Longstreet was at his best in his defense behind a stone wall on Marye's Heights, allowing Lee to focus attention at the other end of his line.

Afterwards, Lee left Longstreet in charge. Behind Fredericksburg, in his typically methodical way, Longstreet laid out a defensive system capable of being held by half the men that had been required before. This enabled him to move Hood's and Pickett's divisions and Dearing's and Henry's artillery battalions near Petersburg to find food for the winter.

Longstreet was not present at Joseph Hooker's defeat at Chancellorsville (1–4 May 1863) but later called Chancellorsville "an instance of an offensive battle, where we dislodged the Federals, it is true, but at such a terrible sacrifice that half a dozen such victories would have ruined us." He was in the Suffolk area with Pickett's and Hood's divisions as commander of the Department of North Carolina and Southern Virginia (February–May 1863). Displaying little ability for independent command, he soon rejoined Lee.

Despite the death of the irreplaceable Jackson at Chancellorsville and Longstreet's aversion to an offensive campaign in the North, Lee decided to advance into Pennsylvania. After the war Longstreet wrote, "[W]hile I first suggested to General Lee the idea of an offensive campaign, I was never persuaded to yield my argument against the Gettysburg campaign, except with the understanding that we were not to deliver an offensive battle, but to so manoeuvre that the enemy should be forced to attack us—or, to repeat, that our campaign should be one of offensive strategy, but defensive tactics."

When Lee suffered a major defeat at Gettysburg (1–3 July 1963), Longstreet, in command of one of Lee's three corps, was proved right. Longstreet's I Corps, now consisting of McLaws's, Pickett's, and Hood's divisions, was heavily involved in fighting on both 2 and 3 July. With little knowledge of Union movements and strength, late in the morning of 2 July, Lee finally ordered Longstreet to make a frontal attack on the Union's southern flank; but Longstreet did not attack until almost four that afternoon. Losing several thousand men to an overwhelmingly superior enemy, his two divisions under Hood and McLaws fought for more than three hours, one unit briefly reaching Cemetery Ridge, before being driven back at Little Round Top. They did take the Peach Orchard.

Two years after Lee's death, in a speech at Washington and Lee College (19 January 1872), Jubal A. Early, a divisional commander at Gettysburg, opened a campaign against Longstreet, blasting him for not participating in a coordinated attack on 2 July and thus causing the Gettysburg defeat. Although Lee's own staff officers refuted this claim, Early's description of Longstreet's unreasonable delay has continued to hurt his reputation.

Searching for a scapegoat, hostile "Lost Causers" like Early and William Nelson Pendleton also blamed the defeat on Longstreet's performance on 3 July. Over Longstreet's urgent objections, Lee ordered him to attack George G. Meade's center on Cemetery Ridge with Pickett's division, which had arrived from Chambersburg late in the previous evening, supporting this drive with other units from his corps and Hill's III Corps. After delaying until 2 P.M., Longstreet reluctantly ordered Pickett's hopeless charge. With less than one fourth of the men surviving the action, this Confederate disaster is considered a major turning point in the war, despite the North's failure to follow up the advantage of this decisive battle.

In a letter to his Uncle Augustus (24 July 1863), Longstreet complained, "The battle was not made as I would have made it. My idea was to throw ourselves between the enemy and Washington, select a strong position and force the enemy to attack us." He added, "As General Lee is our commander, he should have the support and influence we can give him. If the blame (if there is any) can be shifted from him to me, I shall help him and our cause by taking it."

Instead of endorsing the move into Pennsylvania, Longstreet had argued for an offensive in the west. After Gettysburg he received permission to move McLaws's and Hood's divisions and a brigade of Pickett's division to the west, arriving in Georgia just in time to reinforce Braxton Bragg's Army of Tennessee at Chickamauga (19–20 September 1863). On the battle's second day, his left wing made a magnificent attack against William S. Rosecrans. This great and bloody battle was a Pyrrhic victory, however, because Bragg failed to exploit what Longstreet, now called the Bull of the Woods, had accomplished.

As Longstreet continued to quarrel with the difficult Bragg, he was given independent command of the Department of East Tennessee (5 November 1863–12 April 1864). After his unsuccessful siege of Burnside at

strongly fortified Knoxville, the depressed Longstreet rejoined Lee. When Grant forced a bloody but inconclusive battle at the Wilderness in northern Virginia (5–6 May 1864), Longstreet led fresh troops to drive back his old friend's attack. Then the Confederate assault was delayed for two hours because Longstreet was shot by mistake by his own men. This nearly fatal wound in his neck and right shoulder put him out of action until 19 October 1864. Returning to duty with a paralyzed right arm, he eventually suggested to Lee in a now raspy voice that he meet with Grant and remained with Lee through the surrender. After the Appomattox surrender (9 April 1865), Grant sought out Longstreet to recall their past friendship.

After the war Longstreet went into business in New Orleans with the Owen brothers—William, Miller, and Edward—as cotton factors. Lee wrote to him (19 January 1866), "If you become as good a merchant as you were a soldier, I shall be content. No one will then excel you, and no one can wish you more success and more happiness than I." Within a few months he was also president of an insurance company. His affairs remained prosperous until he joined the Republican Party and openly criticized Lee's actions during the war. Now considered a traitor in the South, he had to rely upon federal offices for a living. President Grant nominated him as surveyor of customs at New Orleans, an office he held until 1873. Also appointed Louisiana adjutant general (1870), he was shot and held prisoner during a riot in New Orleans (1874). He served briefly as deputy collector of Internal Revenue in Georgia (1878) and postmaster for Gainesville (1879). After serving as United States minister to Turkey (1880–1881), he returned to Gainesville to operate a hotel and served as U.S. marshall (1881–1884) and later as a U.S. railroad commissioner (1898).

Outliving most of his high-ranking postwar detractors, Longstreet struck back against former colleagues in articles, lectures, and a book entitled *From Manassas to Appomattox* (1896). Despite the Lee cult's efforts to smear his reputation, which had an influence on many later historians, Longstreet is now usually regarded as one of the Civil War's best battlefield tacticians.

Longstreet's wife of over forty years died on 29 December 1889. Eight years later (8 September 1897) at the age of seventy-six he married thirty-four-year-old Helen Dortch (d. 1962) in the governor's mansion in Atlanta.

Longstreet died in Gainesville on 2 January 1904 and was buried in the Alta Vista Cemetery in Gainesville.

—*Charles Ellis Dickson*

See also Army of Northern Virginia; Bull Run, Second Battle of; Chickamauga, Battle of; Fredericksburg, Battle of; Gettysburg, Battle of; Lee, Robert Edward.
For further reading:

Longstreet, Helen D. *Lee and Longstreet at High Tide: Gettysburg in the Light of the Official Records* (1904; reprint, 1989).
Longstreet, James. *From Manassas to Appomattox: Memoirs of the Civil War in America* (1896; reprint, 1960).
Piston, William Garrett. *Lee's Tarnished Lieutenant: James Longstreet and His Place in Southern History* (1987).
Sanger, Donald Bridgman, and Thomas Robson Hay. *James Longstreet* (1952).
Southern Historical Society Papers. Volume 5 (1878).
Sorrel, Gilbert Moxley. *Recollections of a Confederate Staff Officer* (1959).
U.S. War Department. *The War of the Rebellion: A Compilation of the Official Records of the Union and Confederate Armies* (1880–1901).
Wert, Jeffry D. *General James Longstreet: The Confederacy's Most Controversial Soldier, A Biography* (1993).

LOOKOUT MOUNTAIN, BATTLE OF
(24 November 1863)

Despite its legendary status as "the battle above the clouds," the battle of Lookout Mountain was actually nothing more than a sideshow in the overall battle for Chattanooga in November 1863. After the Union defeat at Chickamauga and the Union's subsequent retreat into Chattanooga, Confederate general Braxton Bragg's Army of Tennessee had not been able to surround the embattled Union Army of the Cumberland, then still commanded by General William Rosecrans. When Union general Ulysses S. Grant took charge of operations in Chattanooga, replacing Rosecrans with General George Thomas, Grant immediately changed the mentality of his army from a defensive into an offensive force. Grant's plan to break out of Chattanooga had his trusted subordinate General William T. Sherman attack the northern flank of the Confederate line along Missionary Ridge, General Thomas demonstrate against the Confederate center at Orchard Knob, and General Joseph Hooker clear the area around Lookout Mountain. Hooker was then to move through the Rossville Gap and finally turn the Confederate's southern flank on Missionary Ridge.

On 23 November, Thomas's demonstration had miraculously turned into a complete victory, while still by the 25th Sherman was finding his objective far more difficult to obtain. Like Thomas, Hooker also found that reaching his goal was easier than had been originally contemplated. The summit of Lookout Mountain, with its craggy granite face, appeared too difficult to capture in the amount time available, so Hooker originally planned to attack only the middle and lower parts of the mountain. On the 24th the top half of Lookout Mountain was completely covered by a dense fog, an unusual micro weather formation that often gathers on this mountain range. The fog served as a cover for Hooker's men as they maneuvered around the mountain peak, which stands guard over Chattanooga at a spot where the Tennessee River bends toward and around the city. Although delays and confusion from the fog wreaked havoc with early operations, Hooker's troops soon found that the fog's

The summit of Lookout Mountain, ca. 1864 (*Library of Congress*)

cover had made their operations undetected. By 9:00 A.M., Hooker's men were advancing in attack formation up the ridge seemingly unopposed until they reached the point up the mountain where the Confederates had dug defensive positions. The emplacements, however, proved insufficient to halt the Union advance.

Commanding the Confederate forces on Lookout

Mountain was General Carter Stevenson, who had just been put in charge of these forces when General William J. Hardee was moved to Missionary Ridge. Stevenson had only 1,200 men on the mountain to defend against Hooker's 12,000. Stevenson barely had had time to understand where his men were positioned when Hooker began his offensive. Using well-concentrated

The capture of Lookout Mountain, 24 November 1863 (*Library of Congress*)

artillery on the mountain peak, the Confederates were able to hold off the numerically superior troops until the Union advance up the summit made the artillery ineffective and the guns had to be removed. By the early afternoon, Stevenson's forces were in serious trouble, with Hooker's men now pushing what was left of a Confederate defense off the summit; the only force that had kept the Union troops from an uncontested victory was at Cravens House on the east side of the mountain. Although Cravens House itself was soon lost, the Confederates were able to maintain a high ridge above it and kept the Union troops at bay for several hours. With the fog still clinging to the ground, the vastly outnumbered Confederates menaced their opposition by rolling boulders down below, which crashed into Union troops without much warning. Meanwhile, Stevenson discovered that the reinforcements that he hoped were coming would never be sent, as Bragg was more concerned about his exposed left flank on Missionary Ridge than he was about a mountain summit of dubious value. So Stevenson was ordered to withdraw his troops from around the mountain peak, destroying bridges and holding the enemy as he retreated. Stevenson's primary concern became to avoid being separated from the main Confederate force on the other side of Rossville Gap

atop Missionary Ridge. Fearing a loss of his easy gains, Hooker waited until the next morning to capture Point Lookout, the very top of Lookout Mountain.

Hooker, having cleared Confederate opposition from the northeastern end of the Lookout Mountain chain, then moved toward Ringgold Gap to participate in the Union's stunning victory on Missionary Ridge and the breaking of the siege of Chattanooga.

—*James Meredith*

See also Chattanooga Campaign; Hooker, Joseph; Stevenson, Carter Littlepage.
For further reading:
Grant, Ulysses S. *Personal Memoirs of U. S. Grant* (1885).
Roland, Charles P. "Chattanooga-Ringgold Campaign: November 1863." *The Civil War Battlefield Guide* (1998).
Sword, Wiley. *Mountains Touched with Fire* (1995).

LOPEZ, NARCISO
(1797–1851)
Filibuster

Narciso Lopez's attempts to overthrow Spanish rule in Cuba received support from American annexationists in the North and South and intensified the national debate over the question of the expansion of slavery.

General Grant (*far left*) on Lookout Mountain, 25 November 1863. Also present (*left to right*) are General J. A. Rawlins, General Webster, Colonel Clark Lagow, Colonel William Hillyer, and an unidentified orderly. (*Library of Congress*)

Narciso Lopez was born in Venezuela on 29 October 1797. He joined the Spanish army in 1814 and rose to the rank of colonel. In 1823, he had to leave Venezuela, which had fallen to the revolutionary army of Simón Bolívar. Lopez went to Spanish-held Cuba. There he married Dolores Frias y Jacott, the daughter of a prominent Creole planter, became active in Liberal political circles, quit the army, and continued to live in Cuba until deciding to move to Spain in 1827. He rejoined the army in 1833 to fight for the Liberal cause in Spain's first Carlist War. By the time of the Liberal victory in 1839, Lopez was a general and a member of Spain's parliament, the Cortés.

He eventually returned to Cuba without his wife, who had separated from him in 1836, and served in a number of important administrative and military posts in the island's colonial government. When the Liberal regime ended in 1843, Lopez lost his position and entered private business. After his investments failed, he turned to revolutionary politics as a way to strike out against the Conservative government that had destroyed his former privileged status. His Liberal contacts put him in touch with the wealthy Creole members of the Havana Club, who were plotting for Cuban independence from Spain and annexation to the United States. Lopez agreed to coordinate his own plan for an uprising with the scheme of the Havana Club, whose members were trying to enlist an American general, William Jenkins Worth, to lead an expedition of Mexican-American War veterans in an invasion of the island. Both plans were foiled, however, when President James K. Polk, who was secretly working to purchase Cuba from Spain, informed the Spanish government of the rebels' intentions because their designs threatened to upset his own delicate negotiations. The Spanish sought Lopez's arrest, but he managed to flee to the United States in July 1848.

Lopez made his way to New York, the headquarters of the Cuban annexationist movement, to raise funds for a return to Cuba. For funds, he turned first to the Havana Club, which had an office in New York. Although he receive moneys from that organization, he did not enjoy its members' full confidence. Aware of this attitude, Lopez moved to establish his own Cuban independence junta in New York. He then used Havana Club funds and money raised by his own efforts and those of the vociferous American expansionist, John L. O'Sullivan, to recruit men and charter vessels. By August 1849, several hundred mercenaries had signed on to the venture. This initial expedition died a premature death, however, when the antiannexationist administration of President Zachary Taylor moved quickly to stop the filibustering fleet before it could leave U.S. waters.

Embarrassed by Lopez's failure, the Havana Club broke its ties to the hapless general. Undeterred, Lopez began a new recruiting drive for another expedition in 1850. This time, he concentrated his efforts in the South, eventually relocating his headquarters to New Orleans, and enlisted more than 500 volunteers. After a rendezvous on Contoy Island off the Yucatán coast, the entire force sailed for Cuba on 16 May. When they landed at Cárdenas on 19 May, Lopez's men met unexpectedly stiff resistance that delayed their advance and allowed Spanish reinforcements to arrive at the invasion port. Lopez had to evacuate Cárdenas and return to the United States by way of Key West, which his ship, the *Creole*, reached on 21 May after narrowly escaping capture by Spanish vessels.

When he returned to New Orleans, Lopez was arrested and indicted on a charge of conspiring to break U.S. neutrality laws. After a series of mistrials, the charges were dropped in March 1851, and he began to organize yet another invasion force. He raised an army of 500 men and, after reading reports of pro-independence revolts breaking out all across Cuba, he decided to launch the expedition, which landed on the Cuban shore at El Morrillo near Havana on 12 August. Lopez then divided his army into two battalions. One under the command of Colonel William L. Crittenden remained at the landing site. Lopez himself led the other battalion on a march to the village of Los Pozas to find transport for the filibusters' supplies and artillery. On 13 August, superior Spanish forces attacked the isolated battalions—the rumored Cuban revolt had never risen. The Spanish captured Crittenden and his fifty remaining men on 16 August, marched them to Havana, and shot them the same day. They rounded up Lopez's depleted and scattered forces during the next two weeks. Now a prisoner, Lopez was moved to Havana and garroted outside Morro Castle on the morning of 1 September 1851.

—*R. Boyd Murphree*

For further reading:
Brown, Charles H. *Agents of Manifest Destiny: The Lives and Times of the Filibusters* (1980).
Chaffin, Tom. *Fatal Glory: Narciso Lopez and the First Clandestine U.S. War against Cuba* (1996).

LORING, WILLIAM WING
(1818–1886)
Confederate general

Born to Reuben Loring and Hannah Kenan Loring in Wilmington, North Carolina, William Wing Loring moved with his family to St. Augustine, Florida, when he was a small child. As a teenager he fought in the Second Seminole War and rose to the rank of second lieutenant. His parents then sent him to the District of Columbia to attend Georgetown College. After leaving that institution, he studied law and was admitted to the Florida bar. He was also interested in the new state of Florida's political situation and was elected to the state legislature in the early 1840s.

At the outbreak of the Mexican-American War, Loring received a captain's commission and commanded a company of mounted rifles. He was promoted to major shortly before Winfield Scott's Mexico City campaign. On the march to Mexico City, Loring participated in all of the major engagements. He received two brevet promotions and lost his arm in the battle of Chapultepec. At the end of the war, he remained in the regular army and was promoted to lieutenant colonel in March 1848. With his regiment he made a heroic march from Texas to Oregon and assumed command of the Department of Oregon in 1849. He remained there for two years before being transferred to Texas in 1851. He was promoted to colonel in 1858.

At the end of 1860, Loring assumed command of the Department of New Mexico, headquartered at Santa Fe. During March 1861, after the secession of Texas, he grew increasingly concerned for the security of his department. At the same time, he was wrestling with his own decision about whether to follow Florida out of the Union. He expressed views against the doctrine of secession, but apparently the impending secession of his native state of North Carolina decided him on the issue. He resigned his commission on 13 May 1861 and offered his services to the Confederacy. He was commissioned a brigadier general in the Confederate army on 20 May 1861.

In July 1861, Loring was given command of the Army of the Northwest in western Virginia. Throughout the remainder of the summer and fall of 1861, Loring led his men in a futile attempt to prevent Union forces from gaining a foothold in that area. In early August, General Robert E. Lee, who had been sent to western Virginia to advise the commanders there, urged Loring to attack the Federal position at Cheat Mountain. Loring resisted. Finally, because of the discovery of a route that would allow a secret approach overlooking the Federal position, Loring, with Lee present as an advisor, advanced on the position. The attack, planned for 12 September 1861, was never completed because of faulty intelligence.

At the end of the year, his Army of the Northwest was brought under the overall command of Thomas J. "Stonewall" Jackson. From the very beginning, Loring chafed under this arrangement, and when the ensuing campaign produced few results and it appeared his disgruntled army would be spending the remainder of the winter in comfortless Romney, Loring and his officers requested that they be removed from Jackson's command. To Jackson, such action smacked of insubordination and threatened to tear his entire army apart. It was truly a thorny situation for the War Department. In February 1862, Loring was promoted to major general and shortly afterward was summoned east so that a more suitable command could be found for him. Temporarily placed in command of the Confederate defenses at Suffolk, Virginia, on 8 May 1862 Loring was given command of the Department of Southwestern Virginia.

Through the summer of 1862, Loring defended his department against Union invasion from the Kanawha Valley. In August 1862 he defeated a Union force at Pack's Ferry on the New River, and in September he launched a short, though relatively successful, invasion into the Kanawha Valley. On 27 November 1862 he was transferred to the command of Lieutenant General John C. Pemberton at Jackson, Mississippi.

During the next six months Loring commanded a division under Pemberton in defense of Vicksburg. In March 1863, Pemberton sent Loring north of the city to stop the Federal movement against Yazoo Pass. Loring built Fort Pemberton and repelled the Union offensive. In April 1863, Loring used his division to combat Union colonel Benjamin Grierson's raid into Tennessee, and on 25 April he prevented the town of Enterprise, Mississippi, from falling to Grierson.

By May 1863, relations between Loring and Pemberton were somewhat strained. Loring disagreed with many of Pemberton's decisions regarding the defense of Vicksburg, and during the battle of Champion's Hill on 16 May, he failed to carry out Pemberton's orders to attack the Union left flank. Loring, charged with guarding the subsequent Confederate retreat back to Vicksburg, managed to separate his division from the remainder of the army and was forced to join General Joseph Johnston's force outside of Jackson, Mississippi. As a result, Loring missed the siege of Vicksburg and the surrender of the remainder of Pemberton's army.

Loring served under Johnston for the remainder of the summer, fighting at Jackson after the surrender of Vicksburg. For the remainder of the year into early 1864, Loring and his division were headquartered at Canton, Mississippi. In early 1864, serving under Lieutenant General Leonidas Polk, Loring commanded his division in the attempt to stop William T. Sherman's Meridian campaign. Failing to stop Sherman, Loring moved his division to Montevallo, Alabama.

As part of Polk's Army of Mississippi, Loring moved into north Georgia in May 1864 to join Joseph Johnston's efforts to stop Sherman's move toward Atlanta. He commanded his division in the early phases of that campaign, and when Polk was killed on 14 June, Loring assumed command of the Army of Mississippi, effectively a corps in Johnston's army.

Loring led his corps through the remaining engagements of the campaign and moved north with General John Bell Hood after the fall of Atlanta. He fought under Hood in the disastrous battles of Franklin and Nashville. In early 1865 he took what was left of his army to join Joseph Johnston in the attempt to slow Sherman's march through the Carolinas. In April 1865 he surrendered with Johnston in North Carolina.

After the war, Loring engaged in various business activities in New York City, but, missing the military life, in 1869 he accepted a brigadier general's commission in the Egyptian army. For ten years he fought with distinction in several Egyptian campaigns. He returned to the United States in 1879. In retirement in New York City, Loring wrote extensively about his varied military career. He died of a heart attack in New York City on 30 December 1886.

—*David S. Heidler and Jeanne T. Heidler*

See also Atlanta Campaign; Champion's Hill, Battle of; Jackson, Thomas Jonathan; Vicksburg Campaign.

For further reading:

Raab, James W. *W. W. Loring—A Biography* (1997).

Wessels, William L. *Born to be a Soldier; the Military Career of William Wing Loring of St. Augustine, Florida* (1971).

LOST CAUSE

Defeat in the Civil War left feelings of inferiority within the Southern psyche and in turn induced a desire to justify the Confederacy's losing effort and the South's antebellum culture. In reaction, many white Southerners mixed myth and reality in what became known as the Lost Cause.

The term first appeared in Edward Pollard's 1866 book *The Lost Cause: A New Southern History of the War of the Confederates*. Among other reasons for writing the book, Pollard wanted to preserve Southern identity. The concept of the Lost Cause became particularly popular beginning in the 1880s. Many Southern writers, organizations, politicians, and commoners firmly believed that despite valiant resistance, the Confederacy was primarily defeated because of the Union's overwhelming superiority.

The Lost Cause was thus as much about how the conflict's generation dealt with defeat as how the successive generations of Southerners interpreted this defeat. Many whites in the South needed this sort of rationalization because the alternative meant that they had to take more responsibility for their lack of success in the Civil War. Worse still, they also may have been forced to question their culture and their motivation for fighting to preserve it. Such soul searching could be painful, as evidenced by works such as W. J. Cash's 1941 book *The Mind of the South*.

Belief in the Lost Cause allowed white Southerners to revel in the glories of the Civil War. From the conflict's end until World War I, many organizations such as memorial associations, the Southern Historical Society, the United Confederate Veterans, and the United Daughters of the Confederacy promoted the collective memory of the South's defeat in the Civil War. Confederate war heroes such as Jubal A. Early and John B. Gordon led these groups. Perhaps it is not too much of an exaggeration to say that white Southerners were more unified in looking back at the Civil War than they had been during it.

Lamenting defeat in the Civil War provided a means to cope with changes in the postbellum South. As Reconstruction attempted to finish the transformation of the South that the Emancipation Proclamation and the Civil War had started, the region experienced significant social, political, and economic changes. Slavery was abruptly ended, parts of the region gradually industrialized, and planter power slowly decreased. In many ways, the "New" South looked much different from the "Old" South.

A minority of white Southerners took the Lost Cause's rhetoric much more literally, glorifying the conflict that had been fought to preserve the Old South and slavery. For example, Nathan Bedford Forrest, a Confederate cavalry general and first leader of the Ku Klux Klan (KKK), embraced a nostalgia for antebellum life. Through intimidation and violence, the KKK and other white supremacist groups worked to restore a semblance of the Old South's racial order and social stability. With the end of Reconstruction in 1877, freed slaves found themselves again at the bottom of another hierarchical construct. Many white Southerners tragically chose to ignore lynchings and other cruelties because they believed that a hierarchical racial system remained the only viable way to maintain order and stability. Without slavery, white Southerners believed that some new system of racial control would have to take its place. Discrimination took on new forms of segregation in Jim Crow laws and other racist policies.

In the years between the end of Reconstruction in 1877 and the turn of the century, the Lost Cause continued to play an integral part in the South's ever-evolving self-identity. Its most powerful images and symbols were Robert E. Lee and Pickett's Charge. Burned into the collective memory of Southerners, and not a few Northerners, such symbols helped Southerners to blur myth and reality.

Already revered during the war, Robert E. Lee acquired a divine mystique within Southern culture after it. Remembered as a leader whose soldiers would loyally follow him into every fight no matter how desperate, Lee emerged from the conflict to become an icon of the Lost Cause and the ideal of the antebellum Southern gentlemen, an honorable and pious man who selflessly served Virginia and the Confederacy. Lee's tactical brilliance at Second Bull Run and Chancellorsville took on legendary status, and despite his accepting full responsibility for the defeat at Gettysburg, Lee remained largely infallible for Southerners and was spared criticism even from historians until recent times. Other Confederate generals—James Longstreet, Richard S. Ewell, or J. E. B. Stuart—were blamed for Gettysburg, because Lee was seen as unbeatable except by crushing enemy numbers or perhaps by ugly twists of fate. After the Confederate surrender at Appomattox, such explanations of Lee's ultimate failure foreshadowed the Lost Cause's rationalizations of Confederate defeat.

The third day at Gettysburg emerged as a tragically heroic symbol for the Lost Cause. On 3 July 1863, a doomed assault known as Pickett's Charge began in splendid glory but ended in utter failure. Southerners came to consider Pickett's Charge as the defining moment of their Lost Cause in the Civil War, and the battlefield itself developed into a symbol of civil religion—a shrine where veterans paid homage to the Lost Cause.

By the time the United States entered World War I, the Lost Cause had smoothed the harsher edges of white Southerners' bitterness, allowing even unreconstructed Southerners to accept the American nation as a whole. As many firsthand memories died with the war's veterans in the 1920s, the Lost Cause grew more mythical and less real. World War II went still further to heal the Civil War's wounds in the South and help bring the region back into the Union. As time provides distance for historians, the Confederacy's defeat becomes better understood, yet the Lost Cause still retains some hold on Southern culture, remaining a nostalgic and romantic recollection that is as resilient as it is persistent.

—*David Ulbrich*

See also Ladies Memorial Associations; United Daughters of the Confederacy; Veterans' Organizations.
For further reading:
Cash, W. J. *The Mind of the South* (1941; reprint, 1991).
Foster, Gaines M. *Ghosts of the Confederacy: Defeat, the Lost Cause, and the Emergence of the New South, 1865–1913* (1987).
Pollard, Edward A. *The Lost Cause: A New Southern History of the War of the Confederates* (1866).
Reardon, Carol. *Pickett's Charge in History and Memory* (1997).
Wilson, Charles Reagan. *Baptized in Blood: The Religion of the Lost Cause, 1865–1920* (1980).
Woodward, C. Vann. *Origins of the New South, 1877–1913* (1951).

LOUISIANA

One of the most strategically significant of the Confederate states, Louisiana was the scene of much a great deal of fighting during the Civil War. Union troops—seeking control of the Mississippi

River, Louisiana's fabulous agricultural wealth, and the decisively important commercial center of New Orleans—would begin invading the state in 1862 and would turn it into one of the major battlegrounds of the war. In addition, its patchwork population of Creoles, Acadians, poor whites, foreigners, and Northern capitalists made it a confusing stew of divided loyalties, simmering animosities, and wartime profiteering that put a sinister and embittered edge on the war in Louisiana.

Politically and socially, Louisiana was a divided state. Whig sugar planters, with their opulent estates, dominated the lower parishes of the state, a symbol of outside domination to the poor, French-speaking Cajuns. Traditional Southern democrats controlled the northern parishes and their rich cotton fields. Poor whites roamed the woods and canebrakes, equally suspicious of their rich neighbors and the "foreign" Cajuns.

During the secession crisis of 1861, arguments waxed hot, and the measure passed by a narrow margin. Disappointed Unionists returned home from the convention determined to weather the coming storm however they could. Even though the state had a large slave population, its divided loyalties conspired to create a lukewarm support of the Confederacy. In the election of 1860, Southern Democratic candidate John C. Breckinridge had gathered only 45 percent of the vote. Protective tariffs, long a point of contention in the cotton South, benefited the Louisiana sugar industry. New Orleans, perhaps the most cosmopolitan city in the nation, boasted a largely Northern-born or foreign-born population who did not identify with the politics of secession and slavery.

Even so, rebel planners quickly moved to put Louisiana in a defensive posture. Leaders relied on the masonry Forts Jackson and St. Philip downstream to protect New Orleans from Union naval attack up from the Gulf of Mexico. A flotilla of wooden gunboats would aid in the defense, augmented by several proposed casemate ironclads. With most of his state's strategic worries addressed, Governor Thomas O. Moore authorized the vast majority of Louisiana's 56,000 fighting men to leave the state and serve on distant Confederate battlefields. An almost equal number, however, did not enlist or chose instead to join the more mercurial state militia. In addition, the state provided military leadership to the Confederacy, including Generals P. G. T. Beauregard, Leonidas Polk, Braxton Bragg, and Richard Taylor. Louisiana had its stamp on the political leadership as well, sending men like Judah P. Benjamin and John Slidell to prominent national posts.

In April 1862, with much of the Confederacy's attention focused on Virginia and Tennessee, Union warships surprised the rebel leadership by easily passing the Mississippi River forts, destroying the river flotilla, and putting New Orleans under the guns of the U.S. Navy. The state capital, Baton Rouge, fell soon afterward. Union ground troops under the command of General Benjamin Butler followed, and Louisiana lay open to Union invasion. By early summer, Federal troops patrolled or controlled most of lower Louisiana, including the vastly wealthy LaFourche District. Governor Moore called out the militia to defend their homes, but the men responded sporadically and without enthusiasm. In the face of this hostility from his state forces, the governor turned to semi-irregulars bands of partisan rangers to harass Union shipping on the Mississippi while begging Confederate authorities for reinforcements from other theaters. The bitter skirmishing in the summer of 1862 resulted in swift and decisive responses from the navy. Union sailors put both Baton Rouge and Donaldsonville to the torch as a result of partisan forays.

The Confederacy responded to Louisiana's crisis in a number of ways. East of the Mississippi, an army under General John C. Breckinridge attacked Baton Rouge on 5 August and rattled, but did not dislodge, the Union defenders. The Confederates retreated upstream and began fortifying the bluffs at Port Hudson while Union troops sacked and looted the town, destroying many of its buildings and its monumental live oaks before retreating to New Orleans. The Confederates ordered Major General Richard Taylor, a veteran of Thomas J. "Stonewall" Jackson's corps in the Army of Northern Virginia, to return home and assume command of troops in southwestern Louisiana, west of the Mississippi. He organized recruiting depots, created supply centers, and built forts at key points on Louisiana's river, but his army remained small. His collection of shoddy militia, wild partisans, Texas cowboys, some shot-up survivors of Shiloh, and a few wheezing gunboats were soundly defeated in the last months of 1862 and were driven west of the Atchafalaya Basin.

In 1863, a change in Union command heralded an active year of campaigning in Louisiana. General Nathaniel P. Banks arrived at the head of a 20,000-man army, replacing Butler. This large assembly, composed mostly of nine-month volunteers from New England, was to act in concert with Ulysses S. Grant's campaign against Vicksburg. In April, Banks led his army against Taylor's small command along the banks of Bayou Teche, defeating the rebels at Bisland and Irish Bend and occupying the state as far north as Alexandria in early May and as far west as the Attakapas Prairie. After making arrangements for depots and garrisons west of the Mississippi, Banks led his command against Port Hudson, which he besieged for the next seven weeks.

Confederate general Edmund Kirby Smith, now in command of the newly created Confederate Department of the Trans-Mississippi, sought to aid his compatriots at

Vicksburg and Port Hudson by active campaigning on the west bank. Against Taylor's advice, Texas troops called in from Arkansas led a fruitless campaign against Grant's outposts at Milliken's Bend in late May and early June. In light of this failure, Kirby Smith allowed Taylor to launch his own campaign using his own battered army supplemented by reinforcements from Texas. Wildly successful at first, Taylor's troops not only managed to capture Banks's principal depots, but they overran the LaFourche District, interdicting traffic on the Mississippi and sending scouts to within eyesight of Jackson Square in New Orleans.

All of these efforts were futile. East of the river, Banks's army had a four-to-one advantage over Confederate general Franklin Gardner's forces at Port Hudson, and eventually they wore the Confederates down. The Confederate citadel fell on 9 July, prompting Taylor's Confederates to abandon their gains and withdraw to the vicinity of Lafayette.

In late 1863, Union leaders urged Banks to invade Texas for a variety of political, strategic, and economic reasons even though he opposed such a move. Even so, he massed an army of Port Hudson and Vicksburg veterans and moved up Bayou Teche to Washington and Opelousas while ordering an amphibious assault against the Texas coast. After the defeat of the naval expedition to Sabine Pass, and faced with increasing resistance by Taylor's forces, Banks decided to withdraw his army to New Iberia and beyond, stripping the area bare as it went. Banks eventually sent troops to occupy the Texas coastal islands, but without strategic benefit.

During the fighting of 1863, southern Louisiana suffered destruction equal or surpassing that of any Confederate region during the war, and the passing of the armies had knocked loose any of the social restraints that remained. As a result, the state faced a huge problem of displaced persons, free black contrabands, and guerilla activity. While Confederates battled bushwhackers and bandits west of Washington, Federals combated guerrillas along both banks of the Mississippi. The Confiscation Acts of 1862 had caused many fine plantations to be forfeited, and U.S. troops forced the large, recently emancipated black population to return to their agricultural tasks as wage laborers on the now government-owned farms. The other alternative was conscription into Banks's pet project, the Corps D'Afrique. Likewise, many white Louisianians, thankful to be back under the Stars and Stripes (or generally apathetic to all politics) now found themselves subject to conscription. Some served; others took to the swamps and joined guerrilla bands. The coming months would see an escalation in personal violence in the LaFourche District that would taint the war in Louisiana with an unseemly and bitter nature.

In 1864, Banks yielded to pressure and launched yet another massive invasion of Louisiana, this time by following the Red River to Shreveport and moving into northeast Texas. Aided by a huge flotilla of warships going up the Red River, and coordinated by an invasion column from Little Rock, Arkansas, the campaign was supposed to be a final decisive blow to Confederate prestige and power in Louisiana. Instead, Confederates from Arkansas, Louisiana, and Texas concentrated at Mansfield and ambushed Banks's army on 8 April 1864, rolling back his column. After a furious battle at Pleasant Hill the following day, Banks ordered a retreat to Alexandria, and, in the face of an aggressive Confederate pursuit, eventually all the way to the Mississippi River. By midsummer, Banks and his army were gone from Louisiana, replaced by garrisons of black troops and a smattering of white regiments. Taylor, too, had gone, having requested a transfer east of the Mississippi. The army he had massed against the Federals moved to other fields in Arkansas or Texas, or strengthened their positions along the Red River or Bayou Teche. The lines between Union and Confederate zones of control reverted to where they had been since late 1862, but the widespread devastation revealed that the state was no longer much of a prize.

—*Donald S. Frazier*

See also Moore, Thomas Overton; New Orleans; Port Hudson, Louisianna Campaign; Red River Campaign.

For further reading:

Frazier, Donald S. "Outside Stinking Distance: The Guerilla War in Louisiana." In Sutherland, Daniel (ed.) *Guerrillas, Unionists, and Violence on the Confederate Home Front* (1999).

Parrish, T. Michael. *Richard Taylor: Soldier Prince of Dixie* (1992).

Taylor, Richard. *Destruction and Reconstruction: Personal Experiences of the Late War* (1879; reprint, 1983).

Winters, John D. *The Civil War in Louisiana* (1963).

LOVEJOY, GEORGIA, BATTLE OF
(16 November 1864)

This engagement occurred near the beginning of Major General William Tecumseh Sherman's March to the Sea, which followed the series of battles and maneuvers against Confederate general Joseph E. Johnston from Dalton to Atlanta. As with an earlier engagement fought at Lovejoy's Station in August 1864, Sherman's objectives during the November battle centered on the destruction of the Macon & Western Railroad. This rail line ran south of Atlanta and linked that important stronghold, via the town of Macon, with the vital seaport of Savannah, Georgia.

Even after the fall of Atlanta, on 2 September 1864, the destruction of this supply line had a twofold purpose. First, the Macon & Western Railroad served as one of the most important sources of supply for the Army of Tennessee, then under the command of Lieutenant

General John Bell Hood, after the removal of Joseph E. Johnston. Destruction of this function, even temporarily, would deprive Hood's army of both food and ammunition, commodities increasingly difficult for the Confederate authorities to replace. Second, the destruction of the Macon & Western Railroad would also eliminate any remaining strategic importance of Atlanta for Federal forces under Sherman. With no reason to hold the city after its capitulation, Sherman would be able to concentrate his armies more thoroughly in his southeastward movement toward Savannah. With these goals in mind, Sherman increasingly used his cavalry to strike at the various rail systems throughout Georgia.

On 16 November 1864, the 8th Indiana Cavalry, a veteran regiment in Brigadier General Hugh Judson Kilpatrick's 3d Division of the Military Division of Mississippi, made a dismounted attack against a combined Confederate force of cavalry and artillery under the command of Confederate major general Joseph Wheeler. The Federal troops pushed the Rebels from their defensive position and pursued the retreating Southern force toward Beaver Creek, near the city of Macon. During the rather brief engagement, the Union troops took approximately fifty Confederate soldiers as prisoners of war and captured two Rodman cannon. The brevity of postbattle reports does not reveal how many casualties the Union forces suffered.

In the end, the November battle of Lovejoy proved of little direct importance to the larger strategic objectives of the campaign. Hood marched his forces north into Tennessee to draw General Sherman away from his objectives. Hood's ploy not only failed, it also took his army beyond the operative sphere of the Macon & Western Railroad. Because of the light number of casualties, the brevity of the battle reports, and the general lack of strategic significance, the battle of Lovejoy remains nearly forgotten or overlooked in the history of the campaign. The importance of the battle, however, is that it demonstrates how Sherman's use of cavalry troops evolved during the March to the Sea. Limited by numbers too small to engage the enemy in large battles, the Federal cavalry of this campaign served primarily as a mobile raiding force. Sherman, who believed intuitive aggressiveness to be the most important leadership characteristic needed in his cavalry commanders, assigned the cavalry to strike quickly and frequently at targets of supply and communication. Having used cavalry raids with great success in the campaign against Atlanta, Sherman continued to refine the strategy during the March to the Sea and, later, in the march through the Carolinas. Kilpatrick, whom many contemporaries then considered and historians since have regarded as more reckless than effective, nonetheless won Sherman's confidence as a cavalry commander through an ability to lead in an aggressive and instinctual way. Kilpatrick's

victory against Joseph Wheeler, one of the finest Confederate cavalry leaders in the Western theater, helped sustain Sherman's assessment of Kilpatrick.

Despite its relative obscurity, the battle of Lovejoy did not soon fade from the memory of those who fought there in November of 1864. In later years, veterans mentioned the struggle at Lovejoy in descriptions of events that followed the fall of Atlanta. G. W. Crocker of the 1st Texas Legion, for example, remembered it as the time when Kilpatrick "ran over us." In a reminiscence published in the *Confederate Veteran* magazine in 1908, John H. Ward, a veteran of the 11th Tennessee Infantry, remembered Lovejoy as a place "where we suffered severely."

—Robert Patrick Bender

See also Atlanta Campaign; Sherman's March to the Sea.
For further reading:
Evans, David. *Sherman's Horsemen: Union Cavalry Operations in the Atlanta Campaign* (1996).
Kennett, Lee. *Marching Through Georgia: The Story of Soldiers and Civilians during Sherman's Campaign* (1995).

LOVEJOY, OWEN
(1811–1864)
Abolitionist and congressman

Owen Lovejoy was born on 6 January 1811, in Albion, Maine. His parents were Reverend Daniel and Elizabeth Pattee Lovejoy, and his older brother was Elijah Parish Lovejoy, who later became an abolitionist martyr. The Lovejoys were devout Presbyterians. Owen Lovejoy attended Bowdoin College from 1830 to 1833, when his father died. Lovejoy taught school to pay his tuition, studying law but choosing not to practice. Instead, he committed himself to a career in the clergy like his brother Elijah Lovejoy. Inspired by the abolitionist Theodore Dwight Weld, Owen Lovejoy moved to Alton, Illinois, in 1836 to prepare for the ministry with his brother's guidance. Elijah Lovejoy had settled in Alton to establish an Illinois chapter of the American Anti-Slavery Society and distribute abolitionist propaganda.

Joining the antislavery effort, Owen Lovejoy supported his brother's work, publishing abolitionist materials and speaking publicly. Elijah Lovejoy had published his first newspaper, a religious, antislavery periodical called *The Observer*, in St. Louis, relocating his press across the Mississippi River in Alton in 1836 because of threats in Missouri. The proslavery faction in Illinois resented the Lovejoys' actions and threatened them, destroying their presses several times. Owen Lovejoy encouraged Elijah Lovejoy to publish the *Alton Observer* despite local antagonism. After the arrival of a new press on 7 November 1837, a riot ensued. When the mob murdered Elijah Lovejoy, Owen Lovejoy, standing by his brother's body, vowed to continue his work. The murderers were found not guilty at a trial, and Elijah Lovejoy became an abolitionist martyr, symbolizing the rights of free speech and press. Owen Lovejoy and his brother Joseph Lovejoy prepared a memorial publication dedicated to their slain sibling. John Quincy Adams wrote the introduction for *Memoir of the Rev. Elijah P. Lovejoy; Who Was Murdered in Defence of the Liberty of the Press, at Alton, Illinois, Nov. 7, 1837*, published in 1838.

Completing his theological studies, Owen Lovejoy accepted a position in 1839 as minister of a Congregational church in Princeton, Illinois, where he served for seventeen years. He had sought Anglican ordination, but that church insisted that he promise not to preach about abolitionism. In January 1843, he married Eunice Storrs Dunham, a widow, and the couple had seven children. To honor his brother, Lovejoy intensified his abolitionist efforts and became Illinois's leading antislavery spokesman. From the pulpit, he preached about the evils of slavery. A popular minister and speaker, from 1840 to 1850 Lovejoy traveled around Illinois to lecture about abolition. At that time, an Illinois state law forbade abolition meetings, but Lovejoy ignored the edict. Although he encountered some violent people, he boldly persisted in his efforts and was not injured. Although other preachers were more gifted at dramatic oration, Lovejoy's sincerity and identity as Elijah Lovejoy's brother were responsible for persuading people to accept abolition in Illinois. He also helped fugitive slaves escape to Canada and was acquitted in a trial for protecting runaways.

Lovejoy lost a congressional campaign in 1846 as a representative of the Liberty Party and in 1848 as the Free Soil candidate from his district. He revised his antislavery tactics, moderating his public views to support the Wilmot Proviso's containment but not the elimination of slavery. Elected to the state legislature in 1854, Lovejoy assisted in organizing the fledgling Republican Party in Illinois. The Illinois Republican Party attracted a conglomeration of antiforeign Know-Nothings, German immigrants, Whigs, and abolitionists. Lovejoy believed that his new friend Abraham Lincoln was the only person who could unite and lead these groups within the party, but Lovejoy was unsuccessful in his efforts to urge Lincoln to direct the party in Illinois. Lincoln declined, saying it was not the right time for him. By 1856, Lovejoy was a delegate to the state and national Republican Conventions and won a seat in the U.S. Congress, being reelected three times. In this more influential position, Lovejoy was a powerful, outspoken leader and was chairman of the Committee on Agriculture and a member of the Committee on the District of Columbia.

In Congress, Lovejoy staged verbal attacks on slavery and the South that were compared to the vehemence of Thaddeus Stevens and Charles Sumner. He opposed admitting Kansas as a slave state and annexing Cuba for slavery and supported the Homestead Act. Critical of President James Buchanan's administration, Lovejoy campaigned for Lincoln and loyally supported him when he became president, minimizing his antislavery rhetoric to assist in securing Lincoln's conservative programs during the war. When William Lloyd Garrison politically attacked Lincoln in 1862, Lovejoy rebuked him. He reminded his colleagues to retain the humanitarian aspects of Lincoln's reconstruction plans when Thaddeus Stevens suggested that the South should be considered a conquered territory. Lovejoy pressed Lincoln and Congress to emancipate the slaves and defeat the Confederacy quickly. He sponsored a bill to free slaves that lost by two votes in the House. For a short time, Lovejoy was a colonel in the Western Department of the Army in Missouri under General John C. Frémont and supported the mobilization of African-American soldiers. Lovejoy was selected by his party to introduce a bill calling for the permanent abolition of slavery in the territories. He helped the passage of the Pacific Railroad Bill and was ecstatic when Lincoln signed the Emancipation Proclamation. Before slavery was abolished by the Thirteenth Amendment, Lovejoy died on 25 March 1864, in Brooklyn, New York, and was buried in Oakland Cemetery at Princeton, Illinois.

—Elizabeth D. Schafer

See also Abolitionist Movement; Abolitionists; Emancipation Proclamation.

For further reading:
Dillon, Merton Lynn. *Elijah P. Lovejoy, Abolitionist Editor* (1961).
Haberkorn, Ruth E. "Owen Lovejoy in Princeton, Illinois." *Journal of the Illinois State Historical Society* (1943).
Lovejoy, Joseph C., and Owen Lovejoy. *Memoir of the Rev. Elijah P. Lovejoy; Who Was Murdered in Defence of the Liberty of the Press, at Alton, Illinois, Nov. 7, 1837* (1838).
Magdol, Edward. *Owen Lovejoy: Abolitionist in Congress* (1967).
———. "Owen Lovejoy's Role in the Campaign of 1858." *Journal of the Illinois State Historical Society* (1958).

LOVELL, MANSFIELD
(1822–1884)
Confederate general

Born in Washington, D.C., to Joseph Lovell, surgeon general of the U.S. Army, and Margaret Mansfield Lovell, Mansfield Lovell was educated in local schools before accepting an appointment to the U.S. Military Academy. He graduated ninth of fifty-six in the class of 1842. After being commissioned in the 4th Artillery, he served in a variety of posts before being sent to Texas in 1846. He fought in the Mexican-American War under Zachary Taylor in northern Mexico, where he was wounded at Monterrey, and under Winfield Scott in

Mansfield Lovell (*Library of Congress*)

the Mexico City campaign, where he received a brevet promotion to captain for his actions in the storming of Chapultepec. After the war he served on the frontier and in New York before resigning his commission in 1854. He worked in private industry and as an engineer for the New York City government.

At the outbreak of the Civil War, Lovell went south in September 1861 to accept a Confederate commission as brigadier general and assignment to assist David E. Twiggs in command of Confederate Department Number One, headquartered at New Orleans. He received promotion to major general on 7 October 1861 and was given command of the department. Over the next few months he fought a losing battle to make New Orleans defensible.

Working with a limited force and even more limited equipment and supplies, Lovell had no control of the naval forces near New Orleans. As a result, he ordered the evacuation of his meager force in April 1862 as the city was approach by the naval force of David Farragut.

While fighting in the Western theater for the next year, including by all accounts a highly commendable performance at Corinth in October 1862, Lovell tried to ward off increasing criticism of his handling of the defense of New Orleans. Finally exonerated in a board of inquiry in November 1863, Lovell was considered politically too risky to give another field command. His only other position for the remainder of the war was a brief stint in 1864 as a member of Joseph Johnston's staff.

After the war Lovell lived to New York City, where he worked as an engineer. He returned south briefly to try farming but returned to New York, where he died.

—*David S. Heidler and Jeanne T. Heidler*

See also Corinth; New Orleans.

For further reading:

Hearn, Chester G. *The Capture of New Orleans, 1862* (1995).
Smith, Brier R. *Major General Mansfield Lovell and the Fall of New Orleans: The Downfall of a Career* (1973).

LOWE, THADDEUS SOBIESKI CONSTANTINE
(1832–1913)
Chief of army aeronautics

Thaddeus Sobieski Constantine Lowe served as the Union army's chief of army aeronautics from 1 October 1861 until his resignation on 8 May 1863. During this period, Lowe maintained a civilian status and was responsible for designing, manufacturing, and deploying gas-filled balloons and portable gas generators for the purpose of gathering intelligence. In his capacity as chief of army aeronautics, Lowe supervised several aeronauts using balloons and gas generators of his design.

Lowe was born at Jefferson Mills, New Hampshire, on 20 August 1832. His parents, Clovis and Alpha Green Lowe were established members of the community and Clovis had served in the New Hampshire legislature. Lowe had an early interest in aeronautics, sending the family cat aloft in kites. Commonly know as "Professor" during the Civil War, Lowe was basically a self-educated man having completed only grammar school. He had served as a magician's assistant and, developing a sense of showmanship and a keen interest in the sciences, he embarked on an intense period of reading everything he could on chemistry and aeronautics.

Lowe decided to become an aeronaut and built his first balloon in 1858. Within a year, he had earned a considerable reputation as an aeronaut and became interested in crossing the Atlantic in one of his creations. In 1859, Lowe built a huge balloon, the *City of New York*, for the expressed purpose of conducting a transatlantic flight. Crossing the Atlantic had become a popular goal and Lowe had several competitors, including John Wise and John La Mountain. After several unsuccessful trials, Lowe changed the name of this balloon to the *Great Western* and solicited support and financial aid from prominent citizens. Faced with additional disappointments, Lowe became convinced that the *Great Western* was not capable of the flight and, with the support of a citizens' committee from Philadelphia and with the advice of the secretary of the Smithsonian Institution, Professor Joseph Henry, Lowe proceeded to Cincinnati, Ohio, with a new balloon named *Enterprise* for inland trials. On 19 April 1861, championed by Murat Halstead, editor of the *Cincinnati Commercial*, Lowe ascended for a trial from Cincinnati to the east coast. Due to unexpected southerly air currents, he ended up near Unionville, South Carolina, setting a distance record of more than 900 miles in nine hours. After being jailed twice by Carolinians who thought he was a Yankee spy, Lowe luckily received aid from some local academic admirers and made his way by train back to Ohio.

With the outbreak of the war, Lowe, like his competitors Wise and La Mountain, was determined to offer his services to the government and use aeronautics to gather intelligence by observation. With the encouragement of Professor Henry from the Smithsonian, Lowe traveled to Washington, where he conducted a trial in his balloon *Enterprise*. On 18 June 1861, Lowe lifted off from the Columbian Armory in Washington. The balloon was inflated with "street gas" from one of the gas mains on the armory grounds and Lowe made several ascensions from the armory, the Smithsonian grounds, and the south lawn of the White House. Lowe was equipped with telegraphic equipment and an operator provided by the American Telegraph Company and he telegraphed to President Lincoln: "I have pleasure in sending you this first dispatch ever telegraphed from an aerial station...."

The responsibility for aeronautics was given to the Topographical Engineers, and Captain A. W. Whipple was assigned to make decisions as to which aeronauts would be used to support the army. Whipple sent Lowe to Arlington, Virginia, to make aerial observations but, when it came time to order a balloon for the army, Whipple chose to use the services of John Wise, who had promised to deliver a balloon for $200 less than the one proposed by Lowe. Distressed by this turn of events, Lowe continued to prepare his balloon for service at his own expense, but when he attempted to fill his balloon with gas to support the upcoming battle of Bull Run, he was directed to remove it from the gas main so that Wise's balloon might be filled. Wise's balloon was destroyed as it was being transported to the battlefield and Whipple directed Lowe to move his balloon to the area of operations, where he made significant observations of troop movements after the battle.

Lowe eventually prevailed over Wise as well as La Mountain, who was performing as a freelance balloonist for Major General Benjamin Butler at Fort Monroe. Lowe was ordered to deliver several balloons for the army. He produced two large balloons, the *Union* and

the *Intrepid*, and two smaller ones, the *Constitution* and the *Washington*. Ordered to Fort Monroe to support the Army of the Potomac, Lowe and his aeronauts performed admirably during the Peninsula campaign. Lowe made many flights in his balloons, telegraphing the positions of the Confederates. He discovered the evacuation of Yorktown and made significant observations during the battle of Fair Oaks discerning the main attacks from feints. Lowe contracted malaria on the peninsula and his Balloon Corps lost the momentum and favor it had acquired during the early part of the campaign. Lowe never enjoyed the support of the army commanders who followed Major General George McClellan. After squabbling with his new supervisor, Captain C. E. Comstock of the Corps of Engineers, over a reduction in his pay and the dismissal of his father from the corps, Lowe resigned on 8 May 1863. The Balloon Corps was disbanded shortly after Lowe's resignation.

Lowe became successful in business and as an inventor after his wartime service. He was responsible for developing designs for refrigerated shipping, and his numerous patents included one for carbureted water gas. Moving to California in 1887, Lowe took on endeavors in astronomy and airship design. He died on 13 January 1913.

—*Bill Cameron*

See also Ballons.
For further reading:
Evans, Charles M. "Air War over Virginia." *Civil War Times* (1996).
Haydon, F. Stansbury. *Aeronautics in the Union and Confederate Armies with a Survey of Military Aeronautics Prior to 1861* (1941).
Lowe, T.S.C. "The Balloons with the Army of the Potomac." In *The Photographic History of the Civil War* (1987).
Raines, Rebecca Robbins. *Getting the Message Through, A Branch History of the U.S. Army Signal Corps* (1996).

LOWELL, CHARLES RUSSELL
(1835–1864)
Union general

Born in Boston into the prominent Lowell family, Charles Russell Lowell attended Harvard, where he graduated first in his class in 1854. After graduation Lowell traveled to Europe and then moved to Maryland to accept a position running an iron foundry. At the outbreak of the Civil War, he obtained a regular commission as a captain in the 3d Cavalry.

Lowell served in the Army of the Potomac and gained the attention of its commander, George B. McClellan, during the Peninsula campaign. McClellan made Lowell one of his aides, a position that Lowell held until McClellan was removed from command in November 1862.

During the Maryland campaign in September 1862, Lowell's expert equitation proved very useful in carrying messages between the different parts of McClellan's army. Even when under heavy Confederate fire during the battle of Antietam, Lowell always managed to reach his destination. En route he was observed admonishing and reorganizing retreating Union troops, actions that gained him tremendous praise. Before his removal from command, McClellan recommended that Lowell be given command of a cavalry regiment.

Upon McClellan's dismissal, Lowell returned home to raise a regiment. In May 1863 he became the colonel and commander of the 2d Massachusetts Cavalry. Lowell and the 2d were assigned to the Department of Washington, D.C., and were primarily charged with patrolling the city's outer defenses and surrounding territory.

For the next year, Lowell and his brigade were almost in constant motion around the city, particularly in northern Virginia. His biggest challenge by the fall of 1863 and through the coming winter was monitoring the movements of Confederate raiders, most notably, John Singleton Mosby. Lowell had little success in tracking down Mosby or his main force, but did manage to capture some of Mosby's men in the spring of 1864.

In July 1864 Lowell was summoned with his brigade from his primary headquarters at Vienna, Virginia, to Washington to aid in the defense of the city against Jubal Early. During the few days during the second week of the month when Washington was seriously threatened, Lowell and his men moved around, plugging vulnerable holes in the defenses. Lowell spent much of his time at Tennallytown during the defense. At the end of the month, Lowell and his men were slated to move into the Shenandoah Valley to operate against Early.

In Philip Sheridan's campaign against Early, Lowell commanded the reserve brigade of the 1st Division of Sheridan's Cavalry Corps. During the campaign, Lowell early distinguished himself for bravery in battle, having several horses shot out from under him. He was commended for his actions at the battle of Winchester on 19 September. A month later at the battle of Cedar Creek on 19 October, Lowell demonstrated tremendous bravery. When seriously wounded, he refused to leave the field and instead led his men in an attack on the Confederates. In that attack he was mortally wounded. Carried from the field, he died the next day. His body was returned to Massachusetts for burial. General Sheridan, knowing that Lowell had been mentioned for promotion to brigadier general, arranged for a commission to be signed dating from 19 October 1864.

—*David S. Heidler and Jeanne T. Heidler*

See also Cedar Creek; Washington, D.C.

For further reading:
Emerson, Edward W. *Life and Letters of Charles Russell Lowell—Captain, Sixth United States Cavalry; Colonel, Second Massachusetts Cavalry; Brigadier-General, United States Volunteers* (1907).

LOWELL, JAMES RUSSELL
(1819–1891)
Poet, editor, critic, professor, and diplomat

As coeditor of the *North American Review* and author of *The Biglow Papers, Second Series*, James Russell Lowell was a prominent literary supporter of Abraham Lincoln's administration. Lowell's "Ode Recited at the Harvard Commemoration" (1865) was once regarded as the greatest interpretation of the Civil War in verse.

Lowell graduated from Harvard in 1838 and studied law, but he adopted journalism as a career, contributing to *The Dial* and *Graham's* and editing *The Pioneer*. Lowell was a zealous, sophisticated, pro-Union abolitionist, and his satire, *The Biglow Papers, First Series* (1848), brought him to national prominence. It was one of the earliest and most notable renderings of Yankee dialect in verse. It was also a critique of both Southern expansionism via the Mexican-American War and liberal racism among Northern abolitionists who regarded Africans as an inferior race.

Lowell was the editor of the *Atlantic Monthly* and the Smith professor of modern languages at Harvard College when the Civil War broke out. He supported Lincoln's election with enthusiasm, encouraging the Republican Party to cling to its idealism at all costs. In an influential *Atlantic* essay, "The Election in November," Lowell argued that slavery had corrupted American democracy, North and South, and that the election of 1860 would be a national referendum on the future of the institution.

In another *Atlantic* article, "E Pluribus Unum," Lowell argued against separation of the North and South because they were essentially the same culture by language, law, and religion. President James Buchanan's weakness, he argued, had failed to sustain the indivisibility of the Union, giving comfort to potential Rebels and weakening the firmness of pro-Union Southerners. Lowell misjudged the extent of Southern resentment, arguing that only a minority of Southerners supported secession, whereas the majority would support the Federal government if it asserted its authority.

During the confrontation over Fort Sumter, Lowell advocated sustaining the fort even at the risk of violence. When the actual war began, Lowell welcomed it with a sense of relief, assuming, like most, that it would be a brief conflict that would hasten abolition. He believed correctly that the industrial economy of the North could continue the war, if need be, until the South was exhausted.

Late in 1861 Lowell began *The Biglow Papers, Second Series*, which were serialized in the *Atlantic* (1862–1863, 1865–1866). While Lowell's satire struck the wrong note in a climate of moral earnestness, his second installment, "Mason and Slidell: A Yankee Idyll," was most effective in its attack on England for its support of the Confederacy. One of the subsequent installments, "Sunthin' in the Pastoral Line," reflected Lowell's lingering uncertainty about the war in a dialogue between Nature and the Puritan, one representing rejuvenation, the other representing stern moral duty.

Lowell joined Charles Eliot Norton as coeditor of the *North American Review* in 1863. In the first issue, January 1864, Lowell contributed "The President's Policy," in which he praised Lincoln's gradual approach to emancipation as a means of securing popular support. This was in contrast to Lowell's uncompromising absolutism in 1860. With this essay, Lowell was among the first influential critics to proclaim Lincoln's greatness as a leader for his personal character. The article was widely praised and attracted the attention of Lincoln, who wrote a letter to the editors of the *Review* thanking them for the article.

Though Lowell did not serve in the military, he was affected by the deaths of friends and relatives who did. Three of Lowell's nephews were killed. And Robert Gould Shaw, who died in the assault on Battery Wagner, was the son of close friends. As the war progressed, Lowell grew increasingly conservative about the expenditure of human lives and poured out his private grief in verse.

Lincoln's death inspired Lowell to write "The Ode Recited at the Harvard Commemoration," which was delivered on 21 July 1865, in memory of Harvard's many graduates who had died for the Union. Though many contemporaries praised the "Commemoration Ode," Lowell was very unhappy with it. Though it is technically flawed, the poem is a deeply felt evocation of the mood of the time. Lowell's description of Lincoln, for example, is particularly memorable: "dreading praise, not blame, new birth of our new soil, the first American." The poem was soon the most famous inspired by the Civil War with the possible exception of Walt Whitman's "O Captain! My Captain!"

Lowell's career as a poet dwindled after 1865, but his proadministration prominence during the war and staunch Republicanism afterward eventually led to a diplomatic post. He served as ambassador to Spain from 1877 to 1880 and Great Britain from 1880 to 1885. He died at his home in Cambridge, Massachusetts, securely ranked as of the major literary figures of his time.

—*William A. Pannapacker*

See also Abolitionist Movement; Emerson, Ralph Waldo; Thoreau, Henry David; Whitman, Walt; Whittier, John Greenleaf.

For further reading:
Aaron, Daniel. *The Unwritten War: American Writers and the Civil War* (1973).
Duberman, Martin. *James Russell Lowell* (1966).
Lowell, James Russell. *Letters of James Russell Lowell* (1894).
———. *The Writings of James Russell Lowell* (1890).
Wilson, Edmund. *Patriotic Gore: Studies in the Literature of the American Civil War* (1962).

LOYALTY OATHS

Although the use of loyalty oaths in America dates back to the anti-Tory laws of the Revolution, "test oaths" proliferated during the Civil War. Faced with the nearly impossible task of distinguishing friend from foe in a population with a common culture and language, states such as Missouri, Tennessee, Maryland, and Louisiana passed rigorous loyalty oath statutes that required individuals to swear their loyalty to the Union before they could participate in public or professional life. The U.S. Congress also passed a similar law. In August 1861, Congress required that all federal officeholders and military officials pledge their intent to remain loyal to the Union. A year later, Congress switched to a tougher "iron-clad" oath that required declarations of both past and future loyalty. The "iron-clad" oath not only disqualified ex-Confederates, it also penalized Northerners and border-state residents who gave "countenance, counsel, or encouragement" to the Confederacy. Throughout the war, anyone wishing to hold federal office or even transact business with the federal government had to take this pledge. The Union military also administered oaths throughout the South during the war in an attempt to find a critical mass of loyal whites with which to assemble Reconstruction governments.

In some locales, the loyalty oaths proved remarkably effective. In Missouri—a state plagued throughout the war by internecine fighting—"test-oaths" became an indispensable wartime policy of the loyal state government. In the crucial 1864 election, for example, loyalty oaths kept many Southern sympathizers from the polls and allowed Lincoln to receive 70 percent of the vote. At the end of the war, Missouri toughened its test-oath requirements by expanding the definition of disloyalty to include anyone who had ever indicated any "disaffection to the Government of the United States in its contest with rebellion." Eventually, both the federal and state loyalty oaths faced legal challenges—challenges that led to two landmark rulings by the U.S. Supreme Court.

In the 1867 decisions *Ex parte Garland* and *Cummings v. Missouri*, the Supreme Court declared that both the federal "ironclad" oath and the Missouri test oath were unconstitutional. The *Cummings* case resulted from the wartime indictment and conviction of a Roman Catholic priest from St. Louis, John Cummings, for preaching without first taking Missouri's loyalty oath. Although the links between urban Roman Catholics and Copperhead Democrats often made priests in the North objects of suspicion, the state had no direct evidence of Cummings's alleged disloyalty. Cummings, however, did continue to preach after refusing to swear an oath and for that he was arrested, tried, and convicted. *Ex parte Garland* involved an ex-Confederate general, Augustus H. Garland, who was prevented from arguing before the

U.S. Supreme Court by the federal "iron-clad" oath. President Johnson had pardoned Garland in the summer of 1865 and Garland hoped to reclaim the position he had held before the war as a member of the federal bar. In the end, the Supreme Court sided with both Cummings and Garland. The oaths, the Court ruled, amounted to ex post facto laws and bills of attainder that unjustly denied individuals their right to practice their professions. These Supreme Court decisions emasculated the loyalty oath statutes and helped undermine Republicans' postwar efforts to prevent ex-Confederates from restoring their political and professional hegemony in the South.

—*Michael A. Ross*

See also Civil Liberties, U.S.A.; Supreme Court, U.S.
For further reading:
Cummings v. the State of Missouri, 71 U.S. 277 (1866).
Ex parte Garland, 71 U.S. 333 (1866).
Hyman, Harold M. *To Try Men's Souls: Loyalty Oaths in American History* (1959).
Hyman, Harold M., and William Wiecek. *Equal Justice under Law: Constitutional Development, 1835–1875* (1982).

LUBBOCK, FRANCIS RICHARD
(1815–1905)

Governor of Texas; Confederate officer

Born to Henry T. W. Lubbock and Susan Ann Saltus Lubbock in Beaufort, South Carolina, Francis Lubbock left school at fourteen upon his father's death to accept a position as a clerk in Charleston. Five years later he moved to New Orleans, where he operated a drugstore for two years before moving to the new Republic of Texas. In Texas Lubbock briefly reentered the mercantile business before accepting a position as the clerk for the Texas legislature and then as comptroller for the nation. In the meantime, he had acquired a ranch outside Houston where he spent most of his time.

When Texas became a state, Lubbock remained active in government, serving as county clerk and as lieutenant governor from 1857 to 1859. A strong Democrat, he served as one of the state delegates to the Democratic National Convention in Charleston in 1860. Upon the election of Abraham Lincoln, Lubbock strongly supported the secession of Texas and the following summer was elected governor.

Like other Confederate governors, Lubbock's primary concern was the defense of his state. Unlike other governors, however, he also had the added threat of a large Indian frontier that even before the war had been unstable at best. Along with the usual complaints about pulling men out of the state for service in other parts of the Confederacy, Lubbock also worried about the lack of military supplies in the state. To alleviate this problem, he convened a military board to advise him on the best

way to mount state defenses. Lubbock and the board encouraged the local manufacture of arms and ran a foundry and percussion cap factory.

Lubbock worked closely with Confederate officers to protect the Texas coastline and the Indian frontier and to ferret out disloyal people that might aid in a Union invasion. Lubbock found Major General John Bankhead Magruder congenial, and their relationship possibly influenced Lubbock to offer his services to Magruder after leaving the governorship. Lubbock, with the rank of lieutenant colonel, thus acted as Magruder's aide and assistant adjutant general at the end of 1863. In the spring of 1864, during the Red River campaign, Lubbock served as an aide to Major General John A. Wharton.

In September 1864, Jefferson Davis summoned Lubbock to Richmond to join the president's staff at the rank of colonel. In that capacity, Lubbock acted as a liaison between Davis and high ranking officers on the Petersburg front. When Davis fled Richmond in early April 1865, Lubbock traveled with him and was captured with the president in Georgia. After his capture, Lubbock was imprisoned in Fort Delaware until President Andrew Johnson authorized his release in November 1865.

Lubbock returned to Texas to find his fortunes ruined. For the next few decades he engaged in a variety of business ventures and served in several political posts, including state treasurer. In his later years he wrote his memoirs, published in 1900. He died in Austin, Texas, on 22 June 1905.

—*David S. Heidler and Jeanne T. Heidler*

See also Texas.
For further reading:
Lubbock, Percy, ed. *Six Decades in Texas: The Memoirs of Francis R. Lubbock* (1968).

LYNCH, PATRICK NEISON
(1817–1882)

Catholic bishop of Charleston; commissioner of the Confederate States to the States of the Church

Patrick Neison Lynch was born in 1817 in Clones, County Monaghan, Ireland. In 1819 his family emigrated to America, settling in Cheraw, South Carolina, where Patrick grew up. The Lynches were a prominent Catholic slaveholding family. Patrick studied for the priesthood at seminaries in Charleston and Rome. In 1840 he was ordained in Rome and received a doctorate of divinity. He served the church in Charleston in various posts under Bishops John England and Ignatius A. Reynolds. In 1858, he was consecrated bishop of the Diocese of Charleston, then comprising the states of North and South Carolina.

When war came, Lynch supported the Confederacy. In 1861 he defended the South in a public exchange of letters with Archbishop John Hughes of New York. When Fort Sumter fell to the Confederates, Lynch ordered a "Te Deum" sung in his cathedral. The bishop, his clergy, and religious—especially the Sisters of Our Lady of Mercy—helped impoverished families, tended sick and wounded servicemen, and cared for Northern prisoners of war, irrespective of race or creed. In December 1861 a terrible fire consumed Lynch's cathedral and residence, Catholic institutions, and much of Charleston. Further losses to the diocese resulted from the bombardment of Charleston (1863–1865) and Sherman's invasion of the Carolinas (1865).

After an exchange of letters between President Jefferson Davis and Pope Pius IX in 1863, expressing a mutual desire for a peaceful settlement to the conflict, the Confederate government decided to send a diplomatic envoy to the Holy See and who would reside in Rome. In 1864 Davis appointed Lynch Confederate commissioner to the States of the Church. Secretary of State Judah P. Benjamin instructed Lynch to seek diplomatic recognition, if possible, and to try to influence European public opinion in the South's favor.

In April 1864 the bishop ran the blockade and sailed for Europe. He stopped in Ireland, where he urged Catholic bishops to dissuade Irishmen from emigrating to enlist in the Union army, and then went on to England, France, and Italy, taking along as his chaplain, Father John Bannon, Confederate agent in Ireland. They reached Rome in June 1864.

The Vatican refused to accord diplomatic recognition because Pius IX was unwilling to support the institution of slavery, even indirectly. To sway European opinion, Lynch wrote a lengthy pamphlet on slavery. He condemned the trans-Atlantic slave trade, but defended "domestic slavery" as legitimate and benign. He did not employ scriptural or theological arguments, instead presenting his views as those of an observer. The pamphlet was published in Italian, German, and French, but not in English. Lynch was himself the owner of about ninety-five slaves, purchased mainly to protect black Catholic families. It is uncertain whether they were personal or diocesan property. The pamphlet appeared too late to affect the war's outcome.

After Appomattox, the bishop obtained a pardon from President Andrew Johnson and returned to Charleston in December 1865. War had devastated his diocese, and he was to spend the remainder of his life raising funds to rebuild. Lynch died in Charleston in 1882.

—*David C. R. Heisser*

See also Catholics; South Carolina.

For further reading:

Alvarez, David J. "The Papacy in the Diplomacy of the American Civil War." *Catholic Historical Review* (1993).

Heisser, David C. R. "Bishop Lynch's Civil War Pamphlet on Slavery." *Catholic Historical Review* (1998).

Madden, Richard C. *Catholics in South Carolina: A Record* (1985).

LYNCHBURG CAMPAIGN
(June 1864)

In 1864 Lynchburg, Virginia, was a major transportation center. The Virginia & Tennessee, the Southside, and the Orange & Alexandria railroads all went through the city. In addition, the James River & Kanawha Canal served as a major east-west supply artery. Union lieutenant general Ulysses S. Grant recognized that disrupting the flow of materiel through this area would seriously hamper Confederate general Robert E. Lee's ability to defend Richmond and Petersburg.

On 25 May 1864, Grant sent instructions to Major General David Hunter to move south of the Shenandoah Valley and interrupt Confederate communications by destroying the railroads and the canal at Lynchburg. Grant directed Hunter to Lynchburg and Charlottesville, where he would be moving beyond his supply lines. Hunter's army was to live off the land.

After a small action at Piedmont, Virginia, on 5 June, Hunter moved to Staunton, Virginia. There he consolidated several commands into the newly formed Army of West Virginia. His new command totaled upward of 25,000 troops spread as far north as Harper's Ferry.

Although Grant's directive was to move toward Charlottesville, Hunter interpreted these orders as discretionary. He elected to march on Lynchburg by staying on the west side of the Blue Ridge Mountains, crossing his army over them at the Peaks of Otter just east of Buchanan. He then marched to Liberty (now Bedford) to attack Lynchburg from the south. Between Staunton and Buchanan, Hunter interrupted his march from 11 to 14 June to pause at Lexington. This delay gave Lee time to assess the situation and order Major General Jubal Early's corps from its position near Gaines' Mill to defend Lynchburg.

Early had about 16,000 men. His II Corps totaled 8,000, and he had an amalgamation of infantry and cavalry from various small commands. He reached Charlottesville on 16 June when Hunter was at Liberty, only twenty-five miles south of Lynchburg. Union brigadier general Alfred Duffié's cavalry had cut the railroad between Charlottesville and Lynchburg, but the Confederates had quickly repaired it. Travel was still slow, however, and Early could move only half his troops to Lynchburg on the 17th. The rest followed on the 18th, arriving too late in the afternoon to participate in the engagement that day.

The action opened on the afternoon of 17 June, with the Union army moving troops north from Liberty toward Lynchburg on the Salem road. The combined forces of Confederate brigadier generals John Imboden and John McCausland delayed them by making a stand at the Old Quaker Church about four miles from town. Hunter brought up Brigadier General George Crook's infantry and Captain Henry Du Pont's artillery, and the action intensified. This forced Imboden back toward hastily prepared but strong entrenchments on the outskirts of Lynchburg. At this time, units of Major General Stephen Ramseur's division arrived to support Imboden at the redoubt on the Salem Road.

Meanwhile, to the west on the Forest Road, Duffié's cavalry was advancing. About 3:00 P.M., Early detached McCausland from the Salem Road engagement to intercept Duffié. That night Duffié halted about five miles from Lynchburg.

Though Hunter was confident of success, he was also uncertain about the strength of Early's forces. During the night, Early had one Southside Railroad engine continuously pull a few cars in and out of town while crowds cheered and a band played. The ruse helped to confuse an already concerned Hunter.

The next morning, 18 June, Hunter began probing the Confederate lines looking for a weakness. Duffié was on the left flank along the Forest Road, and Brigadier General Jeremiah Sullivan was on the Salem Road, supported by Brigadier General William Averell, demonstrating against Early's center. Meanwhile, Crook moved three to four miles eastward, extending the Union right to test the Confederate left flank. Finding it impracticable to turn the Confederate flank, Crook returned to the east side of the Salem Road around noon. In his absence, a lively artillery duel had erupted with the Confederates showing unusually good marksmanship against Du Pont's experienced artillerists. Sullivan's demonstration grew in intensity, and he had drawn back to avoid a general engagement. On his return, Crook found Sullivan under a counterattack with the Confederates beginning to drive him. Another lively artillery duel broke out, and Crook deployed his infantry to stop the Confederate advance.

Over on the Forest Road, Duffié was encountering such strong resistance that he overestimated enemy strength. He did, however, keep up a long-range fight until he exhausted his ammunition.

By midafternoon the battle for Lynchburg was essentially over. Far from his supply base and fearful about his severe shortage of ammunition, Hunter erroneously believed that Early had superior numbers, so he withdrew under cover of darkness, retreating toward Liberty and then farther southwest to Salem. Early pursued him to the vicinity of Salem. Hunter then continued through West Virginia, eventually returning to the northern Shenandoah Valley. The Union withdrawal left the valley open to Early, and he promptly moved on Washington to commence one of the most famous raids of the war.

Although Hunter's actions did serve to weaken Lee's defenses around Richmond, his circuitous retreat gave control of the valley back to the Confederates. Hunter's unnecessarily long delay at Lexington and Early's aggressive tactics combined to make the battle of Lynchburg a Confederate victory.

—*Richard C. Halseth*

See also Early's Washington Raid.

For further reading:

Blackford, Charles M. *Campaign and Battle of Lynchburg, Virginia* (1994).

Morris, George S. *Lynchburg in the Civil War* (1984).

Pond, George E. *The Shenandoah Valley in 1864* (1883).

LYON, NATHANIEL
(1818–1861)
Union general

Although Nathaniel Lyon served only a few months during the Civil War, he proved instrumental in preserving Missouri for the Union. Born on 14 July 1818 to Amasa and Kezia Knowlton Lyon in Ashford, Connecticut, Lyon graduated from West Point in 1841. He served fighting the Seminoles in Florida and he fought in the Mexican-American War. Promoted to first lieutenant in 1847, he commanded Company D, 2d Infantry, through the battles of Contreras and Churubusco in Mexico and received a brevet to captain. At Mexico City he received a slight wound. Lyon was promoted to captain in 1851, and his pre–Civil War career for the rest of the decade consisted mostly of garrison duty in California and Kansas.

Lyon's fiery temper surfaced occasionally in his early career. He faced a court-martial on more than one occasion, once for overzealously punishing a soldier. He served with a fanaticism and unwillingness to bend his own personal sense of righteousness, even when it conflicted with his duty. During the seven years he served in Kansas, he developed a disdain of slave society and eagerly joined the Republican Party. By 1860, he was violating his orders in order to support the free-state cause in Kansas. In January 1861 writing about the secession crisis, he proclaimed "It is no longer useful to appeal to reason, but to the sword." That month, Lyon was ordered to reinforce the U.S. arsenal in St. Louis, Missouri.

When Captain Lyon arrived in St. Louis with Company D on 6 February 1861, he found the situation in Missouri critical. Governor Claiborne Jackson and a portion of the state government wanted to take Missouri out of the Union, and they hoped to capture the St. Louis arsenal when Missouri seceded. Lyon found the arsenal defenses inadequate to face this threat. When he attempted to strengthen them, however, he came into conflict with his superiors, including General William Harney who commanded the Department of the West. With the aid of Francis Blair, Jr., a leading St. Louis Republican and unconditional Unionist, Lyon gained immediate command of the arsenal and quickly improved its defenses. On the night of 26 April, he secretly removed most of the arsenal's ordinance to Illinois to secure it from secessionist hands. When Governor Jackson refused to provide Missouri troops for Lincoln's call of 75,000 volunteers, Lyon received the authority to enroll a number of local home guard units that he and Blair had secretly organized to face the secessionist threat.

By May 1861, Lyon had effectively neutralized secessionist chances of capturing the arsenal; however, tensions continued to rise. When Jackson called out the state militia for its annual training, one section encamped at Camp Jackson, just outside of St. Louis. Worried that the militia's pro-Southern elements would attack the arsenal, Lyon arrested them on 10 May. The militia capitulated without a struggle, but, as they were marched toward the arsenal, a riot broke out among the civilians watching the procession and twenty-eight persons were killed. This catastrophe along with Lyon's use of Federal troops to patrol state property enraged many pro-Southern citizens.

On 11 June 1861, Lyon and Blair met Jackson and Sterling Price to settle tensions between the factions. By then Lyon had been commissioned brigadier general of Missouri volunteers and brigadier general of U.S. volunteers, and on 31 May, he had succeeded William Harney in command of the Department of the West. Lyon refused to compromise with Jackson, would not accept limits on his use of Federal troops, and refused to disband the home guards he had enrolled. Lyon ended the meeting by declaring, "This means war!"

Lyon quickly set out after Jackson, who had returned to the capital. On 13 June, Lyon occupied Jefferson City. On 17 June, his army routed Jackson's Missouri State Guard at Boonville. Lyon continued to follow Jackson's retreating forces southward. In July, John C. Frémont succeeded Lyon, who was still in the field, as commander of the newly reorganized Western Department. Lyon's force became the Army of Southwest Missouri. On 10 August 1861, he attacked the Confederate forces at Wilson's Creek. Although, outnumbered two to one, his army fought well until Lyon was killed leading a charge, and the Union army was forced to retreat. Many accused Frémont of failing to reinforce Lyon before the battle. Although defeated at Wilson's Creek, Lyon's quick action had pushed the pro-Southern forces from the state, allowing Union forces to secure the state. On 24 December 1861, Lyon received the Thanks of Congress for his role in saving Missouri for the Union.

—James G. Downhour

See also Boonville Missouri, Battle of; Camp Jackson; Missouri; Wilson's Creek, Missouri.

For further reading:
Peckham, James. General Nathaniel Lyon and Missouri in 1861 (1866).

Phillips, Christopher. Damned Yankee: The Life of General Nathaniel Lyon (1990).
Price, Richard Scott. Nathaniel Lyon: Harbinger from Kansas (1990).

LYONS, RICHARD BICKERTON PEMELL, SECOND BARON AND FIRST EARL LYONS
(1817–1887)
British minister to the United States

As Britain's minister to the United States for most of the American Civil War, Lord Lyons found himself confronted by many vexing diplomatic questions that threatened to disrupt Anglo-American relations. Although his understanding of U.S. affairs proved superficial, his cautious diplomacy did much to ease tension between Great Britain and the United States, preventing the outbreak of a war that would surely have redounded to the Confederacy's advantage.

Born in Hampshire, England, on 26 April 1817, Lyons was the eldest son of Captain Edmund Lyons, a prominent naval officer who later became an admiral, and Augusta Louisa Lyons, the daughter of a naval officer. Originally destined for a career in the Royal Navy, Lyons proved incapable of overcoming his susceptibility to seasickness. He went to the famous public school at Winchester instead and thence to Oxford. A studious young man, he took a degree in 1838.

In the next year, Lyons entered the foreign service as an unpaid attaché at the Athens legation, where his father served as minister. Over the next two decades, Lyons gradually rose through the diplomatic ranks while laboring in a variety of European capitals—Dresden, Rome, and Florence. By 1858, Lyons had become Britain's minister to the Grand Duchy of Tuscany. In the same year, he accepted an offer from the Foreign Office to become minister to the United States.

Presenting his credentials to President James Buchanan in April 1859, Lyons tried his hand at the difficult task of maintaining good Anglo-American relations. He got off to a rocky start, inheriting disputes from his predecessor concerning San Juan Island (Puget Sound), the Bay Islands (off the coast of Honduras), and the Mosquito Coast. It would be the American Civil War, however, that provided him with his most thorny diplomatic problems.

Lyons's calm and measured diplomacy helped prevent Anglo-American disputes from escalating. Generally, he advised the British government to give as little offense as possible to the United States. During the Trent Affair in late 1861, Lyons's discretion, good sense, and moderation made it easier for the United States to meet Great Britain's demands, thus minimizing the risk of war between the two. When the British cabinet considered intervening in the conflict in the fall of 1862, Lyons, who was on vacation in England at the time, threw his weight behind those who opposed the move. Even without momentous diplomatic issues of this sort, Lyons had many other problems with which to deal. Because most of the vessels that sought to run the Federal blockade of the Confederacy were British, he found himself involved in interminable negotiations with Secretary of State William Seward regarding the legality and operation of the blockade. Lyons also devoted a great deal of his time to preventing the illegal conscription of British subjects in the Union army. Always tactful, he contributed to the swift resolution of most diplomatic differences (except for the *Alabama* claims) between the United States and Great Britain throughout the Civil War.

At the same time, however, Lyons's dispatches did much to reinforce the British government's exceedingly dim view of the North. Although he found slavery loathsome and opposed British intervention in the conflict, Lyons did not sympathize to any great extent with the United States. Believing that demagogues and incompetents led the North, he constantly feared that an unstable and unpredictable federal government would pick a war with Britain to pander to the U.S. democracy. For this reason, he constantly feared for British North America's safety. Unsuited to gathering intelligence and inexperienced in U.S. affairs, Lyons did not prove a particularly perceptive observer of the war, peppering his dispatches with traditional British prejudices regarding Americans and democratic institutions.

A combination of stress with overwork led Lyons to suffer from prostrating headaches. These became so intolerable by the summer of 1864 that Lyons handed the day-to-day oversight of the legation to Hume Burnley, the charge d'affaires. After asking the Foreign Office to recall him for health reasons, he finally received the order to go home in November 1864. Unfortunately, Lyons did not recover his health in England, and in February 1865 he finally resigned as Britain's minister to the United States.

Lyons's health improved enough, however, for him to become head of the British legation at Constantinople in August 1865. Only two years later, he received a most desirable assignment, becoming Britain's ambassador to France, a post he occupied for almost twenty years. He was held in such high esteem that in 1886 Lord Salisbury, the prime minister, offered Lyons the position of foreign secretary in the cabinet. Although such an honor was most unusual—politicians, not civil servants, usually sat in the cabinet—Lyons declined. He resigned from the foreign service in November 1887 and was made an earl. Only days later, he suffered a stroke. After lingering for about a week, he died in London on 5 December 1887.

—*Hubert F. Dubrulle*

See also Great Britain; Seward, Frederick W.; *Trent* Affair.
For further reading:
Gallas, Stanley. "Lord Lyons and the Civil War, 1859–1864: A British Perspective" (Ph.D. dissertation, 1982).
Newton, Thomas Wodehouse Legh, 2d Baron. *Lord Lyons: A Record of British Diplomacy* (1913).

LYTLE, WILLIAM HAINES
(1826–1863)
Union general

William Haines Lytle, the only son and oldest child of Robert Todd Lytle and Elizabeth Haines Lytle, was born on 2 November 1826 in Cincinnati, Ohio. Lytle had a proud legacy to uphold. His Scot-Irish grandfather William Lytle (1770–1831), a Pennsylvania native, accompanied his parents, brother, and sisters to Kentucky in 1780. A surveyor, entrepreneur, civic leader, and general in the Ohio militia, he moved his family to Ohio in 1801 and Cincinnati in 1809. His third son, Robert Todd Lytle was a lawyer, Democratic politician, and gifted orator who died from consumption in 1839.

As a child, William Haines Lytle frequently visited Kentucky relatives and spent one year in New Jersey and several months in Washington, D.C., during early 1835 while his father completed a term in the U.S. House of Representatives. In Washington, young Lytle met President Andrew Jackson and other political leaders of the day. A quick student, Lytle entered Cincinnati College in 1840 and graduated first in his class in 1843. After graduation he read law with his maternal uncle, Ezekial Smith Haines. Imbued with a sense of adventure and love of the military, Lytle enlisted in the army in September 1847 and was promptly elected lieutenant of Company L, known as the Montgomery Guards, of the 2d Ohio. His company shipped to Mexico in November 1847, arriving after fighting had ceased. When the captain of Company L died in December 1847, Lytle was elected to that position. Most of his Mexican-American War service consisted of garrison duty. Remaining in Mexico until after the signing of the treaty ending the war, Captain Lytle and his company returned to Cincinnati in July 1848.

Between the Mexican-American and Civil Wars, Lytle practiced law, participated in politics, wrote poetry, and enjoyed several romances. In 1851 he won a term in the Ohio House of Representatives. A pro–states' rights Democrat, Lytle was his party's candidate for lieutenant governor in 1857 but lost in a close election. He received appointment as a lieutenant colonel in the Ohio Militia in 1855 followed by election to major general in 1857, a position he held at the outbreak of the Civil War. During this period he gained widespread renown for his poetry, writing his most famous poem "Antony and Cleopatra" in 1858.

When the Civil War broke out in April 1861, Ohio governor William Dennison ordered Lytle to establish an assembly for Hamilton County troops. Lytle selected the Cincinnati Trotting Park, seven miles from the center of Cincinnati, and named it Camp Harrison. Not wanting to miss action in the field, he resigned his post in the Ohio Militia to accept the position of colonel of the 10th Ohio Volunteer Infantry. Originally a three-month unit, the 10th was re-formed in June 1861 as a three-year regiment. Raised in Cincinnati, the 10th Ohio consisted of mostly Irish troops with two German companies, B and F. Although the 10th was a hard drinking regiment, Lytle's Mexican-American War experiences stood him in good stead and he gained control of the 10th in short order.

Despite lacking supplies and training, the 10th was ordered to western Virginia in late June 1861. After several months of skirmishes and marches throughout western Virginia, Lytle and the 10th saw action at Carnifex Ferry on 10 September 1861. He was wounded leading a charge; the minié ball that passed through Lytle's leg entered and killed his horse, Faugh-a-Ballaugh. At Carnifex Ferry the 10th earned the sobriquet "the bloody Tenth," and its commander gained a reputation for gallantry and bravery, almost to the point of rashness.

Lytle's wound kept him at home until January 1862, at which time he was given orders to assume command of Camp Morton, a camp for recruitment and training, in Bardstown, Kentucky. For several months in addition to his military duties Lytle enjoyed the pleasantries of Bardstown social life including dinners with his relatives, the Rowan family, who owned "My Old Kentucky Home." In late March, his leg having finally healed, Lytle regained his regiment and the Army of the Ohio at Murfreesboro, Tennessee. Although still a colonel, Lytle received command of the 17th Brigade, 3d Division, in the Army of Ohio in late March 1862. Ordered to occupy Huntsville, Alabama, he was stationed there from 14 April until the end of August. During September, Lytle marched his brigade to Kentucky, where he joined the rest of Don Carlos Buell's army. When the two sides clashed in the battle of Perryville on 8 October, Lytle was shot in the head and left for dead on the battlefield. Shortly after capture by the Confederates, he was released on parole to wait for exchange before returning to active duty. While at home in Cincinnati, he testified during December at the Don Carlos Buell court of inquiry. That November he penned "Lines on My Thirty-Sixth Birthday," a melancholy poem anticipating his soldier's grave.

Lytle returned to action in March 1863. Arriving in Murfreesboro, Tennessee, he soon learned that his promotion to brigadier general had come through effective 17 March 1863 with rank dating to 29 November 1862. General William S. Rosecrans placed Lytle in command of the 1st Brigade, 3d Division, XX Army Corps, under Generals Philip Sheridan and Alexander McDowell McCook. During the summer of 1863, Lytle was part of the Tullahoma campaign as Rosecrans pursued the Confederates commanded by Braxton Bragg toward Chattanooga. Lytle occupied his time with picket and outpost duty along with supervising the building of a bridge over the Tennessee River. On 9 September at Bridgeport, Alabama, the officers of the 10th Ohio presented their first colonel with a Maltese Cross. Lytle made a stirring speech urging recognition of both Southern and Northern valor. Finally the two armies collided at Chickamauga on 19 September. On 20 September, the second day of fighting, Lytle on horseback led a charge to cover a gap in the Union lines and was shot several times. After being eased to the ground by an aide, Lytle died on the battlefield.

The Confederates, who respected General Lytle, willingly returned his body to the Union forces. Before shipping Lytle's body by boat to Cincinnati, the 10th Ohio held services for him in Tennessee. When it came to Cincinnati's turn to commemorate its heroic native son, the largest crowd ever participated in his funeral observances. William Haines Lytle is buried in Spring Grove Cemetery in Cincinnati, Ohio. Never married, he was survived by two sisters.

—*Ruth C. Carter*

See also Chickamauga, Battle of.
For further reading:
Brill, Ruth. "Cincinnati's 'Poet-Warrior': William Haines Lytle." *Historical and Philosophical Society of Ohio Bulletin* (1963).
Carter, Ruth C. *For Honor, Glory, and Union: the Mexican and Civil War Letters of Brigadier General William Haines Lytle* (1999).
Lytle, William Haines. *Poems of William Haines Lytle* (1894).
Morris, Roy, Jr. "I Am Dying, Egypt, Dying." *Civil War Times* (1986).

M

MACARTHUR, ARTHUR, JR.
(1845–1912)
Union officer

Born in Springfield, Massachusetts, on 2 June 1845, Arthur MacArthur, Jr., moved with his family to Milwaukee, Wisconsin, in 1849. After the outbreak of the Civil War, MacArthur attempted to get an appointment to West Point but was unable to do so. His politically influential father, Judge Arthur MacArthur, Sr., managed to have him commissioned a second lieutenant and named the adjutant of the 24th Wisconsin Infantry Regiment on 4 August 1862.

MacArthur distinguished himself at the battle of Stones River (31 December 1862–3 January 1863) and at Missionary Ridge (25 November 1863) during the Chattanooga campaign. At Missionary Ridge, he seized the regimental colors at a critical moment and led his regiment to the crest of the ridge. The 24th Wisconsin's colors were the first to be planted on the enemy's former breastworks and, for his daring action, MacArthur would be awarded the Medal of Honor on 30 June 1890. Promoted two grades to major on 25 January 1864, he led the regiment, as part of the Army of the Cumberland, at the battles of Kennesaw Mountain and Jonesboro during the Atlanta campaign. Severely wounded in hand-to-hand combat at Franklin, Tennessee, on 30 November 1864, MacArthur was breveted lieutenant colonel and colonel in March 1865, and promoted to lieutenant colonel on 18 May 1865. Because he was not yet twenty years old when he was promoted to lieutenant colonel, MacArthur was dubbed the "Boy Colonel of the West."

After being mustered out of the volunteers in June 1865, MacArthur was commissioned a first lieutenant in the regular army in February 1866 and was promoted to captain in July 1866. For the next thirty years, he served on the frontier, being promoted to major in July 1889 and lieutenant colonel in May 1896. After the outbreak of the Spanish-American War, MacArthur was promoted to brigadier general of volunteers in May 1898 and commanded a brigade during the capture of Manila. Promoted to major general of volunteers in August 1898, he was given command of the U.S. forces in the Philippines, forces that were fighting against the insurrectionist army of Emilio Aguinaldo. MacArthur was promoted to brigadier general in the regular army in January 1901 and major general in February, which was followed by an appointment as the military governor of the Philippines in May 1901.

During the Russo-Japanese War, MacArthur was an observer with the Japanese forces. That assignment was followed by service as the U.S. military attaché in Tokyo. In September 1906, MacArthur was promoted to lieutenant general and given command of all U.S. Army personnel in the Pacific. Despite being the highest ranking officer in the U.S. Army, however, he was passed over for the position of chief of staff and retired in June 1909. MacArthur died when a blood vessel in his brain burst while he was giving a speech at the 24th Wisconsin's Fiftieth Reunion in Milwaukee on 5 September 1912.

Both of MacArthur's sons followed their father into the military: Captain Arthur MacArthur III, U.S. Navy, was awarded the Navy Cross and Distinguished Service Medal (Navy) during World War I and died from appendicitis at age 47; Douglas MacArthur rose to the rank of general of the army and was awarded the Medal of Honor during World War II. As of this writing, Arthur MacArthur, Jr., and Douglas MacArthur are the only father/son combination to win the Medal of Honor.

—*Alexander M. Bielakowski*

See also Franklin, Battle of; Jonesboro, Battle of; Kennesaw Mountain, Battle of; Missionary Ridge, Battle of; Stones River, Battle of.

For further reading:
James, D. Clayton. *Years of MacArthur: 1880–1941* (1970).
MacArthur, Douglas. *Reminiscences* (1964).
Young, Kenneth R. *General's General: The Life and Times of Arthur MacArthur* (1994).

MACKENZIE, RANALD SLIDELL
(1840–1889)
Union general and Indian fighter

Ranald Slidell Mackenzie is best known as one of the most capable officers in the Indian Fighting Army but, like George Armstrong Custer, he first gained fame in the Civil War. The son of Alexander Slidell Mackenzie, a naval officer, he seemed destined for

a military career from an early age. He began his primary education at a military school and, after attending Williams College for two years, gained an appointment to the United States Military Academy at West Point. Mackenzie graduated first in the class of 1862 and was appointed a second lieutenant of Engineers. He served in this capacity until June 1864, being wounded twice and promoted to the brevet rank of captain.

In June 1864 Mackenzie was promoted to colonel and assigned command of the 2d Connecticut Heavy Artillery, which had been trained to fight as infantry. The regiment had just been through the battle of Cold Harbor and was badly demoralized. Mackenzie applied harsh discipline, earning the hatred of the enlisted men, but turning the 2d into a first-class fighting unit. The regiment served at Petersburg where Mackenzie suffered the loss of two fingers of his right hand. After returning to duty, Mackenzie and his regiment were shifted to Washington, D.C., to aid in its defense against a raid by Confederate general Jubal Early. Assigned next to General Philip Sheridan's Army of the Shenandoah, Mackenzie led the 2d Connecticut Heavy Artillery with distinction in the battles of Winchester, Fisher's Hill, and Cedar Creek, where he was again wounded. His bravery and leadership ability earned him promotion to brigadier general.

After their return to the Petersburg front, Sheridan helped to arrange the appointment of Mackenzie as commander of the Cavalry Division of the Army of the James. Mackenzie participated in the pursuit of Lee's army in the spring of 1865 and played an important role in the battle of Five Forks. He finished the war with the rank of major general. Considering that he did not receive a combat command until the last year of the war, his rise in rank had been remarkable. No wonder General Ulysses S. Grant referred to him as "the most promising young officer in the artillery."

Mackenzie was assigned the permanent rank of captain and reassigned to the Engineers in the reorganization following the war. Not content with working on harbor fortifications, he maneuvered for a field command and was rewarded in 1867 when he was appointed to command the 41st Infantry Regiment, one of the new African-American regiments authorized by Congress. The new colonel improved the quality of recruits and his emphasis on discipline brought his regiment to a high level of efficiency. In 1871 Mackenzie was given command of the 4th Cavalry Regiment, and it was with this regiment that he gained his lasting reputation.

Mackenzie became known for strict discipline and vigorous action. He pioneered the use of large bodies of troops on the Llano Estacado of Texas, led an unauthorized raid across the Rio Grande, and played a major role in the defeat of the Southern Plains Indians in the Red River War. Assigned to command Fort Sill following this war, Mackenzie demonstrated that the Indians might have been better off with army officers rather than civilians as agents. Mackenzie and the 4th Cavalry Regiment were assigned to the Northern Plains following Custer's defeat and fought the only combat action of General George Crook's winter campaign, defeating Dull Knife's Cheyennes on the Powder River. Following his service with Crook, Mackenzie served as a kind of roving fireman assigned to deal with flare-ups throughout the Southwest. He served again on the Rio Grande trying to suppress raids from Mexico into Texas, fought Apaches in Arizona and New Mexico, and helped to force the Utes onto their new reservations in Utah in 1880–1881.

Mackenzie seemed to reach the peak of his career when he was promoted to brigadier general and assigned to command the Department of Texas in 1883. After arriving in San Antonio to take up his new post, Mackenzie began to show signs of mental aberration. His condition deteriorated rapidly, and in December he was removed from his position and sent to New York, where he was judged to be insane. His mental state varied over the next few years, but his physical condition declined steadily. He died 19 January 1889 of a condition diagnosed as "progressive paresis" and was buried at West Point.

—*Michael D. Pierce*

See also Cedar Creek; Five Forks.
For further reading:
Pierce, Michael D. *The Most Promising Young Officer: A Life of Ranald Slidell Mackenzie* (1992).
Wallace, Ernest. *Ranald S. Mackenzie on the Texas Frontier* (1964).
Wert, Jeffry D. *From Winchester to Cedar Creek: The Shenandoah Campaign of 1864* (1987; reprint, 1997).

MAFFITT, JOHN NEWLAND
(1819–1886)
Confederate naval officer

Born to John Newland Maffitt and Ann Carnick Maffitt during his parents' trans-Atlantic voyage immigrating from Ireland to the United States, the younger Maffitt grew up at his uncle's home in North Carolina and was educated in North Carolina and New York. He accepted a midshipman's appointment in 1832 and went to sea in 1835 aboard the USS *Constitution*. From 1842 until 1858 he worked charting the East Coast of the United States for the U.S. Coastal Survey. From 1858 to 1861 he held two commands of the USS *Dolphin* and the USS *Crusader*, looking for slave smugglers along the east coast. He resigned his commission in April 1861 to accept one in the Confederate Navy. During the war he commanded combat vessels and blockade runners.

Maffitt's initial assignment was to Charleston, South Carolina, where he served as the naval aide to Robert E. Lee in preparing the city's defenses and creating obstructions in the Coosa River. In January 1862 Maffitt was promoted from lieutenant to captain. On the recommendation of Charleston merchants Fraser, Trenholm & Company, Maffitt was given command of the blockade runner *Cecile*. Operating out of Nassau he brought arms, ammunition, and other supplies into the Confederacy using New Smyrna, Florida, as his primary port of entry.

Later in 1862, Maffitt assumed command in England of the combat steamer CSS *Florida* in Nassau. Attempting to bring the ship to the Confederacy to be outfitted for combat, Maffitt and his yellow fever-ravaged crew had to fight their way through the Union blockade at Mobile Bay on 4 September 1862, a feat for which Maffitt was lauded throughout the Confederacy. After recovering from his bout with yellow fever and having the ship repaired, he took the *Florida* back out through the blockade in January 1863. For the next several months, operating off the coast of New York City all the way down to Latin America, Maffitt became the scourge of Union merchant vessels.

In the fall of 1863, Maffitt took command of the blockade runner *Florie*; in 1864 he took command of the ironclad combat vessel *Albemarle*. As commander of the *Albemarle*, Maffitt operated off the North Carolina coast, attacking smaller Union vessels. In late 1864 he assumed command of the CSS *Owl* with instructions not to surrender the vessel under any circumstances. After the surrender of Robert E. Lee's and Joseph E. Johnston's armies in April 1865, Maffitt made his way to England, where he put into port in Liverpool, releasing his crew from duty in July 1865.

In the fall of 1865, Maffitt accepted command of the British merchant vessel *Widgeon*. He commanded this vessel for two years before briefly serving in the naval forces of the Cuban revolutionaries. Around 1870 he came back to the United States, where he tried farming around Wilmington, North Carolina. He spent much of the rest of his life farming and writing about his adventures. He died near Wilmington.

—*David S. Heidler and Jeanne T. Heidler*

See also *Florida*; Navy, C.S.A.

For further reading:
Boykin, Edward. *Sea Devil of the Confederacy: The Story of the Florida and Her Captain* (1959).
Maffitt, Emma Martin. *The Life and Services of John Newland Maffitt* (1906).
Shingleton, Royce. *High Seas Confederate: The Life and Times of John Newland Maffitt* (1994).

MAGOFFIN, BERIAH
(1815–1885)

Governor of Kentucky

Beriah Magoffin, Kentucky's governor during 1859–1862, was born in Harrodsburg on 18 April 1815. His father, Beriah Magoffin, Sr., was an Irish immigrant; his mother, Jane McAfree Magoffin, came from one of Kentucky's famed pioneer families. The young Magoffin attended local schools and graduated from Centre College in 1835 and from the Transylvania University law course in 1838. He practiced law briefly in Mississippi and then returned to Harrodsburg in 1839. He married Ann Nelson Shelby in 1840; ten children survived infancy. Active in the Democratic Party, Magoffin was elected to the state senate in 1850. He lost the contest for lieutenant governor in 1855, but was elected governor in 1859. His administration was dominated by the secession crisis and the Civil War.

Magoffin believed that slavery was a positive good for everyone connected to it. He was convinced that Southern rights had been violated in the territories and regarding fugitive slaves, and he accepted the right of secession. He hoped to avoid dissolution of the Union by having the slave states present collective demands that the free states would have to accept. If this failed, he predicted that Kentucky would join the other slave states. Kentucky Unionists were able to prevent the calling of a convention that might have voted for secession, and the legislature stripped the governor of many of his constitutional powers. After Fort Sumter fell, Magoffin rejected President Lincoln's request for troops to put down the rebellion, but he also refused to supply troops to the Confederacy. With state sentiment badly divided, Magoffin supported the movement to adopt armed neutrality, which he proclaimed on 20 May 1861. Unionists did not trust him to be neutral, and his powers to govern continued to be eroded, although he insisted that he would carry out "the lawful will of the people, whether the policy they prefer accords with my own sense or not." He surprised many Unionists by denouncing the Confederate Government of Kentucky that was established in November 1861.

Two elections in the summer of 1861 showed that most Kentuckians were Unionists. On 20 June, Unionists won nine of ten seats to the U.S. House; after August 5, Unionists held majorities of seventy-six to twenty-four in the state House and twenty-seven to eleven in the Senate. Magoffin's vetoes were easily overridden after Kentucky's neutrality ended in early September. His situation became untenable, and in August 1862 a bizarre political agreement led to his resignation. He insisted that he must be succeeded by a sound conservative man who would protect the rights of all citizens. The lieutenant governor had died in office, and Speaker of the Senate John F. Fisk was not acceptable to be the governor. On 16 August 1862, Fisk resigned as Speaker of the Senate; James F. Robinson, who was acceptable to Magoffin, was elected to replace him. On 18 August Magoffin resigned, Robinson became governor, and Fisk was reelected Speaker.

Magoffin retired to his legal practice and farm at Harrodsburg. Real estate investments in Chicago made

him wealthy. He remained interested in politics and served in the state House in 1867–1868. He urged Kentuckians to accept the outcome of the war, to ratify the Thirteenth Amendment, and to grant civil rights to the blacks. Magoffin died at his home on 28 February 1885 and was buried at Harrodsburg.

—*Lowell H. Harrison*

See also Kentucky.
For further reading:
Coulter, E. Martin. *The Civil War and Readjustment in Kentucky* (1926).
Dues, Michael T. "Governor Beriah Magoffin of Kentucky." *Filson Club History Quarterly* (1966).
———. "The Pro-Secessionist Governor of Kentucky: Beriah Magoffin's Credibility Gap." *Register of the Kentucky Historical Society* (1969).
Harrison, Lowell H. "Governor Magoffin and the Secession Crisis." *Register of the Kentucky Historical Society* (1974).
Turner, Wallace B. "The Secession Movement in Kentucky." *Register of the Kentucky Historical Society* (1968).

MAGRATH, ANDREW GORDON
(1813–1893)
Confederate judge and governor of South Carolina

Born in Charleston, South Carolina, to John MaGrath and Marie Gordon MaGrath, Andrew MaGrath was educated at South Carolina College and Harvard Law School. He practiced law in Charleston and became active in South Carolina politics. He served in the state legislature and in 1856 accepted appointment by Franklin Pierce as U.S. district judge for South Carolina. The election of Abraham Lincoln in November 1860 brought about MaGrath's resignation from the federal court and his election to the South Carolina secession convention. He supported secession.

After the secession of South Carolina, MaGrath accepted the position of South Carolina's secretary of state. In that position he handled Governor Francis Pickens's negotiations with the Buchanan administration and Major Robert Anderson regarding the Union occupation of Fort Sumter. Appointed by Jefferson Davis to the Confederate district court, MaGrath declared tax on state bonds unconstitutional and incurred Davis's disfavor as a result. In 1864 MaGrath was elected governor of South Carolina.

As governor, MaGrath continued his criticism of the Davis administration. He tried to resist Davis's efforts to remove South Carolina state troops from the state. As the collapse of the Confederacy loomed in 1865, MaGrath worked with neighboring governors to organized a military force that could continue to resist the United States in the event the Confederate government disintegrated. With William Sherman's invasion, however, it became increasingly difficult to organize the state's forces. Finally giving up any hope of further resistance, MaGrath advised the citizens of the state to cease further resistance in May 1865. He was arrested on 28 May partly because he had tried to bring all Confederate property in the state under state government control. Incarcerated at Fort Pulaski with other high-ranking Confederates until November 1865, he wrote candid letters that did not deny the South's right of secession, but did say that Southern leaders' desire to protect slave property had caused the withdrawal from the Union. After his release, he resumed the practice of law in Charleston, where he spent the rest of his life.

—*David S. Heidler and Jeanne T. Heidler*

See also Courts, C.S.A.; South Carolina.
For further reading:
Cauthen, Charles Edward. *South Carolina Goes to War, 1861–1865* (1950).
Williamson, Joel. "The Disruption of State Government in South Carolina during the MaGrath Administration" (M.A. thesis, 1951).

MAGRUDER, JOHN BANKHEAD
(1807–1871)
Confederate general

John Bankhead Magruder was a Confederate officer whose Civil War service was punctuated by both successes and failures. He was born to Thomas Magruder and Elizabeth Bankhead of Maryland. Historians have disagreed about the time and location of his birth, but reliable evidence suggests that it occurred in May 1807 at a small Caroline County community near Port Royal, Virginia. Although Thomas Magruder was an attorney, he prepared his son for a military career by sending him to Rappahannock Academy and then to the newly opened University of Virginia for two terms. In 1826 John entered the U.S. Military Academy and graduated fifteenth of forty-two in the class of 1830. More than a year later, he received his military commission.

Magruder began his military career as a second lieutenant in the infantry, transferring eventually to the artillery. His assignments included service in Florida during and after the Second Seminole War and duty along the U.S.–Canadian border. Frustrated by missed promotions and limited professional progress, Magruder found an opportunity to distinguish himself during the Mexican-American War. He commanded a company during Winfield Scott's campaign from Vera Cruz to Mexico City and, after the battle of Chapultepec, was brevetted a lieutenant colonel for meritorious service. He held a variety of assignments in the years that followed, including commanding the garrison at Fort Leavenworth, traveling to France in late 1860 and early 1861 to observe French artillery practices, and taking charge of a battery in the Washington defenses.

During these years, Magruder earned the sobriquet "Prince John" for his flamboyant behavior, high fashion, and lavish entertainment, which included the bountiful consumption of alcohol. His excessive drinking repeatedly drew comment and possibly contributed to his mixed military reputation and failed marriage. He wed Henrietta Von Kapff on 18 May 1831, and together they had three children (Isabell, Kate, and Henry). Much of their lives were spent apart, however, as she and the children moved to Italy.

Secession and Civil War brought to an end Magruder's U.S. military career. On 20 April 1861, he submitted his letter of resignation and a month later, on 21 May, received a commission as a colonel in the new Confederate army. In addition, Robert E. Lee gave Magruder command of the strategic Virginia Peninsula between the York and James rivers. Magruder set about organizing his forces, preparing the region's defenses, and assembling his staff, which included his brother, Allan, and his nephew, George A. Magruder, Jr. On 10 June, Major General Benjamin F. Butler's Union forces attacked Magruder's line in the vicinity of Big Bethel Church. The assault was mismanaged and served to give the Confederates a victory in the war's first land battle. The conflict was small in terms of the numbers involved but enormous in the attention it drew for Magruder. Southerners eagerly praised the colorful "Prince John," and the Confederate government promoted him to brigadier general, effective 17 June, and then to major general on 7 October.

Magruder continued to prepare the peninsula's defenses and to skirmish occasionally with the enemy, but he drew his greatest praise and greatest criticism for events of the following spring and summer. In April 1862, Major General George B. McClellan led his Army of the Potomac up the Virginia Peninsula toward the Confederate capital at Richmond. He soon found his path blocked at Yorktown, where Magruder entrenched a 13,000-man force behind the Warwick River. It was badly outnumbered by 55,000 Federals, but the dilatory McClellan refused in characteristic fashion to push the initiative. Eager as always for a grand display, "Prince John" ordered his men and artillery to shift between various points in the line to create the illusion of greater numbers, thereby convincing McClellan that a ponderous siege was required. By early May, the Army of the Potomac was ready for the assault, but, during the night of the 3d, Confederate troops evacuated. McClellan won the battle, but Magruder's antics served to slow the Union advance for a month, giving Major General Joseph E. Johnston valuable time to prepare Richmond's defenses.

Magruder executed a similar ploy toward the end of June during the Seven Days' battle. As McClellan shifted his base of operations to the south side of the

John B. Magruder (*Library of Congress*)

peninsula, his forces straddled the Chickahominy River and were exposed to attack. Lee, who now commanded operations around Richmond, unleashed an assault on the Federal troops north of the river. To keep McClellan from reinforcing one wing with the other, Lee ordered Magruder to launch diversionary attacks against Union forces south of the Chickahominy. Magruder's soldiers skirmished, kept their artillery active, and paraded along the lines to distract the Federals and prevent them from shifting forces northward to counter the Confederate attack.

If Magruder's deceptions of McClellan earned him praise, his generalship during the latter stages of the Seven Days' battle drew increasingly loud disapproval. Fatigue and illness impaired his effectiveness. Critics complained that his lack of aggressiveness and erratic behavior (possibly caused by an allergic reaction to medication) prevented Lee from striking a more costly blow to the Army of the Potomac as it retreated across the peninsula. In addition, they claimed that drunkenness had compromised Magruder's leadership.

As Magruder defended himself from these accusations, he prepared for his new assignment in the Trans-Mississippi Department, which he assumed on 7 October 1862. He shortly thereafter found an opportunity to improve his tarnished image. On 1 January 1863, he

orchestrated the reoccupation of Galveston, the second-largest city in Texas and an important port of entry for blockade runners. The victory won him the adoration of Texans. For the remainder of the war, he continued to serve in the Trans-Mississippi Department, eventually expanding his command to include the District of Arkansas, but never again drawing the national attention he had received in Virginia.

At the war's conclusion, Magruder fled to Mexico and became head of the land office in the French-backed government under Maximilian. He returned to the United States in early 1867, traveled, and lectured until his death from heart disease on 19 February 1871.

—*J. Mark Thompson*

See also Big Bethel, Battle of; Galveston, Texas; Seven Days' Battles; Yorktown.

For further reading:
Casdorph, Paul D. *Prince John Magruder: His Life and Campaigns* (1996).
Gallagher, Gary W. "The Undoing of an Early Confederate Hero: John Bankhead Magruder at the Seven Days." In *Lee and His Generals in War and Memory* (1998).

MAHAN, DENNIS HART
(1802–1871)

Union officer and United States Military Academy professor

Born on 2 April 1802 in New York City to Irish immigrants, Mahan was a frail boy who wanted to be an artist. His family moved to Virginia and Mahan grew up in Norfolk. He sought admission to the United States Military Academy at West Point because drawing was part of the curriculum instituted by Superintendent Sylvanius Thayer. Entering West Point in 1820, Mahan soon attracted Thayer's attention as a brilliant student and, from his second year, Thayer made him acting assistant professor of mathematics.

Mahan graduated first in his class of thirty-two in 1824 and was commissioned in the Engineers. He remained at the Academy to teach, but in 1826 Thayer selected him to go to Europe to study both military and civil engineering, with an emphasis on waterways and roads. Mahan spent much of his time in France, then the world's center for military engineering. In France he inspected military fortifications and also completed a course in the School of Application for Engineers and Artillery at Metz. When he returned to West Point in 1830, Mahan became acting professor of engineering. Two years later he was professor of civil and military engineering, and in 1838 he became dean of the faculty.

Mahan taught the capstone course in Thayer's curriculum, the fourth-year class in civil and military engineering, known by 1843 as Engineering and the Science of War. This included civil and military architecture, field fortification, and artillery science. Significantly, Mahan insisted that there be added to his professorial title the phrase "and the Art of War," for he initiated the American branch of the study of military theory.

Mahan was an exacting professor, but a most unmilitary figure who refused to wear a uniform. In his classes Mahan stressed the necessity of officers acquiring a broad historical and theoretical knowledge of war. Because no textbooks in English were available, Mahan produced his own. His many published books helped establish military engineering in the United States. They include *Complete Treatise on Field Fortification* (1836); *Elementary Course of Civil Engineering* (1837); *Summary of the Course of Permanent Fortification and of the Attack and Defense of Permanent Works* (1850); and *An Elementary Course of Military Engineering* (1867). His most important book, however, was *An Elementary Treatise on Advanced-Guard, Out-Post, and Detachment Service of Troops*. It first appeared in 1847, and cadets knew it simply as "Out-Post." In addition to its use at West Point, the book was widely used for militia and volunteer training before the Civil War. The year before, in 1846, one of Mahan's favorite students, Henry W. Halleck (Class of 1839), published his own book, *Elements of Military Art and Science*, stressing the importance of fortification. These two books are the keys to pre–Civil War U.S. Army tactics.

Mahan and Halleck both stressed that war was a science and could be learned. Knowledge of military history was the key, in their opinion. As Mahan recognized, there were exceptions and "It is in discovering these cases that the talent of the general is shown." Mahan was heavily influenced by French writer and admirer of Napoleon, Antoine Henri Jomini. Mahan and Halleck both stressed the Napoleonic principle of fire and maneuver, which culminates in one big battle. To ensure knowledge of the enemy and deprive him of information in turn, up to one-fifth of a force should be in guards, outposts, and reconnaissances that could screen maneuver by the main body. Virtually all important Civil War commanders, with the exception of Robert E. Lee who graduated in the class of 1829, sat in Mahan's classroom.

In addition to making West Point a model among American schools of engineering, Mahan also helped nourish the military tradition in Virginia. He encouraged the founding in 1839 of the Virginia Military Institute, which used his texts and until 1860 called its summer encampment Camp Mahan. A staunch Unionist, Mahan continued as professor of engineering at the Academy until 1871, when the academic board decided that his age necessitated his retirement. He died shortly thereafter when he fell off a boat and drowned in the Hudson River near West Point on 16 September 1871.

—*Spencer C. Tucker*

See also Halleck, Henry W.; Virginia Military Institute.

For further reading:

Ambrose, Stephen E. *Duty, Honor, Country: A History of West Point* (1966).

Dupuy, R. Ernest. *Men of West Point: The First 150 Years of the United States Military Academy* (1951).

Spiller, Roger J., and Dennis Hart Mahan. In *Dictionary of American Military Biography*, vol. 2 (1984).

MAHONE, WILLIAM
(1826–1895)
Confederate general

William Mahone was born on 1 December 1826 in Southampton County, Virginia, the son of Fielding Jordan and Martha Drew Mahone. He graduated from the Virginia Military Institute in 1847, after receiving an appointment as a state cadet. He taught for two years to satisfy his scholarship requirements and worked thereafter as a surveyor and engineer. Hard-driving and ambitious, by 1860 Mahone was president and superintendent of the Norfolk & Petersburg Railroad Company and married to Otelia Butler, the daughter of a prominent Democratic politician.

With the outbreak of hostilities, Mahone advanced rapidly from quartermaster general of Virginia state troops to colonel of the 6th Virginia Infantry. On 16 November 1861, he received an appointment to the rank of brigadier general. He briefly commanded the Department of Norfolk and helped establish the defenses at Drewry's Bluff before joining General Joseph E. Johnston's army, in May 1862, at Richmond.

Assigned to the division of General Benjamin Huger, Mahone showed flashes of brilliance and incompetence that characterized his early service with the Army of Northern Virginia. His Virginians fought well at Seven Pines, but General D. H. Hill criticized Mahone for withdrawing "his Brigade without any order," thereby creating a gap in the Confederate lines. His record was little better during the Seven Days' battles. While moving through the White Oak Swamp on 30 June 1862, to support General Robert E. Lee's troops, Mahone became embroiled in a wood-chopping contest with Federal troops in one of the most ludicrous episodes of the entire war. The next day Mahone's Virginians gallantly charged a strong Union position at Malvern Hill.

In the July reorganization of the Army of Northern Virginia, Mahone's command, comprising the 6th, 12th, 16th, 41st, and 61st Virginia, was assigned to General R. H. Anderson's division of James Longstreet's corps. At Second Bull Run, Mahone received a serious wound, incapacitating him for several months. Longstreet lobbied for Mahone's promotion to major general, calling him "one of our best brigadiers," but the recommendation failed to receive congressional approval.

With Mahone once more in command, his Old Dominion soldiers fought well enough to earn praise from both Anderson and Lee. Unfortunately, Mahone's adamant refusal to support the 2 July charge of Anderson's other brigades at Gettysburg again tarnished the command's reputation and created hard feelings in the corps. Even admirers admitted that Mahone could be "irritable and in some instances tyrannical."

Such criticism enraged the bantam Virginian. Short of stature and emaciated to the point of starvation, Mahone was an eccentric of the first order. He exhibited a hypochondriac fixation on his digestion, and his headquarters wagon resembled a rolling barnyard with milk cow and chicken to provide the sole ingredients of his diet—fresh milk and eggs.

Beginning with the 6 May 1864 fight in the Wilderness, Mahone began building his reputation as one of Lee's hardest-hitting and most reliable lieutenants. Mahone's brigade spearheaded the flank attack along the Orange Plank Road, which hurled the stunned Federals back in confusion. Longstreet was severely wounded during the assault, and when R. H. Anderson assumed command of his corps, Mahone took over as commander of Anderson's division in General A. P. Hill's III Corps.

At Spotsylvania, Mahone's division gave distinguished service, both along the Po River and in retaking the Mule Shoe salient on 12 May. A few days later, his division repulsed a Federal assault along the North Anna River. At Cold Harbor, troops from Mahone's division retook the one section of the Confederate lines where the Union troops had managed a breakthrough.

Mahone's star shone even brighter during the siege of Petersburg. On 22–23 June 1864, Mahone twice directed his troops in daring assaults against the Federals, temporarily driving the Unionists from the Weldon Railroad, inflicting casualties totaling almost 3,000 men. A week later, Mahone's men aided General Wade Hampton's cavalry in destroying the remnants of the Wilson-Kautz Raid.

On 30 July, Federals exploded 8,000 pounds of powder under the Elliott Salient, creating a wide gap in the Confederate defenses. Several thousand members of the Federal IX Corps charged into the resulting crater and began slowly moving toward Petersburg. Mahone rushed his Virginians forward, closely followed by "Rans" Wright's Georgians. These two units confined the Yankees to the Crater, but were unable to dislodge them. Mahone then dispatched General J. C. C. Sander's Alabamians, who drove the Unionists back to their lines with great slaughter. Mahone's prompt action finally motivated the Confederate Congress to confirm his appointment as major general.

For the remaining few months of the war, Mahone was indefatigable. His division fought at Deep Bottom (16 August) and again at Weldon Railroad (21 August).

A few days later, at Reams Station, Mahone joined General Henry Heth in driving the vaunted Federal II Corps from their fortifications. Mahone again fought at Burgess' Mill (27 October) and conducted a brutal winter march south toward Bellfield in an unsuccessful attempt to trap Union raiders. Despite desertions and flagging morale, in early 1865, Mahone's division fought with its usual valor along the frozen banks of Hatcher's Run (5–7 February).

After the Union breakthrough at Five Forks, Mahone held his unit together on the road to Appomattox, successfully defending the route of retreat at Sayler's Creek (6 April) and Cumberland Church (7 April). Two days later, Mahone surrendered 3,537 officers and men, the largest organized infantry unit in Lee's army.

After the war, Mahone returned to railroading and by 1870 had obtained control of three railroads. In 1869 he threw his support to the Republican candidate for governor of Virginia and built a political base as leader of the "Readjusters." Mahone won election to the U.S. Senate in 1880 and became a Republican ally, much to the disgust of many white Southerners.

Mahone died in Washington, D.C., on 8 October 1895. He was buried in the Blandsford Cemetery at Petersburg, near the site where he had repulsed the Union forces in the Crater.

—*Zack C. Waters*

See also Crater, Battle of the; Deep Bottom Run, Battle of; Glendale, Battle of; Hatcher's Run, Battle of; Malvern Hill, Battle of; Petersburg Campaign; Reams's Station, Virginia; Wilderness, Battle of the.

For further reading:
Bernard, George S., comp. *War Talks of Confederate Veterans* (1892).
Blake, Nelson M. *William Mahone of Virginia: Soldier and Political Insurgent* (1935).
DePeyster, J. W. "A Military Memoir of William Mahone, Major General in the Confederate Army." *Historical Magazine* (1871).
Harris, Nathaniel H. Report. William Mahone Collection, Virginia State Library, Richmond (n.d.).

MALLET, JOHN WILLIAM
(1832–1912)
Confederate scientist

Born in Dublin, Ireland, the son of Robert Mallet and Cordelia Watson Mallet, John Mallet was educated in Germany and at Trinity College, in Dublin, in chemistry. He immigrated to the United States in 1854 to accept an appointment to the faculty of Amherst College. He moved to Alabama, where he became professor of chemistry at the University of Alabama in 1855. Over the next few years he made a geological study of Alabama and made comparisons between American and foreign cotton.

At the start of the Civil War, Mallet enlisted in the Confederate army. Though initially a private, he was promoted colonel of artillery in November 1861 and placed on the staff of Brigadier General Robert Emmett Rodes. Demonstrating his tremendous knowledge of the chemical properties of ordnance, Mallet was transferred to Richmond in 1862 where he was made the superintendent of all ordnance laboratories there. Working with limited resources, Mallet spent the remainder of the war maximizing Confederate artillery capabilities.

After the war, Mallet taught chemistry at the University of Louisiana until 1868. In that year, he accepted an appointment to the University of Virginia, where he taught until his retirement in 1908. During his time at the University of Virginia, Mallet gained world-wide notoriety as a scientist and founded the American Chemical Society. He remained in Charlottesville after his retirement and died there.

—*David S. Heidler and Jeanne T. Heidler*

See also Artillery; Ordnance, Naval.
For further reading:
Eisenschiml, Otto. *John W. Mallet, ACS President in 1882* (1951).

MALLORY, STEPHEN RUSSELL
(ca. 1813–1873)
Confederate secretary of the navy

Born on Trinidad Island around 1813, Stephen R. Mallory moved to Key West, Florida, with his family in 1820. Two years later his father died of tuberculosis. When Stephen was fourteen, his mother sent him to the Moravian school for boys in Nazareth, Pennsylvania. His three years there constituted his formal education. He then assisted his mother in running a boarding house. In 1833 he was appointed customs inspector at Key West. At about the same time he read law with a local judge, was admitted to the bar before 1840, and specialized in maritime cases. During the 1836–1842 Seminole War, Mallory served as a volunteer aboard a gunboat. In 1845 President James Polk appointed him collector of customs at Key West.

In 1851 the Florida legislature elected Mallory to the U.S. Senate. Throughout his years in the Senate, Mallory served on the Naval Affairs Committee and became its chairman in 1857. He used this position to push for naval expansion and technical innovations. He also sought to reinstitute flogging, a move favored by many professional naval officers.

Aware that secession could lead to war, Mallory was one of the important Southern leaders (Jefferson Davis was another) who urged caution in handling the crisis over Fort Pickens at Pensacola. He resigned his Senate seat when Florida seceded, and despite some opposition from die-hard secessionists angry about his stand on Fort Pickens, he was appointed the Confederate secretary of the navy in February 1861 by President Davis. Mallory was the only Confederate cabinet officer to keep his same position throughout the entire war, in large part because he got along well with Davis, whom he had known in the U.S. Senate.

Mallory soon established a Confederate States Navy Department patterned after the U.S. Navy Department. Before the outbreak of hostilities, he sent naval agents to purchase supplies in the North, in Canada, and in Europe. He is credited with making the most of the meager resources available to him.

Mallory was a staunch advocate of commerce raiding, which he hoped would disrupt the North financially, bring pressure on Washington to end the war, and divert Union warships from the blockade of Southern ports. He sent Raphael Semmes to sea in the CSS *Sumter*, the first Confederate commerce raider. He also dispatched naval agents to Europe to purchase cruisers and contract for the construction of others; the most successful of these was James D. Bulloch, who arranged for the construction of the commerce raider CSS *Alabama*.

Mallory's other great goal was the construction of ironclad vessels to help break the Union blockade and even to attack Northern ports. As early as May 1861 he had written that the South should fight wood with iron. For this task, the South, with its limited industrial base and scattered resources, was at a great disadvantage, although Mallory hoped to offset this partially with purchases in Europe. Mallory also established the Torpedo Bureau, which experimented with torpedoes (naval mines) and the means to deliver them against Union warships. In addition, Mallory had the good sense to recognize innovative subordinates, such as Lieutenant John Mercer Brooke. He assigned Brooke to the Bureau of Ordnance and Hydrography, even though Brooke had no prior experience in ordnance design. Brooke became the South's leading designer of naval ordnance; his rifled guns were some of the most successful on either side in the war.

Mallory came under increasing criticism after the loss of the Confederate ports of New Orleans, Memphis, and Norfolk, and the destruction, to avoid capture, of the CSS *Virginia* (formerly the USS *Merrimack*). A Confederate congressional committee, however, cleared him of all charges.

Mallory resigned his post on 2 May 1865. On 20 May Federal troops arrested him, and until March 1866 he was imprisoned at Fort Lafayette in New York harbor. On his release he returned to Florida to practice law. He also spoke out in public and in newspapers against the radical Republican Reconstruction program. He died in Pensacola on 9 November 1873.

—*Spencer C. Tucker*

See also Bulloch, James D.; Davis, Jefferson; Florida; Navy, C.S.A.

For further reading:
Durkin, Joseph T. *Confederate Navy Chief: Stephen R. Mallory* (1954).
Patrick, Rembert W. *Jefferson Davis and His Cabinet* (1944).
Wells, Tom H. *The Confederate Navy: A Study in Organization* (1971).

MALVERN HILL, BATTLE OF
(1 July 1862)

The culminating event of the Seven Days' battles on the Virginia peninsula occurred at Malvern Hill on 1 July 1862. After Confederate forces bungled an opportunity to destroy a part of General George B. McClellan's Army of the Potomac at Glendale the day before, General Robert E. Lee desperately sought one last chance to deal the Federal army a crippling blow before it escaped to the safety of Union gunboats in the James River.

On the morning of 1 July, the Confederate army found that the Union army had developed a nearly impregnable position on the high ground of Malvern Hill, five miles from their new supply base at Harrison's Landing. Union troops under General Fitz John Porter had been preparing the position since the previous day. Nearly 100 cannon lined the crest of the plateau, while 150 more lay in reserve. To complement the artillery, Porter had three divisions of infantry in line of battle, with parts of three corps in supporting distance. Further strengthening the position were creeks and ravines on the east and west sides of the fields, which ensured that Confederates would have to commit a frontal assault.

General D. H. Hill, skeptical of success against such a position, advised Lee that morning, "If General McClellan is there in strength, we had better let him alone." However, General James Longstreet suggested that massed artillery on the Confederate right and left would catch the Union batteries in a crossfire and weaken the defensive line enough that Southern infantry could storm the hill. At 1:30 P.M., in an ambiguous order sent to all division commanders, Lee advocated that the plan be attempted. But the Confederates could never mass more than sixteen guns at either location, and the Union batteries quickly scattered and silenced them before they could cause any real damage to the Union lines.

However, poor communication and unclear orders prompted General John Magruder to launch an attack into the face of tremendous cannon fire. "Prince John" misinterpreted General Lewis Armistead's brigade's overzealous pursuit of sharpshooters as the signal to advance. Any hesitation Magruder had vanished when a second attack order came from Lee, who misunderstood the tactical situation on his right. Believing that he had received unequivocal orders to attack, and

The battle of Malvern Hill, from a battlefield sketch by Alfred R. Waud (*Library of Congress*)

sensitive to rebukes from Lee for his failures at Savage's Station two days earlier, Magruder made certain he would not disappoint again. At 4:45 P.M. he ordered the attack to proceed, first with three brigades of General Benjamin Huger's division, followed by six of his own brigades.

As Magruder's troops marched across a half mile of open field on the Union left, D. H. Hill, who had reasoned that the attack would not materialize and had begun to bivouac, ordered his brigades to join in the assault. The attacks lacked cohesion and concert of action. The Confederate brigades advanced into a near blinding storm of shot and shell and had their lines shattered in the maelstrom before most of them had come within 100 yards of the Federal line. Though one group reached the Union lines near the center of the position on the Quaker Road, they were quickly forced to retreat, and the fighting all along the lines had ended by 8:30 P.M. The Confederate brigades had attacked piecemeal and were defeated in detail by the massed Federal firepower.

Confusing orders had caused the battle to begin against Lee's intentions. Lee confronted Magruder after the battle and asked him why he had attacked, but Magruder pointed to Lee's two orders in his defense.

Magruder, who would later be unfairly accused of drunkenness during Malvern Hill, received a transfer to the Trans-Mississippi soon after the battle. Benjamin Huger, who never commanded his own brigades on the field during the battle, was also removed from Lee's army to the distant Western theater. General "Stonewall" Jackson continued his poor performance in the campaign. Jackson failed to commit any of his troops, excepting D. H. Hill, to the attack.

The Union army suffered 3,007 casualties (314 killed, 1,875 wounded, 818 missing), while the losses were inordinately high for the Confederates, who lost 5,650 men (869 dead, 4,241 wounded, 540 missing). After the war, D. H. Hill reflected on the futile and sanguinary assaults: "It was not war—it was murder."

Though the battle was tactically a defeat for Lee, it proved to be the final battle of his successful campaign to drive the Union army from the Confederate capital. Some of McClellan's generals, especially Porter, whose V Corps bore the brunt of the day's attacks, lobbied the Union commander to hold his position and even initiate another drive to Richmond from their position of strength. But the "Young Napoleon" had seen enough. The beaten Union commander ordered the army to retreat to Harrison's Landing on the James River that night. Lee's inaugural campaign as leader of the Army of Northern Virginia had cost an astonishing number of casualties but proved to be successful. In one week, he had driven a superior enemy from the Confederate capital and extended the life of the breakaway Southern republic.

—*Judkin Browning*

See also Battle of Glendale (White Oak Swamp), Harrison's Landing, Virginia; Peninsula Campaign; Seven Days' Battles.
For further reading:
Dowdey, Clifford. *The Seven Days: The Emergence of Lee* (1964).
Freeman, Douglas Southall. *Lee's Lieutenants: A Study in Command* (1942–1944).
Hill, Daniel Harvey. "McClellan's Change of Base and Malvern Hill." In *Battles and Leaders of the Civil War* (1888; reprint, 1982).
Porter, Fitz John. "The Battle of Malvern Hill." In *Battles and Leaders of the Civil War* (1888; reprint, 1982).
Sears, Stephen W. *To the Gates of Richmond: The Peninsula Campaign* (1992).

MANIGAULT, ARTHUR MIDDLETON
(1824–1886)
Confederate general

The son of Joseph Manigault and Charlotte Drayton Manigault, born in Charleston, South Carolina, Arthur Manigault was educated at the College of Charleston before becoming a businessman in Charleston. During the Mexican-American War, he served as an officer in the Palmetto Regiment and saw combat at Buena Vista. Upon his return to the United States, he continued his business activities until 1856, when he inherited a plantation in Georgetown County.

When South Carolina seceded, Manigault offered his military services to the state and then to the Confederacy when it was formed in 1861. He served on P. G. T. Beauregard's staff during the Fort Sumter crisis. After the fall of Fort Sumter, Manigault became the colonel of the 10th South Carolina and commanded the First District of South Carolina until March 1862, when he was transferred to Corinth, Mississippi.

Manigault commanded a brigade of Braxton Bragg's division at Shiloh in April 1862. Even though not promoted to brigadier general until April 1863, Manigault continued in command of his brigade at Stones River in December 1862 in Leonidas Polk's division. Manigault fought at Chickamauga in September 1863 and in the Chattanooga campaign of the fall of that year.

In the Atlanta campaign as part of Thomas Hindman's division, Manigault was wounded at the battle of Resaca. After returning to command his brigade, Manigault and his brigade were part of John Bell Hood's Tennessee campaign in the fall and winter of 1864. At the battle of Franklin, Manigault received a serious head wound and never saw active service for the remainder of the war.

After the war, Manigault returned to his plantation. In 1880 he was elected adjutant and inspector general of South Carolina. He remained in that position until his death near Georgetown.

—*David S. Heidler and Jeanne T. Heidler*

See also Franklin, Battle of; Resaca.
For further reading:
Manigault, Arthur Middleton. *A Carolinian Goes to War: The Civil War Narrative of Arthur Middleton Manigault, Brigadier General, C.S.A.* (1983).

MANN, AMBROSE DUDLEY
(1801–1889)
Confederate diplomat

Born in Hanover Court House, Virginia, Ambrose Dudley Mann was educated locally and spent some of his youth in Kentucky before accepting an appointment to the U.S. Military Academy. Toward the end of his four years at West Point, he resigned so that he would not incur the military obligation that came with graduation. After leaving the academy, he studied law and opened a practice in Kentucky. An active Whig in Kentucky politics, Mann used his political connections to secure a variety of diplomatic posts in the 1840s and 1850s. In 1850 he accepted the position as U.S. minister to Switzerland. After his return to the United States in 1853, he served in the State Department as assistant secretary until 1856.

With increasing tensions between North and South in the late 1850s, Mann became an enthusiastic advocate of Southern rights and Southern economic independence. He lobbied extensively for direct trade between the South and Europe and the elimination of Northern middlemen. Because of his previous diplomatic experience and his interest in trade, Mann was selected by the new Confederate government in 1861 to act as one of several emissaries to Europe.

In 1861 Mann traveled to Great Britain, where he tried to persuade the British government to recognize the Confederacy and lend material aid to the Southern cause. He managed toward the end of the year to secure the transport to the West Indies and then to the Confederacy one shipment of British Enfield rifles. His mission in London largely unsuccessful, however, he traveled to Belgium, where he spent the remainder of the war at the court of King Leopold. Mann made one extended trip out of Belgium in the winter of 1863–1864; he traveled to the Vatican to meet with the Pope. This visit did secure the Pope's opposition to U.S. recruiting efforts among German and Irish Catholics, but that opposition apparently did little to discourage foreign enlistments.

In addition to Mann's attempts to secure foreign recognition and aid for the Confederacy, he also worked extensively to influence the European press for the Southern cause. In this effort he successfully planted Southern propaganda in British newspapers.

After the war, Mann chose to remain in Europe. He worked as a journalist in several countries before settling in France. He died in Paris.

—*David S. Heidler and Jeanne T. Heidler*

See also Diplomacy, C.S.A.
For further reading:
Benjamin, Judah P. "The Letters of Judah Philip Benjamin to Ambrose Dudley Mann, Minister of the Confederacy to Belgium and Special Commissioner to the Vatican, together with the Correspondence with the Pope." *Louisiana Historical Quarterly* (1937).
Cullop, Charles P. *Confederate Propaganda in Europe, 1861–1865* (1969).
Moore, Samuel Preston, ed. "*My Ever Dearest Friend*"; The Letters of A. Dudley Mann to Jefferson Davis, 1869–1889 (1960).

MANSFIELD, JOSEPH KING FENNO
(1803–1862)
Union general

Born to Henry Mansfield and Mary Fenno Mansfield in New Haven, Connecticut, Joseph King Fenno Mansfield was educated locally before gaining admission to the U.S. Military Academy in 1817. He graduated second of forty in the class of 1822 and was commissioned into the Corps of Engineers. His primary duty for the next twenty years was working on coastal defenses in the Southern states, one of his most important projects being Fort Pulaski, guarding the entrance to the Savannah River.

At the outbreak of the Mexican-American War, Mansfield had achieved the rank of captain. He was assigned to Brigadier General Zachary Taylor as Taylor's chief engineer. In that capacity he designed Fort Brown on the northern bank of the Rio Grande. Later, during the campaign in northern Mexico, he conducted a dangerous reconnaissance of Monterrey and commanded part of the attack on the city. He also fought with distinction at the battle of Buena Vista. As a result of his war service he received three brevet promotions. In 1853 he was promoted from captain to colonel, an almost unprecedented occurrence, and was named by Secretary of War Jefferson Davis as inspector general of the army. He remained in that position during the next eight years, traveling to almost every area occupied by the army.

Mansfield still held the position of inspector general at the outbreak of the Civil War. Two weeks after the firing on Fort Sumter, however, he was given command of the Department of Washington and on 14 May 1861 was promoted to brigadier general. Mansfield remained in command of that department until March 1862. During his time in Washington, he worked to secure the city against Confederate bombardment by ordering the military seizure of the high ground south of the Potomac River. Mansfield also created some controversy during his tenure in the department by ordering the arrest of suspected Confederate sympathizers in the district and in the area of Maryland close to Washington.

In the spring of 1862, Mansfield was sent to Fort Monroe, Virginia. From there he led a division in the occupation of Suffolk, Virginia, and commanded there until 8 September 1862. On 8 September, Mansfield was ordered to join Major General George McClellan in Washington for the upcoming campaign against Robert E. Lee. Upon arrival in Maryland with the Army of the Potomac on 15 September, McClellan gave Mansfield command of XII Corps, Army of the Potomac. Mansfield led his men toward Sharpsburg, Maryland, where Lee waited.

Mansfield's corps was placed on the Federal right to the left of Joseph Hooker's I Corps. He came in to support Hooker's attack through the West Wood at about 7:30 A.M. Early in his corps' move through the cornfield, Mansfield was struck and killed by a Confederate bullet.

—*David S. Heidler and Jeanne T. Heidler*

See also Antietam.
For further reading:
Gould, John Mead. *Joseph K. F. Mansfield, Brigadier General of the U. S. Army; A Narrative of Events Connected with his Mortal Wounding at Antietam, Sharpsburg, Maryland, September 17, 1862* (1895; reprint, 1991).
Taylor, Jeremiah. *Memorial of General J. K. F. Mansfield, United States Army, Who Fell in Battle at Sharpsburg, Md., Sept. 17, 1862* (1862).

MANSFIELD, LOUISIANA, BATTLE OF
(8 April 1864)

Also known as the battle of Sabine Crossroads, this clash was the decisive battle in northwestern Louisiana that effectively halted the Union's Red River campaign of 1864. In early 1864, Federal commanders devised the invasion of Texas by way of the Red River in Louisiana. Major General Nathaniel Banks assumed command of the Red River Expeditionary Force and by late March had taken the strategic town of Alexandria in central Louisiana. Banks next planned to push up the Red River to Shreveport, headquarters of the Confederate commander of the Trans-Mississippi Department, General Edmund Kirby Smith. There he planned to link up with a force under Major General Frederick Steele for the final drive into Texas.

Rather than risk a disastrous defeat, Smith, with fewer than 10,000 available troops under Major General Richard Taylor, ordered Taylor to fall back toward Shreveport. As a reluctant Taylor grudgingly marched his small force northward toward the village of Mansfield, Banks made a fateful decision. Two roads led north to

Shreveport. The longer hugged the riverbank, thus offering his troops the protection of the guns of Admiral David D. Porter's gunboat fleet steaming up the river. Banks, however, eager to reach Shreveport as quickly as possible, chose the more direct overland route. Although the road passed through Mansfield and Pleasant Hill, occupied by Taylor's main force, Banks evidenced little concern, convinced that the Confederates were unwilling to fight. On 6 April the Federal army abandoned the protection of the river to march through the "howling wilderness" of northwestern Louisiana.

Taylor soon decided to ignore Smith's orders and confront Banks near Mansfield, a small village south of Shreveport. During the early morning hours of 8 April, Taylor formed his 5,300 infantry into a line at Sabine Crossroads, a strategic intersection three miles southeast of Mansfield. Partially concealed in the edge of a pine forest, Brigadier General James T. Major's dismounted cavalry anchored the left of the line next to Brigadier General Alfred Mouton's division as Major General John G. Walker's Texas Division formed on the right. Twelve artillery batteries and 3,000 cavalry brought Taylor's strength to about 8,800.

Ignoring warnings from his cavalry commander, Brigadier General Albert L. Lee, Banks continued to Sabine Crossroads. Although the Federals numbered nearly 18,000, their deployment was dictated by the narrow road, barely wide enough for a single wagon. Lee was particularly concerned over the placement of the supply trains. His own, numbering three hundred wagons, stretched three miles to his rear and blocked both retreat and reinforcements. Still, Lee continued his advance and, pushing back Confederate skirmishers, reached Honeycutt Hill, a low wooded ridge, late in the morning. Supported by two infantry brigades, Lee's forces numbered some 4,800 men.

By noon Union and Confederate troops faced one another across a broad field from positions along opposing tree lines. As more Union troops and artillery arrived, the afternoon began to unfold into a series of probing cavalry actions interspersed by artillery duels. Shortly after 4 P.M. an impatient Taylor finally ordered his men forward. Crossing the field under a "murderous fire of artillery and musketry" Mouton's and Walker's Divisions crashed into the Federal positions, which soon crumbled in the ensuing hand-to-hand fighting. Mouton was killed in the assault and command of his division passed to the commander of his Texas Brigade, the French-born brigadier general Camille de Polignac. As Polignac and Walker continued their attack, the Union resistance collapsed and soon deteriorated into a rout with Confederate troops enveloping both flanks. Panicked troops poured to the rear along the already wagon-jammed road, abandoning their transports to the advancing Confederates.

The timely arrival, however, of Brigadier General William H. Emory's division some three miles to the rear of the initial battle saved Banks's force from complete disaster. Shortly before dusk he expertly deployed his troops along Chapman Hill, a steep ridge fronted by an orchard known as Pleasant Grove. Despite repeated Confederate attacks, Emory held his position, thus protecting the remainder of the Federal train and the troops trapped by the narrow road.

Taylor was convinced he had won a decisive victory. The action had cost Banks 113 killed, 581 wounded, and 1,541 missing—a total of 2,235 men. In addition, the Confederates captured hundreds of small arms, twenty artillery pieces, nearly 1,000 draft animals, and 250 wagons.

Taylor's losses were also heavy—approximately 1,500 out of his original 8,800 men. Yet the battle of Mansfield had shaken Banks and convinced him to terminate his invasion plans and return to Alexandria. Although the Federals would win the battle the following day at Pleasant Hill, the Red River campaign had failed at Mansfield.

—*Jeff Kinard*

See also Banks, Nathaniel P.; Pleasant Hill, Battle of; Red River Campaign.

For further reading:
Barr, Alwynn. *Polignac's Texas Brigade* (1964).
Johnson, Ludwell H. *Red River Campaign: Politics and Cotton in the Civil War* (1958).
Kerby, Robert L. *Kirby Smith's Confederacy: The Trans-Mississippi South, 1863–1865* (1972).
Parrish, T. Michael. *Richard Taylor: Soldier Prince of Dixie* (1992).

MARINE CORPS, C.S.A.

The Confederate States Marine Corps was legislated into being by the Act of 16 March 1861, by the Provisional Congress of the Confederate States of America at Montgomery, Alabama. The organizational instructions of the act called for six (later amended to ten) distinct companies.

Nineteen of the twenty officers of United States Marines who resigned their commissions in 1861, or were dismissed for attempting to do so, became the nucleus of the Confederate States Marine Corps. The rest of the fifty-seven men who held commissions as officers of the Confederate States Marines were appointed from the U.S. Navy, from civilian life, or from volunteer regiments of the Provisional Army. Lloyd James Beall, a graduate of West Point, Class of 1830, was appointed colonel and commandant of the Confederate States Marine Corps on 23 May 1861, and he held that post until the end of the war. Due to the loss or destruction of most official records of the Corps, no accurate tally of enlisted Marines is possible. However, what records that have survived indicate that upwards of 1,200 men were recruited.

During the course of the war, Confederate States Marines performed duties normally associated with their

service. The naval stations at Richmond and Norfolk, Virginia; Wilmington and Charlotte, North Carolina; Charleston, South Carolina; Savannah, Georgia; Pensacola, Florida; Jackson, Mississippi; and New Orleans, Louisiana, all at one time or another had the protection of Marine sentries.

Nearly every major Confederate States man-of-war, including the commerce raiders CSS *Sumter*, *Florida*, *Georgia*, *Tallahassee*, *Chickamauga*, and *Shenandoah*, carried a Marine Guard to enforce discipline among the crew and to man one or more of the ship's guns. Marines assigned to warships took part in the battle of Port Royal, South Carolina, 7 November 1861 (CSS *Savannah*, *Sampson*, and *Huntress*); the battle of New Orleans, 24 April 1862 (CSS *McRae*); the battles of Hampton Roads, 8–9 March 1862 (CSS *Virginia*, *Jamestown*, and *Patrick Henry*); the battle of Wassaw Sound, Georgia, 17 June 1863 (CSS *Atlanta*); the engagement at New Inlet, North Carolina, 6–7 May 1864 (CSS *Raleigh*); the Battle of Mobile Bay, 5 August 1864 (CSS *Tennessee*, *Morgan*, and *Gaines*); and the operations against Federal forces at Spanish Fort and Fort Blakely, Alabama, 27 March–9 April 1865 (CSS *Nashville* and *Morgan*).

Marines were also trained as naval artillerists and manned heavy ordnance on Ship Island, Mississippi; Pensacola, Florida; Drewry's Bluff, Virginia; Battery Semmes on the James River, Virginia; and the Shell Bluff Battery on the Savannah River, Georgia.

Confederate States Marines were utilized as a rapid deployment force, being detached from their main post at Drewry's Bluff and sent to the defense of Charleston Harbor in February 1863. They also took part in the proposed expedition to liberate the Confederate prisoners of war at Point Lookout, Maryland, in July 1864.

On four occasions, Marines were part of "cutting out" operations launched against Federal warships: the abortive January 1863 expedition to capture a blockader off Mobile, Alabama; the capture of USS *Underwriter* at New Bern, North Carolina, on 2 February 1864; the capture of USS *Water Witch* off Savannah, Georgia, on 3 June 1864; and the failed attempt of February 1865 to cut through Federal lines at Petersburg and capture a gunboat to bombard the supply base of the Army of the Potomac at City Point, Virginia.

Battle honors were won by Marines acting as infantry at the battles of Drewry's Bluff, 15 May 1862 and 12–14 May 1864; the engagement at Fort Johnson on James Island, Charleston Harbor, 10 July 1864; the fight at Fort Gaines, Mobile Bay, 5 August 1864; the defense of the Ogeechee Battery near King's Bridge on the Ogeechee River outside Savannah, Georgia, 10–20 December 1864; the battles of Fort Fisher, 23–25 December 1864 and 13–15 January 1865; the battle of Sayler's Creek, Virginia, 6 April 1865; and the battle of Fort Blakely, Alabama, 9 April 1865.

Although there were never more than 550 men in its ranks at any given time, the value of the Confederate States Marine Corps as a force in readiness capable of passing from its traditional role to whatever the military situation demanded at a moment's notice far exceeded its small numbers.

—*David M. Sullivan*

See also Blakely, Alabama; Drewry's Bluff, Battle of; Marine Corps, U.S.A.; Sayler's Creek/Harper's Farm, Battle of.
For further reading:
Donelly, Ralph W. *Biographical Sketches Of The Commissioned Officers Of The Confederate States Marine Corps* (1983).
———. *The Confederate States Marine Corps: The Rebel Leathernecks* (1989).
Pacious, Daniel M. "Seawolves of the Confederacy: The Origin, Development, and Operations of the Confederate States Marines Corps" (Thesis, 1993).
Still, William N., ed. *The Confederate Navy: The Ships, Men And Organization, 1861–65* (1997).

MARINE CORPS, U.S.A.

The U.S. Marine Corps' crucial problem in the Civil War was the quality of its officer corps, a problem aggravated by the defection of its Southern officers. Like the other services, the Marine Corps lost one-third (twenty of sixty-three) of its officers. For many, loyalty to state or region meant more than loyalty to country. Very few enlisted men quit, but four of its thirteen captains resigned or were dismissed, including George H. Terrett, who had received a brevet promotion to major for gallantry in action during the Mexican-American War. Terrett, the hero of the battle for Mexico City during the war with Mexico, submitted his resignation on 22 April. It was declined, and he was dismissed by order of the president on 6 May. Terrett accepted a commission as a colonel in the provisional Army of Virginia, which he held until 22 August 1861. In the meantime, he was commissioned a major of Confederate States Marines to rank from 20 June 1861, and he commanded the Confederate States Marine Battalion at Drewry's Bluff for most of the war. Eight of the twenty first lieutenants and seven of the twenty second lieutenants resigned or were dismissed, including John Simms, who had been brevetted for his service in the Mexican-American War (at Chapultepec), and Israel Greene, who struck down John Brown at Harper's Ferry in 1859.

Many Virginians who "went South" were on sea duty when their state left the Union. Captain Robert Tansill, commanding the Marine Guard aboard the USS *Congress*, forwarded his resignation when word of secession reached the southern hemisphere. Upon the return of the *Congress* from Brazil on 23 August 1861, Tansill was notified that his resignation had been declined, that he had been dismissed, and that he was under arrest. He was soon confined at Fort Warren in Boston harbor as a

A Marine battalion in front of the Commandant's House at the Washington Marine Barracks, April 1864 (*Library of Congress*)

prisoner of war. Tansill was held until 10 January 1862. After his release, he went to Richmond and accepted a commission as captain of Confederate States Marines to rank from 22 January 1862, which he held until 15 February 1862. He then resigned to become colonel of the 2d Virginia Battalion.

The Marine Corps senior officers were an even greater problem. Although Congress increased the number of field-grade officers in 1861, these officers had learned too much and forgotten too little to be of much value in a new "modern" war. All were in their sixties, too old for field service, but there were both army and navy officers of similar age who served with great valor and imagination. The problem with the senior Marine officers was that they saw their role as that of administrators; of this group only John G. Reynolds and Jacob Zeilin, both combat veterans of the Mexican-American War, served as battalion commanders in the field. (The others did little beyond their routine duties and returned to such habits as court-martialing one another on petty charges.)

When John Harris died in 1864, Secretary of the Navy Gideon Welles, in despair, selected Zeilin, a junior major at fifty-nine, as commandant and retired the rest, although they actually remained on active duty in their comfortable jobs throughout the war. Zeilin was an improvement over Harris, but neither he nor his senior officers had much influence in the Navy Department.

To recoup corps losses and meet expanded wartime requirements, Congress increased the strength of the corps from 43 to 91 officers and from 1,800 to 3,074 enlisted men. (The corps' numbers never exceeded 3,900 men at any one time during the war.) Unfortunately, these numbers were never adequate to meet the demands made on the corps throughout the Civil War. By the war's end in 1865, 65 Marines had been killed in action, 13 had died of wounds suffered in battle, 203 had died of disease, 30 had died as the result of accidents, 175 had been wounded in action, 280 had been taken prisoner, and 24 had died while in the hands of the enemy. Of the 2,210 who had deserted, 573 had returned to duty on their own accord or by apprehension.

Early in January 1861, President James Buchanan tried to send reinforcements to the beleaguered Federal garrison at Fort Sumter in Charleston harbor. The relief expedition, partly composed of marines, was turned back by the Confederate defenses in the outer harbor. When the war broke out in April, a force of marines together with Union soldiers landed and occupied Fort Pickens in Florida until a larger garrison of troops arrived. (Fort Pickens remained in Union hands throughout the rest of the war.) And on 20 April, sailors, with the help of

marines from the Norfolk, Virginia, barracks and from the *Cumberland, Pennsylvania,* and *Pawnee* were forced to destroy the Norfolk navy yard as a result of Virginia's secession. Other marines who were garrisoned at Fort McHenry, Baltimore, and Fort Washington, Maryland, were assigned to defend the Washington Navy Yard.

In July 1861, Irvin McDowell's force of 35,000 troops included a battalion of marines under the command of Major John G. Reynolds when it left Washington to fight the battle of First Bull Run. Marines went into the fight at Bull Run three times, and were prepared to return to the battle a fourth time when the Union line was rolled up. According to Daniel M. Conrad, surgeon of the 2d Virginia Infantry, the marines made the farthest penetration of the Confederate lines that day. Marines also formed the first rear guard when the Federals eventually retreated.

The first major operation undertaken by the U.S. Navy was to check Confederate privateering and blockade running out of Pamlico Sound, North Carolina. To accomplish this, the two forts guarding Hatteras Inlet, Forts Clark and Hatteras, had to be taken. The army attempted a landing near Fort Clark, but the weather prevented it. Instead, on 28 August 1861, an assault force composed of marine guards from several ships of the fleet and soldiers stormed Fort Clark. With bombardment support from the navy, the fort fell. The next day, Fort Hatteras capitulated.

The Union's next objective was Port Royal, South Carolina, a haven for blockade runners. If captured, it could serve as an advance base for Union forces blockading Charleston and Savannah. Fort Walker on Hilton Head and Fort Beauregard opposite it on Bay Point defended the entrance to Port Royal Sound. Admiral Samuel F. Du Pont was put in charge of an armada composed of ships, soldiers, and a battalion of marines, who were on the Union transport vessel *Governor*. Yet nobody will ever know what would have developed from grouping a fleet marine battalion with a naval amphibious operation, for on 3 November a storm raked the force and sank the *Governor*. The marines from the battalion may not have participated in the actual attack on Port Royal, but they did play important roles. They manned the guns on their respective ships, and marines from the USS *Wabash* were among the landing force that took possession of Fort Walker.

In other November 1861 operations, marines from the *Santee* were part of a raiding party that boarded and destroyed the Confederate schooner *Royal Yacht* in the harbor of Galveston, Texas. Marines from the American steamer USS *San Jacinto,* operating in the Atlantic, boarded the British ship *Trent* and seized Confederate diplomats John Slidell and James Mason. During December 1861, marines from the *Dale* landed and destroyed a Confederate base in the Charleston area

after Union naval guns bombarded it. Later that month, the *Dale*'s marines tangled with Southerners in a brief fight on the South Edisto River in South Carolina.

In the early months of 1862, marines were serving in Florida. On 4 March, marines occupied Fernandina without opposition. Two weeks later, St. Augustine likewise fell without a fight to the marines of the *Wabash* and *Mohican*.

On 8 March, marines were on board the vessels in the waters off Hampton Roads that were attacked by the *Virginia* (the refitted *Merrimack*). The *Virginia* delivered devastating blows to the Union ships *Congress* and *Cumberland* that caused the deaths of several sailors and marines. (Throughout the attack on the *Cumberland*, its marines remained faithfully at their guns. The *Virginia* retired until the following day when it returned to do battle with the *Minnesota*. By that time, the Union's ironclad *Monitor* had arrived. A five-hour battle ensued between the two vessels, ending in a draw. Deprived of its base by the Confederate army's evacuation of Norfolk and with too much draft to retreat up the James River, the *Virginia* was run aground and blown up on 11 May.

Four days later, Union ships approached Drewry's Bluff on the James River about eight miles below Richmond. There they came under the fire of the Confederate shore batteries mounted on the bluff. The Union ship *Galena* was returning their fire when it received a hit that caused an explosion. Marine corporal John Mackie rallied the survivors, carried off the dead and wounded, and got one of the *Galena*'s guns back in action. As a result of Mackie's heroic actions, he became the first marine to be awarded the Medal of Honor. By the time the Civil War ended, 17 marines were awarded this prestigious medal.

In other actions during 1862, marines were on board the vessels commanded by Captain David G. Farragut that took New Orleans. Once Farragut's force had run the batteries along the Mississippi, he dropped anchor and ordered a marine detachment ashore. The next day, the marines landed, marched through a crowd of hostiles, and occupied the U.S. mint. There, they lowered the Confederate flag and replaced it with the flag of the United States. On 29 April, all the marines landed and formed a battalion. The battalion then proceeded to seize the customs house and the city hall. By 1 May, General Benjamin F. Butler occupied the city, and the last of the marines left. With New Orleans in their hands, Union forces could increase their activities along the Mississippi River.

During August 1863, the marines were called upon to assist Union forces in an attack on Fort Wagner, South Carolina. The marines were to make an amphibious assault to the rear of Fort Wagner while the army assaulted from the front. The plan was changed, and the marines were sent ashore to protect the troops digging the parallels to the fort in preparation for a frontal assault. After the Confederates evacuated Fort Wagner and word reached the Union lines, the marines were the first to enter the work.

In September, marines formed part of an expeditionary force organized by Rear Admiral John A. Dahlgren to assault Fort Sumter. The attack itself took place during the night of 8–9 September, and marines constituted one-fourth of the attacking force, 133 officers and men, suffering 44 casualties.

Throughout 1864, marines continued to remain active by serving on board ships. Marines landed at Murrell's Inlet near Charleston and destroyed a Confederate schooner, and they were on the *Kearsarge* when it destroyed the commerce raider *Alabama*. (The marine guard assigned to the *Kearsarge* fired the first and last shots of the engagement against the *Alabama*.) During July, marines helped defend Washington against Jubal Early's forces while other marines from Philadelphia were protecting the railroad bridge over the Susquehanna River at Havre de Grace, Maryland, which linked Baltimore with Washington and Philadelphia. In land actions during November and December, marines joined the army in an attempt to cut the Charleston-Savannah railroad line. (The actions against the Charleston-Savannah rail line were named the battle of Honey Hill and the battle of Tulifinney Crossroads, both taking place in South Carolina.) After several futile attempts, the army abandoned its efforts, and the marine battalion disbanded and the men returned to their ships.

With Union forces controlling the harbors at Mobile, Charleston, and New Orleans, there was only one major port open to Confederate blockade runners in December 1864: Wilmington, North Carolina, which was protected by Fort Fisher. In January 1865, the Union launched an attack against Fort Fisher in a combined operation of soldiers, sailors, and marines. After confusion and hard fighting, the army finally took the fort. With the fall of Fort Fisher, the Union's blockade sealed off the Confederacy, and defeat was imminent.

The American Civil War demonstrated that marines had no consistent role in battle. Many fought aboard ships as gun crews and as sharpshooters. Only in a few isolated incidents did the marines fight on land, and then only in small numbers. Those who did fight on land were either part of a ship's landing force or directly assigned to the Union army. These "land units" had neither the doctrine nor the training for amphibious assaults under fire. The Marine Corps' position was that its purpose remained what it had always been: to furnish ship's guards for naval vessels to enforce shipboard discipline, operate the guns, and join landing parties for very limited operations ashore. To assume any other mission would be to risk amalgamation with the army, which actually was considered by Congress in 1863 and 1864.

Thus, the Marine Corps failed to find a wartime function for itself, a failure that threatened its very existence.

—*Michael S. Davis*

See also Blockade of C.S.A.; Navy, U.S.A.

For further reading:
Hayes, John D. "The Marine Corps in the American Civil War." *Shipmate, U.S. Naval Alumni Association Monthly* (1960).
Millett, Allan R. *Semper Fidelis: The History of the United States Marine Corps* (1980).
Moskin, J. Robert. *The U.S. Marine Corps Story* (1992).
Nalty, Bernard C. *United States Marines at Harper's Ferry and in the Civil War* (1966).
Ryan, Jeffrey T. "Some Notes on the Civil War Era Marine Corps." *Civil War Regiments* (1992).
Sullivan, David M. *The United States Marines in the Civil War* (1997–1999).

MARKS' MILLS, BATTLE OF
(25 April 1864)

The Confederate victory at Marks' Mills, Arkansas, forced Major General Frederick Steele's Union army to abandon its most recent conquest, the fortified city of Camden, and retreat hastily to Little Rock.

The defeat of a Union foraging expedition at Poison Spring on 18 April 1864 posed a grave threat to Steele and his 13,500 remaining troops at nearby Camden. The Federals were seventy miles inside enemy territory and running short of food. Partial relief came on 20 April, when a Union supply train from Pine Bluff arrived with ten days' worth of provisions. Two days later, Steele ordered an enlarged train of 240 wagons to return to Pine Bluff for more rations.

To avoid a repetition of the Poison Spring disaster, Steele assigned Lieutenant Colonel Francis M. Drake and a reinforced brigade of 1,420 men to guard the train. Drake commanded 1,200 infantry from the 43d Indiana, 36th Iowa, and 77th Ohio Regiments; 240 troopers from the 1st Indiana and 7th Missouri Cavalry; and four artillery pieces. The size of his column was swollen by 300 runaway slaves and a large number of white sutlers, cotton speculators, and Unionist refugees. A relief party of 150 cavalry from Pine Bluff rendezvoused with Drake on the morning of 25 April, raising his total fighting force to 1,690 personnel.

By then, thousands of other cavalrymen were hot on Drake's trail, but they wore Rebel gray or butternut. Learning of the supply train's movements on 24 April, Brigadier General James F. Fagan moved to interpose his 4,000 Confederate troopers between Drake and Pine Bluff. Racing along a parallel route, the Confederates succeeded in passing Drake and heading him off in less than twenty-four hours.

Early on 25 April, Fagan ordered Brigadier General William L. Cabell and his Arkansas division to block the Federals at Marks' Mills near where the Warren Road

joined the Camden–Pine Bluff Road. Fagan also directed Brigadier General Joseph O. Shelby to take a provisional division of Missourians and Arkansans on a wide arc to strike the Union column in the flank and rear. Although Cabell's two brigades attacked in an uncoordinated fashion, Fagan succeeded in pulling off a classic pincers movement.

One of Cabell's brigades collided with the 43d Indiana, the Union advance guard, at 8:00 A.M. Drake brought up the 36th Iowa and all his cavalry to meet this threat, but the impetuous Arkansans, fighting dismounted, managed to push the Federals back on their wagons. Stationed at the rear of the train, the 77th Ohio found itself isolated from the other Union units when elements of Cabell's division lapped around Drake's right flank. As Drake tried to organize a cavalry counterattack to open communications with the 77th Ohio, a bullet tore through his left thigh. He soon fell from his horse in a faint from loss of blood and was taken prisoner. Around the same time, Shelby pounced on the disorganized Federals from the north in an unstoppable mounted charge and completed Fagan's triumph.

The Confederates probably killed no more than 100 Union soldiers at Marks' Mills, but they captured at least 1,300 more and all 240 of Drake's wagons. Fagan's losses included 41 killed, 108 wounded, and 144 missing.

Of the 300 runaway slaves who had hoped to follow Drake to freedom, only 150 were taken into Confederate custody. A surviving officer from the 36th Iowa Infantry revealed what the victorious Arkansans and Missourians did to the others: "They shot down our Colored servents & teamsters & others what ware following to get from bondage as they would shoot sheep dogs....The Rebs pointed out to me a point of woods where they told me they had killed eighty odd negroes men women & children." This report received confirmation from Shelby's adjutant, who recalled: "The battle-field was sickening to behold. No orders, threats, or commands could restrain the men from vengeance on the negroes, and they were piled in great heaps about the wagons, in the tangled brushwood, and upon the muddy and trampled road."

Marks' Mills rendered Camden an untenable position for Steele's Union army. Informed that 8,000 enemy infantry had come up from Louisiana, Steele now realized that to linger at Camden meant that his army could be encircled and starved into surrender.

Interestingly, Marks' Mills did not harm Francis Drake's reputation. He left the Union Army a brevet brigadier general. In 1895, Iowa voters elected him to a term as governor. Today, Drake University in Des Moines bears his name.

—*Gregory J. W. Urwin*

See also Fagan, James F.; Shelby, Joseph O.; Steele, Frederick.
For further reading:
Bearss, Edwin C. *Steele's Retreat from Camden and the Battle of*

Jenkins' Ferry (1967).
Christ, Mark K., ed. *Rugged and Sublime: The Civil War in Arkansas* (1994).
Kelly, Orr, and Mary Davies Kelly. *Dream's End: Two Iowa Brothers in the Civil War* (1998).
Richards, Ira Don. "The Engagement at Marks' Mills." *Arkansas Historical Quarterly* (1960).
Urwin, Gregory J. W. "'We Cannot Treat Negroes…as Prisoners of War': Racial Atrocities and Reprisals in Civil War Arkansas." *Civil War History* (1996).

MARMADUKE, JOHN SAPPINGTON
(1833–1887)
Confederate general

John Marmaduke was born in Arrow Rock, Missouri, the son of Meredith Miles Marmaduke and Lavinia Sappington Marmaduke. John Marmaduke's father was active in Missouri politics and served a term as governor while John was a boy. The younger Marmaduke was educated in local Missouri schools and attended Yale and Harvard Universities before accepting an appointment to the U.S. Military Academy. He graduated thirtieth of thirty-eight in the class of 1857. After being commissioned into the 7th Infantry, Marmaduke participated in Albert Sidney Johnston's Utah expedition.

After this campaign he was posted in New Mexico, where he was when the Civil War began. After returning home on leave, Marmaduke resigned his commission and accepted a colonelcy in the pro-Confederate state militia. Soon fighting at the battle of Boonville, he accepted a commission in the Confederate army and was stationed in Arkansas. He rose quickly from lieutenant to lieutenant colonel and became colonel of the 3d Missouri by the end of 1861. He was commended for his actions in leading his regiment at Shiloh in April 1862. He was wounded at Shiloh, and for his bravery there and at Corinth in October he was promoted in November 1862 to brigadier general.

In December 1862, Marmaduke commanded a cavalry brigade of Thomas Hindman's division at Prairie Grove, where he distinguished himself in an enveloping maneuver of one of the Federal positions early in the battle. The following month, Marmaduke led his brigade in a raid out of Arkansas into southern Missouri. He repeated the feat in April 1863. On 4 July 1863, Marmaduke commanded a cavalry division in Sterling Price's unsuccessful attack on Helena, Arkansas, and commanded his division in the unsuccessful defense of Little Rock in September 1863. On 6 September 1863, Marmaduke fought a duel with one of his own brigade commanders, Lucius March Walker. Walker was killed in the duel, and Marmaduke was temporarily incarcerated for the action. He was released and never charged with an offense. The cause of the duel was never officially reported, though there had been aspersions regarding

Walker's courage since the fall of 1862. In October 1863, Marmaduke was back in action at Pine Bluff, Arkansas.

In the spring of 1864, Marmaduke commanded his division in the Red River campaign and in the fall accompanied Sterling Price in his raid into Missouri and eastern Kansas. Marmaduke fought at Big Blue on 22 October, but was captured on 25 October at Marais des Cygnes. He remained a prisoner of war until the summer of 1865. During his incarceration, Marmaduke was promoted to major general.

After the war, Marmaduke traveled for a while in Europe before settling in St. Louis. He worked in the insurance business and edited an agricultural journal before being elected governor in 1884. He died in office.

—*David S. Heidler and Jeanne T. Heidler*

See also Helena, Battle of; Prairie Grove; Price's Missouri Raid.
For further reading:
Marmaduke, John S. *The Battle of Chalk Bluff: An Account of General John S. Marmaduke's Second Missouri Raid* (1994).

MARSHALL, HUMPHREY
(1812–1872)
Confederate general and congressman

Born to John James Marshall and Ann Reed Birney Marshall in Frankfort, Kentucky, Humphrey Marshall attended the U.S. Military Academy and graduated forty-second of forty-five in the class of 1832. Not finding the military life to his liking, Marshall resigned his commission in 1833 to study law. He began his practice in Louisville and became a planter outside that town. He was also active in local politics and militia. At the outbreak of the Mexican-American War, his militia ties enabled him quickly to raise a cavalry regiment that became the 1st Kentucky Cavalry. As it colonel, Marshall led the regiment to a magnificent showing at the battle of Buena Vista in February 1847.

Marshall's Mexican-American War service propelled him into larger political circles, and from 1849 to 1852 and from 1855 to 1859 he served terms in the U.S. House of Representatives. From 1852 to 1854 he served as U.S. minister to China.

Back in Kentucky, Marshall was a strong supporter of states' rights but an opponent of secession. Upon the secession of the lower South in early 1861, he worked to maintain Kentucky neutrality, though he had been a supporter of John C. Breckinridge in the election of 1860. By the fall of 1861, Marshall despaired of maintaining Kentucky neutrality, and when offered a brigadier general commission in the Confederate army, he accepted. Marshall was given command of the Confederate Army of Southwestern Virginian, later the Army of East Tennessee, and operating out of that area he sought to secure the eastern part of Kentucky for the

Confederacy. He fought James Garfield at Pound Gap in March 1862. Preferring to operate alone, Marshall pestered Jefferson Davis in the early summer of 1862 for a completely independent command but was told that was not possible. Marshall resigned in a pique, but was persuaded to withdraw his resignation. He fought in Braxton Bragg's Kentucky campaign of the fall of 1862 and then returned to southwestern Virginia and eastern Kentucky. When sent to Chattanooga in late April 1863, he resigned again and in the fall was elected to the second Confederate Congress.

In the Confederate Congress, Marshall became part of the Davis opposition, especially as a member of the House Military Affairs Committee. He was very critical of Bragg's handling of Kentucky and agitated for a greater Confederate effort to take control of the state.

With the evacuation of Richmond in the spring of 1865, Marshall fled to Texas to avoid capture. After the war, he returned to Louisville and resumed his law practice. He died in Louisville.

—*David S. Heidler and Jeanne T. Heidler*

See also Congress, C.S.A.; Kentucky.
For further reading:
Harrison, Lowell H. *The Civil War in Kentucky* (1975).
Marshall, Humphrey. *Speeches of Hon. Humphrey Marshall & Hon. B. F. Hallett, in the City of Washington on the Nomination of Breckinridge and Lane: Speech of Hon. Humphrey Marshall, of Kentucky* (1860).

MARTIN, WILLIAM THOMPSON
(1823–1910)
Confederate general

Born in Glasgow, Kentucky, to John Henderson Martin and Emily Monroe Kerr Martin, William Martin was educated at Centre College in Kentucky before studying law and opening a practice in Natchez, Mississippi. He became active in state Whig politics and served as the district attorney in Natchez until 1860. As secession loomed, he urged restraint, but when the state seceded he raised a cavalry company and became its captain. In August 1861, he and his company were sent to Manassas, Virginia.

During the fall of 1861, Martin was promoted to major and given command of the Jeff Davis Legion that consisted of six Mississippi cavalry companies. The following spring he was promoted lieutenant colonel and commanded the legion in the Peninsula campaign particularly in "Jeb" Stuart's ride around George McClellan's army. During that raid, Martin and his legion brought up the rear of the ride, and for his actions during the expedition, Stuart recommended that Martin be promoted to colonel.

For the remainder of the summer, Martin commanded a regiment of Stuart's cavalry, though at the battle of

Antietam, he served as an aide to Robert E. Lee. On 2 December 1862, Martin was promoted to brigadier general, and at the end of the month participated in the raid on Occoquan, Virginia, which scattered Union cavalry. Shortly thereafter, he was transferred west to command a cavalry brigade.

After reporting to Major Joe Wheeler in March 1863, Martin led his brigade in the raids on Louisville and Nashville in April and then in the Tullahoma campaign in June through July 1863. In September 1863, he fought at Chickamauga and through the remainder of the year screened the movements of Confederates under James Longstreet in eastern Tennessee. During that time, in November 1863, Martin was promoted to major general.

In February 1864, Martin was ordered to report to Lieutenant General Joseph E. Johnston at Dalton, Georgia, where he would command a cavalry division of Joe Wheeler's cavalry corps. Through the spring and summer of 1864, Martin led his division in the Atlanta campaign and then accompanied John Bell Hood into Tennessee in the fall. He fought at the battle of Spring Hill at the end of November 1864. Shortly after that engagement, Martin was sent to command the District of Northwest Mississippi, a command he held for the remainder of the war. The primary job of Martin and his division during those last months was to protect the local citizens from the scavengers and bandits who had descended on the area.

After the war, Martin resumed his law practice in Natchez and became involved in state Democratic politics. He participated in several state constitutional conventions over the remainder of his life and served in the Mississippi state senate. He also became prominent in the railroad industry. He died in Natchez.

—*David S. Heidler and Jeanne T. Heidler*

See also Peninsula Campaign; Stuart's Ride around McClellan; Wheeler, Joseph.

For further reading:
Dyer, John P. *"Fightin' Joe" Wheeler* (1941).
Miller, William J., ed. *The Peninsula Campaign of 1862: Yorktown to the Seven Days* (1993–1996).

MARTINDALE, JOHN HENRY
(1815–1881)
Union general

Born the son of U.S. congressman Henry C. Martindale in Sandy Hill, New York, John Henry Martindale was educated locally before receiving an appointment to the U.S. Military Academy in 1831. He graduated third of fifty-six in the class of 1835 and was commissioned into the dragoons. Because of his desire to serve in the engineers and his opportunity to become an engineer with a New York railroad company, he resigned his commission in 1836. Not finding engineering to his liking after leaving the army, he entered the legal profession. Over the next two decades, he became one of New York's most prominent attorneys, practicing first in Batavia and then in Rochester.

At the outbreak of the Civil War, Martindale traveled throughout the state recruiting volunteers for Federal service. He also wrote to the Abraham Lincoln administration, initially to Postmaster General Montgomery Blair, making a number of suggestions that he believed would bring a quicker end to the war. First, he suggested that regular officers be detailed to volunteer units to speed the training process. Second, he recommended that as many merchant vessels as possible be brought into the Union navy to allow for a swift implementation of the blockade of the southern coast. Third, he counseled that the defense of Washington should be paramount in the administration's plans. Fourth, he advised the administration to graduate the two upper classes at West Point so that the new second lieutenants could be sent home to train volunteers. Blair passed Martindale's letter to Secretary of War Simon Cameron, who wrote a dismissive reply to Martindale. The suggestions, however, were later implemented in one form or another by Cameron's successor, Edwin Stanton.

Martindale continued his recruiting efforts and in August 1861 accepted a brigadier general's commission in the volunteer army. Initially Martindale commanded a brigade in Washington's defenses, and in October was transferred to command of a brigade of Fitz John Porter's division of the Army of the Potomac. Martindale commanded this unit throughout the Peninsula campaign in the spring and summer of 1862. He fought at the siege of Yorktown and at Hanover Court House and the Seven Days' battles. During the latter part of that series of battles, Confederate forces at Malvern Hill pinned him and his brigade down. For a time during the twenty-four hours that he and his men were under fire, it appeared that they would have to surrender or face annihilation. Finally an opening presented itself, and they were able to evacuate their position on 2 July. After the battle, however, Porter, now commander of V Corps, heard rumors that Martindale had tried to persuade his senior officers to surrender. As a result of the rumors, Porter requested that Martindale be relieved of his command.

By the time Porter proffered charges against him, Martindale was dangerously ill with typhoid fever that he had contracted shortly after retreating with his brigade to Harrison's Landing. He was unable to return to duty until the fall, at which time a court of inquiry cleared him of all charges. Shortly thereafter he requested that he be relieved of duty under Porter who was soon to undergo a court-martial of his own that would remove him from the army.

After leaving the Army of the Potomac, Martindale was assigned to the defenses of Washington. For the first few months of this new assignment, Martindale served on boards including the Irvin McDowell Court of Inquiry and the board that was convened in December 1862 to revise the Articles of War. In February 1863, he was made the military governor of the District of Columbia, a position he would hold until the spring of 1864.

As military governor, Martindale had a number of duties, not the least complicated of which was acting as a liaison between the military and the civilian sector of the city. His extensive legal background was beneficial to him in these activities. In addition, he also aided in the administration of the prison facilities for civilian political prisoners, a task that had him constantly working to alleviate the overcrowding in such places. Still smarting under the accusations made by Fitz John Porter, Martindale also spent much of his time in Washington soliciting written versions of what had transpired at Malvern Hill from the other officers who had been present.

Even though his health had never fully recovered from his bout with typhoid fever in 1862, Martindale longed for another field command and in May 1864 was given his wish when he was transferred to command a division of the Army of the James. Commanding 2d Division, XVIII Corps, Martindale fought at Bermuda Hundred in May before being sent with this division to join the Army of the Potomac. He led them at Cold Harbor and then in the initial stages of the siege of Petersburg. Briefly in July 1864 he commanded XVIII Corps. The constant movement and campaigning since his return to field service, however, had taken their toll, and Martindale's health failed. In September 1864 he was forced to resign his commission and return home to recover his health. After the war was over, he was breveted major general of volunteers for war service and gallantry at Malvern Hill.

Martindale returned to Rochester, New York, where after convalescing he resumed his law practice. In 1866 he became the state's attorney general, a position he held for one term. He also served on the board of the National Asylum for Disabled Volunteer soldiers. His health, however, was still precarious, and in 1881 he traveled abroad in an effort to recover. He died on 13 December 1881 in Nice, France. His remains were returned to Batavia, New York, for burial.

—*David S. Heidler and Jeanne T. Heidler*

See also Bermuda Hundred Campaign; Malvern Hill, Battle of.
For further reading:

Robertson, William Glenn. *Back Door to Richmond: The Bermuda Hundred Campaign, April–June 1864* (1987).
Schiller, Herbert M. *The Bermuda Hundred Campaign* (1988).
Sears, Stephen W. *To the Gates of Richmond: The Peninsula Campaign* (1992).

MARTINSBURG, VIRGINIA
(14 June 1863)

As Robert E. Lee put the Army of Northern Virginia on the move for his second invasion of the North, Richard Ewell's corps led the march behind the Blue Ridge and upon Union garrisons in the mountainous terrain. Major General Robert E. Rodes's division drove Union forces out of Berryville on 13 June and the next day proceeded to Martinsburg, Virginia (now West Virginia) to cut communications between Harper's Ferry and the main Federal force at Winchester. In the move to Martinsburg, Confederate cavalry under Brigadier General Albert G. Jenkins pushed into Bunker Hill on the night of 13 June and fought a small skirmish there with Union soldiers barricaded in some houses. The cavalry moved on Martinsburg the next morning.

At Martinsburg, Colonel Benjamin F. Smith of the 126th Ohio Volunteer Infantry was in command of the 3d Brigade, 1st Division, VIII Corps, numbering about 1,500 men. Smith had made preparations for an attack by sending most of the provisions stored in the town by rail to Harper's Ferry and Baltimore. The place was not nearly as important as its contents, and that was evidenced by the dispatching of Brigadier General Daniel Tyler and his staff from VIII Corps headquarters in Baltimore. As chance would have it, Tyler arrived on the morning of 14 June about the same time rebel troopers did. Because Smith's forces were already engaged, Tyler deferred command and assumed the role of advisor.

Smith had his hands full. At 8:00 A.M. Jenkins had come upon Smith's mounted sentinels, who rushed into Martinsburg with the alarm that a large Confederate force was arriving from the south. Smith hastily took two infantry regiments, a battery of artillery, and a company of cavalry a mile out of town and placed them across the Winchester Road. His pickets, about another half-mile forward, were already taking fire. Jenkins might have overrun this hastily contrived defense—both Smith and Tyler expected him to—but Captain Thomas A. Maulsby's six-gun Independent West Virginia Battery fired with such effect that Jenkins paused and fell back out of range. At most, both sides exchanged scattered fire as Smith himself fell back to higher ground.

When news arrived about Confederates occupying Bunker Hill, Tyler concluded that Federal forces were trapped in Winchester and the best the Martinsburg garrison could now do was save itself. He ordered the baggage train to evacuate to Williamsport and into Pennsylvania. At noon, the Union commanders had decided to quit the region, but they wanted to give their baggage train a head start. In any case, they did not intend to surrender. When Jenkins sent a note demanding Smith's capitulation and pledging that rebel artillery would open on the town in an hour, Smith tersely replied that Martinsburg would not be surrendered. Jenkins could begin shelling whenever he liked, mused Smith, who added that he would "inform the inhabitants of your threats." When he did so, Martinsburg's citizens began streaming out of town. Jenkins, however, did not make good on his threat. Meanwhile, news from Winchester told of an attack underway there, so the Martinsburg garrison decided to retreat as soon as it could. Tyler was chagrined to discover, however, that all locomotives and railroad cars had been sent out of reach; those not lucky enough to be mounted would have to make it on foot.

Rodes arrived ahead of his infantry to find Jenkins stalled outside of town in front of Smith's defenses. Finally, by 5:00 P.M. Rodes had most of his infantry in place. Sending Jenkins to the left to enter Martinsburg and cut off Smith's retreat, he placed the Alabama Brigade on the right, George Doles and Alfred Iverson in the center, and Stephen Ramseur on the left. The Rebel artillery had already opened on Smith, though, and his tired, edgy men broke. The 106th New York threatened to panic the entire Union position, but Smith got them under control and managed a retreat toward Shepherdstown that at least was more confused than frantic. Maulsby's battery that had done so much good that day also succumbed to the sense of urgency. One gun was left dismounted, and the other five split up to get to the Potomac the best as everybody could. Four of the guns fell to Confederate capture. Most of the Union infantry finally collected on the Shepherdstown Road (the cavalry had headed for Williamsport) and reached the Potomac ford after midnight to pull into Harper's Ferry at 7 A.M. on 15 June. The night march had allowed them to slip Jenkins's pursuit.

Smith had held Martinsburg for most of the day against a superior force and had managed to clear almost everything of value from the town. Rodes took inventory of 6,000 bushels of grain, 400 rounds of rifled artillery ammunition, a couple of ambulance wagons, and about 200 prisoners, but that was all. The next day, as he moved his division toward Williamsport, he noticed that many of his men had no shoes. It was a widespread condition in the Army of Northern Virginia as it began the march into Pennsylvania. There was reportedly a shoe factory at Gettysburg.

—*David S. Heidler and Jeanne T. Heidler*

See also Berryville, Virginia; Jenkins, Albert G.; Milroy, Robert H.; Rodes, Robert E.; Winchester, Second Battle of.

For further reading:

Adams, Owen E. "Confederate Major General Robert E. Rodes: A Civil War Biography" (M.A. thesis, 1995).

Johnson, Freddie L., III. "Mountain Warrior: The Political and Military Career of Albert Gallatin Jenkins" Thesis (1993).

Steward, Michelle Lee. "Robert E. Rodes: Lee's Forgotten General" (M.A thesis, 1997).

Strother, David Hunter. *A Virginia Yankee in the Civil War: The Diaries of David Hunter Strother* (1961; reprint, 1998).

MARYLAND

A border state with divided loyalties that controlled Northern access to Washington, D.C., Maryland was a tumultuous place during the Civil War.

Secessionist sentiment was strongest on the eastern shore, along the western shore on the Chesapeake Bay south of the Susquehanna River, and along the Potomac border with Virginia. Unionism was strongest in northern, central, and western Maryland. The war's divisive nature and the skewing of the public record toward the Union make a precise accounting of Maryland residents who served in the Confederacy impossible. While 46,638 Marylanders served the Union, estimates of the total who served the Confederacy range from 4,580 to 25,000.

The firing on Fort Sumter, Lincoln's call for volunteers to protect Washington, D.C., the secession of Virginia, and the initial passage of Union troops through Maryland precipitated a series of events that fell like dominoes. To his credit, square-jawed, sixty-two-year-old Governor Thomas H. Hicks tried to steer a middle ground, but to no avail. The Baltimore riot on Friday, 19 April 1861 saw civilians attack Union troops who were moving through the city on their way to Washington. Three days later Union troops were sent to Annapolis to act as a police force and to secure an alternative rail line so that steamboats could bypass Baltimore to bring troops from Perryville on the north side of the Susquehanna River to Annapolis. On 27 April, Lincoln suspended the writ of habeas corpus between Washington and Philadelphia, and Union soldiers arrived in Baltimore on 13 May.

Over the next several months, Federal forces fanned out along the rail and telegraph lines, encamping at switching or relay stations, along canals, and at ferries and bridges. Simultaneously, they moved to quash all expression of support for, or sympathy with, secession and the Confederacy. Martial law was declared in Baltimore and Annapolis. Regardless of their station in life, Maryland residents were arrested or forcibly sent behind Confederate lines. Prosecession newspapers were shut down and their editors imprisoned or banished. Even churches were required to fly the Stars and Stripes. Hastily cobbled together during summer 1861, the Union Party nominated Augustus W. Bradford for the governorship and defeated the Democratic Party's states' rights candidate, Benjamin C. Howard, in November's election presided over by the military. Thereafter, Maryland's government cooperated with military and Federal officials.

In 1862 the war came to Maryland when the Army of Northern Virginia mounted an invasion that culminated in the battle of Antietam Creek (Sharpsburg). The invasion and its aftermath intensified and focused Maryland's feelings about the war. The state had to rebuild its infrastructure, increase hospital and prison capacities, stream-

General McClellan and the Army of the Potomac passing through Frederick, Maryland, on 12 September 1862
(*Library of Congress*)

line transportation and communication facilities, and provide more materiel for the war effort. But Antietam especially generated a wider public debate about maintaining the institution of slavery in Maryland.

During 1863, as Maryland was drawn more closely to the Union cause, this debate intensified. Most Marylanders became supporters of the Union in 1863 for three reasons. One was the continuing regulation by the military of public behavior. Loyalty oaths and flying the Stars and Stripes were required, and expressions favoring the Confederacy were prohibited. The second reason was that Maryland was not the battleground that it had been in 1862, nor would be again in 1864. Apart from Lee's army passing through Washington County on his way to Gettysburg and back, and relatively minor Confederate attacks on transportation and communication lines in Maryland close to the Virginia border, the state largely experienced the war as a repository for prisoners and infirmary for the wounded, especially after Gettysburg. Both situations strengthened the Union presence in the state. The third reason was the new prosperity that many Marylanders enjoyed by supplying the

Union military. Government contracts also had a salutary effect on employment. A voluntary Union League, formed to reflect and promote civilian support of the war effort, immediately took on a political character.

By 1864 Maryland's support for the Union had prepared her citizens to become the first in a slave state to discuss abolition seriously. Slave valuations had steadily declined since July 1863, when free blacks were recruited into the Union army, and by 1864 had virtually collapsed. Then in July, as seeming punishment for the Unionist convention in Annapolis that was drafting a new constitution, Confederate general Jubal Early raided the western part of state, ranging north of Baltimore and scouring the region between Annapolis and Washington. Early's men destroyed property, held small towns for ransom, and even defeated a Union force commanded by General Lew Wallace. Nevertheless, the Union cause prevailed. In October, carefully guarded polling stations admitted only those who took strict loyalty oaths. Union soldiers were given furloughs so they could return to cast their votes, and still others remaining in the field were allowed to vote by absentee

Confederate troops crossing the Potomac into Maryland, 11 June 1863 (*Library of Congress*)

A pontoon bridge across the Potomac at Berlin (present-day Brunswick), Maryland, October 1862
(Photograph by Alexander Gardner / *Library of Congress*)

ballot for the first time. By a meager margin of 375 votes, Maryland adopted its new constitution abolishing slavery. Only those counties situated in the southern parts of the western and eastern shores and containing abundant slave populations opposed emancipation. But

perhaps the most telling indicator of Maryland's ultimate Unionism were the 40,171 votes out of a total of 72,910 cast for Lincoln's new Union Party in November, a far cry from 1860 when Lincoln received a mere 2,294 out of 91,841 votes.

As in most Union states, by 1865 Marylanders were sick of the war and eager for it to end. Newspapers continued to print the mind-numbing casualties and to follow the Union military invasion of the South, but there now appeared reports of starvation and devastation that were absent before. The Sanitary Commission and the Christian Commission increasingly addressed the plight of civilian Southerners. Even as they celebrated the fall of Richmond, Marylanders were every bit as outraged as other Union states by the assassination of President Lincoln by the Marylander, John Wilkes Booth, and his Maryland accomplices.

Businesses closed and Southern sympathizers were arrested and imprisoned. Thousands upon thousands of people attended Lincoln's funeral procession when it stopped for five hours in Baltimore on Friday, 21 April 1865.

—Gary L. Browne

See also Antietam, Battle of; Baltimore Riot; Early's Washington Raid; Habeas Corpus, Writ of U.S.A.; Hicks, Thomas H.

For further reading:

Manakee, Harold R. Maryland in the Civil War (1961).
Newman, Harry Wright. Maryland and the Confederacy (1976).
Talbert, Bart Rhett. Maryland: The South's First Casualty (1995).
Toomey, Daniel Carroll. The Civil War in Maryland (1983).
Wagandt, Charles Lewis. The Mighty Revolution: Negro Emancipation in Maryland, 1862–1864 (1964).

MASON, JAMES MURRAY
(1798–1871)
Confederate envoy to Britain

James Murray Mason was born the second of ten children to John and Anna Maria Mason on 3 November 1798 in Georgetown, District of Columbia. The family's wealth and influence allowed him to obtain an elite education at the University of Pennsylvania and the College of William and Mary, where he studied law. He married Eliza Margaretta Chew in 1822, and they made a home in Winchester, Virginia, where Mason had practiced law since 1820. They had the first of their eight children in 1825.

In 1826, Mason won election to Virginia's House of Delegates, where he spoke against Federal subsidies for state transportation improvements. Unfortunately, his Shenandoah constituents welcomed the Federal support—they voted him out of office in 1827. Two years later, he regained his seat in the House of Delegates as a Jacksonian Democrat and served as a delegate to the Virginia Constitutional Convention. In 1837, he won election to the U.S. House of Representatives, but the Democrats refused to renominate him in 1839, as he had fought against President Martin Van Buren's federal economic initiatives. He finally returned to politics when the Virginia legislature elected him to the U.S.

Senate after the death of Senator Isaac Pennybacker, whom he succeeded on 27 January 1847.

Senator Mason continued to fight for a strict interpretation of the U.S. Constitution: he fought against any increase in federal power relative to the states, and he staunchly defended slavery as an institution legally protected by the Constitution. He authored the Fugitive Slave Act of 1850, praised the Dred Scott decision, and supported the expansion of slavery into the territories. Despite his role in these controversies, Mason focused most of his time in the Senate on foreign policy matters as chairman of the Senate Foreign Relations Committee, a position he obtained in 1851. Over the next decade, he fought for strict observance of treaties, open commerce with all nations, and a negotiated annexation of Cuba.

By 1860, Mason, like other Southern Democrats, was convinced that Southern independence was the only recourse to a Republican presidential victory. He supported South Carolina's secession in December 1860 and the secession of the states that followed it in January 1861. After Virginia voted to leave the United States in April, Mason served as a representative in the Confederacy's Provisional Congress. President Jefferson Davis appointed him Confederate envoy to Britain on 24 August 1861.

The USS San Jacinto captured Mason and John Slidell, the Confederate envoy to France, on 8 November 1861, as they tried to make their way to Britain via Cuba aboard the Trent, a British mail steamer. The Federals locked them up in Fort Warren in Boston harbor until President Abraham Lincoln, who realized that British anger over the affair could lead to war, ordered their release by the end of the year.

Mason arrived in Britain on 29 January 1862 and met with Lord John Russell, Britain's foreign secretary, for the first time on 10 February. Russell spoke little as Mason explained that the Confederacy could never be reconciled with the North and could defend itself indefinitely; Mason's emphasis on Southern independence went too far, however, when he injudiciously assured Russell that the Confederacy, while welcoming British recognition, did not seek a military alliance with Britain or even need its material support. This blunder was the result of two handicaps that would severely limit his effectiveness for the duration of his mission in Britain: his own diplomatic inexperience—he had never visited another country during his tenure on the Foreign Relations Committee—and the mistaken belief in "King Cotton" diplomacy. The Confederate state department believed that Britain would soon recognize the Confederacy because the British refusal to force the Union naval blockade and the South's intentional destruction of excess cotton would create a shortage. Such would force Britain to break the blockade and stop the war for the sake of its depleted, textile-driven, industrial cities. Unfortunately for Mason and the Confederacy, Britain had enough cotton on hand from its prewar trade with the South to maintain its factories into 1862, and when the supply eventually fell that year, the British simply imported more from Egypt and India.

While Mason patiently awaited the cotton crisis, Confederate military victories in the summer of 1862 created the most favorable atmosphere for British recognition that the South would ever enjoy. The cabinet of Prime Minister Palmerston watched for a Confederate victory on Northern soil as the prerequisite to begin a parliamentary debate on recognition and intervention; Palmerston tabled that discussion after learning of the Army of Northern Virginia's defeat at Antietam on 17 September 1862. Disappointed by this reaction, Mason nevertheless continued to believe that the British government would change its mind once the cotton shortage became acute and Southern armies won new battles. Meanwhile, he worked to arrange financing for the Confederate navy, which sought to purchase ships and construct new vessels, such as the famous Laird Rams, in British ports. These efforts became futile, however, when news of the Confederate disasters at Gettysburg and Vicksburg in July 1863 made Britain's continued neutrality certain.

In September 1863, the Confederate government ordered Mason to protest British inaction by having him leave Britain for France. He returned to London in February 1864, but left for France again in April after President Jefferson Davis made him the Confederacy's special ambassador to the Continent. Buoyed by rumors of a potential British mediation effort, Mason was back to London in June 1864. He met with Palmerston in July, but nothing came of their discussions; the British remained reluctant to do anything for the South that might lead to war between themselves and the United States. After the fall of Richmond in April 1865 and the ensuing end of the war in May, Mason remained in exile in Britain. He crossed the Atlantic in May 1866 to reunite with his family in Canada, where they would live for three years. In May 1869, Mason, now amnestied by the U.S. government and in increasingly failing health, returned to Virginia. He died at home on 28 April 1871.

—*R. Boyd Murphree*

See also Diplomacy, C.S.A.; Fugitive Slave Act; Great Britain; Palmerston, Viscount; Russell, Lord John; Slidell, John; *Trent Affair.*

For further reading:
Jenkins, Brian. *Britain and the War for the Union* (1974).
Jones, Howard. *Union in Peril: The Crisis over British Intervention in the Civil War* (1992).
Owsley, Frank L. *King Cotton Diplomacy: Foreign Relations of the Confederate States of America* (1959).
Young, Robert W. *Senator James Murray Mason: Defender of the Old South* (1998).

MASONS

Freemasonry (or Masonry—the terms are interchangeable) is a fraternal organization that developed in its modern form during the period of the Enlightenment, the 1700s. It teaches its members to support the tenets of friendship, morality, and brotherly love, and presents its lessons in morality plays called degrees. Very close ties are established among Masons, and this spirit of brotherhood continued even among Masons who fought on different sides in the Civil War.

Benjamin Franklin and George Washington were among the prominent early Americans who were Freemasons. Masonry expanded in membership and influence in the United States in the 1800s, despite the setback of the anti-Masonic movement and political party that was active in the 1830s. By the time of the Civil War, Freemasonry was again an important part of the lives of many American men.

Many of the political leaders and soldiers in the Civil War, on both sides, were dedicated Freemasons. Some of the prominent men of the Civil War era who were Masons are Turner Ashby, Nathaniel P. Banks, P. G. T. Beauregard, F. P. Blair, John C. Breckinridge, James Buchanan, Simon B. Buckner, Daniel Butterfield, Lewis Cass, Joshua Chamberlain, Patrick R. Cleburne, Howell Cobb, Andrew G. Curtin, John A. Dahlgren, Stephen A. Douglas, David G. Farragut, James D. Fessenden, Nathan B. Forrest, John B. Gordon, Winfield S. Hancock, Henry Heth, Sam Houston, Albert S. Johnston, John A. Logan, John B. Magruder, George B. McClellan, John A. McClernand, Nelson A. Miles, John Hunt Morgan, George Pickett, Albert Pike, Sterling Price, James A. Reynolds, Winfield Scott, James Shields, Edwin M. Stanton, George H. Thomas, Lorenzo Thomas, Robert Tombs, Zebulon B. Vance, Gideon Welles, Joseph Wheeler, and Henry A. Wise. Abraham Lincoln had many ties with Freemasons. Robert E. Lee's father was a Mason, as was Stonewall Jackson's, whose family was aided by his father's lodge after his death.

There are thousands of recorded incidents of Masons helping brother Masons during the Civil War. For example, the Little Rock, Arkansas, Masonic library of Confederate general Albert Pike was saved from destruction when Thomas H. Benton, Jr., the Grand Master of Iowa, a Federal colonel, placed a guard around the building to keep it from being burned.

In 1861, the National Zouave Lodge was stationed near Hampton, Virginia, where many Southern prisoners were being held. One of the members of the lodge said of its meetings, "Here all passion was laid aside, and with them frequently met the gray clad soldiers from the South, a prisoner without our military lines, but a brother within our Masonic limits. Within our crowded walls the private soldier and the general officer met on the level of equality. Here the beautiful tenets of our institution tempered the rough and rugged life of the soldier."

Joseph Fort Newton, a great Masonic author, wrote that his father, who was a Confederate soldier and a Mason, was captured and imprisoned in Illinois, where he became deathly ill. He gave a Masonic sign of distress to a Northern officer, who took him to his own home, nursed him back to health, and when the war was over gave him money and a gun and saw him off to his home in Texas. Newton wrote, "The fact that such a fraternity of men could exist, mitigating the harshness of war, and remain unbroken when states and churches were torn in two, became a wonder; and it is not strange I tried for years to repay my debt to it."

In 1863 when the North attempted to capture Galveston, Texas, a Mason who was captain of one of the Northern boats was killed. A Galveston lodge met the next day, and Union prisoners who were Masons asked for a Masonic burial for their captain. The minutes of the Galveston lodge recorded that they said they would "administer the last rite of the Order to the remains of a Mason of moral worth, although yesterday they met as an armed enemy in mortal combat in which the deceased parted with his life." A public procession was formed, with both Southern Masons and Northern Masons who were their prisoners, all wearing the insignia of the Order, and accompanied by a proper military escort including Major General John Bankhead Magruder, a Mason. The body of the dead Northern captain was buried with the ritual still used today by Masons for deceased brethren.

In 1993 a Masonic "Friend-to-Friend" monument was dedicated at the Gettysburg National Cemetery. This statue depicts Confederate general Lewis A. Armistead after he was mortally wounded during Pickett's Charge and being assisted by Union colonel Henry H. Bingham. Armistead, a Mason, gave a sign to indicate to fellow Masons that he needed assistance. Bingham, also a Mason, recognized this sign and came to help Armistead. This Friend-to-Friend monument in Gettysburg conveys the fundamental spirit of Masonry, showing one Mason helping another regardless of danger or their involvement on different sides in the Civil War.

—*Paul M. Bessel*

For further reading:
Fraysse, Olivier. "Chicago 1860: A Mason's Wigwam?" *Lincoln Herald* (Fall 1985).
Havlik, R. V. "Is This of Your Own Free Will and Accord?" *Lincoln Herald* (Fall 1985).
Motts, Wayne E. *"Trust in God and Fear Nothing": General Lewis A. Armistead, C.S.A.* (1994).
Munn, Sheldon A. *Freemasons at Gettysburg* (1993).
Roberts, Allen E. *House Reunited: Masonry Aids Reconstruction* (1961; reprint, 1996).
———. *House Undivided: The Story of Freemasonry and the Civil War* (1961).
Shields, Richard Eugene, Jr. *Befriend and Relieve Every Brother: Freemasonry during Wartime* (1994).

MATAMOROS, MEXICO

Matamoros, a Mexican port located across the Rio Grande from Brownsville, Texas, became an important trading center for the Confederacy due to its proximity to Texas. As a foreign port, it lay beyond the reach of the United States. Although it offered only limited facilities and could accommodate only shallow-draught vessels due to a bar at the mouth of the river, it soon became a major entrepôt, especially for the trans-Mississippi Confederacy.

While the Richmond government sought to withhold cotton from the world market, independent-minded Texans defied the nonexport and cotton destruction edicts. On 21 May 1861, the Confederate Congress acknowledged this and exempted cotton shipments to Mexico. Jose Augustin Quintero, a Cuban-born Confederate agent based in Mexico, reported to Richmond on the advantages of using Matamoros. Santiago Vidaurri, the Mexican governor of the provinces of Nuevo Leon and Tamaulipas, assured Quintero that the border would remain open for trade. By 1862 large trains of up to 500 wagons were carrying cotton from the Confederacy to Mexico. The trade was lucrative. At its peak, an estimated four million dollars in cotton went through Matamoros monthly.

In 1862 military authorities in the Confederate Trans-Mississippi Department created a Cotton Bureau, which began issuing export permits to ensure itself a supply of military goods rather than more profitable consumer items. Those holding permits were allowed 100 percent profit on the cost of their imports, provided they benefited the army. The plan aroused great criticism and was modified but remained unpopular. The whole affair was badly managed; profiteers drove out the competition and then cut deals with inexperienced army negotiators and reaped large profits. As many profiteers were based in Mexico, there was little recourse for the cheated Confederates. The army meanwhile was unable to meet its obligations to foreign shippers and began impressing cotton, which elicited civilian protests. In August 1864 the Confederate Treasury Department assumed control of the Cotton Bureau and disbanded it in February 1865.

Meanwhile the Texas Military Board also sought to organize the cotton trade. This largely duplicated the efforts of the Confederate government. Soon both were accusing the other of shipping cotton illegally. The board sought to buy cotton through its agents, who then shipped it overseas on behalf of Texas. Initially the board sought to purchase cotton with 8 percent bonds, rather than cash or specie. The board also capped its price at ten cents a pound—as a result it was often outbid. Moreover, agents were hard to find as the positions were not salaried. In spite of such shortcomings, the board did raise enough to help pay for improvements in the defense of the state.

In spite of his amicable relations with the South, Vidaurri closed Matamoros in April 1862 and then reopened it with a duty of two cents per pound placed on cotton. The Mexican governor explained that the increase was necessary to support his army, which was engaged in fighting insurgents whom he suspected were being aided by Texans. Vidaurri agreed to cut the duty in half when the Confederacy promised to crack down on cross border raids from Texas.

The United States sought to close what amounted to a Southern port of entry. In April 1861, President Abraham Lincoln proclaimed a blockade of the Confederacy. Matamoros had already caught the attention of the Union navy. In February, the USS *Portsmouth* seized several British ships in waters north of the Rio Grande. London protested on the basis that there had been no prior notification. For the British, the blockade represented a reversal of the traditional U.S. policy of advocating maritime rights of neutrals. At the same time, the British were willing to accept the U.S. paper blockade on the basis that it would allow the United States to set precedents for belligerent rights. This was to be the first of a number of international incidents surrounding Matamoros, the best known of which involved the *Peterhoff*. In February 1863 the USS *Vanderbilt* captured the British screw steamer off the Virgin Islands. Aboard were two British subjects and their Texan partner with goods for a trading house that they planned to open in Matamoros. The case eventually made its way to the U.S. Supreme Court, which in 1867 condemned the cargo as contraband but ordered the release of the ship. More significantly, the Court upheld the doctrine of continuous voyage in spite of the U.S. long-standing aversion to the doctrine since the Napoleonic Wars.

In spite of such incidents, the appearance of a blockading Federal gunboat did little to curtail the Matamoros trade. Indeed with up to 200 vessels reported off the mouth of the Rio Grande at any given time, it was difficult to stop. For example, when the U.S. Navy tried to intercept the lighters ferrying goods between the larger vessels and port, these small craft were placed under Mexican registry. In the same vein, it was not uncommon for British consuls across the Caribbean to place Rebel ships under British registry. Surprisingly, a number of ships sailed between Matamoros and New York facilitating a trade in Northern civilian and military goods for the Southern states.

In light of the flourishing trade, the United States sought to move into southern Texas. In October 1863, twenty transports escorted by three warships carried 7,000 troops under the command of General Nathaniel Banks from New Orleans to Brazos Island, which the Confederates had abandoned. In the face of superior Federal numbers, the Confederates under General Hamilton Bee withdrew inland, destroying cotton in their wake. Fort Brown was also destroyed, and fire destroyed two blocks of the town of Brownsville, which Banks occupied on 6 November. The occupation of Brownsville only diverted the trade to crossings further west, such as Eagle Pass some 300 miles upriver. Confederates under John S. "Rip" Ford retook Brownsville on 30 July 1864 and that action reopened the cotton trade. However, with Robert E. Lee's surrender the following year, Federal forces again advanced on Fort Brown only to be driven off by Ford. Finally, on 2 June 1865, Edmund Kirby Smith surrendered the Trans-Mississippi Department to the Union, thus ending the Confederates' trade through Matamoros.

Historians disagree as to the importance of Matamoros to the Confederacy. Frank L. Owsley in his book, *King Cotton Diplomacy*, says that the Union effectively stopped the Matamoros connection, whereas Tom Lea, in *The King Ranch*, and other regional historians tend to overestimate the importance of the trade. Hampering this debate is the fact that the port records did not survive the war. Although Matamoros was important, it contributed in only a limited way to the overall Confederate war effort. Its isolation and marginal port facilities curtailed its effectiveness. In addition, rivalry between Texans and the Confederacy and upheaval in Mexico further hampered trade though the port. Nonetheless, Matamoros did provide a unique focus of international attention in the Civil War.

—Daniel Liestman

See also Brownsville, Texas; Texas.

For further reading:

Daddysmith, James W. *The Matamoros Trade: Confederate Commerce, Diplomacy, and Intrigue* (1984).

Delaney, Robert W. "Matamoros: Port for Texas during the Civil War." *Southwestern Historical Quarterly* (1955).

Larios, Avila. "Brownsville-Matamoros: Confederate Lifeline." *Mid-America* (1958).

Lea, Tom. *The King Ranch* (1957).

Owsley, Frank L. *King Cotton Diplomacy. Foreign Relations of the Confederate States of America* (1959).

Tyler, Ronnie C. "Cotton on the Border, 1861–1865." *Southwestern Historical Quarterly* (1970).

MAUM GUINEA
Popular antislavery novel

Harriet Beecher Stowe's *Uncle Tom's Cabin* may have been the novel that most influenced Northern public opinion about slavery before the Civil War began, but *Maum Guinea*, by Metta

Victoria Fuller Victor, was the novel most likely to be found in the backpacks of Union—and Confederate—soldiers and in the parlors and pockets of readers in both North America and Europe in the early days of the war. This novel was so popular and sold so steadily that contemporary historians estimated that sales during the war years exceeded 100,000 copies. Contemporary observers also claimed that *Maum Guinea* had been important in creating pro-Union sentiment in the British Isles. While these assertions, along with the origin of the contention that Lincoln had read the novel and called it "as absorbing as *Uncle Tom's Cabin*," cannot be verified today, in the nineteenth century they were frequently repeated.

Maum Guinea was published in the United States in December of 1861, as Beadle's Dime Book No. 33. Though published as part of the dime-novel series, *Maum Guinea* was longer than any of the previous thirty-two volumes in the series, and the novel was sold for twice as much: twenty cents, not a dime. The novel was published simultaneously in London, where it was issued in two editions. The British paper-covered version sold for 1 shilling 6 pence; the cloth edition cost 2 shillings 6 pence. The inclusion of the word "American" in the full title of the book, *Maum Guinea and Her Plantation "Children." A Story of the Christmas Week with the American Slaves*, may indicate that the English market had been a prime consideration from the novel's (or at least the title's) inception.

Victor had traveled to England with her husband Orville (editor for the Beadle Dime Book Series) during 1860–1861, and while there would have had confirmed at firsthand the British appetite for antislavery fiction. Her fictional representation of the arguments against slavery and for the Union cause might be seen as a complement to Orville Victor's nonfiction polemic, *The American Rebellion: Some Facts and Reflections for the Consideration of the English People*, which was written and published in London around the same time as *Maum Guinea*.

Metta Victor was a veteran writer of mass fiction. She had previously satisfied the American (and British) reading public's appetite for romantic and sensational fiction without much regard for the "facts" or for realism. Before her marriage, writing as Metta Victoria Fuller and published by a variety of firms including those of J. C. Derby, she had written several popular novels that variously combined romance, violence, and comedy within a framework of a plot drawn from the main topics of the day. She had already been successful with the temperance novel plot (*Fashionable Dissipation* and *The Senator's Son*) and with a novel in which the plot revolves around Mormon polygamy but also manages to discuss "free love" and "the Woman Question" (*Mormon Wives*).

Maum Guinea begins with the author's introduction in which Victor informed readers that she had "sought to depict [African-Americans] to the life" and stressed her use of historical sources, mentioning specifically the historical records of early slave rebellions, including that of Nat Turner. But the high goals for verisimilitude asserted in the introduction of the novel are not achieved. As in her earlier novels, Victor embellished and sometimes simply ignored realism and fact in favor of incidents and descriptions that would appeal to her readers' taste for the sensational and the dramatic.

In *Maum Guinea*, as in *Uncle Tom's Cabin* and the majority of other antislavery novels by women writers, slavery is discussed primarily through two intertwined themes: the effect of slavery on personal relationships, especially the effect on male-female relationships, and the abuse and torture of women and children. *Maum Guinea* includes several sets of star-crossed lovers, white and black, offering readers a rich supply of romance along with the antislavery message. Four different love stories are told. Victor contrasts the easy path of the love between Phillip and Virginia, the (white) children of Southern planters, with the difficulties faced by Rose and Hyperion (their personal slaves); Maum Guinea's love and relationship with the son of her "owner," that led to the birth of her daughter Judy; and Judy's own story of growing up, escaping from slavery, and falling in love with a white sea captain. Victor uses these stories to illustrate some of the ways in which slavery perverted relationships and threatened the autonomy of black women. Some of the stories-within-the-story that are told, by Maum Guinea and by other women, are indeed horrific. But the novel ends with a flurry of happy endings, including a blissful marriage for Judy. The overall positive outcomes are something of a reversal of the more common antislavery novel plot resolution in which death or exile were the only possibilities for lovers of different races. Mixed into the novel's love story plots is another thread, in which Victor weaves a discussion of African-American males' revolt against slavery, including a long flashback that retells the story of the Nat Turner rebellion.

Although there is much in the novel that supported the antislavery position, there are also elements that are very uncomfortable for a reader today. Victor has her African-American characters speak in an invented and demeaning dialect. She includes scenes in which African-Americans are portrayed as childlike and fawning over their white "masters" that would have been comfortable and familiar to the most proslavery of Southern writers. And, although some of her African-American characters strive for and choose freedom, she ends the novel with one pair of African-American lovers, Hyperion and Rose, content to remain with their former owners.

Victor's genius in creating a book that confirmed the

Union antislavery position and at the same time included nonthreatening recapitulation of current stereotypes helped to make the novel popular in its time, as did the vigorous distribution efforts of the Beadle firm, which shipped thousands of copies to the troops, as well as to every possible sales venue in cities and towns of every size. At the same time, the limitations of the novel's vision ensured that it would not outlive its first popularity. Today it is Uncle Tom, not Maum Guinea, who has entered the popular imagination and mythology of the Civil War.

—JoAnn E. Castagna

See also Stowe, Harriet Beecher; *Uncle Tom's Cabin*.

For further reading:

Carby, Hazel. *Reconstructing Womanhood: The Emergence of the Afro-American Woman Novelist* (1987).

Castagna, JoAnn. "Women, Sexuality, and Popular Culture: Gender Identity in Sensation Novels of the 1850s" (Ph.D. dissertation, 1989).

Evans, Clark. "*Maum Guinea*: Beadle's Unusual Jewel." *Dime Novel Roundup* (1994).

Harvey, Charles M. "The Dime Novel in American Life." *Atlantic Monthly* (1907).

Johannsen, Albert. *The House of Beadle and Adams* (1950).

Simmons, Michael K. "*Maum Guinea*: or, A Dime Novelist Looks at Abolition." *Journal of Popular Culture* (1976).

MAURY, DABNEY HERNDON
(1822–1900)
Confederate general

The son of John Minor Maury and Eliza Maury, Dabney Herndon Maury was born in Fredericksburg, Virginia. He was educated at the University of Virginia before accepting an appointment to the U.S. Military Academy. He graduated thirty-seventh of fifty-nine in the class of 1846. After graduation, Maury was sent immediately to the Mexican-American War. He was brevetted for bravery for his actions at the battle of Cerro Gordo, where he was wounded. After the war he returned to West Point as an instructor. From 1852 to 1858 Maury served in Texas. He returned east in 1858 to become the superintendent of the cavalry school at Carlisle Barracks, Pennsylvania. During his time there he wrote a manual for cavalry skirmish drill. In 1860 he was transferred to New Mexico, where he was when he learned of Virginia's secession. He resigned his commission and traveled to Richmond.

Serving first in the Confederate Army as a cavalry captain, in the fall of 1861 he became adjutant general to Brigadier General T. H. Holmes at Fredericksburg. Maury remained in that position until early 1862, when he was transferred west and became adjutant general to Earl Van Dorn at the rank of colonel. Maury fought at Pea Ridge, for which he was commended by Van Dorn and promoted to brigadier general.

During the siege of Corinth, April–May 1862, Maury commanded the third division. In the battle of Corinth in October 1862, Maury commanded Van Dorn's center. For his actions there, he was promoted to major general in November 1862. At the end of 1862, he was sent with his division to Jackson, Mississippi, to aid in the defense of Vicksburg. He fought against William T. Sherman in his Yazoo expedition. In the spring he was transferred to Knoxville, Tennessee, to command the Department of East Tennessee.

Only in Tennessee briefly, in June 1863 Maury was transferred to command the District of the Gulf, headquartered at Mobile. He remained in that command for the remainder of the war. At Mobile, Maury's biggest concern was the defense of the harbor of Mobile. One of the few ports Confederate blockade runners could still sneak into, Mobile presented an important challenge to its new commander. For the next year, he worked diligently to strengthen the entrance to the bay and staff its protecting forts. This task became increasingly difficult in the spring and summer of 1864 when his personnel were used to aid in the Confederate attempt to thwart Sherman's Atlanta campaign. In August 1864, in spite of Maury's best efforts, the bay fell under control of David G. Farragut. For the remaining months of the war, Maury struggled to defend the city of Mobile. Northern officers criticized him for using captured black Union soldiers to work on the defenses of the city. In March of 1865, he was finally forced to abandon the city and retreat with his remaining army toward Mississippi.

After the war, Maury taught school in Fredericksburg and wrote. He was one of the organizers of the Southern Historical Society and in 1885 received appointment as U.S. minister to Colombia. He held that position until 1889. He died in Peoria, Illinois.

—David S. Heidler and Jeanne T. Heidler

See also Mobile Bay; Mobile Campaign; Pea Ridge.

For further reading:

Maury, Dabney H. *Recollections of a Virginian in the Mexican, Indian, and Civil Wars* (1894).

MAURY, MATTHEW FONTAINE
(1806–1873)
Confederate naval officer

The son of a Tennessee farmer who had migrated from Virginia, Maury enlisted in the U.S. Navy as a midshipman in 1825. Over the next nine years, he served aboard warships and demonstrated considerable talent in navigation. In 1836 he published *A New Theoretical and Practical Treatise on Navigation*. Two years later, using the pseudonyms Harry Bluff and Will Hatch, he published twelve articles in the *Richmond Whig and Public Advertiser* criticizing the inefficiency of the navy and calling for reforms.

Maury was badly injured in an 1839 stagecoach accident, which left him lame and, according to the navy, unfit for sea duty. During a lengthy convalescence, he published a number of articles in the *Southern Literary Messenger* (again under the name Harry Bluff) in which he called for naval reform. He advocated establishing a naval academy and placing surplus officers on a half-pay reserve list, and he exposed corruption in the building and repair of naval vessels.

In 1842 Maury became superintendent of the navy's Depot of Charts and Instruments in Washington, D.C. The depot (later renamed the Naval Observatory and Hydrographic Bureau) contained a wealth of oceanographic information collected from ships' logs over the years. Maury began collating the data in the logs and issued blank charts for captains to fill in and return to the depot. In 1847 the result was published as *Wind and Current Charts of the North Atlantic*, which showed wind directions and currents with their strengths and speeds, ocean temperatures, and areas of storms, calms, and fog. It was the most complete map of the Atlantic ever produced and had an immediate impact on ocean voyages. Using Maury's charts, captains cut weeks, and even months, off sailing times. Over time Maury expanded his studies to other waters and became known as the "Pathfinder of the Seas."

In the 1850s Maury was known as the preeminent ocean scientist in the world. He was instrumental in convoking the first International Maritime Meteorological Conference in Brussels in 1853. Representatives from ten nations attended and agreed to exchange ships' logs and other information. In 1855 he published *The Physical Geography of the Sea*, the first modern textbook on oceanography. He defended the practicality of a trans-Atlantic cable and posited the existence of a "telegraphic plateau" on the Atlantic floor. Maury supported the expansion of Southern commerce into the Amazon River basin and publicized the Amazon expedition of his brother-in-law William L. Herndon in *De Bow's Review* and other publications.

Despite Maury's international reputation, a navy review board removed him from active duty in 1855 because he was deemed unfit for sea service and placed him on half-pay reserve. The disgruntled officer demanded a court of inquiry and used political and newspaper connections to overturn the decision. In 1858 he was restored to active duty at the rank of commander, but he retained an animus against Stephen R. Mallory, then chairman of the Senate Naval Affairs Committee, whom he blamed for his reduction.

When Virginia seceded in 1861, Maury resigned from the U.S. Navy and offered his services to his home state. Governor John Letcher placed him on his advisory council. Maury was subsequently commissioned a commander in the Confederate navy and ordered to England, where he experimented with electric torpedoes, lobbied British politicians and the press on the Confederacy's behalf, and joined Captain James D. Bulloch in seeking ships that could act as commerce raiders. In 1863 Maury was responsible for commissioning the iron steamship CSS *Georgia*, which captured U.S. vessels totally valued at $406,000. A second ship he commissioned, the CSS *Rappahannock*, was at sea only forty-eight hours before it was detained at Calais, France.

Maury left England in May 1865 with torpedoes intended for use against Federal ships blockading Galveston, Texas, but learned when he reached Havana that the war was over. Maury took refuge in Mexico, where he convinced Emperor Maximilian to make him imperial commissioner of immigration to persuade Southerners to immigrate there. This plan proved unsuccessful, however, and Maury returned to England in 1866.

Maury returned to the United States in 1868 and became a professor of meteorology at the Virginia Military Institute in Lexington. He advanced a number of causes during this period, including a state agricultural school, a geographic survey of Virginia, and a national weather bureau. He died in Lexington, Virginia, on 1 February 1873. He is buried in Richmond, Virginia, near former presidents James Monroe and John Tyler.

—*Kenneth R. Stevens*

See also Bulloch, James D.

For further reading:

Corbin, Diana Fontaine. *A Life of Matthew Fontaine Maury* (1888).

Jahns, Patricia. *Matthew Fontaine Maury and Joseph Henry: Scientists of the Civil War* (1961).

Spencer, Warren F. *The Confederate Navy in Europe* (1983).

Wayland, John W. *The Pathfinder of the Seas: The Life of Matthew Fontaine Maury* (1930).

Williams, Francis L. *Matthew Fontaine Maury: Scientist of the Sea* (1963).

MAXEY, SAMUEL BELL
(1825–1895)
Confederate general

The son of Rice Maxey, Samuel Bell Maxey was born in Tompkinsville, Kentucky. He was educated locally before accepting appointment to the U.S. Military Academy. He graduated fifty-eighth of fifty-nine in the class of 1846 and was sent to join Winfield Scott's army in preparation for its landing at Vera Cruz in the Mexican-American War. He fought at Cerro Gordo and received a brevet for his actions in the battles around Mexico City. After the war he resigned his commission to study law. He began his practice in Albany, Kentucky, where he also served as the county and circuit court clerk. In 1857 he moved to Texas, where he continued to practice law and became active in Democratic politics. He served briefly as a district attorney before the Civil War.

At the beginning of hostilities, Maxey organized and became the colonel of the 9th Texas Infantry. In December 1861, he was sent with his regiment to Memphis, Tennessee. In March 1862 he was promoted to brigadier general. During the spring of 1862, his brigade staffed the defenses of Chattanooga, Tennessee, and during the summer he acted almost independently, patrolling central Tennessee. In December 1862 he was sent with his brigade to Jackson, Mississippi, to aid in the defense of Vicksburg and in the spring of 1863 participated in the defense of Port Hudson. Back in Chattanooga in the fall of 1863, Maxey learned while there that he had been named the commander of the Indian Territory.

Traveling quickly to his new command, Maxey worked diligently through the early months of 1864 recruiting, supplying, and training members of the Creek, Cherokee, and Choctaw nations for combat. On 18 April 1864, he commanded his new recruits, who had been organized into a cavalry division, at the battle of Poison Spring, Arkansas, in the Camden campaign.

As the war in the West began to disintegrate for the Confederacy in the early months of 1865, Maxey was relieved of command of the Indian Territory in February 1865. He reported to Houston, Texas, where he was given command of an infantry division for the last months of the war.

After the war he resumed his law practice and from 1875 to 1887 served in the U.S. Senate. In the Senate he advocated fiscal conservatism and became an outspoken advocate for individual property rights for Native Americans. He died in Eureka Springs, Arkansas.

—David S. Heidler and Jeanne T. Heidler

See also Cherokee Indians; Choctaw Indians; Creek Indians; Indian Territory; Poison Spring.

For further reading:
Horton, Louise. *Samuel Bell Maxey, A Biography* (1974).
Kerby, Robert L. *Kirby Smith's Confederacy: The Trans-Mississippi South, 1863–1865* (1972).
Waugh, John C. *Sam Bell Maxey and the Confederate Indians* (1998).

MAXIMILIAN, FERDINAND
(1832–1867)
Austrian archduke and emperor of Mexico

Austrian archduke, and younger brother of Austrian emperor Francis Joseph, Maximilian reigned as emperor of Mexico from 1864 to 1867. He entered the Austrian navy in 1850 and, becoming its commander in chief by 1854, proved to be outstandingly successful in its reorganization. In 1857 he married Princess Charlotte, the ambitious daughter of the monarchical conspirator Leopold I, King of the Belgians.

From 1857 to 1859, Maximilian served as the popular Austrian governor-general of Lombardy-Venetia, but his liberalism prompted his brother to remove him from office. Bitterly disappointed, Maximilian decided to visit Brazil in 1859. He became enamored with Latin America, and he was also impressed with the apparent success of the benign role of the emperor Pedro of Brazil. When Napoleon III first unofficially approached Maximilian on October 1861, through the Austrian foreign secretary Count Reichberg, regarding a Mexican throne, Maximilian may have had dreams of his own about creating a utopian state in the New World. Both his wife and father-in-law strongly urged him to accept; his brother had serious and, as it turned out, realistic reservations.

Since achieving independence from Spain in 1821, Mexico had labored under the threat of foreign intervention. In 1821, Mexican Conservatives had offered the throne of Montezuma to the Austrian Hapsburg, archduke Karl, who refused. The liberator of Mexico, General Agustín de Iturbide, briefly had reigned as Agustín I, but his liberalism led to his overthrow and murder. The constant conflict between Liberal-Conservative factions created chronic political instability. When Mexico's own three-year civil war, the War of the Reform, ended in the triumph of the Liberals under Benito Juarez, just three days after South Carolina seceded from the Union on 20 December 1860, many Conservatives fled to Europe. Washington quickly recognized Juarez, but President Abraham Lincoln was powerless to prevent an Anglo-French-Spanish occupation of Veracruz in January 1862 in response to Mexico's failure to repay its European loans. Both Britain and Spain soon realized that occupation would not result in payment and in May 1862 withdrew their forces. Napoleon III kept his forces in Veracruz and gradually increased their number to 30,000 troops.

Exiled Conservatives, especially the ex-diplomats Jose Hidalgo and Gutierrez de Estrada, interested Napoleon III in restoring the Mexican monarchy: Napoleon III was also interested in taking advantage of the American Civil War to break up the Union, weaken republicanism, exploit Mexican mineral resources, and, rather fancifully, regenerate the Latin American nations by the reintroduction of monarchy. Actively aiding the Conservatives to overthrow Juarez, the long campaign finally resulted in French troops entering Mexico City under General Forey in June 1863 and the restoration of the monarchy in July 1863. With some misgivings, Maximilian finally accepted the offer of a Mexican throne from Gutierrez de Estrada on 10 April 1864. He sailed for Mexico, without the support of his brother, on 14 April 1864, perhaps blind to the fact that the military tide had turned against the Confederacy, that Washington would never accept the reintroduction of a monarchy in America, that he was not really the emperor-elect of the Mexican people, and that Napoleon III, who Maximilian had first met in 1856, would renege on his promises of financial and military support when it became expedient for him to do so.

Arriving in Mexico on 28 May 1864, Maximilian was initially heartened by his reception, yet his brief, tragic rule was impossible from the beginning and his liberal plans were doomed with the collapse of the Confederacy on April 1865. Romantically seeing himself as the protector of his people, he upheld Juarez's sweeping land reforms, antagonized the Catholic Church by refusing to restore its vast confiscated church holdings, and alienated Conservatives by his determination to abolish peonage. His attempt to stabilize the dynasty by formally adopting the grandson of Agustín I also enraged traditionalists. The Liberal military opposition to his reign increased and, although Maximilian was happy about the arrival of a Belgian Brigade and an Austrian Corps to be under his direct imperial command, he signed his own death warrant on 3 October 1865 by issuing the Black Decree, which condemned to death the supporters of Juarez and all individuals found in arms against his reign. When President Andrew Johnson sent General Philip Sheridan with a force of 42,000 battle-hardened troops to Texas in May 1865, Maximilian attempted, unsuccessfully, to appease Washington. Initially welcoming Confederate veterans to Mexico to support his throne, he actively discouraged their continued emigration to deflect Washington's continued displeasure early in 1866.

Faced with increasing pressure from the United States that the French presence in Mexico was a violation of the Monroe Doctrine, Napoleon III began to waver in his support for Maximilian. With Liberal forces, supplied by Washington, closing in on Mexico City, Charlotte rushed to Europe to remind Napoleon III of his promises to support her husband. Having failed, she met with Pope Pius IX, urging his support; her failure led to a mental collapse in September 1866. Gradually reducing the French garrison in Mexico, Napoleon III withdrew his last troops in March 1867. Idealistically refusing to leave his people or abdicate, Maximilian personally took command of the imperial army opposing the forces of Juarez. At Querétaro on 15 May 1867, betrayed and defeated, Maximilian was captured.

Mistreated in captivity, he was tried, and, much to the horror of Europe, he was executed by a firing squad on 19 June 1867 near Querétaro. After constant pressure from Europe, Juarez finally allowed Maximilian's body to be transported back to Austria. Admiral Wilhelm von Tegetthoff aboard the *Novara*, the same Austrian warship that had brought Maximilian to Mexico in 1864, finally brought Maximilian's corpse back to be buried in Vienna in January 1868.

Charlotte, remaining mentally ill, died in 1927. She was not the last survivor of this illusionary Mexican adventure. One of the young soldiers in Maximilian's firing squad was, at the age of 111, still alive in 1952. Maximilian, a man of naive liberalism, proved unequal to the task of restoring monarchy on the American continent and never really understood the forces that led to his execution.

—*Rory T. Cornish*

See also Diplomacy, U.S.A.; Mercier, Henri; Mexico; Napoleon III; Seward, William Henry.

For further reading:

Anderson, William Marshall. *An American in Maximilian's Mexico, 1856–1866: The Diaries of William Marshall Anderson* (1959).

Barker, Nancy Nichols. "Empress Eugenie and the Origins of the Mexican Venture." *The Historian* (1959).

Blasio, Jose Luis. *Maximilian, Emperor of Mexico: Memoirs of His Private Secretary* (1934).

Hanna, Alfred J., and Kathryn Abby Hanna. *Napoleon III and Mexico: American Triumph over Monarchy* (1971).

Harding, Bertita. *Phantom Crown: The Story of Maximilian and Carlota of Mexico* (1934).

Haslip, Joan. *The Crown of Mexico: Maximilian and His Empress Carlotta* (1971).

Hendrick, Burton J. *Statesmen of the Lost Cause: Jefferson Davis and His Cabinet* (1939).

Pitner, Ernst. *Maximilian's Lieutenant: A Personal History of the Mexican Campaign, 1864–67* (1993).

Ridley, Jasper. *Maximilian and Juarez* (1993).

Salm-Salm, Prince Felix. *My Diary in Mexico in 1867 including the Last Days of Emperor Maximilian with Leaves from the Diary of the Princess Salm-Salm* (1868).

Tyrner-Tyrnauer, A. R. *Lincoln and the Emperors* (1962).

MCARTHUR, JOHN
(1826–1906)
Union general

Born to John McArthur and Isabella Neilson McArthur in Erskine, Scotland, the younger John McArthur was educated in the local parish school and immigrated to the United States in 1849. Settling in Chicago, Illinois, he went to work with his brother-in-law in the iron industry, ultimately gaining a partnership in a successful iron works. During the years before the Civil War, McArthur also demonstrated an interest in local militia activities, rising to the rank of captain of the Chicago Highland Guards, a unit made up primarily of Scot immigrants.

At the outbreak of the Civil War, McArthur helped to raise a regiment for federal service and in May 1861 was commissioned colonel of the 12th Illinois Infantry. In the first months of the war, McArthur was stationed with his regiment at Cairo, Illinois, where he and his men occupied themselves primarily with protecting rail lines in the area and patrolling across the state line into Kentucky. At the end of the year, he was given command of the 1st Brigade, 2d Division, District of Cairo, under Ulysses S. Grant. In early 1862, McArthur was stationed with his brigade at Fort Heiman,

Kentucky, but on 12 February set out on the short journey to Fort Donelson to join Grant's assault on that Confederate position. Grant was so impressed with McArthur's performance at Fort Donelson that he recommended McArthur's promotion to brigadier general, a promotion that occurred in March 1862.

In April 1862, McArthur led his brigade (William H. L. Wallace's 2d Division) at the battle of Shiloh. He received a wound in his foot on 6 April and was forced to leave the field. However, shortly after his departure, Wallace was mortally wounded (he died on 10 April), and McArthur returned to assume command of the division. He remained in temporary command of the division through the conclusion of the battle and during the subsequent advance on Corinth, Mississippi.

McArthur remained at Corinth through much of the summer of 1862 before leading his brigade in the engagement at Iuka and then during the siege of Corinth in the fall of 1862. In November he was given command of a division, which became 6th Division, XVII Corps in December. McArthur and his men occupied their time at the end of the year with patrols in the area of Waterford, Mississippi, and LaFayette, Tennessee.

During the Vicksburg campaign in the spring and summer of 1863, McArthur continued to command his division under James B. McPherson, though because McArthur and his men were deemed a very mobile force, he often found himself under other corps commanders to meet emergency situations. After the fall of Vicksburg, McArthur was placed in command of the city and remained in that position through July 1864. During this time, he was awarded one of the gold medals bestowed on officers of the Army of the Tennessee who had been especially conspicuous in the army's campaigns. Ulysses S. Grant also tried but failed to secure McArthur's promotion to major general for his actions during the Vicksburg campaign.

While in command at Vicksburg, McArthur conducted reconnaissance missions throughout the area. One such expedition to Yazoo City in May 1864 resulted in sharp skirmishes with Confederate forces at Benton and Luce's plantation. The overall result of the mission, however, was to clear Confederates from the area for at least a while.

In early August 1864, McArthur was ordered to report to William T. Sherman outside Atlanta, Georgia. Sherman too had been impressed with McArthur's performance during the Vicksburg campaign and wanted to use the Scotsman's skills to protect his communication lines back to Tennessee. Therefore, when McArthur arrived on 5 August, he was given command of a district that stretched from Kennesaw to Marietta to Roswell to the Chattahoochee River. His tasks were to guard the railroads coming through his district and to prepare camps there for convalescing soldiers and new recruits being sent down from the North.

After the surrender of Atlanta in September 1864, McArthur continued to manage the defenses of the railroads for another few weeks. At the end of September, the communications lines were deemed safe enough to move McArthur to a more active command. He was transferred to the Districts of Memphis and Vicksburg and given command of 1st Division, XVI Corps. His task was to take his new division immediately to Missouri to help combat the threat posed by Sterling Price's Missouri raid. McArthur arrived, however, after Price had already departed the state.

In December, XVI Corps (commanded by Andrew Jackson Smith) was ordered to Nashville, Tennessee, to aid in the defense of that city. On 16 December, McArthur led the attack on John Bell Hood's left flank that resulted in the retreat of the Confederate army and its virtual annihilation as a fighting force. McArthur received a brevet promotion to major general for his actions at Nashville.

In early 1865, McArthur and his division were transferred to the command of E. R. S. Canby for the upcoming campaign against Mobile. Not only did he fight in the battles around Mobile, but during the campaign he designed and supervised the building of several wooden mortars made from the gum trees in southern Alabama. No doubt using his experience from his foundry days, McArthur was able to produce workable guns that proved very effective at short range against Confederate fortifications.

McArthur remained in Alabama after the war, commanding the garrison at Selma until he was mustered out in August 1865. He returned home to Illinois to try to rebuild his prewar business. His iron works failed, and his stint in government service proved equally disastrous when, while serving as Chicago's postmaster, a bank failure lost the post office more than $70,000 that he was expected to repay. Still he managed to muddle through these problems, remaining active in the community, his church, and the Grand Army of the Republic. He died in Chicago on 15 May 1906.

—*David S. Heidler and Jeanne T. Heidler*

See also Nashville, Battle of; Shiloh, Battle of; Vicksburg Campaign.
For further reading:
Bearrs, Edwin C. *The Campaign for Vicksburg* (1985–1986).
Horn, Stanley F. *The Decisive Battle of Nashville* (1956).

MCCALLUM, DANIEL CRAIG
(1815–1878)
Union railroad superintendent

Born in Renfrewshire, Scotland, Daniel Craig McCallum immigrated to the United States with his parents when he was a small child. The family settled in Rochester, New York, where McCallum received his education in local schools. After leaving school, he trained as a builder, displaying considerable aptitude for engineering. After serving an apprenticeship in that area, he became an accomplished architect and railroad engineer in New York. He designed a bridge called an inflexible arched truss bridge that, once patented, made McCallum a small fortune.

After moving to New York City in 1852, McCallum continued his work designing and supervising construction of railroad bridges and began doing consulting work for the New York and Erie Railway. For a year in the mid-1850s he served as general superintendent of the railroad. Still his first love was bridges, and his company was responsible for bridge construction all over the country.

The outbreak of the Civil War and the early combat in the summer of 1861 quickly convinced many in Washington that the efficient, coordinated running of the nation's railroads would be an integral part of a Union victory. Furthermore, because most of the operations in the Eastern theater were taking place in Northern Virginia and the rails in that state had been owned primarily by people who supported the Confederacy, many of those lines had been confiscated by the federal government as territory was occupied by the Union. There was obviously a need to utilize these lines for the transportation of troops and materiel. At the urging of the War Department, Congress tackled this problem and in February passed an act giving the government supervisory control over all railroads, but most importantly over those that would receive the most use in former Confederate territory. On 11 February 1862, Secretary of War Edwin Stanton appointed Daniel McCallum military director and superintendent of the railroads of the United States at the rank of colonel.

For the first year in his new position, McCallum spent most of his time in Washington establishing the bureaucracy that would be necessary to keep railroads repaired and running to support the monumental needs of the Union army. He established two departments to operate in Virginia, one to handle day-to-day maintenance and train operations and the other to do large repair jobs. These departments would become the model for his activities throughout all theaters of operation before the war was over.

For that first year, McCallum concerned himself primarily with Virginia, leaving the commanding generals in the other theaters to handle the railroads in their areas. He worked diligently to procure the rolling stock necessary to move primarily the Army of the Potomac and its supplies around northern Virginia and to hire the construction crews necessary to keep the tracks in repair in spite of the best efforts of Confederate raiders to destroy them. With McCallum's expertise in bridge construction, this activity became a major focus of his

General Daniel McCallum (*right*) and another officer on Lookout Mountain, Chattanooga, Tennessee (*Library of Congress*)

efforts just as destroying bridges occupied a great deal of the time of Confederate raiding parties. McCallum's construction crews became so adept at repairing and rebuilding railroad bridges that, within a few months of McCallum assuming office, they could construct a usable railroad bridge within forty-eight hours.

During the fall of 1863, McCallum left Washington to supervise personally the construction crews who followed George Gordon Meade and the Army of the Potomac in its pursuit of Robert E. Lee and the Army of Northern Virginia. McCallum and his men were able to provide the logistical support for an army of more than 100,000 men with scarcely any interruption in railroad service.

At the end of the year, McCallum's expertise was needed in Chattanooga. With the repulse of the Southern attempt to retake the city in the fall of 1863 and in the hope of expanding Union control over much of Tennessee, north Georgia, and north Alabama, the rail links to Chattanooga and Nashville were essential. Earlier in the Chattanooga campaign, a civilian railroad official, John B. Anderson, had been fulfilling the same function regarding the railroads as McCallum in the East, but his administration of the lines had been less that satisfactory. When McCallum arrived in Chattanooga, he dismissed Anderson and immediately began reorganizing the railroad workers and construction crews as he had in Virginia. Again, he created two departments, one to handle day-to-day operations and the other to handle major construction jobs on tracks and bridges. McCallum was solicitous of his workers, who often did their jobs under great danger from attack from Confederate raiders, and his treatment of these men made recruiting much easier under his leadership.

Once the railroads were running efficiently in Tennessee, McCallum returned to Virginia to supervise the preparation of the railroads in anticipation of Ulysses S. Grant's overland campaign against Robert E. Lee. Tracks and bridges were repaired, or in some cases added, to handle the massive movement of men, equipment, and supplies that would be needed for this campaign.

By early summer, however, McCallum was again needed in Tennessee and north Georgia to oversee the massive logistical undertaking of keeping the railroads running to support William T. Sherman's Atlanta campaign. McCallum's achievements during that campaign were nothing short of miraculous. Not only did the railroads run, but by keeping his construction crews working almost twenty-four hours a day, McCallum was able to keep pace with the damage being done to the lines by the likes of Nathan Bedford Forrest. For his achievement, McCallum received a brevet promotion to brigadier general in September 1864.

McCallum returned to Washington in the fall, again to supervise the repairs to Virginia railroads made necessary by the activities of Confederate raiders there. He returned south at the commencement of Sherman's Carolina campaign in early 1864, however, to aid in railroad repairs and rolling stock procurement to support Sherman's efforts. McCallum then returned to Washington in the early spring.

The end of the war did not see the end of McCallum's responsibilities. He provided the logistical support for the transportation of Abraham Lincoln's body back to Springfield, Illinois, and personally accompanied the body to see to all the minor details of the rail transport. Returning to Washington, for the next year McCallum oversaw the repairs necessary to Southern railroads to support the Federal occupation of that region. With that task complete, in April 1866 he submitted his final report. For war service he was breveted major general of volunteers.

McCallum was mustered out of the volunteer army in 1866 and returned briefly to the railroad industry. For the remainder of his life, however, he lived mostly in retirement, serving occasionally as a consultant on various railroad projects. He died in Brooklyn, New York, on 27 December 1878.

—*David S. Heidler and Jeanne T. Heidler*

See also Railroads, Union.

For further reading:
Turner, George Edgar. *Victory Rode the Rails: The Strategic Place of the Railroads in the Civil War* (1953).
Weber, Thomas. *The Northern Railroad in the Civil War, 1861–1865* (1952).

McCAUSLAND, JOHN A.
(1836–1927)
Confederate general

John A. "Tiger John" McCausland was one of the most colorful characters in the Civil War. Born of Irish immigrants in 1836 in St. Louis, Missouri, McCausland moved with his brother in 1849 to Point Pleasant, Virginia, where he received his formal education. He attended the Virginia Military Institute and graduated with first-class honors in 1857. He subsequently stayed at the institute and taught until the beginning of hostilities in 1861.

When Virginia seceded, McCausland offered his services to his state and organized the Rockbridge Artillery. Governor John Letcher later assigned McCausland the responsibility for recruitment of troops in western Virginia. He organized the 36th Virginia Regiment and became its colonel. McCausland and his Virginians served under Generals Albert Sidney Johnston, John Floyd, William Wing Loring, John Echols, and Samuel Jones in numerous campaigns in southwestern and western Virginia and in the Shenandoah Valley.

In the spring of 1864, General Albert Gallatin Jenkins ordered McCausland to move his brigade to the Kanawha Valley, where he met Union general George Crook at Cloyd's Farm on 9 May. When Jenkins fell, McCausland took command and performed well enough to earn promotion to brigadier general.

McCausland will forever be remembered in the annals of the war for two actions: his repulse of David Hunter from Lynchburg and the burning of Chambersburg. The first earned him the laurels of a Virginia city and the second, the abiding hatred of a community in Pennsylvania.

Fighting a superior force under Major General David Hunter, McCausland routed Hunter at Lynchburg in mid-June 1864. McCausland held off Hunter's force for three days, giving the city the time it needed before reinforcements under Jubal Early arrived, forcing Hunter to retreat into western Virginia. The city of Lynchburg was grateful enough to bestow McCausland a gold engraved sword, a pair of silver spurs, and a new horse.

After the battle at Lynchburg, McCausland and his men united with General Early and invaded Maryland. Early sent McCausland into Hagerstown and ordered him to demand a $200,000 ransom in retaliation for the burning of the Shenandoah. In the excitement of battle, the former mathematics professor forgot to insert the final digit and was promptly given the $20,000 he requested.

McCausland drove Lew Wallace's inexperienced troops from the field at Monocacy on 9 July 1864 and advanced as far as Georgetown before Federal reinforcements forced both him and Early to retreat into Virginia.

Early received word of Hunter's continued mayhem among the civilians of Virginia and vowed revenge. He ordered McCausland and General Bradley Johnson to demand ransom from Chambersburg, Pennsylvania. The two generals entered the town on 30 July 1864 with a force of 2,800 men and demanded a ransom of $100,000 in gold or $500,000 in greenbacks from the leading citizens of the community. When the city fathers refused to pay the ransom, McCausland burned the town.

After burning Chambersburg, McCausland's brigade fought a few minor skirmishes in Maryland and then withdrew to Moorefield, West Virginia. At Moorefield on 7 August 1864, McCausland's command was shattered as he lost 400 men in the encounter against Union cavalry bent on revenge for the burning of Chambersburg.

After the debacle at Moorefield, McCausland's brigade participated in the final campaigns in the Shenandoah Valley, including Cedar Creek. In March 1865, McCausland joined Robert E. Lee's embattled Army of Northern Virginia at Petersburg and stayed with Lee until the surrender at Appomattox. Rather than surrender, McCausland broke through the lines and was later paroled at Charleston, West Virginia.

The new Union state of West Virginia did not suit the former Confederate general. After he learned of an indictment against him for the burning of Chambersburg, McCausland fled for Canada, the British Isles, and Mexico. He returned in 1868 after the federal government assured him that he would not receive prosecution as a war criminal.

McCausland married in 1878 and began life as a gentlemen farmer, tending his 6,000-acre estate in the Ohio River county of Mason, West Virginia. After the death of his wife in 1891 he lived the rest of his life as a recluse. McCausland died in 1927 in his ninetieth year, unapologetic and unreconstructed. His death followed close enough to the end of the Great War in Europe that many Northern obituary writers could not resist referring to the deceased Confederate as the "Hun of Chambersburg."

—*Jim Baugess*

See also Cedar Creek, Battle of; Chambersburg; Cloyd's Mountain, Battle of; Early, Jubal Anderson; Lynchburg; Monocacy, Battle of; Moorefield, West Virginia, Battle of.
For further reading:
Brown, James Earl. "Life of Brigadier General John McCausland." *West Virginia History* (1943).
Pauley, Michael J. *Unreconstructed Rebel: The Life of General John McCausland, C.S.A.* (1992).
Phillips, David L. *Tiger John: The Rebel Who Burned Chambersburg* (1993).

MCCLELLAN, GEORGE BRINTON
(1826–1885)
Union general

Few figures provoked as much controversy during the Civil War as did George B. McClellan. Dubbed the "Young Napoleon" by his early admirers, McClellan seemed the hope of the Union in the desperate days after the debacle at First Bull Run. In time, however, that hope faded as McClellan's campaign against Richmond, Virginia, in 1862 faltered, and questions about his military competence and political loyalties surfaced. Relieved of his command by Abraham Lincoln after the battle of Antietam, McClellan would unsuccessfully challenge him for the presidency in 1864. His reputation undone by failure, one of the Union's first war heroes would thus end the war rebuffed by the nation.

George McClellan was born in Philadelphia, Pennsylvania, on 3 December 1826. The son of a prominent medical doctor, McClellan enjoyed the advantages of a privileged upbringing. Possessed of a keen mind, he excelled in school. In 1840, at the age of thirteen, he enrolled at the University of Pennsylvania and two years later transferred to West Point, where he finished second in the graduating class of 1846. The advent of the Mexican-American War that year afforded McClellan an immediate opportunity to test his skills on the battlefield. Commissioned as an engineer, he saw extensive action under Winfield Scott's command and won two brevets for distinguished service. After the war, McClellan engaged in survey and construction work for the army, including the construction of Fort Delaware. In 1855, he was sent to Europe as part of a commission to observe the Crimean War, where he witnessed the siege of Sevastopol. Despite having risen to the rank of captain, McClellan by 1857 found life in the military unsatisfying. In that year, he resigned his commission to pursue lucrative engineering work for the Illinois Central Railroad in Chicago. While there, he became acquainted with one of the railway's attorneys, Abraham Lincoln.

McClellan's career with the railroads proved to be as successful as his earlier stint in the military had been. He left the Illinois Central to become president of the Ohio & Mississippi Railroad and was serving as president of the St. Louis, Missouri & Cincinnati Railroad when war broke out in 1861. The Lincoln administration's call for volunteers after the fall of Fort Sumter renewed the former officer's military career. McClellan's military background and political connections prompted Ohio governor William Dennison to appoint him on 23 April 1861 a major general in charge of the state's volunteers. Shortly thereafter, McClellan received a commission in the regular army to command the newly created Department of the Ohio. In that capacity he launched a

McClellan with Lincoln following the battle of Antietam,
3 October 1862
(Photograph by Alexander Gardner / *Library of Congress*)

campaign to wrest western Virginia from Confederate control. In the first land battle of the war, McClellan routed rebel forces near Philippi on 3 June 1861 and followed it up with victories at Rich Mountain and Carrick's Ford. Though historians still question his leadership in the campaign, this series of triumphs garnered McClellan national recognition and the gratitude of a nation. On 16 July 1861, the U.S. House of Representatives passed a resolution of thanks to the young general for his service in defense of the Union. Less than a week later, in the aftermath of First Bull Run, he would be called upon by the Lincoln administration to reassemble the shattered remains of Union forces around Washington, D.C.

McClellan arrived at the nation's capital on 26 July 1861 to find the city in turmoil and the army disheartened. He immediately set about replenishing the ranks and restoring morale. In so doing, he created the renowned Army of the Potomac and established a fine rapport with his soldiers. The same cannot be said for his relationships with political and military superiors, however. Pressured to take the offensive as early as September, the general would not be hurried in his mission to crush the rebellion in a single blow. He

quickly clashed with General-in-Chief Winfield Scott, until the latter's retirement in November of 1861. A formerly cordial relationship with Secretary of War Edwin Stanton and his allies in Congress later turned sour. President Lincoln remained a supporter, but McClellan held him in little regard. Wary of possible leaks, General McClellan rarely shared his strategic thinking with the administration. When he finally did reveal his plan for an amphibious assault against the Confederate capital at Richmond, it was met with concern by Lincoln and outright resistance by others in the administration who favored an overland route. After much debate, McClellan received approval for his Peninsula campaign.

The Peninsula campaign got under way in March 1862, long after the Lincoln administration and the Northern public had wanted. It was a massive undertaking. Nearly 400 vessels transported 121,500 Union troops and their supplies from the area around Washington, D.C., to the staging ground at Fort Monroe on the Virginia peninsula. From there, plans were to advance overland toward Richmond, using naval vessels to protect the army's flanks while it marched down the peninsula. Members of Congress and the Lincoln administration worried, however, that McClellan's campaign would leave Washington, D.C., dangerously exposed to Confederate counterattack, despite the general's assurances to the contrary. For the safety of the city, the decision was made to detach Irvin McDowell's I Corps from McClellan's command and retain it at the capital for defensive purposes. McClellan would later point to this decision as a crippling blow to his chances for victory, but even without McDowell's troops the Army of the Potomac remained formidable. The Confederates certainly believed it so.

McClellan met his first serious resistance of the campaign near Yorktown, site of the Revolutionary War battle. There Confederate troops numbering around 15,000 under the command of General Joseph Johnston had entrenched themselves in the hope of stalling the Yankee advance. It worked. Through false reports and rebel ruses, McClellan believed that he faced a superior force and on 5 April 1862 settled in for a month-long siege of the Confederate works. Though successful, the siege slowed McClellan's advance and gave the Confederates valuable time to concentrate their forces in defense of Richmond.

Other factors also slowed McClellan's advance to a snail's pace. Heavy rains proved to be the bane of the campaign, soaking the soldiers and ruining the roads. Naval support was sporadic at best, as a result of the harassment of the Confederate ironclad *Virginia* (originally the *Merrimack*). Yet by the end of May, the Army of the Potomac had reached the outskirts of Richmond and, true to form, McClellan began preparations for a siege of the Confederate capital. The general pursued a conservative strategy designed to subdue the South with minimal bloodshed by capturing its capital rather than destroying its military might. Radical Republicans in Congress who favored a punitive strategy cried foul, but Confederate leaders understood the danger presented by McClellan's siege and moved to disrupt it. On 31 May 1862, Joseph Johnston initiated an attack on elements of McClellan's army positioned south of the Chickahominy River near Fair Oaks Station. Initially successful, the battle of Fair Oaks (Seven Pines) would finish badly for the rebels when the attack went astray and Johnston fell seriously wounded. Having survived Johnston's challenge, the Army of the Potomac resumed its siege operations. However, Johnston's replacement, Robert E. Lee, sensed McClellan's cautious character and determined to resume the offensive. Recalling Thomas J. "Stonewall" Jackson from his Shenandoah campaign, Lee launched a series of attacks, collectively known as the Seven Days' battles, against McClellan's troops in late June. Suddenly McClellan was put on the defensive and systematically driven away from Richmond.

The abrupt shift in fortunes unnerved McClellan. He began casting about for ways to exculpate himself for what was happening to his army. He denied that he was in retreat, preferring to describe it as a change of base. After a defeat at the battle of Gaines' Mill on 27 June, McClellan fired off a scathing dispatch to Secretary of War Edwin Stanton blaming the Lincoln administration for his recent reversals. "If I save this army now," the general impugned, "I tell you plainly I owe no thanks to you or to any other persons in Washington. You have done your best to sacrifice this army." By all accounts, McClellan's language was not only inconsiderate, but insubordinate as well. The farther McClellan's forces receded from the gates of Richmond, the more any vestige of support he maintained from Lincoln eroded. After a successful defense of his remaining toehold on the peninsula at the battle of Malvern Hill on 1 July, McClellan's hope of resuming the offensive was dashed when he was ordered to return the Army of the Potomac north for the defense of Washington, D.C.

The failure of the Peninsula campaign stripped McClellan of his authority and influence, and he was instructed to support the command of John Pope's newly created Army of Virginia. Throughout the campaign, the general had done much to alienate support at home. His incessant demands for reinforcements along with his dire reports from the front bespoke a lack of will to pursue the enemy. The slow pace of his advance, in part caused by inclement weather, seemed only to confirm this growing perception among the Northern public. He even appeared to be procrastinating in returning his troops to Washington, though he denied such charges.

Indeed, McClellan's formerly shiny image had become badly tarnished.

When Pope's forces were soundly defeated at the battle of Second Bull Run in late August, however, a reluctant Lincoln again turned to the man who had earlier mended a broken army. Historians generally agree that McClellan was a strong organizer and skilled trainer of troops. In the weeks after Second Bull Run he marshaled these skills in defense of a beleaguered capital, much as he had done the previous summer. There was great fear that a Confederate invasion of the North was now imminent, so there was little time to waste. McClellan quickly retooled the disorganized lot of troops for military operations. In the meantime, he fought off allegations that he had maneuvered behind the scenes to subvert Pope's command and had thereby imperiled the safety of the republic. Such charges would plague McClellan throughout the remainder of the war.

On 5 September 1862, McClellan learned that Robert E. Lee's Army of Northern Virginia had crossed the Potomac River and begun an invasion of the North. As McClellan moved the army away from Washington to meet the enemy, he again began demanding reinforcements. The Federal garrison defending Harper's Ferry, Virginia, soon became a point of friction in this regard. An important railroad junction, Harper's Ferry also held symbolic importance for Radical Republicans as the site of John Brown's 1859 raid. In September 1862, approximately 13,000 Union troops under the command of Colonel Dixon S. Miles were occupying the

General George McClellan (*standing to right of stump*) and staff (*Library of Congress*)

town. McClellan wanted these soldiers removed for service in his campaign against Lee. His request was refused. When Confederate troops under "Stonewall" Jackson laid siege to Harper's Ferry, McClellan only reluctantly and irresolutely sent reinforcements, which arrived too late to prevent surrender of the garrison on 15 September. The general's priorities were elsewhere.

On 13 September 1862, Union soldiers had stumbled across a misplaced copy of Lee's operational plans for the current campaign. Dubbed the "Lost Dispatch," it was immediately forwarded to McClellan, who initially approached it with caution. Once convinced of its authenticity, however, he molded his campaign around its every word. At the battle of South Mountain the following day, Union forces pushed elements of Lee's army away from important approaches to the main rebel force in western Maryland. Lee concentrated his army on the banks of Antietam Creek near Sharpsburg, Maryland, and awaited McClellan's assault.

The assault came on 17 September at the battle of Antietam. On that one bloody day, Union and Confederate forces waged war on a titanic scale, producing casualties at an astonishing rate. Indeed, 17 September 1862 stands as the single bloodiest day of the Civil War. Lee battered McClellan's assailing forces, but determined the following day that his army had suffered too greatly to continue the fight. Under cover of darkness, Lee's Army of Northern Virginia removed across the Potomac and abandoned its invasion plans. Ever cautious, McClellan delayed his pursuit of the retiring Rebels until his own forces had sufficiently recovered. In so doing, however, he sacrificed a rare opportunity to deliver final defeat to the Confederate army. Questions regarding his will to fight reemerged. Moreover, there was increasing concern about his loyalty to the Lincoln administration.

President Lincoln arrived at McClellan's headquarters on 1 October to judge for himself the disposition of General McClellan and his troops. Over the course of McClellan's command, Lincoln and McClellan's initially courteous relationship had become increasingly antagonistic. The general resented and often resisted the president's military advice, yet freely offered his own unsolicited political advice. When reinforcements failed to reach him, he disparaged Lincoln's administrative capacities. He began to question the president's commitment to him, particularly after Lincoln queried the general about rumors of treasonous conduct in March 1862. Similarly, Lincoln had come to doubt McClellan's will to fight. During the Peninsula campaign, the president had defended McClellan against critics within the administration. And as long as the general produced results, he was willing to endure McClellan's reproaches of him. It was McClellan's mediocre performance on the battlefield that gave him pause. First, the Peninsula campaign had been repulsed and now McClellan had squandered a chance to deal the deathblow to Lee's battered army. The general's constant delays and cautious ways were testing Lincoln's patience. As such, the president spent four days with the Army of the Potomac after Antietam, buoying the mens' spirits and urging their commander to take the offensive. Decisive military action was needed now as much as ever because Lincoln had just upped the ante on the Confederates by issuing a preliminary Emancipation Proclamation.

Lincoln's proclamation after Antietam fundamentally altered the war in a way that McClellan little approved. Like his military strategy, the general's politics were conservative. He believed that a small cadre of planter elite, whose machinations had imperiled the Union, had foisted secession upon a reluctant South. He wished to see that Union restored with as little revision as possible, believing it to be essentially sound. Unlike Lincoln, he could not conceive that slavery was the true malady threatening the Union. McClellan repeatedly warned against converting the war into a crusade against slavery, but in this respect events passed him by. In the wake of Antietam, McClellan's conservative sentiments became incongruous with administration policy; his cautious generalship, incompatible with the demands of the war. When all hope of capturing the retreating Lee faded by October, so too did any hope of McClellan retaining his command. On 5 November 1862, McClellan was ordered to turn over his command to General Ambrose Burnside, a favorite of the Radical Republicans, and report to Trenton, New Jersey, for a reassignment that never came. The friction between McClellan and the Lincoln administration did not end there, however.

While nursing his wounded pride in Trenton, the deposed general began making serious contacts with Democratic Party representatives. McClellan's well-publicized break with the Lincoln administration afforded Democrats an opportunity to exploit an already intense rivalry for political advantage. His name recognition and states rights' position also made him an attractive candidate to challenge Lincoln in the 1864 presidential election. The result of that election, which Lincoln won handily, does not adequately reflect the concern that many Republicans actually felt upon learning of McClellan's nomination by the Democratic Party.

The general's dismissal by the administration in 1862 had been followed by an emotion-laden farewell ceremony among his troops. The Army of the Potomac maintained great affection for its creator, and Republicans in 1864 worried that lingering loyalties to McClellan might cost Lincoln thousands of soldiers' votes. Moreover, they feared that McClellan would appeal to elements of the Northern population who resented emancipation as a war aim. Although McClellan flatly repudiated the charge that he would as president accept a peace that recognized the

Confederacy, there was a belief among Republicans that McClellan would negotiate a settlement with the Confederacy that would negate their reforms and return the status quo. But McClellan's passive positions, along with signal Union victories in the weeks preceding the election, helped ensure Lincoln's reelection. McClellan captured but 21 of 233 electoral votes and carried only the states of Delaware, Kentucky, and New Jersey.

The presidential campaign whetted McClellan's appetite for politics, despite his lackluster performance. After having administered several engineering firms in the postwar years, McClellan was elected governor of New Jersey in 1878 and by all accounts ran a successful administration. Still, his earlier failures as a Union general haunted him, and the slander he believed he had endured at the hands of his political opponents prompted him to compose toward the end of his life a provocative, self-serving set of memoirs entitled *McClellan's Own Story*. Its pages have added to the controversy surrounding McClellan's tenure as commander of the Army of the Potomac, but the general did not live to see his story published. He died on 29 October 1885, in Orange, New Jersey.

The ambiguity of George McClellan's Civil War service admits both praise and criticism. He forged a powerful weapon of war, the Army of the Potomac, yet wielded it weakly. He roused both the admiration of his troops and the ire of his superiors. He parried Lee's thrust into the North, but was himself checked at the gates of Richmond. Indeed, McClellan's legacy defies easy categorization and simple judgment. Perhaps Ulysses S. Grant expressed it best when asked after the war to evaluate McClellan as a general. "McClellan," he replied, "is to me one of the mysteries of the war."

—*Jonathan M. Beagle*

See also Antietam, Battle of; Ball's Bluff, Battle of; Joint Committee on the Conduct of the War; Election of 1864; Peninsula Campaign; Philippi, Battle of; Seven Days' Battles.

For further reading:

Hassler, Warren W., Jr. *General George B. McClellan: Shield of the Union* (1957).

Rowland, Thomas J. *George B. McClellan and Civil War History: In the Shadow of Grant and Sherman* (1998).

Sears, Stephen W. *George B. McClellan: The Young Napoleon* (1989).

Williams, T. Harry. *McClellan, Sherman, and Grant* (1962).

McCLERNAND, JOHN ALEXANDER
(1812–1900)
Union general

When President Abraham Lincoln appointed general officers for the U.S. Army in 1861, he considered many factors, including military experience and political persuasion. Those men with a military background were needed to fight the war, but influential politicians were also important. A powerful politician might receive a general's commission for his abilities to recruit troops and speak in defense of the war effort. The latter was particularly important in the border state areas that might have strong Southern sentiment. One such individual was John Alexander McClernand of Illinois.

John A. McClernand was born in Kentucky in 1812, and his family moved to the southern Illinois town of Shawneetown shortly thereafter. His only military experience before the Civil War was during the Black Hawk War in 1832. He enrolled for ninety days and served in Captain Harrison Wilson's company, 1st Regiment, 1st Brigade, Illinois Mounted Volunteers. Shortly after enlisting, McClernand was appointed assistant brigade quartermaster with the temporary rank of colonel. He

Major General John McClernand with Lincoln following the battle of Antietam, 3 October 1862 (Photograph by Alexander Gardner / *Library of Congress*)

saw virtually no action and was mustered out after serving about sixty days.

McClernand began his political career in 1836 when he was elected to the Illinois House of Representatives as a Jacksonian Democrat. After several terms in the Illinois General Assembly, he was elected to the U.S. House of Representatives in 1843. As a congressional representative in the 1840s and early 1850s McClernand was in the middle of some of the most important legislative battles that led to the Civil War. He was Illinois senator Stephen A. Douglas's spokesman in the House, and the two played pivotal roles in negotiating the Compromise of 1850. McClernand left Congress in 1851, but returned in 1859 and was a central figure in the contentious 1859 speakership battle. Throughout the 1860 election and the early period of the secession crisis McClernand worked for compromise and conciliation. When that failed, he supported war.

McClernand received a general's commission for his support of the war. President Lincoln needed men like McClernand, a Democrat, to recruit troops and speak for the war effort. His commission came through on 7 August 1861 to date from 17 May 1861. McClernand was assigned to the Western Department, which was commanded by Major General John C. Frémont. He was given command of a brigade of Illinois regiments and stationed at Cairo, Illinois, part of the District of Southeast Missouri, which was commanded by General Ulysses S. Grant. McClernand was Grant's second-in-command. Although both Grant and McClernand fought on the same side, by the end of their association the two men were bitter enemies.

The first combat experience for General McClernand was the battle of Belmont on 7 November 1861. McClernand commanded the 1st Brigade, which consisted of 2,072 men, fully two-thirds of the expeditionary force. During the engagement, a rebel ball struck one of McClernand's pistols and two of his horses were shot from under him. After capturing the Confederate camp, the Federal troops retired from Belmont and returned safely to Cairo. McClernand's first combat experience was successful, and his superior, General Grant, commended him in his official report.

The day after the engagement, McClernand wrote directly to General-in-Chief George B. McClellan in Washington. This was a disturbing habit that McClernand continued throughout the war—disregarding the official chain of command. When this happened, McClernand most frequently corresponded with President Lincoln. Yet another disturbing habit McClernand started after Belmont was his writing congratulatory orders to his troops. After every battle, McClernand congratulated his men and often failed to mention that any other troops participated in the fight. These two habits served to alienate many officers in the Federal army and ultimately

caused Grant to remove McClernand from his command in June 1863. From the very beginning of the war, McClernand mixed war and politics and was unable to separate politics from the military.

General McClernand next commanded Grant's 1st Division in capturing Forts Henry and Donelson in February 1862. After the surrender of Fort Donelson, McClernand, promoted to major general, led his division to Pittsburg Landing, where Grant was concentrating his army for an invasion into the Confederate heartland. It was McClernand who warned General William T. Sherman of the presence of Confederate troops nearby. Precautions were not taken, and the Federal Army of the Tennessee was surprised on 6 April 1862, beginning the two-day battle of Shiloh. After ably leading his division during the battle, McClernand was given command of the Reserve Corps when General Henry Halleck assumed control of the army. McClernand held that position throughout the snail-like advance on Corinth.

After the capture of Corinth, McClernand served garrison duty in Bolivar, Mississippi, and Jackson, Tennessee. This did not suit McClernand, as he was restless and wanted to fight. He finally received orders to report to Illinois governor Richard Yates in Springfield to aid in recruiting troops. Yates requested McClernand to accompany him to the East and the general gladly agreed. This gave McClernand an opportunity to lobby in person for the one thing he wanted badly—an independent command. By September 1862 McClernand had presented a plan to President Lincoln for the capture of Vicksburg. After considerable politicking, on 21 October General McClernand was given command of an independent expedition to capture the formidable Confederate fort.

After spending two months recruiting troops in the Midwest, McClernand assumed command of his troops, styled the Army of the Mississippi, on 2 January 1863. Instead of moving immediately upon Vicksburg, McClernand captured the Confederate outpost on the Arkansas River called Arkansas Post. The capture of the fort on 11 January 1863 was the zenith of McClernand's Civil War career. By the end of January, McClernand's command was reduced to the XIII Army Corps, Army of the Tennessee. In that capacity he participated in the capture of Vicksburg. Throughout this campaign, the relations between McClernand and Grant deteriorated to the point where Grant removed McClernand on 18 June 1863. The reason: McClernand wrote a congratulatory order and published it in the newspapers without first sending it through command channels.

After six months of inactivity, McClernand was reassigned to his XIII Corps in January 1864. His troops were part of General Nathaniel Banks's Department of the Gulf in Texas. Playing almost no role in the Red River campaign, McClernand became ill with malaria in May 1864 and returned home, never again to fight in the war.

John A. McClernand's Civil War experience was dominated by mixing politics with war. He never separated the two and that alienated many high-ranking civil and military officials. It ultimately led to his removal in June 1863. He habitually circumvented the military chain of command and wrote directly to political figures, most frequently to President Lincoln. The most common theme in this correspondence was to request an independent command. In spite of his insubordinate activities, McClernand was a competent commander; he made no great blunders and was always willing to fight the enemy.

—*Christopher C. Meyers*

See also Arkansas Post, Battle of; Army of the Mississippi; Belmont, Battle of; Grant, Ulysses S.

For further reading:

Hicken, Victor. "John A. McClernand and the House Speakership Battle of 1859." *Journal of the Illinois State Historical Society* (1960).

Kiper, Richard L. "Prelude to Vicksburg: The Louisiana Campaign of Major General John Alexander McClernand." *Louisiana History* (1996).

Meyers, Christopher C. "'Two Generals Cannot Command This Army': John A. McClernand and the Politics of Command in Grant's Army of the Tennessee." *Columbiad* (1998).

McCOOKS OF OHIO

The "Fighting McCooks" of Ohio numbered seventeen: eleven from the "tribe of Dan," six from the "tribe of John." Of these, seven eventually reached the rank of general officer or were promoted to that rank for their war service. Five others served either as officers of varying rank, doctors, or chaplains. Little is known of the remaining members.

Daniel McCook (1798–1863) was head of the "tribe of Dan." He served as a volunteer nurse at the battle of Bull Run, where the death of his son Charles perhaps

Major General Alexander M. McCook (*center*) and staff at their quarters near present-day Sheridan Street, Washington, D.C., July 1864 (*Library of Congress*)

influenced him to join the army. At any rate, he received a commission in 1862. On 19 July 1863, he suffered a mortal wound during the pursuit of Confederate raider John Hunt Morgan.

George W. McCook (1821–1877) was a veteran of the Mexican-American War and one-time law partner of Secretary of War Edwin M. Stanton. Poor health kept him from active field duty during the Civil War, but he served the Union cause by recruiting and training new Ohio regiments.

Robert Latimer McCook (1827–1862) served as colonel of the 9th Ohio Cavalry. Promoted to brigadier general in March 1862, he was wounded by guerrillas near Decherd, Tennessee, on 5 August 1862 and died the following day.

The highest ranking member of the family, Alexander McDowell McCook (1831–1903) graduated from West Point in 1852. After frontier duty, he returned to the military academy as an instructor. Appointed colonel of the 1st Ohio in 1861, he saw action in most of the major battles and campaigns in the Western theater of the Civil War. At Chickamauga he commanded the XX Corps Army of the Cumberland and was one of several who were charged with responsibility for the disaster that befell the Union army, though he was later cleared of any culpability. McCook proved able enough as a division and brigade commander, but left much to be desired as a corps commander. A professional soldier, he remained in the army after the war and eventually retired as major general.

Daniel McCook II (1834–1864) was a former law partner of William T. Sherman. He received a commission in the Kansas volunteers in 1861 and saw action at Wilson's Creek. Later, he commanded a brigade during the Atlanta campaign, where he was mortally wounded in the assault on Kennesaw Mountain. He was promoted to brigadier general of volunteers the day before his death.

Edwin Stanton McCook (1837–1873) graduated from the U.S. Naval Academy and spent two years as a midshipman (1854–1856). In 1861, he accepted a commission in the 31st Illinois. He saw extensive service in the Western theater, including the Atlanta campaign and the March to the Sea. He was promoted to brigadier general of volunteers for his war-time service.

Charles Morris McCook (1843–1861) left Kenyon College and joined the 2d Ohio in 1861. He was killed in action at First Bull Run.

John James McCook (1845–?) followed his brother Charles and left Kenyon College to join the army. He was commissioned captain in the 6th Ohio Cavalry in 1863. After the war he practiced law.

John McCook (1806–1865) was head of the "tribe of John." A surgeon, he volunteered his services as a doctor during the Civil War and died while visiting his son, Anson, in 1865.

Edward Moody McCook (1833–1909) was a former Kansas legislator, and a member of the secret service at the outbreak of the Civil War. He accepted an army commission in May 1861. After a series of promotions in the volunteers, he commanded first a cavalry brigade and then a division in the Western theater. After the war, he was U.S. minister to Hawaii and was twice governor of Colorado Territory.

Anson George McCook (1835–1917) was appointed captain in the 2d Ohio in 1861. He rose to be colonel of the regiment and was promoted to brigadier general of volunteers for his war service. He was an editor and legislator after the war.

Henry Christopher McCook (1837–1911) was a Presbyterian minister who served as a chaplain during the Civil War. After the war he published extensively in the field of theology and on the subject of ants.

John James McCook (1843–1927) was the second of this name, being the first cousin of John James McCook of "Dan's tribe." He was commissioned lieutenant in the 1st Virginia regiment, which was comprised mainly of Ohioans. After service in Virginia, he left the army and was ordained an Episcopal minister. He taught at Trinity College and, like his brother, Henry, was also the author of numerous books and articles.

It is often said that the Civil War was an intensely personal sort of war that pitted brother against brother, friend against friend. The story of the Ohio McCooks serves as a notable example of familial sacrifice.

—Jerry Keenan

For further reading:
Cozzens, Peter. *No Better Place to Die* (1990).
———. *This Terrible Sound: The Battle of Chickamauga* (1992).

McCULLOCH, BEN
(1811–1862)
Confederate general

Born in Rutherford County, Tennessee, on 11 November 1811, Ben McCulloch was the fourth son of Alexander McCulloch and Frances S. Lenorr. The family also included a younger brother, Henry E. McCulloch, who—like Ben—became famous as a Texas Ranger, U.S. marshall, and brigadier general in the Confederate army. Between 1812 and 1830 the McCulloch family moved frequently, finally settling near Dyersburg, Tennessee, where Sam Houston and Davy Crockett became influential family friends.

In 1835 McCulloch agreed to follow Crockett to Texas, but he arrived late for a rendezvous in Nacogdoches. Falling ill with measles, he missed the massacre at the Alamo, but joined Houston's army as it retreated into east Texas. For McCulloch's actions commanding one of the famed "twin sisters" at the battle of San Jacinto, Houston promoted him to first lieutenant. Shortly after San Jacinto, McCulloch left the army to become a surveyor and Texas Ranger along the frontier. He earned a noteworthy reputation as an Indian fighter while serving as a first lieutenant in John Coffee "Jack" Hayes's Ranger company.

In 1839 McCulloch won a seat in the legislature of the Republic of Texas. In a rifle duel during the contentious campaign, McCulloch received a wound that partially disabled his right arm for the remainder of his life. In August 1840 at the battle of Plum Creek, he justified his reputation as an Indian fighter while commanding the right flank of a force of Rangers and volunteers that attacked a large band of raiding Comanches. Deciding not to run for reelection in 1842, Ben returned to surveying and a quasi-military career with the Rangers. In February and September 1842 he enlarged his reputation as a scout and soldier by constantly harassing two invasion forces sent by the Mexican government to capture San Antonio.

Subsequent to Texas's annexation, McCulloch won a seat in the state legislature. During the Mexican-American War he led Company A of Hayes's 1st Regiment of Texas Mounted Volunteers. Appointed Zachary Taylor's chief of scouts, McCulloch earned his commander's respect and a promotion to major at the battle of Buena Vista by conducting a bold reconnaissance of the Mexican lines, a deed that saved Taylor's army from disaster. McCulloch returned to Texas after the war and served as a scout for Brevet Major General David E. Twiggs, commander of U.S. troops in Texas. On 9 September 1849 McCulloch departed for the California gold fields. Unsuccessful at prospecting, he served as sheriff of Sacramento County from 1850 through 1852. McCulloch's lack of formal education foiled Houston's attempts to secure him command of the elite 2d U.S. Cavalry Regiment on the Texas frontier. In 1852 Secretary of War Jefferson Davis awarded the command to his friend Albert Sidney Johnston. McCulloch, however, received an appointment as U.S. marshall for the Eastern District of Texas, where he served until 1861. In 1858, as a peace commissioner, he won acclaim for preventing armed conflict between the United States and the Mormon Church in Utah.

As Texas's secession from the Union neared, McCulloch received a Confederate commission as a colonel of cavalry, which he passed on to his brother Henry. Accepting a commission as a colonel of state troops, Ben rode into San Antonio at the head of about 1,000 mounted volunteers and demanded the surrender of all Federal troops near the city. On 18 February 1861 Twiggs responded to this show of force by surrendering the Federal arsenal and all other U.S. property in San Antonio. As Twiggs capitulated, Henry McCulloch was taking control of all Federal posts on the northwestern frontier of Texas.

Ben McCulloch (*Library of Congress*)

On 11 May 1861 Jefferson Davis appointed Ben McCulloch the second ranking brigadier general in the Confederate army, the first general commissioned from the civilian community. Assigned to command the Indian Territory, McCulloch established his headquarters at Little Rock, Arkansas, and began organizing the Army of the West with regiments from Arkansas, Louisiana, and Texas. Even though hampered by logistical shortages and incessant quarreling over strategic objectives with Missourian Sterling Price, with whom he had been ordered to cooperate, McCulloch orchestrated the formation of a formidable military force. Assisted by Confederate Indian Commissioner Albert Pike, McCulloch established valuable alliances with several Indian tribes inhabiting present-day eastern Oklahoma.

On 10 August 1861 McCulloch's 12,000 troops defeated an army of approximately 7,000 effectives under Brigadier General Nathaniel Lyon at Wilson's Creek, or Oak Hill, in southwest Missouri. Unknown to McCulloch, Lyon had planned a double envelopment of the Rebel camp near Wilson's Creek. Lyon's initial assaults surprised the Southerners and drove them back at both points of the Union attack. Undaunted, McCulloch personally led an infantry counterattack that routed Colonel Franz Sigel's 1,200 men south of the Confederate camp. Halted by artillery fire north of the Confederate positions, Lyon concentrated his defense on Bloody Hill and, despite Lyon's death, the Federals withstood three attacks by Price's troops. Outnumbered, outflanked, and short of ammunition, the Union force abandoned the battlefield to McCulloch's exhausted troops.

On 10 January 1862, because of the bitter animosity between McCulloch and Price, Davis appointed Major General Earl Van Dorn to command both men in the newly created District of the Trans-Mississippi. Van Dorn combined both of the recalcitrant generals' divisions to form the 16,400-man Army of the West. In early March, Van Dorn insisted on a campaign to destroy the Federal army then marching into Arkansas and subsequently push on to St. Louis.

When the Confederates met Union major general Samuel R. Curtis's 10,500 soldiers of the Southwestern District of Missouri on 6 March 1862 along Little Sugar Creek in northwest Arkansas, McCulloch's knowledge of the terrain allowed Van Dorn to flank his adversary and threaten Curtis's lines of communication. Curtis fell back and established strong defensive positions from Pea Ridge to an inn called Elkhorn Tavern. During the night of 6–7 March, McCulloch led his division on a cold, dismal march around the Union right flank. Curtis, however, discovered the flanking movement and maneuvered a major portion of his army to attack McCulloch near Leetown.

The following morning, at the battle of Pea Ridge, or Elkhorn Tavern, McCulloch commanding Van Dorn's right flank overran an artillery battery and drove the Federals from their positions. About 1:30 P.M., when Federal resistance stiffened, McCulloch rode forward to determine the exact location of the Union positions. Eschewing a uniform, McCulloch wore his usual black velvet suit. As he rode through the thick underbrush McCulloch unknowingly approached to within seventy yards of a line of Union skirmishers who fired a ragged volley at him. He died instantly with a bullet through the heart. His successor, Brigadier General James M. McIntosh, died only a few minutes later, leading a charge previously planned by McCulloch. Leaderless, McCulloch's division lost confidence and drifted to the rear.

Many participants and historians attribute the disaster at Pea Ridge and subsequent Confederate loss of northern Arkansas to McCulloch's untimely death. McCulloch's men buried him on the battlefield, but his body was later moved to Little Rock and finally to the State Cemetery in Austin.

—*Stanley S. McGowen*

See also Pea Ridge (Elkhorn Tavern), Battle of; Pike, Albert; Price, Sterling; Texas; Wilson's Creek, Missouri.
For further reading:
Cutrer, Thomas W. *Ben McCulloch and the Frontier Military Tradition* (1993).

Nunn, W. C., ed. *Ten More Generals in Gray* (1980).
Ray, Victor Marion. *The Life and Service of General Ben McCulloch* (1958).
Shea, William L., and Earl J. Hess. *Pea Ridge, Civil War Campaign in the West* (1992).

McCULLOCH, HUGH
(1808–1895)
United States secretary of the treasury

Born to Hugh McCulloch and Abigail Perkins McCulloch in Kennebunk, Maine, the younger Hugh McCulloch was educated at Bowdoin College, but never graduated. He tried a variety of jobs after leaving college, including school teaching, before choosing a career in law. He went to Boston to study in some of the law offices there. Rather than practice in Boston after his admission to the bar, McCulloch saw greater economic opportunities in the west and moved to Fort Wayne, Indiana.

Still unable to make a steady living through the law, McCulloch accepted a position that would forever change the course of his life when he became the manager of the Fort Wayne branch of the State Bank of Indiana. Though he had no experience in banking, McCulloch soon showed an aptitude for financial affairs. He managed the Fort Wayne branch for over twenty years. In 1856, on the eve of one of the worst panics in American history, McCulloch accepted promotion to manage the State Bank of Indiana. During the Panic of 1857, his astute management and the sound footing on which he had placed the bank, made it one of only a handful of banks in the entire country that did not have to suspend specie payments on its obligations.

The strength of the Bank of Indiana naturally led McCulloch to oppose legislation during the Civil War that would put increased regulations on state banks. He considered such legislation unfair to those institutions that engaged in sound financial practices. McCulloch personally went to Washington in 1862 to urge the government to postpone such actions. He was unsuccessful in the attempt, though later in life he would see the wisdom of government regulation of state banks. While in Washington he came to the attention of Secretary of the Treasury Salmon Chase. The secretary admired the logic of McCulloch's arguments and quickly saw that McCulloch possessed a keen financial mind. The following year Chase offered McCulloch the appointment of comptroller of the Treasury, and McCulloch accepted.

One of McCulloch's duties was to implement some of the regulations that had been passed by Congress. He was able to do so with a minimum of protests from the state banks and with maximum efficiency. Over the next year he also developed a very positive working relationship with Salmon Chase and Chase's successor William P. Fessenden. Upon Fessenden's resignation in March 1865, Abraham Lincoln offered the cabinet post to McCulloch. Though certainly not Lincoln's first choice and considered by many to be a lackluster addition to the cabinet, McCulloch proved to be a competent and sometimes innovative secretary. He continued to serve as secretary after Lincoln's assassination in April and served as Andrew Johnson's secretary throughout Johnson's presidency.

With the war over, McCulloch had a number of concerns. He purchased United States bonds to prop up the price following the assassination, but considered his primary duty with the end of hostilities to be the redemption of the millions of dollars of greenbacks still in circulation. He had never approved of the government's tremendous reliance on paper money during the war and considered it imperative that such currency be redeemed as soon as possible. During his time as secretary, however, he was only able to persuade Congress to retire approximately one-fourth of the greenbacks in circulation.

Along with these very weighty concerns, McCulloch also had to deal with the disposition of confiscated Confederate property like ships and other items that came into United States government possession. Though of relatively small financial consideration, one of these possessions was a collection of sterling bills of exchange that had been taken from Jefferson Davis upon his capture by the army. McCulloch even traveled down from Washington to Fort Monroe where Davis was imprisoned to interview the former Confederate president regarding the ownership of the bills.

Though he quietly went about the job of rebuilding a peacetime treasury and did so with competent efficiency, McCulloch's efforts largely went unnoticed. He left office to return to the banking industry upon the end of Johnson's term in March 1869. He acquired a partnership in the firm of Jay Cooke, McCulloch & Company headquartered in London. He was eventually able to buy a controlling interest in the company, making it McCulloch & Company.

He enjoyed his business activities and shunned public life until his sense of duty compelled him to accept appointment in 1884 as outgoing President Chester Arthur's secretary of the Treasury. During his less than six months in Arthur's cabinet, he again urged an effort to stabilize the currency, but had little time to accomplish this goal himself. After leaving the cabinet, McCulloch lived quietly in retirement on his estate outside Washington in Prince George's County, Maryland. He wrote and published his memoirs, which reflected his conservative financial philosophy. He died at his estate on 24 May 1895.

—*David S. Heidler and Jeanne T. Heidler*

See also Financing, U.S.A.
For further reading:
McCulloch, Hugh. *Men and Measures of Half a Century* (1888).

McDOWELL, IRVIN
(1818–1885)
Union general

Irwin McDowell was born in Columbus, Ohio, on 15 October 1818 and educated in France. Adept as a student, he gained admittance to West Point in 1834 and graduated from there four years later, twenty-third in a class of forty-five. He was commissioned a second lieutenant in the 1st U. S. Artillery and performed garrison duty along the Canadian border until 1841. That year he returned to West Point as an instructor of tactics, rising to first lieutenant in 1844. The following year, McDowell joined the staff of General John E. Wool in Texas as his aide-de-camp. In this capacity, he fought with gallantry at the February 1847 Battle of Buena Vista, winning brevet promotion to captain. Three months later, McDowell rose to full captain and transferred to Washington, D.C., as part of the adjutant generals' department. McDowell by this time had acquired the reputation of an efficient officer as he served on the staff of General Winfield Scott. Impressed by his abilities, Scott arranged for him to study European military establishments in 1858–1859. His final rank before the Civil War commenced in April 1861 was major.

Prior to the commencement of hostilities, the Union Army was short of experienced and capable senior officers to lead armies in the field. McDowell, by dint of his reputation and Scott's continuing patronage, seemed ideally suited for high command, so he was promoted three grades to brigadier general in May 1861. This was despite of his blunt, abrasive personality, which won him few friends in Washington. Nonetheless, as head of the Department of Northeastern Virginia, McDowell was responsible for raising, equipping, and training a sizable force from scratch. The assignment would have daunted a lesser man, by McDowell threw himself into the task with energy and ability. By July he commanded 50,000 regulars and raw volunteers, deployed in defensive positions about the nation's capital. Enthusiasm for war ran high in the ranks, and had McDowell possessed sufficient time to properly train his charge, they undoubtedly would have become a formidable fighting force. But, in reality, he had little control over the decision to attack the Confederate capital at Richmond, which was decided more by political than military expediency.

Well into the summer of 1861, politics continued to dominate the military agenda. Goaded on by President Abraham Lincoln and others, McDowell was forced to draw up offensive operations before his army was sufficiently competent to enact them. He therefore concocted a viable scheme for advancing into Virginia, outflanking the Confederate army of former classmate Pierre G. T. Beauregard at Manassas Junction, and severing the supply line to Richmond. Union leadership anticipated that a quick, crushing victory would end the war without further bloodshed.

On 16 July 1861, McDowell led his blue-clad columns south along the Warrenton Turnpike as crowds cheered "On to Richmond!" Two days later he arrived at Centreville and paused to reorganize his 37,000-man force and to scout enemy lines. Three days lapsed before the advanced was resumed, but McDowell enacted a plan that, at the time it was conceived, was excellent. A small force was dispatched to Stone Bridge on Bull Run Creek to divert Beauregard's attention. That leader, possessing only 22,000 men, had no idea that McDowell was about to lead the bulk of his army around the Confederate left, flanking him. Unfortunately, the green nature of Union forces was manifested in the slow and unsure advance it made towards its objectives. When Beauregard finally perceived the Union objective, McDowell's tardiness allowed Beauregard to redeploy to meet the attack. Worse, McDowell received no help from the army of General Robert T. Patterson, who was supposed to pin down the army of Joseph E. Johnston in the Shenandoah Valley. Consequently, by the time the battle began on 21 July 1861, Johnston had effectively transferred 10,000 men by rail to the beleaguered Beauregard, tipping the first battle of Bull Run in favor of the Confederates. Furthermore, the inexperienced McDowell compounded his misfortunes by committing his attacks piecemeal, allowing them to be repulsed in detail. At length the sudden infusion of enemy strength caused the Union army to buckle and break, and it fled precipitously toward Washington. The Confederates, equally disorganized, failed to pursue, but defeat became a national disgrace. Lincoln had no choice but to order McDowell summarily relieved and replaced by General George B. McClellan.

McDowell's subsequent Civil War career was anticlimactic. Lincoln, perhaps cognizant of his mistake of rushing the general into combat, allowed him to command I Corps in McClellan's newly constituted Army of the Potomac. He also gained promotion to major general of volunteers in March 1862. Assigned to the defense of Washington, McDowell took no part in McClellan's ill-fated Peninsula campaign. However, he bore a conspicuous role in the August 1862 defeat at Second Bull Run, which terminated his active career. McDowell spent the rest of the war in administrative exile, commanding the Department of the Pacific through July 1864, and the Department of California in 1865.

After the war, McDowell was given a chance to resuscitate his reputation. He was appointed commander of the Department of the West in July 1868, and there he rose to major general in November 1872. Following a four-year stint in charge of the Division of the South, McDowell transferred back to the Department of the Pacific in June 1876, retiring six years later.

He died in San Francisco on 4 May 1885, widely regarded as a capable administrator, but unable to erase the stigma of having lost the Civil War's first great encounter.

—*John C. Fredriksen*

See also Bull Run, Battle of.
For further reading:
Davis, William C. *The First Battle of Manassas* (1995).
Hennessy, John J. *Return to Bull Run: The Campaign and Battle of Second Manassas* (1993).
McDonald, JoAnna M. *We Shall Meet Again: The First Battle of Manassas, July 18-21, 1861* (1999).

McDOWELL, VIRGINIA, BATTLE OF
(8 May 1862)

Confederate major general Thomas J. "Stonewall" Jackson's Valley campaign began with his inauspicious 23 March 1862 defeat at Kernstown. In the weeks after the battle, Brigadier General Edward Johnson and his small Army of the Northwest gradually retired eastward, from Alleghany Mountain, before the advance of Union Major General John C. Frémont. Jackson and his Army of the Valley remained at Swift Run Gap, immobilizing Major General Nathaniel P. Banks's army in the Shenandoah and awaiting reinforcement under Major General Richard S. Ewell. Once these troops arrived, Jackson intended to leave Ewell at Swift Run Gap, neutralizing Banks. He would then unite with Johnson, and the two armies would move against Union brigadier general Robert H. Milroy's command. Jackson's plan would then concentrate all the Southern forces, including Ewell, and turn on Banks.

On 20 April Johnson and his army withdrew from Shenandoah Mountain to West View, seven miles west of Staunton. There, Johnson's command, some 3,000 in all, prepared to withdraw from West View contingent upon the movements that Jackson might be forced to make or if advanced upon by Frémont's force.

Around 1 May 1862, Ewell and his 8,500-man division relieved Jackson at Swift Run Gap. On 4 May, Milroy and his 6,000 troops crossed over the Shenandoah River and encamped within 15 miles of Staunton. This was done, according to Milroy, "for the purpose of observing the traitor army under General Johnson." Johnson's army withdrew, uniting with Jackson at Staunton on 5 May. Two days later the Confederate forces moved toward Milroy. Johnson led the 9,000 troops, because of his familiarity with the region and because his "high qualities as a soldier admirably fitted him for the advance." Milroy withdrew toward McDowell. Learning of the Confederates' advance, Brigadier General Robert Schenck raced to Milroy's support. The Southern army bivouacked on the western base of Shenandoah Mountain, and the next morning, 8 May 1862, the Confederates ascended Bull Pasture Mountain.

Early in the day, Johnson and a small party made their way to the top of Sitlington's Hill, a commanding elevation on the western side of the mountain, to reconnoiter Milroy's position. The Federals made a half-hearted attempt to drive them off and were repulsed. Johnson called forward his army and deployed for battle. Leaving the 31st Virginia Infantry to protect his right flank, the other five regiments scrambled up the hill and took their positions on the rugged crest of Sitlington's Hill. The 12th Georgia took the center, with the 52d Virginia on the left and the 44th Virginia on the right above the 31st Virginia. The 58th Virginia was placed behind the 52d, with the 25th Virginia held in reserve. As the Confederates settled in, the Federals hurled shells over their heads.

Schenck and his 2,400-man brigade arrived later that morning, boosting Union strength to more than 8,000. Although Schenck was senior officer, he deferred to Milroy. Initially, Milroy concluded that his position was indefensible and determined to withdraw. After mistakenly learning that the Confederates were placing artillery on the hill overlooking their position, Milroy and Schenck reconsidered the offensive.

At 4:30 P.M., Milroy attacked Johnson's well-formed line. The 25th and 75th Ohio moved against the center. Johnson personally directed the fighting, his "men holding the line upon the crest of the hill and driving back the enemy with great loss." At one point, as the Federals were pressing on the right, some of Milroy's men, recognizing the Confederate brigadier from the battle of Alleghany Mountain, called out, "There's old Johnson; let's flank him!" Waving his club in the air, Johnson replied, "Yes, damn you, flank me if you can."

Jackson ordered reinforcements under Brigadier General William B. Taliaferro to go to Johnson's support. Milroy threw the 32d and 82d Ohio against the Confederate right, while the 3d western Virginia moved against the 31st Virginia. As the Union troops pressed along the Southern line, the Confederates recoiled and counterattacked. Every Northern thrust was pushed back.

Around 8:00 P.M., a bullet shattered Johnson's ankle and he was removed to the rear. After consulting with the wounded Johnson, Jackson ordered Taliaferro, the ranking officer on the field, to hold the Confederate position. By 8:30, the opposing forces could see each other only by the flame that sparked from their weapons as they fired. The Federal firing soon ceased. "The enemy withdrew from the field in haste, leaving their dead unburied, burned his stores at McDowell, destroyed large quantities of ammunition, camp equipage, &c., and precipitately retreated in the direction of Franklin."

The Confederates lost 146 killed, 382 wounded, and 4 missing, totaling 532 casualties. The Northwestern Army, especially the 12th Georgia in their pivotal position, suffered most of these casualties with 116 killed, 300 wounded, and 4 missing. The Federals lost 34 killed, 220 wounded, and 5 missing. Although the Confederates could claim a very important strategic and tactical victory, their losses more than doubled those of their opponents.

In his final report, Jackson wrote, "General Johnson, to whom I had intrusted the management of the troops engaged, proved himself eminently worthy of the confidence reposed in him by the skill, gallantry, and presence of mind which he displayed on the occasion." The wounding of Johnson signaled the end of the Confederate Army of the Northwest that was absorbed into Jackson's Army of the Valley. A year later, Jackson would be dead and through the reorganization of the Army of Northern Virginia, Johnson would be leading these same troops again.

—Eddie Woodward

See also Frémont, John C.; Jackson, Thomas J.; Johnson, Edward; Milroy, Robert H.; Schenck, Robert C.; Shenandoah Valley Campaign (August 1864–March 1865).

For further reading:

Armstrong, Richard L. *Jackson's Valley Campaign: The Battle of McDowell, March 11–May 18, 1862* (1990).

Freeman, Douglas Southall. *Lee's Lieutenants: A Study in Command* (1942–1944).

Hotchkiss, Jed. *Virginia.* Vol. 4 of *Confederate Military History* (1899, reprint, 1987).

Paulus, Margaret Babcock, comp. *Papers of General Robert Huston Milroy* (1965).

Richardson, James H. *"Old Jack" and His Foot Cavalry; or, a Virginian Boy's Progress to Renown* (1864).

Tanner, Robert G. *Stonewall in the Valley: Thomas J. "Stonewall" Jackson's Shenandoah Valley Campaign, Spring 1862* (1976; reprint, 1996).

Wert, Jeffry D. "A Single Step." *Civil War Times Illustrated.*

McGOWAN, SAMUEL
(1819–1897)
Confederate general

Born 9 October 1819, in Laurens District, South Carolina, Samuel McGowan was the son of Presbyterian Scots-Irish immigrants. In 1841 he graduated from South Carolina College and began the study of law in Abbeville. Admitted to the bar in 1842, he opened his own law practice there. During his political career, McGowan served thirteen years in the South Carolina House of Representatives.

Enlisting as a private in the Palmetto Regiment during the Mexican-American War, McGowan rose to the rank of captain. At the storming of Chapultepec, he received a citation for personal gallantry. After the war he returned to his law practice, but maintained his interest in military affairs, receiving a commission as a major general in the state militia.

Following South Carolina's secession, McGowan accepted a commission as brigadier general of state troops. In this capacity he commanded a brigade under General P. G. T. Beauregard during the capture of Fort Sumter. At Blackburn's Ford and First Bull Run, he served as a volunteer aide to Brigadier General Milledge L. Bonham.

After McGowan returned to South Carolina, the 14th South Carolina Infantry elected him lieutenant colonel on 1 September 1861. Promoted to colonel on 10 May 1862, McGowan joined Maxcy Gregg's South Carolina Brigade in the Army of Northern Virginia. As part of Major General A. P. Hill's division, McGowan's regiment participated in the bloody fighting at Second Bull Run and Antietam. On 29 August 1862 at Second Bull Run, McGowan stood boldly at the crucial railroad embankment on the left of General Thomas J. "Stonewall" Jackson's beleaguered line. Although part of Gregg's brigade fell back under heavy pressure, McGowan's Regiment held firm even though many of the men, out of ammunition, resorted to hurling rocks and insults at the advancing Union infantrymen.

Known for his steadfast courage, "quick perception and prompt, energetic action," except when disabled by wounds, McGowan, took part in every major battle from the Seven Days' to Appomattox. After Gregg died at Fredericksburg, several influential South Carolinians conducted a spirited campaign for McGowan to ascend to the brigade's command. In letters to Secretary of War James A. Seddon, they indicated that Major General A. P. Hill also desired McGowan to lead the brigade. On 23 April 1863 McGowan received his commission as brigadier general, backdated to 17 January.

On 2 May 1863 leading a charge in Jackson's flanking attack at Chancellorsville, McGowan toppled over with a gunshot wound to his left leg. Seriously wounded and forced to recuperate until February 1864, he missed Lee's northern invasion that culminated at Gettysburg. Brigadier General J. Johnston Pettigrew, and then John K. Marshal, commanded McGowan's brigade at Gettysburg, including Pickett's Charge.

Consistently at the head of his men, McGowan fell victim to Union gunfire at Gaines' Mill, Second Manassass, Chancellorsville, and Spotsylvania. On 12 May 1864, during the murderous fighting at Spotsylvania, McGowan led his men in a desperate counterattack that drove exuberant Federal infantry out of the captured Confederate trenches. During the bloody hand-to-hand fighting, McGowan fell with his fourth, and last, wound of the war. He returned to his brigade in

August and led his men through the final battles. At Dinwiddie Court House in 1865, he led a charge with the élan of A. P. Hill's old Light Division, but his men were too tired and too few to recapture bygone glory.

Paroled after Appomattox, McGowan returned to his Abbeville law practice. In 1865 he participated in the state constitutional convention and was elected to the U.S. House of Representatives. As it did with many other former Confederates, however, the U.S. Congress refused him his seat. In 1878 he again attained a seat in the state legislature.

The next year McGowan won a position on the bench as an associate justice of the South Carolina Supreme Court, but lost his bid for reelection in 1893. On 9 August 1897, he died in his home at Abbeville and was buried in Long Cane Cemetery.

—*Stanley S. McGowen*

See also South Carolina.

For further reading:

Caldwell, J. F. J. *The History of a Brigade of South Carolinians First Known as Gregg's and Subsequently as McGowan's Brigade* (1866).

Compiled Service Records of Confederate Veterans. Samuel McGowan, Record Group 109, microfilm M331, roll 171. National Archives and Record Service, Washington D.C.

Evans, Clement A, ed. *Confederate Military History: A Library of Confederate States History* (1899; reprint, 1987).

Warner, Ezra J. *Generals in Gray: Lives of the Confederate Commanders* (1959; reprint, 1987).

McGUIRE, HUNTER HOLMES
(1835–1900)
Confederate physician

Born to Hugh Holmes McGuire and Ann Eliza Moss McGuire in Winchester, Virginia, Hunter McGuire decided to follow in his father's footsteps by entering the medical profession. He received his training at Winchester Medical College, the University of Pennsylvania, and Jefferson Medical College. He began his practice in Winchester and taught at the medical college there.

McGuire was an avid supporter of states' rights and became especially incensed after John Brown's raid in 1859. When the raid occurred, McGuire was studying again in Philadelphia, and he organized the repatriation of Southern medical students in protest. Shortly afterward, McGuire accepted a position on the faculty of the University of Louisiana in New Orleans, but at the outbreak of the war, he returned to Virginia to enlist in the Confederate army. After serving briefly as a private, he was appointed medical director of the Army of the Shenandoah by its commander, Thomas J. Jackson. He continued as the surgeon for the 1st Virginia Brigade, Jackson's division in the valley, and for II Corps when Jackson became a corps commander. When Jackson was

wounded at Chancellorsville, McGuire was his physician and the chief surgeon when Jackson's left arm was amputated at the shoulder. McGuire remained with Jackson until his death on 10 May 1863. Upon Jackson's death, McGuire continued in that position under Richard Ewell until given the position of medical director for the Army of Northern Virginia. Given an opportunity to serve closer to home in the summer of 1864, McGuire accepted the medical directorship of Jubal Early's Valley army.

In his various positions throughout the war, McGuire gained the reputation of a reformer. He was especially active in organizing the Confederate Ambulance Corps to ensure fast removal of wounded Confederate soldiers from the battlefields. He also gained a reputation for kindness toward wounded Union officers and soldiers who fell into Confederate hands. Upon his capture in March 1865, his reputation had preceded him and he was quickly released.

After the war, McGuire taught surgery at the Medical College of Virginia and became active in various medical organizations in the state of Virginia and the nation. In 1892 he became the president of the American Medical Association. He died in Richmond.

—*David S. Heidler and Jeanne T. Heidler*

See also Jackson, Thomas J.; Medicine.

For further reading:

Cunningham, Horace Herndon. *Doctors in Gray; The Confederate Medical Service* (1958).

Shaw, Maurice. *Stonewall Jackson's Surgeon, Hunter Holmes McGuire: A Biography* (1993).

McINTOSH, JOHN BAILLIE
(1829–1888)
Union general

Born to Colonel James Simmons McIntosh of the U.S. Army and Eliza Matthews Shumate McIntosh at Fort Brooke, Florida, John Baillie McIntosh entered the U.S. Navy as a teenager. He served as a midshipman aboard the USS *Saratoga* during the Mexican-American War. His father was killed during Winfield Scott's Mexico City campaign in that conflict. After the war, McIntosh resigned from the navy. Between his resignation and the outbreak of the Civil War, McIntosh was a businessman in New Brunswick, New Jersey.

At the commencement of the war, McIntosh used his military connections to gain a second lieutenant's commission in the cavalry. During the early months of the war, he served in western Virginia and then with the Army of the Potomac during the Peninsula campaign, particularly distinguishing himself during the Seven Days' battles. He received a brevet promotion to major in the regular army for his performance on the peninsula.

McIntosh fought at South Mountain and again distinguished himself at Antietam in September 1862. Shortly afterward, he was promoted to colonel of volunteers and given command of the 3d Pennsylvania Cavalry. During the Fredericksburg campaign, he served in William W. Averell's cavalry brigade of George Gordon Meade's corps.

In March 1863, McIntosh received command of a brigade and led it in the battle of Kelly's Ford on 17 March. While Averell eventually withdrew his division in spite of his larger numbers, McIntosh, commanding on the Federal right, forced the withdrawal of Confederates attacking on his flank. A month and a half later, still serving in Averell's division, McIntosh participated in one of the diversionary cavalry moves preceding Chancellorsville, but took little part in the actual battle. During the battle of Gettysburg, particularly on 3 July, McIntosh distinguished himself and was commended for his actions by Brigadier General David McMurtrie Gregg. McIntosh participated in the cavalry pursuit of Robert E. Lee's Army of Northern Virginia and skirmished with Confederate forces for the remainder of the summer until a fall from his horse temporarily disabled him.

After he was able to return to light duty, McIntosh was placed in command of the Washington Cavalry Depot. He returned to active brigade command in the Army of the Potomac just in time for the battle of the Wilderness, and Brigadier General James H. Wilson commended him for bravery during that battle. On 9 June 1864, George Gordon Meade, commander of the Army of the Potomac, recommended McIntosh for promotion to brigadier general.

McIntosh fought under Wilson through the summer, fighting at Yellow Tavern and in Wilson's raid against the Southside Railroad at the end of June. In August, Wilson's division, and hence McIntosh's brigade, became part of the Army of the Shenandoah created to combat Jubal Early in the valley. McIntosh fought in all the early engagements of the campaign, but at the battle of Winchester on 19 September was severely wounded in the right leg. Doctors amputated the limb, effectively ending McIntosh's Civil War career.

At the end of the war, McIntosh received a brevet promotion to major general in the regular army. During the reorganization of the army in 1866, he chose to remain in the army, a missing limb being no obstacle to military service at the time. He was made lieutenant colonel of the 42d Infantry. He remained in that command for one year, when physical considerations led him to accept the post of governor of the Washington Soldier's Home. In 1869, President Ulysses S. Grant appointed him superintendent of Indian Affairs for California. McIntosh retired the following year at the rank of brigadier general.

In retirement McIntosh returned to his prewar home of New Brunswick, New Jersey, where he lived until his death on 29 June 1888. McIntosh's brother was Confederate general James McIntosh who was killed at Pea Ridge.

—*David S. Heidler and Jeanne T. Heidler*

See also Cavalry, U.S.A.; Kelly's Ford, Battle of; Wilson, James Harrison; Winchester (Opequon), Third Battle of.

For further reading:
Starr, Stephen Z. *The Union Cavalry in the Civil War* (1979–1985).

MCKAY, CHARLOTTE JOHNSON
(1818–1894)

Union army nurse

Charlotte McKay was on hand to minister to wounded soldiers at every major battle in the Eastern theater beginning in 1862. Widowed in 1856 after two years of marriage, the subsequent death of her daughter in 1861 prompted McKay to lose herself in hospital work. In the spring of 1862, the Maine native traveled to Frederick, Maryland, where she remained for eight months distributing supplies and caring for the wounded of Winchester, Second Manassas, and Antietam. She attended Confederate soldiers after Union troops abandoned Frederick in September, and found to her surprise that many "were by no means ruffians," but "good, intelligent, thoughtful men."

McKay became a field nurse in January 1863, after caring for the wounded of Fredericksburg in Washington for six weeks. Stationed near Falmouth during the winter months, she rode atop boxcars, supply wagons, and ambulances, to transport food to the troops. At Chancellorsville in May, McKay made the perilous trip to a field hospital within three miles of the fighting by crossing the Rappahannock on pontoons. No sooner had she learned that her brother, a lieutenant in the 17th Maine, had been mortally wounded than an evacuation order mobilized the medical staff, which was now in the line of artillery fire. McKay, surgeons, and wounded men retreated thirteen miles to Fredericksburg, where she remained until the Army of the Potomac began its summer march into Pennsylvania in pursuit of the Army of Northern Virginia. In recognition of her bravery at Chancellorsville, her brother's regiment awarded her the Kearny Cross.

McKay was on hand at Gettysburg, where want of a stove meant that she served cold food to the thousand patients under her care. Here and elsewhere, she complained that medical officers' stinginess increased the suffering of wounded men. Once a supply box she had packed arrived filled with rusty chains, its nutritious contents having been pilfered by hungry teamsters. Cases of cupidity and graft convinced McKay and her

white middle-class peers that vigilant women could keep avarice in check. Transmitting the belief that women had the power of moral suasion because they reminded men of their mothers, she did not hesitate to intercede when "the boys" descended to fisticuffs.

In 1864 and 1865, McKay remained in Virginia, returning to Washington and Fredericksburg and serving at Brandy Station, Port Royal, and White House Landing through the battles of the Wilderness, Spotsylvania Court House, and Cold Harbor. A seasoned field nurse, she moved to Cavalry Corps Hospital at City Point later that summer, where along with two white and twelve African-American women, she tended casualties of the Petersburg trenches. Well known in the east for organizing food service, McKay established a special diet kitchen in Petersburg after Lee's surrender in April. The next winter she distributed supplies and taught literacy to the freedmen of Petersburg and Poplar Springs, drawing on prewar teaching experience.

Supported neither by husband nor military pension, McKay moved to Massachusetts when her freedmen's relief work ended in the spring of 1866. In the village of Wakefield she settled down to write memoirs, which she published in 1876. It is likely that, as one of a successful New England physician's seven children, McKay lived in proximity to family members during the final decades of the nineteenth century. By the 1890s, she had moved to San Diego, where she died far from home at age seventy-five.

—*Jane E. Schultz*

See also Nurses.
For further reading:
Brockett, Linus P., and Mary Vaughan. *Woman's Work in the Civil War* (1867).
Carded Service Records of Hospital Attendants, Matrons, and Nurses, 1861–1865. National Archives, Washington, D.C.
Conklin, Eileen. *Women of Gettysburg, 1863* (1993).
Dannett, Sylvia G. L. *Noble Women of the North* (1959).
Moore, Frank. *Women of the War: Their Heroism and Self-Sacrifice* (1866).

MCKINLEY, WILLIAM
(1843–1901)

Union officer; U.S. president

William McKinley was born on 23 January 1843, in Niles, Ohio. After studies in local schools in Niles and Poland, Ohio, McKinley enrolled at Allegheny College in Pennsylvania in 1860. Illness forced him to drop out after only a few months, but he quickly thereafter found work as a school teacher. In June 1861, the seventeen-year-old McKinley enlisted in the Union army and was mustered into the service as a member of the 23d Ohio Volunteer Infantry Regiment. After a few weeks of training at Camp Chase near Columbus, the unit was dispatched to western Virginia to deal with guerrillas. On 10 September 1861, McKinley saw his first significant combat at the battle of Carnifex Ferry.

In April 1862, McKinley was promoted to commissary sergeant. His diligence and attention to detail in this position brought him to the attention of regimental commander (and future president of the United States) Rutherford B. Hayes, who took the young man under his wing. After several frustrating months of hard marching and dealing with guerrillas, the 23d Ohio was ordered to eastern Virginia in August 1862. They reached Washington on the 26th, but missed the battle of Second Bull Run. During the Maryland campaign, they saw action at South Mountain and Antietam as part of Ambrose Burnside's IX Corps. During the latter battle, McKinley won praise for his conspicuous courage driving his commissary wagon through shot and shell to bring food and coffee to the men on the front line.

After Antietam, Hayes recommended McKinley for promotion to second lieutenant, which was conferred on 3 November 1862, to date from 24 September. In March 1863 McKinley was promoted to first lieutenant. That summer, the 23d Ohio was assigned to George Crook's corps in western Virginia, where they participated in operations against John Hunt Morgan's raiders, battled guerrillas, and, in May 1864, fought at the battle of Cloyd's Mountain.

Two months after the fight at Cloyd's Mountain, Crook's command was ordered to Harper's Ferry to participate in Union operations in the Shenandoah Valley. As a captain on General Crook's staff, McKinley saw action at the battles of Winchester, Fisher's Hill, and Cedar Creek in 1864. For his distinguished service under fire at those battles, he was breveted major on 13 March 1865. After participating in the Grand Review at Washington, McKinley and the rest of the 23d Ohio were mustered out of the service on 26 July 1865. Ironically, the young man who had dropped out of college as a result of poor health managed to endure four years of ardent military service without suffering a wound or a major illness.

After the war, McKinley practiced law in Canton, Ohio, before winning election to Congress as a Republican and close associate of Hayes in 1876. During his service in Washington, McKinley rose to national prominence as an authority on the tariff. After two terms as governor of Ohio, he was selected to be the Republican Party's presidential nominee in 1896. In one of the pivotal presidential contests in U.S. history, he defeated William Jennings Bryan, thanks to an effective campaign managed by his close friend Marcus Hanna.

Having developed a deep hatred of war during his Civil War service, McKinley very reluctantly yielded to popular clamor for war with Spain in 1898. Once the conflict began, however, he proved himself a forceful

and effective commander in chief. Viewing the war as an opportunity to advance the cause of sectional reconciliation, he also made a point of giving high commissions to a number of former Confederates. After leading the nation to victory over Spain, McKinley easily won reelection in 1900. He was mortally wounded by an assassin during a public event in Buffalo, New York, on 6 September 1901 and died eight days later. He was the last veteran of the Civil War to serve as president.

—Ethan S. Rafuse

See also Hayes, Rutherford B.
For further reading:
Morgan, H. Wayne, ed. "A Civil War Diary of William McKinley." *Ohio Historical Quarterly.*
——— *William McKinley and His America* (1963).
Olcott, Charles S. *The Life of William McKinley* (1916).
Porter, Robert P. *Life of William McKinley, Soldier, Lawyer, Statesman* (1896).

MCLAWS, LAFAYETTE
(1821-1897)
Confederate general

Lafayette McLaws was born at Augusta, Georgia, on 15 January 1821. In July 1838 he entered West Point and graduated forty-eighth in his class of 1842. McLaws's first appointment was with the Sixth Infantry as a second lieutenant. In March 1844 he was transferred to the Seventh Infantry. He was promoted to first lieutenant on 16 February 1847. McLaws served in the Mexican-American War and was promoted to captain 24 August 1851. For about ten years McLaws served as an Infantry Captain at various frontier posts.

On 23 March 1861, McLaws resigned his commission in the army and joined the forces of the South. He was promoted to major in May 1861 before organizing the 10th Georgia Infantry and being promoted to colonel in June 1861. In September of that same year, he was promoted to brigadier general and given command of the First Brigade, Department of the Peninsula. McLaws was in action during the Seven Days' Battles. He was later given command of the Second Division, Department of the Peninsula, and was later promoted to major general, commanding a division of the First Corps, Army of Northern Virginia. In September 1862 his command took part in the battle of Antietam.

McLaws was the division commander on Marye's Heights 13 December 1862, at Fredericksburg. McLaws deployed Cobb's Georgia Brigade in the Sunken Road. McLaws had 2,000 men on the line and 7,000 more in reserve. His troops were well protected by the stone wall and the sunken road by which they were deployed. In addition, McLaws's position was supported by artillery. Seven Federal divisions were sent against McLaws, but none succeeded in pushing him back. Total casualties for the battle numbered 12,535 for the Federals and 5,000 for the Confederates. General Robert E. Lee described the repeated federal assaults being repulsed in "gallant style" by McLaws's troops, while General James Longstreet was even more complimentary: "Much credit is due Major General McLaws for his untiring zeal and ability in preparing his troops and his position for a successful resistance, and the ability with which he handled his troops after the attack."

At Chancellorsville in May 1863, McLaws was on the far right of Lee's line, opposite Jackson's position. While Jackson made his famous march around Joseph Hooker's left, McLaws and Major General Richard Anderson were to hold Hooker in check. Once Jackson's march was completed, Hooker faced an entire column flanking his left. The result was Lee's greatest victory of the war. At Gettysburg in July 1863, McLaws's command participated in some of the most furious fighting of the battle at the Peach Orchard and the Wheatfield.

Later in December 1863, McLaws was embroiled in a dispute with General James Longstreet. Longstreet relieved McLaws of command and brought charges against him for his performance at Fort Sanders, Tennessee. Longstreet had ordered McLaws to make an assault. McLaws delayed and asked for the proposed assault to be reconsidered. Longstreet refused and again ordered the assault. After the action and failed attack, Longstreet relieved McLaws of command. Lieutenant Colonel G. Moxley Sorrel transmitted the order for Longstreet and also the explanation McLaws requested. The explanation follows:

> Major General McLaws,
> General,
> I have the honor to acknowledge the receipt of your note of today, asking for the particular reason for the issue of the order relieving you of command from duty with this army. In reply I am directed to say that throughout the campaign on which we are engaged you have exhibited a want of confidence in the efforts and plans which the commanding general has thought proper to adopt, and he is apprehensive that this feeling will extend more or less to the troops under your command...
> G. Moxley Sorrel
> Lieutenant Colonel and Assistant Adjutant General

Charges were brought against McLaws for misconduct, which resulted in reprimand being suggested by the court. President Davis intervened and had the charges dismissed and McLaws transferred to General Joseph Johnston's staff in Georgia and the Carolinas.

Following the war McLaws became an insurance agent, tax collector, and postmaster. He died on 24 July 1897 and is buried in Savannah Georgia.

—*Thomas A. Wing*

See also Antietam, Battle of; Army of Northern Virginia; Chancellorsville, Battle of; Fredericksburg, First Battle of; Gettysburg, Battle of; Fort Sanders, Battle of; Longstreet, James.

For further reading:
Freeman, Douglas Southall. *Lee's Lieutenants: A Study in Command* (1943).
Longstreet, James. *From Manassas to Appomattox: Memoirs of the Civil War in America* (1991).
Sears, Stephen W. *Landscape Turned Red* (1983).
Warner, Ezra J. *Generals in Gray, Lives of Confederate Commanders* (1959).

McLEAN, JOHN
(1785–1861)
U.S. Supreme Court justice

Renowned for his role in the *Dred Scott* case and for his perennial presidential aspirations, John McLean was born in New Jersey and moved with his family to Ohio in 1797. After studying law and editing a newspaper in the early 1800s, McLean entered politics, first as a Jeffersonian Republican and later as a Jacksonian Democrat. After two terms in Congress from 1813 to 1816, McLean accepted a seat on the high court of Ohio. In 1823 President James Monroe appointed McLean postmaster general, in which office he continued under John Quincy Adams. When Andrew Jackson took office in 1829, he named McLean an associate justice of the Supreme Court.

Undisguised presidential ambitions soon earned McLean the moniker "Politician on the Supreme Court," although his incessant political maneuvering and shifts in party allegiance failed to secure the presidential candidacy he coveted. During his thirty-one years on the Supreme Court, from 1830 to 1861, McLean proved to be a nationalist on most questions of federalism. He subscribed to John Marshall's national-supremacy mandates in the Cherokee cases in 1831 and 1832, while consistently championing the exclusive commercial power of the central government. He did favor state banking, however.

McLean's greatest judicial impact came in cases concerning slavery, an institution he abhorred, as evidenced by his antebellum politics. From the 1840s onward, he aligned himself with the antislavery wing of the Whig Party, the Free Soilers, and the Republicans—all of whom sought to arrest the expansion of slavery. Not surprisingly, an antislavery ethos animated McLean's jurisprudence. He filed a dissent in *Prigg v. Pennsylvania* (1842), in which the Court's majority struck down a state personal liberty law as repugnant to the fugitive slave provisions of the Constitution. McLean upheld the anti-kidnapping statute, asserting the right of the free states to protect alleged runaways from arbitrary and unwarranted seizure.

Yet McLean did not place personal sentiments ahead of constitutional fidelity. In *Jones v. Van Zandt* (1847), antislavery attorneys William H. Seward and Salmon P. Chase argued that their client committed no offense in harboring runaway slaves because a "higher law than the Constitution" condemned slavery and all ordinances recognizing property rights in humans. McLean rejected this higher-law moralism and concurred in the Court's decision, which sustained the Fugitive Slave Law, affirmed the right of property in humans, and acknowledged slavery as one of the "sacred compromises" embedded in the Constitution.

McLean's most significant opinion came in *Scott v. San[d]ford* (1857), which concerned both Dred Scott's, a Missouri slave's, claim to freedom based upon prolonged residence in free territory, as well as the thorny issue of congressional interference with slavery in the territories. Initially, the Court majority of five slave-state justices and two Northern Democrats elected to dismiss the case on narrow jurisdictional grounds. But the two Republican (and antislavery) justices—McLean and Benjamin R. Curtis—determined to draft opinions touching the constitutional merits of the suit. This prompted Chief Justice Roger B. Taney to issue the Court's infamous proslavery ruling, which declared that Congress had no power to regulate slavery in the territories, that temporary residence in free territory did not abrogate slave status, and that African-Americans could not sue in federal court because they were not citizens within the meaning of the Constitution.

McLean's dissent refuted Taney's decision point by point. Citing an impressive array of state and federal precedents, McLean held that slavery existed only where sanctioned by positive law, so that when slaveholders carried slaves into free territory, an entitlement to freedom ensued. He also adduced evidence showing that free blacks were considered citizens in several non-slaveholding states. Most important, McLean insisted that Congress possessed full constitutional authority to exclude slavery from the territories.

The *Dred Scott* decision inflamed sectional hostilities and propelled the nation toward Armageddon. In the sense that the Republican justices forced the issue, McLean helped chart a course toward civil war. In the North, McLean's *Dred Scott* dissent met with applause, which he hoped to parlay into a presidential nomination. Thaddeus Stevens advanced McLean's candidacy at the Republican Convention in 1860, but his name was dropped after a poor showing on the first ballot. During the secession crisis, McLean hoped for a compromise to avert disunion, but failing health denied him an active role in the North-South dialogue. He died of pneumonia in Cincinnati in April 1861.

Though McLean failed to attain his ultimate goal of the presidency, his antislavery jurisprudence embodied a spirit of equal justice that later found constitutional expression in the Fourteenth Amendment.

—Eric Tscheschlok

See also Dred Scott Case; *Prigg v. Pennsylvania*; Supreme Court, U.S.

For further reading:

Dougan, Michael B. "John McLean." In *The Oxford Companion to the Supreme Court of the United States* (1992).

Fehrenbacher, Don E. *The Dred Scott Case: Its Significance in American Law and Politics* (1978).

Gatel, Frank Otto. "John McLean." In *The Justices of the United States Supreme Court, 1789–1969: Their Lives and Major Opinions* (1969).

Weisenburger, Francis P. *The Life of John McLean: A Politician on the United States Supreme Court* (1937).

McLEAN, WILMER
(1814–1882)
Farmer

Wilmer McLean had the distinction of having his home serve as headquarters to General P. G. T. Beauregard during the battle of First Bull Run and yet another home at Appomattox Court House serve as the site where General Robert E. Lee surrendered to General Ulysses S. Grant.

A moderately successful farmer near Manassas, McLean was born on 3 May 1814. The Civil War in northern Virginia began in the immediate vicinity of McLean's home. Because General Beauregard used the McLean home as his headquarters during the first major engagement of the war, much of the Confederate battle plan was laid out in the house. McLean's home sustained considerable damage during the battle when an artillery round entered the kitchen area, reportedly while dinner was being cooked.

Early in the battle, McLean left town with his family. Little is known of his whereabouts over the course of the following two years, but it is assumed that he lived with various family members in the area and supported his family by speculating in sugar. While he did periodically return to the home until spring 1862, he never brought his family back. In the fall of 1863, McLean bought a farm with a two-story brick house fronted by a porch and relocated his family to the isolated central Virginia town of Appomattox Court House, where he expected he would avoid the remainder of the war. Although he did avoid the hostilities associated with war, he would again see armies forming at his doorstep.

During Lee's retreat from Petersburg in early April 1865, Colonel Charles Marshall, who served as General Lee's secretary, approached McLean concerning a fitting venue for the surrender ceremony. After being shown an abandoned house, Marshall deemed it unfit, and then McLean offered the use of his own home.

On 9 April 1865, Generals Grant and Lee met

together in the parlor of the McLean house. It was here that General Lee surrendered his Army of Northern Virginia. After the ceremony ended, McLean, hoping his life would return to normality, saw his home ransacked by soldiers looking for a memento of that historic day. Some men took small relics but others removed the furniture from his sitting room, where the surrender was signed. Others even demolished furniture hoping to allow many tiny souvenirs. Although some of the men offered to pay for their keepsakes, McLean's purpose had never been to sell his possessions.

McLean's considerable supply of Confederate currency was worthless by the end of the year. The McLean house was sold sometime during the later 1860s, at which time the family returned to the Manassas area. Financially ruined, McLean struck up a friendship with former Confederate raider John Singleton Mosby that would last until his death. Mosby, who had befriended Grant during the years after the war, had benefited from Grant's patronage, and McLean was obviously aware of this connection. In 1872, McLean supported Grant's reelection bid and was rewarded with a position in the U.S. Treasury Department. McLean held various government positions until his death on 5 June 1882.

—*Brian D. McKnight*

See also Appomattox Court House; Bull Run, First Battle of.
For further reading:
Cauble, Frank P. *Biography of Wilmer McLean* (1987).

McNEILL, JOHN HANSON AND JESSE
(1815–1864; 1841–1912)
Confederate partisan rangers

John Hanson McNeill and his son Jesse commanded McNeill's Rangers, one the Civil War's most noted Confederate partisan ranger units. A native of Hardy County in western Virginia (now West Virginia), John McNeill migrated with his family to Missouri in 1848, where he successfully raised cattle and farmed. At the war's outset, the elder McNeill raised a company of men, which included three of his sons, and volunteered with the Confederate Missouri State Guard. The McNeills fought in the battles of Carthage, Wilson's Creek, and Lexington. At the last engagement John received a wound that hindered him from moving south with the rest of the Missourians; his son Jesse also remained behind to tend to his father.

Before the two McNeills could rejoin the rest of the Confederate forces, they were captured and sent first to Columbia and then to St. Louis. In June 1862, the two escaped and headed east by way of Illinois, Indiana, and Ohio toward friends and family in Virginia. Once back in Hardy County, John raised an outfit of independent cavalry and offered its services to John D. Imboden and

his partisan rangers, a unit raised under the Partisan Ranger Act of 1862. During the winter of 1863, Imboden's partisans were mustered into regular service as the Northwestern Brigade. At the same time, McNeill received permission to raise and command his own partisan unit, with his son Jesse as his second in command. McNeill's Rangers would soon make a name for itself for its daring exploits in northwestern Virginia.

McNeill's Rangers spent much of the rest of the war disrupting the Baltimore & Ohio Railroad, harassing communication and supply lines in northwestern Virginia, and scouting for Confederate operations in the region. In January 1863 the horsemen scouted the advance and withdrawal of Confederate brigadier general William E. Jones's raid into Hardy County and accounted for one-third of the raid's ninety-nine captured Federals. Their contribution to the incursion evoked the compliments of Jones and Robert E. Lee. During Jones's April Cheat River raid, Captain McNeill and his men occupied the town of Oakland, Maryland, and netted another fifty-seven prisoners. Although the rangers did not participate in the battle of Gettysburg directly, they did contribute to Lee's Pennsylvania campaign by foraging nearly 1,000 head of livestock. In the aftermath of the campaign's climactic engagement, the partisans joined with the Northwestern Brigade to protect the withdrawal of the wagon train carrying wounded back across the Potomac.

McNeill and his command spent the rest of 1863 scouting and foraging for the Confederates and harassing Federal supply lines in northwestern Virginia. These activities continued into the next year, but in April 1864 McNeill nearly lost his command. Several recent recruits to the rangers had been deserters from other Confederate regiments. When McNeill refused to deliver the men to the proper authorities, a court-martial ensued. The court acquitted McNeill of any wrongdoing, a decision certainly influenced by the captain's considerable service record. Just days after his acquittal, McNeill avoided a second threat to his command. On 12 April 1864, Confederate secretary of war James Seddon revoked the Partisan Ranger Act in response to complaints that the partisan units were undisciplined, attracted deserters, and caused mischief by stealing from civilians, friend and foe alike. Seddon included only two exemptions to the revocation: the commands of John Singleton Mosby and John McNeill.

McNeill rejoined his men in time to confront Union Major General Franz Sigel's advance into the lower Shenandoah Valley, a campaign launched in conjunction with Ulysses S. Grant's "Grand Assault" on the Army of Northern Virginia. On 4 May, Captain McNeill struck the B & O Railroad at Piedmont, destroying or damaging several engines, railcars, and machine shops. One week

later, he occupied Romney with little resistance. McNeill's activities in the path of the approaching Federals slowed the cautious Sigel's advance and provided time for Confederate major general John C. Breckinridge to organize his forces to confront and rout Sigel's substantially larger army at the battle of New Market on 15 May.

During the summer and into the fall of 1864, McNeill's Rangers continued their activities in northwestern Virginia and West Virginia, using Moorefield in Hardy County as their base of operations. During a skirmish at Meem's Bottom near Mount Jackson on 3 October 1864, John McNeill received a wound that would take his life. He lingered for more than a month before dying on 10 November. After the elder McNeill's demise, command of the Rangers fell to his son Jesse, although not without controversy. Many of the men exhibited initial hesitancy in allowing the young lieutenant to take command, fearing that he lacked the necessary leadership qualities and that his occasional impulsiveness could prove detrimental to their safety. Nevertheless, Jesse took command and proved up to the task. The Rangers provided crucial intelligence for Thomas Rosser's devastating 28 November raid on the Federal garrison at New Creek. They also helped to fend off an attack on Moorefield on 27 and 28 November that, if successful, could have halted Rosser's moves.

With only months left in the war, Jesse McNeill and his men performed the single accomplishment that would secure the place of McNeill's Rangers in Civil War lore. In the early hours of the morning of 22 February 1865, McNeill and sixty-five men entered Cumberland, Maryland, about sixty miles behind the lines. From their beds in two separate hotels they kidnapped Major General George Crook and Brigadier General Benjamin Kelley and fled the town before being detected. The rangers eluded pursuing Federal cavalry and delivered their prizes to Lieutenant General Jubal Early, who forwarded the generals to Richmond.

With the war in its waning weeks, McNeill's Rangers continued to resist the inevitable, and after the surrender at Appomattox, they hesitated to lay down their arms. While some of the men refused to turn themselves over to the Federal troops for parole, Jesse and thirty-six other rangers formally surrendered on 8 May 1865, in Romney. After the war, Jesse migrated to Illinois, where he lived until 1912.

—*Thomas F. Curran*

See also Crook, George; Imboden, John D.; Kelley, Benjamin Franklin; New Market, Battle of; Rosser, Thomas L.
For further reading:
Bright, Simeon Miller. "The McNeill Rangers: A Study in Confederate Guerrilla Warfare." *West Virginia History* (1951).
Curran, Thomas F. "Acclaim, Blame, and Civil War Memory: The Case of the Kidnapping of Two Union Generals." *West Virginia History* (1998).
Delauter, Roger U., Jr. *McNeill's Rangers* (1986).

McPHERSON, JAMES BIRDSEYE
(1828–1864)
Commander, Army of the Tennessee

James Birdseye McPherson was born near Clyde, Ohio, on 14 November 1828. He obtained an appointment to West Point, where he graduated first in his class of fifty-two cadets. Upon graduation, McPherson accepted the commission of second lieutenant in the Corps of Engineers. His first assignment found him back at West Point teaching engineering courses for the 1853–1854 school year. A three-year tour (1854–1857) in New York City found McPherson involved in numerous engineering duties, such as fortifying the harbor and its approaches along with making navigational improvements. McPherson's next assignment was on the West Coast (1857–1861), where he spent the next three years working on Alcatraz Island, strengthening the federal fort. In 1858, McPherson was promoted to first lieutenant.

McPherson perceived the tensions that were continually mounting between the Northern and Southern states. He believed that if war broke out, it would not be short in duration. Such a civil war would be fought to the bitterest of ends. He correctly foresaw many of the obstacles the South would have to try to overcome if they were to make the transition to modern war. Challenges included a smaller population, no army, no navy, no treasury, and a general lack of machine shops and industry. He believed that the United States, in the event of war, would have to rely on a naval blockade in the subjugation of the South.

McPherson stayed in California until the beginning of August 1861. He arrived in New York at the end of the month, where he received word of his promotion to captain. Hoping for an assignment near the fighting, he was disappointed with his orders to report to Boston. Here his responsibilities included the forts of Boston Harbor and the recruitment of a regiment of engineers, miners, and sappers. Not pleased with these duties, he sought out an acquaintance from San Francisco, Major General Henry W. Halleck. Halleck was now in command of the Department of the Missouri and remembered the capable young officer. He ordered McPherson to report at once to his command, where he would join Halleck's staff as an aide-de-camp.

McPherson was promoted directly to lieutenant colonel and also given the responsibility of assistant chief engineer. His duties, working under Halleck, included establishing recruiting stations, inspecting the defenses of certain towns in Missouri, and determining the strength of the Confederate Army under General Sterling Price.

As Brigadier General Ulysses S. Grant prepared his move on the Confederate strongholds of Forts Henry and Donelson, Halleck transferred McPherson to Grant's Army on 1 February 1862. Grant was pleased to have such a highly rated officer as his chief engineer, since trained engineer officers of his caliber were hard to acquire in the Western theater. Almost immediately his talents became known to Grant. After the fall of Fort Henry, McPherson reconnoitered the terrain in front of Fort Donelson. He identified the best places to deploy the Union troops in the advance on the Rebel fort and provided Grant with a detailed map of the fort and its environs. McPherson, serving again with distinction during the battle of Shiloh on 6 and 7 April 1862, received a promotion to colonel on 1 May 1862 and another promotion to brigadier general of volunteers two weeks later.

After the near defeat of the Union forces at Shiloh, Halleck chose personally to take command of Grant's army, relegating Grant to the powerless position of second-in-command. On the march on Corinth, where the Confederates were located, Halleck advanced painfully slowly. He did not want to be surprised by a Confederate attack as Grant had been and ordered defenses to be constructed along the way. On some days, the Army of the Tennessee only traveled a quarter of a mile. McPherson knew that this over-cautious advance caused needless delays and the goal should be a rapid march on the enemy's position.

McPherson's next assignment was military superintendent of railroads in western Tennessee, where he spent the summer of 1862 repairing the railroads. In September, upon receiving orders, he hastily collected four regiments and arrived in Corinth to aid the besieged position of General William S. Rosecrans. With the arrival of the reinforcements under McPherson, the Confederates were forced to retreat. In October 1862, McPherson was promoted to major general of volunteers. The following month, McPherson switched from staff to line duty.

McPherson took command of the 2d Division, Army of the Tennessee on 16 October and led the same division in the XIII Corps between 24 October and 2 November. With the XIII Corps, he commanded the Right Wing of Grant's Corps and performed well during Grant's Northern Mississippi campaign, an early attempt to capture Vicksburg. He proved to Grant that he was adept at leading an attack during the march into Mississippi and was as capable of conducting a successful rearguard action. The capture of the Federal supply base at Holly Springs caused Grant to cancel this move on Vicksburg. On 18 December 1862, McPherson took command of the XVII Corps in Grant's reorganized Army of the Tennessee.

McPherson and his growing corps wintered in Memphis, preparing for the upcoming campaign against Vicksburg. In March, Grant ordered McPherson's corps to attempt to bypass Vicksburg, which became the ill-fated Lake Providence Expedition.

McPherson's corps played a significant role in many of the battles of the Vicksburg campaign. McPherson would prove to be a cautious general. His performance during the Vicksburg and later campaigns would support this character observance. During the battle of Raymond (12 May), although a Union victory, he did not coordinate the counterattack against the Confederates well. Instead, he sent in his forces in a piecemeal fashion. He did not use to its fullest potential his three-to-one superiority during the second half of the battle.

During the fighting on the outskirts of Jackson, McPherson delayed his attack until he was sure of the number and location of the Confederates opposing him. McPherson's XVII Corps held the center during the siege of the Vicksburg line, and his corps was awarded the honor of entering the city first after the city surrendered. For his accomplishments, McPherson was promoted to brigadier general in the Regular Army. Remaining in Vicksburg until February 1864, McPherson and his troops took part in Sherman's Meridian Expedition in February–March 1864. On 26 March 1864, McPherson took command of the Army of the Tennessee, replacing Sherman, who replaced Grant as commander in the West.

The Army of the Tennessee was no longer an independent force, but one of three elements of Sherman's Division of the Mississippi. It was this organization that Sherman used in the campaign against Atlanta. The inherent cautiousness of McPherson can be observed in his slow advance against Johnston's Army of Tennessee at Dalton (8–9 May 1864), allowing the Confederate army to escape. At Resaca (13–15 May), again McPherson failed to entrap the Rebel army. In McPherson's defense, he did not have the numbers to successfully carry out his assignment. However, McPherson performed well at Dallas (26 May) and Kennesaw Mountain (27 June).

Sherman's force kept moving in the direction of Atlanta. Upon receiving word that Lieutenant General John B. Hood replaced Johnston as commander of the Army of Tennessee, McPherson correctly predicted the action of his former classmate. He warned Sherman that an attack was imminent and deployed his soldiers to meet the assault. This began the battle of Atlanta on 22 July. In attempting to close a gap in the Union line, McPherson ran into a skirmish line of Confederates, near Peachtree Creek, who ordered him to surrender. In attempting to escape, he was mortally wounded. Thus, McPherson became the highest-ranking Union officer to be killed in battle.

Both Grant and Sherman, who considered McPherson to be one of their most talented subordinates, were disheartened upon receiving word of

McPherson's death. McPherson's rapid rise through the ranks illustrates the high regard his superiors had for his ability. Although at times cautious, he proved to be one of the most capable Union officers. His early death and his lack of truly independent commands prevented McPherson from becoming one of the more celebrated Civil War generals.

—James L. Isemann

See also Atlanta Campaign; Visksburg Campaign.
For further reading:
Johnson, Robert Underwood, and Clarence Clough Buel, eds. *Battles and Leaders of the Civil War* (1887–1888).
Macartney, Clarence Edward. *Grant and His Generals* (1953).
Welcher, Frank J. *The Union Army, 1861-1865: Organization and Operations* (1993).
Whaley, Elizabeth J. *Forgotten Hero: General James B. McPherson: The Biography of a Civil War General* (1955).

MEADE, GEORGE GORDON
(1815–1872)
Union general

George Gordon Meade, the son of a wealthy Philadelphia merchant, was born in Cadiz, Spain. After Meade's father died suddenly in 1828, Meade's mother decided to send her son to West Point to secure a proper education. Meade graduated nineteenth of fifty-six in the class of 1835. Lieutenant Meade was assigned to Battery G, 3d U.S. Artillery. He saw brief action in the Second Seminole War before resigning his commission to pursue a career in civil engineering.

Meade reentered the army in 1842 and participated in the Mexican-American War as a topographical engineer on the staff of Zachary Taylor. During the years preceding the Civil War, Meade worked on a variety of projects, most notably lighthouses along the Atlantic seaboard. In 1861, he was in charge of the Great Lakes engineering survey when war broke out.

Pennsylvania governor Andrew G. Curtin used his influence to have Meade promoted to brigadier general of volunteers on 31 August 1861. The new general was assigned to the 2d Brigade of the Pennsylvania Reserves. As commander of this brigade, Meade ably led his regiments during the Seven Days' battles and the fighting at Mechanicsville, Gaines' Mill, and Glendale. In this latter engagement, Meade was badly wounded in the back and arm. However, he recovered to lead his brigade at Second Bull Run.

When John F. Reynolds was called to command the Pennsylvania militia during the opening stages of the Maryland campaign, Meade succeeded to the command of the Pennsylvania Reserves, which he directed at both South Mountain and Antietam. When Joseph Hooker was wounded at the latter battle, Meade temporarily was placed in charge of I Corps.

Meade then returned to divisional command, but was promoted to major general on 29 November 1862. At Fredericksburg on 13 December, the reserves broke into "Stonewall" Jackson's position at Hamilton's Crossing but had to retreat when reinforcements failed to support the breakthrough. Recognizing Meade's talents, General Ambrose Burnside on 23 December promoted Meade to command of V Corps.

Although not actively engaged during the Chancellorsville campaign, Meade performed well and was quite vocal about wanting to continue the battle when Hooker decided to withdraw. Meade led his corps north during the opening stages of the Gettysburg campaign. When the War Department accepted Hooker's resignation, Meade, in spite of his protests, was placed in command of the Army of the Potomac on 28 June 1863. He was given a free hand to appoint or relieve any officers he so chose; before ordering Meade to the command, the War Department ascertained that corps commanders junior to Meade would willingly serve under him.

Meade's greatest test came three days later, at Gettysburg, Pennsylvania. Pushed into an accidental battle, Meade, who wished to fight a defensive engagement against Robert E. Lee's troops, quickly ascertained the state of affairs on the field and brought the entire army to the battlefield. On 2 July, even though III Corps advanced without orders and had to be reinforced by sending troops from other parts of the line, Meade managed the troop movements well and staved off possible disaster. When Lee retreated on 4 July, the wounded Army of the Potomac followed. However, Lee managed to cross the Potomac before Meade's army could engage him; the failure to crush Lee's army haunted Meade the rest of his life.

Shortly after the Gettysburg battle, a London newspaperman described the victor: "He is a very remarkable looking man—tall, spare, of a commanding figure and presence, his manner pleasant and easy but having much dignity. His head is partially bald and is small and compact, but the forehead is high. He has the late Duke of Wellington class of nose, and his eyes, which have a serious and almost sad expression, are rather sunken, or appear so from the prominence of the curved nasal appearance. He has a decidedly patrician and distinguished appearance."

Meade was also outwardly modest, although his voluminous correspondence with his wife Margaret (whom he married in 1840) suggests otherwise. The general was also nicknamed the "old snapping turtle" in honor of his temper, which occasionally flared when a subordinate failed to perform as expected.

After Gettysburg, Meade parried Lee's northward movement in October at Bristoe Station, then launched an offensive that culminated in frustration at Mine Run

General George Meade and corps commanders near Washington, D.C., June 1865. From left to right are Horatio G. Wright, John A. Logan, Meade, John G. Parke, and Andrew A. Humphreys. (Photograph by William Morris Smith / *Library of Congress*)

in November, when General Gouverneur K. Warren called off an attack because he thought the enemy earthworks too strong.

During the winter of 1863–1864, the Joint Congressional Committee on the Conduct of the War, aided and abetted by various malcontent officers such as Daniel E. Sickles, Abner Doubleday, and Alfred Pleasonton, tried to deprive Meade of the credit for Gettysburg and blacken his reputation. Although their bid to have him removed from army command failed, their testimony, coupled with voluminous postwar writings, succeeded in casting a shadow over Meade's reputation.

When Ulysses S. Grant came to Washington in the spring of 1864, Meade offered to resign, but Grant kept him in command. During the campaign against Richmond and Petersburg, Meade remained in control of the Army of the Potomac, but Grant's presence with the army overshadowed the Pennsylvanian's contributions. In early June, as a result of false press stories that enraged

the general, Meade expelled reporter Edward Cropsey from the army; resulting furor by other reporters caused further problems for Meade's reputation. When the army launched its first attacks on Petersburg later that month, Meade was unable to persuade his corps commanders to coordinate their assaults; his frustration was vented on Warren, who had not lived up to his Gettysburg accolades during the 1864 battles.

Meade grew increasingly frustrated, endured the barbs of Grant's staff officers, and chafed under Grant's control. He was bitterly disappointed when he was not chosen to command the troops assembled in the Shenandoah Valley and got into a heated argument with Burnside during the failed 30 July 1864 attack on the Crater. Still, Meade performed his duties competently during the Petersburg operations. During the Appomattox campaign, Meade was thrust into the background and was not present in the McLean house when Lee surrendered the Army of Northern Virginia to Grant.

Meade's headquarters near Culpeper, Virginia, 1863 (*National Archives*)

After the end of hostilities, Meade was placed in command of the Division of the Atlantic, headquartered in Philadelphia. He also served as temporary commander of the Third Military District. The general went to the Canadian border and helped to thwart the abortive Fenian invasion of Canada in 1866. When Grant became president in 1868, he named William T. Sherman to succeed him as full general and then promoted his friend Philip H. Sheridan, two months Meade's junior as major general in the regular army, to lieutenant general. Snubbed, Meade yet resumed his duties without public complaint. He died of pneumonia on 6 November 1872 and was buried in Laurel Hill Cemetery, Philadelphia.

—*Richard A. Sauers*

See also Crater, Battle of the; Fredericksburg, Battle of; Gettysburg, Battle of; Joint Committee on the Conduct of the War; Petersburg Campaign; Warren, Gouverneur K.

For further reading:
Cleaves, Freeman. *Meade of Gettysburg* (1960; reprint, 1980).
Coddington, Edwin B. "The Strange Reputation of George G. Meade: A Lesson in Historiography." *The Historian* (1962).
Meade, George G., ed. *The Life and Letters of George Gordon Meade, Major-General United States Army* (1913; reprint, 1994).
Sauers, Richard A. *A Caspian Sea of Ink: The Meade-Sickles Controversy* (1989).

MEAGHER, THOMAS FRANCIS
(1823–1867)
Union general

Thomas Meagher was born in the city of Waterford, Ireland, on 3 August 1823. His family had prospered in the Newfoundland provision trade. A collateral ancestor, Thaddeus De Meagher, had served in the French army during the eighteenth century, rising to become the court chamberlain to Frederick Augustus II, elector of Saxony and king of Poland. Meagher's father represented Waterford in the British House of Commons, 1847–1857. A Catholic, Meagher was privately educated by the Jesuits at their prestigious school, Stoneyhurst College, Lancashire, England. Never losing his upper-class lisping accent, nor his affected aristocratic manners, Meagher returned to Dublin to study law. A prominent member of Young Ireland, a nationalistic organization, Meagher became noted for his anti-British oratory and his design of the Irish tricolor, the present flag of the Irish Republic. William Makepeace Thackeray sarcastically called him "Meagher of the Sword," an appellation Meagher proudly used during his life.

Meagher's seditious speeches attracted the authorities.

He became involved in the abortive Irish rebellion of 1848 and he was prosecuted for high treason in August 1848. Because of his youth, his death sentence was commuted to hard labor and exile to Tasmania. In January 1852 Meagher engineered his escape, and his arrival in New York City in May 1852 made him an instant hero among the city's Irish community. Having married the daughter of a prosperous American merchant and being called to the New York bar, Meagher became the editor of the pro-Democrat and pro-Southern *Irish News* in 1856.

A revolutionary in Ireland, he became a conservative in his adopted country. After the attack on Fort Sumter in April 1861, Meagher came to support President Lincoln's call for volunteers. Commissioned captain of a company of Irish Zouaves that he raised to become company K of the Irish 69th New York Militia, Meagher fought at First Bull Run in July 1861. When the regiment, a thirty-day unit, returned to New York, Meagher defended its military reputation against nativist attacks in *The Last Days of the 69th in Virginia*. After the 69th reenlisted for the duration of the war, it became the nucleus for the projected Irish Brigade.

Never a Fenian, Meagher nonetheless saw the new brigade as a symbol of Irish glory rather like the Irish brigades who had fought for France, Spain, and even Austria. Tireless in promoting the unit, he was commissioned colonel, and when James Shields, an Irish born veteran of the Mexican-American War, refused command, Meagher was appointed its first brigadier general in February 1862. Despite his lack of previous military experience, he proved to be a courageous commander, and he helped shape the brigade into one of the Army of the Potomac's finest combat units.

Its birth of fire was during the Seven Days' campaign. At Malvern Hill on 1 July 1862, it engaged Irish-born Louisiana Confederates. During the battle of Antietam in September 1862, Meagher had his horse shot from under him while the brigade won further battle laurels in attacking the strong Confederate position at the Bloody Lane. Under his command, the brigade's finest hour came during its attack at Marye's Height, Fredericksburg, in December 1862. Decimated by its heroic action, the brigade was a skeleton command during the battle of Chancellorsville in May 1863. When General Joseph Hooker refused Meagher permission to return north to recruit more Irish to its ranks, Meagher resigned his commission, and his resignation was accepted 14 May 1863. As a Democrat, Meagher had made political enemies, though his critics, perhaps unfairly, had attributed the command's high casualty rate to Meagher's heavy drinking. Meagher returned to New York to another hero's welcome.

Becoming frustrated with inactivity, he petitioned constantly for reinstatement. Political reasons led to his being recommissioned brigadier general of volunteers on 23 December 1864. Ordered to Nashville, Meagher was finally given command of fragmented units and convalescent troops rather grandly called the Provisional Division, the Army of the Tennessee. After garrison duties and brief command of the district of Etowah, in January 1865 Meagher was ordered to transport his command to Savannah to support General William T. Sherman. Meagher so mismanaged his command's transfer—as a result of his drinking, his enemies claimed—that, once he had finally rounded up his unit, he was relieved by General Grant and sent home to New York on 24 February 1865 to await further orders. Disappointed at not being commissioned a major general nor permitted to lead his Irish Brigade during the Army of the Potomac's Grand Review in Washington D.C., he resigned his commission on 12 May 1865.

For his past service, he was appointed the secretary of Montana by President Andrew Johnson. Arriving in the territory in September 1865, he was faced with political disorder as well as the hostility of the Sioux under Red Cloud. Becoming the de facto governor in 1866, Meagher attempted to restore order and prepare the region for defense. While waiting for a shipment of arms for the recently raised Montana Volunteers at Fort Benton, Meagher mysteriously fell from the deck of the *G. A. Thompson* into the Missouri River on 1 July 1867. His body was never recovered, nor his death adequately explained. Considered a hero by the Irish-American community and in his homeland, General Meagher is remembered by a monument outside his birthplace, now the Granville Hotel, Waterford, and by a fine equestrian statue outside the Montana state capital, Helena.

—*Rory T. Cornish*

See also Antietam, Battle of; Irish-Americans; Irish Brigade; Zouaves.

For further reading:

Athearn, Robert G. *Thomas Francis Meagher: An Irish Revolutionary in America* (1949).

Cavanagh, Michael. *Memoirs of General Thomas Francis Meagher* (1892).

Hernon, Joseph M., Jr. *Celts, Catholics and Copperheads: Ireland Views the American Civil War* (1968).

Lonn, Ella. *Foreigners in the Union Army and Navy* (1951).

Lyons, W. F. *Brigadier General Thomas Francis Meagher: His Political and Military Career* (1870).

O'Brien, Kevin E., ed. *My Life in the Irish Brigade. The Civil War Memoirs of Private William McCarter, 116th Pennsylvania Infantry* (1996).

Seagrave, Pia Seija, ed. *The History of the Irish Brigade: A Collection of Historical Essays* (1997).

MECHANICSVILLE, BATTLE OF
(26 June 1862)

Also known as Ellison's or Ellerson's Mill, Beaver Dam Creek, or Meadow Bridge, the clash at Mechanicsville, Virginia, was the first of the

Seven Days' battles and the first battle fought by the Army of Northern Virginia under the command of Robert E. Lee. Major General George B. McClellan's 100,000-man Army of the Potomac had advanced to within five miles of Richmond before stalling after Confederate forces under General Joseph E. Johnston attacked them at Seven Pines on 31 May and 1 June. Johnston, severely wounded at Seven Pines, relinquished command to Lee on 1 June.

By late June, McClellan had made little progress since Seven Pines. His forces were divided, with Fitz John Porter's V Corps isolated on the north bank of the Chickahominy River. J. E. B. Stuart, during his famous "ride around McClellan" (12 June–15 June 1862) learned that Porter's right was "in the air" (not protected by natural obstacles) and could be flanked. On 23 June Lee informed his division commanders of a

daring plan, in which he would risk dividing his outnumbered forces in an attack on Porter's 30,000-man corps. He planned to overwhelm Porter with most of his army, using the divisions of Longstreet, A. P. Hill, and D. H. Hill, along with "Stonewall" Jackson's force, which was marching from the Shenandoah Valley. About 55,000 men were to be brought to bear against Porter at Mechanicsville. John Magruder with the remaining 25,000 Confederates, would hold McClellan's other troops south of the Chickahominy by making noisy demonstrations.

McClellan planned an attack of his own; on 25 June Heintzelman's corps advanced from Seven Pines and fought a small battle known as Oak Grove. At the end of the day, the Federals were less than five miles from Richmond, the closest they would get during the campaign. McClellan, however, had heard of Jackson's

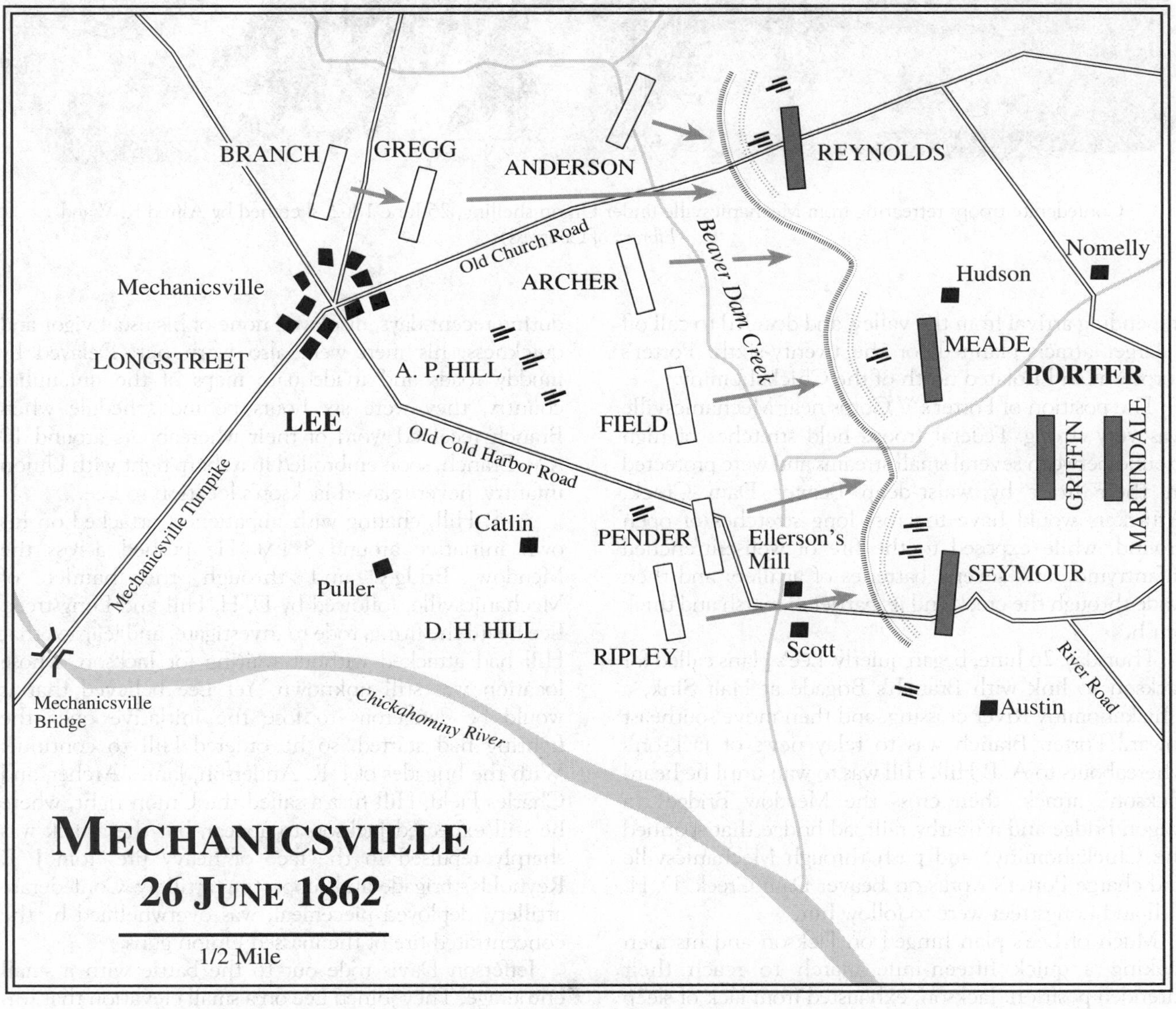

MECHANICSVILLE
26 JUNE 1862

1/2 Mile

BRANCH GREGG ANDERSON REYNOLDS

Old Church Road

Mechanicsville

ARCHER

Nomelly

Hudson

LONGSTREET

Beaver Dam Creek

MEADE

PORTER

A. P. HILL

LEE

FIELD

Old Cold Harbor Road

GRIFFIN

MARTINDALE

Catlin

PENDER Ellerson's Mill

SEYMOUR

Puller

D. H. HILL

Scott

Mechanicsville Bridge

RIPLEY

River Road

Chickahominy River

Austin

Confederate troops retreating from Mechanicsville under Union shelling, 26 June 1862, sketched by Alfred R. Waud
(*Library of Congress*)

impending arrival from the valley, and decided to call off a larger attack planned for the twenty-sixth. Porter's corps was still isolated north of the Chickahominy.

The position of Porter's V Corps near Mechanicsville was very strong. Federal troops held stretches of high ground between several small streams and were protected in their front by waist-deep Beaver Dam Creek. Attackers would have to cross long stretches of open ground, while exposed to the fire of well-entrenched infantrymen and several batteries of artillery and then wade through the creek and its barrier of marsh and thick brush.

Thursday, 26 June, began quietly. Lee's plans called for Jackson to link with Branch's Brigade at Half Sink, a Chickahominy River crossing, and then move southeast toward Porter. Branch was to relay news of Jackson's whereabouts to A. P. Hill. Hill was to wait until he heard Jackson's attack, then cross the Meadow Bridges (a wagon bridge and a nearby railroad bridge that spanned the Chickahominy) and push through Mechanicsville and charge Porter's works on Beaver Dam Creek. D. H. Hill and Longstreet were to follow him.

Much of Lee's plan hinged on Jackson and his men making a quick fifteen-mile march to reach their intended position. Jackson, exhausted from lack of sleep during recent days, displayed none of his usual vigor and quickness; his men were also worn out. Delayed by muddy roads and inadequate maps of the unfamiliar country, they were six hours behind schedule when Branch received word of their whereabouts around 10 A.M. Branch, soon embroiled in a sharp fight with Union infantry, never relayed Jackson's location to Lee.

A. P. Hill, chafing with impatience, attacked on his own initiative around 3 P.M. He pushed across the Meadow Bridges and through the hamlet of Mechanicsville, followed by D. H. Hill and Longstreet. Lee heard the firing, rode to investigate, and learned that Hill had attacked without waiting for Jackson, whose location was still unknown. Yet Lee believed that it would be dangerous to lose the initiative once the fighting had started, so he ordered Hill to continue. With the brigades of J. R. Anderson, James Archer, and Charles Field, Hill first assailed the Union right, where he still expected Jackson to appear, but the attack was sharply repulsed in the face of heavy fire from J. F. Reynolds's brigade and supporting artillery. Confederate artillery, deployed piecemeal, was overwhelmed by the concentrated fire of the massed Union guns.

Jefferson Davis rode out to the battle with a small entourage. They joined Lee on a small elevation that was

Ellerson's Mills, Mechanicsville, Virginia (Photograph by John Reekie / *Library of Congress*)

exposed to enemy shellfire until Lee convinced Davis to withdraw to a less dangerous place.

Jackson arrived at last around 5 P.M. at Pole Green Church, the place where he expected to find the divisions of A. P. Hill and D. H. Hill. Finding none of the units he had expected to join, Jackson ordered his men to make camp, intending to continue on the next day. Under the impression that A. P. Hill's attack would not begin until their forces established contact, Jackson showed little concern about the firing that was heard from the battle three miles distant.

Near dusk, Hill launched a final attack in spite of orders from Lee to hold his position. He sent Dorsey Pender against Truman Seymour's brigade on the Union left near Ellerson's Mill. Pender's men, stalled by the overwhelming fire and blocked by abatis, could neither advance nor retreat. Roswell Ripley's Brigade, fed into the fight to help them, was also trapped, and survivors were unable to leave the field until dark. Artillery fire continued until around 10 P.M.

The misfire of Lee's plans left only 11,000 men, instead of more than 55,000, to strike Porter. Lee lost about 1,475 men; Porter lost only 361. Mechanicsville was a Confederate defeat, but it signaled a turning point in the war in Virginia. Lee's bold, aggressive style contrasted with Johnston's caution, and shocked McClellan into halting his advance toward Richmond. About 2 A.M. on 27 June, Porter received orders from McClellan to fall back four miles to a new position, where the battle of Gaines' Mill was fought twelve hours later.

—*David A. Norris*

See also Gaines' Mill, Battle of; Seven Days' Battle.
For further reading:
OR, Series I, Vol. 11, pt. 2
Robertson, James I., Jr. *General A. P. Hill: The Story of a Confederate Warrior* (1987).
Sears, Stephen W. *To the Gates of Richmond: The Peninsula Campaign* (1992).

MEDAL OF HONOR

Before the Civil War, military decorations for a soldier's act of valor were limited. Some military administrators considered decorations for bravery to be undemocratic and associated with European aristocracy and elitism similar to rewards kings gave to knights and nobility. Some medals had been distributed for leadership in the American Revolution, and foreign awards were given to officers. On 7 August 1782, George

Washington created the Purple Heart to recognize bravery of soldiers, sailors, and marines, but only three men had received it by 1800. The Certificate of Merit was awarded during the Mexican-American War, allowing recipients extra monthly pay. Officers also received brevet promotions generally to reward gallantry. Many officers were breveted for political loyalty, leading to abuse of the system. During the first year of the Civil War, no award existed to recognize outstanding courage and service.

Several congressmen wanted to honor Union servicemen with a tribute that would be acknowledged as the United States' highest honor for valor. Previous efforts had been thwarted by General Winfield Scott, who thought such a medal was unnecessary. After he retired, medal proponents renewed their efforts. Iowa senator James W. Grimes, chairman of the Senate Naval Affairs Committee, introduced a bill asking that a Medal of Honor be presented by the secretary of the Navy to selected enlisted personnel of the U.S. Navy and Marine Corps who "shall most distinguish themselves by their gallantry in action, and other seamanlike qualities during the present war." The medal was intended to inspire servicemen. After the bill passed both houses of Congress, President Abraham Lincoln signed it into law on 21 December 1861. Massachusetts senator Henry Wilson introduced legislation for a similar Medal of Honor for enlisted U.S. Army and Volunteer Forces personnel. This medal was created in an effort to reform the brevet promotion system and to honor soldiers whose actions exceeded the ordinary bravery expected of all combatants. On 12 July 1862, the second Medal of Honor was approved.

The Medal of Honor was declared retroactive to the beginning of the Civil War to recognize earlier acts of courage. Army officers were eligible for Medals of Honor when the law was amended on 3 March 1863; naval officers did not qualify until World War I. Like England's Victoria Cross and Germany's Iron Cross, the Medal of Honor was intended to honor only individuals who displayed extraordinary bravery. At the time of its creation, the Medal of Honor was the only U.S. armed forces medal. In cooperation with the U.S. Mint, William Wilson & Son Company, Philadelphia silversmiths, designed the first Civil War Medal of Honor, and Secretary of the Navy Gideon Welles approved its style. Cast as a five-pointed star, the Civil War Medal of Honor depicted mythic images of the Union defeating secession. The reverse side of each medal had space to be engraved with the recipient's name, unit, and date and place of action. A red, white, and blue ribbon adorned the medal.

Secretary of War Edwin M. Stanton presented the first Medals of Honor to six surviving Andrews's Raiders on 25 March 1863. Nine days later, the first Navy Medal of Honor was given to sailors who had secured crucial forts. Francis E. Brownell eventually would hold the distinction of having committed the first act worthy of a Medal of Honor. In May 1861, he accompanied Colonel Elmer E. Ellsworth to remove a Confederate flag at the Marshall House in Alexandria, Virginia. Trying to stop the proprietor, James T. Jackson, from attacking Ellsworth, Brownell became a hero for bayoneting Jackson. Brownell nominated himself twice for a Medal of Honor and finally received one in 1877 as a result of the insistence of his congressman. Sergeant William H. Carney, Company C, 54th Massachusetts Colored Infantry, was the first African-American to earn a Medal of Honor. Dr. Mary Edwards Walker was the only woman ever to receive a Medal of Honor for serving in the front lines, where she provided medical care for the wounded under fire. Although a committee revoked her medal in 1917, Walker continued to wear it, and President Jimmy Carter issued a citation legally restoring it to her posthumously. The last action meriting a Medal of Honor in the Civil War occurred at Sayler's Creek, Virginia. Sergeant Francis Cunningham procured a Confederate mule and rode up to the enemy's breastworks to seize the flag, returning unscathed. His commander, General George Armstrong Custer, ordered him to deliver the flag to Stanton, who presented Cunningham a Medal of Honor for the final Confederate flag captured in the war.

A total of 1,527 Medals of Honor were given during the Civil War, five times more than awarded in any other war since. Of those, 1,195 medals were presented to 1,194 army soldiers (Lieutenant Tom Custer, brother of General Custer, received two for separate actions), 307 were awarded to navy sailors, and 17 were presented to marines. Many medals recognized individual acts such as capturing or protecting a battle flag, saving a life, or hand-to-hand combat. Some medals were presented to groups such as the 864 members of the 27th Maine Infantry for standing ready to defend Washington, D.C., during the first week of July 1863, when the Confederates invading southern Pennsylvania might have threatened the capital.

Soldiers of all ranks and ages were awarded the Medal of Honor. Some soldiers, such as Brownell, did not receive their medals until years after their act of bravery. Applications submitted after the Civil War were difficult to document, and policies stipulating what should merit a Medal of Honor were questioned. From 16 October 1916 to 17 January 1917, a U.S. Army review board of five retired generals evaluated all 2,625 Medals of Honor awarded to combatants in the Civil War and other military actions afterward. On 15 February 1917, 911 Medals of Honor were revoked, including the 864 presented to the 27th Maine Infantry. The review board withdrew medals that had been offered as an incentive to reenlist or that had been awarded for relatively undistinguished service. Because many commanding officers had not envisioned the medal's uniqueness, many had been liberally bestowed for lesser acts of bravery.

A new medal, the Certificate of Merit, was presented from 1905 to 1918, and then the Distinguished Service Cross was created to protect the special status of the Medal of Honor as the highest distinction possible. Also, Major General George L. Gillespie redesigned and patented the Medal of Honor's design because veterans' groups had copied the original U.S. Army medal's design for wide distribution.

In the twentieth century, the Medal of Honor legislation was amended to clarify the vague language of the original acts and specify who was eligible for the award. The legislation's wording stressed that only military personnel who had exhibited courage above the call of duty and in actual combat should be recognized. The risk of life and conspicuous self-sacrifice distinguishable from that of others would require irrefutable proof thoroughly documented through eyewitness accounts and official reports.

In 1956, the Medal of Honor was approved for service members in the U.S. Air Force. The Medal of Honor has recognized hundreds of heroic participants in twentieth century wars. Medals have been awarded retroactively to African-American World War II veterans originally denied recognition because of racism. Recipients receive increased salaries and pensions and special rights to travel on military planes. The Medal of Honor Historical Society preserves information about Medal of Honor winners and marks their graves with special headstones.

—*Elizabeth D. Schafer*

See also Brevet Rank; Decorations.

For further reading:
Beyer, W. F., and O.F. Keydel. *Deeds of Valor: How America's Civil War Heroes Won the Congressional Medal of Honor* (1903).
Cooke, Donald E. *For Conspicuous Gallantry…Winners of the Medal of Honor* (1966).
Lang, George M. H., Raymond L. Collins, and Gerard F. White, comps. *Medal of Honor Recipients, 1863–1994* (1995).
Lowry, Timothy S. *And Brave Men Too* (1985).
Proft, R. J., ed. *United States of America's Congressional Medal of Honor Recipients and Their Official Citations* (1997).

MEDICINE

The Civil War gave birth to a staggering amount of disease and mayhem. Coping with it was an especially difficult task, as the state of medical arts in the mid-nineteenth century was more medieval than modern. Pharmacology was primitive and largely homeopathic, except for several outright poisons, such as mercury. Modern antibiotics remained over a half-century away, and heat sterilization for asepsis was unknown. It is little wonder that soldiers hid all but the direst diseases from physicians, for to come under a doctor's care tested fate. Diseases caused ten times the

death of wounds. Wounds, however, were double jeopardy because the tissue damage done on the battlefield made them sure to become infected and also because they put the casualty into the clutches of surgeons, some of doubtful competence.

Before the Civil War, older doctors usually had received their training through apprenticeship to a mentoring physician. This practice had merit if the teacher was competent, but it did tend to freeze knowledge into hidebound traditions. The lamentable persistence of dubious medical practices such as bleeding and purging were examples. Even younger physicians, who often received instruction at medical colleges and universities, had the same superstitions, especially when some of these schools were little better than barber colleges. Most colleges taught one yearly standard set of lectures. Sitting through the same set twice in two years resulted in graduation. The most prestigious of them still eschewed clinical and laboratory work. The era's doctors persisted in medical practice fixated on bodily fluids and dating from the time of Aristotle. Diagnoses were observational. They were based heavily on how vigorously the patient voided urine, excreted feces, the condition of the blood, and the nature of suppurations from wounds. In a time when doctors dismissed a serious infection as "laudable pus," the prevailing medical opinion was that the toil of the body was to rid itself of toxins and cure what ailed it. The doctor's helping that process along with emetics and purgatives usually helped the patient along to the grave.

At the start of the Civil War, the Union's Army Medical Bureau was the special preserve of Surgeon General (Colonel) Thomas Lawson, who had been in the job over four decades. He prided himself on never spending the entire allotted annual budget. Lawson's ineptitude was compounded by ill health, and in fact, he died in May 1861. His successor, Clement A. Finley, was possibly worse in that he was robustly incompetent. As volunteers and recruits swelled Union ranks, medical problems became apparent immediately. Health examinations for enlistees were cursory if conducted at all, allowing all but the most obviously feeble to enlist. At least a quarter of Union recruits would never have passed any competent medical examination and many were soon invalided out of the army. For those who remained, persistent good health was rare. In both armies, North and South, men were thrown together in large groups living in squalid camps, exposed to a plethora of new and irresistible diseases, and they died by the hundreds and were sick by the thousands. When the war broke out in earnest in the summer of 1861, the woeful inadequacies of both medical services were underscored with a vengeance. The Union army had only about a hundred physicians in the rank of surgeon (major) or assistant surgeon (captain), so most doctors on the field at First Bull Run were regimental

Dr. Jonathan Letterman, medical director of the Army of the Potomac, and staff near Warrenton, Virginia, November 1862 (*Library of Congress*)

surgeons supplied by the states. There were precious few of those anyway in both Northern and Southern ranks, so the wounded from this first great clash of the war largely had to fend for themselves. Ambulances were a rarity, rarely used, and of wretched design more suited for torture than transportation.

Addressing this intolerable situation became a high priority for both sides. Even before Bull Run, the United States Sanitary Commission had been created on 13 June 1861 by executive order. Originally opposed by the Medical Bureau, secretary of War Edwin Stanton, and

even Lincoln, its official function was limited to providing advice and conducting investigations. Yet the "Sanitary" performed services similar to those of the later USO, and its helpful work was crucial in improving the health of military camps. The commission's September 1861 report included a scathing criticism of Clement Finley's Medical Bureau and persuaded Congress on 18 April 1862 to adopt a bill reorganizing the army's entire medical establishment. Dr. William A. Hammond soon replaced Finley, perhaps because of Sanitary Commission lobbying with the War Department, and he commenced

A Zouave ambulance crew demonstrating removal of wounded soldiers from the field (*Library of Congress*)

a complete overhaul of his department while encouraging a more cooperative relationship with the Sanitary Commission. In one important move, he appointed Jonathan Letterman the medical director for the Army of the Potomac after McClellan's Peninsula campaign. Letterman established an ambulance corps that performed outstanding service in moving wounded to field hospitals at the battle of Antietam. Congress would institutionalize this innovation for all Union armies in 1864. The system remains relatively unchanged in modern armies today.

Samuel Preston Moore built the Confederate Medical Department from the ground up with a handful of former Union army doctors who "went South." Coping with shortages of almost everything, Moore managed to erect a medical establishment comparable to the North's, but it was understandably less effective in contending with the enormous problems of treating the sick and tending the wounded. Many medical problems faced the new Confederacy. Doctor Moore recruited and examined new physicians, developed domestic pharmaceutical resources, established a military evacuation and hospital system, recruited and trained nurses, established a systematic method of treating war wounds, and attempted to manufacture surgical instruments and appliances.

Swelled by enthusiastic Southerners ready to end the war in thirty days, the ranks contained many potential surgeons and assistant surgeons. Neither the Confederate government nor the individual states had a mechanism to identify and commission physicians. Many physicians joined the ranks as common soldiers because they thought that the war would be over shortly, others because it was the way to more rapidly achieve military fame. One company in the 1st South Carolina Infantry started the war with nearly thirty physicians among its one hundred men. Only twenty-four of the 3,000 physicians in the fully constituted Medical Corps of the Confederacy had served in the United States Army. Six physicians achieved Confederate general officer rank as line officers, including Commissary General Lucius Bellinger Northrop. Many served as field grade officers and successful commanders. In Texas, Colonel John Salmon "RIP" Ford, M.D., fought the last battle of the war, Palmito Ranch.

While both the Northern and Southern governments established a system of field hospitals where immediate treatment of the wounded could be accomplished near the battle's rear, the Confederacy got a late start in setting up convalescent facilities and was slow in completing them. During the Seven Days', Richmond was overwhelmed with the wounded that sought shelter in places ranging from private homes to abandoned warehouses. In contrast, a massive hospital construction program in the North raised 151 hospitals by 1863 and added another 53 by war's end with a total capacity of almost 137,000 beds. Eventually about 150 general hospitals would dot the Confederacy, yet some of them were nothing more than improvised sheds. The best were situated in Richmond, where the highest concentration of hospitals included the vast 8,000-bed establishment at Chimborazo Heights, perhaps the largest military hospital ever to exist.

Providing emergency treatment to wounded soldiers during and immediately after a battle direly taxed both medical departments, as statistics show. Although the methods of counting them can result in varying numbers (Confederate medical records burned in Richmond in 1865), the mortality rates of wounded Union and Confederate soldiers was appallingly high by modern standards. About 14 percent of Northern soldiers would not survive a battlefield injury; the figure for Confederate mortality is uncertain only in how much greater it is. The projectile of the rifled musket moved a long distance at relatively low velocity, resulting in mangled flesh and bone and often remaining within the victim's body. Head, chest, and stomach wounds were usually regarded as fatal and often

not treated, while injuries to arms and legs usually resulted in amputation, early, to prevent the onset of gangrene. Field hospitals were filthy places where septic conditions were the norm and surgeons washed their hands and instruments only after an operation. Convalescence was a grueling ordeal in which the defenses of the body were on their own in fighting off bacterial infection and sometimes hobbled by barbaric medical treatments. Yet for all that, it is a testament to the skill and dedication of these overwhelmed surgeons that mortality rates of wounded soldiers in the Civil War were lower than those of the Mexican-American War. Only in the twentieth century with the discovery of powerful antibiotics and sulfa drugs would survival rates of combat casualties markedly improve.

For all the horrible trauma of wounds, disease was the Civil War soldier's greatest and invincible enemy. Disease continued to take a greater toll than wounds, sometimes 10:1. The fate of campaigns hinged on the collective vitality of the army, and epidemic sickness could fell a force more thoroughly than any human opponents could. Robert E. Lee's first field command in western Virginia slogged around in incessant, bone chilling rain and was so wracked by resultant maladies that it was good for little else but losing battles. George McClellan's Peninsula campaign faltered in part because the fetid swamps of the Chickahominy (the

Ambulance drill of the 57th New York Infantry, 1864 (*National Archives*)

"Chicky Bottom" to those mucking about in it) assailed Yankees as much as Rebels did. By the time the Army of the Potomac had been driven into Harrison's Landing, typhus and diarrhea had an alarming companion in scurvy. Similarly, Ulysses S. Grant's grand advance on Vicksburg hesitated as widespread sickness felled so many of his troops that the campaign was subjected to frustrating delays. Doctors armed with only a limited pharmacological arsenal were helpless. The most common and insidious complaint was chronic diarrhea brought on by bad diet, poor hygiene, and foul living conditions. Cleaning up the camps helped some, but poor standards of personal cleanliness and the vagaries of a soldier's diet made diarrhea and dysentery an inescapable certainty of life and a frequent cause of death. Treating the fluxes, as they were called, consisted of dosing the victim with mercurous chloride, a cathartic popularly known as calomel. The prescription not only abetted diarrhea's depletion of essential fluids and electrolytes, but when frequently administered it also dosed the body with lethal levels of mercury.

More benign were the homeopathic remedies that might not have done much good but were salutary in that they did little harm. Some drugs, however, were truly therapeutic and essential. Quinine could prevent malaria and tame it in those already afflicted. Opium had long been used as a painkiller, and some soldiers, mostly Northern, emerged from the war hopelessly addicted to it. The widespread use of anesthetics such as ether and chloroform, the latter of which is noncombustible, made grisly operations more bearable, although when occasional shortages deprived Southern surgeons of these drugs, a couple of shots of whiskey had to suffice. Most times, Confederate surgeons had a sufficiency of captured Yankee anesthetics.

The Civil War did not produce a pharmacological breakthrough in the form of a new wonder drug, but it did give birth to the pharmaceutical industry in which firms such as Squibb and Pfizer would contribute to the medical revolution of the twentieth century. With the implementation of the Northern blockade of Southern ports, medicine and medical supplies became a problem. These items were on the forbidden contraband list and not exempted from the blockade. Confederate surgeon general Moore commissioned several scientist-physicians to forage for natural plants and other ingredients to replace unobtainable medicines. These included Francis

Preparing to amputate at a Union field hospital, 1863 (*Library of Congress*)

Ward at Harewood Hospital in Washington, D.C., early 1860s (*Library of Congress*)

Peyre Porcher who wrote *Resources of Southern Fields and Forests, Medical, Economical and Agricultural, Being Also a Medical Botany of Southern States with a Practical Information on the Properties of the Trees, Plants and Shrubs*. He found substitutes for digitalis, quinine, calomel, belladonna, and other drugs. The war also led to a better understanding of the relationship between cleanliness, health, squalor, and disease.

Several medical firsts should be noted. Dentistry was first recognized as an allied health profession during the war. Early in the war, the Confederacy arranged special pay for dentists serving as soldiers in the ranks. In 1863, it approved a petition requesting exemption from the conscription laws for civilian dentists. The next year, Moore commissioned several dentists into the medical corps. One of these was James Baxter Bean who had developed a system of interdental wiring and splinting for immobilizing fractured jaws. In addition, the first female officers were commissioned. In the South, trained nurses were severely needed as the war progressed. Various newly created women's organizations came to help in hospitals or established private hospitals themselves. Because of "lax practices" in some of these hospitals, a law was passed to ensure quality by requiring that

Confederate soldiers be cared for only in hospitals directed by commissioned military officers with a rank not lower than that of a captain. This led to the commissioning of Captain Sally Louisa Tompkins on 9 September 1861. This was to allow her to continue her excellent hospital under her control. The letter of appointment from the Secretary of War to her begins: "Sir: You are hereby informed that the President has appointed you Captain in the army of the Confederate States...." Doctor Moore, therefore, may have scored another first, as the first surgeon general to commission and command female officers. The Union's Lieutenant Mary Walker, a physician winner of the Medal of Honor, was commissioned in October 1864. Modern public health started as specialized doctors, both North and South looked for the causes of disease outbreaks in troops. Surgeon Joseph Jones roamed the Confederacy like a modern epidemiological investigator, searching out the causes of unusual infections and diseases in the Southern military and Union prisoners. Jones was the first physician in America to use a clinical thermometer and one of the first to use a microscope for clinical research. His orders from the surgeon general were "access to every medical facility...to purse these investi-

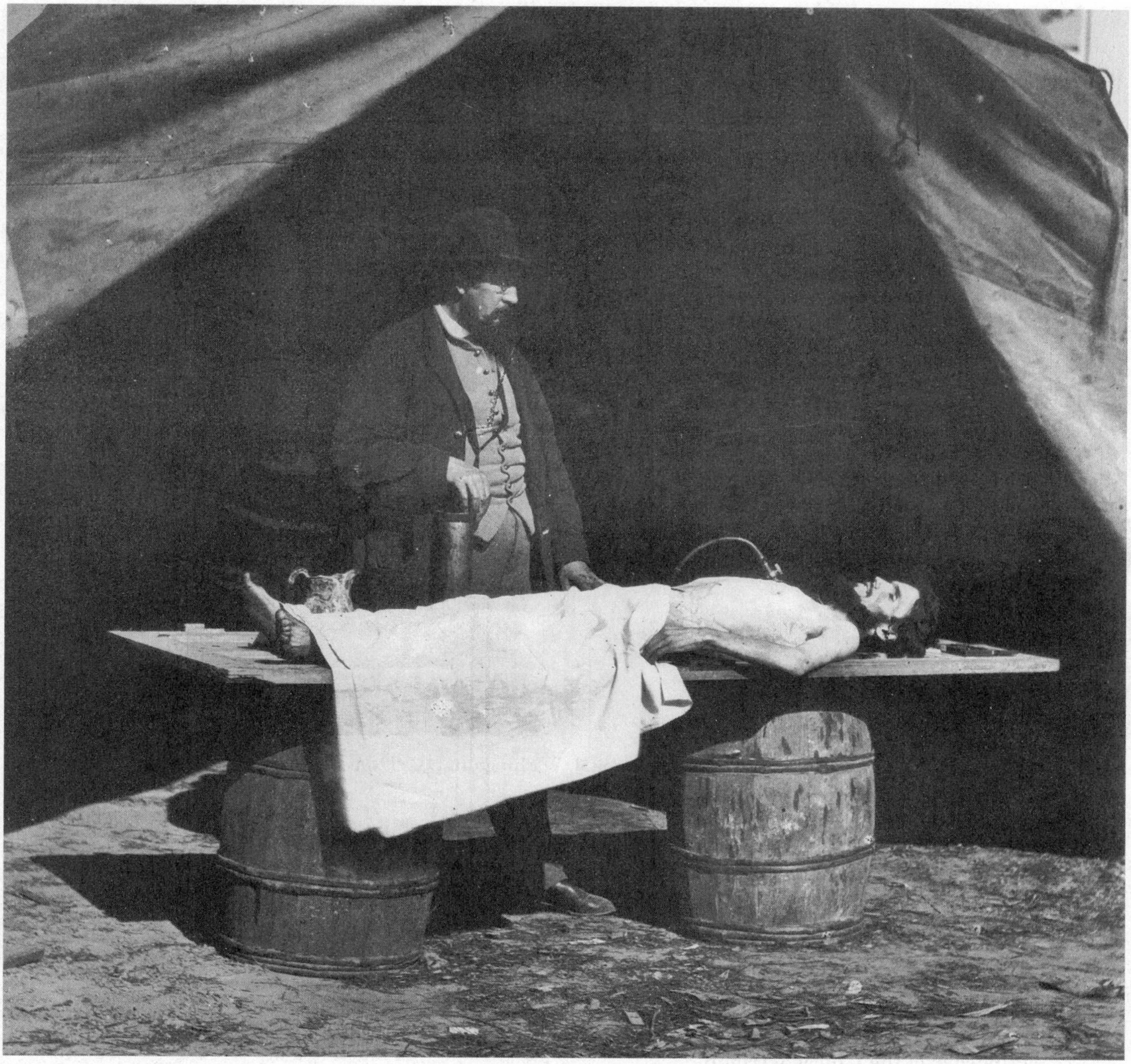

An embalming surgeon at work on a soldier's body, location unknown (*Library of Congress*)

gations according to his own plan and own pace...." Major Jones testified at the trial of Major Henry Wirz, the Andersonville camp commander.

In addition to these advances, the war provided ghastly but invaluable clinical experience to a generation of surgeons. With the advent of the germ theory only a few decades after the Civil War, these surgeons would begin to transform operating rooms from butcher shops into corrective and curative facilities. As the saying goes: "Only young surgeons profit from war."

—*David S. Heidler and Jeanne T. Heidler;*
Warner Farr contributing

See also American Red Cross; Barton, Clara; Casualties; Disease; Finley, Clement A.; Hammond, William; Moore, Samuel Preston; Nurses; Sister Nurses; United States Christian Commission; United States Sanitary Commission.

For further reading:
Bartholomees, J. Boone, Jr. *Buff Facings and Gilt Buttons. Staff and Headquarters Operations in the Army of Northern Virginia, 1861-1865* (1998).

Brooks, Stewart. *Civil War Medicine* (1966).

Cunningham, Horace Herndon. *Doctors in Gray; the Confederate Medical Service* (1958).

Fox, William F. *Regimental Losses in the American Civil War, 1861–1865* (1889).

Livermore, Thomas L. *Numbers and Losses in the Civil War in*

Ward in the Carver General Hospital, Washington, D.C. (*National Archives*)

America, 1861–1865 (1996).

Wiley, Bell Irvin. *The Life of Billy Yank: The Common Soldier of the Union* (1952; reprint, 1993).

———. *The Life of Johnny Reb: The Common Soldier of the Confederacy* (1978; reprint, 1997).

MEDILL, JOSEPH
(1823–1899)

Publisher of the Chicago Tribune

An important force in both journalism and politics, Joseph Medill turned the *Chicago Tribune* into one of the nation's most important newspapers and a dynamic voice in Republican politics, whose party he helped found and to which it is said he gave its name. He was one of Abraham Lincoln's closest friends in the newspaper world, and he was one of the president's most dedicated and forceful advocates.

The Canadian-born Medill came to the United States with his family at the age of nine. Educated in Ohio, he became a lawyer in 1846. Three years later he and his brothers bought the *Coshocton Whig* and renamed it the *Republican*. In 1851, after moving to Cleveland, Medill founded the *Daily Forest City*, which eventually became the *Cleveland Leader*. At the age of thirty-two, he purchased an interest in the *Chicago Tribune* and was named its managing editor. He took majority control of the paper in 1874 and ran it until his death.

Medill was among the founders of the Republican Party, and it was at its state founding conference in 1856 that he first heard Abraham Lincoln speak. He was so mesmerized by the lanky Springfield lawyer—indeed, Medill later wrote, he found himself in "sort of a hypnotic trance"—that he forgot to take notes. (Historian Robert S. Harper, however, has suggested that Medill and the other Republican editors conveniently "forgot" to take notes because Lincoln's radical abolitionist speech did not serve the fledgling party's political interests.)

Regardless, Medill found himself a staunch Lincoln man and began to push for his nomination for president in the 1860 election. Medill switched his support from his onetime ally, Salmon P. Chase, to head off the efforts of an eastern group, led by Henry Raymond of the *New York Times*, to put William Seward at the head of the ticket. Medill's behind-the-scenes maneuvering at the national convention in Chicago caused enough Ohio votes to switch from Chase to give Lincoln the nomination. In fact, it was Medill who pushed the reluctant candidate into seeking the presidency. When Lincoln suggested that he should seek the vice presidency, Medill replied that, "[I]t is president or nothing. Else you may count the *Tribune* out. We are not fooling away our time and science on the vice presidency."

A fervent abolitionist, Medill was aligned with the radical wing of the Republican Party and pressed for vigorous prosecution of the war. But Medill and his partner, Charles F. Ray, split over the question of slavery. Ray fervently endorsed General John Frémont's declaration of martial law and order of immediate emancipation in the areas under his army's control. Medill, however, endorsed Lincoln, who—fearful of losing the border states to secession—directed Frémont to withdraw his order. When the *Tribune*'s news columns, under Medill, continued to attack Frémont, earning the paper the ire of the abolitionist press, the *Tribune* responded that "We know of no reason that exempts the military man from criticism and, if necessary vigorous denunciation. ... It would be as recreant and cowardly not to speak out plainly as on the field of battle to refuse to fire at the foe."

Under Medill's leadership, the *Tribune* became one of the most recognized sources of credible news from the front, rivaling James Gordon Bennett's *New York Herald*. In the words of its historian, Philip Kinsley, the *Tribune* during the Civil War "attained maturity as a newspaper and became the strongest editorial voice of the Northwest for the preservation of the Union and the emancipation of slaves." The paper fielded more correspondents than any other paper—twenty-seven by its own estimate. The *Tribune* also specialized in news from the South, which was referred to in its papers as Secessia. But Medill, typical for the times, did not take the role of dispassionate observer: When Lincoln called for 500,000 volunteers in the summer of 1861, Medill actively recruited a company of soldiers for the 8th Illinois Cavalry. Virtually alone among newspapers, the *Tribune* urged Lincoln to immediately "draft 300,000 men without delay and march them to camps of instruction." Yet Medill vigorously protested in August 1864 when Lincoln demanded that the city of Chicago produce a quota of 6,000 men in a new draft. "You, Medill, are acting like a coward," the president berated him at a White House meeting. "You and your *Tribune* have had more influence than any paper in the Northwest in making this war. You can influence great masses, and yet you cry to be spared at a moment when your cause is suffering. Go home and send us those men."

Eventually, Medill gave in: the *Tribune* wrote that "there seems to be nothing left for the people of Cook County to do but to fill the quota assessed of them and to rely on a ... future draft, if there be one, to relieve them of their disproportionate share of the burden."

Otherwise, the relationship between Medill and Lincoln remained close throughout the war, and Medill rarely wavered in his support of the president and his policies, although the *Tribune* remained a critic of his generals and their strategy, save for Ulysses S. Grant, in whom Medill early saw signs of promise. The historian Tracey Elmer Strevey, in an early work on the *Tribune*'s history, said the paper's policy "was that of a radical and aggressive newspaper; radical in that it was ultra-Republican and continually urged upon the administration the most extreme Republican views." When Horace Greeley pressed Lincoln for an immediate emancipation proclamation in his editorial "The Prayer of Twenty Millions," the president turned to Medill and the *Tribune* to publish his famous reply: "My paramount object in this struggle is to save the Union. ... If I could save the Union without freeing any slave, I would do it, and if I could save it by freeing all the slaves I would do it." When Lincoln finally did issue a proclamation in late 1862, the *Tribune* was ecstatic, calling it "a late but grateful recognition of the finger of God."

One of the few times in which the *Tribune* did not rally behind Lincoln came when the president in June 1863 lifted General Ambrose Burnside's order to suppress publication of the *Tribune*'s hated Democratic rival, Wilbur Storey's *Chicago Times*. "The revocation is felt to be a most unfortunate blunder," the *Tribune* indignantly editorialized. "As the matter stands, it is a triumph of treason." That fall, however, when the *Times* dismissed Lincoln's Gettysburg Address as "silly, flat, dishwatery utterances," the *Tribune* declared that "the dedicatory remarks of President Lincoln will live among the annals of war."

Following the war, Medill was effectively relieved of control of the *Tribune*'s policies by his fellow shareholders, although he continued to hold 20 percent of the stock. Disillusioned as the paper strayed from traditional Republican policies, Medill offered to buy the *Times* and convert its editorial stance, but was rebuffed. After a term as mayor of Chicago, Medill bought a majority interest in the *Tribune* in 1874 and took sole control of its operation. Under his leadership, the *Tribune* solidified its position as the Midwest's most powerful paper.

—*Eric Fettmann*

See also Chicago Tribune; Newspapers; War Correspondents.
For further reading:
Harper, Robert S. *Lincoln and the Press* (1951).
Kinsley, Philip. The Chicago Tribune: *Its First Hundred Years* (1943).
Nicolay, John G., and John Hay. *Abraham Lincoln: A History* (1890).
Pollard, James E. *The Presidents and the Press* (1947).
Wendt, Lloyd. Chicago Tribune: *The Rise of a Great American Newspaper* (1979).
The WGN: A Book About the Chicago Tribune, *The World's Greatest Newspaper* (1922).

MEIGS, MONTGOMERY CUNNINGHAM
(1816–1892)

U.S. Army quartermaster general

Born on 3 May 1816, in Augusta, Georgia, Montgomery C. Meigs spent a year at the University of Pennsylvania in 1831 and then transferred to the U.S. Military Academy, where he graduated fifth in his class of forty-nine cadets in 1836. After a brief stint in the artillery, he served with distinction in the Army Corps of Engineers and was promoted to first lieutenant in 1838. Among other assignments, Meigs assisted with the construction of Fort Mifflin on the Delaware River and Fort Wayne on the Detroit River. He also worked with then Lieutenant Robert E. Lee to make navigational improvements on the Mississippi River. Regarded as a highly intelligent officer, Meigs demonstrated impressive skills of management and organization while serving as assistant to the chief of engineers and rising to the rank of captain in 1853.

Beginning in 1852, he directed the construction of the Washington Aqueduct and supervised the erection of the wings and dome of the Capitol in Washington, D.C. Meanwhile, the uncompromisingly honest Meigs became embroiled in a dispute with Secretary of War John B. Floyd over scandalous contracting and financing of public works. In the political fallout, Floyd sent Meigs to Fort Jefferson on the Dry Tortugas in the Florida Keys for a few months in late 1860. Despite this brief setback, Meigs's successful prewar career provided him with invaluable experience in planning and managing complex projects.

When the Civil War broke out in April 1861, Meigs had returned to Washington, where he planned and helped carry out a seaborne relief expedition to Fort Pickens at Pensacola, Florida. He soon found himself promoted to the rank of colonel in the infantry. However, Meigs's administrative talents were needed elsewhere. In this early stage of the conflict, the U.S. Army did not possess the sufficient staff to manage the logistical challenges faced in the conflict. Federal, state, and local governments attempted to train, cloth, arm, equip, transport, and house Union soldiers. Initially, they carried out these supply functions. However, the task of supporting several hundred thousand soldiers in the long term became too great for an uncoordinated civilian infrastructure.

Increasing the Union army's logistical capabilities to match the needs of its ever-increasing size and complexity fell in large part to the Quartermaster Department. With the exception of weapons, food, and medicine, the Quartermaster Department was responsible for the Union army's procurement, transportation, storage, and distribution of everything from uniforms and horseshoes to locomotives and tents.

Promoted to brigadier general and appointed quartermaster general by Secretary of War Simon Cameron in June 1861, Montgomery Meigs immediately set about to create a centralized organization to manage the army's logistical situation. Meigs expanded his Quartermaster Department from 60 staff members to more than 300 staff members, including six departmental inspectors of colonel's rank to oversee quality control. Of all the basic necessities, clothing and footwear proved to be the most difficult to procure. By 1862, Meigs established policies and procedures to ensure consistent size, quality, and even color of uniforms.

To facilitate efficient logistics in the field and across half a continent, Meigs created what eventually became a three-tiered supply depot system. Several general or principal depots sprang up around St. Louis and Washington where supplies were purchased. Chief Quartermasters Robert Allen and Rufus Ingalls ably directed activities in St. Louis and Washington, respectively. From these central logistics bases, supplies were distributed by railroad, river, and wagon to advance depots such as Nashville, Tennessee, or City Point, Virginia. Finally, supplies found their way to temporary depots near the front lines, where they were distributed to the combat units. At each level, careful coordination was necessary to avoid bottlenecks that would result in idled wagons or trains. Meigs and his subordinates also made significant advances in standardizing identification and assignment of baggage, food, and other essential equipment.

By July 1864, the newly breveted Major General Meigs also revamped the Quartermaster Department's internal structures and functions. He created nine departmental subdivisions responsible for important activities such as animal care, barracks construction, record keeping, and rail and ocean transportation. Each division purchased material according to Meigs's specific guidelines. To deter the abuses from fraud and profiteering, Meigs demanded competitive bidding among contractors whenever possible.

Throughout the Civil War, Meigs and his subordinates performed many logistical feats. The Union rarely suffered from lengthy supply shortages. The Peninsula campaign in the spring of 1862 stands as one of the Quartermaster Department's greatest logistical triumphs. Union general-in-chief George B. McClellan planned to land his Army of the Potomac on the peninsula formed by the James' and York rivers' fork and then march 70 miles west to Richmond, the Confederacy's capital. However, McClellan would need more than 1,000,000 pounds of supplies each day to support his army of 100,000 men, 300 pieces of artillery, and 25,000 mules and horses. Meigs amassed 400 boats and barges to transport this massive army; afterward, this flotilla kept up a waterborne supply line. Several hundred wagons also transported supplies when McClellan's army had landed. The military failure of the Peninsula campaign was not caused by a failure of the Union army's supply system. Throughout the Civil War, Union commanders such as George Gordon Meade at Gettysburg and William Tecumseh Sherman on his March to the Sea could always count on Meigs and the Quartermaster Department for timely and adequate logistical support.

After the haphazard situation in 1861, Montgomery C. Meigs had successfully reorganized the Quartermaster Department and maintained a steady flow of supplies to Union forces in all theaters. Under his scrupulously conscientious supervision, more than $1 billion was spent on supplying the Union war machine. This sum amounted to approximately one-half of the Civil War's direct cost for the Union and more than forty times more than the Quartermaster Department's prewar peacetime budget. After the Civil War ended, Meigs continued to serve as the U.S. Army's quartermaster general until his retirement in 1882. During these years, he made few changes in the Quartermaster Department that suffered from the post–Civil War doldrums like so much of the U.S. military. Montgomery C. Meigs died on 2 January 1892 in Washington, D.C.

—*David Ulbrich*

See also Ingalls, Rufus; Quartermaster.

For further reading:
East, Sherrod D. "Montgomery C. Meigs and the Quartermaster Department." *Military Affairs* (1961).
Nevins, Allan. "A Major Result of the Civil War." *Civil War History* (1959).
Shannon, Fred A. *The Organization and Administration of the Union Army, 1861–1865* (1928).
Weigley, Russell F. *Quartermaster General of the Army: A Biography of M. C. Meigs* (1959).

MELVILLE, HERMAN
(1819–1891)
Poet and novelist

Now considered one of the great writers in American literature, Melville died in relative obscurity, appreciated by only a few of his close contemporaries. Melville's early career did find moderate success, as he wrote popular adventure novels based on his own experience as a sailor. His great masterpiece, *Moby Dick*, was published in 1851, and it not only marked a dramatic departure in his narrative style, it also signaled his decline in popularity and critical approval. Although life became more difficult for Melville, he continued to write important works until the end of his life, including remarkable poetry and the posthumously published *Billy Budd, Foretopman*.

In 1866 Melville published his collection of poetry about the Civil War, *Battle-Pieces and Aspects of the War*. In this volume of poetry, Melville describes his personal

reaction to the bloody conflict that raged around him. Unable himself to participate in the war because of his age and an assortment of physical ailments, Melville spent most of the war years either in the Berkshires or in New York City, where he witnessed the fierce antidraft riots of 1863. He did, however, have one occasion to visit the U.S. Army at the front, at the prelude to Grant's decisive Wilderness campaign. In the spring of 1864, Melville and his brother Allan decided to visit their first cousin, Lieutenant Colonel Henry Gansevoort, who was bivouacked with his regiment at Vienna, Virginia. The camp commander turned out to be Colonel Charles Russell Lowell, nephew of James Russell Lowell, the editor of the *Atlantic*, and friends with other prominent literary figures around Boston. Melville was subsequently given permission to join a scouting party in search of Mosby's Raiders, who were harassing Union supply lines throughout northern Virginia.

Borrowing a horse and more proper clothing from an admirer, private citizen Melville temporarily joined the ranks of the 2d Massachusetts Cavalry. Although this scouting mission failed either to capture Mosby or to defeat him in battle, it did occasion the only poem written by Melville to be based on actual experience, "The Scout toward Aldie," the longest narrative poem in his Civil War collection. Although the remaining poems about the war were garnered primarily from his reading about the events in the newspapers that were collected in the *Rebellion Record*, Melville nonetheless wrote some of the most inspiring poetry about the war. Because of the rise of photography and the ever-building numbers of the severely wounded men on the home front, not much of the war's realism was kept from private citizens, and Melville's fertile imagination and literary sensibilities did the rest. The importance of photography on shaping the nation's understanding of the war is evidenced by Melville's poem, "On the Photograph of a Corps Commander."

Battle-Pieces and Aspects of the War is divided into two main sections, Poems and Verses Inscriptive and Memorial. Melville dedicated his book of poetry "To the memory of the Three Hundred Thousand who in the war for the maintenance of the Union fell devotedly under the flag of their fathers." These poems reflect a blend of Melville's romantic vision and his appreciation of a new reality based on industry and the machine. For example, in "Apathy and Enthusiasm," Melville uses nature and the cycle of time as a reassuring backdrop to this bitter human conflict and drama: "So the winter died despairing,/And the weary weeks of Lent;/And the ice-bound rivers melted,/And the tomb of Faith was rent,/O, the rising of the People/Came with springing of the grass,/They rebounded from dejection/After Easter came to pass." On the other hand, Melville understood

that the side with the best science would win the war. In "A Utilitarian View of the Monitor's Fight," he writes: "Yet this was battle and intense—/Beyond the strife of fleets heroic;/Deadlier, closer, calm 'mid storm;/No passion; all went on by crank,/Pivot, and screw,/And calculations of caloric."

Lee Rust Brown notes that fewer than 500 copies of Melville's collection of Civil War poems were sold, another sign that Melville's literary vision remained ahead of his contemporary readership. But regardless of its immediate lack of popularity, *Battle-Pieces and Aspects of the War* remains a significant literary achievement and view of the war.

—*James Meredith*

See also Photography.
For further reading:
Melville, Herman. *Battle-Pieces and Aspects of the War* (1995).
Robertson-Lorant, Laurie. *Melville: A Biography* (1996).

MEMMINGER, CHRISTOPHER GUSTAVUS
(1803–1888)
Confederate secretary of the treasury

Born to Christopher Godfrey Memminger and Eberhardina Kohler Memminger in Nayhingen, Würtemberg, Christopher Gustavus Memminger immigrated to the United States with his widowed mother when he was a small child. The family settled in Charleston, South Carolina, but the young Memminger soon found himself in the city orphanage when his mother died shortly after their arrival. He was four years old. When he was eleven, Memminger went to live in the home of prominent local attorney Thomas Bennett. In the orphanage Memminger had demonstrated a keen intelligence, and Bennett supervised its development through an excellent education. At about the age of thirteen, Memminger was deemed ready for a college education, and Bennett enrolled him in South Carolina College. He graduated at the age of sixteen. Following graduation from college, Memminger studied law and before the age of twenty-one was practicing in Charleston.

Along with his legal practice, Memminger took an early interest in South Carolina politics. Considered a moderate on the growing issue of states' rights, he wrote extensively against the theory of nullification and opposed its implementation in 1832. In the 1830s Memminger was elected to a seat in the lower house of the South Carolina legislature. He quickly demonstrated a talent for the state's financial issues and was appointed chair of the Committee on Finance. He made it a personal crusade while in that position to regulate the state's banking industry to promote sound financial practices.

Besides his political activities and legal practice, Memminger became an active voice for educational reform in the state. As commissioner of schools for Charleston he advocated an expansion of public schools in the city and vicinity. As a long-time member of South Carolina College's board, he also urged increased funding and expansion of that educational institution.

By the 1850s the divisive politics of the day drew Memminger's attention away from these other pursuits. Still a moderate Democrat in a state of increasingly vocal fire-eaters, Memminger, although certainly concerned about the attacks on slavery from the North and what he perceived to be Northern hostility toward the South, strongly supported cooperation with other Southern states to seek redress of Southern grievances. To that end he traveled to Virginia in early 1860, in the wake of John Brown's raid and execution, to urge that state's legislature to work with other Southern states to defend against further abolitionist aggression.

The election of Abraham Lincoln in the fall of 1860 convinced Memminger that moderation would no longer serve. He was chosen as a delegate to South Carolina's secession convention and strongly supported that state's secession from the Union. In January 1861 he was selected one of South Carolina's delegates to the Provisional Confederate Congress. Among his other activities there, he chaired the provisional constitutional committee. This was an activity he sought. He had a number of ideas regarding such a document and had actually drawn up a draft constitution before he left Charleston. He also served on the flag committee in

Christopher Memminger (*Library of Congress*)

Montgomery and while in Alabama purchased powder for South Carolina with state funds.

With the formation of the Confederate government and the selection of Jefferson Davis as provisional president, Memminger was mentioned by many of the politicians in the new Confederate capital for a cabinet appointment. While conferring with Davis regarding possible cabinet appointments, South Carolinian Robert Barnwell strongly urged the new Confederate president to appoint Memminger secretary of the treasury. Davis concurred, and Memminger quickly accepted the appointment.

After his confirmation Memminger became secretary of an empty treasury. He immediately went to work organizing his department and suggesting ways the new government could finance itself and its military. Credited with little imagination regarding creative financing for the Confederacy, Memminger's initial rather short-sighted recommendations for increasing revenue were based on his belief that any war that might take place between the United States and the Confederacy would be a short one. As a result his initial requests were somewhat modest.

Though he did not approve of relying strictly on treasury notes, he believed that such notes could be funded through the sale of government bonds. He also successfully proposed to the Confederate Congress the passage of a revenue tariff that he mistakenly assumed would bring in a steady government income. The Union blockade made such a possibility impossible within two years. By taking control of former United States government lands and continuing to collect revenue on them, some money was raised. All of these money-making ventures, from bonds to tariffs to miscellaneous revenue, however, proved very disappointing, and increasingly Memminger went to Congress asking for taxes to augment his dwindling treasury. Such measures were very unpopular, and even when Congress obliged with some semblance of what Memminger asked for, it was never enough.

To make matters worse for Memminger and Confederate financing, Memminger was considered by many to be arrogant and dictatorial in his hold over the treasury. Military officers especially resented what they considered his parsimony, and some like E. Kirby Smith in Texas threatened to establish their own treasury departments if the secretary were not more vigilant in getting money to their departments.

Part of Memminger's problem in raising money were his strong constitutional scruples. He successfully opposed a proposal for the government to sell cotton on the international market, arguing that the government could not legally become a cotton merchant because of the threat to private farmers. He also offered the opinion in June 1863 that military authorities in Texas did not have the right under the doctrine of military necessity to confiscate cotton to sell in Mexico to buy supplies.

By 1864 inflation had become rampant in the Confederacy as states continued to pay taxes in treasury notes and their own state bank notes. Memminger in frustration wrote to Secretary of War James Seddon to stop asking for money; there was none. Seddon instead, according to Memminger, would simply have to use promissory notes to pay for war supplies. With the economy all but in collapse and Congress being more uncooperative than ever, Memminger resigned in June 1864.

Memminger went to Flat Rock, North Carolina, where he maintained a summer home. From there he followed the last months of the war with growing trepidation. He wrote to the president and other government officials offering encouragement and advice. One of his major concerns, however, became his and his family's personal safety as outlaws and deserters swarmed the North Carolina hill country during the death throes of the Confederacy. He survived and remained in his North Carolina retreat until receiving amnesty in 1867. At that time he returned to Charleston, where he lived quietly practicing law. He continued his work toward the reform of public schools, though he took little interest in the politics of the state. He died in Charleston on 7 March 1888.

—David S. Heidler and Jeanne T. Heidler

See also Financing, C.S.A.; Impressment; Tax-in-Kind.
For further reading:
Capers, Henry D. *The Life and Times of C. G. Memminger* (1893).

MEMORIALS, C.S.A.

The memorials to the Confederate dead stand forever as monuments to the Lost Cause. In dozens of sleepy little southern hamlets are generic statues of Confederate soldiers that have as inscription on their base, "To our Confederate dead." Such was not the case in the years immediately following the Civil War. In the early days after the war, the memorials reflected defeat, despair, and death. Obelisks and other simple stone monuments on the edge of remote cemeteries dotted the Southern landscape. Many historians believe the cemetery locations represent a desire on the part of Southerners to distance themselves from the war and its painful memories.

Confederate memorials sprang up immediately after the war in Winchester, Virginia, and Columbus, Georgia. The memorial movement moved slowly throughout the 1870s, but it gained strength in the celebration of Confederate Memorial Day.

After returning from a gravesite in 1866, Lizzie Rutherford of Columbus, Georgia, suggested having a public ceremony in remembrance of the soldiers. After reading a European novel in which the Catholic custom

Confederate graves in Hollywood Cemetery, Richmond, Virginia, 1865 (*Library of Congress*)

of decorating churchyard's graves on All Saints Day was described, Rutherford drew inspiration from the fictional account and decided to institute such a practice for the deceased Confederates. Rutherford urged other towns to follow suit. Soon, 26 April, the day Johnston surrendered to Sherman, and 10 May, the anniversary of Stonewall Jackson's death, were set aside as Confederate Memorials Days.

The driving force behind the memorials was the Ladies Memorial Associations. A war widow or bereaved mother usually led the ladies' groups. Though the ladies conducted business in a professional and dignified manner, they enjoyed the financial support of local males who believed that sentimental work was the purview of

women. The initial task of the Ladies' Associations was the proper and dignified burial of the Confederate dead. After burial, the ladies assumed responsibility for the maintenance of the plots. Hollywood Cemetery in Richmond is a prime example. Immediately upon proper interment of the Confederate dead, the drive to raise funds for monuments began in earnest.

By the 1880s, the motifs of the memorials took a turn toward upbeat and celebratory. The statues to Lee, Jackson, and Davis, sprang up across the Southern landscape, as did the statues to the simple Rebel soldiers who gave their lives gallantly for the Confederate cause. Courthouse lawns became the favorite locale for statues dedicated to Johnny Reb. Dozens of statues and memorial sites sprang up between 1885 and 1915. Partly out of need for vindication, and partly out of desire to honor the thinning ranks of the Rebel soldiers, monuments rose dramatically in number.

A significant individual in the building of Confederate monuments was S. A. Cunningham of Tennessee. Cunningham served as editor of the influential *Confederate Veteran*, the unofficial news magazine of the United Confederate Veterans. He worked tirelessly to have the Confederates recognized through a memorial at the Chattanooga National Military Park. He began to build a reputation as one who could get the memorials built. He led in the effort to raise funds for the Jefferson Davis memorial in Richmond, the Sam Davis memorial in Nashville, and many other projects across the South.

Between 1865 and 1885, Southerners placed 70 percent of the Confederate monuments in cemeteries. Most of the memorials evoked a sense of death and grief. At the unveilings, speeches given on the occasion defended the nobility of the cause and the purity of southern motives for fighting the war.

The 1880s witnessed a shift in the themes surrounding the statues and memorials. Rather than death and grief, they stressed vindication of the South's role in the nation's history. Between 1886 and 1899, more monuments were built than in the twenty years following the war. Rather than obelisks, the common subject was that of the Confederate soldier. The number of monuments placed in cemeteries declined to just over 55 percent. The statues and monuments became likenesses of a typical Confederate soldier, and they found their home in the public squares. Though the glorification of the common Confederate soldier grew in popularity, the statues lacked passion. After a short time, they looked remarkably similar.

The redundancy of the statues was in part due to the success of the McNeal Monument Company of Marietta, Georgia. The firm promised local United Daughters of the Confederacy chapters various promotion items for their support in helping to drum up business. Despite the success of the McNeal firm, after 1915 the memorial building declined.

Like the change in the artistic symbols, the speeches also changed. Twenty years after the war, the orators mourned less and praised the cause and the heroes of the Stars and Bars. The further away from the din of battle the old soldiers drew, the nobler the Lost Cause became. Their belief in the war fought in their youth was embodied in the statues and memorials they built.

By the time of the United States' entry in the Great War in 1917, Confederate memorials declined in importance. This is not to say that the monuments ceased to spring up; over three dozen such works have been unveiled since the Civil War centennial celebration. The most recent memorial was dedicated in 1980.

Most of the Confederate memorials are not great works of artistic creation, though some are sensational in either scope or size. The recumbent likeness of Robert E. Lee in the chapel at Washington and Lee University, Battle Abbey in Richmond—which has the pantheon of Confederate heroes on horseback on Monument Avenue in Richmond, and Stone Mountain in Georgia, are the three most well-known monuments to the Confederate past. The three memorials evoke memories of valor and courage, but also of defeat and the Lost Cause.

There is no doubt that the monuments served to both indoctrinate and educate, and it would be difficult to imagine a Southland without a lone bronze or stone likeness of Johnny Reb with an inscription beneath his feet that read "To Our Confederate Dead."

—*James S. Baugess*

See also: Ladies Memorial Associations; Lost Cause; Memorials, U.S.A.
For further reading:
Foster, Gaines M. *Ghosts of the Confederacy: Defeat, the Lost Cause, and the Emergence of the New South, 1865–1913* (1987).
Simpson, John A. *S.A. Cunningham and the Confederate Heritage* (1994).

MEMORIALS, U.S.A.

In 1903 Virginia announced its intended gifts for Statuary Hall in the United States Capitol: bronze portraits of Generals George Washington and Robert E. Lee. At the same time, a move was afoot by a group of Southerners to erect an outdoor statue of Lee in Washington. The outcry from the North was instantaneous. The Grand Army of the Republic flexed every political muscle it possessed, and a tidal wave of angry letters swamped congressional offices. Virginia bided its time for three decades before successfully offering the statues again, but groups trying to erect outdoor monuments to Lee in the capital have fared less well. Each of their half dozen attempts to date has failed, smothered under sacks of opposition mail. Many public officials were taken by surprise by the intensity of the backlash in 1903, but the high stakes for which they were playing were clear to the proponents and opponents of the Lee statues, who understood that statues were, and are, more than the sum of their metal and stone parts. Public monuments impose a memory of an event or individual on the public landscape and confer legitimacy upon the memory they embody. At the 1903 dedication of the Sherman monument in Washington, General David Henderson summed up the raison d'etre of all memorials: "The statues of the world are silent historians."

Seen in this light, it is not surprising that the Civil War should prove the catalyst for more public monuments in Washington and across the nation than any other American war. A civil war between countrymen

Union graves in Soldier's Cemetery, Alexandria, Virginia, 1865 (*Library of Congress*)

who shared a common past and a common ground was a war ripe for memorials that would tell its story from each side's perspective to future generations.

The desire to honor their dead seized towns throughout the North and South while bodies still lay in the fields. The first tributes to the dead were uncomplicated shafts or obelisks, but the most common were the lone Union and Confederate soldiers atop simple pedestals that, by the turn of the century, stood guard over hundreds of town greens and courthouse squares.

These local monuments spoke to local people. But national monuments, erected in a nation's capital, bespeak legitimacy and collectivity on a grand scale. Whether in Washington or Richmond, where the pantheon of Southern heroes resides, national monuments lay claim to the memories of an entire nation or would-be nation. While European countries have long chosen symbolic monuments honoring collective action to memorialize their wars, the very different approach

taken by Americans to memorialize the Civil War is vividly evident in Washington and Richmond. There the nation is quite literally embodied in likenesses of real individuals. The Union chose as its personifier Abraham Lincoln, the Confederacy Robert E. Lee, each with a supporting cast of generals. While more than two dozen national monuments immortalize individual Civil War Union heroes in Washington, only four honor the collective "everyman" or "everywoman" of the Civil War: the Peace Monument, a tribute to Union sailors and marines; Nuns of the Battlefield, honoring the nursing nuns of several orders; the Grand Army of the Republic Monument, a tribute to its founder Benjamin Stephenson and to all Union soldiers and sailors; and the African-American Civil War Memorial, honoring all black Civil War servicemen and their white officers.

While citizens of the capital erected local tributes to the young women killed in a horrible explosion at the Washington arsenal in 1865 and a touching tribute to

Abraham Lincoln in 1868, the first two national Civil War monuments to arise in downtown Washington were statues of Major General John A. Rawlins and Lieutenant General Winfield Scott, both erected at the government's expense in 1874. The equestrian statue of General Winfield Scott, by Henry Kirke Brown, was the first of what one wag called the Civil War "galvanized heroes on horseback" to trot into one of the postwar capital's new traffic circles. It is also widely regarded as the worst.

There are more equestrian statues in Washington proper than in any other city in America. Nine (twenty-one if one counts the twelve straining, crashing horses in the Ulysses S. Grant Memorial) are of Civil War heroes. Following Scott, generals James Birdseye McPherson, George H. Thomas, Winfield Scott Hancock, John A. Logan, William Tecumseh Sherman, George B. McClellan, Philip H. Sheridan, and Ulysses S. Grant took their places in city parks astride their horses. Thomas's watchful horse, by sculptor John Quincy Adams Ward, is considered the best.

In a neat twist of the swords-into-plowshares theme, the Scott statue was cast from condemned cannon from the Mexican-American War, his finest hour. Eighty-eight condemned bronze cannon were melted down and transformed into Thomas and his horse. The McPherson statue was cast from Confederate cannon captured at the battle of Atlanta, the battle in which he was killed. The statue of Admiral David Farragut in Farragut Square was cast from the propeller of his flag-ship, the *Hartford*, from whose rigging he shouted, "Damn the torpedoes. Full speed ahead."

These equestrian statues give the lie to the conventional wisdom that one can divine the fate of the rider by the stance of his horse. McPherson is the only one of the nine killed in action. He rides a horse with a raised right foreleg. But so do Logan and McClellan, who survived the war and died in their beds. Grant, Scott, Thomas, and Sherman also died of natural causes, and their horses have all four feet firmly planted on the ground.

While many of these statues were erected entirely at the government's expense, six equestrian monuments

Dedication of the Bull Run battle monument, 10 June 1865 (Photograph by William Morris Smith / *Library of Congress*)

and the Garfield monument were initiated by army reunion societies. The Society of the Army of the Cumberland sponsored the Garfield, Thomas, and Sheridan statues; the Society of the Army of the Tennessee those of Logan, McPherson, and Sherman; and the Society of the Army of the Potomac honored McClellan. Although the Du Pont family paid for the fountain in memory of Rear Admiral Samuel Francis Du Pont, the other Civil War–related monuments in the capital were erected by private groups that raised funds nationally. Freedmen and women contributed their first earnings to erect the remarkable Emancipation monument. Scandinavian-Americans raised funds for the monument to Swedish-born John Ericsson, designer of the *Monitor*; Catholic women for Nuns of the Battlefield; the men and women of the navy for the United States Naval Memorial; Masons for the statue of Albert Pike, the only Confederate in Washington's parks; and African-Americans for the newest Civil War monument in the capital, the African-American Civil War Memorial.

The process of erecting these Civil War monuments in the capital became a sort of ritual that began with the idea for the memorial, moved through securing congressional authorization, selecting a site and a design, and raising funds, and culminated in a glorious dedication ceremony. Raising money was always the hardest part. Some organizations held raffles and bazaars. In 1882 the wives of members of the Society of the Army of the Cumberland raised $15,000 at the Garfield Memorial Fair in the Capitol Rotunda. The army reunion societies relied heavily upon long, emotional, written appeals to their members evoking the old camaraderie of the camps.

The final and most public stage of the ritual, the dedications, often drew crowds of 50,000 to 100,000 people, and were among the largest public gatherings in the late nineteenth century. The dedication of the Emancipation statue in April 1876, which drew a crowd of 50,000 black men and women, was the largest formal gathering of African-Americans that had ever taken place in America.

Until the 1920s, when their numbers had thinned dramatically, these dedications brought out Union veterans by the thousands and always a handful of Confederates. The Union men never tired of hearing their brave deeds and those of the bronze heroes before them recounted by politicians who knew the value of their votes. Occasionally, speakers would wave the bloody shirt, but for the most part these were not occasions for castigating old enemies. These veterans wanted to believe that all the Civil War monuments in the capital would be aides memoire to perpetuate forever the story of their bravery and sacrifice.

Each of the Civil War monuments in Washington,

and every war memorial everywhere, was, and is, designed to be a "silent historian." Each Civil War statue in the capital that honored the men and women who worked for the Union's cause was planned to remind future generations that, as President Theodore Roosevelt told his audience in 1903 at the dedication of the Sherman monument, we are "forever their debtors."

—*Kathryn Allamong Jacob*

See also Memorials, C.S.A.

For further reading:

Jacob, Kathryn A. *Testament to Union: Civil War Monuments in Washington, D.C.* (1998).

Mayo, James. *War Memorials as Political Landscape: The American Experience and Beyond* (1988).

MEMPHIS, NAVAL BATTLE OF (6 JUNE 1862)

In mid-May 1862, U.S. Navy flag officer Charles H. Davis's Mississippi flotilla lay above Fort Pillow, located on the Mississippi River some forty miles above Memphis, Tennessee. The flotilla subjected Confederate positions to a steady bombardment from mortar boats. During the period 18–27 May, the seven steamers of Union colonel Charles Ellet's Army Mississippi Ram Fleet arrived. These tall, converted Ohio River steamers, conceived solely as rams with no ordnance, were the Union answer to the Confederate river rams, which had won the 10 May battle of Plum Point Bend.

Ellet was keen for an immediate blow against the Confederate rams below Fort Pillow. As Davis resisted this, Ellet laid plans to act alone. Davis questioned Ellet's authority to do so, but Ellet answered with authorization from Secretary of War Edwin Stanton. Davis had planned his own attack on Fort Pillow to take place on 5 June in concert with army troops, but the Confederates preempted both Ellet and Davis. On 29–30 May, Confederate General P. G. T. Beauregard, deciding to save his 50,000 men at Corinth, abandoned that railhead to general Henry W. Halleck's 120,000-man army and retired to a new line along the Tuscumbia River in Alabama. This left Fort Pillow outflanked and untenable, and on the night of 4 June, explosions announced that the Confederates were blowing up their guns and evacuating Pillow.

On 5 June 1862 Davis's flotilla and Ellet's rams moved south past Fort Pillow to attack the Confederates at Memphis, arriving above the city that same evening. Memphis, situated on bluffs above the river, was not fortified. Its defense rested on the eight vessels of Commodore James E. Montgomery's River Defense Fleet, now anchored at the Memphis levee.

The Confederate warships were badly outgunned by the warships of the Union flotilla, but, unlike the five Union ironclads (the flagships USS *Benton*, *Carondelet*,

St. Louis, Cairo, and *Louisville*), they had been converted expressly as rams and were more numerous than the two Ellet rams that would participate in the subsequent battle. They were not as strong as the Ellet rams, however. Their boilers had been lowered into their hulls, whereas the Ellet vessels had their boilers above the decks. Although the Union vessels were thus more vulnerable to enemy fire, their hulls could be greatly reinforced.

The battle for Memphis began early on the morning of 6 June. Thousands of Memphis citizens lined the shores to watch the battle that would decide their city's fate. At 4:20 A.M. David signaled his flotilla to raise anchor, and slowly the ironclads dropped downriver by their sterns. At 4:50 the Confederates also got under way and opened fire, which was returned by the stern guns of the Union flotilla. Although the day was clear, vision was soon obscured both by gun and coal smoke.

Montgomery had hoped to duplicate Plum Point Bend by ramming and sinking the Union ironclads, but then out of the smoke emerged two of the Ellet rams. Ellet had arranged four of his rams in line, above the ironclads, and when the Confederates first opened fire he signaled the others to follow his flagship, the *Queen of the West*. But only his brother, Alfred Ellet, on the *Monarch* responded. These two Union rams, one following the other, now made for the advancing Confederate vessels.

The leading Confederate ram, the *Colonel Lovell*, and the *Queen of the West* seemed headed for a bows-on collision when one of the Confederate's engines suddenly stopped and she veered. Moments later the *Queen of the West* smashed into her side, inflicting a mortal wound. The Confederate ram *Sumter* then struck the *Queen of the West*, crashing into her port wheelhouse. Foolishly, Ellet ran out on deck, where he was wounded in the leg by a Confederate pistol shot. Alfred Ellet's *Monarch* then smashed into the *Lovell*, which promptly sank with all but five of her crew. The *Queen of the West*, meanwhile, was able to ground on the Arkansas shore. The remaining Confederate rams then concentrated on the *Monarch*. The CSS *Price* got in a glancing blow, while the CSS *Beauregard* came up from the other side. But at the last possible moment Alfred Ellet was able to slip his vessel between the two Confederates, which then collided with one another. The *Monarch* then rammed the *Beauregard*.

By this time accurate fire from the Federal ironclads was exacting a toll. One shell burst the *Beauregard*'s boilers and she sank. The disabled *Price* also went down in shallow water. The remaining five Confederate vessels now attempted to escape. With the Union vessels pursuing, the battle moved downriver. During the running fight over about ten miles, the CSS *Little Rebel* was hit below the waterline. As she made for shoal water, the *Monarch* rammed her; the blow pushed her up on the shore, enabling Montgomery and her crew to escape. Union cannon fire disabled both the CSS *Bragg* and *Sumter*. The commander of the CSS *Thompson* grounded his vessel on the Arkansas shore, where he set her afire. All but one of the eight Confederate vessels had been destroyed. Only the CSS *Van Dorn* managed to escape to Vicksburg. Meanwhile Memphis surrendered to the Union.

The naval battle of Memphis was perhaps the most lopsided Union victory of the war. The Union suffered only four casualties and one badly damaged ram. Unfortunately for the Union, Charles Ellet died two weeks later, his superficial wound complicated by dysentery and measles.

At slight cost the Union had ended Confederate naval power on the Mississippi River and added additional vessels to the Union flotilla. The battle also gave the Union the fifth largest city in the Confederacy, along with important manufacturing resources. The latter included a former Confederate naval yard, which soon became a principal Union base. The Confederates had also been forced to destroy the one ironclad, the *Tennessee*, that they had been building. A second uncompleted ironclad, the CSS *Arkansas*, had been removed downriver before the battle to prevent its capture. Control of Memphis also brought the Union control of four key rail lines and the mighty river was now open all the way to Vicksburg.

—*Spencer C. Tucker*

See also Davis, Charles H.; Ellet, Charles; Montgomery, James.
For further reading:

Browne, Junius Henri. *Four Years in Secessia* (1865).
Milligan, John D. *Gunboats Down the Mississippi* (1965).
U.S. Department of the Navy. *Official Records of the Union and Confederate Navies in the War of the Rebellion* (1910).

MERCIER, HENRI
(1816–1886)
French minister to the United States

Born in Baltimore, Maryland, to Marie-Philippe Mercier (the French consul to Baltimore) and Henriette Adèle Leroy, Henri Mercier went to Europe with his parents while he was still a small child and was educated in Switzerland. As a young man, Mercier determined upon a diplomatic career and served in various diplomatic posts in Mexico, Spain, Portugal, and Russia. During these years he developed a close friendship with Edouard Thouvenel, who would serve as Napoleon III's foreign minister during the first years of the Civil War. In 1857, Mercier became minister to Sweden and two years later was named minister to the United States. He and his family arrived at their new posting in June 1860.

Upon his arrival, Mercier established contact with the various consuls in American cities. Once he had received information regarding the state of the country, he wrote frequently to Thouvenel, informing the foreign minister especially regarding the growing sectional crisis. Even though he had been in the country only a few months at the time of Abraham Lincoln's election as president, Mercier predicted the secession of the entire South as a result. During the secession crisis he continued to monitor the situation and reported frequently to Thouvenel.

In early 1861, Mercier also tried to determine the chances of war between the two American sections. In February 1861 he had William Henry Seward and Stephen Douglas to dinner to pry information and insight from these two statesmen. During the next few months, Mercier consulted closely with Lord Richard Lyons, British minister to the United States, on the British government's possible response in the event of war.

After the war began, Thouvenel instructed Mercier in May 1861 to be neutral in all actions. The emperor signed a neutrality proclamation in June and like Great Britain recognized the belligerent status of the Confederacy. This action caused Seward, as Lincoln's secretary of state, to behave very coolly toward Mercier and Lyons. In a conference with Seward in June, Mercier broached the subject of informally dealing with the Confederacy on maritime issues and later in the summer protested to Seward regarding what amounted to a paper blockade of the Southern coastline.

Despite these very serious issues, one of Mercier's primary responsibilities in the early summer of 1861 was to prepare for the visit of the emperor's cousin, Prince Napoleon. Upon the prince's arrival, Mercier accompanied him on a tour of the United States as far as St. Louis. So when Mercier returned to the East in September 1861, he had much work piled up.

The French government at home was very interested in getting cotton out of the United States (or the Confederacy) for the mills in France. This hope proved futile and was complicated in the fall of 1861 by several diplomatic crises. First, at a conference in London in the fall, France, Great Britain, and Spain agreed on a joint expedition to Mexico to force that country to pay its debts. Complicating this plan was the strong opposition of the United States and the rumored plan of Napoleon III to use the French foothold in Mexico to establish a puppet regime there. In addition to this potential rupture with the United States, the British government was faced with the *Trent* Affair. The French government expressed sympathy with the British position, which of course for a time put Mercier again at odds with Seward.

During the spring of 1862, Mercier was once again pressed by his government to try to secure some cotton. When he approached Seward regarding the request, the secretary replied that it was unnecessary to try to ship cotton out of captured Southern ports because Federal victories would soon restore the Union. Mercier replied that he could not be sure of that occurring unless he were permitted to visit Richmond and observe the situation there. As a result, Seward gave Mercier permission to travel to Richmond. While there in mid-April 1862, Mercier conferred with Confederate secretary of state Judah Benjamin and expressed his belief to the Southerner that the South could not win the war. He also took the time while there to inquire into the status of French government-owned tobacco stored in Richmond. He found that it was safe, but also that there was no way to move the tobacco past the Union blockade.

Upon his return to Washington Mercier brought up the possibility of bringing the tobacco out of Richmond and shipping it to France. It would remain a topic of negotiation for the remainder of his time in the United States.

While the tobacco was certainly a concern for Mercier's government, the cotton shortage was far more acute in the fall of 1862. As a result, Mercier was instructed to propose a mediation plan to Seward that might bring an end to the conflict. Seward and Lincoln were not interested, and furthermore were growing more and more nervous about French plans in Mexico. During the next year, Mercier became increasingly frustrated about his inability to wring concessions from Seward regarding the tobacco or cotton. Seward instead preferred to discuss Mexico. As a result of this frustration, Mercier requested to be relieved in the fall of 1863. Although he saw little hope for a Southern victory, especially after Gettysburg and Vicksburg, he believed the war could last much longer. His request was granted in December 1863.

Mercier arrived in France in January 1864. Later that year he was made ambassador to Spain. During his tenure there, his most challenging task was representing his country's interests during the so-called Hohenzollern Candidature for the throne of Spain. He left the diplomatic service upon Napoleon III's abdication. Mercier had inherited his father-in-law's title and estate and died there in retirement on 16 October 1886.

—*David S. Heidler and Jeanne T. Heidler*

See also Lyons, Lord Richard; Mexico; Napoleon III; Seward, William Henry.

For further reading:
Carroll, Daniel B. *Henri Mercier and the American Civil War* (1971).

MEREDITH, SOLOMON
(1810–1875)
Union general

Solomon Meredith was born on 29 May 1810 in Guilford County, North Carolina. In 1829 he moved to Wayne County, Indiana, where he soon pioneered the breeding of prize short-horn cattle. His imposing height of six feet, six inches, as well as his proclivity towards public oratory, made him hard to ignore. Popular in the area, he was elected county sheriff for two terms at the age of twenty-four and to the state legislature for four terms. In 1849 he was appointed U.S. marshall for the District of Indiana.

Meredith was an ardent Democrat who joined the Republican Party during the 1850s. In this he had much in common with Indiana governor Oliver P. Morton, who was also from Wayne County. The two were intimate friends, and in July 1861 Morton commissioned Meredith as colonel of the 19th Indiana Volunteer Infantry Regiment.

The 19th Indiana was first assigned to the Washington, D.C., area, but did not see significant action until the battle of Brawner's Farm during the Second Bull Run campaign. Meredith was severely wounded and the 19th Indiana, suffering 210 casualties, gained fame as part of what would become celebrated as the Iron Brigade.

In October 1862, while Meredith recovered from his wounds, he was promoted to brigadier general of United States volunteers and given overall command of the Iron Brigade, the only unit in the east made up entirely of western regiments. Meredith led the Iron Brigade at Fredericksburg, Virginia, in December 1862 and saw limited service at Chancellorsville, Virginia, in May 1863.

During the first day at Gettysburg, General Abner Doubleday told Meredith to hold his position at all costs. Although he was knocked out before the action was half over, Meredith came close to following these instructions to the letter. The Iron Brigade under Meredith magnificently resisted the Confederate assault near Seminary Ridge. The brigade lost two-thirds of its number, and Meredith received a disabling wound. The Iron Brigade never fully recovered, and Meredith was so badly wounded at Gettysburg that he was unfit for field service thereafter.

The fifty-three-year-old Meredith, having been wounded several times and thoroughly prostrate with exhaustion, was given garrison assignments at Cairo, Illinois, and Paducah, Kentucky. He finished the war as commander in Kentucky, far from the scene of conflict. In August 1865 his noble efforts and service to his country were rewarded with a much-deserved brevet to major general of volunteers.

In 1867 Meredith was named the surveyor general of Montana, but he resigned in 1869, returned to Indiana, and farmed until his death on 2 October 1875. He is buried in Riverside Cemetery in Cambridge City, Indiana.

Meredith was described as a commanding presence and an accomplished speaker. He had two sons in the Union army, both of whom were killed. He was fearless in battle and earned the respect of those men who served

Solomon Meredith (*Library of Congress*)

under him. They knew he would not ask them to go anywhere that he refused to go himself.

—*Ron Hamilton*

See also Gibbon, John; Iron Brigade.

For further reading:

Dunn, Craig. *Iron Men Iron Will, The Nineteenth Indiana Regiment of the Iron Brigade* (1995).

Hunt, Roger D., and Jack R. Brown. *Brevet Brigadier Generals In Blue* (1990).

Lavery, Dennis S., and Mark H. Jordan. *Iron Brigade General* (1993).

Nolan, Alan. *The Iron Brigade: A Military History* (1961).

MERIDIAN CAMPAIGN
(3 February–4 March 1864)

The Meridian campaign was an important, though often overlooked, expedition. Led by total war advocate Major General William T. Sherman, the campaign was the first concerted, organized effort at total warfare, wherein the military might of the North was launched against the will of the Southern people as well as military and transportation facilities. This campaign led in part to the later total war marches by Sherman in Georgia and Philip Sheridan in Virginia.

Sherman organized the campaign for two basic military reasons. One, Sherman desired to wreck the crossroads town of Meridian, Mississippi, where the Mobile & Ohio Railroad met the Southern Railroad of Mississippi.

Second, Sherman saw that in wrecking the crossroads he could clear Mississippi of Confederate resistance, thereby allowing a major transfer of troops to Georgia for the upcoming campaign. In the midst of such military efforts, Sherman realized the potential of total warfare.

The Union effort began on 3 February 1864, when Sherman led two corps of the Army of the Tennessee eastward from Vicksburg, Mississippi. Major General James B. McPherson led XVII Corps, while Major General Stephen A. Hurlbut commanded XVI Corps, together totaling 25,000 men. In addition, Sherman ordered Brigadier General William Sooy Smith to march from Memphis with 7,000 cavalry. Sherman and Smith would meet in Meridian and contemplate further action; Sherman mentioned Mobile, Selma, and Demopolis, Alabama, as future targets.

The Confederates countered the Union thrust, but had little with which to defend Mississippi. Several small cavalry units hampered the Federal advance, but could not stop the march. Confederate commander Lieutenant General Leonidas Polk commanded two small infantry divisions, led by Major Generals Samuel G. French and William W. Loring, but was likewise unable to stop Sherman.

The Federals soon reached Jackson, the Mississippi capital, and almost cut off one Confederate division. It hurriedly scampered across the Pearl River, however, leaving Sherman an almost intact bridge. Sherman continued, marching through many small Mississippi towns before reaching the outskirts of Meridian. Several small Confederate offensives by roaming cavalry did little to thwart Sherman's advance.

The Union columns reached the vicinity of Meridian on 13 February, but realized the Confederates had opted to evacuate to Demopolis, Alabama. To delay Sherman while all stores and goods were taken out of the city, Polk ordered obstructions placed in Sherman's way. The Federal commander realized the ploy and hurried his men onward, entering Meridian in a driving rain on 14 February. Polk had succeeded, however, in removing the valuable stores from Meridian; Sherman captured an empty town. Nevertheless, Sherman began his destruction while waiting for Smith from Memphis. Each corps was given a segment of railroad to destroy, and much of the city likewise ceased to exist.

By 20 February, Sherman had done all he could. Because he could not move forward without cavalry support from Smith, who had not arrived, Sherman decided to abandon a thrust into Alabama and turned back toward Vicksburg. He marched north of his earlier route, in hopes of locating Smith's missing command. Such hope faded, however, as the columns reached he Pearl River at Canton. After crossing the Pearl on 25–26 February, the Union forces made their way to Vicksburg, crossing the Big Black River on 4 March.

Meanwhile, Sooy Smith had troubles of his own. He did not leave Memphis until 11 February, the day Sherman had expected to meet him in Meridian. (Sherman was also late.) Then, Smith met Confederate cavalry under Nathan Bedford Forrest at West Point, Mississippi. In a running battle, Smith was turned back and badly defeated by half his numbers. Smith retreated to Memphis.

Sherman succeeded in reaching and destroying Meridian, but his overall goals were not achieved. He had hoped to destroy the Confederate transportation system in Mississippi, but the Southerners had each rail line back in service within a month. Also, Sherman hoped to clear Mississippi of Confederates, but he also failed to meet that goal. Polk escaped and later provided the Confederate Army of Tennessee in Georgia much needed reinforcements during the Atlanta campaign.

Sherman's success in the Meridian campaign came from the knowledge gained from the use of total war. Sherman cut a swath through Mississippi, living off the land. He learned the military and psychological uses of such raids, and put what he learned to good use later in the war.

—*Timothy B. Smith*

See also Big Black River, Second Battle of; Mississippi; Smith, William S.; West Point, Battle of.

For further reading:
Bearss, Margie Riddle. *Sherman's Forgotten Campaign: The Meridian Expedition* (1987).

MERRITT, WESLEY
(1837–1910)
Union general

Wesley Merritt was born in New York City. He lived in Illinois from the time he was three until July 1855, when he left for the U.S. Military Academy at West Point. He graduated from West Point in July 1860 and was assigned as a brevet lieutenant, 2d Regiment Dragoons. He was promoted to second lieutenant on 28 January 1861 and to first lieutenant, 2d U.S. Cavalry, on 13 May 1861.

In the spring of 1862, Merritt participated as a cavalry officer with General George McClellan in the Peninsula campaign and served as aide to McClellan's cavalry commander, Major General George Stoneman. Assigned as a staff officer in Washington, Merritt participated in the defense of the capital until April 1863. On 5 April, he was promoted to captain. Perhaps Merritt's greatest Civil War triumph was at the battle of Brandy Station on 9 June 1863. This engagement occurred soon after a reorganization of the Federal cavalry that finally made it possible for Union troopers to handle their Confederate counterparts. Merritt's bravery at Brandy Station and later that month at Middleburg led to his promotion to brigadier general of volunteers, a promotion he accepted the next month.

Merritt participated in the battle of Gettysburg, where he commanded the Army of the Potomac's Reserve Cavalry Brigade composed of four regular army regiments and one volunteer regiment. Merritt was awarded a brevet rank of major in the regular army for gallant and meritorious service.

Merritt first served under General Philip Sheridan as a cavalry brigade commander in the Army of the Potomac in March 1864, when Sheridan took command of that army's cavalry corps. Sheridan gave him temporary command of a division in May 1864 at Todd's Tavern. Merritt participated in the battle of the Wilderness on 4–6 May; the battle of Yellow Tavern on 11 May, which earned him a brevet promotion to lieutenant colonel; and the expedition from Spotsylvania Court House to the Meadow Bridge at Richmond on 12 May. His role at the battle of Haw's Shop on 28 May won him a brevet to colonel. Subsequently, he participated in the battles of Matadequin Creek (30 May), Cold Harbor (31 May–1 June), Trevillian Station (11 June), St. Mary's Church, Mallory's Ford Crossroads (12 June), and Weldon Road and Darbytown (28 June). His success led Sheridan to make his temporary appointment permanent as commander of the 1st Cavalry Division in August 1864.

Accompanying Sheridan to the Shenandoah Valley, Merritt participated in the battles of Opequon (Winchester), Fisher's Hill, Tom's Brook, and Cedar Creek. The battle of Tom's Brook was especially noteworthy, for there Merritt won a decisive victory against Confederate cavalry when he bested Confederate forces led by Major General Thomas L. Rosser. On the march from Winchester to Petersburg, Merritt commanded two divisions of cavalry, destroying all railroads and canals north of the James River, for which he was breveted a major general of volunteers. He was also with Sheridan at Dinwiddie Court House, Five Forks, Sayler's Creek, Appomattox Junction, and Appomattox Court House. Sheridan would later praise Merritt's exploits as marking a peerless soldier.

After the Civil War, Wesley Merritt went on to more success as a soldier. He served as executive officer of the 9th Cavalry, an all-black Buffalo soldier regiment, and later fought with the 5th Cavalry in such Indian wars as the Sioux campaign of 1876. His march to the relief of an army unit surrounded by hostile Indians near White River, Colorado, prompted praise from Sheridan for meritorious frontier service.

From August 1882 to June 1887, Merritt served as superintendent of West Point. At the end of his services there in 1887, he was made a brigadier general by President Grover Cleveland. Merritt then served as commander of the Department of Dakota to May 1895, as commander of the Department of Missouri to April 1897, and as commander of the Department of the East to May 1898.

In July 1898, he commanded the U.S. Army's expeditionary force to the Philippines and forced the Spanish to surrender their control of the islands. His success led to his appointment as head of the Department of the Pacific and the VIII Army Corps in the Philippine Islands to August 1898. He was then selected to serve on special duty with the Peace Commission that met with the Spanish in Paris, France, during the last months of 1898.

Merritt's last position was as commander the Department of the East, a post he kept until his retirement in 1900. On 1 May 1900, Daniel Butterfield, former chief of staff of the Army of the Potomac, wrote Secretary of War Elihu Root requesting Merritt be awarded the Medal of Honor for his distinguished service at the battle of Brandy Station. Butterfield's letter was supported by other participants at Brandy Station, including W. A. Harrison and T. F. Rodenbough.

Wesley Merritt died on 3 December 1910 at Natural Bridge, Virginia.

—*Alan K. Lamm*

See also Brandy Station, Battle of; Cavalry, U.S.A.; Sheridan, Philip Henry.
For further reading:
Alberts, Don E. *Brandy Station to Manila Bay: A Biography of General Wesley Merritt* (1980).

MERRYMAN, JOHN
(1824–1881)
Supreme Court plaintiff

The name John Merryman is best known in connection with Supreme Court Chief Justice Roger Brooke Taney. In the midst of Southern secession, the paths of these two men crossed and, in doing so, left an indelible mark on U.S. constitutional law.

A farmer from Cockeysville, Maryland, Merryman was president of the Maryland Agricultural Society, a lieutenant in the local militia, and a Southern sympathizer. It was in the latter roles that Merryman found himself embroiled in the beginnings of secession. On 19 April 1861, the 6th Massachusetts Infantry attempted to cross through Baltimore on their way to the nation's capital. Pro-Southern mobs greeted the soldiers with a shower of rocks and bottles. During the ensuing melee, four soldiers and eleven civilians died. Merryman's involvement came after a meeting at which the mayor, governor, and leading citizens discussed the conflict and wrote to President Abraham Lincoln requesting that troops no longer travel through Baltimore. Merryman allegedly took part in burning several bridges on the Northern Central Railway to ensure that Union soldiers could not travel South, although it is unclear whether he was ordered to do so as part of the militia or took it upon himself. (Some historians have also noted that Merryman was supposedly drilling Marylanders in preparation to join the Confederate army.)

President Lincoln reacted decisively to the trouble in Maryland, ordering the military on 27 April to suspend the writ of habeas corpus if the public safety required it. Shortly thereafter, John Merryman was arrested. At 2:00 A.M. on Saturday, 25 May, Union soldiers under the command of General William H. Keim entered Merryman's home and removed him to Fort McHenry.

Merryman's friends lost no time in coming to his aid. Baltimore attorneys George M. Gill and George H. Williams petitioned for a writ of habeas corpus and presented it to Chief Justice Taney in Washington. The next day, Sunday, 26 May, Taney issued a writ calling for General George Cadwalader, the commander at Fort McHenry, to bring Merryman to the U.S. Circuit Court at 11:00 A.M. on Monday, 27 May, to show cause for his incarceration.

At the appointed hour, General Cadwalader's aide presented the chief justice with a letter declaring that Merryman was arrested for treason and, citing Lincoln's 27 April order, noted that the writ of habeas corpus was suspended. Attempting to flex his judicial muscle, Taney quickly issued a writ of attachment ordering the general to appear in court on the following day to explain why he should not be held in contempt. Taney's demand was in vain. Cadwalader did not appear in court nor did he bring John Merryman before the chief justice.

Taney responded in *Ex parte Merryman*, insisting that Congress alone possessed the authority to suspend the writ of habeas corpus. He also chastised General Cadwalader's conduct, noting that a "military officer has no right to arrest and detain a person not subject to the rules and articles of war, for an offense against the laws of the United States, except in aid of judicial authority, and it is the duty of the officer to deliver him over immediately to the civil authority, to be dealt with according to the law."

The chief justice aimed his most fiery criticism at the very notion of usurping civil liberties. "The military in this case has gone far beyond the mere suspension of the privilege of the writ of habeas corpus," insisted Taney. "It has, by force of arms, thrust aside the judicial authorities and officers to whom the constitution has confided the power and duty of interpreting and administering the laws, and substituted military government in its place. I can only say that if the authority which the constitution has confided to the judiciary department and judicial officers, may thus, be usurped by the military power, at its discretion, the people of the United States are no longer living under a government of laws."

Chief Justice Taney's ruling, though forceful, had little effect on the military's future conduct nor did it gain the immediate release of John Merryman. President Lincoln ultimately authorized the declaration of martial law in a number of states, and Merryman was released to the U.S. Marshals on 12 July only after Secretary of War Simon Cameron had conducted an interview eight days earlier.

Appearing in court, Merryman was charged with treason and released on bond, but never brought to trial. After a long series of prosecution attempts, the case was ultimately closed on 23 April 1867 after the clerk of the district court entered a nolle prosequi by order of the attorney general's office in Washington.

Merryman continued his active involvement in Maryland life, serving as the Maryland state treasurer and as a member of the legislature. Yet the role for which he is most known remains the *Ex parte Merryman* case. In the midst of Southern secession, Merryman's path became intertwined with that of Chief Justice Roger Taney's. Nor did Merryman forget the fight that the Supreme Court judge had waged. Revealing his reverence for the chief justice who had defended his liberties, Merryman named his fifth son Roger Brooke Taney Merryman on 5 December 1864.

—*Matthew S. Warshauer*

See also Baltimore Riot; *Ex parte Merryman*; Habeas Corpus, Writ of (U.S.A.).

For further reading:
Anderson, Eric Paul. "The Body of John Merryman: *Ex Parte Merryman*, A Case of Executive-Judicial Conflict over the Suspension of Habeas Corpus" (M.A. thesis, 1979).
Brugger, Robert J. *Maryland: A Middle Temperament, 1634–1980* (1988).
Culver, Francis. "Merryman Family, Part II." *Maryland Historical Magazine* (1915).
Ex Parte Merryman, Fed. Case No. 9487.
Lewis, Walker. *Without Fear or Favor: A Biography of Chief Justice Roger Brooke Taney* (1965).
Neely, Mark E., Jr. *The Fate of Liberty: Abraham Lincoln and Civil Liberties* (1991).
Siegel, Martin. *The United States Supreme Court: Volume 3, The Taney Court, 1836–1864* (1995).
Swisher, Carl B. *History of the Supreme Court of the United States: The Taney Period, 1836-1864* (1974).

MEXICO

In the midst of the secession crisis of the winter of 1860–1861, Mexico was concluding a three-year civil war that had pitted the republicans of Benito Juárez against the Conservative Party made up primarily of the wealthy landowners. Immediately before the inauguration of Abraham Lincoln, Juárez had ousted the Conservatives from power and confiscated much of their land. Many of the Conservatives then went to Europe, where they tried to persuade the monarchies there to establish a monarchy in Mexico to help them regain their lands. One of these displaced Conservatives, Don José Manuel Hidalgo y Esnaurrizar, attached himself to the French empress Eugénie to gain her support. She became intrigued with the project and encouraged her husband, Napoleon III, to support the plan.

In the meantime, the United States government had recognized the new Republic of Mexico and saw any efforts on the part of European powers to undermine that government as a threat to the United States. Nonetheless, certain European powers planned to do just that, and after a meeting between Great Britain, France, and Spain in the fall of 1861 dispatched at the end of October a joint military expedition to Mexico, ostensibly to collect debts. Both Lincoln and his secretary of state, William Henry Seward, believed that the real purpose of the expedition was to establish a monarchy. They were concerned that if such a government were established, it would naturally ally itself with the Confederacy because the United States had supported the republic. The European governments involved, however, assured the Lincoln government that they merely intended to land at Vera Cruz and take control of the customs house.

Because their expedition had been sent from nearby Cuba, the Spanish arrived first, on 17 December 1861. The French and British did not arrive for three more weeks. The French and Spanish military forces had been told by their governments that they could go into the interior (the French in fact had been instructed to work with the Conservatives to overthrow the republic), though the British were instructed to remain at the coast. In March 1862 Seward issued a strong admonition to the European powers, warning them to withdraw the invaders from Mexico.

By that time the invaders were squabbling among themselves, and shortly thereafter, the British and Spanish withdrew. The French remained and Napoleon III began actively working to overthrow the Juárez government and place the younger brother of Austrian emperor Francis Joseph, Ferdinand Maximilian, on the throne of Mexico. Napoleon III naturally had the support of the Austrian emperor in this endeavor.

The Confederate government came quietly to support this prospect. It had made overtures to the Juárez government, but when Confederate secretary of state Robert Toombs sent John T. Pickett to offer a treaty of alliance and friendship, he had been rejected. As a result the Confederate government saw a decided advantage in a new Mexican government with strong ties to France and Austria. The Confederate military commander in Texas, John Bankhead Magruder, was already using the Mexican border as a convenient place over which to transport cotton to sell abroad and use the money to buy war supplies in foreign markets. Such a practice could be conducted more openly and hence bring greater profit with a friendly government in place in Mexico City. To that end, the Confederate emissary to Paris, John Slidell, supported Napoleon's plans and did not protest when he learned that Napoleon III also planned to create a buffer state out of Texas.

In June 1863 French soldiers took Mexico City, putting the government back in the hands of the Conservatives, who later in the year issued an invitation to Maximilian to accept the crown of Mexico. Juárez was

forced to flee to northern Mexico, where he conducted a guerrilla war against the French military forces.

On 12 June 1864 Maximilian and his wife Charlotte were crowned emperor and empress in Mexico City. Confederate president Jefferson Davis immediately sent William Preston to negotiate an alliance. At the same time Major General John Magruder in Texas asked for military aid from Maximillian's government to repel a threatened Union invasion of Texas. Because the Confederacy was doing so badly militarily in the summer and fall of 1864, Maximilian thought it impolitic to offend the United States in a losing cause. Therefore he refused to aid the Confederates. Instead he sought recognition of his government from the United States, but was refused.

By then the war was drawing to a close and refugee Confederates saw Mexico as a haven from Federal pursuit and possible prosecution. Two groups of former Confederates began moving into Mexico in the spring and summer of 1865. Many were Confederate guerrillas who had operated in the Western theater during the war and were afraid of legal and personal retribution for some of their actions. Many of these men joined with Juárez's guerrillas to have something to do and to be fed. The other group consisted of Confederate officers, politicians, and their families who refused to live under the United States government. These men made their way to Mexico City, where they were received by Maximilian and initially offered land in Córdoba in return for military or other government service. At the end of the year, however, Maximilian reneged on the agreement to avoid offending the United States.

By that time Maximilian was under increasing pressure from Juárez's guerrillas and was losing the support of his European sponsors. In the late spring of 1867 he was captured by Juárez and on 19 June 1867 executed by firing squad.

—*David S. Heidler and Jeanne T. Heidler*

See also Diplomacy, C.S.A.; Diplomacy, U.S.A.; Maximilian, Ferdinand.

For further reading:
Tyrner-Tyrnauer, A. R. *Lincoln and the Emperors* (1962).

MIDDLEBURG (JUNE 1863)
See Aldie, Virginia, Battle of

MILES, NELSON APPLETON
(1839–1925)

Union general, Indian fighter, last commanding general of the U.S. Army

Born in Westminister, Massachusetts, Nelson Appleton Miles moved as a teenager to Boston, where he organized a company of volunteers after the first battle of Bull Run and was commissioned a first

lieutenant. Although his military training had consisted of but a few lessons from a private tutor, Miles quickly proved an outstanding combat commander. In the battle of Fair Oaks, Virginia, he dismissed a minor foot wound to help check a Union retreat. With the support of Francis C. Barlow, a splendid officer with strong New York political connections, Miles was named lieutenant colonel of the 61st New York Regiment. In a furious assault during the battle of Antietam, his men helped to break the Confederate position in the Bloody Lane.

Now a full colonel, Miles's aggressiveness bordered on the foolhardy during the battle of Fredericksburg, where his unit took heavy casualties in futile assaults against Marye's Heights. Miles himself suffered a painful neck wound. He returned to action in time for the battle of Chancellorsville, where he received a near-fatal abdominal wound during the second day of the fighting. Thirty years later, he would receive a Medal of Honor for his heroism there.

After several months' convalescence, Miles took command of the 1st Brigade, 1st Division, II Corps, winning appointment to brigadier general of volunteers for his actions at the Bloody Angle. Decimated by the losses suffered there and in the subsequent assault at Cold Harbor, the performance of Miles's brigade deteriorated, as did that of II Corps in general. In the battle of Reams' Station, a Confederate attack broke through what should have been very defensible Union positions. Only the charismatic leadership of several Union officers, including Miles, prevented a complete collapse. For his efforts, Miles secured a brevet major generalship and command of the 1st Division.

A winter's respite gave the division time to recoup, and Miles again proved his mettle in the final campaigns on the eastern front. A breakthrough was achieved at Sutherland Station, Virginia, with Miles's 1st Division bagging 1,000 prisoners in this single action alone. "Miles has made a big thing of it and deserves the highest praise for the pertinacity with which he stuck to the enemy until he wrung from them the victory," wrote a delighted Ulysses S. Grant. Similar success came at Sayler's Creek, when II Corps ripped into the enemy's rear. In recognition of his extraordinary war record, Miles was later named a major general of volunteers.

After Appomattox, Miles was charged with overseeing the security of former Confederate president Jefferson Davis at Fort Monroe, Virginia. His order that Davis be chained in his cell was sharply criticized and won him the lasting enmity of many Southerners. Miles left this thankless task in September 1866, having been named colonel of the 40th Infantry Regiment (comprised entirely of black enlisted personnel) in the much-reduced postbellum regular army. After Reconstruction duty in North Carolina, Miles wangled a transfer to the all-white 5th Infantry. Miles then carved out an impressive record in the wars against the Indians, participating in the Red River War (1874–1875), helping to force the surrender of the Sioux and Northern Cheyenne followers of Sitting Bull and Red Cloud (1876–1878), blocking the attempted escape of Chief Joseph and the Nez Perce into Canada (1877), overseeing the defeat of Geronimo (1886), and preventing even greater bloodshed in the wake of the disastrous battle of Wounded Knee (1890–1891).

In 1895, Miles was named commanding general of the U.S. Army. He led a model occupation of Puerto Rico during the Spanish-American War. But his refusal to support significant military reform in the wake of the army's embarrassing performance in that conflict led to his complete break with the Theodore Roosevelt administration, and in 1903 Miles retired at the rank of lieutenant general. The office of commanding general was abolished shortly thereafter. In 1925, Miles died of a heart attack while taking his grandchildren to the circus.

Fearless in combat and a natural tactician, Nelson Miles had ranked among the Army of the Potomac's best brigade and division commanders. His determined pursuits of the enemy had also served him well in the later wars against the Indians. As a strategist and policymaker, however, Miles showed less ability. His overweening ambition, inability to get along with other officers, and willingness to take his complaints to the public arena infuriated virtually all of his superiors after the Civil War, rendering a splendid military record somewhat less admirable.

—*Robert Wooster*

See also Antietam, Battle of; Sayler's Creek, Battle of.
For further reading:
DeMontravel, Peter R. *A Hero to His Fighting Men: Nelson A. Miles, 1839–1925* (1998).
Miles, Nelson A. *Personal Recollections and Observations of General Nelson A. Miles* (1896; reprint, 1992).
Wooster, Robert. *Nelson A. Miles and the Twilight of the Frontier Army* (1993).

MILES, WILLIAM PORCHER
(1822–1899)
Confederate congressman

Born to James Saunders Miles and Sarah Bond Worley Miles in Walterboro, South Carolina, William Porcher Miles was educated at the College of Charleston before studying law and opening a practice in Charleston. He practiced only a short time before accepting a faculty position at the College of Charleston. He resigned that position in 1855 to become the mayor of Charleston. From 1857 to 1860 he served as a member of the U.S. House of Representatives, speaking frequently regarding the right of secession. He resigned his seat following the election of Abraham

Lincoln to the presidency. Before his departure, Miles represented the state to the Buchanan administration in its efforts to have the federal garrison removed from Charleston harbor.

Upon his return to South Carolina, Miles served in the South Carolina secession convention, where he was a strong advocate for secession. After secession, he served on the foreign affairs committee of the convention.

In February 1861, he was sent as one of South Carolina's delegates to the Montgomery convention that formed the Confederate States of America. As a member of this Provisional Confederate Congress, Miles was a strong advocate of the term limitation ultimately placed on the president and vice president in the Confederate Constitution.

After the formation of the Confederacy and the movement of Confederate military forces to Charleston, Miles volunteered his services as an aide to the Confederate commander in Charleston, P. G. T. Beauregard. During the Fort Sumter crisis, Miles served in that capacity with the rank of colonel. On 11 April, Miles was one of Beauregard's aides who was sent to persuade Major Robert Anderson to surrender Fort Sumter before firing commenced. Miles returned to Sumter after the bombardment to negotiate the final surrender terms. After the surrender of Fort Sumter, Miles accompanied Beauregard to Virginia, where he continued to serve as his aide at the battle of First Bull Run. This engagement ended Miles's military service and he returned to the Confederate Congress. In the fall, Miles was elected to the first regular Confederate Congress and continued to represent Charleston in that body for the remainder of the war.

In the Confederate Congress, Miles served as the chairman of the House Military Affairs Committee. In that capacity he supported the institution of conscription and a stronger, more centrally organized army. He also worked diligently to procure as many heavy pieces of artillery for Charleston as possible. For the most part, he was considered a supporter of the administration except in his strong criticism of Braxton Bragg. Miles was also a strong supporter of his former commander, P. G. T. Beauregard when charges were made about Beauregard's competence in late 1863.

Toward the end of 1864, Miles became less supportive of Jefferson Davis. The threat to Charleston brought by the activities of William T. Sherman in Georgia caused Miles to break with the administration over what he perceived to be its neglect of South Carolina's defenses. By that point in the war, however, one more voice of dissent probably mattered little to Davis.

After the war, Miles lived on his wife's family plantation in Virginia before accepting the post as the president of the University of South Carolina in 1880. He held the position for only two years before moving to Louisiana to manage his wife's family holdings there. Before his death, he was one of the largest sugar planters in the country. He died near Burnside, Louisiana.

—*David S. Heidler and Jeanne T. Heidler*

See also Congress, C.S.A.; Fort Sumter, Bombardment of; South Carolina.
For further reading:
Daniel, Ruth McCaskill. "William Porcher Miles, Champion of Southern Interests" (M.A. thesis, 1943).

MILLIGAN, LAMBDIN P.
(1812–1899)
Peace Democrat

Lambdin P. Milligan was born 24 March 1812 on a farm in Belmont County, Ohio. Despite a limited formal education, he became a school teacher at nineteen, from which he turned to a study of law. Milligan was admitted to the bar and married in 1835. After practicing law in Ohio until 1845, he moved to Huntington County, Indiana.

He became one of the ablest lawyers in northern Indiana and by 1863 had an average annual income of about $3,000, which was quite sizable for that time. Milligan lived the life of a gentleman farmer near the community of Huntington, Indiana, and kept a stable of thoroughbred race horses.

Milligan has been described as a slender six feet four inches tall, with a light complexion and blue eyes. He was a fastidious dresser, seldom seen without his frock coat and high hat. Often in poor health—he suffered from epilepsy and the effects of a bout of spinal meningitis—he was known for idiosyncratic behavior and took great delight in besting younger members of his profession. Milligan fancied himself a politician, but more often than not his opponents profited from his offensive behavior and wild opinions.

Despite Milligan's lack of political success, local Democrats were resigned to his erratic conduct. A Douglas Democrat in 1860, he frequently spoke about issues in the Huntington area and was a strong advocate of compromise before the war. In 1861 Milligan became chairman of the Huntington County Democratic Central Committee and began describing Abraham Lincoln as a tyrannical usurper and the war as illegal. He declared that only a strict construction of the Constitution and a faithful observance of every section's rights could save the Union. In 1862 he unsuccessfully sought the Democratic nomination for Congress, and in 1864 his bid for the party's nomination for governor came to nothing. He did earn a place as a delegate to the Democratic National Convention in Chicago.

Espousing an extreme states' rights position, he was unstinting in his criticism of Republican policies from the start of the war. Soon his comparing of Confederates to the Revolution's patriots created the impression that he might be a traitor. By 1864 Milligan regarded civil liberties in Indiana as so suppressed that he saw little hope for the restoration of the Union. His deep belief in agrarianism fostered extreme contempt for New England, and he insisted that the South had been driven to secession and war to divide the agrarian states and subject them to Yankee rule.

Milligan represented only the most radical element of the Democratic Party in Indiana, and his outspoken criticism of Republican policies early attracted the attention of state authorities. He began associating with secret societies in November 1863, when he attended a grand council meeting of the Order of American Knights (OAK) in Indianapolis. Although he periodically attended OAK meetings after that, his position in the organization was never clear.

Nonetheless, Milligan was arrested with others in October 1864 and charged with treason. His trial that fall was among those that constituted the famous Indianapolis Treason Trials, proceedings that were politically motivated and from which Governor Oliver Morton of Indiana reaped huge political benefits. A military tribunal found Milligan guilty of treason and sentenced him to hang. Evidence suggests that Lincoln was inclined to stay the execution, but he was assassinated in April 1865 before he could do so. Even Governor Morton, who saw no additional political advantage from the trials, tried to get the execution stopped, but Milligan's appeals to Secretary of War Edwin Stanton for leniency were fruitless.

On 20 May 1865 President Andrew Johnson finally commuted Milligan's sentence to life imprisonment, and he was sent to a Federal prison in Columbus, Ohio. In the meantime, however, his case had been taken to a Federal district court in Indianapolis, where a petition for a writ of habeas corpus was heard on the basis that because the civil courts were open at the time of his arrest, the military commission had been without jurisdiction. The United States Supreme Court rendered the famous *Ex parte Milligan* decision on 3 April 1866, in which it ruled that Milligan's trial and those of others arrested with him were illegal because the civil courts had been operating and unobstructed.

Milligan returned to Huntington to great ovations from the locals. His legal expenses and two years without an income had impoverished him, and he was assailed by chronic illness and daunted by the prospect of rebuilding his law practice. By the time he retired in 1893, however, his financial situation had recovered. Ironically, he became a Republican in 1880 and supported James Garfield's presidency. He died 21 December 1899 at the age of eighty-seven.

—*Ron Hamilton*

See also Copperheads; *Ex parte Milligan*; Order of American Knights; Peace Democrats; Supreme Court, U.S.
For further reading:
Fesler, Mayo. "Secret Political Societies in the North during the Civil War." *Indiana Magazine of History* (1918).
Klaus, Samuel, ed. *The Milligan Case* (1929; reprint 1970).
Klement, Frank L. *Dark Lanterns, Secret Political Societies, Conspiracies, and Treason Trials in the Civil War* (1984).
Tredway, G. R. *Democratic Opposition to the Lincoln Administration in Indiana* (1973).

MILLIKEN'S BEND, BATTLE OF
(7 June 1863)

During the spring of 1863, Confederates west of the Mississippi River launched against Federal troops in northeastern Louisiana an assault designed to aid John C. Pemberton's besieged garrison in Vicksburg. Trans-Mississippi commander Edmund Kirby Smith, acting in response to requests from both Pemberton and Jefferson Davis, sought to destroy Federal supply lines west of the Mississippi and establish a strong position to cut off an anticipated Federal retreat. In late May, Smith ordered Louisiana general Richard Taylor to take John G. Walker's division of Texans along with James C. Tappan's Arkansas brigade and strike the Federals between New Carthage and Milliken's Bend. Confederate intelligence reports that provided the strategic basis of the operation, however, were several weeks out of date. The Federals no longer used Milliken's Bend as a staging area for resupply, but had relocated several miles away at the Yazoo River. Because Ulysses S. Grant no longer needed these troops to guard supply lines, their primary responsibility became the protection of cotton plantations under Federal control.

Another Confederate intelligence communiqué reported that convalescents and black troops guarded Federal outposts along the Mississippi. This prompted the Confederates to underestimate the resolve of the Union defenders. Consequently, Taylor divided his 4,500-man force, sending one brigade to Milliken's Bend, another to Young's Point, and a third to Lake Providence. The decision not to concentrate against any one of the Federal positions proved a costly error for the Confederates.

Federal command west of the river fell to Brigadier General Elias Dennis. Dennis's command consisted primarily of Midwesterners, but also included several newly established black regiments made up of men from Louisiana, Mississippi, and Arkansas. Dennis established a basic training camp at Lake Providence for the freedmen and stationed most of the raw black regiments at Milliken's Bend. The Federal post at Milliken's Bend, under the command of Colonel Hermann Lieb, was at the center of the Federal position that stretched south from Lake Providence to Young's Point.

On 6 June, Lieb sent the 9th Louisiana (Colored) and the 10th Illinois Cavalry to investigate reports of a Confederate movement toward the river. Three miles outside Richmond, Louisiana, the Federals engaged in heavy skirmishing with Confederate cavalry. Although the Federal troops hastily retreated, the reconnaissance mission confirmed that an enemy advance was under way. Dennis immediately requested support from Admiral David D. Porter, and two gunboats, the *Choctaw* and the *Lexington*, steamed toward Milliken's Bend.

Also advancing on Milliken's Bend was a brigade of 1,500 Texans under Henry McCulloch. At 4:00 A.M. on 7 June, McCulloch encountered Federal pickets and steadily drove them back behind their breastworks. A Southern soldier recalled, that "with the first streak of daylight visible through the light mist that ascended from the river, the battle became general." The Confederates continued to push the Federals to an area between two levees, where, in bloody hand-to-hand combat, the defenders slowly broke. Reportedly, one Texas regiment waved a black flag with a skull and crossbones in a call for no quarter. The advance continued beyond the second levee until 7:00 A.M., when Union gunboats churned into action, spraying the attackers with grape and canister. The Confederates withdrew to safety behind the first levee, and McCulloch called for reinforcements. Reserves reached the field at 10:00 A.M. only to discover McCulloch in full retreat. The planned simultaneous assaults on Young's Point and Lake Providence also failed. At Young's Point, Union gunboats drove off the rebels before the attack could develop, while at Lake Providence the assault sputtered into skirmishing.

The battle at Milliken's Bend cost the Confederates 44 killed, 131 wounded, and 10 missing. The lack of pursuit by the Federals was in part a result of their heavy casualties. The defenders suffered 101 killed, 285 wounded, and 266 missing of 1,061 engaged. The black regiments suffered an unusually high casualty rate of 35 percent and the 9th Louisiana lost 45 percent, the highest ratio of any unit during the war.

After Milliken's Bend the disposition of black soldiers captured in battle became a point of contention between Federal and Confederate commanders as well as among Confederate leaders. When Smith learned that fifty black Federals had been taken prisoner, he urged Taylor to give no quarter to armed black soldiers and their white officers. Taylor requested specific orders for the disposition of black prisoners of war, and Smith turned to Secretary of War James Seddon for clarification. Seddon instructed Smith to return black prisoners of war to their owners. Grant, in response to rumors of atrocities against black prisoners of war, requested clarification from Taylor. During an exchange of correspondence with Grant,

Taylor gave assurances that no executions had or would take place. Accordingly, the significance of Milliken's Bend is not in its strategic military value but rather in establishing credibility of black troops as fighting men in the front lines of Federal armies.

—*Jeffery S. Prushankin*

See also Prisoners of War; United States Colored Troops; Vicksburg Campaign.

For further reading:

Bearss, Edwin C. *The Campaign for Vicksburg* (1985–1986).
Blessington, Joseph P. *The Campaigns of Walker's Texas Division* (1875).
Glatthaar, Joseph T. *Forged in Battle: The Civil War Alliance of Black Soldiers and White Officers* (1990).
Parrish, T. Michael. *Richard Taylor: Soldier Prince of Dixie* (1992).
Winters, John D. *The Civil War in Louisiana* (1963).

MILROY, ROBERT HUSTON
(1816–1890)
Union general

Born to Samuel Milroy and Martha Huston Milroy in Washington County, Indiana, Robert Huston Milroy was educated locally before entering Norwich University in Vermont. After graduation, Milroy returned home, but the outbreak of the Mexican-American War led him to raise a company. He was commissioned captain in the 1st Indiana and served until June 1847.

Returning to Indiana, Milroy studied law and in the years before the Civil War practiced law primarily in Rensselaer, Indiana, and served a brief stint as a judge. Angry over the secession of the Gulf States, Milroy began raising a company of volunteers even before the firing on Fort Sumter. At the end of April 1861, he was made colonel of the 9th Indiana, a three-month regiment that was converted to a regular volunteer unit during the summer. In September 1861, Milroy was promoted to brigadier general of volunteers.

Milroy spent much of the first two years of the war in western Virginia. On 30 September 1861, Milroy's brigade was assigned to the Department of Western Virginia, and throughout the remainder of the year he skirmished with Confederate units there. In early 1862 he received command of the Cheat Mountain District of the department. During the spring Milroy fought against "Stonewall" Jackson in the Shenandoah Valley campaign, most notably at McDowell on 8 May.

Later in the summer Milroy commanded his brigade as an independent brigade in the Army of Virginia. He led his men at the battle of Cedar Mountain, after which he helped arrange the truce that allowed both sides to retrieve their dead and wounded. He continued in command of his independent brigade in the Second Bull Run campaign at the end of the month before returning to western Virginia in the fall to serve under Major General Jacob Cox.

Stationed along the upper Potomac River for the remainder of 1862, Milroy was given command in early 1863 of the District of Winchester, headquartered at that town. He was promoted to major general in March 1863 with a date of rank of 29 November 1862. During these months in the Shenandoah Valley, Milroy made it his special mission to ferret out Confederate sympathizers. He did not believe in erring on the side of caution, and many noncombatants, including widows with children, were turned out of their homes for the mere suspicion of Confederate leanings. He complained to his superiors that his orders keeping him around Winchester constrained him in dealing properly with disloyal people. Milroy became so unpopular in the area that the state of Virginia put a $1,000 price on his head, a price that many soldiers from the area serving in the Confederate army were eager to collect.

After Joseph Hooker's defeat at Chancellorsville in early May 1863, rumors started to spread around Winchester of possible Confederate moves in the area. As these rumors became more credible in early June, Henry Halleck in Washington became increasingly nervous and ordered Milroy's superiors, Robert Schenck and Benjamin F. Kelley, to have Milroy move from his exposed position at Winchester back to the security of Harper's Ferry. This order was never passed verbatim to Milroy; in fact it was only suggested to him that he remove to Harper's Ferry. In the meantime, Confederate lieutenant general Richard Ewell and his entire corps were bearing down on Milroy, while Milroy's intelligence reported only Confederate cavalry nearby. Milroy, while his position became increasingly untenable, was writing his superiors that he could defend his position against all comers. On 14 June, he discovered this was not the case when Ewell attacked and it quickly became apparent that, if Milroy stayed in place, he would lose his entire command.

Soon after midnight on 15 June, Milroy conferred with his officers and decided on an immediate retreat. Ewell pursued and caught much of Milroy's force at about 3:00 A.M. In the ensuing fighting, Milroy lost more than half his force, most of whom were captured. Milroy, leading the retreat, made it safely to Harper's Ferry.

The defeat was significant enough to warrant a court of inquiry that was held in August. Milroy was not found culpable in the disaster, and a few months later, President Abraham Lincoln exonerated him. Milroy had written personally to the president in July pleading his case. However, Milroy would find it difficult over the next year to obtain another command. He wrote plaintively and unsuccessfully to Ambrose Burnside in May 1864, begging to be given some position in Burnside's IX Corps. Finally in July 1864 he was given command of the

defenses around the Nashville & Chattanooga Railroad, headquartered at Tullahoma, Tennessee.

Serving under George H. Thomas as part of the Army of the Cumberland, Milroy's biggest worries came from guerrilla bands operating along the rail line, though at times he did have to contend with more regular forces such as Nathan Bedford Forrest's cavalry. As in western Virginia, he resented orders that limited his ability to deal with those people who might be aiding the guerrilla bands. By early 1865, he had the added burden of numerous Confederate stragglers and deserters from John Bell Hood's army after its virtual annihilation at Nashville. Still, he did the best with what he had and remained in this command until the end of the war.

With the end of hostilities, Milroy believed that he could perhaps finally deal with those people he viewed as outlaws the way he believed they deserved. One can only imagine his dismay when he received orders from Thomas in May 1865 instructing him to offer amnesty to guerrillas. He fired back several indignant letters to his commander, the tone of which bordered on insubordination. Thomas, having had quite enough, sent Milroy home to Indiana to be mustered out in July 1865.

After the war, Milroy worked for a time as a promoter of the Wabash & Erie Canal before accepting appointment in 1872 as Indian Superintendent in Washington state. He also served a stint as Indian agent at Olympia, Washington. He died there on 29 March 1890.

—*David S. Heidler and Jeanne T. Heidler*

See also Winchester, Second Battle of.

For further reading:

Lopp, Larry G. "The Campaigns of General Robert H. Milroy, 1862–1863" (M.A. thesis, 1970).

Paulus, Margaret Babcock, comp. *Papers of General Robert Huston Milroy* (1965).

MILTON, JOHN
(1807–1865)
Governor of Florida

John Milton served as governor of Florida from 1861 until 1865. Referred to by a biographer as a "loyal Confederate," Milton was a strong wartime governor who did what he could to defend his state from Union incursions as well as to provide foodstuffs and personnel to the Confederacy. At the war's end, ill and worn down from his exertions, Milton took his own life.

A native of Louisville, Georgia, Milton was born on 20 April 1807. He studied at a local academy before matriculating from the University of Georgia. Milton then studied law, was admitted to the Georgia bar, and moved to Columbus, where he opened a law practice and ran unsuccessfully for Congress. The future governor also became involved in a political dispute with Major Joseph Camp, whom he shot and killed on a Columbus street.

Milton was subsequently tried for murder but acquitted on the grounds of self-defense. Milton then moved to Mobile, Alabama. He commanded a militia company in the Second Seminole War, and in 1845 or 1846, after a period spent practicing law in New Orleans, he moved permanently to Florida. Settling near Marianna in Jackson County, Milton operated a large plantation named Sylvania that eventually grew to more than 7,300 acres, and by the time of the Civil War he owned more than fifty slaves. The transplanted Georgian also raised a large family. While living in Georgia he had married Susan Amanda Cobb, with whom he fathered four daughters and a son. After his first wife's death, he married an Alabamian, Caroline Howze, and fathered ten more children; two sons and eight daughters.

Milton also became active in Florida politics. He served in the state legislature in 1850, and ten years later he led the Florida delegation at the Democratic Convention in Charleston. After the split in the Democratic Party, he attended the convention of Southern Democrats that nominated John C. Breckinridge for president. In early June 1860, after twenty-three ballots, Milton won his party's nomination for governor. In explaining his position in the sectional dispute, he wrote "I am not a Disunionist," but he added "if the people of the South do not become united...the Black Republican party will continue to triumph in a course of aggression, until civil war will come upon us." In the election that followed, Milton defeated his Constitutional Unionist opponent, Edward Hopkins, by 2,000 votes.

Under the provisions of the Florida constitution, Milton remained as governor-elect for a full year. He would not take office until October 1861. In the meantime, lame duck Madison Starke Perry, a political enemy, would lead Florida out of the Union and into the new Confederacy. When he finally assumed the duties of governor, Milton faced a variety of problems arising from the war.

Early in his term, Milton's political opponents in the Florida legislature moved to limit the governor's authority. In early 1862, the Secession Convention reconvened and established a four-member executive council to share power with the governor. The council, however, met only a few times and generally supported Milton's actions. At the same time, Milton also faced a military crisis when Confederate authorities withdrew most of the troops defending Florida's long coastline. This led to the eventual abandonment of Fernandina, St. Augustine, and Jacksonville on the east coast, as well as Pensacola and Apalachicola on the Gulf Coast. Union troops permanently occupied the two former locations, while Jacksonville would be occupied four separate times during the remainder of the war. The region around Pensacola also became a Union base, and

Apalachicola was destined to remain a largely deserted land. Milton strove to raise additional troops for the defense of the state and urged the return of Florida units serving in other theaters, but by the end of the war, Confederate control over Florida had shrunk to the north-central interior portion of the peninsula. Still, at the February 1864 battle of Olustee, Confederate forces were able to stop the major Union invasion of the state.

Other issues facing Governor Milton included the depletion of the state's finances, the military draft and subsequent requests for exemptions (of which Milton granted very few), the growing Unionist sentiment among elements of the population, and the impressment of supplies by Confederate authorities. Though an ardent Southern nationalist, Milton did criticize the excessive seizure of property. Despite these difficulties, during the latter stages of the war, Florida cattle, salt, sugar, and other foodstuffs helped sustain the Southern armies.

In his last message to the Florida legislature, the governor had stated that "The Reconstruction of the American Union, as it existed...is now impossible....In this conflict the baseness, cruelty, and perfidy of our foe have exceeded precedent; they have developed a character so odious that death would be preferable to reunion with them." Milton left the capitol at Tallahassee in late March 1865, to visit Sylvania. Shortly after arriving home on the evening of 1 April, the governor ended his life with a shotgun blast to the head. "It has been known for some weeks past, that he had been suffering from mental disease," a newspaper reported, "but we had not supposed it to be serious, and certainly not such an attack as could hurry him to the dread resort by which he ended his life."

—*David J. Coles*

See also Florida.
For further reading:
Gammon, William Lamar, II. "Governor John Milton of Florida, Confederate States of America" (M.A. thesis, 1948).
Parker, Daisy. "John Milton, Governor of Florida: A Loyal Confederate." *Florida Historical Quarterly* (1942).
Yearns, W. Buck, ed. *The Confederate Governors* (1985).

MINE RUN CAMPAIGN
(26 November–1 December 1863)

By October 1863, Major General George Gordon Meade, commanding the Army of the Potomac, was under pressure from the Lincoln administration to move against Robert E. Lee's Army of Northern Virginia. Since Gettysburg, Meade, preferring the defensive to the offensive, had contented himself with monitoring Lee in the region between Washington and the Rappahannock River.

Finally stirring in November 1863, Meade hoped to

surprise his adversary and defeat a portion of Lee's army. Meade's plan began well, his army aggressively crossing the Rappahannock on 7 November and forcing Lee to retreat south of the Rapidan River.

Meade spent several weeks improving his railroad supply lines before advancing. By late November, though, Lee had erected defenses along the Rapidan that reminded Meade of the debacle at Fredericksburg in December 1862. Meade's choices were limited because the government had insisted that he move forward but had also prohibited a broader flanking move to the east. Meade therefore could either launch a suicidal frontal assault on Lee's position or attempt a more modest turning of Lee's right flank by moving southeastward. Meade opted for the latter, devising a plan whereby he would cross the Rapidan east of Lee's position, then swing across a little creek known as Mine Run. Meade envisioned either crushing a portion of Lee's army before Lee could respond or standing on the defensible high ground west of Mine Run for the anticipated Confederate attack, thus allowing Meade to fight a tactically defensive battle during a strategically offensive campaign. Meade's plan had potential for success, but also had weaknesses in that it required his army to execute timely movements in a thickly wooded area with poor roads.

When the operation began on 26 November, Gouverneur K. Warren's II Corps and George Sykes's V Corps executed their parts of it promptly, but William Henry French's III Corps began its march several hours late and then had trouble crossing the Rapidan, causing a domino effect of difficulties for the Federals. French finally crossed the Rapidan, but promptly headed down a wrong road. Thus, instead of being ready to launch a multicorps attack toward Mine Run on 27 November, Meade did not even have all of his army across the Rapidan.

Lee moved his army eastward toward Mine Run to counter Meade. On 27 November, Warren's II Corps skirmished with Confederate units east of Mine Run, but could do little else until the arrival of III Corps, which had only to march four miles to join Warren. Unfortunately, French (who may have been drinking) allowed his least competent division commander to lead the march and did not exercise sufficient oversight. As a result, III Corps became lost, then halted to gain its bearings, and in the interim allowed Edward Johnson's Confederate division to gain position to block III Corps.

French finally engaged Johnson's division near Payne's Farm in a sometimes heavy but generally confused action that resolved little while resulting in 545 Confederate and 950 Union casualties. However, Johnson's halting of French's III Corps had also stalled Sedgwick's following VI Corps and allowed Lee time to improve his position. On the night of 27–28 November, despite a cold rain, Lee moved his forces to high ground west of Mine Run and fortified his position heavily.

The Federals spent 28 November reconnoitering Lee's position and saw another Fredericksburg developing. Warren offered to move II Corps against Lee's right flank, but Lee effectively countered him on 29 November. Undeterred, Meade planned an assault on Lee's position for 30 November.

Daylight on 30 November showed that Lee had fortified his position so thoroughly that any Union attack would be suicidal. Warren surveyed the line and, knowing that his troops had not slept because of a freezing overnight rain, called off the assault, saying "I would sooner sacrifice my commission…[than] my men." Recognizing that Warren was right, Meade canceled operations, slipped away from Lee's impending counteroffensive on the night of 1–2 December, and went into winter quarters across the Rappahannock.

Blame fell chiefly on French, who eventually lost his command, but other factors contributed, including the complexity of the movements, insufficient reconnaissance, poor roads, bad weather, effective Confederate countermoves, and the "fog of war." Had any of these circumstances differed, Meade's theoretically sound plan might have succeeded. Ironically, Meade's original proposal to make a much wider turn to the east, which the government rejected, foreshadowed what Grant would do months later in launching the Wilderness campaign. In failure, though, the Mine Run campaign became a nearly forgotten operation.

—*Broeck N. Oder*

See also French, William Henry; Johnson, Edward; Meade, George Gordon; Sykes, George; Warren, Gouverneur K.
For further reading:
Freeman, Douglas Southall. *Lee's Lieutenants: A Study in Command.* Vol. 3 of *Gettysburg to Appomattox* (1942–1944).
Johnson, Robert Underwood, and Clarence C. Buel, eds. *Battles and Leaders of the Civil War: Being for the Most Part Contributions by Union and Confederate Officers* (1956).
Luvaas, Jay, and Wilbur S. Nye. "The Campaign That History Forgot." *Civil War Times Illustrated* (1969).

MINIÉ BALL

More properly termed the "minié bullet" after its inventor, the minié ball was a standard rifle projectile, not a spherical projectile as its name implies. It was cylindro-conoidal in shape, much like a modern bullet. Invented in 1848 by Captain Claude Étienne Minié of the French army, it was adopted by the United States in caliber 0.58 for use in the new Model 1855 rifle-musket. Both arsenals and individual soldiers also fabricated scores of variations of minié bullets to accommodate both the imported and updated American weapons pressed into service in the early stages of the war. Significant numbers of caliber 0.54 bullets were manufactured for the popular U.S. Model 1841

"Mississippi Rifles," as well as the less popular imported Austrian "Lorenz Rifles." Massive caliber 0.69 miniés also saw use in refurbished and rifled older American smoothbores.

Minié solved the long-standing dilemma of mating a quickly loaded bullet with a rifled barrel. Arms designers had long been aware of the advantages of the rifled barrel—a barrel with spiraled grooves cut into its bore. Rifling imparted a spin to the projectile that greatly improved both its accuracy and range compared to the conventional smoothbore weapons of the day. Despite this formidable advantage, rifled arms suffered two linked and difficult liabilities. To grip the rifled grooves properly, the soft lead bullets had to be slightly larger than the muzzle of the gun and thus had to be rammed down the barrel with considerable force. Coupled with the tendency of the black powder propellant to foul the bore with unburned residue, the rifle's loading process became progressively more difficult after each shot.

The traditional smoothbore in common use avoided such problems by utilizing a round ball significantly smaller than the musket's bore. The size differential between the ball and bore reduced the effort of loading but significantly reduced accuracy to an optimistic maximum of some 100 yards, as the ball rattled erratically down the barrel upon discharge. Under normal circumstances the smoothbore's effective range was more typically around fifty yards.

Minié's invention combined the best qualities of the rifle and smoothbore, while simultaneously minimizing their deficiencies. To facilitate loading, Minié designed his bullet to be slightly smaller than the rifle's bore. He then introduced a cone-shaped cavity in the base of his bullet. The resultant gasses from the weapon's discharge would then expand the thin walls of the cone into the rifling for a snug fit. A trained rifleman could thus fire three aimed shots per minute and easily hit a man-size target at 100 yards. With more time to aim, he could be deadly at ranges up to 500 yards.

The new bullet weighed nearly one ounce and was propelled by sixty grains of black powder. Both bullet and powder were contained in a paper cartridge that eliminated the separate powder and patched ball load of earlier rifles. American-made minié bullets were also cast with three distinct rings in their bearing surfaces to aid stability.

Tests proved that the minié bullet could penetrate eleven inches of pine boards at 100 yards and nearly six inches of pine at 500 yards. The minié's effect on the human body was predictably devastating. The soft lead bullet's velocity, coupled with its tendency to distort upon impact, pulverized tissue and shattered any bones it struck. Most body and head wounds thus usually resulted in death. If not fatal, wounds to the extremities typically resulted in amputation. Postwar studies revealed that rifle bullets effected fully 90 percent of all Civil War casualties, the majority inflicted by some variant of the minié bullet.

During the war both sides imported large numbers of British caliber 0.577 Enfield rifles as well as their ammunition. Although the British-style minié bullet can be distinguished from its American cousin by its lack of rings, it was interchangeable in both Springfield and Enfield weapons. The minutely larger diameter American 0.58 bullet, however, was not always compatible in somewhat fouled British rifles.

Fouling is an inherent problem with black-powder weapons, and American ordnance experts introduced the ingenious Williams cleaner bullet as a means of overcoming it. The Williams bullet featured a zinc disc attached to the rear of the projectile by a short pin rather than the standard cone-shaped hollow base. The disc acted as a scraper to clean the accumulated residue from the rifle's bore. One blue-paper-wrapped Williams cleaner cartridge was generally included in every forty rounds of tan or white paper-wrapped standard cartridges issued to each soldier.

—*Jeff Kinard*

See also Minié, Claude E.; Rifles; Springfield Rifle.

For further reading:
Edwards, William B. *Civil War Guns: The Complete Story of Federal and Confederate Small Arms: Design, Manufacture, Identification, Procurement, Issue, Employment, Effectiveness, and Postwar Disposal* (1962; reprint, 1997).
Lord, Francis A. *Civil War Collector's Encyclopedia* (1995).
McKee, W. Reid, and M. E. Mason, Jr. *Civil War Projectiles II: Small Arms & Field Artillery* (1980).
McWhiney, Grady, and Perry Jamieson. *Attack and Die: Civil War Military Tactics and the Southern Heritage* (1982).

MINIÉ, CLAUDE ÉTIENNE
(1804–1879)
Inventor of the minié ball

Claude Étienne Minié, who was born in Paris on 13 February 1804, perfected the conoidal bullet that dramatically increased the distance and accuracy of the infantryman's weapon. This improved bullet, dubbed the minié ball, is considered by many to be the most revolutionary technological breakthrough in warfare in the 19th century.

No stranger to mechanical devices, Minié was employed as a machinist before his entry into the French army. While serving as a captain in the Chasseurs d'Orleans, he began to tinker with the idea of a rifle that could be fired as rapidly as a musket. Although the rifle was far more accurate and had a much greater effective range, the difficulty of loading a nineteenth-century rifle excluded their use on any large scale.

The problem with the rifle lay in the necessity to maintain a tight seal around the projectile that allowed the rifling within the barrel of the gun to put a spin on the bullet, thereby improving its accuracy and velocity. A tight-fitting bullet made the rifle difficult to load through its muzzle, so Minié began working on the idea of using a conoidal bullet that would expand in the barrel after the powder had been ignited. This idea originated in 1832 with a Captain Norton of the British 34th Regiment. While serving overseas in the Indian subcontinent, Norton was intrigued by hollow ended projectiles used in blowguns by indigenous hunters.

In 1849 Minié perfected Norton's idea. Along with a rifled barrel that he designed, Minié devised a conoidal-shaped bullet with a hollow base that deformed and expanded when the rifle was fired. This created the desired tight seal around the projectile that increased its accuracy and velocity, but at the same time, allowed it to be easily dropped into a barrel. Rifles equipped with the minié balls had the same reloading capability as a smoothbore musket, but they boasted a range four to five times greater. For Minié's work on the ball, Napoleon III conferred money and honors upon the captain.

The impact that the minié ball had on warfare was significant. The ability to shoot farther, faster, and with more devastation changed the face of modern war. European armies began testing the new technology, and its performance in the Crimean War (1853–1856) created a large demand for precision-made rifles. By 1860, nearly all European and North American armies were equipped with minié rifles and bullets.

Overwhelmed by all the new technological advances, most army officers thought little of changing infantry tactics. Nearly all senior ranking officers on both sides of the Civil War, including Grant, Lee, McClellan, Longstreet, Jefferson Davis, Hooker, Bragg, and many others, had gained their combat command experience in the Mexican-American War. In that war, commanders had won stunning victories using closed-rank linear infantry formations and aggressive Napoleonic bayonet charges. Many leaders entered the Civil War with the assumption that the tactics that worked in the Mexican-American War would work in the Civil War. Predictably, the death tolls were horrific. The advent of technologically improved infantry weapons with greater velocity and accuracy, combined with tactics better suited to weapons of a previous generation, sent casualty rates soaring.

Throughout the Civil War, leaders struggled to adjust infantry tactics to the new weapons technology. Two key adjustments were made during the war. The first was the increased use of trenches that would lengthen as troops caught in them tried to outflank their opposition. The second tactical adjustment was to close with opposing forces quickly to avoid prolonged exposure to withering long-range rifle fire.

Claude Minié continued throughout his life to tinker with military arms. None of his future inventions had nearly the impact of the minié ball, however. His perfecting of the conoidal bullet so changed the nature of battle that it could be argued that Claude Étienne Minié determined the way the Civil War was fought as much as anyone did.

—*Lincoln Bramwell*

See also Ordnance; Rifles; Tactics.
For further reading:

Brodie, Bernard, and Fawn M. Brodie. *From Crossbow to H-Bomb* (1973).
Dupuy, Trevor N. *The Evolution of Weapons and Warfare* (1980).
Mahon, John K. "Civil War Infantry Assault Tactics." *Military Affairs* (1961).
O'Connell, Robert L. *Of Arms and Men: A History of War, Weapons, and Aggression* (1989).

MISSIONARY RIDGE, BATTLE OF
(24–25 November 1863)

On the afternoon of 23 November 1863, the Confederate Army of Tennessee under General Braxton Bragg began its retreat from Lookout Mountain to form a defensive line running north-south along the crest of adjacent Missionary Ridge. The Union forces under Major General Ulysses S. Grant occupied the Chattanooga Valley between Missionary Ridge and Lookout Mountain. Grant's forces consisted of the Army of the Cumberland under command of Major General George Thomas in the center, and the Army of the Tennessee under Major General William Tecumseh Sherman holding the Union left. The Union right consisted of the Union XI and XII Corps under Major General Joseph Hooker. Grant's strategy was to hit both Confederate flanks, turn them, and attack the Confederate rear, crushing and destroying Bragg's line of retreat and capturing his army.

By mid-morning on 25 November, Bragg had his troops ranged along Missionary Ridge, staffing rifle pits at its foot while more troops moved along the crest. At Bragg's headquarters, the bedeviled Confederate commander was receiving intelligence of Grant's pincer plan when cavalry under Warren Grigsby reported advance elements of Sherman's troops at South Chickamauga Creek. Bragg had no troops on the north end of the ridge, and the only ones in reserve were those of Irish-born division commander Major General Patrick R. Cleburne, then at Chickamauga Station loading onto rail cars to be transferred to Knoxville, Tennessee. Bragg quickly recalled Cleburne, who rushed with five brigades to arrive at the northern end of Missionary Ridge just in time to oppose Sherman.

The first action began on the Confederate right, where Chickamauga Creek set the boundary and the ridge ended abruptly in a steep series of hills. Sherman

The battle of Missionary Ridge, depicted in an 1886 print copied from the Missionary Ridge Cyclorama (*Library of Congress*)

arrived that morning and by 1:00 P.M. gained a toehold on what he thought was Missionary Ridge, driving in some of Cleburne's pickets. However, Sherman discovered that he was not on the actual ridge, but a separate hill known as Billy Goat Hill, cut off from the main ridge by a deep ravine.

Sherman already had a division in line opposite Tunnel Hill, with a second division crossing the Tennessee River as support. Cleburne was instructed to hold the hill with its vital railroad bridge to the rear "at all hazards." When Cleburne, the best division commander Bragg had, arrived on the hill, he realized his critical position and difficult orders. He discovered that he was not just to defend the last section of the ridge, but a series of detached hills, with only three brigades. Grasping the situation of the terrain, he skillfully and rapidly deployed his troops as Sherman's leading elements were occupying Billy Goat Hill. It would be the Confederate Irishman's greatest military challenge of his career. Grant and Bragg had unwittingly pitted their best commanders against each other on Tunnel Hill. Yet the odds were much less equal. Cleburne had perhaps 4,000 effectives, whereas Sherman could count 30,000 Union troops at his disposal.

The night of the 24th and early hours of the 25th were crucial for preparations. A lunar eclipse was an added obstacle. Cleburne had difficulty surveying the ground for troop placement, but by sunrise he was ready. The first Union probe came early. Instead of a flanking attack, as Cleburne had expected, Sherman ordered an all-out frontal assault. Desperate hand-to-hand fighting ensued, but Sherman could not break Cleburne's tight-knit defensive line atop the 500-foot high, steep ridge. On a front of only forty yards, the afternoon of 25 November was filled with repeated attacks and repulses, making the line "one continuous sheet of hissing, flying lead." Out of ammunition, the Confederates made a desperate bayonet assault down the steep ridge, driving Sherman back conclusively from the Confederate right. The fighting ended at 4:00 P.M. as the winter sun began its descent.

Grant watched from the Union center at Orchard Knob. Expecting Hooker to have taken the Confederate left, Grant was astounded to learn that his commander had encountered difficulties crossing Chattanooga Creek and was nowhere near his position. Hooker arrived about 4:00 P.M., having little effect on the outcome other than mopping up operations. By the time

A 200-pound battery on Missionary Ridge, ca. 1864 (Photograph by Mathew Brady Studio / *National Archives*)

Sherman's assault had turned for the worst, Hooker was still advancing, and George Thomas awaited orders in the center. Grant ordered a strong attack on Bragg's center, where Confederate rifle pits hugged the base of Missionary Ridge.

Misunderstandings arose at both Union and Confederate command headquarters. Some of Thomas's troops thought the orders were to take the rifle pits at the foot of the ridge and halt, while others understood that their mission was to advance to the top of the ridge. The Confederate troops occupying the center and in those rifle pits were the victims of the same conflicting orders. Some thought they were to hold the pits, while others received orders to fall back up the ridge when the Union attacked. Those who did so were too exhausted when they reached the crest to re-form an effective battle line.

The result was the Union breakthrough at the Confederate center held by Major General Thomas C. Hindman's division under Brigadier General Patton Anderson. A brigade, unsupported on its left, received Thomas's first assault. When the Union troops captured a Confederate battery, they quickly turned the guns on the bewildered soldiers on either flank. The Confederate line crumbled from its center out, despite valiant attempts to rally. Poor planning on Bragg's part by placing breastworks on top of the ridge instead of on the crest below added to the disaster. He had prepared for a siege, not a frontal assault. The result was that men in the trenches above could not fire on the enemy for fear of hitting their men retreating from the rifle pits at the bottom.

Bragg was able to fall back intact as a result of a competent rear-guard action fought by Cleburne's division, which had won its part of the line, and poor coordination by Grant's larger army to follow up its breakthrough. Casualty figures for the Confederate army totaled 6,687 (about 15 percent); the Union loss was 5,824 (nearly 10 percent).

After Missionary Ridge, Bragg had completely lost the confidence of his army and was compelled to resign. Grant's chance to destroy Bragg's army was lost as a result of failure to pursue the Confederates. It would be six months before operations resumed in May 1864 with the Atlanta campaign.

—*Mauriel P. Joslyn*

See also Bragg, Braxton; Chattanooga Campaign; Cleburne, Patrick; Grant, Ulysses S.; Sherman, William Tecumseh.

For further reading:

Buck, Irving A. *Cleburne and His Command* (1995).
Cozzens, Peter. *The Shipwreck of Their Hopes: The Battles for Chattanooga* (1994).
Sword, Wiley. *Mountains Touched with Fire* (1995).
Woodworth, Steven E. *Six Armies in Tennessee: The Chickamauga and Chattanooga Campaigns* (1998).

MISSISSIPPI

Mississippi was one of eleven states that formed the Confederate States of America. The second state to leave the Union, Mississippi passed its Ordinance of Secession on 9 January 1861. Mississippi's departure sparked a rash of secession actions, with three more states following within the next three days. Immediately after secession, Mississippi became an important strategic location. The geography of the state and the internal transportation and communication lines dictated that Mississippi would play a major role in the upcoming war.

The Mississippi River stood as perhaps the most important avenue of transportation in North America. Mississippi's location on the east bank of the river afforded the state a major prewar privilege regarding transportation and shipping, but with the coming of war, the river also decreed for the state a major responsibility concerning defense. The most obvious and indeed strongest position on the river was Vicksburg, which Mississippi governor John J. Pettus began fortifying as early as December 1861.

Mississippi also contained other important transportation routes and hosted several major crossroads. Jackson, the state capital, was the crossing point of the north-south Mississippi Central and the east-west Southern Railroad. Grenada hosted the meeting point of the north-south Mississippi Central and the north-south Mississippi & Tennessee Railroad. The east-west Southern Railroad and the north-south Mobile & Ohio met at Meridian. Perhaps the most important rail crossing in Mississippi and arguably in the South lay at Corinth, where the vital east-west Memphis & Charleston met the north-south Mobile & Ohio. These two lifelines stretched the entire distance of the Confederacy in their respective directions.

Along with the Mississippi River and railroads, many other transportation routes made Mississippi a strategic necessity. The Gulf Coast afforded access to the Gulf of Mexico, while several inland rivers such as the Big Black, Yazoo, and Tombigbee provided lateral communication between the railroads and in areas where rails did not venture.

Because of these important transportation routes and their crossing points, Mississippi witnessed much fighting between 1861 and 1865. The state managed to avoid the bulk of action early in the war as Federal efforts necessarily hinged on states to the north. Some action did take place on the Gulf Coast, however, in association with Union efforts to reach and capture New Orleans. The first major action in Mississippi resulted from the Union thrust down the Tennessee River in the spring of 1862.

In March 1862, portions of the Federal Army of the Tennessee ventured as far as Eastport, Mississippi, before turning back. High waters rather than Confederate activity ended this reconnaissance, and the Union columns settled into camp at Pittsburg Landing, some twenty miles northeast of Corinth. To attack before a concentration of Union armies could occur, Confederate general Albert Sidney Johnston gathered all available forces at Corinth. After much delay, he attacked Major General Ulysses S. Grant at Pittsburg Landing on 6 April 1862. Johnston achieved total surprise, but fell in the day's fighting. Second in command General P. G. T. Beauregard assumed control of the army and fought a hopeless fight against reinforced Union ranks. On 7 April 1862, Beauregard withdrew to Corinth. The battle of Shiloh, fought essentially for the possession of Corinth, ended in Confederate defeat. The Federals soon followed and laid siege to Corinth. Before any major action, however, Beauregard withdrew to Tupelo on 29 May, leaving the crossroads in Union hands.

Between the fall of Corinth and the action around Vicksburg in the summer of 1863, several small but important campaigns took place in Mississippi. Union gunboats sailed up the Mississippi River and reached Vicksburg, only to be driven away by the Confederate ironclad *Arkansas*. In north Mississippi, Major Generals Earl Van Dorn and Sterling Price fought actions at Iuka on 19 September and Corinth on 3 and 4 October 1862. In concentration with the broad sweep north by other Confederate armies in the fall of 1862, Van Dorn focused on retaking Corinth and its crossroads as a precursor to a third invasion. His failure, however, only steadied the Union position in north Mississippi.

With the advent of 1863, major fighting arrived in Mississippi. Major General Ulysses S. Grant led a relentless assault on Vicksburg, the major citadel closing the Mississippi River to Union traffic. Grant attempted some six approaches between November 1862 and April 1863, many of which lay in Mississippi. Most notable were the Chickasaw Bayou assaults in December 1862, the Yazoo Pass expedition between February and April 1863, and the Steele's Bayou expedition in March 1863. All failed to give Grant access to Vicksburg.

On 30 April, Grant put into action a daring plan by crossing the Mississippi River south of Vicksburg and marching inland. He succeeded in his maneuver, fighting battles at Port Gibson on 1 May, Raymond on 12 May, Champions Hill on 16 May, and Big Black River Bridge on 17 May. In the process, Grant captured Jackson, the Mississippi capital, on 14 May. The battle of Champions Hill sealed the fate of Vicksburg, to which Grant laid siege on 22 May, after two deadly and unsuccessful assaults. On 4 July 1863, Confederate commander Lieutenant General John C. Pemberton surrendered Vicksburg, opening the Mississippi River to Union forces.

After the Vicksburg campaign, only smaller actions took place while the scene of fighting shifted to Georgia. William T. Sherman, in practice for his later March to the Sea, led the Meridian campaign in February 1864, which destroyed Meridian's transportation routes. Other actions, during the Atlanta campaign of the summer of 1864, took place in north Mississippi as Sherman endeavored to keep Confederate cavalry off his supply lines in Tennessee. The battles at Brice's Crossroads on 10 June and Tupelo on 14 July succeeded in keeping Confederate cavalryman Major General Nathan Bedford Forrest neutralized in Mississippi. At the end of the war, Lieutenant General Richard Taylor surrendered the forces in Mississippi on 4 May 1865.

Thus, the story of Mississippi in the Civil War is one of control of transportation routes. To defend Mississippi in this lost cause, the state sent some 80,000 troops to Confederate armies, a number totaling more men than the military age population living in the state in 1860.

—*Timothy B. Smith*

See also Big Black River, First Battle of; Brice's Crossroads, Battle of; Champion's Hill, Battle of; Chickasaw Bluffs, Battle of; Corinth, Battle of; Corinth, Siege of; Iuka, Battle of; Jackson, Mississippi, Capture of; Meridian Campaign; Pettus, John J.; Port Gibson, Battle of; Secession; Shiloh, Battle of; Tupelo, Battle of; Vicksburg Campaign; Yazoo Expedition.

For further reading:

Bearss, Edwin C. *Decision in Mississippi: Mississippi's Important Role in the War between the States* (1962).

Bettersworth, John K. *Confederate Mississippi: The People and Politics of a Cotton State in Wartime* (1943).

Bettersworth, John K., and James W. Silver, eds. *Mississippi in the Confederacy* (1961).

MISSOURI

Missouri, the second state west of the Mississippi River admitted to the Union, gained statehood in 1821. It lies west of the junction of the two largest rivers of North America. The Missouri River crosses the state from west to east. Near its entrance into the Mississippi, St. Louis grew to more than 160,000 by 1860. From St. Louis, railroads fanned out, cutting across the northern half of the state, moving along much of the south bank of the Missouri, angling southwest as far as Rolla, and going south to Pilot Knob. Beyond Rolla, a telegraph road continued to Springfield

and on into Arkansas with connections to the military bases at Forts Scott, Gibson, and Smith. Although the *Official Records* underreported battles, skirmishes, and wartime incidents, they credited the state with 1,162 of the war's 10,422 encounters, placing it behind only Virginia and Tennessee as contested ground. Few communities were spared.

Few of the adult men did not bear arms. On the eve of the war, the state's population was 1,182,012, including its 24,320 slave owners and their 114,931 slaves. In the course of the Civil War, the secessionist Missouri State Guard and the Confederacy mobilized perhaps 40,000, whereas more than 160,000 served the Union, about a third of them in the Enrolled Missouri Militia. In addition to the problem of overlapping service among the units on either side, an indeterminate number of Missourians actually served in both armies.

The severity of the war in Missouri was due not only to the division of its peoples but to the complexities of those divisions. Aside from a smattering of French and Spanish pioneers, the first settlers to Missouri Territory came very disproportionately from the South, and their requests for admission to the Union as a slave state provoked the first sectional crisis requiring an open arrangement, the Missouri Compromise (1820). However, through the 1850s, Missouri's population had grown by nearly 75 percent. Many of the newcomers arrived from the more populous North and from Europe, particularly Germany. The 1860 census showed that, for the first time, Missourians of Northern or foreign birth had come to outnumber natives of the South. The coincidence of this crisis in the state's affairs with that of the crisis in the nation intensified the conflict.

Antebellum Missouri politics was personified by former Senator Thomas Hart Benton, a Democrat who had grown independent of the dominant Southern faction in that party in the U.S. Senate. The "Jackson resolutions" of Claiborne Fox Jackson had rallied a powerful anti-Benton faction, including Sterling Price, to unseat Benton. This faction's dominance in the Missouri Democratic Party left the most ardent proslavery leaders in what was nationally the more moderate faction of the party headed by Stephen Arnold Douglas. The tactic enabled Jackson and his allies to win many western and foreign-born voters and establish a state government in 1860–1861 that was far more favorable to secession than were most of the electorate.

The state divided with the nation. A state convention rejected secession in February 1861, but the governor refused to provide Federal troops, mobilized his Missouri State Guard, and seized the U.S. Arsenal at Liberty. Based at the more important U.S. Arsenal at St. Louis, alarmed local Unionists raised their own volunteers and on 10 May 1861 seized Camp Jackson, a Missouri State Guard encampment within striking distance of that arsenal. By June, the war in Missouri assumed the form of an internal civil war in which the Unionist state convention replaced the secessionist state government with a provisional government.

Nearly a dozen major campaigns by regular troops crossed the state throughout the war. Although the early fighting at Boonville (17 June 1861) went well for the Union, later clashes in southwestern Missouri at Carthage (5 July) and Wilson's Creek (10 August) were Confederate victories. A subsequent Confederate thrust toward Jefferson City resulted in the capture of Lexington (20 September) and sufficient political prestige to reassemble the remnants of Jackson's government and declare the state out of the Union (28 and 31 October, respectively), leaving the state with two rival governments. The renewed Union offensive into southwestern Missouri and beyond brought victory at Pea Ridge, Arkansas (6–7 March 1862), and seemed to end Confederate aspirations toward the north. Successful Mississippi River operations against Island No. 10 (28 February–8 April) secured southeastern Missouri. Nevertheless, new recruits supplemented raiders to create a large Confederate force that clashed at Lone Jack (15–16 August) and around Newtonia (30 September–4 October). Similar incursions by thousands of Confederate raiders threatened Springfield (8 January 1863) in the southwest and Cape Girardeau (26 April) in the southeast, and hundreds of cavalry raided as far north as Marshall (13 October). The following year, Price's Missouri Raid (19 September–30 October 1864) brought a large Confederate army back into areas thought secured in the first weeks of the war.

Western realities clearly shaped the realities of the war in Missouri. Both the Union and the Confederacy fed the battles in the east by raising and transferring troops from farther west. With the Union seizure of the Mississippi River, fewer Missouri soldiers went east leaving it with regionally more viable numbers and resources than eastern states and an ability to push the fighting back and forth several times between the Missouri and Arkansas rivers. All this took place against the innovative brutalities of a guerrilla war that continued in the absence of regular troops; it blurred distinctions between civilians and combatants. Few counties south of the Missouri River survived with their records and treasuries intact. The conflict, outside the garrison towns, virtually depopulated the area along the western and southern borders, along with the adjacent areas of Arkansas, Indian Territory, and Kansas.

The particular intensity of the conflict polarized both Unionists and secessionists among themselves. While some Confederate officers struggled to maintain the standards of civilized warfare with regard to prisoners and civilians, others engaged in savage reprisals. Still others maintained a policy of virtual extermination.

Dealing with the latter, along with addressing slavery in Missouri, which was not covered by the Emancipation Proclamation, created an increasing tension between conservatives who sought an ineffectual constitutionalism and radicals driven to ever more draconian measures. Such incongruities shaped the speed and scope of Reconstruction in Missouri.

—*Mark A. Lause*

See also Camp Jackson; Price's Missouri Raid; Wilson's Creek.
For further reading:
Parrish, William E. *A History of Missouri, Volume III: 1860 to 1875* (1971).

MITCHEL, ORMSBY MACKNIGHT
(1809–1862)
Union general, astronomer

Born on 28 August 1809, in Morganfield, Kentucky, Ormsby M. Mitchel grew up in Lebanon, Ohio. Educated in the local schools, he was appointed to West Point at the age of fifteen, becoming a member of the noted class of 1829 that included Robert E. Lee and Joseph Johnston. Mitchel proved himself a talented scholar, especially in mathematics, graduating fifteenth in his class of fifty-six cadets and serving as an assistant professor of mathematics after graduation. He also worked as a surveyor for the Pennsylvania & Ohio Railroad, but this employment provided only a meager subsistence for himself, Louisa Clark Trask, whom he had married in 1831, and their growing family. Consequently, Mitchel accepted a lieutenancy and assignment to St. Augustine, Florida.

Within a year Mitchel resigned from the army and moved to Cincinnati, where he taught mathematics and studied law. In addition, he worked as chief engineer of the Little Miami Railroad and commanded a company of Cincinnati militia. But when Cincinnati College opened in 1836, Mitchel found his vocation when he inaugurated lectures on astronomy that proved popular and led to the founding of the Cincinnati Astronomical Society and the Cincinnati Observatory. Mitchel helped finance the observatory by lecture tours of eastern cities and Europe and was named director of the observatory when it opened in 1845.

Had the Civil War not intervened, Mitchel likely would have continued as an astronomer, but as a West Point graduate, he felt bound to military service. On 20 April 1861, he addressed a crowd at Union Park in New York and, like people throughout both North and South, Mitchel was inflamed by the prospect of war, promising to punish the Union's traitors and proclaiming, "I only ask to be permitted to act, and in God's name give me something to do." But Mitchel waited until August 1861, when Secretary of the Treasury Salmon P. Chase secured his commission as brigadier general. Ordered to

Cincinnati, Mitchel took command of the rendezvous camp and local defenses but was dissatisfied and tried to tender his resignation. Instead, in December 1861, he was assigned to the Army of Ohio, under the command of Don Carlos Buell, and took command of the 3d Division at Elizabethtown, Kentucky.

With the fall of Forts Henry and Donelson in February 1862, Brigadier General Mitchel advanced to Nashville and occupied the city. During this period, Mitchel came to oppose the policy of limited warfare and its conciliatory approach toward Southern civilians that was advocated by Buell. When Mitchel advanced into northern Alabama and captured the city of Huntsville and the Memphis & Charleston Railroad in April of 1862, he gained both a promotion to major general and the opportunity to diverge from limited warfare by punishing Confederate civilians, undermining slavery, and supporting local Unionists. Mitchel confiscated prominent Confederates' property and arrested local leaders in retaliation for guerilla attacks on his extended lines. He also pushed ahead of official policies by protecting slaves who aided the Union army and opening the cotton trade in northern Alabama by utilizing local Unionists as agents. These policies, along with the sacking of Athens, Alabama, by one of his junior officers, brought him into conflict with Buell and made him subject to criticism in conservative Northern papers.

In July 1862, he traveled to Washington to request reassignment and replaced Major General David Hunter as head of the Department of the South in September. Taking up his assignment on the Sea Islands of South Carolina, Mitchel ordered expeditions against Confederate positions at St. John's Bluff, Florida, and Confederate salt works at Blufton. He also sought control of the railroad linking Charleston and Savannah in a failed advance on Pocotaligo. An early advocate of emancipation for its military benefits, Mitchel continued his predecessor's policies toward the Sea Island contrabands, presiding over the construction of shelter and schools, employing the former slaves as laborers, and overseeing their drill as soldiers. But Mitchel's death from yellow fever on 30 October 1862 ended his brief participation in the abolitionist experiments on the Sea Islands.

Laid to rest in the cemetery of the Episcopal Church in Beaufort, South Carolina, Mitchel was eulogized by the Northern press as a learned astronomer and worthy general who had meritoriously abandoned the policies of limited warfare early in the war. At the same time, he was reviled in the Southern press as a participant in the Union's plan to destroy both the institution of slavery and the freedom of the Confederate people.

—*Christine Dee*

See also Huntsville, Alabama.
For further reading:
Headley, Phineas C. *The Astronomer and Soldier* (1870).
Mitchel, Frederick A. *Ormsby Macknight Mitchel, Astronomer and General* (1886).

Niven, John, ed. *The Salmon P. Chase Papers* (1988–1993).

Shoemaker, Philip S. "Ormsby Macknight Mitchel." In *American National Biography* (1999).

U.S. War Department. *The War of the Rebellion: A Compilation of the Official Records of the Union and Confederate Armies* (1880–1901).

MOBILE BAY
(August 1864)

Mobile Bay and the city of Mobile, Alabama, became prominent Union military targets in the summer of 1864. The attack on Mobile Bay was part of a larger plan designed by newly appointed General-in-Chief Ulysses S. Grant. Grant's intention was to deliver a coordinated strike against the Confederacy with General William T. Sherman attacking Atlanta and General George Gordon Meade applying continuous pressure on Robert E. Lee's Army of Northern Virginia. If successful, the attack on Mobile and its large waterways would provide a staging area for further advances into the Deep South and would also alleviate some of the pressure on Sherman's attack on Atlanta. Mobile would also provide the Union with a supply base and a secure destination if Sherman decided to move south after seizing Atlanta.

The fall of New Orleans in April 1862 left Mobile as the leading port on the Gulf of Mexico. Trade was conducted by blockade runners, which primarily shipped cotton to Havana in exchange for both military supplies and other items for Gulf Coast communities. A small Confederate navy under the command of Admiral Franklin Buchanan aided blockade runners. The fleet included both ironclads and gunboats and was responsible for distracting Union gunboats for blockade runners coming in and out of Mobile Bay.

By the summer of 1864 Union admiral David G. Farragut had assembled a fleet of seventeen vessels to break through both Forts Gaines and Morgan at the entrance of Mobile Bay. This gave the Union navy a four to one advantage in firepower over Buchanan's smaller squadron. On 3 August, under the command of Union general Gordon Granger, 1,500 troops landed on the western end of Dauphin Island. Though the Confederate garrison was driven back, it was able to buy time to bring in reinforcements from Mobile to Fort Gaines. With the Confederate garrison distracted on Dauphin Island, Farragut prepared his fleet to run the entrance of Mobile Bay. He placed four ironclad monitors in the lead to protect his additional wooden-hulled frigates from the estimated 180 mines protecting the bay.

Confederate colonel Charles Anderson, who commanded approximately 800 men at Fort Gaines, observed Farragut's fleet closing in at 6:30 A.M. on 5 August. Fort Morgan's smoothbore howitzers and Columbiads opened up a steady fire on the advancing fleet. The first victim was the USS *Tecumseh*, which hit

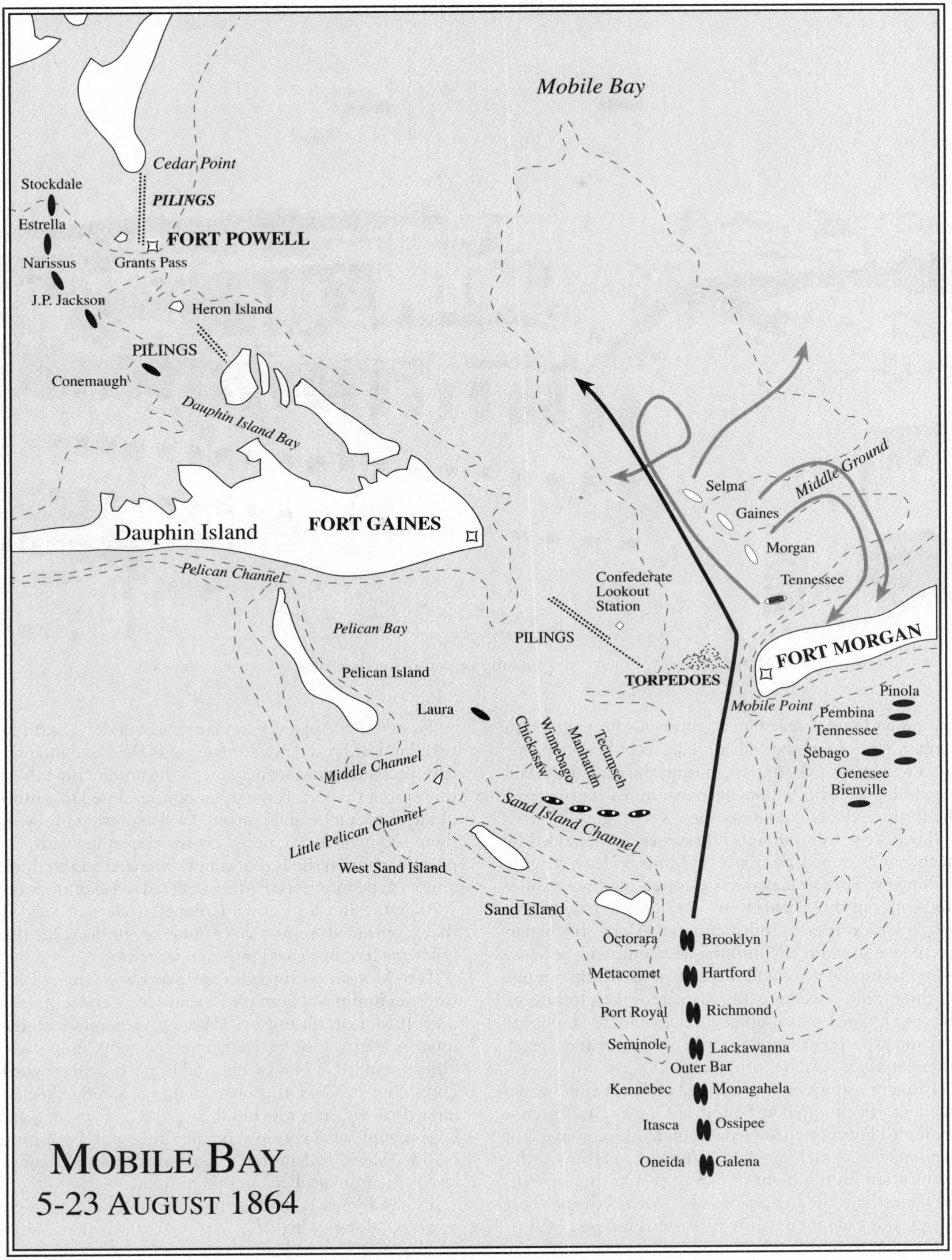

Mobile Bay

Cedar Point

PILINGS

Stockdale

Estrella

FORT POWELL

Narissus

Grants Pass

J.P. Jackson

Heron Island

PILINGS

Conemaugh

Dauphin Island Bay

Selma

Gaines

Middle Ground

Morgan

Tennessee

Dauphin Island

FORT GAINES

Confederate
Lookout
Station

Pelican Channel

FORT MORGAN

Pelican Bay

PILINGS

Mobile Point

Pelican Island

TORPEDOES

Pinola

Pembina

Laura

Tennessee

Chickasaw

Winnebago

Manhattan

Tecumseh

Sebago

Genesee
Bienville

Middle Channel

Little Pelican Channel

Sand Island Channel

West Sand Island

Sand Island

Octorara   Brooklyn

Metacomet   Hartford

Port Royal   Richmond

Seminole   Lackawanna

Outer Bar

Kennebec   Monagahela

Itasca   Ossipee

Oneida   Galena

MOBILE BAY
5-23 AUGUST 1864

Fort Morgan, showing damage to the south side of the structure, 1864 (*National Archives*)

a mine and sank immediately. Farragut's fleet stalled in confusion, only to be galvanized, according to some accounts, by his exhortation, "Damn the torpedoes. Full speed ahead." The Union fleet continued its trek past the forts to a location out of range of their guns.

The Confederate ironclad *Tennessee*, commanded by Buchanan, steamed out from Fort Morgan's lee to engage the enemy. The *Tennessee* was escorted by three smaller gunboats, but these boats were soon rendered ineffective by the Union frigates' rifled cannon. Alone, Buchanan steered his ship directly into the fleet, engaging as many as seven ships at once and firing at times within a range of three feet. Accurate fire damaged the *Tennessee*'s steering chains, which forced Buchanan to disengage and run to a point a mile north of Fort Gaines' guns, where at 10:00 A.M. he surrendered.

Farragut's attention now focused on Fort Gaines and a smaller fortification, Fort Powell, at Grant's Pass. Intense fire forced Fort Powell's defenders under the command of Lieutenant Colonel James M. Williams to abandon the fortification on the night of 6 August. On the way out, Williams had the magazines destroyed because Fort Powell was outgunned with its eastern face exposed to intense fire from nearby monitors.

From 6 to 8 August, Fort Gaines was under siege from both land and sea. Approximately 3,000 Federal infantry with accompanying artillery lay in the entrenchments to the west of the fort. Farragut's monitors closed to within point blank range and delivered a devastating fire with their 100-pounder cannons. Gaines responded with 32-pounder cannon shells that simply bounced off the thick armor of the monitors. Farragut offered a flag of truce on 7 August. After a meeting, Colonel Anderson decided that continued resistance would be futile. On the following day, he agreed to surrender terms.

Fort Morgan withstood a two-week siege from land batteries and naval gunfire. Federal forces concentrated on Fort Morgan starting on 9 August. General Granger's infantry with newly arrived reinforcements from New Orleans landed at Navy Cove and began moving toward Fort Morgan. Over the next few days, Granger's men moved to within a few hundred yards of Fort Morgan. Union gunboats kept up sporadic firing and, beginning on 15 August, Federal forces on the peninsula began a steady fire from artillery and sharpshooters.

By 21 August, twenty-five cannon and sixteen mortars along with the entire Union fleet were bombarding Fort Morgan. As a precautionary measure, the commander of Fort Morgan's garrison, General Richard L. Page, ordered his powder destroyed for fear that a direct hit on the magazine would blow up the fort. Finally, on the morning of 23 August after a discussion with his officers, Page decided to surrender Fort Morgan.

Farragut's relatively easy victory can be explained primarily by weaknesses in the Confederacy's coastal defenses around Mobile. The Confederacy lacked an adequate fleet to defend the forts and to counter Union vessels. Mobile Bay's forts were too far from each other for adequate support, and their small garrisons were unable to prevent Federal forces from gaining footholds and laying siege lines against their defensive positions. Significant reinforcements from outside the Mobile area were not available, so Confederate forces in the lower bay were isolated.

The Union victory in Mobile Bay ended blockade running in and out of Mobile. Though it is difficult to measure the extent to which the flow of supplies was reduced, the lower South surely suffered as a result. The battle achieved little in terms of military value, however. Mobile remained in Confederate hands until April 1865. The victory in Mobile Bay nonetheless gave the Union a psychological victory, which aided President Abraham Lincoln in his bid for reelection in November.

—*Kevin M. Levin*

See also Buchanan, Franklin; Farragut, David Glasgow; Granger, Gordon.

For further reading:

Bergeron, Arthur W. *Confederate Mobile* (1991).

Symonds, Craig L. *Confederate Admiral: The Life and Wars of Franklin Buchanan* (1999).

Wise, Stephen. *Lifeline of the Confederacy: Blockade Running during the Civil War* (1988).

MOBILE CAMPAIGN
(17 March–12 April 1865)

Even before he became general-in-chief of the Federal armies, Ulysses S. Grant had recommended an operation against Mobile, Alabama. After assuming that rank, Grant still had to accede to Nathaniel Banks's Red River campaign, a diversion of resources that not only proved unsuccessful, but also postponed any move against Mobile. David Farragut's August 1864 naval action in Mobile Bay closed the port by placing the entrance of the bay in Federal hands, but the city itself remained a Confederate bastion into the spring of 1865. By then Mobile had lost much of its importance as a strategic target and had become a place on the way to somewhere else, specifically Selma and Montgomery.

Until the last spring of the war, Major General Edward R. S. Canby's Military Division of West Mississippi had a variety of tasks that precluded assailing Mobile. Directing operations from his headquarters in

New Orleans, Canby deployed forces to keep Edmund Kirby Smith from crossing the Mississippi River after the fall of Atlanta. His department also prevented Alabama or Mississippi from sending reinforcements to John Bell Hood's crippled army as it prepared to invade Tennessee. These chores had scattered Canby's forces across a vast area, ranging from the Gulf of Mexico to the Mississippi and Ohio rivers. Once Hood was defeated in Tennessee, however, Canby was instructed to collect his people for a move on Selma or Montgomery, and if Canby thought it possible, he was to capture Mobile.

Such a capture, given the relative weight of Union and Confederate forces, was more than possible—it was inevitable. The garrison defending Mobile was small, an example of Confederate shortages that were becoming acute everywhere, including northern Virginia and the Carolinas. Mobile's role as a guardian of Mississippi and Alabama was not lost on Confederate lieutenant general Richard Taylor, commander of the Department of Alabama, Mississippi, and East Louisiana. Yet there was not much Taylor could do in the face of dwindling resources, eroding morale, and state laws that made it almost impossible to draw upon local militia. Taylor had warned in November 1864 that a serious Federal effort would conquer the city. Now in the spring of 1865 as that threat materialized, Taylor hoped that Nathan Bedford Forrest's cavalry could relieve the city's besieged garrison when the time came. That hope too proved fruitless. Forrest himself would be in dire trouble resisting the 12,500-man cavalry force that James Wilson led into the state at the same time Canby moved on Mobile. What happened in Alabama in early 1865 was simply another demonstration of the Confederacy collapsing before overwhelming and multiplying Federal military operations.

Canby gathered 45,000 men to challenge the Mobile garrison of 10,000. Andrew J. Smith's XVI Corps (16,000 men) and Brigadier General Joseph F. Knipe's cavalry division, both detached from the Army of the Cumberland, joined Gordon Granger's XIII Corps of 18,500 men, Brigadier General John P. Hawkins's Colored Division of 5,500 African-American troops, Brigadier General Thomas J. Lucas's cavalry division, an engineering brigade commanded by the intrepid Brigadier General Joseph Bailey, and a siege train for good measure.

Canby planned to move on Mobile by attacking fortifications on the east side of Mobile Bay (Spanish Fort and Fort Blakely) and Batteries Tracy and Huger that commanded the Tensas and Alabama rivers. Two columns would originate from different locations to converge on these objectives. The larger one under Canby would be ferried by the navy up the bay from Mobile Point and Dauphin Island. The other column under Major General Frederick Steele would set out

from Pensacola. Canby would have 32,500 men—two divisions and one brigade of XIII Corps, XVI Corps, and 3,000 assorted engineers, artillerists, and scouts—to throw against Spanish Fort. Steele's 13,000 men—two brigades of Christopher C. Andrews's division, XIII Corps, Hawkins's black infantry, and Lucas's cavalry—would descend on Fort Blakely.

Appalling weather delayed everything on both land and water until mid-March, but the weather was all that hampered Federal plans. Major General Dabney Maury, commanding at Mobile, watched helplessly as the Union host conducted siege operations that ultimately overpowered Spanish Fort on 8 April and Fort Blakely the following day. Canby's success was not without penalty, however, for it cost about 1,400 Union casualties to reduce the forts, a loss that Grant later bemoaned as ironically unnecessary, given the operation's relative unimportance. Maury abandoned his batteries and after declaring Mobile open, fled the city with 4,500 soldiers and only 27 of his 300 artillery pieces. The five gunboats that remained of the Confederate Mobile Squadron escaped up the Tombigbee River as Maury led his bedraggled soldiers toward Meridian, but the war was over. Richard Taylor surrendered these men to Canby forty miles north of Mobile at Citronelle on 4 May.

—*David S. Heidler and Jeanne T. Heidler*

See also Blakely, Alabama, Battle of; Canby, Edward R. S.; Maury, Dabney Herndon; Mobile Bay; Spanish Fort, Battle of; Taylor, Richard; Wilson's Selma Raid.

For further reading:

Hearn, Chester G. *Mobile Bay and the Mobile Campaign: The Last Great Battles of the Civil War* (1993).

Heyman, Max L. *Prudent Soldier: A Biography of Major General E. R. S. Canby, 1817–1873* (1959).

Maury, Dabney H. *Recollections of a Virginian in the Mexican, Indian, and Civil Wars* (1894).

Parker, Prescott A. *Story of the Tensaw: Blakely, Spanish Fort, Jackson Oaks, Fort Mims* (1922). Taylor, Richard. *Destruction and Reconstruction: Personal Experiences of the Late War* (1879; reprint, 1983).

MONITOR
Union ironclad

Hearing rumors of the construction of a Confederate ironclad, Union secretary of the navy Gideon Welles created a three-member Ironclad Board to review projects and interview prospective ship constructors. On 15 September 1861, Swedish-born engineer John Ericsson won the approval of the board and from Welles to begin construction of an ironclad ship.

On 25 October 1861, workers laid the wooden keel for an ironclad warship at the Continental Iron Works in Greenpoint, Long Island, New York. That same late October day, Ericsson also signed with his subcontractors. The Rensselaer Works would provide the bar iron and rivets for the main deck; the Albany Iron Works, New York's Holdane & Company, and H. Abbot & Company in Baltimore would roll the armor plating; other companies from Buffalo, New York, and Nashua, New Hampshire, would fashion vital special parts. Ericsson's intricate designs allowed him to save valuable time through simultaneous manufacturing. It also allowed him to bring the parts together for rapid assembly with little if any alteration.

The novel warship began to take shape under Ericsson's careful eye during the fall of 1861. Carpenters worked around the clock to complete the hull and prepare it for an iron sheathing, and the various parts arrived in the foundry yard and were assembled to the ship. It was a small vessel by the standards of the day—only 172 feet from bow to stern and 41 feet wide. Its flat deck, comprised of solid wood covered with 1-inch-thick iron plating, extended only 18 inches above the waterline. At the center of the deck stood the 20-feet-wide 9-feet-high gun turret, housing two 11-inch Dahlgren guns and encased in 8 inches of iron plating. Other than the turret, only a 3-foot 10-inch pilothouse rose above the deck. The vessel displaced about 1,000 tons, which meant that it drew only 10 and a half feet of water, a draft that would allow it to operate in virtually any harbor.

Although Ericsson had promised the Navy Department that the ship would be ready for service by 12 January 1862, a series of delays postponed its launching until eighteen days later; on 30 January 1862 the ironclad, christened *Monitor* by its builder, slid out of its dock at Greenpoint into the East River. The following day its captain, Lieutenant John Worden, fired up the ironclad's boilers and made steam for the first time.

The *Monitor* was ready for sea, but it still awaited the two Dahlgren guns for its turret. Because there were no guns available, Worden had to remove the 11-inch cannon from a ship docked at the Brooklyn Navy Yard. By 15 February, the guns had been installed and sighted in; four days later, Ericsson turned the ship over to the U.S. Navy. At 2:00 P.M. on 19 February 1862, the *Monitor* moved from its moorings at Greenpoint toward the Brooklyn Navy Yard. The ironclad's first official voyage was inauspicious as it experienced engine and boiler problems and had to be towed into wharf at 7:30 P.M. Repairs were quickly completed and the ironclad was commissioned in the U.S. Navy on 25 February 1862.

The *Monitor* departed the Brooklyn Navy Yard for Chesapeake Bay on 6 March 1862. After a two-day tumultuous voyage in which the ship almost capsized in stormy seas, the Union ironclad arrived off Hampton Roads. The following day the *Monitor* fought its momentous duel against the Confederate ironclad *Virginia*. Beginning at about 8:45 A.M., the two ships

Sailors on the deck of the USS *Monitor* in the James River, 9 July 1862 (Photograph by James F. Gibson / *Library of Congress*)

began circling one another while trying to gain an advantageous position. The two ironclads battled furiously at close range for the next four hours, but they did minimal damage to each other; neither vessel could claim a clear victory.

On 12 May the *Monitor* and the ironclad *Galena*, accompanied by three wooden ships, unsuccessfully steamed up the James River toward Richmond. The *Monitor* remained off Norfolk for the remainder of the summer. Throughout the fall of 1862, the ironclad underwent extensive renovations: retractable smokestacks and new lifeboats were fitted, and the dents incurred during the battle with the *Virginia* were patched with iron. On 29 December, the *Monitor* departed for Beaufort, North Carolina, where it would assist the Union blockading squadron. During the next day and a half, the ironclad encountered stormy seas that tossed the tiny ship, producing cracks along the vessel's iron seams through which water began to gush. Finally at about 1:00 A.M. on 31 December 1862, the *Monitor* sunk some fifteen miles south of Cape Hatteras, North Carolina; sixteen men went down with the ironclad.

—*Gene A. Smith*

See also Dahlgren Guns; Ericsson, John; *Monitor* versus *Virginia*; Welles, Gideon; Worden, John Lorimer.

For further reading:

Bennett, Frank M. *The Monitor and the Navy under Steam* (1900).

Cracknell, William H. *Warship Profile: United States* Monitors *of the Civil War* (1973).

Davis, William C. *Duel between the First Ironclads* (1975).

Smith, Gene A. *Iron and Heavy Guns: Duel between the Monitor and Merrimac* (1996).

Wheeler, Francis B. "The Building of the Monitor." *Magazine of American History* (1895).

Wilson, Herbert W. *Ironclads in Action: A Sketch of Naval Warfare* (1896).

MONITOR VERSUS VIRGINIA
(8 March 1862)

Confederate captain Franklin Buchanan steamed his ironclad *Virginia* (formerly the USS *Merrimack*) from the Gosport Navy Yard into the Chesapeake Bay to confront the Union fleet there on blockade duty. Anchored in the bay were three coal ships and a hospital vessel; five tugboats and a side-wheel steamer; twelve gunboats mounting one to five guns; the screw frigates *Roanoke* and *Minnesota*; the storeship *Brandywine*; and the sailing frigates *St. Lawrence, Congress,* and *Cumberland.* The Union detachment had 188 guns and more than 2,000 seamen.

At 1:08 P.M. a lookout aboard the *Roanoke* spotted the approach of the slow-moving Confederate ironclad and raised the signal for the Union fleet. Within minutes the *Cumberland,* the *Congress,* and the shore batteries at Newport News opened fire. Because the Union squadron was dispersed, Buchanan decided to close on the becalmed *Cumberland* first and then move against the other Union ships. At about 2:30 the *Virginia* fired its first devastating broadside into the *Cumberland.* After firing several more rounds, Buchanan rammed the wooden frigate and for thirty minutes maintained a murderous fire; shortly after 3:30 P.M. the *Cumberland* sank.

Next, Buchanan turned his ironclad against the frigate *Congress,* which had been towed into shoal waters to prevent the *Virginia* from ramming it. Within minutes the Confederate ironclad was about 200 yards from the grounded frigate and firing continuously into it. At 4:45 P.M., after enduring almost an hour of bombardment, the *Congress* struck its colors and raised a white flag. Even so, Union sharpshooters on shore continued firing on Confederates as they prepared to take the ship; one shot wounded Buchanan in the leg and he had to be carried below to his quarters. Almost instantly, Confederate shot struck the helpless frigate. By 5:00 P.M. the *Congress* was fully ablaze and out of commission. With dark approaching, Lieutenant Catesby ap Roger Jones, the executive officer who had assumed command because of Buchanan's injury, anchored the ironclad under Confederate guns at nearby Sewell's Point.

In only five hours, the *Virginia* sank two Union frigates (USS *Cumberland* and *Congress*), drove three steam frigates aground in shoal waters (*Minnesota, St. Louis,* and *Roanoke*), and exchanged fire with several small armed steamers and shore batteries while suffering virtually no damage. The Confederate ironclad had been responsible for killing almost 300 Federal sailors and wounding 100 more. The day's battle proved conclusively that wooden warships had become obsolete.

Shortly after sunrise on 9 March 1862, Jones noticed that the *Minnesota* was still stranded and that it was not alone. During the previous evening, the strange-looking experimental ironclad *Monitor,* commanded by Lieutenant John Lorimer Worden, had arrived from New York to protect the Union fleet. Even so, Jones intended first to finish off the *Minnesota* and then turn to the remainder of the Federal fleet in the Bay.

As the *Virginia* made its way the two miles from Sewell's Point toward the Union fleet, Worden moved the *Monitor* into a defensive position between the grounded *Minnesota* and the approaching Confederate ironclad; the wooden frigate began firing broadsides that bounced harmlessly off the *Virginia.* Jones continued steaming toward the *Minnesota* until the pilots informed him that the ironclad could not close on the frigate because of shallow water. With that information Jones instead chose to fight the *Monitor.*

It was now about 8:45 A.M. as the two ships closed to within 50 yards, circling one another while trying to gain an advantageous position. The *Virginia's* deep draft, poor steering, and slow speed left it at a disadvantage. The *Monitor,* with its shallow draft and efficient engines, was able to steam circles around the Confederate vessel. The ships moved as close as a few feet from one another and as far apart as 100 yards, all the while maintaining a constant fire. The eleven-inch solid shot from the *Monitor's* guns dented the rebel vessel's iron casemate and splintered its oak backing.

At about 10:30 A.M., after about two hours of almost continuous combat, disaster struck the *Virginia.* With all the circling and maneuvering, the pilots aboard the Confederate ironclad became disoriented and allowed it to run aground. With its 22-foot draft, the *Virginia* became mired in the muddy bottom of the Chesapeake Bay and was helpless against the *Monitor.* For the next fifteen minutes, the *Monitor* maintained against the *Virginia* a ceaseless fire, which cracked the iron sheathing and bent the timbers behind.

As Jones tried to extricate the *Virginia,* he realized that the Confederate cannon could not penetrate the *Monitor's* turret or iron sheathing nor could his armor continue to withstand the pounding of the enemy's guns. Jones concluded that his only recourse was to ram the Union ship. Aboard the *Monitor,* Worden realized Jones's intentions, tried to avoid a direct collision, and instructed his men to continue firing on the Confederate vessel. The Confederate ship was too large, too unresponsive, and too slow to build up the speed necessary to inflict severe damage on the Union vessel. Moreover, shortly before the two ships made contact, Worden turned the helm hard, away from the *Virginia.* Nothing had penetrated the *Monitor's* half-inch iron hull, and no water flooded into the ironclad.

For fifteen minutes, as the *Monitor* withdrew from the fight to replenish its ammunition supply, Jones turned his

The USS *Monitor* (*right foreground*) and the CSS *Virginia* (*left foreground*) (*National Archives*)

attention again to the *Minnesota*. Worden decided, because his ship was faster and more maneuverable, that he should ram the *Virginia*'s stern; such a collision would damage the Confederate ironclad's rudder and propeller, leaving it at the whim of the currents or at the mercy of the Union navy. Worden was able to maneuver his vessel to Jones's stern and closed at full speed for the *Virginia*'s hull. But at the last moment, the *Monitor*'s steering failed and the ironclad missed its target by only a few feet.

Jones's guns concentrated on the *Monitor*'s pilothouse as the Union ironclad approached, and at about 11:30 A.M. a shot struck one of the sight holes on the pilothouse and sent particles of paint and iron into Worden's face. For the next twenty minutes, while Union officers attended Worden, the *Monitor* moved away from the *Virginia*. Although no one realized it at the time, the first battle between two ironclad ships had ended.

The two ships had sparred for almost four hours and had done minimal damage to each other. The engagement did provide a tactical victory for the Federals, as the *Monitor* had fulfilled its primary objective of saving the frigate *Minnesota*. The battle allowed the Confederates to maintain strategic control over Hampton Roads and the James River; Union forces could not move against Norfolk, and General George B.

McClellan had to modify his spring 1862 campaign against Richmond. Although many realized that neither side could claim outright victory, they did acknowledge that history had been made as the two ships had helped to revolutionize naval warfare.

—*Gene A. Smith*

See also Buchanan, Franklin; Jones, Catesby ap Roger; *Monitor*; *Virginia*, CSS; Worden, John Lorimer.
For further reading:
"Battle of Hampton Roads—Confederate Official Reports." *Southern Historical Society Papers* (1879).
Davis, William C. *Duel between the First Ironclads* (1975).
Eggleston, John R. "Captain Eggleston's Narrative of the Battle of the *Merrimac*." *Southern Historical Society Papers* (1916).
Scharf, Thomas J. *History of the Confederate States Navy: From Its Organization to the Surrender of Its Last Vessel* (1877; reprint 1996).
Smith, Gene A. *Iron and Heavy Guns: Duel between the Monitor and Merrimac* (1996).
White, E. V. *The First Iron-Clad Engagement in the World* (1906).

MONOCACY, MARYLAND, BATTLE OF
(9 July 1864)

After moving down the Shenandoah Valley and crossing into Maryland near Sharpsburg on 5 July 1864, Major General Jubal Early planned to move his Confederate army on Washington, D.C. Not until this time did Ulysses S. Grant, busy with the

opening of his siege of Petersburg, Virginia, begin to take Early's movements seriously and begin preparations to reinforce Washington.

When Union major general Lew Wallace, commanding the Middle Department headquartered at Baltimore, learned that Early had crossed the Potomac River, he left Baltimore and established an observation position at Monocacy Junction on the Monocacy River about three miles southeast of Frederick, Maryland. Over the next few days, Wallace gathered as many men as possible, including the 8th Illinois Cavalry. By 7 July he had about 2,300 men.

On that same day, a Confederate cavalry brigade approached Frederick and skirmished with the 8th Illinois. The Confederates pulled back from Frederick just as Wallace received word that Grant had sent a division of VI Corps commanded by Brigadier General James Brewerton Ricketts that would be arriving in Baltimore that night. Wallace sent word to Baltimore for Ricketts to come to Monocacy Junction as soon as he arrived. Wallace intended to make a stand at the river, therefore stopping or at least delaying Early's move down the Washington Pike, which moved south out of Monocacy Junction.

Most of Early's Army of the Valley was still west of South Mountain. He marched on the morning of 8 July through South Mountain's passes and stopped that night just west of Catoctin Mountain. He planned to move on Frederick the following morning.

Starting out before dawn, the Confederate division under Major General Stephen Dodson Ramseur, part of Robert Emmett Rodes's corps, pushed Union skirmishers through Frederick about 8:00 A.M. Early sent Major General John C. Breckinridge's corps around the south of town while the remainder of Rodes's corps moved along Ramseur's left. As Early's entire army moved beyond town at about 9:00 A.M., the Confederates began to perceive Wallace's positions on the other side of the Monocacy River.

Along the northern end of his lines, Wallace had a force guarding the bridge over the river on the road to Baltimore. In the center of his line were two bridges, one of which was the Baltimore & Ohio Railroad bridge. There he placed much of his artillery. Guarding the south or left of his lines and the key to the Washington Pike were the veterans of Ricketts's division who had arrived during the night.

Once positioned, the Confederate artillery opened up on the Union lines and were answered by the Union guns. While the artillery of both sides tested each other's strength, Early extorted $200,000 from the town officials of Frederick in return for not burning the town. Leaving part of his staff to collect the money, Early left town and moved toward the firing.

What Early saw as he left Frederick was part of Rodes's corps moving along the road to Baltimore and Ramseur's

division moving toward the Baltimore & Ohio bridge. While skirmishers on both sides moved toward each other at these positions, Early determined that, if he were to proceed to Washington, he would have to turn the Union left flank. To turn that flank, he would have to find a ford across the Monocacy southwest of Monocacy Junction. Confederate cavalry under Brigadier General John McCausland stumbled upon one at about 11:00 A.M. Early immediately sent word to Breckinridge, who he had been holding in reserve, to move south toward the ford.

The division of Major General John Brown Gordon took the lead, crossed the ford, and began arraying to move against Ricketts's flanks. As Gordon tried to move around Ricketts, Wallace moved reinforcements to that part of the field. In the meantime, Ricketts was shifting his lines to meet Gordon's threat. At about 2:30 P.M. Gordon made one attack but was stopped. Ricketts tried to shift again, and at that point Gordon brought in the relatively fresh brigade of Brigadier General William Richard Terry to attack Ricketts on the right of the Union general's lines. With a furious charge, Terry's men went in, emitting the earsplitting rebel yell. Ricketts's line collapsed in panic, falling back on the Union defenders at the Baltimore & Ohio bridge. A general Union retreat toward Baltimore ensued.

The Confederate pursuit was relatively brief because Early knew that he needed to move quickly on Washington along the now open Washington Pike. The delay at Frederick and the Monocacy had been costly for the Confederates. It would provide enough time for adequate reinforcements, including the remainder of VI Corps, to reach Washington before Early was in a position to attack.

Losses for the day were about 1,880 of the approximate 6,000 Federals engaged and 700 of Early's 14,000 total force.

—David S. Heidler and Jeanne T. Heidler

See also Breckinridge, John Cabel; Early's Washington Raid; Gordon, John Brown; Ricketts, James Brewerton; Rodes, Robert Emmett; Wallace, Lewis.

For further reading:

Cooling, Benjamin Franklin. *Monocacy: The Battle That Saved Washington* (1997).

Vandiver, Frank E. *Jubal's Raid: General Early's Famous Attack on Washington in 1864* (1960).

MONTAGUE, ROBERT LATANE
(1819–1880)
Confederate congressman

Born in Middlesex County, Virginia, to Lewis Brooke Montague and Catherine Street Jesse Montague, Robert Montague was educated at the College of William and Mary and studied law. He practiced law in Saluda, Virginia, and became active in Democratic state politics. He served one term in the

state legislature and became lieutenant governor in 1860 in the administration of Governor John Letcher.

In early 1861, Montague was elected to the Virginia secession convention, where he was selected its president. As the presiding officer of the convention, Montague was a supporter of secession, but could do little to secure the necessary votes until after the Fort Sumter crisis and President Abraham Lincoln's call for volunteers. Once the state seceded, however, at the end of April 1861, Montague became one of Governor Letcher's primary advisers on the defense of the state. At the governor's urging, Montague was made a member of the governor's Advisory Council. The primary duty of this small group was to serve as a type of executive council to the governor on military affairs. Montague served in that capacity until his election to the second Confederate Congress in 1863.

In the Confederate Congress, Montague served as a member of the House Ordnance Committee. He strongly supported Jefferson Davis's administration's efforts to maintain a strong centralized defense and became known as an administration man. Because of his strong stand on defense, Montague was a target for military officers' lobbying efforts for more power to confiscate needed goods and supplies. After the war Montague resumed his law practice and again became involved in state politics. He served again in the state legislature and in his last years as a judge.

—*David S. Heidler and Jeanne T. Heidler*

See also Congress, C.S.A.; Virginia.
For further reading:
Alexander, Thomas Benjamin, and Richard E. Beringer. *The Anatomy of the Confederate Congress: A Study of the Influences of Member Characteristics on Legislative Voting Behavior, 1861–1865* (1972).

MONTGOMERY, JAMES
(1814–1871)
Union officer

James Montgomery first gained notoriety in the Kansas border wars of the 1850s, in which he led a band of antislavery jayhawkers. During the Civil War he served first in Kansas before organizing a regiment of contrabands known as the 2d South Carolina Colored Infantry that served in the Union army's Department of the South. He rose to the rank of colonel and command of a brigade, but his controversial nature precluded higher rank. He ended the war with neither a promotion nor brevet to general.

Of Scots-Irish ancestry, James Montgomery was born in Ashtabula County, Ohio, on 22 December 1814 (although one source lists the year of his birth as 1813). Educated in his native state, he eventually moved to Kentucky, where he taught school and became a Campbellite minister. In

the early 1850s, Montgomery moved with his wife to Missouri and then to Mound City, Kansas.

The area where he settled contained a majority of proslavery settlers, although Montgomery was a committed abolitionist. In 1856 his home was burned, allegedly by his political enemies. The following year he organized a company of Free-State Kansans that skirmished with both proslavery irregulars and federal troops. Montgomery's force drove most of the proslavery settlers out of Linn County, raided into Missouri on a number of occasions, and planned several attacks against Fort Scott, Kansas. In addition to his military activities, Montgomery also served in the Missouri legislature and was a member of the 1860 Republican state convention in Kansas. Along with John Brown, James H. Lane, and Charles Jennison, Montgomery was among the most prominent, yet controversial Free-State leaders in Kansas during the border conflicts of the 1850s.

Shortly after the beginning of the Civil War, Montgomery received a commission as colonel of the 3d Kansas Infantry. During the summer and fall of 1861, Montgomery's regiment was stationed at Fort Scott as part of a brigade, commanded by Lane, that guarded the Kansas border. In August 1861 his regiment skirmished with elements of Sterling Price's army that were on their way to capture Lexington, Missouri. In April 1862, Montgomery's regiment, which had never fully organized, was consolidated with another unit and renamed the 10th Kansas Infantry. It was stationed for a time at Fort Scott and conducted raids and scouts into Missouri and Indian Territory, while "gain[ing] a reputation for jayhawking or plundering."

Montgomery remained in Kansas until December 1862 when, after continued disputes between himself, Lane, and Jennison over the command of a newly organized black regiment, he left the state and traveled to Washington, D.C. After meetings with abolitionist George Stearns, Kansas senator Samuel Pomeroy, and President Lincoln in January 1863, Montgomery received authorization from the War Department to recruit, organize, and command an African-American regiment in the Department of the South. This unit, eventually known as the 2d South Carolina Colored Infantry, was organized in Beaufort and Hilton Head, South Carolina, during the spring of 1863, principally from the ex-slaves who had flocked to the Union-occupied coastal regions.

Montgomery's regiment took part in the March 1863 occupation of Jacksonville as well as several raids and skirmishes along the South Carolina, Georgia, and Florida coast. Most notorious of these was the June 1863 expedition to Darien, Georgia, when his troops looted and then burned the deserted town. Montgomery, according to the shocked Colonel Robert Gould Shaw, stated that "Southerners must be made to feel that this is a real war, and that they were to be swept away by the

hand of God, like the Jews of old." In his classic work *The Sable Arm*, historian Dudley Taylor Cornish described Montgomery as "A primitive patriarch uninhibited by any effete Eastern notions of the rules of civilized warfare, and his Old Testament kind of warfare was completely at odds with the Harvard tradition of fair play. To New England romantics, war was a kind of game, played according to definite rules. Montgomery, with fanatic realism, made his own rules."

By August 1863, Montgomery was placed in command of a brigade of Alfred Terry's division, consisting initially of the 54th Massachusetts and the 2d and 3d South Carolina Colored Infantry. He served with his brigade on Folly and Morris islands, South Carolina, until January 1864, when he was transferred to Hilton Head. In the 1864 Florida campaign, Montgomery led a small brigade composed of the 1st North Carolina Colored Infantry and the 54th Massachusetts. During the bloody 20 February 1864 battle of Olustee, Montgomery's brigade remained in reserve until late in the day, when Brigadier General Truman Seymour ordered them forward to stop a Confederate advance and gain time for the remainder of the Union forces to withdraw. "The colored troops went in grandly," a white veteran later reported, "and they fought like devils." During the retreat, the 54th served as part of the Union rear guard. Soldiers from the regiment gained fame when they manually dragged a trainload of wounded Union soldiers to prevent their capture by Confederate forces.

Olustee was the last major battle of Montgomery's career, although for a time he commanded a brigade of black troops in the District of Florida and again at Morris Island. He returned to Kansas later in 1864 and briefly led the 6th Kansas Militia, which saw service in October during Sterling Price's invasion of Missouri. After the war he farmed at Mound City and joined the First-Day Adventist Church. Montgomery preached throughout the state, but otherwise lived quietly until his death on 6 December 1871.

—*David J. Coles*

See also Kansas; Olustee, Battle of; United States Colored Troops.
For further reading:
Cornish, Dudley Taylor. *The Sable Arm: Negro Troops in the Union Army, 1861–1865* (1966).
Duncan, Russell, ed. *Blue-Eyed Child of Fortune: The Civil War Letters of Colonel Robert Gould Shaw* (1992).
Looby, Christopher, ed. *The Complete Civil War Journal and Selected Letters of Thomas Wentworth Higginson* (2000).

MOORE, ANDREW BARRY
(1807–1873)
Governor of Alabama

Born in Spartanburg, South Carolina, the son of Charles Moore and Jane Barry Moore, Andrew Moore moved as a child with his family to Alabama. He was educated in Alabama and read law there. After beginning his practice, he became active in Whig state politics. He served in the state legislature and was a Zachary Taylor elector in the presidential election of 1848. Moore served as a state judge in the 1850s. The disintegration of the Whig Party caused Moore to switch to the Democratic Party, and as a Democrat he was elected governor for the first of two two-year terms in 1857.

Early in 1860, Moore, in response to the John Brown raid on Harper's Ferry, began increasing defensive measures in Alabama. He encouraged the formation and drilling of local militia troops and urged the citizenry to constant vigilance. He also wrote to neighboring governors urging them to take similar measures and advocating greater cooperation between Southern states.

To Moore, as for many people in the Gulf states, the election of Abraham Lincoln to the presidency was the last straw. He called for a secession convention, but before secession had been accomplished he encouraged the seizure of federal property within the state. He also began preparations for sending a military force to seize Pensacola, Florida.

Still a strong proponent of Southern cooperation, Moore sent emissaries to other Southern states urging joint action and the formation of a Southern confederacy. After the secession of Alabama, he became a driving force behind the formation of the Confederate States of America. For the next year, Moore was tireless in his military preparations for the state and in raising military forces for the Confederacy. When he left office at the end of 1861, he began serving on the staff of incoming governor, John Shorter. In that capacity, Moore continued to work to strengthen the state.

At the end of the war, Moore was arrested by Union troops and held in confinement in Selma, Alabama, until he was transported to Fort Pulaski, Georgia, for imprisonment. He remained at Fort Pulaski with other high-ranking Confederates until November 1865. After his release, he resumed his law practice. He died in Marion, Alabama.

—*David S. Heidler and Jeanne T. Heidler*

See also Alabama.
For further reading:
Fleming, Walter Lynwood. *Civil War and Reconstruction in Alabama* (1905).
Yearns, W. Buck, ed. *The Confederate Governors* (1985).

MOORE, SAMUEL PRESTON
(1813–1889)
Confederate surgeon general

The highest-ranking Southern medical officer, Samuel Preston Moore was born in 1813 and received his education from the Medical School of South Carolina. In March 1835, the U.S. Army surgeon general appointed him an assistant surgeon (captain).

Between 1835 and 1845, Moore served on the frontier at several small military posts. Upon the invasion of Mexico in 1846, he took charge of the wounded on Brazos Island, Texas. In February 1847, he transferred to Camargo, Mexico, and headed the American General Hospital there. During this time, he met Jefferson Davis. He impressed Davis with his ability as an organizer and disciplinarian. Later assignments included West Point.

After appointment as the Confederate surgeon general on 30 July 1861, Moore faced a huge task, which he attacked with his usual authoritarian style. Some of the medical problems facing the Confederacy included recruitment and examination of new physicians, development of domestic pharmaceutical resources, establishment of a military evacuation and hospital system, and recruitment and training of hospital personnel.

To deal with the diversity of civilian medical training, Moore formed the Army Medical Board to test applicants. An associated issue, of particular interest today, was quality assurance. Moore showed his forward thinking in promulgating a circular stating: "Medical directors of hospitals will organize at each hospital station a board of medical officers, to be consulted by the surgeon…when an operation is deemed necessary;…no important operations will be performed without the sanction of this board." Another innovation was to enlist young men and assign them to attend classes at the Richmond Medical College. Upon graduation, they sat for the Army Medical Board's examination. This is remarkably similar to modern U.S. military medical education programs.

Moore fielded a medical corps of 3,000. With the implementation of the Northern blockade of Southern ports, medical supplies were on the contraband list and not exempted from the blockade. Moore commissioned several scientist-physicians to forage for natural plants to replace unobtainable medicines. With the ordinance bureau, he established an agency in London to purchase necessary supplies and ensure passage through the blockade. To disseminate medical information, General Moore organized the Association of Army and Navy Surgeons of the Confederate States. This organization, perhaps the first military medical organization, outlasted the war and its organizer. It merged with the Association of Military Surgeons of the United States in 1914 and still exists today. Moore also instituted a professional journal, *The Confederate States Medical and Surgical Journal*. It appeared monthly until Richmond fell.

Moore personally supervised by letters and directives the medical directors in the field armies, the chiefs of medical bureaus, and the hospital medical directors. He developed a reserve surgical corps of officers working at army hospitals in the rear. They could be quickly pulled for front-line combat service. This is similar to the system used in the army today for mobilization.

Moore designed and built the "hospital hut," a 32-bed ward that could be connected in groups of 45 or more to form a general hospital. Five of these general hospitals eventually dotted Richmond. The largest was Chimborazo, the largest military hospital ever built, which treated 76,000 patients in four years. Various women's organizations established private hospitals. Because of "lax practices," a law was passed requiring that Confederate soldiers be cared for only in hospitals directed by commissioned military officers with a rank not lower than captain. This led to the commissioning of a nurse, Captain Sally Louisa Tompkins, on 9 September 1861. Moore was the first surgeon general to commission and command a female officer. He was the first to recognize dentistry as an allied health profession and commissioned several dentists into the medical corps.

He made his last report to the secretary of war on 9 February 1865. It was in answer to a question about the remaining means to continue the war. In the midst of a failing Confederacy, after four long years of war, Moore reported: "The department has on hand a twelve months' supply…no fear need be entertained that the sick and the wounded of the army will suffer for the want of any of the essential articles."

The surgeon general's importance was illustrated upon the issuance of Confederate bonds. On 19 August 1861, the Confederacy issued the $100,000,000 produce loan. Surgeon General Moore's picture was on 1,093 issues of a $1,000 bond. The only other noncabinet officials depicted were Brigadier General John Henry Winder and General P. G. T. Beauregard.

The surgeon general left Richmond with President Davis but soon returned to take the oath of amnesty on 22 June 1865. Moore remained for the rest of his life in the former capital of the Confederacy, never practicing medicine again. He sat on the Richmond School Board as the chair of the Committee on Teachers and Schools. After completing one of his normal days in which he attended to arrangements for the upcoming high school commencement, he had a violent attack of coughing and died in the early hours of 31 May 1889. At his request, there were no flowers at his funeral, just a Confederate flag and his Confederate Veteran's badge. He was buried near his old commander in chief, Jefferson Davis, in Hollywood Cemetery in Richmond.

—*Warner D. Farr*

See also Davis, Jefferson; Medicine; Tompkins, Sally Louisa.

For further reading:
Burroughs, William Berrien. "A Lady Commissioned Captain in the Army of the Confederate States." *Southern Practitioner* (1909).
Cunningham, Horace Hendron. *Doctors in Gray: The Confederate Medical Service* (1958).
Franke, Norman H., and Laura Webb Stone. "A History of the Association of Medical Officers of the Army and Navy of the Confederacy." *Military Medicine* (1966).

Hume, Edgar Erskine. *The Golden Jubilee of the Association of Military Surgeons of the United States. A History of Its First Half-Century, 1891–1941* (1941).

Lewis, Samuel E. *Surgeon General Samuel Preston Moore and the Officers of the Medical Department of the Confederate States Army* (1911).

McIlwaine, H. R. "Master Surgeons of America. Samuel Preston Moore." *Surgery, Gynecology and Obstetrics* (1924).

Moore, Samuel Preston. "Address of the President of the Association of Medical Officers of the Confederate States Army and Navy." *Southern Practitioner* (1909).

Sharpe, William D. *Confederate States Medical and Surgical Journal* (1976).

Wiese, E. Robert. "Life and Times of Samuel Preston Moore, Surgeon General of the Confederate States of America." *Southern Medical Journal* (1930).

Williams, Carrington. "Samuel Preston Moore, Surgeon General of the Confederate States Army." *Virginia Medical Monthly* (1961).

MOORE, THOMAS OVERTON
(1804–1876)
Governor of Louisiana

The son of John Moore and Jean Overton Moore, Thomas Moore was born in Sampson County, North Carolina and educated locally. As a young man, he moved to Louisiana to run his uncle's sugar plantation. Able to acquire land over the next few years, Moore became a prominent sugar planter and turned his interests to state Democratic politics. He served in both houses of the state legislature in the late 1840s and 1850s, becoming over the years a strong advocate for states' rights.

In 1860 he became governor of Louisiana and through the summer and fall of 1860 used his office to campaign for the John Breckinridge ticket for president. Upon the election of Abraham Lincoln in November 1860, Moore vigorously advocated the secession of the state. Even before the secession convention acted, Moore had state forces seize federal installations and ordered that all federal property within Louisiana be turned over to state officials. In March 1861, before the outbreak of the war, Moore declared martial law in the southern parishes.

For the next year, Moore worked steadily to supply men, equipment, and supplies to the Confederate military. In spite of his best efforts, however, New Orleans fell in the spring of 1862, and Moore was forced to flee with the remainder of his government northward. He temporarily established a new capital at Opelousas before moving it to Shreveport. While the Union established a new state government in the south at New Orleans, the Confederate state government remained at Shreveport for the remainder of the war. Moore continued to govern the northern part of the state until his term expired in 1864.

At the end of the war, Moore left the state and made his way to Cuba rather than submit to arrest by Union authorities. After learning that he had been pardoned in 1866, he returned. Union forces had destroyed his plantation, so he spent the remainder of his life trying to rebuild his fortune. He died outside Alexandria, Louisiana.

—*David S. Heidler and Jeanne T. Heidler*

See also Louisiana; New Orleans.

For further reading:

Bragg, Jefferson Davis. *Louisiana in the Confederacy* (1941).

Moore, Claude Hunter. *Thomas Overton Moore: A Confederate Governor* (1960).

Moore, Thomas Overton. *Thomas O. Moore Papers, 1832–1865, Rapides Parish, Louisiana* (1989).

Odom, Van D. "The Political Career of Thomas Overton Moore, Secession Governor of Louisiana" (M.A. thesis, 1942).

MOOREFIELD, WEST VIRGINIA, BATTLE OF
(7 August 1864)

During General Jubal A. Early's second invasion of Maryland in 1864, Early was determined to exact retribution from the North for the destruction of parts of the town of Lynchburg and of the Virginia Military Academy at Lexington, Virginia, wrought by Union general David Hunter during the latter's sojourn there in June of that year. Early's target was Chambersburg, Pennsylvania, in the southern part of that state. For this mission the general picked Brigadier General John McCausland. The raiding force was to consist of McCausland's and General Bradley Johnson's cavalry brigades.

McCausland was given his orders for the raid on 28 July; he moved out the next day. McCausland and Johnson were chosen due to their apparent ability shown in Early's previous operations in the Shenandoah Valley and during his first incursion into Maryland. The performance of the cavalry during this operation would, in Early's eyes, confirm the worth of his mounted arm. It had not done its part, as far as Early was concerned, up to this time.

The Confederates occupied Chambersburg on 30 July. Before they left, the Rebels fired the town, causing immense damage to private and public property. Union general William Averell's cavalry division was at Greencastle, a dozen miles from Chambersburg, but the raiders were allowed to leave and move twenty-three miles to the west without any interference from Averell. It was not until near dark that the Federals entered Chambersburg.

From McConnellsburg, Pennsylvania, McCausland and Johnson moved to Hancock, Maryland. Their stay was cut short when rebel scouts reported that Averell's blue column was close by and coming on fast. The Confederates then rode to Cumberland, Maryland, reaching that vicinity on 1 August. Near Cumberland the raiders met a Union force of less than two infantry regiments and a battery of artillery determined to stop

the Confederate cavalry from destroying the railroad equipment located in the area.

But the Union defenders need not have worried about an enemy attack; McCausland at this point just wanted to find a crossing over the Potomac River in order to escape to Virginia. After a spirited six-hour battle, known as the battle of Green Spring Run Depot, on 2 August against a few scattered Federal units and defenders at a blockhouse guarding the ford that was to be used, the Rebels were able to cross the river. They camped at Springfield that night.

The next day McCausland decided to continue his operations by seeking out Federal railway equipment to eliminate. He was under the impression that Averell had given up the chase and was no closer than Hancock. The result was the battle of New Creek on 4 August.

New Creek was a strongly Union-held station along the rail line between Harper's Ferry and Parkersburg, West Virginia. The Confederate attack against the enemy position failed, and the Confederate cavalry retired to Moorefield, West Virginia, reaching it on the 5th. Meanwhile, Averell, who had spent the last four days refitting at Hancock, marched to Springfield on the 5th.

On the 6th, the Union cavalry leader received reports that the raiders were at Moorefield, almost thirty miles south of his position. Averell hoped to catch the enemy there and he formulated his plan of attack. He would lead the better part of his force directly to Moorefield along the main road leading to that place; a detachment would move to the east of the town and attack when they heard Averell initiate his assault from the north. The morning of 7 August saw the two Federal columns move toward their objective.

Twelve miles away the Confederates were camped and unaware of the threat that was approaching. McCausland's brigade was bivouacked about a mile north of Moorefield, while Johnson's was about a mile to the rear. A Southern partisan member arrived in town during the night of 6–7 August and warned that Federal cavalry was headed for Moorefield, but after three hours of standing at the alert, the Rebels concluded that the story was false and returned to bed.

The early morning of 7 August was wet, dark, and misty, and out of the mist and dark Averell came trotting into the fields surrounding Johnson's camp. Upon seeing the Rebel encampment, he ordered his men to charge. The Confederates were taken completely by surprise, many being asleep when the Federals came. As the enemy rolled over them, Southern troopers on foot and on horseback tried to make their escape up the road to Moorefield. The attempt quickly turned into a rout. The 8th Virginia almost withdrew in good order but was ridden down by a Union brigade.

By now the men of McCausland's unit knew that their compatriots to the south were under attack, but with Johnson's men streaming through their camp, and no officers able to organize a defense, they could not stop the Union attackers. Averell's regiments rushed the river crossing of the South Branch of the Potomac, which separated the two Confederate camps. Once across, the Federals scattered the confused and dispersed men of McCausland's brigade. Soon the Confederate cavalry was splintered into fragments and was panic-stricken, running for the surrounding mountains. McCausland and Johnson were able to escape in the confusion of the rout.

Averell pushed elements of his forces along the two main roads leading out of Moorefield, hoping to catch as many of the fleeing enemy as possible. But the rebels were too scattered and too fast to be caught, and Averell stopped the pursuit. Averell had taken 420 prisoners, four enemy artillery pieces, three battle flags, and more than 400 horses and their equipage. The Union cavalry lost nine killed and thirty-two wounded.

The encounter at Moorefield greatly weakened Early's cavalry force, both in numbers and in its confidence to meet the enemy in battle. The fight also strengthened Early's opinion that his mounted arm was unfit and unreliable. He never fully relied on it for battle or even intelligence gathering again.

—*Arnold D. Blumberg*

See also Averell, William Woods; McCausland, John.
For further reading:
Bennette, J. Kelly. *Diary and Letters*. Southern Historical Collection, University of North Carolina Library.
Dickinson, Jack L. *8th Virginia Cavalry* (1986).
Phillips, David L. *Tiger John: The Rebel Who Burned Chambersburg* (1993).

MORGAN, EDWIN DENISON
(1811–1883)
Governor of New York, U.S. senator, and Union general

Born to Jasper Morgan and Catherine Copp Avery Morgan in Washington, Massachusetts, Edwin Denison Morgan moved with his family when he was a child to Windsor, Connecticut. Educated locally, Morgan at an early age decided on a career in business. First working with his uncle and then moving to New York City and going into business for himself, Morgan by the 1850s had become one of the city's most important merchants and bankers.

During Morgan's early years in New York, he had also become interested in local and eventually state and national politics. A confirmed, moderate Whig, Morgan served as president of the city board of assistant aldermen and two terms in the state senate. Switching to the Republican Party and becoming chairman of the Republican National Committee in 1856, Morgan

successfully ran for governor in 1858 and was reelected in 1860.

As New York's first wartime governor, Morgan devoted virtually all of his time to aiding the war effort. Morgan corresponded frequently with Abraham Lincoln's first secretary of war, Simon Cameron, and his second, Edwin Stanton, making recommendations on a variety of ways to raise more troops and to defend the coastline. At one point his enthusiasm somewhat angered Cameron when the secretary of war discovered that Morgan was making similar suggestions to Secretary of State William Henry Seward. Morgan argued early that, for him to fulfill adequately his military duties to raise troops in New York, the state needed to be designated a military department with him at its head. To aid him in his initial efforts to raise and organize troops, Washington dispatched Lieutenant Colonel Erasmus Keyes to serve as a military aide to the governor. In September 1861, seeing the wisdom of giving the governor greater military authority and not wanting to offend such an important supporter of the war effort, Lincoln created the Department of New York and appointed Morgan its commander at the rank of major general.

Morgan used his new power judiciously, working tirelessly to raise, equip, and arm troops. During his two years as New York's wartime governor, he sent 223,000 men to fight for the Union army. He was so successful that General George B. McClellan wrote directly to Morgan from the Peninsula campaign requesting more troops be raised in New York.

Morgan declined to run for a third term, and at the end of his second, he resigned his major general's commission. Shortly thereafter, he was chosen by the New York legislature as one of the state's U.S. senators. He remained in that seat until 1869. During his time in the senate, Morgan was a friend of the Lincoln administration but less so of Lincoln's successor, Andrew Johnson. While considered a moderate Republican, Morgan voted for Johnson's conviction in the impeachment trial in 1867.

Morgan was defeated for reelection in 1869 and returned to his business activities in New York. Not losing his interest in politics, Morgan headed the Republican National Committee from 1872 to 1876. In the early 1880s, President Chester Arthur nominated Morgan as secretary of the treasury, but Morgan declined the appointment. Morgan spent much of his later life dedicated to various philanthropic causes, donating large sums of money to educational institutions and medical facilities. He died in New York on 14 February 1883.

—*David S. Heidler and Jeanne T. Heidler*

For further reading:
New York State Library Annual Report. *The Governor Edwin D. Morgan Papers* (1943).
Rawley, James A. *Edwin D. Morgan, 1811–1883; Merchant in Politics* (1955).

MORGAN, GEORGE WASHINGTON
(1820–1893)
Union general

Born to Thomas Morgan and Katherine Duane Morgan in Washington County, Pennsylvania, George Washington Morgan was educated at Washington College before leaving school as a teenager to fight for Texas independence. After rising to the rank of captain in the Texas army and after the fighting had ended, he returned to Pennsylvania, from where he received an appointment to the U.S. Military Academy. He remained at the academy only a little over a year.

Morgan then moved to Ohio, where he studied law. He served as a prosecutor for a short time before the outbreak of the Mexican-American War. That conflict inspired him to raise a company, his own experiences in Texas no doubt helping to inspire his recruits. He was commissioned a captain but was shortly promoted to colonel of volunteers and fought with Zachary Taylor in northern Mexico. Transferred to Winfield Scott's army for the Mexico City campaign, Morgan was wounded in the approach to the Mexican capital. He received a brevet promotion to brigadier general for his actions in the war.

After the Mexican-American War, Morgan returned to Ohio to practice law. In 1856, his former commander, Franklin Pierce, appointed Morgan U.S. consul to Marseilles. President James Buchanan in 1858 appointed him minister to Portugal. Morgan held that diplomatic post until the commencement of the Civil War.

Returning to the United States, Morgan accepted a commission as brigadier general of volunteers in November 1861. In March 1862 Morgan was sent to Don Carlos Buell's Army of the Ohio to command the 7th Division. He was immediately dispatched to take control of Cumberland Gap. Morgan outnumbered the Confederate defenders about 8,000 to 4,000, so after threatening the Southerners' communication lines, he was able to force their evacuation and occupy the gap on 18 June 1862.

During the summer of 1862, Morgan skirmished frequently with Confederates, finding himself increasing isolated from other Federal positions. In July 1862 he tried to resign his position, primarily due to the serious illness of his wife, but her recovery caused him to reconsider. In August, however, his position became increasingly untenable, with Edmund Kirby Smith attempting to cut him off completely from any avenue of retreat. By September his situation was growing desperate, and on the morning of 14 September he held a council of war of his senior officers who recommended evacuation of the position. Morgan was able to accomplish his retreat with minimal losses of men or supplies, and his decision to leave his position was upheld by the new commander of the Army of the Ohio, Major General Horatio G. Wright. In spite of Wright's endorsement of his actions, Morgan detected some stigma attached to him because of the retreat and became increasingly angry over the next months that the War Department refused officially to vindicate him.

Sent to serve under William T. Sherman in the Vicksburg campaign, Morgan commanded a division in the attempted penetration of Confederate lines at Chickasaw Bluffs. Shortly after the battle, relations between Sherman and Morgan became somewhat strained when it became apparent that Sherman believed that Morgan had not performed well in the battle.

On 4 January 1863, Morgan was given command of a corps in John A. McClernand's new Army of the Mississippi. Sherman was given command of the other corps, and both fought more or less as equals in McClernand's Arkansas Post campaign.

When McClernand's force was brought under the control of Ulysses S. Grant for the final push against Vicksburg, Morgan was given command of a division. By spring of 1863 his health had begun to deteriorate and his anger began to grow over his dispute with Sherman and his failure to gain complete vindication for the evacuation of Cumberland Gap. Further, the employment of African-American soldiers, a policy of which he strongly disapproved, added to his dissatisfaction with military service. As a result of all of these factors, Morgan resigned his commission in June 1863.

Returning to Ohio, Morgan became increasingly involved in Democratic politics and was a strong supporter of George B. McClellan for president in 1864. Morgan failed in an attempt to win the Ohio governor's chair in 1865, but the following year he was elected to Congress. In the House of Representatives, Morgan strongly opposed congressional Reconstruction. He was also a vigorous supporter of President Andrew Johnson during his impeachment ordeal. Defeated for reelection in 1868, Morgan won election again in 1870 and served two terms. He remained active in the Democratic Party for the remainder of his life. He died on 26 July 1893 at Fort Monroe, Virginia, and was returned to Ohio for burial.

—*David S. Heidler and Jeanne T. Heidler*

See also Arkansas Post, Battle of; Chickasaw Bluffs, Battle of.
For further reading:
Morgan, George Washington. *Reconstruction of Georgia* (1869).
Smith, Gene. *High Crimes and Misdemeanors: The Impeachment and Trial of Andrew Johnson* (1976).

MORGAN, J. PIERPONT
(1837–1913)
Financier

John Pierpont Morgan was the son of Junius Spencer Morgan, an American banker who worked in London after 1854 attempting to establish a world-

class private bank. Pierpont's education, after graduation in 1854 from the prestigious English High School in Boston, included a period at Institut Sillig in Switzerland to improve his French and at the University of Göttingen to become fluent in German. Junius then arranged for Pierpont to become a clerk in Duncan, Sherman & Co. in New York. He arrived in time to witness firsthand the Panic of 1857.

The Civil War greatly diminished trade between the United States and Britain, and that trade was the mainstay of the family's profits before the war. While Junius cultivated international connections, Pierpont formed J. Pierpont Morgan & Co. in New York in 1861, trading in foreign exchange and gold. On at least two occasions, he engaged in speculations taking advantage of the difficulties of the Union.

In the Hall Carbine Affair, Pierpont's culpability is debatable. In August 1861 he lent $20,000 to lawyer Simon Stevens of New York. Stevens in turn made partial payment to an arms dealer (Arthur M. Eastman) for purchase of 5,000 Hall carbines at $11.50 each. Eastman had previously bought the unused but obsolete carbines from the Department of War for $3.50 each. Before receiving the guns from Eastman, Stevens arranged for resale to General John Frémont, commander of the Department of the West, at $22 each. Stevens's contract with Pierpont gave the latter title to the carbines and responsibility for having them rifled, thus improving the guns' range and accuracy. When Frémont paid for the first 2,500 carbines, Pierpont deducted the loan's cost, shipping costs, and a commission. He gave the rest of the money to Stevens's bankers. Congress investigated the administration of the War Department, including the Hall Carbine Affair. At no time did the investigators condemn Pierpont because no evidence suggested that he had been aware of Stevens's resale contract at the time of the loan. However, the government undoubtedly bought its own carbines at a price well above the cost of rifling in a transaction Pierpont financed.

The second occasion involved trade in gold. Although the U.S. government suspended specie payments in 1861, gold was still used to pay interest on government bonds and settle international accounts. Gold prices fluctuated with the fortunes of Union armies, falling whenever they did well. After the summer 1863 victories, Pierpont joined Edward B. Ketchum in buying gold slowly and quietly. They shipped $1.15 million to England in October, surprising many traders. The price of gold immediately rose, which allowed the two to sell the remainder they had for a profit of about $132,000. (*The New York Times* mistakenly reported shipment of $2.3 million and profit of $160,000.) The surprise this operation caused among financiers must have been a result of the small size and newness of J.

Pierpont Morgan & Co., since other well-known banks executed similar transactions. However, there is little doubt that Pierpont was more interested in the war as a source of profit than as a chance for service. When he was drafted, he hired a substitute for $300.

Wishing to strengthen his international connections, Junius convinced Pierpont to become a partner in Dabney, Morgan & Co. in 1864. Later, in 1871, Junius encouraged Pierpont to join Drexel & Co. (Philadelphia), Drexel, Morgan & Co. (New York), and Drexel, Harjes & Co. (Paris). Until the organization of Drexel, Morgan, Pierpont was not a leading banker in New York, and not until the 1890s did Pierpont Morgan become a nationally known figure. After his father's death in 1890 and Tony Drexel's death in 1893, Pierpont reorganized the New York and London houses, which became J. P. Morgan & Co. and Morgan, Grenfell & Co., respectively. He floated an issue of $65 million of U.S. government bonds in 1895, and he organized U.S. Steel and issued its $1.1 billion in securities in 1901. After 1885 he participated in six railroad reorganizations. He also played a pivotal role in halting the Panic of 1907. Because of his increasing influence on Wall Street, Morgan became the primary suspect in the money trust investigation conducted by a House Banking and Currency Subcommittee in 1912–1913. The inquiry proved conclusively that Pierpont was influential in U.S. finance, but did not prove that his actions had damaged the U.S. economy.

Always a victim of frail health, Pierpont died in 1913 while abroad. Even after donating millions of dollars to various causes over the years, he left an estate of approximately $118 million. His wife (Francis Louise Tracy), one son, and three daughters survived him.

—*Sue C. Patrick*

For further reading:
Carosso, Vincent P. *The Morgans: Private International Bankers, 1854–1913* (1987).
Chernow, Ron. *The House of Morgan: An American Banking Dynasty and the Rise of Modern Finance* (1990).
Satterlee, Herbert L. *J. Pierpont Morgan: An Intimate Portrait* (1939; reprint, 1975).

MORGAN, JAMES DADA
(1810–1896)
Union general

James Dada Morgan was born in Boston, Massachusetts, on 1 August 1810. The son of a sea captain and trader, James Morgan went on his first sailing cruise around the age of twenty. On this voyage, the crew mutinied and burned the ship. Morgan and several companions were forced to spend two weeks in a small boat before reaching the shores of South America. Morgan made his way back to Boston and remained in the city until 1834. In that year, Morgan moved to Quincy, Illinois, and opened a mercantile business. He soon married Jane Strachan and had two sons. Morgan became interested in the local militia, and he soon helped to form two militia companies. He led one mounted rifle company (the "Quincy Riflemen") in the Mormon War of 1844–1845.

With the outbreak of the Mexican-American War, Morgan's rifle company became Company G, 1st Illinois Volunteers, with Morgan as captain. The regiment was soon fighting with Major General Zachary Taylor's army in northern Mexico. Morgan was promoted to major for his gallantry during the battle of Buena Vista, Mexico. At the end of the conflict, Morgan returned to his business interests in Quincy, Illinois, but unfortunately his wife died in 1855.

With the coming of the Civil War, Morgan again helped to raise another unit for state service. This time, the unit was the 10th Illinois Volunteers, and Morgan became its colonel by the year's end. By February 1862, Colonel Morgan was leading a brigade in Major General John Pope's forces during the engagement at Island No. 10, Missouri. On 17 July 1862, Colonel Morgan was promoted to brigadier general for meritorious services at the battles of New Madrid, Missouri, and Corinth, Mississippi. General Morgan's brigade was assigned to the center wing of the Army of the Cumberland, but it did not participate in the battle of Stones River in Tennessee.

Before the Tullahoma campaign of 1863, General Morgan's brigade was assigned to the reserve corps of the Army of the Cumberland. In this assignment, General Morgan's brigade guarded the Federal supply lines through Bridgeport, Alabama, during the battle of Chickamauga, Georgia, in September 1863. In October 1863, General Morgan's brigade was assigned as the 1st Brigade of Brigadier General Jefferson C. Davis's 2d Division, XIV Army Corps. Through the Chattanooga campaign in November 1863, General Morgan's brigade served with this division as it supported Major General William T. Sherman's advance on Tunnel Hill, and the expedition to relieve Knoxville, Tennessee, in December 1863.

During the Atlanta campaign in 1864, General Morgan's 1st Brigade continued to serve with XIV Corps at engagements such as Rocky Face and in a supporting role at the ill-fated assault at Kennesaw Mountain, Georgia, on 27 June 1864. With the promotion of General Davis to the command of XIV Corps, General Morgan was advanced to the command of the 2d Division in August 1864. On 1 September 1864, General Morgan's division participated in the successful assault on William J. Hardee's corps during the battle of Jonesboro, Georgia.

General Morgan and his division continued to play

an active role in the Savannah campaign (Sherman's March to the Sea) and the first stages of the Carolinas campaign from Savannah, Georgia, to Fayetteville, North Carolina, on 8 March 1865. At the battle of Averasboro, North Carolina, on 16 March 1865, General Morgan's division was unsuccessful in attempting to turn the Confederates' third defensive line. Two days later, on 18 March, General Morgan's division was instrumental in clearing away Confederate cavalry from the advance of the Army of Georgia (left wing). The next day, General Morgan advanced his division in support of the 1st Division, XIV Corps along the Goldsboro Road. In midafternoon on 19 March 1865, General Joseph E. Johnston launched a surprise assault on the Union line, and General Morgan's division became nearly surrounded on three sides by elements of two Confederate corps. Despite having to fight on both sides of his works, General Morgan's division successfully maintained its position and enabled the Army of Georgia to restore its lines by nightfall. For this successful action, General Morgan was awarded a brevet promotion to major general. General Morgan remained with the army until he was mustered out on 24 August 1865.

General Morgan returned to Quincy, Illinois, and took up banking as a profession. He remarried on 14 June 1869 to Harriet Evans. He was appointed as treasurer of the Illinois Soldiers and Sailors Home in 1887. He also served as vice president of the Society of the Army of the Cumberland. General Morgan died on 12 September 1896 in Quincy and was buried in Woodland Cemetery.

—*William H. Brown*

See also Atlanta Campaign; Averasboro, Battle of; Carolinas Campaign; Chattanooga Campaign; Goldsboro, North Carolina; Island No. 10, Battle of; Sherman's March to the Sea.

For further reading:

Cannan, John. *The Atlanta Campaign, May–November, 1864* (1991).

Castel, Albert. *Decision in the West: the Atlanta Campaign of 1864* (1992).

Daniel, Larry J. and Lynn N. Bock. *Island No. 10: Struggle for the Mississippi Valley* (1996).

Glatthaar, Joseph T. *The March to the Sea and Beyond: Sherman's Troops in the Savannah and Carolinas Campaigns* (1985).

McDonough, James L. *Chattanooga—A Death Grip on the Confederacy* (1984).

MORGAN, JOHN HUNT
(1825–1864)
Confederate general

John Hunt Morgan was born in Huntsville, Alabama, on 1 June 1825 and spent his childhood near Lexington, Kentucky. He briefly attended Transylvania University before being ejected for boisterous behavior. He joined the 1st Kentucky Cavalry as a lieutenant, and in this capacity he fought in the Mexican-American War under General Zachary Taylor and distinguished himself at Buena Vista in 1847. After that war, Morgan returned to Kentucky and established himself as a successful hemp manufacturer with deep economic links to the South. He also maintained his military connections by equipping a militia company, the "Lexington Rifles," at his own expense in 1857. Despite Kentucky's neutrality in the early days of the Civil War, Morgan was an unabashed Southern sympathizer, and he openly flew the Confederate flag from his factory. He moved south in the fall of 1861 when his state remained with the Union, and that October he took his oath to the Confederacy as a cavalry captain.

In time, Morgan became revered as the "Thunderbolt of the Confederacy" and personified in the minds of contemporaries the romantic ideal of Southern cavalry. He rose to colonel in April 1862 and commanded a squadron during the bloody battle of Shiloh. The slaughter apparently made an indelible impression on Morgan; hereafter he sought to avoid outright combat in favor of stealth, mobility, and surprise. For this reason his columns always traveled light, living off the land. He also believed that firepower was intrinsically superior to shock action and consequently discarded cavalry sabers in favor of infantry rifles and Colt repeating pistols. Most of his command fought on foot as mounted infantry.

Shortly after Shiloh, Morgan was attached to Joseph Wheeler's division in the army of General Braxton Bragg. Throughout the summer and fall of 1862, Morgan made headlines in the United States and the Confederacy by commencing his trademark, lightning raids behind Union lines. On 4 July 1862, he began a 1,000-mile trek across Kentucky, burning supplies, cutting railroads and telegraph lines, and greatly harrying Northern lines of communication. For a loss of 100 of his men, Morgan took 1,200 prisoners and delayed the advance of General Don C. Buell's army by several weeks. Buell countered by dispatching 700 troopers under General Richard W. Johnson to pursue the marauders. Johnson cornered Morgan near Gallatin, Tennessee, on 21 August 1862, but in the ensuing scrape, Johnson was captured and his men scattered.

By October 1862, Morgan had again penetrated Union lines and briefly held his hometown of Lexington with 1,800 men. Two months later, a speedy foray against Hartsville, Tennessee, netted another 1,700 prisoners and a promotion to brigadier general. Moreover, Morgan's actions greatly hindered the advance of General William S. Rosecrans by several weeks, relieving pressure on the badly outnumbered Bragg. Morgan's success, and the apparent ease with which he achieved it, sent shock waves throughout the Northern press. An exasperated

John H. Morgan (*Library of Congress*)

President Abraham Lincoln once berated his military commanders, exclaiming "They are having a stampede in Kentucky. Please look at it." By December 1862, no less than 20,000 sorely needed Union combat troops had been diverted from field operations to guard communications and supply lines. This fact, and not his celebrated raids, was Morgan's greatest military accomplishment.

In July 1863, the deteriorating strategic condition of the Confederacy induced Morgan to initiate one of the Civil War's wildest rides. Against Bragg's explicit orders, he crossed the Ohio River with 2,400 men and rode 1,100 miles across the length of southern Indiana and Ohio. For three weeks his troopers raided local defenses and panicked the populations of two states. The Confederates also baffled their pursuers by covering 50 miles and spending up to 20 hours in the saddle per day. Morgan's command rode full tilt through Cincinnati's suburbs before Union cavalry under General Edward H. Hobson finally cornered him at Buffington Island in the Ohio River. On 19 July 1862 the raiders were defeated and Morgan himself was captured at Salineville one week later. He and most of his officers were then summarily sent to the Ohio State Penitentiary in Columbus, where they were treated like common criminals. However, on 26 November 1863, Morgan staged a spectacular escape and returned to Confederate lines.

In 1864 Morgan gained appointment as head of the Department of Southwestern Virginia. Although subsequent raids continued to make headlines, they did little to improve Confederate fortunes in Tennessee or elsewhere. Union forces had also made great strides in their cavalry and intelligence-gathering capabilities and could offer stauncher resistance. Moreover, discipline and leadership among Morgan's troops had deteriorated, and there were several incidents of plundering. Complaints about looting resulted in an investigation of Morgan, and calls were made for removing him from command. Nonetheless, he elected to mount one final raid against Knoxville, Tennessee, long a bastion of Union sympathizers. After several successful skirmishes, Morgan encamped his men at nearby Greeneville. A body of Union cavalry under General Alvin C. Gilem was alerted to his presence and launched a surprise attack of their own. On 3 September 1864, Morgan was shot and killed by a Union private who had previously served under him. By the time of his death, Morgan's raids were of questionable use to the Confederacy, but Morgan still ranks with John S. Mosby and Nathan Bedford Forrest as a symbol of Southern military prowess.

—*John C. Fredriksen*

See also Cavalry, C.S.A.; Morgan's Raids.
For further reading:
Brewer, James D. *The Raiders of 1862* (1997).
Ramage, James. *Rebel Raider: The Life of John Hunt Morgan* (1986).
Southworth, Samuel A., ed. *Great Raids in History: From Drake to Desert One* (1997).

MORGAN'S RAIDS

Beginning in July 1862, Confederate cavalry officer John Hunt Morgan led a series of cavalry raids into Northern and Northern-held territory, disrupting Union communications and capturing much-needed supplies for the Confederacy.

Morgan's First Raid (4 July–1 August 1862) — In response to Union major general Don Carlos Buell's move toward Chattanooga, Tennessee, in the summer of 1862, Colonel John Hunt Morgan took two cavalry regiments, totaling 867 men, from Knoxville, Tennessee, on 4 July 1862 into Kentucky. On 9 July he captured approximately 400 Union cavalrymen at Tomkinsville, Kentucky, by entering the town from two sides at about dawn. The skirmish lasted only about ten minutes. The following day Morgan took a supply depot at Glasgow, Kentucky. From Glasgow he issued a proclamation to the people of Kentucky, calling for them to join the Confederate cause. He had many copies of the proclamation printed and posted in the towns he passed through.

After fighting his way across the Rolling Fork River, on 11 July Morgan captured more supplies and another small garrison at Lebanon, Kentucky. The day after leaving Lebanon, Morgan and his men entered Harrodsburg, Kentucky, where the citizens seemed to welcome them. Leaving Harrodsburg, Morgan's raiders made their way toward the Kentucky capital at Frankfort, stopping at Lawrenceburg on 14 July. Thus far, Morgan and his men had been able to supply themselves with plenty of guns, ammunition, and horses.

At Lawrenceburg, Morgan learned that Union forces were gathering to stop him. He managed to deceive the converging units by sending misleading telegrams to several of the surrounding towns. As a result he was able to move to Georgetown, Kentucky, and give his men a much needed rest. From Georgetown he took a circuitous route out of the state by attacking the Federal garrison at Cynthiana on 18 July, capturing 400 prisoners, and then moving to Richmond, Kentucky, and reentering Tennessee near Sparta on 1 August 1862. During the raid he had captured more than 1,200 Union prisoners, whom he had paroled because of his need for mobility. He suffered approximately 100 casualties during the raid.

Morgan's Second Raid (18 October–1 November 1862) — By September 1862, Morgan commanded a brigade of cavalry under the overall command of Lieutenant General Edmund Kirby Smith. After operating in Tennessee during August 1862 while Kirby Smith moved into Kentucky in coordination with General Braxton Bragg's invasion of the state, Morgan and his men were summoned to Lexington, Kentucky, to join with Kirby Smith in early September.

After spending about a month in his home state, Morgan screened Kirby Smith's retreat from Lexington. Once he was no longer needed, Morgan asked to be allowed to stage a raid behind Union lines in Kentucky in order to slow Union movement back into Tennessee. Given permission, he set out with about 1,800 men on 18 October 1862. Morgan returned to Lexington, which he captured on 19 October, taking about 300 prisoners. From Lexington, he rode to Versailles, Bardstown (where he destroyed a Union wagon train), and Elizabethtown. At that point Morgan and his men spent most of their time destroying railroad track. That task accomplished, he led his men to Leitchfield and then Hopkinsville, arriving at Springfield, Tennessee, on 1 November 1862.

Morgan's Third Raid (21 December 1862–1 January 1863) — Having been promoted to brigadier general, John Hunt Morgan had command in December 1862 of a cavalry division consisting of two brigades under Colonel Basil Wilson Duke and Colonel Adam R. Johnson and totaling more than 3,000 men. In anticipation of the Stones River campaign in which Union major general William Starke Rosecrans threatened Confederate general Braxton Bragg's position at

Murfreesboro, Tennessee, Morgan was given permission to take his division into Kentucky to threaten Rosecrans's supply and communication lines.

Morgan departed from Alexandria, Tennessee, on 21 December 1862. He skirmished with a Federal detachment at Glasgow, Kentucky, on Christmas Eve and spent Christmas night outside of Hammondsville, Kentucky. Morgan had married only eleven days before. He moved north toward Munfordville, Kentucky, destroying railroad track and bridges of the Louisville & Nashville Railroad along the way. On 27 December, Morgan's raiders attacked the Federal garrison of 600 men at Elizabethtown, Kentucky. The Union force surrendered. Morgan and his men then concentrated on destroying the railroad trestle bridges between Elizabethtown and Louisville.

Morgan and his men then moved to Bardstown and Springfield, Kentucky. At Springfield, Morgan learned that there was a major Union force of as many as 8,000 men waiting in his path at Lebanon, Kentucky. He moved around the town on the night of 30 December, entering Columbia, Tennessee, on 1 January 1863. On this raid Morgan had suffered twenty-six casualties and destroyed several million dollars worth of Federal property. For his actions he was given the thanks of the Confederate Congress.

Morgan's Ohio Raid (2–26 July 1863) — Perhaps Brigadier General John Hunt Morgan's most famous raid, in this the last of his major raids, Morgan, contrary to orders from General Braxton Bragg, crossed the Ohio River into Indiana and Ohio.

Morgan left Tennessee on 2 July 1863 with about 2,460 men divided into two brigades under Duke and Johnson. The purpose of this raid was to hamper Rosecrans's movement toward Chattanooga. On 4 July, Morgan fought Federal cavalry at a crossing of the Green River. From the very beginning, this raid did not start as smoothly as the others. Morgan suffered heavy casualties at Green River and was forced to disengage to cross the river at another point.

On 5 July, Morgan defeated a Federal garrison at Lebanon, Kentucky, capturing several hundred Union soldiers. Although the raiders also captured much-needed supplies, the action had not been without cost. The Federal regulars put up a stiff fight that cost Morgan many casualties. Worst of all for Morgan was the death of his younger brother Tom.

The following day Morgan and his men arrived at Bardstown, and from there they moved toward the Ohio River. Morgan sent several companies in different directions to make it appear that he was not headed for the river. He then sent men ahead to Brandenburg to steal the steamboats necessary to make the crossing. All of his men rendezvoused at Brandenburg on 8 July and began

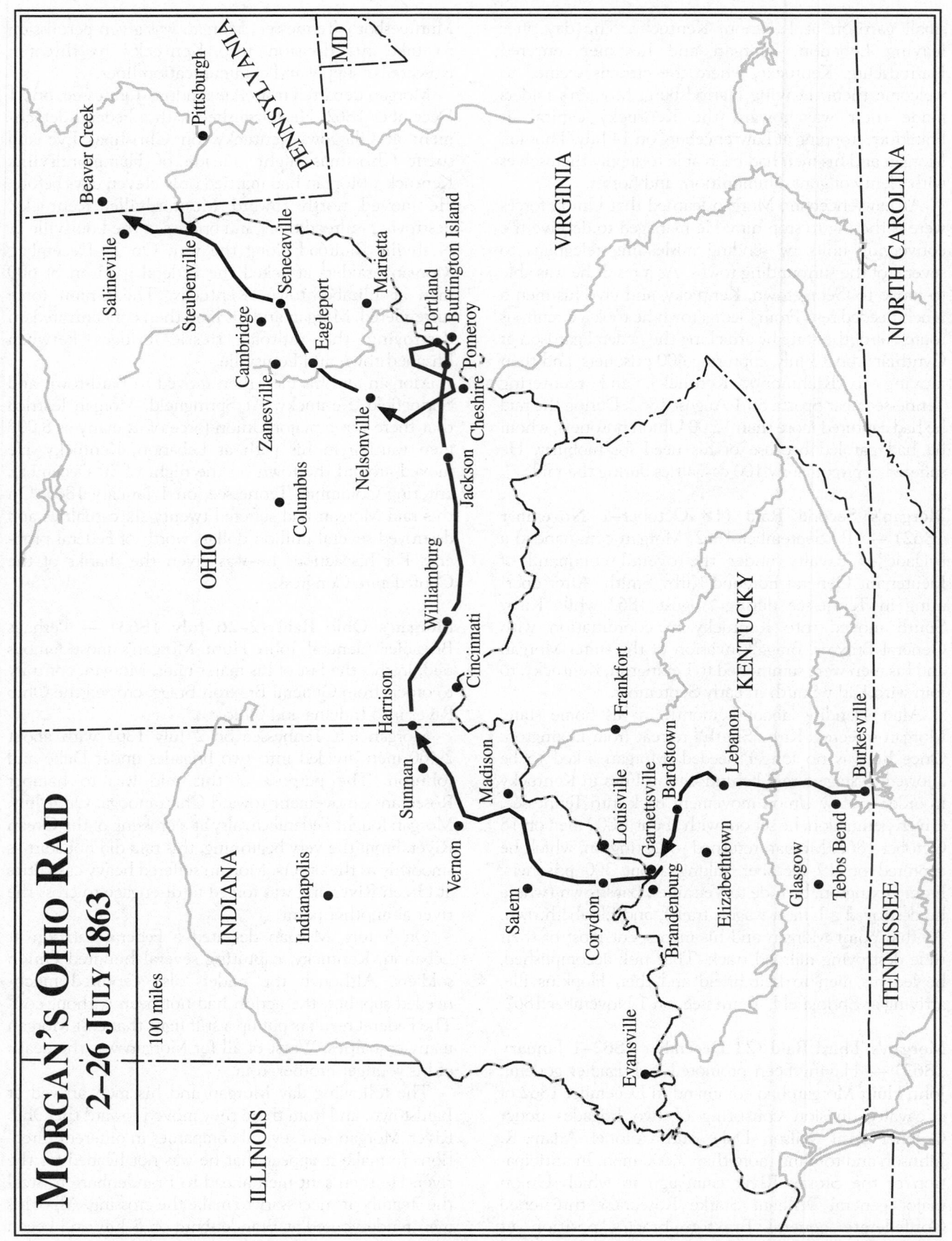

MORGAN'S OHIO RAID
2–26 JULY 1863

100 miles

the crossing. After running off some Home Guard militia with his artillery, Morgan crossed the river successfully and destroyed the boats after reaching the other side.

Now on Indiana soil, Morgan and his men caused a stir through southern Indiana and also Ohio. Home Guards were activated and regulars rushed to those states. Most citizens, fed by the sensational press reports, were convinced that Morgan's raid was part of some Copperhead conspiracy. As Morgan and his men moved east through Indiana, they did little to calm the concerns of the citizens as they looted through the towns and stole whatever horses they could find. On the other hand, Morgan insisted that his men do no physical harm to civilians.

After clashing with Home Guards along the way, Morgan stopped for a brief rest at Lexington, Indiana, where he was almost captured. On 13 July, he and his men crossed into Ohio, stopping briefly at Harrison, and then moved toward an alarmed Cincinnati. By then Morgan was in a hurry. He knew that Union cavalry was in hot pursuit, and as a result, but unknown to the citizens, Cincinnati was in no danger. Morgan skirted around the city and headed for Williamsburg, Ohio, and then Pomeroy on 18 July. By then his men were exhausted, having for the last week been in the saddle twenty-one hours a day.

Outside Pomeroy, Morgan faced not only Home Guard but also regulars guarding the fords at Buffington. Arriving at night, Morgan decided to wait till morning to try to force his way across. While many of the defenders were gone the next day, Morgan and his men were caught by the Federal cavalry that had been pursuing them for days. In the ensuing fight Morgan lost more than 800 men, including 700 captured. Morgan and the remainder of his cavalry tried to outride the Federals but were pursued over the next week and, unable to cross the rising Ohio, were forced to surrender on 26 July.

This raid had accomplished little. Morgan's division was destroyed (only about 400 of his men escaped capture and made it back to the Confederacy). The captives were spread throughout Northern prison camps. Some of those men placed in Camp Douglas in Chicago escaped later in the summer and made their way back to Tennessee. Morgan, deemed a greater security risk than his men, was placed in the Ohio State Penitentiary in Columbus, Ohio. He escaped on 26 November 1863 and returned south. He was killed in battle the following year.

Although it could be argued that Morgan's raids were of little military value, they did disrupt Union war efforts in some areas and lifted Confederate morale, sometimes when it was needed the most.

—*David S. Heidler and Jeanne T. Heidler*

See also Bragg, Braxton; Duke, Basil Wilson; Morgan, John Hunt.
For further reading:
Holland, Cecil Fletcher. *Morgan and His Raiders: A Biography of the Confederate General* (1942).
Keller, Allan. *Morgan's Raid* (1961).
Ramage, James A. *Rebel Raider: The Life of John Hunt Morgan* (1986).

MORMONS

Utah's importance in the Civil War lay in its strategic location on the communication route between California and the rest of the nation. If Utah were to side with the Confederacy, the Union would have to move mail and telegraph lines to a more northerly location. Fears that Utah would join the Confederacy were understandable, given the strained relations between the Mormon Church and the federal government as a result of the 1857 Utah War and earlier persecutions in Missouri and Illinois. In addition, the victorious Republicans had promised in the 1856 presidential campaign to eliminate polygamy, one of the "twin relics of barbarism." However, despite early Confederate hopes of Mormon sympathy for their cause, the predominant number of Utah settlers were of New England ancestry and loyal to the Union. Mormon support for slavery was unlikely; in 1860 there were only thirty free blacks and twenty-nine slaves in the territory. In 1832 after the South Carolina nullification crisis, church founder Joseph Smith had predicted the outbreak of war in that state, so Mormons saw the rebellion as a fulfillment of prophecy. Church president Brigham Young's denunciations of national political leaders from the pulpit brought him under suspicion of disloyalty, but he rejected secession and made statements of loyalty to the Constitution.

The uneasy relationship between Mormons and the federal government was worsened by Utah's status as a territory governed by mediocre presidential appointees. Governor John Dawson of Indiana, who arrived in December 1861, was driven out of town after a Mormon woman accused him of sexual assault. Frustrated by inept territorial leadership, Mormons submitted a petition for the state of Deseret in spring 1862, but it was unsuccessful. Instead, in April 1862 Congress passed the Morrill Act outlawing polygamy. But the law was not enforced, and when newly appointed governor Stephen S. Harding publicly attacked polygamy, Mormons petitioned President Abraham Lincoln for his removal. Relations improved after Lincoln appointed James Duane Doty, superintendent of Indian affairs in Utah and friend to the Mormons, who governed until his death in 1865.

The defeat of the Confederates after early victories in the Southwest diminished concern over Mormon disloyalty to the more immediate problem of containing the Indians who were destroying property along the overland mail routes. At the request of the War Department, in the summer of 1862 Young sent a full cavalry company of 100 men and ten supply wagons from the Utah Militia for a

ninety-day stint to guard the overland mail route between Salt Lake City and Green River, Wyoming. Under the command of Mexican-American War veteran Colonel Patrick Edward Connor of Stockton, California, 700 men in the 3d California Volunteers arrived in Salt Lake City in October 1862 to defend Union territory. In the foothills east of the town, Connor established Camp Douglas, a model army reservation with a commanding view of the city. Connor and his men are best known for the January 1863 battle of Bear River, an attack on Shoshone and Bannock Indians camped on Bear River near Franklin in southern Idaho. In the largest massacre of Indians in the West, U.S. soldiers killed approximately 250 Indians and then raped Indian women and pillaged Indian property. Twenty soldiers were killed in the battle or died later of their injuries, and fifty-four more were wounded. After a series of confrontations between Indians and the army in Utah, peace councils in 1863 quieted the Indians for the remainder of the war.

Connor was less successful in his attempt to dilute the political power of indomitable Mormon leader Brigham Young, who maintained a shadow government throughout the war. Connor established the *Union Vedette* newspaper, which published frequent attacks on Mormon leaders. His attempts to challenge Young culminated in his posting an armed guard in downtown Salt Lake City in July 1864, only to be called off by his superior, Major General Irvin McDowell. Connor then relented in his campaign against the Mormons and concentrated his efforts on locating and developing mineral deposits, employing his soldiers as miners in uniform.

During the Civil War, the army in Utah established a major military installation, secured communications lines, diminished the presence of native peoples, and challenged the political power of the Mormon Church. Nevertheless, because of the Mormon Church's practice of polygamy, not for another thirty years would Utah achieve statehood.

—*Susan Sessions Rugh*

See also Connor, Patrick Edward; Young, Brigham.
For further reading:
Colton, Ray Charles. *The Civil War in the Western Territories: Arizona, Colorado, New Mexico, and Utah* (1959).
Long, E. B. *The Saints and the Union: Utah Territory during the Civil War* (1981).
Madsen, Brigham D. *Glory Hunter: A Biography of Patrick Edward Connor* (1990).

MORRILL, JUSTIN SMITH
(1810–1898)
U.S. representative and senator

Justin Smith Morrill, the oldest child of Nathaniel and Mary Hunt Morrill, was born in Vermont on 14 April 1810. Later dubbed the "Father of Land-Grant Colleges," Morrill left school when he was fifteen and

began working in a general store because his blacksmith father could not afford to send him to college. In 1834, after gaining valuable experience as a merchant, Morrill and a former employer opened their own firm. Their business thrived and expanded, and in 1848, when Morrill was thirty-eight, he sold his interest in the firm and retired, satisfied that he had achieved financial stability.

After his retirement, Morrill focused his attention on his orchard and sheep, but he concluded that farming was not a wholly satisfying endeavor. Subsequently, he turned his attention to politics. In 1854, after the incumbent congressman from the Second District of Vermont announced that he would not stand for reelection, Morrill, at the urging of friends, entered the race. Although he had served as the chairman of the Orange County Whig Committee in 1844 and as a member of the State Committee of the Whig Party in 1848, Morrill had only minimal political experience. However, in this his first national election, the Whig Morrill defeated his Free-Soil opponent by fewer than 100 votes. Morrill was seated in Congress on 3 December 1855, and there he remained for the next twelve years.

Morrill distinguished himself in the House of Representatives as a member of the Ways and Means Committee, and he eventually became its chairman. On 17 December 1857, he introduced the bill for which he is best known. Because Morrill himself had received very little formal education, he wanted to ensure that higher education was available to all Americans, including laborers and their children. He noted that most colleges prepared students for learned professions, while they neglected farmers and mechanics. Consequently, he proposed legislation that called for the establishment of at least one agricultural and mechanical college in each state. This bill, which was supposed to be funded through the sale of public land in the West, passed the Senate and the House in 1859, but President James Buchanan vetoed it.

In December 1861, Morrill reintroduced his college land bill, and on 2 July 1862, President Abraham Lincoln signed it into law. The Morrill Land Grant Act provided 30,000 acres of public land per state per member of Congress from that state for every state that had remained in the Union during the Civil War. The states were expected to sell their land grants for the "endowment, support, and maintenance of at least one college where the leading subject shall be, without excluding other scientific and classical studies and including military tactics, to teach such branches of learning as are related to agriculture and mechanic arts." In 1890, Morrill pushed through a supplementary act that provided direct federal grants to these colleges and encouraged the establishment of colleges for African-Americans. In the end, the Morrill Land Grant Act led to the founding of more than seventy colleges.

In 1867, Morrill, by this time a Republican, left the House after his election to the Senate. He remained in the Senate for the rest of his life, and his expertise on domestic finance matters led him to a seat on and the eventual chairmanship of the Senate Finance Committee. He also served as a member and later as chairman of the Committee on Building and Grounds, where he played a significant role in the beautification of Washington, D.C. Morrill secured numerous appropriations to enlarge and perfect the grounds around the U.S. Capitol with gardens, fountains, and terraces; he voted in favor of completing construction on the Washington Monument; he supported construction of the Library of Congress' Thomas Jefferson building; and shortly before he died, he voted for the purchase of land on which the Supreme Court building was constructed.

On 28 December 1898, Justin Smith Morrill died of pneumonia at age eighty-eight after serving almost forty-four years in Congress. During Morrill's tenure in office, Charles Sumner was caned on the floor of the Senate, John Brown led his ill-fated raid at Harper's Ferry, the Civil War started and ended, fourteen states were admitted to the Union, eight presidents took the oath of office, one president was impeached, and the Republican Party replaced the Whig Party. Ultimately, however, it was Justin Smith Morrill's commitment to higher education that ensured him a lasting legacy.

—*Jennifer L. Bertolet*

See also Morrill Land Grant Act.
For further reading:
Parker, William Belmont. *The Life and Public Services of Justin Smith Morrill* (1924).

MORRILL LAND GRANT ACT

Land legislation benefited from Civil War politics. In 1862, Congress passed significant laws that aided farmers. The act establishing the U.S. Department of Agriculture, the Homestead Act, and the Morrill Land Grant Act expanded Americans' access to natural and intellectual resources. The Morrill Land Grant Act not only enabled more people to receive college educations but also initiated scientific approaches to agricultural issues. Before this legislation, higher education modeled the European classical approach. Few Americans were able to afford the tuition or time to study Latin and other obscure subjects that they considered unimportant. White males attended elite institutions to become lawyers, physicians, educators, and theologians. Members of the working classes were excluded from such institutions. As the industrial revolution reinforced the importance of technology and workers in the early nineteenth century, reformers began to demand that education be made available to more people. They insisted that the purpose of education was to transfer knowledge to improve conditions, not to scrutinize and criticize irrelevant topics.

The antebellum United States consisted of vast quantities of land and resources, but few people had the knowledge to develop this potential. Most private colleges were unable and uninterested in providing information about agricultural development to the average person. Unhappy with the status quo, farmers began demanding the right to an education. Before the Morrill Land Grant Act, the eighteenth-century Northwest Ordinance of 1787 had designated parcels of public land to support public schools for children but not colleges for adults. In the early nineteenth century, a few essayists and educators publicly promoted the creation of agricultural colleges to conduct practical research helpful to the general population. By 1851, American reformers were aware that European agricultural experiment stations used science to solve agricultural problems and demanded similar institutions in the United States. Three agricultural colleges operated in Maryland, Pennsylvania, and Michigan before the Civil War, and the 1860 census estimated that 3 percent of the 397 colleges in the United States had a department of science and agriculture.

Efforts to secure legislation to educate agricultural and industrial workers began in the 1850s. Jonathan Baldwin Turner, a Yale University graduate who taught at Illinois College, believed that colleges should offer courses that met the needs of Americans. He was critical of educators who suggested that members of the industrial classes were uneducable, and he noted the prohibitive expenses of private colleges. Defending the rights of the average man to higher education, Turner promoted access for American males to learn practical subjects, choose what they wanted to study, and to participate in experiments and research to improve themselves, their families, and communities. Turner petitioned Congress on 8 February 1853, asking for each state to receive profits from public land to form endowments for such industrial universities.

In Congress, Justin Smith Morrill, a Vermont senator, supported Turner's plan for practical, scientific education. Believing that public lands were misused and worn out, Morrill thought that scientific agriculture would prevent such wastage and that public colleges would provide an opportunity for farmers' children to receive an affordable education. In December 1857, Morrill introduced a bill, calling for a new form of college. Each state would have at least one agricultural school supported by the sale of public lands and investment of those funds. At that time, western congressmen opposed the plan because their states contained most of the public lands that would be distributed, and they did not want to share profits with eastern states. Southern congressmen protested that the plan violated states'

rights. Morrill lobbied for the bill, which passed by a few votes in February 1859, but President James Buchanan vetoed it, explaining that he thought it would prove too costly and was unconstitutional.

Morrill reintroduced the bill in December 1861, and the Committee on Public Lands urged congressmen to reject it. Supported by the influential Senator Benjamin F. Wade, state legislators, farm groups, educators, and the press, the bill passed thirty-two to seven in the Senate and ninety to twenty-five in the House. The absence of Southern opponents in Congress helped the bill's passage. President Abraham Lincoln signed the Morrill Land Grant Bill into law on 2 July 1862. Each state was permitted 30,000 acres per senator and representative to fund agricultural and mechanical schools. The Confederate states were granted land after they declared their loyalty to the Union. Each state could choose its acreage from public lands and tried to select rich timberland and farmland. By 1863, nine states used the land grant act to create or enhance existing schools, including Iowa State University, Kansas State University, Michigan State University, the University of Minnesota, the University of Missouri, the University of Wisconsin, the State University of New Jersey (Rutgers), Pennsylvania State University, and the University of Vermont. The scarcity of agricultural textbooks and qualified teachers hindered the early land grant schools, but in time the problems were resolved. Also, the wording "mechanical arts" created some controversy regarding whether this meant engineering, and if agricultural and mechanical arts were to be pursued separately or together, with mechanical applications to agriculture.

The act offered the average American man opportunities for self-improvement as well as professional, geographical, and social mobility. The legislation affirmed the federal government's faith in the nation's future after the war. Land grant colleges embraced the concept of serving the growing population through practical education and scientific achievements that were applied to improving agricultural production and consumer goods. Society slowly changed as more people attended colleges aided by federal funds and pursued different careers than their ancestors or performed familiar jobs such as farming using different techniques and approaches. The act also offered dignity to agriculture and mechanical arts as they gradually were taken more seriously by members of other professions.

Additional legislation in the late nineteenth and early twentieth centuries funded experiment stations, extension services, and vocational training for high school students at land grant schools. The second Morrill Land Grant Act of 1890 created segregated land grant colleges for African-American students. Millions of acres provided money for at least one land grant school in every state, with some states having two, and North

Carolina established three land grant colleges. Land grant colleges were pioneers in admitting women. These schools incorporated courses in liberal arts and business and supported Reserve Officers Training Corps on campus. Cooperating with industries, land grant institutions have provided resources for faculty and students to innovate new technologies and enhance productivity in fields ranging from agriculture and engineering to pharmaceutical and space sciences.

—*Elizabeth D. Schafer*

See also Morrill, Justin; Wade, Benjamin.

For further reading:
Allen, Herman R. *Open Door to Learning: The Land-Grant System Enters Its 2d Century* (1963).
Eddy, Edward Danforth, Jr. *Colleges for Our Land and Time: The Land-Grant Idea in American Education* (1957).
Halliday, Samuel Domont. *History of the Agricultural College Land-Grant of July 2, 1862* (1890).
Nevins, Allan. *The Origins of the Land-Grant Colleges and State Universities: A Brief Account of the Morrill Act of 1862 and Its Results* (1962).
Ross, Earle Dudley. *Democracy's College: The Land-Grant Movement in the Formative Stage* (1942).

MORTON, OLIVER PERRY
(1823–1877)
Governor of Indiana

Born in Wayne County, Indiana, on 4 August 1823, Oliver P. Morton was the son of James and Sarah Miller Throck Morton. After the death of his mother, Morton was raised for a time by relatives in Ohio, but he returned to Indiana at age fourteen to attend a seminary at Centerville in his native Wayne County. Leaving the seminary after one year, he served as an apprentice to his brother, a hatter. In 1843 Morton enrolled at Miami University in Oxford, Ohio. He returned to Centerville and read law in the office of Judge John S. Newman. Morton married Lucinda M. Burbank in 1845 and was admitted to the bar in 1846.

In addition to practicing law, Morton, a Democrat, became heavily involved in politics and ran unsuccessfully for the prosecuting attorney position in Wayne County in 1848. Four years later, he served out a term as a circuit court judge for an official who had died in office. In 1854, after the Democratic Party's decision to drop its support of the Missouri Compromise and back the Kansas-Nebraska Act, which allowed states to vote on whether to allow slavery, Morton, disagreeing with this stance, abandoned his Democrat affiliation and helped found the People's Party, which became the basis for Indiana's Republican Party. Morton served as the People Party's candidate for Indiana governor in 1856, but lost to a Democrat.

In 1860, Morton ran as the candidate for lieutenant governor on the Republican ticket with gubernatorial nominee Henry Smith Lane. Shortly after his inauguration as governor, however, Smith was elected by the state legislature to serve as U.S. senator, and Morton assumed the governorship (the two men had agreed to the arrangement before the election). Quickly asserting his control of the state Republican Party, Morton staunchly supported the Union's preservation, even if it led to war with the Southern states.

With the war's outbreak after the bombing of Fort Sumter, Morton became one of the Lincoln administration's key supporters, fulfilling a pledge he made at the war's start to raise 10,000 men for the Union army. Morton subsequently worked tirelessly to fill Indiana's troop quotas and even established an arsenal to supply Indiana soldiers with ammunition (the arsenal later sold supplies to the federal government). Although his concern for Indiana troops won him acclamation as "the soldier's friend," Morton also earned himself numerous enemies for his sometimes dictatorial style of governing, which included subverting civil liberties and painting opponents (especially Democrats) as Southern sympathizers and even Copperheads. The governor even charged that secret societies (the Knights of the Golden Circle and the Sons of Liberty) were being organized in the state, particularly in Indiana's southern portion, and were planning to overthrow his administration by force and withdraw from the Union.

Indiana Democrats, incensed by Morton's methods and by such issues as the federal government's institution of the draft and Lincoln's Emancipation Proclamation, had their revenge in 1862. Indiana voters gave Democrats control over both houses of the state legislature and chose Democratic candidates in seven of the state's eleven congressional districts. Partisanship ran high during the 1863 legislative session as Democratic lawmakers issued numerous proposals to nullify Morton's executive authority. Matters came to a head over the Military Bill, which would have stripped control of the state militia from the governor and placed it with a panel controlled by Democratic officeholders. Vowing the bill would never pass, Republicans fled Indianapolis for Madison. They thus prevented the legislature from having a quorum to conduct its business, including passing appropriations to fund state government for the next biennium.

Although their proposals had failed due to the Republicans' drastic efforts, Democrats were delighted at the legislative stalemate, reasoning that Morton would have to call a special session to garner the necessary funding to run state government. The governor, however, refused to call a special session and instead worked to find other funding sources. Morton succeeded by using a combination of private sources, proceeds from ammunition sales at the state arsenal, and loans from Republican county officials. Because neither the state treasurer nor auditor could legally distribute funds without an appropriation, the governor kept the money he raised in his office safe and established a Bureau of Finance to handle the state's financial needs. To fund the interest on the state debt, Morton turned for assistance to James F. D. Lanier, a former Madison business executive who operated a banking and investment firm in New York City. Lanier had aided the governor earlier in the war when Indiana needed funds to equip its troops. Lanier's subsequent loans to the state during the legislative crisis totaled $640,000, an amount that the state managed to pay back to its benefactor over the years.

Morton's success at running Indiana's government with limited funds, the arrest of the Sons of Liberty grand commander Harrison H. Dodd for plotting to overthrow the governor, and Union triumphs on the battlefield helped propel Morton to a second term as governor. The Republican Party also recaptured a majority in both houses of the General Assembly in the 1864 election. Although the Indiana Constitution then limited governors to one term in office, Republicans argued that Morton had been elected lieutenant governor, not governor, in 1860 and was therefore eligible for election.

Although he suffered a stroke in 1865, Morton continued to play a leading role in the state Republican Party, winning election by the 1867 state legislature to serve in the U.S. Senate. During his Senate career, Morton fought on behalf of the Fifteenth Amendment and allied himself with those Republicans who argued for firm measures against the South during Reconstruction. Although a leading candidate for the Republican nomination for president at the 1876 convention, he lost the honor to Rutherford B. Hayes. Morton was hit by another stroke in August 1877. He died in Indianapolis on 1 November 1877.

—*Ray E. Boomhower*

See also Knights of the Golden Circle; Republican Party; Sons of Liberty.

For further reading:
Calhoun, Charles W. "Oliver P. Morton." In *Encyclopedia of Indianapolis* (1994).
Madison, James H. *The Indiana Way: A State History* (1986).
Sylvester, Lorna Lutes. "Oliver P. Morton and Hoosier Politics during the Civil War" (Ph.D. dissertation, 1968).
———. "Oliver P. Morton and the Indiana Legislature of 1863." In *Gentlemen from Indiana: National Party Candidates, 1836–1940* (1977).
Thornbrough, Emma Lou. *Indiana in the Civil War Era, 1850–1880* (1965).

MOSBY, JOHN SINGLETON
(1833–1916)

Confederate partisan leader

John Singleton Mosby was born on 6 December 1833 to Alfred Mosby and Virginia McLaurine in Powhatan County, Virginia. When Mosby was a boy, the family moved to Albemarle County, where John attended local schools. In 1850, he enrolled at the nearby University of Virginia, where he displayed significant academic talents. While still a student at the university, he and another student became engaged in an argument, whereupon Mosby shot the student. Tried and convicted of the crime, Mosby was sentenced to one year in jail and fined $500. After serving more than seven months of his sentence, he was pardoned by Governor Joseph Johnson on 23 December 1853 as a Christmas present. Shortly after his sentence was commuted, Mosby began to read law in the office of William J. Robertson, the man who had prosecuted his case, and they became close friends.

After being admitted to the Virginia bar, Mosby set up a small practice near Charlottesville and met Pauline Clarke, a Kentuckian visiting in the area. They were married in Nashville, Tennessee, on 30 December 1857, reportedly in the presence of Senator Andrew Johnson. In 1858, Mosby and his new bride moved to the railroad town of Bristol in Washington County, Virginia.

With Virginia drifting toward war, Mosby abandoned his law practice and joined the Confederate cause. After a short time at a makeshift Confederate training camp in Ashland, he was sent to the Shenandoah Valley, where

John S. Mosby (*Library of Congress*)

he, a private, reported to Lieutenant Colonel J. E. B. Stuart, commander of the 1st Virginia Cavalry.

Stuart took an immediate liking to Mosby, trusting him to carry out any order and rewarding him with promotions. After spending late 1861 and nearly all of 1862 riding with Stuart in defense of Manassas and Richmond, Mosby resigned for unknown reasons and secured from Stuart authorization to recruit men for a small autonomous command in northern Virginia. This group would grow in number and reputation and become the famed Mosby's Rangers. In his capacity as commander of the Rangers, Mosby planned and orchestrated raids on small but important Federal outposts in northern Virginia, always reporting back to Stuart as to his degree of success. While sometimes engaging in general harassment of the Union army from his usual base in Warrenton, Mosby concentrated on the capture of Federal resources. Over the course of the war, he was estimated to have taken well over 1,000 prisoners of war, more than 1,500 horses, an incalculable number of weapons and ammunition, and hundreds of thousands of dollars in U.S. currency.

Although immensely successful in his early operations, Mosby's celebrity appeared in the late winter of 1863. On the night of 8 March, Mosby and twenty-nine of his men rode far behind enemy lines to Fairfax Court House. Once in town and in the midst of an entire Federal division, they captured several soldiers, one of whom was a guard for Brigadier General Edwin Stoughton, commander of the division. Mosby pressed the man for details and was given directions to Stoughton's headquarters, where Mosby and a handful of his men entered the general's bedroom. Mosby threw off the blankets and woke the general from his sleep with a sharp slap on the buttocks. By daybreak, Mosby, Stoughton, more than thirty prisoners, and nearly sixty horses were safely within the area of northern Virginia now referred to as Mosby's Confederacy.

While not nearly as theatrical, Mosby's Greenback Raid of 1864 was perhaps his greatest strategic victory. In the predawn of 14 October, Mosby and his men loosened and pulled the tracks from beneath a westward bound Baltimore & Ohio train out of Baltimore. Just west of Harper's Ferry, the train came to a calamitous stop. Mosby and his men emerged from the woods, forced the passengers to disembark, plundered the train and its passengers, and set the train afire. Later that night Mosby's men met up to divide the booty, $173,000 between eighty-four men, more than $2,000 per man. Mosby refused his share, as was his custom.

Although Colonel Mosby was a great friend and loyal subordinate of General Robert E. Lee, Mosby's war did not end on 9 April 1865. Mosby, insistent on the possibility of Joseph Johnston's success in North Carolina and wary of the treatment he and his men might receive from the Federals, refused to disband his Rangers until 21 April.

Although history will record Mosby for his wartime exploits, he outlived the war by more than fifty years. After his pardon, he became a close friend and loyal supporter of President Ulysses S. Grant and received from President Rutherford B. Hayes an appointment as minister to Hong Kong, where he served from 1878 to 1885. With the change in administration in 1885, Mosby was relieved of his assignment in the Orient and arrived in San Francisco, where he spent more than fifteen years as an attorney with the Southern Pacific Railroad. In 1901, Southern Pacific reorganized, leaving Mosby unemployed. President William McKinley appointed him a special agent in the General Land Office in Sterling, Colorado, and in 1904, President Theodore Roosevelt secured for Mosby a post as an assistant attorney with the Department of Justice, allowing Mosby to return to his native area.

John Singleton Mosby died on 30 May 1916. The man who wore a plumed hat and a red cape during his gallant cavalry raids lived to be eighty-two-years old and was buried in Warrenton near his wife and three of his sons. Mosby, although highly effective in the saddle, was renowned for his frequent wounds. During his military service, he was shot several times and incurred several other wounds, and as an old man he was kicked in the face by a horse.

—*Brian D. McKnight*

See also Guerrilla Warfare.
For further reading:
Jones, Virgil Carrington. *Ranger Mosby* (1944).
Mosby, John S. *Memoirs of Colonel John S. Mosby* (1959).
Scott, John. *Partisan Life with Colonel John S. Mosby* (1867).

MOTT, GERSHOM
(1822–1884)
Union general

Born to Gershom Mott and Phoebe Rose Scudder Mott in Lamberton, New Jersey, near Trenton, the younger Mott was educated locally before going to work as a young teenager in the mercantile business in New York City. He entered the army at age twenty-five as a second lieutenant and fought in Winfield Scott's Mexico City campaign in the Mexican-American War. He left the army after the war, returned to New Jersey, and over the next decade engaged in a variety of employment, including a job as a bank teller.

At the outbreak of the Civil War, Mott helped raise a regiment for Federal service and in August 1861 was commissioned the lieutenant colonel of the 5th New Jersey volunteers. This regiment became part of the Army of the Potomac, and Mott remained with it through the early days of the Peninsula campaign. Shortly after fighting in the battle of Williamsburg,

Mott was promoted to colonel and given command of the 6th New Jersey Infantry.

Mott fought at Seven Pines and was commended for his bravery during that battle. He and his regiment saw relatively little action during the Seven Days' battles, and in August 1862 were sent to join John Pope's Army of Virginia. On 29 August at Second Bull Run, Mott was seriously wounded and did not see active service again for several months. During his recuperation, he was promoted to brigadier general of volunteers.

In December 1862, recovered from his wounds, Mott was ordered to return to the Army of the Potomac to command a brigade in Daniel Sickles' division of III Corps. He arrived shortly after the debacle at Fredericksburg. As Joseph Hooker worked to reorganize the Army of the Potomac in early February 1863, Mott and his brigade skirmished with Confederates at Rappahannock Bridge. Mott also fought at Chancellorsville as part of Sickles' III Corps and was again seriously wounded.

Unable to participate in the summer campaign at Gettysburg because of his injuries, Mott did not return to active service until the fall of 1863. He returned to his brigade in time to command it during the Bristoe Station and Mine Run campaigns. On 3 May 1864 he assumed command temporarily of the 4th Division, II Corps, before being given command of the 3d Division, II Corps, to restore the morale of this decimated division. Because of its reduced size, the division was temporarily reduced to a brigade, but over the next few months Mott restored its fighting capability and division status.

From the commencement of the Petersburg campaign until Robert E. Lee's surrender at Appomattox, Mott was an active division commander. He was one of the few Union generals who was lauded for his performance during the battle at the Crater at the end of July 1864, and for his performance there, he was given a brevet promotion to major general. Through the remainder of the campaign around Petersburg, Mott performed with admirable courage and efficiency. For Mott's actions during the campaign, George Gordon Meade recommended him for promotion to major general of volunteers. He received that promotion on 1 December 1865 with a date of rank of 26 May 1865.

After the war, Mott was mustered out of volunteer service in early 1866, but in 1868 was offered a regular colonel's commission. He decided instead to remain in civilian life. After a brief stint in the railroad industry, Mott, for the remainder of his life, occupied a number of state offices including New Jersey state treasurer. Mott also became involved in the state banking industry. He never lost his interest in military pursuits and from 1873 until 1884 served as the commander of the New Jersey National Guard. He died while on a trip to New York City on 29 November 1884.

—*David S. Heidler and Jeanne T. Heidler*

See also Petersburg Campaign.
For further reading:
Sommers, Richard J. *Richmond Redeemed: The Siege of Petersburg* (1981).
Stratton, James Newbold. *A Sketch of the Life of Major General Gershom Mott: Read Before the Society of the Cincinnati in the State of New Jersey, at Princeton, July 4, 1885* (1885).

MOTT, LUCRETIA
(1793–1880)
Abolitionist

Known as the "Black Man's Goddess" for her role in the antislavery movement, Lucretia Mott was a tireless advocate for women's rights and other reform measures. Her poise and unquestionable authority, as well as her inner spirit, made her a symbol of the currents of reform in nineteenth-century America. Her birth in 1793 into a Quaker community in Nantucket, Rhode Island, helped shape her identity, and Mott remained a devout Quaker until her death. Educated at Nine Partners, a Quaker boarding school in New York, she learned early on about the inequality of the sexes. Distressed by the fact that male instructors received higher salaries than their female counterparts, she vowed to claim the natural rights that God had ordained for women. During her time as a student at Nine Partners, she met James Mott, and the couple soon married, committing their lives to the reform of American society. Together they weathered a schism in the Quaker faith, turning toward the Hicksite belief in a boycott of all slave-made goods and products. This disavowal of slave products influenced Mott until her death, particularly during the antebellum period and the early years of the Civil War.

Mott's antislavery sentiments led her to take an active part in the movement against racial prejudice. Through her involvement in this movement, she met William Lloyd Garrison in 1830 and supported him in his belief in the immediate emancipation of all slaves. Along with Garrison and her husband, Mott felt that social change could be achieved only through intellectual and moral action, rather than force or violence. The central theme in all of Mott's discourse was the moral nature of human life. Humans, Mott argued, were moral beings, but they had stumbled along the path of righteousness and truth. This belief led to her involvement in antislavery, which in many ways was also the birth of the woman's rights movement, with its nineteenth-century pinnacle, the 1848 Seneca Falls Convention.

Her Quaker beliefs in morality influenced her political beliefs. She remained a true nonresistant and professed nonsupport of John Brown's violent raid in 1859 at Harper's Ferry in the midst of the free state controversy. However, in an 1860 speech at the meeting of the Pennsylvania Anti-Slavery Society, she noted that she did not honor John Brown the soldier, but rather John Brown the moral martyr. Mott also feared that Abraham Lincoln would prove agreeable to compromise with the South after his election to the presidency in 1860, especially since seven Southern states had seceded from the Union by the time of his inauguration in March 1861. As the war approached, the Motts greeted it with mixed emotions. After the Quaker disavowal of fighting, Mott disliked the thought of attempting to solve problems by force. The war soon hit home, however, when her son-in-law, Edward M. Davis, responded to a commission as a captain in the army of General John Charles Frémont in the Western theater. In a letter home, Davis wrote that Frémont noted that Lincoln had been "sold to the border states—and that we shall never succeed until universal emancipation is proclaimed." Originally distrustful of the efforts of Lincoln, whom she referred to as "our imbecile President," she urged her listeners to petition Washington "so that poor Abe, McClellan, and the others may see how unavailing all their pro-slavery conservatism is." She was not appeased by the abolition of slavery in the District of Columbia, nor by the 1863 Emancipation Proclamation, arguing that the latter document was only a superficial attempt. When read closely, the proclamation freed slaves only in the Rebel areas, which were specifically those areas over which the federal government already had no control. Furthermore, it did nothing to disturb slavery in the loyal border states and exempted all areas under federal military occupation.

Not to be outdone, Lucretia Mott redoubled her efforts in support of emancipation. Early in January 1863, the Union army leased a portion of a farm owned by Edward Davis to use as a training camp for black soldiers. Known as Camp William Penn, it was located less than a mile from Mott's home, and despite her dislike of the military, Mott was a tireless supporter of this training camp. In addition, in December 1863, the American Anti-Slavery Society held its thirtieth anniversary celebration, but support was waning for the Garrisonian belief (also held by the Motts) that racial prejudice would be annihilated with the end of slavery.

The war seemed to be dragging on with no end in sight, with Ulysses S. Grant's army making little progress against Robert E. Lee's forces. In Philadelphia, Mott helped organize a Freedmen's Relief Association, and the introduction of the Thirteenth Amendment in February 1865 seemed to lift her spirits. With the surrender of Lee's troops on 9 April, Mott was somewhat hopeful that prejudice would be eradicated, but she wondered whether good could come out of the evil. By this point, Lucretia's health was failing, but she turned her attention to aiding the newly freed blacks and she resumed her avocation of women's rights. The death of her husband in 1867 was a blow, but she threw her efforts into the establishment of a coeducational institution funded by James Swarthmore College. At her death on 11 November 1880, she left a legacy of support for the underdog and a tireless advocacy of the moral righteousness of humanity.

—*Jennifer Harrison*

See also Abolitionist Movement; Abolitionists; Emancipation Proclamation; Quakers; Stanton, Elizabeth Cady.
For further reading:
Bacon, Margaret Hope. *Valiant Friend: The Life of Lucretia Mott* (1980).
Greene, Dana, ed. *Lucretia Mott: Her Complete Speeches and Sermons* (1980).
———. "Quaker Feminism: The Case of Lucretia Mott." *Pennsylvania History* (1981).
Sterling, Dorothy. *Lucretia Mott: Gentle Warrior* (1964).

MOWER, JOSEPH ANTHONY
(1827–1870)
Union general

Born to Nathaniel Mower and Sophia Holmes Mower in Woodstock, Vermont, Joseph Anthony Mower moved with his parents to Lowell, Massachusetts, when he was a small child. He was educated locally before attending Norwich University in Vermont. At the outbreak of the Mexican-American War, Mower enlisted as a private and served until 1848. Not finding a niche in civilian life, he sought a commission in the army and was appointed a second lieutenant in 1855. He had achieved the rank of first lieutenant at the commencement of the Civil War.

Mower's Civil War career was characterized by conspicuous bravery throughout. He was mentioned constantly in many engagement reports for his gallantry in battle. Because of these actions he was rapidly promoted and given ever-greater responsibilities.

His first promotion in September 1861 to captain came because of the need for experienced regular officers. He served that first year in the West, primarily in Missouri, fighting under John Pope at New Madrid and Island No. 10 in early 1862. On 3 May 1862 he was promoted to colonel of volunteers and given command of the 11th Missouri Infantry.

Mower commanded a brigade beginning in August 1862 and received a brevet promotion to lieutenant colonel in the regular army for the gallantry he displayed in leading his men at the battle of Iuka on 19 September. Two weeks later, Mower was wounded and captured at Corinth and managed to escape but was recaptured.

After his exchange, Mower was given command of a brigade in William T. Sherman's corps during the Vicksburg campaign. During this time, he came increasingly to the attention of his commander, who came to view him as one of the most promising of the younger generals in the army. Mower was promoted to brigadier general in March 1863.

Mower was commended again for his bravery in leading a charge deemed responsible for the fall of Jackson, Mississippi on 14 May 1863, and as a reward for his actions there he was given command of the garrison that occupied the town. He did not remain on garrison duty long, however. Mower returned to the front and participated in the formal siege of Vicksburg until its conclusion.

During the summer of 1863, Mower operated out of Vicksburg and at the end of September was put in command of guarding the Black River railroad bridge. The following spring, Mower was given command of a division in Nathaniel P. Banks's Red River campaign. On 14 March 1864 he led on horseback the charge of his division that resulted in the capture of Fort De Russy. On 30 May 1864 he was relieved from duty with the Army of the Gulf and sent to Memphis. During the summer of 1864, he participated in several expeditions from Tennessee into Mississippi and Arkansas in an effort to stop Confederate raids. All the while, William T. Sherman was trying to arrange his transfer to participate in Sherman's Atlanta campaign. Mower was promoted to major general of volunteers in August 1864.

In September 1864 Sherman finally accomplished Mower's transfer, but before receiving the order to report to Atlanta, Mower received orders to move his division to Missouri to combat Sterling Price's raid there. As a result, Mower did not report to Sherman until November 1864, just in time to receive command of a division in Sherman's March to the Sea. Mower led his division south to Savannah and then up through the Carolinas. His division underwent considerable hardship in the early phases of the march into South Carolina, particularly in the passage through the swamps around the Salkehatchie River. On 7 April 1865, he assumed command of XX Corps of the Army of Georgia. He held that command until early June, when he was granted a much-needed leave of absence.

At the end of July 1865, Mower was sent to command the Eastern District of Texas in the Department of Texas. His primary responsibility was to guard the railroads around Galveston from disgruntled former Confederates. Upon the reorganization of the army the following year, Mower stayed in the army as colonel of the 39th Infantry, an African-American unit. In 1869 he was given command of the Department of Louisiana as the commander of the 25th Infantry, another African-American regiment. He contracted pneumonia during the winter of that year and died on 6 January 1870 in New Orleans.

—*David S. Heidler and Jeanne T. Heidler*

See also Corinth, Battle of; Red River Campaign; Sherman's March to the Sea;.
For further reading:
Glatthaar, Joseph T. *The March to the Sea and Beyond:*

Sherman's Troops in the Savannah and Carolinas Campaigns (1985).
Johnson, Ludwell H. *Red River Campaign: Politics and Cotton in the Civil War* (1958).

MUD MARCH
(20–23 January 1863)

Following the grim fiasco at Fredericksburg on 13 December 1862, Major General Ambrose E. Burnside, commander of the Army of the Potomac, planned another offensive to recoup his army's fortunes. Despite President Abraham Lincoln's reservations, Burnside proposed to swing around the Confederate left to force General Robert E. Lee's Army of Northern Virginia out into the open, where the superior Union numbers could be brought to bear.

Speed and surprise were essential elements in the Union plan. To cross the Rappahannock River, Burnside intended to move quickly to Banks' Ford and erect there five pontoon bridges. His orders to his troops forecast "a great and mortal blow to the rebellion."

With the weather in early January mild and dry enough for the Union army to enjoy baseball, the plan seemed promising. But soon after the Grand Divisions of Major Generals Joseph Hooker and William B. Franklin set off on 20 January from their camps around Falmouth, a drizzle began that worsened by nightfall to a steady downpour. The rain would continue for the next four days. Compounding Burnside's difficulties, the wagons transporting the large pontoons started late and soon became entangled in the formations that they should have preceded. A two-mile-long traffic snarl ensued. The going was slow, with one regiment (5th New York) reporting progress for the day at 1.5 miles. Moreover, the Confederates quickly spotted the Union movement and Lee accurately predicted Burnside's purpose, if not his crossing point.

On 21 January the movement of the Union army was slowed further by a confusion in orders that sent two corps marching across each other at a road junction. Worse, under the feet of thousands of men and hundreds of horses, and the wheels of artillery pieces, quartermaster wagons, and ambulances, the dirt roads turned liquid and were churned into morasses. As the army's trains bogged down, teams were doubled and then tripled. Horses or mules floundering in the mud were cut from their traces and trodden underfoot until they disappeared completely from view. Groups of 150 infantrymen worked on ropes pulling a single cannon or a pontoon yard by yard along the line of march. At any halt, troops quickly shoved fence rails under gun carriages or wagon beds so that they would not sink to the axles.

Any lingering chance for surprise disappeared as the army's nighttime campfires gave the appearance of a "sea

of fire," while the wet wood emitted vast low-hanging clouds of smoke. The Confederates, thoroughly alerted, watched from across the Rappahannock and expressed their amusement with catcalls, feigned offers of assistance, and mocking directions to Richmond scrawled on homemade signs.

Despite this dispiriting situation, Burnside on the afternoon of 21 January ordered the march resumed the next morning. To reward the exhausted troops, he directed the dispensation of liquor, which many of the soldiers poured into empty stomachs at daybreak on 22 January. Drunken men fell to scrapping in the mud, with one fistfight (between the 118th Pennsylvania and 22d Massachusetts, with the 2d Maine joining in) assuming epic proportions.

Hooker soon reported that his troops were running short of rations with no prospect of reprovisioning unless the roads were corduroyed. About midday, Burnside came to the belated conclusion that the campaign should be terminated and ordered his army back into its Falmouth encampments. This retrograde step was quite as difficult to execute as the forward one had been, and Burnside's discomfort was heightened by his fears that his trains would be frozen in place and then destroyed by Confederate cavalry. Burnside later confessed to a friend that the strain of the march had driven him almost frantic.

The costs of the Mud March, as it was known even in official reports, were substantial, evident partially in sickness and desertion rates so severe that some observers concluded the army had lost as many men as if it had fought a battle. Recriminations flowed at Burnside's headquarters. Criticism of the commander reached a crescendo, with Franklin charging that Burnside had lost his mind. Hooker made widely reported remarks that the country needed a dictator.

In frustration, Burnside drafted General Order No. 8 stripping Hooker, Franklin, and others of their commands and even commissions. Without authority to execute such drastic action himself, on 23 January Burnside personally journeyed to the White House and appealed to Lincoln for support. Instead, the president two days later relieved Burnside as commander of the Army of the Potomac and elevated in his place Hooker.

—Malcolm Muir, Jr.

See also Burnside, Ambrose Everett.
For further reading:
Marvel, William. *Burnside* (1991).
Sears, Stephen W. *Chancellorsville* (1996).

MUDD, SAMUEL ALEXANDER
(1833–1883)

Convicted Lincoln assassination conspirator

Born in Maryland, Samuel Mudd was the son of wealthy, slave-owning parents. He graduated from Georgetown College (later University) and then from Baltimore Medical College in 1856. After graduation, Mudd received a gift of 218 acres of land and 11 slaves from his father, and in 1857 he was married to Sarah Francis Dyer. Like many people in Maryland, Mudd supported the Southern cause when the Civil War came. He thought both secession and slaveholding were rights guaranteed by the Constitution. However, he did not enlist in the Confederate army.

Mudd's first meeting with John Wilkes Booth, the man who would make Mudd infamous, occurred in November 1864, when Booth spent the night at Mudd's house. They met again in Washington, D.C., apparently by accident, in December of that year. Their third and final meeting occurred at about 4 A.M. on 15 April 1865. Earlier the previous evening, Booth had assassinated President Abraham Lincoln in his box overlooking the stage at Ford's Theater in Washington. After firing the fatal shot, Booth leapt to the stage below, breaking his leg in the process. Mudd set Booth's leg.

Three days later, detectives arrived to question Mudd. Shortly thereafter, he was arrested. Though Mudd likely did not realize it at the time, he was in a very unfortunate position. Government officials, and the nation at large, were desperate to blame the president's assassination on someone. As would be the case with the assassination of John F. Kennedy a century later, people found it unbelievable that the assassination of a president could be the work of a single man. As such, government investigators proceeded with the assumption that the assassination was the product of a conspiracy undertaken by the Confederate government. Mudd was to be tried in front of a military court as a coconspirator.

Mudd did not help himself with his behavior in court. He was uncooperative while testifying. He also lied while on the stand, claiming that he had only met Booth once prior to the night of 15 April, when in fact they had met at least two times. This undermined Mudd's credibility, and when he tried to claim that he did not recognize Booth on the night of the 15th, he was not believable. He was sentenced on 30 June 1865 to life in prison doing hard labor.

Mudd was imprisoned at Fort Jefferson, Florida. Initially, he was treated with great leniency. He was allowed to exchange letters with his wife, and despite his sentence, he did not do hard labor but instead worked in the prison hospital. However, around the time that African-American soldiers arrived to guard the prison, Mudd tried to escape. After that, he suffered more severe treatment—leg chains, confinement, and hard outdoor labor. Mudd complained bitterly to his wife about the "degraded condition" of prisoners guarded by a "set of ignorant, prejudiced and irresponsible beings of the unbleached humanity."

In 1866, the Supreme Court in *Ex Parte Milligan* declared illegal the trials of civilians by military courts when civilian courts were in session. Mudd attempted to use the Court's ruling to gain his release, but he was denied. His hopes were again raised in 1867 when John Surratt, one of the men identified as a coconspirator in the president's assassination, was finally captured and put on trial. Mudd felt certain that if he were called on to testify at the trial, he would be able to prove his innocence. He did not testify, however, and he remained in prison. Mudd finally secured a presidential pardon from Andrew Johnson in February 1869. He returned to his farm in Maryland to resume his practice, but he was never able to recreate what he had before his imprisonment. He was elected to the Maryland legislature as a Republican in 1876 and after serving one term he went back to his farm, where he died of pneumonia on 10 January 1883.

—*Christopher Bates*

See also Lincoln Assassination.
For further reading:
Higdon, Hal. *The Union vs. Doctor Mudd* (1964).
Jones, John Paul. *Dr. Mudd and the Lincoln Assassination: The Case Reopened* (1995).
Mudd, Nettie. *The Life of Dr. Samuel A. Mudd: Containing His Letters From Fort Jefferson, Dry Tortugas Island, Where He Was Imprisoned Four Years For Alleged Complicity in the Assassination of Abraham Lincoln* (1906; reprint, 1975).

MUNFORD, THOMAS TAYLOR
(1831–1918)
Confederate general

Thomas Taylor Munford was born in Richmond on 29 March 1831. In 1848, he enrolled at the Virginia Military Institute and graduated in 1852, fourteenth in a class of twenty-four. The next year he became a farmer and married Elizabeth Henrietta Tayloe. As war approached, Munford responded by joining the 30th Mounted Rifles and was mustered in on 8 May 1861 with the rank of lieutenant colonel.

Munford served at the battle of First Bull Run, helping to turn the retreat into a rout by attacking the broken Union lines as they fell back across Cub Run. In September the Confederate cavalry was organized into a brigade and the 30th was redesignated the 2d Virginia Cavalry. Munford was elected its colonel the next year. He first led the command during Major General Thomas "Stonewall" Jackson's Shenandoah Valley campaign, eventually leading all of Jackson's cavalry. After months of excellent service, Jackson's command left the Shenandoah and headed toward Richmond in time to participate in the Seven Days' battles. Upon rejoining the main army, Munford reverted to regimental command, an all too common pattern.

Next Munford skillfully led his regiment in the Second Bull Run campaign, again working closely with Jackson, protecting his infantry as it moved toward the old Bull Run battlefield. During the fighting on 30 August, Munford received a slight saber wound to the head. During the Antietam campaign, he again commanded a brigade. On 14 September, Munford held Crampton's Gap through South Mountain in dramatic fashion, fending off assaults by a greatly superior Union force. On 24 October, Brigadier General J. E. B. Stuart recommended Munford for promotion. Again, he was passed over.

In March 1863, Munford ably assisted in repelling a Union attack at the battle of Kelly's Ford. Less than two months later, he was back serving with Jackson, protecting the infantry as it flanked the Union army at Chancellorsville on 2 May. The following month, General Lee invaded the North again. As preparations were made, Munford again was in brigade command, temporarily replacing Brigadier General Fitz Lee.

The Gettysburg campaign began poorly for the Confederates when they were surprised at Brandy Station on 9 June. Although Stuart held his ground at the end of the day, the battle was a tactical draw. Munford had remained away from the battle guarding a ford, thereby failing to assist in the struggle until it was nearly over. Eight days later, however, he performed excellent service, soundly defeating Union cavalry under Brigadier General H. Judson Kilpatrick at Aldie, Virginia, before being ordered to withdraw toward Middleburg. A few days later, Munford returned to the 2d Virginia when Lee resumed command and led it in Stuart's arduous and, for the most part, fruitless raid. During the remainder of the campaign, Munford satisfactorily led his regiment, but never distinguished himself. The remaining months of 1863 were routine, broken only by another cavalry battle at Brandy Station in October. This time, however, Confederate success was undisputed. Before the battle, Thomas Rosser, whom Munford disliked intensely, was promoted to general.

The following year was spent in almost constant activity. Beginning in April 1864, Munford spent the following six months attempting to counter Major General Philip Sheridan's cavalry, first in the Wilderness and later in the Shenandoah Valley. Despite the efforts of officers such as Munford, the Union cavalry defeated its Confederate counterparts up and down the valley. Late that summer, Munford was put back in command of a brigade. Although he spent part of the fall ill in Richmond, he was back in command before the year was out. Also he was finally promoted to brigadier general in November 1864.

Munford continued to lead his brigade in 1865. In the midst of the crushing defeat at the battle of Five Forks on 1 April, he was one of the few senior commanders to have performed skillfully. During the subsequent retreat to Appomattox, he performed excellently against increasing odds. On the morning of 9 April, Munford,

and many of the mounted commands, fought their way out and were not on the immediate field when Lee surrendered. The following day, Munford disbanded his command at Lynchburg. Six weeks later, he turned himself over to Union authorities and was paroled.

After the war, Munford returned to farming and remarried in 1866, his first wife having died in 1864. Although primarily a farmer, he participated in a number of unsuccessful ventures throughout the next fifty years. Over the years, he wrote extensively on the war and maintained a voluminous correspondence with former comrades and foes alike. After his second wife died in 1910, he moved to Alabama permanently, dying there on 27 February 1918.

—*James Robbins Jewell*

See also Aldie, Virginia, Battle of; Cavalry, C.S.A.; Crampton's Gap, Battle of.

For further reading:

Allardice, Bruce. *More Generals in Gray* (1995).
Driver, Robert. *2d Virginia Cavalry* (1995).
Hotchkiss, Jed. *Confederate Military History*. Vol. 3 (1899).
Krick, Robert K. *Lee's Colonels: A Biographical Register of the Field Officers of the Army of Northern Virginia* (1992).
Wert, Jeffery D. "His Unhonored Service." *Civil War Times Illustrated* (1985).

MUNFORDVILLE, BATTLE OF
(14–17 September 1862)

The Confederate invasion of Kentucky in the summer of 1862 was poorly planned and coordinated. E. Kirby Smith had advanced into Kentucky and fought the battle of Richmond while Braxton Bragg's army was still in Tennessee. Bragg wanted to defeat Don Carlos Buell's army in Tennessee and then move into Kentucky, but when Kirby Smith reached central Kentucky Bragg feared that Smith might be trapped between Buell's army and the Union forces being assembled at Cincinnati. Bragg's 32,000 men left Chattanooga on 28 August 1862 and marched northward through middle Tennessee. By 19 September, they were in Glasgow, Kentucky, thirty miles east of heavily fortified Bowling Green. Bragg was between Buell and Kirby Smith, and he was in position to cut Buell's line of retreat to Louisville.

A vital bridge on the Louisville & Nashville Railroad spanned the Green River near Munfordville, some forty-five miles northeast of Bowling Green. It was protected by the command of Colonel John T. Wilder, a businessman from Greenburg, Indiana. When 450 reinforcements reached Munfordville on 14 September, Colonel Cyrus L. Dunham outranked Wilder and assumed command. Confederate cavalry commander Colonel John Scott had been sent by Kirby Smith to find Bragg and urge him to combine his army with that of Smith. Mistaken in his information about the strength of the

Federal force at Munfordville and its determination to resist, Scott demanded surrender on 13 September. When Wilder refused, Scott requested aid from Brigadier General James R. Chalmers whose brigade was at Cave City. Acting on his own initiative, Chalmers advanced to Munfordville on the night of 13–14 September.

Wilder had strengthened the Union defenses of the bridge on the south side of Green River. A strong stockade and Fort Craig were connected by a line of rifle pits and trenches. After Dunham arrived, the defenders numbered about 4,000 men. The 89th Indiana held the stockade; the 67th Indiana occupied Fort Craig.

Chalmers's poorly coordinated attack early on the morning of 14 September was repulsed by massed fire. Among the casualties was Colonel Robert A. Smith of the 10th Mississippi. When Wilder rejected another demand to surrender, he wrote: "If you wish to avoid further bloodshed, keep out of the way of my guns." A truce allowed the wounded to be removed and the dead buried. Chalmers asked Bragg for help. Because the action had been started, Bragg decided that the Federal position must be taken. He moved his army to Munfordville and surrounded the Federals on both sides of the river.

On the afternoon of 16 September, Bragg demanded that the Federals surrender to overwhelming force. When Dunham telegraphed Louisville that he could not hold his position without reinforcements, he was ordered to turn command over to Wilder. Dunham refused to serve under one inferior in rank; he was ordered to report himself under arrest. Inexperienced in military affairs and eager to do what was correct, Wilder took the unusual step of asking an opponent for advice. Late in the evening of 16 September, under a flag of truce, Wilder surprised General Simon Bolivar Buckner, whose home was nearby, by asking him what he should do. Wilder and his adjutant were taken on an inspection of the Confederate lines, where they saw the overwhelming numbers backed by heavy concentrations of artillery. Wilder decided to surrender, and details were worked out at Bragg's headquarters. At 6:00 A.M. on 17 September, the 3,921 Union troops and 155 officers marched to Rowlett's Station, where Buckner accepted their surrender. They were paroled and released to do no fighting until exchanged. The affair had cost the Confederates 288 casualties; the Federals had 72 casualties, not counting the prisoners.

This episode delayed Bragg several days, regardless of what his objectives were. He could advance to take Louisville, he could double back to seize Nashville, or he could force battle with Buell south of the Green River. His decision was to unite his army with that of Kirby Smith and install the Provisional Government of Confederate Kentucky in Frankfort. Bragg scattered his army around the Bardstown region, leaving the path to

Louisville open to Buell. Then Bragg went to Lexington to confer with Kirby Smith about the installation of Governor Richard Hawes. The two Confederate armies were still separated when events moved toward a climax at Perryville.

—*Lowell H. Harrison*

See also Bragg, Braxton; Buckner, Simon Bolivar; Chalmers, James Ronald; Kentucky; Wilder, John T.

For further reading:
Engerud, Hal. *The History of the Siege of Munfordville, September 14–17, 1862* (1984).
Harrison, Lowell H. "'Should I Surrender?'—A Civil War Incident." *Filson Club History Quarterly* (1966).
McDonough, James L. *War in Kentucky: From Shiloh to Perryville* (1994).
Stickles, Arndt M. *Simon Bolivar Buckner: Borderland Knight* (1940).
Williams, Samuel C. *General John T. Wilder, Commander of the Lightning Brigade* (1936).

MURRAH, PENDLETON
(c.1828–1865)
Governor of Texas

Pendleton Murrah was born in Alabama or South Carolina, probably out of wedlock, and was reared in an orphanage. Fortunately for him, a Baptist charity funded his education at Brown University, where he graduated in 1848. He was admitted to the bar in Plantersville, Alabama, but in 1850 moved to Texas, hoping for relief from tuberculosis. He settled in Marshall, a flourishing east Texas community, reopened his law practice, and within a few months had married Sue Ellen Taylor of South Carolina–born daughter of Bayliss Taylor, a prosperous cotton planter.

Murrah was successful as a lawyer and, after dabbling in Democratic politics as an advocate for others, ran unsuccessfully for the legislature in 1855 against a Know-Nothing candidate. In a second attempt, in 1857, he was elected. Still physically frail, he announced himself, then withdrew, as a candidate for the Confederate Congress in 1861. The following year he served briefly as a quartermaster officer in the 14th Texas Infantry before ill health forced his resignation. When the popular Francis R. Lubbock left the governorship in 1863, numerous contenders presented themselves, but only Murrah and Thomas Jefferson Chambers emerged as serious candidates. Chambers was better known and had run twice before, but was perceived as not only unpredictable but, more importantly, an enemy of the Confederate government. After a lackluster campaign resulting in a low voter turnout (31,000), Murrah was elected by a 5,000-vote margin.

Texas remained largely outside the Confederacy's power to control and faced ongoing threats from hostile Indians in the western part of the state and raids from

Mexico in addition to Federal armies. Conducting state affairs during the last eighteen months of the Civil War, Murrah faced daunting problems, particularly in the realms of defense and finances. Texans generally opposed Confederate conscription and impressment laws anyway and felt neglected and misused by the central government. Morale spiraled downward with each military defeat, exacerbated by the state's distance from the major battlefields. A stern advocate of states' rights, Murrah sought to keep Texas soldiers at home, particularly during the 1864 Red River campaign. His views led to clashes with J. Bankhead Magruder, the Confederate commander in Texas, and with Magruder's superior, Edmund Kirby Smith. Both conferred and corresponded often with Murrah, insisting that Confederate laws and regulations, particularly regarding army enlistments, took precedence over those of Texas. Another major point of contention was control of the lucrative cotton trade since Murrah's Texas Cotton Office and its agents acted in direct competition with the Confederate Cotton Bureau under Smith's jurisdiction.

Still, Murrah remained loyal to the war effort, urging resistance to the end. In the spring of 1865 he attempted to negotiate separate terms for Texas with Union officials in New Orleans. When he realized the cause was lost, Murrah hoped for the state's early restoration to the United States, but in mid-June, fearing imprisonment and witnessing the pillage of government buildings in Austin, he joined Confederate general Joseph O. Shelby and his entourage in flight across the border. One of his traveling companions remembered that the ravages of consumption marked "the large, mournful eyes, the tall, bent frame that quivered as it moved. Murrah was a gifted and brilliant man, but his heart was broken....He knew death was near to him, yet he put on his old, gray uniform, and mounted his old, tried war-horse, and rode away." The rigorous trip proved to be Murrah's final journey; he died in Monterrey, Mexico, only six weeks after leaving Texas.

—*Lynda Lasswell Crist*

See also Confederate Diaspora; Magruder, John Bankhead; Smith, Edmund Kirby; Texas.

For further reading:

DeShields, James T. *They Sat in High Places: The Presidents and Governors of Texas* (1950).

Deuson, Benny E. "Pendleton Murrah." In *Ten Texans in Gray* (1968).

Smith, David P. "Conscription and Conflict on the Texas Frontier, 1863–1865." In *Lone Star Blue and Gray: Essays on Texas in the Civil War* (1995).

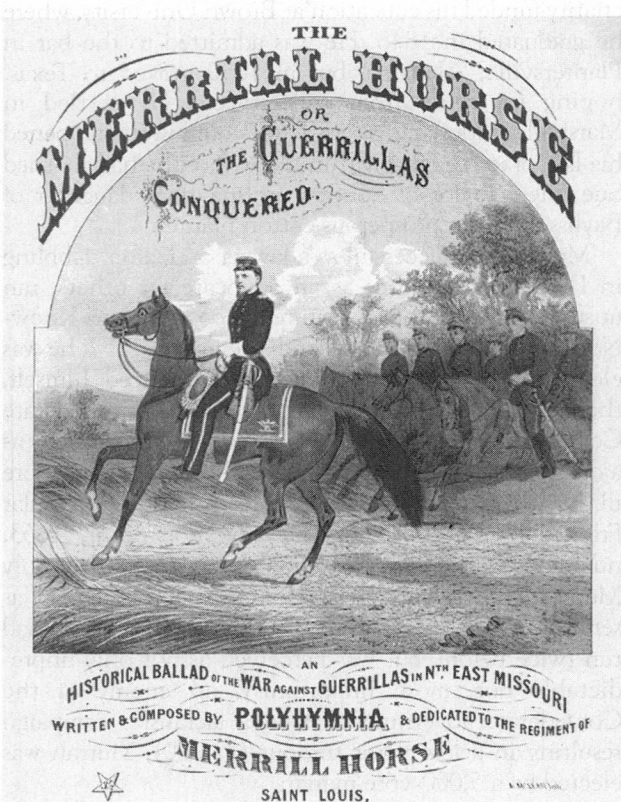

"The Merrill Horse," published in St. Louis in 1863; and "Pea Ridge March," published in Milwaukee in 1862 and dedicated to Major General Franz Sigel (*Library of Congress*)

Band of the 114th Pennsylvania Infantry (Zouaves) at Brandy Station, Virginia, April 1864
(Photograph by Timothy O'Sullivan / *Library of Congress*)

MUSIC

Music was a pervasive and distinctive element of the overall atmosphere surrounding the Civil War. As an art form it reflected the national obsession with every facet of the conflict, and as a commodity it was used by participants and nonparticipants alike for a myriad of purposes. Within the military of both sides, music was used to provide signals, enhance the formality of ceremonies, and sustain morale among soldiers. At home, it served to help recruit volunteers and create public consensus for the war effort. The war itself also had profound effects on the new music of the day, as it provided a wealth of inspiration for folk singers and composers, especially those involved in the booming industry of sheet-music publishing.

Military music comprised two distinct types: field music and band music. The field musicians included the company drummers and fifers, as well as the cavalry buglers, who signaled troops during operations and in daily routine. At times, such as on the march, the infantry musicians came together to form regimental fife-and-drum corps. Classified as noncombatants, the company musicians were often too young to enlist as regular soldiers. Sometimes as young as twelve or thirteen, these were the drummer boys celebrated in postwar battle lore and such popular parlor songs as "The Drummer Boy of Shiloh" (composed by Will Hays, 1863).

The band of music was a brass-and-percussion ensemble of from eight to twenty-four instrumentalists, usually attached to a regiment or brigade. The musicians' pay, which averaged seventeen dollars for those in Union bands, was usually supplemented by contributions from the unit's officers. It is estimated that over the course of the war more than 400 bands saw service in the Federal army, while the Confederate forces included as many as 125. An excessive number of volunteer bands

Band of the 107th U.S. Colored Infantry at Fort Corcoran (Arlington, Virginia), 1865 (*Library of Congress*)

and musicians in the first year of the war caused the U.S. War Department in July 1862 to limit the size of the ensembles to sixteen musicians and restrict their use from the regimental to the brigade level. Confederate army regulations allowed for bands of up to sixteen musicians to be attached to regiments.

Although many combinations could be found, the most common instrumentation for a full military brass band included two E-flat cornets (or saxhorns), two B-flat cornets (or saxhorns), two alto horns, two tenor horns, one baritone horn, one bass horn, and a percussion section of one side (snare) drum, a bass drum, and cymbals. Some bands employed more brass instruments, while a few included woodwind instruments, such as a piccolo or clarinet.

The most prevalent brass instruments in the bands of both sides were the upright valved bugles known as saxhorns. Developed in Paris in the 1840s by Adolphe Sax, these instruments were available in all of the neces-

sary sizes, offered great carrying power, and were comparatively easy to play. A popular version of the saxhorn incorporated a bell pointing back over the performer's shoulder, so that music could be heard by troops on the march behind the band.

Besides playing as troops marched into battle, bands entertained during periods of recreation and supplied music for ceremonies and special events. A favorite pastime was the serenade, a special performance given for a particular honoree, usually an officer, and paid for by a group of friends. The bandsmen also performed nonmusical duties; for example, in the latter stages of battles they generally carried stretchers and assisted with medical operations in field hospitals.

The repertoire of Civil War bands included marches and patriotic music, quickstep versions of popular melodies, polkas, waltzes, and funeral dirges. The more accomplished ensembles often performed concert arrangements of classic overtures and opera arias.

An unidentified regimental fife-and-drum corps (*National Archives*)

Although many pieces were popular with bands of both sides, several were used to express partisan sentiments. Such favorites among northern bands included "Yankee Doodle" and "Battle Hymn of the Republic." Southern bands countered with melodies like "Dixie," "La Marseillaise," and "The Southrons' Chaunt of Defiance."

The level of musicianship among Civil War bandsmen varied widely. Some, like the members of the band of the 25th South Carolina Infantry regiment, had worked as professional musicians before the war, while others had obtained instruments and learned to play only after volunteering for enlistment. Many of the best musicians were Irish, German, or Italian immigrants. Notable bandleaders included Patrick S. Gilmore of the band of the 24th Massachusetts Volunteer Infantry, and Francis M. Scala, director of the U.S. Marine Band.

In addition to the band music, Civil War soldiers enjoyed singing and dancing to music provided by peers on banjos, fiddles, fifes, Jews' harps, and other portable instruments. Among the most popular songs in camp were such sentimental favorites as "Lorena," "Home, Sweet Home," and "Kathleen Mavourneen." Music for dress balls was often supplied by civilian orchestras or, in the South, ensembles made up of slaves.

At home, music served to foster patriotism. Civic brass bands in cities like Philadelphia, Detroit, and Chicago led parades and performed martial airs at recruiting rallies and political gatherings. The published sheet music of the period—parlor songs and works for solo piano—often reflected themes associated with the war. Some songs, like "Tenting On the Old Camp Ground" (Walter Kittredge, 1864), offered images of the soldiering life, while others, such as "The Children of the Battlefield" (James G. Clark, 1864), related sentimental stories of fallen heroes. Another genre celebrated the advent of emancipation; examples include "Kingdom Coming" (Henry Clay Work, 1862) and "Sixty-Three Is the Jubilee" (J. L. Greene and D. A. French, 1863). Both of the latter show close kinship to the music of blackface minstrelsy.

Many piano pieces glorified military leaders or commemorated battles, such as the "Beauregard Bull Run Quickstep" (J. A. Rosenberger, 1862) or "General Bragg's Grand March" (P. Rivinac, 1861). The war also contributed material to a type of concert music popular since the time of the American Revolution: the "battle-piece," an extended composition that depicted the progression of a specific engagement. Examples include "The Fall of Fort Sumter" (E. Menger, 1861) and "The Battle of Gettysburg, July 3d, 1863" (James C. Beckel, 1863), both published for piano.

—*Charles E. Kinzer*

See also "Battle Hymn of the Republic"; "Dixie."
For further reading:
Crawford, Richard, comp. *The Civil War Songbook* (1977).
Currie, Stephen. *Music in the Civil War* (1992).
Garofalo, Robert, and Mark Elrod. *A Pictorial History of Civil War Era Musical Instruments and Military Bands* (1985).
Olson, Kenneth E. *Music and Musket: Bands and Bandsmen of the American Civil War* (1981).

MYER, ALBERT JAMES
(1828-1880)
Union chief signal officer

Colonel Albert James Myer served as chief signal officer of the Signal Corps, which he had founded on 21 June 1860. Myer was born in Newburgh, New York, on 20 September 1828. Raised by an aunt in Buffalo, Myer attended Geneva College at the age of thirteen. After gradation, he attended medical college at the University of Buffalo. To support himself, he worked as a telegrapher for the New York State Telegraph Company. This experience helped him develop his medical college thesis, which was a sign language for people with hearing and speech loss.

After graduation from medical college, Myer practiced medicine for three years and then joined the army as an assistant surgeon. He was assigned to Fort Duncan, Texas, where he used his sign language as the basis for the development of a system of signaling with flags. An early biographer, J. Willard Brown, claimed that Myer saw Comanches signaling each other by waving their lances, giving him the idea for developing his wigwag system. Myer's signaling system consisted of a signal flag that was waved to the left or right, forming a four-element code. The four-foot-square flag could be seen with the aid of telescopes at distances up to fifteen miles by day, and similar distances were achieved at night with the use of torches.

While serving at Fort Duncan, Myer corresponded with Secretary of War Jefferson Davis in order to get the army to adopt his signaling system. Davis failed to act on Myer's request, but Myer continued in his pursuit, and in 1859 he appeared before a board chaired by Lieutenant Colonel Robert E. Lee in order to present his system to the army. Lee thought the system might serve to augment the existing battlefield communication systems and ordered trials to be conducted to further evaluate it. Myer was given several assistants including Lieutenant E. P. Alexander, and he started conducting trials at Fort Monroe, Virginia, in April 1859.

Upon conclusion of trials at Fort Monroe, New York harbor, West Point, and Washington, D.C., Myer's system won the approval of Secretary of War John B. Floyd, who recommended to Congress that the army adopt Myer's system and that Myer be appointed as chief signal officer. Although initially resisted by then-senator Jefferson Davis from Mississippi, Congress approved Myer's appointment as major and chief signal officer and the Signal Corps was formed on 21 June 1860. Major Myer was assigned to a post in New Mexico to further test his system in a campaign against the Navajos.

As the army began preparations for the Civil War, Myer was recalled from New Mexico and sent to Fort Monroe, Virginia, where he established a temporary signal camp of instruction. The authorization from Congress in June 1860 did not provide for any personnel other than Myer so that all signal personnel had to be detailed to the corps. Myer trained a nucleus of officers and enlisted men at Fort Monroe and later moved the camp of instruction to Red Hill, north of Georgetown, District of Columbia. Myer attempted to move signal personnel from Fort Monroe to participate in the battle of Bull Run, but was unable to do so in time to support the engagement. His attempt to move a balloon to the battlefield was also unsuccessful.

Myer continued to receive detailed officers and enlisted men, primarily from the Pennsylvania Reserves, and trained them at Red Hill and smaller camps of instructions led by the early graduates. As the chief signal officer of the army, Myer accompanied the Army of the Potomac and personally directed signal activities during the Peninsula campaign. Upon the Army's return from the peninsula, Myer established a line of signal stations along the Potomac River for the purpose of observation and communications. Some of the key positions included Maryland Heights above Harper's Ferry, Point of Rocks, and Sugar Loaf Mountain. Myer eventually gave up his field duties with the Army of the Potomac and concentrated on the development of the Signal Corps.

Myer recognized the need for a field telegraph to supplement communications by flag signals and developed a field telegraph train (wagons), which used a device consisting of a dial instead of the normal key. The Beardslee telegraph device, intended to be used by signal personnel and not requiring the extensive training that Morse operators received, was used with limited success during the Peninsula campaign. Myer had a succession of difficulties with the Military Telegraph Service, which was primarily a civilian organization that used the commercial equipment of the day. On several occasions, Myer had attempted to take control of all telegraphic operations. When he attempted to remove the less than dependable Beardslee device and recruit trained telegraphers, Secretary of War Edwin Stanton removed him from his position as chief signal officer.

Banished to Memphis, Myer wrote *A Manual of Signals: For the Use of Signal Officers in the Field*. Myer continued an acrimonious relationship with Stanton and worked with various political contacts to regain his original position. On 30 October 1866, due to the influence of General Ulysses Grant and President Andrew Johnson, Myer was reinstated as chief signal officer.

Under Myer's guidance, the Signal Corps assumed responsibility for weather duties on 15 March 1870. By 1873 Myer began to recognize his dream of controlling military telegraphy, and the Signal Corps constructed an extensive telegraph network. Brigadier General Myer died in office in 1880. Fort Whipple, in Virginia, was renamed Fort Myer in his honor on 4 February 1881.

—Bill Cameron

See also Signal Corps.
For further reading:
Brown, J. Willard. *The Signal Corps, U.S.A. in the War of the Rebellion* (1896).
Coker, Kathy R., and Carol E. Rios. *A Concise History of the U.S. Army Signal Corps* (1988).
Raines, Rebecca Robbins. *Getting the Message Through: A Branch History of the U.S. Army Signal Corps* (1996).
Scheips, Paul J. "Union Signal Communications: Innovation and Conflict." *Civil War History* (1963).

MYERS, ABRAHAM CHARLES
(1811–1889)
Confederate quartermaster general

Born to Abraham Myers in Georgetown, South Carolina, the younger Myers grew up in Charleston. He graduated from the U.S. Military Academy thirty-second of forty-three in the class of 1833. After graduation he served in Louisiana before the outbreak of the Second Seminole War. He fought in Florida for two years before accepting a position in the Quartermaster Department. He returned to Florida as quartermaster in the last year of the war. During the Mexican-American War, he left the Quartermaster Department to fight in northern Mexico under Zachary Taylor and under Winfield Scott in the Mexico City campaign. Myers was brevetted twice for bravery, before returning to the Quartermaster Department as chief quartermaster in Mexico during the withdrawal of U.S. forces from there.

During the 1850s, Myers continued in the Quartermaster Department and was stationed in several Southern states. Also in the 1850s, he married Major General David E. Twiggs's daughter, Marion Twiggs. This led the general to take an active interest in the career of his new son-in-law. During the growing tensions between the Southern states and the federal government at the end of 1860, Myers, stationed in New Orleans, and Twiggs, commander of the Department of Texas, corre-

sponded frequently about the crisis. When state officials in New Orleans demanded that Myers turn over all the federal army stores in the city, he did so on 28 January 1861 and resigned his commission the same day.

During February 1861, Myers acted as quartermaster general of Louisiana. Upon the formation of the Confederate States of America, Myers offered his services and was appointed acting quartermaster general on 31 March 1861 at the rank of lieutenant colonel. Myers continued in that capacity until December 1861, when he was named quartermaster general. In February 1862 he received a promotion to colonel, the rank designated by Confederate law for his position.

Over the next year and a half, Myers built a fairly efficient bureaucracy of deputies spread throughout the country. The inferior railroad network of the Confederacy, the scarce manufacturing resources, and the tightening Union blockade, however, made his job of supplying the Southern armies increasingly difficult. Most commanders, especially those whose men suffered from insufficient clothing and other supplies, excoriated him. In the summer of 1863, his problems came to a head when he lost the support of President Jefferson Davis. While Davis was certainly cognizant of his commanders' frustrations, rumors circulated throughout Richmond that his growing dislike of Myers stemmed as much from a feud between the two men's wives as from Myers's inability to supply the armies. Whatever the reason, Davis replaced Myers with Brigadier General Alexander R. Lawton on 7 August 1863. Myers later protested his replacement, claiming that Davis had failed to consult the Confederate Senate regarding Lawton's nomination. The Senate agreed, forcing Davis to make the formal nomination in early 1864. Myers, now jobless within the army, left for Georgia, where he spent the remainder of the war.

After the war, Myers and his wife traveled in Europe for a while before returning to live in the Washington, D.C., area. During the last years of his life, Myers helped his wife fight in the courts for the return of some of her father's property that had been seized by General Benjamin Butler when Union forces took New Orleans. Myers died in Washington.

—David S. Heidler and Jeanne T. Heidler

See also Quartermaster; Twiggs, David E.
For further reading:
Burke, Walter E. *Quartermaster: A Brief Account of the Life of Colonel Abraham Charles Myers, Quartermaster General, C.S.A.* (1976).

N

NAMOZINE CHURCH, BATTLE OF
(3 April 1865)

The cavalry fighting around Namozine Church, Virginia, was the opening clash in General Robert E. Lee's desperate retreat from Richmond and Petersburg. It also provided Major General George Armstrong Custer with the first of many opportunities to distinguish himself in the Appomattox campaign.

Major General Philip H. Sheridan's crushing victory at Five Forks on 1 April 1865, followed a day later by heavy Union attacks on Lee's Petersburg lines, placed the Confederate Army of Northern Virginia in an untenable position. Rather than see his army trapped and destroyed, Lee decided to abandon Richmond and Petersburg. On the evening of 2 April, Lee's troops began evacuating their extensive defenses under the cover of darkness. Lee directed the remnants of his army to rendezvous at Amelia Court House, a junction thirty-nine miles southwest of Richmond and thirty-six miles northwest of Petersburg. From there he planned to follow the Richmond & Danville Railroad to Burkeville and then on to Danville.

Anticipating Lee's moves, Sheridan ordered the forces under his immediate command, four cavalry divisions and the Army of the Potomac's V Corps, to lunge west and block the enemy's line of retreat. Commanding two cavalry divisions from Sheridan's Army of the Shenandoah, Major General Wesley Merritt set out on the morning of 3 April, following the Rebels along the Namozine Road toward Amelia Court House. The energetic Custer and his 3d Cavalry Division, the best mounted command at Sheridan's disposal, spearheaded Merritt's pursuit.

Approaching Namozine Creek later that morning,

Custer encountered the Confederate rear guard, a few infantry, and Brigadier General William P. Roberts's small brigade from Major General W. H. F. "Rooney" Lee's cavalry division. Roberts had dismounted the 4th North Carolina Cavalry Regiment and the 16th North Carolina Cavalry Battalion and occupied entrenchments on the west bank. Custer brought up an artillery battery to pepper Roberts's position with canister while the 1st Vermont Cavalry splashed across the creek out of the defenders' sight to strike their flank. As soon as the Confederates discovered this threat, they beat a hasty retreat.

Having secured the ford, Custer crossed the rest of his division and headed toward Namozine Church, roughly five miles away. Another Confederate cavalry brigade under Brigadier General Rufus Barringer deployed near the church to check the oncoming Federals. Barringer formed the 1st and 2d North Carolina Cavalry in a battle line supported by a single gun and stationed the 5th North Carolina Cavalry in reserve at the church.

Custer's leading regiment, the 8th New York Cavalry, discovered Barringer's dispositions and conducted a quick reconnaissance in force. After the 1st Vermont Cavalry reached the scene, the Federals attacked in earnest. The 8th New York worked its way around the Confederate left, flanking the 1st North Carolina. As Barringer tried to organize a fighting withdrawal, Custer committed a third regiment, the 15th New York Cavalry, and transformed the North Carolinians' retreat into a rout.

Custer's victorious troopers took 350 prisoners, 100 horses, and a gun. Leading one Union charge, 2d Lieutenant Thomas W. Custer, an aide on his older brother's staff, captured the battle flag of the 2d South Carolina Cavalry and fifteen prisoners. For this feat, Custer received his first Medal of Honor. He would earn his second three days later.

Custer chased after the fleeing rebels, skirmishing with various formations throughout the day. He ran into substantial infantry opposition at Sweathouse Creek near dark and halted for the night. That freed the Confederates to continue their retreat, but Sheridan and his fast-moving cavalry would resume their merciless pursuit with the return of daylight.

—*Gregory J. W. Urwin*

See also Appomattox Court House; Barringer, Rufus; Custer, George Armstrong; Five Forks; Lee, William Henry Fitzhugh; Merritt, Wesley.

For further reading:

Calkins, Chris M. *The Appomattox Campaign, March 29–April 9, 1865* (1997).

———. *From Petersburg to Appomattox: A Tour Guide to the Routes of Lee's Withdrawal and Grant's Pursuit* (1983).

Starr, Stephen Z. *The Union Cavalry in the Civil War* (1979–1985).

Urwin, Gregory J.W. *Custer Victorious: The Civil War Battles of General George Armstrong Custer* (1990).

Wert, Jeffry D. *Custer: The Controversial Life of George Armstrong Custer* (1996).

NAPOLEON III
(1808–1873)
Emperor of France

Charles Louis Napoleon Bonaparte was born in Paris on 21 April 1808 to Louis Bonaparte, brother of Napoleon I, and Hortense Beauharnais, daughter of Josephine Beauharnais and stepdaughter of the emperor. After the fall of the First Empire in 1814, Louis Napoleon (the name by which he was known until he became emperor) lived with his family in exile in Germany, Switzerland, and Italy until 1836. In that year he returned to France in what would be the first of two failed attempts to overthrow King Louis Philippe by inciting Bonapartist rebellions within the ranks of the French army. For the second attempt, made in 1840, the government sentenced Louis to life imprisonment in the fortress of Ham, where he remained for six years until managing an escape to Britain. When revolution toppled Louis Philippe in February 1848, Louis Napoleon, whose name and past exploits had since made him famous in France, returned to his homeland in September after winning election to a seat in the assembly. He used his new position as a platform to run for the republican presidency, which he won in December. Determined to restore the empire of his uncle, President Louis Napoleon gained control of the army and undermined the assembly. On 2 December 1851, he ended the republic by military coup and one year later proclaimed himself emperor of the Second Empire. He took the title of Napoleon III in deference to the memory of the original emperor's deceased son.

The first decade of Napoleon's reign produced a number of substantial domestic and foreign policy achievements. His government promoted the expansion of credit, industrialization, railroad and telegraph construction, and the renovation of Paris.

In foreign affairs, Napoleon returned France to the ranks of the great powers. He successfully intervened against Russia in the Crimean War, defeated the Austrians in Italy, completed the conquest of Algeria, acquired Nice and Savoy from Piedmont, established French rule over Indochina, and undertook the construction of the Suez Canal.

Despite this position of strength, Napoleon was worried about the outbreak of civil war in America. It threatened to disrupt or end the flow of Southern cotton to French textile factories and the shipments of Northern wheat to French ports. The resulting economic crisis could produce social unrest, even revolution. Napoleon chose a policy of neutrality for France and hoped for a quick resolution of the American conflict; however, he tempered France's official neutrality with a personal sympathy for Southern independence, which fitted his traditional policy of support for national self-

determination movements in Europe. Following Britain's lead in 1861, he declared France's neutrality and upheld the British position in the *Trent* Affair. A string of Southern victories in the summer of 1862 tempted Napoleon to entertain the possibility of mediating the conflict and granting official recognition to the Confederacy. However, eventual Federal victories and his fear of war with the United States precluded these steps.

In 1862, Napoleon, who had sent troops to Mexico in 1861 as part of an international debt collection force, seized the opportunity offered by America's preoccupation with its war to intervene further in Mexican affairs. He dreamed of creating a French Latin American empire by first overthrowing the revolutionary Mexican government of Benito Juárez. French honor was also at stake after Juárez's army defeated the French expeditionary force near Puebla on 5 May 1862. Napoleon reinforced the French commitment with 23,000 troops, and his men captured Mexico City on 7 June 1863. Mistaken in his belief that the Mexicans would embrace a foreign monarchy, Napoleon established Archduke Maximilian of Austria as emperor of their country.

Southern leaders hoped that Napoleon would seek Confederate recognition and support for Maximilian's regime in return for Maximilian's recognition of their government. This would have constituted de facto French recognition of the Confederacy. Yet Napoleon rejected Southern overtures to court continued U.S. neutrality in Mexican affairs and eventual U.S. recognition of Maximilian's government. The Lincoln administration, however, never recognized Maximilian, but it acted as if it might to keep him from establishing relations with the Confederacy.

When the Civil War ended, the United States no longer had to appease the French, and Secretary of State William H. Seward applied diplomatic pressure to encourage Napoleon to leave Mexico. By 1866 Napoleon no longer believed that he could support the costs of the Mexican expedition, especially in the face of Prussia's disturbing success in central Europe. Consequently, he pulled all of his troops out of Mexico by the spring of 1867. Maximilian's regime collapsed in May, and the Mexicans executed him a month later.

Three years later, Napoleon, angered at being left out of the German settlement that came in the wake of Prussia's defeat of Austria in 1866, let himself be drawn into war against Prussia in July 1870. Unprepared, the French nevertheless fought bravely and inflicted heavy losses on the enemy in the initial border battles. The Prussians, however, maintained their advance, while the poorly led French retreated in two large armies. One army, accompanied by the emperor, concentrated at Sedan, where the Prussians surrounded it and forced Napoleon to surrender on 1 September 1870. The

Second Empire fell two days later to the forces of a resurgent republicanism. After a brief captivity, Napoleon joined his family in exile in Britain, where he died in January 1873 as a result of complications from a kidney operation.

—*R. Boyd Murphree*

See also Cotton; Diplomacy, C.S.A.; Diplomacy, U.S.A.; Maximilian, Ferdinand; Mexico; Slidell, John.

For further reading:

Case, Lynn M., and Warren F. Spencer. *The United States and France: Civil War Diplomacy* (1970).

Gooch, Brison D. *The Reign of Napoleon III* (1969).

Hanna, Alfred J., and Kathryn Abby Hanna. *Napoleon III and Mexico: American Triumph over Monarchy* (1971).

NASHVILLE, BATTLE OF
(15–16 December 1864)

On 30 November 1864, Confederate general John Bell Hood launched a hastily planned, ill-advised frontal assault against two Union corps, under Major General John M. Schofield, at Franklin, Tennessee. Despite suffering casualties that numbered 7,000 (some three times those of the Federals), Hood followed Schofield, who withdrew 20 miles to Nashville during the night. At Nashville, Schofield joined forces with Major General George H. Thomas behind the formidable defenses of Tennessee's capital city. Thomas then commanded some 55,000 effective soldiers, having pulled in garrison troops from many parts of the state, as well as being reinforced by 12,000 men led by Andrew Jackson Smith, just arrived from Missouri. Hood approached Nashville with less than half the number of troops commanded by Thomas.

The Confederate commander's options after the battle of Franklin left much to be desired. Obviously, he might launch an assault at Nashville. But Nashville, one of the most heavily fortified cities in America, was even more formidable defensively than Franklin, and Hood's forces could not endure another bloodletting like that. To move around the Union army at Nashville, crossing the Cumberland River and marching for Kentucky and the Ohio, as winter neared and without wagon transport, was not feasible. Also, Thomas's army would be behind Hood, while enemy reinforcements could be expected to gather in his front. A third option was to retire south, but that would be an admission of defeat. Thus Hood came on to Nashville.

He positioned his army across the two railroads leading south and southeast from the city, severing any possible communication by rail between Thomas and Sherman, and hoped to entice Thomas into making an assault—perhaps an assault coupled with major blundering. (Originally Hood had thought his Tennessee campaign might provoke a counter-march by Sherman, but the latter was well on his way to Savannah, living

without rail supply and hardly concerned about communicating with Thomas.)

Actually it was Hood who blundered—again. Weakening his already depleted forces, Hood sent off Forrest with most of the cavalry and two brigades of infantry to attack the Federals who held Murfreesboro, thirty miles to the southeast. The Confederates at Nashville were left with less than 20,000 effectives, possibly as few as 15,000. What Hood was thinking is a curiosity. Perhaps he had no idea how strong Thomas's army was. If he did know, as he claimed after the war, he was taking a great risk in so weakening his own army in the face of the enemy. Maybe he expected an easy victory at Murfreesboro (which was not to be) that would lift the morale of the Army of Tennessee following the devastation at Franklin. Was he simply seeking to prevent the Murfreesboro Federals from joining Thomas? Or did he seek to compel Thomas to march to the relief of the Murfreesboro garrison so the Southern army might attack the Federals in flank? Whatever Hood had in mind, the Yankee troops at Murfreesboro held their ground and the Rebel line at Nashville was stretched dangerously thin.

The Confederate line extended for almost five miles, from the Hillsboro Pike on the west, held by the corps of A. P. Stewart, across the Franklin Pike to the east, where

NASHVILLE CAMPAIGN
DECEMBER 1864
Fifty Miles

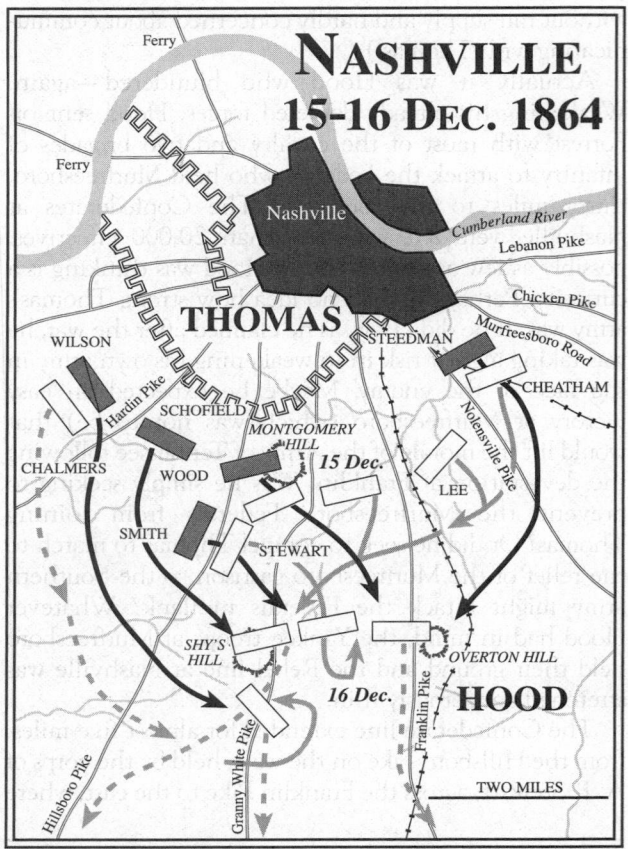

NASHVILLE
15-16 DEC. 1864

of the Union force, fierce fighting erupted and Steedman's men took rather heavy casualties. Meanwhile, the main Federal assault went in against the Confederate left along the Hillsboro Pike. Those Rebels, soldiers of Stewart's corps, fought valiantly, but they were overwhelmed by superior numbers of blue infantry, supported by General James H. Wilson's strong cavalry command. The Southern left was overlapped, their five redoubts overrun, and the men who escaped becoming casualties retreated southeastward toward the Granny White Pike. Reinforcements sent by Hood from Lee and Cheatham were the proverbial too little and too late.

That night the Confederates formed a new line about a mile and a half to the south of their first position. This line was shorter and more compact and did not have the exterior line problem of the first location. The southern line stretched eastward from an eminence soon to be known as Shy's Hill, located just west of Granny White Pike, to Peach Orchard Hill, slightly east of Franklin Road. In a straight line this was about two miles, but the line meandered somewhat, making it considerably more than two miles altogether. Lee's corps held the right flank with Stewart in the center and Cheatham on the left on top of Shy's Hill.

On December 16, Thomas continued to apply pressure against the Rebel right, while planning for the decisive attack on the enemy's left. Again black troops charged the Confederate right and suffered heavy casualties. Their white officers did not serve these brave troops well in mounting this attack. On the opposite end of the line, decisive action came late in the afternoon when the infantry corps of A. J. Smith and Schofield and Wilson's cavalry converged on the Rebels from three directions, after Union artillery had pounded the Confederate position for much of the day. A badly positioned and rather weakly manned southern salient was overwhelmed by charging Yankees as Colonel William Shy died atop the hill that bears his name. Cheatham's entire position collapsed, and so did the rebel center under Stewart. With Wilson's Federal troopers holding the Granny White Pike in their rear, the situation for the Confederates appeared bleak indeed.

The Southerners streamed across the fields east of Granny White toward the Franklin Pike, some of them struggling over the rugged Overton Hill range. Only a capable defense by Lee's corps, who held on until the other two Rebel corps could reach the Franklin Pike, prevented a complete rout of the Confederate forces. Lee continued his rear guard actions until Forrest's cavalry, returned from the Murfreesboro venture, took over that duty, enabling Hood to get the remnants of the once powerful Army of Tennessee back across the Tennessee River into northern Alabama and eventually into Mississippi at Tupelo, where he requested to be relieved from command—a request with which Richmond complied.

Stephen D. Lee's corps manned the center, finally to the Nolensville Pike, where B. Franklin Cheatham's corps occupied the right flank of the position. Yet the rebels did not cover all the major roads into Nashville on the south bank of the Cumberland, had to operate on exterior lines, and were vulnerable to a flanking attack. Hood simply did not have sufficient strength to warrant accepting battle at Nashville.

By 9 December, Hood faced another problem. Bitterly cold weather descended on the region and Nashville was covered with ice and snow. With the ground frozen hard, the poorly clad Southerners, many of whom were without shoes and suffered severely, could not strengthen their line of earthworks as planned. The bad weather, of course, also had an impact on the Federals. General Thomas, whose preparations for battle had just been completed, was compelled to delay his attack until the weather moderated. Undoubtedly Thomas made the correct decision; however, General Grant, who had urged Thomas to attack earlier, became highly impatient, first considering replacing Thomas and then preparing to go to Nashville himself. Fortunately for Thomas, a thaw set in and on 15 December the Union army moved to the attack.

Early in the morning, General James Steedman made a feint against the Confederate right flank. When the Confederates realized that black soldiers composed part

The battle of Nashville, fancifully depicted in an 1891 Kurz & Allison print (*Library of Congress*)

The Federals in the battle of Nashville had inflicted more than 6,000 casualties, at a cost of just over 3,000 to themselves. They narrowly missed destroying the entire Southern army, which had been so seriously weakened by the battle of Franklin only a short time earlier. That army, after Nashville, was damaged to a degree from which it could never recover. Finally, General Thomas, the "Rock of Chickamauga," had proved he could handle an army admirably on the attack as well as on the defense.

—*James L. McDonough*

See also Franklin, Battle of; Hood, John Bell; Schofield, John McAllister; Thomas, George Henry.

For further reading:
Horn, Stanley F. *The Decisive Battle of Nashville* (1956).
Sword, Wiley. *Embrace an Angry Wind* (1992).

NASHVILLE, TENNESSEE

Settled on a bend of the Cumberland River, Nashville, Tennessee, was the main supply depot and rail link for Confederate forces in the West. Captured by the Union in 1862, the city remained in Union hands for the remainder of the war, despite the attempts by Confederate general John B. Hood to liberate it in the battle of Nashville in 1864. The Confederate Army of Tennessee was nearly annihilated in this unsuccessful attempt.

Designated as the state capital in 1843, Nashville grew exponentially when the Nashville & Decatur Railroad linked the city to lucrative trade routes from Ohio to Atlanta. Antebellum Nashville was a burgeoning trading depot whose prosperity was bound not only to trade but also to slave-produced agricultural products from its hinterland. Even though the city had served as the site of the secessionist Nashville Convention during the crisis of 1850, antebellum Nashville was surprisingly Unionist, as evidenced by its being the birthplace of the Constitutional Union Party. Committed to preserving the Union and with no stance on slavery, the party won 59 percent of Nashville's vote for its presidential candidate of 1860. However, once war broke out in 1861, Nashville sided with the Confederacy, becoming a major producer of gunpowder and the main supply depot for Confederate operations in the West.

Nashville in 1862 was part of Confederate general Albert Sydney Johnston's Western Military Department that stretched from Arkansas to the Appalachian

The statehouse at Nashville, 1864 (*National Archives*)

Mountains. Johnston commanded over 70,000 troops in this theater, while his opposite numbers, Union generals Henry Halleck and Don Carlos Buell, commanded nearly the same number. Early in 1862, a little-known Union commander, Ulysses S. Grant, struck out from Cairo, Illinois, toward Fort Henry on the Tennessee River.

Maneuvering in conjunction with Union gunboats, Grant attacked Fort Henry on 6 February, overwhelming the 2,500 defenders. Swinging east, Grant then moved toward Fort Donelson, a much more heavily defended position located north of Nashville on the Cumberland River. Grant took this fort on 16 February, capturing over 13,000 Confederate soldiers and effectively cutting Johnston's remaining army in two. Faced now with Buell's fresh Army of the Ohio marching toward Nashville from the north and Grant's victorious army marching from the northwest, Johnston made the decision to abandon Nashville without a fight on 23 February 1862.

Thus fell the first Southern capital and major indus-

trial center to Union forces during the war. Nashville remained occupied for more than three years. Andrew Johnson, then military governor of Tennessee, conducted government from the city. As a telling sign of the city's antebellum Union sympathies, there was no organized attempt at rebellion or guerrilla warfare within the city during its occupation.

Nashville was an invaluable supply and rail center for the Union army. The Nashville & Decatur Railroad connected to the Memphis & Charleston Railroad, together forming a direct line of supply from Louisville to Nashville, from there to Chattanooga, and from Chattanooga to Atlanta. This invaluable supply link made it possible for William Tecumseh Sherman's army to capture Atlanta on its famous March to the Sea. The seizure of this prize in 1864 came as Abraham Lincoln was running for reelection and needed an impressive victory to overcome the opposition of the peace movement in the North.

Fortified railroad bridge across the Cumberland River at Nashville, 1864 (Photograph by George N. Barnard / *Library of Congress*)

Late in 1864, Nashville became the site of the last great battle of the West. The battle of Nashville destroyed the Army of Tennessee and decided the fate of the western Confederacy. With Lee mired in the Richmond-Petersburg area and Atlanta having fallen to Sherman's army, the chances of the Confederacy surviving the military contest grew slimmer each day. It

was at this time that General John Bell Hood made the decision to lead the Army of Tennessee toward Nashville in an attempt to divert Sherman out of Georgia and possibly capture the rich supply depot there.

As Hood moved closer to Nashville, Union general John Schofield prepared to meet him near Franklin, thirty miles south of Nashville. After skirmishing with

Hood for several days, Schofield's 30,000 troops fortified their entrenched position and waited for Hood's next move. On 30 November, Hood ordered his infantry to make a frontal assault on the works. The fighting at the battle of Franklin was fierce and lasted long into the night. General Schofield ordered his troops to abandon their positions and move toward Nashville. Hood's pyrrhic victory cost him dearly. The Confederate Army of Tennessee suffered more than 7,000 casualties, over one-quarter of its strength. Even more damaging to their cause, the army lost twelve generals and half of its regimental commanders, fifty-four in all. With his command structure shattered, Hood ordered his troops to pursue the Union army to Nashville.

By the time Hood reached Nashville, General George H. Thomas was waiting for him. When Hood neared the fortified capital he entrenched his own troops along the hills south of the city and waited for Thomas to attack. After repeated prodding from Grant, Thomas finally moved out of Nashville with his 50,000 troops and attacked Hood's army of 25,000 on 15 December. After barely hanging on the first day, Hood retreated to a shorter defensive line two miles south. On 16 December his army completely collapsed under the weight of the Federal attack. Confederate troops resembled a mob as they fled the vicinity of the capital city. The Army of Tennessee, once 40,000 strong when Hood took command, now limped out of Tennessee, through Alabama, and finally into Mississippi. When the army mustered in Tupelo, Mississippi, just under half of its original force remained. Devastated by the losses, Hood resigned his command on 13 January 1865. Nashville remained in Union hands for the remainder of the war.

—Lincoln Bramwell

See also Fort Donelson, Battle of; Fort Henry, Battle of; Franklin, Battle of; Nashville, Battle of.

For further reading:

Burt, Jesse C. *Nashville: Its Life and Times* (1959).
Goodstein, Anita Shafer. *Nashville: 1780–1860* (1989).
Stockdale, Paul H. *The Death of an Army: The Battle of Nashville and Hood's Retreat* (1992).

NAST, THOMAS A.
(1840–1902)
Cartoonist

The father of American political cartooning and, by most accounts, its greatest practitioner, Nast gained national fame in his early twenties during the Civil War when his evocative, emotional drawings rallied the North behind the Union cause. Many of his creations—the Democratic donkey, the Republican elephant, the Tammany tiger, even Santa Claus—are still used by cartoonists today.

Born in Breslau in present-day Germany, Nast immigrated to the United States with his mother in 1846. At the age of fifteen he began drawing for *Frank Leslie's Illustrated Newspaper*, where he first gained notice with his pictures of the Heenan-Sayers championship boxing match and his coverage of Garibaldi's campaign in Italy. Nast moved to the *New York Illustrated News* after Leslie cut his salary. In 1862, at the height of the Civil War, he was hired by *Harper's Weekly* just as it was becoming the nation's most important magazine. Rather than simply reproducing war scenes, he began drawing elaborate centerfold woodcuts that portrayed passionate emotional themes and made telling political points. One such illustration, "Compromise with the South," depicted a grinning Confederate shaking hands with a weeping, one-legged Northerner over the grave of "Our Union heroes who fell in a useless war." Aimed at the Peace Democrats who favored a negotiated truce with the South, it was widely circulated by Abraham Lincoln's supporters during the 1864 election. *Harper's* later boasted that its effect "upon the glorious results of the campaign was undeniable."

An intense Radical Republican and a fervent Lincoln supporter, Nast saw himself as the voice of the Union cause and his drawings were aimed at shoring up support for the president during the long and harsh Civil War. "Thomas Nast has been our best recruiting sergeant," Lincoln himself said near the end of the war. "His emblematic cartoons have never failed to arouse enthusiasm and patriotism, and have always seemed to come just when these articles were getting scarce." Nast's 1863 sentimental centerfold "Christmas Eve"—two scenes showing a soldier sitting at a campfire looking at pictures of his family and that same family at home pining for the absent soldier—touched hearts around the country. One colonel wrote to *Harper's* that he couldn't stop weeping after seeing the drawing. "It was only a picture," he wrote, "but I couldn't help it."

Equally powerful were Nast's attacks on the South, condemning its methods of warfare and, particularly, its treatment of slaves. "Southern Chivalry" inflamed passions across the North, precisely as Nast had intended. Nast, said his biographer Albert Bigelow Paine, did not consider his drawings works of art; he believed his role was to strike savage and fatal blows at the enemy during a time of war. By the end of the war, many people were buying *Harper's Weekly* primarily for Nast's illustrations.

Nast's greatest personal and political triumph, however, came after the Civil War. In 1870, he set his sights on the New York City political ring led by Tammany Hall boss William M. Tweed, which was believed to have stolen $200 million through inflated construction costs. Nast launched a dramatic frontal attack on Tweed, which included such classics as "Let Us Prey," "Who Stole the People's Money?", and "The Tammany Tiger Loose."

Nast was threatened repeatedly, to the point that he moved his family out of New York. A pro-Tammany banker offered him $200,000 to "go to Europe and study art." Nast refused the offer, saying, "I shall be busy here for some time getting a gang of thieves behind the bars." After the *New York Times* in 1871 published secret Tammany ledgers dramatically proving the massive fraud, Tweed and his conspirators were arrested and the ring was broken.

"Nast," said the humorist David Ross Locke in an 1871 interview, "is a man of indomitable courage and rare intelligence" and a "moralist" who "must have an idea." His pencil "is savage and bitter and cuts like a knout. He tells in ten strokes of his pencil what it would take volumes to express." Few, however, criticized Nast's vicious anti-Catholic cartoons; he was an ardent nativist who feared a papal plot to seize control of America. In "The American River Ganges," he portrayed Catholic priests as crocodiles emerging from the river to devour the nation's children.

Nast left *Harper's* in 1887 to become chief cartoonist for *America,* an anti-Catholic magazine whose chief causes were limitations on suffrage and opposition to liberal immigration. In 1892 Nast launched his own magazine, *Nast's Weekly,* but it folded after just thirteen weeks. Ten years later, friends prevailed on President Theodore Roosevelt to name Nast as U.S. consul in Guayaquil, Ecuador, as a way to provide some financial security for the aging artist after a series of business setbacks. Unfortunately, Nast died of yellow fever just weeks after his arrival.

—*Eric Fettmann*

See also Art; *Harper's Weekly.*
For further reading:
Hudson, Frederic. *Journalism in the United States from 1690 to 1872* (1873; reprint, 1968).
Mott, Frank Luther. *A History of American Magazines* (1938).
Paine, Albert Bigelow. *Thomas Nast, His Period and His Pictures* (1904).

NATIONAL TRIBUNE

The *National Tribune,* a newspaper for Union veterans, was easily the most influential and widely read sheet of its day. The *National Tribune* was the brainchild of George E. Lemon, a wounded veteran of the 125th New York Regiment. Lemon started the paper in late 1877 to provide pension information to Union veterans. He was especially interested in lobbying Congress to pass more liberal pension laws that would benefit not only wounded and disabled veterans but also their widows and families. Lemon also wanted to include on the pension rolls veterans from the War of 1812 and the Mexican-American War.

The *National Tribune* began as an eight-page monthly newspaper. Its masthead carried a quotation from Abraham Lincoln's second inaugural address: "To care for him who has borne the battle, and for his widow and orphans." In March 1879, the National Tribune Company, based in Washington, D.C., took over publishing the paper, which continued as a monthly until June 1881. After a month's hiatus, the *National Tribune* became a weekly paper, with the edition of 20 August becoming volume 1, number 1 of this new series.

Lemon continued as editor, and in the 20 August edition asked readers to submit for publication their recollections of the Civil War. Although the response was slow at first, by mid-1882 the paper was being flooded with articles from Union veterans. To fill space, Lemon copied from other contemporary papers, added a weekly page of Grand Army of the Republic News, and inserted news from other organizations such as the Sons of Union Veterans and Women's Relief Corps. Pension information remained a chief concern of the growing paper.

In 1884, Lemon brought John McElroy to Washington to serve as editor. McElroy was a veteran of the 16th Illinois Cavalry and editor of the *Toledo Blade* at the time. He had been captured during the war and in 1879 had penned a memoir, *Andersonville: A Story of Rebel Military Prisons, Fifteen Months a Guest of the So-called Southern Confederacy.* McElroy piloted the paper to national prominence and remained its editor until his death in 1929. After Lemon died in 1896, McElroy also became the publisher.

The chief value of the *National Tribune* to today's researchers is the gold mine of reminiscences that appeared each week in the *Tribune.* McElroy enticed prominent officers to contribute as well as privates. John Pope, Abner Doubleday, William P. Carlin, Green B. Raum, Oliver O. Howard, and a host of other subalterns contributed to the success of the paper. Their comrades closely scrutinized every entry, and the weekly "Fighting Them Over" column included entire letters as well as highlights of others bantering back and forth regarding the validity of previous articles.

Subjects ranged from Chickamauga and Gettysburg to obscure skirmishes and engagements unreported in the *Official Records.* Veterans argued over who fired the first shot at Gettysburg, whether Grant's army was surprised at Shiloh, who raised the first flag over Atlanta, who the youngest and oldest veterans were, and where the phrase "grab a root" came from. Confederate soldiers occasionally sent in letters or articles; J. P. Cannon of the 27th Alabama and George D. Mosgrove of John Hunt Morgan's cavalry serialized their memoirs in the *Tribune.*

McElroy himself took over the serialization of the adventures of Si Klegg, a fictional Union soldier whose bumbling and humorous tales delighted the old veterans.

The paper also published three volumes of the *National Tribune Scrapbook*, which consisted of articles not published in the paper.

By 1906, Civil War articles had disappeared from the front page as the *Tribune* began printing tales from other veterans as well. A title change reflecting the paper's broadening scope—*The National Tribune/The National Guardsman/The American Standard*—began with the 19 July 1917 issue. On 7 January 1926, the *Tribune* became the *National Tribune/Stars and Stripes* when it incorporated the newspaper of the World War I veterans; the papers combined to present a united front in seeking care for America's veterans. The paper remained with this title until 7 January 1963, when it became the *Stars and Stripes/National Tribune*. Today, the successor to George Lemon's *National Tribune* continues to carry news of interest to active and retired American military personnel.

—*Richard A. Sauers*

See also Pensions; Veterans' Organizations.
For further reading:
Sauers, Richard A. *"To Care For Him Who Has Borne the Battle": Research Guide to Civil War Material in the National Tribune, Volume 1: 1877–1884* (1995).

NATIVISM

Nativism was the term that mid-nineteenth-century Americans used to describe the movement that favored restricting the political rights of immigrants. Nativism had risen sharply in the 1850s as immigration rose, manifesting itself for a time in the American Party (known as the Know-Nothings because it was organized with all the secrecy and ritual of the Masons). The roots of this movement lay in a fear of the consequences to American society posed by the presence of large numbers of largely unskilled workers, many of whom were Catholic. Republican anxiety about a permanent wage-earning class, the desire of existing workers to protect their jobs, and a powerful anti-Catholicism gave great political strength to nativism.

Historians have debated the extent to which the Republican Party adopted nativist rhetoric in order to replace the Know-Nothings as the dominant non–Democratic Party in the free states. Dependence on building coalitions with nativists varied from state to state and there were many prominent Republicans (such as Abraham Lincoln and William Henry Seward) who firmly resisted using crude nativist appeals on both pragmatic and ideological grounds. Nevertheless, it remains true that the Republican Party drew on similar cultural and socioeconomic impulses to the Know-Nothings: Protestantism, class prejudice, and an Anglo-Saxon conception of American identity. As a result, implicit and sometimes quite crude nativism was evident in Republican Party appeals.

The pace of immigration slowed during the war, but hostility to immigrants was in some ways intensified. Some communities of new immigrants, who were brought immediately into the political orbit of the Democratic Party were the most opposed to conscription. In July 1863, three days of rioting in New York City, in part by Irish workers opposed to the draft, intensified the anti-Irish feeling of the city's "respectable" community. A typical reaction was that of the Republican banker George Templeton Strong, who concluded that "England is right about the lower class of Irish. They are brutal, base, cruel, cowards." Union Party leaders were hostile to new immigrants who tried to avoid the draft by claiming exemption as aliens, but who also voted or who declared intentions to become citizens. It was commonly observed in the Republican Party press that "ethnic" immigrants were not represented in the Union army in proportion to their numbers.

One of the most revealing of many didactic images produced by the pro-Lincoln cartoonist Thomas Nast during the 1864 election campaign was subtitled "Citizens Voting." It depicted a respectable, bearded gentleman voting for Lincoln, while a dirty, scruffy, apelike Irishman voted for McClellan. The crude nativist prejudices that this image revealed were linked to allegations that the Democratic Party was controlled by foreign, anti-Republican interests. Tempting the simian Irishman with a bag of gold was a rotund John Bull figure with a copy of the *London Times* in his pocket. The Democratic Party, it was claimed, was "engaged in exciting sedition, employing...as its principal instruments aliens, and recently naturalised aliens." In another cartoon, an Irishman was depicted with Neanderthal features and carrying a club. He responded to McClellan with the words "All right General! If yere in favor of resistin' the draft, killing the nagurs and pace wid the Southerners, Ill knock any man on the head that'll vote agin ye."

Immigrants, especially Irish Catholics and those in laboring jobs in the Eastern cities, were overwhelmingly Democratic. By their actions in resisting fighting for the Union and by their visible lack of conformity with the cultural norms of ethnically defined Protestant-American nationalism, these communities represented an important internal challenge to the nationalizing effects of the war in the North.

—*Adam I. P. Smith*

See also American Party; Election of 1864; Immigration; Irish-Americans; New York City Draft Riots.
For further reading:
Anbinder, Tyler. *Nativism and Slavery: The Northern Know Nothings and the Politics of the 1850s* (1992).
Bernstein, Iver. *The New York City Draft Riots: Their Significance for American Society and Politics in the Age of the Civil War* (1990).

NATURAL BRIDGE, FLORIDA, BATTLE OF
(4–6 March 1865)

The last fighting of any significance to occur in Florida took place during the St. Marks expedition of early March 1865, which culminated in the battle of Natural Bridge. In this engagement, a motley Confederate force repulsed a Union attempt to cross the St. Marks River below Tallahassee. The defeat ended Federal efforts to capture the blockade-running port of St. Marks and possibly threaten Florida's capital.

Brigadier General John Newton had originated the idea of a joint army-navy expedition directed against St. Marks, which was located on the Gulf Coast about twenty miles south of Tallahassee. Appointed to command of the District of Key West and Tortugas in the fall of 1864, Newton undoubtedly hoped that even a small victory in a minor theater of the war might rejuvenate his flagging career. Skirmishes in February at Fort Myers and at Station No. 4 near Cedar Key evidently convinced Newton to strike against St. Marks. He believed that Confederate forces had been sent from northern to southern and central Florida and that St. Marks and perhaps Tallahassee were vulnerable to attack. An operation hundreds of miles from the army's headquarters at Key West would require naval support, which came from Admiral Cornelius Stribling's East Gulf Blockading Squadron (EGBS).

Immediate planning for the operation began on 21 February 1865. Stribling chose the naval vessels and transports to be utilized, while Newton began organizing the land forces. Eventually he selected parts of the 2d Florida Union Cavalry and the 2d U.S. Colored Infantry (USCI), along with the 99th USCI. Newton's forces sailed from Key West on February 22–23. After a brief stop at the mouth of the Caloosahatchee River, the vessels traveled northward to Union-occupied Cedar Key, where additional troops were loaded for the voyage to St. Marks.

The transports arrived off St. Marks on 28 February, and during the next several days they were joined by nine EGBS ships under Lieutenant Commander William Gibson. Commander Robert Shufeldt arrived later with additional vessels and assumed command of the naval contingent. The Union plan was to land the army forces near the St. Marks lighthouse on the night of 3–4 March. The Federals would then march to the town of Newport, cross the St. Marks River, and attack the town of St. Marks and its small fort from the rear. Before the main landing, parties would be sent ashore to burn railroad bridges over the Aucilla and Ochlockonee rivers to isolate any Confederate forces in the area. The naval forces, meanwhile, were to ascend the St. Marks River, bombard the Rebel positions, and land a force of about 500 sailors to support the land operations.

The grounding of several ships delayed the landing of Newton's main force until the afternoon of 4 March. The next morning, the Federals advanced toward a bridge crossing the East River, where they skirmished with Confederate troops from the 5th Florida Cavalry Battalion and Dunham's Artillery. Two companies from the 2d USCI captured the bridge and an artillery piece after a brief fight. Newton's troops next advanced to Newport, where they hoped to cross the St. Marks River. Troopers from Lieutenant Colonel George W. Scott's 5th Florida Cavalry, however, had destroyed the bridge there and prepared defensive works on the far side of the stream. During the rest of day the two forces skirmished, while a trickle of Confederate reinforcements began arriving. Major General Samuel Jones, who commanded the District of Florida, had learned of the Union landings the previous evening, when a special train reached Tallahassee bearing the news. He quickly gathered together a force of militia and reserves and sent them southward under Brigadier General William Miller to resist the advance. Included among these was a company of cadets from the West Florida Seminary, today's Florida State University. Miller and the first batch of reinforcements reached Newport by 5:00 P.M. on 5 March.

Seeing that he could not cross the St. Marks at Newport, Newton learned from local guides of another crossing to the north. Known as the Natural Bridge, it was a point where porous limestone caused the river to flow underground for a short distance. During the night of 5–6 March, Newton left a detachment at Newport and marched the bulk of his force to Natural Bridge. The distance was greater than expected, and the Confederates had anticipated just such a movement. Consequently, when the 600-man Federal force reached Natural Bridge shortly before daybreak, it found the Confederates already there and dug in along the west bank of the river. During the day, Southern reinforcements arrived until their numbers reached about 1,000 men with six cannon.

Skirmishing continued throughout the morning, with the Federals making several attempts to outflank the Confederates. Finding his opponent's position too strong, by midafternoon Newton withdrew his forces several hundred yards to an open pine barren, where the men prepared several lines of earthworks. After the repulse of a rash Confederate attack, Newton ordered a retreat back to the coast. While the land forces were meeting defeat, the Union navy's attempts to ascend the St. Marks River had also failed, a victim of the stream's shallow, twisting bends.

During the campaign, the Federals suffered 148 casualties, mostly from the two black regiments. Confederate losses were only 6 killed or mortally wounded, with between 20 and 30 suffering lesser wounds. The

Confederate victory at Natural Bridge improved morale in Florida and assured that Tallahassee would remain in Southern hands for two additional months, but it had no other impact on the outcome of the war.

—*David J. Coles*

See also Florida; Newton, John.
For further reading:
Boyd, Mark F. "The Joint Operations of the Federal Army and Navy near St. Marks, Florida, March 1865." *Florida Historical Quarterly* (1950).
Coles, David J. "Far From Fields of Glory: Military Operations in Florida during the Civil War, 1864–1865" (Ph.D. dissertation, 1996).
Graetz, Robert Bruce. "Triumph Amid Defeat: The Confederate Victory at Natural Bridge, Florida, March 1865" (Bachelor honors thesis, 1986).

NAVY, C.S.A.

The Confederacy faced the daunting challenge of ensuring the export of cotton, its main salable commodity, to European buyers and the import of critical goods, military and otherwise, into the country, while at the same time providing maximum distraction to Northern business enterprises. Much of this responsibility fell to the Confederate navy, an almost nonexistent fleet that had to be built or purchased by a nation with virtually no industrial base, no legal standing in the international community, and few sources of international credit.

From the outset, Confederate secretary of the navy Stephen R. Mallory planned to pursue Southern naval strategy by taking advantage of the technological

Deck of the Confederate gunboat *Teaser*, showing damage following its capture by the USS *Maratanza*, July 1864
(Photograph by James F. Gibson / *Library of Congress*)

Bow of the Confederate gunboat *Teaser* in the James River, Virginia, July 1862
(Photograph by James F. Gibson / *Library of Congress*)

changes that had revolutionized naval warfare at mid-century. Confederate naval strategy, therefore, depended on the steam engine and screw propeller, new and powerful naval ordnance, armored warships, and underwater warfare. This technology translated into blockade running and blockade breaking, economic warfare against the merchant ships of the United States, and the defense of shore installations. Blockade running was undertaken by specially designed and technologically advanced blockade runners and Confederate cruisers. For economic warfare, at first the Confederacy authorized privateers, following the model of the Revolutionary War and the War of 1812. But only about thirty letters of marque were actually issued; the technique was high risk and low profit, privateering being illegal by international treaty after 1856. As a result, from 1862 onward economic warfare was conducted largely by official cruisers of the Confederate States of America.

The Confederacy was well-served by Mallory, formerly a senator from Florida and chairman of the Senate Naval Affairs Committee. He oversaw virtually all Confederate naval and maritime policy and strategy. He has been judged an able navy secretary who did the most with limited resources, who succeeded in formulating and implementing naval strategy, and who had vision and the ability to select competent subordinates. Mallory was restricted mainly by the structural limitations of the Confederacy and the lack of an assistant to manage day-to-day operations of his department or fleet.

In the early months of the war, more than 200 American naval officers "went south" and joined the secessionist states. In all, more than 1,500 officers resigned the U.S. Navy and joined the Confederate counterpart. As a result, the Confederate States Navy was blessed with many exceptional officers, the most prominent among them being: John Mercer Brooke,

Franklin Buchanan, Duncan Ingraham, Catesby ap R. Jones, John Newland Maffitt, Matthew F. Maury, Raphael Semmes, Josiah Tattnall, and James Iredell Waddell. These officers and hundreds of others took the Confederate cause to the inland rivers, coastal waters, and high seas and served that cause well. In addition, naval agent James D. Bulloch was sent in May 1861 to London to buy ships and materiel.

The first challenge facing the Confederacy was how to finance and create a navy. The Confederate States of America began the Civil War with a virtually nonexistent navy and with inadequate facilities for building one. Most American naval facilities—and with them the warships—remained within the United States at the outset of the war. The Confederacy, lacking a sufficient industrial base to build both an army and a navy, was not in a position to build a fleet from scratch as quickly as necessary. Consequently, the Confederacy's initial approach was to try to buy a fleet in Europe. Confederate envoys negotiated contracts for the construction of warships in both Great Britain and France, but diplomatic complications arising from such efforts (violations of neutrality laws) slowed the process. In the end, only a few ships were ever completed or delivered. In the fall of 1863, after the Confederate defeats at Gettysburg and Vicksburg, Britain confiscated rams that were under construction for the Confederacy.

Many of the ships that were completed, however, became famous. Ultimately, the Confederacy could claim numerous innovative naval designs, especially the casement ironclad ram (for example, the *Virginia*, the ex-*Merrimack*), early submarines, and underwater mines (called torpedoes). Over its four-year existence, the Confederate navy included vessels that were purchased, specially built, or converted for the challenges of the war: five seagoing ironclads (although only one, the *Stonewall*, was ever commissioned); thirty-four casement ironclads, of which twenty-one were actually commissioned; twenty cruisers, of which the most famous were the *Alabama*, *Florida*, *Nashville*, *Shenandoah*, and *Sumter*; ten spar torpedo boats; forty-three government-owned blockade runners; and a host of river and coastal defense vessels.

The Confederacy's key internal waterway was the Mississippi River. Other significant water routes were the Ohio, Cumberland, Tennessee, and Red rivers. On the Mississippi in particular, the Confederacy was at a disadvantage, with naval forces weaker than the Union's river fleet. To counter the Union challenge there, the Confederate navy marshaled a fleet of armed river steamers and casement ironclads. After the Union capture of Vicksburg on 4 July 1863, however, the war on the Mississippi River was over for the Confederacy. With the loss of the Mississippi, New Orleans, and various Atlantic ports (especially eastern North Carolina), the Confederacy focused on a defensive strategy against Union amphibious operations.

Two Confederate naval strategies have traditionally received the most study: blockade running and commerce raiding. In April 1861, President Abraham Lincoln announced a blockade of the Confederate coast. For the Confederate cause to succeed, it was critical that the blockade fail, because the Confederacy desperately needed to import basic manufactured products and was staking its survival, in part, on its ability to export cotton. At the same time, the Confederacy lacked the ships necessary to actually destroy the blockade. Ironclads such as the CSS *Virginia* or rams such as those the Confederacy contracted to have constructed in Britain were ultimately confiscated by the British government.

Blockade running, therefore, became the only option and the Confederacy's lifeline. It was a most successful option, too, because profits were high. Most blockade runners were privately owned and usually of British registry. Many had been built especially for the purpose of blockade running. The main Confederate ports for blockade-running activities were Wilmington, Charleston, Savannah, New Orleans, Galveston, and other ports in Florida and Texas. From those ports, Confederate blockade runners typically headed to Bermuda, Nassau, or Havana. As the North gained increasing control of key coastal points, however, blockade running became increasingly more difficult.

Because successfully running the blockade could yield high profits, Confederate entrepreneurs built many vessels specially for the purpose. They were small, low, shallow-draft vessels, equipped with collapsible funnels, and fast. Whenever possible, they used clean-burning anthracite coal rather than bituminous, although Confederate coal supplies of either variety were limited. Typical cargoes on inward-bound runs were arms, ammunition, and other essential war products, in addition to luxury goods for wealthy Southerners. In exchange, Confederate traders were able to provide tobacco and especially cotton. In all, the trade was very profitable. According to modern estimates, about 92 percent of all the attempts to run the blockade succeeded, but that success rate declined significantly as the war progressed and the blockade itself became more effective.

Confederate naval efforts on the high seas focused primarily on commerce raiding. At first, the government authorized privateers for the purpose, even though privateering had been outlawed by the Treaty of Paris of 1856. But as blockade running became increasingly profitable, siphoning capital away from privateers, commerce raiding became a Confederate naval responsibility. Confederate commerce raiders were, for the most part, vessels that had been built or fitted in Britain—until, under pressure from the Lincoln administration, that nation ended the practice. Raiders typically sailed out of their European port as merchant vessels and then, on the high seas, were armed and commissioned for their official purpose.

Confederate commerce raiders were statistically successful in damaging U.S. shipping, although the impact that such damage might have had on the outcome of the Civil War was probably negligible. Because privateering had been outlawed, privateers had no prize courts available to them and therefore found it difficult to profit from the fifty Northern merchant vessels that they were able to capture during the second half of 1861. Afterward, as commerce raiding became a responsibility of the Confederate States Navy, it was still difficult to profit directly from captures because the Confederacy remained, throughout its existence, a political entity with no official international recognition. Ports into which prizes could be brought, therefore, were few.

In the end, the Confederacy benefited from commerce raiding only in a negative and indirect way. The Union felt some amount of pressure to divert its naval strength away from riverine, coastal, and blockading duties and toward the protection of U.S. merchant shipping. But President Lincoln, Secretary of State William Henry Seward, and Secretary of the Navy Gideon Welles resisted such pressures and focused the navy on its primary tasks. Confederate commerce raiding, therefore, succeeded mainly in contributing to the long-term decline of the U.S. merchant marine—a process that had begun before the war but that was exacerbated as Northern ship owners transferred their ships to foreign flag registry.

In addition, however, the activities of Confederate cruisers or commerce raiders threatened the security of the North much more directly than did the blockade runners because the cruisers and commerce raiders threatened to disrupt the Union's links with the rest of the world through its foreign trade and merchant marine. As a result, the activities of those Confederate vessels were the cause of considerable diplomatic friction, particularly between the Union and Great Britain, much more than any other point of disagreement during the war. It is not too much to say that Confederate high seas activities, or plans for such activities, brought the United States and Great Britain close to war on several occasions from 1861 to 1865. The cruisers severely tested British neutrality, as the British government, through its frequently pro-Confederate colonial administrators in the Western Hemisphere, turned a blind eye to Confederate violations of international regulations and thereby benefited the Confederacy.

In particular, Nassau, Bahamas, was known as a hotbed of pro-Confederate sentiment and activity and the most important center for all Confederate merchant and naval shipping. Southern privateers, cruisers, commerce raiders, and blockade runners were ubiquitous at Nassau, and in every instance they were accorded the hospitalities of the port and were granted almost unrestricted access to facilities for repairing, coaling, and fitting. The colonial government took no action to limit Confederate warships, even as they limited the movements of comparable Union vessels.

The four most famous of the Confederate commerce

The Confederate ram *Atlanta* after being captured on the James River, Virginia, 1863 (*National Archives*)

raiders were the *Florida* (*Oreto*), *Shenandoah, Sumter,* and *Alabama*. The *Shenandoah* captured thirty-six prizes during its career, and the *Alabama*, which became emblematic of (but was not typical of) the commerce raiders, captured seventy-one vessels. Under Raphael Semmes, who had a reputation for "humane gallantry," the *Alabama* in twenty-two months took sixty-eight Northern merchant vessels. Its reign of terror ended in June 1864 when it was sunk by the USS *Kearsarge* off Cherbourg, France.

The record of the Confederate States Navy during the Civil War was mixed, yet its contributions were significant. The Confederate navy never succeeded in breaking the blockade, which, in reality, became more effective as the war progressed, and it never succeeded in gaining command of the sea. Nevertheless, its major contribution lies in assisting Confederate armed forces in resisting Union amphibious invasion. It was the navy that helped the Confederacy hold on to key locations as long as it did. Beginning with virtually nothing, the Confederacy accomplished a great deal, but ultimately was overwhelmed by the navy of a nation that was the Confederacy's industrial and technological superior in every way.

—Kenneth J. Blume

See also Alabama, CSS; Blockade Runners; Mallory, Stephen Russell; *Monitor* versus *Virginia*; Navy, U.S.A.

For further reading:

Luraghi, Raimondo. *A History of the Confederate Navy* (1996).
Official Records of the Union and Confederate Navies in the War of the Rebellion (1894–1922).
Scharf, J. Thomas. *History of the Confederate States Navy* (1887; reprint, 1996).
Spencer, Warren F. *Raphael Semmes. The Philosophical Mariner* (1997).
Still, William N., Jr. *Iron Afloat: The Story of the Confederate Armorclads* (1985).

NAVY, U.S.A.

Naval power played a central role in federal war planning and contributed to the Union's defeat of the Confederacy, even as the war itself proved a defining event in the history of the nineteenth-century U.S. Navy. "At all the watery margins," President Abraham Lincoln commented, "they have been present. Not only on the deep sea, the broad bay, the rapid river, but also up the narrow muddy bayou, and wherever the ground was a little damp, they have made their tracks."

Part of the story of the U.S. Navy during the Civil War is its growth in terms of ships, materiel, and personnel. The navy began the war in 1861 with ninety vessels on the Navy Register, of which twenty-one were unseaworthy, twenty-seven laid up in naval yards for extensive repairs or not yet launched, and twenty-eight on foreign stations, far from the rivers, harbors, and coastlines of the United States. Only fourteen vessels

were actually on the Home Station: seven screw steamers, three sailing frigates, one side-wheeler, two store ships, and one steam tender. During the war, the Navy Department ordered some 200 new warships (not all were completed during the war) and purchased or leased another 418 vessels. By the end of 1861, the fleet had swelled to 264 vessels; by the end of the war, to 671. Demobilization was rapid: half of the fleet was sold off before the end of 1865, and the squadrons were quickly disbanded or merged.

The Civil War occurred in the middle of a century of great change in naval technology. Armored warships, steam power, and more powerful ordnance were transforming naval warfare. To meet the crisis of secession, the navy expanded rapidly, building many technologically advanced or innovative warships. Most famous was the revolutionary *Monitor*, a design that was successful for its purpose but of only limited use outside coastal waters. Other noteworthy designs were the "90-day gunboats" (which wore out quickly because they had been built rapidly); "double-enders" (side-wheel gunboats with rudders at each end so that the vessel could operate backward or forward in narrow and shallow coastal waters); the experimental ironclad *New Ironsides* (which was never damaged under fire); the *Galena* (which had inadequate armor); the *Keokuk* (which sank the first time it was fired on); and the monster ram *Dunderberg* (which was completed after the war's end and was then rejected by the navy and sold to France). Wartime requirements spurred technological innovations, although in the postbellum era the naval establishment's dependence on such innovations quickly became technological conservatism.

In addition to a rapid expansion of the fleet, the naval ranks swelled rapidly, from 7,600 in 1861 to 51,000 in 1865. The war, in effect, solved the long-standing promotion bottleneck that had plagued the antebellum navy but, in turn, created a postbellum "hump" that remained an unsolved problem for the rest of the century. Among noteworthy officers, whose fame was reinforced or ensured as a result of the war, were David Glasgow Farragut, Samuel F. Du Pont, David Dixon Porter, John Dahlgren, Charles Wilkes, and John Worden.

The navy's chief administrator was Secretary of the Navy Gideon Welles. A journalist from Connecticut, Welles was excoriated throughout the war for the supposed impotence of his policies but has been seen more recently as an effective secretary who accomplished great things in short amounts of time with limited resources. It was Welles who was responsible for implementing the blockade, even though he personally opposed the policy. Throughout the war he carried out the policies of Lincoln and Secretary of State William Henry Seward even more strenuously than the secretary

Deck and officers of the USS *Catskill* in Charleston Harbor, South Carolina, 1865. Lieutenant Commander Edward Barrett is seated on the turret. (*Library of Congress*)

of state himself advocated. In cases where Union naval officers were overzealous in pursuing their duty, and less sensitive than appropriate on issues of belligerent and neutral rights, it was Welles who had given approval and encouragement.

Welles's principal assistant in the Navy Department was Assistant Secretary of the Navy Gustavus V. Fox. A former naval officer, Fox had been chief clerk of the Navy Department and in March 1861 had been involved in planning for the resupply of Fort Sumter. Fox believed that Sumter could be resupplied by sea, and

in April he was sent aboard the steamer *Baltic* on that mission. Fox's day-to-day administration of the Navy Department kept the navy functioning smoothly throughout turbulent times. As one of the main contacts for American consuls abroad, Fox played an important role in funneling diplomatic, military, and economic information to the State Department.

The navy's tripartite strategic mission was shaped by geographical realities, military necessities, political and diplomatic limitations, and Confederate policies. First, the Anaconda Plan, General Winfield Scott's plan to

Crew members, quarterdeck, and starboard battery of the USS *Pawnee* in Charleston Harbor, South Carolina, ca. 1865
(*Library of Congress*)

starve the South into submission by controlling the Confederacy's three main maritime borders (the Atlantic and Gulf coasts and the Mississippi River), required that the navy devote the bulk of its energies to blockading 3,000 miles of the Atlantic and Gulf coasts and to gaining control of the Mississippi River and its tributaries. Second, to gain control of the sea-lanes to and from both Northern and Southern ports, the Union navy engaged in high seas operations that ranged throughout the Caribbean Sea and the Atlantic and Pacific oceans. Third, the navy engaged in combined operations with the Union army, including amphibious landings and preliminary shelling to prepare for army land attacks. At no point, however, did the navy function as a classic "line-of-battle" fleet. Throughout the war, the navy fulfilled its mission well—and, arguably, enabled the North to win.

The Union navy's riverine operations were a crucial

The USS *Commodore Perry*, a ferryboat converted into a gunboat, on the Pamunkey River, Virginia, 1864 (*National Archives*)

part of the Anaconda Plan. River duties typically included operations against Confederate gunboats, the reduction of Confederate forts and batteries, transportation of troops, and amphibious raids against Confederate lines of communication. Important naval support of army operations occurred on the James, York, Potomac, Ohio, Tennessee, Cumberland, and Red rivers. Strategically, the most critical riverine operations took place on the Mississippi, a central objective of the Anaconda strategy. The Western Gunboat Flotilla was under army control until 1 October 1862, after which it was transferred to the Navy Department and placed under the command of David G. Farragut and David D. Porter. The basic strategy was for Federal naval forces to attack from both the northern and southern ends of the Mississippi, meeting midway and thereby splitting the Confederacy. With the fall of Vicksburg on 4 July 1863, the Union achieved full control of the Mississippi River and hence effective control of all major Confederate waterways. Modern assessments suggest, however, that the Mississippi River campaign showed that only an army could take strong land fortifications—not a navy.

On 19 April 1861, President Abraham Lincoln announced a blockade of the Gulf and Atlantic coasts.

The navy had the responsibility of turning a "paper" blockade into an effective one, and to accomplish that task, the Union constructed a fleet of heavily armed wooden frigates. In September 1861, the fleet was divided into four blockading commands: the North Atlantic, South Atlantic, East Gulf, and West Gulf Blockading Squadrons. From mid-1861 until the effective end of the naval war in 1864, therefore, Union blockading operations focused systematically on closing off centers of Confederate blockade running and trade. Important blockade-related naval operations included Hatteras Inlet in August 1861; Port Royal in November 1861; the capture of New Orleans in April 1862; the battle of Mobile Bay in August 1864; and amphibious operations against Charleston (1863–1865) and Fort Fisher (December 1864–January 1865). In all, Union blockaders captured or destroyed 1,500 vessels of all kinds, although the effectiveness of the blockade remains a subject of debate. For Union sailors, blockading typically amounted to extended periods of tedium punctuated by an occasional exciting chase and capture.

Even more critical to the Union war effort were the navy's operations against Confederate cruisers and commerce raiders, which threatened to disrupt the

North's links with the rest of the world through its foreign trade and merchant marine. In addition to enforcing the blockade, therefore, the navy was charged with seeking out and capturing or destroying Confederate cruisers wherever they might be found on the high seas and protecting merchant shipping from the threat of Confederate raiders. The West India Squadron, for example, was sometimes designated a "flying" squadron because of its broad orders to search out and pursue Confederate cruisers wherever they might lurk in the West Indian waters.

The activities of Union warships on the high seas had diplomatic implications that often complicated Northern war goals. For much of the war, Secretary of the Navy Welles encouraged his officers to take an active and overzealous role in pursuing their tasks. Conflict with other nations was inevitable. The first, and possibly most serious, conflict occurred in November 1861. Captain Charles Wilkes of the USS *San Jacinto* precipitated a major diplomatic crisis by overhauling the British mail steamer *Trent* and removing two Confederate

All able-bodied men not in the employment of the Army, will be enlisted into the Navy upon application at the Naval Rendezvous, on Craven Street, next door to the Printing Office.

H. K. DAVENPORT,
Com'r. & Senior Naval Officer.

New Berne, N. C.,
Nov. 2d, 1863.

A federal recruiting poster issued at New Berne, North Carolina, November 1863 (*National Archives*)

envoys, James Mason and John Slidell. Despite initial British saber rattling, the *Trent* Affair was ultimately resolved peacefully. Thereafter, conflicts occurred occasionally because Union warships interfered with neutral shipping.

In addition, the need for coal for naval steamships—particularly Union attempts to maintain supplies of coal—led to diplomatic complications and conflicts with Great Britain and other nations over neutrality regulations. The Union fleet was predominantly steam, and the percentage that was steam grew as the war progressed. It had become imperative to maintain safe and guaranteed sources of coal in strategic locations. But both the Union and the Confederacy, without colonies, could store or acquire coal supplies only at the sufferance of local colonial administrators. As a result, much of the history of Northern and Southern naval activity in the Caribbean during the Civil War—and the resulting diplomatic complications—can be told through the efforts to locate, secure, and maintain supplies of coal.

The Civil War produced its share of naval heroes who distinguished themselves in well-publicized naval battles. The most famous naval battle of the war occurred at Hampton Roads on 9 March 1862, between two vessels representing the dawn of a new age of navy technology: the USS *Monitor* and the CSS *Virginia*. The *Virginia* had been the steam frigate *Merrimack*, now clad in iron and armed with eleven guns and an iron ram. The revolutionary *Monitor,* designed by naval architect John Ericsson, had a single turret and two 11-inch smoothbore Dahlgren guns, drew only twelve feet, and presented an exceptionally low profile. Despite four hours of heavy fire, neither vessel was seriously damaged, and the battle was deemed a draw. Nevertheless, the *Monitor* had at least succeeded in forcing the *Virginia* to withdraw.

Other significant naval engagements were the capture of New Orleans (27–28 April 1862); Mobile Bay (5 August 1864); Fort Henry (6 February 1862), Fort Donelson (14–16 February 1862), Island No. 10 (7 April 1862), and Memphis (6 June 1862) on the Mississippi; and the battle between the notorious Confederate raider *Alabama* and the USS *Kearsarge*, off Cherbourg, France on 19 June 1864.

The naval role in the Civil War was both significant and illustrative. The activities of the U.S. Navy enabled the Union to win the war by assisting in amphibious operations against the Confederacy, by choking off commerce in and out of the Confederacy, by at least trying to protect U.S. commerce on the high seas, and by maintaining an international presence that helped to keep foreign nations out of the conflict. At the same time, however, the navy alone could not have won the war. In addition, naval activities on the high seas complicated the diplomatic aspects of the war. Finally, the navy that fought for the Union illustrated the new shape of naval warfare: warfare determined by technological realities and dependent on a high-level of industrial development. The U.S. Navy during the Civil War was the navy of a major industrial power, and its accomplishments and challenges reflected that reality.

—*Kenneth J. Blume*

See also Ericsson, John; *Kearsarge*, USS; *Monitor*; *Monitor* versus *Virginia*; Navy, C.S.A.; *Trent* Affair; Welles, Gideon.

For further reading:

Anderson, Bern. *By Sea and by River: The Naval History of the Civil War* (1962).

Merrill, James M. *The Rebel Shore: The Story of Union Sea Power in the Civil War* (1957).

Musicant, Ivan. *Divided Waters: The Naval History of the Civil War* (1995).

Official Records of the Union and Confederate Navies in the War of the Rebellion (1894–1922).

Porter, David D. *The Naval History of the Civil War* (1886; reprint 1984).

NEGLEY, JAMES SCOTT
(1826–1901)
Union general

Born to Jacob Negley and Mary Ann Scott Negley in East Liberty, Pennsylvania, outside of Pittsburgh, James Scott Negley attended Western University of Pennsylvania (the future University of Pittsburgh). He was active in the local militia and eagerly joined the 1st Pennsylvania volunteers at the commencement of the Mexican-American War. He served for the duration of the conflict. Upon returning to Pennsylvania, Negley became interested in scientific agriculture and was locally celebrated for his work. He also remained involved in the western Pennsylvania militia and rose to the rank of brigadier general, commanding the 18th Pennsylvania militia by the outbreak of the Civil War.

Initially occupying a three-month appointment as a brigadier general of Pennsylvania volunteers, Negley fulfilled many roles in the spring and summer of 1861. He served as a recruitment agent first in Pittsburgh and then in Philadelphia. In mid-summer he was placed under Major General Robert Patterson and headquartered at Hagerstown, Maryland, where his primary responsibility was to prevent Confederate movements toward Harper's Ferry.

At the end of his three months, Negley returned home, where he engaged in full-time recruiting. In early 1862 he received another commission, this time as a brigadier general of U.S. volunteers with his date of rank as 1 October 1861. Sent to Tennessee, Negley commanded first an independent brigade and then an independent division under Don Carlos Buell, Army of the Ohio.

During the summer of 1862, Negley operated primarily against guerrilla groups, but also protected communication lines against mobile Confederate units commanded by officers such as Nathan Bedford Forrest. When much of the Army of the Ohio was pulled back into Kentucky to deal with Braxton Bragg's invasion of the state in the fall of 1862, Buell left Negley behind in Nashville to protect that city. He did so in spite of repeated Southern probes against his defenses. On 7 October 1862, Negley skirmished with Confederates trying to gain a foothold near La Vergne, Tennessee, in order to allow Forrest to concentrate forces for an attack against Nashville. Negley prevented the concentration of Confederate forces.

At the battle of Stones River at the end of 1862, Negley commanded a division near the center of the Union defenses. For his bravery in defending his position, he was commended by William S. Rosecrans, and on 24 February 1863 Rosecrans recommended Negley for promotion to major general. When that promotion was forthcoming, it was with a date of rank of 29 November 1862.

During the spring of 1863, Negley commanded his independent division out of Murfreesboro, Tennessee, conducting reconnaissance operations from that location to determine Confederate positions. In June 1863 he led his division under Rosecrans in the Tullahoma campaign. At Chickamauga in September 1863, Negley commanded a division under George H. Thomas. In the Confederate attack on the Union right, Negley, along with most Union forces, was pushed back. Other division commanders, especially Thomas J. Wood and John M. Brannan, accused Negley, Thomas L. Crittenden, and Alexander M. McCook of retreating too soon. Negley was relieved of command. In December 1863 he was sent to Cincinnati to aid in recruiting there. His request for a court of inquiry was finally granted by the president in January 1864, and the court found that Negley had not acted cowardly nor deserted his position.

After the finding of the court of inquiry, Negley attempted to gain a new field command but his efforts proved fruitless. He was appointed to several positions in the North on recruiting duty and served on several investigatory boards. Finding such duty tedious and his treatment humiliating, he resigned from the army in January 1865 and returned home to Pittsburgh. He believed that the army's attitude toward him had been the result of U.S. Military Academy graduates' prejudice toward officers from the civilian world.

In civilian life, Negley engaged in a number of business activities. He became especially interested in promoting the transportation industry in and around Pittsburgh. Politics also beckoned, as Negley became first an active local Republican and then in 1868 was

elected by his district to the U.S. House of Representatives. He served three consecutive terms before returning to his business pursuits. He was elected again in 1884 and served one term. In Congress, Negley pursued his interest in the promotion of railroad and water transportation and tariff legislation to promote Pittsburgh's growing industries. In the late 1880s he moved to New York to pursue new business interests. He lived outside the city in Plainfield, New Jersey, where he died on 7 August 1901.

—*David S. Heidler and Jeanne T. Heidler*

See also Chickamauga, Battle of; Nashville, Tennessee; Stones River, Battle of.

For further reading:

Cozzens, Peter. *No Better Place to Die: The Battle of Stones River* (1990).

———. *This Terrible Sound: The Battle of Chickamauga* (1992).

NELSON, SAMUEL
(1792–1873)
U.S. Supreme Court justice

Born to John Rogers Nelson and Jean McArthur Nelson in Hebron, New York, Samuel Nelson was educated locally and at several New York academies before graduating from Middlebury College in 1813. Upon graduation from college he studied law and began practice in 1817 in Cortland, New York. Along with his law practice, Nelson was also active in New York politics. He received the postmastership of Cortland in 1821.

Increasingly throughout the 1820s Nelson became associated with the more Democratic elements in New York politics and by the end of the decade was active in the New York Democratic Party. During the 1820s Nelson also began a long career on the bench when he was appointed a judge of one of New York's circuit courts. In 1831 he was elevated to the state's supreme court. President John Tyler nominated Nelson to the United States Supreme Court in early 1845, and he was confirmed.

While not a brilliant justice, Nelson was known for his clear, logical deliberations, and he quickly carved out a niche for himself on the Court by becoming its expert on such specialties as patent, admiralty, and international law. Both as a Supreme Court justice and a federal circuit judge, Nelson's rulings were well respected.

Like the other justices on the Roger B. Taney Court, Nelson's opinion in the *Dred Scott* case in 1857 became one of his most famous. Initially, Nelson doubted that the Court even had jurisdiction over the case, if earlier rulings denying citizenship to slaves were upheld. He ultimately relented on the jurisdictional issue to reiterate earlier rulings on the status of slaves who were taken into free areas and then returned to slave states. As a result, he was one of two Northern justices who ruled that Scott was still a slave.

Because Nelson agreed with the Southern majority on the Court that Scott was still a slave and because his opinions were generally very well reasoned, he was initially, in February 1857, selected to write the majority opinion. The majority's desire, however, to settle the issue of slavery in the territories conclusively in the face of growing Northern opposition to slavery's expansion, including among the Court's two dissenting justices, caused them to change to Chief Justice Taney as the author of the majority opinion. Eventually, however, there would be variations in virtually every opinion offered by the Court, including Nelson's.

Nelson's opinion was perhaps the most narrow of those justices who ruled against Scott. Because he held that once Scott returned to a free state, the laws of that state applied to him, Nelson did not believe that even though Scott had been taken into a territory north of the Missouri Compromise line, that slavery in the territories was an issue in the case. Therefore, his ruling was simply that the laws of Missouri governed Scott's status, and that he was still a slave.

Even given the narrowness of Nelson's decision, he was roundly criticized in the North. He weathered the storm, however, and remained on the Court throughout the Civil War. Privately, he expressed the view that secession was unconstitutional, though he also believed that the Constitution did not give the national government the power to force the seceded states to remain in the Union. Informally, during the secession crisis of early 1861, he tried to intervene with the new administration to reach a peaceful solution. His wartime decisions reflected his strong belief in limited government and his opposition to the growth of executive power. He voted with the majority in the case of *Ex parte Milligan* and in the original decision against the Legal Tender Acts.

After the war Nelson remained on the Court, although he became less and less active. His expertise on international law gained him an appointment in 1871 to sit on the joint American and British commission that decided the outcome of the *Alabama* claims. During the deliberations he became ill and retired from the Court in late 1872. He died of a stroke a year later at his home in Cooperstown, New York, on 13 December 1873.

—*David S. Heidler and Jeanne T. Heidler*

See also *Dred Scott* Case; *Ex parte Milligan*; Legal Tender Acts; Supreme Court, U. S.

For further reading:

Fehrenbacher, Don E. *The Dred Scott Case: Its Significance in American Law and Politics* (1978).

Friedman, Leon. *The Justices of the United States Supreme Court* (1969–1978).

NEW BERN, BATTLE OF
(14 March 1862)

New Bern, North Carolina's second-largest city, was a major objective of the Burnside expedition. Possession of New Bern would give the Union the key to control of North Carolina's sounds and coast, bottle up the Neuse River, cut the North Carolina Railroad, and give the Union a strong base to launch further attacks into the state.

After the capture of Roanoke Island, Burnside turned on New Bern. On 13 March, about 12,000 Union troops in transports accompanied by thirteen gunboats landed at Slocum's Creek on the Neuse River about seventeen miles from New Bern. The Union forces met little resistance, but rain and muddy roads delayed their advance until the next day.

Brigadier General Richard C. Gatlin commanded Confederate forces in the Department of North Carolina; however, he remained at his headquarters in Kinston, and the 4,000 Confederates at New Bern were commanded by Brigadier General Lawrence O'Bryan Branch. Defensive works below New Bern were begun in 1861, but the extensive works required more staff

than Branch had, and they were planned to repel attack from the river, not from the land.

Branch chose to defend an inner line of works about six miles south of New Bern. Fort Thompson, on the Neuse, anchored the Confederate left. From the fort, a mile of entrenchments stretched west toward a brickyard along the North Carolina Railroad. Some artillery units and four regiments of infantry held the lines from left to right, with the 35th North Carolina nearest the railroad. The 33d North Carolina was held in reserve. At the railroad, Branch's line shifted 150 yards to the north, where the Confederates had built a line of redans behind a stream called Bullen's Branch. General Branch made a fatal mistake by filling a crucial spot in his line, the gap at the brickyard, with his weakest troops, a poorly trained and armed militia battalion.

Burnside's assault began on the morning of 14 March. A heavy fog shrouded the battlefield as the firing started about 7:30 A.M. Burnside's force was divided into three brigades under Brigadier Generals John G. Foster, Jesse L. Reno, and John G. Parke. Foster moved first against Fort Thompson and the Confederate left with a direct attack, which gained little headway in three hours of heavy fighting.

The battle of New Bern, from a Currier & Ives lithograph (*Library of Congress*)

Reno's brigade followed the railroad tracks and hit the Confederate center. Under Reno's attack, the militia broke, leaving a gap in the Confederate line and exposing the right flank of the 35th North Carolina, which began to crumble. The 26th North Carolina, aided by the 33d, kept the Yankees from exploiting the gap in the center until Parke's Brigade joined the fighting. Seeing the added pressure on the rebel center, Foster ordered a charge. The combined assaults overwhelmed the Confederate lines. With his command breaking up and Union troops pouring into his works, Branch ordered a general withdrawal around midday.

The 26th and 33d North Carolina, holding the Bullen's Branch redans, never received orders to withdraw. It was too late for them to retreat by the time they realized that the battle was lost. Part of the 33d and its colonel were captured, but the remaining soldiers from the redans withdrew in good order. They reached the Trent River bridges only to find that they had been set afire by the defeated army. The 26th, under Colonel Zebulon B. Vance, moved up the Trent until their way was blocked by Brice's Creek, which was too deep to ford. They reached safety by finding a few small boats to ferry their men and the remnants of the 33d, under Lieutenant Colonel Robert F. Hoke.

On the afternoon of 14 March, Burnside's men and the navy gunboats reached New Bern. Most of the town's white citizens fled toward Kinston with the army, leaving many slaves to greet the Union forces.

Richmond's seeming indifference to and neglect of New Bern angered many North Carolinians. After the fall of New Bern, the South soon lost control of North Carolina's sounds and coast, excepting only the region around Wilmington. General Gatlin was removed from command after the disaster. Vance and Hoke received wide recognition for their leadership and for saving their regiments from capture. Vance was elected governor in August 1862 and Hoke later rose to the rank of major general. New Bern remained in Union hands for the rest of the war.

Union casualties at New Bern numbered 90 dead, 380 wounded, and 1 missing from the army, and 2 dead and 11 wounded from the navy; Confederate casualties numbered 64 dead, 101 wounded, and 413 captured or missing.

—*David A. Norris*

See also Burnside, Ambrose E.; Hoke, Robert Frederick; Parke, John Grubb; Reno, Jesse Lee; Vance, Zebulon.

For further reading:

Barrett, John G. *The Civil War in North Carolina* (1963).

Official Records of the Union and Confederate Navies in the War of the Rebellion (1894–1922).

Sauers, Richard A. *"A Succession of Honorable Victories": The Burnside Expedition in North Carolina* (1996).

Sauers, Richard A., and William D. Gorges. *The Battle of New Bern and Related Sites in Craven County, N.C., 1861–1865* (1994).

U.S. War Department. *The War of the Rebellion: A Compilation of the Official Records of the Union and Confederate Armies* (1880–1901).

NEW IRONSIDES
Union armored frigate

New Ironsides, one of the first three Union ironclads, was the only seagoing ironclad to see combat in the Civil War. Rear Admiral David D. Porter observed that the ship had been hammered more thoroughly during the war than any other Union vessel. Although in hindsight some deride the navy's decision to build an armored frigate, the choice showed keen awareness of technological risk; *New Ironsides'* conservative design was the nation's ironclad insurance policy against failure of the more novel *Monitor*. Once completed, *New Ironsides* displayed advantages over the *Monitor* type in gunnery, crew protection, and seaworthiness. Its large battery made it the navy's most formidable offensive weapon. Its solid armor was considerably more resistant than the laminated armor used on the monitors, and *New Ironsides* never lost a man to enemy cannon fire. Its high freeboard and seaworthiness allowed it to remain at Charleston for sixteen uninterrupted months, protecting the wooden blockading fleet from ironclad raids, and would have been vital for operations in the open sea against European or European-built Confederate ironclads.

The navy contracted for *New Ironsides* on 15 October 1861, specifying delivery by 15 July 1862. The firm of Merrick & Sons of Philadelphia designed and built the ship, subcontracting its wooden hull to William Cramp & Sons. Measuring 232 feet between perpendiculars and 57 feet 4 inches in beam, its blocky shape sacrificed speed for a shallow draft of 15 feet. Above the belt of 3-inch-thick armor plate that ran all along and somewhat below its waterline, 4-inch armor covered 170 feet on each side of the ship to protect the gun battery. In service, *New Ironsides* carried fourteen 11-inch Dahlgren smoothbores and two 150-pound Parrott rifles on its gun deck, with two 50-pound Dahlgren rifles on the spar (upper) deck. The ship's best speed was about seven knots. Although designed with a full sailing rig, during most of its active service it carried only pole masts for signaling.

New Ironsides was launched on 10 May 1862 and delivered on 10 August 1862. Captain Thomas Turner placed the ship in commission on 21 August 1862, after which it spent nearly four months in Hampton Roads, Virginia. In January 1863, the ship joined the South Atlantic Blockading Squadron, commanded by Rear Admiral Samuel F. Du Pont. Sent to Charleston in February 1863 to protect the Union blockaders from Confederate ironclads, it participated in Du Pont's unsuccessful attack on Charleston harbor on 7 April 1863.

New Ironsides remained at Charleston, resuming offensive operations under a new commanding officer,

Captain Stephen C. Rowan, when Rear Admiral John A. Dahlgren relieved Admiral Du Pont in July 1863. *New Ironsides* repeatedly bombarded Charleston's fortifications, firing more than 4,400 rounds (more than that of all Dahlgren's monitors put together) between 18 July and 8 September 1863 and receiving innumerable hits by Confederate projectiles without significant damage or injury to its crew. A Confederate offer of $100,000 for sinking it led Captain James Carlin to attack *New Ironsides* with a spar torpedo boat on 21 August 1863. Carlin missed, but on 5 October 1863, the spar torpedo boat CSS *David* succeeded in torpedoing the ironclad. The effects of the explosion were slight, and the ship remained at Charleston throughout the winter of 1863–1864. Having spent sixteen uninterrupted months on station, in June 1864 it departed for Philadelphia, where it was decommissioned on 30 June 1864.

New Ironsides enjoyed a refit at Philadelphia before recommissioning on 23 August 1864 under Captain William Radford. In October 1864 it joined the North Atlantic Blockading Squadron, commanded by Admiral Porter. The ship participated in the unsuccessful army-navy assault on Fort Fisher, North Carolina, in December 1864 and then returned to help shell the fort into submission in January 1865. In its final active service, it steamed up the James River in January and February 1865 to protect the army's supply base at City Point from the Confederate ironclads of the Richmond squadron.

In March *New Ironsides* returned to Philadelphia, where it was decommissioned on 6 April 1865 and laid up at League Island, near the Philadelphia Navy Yard. A guard's unauthorized stove in the engine room set the wooden structure afire on the night of 15 December 1866, and the ship burned to the waterline and sank early on the morning of 16 December 1866. Although its contributions have been overshadowed by the publicity afforded to the "revolutionary" monitors, *New Ironsides* was the precursor of the seagoing armored ship in the U.S. Navy.

—*William H. Roberts*

See also *Monitor*; Navy, U.S.A.

For further reading:

Belknap, George E. "Reminiscent of the 'New Ironsides' off Charleston." *United Service Magazine* (1879).

Canney, Donald L. *The Ironclads, 1842–1885*. Vol. 2 of *The Old Steam Navy* (1993).

Merrick, J. Vaughn. "Editorial. The U.S.S. Armored Frigate *New Ironsides*." *Journal of the Franklin Institute of the State of Pennsylvania for the Promotion of the Mechanic Arts* (1867).

Roberts, William H. "The Neglected Ironclad: A Design and Constructional Analysis of the U.S.S. *New Ironsides*." *Warship International* (1989).

———. *New Ironsides in the Civil War* (1999).

NEW JERSEY

New Jersey's experience in the Civil War paralleled that of other Northern states. Military recruitment went through different stages, as elsewhere. The year 1861 saw a tidal wave of enlistments, but that wave receded as war weariness took hold. Army recruits received rudimentary training in camps in Hoboken, Jersey City, Newark, Flemington, Freehold, Trenton, Burlington, Beverly, and Woodbury. During the war, 74,300 of its men served in the armed forces.

New Jersey's contribution consisted of thirty-five regiments of infantry (including the force for the Pennsylvania emergency in 1863), three regiments of cavalry, and five batteries of light artillery. Three thousand African-American New Jerseyites served in special army units organized by other states or in the U.S. Colored Troops. Eight thousand New Jerseyites served in the navy and the marines. Another 1,000 belonged to the regular army.

New Jersey units mainly but not exclusively participated in campaigns in the Eastern theater of operations, mostly in Virginia and Maryland. Of the 300 Union regiments that bore the brunt of the fighting in the war, New Jersey contributed twelve. Notable unit commanders included infantry generals George Bayard, Charles Harker, Philip Kearny, Robert McAllister, George Mindil, Gershom Mott, William Sewell, Alfred Torbert, and William Truex; cavalrymen Joseph Karge and Judson Kilpatrick; and admiral Samuel Du Pont.

The death toll for New Jersey troops reached 6,300, a figure that represented nearly 1 percent of the state's total population. More soldiers died from infections than from combat, and 419 died in Confederate prisons.

State wartime politics reflected the interplay of three forces: competition between evenly divided parties, jockeying of factions within each party, and rivalry between north and south New Jersey. As to sources of support, Republican core constituencies consisted of small farmers in the southern part of the state and members of the upper and middle classes and also industrial workers in the northern cities and towns, particularly those in Passaic, Morris, and Essex counties. Most Republicans were native-born Protestants, but some were immigrant British and German Protestants.

Democrats were strongest in north New Jersey, especially in Hudson County. The Democratic Party attracted poor immigrants, especially Irish and German Catholics, who were concentrated in the state's northeastern cities. Other Democratic supporters were prosperous Dutch and German farmers in the northwestern counties of Sussex, Warren, Hunterdon and in the northeastern counties, including Bergen County.

In elections held in the 1850s, New Jerseyites opposed candidates who wished to expand slavery in the western territories. Opposition candidates won elections

for Congress in 1854 and 1858 as well as for the governorship in 1856 and 1859. In the 1860 presidential election, state voters backed two Northern Unionist candidates, Abraham Lincoln, who received four electoral votes and Stephen Douglas, who won three. This pattern was unlike the border-slave states, which selected John Bell, and the Southern states, which supported John Breckinridge.

In 1864, the Democratic presidential candidate George McClellan of Orange won narrowly as a home favorite. McClellan in his acceptance letter repudiated the dovish national party platform by substituting his hawkish pledge to seek reunion before peace. But, if New Jersey servicemen had voted by absentee ballot, New Jersey would have chosen Lincoln by a razor-thin margin.

New Jerseyites and their leaders strongly supported suppression of the rebellion and a vigorous prosecution of the war. Republican Charles Olden, who during the war served twenty-one months in the statehouse between April 1861 and January 1863, and Democrat Joel Parker, who served twenty-nine months between January 1863 and the spring of 1865, were outstanding war leaders and truly great war governors. They worked tirelessly, resourcefully, and effectively to back the Union cause. Both received support from the legislature when Democrats controlled it in 1861, 1863, and 1864 and also when the parties shared control in 1862 and 1865. Prominent War Democrats, who backed the war effort and joined the Union Republican Party, were George Cobb, Joseph Crowell, and Martin Ryerson. Major Republican leaders included Horace Congar, William Dayton, Thomas Dudley, Richard Field, Frederick Frelinghuysen, and John Ten Eyck.

Most New Jersey Democrats rejected secession, remained loyal to the Union, supported the war effort, but still remained Democrats and criticized the way the war was conducted by Lincoln's administration. Major Democratic leaders were George Middleton, Theodore Randolph, John Thomson, and Jacob Vanatta.

An iconoclastic minority of Democrats formed the antiwar Copperheads, who championed untrammeled individual and states' rights even in wartime. Copperheads favored immediate peace and recognition of the Confederacy. They opposed both the war and the war effort and rejected any cooperation with Republicans.

None of the editors of the leading antiwar dailies was a native New Jerseyite. David Naar migrated from the West Indies. Andrew Mead hailed from Connecticut. Edward Fuller came from New Hampshire. Eben Wiuton immigrated from England. Chauncey Burr moved from New York.

Copperhead members of Congress were James Wall, Nehemiah Perry, and Andrew J. Rogers. Rodman Price, the former governor, was also an active Copperhead.

Two Bergen County politicians led the Copperheads in the state legislature: Senator Daniel Holsman, a former Philadelphian, and Assemblyman Thomas Dunn English, an ex-New Yorker.

Copperhead assemblymen hailed from twelve counties, mainly rural areas and mostly Democratic strongholds in northern New Jersey. In the middle of the war, Copperheads monopolized the delegation from Bergen, Warren, Union, and Salem Counties and accounted for two-thirds of the delegation from Hunterdon and Monmouth Counties. Located mostly on the geographical periphery of the state, Copperheads remained on the political periphery as well.

Thus, the Copperhead faction never seized control of the legislature or the governorship. They failed to sabotage the state's war effort; to wreck military recruitment; to pass a legislative resolution in 1863 calling for a unilateral armistice championed by Holsman; and to get other proposals enacted, including that for a massive buildup of the state militia. They failed to get Copperhead James Wall elected federal senator for a full term of six years. In January 1863, however, during one of the low points of the war, New Jersey Democrats elected Wall federal senator for the short term of six weeks. But that election outcome was a fluke. Other Northern states during the war did elect prominent Copperheads to serve in Congress.

Yet New Jersey Democrats never nominated a Copperhead as their gubernatorial candidate, as occurred in New Hampshire, Connecticut, Pennsylvania, and Ohio. New Jersey's Democratic legislators never adopted the explicit antiwar resolutions that Delaware's legislature did and the House of Representatives of both Pennsylvania and Illinois did. New Jerseyites never resorted to violent protest as New Yorkers and other Northerners did in 1862 and 1863.

To be sure, at election time Democratic politicians of every faction in New Jersey, as elsewhere in the North, hoping to defeat Republican candidates, exploited issues that might be useful. Democratic candidates attacked infringements of civil liberties, rising taxes, raging inflation, increasing conscription, mounting battle casualties, interminable military defeats, and recurring stalemate. Yet most Democrats still backed the war. New Jersey's wartime political pattern, then, was typical of other Northern states.

—*William Gillette*

See also McClellan, George Brinton; Parker, Joel.
For further reading:
Bilby, Joseph G., and William C. Goble. *"Remember You Are Jerseymen!": A Military History of New Jersey's Troops in the Civil War* (1998).
Gillette, William. *Jersey Blue: Civil War Politics in New Jersey, 1854–1865* (1994).
Sinclair, Donald A. *A Bibliography: The Civil War and New Jersey* (1968).

NEW MARKET, BATTLE OF
(15 May 1864)

The farming community of New Market was located on the macadamized Valley Pike, fifty miles south of Winchester, Virginia, in the Shenandoah Valley. The valley, situated between the Allegheny Mountains to the west and the Blue Ridge Mountains to the east, was of immense importance for its agricultural products and livestock. It was also an important invasion route south and north for both the Union and the Confederacy. In the spring of 1864, Union forces mounted a multipronged offensive in Virginia, and one prong of this was a thrust to secure the valley.

On 2 May 1864 troops under Union major general Franz Sigel began an advance south from Winchester. Confederate general Robert E. Lee, his resources stretched to contain the Union offensive, assigned "general direction of affairs" beyond the Blue Ridge to John C. Breckinridge, former U.S. vice president and electoral runner-up to Abraham Lincoln in the 1860 election. "I trust you will drive the enemy back," Lee told him. Breckinridge mustered all available resources in southwest Virginia. He ordered out militia and even sent out an appeal to the Virginia Military Institute (VMI) in Lexington. Superintendent Francis H. Smith responded by sending 279 members of the Corps of Cadets, some as young as fifteen.

By the second week of May, Breckinridge had gathered 5,000 men: 2,500 in two brigades of infantry, Brigadier General John D. Imboden's 1,500-man cavalry, 750 militia men, and the cadets. He also had fourteen cannon.

Breckinridge was aided by Sigel moving south very slowly, in part because of Imboden's harassment. On 11 May, Imboden surprised and took 464 Union cavalry on outpost duty near Port Royal. On 12 May, Breckinridge reached Staunton as Imboden skirmished with Union advance elements to the north.

On 14 May, the Federal column reached Mount Jackson, the terminus of the Massanutten Gap Railroad that was seven miles north of New Market. Possession of New Market would give Sigel control of the single road across Massanutten Mountain. Sigel then sent his cavalry ahead to seize the bridge over the north fork of the Shenandoah River, two miles south of Mount Jackson. There they came under fire from a Confederate battery about a mile beyond the bridge. The two sides then exchanged long-range artillery fire, but Sigel delayed a crossing until his infantry could come up the next day.

Sigel resumed his march south at daylight on the fifteenth, crossing the north fork of the Shenandoah River and then halting about a mile north of New Market astride the Valley Pike. Despite having to leave troops to protect his supply lines, Sigel had some 6,500 infantry and cavalry, and 28 guns. He deployed his forces in line to wait for a Confederate attack. At the same time Breckinridge had also deployed into line south of New Market to meet a Federal attack. Both sides now opened up a long-range artillery fire across the town of New Market.

When Sigel did not advance, Breckinridge took the offensive. He sent forward his two infantry brigades with a regiment of dismounted cavalry between them. They moved north through New Market to the cheers of the townspeople. Imboden also struck the Union positions from the flank. Sigel then disengaged and fell back about a half mile, deploying eighteen guns in three batteries on the forward-sloping crest of a ridge. One battery in particular wreaked havoc on the advancing Confederate center, and Breckinridge ordered it taken.

Breckinridge had hoped to keep the VMI cadets in reserve and avoid what Jefferson Davis had referred to as "grinding the seed corn of the nation," but at this critical moment he believed he had no choice and ordered, "Put the boys in." The cadets then moved forward to fill a gap in the Confederate line and immediately attacked, despite furious Union canister and grapeshot. Many of the cadets were shoeless, the consequence of a muddy depression, later dubbed the "Field of Lost Shoes."

In the general Confederate advance, the cadets took two guns of the Union battery. Sigel, meanwhile, skillfully deployed his forces again. Soon he decided in favor of a general retirement down the valley back toward Winchester, burning the bridge over the North Fork of the Shenandoah River as he withdrew.

The battle of New Market resulted in 831 Union casualties. The Confederacy lost 577, of whom 57 were cadets (5 killed, 4 mortally wounded, and 48 wounded: a 20 percent casualty rate). Sigel was relieved of his command on 19 May, and Breckinridge and his troops went east to reinforce Lee. The cadets went with Breckenridge to Richmond, returning to VMI on 10 June. Two days later, another Union army under Major General David Hunter penetrated the valley. It took Lexington, and Hunter ordered the destruction of the institute.

—*Spencer C. Tucker*

See also Breckinridge, John C.; Imboden, John D.; Lee, Robert E.; Sigel, Franz; Virginia Military Institute.
For further reading:
Conrad, James Lee. *The Young Lions: Confederate Cadets at War* (1997).
Davis, William C. *The Battle of New Market* (1976).
Wise, Jennings C. *The Military History of the Virginia Military Institute from 1839 to 1865* (1915).

NEW MARKET HEIGHTS/CHAFFIN'S FARM/ FORT HARRISON, BATTLE OF
(28–30 September 1864)

During the Union army's siege of Petersburg and Richmond in the fall of 1864, General Ulysses S. Grant launched a series of attacks trying to break through the Confederate defenses guarding the two cities. In late September, the Union commander launched the fifth of these offensives. According to Grant's plan, one part of his army would attempt to break through the Confederate works defending Richmond while the other part assaulted the defenses of Petersburg, twenty-five miles to the south. The general hoped that one of the two attacks would find a weak spot in the Southern lines that could be exploited. Grant also believed that these assaults would also prevent Confederate general Robert E. Lee from sending reinforcements to General Jubal Early, who was then operating in the Shenandoah Valley.

The first part of the new offensive began in late September, when General Benjamin Butler (commanding the Army of the James) prepared to assault the fortifications guarding the Confederate capital. In a move unusual for the normally inept general, Butler had been scouting the Rebel defenses around Richmond since August and initiated a plan to exploit what he believed were weaknesses in the enemy's lines. He was even more correct than he realized. Lee had removed troops from Richmond defenses to support his forces around Petersburg. He had only three brigades from the Army of Northern Virginia in line. These units were supported by a small cavalry brigade and various battalions of reserve troops from Richmond. In total, Lee had approximately 4,000 men guarding the defenses to the capital.

On the night of 28 September, Butler moved General E.O.C. Ord's XVIII corps from its position at Bermuda Hundred north across the James River. There, it would link up with General David Birney's XVIII corps and a cavalry division under the command of General August V. Kautz. These units would then launch a three-pronged attack against the outer defenses of Richmond, less than ten miles from the capital. Ord's men took up a position on the left of the Union line and were to assault Fort Harrison. On the right, the XVIII corps (supported by a division from the X corps) was to attack the Confederate left at New Market Heights. Kautz's cavalrymen would wait on the far right until Birney's troops had cleared the heights, then would attack down the Darbytown Road straight toward Richmond.

Birney closed with the enemy first. His troops pushed toward the defenses at New Market Heights which had repulsed a number of Union thrusts before. Leading the assault were the men of General Charles Paine's African-American division (from the X corps). The black troops boldly charged through the abatis-covered field and reached the Confederate earthworks. After a thirty-minute fight, the 1,800 Rebel defenders realized they soon would be overrun and abandoned their defenses.

As the Confederates gave up the fight on New Market Heights, firing could be heard to the west where Ord's troops had begun their attack on Fort Harrison. Inside the garrison were 800 inexperienced Confederate heavy artillerymen. Although they held a strong position, their lack of training and experience made them vulnerable. General George S. Stannard's division led the Union attack against the fort. As the Federal troops swarmed over the walls of the fort, the defenders panicked and fled. Stannard's men had captured Fort Harrison just in time, because the Confederates who had abandoned New Market Heights were rushing to reinforce the garrison.

Ord and Birney tried to push their respective corps forward after the initial victories. But heavy casualties among the lead units, particularly among officers, and the swampy terrain prevented either general from launching coordinated attacks. Ord personally led a small group of troops in an assault on Fort Gilmer at Chafin's Bluff which guarded a vital Confederate pontoon bridge across the James River. The unsuccessful attack only added to the rapidly growing list of Federal casualties, including a leg wound for Ord that left him incapacitated. On the far right, General Kautz's cavalry division penetrated the Confederate lines along the Darbytown Road and advanced to within two miles of Richmond. But a determined battery of artillery held his men at bay until a large body of Confederate militia came up to support it. By the time Federal infantry came up to assist Kautz, the cavalrymen had been forced to withdraw.

Being unable to advance any further, General Butler ordered his corps commanders to consolidate their gains. The Union troops worked through the night of 29 September preparing for the expected Confederate counterattack. They closed off the open end of Fort Harrison (the side facing Richmond) and strengthened the other earthworks they had captured that day.

While the Federal soldiers fortified their positions, Lee rapidly rushed reinforcements from Petersburg to the Richmond defenses. By dawn of 30 September, Lee had massed eight brigades of infantry within the protected confines of Fort Gilmer. By 2:00 P.M., the Confederates were ready to launch their counterattack. General Charles Field and General Robert F. Hoke commanded the two divisions that would make the attack. The plan called for Hoke's men to move in close to a lightly guarded wall of the fort, then wait for Field's troops to launch a frontal assault. At that time, the two divisions would attack simultaneously and overwhelm the defenders who would have to divide their fire. However, when Hoke began advancing his division, he found that his men would not stop in the designated spot, but instead attacked the fort immediately. The Federal forces easily beat them off. By the time Field's troops advanced, the Union troops could turn their full attention to this new threat. This second Confederate attack met the same as the first. Lee sent his troops in twice more, but they could not come close to breaching the walls of Fort Harrison. By 4:00 P.M., all serious fighting around the fort had ended. Of the 20,000 Union troops involved in the fighting at New Market Heights, Fort Harrison, and Chafin's Bluff, more than 3,300 became casualties. The Confederates lost approximately 2,000 of the 11,000 men engaged.

Following the failure to recapture the lost positions along the exterior lines of the Richmond defenses, Lee had his troops begin constructing new earthworks closer to the city. Grant set his men to strengthening the lines they held while he planned his next move to capture the Confederate capital. His fifth offensive had failed to achieve the objectives of capturing either Richmond or Petersburg, but continued the significant weakening of the Confederate defenses. A few days after the battle, Lee informed Confederate secretary of war, James Seddon, that he could not continue this type of fight for very long. For the first time, the commander of the Army of Northern Virginia began to talk openly about the possibility of losing the Confederate capital.

—David McGee

See also Butler, Benjamin Franklin; Field, Charles William; Hoke, Robert Frederick; Ord, Edward Otho Cresap.

For further reading:

Davis, William C. *Death in the Trenches: Grant at Petersburg* (1986).

Horn, John. *The Petersburg Campaign, June 1864-April 1865* (1993).

Sommers, Richard J. *Richmond Redeemed: The Siege at Petersburg* (1981).

Trudeau, Noah Andre. *The Last Citadel: Petersburg, Virginia, June 1864–April 1865* (1991).

NEW MEXICO TERRITORY

Organized out of territory gained in the Mexico Cession in 1848, New Mexico underwent a variety of changes in the years preceding the Civil War. Its largely Hispanic population had little stake in the national sectional politics and remained lukewarm and even apathetic over issues such as states' rights and slavery. As settlers from the eastern states began to filter into New Mexico Territory, though, they brought their views with them. As a result, New Mexico became an ideologically divided territory.

In the north, around Santa Fe, sentiment resembled that of Missouri and the Midwest and mirrored that of Colorado. The Anglo population had commercial ties to Kansas City and the Missouri River Valley and was largely antislavery in outlook. White settlers in southern New Mexico were mostly Southerners, and they instead reflected Texas and the South in their world view. When the Gadsden Purchase of 1853 added a Tennessee-sized piece of land, including the city of Tucson, to the southern portion of New Mexico Territory, many anticipated that this additional land would be organized into a separate political unit since it was remote from the capital at Santa Fe. These hopefuls began referring to the southern half of New Mexico Territory as Arizona and most saw the area as the logical route for a transcontinental railroad from New Orleans.

The U.S. Congress, reacting to the realities of the sectional crisis, dashed the hopes of the "Arizonans" by annexing the Gadsden Purchase lands to New Mexico Territory, and this led to much resentment among the region's Southern-born settlers. In subsequent years, voters elected Southern sympathizers to the territorial government, and New Mexico appeared to be drifting into the proslavery camp, spreading alarm among free-state proponents. The question of the extension of slavery into the western territories would quickly become one of the principal issues that would dissolve the Union.

During the secession crises of 1861, New Mexico fell into turmoil. U.S. troops abandoned most of the forts in the region, having been ordered to Missouri to help defend that state from secessionists. As a result, Apache and Navajo Indians stepped up their raids. Meanwhile, many frustrated New Mexican Southerners claimed common cause with the Confederacy. Proclaiming the Territory of Arizona, delegates and leading citizens from Tucson and Mesilla traveled east to make their case to the emerging nation. Along with them rode small groups of army officers who had resigned their commissions and left their New Mexico forts and were offering their swords to the South.

Based on the opinions of these soldiers and secessionists, the Confederacy recognized and annexed Arizona Territory, dispatching a few hundred Texas troops under Lieutenant Colonel John Robert Baylor in July 1861 to occupy the region and augment local forces. Baylor's men quickly captured or expelled all U.S. troops in the area. That fall, 2,000 additional Texas troops under Confederate brigadier general Henry Hopkins Sibley arrived in camps near Mesilla. Early in 1862, the combined Confederate forces launched an invasion of New Mexico, north up the Rio Grande, preliminary to a more ambitious move to seize the entire American West.

The Confederate invasion failed. Colonel Edward R. S. Canby, commander of Union forces in New Mexico, successfully collected more than 1,000 U.S. regulars and more than 2,000 volunteers and militia to resist the Confederate invasion. In addition, reinforce-

ments were on their way from Colorado, California, and Kansas. After an indecisive battle at Val Verde in February, Sibley's battered Southerners cut loose from their supply lines to Texas and captured Albuquerque and Santa Fe but suffered a major strategic reverse at Glorieta in March. Short of ammunition and rations, and with Union strength growing, the rebels retreated, never to return. Several hundred secessionist refugees followed them to Texas, where they established an Arizona Territory government-in-exile in San Antonio. From there, these displaced persons maintained a constant lobby for a renewed Confederate offensive, but to no avail.

Having defended the territory from the Confederate threat, the Union army in New Mexico Territory moved to suppress the Indians in the area while government leaders sought to prevent future political agitation. In 1863, the U.S. Congress created Arizona Territory out of the western half of New Mexico Territory. By 1864, most of the remaining Rebels in the area had been imprisoned, killed, or driven out.

—*Donald S. Frazier*

See also Baylor, John Robert; Canby, Edward Richard Sprigg; Glorieta Pass, Battle of; Sibley, Henry Hopkins; Val Verde, Battle of.

For further reading:

Finch, L. Boyd. *Confederate Pathway to the Pacific: Major Sherod Hunter and Arizona Territory, C.S.A.* (1996).

Frazier, Donald S. *Blood and Treasure: Confederate Empire in the Southwest* (1995).

Josephy, Alvin M. *The Civil War in the American West* (1991).

NEW ORLEANS, CAPTURE OF
(April 1862)

The Union capture of New Orleans in April 1862 had tremendous consequences for the Confederacy. With the fall of New Orleans, the Confederacy lost its largest town and busiest port. Union control of the harbor eliminated an important ingress for desperately needed war supplies and restricted commerce along the southern Mississippi Valley. Finally, the South's inability to protect one of its most significant economic assets hindered efforts at achieving diplomatic recognition from Europe.

U.S. secretary of the navy Gideon Welles made the highly unorthodox move of appointing Captain David G. Farragut to lead the expedition to New Orleans. Farragut's selection above so many older, more experienced officers signaled a dramatic change for the Navy Department's civilian leadership. Welles and Assistant Secretary of the Navy Gustavus V. Fox aggressively selected officers with the initiative to carry out the department's strategy. Welles instructed Farragut to take the city and turn control over to Major General Benjamin F. Butler and then proceed up the Mississippi to capture important ports, disrupting commerce during the process.

On 20 January 1862, Farragut issued orders for the capture of New Orleans. His fleet consisted of seventeen steam ships, twenty-one mortar boats (under the command of Farragut's foster brother, Lieutenant David D. Porter), and 13,000 troops (commanded by Butler). The heaviest ship in the fleet was the forty-gun frigate USS *Colorado*. In support were the four steam sloops of the Hartford class, each armed with twenty-two or twenty-four guns. Also in support were tugboats, supply ships, colliers, and other ancillary vessels. Theater operations began with Ship Island's conversion to a base of operations. The navy initially seized the island in September for use as a blockade base.

New Orleans had formidable seaward defenses. Ninety miles south of the city, straddling the waterway just miles from the mouth of the Mississippi, sat Forts Jackson and St. Philip. The former occupied the left bank; the latter held the right. Within Fort Jackson's star-shaped stone walls were sixty-seven guns, including 10-inch Columbiads, 8-inch guns, 42-pound guns, and one 7-inch rifled gun. Fort St. Philip, 700 yards upstream, boasted a modest nineteen-gun arsenal, including 8-inch guns, 42-pound guns, six mortars, and one 7-inch rifled gun. A few miles south of New Orleans lay batteries Chalmette and McGee. Unfortunately for the Confederates, they offered only token resistance.

Confidence in the forts' abilities to prevent Federal ships from passing caused the Confederates to remove the batteries' heaviest weapons (42-pound guns) to arm gunboats on Lake Pontchartrain. Beyond these works, Commodore George N. Hollins commanded six vessels to aid in the city's defense. His "Mosquito Fleet" consisted of the gunboats CSS *Ivy*, CSS *Jackson*, CSS *McRae*, and CSS *General Quitman*. Together they had a combined armament of only ten 32-pound guns and one 9-inch shell gun. The ram CSS *Manassas* had no weapons to speak of, while the vessel with the most firepower, the CSS *Louisiana*, had no engines. Subsequently, the Confederates could only use it as a floating battery. To slow approaching vessels and keep them within Fort Jackson's zone of fire, defenders constructed a makeshift raft of cypress logs. Iron cables two and a half inches thick stretched across the entrance, securing the raft in place.

Porter believed that his mortars could force the garrison's surrender or make it uninhabitable within forty-eight hours. Farragut disagreed. During the War of 1812, a British fleet turned away from New Orleans in the face of only one poorly designed, half-finished fort; now there were two forts, both well constructed. Nonetheless, Farragut permitted Porter the opportunity to force a surrender. Porter ordered twenty of the schooners, each armed with a 13-inch mortar, to bombard the forts around the clock. On 18 April, the bombardment began. For five days the mortar flotilla rained 200 85-pound projectiles upon the forts. Despite

The demand for the surrender of New Orleans (*Library of Congress*)

the intense psychological pressure and an averted mutiny, the Confederates resisted. Farragut called a meeting on 22 April to inform his captains that the fleet would steam past the forts. Porter ardently disagreed with the idea and even wrote a letter officially warning against the plan should disaster occur. Two days later, under the cover of darkness, the USS *Itasca* and USS *Pinola* chiseled through the chains that secured the barricade. Shortly thereafter, Federal ships steamed past the forts two by two as Confederate cannons roared.

The exchange of gunfire was so heavy that smoke obscured visibility. Confederate gunners had to wait for muzzle flashes from Federal guns before returning fire. As Farragut's force passed the works, Hollins engaged his squadron. The resulting naval battle proved that the squadron was aptly nicknamed; Union ships swatted the force aside, destroying or disabling all vessels save one. Porter received the forts' surrender the following day. His timely acceptance both offended and enraged Butler, who had landed his troops a few miles away and was en route to the works.

Damage to the forts was light. Union gunfire disabled just nine of the eighty-six guns. The 1,100-man garrison suffered eleven killed and thirty-seven wounded. Although Porter wrote a glowing report suggesting that the mortar attack nearly crippled the forts, Butler's and Lieutenant Godfrey Weitzel's (U.S. Engineer Corps) examination revealed them to be as strong after the mortar attack as before. They concluded that most of the damage occurred during the duel against Farragut's fleet. As Federal ships steamed toward New Orleans, Major General Mansfield Lovell (commander of Confederate forces) chose to abandon New Orleans rather than risk the heavy collateral damage that would surely result from a battle. Confederates destroyed considerable government property that they could not remove, including the scuttling of the CSS *Louisiana*. Farragut arrived at New Orleans on 25 April, demanding its surrender; Butler arrived on 1 May to officially assume control.

The capture of New Orleans had many concomitants. First, capture of the city led to Farragut's promotion as the navy's first rear admiral. Second, the city's loss had an adverse impact on Confederate commerce. Third, the loss came as a psychological and political blow. Finally, on a more personal note, the disagreement between Porter and army officers regarding the cause of the forts' capture had a detrimental effect on joint operations until Porter began working with Major Generals Ulysses S. Grant and William T. Sherman the following year.

—*David P. Eldridge*

See also Butler, Benjamin Franklin; Farragut, David Glasgow; Hollins, George Nichols; Lovell, Mansfield; Porter, David Dixon.
For further reading:
Dufours, Charles. *The Night the War Was Lost* (1960).
Hearn, Chester G. *The Capture of New Orleans, 1862* (1995).
Milligan, John D. *Gunboats Down the Mississippi* (1965).
Nash, Howard P., Jr. *A Naval History of the Civil War* (1972).

NEW YORK, ATTEMPT TO BURN
(25–26 November 1864)

I hereby direct you to proceed at once to Canada," wrote Jefferson Davis to one of his agents, "there to carry out such instructions as … shall seem most to conduce to the furtherance of the interests of the Confederate States of America." Davis stationed Confederate agents in Canada in a plan to use them to influence Northern politics. During the 1864 presidential campaign, for example, agents tried to rally enough Copperhead support to vote Abraham Lincoln out of office. After the attempt to influence the presidential contest failed, agents turned their energies to revenge for the destruction of the South. On 25 November, the headlines of the *New York Times* reported on General William T. Sherman's triumphant march through Atlanta. That night, Confederate agents carried out another of a number of failed escapades against Northern morale: the attempt to burn New York City.

Confederate agents checked into hotel rooms. At a predetermined time, they piled furniture and sheets, poured a chemical substance over it, set it on fire, locked the doors behind them, and left the area. At 8:43 P.M., the St. James Hotel was the first building reported to be on fire. A few minutes later, Barnum's Museum was also burning. At 8:55 it was discovered that four rooms at the St. Nicholas Hotel were in flames. Fifteen minutes later, yet another hotel was burning. This process continued through the night and into the early morning hours as buildings were set on fire one after the other. Some sites were set on fire more than once. By the end of the ordeal, at least thirteen hotels, Barnum's Museum, Tammany Hall, hay barges, and the shipping harbor fell victims to fire.

The *New York Times* assessed that had the plan "been executed with one-half the ability with which it was drawn up, no human power could have saved this city from utter destruction." But, unfortunately for the conspirators, there was a problem with the mixture of combustible chemicals used to set the fires, and although the extent of the damage varied from place to place, all fires were put out in time to save the buildings, and not a single life was lost.

The New York City Police Department arrested a woman who had been seen going from hotel to hotel as the fires were being set, but she was later released when it was determined that she had no connection to the crime. Shortly afterward, Major General John A. Dix transformed the investigation from a civilian to a military matter by issuing General Order No. 92. The order made the conspirators "subject to martial law and to the penalty of death." Only one man, Robert Cobb Kennedy, was captured, tried, and hanged for trying to burn New York City.

—*Rolando Avila*

See also Covert Action, Confederate
For further reading:
Bates, David Homer. *Lincoln in the Telegraph Office: Recollections of the United States Military Telegraph Corps during the Civil War* (1907).
Brandt, Nat. *The Man Who Tried to Burn New York* (1986).
"The Plot, Full and Minute Particulars." *New York Times* (1864).
"The Rebel Plot, Attempt to Burn the City." *New York Times* (1864).

NEW YORK CITY DRAFT RIOTS
(13–17 July 1863)

On 13 July 1863, two abrasive innovations of Abraham Lincoln's administration sparked in the charged atmosphere of New York City. Military necessity required a readily available personnel pool, which the early enlistment acts, full of legal loopholes, failed to provide. With the Enrollment Act of 3 March 1863, the federal government assumed primary control over the conscription of citizens into the army. Similar military necessity also dictated the Emancipation Proclamation, which Lincoln issued provisionally on 22 September 1862, and officially on 1 January 1863. He had hopes that it would raise the morale of the Union army, send fugitive slaves flocking to the Union lines to fight against the Confederacy, and revitalize pro-Union opinion in England and France.

While the states had managed to control the machinery of enlistment, there always was the possibility that potential draftees could avoid service in one way or another, but when the federal government stepped in, the means of evasion narrowed sharply. To hostile and unenthusiastic civilians, these measures were merely signs of an increasingly tyrannical administration, particularly evidenced by the Enrollment Act's provision for a commutation fee of $300. Republicans thought that the commutation fee provided the working class with an exemption within reach of their means. However, to the average factory worker in New York, already beset by a seasonal drop in employment and war-caused inflation, $300 was most of a year's pay. Likewise, New York governor Horatio Seymour's well-known opposition to the act, the several postponements of its execution in New York, and the relatively large number of enrollees to be drawn from the state helped intensify obstructionist pressure against the draft.

At the same time, antiblack violence was also occurring in many Northern cities. In New York, the large, overwhelmingly Democratic Irish population was generally under the perception that the war was being forced by Protestants in New York for the freedom of blacks. To further magnify tensions, these working men were told by their leaders that not only were they being drafted to fight for the black man's freedom, but that these same black men would take their jobs at lower wages. These fears soon became reality when, in June 1863, striking Irish dockworkers were replaced by black stevedores under police protection.

It is within this contentious milieu that on 11 June 1863 the first names of the draftees were drawn. Although no disturbances occurred on that Saturday, the resumption of the draft on the following Monday was met by the rapid gathering of an unruly crowd, which soon attacked and burned the draft office and nearly beat the superintendent to death. The crowd kept fire apparatus from the building, and flames quickly spread to the entire block. Although most of the men looted—vandalizing many of the homes of the wealthy on Lexington Avenue—they quickly turned violent, killing a police captain, burning the ground floor of the *Tribune*, and attacking any well-dressed man they saw in the street, with shouts of "There goes a $300 man." In addition were the assaulting of antilabor employees and burning of Protestant churches. The rioters then turned their attention on blacks. Rioters beat any black person they could find. A half dozen caught by the crowd were lynched, some were burned alive, and a few others were beaten to death. Businesses that employed blacks were burned to the ground, as was the Colored Orphan Asylum on Fifth Avenue, while the children escaped out back.

The rioting subsided late Monday night, but was resumed with even greater violence on Tuesday, 14 July. Now a new reaction began to set in among early rioters. Through early afternoon on Monday, much of the violence bore the stamp of rioters who were conducting a one-day demonstration against the administration and the inequities of conscription. The earlier rioters included artisans, some of whom were Germans and even native-born Protestants in older trades. Such rioters left the streets by late Monday and in many instances joined the effort to restore order. By midweek the mob was overwhelmingly Irish and Catholic workers in newer industrial occupations and common laborers. The midweek rioters proceeded to connect the draft to many of its social bases in the community. Only the offensive behavior of several social forces, these rioters believed, could account for the tyrannies and unprecedented power of the Republican Party. Midweek crowds aimed to solve this problem simply, by isolating and eradicating all manifestations of the Republican social presence in New York City.

A rage against well-known Republicans, abolitionists, and their property remained a dominant theme of the midweek violence as well as the racial purging of black communities. As the week progressed, the attention of such crowds drifted from the Republican government and its works to other community institutions that the rioters suspected of exploitative behavior, moral reform, or hostility to the insurrection. Likewise, rioters continued to attack those whom they suspected of having political and social allegiances to the Protestant middle and upper classes. Several police stations were burned, as well as a home for aging prostitutes, a product of many of the moral reform projects among the evangelical Protestant middle class during the 1830s.

In the meantime, police, aided by small detachments of troops stationed in and near the city, made vain attempts to disperse the mob. Unrestrained rioting continued until 15 July, when military detachments reached the city from Pennsylvania and from West Point, New York. Temporary suspension of the draft was announced the same day. By Wednesday, 17 July, law and order had been restored. Estimated fatalities during the five days of violence totaled more than 1,000. More than fifty large buildings were destroyed by fire, and property damage was about $2 million. By August a reinstated draft proceeded smoothly as leaders of both parties endorsed the process. The city came up with more than $300,000 to pay for substitutes or commutation. Few New Yorkers were forced to fight for their country.

—*Samantha Jane Gaul*

See also Conscription, U.S.A.; Immigrants.

For further reading:
Barnes, David M. *The Draft Riots in New York, July, 1863, The Metropolitan Police: Their Services during Riot Week, Their Honorable Record* (1863).
Bernstein, Iver. *The New York City Draft Riots, Their Significance for American Society and Politics in the Age of the Civil War* (1990).
Cook, Adrian. *The Armies of the Streets: The New York City Draft Riots of 1863* (1974).
Dupree, A. Hunter, and Leslie H. Fishel, Jr., eds. "An Eyewitness Account of the New York Draft Riots, July, 1863." *Mississippi Valley Historical Review* (1960).
Fletcher, Winona L. "Speech-making of the New York Draft Riots of 1863." *Quarterly Journal of Speech* (1961).
Fried, Joseph P. "Story of the New York Draft Riots." *Civil War Times Illustrated* (1965).
Hyman, Harold M., ed. "New Yorkers and the Civil War Draft." *New York History* (1955).
Lader, Lawrence. "New York's Bloodiest Week." *American Heritage* (1959).
McCague, James. *The Second Rebellion: The Story of the New York City Draft Riots* (1968).
Werstein, Irving. *July, 1863* (1957).

NEW YORK HERALD
See Bennett, James Gordon

NEW YORK TIMES

By the commencement of the Civil War, the decade-old *New York Times*, although not yet considered America's most important newspaper, already had won the reputation as one of its greatest and most prosperous. Its circulation of 75,000 was second only to the *New York Herald*, and it began publishing a Sunday edition just a week after Fort Sumter was fired upon in 1861.

Founded in 1851 by Henry J. Raymond, the paper stressed moderation in all things political and journalistic; the *Times* under Raymond launched no great crusades and was cautious in its political opinions. Raymond himself vowed to "make it a point to get into a passion as rarely as possible." But neither was the paper shy about its politics. Raymond, who had served as speaker of the New York state legislature as a Whig, was one of the founders of the Republican Party, although he was decidedly opposed to the abolition movement. Indeed, he felt that slavery was primarily a Southern problem, and he attacked John Brown's raid at Harper's Ferry as either "irresponsible anarchy or wild and reckless crime."

Under Raymond, the *Times* became noted during the war for its comprehensive reporting, its literate style, and its dispassionate tone. "There are very few things in the world which it is worthwhile to get angry about," Raymond wrote, "and they are just the things that anger will not improve." Raymond himself covered the battle of First Bull Run, filing an erroneous report of a Union victory. The paper scored some important exclusives: it disclosed the Confederate defeat at Franklin, Tennessee, days before even the War Department learned of it; the paper also broke the story of Sherman's plan to march through Georgia. According to one account, Generals Grant and Meade, while conferring in a tent during the battle of the Wilderness, heard noises outside, which turned out to be *Times* correspondent William Swinton taking notes in the nearby bushes. At Cold Harbor General Ambrose Burnside actually had Swinton arrested and ordered him shot. Only Ulysses S. Grant's intercession saved the *Times* reporter's life, although he expelled Swinton permanently from the front.

Raymond chose as field correspondents men who knew the South: Major Ben Truman was the paper's leading reporter, while Swinton and Lorenzo Crounse followed the Army of the Potomac. Mosby's Rangers captured Crounse in 1862 and, after nearly hanging him as a spy, turned his notebooks over to Confederate newspapers, which published them. Crounse also filed the first account of the impending battle at Gettysburg, after mistakenly running into an oncoming Confederate column. The paper stopped the presses and published an extra edition with his dispatch. After a short stint as the paper's night editor, Crounse was sent back into the field in time to cover Lee's surrender at Appomattox. Among the paper's feature writers was Walt Whitman, among whose most notable dispatches was a lengthy and evocative 1864 piece on his visit to an army hospital.

"What a busy place the editorial office of *The Times* was [during the war]!" recalled William Swinton's brother John, who was the paper's managing editor during the war. "We were constantly receiving packages from correspondents at all points of the compass, special dispatches from the front, or from many a front, official documents or advices; covert news from army officers ... and gratuitous suggestions from men of all sorts and conditions."

The *Times* strove to be impartial in its reporting, which led to charges in some quarters—despite Raymond's support of the administration—that it was pro-South. In the fall of 1860, the paper's correspondent in Charleston, George Salter, a Charleston-raised physician who signed his dispatches "Jasper," filed full and dispassionate accounts of the growing anti-Union feeling. Raymond was forced to defend his reporter, who was being berated as a "secessionist," writing that Jasper "went to Charleston with instruction to write strictly what was true, and to give the facts as they might fall under his observation, whether favorable to secession or not." Following the bombardment of Fort Sumter, Jasper was arrested as a Federal spy and put on a train for the North, but not before complaining that he'd been held in a prison "that was fit only for negroes."

The *Times*, like Horace Greeley's *Tribune*, came under physical attack during the 1863 New York City draft riots, which Raymond defied in print, writing that "This mob is not our master. It is not to be compounded with by paying blackmail. It is not to be supplicated and sued to stay its hand. It is to be defied, confronted, grappled with, prostrated, crushed." The paper installed three Gatling guns (one in the business office, which was under the command of Leonard Jerome, Winston Churchill's grandfather) and outfitted the entire staff with rifles.

Despite his support of Lincoln, Raymond continually pressed the president to go slowly on the question of emancipation; he had publicly opposed the March 1862 recommendation for compensated emancipation as too expensive. Shortly after the president issued his historic proclamation, Raymond wrote him that "any attempt to make this war subservient to the sweeping abolition of slavery will revolt the Border States, divide the North and West, invigorate and make triumphant the opposition party and thus defeat itself as well as destroy the Union."

During the 1864 campaign, Raymond was involved as much in political work as in journalistic efforts: he was named chairman of the Republican National Committee and directed Lincoln's reelection campaign. He was also largely responsible for the selection of Andrew Johnson as Lincoln's running mate, a choice he later came to regret. At the same time, Raymond stood for office himself and was elected to the House of Representatives.

After the war, Raymond continued to espouse the policy of reconciliation proposed by Lincoln in his second inaugural address and that his successor, Andrew Johnson, tried to implement. But the radicals had taken control of the Republican Party, and Raymond was ousted from his post as chairman of the Republican National Committee and the paper lost thousands of readers. He was in the process of rebuilding the paper when he died of a heart attack in 1869.

Under Raymond's partner, George Jones, the paper foundered for several decades, although it achieved a notable triumph with its 1871 disclosures that helped smash the Tweed Ring. Finally, hovering near bankruptcy, it was sold in 1896 to a young Tennessee publisher, Adolph Ochs, who shaped the paper into the respected institution it is today.

—*Eric Fettmann*

See also Newspapers; Raymond, Henry; War Correspondents.
For further reading:
Andrews, J. Cutler. *The North Reports the Civil War* (1955).
Davis, Elmer. *History of The New York Times, 1851–1921* (1921).
Shepard, Richard. *The Paper's Papers: A Reporter's Journey through the Archives of The New York Times* (1996).
Starr, Louis M. *Bohemian Brigade: Civil War Newsmen in Action* (1954; reprint, 1987).

NEW YORK TRIBUNE
(1841–1924)

Established by Horace Greeley in 1841, the *New York Tribune* had become the nation's most important Republican newspaper by the eve of the Civil War. Its various editions—daily, weekly, and semi-weekly—helped form the opinions of nearly 300,000 readers in the Northern states, and its editorials influenced military and political deliberations in the Lincoln administration.

The *Tribune* published comprehensive reports of national and international events as well as editorials, reviews, and correspondence. Greeley surrounded himself with a brilliant staff that included Charles Dana (and later Sidney Howard Gay) as managing editor, George Ripley and Margaret Fuller as literary critics, Bayard Taylor as travel writer, and James S. Pike and Samuel Wilkeson as political commentators in Washington. Among the paper's foreign correspondents was Karl Marx, who wrote about European events from 1851 to 1862.

Greeley shaped the *Tribune*'s editorial policy to reflect his interest in social reforms and, after the Mexican-American War, his growing opposition to slavery. The *Tribune* opposed the Fugitive Slave Law and condemned the Kansas-Nebraska Act as an extension of the "slaveocracy" to the West. In 1854 Greeley helped to form the Republican Party; thereafter the *Tribune* supported its presidential candidates and pressured party leaders to forswear compromise on slavery in the territories. Although Greeley equivocated on the Southern states' right to secede, the *Tribune* urged reinforcement of Fort Sumter and rallied to the Union cause when war broke out.

Like other major Northern dailies, the *Tribune* sent reporters to cover Civil War battles and to rush telegraphic reports from the front. Rival papers sometimes scooped its small corps of "specials," but on the whole the *Tribune* produced the clearest and most accurate battle coverage in the North. Greeley's and Dana's friendship with cabinet members gave the paper privileged access to government information until protests by competitors and cooler relations with the Lincoln administration stopped the practice.

Although Lincoln and the Republicans counted on the *Tribune* for editorial support, Greeley waxed hot and cold toward the war. The *Tribune* pushed the administration to march on Richmond, then recanted after the Union debacle at Bull Run. Generally Greeley urged vigorous prosecution of the war, but his paper floated peace feelers when the Union military offensive bogged down in January 1863 and again in July 1864. The *Tribune* was more consistent as a voice for emancipation, urging Lincoln in a famous editorial of August 1862 to liberate the slaves and advocating enlistment of African-American soldiers in the Union army. By Lincoln's reelection, which the *Tribune* belatedly endorsed, the president looked to the *New York Herald*, the *New York Times*, and other Republican newspapers for surer support.

Ironically, the *Tribune* came closest to Lincoln's position at the time of the president's death, when Greeley announced the paper's Reconstruction policy of leniency toward former Confederates combined with guarantees of civil and political rights for African-Americans in the South. The *Tribune* backed the Fourteenth and Fifteenth Amendments and called for President Andrew Johnson's impeachment, but like many moderate Republicans its editor gradually sacrificed the ex-slaves' claims to justice so that Northern and Southern whites could (according to Greeley's infamous phrase) "clasp hands across the bloody chasm" created by the Civil War.

—*Carl J. Guarneri*

See also Dana, Charles A.; Greeley, Horace; *New York Times*; War Correspondents.
For further reading:
Fahrney, Ralph Ray. *Horace Greeley and the* Tribune *in the Civil War* (1936).
Kluger, Richard. *The Paper: The Life and Death of the* New York Herald Tribune (1986).
Starr, Louis M. *Bohemian Brigade: Civil War Newsmen in Action* (1954; reprint 1987).

NEWSOM, ELLA KING
(1838–1919)
Confederate relief worker

With the possible exception of Kate Cumming, who logged thousands of miles with the hospital train of the Confederate Army of Tennessee, Ella King Newsom was the Confederate nurse most often in transit. Married at fifteen to a physician with a plantation of more than a thousand acres of cotton and the slaves to farm it, Newsom was widowed seven years later. Twenty-two when the war began, she devoted her wealth, time, and youthful energy to Confederate sufferers by setting out for the western front in the summer of 1861. After receiving instruction in nursing from surgeon James Keller and the Sisters of Mercy in Memphis, the young widow became matron at the local Overton Hospital, the first of eleven with which she would be associated during the war.

The second of seven children, Ella King spent her girlhood in Mississippi and Arkansas. Her father, Thomas King, was a Baptist minister who had married a Georgia aristocrat. Julia King's four daughters were educated at Mary Sharpe College in Winchester, Tennessee, where Ella absorbed the Christian lessons of selflessness and philanthropic service to humanity. Ella was supervising her sisters at Mary Sharpe when the war began. After dispatching them to her parents' home near Helena, Arkansas, she brought her slaves and a supply wagon to Memphis, where she plunged into hospital work. As well known for her executive ability as Alabama's Juliet Opie Hopkins, Newsom left for Bowling Green, Kentucky, by December 1861, where the illness of soldiers in the field was drastically reducing Confederate troop strength. "The scenes of destitution at that place beggar description," she wrote. "Want of organization, lack of suitable buildings, scarcity of supplies, and the exceedingly cold weather produced untold suffering." Aided by field surgeons, her slaves, and the supplies they collected along the way, she established a hospital but was obliged to leave when the Federal advance on Forts Henry and Donelson along the Tennessee and Cumberland rivers called her south again.

Evacuating patients approximately a hundred miles to Nashville, where she set up shop in Howard High School, Newsom helped the Confederate Army of Tennessee organize transportation of the wounded to its closest hospital center in Atlanta. Proceeding to Atlanta via her beloved Winchester—a distance of nearly two hundred miles over rugged terrain—she no sooner arrived than the battle of Shiloh began and she was recalled to the West. At Tishomingo Hotel and Corinth Hospital in northern Mississippi, Newsom encountered misery even worse than that at Bowling Green. She and Kate Cumming worked around the clock in pools of blood, making patients comfortable after amputations and ball extractions, delivering food and medicine, and looking after clothes and bedding. As patients died or recovered and the hospital mayhem stabilized later that summer, Newsom moved on to Chattanooga, where Confederate officials had been lamenting the inadequacy of medical facilities.

With a track record already established at Memphis, Bowling Green, Nashville, Atlanta, and Corinth, the twenty-four-year-old became administrator of Foard and Academy hospitals at the request of local surgeons. A third Chattanooga hospital opened that year was named in Newsom's honor. By 1863, as the Confederate entourage retreated southward to Marietta, Georgia, and later to Atlanta, Newsom again played a pivotal role in organizing hospitals. The responsibilities entrusted to her were unusual considering surgeons' objections to youthful workers, as Virginia's Fannie Beers chronicled in her *Memories* (1888). There is some suggestion that Confederate officers found her charming and compliant, which may have fueled their cooperation. Though Newsom claimed that "the attentions of men had no charms for me," a year's worth of letters to her from Confederate general William Hardee, whom she met at Bowling Green, indicate otherwise.

Late in 1864, Newsom heard rumors of family trouble in Arkansas. Against the advice of hospital friends, she and a female companion set out in February 1865, hopeful that they could breach the Union lines around Memphis. Over the 213 miles from Jackson, Mississippi, to Memphis in bitter weather, Newsom rode in wagons, slept in boxcars, crossed a trestle on foot, and waited hours for a ferry to carry her across the Mississippi. Told that she must not stay the night lest she be taken into Federal custody, Newsom fled to the shelter of friends outside the city. Unaware that Federal control had reached all the way into Arkansas, Newsom found the family home near Helena deserted. Upon learning that her parents had "refugeed" to Pine Bluff, 150 miles farther west, she determined to press on. Meeting one of her brothers in Helena, the siblings rode horseback the rest of the way, Newsom's childhood skill in horsemanship serving her well. Ascertaining that her family was well, Newsom made her way back to Atlanta, where she resided until Confederate hospitals were disbanded in the summer of 1865.

One for whom the "altars of sacrifice" had proved costly, Newsom was reduced to poverty after the war. Even though she married a Confederate colonel, William Trader, in 1867, much of her property had been confiscated. Then poor investments on the part of Colonel Trader resulted in Newsom losing her first husband's cotton plantation. In an attempt to raise funds for the Traders, Kate Cumming and other Lost Cause devotés published in 1880 an unsuccessful "Appeal to the Patriotic People of the South." In 1886 Newsom found civil service work in Washington following the death of Colonel Trader the year before. For thirty years, in the company of other Confederate women who had managed to secure government jobs, she was an employee of the land, patent, and pension offices. Eager to publish her memoirs in the hope of generating more income, Newsom struggled from 1910 to 1914 before finding a publisher. Two years later, this "Florence Nightingale of the Southern Army," then eighty, succumbed to bronchitis.

—*Jane E. Schultz*

See also Cumming, Kate; Hopkins, Juliet Opie; Nurses.
For further reading:
Andrews, Matthew Page. *The Women of the South in War Times* (1920).
Richard, J. Fraise. *The Florence Nightingale of the Southern Army: Experiences of Mrs. Ella K. Newsom, Confederate Nurse in the Great War of 1861–1865* (1914).
Simkins, Francis Butler, and James Welch Patton. *The Women of the Confederacy* (1936).

NEWSPAPERS

Newspapers played a pivotal role in the Civil War, even more so than they had in the American Revolution. From agitating for or against slavery to reporting battlefield details, they served as lightning rods for public opinion as they informed both governmental leaders such as Abraham Lincoln and citizens. In the process, they changed forever as they covered the greatest news story in American history, the Civil War.

Mainly white abolitionists made diligent use of newspapers beginning in the 1830s to agitate for an end to slavery. William Lloyd Garrison's *The Liberator* never had more than 3,000 subscribers, but his fanaticism created the most violent public reaction since the Revolution. A one-time Presbyterian minister named Elijah Lovejoy became the first American journalist to be murdered when he was killed by a mob opposed to his St. Louis *Observer* in 1837. White abolitionists like Garrison and Lovejoy were aided by African-American slavery opponents, including Frederick Douglass, whose *North Star*, which was first published in 1847 and

A newspaper vendor in camp near Meade, Virginia, November 1863 (Photograph by Alexander Gardner / *Library of Congress*)

The *New York Herald*'s wagon in the field near Bealton, Virginia, August 1863
(Photograph by Timothy H. O'Sullivan / *Library of Congress*)

continued as *Frederick Douglass' Paper* into the 1860s. Other, less literate blacks used the power of the spoken word to advocate an end to the holocaust of slavery.

Technological improvements, an increase in literacy, and changing attitudes toward democratic participation inspired the invention of the first mass medium, the penny newspaper press, in antebellum America. By 1852, Horace Greeley's penny-press *New York Tribune* had a circulation of more than 200,000. The antislavery *Tribune* helped inspire the Republican Party and supported Abraham Lincoln for president in 1860. During the war, certain *Tribune* editorials were rightly or wrongly accepted as Lincoln's own pronouncements. The *Chicago Tribune*, edited by fellow Republican and abolitionist Joseph Medill, joined Greeley's *Tribune* in supporting the Republican cause during the 1850s. The *Chicago Tribune* was one of the earliest supporters of Lincoln and helped popularize the Illinois politician by reporting and reproducing his speeches. A one-time Greeley employee, Henry Raymond, made the *New York Times* a firm Lincoln supporter and a reliable chronicler of the war. Other influential Northern newspapers included the *New York Evening Post* and the *Springfield (Massachusetts) Republican*.

The antebellum South produced counterparts to Northern abolitionist editors in the form of "fire-eaters," newspapermen such as Robert Barnwell Rhett and Edmund Ruffin. Restricted by state laws that prohibited newspapers from advocating abolitionism for fear of slave riots, Rhett was a tireless and indomitable Southern patriot who was called the "father of secession." His *Charleston Mercury* declared for separation from the North as early as 1832. Ruffin wrote for Rhett, including "The Political Economy of Slavery," which argued that blacks were genetically inferior, that government should be by and for the elites only, and that secession was the only way to preserve the "glories of an independent South." Ruffin committed suicide rather than take the oath of allegiance after Appomattox. *De Bow's Review*, started in 1846 by James De Bow, was a vigorous defender of the South and slavery. The South had no newspapers to compare to the *New York Tribune*. The largest circulating newspaper in the South at the time of the war was the *Richmond Dispatch*, with a daily readership of 8,000.

There was newspaper opposition to the Civil War and President Lincoln in the North as well. The penny press *New York Herald* argued against the war until at least 1862. Editor James Gordon Bennett sided with the South on the states' rights issue. Few presidents suffered more editorial abuse than Lincoln did. Newspapers such as the *La Crosse (Wisconsin) Democrat* called Lincoln a murderer and instigated for his assassination. General Ambrose Burnside suspended the *Chicago Times* from publication in June 1863 when editor Wilbur F. Storey used violent language to attack Lincoln for the Emancipation Proclamation. Lincoln rescinded the order when he learned about it three days later. The *New York World* and *Journal of Commerce* were suppressed for two days in May 1864 by General John A. Dix for publishing a forged presidential proclamation. Samuel Medary, editor of the Columbus, Ohio–based *Crisis* and *Ohio Statesman*, was indicted for subversive activities by a federal grand jury in 1864 but died before his case could be tried.

Climbing circulation and increasing advertising revenues allowed extensive war coverage in metropolitan Northern newspapers. The Civil War was one of the first wars in which the telegraph was used to transmit stories, allowing editors to provide up-to-date information in "extra" editions. The *New York Herald*, which featured the most aggressive war coverage, spent as much as $1,000 for the telegraphed account of the capture of New Orleans, a substantial amount at the time. More than 200 full-time correspondents on both sides dodged bullets, generals, and military censors to report the war. They also covered the war from the political capitals of Washington, D.C., and Richmond, Virginia. One female correspondent, Jane Grey Swisshelm, reported on the conditions of Union hospitals in Washington, D.C. Artists and photographers roamed the fronts, providing the first visual war reporting. Technological limitations did not permit the publication of actual photographs, but photographers such as Mathew Brady sold their work to the public through stores. Engravings based on photographs were common in weekly publications such as *Frank Leslie's Illustrated Newspaper* and *Harper's Weekly*, as were detailed maps and other graphical aids. The maps, with their detailed battlefield information, posed a previously unknown security problem, especially since newspapers could and did fall into enemy hands during times of rapidly changing troop positions.

The Civil War changed American journalism forever. The idea of immediate reporting had been born with the invention of the telegraph in the 1840s but became commonplace during the war. A reading public that had previously tolerated war dispatches that were weeks or even months old began to demand immediate information. News writing, which often imitated ornate spoken rhetoric before the war, became better organized, more concise, and easier to read. The Civil War posed new questions about the people's right to know, the need to protect sensitive military information, and even the right to criticize government leaders during wartime. And American Civil War newspaper coverage began to change

forever how democracies viewed war. On-the-scene reporting and visual coverage, especially photographs, turned war from a romanticized or otherwise idealized dispute between gentlemen into the dirty, ugly, and deadly middle and lower class reality that it had become.

—*Richard Digby-Junger*

See also Bennett, James Gordon; *Charleston Mercury*; *Chicago Tribune*; Civil Liberties, U.S.A.; De Bow, James Dunwoody Brownson; *De Bow's Review*; *Frank Leslie's Illustrated Newspaper*; Greeley, Horace; *Harper's Weekly*; Medill, Joseph; *New York Times*; *New York Tribune*; Photography; Raymond, Henry; Reid, Whitelaw; Richardson, Albert Deane; *Richmond Examiner*; *Richmond Whig*; Smalley, George W.; Telegraph; Villard, Henry; War Correspondents.

For further reading:
Andrews, J. Cutler. *The North Reports the Civil War* (1955).
———. *The South Reports the Civil War* (1970).
Dickerson, Donna Lee. *The Course of Tolerance: Freedom of the Press in Nineteenth-Century America* (1990).
Harper, Robert S. *Lincoln and the Press* (1951).
Hughes, Thomas Andrew. "The Civil War Press: Promoter of Unity or Neutral Reporter?" *American Journalism* (1989).
Mathews, Joseph J. *Reporting the Wars* (1957).
Starr, Louis M. *Bohemian Brigade: Civil War Newsmen in Action* (1954; reprint, 1987).
Weisberger, Bernard A. *Reporters for the Union* (1953).

NEWTON, JOHN
(1822–1895)
Union general

John Newton, a native Virginian and regular army officer who remained loyal to the Union, rose to corps command in the Army of the Potomac and later led a division in the Army of the Cumberland. Unfortunately, his harsh criticism and political intrigues against Ambrose Burnside in the aftermath of the Fredericksburg debacle dogged his subsequent career, and he ended the war commanding a minor department in Florida. Despite a checkered Civil War career, Newton would earn recognition for the numerous engineering projects that he supervised during his forty-four years of military service, and he retired as chief of the army's Corps of Engineers.

John Newton was born in Norfolk, Virginia, on 24 August 1822. His father was fourteen-term congressman Thomas Newton. John Newton attended the U.S. Military Academy and graduated second in his class in 1842. This high ranking earned him a commission in the Corps of Engineers, in which he served throughout his antebellum career. After assisting the Board of Engineers and returning to West Point as an instructor, Newton worked extensively on navigational projects and fortifications. He assisted in or supervised the construction or renovation of Forts Warren, Trumbull, Wayne, Porter, and Ontario and on lighthouses or other navigational improvements from Maine to Florida. Newton saw little field duty during the antebellum years, other than serving in the 1858 Mormon Expedition.

Like many regular army officers, Newton joined the volunteers upon the outbreak of the Civil War. He received a commission as brigadier general in September 1861 and, over the next few months, supervised the construction of fortifications around Washington, D.C. He then received an appointment to command a brigade in XI Corps in time to participate in the Peninsula campaign. Despite his lack of combat experience, he performed well enough during the Seven Days and at Crampton's Gap and Antietam to be promoted to command of a division, which he led during the Fredericksburg campaign.

After Fredericksburg, Newton, along with his superiors William F. Smith and William B. Franklin, were harshly critical of commanding general Ambrose Burnside's performance. Newton asked for and received a leave of absence to visit his family and also to meet with politicians in Washington to inform them of the army's condition. Brigadier General John Cochrane accompanied Newton on a visit to President Abraham Lincoln, to whom the two officers outlined the army's discontent and low morale and argued against Burnside's new planned offensive. Their visit apparently convinced the president to order Burnside to cancel his plans to recross the Rappahannock River. Newton later testified before the congressional Joint Committee on the Conduct of the War "that the troops of my division and of the whole army had become entirely dispirited," and that there was a general "want of confidence in General Burnsides's military capacity." "That conviction," he added, "was absolute in my mind." Burnside suspected that Newton was one of a number of officers who had conspired against him. He attempted to dismiss these disloyal subordinates, but the president removed Burnside instead.

Though Newton continued to serve in responsible positions in the Army of the Potomac for the next year, it appears evident that his machinations against Burnside eventually hurt his career. Nevertheless, the Virginian earned promotion to major general in early 1863, and his division was heavily engaged in the Chancellorsville campaign. Newton commanded I Corps at Gettysburg after the death of John Reynolds. He remained in this position until early 1864, when his command was dissolved in the reorganization of the Army of the Potomac. Shortly thereafter, Newton learned that his promotion to major general had not been confirmed, undoubtedly a belated response to his actions against Burnside. A general without a command, Newton eventually wound up leading a division in the Army of the Cumberland during the Atlanta campaign. Though he performed well during most of the campaign's major battles, he was transferred in the fall of 1864 to the remote District of Key West and Tortugas.

While in this position, Newton led the army portion of a combined operation against St. Marks, Florida, a small town and blockade-running center on the Gulf coast south of Tallahassee. The expedition ended in failure at the battle of Natural Bridge on 6 March 1865, when a hastily gathered Confederate force inflicted about 150 casualties on the Federals and forced them to retreat. This unnecessary operation, perhaps undertaken in an effort to revive his flagging career, was Newton's last of the war. One honor that he did receive that same month was a brevet rank of major general in both the volunteers and the regular army. After the Confederate surrender, the Virginian held various district commands in Florida through early 1866.

Newton was mustered out of volunteer service at this time, reverting to his permanent rank of lieutenant colonel in the Corps of Engineers. For the next twenty years he worked on a large number of engineering projects, many in the vicinity of New York and others along the Mississippi River and the Gulf coast. Perhaps the most prominent was the removal of navigational hazards in the East River. Newton returned to the general officer ranks in 1884, when he was appointed chief of engineers. He retired two years later and died in New York on 1 May 1895.

—*David J. Coles*

See also Burnside, Ambrose Everett; Natural Bridge, Florida, Battle of.

For further reading:
Gallagher, Gary, ed. *The Fredericksburg Campaign: Decision on the Rappahannock* (1995).
Marvel, William. *Burnside* (1991).
United States Congress. *Report of the Joint Committee on the Conduct of the War. Part 1*. 37th Cong., 3d sess., Rept. Co. 108 (1863).

NICOLAY, JOHN GEORGE
(1832–1901)

Writer, personal secretary to President Abraham Lincoln, and U.S. consul

John George Nicolay at the age of five moved with his parents and four siblings from his birthplace in Bavaria, Germany, to the United States, eventually settling in Pike County, Illinois. In 1848 he applied for employment at the *Free Press*, a Whig paper published in Pittsfield, Illinois. This printing office served as his school, workshop, and college; it exposed him to opportunities for political training and observation. It was also in Pittsfield that Nicolay began his lifelong friendship with John Hay.

Nicolay worked his way up at the paper, eventually becoming editor and owner. As editor, he devoted the paper to the country's growing absorption with the slavery issue. Political leaders touring Illinois could ill afford to overlook an important county seat such as Pittsfield. The

Free Press reported their speeches, and the young editor applauded those opposing the extension of slavery. In 1856 Nicolay joined other antislavery editors in the call for a convention in Bloomington, where the Republican Party in Illinois formally came into existence.

Nicolay sold the *Press* to take a larger part in the coming political battle. O. M. Hatch, the newly elected Republican secretary of state, invited Nicolay to Springfield to clerk in his office. Nicolay accepted and through his work came into daily contact with the best-known Illinois Republicans, including Abraham Lincoln. The relationship between Nicolay and Lincoln flourished, prompting Lincoln to recommend Nicolay for the position of correspondent for Horace Greeley.

Nicolay returned the favor during the Lincoln-Douglas debates. He authored *The Political Record of Stephen A. Douglas*, comparing Douglas's concessions to the Southern slave interests to Lincoln's republican beliefs in the need to protect the advancement opportunities of hired laborers. The following year, a congressman asked for copies of Nicolay's discourse to be used in a forthcoming Senate debate. Because of this, Nicolay believed that he had played a small part in making Lincoln's views better known.

By 1860, the slavery issue had completely disrupted the established political parties. As correspondent for the *Missouri Democrat*, Nicolay attended the Chicago Republican Convention in May and witnessed William M. Evarts's motion that Lincoln's nomination be made unanimous. Nicolay returned to Springfield pleased in thinking that, as a journalist, he had helped bring about this great event. He hoped to render Lincoln a greater service by writing a campaign biography. As an experienced writer, personal friend, and a thorough believer in the Republican Party's principles, Nicolay thought he was a natural choice. His hopes were crushed when he learned that the job was already promised to William D. Howells, but Nicolay's disappointment was soon salved when Lincoln chose him to be his personal secretary. While serving in this post, Nicolay frequently wrote his fiancée, leaving behind a record of Lincoln's administration from Springfield to Washington.

In June 1860, Lincoln and Nicolay moved into the Governor's Room of the State House and began to meet visitors daily. In his description of a woodcut published in *Frank Leslie's Weekly*, Nicolay offered his perspective on the people's mood after Lincoln's election. In the woodcut, Lincoln stood in the middle of the room; Nicolay was at his desk in the corner. One man with a fanatical expression represented an abolitionist. A calm, seated man was Uncle Sam. A third shadowy character wore a military coat. To Nicolay, this man represented either the South's determination to resist Republican policy or the North's determination to uphold those principles. Either way, this figure proved truly prophetic

as tensions increased and political lines were drawn ever deeper. Nicolay did not fear secession. He believed that there was no more reason to secede in 1860 than there had been in 1856. Nicolay doubted that the Southern states could support themselves if they did leave. But if the Union could be dissolved, then the sooner the revelation of such was made the better. Nicolay would be happy with either result because he would still belong to the most magnificent empire on the globe—the Northern states.

Before leaving for Washington, Nicolay asked if John Hay, who had been brought on to help with the increasing workload, could continue as his assistant. Lincoln agreed, and Hay remained to help Nicolay with his secretarial duties. Despite the great amount of work awaiting him, Nicolay was captivated by the promise of continual excitement in the new administration and in being among the first to witness any new developments. Beyond his office duties of greeting visitors, sorting and answering mail, and serving as liaison officer between the new administration and a highly critical local society, Nicolay was expected to be at the president's service whenever and wherever Lincoln might need him. Nicolay took great pride in the fact that Lincoln reposed entire confidence in him and that their relationship had developed into that of father and son.

Proof of such confidence came in October 1861 when Lincoln sent Nicolay to Missouri to report on the trouble developing with General John C. Frémont, Federal commander of the Department of the West. Nicolay was again called upon to serve as the administration's liaison to western Indian tribes. Nicolay assisted William P. Dole, commissioner of Indian Affairs, in an attempt to conclude a treaty with the Ojibwa Indians. In 1862, Nicolay worked with Dole again, this time in gaining a treaty with the Tabequaches Indians.

Nicolay decided not to serve as Lincoln's personal secretary for the second term and instead became consul to Paris. After Lincoln's second inaugural, Nicolay went to Cuba on official business and was thus out of the country when Lincoln was assassinated.

In May 1865, Nicolay and Therena Bates married and left for Paris. Nicolay served as consul until 1869 and was constantly plagued by false accusations about mishandling funds, charges that were nothing more than incidents of political intrigue. Nicolay returned to Washington, D.C., and from 1872 until 1887 held the position of marshal of the Supreme Court. This post left him plenty of free time in which to finally begin writing, in collaboration with Hay, an authoritative biography of Lincoln. Lincoln's eldest son Robert was a close friend of Nicolay and Hay and granted them exclusive access to Lincoln's personal and official papers. In fact, these three would be the only ones to examine the papers for nearly three-quarters of a century. Nicolay published other military and historical works, but the comprehensive *Abraham Lincoln: A History* was his greatest work and the one for which he is remembered. The widowed Nicolay died in September 1901 in the Washington home he shared with his only daughter, Helena.

—*Katherine L. Swimm*

See also Hay, John; Lincoln, Abraham.

For further reading:

Burlingame, Michael, and John R. Turner Ettlinger, eds. *Inside Lincoln's White House: The Complete Civil War Diary of John Hay* (1996).

Mearns, David. *The Lincoln Papers: The Story of the Collection* (1948).

Nicolay, Helen. *Lincoln's Secretary: A Biography of John G. Nicolay* (1949).

NORTH ANNA, BATTLE OF
(23–25 May 1864)

Just as landforms constricted the conduct of operation at the Wilderness and Spotsylvania, the rivers that divide Virginia served to frame the battle along the North Anna in May 1864 and limit the armies' abilities for adequate tactical maneuvering. Virginia's tidal rivers follow a southeasterly route to Chesapeake Bay. From north to south, they are the Potomac, Rappahannock, York, and James rivers. These rivers provided supply lines to reinforce Federal units as they pushed southeast away from their protected rail lines and Washington. Along the fall line, the Rapidan (which feeds the Rappahannock River), the North and South Annas, and the Pamunkey Rivers (all of which feed the York) provided Robert E. Lee with formidable defensive lines. Throughout the 1864 campaign, Union supply and communications needs required that Ulysses S. Grant maintain unfettered access to Virginia's tidal rivers. This meant that his strategic considerations always focused on turning Lee's right flank. By placing his emphasis there, Grant could probe Lee's defenses, searching for an opening to Richmond, while keeping his river-based supply lines to his rear.

Rail lines were a significant tactical consideration during the Civil War as well. Access to railroads influenced troop movements and battles throughout Virginia in May 1864. The Orange & Alexandria Railroad ran northeasterly from Charlottesville, through Gordonsville, Orange Court House, Culpeper, and eventually into Alexandria. Lee's retreating army had destroyed much of the line from Culpeper south in the fall of 1863. Grant held firm control of the line from Culpeper northward toward Washington, D.C. It formed a vital supply line and a critical defensive line for the Army of the Potomac and the Union capital. Southeasterly from Gordonsville, the unfinished Virginia Central Railroad followed the south banks of the North Anna and Pamunkey rivers on its way to

Cold Harbor. The Virginia Central was critical to Lee's continued success. The line gave Lee access to supplies and reinforcements from the west, and, in many respects, it became a defensive line for Lee as Grant tried to slip around Lee's right flank and make a run at Richmond.

After two weeks of some of the hardest fighting of the war, the Federal army moved east from Spotsylvania Court House. On 22 May, they turned south along Telegraph Road and the Richmond, Fredericksburg & Petersburg rail line toward its intersection with the Virginia Central line at Hanover Junction, twenty-five miles from Richmond.

Watching the movements across Grant's line, Lee was able to ascertain where Grant was going next. Lee's challenge was to get there first. After riding through much of the night, on the morning of 22 May, Lee established his new headquarters at Hanover Junction and anticipated Grant's next move. Personnel concerns were at the top of Lee's agenda. Rather than having his troops construct defensive barricades, he ordered them to rest. As Lee's aide Walter Taylor noted, "For the first time since the 4th of the month, we were…spared the sight of the enemy." Meanwhile, reinforcements from the Shenandoah Valley under Major General John Breckinridge arrived to guard Hanover Court House farther to the south.

Grant continued his trek south and established a front of five miles along the north bank of the North Anna River. Major General Winfield Hancock's II Corps was positioned in the east along Grant's left; Major General Ambrose Burnside's IX Corps occupied the center; and Major General Gouverneur Warren's V Corps formed Grant's right flank in the west. Grant's aide, Horace Porter, said that the "purpose was to cross the North Anna west of the Fredericksburg Railroad [and Hanover Junction], and to strike Lee wherever he could be found."

On Monday afternoon, 23 May, Grant found Lee in two places. On Grant's left, Warren forded the North Anna at Jericho Mill and established a small pocket on the south bank near the Virginia Central rail line, a bold move given that his corps was now split on two sides of the North Anna. Unaware that Warren's force on the south bank was already more than 15,000 strong, Confederate lieutenant general A. P. Hill sent only one division of 6,000 from his III Corps to stop Warren's crossing. In the two hours of pitched battle that followed, V Corps held their ground, moving reinforcements and close-range artillery across the river into their earthworks. To the west, meanwhile, Hancock's men gained control of the Chesterfield Bridge almost unopposed.

II Corps began to cross the North Anna on Tuesday morning with little resistance. Also, V Corps awoke to

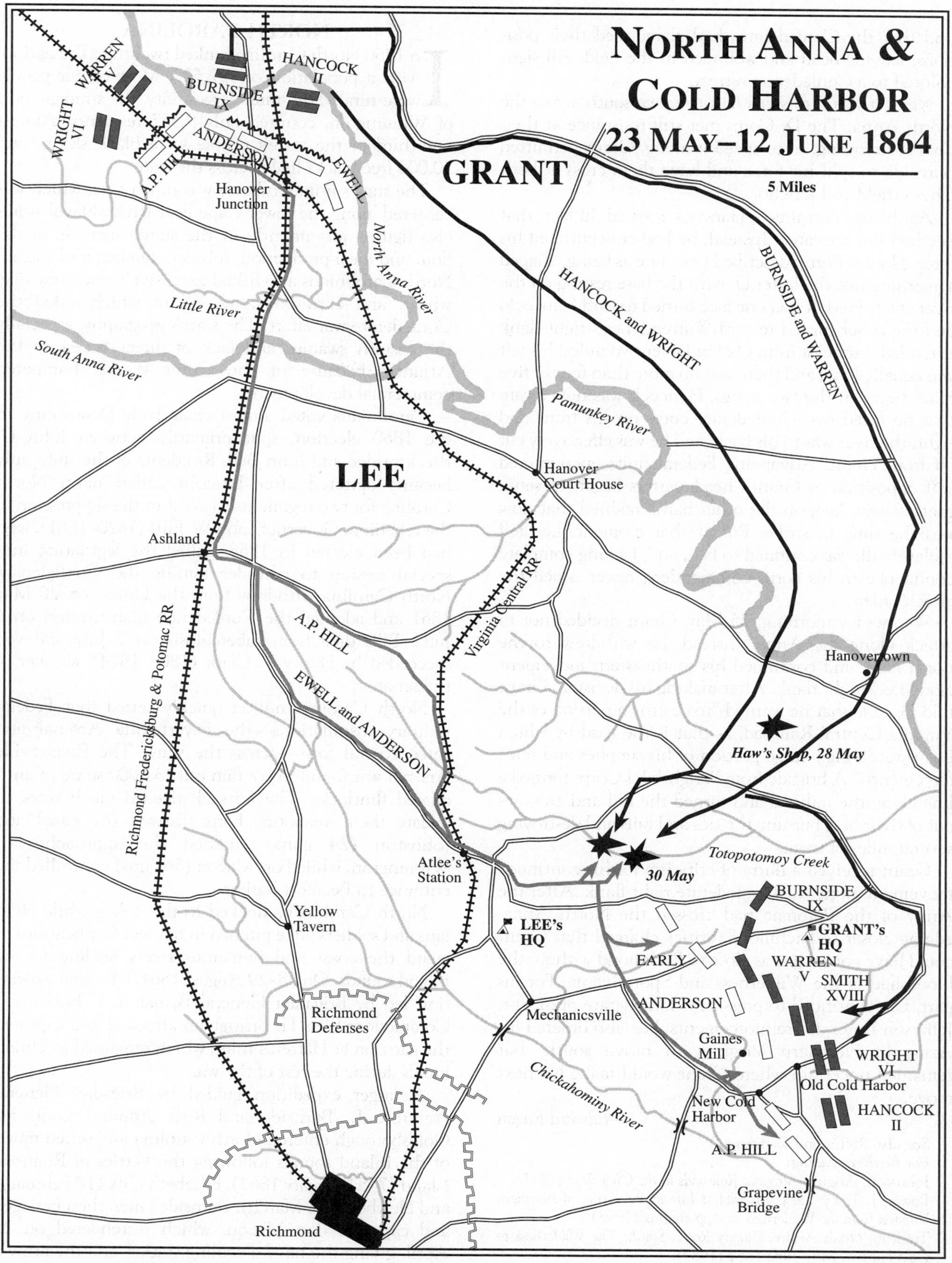

NORTH ANNA & COLD HARBOR
23 May–12 June 1864

5 Miles

GRANT

WARREN V

WRIGHT VI

BURNSIDE IX

HANCOCK II

A.P. HILL

ANDERSON

EWELL

Hanover Junction

HANCOCK and WRIGHT

BURNSIDE and WARREN

North Anna River

Little River

South Anna River

Pamunkey River

Hanover Court House

LEE

Ashland

Hanovertown

Haw's Shop, 28 May

Totopotomoy Creek

30 May

Virginia Central RR

A.P. HILL

EWELL and ANDERSON

Atlee's Station

Richmond Fredericksburg & Potomac RR

Yellow Tavern

LEE's HQ

BURNSIDE IX

GRANT's HQ

EARLY

WARREN V

SMITH XVIII

ANDERSON

Richmond Defenses

Mechanicsville

Gaines Mill

WRIGHT VI

Old Cold Harbor

HANCOCK II

Chickahominy River

New Cold Harbor

A.P. HILL

Grapevine Bridge

Richmond

find that the Confederates had abandoned their positions, leaving dead and wounded in the field. All signs pointed to a Confederate retreat.

Next, it was Burnside's task to move south across the North Anna. The IX Corps met stiff resistance at their Ox Ford crossing, so to speed it along, Grant permitted Burnside to split his force and have them cross at both Chesterfield and Jericho.

As the day continued, Hancock learned, in fact, that Lee had not retreated. Instead, he had concentrated his force. Horace Porter described Lee's line as being "shaped something like the letter U, with the base resting on the river at Ox Ford. It had one face turned toward Hancock, and the other turned toward Warren." Lee's right flank extended southeast from Ox Ford over two miles; his left was equally long; and there was no more than four or five miles between the two wings. Hancock was now aware that he faced two Confederate corps on his front and right, the river was to his back, and he was effectively cut off from Grant. Advancing Federal units encountered stiff opposition as Grant's headquarters began to sense their danger. Lee, on the other hand, realized that now was the time to strike. But at that moment, Lee fell violently ill, was confined to bed, and, lacking complete confidence in his corps commanders, never issued the attack order.

Wednesday morning, 25 May, Grant decided not to attack along the Anna. Instead, he withdrew to the north bank and continued his southeastern movement along Lee's right flank. After making his decision, Grant told his aide that he wanted "to destroy a portion of the Virginia Central Railroad, as that is the road by which Lee is receiving a large portion of his supplies and reinforcements." A brigade from Wright's VI Corps formed a line along the railroad and turned the rail and crossties out of their bed, burning the ties and rails and destroying several miles of track.

Grant received a flurry of criticism for his continued movement along the Confederate right flank. After the Army of the Potomac had crossed the North Anna, edging closer to Richmond, critics charged that Grant could have gotten just as close to Richmond without the bloodshed of the Wilderness and Spotsylvania. For his part, Lee continued to press the Confederate president, Jefferson Davis, for reinforcements. Lee also ordered his Army of Northern Virginia to move south, but remained uncertain where Grant would make his next move.

—Edward Ragan

See also Richmond Campaign.

For further reading:
Johnston, Angus J. *Virginia Railroads in the Civil War* (1961).
Power, J. Tracy. *Lee's Miserables: Life in the Army of Northern Virginia from the Wilderness to Appomattox* (1998).
Trudeau, Noah Andre. *Bloody Roads South: The Wilderness to Cold Harbor, May–June 1864* (1989).

NORTH CAROLINA

In 1860 North Carolina ranked twelfth in the nation, with a population of 992,622. Most of her people were rural. The state's largest city, the strategic port of Wilmington, counted only 9,552 residents. Almost one-third of the state's people were black slaves, and 30,000 free blacks lived across the state.

The state's prime industry was turpentine, which was centered along the lower Cape Fear River. Naval stores also figured prominently in the state's income, as did flour and meal production, tobacco, lumber, and cotton. North Carolinians also fished extensively and grew rice, wheat, and corn on farms, all of which aided the Confederate war effort. The state's geography, especially the eastern swamps and lack of direct access to the Atlantic because of the Outer Banks, hampered commercial development.

Carolinians voted almost exclusively Democratic in the 1860 election, split primarily between John C. Breckinridge and John Bell. Residents of the state only became agitated after Lincoln called upon North Carolina for two regiments to assist in the suppression of the rebellion. Governor John W. Ellis (1820–1861), who had been elected in 1858, called the legislature into special session to consider joining the Confederacy. North Carolina withdrew from the Union on 20 May 1861 and adopted the Confederate Constitution on 6 June. Ellis died from tuberculosis on 7 July and was succeeded by Henry T. Clark (1808–1874), speaker of the senate.

North Carolina militia quickly seized four Federal military installations—the Fayetteville Arsenal and three coastal forts—across the state. The Fayetteville Arsenal was found to contain only 37,000 stand of antiquated flintlocks. The forts all needed much work to update their weaponry. Forts Caswell (61 guns) and Johnston (24 guns) guarded the approaches to Wilmington, while Fort Macon (56 guns) controlled the entrance to Beaufort harbor.

North Carolinians flocked to the colors while civilians and soldiers alike pitched in to erect fortifications to guard the coast and numerous rivers leading to the inland sounds. On 28–29 August 1861, a Federal expedition led by Brigadier General Benjamin F. Butler and Commodore Silas H. Stringham attacked and captured the garrison at Hatteras Inlet, which remained in Union hands during the rest of the war.

A larger expedition guided by Brigadier General Ambrose E. Burnside and Rear Admiral Louis M. Goldsborough entered North Carolina and seized much of the inland sounds following the battles of Roanoke Island (7–8 February 1862), Elizabeth City (10 February) and Newbern (14 March). Burnside's men then besieged and captured Fort Macon, which surrendered on 26 April, giving the navy a coaling station and the army a

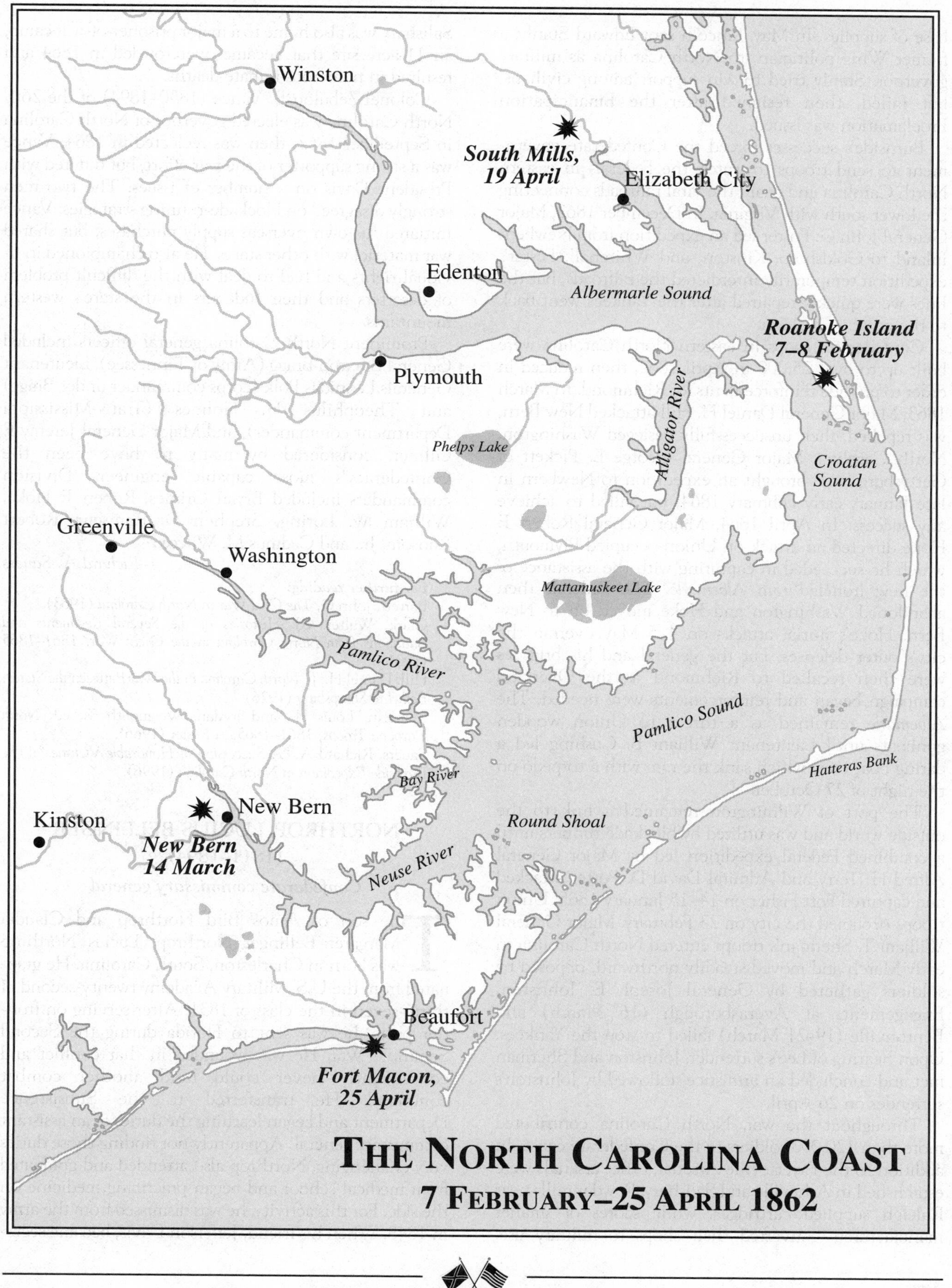

**South Mills,
19 April**

Elizabeth City

Winston

Edenton

Albermarle Sound

Plymouth

*Roanoke Island
7–8 February*

Alligator River

*Croatan
Sound*

Phelps Lake

Greenville

Washington

Mattamuskeet Lake

Pamlico River

Pamlico Sound

Hatteras Bank

Bay River

Kinston

New Bern

*New Bern
14 March*

Round Shoal

Neuse River

Beaufort

*Fort Macon,
25 April*

THE NORTH CAROLINA COAST
7 FEBRUARY–25 APRIL 1862

base of supplies. In May, Lincoln sent Edward Stanly, a former Whig politician, to North Carolina as military governor. Stanly tried to win support among civilians, but failed, then resigned after the Emancipation Proclamation was issued.

Burnside's successes forced the Confederate government to send troops to watch the Federals in eastern North Carolina and guard the vital railroads connecting the lower south with Virginia. In December 1862, Major General John G. Foster led an expedition from Newbern inland to Goldsboro, Kinston, and Whitehall. Foster's expedition temporarily interdicted the railroads, but the lines were quickly repaired after the Yankees went back to the coast.

Confederate troops in eastern North Carolina were built up to over 25,000 in April 1862, then reduced in order to provide reinforcements for Richmond. In March 1863, Major General Daniel H. Hill attacked New Bern, was repelled, then unsuccessfully besieged Washington, North Carolina. Major General George E. Pickett of Gettysburg fame brought an expedition to Newbern in late January-early February 1864, but failed to achieve any success. In April 1864, Major General Robert F. Hoke directed an attack on Union-occupied Plymouth, which he succeeded in capturing with the assistance of the new ironclad ram *Albemarle*. The Federals then abandoned Washington and Hoke moved on to New Bern. Hoke's initial attacks on 4–5 May overran the city's outer defenses, but the general and his brigades were then recalled to Richmond as the Overland campaign began and reinforcements were needed. The *Albemarle* remained as a threat to Union wooden gunboats until Lieutenant William B. Cushing led a daring boat crew which sank the ram with a torpedo on the night of 27 October.

The port of Wilmington remained a link to the outside world and was utilized by blockade runners until a combined Federal expedition led by Major General Alfred H. Terry and Admiral David D. Porter attacked and captured Fort Fisher on 14–15 January 1865; Union troops occupied the city on 23 February. Major General William T. Sherman's troops entered North Carolina in early March and moved steadily northward, opposed by soldiers gathered by General Joseph E. Johnston. Engagements at Averasborough (16 March) and Bentonville (19–21 March) failed to stop the Yankees. Upon hearing of Lee's surrender, Johnston and Sherman met and concluded an armistice, followed by Johnston's surrender on 26 April.

Throughout the war, North Carolina contributed more than 120,000 soldiers to the Confederate cause. In addition to the Fayetteville Arsenal, other arsenals were established in Asheville and Salisbury. Powder mills near Raleigh supplied cartridges, while scores of smaller manufacturers converted their shops to military use.

Salisbury was also home to a major prisoner-of-war camp, an 11-acre site that became overcrowded in 1864 and resulted in numerous inmate deaths.

Colonel Zebulon B. Vance (1830–1894) of the 26th North Carolina was elected governor of North Carolina in September 1862, then was reelected in 1864. Vance was a strong supporter of the war effort, but differed with President Davis on a number of issues. The two men strongly disagreed on blockade-running strategies; Vance initiated his own overseas supply purchases, but shared war materiel with other states. He also championed individual rights and had to deal with the difficult problem of deserters and their hideouts in the state's western mountains.

Prominent North Carolina general officers included General Braxton Bragg (Army of Tennessee), Lieutenant Generals Leonidas Polk (corps commander under Bragg) and Theophilus H. Holmes (Trans-Mississippi Department commander), and Major General Jeremy F. Gilmer, considered by many to have been the Confederacy's most capable engineer. Division commanders included Bryan Grimes, Robert F. Hoke, William W. Loring, Stephen D. Ramseur, Robert Ransom, Jr., and Cadmus M. Wilcox.

—*Richard A. Sauers*

For further reading:
Barrett, John G. *The Civil War in North Carolina* (1963).
Clark, Walter, ed. *Histories of the Several Regiments and Battalions from North Carolina in the Great War, 1861–1865* (1901).
Hill, Daniel H., Jr. *North Carolina in the War Between the States, Bethel to Sharpsburg* (1926).
Manarin, Louis H., and Jordan, Weymouth T., ed. *North Carolina Troops, 1861–1865: A Roster* (1966).
Sauers, Richard A. *"A Succession of Honorable Victories": The Burnside Expedition in North Carolina* (1996).

NORTHROP, LUCIUS BELLINGER
(1811–1894)
Confederate commissary general

The son of Amos Bird Northrop and Claudia Margaret Bellinger Northrop, Lucius Northrop was born in Charleston, South Carolina. He graduated from the U.S. Military Academy twenty-second of thirty-seven in the class of 1831. After serving on frontier posts, he was sent to Florida during the Second Seminole War. He was wounded in that conflict and consequently never could hold another combat command. He transferred to the Subsistence Department and began learning the duties of an assistant commissary general. Apparently not finding those duties very challenging, Northrop also attended and graduated from medical school and began practicing medicine on the side. For this activity, he was dismissed from the army in 1848. When his friend, Jefferson Davis, became secretary of war in 1853, Northrop was returned to the Subsistence Department and allowed to practice medicine while stationed in Charleston.

When South Carolina seceded, Northrop resigned from the army and, upon the formation of the Confederate States of America, accepted his old friend Davis's offer to become acting commissary general of the Confederacy at the rank of lieutenant colonel. He was promoted colonel and became commissary general in June 1861.

In spite of the tremendous agricultural production of the South, Northrop had to contend with a poor transportation network and initially a nonexistent bureaucracy in his efforts to feed dispersed Confederate armies. In his effort to bring efficiency to the system, he insisted that all commissary agents answer directly to him, a practice that may have promoted greater efficiency but angered all military commanders throughout the Confederacy. To complicate his already difficult job, Northrop's department also had the responsibility of providing food for all prisoners of war. He complained bitterly that he could not provide adequate rations for such prisoners when Confederate officials placed prisoner-of-war camps nearby the armies he had to feed.

From almost the very beginning of the Northrop's tenure, Confederate army officers criticized the methods and performance of his department. Northrop took such criticism personally and fought back with petulant letters to Davis and the offending officers. As the war moved into its last year, Northrop earned the enmity of Robert E. Lee, who made a personal request that Northrop be replaced. Most people assumed that Northrop's personal friendship with Davis was the only thing that kept him in office. In the meantime, Northrop struggled against rampant inflation that caused farmers and merchants to hide goods rather than sell to the government. Finally when in February 1865 the Confederate House of Representatives voted that he be removed from office, Northrop resigned. Even as he was preparing to flee Richmond, however, Davis wrote to his old friend expressing sympathy with his embarrassment.

When Union forces entered Richmond in April 1865, Northrop's arrest was ordered. It took some days to locate him; he was arrested but held only until October 1865.

After the war, Northrop was a farmer in Virginia until old age forced him to enter a soldiers' retirement home. He died in Pikesville, Maryland.

—*David S. Heidler and Jeanne T. Heidler*

See also Commissary.

For further reading:
Brown, Alfred Milton. "Lucius B. Northrop, Commissary-General of the Confederacy" (M.A. thesis, 1939).
Moore, Jerrold Northrop. *Confederate Commissary General: Lucius Bellinger Northrop and the Subsistence Bureau of the Southern Army* (1996).

NURSES

More than 20,000 women and 30,000 men took on nursing and relief work during the American Civil War. Hospitalized soldiers were commonly detailed as nurses until they were well enough to return to their units. The men they served vastly preferred female nurses to debilitated and transient convalescents. Not all male nurses were convalescents, however, as poet Walt Whitman's service at Armory Square Hospital attests.

Even before the first battle of Manassas, women began volunteering to nurse. Alabama's Juliet Opie Hopkins advertised in Richmond and Mobile newspapers as early as June 1861 for nurses to staff her hospital for Alabama soldiers in the Confederate capital. Hundreds of women served in makeshift hospitals before the Confederate Congress authorized their work in September 1862 and granted them wages. The Union surgeon general appointed Dorothea Dix, a fifty-nine-year-old activist in the reform of mental health, to superintend an office of female nurses beginning in June 1861. Her mandate that nurses be over thirty and dress plainly was calculated to discourage thrill seekers and romantics, but many younger women, such as New Jersey's Cornelia Hancock, slipped into service after battles when medical exigency was greatest. Clara Barton of Massachusetts never desired to go through channels and appeared with wagons of supplies just after the battles of Antietam and Fredericksburg. Dix appointed more than 3,000 white women to nursing positions until Surgeon General William Hammond authorized surgeons to make staff appointments in October 1863, and thus circumvented Dix's power.

Early in the war, opponents of women's service in military hospitals discouraged would-be nurses from volunteering, suggesting that such work would compromise virtue. A friend of Connecticut's Harriet Foote Hawley, who was considering service herself, heard rumors that hospital women were "closeted" with surgeons for hours at a time and worried that Hawley would mutate into an Amazon. A woman from Castalia, Alabama, asked whether "young ladies" were expected to dress abdominal wounds and witness amputations. So eager were Southern patriarchs to speak in disapproving terms, that Alabama's Kate Cumming and South Carolina's Phoebe Yates Pember would assail the reticence of women to volunteer. As Pember put it, "A woman *must* soar beyond the conventional modesty considered correct under different circumstances." As early as 1862, *Harper's Weekly* published a two-page spread endorsing the active roles women could play in the service, and by midwar, even Confederate doubters were silenced by the track record that female hospital workers had compiled.

The typical nurse was white and middle class, an

unmarried woman or a widow. Mothers of young children also served: Illinois' Mary Ann Bickerdyke dispatched her offspring to relatives; Bostonian Mary Livermore hired a housekeeper. Well-to-do Southerners Ella Newsom and Emily Mason took slaves with them to the front to do the heavier labor. Slaves also aided mistresses who nursed soldiers—Union and Confederate—on their plantations when battles were remote from Confederate hospitals. In both sections, working-class women and free blacks, who often served as regimental nurses, cooks, or laundresses, brought children with them out of economic necessity. Women hired as nurses in the North earned $12 per month (roughly 40 cents per day) and a daily ration; cooks and laundresses were paid from $6 to $10 per month. The Confederacy was more generous in its pay for women, although the effects of inflation were considerable by midwar. Juliet Opie Hopkins paid workers $20 per month in 1861. By 1863, women superintendents at the Confederacy's largest hospital, the Chimborazo in Richmond, earned $40, $35, and $30 per month, depending on their level of responsibility, but they had little purchasing power when chickens cost $3; butter, $2 a pound; and flour, $75 a barrel.

Nursing covered a wide range of custodial duties, including cleaning hospital wards and transport vessels, bathing soldiers, distributing food and medicines, cooking and doing laundry, and occasionally dressing wounds or assisting at amputations. Surgeons and hospital administrators regularly shunted slaves, contrabands, and working-class women into positions of lesser responsibility, although as "cooks" and "laundresses" their duties might overlap with those of elite whites. When Susie King Taylor, a runaway from South Carolina, became a regimental laundress with the 33d U.S. Colored Troops, she did more than wash clothes: she took care of livestock, cleaned guns, nursed soldiers with typhoid and smallpox, and taught soldiers to read and write. Literate women were expected to write letters for soldiers and to read mail to them when not otherwise occupied; surgeons had little time for correspondence with families and gladly gave up this chore to women. In keeping with the evangelical values that sustained war relief work, some nurses took on the ex officio role of clerics, performing deathbed conversions and administering last rites. Those who nursed the enemy occasionally boasted that they had persuaded men to renounce their sectional allegiances and join the other side.

Inevitably female nurses and surgeons sparred over patients' diet and treatment, making the soldier's body a symbolic site for conflict. Women fretted that surgeons would not treat the wounded as individuals because of sheer quantity. When surgeons triaged patients near battlefields, nurses refused to give up on men whose deaths, surgeons believed, were imminent. Mary Edwards Walker, a physician from upstate New York, and Chicagoan Mary Newcomb interceded with surgeons to halt amputations that they believed unnecessary. Surgeons resented zealous nurses who imposed their moralism by way of prohibitions on alcohol and tobacco. When Massachusetts reformer Hannah Ropes charged the surgeon and steward of Union Hotel Hospital with cruelty, graft, and philandering, the rest of the staff shunned her. Still most women managed to negotiate peacefully with their medical superiors, and many admired the surgeons; those who could not avoid quarreling were fired or left the service on their own.

By the end of the war, hundreds of women could claim the status of veterans, having served four years or more. White women who were still vital would go on to seek work in education, journalism, social activism, government service, medicine, nursing administration, and philanthropy. Black women had fewer options: agricultural labor, factory work, or domestic service. By the 1880s, former nurses began to lobby Congress for pensions. Dozens of women recognized for extraordinary service (New Hampshire's Harriet Patience Dame was one) had been pensioned by special acts of Congress in the 1860s and 1870s. By 1892, legislators approved a $12 monthly pension for nurses who could prove that they had served for six months. Although veteran nurses lauded this policy, its political implications were more ambiguous because cooks and laundresses, primarily black and working-class women, were ineligible. Southerners were excluded altogether in the pension stakes, making reconciliation, despite upbeat Northern rhetoric, a bitter pill to swallow.

—*Jane E. Schultz*

See also Barton, Clara; Dix, Dorothea Lynde; Hopkins, Juliet Opie.

For further reading:
Brockett, Linus P., and Mary Vaughan. *Woman's Work in the Civil War* (1867).

Leonard, Elizabeth D. *Yankee Women: Gender Battles in the Civil War* (1994).

Massey, Mary Elizabeth. *Bonnet Brigades* (1966).

Moore, Frank. *Women of the War: Their Heroism and Self-Sacrifice* (1866).

Schultz, Jane E. *Women at the Front: Female Hospital Workers in Civil War America* (2001).

OAK GROVE (HENRICO), VIRGINIA
(25 June 1862)

The first battle of the Seven Days, the battle of Oak Grove, occurred as part of George McClellan's offensive against Richmond. Leaving only Fitz John Porter's V Corps north of the Chickahominy River, McClellan hoped to concentrate most of his army in an assault on Richmond south of the river. On the morning of 25 June 1862, he ordered Samuel Peter Heintzelman's III Corps forward from its position at Fair Oaks to attack Confederate positions commanded by Major General Benjamin Huger.

Joseph Hooker and his division of Heintzelman's corps were slated to lead the attack, followed by Phil Kearny's division. Daniel Sickles's brigade of Hooker's division assumed the Federal right aimed at Lewis Armistead's brigade of Huger's division. To Sickles's left was the brigade of Cuvier Grover to attack the Confederate center, manned by the brigade of Ambrose Ransom Wright, and to Grover's left was one of Kearny's brigades, commanded by John Cleveland Robinson. Robinson was to attack between the brigades of Wright and William Mahone.

Sickles began the attack at about 8:30 A.M. with Grover beginning his movement at approximately the same time. Sickles, moving along the Williamsburg Road east toward Richmond, fanned out beyond the road to maintain contact with Grover's brigade and as a result had to travel through Oak Grove, an approximately half-mile thick, swampy forest traversed by a stream. As a result of the terrain, his brigade moved slower that Grover's. When Grover attacked Wright's brigade, he was completely unsupported on his right flank. Wright's men put up very stiff resistance to the

Union attack, resulting in very heavy fighting back and forth throughout the morning. About midmorning Wright was reinforced by the lead elements of Robert Ransom's brigade from Richmond.

By the time part of Ransom's brigade arrived on the field, the left of Sickles's line had caught up to Grover's right, but when Sickles's men were attacked by Ransom's fresh troops, the Union soldiers ran. Hooker reported this development to Heintzelman, who sent reinforcements forward and telegraphed McClellan, who was monitoring the situation three miles to the rear of the action. The retreat of part of Sickles's brigade worried McClellan, and he telegraphed Heintzelman to withdraw everyone back to their original lines and await McClellan's arrival at the front. Both Hooker and Heintzelman thought McClellan's order premature, but obeyed his instructions.

McClellan arrived on the field about 1 P.M. and, after surveying the situation and ordering more artillery and canister shot brought forward to support the infantry attacks, instructed Heintzelman to renew the attack. Sickles's and Grover's brigades then moved out along the same ground they had marched over that morning and attacked the Confederate positions. With the canister shot raking the Confederate lines, the Southern forces gradually fell back, but darkness halted the battle. McClellan, however, expressed satisfaction at the success of the day, having moved his lines 600 yards forward in the day's fighting. Casualties at Oak Grove were 626 for the Union and 441 for the Confederacy. The following day Robert E. Lee struck Porter's position north of the Chickahominy at Mechanicsville. McClellan never regained the initiative for the remainder of the Seven Days battles.

—*David S. Heidler and Jeanne T. Heidler*

See also Grover, Cuvier; Heintzelman, Samuel Peter; McClellan, George Brinton; Seven Days; Sickles, Daniel
For further reading:
Dowdey, Clifford. *The Seven Days: The Emergence of Lee* (1964).
Sears, Stephen W. *To the Gates of Richmond: The Peninsula Campaign* (1992).

OFFICIAL RECORDS
See War of the Rebellion: Official Records

OGLESBY, RICHARD JAMES
(1824–1899)
Union general

Born to Jacob Oglesby and Isabella Watson Oglesby in Oldham County, Kentucky, Richard James Oglesby spent his early years on his father's farm. The family was a moderately prosperous one, owning a

handful of slaves. Young Oglesby's life, however, rudely changed in his ninth year when cholera swept the county. His parents and siblings perished, and the family property, including slaves, was sold for debt. In later years, Oglesby claimed that seeing the old family servants sold at auction forever turned him against the institution of slavery. After the auction, he was taken to Illinois to live with an uncle.

As a youth Oglesby worked at a number of jobs, becoming somewhat of a jack-of-all-trades. He saved his meager earnings, however, and used them to begin the study of law. He began his law practice in 1845. At the outbreak of the Mexican-American War, however, he accepted a lieutenant's commission in an Illinois volunteer unit and headed for Mexico. He fought in Winfield Scott's Mexico City campaign. He returned home to his practice after the war, but the wanderlust gripped him again at news of the California gold rush. He headed west, but failing to make his fortune, returned to Illinois in 1851. He practiced law for a few years and then, after saving enough money, made an extended trip to Europe and the Middle East. Upon his return, things were becoming increasingly exciting in the United States with the agitation surrounding the sectional crisis, and Oglesby entered the fray as an active Republican.

In the elections of 1860, Oglesby was elected to the Illinois state senate but remained in that body only briefly. The firing on Fort Sumter brought Oglesby's resignation and his volunteering for federal military service. On 25 April 1861, Oglesby was commissioned the colonel of the 8th Illinois Regiment.

During the summer and fall of 1861, Oglesby operated out of Cairo, Illinois, into eastern Missouri. By the end of the year he was commanding a brigade under Ulysses S. Grant and fought in the campaigns that resulted in the fall of forts Henry and Donelson in early 1862. He was promoted to brigadier general of volunteers in March 1862.

Oglesby's next major action was at the battle of Corinth in October 1862. In the battle, Oglesby was severely wounded. His convalescence took many months. Upon his return to duty the following spring, he was sent to serve under Grant, who was then undertaking operations against Vicksburg. Oglesby was promoted to major general of volunteers in March 1863 with a date of rank of 29 November 1862. He was given command of the left wing of Major General Stephen A. Hurlbut's XVI Corps in the Vicksburg campaign.

Following the successful conclusion of that campaign, Oglesby, still not sufficiently recovered from his wounds, asked to be relieved of his command. He returned home, where he came to the conclusion the next year that he could never resume field service. He formally resigned on 26 May 1864, having been persuaded by Illinois Republicans to run for the governorship of the state.

Oglesby's successful campaign over the summer and fall of 1864 was as much a defense of his friend Abraham Lincoln's conduct of the war as it was an effort on Oglesby's part to get elected. He traveled the state praising Lincoln's policies and urging voters to return the president to the White House. The campaign was a success, and it certainly did not hurt Oglesby's chances that his managers never wasted an opportunity to mention his wounds. Once inaugurated, Oglesby did everything in his power to support Lincoln's policies in Illinois.

In the spring of 1865, Oglesby traveled to Washington to confer with the Illinois congressional delegation and the president. Coincidentally, he visited with the president on a purely social call the evening of 14 April, shortly before the president left for Ford's Theater. He accompanied the family on the funeral train back to Illinois later that month. In the immediate aftermath of the assassination, Oglesby offered a reward from the state of Illinois for John Wilkes Booth's capture.

During his administration, Oglesby became a bitter opponent of the policies of President Andrew Johnson. Within the state, however, he was a voice of reform, pushing through a number of philanthropic measures aimed at the physically and mentally impaired. Upon the expiration of his term, he returned briefly to private life but was lured from retirement in 1872 by the state Republican Party. Many in the party leadership believed that Oglesby was the only Republican capable of being elected governor. Oglesby, however, was not particularly interested in being governor again. An arrangement was made whereby Oglesby would run for governor and, if he won, would resign after the inauguration in favor of the lieutenant governor, who would then arrange for Oglesby to take the vacant United States Senate seat of Lyman Trumbull. The plan worked, and Oglesby served a term in the United States Senate. Upon his return home, he was elected in 1884 for an unprecedented third term as governor of the state. It would be his last public office. He retired to an estate outside Elkhart, Illinois, where he died on 24 April 1899.

—*David S. Heidler and Jeanne T. Heidler*

See also Corinth, Battle of; Election of 1864; Lincoln Assassination.

For further reading:
Johns, Jane Martin. *Personal Recollections of Early Decatur. Abraham Lincoln, Richard J. Oglesby and the Civil War* (1912).
Plummer, Mark A. "Richard J. Oglesby, Lincoln's Rail-Splitter." Illinois Historical Journal (1987).

OLD CAPITOL PRISON

Constructed in 1800, the brick building that housed the Old Capitol Prison, a federal military prison beginning in 1861, first served as a tavern and a boarding house. In 1814, after British troops burned the Capitol during the War of 1812, the U.S. government purchased the building to house Congress while a new

Old Capitol Prison at 1st and A Streets NE, Washington, D.C. (*Library of Congress*)

capitol was being designed and constructed. After Congress abandoned the building, it served once more as a boarding house. Famous boarders included Abraham Lincoln, who lived in the building while serving as a young congressman, and John C. Calhoun, who died in the building. The building also housed a school at one point. After Congress ceased using the edifice, Washington residents referred to the structure as the Old Capitol building.

In August 1861, by the time officials acquired the building to house the penitentiary, the three-story structure had fallen into disrepair. To furbish the building to serve as a prison, authorities enclosed the structure with a fence, added buildings, and expanded the original brick edifice. Additional houses added in May 1862 near the prison, called Duff Green's Row, served as an annex to the main prison. This annex became known as Carroll Prison.

Between 1861 and 1865, the Old Capitol Prison and its annex held a total of 5,761 prisoners. Its inmates included men as well as women, with women occupying a portion of the Carroll annex. Most of the women held at Old Capitol were imprisoned as Confederate spies. Perhaps sixteen inmates escaped from the penitentiary, and at least 457 inmates died while at the prison or its annex. Those who died while in the Old Capitol Prison were buried on the grounds of Robert E. Lee's sprawling estate, Arlington (now Arlington National Cemetery).

Inmates included political prisoners, Confederate spies, and Union soldiers convicted of various crimes, including desertion. Prisoners of war were held in the penitentiary as well, but the prison was best known for its Confederate spies and sympathizers. The prison is notable for some of the high-profile inmates it housed. Among those held at the Old Capitol Prison were Belle Boyd and Virginia Lomax, who were Confederate spies; some of the Lincoln's accused conspirators, including Mary Surratt; and Confederate captain Henry Wirz, commander of the interior of Georgia's infamous military prison, Andersonville. Wirz was hanged in the Old Capitol Prison courtyard in November 1865.

Like all Civil War prisons, conditions at Old Capitol were cramped, uncomfortable, and dirty. The Old Capitol Prison was expected to house some 500 inmates while the Carroll annex was constructed to accommodate an additional 1,000 prisoners. At times, however, the population exceeded the capacity that the prison and its annex were designed to hold. During summer months, tents were erected in the courtyard to provide additional housing to inmates and to relieve overcrowding. Most male inmates were confined to the second floor of the Old Capitol Prison, which had been divided into five large rooms. At least eighteen to twenty-five men were crowded into each room, along with their few personal belongings, cots, and tables. At night, the floors of the rooms were covered with sleeping men. The third floor of the prison was reserved for solitary confinement. At one point, the two facilities held at least 2,763 inmates. The prison population, however, fluctuated at any given time as inmates were transferred to and from the prison. Female prisoners were housed in slightly better confines in the annex, received better treatment than their male counterparts, and ate food of a slightly higher quality, though no more appetizing, than that eaten by the men.

The strict discipline imposed on the inmates was well-remembered by former prisoners. Convicts were not allowed to touch the iron bars that covered the windows of their cells. Those who did so—or who stood too close to the windows—risked being shot by the guards, who patrolled the interior corridors of the prison as well as the exterior. It appears however, that Union and Confederate convicts were treated similarly.

The prison was plagued by vermin and rodent infestations, and sanitary facilities were primitive. Bedbugs, lice, rodents, and cockroaches constantly tormented the inmates at Old Capitol Prison. Although some straw-mattress beds were provided, inmates preferred sleeping on the floors or tables to avoid the vermin-infested beds. The crude toilet facilities available to inmates were located at the back of one of the prison's buildings. These "sinks" were in essence long, open trenches featuring wooden rails in front. Although these open sinks were similar to what men would find in a military camp, those in camps would be covered with earth and new trenches dug periodically. New sinks were not regularly constructed at Old Capitol, resulting in a constant stench wafting through the prison's yard, contributing to inmates' misery. The open trenches also served as a breeding ground for vermin.

As foul and uncomfortable as the prison was, prisoners at Old Capitol were better off than many inmates housed at other penitentiaries. Unlike many Civil War prisons, inmates at Old Capitol were served meals three times a day. And, although the meals served in the dirty mess hall were said to have varied little from day to day, captives in Old Capitol Prison suffered less from malnutrition and from intestinal tract disorders than did inmates in other Civil War prisons. Additionally, prisoners could purchase food, tobacco, liquor, and cigars with their own money.

In November 1865, less than a year after the war was over, and soon after Captain Henry Wirz was hanged, government officials began dismantling operations at Old Capitol Prison. Eventually, the prison and its annex were torn down. The U.S. Supreme Court now occupies the property where the prison once stood.

—*Alicia Rodriquez*

See also Andersonville; Libby Prison; Prisons, U.S.A.; Surratt, Mary E.; Wirz, Henry.

For further reading:
Speer, Lonnie R. *Portals to Hell: Military Prisons of the Civil War* (1997).
Williamson, James J. *Prison Life in the Old Capitol and Reminiscences of the Civil War* (1911).

OLMSTED, FREDERICK LAW
(1822–1903)
Landscape architect, author, reformer

A native of Hartford, Connecticut, Frederick Law Olmsted briefly attended Yale University, where his circle of friends included Charles Loring Brace, a philanthropist who founded the Children's Aid Society in the 1850s. The education that became the foundation of Olmsted's fame and success, however, came largely through travel, observation, and self-study. Olmsted first gained national attention in the 1850s with the publication of a series of travel journals. These journals consist of Olmsted's observations on life in the antebellum South. They are characterized not only by Olmsted's disgust with slavery, but also by what he saw as the institution's negative social consequences upon the South's development; Olmsted characterized Southern life as disordered and inefficient and, therefore, uncivilized when measured against the more structured and urban eastern states.

Because of his emphasis on the idea that order is the foundation of modern society, Olmsted soon gained a national reputation as a social reformer, which, in turn, led him into the burgeoning profession of landscape architecture. To Olmsted, by creating areas for structured public recreation, landscape architecture represented a way to provide symbolic structure to the lives of the general public. In 1857 Olmsted established a partnership with Calvert Vaux. The association quickly proved a financial and artistic success; in 1858, the pair won the Central Park design competition in New York City.

Throughout his career, Olmsted received the highest accolades for his work, although some debate exists concerning the degree of credit rightly due his partner and sons. Most noted for numerous city park designs, Olmsted also designed several college campuses, including Stanford University. These designs drew heavily upon the same themes as his city park designs, namely, the English garden style, and are characterized by their balance of pastoral settings in harmony with structure fitted to precise function. As the principal advocate for such visual representations of an orderly and civilized society, Olmsted remains a preeminent influence on the profession of landscape architecture.

With the outbreak of war in 1861, the recently organized U.S. Sanitary Commission (USSC) offered Olmsted the position of general secretary. Olmsted resigned as chief architect of Central Park to accept the USSC offer. In this role, Olmsted chose personnel and supervised the collection

and distribution of food, clothing, and medical supplies among Union troops and civilians. He also managed the numerous USSC branch offices. Olmsted approached his responsibilities with the same zeal, and philosophical convictions, that characterized his career as a landscape architect; order, efficiency, and a strictly centralized hierarchy served as the foundation of Olmsted's vision of how public philanthropy could create a civilized society.

Although the USSC's executive committee shared many of his beliefs about the need for social reform via centralized management, Olmsted immediately ran into difficulties in his effort to unite practice and theory. Branch offices of the USSC, particularly such midwestern branches as Chicago and Cincinnati, proved far more independent-minded than Olmsted could tolerate. Always suspicious of localized efforts, no matter how well-intentioned, Olmsted fought to maintain strict subordination among the branch offices. The popularity and undeniable financial success of such localized techniques as sanitary fundraising fairs, coupled with western suspicions of eastern motives, made centralized control almost impossible to achieve.

Along with these internal difficulties, Olmsted also fought to limit the influence of competing organizations, such as the U.S. Christian Commission (USCC) and the Western Sanitary Commission (WSC). United with the USSC's executive committee in opposition to philanthropic sectionalism, Olmsted, known within the USSC as "Old Boss Devil," attempted to foster political alliances intended to bolster USSC claims to a monopoly of volunteer relief efforts. The bitterness Olmsted felt for the USSC's inability to obtain this monopoly, however, was matched by his anger at the USSC executive committee for their failure to insist on strict adherence to centralized policies. Olmsted believed that inconsistent enforcement of centralized policies encouraged decentralized philanthropic activities and impinged on the organization's efficiency. He, therefore, resigned from the USSC in September 1863.

Olmsted immediately accepted the position of superintendent of the Mariposa Mining Estate, a California venture that offered the prospect of financial stability. By 1865, however, the project proved beyond salvage. Disillusioned again over his inability to fashion a highly centralized organization, Olmsted resigned early in 1865.

After the war, Olmsted reestablished his partnership with Calvert Vaux. The partnership remained highly successful and influential before being dissolved in 1872. Olmsted eventually moved his practice to Brookline, Massachusetts, where his sons took over its operation.

—*Robert Patrick Bender*

See also United States Sanitary Commission; Western Sanitary Commission.
For further reading:
Censer, Jane Turner, ed. *Defending the Union: The Civil War and the U.S. Sanitary Commission*. Vol. 4 of *The Papers of Frederick Law Olmsted* (1986).
Kalfus, Melvin. *Frederick Law Olmsted: The Passion of a Public Artist* (1990).
Stille, Charles J. *History of the United States Sanitary Commission* (1997).

OLUSTEE, BATTLE OF
(20 February 1864)

The battle of Olustee, which took place about a dozen miles east of Lake City, was the largest Civil War engagement to occur in Florida. In the battle, Union troops were decisively defeated, and Confederate control over the interior of the state was secure until the war's end.

Both political and military considerations played a role in the campaign that culminated in the battle of Olustee. Various factions within the Republican Party hoped to organize a loyal Florida government in time to send delegates to the 1864 Republican nominating convention. Treasury secretary Salmon P. Chase was intrigued with this possibility and lobbied for an increased Federal military presence in the state. President Lincoln, who became aware of Chase's machinations, also hoped to see a loyal Florida government returned to the Union under the terms of his December 1863 Reconstruction Proclamation.

In addition to the political objectives, legitimate military concerns also played a role in the decision to occupy east Florida. Major General Quincy Gillmore, who commanded the Union army's Department of the South, wrote in a letter dated 31 January 1864 that the expedition would provide Northern access to Florida products; prevent the flow of salt, sugar, and cattle to the Confederate armies; and obtain recruits for the Union army's black regiments.

By early February 1864, Gillmore received approval from Washington regarding his plans to occupy Jacksonville and other portions of northeast Florida. About 6,000 troops were selected for the operation, with Brigadier General Truman Seymour in direct command. The Union troops landed at Jacksonville on 7 February and quickly gained control of the town. During the next several days, Union mounted forces raided westward to the outskirts of Lake City and southward to Gainesville. Meanwhile, John Hay, Lincoln's private secretary, arrived in Florida to begin taking oaths of allegiance from Florida Unionists as a preliminary step in organizing a loyal state government.

The Confederate commander of the District of East Florida was Brigadier General Joseph Finegan, who at the time of the Federal landings, had only about 1,500 troops to defend the state. He called for reinforcements from South Carolina and Georgia, but the lack of a direct rail

link between Florida and Georgia hampered these efforts, and, by 11 February, Finegan had only been able to assemble about 600 troops at Lake City. Meanwhile, he did what he could to hinder the Federal advance. During the next week Brigadier General Alfred H. Colquitt and his brigade of battle-hardened Georgians arrived to bolster the defenses, as did additional troops under Colonel George Harrison. By the time of the main Union advance on 20 February, the Confederate force facing them numbered more than 5,000.

While the Confederates were being reinforced, the Federal commanders were bickering over their next movement. Apparently, no firm decision had been made as to how far westward the Union advance should be undertaken. Truman Seymour wrote a pessimistic letter to Gillmore on 11 February, stating that he was "convinced that a movement upon Lake City is not, in the present condition of transportation, admissible." He further argued that Unionist sentiment in Florida was less than the Federals had been led to believe, and that "...the desire of Florida to come back [into the Union] now is a delusion." The two generals met in Jacksonville on 14 February to discuss future operations. Gillmore ordered that defensive works be constructed at Jacksonville, Baldwin, and Barbers and that no advance be made westward without his consent. He left Florida the next day, returning to his headquarters at Hilton Head, South Carolina.

Within several days of Gillmore's departure, Seymour's confidence seems to have returned. He wrote to his superior that he now intended to advance to the Suwannee River to destroy a railroad bridge. The shocked Gillmore dispatched an officer to stop the movement, but the battle of Olustee occurred before he reached Florida.

Early on 20 February, General Seymour's army, consisting of between 5,000 and 5,500 men, left Barbers Station and moved westward toward Lake City. The small army was divided into three brigades of infantry, one brigade of mounted troops, and supporting artillery. The Federals advanced along the Lake City and Jacksonville Road, which ran roughly parallel to the Florida Atlantic & Gulf-Central Railroad. In the early afternoon of 20 February, the advance elements of the Union cavalry began skirmishing with a few Confederate horsemen. This intensified as the Federals came within a few miles of the railroad station at Olustee, about ten miles east of Lake City.

After assembling his troops at Lake City, in the previous days General Finegan had moved his force to Olustee. There the Confederates built strong earthworks where the railroad passed through a narrow corridor of dry ground bordered by impassable swamps and bays to the south and a large body of water known as Ocean Pond to the north. When Finegan learned of the enemy's approach, he ordered his cavalry forward to draw the Federals toward his main line. The fighting east of his main line intensified, however, and Finegan had to send out additional troops to help those already deployed.

These included elements of both Colquitt's and Harrison's brigades, with the former in overall command. Finegan, still hoping to fight behind his prepared defenses, remained at Olustee with the main body.

General Seymour, meanwhile, had deployed Colonel Joseph Hawley's brigade, and by midafternoon the skirmishing has escalated into a major battle. While Hawley was positioning one of his regiments, a wrong command was given and the 7th New Hampshire fell into confusion. The unit quickly fell apart, with some men running to the rear and others milling about in a disorganized mob. This disaster directed Southern attention toward the 8th U.S. Colored Infantry, which occupied the left of the Union line. The 8th was an untried unit, having been organized only several months before. Colonel Charles Fribley tried to steady his men, but he soon fell mortally wounded. The raw troops of the 8th held their ground for a time, suffering more than 300 casualties before retreating.

With the destruction of Hawley's brigade, General Colquitt ordered a general advance. By now the Confederate lines stretched for about one mile, north to south, with Harrison commanding the Confederate left and Colquitt the right. To stop this advance, General Seymour ordered forward Colonel William Barton's brigade. It stopped the Confederate advance, and the battle lines stabilized for a time. The Union commander would later be criticized for reacting slowly and for deploying his forces piecemeal. The terrain, however, somewhat limited his options. Swamps bordered both flanks, and the field itself was an open pine barren with little cover.

The fighting during this middle phase of the battle was particularly severe. Confederate forces captured several Union artillery pieces and threatened to overwhelm the Federal infantry, but at a critical moment the surging Confederates ran low on ammunition. After a long delay, cartridges were brought forward, along with the remaining Southern reserves. General Finegan also reached the battlefield at about this time, and the Confederates pressed forward, threatening to outflank the Federals.

By late afternoon, Seymour realized the battle was lost and sent forward his last reserves. Colonel James Montgomery's brigade, which consisted of the 35th U.S. Colored Infantry and the famous 54th Massachusetts, stopped the Confederates for a brief time, enabling Seymour to begin withdrawing his other forces. By dusk, the Union forces had begun their long retreat to Jacksonville. Many wounded and a large amount of equipment had to be abandoned in the hasty withdrawal.

In the battle's aftermath, roaming bands of Southern troops killed or mistreated some of the black soldiers left on the field. Fortunately for the Federals, the Confederate pursuit was poorly conducted, enabling most of the Yankees to escape. By 22 February, Seymour's battered army was back in Jacksonville.

The Federals suffered 1,861 killed, wounded, and missing in the battle, while rebel casualties numbered 946. For the North, the casualty percentage was among the highest of the war, and opposition newspapers in the North bitterly attacked the Lincoln administration. The Olustee defeat ended Union efforts to organize a loyal Florida government in time for the 1864 election. The Federals were somewhat more successful in meeting the expedition's military objectives, which included disrupting the flow of Florida cattle and other foodstuffs to the rest of the Confederacy and gaining recruits for the Union's black regiments. Of course, these could have been met simply by the occupation of Jacksonville and without the loss of nearly 2,000 troops at Olustee.

—*David J. Coles*

See also Florida.
For further reading:
Boyd, Mark F. *The Federal Campaign of 1864 in East Florida* (1956).
Coles, David J. "Far From Fields of Glory: Military Operations in Florida during the Civil War, 1864-1865" (Ph.D. dissertation, 1996).
Nulty, William H. *Confederate Florida: The Road to Olustee* (1990).

OPDYCKE, EMERSON
(1830–1884)
Union general

Emerson Opdyke (*Library of Congress*)

Born in Trumbull County, Ohio, Emerson Opdycke as a young man moved briefly to California in search of gold but soon returned to Ohio. Opdycke made his living as a merchant, but he also contributed time to the abolitionist cause.

At the outbreak of the Civil War, Opdycke accepted a commission on 26 August 1861 as a lieutenant in the 41st Ohio. In January 1862 he was promoted to captain and spent much of his time instructing other volunteer officers in the rudiments of officership. In April 1862 he fought at Shiloh. He resigned his commission at the end of the summer to returned to Ohio to recruit. He returned in October 1862 as the lieutenant colonel of the 125th Ohio and became the colonel of the regiment in January 1863. That month the 125th was dispatched to the District of Western Kentucky. In the summer his regiment participated in the Tullahoma campaign, and in September 1863 Opdycke won praise for his conduct at Horseshoe Ridge at the battle of Chickamauga.

During the Chattanooga campaign in October and November 1863 Opdycke commanded a demibrigade, and in the latter part of the campaign at Missionary Ridge, he was credited with being at least partially responsible for Union troops achieving the crest of the ridge.

The following spring Opdycke received a brigade command at the beginning of the Atlanta campaign. He led this unit through the early phases of the campaign at Rocky Face Ridge and Resaca. Opdycke was wounded at the latter engagement and was briefly out of action but returned in time to fight at Kennesaw Mountain and the last part of the campaign, especially gaining notice at Peachtree Creek.

After the surrender of Atlanta, Opdycke took his brigade north with the Army of the Cumberland. At the battle of Franklin on 30 November 1864, he led a countercharge after the Confederates had penetrated Union lines that not only turned the tide of battle in that quarter but succeeded in recapturing eight Union artillery pieces and ten Confederate battle flags. For this

action, Opdycke was given special commendation by Brigadier General Thomas J. Wood, was recommended for promotion by Brigadier General George D. Wagner, and was praised for conspicuous gallantry by Brigadier General Jacob Cox. Less than a month later, Opdycke distinguished himself at the battle of Nashville. For all of these actions, he was brevetted to the rank of major general and promoted in July 1865 to the rank of brigadier general of volunteers.

After being mustered out of the service at the end of the war, Opdycke moved to New York City, where he worked as a merchant. He died on 25 April 1884 after accidentally shooting himself while cleaning his gun.

—*David S. Heidler and Jeanne T. Heidler*

See also Chickamauga; Franklin, Battle of; Missionary Ridge; Nashville, Battle of.

For further reading:
Castle, Henry A. *Opdycke's Brigade at the Battle of Franklin* (1908).

ORD, EDWARD OTHO CRESAP
(1818–1883)
Union general

Born the son of James Ord in Cumberland, Maryland, Edward Ord moved with his family to Washington, D.C., while he was still a small child. Educated locally and at home, Ord accepted an appoint-

ment to the U.S. Military Academy in 1835. He graduated seventeenth of thirty-one in the class of 1839. Commissioned an artillery officer, Ord went to Florida to fight in the Second Seminole War as his first assignment. He distinguished himself there, after which he served at a variety of frontier posts before being sent to California during the Mexican-American War. He spent the years remaining before the Civil War on the Pacific coast, with only a brief stint in 1859 at the artillery school at Fort Monroe, Virginia. John Brown's raid on Harper's Ferry occurred during Ord's duty at Fort Monroe, and Ord was part of the party sent to capture Brown.

Returning to California in 1860, Ord was stationed in San Francisco, where he served as captain in the 3d Artillery at the outbreak of the war. In September 1861, Ord was promoted to brigadier general of volunteers and transferred to Washington, D.C. From October 1861 to March 1862, Ord commanded the 3d Brigade of George McCall's division in the Army of the Potomac. As part of the defensive force for the capital, Ord routed four regiments of Confederate troops under Brigadier General J. E. B. Stuart at Dranesville, Virginia, on 20 December 1861.

During the early part of the Peninsula campaign, Ord commanded a division in Irvin McDowell's corps, but in May 1862 he was promoted to major general of volunteers and sent to the Army of the Tennessee. He arrived west in time to witness the Confederate evacuation of Corinth, and he took command of that town on 22 June 1862.

General Edward Ord (*center*) and staff at the Jefferson Davis house, Richmond, Virginia (*Library of Congress*)

In October 1862, Ord was part of the pursuit of Earl Van Dorn after the battle of Corinth and was wounded near Pocahontas, Mississippi. He was unable to return to field command until June 1863 in the midst of the siege of Vicksburg. He commanded the XIII Corps during the remaining weeks of the siege and beginning on 5 July participated in the Jackson, Mississippi, campaign. In August 1863, Ord was transferred to Nathaniel P. Banks's command in the Department of the Gulf and fought in Louisiana in the fall of 1863, most notably at Bayou Bourbeau on 3 November.

In the spring of 1864, Ord was ordered east to serve under Franz Sigel in the Department of West Virginia. Ord served in this command for less than a month, being relieved at his own request at the end of April 1864. Sent to Washington to receive a new assignment, he received command of VIII Corps in the siege of Petersburg. He served as support during the battle of the Crater before being transferred to the command of XVIII Corps. On 29 September 1864, while in command of XVIII Corps, Ord was seriously wounded in the attack on the Confederate position at Fort Harrison.

When Ord returned for duty in January 1865, Ulysses S. Grant replaced Benjamin F. Butler with Ord as commander of the Army of the James and Department of Virginia. Ord continued in this command for the remainder of the war. After the Hampton Roads Peace Conference in February 1865, Ord told his men to throw Northern newspapers describing the conference's failure into Confederate lines to demoralize Southern troops.

Ord remained in the army after the war. He took command of the Department of the Ohio in June 1865 and then the Department of Arkansas in 1866. During the reorganization of 1866, he became a brigadier general in the regular army. He retired as a major general in 1881. He died two years later on 22 July 1883 in Havana, Cuba, after contracting yellow fever on a trip to Vera Cruz. His body was returned to the United States and buried in Arlington Cemetery.

—*David S. Heidler and Jeanne T. Heidler*

See also Corinth, Battle of; Dranesville, Battle of; Petersburg Campaign.

For further reading:
Cresap, Bernarr. *Appomattox Commander: The Story of E.O.C. Ord* (1981).

ORDER OF AMERICAN KNIGHTS

During the 1850s, Americans enjoyed the fellowship of secret societies. These organizations were fraternal or political in nature and frequently both. As the Civil War erupted, the political nature of these societies absorbed the highly charged sympathies that divided the nation. One of the most fearsome of these societies, for reasons both real and imagined, was the Order of American Knights.

The Order of American Knights, or O.A.K., was the brainchild of Copperhead attorney Phineas C. Wright. After moving to New Orleans from Oneida, New York, in 1850, Wright became captivated by the cause of states' rights. He enthusiastically followed the efforts of filibusters such as William Walker, who endeavored to further the South's interests in Central America and the Caribbean. Wright developed the idea of the O.A.K. in the winter of 1856–1857, patterning it after other societies such as the Knights of the Golden Circle, which shared his Southern sympathies. The group remained in a planning stage for several years. Wright moved to St. Louis in 1857 and spent his time there pamphleteering against the Union.

After the onset of the Civil War, Wright labeled himself a Peace Democrat, opposed to Lincoln's handling of secession and the war. Melding his interest in states' rights with his displeasure over the direction in which the Union was headed, Wright implemented his dreams of the O.A.K. in February 1863. Several local Democratic friends soon joined him in his efforts to create the society.

Their chief goal was to counteract the work of the Union Leagues, secret societies that endorsed Unionist behavior and loyalty. Led by a "Supreme Council," the purpose of the O.A.K. was to educate the public to be good, faithful Democrats. Hearkening back to his early interest in filibustering and Southern expansion, Wright also declared his intent to provide a haven in Central America for Democrats exiled from the United States.

Most reputable Democrats in St. Louis kept their distance from the group. Nevertheless, the American Knights managed to establish several lodges across Illinois and northern Missouri. The O.A.K. quickly overtook the Knights of the Golden Circle as the primary Copperhead society in the Midwest.

Wright traveled across the North in 1863 as he worked to plant new branches of the O.A.K. He persuaded James A. McMaster to head the organization in New York, and Harrison H. "H. H." Dodd led the group in Indiana. Despite the O.A.K.'s presence in four states, its membership remained limited. One exposé of the society later estimated its peak membership as between 800,000 and one million, but this was never confirmed and was probably exaggerated.

In December 1863 the Supreme Council met in Chicago for its national conference. During the meeting, Wright released the "Occasional Address of the Supreme Commander" under the name of P. Caius Urbanus. In his address, Wright championed states' rights and harshly criticized Lincoln's actions as unconstitutional, despotic tactics. To prepare for the military dictatorship that he was certain loomed ahead, he called all Peace Democrats to be prepared to take up arms against the Union in the imminent crisis. The Council decided to meet again the next February on Washington's birthday.

In January 1864 Wright took an editorial position in the *New York Daily News*. The chief editor of the *News*, Benjamin Wood, held many similar beliefs and was willing to allow Wright to spread his message. On 18 January he published Wright's "Occasional Address" in the paper in the hope of attracting new members to the O.A.K.

Yet the organization was already in a state of decline. The Supreme Council met again in February and expressed its misgivings regarding Wright and his tactics. By the end of the meeting, the Council had dissolved the O.A.K. and allied with the Sons of Liberty, another Copperhead society founded by H. H. Dodd. The group also asked Democrat Clement L. Vallandigham, who was currently in exile in Canada, to be its new leader. Wright was arrested on 27 April 1864 for his activities and imprisoned without trial for the duration of the war. He was released in August 1865 and continued to work toward creating a refuge for exiled Democrats in Central America.

The strange history of the O.A.K. continued, however. In March 1864 Colonel John P. Sanderson had written an exposé of the secret society. Sanderson had undertaken this work primarily hoping that it would win him a promotion. He described the Order's efforts to resist the Union draft, to form a confederacy in the northwest, and to encourage desertions from the army. He portrayed the O.A.K. as a dire threat, saying that lodges across Missouri were running military drills as members prepared for the potential conflict between Union troops and Copperhead resistance. Whether or not these charges ever were legitimate, by mid-1864 the society had actually become only a straw man. Its primary influence was through rumors, although these prompted great concern. The exposé emerged just in time to help Republicans win the elections in 1864, including securing a second term for Lincoln. Sanderson, however, never received his promotion and died not long after the exposé's publication.

—*Adrienne Caughfield*

See also Copperheads; Knights of the Golden Circle; Union League.

For further reading:

Klement, Frank L. *Dark Lanterns: Secret Political Societies, Conspiracies, and Treason Trials in the Civil War* (1984).

Marshall, John A. *American Bastille: A History of the Illegal Arrests and Imprisonment of American Citizens during the Late Civil War* (1878).

Milton, George Fort. *Abraham Lincoln and the Fifth Column* (1942).

ORDNANCE, NAVAL

Virtually all Civil War naval ordnance was muzzle loading, and most of it was smoothbore. In previous decades, a shift had taken place from a battery of many guns mounted in broadside to a few heavier guns in pivot mounts bow and stern. These guns could fire over a wide arc and were designed to project heavier shot and shell before an enemy could close and engage with more numerous, but smaller broadside guns. This process was accelerated by the introduction of early steam warships, the sidewheels of which precluded extensive broadside batteries. Civil War naval ordnance arrangements called for both broadsides and pivot guns.

By the Civil War, two basic kinds of guns were found aboard warships: those that fired solid shot and those for the projection of shell. Solid shot had been the mainstay at sea for centuries, but wooden warships with their thick oak sides could absorb a tremendous number of hits; indeed, it was unusual for a warship to be sunk in combat by being holed. Warships usually succumbed to the explosion of a powder magazine, were taken by boarding parties, or, more often, were forced to strike their colors because of excessive casualties among the crew.

Shell was, however, much more destructive in its effects than shot, and all major naval powers introduced guns specifically to fire fused shell in a flat trajectory and at a velocity sufficient merely to lodge it in the opposing vessel's side, where it would explode. Its detonation created a large irregular hole and inflicted casualties from the shower of wooden splinters. This was an advantage over the old solid shot, which often made a clean hole that would close somewhat on the egress of the shot and was relatively easy to plug.

Shell guns also had the advantage of being lighter than guns that fired shot because shell required smaller charges. This meant that a warship's weight of metal in a broadside might actually be increased at the same time its ordnance weight was reduced. Guns that fired shot were heavier, designed to take large powder charges, and to project shot at a high velocity and longer range. They were designated by the shot's weight, whereas shell guns were designated by size of their bore. A gun of the same caliber might therefore be a 64-pounder if it were a shot gun or an 8-inch if it were a shell gun. By comparison, an 8-inch shell gun of 1856 weighed 63 cwt (hundred weights of 112 lbs., or 7,056 lbs); its counterpart 64-pounder shot gun weighed 105 cwt or 11,760 lbs. Introduced in the 1850s, the new Dahlgren shell guns (named for their inventor, Commander John A. Dahlgren) were distinguished from predecessors by their designation in Roman numerals, such as the most popular Dahlgren broadside gun, the IX-inch. Many contemporaries extended this designation with Roman numerals to the older shell guns as well.

Shell guns were not only lighter, but many had chambered bores for the smaller powder charges. Although designed to fire shell, they were also fully capable of firing shot. By the time of the Civil War, the U.S. Navy had adopted the shell gun exclusively. It is thus ironic that in Civil War naval engagements the most effective weapon against an ironclad vessel was often a shell gun

firing solid shot with a much heavier charge than originally thought possible.

By the 1850s, in part because of the Crimean War, there was renewed interest in rifling large guns for use at sea. The rifle offered the advantages of longer range, greater projectile penetration, and more accurate fire. However, difficulties arose in developing larger rifled guns. For one thing, they had to be quite strong to sustain the higher pressures created by the smaller windage (the difference between the diameter of the projectile and that of the bore). A gun blowing up could be disastrous, particularly in the close confines of a ship. An example of this was the bursting during the 1862 Union siege of Island No. 10 of an old army 42-pounder converted to a rifle on board the *St. Louis*. It killed or wounded fifteen officers and men. Rifled guns were also hard to aim accurately on the heaving deck of a vessel underway and then could not fire in ricochet—that is, the practicing of skimming shot across the water toward a target. The latter capability was important at sea because gunners were routinely instructed to fire low for fear that shot would go high and miss the target vessel entirely. Ricochet fire also greatly increased the range of shot; on hitting the water, the round ball from a smoothbore gun would continue on line to the target, whereas a rifle projectile might take off at any angle. Early rifle projectiles also tended to tumble in flight. Finally, rifled guns were very expensive.

Rifled guns were not a part of U.S. Navy ordnance until the Civil War, when the Parrott gun, named for its designer and manufacturer Robert P. Parrott of the West Point Foundry, was introduced. But rifled guns constituted the minority in ships' batteries during the war and, where they did appear, it was in tandem with shot guns. By the end of the war, the Union navy had only perhaps one-fifth of its ordnance inventory in rifled guns. John Dahlgren also designed rifled guns for the Union; but, in contrast to his smoothbores, they were not successful, and in February 1862 most were withdrawn from service. By 1864 Robert Parrott was the only founder producing rifled guns for the U.S. Navy. The Confederates, on the other hand, particularly favored rifled guns. They converted a number of smoothbores to rifles and they purchased rifled guns in Europe. Lieutenant John Mercer Brooke of the Confederate navy also designed highly effective rifled guns.

The North had many more foundries capable of producing the heaviest guns. The sole prewar source for the manufacture of heavy guns in the South was the Tredegar works (J. R. Anderson & Co.) at Richmond, Virginia, and during the conflict it produced the bulk of ordnance for the Confederacy. The Tredegar, however, was not able to cast heavy guns hollow on the Rodman method, which produced guns of greater strength. Not until February 1863 did the Confederate government purchase a new facility, which became the Selma, Alabama, Naval Works. It cast ordnance, chiefly for use against Union ironclads.

A principal difference between Union and Confederate naval guns was that Confederate pieces were not turned smooth. Thus, the exteriors of Confederate guns were often the same as when they left the molds. Turning gun exteriors contributed nothing to their functioning and was a costly operation. By contrast, all U.S. Navy guns were turned smooth.

Despite some problems, Confederate naval ordnance production was sufficient to meet the Confederacy's more modest requirements, although the lack of manufacturing facilities and skilled labor led to difficulties in mounting guns, and shortages in shells and wrought-iron bolts were chronic.

Confederate navy ordnance practices were the same as the U.S. Navy; the 1864 Confederate navy ordnance manual is almost a word-for-word copy of that of the U.S. Navy. Contrary to what some Union naval officers thought at the start of the conflict, Confederate naval ordnance arrangements during the war were on a par with their own.

—*Spencer C. Tucker*

See also Brooke; John M.; Dahlgren, John A.; Tredegar Iron Works.

For further reading:
Olmstead, Edwin, Wayne Stark, and Spencer Tucker. *The Big Guns: Civil War Siege, Seacoast and Naval Cannon* (1997).
Tucker, Spencer C. *Arming the Fleet: U.S. Navy Ordnance in the Muzzle-loading Era* (1989).

ORPHAN BRIGADE
Confederate Kentucky troops

In response to John Brown's raid on Harper's Ferry in October 1859, the Kentucky militia was reorganized in the spring of 1860. Called the Kentucky State Guard, Simon Bolivar Buckner was placed in charge of training the new recruits. During the secession crisis of the winter of 1860–1861, Southern sympathizers seemed to dominate the guard, and as a result it was looked on suspiciously by supporters of the Union.

In May 1861, after the firing on Fort Sumter and the call for volunteers by President Abraham Lincoln, Kentucky declared its neutrality. A new group, made up of Union supporters, the Home Guard, was formed ostensibly to protect the state's neutrality. The rival groups, the Kentucky State Guard and the Home Guard, vied for recruits through the summer of 1861.

During the summer, pro-Confederate Kentuckians James Hewitt, Robert Johnson, and William T. Withers established a Confederate training and recruiting camp for Kentuckians just across the state line in Montgomery County, Tennessee. They began by organizing the 2d Kentucky Infantry for the Confederacy, but soon they had a lot more than a regiment's worth of recruits. As a result, they were able to organize the 3d Kentucky Regiment which was placed under the command of Colonel Lloyd Tilghman. Recruiting continued, and at the end of August the 4th Kentucky was organized and placed under the command of Colonel Robert Trabue. In the meantime, artillery pieces were contracted for from a Memphis foundry.

The biggest problem faced by the recruiters and officers was procuring enough arms for all of the men. A raid of 100 men, commanded by Captain Philip Lightfoot Lee, was dispatched on 20 August into Kentucky to take weapons from the Home Guard. Lee was unsuccessful primarily because he could not catch any of the guard. Shortly thereafter, another, less ambitious, raid was made that did capture one piece of artillery.

Kentucky neutrality ended on 3 September when Confederate brigadier general Gideon Pillow occupied Columbus, Kentucky. His move was followed on 6 September when Union general Ulysses S. Grant occupied Paducah, Kentucky. On 11 September the Kentucky legislature officially ended the state's neutrality and sided with the Union. This move caused Simon Bolivar Buckner to offer his services to the Confederacy, and he was given a brigadier general's commission.

Confederate major general Albert Sidney Johnston, commanding Confederate forces in the West, ordered Buckner to take command of the Kentucky regiments and take Bowling Green, Kentucky. When Buckner arrived, he took control of one of the Louisville & Nashville Railroad's trains, and on 18 September he loaded those men aboard who had guns and headed for Kentucky. Within a day they had invested Bowling Green.

Bowling Green became a recruiting depot for pro-Confederate Kentuckians. Within a short time, the 1st Kentucky Cavalry was formed under the command of Colonel Benjamin Hardin Helm, Mary Todd Lincoln's brother-in-law. Buckner also recruited more infantry and artillery. By the fall of 1861, the various Kentucky regiments and batteries were beginning to resemble a brigade, and when Buckner was given a divisional command, temporary command of the troops was given to Colonel Roger Weightman Hanson. When the unit was formally designated the 1st Kentucky Brigade in November, command was given to Brigadier General John C. Breckinridge, former vice president of the United States. Breckinridge's son was already a part of the brigade.

The authorized strength of the brigade was 5,000, but it only had about 3,700 when Breckinridge assumed command. Other than recruiting, however, the new commander's biggest problem remained supplying his men with arms, food, and clothes. He also had to increase their training and try to instill some semblance of military discipline in the wild Kentuckians. The brigade remained throughout its service one of the most unruly units in the Confederate army, and in spite of

Breckinridge's efforts to curb its wilder side, they grew to love him with an almost religious devotion.

During the autumn of 1861, the 1st Brigade did not do any real fighting. A few of the men fought a small skirmish on 10 October in Barron County while protecting a pro-Confederate's house when it was fired on by Union soldiers. Another skirmish occurred on 5 December 1861 when a group of thirteen members of the 1st tried to protect the Whippoorwill Bridge over the Louisville & Memphis Railroad. They were terribly outnumbered by a force of Home Guard and most of the thirteen were captured.

In January 1862 the 2d Kentucky Regiment was sent to Brigadier General John Floyd to bolster the defenses of Fort Donelson, Tennessee. The men were taken to their new post by Buckner. During the second week of February 1862, Albert Sidney Johnston issued orders to Breckinridge to begin withdrawing the remainder of the brigade from Kentucky. The men left the state on 14 February and marched through Nashville. Most would not return to Kentucky until after the war. In the meantime, the 2d Kentucky and Buckner had been captured with the fall of Fort Donelson. On 14 March, Breckinridge and the rest of the brigade were at Decatur, Alabama; five days later they were with the bulk of Johnston's army at Corinth, Mississippi.

The brigade was made a part of Johnston's reserve corps, and Breckinridge was placed in command of the corps. The brigade marched out of Corinth on the morning of 5 April. The following morning during the attack on Ulysses S. Grant's position at Pittsburg Landing, the Orphan Brigade was placed on the left flank of Major General Leonidas Polk's attack on the Federal left. They were in the thick of the fighting on that part of the battlefield through the day. The following morning the brigade was sent back into battle and suffered very severe casualties. When the withdrawal was finally ordered, the brigade was fighting near Shiloh Church. It had been the first battle for most of the men.

The brigade went back to Corinth with the rest of the army, and while there, Breckinridge was promoted to major general and was given command of the division of which the 1st Kentucky would become a part. In the meantime, because of the casualties suffered at Shiloh, the brigade was reorganized, with the Kentucky regiments separated into two brigades with units from other states. They all evacuated Corinth at the end of May in the face of Major General Henry Halleck's offensive against the town. At the end of June, Breckinridge's division, including the Kentuckians, was sent to Vicksburg.

During the summer of 1862 many of the men were sick and unfit for duty. Led by Breckinridge, those men who could fight were sent against Baton Rouge on 27 July. It was a very miserable expedition in extreme heat over difficult terrain. Breckinridge and his men attacked

the Federal positions at Baton Rouge on 5 August and pushed them back to the Mississippi, where they took shelter under the guns of their gunboats. Breckinridge, his job done, returned to Vicksburg.

In August, Breckinridge's division was ordered to join Braxton Bragg in Tennessee for the anticipated invasion of Kentucky. Bureaucratic difficulties and the reluctance of Breckinridge's commander in Vicksburg, Major General Earl Van Dorn, to let the division go, caused so many delays that the division did not arrive in Knoxville until 2 October. Bragg was already in Kentucky and angry at Breckinridge's delay. After supplying his men and arranging for a baggage train, Breckinridge and his men left for Kentucky on 14 October. En route on 17 October within a few miles of Kentucky, Breckinridge received word that the campaign was over and that he was to return with the men to Knoxville. Shortly afterward, the division joined Bragg in Murfreesboro, Tennessee.

At the end of October, Breckinridge took the Kentucky regiments that remained in his division and recreated the 1st Kentucky Brigade. He placed it under the command of Roger Weightman "Bench-leg" Hanson. On 5 December 1862 Hanson led the brigade with Colonel John Hunt Morgan's cavalry brigade on a mission to surprise the Federal camp at Hartsville, Tennessee. The Union garrison was not entirely surprised when the attack occurred on 7 December, but were almost totally overwhelmed. After taking almost 2,000 prisoners, the brigades returned to Murfreesboro.

By the time the 1st Kentucky returned to the remainder of Bragg's army, a feeling of mutual hatred had developed between Bragg and the Kentuckians. Apparently because of the failure of the Kentucky invasion and Bragg's anger over the state's less than enthusiastic reception of his army, he had come to hate all Kentuckians. Further, he still blamed Breckinridge for not arriving in time to help with the campaign.

During the Stones River campaign in late December and early January, the 1st Kentucky was initially ordered to defend a hill in front of some of the Confederate positions. The men were not heavily engaged during the fighting of 31 December, but in the early afternoon of 2 January, Bragg ordered Breckinridge to take a strongly defended Federal position in front of him. Breckinridge argued that Federal artillery commanded the position, but Bragg insisted on the attack. During the assault, Hanson, who had been promoted to brigadier general just a few weeks before, was struck in the leg by one of the artillery shells during the assault and died the next morning. Command devolved to Colonel Robert P. Trabue, and during the rest of the day, the brigade suffered 25 percent casualties. Bragg retreated from Murfreesboro with the army on 4 January 1863. In his final report of the battle, he blamed Breckinridge for much of the army's failure in defense of its position.

Trabue unexpectedly died of a fever in February 1863, and command of the brigade was given to Brigadier General Benjamin Hardin Helm. Shortly after that development, Breckinridge was ordered to take his division to General Joseph E. Johnston in Mississippi to join in the effort to bring relief to beleaguered Vicksburg. Breckinridge and his men arrived outside of Jackson, Mississippi, on 31 May 1863 and camped there for a month. On 1 July the division was sent toward Vicksburg. They approached the city on 5 July, not knowing of the surrender of the army there. They were ordered to retrace their steps and arrived at Jackson on 7 July, where they immediately began helping to prepare the defenses of the city. The 1st Kentucky fought in the defense of Jackson and then retreated with the army on the night of 16–17 July. At the end of August, much to the Kentuckians' disappointment, they were sent back to Bragg.

Breckinridge's division, including the 1st Kentucky, was made a part of D. H. Hill's corps and initially were placed on the left of the Confederate position at Chickamauga on 19 September 1863. Later, on the afternoon of that day Breckinridge was ordered to shift his division all the way to the far right of the Confederate line. On the 20th, his and Patrick Cleburne's divisions were to assault the Union left. When the attack occurred, Cleburne was not yet in position and the 1st Kentucky was on the left of Breckinridge's division, its flank exposed to heavy Union fire. Helm was killed in one of the assaults, and command was given to Colonel Joseph H. Lewis.

Union major general George Thomas, commanding the Federal position, received reinforcements because of Breckinridge's furious attacks. That repositioning of Federal troops weakened the Federal center. That weakness was exploited by the Confederates, and a general Union retreat occurred. The 1st Kentucky Brigade participated in the last assault that afternoon against Thomas's position that resulted in Thomas's withdrawal. The 1st Kentucky suffered about 33 percent casualties that day.

In late September, the brigade took up a position on Missionary Ridge overlooking Federal-occupied Chattanooga. They remained there until 21 October and then marched to Tyner's Station, where they remained until 23 November. On that date the brigade returned to Missionary Ridge on the left of the Confederate line. On 24 November the brigade moved to Lookout Mountain, where it repulsed a Federal attack on its position. On 25 November the army retreated toward Dalton, Georgia, with the 1st Kentucky guarding that withdrawal. The men spent the winter outside Dalton, Georgia.

During that winter, the men of the 1st Kentucky lost the man who had become like a father to most when

Breckinridge was given command of the Department of Southwestern Virginia. In December the army at Dalton had been placed under the command of Joseph E. Johnston, and Johnston had told Breckinridge that he could take the 1st Kentucky with him to Virginia if another brigade was assigned to Johnston. No brigade was found, and the 1st Brigade remained in Georgia.

At the commencement of the Atlanta campaign in the spring of 1864, the brigade was down to about 1,500 men. During the upcoming campaign it would suffer its worst casualties of the war.

After the army retreated to Resaca, Georgia, the 1st Brigade occupied part of the Confederate left. It suffered heavy casualties in the fighting on 14 May and then retreated with the rest of the army. Over the next week, the men engaged only in skirmishing with the Federal army, but once again saw its numbers seriously depleted in the attack at Dallas, Georgia, on 28 May. After the fight at Kennesaw Mountain on 27 June, the brigade pulled back to the Chattahoochee River on 4 July. By then the brigade was down to 974 men and would be reduced to 809 after the battle of Atlanta on 22 July. A month later, on 31 August at Jonesboro, the brigade was destroyed as an infantry unit when its numbers fell to 513.

What was left of the Orphan Brigade was ordered to be mounted, but not enough horses were supplied. As the wounded recovered, the numbers of the brigade increased to 945, but only about two-thirds of the men were ever mounted. The remainder were put on guard duty. Those men who did have horses (or mules in some cases) were made a part of the cavalry force that attempted to hamper William Tecumseh Sherman's March to the Sea and were eventually made part of the defenses of Savannah. The remnant of the 1st Brigade then followed Sherman into South Carolina.

For the remainder of the war, the men operated in South Carolina, trying to protect isolated communities from Federal raiders. At Camden, South Carolina, beginning on 18 April they fought for several days to defend the town until word arrived on 21 April of Johnston's surrender in North Carolina. The notification of the surrender also instructed the men to stop fighting and to go to Washington, Georgia, to surrender. On 7 May 1865, the 600 remaining men of the 1st Kentucky Brigade surrendered and were paroled. Over the next few weeks and months, members of the brigade made their way back to their homes in Kentucky for the first time since early 1862.

—*David S. Heidler and Jeanne T. Heidler*

See also Atlanta Campaign; Breckinridge, John Cabell; Chickamauga; Helm, Benjamin Hardin; Kentucky.

For further reading:

Davis, William C. *The Orphan Brigade; The Kentucky Confederates Who Couldn't Go Home* (1980).

OSTEND MANIFESTO
(1854)

Ever since the Polk administration had attempted to purchase Cuba for $100 million during the late 1840s, the idea of annexing the island had been important in the mind of the nation. After his inauguration in 1853, President Pierce sought Alaska as a buffer between east and west and pursued Hawaii and Cuba for their agricultural possibilities. In his dealings for Cuba he was most diligent. Although a native of New Hampshire, Pierce held strong sympathies for the South and felt that the annexation of Cuba would have a favorable effect on the Southern economy. With the Southern frontier steadily shrinking, America looked at Cuba as the next great agricultural area, but the questions over slavery loomed large.

Even before the Pierce administration arrived at the White House, the groundwork for annexation was being laid. The departing Fillmore administration, along with the governments of Great Britain and France, refused to condemn efforts to acquire Cuba. In the hope that the recent happenings in Texas could be repeated in Cuba, General John Quitman (a veteran of the Mexican-American War and a friend of President Pierce), with the knowledge of the president, planned to lead an expedition onto the island. Quitman hoped to combine his force with a group of pro-American Cubans and propel a pro-American junto into the seat of Cuban government. He then expected the junto to ask for admission to the Union as a slave state. With the Spanish hand in Cuba being forced, rumors of Spain's freeing of Cuban slaves and Africanizing the island began to appear.

As president, Franklin Pierce was decidedly expansionist and supported Cuban annexation on behalf of Southern interests. Shrouded in the excuse of American security, Cuba was intended as another slave state. To support the expansionist intentions Pierce had outlined in his inaugural address, he appointed future president and ardent expansionist James Buchanan of Pennsylvania as minister to England; John Mason as minister to France; and for Spain, Pierre Soulé of Louisiana, who had championed Cuban annexation while in the Senate.

Pierce seemed to have found the opportune moment for dealing with the Cuban question. The Crimean War was occupying Britain and France, Spain was in her declining days, and pro-American planters in Cuba had pledged their support for an American invasion. Pressures heightened with the harassment of the *Black Warrior* in Havana harbor, and Pierce began to prepare for negotiations with Spain. At Pierce's urging, Soulé met with Buchanan and Mason to consider the issue of Cuba. From 9 to 11 October 1854, the group met in Ostend, Belgium, and then adjourned to meet in Aix-la-

Chapelle from 12 to 18 October. The result of this meeting was the Ostend Manifesto, which was an analysis of the Cuban situation for Secretary of State William Marcy and President Pierce. Simply stated, it suggested that the United States should make an effort to purchase Cuba from Spain. If rebuffed, the United States would have to consider the question of whether Cuba, as a Spanish possession, was a serious threat to American security. If it was determined to be a threat, forced annexation of Cuba would be necessary.

The timing of the manifesto could not have been worse. Antislavery forces were gaining momentum daily due to the perceived administrative impropriety of the recently passed Kansas-Nebraska Act. While the manifesto was more a study of the Cuban question than a call to arms, when an accurate summary was published in the *New York Herald*, shocked Northerners completely abandoned their already waning faith in Pierce.

With Pierce's initial popularity in shambles, he was forced to abandon all plans for Cuba. Secretary of State Marcy then reversed the administration's Cuban policy in a letter to Soulé. A disgusted Soulé immediately resigned and left Spain. As the War of 1812 concluded American efforts to annex Canada, the Ostend Manifesto would end American efforts to gain Cuba.

—*Brian D. McKnight*

See also Buchanan, James; Kansas-Nebraska Act; Pierce, Franklin; Soulé, Pierre.

For further reading:

Ettinger, Amos A. *The Mission to Spain of Pierre Soulé, 1853–1855: A Study in the Cuban Diplomacy of the United States* (1932).

Nichols, Roy F. *Franklin Pierce: Young Hickory of the Granite Hills* (1958).

OSTERHAUS, PETER J.
(1823–1917)
Union general

Born on 4 January 1823 in Coblenz, Westphalia, Peter J. Osterhaus was one of four German-Americans to reach the rank of major general in the American Civil War. After brief service in the landwehr, Osterhaus joined in the 1848 uprisings, serving with the largest revolutionary army in Baden. When the rebellion failed, Osterhaus was forced to flee to the United States in 1849, where he finally settled in St. Louis, Missouri.

During the early months of 1861, Osterhaus worked as a hardware store clerk and drilled the students at the Humboldt Medical Institute to prepare them for the coming war. On 24 April 1861, heeding President Abraham Lincoln's call for 75,000 volunteers, Osterhaus mustered into the U.S. Army commanding Company A, 2d Missouri Volunteer Infantry, a primarily German-American unit.

Osterhaus began his Civil War career serving under General Nathaniel Lyon during early skirmishes in Missouri in 1861, and for his service, Osterhaus was promoted to major. Osterhaus fought with distinction at the battles of Wilson's Creek on 10 August 1861 and Pea Ridge on 7–8 March 1862, where his battlefield abilities brought him to the attention of his superiors. Osterhaus rose rapidly to the rank of brigadier general by June 1862.

After Pea Ridge, Osterhaus commanded the 1st and 2d Divisions in the Army of the Southwest. The summer of 1862 was filled with minor skirmishes as General Samuel Curtis led the army throughout eastern Arkansas. In the fall, Osterhaus left his command for a brief period while on sick leave. He recovered by January 1863 and received orders transferring him to General Ulysses S. Grant's army in Memphis.

In the Army of the Tennessee, Osterhaus commanded the 9th Division of Major General John McClernand's XIII Corps at the battles of Arkansas Post, Port Gibson, and Jackson, Mississippi. On 16 May 1863, he joined the attack on Champion's Hill east of Vicksburg, Mississippi, followed by the battle of Big Black River, where Osterhaus received his only wound during the entire war. It was a minor injury, and he quickly returned to his command.

After Vicksburg, Osterhaus was given command of the 1st Division, XV Corps, under General William T. Sherman. They were ordered to the Chattanooga area in the fall of 1863 and temporarily transferred to the command of General Joseph Hooker along the southern side of Lookout Mountain. Osterhaus and the 1st Division were among the victorious Federals involved in the "Battle above the Clouds" at Lookout Mountain on 24 November 1863 and participated in driving the Confederates from Missionary Ridge the following day.

In the spring of 1864, Osterhaus's 1st Division rejoined the XV Corps and took part in the capture of Atlanta that September. As reward for his service during the campaign, both Grant and Sherman recommended that Osterhaus be promoted to the rank of major general.

During Sherman's March to the Sea, Osterhaus led the XV Corps and took part in the capture of Savannah on 21 December 1864. In the final months of the war, Osterhaus was transferred to the Army of the South to serve as chief of staff under General Edward R. S. Canby commanding in New Orleans, Louisiana. Osterhaus remained in this position until May 1865, when Canby placed Osterhaus in command of the Military District of Mississippi. He held this position for nearly one year, working to establish peaceful relations between the local populace and the Union forces occupying the state. He was mustered out of service in February 1866.

After the war, President Andrew Johnson appointed Osterhaus U.S. consul to France, where he served from 1866 through 1868. After a period as a private businessman, Osterhaus returned to diplomatic service in

1898 as U.S. vice consul and later deputy consul at Mannheim, Germany, before retiring in November 1900. He lived in Mannheim for the last seventeen years of his life, enjoying several trips to the United States to visit family and attend Civil War reunions. After the outbreak of the Great War in 1914, Osterhaus watched events anxiously, hoping that the United States and Germany would become allies. Peter J. Osterhaus died on 2 January 1917, three months short of witnessing the U.S. declaration of war on the German Empire.

—*Susannah U. Bruce*

See also Atlanta Campaign; German-Americans.

For further reading:
Hess, Earl J. "Osterhaus in Missouri: A Study of German-American Loyalty." *Missouri Historical Review* (1983).
Lonn, Ella. *Foreigners in the Union Army and Navy* (1951).
Zucker, A. E., ed. *The Forty-Eighters: Political Refugees of the German Revolution of 1848* (1950).

O'SULLIVAN, TIMOTHY H.
(1840–1882)
Photographer

Timothy H. O'Sullivan was one of the foremost photographers of the Civil War and, later, of the American West before it was "civilized" by white Americans and new immigrants to the country from abroad in the nineteenth century. In his early twenties he already enjoyed the reputation of an expert technician, capable of working under impeding circumstances even without an assistant, and of an "artist in the field." And yet, for decades after his death he remained unnoted and unappreciated. This partly explains why information about his personality and his life is lacking.

Little is known about O'Sullivan's early life; even the place of his birth cannot be named with accuracy. Whereas O'Sullivan wrote that he had been born in Staten Island, New York, his death certificate, filled out by his physician who relied on information by his father, says that O'Sullivan had been born in Ireland in 1840. Details of his childhood are beyond recall, though it is assumed that he received a formal education, perhaps at a church school. The first reliable information tells of his beginning his apprenticeship in the craft of photography at the age of sixteen.

Like Alexander Gardner, O'Sullivan began his career at the gallery of Mathew Brady, first in New York and soon afterward in Washington D.C., where O'Sullivan was Gardner's assistant. O'Sullivan was not only introduced to the high technical and aesthetic standards of Brady's business, but to the wealthy clientele of the capital. When the Civil War broke out, Brady decided to attempt a photographic coverage as comprehensive as possible. He assembled expert operators in a Photographic Corps, of which O'Sullivan became a member. On 21 July 1861, Brady, O'Sullivan, and many other onlookers traveled to Bull Run to witness what was supposed to become a decisive victory for Union troops. Instead, the photographers and other civilians hurried back to Washington in panic. This was one of the first contacts with war for O'Sullivan, who soon turned out to be one of the most daring of photographers active during the conflict.

From December 1861 to May 1862, O'Sullivan followed General Thomas West Sherman through South Carolina, seizing the opportunity to make his own record of the war in that area. He photographed Union operations at Beaufort, Port Royal Island, Bay Point, Hilton Head, and Fort Pulaski. Military activities were recorded just as much as spots of scenic interest. When Gardner left Brady to set up his own company in 1862, O'Sullivan soon followed him and became Gardner's employee, the most prolific during the war. He was assigned to copy maps and to make prints, but the more important work, seen from the standpoint of generations to come, was done in the field. For three years he photographed soldiers before and after battle, the machinery of war, construction work for military purposes, as well as the devastating aftermath of battles such as Antietam, Fredericksburg, Aquia Creek, Gettysburg, Petersburg, and Appomattox. The images he produced were sold through Gardner's studio; the one's for Brady, through his studio or E. H. & T. Anthony, so that they circulated fairly widely throughout the country. When Gardner published his *Photographic Sketchbook of the War* in 1866, forty-four of the hundred photographic prints were O'Sullivan's and were credited to him.

When O'Sullivan tried to show artillery in action, as he did at Fredericksburg in 1863, it is said that the soldiers had to tell him to withdraw to a safe distance. One of his best-known pictures—in fact, one of the best known of all war photographs—shows bloated corpses at Gettysburg in the morning mist of 4 July 1863. It was titled "A Harvest of Death." That caption, according to Alan Trachtenberg, embodies the central motive of the *Sketchbook* and, in fact, of many war photographs: the photographers' attempt to transform scenes of war into memories or monuments. Gardner described the picture as conveying a "useful moral": "It shows the blank horror and reality of war…. [Let it] aid in preventing such another calamity falling upon the nation."

After the war, O'Sullivan participated in several important scientific and military surveys of the American West, traveling tens of thousands of miles between 1867 and 1874. Even under the most physically strenuous circumstances he was able to produce powerful and compelling images that make him, next to William Henry Jackson, the most outstanding photographer of the American West. He dealt extensively with massive rock formations for geological purposes and photographed the wild and awesome scenery still to be discovered by the European settlers of America in what was (or was to become) Nevada, Arizona, New Mexico, Colorado, Utah, Wyoming, and Idaho, including the Shoshone Falls of the Snake River, Idaho; towering white dunes in the deserts of Nevada; Death Valley; the Colorado River; the Grand Canyon; and the area now known as the Canyon de Chelley National Monument in Arizona. He even turned to record the already dying ways of life of the Native Indians. In 1867 he documented subterranean mining operations in Virginia City, a great technical achievement, as these photographs were the first subterranean mining pictures ever made in the United States.

O'Sullivan was married to Laura Virginia Pywell in 1873. Their son was stillborn in 1876, and five years later, Laura O'Sullivan died of tuberculosis. Timothy O'Sullivan, who had been appointed chief photographer for the Department of the Treasury only a few months before, had contracted the disease, too, and died of it in his parents' home on Staten Island, New York, on 14 January 1882.

—*Angela Schwarz*

See also Brady, Mathew B.; Gardner, Alexander; Photography.
For further reading:
Dingus, Rick. *The Photographic Artefacts of Timothy O'Sullivan* (1982).
Newhall, Beaumont, and Nancy Newhall. *T. H. O'Sullivan: Photographer* (1966).
Snyder, Joel. *American Frontiers: The Photographs of Timothy O'Sullivan, 1867–1874* (1981).
Trachtenberg, Alan. *Reading American Photographs. Images As History—Mathew Brady to Walker Evans* (1990).

OULD, ROBERT
(1820–1882)
Confederate bureaucrat

Born in Georgetown, District of Columbia, and educated there, in Pennsylvania, and at the College of William and Mary, Robert Ould studied law and became a successful Washington attorney and local political figure before the Civil War. Upon the formation of the Confederacy, Ould offered his services and for the first year of the war served as Confederate assistant secretary of war. In July 1862 he was appointed Confederate commissioner for the exchange of prisoners at the rank of colonel, a position he would hold for the remainder of the war.

Besides the routine duties of meeting with Union commissioners to negotiate exchanges, Ould held a variety of temporary appointments and assignments throughout the war. As part of his exchange duties, he was responsible for getting money and goods sent by family and the federal government to prisoners in Southern prisoner-of-war camps. He also handled complaints from Union officers regarding the treatment of prisoners and especially accusations that federal troops held in Southern prisons were used to labor on Confederate entrenchments. This practice, though recognized by both sides as inappropriate, did occur in some Southern cities, especially when the Union prisoners were African-American. Ould also transmitted complaints to the Federal government regarding the treatment of civilians in New Orleans after that city fell to the Union in 1862. In the last year of the war, Ould was a part of the Confederate Secret Service.

After the war, Henry Halleck ordered Ould's arrest on charges that he used money sent for Union prisoners for other purposes. While Ould had privately expressed sentiments during the war that Union prisoners should not be supplied with food as long as Confederate soldiers were hungry, a board of Union officers found after an investigation in June 1865, that Ould had not misappropriated funds during the war, and he was released.

After the war, Ould resumed his law practice, now in Richmond, Virginia. He lived there for the remainder of his life.

—*David S. Heidler and Jeanne T. Heidler*

See also Prisoner Exchanges; Prisoners of War.
For further reading:
Bar Association of the City of Richmond. *Proceedings in Memorium of R. C. L. Moncure and Robert Ould* (1883).

OVERLAND CAMPAIGN
See Richmond Campaign

P

PAGE, CHARLES ANDERSON
(1838–1873)
Journalist

Born to a farm family in Lee County, Illinois, Charles Anderson Page graduated from Cornell College in Mount Vernon, Iowa. After graduation he went to work for a small Iowa Republican newspaper. Upon the election of Abraham Lincoln, he hoped to acquire a government job. He traveled to Washington in February 1861 to plead his case. While preferring a postmaster's position back in Iowa, he had to settle for a clerk's job in the fifth auditor's office of the Treasury Department.

While working in the Treasury Department, the excitement of the war made him want to return to journalism, and Page approached Adams Sherman Hill, the second man in the *New York Tribune*'s Washington office, for a position as war correspondent. Hill hesitated because of Page's relative inexperience, but soon relented, sending Page down to the York Peninsula during the Seven Days' battles on a trial basis.

Page arrived on the battlefield in late morning 27 June 1862. He found himself in proximity to the fighting and watched the events unfold in ever increasing awe. In his dispatches back to Washington he painted vivid word pictures of the raging battle and was especially effective when he reported seeing a riderless horse flee the battlefield with a perfectly intact human leg in the stirrup.

After the campaign the *Tribune* editors were so impressed with his stories from the peninsula that he was allowed to continue to report on the war. Because he was not considered a full-time correspondent of the paper, however, he was forced to remain in the Treasury Department and obtain leave for his trips to the front.

His next big chance came with the creation of John Pope's Army of Virginia and its movement out of Washington later in the summer of 1862. He almost missed the campaign that would become Second Bull Run, however, because the new commanding general of the army, Henry Halleck, issued an order banning reporters from traveling with Pope's army. Perhaps using his contacts in the government from his year at treasury, Page obtained a position as hospital assistant with the Army of Virginia and was present throughout the battle. He was able to send his reports in to the paper, making the *Tribune* one of the few papers in the country to carry early firsthand accounts of Second Bull Run.

Following the battle, Page returned briefly to his treasury job, but was sent out in the middle of September to cover the campaign resulting from Robert E. Lee's first invasion of the North. He arrived in time to witness the battle of Antietam and to acquire interviews with many of the Union officers afterwards. One such interview, conducted with other reporters, was with the wounded Joseph Hooker, and Page was witness to some of Hooker's intemperate remarks. The ability to gain access to high-ranking officers became one of Page's strengths, and he attributed it to always having a ready supply of liquor available after a battle.

Although Page's stories were becoming increasingly popular with readers, Hill still believed him too inexperienced to become a full-time correspondent. When Page was unable to get time off from his treasury job in the summer of 1863, he was forced to miss the battle of Gettysburg. However, shortly afterward he was offered a regular correspondent's job.

Page's abilities and popularity soon gained him his own by-line and increased recognition from other journalists for his engaging style and dedication to accuracy. He insisted on reporting battles as realistically as possible, rather than dressing his stories in the trappings of patriotism. When men did not show enthusiasm for fighting, which was often, he reported it to his readers. He also reported about the actions of individual units, especially when he felt that such units did not receive the proper credit for their performance in a battle.

While becoming one of the more respected war correspondents in the Eastern theater, Page continued his creative efforts to put himself close to the scene of action. He, with other reporters, traveled a rather dangerous route to arrive at the Wilderness in the early stages of Ulysses S. Grant's Virginia campaign against Lee. He covered some of the most exciting actions of that campaign and then settled down to report the opening phases of the siege of Petersburg. His insistence on being present during the establishment of the siege in June 1864 took him into the hot Virginia sun once too often, and at the end of the month he suffered sunstroke.

Never in robust health, he was incapacitated for some weeks by this incident.

At the end of the war, Page again defied efforts to restrict the movement of reporters by making his way to Richmond after it had fallen to the Federal army. He reported back to the *Tribune* about the devastation the city had suffered and the plight of Richmond's civilians.

During the war, Page had become very well known in various government circles and this notoriety gained him an appointment from Andrew Johnson in 1865 as United States consul to Zurich, Switzerland. He enjoyed his stay in Switzerland so much that he decided to remain there at the expiration of his appointment. He engaged in various business activities there, but his poor health took him to London in 1873, where he died at the age of thirty-five.

—David S. Heidler and Jeanne T. Heidler

See also *New York Tribune;* Newspapers; War Correspondents.
For further reading:
Andrews, J. Cutler. *The North Reports the Civil War* (1955).
Crozier, Emmet. *Yankee Reporters, 1861–65* (1956).
Page, Charles P. *Letters of a War Correspondent* (1899).
Starr, Louis M. *Bohemian Brigade: Civil War Newsmen in Action* (1954; reprint 1987).

PAINE, HALBERT ELEAZER
(1826–1905)
Union general

Born to Eleazer Paine and Caroline Hoyt Paine in Chardon, Ohio, Halbert Eleazer Paine was educated locally before graduating from Western Reserve University. For a time after graduation, Paine taught school, including for a short time in Mississippi. After returning to Ohio, he studied law and opened a practice in Cleveland. In 1857 Paine moved to Milwaukee, Wisconsin, where he went into practice with local attorney and politician Carl Schurz. Before the outbreak of the Civil War, Paine took some interest in politics, primarily to advance his strong opposition to slavery.

At the beginning of the war, Paine closed his law practice and raised the 4th Wisconsin Cavalry and became its colonel. During July 1861 he led his men to Washington. En route at Harrisburg, Pennsylvania, he responded to the offer of a cattle car to transport his men by commandeering a passenger train.

One of Paine's first duties in the army was to take him in November 1861 to the Eastern Shore of Maryland. His regiment was to cross Chesapeake Bay, land at White Haven on the Wicomico River, and march into the interior to Princess Anne and then to Snow Hill, all to intimidate Confederate sympathizers and protect pro-Union men on the eve of a local election. Any troublemakers would be sent to Fort McHenry in Baltimore. The Eastern Shore's large number of Confederate sympathizers required its occupation by Union troops for much of the war, but Paine was sent west in 1862. In Louisiana that summer, he refused orders from the War Department to return runaway slaves to their owners. His most conspicuous action during this campaign came in August when the 4th Wisconsin relieved the Federal defenders of Baton Rouge. He defied, however, the order from Benjamin Butler commanding in New Orleans to burn Baton Rouge to prevent its future capture.

On 13 March 1863, Paine was promoted to brigadier general of volunteers and commanded a brigade in the siege of Port Hudson, Louisiana. In one of the assaults on 14 June 1863, Paine suffered such a serious wound to his leg that it had to be amputated. Unable to return to duty until the next year, he then served primarily as a member of military boards.

In July 1864, Paine was called away from one of those boards to help defend Washington against Jubal Early's raid. Following Early's repulse, Paine was given command of the District of Illinois. One of his most important duties in that command was when he recruited and supplied 100-day troops to fight Sterling Price during Price's Missouri raid in the fall of 1864. Later in the fall, however, Paine was relieved from this command at his own request. In the last months of the war he served as a prison commissioner in New York City. He resigned from the army on 15 May 1865, having been brevetted to major general of volunteers for his service at Port Hudson.

After the war Paine was elected to the House of Representatives. He served three terms as a Radical Republican and for a time sat on the Committee on Elections that determined the status of Southern congressmen. After leaving Congress in 1871, he opened a law practice in Washington, D.C. He also served for eighteen months during the Rutherford B. Hayes administration as commissioner of patents and was credited with instituting many reforms in that bureau. Later in his life he published *A Treatise on the Law of Elections to Public Office,* which remained for many years an important legal reference on that subject. He died on 14 April 1905, when he was still an active Washington attorney, and was buried at Arlington National Cemetery.

—David S. Heidler and Jeanne T. Heidler

See also Port Hudson.
For further reading:
Ladd, Story Butler. *Halbert Eleazer Paine, February 4, 1826–April 14, 1905* (1920).

"PAINE" / "PAYNE," LEWIS
See Powell, Lewis Thornton

PALMER, JOHN McCAULEY
(1817–1900)
Union general

John McCauley Palmer was born in Scott County, Kentucky. Palmer's father, an antislavery Democrat, moved the family to Illinois in 1831. Palmer attended Shurtleff College, studied law, and entered the bar in 1839. He entered politics with election as a state senator in 1851. Palmer contributed to the formation of the Illinois Republican Party in the 1850s and lost a bid for a congressional seat in 1859. In 1860 he served as a delegate to the Republican national convention.

Palmer served in the Union army during the Civil War. As a friend of Abraham Lincoln, he received high rank despite his dearth of military experience. He fought in the Island No. 10, Stones River, Chattanooga, and Atlanta campaigns, rising to the rank of corps commander.

During the Island No. 10 campaign, Palmer became deeply resentful of the favoritism shown to West Point graduates. Palmer's troops did not participate in the battle of Shiloh. Later, he received divisional command of the 2d Division of the Left Wing (later XXI Corps) in the Army of the Cumberland. The division consisted of the brigades of Charles Cruft, William B. Hazen, and William Grose. Cruft and Grose, Indiana lawyers, had fought capably at Fort Donelson and Shiloh. Hazen, a West Pointer, was arguably the best brigade commander in the Army of the Cumberland. Palmer led these troops during the Stones River, Tullahoma, and Chickamauga campaigns.

During the Stones River, Tullahoma, and Chickamauga campaigns, Palmer's forces fought well. At both Stones River and Chickamauga, Palmer's division withstood intense attacks and suffered high casualties. At the Round Forest it was one of Palmer's brigades—Hazen's—that probably saved the day for the Union forces. At Chickamauga, Palmer's division participated in Thomas's heroic stand.

Promotion to the position of commander of XIV Corps followed Palmer's performance at Chickamauga. His new command consisted of the divisions of Richard W. Johnson, Jefferson C. Davis, and Absalom Baird. The Illinoisan felt proud of his promotion but believed that the army had wronged his former superior Thomas L. Crittenden after Chickamauga. Palmer believed that the West Pointers had unfairly removed Crittenden because he was a political general.

Palmer commanded XIV Corps during the Chattanooga and Atlanta campaigns. He performed adequately, but not brilliantly. He did not have a close relationship with his new commander, William T. Sherman. Palmer became enraged over the issue of rank with John Schofield. Not surprisingly, Sherman did not back Palmer's position, and Palmer resigned in disgust.

In February 1865 Palmer became commander of the Department of Kentucky. Palmer's encouragement of slave emancipation and African-American enlistment in the Union army brought him into deep conflict with Kentuckians. He resigned from the army in April 1866, and the Kentucky courts indicted him in November 1866 for aiding the escape of slaves. The indictment was voided.

Palmer reentered politics after the war. He served as the Republican governor of Illinois from 1868 to 1872. Becoming disenchanted with the Republican Party, he joined the Liberal Republicans in 1872 and eventually the Democratic Party. Palmer was defeated as a Democratic candidate for governor in 1888 but won election to the Senate in 1891. He served a full term. A conservative, he was the presidential candidate of the Gold Democrats in the 1896 election. Throughout his career Palmer had an independent mind. He defended his political stance in his book *Personal Recollections of John M. Palmer: The Story of an Earnest Life*, published in 1901. He is buried at Carlinville, Illinois.

Palmer exemplified the best and the worst of Union political generals. He had aggressive instincts in battle, and his subordinates served him ably throughout the war. However, the general could not forget he was a civilian and a politician by trade. He resented the military professionals' condescending attitude toward political appointees and believed that he and other civilians had lost promotions because of their background.

As a politician, Palmer never followed the party line, and he was an independent during the height of partisanship. As a result, he never achieved the political aspirations that his considerable abilities seemed to justify.

—*Damon R. Eubank*

See also Grose, William; Hazen, William Babcock; Island No. 10.

For further reading:

Castel, Albert. *Decision in the West: The Atlanta Campaign of 1864* (1992).

Cozzens, Peter. *The Civil War in the West: From Stones River to Chattanooga* (1996).

Daniel, Larry J. *Island No. 10: Struggle for the Mississippi Valley* (1996).

Lamers, William M. *The Edge of Glory: A Biography of William S. Rosecrans, U.S.A.* (1999).

Palmer, George T. Palmer. *A Conscientious Turncoat: The Story of John M. Palmer, 1817–1900* (1941).

Palmer, John M. *Personal Recollections of John M. Palmer: The Story of an Earnest Life* (1901).

PALMER, WILLIAM JACKSON
(1836–1909)
Union officer and railroad builder

Born in Leipsic, Delaware, on 17 September 1836, Palmer grew up in a middle-class environment. His father, a Quaker farmer and teacher, provided public and a private education for his son. At age seven-

teen, Palmer joined the engineering crew of the Hampfield Railroad, starting a career that would go past the end of the century. In 1855 he visited England to study railroads and mines.

On his return in the next year, Palmer joined the Westmoreland Coal Company and a year later became the confidential secretary to J. Edgar Thomson, president of the Pennsylvania Railroad. Using this opportunity, from 1858 to 1861 Palmer learned all aspects of railroading.

When the Civil War broke out, Palmer organized a cavalry troop that was sent to the Western theater and saw service at the crucial battle of Shiloh. Returning east, he recruited the 15th Pennsylvania Cavalry. Captured after the battle of Antietam while on a scouting patrol, Palmer spent several months in a Confederate prison before being exchanged in January 1863. He then rejoined his regiment, which by that time had been transferred to the Western theater, and fought in some of the war's major campaigns and battles in the West, including the campaign for Chattanooga, Missionary Ridge, Chickamauga, and Sherman's 1864 Atlanta campaign. His regiment did not participate in the March to the Sea, however.

Mustered out of service in June 1865, Palmer retired from the army as a brigadier general of volunteers. Throughout the rest of his life, he would be referred to as General Palmer. He received the Medal of Honor in 1894 for his meritorious service during the war.

Few former soldiers returned to civilian life with better prospects. Using his previous railroad experience, Palmer went to work for the Kansas Pacific. While treasurer of the company, he also was placed in overall charge of surveys through Colorado in anticipation of the line going to the West Coast.

Palmer quickly saw the economic promise of the southern part of the territory. His experience in mining and railroading opened the possibilities of the natural resources of this richly blessed, but isolated, region. The potential seemed limitless once a railroad arrived. A man of ambition and vision, he left the Kansas Pacific to organize his own railroad, the Denver & Rio Grande (D&RG, founded in 1870). The goal was to build southward from Denver along the foothills and eventually to Mexico. He hoped the D&RG would serve as a feeder line for the east-west transcontinental lines.

The D&RG would be a narrow-gauge railroad (three feet between rails), and Palmer planned to develop towns along the route. His first, and most successful, was Colorado Springs, followed by Salida and Durango, among others. He also planned to have his workers share in the development by encouraging them to buy stock and partake in the cultural activities the railroad planned. The railroad never got as far as Mexico, but it did open southern and western Colorado and eventually reached Salt Lake City.

After surviving the depression of the 1870s, the D&RG won the race to Leadville but lost out to the rival Santa Fe Railroad for New Mexico. The railroad then turned into the mining regions of the Colorado Rockies, reaching Silverton in 1882, and Aspen and Ouray in 1887. Palmer eventually lost control of his "baby line," regained it, and finally retired to Colorado Springs in 1901 a millionaire. Continuing his interest in his workers, Palmer shared a large portion of his profit from the sale of his stock with those who had been with the company through his years. Meanwhile, he took a deep interest in developing Colorado Springs, the community his railroad had given birth to in 1871. He also helped support Colorado College, one of the features that made the town Colorado's most cosmopolitan community. Palmer died in Colorado Springs on 13 March 1909.

—*Duane A. Smith*

For further reading:
Athearn, Robert G. *Rebel of the Rockies* (1962).
Clothier, Isaac. *Letters, 1853–1868, William Jackson Palmer* (1906).
Fisher, John. *Builder of the West: The Life of General William Jackson Palmer* (1939).

PALMERSTON, JOHN TEMPLE, THIRD VISCOUNT
(1784–1865)
Prime minister of Britain

Third Viscount John Temple Palmerston was prime minister of Britain during the American Civil War. As his peerage was Irish rather than British, he did not have a seat in the House of Lords, but followed a successful career in the Commons, where he served for more than fifty-eight years. First elected in 1807, his jovial character and patriotic, if not jingoistic, foreign policy had made him widely popular in Britain. Almost constantly in office, between 1859 and 1865 he headed a Liberal-Whig coalition government and was undoubtedly the most important politician of mid-Victorian Britain. Clearly pro-Confederate during the war, he nonetheless kept Britain out of the conflict and followed a policy closely related to British interests.

Palmerston was born a year after the 1783 Peace of Paris, which established U.S. independence, and he was five years old when George Washington was inaugurated in 1789. During the War of 1812, Palmerston served as secretary for war and his marked anti-Americanism was increased by decades of U.S. expansionism. Convinced that the United States was a nation of self-righteous, swaggering bullies he was, as a confirmed constitutional monarchist of the old school, no friend to American republicanism. He fumed at the Webster-Ashburton Treaty of 1842, would have gone to war over the Oregon

question, and was openly hostile to continued U.S. involvement in Cuba, the Mosquito Coast, and Latin America. An important, and early, opponent of slavery, Palmerston considered the United States hypocritical regarding the continuation of the institution. His attitude toward Abraham Lincoln's administration was colored by its ambiguous attitude toward slavery in 1861, and the timing of the Emancipation Proclamation only tended to increase his distrust of Northern ambitions. His attitudes were also clearly affected by a personal dislike of Secretary of State William H. Seward and his own friendship with New York's Anglophobic Irish-American journalists. Fortunately for the United States, Palmerston's anti-American feelings were balanced by a dislike of all things French and his deep distrust of Napoleon III's ambitions in both Europe and Mexico, a viewpoint which made any joint Anglo-French intervention in the Civil War unlikely.

Before the outbreak of the war, Palmerston had strongly supported the national aspirations of the Belgians, the Greeks, and the Italians and saw the secession of the South as another example of an oppressed people justifiably resisting aggression. Together with Lord John Russell, the British foreign secretary, Palmerston believed, at least until 1863, that Southern independence was a fait accompli, yet both men became increasingly horrified at the growing violence of the conflict. Believing that Britain should be allowed to trade with each warring faction, Palmerston hoped for an end to the war, thinking that the independence of the Confederacy was a reasonable price to pay for peace. He also hoped that a decisive Southern military victory would convinced the Lincoln administration of the futility of further aggression, and he advocated a policy of nonintervention. Palmerston believed also that Britain should ignore Napoleon III's almost constant overtures for intervention and "rest upon her oars." His policy of neutrality would be severely tested by developments on both sides of the Atlantic.

After the outbreak of hostilities in April 1861, Lincoln declared a blockade of Southern ports, an act Palmerston thought clearly in violation of the 1856 Declaration of Paris, an international agreement that the United States had refused to ratify. Lincoln's actions, he thought, had recognized Southern belligerent status, and to protect neutral rights Palmerston's government recognized the Confederacy's belligerent status on 13 May 1861, a move that Lincoln saw as hostile. The removal of the Confederate envoys from a British ship, the *Trent*, by Captain Charles Wilkes upon the high seas on 8 November 1861 struck Palmerston as an act of blatant piracy. In an emergency cabinet meeting Palmerston declared that, although members of his divided cabinet may accept this affront to British neutral rights, he would "be damned" if he would. British troops were sent to

Canada, British pro-Southern politicians demanded action, and a strongly worded ultimatum to Washington was drawn up by Russell. Only the intervention of Prince Albert, who toned down the diplomatic note to Lincoln, defused the situation, and Lincoln released the Confederate envoys John Slidell and James M. Mason.

As the Union blockade began to starve British cotton mills of supplies and created real economic hardships among the British working class, some in Palmerston's cabinet, especially William Gladstone, feared political violence in Britain. While Gladstone became openingly sympathetic to intervention, an opinion ably countered by the secretary for war, George Cornewall Lewis, Palmerston continued to hope for a decisive Southern victory, which would invite British mediation to end the war. Disappointed that the capture of New Orleans in April 1862 did not end the conflict, Palmerston became enraged at General Benjamin Butler's infamous "Woman Order" of June 1862, and he sent the U.S. minister, Charles Francis Adams, an angry private note. Palmerston refused to speak to Adams for sometime and instructed Lady Palmerston not to invite him to future official receptions.

In the first two years of the war, Palmerston's most decisive action, perhaps paradoxically, was in preventing British intervention. On the evening of 18 July 1862, he rose in the Commons to defeat William Lindsay's motion to recognize the Confederacy. Palmerston's intervention forced Lindsay to withdraw his motion without a vote. Palmerston remained equally unsympathetic to J. A. Roebuck's similar motion in June 1863. As British business interests continued to profit from its wartime trade with the United States and the cotton famine gradually eased, the threat of intervention, without a conclusive Southern military victory, receded. The Union victories at Gettysburg and Vicksburg in July 1863 virtually sealed the fate of the Confederacy, and although Palmerston may have made threatening noises throughout 1864, especially over Adam's behavior regarding the Southern rams being built in the Laird shipyards, there was faint hope that he would deviate from his course of neutrality. In 1864 he refused to listen to Lindsay's idea about joint European intervention to stop the war upon humanitarian grounds. In early 1865, aware of the crumbling Southern resistance to Ulysses S. Grant and William Tecumseh Sherman, Palmerston refused to consider the offer made to him by Duncan F. Kenner, the Confederate commissioner of 1865, of recognition in return for the abolition of slavery in the South. Increasingly after the summer of 1863, Palmerston's attention was drawn to European affairs, especially the growing power of Prussia under Otto von Bismarck.

The collapse of the Confederacy came as no surprise to Britain, although the public was shocked by Lincoln's assassination on 14 April 1865. Palmerston was too ill to

attend the House of Commons to join in the glowing tributes paid to Lincoln, but he did lead the Liberal Party to an overwhelming electoral victory in July 1865. Palmerston died of a fever on 18 October 1865, and Charles Francis Adams rather caustically reflected that he had left nothing behind him except a widow who would have to adjust to playing a less prominent role in public affairs. This is somewhat unfair. Palmerston's decision to maintain a policy of nonintervention throughout the American Civil War was of crucial importance; similarly, if Britain had intervened, Palmerston's role would have been equally decisive.

—*Rory Cornish*

See also Butler's Proclamation; Mason, James Murray; Slidell, John; *Trent* Affair; Wilkes, Charles.

For further reading:

Adams, Ephraim D. *Great Britain and the American Civil War* (1925).

Crawford, Martin. *The Anglo-American Crisis of the Mid-Nineteenth Century: "The Times" and America, 1850–1862* (1987).

Crook, D. P. *Diplomacy during the American Civil War* (1975).

Ferris, Norman B. *The Trent Affair: A Diplomatic Crisis* (1976).

Guedalla, Philip. *Gladstone and Palmerston: Being the Correspondence of Lord Palmerston with Mr. Gladstone 1851–1865* (1928).

Jenkins, Brian. *Britain and the War for the Union* (1974).

Jones, Howard. *Union in Peril: The Crisis over British Intervention in the Civil War* (1992).

Ridley, Jasper. *Lord Palmerston* (1971).

Vanauken, Sheldon. *The Glittering Illusion: English Sympathy for the Southern Confederacy* (1988).

PALMITO RANCH, BATTLE OF
(12–13 May 1865)

In January 1865, the federal government sent Major General Lew Wallace (who after the Civil War gained fame as the author of *Ben Hur*) to Texas. Ostensibly he was on an inspection tour, but his true goal was to negotiate with the Confederate forces along the Rio Grande and try to elicit their military support for the Mexican government of Benito Juárez.

With that end in mind, on 11 March Wallace met with the two Confederate commanders in the Rio Grande region: Brigadier General James Slaughter, who made his name as an artilleryman, and Colonel John "Rip" Ford, a former Texas Ranger. During their meeting Wallace noted that the war situation was such that any fighting along the Rio Grande would be pointless. As a result, the three commanders agreed to an unofficial truce. After their meeting, General Wallace left for Galveston. For two months the unofficial truce maintained peace along the Rio Grande.

May 1865 saw Colonel Theodore Barrett of the 62d Colored Infantry in temporary command of the Federal garrison at Brazos Island, located north of the mouth of the Rio Grande. Barrett had only limited combat service and was eager to gain a measure of military fame before the war ended. With that in mind, he requested—and was denied—permission from departmental headquarters to lead a demonstration against the Confederates at Fort Brown, near the city of Brownsville.

Ignoring both his orders from headquarters and the advice of his own subordinates, Barrett decided to attack the Confederates. Early on the morning of 11 May, Barrett ordered Lieutenant Colonel David Branson and a force consisting of 250 men from the 62d Colored and 50 men from the 2d Texas (Federal) Cavalry to cross the Rio Grande opposite Brazos Island at Point Isabel and attack the Confederate outposts. Owing to a breakdown on the steamer that was to ferry his troops across the river, Branson was forced to divert his crossing to Boca Chica. After great difficulty due to a storm, Branson's force finally completed its crossing at 9:30 P.M.

Having heard reports of a Confederate outpost at White's Ranch, Branson led his men on a long march in that direction. They arrived at 2:00 A.M. only to discover that the outpost had been abandoned for several days. With his men exhausted from the river crossing and their long march, and with no chance of launching a surprise attack on the Confederate outpost at Palmito Ranch (located along the road to Brownsville), Branson decided to hide his men in a thicket along the Rio Grande for the night.

At 8:30 A.M. on 12 May, when people on the Mexican side of the river detected Branson's force, they promptly alerted the Confederates. Having been discovered, Branson immediately set out for Palmito Ranch, skirmishing with Confederates along the way. Around noon his force defeated a force of 200 to 300 Confederates under the command of Captain W. N. Robinson and captured Palmito Ranch, burning it.

Branson halted his men near Palmito to allow them time to rest and eat. During this time Robinson regrouped, and at 3:00 P.M. he counterattacked, driving Branson back to White's Ranch.

Night provided an opportunity for both commanders to reinforce their commands. Barrett personally assumed command from Branson early on 13 May, bringing with him 200 men from the 34th Indiana. The Confederates at Fort Brown did not receive word of the fighting until the evening. Colonel Ford, the Confederate second in command, immediately dispatched couriers to recall his scattered detachments to Fort Brown. General Slaughter then informed Ford of his intention to retreat. This enraged Ford, who persuaded his commander to engage the enemy. The two Confederates then agreed to meet the next morning to start the expedition.

On the morning of 13 May, Barrett led his forces from White's Ranch back to Palmito Ranch, skirmishing along the way. His forces paused at Palmito to finish burning what had escaped the previous day's flames and then pushed onward. After advancing two miles, they again engaged the enemy in a sharp contest. As a result, Barrett withdrew his troops a mile and a half to Tulosa, a bluff along the Rio Grande.

While Barrett's troops were making their morning march to Palmito Ranch, Ford was busy assembling his forces. When Slaughter did not appear at the agreed-upon time, Ford took matters into his own hands. At 11:00 A.M., he took command of the available troops and marched them to just below San Martin Ranch. Sighting the enemy's line running perpendicular to the road half a mile below his position, Ford determined to fight. He formed a line along the road and positioned his artillery forward of that line. In addition, he sent a detachment to flank the enemy's right.

Around 4:00 P.M., the Federal forces spotted the Confederate cavalry attempting to gain their rear. As the Federals turned around to meet the flanking maneuver, Ford opened up with his artillery. To avoid the Confederate flanking movement, Barrett ordered a detachment of 140 men to form a rear guard skirmish line while the rest of his command retreated.

Observing that this skirmish line was unsupported, Ford ordered his entire line to advance. The Confederates drove the Federal forces back in a seven-mile pursuit. The Federals attempted to make a stand at several points along the route, but Ford's artillery was able to find high ground and drive them away. Fearing that the Federals might be reinforced when they reached White's Ranch and with his men and horses exhausted from the march, Ford ordered his men to withdraw.

At this point, Slaughter finally arrived on the field along with a fresh battalion. He ordered Ford to resume the pursuit, which Ford declined to do until he could explain to Slaughter the reasons for his withdrawal. Ignoring Ford, Slaughter threw out a skirmish line. The Federals countered and brief, inconsequential skirmish ensued. After about ten minutes, Slaughter withdrew his men.

The battle of Palmito Ranch was over. The Federals had slightly over 100 casualties, while the Confederate figure is unknown. The battle would have been insignificant had it not been the last of the Civil War. Interrogating their prisoners after the battle, the Confederates learned for the first time of Lee's surrender in Virginia. With that news, Confederate forces along the Rio Grande disbanded.

—*Jonathan L. Mahaffey*

See also Texas; Wallace, Lewis (Lew).
For further reading:
Ford, John S. *Rip Ford's Texas* (1963).
Hughes, W. J. *Rebellious Ranger* (1964).

PARKE, JOHN GRUBB
(1827–1900)
Union general

Born in Chester County, Pennsylvania, near the town of Coatesville, to Francis Parke and Sarah Gardner Parke, John Grubb Parke moved with his family to Philadelphia when he was eight. He was educated at Samuel Crawford's school and the University of Pennsylvania before accepting an appointment to the U.S. Military Academy. He graduated second of forty-three in the class of 1849. Commissioned into the Topographical Engineers (which during the Civil War merged into the Corps of Engineers), Parke helped conduct several boundary surveys before the Civil War. At the outbreak of the war, he was in the Pacific Northwest surveying the boundary between the United States and Canada.

In the fall of 1861, Parke was ordered to return east, where in November 1861 he was made a brigadier general of volunteers. Parke's first assignment was to report to Ambrose Burnside in Annapolis, Maryland, where he was given command of the 3d Brigade in Burnside's upcoming North Carolina campaign. In that campaign, which departed on 9 January 1862, Parke participated in the captures of Roanoke Island and the port city of New Bern and in the siege of Fort Macon.

In the spring of 1862 Parke and most of the division left North Carolina to join the Peninsula campaign. By the time Burnside had named Parke his chief of staff, Parke had received promotion to major general of volunteers (18 July 1862). He served as Burnside's chief at the battles of South Mountain and Antietam and received Burnside's praise after the Maryland campaign for professionalism and competence. When Burnside was named commander of the Army of the Potomac in November 1862, Parke remained his chief of staff, and when Burnside was removed from command and made commander of the Department of the Ohio, Parke traveled with him and became the commander of IX Corps in the department.

In early June 1863, IX Corps was sent to reinforce Ulysses S. Grant at Vicksburg, where it participated in the final stages of the siege. After the fall of Vicksburg, Parke and IX Corps fought in the Jackson, Mississippi, campaign before being sent to rejoin Burnside in Cincinnati at the end of July 1863. Parke was forced to take a medical leave until early fall but returned to his command in time for the Knoxville campaign. Parke fought in the siege at the end of the year and then commanded the pursuit of James Longstreet in December.

In early 1864, Burnside was ordered to bring IX Corps to Annapolis, Maryland, to be reorganized under his command. Parke resumed his role as Burnside's chief of staff. Because Burnside was senior to George Gordon Meade, the commander of the Army of the Potomac,

when IX Corps joined that army in preparation for Grant's Overland campaign, it was placed directly under Grant.

Parke was ill again during the planning stages of the campaign and did not report to the corps until the battle of the Wilderness had commenced, but he remained thereafter as Burnside's chief of staff through the beginning of the siege at Petersburg. When Burnside was removed as commander of IX Corps—the failure of the mine assault on the Confederate works (the Crater) was his undoing—Parke assumed command of IX Corps on 15 August 1864, and the corps was brought officially into the Army of the Potomac. With the exception of a couple of times when he assumed command of the Army of the Potomac in Meade's absence, Parke served as the corps' commander for the remainder of the war.

During the siege of Petersburg, Parke and IX Corps operated primarily south of the city helping to extend Federal siege lines westward. He fought at Hatcher's Run on 27 October, but his most notable engagement was the Federal counterattack at Fort Stedman on 25 March 1865, when he was temporarily in command of the Army of the Potomac.

After Lee's surrender at Appomattox Court House, Parke commanded the District of Alexandria and then in June the Department of Washington. In 1866 he returned to the Corps of Engineers. By 1884 he had reached the rank of colonel in the regular army and three years later was named the superintendent at West Point. He remained in that position until his retirement from the army two years later. During his retirement Parke lived in Washington, D.C., where he died on 16 December 1900.

—David S. Heidler and Jeanne T. Heidler

See also Burnside, Ambrose; Fort Stedman; Hatcher's Run, Battle of; Knoxville Campaign; Petersburg Campaign; Vicksburg Campaign.

For further reading:
Marvel, William. *Burnside* (1991).
Trudeau, Noah Andre. *The Last Citadel: Petersburg, Virginia, June 1864–April 1865* (1991).

PARKER, ELY SAMUEL
(1828–1895)
Union general

Ely S. Parker was born on the Tonawanda Reservation near Indian Falls, New York, the son of William and Elizabeth (Johnson) Parker. Parker's lineage was pure Seneca, and he was the last grand sachem of the Iroquois League of the Five Nations. His Seneca name was Do-ne-ho-ga-wa, or Keeper of the Western Door. His early schooling took place at the Baptist Mission School of Tonawanda, followed by entrance into Cayuga Academy at Aurora, New York, in the fall of 1845. At the age of eighteen he journeyed to Washington, D.C., with a number of tribal leaders to meet with President James Polk and advocate claims on the tribes' behalf. Returning to New York, Parker undertook the study of law, yet he was refused admission to the bar because New York allowed only white males to enter practice.

Parker then turned to the study of civil engineering at Rensselear Polytechnic Institute in 1849. After graduation in 1851, Parker was named first assistant engineer, in which capacity he supervised improvements on the western terminus of the Erie Canal. Four yours later he became chief engineer for the Chesapeake & Albemarle Ship Canal, located in Virginia. In 1857 he was appointed superintendent of construction for the custom house and marine hospital being constructed in Galena, Illinois. While in Galena, Parker became acquainted with a local store clerk and ex-soldier, Ulysses S. Grant.

By 1861, after the fall of Fort Sumter, Parker became interested in the Union cause and returned to New York to seek a military commission. As had happened with the bar appointment, the governor rebuffed him because of his race. Parker then journeyed to Washington, D.C., where the War Department also refused his services. In May 1863 President Abraham Lincoln offered him a commission as a captain of engineers, with assignment to XVII Corps of the division under the command of General John E. Smith. While with the division, Parker played a role in the battles of Lookout Mountain and Missionary Ridge. Later, he supervised the construction of the breastworks and entrenchments in the Wilderness campaign.

In August 1864 Parker was named military secretary to Ulysses S. Grant, with the rank of lieutenant colonel. As secretary, he transcribed most of Grant's correspondence as well as prepared orders, letters, and reports for the commander's signature. On 9 April 1865, when General Robert E. Lee surrendered at Appomattox Court House, Virginia, Parker joined Grant and his staff at the McLean House. Calling for his order book, Grant transcribed the letter for surrender and passed it to Parker for review. After review, Parker passed the book to Lee. Lee suggested a few additions, which Parker was able to transcribe as the official copies of the document ending the Civil War. He was promoted to brevet brigadier general of volunteers at Appomattox, and later first and second lieutenant in the regular army. On 2 March 1867 he was brevetted brigadier general in the regular army for gallant and meritorious service. He continued to serve as aide-de-camp to General Grant until March 1869.

After Grant's presidential inauguration, Parker was appointed commissioner of Indian affairs, the first Native American to hold the post. He instituted several reforms while commissioner, yet earned the enmity of some members of the House of Representatives, who accused him of fraud in the purchase of agency supplies. Although cleared of all charges, Parker left his commissioner post in

August 1871 to return to private life. For several years Parker participated in Wall Street investments and ventures with mixed success. In 1876 he found employment with the New York Board of Police Commissioners and occupied several positions in that capacity until his death on 30 August 1895 in Fairfield, Connecticut.

—*Frank R. Levstik*

See also Appomattox Courthouse.

For further reading:

Armstrong, William H. *Warrior in Two Camps: Ely S. Parker, Union General and Seneca Chief* (1978).

Parker, Arthur Caswell. *The Life of General Ely S. Parker* (1919).

PARKER, JOEL
(1816–1888)
Governor of New Jersey

Born to Charles Parker and Sarah Coward Parker outside Freehold, New Jersey, Joel Parker was educated locally before entering the College of New Jersey (Princeton). After graduating from college, Parker studied law and began practicing in 1842 in his hometown of Freehold. With what quickly became a successful practice, Parker also became involved in New Jersey politics. A staunch Democrat, Parker was elected to represent his district in the state legislature. He also served as a county prosecutor.

Parker's political activities led to involvement in the state militia. By 1857 he had risen to the rank of brigadier general of the militia and used his new position to inaugurate organizational changes. He enacted further reforms when he was promoted to the rank of major general in 1861.

During the presidential campaign of 1860, Parker openly supported the election of Stephen Douglas. He stood for election and won a position as one of Douglas's electors for the state. Once Abraham Lincoln was elected and the secession crisis began, Parker opposed coercing the seceded states until Fort Sumter fell. From that point on he became a supporter of most administration policies to prosecute the war.

In 1862 Parker received the Democratic nomination for governor, and in the fall of that year he was elected. He began his term in early 1863 and served for three years. As governor Parker continued to support the war effort though he did not relinquish the belief that the Southern states had been wronged by the abolitionists before the war. He firmly believed in upholding the prerogatives of the states and opposed such measures as the Emancipation Proclamation as an unnecessary abuse of war powers by the executive.

Parker spent most of his time, however, doing what he could for the war effort. An excellent recruiter, he prevented the state from having to implement conscription for a year after the passage of the Federal draft. He also maintained almost constant contact with New Jersey officers in the field so that he could be apprised of the activities and needs of New Jersey troops. He established hospitals for New Jersey wounded soldiers and provided for the families of those New Jersey soldiers killed in action.

Along with these activities, Parker was attendant to the needs of neighboring states. When Pennsylvania governor Andrew Curtin called for aid in the wake of Robert E. Lee's invasion in June 1863, Parker was quick to respond. He went to several nine-month regiments recently sent home to be mustered out of service and asked for volunteers to go to Pennsylvania. His amazing persuasive power and popularity caused the majority of the men to agree. He next issued a proclamation to the state asking for additional volunteers and received a very strong response. By the end of the month, however, Parker and many of New Jersey's citizens were concerned that if Lee were successful in Pennsylvania, New Jersey might be invaded. As a result, the governor wrote directly to President Lincoln informing him that the people of New Jersey wanted George McClellan returned to the command of the Army of the Potomac and if that were not possible, that McClellan be given command of a new army to protect the northeast.

The following year Parker remained hard at work raising more troops to meet the state's quotas before the draft had to be used. He also tried to answer emergency situations, as was the case in early July 1864 when he issued another proclamation asking for volunteers to meet the crisis of Jubal Early's raid on Washington. Later in the month, however, he protested to the president that the draft was not being conducted fairly in New Jersey. A few months later he protested again because a draft was called without giving state officials enough time to fill the quota through recruiting.

Parker left office in early 1866 and returned to his law practice. He received the party's nomination again for governor in 1871 and was elected. After the end of his term, he served briefly as state attorney general before again entering into private legal practice. In 1880 he was prevailed upon to accept a spot on the state supreme court. He was still serving on the bench when he died of a stroke on 2 January 1888 while on a visit to Philadelphia.

—*David S. Heidler and Jeanne T. Heidler*

See also New Jersey.

For further reading:

Gillette, William. *Jersey Blue: Civil War Politics in New Jersey, 1854–1865* (1994).

Washburn, Emory. *Memoir of the Hon. Joel Parker* (1876).

Yard, James S. *Joel Parker: "The War Governor of New Jersey": A Biographical Sketch* (1962).

PARKER, THEODORE
(1810–1860)
Abolitionist and theologian

Theodore Parker was born into a farming family in Lexington, Massachusetts, where his grandfather had once led colonial militia against the British. Although Parker's prodigious intellectual abilities surfaced at an early age, his family's financial status initially prevented him from attending Harvard. Instead, he supported himself as a schoolteacher. Private study enabled him to pass the school's examinations, however, and in 1834 he entered Harvard Divinity School. He graduated two years later, having won a reputation among classmates and faculty for great energy and impressive scholarly accomplishments (Parker eventually mastered twenty languages.) In 1837 the Congregational Church ordained Parker as a minister, and he accepted a position as a pastor in West Roxbury, Massachusetts. He married Lydia Dodge Cabot the same year. The Parkers had no children.

Parker's unique brand of transcendentalist theology and social activism could not be contained within the orthodox bounds of the Congregational Church. Parker particularly disagreed with the contention that salvation required supernatural inspiration. This doctrine, he felt, created a false barrier between God and mankind. Living a virtuous life in keeping with God's wishes, in Parker's view, laid the foundation for salvation. Parker also occasionally delivered sermons not based on scriptural text, another break with orthodoxy.

Along with other liberal New England Congregationalists, Parker joined the new Unitarian denomination in the early 1840s. Parker's distinctive views and often militant attitude soon alienated many conservative Unitarians, however, and in 1846 he broke with the new denomination. With the assistance of loyal supporters, Parker founded his own, nominally Congregational church in Boston. By the 1850s, he firmly established himself as that city's most popular minister. Thousands flocked to hear his sermons, eventually making it necessary for the congregation to move to a larger building. Along with his sermons, Parker embarked on extensive lecture tours, sometimes making as many as 100 appearances per year in cities and towns throughout the Northern states. The South, however, proved unfriendly to the zealous reform ideals Parker espoused—particularly his advocacy of the antislavery movement.

Always mindful of social causes such as temperance and education reform, Parker especially dedicated himself to condemning the barbarity and injustice of slavery. The passage of the Fugitive Slave Act as part of the so-called Compromise of 1850 particularly outraged Parker, who felt that this act, which made Northerners legally responsible for returning runaway slaves to their owners, subjected the North to the ignominious position of having to support slavery actively. Parker vilified Massachusetts senator Daniel Webster for voting in favor of the Fugitive Slave Act, thereby, in Parker's view, revealing himself as a mercenary willing to betray his ideals to maintain his public prominence. Not even Webster's death halted Parker's attacks; the minister delivered, instead of a standard tribute for that occasion, a stinging assessment of Webster's shortcomings.

Parker gained even more notoriety for his participation in two other controversial episodes on behalf of the abolitionist cause in the 1850s. In 1854 he openly called for citizens to forcibly resist the return of former slave Anthony Burns from Boston to Virginia. After rioting subsequently led to the death of a jailer, a Massachusetts grand jury indicted Parker, although the charges were quickly dismissed. Parker also raised money and provided encouragement for John Brown's raid on Harper's Ferry in 1859. Although he doubted such a project could succeed, Parker nevertheless hoped that it might eventually inspire other, larger slave insurrections. After Brown's capture, the names of Parker and the other "Secret Six" became public knowledge after their correspondence fell into the hands of Virginia authorities. By this time, however, Parker was dying of tuberculosis. He had already embarked on a lengthy ocean voyage in a futile attempt to restore his health. He died in Florence, Italy, bringing a premature end to one of the most influential careers in the history of American religion.

—*Michael Thomas Smith*

See also Abolitionist Movement; Abolitionists; Brown, John; Burns, Anthony; Churches.
For further reading:
Commager, Henry S. *Theodore Parker: Yankee Crusader* (1936).
Dirks, John E. *The Critical Theology of Theodore Parker* (1970).
Grodzins, Dean, and Joel Myerson. "The Preaching Record of Theodore Parker." *Studies in the American Renaissance* (1994).

PARKER'S CROSSROADS
(December 1862)

In December 1862, Confederate brigadier general Nathan Bedford Forrest crossed the Tennessee River at Clifton and embarked on his first raid into western Tennessee. His purpose was to demolish the supply lines in the region and disrupt Union operations that depended on those supplies.

Forrest put his men across the river on flatboats and marched for Lexington, encountering 800 Federals under Colonel Robert G. Ingersoll. These men broke and fled following a brief firefight, leaving Ingersoll, 147 men, and two prized three-inch Rodman guns in Forrest's possession.

The Confederates next moved to the railroad north of Jackson, convincing the Union commander, Brigadier General Jeremiah C. Sullivan, that he was badly outnum-

bered when the opposite was true. This enabled Forrest and his men to have a free hand in capturing several small garrisons and disabling the rail lines, depots, and bridges in the region. By 20 December, the Southern raiders had ruined miles of track, including much of the trestlework over the Obion River. On Christmas Eve, an exultant Forrest reported, "We have made a clean sweep of the Federals and [rail]roads north of Jackson."

Although more destruction followed as Forrest and his raiders turned eastward, Union forces were beginning to bear down on them, urged on by General Sullivan. The Confederate commander headed for his crossing at Clifton and the safety of Southern lines. By 30 December, they had reached the vicinity of the small community of Parker's Crossroads or Red Mound. When scouts detected a body of Union troops blocking his path, Forrest decided to defeat them so that he could refloat his sunken flatboats and cross the river without resistance.

For his part, having made contact with the raiders, Union colonel Cyrus Dunham sent word for the other pursuing forces to converge on the crossroads. Dunham's lead forces reached the crossroads and passed on, running into Confederates about a mile beyond. Following a brief artillery exchange, and feeling pressure from Forrest, Dunham pulled back beyond the crossroads but continued to block the most direct route for Forrest to take to reach Clifton.

Seeing the Union forces positioned behind a split-rail fence, Forrest sent forces under Colonels James A. Starnes, A. A. Russell, and Thomas G. Woodward to flank the Federals. He also brought up his artillery, determined to use it to clear the way and spare his men the casualties that would result from a frontal assault. The Confederate field pieces repelled feeble Union efforts to advance against them and smashed the fence, sending canister and shards of fence rail into the Union defensive position. Except for an impetuous charge by Lieutenant Colonel A. T. Napier, which resulted in Napier's death, the Southern general's tactic worked to perfection. White flags began to appear, and Forrest prepared to finish his business with Dunham by negotiating his surrender.

Suddenly, firing occurred in an unexpected quarter of the battlefield. Forrest had detached a force of scouts under his brother William to guard the avenue of approach from the Confederate rear, but they had mistakenly taken the wrong road. Federal forces under Colonel John W. Fuller hit the unguarded Southern rear, scattering the horseholders. The first notion that Forrest had that something had gone wrong was when some of those horseholders dashed past him in an effort to escape.

Seeing the panic but failing to understand it, Forrest rode to reconnoiter the situation personally. He came upon Union troops, who demanded his surrender. He agreed to do so but asked to be allowed to bring up his men to surrender as well. As soon as he had ridden out of range, he raced to his men to direct them to renew the fight. When asked what he planned to do, Forrest is supposed to have proclaimed: "Charge them both ways."

Whether or not Forrest gave such a command, this was what he had to do in order to have any chance to escape death or capture. Consequently, he assembled his command and sent them against Fuller, while the detached flanking units assaulted Dunham. The attacks froze the advancing Union troops and kept the others from regrouping, which allowed Forrest to ride out from between them. However, this narrow escape from the trap cost Forrest some 300 dismounted men, who were captured. Federal losses amounted to 237, although the Confederates paroled as many as 300 prisoners at Lexington, Tennessee, before crossing the river. Forrest listed his casualties at 163, which was surely low given the number of his men captured. Still, the "Wizard of the Saddle" had lived to fight another day, taking the bulk of his command to safety across the Tennessee River and back into Confederate lines. In addition, despite his rough handling at Parker's Crossroads, Forrest had wreaked enough havoc in western Tennessee that—coupled with Major General Earl Van Dorn's raid against the forward Union supply base at Holly Springs, Mississippi—it convinced Major General Ulysses S. Grant to abort his first drive toward Vicksburg.

—*Brian S. Wills*

See also Forrest, Nathan Bedford; Forrest's Raids; Holly Springs Raid.

For further reading:
Henry, Robert Selph. *"First with the Most" Forrest* (1944).
Kennerly, Dan. *The Dawn of Lightning War—General Forrest and Parker's Crossroads* (1982).
Maness, Lonnie E. "Forrest and the Battle of Parker's Crossroads." *Tennessee Historical Quarterly* (1975).
Wills, Brian Steel. *A Battle from the Start: The Life of Nathan Bedford Forrest* (1992).
Wyeth, John Allan. *Life of General Nathan Bedford Forrest* (1899; reprint, 1989).

PAROLE
See Prisoner Paroles

PARSONS, EMILY ELIZABETH
(1824–1880)
Union army nurse

Emily Parsons was the first hospital worker to establish a nurses training program for African-American women during the Civil War. Born to a family of legal luminaries and liberal thinkers, Parsons grew up amid the abolitionist ferment of Boston and Cambridge. Her experiences among black soldiers and

workers in the Western theater made her all the more dedicated to the principles of racial equality. Like other patrician women of her generation, Parsons found medical relief work the perfect outlet for these energies.

A series of childhood accidents made Parsons an unlikely candidate for the rigors of hospital work. At five she was blinded in one eye, at seven scarlet fever damaged her hearing, and at nineteen an ankle injury nearly crippled her. These disabilities gave her unusual powers of sympathy, however.

Parsons's father opposed her plan to become a nurse, fearing that her infirmities would lead her to an early grave. In time he relented and used his professional connections (he held an endowed chair in law at Harvard) to arrange an eighteen-month course of study at Massachusetts General Hospital for his oldest child. Beginning in April 1861 the thirty-seven-year-old spinster learned how to dress wounds, to assist in surgeries, and to manage the diet and comfort of patients.

Perhaps the best prepared of any Civil War nurse, Parsons assumed responsibility for forty-eight sick soldiers and four attendants at Fort Schuyler on the Long Island Sound in October 1862. Ever anxious to please the surgeon who was "fearfully particular," Parsons relished the work and wrote home to her mother that she had found her calling: "It is as if my former life lay away back, out of my reach, and this was my real life." By December the strain of sixteen-hour workdays had taken its toll and Parsons went to Boston to recuperate. An even better opportunity presented itself in January, when nursing superintendent Dorothea Dix asked Parsons if she would like to take charge of Lawson Hospital in St. Louis. After only three weeks at Lawson, Parsons was selected by the surgeons for duty aboard the *City of Alton*, where she assisted 416 sick and wounded men on their journey from Vicksburg to Memphis. During this, her most strenuous labor yet, Parsons contracted malaria and would suffer from it throughout the rest of the war.

Having proved her mettle with medical officials and sanitary commissioners, Parsons took charge of Benton Barracks outside St. Louis in the spring of 1863. The largest hospital in the Western theater at the time, Benton Barracks could house over 2,000 patients in twenty wards. It also hired more women than any other facility in the region—209 between 1863 and 1865, of whom thirty-one were black. Here, in addition to managing a large nursing staff of women and men, Parsons worked closely with surgeon Ira Russell, who believed that she had "a rare combination of zeal and executive ability." Parsons confessed that keeping discipline was the "most wearisome" part of her job, but she loved to work with patients who were grateful for even the smallest attentions. Within several months, Parsons's nurses were teaching literacy skills to black soldiers, whose segregated wards Parsons made as comfortable as

those for white soldiers. She also instituted the nurses training program for contrabands who, with their children, had come upriver looking for work.

In October Parsons took a leave of absence when her malaria flared up, but returned to work in the spring of 1864. Delighted with the progress that African-American soldiers and nurses were making at Benton Barracks, she visited Freedman's Hospital to see how her systems might be useful. Much to her consternation, she discovered that members of the Colored Ladies Union Aid Society, who wanted to donate their services, were prevented from doing so by public streetcar laws that barred blacks from riding six days a week. Six months later Parsons fell ill again and returned permanently to Cambridge. In the spring she began doing relief work for the black hospitals within the purview of the Western Sanitary Commission, packing food and clothing for needy people more than twelve hundred miles away. She also collected goods to be auctioned at the Chicago Sanitary Fair of 1865.

The armistice found Parsons making good on her promise to "always be working somewhere or other," as she raised money to build a charity hospital for women and children in Cambridge. By 1867 she was assisting the hospital's two physicians as superintendent and matron. She continued to seek funds in the 1870s in the hope of establishing a foundation and buying a building for the hospital, which had started in a rented house. Parsons's letters were published in 1880 in an effort to augment the hospital's endowment. It was the same year that Parsons died of a stroke. Only fifty-six at the time of her death, Parsons would have been gratified to know that her work went on. By 1886 the Cambridge Hospital (later known as Mount Auburn) became a permanent light in the Boston medical firmament.

—*Jane E. Schultz*

See also Nurses.
For further reading:
Brockett, Linus P., and Mary C. Vaughan. *Woman's Work in the Civil War* (1867).
Carded Service Records of Hospital Attendants, Matrons, and Nurses, 1861–1865. Record Group 94. National Archives, Washington, D.C.
Moore, Frank. *Women of the War: Their Heroism and Self-Sacrifice* (1866).
Parsons, Emily Elizabeth. *Memoir of Emily Elizabeth Parsons* (1880).

PARSONS, LEWIS BALDWIN
(1818–1907)
Union general

Born in Perry, New York, and a graduate of Yale (1840), Lewis B. Parsons's first employment as a young man was teaching school in Mississippi. After a year and a half, he entered Harvard Law School, from which he graduated with an LL.B. He opened a

practice in Alton, Illinois, where his abilities as an attorney became highly regarded, and his reputation became widespread throughout the Midwest. That brought him to the attention of the directors of the Ohio & Mississippi Railroad, who appointed him to the general managership of the western section of that line in 1853. The Ohio & Mississippi shortly thereafter was corporately joined to the Baltimore & Ohio Railroad.

When the Civil War broke out, Parsons—by then 43 years of age—resigned from the B&O to accompany Nathaniel Lyon as a volunteer aide during early operations against guerrilla bands in Missouri. After that campaign ended, Parsons applied for and was granted a commission as captain of U.S. volunteers. His initial assignment during the summer of 1861 was as a quartermaster officer dealing with rail and water transportation at the headquarters of Brigadier General John C. Frémont at St. Louis. His ferreting out of dishonest practices by steamboat operators in their dealings with the Quartermaster Department was noted favorably by Quartermaster General Montgomery Meigs, which brought Parsons rapid promotion and an enlargement of his transportation responsibilities.

The railroad companies of the mid-nineteenth century were comparatively large firms whose sophisticated management adjusted quickly to wartime requirements. Not so the steamboat industry, which by contrast consisted of literally hundreds of separate ownerships. Whenever steamboat companies of any size did exist, these management units often proved nothing more than a combination of single boat owners temporarily banded together for purposes of providing economic leverage in the marketplace. As Parsons was to discover, many such mergers could and did dissolve overnight, leaving any prior agreements made between such companies and the army Quartermaster Department automatically invalid. Parsons soon overcame this by working out a charter system based on contractual formats that applied directly to the vessel and not to the company.

As the war went into 1863 and Union conquest reached southward on the Mississippi, it became necessary for Parsons to establish and maintain a logistical support system for the steamboat operators, a facet of which was the supply of fuel for the boats' boilers. Parsons's system included the development of both coal and wood depots strategically located along the Mississippi, encompassing arrangements for infantry guard units that were assigned to protect the civilian woodcutters against attack from Confederate partisans. Another problem was labor discord on the steamboats. Parsons dealt with it effectively—and at times arbitrarily—depending on the exigency of the moment. His dictatorial approach often brought him difficulties, but in most instances the army's high command supported him.

In December 1863, Parsons was appointed chief of river transportation for the entire Western theater. Taking January to May 1864 as an example of the heavy traffic volume for which he was responsible, the Quartermaster Depot at Nashville received by river boats alone 200,000 tons of supplies and nearly 10,000 animals—a tonnage requiring the services of nearly 100 steamboats. Most supplies into Nashville were transshipped from there to the East by rail for the use of the Army of the Potomac. That January, Parsons also was responsible for rapidly transporting by rail the Army of the Ohio to Washington, D.C.

During this 4-month period, Parsons had the responsibility for supplying operations on the Red River that utilized 40 transports while an additional 60 transports were then currently employed on the lower Tennessee, on the Arkansas, and on the main Mississippi system. By 1865 the Quartermaster Department's ownership of steamboats on the western rivers numbered 105 vessels, but these were only a partial indication of the overall role steamboats played within the zones of Parsons's responsibility. From 1861 through the war's end, a total of 615 additional steamboats were at one time or another under the charter or affreightment hire of the Union army. The heaviest employment was from the spring of 1863 to mid-1864.

In discussing the logistical achievements of the Quartermaster Department in his report of 1864 submitted to the secretary of war, Quartermaster General Montgomery Meigs mentioned Parsons, then a colonel, as being owed a debt of gratitude for the outstanding way river transportation management had contributed to the western campaigns. To recognize that service, Meigs suggested a brevet to brigadier general. The brevet was improved upon in May 1865 when Parsons was promoted to brigadier general of U.S. volunteers.

After the Confederate surrender, Parsons remained in the army until he was able to complete the disposal of the army's wartime fleets located on the rivers as well as on the Atlantic and Gulf coasts. With that assignment accomplished, he resigned from the army, effective 10 April 1866. During the postwar years, Parsons served as president of a St. Louis bank until his health began deteriorating. He retired to his 3,000-acre farm at Flora, Illinois, where he died on 16 March 1907 at age 89.

—*Charles Dana Gibson*

See also Meigs, Montgomery; Quartermaster.
For further reading:
Annual Reports. *Quartermaster General to the Secretary of War* (1862–1866).
Gibson, Charles Dana, with E. Kay Gibson. *Assault and Logistics: Union Army Coastal and River Operations, 1861–1866* (1995).

House Executive Documents, 37th Congress, Second Session, vol 7 (1862).

Records of Third Auditor's Office for 1865, Treasury Department.

Schottonhamel, George Carl. "Lewis Baldwin Parsons and the Civil War Transportation" (Ph.D. dissertation, 1954).

U.S. War Department. *War of the Rebellion: A Compilation of the Official Records of the Union and Confederate Armies* (1880–1901).

PATRICK, MARSENA RUDOLPH
(1811–1888)
Union general

Born to John Patrick and Miriam White Patrick in Watertown, New York, Marsena Rudolph Patrick was educated locally before running away from home as a youth to make his fortune. He worked at a variety of jobs and even began the study of medicine before coming under the patronage of General Stephen van Rensselaer, who secured Patrick an appointment to the U.S. Military Academy. Patrick graduated forty-eighth of fifty-six in the class of 1835. After being commissioned into the infantry, Patrick was sent to Florida where he fought in the Second Seminole War. During the Mexican-American War, Patrick served as commissary on the staff of General John Wool.

Long a devotee to more scientific approaches to agriculture, Patrick resigned his commission in 1850 to try some of his ideas as a farmer outside Geneva, New York. Patrick publicized some of his findings statewide, which gained him the position of the president of the new New York State Agricultural College in 1859. At the outbreak of the Civil War, he resigned his presidency to offer his services to the Union.

During the first year of the war, Patrick served as inspector general for New York State. In March 1862, Major General George McClellan, commander of the Army of the Potomac, requested that Patrick accept a brigadier general's commission in the volunteers. Patrick agreed and was given a brigade in the Irvin McDowell's Department of the Rappahannock.

Patrick quickly gained the reputation of being an extremely strict though fair disciplinarian. His brigade was one of the best organized in the army, and while his men knew that Patrick could be stern, his kindness also made him popular.

He led his brigade in the battle of Second Bull Run and during the Maryland campaign at South Mountain and Antietam. After the latter battle, the Army of the Potomac had suffered appalling casualties and was in some disarray. Patrick's reputation as a fair disciplinarian earned him the appointment as the army's provost-marshal-general. He remained in that position for the Army of the Potomac until 4 July 1864, when Ulysses S.

Grant named him provost-marshal-general for all armies operating against Richmond.

Patrick had a wide range of duties in his new position. Overall, he was in charge of security and hence had to deal with intelligence-gathering agents; he supervised all unit provost marshals and reminded them of their various duties and how best to carry them out. The biggest job on that level was to prevent desertion and apprehend those who accomplished it. Patrick established procedures that unit provost marshals should always ride on the periphery of the unit to watch where men went. They also would visit nearby towns frequently to look for soldiers trying to extend visits and to visit army hospitals to distinguish between malingerers and those who were genuinely ill or injured. Finally, Patrick labored to fulfill the important goal of maintaining order within the camps, which proved no small task. He finally had to prohibit alcohol in areas held by the Army of the Potomac.

In recognition for his many accomplishments during the war, Patrick was promoted to major general of volunteers on 13 March 1865. At the end of the war he was relieved from his position and on 25 May 1865 given command of the District of Henrico, which included Richmond. This "stern disciplinarian" quickly came under criticism for being too kind and charitable toward the poor of Richmond. Undoubtedly the criticism stung, for Patrick asked to be relieved. The request was granted on 9 June 1865, and he resigned from the army three days later.

Returning home to New York, Patrick briefly entered politics as a Democrat to oppose the Radical Republicans, but failing in that effort returned to farming. He became very prominent in New York agricultural circles. In 1880 he moved to Ohio to accept the governorship of the Dayton Soldiers' Home. He died there in that position on 27 July 1888.

—*David S. Heidler and Jeanne T. Heidler*

See also Army of the Potomac; Desertion.
For further reading:
Patrick, Marsena Rudolph. *Inside Lincoln's Army: The Diary of Marsena Rudolph Patrick, Provost Marshal General, Army of the Potomac* (1964).

PATTERSON, ROBERT
(1792–1881)
Union general

Born to Francis Patterson and Ann Graham Patterson in County Tyrone, Ireland, Robert Patterson came to the United States with his parents when his father was banished for his role in the Irish Rebellion of 1798. Patterson grew to adulthood in Delaware County, Pennsylvania, and was trained as a businessman. During the War of 1812 he served in the

Pennsylvania militia, rising to the rank of colonel before being offered a commission in the regular army. He rose to the rank of captain in the 32d Infantry. He left the army at the end of the war.

After the war, Patterson expanded his business interest, becoming a wholesale grocer and shipper. He also became interested in Pennsylvania Democratic politics and was an ardent supporter of Andrew Jackson. At the outbreak of the Mexican-American War, Patterson received a volunteer commission as a major general. He fought in Winfield Scott's Mexico City campaign. His services were especially valuable in the battle of Cerro Gordo, where he prevented a premature American attack against a strong Mexican position. General Scott also commended him for his conduct at the taking of Jalapa.

Patterson was mustered out of service at the end of the war, and he returned to Pennsylvania. His business interests had become so diversified by that point that his interest extended all the way to Southern cotton and sugar plantations. He remained active in the Pennsylvania militia, however, commanding a division as a major general.

At the outbreak of the Civil War, Patterson offered his services to the federal government. Even though he was almost seventy years old, Patterson was popular in Pennsylvania, particularly among the militia, and could not be ignored by the government in Washington. To help with recruiting in Pennsylvania, Patterson was given a three-month volunteer commission as a major general dating from 27 April 1861. He was given command of Delaware, Pennsylvania, Maryland, and the District of Columbia. On 29 April the command was formalized with the designation of Department of Pennsylvania with headquarters at Philadelphia. Initially concerned primarily with recruiting, Patterson's role changed in June 1861, when he was ordered to take his men across the Potomac River into western Virginia to guard the approaches from that quarter toward Washington.

Patterson crossed the Potomac at Williamsport, Maryland, in the middle of June. He moved toward Martinsburg, Virginia, in pursuit of a brigade commanded by Thomas J. Jackson. He fought a skirmish with Confederates on 9 July at Falling Waters and then occupied Martinsburg.

By that time the early movements of Union general Irvin McDowell's advance toward P. G. T. Beauregard's position at Manassas Junction had begun. In an attack on Beauregard, McDowell would have significant numerical superiority if Confederate reinforcements could be prevented from reaching Manassas. The most likely source of reinforcements was the force commanded by Joseph E. Johnston in the Shenandoah Valley. Orders were sent to Patterson at Martinsburg to prevent Johnston from moving toward Manassas. When

Johnston began advancing toward Beauregard's position, however, Patterson made no effort to stop him. Later he explained his inactivity by saying that he had not been given specific orders to attack Johnston. The reinforcements Beauregard received proved instrumental in the Confederate victory at First Bull Run.

When Patterson's commission expired on 27 July, it was not renewed, an exception to the rule with most volunteer officers early in the war, and he was replaced by Nathaniel P. Banks. Patterson requested a court of inquiry into his conduct in western Virginia, but it was not granted. He remained a major general of the Pennsylvania militia for the remainder of the war but never again occupied a combat command.

Along with his militia activities through the rest of the war, Patterson remained very involved with his business activities. His son, a brigadier general of volunteers, was killed in an accident near Fairfax, Virginia in 1862. Toward the end of the war, Patterson wrote a memoir of his activities in 1861. After the war, he remained an active businessman; he died in Philadelphia on 7 August 1881.

—*David S. Heidler and Jeanne T. Heidler*

See also Bull Run, First Battle of.
For further reading:
Patterson, Robert. *A Narrative of the Campaign in the Valley of the Shenandoah, in 1861* (1865).

PAUL, GABRIEL RENÉ
(1813–1886)
Union general

Born in St. Louis, Missouri, to a family of recent French immigrants, Gabriel René Paul was educated locally before receiving an appointment to the U.S. Military Academy. He graduated eighteenth of thirty-six in the class of 1834. After graduation he fought in the Second Seminole War in Florida and was stationed at frontier posts. During the Mexican-American War he participated in Winfield Scott's Mexico City campaign and fought in the taking of Chapultepec outside the city, winning a brevet promotion to major. After the war, Paul occupied several posts in the Southwest and was serving at Fort Fillmore, New Mexico, at the outbreak of the Civil War as a major in the 7th U.S. Infantry.

Paul's biggest problem after the onset of hostilities in the East was to deal with the numerous Southern sympathizers in New Mexico and their threats to seize control of Federal property in the territory. By June, he had the added worry of Confederates in neighboring Texas and the need to guard the territory's frontier from them as well as Texas's attempts to persuade Federal soldiers in New Mexico to desert to the Confederacy. As acting inspector general of the Department of New Mexico, Paul was especially vexed by this Confederate effort.

At the end of the year, Paul was promoted to colonel of the 4th New Mexico Infantry. Commanding Fort Union north of Santa Fe, Paul's situation became increasingly critical in early 1862 when he was confronted by the Confederate campaign of Henry Hopkins Sibley out of Texas into New Mexico. After the battle of Val Verde on 21 February 1862 and the subsequent Union abandonment of Santa Fe, Paul began concentrating men and supplies at Fort Union to prevent a Confederate invasion of Colorado Territory. His plans for a major concentration of his forces with those of the department's commander, Edward R. S. Canby, were thwarted in March 1862 with the arrival of the 1st Colorado volunteers and their commander, John P. Slough. Senior to Paul, Slough took command at Fort Union and insisted on proceeding against the Confederate forces. His actions resulted in the battle of Glorieta Pass and the retreat of the Confederate forces. Paul tried to persuade the War Department to promote him so he would outrank Slough, but his efforts came too late to prevent Slough's campaign.

In the pursuit of the retreating Confederates, Paul commanded the 4th New Mexico at Peralta on 15 April. He was promoted to lieutenant colonel in the regular army later in the month. During the summer he was sent east, where he was promoted to brigadier general of volunteers in September 1862. The promotion expired, unconfirmed by the Senate, but Paul was reappointed in the spring of 1863.

In the meantime, commanding a brigade of I Corps, Army of the Potomac, Paul missed the battle of Fredericksburg while on temporary duty in Washington, D.C. He commanded his brigade at Chancellorsville but saw little fighting there. He continued in I Corps for the move into Pennsylvania in June 1863.

At Gettysburg on the first day of the battle, 1 July, Paul, like all members of I Corps, saw considerable action. While leading his brigade as a part of John Cleveland Robinson's division in the efforts to hold the ground around the Lutheran Seminary on Seminary Ridge, Paul was struck by a bullet in the right temple that traveled through his head, exiting his left eye socket. He lost complete sight from his left eye and most of the sight in his right. He suffered other brain damage but survived to attend to minor administrative activity toward the end of the war. He received a brevet promotion to brigadier general in the regular army for his actions at Gettysburg.

Before the end of the war, Paul's disabilities forced his retirement because of wounds in February 1865 at the rank of colonel. The following year Congress approved his retirement at the rank of brigadier general. In retirement, Paul lived in Washington, D.C., where he died on 5 May 1886.

—David S. Heidler and Jeanne T. Heidler

See also Gettysburg, Battle of; Glorieta Pass, Battle of; New Mexico; Val Verde, New Mexico, Battle of.

For further reading:
Alberts, Don E. The Battle of Glorieta: Union Victory in the West (1998).
Coddington, Edwin B. The Gettysburg Campaign: A Study in Command (1968).
Edrington, Thomas S. The Battle of Glorieta Pass: A Gettysburg in the West, March 26–28, 1862 (1998).
Frazier, Donald S. Blood and Treasure: Confederate Empire in the Southwest (1995).

PAY, C.S.A.

The pay structure for the Confederate military was patterned on that of the U.S. Army, with some modifications in procedure and amounts. Usually the Confederate soldier was paid less than his Union counterpart, both in the officer and enlisted ranks. The exception was the pay for Confederate lieutenant colonels, who received $185 per month compared with the Union lieutenant colonel's $181. Also, reflecting the inability of the Confederate quartermaster to provide adequate uniforms, the Southern soldier was originally paid $50 a year in cash if he clothed himself, but that policy was changed in October 1862 when requisitions and manufacturing became sufficient to establish a better uniformity of military apparel. Under the new policy, a soldier was granted an annual clothing allowance, with the provision that if he did not exhaust it, he would be credited for the balance. Correspondingly, if he exceeded it, his pay would be charged the difference.

Early in the war, when the rush of enthusiasm saw volunteers flocking to the colors, there were instances of Southern soldiers refusing pay because they felt patriotism should be a sufficient incentive for doing one's duty and service to the cause compensation in itself. The realization that the conflict would be protracted, however, soon dulled such altruism. Poorer soldiers could not afford to serve as unpaid volunteers because their absence worked hardship on their families.

The rate of pay for enlisted men was paltry even for the standards of the time, but the Confederacy was following the norm rather than posing as an exception in that regard. Originally, privates were paid $11 per month, a figure low enough to animate the Georgia legislature to petition Congress in April 1863 for an increase to $20 a month. Not until 9 June 1864, though, did Congress approve a $7 increase to bring the private's pay to $18 per month. Corporals received $13 per month; sergeants, $17 per month; first sergeants, $20 per month; and engineering sergeants, $34 per month.

Officers were better compensated and were assigned a

different scale of pay depending on their branch of the service. Cavalry and engineering officers were paid at a rate higher than those of artillery and infantry officers. Infantry second lieutenants received $80 per month, while both first and second lieutenants in the cavalry or engineer branch received $100 per month. Artillery or infantry first lieutenants received $90 per month. A captain in the cavalry or engineers would receive $140 per month; his corresponding rank in the artillery or infantry, $10 less. Engineer or cavalry majors received $162 per month; artillery or infantry, $150. Colonels in the artillery, engineers, or cavalry received $210 per month, and in the infantry they were paid $195. A brigadier general received $301 per month.

As in the Union army, receiving pay was an irregular and infrequent event. It was not unusual to go months without pay, and in some instances such droughts stretched to a year or more. Such austerity mainly caused complaints, but it was always a drain on morale, and there are two reported occasions when soldiers refused to follow orders until they were at least partially given what was owed them. It should also be noted that Southern rates of pay, while not significantly at face-value variance with those of the Union, were provided in Confederate dollars. As inflation ravaged the value of the Confederate currency, severe burdens were placed on infrequently paid soldiers who at best received worthless paper. By the end of the war, even officers were complaining that letters had become a luxury given the exorbitant price of notepaper, remarking the irony that stationery of any quality had become more valuable than their money.

—*David S. Heidler and Jeanne T. Heidler*

See also Currency, C.S.A.; Pay, U.S.A.
For further reading:
———. *The Life of Johnny Reb: The Common Soldier of the Confederacy* (1978; reprint 1997).

PAY, U.S.A.

Patriotism may have motivated men to join the Union war effort, but the assurance of monthly pay kept men in the service. While many Union soldiers and sailors joined their respective services for monetary gain, undoubtedly many others joined the fight confident that their monthly pay would sustain themselves and the families they left behind.

Pay in the Union army remained relatively stable for most of the war, changing significantly only in the last months of the conflict. When the war began, army privates received $13 per month; corporals, $14; sergeants, $17; first sergeants, $20; and sergeant majors, $21. To counter growing currency inflation, Congress authorized on 22 June, 1864, a pay raise for the army. Privates were then paid $16 per month, with all higher

ranks receiving similar increases. Pay would be disbursed every two months (although the schedule was seldom met), and a soldier taken prisoner continued to receive his pay even in captivity.

African-American troops, however, received less pay for most of the war. Before June 1864, African American troops received only $10 per month. Also, the $3 per month clothing allowance granted to white troops was denied to African-American troops and was deducted from their pay. After June 1864, wages to African-American troops were equalized with white troops, but retroactive to only January 1, 1864. Any African-American soldier who enlisted before 1864 could claim back wages only to the first of the year. Moreover, the pay increase applied only to African-American troops who could prove their status as free men before the war. Thus, the thousands of former slaves who filled the Union army's ranks were denied the pay raise.

Army officers received their higher pay on a monthly schedule. Lieutenant generals received $270 per month; major generals, $220; brigadier generals, $124; colonels, $95; lieutenant colonels, $80; majors, $70; captains, $65; first lieutenants, $50; and second lieutenants, $45. Officers in the specialized branches, such as Engineers or Ordnance, received slightly higher pay. All officers received camp pay to defer the expenses of uniforms, equipment, and living in the field. Also, officers received their full pay whether in the field or in the rear areas.

Navy pay was significantly different. With a wider range of enlisted ranks, the navy paid its sailors relative to their skill level. Boys (recruits under age eighteen) were paid $8 per month; landsmen (untrained recruits over age eighteen), $12; ordinary seamen, $14; seamen, $18; coal-heavers, $18; second-class firemen, $25; and first-class firemen, $30. Enlisted men with specialized skills, such as coxswain or cook, received wages in the range of $20 to $24 per month. Unlike the army, the navy did not make payment in scrip or cash. Rather, wages were entered into the ship's paybook for disbursal when the sailor was discharged. Also, the navy did not discriminate against African-American crewmen, paying equal wages to all sailors for the duration of the war.

Navy officers were paid on a yearly rather than monthly pay schedule, and various pay scales existed for line officers, deck officers, and acting officers. Among the line officers of the regular U.S. Navy, rear admirals received $5,000 per year; commodores, $4,000; captains, $3,500; commanders, $2,800; lieutenant commanders, $2,343; lieutenants, $1,875; and ensigns, $1,200. Deck officers with specialized training had their own pay range. Surgeons received $3,000 per year, paymasters, $3,100; engineers, $2,600; assistant engineers, $1,250, and clerks, $1,500. Acting officers—merchant ship officers volunteering for naval service—typically received about two-thirds the pay of their regular navy counterparts. Whereas the army paid its officers the same regardless of their duty assignment, the navy reduced the wages for officers on shore duty. An officer at sea received his full wages, but the same officer on shore duty typically received only about half his scheduled pay.

Navy pay was also unique because of the opportunity for prize money. Upon capturing an enemy ship or blockade runner, the capturing vessel would send its prize to a northern port for adjudication, auction, and sale. The Navy Department claimed half the profits, and of the remaining half the squadron commander received 5 percent, the commander of the capturing vessel received 10 percent, and the officers and crew divided the rest with shares based on rank. Crewmen aboard fast and/or lucky Union warships could quickly amass huge sums, often the equivalent of several years' wages in a matter of minutes.

—*Steven J. Ramold*

See also Pay, C.S.A.

For further reading:

Hargrove, Hondon B. *Black Union Soldiers in the Civil War* (1988).
Lord, Francis A. *They Fought for the Union* (1960).
Ringle, Dennis J. *Life in Mr. Lincoln's Navy* (1998).
Wiley, Bell I. *The Life of Billy Yank: The Common Soldier of the Union* (1952; reprint, 1993).

PEA RIDGE, BATTLE OF
(6–8 March 1862)

The battle of Pea Ridge, also known by Southerners as the battle of Elkhorn Tavern, was the most famous engagement fought in the trans-Mississippi region. It also was the key to Union domination of that area, for Federal forces cleared Missouri of Confederate troops, turned back the most powerful Confederate army ever raised in the trans-Mississippi when it tried to invade the state, and opened the way for Union invasion attempts into the heart of Arkansas. The Federal victory at Pea Ridge also supported the much more significant Union drive down the Mississippi River valley that split the Confederacy in two with Grant's capture of Vicksburg.

Missouri was a battlefield from the very beginning of the war. Brigadier General Nathaniel Lyon's defeat and death at the battle of Wilson's Creek on 10 August 1861 allowed Confederate major general Sterling Price's Missouri State Guard to occupy southwestern Missouri and threaten Union control of the Missouri River valley and the all-important city of St. Louis. Major General Henry W. Halleck, commander of Union forces in the state, organized a field force named the Army of the

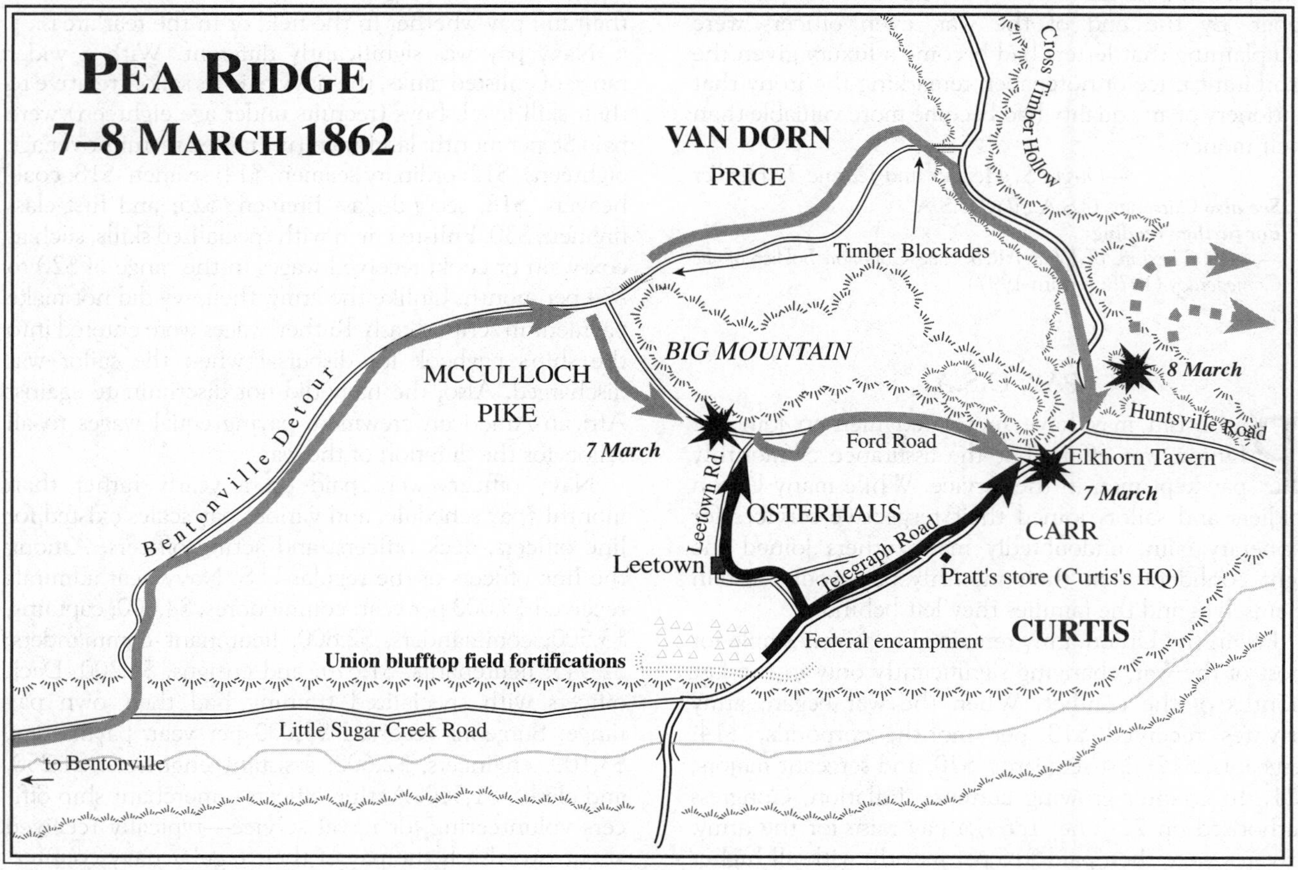

PEA RIDGE
7–8 MARCH 1862

VAN DORN
PRICE

Timber Blockades

BIG MOUNTAIN

MCCULLOCH
PIKE

Bentonville Detour

7 March

Ford Road

Leetown Rd.

8 March

Huntsville Road

Elkhorn Tavern

7 March

OSTERHAUS

Leetown

CARR

Telegraph Road

Pratt's store (Curtis's HQ)

Federal encampment

CURTIS

Cross Timber Hollow

Union blufftop field fortifications

Little Sugar Creek Road

to Bentonville

The battle of Pea Ridge (*Library of Congress*)

Southwest at Rolla to deal with Price. Brigadier General Samuel Ryan Curtis was appointed its commander and given the task of driving Price out of the state.

Curtis started his campaign on 11 February 1862 with more than 12,000 men. His army was divided into four small divisions, two of which consisted mostly of regiments dominated by European immigrants and under his second in command, Brigadier General Franz Sigel. Price's 8,000 poorly trained and supplied Guardsmen could not hold Springfield alone, so Price evacuated the city and retreated along the Telegraph Road into northwestern Arkansas. There he hoped to join forces with Brigadier General Benjamin McCulloch's 8,000 Confederate troops who had already cooperated with Price to win the bloody battle of Wilson's Creek.

Curtis hotly pursued Price into Arkansas, hounding his fast-marching column day and night. Several skirmishes occurred along the Telegraph Road, including two fought on Arkansas soil near a hostelry called Elkhorn Tavern. Price joined with McCulloch just south of the tavern and the two retired all the way to the rugged Boston Mountains, forty miles away. Curtis ended his pursuit two miles south of Elkhorn Tavern and established a fortified defensive position on the northern bluff of Little Sugar Creek, astride the Telegraph Road. He had accomplished his primary task of clearing Missouri of Price's Rebels and preventing them from interfering with Halleck's push down the Mississippi valley, but Curtis had to stop and await developments because his extended supply line from Rolla was stretched to the breaking point.

Price and McCulloch then received a new commander, Major General Earl Van Dorn, who was appointed to lead Confederate forces in the trans-Mississippi. An aggressive, ambitious general, Van Dorn reached Price and McCulloch on 2 March and immediately ordered an advance. With inadequate logistical and administrative preparation, the newly named Army of the West set out to gobble up Curtis's army. The Federals received word of the advance in time to concentrate most of their army at Little Sugar Creek, except that Sigel's rear guard of 600 infantry, artillery, and cavalry was nearly caught by Van Dorn's mounted advance as it retreated from Bentonville on 6 March. Sigel, who personally led the rear guard, was able to cut his way through.

Rather than attack Curtis's fortified position head on, Van Dorn marched around his right flank on a road known as the Bentonville Detour. This took him more than two miles to the rear of Curtis's army and allowed him to place Price's command on the Telegraph Road to cut off the Federal retreat. But the exhaustion of his troops forced Van Dorn to detach McCulloch's command and send it advancing toward the Federal rear two miles to the west, with the imposing bulk of Pea Ridge between the two Confederate wings. Thus the battle of Pea Ridge, as it was fought on 7 March, took place on two widely separated fields with neither wing of Van Dorn's command being able to support the other.

Curtis masterfully handled his army to take advantage of this mistake. He sent sufficient forces to oppose McCulloch near the village of Leetown, while placing a small delaying force in Price's path at Elkhorn Tavern. The fighting at Leetown was a swirling, seesaw affair in which McCulloch and his second in command were killed before they could fully deploy their forces. The third in command was then captured. The resulting breakdown of the chain of command immobilized a large part of this powerful division and greatly contributed to

the smashing Union victory at Leetown. The action here was marked by the involvement of two regiments of Cherokee troops serving in Van Dorn's army. Members of these units scalped and mutilated about a dozen dead and wounded Federal soldiers on the battlefield.

The fighting at Elkhorn Tavern was far more costly, sustained, and bitter than that at Leetown. The outnumbered Federals here, commanded by Colonel Eugene A. Carr, barely held their own under great pressure, and eventually they were forced to retreat after exacting a heavy price in blood from the Confederates. Nightfall and the exhaustion of Price's men enabled Curtis to stabilize his position a few hundred yards south of the tavern.

That night, Curtis managed to concentrate his army to support Carr, bringing his entire force together for the first time in the battle. Van Dorn's ability to control his shattered army broke down. His ammunition train had strayed away from the battlefield the previous day and there was no reserve ordnance available, and much of McCulloch's division had already retreated southward. Faced with a powerful artillery barrage directed by Sigel and a nearly general advance of Curtis's infantry, Van Dorn ordered his men to retreat before noon on 8 March. He managed to escape the battlefield and marched eastward and southward, thus making a complete circuit around Curtis's army until he reached Van Buren, Arkansas.

The three days of fighting at Pea Ridge led to the loss of 1,384 of the 10,250 Federals who actually were engaged. Van Dorn lost about 2,000 of the roughly 14,000 Confederates engaged. It was a decisive Union victory. Van Dorn soon after transferred his army east of the Mississippi to reinforce the Army of the Mississippi at Corinth. Curtis later marched his army across northern and central Arkansas and nearly captured Little Rock before occupying Helena on the Mississippi River, which was the southern-most town on the river held by the Union for many months to come. The long struggle to dominate the upper Trans-Mississippi was over.

—*Earl J. Hess*

See also Arkansas; Carr, Eugene A.; Curtis, Samuel R.; McCulloch, Benjamin; Missouri; Price, Sterling; Sigel, Franz; Van Dorn, Earl.

For further reading:
Shea, William L., and Earl J. Hess. *Pea Ridge: Civil War Campaign in the West* (1992).

PEABODY, GEORGE
(1795–1869)
Merchant, financier, philanthropist

George Peabody was born as the third oldest child of Thomas and Judith (Dodge) Peabody on 18 February 1795 in Danvers, Massachusetts. George received a rudimentary education, yet he revealed a great interest in working, for his family did not have much money. The young Peabody worked in his brother David's dry-goods store until a fire destroyed it in 1811. Having served with his uncle John Peabody as a peddler in Washington between 1812 and 1813, the ambitious George in 1814 served as manager of the Georgetown wholesale dry-goods house of Elisha Riggs; the firm of Riggs & Peabody was set up as a partnership the next year, was moved to Baltimore, and became one of the leading merchant houses of the city. For thirteen years, Peabody sold English and European merchandise to retail firms in Maryland, in Virginia, and in Pennsylvania. After Elisha Riggs's retirement, Peabody in 1829 became the senior partner in the merchant house of Peabody, Riggs & Company, a firm he established with Samuel Riggs, Elisha's nephew. By the late 1820s, the aggressive Peabody believed that Anglo-American trade and finance offered great potential.

Between 1830 and 1860, Peabody was to distinguish himself in London as a prominent American merchant and financier. The shrewd Peabody, who obtained short-term and long-term credits from London banks and deep discounts from British wholesale firms for the purchase of goods in massive quantities, sent an array of merchandise to Baltimore. By the early 1840s, he had earned a solid reputation as a skilled investment banker; in 1836 Peabody marketed in London Chesapeake & Ohio Canal Company bonds, which paid a 6 percent coupon. Between 1838 and 1840, he sold bonds from the states of Maryland, Virginia, and Ohio to his British clients.

With a large business network and with self-confidence, in 1844 Peabody set up his own investment firm (the previous year he had terminated his partnership with Riggs). George Peabody & Company became known for dealing in futures, American securities, and foreign currencies. In an effort to finance the Mexican-American War, in 1848 he marketed in England treasury bonds with a six percent coupon. Among other things, between 1849 and 1853 Peabody shipped massive amounts of British iron to America for the building of railroads in Ohio, Indiana, Illinois, and Tennessee. In 1854, he entered into partnership with Junius Spencer Morgan and for approximately a decade left many responsibilities of this lucrative operation to him.

Peabody became involved in the Civil War in several ways. Despite disruptions caused by the war, he encouraged Morgan to engage in the financing of exports to and imports from both Northern and Southern firms; Robert Garrett & Sons of Baltimore, one of Peabody's leading accounts for many years, continued during the early 1860s to utilize the services of Peabody & Company to collect bond coupon payments and to purchase and sell British and European currencies. Another aspect of Peabody's life, which was spent in London during the war, concerned Union and Confederate leaders who looked to the elderly financier for political support.

Peabody, who was privately an abolitionist, adopted a stance of nonalignment, for he believed that the war was destroying American political and economic institutions. On the one hand, Peabody continued to provide personal assistance to his friend William Wilson Corcoran, who was a Confederate supporter. On the other hand, Peabody developed cordial relations with Charles Francis Adams, Thurlow Weed, and other Union leaders.

The elderly Peabody, who retired from investment banking in September 1864, contributed significantly to American philanthropy after the Civil War; he established endowments to encourage the promotion of the liberal arts and sciences. Peabody made large donations to two Northern universities: $150,000 for the establishment of the Peabody Museum of Natural History at Yale and the same amount for the creation of the Peabody Museum of Archaeology and Ethnology at Harvard. However, the greatest contribution of Peabody came in 1867, for he designated $3,500,000 for the creation of the Peabody Education Fund; this endowment was set up to advance education in the South and to improve relations in America after the Civil War. Monies from this fund were to be allocated to support southern tax-supported schools, were to provide aid to black colleges in the South, and were to be used to set up George Peabody College for Teachers and other normal schools in Southern states.

The career of Peabody illustrates several major themes about nineteenth-century America. Peabody became a symbol of the Protestant work ethic; he effectively used connections, credit, and capital to accrue vast wealth. Moreover, his achievements in the world of merchant and finance capitalism permitted him to emerge as a pioneer in the realm of cultural philanthropy. His funding of Southern educational institutions was especially intended to improve interregional relations after the Civil War. This eminent merchant and financier died in London on 4 November 1869; his remains were brought to America in December of that year. Final burial occurred on 8 February 1870 in Harmony Grove Cemetery in Salem, Massachusetts.

—*William Weisberger*

See also Financing, U.S.A; Garrett, Robert & Sons; Morgan, J. P.

For further reading:
Carosso, Vincent P. *The Morgans: Private International Bankers, 1854–1913* (1987).
Chernow, Ron. *The House of Morgan: An American Banking Dynasty and the Rise of Modern Finance* (1990).
Hanaford, Phebe A. *The Life of George Peabody* (1870).
Hidy, Muriel E. *George Peabody: Merchant and Financier, 1829–1854* (1978).
Hoyt, Edwin P. *The Peabody Influence: How a Great New England Family Helped to Build America* (1968).
Parker, Franklin. *George Peabody: A Biography* (1995).

Peabody, George. Manuscripts. Essex Institute, Salem, Massachusetts.
Riggs Manuscripts. Library of Congress, Washington, D.C.

PEACE DEMOCRATS

Peace Democrats were those members of the Northern Democratic Party who most vehemently opposed Republican war policies and who advocated (naively) a cease-fire so that restoration of the Union could proceed through peaceful negotiations. They were convinced that the war was centralizing national power and subverting state and local prerogatives in the North, and that such developments ultimately posed greater dangers to the nation than the military challenge of Southern Rebels. As a minority in their own party, they reflected the most extreme conservative position on the Northern political spectrum. One historian has described them as "purists," who considered faithfulness to traditional Democratic ideology as being paramount to pragmatic efforts to strengthen Democratic electoral chances by supporting the war (while still opposing the administration). Peace Democrats feared that because the war had become "revolutionary," it was impossible to prosecute it and still preserve the Constitution "as it is" and the Union "as it was." In most cases their opposition to President Lincoln and the Republicans assumed a constitutional posture and employed constitutional arguments, though many also expressed the fear that Northerners were becoming morally desensitized by what they considered the brutality of Northern war measures.

Peace Democrats could be found throughout the North, though conservative opposition to Republican policies was especially strong in the agrarian states of the old Northwest—particularly in Illinois, Indiana, and Ohio. Antiwar dissent was initially stimulated early in the war by what conservatives deemed Lincoln's apparent disregard for the civil liberties of Northern citizens. By 1862 many conservative Democrats were bitterly complaining that Lincoln was a despot who was leading the country into military dictatorship. They accused him of trampling on the constitutional rights of dissenters and of throwing political opponents into Northern prisons without civil trials or due process protections. They were unpersuaded that the exigencies of civil war necessitated the suspension of the writ of habeas corpus, the arrest of war critics, the suppression of dissenting Democratic newspapers, or the passage of a national conscription law. Most significantly, they opposed Lincoln's Emancipation Proclamation, which they believed had turned a political war to save the Union into a social revolution to free the Negro. Some expressed agrarian dissent against Republican economic policies such as protective tariffs and efforts to establish a national centralized banking

system. They were buoyed in their hopes by the 1862 elections, when many Democratic candidates were victorious and Republican majorities in Congress and in state governments were considerably weakened.

By early 1863 Peace Democrats such as Ohio's Clement L. Vallandigham were openly condemning the war. Others had begun condemning the government for conducting what they considered an unnecessarily ruthless military campaign against the people of the South—adopting measures they deemed uncivilized, immoral, un-Christian, and ultimately counterproductive. They complained that Northern war policies were eroding the nation's moral base, corrupting Northern churches, and turning Northerners into "bloodthirsty infidels" devoid of religious sensitivities. As the year progressed, conservative critics increased the frequency and fury of their attacks against Northern military coercion. They demanded that the fighting be stopped and negotiations be opened with the Rebels for peaceful reunification. Peace Democrats in several state legislatures that year introduced "armistice resolutions" calling for a halt to hostilities and peace negotiations. Union victories at Gettysburg and Vicksburg in July 1863 helped to check their momentum temporarily, and several prominent Peace Democrats were defeated in their bids for state governorships that year.

The fortunes of Peace Democrats revived, however, during the important presidential election year of 1864, when by midsummer the military situation settled back into a seeming stalemate. At the 1864 Democratic National Convention in Chicago, the Peace wing of the party succeeded in writing its sentiments into the so-called Peace Plank of the Democratic platform, calling for immediate cessation of hostilities followed by political reunion through a convention of the states or "other peaceable means." (The Democratic Party nominee, General George B. McClellan, subsequently repudiated this plank.) Lincoln's reelection in November 1864 signalled the Northern electorate's ultimate rejection of the Peace Democrats.

Many Northerners strongly suspected unpatriotic motives lay behind the scathing attacks leveled by Peace Democrats against the war and the administration. Republicans branded them as disloyal "Copperheads." Indeed, the activities of some Peace Democrats seemed to border on the treasonable, causing Lincoln such concern that he once expressed his fear of a "fire in the rear." Peace Democrats were often stigmatized and suffered persecution in their communities, such as being ostracized from their church congregations. Reports of antigovernment conspiracies and several highly publicized treason trials involving Copperheads during 1864 also tarnished the cause of Peace Democrats in that important election year.

—*Byron Andreasen*

See also Civil Liberties, U.S.A.; Copperheads; Democratic Party; Election of 1862; Election of 1864; Peace Movements; Vallandigham, Clement L.; War Democrats.
For further reading:
Baker, Jean H. *Affairs of Party: The Political Culture of Northern Democrats in the Mid-Nineteenth Century* (1983).
Klement, Frank L. *The Copperheads in the Middle West* (1972).
———. *The Limits of Dissent: Clement L. Vallandigham & the Civil War* (1970).
———. *Lincoln's Critics: The Copperheads of the North* (1999).
Silbey, Joel H. *"A Respectable Minority": The Democratic Party in Civil War Era, 1860–1868* (1977).

PEACE MOVEMENTS
(1861–1865)

The advent of civil war in April 1861 witnessed a minority of pacifists, North and South, clinging to their opposition to all war. The Historic Peace Churches—Society of Friends, Mennonites, Church of the Brethren—officially refused to condone military service. Both the Union and Confederate governments provided limited exemption from military service for religious objectors from traditionally pacifist sects, but their concessions were considered insufficient in many cases. In the South, particularly, state laws contained no provision for exemption from militia service, and Jefferson Davis was less sympathetic to the pacifist cause than Abraham Lincoln. In both the North and the South, conscientious objectors were jailed for refusing to serve or to obey military orders when forcibly inducted into the army. Cyrus Pringle, a Quaker from Vermont, for instance, was made to lie spread-eagled on the ground for several hours in the hot sun, and objectors in the Confederacy were treated with even more brutality. Numerous Quakers refused to pay war taxes, and both the Union and Confederacy seized property in place of payment.

In the North the vast majority of peace activists supported the war. The American Peace Society argued that the war was an unlawful rebellion against authority and spoke against any concessions to the Confederacy. In the South, pacifist groups did not exist, nor were any members of the American Peace Society, few in number, supportive of the Unionist cause. Sectionalist sentiment was strong in the South.

However, various Northerners criticized the war. Apart from steadfast and well-known pacifists like Elihu Burritt and American Peace Society treasurer Joshua P. Blanchard, there were others critical of the martial spirit. Lindley Spring wrote a pamphlet entitled *Peace! Peace!* that called on all men to lay down their arms. E. H. Heywood, an associate of William Lloyd Garrison, published an article in *The Liberator* in 1863 criticizing the empire of brute force, while the country's most noted anarchist, Josiah Warren, in *True Civilization, an Immediate Necessity* (1863), condemned the whole war as

barbarian and attributed it to the greed and ambition of war profiteers.

Dislike of military service was fueled by the conscription controversy. The poorer classes were angered by those wealthy enough to buy their way out. In the North the most serious violent resistance took place in New York City in July 1863. New York's governor, Horatio Seymour, a staunch critic of conscription, conducted a vicious letter-writing campaign to President Lincoln and the War Department. He protested the constitutionality of the draft as well as the fairness of the quota assigned to New York City. Rioting in the city lasted three days. Angry over the ability of the rich to purchase exemptions, mobs sacked shops, burned numerous buildings, and fought with troops. More than a thousand lives were lost. Similar outbreaks occurred in neighboring states and in the Middle West, though with much less devastation.

Meanwhile, the upper Northwest became a hotbed of disloyalty. Peace Democrats, or Copperheads, called for a negotiated peace. They were strongest in Ohio, Indiana, and Illinois. They denounced military arrests, conscription, and other wartime enactments. Their primary goal was restoration of the Union; they did not favor emancipation. Clement L. Vallandigham of Ohio became their leader. Before his arrest and conviction in May 1863, Vallandigham declared that the conflict was "a wicked, cruel and unnecessary war" that people should undermine. Other leaders included Alexander Long of Cincinnati, Fernando Wood of New York, and B. G. Harris of Maryland. Newspapers supporting the Copperhead position were the *Columbus* (Ohio) *Crisis,* the *Cincinnati Enquirer,* and the *Chicago Times.*

The Copperheads worked openly or in secret societies like the Knights of the Golden Circle—allied with the Sons of Liberty in 1864—calling for an immediate truce. They took aim at eastern capitalists and emancipation as the twin causes of disruption. In 1864 the pro-Southern wing of the Sons of Liberty was charged with disloyalty in plotting the formation of a "Northwest Confederacy" and planning the release of Southern prisoners at Camp Douglas outside Chicago. Northern military successes terminated the Copperheads' antiwar efforts.

Southern opposition to the war was based primarily on weariness and opposition to conscription. Food riots and draft evasion invited the conclusion that the conflict was "a rich man's war and a poor man's fight." The yeoman and laboring classes sought to avoid taxes and conscription. Georgia's governor, Joseph Brown, exempted more men than any other Confederate head of state; he even fought conscription in the courts. Exasperated by his actions, Jefferson Davis, in November 1862, personally sent his former interim secretary of state, William M. Browne, on a mission to seek the governor's compliance with the conscription law.

Support for the Union and desire for peace was strongest in regions inhabited almost entirely by nonplanters.

The strongest movement for peace took place in North Carolina. The governor, Zebulon Baird Vance, worked hard to defeat conscription. Most notably, W. W. Holden, editor of the Raleigh *Standard,* took up the cause of the common folk. He demanded a general convention to bring about peace and reunification of the states. In July 1863, after the fall of Vicksburg and defeat at Gettysburg, close to 100 peace meetings were held in North Carolina alone. Throughout the Southern states some 100,000 people became part of two secret orders, the Heroes of America and the Peace Society, to end the war by working against the Confederacy. They resorted to violence by killing or driving away recruiting officers, encouraging desertion, and weakening morale at every turn.

Diplomatically, efforts to end the conflict began in July 1864, when Horace Greeley of the *New York Tribune* and Confederate commissioners James P. Holcombe, Clement C. Clay, and Jacob Thompson undertook negotiations at Niagara Falls, Canada. Lincoln's terms, reunion and emancipation, were not met. In August, Jeremiah Black, a friend of Thompson, made a futile attempt at negotiations. In Richmond, James F. Jacques and James R. Gilmore, with Lincoln's permission, interviewed Davis in July 1864. One last attempt was conducted by Francis P. Blair in January 1865. But efforts for a negotiated peace finally ended with the abortive Hampton Roads Conference on 3 February 1865.

Efforts to end the war were largely motivated by class consciousness, economic distress, opposition to conscription, the inability to come to terms with secession, desire for reunion, and resentment against regimentation and nationalism. Except for die-hard pacifists on both sides, the desire for peace was based on dislike for the conflict rather than a genuine belief in nonviolence.

—*Charles F. Howlett*

See also Clay, Clement C.; Conscription, C.S.A.; Copperheads; Greeley, Horace; Hampton Roads Peace Conference; Holcombe, James; Holden, William W.; Knights of the Golden Circle; Peace Democrats; Seymour, Horatio; Thompson, Jacob; Vallandigham, Clement L.; Vance, Zebulon; Wood, Fernando.

For further reading:
Curti, Merle. *Peace or War: The American Struggle, 1636-1936* (1936).
Ekirch, Arthur A. *The Civilian and the Military: A Study of Antimilitarist Thought* (1956).
Kirkland, Edward Chase. *The Peacemakers of 1864* (1927).
Klement, Frank L. *The Limits of Dissent: Clement L. Vallandigham and the Civil War* (1970).
Raper, Horace W. "William Woods Holden and the Peace Movement in North Carolina." *North Carolina Historical Review* (1954).
Tatum, Georgia Lee. *Disloyalty in the Confederacy* (1934; reprint 1970).

PEACHTREE CREEK, BATTLE OF
(20 July 1864)

The battle of Peachtree Creek was the first battle conducted by Confederate general John Bell Hood after he assumed command of the Army of Tennessee on 18 July 1864. With Union major general William Tecumseh Sherman's army bearing down on Atlanta, Hood felt compelled to attack his enemy to keep from losing the city. When Hood assumed command from Joseph E. Johnston, Union forces were located south of the Chattahoochee River, near Pace's Ferry and Roswell, Georgia. When Confederate cavalry were driven across Peachtree Creek on the 18th, Hood formed a line of battle. The next day, the Federal troops began crossing Peachtree Creek, and Hood put in place his plan of attack.

Hood hoped to strike the enemy as they were crossing the creek. Peachtree Creek presented a formidable obstacle to a crossing army, having been described by Union colonel John Coburn as a muddy stream, about forty feet wide, ranging in depth from four to twelve feet, and impassable except by bridges. The Confederates burned most of the bridges spanning the creek, but the Federals quickly rebuilt them. In spite of stubborn Confederate resistance, many of the Union troops had crossed the creek by the morning of the 20th. Hood, however, wanted to strike them while the crossing continued. He placed Alexander P. Stewart's corps on the left of the Confederate line, William J. Hardee's corps in the center, and Benjamin F. Cheatham's corps on the right.

The main target of Hood's forces was Major General George H. Thomas's Army of the Cumberland, composed of V, XIV, and XX Corps. Hood wanted to crush Thomas before he could fortify himself. Cheatham, therefore, was to attack Thomas's left, which was separated from the remaining Union troops by Early's Creek, and thereby prevent them from aiding the remaining Union forces. This would enable Stewart and Hardee to attack the rest of Thomas's army, drive them back toward Peachtree Creek, and trap them in the small area formed by the Chattahoochee River and the creek. Everything on the south side of the Peachtree was to be taken.

On the morning of the 20th, Hood decided to move his troops slightly to the east to protect the approach to Atlanta from Union troops in the vicinity. Cheatham's corps would move to the right about one mile, while the remaining two corps would move only half a mile. The redeployment was to be completed in time for the battle to begin at 1:00 P.M. Cheatham, however, moved slowly and then advanced two miles. Hardee and Stewart followed in order to remain connected to Cheatham, and the battle was delayed until almost 4:00 P.M. At that time, the Confederates advanced.

The battle began on the Confederate right when Bate's, Walker's, and part of Cheatham's divisions of Hardee's corps attacked Brigadier General John Newton's 2d Division of IV Corps. The Confederates managed to flank Newton's left, but were repulsed with the help of artillery. After several other charges, they retreated.

In the middle of the Confederate line, William W. Loring's division of Stewart's corps, commanded by Brigadier General Winfield S. Featherston, tried to exploit a gap between John W. Geary's and William T. Ward's divisions of the XX Corps. Initially, the Confederates forced Ward's skirmishers from an important hill. They then encountered heavy fire from their front and right. When Cheatham's division of Hardee's corp, located to the right of Featherston, did not immediately advance and attack, Featherston's men had to retreat as the Union countercharged. The fighting turned fierce, described by Colonel (and future president) Benjamin Harrison, commander of the Union 1st Brigade as "hand to hand and step by step." On the left of this portion of the Union line, the 26th Wisconsin found itself isolated in the fight for the hill. Attacked from the front and left, they managed to hold their position. During the last half hour of their battle, they had to use the ammunition from dead Confederate soldiers. The extreme heat and the intensity of the fighting caused many of these soldiers to collapse after the battle. Finally, after several charges on the Union position, the Confederates withdrew. Loring's division experienced almost a 50 percent casualty rate, with the 31st Mississippi reporting 164 casualties of 215 soldiers, including seventeen of twenty-two company officers.

To the left of Loring's division, the fighting was equally fierce. Here, Edward C. Walthall's division of Stewart's corps was confronting Brigadier General Alpheus S. Williams's 1st Division of XX Corps and part of Geary's. Attacking the Union along a ridge, the Confederates also sent troops down the ravines running to the right and left of the ridge. Those Confederates moving to the right combined with troops from Loring's division and briefly forced back one of Geary's brigades. The front, right, and rear of Geary's division had been enveloped by Confederates, but after three hours of fighting the Confederates were thrown back, and the Union maintained possession of the ridge. Geary later commented that he had never seen more heroic fighting. Fighting to the right of Geary's troops, every field officer and more than half of the men in the 61st Ohio, XX Corps, were either killed or wounded as some of the Confederates got within ten feet of the Ohioans. Meanwhile the Confederates who went down the left ravine bypassed Williams's right and came upon troops from the XIV Corps. Exploiting a quarter mile gap between Williams and the XIV Corps, the Confederates managed to get on the flank and rear of Joseph F. Knipe's troops of XX Corps. The Southern troops, however, were forced back due in large part to effective artillery fire. After about three hours of fighting, Hood realized that the attack had failed, and he ordered all his troops to withdraw to their former positions.

Despite outnumbering the Union forces, the Confederates suffered severe casualties. Union casualties totaled around 1,700, whereas estimates placed Confederate casualties at 2,500. Hood's resolve to fight, however, had not been defeated. He attacked the Union again just two days later at Bald Hill.

—*Scott M. Langston*

See also Atlanta Campaign; Hood, John Bell; Thomas, George Henry.

For further reading:

Castel, Albert E. *Decision in the West: The Atlanta Campaign of 1864* (1992).

Johnson, Robert Underwood, and Clarence Clough Bell, eds. *Battles and Leaders of the Civil War: Being for the Most Part Contributions by Union and Confederate Officers* (1887–1888).

Kennett, Lee. *Marching through Georgia: The Story of Soldiers and Civilians during Sherman's Campaign* (1995).

Newton, George. "The Battle of Peachtree Creek." In *The Atlanta Papers* (1980).

U.S. War Department. *The War of the Rebellion: A Compilation of the Official Records of the Union and Confederate Armies* (1880–1901).

PEARSON, RICHMOND MUMFORD
(1805–1878)

Chief justice, North Carolina Supreme Court

Born to Richmond Pearson and Elizabeth Mumford Pearson in Rowan County, North Carolina, the younger Pearson was educated in Washington, D.C., and at the University of North Carolina. He studied law and began his practice in Salisbury, North Carolina. He was active in North Carolina Whig politics and served in the state legislature before becoming a judge in 1836. While serving on the superior court of North Carolina and beginning in 1848 on the state supreme court, Pearson also ran a law school that produced some of the best lawyers and judges in the state.

In 1858, Pearson became chief justice of the state supreme court. In that position he made plain his view that secession was unconstitutional. However, upon the secession of North Carolina, his loyalty to his state outweighed his legal opinions and he choice to remain in his position as chief justice.

Pearson's rulings during the war, especially after 1862, made him increasingly unpopular with President Jefferson Davis and Davis's supporters. Pearson ruled the 1862 Confederate conscription law unconstitutional and began issuing writs of habeas corpus to deserters who had entered the Confederate army under that law and who

were apprehended in North Carolina. Pearson's earlier statement regarding the constitutionality of secession naturally made his loyalty suspect in some people's eyes.

President Davis at first tried to work around Pearson's ruling by urging Governor Zebulon Vance of North Carolina to work harder to secure more volunteers from North Carolina so that the conscription law would not have to be invoked so frequently in the state. However, when in early 1864 Pearson ruled the recent Confederate law abolishing substitution unconstitutional, Davis lost patience and instructed government officials to ignore Pearson's ruling. Pearson's actions were seen by North Carolina officers as very damaging to the morale of North Carolina soldiers, and they urged his removal from the bench.

Pearson, however, remained in place and continued to serve as chief justice until his death. Even in that position he became active in the Republican Party after the war, for which he was criticized by his political enemies.

—*David S. Heidler and Jeanne T. Heidler*

See also Courts, C.S.A.; North Carolina.

For further reading:

Hutchens, James Albert. "The Chief-Justiceship and Public Career of Richmond M. Pearson, 1861–1871" (M.A.thesis, 1960).

Wilson, Angley F. *Richmond M. Pearson and the Richmond Hill Law School* (1978).

PEGG, THOMAS
(1806–1866)

Cherokee statesman

Thomas Pegg played an important role in Cherokee politics during the Civil War. In 1861, he was president of the Cherokee National Council and endorsed Chief John Ross's neutrality policy. Pegg was also likely a member of the secret Keetoowah Society, a strongly nationalistic group whose members supported Cherokee sovereignty and strongly opposed those Cherokees who supported the South. Although the Keetoowahs have often been characterized as a "traditionalist" and an abolitionist group, many of them, including Pegg, were Christians who forcefully supported their mixed-blood, slave-owning chief, John Ross. Pegg, Ross, and the Keetoowahs were united by an unwavering commitment to preserving the sovereignty of the Cherokee Nation.

Despite Ross's and the Keetoowahs' desire to remain neutral, by August 1861 Southern pressure and the fear that pro-Confederate Cherokees would divide the nation pushed Ross and Pegg to agree to an alliance with the Confederacy. As the Cherokees prepared for war, Pegg was commissioned a major in John Drew's Mounted Rifles, a regiment consisting mainly of men loyal to Chief Ross and opposed to pro-Confederate Cherokees under the command of Stand Watie. Watie's troops were enthusiastic about the war, while most of Drew's regiment quickly deserted. When Union troops invaded Indian Territory in the summer of 1862, Pegg and more than 600 of Drew's men joined the Union army. Pegg was commissioned a captain in the 3d Indian Home Guard Regiment along with several other officers from Drew's command.

Along with his military service, Pegg also served as acting principal chief of the Cherokee Nation while John Ross was in exile in Washington. In February 1863, Pegg and other pro-Ross Cherokees (many of them Keetoowah Society members) reestablished their government and abrogated the Confederate treaty. In a speech to the Cherokee Council, Pegg argued that the treaty had been coerced but the tribe had always remained secretly loyal to the Union—an argument that Cherokee leaders would frequently repeat.

At the February meeting, the council also abolished slavery in the Cherokee Nation. Pegg and many council members opposed slavery, but their opposition was more political than ideological. Pegg and the council hoped abolishing slavery would hurt their Confederate Cherokee opponents and please the Union, but they also felt that the presence of freed slaves in the Cherokee Nation would undermine Indian sovereignty. The council believed that freed slaves had no right to citizenship and expected them to leave the Cherokee Nation.

For the remainder of the war, Pegg worked to restore Cherokee sovereignty in Indian Territory while simultaneously performing his duties as a Union soldier. He traveled to Washington in 1866 as a delegate in postwar treaty negotiations, but he died before the treaty was signed.

—Trevor M. Jones

See also Cherokee Indians; Indian Brigade; Ross, John; Watie, Stand.

For further reading:
Britton, Wiley. *The Union Indian Brigade in the Civil War* (1922).
Gaines, W. Craig. *The Confederate Cherokees: John Drew's Regiment of Mounted Rifles* (1989).
McLoughlin, William G. *After the Trail of Tears: The Cherokees' Struggle for Sovereignty, 1839–1880* (1993).

PEGRAM, JOHN
(1832–1865)
Confederate general

Born in Petersburg, Virginia, to James West Pegram and Virginia Johnson Pegram, John Pegram graduated from the U.S. Military Academy tenth of forty-six in the class of 1854. He was stationed at frontier posts in California, Kansas, and New Mexico. He resigned his commission upon the secession of Virginia and accepted one at the rank of lieutenant colonel in the Confederate army.

Sent to western Virginia, Pegram fought his first serious engagement against troops commanded by Major General George B. McClellan at Rich Mountain on 11 July 1861. Overwhelmed by superior numbers, Pegram and his men were unable to escape and surrendered to McClellan. During his imprisonment, Pegram commended General McClellan for the kind way he treated his prisoners. Pegram was paroled in January 1862 and shortly thereafter exchanged. Pegram was promoted to colonel in April 1862 and was sent to P. G. T. Beauregard in Mississippi, where he became Beauregard's chief engineer.

During the summer Pegram commanded a brigade under Edmund Kirby Smith and was commended by that officer for his actions at the battle of Richmond, Kentucky, on 30 August 1862. Pegram was promoted to brigadier general of cavalry in November 1862. He commanded his brigade under Joseph Wheeler a month later at Stones River. In March 1863, Pegram was sent with his brigade into Kentucky on a raid to procure beef. After being defeated in a skirmish at Somerset, Kentucky, on 30 March 1863, Pegram was able to drive approximately 500 head into Tennessee. In April he was stationed with his brigade at Tullahoma guarding the Cumberland River crossings there. In August 1863 word was sent from Richmond transferring Pegram to the Army of Northern Virginia, but before he received word of the transfer, he commanded a cavalry division at Chickamauga in September 1863.

Pegram arrived in Virginia in time to participate in the Mine Run campaign of November 1863 as part of Jubal Early's division of Richard Ewell's corps. The following spring, Pegram was wounded at the Wilderness but had recovered sufficiently to fight at Cold Harbor in early June and by midsummer commanded a division of Early's Valley campaign. He returned home to Petersburg to marry in January 1865 and to join the defenses of that key rail junction. He was killed 6 February 1865 at Dabney's Mills (Hatcher's Run).

—David S. Heidler and Jeanne T. Heidler

See also Dabney's Mills, Battle of; Rich Mountain, Battle of Richmond, Kentucky;.

For further reading:
Griggs, Walter S. *General John Pegram, C.S.A.* (1993).

PELHAM, JOHN
(1838–1863)
Confederate officer

John Pelham, the third son of Dr. Atkinson and Martha Pelham, lived and worked on his family's farm near Alexandria, Alabama, until he entered West Point in 1856. Pelham enrolled in an experimental five-year curriculum instituted by Secretary of War Jefferson

Davis and Superintendent of the Academy Robert E. Lee. Pelham's academic standing, thirty-seventh in a class of fifty-two, indicated that he was an average student, yet Pelham excelled in athletics, in artillery studies under the tutelage of Major Henry J. Hunt, and cavalry tactics. From all indications, Pelham was a popular young man who rose to cadet noncommissioned officer and then cadet officer while at the academy.

As Pelham's graduation neared tensions between the North and the South grew, and he was forced to decide whether he would stay at the academy or withdraw. Guided by his loyalty to his home state, Pelham resigned from West Point in April 1861 and returned to Alabama. While there he drilled troops in Jacksonville, until he reported for military service in May 1861. Commissioned a lieutenant, he reported for duty in the army of General Joseph E. Johnston, then encamped near Winchester, Virginia.

Pelham's skill on the battlefield soon won him acclaim. Under General Johnston, Pelham demonstrated courage and gunnery skill during First Bull Run. Johnston quickly promoted him to captain, and Pelham was then assigned to Brigadier General J. E. B. Stuart's first horse artillery battery in November 1861. Commanding this unit, Pelham saw action at Yorktown and during the Seven Days' battles. He commanded all of Stuart's horse batteries at Second Bull Run and was promoted to major following the battle. At Antietam his brilliant use of artillery fire to protect Major General Thomas "Stonewall" Jackson's left flank confused the Union forces, and Jackson remarked that he had never seen a more skillful handling of guns.

Pelham's bravery in combat continued. At Fredericksburg, a Union division under the command of Major General George Gordon Meade advanced on the Confederate right, held by Jackson's corps, threatening the stability of the Confederate position. General Stuart dispatched Pelham with orders to move around the lines and fire upon the advancing Union forces. Pelham successfully moved two guns into position on Meade's flank and opened a murderous fire on the Union division. Soon the young major came under artillery attack, but he refused to leave his position—despite the destruction of one of the guns and repeated orders from Stuart to withdraw. Pelham continued to fire until a final direct order forced him to retire, but legends of the battle report that he refused to leave his position until he expended all his ammunition. This action delayed Meade's attack by more than two hours. After witnessing the barrage, General Robert E. Lee made special reference to "the Gallant Pelham" in his report of the battle.

Ironically, Pelham's final battle was not an artillery engagement, but a cavalry charge. While away from his unit with General Stuart, Pelham and the other officers heard of an impending action at Kelly's Ford, Virginia. On 17 March 1863 both Stuart and Pelham rode to the battlefield to observe, but Pelham found it impossible to avoid the fray. He moved forward into the front of the Confederate lines, and participated in the actions of the 3d Virginia Cavalry. While he was directing troops, a shell exploded overhead and a fragment struck Pelham in the back of the head. He was quickly thrown over a horse and led to the rear of the lines, where he was placed in the care of two soldiers who were instructed to take the unconscious man to the nearest ambulance. The soldiers misunderstood the order and marched for miles with Pelham laid across the saddle. A courier finally recognized the major and had him removed to Culpeper, Virginia. He died later that night. General Stuart, saddened by the death of one he had grown to love, remarked that the loss of Pelham was irreparable and ordered the body laid in state at Richmond. Pelham's body was then placed aboard a train and carried back to Alabama, where the hero was laid to rest in Jacksonville.

—Eric L. Bobo

See also Antietam, Battle of; Fredericksburg, First Battle of; Kelly's Ford, Battle of.

For further reading:

Hassler, William W. *Colonel John Pelham: Lee's Boy Artillerist* (1960).

Mercer, Philip. *The Gallant Pelham* (1929).

Milham, Charles G. *Gallant Pelham: American Extraordinary* (1959; reprint, 1987).

Ward, J. M. "Major John Pelham: Alabama's gift to the Confederate artillery". In *A New Nation, A War, A Young Hero, and a Surrender.* Edited by Albert Burton Moore (1965).

PEMBER, PHOEBE YATES LEVY
(1823–1913)
Confederate nurse

Phoebe Pember served as head matron of Richmond's Chimborazo Hospital No. 2 from December 1862 through the end of the war. She was a shrewd observer of human nature, charming, frank, critical, and witty. Her memoir, *A Southern Woman's Story* (1879), and her unpublished letters show her keenness of mind, her compassion for Confederate soldiers, and her close ties to friends and family.

Phoebe Levy was the fourth of seven children born to Jacob Levy and Fanny Yates, who had lived in one of the New World's oldest Jewish communities—Charleston, South Carolina—since the eighteenth century. Pember's intellect and vivacity were cultivated at home with five sisters and a brother. Two sisters would go on to make their mark in the war. Eugenia Levy Phillips, wife of an attorney who represented Alabama in Congress in the 1850s, was banished to a desert island in the Gulf of Mexico by Union general Benjamin Butler in 1862 for mocking a Union funeral cortege as it passed her New Orleans home. Another sister, Septima Levy Collis,

married a Union officer in December 1861 and spent the war years at his side in military camps. Collis published *A Woman's War Record* in 1889, ten years after sister Phoebe's memoir appeared.

Phoebe also married a Northerner—Thomas Pember of Boston—in the 1840s or 1850s but lost him to tuberculosis in July 1861. From Aiken, South Carolina, Phoebe moved back in with her parents, who had migrated to Savannah in the 1850s but were now living as refugees with relatives in Marietta, Georgia. Not one to tolerate living in close quarters, Pember left after a year when the wife of Confederate secretary of war George Randolph found her a salaried position at Chimborazo. Some looked askance at the thirty-nine-year-old Pember for working, but the onus was preferable to continuing as a dependent. When an acquaintance insinuated that she had entered the hospital service to find romance, Pember was furious. "Who would suppose," she wrote to sister Eugenia, "that days passed among fever wards and dying men, in a hospital away from the city, with no comforts and every privation, was voluntary!" Such encounters prompted Pember to speak plainly about the propriety of military nursing in her postwar memoir: "The circumstances which surround a wounded man, far from friends and home,…dependent upon a woman for help, care and sympathy, hallow and clear the atmosphere in which she labors."

Pember arrived at Chimborazo as the wounded of Fredericksburg came pouring in. In December 1862 this pavilion-style hospital was a world unto itself, with 150 wards, 8,000 beds, an icehouse, a bathhouse, a brewery, and a bakery that could produce up to 10,000 loaves per day. Pember was responsible for 600 to 700 men at a time; by the end of the war she had attended over 15,000 of the more than 75,000 who would come to Chimborazo. Ever aware of the "poisonous sting" of gossip, Pember was loath to socialize with hospital staff. She was not as circumspect, however, about the elite of Richmond whom she prized as companions when she found a flat in the city in 1863.

Pember's work as an executive in the Confederacy's largest hospital led her to expect deference from the genteel men in charge, but she was mistaken. Far from welcoming her, the male staff at Chimborazo groaned when they discovered a woman in their midst. Wardmasters were so uncooperative that it took her over a month to learn how to requisition supplies, and tippling surgeons resented her sovereignty over the medicinal liquor cabinet. When Pember agreed to let a certain Dr. H. play the flute in her room, she discovered wet linens and furniture in disarray. "Since that time," she wryly confided to a friend in Charleston, "I have left one particular towel out for practicing purposes and locked up my tooth brush as a man with such saving propensities might take a 'cheap brush' now and then."

Much to her surprise, Pember found that she preferred the grit and honesty of common soldiers who appreciated her care—even the "crazy" man who disrobed whenever she entered his ward. She took delight in arranging a Christmas feast in 1863 that featured twenty-four gallons of eggnog, a dozen turkeys, gallons of oysters, and cakes, although two months later she lamented that her soldiers went hungry. She was intrigued that men from Maryland and Virginia were jealous of her attentions to the other group and kept up "a constant fuss" after they were brought in from the battles of the Wilderness in June 1864. However, she still believed them to be gentlemen and was happy to accept a gift of kid gloves from the Baltimore delegation.

By contrast, Pember considered women in the hospitals her class inferiors. She found many of them coarse and wanting in tact, especially pipe-smoking Virginians who could not fathom her objection to their habit. An employee who assured Pember that she was a teetotaler had to be fired after she showed up for work drunk in the first week. Pember inveighed at a female visitor who gave birth in a ward, then abandoned her babe on the way home. Like elite women in both sections, she revered fighting men, but saw no heroism in the custodial work of hospital women.

Pember remained at Chimborazo when Richmond was evacuated in April 1865, but eventually made her way back to her family in Georgia. In 1879 she enjoyed a banner year with the publication of a short story in the *Atlantic Monthly* and her war memoir, but later writing ventures proved less successful. Though the eighty-nine-year-old was a resident of Pittsburgh when she died in 1913, her remains were taken to Dixie for burial.

—*Jane E. Schultz*

See also Nurses.

For further reading:
Medical Department List of Employees, Chimborazo Hospital No. 2. Record Group 109. National Archives, Washington, D.C.

———. Letters. Southern Historical Collection. University of North Carolina, Chapel Hill.

Pember, Phoebe Yates Levy. *A Southern Woman's Story: Life in Confederate Richmond* (1959).

Phillips, Philip. Collection. Manuscript Division. Library of Congress, Washington, D.C.

Schultz, Jane E. *Women at the Front: Female Hospital Workers in Civil War America* (in press).

PEMBERTON, JOHN CLIFFORD
(1814–1881)
Confederate general

Born to John Pemberton and Rebecca Clifford Pemberton in Philadelphia, Pennsylvania, John Clifford Pemberton was educated in a local private school. His father traveled much in his business as a merchant, and in his travels he met and became close friends with Andrew Jackson. Both of the younger

Pemberton's parents came from Quaker backgrounds, though they did not practice that religion.

Pemberton entered the University of Pennsylvania in the fall of 1830. While at the university, he determined upon a career in engineering and decided that the United States Military Academy was the best place for an engineering education. He began the application process in 1833, and when it appeared that he may have to wait until 1834 for admission, he used the family's connection with President Jackson to gain his appointment. Pemberton entered West Point in the summer of 1833. During his time at the Academy his roommate and closest friend was George Gordon Meade. After a rather rambunctious four years as a cadet, Pemberton graduated twenty-seventh of fifty in the class of 1837.

Pemberton was commissioned into the 4th Artillery and initially stationed in New York City. Before too long, however, he was transferred to Florida, where he fought in the Second Seminole War. Over his entire career in the United States Army, Pemberton moved almost every year. After a short time in Florida, he was sent to North Carolina to help round up Cherokees for the march west, and then in 1838 he went to the Maine-Canadian border during a border dispute there. From Maine he went back to New York, then to Florida, and then back to New York City. Over the next two years Pemberton served at Camp Washington, New Jersey, on the Michigan frontier, at Carlisle Barracks, and then Fort Monroe, Virginia. While at Fort Monroe he met Martha Thompson, the daughter of a prominent Norfolk shipping family, and became engaged. His marriage to the Virginian Martha is generally believed to be the reason Pemberton sided with the Confederacy at the outbreak of the Civil War.

Before he and Martha could be married, Pemberton was called away to serve in the Mexican-American War. He served under Zachary Taylor in northern Mexico, fighting at Palo Alto and Resaca de la Palma in the early stages of the war. Shortly after these engagements he accepted a position as aide-de-camp to William Jenkins Worth and served in that capacity for the remainder of the war. He received two brevet promotions during the war and was slightly wounded in the Mexico City campaign.

In 1848 Pemberton returned to Virginia and married Martha Thompson. Rather than returning to the 4th Artillery, Pemberton remained on Worth's staff and accompanied the general to Texas at the end of 1848. Not finding Texas to his liking, he decided to return to his old unit in 1849 and served in Norfolk, Florida, and New Orleans by the end of the year. Over the next few years, he and his growing family served at posts near Washington, D.C., in New York, and Florida. Following his last stint in Florida, Pemberton participated in Albert Sidney Johnston's Utah expedition, after which he was stationed in Minnesota.

While Pemberton lived this peripatetic existence, the sectional crisis became more serious. There is no record of his views on slavery, sectionalism, or states' rights during this time. As things worsened in the early months of 1861, however, he was sent to Washington, D.C., where he became part of the defensive force there.

Pemberton remained in those defenses during the Fort Sumter crisis and apparently struggled over whether to join with the Confederacy. After much cajoling from his Philadelphia family, he agreed not to leave the army until Virginia seceded. A week after Virginia seceded, Pemberton resigned his commission at the urging of his wife. He was quickly given a commission in the Virginia state army as a lieutenant colonel. On 17 June 1861 he became a brigadier general in the Confederate army.

Initially, Pemberton was stationed around Norfolk until 1861, when he was sent to Charleston, South Carolina, with Robert E. Lee. Pemberton helped improve the defenses of coastal South Carolina, and on 13 February 1862 was promoted to major general, to date from 14 January 1862. In March, upon Lee's return to Virginia, Pemberton became the commander of the Department of South Carolina and Georgia.

As commander he created an unnecessarily complicated bureaucracy and did not get along well with the state governments of South Carolina or Georgia. He had difficulty procuring enough slaves to work on the coastal defenses, even when threats along the coast worsened in the spring and summer of 1862. Pemberton especially had difficulties with Governor Francis Pickens of South Carolina, and the general's Northern background only exacerbated his problems. He was relieved and recalled to Virginia in September 1862.

On 1 October 1862 Pemberton was given command of the District of Mississippi and Eastern Louisiana and placed under the overall command of Joseph E. Johnston in the Western theater. He was ordered to defend his territory and to retake New Orleans if possible. Pemberton traveled immediately to Mississippi, where he initially established his headquarters at Jackson. Because Major Generals Mansfield Lovell and Earl Van Dorn in his district had been promoted to major general before him, Pemberton was soon promoted to lieutenant general, to date from 13 October 1862. Initially, he had about 30,000 men in his district, although that number would about double over the next six months.

Pemberton had been instructed that Vicksburg was the most important place in the district and that he was to hold it at all costs. Therefore, knowing that Ulysses S. Grant was beginning a movement down from Tennessee, he immediately took steps to improve the defenses of that important river town. He began with improvements to Port Hudson to the south in Louisiana to prevent a movement upriver. He then set about to improve the supply system to his army.

Immediately, problems developed with state govern-

ments, particularly in Mississippi, over the use of militia and the procurement of supplies. These problems were only exacerbated by reports that Grant was pressing down from the north and preparing to send William T. Sherman down the Mississippi River with 40,000 men. To meet Grant's threat and perhaps to force him to withdraw back toward Tennessee, Pemberton sent Van Dorn in December 1862 on a cavalry raid against Grant's supply base at Holly Springs. The raid was a success, and Grant withdrew, but Sherman was still coming. From 27 to 29 December 1862 Sherman was repulsed at Chickasaw Bluffs.

In the early spring of 1863 Grant was back trying to find the best approach to Vicksburg. Union brigadier general Benjamin Henry Grierson's raid south in April and early May 1863 confused Pemberton and his officers as to Grant's intentions, while Grant moved south on the west bank of the Mississippi and was ferried across to approach Vicksburg from the south. Pemberton was very cautious in dealing with these various threats.

Joseph Johnston came to Jackson on 13 May but was defeated and pushed out of the town the following day. On Johnston's orders, Pemberton moved out of Vicksburg and fought Grant at Champion's Hill on 16 May 1863. On the Confederate side there was great confusion, partly owing to Pemberton's indecision and partly because of disputes with subordinates like William Wing Loring. The Confederates were defeated and then suffered another loss the next day at Big Black Bridge. Pemberton then pulled his army back into the defenses of Vicksburg. On 18 May Johnston sent word to Pemberton that he should withdraw from Vicksburg to save the army, but Pemberton replied that he would try to hold it and hope for reinforcements.

The next day, on 19 May, Grant attacked the left side of Pemberton's defenses and was repulsed. He attacked again on 22 May with the same results. Following this attack, Grant settled in for a siege. Through the next few weeks Pemberton sent constant messages to Johnston asking for supplies and reinforcements. He finally received word that Johnston did not have the resources to be of any assistance.

On 3 July Pemberton sent emissaries to arrange terms, but Grant refused to accept anything less than unconditional surrender. The two met later in the day, at which time Pemberton told Grant that he would not surrender unconditionally and lied that the city had enough food to hold out indefinitely. Grant then reluctantly agreed to allow subordinates to arrange terms. The final version of the capitulation paroled Pemberton's army until exchanges could be made. The final surrender took place on 4 July.

After obtaining his parole, Pemberton went to Demopolis, Alabama, where his family waited for him. He requested a court of inquiry into his conduct at Vicksburg, but his request was refused. While before he had been viewed as a traitor in the North, now Southerners called him traitor, with many implying that he had lost Vicksburg intentionally. He returned to Virginia, where he was an officer without an assignment until the spring of 1864.

By early 1864 Pemberton was bored and eager to help his adopted state. He wrote personally to Jefferson Davis, asking for some sort of position. It was politically impossible, however, for Davis to give Pemberton a command suitable for his high rank. As a result, Pemberton resigned his commission and asked to be made a lieutenant colonel of artillery. His request was granted, and he was placed in command of the Richmond Defense Battalion of Artillery. His primary concern was Richmond's eastern defenses. In January 1865 he was made Confederate general inspector of artillery and ordnance. In this position he traveled to what was left of the Confederacy's defenses. In the spring of 1865 he was with Joseph Johnston trying to put together batteries, but most of his artillery was captured before Johnston's surrender. Pemberton was in Newton, North Carolina, at the time of the surrender.

After the war Pemberton's mother helped him buy a farm in Virginia. He farmed and taught school locally. He also engaged in a long-distance feud with Johnston over the latter's behavior concerning Vicksburg. In the mid-1870s Pemberton sold his farm and moved back to Pennsylvania. He was employed in a variety of businesses and had his citizenship restored in 1879. He died at his summer home outside Philadelphia on 13 July 1881.

—*David S. Heidler and Jeanne T. Heidler*

See also Champion's Hill, Battle of; Chickasaw Bluffs, Battle of; Grant, Ulysses Simpson; Grierson's Raid; Johnston, Joseph Eggleston; Vicksburg Campaign.

For further reading:
Ballard, Michael B. *Pemberton: A Biography* (1991).

PENDER, WILLIAM DORSEY
(1834–1863)
Confederate general

Born in Edgecombe County, North Carolina, the son of James Pender and Sarah Routh Pender, William Dorsey Pender graduated from the United States Military Academy nineteenth of forty-six in the class of 1854. He was commissioned an artillery officer, but the following year transferred to the 1st Dragoons. He served in frontier posts and along the west coast. He was on recruiting duty in the east when he resigned his commission in March 1861, more than a month before the secession of his home state of North Carolina.

Pender immediately offered his services to the Confederacy. He was commissioned a captain of artillery and detached to Baltimore to recruit men for the Confederate army. Upon the secession of North Carolina, he returned home to recruit and accepted the colonelcy of the 3d North Carolina Regiment. In August 1862 he transferred to the command of the 6th North Carolina.

Pender fought in the early phases of the Peninsula campaign, culminating with the battle of Seven Pines on 31 March 1862. He was promoted four days later to brigadier general for his actions in that battle. During the Seven Days' battles at the end of the month he commanded his brigade as part of A. P. Hill's division. He fought at Cedar Mountain on 9 August and with Jackson at Second Bull Run, Antietam, Fredericksburg, and Chancellorsville. Frequently seen at the front of his brigade, Pender became somewhat legendary by the spring of 1863 for the fact that he had been wounded three times and yet refused each time to leave the field until the end of the battle.

During the reorganization of the Army of Northern Virginia following the death of Stonewall Jackson, Pender was promoted to major general and given command of a division of A. P. Hill's corps on 30 May 1863. He led that division in the invasion of Pennsylvania the following month. Before departing, however, he wrote to his superiors regarding his concern that North Carolina troops were being encouraged to desert by the recent court decision by North Carolina Supreme Court chief justice Richmond Mumford Pearson that the Confederate conscription law was unconstitutional. Pender was distressed that the morale of the troops would be hurt by the perception that they were not supported at home.

In the first day of the battle of Gettysburg, Pender was commended for his actions in using his brigade to push Union forces through the town of Gettysburg onto Cemetery Hill. In the following day's actions, however, he received a serious wound in his leg from an artillery shell. True to form, he refused to leave the field until carried off by his men. Sent by ambulance back to Virginia, Pender had his leg amputated, but he died of infection on 18 July. His death was lamented by Robert E. Lee in his final reports of the battle.

—*David S. Heidler and Jeanne T. Heidler*

See also Gettysburg, Battle of.

For further reading:

Hassler, William W, ed. *The General to his Lady: The Civil War Letters of William Dorsey Pender to Fanny Pender* (1965).

Rakes, Paul H. "The Military Career of an Ambitious Professional: Confederate General William Dorsey Pender, 1834–1863" (M.A. thesis, 1994).

PENDLETON, GEORGE HUNT
(1825–1889)
Ohio congressman

Born to Nathaniel Greene Pendleton and Jane Frances Hunt Pendleton in Cincinnati, Ohio, George Hunt Pendleton was educated locally by tutors and at Cincinnati College. As a young man, after leaving college, he traveled in Europe and the Middle East for two years. Upon his return to Ohio, Pendleton studied law and began practicing in 1847.

Along with his law practice, Pendleton was active in the Ohio Democratic Party. In 1853 at the age of twenty-eight, he was elected to the state senate. Possessed of a keen legal mind, Pendleton spent most of his first year in office drafting revised state laws that were compatible with the new state constitution. He was nominated by the Ohio Democratic Party for the United States House of Representatives in 1854, but lost the election. He ran again in 1856 and was successful.

Pendleton served in Congress through the latter phases of the sectional crisis and through most of the Civil War. In his early days in that body he was a member of the Stephen Douglas wing of the Democratic Party. He was a strong supporter of Douglas for the Democratic presidential nomination in 1860. Upon the election of Abraham Lincoln in the fall of 1860, Pendleton advocated accommodation of Southern demands to prevent secession. He strongly supported the compromise efforts in early 1861, and when they failed, opposed coercion to keep the seceded states in the Union.

Though a member of the so-called Peace Democrats, Pendleton was no Copperhead and remained loyal to the United States throughout the war. However, he was strong in his opposition to many of the measures of the Lincoln administration, especially those actions that he saw as an infringement of individual and property rights. Not only did he severely criticize the executive suspension of the writ of habeas corpus in his capacity as a member of the Judiciary Committee, but also the tampering with slave property. As early as July 1861 he voted with the minority against a measure that allowed army officers not to return runaway slaves that came within Union lines. As a Peace Democrat and someone with Southern antecedents (Pendleton's family had come to Ohio from Virginia), his speeches on these and other issues in opposition to the war were followed very closely in the South as an indication of the mood of the war's opponents in Congress.

As a member of the House Ways and Means Committee, Pendleton strongly opposed the increased reliance of the government on paper currency. He viewed such actions as not only dangerous to the national economy, but potentially disastrous for American credit abroad.

In 1864 Pendleton accepted the nomination of the Democratic Party for vice president on George McClellan's presidential ticket and hence did not run for reelection to Congress. As he and McClellan lost the election, Pendleton left the House of Representatives in March 1865.

Ironically, after returning to Ohio politics after the war, Pendleton became a proponent of the paper

currency, or "greenbacks," that had been printed during the war. He thought such currency would be especially useful in paying off the war debt without draining the treasury of its specie reserve. Some attributed his failure to secure the Democratic presidential nomination of 1868 to this stand.

While remaining active in politics after the war, Pendleton also became involved in various business activities, including a stint as president of the Kentucky Central Railroad. In 1878 he was elected one of Ohio's U.S. senators. During his one term in Washington, he became famous for the passage of what became known as the Pendleton Act. As the chairman of the Senate Civil Service Committee he pushed through this act in 1883, which began the process of civil service reform in the federal government. In March 1885, shortly after Pendleton left the Senate, President Grover Cleveland appointed him United States minister to Germany. He died in Brussels, Belgium, on 24 November 1889, while still serving as minister to Germany.

—*David S. Heidler and Jeanne T. Heidler*

See also Congress, U.S.S.; Peace Democrats.
For further reading:
Mach, Thomas S. "'Gentleman George' Hunt Pendleton: A Study in Political Continuity" (Ph.D. dissertation, 1996).

PENDLETON, WILLIAM NELSON
(1809–1883)
Confederate general

The son of Edmund Pendleton and Lucy Nelson Pendleton, William Nelson Pendleton was born in Richmond, Virginia. He was educated locally and at the U.S. Military Academy, where he graduated fifth of forty-two in the class of 1830. After serving in South Carolina and as an instructor at the academy, he resigned his commission to become a teacher. He taught at several schools in Pennsylvania, Delaware, and Maryland before entering the Episcopalian clergy. He continued to teach until 1847, when he entered the ministry full time. He eventually settled in Lexington, Virginia, where he became the rector of Grace Church. In this position he became prominent in the local community and in the state governance of the Episcopalian Church.

Upon the secession of Virginia, Pendleton, owing to his military experience, was selected as the captain of a local artillery company, the Rockbridge Artillery. His experience and prominence in the community soon gained him promotion, and by July 1861, Pendleton was a colonel on Joseph Johnston's staff in the Shenandoah Valley. Before the end of the year, Pendleton was serving as Johnston's chief of artillery at Manassas Junction, and he would continue in that capacity when Johnston

moved to the defense of Richmond in what would become the Peninsula campaign. Upon Johnston's replacement by Robert E. Lee on 1 June 1862, Pendleton became the chief of artillery of the Army of Northern Virginia. He remained in that position until he surrendered with Lee at Appomattox.

Although there is some debate about Pendleton's effectiveness as an artillery commander, his performance obviously pleased Lee, whom he strongly resembled, and there seems little doubt that he was a very effective administrator and organizer. On several occasions he was quite innovative. In July 1862, he distracted McClellan's remaining positions on the James River with a night artillery attack that allowed much of the remainder of Lee's army to move out of Richmond without the Army of the Potomac's knowledge. During the invasion of Maryland in September 1862, Pendleton coordinated all the artillery movements of Lee's dispersed force between Harper's Ferry and Sharpsburg. During the Chancellorsville campaign in May 1863, Pendleton remained behind with Jubal Early in Fredericksburg to delay the movement of John Sedgwick across the Rappahannock River. Pendleton was commended by Lee for his actions in the Gettysburg campaign.

Along with his combat activities during the war, Pendleton's main duties were to coordinate artillery movements within the Army of Northern Virginia, to act as liaison with the Confederate War Department on artillery issues, to locate forage for the artillery horses, and to scout roads and bridges capable of handling the transportation of the army's biggest guns. Because of his success in these areas and his knack for getting the most out of his limited resources, he was sent in the early spring of 1864 to inspect Joseph Johnston's artillery in north Georgia and to make recommendations for improvements. He was back with the Army of Northern Virginia by May 1864.

At the commencement of the Petersburg campaign in June 1864, Pendleton was called upon to do a great deal with very limited resources. When Lee's army retreated from its entrenchments the following spring, Pendleton accompanied the army and was chosen by Lee as one of the commissioners to draw up surrender terms in negotiations with Ulysses S. Grant's staff.

After the war, Pendleton returned to the ministry, a job he had never really left, as he never wasted any opportunity to minister to the spiritual needs of the troops during the war. He continued as rector of Grace Church until his death.

—*David S. Heidler and Jeanne T. Heidler*

See also Artillery.
For further reading:
Lee, Susan Pendleton. *Memoirs of William Nelson Pendleton, D. D.* (1893).

PENINSULA CAMPAIGN
(March–July 1862)

Early in 1862 President Abraham Lincoln issued Special Order No. 1, directing General George B. McClellan to lead the bulk of the Army of the Potomac by 22 February in a flanking movement southwest of Manassas, Virginia. Lincoln issued the order to force McClellan to disclose his plans for defeating the South, and to prod the procrastinating general into action. That was precisely its result. Immediately upon receiving the order, McClellan wrote Secretary of War Edwin M. Stanton a twenty-two-page letter that for the first time outlined his plans.

Lincoln's proposal was for a relatively simple, direct overland movement upon Joseph E. Johnston's Confederate army through Manassas, with Washington as its base. McClellan preferred to move the Union army down the Potomac and up the Rappahannock to a point opposite Richmond. His base would be the tiny town of Urbana, which would be supplied from the Chesapeake Bay. McClellan argued that this plan would place the army on the shortest feasible land route to Richmond. In his letter McClellan argued that the roads on the Urbana-Richmond route were passable in all seasons, and that because this area of Virginia typically enjoyed an early spring, it was favorable to offensive operations. A quick march from Urbana would cut off Confederate forces on the peninsula, compel a quick evacuation of Manassas, and enable the Union army to reach Richmond before it was reinforced. He further argued that any assault using Washington as its base would have to wait until the muddy roads of the Washington-Richmond line dried,

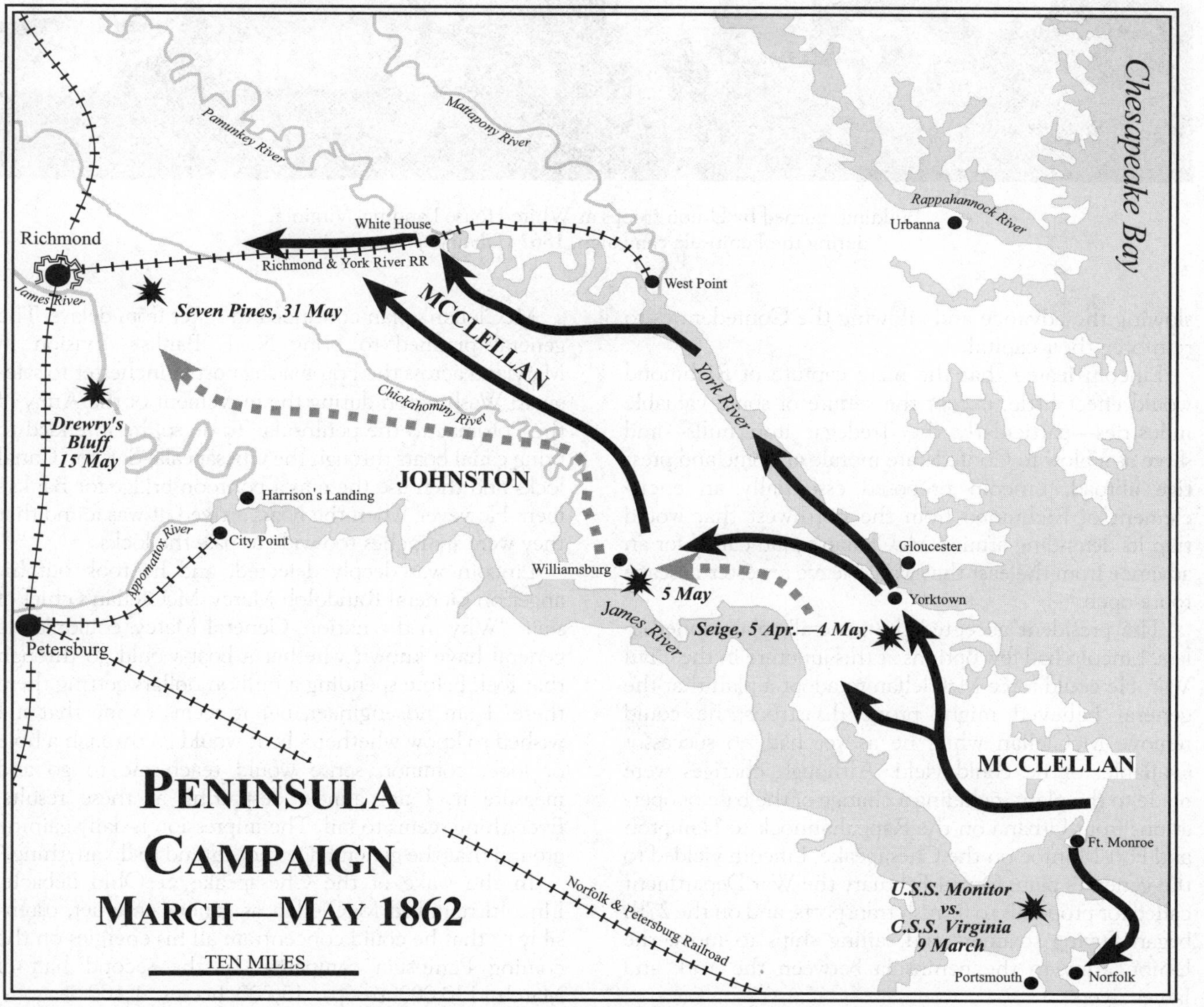

PENINSULA CAMPAIGN MARCH—MAY 1862

TEN MILES

(Map labels: Pamunkey River, Mattapony River, Rappahannock River, Chesapeake Bay, Urbanna, White House, Richmond & York River RR, West Point, Richmond, James River, Seven Pines, 31 May, MCCLELLAN, York River, Chickahominy River, Drewry's Bluff 15 May, JOHNSTON, Harrison's Landing, Appomattox River, City Point, Gloucester, Williamsburg, 5 May, Yorktown, James River, Seige, 5 Apr.—4 May, Petersburg, Norfolk & Petersburg Railroad, Ft. Monroe, U.S.S. Monitor vs. C.S.S. Virginia 9 March, Portsmouth, Norfolk)

Buildings burned by Union troops at White House Landing, Virginia,
during the Peninsula campaign, 1862 (*Library of Congress*)

slowing the advance and allowing the Confederates to reinforce their capital.

Lincoln feared that the mere capture of Richmond would effect little, except the seizure of some valuable industries—particularly the Tredegar iron mills—and serve as a blow to Confederate morale at home and prestige abroad. Lincoln proposed essentially an encirclement of Richmond from the northwest that would trap its defending armies. McClellan's plan called for an advance from the east that would leave a western escape route open.

The president accepted the general's plan nonetheless. Lincoln had few options at this juncture in the Civil War. He could force McClellan to adopt a plan that the general believed might prove disastrous; he could remove McClellan while he as yet had no successor available; or he could yield. Although changes were made to the plan, including a change of the base of operations from Urbana on the Rappahannock to Hampton and Fort Monroe on the Chesapeake, Lincoln yielded to the general's plan. On 14 February the War Department called for proposals to furnish transports, and on the 27th began buying steamers and sailing ships to move the Union army to the peninsula between the York and James rivers.

McClellan's plan continued to suffer from delays. The general planned to bring N. P. Banks's division in Maryland across the Potomac against Winchester to safeguard Washington during the movement of the Army of the Potomac to the peninsula. To do so, he intended to bring canal boats through the Chesapeake & Ohio Canal locks and then use them as a pontoon bridge for Banks's men. However, when the boats arrived, it was found that they were six inches too wide to pass the locks.

Lincoln was deeply dejected, and he took out his anger on General Randolph Marcy, McClellan's chief of staff: "Why in the nation, General Marcy, couldn't the general have known whether a boat would go through that lock before spending a million dollars getting them there? I am no engineer, but it seems to me that if I wished to know whether a boat would go through a hole or lock, common sense would teach me to go and measure it. I am almost despairing at these results. Everything seems to fail. The impression is daily gaining ground that the general does not intend to do anything."

In the wake of the Chesapeake & Ohio debacle, Lincoln removed McClellan as general-in-chief, ostensibly so that he could concentrate all his energies on the coming Peninsula campaign. In the second half of March, 130,000 troops, 15,000 horses, 1,100 wagons, and 44 artillery batteries were loaded aboard ships and barges in Alexandria in order to begin the long-awaited offensive. They sailed down the Potomac, into the Chesapeake, past the mouths of the Rappahannock and York rivers, and on to the peninsula. The transfer was completed by 5 April, bringing the Union army within just seventy-five miles of Richmond.

The advance elements of McClellan's army began to march on 4 April. A cold rain turned the supposedly ever-dry roads of the region into thick mud, slowing the army's progress to a snail's pace. On 5 April the Union force lay siege to Yorktown. McClellan was surprised to discover Confederate fortifications extending completely across the peninsula, from the York to the James. His maps also failed to show that the Warwick River, in places very wide, barred most of his path up the peninsula. The general turned excessively apprehensive, now fearing that Joseph E. Johnston must have reinforced Yorktown. Although it outnumbered the Confederates four to one, for a full month McClellan's army sat outside Yorktown. Instead of attacking, he built batteries and parallels opposite Yorktown, installing nearly a hundred heavy artillery pieces to bombard the Confederates. Then, when McClellan was finally ready to attack on 4 May, J. B. Magruder's small Army of the Peninsula successfully withdrew under cover of darkness toward Williamsburg. McClellan made the most of this "capture" of Yorktown, as he telegraphed Stanton: "The success is brilliant, and you may rest assured that its effects will be of the greatest importance." But he was quick to ask for more troops, as he was certain that Johnston stood between him and Richmond with forces "probably greater a good deal than my own."

In fact, McClellan had some 105,000 men, 85,000 of whom were available for battle. Johnston had a force of just over 60,000, with only some 42,000 available for combat. Despite some setbacks and delays, McClellan's plan to this point had largely succeeded, placing the Union army at the gates of Richmond. Final success would depend upon the rapidity of the final advance, to prevent Johnston from fortifying Richmond too extensively, and on the strategic skills of McClellan.

On 8 May the advance began, but it immediately bogged down. McClellan had insisted that the roads of this region were passable at all times, but spring rains quickly turned them into a thick muck that swallowed up wagons, caissons, and men. The people of the region practiced scorched-earth tactics, burning down structures, filling wells with stones, and running off livestock. Thus slowed, it was not until 21 May that the Union army reached Cumberland, just seven miles from the Confederate capital. But rather than complete his advance, McClellan dug in and began pleading with Washington for reinforcements, even though he outnumbered Johnston's army by some 40,000 men. Not

realizing that McClellan had stopped, Jefferson Davis placed his wife and children, and the Confederate Treasury's gold, on board a special train bound for Columbia, South Carolina.

Despite McClellan's indecision, he still held the upper hand. Then an unexpected element altered the outlines of the situation: the Chickahominy River. On Union maps, the Chickahominy appeared to be little more than a creek that arose in the hills of northwest Richmond, flowed east and south, and emptied into the James River. The main channel was generally easily passable, but if rains raised the river just two feet above normal level, it would spread in channels through the bogs on its edge, quickly overflowing the whole area. Any army advancing on Richmond from the east would have to keep part of its force on the north side in order to hold the line of communications to the James, while the main body moved south of the river to advance toward the Confederate capital. During the period of 20 to 25 May, McClellan moved two of his corps south of the river to maneuver against Richmond, while three corps remained north of the still-passable Chickahominy. But heavy rains beginning on the twenty-seventh caused the river to swell, and by the thirty-first it was no longer passable. On that day Johnston attacked the two corps south of the river. He nearly annihilated the Union forces early in the battle, but the lines held and Johnston was forced to retreat. The Confederates lost over 6,000 men, the Federals lost 5,000 and Johnston was severely wounded in the fighting. But the greatest casualty was McClellan's fragile confidence, which broke—despite the fact that his strategy was sound while circumstances proved unlucky. He would remain immobile for more than three weeks.

The severely wounded Johnston was replaced by Jefferson Davis's military adviser, Robert E. Lee. Lee took command of the renamed Army of Northern Virginia on 1 June, and he immediately began planning an offensive. Lee believed that because of McClellan's superior numbers, any long siege of Richmond would likely lead to a Union victory. Thus, he believed that his forces must strike McClellan's army before the big Union guns were brought to bear on Richmond. First he sent J. E. B. Stuart on a cavalry raid around the entire Union army, gaining the intelligence he needed to make his preparations. Next he pulled Thomas J. Jackson's forces out of the Shenandoah Valley to strengthen his own forces. By 25 June Jackson reached Ashland, just fifteen miles from Richmond, and within striking distance of McClellan. A council of generals that day decided to launch a "pincers" attack against the Union forces at three o'clock the next morning.

The famous Seven Days' battles began at Mechanicsville on 26 June. That battle was a draw, but McClellan ordered a retreat to Gaines' Mill. There on the twenty-seventh Lee smashed the Union right wing, forcing retreats to White Oak and Malvern Hill. At Malvern Hill McClellan dug in on a high plateau, protected at his flank by gunboats in the James River. Confederate forces smashed into the Union lines, but the Confederates lost more than 5,000 men and the Union lines held. Many Union officers felt that it was not yet too late to turn on the severely bloodied Confederates and attempt a new advance on Richmond. When McClellan instead ordered a further retreat to Harrison's Landing, a near mutiny broke out among his officers. One officer, Philip Kearny, asserted that they could easily take Richmond, and that a retreat "can only be prompted by cowardice or treason." Clearly, a bolder general would have renewed the advance. But McClellan believed that his first duty was to the safety of his army, and so he continued his retreat from Richmond.

Lee wrote his wife on 9 July: "Our success has not been as great or complete as we could have desired, but God knows what is best for us." His losses totaled 19,000, as against just over 15,000 on the Union side. But Richmond was secure. Jefferson Davis proclaimed a day of general thanksgiving throughout the South, while before the North stretched the prospect of a prolonged war with all its dangers, complications, and losses.

—*Todd Anthony Rosa*

See also Fair Oaks, Battle of; Johnston, Joseph Eggleston; Lee, Robert Edward; McClellan, George Brinton; Seven Days', Battles; Yorktown.

For further reading:
Catton, Bruce. *Mr. Lincoln's Army* (1951).
Hensel, Howard M. *The Anatomy of Failure: The Case of Major General George B. McClellan and the Peninsular Campaign* (1985).
Sears, Stephen W. *George B. McClellan: The Young Napoleon* (1999).
———. *To the Gates of Richmond: The Peninsula Campaign* (1992).

PENNINGTON, WILLIAM
(1796–1862)
Speaker of the House

During the secession winter of 1860–1861, William Pennington served as the speaker of the U.S. House of Representatives. He had been a compromise candidate for the job and would prove graceless and incompetent in performing almost every aspect of it. Some historians, pointing to his lamentable ignorance of House etiquette and rules, have described him as the worst speaker in congressional history.

Pennington was born on 4 May 1796 in Newark, New Jersey. His family was distinguished, and he attended the College of New Jersey (present-day Princeton University), graduating in 1813. After completing legal studies in 1817, he served as clerk of the district and

circuit courts. His father, William S. Pennington, was a district judge.

Pennington served in the New Jersey legislature beginning in 1828 and subsequently became a member of the Whig Party. In 1837 he was elected governor of the state and thus was intimately involved in the so-called Broad Seal War that concerned disputed congressional election results of 1838. When county clerks vouched that Whigs had won all six congressional districts seats, Democrats insisted that they had taken at least five of the contests. Pennington refused to challenge the results and duly approved the Whig "victors" as legitimate. Taken to the House of Representatives, the issue was finally resolved when Congress seated the Democrats, thus reversing Pennington's decision.

Defeated for reelection in 1843, Pennington wanted a diplomatic post in Europe, but nothing materialized. He was, however, elected to Congress in 1858 and thus entered the House just as it was becoming embroiled in the bitterest debates of its history. As sectional tensions mounted and slavery dominated almost all aspects of discussion, Ohio Republican John Sherman's candidacy for the speakership generated a controversy that threatened to disrupt the national legislature. Finally after eight weeks of acrimony, Sherman withdrew from contention on 30 January 1860, and the next day Pennington was elected Speaker as a compromise. Much of his attraction lay in his murky political affiliations, for his Whig antecedents seemed a more prevailing aspect of his ideology than did any recent political association. He had been elected to the House as a candidate of the People's Party in New Jersey. But even this was not much of an attraction, and his 117-vote victory for the speakership amounted to a majority of one.

To the Democrats' chagrin, especially the Southern wing of the party, Pennington gravitated to the Republicans and made committee appointments along lines suggested by John Sherman. When the secession crisis occurred in the wake of Abraham Lincoln's election, Pennington's crucial but clumsily applied role as Speaker helped to doom any compromise efforts. The special Committee of Thirty-Three authorized by the House to seek a solution for the crisis was in its membership a creation of Pennington's appointive power as Speaker. Pennington did not appoint a single supporter of Stephen A. Douglas. Also, the Southern delegates he chose were not really characteristic of the region's attitudes, and Republican Radicals figured too prominently in the committee's membership. Possibly nobody could have brought the national legislature to a reasonable contemplation of the great menace imperiling the Union in 1861. Yet in his inability to command the House and his remarkable lack of political sagacity, Pennington proved beyond doubt that he could not do so. In the wake of Southern withdrawal, Republicans would in July

elect Pennsylvanian Galusha Grow to the Speaker's chair. Pennington died on 16 February 1862.

—*David S. Heidler and Jeanne T. Heidler*

See also Sherman, John.

For further reading:

Elmer, L. Q. C. *The Constitution and Government of…New Jersey.* Vol. 7 of *New Jersey Historical Society Collections* (1872).

Nixon, J. T. "The Circumstances Attending the Election of William Pennington…as Speaker." *New Jersey Historical Society Proceedings* (1872).

PENNSYLVANIA

As the state with the second-highest population (some 2.9 million in 1860) and significant heavy industry, Pennsylvania's support of the Lincoln administration and the war effort against the South was crucial to Northern success. Owing to the commonwealth's strong Quaker influence, the state also harbored an active antislavery movement as well as extensive Underground Railroad activity.

The chief architect of the state's success was Governor Andrew Gregg Curtin (1817–1894), the first Republican governor of the state, who took office on 15 January 1861 and was reelected in 1863. Curtin was one of Lincoln's staunchest supporters. Nicknamed the "soldier's friend," Curtin also took an active interest in the welfare of the commonwealth's troops. He organized state agencies in Washington and Nashville to look after the men, organized a system of orphan schools to educate the children of slain veterans, personally visited camps to see how the troops were faring, and had the state pay for reinterment of soldiers buried outside the state. To ensure Republican success during the 1864 elections, Curtin authorized the state's troops to vote in the field. Pennsylvania soldiers echoed their governor's confidence by voting overwhelmingly for Lincoln instead of George B. McClellan.

Simon Cameron (1799–1889), a Lancaster, Pennsylvania, native, was Lincoln's first secretary of war. His political feud with Curtin damaged Curtin's political aspirations and led to quarrels that affected promotions of qualified Pennsylvania officers. Galusha Grow (1823–1907), a Democrat representing Susquehanna County, was elected speaker of the House in 1861; he was the principal architect of the 1862 Homestead Act. Thaddeus Stevens (1792–1868) was a Radical Republican and Gettysburg lawyer who was a member of the House of Representatives from 1858 to 1868. As a champion of blacks, Stevens promoted the use of black troops, worked hard to get the Thirteenth Amendment passed, and secured passage of the Civil Rights Act as well as the Freedmen's Bureau bill.

Philadelphia financier Jay Cooke was a key to Northern success. Although his firm had only been formed in 1861, Cooke was an energetic man with the patriotism needed to be successful. After New York bankers failed to support the government's desire to raise money via loans, Cooke approached Secretary of the Treasury Salmon P. Chase and received permission to sell government bonds on a commission basis. It is estimated that Cooke's firm raised more than one and a half billion dollars for the government; Cooke realized a profit of only $220,000 for his efforts.

Pennsylvania industries supplied much war materiel. In Pittsburgh, the Allegheny Arsenal manufactured ammunition and the Fort Pitt Works turned out more than 1,100 cannon. Philadelphia boasted a navy yard, the Frankford Arsenal (ammunition) and the Schuylkill Arsenal (clothing). Coal fields across the state supplied tons of black gold, while factories churned out all sorts of war goods. The Baldwin Locomotive Works in Philadelphia built most railroad engines used by the North during the war.

During the war, Pennsylvania supplied approximately 350,000 white soldiers, including 36,588 militia called into service during the summer of 1863 to oppose the Confederate invasion of the state. Camp Curtin, located in Harrisburg, was one of the major Northern training camps. The state also raised 8,612 black soldiers, ranking the commonwealth first among all Northern states in the recruitment of these troops. All the state's eleven black regiments organized and drilled at Camp William Penn, located on land owned by noted abolitionists James and Lucretia Mott north of Philadelphia.

Five companies of state militia, nicknamed the "First Defenders," were the first troops to respond to Lincoln's call for 75,000 three-month troops to suppress the rebellion. The companies arrived in Washington on 18 April 1861, a full day before the much-heralded arrival of the 6th Massachusetts. After the raising and equipping of twenty-five three-month regiments, Governor Curtin asked the state legislature for permission to raise a new corps of troops to defend the state. The result was the now-famous Pennsylvania Reserve Volunteer Corps, a division of thirteen infantry regiments, one of cavalry, and one of light artillery. Among their number was the Pennsylvania Bucktails, numbered the 42d Infantry (13th Reserves). Keystone State troops fought in most major campaigns of the war.

Pennsylvania furnished a number of notable generals. Chief among them were George G. Meade, the victor of Gettysburg and commander of the Army of the Potomac from 1863 through the end of the war; and George B. McClellan, father of the Army of the Potomac. Pennsylvania-born corps commanders included John F. Reynolds (I Corps), Winfield Scott Hancock (II Corps), Andrew A. Humphreys (II Corps), Samuel P. Heintzelman (III Corps), William B. Franklin (VI and XIX Corps), John G. Parke (IX Corps), David B. Birney (X Corps), Andrew J. Smith (XVI Corps), and John

Gibbon (II and XXIV Corps). Among the outstanding division commanders from Pennsylvania were David M. Gregg, John F. Hartranft, Alexander Hays, and James B. Steedman. Herman Haupt and Thomas K. Scott (assistant secretary of war) were Pennsylvania railroadmen who contributed to the war effort. Naval commander David D. Porter was a Pennsylvanian, as were the Ellet brothers (Alfred and Charles), who developed the Mississippi River ram fleet.

Pennsylvania was invaded three times during the war. The first, in October 1862, involved a cavalry raid by "Jeb" Stuart's horsemen after the Antietam campaign. In 1863, Robert E. Lee brought his Army of Northern Virginia into the state. His invasion was cut short by advancing Union forces, and the result was the climactic battle of Gettysburg on 1–3 July. During Jubal Early's advance on Washington in July 1864, Confederate cavalry under John McCausland and Bradley Johnson entered the state and occupied Chambersburg. When citizens were unable to pay a monetary ransom imposed by McCausland, the town's central district was burned; in all, more than 400 buildings went up in smoke.

—*Richard A. Sauers*

See also Chambersburg Raid; Cooke, Jay; Curtin, Andrew Gregg; Gettysburg, Battle of; Grow, Galusha; Mott, Gershom; Mott, Lucretia; Stevens, Thaddeus; Underground Railroad.

For further reading:
Alexander, Ted, James Neitzel, and William P. Conrad. *Southern Revenge! Civil War History of Chambersburg, Pennsylvania* (1989).
Bates, Samuel P. *History of Pennsylvania Volunteers, 1861–1865* (1868–1871; reprint, 1993).
Gallman, J. Matthew. *Mastering Wartime: A Social History of Philadelphia during the Civil War* (1990).
Sauers, Richard A. *Advance the Colors! Pennsylvania Civil War Battleflags* (1987–1991).

PENNYPACKER, GALUSHA
(1841–1916)
Union general

One of the youngest generals in the history of the U.S. Army and the grandson of a Revolutionary War veteran, Galusha Pennypacker was born in a house called the Mansion House that had been used as George Washington's headquarters at Valley Forge. The only child of Joseph J. Pennypacker and Tamsen Workhizer, Galusha was abandoned by his father after his mother's death in 1846 and raised by his uncle, Elijah Funk Pennypacker, a Pennsylvania legislator and a Quaker abolitionist whose estate was part of the Underground Railroad.

Galusha worked briefly for the *Chester County Times* and studied law before he enlisted in the army (Company A, 9th Pennsylvania) at the outset of the

Civil War in April 1861. He was elected lieutenant but declined because of his youth, serving instead as quartermaster sergeant until he was mustered out at the expiration of his 90-day enlistment.

Attracting recruits in Chester County, Pennypacker organized Company A of the 97th Regiment, Pennsylvania Volunteers, and he was elected captain (22 August 1861). Trusted by the regimental commander, Colonel H. R. Guss, Pennypacker was promoted rapidly to major (7 October 1861). In November, the regiment was sent to Fort Monroe, Virginia, then Hilton Head, South Carolina.

Pennypacker's regiment soon served in operations against Fort Pulaski, Georgia (January–February 1861), and against Fort Clinch, Fernandina, and Jacksonville, Florida (March–April). Pennypacker subsequently led his men at Grimball's Plantation (June 10, 1862), Secessionville (16 June 1862), and the long siege of Charleston (1862–1863), including the assault on Battery Wagner made famous by the 54th Massachusetts Colored Regiment.

Pennypacker was promoted to lieutenant colonel (6 April 1864) and fought with his regiment with the Army of the James at Swift Creek (9 May), Drewry's Bluff (6 May), and Green Plains (20 May), where two-thirds of his men became casualties and he was wounded three times carrying out a hopeless order to charge Pickett's entrenched division. Three months later, Pennypacker returned to duty as a colonel and was placed in command of the 2d Brigade, 2d Division, X Corps (14 September 1864–3 December 1864). He led the brigade in the sieges of Petersburg and at New Market Heights, Fort Harrison, and Fort Gilmer, where he was wounded by a shell fragment in the ankle. He mounted his horse, "Francis Marion," and the horse was shot from under him (29 September 1864). Despite his injury, Pennypacker refused to relinquish command and fought at the Darbytown Road before taking part in the first assault on Fort Fisher in North Carolina (7–28 December).

In the second assault on Fort Fisher (15 January 1865), Pennypacker was severely wounded as he planted the 97th's flag—the first in the charge—on the fort's walls. He was taken by steamer to Fort Monroe and was expected to die. By recommendation of Secretary of War Edwin Stanton, Pennypacker was given the brevet rank of brigadier general (effective 15 January); he was promoted to major general a month later at the recommendation of General Alfred Terry (18 February). Eleven months later, "the hero of Fort Fisher" (as described by division commander General Ames) returned to West Chester as "the boy general." He was discharged from the military (30 April 1866) and resumed his legal studies.

Although he never fully recovered from his wounds, Pennypacker was commissioned in the regular army

(34th and 16th Infantry) as a colonel (November 1866) and served in command positions in New Orleans, Louisville, Nashville, San Antonio, and other cities in the South. He earned a reputation for evenhanded administration and did much to reconcile the former Confederates to the federal government.

In 1872 Pennypacker declined consideration as the Republican candidate for governor of Pennsylvania. Later that year, he accompanied an army delegation led by General Philip Sheridan to Europe and participated in the review of the German army. In 1877 Pennypacker took command of Fort Riley, Kansas, and continued in active service until his final retirement in 1883. For the next thirty-three years, Pennypacker lived a semireclusive life in a townhouse in Philadelphia. His military service had left him in constant pain, with nerve damage, a permanent limp, and bouts of posttraumatic stress. His heroism at Fort Fisher was mentioned in the *Personal Memoirs of U.S. Grant* (1885–1886), and he sometimes received visits from political and military leaders. Nevertheless, he avoided discussing his military service, even after he was awarded the Medal of Honor in 1891.

Pennypacker never married and died alone at the Thomas Jefferson Hospital from complications resulting from his unhealed war injuries (1 October 1916). He was buried in the National Military Cemetery in Philadelphia, and, in 1934, Pennsylvania honored him with a prominent statue in Philadelphia's Logan Circle.

—*William A. Pannapacker and John Marx*

See also Fort Fisher.

For further reading:

Gragg, Rod. *Confederate Goliath: The Battle of Fort Fisher* (1991).

Pennypacker, Galusha. Papers. The Historical Society of Pennsylvania.

Pennypacker, Isaac R. *Galusha Pennypacker: America's Youngest General* (1917).

Price, Isaiah. *History of the Ninety-Seventh Regiment, Pennsylvania Volunteer Infantry, during the War of the Rebellion, 1861–1865* (1875).

The Memorial to Brevet Major General Galusha Pennypacker, Youngest General of the United States Army. The Pennypacker Memorial Commission of Pennsylvania (1934).

PENSACOLA, FLORIDA

Few cities in the United States could boast such a beautiful harbor as Pensacola. It was the home of a major naval yard, three fortifications, numerous lumber mills, and at least eight companies producing bricks. The 1860 census of Pensacola showed a population of 2,876, with many others living in nearby communities like Warrington. Guarding the deep-water harbor were Forts Barrancas, McRea, and Pickens. Of the three fortifications, only Fort Pickens was on neighboring Santa Rosa Island and separated from the mainland by

the waters of Pensacola Bay. Along with the naval personnel in the area, Barrancas Barracks housed Company G, 1st U.S. Artillery. This was the only unit available for the defense of the town and harbor should war commence.

The commander of Company G, Major John H. Winder, was on leave at the time of the Ordinance of Secession, and the only active commissioned officer on duty was Lieutenant Adam J. Slemmer. As pro-Southern sympathies were widely held in Pensacola, Slemmer's position was vulnerable to attack from almost any quarter. Besides the possibility of sudden attack, the man most responsible for the construction of the fortifications, William H. Chase, was commissioned major general of Florida forces by Governor Madison Starke Perry. It was agreed among the political leaders of Florida that one of the first priorities was to take possession of all the fortifications in and around Pensacola. Two companies of local militia had already been organized, and Governor Perry asked for additional troops from neighboring Alabama. Faced with this situation, Slemmer began preparations for the removal of all military materials to Fort Pickens.

On 8 January 1861, just two days before Florida passed its Ordinance of Secession, Slemmer was confronted by about twenty men who failed to heed the guard's call to halt. Shots, maybe the very first fired in the Civil War, were exchanged and the men fled. By daybreak of 9 January, the forces under Slemmer and their gear were being loaded for the trip across the bay to Fort Pickens. Three days later, 12 January 1861, the naval yard and its equipment were surrendered to troops under the command of Colonel Tennant Lomax. Slemmer's timing could not have been better, and he set about placing his batteries in proper order.

At the beginning of events in and around Pensacola, Slemmer had only eighty-one men to handle the guns and repair the abandoned fort. Troops were ordered to reinforce the garrison, and Company A of U.S. 1st Artillery was embarked on the USS *Brooklyn* nine days after the surrender of the naval yard. At this point, a strange arrangement, known as the Fort Pickens Peace, ensued. The agreement was that no reinforcements would be landed unless hostilities broke out. Not until Lieutenant John L. Worden, famed commander of the *Monitor*, brought direct orders to land these troops on 12 April 1861 was this peace broken and hostilities begun in Pensacola.

A number of skirmishes took place in and around Pensacola during the Civil War, but none were of major significance. The battle of Santa Rosa Island, the first of these skirmishes, occurred on the night of 9 October 1861. A force of about 1,200 men landed four miles east of Fort Pickens and divided into three columns and attempted to sweep the island to the encampments

Confederate artillery at Pensacola, 1861 (*National Archives*)

outside the fort. The 6th New York Volunteers had encamped outside the fort and were the first to be engaged. Caught by surprise, many of this unit's men broke and ran but rallied under the command of Major Lewis G. Arnold. The engagement was broken off by rumors of a Federal gunboat approaching. The losses for both sides, killed and wounded, came to a total of only 154.

The fighting around Pensacola was soon reduced to artillery duels and occasional raids. General Braxton Bragg, commanding Confederate forces in Pensacola and Mobile, enjoyed numerical superiority for nearly the entire year he commanded. However, Bragg could not control events elsewhere. News of the disasters at Mill Springs, Kentucky, and Fort Henry, Tennessee, soon led to demands for his troops. As the situation in Tennessee and along the Mississippi River worsened, more of Bragg's forces disappeared to other fronts. It was soon decided that Pensacola was expendable, in part because of the effectiveness of the Union blockade and because of the lack of war materials available in the area. By 10 May 1862, the Confederate presence in Pensacola was no more.

Duty at Pensacola was not always pleasant and

inviting. One officer of the 9th Alabama Regiment complained of being "ordered into a camp in a low swampy place on a disagreeable bayou. … Nearly one hundred of our regiment died in less than three months." Yellow fever, the scourge of the tropics, reared its ugly head in 1863 during the Union occupation and took a number of lives at Warrington and Wolsey. When the Union troops marched into town on the afternoon of 10 May 1862, they were greeted by the "sour looks and downcast faces of the white people who stood in small groups on the corners or furtively peeped out of the closed blinds." They also found the town "very shabby" and had to face the square where the local population had erected a gallows to hang Unionists. This description contrasts with that given by Henry Shorey, who recalled his commanding officer living in the house of former U.S. senator Stephen Mallory, as the lesser officers were "luxuriating in nicely furnished apartments fronting the public squares; while the quarters of the enlisted men were by no means unpretentious." Shorey's account also notes that his unit took advantage of the "deserted private residences," indicating that by the time the 15th Maine arrived in Pensacola, most of the residents had fled inland or quietly melted away into the wilds of West Florida.

Apart from General Alexander Asboth's Marianna campaign, the only military action involved raids on Gonzales' Station and other nearby points. Pensacola was the staging area for many of the attacks on Confederate salt works along the coast, including those on St. Andrews Bay. These raids, while not preventing salt making, did serious damage to the production of this much-needed commodity. It also forced Florida to pass special legislation freeing saltmakers from conscription and allowing special salt protection units to be formed, thus depriving the Confederacy of forces needed elsewhere. Although the Union forces occupied Pensacola for about one year, it was no longer strategically important. For the remainder of the war, Fort Barrancas and Fort Pickens were the focal points of military activity.

—*Joe Knetsch*

See also Asboth, Alexander; Fort Pickens; Slemmer, Adam Jacoby.

For further reading:
Babcock, Willoughby M., Jr. *Selections from the Letters and Diaries of Brevet-Brigadier General Willoughby Babcock of the Seventy-Fifth New York Volunteers* (1923).
Bearss, Edwin C. "Civil War Operations in and around Pensacola, Part 1." *Florida Historical Quarterly* (1957).
Benedict, George G. *History of the Seventh Regiment Vermont Volunteers* (1891).
DeBolt, Dean. "Life on the Front as Reflected in Soldiers' Letters." *Gulf Coast Historical Review* (1988).
Johns, John E. *Florida during the Civil War* (1963).
Jones, James Pickett. "Lincoln's Courier: John L. Worden's Mission to Fort Pickens." *Florida Historical Quarterly* (1962).
Larkin, J. L. "Battle of Santa Rosa Island." *The Florida Historical Quarterly* (1959).
Shorey, Henry A. *The Story of the Maine Fifteenth* (1890).
Taylor, Robert A. *Rebel Storehouse: Florida in the Confederate Economy* (1995).
Yonge, Julian C. "Pensacola in the War for Southern Independence." *Florida Historical Quarterly* (1959).

PENSIONS, CIVIL WAR

At the close of the Revolutionary War, the United States government began administering a limited pension system to soldiers wounded during active military service or veterans and their widows pleading dire poverty. It was not until the 1830s and the advent of universal suffrage for white males and patronage democracy, however, that military pensions became available to all veterans or their widows. Despite these initial expansions, the early U.S. military pension system was minuscule compared to what it became as a result of the Civil War.

Beginning in 1861, the U.S. government generously attended to the needs of its soldiers and sailors or their dependents. Because the Federal government did not implement conscription until 1863, these first Civil War benefits in many ways were an attempt to induce men to volunteer. Although altered somewhat over the years, the 1862 statute remained the foundation of the Federal pension system until the 1890s. It stipulated that only those soldiers whose disability was "incurred as a direct consequence of...military duty" or developed after combat "from causes which can be directly traced to injuries received or diseases contracted while in military service" could collect pension benefits. The amount of each pension depended upon the veteran's military rank and level of disability. Pensions given to widows, orphans, and other dependents of deceased soldiers were always figured at the rate of total disability according to the military rank of their deceased husband or father. By 1873 widows could also receive extra benefits for each dependent child in their care.

In 1890 the most notable revision in the Federal pension law occurred: the Dependent Pension Act. A result of the intense lobbying effort of the veterans' organization, the Grand Army of the Republic, this statute removed the link between pensions and service-related injuries, allowing any veteran who had served honorably to qualify for a pension if at some time he became disabled for manual labor. By 1906 old age alone became sufficient justification to receive a pension.

At the same time that pension requirements were becoming more liberal, several Southern congressmen attempted to open up the Federal system to Confederate veterans. Proponents justified such a move by noting that Southerners had contributed to Federal pensions through the system of indirect taxes since the end of the war. These proposals met with mixed responses in both the North and the South, but overwhelmingly, opposition came from those financially comfortable Confederate veterans and Southern politicians who regarded such dependency on Federal assistance a dishonor to the Lost Cause. It should be noted that impoverished Southern veterans frequently were not averse to the prospect of receiving Federal pensions. In any event, no such law ever passed, and Confederate veterans and their widows never matriculated into the Federal pension system.

Although U.S. Civil War veterans had received pensions since 1862 and Southern state governments had provided their veterans with artificial limbs and veteran retirement homes since the end of the war, it was not until the late 1880s and early 1890s that the eleven states of the former Confederacy enacted what can accurately be called pension systems. The economic devastation of the war and the political upheaval of Reconstruction best explain this long delay. When Southern pension systems did finally emerge, they generally resembled the pre-1890 U.S. system: eligibility depended upon service-related disability or death and indigence, and widows as well as other dependents of

deceased soldiers could receive pensions. Despite these similarities, however, there were striking differences. First, in the South widows collected pensions set at a specific rate for widows of deceased soldiers. These rates were generally lower than those to which their husbands would have been entitled should they have survived. Under the Federal system, there was no separate category for widows. Second, most Southern pension laws determined stipend amounts based only on the degree of disability. No regard was given to military rank. Third, there was never a Confederate equivalent to the 1890 U.S. Dependent Pension Act. Although over time Confederate pension requirements became more liberalized, there was always an income and property limit—pensions were never given simply for service. Fourth, whereas indirect taxes funded Federal pensions, most Southern states financed their pensions through a direct tax. And fifth, because Southern pension systems were on the state level only, they varied as to method and amount and were much less financially generous than U.S. pensions. Though the individual pensions of Southerners were minuscule compared to those of Federal veterans and war widows, as a percentage of state expenditures, Southern pension expenditures were monumental. Of all the former Confederate states, Georgia generally spent the most per year on pensions; Alabama ran a close second.

Both the Federal government and Southern state governments continued to provide pensions for Civil War veterans and their widows well into the middle of the twentieth century. In all, billions of dollars were expended by both sides in an effort to "reward" the survivors of America's costliest war. Because of the high rates of expansion in both the Federal and Confederate systems, critics frequently accused pensioners and officials alike of corruption and fraud. Those pensioners most often labeled as frauds were widows, especially young women who had married veterans much older than themselves, supposed "cowards," and, in the Federal system, black veterans. By the mid–twentieth century, both systems were generally considered devoid of their original integrity.

—*Jennifer L. Gross*

See also Veterans Organizations.
For further reading:
Glasson, William H. *Federal Military Pensions in the United States* (1918).
———. "The South's Care for Her Confederate Veterans." *American Monthly Review of Reviews* (July 1907).
Holmes, Amy E. "Such Is the Price We Pay": American Widows and the Civil War Pension System." In *Toward a Social History of the American Civil War: Exploratory Essays.* Edited by Maris A. Vinovskis (1990).
Morton, M. B. "Federal and Confederate Pensions Contrasted." *Forum* (1893).
Oliver, John William. "History of Civil War Military Pensions, 1861–1885." *Bulletin of the University of Wisconsin* (1917).
Skocpol, Theda. *Protecting Soldiers and Mothers: The Political Origins of Social Policy in the United States* (1992).

PERRY, EDWARD AYLESWORTH
(1831–1889)
Confederate general

Edward Aylesworth Perry, a native of Massachusetts, earned fame as the leader of a brigade of Floridians during the Civil War, and he later served as postwar governor of his adopted state. Born in Richmond, Massachusetts, on 15 March 1831, Perry studied at the nearby Lee Academy and spent two years at Yale in the early 1850s. In 1852 he moved to Georgia, where he taught school. Perry later settled in Greenville, Alabama. He continued to teach while also studying law. In 1856 he moved to Pensacola, Florida, and established a successful law practice.

When the war began, the Northern-born Perry took a secessionist stand. He became captain of the Pensacola Rifle Rangers, an infantry company that eventually became Company A of the 2d Florida Infantry Regiment. In early 1861 the company participated in the Confederate occupation of the Pensacola navy base and nearby Fort Barrancas. Perry took the Rifle Rangers to Virginia in the summer of 1861, but the Floridians missed the battle of First Bull Run. The company was subsequently stationed at Yorktown, Virginia, and it was there that Perry's command and another independent company were formally attached to the 2d Florida Infantry.

The Florida regiment was destined to play a prominent role in the Peninsula campaign. It was part of the Confederate force that defended Yorktown in April–May 1862, and was heavily engaged at Williamsburg, where its colonel, George T. Ward, was killed. Following Ward's death, Perry was appointed colonel of the regiment. He led the 2d Florida at Seven Pines, Gaines' Mill, and Frayser's Farm. In these battles, the Floridians suffered heavy casualties, particularly at Seven Pines. There the Floridians captured a New York artillery battery, the battle flag of a New York infantry regiment, and numerous prisoners. Perry's immediate commander, Brigadier General Samuel Garland, later wrote that Perry "discharged his duty with signal honor to himself." Seriously wounded at Frayser's Farm, Perry missed Second Manassas, but he had recovered sufficiently enough to take part in the Maryland campaign. At Sharpsburg, his small regiment would again suffer appalling losses.

Shortly after the latter battle, Perry received a promotion to brigadier general. He took command of a small, all-Florida brigade, consisting of the 2d, 5th, and 8th Infantry Regiments, and led it with distinction during the Fredericksburg and Chancellorsville campaigns. A

contemporary called Perry a "brave, generous and cool commander...[who] enjoys the full confidence of his entire command."

After Chancellorsville, Perry fell ill with typhoid fever. Consequently, he missed Gettysburg, where his Florida brigade lost more than half its strength during the terrific fighting on 2–3 July 1863. He recovered in time to lead his command at Bristoe Station in October 1863, and at the battle of the Wilderness the following May. Perry, however, was seriously wounded at the Wilderness and forced to relinquish command of the brigade. Brigadier General Joseph Finegan, who had been sent to Virginia with reinforcements from Florida, was eventually placed in command of a reorganized Florida brigade. Perry, meanwhile, with his days of active campaigning at an end, spent the remainder of the war commanding the reserve forces of the state of Alabama.

After the war, Perry returned to Pensacola and resumed the practice of law. Though an ardent Democrat, he did not become active in politics until the 1880s. In 1884 he received the Democratic nomination for governor and defeated a coalition candidate supported by both the Republican Party and disaffected Democrats. During his administration, Florida adopted a new constitution and initiated the payment of pensions to Confederate veterans. A Florida historian has noted that an "important element in the popularity that insured...[Perry's] election was his record as a Confederate general, and his administration was marked by a renaissance of Confederate sentiment."

At the conclusion of his term, Perry returned again to Pensacola. To improve his deteriorating health, Perry visited Texas in the summer and fall of 1889. While in Kerrville on 5 October he suffered a stroke. He died ten days later, and his body was returned to Pensacola for burial in St. John's Cemetery.

—*David J. Coles*

See also Florida.

For further reading:

Hartman, David, and David Coles, comps. *Biographical Rosters of Florida's Confederate and Union Soldiers, 1861–1865*, vol. 1 (1995).
Parker, Daisey. "The Inauguration of Edward Aylesworth Perry." *Apalache* V (1957–1962).
Prince, Sigsbee C. "Edward A. Perry, Yankee General of the Florida Brigade." *Florida Historical Quarterly* (1951).

PERRY, MADISON STARKE
(1814–1865)
Governor of Florida

Madison Starke Perry, governor of Florida from 1857 through March 1861, was a leader of the "South Carolina Faction" in prewar Florida politics. As a state senator from Alachua County, he reflected the very large influx into Florida of settlers from South Carolina and Georgia, many of whom were ardent followers of the political philosophy of John C. Calhoun. Perry himself was born in South Carolina and attended school at the Franklin Academy in Lancaster. He later attended the College of South Carolina. In the latter institution, he was noted for his abilities as an orator and a debater. He left school in 1831, not taking a degree, and returned to the family farm. Although he was reared in a fatherless home (his father died in the year of his birth, 1814) he was well provided for by his mother and stepfather, William Dixon. Prior to his emigration to Florida in 1847, Perry married his first cousin, Martha Peay Starke, and had fathered a son, Madison Starke Perry, Jr.

Within two years of moving to Florida, to a farm near the town of Rachel, Perry entered politics and was elected state senator for Alachua County. During his first term in the Florida senate, Perry strongly endorsed internal improvements, in which he often invested, and served on the important Committees of Taxation and Revenue and Corporations. On the latter, he served as a leader in overriding Governor Thomas Brown's veto of the amendment to the charter of the Atlantic & Gulf Coast Railroad, later known as the Florida Railroad and headed by Florida's powerful United States senator, David Levy Yulee. During his second term as state senator, Perry supported two ventures in which he and Yulee had both invested, a company to drain Orange Lake and the Palatka & Micanopy Plank Road Company. Yulee's alleged changing of the route of the Florida Railroad caused a split between the two men, but not until Perry had won election as Florida's governor.

As governor, he faced the problems presented by the Yulee railroad's change of route. The charter had originally said the road would run from Amelia Island (on Florida's northeast coast) to Tampa, with a branch to Cedar Key. Yulee, who sat on the Postal Committee while in the United States Senate, had arranged a contract for the railroad to carry the U.S. mail across the state. The shortest route available was between Amelia Island and Cedar Key, not Tampa. Perry was most upset because the route change meant a potential loss of income, as the original route had been contemplated through the town of Micanopy, about two miles from Perry's plantation. The important split between the two men, therefore, was not ideological, but political and economic.

Perry also faced the problem of the winding down of the Third Seminole War (1855–1858). Although not as costly or as long as the infamous Second Seminole War (1835–1842), the Third Seminole War nevertheless levied a high cost on the state because it required large numbers of Florida militia troops to patrol the remote interior. In a state greatly retarded in development by the bloody and drawn out Second Seminole War and the lack of adequate transportation, the strain of this new

war placed Florida in an awkward economic position. Perry further had the problem of the Florida-Georgia border dispute and the confused condition of internal improvements to tend to as governor. Added to these substantial problems was the coming of the Civil War.

Under Perry's leadership, the state attempted with its meager resources, to prepare for the war. Perry, a strong advocate of the states' rights school, was in the forefront in this preparation. Lacking a significant tax base or a properly trained and armed militia, Florida was not able to add strength to the Confederate cause. Yet Florida was the third state to vote for leaving the Union, in spite of strong Unionist sentiment in important centers within the state. With the longest coastline and a tiny population, Florida arguably was more vulnerable than any other state in the Confederacy. Perry's attempts to reform and arm the militia by putting its logistics into proper order enjoyed moderate success at best. Although he had reconciled with Yulee, he nevertheless had a weak political base from which to attempt reform and defense preparations. These problems made Perry appear weak and ineffectual as governor.

Perry was replaced as governor in 1861 by John Milton of Marianna, Florida. Milton's well-known personal animosity toward Perry has added to Perry's relative obscurity. Perry, however, served in the Confederate army and was elected colonel of the 7th Florida Infantry. He served in the border campaigns in Tennessee and Kentucky until health problems forced his resignation in April 1863. Madison Starke Perry never fully recovered his health and died at his home in March 1865.

—*Joe Knetsch*

See also Florida.
For further reading:
Knetsch, Joe. "Madison Starke Perry vs. David Levy Yulee: The Fight for the Tampa Bay Route." *Sunland Tribune, Journal of the Tampa Historical Society* (1997).

PERRYVILLE/CHAPLIN HILLS, BATTLE OF
(8 October 1862)

The 1862 Confederate invasion of Kentucky started well, with victories over Federal forces at Richmond and Munfordville. General E. Kirby Smith's army of some 19,000 men captured Lexington and Frankfort and threatened Cincinnati, Ohio, as the Frankfort government fled to Louisville. General Braxton Bragg's 32,000-man Army of the Mississippi moved aside to the Bardstown area after the battle of Munfordville and allowed Union general Don Carlos Buell to reach Louisville uncontested. Buell received 25,000 reinforcements in Louisville, and, moving with unusual speed, he advanced against the Confederates on

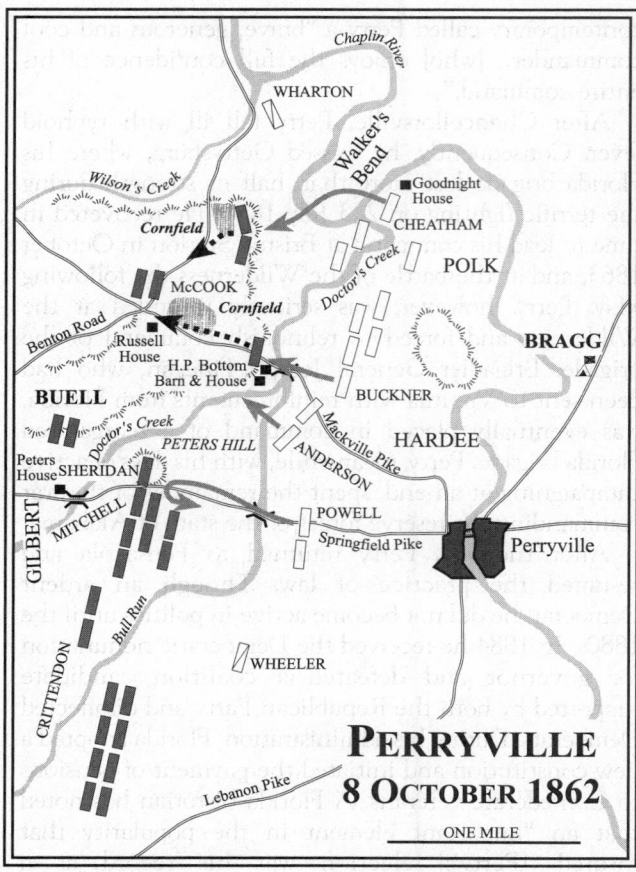

PERRYVILLE
8 OCTOBER 1862
ONE MILE

1 October 1862. He sent 20,000 men eastward to menace Kirby Smith, then led 58,000 men toward Bragg's army.

The failure of large numbers of Kentuckians to volunteer for Confederate service had sorely disappointed Bragg. Most of the few who did enlist wanted to ride with John Hunt Morgan. To get more men, Bragg left his army under the command of Major General Leonidas Polk and went to Lexington to confer with Kirby Smith and to install Governor Richard Hawes of the Provisional Government of Confederate Kentucky in Frankfort. Establishing that government would allow the Confederate Conscription Act of 16 April 1862 to be applied in the state. The installation occurred in Frankfort on 4 October, but the festivities planned for the evening had to be abandoned as Federal troops neared the city.

In the summer and fall of 1862 Kentucky experienced one of the worst droughts on record, and soldiers suffered severely from heat, stifling dust, and poor water as they maneuvered across the state. As Buell advanced toward Bardstown, Polk withdrew through Springfield and Perryville, where some water was available. Bragg ordered the two Confederate armies to concentrate at Harrodsburg; he expected to fight the Federals near

Salvisa, just south of Lawrenceburg. On the afternoon of 7 October three Federal columns approached Perryville. Buell was with Major General Charles Gilbert's III Corps on the Springfield Road, about three miles west of Perryville. Some seven miles to his left, Major General Alexander McCook's I Corps was at Mackville. To Gilbert's right, Major General Thomas Crittenden's II Corps was on the Lebanon Road, nearly ten miles from Perryville. Buell, believing that both Confederate armies were at Perryville, ordered the two flank corps to march at dawn. He intended to attack when all his 58,000 men were up on line.

When Bragg learned on 7 October that a large Union force was nearing Perryville, he ordered Major General William J. Hardee to halt his two divisions at Perryville. Later in the day he told Polk to take another division back to Perryville, defeat the Union force there, then come on to Harrodsburg. Polk reached Perryville during the night of 7–8 October. Learning of the strength of his opposition, he decided to form a strong defensive line instead of attacking. Bragg arrived about 10:00 A.M. on 8 October and was angry because the attack was not under way. He ordered an assault on the Union left flank at 1:00 P.M. With his strength concentrated north of the Springfield Road, he would follow up in echelon, drive the enemy back upon themselves along that road, and destroy it there. Polk, with Major General Benjamin Cheatham's division, would command the right; Hardee, with the divisions of Brigadier General James Patton Anderson and Major General Simon Bolivar Buckner, would direct the fighting on the center and left of the Confederate line.

On the Federal side, Gilbert's III Corps held the center position. McCook's I Corps came up and formed on his left. Crittenden's II Corps was delayed by Colonel Joseph Wheeler's 1,000 cavalry and two guns, so Buell was unable to open his assault as planned. Bragg's artillery opened fire around noon, but McCook's arrival had extended the Federal line so much that Polk had to move troops to the right to outflank it. Cheatham sent his three brigades across the shallow river and up the steep bank on its west side at 2:00 P.M. The Federals were surprised and, after savage fighting, were forced back in considerable disorder. Hardee hit McCook's right flank and drove it back nearly a mile with heavy losses on both sides.

While this desperate struggle was fought, Gilbert's corps beat back an attack by Colonel Samuel Powell's brigade. Bragg still did not realize that he faced more than a corps. Buckner's division, aided by a brigade from Anderson's division, also drove the Federals back. Gilbert did not provide the support that McCook needed, and the II Corps was relatively inactive, although Major General George H. Thomas, Buell's second-in-command, was with it. Because of an acoustic shadow, Buell, some miles in the rear, did not hear the

sound of the battle being waged in his lines. Finally notified of what was happening, he rode forward about 4:00 and sent two III Corps brigades to strengthen McCook's shattered force.

Darkness and exhaustion halted the battle, the largest fought in Kentucky during the war. The Union army had 845 killed and 2,851 wounded; the Confederates losses were 510 killed and 2,635 wounded. Wounded soldiers cried out for water during the night as weary surgeons operated to save as many as possible of the wounded.

Finally aware of the size of the army he faced, Bragg decided that night to move to Harrodsburg, where at last the two Confederate armies united. Buell did not oblige Bragg by attacking any of his strong positions, and Bragg, dismayed by supply problems and recruiting disappointments, decided not to risk the loss of the army that was essential for the defense of the western Confederacy. With Wheeler's horsemen covering the withdrawal from Buell's deliberate pursuit, Bragg and Kirby Smith withdrew through Cumberland Gap. Brigadier General Patrick R. Cleburne performed invaluable service by using his troops to drive the long wagon train through the gap without loss.

Kentucky would be raided often during the rest of the war, but this second and last Confederate invasion of the state had failed to win it for the Confederacy. After his comments about cowardly Kentuckians, Braxton Bragg became the Confederate commander most hated by Kentuckians.

—*Lowell H. Harrison*

See also Bragg, Braxton; Buckner, Simon Bolivar; Buell, Don Carlos; Cheatham, Benjamin Franklin; Hardee, William J.; Kentucky; Thomas, George H.; Wheeler, Joseph.

For further reading:

Connelly, Thomas L. *Army of the Heartland: The Army of Tennessee, 1861–1862* (1967).

Hafendorfer, Kenneth A. *Perryville: Battle for Kentucky* (1981).

McDonough, James L. *War in Kentucky: From Shiloh to Perryville* (1994).

McWhiney, Grady. *Braxton Bragg and Confederate Defeat* (1969).

Parks, Joseph H. *General Leonidas Polk, C.S.A.: The Fighting Bishop* (1962).

PERSONAL LIBERTY LAWS

During the antebellum era, abolitionists and their supporters throughout the North sought means that could be employed to battle slavery and its advocates in every conceivable way. For many of slavery's most zealous opponents, the opportunity to take an active role by assisting fugitives who had escaped, or stolen themselves, from slavery represented the ultimate commitment to the call of social justice and evangelical reform. Motivated by what they perceived to be a higher calling, abolitionists and their supporters mounted one of the earliest campaigns of civil disobedience in the

history of the United States. Taken collectively, the many individual actions of this cohort of reformers fashioned the so-called Underground network that helped fugitive slaves find their way to freedom.

When the states ratified the U.S. Constitution in 1789 they instituted a document that contained a fugitive slave clause (Article IV, Section 2) that stipulated the return of criminal fugitives and fugitives from labor. However, the clause neither stated who was responsible for conducting this action nor did it describe the process of recovering fugitives. Congress later enacted the Fugitive Slave Act of 1793 in an effort to clarify the vague provisions of how this constitutional guarantee should function, but many within the Northern states remained dissatisfied with specific internal weaknesses of this measure. Many believed that the act did not do enough to protect the civil liberties of free blacks who might be falsely accused of being fugitive slaves. Others balked at the act's recognition of the right of reception, the common law provision that Southern slaveowners maintained gave them the right to recapture their property without the burden of using the court system. Between 1780 and 1850, fourteen states enacted Personal Liberty Laws to protect the rights of free blacks within their jurisdictions by imposing a judicial hearing before a suspected fugitive could be removed from the state.

Southern slaveowners and the slave catchers that they hired to recover their fugitives maintained that these Northern laws were impositions that were illegally enacted to stymie their efforts at conducting a constitutionally sanctioned enterprise. Occasionally they used the courts themselves to challenge the validity of Personal Liberty Laws that seemed particularly onerous. In the case of *Prigg v. Pennsylvania*, 41 U.S. 539 (1842), the U.S. Supreme Court struck down an 1826 Pennsylvania law that had added additional hindrances to the process of recaption that were in violation of the Fugitive Slave Act of 1793. The Pennsylvania law had required that slave catchers obtain a "certificate of removal" from a local magistrate before removing a suspected fugitive from the state. The Supreme Court's ruling was a rather hollow victory for proslavery forces in that it asserted the constitutional right of recaption, but also stated that, while local and state officials should enforce the Fugitive Slave Act, the national government could not mandate such compliance. In the wake of the *Prigg* decision, local and state officials began to refuse to cooperate with slave catchers and this systematic noncompliance marked the effectual demise of the Fugitive Slave Act of 1793.

Southerners began to make strident demands for a new and stronger Federal Fugitive Slave Act, and by 1850 there was a discussion of secession from the Union by the slaveholding states if this demand was not met. Henry Clay included a provision for a Fugitive Slave Law

in his Omnibus Bill that the Congress considered in 1850, and this measure eventually won approval as a part of the Compromise of 1850. The Fugitive Slave Act of 1850 was much harsher than the 1793 measure, as it specifically forbade states from interfering with the process of recaption. Although the new act made it easier for the process of recaption to occur, most Northern states maintained their Personal Liberty Laws and urged noncompliance with what they perceived as an unjust law.

Despite Federal efforts to uphold the property rights of Southern slaveowners, many in the Northern states resisted all efforts to assist in the removal of suspected fugitives from their jurisdictions. They were willing to face the possibility of criminal prosecution for their efforts to aid runaway slaves who were seeking freedom, and they often risked life, limb, and reputation to protect the rights of free blacks who were unlawfully accused of being fugitive slaves. Perhaps more than any other example from the antebellum experience, Personal Liberty Laws represent the extent to which the slavery controversy polarized the nation as our constitutional system and our moral compass were set on a collision course with destiny.

—*Junius P. Rodriguez*

See also Abolitionist Movement; Abolitionists; Fugitive Slave Act; *Prigg v Pennsylvania*; Underground Railroad.
For further reading:
Campbell, Stanley W. *The Slave Catchers: Enforcement of the Fugitive Slave Law, 1850–1860* (1968).
Cover, Robert M. *Justice Accused: Anti-Slavery and the Judicial Process* (1975).
Morris, Thomas D. *Free Men All: The Personal Liberty Laws of the North, 1780–1861* (1974).
Rosenberg, Norman L. "Personal Liberty Laws and Sectional Crisis: 1850–1861." *Civil War History* (1971).

PETERSBURG CAMPAIGN
(15 June 1864–3 April 1865)

Petersburg, Virginia, situated on the Appomattox River's right bank twenty-three miles south of Richmond, was the second largest Virginia city and the seventh largest Confederate city in 1861. Nicknamed "the Cockade City," it housed an important lead works manufacturing bullets.

Railroads made Petersburg strategically significant, especially the Southside Railroad (running eastward from Tennessee) and the Weldon Railroad (connecting southward with blockade-runners' ports of Wilmington, North Carolina; Charleston, South Carolina; and Savannah, Georgia). A fifth railroad ran north from Petersburg through Chesterfield County to Richmond. Only one other railroad entered the capital from the south without passing through Petersburg. Petersburg

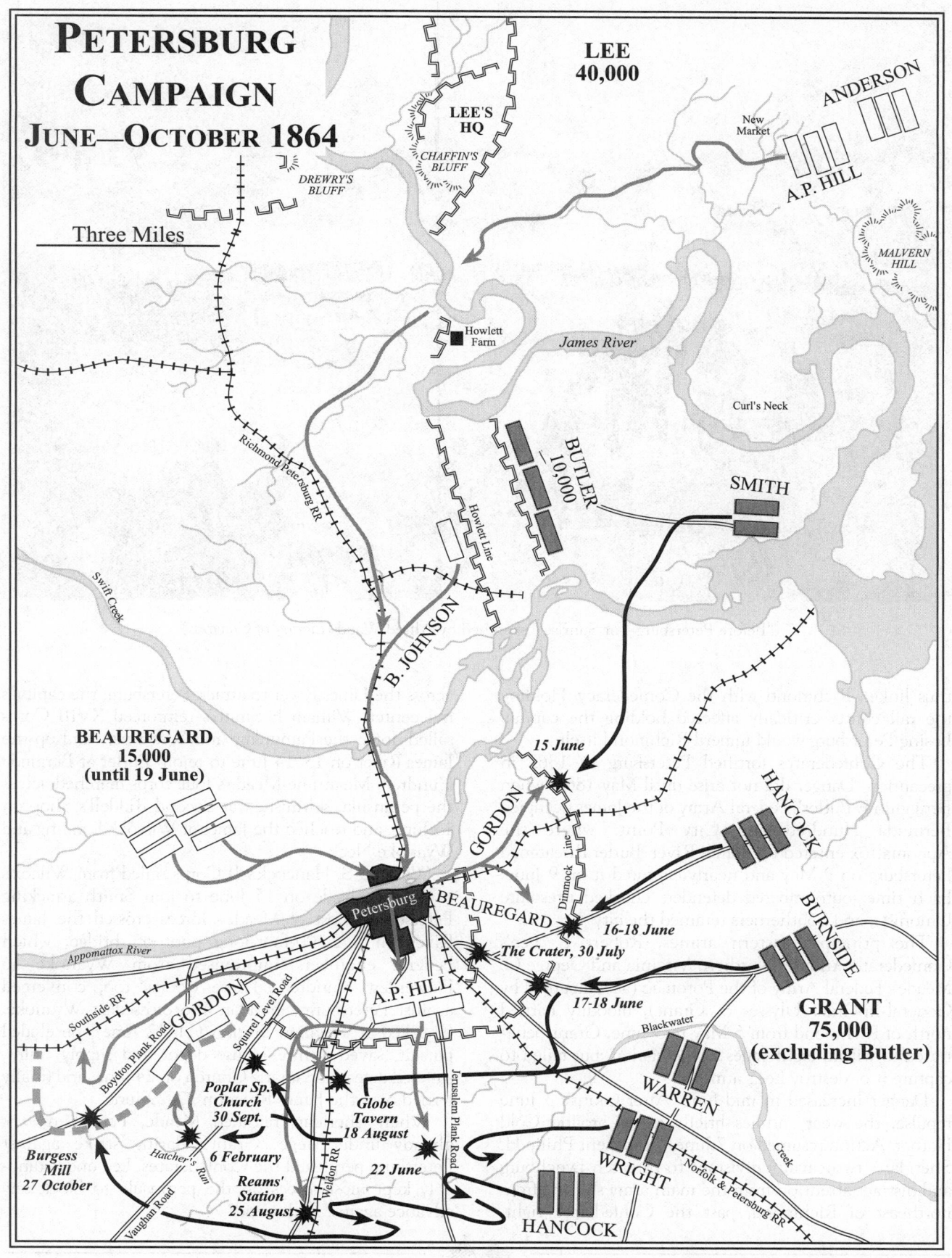

PETERSBURG
CAMPAIGN
JUNE—OCTOBER 1864

LEE
40,000

ANDERSON

New Market

A.P. HILL

DREWRY'S
BLUFF

Three Miles

LEE'S
HQ

CHAFFIN'S
BLUFF

MALVERN
HILL

Howlett Farm

James River

Curl's Neck

Richmond Petersburg RR

BUTLER
10,000

SMITH

Howlett Line

Swift Creek

B. JOHNSON

15 June

HANCOCK

BEAUREGARD
15,000
(until 19 June)

GORDON

Dimmock Line

BURNSIDE

Petersburg

BEAUREGARD

16-18 June

The Crater, 30 July

GRANT
75,000
(excluding Butler)

Appomattox River

Southside RR

GORDON

A.P. HILL

17-18 June

Blackwater

Boydton Plank Road

Squirrel Level Road

WARREN

Poplar Sp.
Church
30 Sept.

Globe
Tavern
18 August

Jerusalem Plank Road

WRIGHT

Burgess
Mill
27 October

Hatcher's Run

6 February

Weldon RR

22 June

Norfolk & Petersburg RR

Creek

Vaughan Road

Reams'
Station
25 August

HANCOCK

"Before Petersburg—at Sunrise," sketched by Alfred Waud (*Library of Congress*)

thus linked Richmond with the Confederacy. Holding the rail center critically affected holding the capital. Losing Petersburg would imperil Richmond itself.

The Confederates fortified Petersburg in 1862 in precaution. Danger did not arise until May 1864, when Benjamin F. Butler's Federal Army of the James occupied Bermuda Hundred and City Point, where the Appomattox entered the James River. Butler threatened Petersburg on 9 May and nearly captured it on 9 June. Each time, outnumbered defenders checked irresolute Unionists, and Southerners retained the city.

The principal eastern armies, Robert E. Lee's Confederate Army of Northern Virginia and George G. Meade's Federal Army of the Potomac (accompanied by General-in-Chief Ulysses S. Grant), bloodily battled north of Richmond from 5 May to 3 June. Grant penetrated to within eight miles of the capital, but failed to capture it or destroy Lee's army.

Danger increased in mid-June. After Grant's 3 June repulse, the weary armies briefly rested around Cold Harbor. Action resumed on 7 June. Grant sent Philip H. Sheridan's two cavalry divisions to threaten Lynchburg and distract attention from the main army shifting from northeast of Richmond, past the Confederate right,

across the James River to attack Petersburg, the capital's rail center. William F. Smith's reinforced XVIII Corps sailed down the Pamunkey and York rivers and up the James River on 13–14 June to rejoin Butler at Bermuda Hundred. Meantime Meade's four corps marched across the peninsula, skirmished at Second Riddell's Shop on 13 June, and reached the James at Wilcox's Landing and Wyanoke Neck.

Winfield S. Hancock's II Corps sailed from Wilcox's to the Southside on 15 June to join Smith attacking Petersburg. Most of Meade's forces crossed the James River on a 2,100-foot-long pontoon bridge, which Federal engineers improvised from Wyanoke to Flowerdew Hundred. Those troops, too, converged against Petersburg. Sheridan also crossed at Wyanoke. Checked at Trevilian Station (11–12 June), he eluded pursuit, saved White House depot and supply trains, suffered defeat at Samaria Church on 24 June, and finally ferried over the James River on 27–29 June.

When Sheridan rejoined Meade, Petersburg was already under siege. Grant's daring strike against Petersburg perplexed the Confederates. Lee understandably kept most forces on the peninsula to block any advance against Richmond.

Even after Smith attacked Petersburg, Lee pondered whether the greater danger lay south or north of the James River. He thus did not immediately comply with Petersburg commander P. G. T. Beauregard's desperate but ambiguous appeals for reinforcements. Beauregard had the equivalent of two brigades at Petersburg when the Union attacked on 15 June. Overnight, he recalled his other five brigades from Chesterfield County and received back four brigades from Lee. Lee also drove Butler back into Bermuda Hundred on 16–17 June. Not until 18 June, however, did the first division of Lee's own army join Beauregard's weary defenders at Petersburg. By then, Beauregard had saved the city. Although Grant's bold blow south of the James River achieved strategic surprise, his subordinates failed to follow through tactically. Smith, admittedly, stormed Petersburg's easterly permanent defenses on 15 June, but neither he nor Hancock captured the city. Reinforced by his own two divisions overnight, Beauregard dug trenches blocking Smith and fought desperately on 16–17 June against increasing Northern forces. Although losing additional permanent defenses and withdrawing to a second trench line, Beauregard saved the city. Victory was confirmed on 18 June, when Beauregard's defenders, now reinforced by Lee's vanguard, bloodily repulsed the onslaught by David B. Birney (Hancock's temporary replacement).

The 18 June debacle ended the frontal assaults that theretofore marked Grant's Virginia campaign. Not until the siege's final day would Grant again attack headlong fortifications considered well staffed. Ever learning from experience, the Illinoisan expressly prohibited frontal attacks. He instead relied on grand tactical and strategic flanking movements.

The first such movement came on 22 June, as he resumed the approach pursued since 4 May: moving his left around the Confederate right. Birney's II Corps advanced beyond the Jeruasalem Plank Road (Meade's left) toward the Weldon Railroad. Meantime Grant's two available cavalry divisions raided the Richmond-Danville Railroad. William Mahone's Confederates surprised and routed Birney on 22 June. The following day, Mahone trounced Horatio G. Wright's VI Corps' attempt to break the Weldon Railroad. On 24 June, however, an attempted Southern counterattack against Grant's right on the lower

Composite sketch by Alfred Waud of scenes from the Petersburg campaign. The center panel shows men digging the Dutch Gap Canal (*Library of Congress*)

Bivouac of the 5th Corps in the rifle pits, Petersburg campaign, sketched by Alfred Waud. (*Library of Congress*)

Appomattox fizzled. The Union cavalry raiders, meantime, failed to destroy Staunton River bridge on 25 June. Then Wade Hampton's Confederate cavalry, having checked Sheridan's Trevilian Raid, routed the Danville raiders at First Reams' Station on 29 June. The failure of Grant's Second Offensive, 22–29 June, ended the mobile warfare that raged in Virginia since 4 May. Operations now stagnated, and the true siege of Petersburg began. Three factors caused this fundamental change. Eight weeks of incessant fighting and staggering casualties had exhausted even veteran soldiers and generals. They needed rest to regain their fighting edge. Semistatic conditions of siege afforded some opportunity to recuperate.

Second, danger elsewhere diverted troops and attention. Before leaving Cold Harbor, Lee dispatched Jubal A. Early's four divisions to relieve Lynchburg. Early eluded Union intelligence until appearing on the upper Potomac River on 5 July. Grant rushed Wright plus the arriving XIX Corps to confront this threat to Washington. In July and August, Sheridan and two cavalry divisions transferred to the Shenandoah Valley. Their departure gave Confederate cavalry at Petersburg

numerical superiority over Union cavalry until Sheridan returned in March.

Grant, as general-in-chief, always heeded Shenandoah Valley operations as well as those at Petersburg and Richmond. Lee, too, oversaw the entire Eastern theater and shifted forces between both fronts. Yet the Virginian was now tied down securing the two cities. After raising the first siege of Richmond in June 1862, he protected the capital best by keeping the Northerners far away, a strategy that succeeded through 1863. Grant denied him that option in 1864 and forced him into the constricting strategic imperative of closely defending Richmond and Petersburg. Lee could afford to abandon outer positions from Orange to Hanover. He could not yield his capital and its communications center. That reality is the third reason why operations stagnated into siege.

Yet the situation at Petersburg was not a classic European tactical siege, where attackers sought either to breach, undermine, or storm walls or else to starve surrounded cities into submission. Petersburg was never surrounded, and its siege was waged strategically. Grant's preexisting position at Bermuda Hundred and his fortified lines from the lower Appomattox to the Jerusalem Plank Road east of Petersburg formed a great entrenched camp from which he launched "offensives," or expeditions, north of the James River against Richmond or south of Petersburg through largely unfortified regions toward the two remaining railroads, the Weldon and Southside (the other two railroads east of Petersburg were captured in mid-June). Meanwhile, Lee from his fortifications at Petersburg and opposite Bermuda Hundred counterattacked expeditions threatening Richmond or his communications. These expeditions and Lee's countermoves characterized the remainder of the siege of Petersburg. The incessant shelling and sharpshooting east of the city were merely background noise as the siege played out elsewhere.

As Early's raid passed crisis but continued threatening, both sides at Petersburg spent July quiescently, trying to regain combat capability. Grant, who controlled the initiative throughout the siege, resumed attacking on 27 July. His Third Offensive opened with Hancock and Sheridan joining Birney, now commanding the X Corps of Butler's army, sallying from the Deep Bottom bridgehead on the north bank of the James River opposite Bermuda Hundred. They overran Joseph B. Kershaw's outer trenches, but stalled before New Market Heights and had to repel Richard H. Anderson's counterattacks on 28 July. The Union withdrawal across the James River on 29 July meant that the First Deep Bottom expedition failed to capture Richmond or cut railroads linking Lee and Early. It

succeeded, however, in drawing four Confederate divisions from the Southside, thus leaving only four divisions protecting Petersburg.

Grant exploited this vulnerability by launching the second prong of his Third Offensive: a massive mine under the secessionist works east of Petersburg. The explosion on 30 July surprised attackers almost as much as defenders. Ambrose E. Burnside's IX Corps failed to pour through the breach into Petersburg but stalled inside the crater. Beauregard contained the breakthrough, and Mahone's counterattacks restored the line. His Crater failure cost Burnside his command. This fiasco, often synonymous with Petersburg, was really an aberration unrepresentative of the siege.

Disgusted but undaunted, Grant waited two weeks and then unleashed his Fourth Offensive. Its purposes again were preventing four divisions from reinforcing Early and also exploiting Confederate weakness around Petersburg. Anderson and Sheridan with two divisions each had already departed, but the offensive forced Lee to detain two other divisions. Hancock, Birney, and David M. Gregg (now commanding Meade's remaining cavalry) again attacked from Deep Bottom on 14 August. They overran outworks and briefly penetrated the Southern left at Fussell's Kill on 16 August. But again, Confederates (under Charles W. Field after Anderson's departure) stopped the Unionists, retained New Market Heights, and recaptured the mill. This time, however, Hancock's force remained on the peninsula until 19 August to distract attention from Meade's attack below Petersburg.

Pontoon bridge across the Appomattox River at Petersburg, 1865 (*Library of Congress*)

Union railroad gun and crew near Petersburg, 1864–1865 (*Library of Congress*)

Gouverneur K. Warren's V Corps led that attack on 18 August, cutting the Weldon Railroad at Globe Tavern and repulsing Henry Heth's counterattacks. Mahone's stronger counterattack on 19 August threatened to sever Warren from Meade, but Orlando B. Willcox's two IX Corps divisions' timely arrival stabilized Warren's position. A massive counterattack by Lee himself on 21 August totally failed, and Meade continued clutching the Weldon Railroad at Globe Tavern for the siege's duration. However, efforts to destroy those tracks southward from the tavern failed, as Hampton's and A. P. Hill's thirteen brigades routed Hancock's nine brigades at Second Reams' Station on 25 August.

Lee now accepted loss of uninterrupted use of the Weldon Railroad. He, however, continued bringing supplies to that line's Stony Creek Depot railhead and then transshipping them by wagon via Dinwiddie County back roads to the Boydton Plank Road and then to Petersburg. Protecting those wagon roads and his one remaining railroad (the Southside) dominated Southern strategy for the remainder of the siege. Cutting those communications comparably claimed Grant's immediate concern.

Heth and Field now dug outer trenches along the Squirrel Level Road confronting Globe Tavern and inner log works paralleling the Plank Road. Extending those defenses southward and southwestward from Petersburg further attenuated Lee's small army. Yet his numerical cavalry superiority afforded mobility in covering threatened sectors, and he also maintained small mobile infantry reserves. Grant, too, had to divert part of his big force garrisoning his gains. The V and IX Corps thus left two brigades each in the new works securing the August conquests when operations resumed in September. Confederates' superior mobility and familiarity with terrain in regions that Grant had not previously penetrated plus the division of Federal forces among large garrisons and two-pronged attacks on each side of the James River affected operations all autumn.

Those factors influenced Grant's fifth offensive, which erupted on 29 September. Sheridan's valley victories on 19 and 22 September hastened that operation, as Lee returned Kershaw to Early and Grant tried to prevent more Confederates from going there. Yet the Illinoisan sought grander goals—Richmond and Petersburg themselves. Federal intelligence showed the lightly guarded capital vulnerable; Butler launched a surprise attack against that city on 29 September. Birney again stalled before New Market Heights, but Edward

Ord's XVIII Corps breached outer defenses at Fort Harrison, rendering the heights untenable and throwing Richmond into its greatest danger during the entire war. Yet Butler's failure to exploit this opportunity plus heroic resistance by Richard S. Ewell's outnumbered defenders saved the city and gave Lee time to lead reinforcements from Petersburg. However, Anderson's grand counterattack against Fort Harrison on 30 September totally failed. Unlike in July and August, the Northerners remained on the peninsula for the rest of the siege. Expanding from their Deep Bottom bridgehead to a full army sector so directly threatened Richmond that Lee had to leave in Henrico County a countering corps, first under Anderson and then under James Longstreet.

Bombproof quarters at Fort Sedgwick, Petersburg, 1865 (*Library of Congress*)

Soldiers in the trenches before battle, Petersburg, 1865 (*National Archives*)

To save Richmond, the Virginian considered abandoning Petersburg on 30 September. Yet he did not yield to threats, but fought for both cities. When Warren stormed the Squirrel Level Line beyond Poplar Spring Church that afternoon, the Boydton Plank Road appeared vulnerable. But when John G. Parke's IX Corps finally groped toward that highway, A. P. Hill (the departed Beauregard's successor as Petersburg's chief defender) counterattacked by surprise, routing Parke. However, Heth's larger counterattack on 1 October failed, and Meade remained secure in his captures around Peebles's Farm.

On both sides of the James River, fighting subsided on 1–2 October. It resumed as Birney repulsed Anderson at First Darbytown Road on 7 October; as Meade and Hill skirmished at Second Squirrel Level Road on 8 October; and as Anderson checked Alfred Terry's X Corps at Second Darbytown Road on 13 October. Basically, however, Grant allowed mid-October's ideal campaigning weather to pass unprofited while awaiting reinforcements. Thirty-two new regiments joined him in September and October, but Sheridan's veterans, detained by their Cedar Creek victory on 19 October, did not arrive until December.

Grant's Sixth Offensive did not wait that long.

Apparently seeking another victory before the presidential election on 8 November, Grant attacked on 27 October. Butler and Meade struck simultaneously in respective hopes of getting around Longstreet's left into Richmond and around Hill's right to the Southside Railroad. Heavy rain, difficult terrain, inaccurate maps, and Confederate resistance delayed them. Longstreet simply shifted leftward up Richmond's Exterior Defense Line and repelled Godfrey Weitzel's XVIII Corps at Second Fair Oaks. Meantime, Hill, who had previously extended his right along the Plank Road to Hatcher's Run, parried Warren and Parke. Hancock and Gregg, advancing south of that stream, hit a hornets' nest at Burgess' Mill. After repulsing Mahone's, Heth's, and Hampton's counterattacks, Hancock was lucky to extricate his isolated strike force. Beaten on each front, both Union armies withdrew to their original lines on 28 October.

The Sixth Offensive's complete failure led the flexible Grant again to rethink strategy. Previously, he launched two-pronged attacks on each side of the James River. Their timing evolved from July's sequential strikes through August's and September's overlapping operations to October's simultaneous sorties. The strategy, however, remained constant: the peninsula push might prove productive, but it at least should draw defenders from Petersburg, where the second strike could achieve greater advantage. After 27 October, Grant changed to massive first strikes with his left against supply lines through Dinwiddie County. Thenceforth, his right wing on the peninsula became like his center east of Petersburg, a static force preventing defenders from countering his left wing. This new strategy emerged on 7–12 December, as Warren led five divisions southward from Globe Tavern, destroying the Weldon Railroad and the Stony Creek Depot railhead. The Federals skirmished at Hicksford-Belfield but eluded Hill's pursuit and returned from this "Applejack Raid" with canteens and bellies much too full of hard cider.

By then, many valley veterans had returned to Richmond and Petersburg: Wright and another infantry division, to Grant; Kershaw and John B. Gordon's II Corps, to Lee. Yet in December and January, each side sent seven brigades to the Carolinas. Those Federal forces under Terry closed blockade runners' access to Wilmington on 15 January. Eight days later, the Confederate naval squadron attempted exploiting Terry's absence by striking down the flooded James River toward Grant's great City Point supply depot. Although the one Union ironclad fled, the Southern ships characteristically malfunctioned or grounded on obstructions, and Federal artillery sank one gunboat. The Confederates withdrew far short of City Point. Fiasco though it was, this battle of Trent's Reach proved the largest naval combat of the siege. It also proved the last battle in Henrico. Thereafter, the siege focused on Southside, Virginia. Grant's Seventh Offensive saw Andrew A. Humphreys's Federal II Corps move southwestward to Armstrong's kill, repulsing Gordon's counterattack on 5 February. Farther southwest, Gordon recaptured Dabney's Mill on 6 February, but could not overcome Warren's final line. When fighting ended on 7 February, Meade's left reached Hatcher's Run.

Grant's slow but seemingly inexorable drive deeper into Dinwiddie County tightened his grip upon Petersburg. The siege had now become grand strategic. As general-in-chief, Grant used armies in the Shenandoah Valley, Tennessee, Georgia, and the Carolinas to devour the Confederacy while he fixed Lee in Virginia. By March, those armies were converging from northwest, west, and south. Still, Lee remained pinned at Petersburg.

Yet now, as throughout the war, the great Confederate commander battled back. Gordon's surprise strike against Parke east of Petersburg on 23 March, Lee hoped, would cause the Union left to recoil upon the threatened center, thus loosening its clutch southwest of Petersburg and allowing his escape to North Carolina. Gordon initially stormed Fort Stedman, but Parke soon recap-

tured it. Meantime, Humphreys and Wright on the Federal left, hardly recoiling, overran Hill's entrenched picket line and fixed their grip even more tightly.

Four days later, Grant's final offensive began. Sheridan, whose two cavalry divisions had raided back from the valley in March, led the new drive on the far left. More importantly, Grant shifted four of six divisions of Ord's (Butler's successor) from Henrico to Dinwiddie, undetected. While Longstreet idled near Richmond, Grant achieved strategic surprise—massing sixteen divisions against seven Confederate divisions guarding Petersburg's communications.

Despite such odds, Lee bravely counterattacked. Anderson slowed Warren near Gravelly Run and White Oak Road on 29–31 March. George Pickett, whose division replaced Mahone's in mobile reserve, and Fitzhugh Lee (the departed Hampton's successor commanding three cavalry divisions) drove Sheridan to Dinwiddie Court House on 31 March. Affairs reversed on 1 April, as Sheridan and Warren together routed Pickett at Five Forks. Tragically, after winning, Sheridan removed Warren, ruining the career of a general so central to Federal success from Globe Tavern to Five Forks.

Five Forks crushed Hill's mobile reserve. Decisive victory came the following day as Grant assaulted the entire line on the Southside. Mahone in Chesterfield and Gordon at Petersburg repelled those onslaughts. Further southwest, Grant fared better. Lee had long lacked sufficient personnel to attack successfully; now his forces were stretched too thin even to defend successfully. Cadmus M. Wilcox's four Confederate brigades could not hold a sector designed for eight brigades. Wright broke this line at Boisseau's house and then swept southward to trap two brigades against Hatcher's Run. Ord, after initially skirmishing with those brigades, passed behind Wright and moved against Petersburg. Two Confederate brigades in Forts Gregg and Alexander repeatedly repulsed Ord's XXIV Corps. By the time those forts fell, Longstreet finally staffed Petersburg's inner defenses with Field's division from Henrico.

Field saved Petersburg but only for one day. Grant now ringed the city from west and, south, as well as east. Also, on 2 April Humphreys drove Heth from the Southside Railroad at Sutherland's Station. The last supply lines southward were now lost. Holding Petersburg longer risked repeating the fate of Fort Donelson and Vicksburg. Overnight on 2–3 April, Lee abandoned Petersburg, Chesterfield, Henrico, and Richmond itself and fled for North Carolina. North Carolina, however, proved too distant. Lee's army was too fatally crippled by the siege. Grant's forces occupied too advantageous a strategic position. One week after the final fighting at Petersburg came Appomattox.

A. P. Hill, long the Cockade City's chief defender, was slain that final, fatal 2 April. Seven other Confederate generals perished in combat during the siege: Victor Gieardey and John Chambliss on 16 August, John Sanders on 21 August, John Dunovant on 1 October, John Gregg on 7 October, Archibald Gracie on 2 December, and John Pegram on 6 February. James Archer died of illness on 24 October. In contrast, four Union generals died: St. Clair Morton on 17 June and Hiram Burnham on 29 September, in battle; and Joshua Howell on 14 September and David Birney on 18 October, from other causes. This discrepancy, however, reflects the reality that colonels led most Federal brigades. Sixteen such Northern brigadiers or brevet brigadiers were killed or died, 11 June 1864–13 June 1865. Union combat casualties throughout the siege totalled approximately 61,500, including 53,000 during Grant's eight offensives. Determining Southern combat losses is harder. A reasonable estimate is 38,000, including 9,700 from 29 March to 2 April.

Yet Petersburg's importance is measured not just in soldiers' lives but in armies' and nations' lives. The siege demonstrated how Lee, through masterful defense and willingness to fight against great odds, prolonged the life of his army and his nation another forty-two weeks. It also demonstrated how Grant, inflexible in resolve and flexible in methods, learned from experience as he eventually found ways to apply the North's potential advantages. He fixed the Southerners in place through a strategic siege, waged a war of strategic (not tactical) attrition, and thereby fatally weakened the once mighty Army of Northern Virginia and, with it, the Confederacy itself.

—*Richard J. Sommers*

See also Bermuda Hundred Campaign; Crater, Battle of the; Deep Bottom Run/Strawberry Plains, Virginia, Second Battle of; Early's Washington Raid; Globe Tavern, Virginia.

For further reading:
Davis, William C. *Death in the Trenches: Grant at Petersburg* (1986).
Humphreys, Andrew A. *The Virginia Campaign of 1864 and 1865; The Army of the Potomac and the Army of the James* (1883).
Sommers, Richard J. *Richmond Redeemed: The Siege at Petersburg* (1981).
Trudeau, Noah Andre. *The Last Citadel: Petersburg, Virginia, June 1864–April 1865* (1991).

PETIGRU, JAMES LOUIS
(1789–1863)
South Carolina Unionist

James Louis Petigru was born on 10 May 1789 in the South Carolina upcountry near Abbeville, the first son of William Pettigrew and Louise Gibert. When Petigru was a boy, his father's inability to provide for his family left young James to shoulder many familial responsibilities, a role he would fill throughout his life. Petigru enrolled in Moses Waddel's academy in Willington in 1804 and entered South Carolina College in 1806. He graduated three years later at the top of his class.

Renouncing his impoverished past, Petigru changed the spelling of his name and became a schoolmaster in the small village of Eutaw. There he met Daniel E. Huger, a local planter who would become a valuable mentor. Huger helped Petigru obtain a teaching position at Beaufort College and arranged for him to study law with a local attorney. Admitted to the bar in 1812, Petigru began his practice in Coosawatchie, the court town of Beaufort District. In 1816 Huger sponsored Petigru's election as the Beaufort District solicitor. The same year Petigru married Jane Amelia Postell, with whom he would have four children.

In 1819 Petigru became the junior partner of James Hamilton, Jr., a powerful Charleston lawyer, and moved his family to that city. When Hamilton left Charleston in 1822 to serve in Congress, Petigru inherited his extensive practice. In the same year, he was elected state attorney general, a post he held for eight years. During the 1820s, Petigru steadily built his reputation as a talented lawyer known for his tightly reasoned arguments and breadth of knowledge. By 1830 he ranked among Charleston's social elite, a status he solidified with the purchase of a Savannah River rice plantation.

Like other aspiring young men of his day, Petigru became embroiled in the controversy over the tariff of 1828. Petigru was no supporter of the so-called "tariff of abominations," but he deplored as reckless and unconstitutional the extreme proposal to nullify federal law, and he quickly became a leading spokesman for the Unionist opposition. Resigning his attorney general post in 1830 to take an active role in the fight, he won a spot on the city council and a legislative seat in a special election. The Unionists, however, proved little match for the politically powerful nullification clique. Nullifiers routed the Unionists in 1832 and swiftly organized a nullification convention. The crisis subsided when a compromise tariff was settled in Congress, but a new controversy soon arose over a nullifier-sponsored test oath requiring all state officers to pledge their primary allegiance to South Carolina. Petigru again played a major role in the conflict. In his March 1834 defense of a militia officer who refused to take the oath, Petigru denounced the oath as an infringement of individual liberties and a threat to the supremacy of the U.S. Constitution. He later negotiated a secret compromise with his former law partner Hamilton that reconciled the oath with the allegiance owed by South Carolina citizens to the United States.

Petigru had defended his principles, but he had fatally injured his political prospects. He was elected to the legislature again in 1836 but lost in 1838; thereafter he largely shunned public office. His political aspirations dashed, Petigru turned his attention toward achieving economic success, a necessity caused partly by his wife's extravagance, his support of his siblings, and a generosity that his longtime friend William Grayson once called "so profuse as to call for restraint." His plans backfired after he engaged in numerous ill-fated ventures in the 1830s that ruined him financially. By the end of the decade, he was forced to sell his plantation; only an 1842 agreement with several banks to settle his outstanding debts for ten cents on the dollar saved him from complete ruin. His financial embarrassment forced him to maintain an extremely active legal practice for the rest of his life.

Petigru continued to be out of step with South Carolina politics throughout his life. In a state decisively opposed to Whiggery, he favored state funding for internal improvements and supported the Whig economic program. As a lawyer, he distinguished himself for his concern for civil liberties and loyalty to the federal Constitution, notably in his representation of the British Consulate in their challenge of South Carolina laws requiring the imprisonment of black sailors while their ships were in port. Despite his persistent Whiggery and Unionism, Petigru retained his professional preeminence. In 1859 he was appointed to codify the state's law, a monumental task that he completed three years later. Rejected by the legislature in 1865, the code was adopted with modifications in 1872.

Petigru watched sadly as the nation careered toward war during the 1850s and secessionist sentiment mounted in his state. He backed the Unionist candidate John Bell in 1860 and was virtually the only vocal opponent of secession in South Carolina. His famous assessment that South Carolina was too small to be a nation and too large for an insane asylum reflected his scorn for the state's radical leadership. Yet Petigru, who had been a slaveholder since marriage and whose Savannah River plantation had 125 slaves at its peak, never questioned slavery. He retained more than 20 slaves at his Charleston residence after the sale of his plantation, and despite financial difficulties he continued to purchase slaves through the 1850s. His feelings toward slavery might be best described merely as "dissent from proslavery exuberance."

Petigru remained in South Carolina during the war but never supported the Confederacy. While he deplored the Confederacy's confiscation acts and defended former clients who had moved north against claims on their property, he was primarily occupied by his exhausting work on the legal code and his grief for family members who were killed or wounded in war. The destruction of his Charleston home by fire in December 1861 dealt another cruel blow. Petigru's health deteriorated rapidly during the war, and he died two months shy of his seventy-fourth birthday. As his body was brought to the St. Michael's Church cemetery, prominent men of Charleston and Confederate officers stationed in the city gathered to pay homage to the brilliant lawyer. In death as in life, his dignity and civility, devotion to justice, and courage to dissent inspired a respect that transcended political differences.

—*Susan Wyly-Jones*

See also South Carolina.
For further reading:

Carson, James Petigru, ed. *The Life, Letters, and Speeches of James Louis Petigru, the Union Man of South Carolina* (1920).
Ford, Lacy, Jr. "James Louis Petigru: The Last South Carolina Federalist." In *Intellectual Life in Antebellum Charleston* (1986).
Pease, William H., and Jane H. Pease. *James Louis Petigru: South Carolina Lawyer, Southern Unionist, and American Conservative* (1995).

PETTIGREW, JAMES JOHNSTON
(1828–1863)
Confederate general

James Johnston Pettigrew was born on 4 July 1828 at Bonarva, the Tyrrell County, North Carolina, plantation of his parents, Ebenezer and Ann Blount Shepard Pettigrew. Young Pettigrew was called Johnston by his friends and family. He was a phenomenally brilliant student and was an especially gifted mathematician. He entered the University of North Carolina at the age of fourteen, and graduated as the class valedictorian in 1847. After graduation, he spent six months as a professor at the Naval Observatory in Washington. From 1850 to 1852 Pettigrew studied law at the University of Berlin and traveled through much of Europe. He became fascinated with Spain and Italy, which he felt had much in common with the chivalric ideals, tradition, and hospitality of the American South.

Returning to America, Pettigrew joined the law firm of a cousin, James Louis Petigru of Charleston. (Petigru had reverted to the French spelling of the name.) Pettigrew flourished in Charleston, practicing law and serving in the legislature. He became convinced that a sectional war was coming, and dedicated himself to serving in the South Carolina militia and teaching himself about military science. In 1859 he returned to Europe to join the war for Italian independence, hoping to help this cause and to gain military experience. The war ended as he arrived, but he spent some time visiting military camps and studying with some French officers. After leaving Italy Pettigrew went to Spain and gathered materials for a book, *Notes on Spain and the Spaniards in the Summer of 1859, with a Glance at Sardinia*, which he published in 1861. Pettigrew spoke several languages, including Hebrew and Arabic. He intended to write a history of the Moors in Spain, but the Civil War ended his plans for that work.

Pettigrew was so well regarded as an authority on military matters that when South Carolina left the Union in December 1860, he was appointed as chief military aide to Governor Francis W. Pickens and became colonel of the 1st South Carolina Rifles. On 27 December, after the Federal garrison at Charleston slipped away to Fort Sumter, Pettigrew was sent with a protest from the governor. Later that day Pettigrew led a small detachment that occupied Castle Pinckney. From January 1861 until the firing on Fort Sumter, he was in charge of various South Carolina army camps around Charleston Harbor.

After Fort Sumter, Pettigrew wanted a post that would allow him to lead men in combat; he avoided service on military boards or staffs. Finding nothing to his liking, he went to Virginia as a private in Hampton's Legion. While there, on 11 July 1861, he learned that he had been elected, nearly unanimously, as colonel of the 22d North Carolina. During the winter of 1861–1862, his regiment took part in the Confederate blockade of the Potomac. Pettigrew refused promotion to brigadier general several times, feeling that he should not accept such rank without having led troops in battle. He finally consented in March 1862.

Pettigrew's Brigade, which included his 22d North Carolina, and units from Georgia, Virginia, Arkansas, and Maryland, fought at Seven Pines on 31 May 1862. Pettigrew was shot through the throat while observing the enemy lines. He thought the wound was fatal and refused to be moved to the rear. Pettigrew was left behind and reported dead on the field when his men withdrew. He was shot again and bayoneted before he was taken prisoner the next day.

Pettigrew was exchanged in August 1862 and given a new brigade, made up of the 11th, 26th, 44th, 47th, and 52d North Carolina Regiments. His brigade was sent to southeastern Virginia and eastern North Carolina from September 1862 to May 1863, where it took part in several small battles around Washington and New Bern.

In May 1863 Pettigrew's brigade was sent to the Army of Northern Virginia and assigned to Henry Heth's Division. At Gettysburg on 1 July, Pettigrew's brigade drove enemy troops, including the famous Iron Brigade, from McPherson's Ridge. Pettigrew took command of the division when Heth was wounded. The brigade lost heavily in officers and men on 1 July. The 26th North Carolina's losses reached 72 percent, the highest loss in a single day of any regiment in the war, according to authority William F. Fox.

On 2 July Pettigrew and Heth's division were granted some rest, but they were called to action again on 3 July. Lee planned a frontal assault on the center of the Union lines on Cemetery Ridge, which has become known as Pickett's Charge. The fresh division of Major General George Pickett made up the right of the assaulting force. Heth's Division, led by Pettigrew, was on the left, with two brigades of Pender's Division behind them. They were unable to break the lines on Cemetery Ridge and withdrew with terrible losses. Pettigrew was wounded in the hand, and led his men on foot after his horse was shot.

In the retreat from Gettysburg, Pettigrew was shot in the stomach on 14 July in a rear guard action near the Potomac at Falling Waters, Maryland. Although told it would be fatal to move him, Pettigrew refused to remain and be captured again. He insisted on going with the army, and was taken to Bunker Hill, in present-day West Virginia, where he died on 17 July.

Pettigrew was buried in Raleigh, but his body was moved to the family graveyard at Bonarva after the war. The fallen general was mourned and honored by his native state. His name was memorialized in Pettigrew Hospital, established in Raleigh in 1864, and the 1912 Battle-Vance-Pettigrew Building at the University of North Carolina. In 1939 much of the land of Bonarva Plantation was incorporated into Pettigrew State Park, North Carolina's sixth state park.

—*David A. Norris*

See also Falling Waters, Battle of; Gettysburg, Battle of.
For further reading:
Tucker, Glenn. *High Tide at Gettysburg: The Campaign in Pennsylvania* (1958).
Wilson, Clyde N. *Carolina Cavalier: The Life and Mind of James Johnston Pettigrew* (1990).
———. *The Most Promising Young Man of the South: James Johnston Pettigrew and His Men at Gettysburg* (1998).

PETTUS, EDMUND WINSTON
(1821–1907)
Confederate general

Born in Limestone County, Alabama, to John Pettus and Alice Taylor Winston Pettus, Edmund Winston Pettus was educated locally and in Tennessee. He studied law and opened a practice in Gainesville, Alabama. He volunteered for service in the Mexican-American War, where he served as a lieutenant in an Alabama regiment. After the war Pettus briefly immigrated to California seeking his fortune. Failing in that endeavor, Pettus returned to Alabama, where he resumed the practice of law in the town of Carrollton. Besides his practice, Pettus became involved in local politics, and from 1855 to 1858 he served as a judge of the state's 7th circuit. Pettus resumed his law practice in 1858 in Cahaba, Alabama.

As the sectional crisis became more intense, Pettus supported states' rights and, after the election of Abraham Lincoln, secession. In early 1861, as the

Alabama Secession Convention met, Governor Andrew Moore sent Pettus to as a commissioner to Mississippi to urge the cooperation of the two states. Moore sent emissaries to all the Gulf states, and Pettus was chosen for Mississippi because his brother, John J. Pettus, was the governor of Mississippi.

With the formation of the Confederacy, Pettus chose the military rather than the political life. He entered the 20th Alabama as a major. Promoted to lieutenant colonel the following year, Pettus continued to fight with the 20th Alabama under Major General Edmund Kirby Smith in eastern Tennessee and went with Kirby Smith in Braxton Bragg's invasion of Kentucky in the fall of 1862. With Vicksburg, Mississippi, threatened at the end of 1862, Pettus and the 20th Alabama were added to its defensive force.

Pettus was captured at Port Gibson on 1 May 1863 but escaped a few days later. A few weeks later, Pettus became the commander of the 20th and was commended by Lieutenant General John C. Pemberton for his actions in the entrenchments outside Vicksburg. A few days later, Brigadier General Stephen D. Lee referred to Pettus's actions in defense of some of Vicksburg's works as the bravest deeds he had ever seen. When Vicksburg fell on 4 July 1863, Pettus surrendered with the rest of Pemberton's army.

Paroled shortly after the surrender, Pettus was promoted to brigadier general in September 1863 and went to Chattanooga commanding a brigade of Major General Carter L. Stevenson's division. The U.S. government held that the entire division, including Pettus, began fighting before they had been legally exchanged, thus violating their parole.

In the fall of 1863, Pettus fought in the battles around Chattanooga, including Lookout Mountain and Missionary Ridge. In December 1863 Pettus became a part of Joseph Johnston's Army of Tennessee headquartered at Dalton, Georgia, after Johnston assumed command from Braxton Bragg. Pettus participated in the Atlanta campaign and led his brigade in John Bell Hood's Tennessee campaign the following fall. When Johnston resumed command, Pettus participated in the Carolinas campaign of early 1865 and was wounded during the Confederate retreat from Bentonville on 21 March 1865. Pettus recovered sufficiently to resume the campaign and surrendered with Johnston's army in April 1865.

After the war, Pettus lived in Selma, Alabama, resuming his law practice and interest in Democratic politics. He was an Alabama delegate to the national Democratic convention six times between 1876 and 1896, and from 1897 until 1907 he served as U.S. senator from Alabama. He died in office while on vacation in North Carolina.

—*David S. Heidler and Jeanne T. Heidler*

See also Bentonville, Battle of; Port Gibson, Battle of; Vicksburg Campaign.
For further reading:
Berry, Thelma Caine. *The Life of Edmund Winston Pettus* (1941).

PETTUS, JOHN JONES
(1813–1867)
Governor of Mississippi

The son of John Pettus and Alice Taylor Winston Pettus and brother of Confederate general Edmund Winston Pettus, John Jones Pettus was born in Wilson County, Tennessee. He moved as a child with his family to Alabama, where he was educated. As a young man, Pettus moved to Mississippi, where he became a successful planter and was active in Democratic state politics. He gained a reputation as a strong supporter of states' rights and carried those beliefs into both houses of the state legislature between 1846 and 1858. The year he left the upper house of the state legislature, he was elected governor of Mississippi. He served in that position from 1859 until 1863.

Upon the election of Abraham Lincoln in November 1860, Pettus supported the secession of Mississippi. That task accomplished, Pettus's primary concern for the next three years was the defense of the state. In January 1861, before the war started, he sent troops to Pensacola, Florida, to help take control of that city. With the formation of the Confederacy, he communicated regularly with President Jefferson Davis and the Confederate War Department in efforts to secure greater protection for the Mississippi coastline and the Mississippi River. Pettus also worked tirelessly throughout the remainder of his term to increase production within the state of supplies for Confederate troops.

During the greatest trial of his governorship, the campaign against and the siege of Vicksburg, Pettus worked closely with Lieutenant General John Pemberton in attempting to shore up the defenses of this strategic city. The cooperation with Pemberton, however, became increasingly difficult as the siege tightened, and Pettus was forced out of the state capital at Jackson by Grant's forces.

When Pettus left office at the end of his term in late 1863, he joined the state's defensive forces at the rank of colonel. He served in that capacity until the end of the war.

After the war, Pettus moved to Arkansas, where he lived in obscurity. He died in Arkansas.

—*David S. Heidler and Jeanne T. Heidler*

See also Mississippi; Vicksburg Campaign.
For further reading:
Dubay, Robert William. *John Jones Pettus, Mississippi Fire-eater: His Life and Times, 1813–1867* (1975).

PHELAN, JAMES
(1821–1873)
Confederate senator

Born to John Phelan and Priscilla Oakes Ford Phelan in Huntsville, Alabama, James Phelan as a young man worked as a journalist, including briefly editing his own paper and serving as state printer for a year. Not finding journalism to his liking and finding it difficult to make a living, Phelan studied law. After his admission to the bar in 1846, he practiced briefly in Huntsville before moving to Mississippi in 1849. He quickly gained the reputation as one of the best attorneys in the state. Along with his legal practice, Phelan also became active in Mississippi Democratic politics. Phelan was a strong advocate of Southern rights and for that reason was elected to the Mississippi senate in 1860.

A very close friend of Jefferson Davis, Phelan used his position in the Mississippi government to keep Davis informed about the situation in the state after Davis was elected president of the Confederacy. In the fall of 1861, Phelan was elected to the First Confederate Congress and took his seat in early 1862.

As a senator, Phelan continued to advise President Davis. He traveled home to Mississippi in the fall of 1862 and wrote Davis frequently about the concerns of the common people of the state. He reported that morale in the state was very low and that there was considerable resentment that the wealthy were not doing their part for the defense of the state. He believed that the only way to increase enlistments and boost morale was for Davis to travel to Mississippi.

Despite his empathy with the people's concerns, Phelan was not a very popular senator with his constituents. His fervent belief that a strong central government, with broad discretionary powers was the only way to win the war conflicted with the states' rights sentiments of many Mississippians. When he proposed in the Senate that all cotton should be purchased with Confederate war bonds and that such sales should be mandatory on pain of death, he was burned in effigy at home and was soon voted out of office (he drew one of the Senate's two-year terms for the First Confederate Congress). However, before his departure, Phelan continued to work to strengthen the Confederates' military through his opposition to conscription substitution and slaveowner exemptions.

After leaving office, Phelan's friendship with Davis gained him appointment as a judge advocate at the rank of colonel. He traveled around the Confederacy hearing military cases.

After the war, Phelan resumed his law practice, first in Alabama and then in Memphis, Tennessee, where he died.
— *David S. Heidler and Jeanne T. Heidler*

See also Congress, C.S.A.; Conscription, C.S.A.; Davis, Jefferson.
For further reading:
Yearns, W. Buck. *The Confederate Congress* (1960).

PHELPS, JOHN WOLCOTT
(1813–1885)
Union general

Born in Guilford, Vermont, John Wolcott Phelps was educated locally before receiving an appointment to the U.S. Military Academy. He graduated twenty-fourth of forty-nine in the class of 1836. Upon graduation he went to Florida, where he fought in the Second Seminole War. There is evidence that this time in the South turned him into the zealous abolitionist he would later become.

After his service in Florida, Phelps served at a variety of frontier posts before being sent to fight in the Mexican-American War. He received a brevet promotion to captain for his actions in this conflict but declined the promotion, possibly because of his growing antislavery views and growing Northern criticism that the war was being fought to advance slavery. After the war he remained in the army, however, again serving on the frontier and in the Mormon expedition. He resigned his commission in 1859. Returning to Vermont, Phelps spent most of the next two years writing pamphlets and newspaper attacks on the institution of slavery and the Masons.

At the outbreak of the Civil War, Phelps raised a regiment of volunteers in Vermont and was commissioned the colonel of the 1st Vermont Volunteers. His previous military experience gained him a promotion to brigadier general of volunteers in August 1861, with a date of rank of 17 May 1861. By the time of his promotion, Phelps had already gone with his regiment to Fort Monroe at Hampton Roads and led his men in the capture of Newport News, Virginia.

Phelps continued in command at Newport News through much of the fall of 1861. In November his commander, Major General Benjamin F. Butler, was in the midst of the planning for an assault against New Orleans and requested of the War Department that Phelps be assigned to the expedition. The War Department granted the request, and by the end of the year Phelps was on his way to the Gulf of Mexico.

In the New Orleans campaign, Phelps commanded the taking of Ship Island, Mississippi, at the end of 1861. In March 1862 he was given command of the 1st Brigade, Department of the Gulf, under Butler. Phelps took possession of Forts Jackson and St. Philip after the fall of New Orleans and the mutiny of the Confederate garrisons.

After the fall of the city, Phelps spent most of his time on the outskirts in command at Camp Parapet. From the very establishment of this encampment, it was inundated

with hundreds of slaves who had fled to Union lines. Some of the slaves were even directed to the camp by their owners, who no longer could feed them. Phelps began ruminating on this unexpected burden on his resources and came to the conclusion that the best way to handle the problem was to enroll the male former slaves in the army. To that end, he began organizing units of African-American soldiers, equipping them the best he could, and training them for military service. He even took the time to write a long treatise on the wisdom of his actions.

When word of Phelps's actions reached the War Department, where the idea of African-American troops had been rejected, orders were sent to the Gulf to cease and desist and immediately to disband any African-American units. When Butler, who was under attack for some of his unrelated actions in New Orleans, refused to come to his defense, Phelps resigned his commission and returned to Vermont. At the time of his resignation, Phelps was considered an outlaw by the Confederate government for arming slaves.

For the remainder of the war and even his life Phelps lived in Vermont, where he continued to write on a number of topics, including history and education. He turned down an offer of a commission of major general of African-American troops after the federal government began organizing them. He died on 2 February 1885 in Guilford, Vermont.

—*David S. Heidler and Jeanne T. Heidler*

See also African-American Soldiers U.S.A.; Butler, Benjamin; New Orleans.

For further reading:

Howard, Cecil Hampden Cutts. *Life and Public Services of General John Wolcott Phelps; A Sketch Read Before the New England Historic Genealogical Society, Dec. 1, 1886* (1887).

PHELPS'S RAID
(6–10 February 1862)

So confident was Navy flag officer Andrew H. Foote of victory in the coming Union assault on Fort Henry on the Tennessee River, that on 2 February 1862, four days before the Union attack, he issued bold special orders to Lieutenant Seth Ledyard Phelps. On his own initiative and without consulting others, Foote instructed Phelps that on the fall of Fort Henry he was to take his division of three timberclad gunboats—the USS *Conestoga* (flagship), *Lexington*, and *Tyler*—up the Tennessee River, disable the key 1,200-foot Memphis, Louisville & Clarksville Railroad drawbridge at Danville twenty-five miles above Fort Henry, and then raid into Confederate territory as far upriver as the depth of water would allow. After the Union capture of Fort Henry on 6 February, Foote himself returned to Cairo with his

ironclads to effect repairs, leaving behind only the iron-clad *Carondelet* to support Union troops ashore.

A fast Confederate steamer, the CSS *Dunbar*, was anchored about a mile upriver from Fort Henry during the battle on the sixth and Captain Gus Fowler kept her there afterward to see what would happen. He did not have long to wait; soon clouds of smoke were seen headed in their direction. Phelps's mission had begun. Fowler quickly ordered the *Dunbar* upriver to the Danville drawbridge. Arriving there about 4 P.M., the *Dunbar*'s crew spread the alarm that Union ships were coming. The Union arrival was delayed, however, when Phelps discovered the camp of the 48th and 51st Tennessee Regiments along the shore and stopped to destroy it. At Danville, meanwhile, the Confederates saved what they could, loading supplies aboard the transport steamers *Appleton Belle*, *Lynn Boyd*, *Samuel Orr*, and *Time*. These vessels then steamed upriver. Fowler also posted sentinels on the bridge and positioned the *Dunbar* along the shore, just beyond the bridge.

The Union ships arrived at the railroad bridge about 8 P.M. Phelps immediately opened fire on the *Dunbar* with one of the *Conestoga*'s 32-pounders. With Union shot splashing around her, the *Dunbar* then fled upriver after the transports.

The few Confederate sentinels on the bridge opened fire at the three Union vessels before escaping aboard a waiting train. The timberclads were held up briefly because the Confederates had disabled the machinery to keep the bridge down. Phelps landed men and in about an hour they succeeded in opening it. He then left behind Lieutenant William Gwin and the *Tyler*, slowest of his gunboats, so that the men might destroy track and telegraph line. Phelps, meanwhile, proceeded upriver with the *Conestoga* and *Lexington*. After accomplishing his assigned tasks and confiscating equipment abandoned by the Confederates, Gwin hurried the *Tyler* after the other two Union gunboats. The Union raiders did not destroy the railroad bridge as Foote had ordered, judging that it would be there when the expedition returned.

Phelps's *Conestoga*, meanwhile, pressed ahead of the slower *Lexington* and gradually gained on the heavily laden Confederate transports. The captain of the *Samuel Orr* decided to fire his vessel rather than see her and her contents fall into Union hands, hoping that the explosion of her cargo of submarine batteries would disable one or more of the Union gunboats, but the *Conestoga* kept at a discreet distance as explosions ripped the Confederate steamer. Farther upriver the captains of the *Appleton Belle* and *Lynn Boyd* realized that they too would soon be overhauled. They then landed their two vessels in front of the home of Judge Creavatt, a Union sympathizer, and fired them in turn. Spotting the burning steamers, Phelps halted the *Conestoga* some 1,000 yards away. No sooner had the Union gunboat stopped than a tremendous

explosion ripped the *Appleton Belle*, which had been loaded with ordnance supplies and 3,000 pounds of powder. The explosion shattered the *Conestoga*'s skylights, lifted her light upper deck, opened doors, and even broke locks. It also shattered the *Lynn Belle* and the Creavatt home and, as Phelps described it, beat up a half-mile stretch along the river.

Phelps decided to halt in order to wait for the other two gunboats, which did not have pilots aboard. At 11 A.M. on 7 February all three gunboats arrived at Perry's Landing, Tennessee, where they discovered strong Union sentiment. Much to the seamen's delight, people on the banks waved hats and handkerchiefs and, on occasion, American flags.

At 7 P.M. the Union gunboats reached Cerro Gordo, Tennessee. Small arms fire on the *Conestoga* produced retaliatory shelling from the flagship and the *Tyler*. The three Union gunboats then hove to and launched their cutters. At the riverbank the Union seamen took possession of the large, 670-ton, 260-feet long steamer CSS *Eastport*, which had been undergoing conversion into an ironclad ram. They also took a great quantity of materials intended for her alteration, including 250,000 feet of "the best quality of ship and building lumber" and iron plating. The *Eastport* had been partially scuttled, but the Union sailors were able to stop the leaks and pump out the water.

Again leaving the *Tyler* behind, this time to guard his prize, Phelps pressed on with the *Conestoga* and *Lexington*. On 8 February, in Mississippi, Phelps took two small steamers, the CSS *Muscle* and *Sallie Wood*, at Waterloo Landing. The *Sallie Wood* was filled with iron destined for the Tredegar Iron Works in Richmond. A prize crew from the *Conestoga* boarded the *Muscle* and used her to tow the *Sallie Wood* back to Cerro Gordo.

Phelps's gunboats got as far south as Florence, Alabama, arriving there on the afternoon of the eighth. Here the raid ended, stopped by Mussel Shoals. The crews of the *Dunbar* and another Confederate steamer, the *Alfred Robb*, managed to prevent their capture by hiding them in a stream. The Confederates fired three other steamers, the *Julius Smith*, *Sam Kirkman*, and *Time*. The *Julius Smith* was cut loose with paddle wheels turning in reverse in the hopes that she would run into and destroy one or more of the raiders, but the Union gunboats easily avoided her mad passage downstream. The other two steamers were fired at the landing, but seamen from the *Conestoga* quickly went ashore and managed to save a quantity of stores from the burning vessels.

A delegation of Florence citizens now approached Phelps, pleading that he not destroy their city or the prized fifteen-pier railroad bridge over the river. Phelps reasoned that because Muscle Shoals impeded him from further passage upriver and that the bridge had little military value, he would leave it intact. He also assured the delegation that the Union seamen were "neither ruffians nor savages" and that they would not destroy private property. Phelps did take an armed party with telegraphers and their equipment to the local telegraph office, where they listened in on telegraph messages until the Confederates learned what was going on and rerouted their messages. At the same time the remainder of the Union shore party was going through warehouses and seizing official Confederate property. They took a quantity of supplies designated for Fort Henry as well as iron plating for the *Eastport*. Phelps ordered private property seized aboard the steamers to be offloaded and returned to its owners.

That same evening the two gunboats departed Florence. Later that night they reached Cerro Gordo, where Gwin and his men had been busy loading captured supplies and getting the *Eastport* ready for her trip downriver. The Union seamen were surprised to find hundreds of local citizens come out to voice their distaste for the Confederacy and support for the Union cause.

On his return to Cerro Gordo Phelps consulted with Gwin and Lieutenant James W. Shirk of the *Lexington*. The three decided they would assault a Confederate regimental camp near Savannah, reportedly containing some 600 pressed men. Leaving the *Lexington* behind to guard the *Eastport*, the *Conestoga* and *Tyler* set out. They soon arrived at Savannah, and 130 sailors and marines with a Dahlgren 12-pounder howitzer stormed ashore, only to find the camp had been hastily deserted. The landing party then removed some stores and fired others, along with the camp's log cabins.

On the night of 9 February the *Lexington* and *Tyler*, on either side of the *Eastport*, took her in tow; the *Conestoga* towed the *Sallie Wood* and the *Muscle*, the latter under steam. But the *Muscle* sprang a leak and had to be abandoned, along with a quantity of lumber on board her.

On 10 February, Phelps's little flotilla returned to Fort Henry. The expedition had been an immense success. It had taken three Confederate steamers and brought the destruction of six others. The large *Eastport* was a particularly valuable capture. She became a Union ironclad of the same name, mounting six 9-inch Dahlgren smoothbores and two 100-pounder rifled guns. The expedition also secured a considerable quantity of lumber, iron plate and other stores, and small arms. News of the raid spread across the South and had a profound psychological impact. In the region it spread panic among Confederates and caused Alabama governor John G. Shorter to call out the militia. At the same time it heartened Union sympathizers, a surprising number of whom had come forward openly to express their sentiments.

—*Spencer C. Tucker*

See also Foote, Andrew H; Fort Henry, Battle of.
For further reading:
Porter, David D. *Naval History of the Civil War* (1886; reprint, 1984).

Slagle, Jay. *Ironclad Captain. Seth Ledyard Phelps and the U.S. Navy, 1841–1864* (1996).

Tucker, Spencer C. *Andrew Hull Foote* (1999).

U.S. Navy Department. Communication of S. L. Phelps to Flag Officer Foote, 10 February 1862. In *Official Records of the Union and Confederate Navies in the War of the Rebellion* (1908, 1910).

PHILIPPI, BATTLE OF
(3 June 1861)

This small and relatively unknown engagement was fought on 3 June 1861 as part of Major General George B. McClellan's campaign to secure the Baltimore & Ohio Railroad (B & O) and control the western part of Virginia. The seat of Barbour County in what is now West Virginia, Philippi is located on the east bank of the Tygart Valley River along a major thoroughfare known as the Beverly-Fairmont Pike. The pike crossed the river on a large covered bridge that still stands today. Phillipi is about fifteen miles south of the town of Grafton, an important rail hub where the B & O and Northwestern railroad lines intersected. The control of Grafton was an important strategic objective for both sides, as it gave access to railroad lines and roads needed for the movement of troops throughout northwestern Virginia.

Confederate forces under Virginia Military Institute graduate Colonel George A. Porterfield occupied Grafton first, on 24 May 1861 with about 500 troops. Discovering that Union forces were about to advance on him, Porterfield ordered two bridges on the B & O burned in an attempt to stall the enemy advance. General McClellan countered these actions by ordering a Union force from Wheeling to advance to Grafton. The initial contingent of the 4,000-man Union force, the 1st Virginia Infantry Regiment (U.S.) under the command of Colonel Benjamin Kelley, reached Grafton on 30 May, but Porterfield already had retreated to Phillipi. Overall command of the Union expedition fell on Brigadier General Thomas A. Morris, who arrived on the scene with a brigade of Indiana troops on 1 June.

The Union plan to strike the Confederates at Philippi called for a simultaneous nighttime advance of two Union columns down both sides of the Tygart Valley River. Colonel Kelley commanded one of the columns, while the other was commanded by Colonel Ebenezer Dumont of the 7th Indiana Infantry. Morris opted to control the operation from Grafton.

Rain, darkness, and unfamiliarity with the local roads upset the Union timetable for the attack, and secessionist-leaning civilians alerted Porterfield of the Union movement. Forewarned, Porterfield instructed his subordinate commanders that their outnumbered force should make an orderly retreat to Beverly, (West) Virginia, in case of a Union attack. As a result of the delays, Kelley's 1,600-man force, which was supposed to block Porterfield's escape, was not in position when Dumont's command of 1,450 troops prematurely attacked. Consequently, most of the Confederates were able to escape. Newspapers called the affair the "Philippi Races."

Although this engagement is sometimes called the first land battle of the Civil War, the action at Philippi can be characterized as nothing more than a skirmish. Only five Union soldiers were wounded at Philippi, Kelley included. Also, during the night march, one of Kelley's soldiers accidently shot himself and bled to death. Confederate casualties, although the record is inconclusive, probably came to less than ten. One of them, an eighteen-year-old Confederate cavalryman by the name of James E. Hangar, fashioned an artificial leg while he was recuperating from the one he lost to a Union cannonball. Private Hangar subsequently made the production of artificial limbs his career, establishing what would become the world-renowned Hangar Limb Company.

The loss of Grafton caused Colonel Porterfield to be relieved of his command, replaced by Brigadier General Robert Selden Garnett. Garnett would be killed a short time later at the battle of Carrick's Ford, thus becoming the first general officer to be killed during the Civil War. Subsequent successes of Union troops in western Virginia propelled Major General McClellan to the command of the Union's premier army, the Army of the Potomac. Colonel Kelley survived his wound and ascended to the rank of brevet major general of volunteers.

The capture and occupation of Grafton allowed additional Federal troops from Ohio and Indiana to be moved into northwestern Virginia, ensuring Union control of this strategic region. Most importantly, the Union success at Philippi gave confidence to politicians from the western section of Virginia to begin the process that eventually would lead to the establishment of West Virginia as the thirty-fifth state.

—*Mark Snell*

See also Kelley, Benjamin Franklin; McClellan, George Brinton.

For further reading:

Bell, Mark E. "A Day at the Races: The First Virginia Infantry (U.S.) at the Battle of Philippi." *Civil War Regiments: A Journal of the American Civil War* (1997).

Newell, Clayton R. *Lee vs. McClellan: The First Campaign* (1996).

PHILLIPS, EUGENIA LEVY
(1820–1902)

Activist in Confederate resistance

Born in Charleston, South Carolina, Eugenia Levy was destined to become a symbol to Federal authorities of Southern women's fierce resistance to the Union. Married in 1836 to South Carolina lawyer

and politician Philip Phillips, Eugenia Levy Phillips spent many years with her husband in Mobile, Alabama, where they established their large family. They moved to Washington, D.C., in 1853, after Philip's election to the United States House of Representatives.

The Phillipses, who eventually had nine children, were living in Washington when the Civil War broke out. Before long Eugenia's passionate prosecession sentiments, and her tendency to express them openly, became a source of worry to her husband and an irritation to various officials in the Federal government. Around the same time that Washington resident Rose O'Neal Greenhow fell under suspicion for espionage that led to the Union rout at the first battle of Bull Run, Eugenia Phillips's outspokenness on behalf of the Confederate cause (along with indications that she had been carrying on an active and treasonable correspondence with the enemy) provoked an official backlash against her. On 23 August 1861 United States Secret Service agents placed both women under house arrest. Within a week they moved Phillips, her two daughters, and her sister to the presumably more secure "Fort Greenhow" (Greenhow's residence), pending an investigation into their activities.

The Phillips women remained at Fort Greenhow for about three weeks, where Eugenia later claimed that the conditions of their imprisonment were appallingly bad. In her unpublished memoir of her wartime experiences, Phillips insisted that all four women had been crowded into an attic room and had been compelled to sleep together on a soiled bed devoid of any sheets or other covering. Phillips complained as well about the rudeness of the soldiers who were assigned to guard them, particularly one who displayed inappropriate interest in one of her daughters. When they were released on 19 September through the intercession of the future secretary of war, Edwin Stanton, the Phillips women's rejoicing was sincere, despite the fact that the conditions of their release required the whole family to remove to the Deep South, where Federal officials hoped they would cause less trouble. This move failed to bring about an end to Phillips's activism on the Confederacy's behalf.

Not long after the Phillipses relocated to New Orleans, Union general Benjamin Butler arrived with Federal troops to occupy the city. Butler took a special interest in eliminating the threat to Federal authority that he firmly believed was presented by the sort of overtly hostile attitude and behavior that Southern women in general—and Phillips in particular—regularly displayed. For example, more than one woman in New Orleans was accused of dumping her chamberpot out of the upstairs window of her home onto the heads of Federal soldiers passing below. Well informed of Phillips's reputation for being a troublemaker, and putting stock in reports that she had been teaching her children to spit on Union soldiers and had herself openly mocked the

remains of one Lieutenant De Kay as his funeral cortege passed by her home (accusations she vehemently denied), on 30 June Butler had Phillips confined in isolation on Ship Island off the Mississippi coast.

The complaints Phillips had about her brief stay at Fort Greenhow are mild in comparison to those she expressed about her accommodations on Ship Island, where she remained for several weeks, until her health seemed likely to give way under the strain. According to Phillips, her "cell" amounted to little more than a large box, the food she received was rancid, she was allowed no exercise and no direct contact with her family, and—worst of all from her perspective—she was surrounded by countless contraband slaves for whom the Union army had recently assumed responsibility. Phillips was convinced that Butler had embarked on a personal mission to destroy her reputation as a woman of honor. By the time Butler allowed her to return home in the fall, Phillips was, by her own account, an emotional and physical wreck.

Following her release from Ship Island, Phillips and her family moved to La Grange, Georgia. There Phillips managed a hospital for Confederate soldiers and brooded over the outrages perpetrated against her by Butler and others. Though she eventually returned with her husband to Washington, D.C., after the war was over, even at the time of her death in 1902 Eugenia Phillips refused to forget or forgive the Federal government's wartime treatment of her, nor did she concede any fault in her own heartfelt Southern nationalism.

—*Elizabeth D. Leonard*

See also Butler, Benjamin; Greenhow, Rose O'Neal.
For further reading:
Kinchen, Oscar. *Women Who Spied for the Blue and Gray* (1972).
Leonard, Elizabeth D. *"All the Daring of the Soldier": Women of the Civil War Armies* (1999).
Morgan, Daniel. "Eugenia Levy Phillips: The Civil War Experiences of a Southern Jewish Woman." In *Jews of the South: Selected Essays from the Southern Jewish Historical Society.* Edited by Samuel Proctor and Louis Schmeirs (1984).

PHILLIPS, WENDELL
(1811–1884)
Abolitionist

Born in Boston, Massachusetts, on 29 November 1811 to a wealthy New England family who dated its arrival in America to John Winthrop's ship *Arbella* in 1630, Wendell Phillips was a product of privilege whose intellect, noted good looks, and charm made him one of the most persuasive and visible of the antislavery orators in antebellum America. Phillips was educated at Boston's Latin School, Harvard University, and Harvard Law School. He practiced law competently

if unenthusiastically from 1834 to 1837. Associated mainly with the Garrisonian wing of the abolitionist cause, he was widely called the "golden trumpet" for his ability to sway audiences. Although through his long public life he would be associated with social and political reforms that would range from Indian rights to prison reform, his fame primarily rests on his uncompromising devotion to the abolition of slavery.

In December of 1837 at Boston's Faneuil Hall, he objected passionately to the state Attorney General James Austin's claim that the murderers of Illinois abolitionist editor Elijah P. Lovejoy were heroes. The young Phillips so stirred the audience with his off-the-cuff speech condemning the murder and Austin's opinion that he instantly became a sensation and had found his life's passion. His marriage that year to Anne Greene, daughter of a wealthy and deceased Boston merchant gave him both an independent income and a partner who encouraged his commitment to reform and abolition activities.

Like William Lloyd Garrison, he believed that the U.S. Constitution was an unholy compromise with slaveholders and that the issue was too central a moral issue to be the property of one political party. Phillips, however often he agreed with Garrison, operated by his own moral compass and at times disagreed openly with Garrison on tactics by being less willing to compromise in any way on the subject. Phillips was also a regular contributor to Garrison's antislavery newspaper *The Liberator,* and in 1840 he served as a delegate to the World Anti-Slavery Convention, where he championed the right of women delegates to speak on the floor of the convention.

Many in Phillips's own family, and undoubtedly even much of the sympathetic public, saw his uncompromising opposition to slavery as fanatical. As the sectional crisis deepened in the late 1840s and into the 1850s, Phillips was among the most inflammatory of the public speakers in his rejection of any wars designed to increase national territory and so to risk the expansion of slavery. And, finally, he was one of the first to call for the division of the nation over the issue.

The advent of the Civil War did not quell Phillips's drive for abolition. He was a harsh critic of Lincoln's policies, which he deemed too slow to abolish slavery. Phillips considered the Emancipation Proclamation as only the first victory in the fight. William Lloyd Garrison, seeing the forces of slavery dealt an unrecoverable blow by the proclamation, suggested the dissolution of the American Anti-Slavery Society, which he himself headed. Phillips, believing that pressure must be kept on the government and the public, argued so persuasively that the society must continue its work that it elected him to the office of president.

The ultimate abolition of slavery did not leave Phillips as a firebrand without a purpose. He saw his role in society as one of an educator who was not above agitating to bring notice to other reforms he believed were important to national moral health. After the Civil War he campaigned against alcohol, for women's rights, for humane treatment of prisoners, for rights of workers, and for better treatment by the government of Indians. In 1870 he ran for governor of Massachusetts as both the Labor Reform and Prohibitionist Parties' candidate. He lost the election but did poll as many as 20,000 votes in his attempt.

Wendell Phillips was to very many the voice of abolition. Yet he left no phrases that eloquently sum up the position of the movement and no speeches that stir the heart when read on the page. Phillips's skill was in communicating the broad ideas and the emotion of the moral rightness of his position to his audience in a simple but never simplistic manner. In a time when a handsome turn of phrase was admired and repeated, Phillips was most effective in person. The descriptions of his deep voice, his sincerity and passion in delivery, and his ability to communicate to his audience their moral duty turned hearts and minds sometimes more effectively than many a more elegant prose stylist.

—*Gretchen A. Adams*

See also Abolitionist Movement; Abolitionists; Garrison, William Lloyd.

For further reading:

Bartlett, Irving H. *Wendell Phillips: Brahmin Radical* (1961; reprint, 1973).

Sherwin, Oscar. *Prophet of Liberty: The Life and Times of Wendell Phillips* (1958).

Stewart, James B. *Wendell Phillips: Liberty's Hero* (1986).

PHILLIPS, WILLIAM ADDISON
(1824–1893)

Union commander of the Indian Brigade

Scottish-born lawyer, author, and abolitionist William Addison Phillips traveled to Kansas in 1855 as a correspondent for the *New York Tribune.* He became active in abolitionist politics and wrote The *Conquest of Kansas by Missouri and Her Allies* in 1856. Phillips was a delegate to the Kansas Free State Convention in 1857 and was a rumored associate of John Brown. In 1862, he was commissioned a major in the 1st Indian Home Guard Regiment and was promoted to colonel and commander of the Indian Brigade in early 1863. In this capacity Phillips commanded over 3,000 Indian troops and was an important military figure in Indian Territory.

Phillips admired his Indian soldiers but was critical of Native American officers and worked to remove them from command. Unlike many Americans, Phillips believed Indians had the potential to achieve equality with whites, but he felt this could only be accomplished

through the destruction of Indian sovereignty. Despite this conviction, Phillips recognized that the Union's success in Indian Territory depended on the good will of Native American soldiers; he was willing to assist the cause of Indian sovereignty to further his own military and political goals.

Under Phillips's command, the Indian Brigade was able to assert nominal control over Indian Territory. Although Phillips launched periodic raids into Confederate territory, the brigade was primarily engaged in maintaining supply lines and protecting an estimated 7,000 Indian refugees near Fort Gibson. Along with his military duties, Phillips remained active in Kansas politics and displayed considerable political ambition. By 1864, Phillips was convinced that Senator Lane of Kansas and his protégé, Major General James G. Blunt, were working to remove him as a political rival. After Blunt issued orders restricting the sale of Cherokee cattle, Phillips claimed that Lane and Blunt were working together to steal cattle from the Cherokee people. Tribal leaders supported Phillips's claim, but in October 1864 he was removed from command and given a minor job overseeing courts-martial in Fort Smith, Arkansas. Phillips's white and Cherokee supporters agitated for his return, and their actions resulted in his reinstatement as the Indian Brigade's commander in January 1865.

After the war, Phillips served three terms in the U.S. Congress and later worked as a lawyer for the Cherokee Nation. In the 1880s, he became a controversial figure among the Cherokees because of his unqualified support of the Dawes Act. He died on a trip to Fort Gibson in 1893.

—*Trevor M. Jones*

See also Indian Brigade; Indian Territory.

For further reading:

Abel, Annie Heloise. *The American Indian as Participant in the Civil War* (1919).
Britton, Wiley. *The Union Indian Brigade in the Civil War* (1922).
Fischer, LeRoy H., ed. *The Civil War in Indian Territory* (1974).

PHOTOGRAPHY

As a modern war in many respects, the Civil War was the first great media event in American history and the first war to be documented by what was then a new technology, photography. Photographers covered a wide range of aspects of the conflict, bringing the war home to Americans with a graphic reality that no other medium at the time possessed. The demand—from both the civilian public and the military—for views of the war remained steady, at least in the North. Nonetheless, the photographic report was fragmented, and it was insignificant as far as strategy and organization of forces were concerned.

The main limitation to comprehensive photographic coverage of the war was the technology itself. The wet-plate process had replaced the daguerreotype, so an almost limitless number of prints could be made from a glass negative, whereas previously only one original image had been possible. Yet the process was still a very elaborate one. The glass plate, kept free of dust, had to be coated with the necessary chemicals in a darkroom, then carried to the camera that had already been planted with the lens brought into focus. After the plate was exposed, it was rushed back to the darkroom while still wet to be developed. A photographer working in the field needed a portable darkroom. Equipment was cumbersome and expensive. Exposure times ranged from about ten to thirty seconds, depending on the light, so photographers were limited to stationary or posed scenes. After the plate was exposed, a variety of things—a breeze, a speck of dust, or an insect on the wet coating, even leaves in a stream where the photographer washed the plates—could ruin the photograph.

It is not surprising, then, that images depicting battles are virtually nonexistent. Most images were produced days after the fighting was over, showing corpse-strewn fields, shattered buildings, and maimed countryside. Also, theaters of war within fairly easy reach got documented heavily, whereas others were neglected. The majority of campaigns, as photographic historian William Frassanito puts it, went completely unrecorded. Generally, outdoor photography focused on inanimate objects such as buildings, fortifications, weapons, ships, and camps. In addition, the U.S. Army Medical Department had photographs taken of extraordinary injuries, medical operations, or peculiar amputations, a collection that was assembled in seven volumes after the war. The overwhelming majority of the images of war, however, were portraits, either of individuals or groups of soldiers. There are no records, but it is safe to assume that several hundred thousand images were produced during the four-year struggle. Some estimates place the number as exceeding a million. More than 90 percent of these were portraits.

On the eve of the Civil War, photography had acquired a mass audience. Firms such as E. & H. T. Anthony in New York catered to an increasing demand for images of persons, events, and scenery, selling such images as paper prints from 25 cents upwards. The Civil War provided a great opportunity to enterprising photographers, recorded by the 1860 census as numbering more than 3,100 in the United States. They followed the armies, put up tents or makeshift studios next to army camps, and offered to take the likeness of soldiers to be sent home as private mementos to family and friends for as little as one dollar per image. It is said that the Bergstresser brothers produced up to 160 portraits every day while with the Army of the Potomac for two years. Others waited until the war came to their hometowns to offer their services to soldiers. For photographers, pecu-

Quarters of photographers attached to the Engineer Corps near Petersburg, Virginia, March 1865 (*Library of Congress*)

niary interests and the hope to enhance one's professional or social standing mingled with patriotism and a sense of the conflict's historical dimensions.

Although a list compiled by the National Archives gives the names of some three hundred photographers who received passes from the Federal military authorities to record images in and around encampments, the actual number of operators producing images of war must have exceeded this number considerably. Possibly as many as 100 additional photographers came from and worked in the South. Possibly as many as 1,500 men and a few women took pictures of the war for the public, the illustrated press, and in a few cases the military.

The Confederacy produced the first photographers of the war. Jay D. Edwards, Osborn and Durbec, Andrew Lytle of Baton Rouge, George S. Cook of Charleston, Charles J. Quinby, Richard Wearn, F. K. Houston, and J.

W. Petty were among the better known. After a few months, supply shortages considerably curtailed their production. Some managed to get fresh supplies from blockade runners or even through more traditional channels. George Cook, for one, could restock the necessary chemicals with the help of the Anthony brothers in New York until the fall of 1863. Others had to ration their materials, with the result that there were markedly fewer photographers in the South and thus fewer images from their point of view.

Among those who supported the Union cause were men like Mathew Brady, the most famous photographer of the war, who busily fostered the image of himself as *the* photographic chronicler of the war. Yet Alexander Gardner, George N. Barnard, and Timothy O'Sullivan also did important work. Gardner left Brady's employ and set up his own business in 1863 because Brady refused to

Wagons and camera of Sam A. Cooley, Union photographer, Department of the South (*Library of Congress*)

give credit to the photographers who had actually taken pictures, insisting instead that the images be publicized under the name of the Brady firm. It is not always easy to ascribe a picture to one photographer, in any case, since the elaborate process required the joint efforts of two or more operators. It is not surprising, however, that some of Brady's best photographers joined Gardner's venture.

A few photographers had semiofficial status by carrying out assignments for the military and thus could charge the War Department for their work. Only one photographer had official status, and he happened also to be a soldier. Captain Andrew Joseph Russell held a commission from the Bureau of the U.S. Military Railroad to record the engineering problems created by the field activities of the army.

Contemporaries were willing to believe that the images were as "truthful as the records of heaven," as a catalogue of Brady's photographs put it in September 1862. Yet the images seen in galleries or as engravings in papers such as *Harper's Weekly, Frank Leslie's Illustrated Newspaper,* or the *New York Illustrated News*—photographs could be reproduced in the press only after the invention of the halftone

process in the 1880s—might be carefully staged scenes or at best represent the subjective views of the photographers. The photographs consequently made people see the war through the eyes of the photographers. The images also allowed people to connect to events in a more immediate way than before and associate those events with the reasons the war was being fought. In any case, war photography deeply moved Americans, and sometimes, as in the case of Brady's first pictures of battlefield dead, it shocked them. The public would never again be able to shut its eyes to the terrible reality of war.

—*Angela Schwarz*

See also Brady, Mathew B.; Gardner, Alexander; O'Sullivan, Timothy.
For further reading:
Carlebach, Michael L. *The Origins of Photojournalism in America* (1992).
Davis, Keith F. "'A Terrible Distinctness': Photography of the Civil War Era." In *Photography in Nineteenth-century America* (1991).
Davis, William C., ed. *The Image of War, 1861–1865* (1981–1984).

Frassanito, William A. *Grant and Lee: The Virginia Campaigns 1864–1865* (1983).

Miller, Francis Trevelyan, ed. *The Photographic History of the Civil War: Thousands of Scenes Photographed 1861–1865* (1911).

PICKENS, FRANCIS WILKINSON
(1805–1869)
Governor of South Carolina

The son of Andrew Pickens, governor of South Carolina, and Susannah Smith Wilkinson Pickens, Francis Pickens was born in Colleton District, South Carolina. He was educated in Georgia and at South Carolina College before studying law. He chose, however, to manage the family plantations rather than practice law. At an early age, Pickens also became interested in state politics and states' rights. He was a strong supporter of nullification in the early 1830s and was elected to the U.S. House of Representatives because of this support in 1834. He served in that body until 1843, becoming one of the strongest supporters of Southern rights during that period.

Pickens's stance on states' rights became even more radical during the next few years. He represented the state at the Nashville Convention of 1850, where he urged strong, united Southern action and secession if necessary. During the 1850s, however, Pickens gradually entered the more moderate camp in South Carolina, urging greater cooperation between the state and the National Democratic Party. In 1856, he supported the James Buchanan candidacy for the presidency. For his loyalty, Pickens was offered, and he accepted, the U.S. ministership to Russia. He served in that position until the fall of 1860. Because of his increasing moderation, while he was still in Russia in the spring of 1860, he was mentioned as a possible compromise candidate for the Democratic presidential nomination in 1860.

While nothing came of his presidential aspirations (Pickens was fully cognizant and in agreement with the efforts to put his name forward), Pickens's concern for the growing crisis in the United States caused him to resign his position and return to the country in the fall of 1860. Upon his return, Pickens continued to urge moderation for a time, arguing that merely the election of Abraham Lincoln should not be cause enough for South Carolina to act alone. When this stance seemed to fall on deaf ears, Pickens accepted the inevitable and supported secession. His change of heart, more than anything else, was probably responsible for his election as governor by the state legislature in December 1860.

As governor of the state in the early crisis days after secession and throughout his two-year term in office, Pickens dedicated himself completely to the military defense of the state. He ordered the taking of Castle Pinckney as soon as secession was official and began negotiations with Major Robert Anderson for the surrender of remaining federal installations in Charleston. Pickens was one of the major figures who urged the reduction of Fort Sumter after the formation of the Confederacy.

Along with the Fort Sumter crisis, Pickens concerned himself directly with the raising of troops in South Carolina. He worked closely with Robert E. Lee when Lee was placed in command of the defenses of coastal South Carolina in the fall of 1861. After Lee's departure, Pickens expressed unhappiness with the work of Lee's replacement, Roswell Sabine Ripley. President Jefferson Davis offered to replace Ripley with P. G. T. Beauregard to placate Pickens.

Besides his dealings with the Confederate government over the defense of the state, Pickens had political problems at home. The fall of Port Royal in the fall of 1861 brought about the creation of an executive council ostensibly to help the governor defend the state, but in actuality it so hindered his efforts that by the end of his term, Pickens felt he had no power at all. Upon leaving office in December 1862, Pickens retired to his plantation for the remainder of the war.

After the war, Pickens tried to recover his fortunes but died in debt at his home, Edgewood.

—David S. Heidler and Jeanne T. Heidler

See also Ripley, Roswell Sabine; South Carolina.

For further reading:

Edmunds, John B. *Francis W. Pickens and the Politics of Destruction* (1986).

Youmans, LeRoy Franklin. *A Sketch of the Life and Services of Francis W. Pickens of South Carolina* (1989).

PICKET

Picket lines were precautionary measures taken by army officers to protect and monitor the boundaries of a camp. Pickets were small groups of soldiers stationed at particular posts throughout the day and night who were used for a variety of purposes. Soldiers or individuals wanting to gain admittance to a camp would be stopped by a picket and asked for identification or a "call sign." Individuals wanting to leave the camp were also questioned by a picket. These measures were taken to protect the camp from enemy soldiers or spies. Pickets were also used as warnings for potential enemy assaults. Warning shots by a picket could arouse a camp to prepare for an attack.

Pickets could also be used to scout enemy positions. A small detachment of men might be sent out to locate an enemy camp. These groups could offer important information to their officers. In response, picket lines could be used to screen camp activities. Scouting parties often bumped into an opposing picket line before finding any useful information concerning enemy size or activity.

Failure or success in battle might be determined by a

picket line. At the battle of Chancellorsville, for example, Union pickets had reported large Confederate activity near the quiet Union camp. Yet the importance of this information failed to impress the higher command, and Stonewall Jackson's assault became a sweeping success.

Picket duty was a job shared by all soldiers. It was usually quiet and uneventful. Soldiers had to be careful not to fall asleep during their shift, or the consequences could be severe. To military authorities, "the picket was the sentinel that held the lives of his countrymen and the liberty of his country in his hands." A court-martial awaited the unlucky soldier who was found asleep at his post.

It was very common for pickets of opposing armies to interact. This included peaceful and friendly interactions, as well as sarcastic and potentially violent confrontations. During campaigns, pickets would sometimes jeer their opponents. Taunts and insults would echo between the opposing lines. However, these events rarely led to physical violence. More common were peaceful meetings between pickets. Soldiers used these opportunities to trade goods. Northern soldiers commonly traded coffee for Southern tobacco. Newspapers were also a favored item, and pickets conversed over news, current events, or even loved ones. When a stream or river divided pickets, soldiers would stand on the opposing banks to talk and would use hand-carved sailboats to ferry the trade goods between the lines. Such boats were so widely used that some soldiers recalled seeing rivers dotted with dozens of such vessels.

Fraternization with the enemy was frowned upon by officers, but enlisted men continued to interact throughout the war. Unlike battle, picket duty was very personal. Opposing pickets often saw each other as individuals, rather than enemies. Feelings of hospitality and brotherhood were shared, and the politics of war were temporarily ignored.

—Ian M. Spurgeon

For further reading:
Griffith, Paddy. *Battle Tactics of the Civil War* (1989).
Robertson, James I., Jr. *Tenting Tonight: The Soldier's Life* (1984).
Watkins, Sam R. Co. *Aytch: A Side Show of the Big Show* (1882; reprint, 1997).
Wiley, Bell I. *The Life of Billy Yank: The Common Soldier of the Union* (1952; reprint, 1993).

PICKETT, GEORGE EDWARD
(1825–1875)
Confederate general

George Edward Pickett was born into the Southern slaveholding elite on 25 January 1825 in Henrico County, Virginia. His parents encouraged him to consider law as a profession, but young George had little interest in the bar. After a short stint studying law,

Pickett obtained admission to the U.S. Military Academy in 1842. He accumulated demerits, showed little aptitude for his studies, and graduated last in his class in 1846.

Pickett next served in the Mexican-American War, marching with Winfield Scott's army into Mexico City. He earned commendation and brevets from his superiors, and at the battle of Chapultepec in September 1847, he triumphantly unfurled the U.S. flag over the ramparts.

The years immediately following the Mexican-American War were difficult ones for Pickett. He spent much of 1848 to 1854 in Texas serving in various isolated posts in the frontier army. He faced low pay and little chance for promotion. In November 1851 his first wife, Sally Minge, and their newborn baby died at Fort Gates, Texas—a loss so devastating that Pickett apparently went absent without leave from the army for several months. He eventually returned to his post, choosing the monotonous existence of the army over any civilian profession.

In 1854, due mainly to the efforts of his father and other well-connected supporters, Pickett gained promotion to captain. After a short stint at Fort Monroe, Pickett went west again, this time to the far Pacific Northwest, where he would remain until the Civil War began in 1861.

Captain Pickett saw limited action in the Yakima War, but by late August 1856, he had a new assignment: to protect white settlers in Bellingham Bay. Over the next three years Pickett frequently found himself caught between whites and natives, often feeling more sympathetic to the plight of the "savage" Indians than to that of the profit-seeking whites.

Pickett also suffered another devastating personal loss while stationed at Fort Bellingham. Although the evidence is spotty, he apparently fell in love with and married an Indian woman, with whom he had a child. Soon after the child's birth, the Indian woman died. Her son, James Tilton Pickett, grew to manhood without ever knowing his father.

In 1859, Pickett was ordered to San Juan Island in the midst of a border dispute between the United States and Britain. Both nations claimed the island, and relations worsened when an American shot a pig owned by a British settler. The resulting "Pig War" never led to open hostilities, but Pickett found himself caught in the middle.

In 1861, when the Civil War began, Pickett left his command in the West to join his native state of Virginia. He arrived in Richmond in September 1861 and quickly obtained a commission as colonel. By the end of the year, he had command of the lower Rappahannock River. In February 1861, he won promotion to brigadier general, largely thanks to his 15 years of professional army experience and the Confederacy's need for brigadier generals. His brigade participated in the siege of Yorktown and the battles of Williamsburg and Seven Pines. Pickett was gaining a reputation as an aggressive brigadier, but at the battle of Gaines' Mill on 27 June 1862, he fell wounded in the shoulder and missed Lee's Maryland campaign, including the battle of Antietam.

It was perhaps during these several months of convalescence that George Pickett began courting LaSalle Corbell. LaSalle claimed she met George when she was a child and he a young army officer before the war. But it seems more likely that George became smitten with the vivacious Sallie early in the war. There is evidence of their budding affair a few months after his return to the army in the fall of 1862. By the spring of 1863, he was leaving his command, often in the middle of the night, to see his lover, returning bleary-eyed the next morning to face the disapproval of many officers and men.

Upon Pickett's return to field command in the fall of 1862, he was promoted to major general in the Army of Northern Virginia's I Corps commanded by Longstreet.

Pickett saw little action for the next several months. During the battle of Fredericksburg, his division was kept in reserve. When Lee and Jackson masterminded their brilliant win at Chancellorsville, Pickett's men were miles away, engaged in the siege of Suffolk.

Pickett's first real opportunity to prove himself as a major general came on 3 July 1863, on the third day of the battle of Gettysburg. After two days of hard but indecisive fighting, Robert E. Lee selected Pickett's fresh division to spearhead a frontal attack on the Union center. The charge failed and Pickett's division was devastated. He never quite recovered from that day.

George and LaSalle married in September 1863, but his military struggles continued. He became commander of the Department of North Carolina, a region vexed by desertion, Unionism, and guerrilla warfare. In February 1864, Lee ordered Pickett to lead an attack on New Bern, North Carolina, and retake the coastal city from Union control. It was another failure. Soon after New Bern, Pickett learned that his men had captured a number of North Carolinians identified as former Confederate soldiers. A court-martial was ordered, and in three separate hangings, 22 men were executed in Kinston, North Carolina. Family and friends watched in horror. Union officials were outraged, and Pickett was blamed.

Pickett next took part in the Bermuda Hundred Campaign in May 1864, and only through sheer desperation did he stave off a strong Union offense. The strain eventually became too much, and Pickett collapsed—mentally and physically exhausted. When he regained his strength, he returned to field command in the Army of Northern Virginia.

Pickett's final ignominy came at the battle of Five Forks on 1 April 1865. Chosen to lead a special task force of infantry, cavalry, and artillery against an expected Union attack on the Confederate line, he initially succeeded in driving back the Federals at the battle of Dinwiddie Court House on 31 March. The next day though, when the Federals resumed the offensive, Pickett left his men poorly positioned as he took a long luncheon. As he and fellow officers ate shad and drank whiskey, the enemy punctured his line. By the end of the day, Federals had rolled up the Confederate flank, and Lee began what was to be his final retreat. Eight days later Lee surrendered to Grant at Appomattox Court House. George Pickett was removed from command just before the surrender.

Pickett returned home to his wife and infant son to try to begin life anew. Soon after the war ended, the U.S. War Department launched an investigation of the Kinston hangings, and George and LaSalle fled to Montreal. They returned a few months later, and eventually the investigation ended, thanks to the timely intervention of U. S. Grant. Pickett spent the remaining years of his life in Virginia, selling insurance and brooding about the charge at Gettysburg. He made few public appearances, and his health continued to deteriorate.

George Pickett died in 1875 at age 50. His wife lived for another five decades, supporting George, Jr. and herself. She worked as a federal employee for several years, and then launched a successful writing and lecturing career. She wrote and spoke mainly about her husband, presenting an idealized image of him vastly at odds with the real man she had married. George Pickett the man became George Pickett the myth.

—*Lesley J. Gordon*

See also Bermuda Hundred Campaign; Five Forks, Battle of; Gaines' Mill, Battle of; Gettysburg, Battle of; Longstreet, James.

For further reading:

Freeman, Douglass Southall. *Lee's Lieutenants: A Study in Command* (1942–1944).

Gordon, Lesley J. *General George E. Pickett in Life and Legend* (1998).

Harrison, Walter. *Picket's Men: A Fragment of War History* (1870).

Pickett, LaSalle Corbell. *Pickett and His Men* (1899).

Reardon, Carol. *Pickett's Charge in History and Memory* (1997).

PIEDMONT, VIRGINIA, BATTLE OF
(5 June 1864)

After Union general Franz Sigel's defeat at New Market, Virginia, on 15 May 1864, David Hunter replaced him. In all, Hunter commanded about 11,000 infantry, including a division under Brigadier General Jeremiah Cutler Sullivan and another under Brigadier General George Crook. Hunter also had about 5,000 cavalry, composed of a division commanded by Brigadier General Julius Stahel and a division commanded by Brigadier General William Woods Averell. Upon assuming command Hunter determined

to move Sullivan's and Stahel's divisions south from his headquarters at Strasburg toward the important rail town of Staunton, Virginia. He sent word to Crook at Lewisburg, West Virginia, to converge on Staunton with his division as well. Opposing Hunter's move southward toward Staunton was John Daniel Imboden's cavalry and artillery totaling about 3,000.

Hunter left Strasburg on 26 May 1864. Imboden established a defensive line at Mount Crawford, but when attacked by Hunter on 2 June was forced to fall back. He sent word to Richmond that he desperately needed reinforcements and more artillery if he was to prevent Hunter from taking Staunton. Various small units from throughout western Virginia, including some recuperating invalids, were sent to his assistance, as well as a brigade under William "Grumble" Jones from Bristol, Virginia, which arrived on 4 June. Upon Jones's arrival the Confederates numbered approximately 5,600.

Jones, senior to Imboden, took command upon his arrival—although he deferred to Imboden, who was far more familiar with the terrain, on the disposition of the troops on a strong piece of high ground near Mount Crawford. Rather than attacking this position, however, Hunter flanked the Confederates to the east at Port Republic with the plan to approach Staunton on the East Road. When the Confederates learned of this flanking maneuver, Imboden took his cavalry to delay Hunter along the East Road north of Piedmont at Mount Meridian, while Jones established a stronger defensive line at Mowry's Hill closer to Staunton. However, when Imboden's position was attacked around 6:00 A.M. on 5 June and the Confederate troopers were driven back toward Piedmont, Jones brought up his entire army to Piedmont instead of remaining at Mowry's Hill.

Jones placed his most seasoned veteran units northwest of Piedmont, anchoring his left flank on the Middle River and keeping his right flank protected by the bulk of his artillery. He placed his reserves just southeast and southwest of town, with Imboden's cavalry farther southeast toward New Hope to prevent a sweeping flanking maneuver from Hunter to the east. Imboden's position guarding the flank, however, left a gap between the infantry and the cavalry that Hunter would exploit later in the day.

At about noon Union colonel Augustus Moor led his brigade in an attack on Jones's left to divert attention from another attack by a brigade commanded by Colonel Joseph Thoburn on the Confederate right. Jones's artillery on the right was able to hold off the initial advances, but during the offensive the Northern troops discovered the gap between the Confederate infantry and cavalry. As a result of this discovery, Stahel's cavalry was sent around the Confederate infantry's right in a wide flanking maneuver to hold Imboden in position and prevent him from closing the gap. The Union

infantry then renewed the attack on the gap and succeeded in knocking out most of Jones's artillery.

Jones attempted to move troops into the gap and in the process was exposed to heavy Union fire at close range. He was struck and killed with a Union bullet to the head, causing his already weakened lines to begin a precipitate retreat southward. The retreat of the infantry left Imboden's left flank exposed, and he too retreated with his cavalry. In the chaotic retreat, approximately 1,000 Confederates were captured by Union troops. During the battle another 600 had been killed or wounded. Hunter suffered about 800 casualties. As a result of the battle, Hunter was able to enter Staunton the next day and was joined by Crook on 8 June. Hunter's victory also opened the upper Shenandoah Valley for Federal occupation.

—*David S. Heidler and Jeanne T. Heidler*

See also Hunter, David; Imboden, John Daniel; Jones, William Edmonson; New Market; Stahel, Julius.

For further reading:

Duncan, Richard R. *Lee's Endangered Left: The Civil War in Western Virginia, Spring of 1864* (1998).

PIERCE, FRANKLIN
(1804–1869)

Fourteenth president of the United States

Born in rural Hillsborough, New Hampshire, in October 1804, Franklin Pierce was the son of Revolutionary War general and New Hampshire governor Benjamin Pierce. A child of privilege, he attended Bowdoin College in the 1820s, began a lifelong friendship with classmate Nathaniel Hawthorne, and became a successful attorney. A diehard Jacksonian Democrat, his interests quickly turned from law to politics in 1829, when he was elected to the New Hampshire House and two years later became its speaker. In 1833, he was elected to the U.S. House of Representatives and, at the age of thirty-two in 1836, was elected to the U.S. Senate as its youngest member.

Pierce's tenure in Washington, D.C., quickly turned sour. His new wife, Jane Appleton Pierce (daughter of the Bowdoin College president) hated the capital. A cool, aloof, aristocratic woman who was related to prominent manufacturing families like the Lawrences and the Aikens, she spent much of her time back in New England. Her unhappiness with her husband's position was compounded in 1836 by the loss of their first child when he was only a few days old. Although Senator Pierce made fast friends of many important national leaders, such as Mississippi senator Jefferson Davis, and developed a reputation as a staunch antiabolitionist, he seldom participated in major debates or proposed legislation. In 1842, he retired from politics and returned to Concord to continue his law practice.

A popular and prosperous attorney, Pierce could not drag himself away from the intrigue of state politics and soon became one of the leaders of a Democratic organization known as the "Concord Regency." He gained the admiration of many national Democrats for his zealous attacks on free-soil elements in the state party, although his enemies soon dubbed him a party "boss" for his tactics. Still respected in Washington, he was offered the attorney generalship by President James K. Polk in 1846, but, wary of a return to life in the nation's capital, he declined and one year later was commissioned a brigadier general for service in the Mexican-American War. Instead of following in his father's footsteps, he incurred laughter for a mishap during the battles outside Mexico City. Pierce's horse, spooked by the noise of the cannon, reared up suddenly and drove the saddle horn into his groin. The pain was so fierce he passed out and was mocked by political foes as a coward. He resigned from the army in 1848 and again returned to his law practice.

Pierce spent much of the early 1850s making money in the law and building his practice among the many manufacturing firms in New Hampshire. An advocate of the Compromise of 1850, he was discussed as a "dark horse" candidate for the presidency in 1852, but few gave him a chance. When New Hampshire Democratic leader and Supreme Court justice Levi Woodbury died in mid-1851 and Democrats bickered on the choice of candidates, however, many spoke of the young Pierce as a compromise candidate. After forty-nine ballots, he was nominated for president in June 1852.

Notified while riding in a carriage with Mrs. Pierce, Pierce was stunned and his wife fainted. Gratified by the high honor yet dreading a return to Washington, he accepted but exerted little effort. Instead, he remained in New Hampshire and met with national leaders, planning strategies and discussing future policies. "Young Hickory," as he was nicknamed, defeated Whig nominee General Winfield Scott easily in the fall and was elected the country's fourteenth president.

Tragedy struck Pierce and his wife when they were traveling south for his inauguration. Their only son, Bennie, was killed before their eyes as their train derailed and crashed down an embankment. Mrs. Pierce never recovered from the trauma. Although Pierce gave an impressive inaugural address promising an expansionist foreign policy, thrift in spending, and procompromise Unionism, the administration began on a sad note for Pierce and an ominous one for the nation. For four years, a glum pall hung over the White House, leading one senator to remark, "I have seen hundreds of log cabins which seemed to contain more happiness."

High hopes quickly gave way to turmoil. A gentle, affable, trusting man by nature, Pierce foolishly tried to satisfy every faction within the Democratic Party with his patronage appointments, but he ended up angering everyone and widening intraparty squabbles. Without friends in Congress, he competed unsuccessfully for control of the Democratic Party with Senate leaders like Stephen Douglas and quickly became one Democratic spokesman out of many. When Douglas proposed his Kansas-Nebraska Bill in 1854—organizing those territories under the concept of "popular sovereignty" and invalidating the 1820 Missouri Compromise—Pierce reluctantly supported the plan, helped ensure its passage, and, in the process, alienated the Northern wing of his party. In addition, when violence broke out in Kansas and a proslavery government was organized there, Pierce horrified antislavery forces by recognizing it as legitimate. Foreign policy further aggravated Pierce's position. Tension with Spain rose throughout 1854 as sentiment grew for seizure of Cuba. Haunted by the violence in Kansas, many Northerners charged that the administration aimed at conquering Cuba and admitting the island as another slave state. Free-soil Democrats were appalled and never again trusted the president.

As the 1856 election loomed, a willing President Pierce offered himself for renomination, but he was a man without a party. Northern Democrats regarded him as a pro-South toady; Southern Democrats thought him weak and unelectable. His rival James Buchanan became the Democratic standard-bearer, and Pierce left office in March 1857 an unhappy, disappointed man.

After a European tour in the late 1850s, Pierce returned to the United States, declined another run for office, and supported John C. Breckinridge for president in 1860. A bitter critic of Lincoln, he received public scorn after giving an antiwar address on 4 July 1863, while news of a Gettysburg victory filtered through the crowd. When his wife and Hawthorne died in the mid-1860s, the broken, outcast Pierce turned to alcohol, began to weaken physically, and in October 1869 died in Concord.

A family man who lost all his children, a general's son humiliated in combat, a temperance advocate who struggled with alcoholism, and a Unionist politician who exacerbated sectional animosity, Franklin Pierce remains one of the most tragic, enigmatic figures of the antebellum and Civil War eras. Like many, he never understood the "moral indignation" of the abolitionists and remained an exacting, rational lawyer, upholding the letter of constitutional law in regard to slavery to the end.

—*Michael J. Connolly*

See also Democratic Party; Election of 1856; Election of 1860; Kansas-Nebraska Act; Ostend Manifesto.

For further reading:
Gara, Larry. *The Presidency of Franklin Pierce* (1991).
Gienapp, William. *The Origins of the Republican Party, 1852–1856* (1987).
Nichols, Roy. *Franklin Pierce: Young Hickory of the Granite Hills* (1958).

PIERPONT, FRANCIS HARRISON
(1814–1899)

*Promoter of West Virginia statehood, wartime
Union governor of Virginia*

Francis Pierpont was born on 25 January 1814 near Morgantown in Monongalia County in western Virginia, and moved with his family to Fairmont, in present-day West Virginia, when he was an infant. As there were no schools of higher education in Virginia west of the Allegheny Mountains at that time, in 1835 Pierpont enrolled at Allegheny College in nearby Meadeville, Pennsylvania. Upon graduation, he taught school in Harrison County, Virginia, and for a short time in Mississippi, before opening a law practice in Fairmont, Virginia, in 1842. While continuing his law practice, Pierpont also opened a coal mine near Fairmont in 1854. At first a Whig, Pierpont supported John Bell and the Constitutional Union Party during the 1860 presidential election. After the election of Abraham Lincoln to the presidency, Pierpont stood adamantly against the secession of Virginia, although he had not been a delegate to the Virginia Secession Convention.

Pierpont was, however, one of the 436 delegates from twenty-seven of Virginia's northwestern counties who attended the First Wheeling Convention in May 1861, where it was determined to resist the secession of the state. At the Second Wheeling Convention less than a month later, an ordinance was enacted establishing a "Reorganized Government of Virginia" that would remain loyal to the Union. The convention delegates subsequently elected Pierpont, by unanimous vote, to be the new governor of the restored government. His immediate tasks were to gain recognition from Washington of the new state government, raise the necessary funds so that the government might function, and recruit and arm volunteer regiments for the state's defense. In these endeavors Pierpont generally was successful. Although he was a lifelong foe of slavery, Pierpont did not become a member of the Republican Party until after the war.

When West Virginia became the thirty-fifth state on 20 June 1863, Pierpont—who had ardently supported West Virginia statehood—yielded to the newly elected governor, Arthur I. Boreman. Moving his office to Alexandria, Pierpont remained the governor of the Restored Government of Virginia. His governing powers, however, were limited to those areas then under Union control: Alexandria, Fairfax, and Loudon counties in northern Virginia; the eastern shore; and the Norfolk region. When the war ended, President Andrew Johnston recognized the legitimacy of the Restored Government and Pierpont moved his office to Richmond, remaining Virginia's governor until the Reconstruction Act of 1868 replaced him with a military governor.

Pierpont returned to his Fairmont law practice in 1868, and was elected to the West Virginia legislature in 1870, serving one term. President James Garfield gave him a patronage appointment as an internal revenue collector in 1881 for the Second West Virginia District. Political enemies in his own Republican Party, however, conspired to remove him from this post, and succeeded in doing so by consolidating his duties with the First West Virginia District and eliminating Pierpont's position.

Francis Pierpont died in his daughter's home at Pittsburgh, Pennsylvania, on 24 March 1899, and is buried in Woodlawn Cemetery in Fairmont. Pierpont's role in the establishment of West Virginia is recognized by his accolade as the "Father of West Virginia," even though he never was the governor of the state. Today, a statue of Pierpont stands in the U.S. Capitol's Statuary Hall.

—Mark Snell

See also Virginia; West Virginia.
For further reading:
Ambler, Charles H. *Francis H. Pierpont: Union War Governor of Virginia and Father of West Virginia* (1937).

PIKE, ALBERT
(1809–1891)

Confederate general

Born 29 December 1809 in Boston, Massachusetts, to Benjamin and Sarah Pike, Albert Pike received his education in Newburyport after the family moved there soon after his birth. After a brief period at Harvard, Pike spent his early professional career teaching at a variety of different schools across Massachusetts.

In 1831, Pike ventured west, traveling with various groups of hunters, trappers, and traders across Missouri, Texas, and New Mexico, dabbling in the fur-trading business. By 1833, Pike had settled in Pope County, Arkansas, where he taught school. There, he built a reputation as a great poet and author, receiving international attention for some of his work.

Along with his poetic prowess, from 1833 to 1861, Pike succeeded in other business ventures. By 1835, he owned a plantation and operated the *Arkansas Advocate*, a successful newspaper. In 1837 he was admitted to the bar and practiced primarily in the Indian Territories, representing Native Americans in disputes with the U.S. government. Pike won several substantial victories in front of the Arkansas Supreme Court during his career.

Throughout the 1850s, Pike, a member of the Whig Party and former clerk of the Arkansas Territorial Legislature, vocally opposed Arkansas' secession. When it became apparent that Arkansas would secede in 1861, however, Pike supported the Confederacy.

The Confederate government commissioned Pike a brigadier general on 15 August 1861, and, because of his

relationship with the Five Civilized Tribes, requested that he recruit support from the Native Americans west of Arkansas in Indian Territory. By November 1861, Pike commanded the Department of Indian Territory and had successfully enlisted over 2,000 natives for the Confederate cause, including Cherokee colonel Stand Watie. For the next few months, Pike trained the new recruits in military maneuvers, readying for possible action.

In early 1862, Major General Earl Van Dorn planned to attack Federal forces in Missouri from northwestern Arkansas. In February, he ordered Pike to move his troops from Indian Territory eastward to unite with regular forces near Elm Springs, Arkansas. On 7–8 March 1862, Pike and his men (about 1,000) fought in the battle of Pea Ridge as the westernmost wing of Van Dorn's army. During the first day's fighting, Pike's three regiments attacked Federal commander Colonel Peter J. Osterhaus's artillery battery across an open field. Union troops, frightened by the brightly painted warriors, broke and ran, abandoning their guns. The victorious Indians, unable to turn the cannon to their advantage and preoccupied with discarded Union equipment and supplies, succumbed to a Federal counterattack. The Confederate Native Americans scattered as they retreated from the scene, making it impossible for Pike to regain control. Some of the men headed back to Indian Territory immediately, while others moved north and then southwest. Within a month, almost all of them as well as Pike had returned to Indian Territory.

When rumors surfaced that some in Pike's regiment had scalped Union soldiers in the melee, a cry went out for retribution. However, Pike had fallen away from Federal forces back into Choctaw country, where he constructed Fort McCulloch a few miles north of the Red River. From his base, he planned to harass any enemy operations into Indian Territory.

In the summer of 1862, the new Confederate commander of the Trans-Mississippi District, Major General Thomas Hindman, ordered Pike's apprehension for disobeying orders. Yet the portly, heavily bearded, longhaired poet proved difficult to capture in Arkansas, where he had many friends. Authorities never arrested him.

Discouraged and unhappy with military politics, Pike resigned in July 1862, although his resignation was not accepted until that November. He remained under suspicion from both sides for the remainder of the war.

Leaving the American Civil War as the only white southerner to lead an all-Native American force in battle, Albert Pike returned to practicing law in Arkansas. He wrote books and became a national figure in Freemasonry, drafting several tracts about the organization. He died in Washington, D.C., on 2 April 1891 and was buried at the Oak Hill Cemetery in that city.

—*Buck T. Foster*

See also Arkansas; Indian Territory; Pea Ridge (Elkhorn Tavern), Battle of; Van Dorn, Earl.
For further reading:
Allsopp, Frederick W. *Albert Pike; A Biography* (1992).
Boyden, William L. *A Bibliography of the Writings of Albert Pike* (1921; reprint, 1957).
Brown, Walter L. *A Life of Albert Pike* (1997).
Duncan, Robert L. *Reluctant General: The Life and Times of Albert Pike* (1961).

PILLOW, GIDEON JOHNSON
(1806–1878)
Confederate general

Gideon J. Pillow engendered controversy throughout his political and military career. Variously labeled cowardly, vain, and quarrelsome, Pillow's personality brought out strong emotions that hindered him from achieving a successful career.

Born 8 June 1806 in Williamson County, Tennessee, Pillow had an inauspicious childhood. At the age of seventeen, he entered Cumberland College in Nashville. His graduation from there in 1827 allowed him to establish a law office in Columbia, Tennessee, some time later. In 1831 he married Mary Elizabeth Martin, a member of an important middle Tennessee family. Pillow spent the next few years engaged in the background of various Tennessee political contests.

During the 1930s Pillow became a friend of James K. Polk. Both men practiced law in Columbia, although not together. Their acquaintance solidified into a lifelong friendship when Pillow served as attorney for Polk's younger brother, who became involved in an unfortunate duel and subsequent court case. As Polk moved within the elite circle of Jacksonian Democrats, Pillow followed. This combination brought success in 1844, when Polk received the presidential nomination of the Democratic convention in Baltimore, Maryland. Pillow's lamentable reputation began at this point. He claimed for himself the recognition of bringing Polk's nomination to fruition. Although Pillow played an important role in the convention, other Tennessee delegates, among them S. H. Laughlin, Cave Johnson, and Andrew Jackson Donelson contributed more substantially to Polk's nomination.

Pillow's loyalty to the eventual winner of the presidential election, James K. Polk, garnered him a military appointment shortly after the United States declared war against Mexico in 1846. He accepted his new position as brigadier general and set off for battle in the west. Pillow performed well enough on the field of battle. It was out of the line of fire that he found himself embroiled in numerous disputes with other officers, including Generals Zachary Taylor and Winfield Scott, for political and personal reasons.

The Mexican-American War ended with Pillow as a major general in the U.S. Army. However, he spent the first few weeks of 1849 before two courts of inquiry defending his conduct during that conflict. The courts exonerated Pillow, but they left him exceedingly irritable. He returned to Tennessee and assisted one of his former staff officers, Captain Roswell Ripley, in writing a history of the recent war. Pillow also attended the two sessions of the Nashville Convention that met in 1850. At both meetings, he stood with the other members of the Tennessee delegation in support of compromise in the face of more radical Southerners and their calls for nullification and secession.

In 1852 Pillow campaigned strongly behind the scenes for a Pierce-Pillow ticket at the national Democratic nominating convention. It was to no avail, as the delegates chose William R. King as vice president over Pillow. His interest in the vice presidency glowed again in 1856, but he abandoned the idea in favor of fellow Tennessee Democrat, Aaron V. Brown. The next year, Pillow failed in his bid to receive one of the two vacant U.S. Senate seats in his home state.

Pillow viewed the presidential election of 1860 with the hope of preserving the Union through his support of Stephen A. Douglas, a favored politician of Unionists in Tennessee. The election of Abraham Lincoln instead of Douglas disillusioned Pillow. He advocated secession from the United States and when Tennessee voters took this action during a special referendum, Pillow quickly went to work to establish a state military unit capable of rendering assistance to the Confederate government. On 9 May 1861, Governor Isham G. Harris named Pillow major general and commander of the Provisional Army of Tennessee. This army grew under Pillow's command to twenty-two infantry regiments, ten artillery companies, and two cavalry regiments. When Tennessee joined the Confederate States in July 1861, Confederate president Jefferson Davis demoted Pillow to brigadier general and placed the Army of Tennessee under Leonidas Polk.

Pillow's conduct during the Civil War recalled that of the Mexican-American War. During the autumn of 1861, Pillow clashed with Leonidas Polk over orders concerning an attack on New Madrid, Missouri. Following the battle of Belmont in Missouri, he resigned his post, only to return a month later. In February 1862 Pillow moved to reinforce Fort Donelson on the Cumberland River in northern Tennessee. Facing a hopeless situation against Ulysses S. Grant's troops, Pillow's determination not to surrender faded and he agreed to retreat with his commanding officer, General John Floyd. Thus, the task of surrendering Fort Donelson fell to Simon Buckner, a subordinate general, instead of to Floyd or Pillow. This decision cost both Floyd and Pillow their military commands.

Pillow spent much of 1862 attempting to regain his position and finally received satisfaction when Jefferson Davis rescinded the Tennessean's resignation. Pillow proceeded to join Braxton Bragg's troops at Murfreesboro, where the Confederate army had encountered Union troops at the battle of Stones River. On 2 January 1863, the last day of the battle, Bragg sent Pillow to John C. Breckinridge, who gave the returning general command of the 2d Brigade. Pillow arrived just as the soldiers began to advance. The defeat of the Confederate army that day cannot, therefore, be attributed to Pillow's actions.

Pillow spent the rest of 1863 and part of 1864 at the head of the Volunteer and Conscript Bureau of the Army of the Tennessee. This organization sought to bring in new recruits for the Confederacy. Pillow succeeded in his position, but he also continued to clash with superior officers over superficial points. In June 1864 Pillow assumed his last field command. His orders were to disrupt William T. Sherman's communications between Atlanta and Chattanooga. The mission failed miserably, and Pillow returned to recruiting soldiers for the remainder of the war.

After the war Pillow practiced law with Isham G. Harris in Memphis. He died of yellow fever on 8 October 1878 and was buried in Helena, Arkansas. His body was later moved to Elmwood Cemetery in Memphis.

—*Mark R. Cheathem*

See also Fort Donelson, Battle of.
For further reading:
Hughes, Nathaniel Cheairs, Jr., and Roy P. Stonesifer, Jr. *The Life and Wars of Gideon J. Pillow* (1993).

PILOT KNOB, BATTLE OF
(27–28 September 1864)

By the late summer of 1864 the Confederate States of America was in serious trouble. The Army of Northern Virginia was entrenched around Petersburg, while William T. Sherman was pressing south upon Atlanta. In the trans-Mississippi west, cut off from the rest of the Confederacy after the fall of Vicksburg, military campaigns had been confined to Louisiana and Arkansas. No major battle had been fought in Missouri since Island No. 10 was overrun in April 1862.

Lieutenant General Edmund Kirby Smith, commander of the Confederate Trans-Mississippi Department, saw Missouri as an opportunity for the Confederacy to strike a blow at the Union. Most of the Union's experienced troops were in the Eastern theater, leaving the state in the hands of often unreliable militia units. Reports of harsh treatment of the civilian population led General Kirby Smith to believe that an invading army would receive popular support and a large number of recruits.

Smith selected Major General Sterling Price to lead

an expedition into Missouri in the autumn of 1864. Three divisions of 12,000 men were assembled at Pocahontas, Arkansas, under the direction of John S. Marmaduke, James F. Fagan, and Joseph O. Shelby. They entered Missouri on 19 September. Six days later, on 25 September, they were in the vicinity of Fredericktown, twenty miles south and east of the southern terminus of the Iron Mountain and St. Louis Railroad at the small village of Pilot Knob. Shelby's division moved north to cut the railroad between Pilot Knob and St. Louis, while Fagan and Marmaduke moved their troops to capture Pilot Knob. As rumors and reports of the Confederate approach reached St. Louis, Union General Thomas Ewing was ordered south to determine the size and location of the enemy troops and to take command of the Union post at Fort Davidson. This small hexagonal earthwork was manned by approximately 1,450 militia, home guards, and new recruits. Rifle pits extended from the fort across the northern end of the narrow Arcadia Valley. Encircled by a dry moat and with substantial armament inside, the fort posed a formidable barrier to enemy forces seeking to pass through the valley. At the first light of day on 27 September 1864, the Confederates moved into the valley with the intention of quickly overrunning and capturing Fort Davidson. Price moved some of his troops and field pieces to the mountains that towered over the fort. He believed that a strong frontal assault supported from the mountain tops would quickly reduce the Union position.

But Price underestimated the difficulty of the terrain, the concentrated firepower from inside Fort Davidson, the determination of the Union troops at the site, and the strength of the earthworks. Confederate troops were spread over a wide area and rough terrain, and instead of one massive assault against the fort, the attack was enacted in uncoordinated waves, permitting the defenders inside the fort and rifle pits to focus a destructive fire upon each successive wave. Some Confederates reached the moat at the edge of the fort, but the intense firing from above and the use of hand grenades tossed into the moat turned them back. They were unable to muster any coordinated attacks upon the fort. Intermittent and sporadic firing from both sides continued throughout the afternoon, ending near dark when Price fell back out of range of the cannon, attended his wounded and dead (more than 1,000), and prepared for a more concentrated attack on the twenty-eighth.

However, General Ewing realized the strength of Price's army and knew that he could not hold out against another such attack. Thus, he ordered a silent, but risky, evacuation of the fort. His men quietly left the fort at 2:30 A.M., passing directly through enemy lines. A small group of men were left behind, and at 3:30 A.M., they ignited the powder magazine—destroying all remaining powder, weapons, and supplies. Price apparently concluded that the explosion was an accident and did not immediately respond. Federal forces, encircled and trapped inside Fort Davidson, walked to safety directly through enemy lines.

Early on the morning of the twenty-eighth, angered that Ewing had slipped out of the fort, Price organized a vigorous pursuit. But Ewing moved north and west, marching sixty-six miles in thirty-nine hours. Near Leasburg he was joined by reinforcements from St. Louis. Price found his "invading" army suddenly on the defensive. He decided to move west across the state in search of men and supplies. But Union forces pressed his army into battle at Westport, Mine Creek, and Newtonia, before he was able to fall back into Arkansas. This was a campaign that failed. The battle at Pilot Knob disrupted Price's efforts and set the stage for his failure to carry out his invasion of Missouri. Here in the tranquil Arcadia Valley, the largest Confederate offensive military campaign west of the Mississippi and the largest mounted raid of the American Civil War was thwarted. This venture was the Confederacy's last chance to pry Missouri from Federal control and influence the presidential election of 1864. The stand made by Thomas Ewing's men on 26–27 September 1864 was the turning point of the campaign and sealed the fate of the Confederacy west of the Mississippi River.

—*Frank Nickell*

See also Ewing, Thomas, Jr.; Fagan, James Fleming; Marmaduke, John Sappington; Missouri; Price, Sterling; Price's Missouri Raid.

For further reading:
Brownlee, Richard S. "The Battle of Pilot Knob, Iron County, Missouri, September 27, 1864." *Missouri Historical Review* (1964).
Castel, Albert E. *General Sterling Price and the Civil War in the West* (1968).
Cole, Birdie Hale. "The Battle of Pilot Knob." *Confederate Veteran* (1914).
Harris, W. D. "Price's Raid Through Missouri." *Confederate Veteran* (1905).
Margreiter, John. "The Battle of Pilot Knob." *Civil War Times Illustrated* (1964).
Peterson, Cyrus A., and Joseph M. Hanson. *Pilot Knob: The Thermopylae of the West* (1914).
Suderow, Bryce. *Thunder in Arcadia Valley: Prices's Defeat, September 27, 1864* (1986).

PINKERTON, ALLAN
(1819–1884)
Union spy

The son of a police sergeant, Allan Pinkerton was born in Glasgow, Scotland, on 25 August 1819. After working as an apprentice barrel maker in Scotland, he came to the United States because of union strikes and political difficulties in 1842, settling in Dundee, Illinois, to become a barrel maker. One day

Allan Pinkerton (*Library of Congress*)

while cutting wood for his barrels, he happened upon the hideout of a group of counterfeiters. Rallying a group of citizens behind him, Pinkerton raided their lair and apprehended the entire gang. Now having a taste for law enforcement, he was named deputy sheriff of Kane County in 1846. Pinkerton gained success quickly, rising to the rank of deputy sheriff of Cook County, the county in which Chicago is located. He later sold his business in 1850 to move to Chicago, acquiring the designation of the city's first detective. Later that year, he organized his own detective agency, involved in the assistance of runaway slaves and the protection of mail and railroad property from thieves. He acquired the position of the first special U.S. Mail agent in this area. In 1852, this organization became his own Pinkerton National Defense Agency. Successful work for the Adams Express and other railroads allowed him to gain national notoriety, giving him the opportunity to expand his operations and services.

In April 1861, Pinkerton was called to Washington by railroad owner Samuel Felton to investigate rumors of a plot by Maryland secessionists to sabotage property belonging to the Philadelphia, Wilmington & Baltimore Railroad. His investigation in this case led to the estab-

lishment of the Federal Secret Service Agency. It was on this case that one of his operatives, Timothy Webster, posing as a secessionist, accidentally discovered a plot to assassinate then president-elect Abraham Lincoln as he passed through Baltimore on his way to Washington, D.C. The president-elect's train plans, intending to stop at most major cities between Indianapolis and Washington, were rescheduled. Lincoln was informed of the plan in Philadelphia as Pinkerton rendezvoused with him on the night of 21 February. Pinkerton took this case into his own hands as he cut short Lincoln's itinerary, rushing him to Washington to arrive on 23 February.

When the war began, Pinkerton offered himself and his agents for secret service work for Lincoln. When the president refused, Pinkerton was called upon by Major General George McClellan, a former railroad president, in May of 1861. Pinkerton was initially hired to tour the South from Kentucky to Mississippi to assess public opinion of the North. He operated under the name of E. J. Allen, the name by which he was known throughout the war. When he returned North, he assumed the rank of chief detective and established a secret service bureau for the Department of the Ohio. Later in the year, when McClellan became the commander of the Army of the Potomac, Pinkerton's agency, through which all intelligence operations for McClellan were conducted during the war, moved to Washington. While there, on 23 August Pinkerton caught one of the South's most famous spies, Rose Greenhow, a "seducer" who had many political and military connections in Washington.

Although Pinkerton was heavily consulted for his intelligence surveys, the most famous use of Pinkerton's reports were during McClellan's attack on Richmond. In the Peninsula campaign, Pinkerton's objective was to determine Confederate troop strength in Virginia. Pinkerton and his men, however, were detectives, not intelligence agents. Being untrained in the arts of spying on armies, they relied heavily on the accounts of frantic civilians and slaves. He reported that he and his agents had identified more than 200 Confederate regiments, 119,000 men, around Manassas. Unfortunately for McClellan, there were actually no more than 50,000 Confederate soldiers there. McClellan accepted his estimates as a result of his confidence in Pinkerton, his best source of information. At Richmond, Pinkerton warned McClellan of Confederate troop sizes of between 180,000 and 200,000. Later reports, however, tell that the South had amassed an army of maybe only a third of that size. Pinkerton also erred in the identification of cannons that turned out to be nothing more than painted tree trunks. McClellan, known for his cautious nature, saw opportunities pass him by as he relied on Pinkerton's reports. McClellan's continual delays in attacking the Confederates allowed for Confederate positions to be fortified and forces to amass, reaching

adequate numbers to oppose the Federals once a strike had finally been initiated. McClellan had started moving his divisions to begin the campaign on 17 March; however, it was not until 3 May that any attack took place. Based on the intelligence reports of Pinkerton, the Peninsula Campaign ended in failure.

When McClellan was removed from command after his inability to complete even a partial victory at the battle of Antietam on 11 November 1862, Pinkerton, losing credibility as a result of his spying blunders, did not continue to work within the military. He did continue to work for the government, however, through the investigation of claims against it. In 1865, he returned to Chicago to his detective agency, which by this time had branched out to offices in New York and Philadelphia. The types of work that Pinkerton's agency was hired for broadened. He now also investigated trade union espionage and provided protective services for businesses and homes. Being in demand, his services allowed for the accumulation of the nation's largest database of information on crime and criminals. Although his agency is best remembered for breaking up strikes and union busting in the 1870s, he is regarded as the most famous American detective.

Pinkerton's later years involved the writing of several popular books about his adventures as a "master-spy" and detective. Although often reading like fiction, there is no doubt to the daringness of his work during the war. Though he portrayed himself as the Union's greatest spy, few Federals were more criticized. The value of his estimates of Confederate troop strengths has been questioned. Among other overestimations and miscalculations, he probably helped in losing the Peninsula campaign, although Pinkerton insisted in the accuracy of his intelligence reports to the very end. Pinkerton died in Chicago on 1 July 1884.

—*Andrew Paul Bielakowski*

See also Espionage; Greenhow, Rose O'Neal; McClellan, George Brinton; Peninsula Campaign.

For further reading:

Axelrod, Alan. *The War between the Spies: A History of Espionage during the American Civil War* (1992).

Fishel, Edwin C. "Pinkerton and McClellan: Who Deceived Whom?" *Civil War History* (1988).

Horan, James D. *The Pinkertons: The Detective Dynasty That Made History* (1968).

Markle, Donald E. *Spies and Spymasters of the Civil War* (1994).

Spies, Scouts, and Raiders: Irregular Operations. Vol. 18 of *The Civil War* (1983).

PLANTER

One of the outstanding military exploits of the American Civil War involved not a soldier, but a slave. Robert Smalls, a sometime waiter, teamster, and sailor, stole the Confederate cotton steamer *Planter*, sailed it out of Confederate waters, and delivered it to Union naval forces, saying, "I thought that the *Planter* might be of some use to Uncle Abe."

Built in 1860 of live oak and red cedar in Charleston, South Carolina, the *Planter* measured 150 feet in length, had a 10-foot beam, a depth of 7 feet 10 inches, drew 3 feet 9 inches of water, and had enough space to carry 1,400 bales of cotton.

Late in 1861 the Confederate war government chartered the *Planter* and converted it into a special dispatch boat for General Roswell Ripley, second in command of Charleston's defenses. The *Planter* could carry 1,000 men, and this fact made her particularly suitable for this enterprise. She was armed with one long 32-pound pivot gun on the foredeck and a 24-pound howitzer on the afterdeck. The *Planter* was also used by the Confederate engineering department to help in the construction of new fortifications in Charleston harbor and in the transporting of supplies to other fortifications in neighboring waters. The *Planter* carried a crew of eleven men, of whom three were white—the captain, the mate, and the engineer. The rest were slaves.

On the night of 13 May 1862, while the captain and his mates were ashore, Smalls set off with his band—including five women and three children—and sailed the *Planter* out of Charleston Harbor towards the Union blockade. He then lowered the Confederate colors and hoisted a bed sheet as a flag of truce.

The bed sheet was not run up a moment too soon, for the *Planter* had come within the range of the guns of the Union ship *Onward*, which was on blockade duty in Charleston harbor. The lookout on the *Onward* called out that a strange vessel was approaching. As the *Onward*'s crew prepared to open fire on the approaching vessel, its captain, J. F. Nickels, caught a glimpse of the flag of truce, and told his gunners to relax. A prize crew was sent aboard the strange vessel, and there they greeted "Captain" Smalls and his crew. The white flag of truce came down and up went the American flag. There in the main ship channel of Charleston harbor, the ownership of the *Planter* was transferred from the Confederate States of America to the Union navy.

News of Smalls's exploits quickly spread throughout the North and many believed that Smalls and his band should be rewarded for their efforts. Congress responded, moving with unusual speed. Two weeks from the day that the *Planter* was abducted, the Senate passed a bill authorizing the appraisal of the *Planter*, and when her value was determined, one-half was to be given to Smalls and his associates. Within another week, the House of Representatives had passed the measure and President Lincoln had signed it.

Robert Smalls assumed correctly that the *Planter* would be of some use to "Uncle Abe." Admirably suited to the shallow waters of South Carolina's Sea Island region, the

The *Planter* at the General Hospital wharf on the Appomattox River at City Point, Virginia, ca. 1865 (*Library of Congress*)

Planter was equipped with musket-proof bulwarks and converted into a Union navy transport, which could carry upwards of seventy men. Exactly one month after the ship's abduction, Admiral Samuel F. Du Pont, commander of the South Atlantic blockading squadron, wrote that he was "glad that the *Planter* has proved so useful a transport, and that we have again been able so materially to aid the army, especially at a critical time, when its generals were almost helpless for want of transports."

Because the army could make much better use out of a wood-burning vessel than the navy, in early September 1862 the *Planter* was sold to the Union army. The Quartermaster's Department welcomed the addition of the *Planter* because the army lacked vessels of light draft. The *Planter* was then used by the army mainly to transport troops, but it saw occasional service as a supply boat as well. She faithfully served the Union until September 1866, when she was decommissioned and sold in Baltimore, Maryland.

—*Michael S. Davis*

See also Blockade of C.S.A.; Smalls, Robert.

For further reading:
McPherson, James M. *The Negro's Civil War: How American Blacks Felt and Acted during the War for the Union* (1965; reprint, 1991).
Quarles, Benjamin. The Abduction of the *Planter*. In *The Black Soldier: From the American Revolution to Vietnam*. Edited by Jay David and Elaine Craine (1971).
———. *The Negro in the Civil War* (1953; reprint, 1989).
Uya, Okon Edet. *From Slavery to Public Service: Robert Smalls, 1839–1915* (1971).

PLEASANT HILL, LOUISIANA, BATTLE OF
(9 April 1864)

Pleasant Hill was the last major battle of the Red River campaign of 1864. Persistent if not talented, Union major general Nathaniel P. Banks still held onto his scheme to take Shreveport, Louisiana, despite his loss to Confederate major general Richard Taylor at Mansfield on 8 April. By rejoining his Red River Expeditionary Force with Admiral David D. Porter's gunboat fleet and Brigadier General Thomas Kilby Smith's detachment of XVII Corps at the Red River, he believed he could salvage his expedition. Under cover of darkness during the night of 8–9 April, Banks evacuated his rear guard positions for Pleasant Hill, some fourteen miles to his rear. To mask his withdrawal, two divisions under Brigadier Generals W. H. Emory and J. A. Mower remained behind.

Although significantly outnumbered, the aggressive Taylor pressed his pursuit in expectation of destroying Banks's forces. At dawn Taylor, accompanying Brigadier General Thomas Green's cavalry, led two brigades of Brigadier General Thomas J. Churchill's division under Mosby M. Parsons and James C. Tappan in pursuit of the Federals' rear guard. Having suffered heavy losses the day before at Mansfield, Major General John G. Walker's and Brigadier General Camille de Polignac's Divisions brought up the Confederate rear.

Arriving at Pleasant Hill's outskirts at about 9 A.M., Taylor was somewhat surprised to find the Federals forming a line of battle. As Taylor waited for Churchill's Division to come up, reconnaissance forays by Brigadier General Hamilton P. Bee's cavalry confirmed that Banks's troops were indeed occupying formidable defensive positions. Attackers would be forced to cross an open field in the face of fire from skirmishers concealed in a ravine that, in turn, fronted a low plateau on which Banks had placed his artillery and main infantry positions. Still, Taylor remained firmly convinced that he could exploit the momentum from the morale advantage he had gained from his success at Mansfield.

Taylor's troops, however, were exhausted. Polignac and Walker's men had fought a pitched battle the previous day and Churchill's had marched forty-five miles in thirty-six hours. Reluctantly, Taylor was forced to allow his troops, now reinforced to some 13,500 men, two hours' rest before opening his attack. At 3 P.M., disregarding his opponent's superior position and numbers, Taylor set his attack in motion. Pinning his strategy on Churchill's relatively fresh troops, he ordered his two divisions southward in a flanking maneuver. Within an hour and a half Churchill's force, led by Tappan and Parsons, stood in line of battle across the Sabine Road. Taylor's plan called for Churchill's troops to launch a decisive attack on the Union southern flank, rolling it upon itself. As the enemy line collapsed, Walker was then to throw his division at Banks's center while Bee's Texas Cavalry was to exploit any breakthrough with a mounted saber attack. Polignac's survivors, who had borne the worst of the fighting at Mansfield, were to rest as reserves on the Confederate far left.

The Confederate attack opened at 4:30 P.M. as Taylor's artillery commander, Major Joseph Brent, ordered his gunners to pull their lanyards and the infantry stepped off into a hail of Union fire. Parsons and Tappan achieved initial success on the Confederate right as they overwhelmed the brigade of Colonel Lewis Benedict who was killed in the fighting. Taylor saw less success on his left as Union troops repulsed savage assaults by Walker's infantry and Bee's ill-fated cavalry charge. After over an hour of desperate and costly fighting, Churchill's command under Parsons and Tappan was making headway on the Confederate right but the Confederate assaults on the Union center had made little progress. As Walker's brigade commanders struggled to maintain their momentum, Taylor ordered up Polignac's Division. Polignac formed his line between General Thomas Green's now dismounted cavalry under Brigadier General James Major and Walker's left brigade under Colonel Horace Randal. Meeting Polignac's, Walker's, and Green's combined onslaught, Colonel William T. Shaw's 2d Brigade of Brigadier General A. J. Smith's XVI Corps's, 3d Division, which had broken every assault Taylor had thrown against them, finally was exhausted and grudgingly gave way in the center. At the same time, the Federal left collapsed under pressure from Churchill's two brigades. Churchill's advantage, however, was short-lived. Just as he sensed victory, a determined counterattack by veteran regiments of A. J. Smith's XVI Corps emerged from the woods to slam into Parson's right flank. As Parson's troops gave way, the momentum shifted to the Federals as Mower led the Union center forward. The Federal counterattack crushed Taylor's critical flanking movement and with it hopes of adding a second victory to Mansfield. Although Taylor continued to press the Union center, fatigue, disorganization, and the approaching nightfall soon dictated the battle's end.

Despite having won a tactical victory at Pleasant Hill, a demoralized Banks withdrew under cover of night to Grand Ecore and eventually on to Alexandria. Taylor, although disappointed in not having destroyed Banks, contented himself with having finally driven the Federals from western Louisiana. Both sides had suffered heavily during the two days' fighting. Federal records added 152 killed, 859 wounded, and 495 captured at Pleasant Hill to the losses of the previous day at Mansfield. Taylor estimated his total losses at 2,200.

—Jeff Kinard

See also Alexandria, Louisiana; Mansfield, Battle of; Red River Campaign.

For further reading:
Barr, Alwyn. *Polignac's Texas Brigade* (1964).
Johnson, Ludwell H. *Red River Campaign: Politics and Cotton in the Civil War* (1993).
Kerby, Robert L. *Kirby Smith's Confederacy: The Trans-Mississippi South, 1863–1865* (1972).
Parrish, T. Michael. *Richard Taylor: Soldier Prince of Dixie* (1992).

PLEASANTS, HENRY
(1833–1880)
Union officer

Born in Argentina in 1833, Henry Pleasants was the son of a Philadelphia merchant and his Spanish wife. His father smuggled arms and ammunition to South American insurgents fighting against a dictator. After his father died in 1846, thirteen-year-old Henry was sent, alone, to be raised by his father's favorite brother, then a physician living in Philadelphia. After overcoming many educational difficulties, Pleasants was graduated from Central High School with a B.A. in 1851.

Upon graduation, Pleasants went to work as an engineer with the Pennsylvania Railroad; by 1853, he was senior assistant engineer. His greatest fame while working for the railroad was his ability to solve the problem of getting fresh air in to the workers digging the 4,200-foot-long Sand Patch Tunnel. Soon after, Pleasants resigned from the company and moved to Pottsville, Schuylkill County, where he became a successful deep mining engineer in the coal fields there. He married a local woman early in 1860, but she died during pregnancy late in the year. Pleasants was overcome by grief and never entirely recovered from this tragedy.

When war erupted in April 1861, Pleasants enlisted in the Tower Guard, a local militia company that became Company H, 6th Pennsylvania Volunteer Infantry. After an uneventful three-month term of service, Pleasants returned home and recruited a new unit. When the men were accepted into service, Pleasants was commissioned as captain of Company C, 48th Pennsylvania Volunteer Infantry, a regiment composed almost entirely of men from Schuylkill County.

Pleasants took an active part in the campaigns of the 48th. After service on the North Carolina coast, the regiment was attached to IX Army Corps and served with the corps its entire term of service. Pleasants was present at the battles of Second Bull Run, Chantilly, South Mountain, and Antietam. On 20 September 1862, he was promoted to lieutenant colonel. Pleasants was wounded in the leg at Fredericksburg, but recovered and accompanied the regiment to Kentucky. In July 1863, Pleasants was appointed provost marshal general of XXIII Army Corps and participated in the Knoxville campaign.

Upon the return of IX Corps to Virginia, Pleasants led the 48th during the battles of the Wilderness, Spotsylvania, North Anna River, Cold Harbor, and Petersburg. In June 1864, shortly after siege operations began at Petersburg, some of Pleasants's men who had been coal miners proposed digging a tunnel under a Confederate fort and then blowing it up. The colonel wholeheartedly agreed with his men, and work started on 25 June. General Meade and other regular army engineers did not support the tunneling effort, believing that the

feat could not be accomplished. In spite of a lack of proper equipment, the tunnel—some 511 feet long—was completed, and two lateral galleries were packed with explosives. The fuse was lit on 30 July and the resulting explosion destroyed the Confederate fort and blew a large crater in the trench line. General Burnside's corps charged into the hole and was supposed to advance beyond to higher ground, but resulting chaos and bold Southern moves confined the Yankees, and the result was a defeat.

Pleasants remained in command of the 48th until late 1864. His health broken by active campaigning, Pleasants asked to be mustered out of service, which occurred on 21 December. Even though General Meade had issued an order (3 August 1864) complimenting Pleasants and his men for the tunnel operation, the colonel was bitter over the lack of respect from army headquarters, and this bitterness probably led to his request to leave military service. On 13 March 1865, Pleasants received a brevet brigadier generalship in recognition of his wartime services.

After the Civil War, Pleasants became chief engineer of the Philadelphia & Reading Coal & Iron Company. The colonel remarried and sired three sons. Wartime exposure had affected Pleasants's health, though, and in 1877 he took a year's leave of absence in Europe to recuperate. Pleasants never recovered full health, and he died in 1880. His tombstone, in Pottsville's Charles Baber Cemetery, is completely devoid of any mention of his military service, a probable intentional oversight on Pleasants's part.

—*Richard A. Sauers*

See also Crater, Battle of the.
For further reading:
Bosbyshell, Oliver C. *The 48th in the War, Being a Narrative of the Campaigns of the 48th Regiment, Infantry, Pennsylvania Veteran Volunteers, during the War of the Rebellion* (1895).
"Obituary. General Henry Pleasants." *Pottsville Weekly Miners' Journal* (1880).
Pleasants, Henry, Jr., and George H. Straley. *Inferno at Petersburg* (1961).

PLEASONTON, ALFRED
(1824–1897)
Union general

Born in Washington, D.C., Alfred Pleasonton attended the U.S. Military Academy and graduated seventh of twenty-five in the class of 1844. Shortly after graduation, Pleasonton was sent to fight in the Mexican-American War as a lieutenant of dragoons. He received one brevet promotion for his actions in that conflict. After the war, he served at a variety of frontier posts, including a stint in Florida during the Third Seminole War and in Kansas during the difficulties known as "Bleeding Kansas."

General Alfred Pleasanton (*right*) and Captain George A. Custer on horseback at Falmouth, Virginia, April 1863
(Photograph by Timothy O'Sullivan / *Library of Congress*)

At the outbreak of the Civil War, Pleasonton was a captain in the 2d Cavalry stationed in Utah. He led that part of the regiment in Utah back east to Washington in the fall of 1861. Once there, Pleasonton served in the Washington area as part of the Army of the Potomac. In February 1862 he was promoted to major.

Pleasonton fought in the Peninsula campaign and distinguished himself in guarding the retreat of the army to the James River at the end of the Seven Days. In July he was made brigadier general of volunteers, and the following month, in command of a cavalry brigade, he protected the retreat of the army as it moved from Harrison's Landing to Williamsburg.

In the Maryland campaign, Pleasonton commanded a cavalry division. He led his division at South Mountain and pursued the retreating Confederates after they were pushed from their strongholds there. During the battle of Antietam a few days later, he provided support for several infantry attacks, particularly on the Union left. In the second week of October he led his division in unsuccessfully combating J. E. B. Stuart's raid into Maryland and Pennsylvania.

During the remainder of the fall of 1862, Pleasonton skirmished with Confederates who ventured across the Rappahannock River and then fought in the battle of Fredericksburg. The following spring he fought at Chancellorsville and grossly inflated his own role in the conflict in his official report. Still, he had impressed the commander of the Army of the Potomac, Joseph Hooker, who had been quite unimpressed with the commander of the army's cavalry corps, George Stoneman. On 7 June 1863 Hooker replaced Stoneman with Pleasonton. Two days later, Pleasonton led his corps forward to attack the Confederate cavalry position at Brandy Station, Virginia.

At Brandy Station, the Union cavalry held its own against what had up to that point been superior Confederate horsemen. Whether deservedly or not, Pleasonton received much of the credit for the Union performance in the battle, and there can be little doubt that the engagement did much to boost the Union cavalry's morale. Pleasonton was promoted to major general of volunteers on 22 June 1863. In the subsequent Gettysburg campaign, however, Pleasonton did little to distinguish himself, with much of the glory of the Union cavalry's success, especially on 3 July, going to other officers.

Pleasonton led his corps forward in the pursuit of Robert E. Lee after Gettysburg in the late summer and fall of 1863. He fought in the Bristoe Station and Mine

Run campaigns. By early 1864, however, because of Pleasonton's perceived lack of aggression (as characterized by his opposition to the Kilpatrick-Dahlgren Raid) and because of the preference of General Ulysses S. Grant, the new commanding general of the army, for more offensive-minded officers, Pleasonton was relieved by David McMurtrie Gregg on 25 March 1864. Pleasonton was sent to the Department of the Missouri to serve as second-in-command to William S. Rosecrans.

In Missouri, Pleasonton was placed in command of the District of Central Missouri. In the late summer of 1864 he secured a leave to New York City but was summoned back frantically by Rosecrans with the threat of Sterling Price's raid into the state with the promise that if he hurried he could command the department's cavalry against Price. Pleasonton returned quickly and was later commended for his actions in repelling Price.

In early 1865, Pleasonton again headed east on leave but was summoned back again in February by the new commander of the department, Major General Grenville Mellen Dodge, to deal with Confederate guerrillas. In March Pleasonton became the department's chief of cavalry. In July after the war, he was sent to the District of Wisconsin.

Pleasonton decided to remain in the army after the reorganization in 1866, reverting to the rank of major of cavalry. He had turned down a lieutenant colonelcy in the infantry, and as a result was junior to several officers whom he had preceded at West Point and whom he had outranked as a volunteer officer. Rather than suffer that indignity he requested retirement at his volunteer rank, but his request was denied. He then resigned. He received several federal appointments over the next two decades, including internal revenue collector. In 1888 he was retroactively retired from the army but at the rank of major. In retirement he lived in Washington, D.C., where he died on 17 February 1897.

—*David S. Heidler and Jeanne T. Heidler*

See also Brandy Station, Battle of; Cavalry, U.S.A.; Chambersburg Raid; Price's Missouri Raid.

For further reading:
Downey, Fairfax Davis. *Clash of Cavalry: The Battle of Brandy Station, June 9, 1863* (1959).
Landrith, Mark S. *The Effect of Personality of Senior Leaders on the Outcome of the Battle of Gettysburg* (1997).

PLUM POINT BEND, NAVAL BATTLE OF
(10 May 1862)

The battle of Plum Point Bend, on the Mississippi River above Fort Pillow, on 10 May 1862 was the war's first real engagement between naval squadrons, one that Union commander Commodore Charles Henry Davis characterized as "a smart affair."

In May 1862 the Union flotilla lay above Fort Pillow, unable to pass and using long-range mortar fire to try to shell the fort into submission. An attempt to take the fort had been stymied by the department commander General Henry Halleck's decision to remove the great bulk of Union army troops for his own campaign against Corinth. Confederate deserters had warned that the Confederate River Defense Fleet would come out, and a Confederate sortie on the eighth should have served as confirmation of this. Flag Officer Andrew H. Foote, who turned over his command to Davis on 9 May, had taken the precaution of ordering the gunboats positioned so they faced downstream, but no lookouts had been posted downriver. Foote claimed the flotilla was prepared for a fight, but that was not true.

The Union gunboats were in two divisions: three on the Tennessee bank and four on the Arkansas side of the river. Since mid-April the flotilla had followed the same routine: a gunboat daily towed one or more mortar boats to just above Craigshead Point, and guarded there by the gunboat, the mortar boats would then fire shells across the point toward Fort Pillow.

At 6 A.M. on 10 May, Union mortar boat No. 16 with a crew of fourteen commanded by Second Master Thomas B. Gregory was in position, along with her covering gunboat, Lieutenant Rodger Stembel's USS *Cincinnati*, the crew of which was nonchalantly going through their usual morning routine.

The Union mortar boat had just fired its fifth shell when shortly after 7 A.M. eight Confederate gunboats suddenly appeared around Craigshead Point. They were the CSS *General Bragg, General Sterling Price, General Van Dorn, General Sumter, General Thompson, General Beauregard, Colonel Lovell,* and the flagship *Little Rebel.* Confederate senior captain James Montgomery hoped to cut out or destroy the mortar boat and possibly her covering gunboat. The two seemed vulnerable, unsuspecting and separated as they were from the rest of the flotilla.

The Confederate flotilla made straight for the *Cincinnati* as her crew desperately struggled to get her underway. Although the *General Bragg* took a broadside at only fifty yards from the *Cincinnati,* she continued on and crashed into the Union gunboat. Stembel swung his bow so that the impact was at an angle, but it still tore a large hole in the *Cincinnati's* starboard quarter, just abaft the armor plate, flooding her magazine. As the *General Bragg* wrenched free, another Union broadside tore into her, and she drifted downstream out of action.

Both the *General Sterling Price* and *General Sumter* also rammed the Union gunboat. The *General Sterling Price* struck her on the port side near her stern, carrying away her rudder, sternpost, and part of her stern. This blow threw the stern of the *Cincinnati* around so that it now caught the entire force of the *General Sumter,* running at her at full speed. The *Cincinnati* was sinking rapidly and Confederate sharpshooters began to pick off her crew,

among them Commander Stembel, who had recklessly exposed himself on deck and fell badly wounded. First Master William R. Hoel of the *Cincinnati* did manage, with the aid of two Union tugs that had appeared, to get the gunboat to the shore, where she went down in twelve feet of water. The crew then made their way to the upper deck with Commander Stembel and two other wounded men, where they watched the rest of the action.

When the first shots rang out the rest of the Union gunboats were at anchor with hardly any steam up. Finally, they got underway, the USS *Mound City* and *Carondelet* in the lead, followed by the slower USS *Benton* and then the *Pittsburg*. The other Union gunboats did not arrive in time to take part in the battle.

Meanwhile the fight continued. As the Confederate ram *Van Dorn* passed by to engage the *Mound City*, she sent two 32-pounder shots, as well as several volleys of musket fire, into Mortar Boat No. 16. The larger shells went completely through the unarmored mortar boat, but miraculously no one on her was injured. Her crewmen had lowered the mortar's elevation and, by firing with reduced charges and dangerously short fuzes, managed to burst shells over the Confederate vessels. Even after the vessel was hit, Gregory's men continued to fire. They expended fifty-two shells that day, including those fired before the battle.

The *Van Dorn* then rammed the *Mound City*. The Union gunboat received a glancing blow, which, however, tore away part of her bow, and she began rapidly shipping water. Commander Alexander H. Kilty managed to get off a punishing broadside before he grounded the *Mound City* to prevent her from sinking. She had only one man wounded.

With the Confederates seemingly enjoying the upper hand, the more powerful Union vessels tipped the balance, leading Montgomery to signal a retirement. As the Confederate vessels fled downriver, a rifled shell from the *Carondelet* smashed into the *General Sumter's* boilers, releasing a great cloud of steam, which her crew desperately attempted to escape. Rifled rounds from the flagship *Benton* also shattered the boilers of first the *Colonel Lovell* and then the *Van Dorn*, disabling both.

During the hour-long battle, the Union side suffered only four wounded, one of whom soon died; deserters later reported up to 108 Confederate dead. But apart from the heavy personnel losses, the South had achieved a tactical victory. Her flotilla had temporarily disabled two of the much more powerful Union ironclads. Refloated, they had to be sent to Mound City for repairs.

In his report to General Beauregard, Captain Montgomery boasted that Union forces would "never penetrate further down the Mississippi" unless they "greatly increase their force." Union commander Davis, meanwhile, informed Secretary of the Navy Gideon Welles that there was every indication that the

Confederates would "come up again." Davis urged that the Union rams being readied upriver now be pressed into service. These Ellet rams proved to be very important in the next engagement between the two flotillas.

—*Spencer C. Tucker*

See also Davis, Charles Henry; Foote, Andrew H.; Montgomery, James.

For further reading:

Milligan, John D. *Gunboats Down the Mississippi* (1965).

Porter, David Dixon. *Naval History of the Civil War* (1886; reprint, 1984).

Slagle, Jay. *Ironclad Captain: Seth Ledyard Phelps and the U.S. Navy, 1841–1864* (1996).

PLYMOUTH, BATTLE OF
(17–20 April 1864)

The Roanoke River port of Plymouth fell to the Union in May 1862. Possession of Plymouth allowed the Union to bottle up the Roanoke River. It also gave the Federals a base for raiding northeastern North Carolina by land or the numerous rivers that emptied into the Albemarle Sound, and deprived the South of much-needed pork and crops raised in a region of several counties.

Following a failed attack on New Bern (February 1864) led by Major General George Pickett, command of Pickett's forces in eastern North Carolina was given to native North Carolinian brigadier general Robert F. Hoke. Hoke proposed an attack on Plymouth, which was partly planned by General Bragg. The attack would combine Hoke's troops with the ironclad CSS *Albemarle*, nearing completion at an improvised shipyard up the Roanoke.

In April 1864 the Union garrison at Plymouth consisted of 2,834 men of four infantry regiments, detachments of cavalry and artillery, and two companies of North Carolina Unionists, all commanded by Brigadier General W. H. Wessells. The town was well protected on its land side. Battery Worth, on the river, anchored a line of earthworks on the western edge of town.

The line ran south, then ran east past a large work called Fort Williams to the edge of a swamp near Conaby Creek. The swamp was thought to be a sufficient defense of the east side of Plymouth with the addition of two redoubts to guard the Columbia Road. The outworks Fort Grey (a mile upriver) and Fort Wessells and a smaller redoubt west of the main works added further protection. In the river were Commander C. W. Flusser's gunboats *Miami* and *Southfield*, and three smaller vessels, *Whitehead*, *Ceres*, and *Bombshell*.

Hoke's 7,000-man force, made up of his brigade (commanded by Colonel John T. Mercer) and those of Matt Ransom and James Kemper (commanded by Colonel William R. Terry) attacked and began to lay siege to Plymouth late in the afternoon of 17 April. That night hundreds of civilians were crowded aboard the steamer *Massasoit*, which took them to safety on Roanoke Island.

At dawn on 18 April, Hoke's artillery pounded Fort Gray and severely damaged the *Bombshell*, which slipped back to town and sank at the wharf. That afternoon, Hoke's Brigade attacked Fort Wessells and Ransom's attacked the lines east of Fort Williams. Fort Wessells fell after several charges were turned back by musketry and hand grenades. Despite this success, Hoke still needed the *Albemarle*, which had not appeared.

Commander J. W. Cooke, captain of the *Albemarle*, had started downstream on 17 April with shipyard workmen still on board. At 2:30 A.M. on 19 April, the *Albemarle* took advantage of a spring freshet to pass over obstructions placed in the river and steamed toward the *Miami* and *Southfield*. The Union gunboats were chained together in hope of trapping the Rebel ram between them. The *Albemarle* rammed and sank the *Southfield*, killed Commander Flusser aboard the *Miami*, and drove off the other vessels. Cooke was then free to turn his guns on Plymouth.

Fighting continued on 19 April, as Ransom shifted his brigade to attack from the east, a maneuver that took until nearly midnight. At dawn on 20 April, Ransom's men pushed into Plymouth and trapped the remaining defenders in Fort Williams, which was heavily bombarded from all sides. General Wessells surrendered at 10:00 A.M.

Hoke captured about 2,500 prisoners, 500 horses, and vast amounts of small arms and supplies. Hoke lost about 163 killed and 554 wounded. The Union troops, protected by fortifications, lost perhaps 150 to 180 killed or wounded. Several hundred Union prisoners from Plymouth died at Andersonville. Hoke was promoted to major general for his victory, which was a tremendous boost to Confederate morale. After learning of the fall of Plymouth, the Union garrison at Washington, North Carolina, set fire to the town and fled to New Bern. Hoke moved on to New Bern, intending a major attack with the cooperation of the *Albemarle*. However, the *Albemarle* was blocked by a flotilla of seven Union gunboats in a fight on Albemarle Sound on 5 May, and Hoke was soon urgently recalled to Virginia to reinforce Lee's army.

Plymouth and Washington remained in Confederate hands until the *Albemarle* was blown up in Plymouth in a daring raid led by Lieutenant William B. Cushing on 27 October 1864. Without the protection of the ram, Plymouth was recaptured by the Union on 31 October.

—*David A. Norris*

See also *Albemarle*, CSS; Albemarle Sound; Hoke, Robert Frederick; New Bern, North Carolina, Capture of; North Carolina.

For further reading:

Barefoot, Daniel W. *General Robert F. Hoke: Lee's Modest Warrior* (1996).
Barrett, John G. *The Civil War in North Carolina* (1963).
Elliott, Robert G. *Ironclad of the Roanoke* (1994).
Jordan, W. T., Jr., and G. W. Thomas. "Massacre at Plymouth." *North Carolina Historical Review* (1995).
Official Records, Naval Records Series I, 9.
———. Series 1, 33.

POINT LOOKOUT PRISON

Before the Civil War, Point Lookout, Maryland, served as a resort for those seeking to escape the heat of Maryland summers. Cooled by bay breezes, the sandy spit of land at the juncture of Chesapeake Bay and the Potomac River featured a hotel, beach cottages, a large wharf, and a lighthouse.

Taking advantage of a precipitous decline in Point Lookout's business after fighting between the North and South began in earnest, the U.S. government leased the resort from its nervous owners for use as a hospital. Army physicians reasoned that the natural ventilation would help the healing process. The first patients arrived at Point Lookout's Hammond General Hospital on 17 August 1862. Early the following year, Point Lookout's first reluctant guests, mostly Southern Marylanders who favored the Confederacy, were confined at the hospital.

After Robert E. Lee's failed 1863 campaign into Pennsylvania, more prison facilities were needed for the thousands of Rebels captured during the three-day battle of Gettysburg. Protected by a navy with almost undisputed control of both northern and southern coasts and rivers, Point Lookout offered an easily defensible site for a detention camp. In a short amount of time, additional administration buildings, guard barracks, and a palisade were erected, and the complex was named Camp Hoffman. By September 1863, a total of 4,000 prisoners had arrived aboard bay steamers from Gettysburg via Baltimore. In addition another 9,000 wounded Federals were shipped to Point Lookout for treatment.

With the coming of fall, the refreshing breezes turned chilly. Willam Hoffman recommended wooden barracks be constructed, but Secretary of War Edwin Stanton ordered that Sibley tents be used to protect the prisoners from winter gales inside the walled prison area, called the "bull pen." To make matters worse, in retaliation for the poor conditions in Southern prisons, Confederates at Point Lookout were forced to survive on short rations. For Christmas, one wrote, "I ...onley got a peace of Bread and a cup of coffee for Breakfast and a small Slice of Meat and a cup of Soop and five Crackers for Dinner and Supper I had non." When Stanton visited Point Lookout with President Lincoln two days later, the camp had almost reached its capacity of 10,000 men.

With the coming of nicer weather the following spring, prisoners were allowed to bathe in the Chesapeake and catch fish, crabs, and oysters to supplement their diets. Nevertheless, imperfect drainage and brackish wells caused diarrhea and smallpox outbreaks.

As could be expected, hundreds of men died every month. To add to the misery, former slaves used as guards responded to reports of a massacre of black troops by Nathan Bedford Forrest at Fort Pillow, Tennessee, on 18 April 1864 by firing random shots into the bull pen, killing several inmates.

Poet Sidney Lanier, captured aboard a blockade runner in 1864, was one of the lucky ones. A friend managed to sneak some gold into Point Lookout and use it to secure his and Lanier's release after a four-month confinement.

In July 1864, Rebel agents in Baltimore, Washington, D.C., and southern Maryland made overly optimistic plans to free the nearly 20,000 prisoners at Point Lookout and join them with Jubal Early's 14,000-man army steamrolling its way up the Shenandoah Valley toward the Northern capital. Details of the escape attempt reached the commandant at Point Lookout, however, and he ordered the construction of three forts to protect the "two necks of land which connect the Point with the mainland." General Early made it to the outskirts of Washington, D.C., where word of the failure of the Point Lookout plot reached him. With reinforcements from Union general Ulysses S. Grant beating him into the city, Early turned back to Virginia, thus ending any hopes for the inmates at Camp Hoffman.

Finally in February 1865, the bulk of those captured at Gettysburg were paroled, too weak to help a mortally wounded South. After Appomattox, the remainder were released. Of the 52,264 men held at various times in the prison, almost 3,400 died.

The state of Maryland dedicated a monument to the memory of those prisoners in 1876, and the U.S. government erected a second in the early 1900s. A century after the war ended, Maryland's Department of Forests and Parks began to redevelop Point Lookout into a place for vacationers. Today, Point Lookout State Park offers a reconstructed section of the bull pen and restored Fort Lincoln as well as camping facilities, a fishing pier, picnic grounds, a beach, and rental boats.

—*Dave Page*

See also Hoffman, William; Maryland; Prisons, U.S.A.

For further reading:

Beitzell, Edwin W. *Point Lookout Prison Camp for Confederates* (1991).

Cottom, Robert I., Jr., and Mary Ellen Hayward. *Maryland in the Civil War* (1994).

Kemmerle, Darlene. "3,384 Who Died." *Oak Leaflets* (n.d.).

POISON SPRING, BATTLE OF
(18 April 1864)

At Poison Spring, Confederate cavalry delivered a major blow to the Arkansas prong of a projected Union thrust up Louisiana's Red River. The Rebels also transformed their victory into a notorious war crime by committing atrocities against captured black Union soldiers.

On 15 April 1864, Major General Frederick Steele occupied Camden, Arkansas, with a 14,000-man Union army that had been on half rations for three weeks since leaving Little Rock and Fort Smith. On 17 April, Steele sent a train of 198 wagons to gather 5,000 bushels of corn that had been discovered sixteen miles west of Camden. To guard the train, he detailed a total of 1,170 men—821 infantry, 291 cavalry, and 58 artillery with four guns. Command of this foraging expedition went to Colonel James M. Williams, whose own regiment, the 1st Kansas Colored Infantry, constituted the largest unit in the escort. Vigilant Confederates destroyed half of the corn before Williams could reach it, but his troops loaded the rest aboard their wagons by midnight.

Williams commenced his return march to Camden at sunrise, 18 April. After covering some five miles, he encountered 3,600 enemy cavalry with twelve cannon astride his route at Poison Spring. Brigadier General Samuel B. Maxey was the senior Confederate officer present, but he entrusted the direction of the coming battle to Brigadier General John S. Marmaduke. Marmaduke had originated the plan to intercept Williams at Poison Spring, and he had reached the ground first. Marmaduke's command included battalions of Arkansans, Missourians, and Texans, plus a Choctaw brigade from Indian Territory. The Confederates fought dismounted and they carried long-range infantry rifles, which increased their hitting power.

As gray skirmishers sniped at the Union advance guard, Williams brought up the 438 officers and men of the 1st Kansas Colored, forming them in an L-shaped line to shield his forage train from the Rebels massing to the east and south. He posted the 18th Iowa to the left of the African-American regiment and assigned his cavalry to guard his flanks.

Thanks to Williams's dispositions, the 1st Kansas Colored would bear the brunt of fighting on the Union side at Poison Spring. Though badly outnumbered and scourged from three directions by enemy artillery, the black soldiers acquitted themselves well. Most were runaway slaves from Missouri and Arkansas, but they were proud to belong to the first black combat unit in the Union army, and they had bested enemy troops the previous year at Cabin Creek and Honey Springs in Indian Territory.

Quick shooting from the 1st Kansas repulsed the first Confederate attack at Poison Spring and checked a second, but they suffered heavy casualties and depleted their ammunition. When Marmaduke pressed home a third onslaught, a portion of the 1st Kansas gave way and then the entire regiment broke, allowing the Confederates to overrun the forage train. With the center gone, the rest of the Union line quickly dissolved.

Colonel Williams rallied a number of men and conducted a fighting withdrawal to the relative refuge of a swamp north of the battlefield. In the meantime, General Maxey, fearing the imminent arrival of a Federal relief column from Camden, called a halt to any further pursuit and had the Confederates remove the captured wagons. Unobstructed by their foes, Williams and other Federal survivors made their way back to friendly lines, the first of them reaching Camden around 8:00 P.M.

In addition to the loss of four cannon and 198 wagons, the Federals suffered 301 killed, wounded, and missing at Poison Spring. Nearly two-thirds of these casualties belonged to the 1st Kansas Colored, which reported 117 dead and 65 wounded. Confederate losses amounted to only 13 killed, 81 wounded, and 1 missing.

Enraged at the sight of ex-slaves fighting against the South, the victorious Confederates killed every black soldier who fell into their hands. "The havoc among the negroes had been tremendous," admitted a Texas artillery officer. "Over a small portion of the field we saw at least 40 dead bodies lying in all conceivable attitudes, some scalped & nearly all stripped...No black prisoners were captured." Some Confederates blamed the worst atrocities on the Choctaw brigade, but the massacre received the endorsement of the *Washington Telegraph*, the voice of Confederate Arkansas, which proclaimed, "We cannot treat negroes taken in arms as prisoners of war without a destruction of the social system for which we contend."

—*Gregory J. W. Urwin*

See also Choctaw Indians; Marmaduke, John Sappington; Maxey, Samuel Bell; Steele, Frederick.

For further reading:
Bailey, Anne J. "Was There a Massacre at Poison Spring?" *Military History of the Southwest* (1990).
Bearss, Edwin C. *Steele's Retreat from Camden and the Battle of Jenkins' Ferry* (1967).
Christ, Mark K., ed. *Rugged and Sublime: The Civil War in Arkansas* (1994).
Fisher, Mike. "The First Kansas Colored—Massacre at Poison Springs." *Kansas History* (1979).
Urwin, Gregory J. W. "'We Cannot Treat Negroes ... as Prisoners of War': Racial Atrocities and Reprisals in Civil War Arkansas." *Civil War History* (1996).

POLIGNAC, CAMILLE ARMAND JULES MARIE, PRINCE DE
(1832–1913)
Confederate general

The only foreign national to achieve high rank on either side in the American Civil War, Camille de Polignac was the son of the president of the Council of Ministers to France's King Charles X. Born in Miltemont, Seine-et-Oise, France, Polignac graduated from the College Stanislaus, where he excelled in mathematics. In 1853 he failed the entrance examination to the French military academy, the École Polytechnique, and enlisted in the 3d Chasseurs as a private. At the outbreak of the Crimean War in 1854, Polignac, having risen to the rank of sergeant, volunteered for duty in the trenches before Sevastopol. His bravery during the heavy fighting in June 1855 quickly earned him promotion to second lieutenant in the 4th Regiment, Chasseurs d'Afrique.

Polignac obtained a discharge in February 1859 and traveled to Central and North America in search of adventure and opportunity. During a visit to New York City he befriended a number of future Confederate luminaries, including Judah Benjamin and P. G. T. Beauregard, who recruited him to their cause. When the American conflict erupted, Polignac immediately offered his services to the Confederacy.

On 6 July 1861 newly commissioned lieutenant colonel of infantry Polignac joined the staff of his sponsor, General P. G. T. Beauregard, then commanding the Confederate Army of the Potomac. Upon Beauregard's transfer to the Western theater in the spring of 1862, Polignac followed, joining the general on 17 April as his assistant inspector general in Corinth, Mississippi. Although Polignac relentlessly pressed his superiors for a combat assignment, he continued as assistant inspector general under General Braxton Bragg when Bragg replaced the ailing Beauregard in June. He was thus with Bragg during the general's 1862 invasion of Kentucky.

Polignac, still eager to gain a field command, next obtained a transfer to the Army of Kentucky, commanded by Major General Edmund Kirby Smith. He was subsequently on temporary duty with the 5th Tennessee Infantry Regiment of Brigadier General Patrick Cleburne's Division during the 29 August 1862 battle of Richmond, Kentucky. During the battle Polignac exhibited extraordinary bravery and leadership, yet nevertheless failed to win his own permanent command. Polignac correctly blamed his lack of advancement on the highly political nature of the Confederate military. He consequently obtained a transfer back to Richmond to lobby President Davis and General Samuel Cooper for promotion.

His efforts were rewarded when he was promoted to brigadier general on 10 January 1863. On 22 May 1863 he arrived in Shreveport, Louisiana, headquarters of General Edmund Kirby Smith's Trans-Mississippi Department. Every unassigned brigadier in the department must have breathed a collective sigh of relief at Polignac's assignment to the 2d Texas Brigade in Major General Richard Taylor's District of West Louisiana. Smith himself considered the brigade "an undisciplined mob, the officers as worthless as the men." Suspicious of outsiders and unable to pronounce their new commander's name, the unruly Texans quickly dubbed the Frenchman "General Polecat." Supported by his immediate superior, General John G. Walker, Polignac

eventually overcame the brigade's resistance to his authority and transformed his Texas Brigade into one of Taylor's most dependable commands. Exhibiting considerable skill and adaptability, he developed unique hit-and-run tactics that effected serious damage to Union admiral David D. Porter's powerful gunboat fleet patrolling Louisiana's numerous waterways.

Polignac and his Texans went on to play a major role in defeating Union major general Nathaniel P. Banks's 1864 Red River campaign. Joined with Brigadier General Alfred Mouton's Louisiana Brigade to form Taylor's 2d Infantry Division, Polignac's Texas Brigade anchored the Confederate left during the 8 April 1864 battle of Mansfield. Mouton was killed during the battle and Polignac assumed his position as divisional commander. It was in this role that he led the division the following day during the battle of Pleasant Hill. Although the battle proved a tactical Federal victory it effectively ended Banks's hopes of success and he was forced to retreat. Polignac continued to harass the Federals during their withdrawal, and on 13 June, was promoted to major general to date from 8 April in recognition of his achievements at Mansfield.

In January 1865 Polignac led a Confederate diplomatic mission to France to gain military aid from Napoleon III. Learning of Lee's surrender shortly after his arrival in Europe, he chose to remain in his homeland and resumed his study of mathematics. He temporarily interrupted his private pursuits to command France's 1st Division during the Franco-Prussian War, winning the Legion of Honor for his service. Polignac, one of the last Confederate major generals, died in Paris 15 November 1913 and was buried in Frankfort-am-Main, Germany.

—*Jeff Kinard*

See also France; Mansfield, Battle of; Pleasant Hill, Battle of; Taylor, Richard.

For further reading:

Barr, Alwyn. *Polignac's Texas Brigade* (1964).

Frankignoul, Daniel J. *Prince Camille de Polignac Major General, C.S.A. "The Lafayette of the South"* (1996).

POLK, LEONIDAS
(1806–1864)
Confederate general

Leonidas Polk was born to William and Sarah Polk on 10 April 1806, in Raleigh, North Carolina. William, a war hero of the American Revolution and an original member of the Order of Cincinnati, benefitted from a close association with prominent Federalists of the early national period. He served as director and president of the State Bank of North Carolina from 1811 to 1819, and as chief surveyor of the central district of Tennessee that enabled him to acquire roughly 100,000 acres of land in that state. Very little is known of Polk's

The death of General Polk (*Library of Congress*)

childhood. He matriculated at the University of North Carolina in 1821 but left in 1823 after receiving an appointment to the United States Military Academy.

Polk compiled an impressive record at the academy. His class rank never fell below ninth, and he graduated eighth in his class of thirty-eight in 1827. He excelled in rhetoric and moral philosophy where he tied George W. Hughes for the highest score in his class, and he earned the second best score in conduct. At the beginning of Polk's third year, West Point implemented the demerit system; he accumulated seventy-nine demerits that year, but in his final year he was one of twelve cadets, along with Robert E. Lee, who tallied zero demerits. In addition, Polk took the unusual step of professing Christianity at West Point, and Chaplain Charles P. McIlvaine, later to become the Episcopal bishop of Ohio, baptized Polk in the academy chapel. Both the profession of faith and the baptism are regarded as the first such cases in Academy history.

Immediately after graduation, Polk resigned from the military, and in the fall of 1828 enrolled at the Virginia Theological Seminary in Alexandria, Virginia. As a seminarian, Polk was active in student organizations and missions projects. After two years of seminary training, he accepted an assignment as assistant to Bishop Richard Channing Moore at Monumental Church in Richmond, Virginia. Bishop Moore ordained Polk as deacon on 11 April 1830, and ordained him as priest on 22 May 1831. On 6 May 1830 Polk married Frances Ann Devereux, the daughter of John and Frances Pollock Devereux, the latter the granddaughter of Puritan theologian Jonathan Edwards. They had eight children. From late summer 1831 to spring 1833, Polk took a sabbatical from the ministry. He then moved to Tennessee, where he began life as a planter and resumed his ministerial career.

Census records indicate that with 111 slaves, Polk was the largest slaveholder in Maury County, Tennessee, in 1840. Generally speaking, Middle Tennessee planters of Polk's class produced an annual yield of 100 bales of cotton and 10,000 bushels of corn. Besides agricultural pursuits, Polk increased his involvement in the Episcopal church and in December 1838 he was consecrated missionary bishop of the southwest. Just three years later, he was chosen bishop of Louisiana, and he relocated to Thibodaux, Louisiana, where he purchased Leighton, a sugar plantation, from James Porter for $100,000. During the ten growing seasons from 1844 to 1854, Polk produced an average of 692 hogsheads or 761,200 pounds of sugar per season, and in 1844 Leighton ranked as the largest sugar plantation in Lafourche Parish. Census records indicate that Polk owned 215 slaves in 1850, but agriculturalist Solon Robinson estimated 370 and Frederick Law Olmsted estimated 400 during their respective tours of 1849 and 1854. Polk's religious beliefs affected his plantation management in that he did not work slaves on Sunday even during the critical rolling season; he hired a chaplain to minister to his slaves; and he personally conducted the marriage ceremonies of his slaves. Under the burden of debt, Polk chose to sell Leighton to John Williams of New Orleans for $307,000 in 1854. Polk purchased a 2,700-acre cotton plantation in Bolivar County, Mississippi, with his remaining resources, and his son Hamilton managed the estate and its 134 slaves. Meanwhile. Polk turned his attention toward the creation of the Episcopal-affiliated University of the South. The Diocese of Louisiana contributed $264,160, roughly 63 percent, to the initial endowment fund.

When the sectional controversy erupted and Louisiana seceded from the Union, Polk responded first by leading his diocese out of the Episcopal General Convention, thereby paving the way for the formation of the Protestant Episcopal Church in the Confederate States of America. He also wrote Confederate president Jefferson Davis about his concern for the safety of the Mississippi Valley. Davis invited Polk to Richmond to discuss military policy, and during the June 1861 visit Davis offered and Polk accepted a commission in the Confederate army. He was commissioned as a major general and promoted to lieutenant general on 10 October 1862. His command, known as Department Number 2, consisted primarily of western Tennessee and the defense of the Mississippi River. After a failed attempt to liberate Missouri from Federal control, Polk seized Columbus, Kentucky. This decision prompted Kentucky to end its declared position of neutrality.

Polk commanded the Confederate forces at the battle of Belmont, and the Confederate Congress passed a resolution of thanks acknowledging Polk, Gideon Pillow, Benjamin Cheatham, and their soldiers for their victory at Belmont. At Shiloh, Polk served as a corps commander. After Shiloh, Polk's military career, which included participation in the battles of Perryville, Stones River, and Chickamauga, was defined by his adversarial relationship with the commander of the Army of Tennessee, Braxton Bragg. The feuding intensified after Stones River when Bragg circulated a ridiculous petition requesting that his subordinates express their views on two questions: the Confederate withdrawal from Stones River and the army's confidence in his leadership abilities. Polk took every opportunity to discredit Bragg and urged Davis to replace him. The climax of their personal war occurred after Chickamauga, when Bragg charged Polk with disobeying orders and stripped the bishop general of his command. Technically, such a move required a court-martial proceeding. Trying to dissipate further controversy, Davis stepped in and transferred Polk to Mississippi. As head of the Department of Alabama, Mississippi, and East Louisiana, Polk offered little resistance to William T. Sherman during his 1864 Meridian campaign. In May 1864 Polk rejoined the Army of Tennessee on the eve of the Atlanta campaign. On 14 June 1864, Polk was struck and mortally wounded by Federal artillery fire while reconnoitering with Joseph Johnston and William Hardee. Polk's good friend, Bishop Stephen Elliott of Georgia, conducted the funeral service—one of the most elaborate during the war. Originally buried in Augusta, Georgia, Polk's remains were reinterred at Christ Church in New Orleans, Louisiana, in 1945.

—*Glenn Robins*

See also Atlanta Campaign; Belmont, Battle of; Bragg, Braxton; Chickamauga, Battle of; Stones River, Battle of.

For further reading:
Connelly, Thomas L. *Army of the Heartland: The Army of Tennessee, 1861–1862* (1967).
————. *Autumn of Glory: The Army of Tennessee, 1862–1865* (1971).
Parks, Joseph H. *General Leonidas Polk, C.S.A.: The Fighting Bishop* (1962).
Polk, William M. *Leonidas Polk: Bishop and General* (1915).
Robins, Glenn M. "Leonidas Polk and Episcopal Identity: An Evangelical Experiment in the Mid-Nineteenth-Century South" (Ph.D. dissertation, 1999).

POLLARD, EDWARD ALFRED
(1831–1872)
Confederate journalist

Born in Albemarle County (a part of the county that is now Nelson County), Virginia, the son of Richard Pollard and Paulina Cabell Rives Pollard, Edward Pollard was educated at Hampden-Sidney

College and the University of Virginia and studied law at the College of William and Mary. After studying law in Baltimore, Pollard traveled west as a journalist, in which profession he also traveled to Latin America and abroad. Upon his return he served briefly as a clerk in Congress. A strong supporter of secession, he wrote extensively in support of that position.

In 1861, Pollard accepted the editorship of the Richmond *Examiner,* a position that would gain him great notoriety and even infamy in some circles of the Confederacy. Pollard used the *Examiner* to espouse the Southern cause and to encourage support for the war effort. Early in the conflict, however, he came to believe that Jefferson Davis was not the man to lead that cause. As a result, he used the *Examiner* to wage a vicious attack upon the Confederacy's president that some considered almost treasonous. Pollard blamed everything that went wrong in the war on what he believed was Davis's mismanagement of the conflict and made the *Examiner* both a forum and rallying point for Davis's critics.

Besides the criticisms he leveled in the *Examiner,* Pollard wrote books during the war that aimed colorful barbs at the Confederate president. His most famous work—written for the most part during the war but finally finished after its conclusion—was the four-volume *Southern History of the War.* In his attempt to publicize this work in Great Britain in 1864, Pollard sailed on the blockade runner *Grayhound* but was arrested when the Union navy captured the ship. Briefly imprisoned in Fort Monroe, Pollard was carried North, where he was allowed the run of both New York and Boston for a time. Eventually authorities incarcerated him in Fort Warren in the late summer of 1864. Pollard returned to Fort Monroe and was exchanged in January for a Northern journalist who had fallen into Confederate hands. Some might have wondered if President Davis was tempted to let Pollard remain in Northern hands until the end of the war.

After the war Pollard continued to edit the *Examiner* until 1867. He failed in efforts to establish several other newspapers, including one in New York City. Along with his editing chores, Pollard continued to write books, most of which blamed Davis for the loss of the war. His most famous postwar work was *The Lost Cause,* published in 1866. Pollard died in Lynchburg, Virginia.

—*David S. Heidler and Jeanne T. Heidler*

See also Newspapers; *Richmond Examiner.*

For further reading:

Andrews, J. Cutler. *The South Reports the Civil War* (1970).
Houston, Michael. "Edward Alfred Pollard and the Richmond *Examiner*: A Study of Journalistic Opposition in Wartime" (M.A. thesis, 1963).
Pollard, Edward A. *The Lost Cause: A New Southern History of the War of the Confederates* (1866).
———. *Southern History of the War* (1862–1865).

POMEROY, SAMUEL CLARKE
(1816–1891)
U.S. senator

Born in Southampton, Massachusetts, Pomeroy briefly attended Amherst College, then taught school, and became a merchant in New York. Returning to Southampton, he embarked on a political career as a member of the abolitionist Liberty Party and served in the Massachusetts legislature in 1852 and 1853. Then, following the passage of the Kansas-Nebraska Act in 1854, he became the financial agent of the New England Emigrant Aid Company, an organization dedicated to making Kansas a free state. In that capacity Pomeroy led a party of antislavery settlers to Kansas, where they established the town of Lawrence and made it the stronghold of the Freestate Party in the territory. On 21 May 1856 a large force of proslavery Missouri "border ruffians" approached the town and demanded that it surrender. Realizing that resistance would be futile, Pomeroy, as chairman of Lawrence's defense committee, complied. The so-called sack of Lawrence followed—an act that provided excellent propaganda for the newly formed Republican Party in the North and touched off a conflict between pro- and antislavery elements in Kansas that caused it to become known as "Bleeding Kansas."

In 1858, by which time the freestaters had gained the upper hand in Kansas, Pomeroy moved to Atchison in the northeast corner of the territory. There he engaged quite lucratively in banking, land speculation, and railroad promotion, while at the same time seeking to further his political ambitions. These received a strong boost in 1860–1861 when he became the agent for the Kansas Relief Committee, a New England-based organization that provided money, seed, and food for large numbers of drought-stricken Kansas farmers, many of whom went about wearing pants made from grain sacks with "S. C. Pomeroy, Atchison, K. T." stencilled on them. The prominence and popularity he thus gained helped Pomeroy win election by the Kansas legislature to the U.S. Senate following Kansas's admission to statehood on 29 January 1861, an outcome that also was greatly aided by the financial backing of Atchison's business interests and in all probability the bribery of legislators.

In the Senate Pomeroy served on the Committee on Public Lands, where he sponsored legislation to promote Kansas railroads, in particular the Atchison, Topeka & Santa Fe, of which he became president in 1863. But his major goal was to supplant Senator James H. Lane as the top leader of the Kansas Republicans and thus the "king" of Kansas politics. Lane's power derived from his prominent role as military commander of the free-state forces during the "Bleeding Kansas" struggle, his great talent as a demagogic orator, and above all from his possessing a virtual monopoly—owing to President Lincoln's friendship—of Federal patronage in Kansas. It was the hope of obtaining this monopoly for himself that motivated Pomeroy's historically most important act during the Civil War, namely the publication early in 1864 of what became known as the "Pomeroy Circular." Bearing the title "The Next Presidential Election," the document contended that Lincoln could not be reelected and that therefore the Republican Party should nominate as its 1864 presidential candidate Secretary of Treasury Salmon P. Chase, whom Pomeroy described in the circular as "an advanced thinker" because of his more radical stance on slavery and the reconstruction of the Southern states.

Many so-called Radical Republicans agreed with Pomeroy privately, but few publicly supported him, with the result that the circular merely strengthened Lane's relationship with Lincoln and thus his power in Kansas. Following Andrew Johnson's accession to the presidency in 1865, Lane sought to preserve this power by establishing the same relationship with him, to which end he became one of the few Republican senators to vote to uphold Johnson's vetoes of the Freedmen's Bureau Bill and the Civil Rights Act in 1866. His votes, though, cost him the support of large numbers of Kansas Republicans and this, along with newspaper exposures of his corrupt dealings, led Lane to commit suicide in July 1866.

With the "Grim Chieftain" out of the way, Pomeroy had no trouble securing reelection in 1867, with bribery again being instrumental. He then attempted to gain from Johnson control of Kansas patronage by secretly offering to vote not guilty when the president was impeached in 1868—an offer Johnson rejected, suspecting (perhaps correctly) a trap.

After Grant became president Pomeroy enjoyed ample patronage, but even so he deemed it necessary when he came up for election in 1873 to resort again to bribery. This time it backfired. Just before the legislature was to vote, one of its members announced that Pomeroy had personally given him $7,000 and promised another $1,000 for his vote. To a man, the legislators renounced "Pom the pious," as he was often sarcastically dubbed because of his pretension to religious piety, and his political career in Kansas abruptly ended.

After the conclusion of his Senate term—his fellow senators refused so much as to censure him—Pomeroy remained for awhile in Washington, then moved to Boston, where he championed women's suffrage and prohibition, becoming in 1884 the presidential candidate of the American Prohibition Party. Seven years later he died in his native Massachusetts, but remains immortalized in Mark Twain's and Charles Dudley Warner's 1873 novel, *The Gilded Age*, as the hypocritical

Senator Dilworthy from a state thinly disguised by the name of "Happy Land of Canaan."

—*Albert Castel*

See also Chase, Salmon Portland; Kansas; Lane, James Henry.
For further reading:
Caldwell, Martha B. "The Attitude of Kansas toward Reconstruction before 1875" (Ph.D. dissertation, 1933).
Castel, Albert. *Civil War Kansas: Reaping the Whirlwind* (1958; reprint, 1997).
Rawley, James A. *Race and Politics: "Bleeding Kansas" and the Coming of the Civil War* (1969).
Strobel, Margaret Lynn. "A Political Biography of Senator Samuel C. Pomeroy of Kansas" (M. A. thesis, 1962).

POOK'S "TURTLES"

The idea of an offensive strike by advancing down the Mississippi River had long been in the minds of Union strategists. This idea was later deemed impractical as Confederate major general Leonidas Polk fortified the bluffs at Columbus, Kentucky, with 140 heavy guns on 19 September 1861. In spite of the guns at Columbus, however, there was a general weakness in the Confederate riverine system. To exploit this line of attack, the Union called upon its increasingly important fresh-water navy. Wooden gunboats, which had made up this force, however, were not able to handle the power of the guns at Columbus. The only solution to this problem was to design a new ironclad vessel focusing on shore battle. On 7 August 1861, contracted by the War Department, James B. Eads, a St. Louis riverman and salvage expert, hired naval constructor Samuel M. Pook and engine designer Thomas Merritt to design and construct an armored vessel that could be used for battle on western rivers.

Construction proved difficult at first because there was no previous concept for an ironclad riverine vessel. The ships had to be strongly protected to withstand the heavy guns of river forts and they also had to be able to defend themselves against these bombardments, mounting cannons as heavy as those fixed on the bluffs. The metal used for protection and firepower created a vessel with a tremendous amount of weight; however, the ships still had to be allowed clearance enough to navigate in less than ten feet of water. To deal with these problems, Pook improvised, using paddle-wheelers as models. The result was basically an ironclad paddle-wheeler that could withstand bombardment while returning fire to Confederate forts.

It took only two months to complete the building of the first "turtle," also known as "mud-turtle," in St. Louis on 12 October. By this time, crews had swelled to nearly 4,000 men working at a hectic pace, often around the clock. Timber was shipped in by barge from seven states, and machine shops and metal foundries worked through the night. Although river operations had remained

constant since August through the conversion of such wooden gunboats into ironclads such as the *Tyler, Lexington,* and *Conestoga,* the river fleet was not complete until 15 January 1862, when the last of the other six turtles was built. The Union riverine naval fleet had finally acquired the offensive weapon for which it had been waiting.

Resembling turtles in shape and form, the craft were round-nosed and flat-bottomed. Each of the seven was 175 feet long and 51.2 feet high at its beam. Although weight seemed to be a problem, the vessels sank a mere six feet, easily clearing most rivers. The casing was slanted at a 35-degree angle to deflect enemy fire and was protected with a 2.5-inch-thick iron plate. Each ship was armed with thirteen smoothbore and rifled cannons and was powered by two high-compression steam engines that moved the 512-ton vessels at five miles an hour upstream and downstream at nine miles an hour.

By design, everything was hidden behind iron, except the smokestack, which was used to distinguish them with painted stripes and colors. Due to their riverine purpose, they were aptly named after western river ports on the Mississippi and Ohio rivers. Pook's turtles consisted of the *Cairo, Carondelet, Cincinnati, Louisville, Mound City, Pittsburgh,* and *St. Louis* (later renamed *Baron De Kalb*), giving them the title of "city class" vessels. Of the seven, four were constructed at Carondelet, Missouri; the other three, at Mound City, Illinois. They were generally based out of Cairo, Illinois; however, they were often placed at strategic areas along the river.

Although professional naval officers ran all the turtles, these unconventional vessels were filled with an uncommon mix of men: salt-water sailors from the East, fresh-water sailors from the Great Lakes, rivermen, regular navy men, volunteers, army personnel, and contract civilians. Although the turtles were slow, hard to maneuver, and structurally unsound, they proved successful and always intimidating. At battles such as those at Fort Henry and Fort Donelson, Island No. 10, Memphis, and Plum Run Bend and the battle and engagements of Vicksburg, the vessels continually proved themselves effective and important. Commanded by Captain Andrew Hull Foote, Pook's turtles proved to be the backbone of western riverine combat.

—*Andrew Paul Bielakowski*

See also Eads, James Buchanan; Navy, U.S.A.; Riverine Warfare, U.S.N.

For further reading:
Anderson, Bern. *By Sea and by River: The Naval History of the Civil War* (1962).
Gosnell, H. A. *Guns on the Western Waters: The Story of the River Gunboats in the Civil War* (1949).
The Road to Shiloh: Early Battles in the West. Vol. 4 of *The Civil War* (1983).
War on the Mississippi: Grant's Vicksburg Campaign. Vol. 12 of *The Civil War* (1983).

POPE, JOHN
(1822–1892)
Union general

John Pope was born in Louisville, Kentucky, on 16 March 1822, the son of a prominent Illinois judge who was also a close friend of Abraham Lincoln. He entered West Point in 1838 and four years later graduated seventeenth in a class of fifty-six. Commissioned a second lieutenant, Pope was assigned to the Topographical Engineers and conducted survey and road work along the Canadian border. In 1846 he joined General Zachary Taylor's army in Texas, winning a brevet promotion to first lieutenant at the battle of Monterrey. The following year he won a second promo-

John Pope (*Library of Congress*)

tion to brevet captain for his role in the victory at Buena Vista. After the war Pope resumed his surveying activities in Minnesota, and in 1850 he demonstrated the navigability of the Red River. From 1851 to 1853 he served as chief engineer of the Department of the New Mexico, and he spent the next six years surveying a route for the Pacific Railroad.

Pope, a captain since 1856, was serving on lighthouse duty when the Civil War seemed imminent. In January 1861, he became one of four officers chosen to escort President-elect Lincoln from Springfield, Illinois, to the nation's capital. Pope wasted no time renewing his old family ties to Lincoln and initially offered to serve as an aide, but in May 1861 he gained appointment as brigadier general of volunteers and was ordered to organize Illinois recruits for war.

For several months Pope served as the unhappy subordinate of the mecurial General John C. Frémont in Missouri, and behind the scenes he helped arrange his removal. Nonetheless, he was also a competent, aggressive commander, and on 18 December 1861 Pope defeated Confederate general Sterling Price at Blackwater taking 1 200 prisoners. Somewhat of a braggart by nature, Pope wildly exaggerated his accomplishments to the press, which brought him to the attention of Frémont's successor, Henry Wager Halleck. In March 1862, Halleck appointed Pope commander of the newly organized Army of the Mississippi, 25,000 strong, with orders to clear Confederate obstacles from the waterway. Moving swiftly, he made a surprise march on New Madrid, Missouri, capturing it on 14 March 1862. He then orchestrated a clever campaign to capture Island No. 10 in the Mississippi River. This was a strongly fortified post in the reverse bend of the river garrisoned by 12,000 men and fifty-eight cannon. However, Pope cut a channel that allowed his troops passage around the island. Then, assisted by the gunboats of Captain Andrew H. Foote, he landed his men on the opposite shore isolating the defenders. When Island No. 10 surrendered on 7 April 1862, it freed Union navigation of the Mississippi as far south as Memphis. Pope's sterling performance gained him promotion to major general of volunteers, and when Halleck commenced his ponderous Corinth campaign in Mississippi, Pope's men formed the left wing.

Eventually Pope's good behavior came to the attention of President Lincoln, who was desperate for better Union leadership in the Eastern theater. In June 1862, Pope assumed command of scattered Union forces in the Shenandoah Valley, a move that prompted his former antagonist Frémont to resign. However, the general won few friends by bragging about his prior accomplishments and by declaring that armies in the West were victorious by showing only their fronts and not their backs to the enemy. At length, General George B. McClellan's unsuccessful Peninsula campaign necessitated his removal from command by Lincoln, who went on to assign much of the Army of the Potomac to Pope's Army of Virginia. By August his command had swollen to 70,000 men, and it advanced cautiously toward Richmond. However, Pope underestimated the guile and audacity of his opponent, Robert E. Lee. The Confederate commander, who only possessed 55,000 men, gauged Pope as indecisive and broke with military convention. He boldly divided his army in the face of the enemy sending General Thomas "Stonewall" Jackson with 24,000 men to engage General Nathaniel Banks at Cedar Mountain as a diversion. Meanwhile, as Lee advanced upon Pope with his main force, Jackson then circled to the north, capturing Pope's main supply base at Manassas Station. The perplexed Union leader, unable to locate the main Confederate body, walked into a trap on the old battlefield of Bull Run. On 29 August 1862, Pope's men initially withstood a pincer attack by Jackson and Lee, but on the following day a surprise flank attack by General James Longstreet decided the issue. The Federals, losing heavily, managed to draw off in good order.

Pope compounded his failure and unpopularity by blaming the talented General Fitz John Porter for the defeat, which also culminated in Porter's court-martial. In a controversial trial decided by officers loyal to Pope, Porter was found guilty and cashiered. Pope, however, was also removed from command and endured administrative exile by commanding the Department of the Northwest. For the next 18 months he organized numerous campaigns, which finally crushed the bloody Sioux uprising under Little Crow. By January 1865 Pope's military reputation was partially revived when he gained control of the Department of the Mississippi and received brevet promotion to major general for his capture of Island No. 10.

After the war Pope enjoyed a wide-ranging and generally successful career in the far West, where he campaigned successfully against the Apache under Cochise and Geronimo. However, he enjoyed less success convincing Washington bureaucrats that peace on the frontier would be better served if the reservation system was administered by the military and not the corrupt Indian Bureau. And, like George Crook and Oliver O. Howard, he gained controversial renown by calling for better and more humane treatment of Native Americans. Pope died in Sandusky, Ohio, on 23 September 1892.

—*John C. Fredriksen*

See also Bull Run, Second Battle of; Island No. 10; Porter, Fitz John.

For further reading:
Cozzens, Peter, and Robert I. Girandi eds. *The Military Memoirs of General John Pope* (1998).

———. *Abandoned by Lincoln: A Military Biography of Major General John Pope* (1990).

Schutz, Wallace J. *Major General John Pope and the Army of Virginia* (1986).

POPLAR SPRINGS CHURCH (PEEBLE'S FARM OR PEGRAM'S FARM)
(29 September–2 October, 1864)

During the Union Army's siege of Petersburg and Richmond, Virginia, in the fall of 1864, General Ulysses S. Grant launched a series of attacks trying to break through the Confederate defenses guarding those two cities. In late September, Grant launched the fifth of these offensives.

The first part of the new offensive came on 28 September, when General Benjamin Butler assaulted the fortifications guarding the Confederate capital. At the same time, Grant told General George G. Meade to be prepared to attack the defenses surrounding Petersburg. Grant hoped that Meade's troops from the Army of the Potomac would accomplish two goals: 1) prevent Confederate commander General Robert E. Lee from sending reinforcements from Petersburg to the defense of Richmond; and 2) exploit the weakened Confederate lines and capture the Southside Railroad if Lee did send troops from Petersburg to Richmond. Grant especially wanted to capture the Southside line, since it was the last major railroad connecting Petersburg (and through it, Richmond) to the rest of the South. If that line could be cut, then it would only be a matter of time before Confederates would be forced to evacuate both Petersburg and Richmond.

On 29 September, Meade moved 20,000 men from General Gouvernor K. Warren's V Corps and General John G. Parke's IX Corps into position to attack recently constructed Confederate earthworks along the Squirrel Level Road, about 5 miles southwest of Petersburg. The next day, the four Union divisions struck near Poplar Springs Church, catching the weak Rebel defenses at a redoubt (sometimes referred to as Fort Archer) guarding their right flank. They easily captured the redoubt and the rest of the Confederate line. However, the two divisions under Parke advanced very slowly after the initial breakthrough. This delay gave General A.P. Hill (who had the responsibility for defending Petersburg) sufficient time to send two divisions under Generals Henry Heth and Cadmus Wilcox to meet the new threat. The Confederates wasted no time in trying to establish a new line less than a mile from the earthworks captured by the Federal troops. By the time Parke ordered General Robert Potter's division to attack in the late afternoon, the Confederates were ready. Wilcox sent his troops on a flanking counterattack that not only stopped the advance of Potter's troops, but forced the rest of the IX

corps to retreat. The defeated Union troops fell back on the support of Warren's V corps, situated at Peeble's Farm. The Confederates attempted to break through the Federal line, but were stopped by massed artillery.

On 1 October, the men of the IX corps (reinforced by another division) advanced a brief distance again. However, their plan was not to attack Hill's men, but to create a forward line of their own nearer the Confederate entrenchments. The Federal troops successfully completed this maneuver and began working to connect a line of earthworks that would connect their new position with existing entrenchments at Globe Tavern on the Weldon Railroad.

The following day, the Confederates launched attacks against the new Union line but were repulsed each time. This would be the last fighting at Poplar Springs Church. Federal casualties numbered around 2,800, including 1,300 men taken prisoner. The number of Confederate casualties is not known precisely, but has been estimated at 1,300 men.

Although the Union offensive south of Petersburg failed to completely achieve either of the objectives Grant set for it, it did result in important gains for his attempt to capture the two cities. First, it prevented Lee from moving additional troops from Petersburg to the defense of Richmond. Second, it forced Lee to extend his already thinly manned defenses another mile to the west. After Poplar Springs Church, Southerners could only hope that cold, wet winter weather would come before Grant could push his lines around Petersburg further westward.

—*David McGee*

See also Hill, Ambrose Powell; Petersburg Campaign.

For further reading:
Horn, John. *The Petersburg Campaign, June 1864-April 1865* (1993).

Sommers, Richard J. *Richmond Redeemed: The Siege at Petersburg* (1981).

Trudeau, Noah Andre. *The Last Citadel: Petersburg, Virginia, June 1864-April 1865* (1991).

POPULAR SOVEREIGNTY

Popular sovereignty was a doctrine employed during the antebellum era to defuse the explosive issue of slavery expansion. The concept of popular sovereignty can be traced to ancient Greece, and it was introduced in the 1840s as a moderate response to the Wilmot Proviso, which called for a congressional prohibition of slavery in any territory acquired as a result of the war with Mexico. The "Father of Popular Sovereignty" was Lewis Cass, a Democratic senator from Michigan. The principle, of course, was not original to Cass. Both supporters and opponents of the Wilmot Proviso had argued that only territorial residents could properly decide the slavery question. Congressmen Caleb Blood Smith of Indiana

and Shelton Leake, a Virginian, disagreed over the efficacy of the proviso, but each spoke in favor of allowing westerners to decide the slavery question for themselves. Vice President George M. Dallas expressed the same opinion at Pittsburgh, in September 1847, and New York senator Daniel Dickinson shortly thereafter presented resolutions supporting territorial self-determination regarding slavery.

While Lewis Cass did not formulate the concept of popular sovereignty, he provided a systematic framework for the doctrine in a letter to Alfred O. P. Nicholson, dated 24 December 1847. Ignoring the legislative precedents established with the Northwest Ordinance and the Missouri Compromise, Cass claimed that the federal government did not possess the authority to interfere with slavery in either the states or the territories. True, the Constitution granted Congress the power to "make all needful rules and regulations, respecting the territory and other property belonging to the United States" (article 4, section 3), but the clause referred to "territory" solely in the sense of "property," not as a governmental entity. According to Cass, the question of slavery should be decided by the settlers of the western territories, not by the federal legislature. Cass did not state when the people of a territory could make this decision, or whether it would be binding until statehood was attained. Popular sovereignty, Cass hoped, would serve as an ambiguous compromise that united Democrats on the dangerous issue of the extension of slavery. As presented by Cass, the doctrine of popular sovereignty was predicated on the principle of self-government and a strict construction of the Constitution. It also secured for Cass the ensuing Democratic nomination for president, but Zachary Taylor defeated him.

The Wilmot Proviso never passed the Senate, but the controversy over slavery expansion continued. The concept of popular sovereignty was embodied in the Compromise of 1850, fashioned by Henry Clay, a Whig senator from Kentucky, and pushed through Congress by the unstinting efforts of Senator Stephen A. Douglas of Illinois. Among its provisions, California was admitted as a free state, as the residents clearly wished, and governments were established for the Utah and New Mexico Territories, tacitly leaving the slavery decision to the affected settlers. Political extremists from the North and South opposed aspects of the Compromise of 1850, but its popular sovereignty solution to the divisive issue of slavery expansion was generally hailed by the American people as the final settlement of the sectional controversy.

Ironically, that avowed disciple of the popular sovereignty creed reignited the slavery extension controversy. The Kansas-Nebraska bill, introduced by Senator Stephen A. Douglas in January 1854, and embraced by President Franklin Pierce as a test of Democratic orthodoxy, repealed the Missouri Compromise Line prohibiting slavery in the region north of 36°30´ and

substituted the popular sovereignty concept. During the debates over the bill, Cass helped strip his doctrine of its carefully contrived ambiguity. In response to critics of "squatter sovereignty," including John C. Calhoun, who demanded to know when the population of a territory was sufficient for its organization, Cass replied that "the smallest number of persons" were entitled to regulate their local affairs. Defenders of slavery expansion contrastingly argued that the western territories were held in trust by the national government, and Congress had no power to undermine the sovereign rights of the states in any territory. By repudiating both the Southern claim that residents could not prohibit slavery prior to statehood and the northern demand that Congress exclude slavery from the territories, the popular sovereignty principle remained acceptable to the vast majority of Democrats. Passage of the Kansas-Nebraska Act, however, triggered a wave of moral indignation that swept through the North and led to the creation of the Republican Party, a sectional organization pledged to oppose the extension of slavery by all constitutional means. Republicans and southern defenders of slavery expansion jointly rejected popular sovereignty.

James Buchanan, a Pennsylvania Democrat, was nominated for the presidency in 1856, on a platform that endorsed popular sovereignty and congressional nonintervention regarding slavery in the territories. The Cass doctrine thus continued to serve as a sectional bridge within the Democratic Party, and Buchanan won the White House. President Buchanan and his secretary of state, Lewis Cass, moved quickly to settle the "Bleeding Kansas" controversy on the basis of popular sovereignty. However, the enflamed political atmosphere, exacerbated by the *Dred Scott* decision, precluded a peaceful compromise. Despite a demonstrated free-state majority in Kansas, Buchanan and Cass ultimately supported the proslavery Lecompton Constitution in an effort to maintain Democratic unity. The Father of Popular Sovereignty spurned his doctrine, although Stephen Douglas remained true to the concept and led the opposition in Congress. The Cass creed no longer functioned as a viable ideological bridge between Democrats. The Buchanan administration failed in its efforts to bring Kansas into the Union as a Democratic slave state; in the process, sectional tensions worsened and party solidarity was shattered. Popular sovereignty, a compromise approach to the explosive sectional issue of slavery expansion, had outlived its usefulness. It tragically failed its final test and pushed the nation closer to disunion.

—*Willard Carl Klunder*

See also Cass, Lewis; Democratic Party; Douglas, Stephen Arnold; Election of 1856; Election of 1860; Freeport Doctrine; Kansas-Nebraska Act.

For further reading:
Conkin, Paul K. *Self-Evident Truths: Being a Discourse on the Origins and Developments of the First Principles of American*

Government—Popular Sovereignty, Natural Rights, and Balance and Separation of Powers (1974).

Klunder, Willard Carl. "Lewis Cass and Slavery Expansion: The Father of Popular Sovereignty and Ideological Infanticide." Civil War History (1986).

[Nicholson] Letter from Hon. Lewis Cass, of Michigan, on the War and the Wilmot Proviso (1847).

PORT GIBSON, BATTLE OF
(1 May 1863)

Early attempts by Union forces to capture Vicksburg, Mississippi, in late 1862 and early 1863 had failed. Ulysses S. Grant then turned his attention south of the city. He planned to march his army down the Louisiana side of the river, cross over, and establish a beachhead on the Mississippi side. The Union victory at Port Gibson secured this beachhead and led to the eventual fall of Vicksburg itself.

Although his first choice of a landing site at Grand Gulf became impossible when his gunboats failed to silence the Confederates' formidable defenses, a local African-American informed the Union troops of a good site farther south at Bruinsburg. Union forces began crossing the river early on 30 April, and by late afternoon, 22,000 troops had landed on Mississippi soil. Grant's inland campaign had begun.

Grant's men faced no resistance while landing at Bruinsburg. A Union cavalry raid through Mississippi led by Benjamin Grierson, and a feint against the bluffs north of Vicksburg by William T. Sherman confused the Confederate commander, John C. Pemberton. Not knowing where the main threat was, Pemberton could not unite his scattered forces to resist the Union landing. General John S. Bowen, Grand Gulf's commander, could only watch as Grant's gunboats passed his batteries on 29 April heading south toward Bruinsburg.

Ecstatic about his peaceful landing, Grant pushed his army forward to secure his beachhead. John McClernand's XIII Corps quickly gained the high ground east of Bruinsburg. His men then continued eastward toward the town of Port Gibson in hopes of surprising the enemy and saving the bridges spanning Bayou Pierre, a stream that passes east of the town.

After notifying Pemberton of the need for reinforcements, Bowen began shifting some Grand Gulf troops southward to Port Gibson to meet Grant's threat. Pemberton began sending troops from other parts of Mississippi, but these men would not arrive in time and Bowen would be forced to fight greatly outnumbered.

Union and Confederate forces first collided after midnight on 1 May. The vanguard of McClernand's corps ran against Confederate pickets near the A. K. Shaifer house. A brief firefight and an artillery duel ensued. The clash quickly subsided, as both sides prepared for the battle they knew would begin by morning.

Terrain played a major role at the battle of Port Gibson. Mazes of ridges and ravines running between tangles of cane and underbrush dominated the landscape. Grant himself described the land as "standing on edge." These features provided Bowen an ideal line of defense. Grant would not be able to utilize his numerical and artillery strengths fully.

The battle of Port Gibson took place along two parallel roads that led into the town. McClernand's troops traveled the Rodney Road. A more northerly route called the Bruinsburg Road eventually joined with the Rodney Road outside the town itself. Ravines separated the two roads, preventing troop coordination. McClernand focused on the Rodney Road but, after spotting enemy troops, ordered one division toward the Bruinsburg Road early on 1 May.

Unsure about which road the Union forces would take, Bowen defended both roads. During the early phase of the battle, Bowen's outnumbered men held their ground, especially those holding the Bruinsburg Road. His forces along the Rodney Road, however, faced the main brunt of the attack where McClernand massed the majority of his corps and stormed the Confederates' first line along a ridge at Magnolia Church. These Southern troops withdrew and reformed a few miles to the rear closer to Port Gibson. Bowen hurriedly placed newly arrived reinforcements along this site and the Bruinsburg Road and awaited the next onslaught.

Federal numerical superiority would eventually take its toll and force Bowen's men to retire. Grant arrived on the scene and funneled more men to flank the Southerners on the Bruinsburg Road while McClernand continued to march ahead on the Rodney Road. Bowen plugged open gaps in his lines with available men and ordered a counterattack on the Rodney Road. The attack went well at first, but Union forces were too numerous. After delaying a numerically superior force for a full day, Bowen ordered a retreat. His men gave up Port Gibson and crossed the Bayou Pierre to safety.

The battle of Port Gibson solidified Grant's landing site, but Bowen and his men could take solace in knowing that they had fought well against enormous odds, 23,000 versus 6,500. When the day had ended, however, the Union army had control of the field. Casualties were approximately 800 on each side.

The Union victory at Port Gibson launched Grant's successful campaign to capture Vicksburg. Pemberton's failure to mass his troops allowed Grant to gain a solid foothold that ultimately spelled doom for Vicksburg.

—*Clay Williams*

See also Bowen, John Stevens; Grant, Ulysses Simpson; Grierson's Raid; McClernand, John Alexander; Pemberton,

John Clifford; Sherman, William Tecumseh; Vicksburg Campaign.

For further reading:
Ballard, Michael B. *Pemberton: A Biography* (1991).
Bearss, Edwin C. *Grant Strikes a Fatal Blow*. Vol. 2 of *The Campaign for Vicksburg* (1986).
Grant, Ulysses S. *Personal Memoirs of U.S. Grant*. Vol. 1 (1885).
Winschel, Terrence J. *Triumph & Defeat, The Vicksburg Campaign* (1999).

PORT HUDSON, LOUISIANA CAMPAIGN
(14 March–9 July 1863)

Located about twenty-five miles by river and seventeen miles overland from Baton Rouge, Louisiana, on the Mississippi River, Port Hudson became a well-fortified, heavily armed Confederate position during the second year of the Civil War. The Confederate commander at New Orleans, Major General Mansfield Lovell, began work on fortifications at Port Hudson in early April 1862 to prevent a Federal move on New Orleans from the north. New Orleans fell by an attack from the south by the end of the month, and Port Hudson, as a further step in gaining control of the Mississippi River, became a logical objective for the Federal military over the next year.

As part of the Confederate effort to strengthen Vicksburg, Mississippi, in the summer of 1862, Major General Earl Van Dorn put the Federals in Baton Rouge on the defensive and strengthened Port Hudson, then under the command of Brigadier General Daniel Ruggles and later in the fall under Brigadier General William Beall. Not a terribly healthy place in the best of times, as the garrison increased at the small town, sickness became a very prevalent problem.

At the end of 1862, Union major general Nathaniel Prentiss Banks was placed in command of the Department of the Gulf. One of his instructions was to secure the line of the Mississippi River as far north as possible. Even with the naval forces of Rear Admiral David Glasgow Farragut, Banks did not seem in much of a hurry to carry out these orders.

Also in late 1862, Port Hudson's command was transferred to Major General Franklin Gardner. He worked steadily to strengthen the defenses and to make room for the reinforcements he received. In spite of Union naval efforts to stop river travel from Vicksburg to Port Hudson, Gardner also received steady supplies from that quarter as well.

Under increasing pressure from the War Department, Banks in late February 1863 launched a tentative campaign against Port Hudson. He had built up forces around Baton Rouge for several weeks and began testing Confederate defenses at the end of the second week of March. He was close enough to Port Hudson by 14 March that he felt confident that Farragut could attack from the river and move past the town.

Farragut began moving upriver with seven boats toward Port Hudson at about 9 P.M. on 14 March. Confederate gunners manning their river batteries were waiting for him. Farragut was spotted by Confederate lookouts at 11:20 P.M., starting the battle. He was able to get only the *Hartford* and the *Albatross* past Port Hudson, losing the USS *Mississippi* in the attempt. The other four Union vessels had to fall back downriver. As a result of Farragut's failure, Banks retreated on 15 March. During the next two months, Gardner worked to strengthen Port Hudson's defenses.

In the meantime, Ulysses S. Grant had moved down the west bank of the Mississippi River and crossed below Vicksburg. In early May 1863 he commenced operations against that river city and instructed Banks to send troops to help with the campaign. While Banks hesitated, preferring an independent campaign of his own, Gardner sent some of his troops to beleaguered Confederate lieutenant general John Pemberton at Vicksburg.

With Vicksburg threatened, Gardner knew that Banks might use that opportunity to move against Port Hudson again. Further adding to his worries came news on 24 April of Colonel Benjamin Henry Grierson's raid into Louisiana toward Baton Rouge. He tried to set several traps for the Federal cavalryman, but failed to nab him. Then on 5 May the Federal gunboats below Port Hudson began shelling the town.

On 11 May Banks began moving his army out of Baton Rouge. He was still unsure whether to move to join Grant or to attack Port Hudson. Within the week, he decided to make Port Hudson his objective.

Banks planned to encircle Gardner's defenses by land, while Gardner worked frantically to prevent the Federals from gaining footholds. The small offensives he was able to mount against the Union forces, though, demonstrated only how desperately he was outnumbered. Possessing only about 3,500 men to defend his positions against over 30,000 Union troops, Gardner had no choice but to withdraw into his works. On 21 May he received orders from Lieutenant General Joseph Johnston to evacuate the town. Gardner refused and asked for reinforcements. By the time he heard from Johnston again, there was no escape.

Over the next five days, the two armies fought a number of small engagements as Banks probed Gardner's defenses, moving closer to the Confederate outer works. While Banks maneuvered, Gardner frantically strengthened his northern defenses, which were his weakest. Banks, meanwhile, was shelling more as he drew closer.

Federal preparations pointed to an imminent attack. Banks consulted his top brigadiers, Christopher Augur,

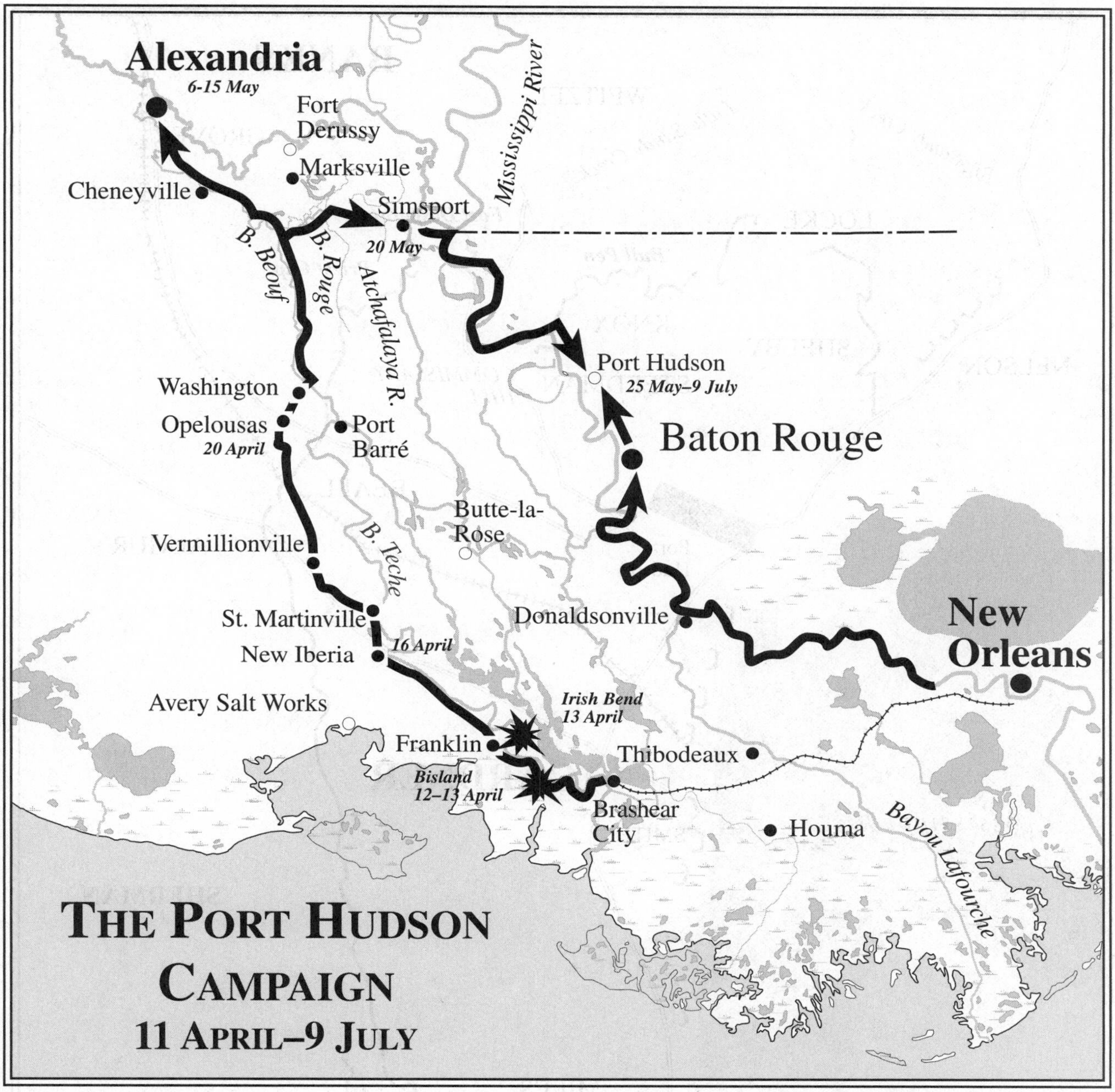

THE PORT HUDSON CAMPAIGN
11 APRIL–9 JULY

Map labels:

Alexandria
6-15 May

Fort Derussy

Marksville

Cheneyville

Simsport
20 May

Mississippi River

B. Beouf

B. Rouge

Atchafalaya R.

Washington

Opelousas
20 April

Port Barré

Port Hudson
25 May–9 July

Baton Rouge

Vermillionville

B. Teche

Butte-la-Rose

St. Martinville

New Iberia
16 April

Donaldsonville

Irish Bend
13 April

New Orleans

Avery Salt Works

Franklin

Bisland
12–13 April

Thibodeaux

Brashear City

Houma

Bayou Lafourche

Godfrey Weitzel, Thomas West Sherman, and Cuvier Grover. All but Grover favored using their numerical superiority to institute a siege and starve out the Confederates. Banks decided to attack.

The Federal batteries opened up at 5:30 A.M. on 27 May and the Federal gunboats at 7 A.M. The latter proved of little value. At 6 A.M. Weitzel moved against Port Hudson's northern defenses, followed by Grover from the northeast. Augur and Sherman on the Union left remained uninvolved during the morning. Weitzel's men had to travel across very rough, uneven terrain, and then over Little Sandy Creek. As a result, units became

broken up and separated. Heavy fighting took place all along Weitzel's line down to Commissary Hill, but because he was unable to concentrate his forces, the Confederates were able to move men around to meet these various threats. Throughout the morning, all of the Federal attacks were uncoordinated. As a result, some of the heaviest casualties were taken by the African-American Native Guards from New Orleans. These troops were sent against the Confederate position to the northwest of Port Hudson and were decimated by Confederate rifle and artillery cross fire.

In the early afternoon, Sherman finally sent his men

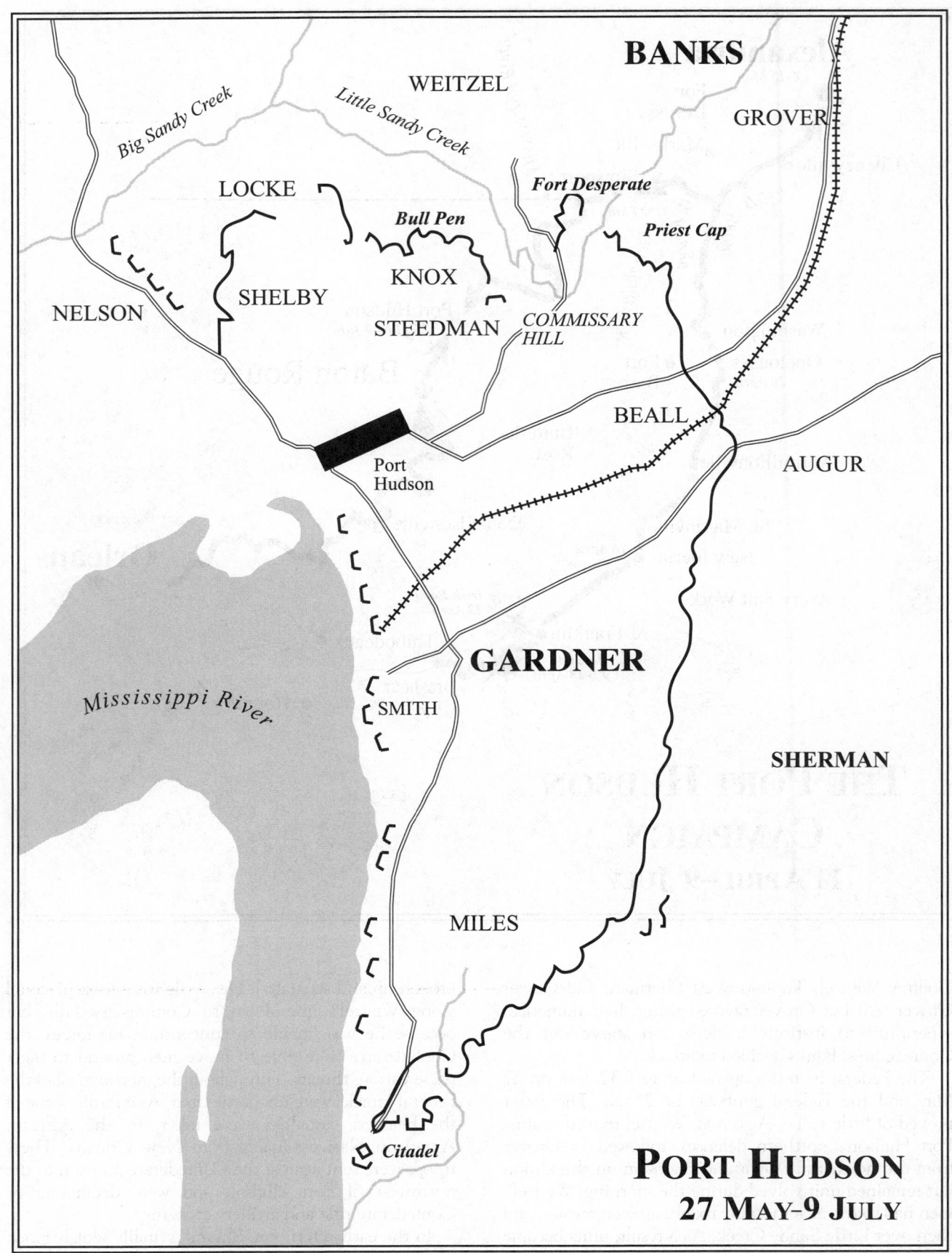

BANKS

WEITZEL

GROVER

Big Sandy Creek

Little Sandy Creek

LOCKE

Fort Desperate

Bull Pen

Priest Cap

KNOX

SHELBY

COMMISSARY HILL

NELSON

STEEDMAN

BEALL

AUGUR

Port Hudson

Mississippi River

GARDNER

SMITH

SHERMAN

MILES

Citadel

PORT HUDSON
27 MAY–9 JULY

Captain Edmund C. Bainbridge's Battery A, 1st U.S. Artillery, at the siege of Port Hudson, 1863 (*National Archives*)

in, followed by Augur. Again, a lack of coordination on the part of the Federals allowed the Confederates to meet these offensives as well. The Confederates repulsed every attack. That night the siege of Port Hudson began.

Over the next few weeks Gardner's garrison experienced shortages of virtually everything it needed, particularly food. Because of malnutrition suffered by the men, illness also increased. In the meantime, Banks was supplied regularly and received regular reinforcements.

Those reinforcements convinced Banks by the middle of June that he should try another assault on Port Hudson's works. On the night of 13 June he began a massive artillery bombardment. Before dawn on 14 June he assaulted Fort Desperate in the northeastern part of the Confederate defenses. This offensive failed.

For the next three weeks the two sides engaged only in light skirmishing. Confederate cavalry harassed Banks's rear, but did little to threaten his positions. Meanwhile, Gardner and his men resorted to eating dogs and rats for sustenance. Finally, when word reached the area that Vicksburg had surrendered, Gardner saw little reason to continue and agreed to surrender. When the formal surrender occurred on 9 July, Gardner capitulated

with 3,000 soldiers at his side. He had suffered about 500 casualties to Banks's 5,000. Further, by holding out as long as he did, Gardner had prevented the use of over 30,000 Union soldiers against other Southern targets for about two months.

—*David S. Heidler and Jeanne T. Heidler*

See also Augur, Christopher Columbus; Banks, Nathaniel Prentiss; Farragut, David Glasgow; Gardner, Franklin; Grover, Cuvier; Sherman, Thomas West; Vicksburg Campaign; Weitzel, Godfrey.

For further reading:
Cunningham, Edward. *The Port Hudson Campaign, 1862–1863* (1963).
Hewitt, Lawrence. *Port Hudson, Confederate Bastion on the Mississippi* (1987).

PORT REPUBLIC, BATTLE OF
(9 June 1862)

The battle of Port Republic was the sixth and final battle of Confederate major general Thomas E. "Stonewall" Jackson's 1862 Shenandoah Valley Campaign, fought the day after the battle of Cross Keys.

At the same time that Union major general John C. Frémont's troops moved from the northwest toward Port Republic via Cross Keys, Union brigadier general James Shields's division of Major General Irwin McDowell's command was crossing the Blue Ridge Mountains from the east. The two Union generals hoped to trap Jackson's force between them.

While Confederate major general Richard Ewell positioned his men near Cross Keys to block Frémont's advance from that direction, Jackson placed his own troops on high ground just north of Port Republic and the confluence of the south fork of the Shenandoah with the South River. Jackson was thus close enough to Ewell at Cross Keys to support him if necessary. His position dominated the road from Conrad's Store to Port Republic, which ran parallel and south of the south fork of the Shenandoah River; this meant he could enfilade Shields's advance toward Port Republic. On the evening of 7 June 1862, as he waited for the Union troops to arrive, Jackson mulled over news of the death of his favorite cavalry commander, Brigadier General Turner Ashby, killed in a skirmish near Harrisonburg.

From Conrad's Store, where he halted to rest his division, Shields sent two brigades to probe Jackson's defenses at Port Republic. He also appealed to Frémont for cooperation against the Confederates.

On the next morning, Sunday, Union troops reached the Confederate lines. In Port Republic, Jackson had just told his chief of staff that he did not plan on any fighting that day ("You know I always try to keep the Sabbath if the enemy will let me"), when musket fire shattered the calm and a rider came up with a report that Federal troops had forded the South River and were in the town. Jackson instructed the messenger to "Go back and fight." Then Jackson and his staff rode hard for the North River Bridge. The general got across it just in time; two officers who brought up the rear were captured. A little more vigor on the part of the Federals and Jackson might have been taken.

Jackson now ordered his artillery to fire into the Federals while Confederate infantry moved forward to clear them from Port Republic at the point of the bayonet. As Jackson's men accomplished this, they could hear distant artillery fire from the battle of Cross Keys, where Ewell was beating back Frémont.

That night Jackson ordered Ewell to leave only Trimble's and Patton's brigades at Cross Keys and move the rest of his men to Port Republic. This would give Jackson four brigades to attack Shields's force. Jackson hoped to defeat it quickly and that same morning turn and complete the destruction of Frémont. Ewell set his men in motion to join Jackson very early on the ninth.

Also early on the ninth, Jackson moved his main body from high ground north of Port Republic across the North River Bridge and through the town. Not without difficulty they then got across the South River on a temporary bridge of wagons driven into the stream. As they moved to attack the Union troops to the northeast, they had the south fork of the Shenandoah to their left and the Blue Ridge to their right. Brigadier General Charles Winder's Stonewall Brigade led. At 7 A.M. the Confederates encountered Federal pickets and Jackson ordered an attack. While Jackson was not certain of the Union strength, he was reassured by knowledge that Ewell was marching to join him. He also believed he could not delay and had to dispatch Shields's troops before Frémont learned of the weak Confederate front at Cross Keys.

As Winder's brigade advanced through wheat fields toward the Union lines, it came under heavy Union fire. Opposing the Confederates were only 3,000 troops under Brigadier General E. B. Tyler, but the Union troops were along a fence line and Tyler had positioned six of his sixteen guns on high ground to the Union left. Their fire exacted a heavy toll from the Confederates.

A bottleneck had developed at the temporary bridge across the South River when the board flooring collapsed, forcing men to come across in single file. The Stonewall Brigade now found itself virtually alone. With all chance of a dual victory lost and his situation desperate, Jackson tried to hurry units forward; he also sent couriers to Ewell to make haste, and he ordered Trimble at Cross Keys to come up through Port Republic and burn the North River Bridge behind him so Frémont could not join the action.

Shelled to a halt, the Stonewall Brigade was just managing to hold on. Confederate brigadier general Richard Taylor's brigade now arrived, having marched to the sound of the guns. Jackson sent Taylor's lead regiment to join the Stonewall Brigade in the wheat fields. When Taylor suggested that he attack the battery on the Union left that was exacting such a toll from Winder's brigade, Jackson agreed instantly. The Louisianans forded the South River to enfilade the Union position. Meanwhile, Jackson personally rallied the Stonewall Brigade, but he could only do so for a time. Out of ammunition, the brigade broke and many of its men streamed to the rear. At this critical juncture, Ewell arrived with Steuart's brigade (temporarily commanded by Colonel W. C. Scott) and blocked the Federal advance, although at some cost. At the same time, Taylor's men struck the Federal left flank. As the Union troops attempted to wheel to engage Taylor, three more of Ewell's regiments arrived and went into action. Now outnumbered three to one, Shields's troops were soon in full retreat. Jackson turned to Ewell and said, "He who does not see the hand of God in this is blind, sir. Blind!"

It was then 11 A.M. Jackson's hopes of pursuit were dashed by the fact that Tyler's men had retreated in good order and Frémont was to his rear. Indeed, Frémont had

finally come up and ordered his artillery to shell the field, although he did not attempt an attack.

Union casualties in the battle of Port Republic came to 1,108 men, most of them in the retreat, including 558 prisoners. Jackson's losses were also heavy—in excess of 800—the most he had suffered in battle thus far.

That same afternoon Jackson put his army in motion toward Brown's Gap by a path beyond the range of Frémont's guns. At the same time, President Abraham Lincoln ordered Shields and Frémont to withdraw. Frémont was glad to go, but Shields said, "I never obeyed an order with such reluctance." Soon Jackson slipped his men out of the valley in trains to Richmond in order to assist General Robert E. Lee in the Peninsula Campaign.

—*Spencer C. Tucker*

See also Ewell, Richard s.; Frémont, John C.; Jackson, Thomas J.; Shenandoah Valley Campaign (1862); Shields, James; Taylor, Richard; Trimble, Isaac; Winder, Charles S.

For further reading:

Collins, Darrell L. *Jackson's Valley Campaign. The Battles of Cross Keys and Port Republic, June 8–9, 1862* (1993).

Tanner, Robert G. *Stonewall in the Valley. Thomas J. "Stonewall" Jackson's Shenandoah Valley Campaign, Spring 1862* (1976; reprint 1996).

PORT ROYAL SOUND/HILTON HEAD, BATTLE OF
(4–5 November 1861)

In the early stages of the Union blockade of Southern ports, available Federal ships were few and spread thinly along the hundreds of miles of Southern coastline. Months into the blockade, the need for a base of operations to repair, refuel, and refit ships on the east coast was viewed as crucial in this increasingly important operation. It was then a strategy of the North to capture a sufficient number of major Confederate sites, converting them into U.S. naval bases. The proximity of these bases in the South, close to ships involved in the blockade, was important because long voyages back to far-off Northern ports for refueling created holes in the Federal defense. On 1 October 1861, President Abraham Lincoln asked for an expedition to the Southern east coast to establish such a station. After review of possible sites, this request was carried out through the Port Royal operation of November 1861. Port Royal, South Carolina, located between Charleston, South Carolina, and Savannah, Georgia, seemed to be the best site suited for the Federals' needs.

The fleet of approximately seventeen warships, twenty-five supply vessels, and twenty-five transports as well as nearly 12,000 troops that made up the Port Royal expedition left Fort Monroe on 29 October. On their way to South Carolina, they experienced a fierce storm off of Cape Hatteras. The ships were scattered and suffered minor damage, and two vessels including the USS *Sabine* went down in the storm on 1–2 November. On 4 November, as the Federal fleet, commanded by Flag Officer Samuel F. Du Pont, assembled outside the sound, three vessels surveyed the port and were fired upon by several small ships of the Confederate naval squadron. The survey found the two-mile-wide entrance to the harbor guarded by Fort Beauregard at Bay Point and Fort Walker on Hilton Head. Although the sound was well armed with forty-one guns, the Union fleet severely outmatched the Confederates in arms as well as troop size. The Confederate garrisons staffing the forts proved to be outnumbered, undertrained, and low on ammunition.

On 5 November, a small and weakly armed Confederate flotilla engaged four Federal naval vessels in Port Royal Sound. The flotilla was overpowered and forced up into the inland streams of the sound, only to emerge later in the following days. Although the survey mission was fired upon and four Federal vessels were engaged, the battle did not start until 9:00 A.M. on 7 November. Du Pont led his Federal naval fleet into Port Royal Sound, steaming straight into the harbor between Fort Beauregard to the north and Fort Walker on Hilton Head. Once again, the small Confederate flotilla of four ships could do little to oppose them. Quickly overpowering the Confederate vessels, the squadron circled the harbor. The 155 guns of the Federal fleet hammered the forts simultaneously at a rate of up to 24 shells per minute, starting with Fort Walker and then circling north to Fort Beauregard. Outgunned, inexperienced, and with at times defective ammunition and guns, the Confederates found it difficult to hit a moving target. Led by Brigadier General Thomas Drayton, the Confederates fought on well into the afternoon. The professional sharpshooters of the Union fleet accurately landed shot after shot into the earthen structures. Ammunition running low, the Confederates finally fled the forts. At 2:00 P.M., forces fled Fort Walker; at 3:30 P.M., Fort Beauregard.

Casualties were light. Eleven Confederates were killed, forty-eight wounded, three captured, and four missing. The Federals recorded eight killed, six seriously wounded, and seventeen slightly wounded, and they experienced no major damage to their vessels.

Brigadier General Thomas W. Sherman's 12,000 Union men were quickly unloaded to take control of the Hilton Head–Port Royal area. Almost immediately, Federal troops from Port Royal carried out expeditions taking possession of land and crops, but only partially exploiting the Union landing.

The capture of Port Royal established a Union hold in Confederate territory between Savannah and Charleston. Although proving no great threat in land-based operations through the duration of the war, it

haunted and intimidated the Confederates as a possible risk. It revived Northern spirits in a year of continued demoralizing defeats. Its greatest importance, however, came in its significance throughout the war, providing a base of operation for the ever-important blockaders, refueling, reloading, and allowing such ships to remain longer at their stations. With such ports being converted to Northern bases, the blockade led to the increased dwindling and stagnation of the Confederate military, quite possibly leading to an earlier end of the war.

—*Andrew Paul Bielakowski*

See also Blockade of C.S.A.; Du Pont, Samuel Francis; Sherman, Thomas West.

For further reading:

The Blockade: Runners and Raiders. Vol. 3 of *The Civil War* (1983).

DuPont, S. F. *The Mission: 1860–1862.* Vol. 1 of *A Selection from His Civil War Letters* (1969).

Headley, J. T. *Farragut and Our Naval Commanders* (1867).

PORTER, DAVID DIXON
(1813–1891)
Naval officer

David Dixon Porter was the third of ten children of the aggressive David Porter who had fought on the sea in every war from 1776 until 1824, when he resigned rather than accept sentencing for insubordination. The younger Porter was every bit as daring, obstreperous, and opinionated as his father and is known for his intrepid exploits during the Civil War.

When he was ten, Porter had gone to sea with his father. His foster brother was Admiral David Farragut, who also sailed with the senior Porter and took the commodore's given name as his own. Porter was wounded while serving with his father, who had accepted an appointment in the Mexican navy after his resignation. David Porter's early education was minimal at best. His appointment as a midshipman in 1829 was the beginning of his U.S. Naval Career. He became a passed midshipman in 1835 and made lieutenant in 1841.

The brightest thing about his career in the period from 1829 to 1845 was his marriage in 1839 to George Ann Patterson, daughter of Commodore Daniel Patterson, who had supported Andrew Jackson in New Orleans in the War of 1812. Porter had been on Mediterranean cruise duty with Patterson, whose daughter was aboard.

Action and promotion were uppermost in Porter's mind. After an assignment with the Coast Survey, Porter sought a combat command, but instead was assigned to recruiting duty in New Orleans. He finally gained a lieutenancy aboard the war steamer *Spitfire*, from which he led a landing party and captured the fort at Tabasco. He was rewarded with command of the ship. He was then assigned once again to the Coast Survey and the Naval Observatory. But it was the sea he wanted, so he took leave to captain a merchant steamer around South America to the Pacific coast and then to captain a mail ship for two years. He then took the captaincy of the Australian steamship *Golden Age*, which sailed from England to Australia and was regarded as the fastest ship afloat at the time.

Porter in 1855 decided to return to duty and was given command of the steamer *Supply* with orders to sail to North Africa for a cargo of camels for experimental use by the U.S. Army in the southwest. He learned something of the war in the Crimea while on this assignment, but upon his return he was given shore duty at the Portsmouth Navy Yard from 1857 to 1860. Once again his career foundered and he looked once more to the merchant fleet. On the eve of the Civil War, he accepted assignment to the Pacific Coast survey in preparation for joining the Pacific Steamship Company. He was forty-eight years old and had spent twenty years as a lieutenant.

The perverse reality of war now worked in his favor and his experience came to the fore. He was selected to captain the ship *Powhatan* to relieve the besieged Fort Pickens at Pensacola, Florida. Porter wrote his own orders and made personnel assignments, which proved embarrassing in that one of his crew, a Samuel Barron, had resigned to join the Confederacy without Porter's knowledge. The Secretary of the Navy now questioned Porter's loyalty as well. President Abraham Lincoln told Secretary of State William H. Seward to remove Porter from command. The redoubtable Porter ignored that order, giving personal preference to the original assignment. Porter wanted to take Pensacola, but the army there refused to cooperate, leaving Porter to spend six weeks cruising on blockade duty in the West Indies and South America and searching for the Confederate ship *Sumter*. The navy, despite its jaundiced concern for Porter, rewarded his audacity with a promotion to commander.

Given his sailing experience, he was asked for an opinion on attacking New Orleans. Always the aggressor, Porter sounded out his foster brother Farragut about a joint venture. The navy was also concerned about the loyalty of Farragut, who had been born in Louisiana and then adopted by the Porters upon the death of his father. Porter suggested that Farragut should lead and he would accompany him with a flotilla of mortars in support.

After a six-day ineffectual bombarding of Forts Jackson and St. Philip, south of the city, Farragut decided to sail past them at night with Porter following. Porter's flagship, *Harriet Lane*, reduced the shore batteries with withering fire and prepared the way for General Benjamin Butler's army to occupy the city. Porter ques-

Rear Admiral David D. Porter and staff aboard his flagship, the USS *Malvern*, at Hampton Roads, Virginia, December 1864
(*Library of Congress*)

tioned Butler's readiness for combat and embarrassed him by declaring that his own sailors would take the city if Butler would not. The two became lifelong enemies.

Porter's flotilla was detached and he proceeded up the Mississippi River toward Vicksburg. The going was slow; he had to remove chained log impediments to shipping as he went. After an ineffective start, Porter worked closely with Generals Ulysses S. Grant and William T. Sherman in a classic coordinated engagement. The three dominant military personalities meshed perfectly to take Vicksburg in the summer of 1863. Porter received the thanks of the two generals and the thanks of the joint Congress. He was promoted to rear admiral over eighty officers his senior in rank. He had taken control of 3,000 miles of water, built a shipbuilding yard at Cairo, Illinois, and commanded eighty war vessels. Unprecedented, he had made admiral without having served as captain or commodore.

In spring 1864, Porter commanded a gunboat expedition in support of Major General Nathaniel P. Banks in a sorry adventure on the Red River. Water levels dropped and Porter's vessels were bogged until engineers could dislodge them. Porter was now called to command the blockading fleet off Wilmington, North Carolina, to prevent Lee from using the port to supply his army. Porter assembled an armada of 120 vessels and organized them in four divisions. He went on the attack against Fort Fisher, which guarded the harbor, bombarding it for three days until there was no retaliatory fire. Once again he was to contend with General Butler, who again was reluctant to attack and instead retired to Hampton Roads to the north. Porter telegraphed a demand for a new army to replace Butler. General Alfred H. Terry arrived with 8,000 men and joined with Porter to reduce the fort that was the last great Confederate coastal stronghold.

In April 1865, Porter took his gunboats up the James River and forced the Confederate commander Raphael Semmes to scuttle his squadron. Porter then received President Lincoln aboard his flagship, *Malvern*, from which they watched Grant's drive to Richmond. The U.S. Congress voted Porter an unprecedented three votes of thanks for his achievements. But Porter was a sailor without a war to fight. He took the superintendency of the Naval Academy, where he stayed until 1869. He was made vice admiral in 1866 while Farragut was made Admiral of the Navy. Upon Farragut's death in 1870, Porter was promoted to Admiral of the Navy.

Porter was an indefatigable worker. He revised the Naval Academy's curriculum to stress steam engineering. When he was made advisor to the secretary of the navy, he created the Board of Inspection and established a regular agenda for repair of all vessels. He also ensured that all steam vessels would be equipped with auxiliary sails. He was appointed head of the Board of Inspection, on which he served until his death in Washington on 13 February 1891. He is buried in Arlington Cemetery close to his grandson and namesake, Major General David Dixon Porter III.

Peacetime had brought little peace to Porter, who after the war led a navy that was reminiscent of the navy of his youth; officers were clamoring for promotion and active duty. Old disputes continued as residue of his experiences with colleagues. Unfortunately, Porter continued his quarrels with Benjamin Butler, who had returned to his seat in the U.S. Senate and made no secret of his dislike for Porter. Their disputes were aired in printed articles at a time when the nation sought to put the war in perspective. Tough, opinionated, brash, and vain, Porter was never one to be easily mollified.

—*Jack J. Cardoso*

See also Fort Fisher; Navy, U.S.A.; New Orleans, Capture of; Red River Campaign; Vicksburg Campaign.

For further reading:

Anderson, Bern. *By Sea and by River: The Naval History of the Civil War* (1962).

Fowler, William M., Jr. *Under Two Flags: The American Navy in the Civil War* (1990).

Milligan, John. *Gunboats Down the Mississippi* (1965).

Porter, David D. *Incidents and Anecdotes of the Civil War* (1885).

Reed, Rowena. *Combined Operations in the Civil War* (1963).

Soley, James R. *Admiral Porter* (1903).

West, Richard S., Jr. *The Second Admiral: A Life of David Dixon Porter* (1937).

PORTER, FITZ JOHN
(1822–1901)
Union general

Born in Portsmouth, New Hampshire, into a family with strong connections to the navy, Fitz John Porter was the son of U.S. naval captain John Porter and a cousin of future admiral David Dixon Porter. He attended Phillips Exeter Academy before receiving an appointment to the U.S. Military Academy. He graduated eighth of forty-one in the class of 1845.

Porter's initial assignment at Fort Monroe was cut short by the outbreak of the Mexican-American War. He was sent to Zachary Taylor's army, in which he fought in northern Mexico until detached with most of the regulars to join Winfield Scott's Mexico City campaign. From Vera Cruz to Mexico City, Porter earned two brevet promotions and was wounded once. After the war, Porter served as an instructor at West Point and at various frontier posts as a member of the adjutant general's office. He also participated in Albert Sidney Johnston's Utah expedition. In the months preceding the outbreak of the Civil War Porter supervised the evacuation of U.S. soldiers from Texas after the department's surrender to Texas secessionists.

On 14 May 1861, Porter became colonel of the 15th Infantry, and during the summer he would be made brigadier general of volunteers, with his date of rank set at 17 May 1861. George McClellan, a major general of Ohio volunteers, had requested Porter's services as his adjutant in April 1861 but had been refused. So Porter served in the Shenandoah Valley in the summer of 1861, first under Major General Robert Patterson and then under Major General Nathaniel P. Banks. When McClellan became commander of the Army of the Potomac, he summoned Porter to Washington.

During the Peninsula campaign of the spring and summer of 1862, Porter held several important positions under McClellan. Initially he commanded a division in the Army of the Potomac. When the army was reorganized into corps, he commanded the 1st Division, III Corps. McClellan named him director of the siege at Yorktown, essentially turning everyday management of that phase of the campaign over to Porter. On 18 May 1862, Porter was named commander of V Corps.

McClellan's cautious approach toward Richmond in June 1862 placed V Corps north of the swollen Chickahominy River and most of the army south of it. Robert E. Lee saw an opportunity to crush the isolated V Corps while he kept the rest of the Army of the Potomac occupied. On 26 June 1862—the second day of the campaign that would become known as the Seven Days'—Lee struck Porter at Mechanicsville. Porter defended his position against staggering odds and fell back to Gaines' Mill. He then took the lead in McClellan's retreat toward the James and established the Union defensive line at Malvern Hill.

On 4 July 1862, Porter was promoted to major general of volunteers, and while he was generally praised for his actions on the Peninsula campaign, his promotion came at a time of growing criticism of his superior, McClellan. Among McClellan's faults, according to some, was that he consulted more with a few loyal officers rather than his staff or his superiors in Washington. As early as 9

May, President Lincoln had written to McClellan on the peninsula, complaining that McClellan confided his plans only to Porter and a few other officers. Porter and McClellan were indeed confidants, and when McClellan was summoned with his army back to Washington so that much of that force could become part of rival John Pope's Army of Virginia, Porter made indiscreet remarks regarding Pope's competence. Unfortunately for everyone, Porter was soon ordered to take his V Corps to join Pope in northern Virginia.

During the battle of Second Bull Run, Porter failed to carry out Pope's orders to attack Stonewall Jackson's flank. Many officers then (and many historians since) regarded Pope's task as impossible, but the worst of it was his failure to attempt any offensive action. Grumbling criticism became a serious matter when Pope officially accused Porter of dereliction of duty and failure to obey orders. The charge shocked Porter when he heard about it on 10 September. He claimed that immediately after the battle, Pope had told him that he had no complaints about the way Porter had conducted himself. Porter asked for an official investigation of his conduct.

In the meantime, Porter rejoined the Army of the Potomac and George McClellan as they attempted to counter Lee's first invasion of the North. McClellan held Porter in reserve during the battle of Antietam. Then on 10 November 1862, Porter was relieved of command of V Corps pending the results of a court-martial. The action ominously came just three days after McClellan's final removal as the commander of the Army of the Potomac.

Porter's court-martial began in December 1862 and lasted until 10 January 1863. Charged with disloyalty to his commanding officer and disobedience of orders, some claimed that Porter was the victim of Secretary of War Edwin Stanton's desire to discredit George McClellan and anger at McClellan among the officer corps. Whatever the motive behind his trial, Porter was found guilty on most counts, and the court recommended that he be cashiered from the army and never be allowed to hold another position in the government. Lincoln endorsed the verdict, and Porter was cashiered on 21 January 1863.

For the remainder of his life, Porter engaged in a variety of business activities, but his primary occupation was gaining a review and reversal of the 10 January 1863 verdict. During Reconstruction, Porter's ties to the Democratic Party made this task an impossibility. Finally, in 1879 an army review board headed by former Civil War general John M. Schofield not only ruled that Porter was totally blameless, it praised him for his actions at Second Bull Run. Two successive Republican administrations refused to act on the board's recommendations, however. In 1886, Democratic president Grover Cleveland restored Porter to the regular rank of colonel,

though he did not authorize back pay. Porter retired two days after his restoration to rank.

Porter retired to Morristown, New Jersey, where he died on 21 May 1901. Historians still debate his guilt or innocence.

—*David S. Heidler and Jeanne T. Heidler*

See also Bull Run, Second Battle of; Malvern Hill, Battle of; McClellan, George Brinton; Mechanicsville, Battle of; Peninsula Campaign; Pope, John; .

For further reading:

Eisenschiml, Otto. *The Celebrated Case of Fitz John Porter, An American Dreyfus Affair* (1950).
Gabler, Henry. "The Fitz John Porter Case: Politics and Military Justice" (Ph.D. dissertation, 1978).

PORTER, WILLIAM DAVID
(1809–1864)
United States naval officer

Born the son of United States naval officer David Porter in Louisiana while his father commanded United States forces in New Orleans, William David Porter was educated to be a naval officer. He was the older brother of future Civil War naval hero David Dixon Porter and grew up in a home where the elder David Porter was rearing David Glasgow Farragut as a foster son. Two of William Porter's sons, reared in the South, chose to fight for the Confederacy during the Civil War.

William David Porter entered the navy as a midshipman in 1823. Throughout a long and distinguished naval career, Porter served at a variety of stations around the world. When the Civil War broke out, Porter was serving in the Pacific. He was quickly summoned east and then put on station at St. Louis.

In October 1861 Porter was ordered to take command of the gunboat *New Era*. One of his first tasks as the ship's new commander was to supervise its conversion to an ironclad vessel. That mission accomplished by the end of the year, the boat was renamed the *Essex*. Once the *Essex* was ready for action, Porter took it to join Andrew Foote's flotilla cooperating with Ulysses S. Grant's expedition to take Fort Henry on the Tennessee River.

A few days before the actual attack began on the fort, Porter took Grant aboard the *Essex* to reconnoiter the fort and to determine the range of its guns. When the fort was attacked on 6 February 1862, the *Essex* played a conspicuous part. She was hit a number of times by the fort's guns and suffered serious damage when one of the shots struck the boiler, causing a large explosion and a large number of casualties. Porter was one of those casualties, when he was burned by steam from the boiler. When he and the other surviving crewmembers were forced to jump into the water to escape the heat from the boiler, his sailors kept him afloat.

After a lengthy convalescence, Porter returned to duty during the summer of 1862, still in command of the *Essex*. Charged with supervising the ship's repairs, Porter took the opportunity virtually to rebuild the ship, incorporating many of his ideas to make it more maneuverable and less vulnerable to Confederate fire. All of this construction was accomplished at St. Louis, after which Porter took the *Essex* to join other Union gunboats on the Mississippi above Vicksburg. While at St. Louis, Porter was promoted to commodore.

One of the primary goals of the Union fleet above Vicksburg was the destruction of the Confederate ironclad *Arkansas*. Porter commanded the *Essex* in an engagement on 22 July 1862 that sought to trap the Confederate ship, but Union forces failed in their attempt to destroy her. The *Essex* and some of the other ships pursued the *Arkansas* south toward Baton Rouge in early August, but she eluded their grasp. Then on 5 August she ran aground and was destroyed by her crew. Porter later had to defend himself against criticism leveled at the officers in this expedition.

Over the next year of the war Porter commanded the *Essex*, primarily along the Mississippi, and participated in the bombardment of Port Hudson, Louisiana, in the spring of 1863 and in the Vicksburg campaign. His health, however, had never fully recovered from his injuries at Fort Henry, and after Vicksburg he was forced to leave active service. For the next year he served on a variety of naval boards, until even this duty became too much of a strain. He died in 1864.

—*David S. Heidler and Jeanne T. Heidler*

See also Arkansas, C.S.S.; Fort Henry; Port Hudson Campaign.
For further reading:
Milligan, John D. *Gunboats Down the Mississippi* (1965).
Porter, William David. *Defence of Commodore W. D. Porter before the Naval Retiring Board, Convened at Brooklyn Navy Yard, November, 1863* (1863).

POTTER, ROBERT BROWN
(1829–1887)
Union general

Born in Schenectady, New York, Robert Brown Potter was educated at Union College and studied law before opening a practice in New York City. At the outbreak of the Civil War, Potter was a militia private in New York but was quickly elevated to a lieutenant in his company. In October 1861 he was mustered into Federal service as a major in the 51st New York Infantry. He was promoted to lieutenant colonel of the regiment two weeks later.

With the organization of Ambrose Burnside's expedition to the North Carolina coast at the end of 1861, the 51st New York was incorporated into Burnside's independent division. Potter fought in the successful assault at New Bern on 14 March 1862 but was wounded early in the battle and had to leave the field. He was commended for his bravery in the engagement.

The 51st traveled to Virginia with Burnside in July to augment George B. McClellan's force on the York Peninsula. At that time the IX Corps was created under Burnside's command and the 51st made a part of it. The 51st would remain part of IX Corps for the remainder of the war, and Potter would be one of the few officers who would remain in the same corps for the duration of the conflict. In September 1862 Potter was promoted to colonel of the 51st New York.

Potter led his regiment in the Second Bull Run campaign and in the Maryland campaign. At Antietam as part of Burnside's corps, Potter was focused on the capture of the bridge on the Union left that would eventually bear Burnside's name. After repeated assaults on the bridge by the Union forces, the Confederate defenders on the opposite side began to run low on ammunition. When they began to fall back, Potter rushed forward with his regiment, finally taking the bridge.

Potter continued to command the 51st at Fredericksburg. After the battle, Burnside recommended him for promotion to brigadier general, a promotion that occurred in March 1863. By that time Burnside had been removed as commander of the Army of the Potomac and ordered with IX Corps to Cincinnati and command of the Army of the Ohio. Potter commanded the 2d Division of the corps and was detached from Burnside's command in June 1863 to fight in the Vicksburg campaign and the Jackson, Mississippi, campaign in July 1863.

Returning to Burnside and the Army of the Ohio in August 1863, Potter assumed command of IX Corps on 25 August and led the corps in the upcoming campaign in eastern Tennessee culminating in the Knoxville campaign. Potter remained in command of IX Corps until 17 January 1864, when he relinquished command to the senior Orlando Bolivar Willcox and resumed command of the 2d Division of the corps.

With the recall of Burnside east and his resumption of command of IX Corps, Potter remained in command of the 2d Division as the corps joined Ulysses S. Grant's campaign against Robert E. Lee in Virginia. In that campaign Potter distinguished himself at Spotsylvania and the North Anna, gaining the attention of many senior officers. During the battle of the Crater at the end of July 1864, Potter was conspicuous in the assault, something that could not be said for any other division commander in IX Corps. He testified at the court of inquiry convened to investigate the disaster that he did not believe that the preparations for the assault had been adequate and that the attacks made after the explosion had been poorly led. Ironically, his testimony contributed to the removal of Burnside, the man he had served under since late 1861.

Potter remained in command of the 2d Division of IX Corps until the last week of the campaign against Lee. He participated in many of the assaults against Lee's works over the next nine months. In the attack on Fort Sedgwick on 2 April 1865, he was seriously wounded and had to relinquish command. For his bravery on that occasion, he was recommended for promotion to major general of volunteers by the commander of the Army of the Potomac, George Gordon Meade. He was promoted to major general of volunteers in September 1865 while serving in the Department of the East under Joseph Hooker.

Potter was mustered out the volunteer army in January 1866 and returned to civilian life. He worked briefly for the railroad industry before going abroad to Europe for his health. Upon his return, he retired to Newport, Rhode Island, where he died on 19 February 1887.

—*David S. Heidler and Jeanne T. Heidler*

See also Crater, Battle of the.

For further reading:

Pleasants, Henry, Jr. *The Tragedy of the Crater* (1938).

Rhea, Gordon C. *The Battles for Spotsylvania Court House and the Road to Yellow Tavern May 7–12, 1864* (1997).

Trudeau, Noah Andre. *The Last Citadel: Petersburg, Virginia, June 1864–April 1865* (1991).

POWELL, LEWIS THORNTON ("PAINE"/"PAYNE")
(1844–1865)

Lincoln assassination conspirator

Lewis Thornton Powell was an important participant in the Lincoln assassination conspiracy. He is most famous for attacking Secretary of State William H. Seward on the night of 14 April 1865, the same night that John Wilkes Booth, the leader of the conspirators, assassinated President Abraham Lincoln.

Lewis Powell, born in Alabama on 22 April 1844, was the son of a Baptist minister and plantation owner named George Cader Powell. George Powell eventually took the family to Florida, where they settled in Hamilton County, located in the Suwannee River valley. The elder Powell began to farm and continued to serve in the Baptist ministry. The youthful Lewis helped with the farm work and developed a strong interest in the church.

When the Civil War broke out, notes the historian Betty Ownsbey, the family was living near the Suwannee County town of Live Oak. Powell, now seventeen years old, quickly enlisted at Jasper in the Hamilton Blues, commanded by Captain Henry Stewart. In June 1861, the Hamilton Blues were added into the 2d Florida Infantry. The Confederate command then dispatched the 2d Florida to Virginia, where the regiment arrived just after the first battle of Bull Run. The 2d Florida was stationed close to Richmond and had the task of guarding Union prisoners.

According to the historian Leon Prior, Powell obtained permission to visit Richmond one evening. While watching a play, he became mesmerized by the performance of an actor named John Wilkes Booth. Powell met Booth after the play, striking up a fateful acquaintance with the actor. As the war continued, Powell and the 2d Florida saw action in numerous battles, including Antietam and Fredericksburg. At Gettysburg, Powell was wounded in the wrist and captured by Union troops. After his recovery, he became a prisoner nurse and helped treat injured soldiers. In late 1863, he escaped from the U.S. Army Hospital in Baltimore, Maryland, and crossed into Virginia, where he joined up with Colonel John Singleton Mosby's Confederate cavalry raiders.

After serving with Mosby, Powell deserted the raiders and Union officers issued him a parole in January 1865. (Powell used the alias "Payne" on his parole documents.) Moving to Baltimore, he encountered John Wilkes Booth at Barnum's Hotel. Booth, who was now making grandiose plans to abduct President Lincoln and the cabinet, brought Powell into his conspiracy. Arrested after fighting with a maid, Powell was ordered by a Union officer to take the oath of allegiance and move north of Philadelphia. (This time, Powell signed the oath using the alias "Paine.") Powell ended up moving to the Washington, D.C., boarding house of Mary Surratt, whose son John was one of Booth's followers. Suddenly, Booth changed his plans and decided to assassinate Lincoln and his cabinet instead of kidnapping them. Apparently, though, he told only Powell about the change.

According to Prior, Booth provided Powell with a gun and a knife and instructed him to kill Secretary of State William Seward. Booth himself would assassinate Lincoln. On the evening of 14 April 1865, Powell went to Seward's home, where the secretary was recovering from a carriage wreck. Seward's daughter Fanny and a military nurse named George Robinson were at his bedside. Seward's sons, Assistant Secretary of State Frederick Seward and Major Augustus Seward, were also in the house. When Seward's servant, William Bell, answered the door, Powell produced a package that he claimed contained medicine and insisted that he be allowed to see Seward. Hearing the commotion,

Frederick came out and denied Powell admittance to Secretary Seward's bedroom. Powell then beat Frederick with his pistol, burst into Seward's room, and stabbed the secretary. Robinson and Augustus Seward engaged in a fierce struggle with Powell (who kept saying "I'm mad! I'm mad!") and managed to get him away from the secretary. Powell fled from Seward's home into a forest, but hunger soon drove him to Mary Surratt's boarding house. The War Department, however, had sent officers to the Surratt house, and they confronted Powell when he knocked on the door. Powell attempted to pose as a workman, but his story collapsed and the officers promptly seized him.

President Andrew Johnson, as the historian Roy Chamlee notes, ordered the assistant adjutant general to establish a military commission that would try Powell and the other conspirators. Powell's court-appointed counsel, William Doster, attempted to portray Powell as insane, but Powell rejected this approach. Doster then tried to show that Powell had been affected by the terrible experience of battle and that he was "penniless and friendless" when he fell under the influence of Booth. Powell had not, Doster pointed out, actually killed anyone. Nevertheless, Powell was found guilty of assaulting Secretary Seward and of conspiring to assassinate President Lincoln. He was hanged along with three of the other conspirators at the Arsenal Penitentiary in Washington on 7 July 1865.

—*David A. Proctor*

See also Booth, John Wilkes; Lincoln Assassination.

For further reading:
Chamlee, Roy. *Lincoln's Assassins: A Complete Account of Their Capture, Trial, and Punishment* (1990).
Ownsbey, Betty. *Alias "Paine": Lewis Thornton Powell, the Mystery Man of the Lincoln Conspiracy* (1993).
Prior, Leon. "Lewis Payne, Pawn of John Wilkes Booth." *Florida Historical Quarterly* (1964).

PRAIRIE GROVE, BATTLE OF
(7 December 1862)

During the late summer and fall of 1862, Confederate major general Thomas C. Hindman assembled a new army in Fort Smith, Arkansas, situated on the Arkansas River only a short distance from the Indian Territory. The nascent Army of the Trans-Mississippi was short of arms, ammunition, food, forage, wagons, and draft animals and possessed only twenty-two light artillery pieces. Nevertheless, Hindman intended to drive north in the spring and reoccupy northwest Arkansas and southwest Missouri, which had been lost during the Pea Ridge campaign several months earlier.

Hindman's timetable was upset by the activities of Union brigadier general John Schofield, whose Army of the Frontier was formed in Missouri at about the same time for the express purpose of preventing the Confederates from returning to their former haunts. Schofield's army entered northwest Arkansas in October. When Schofield became ill and left the scene, command passed to Brigadier General James G. Blunt. At that time Blunt's division was near Maysville in extreme northwest Arkansas; two other divisions under the command of Brigadier General Francis J. Herron were more than seventy miles away near Springfield, Missouri.

The distance between the two widely separated Union forces grew even larger when Blunt recklessly advanced thirty-five miles deeper into Arkansas to intercept Confederate brigadier general John S. Marmaduke's cavalry division. The two forces clashed at Cane Hill, sixteen miles southwest of Fayetteville, on 28 November. Marmaduke was defeated and fell back across the Boston Mountains to the Arkansas River near Fort Smith, where the remainder of Hindman's army was waiting. Blunt had achieved a small tactical victory, but his aggressiveness had placed his division in a dangerous spot.

Barely thirty miles away on the south side of the Boston Mountains, Hindman had a golden opportunity to cut off and destroy Blunt's isolated command. On 3 December Hindman's army of 11,000 men set out for Cane Hill. Blunt detected the Confederate movement in his front, but instead of falling back to a safer location, he placed his 5,000 men in defensive positions around Cane Hill and called on Herron for support. Herron responded magnificently. On the morning of 3 December he put his 7,000 men in motion. Over the next three and a half days Herron's two divisions marched 110 to 115 miles across rocky terrain on primitive roads—by far the most extraordinary march of the Civil War.

The rapid approach of Union reinforcements surprised Hindman. He abandoned his original plan to envelop Blunt at Cane Hill and turned north to intercept Herron. Hindman apparently hoped to drive Herron away, then turn back and bag Blunt. Instead of attacking, however, he inexplicably established a defensive position atop a wooded hill at Prairie Grove on the morning of 7 December and waited for Herron to attack him.

Herron proceeded to do just that. He deployed his two depleted Union divisions—only about 3,500 men were still on their feet—opposite the right wing of the Confederate army. Herron apparently did not realize that he was facing the entire Confederate army and was outnumbered three to one. He ordered his twenty-four rifled cannons to bombard the hilltop. The lighter Confederate guns were wrecked or driven off, and the Confederate infantry was forced deeper into the woods.

Encouraged by this development, Herron sent his infantry forward to take the high ground. Four under-strength Union regiments swept up the hill only to be driven back by overwhelming numbers of Confederate infantry and dismounted cavalry. An ill-advised Confederate pursuit was broken up by a hail of grape and canister from the massed Union artillery. The initial phase of the battle was over and an uneasy lull ensued as both commanders weighed their options.

All morning Blunt had awaited Hindman's attack at Cane Hill. When he heard the roar of battle to the northwest, he surmised what had happened and marched to the sound of the guns. The advance elements of his division reached Prairie Grove during the mid-afternoon lull and deployed opposite Hindman's left wing. Blunt's fresh division fought the second and final phase of the battle without much support from Herron's exhausted troops. He opened fire with thirty guns and sent his infantry up the hill. Heavy fighting raged up and down the slope. The Union troops eventually fell back and the Confederates tried to follow, but were repulsed by another hail of artillery fire. The battle ended as darkness fell.

The Confederates successfully maintained their position atop the hill—no surprise considering their numerical advantage—but their artillery had been shattered and most of their ammunition was gone. During the night of 7–8 December, Hindman ordered a withdrawal across the mountains to Fort Smith. While the Confederates slipped away, as many as 5,000 additional Union reinforcements arrived, many of them footsore stragglers from Herron's divisions. By the next morning the Army of the Frontier was ready to renew the fight, but the enemy was gone.

Prairie Grove was a tactical draw but a strategic Union victory. The Confederate attempt to destroy Blunt's isolated division and recover northwest Arkansas and southwest Missouri had failed. Casualties were extremely heavy on both sides. The Union Army of the Frontier suffered at least 1,233 killed, wounded, and missing. The Confederate Army of the Trans-Mississippi lost at least 1,483 killed, wounded, and missing. A substantial part of the battlefield is preserved today in Prairie Grove Battlefield State Park.

—William L. Shea

See also Arkansas; Blunt, James Gilpatrick; Fort Smith, Arkansas; Herron, Francis Jay; Hindman, Thomas Carmichael.

For further reading:

Banasik, Michael E. Embattled Arkansas: The Prairie Grove Campaign of 1862 (1996).

Christ, Mark K., ed. Rugged and Sublime: The Civil War in Arkansas (1994).

Shea, William L. War in the West: Pea Ridge and Prairie Grove (1997).

PRENTISS, BENJAMIN MAYBERRY
(1819–1901)
Union general

Born in Belleville, Virginia, to Henry Leonidas Prentiss and Rebecca Mayberry Prentiss, Benjamin Prentiss was educated locally and moved with his parents to Marion County, Missouri, when he was seventeen. At twenty-two he moved to Quincy, Illinois. At a young age, Prentiss showed an interest in military pursuits. He served in the Illinois militia, rising to the rank of lieutenant and in that capacity served against the Mormons in the state in 1844 and 1845. At the outbreak of the Mexican-American War, Prentiss raised a company of Illinois volunteers and became its captain. He fought under General Zachary Taylor at Buena Vista.

In the summer of 1847, Prentiss returned to Illinois, where he began the study and then the practice of law. In the 1850s he became interested in politics and in the late 1850s joined the new Republican Party. He ran unsuccessfully for the U.S. House of Representatives in 1860.

In the years after the Mexican-American War, Prentiss had become more involved in the Illinois militia and had risen to the rank of colonel. In April 1861 he commanded at Cairo, Illinois, and used his forces there to prevent the movement of munitions down the Mississippi to Confederate territory. In May 1861, he became colonel of the 10th Illinois Infantry. Still in Cairo in July 1861, Prentiss complained that he did not have enough men or equipment to hold the place if assailed by Confederate forces.

In August 1861 Prentiss was promoted to brigadier general of volunteers, with his date of rank as 17 May 1861. He was given command of the area around the Hannibal & Saint Joseph Railroad with instructions to keep communications open in the northern part of Missouri. Headquartered at Jefferson City, Missouri, and officially commanding the District of North Missouri as of November 1861, for the remainder of the year Prentiss tried to clear that part of the state of secessionists, fighting a number of skirmishes with Southern sympathizers.

In the spring of 1862, Prentiss was ordered to join Ulysses S. Grant's Army of the Tennessee, in which he was given command of the 6th Division. He fought bravely on the first day of the battle of Shiloh but was forced to surrender at the Hornets' Nest about 5:30 in the afternoon. He was held in several Southern prisons for the next six months. Within a month of his release in October 1862, Prentiss was promoted to major general and called to serve on the court-martial of Major General Fitz John Porter.

With Porter's trial over in January 1863, Prentiss went to Helena, Arkansas, where he commanded the District of Eastern Arkansas. From Helena, Prentiss sent out raids into the interior and along the rivers, looking for young male slaves to recruit into the Union army. He was also able to use his position to exert pressure on Confederate positions during Grant's Vicksburg campaign. On 4 July 1863, in a tardy effort to relieve some of the pressure on Vicksburg, Confederate major general Sterling Price attacked Prentiss's position at Helena. Prentiss repulsed the attack.

With the fall of Vicksburg, Union forces in the theater were reorganized, with the result that in the fall of 1863, Prentiss found himself without a command. He was ordered to Washington for reassignment, but citing ill health and family considerations (his wife had died in 1860, leaving him with young children), Prentiss resigned his commission. He practiced law in Quincy, Illinois, for the remainder of the war.

After the war, Prentiss accepted a variety of federal appointments to various jobs. He served as a federal pension agent under President Grant, a land office agent under President James Garfield, and a Missouri postmaster under President Benjamin Harrison. He died in Bethany, Missouri, as its postmaster on 8 February 1901.

—*David S. Heidler and Jeanne T. Heidler*

See also Helena, Battle of; Porter, Fitz John; Shiloh, Battle of.
For further reading:
Victor, Orville J. *Men of the Time: Being Biographies of Generals Halleck, Pope, Siegel, Corcoran, Prentiss, Kearney, Hatch and Augur* (1862).

PRESTON, JOHN SMITH
(1809–1881)
Confederate general

Born to Francis Smith Preston and Sarah Buchanan Campbell Preston outside Abingdon, Virginia, John Smith Preston was educated at Hampden-Sydney College, the University of Virginia, and Harvard Law School. He moved to Columbia, South Carolina, in 1840. Shortly afterward, however, he went to Louisiana for several years to manage his plantation, Homus. He returned to South Carolina later in the decade and became involved in state politics. He served a stint in the state senate and became a proponent of Southern rights. He left the senate in 1856 to take an extended trip to Europe, not returning to South Carolina until 1860. Upon his return he was chosen a South Carolina delegate to the Democratic National Convention in Charleston. There he was a strong supporter of a national slave code and walked out with his delegation when support of such a code was not included in the platform. Early in 1861, after South Carolina's secession, he was sent by the state's government to Virginia to urge that state to secede. Failing in that endeavor, he returned to South Carolina.

Preston traveled to Charleston where he offered his services as an aide to P. G. T. Beauregard, the Confederate commander there. He served in that capacity during the firing on Fort Sumter and during the First Bull Run campaign. Later in the summer he was assigned to the adjutant general's staff at the rank of lieutenant colonel. In the fall he was sent back to South Carolina to recruit for the Confederate army. When Union forces began landing on the South Carolina coast in the latter part of the year, Preston asked for a field command, but it was deemed that his recruiting services were more valuable and he remained at Columbia. Early in 1862, while still on recruiting duty, he was made the commander of the prisoner-of-war camp established at Columbia.

In the spring of 1862, the Confederate Congress passed the first conscription act, and Preston was given the job of mustering in the first draftees from South Carolina. In addition, he commanded the Camp of Instruction established at Columbia to give the conscripts their first rudimentary training. This activity was not exactly the service to the Confederacy Preston would have chosen for himself, but he was so efficient and diligent in his duties that his performance came to the attention of the Confederate War Department. On 30 July 1863 he was appointed superintendent of the Bureau of Conscription in Richmond at the rank of colonel. During the approximately eighteen months Preston headed the bureau, he made it one of the most efficient offices in the Confederate government. While states and officers caviled at his rather dictatorial methods, Preston insisted that the conscription laws be obeyed to the letter. In 1864 he wrote an extensive report explaining the operation of the laws. For his loyal and efficient service, he was promoted to brigadier general on 10 June 1864.

With the Confederacy in a state of collapse in March 1865, the Confederate Congress abolished the bureau on 17 March. Without a job in the army, Preston returned to South Carolina. Once there, he wrote to Confederate secretary of war John C. Breckinridge offering his services against William T. Sherman's army in the Carolinas, offering to raise some local militia for service. By that time Breckinridge and the remainder of the cabinet were in flight (Breckinridge joined Joseph Johnston's army in North Carolina).

With the surrender of Confederate armies, Preston traveled to Great Britain and lived there for several years after the war. Upon his return he proved to be one of the most unreconstructed of the former Confederates, as evidenced in a speech he made in 1868 at the University of Virginia. For the remainder of his life he made speeches urging former Confederates not to accept reunion with the North. Preston died on 1 May 1881 in Columbia, South Carolina.

—*David S. Heidler and Jeanne T. Heidler*

See also Conscription, C.S.A.
For further reading:
Confederate States of America, War Department. *Communication of the Secretary of War Relative to the Number of Able-bodied Men between the Ages of Eighteen and Forty-Five* (1865).
Preston, John S. *Address Before the Washington and Jefferson Societies of the University of Virginia, June 30 1868* (1868).
Seddon, James A., and John Smith Preston. *Report of the Secretary of War* (1864).

PRESTON, WILLIAM
(1816–1887)
Confederate general and minister to Mexico

During the Civil War William Preston served the Confederacy as a colonel, general, and minister to Mexico. Son of a Revolutionary War soldier who was given a vast land grant in Kentucky at the Falls of the Ohio (later Louisville), he was a member of the state's slave-owning aristocracy and an advocate of states' rights. Born in Louisville in 1816, Preston attended Harvard and graduated from Yale University with a degree in law. He was an officer in the Mexican War and a proslavery delegate to the 1849 Kentucky Constitutional Convention. His Lexington-born wife, Margaret Howard Wickliffe, was the daughter of the state's largest slaveholder. In Louisville they reared Preston's namesake, William Preston Johnston, who was the son of Preston's brother-in-law and future Confederate general, Albert Sidney Johnston, while the elder Johnston served as secretary of war for the Republic of Texas.

In the 1850s Preston served as a legislator and diplomat. He represented the Louisville region in Congress as a Whig between 1853 and 1855, championing the Kansas-Nebraska bill to permit the extension of slavery. Having changed his allegiance to the Democratic Party, at the 1856 Democratic National Convention he nominated his cousin, John C. Breckinridge, for the vice presidency. When Breckinridge was elected with James Buchanan, Buchanan appointed Preston minister to Spain. For three years in Madrid he attempted to purchase Cuba for the United States, a mission that the growing abolitionist movement saw as another attempt to create new slave states.

In 1861 Preston returned to Kentucky. Leaving his wife and six children in Lexington, he rode to Bowling Green in September with Breckinridge to join Confederates under Simon Bolivar Buckner. Preston was commissioned a colonel and made aide-de-camp to General Johnston. After the battle of Shiloh, Preston was promoted to brigadier general. He served under Breckinridge and commanded troops in northern Mississippi and at Vicksburg. Preston was transferred to Braxton Bragg's Army of Tennessee in 1862 and participated in the invasion of Kentucky that autumn. He commanded a brigade at the battle of Stones River, December–January 1862–1863, and was one of the group of officers who opposed Bragg's leadership. In spring 1863 Preston was placed in command of 5,000 troops at Abingdon in southwest Virginia guarding a saltworks. He and his troops in the late summer joined Bragg's forces in attempting to halt a Union advance from Chattanooga, Tennessee.

The battle of Chickamauga marked the high point of Preston's military service. There on 20 September 1863 he led a bayonet charge that surprised entrenched Union troops. Buckner, General James Longstreet, Confederate president Jefferson Davis, and even a correspondent for the London *Times* praised his bravery and leadership.

In January 1864 Davis appointed Preston minister to the court of the Emperor Maximilian in Mexico City. The Confederacy believed the new monarch could be persuaded to recognize Southern independence. Maximilian only arrived in Mexico in May 1864 and he never agreed to see Preston. A civil war in Mexico and the need to appease the Emperor Napoleon III, whose troops guaranteed the government, forced the Mexican emperor to avoid the issue of Southern recognition. While optimistically waiting for an invitation to meet with Maximilian, Preston spent time in Cuba, France, England, and finally Canada. When it became apparent that Maximilian would not see him, Preston unsuccessfully attempted to return to Richmond via Bermuda. Able only to reach northern Mexico via Cuba, he joined General Edmund Kirby Smith's troops in defending the Trans-Mississippi Department. Kirby Smith placed him in charge of the Polignac Division and gave him the title of major general, a promotion the Confederate Congress did not confirm.

After the war's end, Preston joined General John B. Magruder and other Confederates who crossed through Mexico to Vera Cruz, where he took passage to England. In December 1865 Preston returned to Lexington. He served two years in the Kentucky legislature, campaigned in 1876 for the Democratic presidential nominee, Samuel Tilden, joined Henry Watterson in helping resolve this disputed election, and was a delegate to the 1880 Democratic Convention. Most of his efforts were devoted to administering the family's large agricultural properties around Lexington. Following years of poor health, Preston died in Lexington in 1887 and is buried in Louisville.

—*Peter J. Sehlinger*

See also Maximilian, Ferdinand.
For further reading:
Dorman, J. Frederick. "General William Preston." *The Filson Club Historical Quarterly* (1969).

———. "'At the Moment of Victory. . .': The Battle of Shiloh and General A. S. Johnston's Death as Recounted in William Preston's Diary." *The Filson Club Historical Quarterly*.

———. "General William Preston: Kentucky's Last Cavalier Fights for Southern Independence." *The Register of the Kentucky Historical Society* (1995).

Sehlinger, Peter J. "William Preston, Kentucky's diplomat of lost causes." In *Kentucky Profiles: Biographical Essays in Honor of Holman Hamilton*. Edited by James C. Klotter and Peter J. Sehlinger (1982).

PRICE, STERLING
(1809–1867)
Confederate general

Born 20 September 1809 in Prince Edward County, Virginia, Sterling Price moved to Missouri in 1831. A young tobacco farmer, he entered politics and held several offices, including legislator, governor, and congressman from Missouri.

During the Mexican-American War, he received a commission as brigadier general and later served as military governor of the New Mexico Territory. By 1860, Price commanded the Missouri state militia. Price initially opposed secession, but the Union capture of Fort Jackson, St. Louis, in 1861, caused him to reconsider. He saw the seizure of the camp as a violation of Missouri's sovereign rights. From that time forward, Price stood unwavering in his support of states' rights. Missouri governor Claiborne Fox Jackson offered Price, known affectionately as "Old Pap," command of the newly recruited and trained state guard in May 1861.

Creating a base in southwestern Missouri, Price recruited and trained 5,000 men for Confederate service. In July 1861, he joined Brigadier General Ben McCulloch to drive the Federals from Missouri. They met Union brigadier general Nathaniel Lyon at Wilson's Creek, Missouri, in early August 1861. After Lyon made a surprise offensive maneuver, the Confederates counterattacked, and the outnumbered Federals retreated, allowing the Rebels to occupy Springfield.

Despite their victory, Price and McCulloch constantly quarreled, so their joint success proved short-lived. Feeling that Price's undisciplined troops illustrated a poor example for his men, and believing that they had not fought well at Wilson's Creek, McCulloch separated from Price and retreated to Arkansas. Price continued northward, determined to retake all of Missouri for the South.

In September 1861, Price captured 3,500 Federal troops and seven guns garrisoning Lexington, Kentucky. Pressure from Union general John C. Frémont's 30,000 men forced Price to withdraw into Arkansas shortly after his triumph. Nevertheless, Lexington proved Price's greatest military victory. Occurring just after Wilson's Creek, the exploit made "Old Pap" a hero across the South.

Because of his concern about Price and McCulloch's constant disagreements, Confederate president Jefferson Davis sent General Earl Van Dorn to the Trans-Mississippi theater to ensure their cooperation. At the battle of Pea Ridge in Arkansas, the three joined in an attempt to push Union forces from Missouri. In March 1862, after a two-day fight, Union general Samuel R. Curtis forced the Confederates to retreat.

Price officially joined the Confederate army as a major general in March 1862 and assumed command of the 1st Division, Army of the West, on 22 March. In the summer of 1862, he gained overall command of the Army of the West and fought two losing battles against General William S. Rosecrans at Iuka and Corinth, Mississippi. In addition, he suffered another defeat when he met Union Brigadier General Benjamin Prentiss at Helena, Arkansas, in July 1863.

On 18 March 1864, Major General Edmund Kirby Smith ordered Price to keep Major General Frederick Steele's men from linking with the main Union forces involved in Nathaniel P. Banks's Red River expedition. Price participated in the successful repulse of Steele and his Camden expedition.

On 4 August 1864, Kirby Smith gave Price the opportunity that he had awaited—the chance to conduct a raid back into Missouri. Throughout the war, Price had searched for a way to take back Missouri from the Federals. Price's Missouri Raid began in August 1864 with 12,000 men (4,000 unarmed) forming the Army of Missouri and concentrating in Pocahontas, Arkansas.

After initially moving successfully into Missouri and capturing ground, the raid shuddered to a miserable halt as hundreds of state militia harassed Price's poorly supplied men. Price's rush to retake Missouri caused him to make poor decisions. He ordered costly frontal assaults, spending precious time and men on smaller battles at Pilot Knob, West Point, and Mine Creek. Underestimating the resolve of the outnumbered Federal troops, he allowed Union men garrisoning the capital city time to organize. As Federal forces in Missouri moved to meet the Confederates, Price retreated more than sixty miles in two days, falling back into Arkansas and eventually into the Texas plains. Price's Missouri Raid ended the South's major military operations in Missouri and the Trans-Mississippi theater.

When the war ended, Price slipped into Mexico, residing in Carlota and then Cordova, until the fall of Maximilian's empire in 1866. Returning to St. Louis, Missouri, in 1867, he died a pauper on 29 September. He was buried at Bellefontaine Cemetery in St. Louis.

—*Buck T. Foster*

See also Corinth, Battle of; Helena, Arkansas, Battle of; Iuka, Battle of; Pea Ridge (Elkhorn Tavern), Battle of; Pilot Knob, Battle of; Price's Missouri Raid; West Point, Battle of; Wilson's Creek, Missouri.

For further reading:

Castel, Albert. *General Sterling Price and the Civil War in the West* (1968).

Rea, Ralph. *Sterling Price: The Lee of the West* (1959).

Shalhope, Robert E. *Sterling Price: Portrait of a Southerner* (1971).

PRICE'S MISSOURI RAID
(September–October 1864)

Confederate general Sterling Price's Missouri raid, the last great campaign west of the Mississippi River, involved greater numbers than those involved a few weeks later in Union general William Tecumseh Sherman's March to the Sea through Georgia. Along with the thousands of new recruits and "conscripts," the Confederate Army of Missouri under General Price likely had 20,000 pass through its ranks, though never at the same time or with adequate arms. The campaign involved between 40,000 and 50,000 Federal volunteers in Arkansas, Missouri, and Kansas garrisons, with an additional 20,000 to 30,000 militia from Missouri and Kansas. However, the logistics of operations over a 1,300-mile route of march kept all but a relatively few from being engaged at any given point.

Confederates hoped to seize one or more key points in the thinly defended state before it would hold its 1864 elections. However briefly or partially accomplished, such a demoralizing reversal for the Union would expand the available resources needed to sustain the rebel armies west of the river, allow for possible raids into adjacent Kansas, Illinois, and Iowa, and doubtless divert needed Union forces from the campaigns that threatened Atlanta, Mobile, and Richmond itself. Of even greater possible importance, carrying the war in 1864 back to areas thought secure since 1861 would provide a powerful argument against continuing the war effort.

Civilians, militia scouts, and even small federal patrols reported the mid-September entry of Price's army into Missouri. However, several thousand rebels had raided parts of the state in 1862 and 1863. Commanding at St. Louis, General William S. Rosecrans discounted reports of both the numbers of troops and the presence of General Price; therefore, he took few measures to reinforce key garrisons or to mobilize the militia. Confirmation of Price's presence at the head of a large army came when Colonel Thomas Ewing took reinforcements to his subdistrict headquarters ninety miles south of St. Louis. Although the Confederate advance had already passed as far north as Potosi, the bulk of Price's men had concentrated at Fredericktown. Two of his three divisions assaulted Ewing's badly outnumbered 1,400 federals around Pilot Knob (26–27 September). The Unionists escaped by forced marches to Leasburg, where they were rescued by cavalry based at Rolla. Behind federal lines, guerrillas engaged in the Centralia Massacre.

Rosecrans concentrated his available troops at district headquarters—notably St. Louis, Jefferson City, and Rolla, leaving the rest of the state to be defended by the militia with its minimal coordination and in the face of daily clashes with rebel troops. Within hours of these belated preparations, Confederate forces turned up at Pacific (30 September–1 October), less than forty miles west of poorly defended St. Louis, while the bulk of Price's men concentrated a short march to the southwest, at the town of Union.

Apparently uncertain of their advantages, the Confederates pivoted their course to the west, closing on the outnumbered Federals at Jefferson City. There, Price's men pushed their way across the Osage River and the Moreau, reaching within two miles of the state capital (6–7 October). As before St. Louis, Price ascribed vastly greater numbers and resources to the defenders and again bypassed a more strategic goal to the west. This decision transformed the invasion into "Price's Raid."

The Confederates moved west into the Great Bend of the Missouri River, the most prosecessionist part of the state. The Confederates virtually surrounded and forced the surrender of the Union garrison at Glasgow (15 October) and won easier surrenders by the outposts at Paris, Ridgely, and Carollton (15–17 October). Thousands joined the rebels during their passage through the area.

However, the mounted Federals under General Alfred Pleasonton operating under Rosecrans, pushed the Confederates from the east, while horsemen under General James G. Blunt—part of the growing Union force on the border under General Samuel R. Curtis—met the westward rebel advance at Lexington (19 October), and along the Little Blue and at Independence (21 October). The next day, as Curtis tried to hold the Big Blue below Kansas City, Pleasonton pushed the Confederate rear through Independence, and the two Union armies converged on the Confederates before Westport (23 October). Thereafter, the shattered rebel column turned south in a desperate bid to reach Texas, while lack of coordination crippled the Union pursuit. Although engaged at Marais des Cygnes (25 October), Newtonia (28 October), and elsewhere, the disintegrating Confederate army faced little armed opposition as it moved between federal garrisons at Fort Smith and Fort Gibson into Rebel territory.

Although Blunt and Shelby demonstrated great skill, their superiors achieved none of their major goals. Kansas politics crippled Curtis's reactions, while Rosecrans ignored early warnings, failed to mobilize or

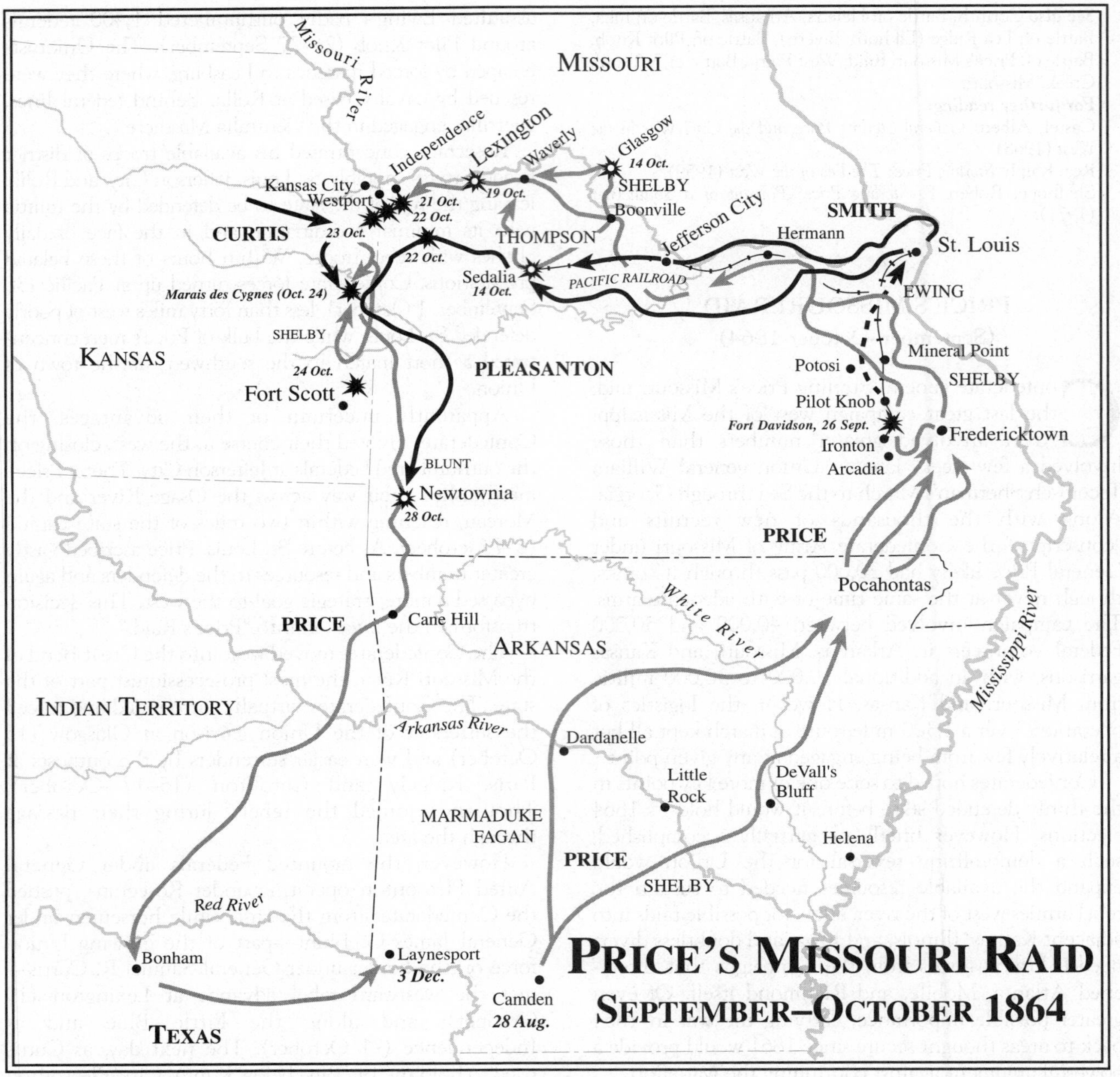

Map

MISSOURI

Missouri River

Independence · Lexington · Waverly · Glasgow
14 Oct.
SHELBY
Kansas City · Boonville
Westport · 21 Oct. · 19 Oct.
22 Oct. · THOMPSON · Jefferson City
CURTIS · 23 Oct. · 22 Oct.
Hermann · SMITH
St. Louis
EWING
Marais des Cygnes (Oct. 24)
Sedalia · PACIFIC RAILROAD
14 Oct.
SHELBY
Mineral Point
Potosi · SHELBY
24 Oct. · PLEASANTON
Fort Scott · Pilot Knob
Fort Davidson, 26 Sept.
Ironton · Fredericktown
Arcadia
BLUNT · PRICE
Newtownia
28 Oct. · Pocahontas

KANSAS

PRICE · Cane Hill · White River · Mississippi River
ARKANSAS

INDIAN TERRITORY · Arkansas River
Dardanelle
Little Rock · DeVall's Bluff
MARMADUKE FAGAN
Helena
PRICE
SHELBY

Red River

Bonham · Laynesport · 3 Dec.

PRICE'S MISSOURI RAID
SEPTEMBER–OCTOBER 1864

Camden · 28 Aug.

TEXAS

---

use the militia sufficiently, and began his pursuit from St. Louis more than a week after the Confederates had gone. Neither the militia nor the infantry of General A. J. Smith blocked Price's retreat south. From a Confederate perspective, Price could have likely seized and held St. Louis or Jefferson City at least for a time, and failed to do so from concern over the overestimated Union troop strength and the political impact of his forces among the civilians, whose response to invasion swept Radical Republicans to power in both Missouri and Kansas.

—*Mark A. Lause*

See also Army of Missouri; Blunt, James Gilpatrick; Centralia

Massacre; Curtis, Samuel Ryan; Ewing, Thomas, Jr.; Glasgow; Pilot Knob, Battle of; Pleasonton, Alfred; Price, Sterling; Rosecrans, William Starke; Sherman's March to the Sea; Smith, Andrew Jackson; Westport, Battle of.

For further reading:

Britton, Wiley. *The Civil War on the Border* (1890–1899).

Hinton, Richard J. *Rebel Invasion of Missouri and Kansas, and the Campaign of the Army of the Border against General Sterling Price, in October and November 1864* (1865).

Monaghan, Jay. *Civil War on the Western Border, 1854–1865* (1955).

Peterson, Cyrus A., and Joseph M. Hanson. *Pilot Knob: The Thermopylae of the West* (1914).

Sallee, Scott E. "Missouri! One Last Time: Sterling Price's 1864

Missouri Expedition, 'A Just and Holy Cause.'" *Blue and Gray Magazine* (1991).
Suderow, Bryce A. *Thunder in the Arcadia Valley: Price's Defeat, September 27, 1864* (1986).

PRIGG V. PENNSYLVANIA (41 U.S. 539) (1842)

The 1842 U.S. Supreme Court case *Prigg v. Pennsylvania* affirmed the constitutional right of slaveholders to capture their escaped slaves when it declared unconstitutional a Pennsylvania statute of 1826 that interfered with this right. Prigg, along with *Scott v. San[d]ford* and *Ableman v. Booth*, was one of the most significant cases in which the Supreme Court addressed slavery.

In 1837, Edward Prigg, a professional slave catcher acting as agent for Margaret Ashmore of Harford County, Maryland, captured alleged fugitive slave Margaret Morgan and her children in free-state Pennsylvania. The Fugitive Slave Act of 1793 provided Prigg the legal means to seize Morgan and her children and return them to Maryland. This vaguely worded act authorized a slaveowner or agent to cross state lines to seize a purported fugitive slave. After the captor produced proof of ownership, a federal judge or local magistrate was supposed to grant him a certificate of removal that allowed him to return home with the captive. However, since the act did not include any penalties for removing the captive without the certificate, kidnapping was common.

On 26 March 1826, Pennsylvania passed a companion statute to the 1793 federal act. This state act required a state-issued certificate of removal for all alleged fugitive slaves before they could be returned to their home state. When Edward Prigg located Morgan in Pennsylvania, he obtained a warrant from a local magistrate and had a state constable apprehend Morgan. Next he returned to the magistrate to secure the certificate of removal, but the magistrate refused to recognize the case. Consequently, on 1 April 1837, Prigg returned Morgan and her children to Maryland without the certificate. Two months later a Pennsylvania grand jury indicted Prigg for kidnapping.

After his indictment, Prigg was extradited to Pennsylvania and tried. Despite his plea of not guilty, on 22 May 1839, the court of oyer and terminer of York County, Pennsylvania, convicted Prigg for violating the 1826 statute by forcibly removing Morgan from the state without the authorized certificate of removal. The case then moved on a writ of error to the Pennsylvania Supreme Court, which affirmed the lower court conviction in a *pro forma* hearing in 1840. From there, the case moved on a writ of error to the U.S. Supreme Court.

The question the U.S. Supreme Court had to consider in the *Prigg* case was twofold. First, the Court had to determine whether a slaveowner had the right to capture and remove a slave from any state in the Union, including free states, as set forth in the Fugitive Slave Act of 1793. Second, the Court had to determine the constitutionality of the Pennsylvania act of 1826.

During the trial, Prigg's counsel argued that the Pennsylvania statute was unconstitutional because it violated the 1793 federal act. Furthermore, counsel claimed that federal enforcement of the Fugitive Slave Act was essential because without it, free states would not enforce the act. Conversely, counsel for the Commonwealth of Pennsylvania argued that the United States was not truly a free country if a free man could potentially be apprehended and removed without due process. Both sides emphasized the impact the Court's decision would have on the future of the Union.

On 1 March 1842, Justice Joseph Story, an antislavery New Englander, delivered the opinion of the Court. Although seven justices wrote separate opinions and no five justices completely concurred with Story, the majority of the Court concluded that a slaveowner had the constitutional authority "to seize and recapture his slave, whenever he can do it without any breach of the peace, or any illegal violence," and that the power to establish procedures for repossession was vested exclusively in Congress. Story further stated that state officials should enforce the Fugitive Slave Act of 1793 but that the federal government could not force them to do so. Accordingly, the Court declared the Pennsylvania act of 1826 unconstitutional because it "purport[ed] to punish as a public offense against that state, the very act of seizing and removing a slave by his master, which the Constitution of the United States was designed to justify and uphold." Thus, the Court ruled in favor of Prigg and reversed the lower court conviction.

Prigg v. Pennsylvania provided the means to resolve the decade-long dispute between abolitionists and slaveowners over the personal freedom of African-Americans. However, in the opinion, the Court addressed neither the constitutionality of the Fugitive Slave Act of 1793 nor the problems that arose when free African-Americans were captured. Ultimately, *Prigg* denied free African-Americans in the North equal protection under the law and it freed states from compulsory enforcement of the 1793 act. The Court's ruling led to calls for a new fugitive slave law, which came to fruition with the passage of the Fugitive Slave Act of 1850.

—*Jennifer L. Bertolet*

See also *Dred Scott* Case; Fugitive Slave Act; Personal Liberty Laws; Supreme Court, U.S.
For further reading:
Cover, Robert M. *Justice Accused: Anti-Slavery and the Judicial Process* (1975).

Finkelman, Paul. *Slavery in the Courtroom: An Annotated Bibliography of American Cases* (1985).

Morris, Thomas D. *Free Men All: The Personal Liberty Laws of the North, 1780–1861* (1974).

PRINCETON, VIRGINIA
(16–17 May 1862)

Part of Union brigadier general Jacob Dolson Cox's operations in western Virginia, the battle of Princeton occurred when Cox was unexpectedly attacked by Confederates under Brigadier General Humphrey Marshall. Cox commanded four brigades in what is now West Virginia in the spring of 1862. William Wing Loring commanded two brigades under Henry Heth and Humphrey Marshall opposed him.

During the second week of May 1862 Cox moved east across the Flat Top Mountains from Raleigh with a goal of cutting the Virginia & Tennessee Railroad. To prevent this move, Marshall moved north from Abingdon and then Tazewell toward Princeton, in western Virginia. Heth, in the meantime was instructed also to move toward Princeton via Pearisburg, southeast of Princeton. Marshall knew that Princeton was the best location for Cox to establish a base and to maintain his line of communication over the Flat Top Mountains and to strike at that location would probably force Cox to withdraw westward.

As he moved north toward Princeton, Marshall collected new recruits, who had been organized for this expedition. By the time he approached Princeton, he had about 2,195 men and one six-gun battery. About half of his men had never seen combat. Heth had about the same number of men. In preparation for striking at the Union position at Princeton, Marshall sent word to Heth to attack the town from the east on the morning of 17 May. Marshall arrived to the south of town on the evening of the sixteenth.

As Marshall approached the town, Cox, who had made Princeton his headquarters, had only about 1,200 men in town. Marshall encountered the Union pickets about four miles outside town and easily pushed them to about one mile from the town center. By that time it was about dusk, and rather than giving up the advantage, Marshall ordered a general infantry assault into the center of town. The Confederate right was the first to encounter resistance, but when supported by the left quickly overcame the Union defenders who fled through the town, leaving most of their belongings behind. Marshall took complete possession of the town about 10 P.M.

Through letters captured at Cox's headquarters, Marshall learned that four additional regiments were expected to arrive in town that night. He immediately became concerned that Cox would join this group and counterattack his position the next morning, in which case Marshall would be outnumbered by a ratio of more than two to one. As a result, rather than remaining in town, Marshall moved his men out of town the way he had come to more defensible terrain. The next morning Marshall learned that more than 2,000 Union soldiers had reoccupied the town.

While it was still early morning, Federal skirmishers began moving out of the town toward Marshall's position. During the night Marshall had been in communication with Colonel Gabriel Wharton, who he knew was approaching the Union left flank with about 800 men, but he still had no word of or any sign that Heth was attacking as planned. When Wharton arrived a sharp engagement ensued, bringing a halt to the Federal offensive. Marshall hesitated to continue the fight, however, until he received some word from Heth.

In the meantime, a local farmer had misinformed Heth that Marshall was in full retreat, so Heth had pulled back from Princeton to avoid being trapped by the superior Union force. In one way, though, Heth's presence on the outskirts of town had produced the desired effect. When Union forces learned of his approach, they feared a trap and withdrew from the town. Cox did not stop his retreat until he had moved back across the Flat Top Mountains, thus giving up any plans to cut the Virginia & Tennessee Railroad. Marshall followed at a distance, but because he was outnumbered, he did not attack. He returned to Princeton shortly, where he took possession of some of the Federal property left in the hasty retreat. In all he captured fourteen tents, five horses, eighteen mules, thirty-five saddles, four wagons, and twenty-nine Union soldiers. Though certainly pleased with the victory, in his final report Marshall criticized Heth for not communicating more frequently and for not implementing the original plan.

—*David S. Heidler and Jeanne T. Heidler*

See also Cox, Jacob Dolson; Heth, Henry; Marshall, Humphrey.

For further reading:
"Princeton." In *Southern History of the War. Official Reports of Battles, As Published by Order of the Confederate Congress at Richmond* (1970).

PRISONER EXCHANGES

The parole or exchange of soldiers captured by the opposing armies occurred on a regular if informal basis until the middle of 1862. The Dix-Hill cartel of July 1862 was designed to formalize such exchange arrangements, but acted mainly to slow and at times to halt exchanges as the cartel became entangled in policy and diplomatic considerations during the war's latter years.

While the Federal government was initially reluctant to deal with their Confederate counterparts for fear of seeming to recognize the legitimacy of the Rebel government, individual commanders in the field felt less constrained. At the beginning of the war, commanders on both sides—presumably motivated in part by notions of chivalry, in part by logistical constraints, and in part by the inertia of customary practice—paroled or exchanged prisoners, sometimes in numbers running into the thousands, within hours, days, or weeks of capture. As the war dragged into 1862, and as Washington authorities fell under some public pressure from the families of prisoners, the Confederates appointed first Benjamin Huger and then Howell Cobb to meet with the Unionist John Wool to discuss a nationwide framework for future exchanges.

After several rounds of negotiations, the Confederate D. H. Hill and the Federal John A. Dix reached such an agreement on 22 July 1862. The Dix-Hill cartel exchanged private soldiers on a one-for-one basis, with noncommissioned officers "valued" at two, second lieutenants at three, and so on up a sliding scale to sixty for a commanding general. All prisoners were to be paroled within ten days of capture at agreed upon locations—usually City Point, Virginia, in the east and in the vicinity of Vicksburg in the west. "Surplus" parolees—those returned to their own forces but not yet able to be offset against an enemy returnee—were not permitted to return to duty until actually exchanged. Many soldiers returned to Union control were held in "parole" camps, where treatment and regimen sometimes resembled those in prison camps. Even in an atmosphere of good will and mutual trust at odds with the whole notion of civil war, the legalities and bureaucratic complexities of such an agreement would have made the operation of such a regime difficult. In the context of an ongoing war, the cartel was doomed to failure. Disputes between Judge Robert Ould, the Confederate agent for exchange, and his changing Union counterpart (for a period after December 1863, Benjamin F. Butler, hardly a conciliatory choice) were constant, as the precise status—captured, paroled, exchanged, returned to duty—of many individuals and groups of prisoners was always open to doubt. Inevitably, each side seemed always to claim that it was owed prisoners. Union leaders, especially Ulysses S. Grant, came to understand that the numerically superior North gained less from exchanges than did the Confederacy.

By the end of 1862, the issues of race raised by black soldiers in blue uniforms added to these legalistic and numerical tangles. The Union decisions for emancipation and the raising of black troops led by white officers infuriated Confederate leaders and raised fears of slave rebellions. From the end of 1862 until the beginning of 1865, exchanges were variously slowed, suspended, canceled, or allowed to continue as the two sides bickered constantly over issues great and small, real and imagined. Confederate authorities repeatedly threatened to execute black Union soldiers and their white officers, even as Lincoln and the Federals insisted that all their soldiers be treated alike by Confederates. Fort Pillow, where besieged black and white Union troops died under unusual circumstances at the hands of overrunning Confederates, was one of many incidents that increased tensions between the two sides.

An April 1864 exchange of especially sick prisoners revealed the worsening supply and nutritional situation of the South as "living skeletons," as they were quickly dubbed by Union publicists and politicians, were returned to Union control. Woodcuts depicting these emaciated ex-prisoners appeared throughout the North in illustration of alleged (and nonexistent) Confederate policies of deliberately starving Union soldiers. These atrocity charges hardened the otherwise war-weary attitudes of some Northerners in a presidential election year, while leading others to push Lincoln, Grant, and other Northern leaders for increased exchanges.

The general resumption of exchanges in January and February 1865 came too late for tens of thousands of Union and Confederate soldiers fated to suffer and often die in Andersonville, Elmira, and the other hellholes of the war's last years. Disputes about exchange and who was responsible for the frequent breakdowns continued long after the war as part of the general postbellum intersectional dispute among whites about wartime prisons and the sufferings of prisoners of war.

—*Douglas G. Gardner*

See also Andersonville; Libby Prison; Old Capitol Prison; Prisoner Paroles.

For further reading:
Thomas, Eugene Marvin. "Prisoner of War Exchange during the American Civil War" (Ph.D. dissertation, 1976).
U.S. War Department. *The War of the Rebellion: A Compilation of Official Records of the Union and Confederate Armies* (1880–1901).

PRISONER PAROLES

Parole, based on the personal honor of the prisoner and the good faith of warring nations, was the traditional means militaries handled captured enemy officers. Typically, the prisoner gave a pledge that he would not attempt to escape or fight against his captors if allowed to await his exchange, either at a designated area in enemy territory or back in his home country. According to this principle, any officer who violated his word, or parole, would no longer be considered a gentleman and could be justly executed if recaptured. While America utilized paroles in all its early wars, its most extensive use occurred during the Civil War. Of the 463,000 Union and 212,000 Confederate soldiers and sailors captured during the war, 248,000 and 17,000 respectively were paroled.

Neither the North nor the South had made any formal

Confederate prisoners of war being led from Gettysburg, 3 July 1863 (*Library of Congress*)

preparations for prisoners of war because both expected a short conflict. Operating under that misconception, the belligerents adopted an informal system of parole and exchange as the most convenient and humane means to dispense with the Union officers and men captured in Texas and the pro-Southern militia held by Federal forces in Missouri, even before actual fighting commenced. From this modest beginning, the number of unofficial paroles sharply increased, as Union generals in the field made parole arrangements with their Southern counterparts eager to rid themselves of burdensome prisoners.

Lincoln avoided giving de facto recognition to the Confederacy that would be implied by making an official agreement on paroles and exchanges until the summer of 1862, when the number of prisoners of war had increased significantly and necessitated the rapid construction of prisoner-of-war camps for both sides. According to the Dix-Hill Cartel, all prisoners held by the North and South would be paroled within ten days of capture (although it often took more than thirty days) and sent to their own lines to await a formal "paper" exchange,

when they would be freed to rejoin the fighting. A triumph of civilized and humane warfare, the passage of the cartel closed most early prison camps. In addition, Lincoln entrusted Prussian-born Francis Lieber with the task of drafting a code of conduct for the warring parties that included numerous sections regarding the care of prisoners, the giving and taking of paroles, and what services (e.g., diplomacy, civil service, recruiting, drilling, fortifying places not besieged, quelling civil disorders, fighting other warring powers not connected to the current hostilities, etc.) that detainees could contribute to their governments while waiting exchange.

Southern parolees generally went to their homes, but the Union housed its returning prisoners in three "parole camps." Whether at Camp Chase (Columbus, Ohio), Benton Barracks (near St. Louis, Missouri), or Camp Parole (Annapolis, Maryland), Union detainees resented confinement. As their numbers increased, their standard of living fell rapidly while they waited for an equal number of Confederates to be captured. The North originally kept its men under light supervision, while compiling the detailed records required by the cartel and Leiber's Code before an exchange could occur. However, parole life became exceedingly more onerous after the War Department charged that large numbers were surrendering in order to wait out their one-year enlistments from the safety of Union lines. Instead of the comfort of a home, Union parolees found themselves quartered in overcrowded and unsanitary facilities with no alcohol, gambling, or town liberty allowed. One camp had only one overflowing latrine, and its inmates were forced to tear down buildings for wood to keep warm. The governor of Pennsylvania claimed that paroled Pennsylvanians fared better in Southern prison camps than at Annapolis. Ironically, although Union officials hoped that the less-than-ideal conditions in their parole camps would keep men fighting and discourage surrenders, in reality such treatment limited the country's manpower base because few wished to reenlist when their exchanges were completed lest they be recaptured.

The parole system helped the Confederate cause greatly by burdening the North with the care of large numbers of bitter detainees, while the South's favorable balance of exchange allowed its men to return promptly to active duty. One Ohio citizen wrote Secretary of War Stanton urging the end of the system. "We will be beaten by the number of paroled prisoners we shall have. It is an inducement not only for cowards but for men discontented with their offices or even homesick to surrender. . . . An order ending all paroling of officers will force upon the South the necessity of feeding or releasing our soldiers, and if our men understand positively that they are to be prisoners in the South if taken they would strike with more energy and desperation." The War Department agreed, and because the South refused to concede to Northern demands regarding the status of black prisoners of war, official paroles and exchanges ceased on 25 May 1863. After that date, the large numbers of prisoners captured by both sides lived and died under the most brutal prisoner-of-war system ever conducted on the North American continent.

—*Lori Bogle*

See also Prisoner Exhanges; Prisoners of War.
For further reading:
Rasner, Gustav Charles. "The Effect of the Breakdown of the Parole and Exchange Cartel of 22 July 1862, on Conditions in Civil War Prisons" (M.A. thesis, 1986).

PRISONERS OF WAR

The American Civil War produced some of the most notorious instances of the alleged abuse of prisoners of war in U.S. history and much inflammatory rhetoric on prisoner issues. Neither side was prepared for war in early 1861, particularly for a war with

Three unidentified Confederate prisoners of war at Gettysburg, July 1863 (*Library of Congress*)

tens of thousands of long-term prisoners. Until the middle of 1863, when informal and formal arrangements of exchange foundered, the problems presented by prisoners proved manageable for both sides, if conditions for individuals and small groups were sometimes uncertain or locally harsh. Many were exchanged immediately after capture or paroled within hours or days after a brief period of uncertainty. Those who found themselves subjected to longer periods of imprisonment—over weeks or months—were generally housed in converted warehouses, civilian jails, or makeshift camps. It was not until 22 July 1862 that the Dix-Hill cartel regulating exchanges on a nationwide basis was concluded. Union authorities were reluctant to deal with their Confederate counterparts for fear of seeming to recognize the Confederacy as a legitimate government, and the cartel was explicitly between contending military forces. Confederate diplomat Robert Ould and various Union generals became the most active agents under the cartel.

Although such agreements are always prolific of disputes and mutual distrust, the cartel broke down in mid-1863 largely because of the growing Union emphasis on emancipation of slaves as a necessary war aim to destroy Southern resistance and because of the resulting Confederate reaction. The Emancipation

Confederate prisoners being conducted to Atlanta from Jonesboro, 1864 (*Harper's Weekly / Library of Congress*)

Proclamation and Union decision to raise black regiments angered Confederates and raised fears of servile insurrection. Confederate officials announced policies of summarily executing white officers leading black troops and turning captured black soldiers over to states to be dealt with as rebellious slaves, even if the soldier had been free before the war. Union authorities insisted that all their soldiers be treated alike, an ironic policy given the pay disparities between white and black troops. While it is difficult to generalize about the fates of blacks taken prisoner by Confederate troops—some ended up as part of the general population in prison camps and others were undoubtedly killed upon or before capture—it is clear that at a series of battles (e.g., Fort Pillow, Poison Spring, Saltville, the Crater) black soldiers died in numbers and under circumstances that suggest that they were much more likely to face dire consequences if overrun or captured than were their white comrades.

The timing of the cartel's suspension proved catastrophic. Caring for, feeding, and guarding prisoners of war is never a top priority for scarce resources in wartime, and tens of thousands of soldiers on both sides were take prisoner during the major battles of 1863 and 1864,

overwhelming the arrangements of both sides, especially the Confederacy. The Union, under the leadership of Colonel William Hoffman, opened or expanded prison camps in Chicago (Camp Douglas); Columbus, Ohio (Camp Chase); Elmira in New York; Indianapolis (Camp Morton); Point Lookout, Maryland; Rock Island, Illinois; and elsewhere. Johnson's Island, in Lake Erie off Sandusky, Ohio, was reserved mostly for officers. The Confederacy, under the leadership of General John Winder, opened or expanded facilities at Richmond's Libby Prison (once a tobacco warehouse); on Belle Isle, outside Richmond; at Salisbury, North Carolina; Macon, Georgia; most notoriously at Andersonville, Georgia; and elsewhere. Conditions often were barely acceptable at best, and the progress of the war helped to guarantee that Southern prison camps for Union soldiers were particularly ill-planned, ill-run, and ill-supplied. Prisoners displayed the full range of human behavior in camps, from making repeated escape attempts to preying on each other to hoping for an end to their captivity. The Union recruited some disaffected Confederates into special "galvanized" units to staff selected frontier outposts. The Leiber Code, Special Orders No. 100 of

Confederate prisoners captured in the Shenandoah Valley, under Union guard, May 1862 *(National Archives)*

the federal army, sought to codify the law of war, including legal guarantees to prisoners, and became a foundational document in international law.

A special April 1864 exchange of the sickest prisoners led to widespread outrage in the North as the "living skeletons" returned by the Confederates seemed to confirm fears that Union troops were particularly suffering in captivity. Engravings of the most emaciated returnees filled the Northern illustrated press. The Joint Congressional Committee on the Conduct of the War and the semiofficial Sanitary Commission seized the opportunity to issue widely reprinted reports that accused the Confederate leaders of deliberately starving Union troops. In May 1864, Union secretary of war Edwin M. Stanton cut rations of Confederates held prisoner in retaliation. Easing of prisoners' perceived plights and punishment of those responsible became an additional Union war aim for some. George F. Root's 1864 popular song, "Tramp! Tramp! Tramp! or, The Prisoner's Hope," reflected the unforgiving hyperpatriotic mood of many Northerners. Others blamed Abraham Lincoln and his advisers for allowing almost all exchanges to end over issues such as the treatment of black troops in Confederate hands. Lincoln feared for a time that the issue might affect his reelection chances in 1864. Some

commentators have argued that General Ulysses S. Grant, from early 1864 commander of all Union troops, urged that exchanges remain suspended to aggravate Southern personnel problems.

In January 1865, the Confederates, perhaps looking to the desperate measure of recruiting large numbers of blacks into their own forces, agreed to rapid exchange of all soldiers, including black Union soldiers. After the major surrenders of April 1865, ex-Confederate soldiers were allowed to return home on parole, and the remaining prisoners on both sides were released. With the final return of prisoners, calls that the (Confederate) perpetrators of perceived abuses against (Union) prisoners grew louder. Henry Wirz, a Swiss-born physician and Confederate captain who had commanded the stockade at Andersonville, was hanged in November 1865 after a trial by a Union military commission. Wirz seems to have been guilty mostly of inefficiency and of being a foreign-born martinet.

The conditions in prison camps and responsibility for them provided the most contentious issue of intersectional debate among whites about the war's conduct; the sufferings and unique perils of black troops dropped out of most white remembrances of the war and its prisoners. Northern commentators, particularly survivors, for a

A baseball game between Union prisoners of war at Salisbury, North Carolina *(National Archives)*

half-century wrote vicious attacks on Confederates on issues related to the wartime experiences of prisoners. Confederate partisans were slower to organize a counterattack because of the greater disruption of life in the South and the facts of Union victory. More than two-thirds of the more than 400 narratives by or about ex-prisoners were from Union soldiers. Many narratives were formulaic, drawing upon each other in sometimes unacknowledged ways and upon the American literary tradition of captivity narratives. Some were exaggerated. Wirz's Andersonville was the camp most commonly pointed to as a place where Union troops suffered at the hands of evil captors; the hellish conditions at Elmira came to provide the favorite Southern riposte.

About 144,000 Union soldiers and 215,000 Confederates were held as prisoners. Approximately 30,000 Union soldiers and 26,000 Confederates died while captive. Almost 9 percent of the war's dead perished in prison camps, mostly during the war's last two years. Andersonville is today the site of a museum honoring all Americans who have been held prisoner or who are missing in action.

—*Douglas G. Gardner*

See also Prisoner Exchanges; Prisoner Paroles; Prisons, C.S.A.; Prisons U.S.A.

For further reading:
Denney, Robert E. *Civil War Prisons and Escapes: A Day-by-Day Chronicle* (1993).

Hesseltine, William B. *Civil War Prisons: A Study in War Psychology* (1930; reprint, 1992).
Mitchell, Reid. *"Our Prison System, Supposing We Had Any":* The Confederate and Union Military Systems. In *On the Road to Total War: The American Civil War and the German Wars of Unification, 1861–1871* (1997).
U.S. War Department. *The War of the Rebellion: A Compilation of the Official Records of the Union and Confederate Armies* (1880–1901).

PRISONS, C.S.A.

Perhaps the most depressing, and certainly one of the more controversial, topics of the Civil War is the treatment of prisoners. The prison camp facilities of both sides were woefully insufficient and could be on occasion every bit as lethal as the battlefield. Such was particularly the case for Northern soldiers in Confederate prison camps. While an official 15.5 percent mortality rate for these Northern prisoners is shocking enough, the statistic is undoubtedly lower than the actual figure because so many Confederate records were lost during the war. Federal prisoner mortality was a tragedy, but it was not, as contemporary Northerners contended, evidence of a Confederate conspiracy to use its prisoner-of-war camps as extermination centers.

The Confederacy, already beset by numerous supply problems, did not want the added burden of feeding and caring for large numbers of Union prisoners. Although the Confederate government pressed for a formal

Libby Prison in Richmond, Virginia, 1865 (*Library of Congress*)

exchange agreement early in the war, the Lincoln administration was reluctant to enter into such an agreement because it would imply recognition of the Confederacy as a separate nation. Yet, as thousands of Northern prisoners poured into inadequate Southern prisons after the battles of First Bull Run, Shiloh, and the Seven Days', pressure intensified from the Northern press and the public to get Union soldiers out of prison camps, where it was believed Confederates abused them. With the war not going well, Lincoln could ill afford to give the Peace Democrats another issue to use against the Republicans in upcoming elections. Consequently, on 22 July 1862 an official exchange agreement based on the agreement between the Americans and British during the War of 1812 was signed. This effectively emptied each side's prisons. Unfortunately for thousands of future prisoners, the arrangement broke down the following spring, slowing exchanges to a trickle.

Ironically, the Confederacy, which had agitated so much for an exchange agreement in the first place, was responsible for that agreement's suspension in the summer of 1863. In May 1863 the Confederate Congress authorized a policy to reenslave or execute black soldiers and their white officers. To protect black soldiers, exchanges were halted and Southern soldiers were held as hostages

against the fulfillment of that policy. Exchanges would begin again as soon as the South agreed to treat all black soldiers as prisoners of war and exchange them on equal terms with whites. Confederate exchange commissioner, Robert Ould, declared the South would "die in the last ditch before giving up the right to send slaves back to slavery as property recaptured." Consequently, tens of thousands of soldiers were doomed to death in captivity. Some have argued that the North used this issue as an insincere pretext for halting exchanges, but the evidence does not support such a claim. The North had to protect its soldiers and as soon as the Confederacy agreed to exchange all black soldiers on equal terms with whites in January 1865, exchanges resumed.

Northern prisoners would die in larger numbers than their Southern counterparts, though this does not in any way indicate that the South was any less humane in its treatment of captured soldiers. Serious resource problems, as well as a lack of planning, doomed thousands of Union prisoners to early graves. Due in large part to the Union blockade and the fact that the war was being fought in the South, the Confederacy had tremendous problems supplying its most basic needs. Confederate soldiers wrote in their diaries, particularly during the last two years of the war, that they were often hungry, shoeless, and clad in rags. In Richmond, Jefferson Davis had to appear personally to quell a food riot begun by hungry and frustrated citizens. If Southern soldiers and civilians got barely enough to eat, Union prisoners got even less, leading to thousands of deaths due to malnutrition.

The South was also unable to provide adequate shelter from the elements. While the region had plenty of cotton, it lacked the industrial capacity to convert it into canvas for tents. In many places the South had wood for barracks, but there were not enough nails, sawmills, or other necessary tools available to construct them. Unfortunately, this situation caused tens of thousands of Union prisoners to die in captivity. Poor food, and not enough of it at that, combined with exposure to the elements to weaken immune systems. Prisoners became susceptible to lethal infectious diseases such as pneumonia, dysentery, and typhoid. Among the most notorious prison camps were Belle Isle in Richmond, Florence in South Carolina, and the most infamous, Andersonville in western Georgia.

—*James Gillispie*

See also Andersonville; Belle Isle; Libby Prison; Ould, Robert; Prisoner Exchanges; Prisoner Paroles; Prisoners of War; Prisons, U.S.A.
For further reading:
Blakey, Arch Fredric. *General John H. Winder, C.S.A.* (1990).
McPherson, James M. *Battle Cry of Freedom: The Civil War Era* (1988).
Speer, Lonnie R. *Portals to Hell: Military Prisons of the Civil War* (1997).

PRISONS, U.S.A.

From the start of the war, Union political and military officials made the practical decision to treat captured Confederate soldiers as prisoners of war, as persons entitled to honorable treatment and protection, rather than as traitors, criminals, or outlaws. To do otherwise would have provoked reprisals against captured Union soldiers. Feeding, housing, and guarding prisoners of war is rarely a top priority for the scarce resources of any combatant. Conditions in some Northern camps became especially grim in 1864, when swelling numbers of prisoners, the sometimes limited competence of responsible officers, and Northern anger at reported conditions in Southern prison camps combined to overwhelm the Union prison system. About 215,000 Confederates (mostly in the latter half of the war, excluding the end-of-conflict surrenders) spent time as prisoners, of whom about 26,000 died while prisoners.

During the first half of the war, most Confederate prisoners were either paroled fairly soon or else were exchanged after a brief sojourn in temporary facilities. These arrangements were generally made in the field on a local basis between commanders acting on their own

authority, though presumably with the connivance of higher commands.

In the summer of 1861, Colonel William Hoffman (who had briefly been a prisoner himself when Federal troops were surrendered to state and Confederate authorities in Texas) was appointed commissary of prisoners by the Union army, with the general responsibility of providing for guarding, housing, feeding, and medically treating captive Confederates. Among Hoffman's initial acts was to lease Johnson's Island, in Lake Erie off Sandusky, Ohio, as a site for what was intended to be the Union's major prison. Hoffman seems to have diligent and competent, if often hamstrung by bureaucratic and political considerations and the low priority afforded the care and comfort of enemy soldiers.

Johnson's Island quickly proved inadequate as a replacement for the makeshift arrangements—civilian jails, areas of Union training camps, the walled interiors of Northern forts—it had been intended to replace. Johnson's Island was therefore reserved mainly for Confederate officers, the exchange of officers being generally a slower process than the exchange of enlisted men due to the technical requirements of most exchange agreements. Hoffman's empire grew throughout the war. Major facilities would be opened or expanded at Chicago (Camp Douglas); Columbus (Camp Chase); Elmira; Indianapolis (Camp Morton); Point Lookout, Maryland; Rock Island, Illinois; and elsewhere. These prison camps would each come to hold thousands of prisoners at a time. Material conditions in early years were adequate— if subject to the vagaries of local conditions, including the rapacity of local contractors who supplied food and other goods to the camps—and at times security was so inattentive as to cause accusations of laxness in host communities. Some disaffected Confederates were recruited into special "galvanized" units of the Union army, which were used for border duty and on the Indian frontier. Treatment of prisoners was among the subjects dealt with in the Leiber Code (General Orders No. 100 of the Union Army), which had significant influence on subsequent international legal documents. It was not until July 1862 that the two opposing militaries formalized and regularized exchanges on a national basis with the Dix-Hill cartel. The result was a virtual emptying of many Northern prison camps by the autumn of that year. They would fill, and overfill, again.

The inevitable disputes over technical and practical issues—who precisely had been paroled or exchanged, under what conditions, and so forth—always threaten prisoner exchange schemes between opposing armies that have every reason to distrust each other. The breakdown and suspension of the Dix-Hill cartel in the middle of 1863 over such issues, and particularly over announced Confederate policies that threatened to treat black Union soldiers as revolting slaves, led to the ending of large-scale exchanges just as Hoffman and the prison camps of the North were swamped with captives from the major battles of that year. While material and medical conditions deteriorated for Confederate captives, conditions in Northern camps—except perhaps at Elmira in the summer of 1864—never approached those found at times in Southern camps such as Andersonville. This is an index of the resource and logistical superiority of the North over the South in the last two years of the war, and perhaps of Hoffman's relative competence as compared to his Confederate counterpart, John H. Winder. Treatment of Northern prisoners by their Confederate captors and the Fort Pillow incident, where black Union troops died in suspiciously large numbers when overrun by Confederate troops commanded by Nathan Bedford Forrest, became issues on the Northern home front during 1864. As a result, in May of that year, Secretary of War Edward M. Stanton cut rations for Confederate prisoners and introduced other severities into camp regimens. By the beginning of 1865, exchanges were resumed. At the end of the war, the remaining prisoners were released, and surrendering Confederate troops were allowed to go home. Prison sites were quickly returned to prewar uses.

The postwar years saw great intersectional controversy among whites about the wartime conditions under which prisoners had suffered and, all too frequently, died. While Northern commentators and ex-prisoners of the Confederacy were always more vocal in condemning conditions in Southern camps, most especially Andersonville, pro-Confederate commentators and ex-prisoners were never silent, and eventually the undoubted suffering of many in the overcrowded Northern camps, especially Elmira, provided a substantial support for "Lost Cause" mythologizing. Eventually, individuals both North and South and various Confederate memorial groups saw to the marking and care of graves at prison cemeteries, and statues and other suitable memorials were erected at many of the former camp sites by survivors. Today, there is a museum at Andersonville honoring all American prisoners of war and missing in action, including those who served the Confederacy in Union camps.

—*Douglas G. Gardner*

See also Elmira Prison; Hoffman, William; Prisoner Exchanges; Prisoner Paroles; Prisons, C.S.A.

For further reading:

Hesseltine, William B. *Civil War Prisons: A Study in War Psychology* (1930).

Mitchell, Reid. "Our Prison System, Supposing We Had Any": The Confederate and Union Military Systems. In *On the Road to Total War: The American Civil War and the German Wars of Unification, 1861-1871,* edited by Stig Förster and Jörg Nagler (1997).

The War of the Rebellion: A Compilation of Official Records of the Union and Confederate Armies, Series II. (1880–1901).

PRIVATEERS

After President Abraham Lincoln requested 75,000 soldiers to suppress the rebellion on 15 April 1861, Jefferson Davis countered and issued a proclamation that allowed civilians of the Confederate States of America to operate "privateers," privately armed commerce-raiders, against Northern merchant ships. The term privateer is used to refer both to privately armed commerce-raiding vessels generally, and to the commanders or crew members of such vessels. Davis's proclamation, referencing Lincoln's de facto declaration of war, indicated that the Confederacy desired privateers in order to "resist so wanton and wicked an aggression." Lincoln reacted to Davis's proclamation in turn by authorizing a naval blockade of Southern ports. Within a month of these precipitous events, began the short-lived operational history of the Confederate privateers.

While Lincoln did eventually authorize the use of Northern privateers in March 1863, Union privateering was an extremely limited affair. In May and June 1861 the *Quaker City,* an armed steamer from New York, took five prizes off Virginia. While the *Quaker City* was never issued a letter of marque (that is, a license to a private citizen from a government authorizing the citizen to seize for his or her private gain the property of other nations or other nations' citizens), the owners of the vessel chartered the ship and crew to the U.S. Navy. In June 1861 the *Quaker City* was assigned to the Hampton Roads squadron and saw action as an unofficial privateer before the navy purchased it in October 1861.

On the Confederate side, privateers should not be confused with the Confederate States Navy's commerce-raiders, such as the infamous CSS *Alabama,* the CSS *Shenandoah,* and the CSS *Florida.* Official Union documents and the Northern and Southern press commonly confused the two types of vessels during the war. Privateers were privately owned and maintained warships, while commerce-raiders like the CSS *Alabama* were operated by the Confederate States Navy. In contrast to "pirates," Confederate privateers were legitimized through a government commission or "letter of marque." Licensed Confederate privateers legally preyed upon merchant ships registered in states loyal to the Union. The privateer owners and crews profited from the sale of prize ships and confiscated cargoes through Confederate Admiralty Courts in Southern ports, often at inflated wartime prices.

Although the European nations had collectively agreed to ban privateering, the activity was still accepted elsewhere as a sanctioned, but somewhat outdated, element of naval warfare by 1861. The 1856 Declaration of Paris, signed by representatives of England, France, and other European naval powers, outlawed the licensure and deployment of privateers by European govern-

ments. The United States had successfully relied on privateers in earlier conflicts and American representatives refused to sign the treaty. Because the United States was not a signatory of the declaration, the Confederacy was not legally compelled to observe the ban.

The Confederacy entered into war with no significant naval forces. A handful of warships operated by the state navies were quickly transferred to the Confederate navy. These vessels and a few Northern merchant ships, trapped and confiscated in Southern ports, became the genesis of the Confederate States Navy. With such limited resources, Jefferson Davis had little choice but to encourage privateering. Tenets of pre-1860 naval warfare traditionally called for a *guerre d'course*, or "commerce-raiding," strategy for nations with limited naval power. Commerce raiding, the destruction of enemy commercial shipping, was an element of naval strategy that was expected to reduce the enemy's ability to make war through the cumulative loss of ships and supplies needed to support both military needs and the home-front civilian population. Privateers contributed to commerce-raiding strategies by supplementing naval fleets with additional warships to roam global shipping lanes. President Davis and his naval planners further hoped that privateers and Confederate naval raiders might render the Union blockade ineffective, as blockade ships would be forced "off station" to hunt down the pesky raiders. This point alone was an important element of the early Confederate naval strategy.

Lincoln quickly claimed that Southern privateers were simply lawless "pirates" and based the piracy claim on the fact that the Confederate States of America was not officially recognized as a political entity by the European nations. As such, Confederate letters of marque were not legal documents. The United States sought to retroactively sign the Declaration of Paris, but the patently hypocritical offer was refused by Great Britain. By mid-May 1861 the Confederate Congress had issued several letters of marque and the privateers thus authorized began to prey upon unsuspecting Northern commerce. Most early war captures involved Northern ship captains who had been at sea for several months and knew nothing of the war. The New Orleans–based *Calhoun* made the first capture, the bark *Ocean Eagle*, on 16 May 1861. This action occurred three days after Great Britain claimed neutrality, but had recognized the Confederacy as a belligerent political entity. Belligerency status, among other things, legalized Confederate privateering in the eyes of the world and allowed Confederate warships and privateers the use of British ports for shelter and maintenance. Such status, however, did not allow privateers to sell prize ships or cargoes in British ports. Similar declarations soon followed from France, Spain, and the Netherlands.

As expectations of abundant prizes and the exhortations of the Southern press mounted, applications for letters of marque by adventurous seamen flooded the Confederate capital. Privateer associations formed in all major Southern port cities to raise funds needed to outfit vessels and "cash in" on the seemingly bountiful Northern commerce. Dreams of glory and profit, mingled with the desire to strike a blow at the Yankees, fueled the privateers' purpose. The fortunes of war soon negated such premature euphoria.

Among Northern newspapers and commercial circles, the reaction to Davis's request for privateers was one of shock and apprehension. Letters from concerned insurance and shipping companies bombarded Lincoln and his cabinet. Northern companies clamored for immediate and aggressive naval action against the perceived menace. As anticipated risks increased, shipping insurance rates climbed. While the Northern press fueled the fires of rumor, suggesting that 3,000 privateers were expected to sail from Southern ports, the U.S. Navy received explicit orders to destroy the privateers and protect Union commerce.

Throughout the summer and fall of 1861 Confederate privateers prowled the Atlantic and Gulf sea lanes with some measure of success. Following the *Calhoun's* first capture, the privateers went rapidly into action. Privateers from ports in North Carolina, South Carolina, and Louisiana captured more than thirty-five vessels by August 1861. The Charleston-based *Jefferson Davis*, a five-gun brig, became the most notorious privateer of the period. After a seven-week odyssey, ranging from the coast of Massachusetts to the West Indies, the *Davis* managed to capture a total of nine vessels. The Northern press anxiously followed the career of the *Davis*, as Union warships were rushed into the Atlantic to apprehend the raider. The intrepid privateer's career abruptly ended when the vessel was grounded in a gale off St. Augustine in August 1861. During this period, privateers and a handful of Confederate navy vessels based at Hatteras Inlet, North Carolina, wreaked havoc on Union merchant shipping and took fifteen recorded prizes in July and August 1861.

During the early months of the war, Union warships captured two Confederate privateer crews. After a short duel, the privateer *Savannah* was surrendered to the USS *Perry*, while the *Petrel* was sunk after a brief engagement with the USS *St. Lawrence*. The badly outgunned privateers quickly succumbed in both instances. The captured crews were shipped to common jails in New York and Philadelphia, respectively, and awaited trial as pirates in the United States Circuit Court system. The trials brought into question Lincoln's condemnation of privateers as pirates and sensationalized newspaper headlines for months. The courts, however, acquitted the captives and simply recognized the privateers as prisoners of war. The judgment dashed Northern hopes that the men would be hanged as pirates to deter other privateers.

During 1861 and 1862 the Confederate privateers continued operations, until such activities became too risky or unprofitable for the owners and crews. By 1863 the increased effectiveness of the Union blockade and the capture of several key Southern ports decreased the opportunity of successfully taking prizes. In 1861 most privateers operated from weakly blockaded ports. They sallied forth under the covering guns of Confederate harbor defenses during hours of darkness to take prize ships that sailed near the coast. By late 1862 the *New York Times* noted: "The small craft that pounced out with impunity…and seized our unsuspecting traders as they passed by have all been quiet lately. They are neither able to get out of their dens nor able to get in again…there are no better times for them in prospect."

The Union blockade slowly tightened its grip on Southern ports and employed faster steamships that could outmaneuver, outrun, and outgun most of the privateers. Even though many privateers were steam powered, all privateers encountered trouble towing or sailing the slower prize vessels into port; most merchant ships were simply not built for speed. A few privateers later resorted to sinking prizes and claiming a token 20 percent of value reward, but such remuneration made for slim profits.

As Confederate war needs expanded, most private entrepreneurs found that they could no longer acquire the armaments and munitions needed for their vessels; the Confederate navy received priority in such matters. In many respects, the technological dilemma faced by privateer outfitters was demonstrative of the end of an era. The rapidly advancing technology of naval warfare, considering the development of ironclads and heavy rifled guns, became too expensive and far too complex for private ventures. Privateering became obsolete, along with the sail-powered warships of a more romantic age, with the advent of the American Civil War. Furthering the demise of the privateers was the fact that several privateer ships were confiscated and pressed into service with the Confederate navy.

With the increased demand for war materiel to supply the Confederate military and the increased demand for manufactured goods by the Southern public, many privateers discovered a more lucrative outlet for their services—blockade running. The principal object of privateering was financial gain and, as one historian noted: "The occupation of commerce destroying . . . however useful and patriotic, is not lucrative; and it was therefore left to the Confederate naval officers, who took it as part of their duties. The privateers . . . diverted to the more profitable pursuit of carrying contraband."

By early 1863 Confederate privateering was essentially defunct. Although letters of marque were issued as late as 1864, few privateers were actually outfitted and no recorded prizes were taken after 1863.

Although they were no more than "a thorn in the flesh"

for the U.S. Navy from a strategic viewpoint, the Confederate privateers sparked the imagination of the Northern and Southern press during the early uncertain years of the war. For the U.S. Navy, privateers were simply a minor nuisance that had to be dealt with; the lightly armed privateers were no match for the Union warships that patrolled Southern shores. For the Southern public, the privateers were heroic adventurers who took the war outside the Confederacy's territorial bounds to threaten Northern institutions. For the Northern public, the privateers were dreaded pirates in sleek, well-armed vessels who jeopardized American maritime interests around the globe.

Generally, historians discount the Confederate privateering effort as ineffective and, as such, of little historic consequence. The Northern press and public, however, fell prey to the deepest fears that could disquiet a nation with such extensive maritime interests. The privateers carried a weapon much stronger than all of their cannon combined: fear. During the first two years of the war, the psychological impact of the anticipated privateer fleet was greater than Confederate strategists could have anticipated. The Northern press eagerly fueled public fears as it exaggerated Southern naval strength and stimulated deep consternation among Northern shipping interests. The *New York Tribune* on 13 May 1861 stated, "It is said that 3,000 applications have been made for letters of marque, some of which are from foreign States." In reality, fewer than fifty Confederate privateers ever put to sea and fewer than half of those vessels were responsible for the damage that was eventually done. The anxiety over commerce-raiders quickly compelled the Northern marine insurers to increase insurance rates far out of proportion with actual losses. Marine insurance companies, fearful of significant monetary losses on insured vessels and cargoes, first doubled, and then tripled, prewar insurance rates before the end of 1861. Rates briefly dropped once the privateers' effectiveness had been negated in late 1862. However, when the Confederate navy's commerce-raiders successfully entered the fray in 1863, rates soon exceeded the 1861 level of 5 percent and then exceeded 10 percent of the insured value of vessel and cargo.

To control costs American exporters were compelled to transfer their cargoes to foreign-flagged vessels to ensure protection from privateers and naval commerce-raiders. To remain competitive against European-owned trading companies, many American shipping companies transferred registry of their ships to foreign flags. Several British firms compounded the problem and purchased a number of American merchant ships at "panic prices." At the time, Northern observers were quite cognizant of the problem, and one Boston financier wrote, "Our commerce will soon be entirely in the hands of foreigners."

And so it came to be. Because Jefferson Davis recog-

nized the neutrality of foreign vessels, only American shipping could be targeted as prizes by the privateers. Thus, the mere change of national registry protected American merchant ships from privateer depredation. Before 1860 there had been only a minimal annual shift in American transfers of registry. In 1861 over 125 American vessels (approximately 75,000 tons) changed flags of registry, a number well in excess of the total amount of tonnage transferred in the three years before the war began. An equal number of tonnage was transferred to foreign flags in 1862. The transferred tonnage quadrupled to some 250,000 tons reregistered in 1863 when the national raiders, such as the CSS *Alabama*, went into action. The initial captures of Northern prizes by privateers during the months of May through December 1861 set the change of national registry in motion, well before the advent of the C.S. Navy's commerce-raiders. The national raiders, with the exception of the CSS *Sumter*, which took nine vessels in 1862, did not begin to make a significant impact on Union commerce until 1863. The Confederate cruisers captured or destroyed over 285 vessels (approximately 100,000 tons). Frightened shippers sold or transferred another 800,000 tons to foreign flags. Confederate privateers accounted for some sixty-five merchantmen captures, or 23 percent of the total Union loss in merchant shipping, between 1861 and 1863. The Confederate privateering effort affected American merchant shipping in no small way by first instigating, and later accelerating, the so-called flight from the flag.

Yet for all this, the Confederate commerce-raiding strategy, to which the privateers contributed, failed to produce the expected results. The Northern war effort was not significantly weakened materially or politically through the loss of merchant ships or cargoes. The strategic ineffectiveness of the Southern "gentleman pirates" in relation to the outcome of the naval war cannot be disputed, but their mere presence and sporadic actions significantly affected American shipping interests well beyond the strategic scope of the Civil War. The privateers, an unwitting psychological weapon, contributed to the later demise of the American merchant fleet in the postbellum era, and the historical legacy of the Confederate privateers lingered for many decades to come.

—*Charles L. Heath, Jr.*

See also Navy, C.S.A.; Navy, U.S.A.
For further reading:
Dalzel, George W. *The Flight From the Flag: The Continuing Effect of the Civil War Upon the American Carrying Trade* (1940).
Hearn, Chester G. *Gray Raiders of the Sea: How Eight Confederate Warships Destroyed the Union's High Seas Commerce* (1992).
Johnson, Emory R. *History of Domestic and Foreign Commerce of the United States*, vol. 2 (1915).
Maclay, Edgar S. *A History of American Privateers* (1899).
Musicant, Ivan. *Divided Waters: The Naval History of the Civil War* (1995).
Robinson, William M., Jr. *The Confederate Privateers* (1928; reprint, 1990).
Scharf, Thomas J. *History of the Confederate States Navy: From Its Organization to the Surrender of Its Last Vessel* (1877).
Soley, James R. *The Blockade and the Cruisers* (1885).
Strivers, Reuben E. *Privateers and Volunteers: The Men and Women of Our Reserve Naval Forces, 1766–1866* (1975).
United States Navy Department. *Civil War Naval Chronology, 1861–1865*, part 4 (1961).

PRIZE CASES [67 U.S. (2 BLACK) 635 (1863)]

President Abraham Lincoln announced his intention to blockade several of the seceded Confederate states on 19 April 1861. Eight days later, he added two more to the list. Congress gave Lincoln authority to take such actions on 13 July 1861, by which time the blockade had already long been in effect; on 6 August 1862, it retroactively covered Lincoln's actions up to that date with the mantle of congressional authority insofar as it could do so.

By a 5-to-4 vote (with all three of Lincoln's appointees sustaining his government's position), the Supreme Court ratified the policy of the Lincoln administration at once to deny that the Confederate States of America legally existed and at the same time to blockade the states subscribing to the Confederacy, thereby—under international law—invoking the law of war. The four cases consolidated here, those of *The Brig Amy Warwick* (owned by Confederate civilians), *The Schooner Crenshaw* (owned by Confederate civilians), *The Barque Hiawatha* (a British vessel), and *The Schooner Brilliante* (a Mexican vessel), raised a number of issues related to the legality of President Lincoln's acts. In a real feat of judicial derring-do, the Supreme Court gave its stamp of approval to all of those acts.

Several important legal questions were at issue in these cases. First, the appellants denied that President Lincoln could impose a blockade and thus bring the federal government into war without a declaration by the Congress. Capture of neutral vessels on the high seas, a war measure, would have required Congress' antecedent authorization if the minority (Justice Samuel Nelson, joined by Chief Justice Roger Brooke Taney, Justice John Catron, and Justice Nathan Clifford) had had its way, but the majority accepted the contention of the counsel for the government that once the government faced a de facto war, the president was at liberty to take suitable war measures. Subsequent ratification by Congress (for which Justice Robert Cooper Grier's majority found a precedent in the Mexican-American War) covered the president's war-making measures with the legitimacy of Congress's sole power to declare war.

Second, the appellants insisted that because only the Congress had power to declare war, and since the law of prize was an incident of war, the state "in the nature of a blockade" declared by President Lincoln had not amounted to an *actual* blockade. Therefore, they concluded, the law of prize had never been invoked and their ships must be returned to them. Again, the Court held that Lincoln's decision to invoke the law of prize without a declaration of war was legitimate.

The Lincoln administration's position regarding prize contradicted the policy of the U.S. government since the first administration of Thomas Jefferson. Then, following on the heels of their arguments against British depredations in the 1790s, Jeffersonian Republicans had insisted that "free ships made free goods." Now that the shoe was on the other foot, the United States seized the ships of neutrals in support of their war effort.

Incidentally, the Supreme Court majority also defined the term "civil war" in its opinion in these cases. In regard to the law of prize, as in regard to this technical term, the Court found a definition consonant with the government's contemporaneous purposes. A "civil war" was not a war for control of the government, as the English and Roman examples might have led one to think; rather, "civil war" existed whenever the courts were unable to function. Thus, the seceded states—totally uninterested in controlling the federal government—might be said to be engaged in "civil war."

The dissenting justices viewed the act of 6 August 1862 as an ex post facto law. Under it, several people had been deprived of their property for violating those of Lincoln's actions that Congress had only retroactively validated. The majority scarcely addressed this question.

Perhaps the most important legacy of this Supreme Court opinion is the impetus it gave to presidential freelancing in matters of war. While we have become accustomed to presidents' essentially untrammeled authority to commit the United States to hostilities, the subordination of the Congress to the executive branch galled the majority of justices not appointed by Lincoln in this instance. As Charles Warren noted, this case underscored the extent to which "the Court was insistent on upholding the arm of the Government in its war operations."

—*K.R. Constantine Gutzman*

See also Blockade of C.S.A.; Blockade Runners; Impressment; Secession.

For further reading:
Bernath, Stuart L. *Squall Across the Atlantic: American Civil War Prize Cases and Diplomacy* (1970).

Newmyer, R. Kent. *The Supreme Court under Marshall and Taney* (1968).

Warren, Charles. *The Supreme Court in United States History* (1926).

PRYOR, ROGER ATKINSON
(1828–1919)
Confederate general

Roger A. Pryor was born in Petersburg, Virginia, to Theodorick Bland Pryor and Lucy Eppes Atkinson Pryor. He was educated locally and at Hampden-Sidney College and the University of Virginia School of Law. Pryor, however, practiced law only briefly before entering a journalism career. He used various Virginia and Washington, D.C., newspapers to espouse his strong states' rights and ultimately secessionist views. He also became active in the Southern wing of the Democratic Party, gaining him in 1854 appointment as a special envoy to Greece.

Upon his return from Greece, he founded the radical secessionist newspaper *The South* in Washington. He used this paper as a platform for his strong support of Southern rights, and it was probably because of his editorials that he was elected to the U.S. House of Representatives in 1858. He was reelected in 1860 but resigned his seat the day before Lincoln's inauguration in protest. Upon his resignation, even though Virginia had not yet seceded, he traveled to Charleston, South Carolina, to offer his services to the Confederate military force watching Fort Sumter.

After arriving in Charleston, Pryor offered his services as an aide to Confederate general P. G. T. Beauregard. He was one of a committee of such aides who was sent to Fort Sumter on 11 April to try to negotiate the surrender of the fort from Major Robert Anderson before the firing commenced. After the bombardment and Anderson's decision to surrender, Pryor was part of the same group who negotiated the final surrender terms.

Even though Pryor was elected by Virginia, once the state seceded, to the Provisional Confederate Congress and then the First Confederate Congress, he preferred the military life. As a colonel Pryor commanded a brigade at Smithfield, Virginia, in December 1861 watching the approaches up the James River. He resigned his seat in the Confederate Congress in April 1862 at the commencement of the Peninsula campaign to devote his full attention to his military command. He was promoted to brigadier general the same month. He was commended for bravery by James Longstreet for his actions at Williamsburg on 5 May 1862 and again by the same officer for his actions at Seven Pines on 31 May 1862.

Pryor fought at the Seven Days and Second Bull Run, where he was almost captured when he became separated from his command. Pryor continued with the main Army of Northern Virginia through the Antietam campaign, but he was detached with a cavalry brigade to the York Peninsula in November 1862 to guard against Union raiders coming up from Fort Monroe. He

remained in this command until the summer of 1863 fighting off numerous Federal probes.

In the summer of 1863, Pryor was relieved of command of his brigade for reassignment. The assignment, however, was slow in coming, and an impatient Pryor resigned his commission and joined the cavalry division of Fitzhugh Lee as a private. Serving as a courier during the Petersburg campaign of the following year, Pryor was captured by Union troops in November 1864 and taken to Fort Lafayette in New York for imprisonment. While in prison, Pryor gave legal counsel to some of his fellow prisoners, especially those who had been accused of espionage. Since his capture took place during a brief truce in the fighting, he was paroled to Petersburg before the end of the war. Once Lee had fled his trenches, Pryor, who remained behind as part of his parole, informed the Union forces who first entered Petersburg of the evacuation of Richmond.

After the war, Pryor, having lost everything, traveled to New York City to try to make a living as a newspaper writer, using at first an assumed name because of his prewar reputation. However, he became successful enough after a while to write under his own name. He also passed the New York bar and became a very successful attorney. He was appointed a state judge in 1890 and in 1894 became a justice on the New York Supreme Court. He retired from the bench in 1899 and practiced law in New York City for the remainder of his life. A fiery supporter of secession and states' rights before the war, Pryor in his postwar career became a model of the spirit of reconciliation.

—*David S. Heidler and Jeanne T. Heidler*

See also Fort Sumter, Bombardment of; Williamsburg, Battle of.

For further reading:
Holzman, Robert S. *Adapt or Perish: The Life of General Roger A. Pryor, C.S.A.* (1976).
Pryor, Sara Agnes Rice. *Reminiscences of Peace and War* (1905).

those manufactured by Southern industries proved defective. To try to mask this deficiency, the army on several occasions affixed painted logs to wheels and strategically placed them in such a way as to present the illusion to Federal scouts that it had a greater number of artillery pieces.

The ruse often proved effective. For example, in the fall of 1861 the Confederates deployed the sham cannon along their line of advance, which was edging dangerously close to Washington. When the Confederates abandoned an exposed portion of their line just southwest of the city, Federal soldiers found the abandoned decoys. The "weapons" were quickly dubbed "Quaker guns" by a newspaper reporter in reference to the traditional pacifism of the Society of Friends. The discovery helped to raise doubts about Army of the Potomac commander Major General George McClellan's claims that he faced a much superior force.

When the Confederates withdrew behind the Rappahannock River in anticipation of McClellan's spring offensive in 1862, Federals found more Quaker guns left behind along the abandoned defensive line. Confederates in the Western theater also used the ploy. For instance, defenders at Corinth placed the wooden weapons along their defensive line before they abandoned the town in May 1862 upon the cautious approach of Major General Henry Halleck. While

QUAKER GUNS

Quaker guns were logs painted black and attached to wheels to resemble cannon. The Confederate army suffered from an inadequate number of artillery pieces throughout the war. During the war's first two years, the Confederate army captured more cannon than the South was able to produce or import. Often

Quaker guns positioned on the heights near Centreville, Virginia, March 1862
(Photograph by George N. Barnard / *Library of Congress*)

Quaker guns posed no real physical threat, their use by Confederates proved at least temporarily effective in concealing their deficiency in artillery.

—*Thomas F. Curran*

See also Corinth, Siege of; McClellan, George Brinton.

QUAKERS

Quakers, known officially as the Religious Society of Friends, began their religious movement in the 1650s to protest the perceived authoritarianism of the Church of England under the Puritan regime. Drawing upon the theology of Baptists, early Quakers such as George Fox preached that the true source of all religious knowledge was the "inner light," God's immediate presence in the human consciousness, as opposed to the Bible or institutional traditions. Christians, believed Quakers, owed complete and active obedience to God as revealed through this inner light. Therefore, no Christian should allow temporal allegiances to interfere with his or her performance of God's will, even in everyday matters of culture or custom. For these reasons, many Quakers refused to take oaths, acknowledge social rank, or bear arms in battle. Their counterculture soon drew persecution from the Restoration monarchy and the Puritan-dominated governments of American New England, where Quakers migrated during the seventeenth century to win converts and establish their way of life.

In spite of royal and Puritan opposition, Quakers in colonial America reached levels of political and social power that quickly challenged their ideals of equality, pacifism, and personal conscience. For example, in Quaker-dominated Pennsylvania political leaders struggled to develop viable policies on law enforcement, civil disobedience, and the French and Indian Wars that were also consistent with their religious beliefs. Also during the eighteenth and nineteenth centuries tensions developed between Quaker anti-institutionalism and the increasing authority and organization of local Quaker groups. Condemning perceived secular tendencies, minister Elias Hicks and his followers withdrew from the yearly meeting of Philadelphia Quakers to form their own meeting, the General Conference, during the 1820s. Additional schisms occurred in the late 1830s, when British Quaker John Gurney toured the United States, promoting revivalism and evangelical practice among Protestants.

Initially, slavery was also a divisive issue, as some wealthy Quaker colonials continued to own slaves, while others condemned slaveholding on moral grounds. These internal disagreements were reflected in the Philadelphia Quakers' 1696 statement, which opposed slave importation but stopped short of outright abolitionism. However, during the 1700s an influx of white indentured labor facilitated the antislavery movement by providing Northern landowners with cheap alternatives to slaveholding. By mid-century many Quaker disciplines forbade slave trading, though not slaveholding. Quaker leaders such as John Woolman and Anthony Benezet argued publicly for abolition; and even Quakers in Maryland, Virginia, and North Carolina emancipated slaves and exerted their organizations' limited powers to protect the freedmen. As tensions increased between North and South during the early 1800s, many Southern Quakers migrated northward to escape the persecution of their proslavery neighbors.

As the Civil War approached, Quakers actively opposed the slave system through leadership in, and contributions to, abolitionist organizations. For instance, Quaker Lucretia Coffin Mott helped to found both the Philadelphia Anti-Slavery Society and the Female Anti-Slavery Society, linking the abolitionist cause to an emerging feminist movement. Influenced by non-Quaker William Lloyd Garrison, abolitionist writers John Greenleaf Whittier and Benjamin Lundy used journalism to erode public support for the Southern position. Other Quakers, such as Levi Coffin, became valuable leaders in the Underground Railroad, a loose organization that secretly aided the escape of slaves from Southern plantations into Canada. The Underground Railroad especially appealed to Quakers in that it enabled them to break unjust laws without violent confrontation, pacifism being one of their central religious tenants.

Indeed, the Quaker peace testimony placed painful limits on members' participation in a Union war effort that, they believed, promoted a just cause. Forbidden to bear arms, the Quakers were also prohibited from supporting violence by paying fees or hiring substitute, non-Quaker soldiers. Still, in spite of these prohibitions, Quaker meetings between 1860 and 1865 gave ample evidence of member participation in the Union army; and the Quakers' reluctance to disown or punish their soldiers showed ambivalence toward their requirement of conscientious objection.

During the war and Reconstruction following it, Quakers also worked to benefit the freedmen through fundraising, teaching, and organizing relief programs. Pennsylvania Quakers, for example, raised money for the National Freeman's Relief Association in 1862; while New England Quakers founded the Washington Mission for Freemen, which raised over $4,000 for relief work in 1867. In addition, Quaker Schools opened in Indiana, Mississippi, and North Carolina for the purpose of educating the emancipated children.

Perhaps as a consequence of the war's religious challenges, after 1865 the Quakers enforced their disciplines less strictly and turned increasingly toward Midwestern "holiness" revivalism for religious inspiration. In the twentieth century Quakers continued their traditions of social and educational reform.

—*Rae Sikula*

See also Abolitionists; Churches.

For further reading
Barbour, Hugh, and J. William Frost. *The Quakers* (1988).
Hamm, Thomas. *The Transformation of American Quakerism: Orthodox Friends, 1800–1907* (1988).

QUANTRILL, WILLIAM CLARKE
(1837–1865)
Confederate guerrilla leader

Born on 31 July 1837 in Canal Dover (now Dover), Ohio, the oldest of eight children of Thomas and Carolina Clarke Quantrill, this future guerrilla chief at the age of 16 began teaching school in his hometown, then in Illinois and Indiana. But in 1857 he began life anew as a farmer in Kansas. Eager for adventure, he joined an army expedition heading for Utah the next year as a teamster. Then, after prospecting for gold near Pike's Peak, he returned to Kansas, taught for a while, and in 1860 moved to Lawrence, Kansas where under the alias of Charles Hart he became a "Jayhawker" against the proslavery "Border Ruffians." Yet he betrayed a group of five abolitionists by warning a Missouri master of their plot to free his slaves. As a result, three of the plotters were shot and killed. Suspected of thievery and charged with horse stealing, he decided to switch over to the Missouri side of the border.

When pro-Confederacy guerrillas began their depredations along the Missouri-Kansas border in 1861, Quantrill emerged as their leader. Although he and his band were not recognized as regular Confederate forces, they began a campaign of raiding communities in both states, robbing mail coaches, and executing anyone suspected of having ties with or aiding either the Jayhawkers or the Union forces sent into the area to control the guerrillas. On 22 December 1861, out of sheer exasperation, Major General Henry W. Halleck issued General Orders No. 32 outlawing all guerrillas and irregulars, stating they would be shot outright whenever caught carrying out unlawful acts.

Leaders of regular Confederate forces eventually and rightly condemned Quantrill's behavior as savage and beyond the code of civilized warfare since it consisted in large measure of cold-blooded executions and other depredations, often against noncombatants. Yet in August 1862, after a successful raid on Independence, Missouri, he and his men were accepted into Confederate service, Quantrill being given the rank of captain in the Confederate Partisan Ranger service. That same year he traveled to Richmond to ask for a command with the rank of colonel under the Partisan

Ranger Law. For whatever reason (the record is unclear), he was turned down, but he often referred to himself as "colonel" thereafter, and Confederate authorities sometimes addressed him by that title.

Quantrill, his band, and many others, plus Confederate recruits, totaling about 450 men, including "Bloody Bill" Anderson, Cole Younger, and Frank James, gained their greatest notoriety on 21 August 1863, when they staged a raid on the proabolitionist town of Lawrence, Kansas. In three hours they killed close to 200 men and teenaged boys in cold blood, Quantrill having ordered his followers to kill every male capable of firing a gun whatever his age, and left most of Lawrence pillaged and burned to the ground. The raid on Lawrence proved to be an embarrassment to the Confederacy and caused such an uproar in the North that concerted action was demanded to clean out the guerrilla bands. The result was Order No. 11 issued by General Thomas E. Ewing, Jr., whereby almost everyone in three Missouri counties and in the Kansas City area was moved out of the area, the harshest measure carried out against civilians during the Civil War.

Quantrill and his band continued to raid and kill. Six weeks after sacking Lawrence, on 6 October 1863, they attacked a small Union outpost at Baxter Springs, Kansas, then turned on the approaching headquarters train of 100 men of Major General James G. Blunt. They slaughtered 89 Federals including 17 musicians and noncombatants. During 1864, however, Quantrill's band began to break up. On returning to Missouri in the spring of 1864, George Todd deposed Quantrill as the band's leader, and Quantrill spent the summer and fall in a hideout in northern Missouri with his mistress. In October both Todd and "Bloody Bill" Anderson were killed. That fall Quantrill pulled together some of his old guerrilla band and led about 30 of them into Kentucky. There, near Taylorsville, on 10 May 1865, he was severely wounded and captured by a Union force.

Reputed to be one of the bloodthirstiest men in American history, he died in a Louisville, Kentucky, prison on 6 June 1865, after a deathbed conversion to the Roman Catholic faith. His body was buried in an unmarked grave in St. Mary's Cemetery in Louisville. His mother recovered his bones in 1887, and parts of his body (some arm and leg bones and a lock of his hair, hitherto kept in the Kansas State Historical Society Museum) were reburied in Dover two years later, then reburied in a fiberglass child's coffin in the Confederate Memorial Cemetery in Higginsville, Missouri, in 1992 with full (Confederate) military honors and Catholic rites. Six days later his skull was buried in the Quantrill family plot in Dover, Ohio.

— *James M. Morris*

See also Anderson, "Bloody Bill"; Baxter Springs, Battle of; Guerrilla Warfare; Lawrence, Kansas; Todd, George.

For further reading:
Barton, O. S. *Three Years with Quantrill: A True Story Told by his Scout John McCorkle* (1992).
Brownlee, Richard S. *Gray Ghosts of the Confederacy: Guerrilla Warfare in the West, 1861–1865* (1958).
Castel, Albert E. *William Clarke Quantrill: His Life and Times* (1962; reprint, 1998).
Connelley, William E. *Quantrill and the Border Wars* (1910).
Goodrich, Thomas. *Black Flag: Guerrilla Warfare on the Western Border, 1861–1865* (1995).
———. *Bloody Dawn: The Story of the Lawrence Massacre* (1991).
Leslie, Edward E. *The Devil Knows How to Ride: The True Story of William Clarke Quantrill and his Confederate Raiders* (1996).
———. "Quantrill's Bones." *American Heritage* (1995).
Monaghan, Jay. *Civil War on the Western Border, 1854–1865* (1955).

QUARTERMASTER

The Quartermaster's Department, commanded by the quartermaster general, was established for the army by an act of 28 March 1812. The department was responsible for purchasing military stores, camp equipage, and other necessities for the troops, as well as providing transportation. One exception to the duties of this office was the role of providing food, which was the responsibility of the Office of the Commissary General of Subsistence. During the Civil War, the quartermaster played a vital part in keeping both the Union and Confederate armies equipped and supplied, a task accomplished with varying degrees of success.

Serving as quartermaster general for the U.S. Army was the very capable Montgomery Meigs. He filled a vacancy created when Joseph Johnston, who served as quartermaster general for less than ten months, resigned his commission and joined the Confederate army. From 22 April 1861, until Meigs took office on 13 June 1861, Maj. Ebenezer S. Sibley was acting quartermaster general. Sibley experienced a frustrating two months in office because of the haphazard way the War Department was managed under Secretary of War Simon Cameron, who appointed his own supply agents with little regard to their experience or qualifications. The Quartermaster's Department would remain hindered until the more competent Edwin Stanton replaced Cameron in 1862.

Initially, the most pressing need of the Union army was procuring adequate supplies and equipment to outfit the volunteers responding to President Abraham Lincoln's calls to service. The War Department had barely enough supplies on hand at their chief depository, the Schuylkill Arsenal, to serve the needs of the small peacetime regular army. The volunteer troops placed an added burden on a department hindered by minimal funds. As a result, state governments were forced to purchase their own supplies, often at inflated prices from unscrupulous merchants. The rush to procure uniforms overworked the mills in the United States, and they were unable to produce the cloth quickly enough to meet demand. This prevented thousands of troops from taking the field until they were issued uniforms.

Desperate to outfit the growing army, the Quartermaster's Department looked to the European market for cloth and a way to stabilize the inflated prices charged by contractors in the United States. This was a short-lived, but successful, experiment, as Meigs determined that the cost was about the same for cloth produced domestically or overseas. Also, domestic suppliers, fearful of losing business to foreign competitors, increased their production in an effort to meet the demands of the army.

Essential to the operations of Quartermaster's Department were the railroads. The Union army relied upon trains to transport troops and move supplies from the depots to the field. In the early part of the war, privately operated railroad companies exploited the War Department's need for their trains by charging exorbitant rates. To resolve this issue, Congress passed the Railroad Act on 31 January 1862, that allowed the government to take control of any railroad line in the United States that was deemed necessary for the operations of the military. In response to the new legislation, representatives of the railroad industry and the War Department agreed upon a reasonable rate for use of the rail lines. Because of the cooperation between the two parties, none of the Northern railroads were seized during the war.

Field operations were the largest and most vital function of the Quartermaster's Department. With the exception of a few officers directing the work of the department in Washington, most of the quartermasters in the field were responsible for either a military department or tactical unit. The field quartermasters were accountable for making the contracts, obtaining the supplies, and ensuring that material was funneled down to the regimental quartermasters. Operating independently from the Quartermaster's Department in Washington, the field staff was self-sufficient, leaving the quartermaster general to serve only as an advisor and supervisor. This was especially true for the Western theater field commanders, who resented interference and wanted to do things their way.

During the first three years of the war, procurement was done by contract or, in emergency situations, through open-market purchase. Consequently, contracts were subject to fraud, and the quality of the materials purchased was often not up to War Department standards. To establish greater control over purchases and standardize the methods used for contracts, the Quartermaster's Department reorganized into nine divisions. Each division related to the varied responsibilities of the office: animals, clothing and equipage, ocean and lake transportation, rail and river transportation, forage and fuel, barracks and hospitals, wagon transportation, inspection, and finance.

Under the reorganized department, the chiefs of the various divisions contracted for all quartermaster supplies and ensured that they were inspected. Payment was not to be made until the division quartermaster received an inspection certificate. The newly organized department allowed for more proficient methods of procurement and the issuance of supplies. By November of 1864, Meigs could confidently report that "all difficulties in providing a sufficient supply of clothing and material for our increasing Army have disappeared. The manufacturing power of the country has so expanded as to fully meet the demands…."

The Confederate Quartermaster General's Department was established by the Provisional Congress on 26 February 1861, as part of the army's general staff. The functions of this office were the same as that of the Union army's quartermaster with one exception: the Confederate quartermasters were also charged with the duties of paymaster. A separate office, the Pay Bureau, was established under the supervision of the quartermaster general with the duty of disbursing pay to military personnel and making bounty payments and expenditures.

Appointed as the first quartermaster general of the Confederacy was Abraham C. Myers. Upon starting his new position, Myers immediately concluded that adequate supplies and equipment needed for the small regular army and the growing ranks of volunteers were not available. Although the volunteers were required to furnish their own uniforms, Myers acknowledged that they would be unable to provide additional clothing once they entered the field. To rectify this problem, Myers established quartermaster depots at Montgomery, San Antonio, Charleston, New Orleans, Mobile (then later at Nashville), Lynchburg, and Richmond to collect the supplies for requisitioning by the field armies. The depots were modeled after the Federal arsenal at Schuylkill.

Thanks to an abundance of cotton, large quantities of shirts, underwear, and lightweight articles were issued to the troops. By October of the first year of the war, the Quartermaster's Department successfully clothed and supplied its army through the depot system, but stockpiles were insufficient for future distribution. A shortage of wool was particularly a problem, and the Confederate mills could not provide the heavy material needed for winter uniforms. As a result, the Confederate government turned to foreign suppliers. Major J. B. Ferguson was sent to England as the official quartermaster purchasing agent. There he purchased large quantities of English army shoes and bulk woolen cloth. Payment was made in cotton, and private speculators were hired to run the uniforms and cloth through the Union blockades. To supplement the foreign purchases, states such as Georgia and North Carolina produced clothing for their own troops.

The Confederate army suffered a severe setback in the spring of 1862, as a shortage of supplies occurred due to the loss of the depots at New Orleans, Memphis, and Nashville to Union hands. The lack of supplies continued into the fall, greatly hampering Robert E. Lee's Maryland campaign and Braxton Bragg's operations in Kentucky. To resolve the crisis, Myers issued more contracts and placed pressure on textile mills in the South to increase production. Another dilemma was the shortage of wagons for field transportation and draft animals, artillery horses, and fodder. A special agent was sent to make purchases from private sources, but the costs and limited supply did little to resolve the problem.

In the spring of 1863, Myers reorganized the bureau. The change occurred because of vastly expanded purchasing and manufacturing activities and a conflict between staff officers reporting to Richmond and field quartermasters. Field officers often ignored bureau regulations for proper requisitioning and distribution, causing unnecessary shortages and waste. Myers divided the Confederacy into eleven purchasing districts, which resulted in a more extensive supply network and tighter control of requisitions. Despite improvements in the procurement and distribution of supplies, Myers was dismissed by President Jefferson Davis on 7 August 1863 and replaced by Alexander R. Lawton.

By the fall of 1863, the summer campaigns depleted stockpiles even further, and efforts to acquire more supplies from overseas contractors were thwarted by the Union blockades of Southern ports. To counteract this problem, the Confederate government contracted to purchase a fleet of specially designed blockade runners. They were used so successfully in the fall and winter of 1864 and 1865 that the army was well supplied and able to begin establishing a reserve by the end of the war.

On the domestic front, production was low because factory workers were needed to fill the ranks of depleted regiments in the field. Early in the war, the Confederates relied upon impressment of private property, such as forage and livestock. But overzealous field commanders confiscated private property with little regard for fair compensation. Property owners constantly complained to the War Department, and the impressment policy was abolished in March 1865.

A chief concern of both Myers and Lawton throughout the war was the management of the rail lines through the Railroad Bureau. Without a reliable transportation system, it was difficult to move supplies from the depots. The Confederacy had roughly 9,000 miles of railroad, but the numerous lines could not be considered a system because of gaps between cities, differences in gauge, and breaks between lines that entered cities. Unlike the federal government, the Confederate War Department did not stockpile supplies for repairs and replacements, and railroad shops in the South were nonexistent. As the war progressed, the condition of the railroads worsened. The Confederate Congress passed an act for public control of railroads in February 1865, but Lawton was reluctant to enforce the law, except in specific instances. So it had little effect, especially this late in the war.

The successful operation of the Quartermaster's Department contributed greatly to the Union victory. The U.S. Army rarely went without supplies and equipment after 1861. Many of the accomplishments of the Quartermaster's Department resulted from the administrative genius of Montgomery Meigs, who directed an operation that expanded significantly as the war progressed. The Confederate army was less successful in its quartermaster operations, mostly because of a lack of coordination between the general staff in Richmond and the commanders in the field. President Davis and his advisors reacted to situations after they occurred instead of planning ahead and appropriating enough funds for purchases in advance. Despite the lack of cooperation and resources received, it is doubtful that quartermaster operations directly attributed to the surrender of the Confederacy in 1865.

—*Mitchell Yockelson*

See also Lawton, Alexander Robert; Logistics; Meigs, Montgomery; Myers, Abraham Charles.
For further reading:
Goff, Richard D. *Confederate Supply* (1969).
Risch, Erna. *Quartermaster Support of the Army: A History of the Corps, 1775–1939* (1989).

QUITMAN, JOHN ANTHONY
(1799–1858)

Mississippi secessionist

John Quitman was born in Rhinebeck, New York, to the Reverend Frederick and Anna Quitman. Little evidence remains concerning John's upbringing except that he was an avid outdoorsman and was educated to be a Lutheran minister. However, John desired a more lucrative career and took up the study of law. He moved to Natchez, Mississippi, and soon established a thriving practice. He quickly endeared himself to the reigning social elite and discovered his ideal lifestyle. Quitman never had any moral qualms about slavery, as he failed to see any proof of slave discontent and believed that the "inferior" blacks would degenerate into mindless animals without white influence. In 1824 Quitman married into a prestigious Mississippi family and purchased the town estate of Monmouth. He later added Springfield, Palmyra, and Live Oaks Plantations to his holdings. Quitman was a paternalistic slaveowner, basing his labor operations on an incentive system with reciprocal concessions being made between master and slave.

Pursuing his political goals, Quitman organized and led a volunteer militia unit, the Natchez Fencibles. He was elected to the state's legislature in 1827, and there gained experience defending minority interests, learning to fashion coalitions to advance his causes. After the session ended, Quitman's appointment as chancellor distanced him from the evolution of partisan politics.

Quitman's emergence as a states' rights radical resulted from his transformation from transplanted Northerner to Southern plantation owner, alienated by Northern events. Fearing outside influence over slavery and believing both national parties to be ideologically tainted, Quitman saw a third party as the South's only hope. Issues of tariff nullification and the Force Bill only reinforced his beliefs and drew him back into politics.

At the 1834 meeting of the States' Rights Association, Quitman insisted that the states were political entities individually joined to a league and not a consolidated government. Unfortunately, John C. Calhoun's (Quitman's ideological hero) cooperation with the anti-Jacksonian Whig Party undercut the movement. Quitman became a states' rights Whig and was elected a state senator. While senator, Quitman served as interim governor and used his office to advance nullification, to revive the state's practice of incorporating private internal improvement companies, to support the Natchez-Jackson railroad project, to encourage chartering of private banks, to support public education, prison, and military reforms, and to propose a constitutional amendment eliminating the need for an interim governor. When Calhoun realigned with the Democratic Party, Quitman announced his own political conversion, describing himself as a true Democrat, a Jefferson-Calhoun strict constructionist. Politically, he stood as a resolute nonpartisan, working within any party that fell in line with his beliefs and that advanced similar ideals.

The annexation of Texas gained Quitman's full support in the 1840s. Quitman acted in Texas-Mexican affairs after Santa Anna's attempt to violate American settlers' property rights by ending slavery in the 1830s. When war broke out Quitman, the planter-politician, became a brigadier general and set off to gain military glory. His adventures brought him into competition with neighboring plantation owner and future Confederate president, Jefferson Davis, as both men hoped to boost their political careers. Quitman served courageously and, after his performance at Chapultepec, was appointed governor of Mexico in September 1847.

By the end of November the national hero was back home, but the growing Free Soil Party and the Wilmot Proviso debates pushed Quitman away from his nationalistic rhetoric and attitudes. His involvement in the states' rights movement gained Quitman the governorship in 1849. His inaugural address spoke of Northern obtrusiveness and denounced restrictions on Southern property holders. Quitman supported revolution in Cuba as a way to preserve it from antislavery Spanish rule.

Quitman was indicted for violating neutrality laws and resigned as governor. Failing to obtain convictions in related cases, United States district attorney Logan Hunton dropped all charges.

Quitman returned to radical politics to find Mississippi's support for Southern rights emasculated. He turned again to filibustering against the Cuban government. Quitman's efforts ended when President Franklin Pierce, placating the North and gaining support for the Kansas-Nebraska Act, issued a proclamation that filibustering against Cuba violated U.S.–Spanish treaties, thus destroying any legitimacy and support associated with Quitman's efforts.

Quitman took his sectional struggle to Congress when he was elected to the House of Representatives in 1855. There he defended the slave trade as a means whereby slaves were transferred from cruel African masters to benevolent white masters, and supported the Kansas-Nebraska Act, claiming it gave equal rights to all portions of the country. Quitman endorsed the Lecompton Constitution in Kansas, though he felt slavery's continuance there was increasingly unlikely. Quitman died in 1858 without realizing his political ambition of securing slavery and the Southern lifestyle within the Union, or of creating a separate Southern nation.

—*Katherine L. Swimm*

See also Davis, Jefferson; Fire-eaters; LeCompton Constitution; Mississippi; Secession.

For further reading:
Franklin, John Hope. *The Militant South, 1800–1861* (1956).
May, Robert E. *John A. Quitman: Old South Crusader* (1985).
McCardell, John. *The Idea of a Southern Nation: Southern Nationalists and Southern Nationalism* (1979).
McLendon, James. "John A. Quitman, Fire-Eating Governor." *Journal of Mississippi History* (1953).
Potter, David M. The Impending Crisis, 1848–1861 (1976).

R

RADICAL REPUBLICANS

The Radical Republicans were a political faction in the North devoted to a vigorous prosecution of the Civil War, immediate emancipation and rights for the slaves, and a thoroughgoing postwar reconstruction of the South.

The unhappiness of antislavery activists with national parties that compromised on slavery led in the prewar years to independent antislavery organizations in the Liberty, Free Soil, and finally Republican Parties. Only the Republican Party reached major party stature, however, and only then by muting its abolitionism and broadening its appeal to include other issues. The party's "radicals" emerged as the conscience of the party, attempting to keep it true to its original antislavery idealism. Tracing their intellectual and often geographical roots to New England and its Puritan past, radicals believed political leaders must pursue morally just policies regardless of their political expediency. Even the Constitution must not be allowed to stand in the way of achieving a just and moral society. While all Republicans shared a dislike of slavery and preference for free labor, only the radicals insisted that correcting the moral wrong of slavery outweighed all considerations of property loss, possible civil war, constitutional objections, and existing racial prejudices.

Democrats, and even some conservative Republicans, found what they perceived as radical self-righteousness and indifference to the Constitution hard to bear. Democrats in particular happily labeled all Republicans "radicals." They recognized that many of the causes championed by individual radicals (racial equality, temperance, labor reform, and women's rights along with abolition) were in fact highly controversial and sure to alarm many voters outside reform-minded New England and the upper North states of Yankee migration. The efforts of moderate Republicans to dissociate the party from extreme stands and radical candidates characterized the period of Republican growth before the war. Moderate Abraham Lincoln's nomination for president in 1860 in preference to the more radical William Henry Seward was just one example of this.

The radicals' extreme stands on issues and unwillingness to compromise led to constant frustration in the prewar era. Only with the secession of the Southern states and the onset of war did the political situation change to accommodate those at the political extremes. Those who had defied the South for years now took positions as chairs of congressional committees (Charles Sumner, Thaddeus Stevens, Zachariah Chandler, and Henry Wilson, among others) or served in the cabinet (Salmon P. Chase). In addition, the revolutionary wartime situation seemed opportune for emancipation. Convinced that the Northern public would support seizure of Southern property, arrests of Northern and border state "traitors," abolition of slavery, and African-American soldiers, radicals challenged those who would proceed more cautiously, including Abraham Lincoln. Although the moderate Lincoln sought to maintain good relationships with radicals in his party, the latter openly cringed at his preference for creating a broad coalition in favor of the war over pursuing a "principled" radical agenda of confiscation and abolition.

In December 1861 Congress authorized a joint investigative committee, the Committee on the Conduct of the War, which was presided over by radical Benjamin F. Wade. It offered a vehicle for radicals to comment on the war's management by Lincoln. Democratic generals such as George B. McClellan were criticized for being overly sympathetic to the South and slaveholders, while ineffective but radical generals such as Benjamin F. Butler found a friendly forum for defending their military actions. The committee issued reports on treatment of Union prisoners of war sure to arouse hatred of the South and calls for a more vigorous prosecution of the war. But although radicals could investigate Lincoln's war effort, the committee produced little legislation and had no direct impact on the military; its main influence was on public opinion. Indeed, radicals may have served the president's cause by preparing the way for some of the more extreme measures the war dictated.

Dissatisfied with Lincoln's avoidance of emancipation early in the war, radicals pursued, over Lincoln's objections, confiscation bills that would free most Southern slaves. They also offered in 1864 an alternative (the Wade-Davis Bill) to Lincoln's reconstruction ideas, which would have permitted those who had supported the Confederacy to assume political roles on the taking of oaths of future loyalty. When the president pocket vetoed the measure, Wade and Davis openly

attacked the president in the Wade-Davis Manifesto for "dictatorial usurpation." Radicals Salmon P. Chase, John C. Frémont, and Benjamin F. Wade all maneuvered for the Republican nomination in 1864. Radicals even spearheaded a drive in August (after the Republican Convention) to replace Lincoln as the party's nominee.

Historians have long debated the radicals' significance. Analysis of congressional votes reveals that consistent radicals never were a majority of their party, much less Congress. Many individuals shifted factional allegiances from session to session. Seward, a prewar radical, took moderate positions during the war. Wartime radical Benjamin F. Butler had been a prewar Democrat, even favoring Jefferson Davis for the Democratic nomination in 1860. Such factional inconsistency suggests that some who favored radical policies did so as a result of political calculation, not solely as a moral imperative. The radical faction was far from unified or stable. Despite the intraparty feuding, Lincoln could normally count on most radicals for support—as his decisive victory in 1864 demonstrated.

Nevertheless, radicals added a distinctive element to Civil War politics. By acting as a faction and threatening to withdraw support at key moments, radicals could gain concessions. Some regard the Emancipation Proclamation itself as an attempt to forestall a boycott of the war by frustrated radicals. When Lincoln removed the scheming Chase from his cabinet in 1864, he compensated radicals by removing a conservative (Montgomery Blair) as well. While radicals may have found many wartime policies regarding race and reconstruction too conservative for their tastes, their contributions to the debates on those topics also guaranteed that the most conservative options would be rejected. In this way they exercised influence.

Some historians have defined the radicals in economic terms as defenders of Northern capitalism. While long discounted, analysis of wartime congressional voting shows radicals disproportionately favored measures promoting economic growth and development at the national level. Such views suggest a linking in radical minds of free labor and capitalism as signs of a modern, progressive nation.

Lincoln's death would lead to the period of greatest radical influence as Andrew Johnson squared off with Congress on Reconstruction. The nation had not been radicalized, however; by 1867 the radicals began a permanent decline.

—*Phyllis F. Field*

General Warren's men making a Greek cross (the Fifth Corps badge) from heated rails of the Weldon Railroad
(*Library of Congress*)

See also Butler, Benjamin F.; Chandler, Zachariah; Chase, Salmon P.; Joint Committee on the Conduct of the War; Seward, William H.; Stevens, Thaddeus; Sumner, Charles; Wade, Benjamin; Wade-Davis Bill; Wilson, Henry.

For further reading:

Bogue, Allan G. *The Earnest Men: Republicans of the Civil War Senate* (1981).

Trefousse, Hans Louis. *The Radical Republicans: Lincoln's Vanguard for Racial Justice* (1968).

Williams, T. Harry. *Lincoln and the Radicals* (1941).

RAILROADS, C.S.A.

When the Civil War began in April 1861, the Confederacy's railroad system lagged far behind the Union's in every category. Only 9,000 miles of track existed in the South, as opposed to 22,000 miles of track in the North. Much of the South's existing track was too cheaply constructed and inadequately maintained to handle the huge volume of traffic necessary to wage a long, modern war. From June 1860 to June 1861, the South shipped only 737,901 tons of freight on its railroads, while the North shipped 13,654,925 tons.

Construction of locomotives and new track also shows the disparity between the South and North. In 1860 the South built only nineteen locomotives; the North built 451 locomotives. During the Civil War, the Confederacy laid less than 400 miles of new track, while the Union laid approximately 4,000 miles of new track.

Despite such serious material handicaps, the Confederacy did enjoy the strategic advantage of interior lines, which might have been successfully exploited by using railroads more effectively. Union forces had to invade the South and then be supported in hostile territory. Even when attacked at several points, railroads potentially increased the Confederacy's strategic mobility; Southern forces could react to the most immediate threats by concentrating and counterattacking. One example of using interior lines in this way followed the Tullahoma campaign, when Braxton Bragg was significantly reinforced with soldiers transported by rail from Virginia. The extra troops helped secure the Confederate victory at Chickamauga. Also, at a tactical level in a given battle, reinforcement could be quicker by transporting troops by rail. Perhaps most importantly, using railroads could have lessened the Confederacy's logistical problems in such a defensive strategy. However, the South in general failed to use railroads effectively for the necessities of the war in the following areas: administrative infrastructure, railway construction, and tactical and strategic application.

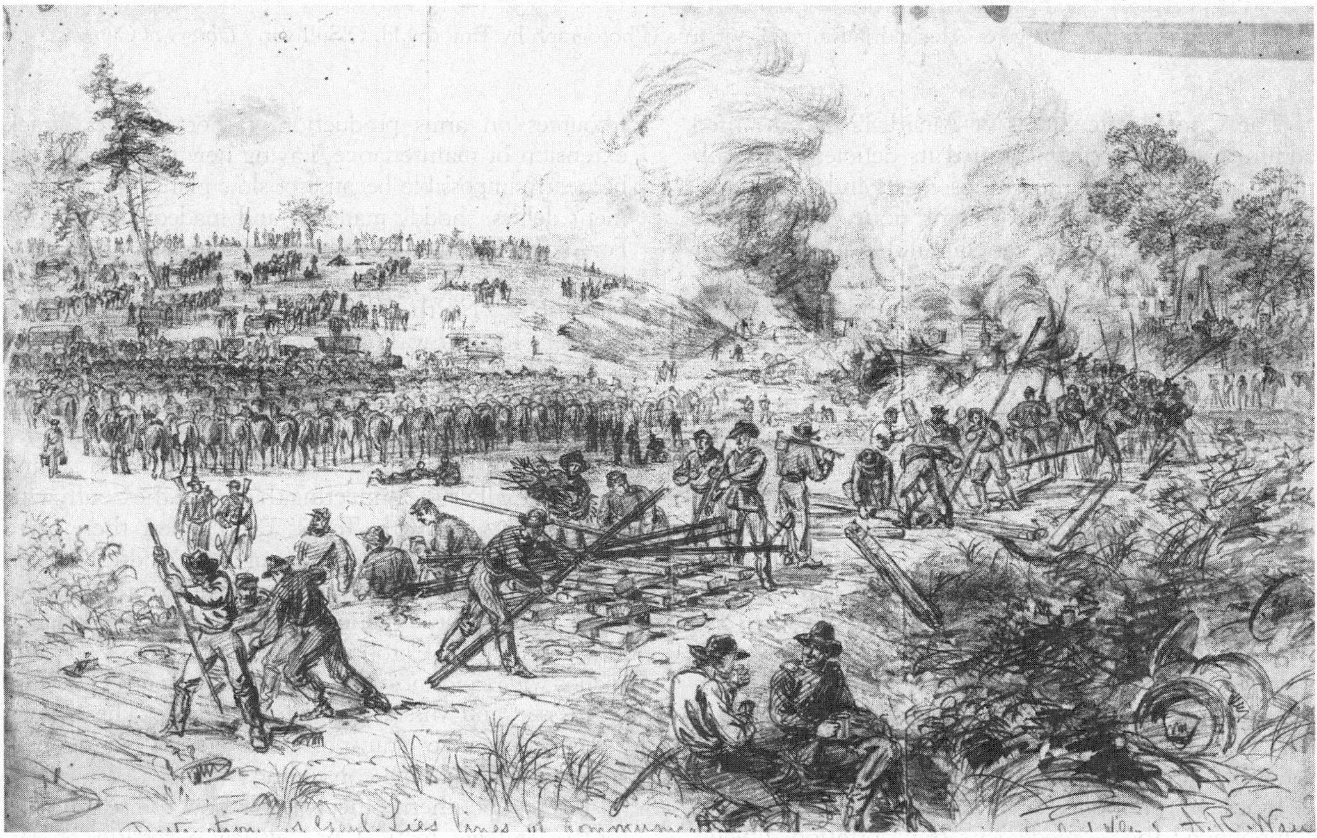

Destruction of a Confederate rail line in Virginia, sketched by Alfred R. Waud (*Library of Congress*)

Locomotive on the Orange & Alexandria Railroad, Virginia (Photograph by Timothy H. O'Sullivan / *Library of Congress*)

The Confederate States of America's decentralized administrative system magnified its deficiency in railroads and its severe limitations in its industrial base. The Confederate War Department, not to mention the civilian government in general, did not regulate or coordinate the South's railroads. Neither Quartermaster General Abraham C. Myers nor Alexander R. Lawton, his successor after August 1863, could ensure cooperation among the government, military, and railroad companies. The approximately 170 railroad companies in the South tended to be short lines that were locally owned and operated. Their owners frequently refused to abide by the Confederate government's standardized shipping rates for military supplies. Furthermore, because of the constitutional issue of states' rights, the tasks of railroad regulation were often left to state governments and local military commands. It was 1864 before the Confederate government began to exercise more centralized control over Southern railways. The new policy proved, however, to be too little and too late to stop the deterioration of the South's railways or affect the war's outcome.

Practical problems such as construction further compounded the Confederacy's transportation difficulties. The South's few manufacturers concentrated their resources on arms production, rather than on track extension or maintenance. Laying new track proved to be nearly impossible because of slow planning, procurement delays, shoddy material, and inadequate funding. For example, the Confederate Congress authorized a loan to finance forty-eight miles of track from Greensboro, North Carolina, to Danville, Virginia, in February 1862. It was not completed until May 1864.

Confederate soldiers and civilians alike needed livestock from Florida and Texas for food and transportation. At the beginning of the Civil War, no rail lines connected either state with the rest of the South. A line was eventually laid connecting the rest of the South with Florida, but not with Texas. Even when there were connecting lines, no standard gauge (the width between tracks) could be found throughout the South: Rails in Texas were 5 feet, 6 inches wide; most rails in Alabama, Louisiana, North Carolina, and Virginia were 4 feet, 8.5 inches wide; and most rails in Georgia, South Carolina, Tennessee, and Mississippi were 5 feet wide. These gauge deviations made transportation across state lines cumbersome and time-consuming.

Too few Southern officers knew how to use railroads for the strategic, tactical, or logistical necessities of war. Because most had little experience with industry of any

The U.S. Military Rail Road's engine "General Haupt" at Devereux Station, Virginia, on tracks of the Orange & Alexandria Railroad (*National Archives*)

kind, Southern commanders often did not understood how to operate a railroad effectively. Those Southern civilians who did understand railroad operation often remained with one of the short, local lines.

Joseph E. Johnston presents a typical example of a Confederate commander who either overestimated the capabilities of railroads or underestimated the requirements to utilize railroads successfully. Several years of experience as a surveyor in the early 1850s had given him some technical knowledge about rail construction. Yet these lessons did not affect Johnston's tactical use of railroads in July 1861 at the battle of First Bull Run.

On 18 July 1861 Johnston commanded a force of some 12,000 soldiers in the Shenandoah Valley. He was ordered to elude Union forces and reinforce Confederate forces under P. G. T. Beauregard at Manassas, fifty miles to the southeast along the Manassas Gap Railroad. After initial success in moving Colonel Thomas J. Jackson's command on this railroad on 19 July, Johnston could not rapidly move his remaining troops on the Manassas Gap because of unreliable crews, frequent derailments, and even harassing saboteurs. This poorly planned and clumsily conducted operation nearly cost the Confederacy

the battle. Still, enough of Johnston's forces did arrive to help Beauregard on 21 July, and their combined forces defeated the Union forces at First Bull Run.

As the war dragged on, Johnston utilized railroads in an inconsistent manner. Although he eventually learned to move his soldiers by rail, Johnston often failed to make effective use of railroads in supplying his troops. Like many other Confederate commanders, he focused too much on battles, without paying enough attention to the logistical support necessary to win those battles. It is also worth noting that Union forces targeted railroads in campaigns such as Sherman's March to the Sea. Union destruction of track, rolling stock, and locomotives crippled Confederate attempts to utilize railroads for transportation and supply.

The Confederacy's confused administrative infrastructure, meager railway construction problems, and misapplication of railroads to strategy, tactics, and logistics reveal many shortcomings. By using interior lines, Confederate soldiers could also have been transported more quickly to the many trouble areas across the South or in a battle. Likewise, local shortages of food, clothing, weapons, ammunition, and other material could have

The engine "Firefly" on a trestle of the Orange & Alexandria Railroad (*National Archives*)

been alleviated by railroads if they had been efficiently employed and maintained.

—*David Ulbrich*

See also Quartermaster; Railroads, C.S.A.; Strategy, C.S.A.
For further reading:
Black, Robert C., III. *The Railroads of the Confederacy* (1952; reprint, 1998).
Johnson, Angus J. *Virginian Railroads in the Civil War* (1961).
Lash, Jeffrey H. *Destroyer of the Iron Horse: General Joseph E. Johnston and the Confederate Rail Transport, 1861–1865* (1991).
Ramsdell, Charles W. "The Confederate Government and the Railroads." *American Historical Review* (1917).
Turner, George Edgar. *Victory Rode the Rails: The Strategic Place of the Railroads in the Civil War* (1953).

RAILROADS, U.S.A.

Northern victory in the Civil War was in part a result of better resources and more sophisticated technology. The railroad system that had been developed in the Northern states during the 1850s was by 1860 far superior in quality and quantity to its counterpart in the South. Had the war broken out ten years before it did, the South's chances of winning would have been markedly better because the inequality between its region's railroads and those of the North would not have been as great. As it was, the North had far outpaced the South in track mileage during the 1850s. Northern improvements in railroad practice had acquainted the region with the requirements of operating long-distance routes as well as satisfying regional needs. No such modernization characterized Southern railroads, where the variety of track gauges was a testament to rivalries between local roads that would prove fatal in the test of war.

In contrast, Northern railroads not only helped the Union win the war, they scored a phenomenal set of accomplishments in their own right. At the start of the Civil War, the North had 21,276 miles of track linking its burgeoning industries and abundant farmlands. Though the rapid pace of construction achieved during the 1850s was dramatically slowed by the war in the early 1860s, the railroads would nonetheless lay 4,000 additional miles of track between 1861 and 1865. Meanwhile the railroads became an integral and indispensable part of the Northern war effort on the home front. They not only met military needs, they also served a growing number of private passengers, increased their freight traffic, and answered the high European demand for grain exports. Traffic dramatically increased by as much

Ruins of the Confederate enginehouse at Atlanta, Georgia, September 1864 (*National Archives*)

as 50 percent and sometimes more. All these burdens required the railroads to increase efficiency by improving old practices and developing new and innovative ones, a circumstance that would make them the engine of America's expansive destiny after the Civil War.

The potential isolation of the nation's capital at Washington, D.C., early illustrated the necessity of securing communications and transportation links to the rest of the Union. By the summer of 1861, when it was apparent that the war would be lengthy, both Congress and the president realized the paramount need to integrate railroads into the war effort. Tense relations between the government and private lines marked early efforts. Constant wrangling over rates of compensation for ferrying troops and materiel only made the War Department suspect the government was being gouged, while the railroads complained they were being driven to insolvency by unreasonable claims on their patriotism. In January 1862 sizeable majorities in both the House and the Senate passed a law providing the president with unprecedented powers over the North's private railroads. Signed by Lincoln on 31 January 1862, the law empowered him to seize any or all railroads when public safety required it. Anyone resisting or impeding

this authority would be tried by a military court, and if found guilty, could be executed. The secretary of war was authorized to supervise and direct the rail transportation of troops and materiel related to the war effort. Within days of the bill's enactment, the War Department created the United States Military Rail Roads (USMRR), and Secretary of War Edwin Stanton appointed former railroad executive Daniel McCallum as its head.

While these actions demonstrated how seriously the government regarded the role of railroads in the war, Lincoln and Stanton rarely applied their sweeping regulatory powers. Both men knew the workings of railroads, having represented them during their legal careers, so they adopted a sensible policy of dealing sternly only with those that would not accommodate the government's military needs. Doubtless the government's potential power to regulate and commandeer encouraged the railroads' cooperation. In February 1862 Stanton called railroad executives to Washington, where they worked out a system of fares for soldiers and military freight. Put into place in May, the rates charged two cents per mile per soldier with eighty pounds of baggage. Freight rates followed existing classifications,

Depot of the U.S. Military Rail Roads at City Point, Virginia, 1864 (*National Archives*)

The railroad depot at Hanover Junction, Pennsylvania, 1863 (*Library of Congress*)

The U.S. Military Rail Roads engine "General Haupt," built in 1863. (*National Archives*)

but the government would receive a 10 percent discount for military shipments.

Such arrangements were not unprofitable for the railroads. Earnings swelled as a consequence of growing traffic and passenger service beyond that supplied by the military, but the lines also suffered from material shortages that made maintenance difficult, especially when the increased traffic accelerated wear and tear on equipment and track. Even when material was available, it was always expensive. Also, men conscripted into military service left the railroads facing labor shortages, and the lines sought draft exemptions for their workers. Stanton refused to make a blanket exception, but he relented at least to exclude engineers from the draft. As for other of their employees who were drafted, if the railroad could prove the loss would impair operations, the army would release them from service.

Railroads revolutionized war making, and the Civil War was the first instance of their widespread use in strategic and logistical operations. Because of their importance, railroads frequently became military objectives themselves, so their extended lines and junctions could dictate strategic decisions. Some commanders, such as William T. Sherman, regarded their vulnerability

to sabotage by local vandals as making them supremely unreliable as a means of supply. Yet the railroads made their most dramatic impact in military theaters by moving soldiers and materiel over long distances, and the Union was thus able to overcome the disadvantages of operating on exterior lines. In 1862 Confederate general Braxton Bragg moved 30,000 men almost 800 miles by rail from Mississippi to Chattanooga in two weeks, and in 1863 James Longstreet moved 12,000 some 900 miles from the Army of Northern Virginia to Chickamauga in twelve days. But nothing could match the stunning transportation feat the Union accomplished after the battle of Chickamauga. To reinforce William S. Rosecrans, the railroads rushed 20,000 men from the Army of the Potomac in Virginia to the environs of Chattanooga, Tennessee, in eleven days. They arrived at the end of their 1,200-mile trip along with all their equipment, artillery, and animals.

The USMRR was an almost invisible presence in the North, but in the occupied South, it became a towering companion of, and assistant to, the Federal armies. Fed, clothed, and armed by rail, those armies could range far from supply depots. Under the leadership of the temperamental but talented Herman Haupt, the

U.S. Military Rail Road's engine No. 137, built in 1864 in the yards at Chattanooga, Tennessee (*National Archives*)

USMRR's Construction Corps achieved prodigious feats of bridge building and track laying, and Haupt's innovative techniques remained to continue the marvels even after he had left the service in late 1863. By the time Sherman was advancing on Atlanta in 1864, the Construction Corps' highly refined methods of operation inspired the observation that Yankees could repair railroads quicker than Rebels could tear them up. The Construction Corps could also destroy with equal effectiveness, having developed a way to make torn-up track useless by twisting and bending heated rails.

Just as railroads changed the way of war, so did the Civil War change the way of American railroading. By the close of the conflict, the same necessities that had led to the creation of hospital cars and rolling batteries had also revealed the advantages of cooperation between competing lines and partnerships with the government. The practices designed to cope with the daunting problems of running long-distance routes to deliver massive numbers of people and goods would facilitate the creation of a continental network of steel. Even during the war the Transcontinental Railroad, that generation's version of landing a man on the moon, was already under way, with track stretching out from both the east and the west. As the country emerged from its bitter struggle, the railroads that had helped give the Union victory would help shape the United States into a world power.

—*David S. Heidler and Jeanne T. Heidler*

See also Commissary; Haupt, Herman; Logistics; McCallum, Daniel Craig; Railroads, C.S.A.

For further reading:
Turner, George Edgar. *Victory Rode the Rails: The Strategic Place of the Railroads in the Civil War* (1953).
Weber, Thomas. *The Northern Railroads in the Civil War, 1861–1865* (1952).

RAINS, GABRIEL JAMES
(1803–1881)
Confederate general

Born in Craven County, North Carolina, to Gabriel M. Rains and Hester Ambrose Rains, Gabriel James Rains was educated locally before receiving an appointment to the U.S. Military Academy. He graduated thirteenth of thirty-eight in the class of 1827. Rains's younger brother, George Washington Rains, would follow him to West Point more than a decade later and would become one of the most important powder producers for the Confederacy.

Rains served in frontier posts until he was transferred to Florida during the Second Seminole War. He received a brevet promotion to major during that conflict. Rains also fought in the Mexican-American War and returned to Florida during a brief uprising of the Seminoles there in 1849. For the remainder of his U.S. Army career, Rains served on the frontier and on recruiting duty. However, during his spare time, he developed a strong interest in explosives and their characteristics. His avocation would become a consuming interest in the upcoming Civil War.

When Rains resigned from the U.S. Army on 31 July 1861, he had achieved the rank of lieutenant colonel. He entered Confederate service as a colonel but remained in that rank only briefly before being promoted to brigadier general. From the fall of 1861 until the spring of 1862, Rains commanded a brigade at Yorktown, Virginia, preparing the defenses of the York Peninsula and planting mines in the waters around Yorktown.

He continued in command of his brigade during the Peninsula campaign, while on the side planting land mines at the battle of Williamsburg. The use of these pressure-detonation devices during this campaign is reputedly the first use of such mechanisms in wartime. Their use at this time was highly controversial on both sides of the conflict, and for a time Rains was ordered to cease their use. He continued to command his brigade, however, and D. H. Hill credited him for directing a pivotal flanking maneuver during the battle of Seven Pines.

After Seven Pines, Rains was detached for service to the War Department, where he spent considerable time trying to convince President Jefferson Davis and the secretary of war of the usefulness and ethics of using land mines. Rains was ultimately successful.

In the meantime, Rains worked to strengthen the mine defenses of the James River and in the spring of 1863 performed the same duties for Joseph Johnston on the Mississippi. Shortly thereafter he traveled to Charleston, South Carolina, where he worked for over six months mining the water approaches to that city and selectively placing land mines in strategic locations. While he worked on his explosive devices, Rains also served briefly as the superintendent of the conscription bureau, after which he became the superintendent of the newly created Torpedo Bureau in June 1864.

Rains continued to manage the operations of the Torpedo Bureau, which handled land as well as water explosives, until the end of the war. He also continued to travel where he was needed. His last major assignment was mining the rivers of both Carolinas in the early months of 1865 to impede Union progress in those states.

After the war, Rains lived in Atlanta, Georgia, before moving to Charleston. He spent his last years primarily

Gabriel J. Rains (*Library of Congress*)

working as a clerk to the U.S. Army's Quartermaster Department. After retiring from this job, he died in Aiken, South Carolina.

—*David S. Heidler and Jeanne T. Heidler*

See also Ordnance, Naval; Torpedoes.
For further reading:
Waters, William Davis. "'Deception in the Art of War': Gabriel J. Rains, Torpedo Specialist of the Confederacy." *North Carolina Historical Review* (1989).

RAINS, GEORGE WASHINGTON
(1817–1898)
Confederate officer

George Washington Rains was born to Gabriel M. Rains and Hester Ambrose Rains in Craven County, North Carolina. His older brother was Confederate explosives expert Gabriel James Rains. Educated locally before accepting an appointment to the United States Military Academy, George Rains graduated third of fifty-six in the class of 1842. Commissioned in the engineer corps, Rains saw his first service in Boston and then Fort Monroe, before returning to West Point as an instructor. In 1846 he joined many of his fellow offi-

cers in Mexico during the Mexican-American War. He saw most of his action during Winfield Scott's Mexico City campaign. He received two brevets for his exploits during that campaign. Following the war he served in New Orleans, along the Mississippi coast, and in Florida.

Rains resigned his commission in 1856, bought a portion of the Washington Iron Works and Highland Iron Works in Newburgh, New York, and became president of the companies. He remained in that position until the secession of North Carolina, when he resigned and returned to the South. Offering his military services to the Confederacy, he became a major of artillery in July 1861.

Rains was attached to the Ordnance Bureau and his first major assignment became his primary duty during the war: producing gunpowder for the Confederacy. After traveling through the South looking for the best place to ship in raw materials and establish a factory, Rains determined that Augusta, Georgia, was the most convenient location. Situating his factory at what had been an old federal arsenal, Rains established one of the Confederacy's most reliable sources of gunpowder.

By April 1862 the Augusta complex was also the site of other important Confederate munitions manufacturing. Rains served as the overall commander of these operations and for his efforts was promoted to lieutenant colonel in May 1862, and colonel in July 1863. His Augusta works produced almost three million pounds of gunpowder, along with small arms, artillery, and ammunition.

In response to rumors of Federal plans to destroy the complex, Rains was told to obstruct the Savannah River in February 1862. Yet it was not until William T. Sherman's invasion of Georgia in the spring of 1864 that the danger to Augusta materially increased. Although the summer of 1864 saw dozens of alarms about Federal cavalry raids bearing down on the manufacturing center, no such raid occurred. Finally, Sherman's occupation of Savannah, Georgia, at the end of 1864 caused P. G. T. Beauregard to order Rains to evacuate whatever he could and destroy the rest on 8 February 1865.

After the evacuation, Rains remained in Augusta. After the war, he settled there and became a professor of chemistry at the Georgia Medical College. While working in this capacity, Rains studied medicine and received an M.D. degree. He also for a time served as dean of the school. He retired from the faculty in 1894 and moved back to Newburgh, New York. Rains wrote extensively during the postwar years, most notably producing a history of Confederate powder manufacturing. He died in Newburgh on 21 March 1898.

—*David S. Heidler and Jeanne T. Heidler*

See also Artillery; Ordnance, Naval.

For further reading:

Milgram, Joseph B. *George Washington Rains: Gunpowermaker of the Confederacy* (1961).
Rains, George Washington. *History of the Confederate States Powder Works* (1882).

RAMSEUR, STEPHEN DODSON
(1837–1864)
Confederate general

Born to Jacob A. Ramseur and Lucy Wilfong Ramseur in Lincolnton, North Carolina, Stephen Dodson Ramseur was educated locally and at Davidson College before accepting an appointment to the U.S. Military Academy. He graduated fourteenth of forty-one in the class of 1860 and was commissioned into the 3d Artillery. He served in Virginia and Washington, D.C., before resigning his commission in April 1861, before the secession of North Carolina.

After his resignation, Ramseur traveled to Montgomery, Alabama, to offer his services to the Confederate army. He accepted a lieutenant's commission, but before he could report to his new unit, he was also offered a position as a lieutenant in a North Carolina artillery unit. He transferred to that unit and traveled to North Carolina.

Within a short time he was promoted to captain of his own battery, and in the spring of 1862, at the commencement of the Peninsula campaign, he led his men to Yorktown, where they became a part of John B. Magruder's defensive force. Shortly after Ramseur's arrival, he was promoted to major, and then in April he became the colonel of the 49th North Carolina Infantry as part of the brigade of fellow North Carolinian brigadier general Robert Ransom, Jr.

Ramseur led the 49th at the Seven Days and gained plaudits from Ransom for bravery. In the last battle of the campaign at Malvern Hill, Ramseur was severely wounded in the upper right arm and never regained full use of it.

Ramseur spent several months recovering from his wound. In the fall, General Robert E. Lee recommended that he be promoted to brigadier general, and he received his promotion on 1 November 1862. Ramseur subsequently commanded the 5th Brigade in Thomas J. "Stonewall" Jackson's corps at Fredericksburg. At Chancellorsville, his brigade in D. H. Hill's division participated in Jackson's sweeping move around Joseph Hooker's right flank and suffered more than 50 percent casualties during the attack. Ramseur was again wounded, this time in the leg by a shell fragment.

When Stonewall Jackson's death after Chancellorsville prompted Lee to reorganize the Army of Northern Virginia into three corps, Ramseur's brigade was placed in Robert E. Rodes's division of Richard Ewell's II Corps. As part of that corps Ramseur and his brigade headed north in June 1863 in Lee's second invasion of the North. At the battle of Gettysburg on the first day, Ramseur's brigade brought up the rear of Ewell's corps as it moved south into Gettysburg from Heidlersburg. Consequently, he did not see much action until late in the day when his brigade was ordered in against the Union right flank on Seminary Ridge. He successfully turned the Union right and drove the Federals through Gettysburg onto Cemetery Hill. For the remaining two days of the battle Ramseur remained roughly in the same location and participated in subsequent attacks from there.

That fall Ramseur's brigade fought at Bristoe Station and Mine Run. In February 1864, the Confederate Congress extended the thanks of a grateful nation to Ramseur and his brigade for their exploits during the previous year and a half.

Ramseur commanded his brigade in the Virginia campaign of May–June 1864. At Spotsylvania he led a counter charge at the Bloody Angle that some credited with saving the battle for the Confederacy. In that attack he had three horses shot from under him and suffered another wound to his right arm. His crucial action in the campaign earned him promotion to major general on 1 June 1864.

Ramseur took command of Robert Rodes's division in Jubal Early's invasion of Maryland and raid on Washington during the summer of 1864 and then in Early's Valley campaign. At the battle of Cedar Creek on 19 October 1864, while trying to rally his men to defend the Confederate position, Ramseur was shot in the chest. Carried from the field and placed in an ambulance as part of the general Confederate retreat, Ramseur fell into Union hands when his ambulance stopped before a destroyed bridge. He was carried to General Philip Sheridan's headquarters, where he was given the best medical care the Union army could provide. The physicians, however, could do little but ease his pain. During the night a series of Union officers who had known Ramseur at West Point came to pay their respects to the dying Confederate. On the morning of 20 October 1864, two days before his first wedding anniversary and just a few days after learning that his young wife had given birth to a daughter, Ramseur died.

The Confederacy greatly mourned Stephen Dodson Ramseur. Many saw him as a rising star in the Confederate Army, and some even compared him to Stonewall Jackson. "No truer or nobler spirit," Brigadier General Bryan Grimes bitterly remarked, "has been sacrificed in this unjust and unholy war."

—*David S. Heidler and Jeanne T. Heidler*

See also Cedar Creek, Battle of; Gettysburg, Battle of; Malvern Hill, Battle of; Spotsylvania Court House.

For further reading:
Gallagher, Gary W. *Stephen Dodson Ramseur, Lee's Gallant General* (1985).

RANDOLPH, GEORGE WYTHE
(1818–1867)
Confederate secretary of war and general

Born at Monticello, the grandson of Thomas Jefferson and son of Thomas Mann Randolph, governor of Virginia, and Martha Jefferson Randolph, George Wythe Randolph was educated at home and in Boston before accepting an appointment as a midshipman in the U.S. Navy. He served for six years before entering the University of Virginia. After two years' study there, he read law and became a practicing attorney in Richmond, Virginia.

Randolph became a prominent Richmond lawyer, and though he had many friends and acquaintances involved in Virginia politics, he took no active role in public life before the Civil War. The John Brown raid in the fall of 1859 so distressed him, however, that Randolph organized an artillery unit known as the Richmond Howitzers.

The election of Abraham Lincoln to the presidency in the fall of 1860 compelled Randolph to support secession. He was elected to Virginia's secession convention in early 1861. Perhaps in spite of rather than because of his disunionist views, he was one of Virginia's emissaries to Abraham Lincoln in April 1861. As a member of the convention, Randolph also worked to improve the military readiness of the state and was the primary author of what would become Virginia's conscription law.

Upon Virginia's secession following the firing on Fort Sumter, Randolph offered the Howitzers' services to the state with him at their head. He was commissioned a major of the state army and was placed under John Bankhead Magruder. When Magruder organized the Army of the Peninsula on the York peninsula, Randolph was promoted to colonel and became Magruder's chief of artillery. Magruder commended Randolph for his actions at Big Bethel in June 1861.

In the fall of 1861 Randolph went on sick leave, showing the early signs of the tuberculosis that would eventually kill him. By November, however, he felt sufficiently recovered to serve in the Virginia Constitutional Convention.

He returned to his military duties by the first of the year, commanding at Suffolk, Virginia, at the rank of brigadier general. Randolph did not enjoy his new command long, however. Jefferson Davis soon appointed him secretary of war on 17 March 1862, and he took office several days later.

Randolph assumed his new job at the beginning of Union general George McClellan's Peninsula campaign. From his months in the army, Randolph was intimately familiar with the terrain, strengths, and weaknesses of the Confederate defensive position on the York Peninsula. He worked closely with Davis, Robert E. Lee, and the Confederate commander on the peninsula, Joseph E. Johnston.

While dealing with the crisis on the peninsula, Randolph also set about to reform the operation of the Confederate War Department, particularly to improve procurement of supplies such as gunpowder, to regularize the department's staff, and to provide the Confederate

army with a steady supply of new soldiers. In dealing with this last need, Randolph had the experience of drafting Virginia's statute of conscription and was primarily responsible for what would become the Confederacy's first conscription law.

After the Peninsula campaign, Randolph continued to work toward greater efficiency in the army while dealing with an army of office seekers. Many of these patronage seekers were distant relatives or friends of friends. Randolph's regular office hours were often consumed by such people, so he had to work late hours tending to the obligations of his job.

His temperament tended to expand those obligations as well. Randolph believed that the secretary should be more than a clerk. He broadly surveyed Confederate strength and weakness to enhance the one and diminish the other. Concluding that his predecessors had sorely neglected the West, he resolved to give that area of the Confederacy more attention. One of his fondest wishes was to mount a campaign to retake New Orleans, an essential port that had fallen during the early days of his secretaryship. It was precisely Randolph's interest in the West, however, that conflicted with Jefferson Davis's strategic emphasis for the war. Davis's insistence that all appointments and decisions be approved by him also irritated Randolph's independent nature. As stress began to erode Randolph's already fragile health, he resigned in November 1862. Despite his short tenure in office, Randolph was hailed as one of the most important and beneficial leaders of the Confederate War Department.

Randolph believed that a brief rest would allow him to return to a field command, but his health only worsened. Even his attempt return to his law practice faltered. By the fall of 1864, he took the advice of physicians and traveled to Great Britain to consult lung specialists. They advised him go to the south of France. For the next two years, Randolph divided his time between France, England, and Ireland while informally acting as a Confederate purchasing agent. After the war, he took the loyalty oath and sought entrance back into the United States. He was allowed to return because of his shattered health. He died at his home, Edgehill, on 3 April 1867.

—*David S. Heidler and Jeanne T. Heidler*

See also Big Bethel, Battle of; Magruder, John Bankhead; Peninsula Campaign; Virginia.
For further reading:
Jones, Archer. "Some Aspects of George Wythe Randolph's Service as Confederate Secretary of War." *Journal of Southern History* (1960).
Shackelford, George Green. *George Wythe Randolph and the Confederate Elite* (1988).

RANSOM, MATT WHITAKER
(1826–1904)
Confederate general

The son of Robert Ransom and Priscilla West Coffield Whitaker Ransom, Matt Ransom was born in Warren County, North Carolina. He was educated locally and at the University of North Carolina, where he studied law. Upon graduation, he practiced law for several years before turning to planting and participation in Whig politics. Upon the demise of the Whig Party in North Carolina in the mid-1850s, Ransom became a Democrat. In the late 1850s, he served in the state legislature, where he advocated a moderate position regarding the sectional crisis. When Abraham Lincoln was elected, Ransom opposed North Carolina's secession, and when the Confederacy was formed in February 1861, the North Carolina state legislature sent Ransom and two other members to meet with that government in Montgomery.

It was President Abraham Lincoln's call for volunteers on 15 April 1861 that changed Ransom's mind about secession. He resigned from the North Carolina legislature and joined the Confederate army as a private. Soon he became the lieutenant colonel of the 1st North Carolina, a regiment in the brigade of his brother Brigadier General Robert Ransom. He saw action during the Peninsula campaign and received a wound at Malvern Hill that removed him from service until late summer 1862. His actions on the peninsula earned him promotion to colonel of the 35th North Carolina.

Ransom led his regiment at the battle of Antietam in September 1862 and at Fredericksburg in December. In early 1863, the entire brigade, including the 35th, was sent to North Carolina to guard the railroad approaches into Virginia. During that summer, Ransom was promoted to brigadier general and succeeded to the command of his brother's brigade when Robert Ransom took command of the Department of Richmond.

During the Gettysburg campaign, Ransom continued to protect the southern approaches to Richmond, particularly the Weldon Railroad, while the Army of Northern Virginia moved north. He repulsed a Union raid on the railroad on 28 July 1863. Over the next year, Ransom commanded his brigade in northern North Carolina and southern Virginia. When Ulysses S. Grant threatened Richmond in the spring of 1864, Ransom took his brigade north, where he fought and was wounded at Drewry's Bluff in May 1864.

Ransom continued to command his brigade during the siege of Petersburg. He fought at the Crater and at Five Forks, and then he led his brigade out of the entrenchments of Petersburg to the surrender at Appomattox.

After the war, Ransom returned to his plantation. He reentered state politics in 1870 because he disagreed with

Governor William Woods Holden's policies. From 1873 until 1895 he served in the U.S. Senate and then spent two years as U.S. minister to Mexico. He retired from public life after his stint in Mexico City and died in Northampton County, North Carolina.

—*David S. Heidler and Jeanne T. Heidler*

See also North Carolina; Petersburg Campaign.

For further reading:

Marlow, Clayton Charles. *Matt W. Ransom, Confederate General from North Carolina* (1996).

RANSOM, ROBERT, JR.
(1828–1892)
Confederate general

Born in Warren County, North Carolina, the son of Robert Ransom and Priscilla West Coffield Whitaker Ransom, and the older brother of fellow Confederate general Matt Whitaker Ransom, Robert Ransom, Jr., was educated locally before accepting an appointment to the U.S. Military Academy. He graduated eighteenth of forty-four in the class of 1850. Ransom was commissioned a dragoon and after training at Carlisle, Pennsylvania, served at several frontier posts before returning to West Point as an instructor. After his tour of duty at the academy, he returned to the frontier, where he served in Kansas during the upheaval there. He had achieved the rank of captain by the outbreak of the Civil War. Upon the secession of North Carolina, he resigned his commission and accepted a captain's commission in the Confederate cavalry.

By the fall of 1861, Ransom had been made the colonel and commander of the 1st North Carolina Cavalry stationed at Vienna, Virginia. The following March he was promoted to brigadier general and was sent to Goldsboro, North Carolina. On 13 April 1862 he led his brigade of North Carolinians (including his brother Matt's 35th North Carolina) in a skirmish against Federal coastal raiders at Gillett's farm. Shortly thereafter, he was ordered to bring his brigade to the York Peninsula to aid in the defense of Richmond. The brigade became part of Benjamin Huger's division and fought ably in the Seven Days.

During the Maryland invasion of late summer 1862, Ransom commanded his brigade at Antietam. The brigade was at first on the Confederate right but was shifted to the left when the first Union attack came there. Ransom commanded a division at Fredericksburg and then was sent to North Carolina, where in the spring of 1863 he fought at the siege of Washington, North Carolina. He was promoted to major general in May 1863.

Through the spring and early summer of 1863, Ransom commanded the area south of Richmond, guarding the railroad approaches to the Confederate capital. Illness forced him to take a leave of absence in July 1863, but he returned to duty in time to accompany James Longstreet to Tennessee and Georgia in the late summer of 1863. He commanded Longstreet's cavalry in the Chickamauga and Knoxville campaigns. He returned to Virginia in April 1864 to take command of the city's defenses in opposition to the threat posed by Benjamin Butler on the York peninsula. He commanded the Department of Richmond until June 1864, when he was sent with Jubal Early on his Maryland and Washington raid. Ill health forced him to relinquish his command in August 1864. Upon his recovery in November 1864 he was sent to command Charleston, South Carolina.

After the war Ransom returned to North Carolina, where he farmed for a while and tried various other jobs before becoming a civil engineer in New Bern, North Carolina. He died in New Bern.

—*David S. Heidler and Jeanne T. Heidler*

See also Butler, Benjamin Franklin; Ransom, Matt Whitaker; Richmond, Virginia.

For further reading:

Marlow, Clayton Charles. *Matt W. Ransom, Confederate General from North Carolina* (1996).

RANSOM, THOMAS EDWARD GREENFIELD
(1834–1864)
Union general

Born in Norwich, Vermont, to Truman Bishop Ransom, president of Norwich University, and Margaret Morrison Greenfield Ransom, Thomas Ransom was educated at Norwich, a military school, and trained as an engineer. His father volunteered for service in the Mexican-American War and was serving as the colonel of the 9th Infantry when he was killed at Chapultepec.

As a young man Thomas Ransom moved to Illinois, where he worked as an engineer. At the outbreak of the Civil War he was living in Fayette County. He volunteered for service and became a major in the 11th Illinois Infantry. He saw his first action 22–23 June 1861 in an expedition from Cairo, Illinois, to Little River, Missouri. In July, he was made lieutenant colonel of the regiment and on 19 August saw further action when the regiment attacked a Confederate position at Charleston, Missouri. Ransom received his first of many wounds during that engagement.

Ransom and the 11th were at the fall of Fort Henry and then participated in the siege of Fort Donelson. At the latter engagement, on 15 February 1862, Ransom was severely wounded while fighting his way out of a potentially disastrous situation. As it was, the regiment suffered almost 50 percent casualties. Ransom was promoted to colonel for his actions that day and led the

regiment at the battle of Shiloh almost two months later, where he was again wounded.

In June 1862, Ransom joined the staff of Major General John McClernand, serving as chief of staff and inspector general of reserves during the siege of Corinth. In the fall he was placed in command of the Union position at Paducah, Kentucky. On 15 April 1863, Ransom was promoted to brigadier general of volunteers with date of rank at 29 November 1862. He commanded a brigade in the siege of Vicksburg, where he distinguished himself and gained the praise of Ulysses S. Grant.

After the fall of Vicksburg, Ransom went on 13 July 1863 to occupy Natchez, Mississippi. He did so without a fight, capturing approximately twenty Confederate soldiers and disarming the civilian population. He remained in command at Natchez through August. During that time he conducted raids into the interior searching for supplies useful to the Federal army. On 30 July 1863 he repulsed a Confederate attempt to retake the town.

In the fall of 1863, Ransom took his brigade to participate in an expedition against the coast of Texas. Operating in Aransas Pass and Matagorda Bay, he remained along that coast until the late winter of 1864, when he was ordered to join Nathaniel P. Banks's Red River campaign. At Sabine Crossroads in April 1864, Ransom suffered a wound to his knee that was serious enough to require an extended medical leave of absence.

When Ransom returned to duty in early August 1864, he reported to William T. Sherman outside Atlanta. Given command of the left wing of XVI Corps, Ransom assumed command of the corps on 19 August when its commander, Major General Grenville M. Dodge, was wounded. Ransom commanded XVI Corps at Jonesboro. After the fall of Atlanta, he was given command of XVII Corps and participated in the pursuit of John Bell Hood through north Georgia. By now quite ill, he was following his corps into Alabama in an ambulance when the cumulative effect of his many wounds forced him to relinquish command. His fever-racked body was en route to Rome, Georgia, when he died on 29 October 1864, one month short of his thirtieth birthday. In September 1864, Sherman had recommended Ransom for promotion to major general of volunteers, but that recommendation had not been acted upon at the time of Ransom's death. As a comrade remarked, "He was an officer of fine promise, universally loved and admired for his amiable disposition and his noble, gallant, and indomitable spirit."

—*David S. Heidler and Jeanne T. Heidler*

See also Fort Donelson, Battle of; Jonesboro, Battle of; Red River Campaign; Shiloh, Battle of.
For further reading:
Proceedings of the First Reunion of the Eleventh Regiment Illinois Volunteer Infantry Held at Ottawa, Ill., Oct. 27, 1875 (1875).

RAPPAHANNOCK STATION, BATTLE OF
(7 November 1863)

After failing to defeat Major General George G. Meade's Union Army of the Potomac during the October 1863 Bristoe campaign, General Robert E. Lee withdrew his Confederate Army of Northern Virginia to positions south of the Rappahannock River, destroying the Orange & Alexandria Railroad as he retreated. Crossing the river on 18 October, Lee quickly established a fortified bridgehead consisting of two redoubts and connecting rifle pits along the stream's north bank near the railroad's ruined bridge at Rappahannock Station. There and at Kelly's Ford, located some five miles downstream, Lee awaited Meade's next move.

The Army of the Potomac soon repaired its damaged supply artery, and Meade, facing considerable pressure from his superiors in Washington, on 7 November determined to attack his foe. He divided his force into two wings. Major General William H. French would force passage of the river at Kelly's Ford with the I, II, and III Corps, while Major General John Sedgwick, leading the V and VI Corps, concentrated on Rappahannock Station. Screening the advance were elements of David M. Gregg's cavalry division.

Defending at the ford and station was Confederate infantry under the command of Major Generals Robert E. Rodes and Jubal A. Early. Kelly's Ford was, in fact, but lightly protected. Lee determined that the steep bluffs along the river's bank precluded an effective defense at that point. Therefore, he would allow French's force to advance from the crossing before himself attacking, all the while keeping Sedgwick's column at bay at Rappahannock Station. If Lee's plan proved successful, Meade's army, its numerical advantage negated, could be beaten in detail.

French engaged Rodes at the ford just after noon on 7 November. Elements of Major General David B. Birney's III Corps division overwhelmed the two North Carolina regiments guarding the ford's meager defensive works. More than 300 rebel prisoners were taken in the brief fight. French had performed his task much to Meade's satisfaction, incurring only thirty-three casualties.

Meanwhile, at Rappahannock Station, Sedgwick's right wing advanced cautiously toward the Confederate bridgehead. Its defenders, Brigadier General Harry T. Hays's vaunted brigade of "Louisiana Tigers" soon were hard pressed, and Early called for reinforcements. Lee, however, convinced that Sedgwick's effort was merely a well-orchestrated feint, limited support to one brigade under the leadership of Colonel Archibald C. Godwin. By late afternoon, 2,000 Confederate soldiers were employed in the redoubts and rifle pits.

The Confederate chieftain's decision proved costly.

Burning of the Orange & Alexandria Railroad bridge over the Rappahannock River, 13 October 1863, sketched by Alfred R. Waud (*Library of Congress*)

Sedgwick worked his way around both rebel flanks and poured effective artillery and small arms fire into the redoubts. With daylight fading fast and Meade expecting results, "Uncle John" and his officers soon decided upon a bold stroke: a nighttime bayonet assault to carry the works. The VI Corps division of Brigadier General David A. Russell was chosen to make the attack.

Like their commanding general, the Confederates inside the parapet were convinced that further action that day was unlikely. Suddenly, out of the shadows, stormed Russell's lead regiment, the 6th Maine. Many rebels, bewildered by the attack's unexpectedness, broke and ran toward a nearby pontoon bridge leading to the river's south bank. Enough rallied, however, to engage the impetuous 6th in desperate, hand-to-hand combat.

The 6th Maine soon needed help. It came in the form of the 5th Wisconsin, whose arrival balanced the odds within the brimming parapet. Undaunted, Hays's Tigers counterattacked. Finally, more of Russell's Federals advanced, clearing the redoubts and nearly capturing Hays. With the Tigers effectively out of the fight, Russell now focused on Godwin. The result was the same; Colonel Emory Upton's onrushing brigade overran the beleaguered Confederate defenders after a fierce firefight. In all, the exultant Union troops captured more than 1,600 prisoners, including Godwin, along with

numerous regimental colors and four field pieces. For Meade, the day had been a brilliant success. The combined actions at Kelly's Ford and Rappahannock Station resulted in nearly 2,000 Confederate casualties, at the cost of some 400 Federal soldiers.

Generals Lee and Early learned too late of the disaster at the bridgehead. A strong south wind muffled the sounds of battle, preventing Confederate high command from appreciating the contest's severity. Lee, realizing that his advantage was now lost, sullenly retreated toward Culpeper Court House later that evening. Meade slowly followed, hoping that his foe would offer battle on the ridges north of Culpeper. Lee did not oblige. The Army of Northern Virginia withdrew south across the Rapidan River on the night of 10 November. Nearly three weeks hence, Meade would again attempt to bring on general engagement with Lee, resulting in the abortive Mine Run campaign.

—*Christopher S. Stowe*

See also Mine Run Campaign.
For further reading:
Daggett, A. S. "The Battle of Rappahannock Station, Va." In *War Papers, Read before the Commandery of the State of Maine, Military Order of the Loyal Legion of the United States* (1898–1915).
Graham, Martin F., and George F. Skoch. *Mine Run: A Campaign of Lost Opportunities, October 21, 1863–May 1, 1864* (1987).

The battle of Rappahannock Station (*Library of Congress*)

McMahon, Martin T. "From Gettysburg to the Coming of Grant." In *Battles and Leaders of the Civil War* (1887–1888).
Wert, Jeffry D. "Rappahannock Station." *Civil War Times Illustrated* (1976).

RATIONS, C.S.A.

It is one of the great ironies of the American Civil War that, while the Old South took pride in its rich agrarian culture, the Confederate states failed efficiently to feed the army that was sent forth in its defense. The memoirs and recollections of thousands of Confederate veterans clearly indicate that hunger remained the ubiquitous companion of soldiers throughout the war. The meager rations consumed by Southern fighting men served to weaken their effectiveness and quite likely contributed to the demise of the Confederacy.

The task of supplying the Confederate army with food became the responsibility of the Commissary Bureau on 26 February 1861. The bureau quickly established guidelines for the daily ration based on previously existing U.S. Army standards. Initially, a day's supply of food included three-fourths of a pound of bacon or one and one-fourth pounds of fresh or salted beef, eighteen ounces of bread or flour, or one and a quarter pounds of corn meal, or twelve ounces of hard bread, if available. As a supplement to this, soldiers were to be given beans, peas, coffee, tallow, sugar, and salt. Unfortunately for the common soldier, the Commissary Bureau proved most ineffective at consistently providing these items in either quantity or quality. Problems associated with transportation, inflation, the steadily advancing Union army, the large number of farmers and slaves no longer on the farm, and generally inefficient administration all combined to undermine the mission of this Confederate agency.

Despite the shortcomings of the Confederate government, its soldiers still managed to consume a diet that generally remained Spartan in nature. While in camp soldiers ate various combinations of corn meal, beef, bacon, potatoes, occasionally rice, and vegetables in season. A popular dish known as "sloosh" consisted of corn meal immersed in bacon grease, then coiled around a ramrod and baked over the campfire. Southerners employed similar creativeness to find a substitute for coffee, which became scarce early in the war. Men brewed a variety of concoctions containing acorns, rye, potatoes, and chicory (a perennial weedy plant whose root can be roasted and ground into a mixture used as a coffee substitute), all in a vain effort to capture the familiar flavor they craved.

Early in the war some soldiers received boxes of food from home as a supplement to military fare. Items such as hams, pickles, cakes, and a variety of breads certainly eased the hunger of the fortunate recipient. However, as the war continued, such parcels became less frequent as civilians succumbed to harsh food shortages as well.

When marching or during periods of combat, soldiers often ate less than they did in camp. Typically they consumed little more than cornbread and water. One Tennessee private, recalling his regiment's intense hunger on the march, remembered that when a stray heifer emerged from the woods, it was quickly butchered and distributed to his unit. Some men actually consumed their portions raw, as there was no time to stop and build a fire.

The longer the war continued the more difficult it became for the South's fighting men to acquire enough food to sustain themselves. Like their Northern counter-parts, Confederate soldiers often relied on foraging from the local countryside to supplement their diminishing diets. This practice basically consisted of hungry men helping themselves to any edible item within walking distance. Soldiers gathered everything from fresh corn to ripe fruit and occasionally resorted to elaborate measures to steal livestock from local farms. The cumulative effect of four years of foraging created a tremendous burden on farming families who lived in areas containing a high concentration of soldiers.

During the war's final year, the lack of adequate rations strained the dwindling Confederate forces to the breaking point. By the summer of 1864, General Lee's army received a quarter-pound of meat and a few crackers as their entire day's allotment. Increasingly, Southern soldiers everywhere consumed a day's worth of food in one sitting. Without sufficient food, while also suffering from a variety of privations, a steady number of soldiers daily slipped away from the Confederate army until it no longer composed a viable fighting force.

The generally inadequate rations of the Confederate soldier certainly affected his ability to fight, and thus it also had an impact on the war in general. Scholars

A log hut company kitchen, 1864 (*National Archives*)

An African-American army cook at work, City Point, Virginia, ca. 1864–1865 (*Library of Congress*)

continue to debate the significance of this factor, and some even contend that the scarcity of food was a major component of the South's defeat.

—*Gary T. Edwards*

See also Commissary; Logistics; Northrop, Lucius Bellinger; Rations, U.S.A.
For further reading:
Gates, Paul W. *Agriculture and the Civil War* (1965).
Goff, Richard D. *Confederate Supply* (1969).
Robertson, James I., Jr. *Soldiers Blue and Gray* (1988).
Watkins, Sam R. *Co. Aytch: A Side Show of the Big Show* (1882; reprint, 1997).
Wiley, Bell I. *The Life of Johnny Reb: The Common Soldier of the Confederacy* (1943; reprint, 1993).

RATIONS, U.S.A.

One of the truest adages is that an army marches on its stomach, with the most powerful army vulnerable to defeat if its soldiers cannot be fed.

Fortunately for the Union, its superior production and logistic capability more often than not provided its military forces with nutritious, if not varied, sustenance.

Food for the Union army was issued by the army's Commissary Bureau. In 1861, the standard ration consisted of twenty-two ounces of bread (usually in biscuit form known as hardtack) issued daily, either twelve ounces of pork or sixteen ounces of salted beef daily, and eight quarts of beans (replaceable by two hundred fifty ounces of desiccated vegetables), ten pounds of coffee, fifteen pounds of sugar, and four quarts of vinegar twice a week. Fresh meat was generally available only when in camp, and soldiers had to suffice with the canned salted variety. Also, hardtack stored in wooden boxes became infested with insects, forcing soldiers to boil their biscuits in coffee to render them edible. The regular supply of rations became problematic when armies went into the field, as fast-moving armies outstripped commissary wagons and

Noncommissioned officers' mess of Company D, 93d New York Infantry, Bealeton, Virginia, August 1863
(Photograph by Timothy O'Sullivan / *Library of Congress*)

railroad supply lines. On the march, soldiers would receive "iron rations": hardtack, a few ounces of bacon, salt, and all the coffee the soldier could carry. If supplying the army became difficult, only hardtack and coffee, the core of the soldier's diet, would be issued.

Army rations were also supplemented by food packages from home, gifts from the Sanitary Commission, or foraging in the countryside, although large armies would strip the countryside bare. Living off the countryside eventually became a common military practice as a means of destroying Confederate military resources. The best-known example was General William T. Sherman's March to the Sea, led by "bummers," men whose lax

discipline or proclivity for theft made them ideally suited for the acquisition of civilian foodstuffs.

Whatever the source, soldiers prepared their meals themselves. With little culinary skill before the war, most soldiers dined on basic but repetitive meals. Generally, squads of men prepared their meals together. Typical meals featured hardtack fried in the grease left from preparing bacon, basic bread fashioned from flour and water, or a thin soup made with desiccated vegetables. Because cooking implements could not be carried on the march, small frying pans or pots served as field kitchens. When implements were not available, soldiers fried their bacon with their bayonets or ramrods.

Union sailors enjoyed several advantages over their army counterparts. First was a more varied diet. The basic navy diet, proved by the Bureau of Provision and Clothing, amounted to one pound of salt pork, half a pint of peas or beans, half a pound of flour, a quarter pound of dried fruit (to ward off scurvy), half a pound of rice, two ounces of butter, two ounces of cheese, fourteen ounces of hardtack, a quarter ounce of tea, with half a pound of pickles, half a pint of molasses, and half a pint of vinegar issued weekly. Foraging also bolstered the navy diet. Whereas army foraging would soon deplete a region, fish from the oceans and rivers could be had in countless numbers. The navy also benefited from a more reliable logistic system. Along with sizable stores of food aboard the warships themselves, the navy maintained a large force of supply ships to replenish vessels at sea. An extensive system of supply bases encircling the Confederacy meant that navy ships were never more than a few days away from a supply base. Lastly, sailors were granted a spirit ration in the early months of the war. In old navy tradition, sailors received a gill (a quarter pint) of whiskey every day until the practice ended in September 1862. The liquor ban purported to improve discipline, although in practice the ban had no real effect. Quite the opposite, disciplinary crimes related to liquor increased as sailors smuggled alcohol aboard ship or maximized their consumption on shore leave.

—Steven J. Ramold

See also Rations, C.S.A.
For further reading:
Browning, Robert M. *From Cape Charles to Cape Fear: The North Atlantic Blockading Squadron during the Civil War* (1993).
Lord, Francis A. *They Fought for the Union* (1960).
Symonds, Henry C. *Report of a Commissary of Subsistence, 1861–1865* (1888).
Wiley, Bell I. *The Life of Billy Yank: The Common Soldier of the Union* (1952; reprint, 1993).

RAWLINS, JOHN AARON
(1831–1869)
Union general

John Rawlins was born on 13 February 1831 in Galena, Illinois, though his family had originated in Virginia and had moved to Illinois by way of Kentucky in the late 1820s. In 1849 Rawlins's father succumbed to gold rush fever and left his son as the family's sole provider. Rawlins would have a lifelong dislike of alcohol due, in part, to his father's excessive drinking, which he believed was somewhat responsible for the way that he abandoned his family. Although he received only a minimal education in early life, Rawlins studied in a local law office and was admitted to the Illinois bar in 1854. Rawlins practiced law in Galena and became the city attorney in 1857. A staunch Douglas Democrat, he became a candidate for the position of presidential elector during the 1860 presidential election.

With the outbreak of war, Rawlins vehemently supported the defense of the Union. His passion caught the attention of a fellow Galena resident, Captain Ulysses S. Grant. Upon learning of his appointment as a brigadier general of volunteers in August 1861, Grant asked Rawlins to become his aide-de-camp and on 30 August 1861 Rawlins was commissioned a captain and became the assistant adjutant general on Grant's staff. He became Grant's principal staff officer and most intimate and influential advisor. From then until his death, Rawlins would serve as Grant's friend, military and political advisor, sometime editor, and—it was said—his guard against excessive drinking. Of his friend, Grant would say that he came closer than any other officer did to being truly indispensable.

Rawlins's formal duties throughout the Civil War were to serve as Grant's adjutant general. When Grant was promoted, so was Rawlins. Rawlins was promoted to major on 14 May 1862, lieutenant colonel on 1 November 1862, and brigadier general of volunteers on 11 August 1863. On 3 March 1865 he was promoted to brigadier general in the regular army and given the newly created position of chief of staff to the general-in-chief. Interestingly, Rawlins's promotion was the last generalship awarded in the regular army during the Civil War. Brevetted major general of volunteers on 24 February 1865 for war service, Rawlins was also brevetted major general in the regular army on 9 April 1865 for the Appomattox campaign.

Rawlins's wife had died of tuberculosis in 1861, and it was that disease that he, himself, contracted during the last of year of the war. In 1867 he was sent out West with Major General Grenville M. Dodge to examine the proposed route of the Union Pacific Railroad in the hopes that the change in climate might improve his health. Unfortunately, the trip was unsuccessful in this respect. (The city of Rawlins, Wyoming, would eventually grow out of one of the campsites used by Rawlins on his trip.) In March 1869 the newly elected President Grant appointed Rawlins as the secretary of war, but neither of them knew that Rawlins now had less than six months to live. On 6 September 1869, in Washington, D.C., he succumbed to tuberculosis and was eventually buried at Arlington National Cemetery.

—Louis Bielakowski

See also Grant, Ulysses S.
For further reading:
Dana, Charles A. *Recollections of the Civil War* (1898).
Wilson, James H. *Life of John A. Rawlins: Lawyer, Assistant Adjutant General, Chief of Staff, Major General of Volunteers, and Secretary of War* (1916).

RAYMOND, BATTLE OF
(12 May 1863)

After the battle of Port Gibson on 30 April–1 May 1863, the commander of the Army of the Tennessee Ulysses S. Grant's next objective in his operations to capture Vicksburg was northeast toward Edwards Station, about sixteen miles east of Vicksburg. Grant's objective was to isolate the Confederate forces defending Vicksburg by severing the Vicksburg & Jackson Railroad around the vicinity of Edwards Station. The three corps comprising Grant's army (General John A. McClernand's XIII Corps, General William T. Sherman's XV Corps, and General James B. McPherson's XVII Corps) were moving on Edwards Station. McClernand's corps was on the left with the bank of the Big Black River protecting its left flank, Sherman's corps was in the center, and McPherson's corps was on the right, or eastern, flank, moving toward the crossroads town of Raymond, Mississippi.

Confederate brigadier general John Gregg received orders from General John C. Pemberton on 11 May to protect the southwest approach to Jackson. Gregg moved his understrength brigade along with a battery of artillery and other miscellaneous troops to Raymond. If the enemy presented him an opportunity, he was to engage detached troops along the flank of the Union army or, if he encountered overwhelming numbers, he was to retreat back into the defensive positions around Jackson.

Gregg knew that the target of the Federal army was Edwards Station. When he received a report of an unknown number of enemy troops approaching Raymond in the morning of 12 May, he believed that it might be a Union feint, attempting to draw off Confederate strength from the north, or a detached brigade either foraging or on a destroying mission. With either scenario, the confident Gregg believed that he faced only a limited number of Union troops. When he received a follow-up report estimating Federal strength at 2,500, this confirmed his notion. Around 9:00 A.M., Gregg had his brigade deployed along the north bank of the east- to west-flowing Fourteenmile Creek, about a mile and a half south of Raymond. Gregg, an aggressive officer, hoped to defeat this detachment of Union troops, while following this victory up with a reinforced attack on the rear of Grant's army.

The leading element of McPherson's XVII Corps, the 3d Brigade of John A. Logan's 3d Division arrived south of Fourteenmile Creek around 10:00 A.M. The terrain of the battlefield had a large impact on the subsequent engagement. The stream running through dense woods separated the opposing forces. The thick undergrowth made it difficult for the brigades to maintain cohesion; the regiments of each became separated and thus were unable to support one another. The topography also made it difficult for each side to correctly assess the enemy's numbers.

Around noon, Gregg attacked two of Logan's brigades (1st and 2d) that had deployed in the woods. Over the next three hours, the battle degenerated into a melee in which soldiers of both armies employed loaded guns at point-blank range along with bayonets and the wielding of clubs and fists. The badly deployed Union troops that Gregg encountered quickly became disorganized. The 23d Indiana, the only Union regiment to cross to the north bank of the creek, found itself under a withering fire from Gregg's advancing brigade. The attack broke the regiment, forcing it to recross Fourteenmile Creek and panic ensued. The subsequent rout began to negatively affect the 20th Ohio, which it passed heading toward the rear.

At this point, Logan's presence near the front helped to rally his men, halting the advance of the Confederate brigade. He eventually organized his 3d Division sufficiently enough to launch a counterattack. The rebels were now retreating, although the Union forces could not fully press their attack. At this point, Gregg became aware of the increasing number of Union troops and rightly ascertained that he faced more than a single brigade. He proceeded to pull his force back to Jackson, allowing McPherson's corps to cross Fourteenmile Creek and spend the night of the 12th in Raymond.

The casualties for this Union victory amounted to the following: the Confederates lost 72 killed, 252 wounded, and 190 missing; the Union suffered 66 killed, 339 wounded, and 37 missing. In this hotly contested battle, neither Logan nor Gregg knew the exact location of their regiments throughout the engagement.

The significance of the battle was that it altered Grant's strategy. The stubborn defense of Raymond by Gregg's forces indicated to Grant that a considerable Rebel force might be building in Jackson. Grant did not want to risk being caught between two sizable Confederate forces, Pemberton's forces to the west and the growing forces of General Joseph E. Johnston's army in Jackson. Instead of placing his army precariously in the middle, Grant decided to deal with each force in detail before they could unite or jointly attack Grant's army. Grant chose Jackson, the capital of Mississippi, as his next target.

—*James L. Isemann*

See also Jackson, Battle of; Vicksburg Campaign.
For further reading:
Arnold, James R. *Grant Wins the War: Decision at Vicksburg* (1997).
Miers, Earl Schenck. *The Web of Victory: Grant at Vicksburg* (1955; reprint 1983).
Welcher, Frank J. *The Western Theater.* Vol. 2 of *The Union Army, 1861–1865: Organization and Operations* (1993).

RAYMOND, HENRY JARVIS
(1820–1869)
Editor, politician

Henry J. Raymond, the editor and founder of the *New York Times*, born to Jarvis and Lavinia Raymond in Lima, New York, in 1820, was virtually a bellwether of the tumultuous time. The Missouri Compromise marked his birth, and the triumph of the Radical Republicans his death.

At age fifteen Raymond graduated from the Genesee Wesleyan Seminary in his hometown and in 1840 from the University of Vermont, where his tuition was paid by a lien on the family farm. Even before he left the university, he had embarked on his journalistic career, having contributed to the *New-Yorker*, a weekly published by Horace Greeley, his first employer and, in time, severest critic. Raymond's editorial talents were honed by Greeley, when the latter launched the *New York Tribune*. But clashes with Greeley, who considered Raymond a Tory, led Raymond to take a position with James W. Webb's *Morning Courier* and *New-York Enquirer*, a Wall Street paper, in 1843, and simultaneously to edit *Harper's Magazine*.

Still, the peripatetic Raymond found time to court and marry Juliette Weaver in 1844, and, although the two were later estranged, to father six children. In 1880, Henry, his second born would publish extracts from his father's journal in *Scribner's Monthly*.

In 1848, when he was just 28, Raymond wrote platform resolutions for and spoke on behalf of Whig presidential candidate Zachary Taylor. This action permanently linked him to powerful party stalwarts Thurlow Weed and former Governor William H. Seward, who thereafter was regarded as Raymond's patron. A year later, when he was not yet 30, Raymond was elected to New York's lower legislative house, the Assembly, and two years later he was elected its speaker.

His term over, insultingly fired by Webb, and in ill health because of his inveterate tendency to do two things at once, Raymond sailed to England. Aboard ship he developed a prospectus for what would become the *New York Times* and sent it to his friend George Jones, who had been Greeley's business manager when Raymond came to work for the *Tribune*.

The next year Raymond and Jones, with capitalization arranged by Edward B. Wesley, launched their paper. This offered Raymond a venue for his well-articulated views, which, because of their moderation and tolerance, caused many to distrust him. Nonetheless, he was elected New York's lieutenant governor in 1854, and by 1859, Raymond, then regarded as a Republican, had gained a national reputation. However, his support of Stephen Douglas for the Senate a year earlier, brought charges that he was drifting and disingenuous.

These charges were temporarily silenced by the urbane Raymond's active campaigning and unswerving support of Abraham Lincoln, which included writing a campaign biography of Lincoln. In 1862, as a member of the Union Party, he was returned to the New York State Assembly, where again he was elected speaker. Though he chaired the Union Party convention in Syracuse in 1862, his criticism of the radicals and support of compromise alienated party loyalists.

In 1864, when he was elected to Congress, Henry Raymond reached what biographer Francis Brown labeled the "pinnacle" of his political career. However, support of the moderate policies of Lincoln's successor, Andrew Johnson, led to clashes with congressional radicals. Raymond became, in his own words, so estranged "from the majority of the Union party" that he opted against renomination two years later.

The flame that had burned so brightly was prematurely extinguished on 18 June 1869, when the forty-nine-year-old Raymond died. Memorials poured in; some extremely critical. For example, James G. Bennett, Raymond's long-time rival at the *New York Herald*, charged Raymond with trying to serve two masters, journalism and politics, and with failing at both. However, Horace Greeley, Raymond's one-time employer and severest critic during his lifetime, was surprisingly laudatory. Though he acknowledged that Raymond was considered by many a "trimmer," trimming his sails to meet public opinion, he was misjudged. Rather, said Greeley, Raymond was "an admirable reporter, discerning critic, a skillful selector and compiler of the news, as well as an able and ready writer," and was simply "averse to rash or violent changes." Instead, he was what the English would call a "Liberal Conservative."

—*Wayne Mahood*

See also Bennett, James Gordon; Greeley, Horace; *New York Times*; Newspapers; Seward, William H.

For further reading:
Alexander, DeAlva S. *A Political History of the State of New York*, vol. 3 (1969).
Brown, Francis. *Raymond of the Times* (1950; reprint, 1970).
Maverick, Augustus. *Henry J. Raymond and the New York Press for Thirty Years: Progress of American Journalism From 1840–1870* (1870).
Raymond, Henry W. "Extracts From the Journal of Henry J. Raymond." *Scribner's Monthly* (1879–1880).

REAGAN, JOHN HENNINGER
(1818–1905)
Confederate postmaster general

The son of Timothy R. Reagan and Elizabeth Lusk Reagan, John Henninger Reagan was born in Sevier County, Tennessee. He was educated locally and tried several occupations, including a stint in the army of the Republic of Texas, before studying law. After practicing for a short time, he became a judge in the new state of Texas. He also became active in Texas politics. He served in the state legislature and in 1856 was elected to the U.S. House of Representatives.

Though not considered an extremist on sectional issues, Reagan was elected to the Texas Secession Convention and advocated the state's secession. He was next chosen to represent the state in the Provisional Confederate Congress. Upon his arrival in Montgomery, Alabama, to take his seat, he was appointed postmaster general of the Confederacy by President Jefferson Davis. Reagan would occupy the position throughout the Civil War.

Reagan demonstrated excellent administrative skills as postmaster general. The Confederacy's infamous transportation problems made timely delivery of mail an almost impossible goal, but Reagan did make the Confederate post office a self-supporting operation.

Yet the postal service was not Reagan's only concern during the war. Early in the conflict, he encouraged men of the U.S. Army in Texas to join Confederate service after their surrender to pro-Confederate sympathizers. Throughout the war, Reagan monitored Texas defenses not only against Federal forces but also against the Indians on the state's frontier. He was concerned, for instance, that Confederate demands on men and equipment would limit resources to defend against Indians in the western part of the state.

Nevertheless, Reagan proved one of Jefferson Davis's most stalwart defenders. In the last months of the war, he consulted with Davis frequently to make suggestions for the best way to appease the Union and gain a favorable peace. As the Confederacy disintegrated, he also assumed the position of secretary of the treasury. Finally, when Davis fled Richmond, Reagan accompanied the president and his family and was captured with them in Georgia.

Reagan's capture meant jail. He was held in Fort Warren in Boston until the fall of 1865. Returning to Texas, he tried farming for a while but soon reentered politics and became involved in Texas railroad promotion. In 1875 he was elected to the House of Representatives and served there until 1887 when he entered the U.S. Senate. He retired from public life in 1891. He died in Palestine, Texas.

—*David S. Heidler and Jeanne T. Heidler*

See also Davis, Jefferson; Texas.
For further reading:
Reagan, John H. *Memoirs with Special Reference Secession and the Civil War* (1906).

REAMS' STATION, VIRGINIA
(25 August 1864)

By late August 1864, Federal troops commanded by General Ulysses S. Grant had cut the Weldon Railroad approximately six miles south of the city of Petersburg, Virginia. Control of this railroad was vital to operations against both Petersburg and the Confederate capital at Richmond, twenty-five miles to the north, because it was the main supply artery connecting the two cities with the rest of the South. Grant quickly learned that cutting the rail line had brought only partial success. The Southerners simply halted trains on the Weldon line a day's ride south of Petersburg, then sent supplies overland by wagon to Richmond. On 23 August Grant ordered his troops to destroy the line as far as Hicksford, Virginia, forty miles south of Petersburg.

The task of destroying the Weldon Railroad fell upon the shoulders of the men in General Winfield Scott Hancock's II Corps. Less than a week earlier, these troops had participated in action against the Confederate defenses in front of Richmond. Now the Federal high command asked them to march to Globe Tavern about five miles south of Petersburg and begin destroying the railroad. By the evening of 24 August, the two divisions had destroyed eight miles of track. That night the troops set up camp at Reams' Station, among some uncompleted earthworks begun by Federal troops back in June. Exhausted, they made no effort to improve their defensive position.

While the Federal troops slept, General Robert E. Lee sent General A. P. Hill's corps and two cavalry divisions under General Wade Hampton to crush this latest Federal incursion against the railroad. Federal signalmen reported the movement to General George G. Meade, who promptly relayed a warning to Hancock. The next morning, Hancock sent out his cavalry (under General David M. Gregg) to look for the Confederates. When they found only a small body of enemy troops, he ordered the division of General John Gibbon to resume destruction of the railroad. Gibbon's men had just begun their work, when a Rebel attack drove the Union cavalrymen from their positions. Gregg's troopers managed to regain their lines with help from the infantry.

Hancock realized that this was no skirmish, but the beginning of a full-scale assault on his position. He recalled Gibbon's division to the earthworks around Reams' Station, where they took up a defensive position. Gibbon defended the southern half of the line, while the division of General Nelson A. Miles held the northern half of the line. The square-shaped (with the eastern end open) Federal earthworks were so small that bullets and artillery shells that passed harmlessly over one wall could easily hit troops along the opposite wall.

Around 5 P.M., A. P. Hill's artillery opened fire on the northern part of the Federal trenches. Although the barrage inflicted few casualties, it demoralized many of the green troops in Gibbon's division when shells fell among them. Some of the men even moved to the outside of their works to gain protection. Hill then advanced six brigades from the divisions of General

The battle of Reams' Station (*Library of Congress*)

Henry Heth and General Cadmus Wilcox against the portion of the Federal line held by Miles's troops. At first it appeared the line would hold, but the Southerners finally broke through. In the excitement, Heth tried to grab the flag of the 26th North Carolina regiment from its color-bearer and lead the fight himself. But the man refused to let go, so he and the general both carried it. The Confederates continued to advance despite galling artillery and infantry fire. Hancock tried to get the men of John Gibbon's division to plug the gap, but they were under attack by dismounted troopers from Hampton's cavalry. The Federal troops became completely disorganized and unnerved and abandoned their earthworks.

Hancock quickly polled his commanders to see if they could retake the position. Miles and Gregg expressed their desire to attack, but Gibbon felt his troops were not up to the task. Reluctantly, Hancock gave the order to retreat. As his men began to do so, reinforcements from General Orlando Willcox's IX Corps division came up to cover the movement.

The action at Reams' Station left a deep scar on the commander of the II Corps and his troops. Hancock lost over 2,700 men (including 2,150 prisoners), nine cannon, twelve regimental flags, and over 3,000 rifles. Finger-pointing after the battle destroyed the close working relationship between Hancock and Gibbon. By

October both men had left their positions with the II Corps, which was no longer the preeminent fighting unit in the Army of the Potomac. The operation at Reams' Station had failed to achieve all that Grant hoped, but it had destroyed eight more miles of the Weldon Railroad. This forced Lee to move his supply route even farther south, making it more difficult to supply his besieged army at Petersburg.

—David McGee

See also Gibbon, John; Globe Tavern, Virginia; Hampton, Wade; Hancock, Winfield Scott.
For further reading:
Davis, William C. *Death in the Trenches: Grant at Petersburg* (1986).
Horn, John. *The Destruction of the Weldon Railroad: Deep Bottom, Globe Tavern, and Reams Station* (1991).
———. *The Petersburg Campaign, June 1864–April 1865* (1993).
Trudeau, Noah Andre. *The Last Citadel: Petersburg, Virginia, June 1864–April 1865* (1991).

REBEL YELL

Originally heard at First Bull Run, the unique Confederate war cry, known as the Rebel yell, accompanied hundreds of Confederate charges throughout the Civil War. Probably not initially calculated to intimidate the enemy, the psychological effects of the yell on both friend and foe soon became apparent. Confederate officers discovered the bold exultation the yell imbued in their men, and the fear it often spread through Union ranks, and actively encouraged their troops to interject the yell in every charge. At Lovejoy's Station a Mississippi colonel urged his men, "Fire and charge with a yell." The historian Bell I. Wiley asserted that the yell became as important to the Confederate soldier as his musket. In 1864, when General Jubal Early ordered a charge near Richmond and his men answered that they were out of ammunition, he snapped back, "Damn it, holler them across." His men immediately charged with only a yell and bayonets.

The ululating howl may not have frightened all Union soldiers, but many recounted how the eerie screams affected them. The grey-and-butternut-clad Rebels seemed to elicit demons from hell when they advanced "yelling like fiends." One Federal infantryman recalled that hearing it "made the hair stand up on his head." Another Yankee remembered "that terrible scream and barbarous howling . . . loud enough to be heard a mile off."

Various sources ascribe the origins of the yell to sundry ethnic and cultural backgrounds. The yell seemed to be a mixture of certain Celtic calls, brought by immigrants from Scotland and Ireland and used to gather cattle, hogs, and hunting dogs, combined with pent up nervousness, hatred, exultation, and "a pinch of pure deviltry." Some veterans described the yell as a variation on the Southern fox hunter's exclamations. Adrenaline and the excitement of imminent personal combat obviously influenced the volume and timbre of the yell. Certainly, ferocious shouts are not unusual in warfare. Histories of massed battles of the Greeks and Romans, as well as the Civil War, seldom fail to mention the tumult created by warriors' shouts. A high-pitched clan war cry of the Highland Scots was an intrinsic part of their warfare. States of origin also influenced the Southern battle cry. For example, Mississippians yelled differently than did soldiers from Virginia or Texas. In the Trans-Mississippi Department, a blend of Indian war cries and Texas cattle drovers' shouts made the yell even more terrifying. Colonel Tandy Walker, commander of the 2d Indian Brigade, reported that during an action in Arkansas when one of his Choctaw privates jumped astride a captured enemy cannon and gave a whoop, his comrades brought forth a succession of cries "as to make the woods reverberate for miles around." The fact that Indian troops also took scalps probably encouraged the Union soldiers to flee before the brightly painted warriors.

The Texas yell, which intermingled Comanche Indian war whoops with the Rebel yell, so demoralized several Federal units that they bolted from the field of battle. After the 9 April 1864 rout at Mansfield, a Yankee prisoner reported that "it was them durn Texans hollerin' that scared them [Union infantry]" and precipitated the panic that broke Major General Nathaniel P. Banks's line. Another Federal wrote that "they emerged from their concealment in the woods, and yelling as only the steer-drivers of Texas could yell, charged upon our division."

With the passage of time, the actual yell became a lost art. By the time recording equipment became available, old Rebel throats were too weak and feeble to produce their famous battle cry. They could not generate the volume and intensity of a cacophonous yell that could be heard for miles over the roar of cannon and musket fire. One Confederate veteran remembered it as "woh-who-ey! who-ey! who-ey!" The yell began with "the first syllable, 'woh' short and low, and the second 'who' with a very high and prolonged note deflecting upon the third syllable 'ey'." One thing is clear, the Rebel yell was invariably different from the Yankee cheer of "hurrah" (pronounced "hooray" with the emphasis on the second syllable). After the battle of Fredericksburg, Major General Early reported that his men went forward "with the cheering peculiar to the Confederate soldier, and which is never mistaken for the studied hurrahs of the Yankees." English Colonel James Fremantle wrote that the "Southern troops, when charging . . . always yell in a manner peculiar to themselves."

—Stanley S. McGowen

For further reading:

Evans, Clement A., ed. *Confederate Military History: A Library of Confederate States History* (1987).

Lord, Walter, ed. *The Fremantle Diary: Being the Journal of Lieutenant Colonel James Arthur Lyon Fremantle, Coldstream Guards, On His Three Months in the Southern States* (1954).

McGowen, Stanley S. *Horse Sweat and Powder Smoke: The 1st Texas Cavalry in the Civil War* (1999).

McWhiney, Grady, and Perry D. Jamieson. *Attack and Die: Civil War Military Tactics and the Southern Heritage* (1982).

Wiley, Bell Irvin. *The Life of Johnny Reb: The Common Soldier of the Confederacy* (1943; reprint 1997).

RECTOR, HENRY MASSEY
(1816–1899)
Governor of Arkansas

Born to Elias Rector and Fannie Bardella Thurston Rector in Louisville, Kentucky, Henry Rector moved to Arkansas as a young man. He worked at various jobs, including bank teller and U.S. marshal. He became involved in Arkansas state politics, serving in the state senate for four years while also studying law. He opened a practice in Little Rock in 1854. In 1855 Rector was elected to the U.S. House of Representatives. In 1859 he became a justice of the state supreme court, the result of rival Richard H. Johnson's maneuver to remove Rector from Congress. The following year, however, Rector triumphed against the Johnson faction when he was elected governor.

Rector supported secession upon the election of Abraham Lincoln, although the state did not secede until after the president's call for volunteers on 15 April 1861. Before the state secession convention took this action, however, Rector demanded and secured the surrender of the Little Rock Federal Arsenal. When Secretary of War Simon Cameron called for Arkansas' quota of volunteers, Rector refused. Shortly thereafter, the state secession convention voted the state out of the Union.

Rector was naturally concerned with the defense of the state. He wrote to generals serving in the state and made suggestions about the disposition of troops. He also negotiated with Indian leaders to secure their loyalty to Arkansas and the Confederacy, a process he had begun before Arkansas' secession.

Rector strongly supported the secession of the state, but it was this strong states' rights view that also caused him to reject Confederate pleas for Arkansas troops. His political enemies used his failure to cooperate with the Confederacy to push through a measure shortening his term as governor from four to two years. When his shortened term ended in 1862, he failed to win reelection.

Upon leaving office, Rector retired to his plantation. After the war he continued to avoid political involvement except for two stints as a state constitutional delegate. He died in Hot Springs, Arkansas.

—*David S. Heidler and Jeanne T. Heidler*

See also Arkansas.
For further reading:
Ferguson, John Lewis. *Arkansas and the Civil War* (1965).

RED RIVER CAMPAIGN
(March–May 1864)

The Red River campaign in 1864 comprised the final U.S. large-scale riverine operation of the war. Union military and naval leaders believed that a raid up the Red River would grant Federal command of the region and a gateway into Texas. In addition, economic and political concerns surrounding the diminishing supply of cotton, which escalated its value in Northern markets, led Union decision makers to advocate an advance up this inland waterway. Lastly, the French invasion and occupation of Mexico in 1863 influenced leaders in Washington to favor Federal military and naval operations into Texas to discourage any French attempts at annexation of any Trans-Mississippi states.

The overall plan outlined that a naval force, commanded by David Dixon Porter, would penetrate the Red River and provide partial transportation, fire support, and logistical assistance for Major General Nathaniel P. Banks's ground element. Meanwhile, Major General Frederick Steele's army "would move southwest from Little Rock, Arkansas. Together they would form a pincer on Shreveport." On 12 March 1864, Porter, with approximately twenty gunboats, combined forces with Banks in what was to be one of the greatest fiascoes for U.S. military arms during the war.

Ahead of the slower army transports, which carried 10,000 troops commanded by Brigadier General A. J. Smith, Porter's command entered the Red River on 12 March. About eight miles below Fort de Russy, with obstacles barring the approach, it was decided that "Porter would then take most of his fleet up the Atchafalaya [River] and try to get at Fort De Russy from the rear while Smith went overland." Meanwhile, a small component of Porter's command would attempt to destroy the waterborne obstacles and proceed toward the fort. Late on 15 March, Lieutenant Seth Ledyard Phelps, commanding the small gunboat force attacking the fort, fired a few cannon rounds at the rebel emplacements and the defenders of Fort de Russy hoisted a white flag, whereupon, Union brigadier general Joseph Mower rode into the fort. The next day, Alexandria, Louisiana, capitulated after the arrival of four Federal riverboats and the landing of a small detachment of marines and sailors. Almost two weeks lapsed before Banks's army finally reached Alexandria. The remainder of the expedition was not as successful.

As Porter pushed forward to Shreveport with his naval component, Banks slowly marched his troops on the west side of the river almost twenty miles away from any fire support that could be provided by the navy gunboats. On 8 April, Confederate major general Richard Taylor entrapped Banks at Mansfield, Louisiana, or Sabine Cross Roads. Taylor soundly defeated Banks and forced the Union general to retreat to Pleasant Hill, Louisiana. After a brief meeting with his commanders, Banks elected to retreat back to New Orleans, Louisiana.

Banks's action forced Porter to slowly begin the long trip back to the Mississippi. Along the way, Confederate forces lobbed shells and sniped at the passing Federal gunboats, and then the water level fell. Stranded in the river near Alexandria, Porter requested army support. In response, Lieutenant Colonel Joseph Bailey, with the assistance of more than 3,000 sailors and soldiers, constructed several dams below the rapids near Alexandria that permitted Porter's marooned gunboats to run the rapids and proceed to safety, thus ending the Red River expedition.

—*R. Blake Dunnavent*

See also Alexandria, Louisiana; Bailey, Joseph; Jenkins' Ferry, Battle of; Mansfield, Louisiana, Battle of; Pleasant Hill, Battle of; Riverine Warfare; Yellow Bayou.
For further reading:
Anderson, Bern. *By Sea and by River: The Naval History of the Civil War* (1962).
Fowler, William M., Jr. *Under Two Flags: The American Navy in the Civil War* (1990).
Slagle, Jay. *Ironclad Captain: Seth Ledyard Phelps and the U.S. Navy, 1841–1864* (1996).

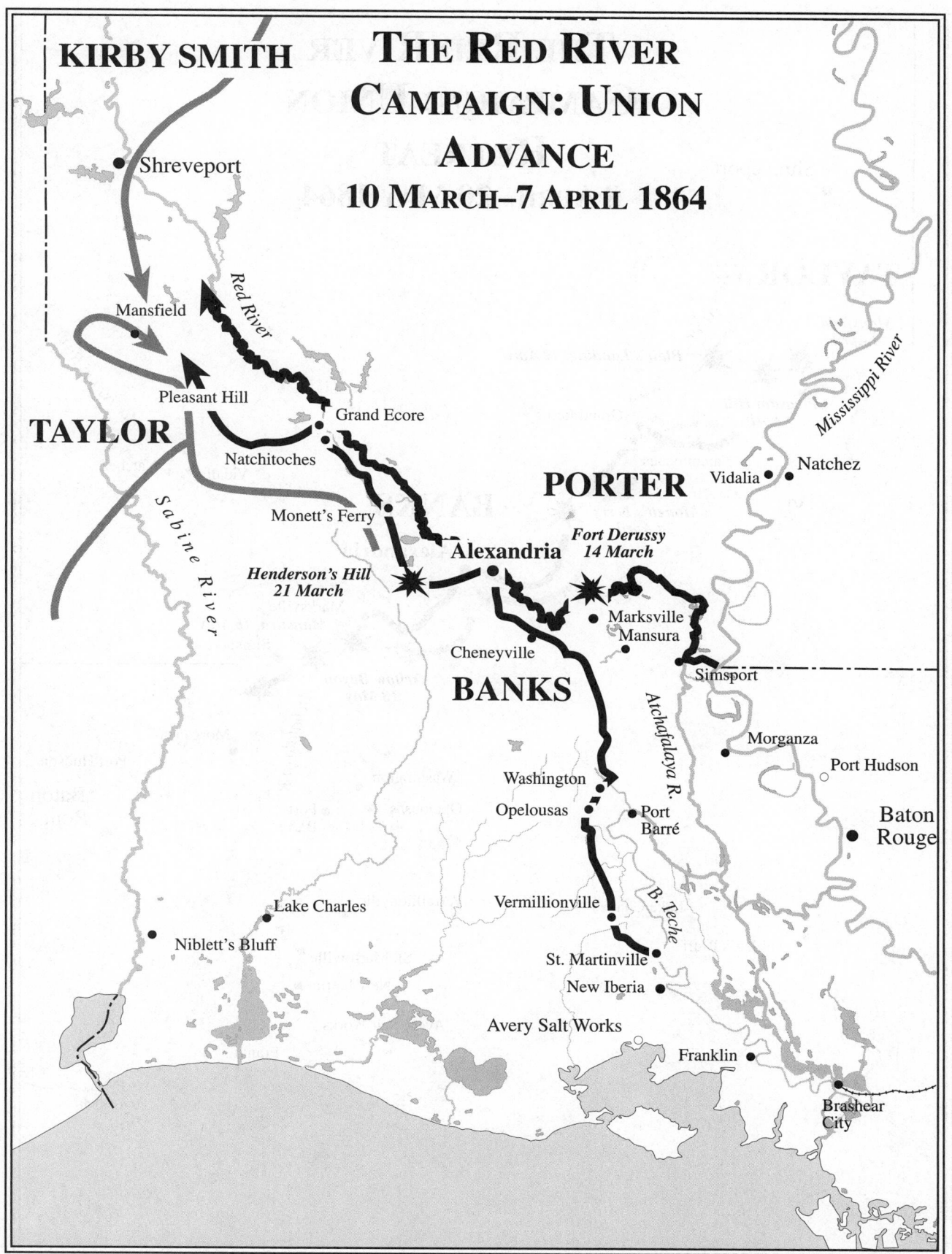

THE RED RIVER CAMPAIGN: UNION ADVANCE
10 MARCH–7 APRIL 1864

KIRBY SMITH

Shreveport

Red River

Mansfield

Pleasant Hill

TAYLOR

Grand Ecore

Natchitoches

Mississippi River

Monett's Ferry

PORTER

Vidalia   Natchez

Fort Derussy
14 March

Henderson's Hill
21 March

Alexandria

Sabine River

Marksville
Mansura

Cheneyville

Simsport

BANKS

Atchafalaya R.

Morganza

Port Hudson

Washington

Opelousas

Port Barré

Baton Rouge

Vermillionville

B. Teche

Lake Charles

St. Martinville

Niblett's Bluff

New Iberia

Avery Salt Works

Franklin

Brashear City

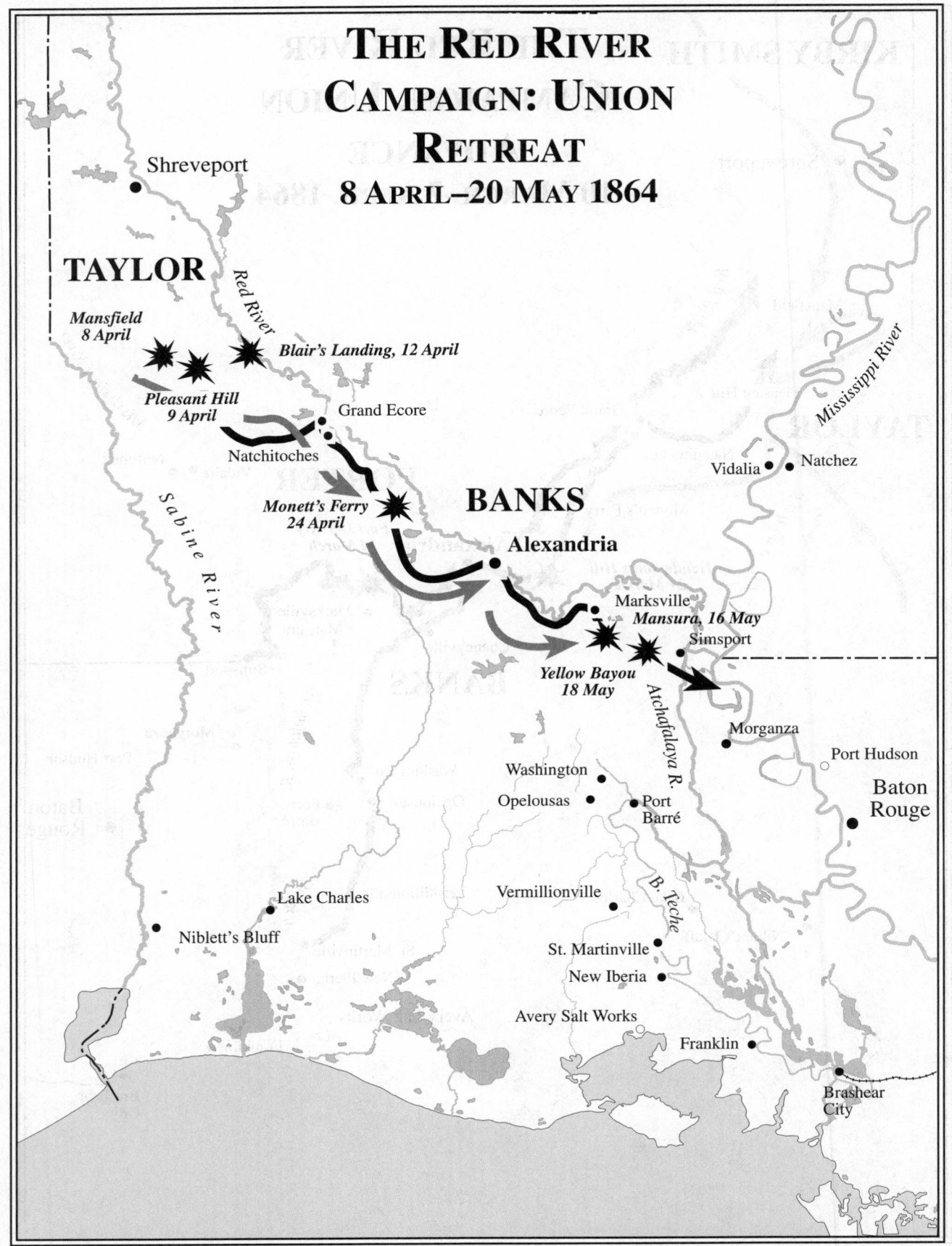

THE RED RIVER CAMPAIGN: UNION RETREAT
8 APRIL–20 MAY 1864

Shreveport

TAYLOR

Mansfield 8 April

Red River

Blair's Landing, 12 April

Pleasant Hill 9 April

Grand Ecore

Natchitoches

Sabine River

Monett's Ferry 24 April

BANKS

Alexandria

Vidalia • Natchez

Mississippi River

Marksville
Mansura, 16 May
Simsport

Yellow Bayou 18 May

Atchafalaya R.

Morganza

Port Hudson

Washington

Opelousas • • Port Barré

Baton Rouge

Lake Charles

Niblett's Bluff

Vermillionville

B. Teche

St. Martinville

New Iberia

Avery Salt Works

Franklin

Brashear City

REEDER, ANDREW HORATIO
(1807–1864)
Territorial governor of Kansas

Born to Absalom Reeder and Christiana Smith Reeder in Easton, Pennsylvania, Andrew Horatio Reeder was educated locally and at an academy in New Jersey before beginning the study of law in 1825. He began practicing law in 1828 in Easton. Over the next twenty-five years, Reeder was a prosperous lawyer and active Democrat in his community. He showed no interested in holding political office but worked hard for local and state Democratic candidates.

In the early 1850s, Reeder became a strong supporter of the doctrine of popular sovereignty as the best solution to the question of slavery in the territories. His assistance to Democratic candidates and vocal belief in popular sovereignty led in 1854 to his appointment as the first territorial governor of Kansas. President Franklin Pierce appointed Reeder to this position, even though the Pennsylvanian had no previous experience in political office. Reeder's reputation for honesty and long-time loyal support for the Democratic Party no doubt influenced Pierce's decision.

Reeder arrived in the territory in October 1854 and temporarily established his headquarters at Leavenworth. After settling in, he traveled throughout the territory trying to measure the mood of the people and to allow them to ask him questions about the territorial process. Through these travels, Reeder determined that the territory's divisions over the issue of slavery already had the potential to lead to violence. As a result, he decided to postpone the election of a territorial legislature until March, but to go ahead with the election of a territorial delegate to Congress. In the meantime he established a temporary capital at Shawnee Mission.

In March the legislative election was held. There was open fraud, particularly on the proslavery side, but to keep the peace, Reeder allowed all but some of the most blatantly fraudulent results to stand. That he tried to disallow any results antagonized the proslavery element and that he did not disallow virtually all the returns antagonized the free-state element. Reeder traveled to Washington to confer with the president about the divisions within the territory, but received little encouragement from Pierce. The governor left angry, but returned to the territory determined to implement popular sovereignty.

The new legislature that convened in July was heavily proslavery and immediately began passing laws protecting the institution of slavery in the territory and trying to limit the freedoms of antislave forces, particularly by making it a crime to speak out against slavery. Under the legislature's extremely strict slave code,

helping a slave escape his owner was a capital offense. Feeling that these laws were too extreme, Reeder vetoed them, but the legislature overrode his vetoes. Within a very short time Reeder was at an impasse with his own legislature, which passed a resolution calling for his removal. The president, thinking that Reeder's removal would calm the situation, complied.

Rather than return to Pennsylvania after his removal, Reeder opted to stay in the territory, where he had bought much land since his arrival. He joined the free-state element in Kansas politics. He initially encouraged the free-staters to establish their own territorial legislature (he would later advise against separate action) and was elected by the body that was created as one of the territory's delegates to Congress. He was not seated, however. In early 1856 that same legislature applied for statehood as a free state and chose Reeder as one of its first United States senators. Again, this government was not recognized in Washington as the legitimate Kansas government.

Reeder's actions with the free-staters caused the proslavery state government to indict him for treason. After several close calls in which he was almost arrested, he escaped the territory and went on a speaking tour of the Midwest, describing the abuses perpetrated by the proslavery government of Kansas. Perhaps his most famous speech of the tour occurred at the Republican state convention in Bloomington, Indiana. Until November 1856 he campaigned vigorously for the election of the first Republican candidate for president, John C. Frémont. Although he failed in the effort, he was especially eager to help Frémont carry Pennsylvania.

At the end of the year Reeder returned to his law practice in Pennsylvania, though for the next four years he remained active in Republican Party activities. In 1860 he was a Pennsylvania delegate to the Republican National Convention in Chicago and received fifty-one votes for the vice presidential nomination on the first ballot. He actively campaigned for Abraham Lincoln through the summer and fall of 1860, after which he again returned to his law practice. In 1864 he was again a delegate to the nominating convention, this time in Baltimore, Maryland. He died shortly afterward at home on 5 July 1864.

—*David S. Heidler and Jeanne T. Heidler*

See also Kansas.

For further reading:

Gardner, Theodore. "Andrew H. Reeder, First Territorial Governor." *Collections of the Kansas State Historical Society* (1923–1925).

Monaghan, Jay. *Civil War on the Western Border, 1854–1865* (1955).

Youngstrom, Gustaf Adolph. "The Official Career of Andrew Reeder in Kansas" (M.A. thesis, 1931).

REFUGEE HOME SOCIETY
(1851–1865)

African-Canadian colonization society

In reaction to the continued successes of African-Americans escaping from slavery, the U.S. Congress passed the Fugitive Slave Act and President Millard Fillmore signed it into law on 18 September 1850. Alongside white abolition societies, a multitude of black self-help groups geared up to oppose the effects of the new federal support for slave owners. One of these groups was the controversial Refugee Home Society, founded in 1851 by a Kentuckian, Henry Bibb, and his wife, Mary Elizabeth Bibb.

Born in Shelby County, Kentucky, Henry Bibb (1815–1854) was the son of an enslaved black woman and a white man he never knew. His narrative, published in 1849 and reprinted many times, described his early life, first marriage, and harrowing escapes from slavery. He traveled extensively on the abolitionist lecture circuit, traveling through Michigan, Ohio, New York, and Canada West (now known as Ontario), and he organized many antislavery groups. Black historian William Wells Brown described the orator Bibb: "In personal appearance he was tall and slim, a pleasing countenance, half white, hair brown, eyes gray, and possessed a musical voice, and a wonderful power of delivery."

In 1848 he married Mary Elizabeth Miles (1820–?), a free black Quaker and teacher from Rhode Island. With the passage of the 1850 Fugitive Slave Act, they moved to Windsor, Canada. There they organized an antislavery society and started a printing press. Their first issue of the abolitionist newspaper *The Voice of the Fugitive* came out on 1 January 1851. The Bibbs advocated agriculture as the basis of success for new arrivals, and they chronicled the development of the Refugee Home Society's colony for escaped slaves.

The Refugee Home Society supplanted the Sandwich Mission, which had sold some land in the area to fugitive African-Americans between 1846 and 1851. The mission fell apart due to quarrels between the black ministers who served as agents and their financial backers, white philanthropists in Detroit. The Bibbs established the Refugee Home Society along with another Kentuckian, Josiah Henson (1789–1883), and American Missionary Association agent David Hotchkiss. Henson had escaped to Canada with his family in 1830 and established the Dawn Settlement in 1842. This black community was situated near Dresden, Ontario, and centered around a vocational education center called the British North American Institute on the River Sydenham.

Fugitive slaves entering Union lines (*Corbis-Bettman*)

The constitution for the American Refugees' Home, written in 1852, recorded the society's pledge to purchase 50,000 acres of Canadian land for the use of fugitive slaves. The sale of these lands in 25-acre lots would provide funds to purchase more land and to establish and support community schools and churches. A temperance bylaw forbade the sale or manufacturing of liquor on settlement lands. Five acres of each lot were free if the settler cleared and cultivated it within three years. The remainder of the purchase price was to be paid off in nine equal payments, and not until all payments were made would the society trustees turn over the deed to the land. The lot ownership would return to the society if the settler migrated elsewhere or died.

One of the most controversial stipulations of the project was that only landless fugitives could purchase settlement lands, and settlers could not sell or even transfer the land as a gift for fifteen years after the original purchase. Opponents of the Bibbs complained that this effectively turned away industrious black settlers who would have served as important African-Canadian community leaders. Clearly, from the name choice of the society and from editorials in *The Voice*, the Bibbs envisioned that these settlement farms would be temporary at best, and that the refugees would return to the United States once slavery was abolished.

Fundraisers had already collected enough U.S. dollars in 1851 for the society to purchase 680 hectares (1,680 acres) in Essex County, Canada West. The main tract lay about 10 miles from the Detroit River, southeast of Windsor in the Townships of Sandwich and Maidstone. By 1855, half of the original lands had been resold to 20 families, about 150 settlers. However, the varying distances between the settled lots frustrated any attempts to create a strong African-Canadian community, such as the more widely known Buxton Mission in the Elgin Settlement.

In its heyday during the early 1850s, the community could boast of many crops, and the settlers' homes were reportedly sturdy and comfortable. Although some families were more successful than others, all had enough to eat and wear. Mary Bibb set up a classroom in her home in Sandwich, since the common school was closed to the area's black children. The Bibbs's supporters in Michigan donated schoolbooks and Bibles for a Sabbath school in which both Mary and Henry taught literacy skills for all ages. The Bibbs struggled to establish a continental black unity—from the British West Indies and Haiti to Canada—as well as to encourage black commercial enterprises and emigration.

An organized opposition to the society and its settlement efforts soon surfaced, and two abolitionist newspapers, the *Western Evangelist* and the *Provincial Freeman*, set the stage for scandals. Mary Ann Camberton Shadd Cary (1823–1893), an American-Canadian black abolitionist, had served on the executive committee for the Anti-Slavery Society of Windsor under its first president, Henry Bibb. Shadd Cary used her editorship of the *Provincial Freeman*, the second black newspaper in Canada, to rail against injustices such as segregated schools and the paternalism of the American Missionary Society. In a militant effort to expose the inadequacies of black organizations that relied on white supporters, she and Samuel R. Ward, another prominent Garrisonian, voiced their suspicions of the activities of Henry Bibb and Josiah Henson with the finances of the Home Refugee Society. She exposed the fact that although the society continued to solicit funds to operate relief centers, there were no new settlers who required such support. In addition, Shadd Cary claimed that the society offered no advantages to fugitives that the Canadian government did not provide already. She quoted Theodore Holly, a junior editor of *The Voice*, who told her that in 1858 a society board member and Detroit philanthropist, Horace Hallock, sold to the society 120 hectares (297 acres) along the Puce River at a profit. George Cary, another executive committee member, admitted to her that he still held the deed for the first 80 hectares bought with donations—he and Henry Bibb had never turned it over to the society.

Henry Bibb died in August 1854 and the Refugee Home Society lost much of its forward-looking energy. Charles Foote took over the leadership of the society and tried to defend its strict regulations on the basis that the new settlers needed protection from bootleggers and land speculators. Mary Bibb married Isaac N. Cary the following year, and she opened a new school where she taught until 1865.

By 1861, the Refugee Home Society had settled a total of 60 families on 100 lots. However, as the American Civil War wore on, the U.S. military strategies changed and federalized emancipation slowly became a reality for African-American slaves. By 1865 the Bibbs's original purpose for the Refugee Home Society was no longer needed: the Thirteenth Amendment abolished slavery in the United States. The American Missionary Association eventually withdrew its financial support from the society, and Foote returned to the United States. Many of the settlers migrated to Haiti, and some families moved to other parts of Canada West in search of a more vibrant black community.

Canadian historians find few positive aspects to the story of the Refugee Home Society. Detractors assess its settlement policy as paternalistic and narrow-minded, attracting the apathetic and excluding many potentially able settlers. The society seemed to make no attempt to organize self-government or leadership among the settlers. The powerful effects of Shadd Cary's series of exposés badly discredited the Society's reputation then and now. Henry and Mary Bibb, however, are important

figures in the search for a black nationalism and the black self-help movements of the nineteenth century.

—*Randolph Hollingsworth*

See also Abolitionist Movement.
For further reading:
Carlesimo, Peter. "The Refugee Home Society: Its Origin, Operation and Results, 1851–1976" (M.A. thesis, 1973).
Cooper, Afua. "The Search For Mary Bibb, Black Woman Teacher In Nineteenth-Century Canada West." *Ontario History* (1991).
Drew, Benjamin. *The Refugee: A North-side View of Slavery* (1855; reprint, 1969).
Hill, Daniel G. *Freedom-Seekers: Blacks in Early Canada* (1981).
Kimmel, Janice Martz. "Break Your Chains and Fly for Freedom." *Michigan History* (1996).
MacDonald, Cheryl. "Last Stop on the Underground Railroad." *Beaver* (1990).
Pease, William Henry, and Jane Pease. *Black Utopia: Negro Communal Experiments in America* (1963).
Quarles, Benjamin. *Black Abolitionists* (1969).
Rhodes, Jane. *Mary Ann Shadd Cary: The Black Press and Protest in the Nineteenth Century* (1998).
Stouffer, Allen. *The Light of Nature and the Law of God: Anti-Slavery in Ontario 1833–1877* (1992).

REID, WHITELAW
(1837–1912)
Civil War journalist and author

Born near Xenia, Ohio, in 1837, Whitelaw Reid first gained national attention as a war correspondent for the *Cincinnati Gazette*, covering both battles and Washington, D.C., politics. In later life he would serve as editor of the *New York Tribune*, the paper made famous by Horace Greeley, run for vice president in 1892, and serve as minister to both England and France. An ardent Republican, Whitelaw Reid graduated from Miami University (Ohio) in 1856 and worked for several Ohio newspapers during the late 1850s. Following the outbreak of war in 1861, he went to Washington as the *Cincinnati Gazette*'s war reporter, writing under the pseudonym "Agate."

Described by one of his biographers as "a penetrating observer and a severe critic," Reid's first letters described life in camp from the perspective of Ohio troops. He spent several months in 1861 and 1862 as an aide-de-camp to Union general William S. Rosecrans in western Virginia. Reid mingled stories of the men's high spirits and excitement with piercing complaints about waste and inefficiency, poor-quality uniforms, and ill-trained and irresponsible officers. His critiques sometimes backfired, resulting in Reid's being banned from certain camps, but he continued to report what he saw. Early on, Reid became frustrated with George McClellan's lack of aggressiveness, and he never shied from attributing Union defeats to their own incompetence.

In April 1862 Reid found himself in Tennessee and a

witness to the grim fighting at Shiloh. His 19,000-word story became the classic newspaper account of the battle, uniformly praised for both its accuracy and its emotive power. Reid's report mingled tactics and topography, accounts from soldiers and officers with those of stragglers and refugees, and included a critical appraisal of Grant's leadership. It gave Reid, or at least his alter ego Agate, a national profile. The *Cincinnati Gazette* then sent its star reporter to Washington, where Reid continued to cover and analyze military affairs, although primarily using other reporters' dispatches. He did, however, travel to Gettysburg to report firsthand, and, despite his criticism of Grant at Shiloh, provided his readers with both an explanation and an endorsement of Grant's strategy following the battle of the Wilderness in 1864. Reid was also one of the first journalists to visit Richmond after it fell to the Union on 3 April 1865.

Most of Reid's Washington writings were about politics, and Reid made the most of his Republican connections. He was well acquainted with such congressional leaders as Charles Sumner and John Sherman, and struck up a close friendship with Secretary of the Treasury Salmon P. Chase. Reid's relationships with Republican leaders not only meant increased access for the reporter, but also translated into patronage posts: Reid served as the librarian for the House of Representatives from 1863 to 1866 and briefly as the clerk of the House Military Committee. Reid's dispatches from his Washington years reached not only Ohio readers, but were regular features in several other papers, including the *New York Times*, *New York Tribune*, *Chicago Tribune*, *Detroit Tribune*, and the *St. Louis Democrat*.

Immediately after the war, Reid eagerly accepted an invitation from Salmon Chase, now chief justice of the Supreme Court, to accompany him on an inspection tour of Southern cities. He and his party had carte blanche to visit any place within the lines of military occupation from Washington to New Orleans and back. They traveled on a Navy cutter, stopping at places like Fort Fisher, Charleston, Savannah, Key West, Havana, Mobile, and New Orleans, greeted everywhere with parades, troop reviews, and elaborate dinners. While in New Orleans, Reid became interested in the possible profits to be made in cotton, and the party traveled up the Mississippi River, stopping at Jefferson Davis's plantation on the way home.

The rosy picture Reid painted in his dispatches during the summer of 1865 was dispelled by a second trip he took that fall and winter. Reid no longer had the privileges of an official party and found himself traveling on worn-out, creaky, and uncomfortable Southern trains, passing through a seemingly endless landscape of ruined buildings, desolate fields, and suffering people. Reid was sympathetic to the Southern freedmen, though cautious in estimating the degree to which they might be able to succeed and prosper on their own. He was equally sensitive to the shifting emotions of postwar Southerners and the uncertainty that permeated the first months of Reconstruction. He was struck by "the spirit of unconquerable hate" that persisted among most Southerners and thought that Andrew Johnson's Reconstruction terms and frequent pardons were entirely too generous to the former Rebels.

Reid's dispatches from his two trips were collected and published in 1866 in *After the War: A Southern Tour*, which quickly became a classic travel account of the postwar South. Reid invested in cotton land in Louisiana in 1865, and after making a little money there moved on to a property in Alabama, where he lost most of it. While in the South he also compiled his two volume account *Ohio in the War*. In 1867 Reid returned to the North, and in 1868 joined the staff of the *New York Tribune*. Following Horace Greeley's defeat in the 1872 presidential election, the thirty-five-year-old Reid took over as editor of the paper. Reid remained a staunch Republican throughout his life, running unsuccessfully on the ticket with Benjamin Harrison in 1892. An advocate of American expansionism, Reid served as minister to France in the late 1880s and to Great Britain in the early 1900s. He died in London on 15 December 1912.

—*Anne Sarah Rubin*

See also New York Tribune; Newspapers; War Correspondents.
For further reading:
Cortissoz, Royal. *The Life of Whitelaw Reid* (1921).
Duncan, Bingham. *Whitelaw Reid: Journalist, Politician, Diplomat* (1975).
Reid, Whitelaw. *After the War: A Southern Tour*. Cincinnati: Moore, Wilsatch and Baldwin, 1866; *Ohio in the War: Her Statesmen, Her Generals, and Soldiers* (1868).
———. *Ohio in the War: Her Statesmen, Her Generals, and Soldiers* (1868).

RELIGION

Religion in the Civil War pervaded virtually all aspects of American society. Not all Americans held religious beliefs and values, but many did. Religion was not confined to one particular group, but soldiers and civilians, Northerners and Southerners, freed and slave, males and females, and Jews and Christians all made use of religion. Furthermore, a reciprocal relationship existed between the Civil War and religion, with both influencing and being influenced by each other. As a result, religion during the Civil War did not remain a static entity during 1861–1865; instead, it became an institution that constantly changed and adapted itself, as well as its devotees.

Americans used religion to interpret their experiences during and after the war. People on both sides of the conflict believed in a God who was actively involved in their affairs. To them, the war was not a secular event,

Religious services on the deck of the monitor USS *Passaic*, 1864 (Photograph by Samuel A. Cooley / *National Archives*)

A chaplain conducting mass for the 69th New York State Militia encamped at Fort Corcoran, Washington, D.C., 1861
(*National Archives*)

but one guided by God. The God of the Civil War judged, chastised, and liberated people. Northerners and Southerners alike believed that their cause was a just cause, and because God was a just God, they each considered their nation to be God's nation. Naturally, their enemies were unrighteous and needed correction by God. Victories in battle, therefore, signaled God's activity on their behalf and foreshadowed their ultimate success. Defeats, however, needed explaining.

The faithful of the North and South distinguished between chastisement and judgment. The righteous experienced chastisement, while the unrighteous encountered judgment. Whenever their armies suffered defeat or their civilians experienced hardship, it was due to God's chastisement and his efforts to purify his people. Greed, the neglect of the Sabbath, inhumane treatment of slaves, and drunkenness often were singled out as examples of unrighteousness. Accordingly, national days of prayer and fasting were proclaimed in an effort to regain God's favor and call his people back to righteous living. Suffering by God's people, however, was not always explained in terms of sin. In God's mysterious providence, sometimes the righteous suffered

at the hands of evildoers. Yet, ultimately, the righteous would overcome.

Defeat of the enemy not only indicated God's blessing on the part of the victor's cause. It also demonstrated that God was judging the enemy nation in an effort to stamp out their evil society. Accordingly, the victor often proclaimed national days of thanksgiving to celebrate God's blessing. As the Confederacy collapsed, Northerners understood it as evidence of God's judgment upon the unrighteous South. Many Southerners, however, continued to believe even after the war that God had not abandoned them, but was chastening the country to purify it. Slaves, however, viewed God as the great liberator. While they believed that God was judging the South, of prime importance was God's freeing of the slaves. As they were regarded as God's children in bondage, He had intervened on their behalf.

Religion not only interpreted the war experiences, but it strengthened and consoled its adherents. Soldiers often found the courage to enter battle knowing that a providential God controlled their destiny. Faith could give comfort, encouragement, and hope to those who were grieving. Civilians used religion to cope with the death of a loved one or with the destructive consequences of the war.

While religion interpreted the war, the war also changed interpretations of religion. Oftentimes, one's understanding of the biblical teaching on slavery was greatly influenced by Southern or Northern affiliations. Interest in heaven grew markedly after the Civil War, with it often being described in domestic terms. Structural changes in religion also occurred. As local congregations saw their ministers become soldiers, the laity, especially women, took on more religious responsibility. Through Christian organizations, women actively became involved in the war effort. Slaves were able to free themselves from white-controlled churches and establish their own form of piety. Some people lost faith all together. Dramatic religious changes, therefore, were wrought by the war.

While religion during the Civil War reflected a largely Protestant understanding, not all participants embraced these values. Several thousand Jews fought on both sides and debated the biblical basis of slavery. Dr. Morris J. Raphall, a New York City rabbi, gave one of the most highly publicized sermons on slavery, arguing that the Bible did not prohibit it. Other rabbis strongly disagreed. Yet, as with Protestants and Catholics, Jews often were influenced more on the subject of slavery by the section of the country in which they resided.

Religion played a major role in the Civil War. It united and divided the North and South. It, however, would not be the same after the war, yet still would offer many Americans a way to integrate their experiences.

—*Scott M. Langston*

See also Abolitionist Movement; Chaplains; Chaplains, African-American; Churhes; Jews; Quakers; United States Sanitary Commission; Western Sanitary Commission.

For further reading:

Genovese, Eugene D. *A Consuming Fire: The Fall of the Confederacy in the Mind of the White Christian South* (1998).

Korn, Bertram Wallace. *American Jewry and the Civil War* (1951).

Miller, Randall M., Harry S. Stout, and Charles Reagan Wilson, eds. *Religion and the American Civil War* (1998).

Moorhead, James H. *American Apocalypse: Yankee Protestants and the Civil War, 1860–1869* (1978).

Stowell, Daniel W. *Rebuilding Zion: The Religious Reconstruction of the South, 1863–1877* (1998).

RENO, JESSE LEE
(1823–1862)
Union general

Born in Wheeling, Virginia (now West Virginia), to Louis Reno and Rebecca Quinby Reno, Jesse Lee Reno moved with his family to Pennsylvania when he was a child. He was educated locally before receiving an appointment to the U.S. Military Academy. He graduated eighth of fifty-nine from what would become the very distinguished class of 1846.

Upon graduation, Reno went with most of his classmates to join Winfield Scott's Mexico City campaign. Reno received brevets for his actions at the battle of Cerro Gordo and the storming of Chapultepec. After the war, he served as an instructor at West Point, on various ordnance boards and surveys, and in Albert Sidney Johnston's Utah expedition. Upon his return from the West, Reno, who had reached the rank of captain, was given command of the Mount Vernon, Alabama, Federal arsenal. On the morning of 4 January 1861, Reno awoke to find secessionists, on orders from Alabama's governor, scaling the walls of the arsenal. His tiny force overwhelmed, Reno surrendered.

Reno was sent to Kansas to command the Leavenworth arsenal, where he remained until being made a brigadier general of volunteers in November 1861. Transferred to the Army of the Potomac, Reno received orders in December 1861 to report to Annapolis, Maryland, to join the expedition being organized by Ambrose Burnside against the coast of North Carolina. Reno saw action commanding his brigade at Roanoke Island on 8 February 1862, at New Bern on 14 March 1862, and at South Mills on 19 April 1862. By the last engagement, Reno commanded a division in what had been designated the Department of North Carolina.

In early August 1862, Reno and his division were called to Washington to become part of John Pope's Army of Virginia. Reno commanded the 2d Division of Burnside's IX Corps. On 18 August 1862, his division skirmished with Confederates at Clark's Mountain, Virginia. Less than two weeks later he moved forward as acting commander of IX Corps while Burnside commanded the right of Pope's army moving toward Manassas Junction. On 20 August Reno had been promoted to major general of volunteers with a date of rank of 18 July.

Reno was commended for his handling of the IX Corps during the battle of Second Bull Run on 29–30 August and for his actions at the battle of Chantilly on 1 September. Returning to Washington, Reno found himself again a part of the Army of the Potomac under George McClellan. Again as acting commander of IX Corps as the army moved in pursuit of Robert E. Lee, Reno and his corps passed through Frederick, Maryland, on 12–13 September 1862. While there, Reno apparently investigated the Barbara Frietschie incident that had occurred a few days earlier and came away with what he presumed to be the already legendary flag. It was this very artifact, it is said, that draped his coffin when he was buried a few weeks later.

While trying to dislodge Confederate defenders in Fox's Gap at South Mountain on 14 September, Reno was mortally wounded. He died that day and was taken for burial to Boston, where his wife lived during the war. After the war his body was moved to Georgetown, in the District of Columbia.

—*David S. Heidler and Jeanne T. Heidler*

See also Alabama; Freitchie, Barbara; New Bern, Battle of; Roanoke Island; South Mountain, Battle of.

For further reading:
McConnell, William F. *Remember Reno: A Biography of Major General Jesse Lee Reno* (1996).

REPUBLICAN PARTY

When the founding fathers were framing the Constitution, they hoped to fashion a political system without parties. On that count they failed; as early as George Washington's second term the Federalist and Democratic-Republican parties were beginning to coalesce. America's first party system lasted until the 1820s, when the Democratic-Republicans became known as the Democrats, and the Federalists faded from the scene, to be replaced by the Whig Party.

The Whig Party was a factor on the national level for only about two decades, but in that time its membership included a diverse and distinguished group of political leaders, including Henry Clay, Alexander Stephens, and Abraham Lincoln. There was wide variance in the individual political philosophies of the men who made up the Whig Party, but they all believed in the importance of individual initiative and opportunity. To that end, most Whigs favored energetic government in the pursuit of progress and the promotion of economic growth. The ultimate expression of this agenda was Henry Clay's American System, a plan for government-sponsored construction of roads and canals. The Whig Party was a minority party, however, and was never especially successful on the national level, capturing the presidency only twice.

For most of their existence, the Whigs endeavored to minimize the slavery issue. They kept it off the agenda as much as possible, and when that was not possible, they compromised. By the late 1840s, however, their position was increasingly tenuous. The Liberty and Free Soil Parties, both dedicated to halting the advance of slavery, began to siphon off a part of the Whig vote. In response to increased immigration, the antiforeign American (Know-Nothing) Party came into being, and it also took votes away from the Whigs. By the 1850s the slavery issue could be ignored no longer, as the Congress and the nation debated over whether the territories would have slave labor or free labor. Northern Whigs, who were in the numerical majority, focused on the party's central theme of opportunity, and insisted that the very survival of the republic depended on the spread of free labor across the continent. This was unacceptable to Southern Whigs, who bolted the party. This was the final blow, and the Whig Party disappeared by the mid-1850s.

From the ashes of the Whig Party rose the Republicans. In order to compete with the Democrats, who were still the majority party, the Republicans had to bring together all of the groups who opposed the Democrats; abolitionists, free-soilers, former Whigs, antiforeigners, and so forth. To do so, the Republicans staked out a fairly narrow agenda, focusing on the importance of free soil—limiting slavery to those states where it existed and preserving the territories exclusively for free labor. They also supported government assistance in this area, through grants of land and the construction of a transcontinental railroad.

By shrewdly adjusting their message to suit the needs of local constituencies, the Republicans were quickly able to develop into a force on the national political scene. The first meeting of members of the new party occurred in 1854, and by 1856 they were ready to field a presidential candidate. Mexican-American War hero John Frémont ran against Democrat James Buchanan, a Northerner well known for his record of public service and his tendency to sympathize with the Southern position on slavery. The Republican platform quoted both the Declaration of Independence and the Constitution, emphasizing the importance of free soil and outlining what Republicans viewed as Southern transgressions against the American people, including the events in "Bleeding Kansas," and the repeal of the Missouri Compromise. Frémont was defeated fairly soundly, capturing 33 percent of the vote compared to Buchanan's 45 percent. Republican leaders were heartened, however, by their many victories in local contests, and by their realization that the party would be much better organized by the time of the next presidential election in 1860.

The Republican message in the election of 1856 had a strong anti-Southern strain to it, a theme that became increasingly dominant as the election of 1860 approached. As a counterpart to their arguments about the importance of free labor in the territories, the Republicans warned Americans about a national conspiracy, promulgated by the "Slave Power." Each of the events that pushed America closer to civil war were part of this conspiracy, according to the Republicans. The notion that slavery presented a threat to the American way of life was crystallized in an 1858 speech by Republican William Seward, in which he said that there was an "irrepressible conflict between opposing and enduring forces" of slavery and free labor.

In that same year congressional elections were held, and Republican leaders hoped to substantially expand their membership in the legislature. One race in particular, the contest for Illinois's open Senate seat, captured national attention. Republican Abraham Lincoln and Democrat Stephen A. Douglas waged a spirited campaign in which they focused almost exclusively on the issue of slavery. Douglas saw no tension between free and slave labor, while Lincoln argued that a "house divided upon itself cannot stand." Lincoln eventually lost this contest by a close margin, but he had helped to outline the Republican agenda for a national audience, while achieving national stature for himself. Nationally, the Republicans did well, moving much closer to parity with the Democratic Party, especially in the House of Representatives.

The Republicans were still in the minority, but they had high hopes going into the election of 1860. Continued conflict across the nation, especially in Kansas, won many new converts for the party. The election of 1856 had hinged on only a few states, notably Pennsylvania, Illinois, and Indiana, and in each of those states the vote had been close. The greatest boon of all for the Republicans came when the Democrats were unable to nominate a candidate at their first convention in Charleston, South Carolina, in April 1860. As a result, when the Republicans convened for their convention in 1860, they knew they could win if they chose the right candidate.

Entering the convention, the front-runner for the nomination was William Seward of New York. However, there was concern that he would not attract antiforeigner votes due to his strongly antinativist stance. His "irrepressible conflict" speech had also caused him to be branded somewhat of a radical, even though he really was not. In addition, years of partisan warfare in New York had made Seward a lot of enemies, most notably the important newspaper publisher Horace Greeley.

Seward's best hope was to wrap up the nomination quickly, based on his strength in the states of the upper North. In view of this, anti-Seward pragmatists organized quickly to stop his nomination. They had several promising alternatives, notably Salmon P. Chase of Ohio, Simon Cameron of Pennsylvania, Edward Bates of Missouri, and Abraham Lincoln of Illinois. But Chase, like Seward, had a reputation as a radical and did not have unanimous support even in his own state. Cameron's reputation as a spoilsman and his frequent shifting of political allegiance from Democrat to Whig to Know-Nothing to Republican concerned delegates who wanted the party to appear ideologically pure. Bates had the support of many powerful Republicans, notably the Blair family in Missouri and Horace Greeley, but had been a slaveholder and a nativist and thus had alienated too many key constituencies, most notably German Protestants.

This left Lincoln. Party leaders realized that Lincoln had most of the strengths of the ideal candidate and few of the weaknesses of the other contenders. He was an antislavery former Whig in a party made up mostly of antislavery former Whigs. He had a reputation as a moderate. Lincoln had opposed the Know-Nothings

enough to win the German vote, but not so much as to alienate former members of the party. Lincoln was from Illinois, a state that was crucial to Republican hopes, particularly given the Northern Democrats' nomination of Stephen A. Douglas, also from Illinois. Lincoln had a reputation for honesty and integrity. Finally, and perhaps most significantly, because Lincoln was of humble origins, he personified the Republican ideology of equal opportunity and upward mobility. He had been born in a log cabin, and, in a stroke of genius, one of Lincoln's managers at the convention acquired two rails that Lincoln had supposedly split thirty years before. Lincoln secured the nomination on the third ballot, and from then on, Lincoln the rail splitter became the symbol of frontier, farm, opportunity, hard work, rags to riches, and other components of the American dream embodied in the Republican message.

The election of 1860 was unique in the history of American politics. The campaign became two separate contests; Lincoln versus Douglas in the North, and John Bell versus John Breckinridge in the South. Republicans did not even have a ticket in the ten states of the lower South. In order to capture the Northern states, the Lincoln camp mounted a spirited campaign. Though Lincoln observed the silence customary of presidential candidates at the time, writing only a few private letters, his supporters delivered some 50,000 speeches on his behalf. They continued to portray the Democrats as the party of slavery, disunion, and corruption. To counter this effort, Douglas took the unprecedented step of taking to the campaign trail. He undertook an exhausting tour that undoubtedly contributed to his death a year later. His message was that he was the only national candidate, but this was scarcely true, as he had almost no support in the South.

In the end, though, the only hope the Democrats really had was to deny Lincoln an electoral majority and get the election thrown into the House of Representatives. This did not happen. Despite not being on the ballot in the South, Lincoln won 180 electoral votes, considerably more than the 152 needed for election. Charles Francis Adams, whose grandfather John Adams and father John Quincy Adams had been defeated for reelection by slaveowners, wrote in his diary the day of Lincoln's election: "The great revolution has actually taken place. . . . The country has once and for all thrown off the domination of the slaveholders." Six weeks later, on 20 December, South Carolina seceded from the Union.

When Lincoln took office in March 1861, he faced a Congress that was dominated by members of his own party. Most congressional Democrats were from the South and had resigned their seats to serve in the Confederate government. Thus, the new president was in an excellent position to work harmoniously with

Congress. The honeymoon lasted for most of the early part of the war, through the first few months of 1862, with Congress essentially approving whatever requests were made by Lincoln. The Congress also enacted several major parts of the Republican platform, including the Pacific Railroad Act and the Morrill Land Grant Act.

The Republican Party was still essentially a collection of political factions, however, and by 1862 a vocal and powerful group of Republicans, known as the radicals, had emerged. The Radical Republicans rarely saw eye to eye with Lincoln, and they were especially critical when it came to the conduct of the war or Lincoln's progress on the slavery question. The radicals believed in vigorous prosecution of the war. This meant, among other things, confiscation of Southern property, which meant, in turn, emancipation. This was a step Lincoln was unwilling to take in the early part of 1862. Most of the radicals disagreed with Lincoln's view that the prosecution of the war was the responsibility of the executive, and instead felt it was the province of Congress. In addition, most of the radicals were experienced Washington insiders, and they viewed Lincoln as an outsider.

The radicals included an extremely militant element known as the Jacobins, after the French political party of the 1780s that had been responsible for the Reign of Terror after the French Revolution. The Jacobins were few in number, but due to their seniority they held some of the most prestigious and important positions in the Congress. These men were sometimes ferociously hostile, and occasionally they went out of their way to insult the president. In part this behavior was the result of the Jacobins' disappointment. Many of them were thoroughly disappointed at how their political careers were going, either because they had not received the presidential nomination in 1860 or because they had not gotten an adequate amount of patronage. A more significant cause of conflict between Lincoln and the Jacobins was their basic personality differences. The Jacobins were inflexible doctrinaires, firmly committed to a fixed position, and Lincoln's flexibility and pragmatism were anathema to them.

Occasionally, relations between Lincoln and the radicals improved, most notably around the time that he issued the Emancipation Proclamation and after military victories. For the majority of the war, however, the radicals were unfriendly to the president. They tried to block his renomination in 1864, and when that failed, they tried to get a new convention called. Lincoln easily managed to quash these challenges, which infuriated the radicals even more.

Some of the Radical Republicans eventually came to respect Lincoln, albeit grudgingly, but a few were not all that upset to see him die. When Andrew Johnson replaced him, many of the radicals felt that they had the man they wanted in the White House. When they found out otherwise, they savaged Johnson as badly as they had Lincoln. Johnson, however, proved far less adept at handling the situation, and the conflict nearly led to his removal from office. In the two years following Johnson's impeachment trial, the radicals were at the height of their power. They managed to impose a rather punitive and harsh Reconstruction on the South and to pass an impressive body of civil rights legislation. The elections of 1868 marked the end of their power, however, as several of their leaders were defeated and others died. The decline of the radical faction of the Republican Party marked the end of Congressional Reconstruction.

One of the primary goals of Congressional Reconstruction had been to establish a foundation for the Republican Party in the South, and by 1868 Republican congressmen were seeing their plans put to the test. There were three parts of the Republican coalition in the South. The first were the carpetbaggers, Northerners who either had moved South or remained in the South after the war, sometimes for humanitarian reasons and sometimes because they saw it as an area of great opportunity. They were only 16 percent of the Republicans in the South, but they dominated Republican politics in the region. They depended on black constituencies, and as such were big proponents of civil rights, education, and social services. This meant that they had to be big proponents of tax increases as well.

African-Americans were the second group of Southern Republican voters. They were the large majority of the party, but they did not hold office very often because whites tended to seize offices for themselves, and also because they were hesitant to identify themselves too readily with the party that Southern whites hated. Some did gain office, though. There were fourteen African-Americans in the House of Representatives, two in the Senate, and several black lieutenant governors. Nonetheless, blacks were very underrepresented, especially on the local level. The third segment of the Republican coalition was the scalawags. These were the native whites who chose the Republican Party as their political vehicle after the war. They were the pivotal members of the coalition, for the survival of the party in the South depended on the ability of these individuals to convert their fellow white Southerners. The problem was that the scalawags were themselves a diverse group; some were former Whigs who joined just because they hated the Democrats, some were former Democrats who resented the Confederacy for seceding and provoking a war, and some were dissenters who wanted reform. The Republicans tried to appeal to all of these groups, but because they had such different interests, this meant that the Republican identity in the South was ambiguous and unfocused.

Because of the divided nature of the Republican coalition, as well as the other impediments that Republican state governments faced, the party had a mixed record in the South. Among the positives was the establishment of a public education system in every state and the passage of much civil rights legislation. Southern Republicans were less successful in making internal improvements and they had considerable difficulty dealing with issues related to land and labor policies. In the end, the Republicans failed to establish a unified, politically viable coalition in the region. The era of Reconstruction left most Southern whites resenting the Republicans, and more than anything else laid the groundwork for the "redemption" of the South by white Democratic politicians.

By the time Reconstruction ended in 1877, the Republicans had achieved the stability that had eluded the party for its first decade of existence. They had grown to become the nation's majority party, focused largely on the creation of economic opportunity by the federal government. As the nation tired of race issues, and as it became clear that the Republicans could win elections without a major presence in the South, the freedmen disappeared from the party's agenda. The Republicans would dominate national politics for the next three decades, while the freedmen would have to wait nearly six decades before a major political party took notice of them again.

—*Christopher Bates*

See also Election of 1860; Election of 1864; Frémont, John Charles; Lincoln, Abraham; Radical Republicans; Seward, William Henry.

For further reading:
Donald, David Herbert. *Lincoln* (1995).
Foner, Eric. *Free Soil, Free Labor, Free Men: The Ideology of the Republican Party before the Civil War* (1970).
Holt, Michael F. *The Political Crisis of the 1850s* (1978).
Howe, Daniel Walker. *The Political Culture of the American Whigs* (1979).
Stampp, Kenneth. *The Era of Reconstruction* (1965).

RESACA, BATTLE OF
(14–15 May 1864)

The battle of Resaca represents a series of firsts: the first major battle in the Atlanta campaign, the first occasion in Georgia in 1864 of Confederate and Federal armies in their entirety facing one another across a field of battle, and the first major encounter between Joseph E. Johnston and William T. Sherman as army field commanders. The two-day battle of Resaca would serve to expose weaknesses in military leadership in each commander and to establish the pattern of maneuver for the entire campaign for Atlanta.

The tactical flow of battle on these two days began with a preliminary flanking movement by the Federals via Snake Creek Gap. This movement forced a Confederate withdrawal on 13 May 1864 from their strong defensive position at Dalton, Georgia. Thirteen miles south of Dalton, at Resaca, the new Confederate line of defense faced west, covering the village and the railroad with each flank of this line anchored on a river. This ill-chosen position by the Confederates offered the larger Federal army an opportunity to destroy its opponent before the campaign had barely begun. Yet Sherman hesitated—his missed opportunity at Resaca would result in another 110 days of marching with daily combat before Atlanta's surrender on 2 September 1864.

The two days of battle at Resaca can best be understood by dividing the action into three zones of combat: (1) the battle at the Angle; (2) Leonidas Polk's battlefield; and (3) John B. Hood's battlefield.

The battle at the Angle involved more than two hours of fighting on 14 May, when two divisions of the 23d Army Corps (Army of the Ohio, John Schofield, commanding) failed to break the Confederate line of defense at the junction of John Bell Hood's and William J. Hardee's corps. Federal casualties, including killed, wounded, and missing exceeded 1,000; Confederate casualties were substantially fewer.

On Leonidas Polk's battlefield, the only significant advantage gained by either side on 14 May was a successful assault by John Logan's XV Army Corps near the south end of the battlefield late in the day. Two Federal brigades of infantry rushed across Camp Creek (a small stream and marsh that divided the two armies) and captured a group of low hills, driving a reinforced skirmish line of Confederate infantry from these earthworks. The Federals managed to hold this position just east of Camp Creek despite repeated, evening-long efforts by Confederate general Polk to dislodge them.

The advantage won here offered the Federals an opportunity to place artillery on these hills—artillery that could control or destroy Confederate rail and foot bridges necessary to an organized retreat less than three quarters of a mile away.

On John B. Hood's battlefield, in action on 14 May the two divisions of Hood's Corps succeeded in winning a temporary advantage late in the day near the Dalton-Resaca wagon road. The understrength and unsupported Confederate infantry were finally driven back east of the wagon road by the timely arrival of Federal reinforcements and the heroic action of the 5th Indiana Battery. The next day (15 May) Joseph Hooker's Federals and Hood's Confederates, each seeking to advance, collided in the maze of ravines and thickets, neither gaining an advantage. The event of the day that attracted most attention was the capture of an abandoned Confederate four-gun artillery battery by an Indiana regiment commanded by future president of the United States,

The battle of Resaca (*Library of Congress*)

Benjamin Harrison. The action at the Confederate battery was especially desperate. Some fighting continued here until near midnight.

When the Confederates learned that their railroad supply line to Atlanta was being threatened by a Federal division crossing the river south of Resaca, they withdrew from the battlefield in the predawn hours of 16 May.

Resaca is said to have been a tactical victory for the Confederate army, but the threat of flanking maneuvers by Sherman forced the Southern army to protect its railroad to Atlanta by abandoning Resaca and subsequent battlefields, always retreating southward along the railroad. At Resaca, an alert and aggressive commander would have seized the opportunity on the fourteenth. Sherman had won a half-mile wide corridor of gentle hills spanning his front from the river on the right to the nearest ridge on his left, and he should have carried the fight to his opponent. Yet with only Polk's newly constituted and untested corps between him and the almost certain destruction of the Confederate army, Sherman chose instead to spend 15 May entrenching artillery.

Sherman thus lost a great opportunity to bag the entire Confederate army at Resaca. When Sherman's victorious army marched into Atlanta on 2 September, it was largely the result of a long campaign of maneuver attended throughout with great uncertainties. Although in retrospect some of his reputation as a great commander seems unwarranted, Sherman does deserve credit for his resourcefulness in adjusting his campaign to accommodate the nature of the army he commanded and his own limitations.

—*Philip Lee Secrist*

See also Atlanta Campaign; Hardee, William J.; Hood, John Bell; Hooker, Joseph; Johnston, Joseph E.; Logan, John A.; Polk, Leonidas; Rocky Face Ridge, Battle of; Schofield, John M.; Sherman, William T.

For further reading:
Cox, Jacob Dolson. *Atlanta* (1882).
McMurray, William J. *History of the Twentieth Tennessee Volunteer Infantry C.S.A.* (1904).
Nisbet, James C. *Four Years on the Firing Line* (1963).
U.S. War Department. *War of the Rebellion: A Compilation of the Official Records of the Union and Confederate Armies* (1880–1901).

REYNOLDS, ARABELLA "BELLE"
(1843– ?)

Union nurse and daughter of the regiment

Arabella "Belle" Macomber was born in Massachusetts in 1843. When she was an adolescent, Belle traveled with her family to the Midwest, where at the age of seventeen she married John G. Reynolds, settling with him in Peoria, Illinois. When the Civil War broke out, John signed up with the 17th Illinois Infantry and, despite much advice to the contrary from friends and family members, his young bride decided to accompany him to war as a regimental nurse. In August 1861 the 17th headed south.

Arriving at the regiment's encampment at Bird's Point, Missouri, Belle Reynolds initially seems to have been less than enthusiastic about military life. In a reminiscence published after the war she recalled her first impression of her new camp home: "No floors, no chairs, the narrow cot my seat, my feet imbedded in the hot sand, the confusion of camp close around me, with but the thickness of cloth between me and the eyes of all." Belle determined to make the best of it, however, cheerfully taking up the work of a nurse and, within short order, earning the love and respect of the men of the 17th.

Reynolds was present with her regiment during Ulysses S. Grant's campaigns against Forts Henry and Donelson, and then at Shiloh in April 1862. It was in connection with that great battle, with its 23,000 casualties, that Reynolds formally earned the designation "daughter of the regiment." On 16 April, in honor of her unstinting care of the sick and wounded at Shiloh and also her bravery in trying to prevent hundreds of frantic soldiers from storming the Union hospital ship, the *Emerald*, which had docked at Pittsburg Landing during the battle, Illinois governor Richard Yates signed a document recognizing Reynolds's courageous service to the regiment and even going so far as to grant her an honorary commission as a "major," above and beyond her already special status as regimental daughter.

After Shiloh the battle-weary Reynolds traveled home to Peoria for a brief period of rest and recuperation, returning to the regiment—and her husband—to continue in military service until the fall of 1864. Most notably during these latter years the 17th participated in Grant's Vicksburg campaign, through all of which Belle Reynolds continued to prove her value to the regiment as both nurse and—in keeping with her "office"—inspiration to the troops. She tended the sick and wounded, wrote letters for them, did their sewing, and sent home reports—often published subsequently in local newspapers—of the regiment's (and the individual soldiers') progress and needs. Soldiers who knew her well recalled that Reynolds asked for no privileges, instead sleeping regularly on the ground and eating the same food as they, even marching long distances on foot when she had the opportunity to ride in an ambulance.

In the fall of 1864 John Reynolds's enlistment expired and with him Belle retired from Union army service. Eventually, the two moved to Santa Barbara, California, where they were active in veterans organizations, she perhaps even more so than he. Reynolds's date of death is unknown, but in 1898 a newspaper article describing an earlier visit by former President Benjamin Harrison to Santa Barbara noted that Harrison, upon meeting this famous daughter of the regiment in 1891, paid more attention to her "than to any of the hundreds of political leaders and rich men of California who gathered around him."

—*Elizabeth D. Leonard*

See also Nurses; Shiloh, Battle of; Vicksburg Campaign; Women; Yates, Richard.

For further reading:

Leonard, Elizabeth D. *"All the Daring of a Soldier": Women of the Civil War Armies* (1999).

Moore, Frank. *Women of the War: Their Heroism and Self-Sacrifice* (1866).

"Only Woman Officer." *Washington Post* (1898).

Young, Agatha. *The Women and the Crisis: Women of the North in the Civil War* (1959).

REYNOLDS, JOHN FULTON
(1820–1863)

Union general

John Fulton Reynolds was born in Lancaster, Pennsylvania, on 21 September 1820. One of nine surviving children, Reynolds was educated in Lititz, Pennsylvania, and later at the Long Green Academy in Baltimore. He graduated from the Lancaster County Academy in 1835. In 1837, Senator James Buchanan, a family friend, secured him admission to the United States Military Academy.

Reynolds reported to West Point in June 1837. He graduated on 1 July 1841, 26 in his class of 52. Reynolds was commissioned brevet second lieutenant in the 3d United States Artillery Regiment. Reynolds was ordered to Fort McHenry following graduation. In 1842, he was sent to St. Augustine, Florida, and then to Fort Moultrie, South Carolina, where he remained until 1845 when his regiment moved to Corpus Christi, Texas, to join Zachary Taylor's army.

After moving to the Rio Grande in 1846, Reynolds helped defend Fort Brown. His baptism by fire came on 21 September 1846 during Taylor's assault on Monterrey. He received a brevet to the rank of captain for gallantry. During the battle of Buena Vista, Reynolds's section of guns prevented Mexican horsemen from outflanking the American left and participated in stemming the final Mexican charge. These actions earned him a second brevet to major.

Reynolds was stationed at Fort Preble, Maine, after the Mexican-American War. In 1853 he was ordered to New Orleans and later was sent to Fort Lafayette, New York. Reynolds marched to Salt Lake City during tensions with the Mormons in 1855. He was stationed at Fort Orford, Oregon, and participated in the Rogue River Indian War in 1856. Reynolds returned to the Utah Territory during the "Mormon War."

Reynolds arrived at West Point as commandant of cadets in 1860. One year later he was offered, but rejected, a position as Winfield Scott's aide-de-camp. With the onset of hostilities, he was given command of Regular Army regiment but before he could raise the unit, was made brigadier general and ordered to report to Washington, D.C. Reynolds received new orders to report to Cape Hatteras Inlet, North Carolina, before he reached the capital, but this raised controversy. General George McClellan was furious about this change in orders. He complained directly to the secretary of war and secured Reynolds's service in the Army of the Potomac, where he was immediately appointed to a military board examining the qualifications of volunteer officers. After release from that duty, Reynolds assumed command of a brigade of the Pennsylvania Reserves.

Reynolds occupied and was military governor of Fredericksburg, Virginia, in June 1862. His brigade was soon ordered to join General Fitz John Porter's V Corps near Mechanicsville, Virginia, during the Peninsula campaign. On 26 June 1862, the Rebels assailed Porter's position, but the defensive line that Reynolds had created held. The V Corps pulled back to Gaines' Mill and on 27 June faced renewed attacks. After fighting a holding action that allowed Porter to retreat, Reynolds was unable to find his way back to Union lines and was taken prisoner at dawn on 28 June. He was transferred to Richmond were he was interred at Libby Prison until he was exchanged on 13 August 1862.

Upon release, Reynolds was given command of the Pennsylvania Reserve division. His division arrived at Bull Run to support General John Pope's Army of Virginia on 22 August. Reynolds was never able to engage the enemy fully until the last day of the battle of Second Bull Run. As Pope's routed army began to flee toward the rear, Reynolds threw a hasty line of defense on Henry House Hill. As Rebels hurled themselves at his position, Reynolds seized the flag of the 2d Regiment and led a downhill charge that halted the Confederate advance. His stand on 30 August at Henry House Hill helped save Pope's army from destruction.

Reynolds missed the opportunity to fight at Antietam. Pennsylvania governor Andrew Curtin insisted that Reynolds be released from the Army of the Potomac in order for him to command the state militia. After the threat of a Confederate invasion of Pennsylvania subsided, Reynolds returned to the Army of the Potomac. He was given command of I Corps and on 29 November 1862 was made a major general. At the battle of Fredericksburg, Reynolds's corps launched several assaults, and one of his divisions nearly broke through the Rebel defenses but was forced to withdraw.

During the battle of Chancellorsville, much to Reynolds's dismay, his corps sat unengaged. General Joseph Hooker refused repeated requests to allow I Corps to join the fray. After the Union failure in the campaign, Reynolds was called to a private meeting with President Abraham Lincoln on 2 June in Washington, D.C. At the conference, Lincoln questioned if he would be interested in command of the Army of the Potomac. Reynolds informed the president that unless given complete independence, he would prefer not to take command. Out of respect, Lincoln did not assign Reynolds to the position. Instead, he ordered George G. Meade to assume command of the Army of the Potomac.

Meade immediately gave Reynolds command of the left wing of the Army of the Potomac, which consisted of I, III, and XI Corps, as well as General John Buford's cavalry. The lead elements of Reynolds's command crossed into Pennsylvania on 30 June. Buford informed him that Confederate forces were converging on Gettysburg. Early on 1 July, Reynolds rode into Gettysburg where Buford requested instructions about whether to stand and fight or retreat. The major general decided to interpose his own command between the scattered Confederate units and prevent the Rebels from concentrating their forces unopposed. It was Reynolds's decision that forced Meade to fight at Gettysburg. Reynolds rushed the 1st Division of I Corps forward and positioned a defensive line across the Chambersburg Pike. Reynolds stayed on McPherson's Ridge and personally directed the onrushing regiments. As the 2d Wisconsin came into line, Reynolds ordered a charge into a Rebel position and riding at its front cried "For God's sake forward!" Shortly after leading the advance, Reynolds was killed by a Confederate volley directed from near McPherson's Barn. Reynolds was laid to rest in Lancaster on 4 July 1863.

John Reynolds was a complex individual whose own family did not learn of his engagement to Kate Hewitt until after his death. He was a consummate professional who was respected by his peers and his troops. Reynolds was a soldier who possessed the ability to command men in battle and had a strong grasp of strategic and tactical operations. As the ranking Union officer on the field at the time, Reynolds committed his command and ultimately the entire Army of the Potomac to fight at Gettysburg. The lack of imaginative Union command, especially at the battles of Fredericksburg and Chancellorsville, helped fuel his desire to engage the Army of Northern Virginia during its invasion of

Pennsylvania. John Fulton Reynolds deserves credit as the "architect" of the battle at Gettysburg.

—*Stephen A. Carney*

See also Bull Run, Second Battle of; Gettysburg, Battle of.

For further reading:

Anderson, Kalina K. "The Girl He Left Behind." *America's Civil War* (1999).

Nichols, Edward J. *Toward Gettysburg: A Biography of General John F. Reynolds* (1958; reprint, 1987).

Riley, Michael A. *"For God's Sake, Forward": General John F. Reynolds, U.S.A.* (1995).

Sanders, Steve. "Enduring Tales of Gettysburg: The Death of Reynolds." *Gettysburg Magazine* (1996).

REYNOLDS, JOSEPH JONES
(1822–1899)
Union general

Born in Flemingsburg, Kentucky, to Edward Reynolds and Sarah Longley Reynolds, Joseph Jones Reynolds moved with his family when he was fifteen to Lafayette, Indiana. He began his college education at Wabash College but in 1839 accepted appointment to the U.S. Military Academy. He graduated tenth of thirty-nine in the class of 1843. Commissioned into the 4th Artillery, Reynolds served at several posts before being sent to join Zachary Taylor's Army of Observation in Texas. Reynolds, however, went to serve as an instructor at West Point before seeing any action in the Mexican-American War. After eight years at the academy, he was sent to Indian Territory. He resigned his commission in 1857 and accepted a teaching position at Washington University in St. Louis. When the Civil War broke out, Reynolds was in business in Lafayette, Indiana, with his brother.

Reynolds's military experience gained him appointment as colonel of the 10th Indiana. He was promoted to brigadier general in May 1861. By late summer 1861, Reynolds had been assigned to the command of William S. Rosecrans in the District of West Virginia. Near Elkwater at Cheat Mountain on 11 September 1861, forces commanded by Robert E. Lee attacked Reynolds's brigade. During several days of fighting and maneuvering, Reynolds was able to repulse the attack. For the remainder of the year he skirmished with Confederates but kept control of the area. In early 1862, he resigned his commission to attend to business concerns.

Reynolds returned to the army in August 1862 as the colonel of the 75th Indiana. Within a month he was promoted to brigadier general and became major general of volunteers by the end of November. At the same time, his former commander, Rosecrans, requested that Reynolds be assigned to Rosecrans's Army of the Cumberland. He was immediately given a division in George Thomas's corps and fought at the end of the year at Stones River. Thomas commended Reynolds for his actions in that battle.

During the early months of 1863, Reynolds and his division conducted several raids into Confederate territory to tear up rail lines and destroy or confiscate supplies. Perhaps his most productive raid was against the Manchester & McMinnville Railroad at the end of April 1863, when he destroyed not only supplies but a large amount of rolling stock as well. In June 1863, Reynolds participated in the Tullahoma campaign, particularly distinguishing himself at the skirmish at Hoover's Gap on 24 June.

In September 1863, Reynolds fought under Thomas at Chickamauga and was again commended by his commander. When Thomas assumed command of the Army of the Cumberland in October 1863, Reynolds became the army's chief of staff. He held that position through the Chattanooga campaign, but in January 1864 he took temporary command of the defenses of New Orleans. During the summer of 1864, Reynolds commanded XIX Corps and the District of Morganza, Louisiana, and participated in the campaign that culminated in the battle of Mobile Bay. In the fall, he became the commander of the Department of Arkansas, a position he held for the remainder of the war.

Joseph Reynolds (*National Archives*)

After the war Reynolds remained in the army. Upon the 1866 reorganization he became the colonel of the 26th Infantry. Reynolds's friendship with his old West Point classmate Ulysses S. Grant may have helped him with his new army career. After transferring to the cavalry in 1870, Reynolds served on the frontier, fighting in various Indian wars. In 1876, while serving under George Crook against the Sioux on the Powder River, Reynolds ordered a retreat that some considered premature, especially since if left men behind to fall into the hands of the Indians. Though he avoided a court-martial conviction, Reynolds did have to face considerable criticism, so he retired the following year. He spent his remaining years in Washington, D.C., where he died on 25 February 1899. He had been brevetted brigadier general and major general for his Civil War service.

—*David S. Heidler and Jeanne T. Heidler*

See also Cheat Mountain, Virginia; Thomas, George Henry; Tullahoma Campaign.

For further reading:
Vaughn, J. W. *The Reynolds Campaign on Powder River* (1983).

RHETT, ROBERT BARNWELL, SR.
(1800–1876)
Southern journalist and Confederate congressmen

No name is more associated with secession than that of the man sometimes called the "Father of Secession." He was born Robert Barnwell Smith, near Beaufort, South Carolina, 21 December 1800. He studied law and went into practice in 1821, achieving some initial success, but quickly showing a tendency to go heavily into debt acquiring rice plantations and slaves, partly to improve his fortune, but also to raise his social status. In 1837 he and several of his brothers changed their name to Rhett for reasons that are still unclear. By then he had already served in the state legislature and spent a term as attorney general.

He early became involved in extreme Southern rights politics as a disciple of John C. Calhoun, but in time became even more strident than his mentor, with whom he broke on occasion. Rhett first publicly issued a call for secession in the 1830s at Bluffton, and though forced to retreat somewhat in the face of the reaction even in South Carolina, he thereafter raised the specter of secession again and again in speaking for states' rights and opposing a Washington government that he felt was increasingly dominated by corrupt Northern moneyed and antislave interests. His six terms in Congress from 1837 to 1849, and his brief term in the Senate when appointed to succeed the deceased Calhoun, were marked by bitter speeches on the floor in which he attacked even Southerners who did not share his views. Rhett resigned from the Senate when an election in

South Carolina repudiated, for a time, prosecession candidates, and spent the next several years working to change the public's views through the Charleston *Mercury*, which he partially owned and which was edited by his son Robert Barnwell Rhett, Jr. Rhett was on the spot to serve in the secession convention in 1860 after the election of Lincoln, and proudly signed the ordinance taking South Carolina out of the Union. It was Rhett, too, who proposed that South Carolina invite other seceding states to meet in convention at Montgomery, Alabama, to decide what steps to take next.

Rhett went to the Montgomery Convention at the head of his delegation, though his position seems to have been little more than honorary, since he exerted no influence over his fellow delegates. In fact, several of them regarded him as an arrogant crank, and he would never formally call them together to caucus. Rhett did go expecting to cast a giant shadow, however. He took with him his own draft of a constitution for the proposed new nation, and apparently had some expectation of a high office, perhaps even the presidency.

His disillusionment commenced almost immediately. It became evident that the convention was firmly in the hands of moderates, and old extremists like Rhett would have very little influence at all. Immediately he railed at deliberations being conducted in secret session, arguing that free government required all debate to be in the open. He was decidedly unhappy with the Provisional Constitution adopted on 8 February, and then chagrined to find that there was no support, even in his own delegation, for making him president. His cousin Robert Barnwell persuaded him to vote for Jefferson Davis, which he afterward maintained was the greatest mistake of his life.

Rhett did exert influence on the framing of the permanent Constitution, securing the chairmanship of the committee selected to draft the document. He stood the same ground that he had for decades, arguing for free trade and governmental noninterference with domestic economy. He proposed and won several of the permanent Constitution's provisions, including a single six-year presidential term, civil service reform, a streamlined means of amendment, and a prohibition on appropriations to encourage industry or to impose duties on imports for the benefit of domestic manufactures. Rhett was active in attempting to manage the debate on the document, but apparently spoke too much, as was his wont, and some tired of him.

A bitter pill for Rhett was his appointment to escort President-elect Davis to his inauguration. From the moment of Davis's election, Rhett seemed determined to oppose him, and quickly became a leader of the anti-Davis faction. As chairman of the Foreign Affairs Committee, he accused the president of moving too

slowly in acquiring arms from abroad, of failing to use the South's cotton reserves to fund arms and especially the acquisition of a fleet of warships abroad, and especially of failing to pursue an aggressive foreign policy promising England and France favored nation status with access to cotton and virtual free trade in return for diplomatic recognition and possible military intervention. These would be Rhett's themes against Davis for the rest of the war, and in time he would blame Davis personally for everything that went wrong in the Confederacy. He compared Davis to Judas Iscariot and eventually asserted that Davis was the only man in the South who could have led the cause to defeat.

Rhett held a seat in the Confederate Congress only during the sitting of that first provisional gathering and did not seek election to the first regular Congress. In 1863, however, he sought a seat and was defeated, South Carolinians themselves realizing that he was now too extreme to do anything but harm. He spent the remainder of the war sniping at every action of the Davis administration, using the pages of his son's newspaper, the *Mercury*, as his podium. At one point he was in correspondence with others to suggest deposing Davis forcibly and putting General Lee at the head of the government. When the Federals occupied Charleston and the Low Country in early 1865, Rhett and his family and slaves barely escaped by night.

After the war Rhett wandered between Charleston, Georgia, and Alabama, before finally settling near New Orleans, where his son Robert took up editing a newspaper after the failure of the *Mercury* in 1868. Utterly ruined financially, Rhett strove heroically to provide for his large family, yet could never escape his debt. His health also deteriorated rapidly. During the war his nose showed the beginnings of a facial cancer that eventually saw his entire nose obliterated and his face so deformed that he would not let his grandchildren see him. He retired to a small house that he called Castle Dismal, and there, with his devoted second wife, Katherine, spent much of his time composing a memoir that would be his final justification of his career and a last salvo at Jefferson Davis. He shared it with Beauregard, Joseph E. Johnston, and anyone else pursuing their own personal feuds with Davis. He died at the home of his son-in-law, Alfred Roman (coauthor of Beauregard's memoirs) on 14 September 1876, and was later buried in an unmarked grave in Magnolia Cemetery near Charleston.

—*William C. Davis*

See also *Charleston Mercury*; Constitution, C.S.A.; Fire-eaters; Secession.

For further reading:
Davis, William C. *Rhett: The Ordeal of a Fire-eater* (in press).
Heidler, David S. *Pulling the Temple Down: The Fire-eaters and the Destruction of the Union* (1994).
Walther, Eric H. *The Fire Eaters* (1992).
White, Laura A. *Robert Barnwell Rhett: Father of Secession* (1965).

RICH MOUNTAIN, BATTLE OF
(11 July 1861)

After the Union victory at the battle of Philippi in early June 1861, Richmond dispatched General Robert Garnett to northwestern Virginia to take command of Confederate forces in that region. Upon his arrival there on 14 June Garnett positioned 4,500 men on Laurel Hill, which commanded the road from Grafton to Lewisburg, and 1,300 men under Colonel John Pegram on Rich Mountain to block the Staunton-Parkersburg Turnpike. From these positions, Garnett hoped to thwart the offensive Union general George B. McClellan, commander of the Department of the Ohio, was planning to launch with an eager but inexperienced 20,000-man army.

Upon learning the disposition of Garnett's forces, McClellan drew up a plan that called for a brigade under Thomas A. Morris to make a demonstration at Laurel Hill, while three brigades under his personal direction operated against Pegram. On 6 July McClellan ordered Morris to move forward from Philippi toward Laurel Hill. McClellan began his own advance from Buckhannon the following day and reached Roaring Fork Flats two miles west of Camp Garnett, Pegram's fortified camp at the western base of Rich Mountain, two days later. A reconnaissance in force conducted by engineer officer Orlando Poe confirmed McClellan's desire to win the battle through maneuver, specifically by using William S. Rosecrans's brigade to turn Pegram's position. Fortunately, on 10 July Rosecrans learned from twenty-two-year-old Unionist David Hart, whose family home was situated on the Staunton-Parkersburg Turnpike near the summit of Rich Mountain, that there was a path that offered a convenient route around the Confederate left flank. With some reluctance, McClellan approved Rosecrans's proposal to use the route described by Hart and assured him that he would move the rest of his command forward when he heard gunfire from Pegram's rear.

With Hart as his guide, Rosecrans began his flanking march at 4:00 A.M. on the morning of 11 July. After a difficult climb through a drenching rain, Rosecrans and his 1,900 men reached the summit shortly after noon. Finding their march had been undetected, Rosecrans called a halt and waited until 2:00 P.M. before pushing forward to seize the turnpike. A half-hour later they encountered a 310-man Rebel force under the command of Captain Julius A. de Lagnel positioned around the Hart homestead on the north side of the turnpike. Although greatly outnumbered, de Lagnel's men, aided by a single artillery piece, managed to repulse several attacks before Rosecrans overwhelmed their position. In all,

The battle of Rich Mountain (*Library of Congress*)

the Union suffered twelve dead and sixty-two wounded, while inflicting an estimated seventy-two casualties during the fight at the Hart farm.

McClellan did not make the promised attack on Pegram's camp when he heard the sound of Rosecrans's guns, but merely contented himself with positioning artillery to shell the Rebels. Nonetheless, after de Lagnel's defeat, Pegram had no choice but to abandon Camp Garnett. Only half of his men managed to escape to Beverly. Pegram and the rest, 555 men altogether, surrendered on the twelfth. Meanwhile, Garnett hastily abandoned Laurel Hill, and on 13 July McClellan smashed Garnett's rear guard at the battle of Carrick's Ford. Garnett was mortally wounded during the battle, but the bulk of his command managed to avoid capture. McClellan nonetheless exulted to Washington the following day that: "Our success is complete and secession is killed in this country."

Rich Mountain and Carrick's Ford made McClellan one of the first great Union heroes of the war. They also secured the Trans-Allegheny region of the Old

Dominion for the Union. Later that summer a convention at Wheeling would create the new state of Kanawha out of the western counties of Virginia. The state was later renamed West Virginia and formally entered the Union in June 1863.

—*Ethan S. Rafuse*

See also Carrick's Ford; Garnett, Robert S.; McClellan, George B.; Pegram, John; Rosecrans, William S.
For further reading:
Cox, Jacob Dolson. "McClellan in West Virginia." In *Battles and Leaders of the Civil War.* Edited by Robert U. Johnson and Clarence C. Buel (1887–1888).
McClellan, George B. *Report on the Organization of the Army of the Potomac, To Which is Added an Account of the Campaign in Western Virginia, With Plans of Battlefields* (1864).
Newell, Clayton R. *Lee vs. McClellan: The First Campaigns* (1996).
Thomas, Joseph W. "The Campaigns of Generals McClellan and Rosecrans in Western Virginia, 1861–62." *West Virginia History* (1944).
U.S. War Department. *War of the Rebellion: A Compilation of the Official Records of the Union and Confederate Armies* (1880–1901).

RICHARDSON, ALBERT DEANE
(1833–1869)
Journalist

Born to Elisha Richardson and Harriet Blake Richardson in Franklin, Massachusetts, Albert Deane Richardson was educated in the local schools and for a time attended Holliston Academy. After leaving school he tried his hand at a variety of jobs, including school teaching, before deciding to make his fortune in the west. He initially went to Pittsburgh, where he entered the field of journalism and then to Cincinnati, where he also wrote for local newspapers. From Cincinnati, Richardson moved farther west to Kansas, where he arrived in the midst of that territory's troubles in 1857.

A staunch opponent of the expansion of slavery, Richardson sent stories detailing the controversies in the territory back to the *Boston Journal*. While in Kansas Richardson also held several minor positions in the free territory government.

Even with all the turmoil in Kansas, Richardson had not seen the Wild West he had hoped for, so in 1859 when given the opportunity to travel with Horace Greeley and Henry Villard to Colorado to see Pike's Peak, he jumped at the opportunity. While in Colorado, Richardson toyed with the idea of settling there and for a brief time published a small newspaper in the territory. After leaving Colorado, he toured New Mexico for a brief time and then moved to New York City, where Greeley had offered him a correspondent's position on the *New York Tribune*.

Richardson started with the *Tribune* in the midst of the secession crisis. One of his first assignments was to travel to the South, specifically New Orleans, to report back to the paper regarding the mood there. He made his way to New Orleans in February 1861 and stayed there for over a month. Richardson found various ingenious means to correspond with the paper without alerting his New Orleans neighbors or anyone who might intercept his letters as to his true identity. He wrote most of his reports as if he were a long-time resident of the city writing to a business friend in the North. He also used various ciphers to communicate some information to the *Tribune* and always sent his letters to intermediaries, rather than directly to the paper. He returned to New York in April 1861, having given the readers a detailed account of life in the new Confederacy.

Upon his return Richardson requested to become a war correspondent, the Fort Sumter crisis having made the possibility of war a reality. He was sent to Missouri to cover the growing hostilities there and arrived in time to cover the battle of Wilson's Creek. While in Missouri Richardson became acquainted with the theater's commander, John C. Frémont. Unlike many who came to know the "Pathfinder," Richardson was favorably impressed, especially with Frémont's unsuccessful efforts to free the slaves belonging to Confederate sympathizers.

Remaining in the Western theater, Richardson went to Tennessee after Shiloh in the spring of 1862 and attempted to cover Henry Halleck's campaign against Corinth, Mississippi. When Halleck, indulging a strong dislike of war correspondents, banned reporters from the campaign, Richardson led the unsuccessful petition campaign launched to overrule Halleck's decision.

Richardson continued to try to cover the war in the west, but with other generals such as William Tecumseh Sherman following Halleck's lead, such coverage became increasingly difficult. He came east in the summer of 1862 and covered the Antietam campaign, but access to battlefields was becoming more difficult. Somewhat of an activist on this issue of access, Richardson and a group of reporters met with the Abraham Lincoln in March 1863 to persuade the president to overrule generals who banned reporters. Lincoln, who had met Richardson before the war when the latter was a correspondent in the Midwest, gave the reporters a friendly hearing, but made no promises.

Shortly after Richardson's interview with the president, Richardson was sent by the *Tribune* to Mississippi to cover Ulysses S. Grant's Vicksburg campaign. Traveling with two other reporters, Junius Henri Browne and Richard T. Colburn, Richardson and his companions tried to make their way past the city by river on a barge. When they were spotted and a party sent out to capture them, the three tried to make their escape on cotton bales thrown into the river. They were overtaken and placed in Vicksburg's jail. From Vicksburg, Richardson and Browne were sent to Libby Prison in Richmond, Virginia, and in September 1863 transferred to Castle Thunder. In February 1864 the two were moved again, this time to the prison at Salisbury, North Carolina. Throughout the time of their imprisonment, great exertions were made by the Northern press and the government to obtain their release, but to no avail. While at Salisbury, Richardson learned of the death of his wife.

In June 1864 Richardson and Browne attempted to tunnel their way out of the prison but were caught when their tunnel was discovered. The following December, however, they successfully escaped and walked several hundred miles overland to Union territory in Tennessee.

After the war, Richardson continued to work as a reporter for the *Tribune*. He traveled west again for the paper in 1866, sending reports back on the economy and cultures of that region. He later compiled his writings from that trip into a book, *Beyond the Mississippi*. Besides that work he wrote an account of his harrowing days in Confederate captivity and of his escape. In 1868 he wrote a very well-received campaign biography of Ulysses S. Grant.

In 1869 Richardson fell in love with Abby Sage McFarland, the estranged wife of Daniel McFarland, an alcoholic, abusive Tammany Hall thug. When Mrs. McFarland's divorce was final, she and Richardson announced their engagement. On 25 November 1869 Daniel McFarland came into the *Tribune* offices and shot Richardson. The wounded man was carried to a nearby hotel where he lingered for a week. During that time Henry Ward Beecher and Octavius Brooks Frothingham performed a marriage ceremony for the two tragic lovers. Richardson died on 2 December 1869. Using his Tammany connections and misplaced sympathy for a wronged husband, McFarland was acquitted of murder.

—*David S. Heidler and Jeanne T. Heidler*

See also *New York Tribune*; Newspapers; War Correspondents.

For further reading:

Andrews, J. Cutler. *The North Reports the Civil War* (1955).

Cooper, George. *Lost Love: A True Story of Passion, Murder, and Justice* (1993).

Richardson, Albert D. *The Secret Service, the Field, the Dungeon and the Escape* (1865).

Starr, Louis M. *Bohemian Brigade: Civil War Newsmen in Action* (1954; reprint, 1987).

RICHARDSON, ISRAEL BUSH
(1815–1862)
Union general

Born in Fairfax, Vermont, the son of Israel Putnam Richardson and Susan Holmes Richardson and a descendent of General Israel Putnam, Israel Richardson was educated locally before receiving an appointment to the U.S. Military Academy. He graduated thirty-eighth of fifty-two in the class of 1841. Upon his commissioning, Richardson went to fight in the last phases of the Second Seminole War. After the end of that conflict, he served on the southwestern frontier. When tensions increased with Mexico over the annexation of Texas, Richardson became part of Zachary Taylor's Army of Observation. He fought in Taylor's opening campaign in the Mexican-American War before transferring to Winfield Scott's command for the Mexico City campaign. During the march to the Mexican capital, Richardson won the nickname that would follow him to the Civil War—"Fighting Dick"—and two brevet promotions.

After the Mexican-American War, Richardson continued to serve on the frontier until he resigned from the army in 1855. He moved to Pontiac, Michigan, and became a farmer until the outbreak of the Civil War.

Abraham Lincoln's call for volunteers prompted Richardson to raise a regiment that became the 2d Michigan. He became its colonel. Richardson led his men to Washington, where they immediately became part of Irvin McDowell's army marching on the Confederate position at Manassas Junction. At the battle of First Bull Run, Richardson commanded the 4th Brigade of the 1st Division, charged with guarding Blackburn's Ford. Although he did not see much action during the battle, Richardson's men remained calm during the precipitous Union retreat and were able to guard part of the withdrawal. During the battle, Richardson had engaged in a dispute with Colonel Dixon S. Miles in which Miles threatened to arrest Richardson for disobedience. Richardson accused Miles of being drunk, an accusation that was later upheld by a court of inquiry.

On 9 August Richardson was promoted to brigadier general of volunteers with the rank to date from 17 May. That fall, Richardson and his brigade patrolled south of Washington as far as the Rappahannock River. In the early months of 1862, he and the rest of the Army of the Potomac prepared for what would become the Peninsula campaign. As a result of the reorganization of the army into corps, on 14 March 1862 Richardson assumed command of Edwin Sumner's division when Sumner became commander of II Corps. Richardson's division was a part of that corps.

In the Peninsula campaign Richardson led his division at the siege of Yorktown and in the battles of Seven Pines and the Seven Days'. His stern discipline tempered by a somewhat casual attitude toward military formality earned him not only the respect but the affection of his men. Moreover, his division gained the reputation as ranking among the army's hardest fighting volunteers; it certainly contained some of the rowdiest, including Thomas Meagher's Irish Brigade. They distinguished themselves on the battlefield, however, and on 5 July 1862 Richardson earned promotion to major general of volunteers dating to the previous day.

During the Antietam campaign of September 1862 as McClellan closed in on Robert E. Lee's position at Sharpsburg, Maryland, Richardson's division led the advance toward Antietam Creek. On the day of the battle, 17 September, Richardson's division of Sumner's corps was held in reserve in the early morning hours of the battle. About 10:30 A.M., it was sent toward the furious fighting at Bloody Lane. Richardson led his men forward and, after fierce exchanges of fire, forced the Confederate retreat. Yet Confederate artillery threatened Richardson's newly won ground. After waiting for Union long-range batteries to join the fray, Richardson in some exasperation began positioning a small battery, the only one at his disposal. He was thus occupied when Confederate case shot struck him. Carried to McClellan's headquarters, he lingered for three weeks and finally died on 3 November 1862. Before his death, Richardson was commended for his bravery by Major General Sumner.

—*David S. Heidler and Jeanne T. Heidler*

See also Antietam; Irish Brigade.

For further reading:

Priest, John M. *Antietam: The Soldier's Battle* (1989).

Sears, Stephen W. *Landscape Turned Red: The Battle of Antietam* (1983).

RICHMOND CAMPAIGN (OVERLAND CAMPAIGN)
(May–June 1864)

The May–June 1864 Overland campaign against Richmond saw the most sustained and ferocious bloodletting of the entire Civil War. From the fighting in the Wilderness on 5–6 May through Spotsylvania, Trevilian Station, North Anna, Totopotomoy Creek, Bethesda Church, Cold Harbor, and the onset of the siege of Petersburg in mid-June, the Army of Northern Virginia suffered approximately 33,500 casualties. Losses in the Army of the Potomac and its attached units, meanwhile, approached 55,000. While the butcher's bill was enormous, the campaign ended Lee's ability to fight a war of maneuver, and forced the Army of Northern Virginia into defensive siege lines around Richmond and Petersburg that would collapse in the spring of 1865.

In March 1864, President Lincoln appointed Lieutenant General Ulysses S. Grant to overall command of the Union Army. Grant planned multiple offensives for the spring of 1864. Primary among these was the advance of George Meade's Army of the Potomac directly against Richmond and Lee's army, and William T. Sherman's multiarmy offensive in north Georgia. Other planned movements included those of Benjamin Butler's Army of the James, which was to advance against the Confederate capital from the south and east; Franz Sigel's troops in western Virginia, which were to clear the Shenandoah Valley; and a proposed offensive against Mobile to be led by Nathaniel Banks. Grant himself would accompany the Army of the Potomac, though Meade was to remain in actual command. Reorganized prior to the opening of the campaign, the eastern army consisted of three army corps, the II, V, and VI. Winfield Scott Hancock led the II Corps, while Gouverneur Warren and John Sedgwick commanded the V and VI Corps respectively. Philip Sheridan, meanwhile, would lead Grant's cavalry. Complicating an already awkward command structure was the fact that the Ninth Army Corps, commanded by Major General Ambrose Burnside, would move with the Army of the Potomac. Because of Burnside's seniority in rank, however, his corps would receive orders directly from Grant. At the campaign's outset, Federal forces numbered about 118,000. Grant received some 64,000 additional troops during the course of the fighting, most prominently William Smith's XVIII Corps. Offsetting this, however, was the loss of 20,000 men whose enlistments would expire.

Robert E. Lee faced this threat with fewer resources. When the Overland campaign began, his Army of Northern Virginia, encamped south of the Rapidan River in the vicinity of Orange Court House and Gordonsville, numbered approximately 66,000, but he would receive some 30,000 reinforcements during the fighting. His veteran army was divided into the I, II, and III Corps, commanded respectively by James Longstreet, Richard Ewell, and Ambrose Powell Hill, while J.E.B. Stuart led Lee's cavalry corps.

In early May, Grant ordered the Army of the Potomac to break camp and move toward the Rapidan. He planned to cross the river to the east of Lee's army and move through the tangled region west of Fredericksburg, known locally as the Wilderness, before the Confederates could react. Grant hoped to ultimately face Lee in open country beyond the Wilderness where his superior numbers could overwhelm the Rebel army. After crossing on 4 May, the leading elements of the Federal army encamped in the Wilderness and waited for their supply trains to reach them. Grant ordered an advance for the next morning, but by this time Lee had sent Hill's and Ewell's corps to contest the advance. On 5 May, bitter, confused fighting broke out along the Orange Turnpike and the Plank Road. The Confederates grimly held their lines until darkness ended the fighting. The next day Grant renewed Hancock's attack on the Confederate right, while sending Burnside's IX Corps into the gap between Hill and Ewell. Hill's exhausted troops were driven back, but Burnside was slow and Longstreet's Corps arrived at a critical moment to blunt the Union advance. By midday, Longstreet launched a counterattack that drove back Hancock's Corps some distance. Later in the afternoon Lee ordered a larger assault against Hancock that was repulsed, while Ewell mounted an attack on the Union right. In the two-day battle, the Federals lost about 17,500 men. A recent study cites Confederate casualties at 11,125.

While his army had suffered heavy casualties, Lee had stopped Grant from moving unimpeded through the Wilderness. After similar defeats in previous campaigns, the Federals had retreated back across the Rapidan. Grant, however, was determined to press his outnumbered foe. During the fighting in the Wilderness, the general had sent word to President Lincoln that "whatever happens, there will be no turning back." On 7 May, he moved around Lee's right toward the important road junction at Spotsylvania Court House. Confederate troops under Richard Anderson, who had succeeded the wounded Longstreet as commander of the I Corps, were able to reach Spotsylvania in time to reinforce a small cavalry force and prevent Union troops from occupying the crossroads. Fighting would continue in the vicinity for nearly two weeks, with Confederate troops establishing strong defensive positions upon which Grant's men repeatedly assaulted. On 10 May, Grant attacked the Confederate left but was repulsed. That evening Colonel Emory Upton led an attack on the "Mule Shoe"

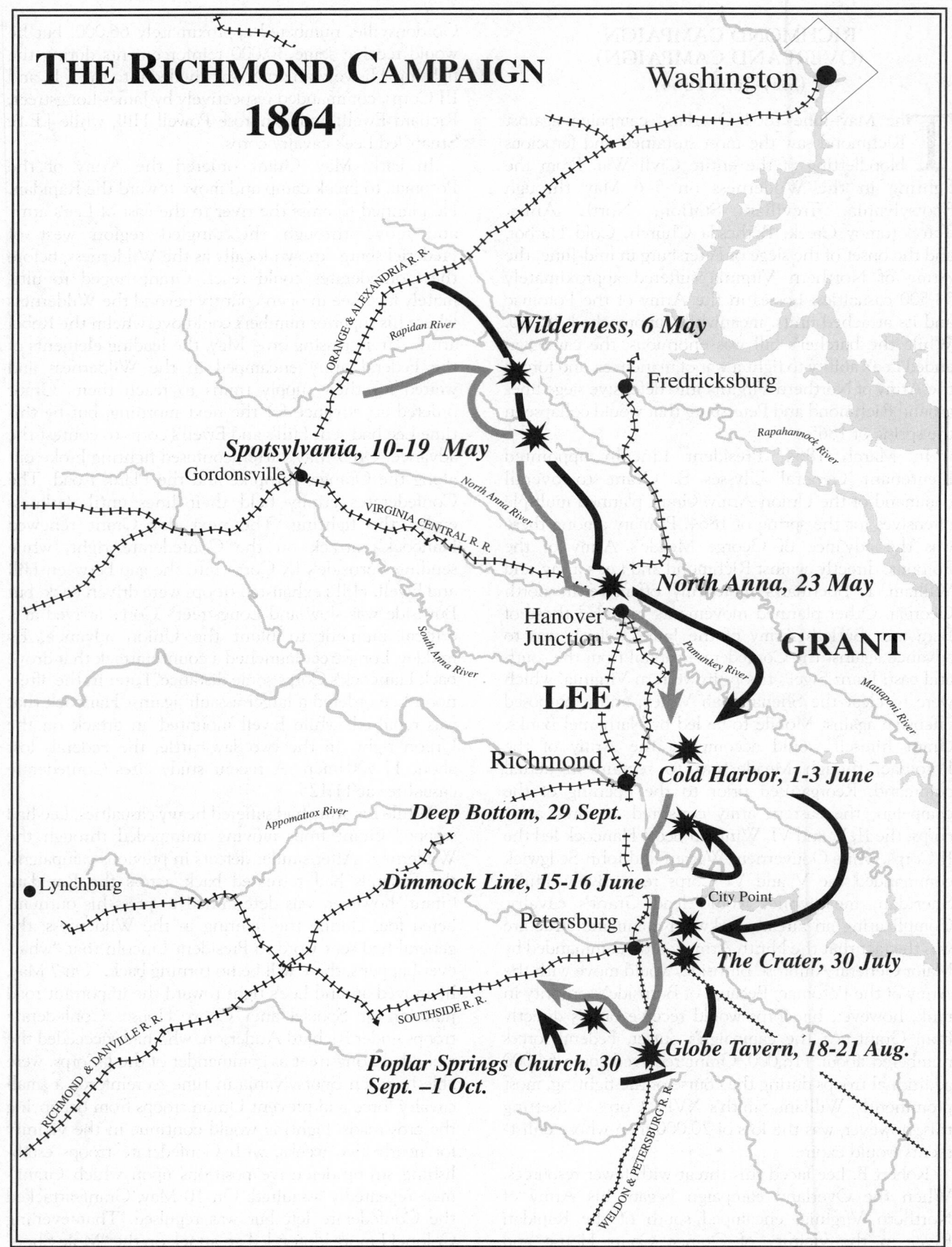

THE RICHMOND CAMPAIGN 1864

Washington

ORANGE & ALEXANDRIA R.R.

Rapidan River

Wilderness, 6 May

Fredericksburg

Rapahannock River

Spotsylvania, 10-19 May

Gordonsville

North Anna River

VIRGINIA CENTRAL R.R.

South Anna River

North Anna, 23 May

Hanover Junction

Pamunkey River

Mattaponi River

GRANT

LEE

Richmond

Cold Harbor, 1-3 June

Deep Bottom, 29 Sept.

Appomattox River

Dimmock Line, 15-16 June

Lynchburg

City Point

Petersburg

The Crater, 30 July

SOUTHSIDE R. R.

Globe Tavern, 18-21 Aug.

Poplar Springs Church, 30 Sept. –1 Oct.

RICHMOND & DANVILLE R.R.

WELDON & PETERSBURG R.R.

salient in the center of Lee's lines. Advancing in columns along a narrow front, Upton's reinforced brigade penetrated the Confederate lines but was eventually forced to withdraw.

On the twelfth, Hancock launched a massive assault of some 20,000 men against the "Mule Shoe." Overwhelming the defenders, the Federals broke the rebel lines, capturing several thousand men of Ewell's Corps and threatening to crack Lee's entire line. Lee frantically established new defensive works at the base of the salient, and further assaults by the corps' of Burnside and Horatio Wright (who had replaced Sedgwick—killed by a sharpshooter on 9 May) were repulsed. The hand-to-hand fighting along the salient, known also as the "Bloody Angle," was among the worst of the entire war. Over the next week each army made probing attacks against the other, most notably at Harris's Farm on 19 May, but the worst of the fighting was over. At Spotsylvania, Lee lost nearly 12,500 men. Among the dead was J.E.B. Stuart, mortally wounded in the 11 May cavalry fight at Yellow Tavern. Grant's losses were significantly higher.

From Spotsylvania, Grant once again shifted along Lee's right, forcing the Confederates to abandon their strong defensive position. The next significant combat occurred along the North Anna River from 20–26 May. This included fights at Milford Station on 21 May, Chesterfield Bridge and Jericho Mill on 23 May, as well as actions at Guinea Station and Milford Station. After these indecisive engagements, Grant crossed the Pamunkey River to the vicinity of Totopotomoy Creek. During the last days of May, Sheridan's cavalry fought several sharp skirmishes in this area, and a Confederate attack was repulsed at Bethesda Church. Here Grant also received reinforcements to bolster his depleted command in the form of the XVIII and a portion of the X Corps.

On 31 May, Grant directed Sheridan to occupy the crossroads at Cold Harbor. The next day Lee attempted to recapture the strategic position, but an attack by elements of the I Corps was repulsed. Later that afternoon Union troops from Wright's VI Corps and William Smith's XVIII struck the Confederate lines near the crossroads. They were repulsed, and Grant then waited for the arrival of Hancock's II Corps before resuming the attack. Unfortunately for the Federals, extreme heat and fatigue slowed Hancock, and a planned attack for 2 June was postponed to the following day. Lee took advantage of the reprieve, establishing an extremely strong line extending past Old Church Road to the north and anchored on the Chickahominy River to the south. Early on 3 June, Grant sent the II, VI, and XVIII Corps against the rebel lines. The Union troops advanced bravely but were repulsed with very heavy losses. A few outer works were captured and in one instance a small

penetration was made in Lee's line, but the Florida Brigade under Joseph Finegan quickly counterattacked and drove the Federals back. Union losses were about 7,000, while Lee suffered only 1,500 casualties.

The two armies remained in the vicinity of Cold Harbor until mid-June when, in a brilliant tactical maneuver, Grant shifted his operations south of the James River. His objective was the city of Petersburg, possession of which would force the Confederates to abandon their capital. The Federal commander's plans to immediately capture Petersburg were frustrated by miscommunication and the failure of subordinates to perform effectively. Nevertheless, by the end of June, Petersburg was under siege and Lee's army had been forced into defensive lines that would be spread ever longer and thinner over the next ten months. The Overland campaign, which had produced nearly 90,000 Union and Confederate casualties, was over.

—*David J. Coles*

See also Cold Harbor, Battle of; Grant, Ulysses Simpson; Lee, Robert Edward; North Anna, Battle of; Spotsylvania, Battle of; Wilderness, Battle of the.

For further reading:
Dowdey, Clifford. *Lee's Last Campaign: The Story of Lee and his Men Against Grant–1864* (1960).
Gallagher, Gary W., ed. *The Spotsylvania Campaign* (1998).
———. *The Wilderness Campaign* (1997).
Matter, William D. *If It Takes All Summer: The Battle of Spotsylvania* (1988).
———. *The Battle of the Wilderness, May 5–6, 1864* (1994).
Rhea, Gordon C. *The Battles for Spotsylvania Court House and the Road to Yellow Tavern, May 7–12, 1864* (1997).
———. *To the North Anna River: Grant and Lee, May 13–25, 1864* (2000).
Steere, Edward. *The Wilderness Campaign* (1960).
Trudeau, Noah Andre. *Bloody Roads South: The Wilderness to Cold Harbor, May–June 1864* (1989).
Young, Alfred C., III. "Numbers and Losses in the Army of Northern Virginia." *North and South* (2000).

RICHMOND EXAMINER

Along with the *Charleston Mercury*, the *Richmond Examiner* was the most outspoken defender of the Confederate position—even as it exceeded the *Mercury* in lambasting President Jefferson Davis's political leadership and military strategy. The *Examiner* was founded in 1847 by twenty-two-year-old John Moncure Daniel, a vehement secessionist and ardent states' rights proponent, who edited the paper until his death just ten days before Lee's surrender at Appomattox. Following the surrender of Fort Sumter, Daniel called on Virginians to march on Washington—anticipating by two months Horace Greeley's "Forward to Richmond!" cry—without waiting for the formal organization of a Confederate army.

Daniel was as flamboyant outside of the *Examiner's* offices as he was in its editorial columns. He defended his

writings in no less than nine pistol duels. His attacks against the North, especially on those elements who Daniel believed harbored secret sympathies to the Southern cause, were no less severe. "The proposition to subjugate (the South)," he wrote in the wake of Fort Sumter, "comes from the Metropolis of the North's boasted conservatism, even from the largest beneficiary of Southern wealth—New York City."

The *Examiner* was known both before and during the war as the South's "school of journalism" because so many prominent writers and correspondents filled its pages. They included George W. Bagby and John Reuben Thompson, both future editors of the *Southern Literary Messenger*, which became the South's most prominent magazine. Basil Gildersleeve, a Princeton-educated philologist with a Ph.D. from Göttingen and later a renowned professor of Greek, also served as an *Examiner* correspondent. Felix Gregory de Fontaine, a French nobleman's son and later editor of the *Charleston Daily Courier*, covered the battle of First Bull Run for the *Examiner*—one of the few Southern correspondents exempted from General P. G. T. Beauregard's order to evacuate all civilians from the area. (After the war, he moved North and worked for James Gordon Bennett's *New York Herald*, for which he had filed the famous first dispatch from Fort Sumter: "Civil War has at last begun.")

Daniel's associate editor, Edward A. Pollard, widely considered the ablest and most prolific Southern writer of the war period, later published numerous lengthy defenses of the Confederacy, one of which, *The Lost Cause*, was considered the standard Southern history of the Civil War. Pollard was captured off the coast of Wilmington, North Carolina, in April 1864 aboard the British-owned ship *Greyhound* while trying to reach England, where he planned to publish a volume about the ongoing war. (Southern presses were no longer capable of such an effort.) He was ordered held at Fort Warren in Boston harbor until the South agreed to release Albert Deane Richardson of the *New York Tribune*, who had himself been taken prisoner. In January 1865 Pollard was granted temporary parole to try to negotiate the release of Richardson, who had been held captive for more than twenty months. Ironically, even as Confederate exchange commissioner Robert Ould was rejecting such a trade, Richardson already had escaped from custody.

In a pamphlet produced shortly before the war's end, Pollard exhorted his fellow Virginians to continued resistance, even as he acknowledged that their cause was lost. "The glory of History is indifferent to events: it is simply Honour," he wrote. "No Submission; No State Negotiations with the Enemy; No Conventions for such objects, however proper for others. Let Virginia stand or fall by the fortunes of the Confederate arms, with her spotless honour in her hands."

The last regular issue of the *Examiner* appeared on 30 March 1865 and carried two major stories: the impending evacuation of Richmond by the Confederate government and the death of the paper's owner and editor, John Moncure Daniel. After a seven-month suspension, the *Examiner* resumed publication on 10 December 1865 and continued until 1867, when it merged with the *Richmond Enquirer*.

—*Eric Fettmann*

See also Bagby, George W.; Newspapers; Pollard, Edward A.; Richardson, Albert Deane; War Correspondents.

For further reading:

Cooley, Raymond K. "John M. Daniel, Editor of the Richmond Examiner and Gadfly of the Confederacy" (M. A. thesis, 1973).

Harwell, Richard B., ed. *The Civil War Reader* (1955).

Houston, Michael. "Edward Alfred Pollard and *The Richmond Examiner*: A Study of Journalistic Opposition In Wartime" (M. A. thesis, 1963).

Mott, Frank Luther. *American Journalism* (1962).

Starr, Louis M. *Bohemian Brigade: Civil War Newsmen in Action* (1954; reprint, 1987).

Synovitz, Ronald William Jozef. "Community Conflict in the Confederacy: An Examination of Coverage by the *Richmond Examiner*, 1861–1864" (M. A. thesis, 1990).

RICHMOND, KENTUCKY, BATTLE OF
(29–30 August 1862)

Confederate generals Braxton Bragg and E. Kirby Smith conferred in Chattanooga, Tennessee, on 31 July 1862 without reaching a definite agreement for taking the offensive against the Federal forces in Tennessee and Kentucky. Although he was the senior commander, Bragg did not exert authority by giving precise orders, and Kirby Smith preferred independent command. There was a vague understanding that Kirby Smith would move against the Federal force under General George Morgan that was holding Cumberland Gap. If successful, he would join Bragg to deal with General Don Carlos Buell's Union army in Middle Tennessee or Kentucky.

Bragg reinforced Kirby Smith to about 19,000 men, and they moved out of Knoxville on 14 August 1862. Bypassing Cumberland Gap, they occupied Barboursville, Kentucky, by 18 August. Kirby Smith then announced that because of the lack of supplies in that area, he would have to advance to Lexington. His cavalry under Colonel John S. Scott defeated a small Union detachment at Big Hill, south of Richmond, on 23 August.

The Kentucky River palisades formed a natural defense line that Union forces under Major General Horatio Wright planned to use. But Brigadier General Mahlon D. Manson did not receive orders from Wright to go there; instead, he decided to make a stand on some high ground south of Richmond. Manson had some 6,500 troops, most of them untrained recruits. Although

Kirby Smith's force was scattered, he had available Irish-born Patrick Cleburne's division with James Churchill's division coming up, as well as Colonel Scott's 850 troopers. In the late afternoon of 29 August, Manson advanced southward to the village of Rogersville. That evening, Colonel Leonidas Metcalfe's cavalry chased some of Scott's detachment into the lines of Cleburne's division.

Early on the morning of 30 August, Manson moved his troops southward and formed a line of battle near Mount Zion Church, about five and a half miles south of Richmond. Cleburne started skirmishing, but Kirby Smith ordered him to avoid a general action until Churchill's division arrived. While Cleburne was preparing to advance, he suffered a severe mouth wound and had to turn command over to Colonel Preston Smith. When the battle began, the more experienced Confederate troops soon routed the Federals.

Manson was able to form a second battle line near Rogersville, about two miles north of his first position. Kirby Smith sent Churchill against the Federal right flank while Preston Smith engaged the Union left elements. A temporary lull in the fighting encouraged the Federals to launch an ill-considered attack that was halted by massed rifle fire. Then the Union line broke again as the Confederates began a general advance.

The twice-routed Federals made another stand at the southern edge of Richmond under the personal direction of General William "Bull" Nelson, who had made a forced ride of fifty miles to reach the scene. In a raging temper, using the flat of his sword to emphasize orders, he rallied some 2,500 men along a line that ran through the cemetery. To encourage the men, Nelson, who stood six feet five inches and was estimated to exceed 300 pounds, stalked along the line saying, "Boys, if they can't hit something as big as I am, they can't hit anything." Moments later, Nelson was struck in a thigh and was forced to leave the line. As Churchill and Preston Smith attacked, the Federal line collapsed for the third time that day. But this time Colonel Scott's troopers had swept behind the battle front to block the roads over which the Union soldiers tried to flee. Nelson was captured but managed to escape; Manson and his staff were captured.

The battle of Richmond was one of the most decisive engagements of the Civil War. Although battle statistics seldom agree, of the 6,850 Confederates engaged, 98 were killed, 492 were wounded, and 10 were missing. Of the 6,500 Federal troops, 206 were killed, 844 wounded, and 4,303 captured. Fewer than 1,200 managed to escape. The Federals also lost their artillery, wagon trains, and supplies. The road to Lexington was open, and on 1 September the mayor surrendered the town to the Confederate advance units.

—*Lowell H. Harrison*

See also Bragg, Braxton; Cleburne, Patrick Ronayne; Kentucky; Smith, Edmund Kirby; Wright, Horatio Gouverneur.

For further reading:

Connelly, Thomas L. *Army of the Heartland: The Army of Tennessee, 1861–1862* (1967).

Lambert, D. Warren *When the Ripe Pears Fell: The Battle of Richmond, Kentucky* (1995).

McDonough, James L. *War in Kentucky: From Shiloh to Perryville* (1994).

Parks, Joseph H. *General Edmund Kirby Smith, C.S.A.* (1954).

Symonds, Craig L. *Stonewall of the West: Patrick Cleburne and the Civil War* (1997).

RICHMOND, VIRGINIA

Before the Civil War, the city of Richmond, Virginia, was not a hotbed of prosecession sentiment. Indeed, the first capital of the Confederate States of America was located at Montgomery, Alabama, and Virginia was still part of the Union when Fort Sumter fell on 14 April 1861. However, the situation changed quickly as popular sentiment for the Confederacy flared following this first military engagement. On 17 April 1861, the Virginia Secession Convention voted to withdraw from the United States, and an alliance with the Confederacy was ratified a week later on 25 April.

A few days later, on 27 April, the convention extended an invitation for the Confederate government to relocate to Virginia. On 20 May the Confederate Congress responded and passed a measure to move the fledgling government to Richmond and reconvene on 20 July 1861. Jefferson Davis signed the act into law the following day, thus moving the new capital to within 106 miles of Washington D.C. From this point on, the conquest of Richmond became an overriding objective of Union military strategy.

Located at the falls of the James River, antebellum Richmond was one of the South's most bustling cities. Unlike most other Southern urban centers, Richmond contained a relatively diversified commercial and industrial base. Among these industries was the Tredegar Iron Works, an invaluable asset to the material war effort of the rebellion. As a consequence of this industrial development, Richmond was well connected by rail lines to other parts of the South and also provided port access via the James River and the Chesapeake Bay. Like most of the South, the economy of the surrounding Virginia countryside was predominantly agricultural. However, the Virginia crops were more diversified than the single-crop agriculture that dominated the Deep South.

As a city at the center of a rebellion, Richmond was constantly involved in a balancing act between three levels of government. Besides the immediate concerns of the Confederacy, Richmond continued as the state capital of Virginia, and was itself managed by its own municipal

African-American refugees on the canal at Richmond, 1865 (Photograph by Alexander Gardner / *Library of Congress*)

government. The needs of the Confederate government, however, dominated those of state and local politics. Although friction between these different administrative levels was inevitable and worsened as the conflict dragged on, the overall goal of self-preservation made the immediate survival of the capital city an area of general agreement.

Life during wartime provided a series of unique challenges to the inhabitants of Richmond. Rampant inflation came first, fueled by the population explosion resulting from the relocation of the Rebel government and a marked shortage of housing. According to the United States census of 1860, a prewar population of 37,910 (11,739 of whom were slaves and 2,576 of whom were free African-Americans) quickly expanded to a total population estimated as high as 100,000. The presence of this large impermanent influx, combined with the instability of Confederate currency and the transformation of Richmond into a military town, led to an overall increase in crime—especially muggings and

prostitution. In an effort to curb these offenses, Jefferson Davis was voted the right to suspend habeas corpus on 27 February 1862. Martial law was declared in Richmond proper and within a ten-mile radius of the city on 1 March 1862.

The overall mood of the Confederate capital remained quite high during the early years of the war, in spite of the conflict that raged around the city. Following the first waves of casualties from the battle of First Bull Run, the citizens of Richmond did their best to take care of the sick and wounded soldiers. With each military engagement, a new flood of dead and wounded arrived in Richmond, and the sight of death and funerals became a daily event. Hospitals sprang up throughout the city, with Chimborazo in Church Hill being the largest. The seemingly endless stream of anonymous war fatalities was broken on occasion by high-profile deaths that rocked the entire city. The deaths of Thomas J. "Stonewall" Jackson on 10 May 1863, J. E. B. Stuart on 12 May 1864, and the tragic fall of Brigadier General John Pegram on

Richmond mills in ruin, April 1865 (Photograph by Mathew Brady Studios / *Library of Congress*)

6 February 1865 were occasions that brought great sadness to the Confederate capital.

Civilian shortages of food and general supplies increased as the war dragged on. The wear and tear on the city and its inhabitants worsened as the Union navy's blockade clamped down on the supply lines to Richmond, and the slow collapse of the Confederate rail system only served to make matters worse. The bread riot of 2 April 1863 was indicative of the pressures with which the people of Richmond dealt on a daily basis. Suffering along with the citizens of Richmond were large numbers of unfortunate Union prisoners held at facilities such as Belle Isle, Castle Thunder, Libby Prison, and Castle Godwin.

As the Confederate capital, Richmond found itself the eventual target of every campaign mounted by the Army of the Potomac, and, as a direct result, many of the war's engagements were fought in the surrounding Virginia countryside. Due to the defensive skill of Confederate commanders such as Robert E. Lee, time

and again these advances were repelled by the Army of Northern Virginia. In late June 1862, during the climax of the Peninsula campaign, Union troops under General George McClellan came within four miles of downtown Richmond, only to be turned away by Lee in the Seven Days' campaign. False alarms and small-scale Federal assaults, however, kept the citizens of Richmond wary. Ulric Dahlgren's cavalry raid in March 1864, for example, electrified the entire community as the ill-fated Federal troopers rode around the outskirts of the city.

With the continuance of the war, the fate of Richmond became inexorably intertwined with that of the rebellion itself. Following the defeat at Gettysburg in 1863, the Army of Northern Virginia spent the last two years of the conflict in a holding action, shifting from one hot spot to the next as Ulysses S. Grant steadily closed in on the capital. With each ensuing battle, Lee's army ran thinner on men and supplies, and even victories came at an unbearable cost. When the defenses of nearby Petersburg were finally breached, the end came quickly for Richmond as well.

Early on Sunday, 2 April 1865, Lee sent word for the Confederate government to evacuate Richmond. Jefferson Davis and his family fled by rail to Danville, and the government quickly packed what it could relocate and attempted to destroy the rest. Many of the city's inhabitants took to the streets, either in an attempt to flee the capital or to join in the rampant looting that quickly broke out. During the ensuing panic, a large fire started in downtown Richmond and raged through the night, effectively destroying the commercial and industrial districts. Approximately 900 buildings were lost in the blaze.

Near dawn the following morning, Captain Clement Sulivane and the last detachment of Rebel troops left the former capital, firing the last bridge across the James River as they withdrew. City council members promptly sent a request for Union general Godfrey Weitzel to enter the city, and Federal troops were marching through downtown Richmond by 7:30 A.M. At 8:15 A.M. the city was officially in the possession of the Union army, which immediately turned its attention to putting out the still raging fire.

The abandonment of Richmond may have freed the Army of Northern Virginia from the task of defending the city, but the respite was short-lived and represented an utterly demoralizing setback for the Confederacy. For the Union troops in the field, the news of Richmond's fall signaled that the end of the conflict was near, and there was "wild rejoicing" amongst the Army of the West as they advanced north through North Carolina. Lee's last-ditch attempt to join forces with General Joseph Johnston was not successful, and the Army of Northern Virginia surrendered at Appomattox on 9 April 1865. For Richmond and the state of Virginia, the war was finally over.

—*Dane Magoon*

See also Peninsula Campaign; Richmond, Virginia, Surrender of; Virginia.
For further reading:
Dabney, Virginius. *Richmond: The Story of a City* (1990).
Pember, Phoebe Yates. *A Southern Woman's Story: Life in Confederate Richmond* (1959).
Thomas, Emory M. *The Confederate State of Richmond: A Biography of the Capital* (1971; reprint, 1998).
Woodward, C. Vann, ed. *Mary Chestnut's Civil War* (1981).

RICHMOND, VIRGINIA, SURRENDER OF
(3 April 1865)

Trying to draw Union attention from his planned flight to the west, Robert E. Lee failed to penetrate Ulysses S. Grant's lines east of Petersburg at Fort Stedman on 25 March 1865. Grant immediately ordered assaults on the Confederate right at Petersburg. At Five Forks on 1 April, Philip Sheridan won a smashing victory that brought further attacks on the crumbling Confederate lines the next day. When Sheridan cut the last rail line into Petersburg on 2 April, Lee knew he would need to leave his lines that night. He sent word during the day to Jefferson Davis in Richmond that the capital could no longer be defended. It was a Sunday, and the message reached Davis while he was in church. He left the services to begin preparations to evacuate the government.

Rumors quickly spread throughout the city that the defenses would be abandoned, and civilians began to flee. Davis, his family, and his cabinet left on a train to Danville, Virginia, shortly before midnight on 2 April. Along with the presidential party were aides who took what Confederate government papers they could carry. Shortly after midnight a train departed for Danville, carrying what was left of the Confederate treasury. The presidential party arrived in Danville the next afternoon and established a temporary capital there.

The commander of the Confederate military forces in Richmond, Lieutenant General Richard Ewell, gave orders during the night to burn the military stores left in the capital. Some of these fires spread to nonmilitary areas, but apparently looters set the most damaging fires as they began moving through the city after dark on 2 April. As more of the military pulled out of the city, the looters became bolder and more numerous. With the limited troops he had left Ewell tried to restore some semblance of order, but he was fighting a losing battle against the lawless elements of Richmond. He finally had to turn most of his attention to securing the evacuation of his own men. To that end, he ordered the destruction of all bridges across the James River, save the Mayo Bridge, and instructed the troops there to hold it as long as possible. Ewell hoped that would be until all troops had left the city.

Many Confederate soldiers could not leave the city immediately because they were still busily trying to destroy anything that could be used by Union forces. At the same time, the minuscule Confederate naval forces just below Richmond on the James were making preparations to destroy their tiny fleet of ironclads. Their commander, Raphael Semmes, gave the order about 3 A.M. on 3 April, and the explosion of the boats could be seen from miles away.

Union soldiers outside Richmond's defenses watched with growing amazement as flames and smoke from the city spread across the night sky. Major General Godfrey Weitzel, commander of the African-American XXV Corps, also commanded all troops belonging to the Army of the James north of the James River. These soldiers included not only XXV Corps, but also parts of XVIII and XXIV Corps. When Weitzel saw the flames, he decided to wait until dawn to enter Richmond to

Ruins at Richmond, with the Capitol building (*center*), April 1865 (*National Archives*)

avoid any potential problems his men might encounter from the chaotic situation in the city.

At 5:30 A.M. Weitzel sent a small party with staff officers, commanded by Major Atherton H. Stevens toward the city. The mayor and his entourage, carrying a flag of truce, met them on the outskirts of town. The last of the Confederate troops had recently left, destroying the Mayo Bridge after crossing to safety. The mayor led Major Stevens and his men to city hall, where he surrendered the city. The United States flag was raised over city hall and Stevens proceeded to the state capitol, where another flag was also raised.

By the time Stevens had received the surrender of the city, Weitzel was already leading the rest of his men toward Richmond. He arrived at city hall about 8:15 A.M. to conduct the formal surrender of Richmond. During his march into town, he had ample opportunity to observe the destruction wrought by the fires that had obliterated approximately twenty city blocks. After receiving the surrender, Weitzel issued orders that those soldiers already in the city should work to control the fires, collect Confederate stragglers, and arrest looters. Weitzel then made his way to the house that had been used by the Davises during their residence in Richmond and established his headquarters there.

During the day the Union army gradually extin-

guished all the remaining fires and restored order to the city. The following day all was eerily peaceful when President Abraham Lincoln, who had been visiting Grant at City Point, came to the town. The town's African-American inhabitants greeted him with great celebration, but its remaining white civilians brooded in stony silence. Lincoln returned to City Point in the late afternoon of 4 April with the knowledge that the former Confederate capital was now firmly in Union hands.

—*David S. Heidler and Jeanne T. Heidler*

See also Davis, Jefferson; Fort Stedman, Battle of; Weitzel, Godfrey.

For further reading:
Trudeau, Noah Andre. *Out of the Storm; The End of the Civil War, April–June 1865* (1994).

RICHMOND WHIG

From its position at the outset of the Civil War as the newspaper least sympathetic to the Confederacy, the *Richmond Whig* became a zealous convert to the cause of Southern independence—albeit with equally healthy doses of both skepticism and criticism of the Jefferson Davis administration. Along with its more enthusiastic Richmond daily competitors—the *Examiner,* the *Dispatch,* and the *Enquirer*—the *Whig*

formed the hub of news reporting for the Confederacy and exerted tremendous influence over newspapers and periodicals throughout the South.

The *Whig* was founded in 1824 by John Hampden Pleasants, who in 1846 was killed in a bloody duel, fought with both pistols and swords, with *Enquirer* editor Thomas Ritchie, Jr. Pleasants was a strong supporter of Henry Clay, and the *Whig* was the leading Southern organ of that short-lived party; as such, it became the natural political rival of the *Examiner,* which, even as Fort Sumter fell, was calling on Southern armies to march on Washington. The *Whig,* in sharp contrast, opposed secession—and its offices were noticeably dark on the night of Sumter's surrender. Unlike the region's other papers, which saw Lincoln's election as a virtual declaration of war, the *Whig* charged that the South had only itself to blame: "To the Breckinridgers, led on by Yancey, and to the corruptions of the Buchanan administration, we attribute the election of Lincoln."

Indeed, the paper clung to its Unionist position until 15 April 1861, when Lincoln issued his first call for a 75,000-strong militia. Overnight, however, the *Whig* abruptly switched sides and was suddenly vowing "vengeance on the tyrants who pollute the capital of the Republic" and promising that Jefferson Davis would soon dine in the White House. In fact, it said, Lincoln could save the country the inconvenience if he stood "in readiness [sic] to dislodge at a moment's notice."

Editor Robert Ridgeway was forced from his position and replaced first by Alexander Mosely and then by the fiery James McDonald; the paper's offices even became a favorite meeting place for Confederate congressmen. The *Whig*'s abrupt political shift was hailed by the Northern Copperhead press: the proslavery *New York Day Book* noted that "the *Richmond Whig,* the ablest paper in the South, which has hitherto opposed secession, has hauled down its Union flag and goes for the new Confederacy. There can be no doubt that the cause of secession is all the time progressing with a sure step in Virginia."

But the *Whig* was not a totally faithful follower of the Confederacy. It became known as a persistent critic of Jefferson Davis, repeatedly advocating sharp restrictions on his executive power. And in the fall of 1862, when the Confederate War Department reversed itself and began censoring articles based on reports in Northern newspapers, the *Whig* openly protested and demanded that the new policy be withdrawn.

Still, like other Southern papers, it advocated anything that might help the Confederacy in the field. In 1864, the *New York Tribune* reprinted on its front page a dispatch from the *Whig* about the petition of one R. O. Davidson, a clerk in the Confederate quartermaster-general's office, who complained that the War Department refused to believe that he had invented a flying machine, with which "all the Yankee armies now upon our soil and their blockading fleets may be speedily driven off or destroyed." The *Tribune* gleefully pointed to the article as evidence of the South's growing desperation.

As the Union army moved into Richmond in April 1865, the *Whig*'s was the city's only newspaper office not to be destroyed by fire. Troops took over the paper, and after a one-day suspension, it resumed publication as a Union organ. Appropriately, it was in the pages of the *Whig* two weeks later that the first news was published in the South of Lincoln's assassination, which the paper bemoaned as "the heaviest blow which has ever fallen upon the people of the South," given that his "benignant and magnanimous policy" promised "a restoration of tranquility."

After the war, Mosely resumed editorship of the *Whig,* which survived until the end of 1888.

—*Eric Fettmann*

See also Newspapers; *Richmond Examiner.*
For further reading:
Andrews, J. Cutler. *The South Reports the Civil War* (1970).
Harper, Robert S. *Lincoln and the Press* (1951).
Starr, Louis M. *Bohemian Brigade: Civil War Newsmen in Action* (1954; reprint, 1987).
Tomlinson, Robert Hume. "The Origins and Editorial Policies of the *Richmond Whig and Public Advertiser,* 1824–1865" (Ph.D. dissertation, 1971).

RICKETTS, JAMES BREWERTON
(1817–1887)
Union general

Born in New York City to George R. A. Ricketts and Mary Brewerton Ricketts, James Brewerton Ricketts was educated locally before accepting an appointment to the U.S. Military Academy. He graduated sixteenth of thirty-one in the class of 1839.

After graduation, Ricketts served for a time on the northern frontier along the Canadian border. At the outbreak of the Mexican-American War he went to Mexico, where he served under Zachary Taylor in the Monterey campaign and the battle of Buena Vista. After the war, Ricketts returned to frontier duty, including a stint in Florida. At the beginning of the Civil War he was a captain in the 1st Artillery.

Attached to Irvin McDowell's army as it marched on the Confederate position at Manassas Junction, Ricketts commanded a battery during the ensuing battle of First Bull Run. He was wounded four times, left behind during the Union flight from the field, and thus fell to Confederate capture. His time as a prisoner—he would be released in January 1862—was especially harrowing. In November 1861, Ricketts was one of several prisoners chosen by lot to be executed in retaliation for any

Confederates executed. He escaped that fate, but his wounds still troubled him after his release, so he was unable to resume active service until April 1862. In that month he was promoted to brigadier general of volunteers dating from 21 July 1861, the day of First Bull Run.

Now commanding a brigade of Major General Edward Ord's division of McDowell's Corps, Ricketts marched his men south from Washington to the Rappahannock. After George McClellan's Peninsula campaign, Ricketts's brigade became part of the force sent to counter Stonewall Jackson's move out of Richmond. As a result, he fought at Cedar Mountain, where he covered part of the Union retreat, at Thoroughfare Gap, and at Second Bull Run, where he commanded a division.

Returning to the Army of the Potomac, Ricketts commanded the 2d Division of I Corps in the Maryland campaign. He fought at South Mountain and the ensuing battle of Antietam. In the latter engagement, Ricketts was injured when he was pinned under the second of two horses shot from under him. He refused to leave the field. During the next few weeks the injury so plagued him that when his division was ordered to Harper's Ferry on 1 November, he was forced to relinquish command.

Put on desk duty, Ricketts was named in December 1862 to sit on the court-martial of Fitz John Porter. Completing that duty in January 1863, he served on a variety of other boards for the next year. Returning to field duty on 4 April 1864, Ricketts commanded the 3d Division of VI Corps of the Army of the Potomac during Ulysses S. Grant's campaign against Robert E. Lee. He fought in the battles of the Wilderness, Spotsylvania, North Anna, and Cold Harbor and in the opening stages of the siege of Petersburg.

In July 1864 his division was sent to Washington to serve as part of the defensive force to counter Jubal Early's Washington raid. At the battle of Monocacy, Ricketts's division suffered more than 50 percent casualties and was commended by Major General Lew Wallace.

After Early's retreat, Ricketts joined Philip Sheridan's Shenandoah Valley campaign. Sheridan commended Ricketts for his actions at Fisher's Hill on 22 September. A month later, on 19 October, while commanding VI Corps at Cedar Creek, Ricketts was shot in the chest. The wound was not mortal, but he never fully recovered. He was unable to return to active duty until two days before Lee's surrender at Appomattox.

After the war, Ricketts tried to remain on active service, but health made fragile by the numerous wounds he had suffered in the war prohibited it. He was retired in January 1867 at the rank of major general. Ricketts spent the rest of his life in Washington, D.C., where he died on 22 September 1887. He was buried at Arlington.

—*David S. Heidler and Jeanne T. Heidler*

See also Monocacy, Battle of; Porter, Fitz John.
For further reading:
United States Congress. Joint Committee on the Conduct of the War. *Supplemental Report of the Joint Committee on the Conduct of the War: Supplemental to Senate Report No. 142, 38th Congress, 2d Session* (1977).

RIFLES

Rifles are longarms manufactured with spiral lands and grooves cut into their bores to impart a stabilizing spin to the bullet. The infantryman's percussion rifle-musket was the weapon most used by either side in the Civil War. It was also the deadliest, accounting for 90 percent of all combat casualties.

The basic rifles were the caliber .58 U.S. Models 1861 and 1863 Springfield Percussion Rifle-Muskets and the caliber .577 Models 1853 and 1856 British Enfields. Although of slightly different caliber, the cartridges for both weapons were generally interchangeable. Both the Springfield and Enfield were percussion, muzzle-loading weapons and accepted a triangular-bladed, socket bayonet.

The federal arsenal at Springfield, Massachusetts, produced more than 800,000 Models 1861 and 1863 rifles. These arms were supplemented by more than 670,000 additional Model 1861s manufactured by civilian contractors. Both the North and the South imported a combined total of more than 800,000 Enfields from Britain. Other rifles such as the caliber .54 U.S. Model 1841 "Mississippi Rifle" and the calibers .54 and .58 Austrian Lorenz rifle also saw significant service.

Southern arsenals such as those at Richmond, Virginia, and Fayetteville, North Carolina, did produce copies of Northern designs, but their production never met demand. Most Confederate troops thus fielded either captured U.S. or imported foreign rifles.

Although most military theorists were initially slow to grasp its implications, the advent of the rifle was to revolutionize warfare. The earlier smoothbore muskets had effective ranges of scarcely 100 yards. Their short range and inaccuracy had thus necessitated the massing of troops into tight formations. Such formations, when marched to within 100 yards or less of one another, could thus, with their massed fire, expect to inflict some damage on their opponent. Military schools had stressed such tactics with an emphasis on the offensive and the bayonet since pre-Napoleonic times.

The rifle, with its projectile, the minié bullet, rendered the massed frontal assault suicidal. In the hands of a skilled marksman, a rifle was capable of hitting a man-sized target at ranges in excess of 500 yards. Significantly fewer riflemen, firing from prepared defensive positions, could thus inflict crippling casualties on attacking troops at previously unheard of ranges. By late

A row of stacked Union rifles at Petersburg, Virginia, 3 April 1865 (*Library of Congress*)

1864 the rifle had dictated a form of defensive fighting foretelling the trench warfare of World War I.

—*Jeff Kinard*

See also Small Arms; Smoothbores.
For further reading:
Evans, William B. *Civil War Guns* (1962).
Flayderman, E. Norman. *Flayderman's Guide to Antique American Firearms* (1987).
Lord, Francis A. *Civil War Collector's Encyclopedia* (1965).

RIO GRANDE CAMPAIGN
(November 1863–July 1864)

Despite the growing effectiveness of the Union blockade of the Confederacy, the long Confederate border with Mexico—beginning at the mouth of the Rio Grande on the Gulf of Mexico and running hundreds of miles to the northwest—allowed trade goods to flow between the seceded states and the outside world. Contrary to the policies of Mexico's president Benito Juarez, the governor of the state of Tamaulipas, Santiago Vidaurri, remained friendly to the Confederacy. As a result, a brisk trade in Texas cotton, as

well as military and other supplies from foreign countries, sprang up. The Union's Rio Grande campaign was intended to interdict that trade and to eliminate the possibility of cooperation between Mexican dissidents and the invading French against the United States. On 2 November 1863 a 6,000-man invasion force from the Union XIII Corps entered Texas. Under the command of Major General Napoleon Dana, the small army advanced on Brownsville, which was soon evacuated by the Confederates. The major battle of the campaign occurred when Federal forces attacked Fort Esperanza, a lightly defended earth-and-timber structure at the northern end of Matagorda Island. Fighting a strong wind as well as Confederate batteries, the Yankees engaged in a generally harmless artillery duel during the brief siege. The Rebels evacuated the fort early on the morning of 30 November 1863. By 1 January 1864 Federal troops, meeting little opposition, had pushed up the Gulf Coast nearly 300 miles to Corpus Christi, Indianola, and Port Lavaca, and up the Rio Grande River as far as Edinburg and Rio Grande City. A small unit got as far as Laredo, but retreated after a sharp skirmish outside the town.

The XIII Corps settled into occupation duty, conducting occasional scouting and foraging expeditions, but generally engaging in drilling, fishing, and other garrison routines. Although Dana and his successor, Major General Francis Herron, made Brownsville their headquarters, posts were also established along the Rio Grande as well as the Gulf Coast. The Yankees built small houses, confiscated fishing huts and boats, took over abandoned warehouses and office buildings, and even used the Brownsville courthouse as a barracks. In the meantime, Brigadier General A. J. Hamilton, a Texas Unionist and one-time congressman who had been appointed military governor by President Lincoln, arrived with a retinue of other Texas refugees to establish a provisional government. They set up a Brownsville chapter of the Loyal League, an auxiliary to the Republican Party. Former newspapermen in the army published the *National Loyal Union Journal* for several months, promoting the reelection of Abraham Lincoln, the abolition of slavery, and soldiers' interests. But mostly the occupying Yankees enjoyed the warm, healthy winter climate and the availability of the gambling houses of Matamoros, where they mingled with Mexicans and Confederates at the gaming tables. In response to recruiting efforts by Federal commanders and Texas refugee leaders, several hundred Unionists, Confederate deserters, German-Americans, and Mexican-Americans joined the 1st and 2d Texas Cavalry Regiments, under the command of Colonels Edmund J. Davis and John Haynes, respectively. The campaign saw perhaps the only instance in the entire Civil War in which Hispanics fought on opposite sides, when troopers in the 2d Texas engaged Confederates under the command of Colonel Santos Benavides near Laredo. The campaign also saw the first entry into Texas of African-American soldiers; two regiments of the Corps d'Afrique were among the troops Dana led to the Rio Grande.

The rather aimless existence—aside from a foray into Matamoros to protect United States property during a battle between warring Mexican factions—of the men posted in south Texas helped end the Rio Grande campaign. Pressure from cotton interests, which, as long as the lower Rio Grande Valley was controlled by Union forces, had to transport their product into Mexico by way of remote Eagle Pass, caused Texas authorities to act. By June 1864 former Texas Ranger colonel John "Rip" Ford had gathered a motley assortment of about 1,300 old men and young boys, outlaws, mercenaries, and Hispanics into the grandly named Cavalry of the West, which began harassing Union patrols and outposts. More importantly, General Nathaniel Banks, commanding the Department of the Gulf, gearing up for his Red River campaign in Louisiana, recalled over half of the Union invasion force and ordered all occupied

territory—aside from Brownsville, Brazos, Santiago, and Port Isabel—to be evacuated.

Ford's cavalrymen won several fights against the retreating Federals, who gave up Brownsville on 29 June 1864. By the end of September, fewer than a thousand Union troops remained at the mouth of the Rio Grande, where at least a small garrison of Federals would remain for the rest of the war. Elements of that force would earn the dubious distinction of losing the last land battle of the Civil War at Palmito Ranch.

—James Marten

See also Banks, Nathaniel P.; Brownsville, Texas; Dana, Napoleon Jackson; Hamilton, Andrew Jackson; Herron, Francis J.; Matamoros, Mexico; Palmito Ranch, Battle of.
For further reading:
Daddysman, James W. *The Matamoros Trade: Confederate Commerce, Diplomacy, and Intrigue* (1984).
Kerby, Robert L. *Kirby Smith's Confederacy: The Trans-Mississippi South, 1863–1865* (1972).
Marten, James. "For the Army, the People, and Abraham Lincoln: A Yankee Newspaper in Occupied Texas." *Civil War History* (1993).
Thompson, Jerry D. *Vaqueros in Blue and Gray* (1976).
Tilley, Nannie M., ed. *Federals on the Frontier: The Diary of Benjamin F. McIntyre, 1862–1864* (1963).

RIOTS, C.S.A.

Women living in the South during the Civil War faced the daunting task of surviving on the home front while their husbands, brothers, sons, and fathers fought battles on distant fields. Families had to deal with an economic system uprooted by speculation and the hoarding of the necessities of life. As the war escalated, prices for salt, bacon, flour, corn, and yarn for clothing became grossly inflated when speculators purchased what supplies were left in warehouses and depots and sold the goods to those who could afford them. Adding to the difficult situation was the Confederate government's impressment of livestock, crops, and other supplies from already destitute families in the South. Promises were made by the planter class in most states to care for soldiers' families, but those promises were not kept. Starvation and destitution loomed ahead. What would become of the women and children in such desperate times? It was not long before desperate times produced desperate acts.

Through the "twenty slave law" and purchases of exemptions and substitutes, many planters were able to avoid military service, claiming that they better served the cause by staying home and managing food production. Men from poor families, unable to afford exemptions and substitutes, were conscripted into the army, after volunteering waned in early 1862. Wives of these soldiers began writing letters to their respective state governors begging for the release of their men so they could return home to work the fields and give their families a chance at survival. While planters and their families had ample supplies of cotton and corn waiting to be sold to speculators and the Confederate government, soldiers' wives, mothers, and daughters resorted to theft and rioting to survive.

Neither small towns nor large cities could escape the wrath of starving women as they conducted their desperate raids for food. As early as July 1861 New Orleans, Louisiana, faced such a mob. In 1862 Georgia's Bartow County reported a raid, as did the Georgia town of Cartersville. In 1863 the pace of rioting quickened. That year saw food riots in Atlanta, Augusta, Milledgeville, Macon, and Columbus in Georgia; Raleigh, Boone, and High Point in North Carolina; and Petersburg in Virginia. Two of the worst riots that year took place in Salisbury, North Carolina, on 18 March, and in Richmond, Virginia, on 2 April.

Responding to an indifferent government and speculators and extortionists, a group of about fifty women entered Salisbury carrying axes and hatchets determined to get salt and flour. They targeted the shops of well-known speculators and demanded goods at current government prices, about half the rate the speculators were offering. After the shop owners refused their demands, the women broke down doors with hatchets and made off with thirteen barrels of flour, a barrel of

Confederate bread riots as depicted in *Frank Leslie's Illustrated Newspaper*, 23 May 1863 (*Library of Congress*)

molasses, two sacks of salt, and twenty dollars in cash. The mob next raided the local railroad depot, where ten more barrels of flour were confiscated. There were no arrests and no prosecutions. As with most such incidents, local sentiments were usually with the soldiers' families that were forced to such actions due to high inflation, loss of missing family members' labor, and increasing food shortages.

After meeting the previous night at a local Baptist church, on 2 April women from Richmond and surrounding counties followed May Jackson, a painter's wife, from the Second Market to the Governor's Mansion. The mob then made its way from Capitol Square down Ninth Street to the business district on Main and Cary streets. In their wake, twenty stores lay ransacked. The mayor tried to restore order by reading the women the Riot Act, but to no avail. Virginia's governor, John Letcher, even called out the Public Guard, a state security force for the capital, when the crowd had grown close to one thousand. It was all over by eleven that morning. Unlike most other such incidents, forty-five women and twenty-nine men were arrested, though not all of them were charged. Twelve women and six of the men were convicted. More crowds gathered on 3 April, and there were rumors of another riot planned for 10 April, but no further riots took place.

Riots continued in 1864 as winter gave way to spring and no relief from destitute conditions was forthcoming. In April Savannah, Georgia, witnessed a mob of women roaming from store to store on Whitaker, Congress, St. Julian, and Bryan Streets, taking what they believed was theirs; bacon, rice, sugar, flour, salt, and other items. As a matter of courtesy to the merchants, Sheriff Cole of Chatham County arrested three women and placed them in jail. The following day they were brought before the courts and charged with theft and disorderly conduct. They were later released because no one came forth to press charges. Two store owners, claiming a loss of approximately $450 worth of bacon, applied for reimbursement with Savannah's city council, but the council tabled the matter.

Riots continued in Georgia, Alabama, North Carolina, Virginia, and even Texas. In February 1865 a mob of about fifty soldiers' wives in Miller County, Georgia, armed themselves with axes and marched on the county seat of Colquitt. They forced open the door of the depot and took fifty sacks of government corn.

As the war drew to a close in 1865, Southern women realized they had not only fought a civil war between the Union and the Confederacy, but also a civil war among those left at home. They drew their battle lines at the doors of government depots and warehouses, and at the doors of well-stocked, overpriced goods stores. From Mobile to Richmond, Atlanta to Salisbury, women resorted to mob warfare to relieve the suffering of their families. The destitution these women faced was in large part due to the selfishness and greed that planters exhibited by speculating in cotton and corn, rather than assisting soldiers' families as promised, and by an indifferent government. For hundreds of women in the South, there was no choice; obtain food for themselves and their children by any means necessary or die. Hoping for any response to their pleas for help, the voices of these angry women cried out through hundreds of letters to governors and through letters to editors of Southern newspapers. With little or no response to speak of, these women made their own history.

—Teresa C. Williams

See also Civil Liberties, C.S.A.; Class Conflict, C.S.A.; Financing, C.S.A.; Impressment; Tax–in–Kind.

For further reading:
Amos, Harriet E. "'All Absorbing Topics': Food and Clothing in Confederate Mobile." *Atlanta Historical Journal* (1978).
Bynum, Victoria E. *Unruly Women: The Politics of Social and Sexual Control in the Old South* (1992).
Chesson, Michael B. "Harlots or Heroines? A New Look at the Richmond Bread Riot." *Virginia Magazine of History and Biography* (1984).
Graham, Christopher A. "Women's Revolt in Rowan County." *Columbiad* (1999).
Williams, Teresa C. "'The Women Rising': Class and Gender in Civil War Georgia" (M. A. thesis, 1999).

RIOTS, U.S.A.

Between 1862 and 1864, thousands of Northern citizens took to the streets in a succession of angry riots that threatened to destabilize the Union war effort. The immediate cause of the riots was the efforts of the federal government to enforce conscription upon a reluctant population. Underlying their opposition to the draft were deep-rooted racial and economic grievances.

The initial outbreak of violence occurred in response to the Militia Act of 17 July 1862. Passed in response to escalating recruitment problems, the act ordered the enrollment of all men aged between eighteen and forty-five and in addition gave the president the power to conscript state militia into Federal service for up to nine months. Opposition to the state militia drafts spilled over into violence in several Northern states. One of the most serious incidents occurred on 10 October 1862 when a mob bearing banners with the inscription "No Draft" marched through the streets of Port Washington, Wisconsin. The mob stormed the courthouse, drove out the draft commissioner, and destroyed the enrollment records. Six hundred troops were needed to restore order after rioters then proceeded to ransack the homes of local public officials.

These disturbances were but the prelude to the dramatic protests that accompanied the imposition of federal conscription the following summer. By 1863 the Union army was confronted with the threat of a serious manpower shortage. The Enrollment Act of March 1863 ordered that all able-bodied men between the ages of twenty and forty-five were to be enrolled in readiness for a federal draft. Anger and resentment at the act escalated into scenes of violence across the North. On 6 March 1863, a riot in Detroit resulted in several deaths and damage to property estimated up to $20,000. Three months later, miners clashed with Federal troops in Rutland, Vermont. In Chicago also, several thousand protesters disrupted the draft and then set upon the police officers who were called in to disperse them. The most spectacular riot occurred between 12 and 15 July in New York City, where four days of rioting resulted in the deaths of at least 105 people. The New York draft riots also served as the catalyst for a series of smaller disturbances. Three people were killed during an attack on the Federal armory in Boston on 14 July 1863. Further disturbances were reported as far afield as Hartford, Connecticut; Troy, New York; Newark, New Jersey; Portsmouth, New Hampshire; Green Bay, Wisconsin; and Wooster, Ohio.

Several factors serve to explain the draft riots. They must first be understood against the general background of military defeat. The Union cause had suffered a series of setbacks the previous winter, including the defeat at Fredericksburg and the failure of Grant's advance on Vicksburg. The call for troops therefore came at precisely the time when popular support for the war was at its lowest ebb. Democrats also denounced the draft as an unconstitutional assault on popular sovereignty and personal autonomy. Distrust of centralized power was not in itself sufficient to precipitate riots. Abstract political issues were less important than pressing personal concerns.

Many of the rioters were poor immigrant laborers whose wages had declined in relative terms as a result of wartime inflation. Between 1860 and July 1863 Northern retail prices rose by 43 percent but wages only by 12 percent. In New York City, Irish immigrants lived on the edge of destitution, crowded into disease-ridden slums. The Enrollment Act aggravated these class tensions by providing exemption to anyone who could afford either to furnish a substitute or to pay a $300 commutation fee. Since $300 represented at least half a year's wages for an unskilled laborer, the exemption clause was denounced as a blatant act of class bias. The resentment of many laborers was compounded in certain instances by the corruption of enrolling officers. In Pennsylvania, for example, the provost marshals responsible for enforcing the draft collaborated with local mine owners to discourage employees from organizing in protest at their appalling working conditions. A parody of a popular recruiting song captured the sentiments of many ordinary laborers: "We're coming, Father Abraham, three hundred thousand more, / We leave our homes and firesides with bleeding hearts and sore, / Since poverty has been our crime, we bow to thy decree; / We are the poor who have no wealth to purchase liberty."

Class tensions were compounded by racial prejudice. Democratic demagogues frightened white workers into believing that the Emancipation Proclamation would force them into economic competition with the former slaves. As one Copperhead newspaper observed, "We are inclined to the opinion that a large majority of the men will make very poor fighters for niggers. They don't believe in the programme. They think that a white man is as good as a nigger, and can see no reason why *they* should be shot for the benefit of niggers and abolitionists." The fear and prejudice of Northern whites were starkly exposed in Detroit, where the riot was precipitated by unsubstantiated rumors that a black man had raped a white orphan girl. In New York, the worst brutalities of the mob were deliberately directed at the black community. Several African-Americans were murdered and hundreds were left homeless as rioters burned and ransacked their neighborhoods.

The draft riots did not have any permanent impact on the Northern war effort. To avert any further unrest, New York City established a fund financed through the sale of bonds to pay the commutation fee for poor draftees. Other cities adopted similar measures. Commutation was finally repealed in March 1864. For a time, the riots offered a renewed sense of hope to the beleaguered forces of the Confederacy. Southern newspapers reported events with unrestrained glee. The riots also raised doubts abroad as to the ability of the Lincoln administration to restore the Union. Events would soon disprove both the hopes of Confederates and the skepticism of foreign governments.

Although order was restored, the riots nonetheless underline the fragile basis of Northern support for the war. Along with these more dramatic incidents, it should be emphasized that there were many other minor acts of resistance against the draft. Across the nation, more than sixty enrolling officers were wounded in the performance of their duties, and in Indiana two more were murdered. Emphasis should also be given to the 16,000 men who simply failed to report to their draft boards for examination. Seen in this larger perspective, the riots serve as a powerful corrective to scholars who emphasize internal troubles within the Confederacy as the central explanation for the outcome of the Civil War.

—*Clive Webb*

See also Charleston, Illinois, Riot; Conscription, U.S.A.; New York City Draft Riots.

For further reading:

Cook, Adrian. *The Armies of the Streets: The New York City Draft Riots of 1863* (1974).
Gallman, J. Matthew. *The North Fights the Civil War: The Home Front* (1994).
Geary, James W. *We Need Men: The Union Draft in the Civil War* (1991).
Gray, Wood. *The Hidden Civil War: The Story of the Copperheads* (1942).
Murdock, Eugene C. *One Million Men: The Civil War Draft in the North* (1971).
Paludan, Phillip S. *"A People's Contest": The Union and Civil War, 1861–1865* (1988).

RIPLEY, JAMES WOLFE
(1794–1870)
Union general

Born to Ralph Ripley and Eunice Huntington Ripley in Windham County, Connecticut, James Wolfe Ripley was educated locally before receiving an appointment to the U.S. Military Academy. He graduated a year later in 1814—Ripley attended the academy before the institution of the class system—and entered the artillery. He initially served at Sackett's Harbor, New York, before being transferred to garrison duty on the U.S. border with Spanish Florida. He served under Andrew Jackson in the First Seminole War in 1818.

After over a decade of garrison duty, Ripley transferred to ordnance and, except for a stint in the Mexican-American War, spent most of the remainder of his pre–Civil War years in command of various arsenals, most importantly the one in Springfield, Massachusetts. He remade the Springfield Arsenal into perhaps the best in the country.

At the beginning of the Civil War, Ripley was named chief of ordnance, a position he held until his retirement in 1863. With meticulous attention to detail, within two months of taking his position, he had made a full report to Secretary of War Simon Cameron concerning the number of weapons and amount of ammunition in government hands. He also reported to Cameron the costs of manufacturing more weapons and the approximate speed with which such manufacturing could be accomplished. Ripley had no doubt that he would be able to supply the needs of the American army in this crisis, but he was distressed that in the heat of President Lincoln's call for volunteers, many of the arsenals in the North had been raided by state forces without authorization or a proper accounting of who took what. In August 1861, Ripley was promoted to brigadier general.

A man of apparently boundless energy, Ripley communicated directly with commanders in the field regarding their ordnance needs. This was especially true with George McClellan during the Peninsula campaign, because McClellan never felt he had enough artillery. Along with these many duties, Ripley also served on boards recommending artillery for U.S. fortifications.

Besides his stamina, Ripley was also known for his integrity. He went far in eliminating waste and graft in his department. His one fault was his resistance to change and innovation. Ripley blocked modernization at almost every turn, particularly opposing the introduction of new weapons such as breechloaders. Perhaps the attitude stemmed partly from his fear that he would not be able to supply enough ammunition for the new weapons. He knew from where and in what quantities he could obtain ammunition for the old ones. His resistance to change and experimentation, however, cost him his job, and he retired on 15 September 1863. He remained attached to the government as inspector of armament until the year before his death. He retired to Hartford, Connecticut, where he died on 15 March 1870.

—*David S. Heidler and Jeanne T. Heidler*

See also Artillary; Ordnance, Naval.

For further reading:

Bruce, Robert V. *Lincoln and the Tools of War* (1956; reprint, 1989).

Davis, Carl L. *Arming the Union: Small Arms in the Civil War* (1973).

RIPLEY, ROSWELL SABINE
(1823–1887)
Confederate general

Roswell Ripley was born in Franklin County, Ohio, not far from Columbus in the community of Worthington. He entered the United States Military Academy at West Point in 1839 and graduated seventh in a class of thirty-nine in 1843. His stateside military service left him a brevetted second lieutenant in the 3d United States Artillery. After serving in various posts in the South, he finished his pre–Mexican-American War service as an assistant professor of mathematics at West Point.

During the Mexican-American War Ripley served on the staffs of generals Taylor and Pillow. His combat service was notable enough to win him a promotion to captain for his leadership at Monterey, and to major for his gallantry at Cerro Gordo. At the end of the conflict while on military leave, he wrote and published the two-volume chronicle *The History of the Mexican War*.

After his retirement from the army, Ripley served in the South Carolina state militia. In 1860 he drew an appointment as major of ordnance, and after the evacuation of the garrison at Fort Sumter by Major Anderson, he earned promotion to lieutenant colonel. His main task in Charleston was to recondition both Fort Moultrie and Fort Sumter after their shelling by Beauregard's men. Ripley, disturbed at the slow pace of his promotions while serving in Charleston, threatened to resign until a group of Charleston's leading citizens begged him to stay on. In August 1862 he was made brigadier general and placed in command of South Carolina. A disagreement with his superiors, in which Ripley proved to be correct, resulted in his leaving Charleston to serve with General Lee in the Army of Northern Virginia. Placed in command of a brigade in D. H. Hill's division of North Carolina and Georgia troops, Ripley served admirably in the battles of Mechanicsville, Gaines' Mill, Malvern Hill, South Mountain, and Antietam. At Antietam he suffered a serious wound to his throat, but immediately upon the dressing of the wound, he returned to the fray. Within a month of his wounding at Antietam, he was sent back to Charleston and placed in command of the 1st Artillery District. Ripley served as commander of the Charleston garrison during the horrific bombardment by Federal gunboats in 1863 and 1864.

Ripley always maintained that South Carolina was not sufficiently defended against Federal invasion. Always low on both men and materiel, Ripley wrote Governor McGrath offering his resignation, but also offered to take command of state troops in an effort to resist the impending invasion of the state by Union general William T. Sherman. In the same correspondence he suggested the enlistment of slaves.

Upon the fall of Charleston, Ripley received orders to join Joseph E. Johnston's Army of Tennessee. He arrived in time for the battle at Bentonville, but was immediately ordered back to South Carolina, where he was stationed at the cessation of hostilities.

When the war ended, Ripley traveled to England and engaged in manufacturing, but success in the venture eluded him. He returned to the United States, where he divided his time between Charleston and New York City. Ripley died of apoplexy on 29 March 1887 in New York City, and later was interred in Charleston.

Despite his reputation as a surly, unreasonable, and contentious individual, Ripley remained popular with the residents of Charleston throughout his life. Henry Timrod wrote the poem "Ripley" in honor of Charleston's gallant defender.

—*James S. Baugess*

See also Beauregard, Pierre Gustave Toutant; Fort Sumter, Bombardment of; Pemberton, John.

For further reading:

Bennett, C. A. "Roswell Sabin Ripley: Charleston's Gallant Defender." *South Carolina History Magazine* (1994).

Burton, E. Milby. *The Siege of Charleston: 1861–1865* (1970).

Frasher, Walter J., Jr. *Charleston! Charleston!: The History of a Southern City* (1989).

RIVERINE WARFARE, U.S.N.

After eleven Southern states seceded and the Civil War broke out, the Federal government sought a suitable strategy that would crush the South's military forces, thus terminating civil conflict and reuniting the country. Commanding General of the Army Winfield Scott devised the plan eventually adopted by the U.S. Army and Navy. In the Anaconda

Plan, as newspapers of the era dubbed it, Scott recommended first the establishment of a naval blockade from Chesapeake Bay to the Gulf of Mexico to prevent European assistance to the Confederacy. Next, Scott advised that American forces penetrate down the Mississippi River which, according to historians Harold and Margaret Sprout, "isolated the Trans-Mississippi Confederate States, extended the blockade along a third side of the military frontier, and seriously disrupted the internal communications of the Confederacy."

As a result, procurement, development, construction, and deployment of a riverine fleet emerged as, and remained, a concern of the Navy Department throughout the war. Although the navy used wooden steamships on America's inland waterways, two new factors added to the complement of the brown-water fleet, the woodenclad and ironclad steam-driven gunboat. With the formation of a navy riverine force, Secretary of the Navy Gideon Welles, to curb potential criticism, initially placed command of all gunboat operations on the western rivers under the authority of the War Department. Subsequently, on 16 May 1861, he ordered Commander John Rodgers to General George McClellan's headquarters in Cincinnati, Ohio, to establish and deploy a riverine fleet to attack, blockade, or interdict Confederate movement on the Mississippi and Ohio rivers. Welles further stipulated that all operations were under army control and that Rodgers was subordinate to the army commander. Although Welles hoped to promote interservice cooperation and a unified command structure, after a year and a half, differing views of naval roles and logistical problems necessitated an independent waterborne component. With these difficulties in mind, Congress authorized the transfer of command of the western riverine fleet to the Navy Department on 1 October 1862. Despite the change, naval commanders were ordered to extend their services to army leaders upon their request, if this did not impede or infringe on previously issued navy orders.

The attacks on Forts Henry and Donelson represented the first large-scale riverine assaults on strategic positions during the war. The "capture of Fort Henry would open the navigable waters of the Tennessee into northern Alabama and sever the northernmost lateral railway—the Memphis, Clarksville, and Louisville line." The elimination of Fort Donelson, in addition, "would remove the only real obstacle to navigation from the mouth of the Cumberland to Nashville." Not only would the capture of these two posts permit river incursions into Confederate territory but also "a successful penetration up the two rivers would turn every confederate position on the Mississippi from Cairo to Memphis and . . . would separate the confederate forces in Missouri from those in Kentucky."

The plan for the strike on Fort Henry included the use of four ironclads and three woodenclads, split into two divisions, to bombard the fort. The flotilla was under Commodore Andrew Foote, who had assumed Rodgers's command on 30 August because of political reasons. Brigadier General Ulysses S. Grant's ground force, after disembarking from transports, would cut off the enemy's escape from the rear. On 6 February, the two-division riverine fleet steamed forward with the ironclads running parallel to the approaching fort, protecting the wooden vessels. About forty-five minutes later, the Federal rivercraft commenced firing on Fort Henry. For an hour and fifty minutes the U.S. gunboats barraged the fort. Shortly thereafter the Confederate commander hauled down the Rebel flag before the U.S. Army reached its objective. With Fort Henry eliminated, the army and navy focused their efforts on the destruction or capture of Fort Donelson. On 10 February, Foote ordered his command up the Cumberland River to cooperate with the army in a combined assault on Fort Donelson. After Federal troops and artillery were in position to lay siege to the fort, General Grant ordered Foote's gunboats to attack the guns at Fort Donelson. On 13 February, as the fleet moved forward and began firing a mile and half from the Confederate guns, the Union sailors noticed the silence from the enemy emplacements. When the ironclads at the front of the small riverine column were within point-blank range, the Confederate batteries unleashed a devastating fire into the Union gunboats. The navy's involvement in the gunnery duel lasted about an hour and fifteen minutes. By the close of the action, all the Union gunboats had sustained casualties and extensive damage that forced their withdrawal. Two days later, without naval assistance, Grant captured Fort Donelson.

As a result of the collapse of Forts Henry and Donelson, the Confederates, now outflanked in Columbus, Kentucky, relocated down the Mississippi to New Madrid, Missouri, and Island No. 10, Tennessee. Subsequent Union operations aimed at the capitulation of both these locations would enable potential future operations against Memphis, Tennessee. After Memphis had been secured, the Federal army and navy on the upper Mississippi could focus all of their attention on Vicksburg.

Despite expected resistance from the defenders of New Madrid, when Union major general John Pope's army marched into the town on 12 March, the Confederate forces had already dispersed during the night. At Island No. 10, Pope counted on naval assistance from Foote to invest the heavily defended positions both ashore and on the island. Initially, Foote was reluctant to deploy his gunboats, insisting that they required repairs following the engagement at Fort Donelson. On 14 March, however, Foote finally got underway from Cairo, Illinois, with his mortar and gunboats and arrived above Island No. 10 on 15 March. The next morning his mortar boats were tied to the bank and began a two-week-long bombardment of the defended position. Despite General Pope's requests that Foote dispatch his gunboats below the island to protect an army assault against the Confederates, Foote stubbornly refused the general. Pope, in frustration, used his engineers to dig a canal near New Madrid that would enable his forces to move to the rear of the enemy's guns. Pope's men completed the canal in nineteen days, only to have the Mississippi's water level lower to the point that the canal was ineffectual for even shallow boat transits. To conclude the military stalemate, Foote authorized Commander Henry Walke to take his gunboat and pass by the Rebel fortifications. On 4 April, Walke successfully carried out his mission, which proved that slipping under the guns was viable. Two days later another gunboat accomplished the same feat. The following day under cover fire from the gunboats, Pope's troops attacked the shore-based garrison and forced its surrender. Observing their precarious position, the island's defenders surrendered to Foote later that day.

The U.S. Navy's riverine force subsequently centered its targets on Fort Pillow, where a Union victory would eliminate the final barrier to the capture of Memphis. Pope and Foote made plans for a combined attack on 14 April, but topographical problems prevented Pope from achieving his part of the operation. Before the two commanders could reorganize for another attack, Pope received orders to join forces with General Henry W. Halleck for operations against Corinth, Mississippi. Foote, with only a small detachment of soldiers, elected not to engage the fort without a larger ground force. Instead, he chose to dispatch one or two mortar boats down the Mississippi with a one-gunboat escort, away from the river fleet and out of range of the bastion's guns, and shell the fort from a distance. Meanwhile, Foote, whose wound that he received at Fort Donelson had never quite healed, requested permission for a leave of absence to convalesce in more peaceful surroundings. On 9 May, Captain Charles H. Davis assumed command of the western river fleet and immediately became engaged in combat with Confederate riverine forces. The following morning, eight enemy craft, armed with cannon and rams, left Fort Pillow and steamed toward the Federal mortar boat and her escort. The hour-long battle that ensued resulted in damage to both Union craft, and before reinforcements could arrive the Confederates safely retired to Fort Pillow. For weeks nothing occurred between the two forces until the battles of Shiloh and Corinth. After the South lost these positions, Confederate commanders chose to evacuate Fort Pillow on 2 June. The next day Davis sent his small detachment of troops into the fort and he and his flotilla departed for Memphis. On 5 June, Davis's gunboats attacked the Confederate flotilla. On this occasion the Federal complement of rivercraft included several rams that, once the fray began, slipped through the Union

gunboats and charged the enemy gunboats. Concurrently, the Union gunboats closed with the enemy and began inflicting serious damage to the Confederate boats. This proved too much for the Confederates and several of their gunboats attempted to flee the engagement, only to be assailed from the Union craft that followed. Following the battle, Davis accepted the surrender of the city. While Foote and his officers secured the upper Mississippi and its tributaries, Flag Officer David G. Farragut prepared for the capture of the port of New Orleans. Forts Saint Philip and Jackson, armed and garrisoned to protect the Crescent City from a southern approach up the Mississippi, were the principal obstacles to the Federal navy. Farragut's plan, according to Navy Department orders, was to bombard and subdue the forts with his mortar boats, then to proceed to New Orleans with his gunboats and deep-draft vessels, there to await ground forces. On 18 April 1862, Farragut's mortar boats began a six-day bombardment of the two Confederate river forts. With mortar ammunition running low, the admiral decided to pass the guns of the forts and take New Orleans. In the early morning hours of 24 April, Farragut's armada, although under continuous fire from enemy cannon, slipped past the forts, successfully engaged a small Confederate naval force, and captured New Orleans.

After the collapse of New Orleans, Secretary of the Navy Gideon Welles directed Farragut to push up the Mississippi, engage the defenders at Vicksburg, and link up with Davis's command above the river town. With knowledge gained from the New Orleans operation, on 28 June Farragut with his gunboats in two columns ascended the river and ran past the guns of Vicksburg with minimal damage to his craft. Regardless of the combined naval force, without a substantial ground element, Davis and Farragut knew that the navy alone could not force the surrender of Vicksburg. Hence, in late July Farragut gathered his fleet and steamed back to New Orleans.

In a continued effort to gain complete control of the Mississippi, Union operations persisted against Vicksburg. Determined to accomplish this goal, Major General William T. Sherman believed securing land between the Black and Yazoo rivers would provide the U.S. Army with a landing place from which he could then launch a ground assault on Vicksburg. On 20 December 1862, seven Navy gunboats proceeded up the Yazoo to obtain a landing site for the army. The Union naval forces also attempted to clear the river of torpedoes, to bombard landing sites, and to provide fire support for the army. For example, David Dixon Porter directed two mortar boats to support operations ashore by firing on both the right and left flank of the army moving against enemy positions.

On many other occasions Union navy rivercraft

directly engaged entrenched Confederate troops and gun emplacements to relieve pressure upon Sherman's ground elements. Although Sherman's troops later were forced to withdraw from the area due to heavy losses sustained in combat at Chickasaw Bluffs, Porter's riverine fleet had proved its worth to the army commanders.

From January to July 1863, the navy continued to assist the army in its efforts to force the surrender of Vicksburg. On 16 April Porter's force, with his gunboats providing protection for army transports, steamed past the guns of Vicksburg, guarded the disembarkation of troops, and took up positions below the well-protected Confederate river town. By May, Union ground forces had laid siege to the entrapped defenders at Vicksburg. From 19–22 May, 27 May, and 20 June, the U.S. riverine fleet above and below Vicksburg rained shot and shell onto the besieged Southerners. With their supply lines cut by river, railroad, and overland routes, combined with increasing military and naval pressure, the Confederates succumbed to Union forces on 4 July 1863. This strategic victory guaranteed Federal control of the South's primary inland waterway from Illinois to the Gulf of Mexico.

The Red River campaign in 1864 was the final U.S. large-scale riverine operation of the war. Union military and naval leaders believed that a raid up the Red River would attain Federal command of the region and a gateway into Texas. On 12 March 1864, Porter, with nineteen gunboats, combined forces with Major General Nathaniel P. Banks in what was to be one of the greatest fiascoes for U.S. military arms during the war. With Porter's command ahead of the slower army transports, some of Porter's craft assisted the army in investing Fort de Russy on 15 March and Alexandria, Louisiana, the next day. Almost two weeks lapsed before Banks's army finally reached Alexandria. The remainder of the expedition was not as successful. As Porter pushed forward with his naval component, Banks slowly moved forward, but was soundly defeated at Mansfield, Louisiana, and began to retreat. Banks's action forced Porter to begin the long trip back to the Mississippi. Along the way, Confederate forces lobbed shells and sniped at the passing Federal gunboats, and then the water level fell. Stranded in the river near Alexandria, Porter requested army support. In response, Lieutenant Colonel Joseph Bailey constructed several dams below the rapids near Alexandria that permitted Porter's marooned gunboats to run the rapids and proceed to safety, thus ending the Red River expedition.

Although the Union navy's primary focus centered around the elimination of key strategic locations, the navy's riverine fleet also performed additional duties. On both western and eastern rivers the navy conducted interdiction operations against enemy supply and manpower routes, established regular patrols, and performed counterguerrilla operations. These roles were, however, of secondary importance to providing support to ground forces attempting to capture significant forts and positions.

—R. Blake Dunnavent

See also Alexandria, Louisina, Destruction of; Bailey, Joseph; Davis, Charles Henry; Farragut, David Glasgow; Foote, Andrew H.; Fort Donelson; Fort Henry; Island No. 10, Battle of; Navy, C.S.A.; Navy, U.S.A.; Porter, David Dixon; Vicksburg Campaign.

For further reading:
Anderson, Bern. *By Sea and By River: The Naval History of the Civil War* (1962).
Bradford, James C., ed. *Captains of the Old Steam Navy: Makers of American Naval Tradition 1840–1880* (1986).
Fowler, William M., Jr. *Under Two Flags: The American Navy in the Civil War* (1990).
Hagan, Kenneth J. *This People's Navy: The Making of American Sea Power* (1991).
Milligan, John. *Gunboats Down the Mississippi* (1965).
Slagle, Jay. *Ironclad Captain: Seth Ledyard Phelps and the U.S. Navy, 1841–1864* (1996).
Sprout, Harold, and Margaret Sprout. *The Rise of American Naval Power 1776–1918* (1944).

RIVES, ALFRED LANDON
(1830–1903)
Confederate engineer

Born to William Cabell Rives (a future Confederate congressman) and Judith Walker Rives, Alfred Landon Rives was born in Paris while his father served as U.S. minister to France. Rives was educated primarily in Virginia, including the Virginia Military Institute and the University of Virginia, where he studied engineering. Travel to France also exposed him to engineering studies there. Upon his return to the United States, he worked briefly in the railroad industry before joining the U.S. Corps of Engineers.

Upon the outbreak of the Civil War, Rives accepted a captain's commission in the Confederate Engineering Bureau. During the summer through the fall of 1861, he was headquartered at Williamsburg, Virginia, and in early 1862 he managed much of the construction of the works on the York Peninsula and the Rappahannock River. He also served briefly as acting chief of the Engineering Bureau before the appointment of a permanent head, Jeremy Francis Gilmer, in October 1862. Throughout the war when Gilmer was away from the Confederate capital, Rives would serve as the bureau's acting chief.

In the fall of 1862, Rives was promoted to major and given the title of assistant to the chief engineer. In the summer of 1863, he was promoted to lieutenant colonel and for almost a year occupied the post of acting chief while Gilmer was in South Carolina. The following spring he was promoted to colonel, the highest rank he would attain during the war.

Rives spent most of his time in Richmond or with the Army of Northern Virginia. His most valuable contributions were in the areas of bridge building and field fortifications.

After the war, Rives worked primarily in the railroad industry in Virginia, although he worked for a while in Panama supervising the construction of an isthmian railroad. He died outside Richmond.

—David S. Heidler and Jeanne T. Heidler

See also Army of Northern Virginia; Gilmer, Jeremy Francis.
For further reading:
Nichols, James L. *Confederate Engineers* (1957; reprint, 1987).

RIVES, WILLIAM CABELL
(1793–1868)

Confederate congressman

Born in Amherst County, Virginia, the son of Robert Rives and Margaret Jordan Cabell Rives, William Cabell Rives was educated at Hampden–Sydney College and the College of William and Mary. After a brief stint as a private in the War of 1812, he read law with Thomas Jefferson and began practicing in 1814. Soon he became involved in Virginia state politics. He represented Nelson County at the state constitutional convention and then a few years later was elected to represent the county in the Virginia House of Delegates. After moving to Albemarle County, he represented Albemarle in the same body.

By the early 1820s, Rives had enough support in the Charlottesville area to be elected to the U.S. House of Representatives, where he became a supporter of Andrew Jackson. In 1829 he left the House to accept Jackson's appointment as minister to France. Upon his return from France, Rives was elected to represent Virginia in the U.S. Senate, where he continued to be a strong advocate of Jacksonian policies.

In the early 1840s, Rives began to lean more toward the Whig Party. In 1844 he officially became a member, but he soon retired to his plantation to write what became a multivolume biography of James Madison. Called in 1849 to serve again as minister to France, he retired to his estates upon his return to the United States. Rives did not emerge from private life until the sectional crisis was destroying the country in early 1861.

A member of the Virginia convention of early 1861, Rives strongly opposed secession. The U.S. government had done nothing to threaten the South, he argued, and only if coercion was used against the seceded states would Virginia be justified in resorting to secession. Because of his opposition to Virginia's secession and his belief in a negotiated settlement, Rives was appointed by the convention to attend the Washington Peace Conference that Virginia had initiated. In the capital, he and several other distinguished men met informally with President-elect Abraham Lincoln to discuss the crisis. Some reports state that Lincoln responded to Rives's entreaties for peace by promising that the government would evacuate Fort Sumter if Virginia would remain in the Union. Some accounts, however, dispute that Lincoln ever made such an unqualified statement. In any event, upon the failure of the peace conference, Rives returned to the Virginia Convention to await the outcome of the Fort Sumter crisis. Abraham Lincoln's call for volunteers to suppress the rebellion after the fall of Fort Sumter caused Rives to abandon his opposition to Virginia's secession.

After the secession of Virginia, Rives accepted selection to the Provisional Confederate Congress. In that body he took a strong interest in the defense of his state, and in May 1861 he traveled to Harper's Ferry to inspect the site of one of the early Confederate triumphs. His caution and early opposition to secession probably cost him his attempt to win a senate seat in the First Confederate Congress the following fall. He again retired but returned in 1863 as a candidate for the Confederate House of Representatives.

Victorious in this election, Rives served in the Second Confederate Congress, though age and infirmities kept him from regular attendance at its sessions. When there, however, he consistently supported the administration, particularly Jefferson Davis's efforts to maintain a strong military. As it became evident that the war was lost, Rives resigned his seat on 1 March 1865 and returned to Albemarle County.

After the war, Rives continued to write, completing his biography of Madison. He died at his wife's family home outside Charlottesville.

—David S. Heidler and Jeanne T. Heidler

See also Congress, C.S.A.; Virginia.
For further reading:
Brown, Alexander. *The Cabells and Their Kin, A Memorial Volume of History, Biography and Genealogy* (1895).

ROANOKE ISLAND, NORTH CAROLINA

In the aftermath of the Federal defeat at the battle of First Bull Run, Northern strategists contemplated a number of alternative avenues of operation against the Confederacy, including a combined land and sea operation aimed at coastal fortifications protecting North Carolina's inlets, sounds, and rivers. The first objective was to prevent Confederate raiders and privateers based in this safe haven from preying upon U.S. vessels. A second, future goal was to establish a foothold in eastern North Carolina, making it possible eventually to cut the Wilmington & Weldon

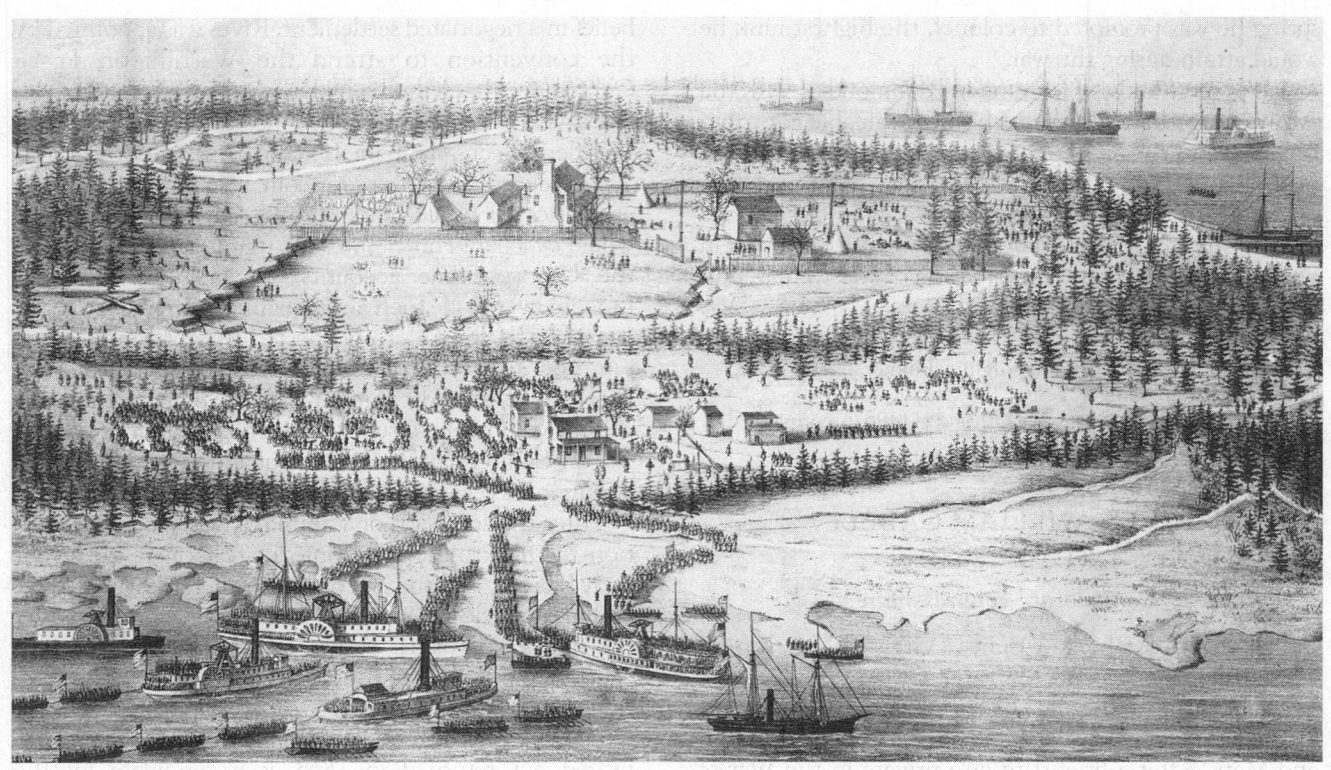

Burnside's troops landing at Roanoke Island, 7 February 1862 (*Library of Congress*)

Railroad running northward with connections to Petersburg and Richmond. Forts Hatteras and Clark, located on the Outer Banks guarding Hatteras Inlet, emerged as the primary Federal targets in the summer of 1861.

Even though authorities in Richmond and Raleigh recognized the strategic importance of North Carolina's shoreline, its defenses were incomplete and undermanned when the Federal operation materialized. The defenders of Fort Clark were overwhelmed by a combined naval and land bombardment and withdrew on 28 August 1861. Fort Hatteras's 700 defenders broke under the weight of a three-hour naval bombardment and surrendered on 29 August. Soon, fortifications guarding the Oregon and Ocracoke inlets were evacuated. By early September, access to the sea from Albemarle and Pamlico sounds was largely controlled by Federal forces, and the initial objective of the operation had been achieved. The North could also claim one of its first significant victories of the war.

Encouraged now to continue operations in North Carolina, strategists in Washington planned for an offensive in January 1862 to capture Roanoke Island, which guarded the immediate entrance to Albemarle Sound. The plan was initially proposed by Colonel Rush C. Hawkins, commander of the Federal occupying force at Hatteras Inlet, and included a proposal to secure the

Pamlico and Neuse rivers as well as the coastal town of Beaufort. Once accomplished, Northern troops could move inland, gain control of the state's eastern counties, and disrupt Confederate communications with Virginia. They also would be available to cooperate with General George B. McClellan's planned operation to capture the Confederate capital from the east.

On 11 January, an expeditionary force consisting of an amphibious division of more than 15,000 troops under Brigadier General Ambrose E. Burnside, commander of the newly created Department of North Carolina, and a flotilla of eighty vessels of varying sizes, set out to sea from Fort Monroe. The vulnerable transport ships were escorted by warships from the North Atlantic Blockading Squadron under the command of Flag Officer Louis M. Goldsborough. The lead ships entered Hatteras Inlet two days later, but bad weather and keels too deep for the shallow inlet waters delayed the attack on Roanoke Island for three weeks.

Owing to the work of busy informants, North Carolina and Confederate officials knew of the impending attack prior to the fleet's departure from Virginia. Brigadier General Henry Wise, the former governor of Virginia now commanding the Chowan District of the Department of Norfolk, made efforts to reinforce Colonel Henry Shaw's 1,435 men on Roanoke Island. While a few men and weapons trickled onto the

The capture of Roanoke Island (*Library of Congress*)

island and to nearby batteries, Confederate forces were outmanned and outgunned when Goldsborough began his naval assault on the morning of 7 February. After losing two gunboats, Confederate captain William F. Lynch's seven-vessel "mosquito fleet" withered and withdrew in the face of superior naval firepower. Water obstacles also proved to be ineffective in retarding the Federal naval advance.

Following Goldsborough's successful naval action, Burnside began landing his force at Ashby's Harbor near the center of Roanoke Island in the late afternoon. Encountering little resistance, 10,000 Federal troops were on shore by the end of the day. The following morning, Burnside's division outflanked and overran the island's defenders. Shaw surrendered 2,580 men after losing 23 men in battle. Federal casualties included 37 killed and 214 wounded. Burnside's successful operation gave the North one of its first significant battlefield victories of the war.

On 10 February, a squadron of vessels from Goldsborough's flotilla destroyed the remnants of North Carolina's navy on the Pasquotank River. With Albemarle Sound open for navigation, Federal detachments began moving up the Chowan River with orders

to destroy railroad bridges and rally Union sympathizers. By 14 March, Burnside had control of the lower Neuse River and the old colonial capital of New Bern—an occupation that would last for the remainder of the war. By May 1862, most of North Carolina's sounds and surrounding counties were under Federal control. Burnside and officials in Washington hoped that supporters of the Union would feel secure enough to condemn the state's Confederate policies openly. Accordingly, Abraham Lincoln appointed Edward Stanly, a former Whig congressman and native North Carolinian, military governor of the state. Stanly's brief tenure at his New Bern capital was controversial, but he did relieve Burnside of the burden of civil administration. Following Stanly's resignation in 1863, a fugitive slave colony was established on Roanoke Island under the supervision of the Reverend Horace James.

—*Alan C. Downs*

See also Hatteras Inlet, Capture of; North Carolina; Stanly, Edward.
For further reading:
Barrett, John G. *The Civil War in North Carolina* (1963).
Marvel, William. *Burnside* (1991).

ROBERTSON, JEROME BONAPARTE
(1815–1891)
Confederate general

The son of Cornelius Robertson and Clarissa Hill Robertson, Jerome Bonaparte Robertson was born in Woodford County, Kentucky. His family's dire financial straits compelled his apprenticeship to a hat maker, but as a youth Robertson began studying medicine with a local doctor and was sent to Transylvania University to complete his medical education. He practiced briefly in Kentucky before moving to Texas in 1836 to join the revolution there. After the revolution he remained in Texas, where he practiced medicine and became involved in state politics. Statewide, he was known largely as an Indian fighter, and he parlayed this reputation into several political offices, including terms in the lower and upper houses of the Texas legislature.

In early 1861, Robertson was elected to the Texas secession convention, where he was an advocate of secession. Upon the secession of the state he raised a company of infantry and became its captain. The company eventually joined the 5th Texas Infantry in John Bell Hood's brigade. By November 1861 Robertson had risen to the rank of lieutenant colonel.

Robertson fought with the regiment in the early phases of the Peninsula campaign and earned promotion to colonel and commander of the 5th Texas on 1 June 1862. He led the regiment during the Seven Days' and Second Bull Run. He received a severe wound at the latter battle but insisted on returning to his command at the commencement of Robert E. Lee's invasion of Maryland. The seriousness of the wound, however, caused his collapse during that campaign.

In October 1862 Lee recommended that Robertson be promoted to brigadier general and assume command of Hood's Texas Brigade when Hood took command of the division. The promotion became official in November 1862, and Robertson commanded the brigade at Fredericksburg and Gettysburg, where he received a minor wound.

In the late summer of 1863, Robertson led his brigade south as part of James Longstreet's move to reinforce Braxton Bragg in north Georgia. Robertson fought with his Texans at Chickamauga and in the Knoxville campaign that followed. During the latter campaign Robertson was criticized by Longstreet, who removed him from command and preferred charges against him for mishandling his brigade at Knoxville. Longstreet made similar charges against Brigadier General E. M. Law. Though neither of the courts-martial took place, Robertson essentially was banished to Texas in June 1864 to take command of the reserve troops there. While his problems with Longstreet certainly contributed to his transfer, Robertson's brigade was so depleted by the campaigns of 1863 that there was scarcely anyone left for him to command. He remained in the trans-Mississippi for the remainder of the war. In March 1865 he came under the command of John B. Magruder, although there is no record that he ever surrendered Texas forces.

After the war, Robertson returned to his medical practice. During the remaining years of his life he also worked for the state government and promoted railroad construction in Texas. He died in Waco, Texas.

—*David S. Heidler and Jeanne T. Heidler*

See also Hood, John Bell; Longstreet, James; Texas.
For further reading:
Touched with Valor: Civil War Papers and Casualty Reports of Hood's Texas Brigade (1964).

ROBINSON, CHARLES
(1818–1894)
Governor of Kansas

Charles Robinson was born in Hardwick, Massachusetts, on 21 July 1818. The Robinson family traced its roots back to the Plymouth colony. Though trained in medicine, Robinson spent more of his life as a politician than a doctor. In 1843 he married Sarah Adams. She died three years later. Neither of the two children she bore survived infancy.

In 1849 Robinson was caught up in the gold fever that swept the country. He embarked for California as physician to an overland company. Once out West he became an advocate for the squatters in contentious disputes over land rights to the public domain. Robinson was wounded in a squatter demonstration. Although he was jailed for murder, conspiracy, and assault with intent to kill arising out of the squatter riots, the case was dropped and Robinson was elected to the California legislature. But Robinson did not intend to remain in California. He returned to Massachusetts, where he married a former patient, Sara T. D. Lawrence, in 1851.

Robinson's westward travels made him useful to wealthy New Englanders who had formed an organization, the New England Emigrant Aid Company (NEEAC), to encourage the settlement of Kansas Territory with people from the free states. Robinson became an agent of NEEAC and helped to found its leading settlement, Lawrence, Kansas. When Missourians crossed the border in March 1855 to vote in territorial elections, Kansas settlers formed an opposition movement to resist the rule of the fraudulently elected territorial legislature. This opposition movement, the Topeka government, was a coalition of New Englanders led by Robinson and westerners led by James H. Lane, formerly of Indiana. Although the coalition was marked by tension, including the personal distaste and distrust Robinson felt for Lane, it remained in effect throughout the territorial period. While Lane served as military commander for the Topeka forces and was a spell-binding orator, Robinson was the most perceptive commentator on its political meaning. In a 4 July 1855 oration in Lawrence, Robinson explained the Topeka government's objections to the territorial government: The denial of political rights to white settlers implicit in the fraudulent elections was intended to force slavery into the territory. Many settlers, including Robinson, found slavery morally objectionable. The territorial government therefore sought, Robinson charged, to make political slaves of Kansas settlers to bring black slavery into the territory.

The Topeka movement elected Robinson as its governor and, during the guerrilla fighting of "Bleeding Kansas" in the summer of 1856, he was jailed for having illegally assumed that office. Sara Robinson made an important contribution as well to the free-soil movement in Kansas by authoring the propaganda tract, *Kansas: Its Interior and Exterior Life* (1856). Her account of the alleged atrocities committed by Missourians upon Kansas settlers went through several editions and did much to shape Northern support for the Topeka movement.

When Kansas achieved statehood in 1861, Robinson was elected the first state governor, but his period in office was marred by continued quarrelling with Lane over control of Kansas troops. Lane, now a U.S. senator, enjoyed the advantage of friendship with President Abraham Lincoln and continually undercut Robinson's authority as governor.

In addition, scandal over the sale of state bonds led to the impeachment of Governor Robinson and other state officials. Although Robinson was acquitted, the taint of corruption remained a charge used by his enemies. He was not renominated for office and later attempts at political comebacks failed.

After retiring from the governorship, Robinson worked with the Greenbacker and Populist movements. He was sympathetic to movements for African-American and women's fights. He wrote a memoir, *The Kansas Conflict* (1892), about territorial Kansas that was part of an ongoing battle for the memory of Bleeding Kansas by old political rivals within the free-soil movement. Robinson's critics charged that his involvement with the state historical society, of which he served as director, was also intended to restored his historical reputation. He was a strong supporter of education, including plans for the state university, and for a period served as director of the Haskell Institute for Indians.

Robinson's correspondence and writings reveal a keen intelligence and acerbic wit, as well as a close, affectionate, and—for that period—remarkably egalitarian relationship with his second wife. The couple had no children. Robinson died on 17 August 1894.

—*Nicole Etcheson*

See also Kansas; Kansas-Nebraska Act; Lane, James H.
For further reading:
Blackmar, Frank W. *The Life of Charles Robinson. The First State Governor of Kansas* (1902).
Clugston, W. G. *Rascals in Democracy: A Case Study of Popular Government* (1941).
Rawley, James A. *Race & Politics: "Bleeding Kansas" and the Coming of the Civil War* (1969).
Robinson, Charles. *The Kansas Conflict* (1892).
Wilson, Don W. *Governor Charles Robinson of Kansas* (1975).

ROBINSON, JOHN CLEVELAND
(1817–1897)
Union general

Born to Tracy Robinson and Sarah Cleveland Robinson in Binghamton, New York, John Cleveland Robinson received his early education at Oxford Academy before accepting an appointment to the U.S. Military Academy. He was dismissed from the academy after three years because of a disciplinary matter. After a year of legal study, Robinson was able to procure a commission as a second lieutenant.

Until the outbreak of the Mexican-American War, Robinson served at a variety of frontier posts. During the war, Robinson served as a quartermaster in northern Mexico under Zachary Taylor and in Winfield Scott's Mexico City campaign. After the war, he again served on the frontier, in Florida during the Second Seminole War, and in the Mormon expedition. In later years, Robinson wrote that the sending of troops to Utah had been a Southern conspiracy to remove the army from the East to make it easier to divide the Union.

At the outbreak of the Civil War, Robinson was a captain commanding Fort McHenry in Baltimore harbor. When the city's pro-Southern mob attacked the 6th Massachusetts as it passed through town and threatened an attack on Fort McHenry, Robinson prepared his 60-man garrison for a siege and turned his artillery toward the city. He was not molested.

During the summer of 1861, Robinson traveled in the upper Midwest recruiting for the army. His success in Michigan gained him selection as the colonel of the 1st Michigan Infantry. The 1st Michigan was made a part of the Army of the Potomac and traveled to the York peninsula with the army in the spring of 1862 to participate in the Peninsula campaign. Robinson commanded his regiment through the early battles of that campaign until assuming command of a brigade in Philip Kearny's division of III Corps in June 1862. Robinson had been promoted to brigadier general with a date of rank of 28 April 1862. Robinson fought in the Seven Days', and then in August with Kearny's division was sent back to Washington to become a part of John Pope's Army of Virginia. Robinson fought at Second Bull Run and at Chantilly, where Kearny was killed. During the

Maryland campaign of September 1862, Robinson's brigade was assigned to the defense of Washington.

Robinson commanded his brigade at Fredericksburg, where his flanking attack on one of the Confederate positions on the Confederate left yielded him 60 prisoners, one of the few positive events for Union forces that day. After the battle of Fredericksburg, Robinson was given command of the 2d Division in John Reynolds's I Corps. He did little fighting at Chancellorsville in May of 1863 but would distinguish himself during the first day's fighting at the battle of Gettysburg.

I Corps was the first to arrive at Gettysburg on 1 July in relief of John Buford's cavalry. Reynolds was killed before the men could start to deploy along the ridgeline west of town. The situation being desperate, Robinson began to gather his men on the high ground around the Lutheran seminary. He was able to amass only two brigades before the Confederates attacked his position, and for four hours he held off attacks by more than twice his number before being ordered back to the ground known as Cemetery Hill. Robinson placed his men in the area to the left of the cemetery, where they did little fighting for the remainder of the battle. Robinson was commended for protecting the Union left flank through the first day's fighting, allowing for an orderly withdrawal back to the more secure ground along Cemetery Hill and Ridge.

The following fall, Robinson and his division fought in the Bristoe Station and Mine Run campaigns. Early in 1864, Robinson and his men were headquartered around Culpeper Court House, Virginia, before being ordered forward in April as part of Ulysses S. Grant's campaign against Robert E. Lee.

Robinson led his men with distinction at the Wilderness in early May 1864 and was one of the first units sent in Grant's flanking maneuver to Spotsylvania Court House. Upon arrival, Robinson was sent forward in one of the first attacks against the Confederate positions. In this attack Robinson received a bullet in his left knee. He was carried from the field, and later that day surgeons removed his left leg.

Robinson spent his recuperation near his wife's home in Janesville, Wisconsin, and by the end of the summer he reported to the War Department that he was fit for duty. While unable to fill a field command position, Robinson was sufficiently recovered to report to the Department of the East in New York City, where he was given command of the Military District of Northern New York headquartered at Albany. While Robinson would no longer lead in combat, this position was anything but an easy desk job. With Confederate agents operating just across the border in Canada, Robinson had to remain vigilant for any actions from that quarter. Furthermore, after the St. Albans raid of October 1864,

Robinson was instructed to prevent any retaliatory raids into Canada by patriotic New Yorkers.

Robinson remained in this command until the end of the war. He opted to remain in the army after the reorganization in 1866. He had already been made the commander of the Freedmen's Bureau in North Carolina. He occupied several department commands before retiring because of his disability at the rank of major general in 1869.

In retirement Robinson remained very active. He served for two years as New York's lieutenant governor and one year as the commander of the Grand Army of the Republic. He remained active in veterans' affairs. In 1894 he was awarded the Medal of Honor for his bravery in a skirmish at Laurel Hill, Virginia, during the war. In his last years he was forced to curtail his activities due to blindness. He died on 18 February 1897 in Binghamton, New York.

—*David S. Heidler and Jeanne T. Heidler*

See also Gettysburg, Battle of; Spotsylvania, Battle of.
For further reading:
New York State Monuments Commission. *In Memoriam, Abner Doubleday, 1819–1893, and John Cleveland Robinson, 1817–1897* (1918).

ROCK ISLAND PRISON

Located on the Mississippi River, Rock Island Prison was one of the largest prisoner-of-war camps in the Union. A total of 12,409 Confederate prisoners were incarcerated at Rock Island. The prison was located on a three-mile-long, half-mile-wide island between Davenport, Iowa, and Moline and Rock Island, Illinois. Owned by the Federal government, Rock Island had been the site of Fort Armstrong from 1816 to 1836 and was selected as a prison because of its distance from the front.

On 14 July 1863 Quartermaster General Montgomery C. Meigs ordered Captain Charles A. Reynolds of the Quartermaster Department to begin construction at Rock Island in August. Meigs stated that "barracks for prisoners on Rock Island should be put up in the roughest and cheapest manner, mere shanties, with no fine work about them." On a twelve-acre site, eighty-four barracks, each twenty-two feet wide and one hundred feet long, were erected and enclosed by a twelve-foot-high board fence with a catwalk for patrolling sentries. Each barrack included a kitchen separated from the sleeping area, which was filled with twenty three-story bunks, each set accommodating six men. Guardhouses were placed by the east and west gates. The prison's maximum capacity was 10,000 prisoners, peaking at 8,594. Colonel Adolphus J. Johnson served as prison commander.

Inspected by Commissary General of Prisoners colonel William Hoffman in November 1863, the Rock Island stockade was still not completed when the first prisoners arrived in early December. Captured during the Chattanooga campaign at Missionary Ridge, Orchard Knob, and Lookout Mountain, some of these prisoners were transferred from overcrowded prisons such as Camp Chase. Others were transported directly from the Chattanooga Depot. On 3 December 1863, 4,196 prisoners reached Rock Island. One thousand prisoners were transferred from Camp Douglas near Chicago, where a fire had damaged facilities. As temperatures reached 32 degrees below zero, the Confederate soldiers suffered from the frigid conditions. Dr. J. J. Temple, the surgeon in charge, and his assistant surgeons, Drs. Marcellus Moxley and T. J. Iles, lacked appropriate medicines to treat the sick. The prison did not have a hospital or sick wards to isolate smallpox cases, and an epidemic broke out among healthy soldiers exposed to sick men. By 1 January 1864, ninety-four prisoners had died from smallpox and were buried 400 yards south of the prison. When Assistant Surgeon General A. M. Clark inspected the prison in February 1864, he criticized the physicians, whom he labeled inept because they had not reported new smallpox cases to the commanding officer and quarantined infected prisoners. Clark requested more vaccine and insisted that wards not be utilized as hospitals. Smallpox cases were removed to pest houses a half mile from the prison.

Differing accounts describe Rock Island in extremes, ranging from a Northern Andersonville to a comfortable prison with ample provisions. Many conditions were beyond the control of Rock Island's officers. The first winter was colder than normal, and the prison did not have enough blankets to give to unacclimated Southerners. Corporal Joseph E. Riley, of Company K, 33d Tennessee, lamented "the hardest service ever tendered by a soldier was to be my lot for the next sixteen months—Rock Island." A Rock Island prisoner told the *Louisville Age*, "In the better days of life there, the bill of fare was generous—coffee, sugar, rice, molasses, boiled meats, and bread in the loaf. After the Andersonville excitement, rations were reduced and the state of affairs began to be painful. A wicked commissary tried a little private retaliation and corn beef got to be abominable." On the other hand, Corporal William Wall of the 2d Kentucky Cavalry wrote his mother that in comparison to life in the Confederate army "this is a rather colder climate, but we have more comfortable quarters and more to eat, altogether a much better place." Stephen J. Stadler, of Company B, 15th & 20th Louisiana, admitted that "the rations were better and more of them than [I] had ever received in the army." Before the prison bakery was completed in June 1864, each prisoner received nine hardtack crackers daily. Rations for each barrack were issued every ten days, and relatives shipped supplemental supplies. Wall asked his mother to send a box of provisions, tobacco, and money.

Elected commander of his barracks, he was expected to enforce cleanliness and discipline, commenting that it was "rather hard work to manage so many men." Prisoners carved clam shells from the river into trinkets that they sold to earn money to purchase soap, paper, and other goods from the post sutler, Albert Dart. Some prisoners helped construct the prison sewers and waterworks, earning credit at the sutler's store. Spare time was also spent creating pen and ink sketches and watercolor paintings of the prison to enclose in letters home. Private E. Purdee of the 7th Florida Infantry made and sold violins. Wall wrote, "I take my fiddle and Dick Cooper, of Covington, who is a capital jig dancer, furnish amusement for our room for an hour or two."

Some prisoners spent their time scheming how to escape by digging tunnels. Forty-one prisoners escaped without being caught. Others drowned crossing the Mississippi or were captured in Illinois. Prisoners were aware that they could be shot if they crossed the deadline around the prison, and a prison commission investigated and acquitted an African-American guard who killed a fleeing prisoner. A former prisoner told the *Louisville Age* that "various punishments were devised against those caught in rebellious ways—riding a rail, hanging by the thumbs, wearing a ball and chain, etc., but on the whole the Federal government was liberal." Several units served as guards, including the 37th Iowa Infantry, elderly soldiers known as the Graybeards who temporarily lived in prison barracks because Johnson believed them to be incompetent; the 4th Regiment Veteran Reserve Corps, who were physically unfit to fight; and the 108th United States Colored Troops, freemen and ex-slaves from Kentucky, whose presence enraged many of the Confederates.

A total of 1,797 prisoners became "Galvanized Yankees" by swearing an oath of allegiance and enlisting in the Union army for frontier garrison service. Delays in transfer resulted in those prisoners remaining in barracks where they were at the mercy of former comrades for food and supplies. Regulations also prevented the quartermaster from issuing food and clothing rations to men who were no longer prisoners because they had elected to serve the Union.

Smallpox, dysentery, and other diseases, as well as accidents and exposure caused deaths among both prisoners and guards. In March 1864 the Confederate dead were reinterred in a plot farther from the cemetery. Union guards and prisoners who had signed the amnesty proclamation were buried in a separate area and eventually moved to the burial ground designated as the Rock Island National Cemetery. A total of 1,960 prisoners died from disease, and 171 guards perished. Prisoners' rations ironically were reduced to save money to fund better health care. A noncontagious diseases hospital was built to accommodate the sick, a laundry boiled

prisoners' clothes, and a reservoir filled with water pumped from the river improved sanitation by flushing the camp's sewage canals.

Nevertheless, in late 1864 newspapers began comparing Rock Island to Andersonville. The local *Rock Island Argus* printed scathing accounts of starvation and torture, provoking Johnson to respond that the papers were not credible "and it would be difficult to imagine it possible to put together a greater amount of error and misrepresentation in the same space." Noting that prisoners' families subscribed to what he considered a pro-Confederate newspaper, Johnson reassured them that prisoners received only two ounces less rations than guards and that deaths from diseases had decreased. Johnson angrily admitted that "had I the power, strict retaliation would be practiced by me. Again, if discretionary power rested with me, I would arrest and confine the known sympathizers with the rebellion residing in Rock Island and Davenport, and quite a large number would be quickly added to our list of prisoners." Johnson wrote the War Department regarding other propagandistic articles, such as the *New York Daily News*'s piece whose headline proclaimed: "Prisoners at Rock Island— Inhuman Treatment—They Feed on Dogs and Rats."

During the twenty months Rock Island Prison operated, 730 prisoners were transferred to other prisons, 3,876 prisoners were exchanged for Union prisoners, and 5,581 prisoners were paroled, including the "Galvanized Yankees." Rock Island also housed 213 civilian prisoners, mostly from nearby Missouri, which caused the additional problem of accommodating numerous visitors. Johnson insisted that all visitors prove their loyalty to the Union before receiving a pass to see prisoners.

By 11 July 1865, the barracks were empty and were later to be sold to the Ordnance Department. Congress had approved the construction of an arsenal on Rock Island in July 1862. Ironically, many Confederates remained at Rock Island as employees. After his release, Private Charles Wesley Parker of Company I, 28th Alabama Infantry, worked in a quarry excavating stones to build the arsenal. Manufacturing military weapons, saddles, and equipment, the Rock Island Arsenal covered the prison site, replacing the barracks with machine shops, offices, housing, and eventually even a golf course. The John M. Browning Memorial Museum preserves artifacts from the prison, and the Confederate and National Cemeteries on Rock Island commemorate veterans' holidays, including Confederate Memorial Day every April.

—*Elizabeth D. Schafer*

See also Disease; Galvanized Yankees; Prisoners of War; Prisons, U.S.A.

For further reading:

Displays and records at the John M. Browning Memorial Museum, Rock Island Arsenal, Rock Island, Illinois.

Minnich, J. W. *Inside of Rock Island Prison, From December,* 1863, to June, 1865 (1908).

Register of Confederate Soldiers and Sailors Who Died in Federal Prisons and Military Hospitals in the North (1912).

Rogan, Lafayette. *Diary of Lafayette Rogan, C.S.A. Prisoner of War at Rock Island Prison Barracks, 1863–1865* (circa 1938).

Walker, T. R. "Rock Island Prison Barracks." In *Civil War Prisons*. Edited by William B. Hesseltine (1962).

Wynn, William O. *Biographical Sketch of the Life of an Old Confederate Soldier* (1916).

ROCKY FACE RIDGE, BATTLE OF
(8–12 May 1864)

The battle of Rocky Face Ridge, Georgia, inaugurated Major General William T. Sherman's Atlanta campaign, and actually consisted of battles that occurred at Dug Gap and Mill Creek Gap (Buzzard's Roost Pass). Sherman's strategy consisted of making a demonstration against the Confederate positions on Rocky Face Ridge with two columns of troops, while a third endeavored to skirt the Confederates and attack the Western & Atlantic Railroad at Resaca. Accordingly, Major General James B. McPherson and his Army of the Tennessee were to pass through Snake Creek Gap, about thirteen miles south of Dalton, Georgia, on their way to Resaca. The Army of the Ohio, under Major General John M. Schofield, and the Army of the Cumberland, led by Major General George H. Thomas, hoped to distract the Confederates by attacking Rocky Face Ridge.

By 7 May, Sherman's troops were positioned for the attack, and the next day, Thomas's army advanced on Mill Creek Gap. The Union troops faced formidable defenses as the Confederates entrenched themselves within the natural barriers posed by the mountain. Union commanders described the defenses on the mountain as impregnable, heavily fortified, and formidable. The Union troops slowly progressed up the steep sides of the mountain. Finally, Brigadier General John Newton, commander of the Second Division of the Fourth Army Corps, managed to capture about three-quarters of a mile of the northern crest. On the night of the 8th, he put two batteries on the crest. By the 9th, Union troops occupied approximately one and three-quarter miles of the crest. Confederates from Lieutenant General John Bell Hood's corps, however, managed to repel several assaults. For the next two days, little happened except some severe skirmishing. On 12 May, however, the Confederates attacked, but once Union reinforcements arrived, they retreated. That night, the rebel troops withdrew from their positions.

While the fighting associated with Mill Creek Gap was taking place, Union troops under Brigadier General John Geary attacked Dug Gap, a pass leading through Rocky Face Ridge and located about five miles southwest of Dalton. Union soldiers conducted their assault up the

The attack on Rocky Face Ridge (*Library of Congress*)

steep and forested slopes in stifling heat and encountered Confederate fire approximately halfway up the mountain; the Confederates also rolled stones down on the attackers. Once they reached the crest, hand-to-hand combat ensued. Union troops often had to attack through narrow passes that would allow no more than four men at a time to pass through them, and the Rebel troops, though few, easily overwhelmed them. Many of the advancing soldiers were forced to jump several feet to safety. To reinforce the Confederate defenders, Brigadier General Patrick Cleburne marched rapidly in the severe summer heat with two brigades. Arriving only about an hour before sundown, Cleburne's troops hurriedly climbed to the pass before the Union attackers could break through the lines. Once the sun set, the attack ceased. Even though Geary's troops failed to take Dug Gap, he believed that they had accomplished their mission. Geary had successfully distracted the Confederates long enough to allow General McPherson's army to enter Snake Creek Gap. They remained in their positions near Dug Gap until 12 May, when they were withdrawn and sent through Snake Creek Gap.

By 9 May, McPherson completely controlled Snake Creek Gap and threatened the rear of General Joseph E. Johnston's Army of the Tennessee. For this reason, the battles associated with Rocky Face Ridge can be considered a Union success, even though their assaults largely failed. Johnston's actions at Rocky Face Ridge have been criticized by his contemporaries and by later scholars. Perhaps most glaring among his mistakes was his failure to place adequate defenses at Snake Creek Gap. General Cleburne commented in his official report, "How this gap, which opened upon our rear and line of communication, from which it was distant at Resaca only five miles, was neglected I cannot imagine." While not overtly placing blame on Johnston, Cleburne nonetheless thought this failure robbed the Confederates of the opportunity to delay their enemies for months and to kill or wound large numbers of Federal soldiers. Johnston apparently believed that Rome, not Resaca, was the primary objective of the Union advance. By the time he realized his error, he had to withdraw to avoid being flanked. McPherson also has been criticized for his lack of aggression once he had obtained possession of Snake Creek Gap. Had he attacked Resaca, he may have been able to cut off Johnston from Atlanta. Instead, he retreated to Snake Creek.

—*Scott M. Langston*

See also Atlanta Campaign; Cleburne, Patrick Ronayne; Johnston, Joseph Eggleston; McPherson, James Birdseye; Resaca, Battle of.

For further reading:

Castel, Albert. *Decision in the West: The Atlanta Campaign of 1864* (1992).

Kerkiss, Sydney C., comp. *The Atlanta Papers* (1980).

RODES, ROBERT EMMETT
(1829–1864)
Confederate general

Born in Liberty, Virginia, the son of David Rodes and Martha Yancey Rodes, Robert Emmett Rodes was educated locally and graduated in 1848 from Virginia Military Institute. For two years after graduation

he taught engineering at the institute before accepting a position as an engineer for the Southside Railroad. Over the next few years he supervised construction for several Southern railroads. In 1860 he decided to return to teaching at Virginia Military Institute. The outbreak of the Civil War cut short this career when he accepted a colonel's commission in the Confederate army.

For the first few months of the war, Rodes served as the colonel of the 5th Alabama. After fighting at First Bull Run, he was promoted to brigadier general in October 1861. In the Peninsula campaign, Rodes commanded his brigade at Seven Pines, where he was severely wounded in the arm. After trying to remain on the field, Rodes lost so much blood that he had to relinquish command to John B. Gordon. Rodes returned too soon to his command during the Seven Days' and became so ill that he was out of action until the Maryland campaign in September 1862.

He mounted a tenacious defense at South Mountain and commanded his brigade in the Confederate center at Antietam, receiving a slight wound in the action. Rodes also commanded his division at Fredericksburg.

In early 1863, Rodes temporarily took command of a division to lead it in Stonewall Jackson's movement around Joseph Hooker's right flank at the battle of Chancellorsville. In the initial attack, Rodes accompanied Jackson and so impressed him that Jackson on his deathbed recommended Rodes's promotion to major general. Robert E. Lee complied, making the necessary recommendation to the Confederate War Department.

In the reorganization of the Army of Northern Virginia following the death of Jackson, Rodes and his division were placed in Richard Ewell's corps. Ewell led the invasion of Pennsylvania in June 1863, and Rodes's division was instrumental in turning the Union right flank in the first day of the battle of Gettysburg and driving Federal forces through the town onto Cemetery Hill. Rodes was commended for his actions on that day by Robert E. Lee.

In the fall of 1863, Rodes commanded his division at Bristoe Station and Mine Run. In the Virginia campaign of the following spring, he fought at the Wilderness, where he repulsed the attack of Major General Gouverneur Warren, and at Spotsylvania, where his division defended the Bloody Angle.

During the summer he was detached to lead his division in Jubal Early's invasion of Maryland, the raid on Washington, and the Shenandoah Valley campaign. At the battle of Winchester on 19 September, while attempting to rally his men for an attack, he was mortally wounded and died before he could be removed from the battlefield. Rodes was known as an especially effective combat general.

—*David S. Heidler and Jeanne T. Heidler*

See also Ewell, Richard Stoddert; Gettysburg, Battle of;

Jackson, Thomas Jonathan; Spotsylvania; Wilderness, Battle of the; Winchester, Third Battle of.

For further reading:
Adams, Owen E. "Confederate Major General Robert E. Rodes: A Civil War Biography" (M.A. thesis, 1995).

Steward, Michelle Lee. "Robert E. Rodes: Lee's Forgotten General" (M.A. thesis, 1997).

RODGERS, JOHN, JR.
(1812–1882)
Union naval officer

John Rodgers, Jr., was born in Havre de Grace, Maryland, the son of Commodore John Rodgers, Sr., the noted War of 1812 hero. He joined the navy as a midshipman in 1828 and, after several Mediterranean cruises, rose to passed midshipman in 1834. The following year he took a leave of absence to study mathematics at the University of Virginia and subsequently served with the Brazilian squadron from 1836 to 1838. In 1839 Rodgers fought in Florida's Second Seminole War while commanding the one-gun schooner USS *Wave*. He rose to lieutenant in January 1840 and two years later took control of the schooner USS *Boxer* as part of the African squadron.

Considered an excellent officer, Rodgers next received command of the sloop USS *John Hancock*, then part of the Asiatic squadron. In this capacity he accompanied Commodore Cadwalader Ringgold on a surveying expedition of the North Pacific. When Ringgold sickened, Rodgers replaced him and led the squadron into the furthest reaches of the Bering Sea. He was residing in Washington, D.C., compiling the official account of his expedition, when the Civil War erupted in April 1861.

On 17 April 1861 Rodgers participated in the botched Union attempt to burn the dry docks at Norfolk, Virginia. Captured and repatriated the following May, he next reported to Cincinnati, Ohio, to construct several shallow-draft gunboats for riverine warfare. However, in October Rodgers was replaced by Captain Andrew H. Foote, and he subsequently transferred to the South Atlantic Blockading Squadron under Commodore Samuel F. Du Pont. Rodgers so distinguished himself in the 7 October 1861 capture of Port Royal, South Carolina, that Du Pont allowed him to personally raise the American flag there. This was the first Union lodging on South Carolina soil since the fall of Fort Sumter in April. Rodgers then garnered additional laurels by capturing Tybee Island off Savannah in November 1861 and Fernandina Island, Florida, the following spring.

In April 1862 Rodgers repaired back to Washington to assume command of an experimental warship, the USS *Galena*, which was heavily armed, but poorly armored. During the ensuing battle of Drewry's Bluff on 15 May 1862, the *Galena* closely engaged a Confederate fort above it and sustained forty hits, but Rodgers remained in action until his ammunition was exhausted. He next assisted in covering the withdrawal of General George B. McClellan's army. He rose to the rank of captain on 16 July 1862.

In consequence of his good service, Rodgers next commanded the USS *Weehawken*, a new and powerful ironclad vessel, and was reassigned to Du Pont's blockading squadron. At that time, doubts were raised as to the seaworthiness of that class of warship, as the original *Monitor* had foundered in a storm and sank. Rodgers deflated these concerns by deliberately sailing the *Weehawken* through stormy seas to Charleston, demonstrating its survivability. He then participated in Du Pont's ill-fated attack against Charleston Harbor on 7 April 1863, which was eventually repulsed. Having received over fifty hits, Rodgers and several other officers prevailed upon Du Pont to withdraw, an act that led to his replacement. Fortunately, the *Weehawken* enjoyed better luck on 17 June 1863, when it engaged and captured the Confederate ram CSS *Atlanta* after a brief running battle. Rodgers consequently received the thanks of Congress, promotion to commodore, and command of a new ironclad, the USS *Dictator*. However, this vessel was plagued with developmental problems, and Rodgers saw no further fighting.

After the war, Rodgers resumed routine land and sea assignments and in 1866 took charge of the Boston Navy Yard. Promoted to rear admiral in December 1869, he transferred his flag to the Asiatic squadron to perform a diplomatic mission. Accompanied by Ambassador Frederick Low, Rodgers attempted to make contact with Korea. This country, which prided itself on being the "Hermit Kingdom," did not seek relations with other nations and resisted them by force. Thus, on 6 June 1871, as Rodgers's squadron ascended the Han River near Seoul, it was fired upon by a barrier fort. The enraged commodore demanded an apology and an explanation and, when none was forthcoming, he landed 700 sailors and marines ashore. These stormed several forts, killing an estimated 243 Koreans, before concluding the first armed American intervention in Korea. The diplomatic mission failed when the Korean king ignored all diplomatic overtures, and Rodgers returned to the United States in 1872. He subsequently served with the Examining and Retiring Boards and also commanded the Mare Island Navy Yard, San Francisco, before becoming head of the Naval Observatory. He died working in that capacity in 1882.

—*John C. Fredriksen*

See also Navy, U.S.A.
For further reading:
Bradford, James C., ed. *Captains of the Old Steam Navy: Makers of the American Naval Tradition, 1840–1880* (1986).

Johnson, Robert E. *Rear Admiral John Rodgers, 1812–1882* (1967).

RODMAN GUN

The Rodman smoothbore gun was a Model 1861 Columbiad, capable of firing either shell or solid shot. Lieutenant Thomas J. Rodman designed and manufactured it according to the revolutionary hollow-casting process he perfected. An ordnance officer and 1841 graduate of West Point, Rodman began working on the problems of cannon barrel design after a 12-inch gun exploded on board the USS *Princeton* in 1844.

Cannon barrels of the time were cast solid from iron and then bored out. Iron was an extremely difficult material, prone to internal casting defects, which often led to gun barrels bursting prematurely. Gun makers prior to Rodman never completely mastered the material. In studying the problem, Rodman noted that as a barrel casting cooled, the outside solidified first. As the cooling process continued, it caused a contraction of the inner material, often resulting in large cracks in the center. Although the cracks were removed when the center was bored out, Rodman realized that the metal on the outer surface of the tube was in a state of compression, while the inside metal surrounding the bore was in a state of tension. Thus, when the explosion from a propellant ignition occurred inside the chamber, the additional tension could cause the barrel to rupture.

Rodman first thought to increase the compression on the barrel by wrapping it with wire. The difficulty of maintaining a constant tension on the wire caused him to reject that approach. Rodman then surmised that he could achieve an even better effect by cooling the cast tube from the inside out. To do this, he developed a method of casting a barrel hollow and then cooling the inside by circulating water through an iron pipe inserted into the cored barrel. Simultaneously, the outside of the casting was kept hot with coals, which were removed gradually as the barrel cooled from the inside out. As the cooling process slowly progressed, each successive layer of metal shrunk one upon another, with each layer being further compressed by the shrinking of the next outer layer. The final barrel wall was in a state of compression throughout its thickness. Rodman compared his revolutionary process to the principle of shrinking an iron tire onto a wooden wagon wheel.

At first Rodman could not convince the Ordnance Department to experiment with his new process. Many

A 15-inch Rodman Columbiad at Fort Monroe, Virginia, 1864 (*Library of Congress*)

The Model 1861 Rodman Guns

	Tube Length (inches)	Tube Weight (pounds)	Projectile Weight (pounds)	Charge Weight (pounds)	Range: 5 degrees elevation (yards)	Maximum Range (yards)
8–inch	124	9,210	65	10	1,813	4,812
10–inch	126	15,400	128	18	1,814	5,600
15–inch	182	50,000	302	40	1,518	4,680

officers and engineers believed that circulating water through a molten casting was too risky, because the pressure of the steam resulting from water hitting the hot iron might cause an explosion. Finally the chief of ordnance, Colonel George Taclott, gave Rodman permission to patent and privately develop the process. In 1845 Rodman entered into a contract with the Pittsburgh firm of Knapp and Totten, who agreed to cover the testing and manufacturing costs in exchange for a half interest in the patent.

Rodman smoothbore siege guns on Battery Magruder at Yorktown, Virginia, June 1862
(Photograph by George N. Barnard / *Library of Congress*)

A 15-inch Rodman gun in Battery Rodgers at Alexandria, Virginia (*National Archives*)

Rodman conducted tests between 1848 and 1859 using eight different pairs of 8- and 10-inch guns. One gun of each pair was cast by conventional methods, the other by the hollow-casting process. The guns were identical in all other respects. Rodman conducted the first test firings in 1849 with a pair of 8-inch guns, firing a 64-pound projectile with 10 pounds of powder. The solid-cast gun burst on the eighty-fifth round while the hollow-cast gun was still intact when the test ended at 251 rounds. In a follow-up test in 1851, the solid-cast gun burst on the seventy-third round, the hollow-cast tube survived 1,500 rounds.

The government finally accepted the hollow-casting process in 1859 and requested Rodman to design and manufacture a 15-inch prototype. Externally, Rodman's design did away with all unnecessary moldings and flourishes. The resulting gun barrel had a streamlined, bottle shape, with a length of 190 inches and a weight of 49,099 pounds. A joint board of engineer, ordnance, and artillery officers, which included Major Robert Anderson, witnessed the test firing in May 1860 at Fort Monroe, Virginia.

The board observed a total of forty-nine firings using both 330- and 450-pound projectiles with a 25-pound propellant charge. On the first round, a complete firing cycle of sponging, loading, and running into battery required one minute and fifty-two seconds. By the sixth round the gun crew had the cycle time down to one minute and three seconds. The prototype gun achieved a maximum range of 5,730 yards.

The board recommended acceptance of the design, which subsequently was adopted as the standard heavy gun for coastal artillery. During the Civil War, the Federal government purchased over 1,500 Rodman guns in 8-, 10-, and 15-inch calibers. Rodman also made two experimental 20-inch monsters in 1864, but neither was ever fired in action.

The Confederate government generally copied the external features of the 1861 design, but they rejected the hollow-casting system. Thus, the term "Confederate Rodman" is something of a misnomer. Also during the war, volunteer Union field artillerymen often erroneously called the 3-inch ordnance rifle a Rodman, because its tapered and smooth lines were similar to Rodman's great Columbiads.

—*David T. Zabecki*

See also Artillery; Ordnance, Naval; Rodman, Thomas.
For further reading:
Peterson, Harold L. *Round Shot and Rammers: An Introduction to Muzzle-loading Land Artillery in the United States* (1969).

Rodman, Thomas J. *Casting the 15-in. Gun* (1980).

———. "Testimony of Major T. J. Rodman, February 6, 1864," in *Report of the Joint Committee on the Conduct of the War* (1980).

Webster, Donald B., Jr. "Rodman's Great Guns." *Ordnance* (1962).

Zabecki, David T. "Father of the Rock Island Arsenal." *Field Artillery Journal* (1981).

RODMAN, THOMAS JACKSON
(1815–1871)
Union officer and artillery designer

Thomas J. Rodman was the most important designer of artillery at the close of the smoothbore era. He was born in Salem, Indiana, on 30 July 1815 and privately educated until he entered the United States Military Academy. He graduated from that institution on 1 July 1841, seventh in a class of fifty-two. Commissioned a brevet second lieutenant in the Ordnance Corps, Rodman's first assignment was as an assistant ordnance officer at the Allegheny Arsenal in Pennsylvania.

In the years prior to the Mexican-American War, Rodman worked as an ordnance officer in Richmond, Boston, and Pittsburgh. While still a second lieutenant, he started working on the problems of cannon barrel design after a 12-inch gun exploded on the USS *Princeton* in 1844. His experiments resulted in the development of a revolutionary hollow-casting process that produced significantly stronger gun barrels.

The Ordnance Department was reluctant at first to adopt the new process. After making three trips to Washington to argue his case, Rodman received permission in 1845 from the chief of ordnance, Colonel George Taclott, to patent and privately develop the process. The U.S. Army finally adopted the hollow-casting process in 1859, and requested Rodman to design and cast a new 15-inch coastal gun. The result was the Model 1861 Columbiad, which became known as the Rodman Gun.

Rodman was promoted to first lieutenant on 3 March 1847 and to captain on 1 July 1855. He continued to serve at various arsenals, commanding the Baton Rouge Arsenal from March 1855 to June 1856. It was during this period that he made his most significant contribution to artillery design. Rodman was the first to realize that the physical configuration of propellant powder should be designed specifically for the gun in which it was used. During test firings in the 1850s, he observed that the rate at which a propellant burned was directly proportional to its surface area. With the conventional grain powder of the period, the greatest surface area existed at the moment of ignition, and then shrunk as the powder grain burned. Hence, the rate of burning

slowed and the subsequently generated pressure decreased. As the projectile moved farther down the cannon's bore, the chamber volume behind the round increased. This, combined with the decreasing rate of powder burn, reduced the pressure behind the projectile as it left the muzzle of the gun.

Rodman reasoned that the optimum artillery propellant would burn at a progressively faster rate, thereby creating more pressure to offset the increasing volume in the chamber as the projectile moved forward. Rodman's solution was to press powder into hexagonal cakes, which then were perforated with longitudinal holes. This configuration caused a cake of propellant to burn from the inside out as well as from the outside in. As the propellant material around the holes burned away, the holes got larger, thereby increasing the exposed surface area—and with it the rate of burning.

Prismatic powder, as Rodman called it, did not increase the chamber pressure in the gun as the projectile moved forward, rather it maintained the pressure at a constant level. The result was an increase in muzzle velocity without an increase in strain on the tube. Increased muzzle velocity brought with it improved range and accuracy. In conjunction with his powder experiments, Rodman also invented the first practical gauge to measure precisely the pressure of the exploding gas inside a gun.

In May 1859 Rodman assumed command of the Watertown Arsenal, outside Boston. He remained at that post throughout the Civil War. While at Watertown, he supervised the casting of 12-, 15-, and 20-inch smoothbores and 12-inch rifled tubes. In 1861 he published his *Reports of Experiments on the Properties of Metals for Cannon and the Qualities of Cannon Powder*. On 1 June 1863 Rodman was promoted to major, and in February 1864 he testified before the Congressional Joint Committee on the Conduct of the War. In September 1864 Rodman started applying his casting methods to the manufacture of artillery projectiles.

A workaholic who drove himself relentlessly, Rodman's health collapsed in the summer of 1864. He returned to duty only after a two-and-a-half-month period of convalescence. As the Civil War ended, Rodman on 13 March 1865 received brevet promotions to lieutenant colonel, colonel, and brigadier general, "for Faithful, Meritorious, and Distinguished Services in the Ordnance Department." That August he was appointed the commander of the Rock Island Arsenal in Illinois. He was promoted to lieutenant colonel on 13 March 1867, the highest substantive rank he was to hold.

The Rock Island Arsenal had been established in 1863, but for most of the Civil War the installation on a large island in the Mississippi River had served as a Union military prison. Upon Rodman's assumption of command, he faced the challenge of turning Rock Island into a major ordnance manufacturing facility. Throwing himself at the task in his characteristic fashion, he drew up the plans for the installation's road system, the commandant's quarters, and ten large shop buildings built out of stone. Working day and night, he ignored repeated warnings from his doctors. His health finally gave out again and he died while in command on 7 June 1871. He lived to see two of his ten great shop buildings completed. Almost 130 years later, most of those shop buildings remained in use. At his own request, Rodman was buried on the Arsenal grounds.

Rodman's great guns proved to be a relatively short-lived military technology, as smoothbore, muzzle-loading, cast-iron artillery gave way to rifled, breech-loading, steel artillery in the years following the Civil War. Rodman's progressive burning propellant, however, remains a basic principle of artillery ammunition design to this day.

—*David T. Zabecki*

See also Artillery; Ordnance, Naval; Rodman Gun.

For further reading:
Rodman, Thomas J. "Testimony of Major T. J. Rodman, February 6, 1864," in *Report of the Joint Committee on the Conduct of the War* (1980).
Zabecki, David T. "Father of the Rock Island Arsenal." *Field Artillery Journal* (1981).

ROEBUCK, JOHN ARTHUR
(1802–1879)
Member of Parliament

A controversial pro-Southern member of Parliament, John Arthur Roebuck attempted both inside and outside the House of Commons to bring about British recognition of the Confederacy during the American Civil War. Attacking the North in characteristically fiery speeches—he referred to Northerners as the "scum and refuse of Europe"—Roebuck also achieved great notoriety by introducing a motion in the House of Commons requesting that the British government consult with the other European powers with the intent of recognizing the Confederacy. The motion backfired spectacularly and destroyed all hope of parliamentary backing for recognition. Indeed, it proved to be Confederate sympathizers' last serious attempt to influence British policy toward the war.

Born on 28 December 1802 in Madras, India, Roebuck was the son of Ebenezer Roebuck, a civil servant, and Zipporah Tickell. Soon after Roebuck and his mother returned to England in 1807, Roebuck's father died in India. Roebuck's mother remarried, but her new husband's unsuccessful business ventures led them to move the family to Canada in 1815. Receiving an education at a variety of schools, Roebuck returned to England in 1824. Associating briefly with James Mill

(father of John Stuart Mill) and Jeremy Bentham's Utilitarians, Roebuck entered the Inner Temple and was called to the bar in 1831.

Although he would continue to pursue a career in law for some years, Roebuck grew increasingly interested in politics. His association with the Benthamites had given him decidedly radical views. Having attained some prominence for his public work on behalf of the Great Reform of 1832 (which extended the franchise and redistributed representation in the House of Commons), Roebuck came to the attention of Joseph Hume, the great radical parliamentarian, who encouraged Roebuck to stand for election in Bath. Roebuck won and in 1833 took his seat in the House of Commons. Roebuck would represent Bath for a total of eleven years (1832–1837 and 1841–1847).

Even for an era when party discipline was lax, Roebuck relentlessly pursued an independent course. A radical, he despised the Tories for their conservatism and loathed the Whigs for their exclusiveness. He supported radical domestic reform, including further extension of the franchise, suspension of the House of Lords' veto, and an end to British oppression in Ireland. Not only his ideas, but his aggressive manner antagonized both fellow legislators and his own constituents. His abrasiveness led a number of politicians to challenge him to duels over the course of his career, and eventually the electors of Bath grew tired of his antics. In 1849 he won a seat from Sheffield, where he enjoyed old family connections.

During this period Roebuck threw his weight behind a strong foreign policy that aggressively defended British interests. A supporter of the Crimean War, Roebuck found the British army's poor performance humiliating. Perhaps his most dramatic intervention in British international politics took place when he introduced a motion calling for an inquiry into the government's conduct of the war on 26 January 1855. When Roebuck's motion passed, Lord Aberdeen's government felt compelled to resign because it had lost the House of Commons's confidence. Roebuck became chairman of the committee of inquiry that released a blistering report condemning the Aberdeen administration's incompetence.

Roebuck increasingly fell out of step with other parliamentary radicals concerning foreign policy. Not only his support of the Crimean War, but his defense of Austria's continued presence in northern Italy during the wars of Italian unification puzzled fellow radicals. His stance on the American Civil War further alienated much radical opinion.

Roebuck feared the United States as a potential great power that could one day threaten Britain's position in the world. At an 1862 banquet in honor of Lord Palmerston, Britain's prime minister, Roebuck took advantage of the occasion to deliver an infamous speech in which he pled on behalf of recognizing the Confederacy. "A divided America will be a benefit to England," he explained before a cheering audience, continuing, "The North will never be our friends. Of the South you can make friends. They are Englishmen; they are not the scum and refuse of Europe."

Aside from making such public pronouncements, Roebuck vigorously worked behind the scenes to push the British government toward recognition of the Confederacy. After the cabinet decided against intervening in the conflict in November 1862, Roebuck and other Southern sympathizers hoped they could achieve their ends by using the House of Commons as a lever against the government. Believing that news of the Confederate victory at Chancellorsville would provide a favorable opportunity, Roebuck and William Lindsay, a fellow member and shipbuilder, met with James Mason, the Confederate envoy to Britain, and concluded the time had come to introduce a motion in the House of Commons asking the government to recognize the South. The British government would not interfere in the conflict alone, but Roebuck and Mason believed France's Emperor Napoleon III still supported intervention. Napoleon III indeed supported such a course of action in conjunction with the British, but having already suggested the idea to the British government and suffering a rebuff, he had no intention of bringing the issue up again only to experience further humiliation. Moreover, he sought to keep his intentions as secret as possible for as long as possible, lest he antagonize the United States without winning British support for his policies.

Roebuck and his friends also believed they enjoyed domestic backing for their project. Hoping to drum up support for his measure in the House of Commons, Roebuck met with Benjamin Disraeli, leader of the Conservative opposition. A master of ambiguity, Disraeli egged Roebuck on without committing himself. In all likelihood, the Conservative leader hoped to use Roebuck to embarrass the Liberal government or possibly even eject it from office. To obtain public backing for their venture, Roebuck and his allies also took care to organize a number of mass meetings in support of recognition.

In late May 1863 Roebuck gave notice that he would introduce a motion asking the government to confer with other European powers preparatory to recognizing the Confederacy. Hoping to avoid a debate in the House of Commons that would only antagonize the North and possibly divide the Liberals, Lord Palmerston sought to kill Roebuck's motion by spreading the rumor that Napoleon III no longer supported intervention. Roebuck countered Palmerston's deviousness with some amateur diplomacy. He and Lindsay crossed the English Channel and on 22 June obtained assurances from

Napoleon III himself that France was still prepared to act with Britain in the matter. The two Englishmen also later claimed Napoleon III promised to provide Baron Gros, the French ambassador to Britain, with instructions to "sound out" the British government on joint intervention.

Thus armed, on 30 June Roebuck initiated debate on his motion by claiming that the Confederacy's survival for two years made it a de facto state, describing how the Federal blockade had imposed great suffering on workers in Britain's textile industry, painting abolitionists as hypocrites, and accusing the United States of being "the great bully of the world." He then revealed the outcome of his conference with Napoleon III. A number of members of Parliament, however, attacked Roebuck, believing intervention would lead to a costly war with the United States. Others feared that even without war, recognition of the South would accomplish little. Still others found Roebuck's personal diplomacy and his aggressive manner distasteful. Lord John Russell, the foreign secretary, and other members of the government dealt the most crushing blow of all when they repeatedly asserted they had received no official communication from Napoleon III indicating that France still wished to act in conjunction with Britain.

In the aftermath of this debate, Roebuck thought either Napoleon III or Russell had lied. Most of the Commons believed Roebuck or the French emperor to be the liar. Although historians have never satisfactorily determined what took place at the meeting between Napoleon III, Lindsay, and Roebuck, it appears that all concerned told the truth. Napoleon III did indeed tell Edouard Drouyn de Lhuys, his foreign minister, to instruct Gros along the lines revealed to Roebuck. Unfortunately, Napoleon III's position on intervention stood far in advance of the French cabinet's. Recognizing this difficulty, Drouyn watered down the instructions to Gros. Instead of a strong, unofficial statement of Napoleon's desire to see the Confederacy recognized, Drouyn sent a message asking Gros simply to inform Lord Palmerston in the course of conversation that France had no objection to recognizing the Confederacy. Seeing no urgency in such a command, Gros eventually met with Russell (Palmerston was ill) on 30 June—the first day of the debate—and let slip this suggestion in an informal way. Russell chose to see Gros's comment as an unofficial communication. Once Roebuck had bungled the motion in the House of Commons, however, Napoleon III and the French government did everything they could to distance themselves from the unfortunate measure.

Whatever the case, Roebuck had discredited himself in the eyes of the House of Commons. Even his fellow pro-Confederate members urged him to drop the motion as an embarrassment to the cause. Further debate on 2

July could not restore Roebuck's credit, and eleven days later he withdrew the motion. The last significant attempt by pro-Southern sympathizers in Britain to obtain recognition of the Confederacy, Roebuck's motion was doomed to failure. The British cabinet had already carefully weighed its options and decided against intervention as a difficult policy whose potential dangers outweighed its potential benefits.

Roebuck's increasingly conservative positions on both domestic and foreign policy alienated his constituents. In 1868 he lost his seat at Sheffield, only to regain it in 1874. By the 1870s Roebuck had completed his transformation to conservatism, even being made a privy councilor by the Conservative government in 1874. He died in London on 30 November 1879.

—*Hubert F. Dubrulle*

See also Adams, Charles Francis; Diplomacy, C.S.A.; Diplomacy, U.S.A.; Great Britain; Lyons, Lord Richard; Mason, James Murray; Napoleon III; Palmerston, Viscount; Russell, Lord John; *Trent* Affair.

For further reading:
Crook, D. P. *The North, the South, and the Powers 1861–1865* (1974).

Jenkins, Brian. *Britain & the War for the Union* (1974).

Leader, Robert Eadon, ed. *Life and Letters of John Arthur Roebuck* (1897).

Owsley, Frank Lawrence. *King Cotton Diplomacy* (1959).

ROOT, GEORGE FREDERICK
(1820–1895)
Northern songwriter

George Frederick Root was a Yankee songwriter whose work became inseparable from memories of the Civil War. Although a native of Sheffield, Massachusetts, he grew up on his parents' farm at North Reading, which the family retained throughout his life. After demonstrating a remarkable facility with music and musical instruments, he entered the employ of a Boston piano instructor, who subsequently began introducing a music curriculum into the local schools. In this rapidly expanding project, Root became a master of his own, continuing in 1844 to teach in Jacob Abbott's School for Young Ladies at New York, and spending 1850 and 1851 in Paris and London.

Upon returning, Root not only resumed teaching, but also pursued a busy career of organizing local, regional, and national musical convocations. At the time the new popularity of professional songwriters like Stephen Foster and performers like the Hutchinson family was beginning to draw American music onto the stage from the classroom, the church, and the parlor. By 1855, Root decided to carve out such a career for himself. In 1858 he got a small interest in Root & Cady, the music publishing company of his younger brother, Ebenezer Towner Root, and Chauncey Marvin Cady. In December

1860 Root physically joined the Chicago enterprise, leaving his wife and children temporarily behind. His knowledge of instrumental music, his improvisational skills, and his heartfelt devotion to the Union made Root the single most important wartime songwriter.

Under George Root's leadership, and aided by writers like Henry Clay Work, Root & Cady anticipated the "Tin Pan Alley" firms that sought to explain (and commoditize) the First World War with an almost uncanny ear for public tastes. On 15 April 1861—within days of the war's outbreak—Root began the process of cranking out tunes and music with "The First Gun is Fired! May God Protect the Right!" The firm completed a new work every few days, sometimes experimenting, as in "Who'll Save the Left?" with telling in song the story of a decisive event on the battlefield. At their best Root's songs successfully tapped the emotions of the soldiers and their families, expressing sources of inspiration, hope, and grief that were individual and personal, as well as part of a shared national experience. First performed by the Lombard brothers at an April 1862 recruitment rally, his "Battle Cry of Freedom" so moved the participants that a thousand voices readily took up the repeating chorus. Through it, legions of volunteers sang of their broadening war goals; months before the Emancipation Proclamation, the song's lyrics insisted that "although he may be more, not a man shall be a slave" and promised to "welcome to our numbers the loyal true and brave," including "a million freemen more." As Root recalled, "the song went into the army, and the testimony in regard to its use in the camp and on the march and even on the field of battle . . . made me thankful that if I could not shoulder a musket in defense of my country I could serve her in this way." A Confederate officer at the war's close responded to this song by telling his victorious counterparts: "Gentlemen, if we'd had your songs we'd have whipped you out of your boots!"

Perhaps as important at the time as this patriotic crowd-pleaser, Root wrote several pieces that, however maudlin and melodramatic to modern ears, attained great and lasting popularity. "The Prisoner's Hope" became better known by its first line: "Tramp! Tramp! Tramp! The boys are marching." "Just Before the Battle, Mother" recalled the frank terror, mingled with determination, of a young soldier going into battle. Highlighting the kind of civilian heroism usually ignored in war, "The Vacant Chair" spoke of the place at the family dinner table of a soldier lost on a distant battlefield. (As with Sullivan Ballou's famous letter, modern listeners frequently forget that these songs arose in an age when spiritualism was popular and in which people believed in the very real and continued presence of spirits among us. Root himself, his brother, and their families formally declared such a belief in 1864.)

After the war Root continued to live in Hyde Park,

south of Chicago. Root & Cady survived, reorganizing after the great fire of 1871 and transferring publishing rights to John Church & Company at Cincinnati. George F. Root continued to produce new songs and songbooks for schools, churches, the temperance movement, and farmers' organizations—notably his "Trumpet of Reform" (1874). After years of success and prominence, Root died at Bailey's Island, Maine.

—*Mark A. Lause*

See also Music.
For further reading:
Crawford, Richard, comp. *The Civil War Songbook* (1977).
Epstein, Dena J. *Detroit Studies in Music Bibliography*, no. 14 (1969).
Root, George F. *The Story of a Musical Life* (1891; reprint, 1970).

ROSECRANS, WILLIAM STARKE
(1819–1898)
Union general

Born on 6 September 1819 in Delaware County, Ohio, William Starke Rosecrans entered the world with the army in his blood. His father had seen action in the War of 1812, had served as an adjutant to General William Henry Harrison, and had even named William in honor of Revolutionary War hero General John Stark (but adding an *e* to his name). In 1838 William Rosecrans opened another chapter in his family's military history when he accepted an appointment to West Point. While a cadet he earned the nickname "Old Rosy" and befriended other classmates destined for service in the Civil War, including Abner Doubleday and James Longstreet. As an upperclassman he once saved plebe Ulysses S. Grant from being hazed by other cadets, an act of generosity he may have come to regret later on. Rosecrans performed well in the classroom and graduated fifth in the Class of 1842, a ranking that garnered him a much-coveted position in the Corps of Engineers. For the next decade he utilized his engineering skills on various projects at such places as Newport, Rhode Island; Bedford, Massachusetts; and the Washington Naval Yard. However, the performance of these important duties precluded his participation in the Mexican War and reduced his chances for more rapid promotion.

Tired of inadequate pay, the glacial speed of advancement, and in ill health, Rosecrans resigned his commission in 1854—despite Secretary of War Jefferson Davis's efforts to dissuade him—and embarked upon a career in the coal and oil business. He was for a time an engineer and superintendent of the Canal River Coal Company in western Virginia before moving into the oil-refining business. By 1861 he was head of a refinery in Cincinnati and had survived an oil lamp explosion that left his face severely scarred and seemingly frozen in what his biographer called "a permanent smirk."

When the Civil War broke out Rosecrans accepted a position on the staff of Major General George B. McClellan, who was then commanding the state troops from Ohio. In June 1861 he gained command of the 23d Ohio Infantry, which had in its ranks future presidents of the United States Rutherford B. Hayes and William McKinley. As part of an effort to gain broad support for his war policies, President Abraham Lincoln commissioned Rosecrans, a prominent Democrat and devout Catholic, as a brigadier general in the regular army. He served with distinction during McClellan's campaign in western Virginia and commanded a brigade in the Union victory at Rich Mountain on 11 July 1861. After McClellan left to command the Army of the Potomac, Rosecrans drove Confederate forces under General Robert E. Lee out of the region, an important step in securing western Virginia for the Union.

After being transferred to the Western theater, Rosecrans participated in Major General Henry W. Halleck's drive on Corinth, Mississippi, in May 1862 and shortly thereafter succeeded Major General John Pope in command of the Army of the Mississippi, one of two

William S. Rosecrans (*Library of Congress*)

armies under the overall command of the plebe "Old Rosy" had once rescued from hazing at West Point, Ulysses S. Grant. Rosecrans played a major role at the battle of Iuka (19 September) and successfully defended Corinth from an attack by Confederates under Earl Van Dorn (3–4 October). After this battle, Grant criticized Rosecrans for a less-than-vigorous pursuit of the retreating Confederates and precipitated a feud that created a permanent rift between the two officers.

After receiving a promotion to major general on 25 October 1862, Rosecrans traveled to Kentucky to assume command of the Army of the Cumberland, then facing General Braxton Bragg's Army of Tennessee. At the hard-fought battle of Stones River (31 December 1862–2 January 1863) outside Nashville, Tennessee, Rosecrans forced the Confederates to retreat to a new defensive line north of the Duck River. Ignoring pleas from Washington to advance, Rosecrans remained stationary for the next six months while he planned and organized his next move. His efforts paid handsome dividends in June and July 1863 when, after a brilliant campaign of deception and maneuver, he drove Bragg from middle Tennessee all the way to the vital rail hub at Chattanooga. Another skillful maneuver forced Bragg to relinquish the town, leaving Rosecrans and the Army of the Cumberland in possession of the "Gateway to the South." The Tullahoma campaign (25 June–4 July) achieved magnificent results with very little loss to Union forces, but never won the accolades Rosecrans believed it deserved.

On the heels of perhaps his greatest triumph, Rosecrans's career and reputation suffered irreversible damage. At the battle of Chickamauga (19–20 September), Bragg soundly defeated Rosecrans's army and forced it into headlong retreat back to Chattanooga. Only Major General George H. Thomas's famous stand at Horseshoe Ridge averted complete disaster. This crushing blow, Bragg's subsequent siege of the town, and the indecisiveness of Rosecrans (whom Lincoln described as resembling "a duck hit on the head") led to his removal from command and the virtual end of his military career. He went on to command the Department of the Missouri (28 January–9 December 1864), but held no other post before war's end. He finally resigned his commission on 27 March 1867, after nearly two years without an assignment.

Rosecrans entered the diplomatic arena in 1868 when President Andrew Johnson appointed him minister to Mexico, a position he held until Johnson's successor, Ulysses S. Grant, removed him in 1869. It would be over a decade before he reentered the public arena, serving two terms in Congress (1880–1885) and as register of the treasury (1885–1893). While in Congress he rose to chair the important Committee on Military Affairs. Rosecrans spent his last years on his ranch near present-day Redondo Beach, California. He died on 11 March 1898 and was buried in Los Angeles. In 1902 his remains were reinterred at Arlington National Cemetery.

—*William B. Feis*

See also Army of Mississippi; Bragg, Braxton; Chickamauga, Battle of; Corinth, Battle of ; Grant, Ulysses S.; Iuka, Battle of; Rich Mountain, Battle of; Stones River, Battle of; Tullahoma, Campaign.

For further reading:
Lamers, William M. *The Edge of Glory: A Biography of General William S. Rosecrans* (1961; reprint, 1999).

ROSS, JOHN
(1790–1866)
Principal chief of the Cherokee Nation

Born in Tennessee near Lookout Mountain, John Ross was also named Cooweescoowe. He was of mixed blood, only one-eighth Cherokee with a Scottish father and a one-quarter Cherokee mother. Ross rose to prominence in Cherokee councils, in part because of the matrilineal nature of Cherokee culture but also because of the renown brought by his service with Andrew Jackson in the War of 1812. As principal chief of the Cherokee Nation after 1828, he resisted removal but was forced to lead his people to Indian Territory in 1838–1839. Under the revised constitution that unified the eastern and western branches of the Cherokee, he also assumed the position of principal chief of the confederated nation.

Thus, when the Civil War began, John Ross had been principal chief of the Cherokee Nation for more than three decades. Long adept at balancing white pressure to "civilize" with a commitment to Cherokee sovereignty, Ross was presented with new challenges by the war. Ross believed the tribe should remain neutral, but other Cherokees, led by his adversary Stand Watie, openly supported the Confederates. Reflecting longstanding political and cultural divisions within the tribe, Watie's supporters were mostly wealthy, mixed-blood Cherokee slave owners. Watie and his followers wanted to preserve slavery in the Cherokee Nation, but they also saw the war as an opportunity to wrest political control away from John Ross. Ross's supporters were primarily poorer full-bloods who desired to stay out of white conflicts and prevent Watie from gaining political power.

By the summer of 1861, Ross's neutrality policy had become untenable. Union forces had pulled out of the area, neighboring tribes had joined the Confederacy, and Watie's faction seemed poised to seize power. After a series of Union defeats, it appeared that the Confederacy would soon win the war. In an attempt to prevent a Confederate invasion and open civil war within the nation, Ross finally recommended an alliance with the South in August 1861.

Despite the alliance, tensions between the Ross and Watie factions increased and the Cherokees formed two distinct regiments to fight for the Confederacy. The first regiment, commanded by Watie, consisted of Cherokees who were loyal to Watie and the Southern cause. The second regiment, commanded by John Drew, included Ross's supporters, who were more hostile toward Watie's followers than they were loyal to the Confederacy. As the war continued, Watie's faction fought with distinction, while Drew's troops deserted in large numbers.

The Cherokee Nation was plunged into open civil war in the summer of 1862 when Union forces moved into Indian Territory and quickly captured key positions. Ross was arrested but was permitted to proceed to Washington with his family. He spent the next three years in Washington attempting to convince the Northern government that the Cherokees had been coerced into joining the Confederacy.

Ross argued that, despite the treaty, the Cherokees had always remained secretly loyal to the North. By convincing the Union of the Cherokees' unbroken loyalty, Ross hoped to preserve the tribe's prewar treaty rights and obtain money and support for thousands of Cherokee refugees. Ross worried that the independence of the Cherokee people was in jeopardy, and he feared that the North would use the issue of Cherokee "disloyalty" as an excuse to destroy their sovereignty.

When the war ended, Ross's worst fears were realized. The United States ignored both his protests and the service of thousands of Cherokees in the Union army, and declared that the entire tribe had been disloyal. Through adroit lobbying and negotiation, Ross was able to minimize the damage, but in 1866 the Cherokees were forced to grant major concessions to the United States. Exhausted by continual lobbying, Ross died in Washington on 1 August 1866.

—*Trevor M. Jones*

See also Cherokee Indians; Indian Territory; Watie, Stand.
For further reading:
McLoughlin, William G. *After the Trail of Tears: The Cherokees' Struggle for Sovereignty, 1839–1880* (1993).
Moulton, Gary E. *John Ross, Cherokee Chief* (1978).
———, ed. *The Papers of Chief John Ross* (1985).
Wardell, Morris L. *A Political History of the Cherokee Nation, 1838–1907* (1938).

ROSSER, THOMAS LAFAYETTE
(1836–1910)
Confederate general

Thomas Lafayette Rosser spent his first thirteen years in Campbell County, Virginia, where he was born on a farm on 15 October 1836. In 1849 his family moved to Panola County, Texas, from whence he was appointed to the United States Military Academy in July 1856. Among his classmates was close friend George Armstrong Custer. Rosser's strong Southern sympathies led him to resign from the academy in late April 1861, just two weeks before graduation.

Rosser immediately offered his services to the Confederacy and was commissioned a lieutenant and assigned to instructional duty with the Washington Artillery. He commanded a company of that unit at the July battle of Bull Run and two months later was promoted to captain.

After months of relative inactivity that followed Bull Run, Rosser led the battery during both the Peninsula campaign and the Seven Days' battles. During the latter, on 26 May 1862, at the battle of Mechanicsville, he was wounded for the first of nine times. While recovering he was promoted to lieutenant colonel of artillery. Two weeks later he was promoted to colonel of the 5th Virginia Cavalry.

Rosser led the regiment throughout 1862, and in December was again wounded. Early the next year in March, he distinguished himself at the battle of Kelly's Ford. Due to wounds he was incapacitated during the spring. Back at his command, he saw limited action at the 9 June battle of Brandy Station, but performed excellent service a week later at Aldie, Virginia, helping fend off Union probes toward the main army then on its way to Gettysburg. Days later he led his regiment on the arduous raid north around the Union army, arriving at Gettysburg only to perform picket duty during the final two days of battle. He skillfully led his regiment during the retreat to Virginia, and three months later was promoted to brigadier general, on 5 October.

Rosser first led his brigade at the battle of Raccoon Ford on 11 October and later participated at the second battle of Brandy Station, where he was again wounded. Like the rest of the Army of Northern Virginia, he spent the remainder of the year relatively inactive.

Beginning in the spring, Rosser spent 1864 in almost constant activity. He first participated in the opening stages of the Overland campaign in April as Major General U. S. Grant's Union forces maneuvered toward the Wilderness. In the following months he led his brigade at the battles of Yellow Tavern and Trevelian's Station. He remained with Lee's main army for the entire summer and early weeks of the fall, battling the Northern cavalry while the main armies fought their way to the Petersburg and Richmond defenses.

Early in October his brigade was ordered to join the Confederates forces in the Shenandoah Valley. He arrived on the third and fought his first battle in the valley six days later. Rosser, who had been dubbed the "Saviour of the Valley" was soundly defeated at Tom's Brook by Union forces led by his old friend Brigadier General George Custer, among others. Despite his best efforts, his depleted ranks presented little challenge to

the Union cavalry at the battle of Cedar Creek and his labors during the remainder of the campaign proved generally unsuccessful.

Rosser was promoted to major general on 1 November 1864 and led his small command in the Shenandoah for the remainder of the year. He finally returned to the main army in March 1865, in time to lead a division at the 31 March–1 April battle of Five Forks. Much controversy surrounds his absence from the field, enjoying a meal of shad while his command was attacked by Union forces. Rosser performed better service during the retreat toward Appomattox and like many cavalrymen fought his way out before Lee surrendered. Like others, he hoped to reorganize his command and join General Joseph Johnston in North Carolina, but he surrendered to Union authorities in May.

After the war, Rosser and his wife, whom he had married in May 1863, moved to Baltimore, but in 1871 he was appointed chief engineer of the Northern Pacific Railroad and moved to the far West. Ten years later he became chief engineer of the Canadian Pacific Railroad. Rosser returned to Charlottesville, Virginia, in 1885 and took up the life of a gentleman farmer. In 1898 he was appointed a brigadier general in the United States Army during the Spanish-American War. He commanded three regiments of infantry that did not finish their training before the war ended. He became postmaster for Charlottesville in 1905, and died there five years later on 29 March.

—*James Robbins Jewell*

See also Aldie, Virginia, Battle of; Cedar Creek, Battle of; Five Forks, Battle of; Kelly's Ford, Battle of; Tom's Brook, Battle of.
For further reading:
Bushong, Millard K., and Dean Bushong. *Fightin' Tom Rosser, C.S.A.* (1983).
Driver, Robert J. *5th Virginia Cavalry* (1997).
Hotchkiss, Jedediah. *Confederate Military History*, vol. 3 (1899).
Tyler, Lyon G., ed. *Encyclopedia of Virginia Biography* (1915).
Warner, Ezra J. *Generals in Gray, Lives of Confederate Generals* (1983).

ROST, PIERRE ADOLPHE
(1797–1868)
Confederate diplomat

Born in Lot et Garonne, France, Pierre Adolphe Rost was educated locally before gaining admission to the Lycée Napoleon in Paris. Upon graduation from that institution, he entered the École Polytechnique. He left school with the other students in 1813 to help in the defense of France and commanded a battery in the defense of Paris in 1814. With the restoration of the monarchy later that year, he returned to school but left to support Napoleon upon the emperor's return in 1815. With the return of the monarchy, he

determined to leave the country and emigrated to New Orleans, Louisiana, in 1816.

From New Orleans, Rost traveled to Natchez, Mississippi, where he made his living teaching school. He also determined upon a career in law and was allowed to study in the office of Joseph Davis, Jefferson Davis's older brother. Upon completion of his studies he moved to Natchitoches, Louisiana, where he was admitted to the Louisiana bar and began his practice.

Along with his law practice, Rost became involved in Louisiana politics. In the 1820s he represented his district in the Louisiana state senate. He moved to New Orleans in 1828, where he hoped to expand his practice. Once there he put his military experience to use by becoming active in the local militia. He eventually rose to the rank of colonel. Meanwhile his law practice flourished, and he gained a reputation as one of the best attorneys in the state.

At the end of the 1830s, Rost served a brief stint as a justice of the state supreme court. A decline in his financial resources brought about his resignation, but he accepted appointment to the same court again in 1846. He remained on the court until 1852 when he again resigned to manage his business affairs. After 1852 he lived for the most part on his plantation, which became one of the richest in the state.

As the sectional crisis worsened, Rost became a strong proponent of Southern rights. Upon the secession of Louisiana and the formation of the Confederate States of America, Rost was approached by the new Confederate president, Jefferson Davis, to serve on a mission with William Lowndes Yancey and A. Dudley Mann to Great Britain and France. Rost's language skills and ties to France no doubt influenced Rost's appointment, though most saw him as not a prominent enough figure for such a mission. He left for Europe with fellow commissioner William Lowndes Yancey in the spring of 1861.

After passing through Havana, Cuba, where they were entertained by the Spanish governor there, the commissioners made their way to Great Britain, arriving in London on 27 April 1861. They sought recognition from the British government and to that end met informally with Lord Russell on 4 May. Rost then traveled to France, where he met with a number of intermediaries who held out hope that at the very least he might be able to purchase weapons for the Confederacy from the French government. This hope proved forlorn, although Rost continued to press the issue through the remainder of the year. Rost also met unofficially with French foreign minister Antoine Edouard Touvenel. The Frenchman held out little hope of immediate recognition of the Confederacy by the French government.

In November 1861 Rost joined with fellow Confederate diplomats Yancey and A. Dudley Mann in writing to Lord Russell regarding the Confederate interpretation of the *Trent* Affair. They claimed that the seizure of James Mason and John Slidell was a violation of international law and should be met forcefully by the British government. Rost returned to France at the end of the year, bringing documents demonstrating the paper nature of the Federal blockade of the Southern coastline. This information failed again to sway the French government toward recognition.

Having failed to gain recognition or aid from either Great Britain or France, Rost was sent in early 1862 to the court in Madrid to attempt to gain recognition from the Spanish government. He realized within a very short time that Spain had no desire to recognize the Confederacy. His dispatches back to Richmond detailing his various failures were captured when the ship they were on fell into Union hands.

Probably feeling that things could not become any worse for him, Rost boarded a ship for home later in 1862. When he arrived back in the Confederate states, he learned that his plantation had been occupied by the Union army and the United States government had declared his property forfeit. His plantation was later used by the Federal government as settlement farms for former slaves. Unable to return home or to New Orleans until the end of the war, Rost spent much of the remainder of the war in Richmond. After the war Rost returned to New Orleans where he lived quietly until his death on 6 September 1868.

—*David S. Heidler and Jeanne T. Heidler*

See also Diplomacy, C.S.A.; *Trent* Affair; Yancey, William Lowndes.

For further reading:
Biographical Sketches of Distinguished American Lawyers (1852).
Case, Lynn M., and Warren F. Spencer. *The United States and France: Civil War Diplomacy* (1970).

ROUSSEAU, LOVELL HARRISON
(1818–1869)
Union general

Lovell Harrison Rousseau was born on 4 August 1818 near Stanford in Lincoln County, Kentucky. His parents' names were not recorded, although it is known that his father was from Virginia and died in 1833, leaving his family impoverished. Rousseau attended some school but had to work to support his mother and siblings. He broke rock that was used to build the turnpike from Lexington to Lancaster, Kentucky. As a young man, he moved to Louisville, where he independently studied law fourteen hours every day, an exhausting regimen that damaged his health. In 1840 he moved to Indiana, where he was admitted to the bar at Bloomfield in February 1841. Elected as a Whig to the Indiana house of representatives, Rousseau served in 1844 and 1845. During the

Mexican War, he was captain of the 2d Indiana Infantry, which was recognized for its part at the battle of Buena Vista. Mustered out on 23 June 1847, Rousseau returned to Indiana, where he was elected to the state senate that year. He moved to Louisville one year before his term was completed and consequently planned to resign his seat, but his constituents insisted that he serve them from Kentucky. Considered a capable criminal lawyer who could skillfully talk to jurors, Rousseau helped stop a riot in 1855 related to the Know-Nothing movement. He was elected to the Kentucky state senate in 1860.

Opposing secession, Rousseau spoke eloquently about why Kentucky should not join the Confederacy and gained national acclaim for his speeches. He resigned his political office and stopped practicing law in 1861 to enlist troops for the Union, establishing a training camp named Camp Jo Holt across the Ohio River in Indiana. He discreetly recruited and equipped volunteers in Kentucky who were not officially mustered into service until the late summer of 1861. His effort to organize soldiers was instrumental in retaining Kentucky, a crucial border state, in the Union.

Rousseau first was named colonel of the 3d Kentucky Infantry on 9 September 1861. By 1 October, he was promoted to brigadier general of United States Volunteers, commanding the 1st Brigade, McCook's Division, Army of the Cumberland until November. Next Rousseau led the 4th Brigade, 2d Division, Army of the Ohio, from November until July 1862. He commanded the brigade as part of General Don Carlos Buell's relief force on the second day of the battle of Shiloh.

From July to November 1862, Rousseau was in charge of the 3d Division, 1st Corps, Army of the Ohio, and was promoted to the rank of major general in October 1862 because of his leadership at the battle of Perryville. From November 1862 through late 1863, he commanded the 1st Division, 14th Corps, Army of the Cumberland, and later in the war and afterward the Districts of Nashville and Middle Tennessee, Department of the Cumberland, until 3 July 1865, where he oversaw garrison forces. Rousseau's jurisdiction included the 3d Division, 12th Corps, and 4th Division, 20th Corps. Rousseau also monitored activity in Alabama, Mississippi, and west Tennessee. In July 1864, he was selected to lead a cavalry raid through Alabama and western Georgia to destroy Confederate railroads. Traveling 400 miles from 10 to 22 July 1864, Rousseau's raid resulted in damage to crucial supplies affecting transportation between Montgomery and Atlanta, as well as crippling citizen morale. Considered one of the most successful Civil War raids, this excursion contributed to General William T. Sherman's victory at Atlanta. Rousseau also conducted smaller raids and protected Fort Rosecrans in Nashville from Confederate forces led by General John Bell Hood.

In January 1865 Kentucky Radical Republicans endorsed Rousseau in the race for a seat in the United States Senate, but James Guthrie defeated him. Rousseau won a seat in the United States House of Representatives and resigned from the army in November 1865. His congressional tenure was controversial as he ignored his radical supporters, supported Andrew Johnson, became more conservative, and protested the Freedmen's Bureau Bill and other legislation he considered too extreme. He served on the Committee on Military Affairs and skillfully debated how Reconstruction should be pursued in the South, criticizing Radical Republicans for their harsh plans and severing ties with them. Rousseau was enraged by congressmen who had not fought in the war, but nevertheless vowed vengeance against the South. When he beat Iowa congressman Josiah B. Grinnell in the face with a cane, the House censured him. Although his colleague Thaddeus Stevens encouraged him to continue his work, Rousseau chose to resign on 21 July 1866. After explaining his behavior to his constituents, Rousseau was reelected to fill his empty seat and remained in the Senate through 3 March 1867. President Johnson rewarded Rousseau for his war service with a regular army commission as brigadier general with the brevet rank of major general. He was placed in charge of occupation troops in the department of Louisiana, where he was known for his empathy toward citizens. Rousseau died in New Orleans, on 7 January 1869. Buried in Arlington National Cemetery, he is also memorialized with a monument in Louisville's Cave Hill Cemetery.

—*Elizabeth D. Schafer*

See also Buell, Don Carlos; Kentucky; Perryville, Battle of.
For further reading:
Abrams, Paul R. "The Assault Upon Josiah B. Grinnell by Lovell H. Rousseau." *Iowa Journal* (1912).
Dawson, Joseph G., III. "General Lovell H. Rousseau and Louisiana Reconstruction." *Louisiana History* (1979).
Schafer, Elizabeth D. "Jaded Mules, Twisted Rails, and Razed Depots." *Civil War* (1991).

RUFFIN, EDMUND
(1794–1865)

Southern nationalist and agriculturist

The son of George Ruffin and Jane Lucas, Ruffin was born into the antebellum Southern planter class. His early years were spent in Prince George's County, Virginia, where he was educated by a private tutor. After the death of Edmund's mother, Ruffin's father married Rebecca Cocke. While isolated for long periods during his youth, Ruffin became an avid reader and mastered numerous great works of literature before reaching his teens.

At sixteen Ruffin entered the College of William and Mary. In less than a year he withdrew from the College, as he was more attracted to romance than academic pursuits. While in Williamsburg he met Susan Travis, the daughter of a well-established local family, and they were married in 1812. Answering the call to military service in the War of 1812, Ruffin enlisted but never engaged in combat. Stationed in Norfolk, he complained of constant military drills and procedures. After six months Ruffin was allowed to return home and he assumed control over his ancestral plantation, Coggin's Point.

Confronting health afflictions on a personal level and soil infertility on a professional level, Ruffin began to ponder the means of revitalizing his mind and his plantation. As a lover of literary pursuits, he combined his writing and agricultural interests, as well as his experimental bent, in an effort to resolve the dilemma over soil infertility. Following years of experimentation, he published an account of his successes and became the publisher of the *Farmers Register*, a respected farm publication. In his successful transitions from agricultural pursuits to journalism and back to farming, Ruffin established himself as a leading student of soil science and American agriculture.

Ruffin's interests eventually turned from agriculture to politics. Although elected to the Virginia state senate in 1823, he did not complete his term of office. Ruffin apparently recognized that he was better suited as a

Edmund Ruffin (*Library of Congress*)

writer and speaker than as a public servant. Earlier in life he had asserted that slavery was an evil, but one that could be eliminated over time. As the years and regional tensions progressed, Ruffin came to endorse the necessity of slavery. As a critic of all tariff measures, he claimed such efforts were a "monstrous anomaly in free government." Ruffin accepted the position of South Carolina in the Nullification Crisis, which affirmed his devotion to state authority. He argued that a state was allowed to assume such a course of action only if the goal was to protect the state's citizens and the Constitution. Recovering this necessary responsibility of the states in relation to the central government might make decision making less efficient, but would allow it to gain vastly in moral power. In Ruffin's assessment, the interposing and amending power of the states implicit in the Constitution could only augment authentic popular rule by allowing for a greater diffusion of authority.

As tensions increased, Ruffin published many articles endorsing the Southern position on slavery, abolitionism, and other disputed concerns. Disgruntled with the inactivity of his native Virginia, Ruffin moved to Charleston in 1861, where on 12 April 1861 the sixty-seven-year-old Ruffin was allowed to fire the first shot, a 64-pound Columbiad, against Fort Sumter. Although the controversy over who actually fired the initial shot remains, Ruffin was received as a patron of the secessionist cause. After Virginia seceded, he returned to his native state and was a tireless defender of the South until the surrender at Appomattox. Ruffin became increasing despondent, wishing that he could be "buried as usually were our brave soldiers who were slain in battle." On 17 June 1865 Ruffin committed suicide by shooting himself.

—H. Lee Cheek, Jr.

See also Fire-eaters.

For further reading:

Craven, Avery O. *Edmund Ruffin, Southerner* (1982).
Mathew, W. M. *Edmund Ruffin and the Crisis of Slavery* (1988).
Scarborough, William K., ed. *The Diary of Edmund Ruffin* (1972–1989).

RUGER, THOMAS HOWARD
(1833–1907)
Union general

Born in Lima, New York, to Jefferson Ruger and Maria Hutchins Ruger, Thomas Howard Ruger moved with his family to Janesville, Wisconsin, when he was an adolescent. In 1850 he accepted an appointment to the U.S. Military Academy. He graduated third of forty-six in the class of 1854. Ruger remained in the army only one year before resigning to study law. For the five years after his admission to the bar before the outbreak of the Civil War, Ruger practiced law in Janesville. With the commencement of hostili-

ties, he accepted a commission as the lieutenant colonel of the 3d Wisconsin Infantry.

He was promoted to colonel of the regiment in September 1861. At the time the regiment was stationed in Maryland, and in the fall of 1861, Ruger spent much of his time suppressing Confederate activity around Frederick. Later in the year, Ruger and his regiment came under the command of Nathaniel P. Banks and the Department of the Shenandoah. In the spring of 1862 they fought under Banks in the Shenandoah campaign against Stonewall Jackson. They continued to serve under Banks at Cedar Mountain in August 1862.

At Antietam, Ruger commanded a brigade and was wounded in the battle fighting on the Union right in the cornfield. He was unable to participate in the Fredericksburg campaign because of his injuries. In the spring of 1863 he was promoted to brigadier general with a date of rank of 29 November 1862. In April 1863 he was given command of a brigade of Alpheus Williams's division in XII Corps. He fought at Chancellorsville and led his brigade in pursuit of Robert E. Lee in June 1863. On the morning of 2 July, Ruger assumed command of the division when Williams became corps commander. Positioned on the barb of the fishhook, Ruger so effectively led his men through the battle that he received a brevet promotion to brigadier general in the regular army.

In August 1863 Ruger and his brigade were sent to New York City to restore calm in the wake of the draft riots there. The city was about to resume drawing names for the draft, and the government had learned its lesson from July and wanted plenty of troops visible on the streets of the city. In the fall Ruger was sent from New York to the Army of the Cumberland in Tennessee, where he was headquartered at Tullahoma dealing with Confederate guerrilla raids. In the Atlanta campaign he commanded a brigade in Alpheus Williams's division, XX Corps. He fought in all the major engagements of that campaign, and after the fall of the city, he was sent back to Tennessee to serve under John M. Schofield in the Army of the Ohio. He distinguished himself at the battle of Franklin, where he commanded a division of XXIII Corps. Schofield commended him for bravery in that battle and recommended that he receive a brevet promotion to major general.

In December 1864, Ruger was sent to Murfreesboro, Tennessee, where he patrolled from the town looking for Confederate guerrilla groups. In February 1865, Ruger and his division accompanied Schofield and XXIII Corps to Alexandria, Virginia, where they embarked for the North Carolina coast to aid William T. Sherman in his Carolina campaign. Ruger was present at the surrender of Joseph E. Johnston's army in April 1865.

After the surrender, Ruger remained in North Carolina and temporarily commanded XXIII Corps in June 1865.

For the next year he commanded the Department of North Carolina and, with the reorganization of the army in 1866, decided to remain in the service. He became the colonel of the 33d Infantry. From 1871 to 1876 he was superintendent of the U.S. Military Academy, after which he served as the commander of the Department of the South. From there he served as a department and field commander in the West and on the Pacific Coast. He rose through the officer ranks to brigadier general in 1886 and to major general in 1895. He retired in 1897. In retirement he traveled extensively for a while and then settled in Stamford, Connecticut, where he died on 3 June 1907. His remains were taken to West Point for burial.

—David S. Heidler and Jeanne T. Heidler

See also Franklin, Battle of; New York City Draft Riots.
For further reading:
Georgia Department of Technical and Adult Education. *Biography of Thomas Howard Ruger* (1900).

RUSSELL, DAVID ALLEN
(1820–1864)
Union general

Born to David Abel Russell and Alida Lansing Russell in Salem, New York, David Allen Russell was educated locally before receiving an appointment to the United States Military Academy. He graduated thirty-eighth of forty-one in the class of 1845. Upon graduation Russell was sent to Kansas and from there to join in Winfield Scott's Mexico City campaign in the Mexican-American War. He received one brevet promotion for his actions in that campaign.

After that war Russell served primarily in the Pacific Northwest and at the outbreak of the Civil War was a captain in command of Fort Yamhill in Oregon. From there he was sent to San Francisco in September 1861, embarking for the east shortly thereafter. He had been promoted to major in the 8th Infantry.

Upon his return east, Russell was named the colonel of the 7th Massachusetts Infantry, which was part of the defenses around Washington, D.C. The regiment became a part of the Army of the Potomac, and Russell led it in the Peninsula campaign and in the battle of South Mountain. Russell and the 7th fought at Antietam, after which, in November 1862, Russell was promoted to brigadier general of volunteers. He commanded a brigade of VI Corps at Fredericksburg, but saw little action in that battle.

Russell remained in command of a brigade of VI Corps, now under John Sedgwick, in the spring of 1863. He remained opposite Fredericksburg with the remainder of the corps while Joseph Hooker and the rest of the Army of the Potomac moved around to Chancellorsville in an attempt to flank Robert E. Lee's position. Russell led his brigade in the attack on Marye's

Heights that dislodged Jubal Early's force there, forcing the Confederates out of the defenses at Fredericksburg on 3 May. For the next day-and-a-half Russell led his brigade, which had sustained serious casualties at Marye's Heights, at Salem Church, before the corps was forced to retreat back across the Rappahannock River.

Russell commanded his brigade at Gettysburg, but did not arrive until the evening of 2 July and was never seriously engaged in the battle. He fought at Bristoe Station in October 1863. On 7 November 1863 Russell gained the attention of the commander of the Army of the Potomac, George Gordon Meade. On that day he led a charge against what the Confederates viewed as an impregnable position at Rappahannock Station. He not only carried the position, but also captured several Confederate artillery pieces and eight battle flags. Because Russell was wounded in the attack and would need some time to convalesce, he was sent to Washington to deliver the battle flags to the War Department personally.

Russell returned to duty in January 1864. In May he was given command of a division in Horatio G. Wright's VI Corps. He led his division in every engagement of Ulysses S. Grant's campaign against Robert E. Lee, through the commencement of the siege of Petersburg. In early July he and his division were sent to Washington to aid in the defense of the capital against Jubal Early's raid. That threat removed, Russell was rejoined with Wright and VI Corps for Philip Sheridan's campaign in the Shenandoah Valley.

Russell fought in all the early engagements of that campaign. On 19 September 1864 at Winchester, Russell led his division in a counterattack on Confederates threatening to penetrate the Union lines. He was shot in the chest, but managed to stay in his saddle, encouraging his men to continue the attack. In the midst of these efforts, a piece of a Confederate artillery shell whistled through the air, striking Russell in the heart. He died instantly. Sheridan personally reported the loss to the War Department. He had been one year ahead of Russell at West Point and was a close friend.

—David S. Heidler and Jeanne T. Heidler

See also Fredericksburg, Battle of; Salem Church, Battle of; Winchester, Third Battle of (Opequon).
For further reading:
Slade, A. D. *That Sterling Soldier: The Life of David A. Russell* (1995).

RUSSELL, LORD JOHN
(1792–1878)
British foreign secretary

Britain's foreign secretary for the entire American Civil War, Lord John Russell rarely took any individual initiative and generally did the bidding of Lord Palmerston, the prime minister. Fussy and indecisive, with a reputation for disloyalty, he did not carry much weight in a cabinet that suspected his judgment and saw him as an agent of Palmerston's aggressive foreign policy. In the fall of 1862, however, Russell proved one of the most enthusiastic proponents of intervention in the Civil War. His bid to convince the cabinet, however, failed. For the rest of the conflict, he sought to keep the peace between Britain and America, succeeding despite a few serious mistakes.

Born on 18 August 1792, Russell was the third son of the sixth duke of Bedford, an aristocrat with liberal tendencies. Entering the University of Edinburgh in 1809, he left three years later without a degree. In 1813 he was elected to the House of Commons from his home district of Tavistock. He would remain in the Commons for nearly fifty years.

As a Whig member of Parliament, Russell quickly proved himself active in the cause of parliamentary reform. Many Whigs were reaching the same conclusion as he: Britain's political system must change to represent the country's changing social and economic situation brought about by the Industrial Revolution. Russell played a pivotal role in drafting and passing the Great Reform Act of 1832, which extended suffrage and redistributed representation in the House of Commons. Russell's association with this legislation earned him national prominence, and he suddenly became an important statesman of the first rank. Throughout the 1830s Russell held a number of positions within the government, most notably home secretary from 1835 to 1839 and colonial secretary from 1839 to 1841, in which offices he continued his efforts to reform the political system.

In 1846 Russell became prime minister. With high hopes for his administration, he embarked on a series of reform efforts. His progress was slowed, and in some cases halted, by poor judgment, lackadaisical administrative practices, divisions within his own party, bad luck, and opposition from the Tories. His government fell in 1852, but he immediately reentered the cabinet as foreign secretary and leader in the House of Commons under Lord Aberdeen's coalition government. As a former prime minister, Russell resented his new subordinate position. Suffering a fit of pique during the Crimean War, Russell resigned from the cabinet in 1855. He thus precipitated the government's collapse and won a reputation for disloyalty. Palmerston called him back as foreign minister later that year, but the widespread belief that Russell had botched the Vienna negotiations settling the Crimean War led him to resign again. In 1859 Russell agreed to serve as foreign secretary in Palmerston's second administration.

Mercurial, erratic, and indecisive, Russell did not prove an effective foreign secretary. Palmerston managed, however, to manipulate his impressionable subordinate. In 1861 Russell was elevated to an earldom. Leaving the rough-and-tumble House of Commons, he now sat in the more staid House of Lords, where he could do the government less damage.

Soon after the Southern states seceded, Russell immediately concluded that the Federal Union had broken irrevocably. Hoping to score a diplomatic coup, he suggested to Palmerston that Britain mediate between the North and South. The more cautious Palmerston quashed Russell's plan and adopted a wait-and-see attitude. Until the summer of 1862, Russell's opinion regarding the United States' prospects changed with great frequency. Lee's successful defense of Richmond during the Seven Days' battles, his victory at the battle of Second Bull Run, and his invasion of Maryland convinced Russell (as it did many other Britons) that the Confederacy did indeed constitute a de facto nation. Russell began considering intervention in the conflict with the intention of bringing it to an end. The Federal victory at Antietam and the appearance of the Emancipation Proclamation only made the situation more urgent. Russell, along with most of the cabinet, believed that Lincoln's decree would only make the conflict more destructive without contributing to Northern victory.

In October 1862 Russell proposed that Britain, France, and Russia jointly recommend an armistice and oversee negotiations between the North and South. In a cabinet memorandum, he argued that neither side could beat the other, that war had created a bitterness of feeling that made reunion impossible, and that emancipation had introduced the appalling prospect of servile insurrection. Cabinet criticism, particularly from Sir George Cornewall Lewis, the secretary of state for war, prompted Russell to amend this proposal by suggesting that Prussia and Austria also take part in the process. Lewis persisted in criticizing Russell's plan, arguing that the risks associated with intervention far outweighed any potential benefit. At a meeting held to decide the issue on 11 November 1862, Lewis rallied the cabinet against intervention, Russell obtaining support only from Palmerston and William Gladstone. Russell postponed any action, hoping that the spring of 1863 might present a more opportune moment. That more opportune moment never came, and neither Russell nor the British cabinet seriously considered intervening in the Civil War again.

Although Russell no longer had to consider the weighty issue of intervention, he still had to handle a number of disputes with the Federal government. The most important of these concerned the construction of Confederate commerce-raiders in British ports. In April 1862, Charles Francis Adams, the American minister to Britain, discovered that a Liverpool shipyard had almost finished a vessel known as the No. 290. Convinced that

the Confederacy had paid for this ship, Adams claimed it violated Britain's Foreign Enlistment Act, which, among other things, stipulated that Britain could not build vessels intended for use against a friendly power. Adams submitted evidence to back up his claim, but the British government responded tardily and the vessel escaped at the end of July 1862—-becoming the CSS *Alabama*, which badly damaged Northern commerce. To add insult to injury, most of the crew was British. The North was outraged and the United States demanded compensation for damages suffered. Despite American pressure, Russell refused to submit the matter to international arbitration. The *Alabama* claims became a cause of incessant dispute until both sides reached a settlement in 1872, when the British government paid $15 million. Nevertheless, the incident made Russell far more vigilant about investigating and seizing suspicious vessels under construction in British ports.

Russell and Adams also found themselves at loggerheads over the Federal blockade of Southern ports. Adams sought to defend the North's aggressive blockading policy to the British, a difficult task considering that most blockade runners were British. Russell sought to curb American excesses, particularly harassment of British trade in the Caribbean, and American violations of British territorial waters off the coast of Bermuda and the Bahamas. Despite this friction, Britain and the United States enjoyed fairly good relations for the last two years of the war.

When Palmerston died in October 1865, Russell became prime minister again. He tried and failed to secure passage of another reform act. With the collapse of his administration in 1866, he retired and ceased to play a major role in politics. Russell died at his home, Pembroke Lodge, on 28 May 1878.

—*Hubert F. Dubrulle*

See also Adams, Charles Francis; *Alabama* Claims; *Alabama*, CSS; Diplomacy, C.S.A.; Diplomacy, U.S.A.; Great Britain; Lyons, Lord Richard; Mason, James Murray; Napoleon III; Palmerston, Viscount; Russell, Lord John; *Trent* Affair.

For further reading:

Cook, D. P. *The North, the South, and the Powers 1861–1865* (1974).

Prest, John. *Lord John Russell* (1972).

Scherer, Paul. *Lord John Russell: A Biography* (1999).

Walpole, Spencer. *Life of Lord John Russell* (1899).

RUSSELL, WILLIAM HOWARD

(1820–1907)

American correspondent for London Times

The most celebrated newspaper correspondent of his time, British journalist William Howard Russell did much to familiarize his countrymen with the Civil War in its early stages. Working for the *Times*, perhaps the most prominent newspaper in the world, Russell exerted a tremendous influence on public opinion in Britain, the neutral power with the greatest interest in the conflict.

Born at Lily Vale in County Dublin in 1820, Russell was the son of John Russell, the Dublin agent of a Sheffield firm, and Mary Kelly Russell. Because his father left for Liverpool to revive the family's declining fortunes, Russell spent his youth passing from relative to relative, all of them living in genteel poverty. After attending grammar school, he entered Trinity College, Dublin, in 1838. He left in 1841 without graduating because his family could no longer bear the cost of his tuition and suggested that he start working.

Shortly thereafter, Russell obtained his first newspaper assignment from the *Times*, which consisted of covering the wild Irish general election of 1841. Vigorously taking the Tory side in this contest, Russell received severe thrashings at the hands of several Irish mobs. His vivacious writing style caught the eye of J. T. Delane, the *Times*'s editor, who provided Russell with additional assignments. In 1843 Russell became a regular member of the *Times* staff, covering a wide variety of important social and political events.

The Crimean War—which pitted Britain, France, Sardinia, and Turkey against Russia—made Russell famous. Sent by the *Times* to the seat of war in 1854, he became the modern world's first dedicated war correspondent. His stirring prose not only made a hero of the British common soldier, but indicted the high command for its military blundering and logistical inefficiency. His columns in the *Times* provoked outrage in Britain and contributed to the fall of the government in January 1855. Shortly after the Crimean War, Russell went to India in 1857 to report on the Sepoy Mutiny. Although his criticism of the brutal repression of the Indians did not strike a popular chord, his account of India enthralled readers. By the time he returned to Britain in 1859, Russell was the most famous journalist alive.

In March 1861, with secession threatening to precipitate civil war in America, the *Times* responded to widespread British interest in American affairs by sending Russell to the United States. Soon after arriving, Russell traveled through both the North and South. When Fort Sumter fell, he headed South toward Charleston and thence through the Gulf States. From New Orleans, he traveled northward, up the Mississippi to Cairo, Illinois, before returning to Washington, D.C. During these travels, Russell provided the *Times* and its British readers with their first images of the Confederacy. A perceptive observer, he proved far more evenhanded than most British correspondents. Russell saw the South as a land of great contrasts, with many strengths and weaknesses. Wealth and poverty, ignorance and erudition, as well as culture and barbarism all seemed to exist side by side. Much as he admired what he described as a Southern

aristocracy, he found slavery abominable. Russell also had misgivings about the North as well. Elements of Northern democracy repulsed and frightened him. He feared that mob rule and incompetent demagogues would lead the North down the path of military dictatorship. In general, Russell viewed American democracy as a great and noble experiment doomed to failure. Although he felt Northern armies would eventually triumph, he did not believe that the Federal government could reconstruct the Union on a democratic basis.

Russell witnessed only one battle in America—First Bull Run. Reaching the battlefield just as the Federal army began to panic, Russell was engulfed in the rout that followed. Russell's correspondence in the *Times*, condemning the Northern army's conduct, made him the most unpopular man in America. Not only did the New York press abuse him remorselessly, but he also received an endless torrent of death threats and hate mail. In April 1862, after Secretary of War Edwin Stanton revoked Russell's pass to accompany the Army of the Potomac, Russell quit his post and boarded a boat for Britain, despite pleas from the *Times* management that he stay.

In later years, Russell continued to serve as a war correspondent, covering the Austro-Prussian War (1866), the Franco-Prussian War (1870–1871), and the Zulu War (1879). Throughout this period, however, he increasingly turned to travel writing. A good friend of the Prince of Wales (later King Edward VII), Russell enjoyed extensive contacts throughout the literary world. Knighted in 1895, Russell died in London on 10 February 1907.

—*Hubert F. Dubrulle*

See also Great Britain; Newspapers.

For further reading:

Atkins, John Black. *The Life of Sir William Howard Russell, the First Special Correspondent* (1911).

Crawford, Martin, ed. *William Howard Russell's Civil War: Private Diary and Letters, 1861–1862* (1992).

Furneaux, Rupert. *The First War Correspondent: William Howard Russell of the* Times (1944).

Hankinson, Alan. *Man of War: William Howard Russell of the* Times (1982).

Russell, William Howard. *My Diary North and South* (1988).

RUSSIAN-AMERICAN RELATIONS

Led by Great Britain and France, the governments of western Europe were not averse to the dismemberment of the United States and the concomitant attenuation of the young republic's commercial and military power. The Southern Rebels, in their efforts to secede from the Union, placed fervent hopes on British recognition prompted by the British belief that, as the primary commercial rival of Washington, Great Britain would profit from the breakup of the United States. In contrast to the Western European maritime powers,

Russia hoped that the United States would avert the internecine strife of a civil war. Russian sympathy for the Union was a continuation of the cordial relations between the two nations that dated back to the American Revolution. The Russian empress Catherine the Great rejected King George III's official request for Cossacks to suppress the rebellion in his American colonies. Although the empress, whom George III affectionately called "Kitty," had little sympathy for the rebellious colonists, she refused his request by alluding to Russia's internal exhaustion from a long war with the Ottoman Empire and a recent large-scale peasant rebellion. She would not allow her Cossacks to act as Hessians. More important, Catherine had already begun to discern the beginnings of what would become an increasingly bellicose Anglo-Russian relationship in the quest for colonies in the nineteenth century.

It was, however, during the Crimean War (1853–1856), when Russia faced the combined military power of France and Britain, that Russo-American relations became much more cordial and led to friendship during the American Civil War. Fearing that a victorious Anglo-French alliance would change the balance of power in a way detrimental to American interests—particularly if it prompted allied intervention in the New World in defiance of the Monroe Doctrine—Washington adopted a benevolently neutral policy towards Russia during the Crimean War. Supporting the traditional American slogan of "free ships make free goods," the Russian government signed a bilateral treaty with the United States that allowed for neutral shipping rights; American traders took advantage of this treaty by selling large quantities of arms and ammunition. In turn, the American government manifested its support for Russia when it informed St. Petersburg of a planned attack by a joint Anglo-French naval squadron in the Russian Far East, which the Russians successfully repelled. The Russians later reciprocated by supporting American efforts to annex the Hawaiian (Sandwich) Islands.

Beyond these tangible considerations, the good relations between the United States and Russia in the middle of the nineteenth century were the result of several factors. The most often cited include the common attitude of the two countries toward Britain, the lack of conflict over territory (the Pacific Northwest notwithstanding), the absence of points of disagreement, and the history of cordial relations. Both the United States and Russia viewed London as their primary territorial and commercial rival, yet it was also true that Britain was the chief trading partner of both countries. Nevertheless, the expansionist Russian and British Empires in the middle of the nineteenth century confronted one another in several parts of the globe, including the Far East, the Middle East, and Central

Asia. The United States, seeking support against British and French designs on the American continent and the Pacific, considered Russia a nation powerful enough and willing to work with Washington in its struggle against the two European powers. Washington and St. Petersburg resolved to establish political and commercial links, initially through the Far East, where the shortest route between the two countries lay. The American government, fully aware of the precariousness of Russia's position in the Far East, hoped to profit from that weakness for its own purposes.

Thus, the outbreak of civil war in the United States elicited dismay in Russia. Fearing the loss of the counterweight to Great Britain, the Russians initially hoped to defuse the crisis. Once St. Petersburg understood that a civil war could not be prevented, the Russian government made it clear that it would exclusively recognize the Union, as Russian foreign minister Prince Alexander Gorchakov made clear in April 1861 to the American minister in St. Petersburg.

As the United States suffered through the difficult early months of the war, only Russia's government offered support for the Union. Russia, like the other powers, professed neutrality, but Gorchakov assured Washington that his government deplored the war and asked the Russian minister in Washington, Eduard de Stoeckl, to work for a speedy reunification. In the name of the emperor, Gorchakov called the United States "an essential element in the political equalibrium [sic] of the world," and referred to the "natural solidarity of interests and sympathies" that Russia and the United States had already displayed toward each other. The American government appreciated the message of friendship during these hard days. In fact, Secretary of State William Seward told Stoeckl that it was the most benevolent and loyal response that the United States had received from any European government and requested the right to publish it.

The Russian government refused to recognize Confederate belligerency and reaffirmed Gorchakov's expression of sympathy and support throughout the war. Seward responded gratefully, addressing Russia as an old and constant friend and expressing hope for "relations of mutual confidence and friendship between the great republican power and a great, enterprising, and beneficent monarchy."

How could an autocracy share "mutual confidence and friendship" with a republican government? St. Petersburg was familiar with the moral and, sometimes, material support that the American republic had provided to various revolutionaries in Europe. Americans had welcomed the Hungarian revolutionary nationalist Louis Kossuth after he had fled Russian armies in the Austrian Empire following the 1848 uprising, and the ex-senator and current Secretary of

State Seward had been foremost among his greeters. In addition, the Russian revolutionary Mikhail Bakunin had used an American ship to escape Siberia and had spent two months in autumn 1861 touring the United States before returning to Europe. Despite these potential points of friction, as early as 1854 William Marcy, secretary of state in Franklin Pierce's administration, had articulated clearly how Washington distinguished between Russia's offensive political system and the United States' international position. "In relation to the political organization of her government," declared Marcy, "the people of the United Sates never can have any sympathy with Russia and will always regret to see her political system extended; but in regard to our international relations no nation on the face of the earth has used us more fairly."

St. Petersburg also made a similar distinction between America's political system and Russia's international position. The Russian minister to Washington, Stoeckl, appreciated the distinction between foreign and domestic politics. His reports highlighted the contradiction between the American tradition of applauding European revolutionary movements and Seward's current policy of asking the powers of Europe to ignore the American Civil War, in essence an American revolutionary movement. In 1862 Stoeckl denounced America's "ultra-democratic system," and described the Civil War as proof of the failure of self-government that should serve as a lesson for European socialists. Nevertheless, the Russian minister did not allow his support for autocracy to diminish America's international value for Russia. In the world of diplomacy, the United States had served as Russia's ally, or at least Britain's enemy. Hostility between the United States and Great Britain was Russia's best guarantee against London's ambitions, and had to be encouraged. Russia remained diplomatically isolated in Europe after the Crimean debacle. Despite the evils and shortcomings of American republicanism, Stoeckl advised close diplomatic cooperation between St. Petersburg and Washington and hoped for an early end to the fratricidal war. In the same dispatch that denounced the American political system, the Russian minister advised that "the deterioration of the U.S. as a power is an event that we must regret. The American federation is a counterweight to English power and as such its existence constitutes an element of world stability." Gorchakov echoed these sentiments almost twenty months later and the official Russian attitude toward the United States for the duration of the war remained friendly.

Thus, while Great Britain remained suspiciously neutral and France sought to exploit American division, Russia cautiously supported the North. Gorchakov pledged his government to recognize Washington as the only legitimate government of all

the states. At a time when other capitals of Europe openly welcomed Confederate agents, St. Petersburg openly supported the Union.

Despite refusing to breach official neutrality, the Russian government manifested its unwavering support for the Union. In November 1862 the French emperor Napoleon III called for a three-power (Russia, France, and England) conference at a neutral site with representatives of the two sides to mediate the American Civil War. Napoleon III sought to reopen Southern cotton ports and, more important, to foster a divided United States to facilitate his dreams of an American empire. Calling for an armistice and suspension of the blockade, the project, which would have confirmed Confederate successes when Northern victory looked doubtful, was rejected by the Union. However brief, an armistice might give the South time to supply for an even lengthier engagement. The secretary of state clearly articulated Washington's outright rejection of any European mediation to Stoeckl and thus to the Russian government. Agreeing to Washington's wishes, St. Petersburg informed Paris that Russia would help mediate only if both parties in the divided United States requested such assistance.

Gorchakov assured the American chargé d'affaires, Bayard Taylor, that Russia would reject participation in any mediation plan that Washington did not favor. When Taylor reported Gorchakov's promise, Congress ordered the foreign minister's words published. The Russian government honored its pledge when approached by French diplomats later that year. Gorchakov explained to the French diplomats that St. Petersburg had no intention of putting any pressure on the Union and refused to join if Britain and France attempted to act. Russia's stand on mediation also persuaded the British cabinet to reject European intervention in the American Civil War.

The United States reciprocated the following year after the outbreak of the Polish rebellion. In January 1863 Polish nationalists in Warsaw began an insurrection aimed at gaining independence from Russia. Napoleon III resolved to make himself the protector of the Poles and spokesman for Europe. Together with Britain and Austria, he hoped to pressure Russia to release Poland by turning the rebellion into an international issue, subject to mediation. The Polish rebellion of 1830 had evoked American sympathy for the oppressed Poles, and criticism of Russia. Could Washington ignore the land of Polish fighters for American independence, Kosciusko and Pulaski, when the same cry for independence sounded in Poland? In addition, Seward as a senator had offered a resolution condemning Russian oppression after the Revolutions of 1848. In the wake of recent Russian support for the North and as Washington's only friend in Europe, St. Petersburg naturally anticipated American support, especially because the European powers that proposed to intervene were also hostile to the Union. Moreover, Seward understood that he would appear a hypocrite when he disapproved of foreign mediation for an American rebellion and approved of it simultaneously in Europe. The secretary of state resolved to be consistent in his support of the Russians, and refused to cooperate with France.

Although he claimed that he relied on the humaneness of Alexander to treat the gallant Poles fairly, the secretary of state confessed to his minister in Paris the real state of affairs. "This government," he divulged, "finds an insurmountable difficulty in the way of any active cooperation with the governments of France, Austria, and Great Britain." The emperor publicly praised Washington's stand, and Gorchakov published the letter as a testament of Washington's good will. Thus, in April 1863, when the French foreign minister asked Washington to join with France, Britain, and Austria on behalf of the Polish rebels and call for an international settlement, Washington refused. Explaining candidly the closeness between Russia and the United States at this time, Seward asserted why Washington refused to participate in the Anglo-French endeavor: "[I]n regard to Russia, the case is a plain one. She has our friendship in preference to any other European power, simply because she always wishes us well and leaves us to conduct our affairs as we think best."

The secretary of state's stand on the Polish question did not prevent intervention. Nevertheless, Seward's rejection of the Anglo-French inspired effort to mediate the Polish rebellion cemented Russian-American friendship for the duration of the American Civil War. St. Petersburg remained wary of a possible Anglo-French war in support of the Poles until the spring of 1864. Expecting a war in the summer with the two maritime powers, the Russian admiralty feared that its fleets in the Baltic and Pacific would be blockaded in their ports as they had been in the Crimean War. Even though the Russian navy could not defeat the combined power of the Anglo-French forces, the emperor's ships, with their maneuverability, could successfully raid enemy commerce on the open seas from neutral ports.

Considering the value of such a strategy, the Russian government ordered two squadrons to find sanctuary in American ports to await war news. Undoubtedly Seward's response to the Polish rebellion and Northern hostility toward Britain and France satisfied the Russians that their ships would be welcome. For Washington, the arrival of these ships to American harbors came at an opportune time. Despite the recent Union victories at Gettysburg and Vicksburg in early July 1863, there remained much uncertainty about the outcome of the war and the possibility of European intervention. The

recent French invasion of Mexico and the arrival of British troops in Canada appeared ominous to Washington. The arrival of Russian ships created the illusion in Paris and London of a possible Russo-American alliance and comforted many Americans. This decision to send the squadrons to the United States, based largely on defensive, strategic considerations and the opportunity to test the Russian navy's newest ships on the open seas, had unexpected consequences for the future of Russian-American relations.

Seven warships from the Baltic fleet commanded by Rear Admiral Nikolai Lesovskii sailed from Kronstadt for New York. Meanwhile, Admiral A. A. Popov led the Pacific squadron to San Francisco to await a possible declaration of war. Although Washington had been notified of the squadrons' visits, the public did not know the purpose. New Yorkers had not expected the ships, but assumed that the Russians had come to demonstrate friendship for the United States and lend support in an hour of need. It would have been difficult for Americans not to respond to any such gesture in this trying period. The Federal government did nothing to discourage this belief.

Thus as Admiral Lesovskii's flagship, the 51-gun, 800-horsepower, 4,500-ton steam frigate *Alexander Nevskii*, approached the harbor in September 1863, crowds lined the shore and cheered. The next two months were filled with receptions for the Russians. At a dinner honoring the navy officers, New York's mayor and aldermen struck the theme of friendship, the former citing common interests in the Pacific, where a telegraph line was expected to join the two powers. Minister Stoeckl and Admiral Lesovskii responded in kind, never hinting at the real purpose of the visit. In fact, the Russian admiral, in an interview with the American editor Thurlow Weed, coyly mentioned that he had arrived in America with "sealed orders," hinting at the possibility of an alliance. The grateful Americans toasted the eagles of America and Russia "Their talons will uphold the weapons of protection over the American continent."

Following the arrival of the Russian squadron, a procession down Broadway opened the festivities, followed by elaborate parties and banquets. New York City staged the grandest ball in its history. The party moved to Delmonico's for a banquet called the "Soiree Russe" that included thousands of game birds, hundreds of turkeys and chickens, a thousand pounds of tenderloin, and 3,500 bottles of wine. For dessert, the assembled received pastry shaped in the likenesses of President Lincoln, Tsar Alexander II, George Washington, and Peter the Great. Before departing, Admiral Lesovskii contributed $4,700 to New York charities.

Washington also offered an official welcome. Secretary of the Navy Gideon Welles, notified of the visit, immediately offered the services of the Brooklyn Navy Yard. When the *Alexander Nevskii* called later at Alexandria, Virginia, President Lincoln honored the Russians with a White House reception. Admiral Lesovskii reciprocated with a ball aboard the flagship. Congressmen, cabinet members, and other notables eagerly inspected the vessel and were entertained. There were numerous toasts for the emperor and president, the emancipators, and a series of speeches of eternal friendship between Russia and America.

American officials suspected why the squadrons had come, but chose to use the visit as a warning to Britain and France, and to play down Russia's true motive for the trip. When informed of the squadron's appearance in New York, Welles concluded that it had left the Baltic to avoid confinement, but "in sending them to this country at this time there is something significant. What will be its effect on France and the French policy we shall learn in due time. It may moderate; it may exasperate. God bless the Russians!"

Admiral Popov's squadron in San Francisco also enjoyed American hospitality. A large crowd greeted the flagship as it reached port. Popov, a frequent visitor to San Francisco, expressed his gratitude to the city by hosting numerous parties. The Russians earned the city's friendship and an official commendation by helping to extinguish a large fire. In addition, when rumors spread that Confederate raiders threatened the port, Popov offered to help defend the city with a standing order that was published in local newspapers and hailed by the local population. If Southern raiders were to come to San Francisco, the admiral ordered his fleet to clear for action and warn the Confederates that "His Imperial Majesty's Pacific Squadron [would] repel any attempt against the security of the place." Although such a gesture was clearly outside his instructions, Admiral Popov won the hearts of the people of San Francisco and gave them a sense of security. Because a Confederate attack never occurred, the Russian squadron's actual readiness to assist was never tested. The visits, however, provided many Americans with proof of Russian sympathy and left behind a profound sense of gratitude and camaraderie. Newspapers in a nation resistant to foreign alliances wrote of Russia as "our natural ally." San Francisco's leading daily noted the rumors that "an alliance has been entered into between our country and Russia. If there has been, it is nothing but a formal recognition of a fact which already exists."

Regardless of the reasons why the ships came to American shores, the presence of two Russian squadrons had several significant implications. After numerous defeats over the previous two years, the Union received a much-needed psychological boost from the arrival of an "ally." The informal alliance also compelled France and England to consider the consequences of a formal

Russo-American entente if the European powers recognized the South.

The Russian government greeted the news of the Union's victory in April 1865 with satisfaction. Because the peace terms were an internal matter and not subject to diplomacy, the Russians played no role in connection with the end of the war. St. Petersburg, however, manifested the bond between the two countries that continued into the immediate aftermath of the Civil War. The assassination of President Lincoln fostered genuine public grief throughout the Russian Empire. The imperial government honored the late president by displaying his picture prominently throughout Russia next to that of the Emperor's oldest son, Grand Duke Nicholas Alexandrovich, who had also recently died.

The United States reciprocated almost a year after John Wilkes Booth's murder of Lincoln. The Emperor Alexander survived an assassination attempt by a young Russian radical, Dmitrii Karakozov. In response, Congress passed a joint resolution that congratulated Alexander on his escape. President Andrew Johnson selected Assistant Secretary of the Navy Gustavus Fox, who was highly regarded by Stoeckl in Washington, to deliver the resolution personally. In reality, the goal of the American government was to thank the Russians for the visits of their squadrons three years earlier and to extend thanks for friendship during the war.

The sending of the delegation marked the first time in American history that such a resolution had been passed and subsequently carried abroad by a high-ranking government official. The mission also stressed Russo-American friendship in Paris and London by publicly passing through both countries en route to St. Petersburg. To impress the Europeans, Fox sailed to Europe on a new American monitor, the *Miantonomah*, accompanied by an older steam frigate, the *Augusta*. Weighed down by a 450-pound Dahlgren cannon mounted in its turret, the 1,200-ton monitor rode unusually low in the water. The trip marked the first time that a monitor crossed the Atlantic.

St. Petersburg anxiously awaited the American delegation. Accompanied by eleven of Russia's most modern ships, the two American vessels arrived in Kronstadt on 6 August to great fanfare. Two days later, the emperor received Fox, who presented the former with the congressional resolution. The report of this ceremony also represented the first message transmitted on the new Atlantic cable from Russia. On the following day, the emperor and other dignitaries toured the American ships and then supped together on the imperial yacht. Shortly thereafter, the Americans toured many Russian cities, including Moscow and Nizhnii Novgorod. Prior to their departure on 15 September, the Americans returned to the Russian capital, where Prince Gorchakov at the English Club feted them. The Foreign Minister gave a toast that exemplified the friendship between the two nations: "I need not insist upon the manifestations of sympathy between the two countries. They shine out in broad daylight. It is one of the interesting facts of our day—a fact which creates between the two peoples—I will venture today, between two continents—the genus of good will and reciprocal friendship; which will bear fruit; which create traditions; and which tend to consolidate between them relations based upon a true spirit of Christian Civilization."

—*Curtis Richardson*

See also Cameron, Simon; Clay, Cassius M.; Diplomacy, C.S.A.; Diplomacy, U.S.A.; Great Britain; Stoeckl, Edouard de.

For further reading:

Dowty, Alan. *The Limits of American Isolation: The United States and the Crimean War* (1971).

Jensen, Ronald J. *The Alaska Purchase and Russian-American Relations* (1975).

Kiniapina, N. S. Russia and the U.S. Civil War. In *Russian-American Dialogue on Cultural Relations, 1776–1914.* Edited by Norman E. Saul and Richard D. McKinzie (1997).

Kushner, Howard I. "The Russian Fleet and the American Civil War: Another View." *Historian* (1972).

SABINE CROSSROADS (APRIL 1864)

See Mansfield, Louisiana, Battle of

SABINE PASS, TEXAS, FIRST BATTLE OF
(21 January 1863)

On 21 January 1863, a small naval battle took place in the waters surrounding Sabine Pass, Texas, that resulted in a Confederate victory. This successful effort allowed the Confederates to retake Sabine Pass from Union troops. As a strategic point, Sabine Pass guarded the entrance to the Sabine River and served Confederate interests in Texas as an important port.

From the early days of the Civil War, Union vessels had blockaded the Texas coast. Soon after the blockade began, preparations were made for the defense of the city, which included the building of a fort. When yellow fever broke out in the summer of 1862, most citizens and soldiers left the city. Only a token force remained with instructions to spike the guns of the fort and retreat if the Federals landed troops. In late September, the Federals landed and destroyed the fort after the small Confederate force retreated toward Beaumont. About a week later, the Union army began threatening Confederate communications with Sabine Pass by setting fire to the railroad bridge across Taylor's Bayou and burning the railroad depot. As yellow fever and measles struck large numbers of their soldiers, Confederate commanders suspected that the Federals would expand their aggression beyond Sabine Pass. Then on 5 October, Union troops took Galveston. Confederate fortunes along the Texas coast, however, began to change beginning on New Year's Day 1863,

when the Confederates retook Galveston and inflicted severe damage on the blockading fleet. Three weeks later, they would reoccupy Sabine Pass.

Major General John Bankhead Magruder assumed command of the Confederate District of Texas, New Mexico, and Arizona in late November 1862. When he arrived in Texas, he found the Union in possession of all the coastal harbors from the Sabine River to Corpus Christi. He also discovered that the line of defense formed along the Rio Grande had been virtually abandoned. He immediately devised a plan to recapture the harbors, including Sabine Pass, and reoccupy the Rio Grande Valley. Employing a similar strategy to that used in the recapture of Galveston, the Confederates outfitted two ordinary river steamers, the *Bell* and the *Uncle Ben*, with bales of cotton. These bales would provide protection for sharpshooters stationed on the vessels. In addition, the *Bell* was armed with a rifled cannon, and the *Uncle Ben* carried two cannons.

Early on the morning of 20 January, the small expedition set sail across Sabine Lake under the command of Major O. M. Watkins. Several of the sharpshooters on the *Bell* became seasick and had to be taken off the boat. By daylight on the 21st, the Confederate vessels approached the Union blockading force composed of the *Morning Light*, a twelve-gun ship of war, and the *Velocity*, a schooner man-of-war outfitted with two twelve-pound Napoleon guns. As the Confederate steamboats approached the two Union vessels, the latter retreated into the open sea. The *Bell* and the *Uncle Ben*, however, followed. After disabling the forward gun of the *Morning Light*, the *Bell*, commanded by Captain Charles Fowler, managed to draw close enough for the sharpshooters to inflict heavy damage on the gunners of the *Morning Light*. Meanwhile, the *Uncle Ben*, commanded by Captain William Johnson, pursued the *Velocity*. After a fight that lasted approximately one hour and ranged up to thirty miles at sea, the crews of both the Northern ships surrendered. The Confederates captured them, and later burned the *Morning Light* to keep it from falling back into the hands of the Union.

While this first battle for Sabine Pass has been overshadowed by a second that occurred later that year in September, at the time, General Magruder heralded it as a heroic example of the daring and skill of the Texans that also electrified the whole country. While Magruder may have been guilty of exaggerating the impact of the battle, he nonetheless highlighted the dangerous feat of taking two river steamers onto the open sea to engage in battle. Had the seas not been calm at the time, the Confederates probably would not have met with such success. One month later, Magruder wrote Texas governor F. R. Lubbock and proclaimed that "the coast of Texas is occupied and free for the occupation of our troops from Sabine to the Rio Grande." He cited the

action at Sabine Pass as an important factor in bringing about this state of affairs. Later that year, both the Texas Legislature and the Confederate Congress passed resolutions of thanks to the men involved in the battle.

—*Scott M. Langston*

See also Galveston; Magruder, John Bankhead.

For further reading:

Journal of the Congress of the Confederate States of America, 1861–1865. Vol. 6 (1905).

Keith, K. D. *Military Operations: Sabine Pass, 1861–1863* (1963).

Wiess, William. "First Federal Defeat at Sabine Pass." *Confederate Veteran* (1912).

SABINE PASS, TEXAS, SECOND BATTLE OF
(8 September 1863)

On 8 September 1863, Fort Griffin, manned by First Lieutenant Richard W. "Dick" Dowling and forty-seven boisterous Irish immigrants of Company F, 1st Texas Heavy Artillery Regiment, happened to be in an ideal position to thwart a Federal attempt to invade east Texas and cut the rail line between Beaumont and Houston. Located on the west side of Sabine Pass, about two miles above the Gulf of Mexico, the incomplete earthen fort commanded access to both channels of the Sabine and Neches rivers separating Jefferson County, Texas, and Calcasieu Parish, Louisiana.

With the fall of Vicksburg and Port Hudson, President Abraham Lincoln sought a quick means to plant the United States flag in Texas. Prodded by Lincoln and Washington bureaucrats, Union major general Nathaniel P. Banks conceived a plan to invade east Texas, but remain near Mobile, Alabama. Both Banks and Major General Ulysses S. Grant considered Mobile more significant to the Union war effort than an invasion of Texas. From New Orleans Banks dispatched an amphibious invasion force consisting of four gunboats, the USS *Arizona*, *Clifton*, *Granite City*, and *Sachem*, along with eighteen small transports carrying about 6,000 troops of the U.S. XIX Army Corps. Banks selected Major General William B. Franklin as overall commander of the invasion force, while acting Lieutenant Frederick Crocker, captain of the *Clifton*, would command the naval forces and act as advisor to Franklin.

The twenty-five-year-old Dowling, a successful Houston saloon keeper and businessman, occupied his men, also known as the Davis Guards, with improving Fort Griffin and conducting regular artillery practice. Dowling prepared to defend Sabine Pass by planting a series of aiming stakes across both channels of the rivers and having his men range their six old smoothbore cannon on the poles sticking out of the water. By previously sighting their two 24-pounders and four 32-pounders, Dowling's cannoneers could readily engage any enemy ship steaming into the pass.

On the night of 7 September, after missing a rendezvous at sea, the Union ships finally arrived piecemeal off the pass. Calling his officers together, Franklin issued orders for an invasion the next day. From 6:30 A.M. on the seventh to 7:30 A.M. on the eighth, the *Clifton* shelled Fort Griffin from long range, while Dowling's men crouched under cover in their bombproofs. The Union ships had steamed out of range of his antiquated cannon. Several small Federal landing parties discovered that marshy conditions precluded landings at the mouth of the pass, and Franklin's troops would have to be put ashore in range of the Confederate artillery.

Altering his plans for at least the third time, Franklin ordered the invasion to commence. At 3:40 P.M. the Union flotilla moved up the pass, firing at Fort Griffin as the gunboats advanced. Emerging from cover, the Confederate gunners opened fire at a range of 1,200 yards. Leading the assault force, the *Sachem* and *Clifton* immediately came under accurate Confederate cannon fire. Two well-aimed rounds hit the *Sachem*, disabling the ship and exploding its boiler. Blocked by the *Sachem*, the *Arizona* backed away from the action and grounded on the shallow sandbar at the mouth of the Louisiana channel.

At a range of one-quarter mile, direct hits cut the zigzagging *Clifton*'s rudder controls, causing the ship to run aground on the Texas side of the channel. Another solid shot through its boiler sent scalding steam through the ship, and, their decks littered with dead and wounded, both the *Clifton* and *Sachem* struck their colors. Observing the pandemonium ahead of him, the captain of the *Granite City* lost his nerve and abandoned his compatriots without firing a shot. With his plans in shambles, Franklin ordered a general withdrawal to New Orleans. In the panic to flee the pass, transport commanders ran aground and dumped thousands of rations and hundreds of horses and mules overboard to get over the bar.

In less than an hour the Confederates fired an estimated 137 shot and shell and, except for a few minor wounds from shell splinters and some blisters from handling the hot cannons, suffered no casualties. One cannon, however, ran off its platform and was out of action early in the engagement. The Federals lost two gunboats, at least twenty-eight men killed, seventy-five wounded, thirty-seven missing, and 315 taken prisoner.

As a result of the shocking Rebel victory, Dowling and his men became heroes, Union morale and the U.S. stock market fell temporarily, and Banks abandoned his hopes of an easy invasion of east Texas. He then turned his attention to occupying the lower Rio Grande Valley. Franklin was ridiculed for losing the battle when he possessed an overwhelming combined force of ships and men.

—*Stanley S. McGowen*

See also Banks, Nathaniel P.; Franklin, William Buel; Rio Grande Campaign.
For further reading:
Barr, Alwyn. "Sabine Pass, September 1863." *Texas Military History* (1962).
Connor, Seymour V. *Battle of Texas* (1967).
Tolbert, Frank X. *Dick Dowling at Sabine Pass* (1962).

SACRAMENTO, KENTUCKY, BATTLE OF
(28 December 1861)

The battle of Sacramento, Kentucky, was a skirmish between Confederate and Federal cavalry patrols that was Nathan Bedford Forrest's first combat action. In September 1861, Confederate troops moved into Kentucky along a broad front across the commonwealth's southern boundary from Columbus to the Cumberland Gap. Confederate forces in the Green River area in western Kentucky moved to secure the water approaches to Bowling Green by obstructing the locks and dams along the Green River. In response, Federal forces rushed from Evansville to secure as many of the locks and dams as possible. They were able to secure Lock and Dams No. 1 and No. 2, while Confederate forces seized Lock No. 3 in Rochester, nearer Bowling Green. The Green River became a dividing line between Union and Confederate forces in Kentucky.

Federal general Thomas L. Crittenden was stationed in Calhoun, Kentucky, commanding the 5th Division of the Army of the Ohio, which was protecting Lock and Dam No. 2, located on the opposite side of the Green River at Rumsey. At about the same time, Lieutenant Colonel Nathan Bedford Forrest was leading the Confederate 7th Tennessee Cavalry in guerrilla and recruiting activities south of the Green River. Forrest was securing horses, cattle, and other supplies in the area, which was heavily pro-Confederate. The Confederate command was concerned about a possible advance by Crittenden's troops toward Bowling Green, the center point on their defense line across southern Kentucky. This concern led directly to the battle of Sacramento.

On 27 December 1861, Forrest assembled his troops in Greenville, Kentucky. With reinforcements, he had nearly 300 men for a patrol toward Rumsey the following day to ascertain Federal troop strength and deployment.

The morning of the 28th, as Forrest moved north toward Rumsey, he met his advance scouts eight miles outside of Greenville. The scouts reported sighting a Federal force just south of Sacramento. Forrest pressed quickly toward the small village, approximately nine miles south of Calhoun. Meanwhile, just south of Sacramento, eighteen-year-old Major Eli Murray commanded a Federal scouting party of 168 men. It was one of two scouting parties sent out from Calhoun the previous day. Murray's troops were watering their horses at Garst's Pond, unaware of Forrest's advancing force.

Forrest sent a scout ahead to determine the exact position of Murray's force. Upon the scout's return, Forrest followed him to a steep ridge overlooking Garst's Pond to observe the situation. Murray's troops sighted the men on the ridge. Murray was initially unsure who they were, believing they might be part of the other Union scouting party. All doubts were ended, however, when Forrest seized a private's rifle and fired on the Federal troops.

Forrest attacked without waiting for his full force, part of which was still catching up after the pressed advance. Federal forces fired at 200 yards and Confederate troops returned fire at 80 yards. Realizing his disorganization, Forrest pulled his men back to wait until his entire force had caught up. At the same time, he dismounted some of his men to act as sharpshooters, sent a detachment under Major D. C. Kelly toward the Union right and another under James W. Starnes to the Union left.

Mistaking Forrest's withdrawal as a retreat, Murray began to advance his outnumbered force. But, with the reorganization of his troops complete, Forrest began a second attack on the Federal center at the same time that Kelly and Starnes attacked the flanks. Murray's troops held off the Confederate attack for ten minutes. Due to confusion, or according to some reports a panicked private's call to retreat, the Federals turned and ran toward Sacramento despite their officers' attempts to stop them and maintain order.

Sacramento was not a safe haven. Southern sympathizers in the village fired on the Federal soldiers from their businesses and homes. When Forrest's men caught up with a Union rear guard, there was hand-to-hand fighting, including numerous saber fights, as the Federal troops fought desperately while retreating toward Calhoun.

In the midst of the chase, while Forrest was engaged in hand-to-hand combat he was unaware of a second soldier approaching him from the rear. A Confederate lieutenant Lane shot this soldier just as Forrest brought his initial foe to the ground. Federal captain Arthur Davis killed Confederate private William H. Terry with his sword and then turned and attacked Forrest from behind. Davis's horse fell, however, and Davis was violently dismounted, dislocating his shoulder, and was forced to surrender. Another Federal officer, Captain Albert G. Bacon, next engaged Forrest, but his shot narrowly missed. Forrest turned and returned fire, wounding Bacon, who refused to surrender, fighting to his death. Two Federal officers charged at Forrest with drawn sabers at the same time. He shot one and hit the other with his sword. Their riderless horses collided into a heap. In pursuit of the retreating Federals, Forrest rode into the pile and ended up off his own horse. By the time

Forrest was back on his horse, the Federals were out of sight and closer to the larger force in Calhoun. Forrest decided to abandon his pursuit, which had covered some two miles, and return to Greenville.

As soon as he heard of the engagement at Sacramento, General Crittenden dispatched a 500-man relief column under Colonel James Jackson of the 3d Kentucky Cavalry. By the time they arrived, however, Forrest was gone, well on his way back to Greenville. He camped outside town at the Mount Pisgah Baptist Church for the night and then headed for Hopkinsville, Kentucky, the next day.

Union reports counted eleven dead, including Captain Bacon. They also listed forty men as missing, some of whom had been taken prisoner. Forrest lost two men. While little more than a skirmish, the battle of Sacramento was the first combat engagement of Nathan Bedford Forrest's military career in which he displayed many of the aggressive characteristics and the personal courage that made him one of the Confederacy's premier cavalry commanders.

—*William H. Mulligan, Jr.*

See also Forrest, Nathan Bedford.

For further reading:

Hurst, Jack. *As They Saw Forrest* (1956).

Jordan, Thomas, and J. D. Pryor. *The Campaigns of Lieutenant General Nathan Bedford Forrest, and of Forrest's Cavalry* (1868; reprint, 1988).

Mathes, J. Harvey. *General Forrest* (1902).

Wills, Brian Steel. *A Battle from the Start: The Life of Nathan Bedford Forrest* (1992).

SALEM CHURCH/SALEM HEIGHTS, BATTLE OF
(3–4 May 1863)

On the night of 2 May 1863, as the battle of Chancellorsville raged on, Major General Joseph Hooker ordered Brigadier General John Sedgwick with 19,000 Union troops to push Major General Jubal Early's 9,000 Confederate forces from Fredericksburg. This offensive surprised General Robert E. Lee's forces as Sedgwick attacked from the rear. At what became known as Second Fredericksburg, Sedgwick attacked at Marye's Heights and failed two times. Sedgwick's Federal forces finally pushed through the weakened Confederate line and cross the Rappahannock River at Fredericksburg, taking hold of the old Confederate works at Sunken Road shortly after noon on 3 May. As Early's troops withdrew to the southwest along Telegraph Road, the Union troops continued west, generally unobscured, toward Chancellorsville. Only a single brigade under Brigadier General Cadmus Wilcox, lay between Sedgwick and Lee. Wilcox fell back, sending some of his men forward to skirmish with Sedgwick, slowing the Union advance and allowing Wilcox to strategically position his troops. Seeing the oncoming threat of Union forces, Lee sent a portion of his line from Chancellorsville, under the command of Major General Lafayette McLaws, around to help slow the advance of Sedgwick. Falling back, with Sedgwick following closely, Wilcox was reinforced by McLaws at 4:00 P.M. The two forces met six miles east of Chancellorsville along a low ridgeline, the Confederates having already settled in. Upon this ridge stood a Baptist chapel dating from 1844 called Salem Church.

The elevated view of the battlefield provided the 10,000 Confederate troops with a strategic advantage over the Union army. At about 5:00 P.M., the Federal divisions under Brigadier General William Brooks and Major General John Newton pushed forward, musket fire raining upon them from the ridge. Initially, the Confederate line wavered and broke, making a Union victory seem imminent. Regrouping, Wilcox thrust his remaining forces into the Union line, pushing them onto the plain. With his last two divisions arriving, Sedgwick was able to stabilize his forces in time. The Federal artillery pounded the Confederates, allowing the weakened Union forces slowly to make their way to the base of the ridge; however, as nightfall was fast approaching, another major offensive had to wait until the following day.

Holding off the Union advance on 3 May allowed Lee enough time to reinforce McLaws. Lee, confident, decided that a defeated Hooker, dug in and settled with 75,000 men, would not attack the outnumbered Confederate army. Weighing the risk, Lee boldly decided to divide his army, leaving only 25,000 men to face Hooker; however, Hooker, unlike Lee, made no effort to reinforce Sedgwick's forces or attack Lee at Chancellorsville. Early in the morning on 4 May, Lee ordered Brigadier General Robert Anderson to move against Sedgwick. By dawn, Early's forces, now regrouped and reorganized, reoccupied Marye's Heights. Unable to arrive until 6:00 P.M., Anderson moved into position at the right side of Sedgwick as Early positioned his troops to strike Sedgwick's rear. Lee, leaving the inactivity of Chancellorsville, arrived at Salem Church and decided to take command of the now 21,000 Confederate troops that had amassed.

Fighting throughout the evening, the Federal forces were within striking distance of the ridge. As the Union forces pushed forward by nightfall, a Confederate counterattack was launched. Positioning their forces in a crescent to allow for a riverine escape, the Confederates attacked three sides of Sedgwick's forces, sending Federal troops back onto the open plain and moving closer to the river to the north. Attacking during the night, Lee

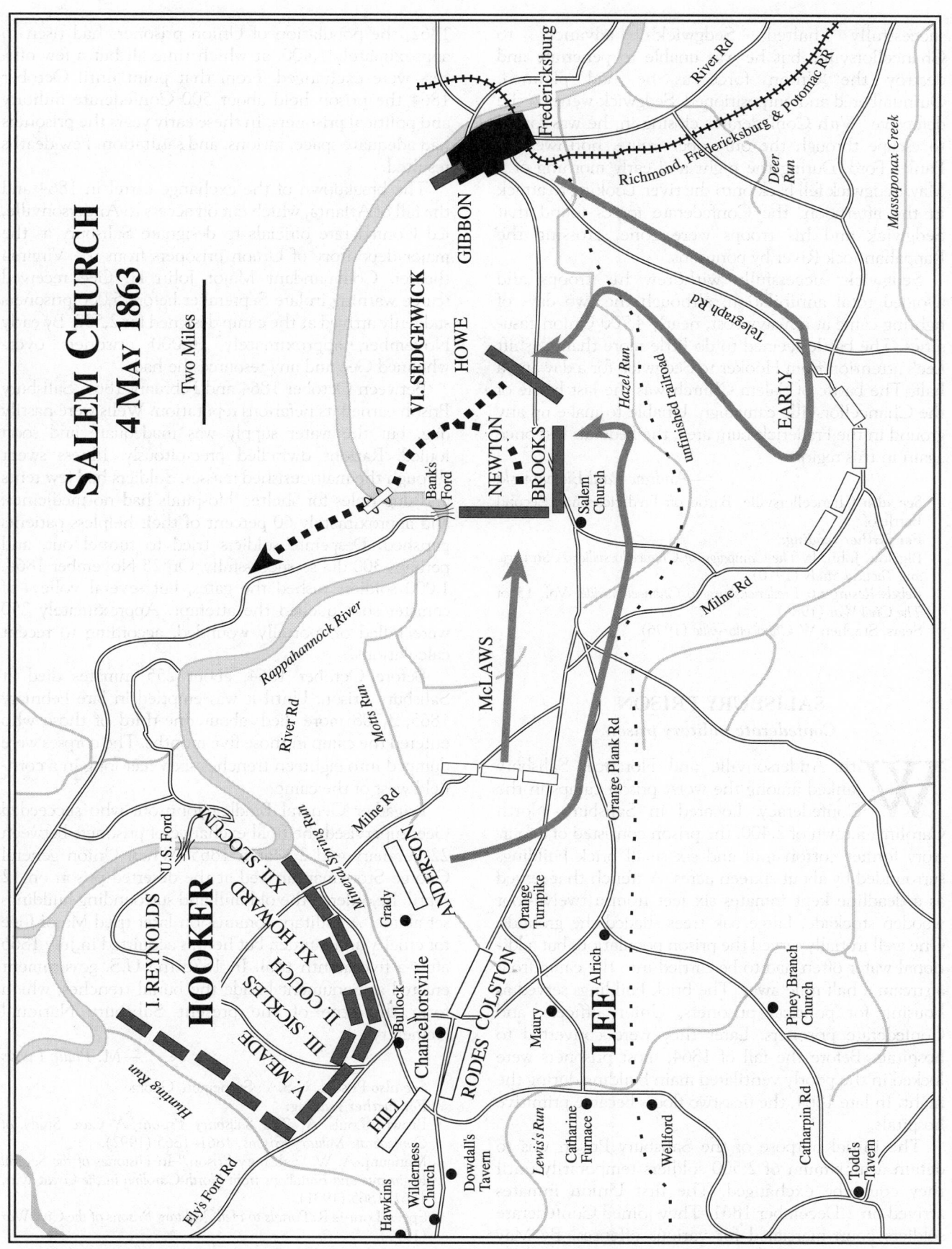

SALEM CHURCH
4 MAY 1863

Two Miles

Fredericksburg

River Rd

Richmond, Fredericksburg & Potomac RR

Massaponax Creek

Deer Run

GIBBON

Telegraph Rd

EARLY

HOWE

SEDGWICK

VI.

Hazel Run

NEWTON

unfinished railroad

BROOKS

Banks Ford

Salem Church

Milne Rd

Rappahannock River

McLAWS

Orange Plank Rd

River Rd

Motts Run

Milne Rd

U.S. Ford

XII. SLOCUM

Mineral Spring Run

Grady

ANDERSON

Orange Turnpike

I. REYNOLDS

HOOKER

XI. HOWARD

II. COUCH

III. SICKLES

V. MEADE

Bullock

Chancellorsville

RODES COLSTON

LEE

Alrich

Maury

Piney Branch Church

HILL

Wilderness Church

Dowdall's Tavern

Hawkins

Ely's Ford Rd

Lewis's Run

Catharine Furnace

Wellford

Catharpin Rd

Todd's Tavern

Hunting Run

successfully halted Sedgwick's advance to Chancellorsville, but he was unable to penetrate and destroy the Union force as he had planned. Outnumbered and outpositioned, Sedgwick went on the defensive. With Confederates closing in, he was forced to escape through the only open route, northwest to Banks' Ford. During the night and early morning of 5 May, Sedgwick fell back onto the river. Looking to attack in the afternoon, the Confederate forces found that Sedgwick and his troops were gone, crossing the Rappahannock River by pontoons.

Sedgwick successfully withdrew his troops and avoided total annihilation, although the two days of fighting came at a heavy cost, nearly 4,700 Union casualties. The battle seemed to do little more than to shift Lee's attention from Hooker to Sedgwick for a day and a half. The battle of Salem Church was the last battle of the Chancellorsville campaign. Unable to make up any ground in the Fredericksburg area, the Federals lost once again in this region.

—*Andrew Paul Bielakowski*

See also Chancellorsville, Battle of; Fredericksburg, Second Battle of.
For further reading:
Bigelow, John, Jr. *The Campaign of Chancellorsville: A Strategic and Tactical Study* (1910).
Rebels Resurgent: Fredericksburg to Chancellorsville. Vol. 13 of *The Civil War* (1983).
Sears, Stephen W. *Chancellorsville* (1996).

SALISBURY PRISON
Confederate military prison

With Andersonville and Florence, Salisbury ranked among the worst prison camps in the Confederacy. Located in Salisbury, North Carolina, a town of 2,400, the prison consisted of a four-story former cotton mill and six small brick buildings surrounded by about sixteen acres. A trench that served as a deadline kept inmates six feet from a twelve-foot wooden stockade. Large oak trees shaded the grounds. One well initially served the prison population, but additional water often had to be carried into the camp from a stream a half mile away. The brick buildings served as housing for political prisoners, Union officers, and Confederate prisoners. Later they were converted to hospitals. Before the fall of 1864, most prisoners were locked in the poorly ventilated main building during the night. In late 1864, the first two floors became primitive hospitals.

The initial purpose of the Salisbury Prison was to detain a maximum of 2,500 soldiers temporarily until they could be exchanged. The first Union inmates arrived on 2 December 1861. They joined Confederate soldiers court-martialed for various offenses. By May 1862, the population of Union prisoners had risen to approximately 1,400, at which time all but a few officers were exchanged. From that point until October 1864 the prison held about 500 Confederate military and political prisoners. In these early years the prisoners had adequate space, rations, and sanitation. Few deaths resulted.

The breakdown of the exchange cartel in 1864 and the fall of Atlanta, which cut off access to Andersonville, led Confederate officials to designate Salisbury as the major depository of Union prisoners from the Virginia theater. Commandant Major John H. Gee received scarce warning in late September before 5,000 prisoners suddenly arrived at the camp designed for 2,500. By early November, approximately 10,000 prisoners overwhelmed Gee and any resources he had.

Between October 1864 and February 1865, Salisbury Prison earned its nefarious reputation. Wells were hastily dug, but the water supply was inadequate and soon fouled. Rations dwindled precipitously. Illness swept through the malnourished masses. Soldiers had few tents and dug holes for shelter. Hospitals had no medicines, and approximately 60 percent of their helpless patients perished. Desperate soldiers tried to tunnel out, and perhaps 300 did so successfully. On 25 November 1864, 1,000 soldiers rushed the gates, but several volleys of canister shot quelled the attempt. Approximately 250 were killed or mortally wounded, according to recent calculations.

Before October 1864, about 255 inmates died at Salisbury Prison. Until it was emptied in late February 1865, 3,708 more died, about one-third of those who entered the camp in those five months. The corpses were dumped into eighteen trenches sixty feet long in a cornfield west of the camp.

Brigadier General Bradley Johnson, who succeeded Gee, supervised the final exchange of prisoners between 22 February and 2 March 1865. When Union general George Stoneman arrived at the deserted prison on 12 April, he ordered the old mill and surrounding buildings set ablaze. A military commission later tried Major Gee for cruelty and murder, but he was acquitted in July 1866 after a five-month trial. In 1876 the U.S. government erected a monument beside the burial trenches, which form the core of the present Salisbury National Cemetery.

—*M. Philip Lucas*

See also Prisons, C.S.A.; Stoneman, George.
For further reading:
Brown, Louis A. *The Salisbury Prison: A Case Study of Confederate Military Prisons, 1861–1865* (1992).
Mangum, A. W. "Salisbury Prison." In *Histories of the Several Regiments and Battalions from North Carolina in the Great War, 1861–1865* (1901).
Speer, Lonnie R. *Portals to Hell: Military Prisons of the Civil War* (1997).

SALM-SALM, PRINCE FELIX CONSTANTIN ALEXANDER JOHANN NEPOMUK
(1828–1870)
Union officer

Born 25 December 1828 in Alholt, Westphalia, Prussia, Prince Felix Constantin Alexander Johann Nepomuk Salm-Salm was the youngest son of Prince Florentin zu Salm-Salm. A lieutenant in the Prussian Hussars, Prince Felix Salm-Salm was decorated for bravery during the Schleswig-Holstein War. Evading creditors, he fled to Paris and then to the United States.

Arriving in the United States in 1861, shortly after the start of the Civil War, he obtained a position as chief of staff to Brigadier General Louis Blenker. While serving with Blenker, the prince met his future wife, Agnes Joy, an American. The couple married on 30 August 1862 in Washington, D.C.

By the autumn of 1862, it was apparent that the prince's position on Blenker's staff was in danger from Secretary of War Edwin Stanton's efforts to reduce the moribund officer corps. Princess Agnes Salm-Salm used her influence to win her husband a commission in command of the 8th New York Infantry. The regiment was relegated to the rear during December's Fredericksburg campaign and entered winter quarters with the new colonel yet to see battle. Prince and Princess Salm-Salm were among the colorful personages that made up the much-storied Major General Joseph Hooker's winter camp near Aquia, Virginia.

By April 1863, Salm-Salm's commission was again in danger, as the two-year enlistment of the majority of the men in the 8th was concluding. The princess was successful in obtaining for her husband the command of the veteran 68th New York. On 8 June 1864, Prince Salm-Salm finally took command of the regiment in Nashville, Tennessee, where they guarded the Nashville & Chattanooga Railroad from guerrilla attacks as part of the 3d Brigade, 4th Division, XX Army Corps, Army of the Cumberland.

The 68th New York spent the remainder of the fall of 1864 on an island in the Tennessee River, near Bridgeport, Alabama, guarding railroad and pontoon bridges against raids. Hearing of Confederate general John Bell Hood's campaign into Tennessee and desperately wanting in on whatever fighting may be in the offing, Salm-Salm convinced Major General James Steedman to permit him to join his staff. Thus, he left the 68th behind, along with his wife, who was accompanying him in the field, and traveled to Nashville. On 18 December, Salm-Salm ordered his regiment to meet him at Stephenson, Alabama, to chase the retreating Hood. The regiment cleared out Hood's rear guard from Decatur, Alabama, and returned to camp near Bridgeport the day after Christmas.

Salm-Salm remained in the field as commander of a Reserve Brigade ordered to pursue Brigadier General Hylan B. Lyon, whose troops were raiding Federal army stores and destroying rail and telegraph lines throughout the Alabama-Tennessee region. From 7 to 11 January 1865, the prince was on Lyon's trail, never able to overtake him, and succeeded only in capturing an ambulance filled with wounded soldiers.

The prince was recommended for a promotion for his actions during the Franklin and Nashville campaign. Though he had letters of recommendation from his superiors, his promotion to brevet brigadier general did not come until 13 April 1865 and then due in large part to his wife's stubborn and unfailing efforts on his behalf in Washington. His generalship was brief, as the 68th was mustered out in November.

After the Civil War, Prince and Princess Salm-Salm traveled to Mexico, where the prince became embroiled in the overthrow of Maximilian's French-supported regime in 1867. Salm-Salm barely escaped with his life. The couple returned to the prince's ancestral home in Germany, where in 1868 Salm-Salm wrote and published *My Diary in Mexico,* an account of his adventures with Maximilian. Later that year, Salm-Salm was appointed major in the 4th Regiment of Guards in Koblentz. In April 1870, he was promoted to colonel of the Fusilier Battalion and went to war against France. On 18 August 1870, Felix Salm-Salm was killed at the battle of Gravelotte in the Franco-Prussian War.

—*Heidi Campbell-Shoaf*

See also German-Americans.
For further reading:
Salm-Salm, Agnes Elisabeth Winona Leclerq Joy, Prinzessin zu. *Ten Years of My Life* (1877).

SALOMON, FRIEDRICH
(1826–1897)
Union general

Born in Strobeck, Saxony, Friedrich Salomon was educated locally before serving briefly in the Prussian army. After studying architecture in Berlin, he immigrated to the United States during the Revolutions of 1848 with his two brothers. Two of the Salomon brothers became officers in the Union army during the Civil War, and the other, Edward S. Salomon, became governor of Wisconsin.

After coming to the United States, Friedrich Salomon moved to Wisconsin, where he worked as a surveyor and engineer. At the outbreak of the Civil War he accepted a captain's commission in the 5th Missouri Volunteers. As part of Brigadier General Franz Sigel's brigade, Salomon fought at Wilson's Creek in August 1861.

On 26 November 1861, Salomon was promoted to colonel and was given command of the 9th Wisconsin

Infantry. In the spring of 1862, his regiment garrisoned and he commanded Fort Scott, Kansas. In June 1862, Salomon was promoted to brigadier general and was given command of the 1st Brigade of the Kansas Volunteers. For most of the rest of the year he commanded his brigade in Missouri. On 30 September, in a probe out from his headquarters at Sarcoxie, Missouri, Salomon was attacked by Confederates and was forced back to base. Later in the year he was given command of the 1st Brigade, 1st Division, District of Eastern Arkansas. On 7 December 1862, he led his brigade at the battle of Prairie Grove, Arkansas.

Salomon and his brigade remained in the District of Eastern Arkansas under the Command of Major General Benjamin Mayberry Prentiss through the spring and early summer of 1863. In early July, Salomon was given command of 13th Division, XIII Corps, District of Eastern Arkansas, and was commended for his actions at the defense of Helena, Arkansas, against the attack by Major General Sterling Price and Lieutenant General Theophilus Hunter Holmes. In August 1863, he relieved Prentiss as the commander of the District of Eastern Arkansas.

Salomon served only a month in his new command before being sent to Little Rock to serve under Major General Frederick Steele. He was given command of the 3d Division, Army of Arkansas. Not terribly active at first, Salomon and his men would more than make up for this inactivity in the fall of 1863 during the campaigns of 1864.

Salomon commanded his division on Steele's Camden, Arkansas, expedition from 23 March to 3 May 1864. At the battle of Jenkins' Ferry on 30 April, Salomon especially distinguished himself when the army threatened to be overwhelmed by Confederate pursuers under Edmund Kirby Smith while crossing the Saline River. His division suffered severe casualties guarding the retreat of the Union forces, and as a result most of Steele's army was saved.

Upon the return to Little Rock, Salomon remained in command of his division there for the remainder of the war, seeing very little action. At the end of the war he received a brevet promotion to major general of volunteers. He was mustered out the volunteer service in August 1865.

After the war, Salomon served as surveyor general of Missouri for several years. In 1877, President Rutherford Hayes appointed him surveyor general of Utah Territory. He remained in Utah for the rest of life and died in Salt Lake City on 8 March 1897.

—*David S. Heidler and Jeanne T. Heidler*

See also German-Americans; Jenkins' Ferry, Battle of; Prairie Grove, Battle of.
For further reading:
Brancaforte, Charlotte, ed. *The German Forty-Eighters in the United States* (1989).

SALTVILLE, BATTLE OF
(2 October 1864)

Although a minor theater of operations throughout the war, southwestern Virginia possessed strategic significance for the South. Traversed by the Virginia & Tennessee Railroad, a vital link between the Eastern and Western theaters of operation, the mountainous region also embraced the Wytheville lead mines and the crucial salt production facilities at Saltville. Indeed, by the summer of 1863 the salt works in southwestern Virginia supplied most of the embattled Confederacy. Both sides recognized that the loss of Saltville would seriously cripple the South's ability to provision its major armies.

By late 1864, Union forces had made several futile attempts to strike Saltville and other key targets in the region. After he defeated and killed John Hunt Morgan at Greeneville on 4 September 1864, Brigadier General Alvan C. Gillem prepared a Union raid into southwestern Virginia from his base in East Tennessee. On 10 September, he contacted Brigadier General Stephen O. Burbridge, Union commander of the District of Kentucky, and requested that a diversionary force be sent to the Kentucky-Virginia border.

However, Burbridge had no desire to lead a mere diversion. On 11 September he requested permission from both Henry W. Halleck, the army chief of staff in Washington, and Major General John M. Schofield, his departmental commander, to launch a major raid against Saltville. By 18 September, it was determined that Kentuckian Burbridge would strike the main blow at the salt works while Gillem threatened southwestern Virginia from east Tennessee.

More than 5,000 strong, Burbridge's mounted column set out from Mount Sterling, Kentucky, on 20 September. Passing through the mountainous eastern portion of the state, Burbridge sent a small force to threaten Pound Gap on the Kentucky-Virginia line. At the same time, his main column penetrated Virginia via the Louisa Fork of the Big Sandy River. On 30 September, his advance units clashed with a detachment of Colonel Henry L. Giltner's Confederate cavalry brigade at Cedar Bluff in Tazewell County.

Brigadier General John Echols, in temporary command of the Confederate Department of East Tennessee and Southwestern Virginia, had barely 1,000 men to meet the dual Federal threat. The balance of his force, the cavalry brigades of John C. Vaughn, George B. Cosby, and Basil Duke, were able to check Gillem's advance in East Tennessee by 1 October. However, Giltner's 600-man brigade represented the only sizable force between Burbridge and Saltville. Indeed, the town itself was defended by only a single battalion of Virginia reserves.

From his headquarters at Abingdon, Echols called up more reserves and secured the aid of Brigadier General John S. Williams, whose small cavalry division miraculously appeared in east Tennessee. Cut off from "Fighting Joe" Wheeler's command during the latter's recent Tennessee raid, Williams was promptly ordered to march to Echols's aid. In the meantime, Giltner fought a stubborn but futile delaying action against Burbridge at Clinch Mountain on 1 October.

Heavily outnumbered, Giltner fell back to the outskirts of Saltville on the morning of 2 October. Although Williams's force was en route, the town's defenses, which were temporarily commanded by Brigadier General Alfred E. Jackson, remained largely unstaffed. Burbridge's troopers soon drove Giltner and the 13th Virginia Reserves from their advance position at Sanders Hill, forcing the Confederates to fall back across the North Fork of Holston River.

At this critical moment, Williams arrived on the field and established a line of battle that extended from the bluffs above the Holston to Chestnut Ridge. Burbridge, who now faced more than 2,800 rebel defenders, launched a series of determined assaults that hammered the Confederate line until nightfall. However, by the time they carried Chestnut Ridge, the battle-weary Federals were dangerously low on ammunition. Despite that Saltville was now within sight of his command, Burbridge was forced to retreat during the night. Although pursued to the Virginia line by the victorious Confederates, the Federal column escaped into Kentucky.

The Confederate victory was tarnished, however, by reports of the massacre the day after the battle of a large number of wounded prisoners belonging to the 5th and 6th U.S. Colored Cavalry. In this respect, the battle has recently become more significant as Civil War scholars further explore the role African-American units played during the conflict. Although historians such as William C. Davis describe the "Saltville Massacre" as a greater atrocity than the notorious incident at Fort Pillow, other scholars such as William Marvel contend that no evidence exists to support such claims. Nevertheless, all sources agree that Burbridge's black troopers distinguished themselves in the fighting.

A minor clash in the annals of the war, Saltville was a hollow victory for the moribund Confederacy. Nevertheless, the small scratch force of Confederate cavalry worked a minor military miracle by defeating a much stronger opponent. At the moment that victory seemed within reach, Burbridge was defeated by the delaying tactics of Giltner, which cost the Union raider precious ammunition, and by the timely arrival of John S. Williams's command. Union losses numbered more than 329 killed, wounded, and missing. Total Confederate casualties were estimated to be 190.

—*James M. Prichard*

For further reading:
Davis, William C. "The Massacre at Saltville." *Civil War Times Illustrated* (1971).
Marvel, William. "The Battle of Saltville: Massacre or Myth." *Blue and Gray Magazine* (1991).
Mays, Thomas D. *The Saltville Massacre* (1995).

SAND CREEK MASSACRE
(29 November 1864)

Located in southeastern Colorado, fifty miles from present-day Lamar, Sand Creek was the site of a deliberate and unprovoked attack on peaceful Southern Cheyenne and Arapaho Indians by Colorado volunteers. In a little over an hour, 148 Indians lay dead, many of their bodies mutilated for souvenirs.

Included in the land guaranteed to the Cheyenne and the Arapaho in Article V of the Fort Laramie Treaty of 1851 was eastern Colorado, from its border with Kansas and Nebraska westward to the Rocky Mountains and south to the Arkansas River. However, the discovery of gold at the confluence of the South Platte River and Cherry Creek drew a multitude of prospective miners into Cheyenne territory during the latter half of the decade. New trails traversed Cheyenne hunting grounds, opening the way for immigrants, who constructed settlements and towns on land promised to the Indians. Soon the buffalo and other wildlife grew scarce. Tensions mounted as hunger and disease spread through Indian bands.

The United States government sought to relieve the friction by further reducing Indian land. Believing obstinacy and delay would result in a less favorable settlement, Cheyenne leaders Black Kettle and White Antelope, along with an Arapaho delegation led by Little Raven and Left Hand, met with government agents on 8 February 1861, and placed their "X" on the Treaty of Fort Wise. The document ceded to the United States the vast territory granted to the Indians in the 1851 Fort Laramie agreement in exchange for annuity payments and a small reservation of 600 square miles in southeastern Colorado between the Big Sandy and the Arkansas rivers. The treaty was never approved by Cheyenne and Arapaho leaders who were not present at the signing.

The Sand Creek Reservation was unable to sustain the Indians who were compelled to live there. Unsuitable for agriculture, the desolate, gameless terrain proved to be a breeding ground only for epidemic diseases. With the nearest buffalo herd over 200 miles away, young Cheyenne men left the reservation in search of food. Raids on livestock and passing wagon trains became more and more frequent. Between 1861 and 1864, sporadic violence spread across eastern Colorado and the plains of Kansas and Nebraska, as men

from Cheyenne and Arapaho bands clashed with soldiers and volunteer militia units. Fear and panic swept through white homesteaders, who were fully aware of the incidents associated with the Dakota uprising of 1862.

In June 1864, John Evans, who had become the second governor of Colorado Territory two years earlier, issued a proclamation inviting all "friendly Indians" to certain designated forts, where they would be fed and allowed to camp under the protection of the military. Those Indians who chose not to comply with this directive would be considered hostile and subject to punitive raids. With most of the territory's regular troops away fighting the Confederates, Evans called for civilians to join the 3d Colorado Cavalry for 100 days to carry out his plan, stressing "Any man who kills a hostile Indian is a patriot . . . and no one has been or will be restrained from this."

The commander of the Colorado volunteers was Colonel John M. Chivington, a forty-three-year-old Methodist minister turned soldier turned politician. In 1862 Chivington replaced his clerical attire with a major's uniform in the Colorado Volunteer Regiment and won acclaim for his role in defeating Confederate troops at the battle of Glorieta Pass in eastern New Mexico. Now he was to lead an expedition against the Indians, "fully satisfied . . . that to kill them is the only way we will ever have peace and quiet in Colorado."

Black Kettle and six other chiefs decided to accept the governor's invitation and traveled with Major Edward Wynkoop, the commander of Fort Lyon, to Denver to meet with Evans and Chivington. Meeting at Camp Weld on 28 September, the Indians were told to submit to military authority as represented by the garrison at Fort Lyon. Black Kettle believed that he had secured peace and safety for his band and others. Unbeknownst to the Indians, Chivington received an order that same day from Major General Samuel R. Curtis, commanding officer of the Department of Kansas, instructing him not to make peace with the Indians. To this Chivington readily assented, with the blessing of Governor Evans.

On 4 November 1864 Major Wynkoop was relieved of command of Fort Lyon, owing to his benevolent dealings with Black Kettle, Left Hand, and Little Raven. His replacement was Major Scott Anthony, who proceeded to disperse the Indians, sending them away from the fort and north to Sand Creek. Chivington, meanwhile, moved his column of nearly 600 men down the Arkansas River toward Fort Lyon, arriving at the post on 28 November. The enlistment of his 100-day volunteers was about to expire, and the men were already disappointed at having never experienced a battle. Chivington, as well, had been ridiculed in the press for his inactivity. Accompanied by 125 men under Major Anthony and four mountain howitzers, the volunteers started out for Black Kettle's camp at 8 P.M. that evening. Having

covered the forty miles to the village that night, Chivington's men were in position to attack as dawn broke on 29 November.

Black Kettle's camp along Sand Creek was composed of approximately 450 Southern Cheyenne and forty Arapaho, split into separate groups of lodges, each headed by a chief. While a few women were up starting fires for cooking, most of the village was still asleep when the volunteers struck. Major Anthony drove away the herd of Indian ponies and then approached the village from the west. Three companies of the 1st Colorado crossed the mostly dry creek bed and attacked from the east and north, while the 3d Colorado Cavalry under Colonel George L. Shoup charged straight into the center of the encampment. Cheyenne oral history is replete with accounts of confusion and chaos as the Colorado volunteers swept through the village, firing indiscriminately into the lodges. The mountain howitzers positioned on the south bank of the creek began to rain grapeshot down on the fleeing Indians. Black Kettle and others were in a state of disbelief over what was happening. The Cheyenne chief tied an American flag that he had received in Denver, along with a white flag of truce, to one of his lodge poles in an unsuccessful effort to halt the slaughter. Black Kettle, along with Left Hand, was left with no choice but to try and escape with his life. White Antelope chose to remain and face death and was shot in front of his lodge.

The blood-letting continued as Chivington's men chased the remaining Cheyenne and Arapaho for miles up Sand Creek, overtaking and killing as many men, women, and children as they could find. Some of the refugees, including Black Kettle, managed to escape by digging into the sandy soil or hiding under the embankments of the creek. Returning to the village, the Colorado volunteers proceeded to kill all the remaining wounded and mutilate the bodies of the dead—taking scalps, ring-fingers, ears, and even genitalia for souvenirs. Chivington did nothing to halt the carnage. On 1 December the remains of the village and its inhabitants were set on fire, and the Colorado volunteers left the area bound for Denver. Chivington's casualties at Sand Creek were nine killed and thirty-eight wounded. The Cheyenne and Arapaho dead numbered 148—only sixty were men.

At first, Chivington and his volunteers were wildly praised and rewarded for their actions as triumphal celebrations filled the streets of Denver. Soon, however, rumors and testimonials about what really happened at Sand Creek convinced the United States Congress to order a formal investigation of the affair. Although never formally punished for his actions, Chivington nevertheless resigned from military service and withdrew from political life. Black Kettle, having miraculously escaped the carnage with his injured wife, returned to his efforts for

peace on the plains. On 14 October 1865, Cheyenne and Arapaho representatives agreed to a treaty giving up the Sand Creek Reservation in Colorado in exchange for a reservation in southwestern Kansas and Indian Territory.

—*Alan C. Downs*

See also Chivington, John Milton.

For further reading:

Hughes, J. Donald. *American Indians in Colorado* (1977).
Josephy, Alvin M. *The Civil War in the American West* (1991).

SANDERSVILLE, BATTLE OF
(5–26 November 1864)

The Union occupation of Sandersville, Georgia, possessed more of the characteristics of a skirmish than a battle. Beginning on 15 November 1864, Union troops under the command of Major General William T. Sherman left Atlanta and began a march across Georgia that would eventually terminate at Savannah. On their way to Savannah, they passed through the town of Sandersville and encountered relatively light resistance.

Sherman had left Atlanta with the aim of placing his army between Macon and Augusta to force the Confederates to defend both cities, as well as Millen, Savannah, and Charleston, and in doing so, divide their army. As they progressed, both corps of Sherman's left wing approached Sandersville simultaneously. The XX Corps, led by Brigadier General Alpheus S. Williams, entered Milledgeville on the 22d, while XIV Corps, directed by Major General Jefferson C. Davis, arrived the following day. On the 24th, the two corps left the city and advanced on Sandersville, located in Washington County.

To reach Sandersville, the Union troops had to cross Buffalo Creek. At this point, they encountered their first obstacle. Brigadier General John W. Geary, commanding the 2d Division of XX Corps, described the creek as "an extensive, heavily timbered, swampy stream, being nearly half a mile wide where the road passes through it." Here, the creek divided into eight channels, all spanned by bridges with earth causeways built between them. As the retreating Confederates tried to ascertain the intent of the Union army, they needed to delay Sherman as long as possible to concentrate their forces. So General Braxton Bragg ordered Major General Joseph Wheeler, commander of the Confederate Cavalry Corps, to use all possible means to slow Sherman's progress. The Confederates, therefore, burned all the bridges over Buffalo Creek. This action, however, only delayed the Federals for a matter of hours. Geary had arrived at Buffalo Creek around nine o'clock that morning. By 2:00 that afternoon, the bridges had been reconstructed, and by nightfall, Union troops had cleared the road sufficiently to enable Geary himself to cross the creek.

During the reconstruction of the bridges, a party of Confederate cavalry attacked the Union pickets. Five companies of the 101st Illinois Volunteers were sent as reinforcements, causing the Confederates to withdraw and ending the action. By the middle of the afternoon, Union troops were crossing the creek on their way to Sandersville. About three miles beyond Buffalo Creek, the Federals encountered stronger resistance from Wheeler's cavalry. Although some of the Union infantry deployed into a line of battle, they quickly halted and made camp. Again, the Confederate resistance had been easily driven by the Union advance troops. By the end of the day on the 25th, Sherman's left wing had crossed Buffalo Creek and encamped only a few miles from Sandersville.

Around 6:00 A.M. the following day, Union troops resumed their march. Colonel Ezra A. Carman's 2d Brigade of the 1st Division led XX Corps and within a few miles encountered Confederate troops stationed along a small creek. Dislodging them rather easily, the 9th Illinois Mounted Cavalry pursued them to Sandersville. There, Wheeler's cavalry stopped the Union advance and even drove them back for about one mile. Wheeler then advised the citizens of Sandersville to remove any valuables from the town since the enemy would soon enter it. Shortly thereafter, troops from XX and XIV Corps entered Sandersville simultaneously and drove the Confederate cavalry through the town. Sherman ordered the courthouse burned, since Confederate soldiers had used the portico to fire on his troops.

General Sherman characterized the resistance offered by Wheeler as light. Except for burning bridges, felling trees to block roads, burning supplies, and engaging in token skirmishes, the Confederate forces did little to resist the Union advance in and around Sandersville. At this time, however, the Confederates began to discern Sherman's goal. On the 25th, Lieutenant General William J. Hardee remarked, "It seems certain that the enemy is moving toward Savannah." Yet, after Wheeler's skirmish at Sandersville, Bragg remained undecided whether Sherman would move on Augusta or Savannah. Wheeler apparently shared the same uncertainty. On the evening of the 26th, however, Hardee left for Savannah to make preparations for its defense, while Bragg remained in Augusta. Sherman's ability to disguise his intentions prevented the Confederate forces from uniting and deprived them of valuable time to prepare a defense. By the second week of December, Sherman's army had arrived at Savannah.

—*Scott M. Langston*

See also Sherman's March to the Sea.

Further Reading

Glatthaar, Joseph T. *The March to the Sea and Beyond; Sherman's Troops in the Savannah and Carolinas Campaign* (1985).

SANTA ROSA ISLAND

The first significant land fighting in Florida took place at Santa Rosa Island on 9 October 1861. During the engagement, a small Confederate force crossed Pensacola Bay and attacked a Federal camp that had been established outside the walls of Union-occupied Fort Pickens. Although they were able to overrun the camp, the Southerners were unable to threaten the fort or its outlying batteries, and they eventually retired back across the bay. Total losses in the affair numbered about 150.

When the war began, several fortifications in Florida remained in Union hands, including Key West, Fort Jefferson in the Dry Tortugas, and Fort Pickens. The latter was on Santa Rosa Island, a barrier island that guarded the entrance into Pensacola Bay. After Florida's secession in January 1861, state troops occupied Fort Barrancas and the Pensacola Navy Yard, which were on the mainland, and Fort McRee, across the channel from Fort Pickens at the mouth of Pensacola Bay. During the spring and summer of 1861, Confederate troops under Major General Braxton Bragg improved these fortifications and mounted additional batteries facing the Union position. The fort itself was in poor condition and its garrison weak, but in April 1861 Federal officials authorized the landing of two groups of reinforcements. By June more than 2,000 Northern troops were in place to guard Fort Pickens against attack, and the fort's defenses had been greatly improved.

Though it was expected by both sides, no major fighting took place during the summer of 1861. In September, however, the Federals conducted two operations that would break this unofficial truce. On 2 September, Colonel Harvey Brown, who commanded the Union army's Department of Florida with headquarters at Fort Pickens, ordered a picked force to cross Pensacola Bay and destroy a dry dock that the Confederates were preparing to use to block the main entrance to the bay. Twelve days later, the Federals struck again, destroying the Confederate ship *Juda* at its dock near the navy yard.

In retaliation for these acts, General Bragg began planning a raid against Santa Rosa Island. By early October he was ready to proceed. The Confederate force selected for the operation consisted of about 1,200 men, including detachments from Alabama, Florida, Georgia, Louisiana, and Mississippi units. Brigadier General Richard H. Anderson commanded the force, which was divided further into battalions under Colonels James R. Chalmers, J. Patton Anderson, and John K. Jackson. After the troops had assembled on the evening of 8 October, they were loaded aboard barges and towed across the bay by the steamers *Ewing* and *Neaffie*. By 2:00 A.M. on 9 October they had landed on Santa Rosa Island some four miles to the east of Fort Pickens and began their advance on the fort. The Southern force moved in three columns, with one moving along the northern (bay) side of the narrow island, and another along the southern (gulf) side, while the third force constituted the reserve.

The attacking force advanced about three miles before encountering a Federal picket post. They overwhelmed this advanced position, but not before shots were fired that awakened the main camp of the 6th New York Infantry (Billy Wilson's Zouaves), which was located some distance east of Fort Pickens. The sleepy Zouaves put up a brief resistance before fleeing to the safety of the fort. Colonel Brown later reported that the New Yorkers "did not behave well on the occasion." After its occupants had fled, the Confederates torched the camp and much of its contents. Anderson contemplated an advance against the fort and its outlying batteries, but with "daylight appearing, and there being no longer a possibility of surprise of the batteries," he reluctantly ordered a return to the boats for reembarkation.

Colonel Brown, meanwhile, had ordered out four companies of the fort's regular army garrison under Majors Israel Vodges and Lewis Arnold, who, along with remnants of Wilson's command, skirmished sharply with the retreating Confederates. They captured a number of stragglers and fired on the rebels as they reembarked, but most of the Confederates reached the boats safely. Despite a delay caused by a fouled propeller, the attackers were able to cross the bay to the mainland before the arrival of U.S. naval ships.

Union losses in the affair totaled 13 killed, 27 wounded, and 21 missing. The latter included a number of captives, most prominently Major Vodges. Anderson later reported Confederate losses at 18 dead, 39 wounded, and 30 captured by the Federals. One of the dead was Captain Richard Bradford, for whom the Florida legislature would name a newly formed county.

After the raid on Santa Rosa Island, quiet returned to Pensacola Bay, although the Federals did mount a retaliatory artillery bombardment on 22–23 November that severely damaged Fort McRee. A similar bombardment erupted on 1 January 1862. In the spring of 1862, in the aftermath of their defeat at Fort Donelson and the loss of middle Tennessee, Confederate authorities withdrew the garrison at Pensacola, sending the troops to reinforce the main Confederate army in the Western theater. Fort Pickens remained in Union hands throughout the war, with the Federals later occupying Fort Barrancas on the mainland as well.

—*David J. Coles*

See also Florida; Fort Pickens; Pensacola.
For further reading:

Davis, William W. *The Civil War and Reconstruction in Florida* (1913).
Johns, John E. *Florida during the Civil War* (1963).
Larkin, J. L. "Battle of Santa Rosa Island." *Florida Historical Quarterly* (1959).

SAVAGE'S STATION, BATTLE OF
(29 June 1862)

The battle of Savage's Station, Virginia, which included fighting at the Peach Orchard (also called Allen's farm), took place during the Seven Days' battles of the Peninsula campaign. After the Federal defeat at Gaines' Mill on 27 June 1862, General George B. McClellan ordered the Army of the Potomac to withdraw from its position outside Richmond and begin a retreat across the Chickahominy to the James River. The line of retreat moved past Savage's Station, a depot on the Richmond & York River Railroad line and the site of a Federal field hospital established after Gaines' Mill. McClellan ordered three corps to screen the retreat by holding a position in front of Savage's Station until the bulk of the 100,000-man army crossed the White Oak Swamp. This rear guard consisted of Samuel P. Heintzelman's III Corps; VI Corps, commanded by William B. Franklin; and Edwin "Bull" Sumner's II Corps. By 29 June the Federal line of retreat stretched over five miles and ran south from Savage's Station through the White Oak Swamp. Cumbersome

supply trains, poor use of roadways, and McClellan's failure to assign overall command of the rear guard troops left the Federals vulnerable to attack.

Upon learning of the Federal withdrawal, Robert E. Lee shifted his objective from the defense of Richmond to the pursuit and destruction of McClellan. Accordingly, he ordered a series of complex troop movements designed to reposition the Confederates for a sequence of flank attacks. To buy time for these movements, Lee ordered John B. Magruder to move his division east along the York River Railroad line and to attack the Federal rear guard. To support Magruder's right, Lee directed Benjamin Huger to strike the Federal column just south of White Oak Swamp. He instructed Thomas J. "Stonewall" Jackson to secure Magruder's left flank and envelop the Federal rear. Given the widely dispersed Confederate troop positions, however, the plan required precise coordination and left much to chance.

Further complicating Lee's plan was Magruder himself. The flamboyant Virginian had been ill during the campaign and may have suffered from the side effects of morphine. During a conference with Lee on the eve of the battle, Magruder appeared exasperated and did

Field hospital at Savage's Station, Virginia, 30 June 1862 (Photograph by James F. Gibson / *Library of Congress*)

not fully comprehend the nature of Confederate troop movements on his flanks.

Although Lee's plans required swift movement, Magruder chose to wait for Jackson's arrival. Jackson, however, slowed by reconstruction of a bridge across the Chickahominy, informed Magruder that he would be delayed. Magruder also learned that Huger was not marching along his flank on the Williamsburg Road. Instead, Huger's troops were marching several miles farther to the south than Magruder expected. Thus, Magruder's 14,000 troops advanced toward the Federals unsupported on either flank. At 9:00 A.M. on 29 June, Magruder struck Sumner's 26,000 men at Orchard Station, two miles west of Savage's Station. By 11:00 A.M. the attack posed a serious threat to Sumner's exposed flanks. Beseeched by his fellow corps commanders to fall back, Sumner reluctantly withdrew to Savage's Station. Once the Federal rear guard was reunited, Heintzelman, unbeknownst to Sumner and Franklin, resumed his retreat toward White Oak Swamp.

Magruder believed that resistance at the Peach Orchard signaled a Federal assault and hurriedly sent word to Lee asking for reinforcements. Lee reluctantly ordered two brigades from Huger to join Magruder with the understanding that they would be returned if a Federal threat failed to develop by 2:00 P.M. Huger, however, noting that the fighting to Magruder's front had ceased, countermarched the brigades and continued toward his objective south of White Oak Swamp. Magruder's situation worsened with news that Jackson would not arrive until the following day. Thus, with both flanks still exposed, Magruder cautiously resumed pursuit of the Federals at 4:00 P.M.

By 5:00 P.M. Magruder made contact with the enemy. A brigade from Lafayette McLaws's division formed a line of battle along the eastern edge of the woods. From there they launched their attack across an open field in front of Savage's Station. Opposed by a brigade from John Sedgwick's division, the Confederates stubbornly pushed toward the depot. As the fighting intensified, McLaws's other brigade came up on the right. This extended the Confederate line south from Savage's Station to the Williamsburg Road. In danger of being flanked, Sumner hurriedly sent reinforcements to meet the Confederate threat on his left. Fierce fighting continued until 9:00 P.M., when a torrential rainstorm ended the battle. The Federals suffered approximately 1,000 casualties, nearly twice those of the Confederates. That night the Federal retreat continued, culminating at Malvern Hill on 1 July. Despite the lack of organization, the Federal rear guard succeeded at Savage's Station in protecting McClellan's withdrawal. Confederate failure at Savage's Station resulted from weak tactical leadership and poor execution of overall strategy.

—*Jeffery S. Prushankin*

See also Malvern Hill, Battle of; Seven Days' Battles.
For further reading:
Cullen, Joesph P. *The Peninsula Campaign, 1862: McClellan and Lee Struggle for Richmond* (1973).
Dickert, D. Augustus. *History of Kershaw's Brigade, with Complete Roll of Companies, Biographical Sketches, Incidents, Anecdotes, Etc* (1899; reprint, 1973).
Dowdey, Clifford. *The Seven Days: The Emergence of Lee* (1964).
Johnson, Robert Underwood, and Clarence Clough Buel, eds. *Battles and Leaders of the Civil War: Being for the Most Part Contributions by Union and Confederate Officers* Vol. 2 (1887).
Sears, Stephen W. *To the Gates of Richmond: The Peninsula Campaign* (1992).

SAVANNAH, GEORGIA

Savannah, Georgia, is a city and harbor on the Savannah River, which empties on Georgia's northern coast. Known for its Irish influence (the Society of Hibernians has its original lodge there), Savannah is one of the oldest settlements in Georgia, dating back to the 1730s. It grew prosperous thanks to increased Atlantic trade, especially the cotton and Triangular slave trades as well as the commerce of rice and indigo. A thriving city of 20,000 on the eve of the Civil War, it was then the second largest port installation on the nascent Confederacy's Atlantic coast after Charleston. An iconic Southern city with its lush parks, colonial cemeteries, and stately mansions, Savannah was immediately and massively prosecession. On 8 November 1860, over 3,000 of its denizens gathered to express their opposition to the election of Abraham Lincoln. The city was rich in militia units, and it is said that the Confederate armed forces adopted their distinctive cadet gray uniforms in imitation of the city's Oglethorpe Light Infantry. In January 1861, the city's main defensive stronghold, Fort Pulaski, was seized by militia colonel Alexander R. Lawton, and three months later, it was in Savannah that the Georgia Secession Convention ratified the Confederate constitution. Upon the capture of Port Royal by the Union in November 1861, Federal forces invested Savannah and proceeded to pound its defenses, including Wassaw and Thunderbolt islands, with rifled artillery. By spring 1862, Fort Pulaski, reduced to mere rubble, was captured by Union troops.

A primary port of entrance for blockade runners, Savannah actively participated in the Confederacy's naval effort under the energetic command of Commodore Josiah Tattnall. In addition to the armed merchantman named after the city, three ironclads were built in the harbor during the war, while two additional ones were never completed. Despite the blockade, the harbor thus never ceased to play its role as a commercial hub. Because of its strategic importance, Savannah was therefore chosen by General William T. Sherman, who had been stationed in Savannah as a young officer, as the objective for his March to the Sea (a.k.a. the Savannah campaign), which covered the 500 miles from Atlanta to Savannah. Having left Atlanta on 15 November 1864, Sherman reached the coast on 10 December, connecting with Admiral John A. Dahlgren's Atlantic blockading fleet and laying siege to the city. Upon the fall of Fort McAllister, without means of stopping the Union juggernaut, General William J. Hardee evacuated the city on 20 December, making Savannah, in Sherman's words, Lincoln's Christmas gift. The city was thus spared destruction. Confederate president Jefferson Davis stayed briefly in the city after the end of the war en route to his prison of Fort Monroe, Virginia.

—*Laurent Ditmann*

See also Sherman's March to the Sea.
For further reading:
Smith, Derek. *Civil War Savannah* (1997).
Wayt DeBolt, Margaret. *Savannah: A Historical Portrait* (1974).

SAVANNAH, SIEGE OF
(10–21 December 1864)

The siege of Savannah, Georgia, marked the culmination of Major General William Tecumseh Sherman's March to the Sea. Having left Atlanta on 15 November, Sherman's army marched through Georgia and arrived in the vicinity of Savannah on 10 December. By the 21st of that month, Union troops held the city.

Before Sherman approached Savannah, the Confederates constructed a series of defenses that combined human-made fortifications with natural barriers. The advance line of defense sought to protect the Charleston & Savannah Railroad and its bridge across the Savannah River. In addition to putting light artillery and infantry in position, the Confederates felled timber across the main roads leading to the city. They hoped that the Federals would turn away from Savannah when confronted with these obstacles; instead, the Union troops quickly cleared them and drove the Southern troops toward the city.

The main Confederate line of defense ran from the Savannah River across the Central Railroad, to the Atlantic & Gulf Railroad bridge and across the Little Ogeechee River. This line incorporated a series of marshes and rice fields as natural defenses. The Confederates strengthened these natural barriers by flooding the swamps and rice fields, increasing the amount of water in them by several inches to several feet. Interspersed throughout these natural barriers were almost 10,000 infantry, cavalry, and artillery drawn primarily from the Georgia Militia, Georgia State Line, and regular Confederate units. Essential to the successful resistance of Sherman's 60,000 soldiers would be the ability to hold the Charleston &

Savannah Railroad; it provided the only line of communication.

As the Union army approached the main defensive line on 10 December, Sherman ordered his commanders to besiege the city while he personally attempted to establish communications with the Union fleet. The XX Corps took position on the Union left, with its line reaching from the Savannah River to the Georgia Central Railroad. From this point west, the XIV Corps positioned itself and connected with the XVII Corps. The V Corps approached Savannah after crossing the Ogeechee River. These positions prohibited the Confederates from receiving supplies via the Savannah & Charleston Railroad and the Gulf Railroad. Confederate occupation of Fort McAllister, however, still prohibited Sherman from communicating with the Union fleet.

Fort McAllister, located on the Ogeechee River, stopped Sherman's army from being supplied by the Union boats. So, Sherman ordered the fort to be taken. On 13 December, the 2d Division of the XV Corps assaulted and carried the fort. The loss of Fort McAllister dealt the Confederates a major blow. Major General Gustavus W. Smith, commander of the Georgia Militia, later wrote in his official report, "After the fall of Fort McAllister it was clearly only a question of time when Savannah would fall into the hands of the enemy." With limited supplies, no hope of reinforcements, and only one line of communication (across the Savannah River along a narrow rice field dike), the Confederate situation turned grim.

These circumstances led Lieutenant General P. G. T. Beauregard, commander of the Military Division of the West, on 15 December to instruct Lieutenant General William J. Hardee, commander of the troops in Savannah, that it was more important to save the troops and materiel than to engage in a prolonged defense. The next day, Union troops began trying to cross to the South Carolina side of the Savannah River and threaten Hardee's only line of retreat. So, Hardee decided to begin preparations for evacuating the city. On the 17th, Sherman demanded the surrender of Savannah, and on the 18th, Hardee refused. By the 19th, three regiments from the XX Corps reached the South Carolina shore. The evacuation then was ordered for that night, but heavy fog delayed it until the next. Meanwhile, Sherman ordered his troops to prepare to assault Savannah.

Before the Federals could launch their attack, however, Hardee slipped his troops out of Savannah on the night of the 20th. By constructing a pontoon bridge made from rice-field flats lashed end-to-end, the Confederates evacuated Savannah and crossed the river to South Carolina. Union troops had observed the building of the bridge, but did not discover the successful

The evacuation of Savannah on 21 December 1864 (*Library of Congress*)

evacuation until 3 A.M. At that time, they began to move troops into the city.

After leaving Savannah, Hardee went to Hardeeville and then to Charleston. Sherman entered the city on the 22d, happy to have taken it, but disappointed that Hardee got away. The March to the Sea had ended, but Sherman next would direct his attention toward South Carolina.

—*Scott M. Langston*

See also Carolinas Campaign; Fort McAllister, Reduction of; Savannah, Georgia; Sherman's March to the Sea.

For further reading:

Jones, Charles Colcock, Jr. *The Siege of Savannah* (1874; reprint, 1988).

Schiller, Herbert M. *Fort Pulaski and the Defense of Savannah* (1997).

Smith, Gustavus W. "The Georgia Militia during Sherman's March to the Sea." In *Battles and Leaders of the Civil War* (1956).

U.S. War Department. *The War of the Rebellion: A Compilation of the Official Records of the Union and Confederate Armies* (1880–1901).

SAXTON, RUFUS
(1824–1908)
Union general

Born in Greenfield, Massachusetts, Rufus Saxton was educated at Deerfield Academy before receiving an appointment to the U.S. Military Academy. He graduated eighteenth of forty-three in the class of 1849. Between graduation and the outbreak of the Civil War, Saxton had a varied military career. He served on frontier posts, fought in the Third Seminole War in Florida, worked on coastal surveys, taught artillery at West Point, and served as an observer in Europe. When the war began he was stationed in St. Louis as an artillery officer.

On 10 May 1861, Lieutenant Saxton participated in the action directed by Captain Nathaniel Lyon (who

would be promoted to brigadier general of volunteers two days later) in breaking up the pro-Confederate enclave known as Camp Jackson. After Lyon's promotion, he named Saxton his quartermaster. At the same time Saxton was promoted to captain in the regular army. Later in the summer he became chief quartermaster on George B. McClellan's staff in western Virginia.

Much in demand for his services, in the fall of 1861 Saxton was made chief quartermaster for Thomas W. Sherman's expedition to Port Royal. During this trip, Saxton had his first encounter with the group of people the Union soldiers called contrabands. These refugee African-Americans from neighboring plantations flocked to the Federal camps. There Saxton formulated some of the ideas he would later espouse to tap this source of manpower for the Union cause.

Saxton had so impressed his various supervisors during the first year of the war that he was promoted to brigadier general of volunteers in April 1862. The following month the War Department sent him to Harper's Ferry to prevent its capture by "Stonewall" Jackson, who was then engaged in his Shenandoah Valley campaign. Saxton arrived at Harper's Ferry in the wake of Nathaniel P. Banks's defeat at Winchester on 25 May 1862. He and his men worked around the clock to secure the town and arsenal's defenses and successfully repulsed an attack by Richard Ewell on 31 May. Saxton was sent a personal thanks by Secretary of War Edwin Stanton for his success at Harper's Ferry.

In the early summer of 1862, Saxton was sent to the Department of the South, where he would spend the remainder of the war. In one of his early posts, St. Augustine, Florida, Saxton demonstrated his impatience with Southern sympathizers by expelling everyone from the town who refused to take an oath of allegiance to the Union. Given the political views of the citizens of that part of Florida, this order entailed the expulsion of a sizable portion of the town's population, including large numbers of women with no visible means of support if forced from their homes. For that reason, Saxton's order was overturned by department headquarters.

In February 1863, Saxton was placed in command of U.S. forces in Beaufort, South Carolina. He had already come to the conclusion in the fall of 1862 that Federal forces in South Carolina could be considerably augmented with African-American soldiers recruited from the former slave population. The use of such soldiers would not only solve the Federal manpower problem in South Carolina but would also more usefully employ a large part of the former slave population that the government was supporting. With Northern abolitionists coming down to organize the former slave communities, particularly around Port Royal, the employment of many of the men in the army would ease the burden on these new communities.

When Saxton assumed command at Beaufort in early 1863, he was ready to put some of his ideas to the test. In March 1863, Saxton was moved to Port Royal Island, where he insisted that all able-bodied adult African-American men be subject to the draft. For the remainder of the year he trained and equipped his troops and then sent them on expeditions along the South Carolina and Georgia coast, destroying Confederate salt works and lookout stations. He wrote his superiors that the purpose of these expeditions was twofold. The first was to accomplish the military objective of reducing the Confederate ability to make war along the coast and second was to demonstrate to Northern critics that African-Americans could make good soldiers.

In 1864 Saxton spent a brief time on Morris Island leading his troops in some of the late-summer operations there. By early 1865, however, his value to African-American recruiting efforts was deemed more important, and he was made superintendent of Volunteer Recruiting Service, Department of the South. Along with that duty he was also the inspector of settlements and plantations, Department of the South, with headquarters at Beaufort. In March, as he led his army through the Carolinas, William T. Sherman was faced with increasing numbers of refugee former slaves attaching themselves to his army. Hard pressed to feed such large numbers, Sherman ordered that all such refugees be sent to Saxton at Beaufort to be placed in one of the refugee settlements along the South Carolina coast.

When the war was over, Saxton's experience with the former slaves of the South Carolina coast led to his appointment as a Freedmen's Bureau commissioner in that area. He worked at that task until he was mustered out of the volunteer service in 1866. After that, he reverted to the quartermaster service. He remained in the army as a quartermaster at various posts, rising to the regular rank of colonel. He retired to Washington, D.C.,

in 1888. He lived there for twenty years, dying in the nation's capital on 23 February 1908.

—*David S. Heidler and Jeanne T. Heidler*

See also Harper's Ferry, (West) Virginia; United States Colored Troops.
For further reading:
Rose, Willie Lee. *Rehearsal for Reconstruction: The Port Royal Experiment* (1964).
Wise, Stephen R. *Gate of Hell: Campaign for Charleston Harbor, 1863* (1994).

SAYLER'S CREEK/HARPER'S FARM, BATTLE OF
(6 April 1865)

The battle of Sayler's Creek was the last major engagement involving Robert E. Lee's Army of Northern Virginia. On 6 April 1865, Federal forces under Generals Philip Sheridan and George Meade overtook and routed the rear elements of the Confederate column in its flight west from Amelia Court House to Farmville, Virginia. The fighting comprised three separate engagements in the valley of Little Sayler's Creek, a north-flowing tributary of the Appomattox River. All told, the Union forces captured about 7,700 men, almost one-fifth of Lee's army, including corps commander Richard S. Ewell and seven other generals.

As an incident on the march from Amelia to Farmville, the fighting on Thursday, 6 April formed part of the middle segment of Lee's retreat from Richmond and Petersburg to Appomattox. On the 5th, Lee had withdrawn his army from a stalemate with a Union force under Sheridan near Amelia. Cut off from his original plan to retreat directly to Danville via the Richmond & Danville Railroad, Lee now hoped to evade pursuit by dodging west to Farmville, then turning south around the Union flank and heading for the Danville railroad below Grant's position at Burkeville. The Army of Northern Virginia, at this point numbering about 40,000 effectives, began moving during the night, led by General James Longstreet's combined I and III Corps. Following Longstreet in order were General Richard Anderson's "Small" corps, General Richard S. Ewell's reserve corps, and finally General John B. Gordon's II Corps.

The Union troops awoke on the rainy morning of 6 April to find the Confederates gone from their front. By 9:00 A.M., however, the trailing elements of the Southern army had been located, and a pursuing force, made up primarily of Sheridan's cavalry and the II and VI Corps of the Army of the Potomac, was sent out. The first unit to engage the Confederates was the cavalry division of General George Crook, whose delaying action about one mile above the creek crossing caused a sizable gap to open between Anderson and Longstreet.

At about 2:00 P.M., General George Custer discovered the opening in the Confederate column at the crossroads near Harper's Farm, just below the creek crossing. His cavalry immediately swept into the break, routing an enemy artillery battalion and capturing most of its guns. As the rest of Anderson's corps approached, Federal reinforcements also arrived and lines of battle began to form. General Wesley Merritt assumed command as the ranking officer on the Union side.

Meanwhile, apprised of Anderson's situation ahead on the main road, General Ewell decided in the interest of speed to send his wagon trains along a secondary road to the northwest. Gordon's infantry corps also took the alternate route. Once the main body of Ewell's troops had crossed Little Sayler's Creek, Anderson formed a line of battle on either side of the road, facing back along it. Almost immediately, General Horatio Wright's VI Corps, under the field command of Sheridan, appeared in force on the opposite ridge, setting the stage for a second pitched battle scarcely a mile from the first. Ewell's and Anderson's forces stood back to back, facing Federal infantry and cavalry, respectively.

At 6:00 P.M. Merritt attacked Anderson's two divisions of infantry under Generals George Pickett and Bushrod Johnson. When Custer's troops finally pierced Pickett's line after several attempts, most of the Confederates broke for the woods and headed for the main body of Lee's army up ahead. Merritt captured 2,600 men, 300 wagons, and 15 pieces of artillery.

Wright's corps attacked Ewell concurrently with the action at Harper's Farm. After a half-hour artillery bombardment, the nearly 7,000 Federals marched in battle line to the creek, which was swollen to depths of four feet due to spring rains. A Federal assault and Confederate counterattack saw hand-to-hand fighting rage back and forth across the creek, but a second Federal charge overwhelmed the Confederate flanks, and Ewell's troops began to lay down their arms. About 3,400 men, including six generals, surrendered.

As the Confederate rear guard, John B. Gordon's corps had been harassed most of the day by the Federal II Corps under General Andrew A. Humphreys. When Gordon turned off the main road behind Ewell's wagons, Humphreys's men pursued and forced a battle about two miles to northwest, near the creek crossing at the farm of James Lockett. Although darkness halted the Federal advance, the Confederates again suffered heavy losses. Among the spoils for the II Corps were 1,700 prisoners and Ewell's entire train of over 300 wagons.

General Lee had ridden that day with Longstreet's

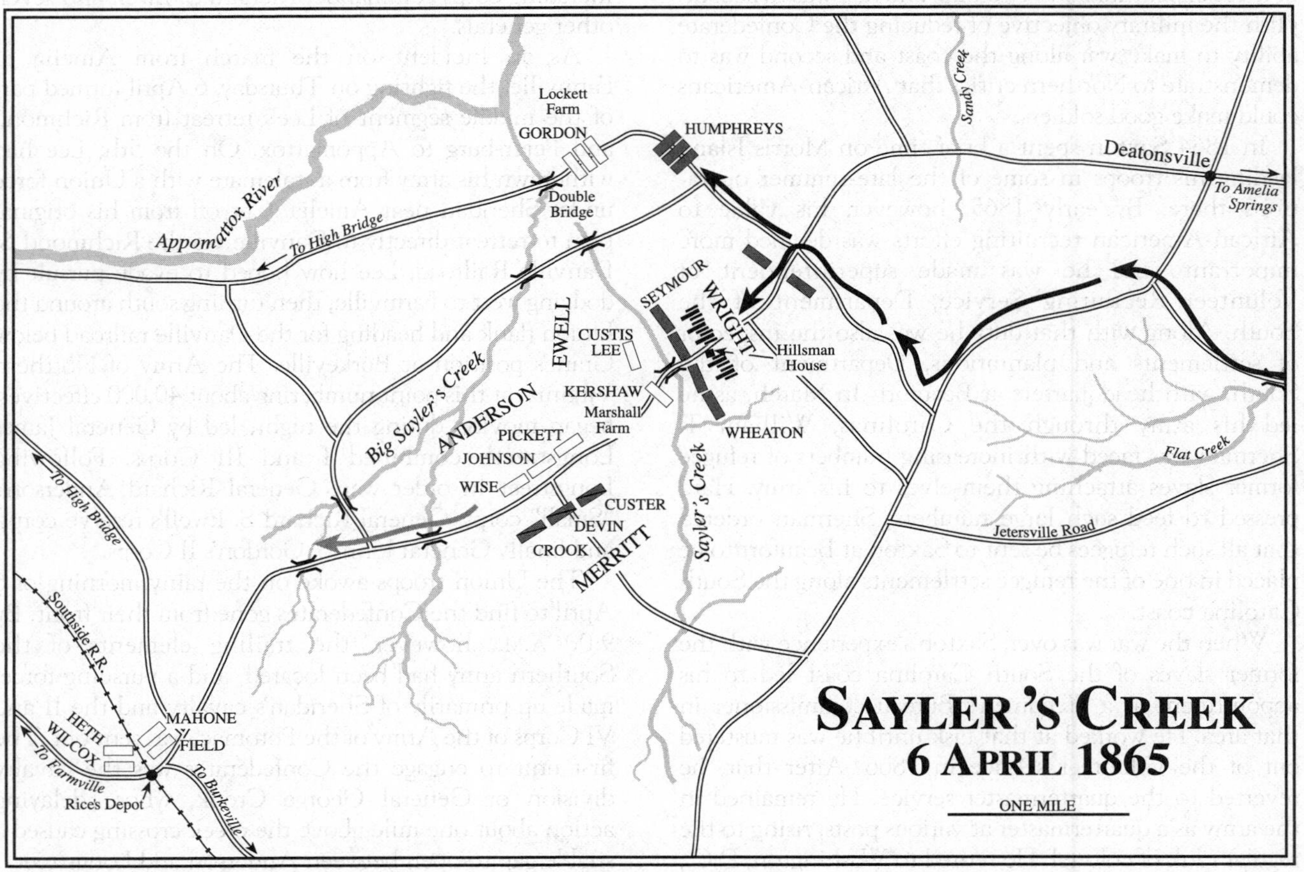

SAYLER'S CREEK
6 APRIL 1865

ONE MILE

corps, which by dark had safely reached Rice's Depot a few miles shy of Farmville. Concerned about the fighting to the rear, Lee rode back to a knoll overlooking the battlefield at Harper's Farm only to see Anderson's refugees streaming through the woods. Alarmed, he exclaimed, "My God, has the army been dissolved?"

Lee's counterpart, General Ulysses S. Grant, forwarded a message to President Lincoln from Sheridan, reporting the rout and saying, "If the thing is pressed, I believe that Lee will surrender." Lincoln replied, "Let the *thing* be pressed."

—*Charles E. Kinzer*

See also Amelia Court House/ Jetersville; Appomattox Court House; Farmville/High Bridge, Battle of.
For further reading:
Calkins, Chris M. *The Appomattox Campaign: March 29–April 9, 1865* (1997).
Davis, Burke. *To Appomattox: Nine April Days* (1959).
Korn, Jerry. *Pursuit to Appomattox: The Last Battles* (1987).

SCHENCK, ROBERT CUMMING
(1809–1890)
Union general

Born into a wealthy and influential Ohio family, Robert Schenck had a distinguished career as a politician, diplomat, and lawyer before accepting President Abraham Lincoln's offer of a commission as major general of volunteers on 5 June 1861. His brother, James Findlay Schenck, was a career naval officer who, during the Civil War, participated in both attacks on Fort Fisher and would retire with the rank of rear admiral.

Robert Schenck had served as U.S. minister to Brazil between 1851 and 1853. His influence with Lincoln stemmed from his support during the 1860 campaign, when he stumped for him in southern Illinois. Schenck's appointment was questioned and rightfully criticized by fellow Ohioans, who worried that political appointees with no military experience would be the downfall of the Union army. The Ohio general later defended his commission by stating that it was Lincoln who said, "I want to make a general out of you."

Placed under Schenck's command was a brigade of the 1st and 2d Ohio Volunteer Infantry Regiments, as well as all Ohio volunteers in east Virginia. Schenck's Ohio troops had their first encounter with the enemy on 17 June 1861 at Vienna, Virginia, and the results were disastrous. He ordered three companies of the 1st Ohio Volunteer Infantry Regiment on a reconnaissance mission along the Alexandria, Loudoun & Hampshire Railroad to search for Confederate troops reported near Fairfax, Virginia. This mission was the first time the railroad had been used for tactical purposes. When rounding a bend along the line, the Ohio troops were ambushed

by Maxcy Gregg's 1st South Carolina Infantry Regiment. As a consequence of the skirmish, the Ohioans suffered twelve casualties, while the remainder of the regiment retreated toward Washington. Ohio newspapers were very critical of Schenck for sending his green troops against the enemy and questioned his ability as a commander.

The following month, the First Manassas campaign was launched and Schenck's brigade was attached to General Nathaniel Tyler's division. After receiving unclear instructions from General Irvin McDowell, the brigade moved slowly toward the Union lines and arrived at the scene of the battle too late to participate.

In the spring of 1862, during Confederate general "Stonewall" Jackson's famous Valley campaign, Schenck was ordered to support Major General Robert Milroy in the Shenandoah Valley and commanded Union forces at the battle of McDowell, Virginia. Federal forces gave a good account of themselves, but the larger Confederate army eventually overwhelmed them. A month later at the battle of Cross Keys, Schenck commanded the right of General John C. Frémont's army, yet another Jackson victory.

During the battle of Second Bull Run, where Schenck's brigade was attached to I Corps, he was severely wounded in the arm by three bullets and was carried from the field unconscious. Promoted to major general of volunteers because of his bravery in action but with his right arm virtually useless, Schenck was removed from field duty. During his period of recovery, he returned to his home state to run against Clement L. Vallandigham in the Third Ohio Congressional District. Schenck easily won the election, but not before he was placed in command of the Middle Department with headquarters in Baltimore, Maryland. The assignment was largely administrative, but during his tenure, Schenck managed to antagonize Maryland's pro-Southern and secessionist population. His biggest mistake during his time in this command occurred before Gettysburg, when Schenck did not act upon intelligence he received that the Army of Northern Virginia was descending on Winchester. When Robert Milroy tried to defend the city without reinforcements and failed, the fall of Winchester tarnished the military careers of both Milroy and Schenck. Later that summer, a court of inquiry investigated the debacle, and both Milroy and Schenck were exonerated. No doubt Schenck's political connection with Lincoln helped sway this decision.

Having won election to Congress, Schenck resigned his commission on 5 December 1863 to devote his full attention to his political activities there. Because of his military background, he was appointed chairman of the powerful Committee on Military Affairs. In this position he was successful in gaining much-needed changes in

the conscription bill that would provide that all able-bodied men between the ages of twenty and forty-five be liable for military service.

After the Civil War, Schenck was vehemently opposed to President Andrew Johnson's Reconstruction policy. After failing to gain reelection to Congress in 1870, he was able to parlay a close relationship with President Ulysses S. Grant into an appointment as U.S. minister to England that year. Before taking on this assignment, Schenck served as a member of the joint high commission that, among other responsibilities, helped negotiate the Treaty of Washington. In addition to his military and political career, Schenck was known for his draw poker skills and published a book on the subject. While in England, Schenck became involved in the notorious Emma Mine fraud and was forced to return to the United States for the investigation. He was acquitted of all charges but never returned to public service. He died in Washington, D.C., on 23 March 1890.

—*Mitchell Yockelson*

See also Cross Keys, Battle of; McDowell, Virginia, Battle of; Winchester, Second Battle of.

For further reading:
Joyner, Fred B. "Robert Cumming Schenck: First Citizen of the Miami Valley." *The Ohio State Archaeological and Historical Quarterly.* (1949).
Therry, James R. "The Life of Robert Cumming Schenck" (Ph.D. dissertation, 1968).

SCHOFIELD, JOHN MCALLISTER
(1831–1906)
Union general

Union general John McAllister Schofield spent most of the Civil War in the Western theater, where he commanded the Army of the Ohio in the Atlanta campaign and at the battles of Franklin and Nashville. He proved to be a levelheaded, efficient commander with considerable organizational abilities.

Born in Gerry, New York, on 29 September 1831, Schofield was the oldest son of James Schofield, a Baptist minister, and Caroline McAllister Schofield. In July 1849, Schofield entered the U.S. Military Academy; he graduated seventh in his class four years later. After stints at Fort Moultrie in South Carolina and Fort Capron in Florida, Schofield returned to West Point in 1855 as an instructor in philosophy. In June 1857, he married Harriet Bartlett; they had five children, three of whom reached adulthood. In the summer of 1860, Schofield took a one-year leave of absence from West Point to teach physics at Washington University in St. Louis, Missouri.

President Abraham Lincoln's call for troops on 15 April 1861 brought an end to Schofield's teaching career. First ordered to muster in men in Missouri, he was soon named adjutant general to Brigadier General Nathaniel Lyon, who commanded Union forces in Missouri. At the battle of Wilson's Creek, in which Lyon was killed, Schofield led a charge that earned him the Medal of Honor. In November 1861, he became brigadier general of volunteers, in charge of all the militia of Missouri. Named commander of the Military District of Missouri in June 1862, Schofield disliked having to deal with the contentious political situation in Missouri and requested a return to the field. In September 1862, he was appointed commander of the Army of the Frontier in Missouri, a post he held until the following spring, when he requested a transfer due to conflict with General Samuel R. Curtis, head of the Department of Missouri.

After one month with the Army of the Cumberland in Tennessee, Schofield was ordered back to Missouri to replace Curtis. The increase in guerrilla warfare along the Kansas-Missouri border in the summer of 1863 gave Schofield considerable trouble. After the burning of Lawrence, Kansas, by Missouri guerrillas in August, Senator James Lane of Kansas and other Unionists wanted to conduct a retaliatory raid into western Missouri. When Schofield refused to allow it, they appealed to President Lincoln for his removal. While Lincoln did not view their charges as legitimate, he also wanted to resolve the Kansas-Missouri situation before the 1864 Republican presidential nominating convention. On 9 February 1864, Lincoln named Schofield commander of the Department and Army of the Ohio, a transfer he accepted with pleasure.

As head of the Army of the Ohio, Schofield joined General William Tecumseh Sherman in Dalton, Georgia, for the advance on Atlanta. After the Confederates abandoned the city, Schofield returned to Tennessee to obtain reinforcements. In October 1864, Sherman ordered him to report to General George H. Thomas, commander of the Army of the Cumberland, to help him defend Tennessee against General John Bell Hood and the Army of Tennessee. During November Schofield kept Hood at bay while Thomas reinforced Nashville. After evading Hood at Spring Hill, Schofield's troops entrenched at Franklin in preparation for crossing the Cumberland River into Nashville. Although prepared for an attack, Schofield did not expect one, but on the afternoon of 30 November, Hood launched a frontal assault on the Union position. Although both sides suffered heavy losses in the two-hour battle, Hood's Army of Tennessee endured a crushing blow, losing six generals and about one-quarter of its strength. Despite the Confederate casualties, Schofield withdrew to Nashville, as Thomas had ordered.

As Hood's army limped toward Nashville, Schofield urged Thomas to attack Hood's weakened forces quickly. Schofield disagreed with Thomas's decision to delay in favor of greater preparedness and may have intrigued to try to replace him as commander. After the Union victory at the battle of Nashville on 15–16 December 1864, Schofield further differed with Thomas's plan for a spring campaign against Hood and asked General Ulysses S. Grant for a transfer to the Eastern theater. In February 1865, Schofield took command of the newly created Department of North Carolina, and his troops entered Wilmington later that month. In April 1865, Schofield wrote up the surrender terms for General Joseph E. Johnston and the Army of Tennessee after Sherman and Johnston had reached an impasse in their negotiations.

In November 1865, Schofield began a seven-month diplomatic mission to France to persuade Emperor Napoleon III to remove the puppet government he had installed in Mexico. After returning to the United States, Schofield in August 1866 was sent to Richmond as commander of the Department of the Potomac. Although he opposed the Fourteenth Amendment's disfranchisement provisions, Schofield encouraged the Virginia legislature to accept the amendment to avoid harsher terms. He gained the support of Virginia conservatives because of his conciliatory stance toward former Confederates and his elitist support for a qualified suffrage based on education. After passage of the Reconstruction Acts of March 1867, Schofield became head of the First Military District, which encompassed Virginia. Although he viewed the Reconstruction Acts as too punitive, Schofield fulfilled his responsibility of setting up voter registration for a constitutional convention and administering the election of delegates. Radical Republicans, for whom Schofield showed great disdain, dominated the convention. Dismayed by the convention's handiwork, he postponed the vote on the proposed constitution because Congress had not appropriated money for it.

Schofield's moderate Republicanism led to his appointment as secretary of war on 1 June 1868, as part of the compromise between President Andrew Johnson and moderate Republican senators that had resulted in the exoneration of Johnson on impeachment charges. Schofield relinquished the office after President Grant's inauguration. Schofield's later posts included superintendent of West Point, commander of the Division of the Pacific, head of the Division of the Missouri, commander of the Division of the Atlantic, and commanding general of the army from 1888 to 1895, when he retired as lieutenant general. In 1897, Schofield published his memoirs, in which he described the Civil War as a destructive conflict that had caused "permanent national injury, irreparable in all future time." Schofield died on 4 March 1906 in St. Augustine, Florida.

—*Antoinette G. van Zelm*

See also Army of the Ohio; Franklin, Battle of; Nashville, Battle of.

For further reading:

Lowe, Richard G. "Virginia's Reconstruction Convention: General Schofield Rates the Delegates." *Virginia Magazine of History and Biography* (1972).

McDonough, James L. *Schofield: Union General in the Civil War and Reconstruction* (1972).

Schofield, John McAllister. *Forty Six Years in the Army* (1897).

Sefton, James E., ed. "Aristotle in Blue and Braid: General John M. Schofield's Essays on Reconstruction." *Civil War History* (1971).

Weigley, Russell F. "The Military Thought of John M. Schofield." *Military Affairs* (1959).

SCHURZ, CARL
(1829–1906)
Union general

Born on 2 March 1829 near Liblar in the Rhineland, Germany, Carl Schurz began secondary school in Cologne in 1839, receiving his diploma in 1847, the year he enrolled as a matriculated student at the University of Bonn. Involved in the failed Revolution of 1848–1849, he immigrated with his wife, Margaretha Meyer, to the United States in 1852. In 1855, they settled in Watertown, Wisconsin, in the midst of a well-populated, mostly Democratic, German area.

Schurz spontaneously sought his future in national politics, as the antislavery movement was the one issue then that he could identify with. Joining the Republican Party shortly after its birth, he felt obligated from the start to bring to it a significant increase of the German-American vote. Faithfully supporting John C. Frémont, their presidential candidate in 1856, Schurz gave his first political speech (in German) on antislavery expansion at a Republican meeting in Jefferson, Wisconsin. (Frémont won a respectable majority of 12,669 votes in the state over James Buchanan, the Democratic candidate.) Invited also by the Republican State Committee of Illinois, he spoke in Chicago (in English), where he passionately made clear and plausible the inherent incompatibility between slavery and democratic government. In his distinguished Boston lecture, "True Americanism" (18 April 1859), Schurz maintained that liberty and equality of rights ensured the stability of democracy.

Rejecting the breakup of the Democratic Party in 1856 into the Northern and Southern factions, Schurz viewed it as a power play between their respective leaders, Stephen Arnold Douglas and James Buchanan. In his speech on 16 October 1857, at Madison, Wisconsin, Schurz gave only minor attention to the Southern Democratic wing, directing his rancor at Douglas, the author of the Kansas-Nebraska Act of 1854 that had popularized his doctrine of Popular Sovereignty. He thought Douglas unprincipled and lacking moral

courage for reopening the dispute over slavery expansion by leaving the decision to approve or disapprove slavery to the Western territories themselves. Schurz argued that the Constitution did not recognize the right of slave ownership, contending that slavery was not a national institution but rather a completely sectional or local one. He repeated his assertion in his Chicago speech, "The Irrepressible Conflict" (28 September 1858), which drew national attention.

Schurz first met Abraham Lincoln—whose central thought in his speeches was that slavery was wrong—at the time of the sixth Lincoln-Douglas debate, held 13 October 1858, in Quincy, Illinois. He campaigned for Lincoln in his race for the U.S. Senate, speaking in both English and German to German immigrants. The legislature reelected Douglas by a vote of fifty-four (Democrats) to forty-six (Republicans). (Schurz, a declared lifelong Independent, whose speeches were not strongly partisan and with hardly any notion of his being a party man in the strict sense of the term, called it a "pernicious" practice for a narrow partisan-controlled legislature to decide the election.)

In 1860, Schurz was named chairman of the Wisconsin delegation to the Republican National Convention in Chicago. Committed to William H. Seward, whom he had first met in Washington in 1854, Schurz wrote to his wife on 9 March 1860, that he "should be very well satisfied with either Seward or Lincoln." Seeing Lincoln's presidential campaign as his fight, Schurz's participation in it was impressive. As a member of the Republican National Executive Committee heading the "foreign department," he helped draft the antislavery expansion plank and reminded the convention to make its opposition to nativism unmistakably clear. Lincoln, who approved Schurz's campaign tactics that included virtually limiting his own activity to the doubtful states, valued the German-American vote. With Schurz's estimate of 300,000 German-Americans already shifted over to the Republican Party, the gifted speaker fought intensely and effectively for Lincoln. Schurz's masterly address, "The Doom of Slavery," delivered in English on 1 August 1860 in St. Louis, was still another accusatory speech aimed at Douglas and was Schurz's first in a slave state. In it, he pointed out the unsuitability of slavery in an industrial age.

Lincoln was affected forcibly by Schurz's labor. On 10 February 1861, the president-elect and Schurz met to review the draft of the inaugural address; it was evident to Schurz that Lincoln had made no concessions to the defiant South. On 6 March 1863, Schurz spoke at the Cooper Institute in New York on "Reconciliation by Emancipation," submitting that an enduring Union required an antislavery policy whose objective would be to restore Southern loyalty to the Union. He made that argument again in "The Treason of Slavery" (7 October 1864) in Brooklyn.

Appointed minister to Spain in 1861, Schurz had already urged Lincoln to implement an emancipation policy that he believed would dissuade European intervention or recognition of the Confederacy and that would also arrest the secessionist movement. Upon his resignation as minister in April 1862, the national Republican leadership commissioned him, an avid student of military history, a brigadier general and in 1863 the "political general" was promoted to major general. He was on the battlefield at the second battle of Bull Run, at Chancellorsville, and at Gettysburg.

Although Schurz was a Radical Republican, he was steadfast in his loyalty to Lincoln. Concluding that Lincoln's course of action pointed toward the achievement of the war's objectives, Schurz believed that the success of the Union cause hinged wholly on the president's winning a second term. He campaigned fervently for Lincoln's reelection in 1864, keeping German-Americans in the ranks of the Republican Party. In his speaking tour in New York, Pennsylvania, and the Middle West, he pleaded for staying the course until victory came. On 28 October 1864, addressing Democrats in Philadelphia, he spoke again on the theme of "Liberty and Union."

Years later, Schurz evaluated President Lincoln thusly: "… his singular power over their [his fellow-men] minds and hearts… fitted him to be the greatest leader in the greatest crisis of our national life." At the request of Andrew Johnson, Schurz visited Southern states in 1865 to assess the impact of the president's Reconstruction program. His well-documented report on the region's social and economic conditions was a harsh criticism of Johnson for emboldening the unrepentant South and thus imperiling the rights of the emancipated slaves. Schurz proposed Republican retention of control over the South until a free-labor society was firmly established that included protection of the civil rights of Southern Unionists of both races and provision for the right of the freed slaves to vote and to elementary schooling. Schurz decided that Ulysses S. Grant should be nominated president, and, after the Republican National Convention of 1868 where Schurz was the keynote speaker, he campaigned for him. By then, Schurz began to veer toward leniency for the South, commensurate with the level of its loyalty to the Union and with public safety. In 1869 Schurz was elected as a Republican by the Missouri legislature to the U.S. Senate, the highest political office he had sought. In 1870 Senator Schurz, by then a civil service reformer, significantly influenced the Liberal Republican movement in Missouri. Its spread resulted in a national convention (over which Schurz presided) in 1872 in Cincinnati to oppose Grant's reelection.

As President Hayes's secretary of the interior, Schurz

applied the merit system to his department. Schurz supported the Democrat, Grover Cleveland, for president in 1884, 1888, and 1892. As a resident of New York City from 1881 on (Schurz's first home in America), he championed the cause of good government. Schurz was president of the National Civil Service Reform League (from 1892 to 1900) and of the Civil Service Reform Association of New York (from 1893 to 1906). He wrote, both as a journalist and a historian, producing in 1887 a notable two-volume biography of Henry Clay. Schurz died in New York City on 14 May 1906.

—Bernard Hirschhorn

See also Abolitionist Movement; German-Americans; Radical Republicans.

For further reading:
Bancroft, Frederic, ed. *The Writings of Carl Schurz: Speeches, Correspondence and Political Papers of Carl Schurz.* Vol. 1 (1913).
Easum, Chester Verne. *The Americanization of Carl Schurz* (1929).
Fuess, Claude Moore. *Carl Schurz: Reformer, 1829–1906* (1932).
Schurz, Carl. "Abraham Lincoln." *Atlantic Monthly* (1891).
Trefousse, Hans Louis. *Carl Schurz: A Biography* (1982).
Wersich, Rüdiger B., ed. *Carl Schurz: Revolutionary and Statesman: His Life in Personal and Official Documents with Illustrations* (1979).

SCOTT, DRED
(ca.1795–1858)
Supreme Court litigant

Dred Scott, a litigant in the famous 1857 U.S. Supreme Court case *Scott v. San[d]ford*, was born to slave parents in Virginia sometime between the years 1795 and 1809. Although the details related to his suit against John Sanford and his earlier suit against Irene Emerson provide information about his adult life, very little can be confirmed about Scott's early years.

Peter Blow of Southampton County, Virginia, owned Scott, but how and when Scott was acquired is unknown. In 1818, Scott accompanied Blow and his family on their move from Virginia to a cotton plantation in Alabama. The Blows and Scott remained in Alabama for twelve years.

In 1830, Peter Blow—along with his wife, Elizabeth, three daughters, four sons, and six slaves—moved to St. Louis, Missouri. There the family opened a boarding house, but tragedy struck when Elizabeth died in 1831 and Peter died less than a year later. Blow left the bulk of his estate to his youngest sons Taylor and William Thomas and to his unmarried daughters Elizabeth and Martha Ella. Realizing that the family had more slaves than it needed in St. Louis, Blow sold one slave before his death and his family sold another after his death. Dred Scott was one of these slaves, but it is not clear which one. Scott later claimed that Blow had sold him to Dr.

John Emerson, but in 1907 the widow of the youngest Blow child stated that Scott had been "assigned" to the younger Elizabeth Blow after her father's death. In this case, Scott would have been hired out and his earnings would have been used to support Elizabeth.

Although no known record of the transaction exists, Dred Scott was sold to John Emerson sometime between 1830 and 1833. In October 1833, Emerson received an appointment as an assistant surgeon in the U.S. Army, effective December 1833. In November of that year, Emerson left St. Louis for Fort Armstrong, Illinois, and Scott accompanied him. In 1836, the army transferred Emerson to Fort Snelling in Wisconsin Territory, near present-day St. Paul, Minnesota. Again Scott accompanied his owner. Consequently, Scott lived as a slave in a free state for more than two years before he moved to a territory that prohibited slavery under the Missouri Compromise of 1820.

Sometime between May 1836 and September 1837, Scott married Harriet Robinson. Major Lawrence Taliaferro, an Indian agent at Fort Snelling, owned Robinson and he either gave Robinson to Scott or he sold her to Emerson. Regardless, upon marrying Scott, Robinson became Emerson's property. The union ultimately produced four children, two boys (both of whom died in infancy) and two girls, and it lasted until Scott's death in 1858. It was the first marriage for Robinson and the second for Scott, the latter having had a wife who was sold away from him. Once they were married, the Scotts worked for Emerson, who also hired them out to others.

In October 1837, the army transferred Emerson from Fort Snelling to Fort Jessup, Louisiana. Instead of accompanying him on this move, the Scotts remained at Fort Snelling, where Emerson hired them out to various officers. In the spring of 1838, however, after his marriage to Eliza Irene Sanford, Emerson sent for the Scotts. The following September, the army transferred Emerson back to Fort Snelling and the Scotts accompanied him and his wife. This marked the second time that Emerson had settled with Scott in an area in which the Missouri Compromise declared slavery illegal.

In the fall of 1842, Emerson finally left his position as assistant surgeon after the army granted him an honorable discharge. Subsequently, he returned to St. Louis, then settled in Davenport in the spring of 1843. Several months later, in December 1843, John Emerson died, leaving the bulk of his estate to his wife. After her husband's death, Irene Emerson hired the Scotts out to several individuals, but there is little documentation concerning the Scotts' whereabouts between 1843 and 1846. By March 1846, the Scotts were definitely back in St. Louis, and it was at that time that Dred Scott attempted to buy freedom for himself and his family. Mrs. Emerson refused his request.

On 6 April 1846, the Scotts filed petitions in the

Missouri Circuit Court in St. Louis, requesting permission to bring suit against Mrs. Emerson for their freedom. They based their request on the fact that they had lived as slaves on free soil for several years. The judge granted them leave to sue.

On 30 June 1847, *Dred Scott v. Irene Emerson* came to trial and the verdict was issued on the same day. Although the attorney could easily prove that Scott had lived on free soil for an extended time, he was unable to establish that Scott was actually owned by Mrs. Emerson. Consequently, the jury ruled in favor of the defendant. In 1850 the case was retried and Scott won, but following Mrs. Emerson's appeal, the Missouri Supreme Court reversed the lower court decision in 1852. Not long after the decision, Mrs. Emerson moved to Massachusetts, married Calvin C. Chaffee, and left the Scotts under the control of her brother, John Sanford. This shift in control enabled Scott's lawyer to initiate a new suit in 1853, against John Sanford. In February 1856, *Dred Scott v. John F. A. San[d]ford* reached the U.S. Supreme Court, and in March 1857 Dred Scott finally lost his eleven-year struggle for freedom.

After the Court's decision, it was revealed that Calvin Chaffee, not John Sanford, owned Scott. Chaffee, an antislavery congressman from Massachusetts who was completely unaware of his connection to Scott until 1857, hastened to rectify this embarrassing situation. In May of that year, he manumitted Scott to Taylor Blow, Scott's longtime friend. This transfer was necessary because Missouri law stipulated that only a resident of the state could free a slave.

On 26 May 1857, Dred Scott was finally emancipated. He and his wife remained in St. Louis, where they worked as a porter and a laundress, respectively. Sixteen months later, on 17 September 1858, Dred Scott, who in seeking his freedom had led the U.S. Supreme Court to declare the Missouri Compromise unconstitutional and who had contributed to the coming of the American Civil War, died a free man.

—*Jennifer L. Bertolet*

See also *Dred Scott* Case.

For further reading:
Ehrlich, Walter. *They Have No Rights: Dred Scott's Struggle for Freedom* (1979).
Fehrenbacher, Don E. *The Dred Scott Case: Its Significance in American Law and Politics* (1978).
Potter, David M. *The Impending Crisis, 1848–1861* (1976).

SCOTT, WILLIAM CAMPBELL
(1809–1865)

Confederate colonel and Virginia politician

A member of Virginia's Secession Convention and a Confederate officer, W. C. Scott, as he signed himself, shared in the creation and the defense of Confederate Virginia.

After graduating from Hampden-Sydney College (1827) and receiving a law degree from the University of Virginia (1829), Scott returned to his Powhatan County birthplace and began the legal career that would occupy most of the rest of his life. At around the same time, he joined a local militia company and was elected its first lieutenant. Subsequently he rose by election to command the company and later the 102d Regiment of Virginia militia. Commissioned a colonel by the governor in consequence of the latter role, he was later promoted to brigadier general of militia.

In civilian politics, Scott served two terms in the Virginia House of Delegates and won the Know-Nothing nomination to represent the Richmond area in Congress in 1856, defeating John Minor Botts for the nomination but losing the general election. A member of the Virginia State Convention of 1861, he voted for Virginia's secession and chaired the Committee on Military Affairs. As chairman, it was Scott who introduced the resolution calling upon the governor to appoint Robert E. Lee commander of the military and naval forces of Virginia.

As the strains of massive mobilization left militia generals without effective commands, Scott secured appointment as colonel of the newly formed 44th Virginia Volunteer Infantry Regiment. Shortly after the 44th and its officers were accepted into Confederate service, it was ordered to Beverly in western Virginia to reinforce Robert Garnett's defense against George McClellan's Union incursion. Positioned at the eastern foot of Rich Mountain to defend against an anticipated flank attack that never came, the regiment was summoned late on 11 July 1861 to march to the top to assist a Confederate detachment resisting a surprise attack. As he approached the site of the action, Scott observed that he had arrived too late: Union forces had already overrun the Confederate position and had seized terrain almost impossible to assault from where he was. Fearing attack and encirclement, he retreated to Beverly, then eastward across Cheat Mountain.

The battle of Rich Mountain, although involving relatively few soldiers, was the first major Confederate reverse of the young war. Observers in the Confederate army and government and in the press, seeking an explanation, fastened upon Scott's failure to enter the fray atop the mountain and his subsequent retreat, which had left much of western Virginia to Union occupation. Robert E. Lee informed Scott that a court of inquiry would be convened to examine his conduct. Statements attacking and defending him appeared in Southern newspapers. The Confederate Congress began its own investigation. Neither the court of inquiry nor the congressional investigation came to fruition, but the battle in the press persisted into the twentieth century.

Scott, meanwhile, continued in command of the

44th, participating in the remainder of the 1861 Mountain campaign and taking leave from time to time to attend further meetings of the Secession Convention in Richmond and to recover from unspecified illness. Appointed to brigade command in the spring of 1862, he fought in that capacity under Thomas J. "Stonewall" Jackson at the battle of McDowell (8 May 1862) and for most of the remainder of the Valley campaign. At Port Republic (9 June 1862), Scott's brigade performed notable service, stalling the major Union thrust with an almost suicidal charge, then regrouping to support Richard Taylor's final successful assault on "the coaling." Praising this remarkable performance, Richard Ewell noted, "It would be difficult to find another instance of volunteer troops after a severe check rallying and again attacking the enemy," and commended Scott's "undoubted courage at a critical moment."

Scott engaged in no significant military action after that, eventually resigning his commission "in consequence of the delicate state of my health." In late 1863, he sought reinstatement, this time as a brigadier general, but his efforts and the support of prominent political and military figures (including Ewell) were insufficient to overcome the opposition of Robert E. Lee. For the remainder of the war, he practiced law in Powhatan, often successfully defending slaves accused of crimes. He expired with Confederate Virginia, dying at his home not fifty miles from Appomattox on the day of Lee's surrender.

—*Thomas Lynwood Powers*

See also Rich Mountain, Battle of; Shenandoah Valley Campaign (1862).

SCOTT, WINFIELD
(1786–1866)
Commanding general of the U.S. Army

After attending the College of William and Mary and spending a year reading law, Winfield Scott's quest for glory led him into military service. Commissioned a captain of artillery in 1808, he emerged from the War of 1812 the youngest general in the army, having garnered fame at the battles of Chippewa and Lundy's Lane (5 and 25 July 1814). After the war he diligently sought to incorporate professionalism into the U.S. Army by writing the first comprehensive set of army regulations and infantry tactical manuals. An admirer of European armies and a student of the Napoleonic Wars, Scott used the French model in his efforts to improve the regular army.

His knowledge of conventional tactics proved of little value in waging war against Indian tribes of the Southeast. His failure to subjugate the Seminoles in Florida and the Creeks in Alabama and Georgia in 1836

resulted in an inquiry into his conduct, but the court eventually cleared him of wrongdoing. He participated in the Trail of Tears in 1838 and skillfully negotiated settlements in border disputes with Canada before his promotion to commanding general of the army in 1841. By this time Scott had acquired the nickname "Old Fuss and Feathers." The first part of the sobriquet resulted from his strict adherence to military discipline as well as his frequent disputes with fellow officers and civilian superiors. The last half derived from his love of ornate uniforms replete with gold sash, sword, shoulder epaulets, and cocked hat.

Scott's crowning achievement came during the war with Mexico. His leadership in the Mexico City campaign in 1847 served as a model of skillful planning and execution. That more than a hundred Civil War generals served as lower-grade officers in Scott's army in Mexico indicates a strong link between the two wars. During his campaign, Scott illustrated the importance of competent staffs, thorough reconnaissance, pacification of local inhabitants, and flank attacks, and the conduct of numerous Civil War battles indicates that many of his subordinates learned the art of war from him.

During the secession crisis in 1861 the seventy-five-year-old Scott, still on active duty as the army's highest-ranking officer, chose to part with his native state of Virginia and remain loyal to the Union. He did not, however, as is often purported, offer Robert E. Lee command of the Union army, despite the fact that he once described Lee as the best soldier he ever saw in the field. In the early weeks of Abraham Lincoln's administration, Scott advised the evacuation of Fort Sumter in Charleston harbor as a goodwill gesture toward the South. Many officials, including the president, rejected such an unpopular proposal as politically unacceptable. Scott's age and physical infirmities caused some to question his mental capacity, and his birthplace made others suspect his true loyalties.

Called on by the president to develop a strategy for subjugating the Confederacy, Scott formulated a comprehensive plan. The strategy called for a naval blockade of Southern ports along the Atlantic and Gulf coasts and an advance down the Mississippi River, capturing that major waterway with a land force of 80,000. The plan's heavy reliance on water for its communication and supply lines took advantage of the fact that the South had no navy with which to disrupt the Northern vessels. This encirclement would gradually crush the Confederacy economically by isolating it from the rest of the world. Critics of the elaborate scheme sarcastically dubbed it the Anaconda Plan after the giant snake that squeezes the life out of its prey. Anticipating a short war, these critics charged that Scott's strategy would take too long to accomplish its goal. Scott,

however, urged patience, and he devised a plan that he believed would create an overpowering advantage for the North while limiting the loss of life. It also reflected the realization that in 1861 the North lacked the troops necessary to mount multiple land offensives to conquer thousands of square miles of enemy territory. Though initially rejected, the North eventually enacted the major components of the Anaconda Plan.

In the summer of 1861, with growing pressure from the administration to act, Scott reluctantly approved an advance in northern Virginia that led to the battle of First Bull Run. A proponent of thorough training and preparation, Scott saw his fears realized when the inexperienced Union troops were defeated and sent running back to Washington. His caution along with his old age gradually caused administration officials to look elsewhere for military counsel. George McClellan, the new commander of the Army of the Potomac, soon began to replace Scott as the administration's chief adviser. By autumn the rigors of the job were more than Scott could manage. At over 300 pounds he suffered from gout, dropsy, and rheumatism; he was unable to mount a horse or to climb stairs unassisted. Because of his failing health, Scott resigned on 31 October.

Although he left public life, Scott's influence on Civil War generalship remained. Many of his subordinates, now commanding their own armies, executed turning movements at places like Chancellorsville, Pea Ridge, and the Wilderness that were reminiscent of those carried out at Cerro Gordo, Contreras, and other battlefields of the Mexican-American War. And McClellan's Peninsula campaign (1862) was remarkably similar to the Mexico City campaign. Scott published his *Memoirs* in 1864, and he died at West Point in 1866.

—*Timothy D. Johnson*

See also Anaconda Plan; Lee, Robert Edward; McClellan, George Brinton.

For further reading:

Elliott, Charles Winslow. *Winfield Scott: The Soldier and the Man* (1937).

Johnson, Timothy D. *Winfield Scott: The Quest for Military Glory* (1998).

SECESSION

The verb "to secede" is derived from the Latin *secedere*, meaning "to withdraw" and referring to any act of withdrawal. Originally introduced in the seventeenth century as a concept of political theory, secession assumed the existence of the modern state, as well as the possibility of dismemberment of that state. In an American context, secession has been understood as the withdrawal by the Southern states from the Federal Union following the election of Abraham Lincoln to the presidency in November 1860.

The structure of the political system, the original intentions of some framers of the Constitution, and the citizenry's prevailing understanding of the political order during the early Republic encouraged a diversity of opinions regarding the fundamental nature of the Union. Concerns arose in many quarters during the Constitutional Convention and ratification process, especially among the anti-Federalists, who feared that an overbearing national government would assume the authority of the states. Article Two of the Articles of Confederation had contained explicit provisions for protecting states, initiating a system whereby "each state retains its sovereignty." Various early state constitutions included provisions outlining the primacy of states in the confederal arrangement, often at the expense of a unified political order. The most popular form of amendment requested during the state ratification conventions for the Federal Constitution and proposed to the First Congress concerned a reserved powers clause. The defenders of the Constitution argued that such a provision was unnecessary. James Madison suggested in *The Federalist* No. 39 that each state was "a sovereign body" only "bound by its voluntary act" of ratification. Other Federalists, including James Wilson, Alexander Hamilton, and John Marshall at the Virginia ratifying convention, held that such a proposal was already present in the Constitution and that the new government would only have the powers delegated to it. Opposition to, and suspicion of, the proposed Constitution on the grounds that it would infringe upon the privileged status of the states was widespread. The defenders of state authority viewed the states as the repository of reserved power, and many believed that states were invested with an equal, and perhaps superior, capacity to judge infractions against the federal government. The most significant assurances to this effect came in the Virginia ratifying convention from George Nicholas and Edmund Randolph. As the spokesmen for the committee that reported the instrument of ratification, they noted that the Constitution would only have the powers "expressly" delegated to it. If Federalists disagreed with the stress on state authority, they generally viewed a reserved power clause as innocuous, and Madison included such a provision among the amendments he introduced in 1789.

In the first Congress, Elbridge Gerry, a founder and anti-Federalist elected to the House of Representatives, introduced a proposal reminiscent of the Articles of Confederation, leaving to the states all powers "not expressly delegated" to the federal government. Gerry's proposal was defeated, in part due to concerns about the similarity between the language of his amendment and the Articles. Others who took a states' rights or strict constructionist view of the Constitution, including Thomas Jefferson, persisted in defending state power. Before ratification of the Tenth Amendment, Jefferson

advised President Washington that incorporating a national bank was unconstitutional, basing his opinion on the Tenth Amendment. Jefferson would later compose the Kentucky Resolutions, which defended the states as the sovereign building blocks of the American nation and noted that the states retained a means of protection when threatened. To describe the process of state action, Jefferson supplied a new term, *nullification*, to note the immediacy and severity of the "remedy" necessary to prohibit the federal government from absorbing state authority.

Defenders of the federal government, sometimes described as nationalists or loose constructionists, argued that the Congress must assume more power if the needs of the country were to be met. Most prominent among the advocates of increased federal authority was Alexander Hamilton. For Hamilton, the explicit protection of state prerogatives, or providing a mechanism against secession, was unnecessary, as the political order already protected states. The Constitution, according to the nationalists, already contained provisions for the exercise of federal power, including the "necessary and proper" and "supremacy" clauses.

The Supreme Court addressed the controversy in its *McCulloch v. Maryland* (1819) decision. The high Court upheld the constitutionality of a national bank, even though such an institution was not specified in the Constitution. In dismissing a strict delineation of state and federal authority, the Court under the leadership of John Marshall extended the powers of Congress at the expense of the states. On the other hand, the Marshall Court affirmed the excepted notion that police powers belonged exclusively to the states. Under Chief Justice Roger Brooke Taney (1836–1864), the Court assumed more of a strict constructionist posture.

The emerging defense of state authority, and ultimately the secession of the South, was an interpretation of the American political experience, with an emphasis upon the perceived original dispersion of authority, sovereignty, and restraint within the Constitution of 1787. According to this interpretation, offered by John C. Calhoun and Robert Y. Hayne among others, the original system was predicated upon reserving the states' sphere of authority, while delegating sufficient authority for particular and limited responsibility to the general government. For Calhoun, this original diffusion, buttressed by a prudent mode of popular rule, was the primary achievement of American politics. A necessary corollary to his understanding of the regime's historical evolution was the need to perpetuate the original vision of the Union for posterity's sake: "The Union: Next to our liberty, the most dear; may we all remember that it can only be preserved by respecting the rights of the states and distributing equally the benefit and the burden of Union," urged Calhoun. If, as Calhoun

suggested, America had "departed" from its "original character and structure," a recovery of the older design was necessary.

For the defenders of states' rights and secession, the Declaration of Independence initiated the legitimate delineation of state and federal authority and a properly constituted mode of popular rule through first articulating the primary nature of the Union. According to this view, which was shared by many Southerners, the Declaration illuminated and explained the foundations of the American republic as also resting upon a political compact. In contradistinction to a social compact, a political compact did not unite individuals or governments. Instead, such an agreement formed a republic with the same equality of rights among the states composing the union, as among the citizens composing the states themselves. The Declaration encouraged a political compact that had developed with "time and experience" into a model of political and social stability. The Declaration preserved the locus of authority within each individual state, and allowed for secession when government "becomes destructive of these ends, it is the right of the people to alter or abolish it." For many Americans, the Declaration of Independence expressed the foundation for popular rule and a territorial republic that came to fruition in the Constitution. While the Declaration appropriately described the status of "Free and Independent States" as intrinsic to the republic, the document also confirmed the conceptional thesis of secessionist political theory: the states "ordained" or created the Republic. If the Declaration of Independence supplied the prologue to the original design for the Republic, it was the Articles of Confederation, the first American embodiment of the design, that incorporated this insight into the fundamental law of the regime. For Southerners, the provisions and language of the Articles served as an authentic precursor to the American Constitution. The Constitution of 1787 was incomprehensible without first assimilating the defense of states' rights contained in the Articles. Drafted in stages from 1776 to 1777, the Articles extended and revised the Declaration's ennobling of diffused authority and the delineation of state autonomy, while establishing popular rule based upon the deliberative, decentralized, community-centered participation of the citizenry. As in the case of the Declaration, the Articles perpetuated the original design for the territorial division of the country, into independent and sovereign states, on which the secessionist argument would later rest.

By strengthening the foundations laid by the Articles, the Constitution provided the final and most profound manifestation of the secessionist view's defense of popular rule and the diffusion of political authority. While the Declaration and Articles contributed to this

evolving discernment, the Constitution presented the definitive maturation from a confederacy to a federal government, resting upon the authentic, organic, and delineatory manifestations of the states, although the citizenry retained final and complete political authority. Such a constitution, in Calhoun's view, was most appropriately identified as a concurrent constitution because it served primarily as an exemplification of the states' role in preserving the regime. The Constitution also provided a careful "enumeration" and "specification" of power consigned to the general government. In other words, by forming a concurrent foundation for the political order, it was argued that in times of crisis the states should exert their concurrent prerogative and repossess certain delegated power from the federal government if needed and in accord with the Constitution—especially in situations in which the federal government had usurped power from the states. Through the adoption of the Constitution, the American people accepted a "joint supplemental government" that retained the states as the primary voice of the people.

In situations in which the general government and the states were in conflict, each possessed a "mutual negative" on the other's actions, according to the secessionist argument. Defenders of secession often cited the record of the Virginia ratifying convention and the Tenth Amendment to the Constitution as primary evidence of the doctrine. The Virginia convention provided, along with its New York counterpart, the most erudite and complete commentary on the interpretation of the fundamental law besides the records of the Constitutional Convention itself. In situations of disputed authority, the states possessed the right of self-protection, with secession serving as the ultimate manifestation of such a response.

Struggles over the basis of the Union arose after the ratification of the Constitution, including Jefferson's and Madison's response to President John Adams and the Alien and Sedition Acts of 1798. Defenders of state and national supremacy often changed positions depending on their political needs. In an effort to reduce the hardships incurred by the War of 1812, some New Englanders held a convention in Hartford, Connecticut, in 1814, as New England states were threatening secession. The first debate over secession in America took place in New England, not in the South.

The ensuing crises over Missouri statehood (1819–1820) and nullification (1832–1833) increased secessionist tensions, but these problems were resolved by compromise. The problem of slavery, compounded by the rise of abolitionism, would intensify the conflict. After Southerners were able to defeat the Wilmot Proviso, the Compromise of 1850 made resolution of the slavery problem more problematic. In 1854 Senator Stephen A. Douglas of Illinois, attempting to garner

support from Southern congressmen for his legislation that would organize the territories of Kansas and Nebraska, reopened the issue of extending slavery into new areas. The passage of the Kansas-Nebraska Act unified resistance to slavery in the North, and by 1854 the Republican Party was dominant in the region. The election of James Buchanan to the presidency in 1856 and the ill-fated ruling of the Supreme Court in the *Dred Scott* case in 1857, widened the sectional divide.

Lincoln's election in 1860 galvanized Southern attitudes in favor of secession. In Lincoln the South saw a threat to its established way of life and fundamental rights. The success of a minority political party, the Republicans, in electing a president was a source of some disdain as well. Agitated by the more radical advocates of secession, known as "fire-eaters," and the failure of other efforts to ameliorate the tension, South Carolina withdrew from the Union, having passed a secession ordinance on 20 December 1860. South Carolina was followed in quick succession by Mississippi, Florida, Alabama, Georgia, Louisiana, and Texas. After the incident at Fort Sumter in April 1861, and Lincoln's call for troops, Virginia, Arkansas, Tennessee, and North Carolina adopted secession ordinances and eventually joined the Confederacy.

—*H. Lee Cheek, Jr.*

See also Calhoun, John Caldwell; Election of 1860; Fire-eaters; Taney, Roger Brooke; Wilmot Proviso.

For further reading:

Berger, Raoul. *Federalism: The Founders' Design* (1987).
Buchanan, Allen. *Secession* (1991).
Freehling, William W. *The Road to Disunion: Secessionists at Bay, 1776–1854* (1990).
Gordon, David, ed. *Secession, State and Liberty* (1998).
Kaminski, John P., and Gaspare J. Saladino, et al., eds. *The Documentary History of the Ratification of the Constitution*, vols. 8–10 (1993).
Lence, Ross M., ed. *Union and Liberty: The Political Philosophy of John C. Calhoun* (1992).

SECESSIONVILLE, BATTLE OF
(16 June 1862)

Federal plans to occupy Charleston, South Carolina, in June 1862 faltered after Union troops landed on James Island. About 9,000 Federals managed to take up positions along the Stono River on the southwestern part of the island, but delays allowed Confederate reinforcements to construct such strong fortifications that Major General David Hunter ordered no general engagement be mounted until he explicitly authorized it. Aside from the Confederate defenses, the Southern commander on James Island was Brigadier General Nathan "Shanks" Evans, a veteran of Bull Run and Ball's Bluff—and he was not to be trifled with.

Evans's Union counterpart on the island was

Brigadier General Henry W. Benham, who had scored some notable achievements himself. Leading the pursuit of Major General Robert Garnett's retreating forces in western Virginia the previous summer, Benham's people had been responsible for Garnett's death at Carrick's Ford. Promoted to brigadier, Benham had commanded the army of occupation in western Virginia that fall. Yet he was headstrong and could irritate superiors: William S. Rosecrans ordered his arrest in November 1861 on the vague charge of "unofficer-like neglect of duty." Yet things were patched up, and in March 1862 Benham became the commander of the northern district of David Hunter's Department of the South. The district contained South Carolina, Georgia, and northeastern Florida, with headquarters at Port Royal. But now Benham was on James Island, and he was apparently eager to move those headquarters to Charleston.

After Hunter's departure from the island on 11 June, Benham proceeded under the vast misimpression that he was authorized to protect his front by capturing a fort and a floating battery at Secessionville. When he held a council of war with his subordinates on the night of 15 September, according to each of them—Brigadier Generals Horatio Wright and Isaac I. Stephens, and Colonel Robert Williams—they told him that an attack on Confederate works at Secessionville would be deadly folly. Nonetheless, Benham ordered an assault to begin before dawn the next day.

If Benham's lieutenants had protested (and at least one additional attendee at the meeting later cast doubt that they had), they were right. Controversy would erupt over why Benham had insisted on the attack, and it still seems strange that he did. True enough, Secessionville was lightly manned with only about 500 Confederates, but it did not need much more than that number to hold out against almost anything thrown at it. From behind a forbidding collection of abatis bristling with artillery, including an 8-inch Columbiad, Colonel Thomas G. Lamar of the 1st South Carolina Artillery surveyed a stretch of relatively firm ground framed and narrowed before his works by marshes on each side. The terrain had the effect of funneling any attacker toward the Confederate parapets, essentially nullifying the advantage an assailant's numbers would provide. Benham arranged for 6,000 men to take part in the attack, and though only a part of these would see action, it probably would not have mattered if all of them had.

When Evans received word at 3:00 A.M. on 16 June that Federal troops were moving on Secessionville, he sent reinforcements to Lamar. Stephens's 2d Division was already closing on the Confederate works. It was about 4:30 and dark enough that the Yankees in rearward lines could not see those in their front. Lamar's artillery soon took care of that. The Columbiad loaded with cannister simply disintegrated soldiers stumbling toward it, tearing holes in the Union line. Those remaining struggled to close ranks and press on, some incredibly reaching the palisades, but the achievement was as empty as it was heroic. Though this first assault was soon joined by Wright's 1st Division, a second and third attempt to breach the fort were repulsed as well. By then, Lamar had grown fat with 1,500 reinforcements and would have killed every bluecoat who came at him had they persisted in doing so. Mercifully, the slaughter stopped when Benham ordered a general withdrawal at 10:00 A.M. The Federal column came back 683 men lighter than when it had started before daylight. Lamar, lauded as "gallant and indefatigable" in the official note of thanks, had lost only 204.

Immediately, everyone—including his subordinates—blamed Benham for the disaster. Hunter was especially livid because Benham appeared to have deliberately disobeyed explicit orders. "You will see," Hunter acidly noted to Secretary of War Edwin Stanton, "that General Benham endeavors to evade the responsibility of having violated his instructions by terming his attack upon the enemy's works a 'reconnaissance in force,' but such a plea is too puerile to deserve consideration." Three days after the attack on Secessionville, Benham was arrested and subsequently the Judge Advocate General's office recommended the revocation of his commission as brigadier general of volunteers. By then the dispute about what actually had happened before and during 16 June 1862 had grown ugly. Some testimony asserted that Benham's council of war had not objected to the attack, and Benham himself accused Isaac Stephens of a tardy and half-hearted performance in the initial assault. Stanton perfunctorily approved the revocation, though, and despite powerful political supporters, such as John Andrew and the governor of Vermont interceding on Benham's behalf, Lincoln let it stand.

Yet Benham, though headstrong, had proved himself aggressive, and such in this protracted war was too valuable an asset to let languish. The administration rescinded the revocation the following January, and Benham again became a brigadier general. He would be at Vicksburg in the summer of 1863, and when Ulysses S. Grant began his march on Richmond the following spring, Benham would be there as well to command the Army of the Potomac's engineering brigade.

—*David S. Heidler and Jeanne T. Heidler*

See also Evans, Nathan; South Carolina.
For further reading:
Brennan, Patrick. *Secessionville: Assault on Charleston* (1996).
"Charleston Battles and Seacoast Operations in South Carolina." In *Civil War Regiments: A Journal of the American Civil War* (1996).

SECOND MANASSAS, BATTLE OF
See Bull Run, Second Battle of

SECRET SERVICE, C.S.A.

When one speaks of Confederate secret service, one speaks of an activity, not an organization. There were a number of different elements of the Confederate government engaged in secret service work. These included a State Department secret service, which actually worked primarily for President Jefferson Davis; a War Department secret service, a foreign clandestine ship procurement program, a Torpedo Bureau in the War Department (which actually dealt with explosive devices, not naval torpedoes); a Submarine Battery Service, which developed underwater mines; and a counterintelligence effort organized originally by the provost marshal of Richmond. Other organizations, such as the Engineer Bureau, took part in clandestine operations as the need arose.

Only nearing the end of the war did the Confederate government try to pull a number of these activities together in a Special and Secret Service Bureau of the Confederate War Department. The act establishing this bureau was finally passed on 6 March 1865, too late to be implemented before the end of the war. This was the first attempt to create a central intelligence organization in North America.

At the beginning of the Civil War, the Confederacy sought to establish diplomatic ties with a number of European nations. The diplomats they sent abroad were furnished with secret service funds to enable them to buy information and influence. The Confederate State Department advanced these funds. Later, the Confederate Congress passed legislation authorizing secret service funds, and the State Department was reimbursed.

In 1862, regular procedures were adopted for the use of gold for secret service purposes. Because gold was in limited supply, the Confederate treasury was authorized to issue gold for secret service purposes only on the specific approval of the president. When such money was needed, the requesting officer submitted a memorandum to Davis outlining the purpose of the funds and the amount needed. If Davis approved, he signed a form used by the State Department, but with the State Department heading crossed out and "Office of the President" written in. The form stated the amount approved, the manner in which to issue the money, and the account to be charged. The account most used was "Necessities and Exigencies," but in February 1864 a new account was added, called simply "Secret Service." This account was to cover funds issued to support a major program of sabotage and other drastic actions to take place behind enemy lines. Together, the two funds

accounted for more than one and a half million dollars in gold.

Along with these funds, the War Department collected Union currency to support its secret service activity. The primary source of these funds was money taken from Union prisoners of war. Additional funds were obtained from time to time, by selling cotton across the lines.

When the Confederate government moved to Richmond in June 1861, it took over an espionage network in Washington established originally by the Commonwealth of Virginia. The famous spy Rose Greenhow belonged to this network, but, contrary to popular belief, she was not its organizer or main spy. Thomas Jordan set up the network when he was a lieutenant colonel in the army of Virginia, before its absorption by the Confederacy. Greenhow was too much of a political advocate to be a good spy. Her main contribution was to warn General P. G. T. Beauregard that the Union army was marching on Manassas. She was arrested in August 1861, primarily because she talked too much. She was sent South the following year, and Jefferson Davis gave her $2,500 in appreciation for her work, charged to the secret service account "Necessities and Exigencies."

Greenhow's arrest did not stop Confederate espionage in Washington. The network continued to operate throughout the war, reporting to both the Confederate government in Richmond and to the Army of Northern Virginia. Several officers in the Confederate army maintained this network. One was the provost marshal of the Army of Northern Virginia, Major Cornelius Boyle, stationed for most of the war at Gordonsville, Virginia, and the other was a principal liaison officer who delivered requirements to the organization and carried back espionage reports to Richmond and the army. The men who performed this function were George Donnellan, who was transferred to the Engineer Corps in 1862; Walter Bowie of Upper Marlboro, Maryland, who held the post until he joined Mosby's Rangers in June 1864; and Edward E. Thompson, an especially trusted officer in Colonel John S. Mosby's unit, who held the post until the end of the war.

Along with these operations in Washington, the Confederate Signal Corps operated the "Secret Line" into Washington and points north. This line operated in one form or another for nearly the entire war through southern Maryland and the Northern Neck of Virginia. Its primary missions were to bring Northern newspapers to Richmond within a day or two of publication, to bring to Richmond reports from agents in the North, and to escort agents or other important persons across the lines into and out of the Confederacy. The Union tried to break up the line on several occasions, but disruptions were temporary.

The Confederate army never developed a highly effective order-of-battle intelligence unit such as that developed by the Union Army of the Potomac under Colonel George H. Sharpe. But Captain (later brigadier general) Edward Porter Alexander, while assigned to signal duty in 1861, constructed a "roster" of the Union army showing its organization and strength in surprising detail. This enabled him to make a good estimate of the force of the Union army. There is no indication of what happened to this effort, but the basic work having been done, it might have been fairly easy for the Army of Northern Virginia to keep the "roster" up to date without attracting attention to its existence.

During General Robert E. Lee's tenure as commander, Lieutenant Colonel Charles Venable had the function of keeping track of intelligence reports as they came in, and maintaining correspondence with the various sources of the reports. He may have kept the "roster" up to date, but we may never know for sure, because most of the papers of General Lee's headquarters were destroyed on the retreat to Appomattox.

Outside the Eastern theater, Confederate secret service activity was more hit-or-miss. During the siege of Charleston, South Carolina, the Confederate army did a first-class job of reading Union signals and taking advantage of the information thus gleaned. In other areas, secret service helped from time to time, and in still other areas, there was little or no useful secret service activity. The Confederate War Department made available secret agents to help various headquarters obtain information as needed. Jefferson Davis also approved secret service gold expenditures for various requesters in the western and southern parts of the Confederacy. In those parts of the Confederacy, however, the main source of funding for secret service work was probably money collected from prisoners of war and clandestine trading with the enemy.

In 1863 the Confederacy adopted a program of covert attacks against targets behind Union lines, advocated by a Louisiana planter named Bernard Janin Sage. As part of this new program, the Confederate army organized "Strategic Corps" in each military district. These were teams of men trained in the use of explosives and other measures, and their mission was to attack targets approved by the district commander. Some of these teams achieved considerable success, but fires and explosions they caused were usually interpreted as industrial accidents and caused little publicity.

Also, as part of the new program the Confederate Congress enacted two bills: one authorizing the expenditure of five million dollars for covert action projects, and the other authorizing Confederate personnel to participate in such projects. These laws were enacted in February 1864, and the major project organized to implement the program was an effort, based in Canada, to influence the 1864 election in the Union and to disrupt the Federal war effort. One million dollars in gold was devoted to this project.

In the summer of 1864, John Wilkes Booth began to recruit a team to capture Abraham Lincoln as a hostage. He went to Montreal, Canada, in October 1864 to discuss the operation with Confederate operatives. Booth was subsequently furnished with other experienced secret service personnel, and the Confederacy prepared to receive a captive Lincoln in the Northern Neck of Virginia. Booth tried to capture Lincoln on 17 March 1864, but failed. The Confederacy then tried to attack Union command authorities in Washington, but their explosives expert was captured. Booth then took it upon himself to try to approximate the damage that an explosion might have caused, and he organized attacks on Lincoln, Vice President Andrew Johnson, and Secretary of State William Seward. In one of these attacks, Lincoln was killed.

Another major effort was devoted to burning steamboats in the Mississippi River and its tributaries. According to Union investigations of this project, about sixty boats were destroyed, but this was not sufficient to affect the outcome of the war in the West.

Toward the end of the war, the Confederacy began a major attack on Union ocean shipping. A number of men had been deployed to foreign ports, and action was about to begin when General Lee surrendered the Army of Northern Virginia on 9 April 1865, and the war wound down to an end.

The Confederacy's secret service efforts may have helped to prolong the Civil War. It is certain, however, that they foreshadowed many of the organizations, techniques, and problems that the United States encountered in intelligence work in the twentieth century.

—*William A. Tidwell*

See also Booth, John Wilkes; Greenhow, Rose O'Neal.
For further reading:
Bakeless, John. *Spies of the Confederacy* (1970).
Fishel, Edwin C. *The Secret War for the Union* (1996).
Tidwell, William A. *April '65: Confederate Covert Action in the American Civil War* (1995).
———, James O. Hall, and David Winfred Gaddy. *Come Retribution: The Confederate Secret Service and the Assassination of Abraham Lincoln* (1988).

SECRET SERVICE, U.S.A.

Secret service in the North during the Civil War encompassed far more than just daring spies undertaking harrowing adventures behind enemy lines. In reality, those engaged in "secret service" work included spies, army scouts, cavalry patrols, government detectives, agents operating abroad, guides, couriers, telegraphers, and Signal Corps personnel. The federal government initiated secret service operations on many

levels but never created a centralized, government-wide bureaucratic agency to handle its secret service needs on the political, diplomatic, and strategic military levels. In the field with the Union armies, secret service operations (primarily operational intelligence gathering) were left to the discretion of individual commanders; no army-wide intelligence organization existed during the war. Like secret service operations on the governmental level, those within the Union armies were neither centralized nor coordinated, and both were mostly ad hoc in nature.

On the national level, two separate organizations handled miscellaneous secret service duties in Washington. Allan Pinkerton ran a detective agency before the war and in 1861 uncovered the plot to assassinate President-elect Abraham Lincoln as he traveled through Baltimore to his inauguration. Pinkerton's reputation and connections netted him a position at Army of the Potomac headquarters in Washington after Major General George B. McClellan assumed command in July 1861. For eighteen months Pinkerton (alias "Major E. J. Allen"), served as McClellan's secret service chief tasked with gathering intelligence on Confederate forces in Virginia. Due to the large number of Southern sympathizers in Washington, his agency also conducted counterintelligence operations. His most famous catch was Confederate spy Rose O'Neal Greenhow. When McClellan's army advanced against Richmond in the summer of 1862, Pinkerton and his detectives followed him into the field.

Pinkerton's departure from Washington, however, did not leave the government without a secret service. From 1861 to 1865 Lafayette Baker, provost marshal of the War Department, ferreted out Confederate spies and subversives and investigated unscrupulous government contractors. Baker arrested a few Confederate spies, most notably Belle Boyd, but was also involved in other forms of law enforcement, including pursuing army deserters, bounty jumpers, corrupt government employees, and prostitutes.

Members of the secret service relaxing at Cumberland Landing, Virginia, May 1862 (Photograph by James F. Gibson / *Library of Congress*)

Secret service activities in the field centered primarily on intelligence gathering, but how much emphasis was placed on this function was left to individual commanders. During the war three prominent organizations emerged—two in the East and one in the West. Although systematic and centralized organizations, they were still ad hoc in nature and not army-wide in scope. The first secret service in the field was established by McClellan in the Army of the Potomac and operated from 1861 to 1862. Headed by Pinkerton, this unit had the task of discovering the strength and dispositions of the Confederate forces in Virginia. During the 1862 Peninsula campaign, Pinkerton's scouts filed numerous reports on the enemy's strength, some of which Pinkerton intentionally inflated to support McClellan's paranoid visions of a vastly superior enemy on his front. This interesting relationship facilitated McClellan's "slows" during the campaign.

Pinkerton's secret service activities ended with McClellan's removal in late 1862 and not until Major General Joseph Hooker took command in early 1863 did that army again possess another intelligence unit. Designated the "Bureau of Military Information" (BMI) and headed by Colonel George H. Sharpe, this new organization developed into an all-source intelligence agency within the Army of the Potomac and eventually established branch offices with other commands in Virginia. Sharpe's men became proficient at gathering information on the order of battle, strength, dispositions, movements, and morale of the enemy. The BMI also maintained contact with the "Richmond Underground," a group of pro-Union citizens in the Confederate capital headed by Elizabeth Van Lew and Samuel Ruth. The BMI remained operational until the end of the war and provided valuable service to Major General George G. Meade at the battle of Gettysburg and to Major General Ulysses S. Grant during the siege of Richmond and Petersburg.

Major General Grenville M. Dodge also created an intelligence network in northern Mississippi in late 1862. Instructed to watch Grant's rear during the 1863 Vicksburg campaign, Dodge assembled a group of 120 scouts and spies to perform this task and used the proceeds from the sale of confiscated cotton to pay for their services. Dodge's agents, culled from the ranks of northern Alabama Unionists (including a future governor of the state), operated primarily in western Tennessee and the northern reaches of Mississippi and Alabama. However, some scouts ranged as far as Atlanta and Richmond. After Vicksburg fell and major operations shifted to eastern Tennessee and northern Georgia, Dodge's intelligence service eventually disbanded.

Other activities that fell under the rubric of secret service included encrypting and decrypting Union telegraph messages and intercepting and decoding enemy transmissions. The telegraph and a new visual signaling system in the field (a wig-wag alphabet transmitted by flag or torch) allowed for speedy communication and offered another source of intelligence through the interception of enemy signal traffic. The U.S. Military Telegraph (USMT) developed secret codes or "ciphers" to protect Union signal transmissions and succeeded in cracking Confederate codes. The most famous USMT employees were Charles A. Tinker, Albert B. Chandler, and David Homer Bates, also known as the "Sacred Three." By 1864 the USMT had "cipher clerks" posted at the headquarters of many major field commanders.

The Union also had secret agents in Europe. Due to their need for financial and diplomatic support from European nations, the Confederacy courted foreign governments and established a covert network to acquire arms and naval vessels. The federal government recognized this potential threat and instructed Henry S. Sanford, the U.S. minister to Belgium, to monitor the activities of Southern agents and to hamper their efforts. Sanford constructed an efficient surveillance network and doggedly pursued Confederate agents throughout the war.

The Civil War was a testing ground for secret service operations on the political, diplomatic, and military levels. However, much of what was learned remained buried in War Department files or died with the chief participants.

—*William B. Feis*

See also Baker, La Fayette Curry; Boyd, Belle; Dodge, Grenville M.; Greenhow, Rose O'Neal; Peninsula Campaign; Pinkerton, Allan.

For further reading:

Feis, William B. "Intelligence Activities." In *The American Civil War: A Handbook of Literature and Research* (1996).
Fishel, Edwin C. *The Secret War for the Union* (1996).
O'Toole, G. J. A. *Honorable Treachery: The History of U.S. Intelligence, Espionage, and Covert Action from the American Revolution to the CIA* (1991).

SEDDON, JAMES ALEXANDER
(1815–1880)

Confederate secretary of war

Born to Thomas Seddon and Susan Alexander Seddon near Fredericksburg, Virginia, James A. Seddon was educated locally before studying law at the University of Virginia. Upon graduation and admission to the bar, Seddon began his practice in Richmond, Virginia. Seddon also became active in Virginia politics during the 1840s. A strong advocate of Southern rights, he stood for election to the United States House of Representatives twice during the 1840s and won each time, first in 1844 and again in 1848.

Upon the expiration of his second term, he refused to run again and retired to his plantation, Sabot Hill, in Goochland County.

The secession crisis of 1861 brought Seddon out of retirement. He served as a Virginia delegate to the Washington Peace Conference, where he argued the constitutionality of secession and not surprisingly failed to support most of the compromise measures.

Upon the secession of Virginia following Abraham Lincoln's call for volunteers, Seddon in June 1861 was appointed to the Provisional Confederate Congress. In that body he proved to be a strong supporter of Jefferson Davis's administration on most issues, although in this early phase of the war, he did not believe that high taxes were yet necessary. He decided not to run for a seat in the first regular Confederate Congress in the fall of 1861, although early in 1862, when a Virginia seat became available, he did run and was defeated. Later in the year, Confederate secretary of war George W. Randolph resigned his post, and Davis, remembering Seddon's loyalty in the Confederate Congress, prevailed upon him to accept the position, the appointment dating from 21 November 1862. Seddon served in the position longer than any other man—until 16 February 1865.

Seddon's tenure as Confederate secretary of war has met with little praise. While demonstrating at times a keen grasp of the importance of unified command and a centralized strategy, Seddon's deference to Davis prevented him from encouraging the adoption of strategies that contradicted Davis's stated wishes. Still, he made some efforts through his communications with his generals to push for more aggressive actions. His belief in the importance of an aggressive military strategy was probably one of the reasons that he got along with Robert E. Lee the best of all of his generals, and Joseph E. Johnston the least. Seddon politely urged Johnston to be more aggressive during the Vicksburg campaign and attack Grant outside of the city. The following year, during the Atlanta campaign, Johnston's lack of assertive action against William T. Sherman, caused Seddon to agree with Davis to remove him from command. Seddon was criticized heavily for this decision.

In addition to Seddon's lack of assertiveness with the president, which earned him much censure from the Confederate Congress, he also had an entire collection of difficult governors to deal with. His largest difficulty with the governors, the procurement of troops, only magnified as the war moved into its final months and Union forces threatened all parts of the Confederacy. Not only were governors not sending fresh troops to the Confederate army, they were asking Seddon to send men back to their home states to defend the home front.

Worn down by constant criticism and bad health, Seddon resigned his post when the Confederate Congress voted in January 1865 that the cabinet needed

reorganizing. Although Seddon was certainly not a very effective secretary, there seems little doubt that with Jefferson Davis's meticulous management of the war, no man would have been able to impose his will on the Confederate War Department.

At the end of the war Seddon was captured by Union forces and briefly imprisoned. Upon his release, he returned to his home at Sabot Hill. He lived much of the remainder of his life in seclusion there, broken somewhat in spirit by the collapse of the Confederacy and ultimately in body by the bad health that had plagued him throughout the war. He died at home and is buried in Richmond.

—*David S. Heidler and Jeanne T. Heidler*

See also Davis, Jefferson; Johnston, Joseph Eggleston; Lee, Robert Edward.

For further reading:

Patrick, Rembert W. *Jefferson Davis and His Cabinet* (1944).
Stearns, Merton Everett. *The Public Life of James A. Seddon* (1924).

SEDGWICK, JOHN
(1813–1864)
Union general

John Sedgwick was born in Cornwall Hollow, Connecticut, on 13 September 1813. After attending the Sharon Academy and teaching school for two years, he received an appointment to West Point, from which he graduated near the middle of a class that included Braxton Bragg, Jubal A. Early, John C. Pemberton, and Joseph Hooker. After being commissioned in the artillery in 1837, Sedgwick saw action in the Second Seminole War in Florida, assisted in the removal of the Cherokees from their eastern homes, and served in the "Aroostook War," a border dispute between Maine and the Canadian province of New Brunswick. During the Mexican-American War, Sedgwick was brevetted to captain for his actions at the battles of Contreras and Churubusco on 20 August 1847 and was brevetted to major for his actions at the storming of Chapultepec on 13 September 1847.

Promoted to captain in the regular army in January 1849, Sedgwick continued to serve as an artillery officer until March 1855, when he was promoted to major and assigned to the newly organized 1st Cavalry Regiment (later redesignated the 4th Cavalry Regiment). After serving in the Mormon War, in "Bleeding Kansas," and seeing action against the Indians in the West, he hoped to retire from the army and return to his boyhood home of Cornwall Hollow to a quiet life of farming. The year 1861, however, saw Sedgwick receiving a rapid series of promotions as the result of resignations by Southern officers (including Lieutenant Colonel Robert E. Lee of the 2d Cavalry Regiment). He was promoted to lieutenant colonel of the 2d Cavalry (later redesignated the 5th Cavalry Regiment) in March and to colonel of the 1st Cavalry (later redesignated the 4th Cavalry Regiment) in April 1861.

After serving as the acting inspector general of Washington, D.C., Sedgwick was promoted to brigadier general of volunteers and given command of the 2d Brigade, Heintzelman's division, Army of the Potomac in August 1861. Affectionately called "Uncle John" by his troops, during the Peninsula campaign, Sedgwick commanded the 2d Division of Major General Edwin V. Sumner's II Corps, Army of the Potomac, and was badly wounded in the Seven Days' battle at Frayser's Farm on 30 June 1862. Promoted to major general of volunteers on 4 July 1862, Sedgwick continued to lead his division until the battle of Antietam (17 September 1862). At Antietam, Sumner rashly ordered Sedgwick to mass his division, which, after a brief advance, was cut to pieces by Confederate artillery. Sedgwick, while attempting to rally his division, was twice wounded and had a horse shot from under him. After being advised by a surgeon to leave the field and refusing to do so, he received a third wound and had to be carried unconscious from the field.

After only three months of recuperation, Sedgwick returned to the Army of the Potomac to command, in quick succession, the II, IX, and finally the VI Corps. Commanding the VI Corps during the Chancellorsville campaign, he was ordered by Major General "Fighting Joe" Hooker (one of Sedgwick's classmates from West Point), the commander of the Army of the Potomac, to storm Marye's Heights at Fredericksburg on 3 May 1863. Hooker was attempting to relieve the pressure on the right flank of the Army of the Potomac caused by a Confederate force under Confederate lieutenant general Thomas J. Jackson (who was mortally wounded by his own men during the battle). Sedgwick stormed Marye's Heights and captured it despite the opposition of a Confederate division commanded by another of his West Point classmates, Confederate major general Jubal A. Early. Later that day at Salem Church, VI Corps was unable to continue the offensive, and Sedgwick was ordered to withdraw his corps the next day.

Though the VI Corps was in reserve during the battle of Gettysburg, Sedgwick would command both the VI and V Corps (the right wing of the Army of the Potomac) at Rappahannock Bridge on 7 November 1863. At Rappahannock Bridge, he again found himself facing a force under the command of Early. Although Sedgwick bombarded Early's position with artillery, it appeared that he would be unable to attack until the following day, as night attacks were rare during the Civil War. At dusk, however, Sedgwick ordered an attack by three brigades, and the decisive moment of the battle would be a bayonet charge by the 6th Maine and 5th Wisconsin Regiments. The bayonet charge would allow

Colonel Emory Upton's brigade to advance into the Confederate defensive positions; as a result of the ensuing debacle, the Union captured almost 2,000 Confederate prisoners, eight regimental colors, and four artillery pieces.

During Lieutenant General Ulysses S. Grant's Overland campaign in the spring of 1864, Sedgwick commanded his corps with his usual skill. On 9 May 1864 at Spotsylvania, Sedgwick was personally positioning his units in preparation for the battle, when he noticed several men attempting to dodge enemy bullets by staying close to the ground. Sedgwick laughed when he saw this and stated, "They couldn't hit an elephant at this distance." He was immediately struck by a bullet in the left cheek and killed. A lifelong bachelor, "Uncle John" Sedgwick has often been described as the most beloved general officer in the Union army. His reputation among his men did not belie his fighting prowess, as Sedgwick's command of his corps was marked by tight discipline and considerable courage.

—*Alexander M. Bielakowski*

See also Antietam, Battle of; Early, Jubal; Fredericksburg, Second Battle of; Salem Church, Battle of; Spotsylvania Court House, Battle of.

For further reading:
McMahon, Martin T. *In Memoriam: Major-General John Sedgwick* (1885).
Sedgwick, John. *Correspondence of John Sedgwick, Major-General* (1902–1903).
Welch, Emily S. *John Sedgwick, Major-General: A Biographical Sketch* (1899).
Winslow, Richard E., III. *General John Sedgwick: The Story of a Union Corps Commander* (1982).

SELIGMAN, JOSEPH
(1819–1880)
Union financier

The oldest child of Fanny Steinhardt Seligman and her husband, David, who was in the wool-weaving business, Joseph Seligman was born in Baiersdorf, Bavaria, on 22 November 1819. Joseph, who did well in literature and in the classics, graduated from the Gymnasium in Erlangen and began to prepare himself for a career in medicine. His dissatisfaction with the economic and political restrictions against Jews in the German states led him to go to the United States in 1837. He lived in Mauch Chunk, Pennsylvania, with his cousin Lewis Seligman, who introduced him to Asa Packer, the owner of a canal boat construction company. Between 1837 and 1839 Joseph learned much about business, serving as a clerk for, and then as a secretary of, Packer's firm.

In 1839 Seligman decided to leave Packer's company and to open a family business. With his brothers, William and James, who were brought from Bavaria to

America, Joseph Seligman in 1839 established a business near Lancaster, Pennsylvania. The Seligmans sold jewelry and clothing to farmers. In 1841 Joseph brought his brother Jesse to Lancaster, but decided that year to dissolve their business as a result of intense competition. With his brothers, Seligman moved the family business to the South and in 1841 set up a dry-goods store in Selma, Alabama. As business began to prosper, Seligman brought more brothers to America: Abraham, Leopold, and Isaac in 1842; and Henry the next year. Following the arrival of these four brothers in Alabama, Joseph established three more stores near Selma. Believing that business would be better in the North than in the South, Seligman in 1848 liquidated his stores in and around Selma. In October of that year, he also married Babette Steinhardt.

In 1848 Joseph went to New York City with his brothers, James and William, and set up J. Seligman & Brothers at 46 Pine Street. Under the direction of Joseph, this firm became one of the city's leading clothing importers. From the profits of this firm, Joseph established during the 1850s branch stores in Watertown (New York), St. Louis, and San Francisco.

Seligman and his firm quickly became involved in the Civil War. On 20 April 1861, eight days after the shelling of Fort Sumter, Seligman, who strongly opposed slavery, was named as a vice president of a large Union meeting in New York City. During the autumn and winter of 1861, he frequently went to Washington and entered into contracts to provide military clothing to Union armies. In July 1862 Seligman received from the Treasury Department $1,437,483.61 in cash and bonds for merchandise supplied.

Joseph, who recognized the potential of profits in the world of finance, formed in 1862 the international banking firm of J. and W. Seligman & Company. He directed this firm in New York City and empowered his brothers to direct the activities of branches in San Francisco, New Orleans, London, and Paris. In the summer of that year, Seligman went to Germany and created the Frankfurt branch of his firm. Known as Seligman & Stettheimer and headed by his brothers, Abraham and Henry, this branch met with great success during the Civil War. It sold in German states between 1862 and 1863 approximately $200 million worth of U.S. Treasury bonds with a coupon of 6 percent. The success of Seligman's firm in marketing these bonds within the German states was of great importance, for there were not many buyers of Union debt either in France or in England.

Seligman in numerous ways contributed greatly to nineteenth-century America during and after the Civil War. As a member of New York City's Committee of Seventy, he became an advocate of municipal reforms and played an active role in bringing an end to the corruption of the Tweed Ring during the 1870s. In 1875 he served as a commissioner for the city's rapid transit system and compiled a report for the establishment of a rapid transit system for the city. He also served as vice president of New York's Union League Club and was active in the affairs of Temple Emanu-El, the center of German Jewry and Reform Judaism in New York. A person of varying cultural interests, Seligman assisted in 1876 Professor Felix Adler in establishing the Society for Ethical Culture. On 25 April 1880 Seligman, during a visit to his daughter and her family in New Orleans, died suddenly. He is best remembered for obtaining needed funds for the Union cause, for giving financial advice to presidents and government leaders, and for being one of the most eminent leaders of the nineteenth-century American German-Jewish elite.

—William Weisberger

See also Financing, U.S.A.

For further reading:
Ashkenazi, Elliot. "Jewish Commercial Interests between North and South: The Case of the Lehmans and the Seligmans." *American Jewish Archives* (1991).
Birmingham, Stephen. *Our Crowd: The Great Jewish Families of New York* (1967).
Carosso, Vincent P. *The Morgans: Private International Bankers, 1854–1913* (1987).
Muir, Ross L., and Carl J. White. *Over the Long Term: The Story of J. and W. Seligman and Company* (1964).
Supple, Barry E. "A Business Elite: German-Jewish Financiers in Nineteenth-Century New York." *Business History Review* (1957).

SELMA, ALABAMA

A town of 1,809 residents in 1860, Selma became one of the Confederacy's most important industrial centers. As such, it was the objective of Union general James Harrison Wilson's raid in the spring of 1865 and the site of a brief battle on 2 April 1865.

When New Orleans fell in April 1862, Chief of Ordnance Josiah Gorgas relocated the Confederate arsenal from Mount Vernon, Alabama, to Selma for greater security. The Tennessee & Alabama River Railroad supplied iron and coal to Selma, and the Alabama & Mississippi Railroad and the navigable Alabama River permitted manufactured goods to be sent to armies east and west. Situated in a very productive agricultural region, Selma also served as a food collection and distribution depot.

By 1863 and to the end of the war, a vast amount of military equipment and ordnance flowed from Selma. Rough estimates suggest the town's population increased by 10,000 as skilled artisans, women and children, and slaves came to work in the various factories. Most important were the arsenal and the naval foundry that produced siege guns, field artillery, caissons, ammunition of all types, and even three ironclads for coastal defenses. Four smaller iron foundries, machine shops, saltpeter and

niter factories, and other private establishments diligently supported the Confederate war effort.

In February 1864, Union general William T. Sherman's expedition to Meridian, Mississippi, led Confederate authorities to begin construction of an extensive set of fortifications around Selma. In March 1865 the threat by the Union became more real. Brigadier General James Harrison Wilson led 13,480 men, mostly cavalry, from Chickasaw Landing on the Tennessee River on 22 March. By 1 April, his main force of 9,000 men pushed Nathan Bedford Forrest's bedraggled cavalry into the fortifications surrounding Selma.

The defensive works were formidable; the defense force was not. The parapets were woefully undermanned. Along with Forrest's 2,000 veterans, approximately 2,000 to 3,000 conscripts from Selma were ordered to defend the center of the line. At dusk on 2 April, Wilson sent General Eli Long with 1,500 dismounted troopers against the Confederate left. Despite such obstacles as a five-foot palisade, a deep ditch, and an eight-foot-high parapet, the Union forces bravely breached the fortifications. Armed with Spencer repeating carbines, Wilson's troopers achieved a breakthrough against the thinly stretched line at a cost of about 20 percent of the attacking force. When a secondary assault led by General Emory Upton pierced the center of the defenses, the untrained conscripts panicked. Forrest's men made a brief but futile stand at an uncompleted inner defensive line, but reinforcements commanded by Wilson put the Confederates to rout. By nightfall Selma was in the hands of the Union army.

The Union losses were 46 killed, 300 wounded, and 13 missing. Confederate casualties were uncounted but were fewer than Wilson's. Wilson did capture approximately 2,700, most of them the conscripted residents of Selma. Forrest and his generals escaped in the confusion and darkness, but for all intents this was the end of Forrest's army and his last battle.

There is no unbiased or convincing contemporary account of the plundering of Selma on the night of 2 April or in the following days. Some 35,000 bales of cotton ignited by retreating Confederates inadvertently consumed several businesses. Other fires started by Union soldiers and slaves destroyed some downtown businesses and homes. Union troopers discovered barrels of whiskey, which led to other atrocities. Wilson would later recall that he stopped the plundering of private homes within a day. Whether Selma was "the worst sacked city," as residents long recalled, will always remain in dispute.

Before Wilson crossed the Alabama River on 9–10 April, he thoroughly destroyed the stores of supplies, railroad equipment, the machinery, and the factory buildings. So much material was dumped into the Alabama that the piles stuck above water. During World War II some of this metal was salvaged for the war effort. After refitting and remounting the cavalry, Wilson ordered the killing of over 1,000 horses and mules, leaving many of the corpses in the streets of Selma for residents to remove.

With the destruction of resources in Selma, Wilson aimed to guarantee that the Confederacy lost the will and the means to fight. His campaign foreshadowed the effectiveness of mechanized infantry in later wars. Nevertheless, the industrialization of Selma demonstrated the Confederacy's ability to mobilize resources to almost revolutionary proportions.

—*M. Philip Lucas*

See also Forrest, Nathan Bedford; Wilson, James Harrison; Wilson's Selma Raid.

For further reading:

Hardy, John. *Selma: Her Institutions and Her Men* (1879).

Jackson, Harvey H., III. *Rivers of History: Life on the Coosa, Tallapoosa, Cahaba, and Alabama* (1995).

Jones, James Pickett. *Yankee Blitzkrieg: Wilson's Raid through Alabama and Georgia* (1976).

McMillan, Malcolm C. *The Alabama Confederate Reader* (1963).

Wilson, James Harrison. *Under the Old Flag: Recollections of Military Operations in the War for the Union, the Spanish War, the Boxer Rebellion, Etc.* (1912; reprint, 1971).

SEMINOLE INDIANS

At the beginning of the Civil War, the Seminoles were a divided and defeated people in the aftermath of the Seminole Wars in Florida and the subsequent removal of a large segment of the tribe to the Indian Territory. Despite being the smallest of the Five Civilized Tribes forced to relocate westward, the Seminoles were courted by the Confederacy through the flamboyant Albert Pike to cut ties with the United States and join the rebellion. Leaders such as Chief John Jumper reluctantly agreed and signed a formal treaty with the Confederates on 1 August 1861. However, several prominent tribal chieftains denounced this act and remained loyal to the federal government for the duration of the war.

As Confederate allies the Seminoles were expected to furnish some five companies of mounted volunteers initially to protect the Indian Territory from any Union attacks from Kansas. Chief Jumper was commissioned a major and given command of a Seminole battalion that saw service until the war's end. Though lacking in modern arms, good horses, and training, they gave a good account of themselves along with other Native Americans at the March 1862 battle of Pea Ridge. The battalion went on to fight in numerous skirmishes with Unionists in the general region. By 1864 this Seminole unit was incorporated into the C.S.A. Indian Cavalry Brigade under the command of General Stand Watie (a Cherokee) until the final surrender in 1865.

A significant number of Seminoles did not bend to Rebel pressures and remained in the Union camp. The strong influence of black members of the tribe, a weak "mixed blood" element, and the position against the secessionists of well-known leaders such as Holata Micco (also known as Billy Bowlegs) and Halleck Tustenugge of the Mikasuki subtribe all played key roles in maintaining a sense of fealty. As the war west of the Mississippi went on, the ranks of the Unionist Seminoles swelled to a majority of the tribe, as Seminoles grew dissatisfied with apparently empty Confederate promises. Many flocked to enlist in two companies made up of fellow tribal members in the Union First Indian Regiment. Chief Bowlegs received a commission as a captain in the Union army and the command of one of these blueclad Native American companies. Like their Rebel counterparts, these Seminoles spent much of the war patrolling and occasionally fighting Confederate units in their western area of operations.

Seminoles remaining in the state of Florida underwent a very different wartime experience than their cousins far away. In 1861, the few members living there survived by staying deep in the swamps and hammocks of south Florida and as far away from whites as possible. Many Floridians feared these scattered people might take the opportunity created by the outbreak of civil war to seek vengeance for past wrongs. Governor John Milton sent several agents far into the sparsely settled interior to confer with chiefs such as Sam Jones and Tiger Tail to learn their wants for trade goods and any grievances they might be harboring. Despite such efforts, rumors continued to abound of Seminole war parties on the loose and of Union forces then in parts of Florida urging them to attack settlers and cut vital supply lines.

State leaders probably overestimated the military potential of the few Seminoles still in Florida. Having already fought three wars with the United States, they surely had little eagerness to go into battle again for any reason. However, many white Floridians believed that a feasible Seminole-Unionist alliance posed a serious menace to the state and its people. State officials worked with great vigor to supply the wandering bands with scarce trade goods, including ammunition, to keep them neutral if not in the Confederate camp. Seminoles would rate highly as late as 1865 with some $8,000 worth of supplies being earmarked for delivery to them. At least one attempt was made to raise a company of south Florida Seminoles for service in the Confederate army. One A. McBride submitted a list of sixty-five Seminole "volunteers" he claimed were ready to enlist. However, no evidence exists that such a unit was ever mustered into service or took the field.

The war's termination found the south Florida Seminoles even more reluctant to interact with whites, and they moved even farther into the wilderness vastness of the Everglades. Both halves of the tribe struggled to survive the white man's war, but in some cases they could not help being caught up in it to endure their own internecine conflicts.

—*Robert A. Taylor*

See also Cherokee Indians; Choctaw Indians; Indian Territory; Pea Ridge, Battle of; Pike, Albert; Watie, Stand.

For further reading:

Abel, Annie Heloise. *The American Indian in the Civil War, 1862–1865* (1992).

Hauptman, Laurence M. *Between Two Fires: American Indians in the Civil War* (1995).

Nichols, David A. *Lincoln and the Indians: Civil War Policy and Politics* (1978).

Porter, Kenneth W. "Billy Bowlegs (Holata Micco) in the Civil War." *Florida Historical Quarterly* (1967).

Taylor, Robert A. "Unforgotten Threat: South Florida Seminoles in the Civil War." *Florida Historical Quarterly* (1991).

SEMMES, RAPHAEL
(1809–1877)
Confederate naval officer

Raphael Semmes was born on 27 September 1809 in Charles County, Maryland. His parents died early in his childhood, and he was raised by relatives in Georgetown, in the District of Columbia. In 1826 Semmes won appointment as a midshipman. Although he had an excellent record, there were too many midshipmen, and it was February 1837 before he made the rank of lieutenant. In long leaves of absence ashore, Semmes took up the study of law, which profession he followed when not at sea.

From 1837 until the Mexican-American War began in 1846, Semmes spent most of his time on survey work along the southern coast and Gulf of Mexico. In 1841 the U.S. Navy ordered him to survey Mississippi Sound, and at that time he established his legal residence in Alabama. During the Mexican-American War, Semmes commanded the brig USS *Somers*. In December 1846, while off the eastern coast of Mexico, she went down in a sudden squall. Half of her crew were lost, but a court-martial found Semmes blameless. In March 1847 he took part in the capture of Vera Cruz; later he participated in the expedition against Tuxpan and accompanied General Winfield Scott's forces to Mexico City as an aide to division commander Major General William Worth, who cited Semmes for bravery.

After the war, Semmes again found himself in a navy with too many officers, and he spent much of his time on leave at the family home in Alabama. In 1852 he published *Service Afloat and Ashore During the Mexican War*. Ironically, in view of later events, Semmes argued that if Mexico had used privateers against U.S. shipping,

they should have been treated as pirates. In 1855 he became a commander and in 1856 was posted to Washington, D.C., as a member of the lighthouse board.

Following his state's secession and creation of the Confederate States of America, Semmes in February 1861 resigned his U.S. Navy commission and traveled to Montgomery, Alabama, to enter Confederate service. President Jefferson Davis immediately sent him into the North to purchase military and naval supplies and manufacturing equipment. Commissioned a commander in the Confederate States Navy, Semmes met in mid-April with Confederate secretary of the navy Stephen R. Mallory. Both men favored commerce raiding as a means of hurting the North financially, weakening resolve, and forcing naval vessels from blockade duties.

Mallory gave Semmes command of the CSS *Sumter*. The first Confederate commerce raider, she was both small and slow, yet between June 1861 and January 1862 Semmes took eighteen Union prizes in her. After six months she was in poor repair and blockaded by Union warships, so Semmes abandoned her at Gibraltar. Mallory was pleased with Semmes's success and in August 1862 the Confederate Congress advanced him to the rank of captain.

Mallory now gave Semmes command of a new ship contracted for by the Confederates and nearing completion at Liverpool, England. Semmes joined the ship at Portuguese Terceira in the Azores. After supervising the mounting of her ordnance, in late August Semmes named her the *Alabama*.

An excellent captain who paid attention to detail and was a stickler for order and cleanliness, Semmes was also extraordinarily lucky. Semmes was an introvert who did not socialize with his officers. A staunch Catholic, he was also opinionated and wordy. Proud and entirely self-satisfied, Semmes never saw any wrong with his own cause and only evil and unfairness on the part of his adversaries. His memoirs reveal great hatred of the North and contempt for the U.S. Navy.

For nearly two years Semmes and the *Alabama* ravaged Union shipping. Through July 1864 she took sixty-six prizes and sunk a Union warship. In the *Sumter* and the *Alabama*, Semmes had captured eighty-four Union merchantmen. He estimated he had burned $4,613,914 worth of shipping and cargoes and bonded others valued at $562,250. Another estimate places the total at nearly $6 million.

Semmes finally put into Cherbourg, but French officials rejected his request that the *Alabama* be allowed into dry dock for repair. On 19 June 1864, despite the fact that his ship was in poor condition and slowed by her foul bottom, Semmes ordered the *Alabama* out to engage the Union third-rate screw steam sloop USS *Kearsarge*. Perhaps it was a matter of pride; there had been little glory in sinking merchantmen. In any case,

Raphael Semmes (*Library of Congress*)

Semmes had little choice, for delay would only bring more Union warships. In the ensuing engagement the *Kearsarge* sank the *Alabama*. Semmes escaped capture and was taken to Southampton on an English yacht. Semmes then traveled to Belgium and Switzerland before returning to London. He then made his way to Richmond via the West Indies, Cuba, and Mexico. Promoted to rear admiral in February 1865, he took command of the James River Squadron of three ironclad rams and seven wooden steamers. This command lasted barely three months. When Confederate forces abandoned Richmond, Semmes was forced to destroy his vessels on the night of 2 April 1865. The men of the squadron then formed into a naval brigade under Semmes as a brigadier general. At Greensboro, North Carolina, it joined General Joseph E. Johnston's army, where it surrendered.

Paroled in May 1865, Semmes returned to Mobile, Alabama, where that December he was arrested and transported to Washington and held there for three months. U.S. secretary of the navy Gideon Welles planned to try him before a military commission on charges that he had violated military codes by escaping from the *Alabama* after she had struck her colors. After the Supreme Court denied the jurisdiction of the commissions, Semmes was released.

Semmes was briefly a probate judge of Mobile County, professor at Louisiana State Seminary (now Louisiana State University) at Baton Rouge, and then editor of the *Memphis Daily Bulletin*. Political pressure cost him all three positions. After a profitable lecture tour, he resumed the practice of law. In 1869 he published *Memoirs of Service Afloat, during the War between the States*. Semmes died on 30 August 1877 and is buried in Mobile.

—*Spencer C. Tucker*

See also Alabama, CSS; *Kearsarge*, USS; Mallory, Stephen R.

For further reading:

Robinson, Charles M., III. *Shark of the Confederacy. The Story of the CSS Alabama* (1995).

Semmes, Raphael. *Memoirs of Service Afloat* (1869; reprint, 1987).

Sinclair, Arthur. *Two Years on the Alabama* (1895).

Taylor, John M. *Confederate Raider: Raphael Semmes of the Alabama* (1994).

Tucker, Spencer C. *Raphael Semmes and the Alabama* (1996).

SEVEN DAYS' BATTLES
(25 June–1 July 1862)

The Seven Days' battles constituted the climax of General George B. McClellan's Peninsula campaign. As commander in chief of the Union army, McClellan decided on the basis of a gross overestimate of both the number of Confederate troops in Northern Virginia and of the abilities of their commander, General Joseph E. Johnston, that he would prefer a Napoleonic plan combining a feint at Manassas with an attack up the Virginia Peninsula on Richmond. After much argument he obtained approval for his plan, on the condition that he leave behind sufficient Federal forces to guarantee the safety of Washington, D.C. He was also moved from overall command to command of the Army of the Potomac only. He planned on bringing about 140,000 troops to the peninsula, leaving 73,000 behind to secure the capital.

On 4 April 1862, when Federal troops disembarked at Fort Monroe at the peninsula's tip, McClellan had only about 58,000 men with him. Others were to follow, but he was upset to find that President Lincoln, on reviewing the troop dispositions, had noted that McClellan had included forces in the Shenandoah Valley and troops yet to be supplied by various states in his estimates of Washington's defenses and had decided that the 35,000 troops commanded by General Irvin McDowell would stay at Fredericksburg, rather than march to join McClellan. This affected McClellan's approach when he discovered that the Rebels had dammed and flooded the Warwick River crossing the peninsula from the York River to the James and strengthened their defensive positions anchored on Yorktown. The Confederate garrison at Yorktown, 13,000 men under General John

Magruder, was in fact an inconsiderable obstacle, but poor intelligence provided to McClellan by his disastrously incompetent director of military intelligence, Allan Pinkerton, led him to assume he was facing between 100,000 and 120,000 foes. If McDowell were coming to join him, McClellan could hope to crush the Confederates between their armies, but now he saw no recourse but a classic siege while waiting for more men to join him. The defenders did their part, brandishing fake cannon made of wood, moving about to create the appearance of great numbers, and loudly issuing orders to nonexistent units. Even when a Vermont regiment broke through Yorktown's defenses on the third day of the siege, McClellan refused to reinforce success. Any chance of an easy victory was lost when the Confederate commander on the peninsula, General Joseph E. Johnston, arrived with enough troops to bring the garrison to 55,000. The siege dragged on for nearly a month, until Johnston slipped away the night of 3–4 May just as McClellan was about to begin a massive bombardment of Yorktown from land and sea.

Always suspicious of politicians, McClellan felt that the withholding of McDowell's corps and delays in the arrival of reinforcements and supplies were part of a political plot to discredit him and turn the war into an abolitionist crusade. Convinced that he was beset on all sides by enemies hidden and apparent, he followed Johnston up the peninsula, setting up a base at West Point and absorbing reinforcements.

The Union force, now swollen to 107,000, with another 21,000 holding the line of communication back to Fort Monroe, arrived before Richmond on 17 May. By this time, Lincoln had given permission for McDowell to move south from Fredericksburg to link up with McClellan, so that McClellan could count upon another 35,000 troops with which to besiege Richmond if the defending force were not caught in the open between his army and McDowell's. This meant that McClellan had no choice but to take a position straddling the Chickahominy River, with the bulk of his forces to the north of the river to facilitate the juncture with McDowell. He organized his forces into five corps, commanded by Generals Fitz John Porter, William Franklin, and Edwin Sumner north of the river, and Samuel Heintzelman and Erasmus Keyes south of it.

But McDowell was not coming after all. General Robert E. Lee, Confederate president Jefferson Davis's military advisor, had conceived the plan of drawing off McDowell by a diversion in the Shenandoah Valley. It was a brilliant move that saw General Thomas "Stonewall" Jackson and a Rebel army of 17,000 lead three Federal armies with an aggregate of nearly twice as many troops on a merry chase for five weeks and win five battles against them. McClellan, expecting to pin down Rebel defenders to the east of Richmond while

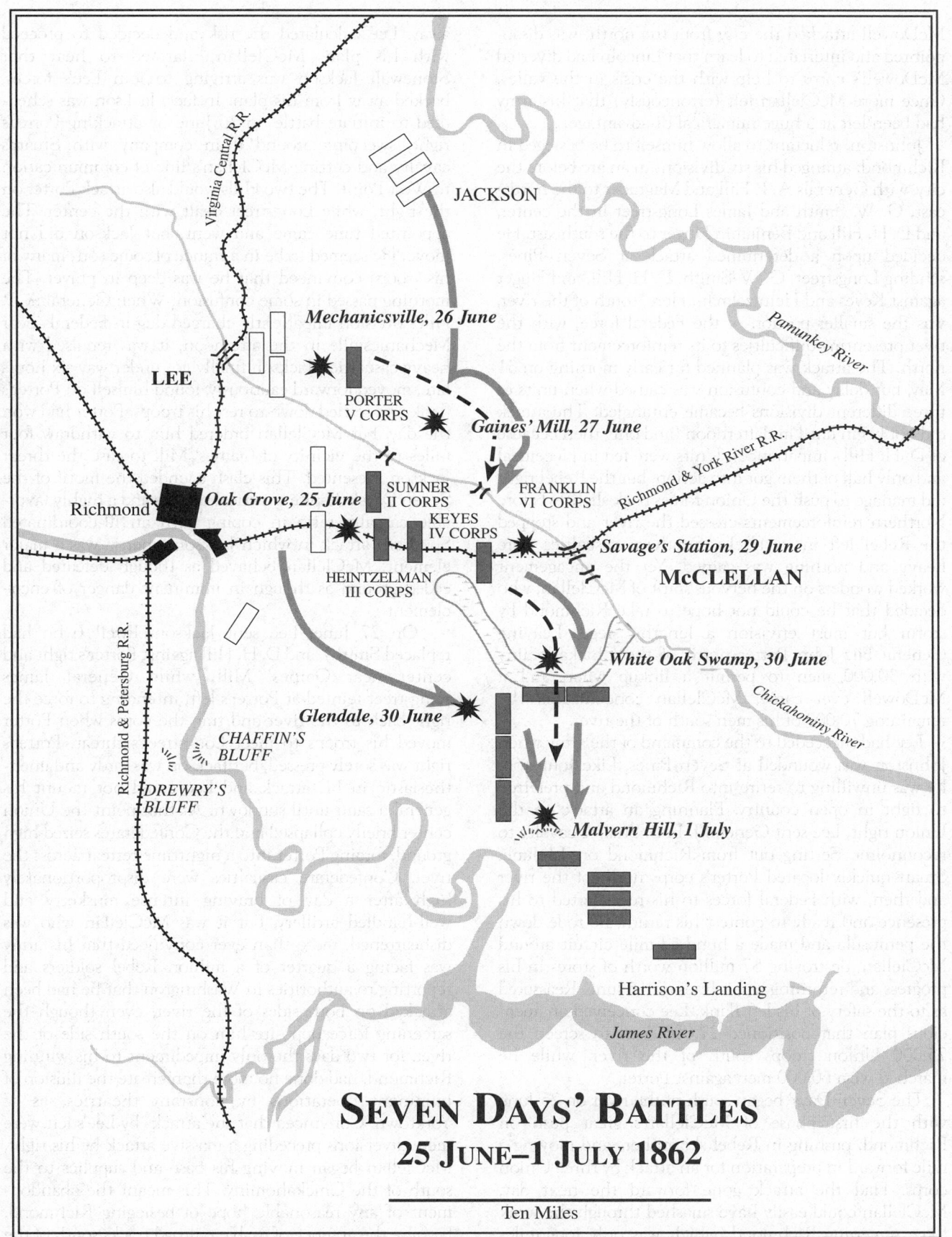

JACKSON

Virginia Central R.R.

Pamunkey River

Mechanicsville, 26 June

LEE

PORTER
V CORPS

Gaines' Mill, 27 June

Richmond & York River R.R.

Richmond

Oak Grove, 25 June

SUMNER
II CORPS

FRANKLIN
VI CORPS

KEYES
IV CORPS

Savage's Station, 29 June

McCLELLAN

HEINTZELMAN
III CORPS

Richmond & Petersburg R.R.

White Oak Swamp, 30 June

Chickahominy River

Glendale, 30 June

CHAFFIN'S
BLUFF

DREWRY'S
BLUFF

Malvern Hill, 1 July

Harrison's Landing

James River

SEVEN DAYS' BATTLES
25 JUNE–1 JULY 1862

Ten Miles

McDowell attacked the city from the north, was disappointed and infuriated to learn that Lincoln had diverted McDowell's corps to help with the crisis in the valley. Once more McClellan felt (erroneously) that his army had been left at a huge numerical disadvantage.

Johnston, reluctant to allow himself to be besieged in Richmond, arranged his six divisions in an arc before the city, with Generals A. P. Hill and Magruder to the northeast, G. W. Smith and James Longstreet in the center, and D. H. Hill and Benjamin Huger to the southeast. He decided upon a determined attack at Seven Pines, sending Longstreet, G. W. Smith, D. H. Hill, and Huger against Keyes and Heintzelman. Here, south of the river, was the smaller portion of the Federal force, with the river presenting difficulties to its reinforcement from the north. The attack was planned for early morning on 31 May, but delay and confusion was caused when units of three different divisions became entangled. The attack did not begin until midafternoon (and only then because of D. H. Hill's impatience). Units were fed in piecemeal and only half of them got into action, but the Rebel right did manage to push the Union forces back slightly before Northern reinforcements crossed the river and stopped the Rebel left in its tracks. Southern casualties were heavy and nothing was gained. Yet the engagement worked wonders on the nervous spirit of McClellan, who decided that he could not hope to take Richmond by storm but must envision a lengthy siege. Leaving General Fitz John Porter north of the Chickahominy with 30,000 men to permit a linkup when and if McDowell ever came, McClellan concentrated the remaining 70,000 of his men south of the river.

Lee had succeeded to the command of the army when Johnston was wounded at Seven Pines. Like Johnston, he was unwilling to retire into Richmond and preferred to fight in open country. Planning an attack on the Union right, Lee sent General J. E. B. Stuart's cavalry to reconnoiter. Setting out from Richmond on 12 June, Stuart quickly located Porter's corps north of the river and then, with Federal forces to his rear alerted to his presence and ready to contest his return, he rode down the peninsula and made a hundred-mile circuit around McClellan, destroying $7 million worth of stores in his progress and returning to his lines on 16 June. Reassured as to the safety of his left flank, Lee conceived an audacious plan that positioned 27,000 men to screen the 75,000 Union troops south of the river, while he marched with 60,000 men against Porter.

The Seven Days' began south of the river on 25 June with the first phase of McClellan's great push on Richmond, pushing in Rebel skirmishers and moving a mile forward in preparation for an attack by three Union corps. Had the attack gone forward the next day, McClellan could easily have smashed through the weak force screening Richmond, which was only four miles away. Lee calculated the risk and decided to proceed with his plan. McClellan, alarmed to hear that Stonewall Jackson was arriving to join Lee's forces, backed away from his plan. In fact, Jackson was scheduled to initiate battle on 26 June by attacking Porter's right, sweeping around it in company with Stuart's cavalry and cutting McClellan's line of communication to West Point. The two Hills would also attack Porter on the right, while Longstreet dealt with the center. The appointed time came and went, but Jackson did not move. He seemed to be in a trance of some sort, many of his troops convinced that he was deep in prayer. The morning passed in some confusion. When General A. P. Hill's division impatiently charged dug-in Federals near Mechanicsville in the afternoon, it was repulsed with heavy casualties. Jackson finally got under way six hours late, moved forward cautiously, found himself on Porter's flank and settled down to rest his troops. Porter had won the day, but McClellan ordered him to withdraw four miles to the vicinity of Gaines' Mill to ease the threat Jackson presented. This clash sounded the motif of the Seven Days': despite a tactical success and a highly favorable casualty ratio in coping with an ill-coordinated Southern attack in which Jackson's inertia was a major element, McClellan behaved as though defeated and ceded ground as though in imminent danger of encirclement.

On 27 June, Lee sent Jackson, Ewell (who had replaced Smith), and D. H. Hill against Porter's right and center near Gaines' Mill, while General James Longstreet feinted at Porter's left, intending to force the right back to the river and trap the corps when Porter moved his troops to meet Longstreet's threat. Porter's right was sorely pressed, but Jackson was tardy and unenthusiastic in his attack and Lee could not mount his general assault until sundown. At that point the Union center briefly collapsed and the Confederates seized high ground, forcing Porter into a nighttime retreat across the river. Confederate casualties were disproportionately high after a day of braving intense musketry and well-handled artillery, but it was McClellan who was disheartened, more than ever convinced that his army was facing a quarter of a million Rebel soldiers and reporting to authorities in Washington that he had been attacked on both sides of the river, even though the screening force opposite him on the south side of the river, for two days the only impediment to his winning Richmond, had done no more than create the illusion of imminent operations by constant theatrics, as at Yorktown. Convinced that the attacks by Lee's left were mere diversions preceding a massive attack by his right, McClellan began moving his base and supplies to the south of the Chickahominy. This meant the abandonment of any reasonable hope of besieging Richmond, because the absence of usable railroad tracks south of the river made it impossible to move his siege train of heavy artillery toward the city. He now burned the bridges over the Chickahominy along with tons of supplies, fired munitions dumps, and pushed or drove his locomotives into the river (in one case an entire ammunition train was set ablaze and driven into the water). The retreat was well executed and orderly, a readjustment rather than a retreat, in McClellan's thinking. The Rebels were delayed for a day because Lee, though he suspected that McClellan was retreating south of the river, had to be assured that he was not retreating on his base at West Point, and had to wait for Stuart's cavalry to reconnoiter and clarify the situation.

When Lee again made contact with the Union army, his project of a flank attack on the retreat was the victim of inept planning and timid execution. During the Seven Days' it became evident that Lee was able to devise plans that his staff and subordinates were not up to carrying out. It would take time for them to get used to his ways and for him to measure and utilize their abilities properly. Moreover, there was the continued problem of Jackson's poor performance, likely due to his exhaustion from his feats of arms in the Shenandoah Valley. An attack on 29 June at Savage's Station achieved nothing. Magruder, sent to attack the retreating Federals, managed to advance five miles against stubborn resistance, but to little avail, because Jackson, who had been ordered to march down the north side of the river with D. H. Hill, cross it at Grapevine Bridge, and attack the Federal right flank, became preoccupied with repairing a bridge rather than seeking a ford and never brought his forces into action. The following day, Lee devised an overly complex concentric attack, consisting of an attack at Glendale by Longstreet and A. P. Hill to sever McClellan's retreating column and threaten his supply train, while Jackson, D. H. Hill, and Ewell came up on the Federal rear, and three other divisions carried out separate attacks. The plan confused the attackers themselves and got rolling too late to catch the supply train. The divisions of Longstreet and A. P. Hill took heavy casualties, but ruptured the Federal line only briefly. Jackson moved forward vigorously to the edge of White Oak Swamp, but again dithered over bridge-building, despite the availability of fords, and finally settled down for a nap. Lee's right was driven back by naval guns firing from ships on the James River and from siege guns on high ground.

On 1 July Lee, frustrated by his inability to force a decisive conclusion, attacked Porter's corps waiting at Malvern Hill to cover the retreat to prepared positions at Harrison's Landing. The Federal forces were numerous, well ensconced on a hillside in a strong defensive position with flanks secured by ravines, and with plenty of artillery, including siege guns. Lee was impatient and convinced that the Union army was ready to crack. The Southern

artillery was simply massacred by the superior Federal firepower and did nothing to prepare the way for the infantry attack. Lee's troops went forward into the teeth of the Northern guns. Delays in the passing on of orders meant that the fourteen attacking battalions were fed in piecemeal, giving the Union cannoneers plenty of time to rake the attackers. As in previous engagements, the Rebels took far more casualties than the Federals, more of them from artillery than musketry in this battle. When the disastrous assaults ceased, the Seven Days' was over: McClellan was relieved to continue his withdrawal to Harrison's Landing, despite recommendations from his subordinates to counterattack. Lee was disappointed not to have destroyed the Union army and taken aback by casualties that amounted to one in four of all the troops in his command. After a desultory attempt late in July to get his army moving toward Richmond once again, McClellan marched his troops to Fort Monroe for reembarkation.

—Joseph M. McCarthy

See also Gaines' Mill, Battle of; Glendale (White Oak Swamp), Battle of; Lee, Robert Edward; Malvern Hill, Battle of; McClellan, George Brinton; Mechanicsville, Battle of; Savage's Station, Battle of.

For further reading:
Cullen, Joseph P. *The Peninsula Campaign, 1862: McClellan and Lee Struggle for Richmond* (1973).
Dowdey, Clifford. *The Seven Days: The Emergence of Lee* (1964).
Garrison, Nancy Scripture. *With Courage and Delicacy: Civil War on the Peninsula: Women and the U.S. Sanitary Commission* (1999).
McClellan, George B. *The Army of the Potomac: General McClellan's Report of Its Operations While Under His Command* (1864).
Miller, William J. *Battles for Richmond, 1862* (1996).
———, ed. *The Peninsula Campaign of 1862: From Yorktown to the Seven Days* (1993–1996).
Newton, Steven H. *The Battle of Seven Pines* (1993).
———. *Joseph E. Johnston and the Defense of Richmond* (1998).
Sears, Stephen W. *George B. McClellan: The Young Napoleon* (1999).
———. *To the Gates of Richmond: The Peninsula Campaign* (1992).
Wheeler, Richard. *Sword over Richmond: An Eyewitness History of McClellan's Peninsula Campaign* (1986).

SEVEN PINES, BATTLE OF

See Fair Oaks/Seven Pines

SEWARD, FREDERICK WILLIAM
(1830–1915)

United States assistant secretary of state

Born to William Henry Seward and Francis Miller Seward in Auburn, New York, Frederick William Seward was educated at Union College and studied law. During his law studies he served as his father's secretary. In 1851 he became an associate editor

of the *Albany Evening Journal*, edited by his father's friend and political associate, Thurlow Weed. While retaining his affiliation with the *Evening Journal*, Seward also assisted his father with his United States Senate duties and during the winter of 1856–1857 became his father's lead legislative assistant. The younger Seward remained in that position until his father was named secretary of state by Abraham Lincoln.

William Henry Seward had come to rely so heavily on his son that upon taking office he named the younger Seward his assistant secretary of state. Along with providing advice and counsel to his father, Frederick's primary duties were handling the myriad correspondence with United States consuls all over the world. This activity could range from the mundane acceptance of annual reports to issuing instructions regarding United States positions on Confederate agents operating abroad. In addition to these very time-consuming duties, Seward also dealt with the State Department's many political prisoner cases.

In his father's absence from Washington, Seward also acted as secretary of state. This occurred periodically for short periods of time throughout the war. For the most part, however, he served as his father's dutiful assistant and in that role proved to be a keen observer of his father's relationship with the president. Frederick came to admire President Lincoln a great deal, and in his numerous writings after the war he expressed his views on the Lincoln presidency.

Perhaps one of the sources of his admiration for Lincoln was an incident in December 1862 when the elder Seward was under attack from congressional leaders and decided to resign. He wrote out his resignation, had Frederick pen a similar resignation, and sent them to the president's mansion. Lincoln not only refused to accept both resignations, but came to the Seward house to persuade the two men to remain in his service.

On 5 April 1865 Frederick went out with his father and sister for a carriage ride, when something startled the horse and it bolted, causing Frederick to drop the reins. His father tried to retrieve them while the carriage was moving at full tilt and he fell, suffering a severe injury. Over the next week and a half Frederick served as acting secretary and attended the president's last cabinet meeting on 14 April.

On the night of 14 April, while his father slept in his sickroom, Frederick went to the head of the stairs when Lewis Powell, posing as a deliveryman with medicine for the secretary, entered the house. When Frederick refused to allow Powell to enter the secretary's room, Paine pulled out a pistol, which misfired when he tried to shoot Frederick. Powell then hit Frederick several times on the head with the pistol, fracturing the younger Seward's skull. Powell then entered the secretary's room and stabbed him several times in the face and neck before

being pulled off by an attendant. This attack, part of the conspiracy to assassinate the president, occurred within a short time of John Wilkes Booth's attack on Lincoln.

Frederick's life was despaired of for several weeks, and he spent a number of days in a coma. He recovered, however, and resumed his duties as his father's assistant by the summer of 1865. Both Sewards remained in office during the presidency of Andrew Johnson. During those years Frederick was sent by his father on diplomatic missions, primarily to acquire naval bases for the United States. He left office with his father in 1869 with the beginning of the Ulysses S. Grant administration.

Frederick moved back to New York after leaving office, but within a few months he and his father, with members of their families, decided to take an extended trip. The elder Seward had always wanted to visit much of the far west and wanted to see, after all of his difficult negotiations for its purchase, Alaska. While in the west, the family also decided on a tour of Mexico. After seeing all of these places, they returned to New York in early 1870.

The elder Seward died in 1872, leaving a major void in Frederick's life. He spent much of his time writing, but in 1874 entered politics and was elected to the New York legislature. He also served another stint from 1877 to 1879 as assistant secretary of state. After leaving office, he spent much of the remainder of his life quietly with his family and writing extensively. His most famous work was a biography of his father. The elder Seward had begun an autobiography but had stopped at 1834. Frederick continued from that point, publishing his work in 1891. He also wrote and published his own memoirs. He died on 25 April 1915.

—*David S. Heidler and Jeanne T. Heidler*

See also Diplomacy, U.S.A.; Lincoln Assassination; Seward, William Henry.

For further reading:

The Assassination of Abraham Lincoln: and the Attempted Assassination of William H. Seward, Secretary of State, and Frederick W. Seward, Assistant Secretary, on the Evening of the 14th of April, 1865 (1867).

Bemis, Samuel Flagg. *The American Secretaries of State and Their Diplomacy* (1963).

Seward, Frederick William. *Reminiscences of a War-Time Statesman and Diplomat, 1830–1915* (1916).

SEWARD, WILLIAM HENRY
(1801–1872)
U.S. secretary of state

One of the most influential figures in the administration of President Abraham Lincoln, William Henry Seward is also one of the more intriguing politicians of his generation. Unlike those of many of his equally high-profile Republican Party contemporaries, Seward's political views were shaped by an instinctive

pragmatism. From antislavery radical to conservative supporter of the archconservative President Andrew Johnson, Seward appears mercurial if he is judged purely in terms of his relative position on the question of the rights of African-Americans. The consistent theme in his political attitudes was a Victorian faith in the progress and prosperity of the American republic through economic development, expansion, and reform.

Born in Orange County, New York, Seward spent time in the South as a young man, earning his living as a schoolmaster before returning to his native state to establish a law practice in Auburn. He entered politics as an Anti-Mason and then became a Whig, serving as a state senator from 1830 to 1834. During this time, he forged a most valuable and enduring political friendship with Thurlow Weed, a political fixer with the name and appearance of a Dickensian clerk and editor of the influential *Albany Evening Journal*. Weed and Seward remained indelibly linked for the next four decades, building a network of correspondents and supporters that sustained Seward throughout his long political career.

In 1838 Seward became governor of New York. In that office, he provided vigorous support for state-funded internal improvements and the extension of public education. He was sympathetic to educational reform initiatives and to projects to create insane asylums, although his sociability made him rather more distant from that other great cause of Whiggish Protestant reformism, temperance. Seward was never a racial egalitarian, and he deeply distrusted what he regarded as the single-issue fanaticism of the abolitionists. Nevertheless, he acquired a reputation as a radical for his defense of fugitive slaves in a number of high-profile court cases. Like many other Whigs, he was instinctively opposed to the extension of slavery into the new territories gained after the Mexican-American War because doing so would not only restrict opportunities for free white migrants, but would make the eventual disappearance of slavery more difficult to accomplish. Like Abraham Lincoln, Seward believed that slavery, while tolerable where it currently existed, should be seen as an aberration to the general rule of freedom in the United States. This concern about slavery in the territories was reinforced by Seward's fervent belief in Manifest Destiny, an enthusiasm for national expansion that was to become an increasingly important element in his political career.

Seward was elected to the U.S. Senate in 1849 and made a dramatic appearance on the national stage during the debates on the Compromise of 1850. To the delight of antislavery Northerners who had felt betrayed by the ageing Daniel Webster's support for, among other things, a strengthened Fugitive Slave Act, Seward boldly announced that a "higher law than the Constitution, the law of God" condemned slavery to eventual death. It was a striking and influential phrase with which he was to be

thereafter associated, earning him a reputation for radicalism, which sat rather uneasily with his more cautious inclinations.

Initially, Seward was reluctant to abandon the old Whig Party, which he saw as the ideal vehicle for advancing the kind of economic policies and social projects he believed in. His embrace of the Republican Party did not represent a rejection of those values, but a recognition that economic and social questions were being overwhelmed by sectionalism. He played an important role from 1855 onward as the old Northern Whig voice in the Republican Party. Unlike many other former Whigs, Seward was never tempted by the Know-Nothing's appeal to anti-Catholic and anti-immigrant prejudice, but as a life-long opponent of Jacksonian Democrats he was distrustful of the influence in the Republican Party of former Democrats. In 1860 he badly wanted the Republican nomination and was widely expected to receive it. But the convention, meeting in Chicago, thought that Abraham Lincoln would be a more effective candidate in the lower North, especially the key states of Indiana, Illinois, and Pennsylvania, which the Republicans had failed to win four years earlier.

Seward prevaricated when Lincoln asked him to become secretary of state, hoping to exercise influence over the new cabinet and to establish his authority over the untested Lincoln. Seward, who was based in Washington throughout the winter of 1860–1861, was far more aware than Lincoln (and most other Republican leaders) of the genuineness of secession threats, and he became convinced that his personal and political contacts with border-state congressmen and upper South politicians were essential to prevent war. Seward pressured Lincoln to appoint old Whigs to his cabinet and to offer a post to a Southerner, John A. Gilmer of North Carolina. Seward was deeply opposed to the appointment of the self-important ex–Free Soiler Salmon P. Chase to the treasury.

Seward's concern to conciliate the South led him to suggest a number of amendments to the draft version of Lincoln's inaugural address. All the suggestions, in the words of James G. Randall, "in their general effect tended to soothe the public mind." Seward took upon himself to make some stylistic improvements as well, inventing a strangely morbid image of "mystic chords proceeding from…so many patriot graves…through all the hearts…in this broad continent of ours." Lincoln's reworking of this image as "mystic chords of memory, stretching from every battlefield and patriot grave to every living hearth and hearth-stone" demonstrated a deftness of expression that Seward's cumbersome prose never approached.

In cabinet, Seward took the lead in opposing the reinforcement of Fort Sumter, arguing that Southern public opinion, which was "feverish" for secession should be given time to calm down. His assumption of superiority within the administration was revealed by a clumsy attempt to persuade three Confederate commissioners that Sumter would not be reinforced—an undertaking given with no authorization at all from the president. In his self-conceived role as the first minister of the administration, Seward underestimated Lincoln's political judgment and skill. On April Fool's Day, 1861, the secretary of state overreached himself. In a rather presumptuous memorandum to the president, he implicitly offered to take control of the administration: "either the President must do it himself, and be all the while active in it; or devolve it on some member of his cabinet....I neither seek to evade nor assume responsibility."

It was typically quixotic of Seward that he suggested a foreign war to remind Southerners and Northerners of their shared interest and common values. Lincoln dryly responded that, if any new policy was to be undertaken, "I will do it." Thereafter, relations between the two men were cordial, even warm. Lincoln was able to calmly discard the most unnecessarily exuberant of his secretary of state's suggestions, while broadly concurring with the thrust of his suggestions. Above all, Lincoln entirely agreed with Seward's insistence that the administration must "Change the question before the public from one upon Slavery or about Slavery for a question upon Union or Disunion. In other words, from what would be regarded as a Party question to one of Patriotism or Union."

As secretary of state, Seward took control of the administration's internal security arrangements. He became notorious for a reported boast about being able to imprison anyone in the Union at the ring of a "little bell." He was certainly zealous in his determination to suppress dissent, but his reputation as a dictator was exaggerated.

In the sphere of foreign policy, Seward was by turns bullish and conciliatory, threatening war against Britain if it recognized the Confederacy in 1861, but backing down over the *Trent* crisis in part after pressure from Lincoln. The extent to which Seward was really in control of foreign policy later became a mater of dispute between wartime U.S. minister to London Charles Francis Adams and Secretary of the Navy Gideon Welles. After Seward's death, Adams published a short work, *Lincoln and Seward* (1873), in which he lauded the secretary of state's pivotal role as advisor to the martyred president. On the other hand, Welles, a grumpy New Englander who was always distrustful of his cabinet colleagues, accused Seward of aggrandizing himself at the expense of Lincoln, who was always the real master of operations. It is certainly true that Seward had less influence than he sometimes liked to think, but equally true that Lincoln relied heavily on his judgment. This was

revealed when the president took Seward's advice about the timing of the Emancipation Proclamation. The secretary of state thought that they should wait for a significant military victory before announcing the policy so that it would appear to be a product of military strength rather than desperation. Seward was overanxious about foreign reaction to the Emancipation Proclamation, but his sensitivity to the conservatism of domestic public opinion was characteristically acute. Lincoln duly waited until after the battle of Antietam before making public the emancipation policy.

While he understood the frustrations of the radical antislavery campaigners, Seward steered the Lincoln administration toward as broad an electoral appeal as possible. Although he was the most effective conservative influence on Lincoln, Seward was genial enough and maintained sufficient contacts throughout the Republican Party and beyond to insulate him from some of the fierce assaults from radicals suffered by more brazen, although less influential, conservative cabinet members, such as Postmaster General Montgomery Blair. Throughout the war, Seward was among those who were unhappy with the apparent dominance of radicals in the party. Thurlow Weed briefly flirted with the idea of a third party "composed of the moderate men of both parties," on the principle that if it was not possible to read the radicals out of the Republican Party, then they should be deserted by the rest. Along with *New York Times* editor Henry J. Raymond, however, Seward believed that the war gave the Republican moderates an unrivaled opportunity to broaden their base, including ex-Whigs and those voters who had supported Constitutional Union candidates John Bell and Edward Everett in 1860. By 1864 Seward and Raymond were looking forward to a settlement of the slavery question in such a way that something resembling the old Whig Party might be reconstructed. They agreed with Weed in his assumption that the Republican Party could not be electorally successful in the future unless it created a base in the South and among "the men of moderation and sound-judgement." As ever, factional struggles over control of patronage, feuds that had their origins in the murky world of antebellum New York politics, intersected with these kinds of strategic political considerations. Seward and Weed saw the threat of radicals within the administration as a direct challenge to their ability to distribute spoils. For instance, it was reported that Seward completely lost his temper about the success of the Loyal National League in New York because he saw it as a threat to his and Thurlow Weed's political control.

Seward's political leadership was crucial in the shaping of the Union Party strategy for the 1864 presidential election. The decision to call a convention to nominate Lincoln for reelection under the name "National Union Party" consciously met the pleas of many conservatives who, since the decline of the Whig Party in the mid-1850s, had been left without a natural political home. Moderate Republican leaders such as Seward saw the Union Party as a strategic step toward a new organization that would embrace a national conservative constituency. Seward spoke enthusiastically of a "great coming together" of the parties once the divisive issue of slavery was dispensed with by the Thirteenth Amendment. For precisely this reason, Seward used his influence to play down publicly the radical implications of emancipation. Although he firmly supported the ending of slavery, he attempted to distance the administration from the taint of prewar abolitionism and repeatedly denied that he had any interest in predetermining the nature of Southern society after the war. Leading Unionists built a campaign that side-stepped the issue of emancipation while not repudiating it, and Seward was a key figure in the articulation of this approach. His correspondence is filled with reports from friends in key electoral states, and throughout the war he maintained close connections with conservatives outside the fold of the Republican Party. Seward and like-minded moderates hoped to distance Lincoln's Union organization from what many conservatives and border state people still regarded as the irresponsible radicalism of the Republican Party, while building on what they saw that party as having accomplished.

The 1864 campaign began in earnest on 3 September with a speech by Seward in his hometown of Auburn that was widely reprinted in the newspapers and as a campaign document. He appealed to those voters who accepted emancipation as a final solution to the sectional crisis, and as a moral advance, but who were fundamentally conservative on the question of race. He made no mention of the Baltimore convention's enthusiastic endorsement of the proposed abolition amendment. Instead, he insisted that while the rebels waged war, military measures affecting slavery—meaning the Emancipation Proclamation—would continue. But, Seward said, as soon as the Confederates laid down their arms, all such questions would "pass over to the arbitrament of the courts of law and to the councils of legislation." To the irritation of many radicals, Seward had neatly set the tone for the campaign. He had not explicitly endorsed the proposed Thirteenth Amendment, but he had declared his faith that constitutional action could solve the slavery problem. Most importantly, he had assured his listeners that a commitment to emancipation would not prolong the war. Hugh McCulloch, Seward's future cabinet colleague, understandably observed that the speech had been "captivating and adroit!"

The Seward speech was delivered two days after the North learned of General William T. Sherman's great victory at Atlanta, and three days after the Chicago convention had committed the Democratic candidate to pursue a policy of an armistice, followed by negotiations with the Rebels. These two developments were a tremendous boost to the credibility of the proadministration arguments. A sudden return of public optimism about the war made the crucial conservative center more receptive to the idea that changing horses while crossing a stream would be folly. No longer forced to be defensive about the military situation, supporters of the administration were free to concentrate their attacks on the Democrats and the threat to the national cause that they represented, especially given the contents of the Chicago platform, which played into the hands of Lincoln supporters, who found it easier than they otherwise would have done to stigmatize all their opponents with copperheadism.

At the Hampton Roads Peace Conference, Seward was apparently prepared to concede the commitment of the administration to abolishing slavery in return for reunion. Although he may well have been willing to concede the temporary effectiveness of the Emancipation Proclamation, the secretary was convinced of the necessity of a constitutional amendment to settle the slavery question. His influence was crucial in persuading wavering congressmen in the lame duck session in January 1865 to support the Thirteenth Amendment.

A grim testimony to the influence of Seward in the administration is that he was also the target of an assassin on Good Friday, 1865. Recovering in bed from a carriage fall, Seward was stabbed by an intruder, Lewis Thornton Powell, an accomplice of John Wilkes Booth. Seward survived and after a summer of convalescence returned to his duties in the State Department under President Andrew Johnson's leadership.

After the war, Seward became one of a minority of Civil War Republicans who continued to support the Union Party project, seeing it as a means of reconstructing something like the old Whig Party, a great conservative cross-sectional organization, that would be nationalist and expansionist in both economic and geographical terms.

The National Union Party emerged from the conflict with such a stock of moral and political capital that *Harper's Weekly* could talk confidently of the "end of parties." During 1865 Seward, Raymond, and their allies tried to exploit antipartisanship to construct a new centrist organization. They saw the National Union Party as the basis for an alliance of the "conservative" men of the country, uniting Southern Whigs with the "moderate men of the north" around a platform of generosity toward the South and support for President Johnson. Building on the successful wartime strategy, the National Union Party of 1865 rallied against the evils of division. Resolutions presented at a Union "mass meeting" at the Cooper Institute in June

contained a sharp attack upon parties now that the contentious issues of slavery and Union were "substantially settled and decided." Still later, in 1866, President Johnson's supporters met in Philadelphia to rally support for the National Union Party. Seward and Raymond were leading figures, but by then the coalition of support that Lincoln had created had collapsed. In war, the divisive issues of Reconstruction could be kept at bay with an appeal to national unity. By this time, with the president in conflict with Congress and the bulk of his own party, claims to represent the entire nation sounded empty. Johnson's men did not have the political authority to dominate the political agenda in the way that Lincoln's supporters could in 1864. Seward's legacy to the Republican Party was an ambiguous one: a vital figure in its early days, he appeared to abandon the party in later years.

William H. Seward was a sagacious political operator and a witty and affable man who greatly enjoyed his challenging public roles. Although committed to the antislavery cause, he was a better representative than his more radical colleagues of the political assumptions of most Northern whites. Seward considered that one of his greatest triumphs in politics was the acquisition in 1867 of Alaska, purchased from Russia and immediately dubbed "Mr. Seward's Ice Box." It is a revealing and highly characteristic final achievement: apparently eccentric, quirkily dramatic, but entirely consistent with Seward's vision of what the United States would become. For Seward, as for many white Northerners of his generation, slavery was not only a moral indecency, it was the great obstacle to that vision.

—*Adam I.P. Smith*

See also Diplomacy, U.S.A.; Great Britain; Lincoln, Abraham; Maximilian, Ferdinand; Republican Party; Seward, Frederick William; *Trent Affair*.

For further reading:
Seward, William Henry. Papers. Microfilm, University of Rochester Library.
Taylor, John M. *William Henry Seward: Lincoln's Right Hand* (1967).
Van Deusen, Glyndon G. *William Henry Seward* (1967).

SEYMOUR, HORATIO
(1810–1886)
Governor of New York

Horatio Seymour was born in Pompey Hill, New York, on 31 May 1810. Educated at Geneva Academy (now Hobart College) and at a military school in Middletown, Connecticut, he gravitated to law and was admitted to the bar in 1832. His association with William L. Marcy integrated Seymour into the Albany Regency, and he served as military secretary for Marcy during Marcy's tenure as New York's governor.

Elected to the state assembly in 1841 and as mayor of Utica in 1842, Seymour revealed a high talent for political maneuver and conciliation. When he returned to the state assembly in 1844, he proved so effective in neutralizing opposition to significant canal legislation that he was elected speaker of the assembly the following year.

Seymour's deft abilities made him an able mediator between Democratic Party factions in New York who had drawn lines over the slavery issue. As the Barnburner and Hunker camps snarled at one another, Seymour remained the picture of moderation, disdaining the extremism of the sectional debate. He denounced Northern abolitionists and Southern fire-eaters with equal scorn. Constant in his preoccupations, however, was the ascendancy of local government, so his opposition to extensive federal authority often overshadowed his free-soil inclinations. Elected governor in 1853, Seymour again played the role of moderate reformer who was a political realist, pushing through important reforms of the state prison system even as he objected to prohibition. His political acumen and restraint made him a potential compromise candidate for the Democratic presidential nomination in 1860, and he was seriously mentioned as such at the fractious convention in Charleston, South Carolina. Yet Seymour was by nature and temperament an admirer of Stephen A. Douglas and a supporter of the local dominion that Douglas's doctrine of Popular Sovereignty espoused. When Abraham Lincoln defeated Douglas, Seymour was among the moderate Northern wing of the Democratic Party that urged calm and supported the Crittenden Compromise as a way of resolving the secession crisis.

Seymour deplored the enhancement of federal power that the Civil War inevitably brought about, but he nonetheless urged a patriotism that supported restoring the Union. Elected governor of New York in 1862, Seymour occupied a key position during the most critical years of the war. For the most part, he sustained Lincoln's policies, although he thought the Emancipation Proclamation and the policy of military arrests were examples of dangerously extended federal authority. He was especially perturbed by federal conscription, not only because he thought it unconstitutional, but also because it struck him as inappropriate. New York's quotas were excessive, he said, and the method of induction provoked civil convulsions. Nonetheless, he labored tirelessly to fill the state's quota for the Union army and reacted with brisk resolve to suppress the New York City draft riots in 1863. It was thus unfair to brand him a Copperhead, as some such as Horace Greeley did, because afterward he was characteristically conciliatory to the rioters and because he continued to take exception to the extraconstitutional powers assumed by the president. Lincoln, at least, knew better. When Seymour lodged a complaint in August 1863 that it was unaccept-

able for the Federal government to keep him in the dark about conscription plans, Lincoln ordered Secretary of War Edwin Stanton to notify Seymour before any future drafts so that he could take measures to prevent domestic disturbances.

Seymour resisted being named the Democratic presidential nominee in 1868, especially because it was clear that his Republican opponent would be the popular war hero Ulysses S. Grant. Yet Seymour was chosen on the twenty-second ballot in a compromise that attempted to mend rifts between eastern and western wings of the party. He afterward marked his acceptance of the nomination as a major political mistake. His instincts were sound, for Grant easily bested him by more than 300,000 popular votes and with a margin of 214 to 80 in the Electoral College.

Seymour's defeat hardly meant that he was finished as a major actor in New York politics, however. He joined the fight against William Tweed's corruptionists and applauded the rise of Grover Cleveland in the state Democratic Party. Seymour found the principled, if impolitic bluntness of Cleveland most congenial and was gratified to the point of vindication to see Cleveland win the presidency in 1884. By the time Seymour died on 12 February 1886 in Utica, he had become an anachronism in the political climate of the Gilded Age, for his dignity and moderation had always made it appear that he found politics slightly embarrassing.

—David S. Heidler and Jeanne T. Heidler

See also New York City Draft Riots.

For further reading:

Murdock, Eugene Converse. *Horatio Seymour and the 1863 Draft* (1965).

Stewart, Mitchell. *Horatio Seymour of New York* (1938; reprint, 1970).

Wall, Alexander J. *A Sketch of the Life of Horatio Seymour, 1810–1886, with a Detailed Account of His Administration As Governor of the State of New York during the War of 1861–1865* (1929).

SEYMOUR, THOMAS HART
(1807–1868)
Connecticut Democrat

Born to Henry Seymour and Jane Ellery Seymour in Hartford, Connecticut, Thomas Hart Seymour was educated locally before attending and graduating from Alden Partridge's military school in 1829. Returning home, Seymour studied law and became active in Connecticut Democratic politics. Beginning in 1836 at the age of twenty-nine, Seymour began a three-year term as a probate judge in Hartford. During that time he also became quite active in the local militia and eventually commanded the local unit.

After leaving the bench in 1839, Seymour spent several years building his law practice and exploring a

career in partisan journalism. He had gained enough of a reputation statewide by 1842 to receive the Democratic nomination for his district's seat in the U.S. House of Representatives. He won the election and served one term in Congress, declining the nomination for a second term in 1844.

The outbreak of the Mexican-American War inspired Seymour to put some of his military training and interest to work, and he helped raise a regiment of Connecticut volunteers for the war. Commissioned a major of volunteers before the regiment joined Winfield Scott's Mexico City campaign, Seymour's military training gained him a transfer as major to the 9th U.S. Infantry early in the campaign. Having fought in all the engagements of the campaign up to that point, in August Seymour was promoted to lieutenant colonel. The 9th was given the lead in the attack on the Mexican stronghold of Chapultepec, and after the regiment's colonel was wounded early in the fighting, Seymour took command and led his men to the summit. For this action he was given a brevet promotion to colonel.

Seymour's service in the war helped his political career back home, and when he returned to Connecticut he received the Democrats' nomination for governor in 1849. Though he barely lost the election in that year, he won in 1850. He was reelected in the next three successive elections, though he resigned early in his fourth term after President Franklin Pierce appointed him minister to Russia. He remained in that position for four years, serving his last year under Pierce's successor, James Buchanan. After resigning, he remained in Europe as a tourist for one year and returned to Connecticut in 1859.

Upon his return home in the midst of the sectional crisis, Seymour met with his old friend Franklin Pierce regarding the future of the Democratic Party. Pierce believed that the best hope for the party in 1860 was the nomination of Jefferson Davis for president. Seymour agreed with Pierce's assessment and pledged to work for Davis's candidacy among Connecticut Democrats. When Stephen Douglas received the nomination at the Baltimore Democratic Convention and John C. Breckinridge received the nomination of a coalition of Southern and Northern opponents of Douglas, Seymour pledged his support to Breckinridge.

While the presidential campaign proceeded throughout the country, Connecticut also had its annual governor's race, and Seymour received the Democratic nomination for that position. In what proved to be one of the closest contests in Connecticut history, Seymour received 49.7 percent of the vote to Republican William Alfred Buckingham's 50.3 percent. Among Democrats in the state, the race between Douglas and Breckinridge was nearly as close, with Douglas receiving 51 percent to Breckinridge's 49

percent. It was estimated that about 10,000 Democratic voters stayed away from the polls in 1860.

During the secession crisis of early 1861, Seymour advocated allowing the Southern states to depart in peace, strongly denouncing any suggestion that force be used to keep the Union together. At the outbreak of the war in April 1861, he remained a proponent of a peaceful solution and made peace proposals in the Connecticut legislature in July 1861. While the Republican majority in the legislature defeated his proposals, Seymour's actions inspired peace meetings throughout the state during the next several months.

As the war progressed, Seymour increasingly became associated with the so-called Copperheads of the North, the Peace Democrats who privately and sometimes not so privately hoped for a Confederate victory in the war. His loyalty was questioned in the state legislature, where his portrait as a former governor was temporarily removed from display. In 1863, on the heels of the overwhelming Union defeat at Fredericksburg, the war was becoming increasingly unpopular in Connecticut, and the Democratic Party in the state nominated Seymour for governor in the hopes of taking advantage of disaffection with the war. He again lost by a narrow margin to Buckingham in what proved to be a very bitter campaign on both sides. Many Democrats, looking at the election later, came to believe that a more moderate Democrat might have carried the election.

In 1864 Seymour was mentioned frequently as a possible presidential nominee for the national party, and at the convention he received several dozen votes on the first ballot. After George McClellan received the nomination, Seymour was frequently mentioned as a possible secretary of state should McClellan be elected.

McClellan's defeat and the subsequent Union victory in the war discredited Northern politicians who had taken stands similar to Seymour's. After the war, as a result, he lived quietly in retirement in Hartford. He died there on 3 September 1868.

—*David S. Heidler and Jeanne T. Heidler*

See also Copperheads; Peace Democrats.

For further reading:
Niven, John. *Connecticut for the Union: The Role of the State in the Civil War* (1965).

SEYMOUR, TRUMAN B.
(1824–1891)
Union general

During the Civil War, Truman B. Seymour served from Fort Sumter through the Appomattox campaign, and rose from the grade of captain to major general. Nevertheless, he earned a reputation as an aggressive, perhaps exceedingly rash, officer who suffered several controversial, well-publicized defeats.

A native of Vermont, Seymour was born in Burlington on 24 September 1824. Son of a Methodist minister, he attended Norwich University, perhaps the North's most prominent private military school, from 1840 until 1842. He then earned an appointment to West Point and graduated in the prestigious class of 1846, which included a number of future Civil War generals, including Thomas J. Jackson and George B. McClellan. Assigned to the artillery, Seymour fought in the Mexican-American War, where he earned two brevets and performed heroically in the battles of Cerro Gordo, Contreras, and Churubusco. In the years after the war the young lieutenant performed garrison duty in New York and returned to the U.S. Military Academy as an instructor. In 1852 he married Louisa Weir, the daughter of a longtime West Point professor. During the late 1850s, Seymour served in Florida in what became known as the Third Seminole War.

During the secession winter of 1860–1861, Seymour, who by then had been promoted to captain, was part of Major Robert Anderson's command occupying the Federal fortifications in Charleston harbor. He defended Fort Sumter during the April 1861 bombardment and earned another brevet promotion. Following the fort's surrender, Seymour returned to the North and joined the volunteer service. Rising rapidly in rank, he received a commission as brigadier general in April 1862. Seymour led a brigade of Pennsylvanians in the Seven Days' battles, and later at Second Bull Run, South Mountain, and Antietam. Following the appointment of a junior officer to divisional command, Seymour penned a scathing letter to his superiors, illustrating a prickly temperament and overdeveloped sense of honor that would be displayed again later in the war. "I respectfully but earnestly protest against the humiliating depreciation expressed by this preference," he complained, "to which no officer of sensibility can submit without the destruction of all stimulant to further usefulness."

Shortly after writing the above, the general requested reassignment for health reasons. Suffering from bronchitis that had exacerbated a previous case of malaria, Seymour was subsequently sent to the Department of the South, which encompassed the Union-held portions of the lower Atlantic seaboard. He would remain in this theater of the war throughout 1863 and early 1864, commanding a division under departmental commander Quincy Gillmore. During this period a fellow officer described him as "[a] trim-built, soldierly-looking officer, with handsome, artistic features, [but] something of a martinet in manner and speech."

In July 1863, Seymour commanded the unsuccessful assault against Battery Wagner, one of the Confederate fortifications defending Charleston. Brigadier General George Strong's brigade, spearheaded by Robert Gould Shaw's African-American 54th Massachusetts, led the attack, which was repulsed with heavy losses. In the battle, a shell fragment wounded Seymour, while Strong was mortally wounded and Shaw killed. In the aftermath, elements of the Northern press criticized Seymour for placing Shaw's regiment in the vanguard, accusing him of a hostile attitude towards African-American soldiers.

Despite these criticisms, Seymour evidently remained on good terms with his department commander, for in January 1864 Gillmore selected him to command an expedition to reoccupy Jacksonville, Florida. Federal officials hoped to organize a loyal Florida government in time for the 1864 election, to cut off the flow of Florida supplies to Rebel armies, and to recruit African-American Floridians into the Union army. The early stages of the campaign went well, but on 20 February, apparently against orders, Seymour advanced his command of about 5,500 men westward into the interior towards Lake City. In a bloody engagement near Olustee Station, the Federals were repulsed with heavy losses and forced to retreat back to Jacksonville. Again, Northern papers bitterly attacked Seymour and accused him of leading his small army, which included a brigade of African-American soldiers, into an ambush.

After his long sojourn along the Atlantic coast, Seymour returned to the Army of the Potomac in the spring of 1864, in time to lead a brigade at the Wilderness. He fell into Confederate hands at this battle and was imprisoned for a time in Charleston, the city he had tried so long to capture. Eventually, the general was exchanged and led a division of the VI Corps in the Shenandoah Valley and Petersburg campaigns. By the end of the war he had earned brevet promotions to major general in both the regular and volunteer service, but when he was mustered out of the volunteers in August 1865, he reverted to his permanent rank of captain in the 5th U.S. Artillery. After a leave of absence, Seymour commanded the garrisons at Key West and later Pensacola. Promoted to major, he subsequently served on the Artillery Board, and in turn commanded Forts Warren, Preble, and Barrancas. The former general also found time to earn a degree from Williams College in Massachusetts. In November 1876 Seymour retired from active service. He lived the remainder of his life in Florence, Italy, where he became accomplished as an artist. The ex-soldier died in Italy on 30 October 1891.

—*David J. Coles*

See also Fort Wagner, Battle of; Jacksonville, Florida.
For further reading:
Poirier, Robert G. *"By the Blood of Our Alumni": Norwich University Citizen Soldiers in the Army of the Potomac* (1999).
Waugh, John G. *The Class of 1846 From West Point to Appomattox: Stonewall Jackson, George McClellan and Their Brothers* (1994).
Wise, Stephen R. *Gate of Hell: Campaign for Charleston Harbor, 1863* (1994).

SHARPSHOOTERS

As early as the Revolutionary War, American military leaders saw the need for special units of marksmen or sharpshooters. In the great tradition of Rogers' Rangers of the American Colonial wars, which had already set the standard for such units, the green jackets of George Washington's special skirmishers were a justifiable cause of alarm to the British. When the American Civil War erupted, Colonel Hiram Berdan organized special sharpshooter regiments for the Union army in 1861. Each man, armed first with the Colt revolving rifle, then later with the preferred Sharps breechloader, had to be able to put seven shots into a ten-inch circle at 200 yards over open sights. These men were specially trained in sniping, stealth tactics, and scouting, not unlike the training of today's Special Forces.

In July 1862, the Confederate Congress passed a resolution calling for such units in the Southern armies. Under this rubric, each brigade commander was empowered to select a small number of men from each regiment who were proven in battle, of good standing, and of good marksmanship. These men would form a corps d'elite for duties much like their Union counterparts. Exempted from onerous duties, they would camp and train together. On the march they were the advance, in retreat the rear guard. In combat, they skirmished with the enemy or scouted; when the assault began, they fell back to serve as file closers for the line of attack. Each man had to be able to hit a target at 600 yards with open or field sights.

Probably since the old code of chivalry was hard to abandon, most Confederate brigadiers did not form such units. Some, on the other hand, were formed but were not officially commissioned by the Confederate Congress. A partial list of official units includes the 17th Battalion, Alabama Sharpshooters; the 1st, 2d, 3d, 4th, and 8th Battalions, Georgia Sharpshooters; the 9th and 13th Battalions, Mississippi Sharpshooters; and the 24th Tennessee Battalion Sharpshooters.

In both armies, the sharpshooter units fought beyond the call of duty, took heavy casualties, and maintained a high standard of conduct as elite troops. Disliked for their sniping and stealth, these units nevertheless continued a vital tradition in American military history that has come full circle in today's highly trained and mobile Special Forces.

—*Gerald J. Smith*

See also Berdan, Hiram.
For further reading:
Anonymous. "Sharpshooting in Lee's Army." *Confederate Veteran* (1895).
Atlanta Southern Confederacy, 19 May 1863.
Cuppell, Charles. *History of Durrell's Battery in the Civil War* (1904).
Hutchins, Nathan L. File, Georgia Department of Archives

and History, Atlanta, Georgia.

Journal of the Congress of the Confederate States of America, 1861–1865 (1904–1905).

McWhirter, A. J. "General Wofford's Brigade in the Wilderness, May 6th, 1864." *Atlanta Journal* (1901).

Montgomery, George, Jr., ed. *Georgia Sharpshooter: The Civil War Diary and Letters of William Rhadamanthus Montgomery* (1997).

Phillips, W. F. "Wofford's Brigade at the Wilderness." *Atlanta Constitution* (1887).

Smith, Gerald J. *"One of the Most Daring of Men": The Life Of Confederate General William Tatum Wofford* (1997).

White, M. E. "The Thomas G. Jordan Family During the War Between The States." *Georgia Historical Quarterly* (1975).

"Wofford's Brigade at Gettysburg." *Richmond Daily Enquirer* (1863).

Young, John D. "A Campaign with Sharpshooters." *Annals of War* (1879).

SHAW, ROBERT GOULD
(1837–1863)
Union general

Born in Boston, Massachusetts, on 10 October 1837 into great wealth with interlocking kinship ties to the Brahmin families of Forbes, Parkman, Cabot, Lodge, Hunnewell, Sturgis, and Lowell, Robert Gould Shaw had a privileged childhood. His parents insisted on perfectionist ideals. They funded the experimental transcendentalist community at Brook Farm—where Robert attended classes—and were outspoken for the abolition of slavery. Shaw learned lessons of noblesse oblige as he met and interacted with his parents' circle of friends, including Harriet Beecher Stowe, William Lloyd Garrison, Henry George, Ralph Waldo Emersen, Sydney Howard Gay, Frances Anne Kemble, and Lydia Maria Child, his mother's closest confidant. Within this circle, Shaw grew up on an ideology of service and principles of moral uplift.

After spending one year at Fordham and five years at schools in Switzerland and Germany, Shaw entered Harvard in 1856. That year he met the Republican Party's first nominee, John C. Frémont, who was attending the wedding of Shaw's oldest sister, Anna, to the well-known national orator and, later, editor of *Harper's Weekly*, George W. Curtis. Shaw had three other siblings, all sisters, who married prominently to Colonel Charles Russell Lowell, General Francis C. Barlow, and Robert Minturn.

In 1859 Shaw quit Harvard to enter business in the New York City mercantile firm of his uncles. He joined the exclusive 7th New York National Guard, a social club. After the firing on Fort Sumter, Shaw mustered with his regiment and marched down Broadway in the glow of war fever—and with sandwiches from Delmonico's and a velvet stool to sit upon. The 7th was the first unit to reach Washington after Lincoln's call for troops and thus won the sobriquet, "the regiment that saved the capital."

When the "Darling Seventh" disbanded after thirty days, without seeing action, Shaw gained a commission as a second lieutenant in the 2d Massachusetts Infantry, commanded by George H. Gordon and stocked with officers from the state's most prominent families. Shaw proved himself a competent soldier and rose to the rank of captain, having suffered battle wounds during the Shenandoah Valley campaign and the battle of Antietam. In the aftermath of Antietam, President Lincoln issued the Emancipation Proclamation.

When Lincoln authorized the enlistment of African-American soldiers, Massachusetts governor John Andrew quickly gained permission to raise a black regiment. To guarantee success, Andrew sought an officer with prominent family ties, and so turned to the well-connected businessman, John Murray Forbes. Forbes suggested the staunch abolitionist Captain Norwood Penrose Hallowell, 20th Massachusetts Infantry. But Hallowell was from Pennsylvania. Agreeing with Forbes's second choice, Andrew offered Shaw the colonelcy of what would become the North's most famous African-American regiment, the 54th Massachusetts Infantry.

Shaw initially declined the offer out of loyalty to his beloved 2d; but his desire for higher rank, the support of his friends, the pressure applied by his mother, his own moral dilemma, and his recent engagement to marry Annie Haggerty of Lenox helped him to change his mind. The pressure from his mother cannot be overstated. When he accepted the position, she wrote him of her "deep and holy joy" that he had been "willing to take up the cross."

Insisting upon success—and fearing ridicule—Shaw organized the regiment. He selected officers with firm antislavery views, including a brother of William and Henry James. Shaw wanted only the most educated and physically fit men possible. Altogether, he ordered the rejection of every third man who arrived at the Camp Meigs training center in Readville, Massachusetts. Furthermore, a "Black Committee" of prominent abolitionists was organized to direct the recruiting of men from all the Northern states and Canada into this one regiment and to supply the best equipment available. This was their showcase unit. Well-known black leaders, such as Frederick Douglass, John Mercer Langston, O. B. Wells, and James Forten, recruited for the regiment. Douglass signed up two of his sons and the grandson of Sojourner Truth. In this manner, the 54th Massachusetts became the most highly selective and well-provisioned regiment of the war.

From the first day in camp, recruits received shoes and uniforms. If they could not read, and there were only a few who could not, they attended reading classes at night. Shaw was a strict disciplinarian who enforced a rigid training schedule. In fact, he was so rigid that he came under criticism from the men, officers, press, and camp commander Colonel Richard Peirce, who ordered Shaw to stop the "severe and unusual punishments not laid down by regulations."

By 2 May, with 1,000 men under arms, trained and ready, Shaw took a furlough to marry. Four days later, the honeymoon was cut short by orders assigning the regiment to Major General David Hunter and the Department of the South. At the flag presentation ceremony on 18 May, Governor Andrew told the men that the world was watching to see if they would fight like white men. He told Shaw that the experiment was one "full of hope and glory." Ten days later, Shaw led the men in a parade through Boston and onto the steamer from which they would debark at Port Royal, South Carolina, on 3 June.

The regiment's first action was a raid into Georgia with Colonel James Montgomery's 2d South Carolina Infantry, a regiment recruited from freed slaves. The seaport town of Darien was looted and burned under orders from Montgomery and protests from Shaw. Press reports hurt the reputation of the black fighting man. The regiment stayed mostly in camp for the next month, while Shaw persistently asked for regular combat duty for his men.

The opportunity came when Major General Quincy A. Gillmore, in charge of the operations to reduce Charleston, directed an assault against Battery Wagner on Morris Island. Ordered to support the assault, Shaw moved his regiment to James Island. On 16 July, the regiment stood firm in the face of a surprise attack by a larger Confederate force, losing forty-six men before marching all night to reach a ferry transporting them to Morris Island.

Understanding his duty to show that black men could fight and die like whites, Shaw volunteered to lead the attack on Wagner. At 7:45 P.M. on 18 July, Shaw and his men charged across the open beach and up the sloping walls, directly into Confederate guns and men unhurt by a day-long artillery barrage directed against them. Shaw died at the top of the parapet. His regiment, and the thirteen white regiments that followed, did not take the fort. The next day, Confederate gravediggers buried 800 Union soldiers in the sand, and made a statement by burying Shaw face up with twenty of his men face down on top of him.

The burial "with his niggers," as Confederate general Johnson Hagood put it, did not have the effect intended. Instead, the charge, the deaths, and the burial were victories for the abolitionist cause. Nearly fifty poems have been written to commemorate the noble sacrifice. Sculptor Augustus Saint-Gaudens crafted a huge bronze monument to the battle set on Boston Common in 1897. A motion picture, *Glory*

(1989), broadcast the story to a wide audience, and books about the young martyr proliferate.

—*Russell Duncan*

See also Fort Wagner, Battle of; Montgomery, James; United States Colored Troops.
For further reading:
Duncan, Russell, ed. *Blue-Eyed Child of Fortune: The Civil War Letters of Colonel Robert Gould Shaw* (1992).

SHELBY, JOSEPH ORVILLE
(1830–1897)
Confederate officer

Joseph Orville "Jo" Shelby was an ostrich-plumed, dynamic, aggressive, and iron-willed leader, deeply steeped in the chivalric lore of Sir Walter Scott. He was born in Lexington, Kentucky, to an aristocratic family from Tennessee and Kentucky. His spent his boyhood years in the company of his Uncle Francis Preston Blair, Sr., and his cousins Francis "Frank" Preston Blair, Jr., and Benjamin "Gratz" Brown. In 1852, after attending Transylvania College, Shelby followed his cousins Frank Blair and Gratz Brown to Missouri. While his cousins pursued politics, Shelby moved down the Missouri River Valley and became one of the richest young men in Missouri as a hemp planter, rope manufacturer, and steamboat owner.

In 1854 Shelby returned to Kentucky. He recruited and outfitted a company of proslavery cavalry to fight free-soil forces in Kansas. Because of Shelby's leadership in this conflict, attacks by free-soil "Jayhawkers" cost him most of the financial fortune he had amassed.

When the Civil War broke out, Frank Blair called Shelby to St. Louis. He arrived on 11 May 1861, the day of the St. Louis Massacre. Shelby later refused a Federal captaincy offered to him by Frank Blair. Instead, he recruited and outfitted a company of pro-Southern mounted rangers and accepted a commission as a captain of cavalry in the Missouri State Guard.

Although Shelby missed the battle at Boonville (17 June 1861), he played a critical part in nearly every battle in Missouri and Arkansas afterward. After fighting at Carthage, Wilson's Creek, Lexington, Springfield, Pea Ridge, St. Charles, and De Vall's Bluff, Shelby and his company were dismounted and transferred east of the Mississippi River to support General Albert Sidney Johnston in northern Mississippi. In June 1862, after uneventful service near Corinth, Shelby accepted a Confederate colonelcy with the requirement that he recruit a regiment of cavalry. He crossed more than 500 miles of Federal territory to central Missouri and recruited 1,000 cavalry troopers in four days. Shelby quickly organized his new regiment and rendezvoused with two other cavalry regiments in southwest Missouri. After skirmishes near Newtonia in southwest Missouri,

Joseph Shelby (*Library of Congress*)

he organized the three regiments into the Missouri Cavalry Brigade. Operating out of northern Arkansas, this unit soon earned the moniker of the "Iron Brigade." In November and December 1862 Shelby's Iron Brigade was indispensable in the battles of Cane Hill and Prairie Grove. At Prairie Grove, a reckless young man named Frank James saved Shelby's life, and Shelby returned the favor in 1883 when he testified as a character witness for Frank who was on trial for murder.

On 31 December 1862 Shelby led his brigade into Federally occupied Missouri on the first of four cavalry raids in which he would participate. The first two raids, commanded by his superior, Brigadier General John Sappington Marmaduke, accomplished their objectives, but were poorly planned. In September 1863 Shelby was given permission to lead a raid from southwestern Arkansas to the Missouri River and back. This raid would be the longest raid of the Civil War and one of the most successful. Although Shelby's arm had been shattered by a musketball at the battle of Helena, Arkansas, he and his men rode 1,500 miles in 41 days and prevented the transfer of large numbers of Federal troops to Major General William S. Rosecrans at Chattanooga, Tennessee.

On 1 April 1864 Shelby received notification of his appointment as a Confederate brigadier general and orders to join the effort to stop the Federal Red River expedition. The following day, Shelby and his brigade fought a series of desperate clashes with Major General Frederick Steele's 15,000-man command, finally forcing it to retire. In September 1864 Shelby led a division on Major General Sterling Price's Missouri expedition. Price's raid was poorly planned and ended in failure. Price praised Shelby, however, as "the best cavalry officer he had ever seen" and Major General Alfred Pleasanton, United States Volunteers, described him as "the best cavalry general of the South."

On 26 May 1865 the Army of the Trans-Mississippi surrendered, but Shelby and 500 men of his Iron Brigade refused to admit defeat. On 2 June 1865 he and his men sank their battle flag in the Rio Grande River and crossed into Mexico to offer their services to Emperor Maximilian. Although Shelby and other expatriates established the Colony of Carlotta in Mexico, their dreams died with Maximilian. In 1867 Shelby returned to Missouri.

In the years following the war, Shelby became one of the most admired men in Missouri and a key figure in healing the wounds left by the Civil War. Although the loyalty of old Iron Brigade troopers to Shelby was legendary, he disenchanted many of them by supporting Republican politics after the war. And Shelby never commanded the success in business that he had enjoyed before the war. Finally, in 1892, President Grover Cleveland appointed him to the office of U.S. marshall, Western Missouri. Shelby served with distinction in this office until his death from pneumonia on 13 February 1897.

—*Mark E. Scott*

See also Cane Hill, Battle of; Helena, Battle of; Prairie Grove, Battle of; Price's Missouri Raid; Red River Campaign.

For further reading:
Edwards, John Newman. *Shelby and His Men, or, The War in the West* (1993).
Gottschalk, Phil. *In Deadly Earnest: The History of the First Missouri Brigade, CSA* (1991).
Hollister, Wilfred R., and Harry Norman. *Five Famous Missourians: Samuel L. Clemens. Champ Clark, Richard P. Bland, James M. Greenwood, and Joseph O. Shelby* (1900).
Oates, Stephen B. *Confederate Cavalry West of the River* (1961).
O'Flaherty, Daniel. *General Jo Shelby: Undefeated Rebel* (1987; reprint, 2000).
Scott, Mark E. "The Forgotten Cavalier: General Joseph Orville Shelby and his Great Missouri Raid of 1863" (Master's thesis, Eastern Washington University, 1996).
Smith, William E. *The Francis Preston Blair Family in Politics*, vol. 2 (1933; reprint, 1969).
U. S. War Department. *The War of the Rebellion: A Compilation of the Official Records of the Union and Confederate Armies* (1880–1901).

SHENANDOAH, CSS

Purchased in England in September 1864 by Confederate agent James D. Bulloch, the CSS *Shenandoah* was the last Confederate cruiser that he got to sea. Initially christened the *Sea King* and launched on 17 August 1863, this ship was the first composite auxiliary screw steamship in the world and was designed for transporting troops to India. Her frames and beams were of iron, and she was planed with East Indian teak wood. She weighed 1,160 tons and was 230 feet long, 32 feet in beam, and 20 feet 6 inches in depth of hold. Capable of nine knots under steam, the *Sea King* had one screw, two boilers, and direct-acting engines.

Flag Officer Samuel Barron, the ranking Confederate officer in Europe, named Lieutenant Commander James I. Waddell the *Sea King*'s captain and ordered him to destroy the Union whaling fleet in the Pacific. On 8 October 1864 the *Sea King* slipped out of the Thames estuary under merchant captain G. H. Corbet on what appeared to be a merchant voyage, but she then proceeded to Funchal on the Island of Madeira to rendezvous with the supply ship *Laurel*, which had sailed from England the same day with Waddell and the remainder of her crew and her armament. Her crew complement was 73 men, and her armament consisted of four 8-inch and two 12-pounder smoothbore cannon, and two 32-pounder rifled guns. On 19 October 1864, Waddell officially commissioned the *Sea King* a Confederate warship under the name CSS *Shenandoah* and began his cruise for Union vessels.

The *Shenandoah* took six Union prizes in the Atlantic. She arrived at Melbourne, Australia, on 25 January 1865, and there underwent repairs. Without the dry docking and machinery repairs at Melbourne, Waddell would not have been able to undertake his subsequent mission. The *Shenandoah* sailed again on 18 February and then cruised the whaling grounds in the Pacific Ocean and off Alaska. Her long stay at Melbourne allowed U.S. whaling vessels in the South Pacific to be warned and disperse, but Waddell then took the *Shenandoah* north and devastated the Union whaling fleet.

For some time Waddell refused to believe reports of the end of the war. Finally, after he had left northern waters, he accepted as proof a report from an English captain on 2 August 1865. Waddell then sailed the *Shenandoah* 17,000 miles without stopping at any port to Liverpool, England, arriving there on 6 November 1865, and surrendering to British authorities. The trip had been made virtually under sail alone. Waddell resorted to steam only once, at night in the mid-South Atlantic to elude the USS *Saranac*. In the process the *Shenandoah* became the only Confederate warship to sail around the world. In all, the *Shenandoah* took 38 Union vessels, of which Waddell burned 32. Damage to Union shipping was estimated at some $1.36 million.

In 1866, the *Shenandoah* was sold to the Sultan of Zanzibar. Renamed the *El Majidi*, she was damaged in a hurricane off Zanzibar in April 1872. That September she sank in the Indian Ocean while on the Zanzibar-Bombay route.

—*Spencer C. Tucker*

See also Bulloch, James D.; Navy, C.S.A.; Waddell, James I.
For further reading:

Hearn, Chester G. *Gray Raiders of the Sea. How Eight Confederate Warships Destroyed the Union's High Sea Commerce* (1992).

Horn, Stanley F. *Gallant Rebel: The Fabulous Cruise of the C.S.S. Shenandoah* (1947).

Morgan, Murray. *Dixie Raider: The Saga of the C.S.S. Shenandoah* (1948).

United States Navy Department. *Civil War Naval Chronology, 1861–1865, Part IV, Special Studies and Cumulative Index* (1961).

Waddell, James T. *C.S.S. Shenandoah: The Memoirs of Lieutenant Commander James I. Waddell.* Edited by James D. Horan (1960).

SHENANDOAH VALLEY CAMPAIGN
(March–June 1862)

The Shenandoah Valley, long known as the bread-basket of the Confederacy, was of immense importance to both the Union and Confederate armies. The valley provided foodstuffs and small manufactures for the Confederacy and an easily defended route to the north. Bounded by the Allegheny Mountains to the west and the Blue Ridge to the east, movement in the valley could go undetected if the mountain passes were secured. At the northern (or lower) end of the valley, Harper's Ferry sits at the confluence of the Shenandoah and Potomac rivers. To the south were the major communities of Winchester, Middletown, Strasburg, Front Royal, Mount Jackson, New Market, Harrisonburg, and Staunton, Virginia. The total distance from Harper's Ferry to Staunton is about 150 miles. The Massanutten Mountains are located in the middle of the valley. The northern tip of the mountain range lies between Strasburg and Front Royal, which are about 12 miles apart. The mountains run south to Harrisonburg, dividing the valley and splitting the north-flowing Shenandoah River into the North Branch on the west side and the South Branch on the east.

In July 1861, Confederate brigadier generals Joseph E. Johnston and Thomas J. Jackson left the lower Valley to join Brigadier General P. G. T. Beauregard at Manassas. Protection of the valley was left to the Virginia militia. In October a Union force moved to Romney, west of Winchester, to threaten the northern end of the valley. Johnston sent Jackson (promoted to major general on 7 October) with his "Stonewall" brigade to take over the valley command. His Army of the Valley was a potpourri of volunteers and militia with a combined total of 5,000 to 6,000 men.

Jackson conducted a winter campaign at Romney and Bath that had undistinguished results. The experience did teach Jackson some valuable lessons that served him well in the coming months. In March 1862, Union major general Nathaniel P. Banks with 18,000 men

moved toward Winchester, causing Jackson's much smaller force to evacuate the city on 11 March. The Federal forces in the area were substantial: Brigadier General John Sedgwick at Harper's Ferry had 7,000 troops; Brigadier General James Shields at Strasburg, had 9,000; Brigadier General Alpheus S. Williams at Winchester, 7,000. Upon departing Winchester, Jackson went to Mount Jackson, 42 miles south, to strengthen his army. Militia units were drawn in from the valley, and recruiting, drilling, and installing discipline was Jackson's priority.

Meanwhile, Union major general George McClellan was moving to the Virginia Peninsula. Having about 200,000 troops at his disposal, he was transferring about 130,000 to threaten Richmond from the southeast. The balance was left to Major General Irvin McDowell for the protection of Washington, D.C., and for a move on Richmond from the north. Against this force General Johnston had 60,000 Confederates at Richmond plus Major General Richard S. Ewell's division of 8,000 at Gordonsville and Jackson's contingent in the valley.

Johnston expected Jackson to oppose and delay any Union advance up the valley and to stay between the valley and the main Union army. Keeping Federal forces occupied in the valley kept them from being shifted to support McClellan. On 20 March, with the objective to reinforce McDowell, Williams began moving his forces toward Manassas and Shields prepared to follow. Upon learning of this move, Jackson made a forced march toward Kernstown, just south of Winchester, to give battle to the weakened Union force under Shields that remained there. Jackson attacked, only to discover that his usually reliable cavalry commander, Colonel Turner Ashby, had given him bad information. Shields had effectively deceived Ashby's sources and positioned his troops so they were not apparent to the Confederates. Colonel Ashby, in the lead of the infantry, charged the Union forces on 22 March thinking it was just the rear guard. The following day, 23 March, was a Sunday, and Jackson, who would normally refrain from fighting on the Sabbath, realized that in front of him was an opportunity that would be gone by Monday.

Jackson's troop deployment had Ashby covering the Valley Pike on the south, supported by Colonel Jessie S. Burks's brigade. Colonel Samuel V. Fulkerson's brigade was aligned on the west side of the pike to attack Shields's right flank and rear. Brigadier General Richard B. Garnett, commanding the Stonewall Brigade, supported Fulkerson. In the center Jackson placed his twenty-seven cannon, which could be moved as needed. Opposing these forces was Union artillery in a commanding position atop Pritchart's Hill west of the pike. Union brigades under Colonel Erastus B. Tyler and Nathan Kimball supported these guns.

Jackson, observing from a hill on his left flank, watched as two Confederate regiments pushed forward, breaking up two enemy attacks. Fulkerson found a stone fence from which his troops leveled a devastating fire. Garnett brought up the Stonewall Brigade, and it looked as though they could turn the Union right flank. The fighting was close in, and the battle raged for hours, but the Union troops stood fast. Jackson moved to the line of battle, only to find his old brigade retreating. Asking what was happening, Jackson was told by Garnett that his men were running out of ammunition and were without any support, so he had ordered the withdrawal. Jackson was furious and arrested Garnett as the action was unauthorized and, in Jackson's mind, not necessary. Once it had started, however, Jackson could not stop the retreat, and the day belonged to the Union army under Shields. Jackson lost 700 men out of 4,200 engaged. Shields's losses were about 600 men out of 9,000. The Army of the Valley retired to Newtown, about 4 miles south of Winchester.

Jackson may have lost the battle, but it was a major psychological victory for the Confederacy. The Federals assumed Jackson would not have made such a bold attack unless his strength was far greater than estimated. This led to some panicked Federal decisions, including the recall of Williams's troops to the valley. Furthermore, Washington transferred Brigadier General Louis Blenker's division, 9,000 strong, to Major General John C. Frémont in western Virginia. President Lincoln ordered McDowell to hold his corps of 40,000 at Manassas to protect the capital. Jackson's action at Kernstown accomplished more than anyone in Richmond could have hoped for.

The War Department now organized the Federal forces into four distinct and separate groups: the Department of the Rappahannock under McDowell; the Department of the Shenandoah under Banks; the Mountain Department under Frémont; and the Army of the Potomac under McClellan. Each reported to Secretary of War Edwin M. Stanton.

Greatly outnumbered, Jackson continued his retrograde movement. He went southward to Swift Run Gap near Conrad's Store, a hard day's march east of Harrisonburg around the southern tip of the Massanutten Mountains. By 26 April, Banks had advanced to New Market with his forward elements at Harrisonburg. Jackson's position at Swift Run Gap kept him in touch with Richmond and prevented Banks from moving any farther south without exposing his flank.

Ewell, at Gordonsville, was now available to Jackson, bringing his total strength up to 17,000. On 18 April General Robert E. Lee had ordered the small army of Brigadier General Edward Johnson to coordinate movements with Jackson. Johnson, commanding about 2,800 troops, had been protecting the passes through the Allegheny Mountains west of Staunton. Technically,

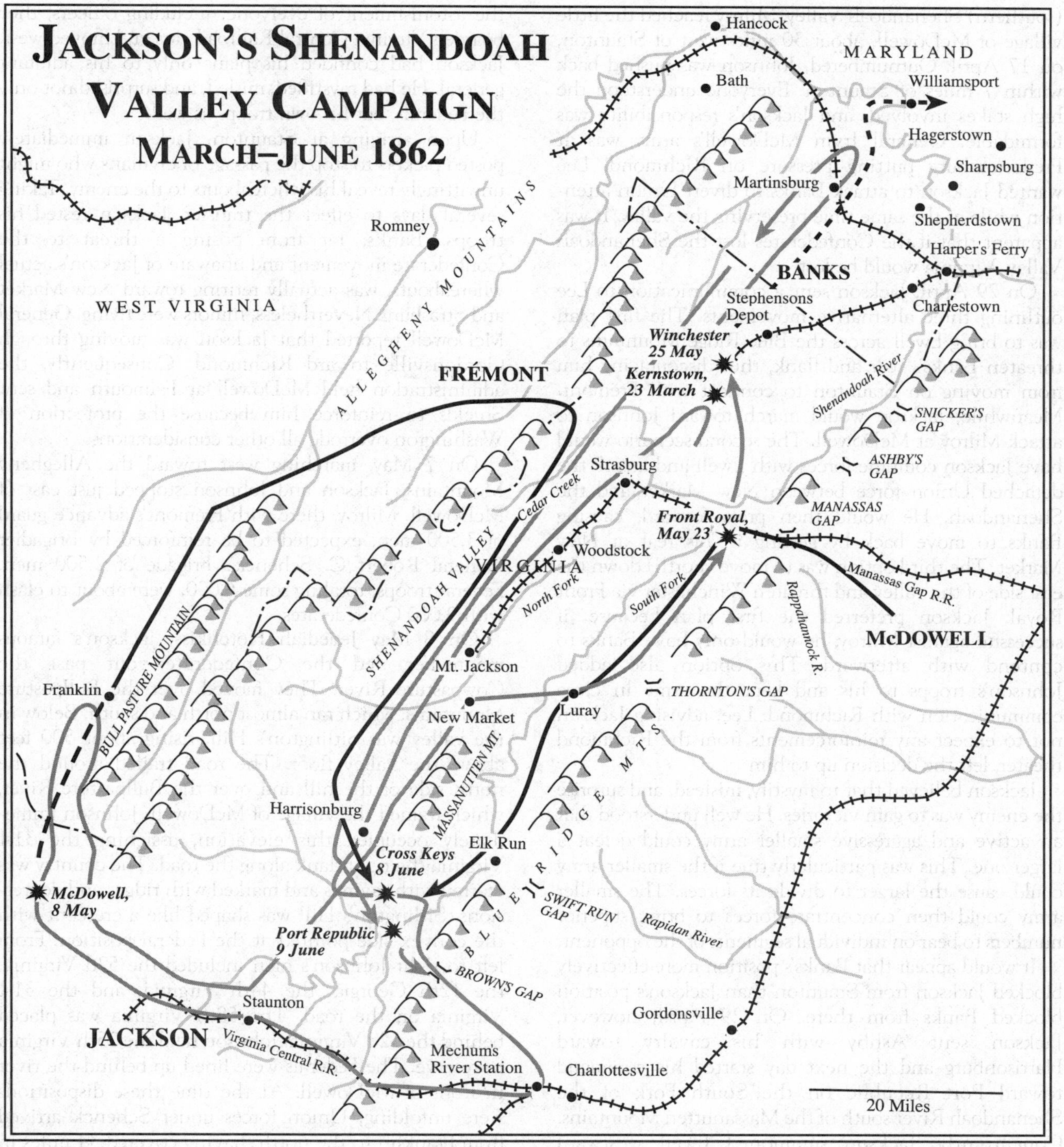

JACKSON'S SHENANDOAH VALLEY CAMPAIGN
MARCH–JUNE 1862

MARYLAND

Hancock

Bath

Williamsport

Hagerstown

Sharpsburg

Martinsburg

Shepherdstown

Harper's Ferry

Romney

BANKS

Charlestown

Stephensons Depot

WEST VIRGINIA

Shenandoah River

Winchester
25 May

Kernstown,
23 March

SNICKER'S GAP

ALLEGHENY MOUNTAINS

FRÉMONT

Strasburg

ASHBY'S GAP

Cedar Creek

MANASSAS GAP

Front Royal,
May 23

VIRGINIA

Woodstock

North Fork

South Fork

Rappahannock R.

Manassas Gap R.R.

BULL PASTURE MOUNTAIN

Mt. Jackson

SHENANDOAH VALLEY

McDOWELL

THORNTON'S GAP

Franklin

New Market

Luray

MASSANUTTEN MT.

Harrisonburg

BLUE RIDGE MTS.

*McDowell,
8 May*

Elk Run

SWIFT RUN GAP

Rapidan River

Cross Keys
8 June

*Port Republic
9 June*

BROWN'S GAP

Staunton

JACKSON

Virginia Central R.R.

Gordonsville

Mechum's
River Station

Charlottesville

20 Miles

Jackson and Ewell were under the command of Joseph E. Johnston, and Lee was just acting as President Jefferson Davis's military advisor. Nonetheless, during the later part of April, Lee sent messages encouraging Jackson to take the offensive.

When Secretary Stanton gave Frémont command of the Mountain Department, embracing the area of western and southwestern Virginia and eastern Kentucky, Frémont promised President Lincoln he would move on Knoxville, Tennessee. It was Frémont's intent to cross the Allegheny Mountains, join with Banks, and advance southwest to Knoxville. To effect the meeting with Banks, he directed Brigadier General Robert H. Milroy to take his 6,000 troops into the upper

(southern) Shenandoah Valley. Milroy reached the little village of McDowell, about 30 miles west of Staunton, on 17 April. Outnumbered, Johnson was pushed back within 7 miles of Staunton. Everyone understood the high stakes involved, and Jackson's responsibility was formidable. General Irvin McDowell's army was at Fredericksburg putting pressure on Richmond. Lee wanted Jackson to attack Banks to divert Union attention while at the same time preserving the valley. It was apparent that if the Confederates lost the Shenandoah Valley, Virginia would be lost.

On 29 April, Jackson sent a communication to Lee outlining three alternative movements. The first plan was to bring Ewell across the Blue Ridge Mountains to threaten Banks's rear and flank, thus discouraging him from moving on Staunton to connect with Frémont. Meanwhile, Jackson would march toward Johnson to attack Milroy at McDowell. The second scenario would have Jackson combine forces with Ewell and attack the detached Union force between New Market and the Shenandoah. He would then press forward, causing Banks to move back by getting in his rear at New Market. The third option was to move (north) down the east side of the valley and threaten Winchester via Front Royal. Jackson preferred the first plan because, if successful against Milroy, he would only have Banks to contend with afterward. This option also added Johnson's troops to his and kept the army in close communication with Richmond. Lee, advising Jackson not to expect any reinforcements from the Richmond theater, left the decision up to him.

Jackson believed that to mystify, mislead, and surprise the enemy was to gain victories. He well understood that an active and aggressive smaller army could defeat a larger one. This was particularly true if the smaller army could cause the larger to divide its forces. The smaller army could then concentrate forces to bring superior numbers to bear on individual segments of the opponent.

It would appear that Banks's position more effectively blocked Jackson from Staunton than Jackson's position blocked Banks from there. On 29 April, however, Jackson sent Ashby with his cavalry toward Harrisonburg and the next day started his command toward Port Republic on the South Fork of the Shenandoah River south of the Massanutten Mountains. Concurrently, Jackson summoned Ewell westward through Swift Run Gap to Jackson's just-vacated position. For three days Jackson's men struggled along roads ruined by terrible rains. Instead of stopping at Port Republic, they turned east away from the valley, toward Brown's Gap in the Blue Ridge. The move discouraged Jackson's men, who believed they were leaving the valley to the Federal forces and moving to join Johnston around Richmond. From Brown's Gap, they moved south to Mechum's River. On Sunday, 4 May, much to

the astonishment of everyone, including officers, they boarded Virginia Central Railroad cars and moved west. Jackson had confided his plans only to his adjutant general. He had mystified, misled, and surprised not only the Federals, but his own troops as well.

Upon arriving at Staunton, Jackson immediately posted pickets to stop the passage of civilians who might unwittingly reveal his whereabouts to the enemy. Taking several days to effect the transfer, Jackson rested his troops. Banks, far from posing a threat to the Confederate movement and unaware of Jackson's actual whereabouts, was actually retiring toward New Market and Strasburg. Nevertheless, rumors were flying. General McDowell reported that Jackson was moving through Gordonsville toward Richmond. Consequently, the administration held McDowell at Falmouth and sent Shields to reinforce him because the protection of Washington overrode all other considerations.

On 7 May, marching west toward the Allegheny Mountains, Jackson and Johnson stopped just east of McDowell. Milroy, there with Frémont's advance guard of 3,500 men, expected to be reinforced by Brigadier General Robert C. Schenck's brigade of 2,500 men. Federal troops, totaling some 6,000, were about to clash with 9,000 Confederates.

On 8 May Jedediah Hotchkiss, Jackson's famous mapmaker, led the Confederates out past the Cowpasture River. They moved over the Bullpasture Mountains, which ran almost north and south. Below in the valley was Sitlington's Hill, rising about 500 feet above the valley floor. The road trailed around the north side of the hill and over the Bullpasture River, which framed the village of McDowell. Johnson immediately occupied this elevation, assigning the 31st Virginia the right flank along the road. The country was scarred with ravines and marked with ridges and depressions. Sitlington's Hill was shaped like a crescent with the convex side pointed at the Federal position. From left to right Johnson's men included the 52d Virginia, the 12th Georgia, the 44th Virginia, and the 31st Virginia on the road. The 58th Virginia was placed behind the 52d Virginia. Johnson held the 25th Virginia in reserve. The Federals were lined up behind the river in front of McDowell. At the time these dispositions were unfolding, Union forces under Schenck arrived from Franklin to the north, having covered 34 miles in just 23 hours.

Although the Union generals decided their position was untenable, they would not retreat without a fight. Late in the afternoon of 8 May, Milroy sent the 25th and 75th Ohio Regiments to the attack, doing so under the false impression that Jackson was moving artillery to the hill, a circumstance that would have compromised the Federal position. The Ohio Regiments managed to make their way across the rugged hillside to meet the 12th

Georgia. Their success caused Milroy to add the weight of the 32d and 83d Ohio against the Confederate right. The 3d West Virginia (Union) was placed on the road facing off against the 31st Virginia (Confederate). These contending regiments had been recruited from Jackson's hometown of Clarksburg, Virginia, (now West Virginia).

The combatants were unwilling to give an inch, and the battle lasted until about 8:30 P.M., when Milroy withdrew his troops. In the very early hours of 9 May, the Federals abandoned their position and started north. Jackson pursued the Union troops as far north as Franklin and on 13 May returned to McDowell.

The battle at McDowell was a marked success for the Confederates even though their loss of 500 men was more than double the Federal casualties of 250. Milroy and Schenck had been forced out of the valley, and Frémont was prevented from joining forces with Banks. The Union commanders were thus completely isolated, allowing Jackson to pursue Banks unmolested. Having effectively dispersed the Union armies, he was now free to pick off the pieces on a more equal footing.

Meanwhile, Banks dug in at Strasburg with only about 8,000 troops. Shields was en route to join General McDowell near Fredericksburg. On 16 May, Lee wrote to Jackson, directing him with his combined forces to make haste in his move against Banks. If successful, he was to threaten the line of the Potomac River. Lee was playing on Lincoln's fears for the safety of the federal capital. Jackson and Ewell, however, were still under the command of Johnston, who wanted Ewell to return eastward. By 17 May, Jackson had camped at Mount Solon, situated about 16 miles south and west of Harrisonburg,

when Ewell came to discuss his conflicting orders: should he remain with Jackson or follow Johnston's order to move east? Jackson telegraphed Lee to suggest that he and Ewell combine to attack Banks. Lee replied that Johnston was in agreement and that Ewell was to remain with Jackson.

Jackson's and Ewell's cavalry shielded their movements effectively, and by 20 May Jackson was at New Market. Meanwhile Ewell had moved north, down the Luray Valley, and was opposite New Market on the east side of the Massanutten Mountains. The Confederate forces now totaled about 17,000 officers and men, and for the most part the units were well led.

On 21 May, Jackson again surprised even his own command. Instead of moving his superior force directly toward Strasburg on the Valley Pike, he crossed the mountains into the Luray Valley and headed north toward Front Royal. Secretary Stanton had dictated Banks's position, which was not strong, and Banks, a politician and an untrained soldier, did not object to it. He had about 8,000 men and sixteen guns at Strasburg and 1,500 infantry and cavalry at Winchester. There were 1,000 men and two guns under Colonel John Kenly of the 1st Maryland at Front Royal, and it was here on 23 May that Jackson attacked. The Confederates vastly outnumbered the Federals, but the bluecoats fought well and displayed good discipline. They set fire to the bridge over the North Fork of the Shenandoah, but the Confederates reached it before too much damage was done. It did, however, serve to slow Jackson's advance. After the cavalry had found a nearby ford, Jackson instantly sent them into the retreating Federals, and they

General Frémont's troops in their march up the Shenandoah Valley (*Library of Congress*)

won the opening action. Banks, thinking this was just a raid, expected Jackson to show up south of him on the Valley Pike. The Union general had difficulty believing that Jackson would put his army between two Federal forces such as the one General McDowell commanded in Fredericksburg and the one Banks had at Kernstown.

At this point, Jackson had to deal with Banks's options: Banks could retreat north to Winchester; he could attack Jackson at Front Royal and try for Manassas to the east; or he could stay in Strasburg and try to get help from Frémont over the mountains. Jackson sent Ashby toward Strasburg and Brigadier General Richard Taylor with his Louisiana Brigade (called the Louisiana Tigers with good reason) to Middletown, 5 miles north of Strasburg. Brigadier General George Steuart was to take two cavalry regiments to Newtown, 8 miles south of Winchester. Jackson held the remainder of his command at Nineveh to the east and at Front Royal. All were within striking distance of the Valley Pike leading to Winchester and the road through Front Royal. Thus with his forces fanned out, Jackson was ideally situated to detect Banks's decision. Banks had his men moving north at dawn, giving him a lead of several hours, but Jackson pushed vigorously. As Jackson's forces moved west, they found Banks on the Valley Turnpike and attacked with the few troops available and in position, not knowing if they had found the nose or the tail of Banks's column. It turned out to be the tail, as reported by the residents of Middletown. Jackson had to move quickly, because time was also his enemy. The Federal troops at Harper's Ferry, Romney, and Washington were only a short train ride away from supporting Banks.

The hills surrounding Winchester were key to the town's defense, and Jackson did not want to give Banks time to entrench on them, so he marched his tired and hungry troops long into the next morning. They renewed the march at dawn after only a few hours of sleep. By that time Banks had positioned Colonel George Gordon's infantry brigade and his artillery on the turnpike and to the west. On the Front Royal road, angling southeast of Winchester, Banks had Brigadier General Dudley Donnelly's brigade. His line ran along a ridge protected by stone fences and by Abraham's Creek. Jackson's plan was to hold Gordon in position while Ewell came up on the Front Royal Road and pressured Donnelly. Jackson would then work around Gordon's right flank.

Although the Federal position was relatively strong and the Union artillery well positioned, Taylor and Brigadier General William Taliaferro's brigades were able to move to the flank and effectively turn the Union line. It became impossible for the Federals to hold their ground, and they retreated through Winchester. A frustrated Jackson, unable to find his cavalry to turn the retreat into a rout, knew he had missed an opportunity to destroy Banks's army, which was retreating toward Martinsburg. Banks would eventually cross the Potomac at Williamsport to reorganize. Yet Jackson again had won both a military and a psychological victory and had also captured an enormous amount of stores. Thereafter, Banks was derisively labeled by everyone "Commissary Banks," supplier of the Confederacy.

Jackson's impressive victories—marked by total surprise, audacity, ferocity and daring—so far had served to bewilder Lincoln and Stanton. Lee directed him to push for the Potomac.

On 24 May, while Jackson was attacking at Middletown and Newtown and before Lincoln knew the outcome of the battle, he had reacted to Jackson's position by ordering General McDowell to halt at Fredericksburg and transfer 20,000 men to the Shenandoah Valley. His aim was to get a Federal army between Jackson and the upper valley to cut his communications. Frémont was to move east toward Harrisonburg to aid in the destruction of Jackson's army. Yet McDowell and McClellan did not support this plan, believing the valley was not worth the disruption of plans to crush the main Confederate army at Richmond. McDowell wrote to President Lincoln, respectfully stating his dissent while advising that he was obeying the command. He felt that coordination with Frémont was not possible and that he was too distant from Jackson and the valley roads to intercept him. McDowell also believed that Banks's withdrawal had been unnecessary and prompted by panic. The observations were not material to Lincoln, however. McDowell and McClellan might think Washington safe, but what counted was that Lincoln did not feel secure. Ultimately his military counselors did not dissuade Lincoln from his desire to take the offensive. He told McClellan to either move his army on Richmond or bring it back to defend Washington. Jackson's aggressive move northward had intimidated Lincoln.

There were problems with Lincoln's plan, though. For one, Frémont was not where Lincoln thought he was. Effectively blocked from the routes through the mountains that would have given him access to Jackson's rear, Frémont moved through the Alleghenies via Moorefield to Strasburg and Middletown.

On 28 May, the Stonewall Brigade moved forward through Charles Town toward Harper's Ferry. Supported by Ewell's troops, the brigade forced Brigadier General Rufus Saxton's troops back from advanced positions to Bolivar Heights, adjacent to Harper's Ferry. To the south, Jackson placed the 12th Georgia at Front Royal, the Louisiana Brigade to the east near Berryville, and Ashby's cavalry to the west to watch Frémont. Although Jackson might have taken Harper's Ferry, he made no attempt to do so other than to send a regiment across the Shenandoah River to occupy Loudoun Heights.

Jackson was by now aware that McDowell and

Frémont were in motion to cut him off. Shields, the lead element of McDowell's forces, was coming in from Manassas toward Front Royal. Frémont was moving north and east from Franklin and was about 35 miles west of Strasburg. On 29 May, Jackson, convinced that he had accomplished as much as he could, started moving south. While the main body returned to Winchester, the Stonewall Brigade remained to watch Saxton. On the way back to Winchester, Jackson learned that Shields had driven back the 12th Georgia at Front Royal and that the bridges that would allow a rapid Federal advance were still intact.

Jackson's situation immediately became critical. Front Royal was only 12 miles from Jackson's route of retreat. He not only had to extricate his troops and move several thousand prisoners, he was also mindful of the Confederacy's great need for the vast stores and medical supplies captured at Winchester, Martinsburg, and Charles Town. The Union armies had reacted quickly to encircle Jackson. Directly behind Shields's 10,500 troops was General Edward Ord with another 10,000. Frémont had 15,000, and from Williamsport and Harper's Ferry there was another 15,000. Within a couple of days, the Federals had the potential of amassing 50,000 troops against Jackson's 16,000 effectives.

The noose was closing. On the evening of 30 May, Jackson ordered his army to move farther south to Strasburg. The Stonewall Brigade still remained in front of Harper's Ferry at Charles Town, about a 35 mile march from Strasburg. Jackson sent Hotchkiss to retrieve the brigade with instructions to conduct it around and through the mountains should the Union army prevent it from rejoining the main body. On the first day, the Stonewall Brigade had reached Newtown, just south of Winchester, with one regiment having marched 35 miles, the rest 28 miles. Frémont, harassed by Ashby, was only 6 miles from Jackson's escape route, but Taylor's Louisiana Tigers had intimidated Shields, freezing him at Front Royal. Neither Shields nor Frémont was in direct communication, and all the Union armies seemed to overestimate Jackson's strength. Again, rumors were rampant, and Confederates fueled them with misinformation.

Lincoln and Stanton tried to keep their armies informed, but effective coordination from Washington was not possible. Jackson correctly judged his enemy as hesitant, and by 31 May he had slipped through the noose. His only remaining concern was his old brigade under Brigadier General Charles Winder at Newtown. To protect the Stonewall Brigade's passage through Strasburg, Jackson sent Ewell westward to help Ashby stall Frémont, who was closest to the line of march. Frémont was checked, and at noon on 1 June the Stonewall Brigade marched through Strasburg.

In a period of two weeks Jackson had lost only 600 soldiers while occupying the attention of virtually every Union soldier not on the peninsula with McClellan. Marching with a huge convoy and not losing a wagon of his own, he had routed Banks's army and relieved the pressure on Johnston around Richmond. Between 19 May and 1 June, his army marched 170 miles.

By the night of 1 June, Jackson had his infantry and artillery consolidated at Woodstock, and Ashby was at Tom's Brook. Frémont was still at Cedar Creek with the Union force closest to Jackson. The Federals, now having a better idea of Jackson's position and strength, began a vigorous pursuit. Shields moved south out of Front Royal up the Luray Valley, and Ord occupied the vacated position at Front Royal. Frémont moved out of Cedar Creek in Jackson's rear. Jackson was moving south through Harrisonburg to Port Republic again, and a quick move by Shields would have positioned him at the pass between Luray and New Market on Jackson's front or flank. If he missed Jackson at this point, he still could continue south and gain the bridges at Conrad's Store and Port Republic to cut Jackson off from the Blue Ridge Mountains. Ever vigilant, Jackson anticipated Shields's intentions and sent the cavalry to New Market Gap. The Confederates won the race, and by the time the Union cavalry arrived, they found the bridges over the South Fork of the Shenandoah burned. This quick action denied the Union army access to Jackson, who was coming up the west side of the Massanutten Mountains.

Frémont was becoming more aggressive, and his cavalry, led by Brigadier General George Bayard, was almost more than Ashby's rear guard could handle. On 2 June, between Strasburg and Woodstock, the Union attack sent the rear guard flying southward up the valley and resulted in the capture of numerous exhausted and poorly fed Confederates. On 3 June, Confederates arrived at Mount Jackson, and on the following day they burned the bridge over the North Fork of the Shenandoah. The deed, combined with heavy rains, bought Jackson a day's march on the pursuing Federals. On 5 June, he sent his sick and wounded to Staunton while his main body moved southeast to Cross Keys, beyond Harrisonburg.

Ashby, still watching the rear, had a hot cavalry fight 3 miles south of Harrisonburg in which he drove the Federals back. When Frémont put forward a stronger group of horsemen and several battalions of infantry, a fierce battle ensued, and Ashby found himself rallying his troops in the thickest part of the fight. His horse was shot from under him and shortly afterward, while he was on foot, a Union marksman killed him. Jackson's respect for his fearless cavalry leader had grown immensely, and Ashby's death was a major loss to the Army of the Valley.

For the next two days the Confederate troops rested. Ewell was at Cross Keys, while the remainder of the army

was near Port Republic. The cavalry was divided to watch for Frémont moving from Harrisonburg and for Shields coming south up the Luray Valley. Jackson established a signal post at the southern tip of the Massanutten range, where the movements of both Federal armies could be observed.

Shields learned of Jackson's whereabouts from Frémont and determined to intercept him at Port Republic. Both Union generals thought they had in front of them a demoralized and disorganized Confederate army that would be easy prey. Cautioned to stay closed up, Shields instead opted for speed and had his troops strung out over a 25-mile length of road. Jackson, ever the aggressor, was eyeing his prey.

Finding that Shields had stopped his pursuit on 5 June, Jackson wrote Lee that he did not see any immediate opportunities to engage the enemy. Shortly afterward, however, he found that Shields was again moving and was again spread out. Jackson, planning to take advantage of Shields's impetuosity, knew he would have to move quickly: if Frémont and Shields were allowed to combine they would outnumber Jackson 25,000 to 16,000. On the other hand, if Jackson could bring them to battle individually, he would enjoy superior numbers and defeat them in detail.

The town of Port Republic sat in the point of a vee formed by the convergence of the North and South rivers, which together formed the South Fork of the Shenandoah. The point of the vee faced east, with the larger of the two streams to the north. Across the North River was the main bridge toward Harrisonburg. The Stonewall Brigade camped up this road. Beyond was Cross Keys, not much more than a rural tavern, 7 miles southeast of Harrisonburg.

The only way over the South River to the Luray Valley was by way of two fords. To the north, down the Luray Valley, ran the newly formed South Fork of the Shenandoah River. On the left or west bank a line of high bluffs commanded the plain to the east of the river where the road led through the valley, the route used by Shields. To move on Shields would require that Jackson expose his left flank to the bluffs along the river, allowing Frémont to control the plain with artillery. To attack Frémont first, though, posed the problem of allowing Shields to gain the Confederate flank or rear and cutting off any line of retreat. Therefore, keeping Frémont back was imperative so the attack could proceed against Shields. Once he defeated Shields, Jackson could then turn and attack Frémont. Jackson also had the option of burning the bridge over the North River and retreating toward Waynesboro and the Virginia Central Railroad, but he chose to hold Frémont at Cross Keys using Ewell's troops.

Cross Keys was rolling but not mountainous country. The Port Republic road ran northwest-southeast and

intersected with the perpendicular Keezletown Road. To the north another road ran parallel to the Port Republic Road. Ewell placed his 5,000 troops astride the Port Republic Road on a high wooded ridge. Initially the 15th Alabama was in the advance at the tee formed at the Keezletown intersection. Behind, from left to right, were Brigadier Generals George H. Steuart, Arnold Elzey, and Isaac Trimble, with Taylor in reserve. Across Ewell's front was a shallow stream known as Mill Creek. In the center of his line, in front of Elzey's brigade, four artillery batteries were directed at the open fields.

On 8 June, between 8:30 and 9:00 A.M., Ewell's pickets traded fire with advance elements of Frémont's army. The ground, a combination of woods and clearings, afforded protection and secrecy. Although the Federal movements were hidden, the picket fire identified the Union position and progress. About 10:00 A.M., Federal artillery was up and dueling with the Confederate guns. Frémont had about 10,500 troops, including ten batteries of artillery and a brigade of cavalry. Commanding his infantry were Brigadier Generals Julius Stahel, Henry Bohlen, Robert H. Milroy, and Robert C. Schenck and Colonels John A. Koltes and Gustave P. Cluseret.

Frémont determined that Ewell's right was his weakness and ordered Stahel supported by Bohlen to move between the parallel roads. Trimble, responsible for the Confederate right, kept his men hidden behind a fence at the edge of the field and withheld his fire until Stahel's men were within about 50 yards. A devastating volley caused the Federals to fall back in confusion. Trimble followed up this advantage with an attack of his own. Using a ravine for cover, he assailed Stahel's left flank and, surprising his adversaries, forced them back on Bohlen's brigade. Reinforced with elements of Elzey's brigade, Trimble pushed toward the Keezletown Road.

Meanwhile, at the center and right Cluseret and Milroy advanced through the woods to the southwest of the Port Republic Road. Here Confederates held firm, and Union troops could not penetrate the line. Schenck assaulted the Confederate left in a flanking effort but gained no advantage. Because Frémont outnumbered Ewell by two to one, Jackson had sent him the brigades commanded by Colonel John M. Patton and Taylor, and Ewell used them to reinforce his left. Frémont, concerned by his lack of progress, moved his command back to a defensive line along the Keezletown Road. Casualties had amounted to about 700 Union and 300 Confederate. That evening Ewell quietly retired to Port Republic.

Jackson had established his headquarters a short distance west of Port Republic at the Kemper house. On 8 June, having just mounted his horse, Jackson was on his way to Cross Keys when a sudden commotion broke out in the streets of Port Republic. A rider hurried to tell Jackson that Union cavalry had surprised the Confederate pickets and were fording the South

River to make their way into town. The situation was critical, because Jackson had parked his trains, including his reserve ammunition, in the open fields southwest of the town. Two guns were supporting the Federal cavalry, one on the opposite side of the river to protect their crossing and the other toward the bridge over the North River.

Jackson raced for the bridge to reach his command encamped on the north side. He barely escaped; some members of his staff were not so lucky. As the Federals brought up more artillery and troopers, Jackson placed himself at the forefront of the action and called for his infantry and artillery. A well-placed shot dismantled the Union cannon at the bridge, and Jackson ordered the 37th Virginia to charge over it. The Federals were swept in disarray, losing four cannons in the process, and though the Union troopers had infantry support behind them, the haste of retreat created a confused mass. Jackson's cavalry pickets had failed him, but with immediate and aggressive action he had saved his command.

At the end of 8 June, Jackson planned his attack for the following morning. In a bold and ambitious plan, he intended to hold Frémont in his current position while he defeated Shields quickly in the morning. He would then turn on Frémont. After that engagement, he would recross the North River, burning the bridge behind him. Jackson gave personal and explicit orders to Patton to hold back Frémont. Jackson told Patton, who had only a small brigade, that the main army would be back to support him by 10:00 A.M.

Jackson now planned to attack Shields over the northerly road into the Luray Valley. To his left would be the South Fork of the Shenandoah River and to the right the foothills of the Blue Ridge with a relatively flat plain between. At 5:00 A.M. the Stonewall Brigade, ably commanded by Winder, started north to intercept Brigadier General Erastus Tyler in the lead of Shields's army. Winder had about 1,200 men and two batteries. Taylor's brigade followed. Four thousand Federals with sixteen guns opposed Winder. The Union right sat on the river with their left anchored on an elevation to the east of the road, where Tyler positioned seven guns. The commanding elevation was called "the coaling" because it had recently been the site of charcoal production. Tyler's position, about a half mile wide, was about two and a half miles north of Port Republic.

Winder had a formidable task. Tyler outnumbered, outgunned, and outpositioned him with experienced, hard-fighting troops. Winder's first order of business was to neutralize the Union artillery. His own artillery was no match for the job, so he sent his infantry to flank the Union guns. The Federals threw them back in some confusion. The Union infantry, strongly positioned along the road, held firm as their artillery inflicted serious injury to Winder's men. Ewell's supporting troops had trouble crossing the South River on a makeshift bridge that would only accommodate a single column. Jackson ordered Taylor to circle the Federal left and silence the guns at the coaling.

Time was critical to Jackson, whose plans called for a quick victory so he could turn on Frémont by midmorning. Tyler attacked, and after a furious battle, the Confederates fell back on their guns. Some of Ewell's command gained the Federal left, but Union reinforcements had stymied the maneuver, when the Union surge suddenly came to a halt. Having worked their way through the woods just in time, Taylor's brigade finally pitched into the Federals at the coaling. Three desperate charges carried the position and the prize of six guns. Ewell's remaining troops were now up, and Tyler, realizing that the Confederates now commanded his rear and threatened his line of withdrawal, ordered a retreat. Jackson sent the cavalry to press the victory, and they followed the retreating Federals for 9 miles down the river. The battle had gone on for five hours.

It was 10:30 A.M. Tyler had so roughly handled Jackson's troops that they were in no condition to assail Frémont. An hour or two before the battle of Port Republic was over, and before Taylor had helped turn the tide, Jackson had realized that his plan to attack Frémont had to be abandoned. So he ordered the troops holding Frémont to fall back and burn the bridge over the North River behind them to secure his flank and line of retreat should he have need to quit the engagement with Shields.

Frémont, following Ewell's retrograde, came upon the bluffs along the South Fork of the Shenandoah just in time to find the Confederates collecting their casualties. His only remaining action was to harass the Confederates with artillery as they returned from pursuing Shields. By midnight, most of Jackson's army was at Brown's Gap 8 miles from Port Republic. Losses were about 800 Confederate and 1,000 Union (about a quarter of Tyler's strength).

The Confederate victories at Cross Keys and Port Republic came as a total surprise to Lincoln and Stanton, who, like Frémont and Shields, had thought Jackson was in disarray. On 6 June, Stanton had sent out communications instructing Frémont to halt at Harrisonburg and Shields to return to Fredericksburg. Confident that Jackson was on the run, McDowell was already shifting his command to the peninsula by water. The stunning Confederate victories caused the Federals to hold Shields at Luray, Frémont at Mount Jackson, and Brigadier General James Ricketts, replacing Ord, at Front Royal. Jackson was close to the Virginia Central Railroad and could move to Staunton, Gordonsville, or Richmond.

Lee, pleased with the effect of the victories, sent six regiments under Brigadier General Alexander Lawton and eight regiments under Brigadier General William Whiting to enable Jackson to crush the forces opposing him, but by the time they arrived, the situation had changed. Federal forces were too far north and following them would have put Jackson out of touch with Richmond. On 12 June, Jackson had moved back west and was encamped at Mount Meridian, 14 miles north of Waynesboro, his men enjoying a well-earned rest. Between 12 and 17 June, Jackson actively spread false and conflicting information about his whereabouts and plans, making himself virtually invisible to the Union army. On 17 June, Lee sent a message agreeing that pursuit of the Federals was not advisable and instructing Jackson to return to Richmond. The Shenandoah Valley campaign was over.

From 22 March to 17 June, Jackson's "foot cavalry" had covered 676 miles in 48 marching days, participated in two actions, four skirmishes, and five battles. He had pinned down 60,000 to 70,000 Federal troops, had demoralized the Union armies opposing him, and had caused considerable confusion in Washington. Most important, he relieved the pressure on Joseph E. Johnston's army protecting Richmond. Jackson had also provided the South with considerable stores. Most significantly, he had emerged as the Confederacy's premier military genius and hero.

Credit goes to Johnston for selecting Jackson to command the valley forces after First Bull Run. Lee must be applauded for his foresight and boldness, for he took the measure of the Union generals, Lincoln, Stanton, and the Northern public with a strategy to worry Washington and reduce or eliminate the pressure on Johnston's much smaller army. He was bold in giving Jackson free reign in the valley, supporting him with troops even when they were difficult to spare from the defense of Richmond.

Jackson's performance still awes military historians. Bold, aggressive, fearless, daring, clearheaded, and secure in the ability and motivation of his army, Jackson took advantage of every opportunity, both those he created and those that bewildered Union commanders gave him. Jackson appointed an effective staff that was loyal and dedicated to him. He had an eye for terrain and used maps to his advantage. Although an artillerist by experience, Jackson understood the use of cavalry to maintain constant contact with the enemy, monitoring their position and movements, and to confuse and misdirect them. His troops knew he cared for them, for although he was a strict and exacting disciplinarian, he minimized casualties and kept his men fed to the best of his ability. Despite marching them long and hard, he ordered regular rest periods that kept up their stamina and minimized straggling.

Still studied for its spectacular use of the fundamental principles of warfare, Jackson's Shenandoah Valley campaign is considered one of the most brilliant operations in military history.

—Richard C. Halseth

See also Ashby, Turner; Banks, Nathaniel Prentiss; Cross Keys, Battle of; Ewell, Richard Stoddert; Frémont, John Charles; Jackson, Thomas Jonathan; Kernstown, First Battle of; McDowell, Virginia, Battle of; Milroy, Robert Huston; Peninsula Campaign; Port Republic, Battle of; Shields, James; Stonewall Brigade; Taylor, Richard; Winchester, First Battle of.

For further reading:

Ecelbarger, Gary L. *The First Battle of Kernstown* (1997).

Henderson, G. F. R. *Stonewall Jackson and the American Civil War* (1988).

Krick, Robert K. *Conquering the Valley, Stonewall Jackson at Port Republic* (1996).

Robertson, James I., Jr. *Stonewall Jackson: The Man, the Soldier, the Legend* (1997).

Tanner, Robert G. *Stonewall in the Valley: Thomas J. "Stonewall" Jackson's Shenandoah Valley Campaign, Spring 1862* (1976; reprint, 1996).

Vandiver, Frank E. *Mighty Stonewall* (1957; reprint, 1988).

SHENANDOAH VALLEY CAMPAIGN
(August 1864–March 1865)

In August 1864 the outlook for the Union was bleak. President Abraham Lincoln was not sure of reelection, the cost of the war was mounting, the loss of men was appalling, and the Confederate forces were far from beaten. Exacerbating this situation was Lieutenant General Jubal Early's raid on Washington, D.C., his burning of Chambersburg, Pennsylvania, and the embarrassing debacle at the battle of the Crater near Petersburg, Virginia. Political pressure for a positive sign that the Union forces would prevail was beginning to bear on Lieutenant General Ulysses S. Grant.

Grant's strategy was to maintain pressure on all fronts and to use the Federal advantage in men and materiel effectively. This included controlling the Shenandoah Valley, which had long been the major north-south access route of the Confederate army. The valley provided foodstuffs, finished goods, and other necessities for General Robert E. Lee's army. The Federals tried in May and again in June to control the valley, but both Generals Franz Sigel and David Hunter failed.

At this point Grant recognized that his forces in the east suffered from an overlapping command structure that prevented effective coordination. He decided to consolidate these forces into a single command. He combined the Department of the Susquehanna, Middle Department, Department of Washington, and Department of West Virginia into the Middle Military Division. Brigadier General Philip Sheridan became temporary commander on 5 August.

Sheridan's command, now called the Army of the Shenandoah, included the following: VI Corps under Major General Horatio G. Wright with the divisions of

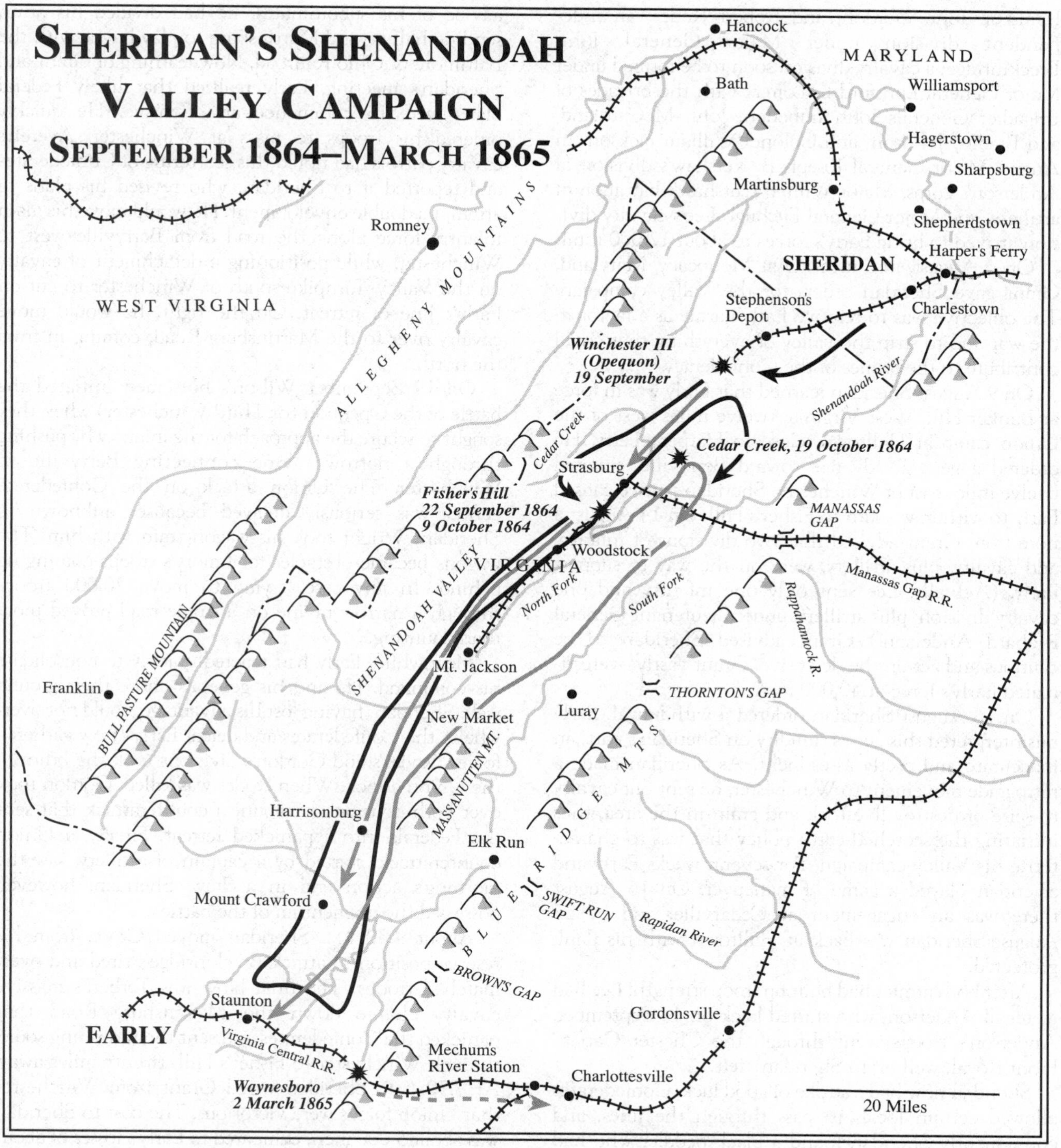

SHERIDAN'S SHENANDOAH VALLEY CAMPAIGN
SEPTEMBER 1864–MARCH 1865

Hancock

MARYLAND

Bath

Williamsport

Hagerstown

Sharpsburg

Martinsburg

Shepherdstown

Romney

SHERIDAN

Harper's Ferry

WEST VIRGINIA

Stephenson's Depot

Charlestown

ALLEGHENY MOUNTAINS

Winchester III (Opequon) 19 September

Shenandoah River

Cedar Creek

Cedar Creek, 19 October 1864

Strasburg

Fisher's Hill 22 September 1864 9 October 1864

VIRGINIA

Woodstock

MANASSAS GAP

North Fork

South Fork

Manassas Gap R.R.

BULL PASTURE MOUNTAIN

SHENANDOAH VALLEY

Mt. Jackson

Rappahannock R.

Franklin

New Market

Luray

THORNTON'S GAP

MASSANUTTEN MT.

BLUE RIDGE MTS.

Harrisonburg

Elk Run

SWIFT RUN GAP

Rapidan River

Mount Crawford

BROWN'S GAP

Staunton

Gordonsville

EARLY

Virginia Central R.R.

Mechum's River Station

Charlottesville

Waynesboro 2 March 1865

20 Miles

Brigadier Generals David A. Russell, George W. Getty, and James B. Ricketts; XIX Corps under Brigadier General William H. Emory with the divisions of Brigadier Generals William Dwight and Cuvier Grover (arrived later); the Army of West Virginia (later the VIII Corps) under Major General George Crook with the small divisions of Colonels Joseph Thoburn and Isaac

Duval; the cavalry divisions of Brigadier Generals Alfred Torbert, William Averell, and James Wilson; and twelve batteries of artillery. The total represented about 40,000 men, who either were in place or would be soon.

Facing off against Sheridan was Lieutenant General Jubal Early. His command consisted of the following: II Corps with the divisions of Major Generals Stephen

Ramseur, John Gordon, and Robert Rodes; an independent division under Major General John Breckinridge; a cavalry division soon to be formed under Major General Lunsford L. Lomax with the brigades of Brigadier Generals John Imboden, John McCausland, and Bradley Johnson, and Colonel William Jackson. In August Major General Joseph B. Kershaw's division of Anderson's corps, Major Wilfred Cutshaw's battalion of artillery, and Major General Fitzhugh Lee's cavalry division arrived to bring Early's forces to about 12,000 total.

On 6 August, at a meeting at Monocacy, Maryland, Grant gave Sheridan orders for the Valley campaign. The objective was to remove Early's army as a factor in the war and to strip the valley of everything that could contribute to the armies of the Confederacy.

On 9 August Sheridan learned that Early was in force at Bunker Hill, West Virginia, twelve miles west of the Union camp at Halltown, close to Harper's Ferry. He ordered a general advance toward Berryville, situated twelve miles east of Winchester. Sheridan's move caused Early to withdraw south to Fisher's Hill. On 14 August a note from Grant advised that two divisions of infantry and cavalry, plus artillery, were on the way to support Early. (Actually, Lee sent only one infantry and one cavalry division, plus artillery, under Lieutenant General Richard Anderson.) Grant advised Sheridan to be cautious and act on the defensive. Grant vastly overestimated Early's force at 40,000 men.

On 16 August Sheridan ordered a withdrawal. Early misinterpreted this act as timidity on Sheridan's part, an inaccurate and costly assessment. As Sheridan made a retrograde movement to Winchester, he sent out cavalry to seize or destroy livestock and grain in the area, thus initiating the scorched-earth policy that was to characterize his Valley campaign. For several weeks Early and Sheridan played a game of maneuver. On 16 August there was an engagement at Cedarville, and by 22 August Sheridan was back at Halltown with his flank protected.

After both armies had built up troop strength, Lee had to recall Anderson, who started back on 14 September. Anderson's troops went through the Chester Gap to Front Royal, well off to Sheridan's left.

Sheridan now had a stroke of good luck. Confederates allowed certain locals to pass through the lines, and consequently Sheridan found a black peddler who had access into Winchester. Crook knew a lady with strong Unionist sympathies, so they sent the peddler to her with an inquiry from Sheridan. When she relayed the valuable information that Anderson had departed, Sheridan knew that he was free to attack. On 17 September, at Grant's request, the two generals met at Charlestown. Grant had his own plan, but when he heard Sheridan's, he said nothing of it and gave him approval to move.

Early had misjudged Sheridan. Acting against the advice of his subordinates, he had divided his army, sending half toward Martinsburg to play havoc with the Baltimore & Ohio Railroad. Now learning of Grant and Sheridan's meeting, Early realized that likely Federal plans were to commence an offensive. He quickly ordered his troops to mass at Winchester. Averell's cavalry patrols had noted this scattering of Confederates and reported it to Sheridan, who revised his plans to attempt a double envelopment. He would move his main infantry force along the road from Berryville west to Winchester, while positioning a detachment of cavalry on the Valley Turnpike south of Winchester to cut off Early's line of retreat. On the right, he would move cavalry over to the Martinsburg Road, coming in from the north.

On 19 September Wilson's horsemen initiated the battle of the Opequon (or Third Winchester) when they sought to secure the approach for the infantry by pushing through a narrow ravine connecting Berryville to Winchester. The Union attack on the Confederate center was seriously delayed because, unknown to Sheridan, Wright took his wagon train with him. The wagons became obstacles for Emory's troops coming up behind. In any case, trying to move 20,000 troops through a narrow ravine on a single road proved more than daunting.

Meanwhile, Early had reacted quickly to consolidate his command. He and his generals chose their ground well. Sheridan, having lost his advantage, could not overwhelm the Confederates and defeat Early's now gathered forces. Rodes's and Gordon's divisions took the brunt of the Union attack. When Rodes was killed, Gordon took over both divisions to mount a counterattack that sent the Federals into a panicked retreat. Finally, a Union counterattack, started by a captain of artillery, saw the morning's action end in a draw. Sheridan, however, possessed the momentum of the battle.

About 4:30 P.M. Sheridan moved Crook from his reserve position to attack Breckinridge's tired and overmatched troops. The final blow was Torbert's massive cavalry charge down the Martinsburg Road that panicked the Confederates and sent them running south through Winchester to Fisher's Hill, twenty miles away. At 7:30 P.M., Sheridan wired Grant from Winchester that Union forces were victorious. The cost to Sheridan was about 5,000 men, compared to Early's losses of about 4,000. Combined with Sherman's taking of Atlanta, the victory at Opequon provided a much-needed political boost for Lincoln. It earned Sheridan the permanent rank of brigadier general in the regular army and permanent command of the Middle Military Division.

Fisher's Hill was a natural defensive position between Massanutten Mountain and North Mountain, so Early established a new line there. At this time, Lee called Breckinridge back to southwest Virginia, and Sheridan on 22 September aggressively attacked Early, after sending cavalry south along the east side of the Blue Ridge. Sheridan's orders were to force a crossing and secure a position across the Valley Turnpike at New Market, cutting Early's retreat route. Early's poorly prepared left flank again gave Crook a significant advantage, causing another rout that cost Early more than 1,300 men, most of them taken prisoner, and eleven guns. Union losses were only about 400 men.

Yet for all that, Union cavalry did not accomplish their mission to cut the line of retreat, and Early got away. Sheridan ordered Averell to follow on the heels of the retreating Confederates, but he failed to do so and Sheridan relieved him of duty. Sheridan was disappointed that the battle had not completely destroyed Early, but Grant was pleased with another victory.

Early went as far south as Port Republic on 25 September. There he had returned to him Kershaw's division and Cutshaw's artillery battalion. Lee thereby replaced most of Early's recent losses. Sheridan followed, stopping at Harrisonburg. On 6 October Sheridan started back north to shorten his supply lines and carry out Grant's directive to destroy the valley foodstuffs. The Federals devastated the valley, destroying 400 square miles of prime farmland. In the forty miles from Harrisonburg to Woodstock they burned 2,000 barns and seventy grain mills, ran off 4,000 cattle, and butchered 3,000 sheep.

On the route back north Brigadier General Thomas Rosser's cavalry harassed the Union troops. Sheridan, fed up with this action, ordered Torbert to turn and engage them. On 9 October a battle took place at Tom's Brook, five miles south of Strasburg. Rosser was routed and his cavalry retreated south twenty miles to the protection of the Confederate infantry.

Sheridan stopped at Cedar Creek, and Early followed as far as Fisher's Hill. Early established a lookout on Three Top Mountain, where he could easily monitor the Union troop dispositions. Gordon decided the Union left was vulnerable. Due to the topography, the Federals were not expecting an attack from that direction. Gordon found what amounted to little more than a pig trail along the base of the mountain that led to Crook's encampment on the Union left flank.

Because Secretary of War Edwin Stanton wanted Sheridan to meet with him to discuss future actions in the valley, Sheridan left for Washington and returned to Winchester on the afternoon of 18 October, assured that all was well. On the next day, Early struck before dawn, catching the Union army in bed. Within two hours the Confederates had routed the Union VIII and XIX Corps, sending many Federals scurrying back north toward Winchester. At about 7 A.M. Sheridan got reports of firing from the direction of Cedar Creek. At 9 A.M. he left Winchester, picking up his cavalry escort south of

town. As Sheridan got nearer to Cedar Creek, the sound of firing became more pronounced and he started seeing his retreating troops. After setting up his escort to stop the retreat, Sheridan arrived on the scene at 10:30 A.M. during a lull in the fighting. He quickly assessed the situation and had reformed his lines by noon. Early's troops lost momentum when they stopped for plunder. This gave Sheridan time to bring the retreating elements of his forces back to the front. Around 4 P.M. he attacked Early, and for a while it was a death lock. Then General Custer's cavalry turned Early's left so that by 5:30 P.M. the battle was over, except for the pursuit. Union losses were about 5,700 and Confederate almost 3,000.

From 19 September to 19 October Sheridan had won three major battles, had earned the permanent rank of major general, and had gained national fame.

The following month, November, Sheridan sent Brigadier General Wesley Merritt's cavalry into Mosby country (Fauquier and Loudoun Counties, Virginia) on a raid of destruction. In four days they did more than a million dollars worth of damage.

Grant kept prodding Sheridan to destroy the Virginia Central Railroad. Sheridan initiated an ill-fated attempt on 19 December. Custer got only as far as Harrisonburg, and Torbert came up short of Gordonsville. Although Sheridan's Valley campaign was essentially over, Early's army would not be truly eliminated until his defeat at Waynesboro on 2 March 1865. After Waynesboro, Sheridan returned his remaining army (about 10,000 cavalry and artillery) to Grant.

—*Richard C. Halseth*

See also Cedar Creek, Battle of; Custer, George Armstrong; Early, Jubal Anderson; Fisher's Hill, Battle of; Gordon, John Brown; Hotchkiss, Jedediah; Sheridan, Philip Henry; Tom's Brook, Battle of; Winchester (Opequon), Third Battle of.

For further reading:

Bushong, Millard K. *Old Jube: A Biography of General Jubal A. Early* (1988).

Heatwole, John L. *The Burning: Sheridan in the Shenandoah Valley* (1998).

Morris, Roy, Jr. *Sheridan: The Life and Wars of General Phil Sheridan* (1992).

Osborne, Charles C. *Jubal, The Life And Times of General Jubal A. Early, CSA* (1992).

Sheridan, Philip. *Personal Memoirs of Philip Henry Sheridan, General, United States Army* (1904).

Stackpole, Edward J. *Sheridan in the Shenandoah: Jubal Early's Nemesis* (1992).

SHEPLEY, GEORGE FOSTER
(1819–1878)
Union general

George Foster Shepley was born to Ether Shepley (a one-time U.S. senator and chief justice of the Maine Supreme Court) and Anna Foster Shepley, in Saco, Maine. George graduated from

Dartmouth College at the age of 18 and began the study of law. After admission to the bar he practiced law first in Bangor, Maine, and then in Portland. Like his father, he was active in Democratic politics and secured an appointment as U.S. district attorney for the state during James K. Polk's presidency. Dismissed by the Whig Zachary Taylor, Shepley was returned to the position under Franklin Pierce and remained in office until the summer of 1861.

In the meantime, Shepley had been selected by the state Democratic Party in early 1860 to serve as one of the state's delegates to the Democratic National Convention in Charleston, South Carolina. Shepley was a supporter of Stephen A. Douglas at that convention and at the reconvened meeting in Baltimore in June. While at both conventions, Shepley became acquainted with one of the Massachusetts delegates, Benjamin F. Butler. This acquaintance would later have a bearing on Shepley's military career during the war.

At the outbreak of the Civil War, Shepley helped to raise what would become the 12th Maine Infantry and was commissioned its colonel in November 1861. At the time, Benjamin Butler was in the process of planning the land phase of a campaign against New Orleans and requested that Shepley and the 12th Maine be assigned to his expedition. In March 1862 he was given command of a brigade in the New Orleans campaign.

After the fall of New Orleans, Butler made Shepley first military commandant of the city and then, in June 1862, military governor of the state of Louisiana. He would hold that post until March 1864. He was promoted to brigadier general in July 1862. Some have argued that much of the corruption that characterized the first months of U.S. administration in New Orleans was as much Shepley's fault as Butler's. Whatever the case, Shepley had his hands full dealing with not only a largely hostile population but also the large numbers of former slaves who flocked to Federal lines and the constant threat of a Confederate attempt to retake New Orleans and any other Federal occupied territory. While handling all of these tasks, he also had to supervise an attempt to establish some sort of loyal civilian government. To that end, the government encouraged Northern civilians to move to Louisiana to establish a base of support for the Union. By early 1864, there was a strong enough Unionist community of transplants and native Unionists to hold elections. With a new civilian government in place by March 1864, Shepley received orders that the commanding general of the army, Ulysses S. Grant, had removed him from command and ordered him to report to Grant in Virginia.

Initially Shepley was placed in the Department of Virginia under his old commander Benjamin F. Butler. Shepley briefly commanded Norfolk before being given command of the District of Eastern Virginia in May

1864. In February 1865 he was relieved of that command and became chief of staff to Major General Godfrey Weitzel, commander of XXV Corps. He was commended by General Weitzel after Robert E. Lee's surrender for the part Shepley had played in bringing about Lee's retreat from Petersburg. Weitzel recommended Shepley for promotion to major general.

Weitzel's corps was charged with the occupation of Richmond after the Confederate evacuation, and, given Shepley's experience in such matters, Weitzel appointed him military governor of the city. He remained in that position until he resigned his commission on 1 July 1865.

Shepley returned to Portland, where he practiced law until 1869, when President Grant appointed him U.S. circuit judge for Maine. Known primarily for his expertise in patent law, these types of cases made up a large part of those heard by his court. He remained on the bench until his death on 20 July 1878.

—*David S. Heidler and Jeanne T. Heidler*

See also Louisiana; New Orleans, Capture of.
For further reading:
Hearn, Chester G. *The Capture of New Orleans, 1862* (1995).
Winters, John D. *The Civil War in Louisiana* (1963).

SHERIDAN, PHILIP HENRY
(1831–1888)
Union general

Philip Henry Sheridan was probably born in Albany, New York, on 6 March 1831, the son of Irish immigrants. He was raised in Somerset, Ohio, and entered West Point in 1848 after lying about his age. Sheridan performed modestly as a student and, on account of his short stature, acquired the moniker "Little Phil." He was exceptionally thin-skinned and short-tempered, and once assaulted a cadet sergeant for placing him on report. Consequently, Sheridan forfeited an entire year and graduated in 1853, ranking thirty-fourth in a class of forty-nine. He then became a second lieutenant in the 1st U.S. Infantry and traveled west to combat hostile Indians along the Rio Grande in Texas. He also performed similar duties in the Oregon Territory, having transferred to the 4th U.S. Infantry in 1854. Sheridan was functioning as an obscure army captain with few prospects of advancement in the peacetime army, when the Civil War commenced in April 1861. Thereafter, the rise of this swarthy, nondescript individual was meteoric.

Reporting to St. Louis, Sheridan gained appointment as quartermaster on the staff of General Henry W. Halleck. He conducted his charge competently, if sullenly, and subsequently accompanied Halleck's botched advance on Corinth, Mississippi. Eager for greater responsibility, Sheridan relentlessly badgered superiors for a combat command and in May 1862 became colonel of the 2d Michigan Cavalry. In his first action on 1 July 1862, Sheridan distinguished himself during a mounted raid against General William J. Hardee at Boonesboro, Mississippi.

The Union army desperately needed commanders possessing the stomach and ability to fight, and Sheridan exuded both traits in abundance. He consequently transferred back to the infantry as a brigadier general and accompanied General Don C. Buell's Army of the Ohio to Kentucky. In this capacity Sheridan bore a conspicuous role in the bloody victory at Perryville on 8 October 1862. In December he performed similar work for General William S. Rosecrans at Murfreesboro, repulsing the determined attacks of General Leonidas Polk. In consequence of his outstanding performance, Sheridan advanced to major general of volunteers at the age of thirty-two.

Throughout the spring and summer of 1863 Sheridan accompanied Rosecrans during his successful Tullahoma campaign in central Tennessee. However, both men came to grief on 18–20 September, when Confederate General Braxton Bragg suddenly turned upon his pursuers at Chickamauga. Sheridan performed well in the initial phases of battle and was maneuvering for position when the corps under General James Longstreet made its sudden, unexpected assault. The entire Union right disintegrated and Sheridan's division dissolved into a mob of fugitives. Undeterred, "Little Phil" rallied most of his men and managed to shore up General George H. Thomas in the vicinity of Snodgrass Hill. Together the two men beat off subsequent Confederate attacks and conducted a well-organized withdrawal back to Chattanooga. The remnants of the Army of the Cumberland were then besieged there by Bragg, and Rosecrans was relieved by George H. Thomas.

By November 1863 General Ulysses S. Grant had taken charge in the west and began preparing an all-out assault on Bragg's position. On 25 November Sheridan, now assigned to William Sherman's army, successfully attacked the rifle pits directly to his front and captured them. That accomplished, Union troops began clambering up the slopes of Missionary Ridge without orders. Sheridan then ordered a formal advance that captured the heights. Union forces next cracked the Confederate center and nearly captured Bragg and his staff before the pursuit was halted. Grant was singularly impressed by Sheridan's performance, so he ordered Sheridan to accompany him back east, where even heavier fighting was anticipated.

Sheridan now found himself chief of cavalry in the Army of the Potomac, a curious appointment considering his background in the infantry. At that time Union cavalry was less a battlefield weapon than an instrument of patrolling, raiding, and guarding supply columns. Sheridan determined to overhaul the tactics and battle-field mission of his charge by equipping his men with the latest rapid-fire carbines and his own aggressive spirit. Within weeks he remolded the Union cavalry into a mobile, hard-hitting strike force.

In May 1864 Grant commenced his Overland campaign against the redoubtable Robert E. Lee. Prior to this he unleashed Sheridan's three cavalry divisions (12,000 men) and thirty-two cannon with orders to raid Richmond. Such a move was calculated to lure the elusive J. E. B. Stuart into the open, where Sheridan intended "to whip his boots off." Union cavalry skirmished incessantly with their Confederate opposites, before Stuart scraped together four brigades and made a stand at Yellow Tavern on 11 May. Sheridan led his larger force in a swirling battle, killing Stuart in the process. He then trotted up to the outer perimeter of Richmond's defenses, judged them too strong to be stormed by cavalry, and withdrew, his mission accomplished. As summer unfolded Sheridan conducted other raids against the Virginia Central Railroad and its hard-pressed defenders. On 11–12 June the Union cavalry brought General Wade Hampton to bay at Trevilian Station, and fought another heavy, inconclusive battle. At this juncture, pressing matters elsewhere forced Grant to pull Sheridan from the line and assign him command of the Army of the Shenandoah.

Since June a force of 14,000 Confederates had been operating in the Shenandoah Valley with near impunity. This region constituted the breadbasket of the Confederacy and was of considerable strategic significance. Moreover, their local commander, the aggressive General Jubal A. Early, had stampeded two Union armies out of his way and made an alarming raid on Washington, D.C. Sheridan now made his appearance at the head of 40,000 well-trained and equipped men and brooked no delays in seeking out his quarry. He tore into the outnumbered Early, inflicting heavy defeats at Third Winchester and Fisher's Hill that September. Union troops then began a systematic despoliation campaign of the fertile valley to deny its resources to the South. Sheridan, who strongly disliked Southerners, accepted the task unflinchingly and authorized the burning of homes and farms, and the confiscation of crops and livestock. It was total war at its fiercest, and closely mirrored the better-known efforts of Sherman in Georgia. As events told, Sheridan proved himself an even more ruthless exponent.

By October the campaign had progressed to Sheridan's satisfaction, so he carelessly encamped his army at Cedar Creek and departed for Washington, D.C., to confer with Grant. But he had totally underestimated the verve of "Old Jube," who marshaled his weary forces for one last lunge at the invaders. On 19 October 1864 the Confederates staged a successful surprise attack against the Union camp along Cedar Creek, routing two of three corps involved. Sheridan,

who heard the fighting when fifteen miles distant, spurred his faithful mount, Rienzi, and rode full gallop back to the scene of the action. As at Chickamauga, "Little Phil" rallied his milling soldiers and promptly counterattacked. The surging blue tide swept Early's victorious men from the field, capturing half his army and most of his artillery. By dint of this victory, the North was in undisputed control of the Shenandoah Valley, and now possessed a back door approach to Richmond. The event also bolstered President Abraham Lincoln's flagging reelection bid that November and, along with the fall of Atlanta, assured his political survival. The very nature of the victory inspired Thomas Buchanan Read to compose a famous poem, "Sheridan's Ride," while Congress granted him thanks and a promotion to major general of regulars.

By the spring of 1865, an iron noose was slowly drawing itself around the Confederate capital. Sheridan, meanwhile, resumed his raiding activities, destroying all railroads and rolling stock in his grasp, while crushing the remnant of Early's army at Waynesboro on 2 March. Several weeks later he suffered a repulse at the hands of General George Pickett at Dinwiddie Court House on 31 March. One day later Sheridan regrouped and stormed Pickett again, catching him unprepared at the battle of Five Forks. The Confederates were decisively shattered, and the defeat compromised the Army of Northern Virginia's left flank. Lee summarily abandoned the capital he had so adroitly defended for three years and marched west before the circle closed around him. Sheridan pursued vigorously and captured 6,000 men and five generals at Sayler's Creek on 6 April 1865. Then three more days of hard riding posited Union forces squarely in the path of Lee's retreat at Appomattox, prompting his immediate surrender. Sheridan, the thunderbolt of the Union, helped close the Civil War in his accustomed, decisive style.

The postwar period afforded Sheridan additional venues for distinction. In 1865 President Andrew Johnson dispatched him to Texas at the head of 50,000 veterans. This show of strength eventually induced French forces to evacuate Mexico. In March 1867 Sheridan next assumed command of the Fifth Military District, encompassing Texas and Louisiana. His strict enforcement of Reconstruction policies rendered him highly unpopular and Johnson removed him six months later. Unruffled, Sheridan openly pronounced his dislike of things Southern and once declared, "If I owned both Hell and Texas, I'd rent out Texas and live in Hell." By September 1867 he was reassigned as head of the Department of the Missouri, a huge tract encompassing all land between the Mississippi River and Rocky Mountains. Here he was responsible for enforcing peace among numerous Plains Indians, grown restless by the pace of white encroachment. When several tribes became

hostile, Sheridan simply adapted his total-war philosophy to frontier conditions. During 1868–1869 Sheridan waged a ruthless winter campaign against warring Cheyenne, Kiowa, and Comanche tribesmen, driving them onto reservations. The expression, "The only good Indians I ever saw were dead," originated with him, although he denied overt hostility towards Native Americans. Sheridan rose to lieutenant general in March 1869. Two years later he served as an observer during the Franco-Prussian War. He returned in time to orchestrate continuing efforts against the Plains Indians and in 1878 directed the final operations that captured the celebrated Chief Joseph. In November 1883 Sheridan supplanted Sherman as commanding general of the army and helped draw the bloody period of Indian wars to a close through the capture of Geronimo. He rose to full general shortly before dying at Nonquitt, Massachusetts, on 5 August 1888, three days after completing his memoirs. Sheridan was one of the most aggressive and all-around successful military commanders of American history.

—*John C. Fredriksen*

See also Cedar Creek, Battle of; Chickamauga, Battle of; Early, Jubal Anderson; Five Forks, Battle of; Lookout Mountain, Battle of; Shenandoah Valley Campaign (1864–1865); Yellow Tavern, Battle of.

For further reading:
Dawson, Joseph G., III. *Army Generals and Reconstruction: Louisiana, 1862–1877* (1984; reprint 1994).
Hutton, Paul A. *Phil Sheridan and His Army* (1985).
Morris, Roy. *Sheridan: The Life and Wars of General Phil Sheridan* (1992).
Sheridan, Philip. *Personal Memoirs of Philip H. Sheridan, General, United States Army* (1904).
Stackpole, Edward J. *Sheridan in the Shenandoah: Jubal Early's Nemesis* (1992).
Wooster, Robert. *The Military and United States Indian Policy, 1865–1903* (1988).

SHERMAN, JOHN
(1823–1900)
U.S. senator

The younger brother of General William Tecumseh Sherman, John Sherman was born in Lancaster, Ohio, on 10 May 1823. He was the eighth child born to Charles Robert and Mary Hoyt Sherman. The famous Sherman brothers, Tecumseh and John, shared a close, affectionate relationship, particularly once their father died in 1829. At age fourteen John Sherman left school but soon began reading the law with his uncle, Judge Jacob Parker, and his eldest brother, Charles Taylor Sherman, in Mansfield, Ohio, in 1840. He passed the bar in 1844 and practiced law in Mansfield for over ten years. Sherman later solidified his position in town by marrying Margaret Sarah Cecilia, the daughter of an influential Mansfield lawyer. The couple had no children but did adopt a daughter.

John Sherman's political career formally began when he served as a delegate to the Whig national conventions of 1848 and 1852. After the repeal of the Missouri Compromise by the Kansas-Nebraska Act in 1854, Sherman won a seat in the federal House of Representatives as an "anti-Nebraska" man. The following year he helped organize the Republican Party in Ohio, and in 1855 was president of the state's first Republican convention. While in the House, Sherman established a record as a political moderate within the Republican Party. A member and eventual chairman of the powerful Ways and Means Committee, Sherman became a prominent supporter of such important Republican programs as free homesteads, the construction of a transcontinental railroad, and strong tariffs to protect domestic manufacturing, while opposing federal interference with slavery in the District of Columbia. Like most moderate and conservative Republicans, Sherman feared the issue of black rights would damage his party's electoral prospects. The young Ohio congressman found national politics to his liking. Indeed, he would spend the next fifty years of his life holding various offices and appointed positions in Washington.

After six years in the House of Representatives, Sherman was elected to the Senate in 1861 to fill the seat vacated by Salmon P. Chase. In a matter of months the secession of the Southern states and civil war forced the junior senator from Ohio to perform a critical role on the national stage. Sherman focused much of his attention on creating an efficient federal bureaucracy to support the Northern war effort. In attempting to achieve his goal, Sherman proved to be a pragmatist when it came to interpreting the Constitution and the power of the federal government. Although he sometimes expressed ambivalence regarding the growing strength of the state, he supported Lincoln's suspension of the writ of habeas corpus and the rapid enlargement of the army. More important, it was as chairman of the Senate Finance Committee that Sherman came to influence most of the financial measures associated with the Civil War and Reconstruction. He helped draft the National Banking Act (1863), which created a national banking system that would eventually replace the decentralized state banking system that had been in place since the 1830s. Sherman also supported the Legal Tender Act, which gave "greenbacks" the status of legal tender. Thus, for the first time, the nation established national paper money as the standard of value. Expediency and the dire need to finance the Union war effort fundamentally swayed Sherman's position on these and other economic positions. Ultimately the senator expected to redeem the new "greenback" currency with gold once the war had been won. Sherman remained sympathetic to many traditional "hard" money ideals both during and after the Civil War.

Along with his important role in shaping legislation regarding the U.S. economic system and the financing of the war, John Sherman also worked hard in support of his brother William Tecumseh's budding military career in the Union army. John Sherman made sure that President Abraham Lincoln and other prominent Republican leaders in Washington noticed and rewarded his brother's genius as an effective and ruthless general in the field. Though their relationship exhibited occasional signs of tension, John and William Tecumseh offered each other emotional and political support throughout their lives.

After the war, Sherman adopted a moderate stance on Reconstruction and opposed the Radical Republican plan for a sustained military government to rule the conquered South. He initially opposed the impeachment of President Andrew Johnson but later voted for his conviction. As secretary of the treasury in President Rutherford B. Hayes's administration, he exhibited great skill in administering the Resumption Act, which provided for the restoration of specie payments—an issue dear to his heart. Sherman supported the Bland-Allison Act of 1878, which provided for the limited coinage of silver. In 1881 he was reelected to the Senate, where he served until 1897. Again he shaped financial legislation by helping to draft the Sherman Antitrust Act (1890) and the Sherman Silver Purchase Act (1890). President William McKinley appointed Sherman secretary of state in 1897, but illness prevented him from meeting his responsibilities, and he resigned in 1898. Shortly thereafter, John Sherman died in Washington, D.C., on 22 October 1900.

—*Frank J. Byrne*

See also Financing, U.S.A.; Greenbacks; Legal Tender Acts; Sherman, William Tecumseh.

For further reading:

Burton, Theodore E. *John Sherman* (1906).

Cimprich, John Vincent. "The Development of John Sherman's Views on Slavery and the Freedmen, 1861–1867" (M.A. thesis, 1973).

Isphording, Stephan M. "The House Years of John Sherman" (M.A. thesis, 1978).

Patrick, John J. "John Sherman: The Early Years, 1823–1865" (Ph.D. dissertation, 1982).

Wheeler, Kenneth W., ed. *For the Union: Ohio Leaders in the Civil War* (1998).

SHERMAN, THOMAS WEST
(1813–1879)
Union general

Born in Newport, Rhode Island, to Elijah Sherman and Martha West Sherman, Thomas West Sherman was educated locally before seeking an appointment to the U.S. Military Academy. Since his father would not allow him to apply through the usual channels, Sherman walked to Washington to apply personally to President Andrew Jackson. The president granted him the appointment. Sherman graduated eighteenth of forty-nine in the class of 1836.

After graduation, Sherman was sent to fight in the Second Seminole War as a second lieutenant in the 3d Artillery. After serving two years in that conflict, Sherman aided with the removal of the Cherokee Indians to the newly designated Indian Territory. He returned to Florida for the conclusion of the Second Seminole War, followed by a variety of duties, including recruiting service, before being sent to join Zachary Taylor at the outbreak of the Mexican-American War. He fought in all the major battles in Taylor's campaign in northern Mexico, earning a brevet promotion for his actions at Buena Vista in February 1847.

Sherman served at several posts after the Mexican-American War, including two in his native New England as well as the Minnesota frontier. He also served in Kansas during some of the troubled times there from 1857 to 1858. At the outbreak of the Civil War, Sherman was a major of the 3d Artillery.

On 21 May 1861 Sherman was given command of all the light batteries in the Department of Washington, D.C. He had been promoted to lieutenant colonel of the 5th Artillery. On 6 August 1861, Sherman was promoted to brigadier general of volunteers with a date of rank of 17 May. By this time he had been designated the commander of land forces for an expedition to the South Carolina coast.

In August, Sherman was sent to New York City to recruit and organize for the expedition. He would have about 12,000 men for the campaign. On 21 October 1861 the expedition left Annapolis, Maryland. After stopping at Hampton Roads, the ships proceeded to the South Carolina coast, where, after a naval bombardment on 7 November, Sherman and his men took possession of Fort Beauregard and Fort Walker at Port Royal Sound.

From Port Royal Sherman operated along the South Carolina and Georgia coasts. He attempted in January 1862 to organize an expedition against Savannah, Georgia, but his plan was vetoed by the commanding general of the army, George B. McClellan, because of the resources that would be necessary for such a campaign's success. Along with his military activities, Sherman also had to cope with the large numbers of coastal slaves who flocked to Union lines. He suggested to the War Department that as the war proceeded, the problems of feeding large numbers of slaves would only increase and therefore some system needed to be established early to supply these people with the necessities of life.

In April 1862, Sherman was transferred to Don Carlos Buell's Army of the Ohio. The following month he was placed in command of what had been George H. Thomas's division in the advance on Corinth,

Mississippi. In this new command, Sherman experienced difficulties with his immediate subordinates. His stern methods of command and insistence on iron discipline rankled the volunteer officers, and a petition was organized among many of the colonels and brigadier generals of his division. As a result of the disaffection among his officers, Sherman was relieved of command in June 1862. While another suitable position was sought for him, he was granted a 60-day leave of absence.

At the expiration of his leave, Sherman was sent to report to Benjamin F. Butler at the headquarters for the Department of the Gulf in New Orleans. In September 1862 he took command of the Federal position at Carrollton, Louisiana. Sherman remained in this command through the end of the year. In January 1863 he was called on to command a division in the Port Hudson campaign.

Serving under Nathaniel P. Banks, Sherman commanded the left of the expedition, leading one of the major assaults on the Confederate works on 27 May 1863. In this attack, Sherman was severely wounded in the right leg, an injury that required the amputation of the leg. It was nine months before he could return to duty.

Upon his return in early 1864, Sherman was placed in command of Forts Jackson and Saint Philip below New Orleans. Shortly thereafter, he briefly joined Banks on the Red River campaign. In June Sherman was placed in command of the defenses of New Orleans, a position he held until the end of the war. In January 1865 the name of his command was changed to the Southern Division of Louisiana.

After the war, Sherman remained in the Department of Louisiana until 1866, when he was mustered out of the volunteer army and reverted to colonel of the 3d Artillery. For the remainder of his army career he commanded posts from New England to Key West. He retired due to his injuries in 1870 at the rank of major general. In retirement he lived quietly in Newport, Rhode Island, where he died on 16 March 1879.

—*David S. Heidler and Jeanne T. Heidler*

See also Port Hudson Campaign; Port Royal Sound, Battle of.
For further reading:

Cunningham, Edward. *The Port Hudson Campaign, 1862–1863* (1963).

Hewitt, Lawrence. *Port Hudson: Confederate Bastion on the Mississippi* (1987).

SHERMAN, WILLIAM TECUMSEH
(1820–1891)
Union general

Born in Lancaster, Ohio, Sherman was the son of Charles Sherman, a leading state judge, and Mary Hoyt, both originally from Connecticut. Charles died suddenly in 1829, and the young William ("Cump"

William Tecumseh Sherman (*Library of Congress*)

as he was universally called) became a member of the neighboring Ewing family. Thomas Ewing, the patriarch, was a leading lawyer and politician. Sherman always felt unsure of his place in this foster family and unhappy at the disintegration of his birth family as a result of his father's death.

At sixteen, through Ewing's influence, Sherman entered the United States Military Academy at West Point. He was an excellent but obstreperous student, finishing sixth in his class of 1840, demerits having dropped him two places in class rank.

Sherman's early army years found him assigned to a variety of locales, almost all in the South. He fought the hard Seminole War in Florida (1840–1842), and he was part of the garrison at Fort Morgan on Mobile Bay (1842) and at Fort Moultrie in Charleston harbor (1842–1846). He traveled throughout the southeast during these years gaining valuable knowledge about Southern people and terrain and developing his network of friends in the region. It was during this period that he fell in love with, and became engaged to, Ellen B. Ewing, one of his foster sisters.

The Mexican War caused his reassignment from a recruiting station in Pittsburgh to occupation duty in California. After a six-month cruise with an artillery company and with future Civil War chief of staff, Henry W. Halleck, aboard a navy ship around the Horn of South America, he arrived in Monterey and served as chief subordinate to Colonel Richard B. Mason, the future state's military governor. Sherman saw no combat, but he experienced the gold rush of 1849, composing the first report to reach Washington about it. He found his time in California exasperating because of separation from his future wife and family, the enervating boredom of much of his existence, and the crushing inflation caused by the discovery of gold. His relationship with Ellen Ewing continued through the mails, despite their disagreement over his refusal to convert to Catholicism and his insistence on remaining in the army rather than taking a civilian job closer to Ohio.

Sherman jumped at the chance to leave California in 1850. He carried messages to President Zachary Taylor and commanding General Winfield Scott in Washington, D.C. In May of that year he and Ellen married in a highly public ceremony attended by the president and his cabinet members. Ewing was secretary of the interior, and the marriage of his daughter was an important Washington social event.

Sherman now faced a crossroads. He was married to a woman who insisted she wanted to live only near her parents in Lancaster, yet he wanted to continue his army career despite his lack of combat experience in the Mexican War. The couple's first child was born in 1851, and Sherman gained promotion to captain in the commissary service. He served in St. Louis and New Orleans until 1853, frequently separated from his wife and growing family. Fearful of the kind of financial collapse his father had experienced, Sherman decided to accept the offer of an army friend and become manager of the San Francisco branch of a St. Louis bank. His wife was unhappy about leaving her father and mother. The couple compromised by leaving their first-born child with the Ohio grandparents.

The Shermans lived in California from 1853 to 1857. Ellen never adjusted to life there, and Cump had major financial difficulties. In 1855 Sherman survived a general run on the banks through astute management. However, in his role as commander of the local militia and despite support from the governor, Sherman could not prevent local vigilantes from taking control of San Francisco. He resigned his militia post in disgust, but he maintained his high banking position in the city. Meanwhile, Ellen returned to Ohio for seven months to visit her parents and daughter, leaving Cump and the two other children behind in California. Throughout his time in San Francisco, the pressure of personal and public problems caused Sherman to suffer from asthma and depression.

Finally in late 1856, the bank directors in St. Louis

decided to close the California branch. Financial concerns and worries about Sherman's frequent pessimistic letters brought about the decision. Sherman was devastated, but Ellen was pleased to be returning to her parents' home. Sherman moved to New York to open a new branch bank, but the Panic of 1857 quickly doomed that project.

Depressed at his failure to make a success of his life and faced with pressure from his wife and family to come home and take over management of the Ewing saltworks, Sherman grappled with his future plans. He was prepared to accept the saltworks position, when two of his brothers-in-law asked him to join them in a real estate law venture in Kansas. Once again Sherman's hopes were dashed. The business failed, and Sherman now desperately tried to get back into the army. There were no openings, but in 1859 army friends helped him obtain the position of superintendent of the newly created Louisiana Military Seminary. Sherman went South alone because there was no available housing for his family, but he expected Ellen and five children to join him when the promised house was constructed. Ellen and the Ewings were not that enthusiastic about the move. Although Sherman was happily and successfully running the school, Ellen and her family pressured him to take a position with a London bank. That way, Ellen could remain in Lancaster.

Louisiana's secession ended the domestic debate. Sherman had determined early on that he would not remain in Louisiana if the state left the Union. His sense of order would not permit him to cooperate even passively in the destruction of the Union. In February 1861 he left Louisiana and went to St. Louis, Missouri, as president of a street railroad company. There Sherman witnessed the horror of conflict between Union and Confederate supporters in the streets of the city. Traveling to Washington, he joined the United States Army as a colonel that May. He served as inspector general for Winfield Scott and then became commander of a brigade in Daniel Tyler's division. Sherman found the volunteer soldiers' lack of preparation and enthusiasm disconcerting, but did heroic work in the Union debacle at Bull Run (Manassas) in July 1861. Once again, however, failure seemed to be dogging his life.

In August 1861 Sherman traveled to Kentucky to become Robert Anderson's chief subordinate in the Department of the Cumberland, taking the position only after Abraham Lincoln promised him that he would never have to command. This promise proved shallow. Anderson, who had gained a national reputation because of his stand at Fort Sumter, resigned his command because of exhaustion, and Sherman found himself in command, despite Lincoln's promise.

Sherman's performance was abysmal. The situation in Kentucky was chaotic, and Sherman overreacted in response. He sent hysterical letters and telegrams to officials in Washington, predicting a Union disaster in his department and demanding to be relieved of command at once. In mid-November, Don Carlos Buell arrived as his replacement, and Sherman went to Missouri to serve under his California colleague, Henry W. Halleck. His pessimistic view of the war continued unabated, however, so Halleck sent him home for a brief rest. While in Lancaster and again forced to accept the help of Thomas Ewing, Sherman suffered the revenge of reporters whom he had accused of being spies while he was in Kentucky. Newspapers accused him of being insane, and rumors to this effect circulated in army and political circles.

Upon his return from leave in January 1862, Sherman was pushed to the backwater of the war: troop training at Benton Barracks, Missouri. Slowly he regained his equilibrium and was given a command in Paducah, Kentucky. He began forwarding troops to U. S. Grant as the little-known Union commander won victories at Forts Henry and Donelson. Commanding a division, Sherman fought under Grant at Shiloh on 6–7 April 1862. Despite Confederates overwhelming his position during the early hours of the battle, Sherman did not crack under the pressure. He helped steel Union soldiers and watched with awe as Grant stubbornly led the Union army to victory on the second day of the battle. Grant helped convince him that the Union cause was not hopeless. Sherman's participation in Halleck's subsequent capture of Corinth in May 1862 made him feel even more hopeful.

Halleck now broke up his victorious army and assigned Sherman to be military governor of the recently captured Memphis, Tennessee. Sherman's experiences here had a major effect on his understanding of the war he was fighting. He experienced no threat from the Confederate army while governing Memphis, but guerrillas proved extremely bothersome. He came to see the war as a conflict not between two armies but between two societies. Before the Union could be preserved, he came to believe, the Confederate people, not simply its armies, had to be defeated. The Union, therefore, would have to wage a new kind of war.

In the fall of 1862 Sherman departed Memphis, pleased with his success in building up Union sentiment in the city and convinced that he had effectively controlled the guerrillas. That December Sherman failed miserably in his attack on Chickasaw Bayou north of Vicksburg, when Grant did not appear to support him as planned. A Confederate raid had crippled Grant's supply base, so he did not march on Vicksburg. Most unhappily, the press once more accused Sherman of insanity and, in response, he court-martialled Thomas W. Knox of the *New York Herald*, one of the few such military actions in American history.

Adding even more to Sherman's frustration, John

General Sherman (*leaning on gun, right*) at Federal Fort No. 7, Atlanta, 1864 (Photograph by George Barnard / *Library of Congress*)

McClernand, a leading Illinois politician turned general, arrived to take command of Sherman's troops. Sherman maintained control long enough to lead his soldiers to victory at Arkansas Post in January 1863, and then he settled in under U. S. Grant in a series of unsuccessful attempts to capture Vicksburg. Finally, in May 1863 Grant initiated his daring plan that, along with a long siege, resulted in the capitulation of the Mississippi fortress on 4 July 1863. During the siege, Sherman set up a defense line along the Big Black River to prevent Confederate general Joseph E. Johnston in Jackson from sending reinforcements to break the Union siege of Vicksburg.

Once again, Sherman's success proved short-lived. After Vicksburg's capture, he allowed his wife and chil-

dren to visit him in his camps along the Big Black River. Tragically, his beloved son Willie died from a fever. Cump and Ellen never really overcame the grief over their loss.

In fall 1863 Grant became commander of the Union war in the West, and Sherman assumed command of the Department and Army of the Tennessee. He helped Grant lift the siege of Chattanooga and then rushed to the aid of Ambrose Burnside, then under siege at Knoxville. In February 1864, Sherman implemented the destructive war he had been planning since Memphis. During this so-called Meridian campaign, he destroyed property as his way of waging psychological warfare against Confederate society. He came away convinced that he did not have to kill and maim people he had long known and admired, but he could help bring about Union victory through property destruction and attacks on the Southern psyche.

Grant's and Sherman's successes in the West resulted in Grant being named commander of all Union armies, while Sherman took overall command in the West. The two men, now personally close, planned a coordinated campaign for the entire Union war effort. On 6 May 1864, Grant moved against Lee in Virginia, while Sherman simultaneously moved against Joe Johnston in Georgia. Sherman used well-designed flanking movements and incredible logistical skill to push Johnston back toward Atlanta. He proved unsuccessful in destroying the Confederate army, however, and foolishly made a frontal attack at Kennesaw Mountain that resulted in heavy casualties. He then returned to flanking movements. When Jefferson Davis replaced Johnston with the more offensive-minded John Bell Hood, who immediately went on the attack, Sherman inflicted terrible punishment on him. In September he captured Atlanta and helped influence the outcome of the 1864 presidential election in favor of Abraham Lincoln.

After forcing the evacuation of Atlanta and torching all its war-making facilities (but not burning the city to the ground, as myth would have it), Sherman took his

General Sherman on horseback near Atlanta, 1864
(*National Archives*)

concept of destructive war to its next level. He marched from Atlanta to Savannah and the sea, moving on a forty- to sixty-mile front and inflicting enormous property damage everywhere he passed. Casualties on both sides were light, however, and personal violence against Georgian civilians was slight. Sherman did not pursue a scorched earth policy, but he used purposeful destruction to plant uncertainty and fear in the hearts and minds of the Confederate populace. Confederate soldiers, deserters, civilians, and fugitive slaves did their share of damage, too, and their activities added to the psychological trauma.

As he marched and destroyed, Sherman kept insisting that, once the South surrendered, he would become its best friend. Upon capturing Savannah in December 1864, he put this promise into practice. Unlike his previous campaign of hard war, he now established a lenient peace in the Georgia city. He did not want to kill and maim, so he destroyed property in order to convince Southerners to end the war as quickly as possible. Once Union victory was secure, he wanted all punishment to end.

Grant now wanted Sherman to board his troops on ships and join him against Lee in Virginia. Sherman did not want to return to the bloodbath of conventional war, so he convinced Grant to let him march through the Carolinas toward Virginia and Lee's army. He argued that his march would weaken Lee's and other Confederate armies as much as if he were facing them on a battle field. And, he pointed out, his method was less bloody.

Sherman's march through South Carolina was even more destructive than his march to the sea because he and his men blamed the Palmetto State for bringing on the war. He did not, however, burn Columbia, the state capital, as was later charged. The destructive fire there was the result of Confederates torching cotton as they retreated, high winds that fanned the cotton fires, and liquor that Union soldiers and white and black Southerners consumed in the city. When the army entered North Carolina, their purposeful destruction grew less harsh, the army feeling more kindly toward the Tarheel State than it had toward the Palmetto State to its south.

Once again Sherman demonstrated his "soft peace" philosophy. After defeating the last-gasp Confederate efforts to defeat his army at Averysboro and Bentonville, North Carolina, Sherman met with Lincoln, Grant, and Admiral David D. Porter at City Point, Virginia, to discuss the ending of the war. In mid-April, he met with Joseph E. Johnston, his Confederate counterpart, in Durham Station, North Carolina. The result was a surrender agreement so lenient that the nation's press and officials of the new Andrew Johnson administration, particularly Secretary of War Edwin Stanton, stunned by Lincoln's assassination, labelled Sherman a traitor.

Sherman was forced into negotiating new surrender terms, and his anger at Stanton and at his old friend Henry W. Halleck for accusations against his loyalty caused him to snub both men. He refused to acknowledge Halleck when his army marched through Richmond, and he refused to shake Stanton's hand on the reviewing stand during the Grand Review of Union Armies in Washington.

During Reconstruction, Sherman showed that his affection for the white South was sincere. He urged a mild Reconstruction policy and, although he reluctantly acknowledged that slavery was finished, he believed that freed people should not have rights equal to his long-time Southern white friends. As his command was now in the trans-Mississippi west, however, he did not have to become involved in the army's difficult Reconstruction battles. In 1869, when Grant became president, Sherman became commanding general of the United States Army.

He served in this office until 1883, but he was never happy in the position. He battled a series of secretaries of war over ultimate command of the military, and he even spent a year touring Europe (1871–1872) and a year and a half in St. Louis (1874–1875) in order to get out of Washington and away from the cabinet and congressional battles. He completed his memoirs in 1875. They were a controversial but literary and commercial success, and in 1879 he toured the sites of his Civil War campaigns in the South, where he was greeted with good humor. Sherman served as president of the Society of the Army of the Tennessee and regularly attended a variety of veterans' reunions. After his retirement in 1883, he became one of the nation's most popular after-dinner speakers and, through his publications in the nation's magazines, he took on the task of presenting to the public what he believed was the true history of the war—that is, the moral superiority of the Union cause. This activity brought him into conflict with a variety of contemporaries, from Jefferson Davis to fellow Union generals. He also enjoyed an active social life, attending the theater regularly. By this time, his family was grown and his wife Ellen was a virtual recluse, with no desire to share in his social life. Sherman developed a reputation for kissing young girls every chance he had, and he had some sort of liaison with Vinnie Ream, a nationally known and beautiful sculptress.

Sherman died in 1891, following Ellen's death in 1888. Obituaries all over the nation praised him for his wartime and postwar activities. He was not yet the brutish villain of later Lost Cause views. In the twentieth century, however, he was inaccurately viewed as a heartless destroyer. He was also frequently quoted because of his aphorisms: "War is hell" and "I will not accept if nominated and will not serve if elected." In military history, however, his fame results from his elevation of destructive and psychological warfare to a major method of waging war. Sherman is one of the most significant figures in all of American military history.

—*John F. Marszalek*

See also Arkansas Post, Battle of; Army of the Tennessee; Atlanta Campaign; Chattanooga, Campaign; Grant, Ulysses S.; Halleck, Henry W.; Johnston, Joseph E.; Meridian Campaign; Sherman's March to the Sea; Vicksburg Campaign.

For further reading:

Fellman, Michael. *Citizen Sherman: A Life of William Tecumseh Sherman* (1995).

Lewis, Lloyd. *Sherman, Fighting Prophet* (1932).

Marszalek, John F. *Sherman, A Soldier's Passion for Order* (1994).

———. *Sherman's Other War, The General and the Civil War Press* (1999).

Sherman, William T. *Memoirs of General William T. Sherman* (1990).

SHERMAN'S MARCH TO THE SEA
(November–December 1864)

From 15 November to 21 December 1864, William Tecumseh Sherman led 62,000 Union soldiers on his "March to the Sea," a sixty-mile-wide path of destruction that stretched 285 miles across Georgia from Atlanta to Savannah. Because Sherman intended to demolish Confederate logistics and crush Southern morale, it has often been argued that Sherman's raid was an example of modern and total war. A war may be considered modern if a nation utilizes its industrial capabilities and arouses nationalism among its citizens to achieve victory. Likewise, a war may be considered total if a nation attempts to harness all its natural and human resources as effective means to achieve victory.

Born on 20 February 1820 in Lancaster, Ohio, William Tecumseh Sherman entered the U.S. Military Academy in 1836 and graduated in 1840. In his first assignment, he went to Florida to fight the Seminole Indians. Much has been made of Sherman's experiences in this conflict, because he came to realize that wars were fought not only between armies but also between the societies that supported them. During the Civil War, Sherman joined Ulysses S. Grant's command and fought under him at Shiloh, Vicksburg, and Chattanooga. When Grant went east as general-in-chief of the Union army in the spring of 1864, Sherman assumed command of the Western theater. In this role, he used the Armies of the Cumberland, Tennessee, and the Ohio to place constant pressure on the Confederacy—especially against Joseph E. Johnston and later John Bell Hood in Georgia. As part of this strategy, Sherman's forces attempted to demolish Confederate logistical infrastructure and hurt Southern morale.

After much maneuvering and fighting in the Atlanta campaign beginning May 1864, Sherman forced the Confederate John Bell Hood to evacuate Atlanta and

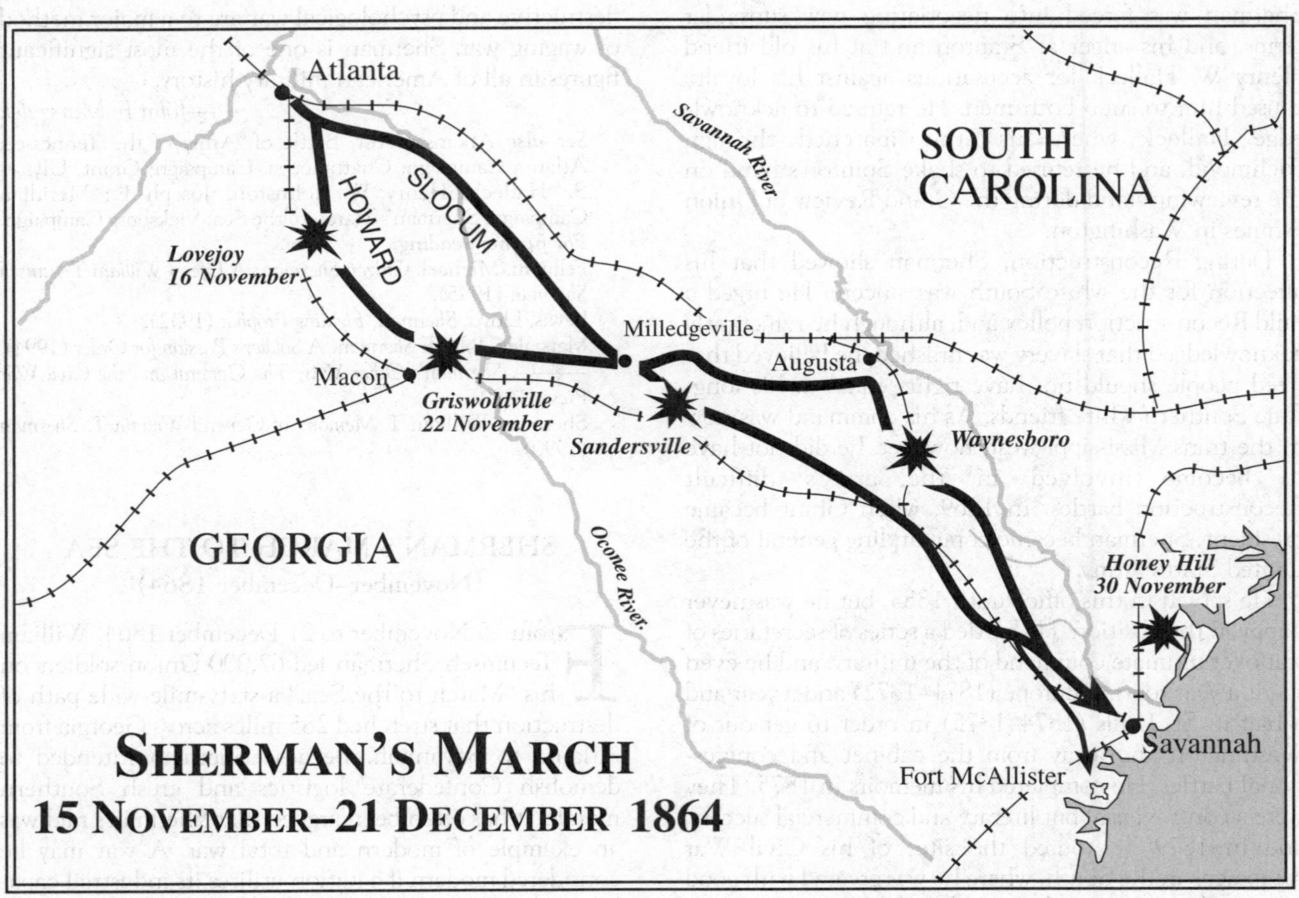

SHERMAN'S MARCH
15 NOVEMBER–21 DECEMBER 1864

Map showing Atlanta, Lovejoy 16 November, Macon, Griswoldville 22 November, Milledgeville, Sandersville, Augusta, Waynesboro, Honey Hill 30 November, Fort McAllister, Savannah; with HOWARD and SLOCUM march routes across GEORGIA toward SOUTH CAROLINA, the Savannah River, and the Oconee River.

relinquish its key railroad hub on 2 September. Hood retreated from Georgia into Tennessee. After briefly pursuing his enemy, Sherman left the task of fighting Hood to his subordinates George H. Thomas and John M. Schofield. Meanwhile, Sherman took his remaining 62,000 soldiers of the Army of the Ohio and 64 cannon further southeast on a campaign across northern Georgia to Savannah; as one of the most important seaports in the South, Savannah remained a key to Confederate transportation between Lee's troops in Virginia and the deep South. Sherman departed from Atlanta on this march to the sea on 15 November 1864.

Sherman's route across northern Georgia initially confused Confederates. He divided his forces into two columns or wings. One of these columns moved as if it were going to attack Augusta, Georgia; this upper column included XIV and XX Corps from the Union's Army of Georgia and was commanded personally by Sherman. The other column moved in a more southerly direction toward Macon, Georgia. This lower column included XV and XVII corps from the Union's Army of Tennessee led by Henry W. Slocum, as well as a cavalry division led by H. Judson Kilpatrick.

Sherman's forces quickly broke away from the Union

supply lines and lived off the land in northern Georgia. Sherman moved so quickly because his troops foraged in the Southern countryside and utilized Confederate resources to supply themselves. What his troops did not consume, they destroyed. The total Confederate losses included more than 13,000 head of cattle, some 6 million rations of bread and beef, and about 90,000 bales of cotton. Many sawmills, cotton gins, foundries, and warehouses also fell into Union hands. Sherman himself estimated his raid had inflicted $100 million worth of damage.

Sherman's strategy of destruction rather than strategy of battle was designed, as his own saying went, to "make Georgia howl." Sherman's forces burned and looted much of the north Georgia countryside. Although he did not condone wanton acts of violence and devastation, he certainly tolerated them. Drawing from experiences fighting the Seminoles in the early 1840s, Sherman believed that destruction or confiscation of Southern property was necessary to cripple Confederate logistics and morale. These actions, however, caused few deaths among Southern civilians.

Sherman's troops faced little opposition during the campaign. The only battle, if it can even be called that, was at Griswoldville on 22 November. Several hundred

Sherman's March to the Sea (*Bettmann/Corbis*)

members of the Georgia militia assaulted elements of Sherman's XV Corps. After 523 Georgians had been

killed or wounded in action, the remaining militia retreated. After this brief engagement, Sherman's

Sherman's troops removing ammunition from Fort McAllister near Savannnah, Georgia, December 1864 (*Library of Congress*)

seasoned veterans wrecked more than 200 miles of Confederate railroad track and deprived the starving Confederate soldiers in Virginia of much-needed rations. By 24 November, Sherman's two columns had converged and sacked the state capital at Milledgeville. Union troops then occupied Sandersville on 26 November, Louisville on 29 November, and Millen on 3 December. Sherman bypassed Augusta, despite the fact that important arms production facilities remained there.

On 9 December 1864, Sherman's forces took up positions outside Savannah and readied their attack against the heavily fortified city with its 10,000-man garrison. Rather than fight a losing battle, Confederate commander William J. Hardee evacuated his troops to South Carolina on the night of 20 December 1864. The next day, Sherman occupied Savannah and effectively isolated the upper South from the lower South. He offered the city to President Abraham Lincoln as a present that Christmas.

In 1865, Sherman took his troops on another destructive raid northward into the Carolinas.

Ultimately, the damage to Confederate logistics affected Southerners' morale because Sherman's March to the Sea showed the region's vulnerability. Consequently, Southerners could not help but realize that the North was going to grind them into dust. Little hope was left.

Herein lies a key to understanding whether William Tecumseh Sherman and his March to the Sea were examples of total and modern warfare. Two intertwined observations can be made. First, Sherman, along with Grant and others, clearly grasped the relationship that linked strategy, logistics, and morale. They attempted to hurt both the Confederacy's psychological will and its material capability to fight. To accomplish these goals, Union strategy called for mobilization of the North's populace, industry, and natural resources as well as for an assault on the Confederacy's populace, industry, and natural resources. Such an understanding indicates an increasingly modern view of warfare. Likewise, Sherman clearly comprehended that the Civil War was fought by opposing militaries as well as the opposing societies. Morale, patriotism, and loyalty both on the front and at home remained crucial to military success. Civilian property, if not the civilians themselves, became viable targets for attack. War between whole societies is also a hallmark of modern and total war.

These two observations notwithstanding, the Civil War remained relatively limited because the North did not wage unrestricted war against the Southern people themselves. Despite rhetoric and legend portraying Sherman's March to the Sea as brutal and vicious, the campaign concentrated on destroying property. Thus, Sherman's raid may be best categorized as part of a transitional stage anticipating total and modern war in the twentieth century.

—*David J. Ulbrich*

See also Atlanta Campaign; Carolinas Campaign; Griswoldville, Georgia, Battle of; Honey Hill, South Carolina, Battle of; Sandersville, Battle of; Savannah, Siege of; Sherman, William Tecumseh.

For further reading:
Glatthaar, Joseph T. *The March to the Sea and Beyond: Sherman's Troops in the Savannah and Carolinas Campaigns* (1985).
Grimsley, Mark. *The Hard Hand of War: Union Military Policy Toward Southern Civilians, 1861–1865* (1995).
———. "Modern War/Total War." In *The American Civil War: A Handbook of Literature and Research* (1996).
Marszalek, John F. *Sherman, A Soldier's Passion for Order* (1994).
Neely, Mark E, Jr. "Was the Civil War a Total War?" *Civil War History* (1991).
Royster, Charles. *The Destructive War: William Tecumseh Sherman, Stonewall Jackson, and the Americans* (1991).
Sherman, William T. *Memoirs of William T. Sherman* (1990).
Williams, T. Harry. *McClellan, Sherman, and Grant* (1962).

SHERWOOD, ISAAC RUTH
(1835–1925)
Union general, editor, and politician

Isaac Ruth Sherwood was born in Stanford, Dutchess County, New York, on 13 August 1835, the son of Aaron and Maria Youmans Sherwood. The family was descended from an early Puritan settler in Connecticut and included several Revolutionary War veterans in the lineage. At Aaron's death, when Isaac was only nine, Isaac's uncle, Daniel Sherwood, a leading Democrat and member of the New York State legislature became the younger Sherwood's guardian and mentor. In 1852 Isaac began studying, first at Hudson River Institute in Claverack, New York, and then in 1854 at Antioch College in Yellow Springs, Ohio, while Horace Mann was president there. Sherwood read law with a judge in New York and studied at the Ohio Law College in Poland, Ohio. There he married Katherine Brownlee, the daughter of a local judge; the couple had three children. In 1857 the Sherwoods removed to Bryan, Ohio, to edit and publish *The Williams County Gazette*, a radical newspaper that inspired controversy in 1859 when it sanctified John Brown as a martyr for the cause. Sherwood was also elected probate judge of Williams County as a Republican in 1860.

After Lincoln's call to arms in April 1861 Sherwood enlisted as a private in the 14th Ohio Infantry Regiment under Colonel James Blair Steedman of Toledo. Sherwood fought in the summer of 1861 to secure western Virginia for the Union in battles at Philippi, Laurel Hill, and Carrick's Ford. He reenlisted in 1862 and served first as adjutant, then major in 1863, of the 111th Ohio. Over the next two years he commanded the regiment in thirty-one engagements until mustered out in 1865.

The 111th saw action in Kentucky chasing the Confederate cavalry raider John Hunt Morgan. In 1863 the regiment took part in Ambrose Burnside's campaign to take Knoxville and later the defense of the city against James Longstreet's assault with engagements at Loudon Creek, Campbell's Station, and Fort Sanders.

Sherwood, by now promoted to colonel, spent most of 1864 in Georgia with the 111th. They took part in more than a dozen engagements between May and September, including major fights at Resaca, Rocky Face Mountain, Dallas, Kennesaw Mountain, Peachtree Creek, Atlanta, and Lovejoy.

In November 1864 Sherwood and the 111th rushed to Tennessee to take part in the campaign against John Bell Hood. They guarded Schofield's retreat from Columbia and Spring Hill to Franklin and played a critical role in defending the Union position from repeated Confederate assaults at the battle of Franklin. After the battles of Franklin and Nashville, for his conspicuous

bravery and leadership Sherwood was appointed brevet brigadier general and then commanded troops in the final engagements of the war in North Carolina in 1865.

Sherwood returned to journalism after the war. He settled in Toledo, where he edited *The Commercial*, and was elected secretary of state for Ohio in 1868 and reelected two years later. He served in Congress as a Republican between 1873 and 1875, but his soft-money views cost him his party's nomination in 1874. In 1878 he was elected probate judge of Lucas County as a candidate of the Greenback-Labor, or National, Party and reelected as a Democrat. He edited the Canton *News-Democrat* in the 1890s, returned to Toledo, and was elected again to Congress in 1906.

As chair of the committee on invalid pensions, Sherwood became nationally known as the author of the "dollar-a-day" pension for Civil War veterans in 1912. When the First World War broke out in 1914, Sherwood turned into a critic of preparedness and any measures that would draw the United States into the war. He was the only Ohio congressman to vote against the declaration of war against Germany in April 1917. His constituents returned him to office in 1918. He lost his seat in the Republican landslide of 1920, but was reelected in 1922. Sherwood was the last Civil War veteran to serve in Congress. He was defeated in 1924. Exactly fifty years elapsed between the end of his first and the end of his last term in Congress. Always something of a radical in his political stances, he was nevertheless enormously popular with the voters. He died of pneumonia in 1925 in his ninetieth year.

—*Gregory R. Zieren*

See also Franklin, Battle of; Nashville, Battle of.
For further reading:
McCormick, Virginia E. "The Talented Sherwoods: Poets and Politicians." *Northwest Ohio Quarterly* (1980).
Sherwood, Isaac Ruth. *Memories of the War* (1923).
Waggoner, Clark. *History of the City of Toledo and Lucas County Ohio* (1888).
Weisenburger, Francis P. "General Isaac R. Sherwood." *Historical Society of Northwest Ohio* (1942).

SHIELDS, JAMES
(1806–1879)
Union general

Born to Charles Shields and Katherine McDonnell Shields in County Tyrone, Ireland, James Shields was educated locally before embarking for Canada from Liverpool at sixteen years of age. He was shipwrecked on the coast of Scotland and spent several years there working as a tutor to earn his passage to North America. He arrived in New York City in 1826. He made his way to Illinois, where he settled in Kaskaskia. There he made his living as a teacher while he studied law. He also became increasingly involved in Illinois Democratic

politics and in 1836 was elected to the state legislature. Sometimes criticized for his policies by rival Whigs, he almost became involved in a duel with young Abraham Lincoln when Lincoln's fiancée, Mary Todd, wrote a letter to a newspaper attacking Shields. The duel never took place and was always shrouded in some mystery. Lincoln refused to discuss it even years later.

In 1843, Shields became a justice of the Illinois Supreme Court, a position he held until 1845 when President James K. Polk sent him as land commissioner to Washington. Never happy doing one thing too long, Shields was rescued from the tedium of the territorial land office by the outbreak of the Mexican-American War. Made a brigadier general of Illinois volunteers, Shields fought in Winfield Scott's Mexico City campaign. He was wounded once in the campaign and was commended by Scott for bravery. Upon being mustered out of the army, he returned to Illinois briefly but left soon afterward when appointed by Polk as governor of Oregon Territory. When elected to the U.S. Senate from Illinois shortly thereafter, Shields returned east to take his seat. The Senate held a majority of Whigs at the time, and they voted to deny Shields his seat because he was just short of the requisite years of citizenship to hold a Senate seat. He returned to Illinois only to be reelected, this time having met the necessary qualifications. After being defeated for reelection, Shields moved to Minnesota, and after the territory became a state, he was elected as one of its senators. Failing reelection, he moved to California and then to Mexico to take a job in the mining industry there. Shields was in Mexico when the Civil War started.

He immediately returned to the United States, where he offered his services to his old friend Abraham Lincoln. In August 1861 Shields was made a brigadier general of volunteers and ordered to report to John C. Frémont in the Western Department. In the spring of 1862, Shields commanded a division of Nathaniel P. Banks's V Corps in the Shenandoah Valley.

Shields's greatest glory during the Civil War came on 23 March 1862, when his superior force was attacked by a far inferior army commanded by Stonewall Jackson at Kernstown, Virginia. Shields was able to repulse the attack but failed to capitalize on the victory, partly because he had been wounded in the battle. That Jackson had attacked at all convinced Shields that the Confederate numbers were much larger than they were. Nevertheless, Shields was lauded in the Northern press and received a personal expression of gratitude from Secretary of War Edwin Stanton.

From that point things went downhill for Shields in the war. After being shifted to command of a division under Irvin McDowell in the Department of the Rappahannock, he was sent back to the Shenandoah Valley on 25 May 1862. He drove the Confederate

James Shields (*Library of Congress*)

garrison out of Port Republic on 30 May but could do little to catch up to Jackson or to join with other Federal armies in the valley because of Jackson's destruction of key bridges. By the time he was able to converge with Frémont between Cross Keys and Port Republic, Jackson was in a position to defeat them in detail. Striking first against Frémont on 8 June at Cross Keys, Jackson then turned on Shields outside Port Republic on 9 June. Both Union armies suffered defeat and were withdrawn from the valley.

Shields held no other command position for the duration of the war and had by the end of 1862 determined to resign his commission. In early 1863 a strange series of events occurred that were perhaps designed by President Lincoln to allow Shields to save face. Since Shields intended to return to California after his resignation, he was ordered to report to Brigadier General George Wright in command of the Department of the Pacific, headquartered in San Francisco. Shields did as ordered, reporting to Wright on 20 March. In the meantime, Wright had received a telegram from Secretary of War Edwin Stanton, instructing him not to assign Shields to any duties when he arrived. A week after reporting, Shields resigned his commission.

For the remainder of the war, Shields served as a state railroad commissioner in California. After the war, he moved to Missouri, where he became involved in state politics. He served in the state legislature and in 1879 was selected to fill an unexpired U.S. Senate term. In doing so he became the only man to have served in the Senate representing three different states. He died shortly after leaving the Senate, while on a speaking engagement in Ottumwa, Iowa. He was returned to Missouri for burial.

—*David S. Heidler and Jeanne T. Heidler*

See also Irish-Americans; Kernstown, First Battle of; Port Republic, Battle of; Shenandoah Valley Campaign (1862).
For further reading:
Tanner, Robert G. *Stonewall in the Valley: Thomas J. "Stonewall" Jackson's Shenandoah Valley Campaign, Spring 1862* (1976; reprint, 1996).

SHILOH, BATTLE OF
(6–7 April 1862)

Fought in the early spring of 1862 on the west bank of the Tennessee River just north of the Mississippi state line, the battle of Shiloh was, up to that time, the biggest battle of American history. For two days in April, Confederates and Federals—100,000 soldiers in all—waged a desperate struggle through the fields, forests, orchards, ravines, creeks, and swampy areas near a steamboat docking point called Pittsburg Landing. Major Civil War commanders such as Ulysses S. Grant, William T. Sherman, Don Carlos Buell, A. S. Johnston, P. G. T. Beauregard, Braxton Bragg, and Nathan Bedford Forrest participated.

The engagement played a significant role in the campaign for control of the Mississippi Valley. It also presented a terrible preview of all the other major battles of the war that were yet to come. For the first time in the conflict, men on both sides came to envision something of the true cost in suffering and death that victory would ultimately entail. People like General Grant, who had thought that perhaps one great battle would bring the war to a conclusion, would sense, after Shiloh, that such was not to be; that the war must go on, draining the nation of men, money, and resources, until either the Confederacy was finally smashed or the Union was divided.

The events that led up to Shiloh commenced in the winter of 1862. In early February, a Federal army-navy offensive, under command of Grant and Andrew H. Foote, penetrated the Confederate defensive perimeter across southern Kentucky. Driving south up the Tennessee and Cumberland rivers, they captured the supposed strongpoints protecting those vital waterways, respectively Fort Henry and Fort Donelson, located near the Tennessee-Kentucky border. The very heart of Tennessee was thereby laid open to the Union forces.

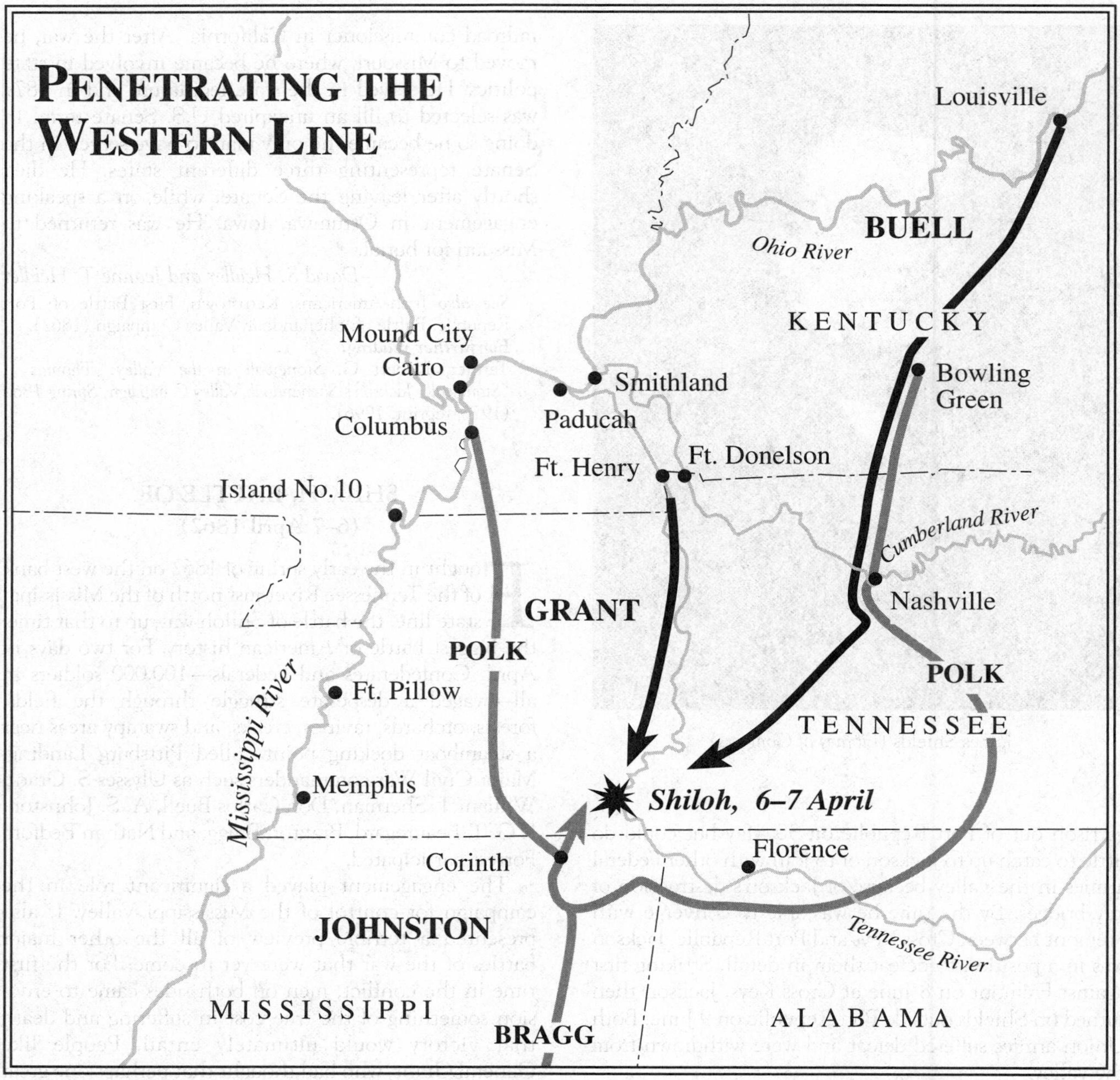

PENETRATING THE WESTERN LINE

BUELL

Ohio River

Louisville

KENTUCKY

Mound City

Cairo

Smithland

Bowling
Green

Columbus

Paducah

Island No.10

Ft. Henry

Ft. Donelson

Cumberland River

GRANT

POLK

Nashville

POLK

Ft. Pillow

Mississippi River

T E N N E S S E E

Memphis

Shiloh, 6–7 April

Florence

Corinth

JOHNSTON

Tennessee River

MISSISSIPPI

ALABAMA

BRAGG

The fall of the two forts began a series of Federal victories that left the Confederacy struggling to stave off disaster.

The Confederate defensive line across southern Kentucky, centered at Bowling Green, collapsed at once and the grayclads retreated from northern Tennessee to Alabama and Mississippi. A Union army under Don Carlos Buell advanced, virtually unopposed, into the capital of Tennessee, a major arsenal, transportation center, and supply depot. Suddenly Nashville found itself the first Confederate state capital to fall to the blueclads.

The fall of Fort Henry opened the Tennessee River as an avenue of Union advance to the Alabama and

Mississippi state lines. It enabled the Federals to immediately break one east-west railroad, the Memphis, Clarksville & Louisville, which crossed the Tennessee only seventeen miles south of Fort Henry. Three gunboats did the work of destroying the bridge. The gunboats then continued (south) up the Tennessee, knocking out other bridges and cutting telegraph lines, all the way to Muscle Shoals, Alabama. Union forces under Major General Grant advanced south past Savannah, which Grant selected for his headquarters, to Pittsburg Landing, a site chosen by Sherman for the army's encampments. There, only twenty miles northeast of Corinth, Mississippi, the Union force was

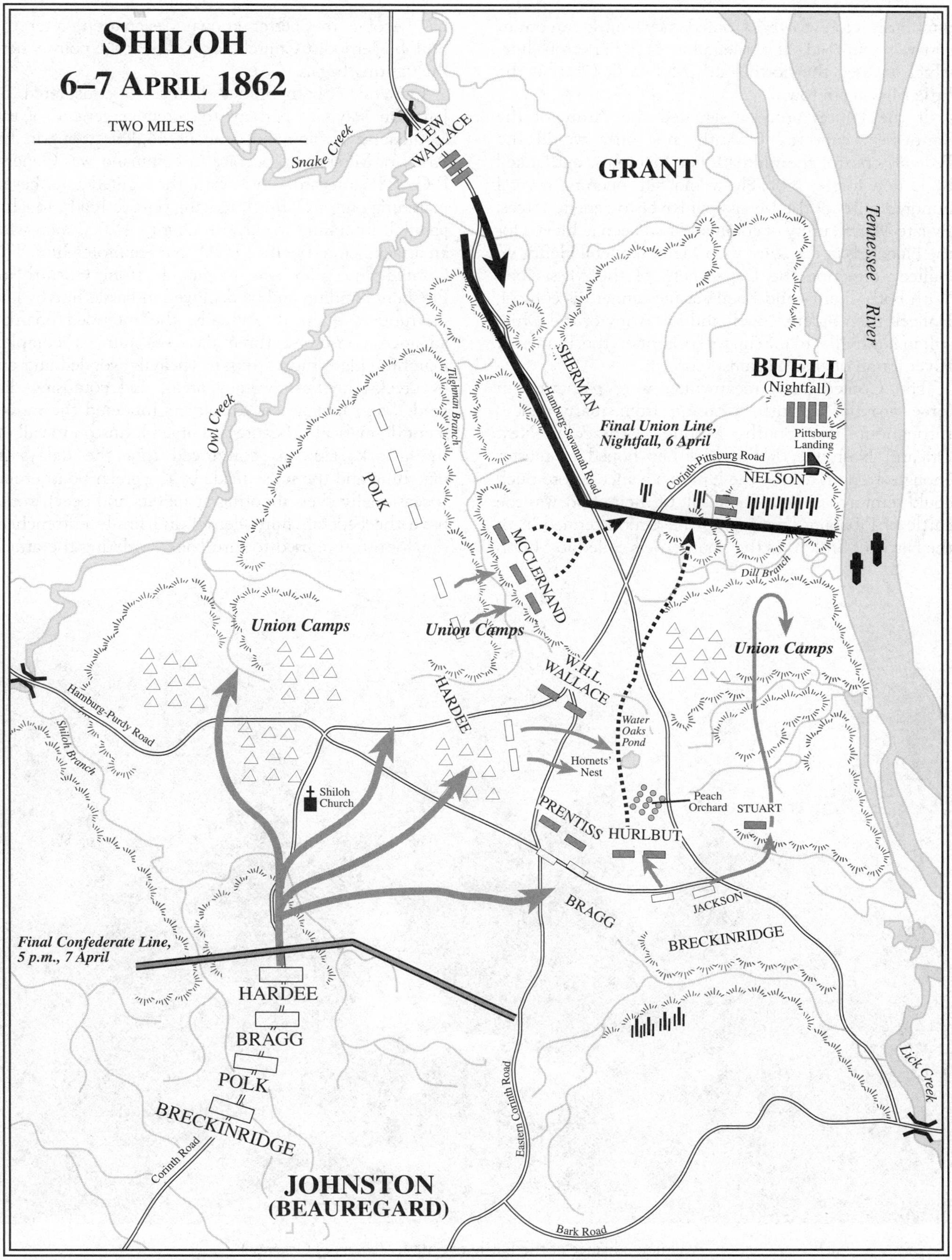

SHILOH
6–7 APRIL 1862

TWO MILES

Snake Creek

LEW WALLACE

GRANT

Tennessee River

SHERMAN

Hamburg-Savannah Road

BUELL
(Nightfall)

Pittsburg Landing

Owl Creek

POLK

Tighman Branch

Final Union Line, Nightfall, 6 April

Corinth-Pittsburg Road

NELSON

MCCLERNAND

Dill Branch

Union Camps

Union Camps

W.H.L. WALLACE

Union Camps

HARDEE

Water Oaks Pond

Hornets' Nest

Hamburg-Purdy Road

Shiloh Branch

✝ Shiloh Church

Peach Orchard

STUART

PRENTISS HURLBUT

JACKSON

BRAGG

BRECKINRIDGE

Final Confederate Line, 5 p.m., 7 April

HARDEE

BRAGG

POLK

BRECKINRIDGE

Corinth Road

Eastern Corinth Road

Lick Creek

**JOHNSTON
(BEAUREGARD)**

Bark Road

ominously close to the Confederacy's most important east-west railroad, the Memphis & Charleston line, which crossed the north-south Mobile & Ohio at the little Mississippi town.

If the Union army, designated the Army of the Tennessee, captured Corinth, not only would the Federals control the railroad, but Memphis, outflanked by Union forces, probably would fall, opening several hundred miles of the Mississippi River to Federal forces. By late March, unity of command had been achieved for the blueclads in the West with Major General Henry W. Halleck directing the Department of the Mississippi. With both Grant's and Buell's armies under his control, Halleck then ordered Buell and his Army of the Ohio, still in Nashville, to join up with Grant on the Tennessee River for an offensive against Corinth.

The Confederates, meanwhile, were gathering in force around Corinth. Coming from many places throughout the South—Mobile, Pensacola, New Orleans, Nashville, Memphis—they hoped to muster enough strength to stop the Union advance before Buell could reinforce Grant. The result of their effort was the battle of Pittsburg Landing, as the Union termed it, or the battle of Shiloh, as the Southerners called it. Shiloh

has become the better known designation, after the Shiloh Methodist Church, located near the point where the fighting began.

General Albert Sidney Johnston, considered by Jefferson Davis as perhaps the premier general of the Confederacy, commanded about 44,000 troops in his Army of Mississippi. Second in command was General P. G. T. Beauregard. On 3 April, the Confederates began marching out of Corinth, moving on two roads, roughly parallel, intending to surprise Grant's 42,000 men with an attack before Buell's 25,000 could reinforce him. The Confederate plan was to march from Corinth to Pittsburg Landing and be deployed in battle line by late morning of 4 April. Actually, the intended one-day advance consumed three days, as rain, a complex marching plan, rugged terrain (heavily wooded and cut by creeks, ravines, swampy areas, and confusing dirt roads), and inexperienced soldiers hindered the movement dramatically. Beauregard urged Johnston to call off the attack. He was convinced that the delays in marching and the noise made by the green Southerners (occasionally even shooting at rabbits and deer) would have the Federals fully alerted and firmly entrenched. But Johnston refused to turn back. Ordering the attack

A Union advance at the Battle of Shiloh (*Library of Congress*)

for the early morning of Sunday, 6 April, the general is said to have dramatically announced something to the effect that on the following evening the army would water its horses in the Tennessee River.

Striking at dawn, the Confederate army achieved a complete strategic surprise. The first fighting occurred as the grayclad skirmishers engaged Federal patrols about three-fourths of a mile south of the Shiloh Church. Fighting a delaying action, the Union troops were compelled to fall back as the Rebel main body came on behind their skirmishers. But many Union soldiers, despite the heavy skirmishing occurring only a short distance away, remained unaware that the Rebels were upon them. Suddenly, screaming Confederates emerged from the woods to the south, and in some sectors, streamed directly into the Union camps.

At first, a Confederate triumph seemed highly probable. The Yankee encampments lacked tactical formation, and inexperienced troops held the advance positions, the first to be struck by the Southern onslaught. Neither Grant, at his headquarters nine miles away, nor Sherman, the camp commander, had expected an attack. Grant had recently told the commander of Buell's advance division that there would be no fight at Pittsburg Landing; he said the Federals would have to go to Corinth, where the Rebels were fortifying. Sherman, on 5 April, had written Grant, expressing his confidence that no attack would be made on the Union position at the landing. Confidence and offense had been the orders of the day for the two key men in the Union army. Thus the Confederates, in spite of their time-consuming and noise-making approach, enjoyed the elements of surprise and momentum as well as a slight numerical advantage. Union miscues added to the Southern advantage, as the Union division of Major General Lew Wallace never got into the battle on 6 April and some 5,000 Union soldiers (perhaps more) fled from the fight in panic.

But the Confederate attack, unfortunately for the Southerners, did not develop as General Johnston had originally planned. Apparently there was confusion (or disagreement) in the high command over whether to drive the Federals back to Pittsburg Landing or away from it. Compounding the confusion was an attack formation in which their corps advanced with one in front of another rather than side by side. Command control was sacrificed as regiments, brigades, and divisions became badly intermingled. All of this slowed the initial momentum that had given the Southerners an advantage at the beginning of the fight. Also, early in the afternoon, General Johnston suffered a leg wound and, in a short time, bled to death. General Sherman thought that a lull in the fighting followed the death of the Confederate commander, further sapping the energy of the Rebel attack. Possibly more important than any other factor, the "Hornets' Nest," as it was called by the

Southerners, was a natural defensive position along a slightly eroded wagon trace that became a rallying point for Union troops, first those of General Benjamin Prentiss's division, as they fell back toward the landing. Soon troops from several divisions joined Prentiss's men in defending the position against repeated Confederate attacks.

Time and again the Confederates attempted to storm this Union strongpoint. They came across the open fields and they came through the timber. Federal major D. W. Reed, who fought in the Hornets' Nest and was a careful student of the battle, said as many as twelve separate charges were made against the line. It was not until about 5:30 in the afternoon that the grayclads succeeded, finally, in reducing the Union position.

The fight at the Hornets' Nest cost the Southerners too much time and too many men—it was while attempting to reduce the Hornets' Nest that Johnston was killed—and drew their attention away from an opportunity earlier in the day, to break through the weak Federal left nearer the river. The Rebel focus on the Hornets' Nest gave Grant, who hurried from Savannah at the sound of battle, a sorely needed opportunity to establish a last line of defense at Pittsburg Landing.

Beauregard took command after Johnston's death and continued the assault until the Rebels, shortly before dark, held the entire battlefield except for the Yankee line covering the landing. Beauregard chose not to make an attack on the Federals at the landing, a decision that has been second-guessed by many. Probably the exhausted and disorganized Southerners, some of whom were out of ammunition, could not have overcome the Union line. That line, shortened and compacted, and supported by artillery, was also being reinforced by the first arrivals of Buell's army. But Beauregard needed either to attack or withdraw because, during the night, Buell came up on the Federal left with thousands of reinforcements and Lew Wallace arrived with his division from Crump's Landing to take a position on the right side of the Union line. Thus the Federals could count an additional 25,000 men on 7 April. Although Beauregard did not know about these fresh enemy troops (indeed, he had false information that Buell was headed elsewhere), there is no evidence that he made any attempt to learn anything about the Federal situation. Like many Confederates, he apparently thought the Yankees were whipped.

Grant struck at dawn and drove the grayclads back across the battlefield and forced them to retreat to Corinth. Battle casualties approached 24,000; each side counted more than 1,700 dead and 8,000 wounded, with those missing accounting for the remainder. The killed and wounded at Bull Run, Wilson's Creek, Fort Donelson, and Elkhorn Tavern, all put together, did not equal the killed and wounded at Shiloh, clearly making it

the bloodiest battle of the war to that time. Moreover, the Union army had turned back a major Southern counteroffensive, maintaining its position on the flank of the line of the Mississippi River, and within a few miles of the strategic Memphis & Charleston Railroad that was soon to be in Federal hands. The battle opened the way to split the Confederacy along the Mississippi, which, in the long run, spelled defeat for the Confederacy.

—James L. McDonough

See also Beauregard, Pierre Gustave Toutant; Buell, Don Carlos; Foote, Andrew Hull; Fort Donelson, Battle of; Fort Henry, Battle of; Grant, Ulysses Simpson; Johnston, Albert Sidney; Prentiss, Benjamin Mayberry; Wallace, Lewis.

For further reading:
Daniel, Larry J. *Shiloh: The Battle That Changed the Civil War* (1997).
McDonough, James L. *Shiloh—In Hell before Night* (1997).
Sword, Wiley. *Shiloh: Bloody April* (1974).

SHORTER, JOHN GILL
(1818–1872)
Governor of Alabama

Born to Reuben Clarke Shorter and Bary Butler Gill Shorter in Monticello, Georgia, John Gill Shorter was educated locally and at what would become the University of Georgia (Franklin College). Upon graduation from college, Shorter moved to Eufaula, Alabama. He studied law there and began to practice. Shorter made his home in Eufaula for the remainder of his life.

Shortly after starting his law practice, Shorter became active in Alabama Democratic politics. He became a district solicitor in 1842 and then in 1845 won election to the state senate. He did not run for a second term. In 1851 he was elected to the lower house, but left that office to accept a position as a state circuit judge.

In the years immediately preceding the Civil War, Shorter increasingly believed in the cause of Southern secession. After Abraham Lincoln's election to the presidency, Governor Andrew Moore appointed Shorter as a commissioner to Georgia to encourage that state's secession convention to withdraw Georgia from the Union. Upon his return he was chosen as an Alabama representative to the Provisional Confederate Congress, where he served on several committees, including the one that designed the executive branch for the Confederate Constitution. With the formation of the Confederate government, Shorter became a strong supporter of executive power, defending President Jefferson Davis against all criticism. His extreme nationalism is at least partly credited for his election as the governor of Alabama in August 1861.

During Shorter's two-year term as governor he continued his staunch defense of the Davis administration and stoutly supported the strong measures it employed for Confederate military preparedness. It was in fact his support for conscription and impressment of war supplies that eroded his popularity in Alabama. He nevertheless took whatever measures he thought necessary to defend the state, especially the coastal area around Mobile.

The sacrifices burdening the average Alabamian began to tell by 1863, and when Shorter stood for reelection in that year he lost by a three-to-one margin. Embittered by the treatment he received from the voters, Shorter returned to Eufaula and took no further part in the war.

After the war, Shorter continued to practice law and refused to reenter politics even when asked by former supporters to do so. He died at his home in Eufaula.

—David S. Heidler and Jeanne T. Heidler

See also Alabama.
For further reading:
Fleming, Walter Lynwood. *Civil War and Reconstruction in Alabama* (1905).

SHOUP, FRANCIS ASBURY
(1834–1896)
Confederate general

Born to George Grove Shoup and Jane Conwell Shoup in Laurel, Indiana, Francis Shoup was educated locally and at what would become DePauw University (Asbury University) before accepting an appointment to the U.S. Military Academy. He graduated fifteenth of thirty-four in the class of 1855. Upon graduation he was commissioned into the artillery and sent to Florida, where he fought in the Third Seminole War. Later he was sent to Fort Moultrie in Charleston, South Carolina. He resigned his commission in 1860. He studied law and practiced briefly in Indiana before moving to St. Augustine, Florida, to open a practice there. Upon the secession of Florida in early 1861, he offered his military services to the state.

Under instructions from the governor of Florida, Shoup helped erect defenses for Fernandina before accepting a commission in March 1861 as a first lieutenant of artillery in the Confederate army. He was sent to Mobile, Alabama.

In October 1861, Shoup was promoted to major and was sent to Kentucky, where he became chief of artillery in the Central Army of Kentucky. He served under William Hardee and had become that officer's chief of artillery by the battle of Shiloh. His handling of his batteries in that engagement won the praise of his superiors. Rapidly promoted over the next few months, he served first as P. G. T. Beauregard's inspector of artillery and chief of artillery under Thomas Hindman. Hindman commended him for his command of the artillery on 7 December 1862 at Prairie Grove, Arkansas.

Shoup had been promoted to brigadier general in September 1862, and after Prairie Grove he was sent to Mobile, Alabama, where he served again as chief of artillery. In the late spring of 1863 he was transferred to Vicksburg, Mississippi, where he commanded an infantry brigade. He was captured in the surrender of Vicksburg on 4 July 1863 but was paroled shortly thereafter.

In the fall of 1863, Shoup became Joseph E. Johnston's chief of artillery and in that capacity commanded all artillery of the Army of Tennessee in the Atlanta campaign of the spring and summer of 1864. He was commended not only for the effective use of his guns, especially at the Chattahoochee River crossings, but also for the amazing feat of not losing any of his pieces in the retreat toward Atlanta. Shoup also designed a series of fortifications on the Chattahoochee River line that not only impressed Union general William T. Sherman but also might have provided an opportunity to maul the Union advance had Johnston exploited them. Upon the replacement of Johnston by John Bell Hood in July 1864, Shoup became Hood's chief of staff, remaining in that position through the Tennessee campaign of the fall and winter of 1864. During that time, Shoup wrote a detailed pamphlet for the Confederate Congress's consideration pointing out the advantages of enlisting African-American troops into the Confederate army.

Upon Hood's removal as commander of the Army of Tennessee, Shoup apparently left the army and moved to Mississippi. After the war, he taught at the University of Mississippi and became an Episcopal priest. For the remainder of his life he taught at a variety of universities, primarily in the South, and served the local parishes of university towns. He ended his career as a professor of engineering at the University of the South in Sewanee, Tennessee, where he died.

—*David S. Heidler and Jeanne T. Heidler*

See also Atlanta Campaign; Prairie Grove, Battle of; Shiloh, Battle of.

For further reading:
Shoup, Francis Asbury. *Policy of Employing Negro Troops* (1865).

SIBLEY, HENRY HASTINGS
(1811–1891)
U.S. general

Henry Hastings Sibley, a long-time fur trader and first governor of Minnesota, had no military experience prior to his commissioning as a colonel of the 6th Minnesota Regiment at the advent of the Dakota uprising in August 1862. Yet the untrained officer played a conspicuous role in his state's effort to subdue the Indians and punish those whom the government deemed responsible for the conflict.

Sibley was no stranger to warfare. Born on 20 January 1811 in Detroit, Michigan, Sibley and his mother were inside Fort Detroit when the garrison was besieged by the British at the beginning of the War of 1812. The two were captured when the fort fell on 16 August 1812 but were later released. Sibley's father, a well-known Detroit lawyer, was away serving in the army at the time. Shunning his father's desire for his son to pursue a career in law, Sibley chose the outdoors instead, acquiring a job in John Jacob Astor's American Fur Company in 1834. Sibley soon rose to the position of partner within the company and was placed in charge of all operations in what are now the states of Minnesota and Wisconsin. He settled in Mendota, Minnesota, married Sarah Jane Steele in 1843, and fathered nine children.

Sibley's rise to prominence was replete with all the trappings of aristocracy—an impressive house, ornate furnishings, and servants. His status in society helped win him a seat in the United States Congress as a Democrat in 1848. While in Congress Sibley campaigned for the establishment of Minnesota as a territory, a goal that was accomplished in 1849. Returning home to go into state politics in 1853, Sibley advocated statehood for Minnesota, which became a reality in 1858. Sibley helped draft Minnesota's constitution and served as its first governor from 1858 to 1860.

When violence erupted along the Minnesota River on 18 August 1862, Governor Alexander Ramsey called upon his political rival to lead a military relief column out of Fort Snelling to smash the warring Dakotas. The appointment came with a colonel's commission, the first military rank Sibley had ever acquired. Ramsey believed that Sibley's experience as a fur trader, his knowledge of Dakota customs and language, and his friendship with many Dakota leaders, including Taoyateduta (Little Crow), a prominent chief of the Mdewakantonwan band, made him the logical choice for the task.

Arriving at Fort Snelling on 19 August, Sibley quickly assembled the 400 inexperienced and ill-equipped men comprising four companies of the recently organized 6th Minnesota and began moving toward the unstockaded Fort Ridgely and the scene of the uprising. The column moved slowly owing to quartermaster problems and Sibley's uneasiness about his untrained men, taking five days to reach the beleaguered post. The expedition was joined en route by six more companies of the regiment, as well as civilian volunteers (some mounted), bringing his total strength to 1,400 men. On 27 August the vanguard of Sibley's force reached Fort Ridgely, the main body arriving the following day.

Sibley's first task was to reconnoiter the area between the fort and the Lower Agency, some sixteen miles up the Minnesota River valley. His intent was also to bury the victims of the uprising, including twenty soldiers

from the fort's garrison who had been ambushed at Redwood Ferry. Accordingly, Sibley assigned an armed burial party of 163 men under Major Joseph R. Brown and Captain Hiram P. Grant to the task. After two days of the grim work, the party went into bivouac at Birch Coulee across the river from the Lower Agency. On 2 September, 200 Dakota warriors attacked the sleeping encampment, killing and wounding half of Brown and Grant's command in an hour.

The sounds of the engagement broke the early morning quiet at Camp Ridgely. Sibley sent 240 men under Colonel Samuel McPhail to aid the besieged burial party. McPhail, however, was stopped short of his rendezvous with Brown and Grant by Dakota warriors. By midmorning Sibley organized the remainder of his command at Fort Ridgely and headed toward his two imperiled detachments. By the time he arrived, the Indians were withdrawing, and the reunited force returned to Fort Ridgely, having lost twenty-four killed and sixty-seven wounded.

Convinced that his troops needed time to be trained, resupplied, and reinforced, Sibley remained at Fort Ridgely for two weeks, amidst loud objections from panicked civilians and critical newspaper editors. Sibley was also concerned that a rapid move might jeopardize the safety of the many white captives within the Dakota camps. When word arrived of growing factions among the Dakota bands over the wisdom of continuing the hostilities, Sibley took the opportunity to advance with his reconstituted force of 1,619 men up the river valley to just below the Upper Agency. There Sibley encamped near Wood Lake, a dozen miles from the Dakota camps. On 23 September some 300 warriors led by Taoyateduta ambushed elements of Sibley's command. The battle lasted for two hours before the Dakota finally withdrew. Sibley, having lost seven killed and thirty-four wounded, chose not to pursue—a move for which he was once again sharply criticized. Taoyateduta now realized the inevitability of failure, at least for the time being, and took his 200 followers west to Devil's Lake in present-day North Dakota.

With the departure of the hostile faction of the warring Dakota, Sibley was able to come to terms with the bands that sought peace. With the intent of caring for released white captives and corralling some 2,000 surrendering Dakota, Sibley established Camp Release northwest of the Upper Agency. There he supervised a five-man commission charged with convicting all the Dakota who took part in the insurrection. After one month of deliberations, Sibley's board had tried 392 Dakota men and condemned 303 to die. Those men who were convicted were transported to Camp Lincoln at Mankato, while the remaining 1,700 men, women, and children were marched to Fort Snelling. President Abraham Lincoln commuted the sentence for all but thirty-eight of the convicted Dakota men. On 26 December 1862 Mankato was the scene of the largest mass execution in United States history as all thirty-eight warriors were hanged simultaneously on a specially built gallows.

Pressure from governors in the states and territories bordering Minnesota to preclude any potential Indian peril for their citizenry led Lincoln to organize the Military Department of the Northwest and name Major General John Pope as its commander. Pope, having lost the battle of Second Bull Run, arrived in St. Paul determined to "utterly exterminate the Sioux." Pope planned a two-pronged offensive through Dakota Territory (present-day North and South Dakota) aimed at driving the remaining hostile Dakota and their allies westward and away from the Minnesota border and at the same time intimidating those bands that were a potential threat to traffic on the upper Missouri River bound for the gold fields of Montana. Sibley was charged with the northern wing of the operation and assigned to march from Camp Pope on the Minnesota River northwest for 600 miles to Devil's Lake, then on to the Missouri River, driving and defeating the Indians before him. The southern wing was to be under Brigadier General Alfred Sully, a West Point graduate and veteran of the battles of Antietam and Fredericksburg. His job was to ascend the Missouri River and cut off and destroy any hostile Indians fleeing southward from Sibley's advance.

After assembling a massive expeditionary force that included 2,200 infantrymen, 800 mounted troops, 1,500 artillerymen, 100 pioneers, and 70 scouts—all supported by 325 wagons carrying supplies and equipment—Sibley left Camp Pope on 16 June 1863, bound for Dakota Territory and determined to give the Dakota "a whipping they would long remember." Moving through unfavorable terrain and dogged by searing daytime temperatures, Sibley reached the vicinity of Devil's Lake on 18 July. Although there were no Indians to be found in the immediate area, Sibley did learn from his scouts that there was a large hunting party to the west. On 24 July Sibley overtook the band of Indians and discovered that it included Wahpetonwan and Sissetonwan under Standing Buffalo, who had refused to follow the lead of Taoyateduta in the Minnesota uprising the previous year. After a botched attempt to talk with the chief, confusion led to panic and the army attacked the camp in the battle of Big Mound. After briefly withstanding the army's onslaught, Standing Buffalo and his followers withdrew to the Missouri River, eventually finding safe haven in Canada.

After resting for a day, Sibley pressed further west in pursuit of another hunting party that included the Sissetonwan chief, Inkpaduta, and his Nakota and Lakota allies. The two groups collided twice, first at the battle of Dead Buffalo Lake on 26 July and then again

two days later at the battle of Stony Lake. In both instances Sibley's force was able to withstand determined Indian attacks (possibly including Tatanka Iyotanka, Sitting Bull) through effective use of artillery. The Indians withdrew across the Missouri River, while being harassed by artillery and small arms fire from elements of Sibley's command. Sibley remained at the river's edge for forty-eight hours, anticipating the arrival of Sully's column, which never came. Deciding against crossing the Missouri and continuing the campaign, Sibley turned his exhausted force around on 1 August and headed back to Minnesota. He had lost only six men during the entire campaign, but never once encountered the hostile Dakota bands from the Minnesota uprising that he had set out to whip.

In 1864, as Pope chose to continue the army's campaign in the Dakota Territory, Sibley requested and received permission to remain in Minnesota. Breveted a major general on 29 November 1865, Sibley soon returned to civilian life, serving as the president of the St. Paul Gas Company, as a member of the University of Minnesota's Board of Regents, and as the founder and president of the Minnesota Historical Society. Henry Hastings Sibley died on 18 February 1891 at his home in St. Paul.

—*Alan C. Downs*

See also Pope, John; Sioux Indians.

For further reading:

Anderson, Gary Clayton. *Through Dakota Eyes: Narrative Accounts of the Minnesota Indian War of 1862* (1988).
Clodfelter, Michael. *The Dakota War: The United States Army Versus the Sioux, 1862–1865* (1998).
Josephy, Alvin M. *The Civil War in the American West* (1991).

SIBLEY, HENRY HOPKINS
(1816–1886)
Confederate general

Born on 25 May 1816 in Louisiana, Henry Sibley graduated thirty-first of forty-five in West Point's class of 1838. Service followed in the Second Seminole War and in Mexico, where he was brevetted major. With the dragoons in the 1850s, Sibley served most notably in operations in "Bleeding Kansas" and on the Mormon expedition. Sibley's chief accomplishment was his invention of the Sibley tent, essentially a large teepee for campaign use on the plains.

In New Mexico at the outbreak of the Civil War, Sibley, motivated equally by Southern pride and hopes for higher rank in Confederate service, resigned his Federal commission in May 1861, accepting a Confederate brigadier general's commission on 17 June 1861. Soon thereafter, Sibley persuaded Jefferson Davis that the New Mexico Territory (now Arizona and New Mexico) could be easily conquered, thus raising hopes of acquiring California's gold fields and seaports. As a few hundred Texans had already occupied southern New Mexico, Sibley's plan seemed feasible, and Davis consented.

At Fort Bliss, Texas, in December 1861, Sibley organized the Army of New Mexico, actually a 3,700-man brigade. Although lacking adequate uniforms and arms, Sibley's army invaded New Mexico in January 1862, planning to live off the land and capture the ample U.S. Army stores in New Mexico.

At Val Verde on 21 February 1862, Sibley attacked 3,800 Federals under Colonel E. R. S. Canby. As the day-long battle raged, Sibley, probably suffering from illness and inebriation, delegated command to Colonel Thomas Green, who finally drove Canby's men into Fort Craig at sunset.

Lacking siege capabilities and supplies, Sibley moved north, seeking the $250,000 worth of Federal supplies in Albuquerque and Santa Fe. Entering Albuquerque on 4 March and Santa Fe on 23 March, the Confederates found the Unionists had destroyed or evacuated nearly everything, leaving Sibley in a worsening logistical nightmare. After Union forces at Glorieta Pass on 26–28 March destroyed his supply train, Sibley had no option but to retreat down the Rio Grande Valley. Shadowed but largely unengaged by Canby, Sibley's 1,700 survivors trudged back to Texas by early May. Their hopes of returning to New Mexico were shattered by the "California Column's" reinforcement of Canby.

Sibley reported to Richmond that his campaign had completely succeeded and that his men were well-fed and equipped. The reality was that his hungry, ill-clothed Texans considered him a drunken fool. Alcohol plagued Sibley throughout the war and thereafter. He had long suffered from a likely renal disorder that caused him severe pain, so Sibley drank for relief, and by forty-five, he was clearly an alcoholic. Consequently, his modest talents progressively eroded. Although accusations about his drinking and military ineptitude reached Richmond, bureaucratic delay and Sibley's friendship with Jefferson Davis resulted in no action.

Sibley and his brigade joined Major General Richard Taylor's forces in Louisiana in early 1863 to oppose the first Federal Red River campaign. At Irish Bend on 13–14 April, Taylor, though outnumbered three to one or more, skillfully led his force out of a potential trap, but Sibley disobeyed Taylor's order to attack the Federal left flank. In the ensuing retreat, Sibley, probably in a fog of pain and alcohol, disobeyed or ignored several other orders, further infuriating the volatile Taylor, who quickly court-martialed Sibley.

The charges against Sibley—disobedience and conduct unbecoming an officer—went before a military court in the late summer of 1863. On 25 September, the court acquitted Sibley of the charges but censured his

conduct. The reasons behind this seemingly paradoxical verdict remain murky because no record of the trial exists. Technically restored to command but unwelcome in Taylor's camp, Sibley spent the remainder of the war "awaiting orders" that never came, his reputation apparently having spread throughout the army.

Sibley spent several years after the war in Brooklyn, New York, with no real prospects. A chance to reestablish his reputation came in 1869, when (on the recommendation of William T. Sherman), Sibley accepted a general's commission in the Egyptian army. Sadly, Sibley failed in this final opportunity at professional redemption, for his constant drinking again caused erratic behavior. Cashiered in 1873, Sibley returned to America, spending his last years in Virginia immersed in poverty and alcohol. He died on 23 August 1886. It has been suggested that if his foray into New Mexico had succeeded, the Confederacy's fortunes might have brightened considerably. Its failure, however, eventually left Sibley in a grave that would not be marked until seventy years after his death.

—*Broeck N. Oder*

See also Army of New Mexico; Canby, Edward Richard Sprigg; Glorieta Pass, Battle of; Green, Thomas; Irish Bend/Bayou Teche; Taylor, Richard; Val Verde, New Mexico, Battle of.

For further reading:

Frazier, Donald S. *Blood and Treasure: Confederate Empire in the Southwest* (1995).

Hall, Martin H. *The Confederate Army of New Mexico* (1978).

———. *Sibley's New Mexico Campaign* (1960).

Parrish, T. Michael. *Richard Taylor: Soldier Prince of Dixie* (1992).

Thompson, Jerry. *Henry Hopkins Sibley: Confederate General of the West* (1987).

SICKLES, DANIEL EDGAR
(1819–1914)
Union general

Daniel Edgar Sickles was born in New York City on 20 October 1819 to Susan Marsh and George Garrett Sickles, a patent lawyer and politician. Sickles elected to study law in the office of Benjamin F. Butler and was admitted to the bar in 1843. Personable and intelligent with a facility for languages that would later serve him well in foreign posts, Sickles also had a reputation as a philander, an embezzler, and one who avoided repaying loans.

A Democrat, Sickles soon began building a successful political career within New York's infamous Tammany Hall machine, where he was a member of the conservative "Hunker" faction opposed to abolitionist efforts. In 1847, he was elected to the New York State assembly, and in 1853 he was appointed secretary to James Buchanan, then minister to England. Sickles formed a close alliance with the future president, and, upon returning home, he was elected to the New York Senate in 1855 and then served in the U.S. House of Representatives from 1857 to 1861.

Sickles's career was marked by personal scandals and outrageous acts. The New York State Assembly censured Sickles for escorting a known prostitute, Fanny White, into its chambers. Sickles also reportedly took her to England with him, leaving his pregnant wife at home, and presented White to Queen Victoria using as her alias the surname of a New York political opponent.

Scandal, with an ironic twist, wrecked Sickles's political ascent shortly before the Civil War. His wife, Theresa, had an affair with Philip Barton Key, son of Francis Scott Key. In 1859, Sickles confronted Key while he was attempting to signal Theresa with a handkerchief and, enraged, shot Key dead. Indicted for murder, Sickles was defended by Edwin Stanton, who argued that Sickles was not guilty by reason of temporary insanity. Sickles became the first defendant in the United States to win acquittal with this defense. The indictment and trial were the talk of Washington, but ultimately had minimal effect on Sickles's standing. Sickles then destroyed his political career when he forgave his wife and took her back into his home. The morality of the day would tolerate Sickles's adultery, but not an act such as this. Ostracized by his social and political contacts, Sickles left office in 1861, but the oncoming war offered him new opportunities.

Sickles had long supported the South's constitutional argument that secession was legal, but he was equally convinced that the South's use of force was illegal. A successful recruiter, Sickles accepted an offer to command his volunteers, the Excelsior Brigade, with the rank of brigadier general. He was forced, however, to relinquish command when, given his political background and scandals, Congress proved reluctant to confirm his commission. Sickles worked diligently among the Washington politicians and reclaimed both his rank and brigade in time to serve with Joseph Hooker's division at Seven Pines and in the Seven Days' battles.

Sickles missed Second Manassas and Antietam, but was promoted to division command in September 1862 and to major general in November. After Fredericksburg, where Sickles and his men were held in reserve, he was promoted to command of the III Corps when Hooker was promoted to command the Army of the Potomac. Sickles proved to be a popular commander. He also employed his personal skills and political contacts to entertain important visitors to Hooker's headquarters, even calling on Lorenzo Delmonico to provide some of the more sumptuous dinners, to the acclaim of guests and other officers. Sickles, Hooker, and Major General Daniel Butterfield, Hooker's chief of staff, became cronies.

Sickles with two Wiard guns at the Arsenal, Washington, D.C., 1862 (Photograph by Mathew Brady Studio / *Library of Congress*)

At Chancellorsville, Sickles's men located and attacked the rear guard of Thomas "Stonewall" Jackson's famous flank march, and the III Corps held the crucial high ground at Hazel Grove until Hooker ordered their retreat. The Confederates then occupied Hazel Grove and massed artillery fire, inflicting heavy casualties on Union troops, especially on the III Corps. This experience would, evidently, influence Sickles's actions on the second day at Gettysburg.

Sickles's III Corps missed the first day's fighting at Gettysburg. Assigned to protect the Union left at Emmitsburg, they arrived at the battlefield that night. On 2 July, Major General George Meade ordered Sickles to form the III Corps on the right of Winfield Scott Hancock's II Corps and extend the Union line southward along Cemetery Ridge onto Little Round Top. The III Corps's line thus included the low-lying portion of Cemetery Ridge that ran between Cemetery

Hill and Little Round Top. This worried Sickles because he could see high ground to his immediate front from which Confederate artillery could shell his position.

Sickles made several unsuccessful appeals to Meade to redeploy the III Corps to the higher ground and sent out Colonel Hiram Berdan's sharpshooters to reconnoiter. When Berdan's men reported a strong enemy presence, Sickles moved the III Corps forward. The new position was weak, a salient that extended along the Emmitsburg Road on the right to the Peach Orchard, where the line turned at a ninety degree angle to extend on the left through woods, the Wheatfield, and into the Devil's Den.

Sickles did not understand that Meade had been constructing a strong defensive position, which the unauthorized forward position of the III Corps severely compromised: Little Round Top was undefended and the

Daniel E. Sickles (*left*) and Samuel P. Heintzelman
(*Library of Congress*)

Union left flank exposed. Meade discovered Sickles's mistake too late, just as James Longstreet's forces attacked, and the III Corps had to fight in place. Meade and Hancock remained in exposed positions using the advantages afforded by Meade's carefully constructed defensive position to maneuver units into action. The III Corps was driven back with heavy losses, but, at the end of the day, the Union held along the line that Meade originally ordered.

Sickles himself was carried from the field, the victim of a rebel cannon ball that nearly tore his right leg from his body. The leg was amputated that evening, and the next morning Sickles began a potentially life-threatening journey to Washington to preempt any charges that Meade might bring. Sickles quickly met with President Abraham Lincoln, asserting that the III Corps's advance from Cemetery Ridge toward the Confederate line prevented Meade from retreating at Gettysburg and forced him to stay and fight. Sickles's assertions apparently helped to undermine Lincoln's confidence in Meade and contributed to Lincoln's dissatisfaction with Meade's supposed failure to destroy the Confederate army as it retreated from Gettysburg.

Meade did not bring charges against Sickles, but used Sickles's wound as justification to remove him from command of his beloved III Corps. Sickles, who continued to level false accusations against Meade in the press, entered into political intrigue with Radical Republicans to remove Meade and reinstate abolitionist Joe Hooker as commander of the Army of the Potomac. Sickles testified against Meade before the Joint Committee on the Conduct of the War, which, while unsuccessful in its efforts to remove Meade, did produce records that have been used extensively, and often uncritically, by historians. Furthermore, Sickles was a central figure in the early years of debate about the battle and merits of individual commanders. For the next half-century Sickles attempted to vindicate his actions and discredit Meade. Sickles's views had a tremendous impact on the historiography of the Gettysburg campaign and damaged Meade's reputation, a legacy that persists to this day.

Sickles did not command troops in battle again. In 1864, Lincoln sent Sickles on a mission to assess the progress of Reconstruction in Union-held areas of the South, and later that year Sickles was vocal among the Democrats supporting Lincoln's reelection. In the last months of the war, Sickles conducted a diplomatic mission for Lincoln and was in South America when the war ended.

After the war, Sickles served as military governor of South Carolina and then of the Carolinas for nearly two years until he was removed in a dispute with President Andrew Johnson. In 1869, President Ulysses S. Grant named Sickles as minister to Spain. Sickles held this post until 1874, again marking his tenure in office with scandal, rumors flying about trysts with Queen Isabella II.

In his waning years, Sickles devoted much energy to preserving the memory of his actions at Gettysburg. He served as chair of the New York State Monuments Commission and won another term as congressman from New York to promote his plans for the Gettysburg battlefield. Sickles successfully pushed a bill through Congress that turned the battlefield over to federal management and began the creation of the park as it exists today. Additionally, he oversaw the placement of many of the early monuments and memorials.

Sickles's impact on the battle of Gettysburg was far greater than that of a corps commander: He altered the course of the second day's battle, shaped the writing of the battle's history, and helped to preserve the battlefield. On 3 May 1914, Sickles died at age ninety-four after a cerebral hemorrhage and was buried in Arlington National Cemetery. His leg, which he had preserved after the amputation, is on display at the Armed Forces Medical Museum in Washington, D.C.

—*W. Robert Beckman*

See also Gettysburg, Battle of.
For further reading:
Coddington, Edwin B. *The Gettysburg Campaign: A Study in Command* (1968).
Pfanz, Harry W. *Gettysburg: The Second Day* (1987).
Sauers, Richard A. *A Caspian Sea of Ink: The Meade-Sickles Controversy* (1989).
Swanberg, W. A. *Sickles the Incredible* (1956).
Tap, Bruce. *Over Lincoln's Shoulder: The Committee on the Conduct of the War* (1998).

SIGEL, FRANZ
(1824–1902)
Union general

Franz Sigel was born in Sinsheim in the Grand Duchy of Baden on 18 November 1824 and was educated at the Classical School at Bruchsal and at the Military Academy at Karlsruhe. He graduated in 1843 and was appointed lieutenant in the 4th Infantry Regiment. During the 1848–1849 insurrections, he was a leader of the revolutionary forces overthrown by the Prussians. He fled first to Switzerland and England, and finally in May 1852 moved to the United States. He settled in New York City, where he worked as a tobacconist, surveyor, teacher, and musician. In 1855, with his father-in-law, Rudolf Dulon, he formed the German-American Institute, where he taught mathematics, history, and languages. He also taught in the public schools and the German Turner Society, belonged to the 5th New York Militia, and wrote for the *New Yorker Staats-Zeitung* and the *New York Times*. In 1857 he moved to St. Louis to teach at the German-American Institute.

When the Civil War broke out, Sigel was instrumental in rallying Germans to join the Union army and was commissioned colonel of the 3d Missouri Infantry. He played a prominent, but undistinguished, part in the battle of Wilson's Creek on 10 August 1861. His bold, but ill-fated, flanking maneuver in this battle, however, became synonymous with Union failure. When Henry W. Halleck, commander of the Missouri Department, replaced him with Samuel R. Curtis in the winter of 1861, Sigel resigned from the army, causing considerable uproar in the German-American community. In early 1862 he returned to the army and partially redeemed himself by playing a prominent role in the Union victory at the battle of Pea Ridge on 7–8 March, for which he was promoted to major general. In May he was transferred to the Eastern theater and took command of a division of Nathaniel P. Banks's troops at Harper's Ferry and fought in the Shenandoah Valley against Thomas J. "Stonewall" Jackson. When the War Department created the Army of Virginia in the summer of 1862, Sigel received his first significant command. He was ordered to take command of the newly designated I Corps of the new army, comprised of troops from John C. Frémont's Mountain Department. He fought in the battle of Second Bull Run and later operated in and around the Shenandoah Valley. In January 1863 the War Department disbanded the Army of Virginia, and Sigel's I Corps was reintegrated into the Army of the Potomac as XI Corps. In February Sigel took an extended leave of absence from the army and travelled to New York City, where he gave numerous political speeches in support of the Republican Party. Though he wanted to return to the army to participate in the upcoming campaign, he lobbied to increase the size of his corps. Henry Halleck, then President Lincoln's chief of staff, refused Sigel's demands and Sigel resigned from the army for the second time. He remained in New York City and continued to lobby for a more prominent command. Finally in April, at the urging of several friends, Sigel rescinded his resignation and planned to return to his old command in Washington. Frustrated over Sigel's pettiness, Halleck had no use for him. Thus, Sigel missed the opportunity to command the XI Corps at Chancellorsville in May. Sigel eventually returned to the army in summer 1863, and was assigned to the District of Lehigh, Pennsylvania, in the Department of the Susquehanna. More political lobbying won him a more significant command in February 1864 with the Department of West Virginia, which included the Lower Shenandoah Valley. On 15 May 1864 Sigel fought John C. Breckinridge's Confederates at the battle of New Market and was defeated. He was then assigned to the defense of Harper's Ferry and the Baltimore & Ohio Railroad, but was unable to keep the Confederates from inflicting serious damage on both. He was relieved of command on 8 July 1864 and spent the last year of the war in Baltimore and Washington, hoping for another command. On 4 May 1865 he resigned his commission in the Union army for the final time.

He returned to New York City after the Civil War and in 1869 worked for the Brooklyn Steamship & Emigration Company and the Metropolitan Railway. In June 1870 he was appointed internal revenue collector for the 9th New York District by President Ulysses S. Grant. Elected to one term as register of the city in 1871, he served during Grover Cleveland's presidency as chief clerk in the county clerk's office (May 1885 to June 1886) and pension agent for the New York District (March 1886 to May 1889). After retiring from politics, Sigel published the *New Yorker Deutsches Volksblatt* and edited the *New York Monthly* from 1897 to 1900. Sigel died in New York City on 22 August 1902.

In 1906 an equestrian statue of Sigel was dedicated at McKinley and Government streets in Forest Park, St. Louis. That same year, Franz Sigel School was dedicated in Lafayette Square in his honor. In New York City a bronze equestrian statue of Sigel was erected at 106th Street and Riverside Drive in 1907, and a park bounded by 158th Street, the Grand Concourse, 153d Street, and Walton Avenue in the Bronx was named for him. More recently, Sigel was one of thirty-three Missourians honored in World War II by having a liberty ship named for him. In 1998 Sigel, along with other Forty-eighters, was honored at the 150th Anniversary of the German Revolution at the Badisches Landesmuseum in Karlsruhe, Germany.

—*Stephen D. Engle*

See also German-Americans.
For further reading:
Engle, Stephen D. *Yankee Dutchman: The Life of Franz Sigel* (1999).
Griffen, Lawrence E. "The Strange Story of Major General Franz Sigel: Leader and Retreater." *Missouri Historical Review* (1990).
Hess, Earl J. "Sigel's Resignation: A Study in German-Americans and the Civil War." *Civil War History* (1980).

SIGNAL CORPS

Albert James Myer, physician and army surgeon, founded the Union Army Signal Corps. Myer had served as a telegraph operator before attending medical school at Buffalo Medical College. His thesis, "A Sign Language for Deaf Mutes," coupled with his experience as a telegrapher, sparked an interest in developing a system for military communication. Myer practiced medicine for three years before accepting a commission in the regular army as an assistant surgeon. Assigned to a post in Texas, Lieutenant Myer devised a system of signals using a single flag that became the basis for Signal Corps' primary means of communications during the Civil War.

Myer obtained patents on his system and in 1858 convinced the army to consider his system for use in providing communications on the battlefield. A board

Central Signal Station atop the Winder Building, Washington, D.C., April 1865 (*Library of Congress*)

was appointed to review the system. Myer's system received a less than enthusiastic endorsement by the chairman, Lieutenant Colonel Robert E. Lee, who deemed it suitable as an "accessory" to the army's existing means for battlefield communications. Lee did recommend additional testing, and Myer was given several assistants, including Lieutenant E. P. Alexander, to help him during formal military trials. The trials began in April 1859 at Fort Monroe, Virginia, and were later moved to New York harbor, West Point, and Washington, D.C. The trials were successful enough to cause Secretary of War John B. Floyd to recommend to Congress that the army adopt Myer's system and that Myer be appointed as chief signal officer. Although initially resisted by Senator Jefferson Davis from Mississippi, Myer's appointment as major and chief signal officer was approved by Congress, and the Signal Corps was formed on 21 June 1860. Major Myer was assigned to a post in New Mexico to further test his system in a campaign against the Navajos.

Myer's system consisted of a single flag, often dubbed "wigwag," which was moved to the left or right, forming a four-element code. The four-foot-square flag could be seen with the aid of telescopes at distances up to fifteen miles by day, and similar distances were achieved at night with the use of torches. Myer formed a school for signaling at Fort Monroe that was later moved to Red Hill, north of Georgetown, where hundreds of enlisted men and officers were trained on the system. The enlisted men were trained to signal with the flag, and the officers were trained in the code and were used to read the distant signals. Myer also incorporated a system of field telegraphy that could be operated by the Signal Corps personnel without extensive training.

Major Myer's involvement in the battle of First Bull Run was limited, but his former assistant, E. P. Alexander, successfully used the flag system to support Confederate forces. Myer personally controlled the Signal Corps support during the Peninsula campaign, where it was used with considerable success. Myer later gave up the field duties to others and assumed staff duties in Washington. By July 1863, Captain Lemuel B. Norton served as the chief signal officer of the Army of the Potomac.

The signal support provided during the Gettysburg campaign was representative of the new corps' service to the Army of the Potomac. During the movement north, two signal officers with their enlisted couriers and signalers were assigned to each corps. They were used to provide intelligence by observation and communications by sending messages by flags and torches. Brigadier General John Buford's signal officer, Lieutenant Arron B. Jerome, provided intelligence from the cupola at the Lutheran Theological Seminary. Jerome later climbed upon Little Round Top early on the morning of 2 July,

Signal tower at Cobb's Hill, near New Market, Virginia, 1864 (*National Archives*)

where he reported Confederate movement on the Union right. Captain James Hall replaced Jerome on the position and signaled intelligence to the signal station at the Leister house describing Lieutenant General James Longstreet's countermarch. The Confederates were aware of the Signal Corps' ability to observe and report intelligence and, having spotted the flags waving on Little Round Top, Longstreet elected to countermarch in order to find a route secure from their observation. In fact, Major General Lafayette McLaws, the lead division commander who halted Longstreet's columns had been supported by Myer's system in New Mexico and had firsthand knowledge of its capabilities. During the Army of the Potomac's pursuit of the Confederates after the battle, the Signal Corps was active during the cavalry engagement at Boonsboro, Maryland. Cavalry commanders used the signal parties to direct the movement of combat soldiers by the use of flags during this engagement. Messages from the battlefield were signaled by flags to Turners Gap, where they were relayed by telegraph to Washington.

In November 1863, Myer was relieved from his duties as chief signal officer in a dispute with Secretary of War Edwin Stanton over the control of the Military Telegraph Service. The Signal Corps continued under a succession of Myer's former subordinates until the end of the war. The Signal Corps evolved into a credible service that provided communications and intelligence in every theater of the war. In 1866, Myer was again appointed chief signal officer, and in 1867, telegraphy became the responsibility of the Signal Corps. The Signal Corps remains a branch of the modern U.S. Army and is deployed worldwide, providing communications and information systems.

—*Bill Cameron*

See also Myer, Albert James.
For further reading:
Brown, J. Willard. *The Signal Corps, U.S.A. in the War of the Rebellion* (1896).
Cameron, Bill. "The Signal Corps at Gettysburg." *Gettysburg Magazine* (1990).
Coker, Kathy R., and Carol E. Rios. *A Concise History of the U.S. Army Signal Corps* (1988).
Raines, Rebecca Robbins. *Getting the Message Through, A Branch History of the U.S. Army Signal Corps* (1996).
Scheips, Paul J. "Union Signal Communications: Innovation and Conflict." *Civil War History* (1963).

SIMMS, WILLIAM GILMORE
(1806–1870)
Author

Born in Charleston, South Carolina, on 17 April 1806, William Gilmore Simms was the son of William Gilmore Simms, Sr., and Harriet Singleton Simms. Simms's mother died in childbirth when his brother was born in 1808, and his father moved to the southwestern frontier to serve with Andrew Jackson. Raised by his maternal grandmother, Jane Miller Singleton Gates, Simms listened to her stories about the American Revolution. He briefly attended the College of Charleston and read law. He purchased and edited the *Charleston City Gazette*, an antinullification newspaper. Marrying Chevillette Roach, a wealthy woman, in 1836, he acquired her plantation, Woodlands, where he was able to focus on his writing.

Twentieth-century scholars cite Simms as one of the most significant Southern antebellum writers. Nineteenth-century critics, however, often described Simms's writing as overly sensational and melodramatic. Although Edgar Allan Poe thought that Simms penned flawed, predictable plots with stereotypical characterizations, Poe praised his imaginative, descriptive passages, especially of the Carolina Low Country. A prolific author, Simms wrote more than eighty books. He also edited journals, promoting Southern literature. He was intrigued by the conflicting loyalties of South Carolinians during the American Revolution. From the 1830s to 1850s, he created an eight-volume series of novels about the American Revolution, which is considered his best work. Many of these stories were first published serially in periodicals and then reissued as books.

Simms represented the voice of influential Southern aristocrats who supported slavery and secession. Yet some critics misinterpreted Simms's anti-Northern comments in his fiction as a propagandistic response to abolitionism. His novel *Woodcraft* (1854) was considered to be Simms's reaction to Harriet Beecher Stowe's *Uncle Tom's Cabin*. In fact, Simms had already written half of his novel when her book was published.

Simms served in the South Carolina legislature from 1844 and 1846 and was defeated in a close race for lieutenant governor. Simms corresponded widely with politicians and intellectuals, especially James Henry Hammond and Edmund Ruffin. He suggested resettlement in Texas or the Caribbean to avoid the dangers of Northern industry and economic power. In 1856, Simms spoke publicly about the sectional crisis during a lecture tour in the North. Sensitive to criticism about his sectional tone, he resolved to secure independence for the South. When Confederate troops attacked Fort Sumter, Simms told William Porcher Miles, who was serving on the Committee on Military Affairs of the Confederate Congress: "You must either starve out or smoke out the garrison … by incessant cannonade, from the landside, wear them out." Urging Miles to defend the coast, Simms acknowledged his frustration at being too old to fight: "I am … like a bear with a sore head, & chained to the stake. I chafe, and roar & rage, but can do nothing." His son enlisted in the Confederate army, but Simms was left to manage Woodlands and dabble in devising military strategies.

Simms asked Miles to "not forget the interests of Literature in the formation of the new Government." Yet the war stifled Simms's creativity. Shortages of paper and supplies, separation from his Northern printers, and the emotional turmoil and work produced by the conflict prevented Simms from publishing much. He did write letters to his son that offered wisdom about military service. He admitted to Miles that he was anxious about his son's well-being and that writing proved little comfort: "My occupation utterly gone, in this wretched state of war & confusion." He also complained that his copyrights were "all confiscated at the North," costing him his profits. Despite his feelings of hopelessness and despair, Simms experienced creative moments during which "my brain is seething with some new conceptions," but he lamented the lack of publishers. He revised some poems and *The History of South Carolina* and completed *Joscelyn; A Tale of the Revolution* that was published after the war. He also gave voice to the character Paddy McGann's anti-Yankee comments in the *Southern Illustrated News*.

During the Civil War, Simms's wife died, his son was wounded, and his finances were devastated. Moving with his children to Columbia, South Carolina, he earned money by writing for local newspapers. When the city burned on 17 February 1865, Simms witnessed the damage and recorded his impressions of the chaos for the *Columbia Phoenix*. He then wrote the book entitled *Sack and Destruction of the City of Columbia, S.C. to Which is Added a List of Property Destroyed* (1865), which is considered one of his strongest works. Simms noted how the city was burned even after the civilian government surrendered to Sherman's military command. He emphasized that Sherman should have taken responsibility for his troops and prevented them from plundering and interfering with firefighters. While living in Columbia, Simms received a letter from the caretaker at Woodlands telling him that the house had been burned and his library looted. "My books! My books!" Simms wrote. "My heart is ready to break when I think of them."

Rebuilding Woodlands, Simms asked his Northern friends for money and to contact publishers about publishing his manuscripts. After the Civil War, many Southern writers' books went out of print, including Simms's volumes. Illness prevented him from writing full time, but he managed to work as associate editor of the *Charleston Daily South Carolinian*. He composed hastily written stories that were serialized in magazines and collected Confederate verses from leading Southern authors, editing the anthology, *War Poetry of the South* (1866). Simms died on 11 June 1870, in Charleston, suffering from overwork. Death notices were published across the South. Simms's Revolutionary War novels were reprinted with scholarly notes for the Bicentennial.

—*Elizabeth D. Schafer*

See also Columbia, South Carolina; Hammond, James Henry; Ruffin, Edmund; South Carolina; *Southern Illustrated News*.
For further reading:
Faust, Drew Gilpin. *A Sacred Circle: The Dilemma of the Intellectual in the Old South, 1840–1860* (1977; reprint, 1986).
Guilds, John Caldwell. *Simms: A Literary Life* (1992).
Oliphant, Mary C. Simms, Alfred Taylor Odell, and T. C. Duncan Eaves, eds. *The Letters of William Gilmore Simms* (1952–1982).
Simms, William Gilmore, ed. *Sack and Destruction of the City of Columbia, S.C.* (1937).
———. *War Poetry of the South* (1866).
Watson, Charles S. *From Nationalism to Secessionism: The Changing Fiction of William Gilmore Simms* (1993).

SIMS, THOMAS
(ca. 1828–?)
Fugitive slave

The first incidence of a runaway slave being returned to bondage from Boston, Massachusetts, under the Fugitive Slave Act of 1850 became a test case in the struggle over the enforcement of the act. The property of James Potter, a rice planter of Chatham

County, Georgia, Thomas Sims lived and worked as a bricklayer in Savannah before his escape. After frequenting the city's wharves and asking questions of the African-American seamen who sailed on ships in the Atlantic coastal trade, he stowed away on 21 February 1851 on the brig *M. & J.C. Gilmore*. Although he remained hidden for most of the vessel's two-week voyage to Boston, he was eventually discovered and locked in a cabin. As the brig lay anchored off Boston, he used a pocketknife to jimmy the lock and jumped ship, successfully reaching land and blending into the city's sizable black community.

For nearly a month he avoided detection, taking odd jobs and lodging in a boardinghouse catering to African-American seamen in Boston's North End. But attempts to contact his free black wife in Savannah brought his whereabouts to his master's attention. On 3 April, Potter's agent, John B. Bacon, arrived in Boston to swear out a warrant for Sims's arrest under the federal Fugitive Slave Act. Local police located Sims on the city streets later that evening; although he resisted capture, stabbing one officer in the thigh, he was eventually overpowered and imprisoned in the jury room of the Boston Court House, where he was closely guarded by U.S. Marshal Charles Devens.

Stung by Southern criticism following the rescue of fugitive slave Shadrach Minkins from federal custody in Boston earlier in the year, the administration of President Millard Fillmore acted quickly to prevent Sims's escape. Devens barricaded the courthouse with chains and posted some 500 special police to guard the slave and patrol the surrounding square. In response to this show of force, the Boston Vigilance Committee—an interracial organization devoted to the aid and protection of fugitive slaves—acted instead to pursue Sims's release through legal means. Robert Rantoul, who represented Massachusetts in the U.S. Senate, and Charles G. Loring, a leading local attorney, were enlisted to represent Sims in extended hearings before George Ticknor Curtis, the local commissioner under the federal Fugitive Slave Act. The committee also attempted to prevent Sims's return to slavery by requesting action from the state legislature and other federal and state courts. These included requests for a writ of habeas corpus claiming that the slave was illegally detained and a writ of *personal replevin* commanding Devens to produce him in court. The committee also challenged the constitutionality of the Fugitive Slave Act, lodged a criminal complaint against Sims for stabbing a policeman during his arrest, and filed a petition for intervention by the state senate. All were denied. Meanwhile, local abolitionists worked to stir and sway public opinion by posting placards, holding impassioned rallies, and continuing to crowd the court square. Thomas W. Higginson, a local abolitionist clergyman, even conspired with Boston's black leaders to

rescue Sims by having him jump out of the courthouse window at a prearranged signal and flee in a waiting carriage. But before it could be put into effect, Devens had iron bars installed over the windows. Finally, on 11 April, Curtis ordered Sims's rendition. Before dawn the following morning, he was marched under guard to the waiting brig *Acorn* for the return to Georgia, as church bells tolled and crowds filled the streets with cries of "Shame!"

Although black congregations in Boston collected some $1,800 toward the purchase of the fugitive's freedom, the amount proved insufficient. Sims was returned to his owner in Savannah, where he publicly received thirty-nine lashes as punishment for his escape. Two months later, Potter sold him into the slave pens at Charleston, South Carolina; from there he was shipped to the auction block at New Orleans and purchased by a brick mason from Vicksburg, Mississippi. Sims lived in bondage in Vicksburg until the Civil War. His next opportunity to escape came in 1863 during the siege of the city by Union forces. After fleeing to Union lines, he was given a pass by General Ulysses S. Grant to return to Boston, where he lived for several years. In an ironic twist, Sims became a messenger in the Department of Justice in 1877 through the efforts of Devens, then attorney general in the administration of President Rutherford B. Hayes. He was still living in Washington, D.C., in 1889 and working as a bricklayer. The facts of his later life and death are unknown.

—*Roy E. Finkenbine*

See also Burns, Anthony; Devens, Charles; Fugitive Slave Act; Higginson, Thomas Wentworth.

For further reading:

Campbell, Stanley W. *The Slave Catchers: Enforcement of the Fugitive Slave Law, 1850–1860* (1968).

Horton, James O., and Lois E. Horton. *Black Bostonians: Family Life and Community Struggle in the Antebellum North* (1979).

Levy, Leonard W. "Sims' Case: The Fugitive Slave Law in Boston in 1851." *Journal of Negro History* (1950).

SIOUX INDIANS

In the summer of 1862 the Minnesota River valley erupted into six weeks of violence generally referred to as the Great Dakota Conflict. When order was restored, over 500 white soldiers and civilians lay dead and approximately 150 Dakota warriors were slain. The conflict led to the largest mass execution in the history of the United States and signaled the beginning of an exile of a people and a twenty-eight-year war for the plains.

Popularly called "Sioux," a derogatory term derived from a fragment of the French and Ojibwa word *nadouessioux*, meaning "little snake," the Dakota ("friends" or "allies") moved with the seasons and food supply in their ancestral homeland—primarily in what is now the state of Minnesota. The Dakota were composed of four bands:

the Mdewakantonwan (People of Spirit Lake), the Wahpekute (Shooters among the Leaves), the Wahpetonwan (Dwellers among the Leaves), and the Sissetonwan (People of the Swamp). In 1819 Dakota leaders granted the United States government permission to set up an outpost, Fort Snelling, near the confluence of the Minnesota and Mississippi rivers. The subsequent influx of white traders brought a new way of living to the Dakota, as well as a constant state of debt.

The United States Congress granted Minnesota territorial status in 1849. Two years later, Governor Alexander Ramsey negotiated the Treaty of Traverse des Sioux on 23 July 1851 and the Treaty of Mendota on 5 August, whereby the Dakota were coaxed into surrendering twenty-four million acres of land in exchange for yearly payments in food and gold and a reservation ranging ten miles on either side of the Minnesota River from Lake Traverse to just west of the Cottonwood River. The Dakota were also promised a large sum of money for removal assistance and to help settle their debt with traders. Governor Ramsey ignored laws prohibiting payoffs to traders in treaties and allowed the predatory entrepreneurs to claim most of the money promised to the Indians. The United States Senate later modified the treaty, striking out the creation of a permanent reservation, but allowing for a temporary reserve along the Minnesota River. Taoyateduta (His Red Nation, also known to whites as Little Crow), a prominent Mdewakantonwan chief, objected to this change, but was forced to give his approval if annuity payments were to commence. The temporary reservation was to be served by two supervisory agencies—an Upper Agency (or Yellow Medicine) for the Wahpetonwan and the Sissetonwan and a Lower Agency (Redwood Creek) for the Mdewakantonwan and the Wahpekute. Fort Ridgely, an unstockaded garrison was erected nearby.

With 8,000 Dakota confined to a temporary reserve, settlers from Europe and the Atlantic seaboard poured into Minnesota Territory, where they fenced off claims, cleared timber, and plowed up fields. The town of New Ulm, formed by German immigrants, sprang up at the mouth of the Cottonwood River on land promised to the Dakota. Missionaries arrived with the aim of changing Dakota religion and culture and turning Indians into self-sufficient farmers. Most importantly, the food shipments bound for the Dakota rarely arrived; those that did were usually spoiled. Consequently, with little money and food, in just a few short years many Dakota had been reduced to penniless beggars.

In 1858 Minnesota officially entered the Union as a state. That same year, twenty-six Dakota elders and chiefs, including Taoyateduta, traveled to Washington to meet with President James Buchanan. On 24 May Commissioner of Indian Affairs Charles E. Mix announced to the delegation that the United States government wanted all the reservation land on the northeast side of the Minnesota River—approximately half of the reservation. Those Dakota families living there would be moved to the south bank, where they were to receive eighty-acre plots. Taoyateduta and the other members of the delegation had little choice but to sign the new agreement. Congress promised to compensate the Dakota thirty cents per acre for the ceded land, but most of the money went directly to the traders to clear debt.

By the summer of 1862 many Dakota families were at the brink of starvation. Cutworms had damaged or destroyed corn crops and game was no longer plentiful. The treaty payment of $71,000 was late and Indian agent Major Thomas J. Galbraith refused to open up the government warehouses containing provisions until the money arrived. Traders, likewise, were unwilling to extend credit and sell their stores of food. On 6 August Taoyateduta and a council of elders met with Galbraith and a group of traders, including the most prominent trader at the Lower Agency, Andrew Jackson Myrick. Denying the council's request for assistance, Myrick retorted, "So far as I am concerned, if they are hungry, let them eat grass." Insulted, Taoyateduta and the other Dakota elders left in anger.

On 17 August 1862 four Mdewakantonwan youths returning from an unsuccessful hunt outside the reservation's boundary passed through the property of a white family and stole some eggs from the henhouse. Emboldened by taunts and dares to each other, the youths attacked the family, killing three men and two women. Their deaths triggered the beginning of six weeks of violence. Mdewakantonwan and the Wahpekute warriors, aware that the whites would seek retribution for the killings, argued that the time was right for war. Taoyateduta, professing that such action was foolhardy, nevertheless agreed to participate.

On 18 August Dakota warriors attacked the Lower Agency, killing twenty people, including Andrew Myrick, whose mouth was then stuffed with grass. Soon the uprising spread the entire length of the reservation, reaching the Upper Agency by midmorning. When word of the revolt reached Fort Ridgely, the commander of the post, Captain John Marsh, a veteran of the battle of First Bull Run, responded by taking forty-six men from Company B of the 5th Minnesota Infantry and heading toward the Lower Agency. As the they prepared to cross the Minnesota River on the Redwood Ferry, Marsh and his men were ambushed by Dakota warriors. Twenty-four soldiers died, including Marsh, who drowned while trying to swim across the river to safety.

Dakota warriors next turned their attention toward the defenders of Fort Ridgely. On 19 August Taoyateduta's 400 warriors attacked the garrison from four directions. Reinforced to a strength of 180 men, Fort

Ridgely's defenders staved off the attack for three days. The garrison lost six killed and twenty wounded while defending the post. The exploding projectiles from Fort Ridgely's four cannons finally compelled the Indians to withdraw. Frustrated, Taoyateduta and his warriors now focused their attention on the German citizens of New Ulm. Surrounding the town on 23 August, Dakota warriors engaged in fierce combat with its barricaded defenders under the command of Judge Charles Flandrau. At midafternoon the Indians began to set the town on fire. Aided by a strong wind, flames swept through 190 buildings, reducing virtually the entire town to ashes. Even this failed to break the resolve of Flandrau and his 300 men, and the Dakota eventually abandoned the attack and withdrew. The citizens of New Ulm suffered thirty-six killed and twenty-three wounded in the defense of their homes—most of which were no longer standing. Consequently, Flandrau decided to evacuate the town's 2,000 residents and head east to Mankato, thirty miles away.

The bold stand of the defenders of New Ulm and, more importantly, that of the soldiers at Fort Ridgely, signaled to many Dakota the folly of continuing the conflict. To make matters worse, Colonel Henry Hastings Sibley and 1,400 troops from Fort Snelling were slowly moving up the Minnesota River toward Fort Ridgely. Wahpetonwan and Sissetonwan elders refused to continue the fight, arguing instead for migration west to the Dakota Territory. Taoyateduta, refusing to capitulate, nevertheless moved his people to safety upriver from the Upper Agency. The move split the Dakota into two factions—one for continuing the war and the other for peace and the return of all white captives.

Taoyateduta and his Mdewakantonwan warriors next chose to return to the fight. At 4 A.M. on 2 September warriors under Wambdi Tanka (Big Eagle) attacked a sleeping camp of soldiers at Birch Coulee, sixteen miles from Fort Ridgely. The soldiers, in the area serving as a burial party, managed to hold back the Dakota for thirty-one hours, until Sibley arrived with reinforcements. The attack served to heighten the panic that had already gripped the white population of the state.

Concern over the uprising spread from Minnesota to its surrounding states and territories. In response to pleas emanating from the governors in this area, on 6 September President Abraham Lincoln organized the Military Department of the Northwest and named Major General John Pope as its commander. Pope, having just lost the battle of Second Bull Run, arrived in St. Paul on 16 September determined to "utterly exterminate the Sioux." Undaunted by Pope's arrival, Taoyateduta struck again, this time as Sibley's army lay encamped on 23 September at Wood Lake near the Upper Agency. The warriors unleashed a determined attack, but were turned back by the equally resolute soldiers and their ever-present artillery.

Taoyateduta recognized the inevitable. After ordering the release of white and mixed-blood captives, the Mdewakantonwan chief and 200 of his followers left Minnesota for Devils Lake in present-day North Dakota, hoping to find allies who would help him continue the struggle. With the departure of the hostile warriors, Sibley moved to meet with the Dakota peace faction. After taking in the 269 liberated whites and mixed-bloods, Sibley began rounding up the Dakota. Soon, over 2,000 men, women, and children had been amassed. Next, Sibley began the process of identifying the Dakota warriors who were responsible for the uprising or who had committed atrocities against whites. Based upon their own cultural values and the honor associated with personal combat, the Dakota were proud to say that they had fought in battles against whites. To Sibley, such boasting was all that was necessary to prove their guilt. In one month 392 Dakota men were tried and 303 were condemned to die. Those men who were convicted were transported to Camp Lincoln at Mankato, while the remaining 1,700 men, women, and children were marched to Fort Snelling, where they were exposed to overcrowded conditions and epidemics that depleted their numbers.

For Abraham Lincoln, the tally of guilty verdicts coming out of Sibley's five-man military court seemed excessive. Persuaded by Bishop Henry B. Whipple, the Episcopal Bishop of the Missionary District of Minnesota and friend of the Dakota, the president reviewed the evidence and, over the objections of Pope and Ramsey, narrowed the number of condemned prisoners to thirty-eight. On 26 December 1862 Mankato witnessed the largest mass execution in the history of the United States, as all thirty-eight men were hanged simultaneously from a specially constructed gallows. Their bodies were buried under a willow tree by the river, only to be exhumed by Dr. William Mayo and other physicians for medical use.

In February 1863 Congress voided all its treaties with the Dakota, thereby abolishing the reservation and ending all annuity payments. Money that had been allocated for Indians was used to aid white victims of the conflict. The Dakota were banished from the state and bounties for Indian scalps were raised to $200. In April 1863 the prisoners at Mankato who were not hanged were transferred by steamer to Camp McClellan in Davenport, Iowa. The remaining Dakota at Fort Snelling were likewise crowded on board steamers and sent to Crow Creek, Dakota Territory.

Concern over the whereabouts and intentions of Taoyateduta and his followers led to outcries from the residents of western Minnesota, Nebraska, Iowa, and the Dakota Territory. In response, Pope organized a

two-pronged punitive expedition in the spring of 1863 to hunt down and crush the Dakota. Sibley commanded one wing of the operation and Brigadier General Alfred Sully, a veteran of the battles of Antietam and Fredericksburg, commanded the other. The operation met little success and the Dakota disappeared into the plains.

Taoyateduta made one last attempt to continue the struggle. Traveling to Fort Garry (Winnipeg), Canada, the Mdewakantonwan chief and eighty of his followers asked the British to honor their alliance dating back to the War of 1812. Meeting with no success, Taoyateduta returned to his home in Minnesota. On 3 July 1863 he was shot dead by a farmer as he was picking raspberries with his son. Taoyateduta's scalp was given to the Minnesota State Historical Society, where it remained on display until 1971. In 1866 the Dakota prisoners at Camp McClellan were reunited with the men, women, and children sent to Crow Creek at a site in northeastern Nebraska near the mouth of the Niobrara River—thereafter referred to as the Santee reservation.

—*Alan C. Downs*

See also Pope, John; Sibley, Henry Hastings.

For further reading:
Anderson, Gary Clayton. *Through Dakota Eyes: Narrative Accounts of the Minnesota Indian War of 1862* (1988).
Clodfelter, Michael. *The Dakota War: The United States Army Versus the Sioux, 1862–1865* (1998).
Josephy, Alvin M. *The Civil War in the American West* (1991).

SISTER NURSES

Among the numerous monuments in Washington, D.C., is one at the corner of Rhode Island and Connecticut Avenues. "Nuns of the Battlefield," erected in 1921, commemorates the approximately 600 Roman Catholic sisters from twenty-one separate communities of twelve different orders of sisters who nursed both Union and Confederate soldiers during the Civil War.

These sisters, or nuns, as they were sometimes called, had a tradition of nursing care, often from their European origins, and a history in the United States of establishing hospitals and reaching out in times of epidemics and other crises. In addition, unlike their female counterparts organized under Dorothea Dix or other hospital matrons, the sisters had written regulations for their community life that served as a training manual for how patients should be treated. This simple "nursing manual," combined with their structured community life and dedication to others, enabled them to be easily and quickly organized for dealing with the demands of a war that left thousands wounded and dead.

Largely unpublished materials from these communities reveal the details of the service of these women. Of approximately 800 Daughters of Charity, whose head-quarters was in Emmitsburg, Maryland, at least 270 sisters serving in about sixty sites have been documented as providing nursing care and spiritual assistance. This was the largest group of sisters nursing in the Civil War. The smallest group consisted of six Ursuline nuns in Galveston, Texas, serving in their own convent, which was twice turned into a hospital. Sixty-three Holy Cross sisters from South Bend, Indiana, whose works had not included nursing prior to the war, were the second-largest group of sisters serving in at least ten different institutions. In the South, Sisters of Charity of Our Lady of Mercy (then called Sisters of Mercy) in Charleston, South Carolina, and Sisters of Mercy of Vicksburg, Mississippi, also provided sisters throughout the war.

Other communities of Sisters of Charity included those from Cincinnati, New York City, and Nazareth, Kentucky, all separate orders, which provided nursing care for extended periods. The Sisters of Mercy from Cincinnati, Baltimore, New York, Pittsburgh, and Chicago supplied over 100 sisters. Although the city of origin of these sisters identifies the community, often their geographic place of service during the war was elsewhere. The actual locations where they nursed are not easily identifiable, as the temporary hospitals often moved from place to place with the soldiers, or the sisters served only a limited time. In addition, Sisters of Our Lady of Mount Carmel in New Orleans, Dominican sisters in Perryville, Kentucky, and Sisters of Mercy in Little Rock, Arkansas, also responded to immediate and short-term battle needs in their own geographic areas. However, these three teaching communities served only a matter of weeks.

Several other communities, with both nursing and teaching backgrounds, also nursed. Of the nursing groups, the Sisters of St. Joseph had sisters in their own hospital in Wheeling, West Virginia, during the entire war, while the Sisters of St. Joseph of Philadelphia nursed in the area around the city. Sisters of the Poor of St. Francis from Cincinnati served in a hospital there and in Columbus, Ohio. In addition, Sisters of Providence, whose headquarters was in St. Mary of the Woods, Indiana, served in two hospitals in that state for most of the war, as did Dominican sisters in hospitals in Memphis, Tennessee. Significantly, these sisters were not engaged in hospital work before the war, although they, like the Holy Cross sisters, have remained in health care work ever since.

Though statistics are difficult to reconstruct, the sisters who nursed during the war probably represented about one-third of all the sisters in the United States at the outbreak of the conflict. Logically, in the early months of the war, both Union and Confederate authorities turned to the hospitals and religious communities who staffed them to take in wounded soldiers, and later, to other communities. Requests for the use of buildings and institutions under the control of various women's religious communities and especially pleas for the services of sisters, often all called "Sisters of Charity" or "Sisters of Mercy," regardless of the specific name of the religious community, came from a variety of governmental, military, medical, and religious leaders. Sometimes the requests went to the primary administrators of the religious community; sometimes to the smaller unit of the community that was in charge of a specific hospital or usable building. Frequently, the requests came through the bishop of the diocese in which the sisters were located. Sometimes, the bishop offered the services of sisters under his jurisdiction, especially when he was sympathetic to the Union or Confederate cause, or simply sensitive to the need for physical and spiritual care for the soldiers of either side.

In mid-nineteenth-century America, nursing was generally done in the home. Only the poor were cared for in hospitals. Classed with low-level menial scrubbing, nursing during the Civil War was not a profession, but consisted of keeping a patient clean, feeding him, or caring for other needs. Most nursing tasks in wartime were performed by other convalescing soldiers; however, some groups of women were organized in various parts of the country for the care of the sick, notably by Dorothea Dix in the North.

Similar to work done by other women nurses, the usual duties performed by the sisters in field or general hospitals were giving medicines, tending wounds, feeding the soldiers, caring for the laundry and linen departments, cooking for special diets, writing letters for the soldiers, and sometimes nursing in the smallpox section. Primary in the sisters' view, though, was their desire and need to be with the soldiers when they were dying, baptizing those who wished, and encouraging repentance and a peaceful death for those who were Catholic. Typhoid, pneumonia, erysipelas (a highly contagious strep infection), measles, and smallpox were among the diseases frequently encountered by the sisters.

The sisters' quietness, good order, cooperation with the doctors (some of whom they had known in their own hospitals before the war), ability to handle the domestic but vital chores of cleaning and cooking, dedication, and willingness to learn and take on extra duties were all qualities praised by the doctors.

Other female nurses of the Civil War sometimes clashed with doctors because the nurses' presence challenged the male authority generally and the medical field specifically. The implication was that sisters were preferred because of their greater conformity to the image and ideals of domesticity or to the fact that some were unpaid. However, the situation was more complex.

The sisters did challenge doctors and other authorities when they felt nursing care, nutrition, cleanliness, good order, and their religious practices demanded it,

and they were often able to get supplies that doctors or military authorities were not able to procure. Some communities also had specific agreements about aspects of their service. However, their lifestyle enabled them to live simply, to be quickly organized under both male and female leaders, to be supported by a group of like-minded women, and to be experienced in various social services, including care of the sick. In addition, because they were unmarried with a vow of celibacy, the sisters were less suspect in their motivations for desiring to serve and work with men. Underlying all their service was the moral and religious vision and values that gave impetus to the quality and universality of their service.

Nursing for all women from 1861 to 1865 was primarily an opportunity to "mother" the "boys" in blue and grey, but for the sisters the demands of the war were also a chance to make more visible the religious imperative and commitment behind such services. The role and image of the nurse in the Civil War stands as a pivotal point both in the recognition of the value and scope of the service performed by female nurses and in the necessity of training needed to develop that service into a profession for women. Of particular significance is the contribution of the sisters, whose dedication and professionalism led to a heightened awareness by the U.S. public of the positive aspects of Catholicism in contrast to the prewar prejudices behind anti-Catholicism, and gave impetus to the rise of professional schools of nursing, some started by these religious communities.

—*Sr. Mary Denis Maher, CSA*

See also Dix, Dorothea; Nurses.
For further reading:
Maher, Sr. Mary Denis, CSA. *To Bind Up the Wounds: Catholic Sister Nurses in the U.S. Civil War* (1989; reprint, 1999).
Schultz, Jane. "The Inhospitable Hospital: Gender and Professionalism in Civil War Medicine." *Signs* (1992).

SLANG

A broad and rich body of slang terms developed during the Civil War. Undoubtedly, several unique characteristics of the war and the armies that fought in it contributed to this development. First, the Civil War was the first American war fought by a large army made up mostly of nonprofessional volunteers. Career men are likely to be trained to use a specific set of terms for all things military; amateurs are much more likely to invent their own terms as needed. Additionally, those amateur soldiers were mostly literate, which meant that they had an affinity for verbiage, as well as an ability to spread new terms via letters and newspapers. Finally, the Civil War was a time of innovation, politically, militarily, and socially, necessitating the development of terms for a variety of things that had been unknown to Americans a generation earlier.

Developments in national politics generated many

new slang terms, some of which entered the lexicon permanently. People spoke of *blockade runners* or *bounty jumpers*. Congressional laws changing postal regulations gave us *first-class* letters, and legislation allowing for the printing of currency gave us *greenbacks*. The establishment of America's first draft added *draftee* and *draft dodger* to the dictionary. The U.S. War Department, which was run very badly in the early part of the war, purchased a great deal of poor-quality equipment that came to be known as *shoddy*. Their adversaries stigmatized Peace Democrats who wanted the war to end at any cost as *Copperheads*.

Soldiers, of course, had a highly developed jargon. They were themselves known as *doughboys*, a term that became popular during World War I, but was first used during the Civil War. They had a wide variety of names for the different weapons issued to them, including *Lincoln rifles*, *coffee-mill guns*, *pumpkin slingers*, *smoke poles*, and *Yankee seven devils*. Other pieces of equipment included *beehives* (knapsacks), *doghouses* (tents), *Sibleys* (tents), *mudscows* (shoes), and *tar buckets* (hats). To have experienced warfare was to have *seen the elephant*, while to beat a hasty retreat was to *skedaddle*.

The afflictions of soldier life led to some particularly colorful lingo. Body lice, the bane of almost every soldier, were called *bodyguards*, *crumbs*, or *graybacks*. Diarrhea and dysentery, known as *quickstep* or the *evacuation of Corinth*, were also common. The soldiers had a low opinion of the food they were given to eat, and so the vocabulary they used to describe it was less than flattering. One might dine on *hellfire stew*, *desecrated vegetables*, *shadow soup*, or *embalmed beef*, all prepared by a *dog robber*. Perhaps the most widely despised culinary creation of the Civil War was the rock-hard biscuit known was hardtack, also called *sheet-iron cracker*, *worm castle*, or *son of a sea dog*. *Goober peas*, known to us as peanuts, had their own song. The soldier's favorite beverage was coffee, sometimes known as *subtle poison*. There were also plenty of terms for more potent drinks. Whiskey alone was called by at least a dozen different names, including *bust head*, *dead shot*, *how come you so*, *knock-em-stiff*, *rot gut*, and *tarantula juice*.

Quite a few Civil War figures inspired their own personal slang terms. To *Butlerize* was to steal, a crime of which Union commander Benjamin Butler was accused while commanding troops in New Orleans. Union general Ambrose Burnside's prominent whiskers gave us *sideburns*. *Sherman's neckties* were railroad rails heated and twisted around trees during William Sherman's marches through Georgia and to the sea. Both presidents lent their names to several slang terms, usually unflattering ones. There were *Davis boots*, *Jeff Davis money*, *Jeff Davis hats*, and *Jeff Davis bread*, as well as *Lincoln flags*, *Lincoln pies*, *Lincoln hirelings*, and *Lincoln pups*.

Of course, many slang terms were discarded when the soldiers discarded their guns. The dozens that remain in use, however, remind us of the extent to which the Civil War influenced modern life.

—Christopher Bates

See also Copperheads.

For further reading:

Dickson, Paul. *War Slang: American Fighting Words and Phrases from the Civil War to the Gulf War* (1994).

Lyman, Darryl. *The Civil War Wordbook: including Sayings, Phrases, and Slang* (1993).

Monaghan, Jay. *Civil War Slang & Humor* (1955).

SLAVES

Almost from the beginning, rather than being "conceived in liberty," as many historians have maintained, the United States was heavily dependent on coerced labor and, from the early eighteenth century until as late as 1865, slavery. Eight of the country's first twelve presidents, including George Washington, Thomas Jefferson, and Andrew Jackson, were slave holders, constituting 49 of the nation's first 61 years. What ended as the Civil War began in many respects as abolitionism, the first serious reform movement in American history. Slavery was so entrenched in the American experience and culture, however, that as late as the 1830s abolitionists were considered raving fanatics whose provocative tirades threatened the well-being of the entire nation, North and South.

The English word *slave* comes from *Slavs*, an ethnic group in Eastern Europe who were captured and sold by Germanic tribesmen. Although the term denotes agricultural laborers in the Western Hemisphere, slavery historically has varied widely in terms of type, purpose, gender, and ethnicity. Some of the earliest American slaves were Native Americans, the victims of military defeat or kidnapping who were eventually bought and sold on the open market. Small numbers of Native American slaves remained into the nineteenth century, but they were deemed inferior because the men refused to cooperate and because it was fairly easy for them to escape and conspire against their captors. Many seventeenth-century slaves were white also—indentured servants who paid for their transportation to the New World by promising to work for free for several years. The number of white indentured servants failed to keep pace with the rapidly increasing populations of the various colonies by the late eighteenth century, and Africa became the primary source of slaves by 1700.

The first African slaves arrived in North America as indentured servants for the Spanish in what would become Georgia in 1526. In 1619, 20 survivors of an original shipment of 100 Africans landed at Jamestown, Virginia, and began providing the stable labor force that was the backbone of large-scale agricultural production. Africans were prized as slaves because of their color and

the fact that they knew little about North America, making it more difficult for them to escape. A black man or woman was presumed to be a slave unless he or she could show otherwise. Literally bound to a life of racism, servitude, and enforced illiteracy, African slaves and their descendants had little choice but to submit to their situation at least temporarily or face death. Estimates vary, but at least ten million Africans were transported to the New World between the seventeenth and nineteenth centuries to become slaves.

At the time of the American Revolution, every colony had slaves. Opponents tried to have the practice declaimed or banned in the Declaration of Independence and Constitution but were defeated, and the Northwest Ordinance of 1787 provided for the return of fugitive slaves as it prohibited slavery in states carved out of the Northwest Territory. Pennsylvania was the first state to emancipate its slaves in 1780, and it was joined by New York, New Jersey, and other Northern states, some grudgingly. Still, the United States became the first nation in the New World to have a self-reproducing slave population by the early nineteenth century. In the Deep South, plantation owners viewed slaves as an economic necessity. Many planters earned a return on their investment in slaves equal to the returns on money Northerners invested in manufacturing or railroads. By the time of the Civil War, the capital investment in slaves exceeded in value all other capital worth in the South, including land.

Subjugated but never defeated, African-Americans resisted slavery any way they could. Escapes, while difficult, were common from the earliest years of slavery. Alliances with Native Americans led some slaves to settle or intermingle with tribes in Florida before the Revolutionary War. In the nineteenth century, the Underground Railroad provided freedom for thousands of slaves even as thousands of others who were unsuccessful perished or were returned into bondage. More organized slave revolts began as early as 1690, but the Nat Turner Rebellion of 1831 was particularly disturbing because it was organized and led by a literate, religiously inspired slave. The South became increasingly paranoid toward and protective of its "peculiar institution" in the wake of the rebellion. Slaves were prohibited by law from becoming literate, gatherings (even religious) of African-Americans were viewed with apprehension, and white abolitionists and their propaganda were driven or prohibited from the South. The Fugitive Slave Act of 1850 and the 1857 Supreme Court decision in the *Dred Scott* case were both inspired by the unfounded paranoia that massive numbers of slaves were escaping to the North. Although slavery was supported as an institution by most of the South before the Civil War, it cut a limited socioeconomic line. Only one quarter of all Southern whites owned slaves in 1860, and of that

Slaves preparing cotton for the gin on Smith's Plantation (Port Royal Island, South Carolina), 1862 (Photograph by Timothy H. O'Sullivan / *Library of Congress*)

number, only ten thousand families owned at least 50 slaves, according to the federal census.

The Civil War meant the end of slavery. During the first months of the war, many white Union supporters worried whether emancipating African-Americans justified the war's deadly toll, but the use of slavery to sustain the Confederacy convinced all but a small minority of the need to eliminate an institution that had been so much a part of the nation. But to slaves, the war meant hardships as it provided deliverance. The Confederate impressment policy of 1863 forced many slaves to work away from their homes building fortifications or performing other heavy tasks, often under debilitating conditions. Wartime shortages cost many slaves even the modest material gains they had made during the prosperous 1850s, especially when renegade Union and Confederate soldiers looted their cabins and took the produce of their gardens, the little livestock they had, and the crops from nearby fields. Slaves not felled by hard labor often died or became ill due to malnutrition and other diseases. The attitude of Union soldiers, supportive yet contemptuous, created distrust among the same slaves they sought to liberate.

There were opportunities as well. White control of slaves eroded as so many slave owners joined the Confederate army and were killed in the fighting. Some white men entrusted slaves with plantation management, and house servants and other faithful slaves often became the protectors of upper-class white women. The postwar myth of the faithful black slave, popularized by

Slave-pen interior, Alexandria, Virginia (*National Archives*)

lawn jockey statues and in movies such as *Birth of a Nation* and novels such as *Gone With the Wind*, was born in the wartime sharing of common interests between slaves and their owners. The war allowed many African-Americans to drop the masks they had been taught to wear as children, revealing their true feelings for the first time. Slaves became openly disobedient and reduced their work throughout the South. They spied and provided military and other kinds of information to the Union armies.

The most dramatic opportunity afforded by the war was to allow more slaves to escape. As their owners fled Union forces, many slaves stayed behind and even migrated toward arriving soldiers. Over 180,000 African-Americans, many former slaves, fought in the Union army during the war, and 37,000 died. Those who were captured by Southern forces were treated worse than slaves were. Many did not wait for the Emancipation Proclamation. At least one-seventh of all the slaves in

the South crossed Union lines to freedom during the war. Others were kept in the dark, even after the end of the war. Juneteenth, or Black Emancipation Day, celebrates the liberation of the slaves of Texas, who received word of their freedom on 19 June 1865, two and a half years after the Emancipation Proclamation was issued.

African-Americans emerged from the Civil War with their own vibrant, definable culture in American society. Their shared experiences, especially religious, during the war helped create leadership institutions. Their new situation as freedmen encouraged them to expand their legal status in society. Most importantly, the folklore, food, language, family, music, and religious institutions they developed as slaves before and during the Civil War helped sustain them through the difficult years of the late nineteenth and twentieth centuries.

—*Richard Digby-Junger*

See also African-American Sailors; Contrabands; *Dred Scott Case*; Emancipation Proclamation; Freedmen's Bureau;

Fugitive Slave Act; Impressment; United States Colored Troops.

For further reading:
Brown, Richard D., ed. *Slavery in American Society* (1992).
Fogel, Robert William. *Without Consent of Contract: The Rise and Fall of American Slavery* (1989).
Franklin, John Hope. *From Slavery to Freedom: A History of Negro Americans* (1996).
Kolchin, Peter. *American Slavery, 1619–1877* (1993).
Mathews, Don. "Wealth and Its Distribution in the Antebellum South: Where Do We Stand and Why Does It Matter?" *Essays in Economic and Business History* (1997).
Oates, Stephen B. "The Man at the White House Window." *Civil War Times Illustrated* (1995).
Ransom, Roger L. *Conflict and Compromise: The Political Economy of Slavery, Emancipation, and the American Civil War* (1989).
Stafford, Tim. "The Abolitionists." *Christian History* (1992).
Tate, Gayle T. "How Antebellum Black Communities Became Mobilized: The Role of Church, Benevolent Society, and Press." *National Political Science Review* (1993).
Wayne, Michael. "The Reshaping of Plantation Society Revisited." *Journal of Mississippi History* (1992).

SLEMMER, ADAM JACOBY
(1829–1868)
Union general

Born in Montgomery County, Pennsylvania, Adam Jacoby Slemmer was educated locally before receiving an appointment to the U.S. Military Academy. He graduated twelfth of forty-four in the class of 1850. Upon graduation, Slemmer served in Florida and then California before being recalled to West Point to teach. In 1859, after his tour of duty at the academy, Slemmer was sent to Pensacola, Florida, where he commanded Fort Barrancas as first lieutenant, 1st U.S. Artillery.

In early January 1861, with secessionist feelings growing in Florida, Slemmer began to worry about the security of his small force in the very vulnerable Barrancas. He telegraphed the War Department on 8 January asking permission to move his men from Barrancas to the more secure Fort Pickens on Santa Rosa Island. When the Florida Secession Convention voted in favor of Florida leaving the Union on 10 January, Slemmer, after spiking Barrancas's guns, quietly moved his 81-man garrison. His efforts made it possible for Federal forces to reinforce Fort Pickens in April 1861 and hence hold Fort Pickens for the duration of the war. While at Fort Pickens, Slemmer tried to maintain good relations with the surrounding population by returning any runaway slaves who tried to take refuge at the fort. He was promoted to major in May 1861 and was commended by Secretary of War Simon Cameron for his actions at Pensacola.

Through the summer of 1861, Slemmer aided in the recruiting and training of the new 16th U.S. Infantry.

Upon completion of this task, he and the 16th were sent to the Army of the Ohio under Don Carlos Buell, whereupon Slemmer became the acting inspector general of the army. He served in expeditions in western Virginia in the fall of 1861.

In 1862 Slemmer served primarily in Tennessee, although he did command a battalion in the repulse of Braxton Bragg from Kentucky in the fall of that year. In December 1862, Slemmer commanded his battalion of regulars as part of George H. Thomas's XIV Corps. Leading his men on the Federal left at Stones River on 31 December, Slemmer was severely wounded and was carried from the field. He was never able to return to active field service for the remainder of the war, though he did remain in the army, serving on boards and courts-martial for the next two years. His most important duty during that time was presiding over the board that examined injured and ill officers to determine fitness for duty. He was promoted from major to brigadier general in April 1863 with a date of rank of 29 November 1862.

After the war, Slemmer decided to remain in the army, continuing his service on boards before being placed in command of Fort Laramie, Wyoming, in 1867. His health had never fully recovered, and in the aftermath of the war he began to show the signs of heart disease. He succumbed to his debilitating illness in 1868 at Fort Laramie at the age of thirty-nine. His remains were returned to Montgomery County, Pennsylvania, where he was buried.

—*David S. Heidler and Jeanne T. Heidler*

See also Pensacola, Florida; Stones River, Battle of.
For further reading:
Cozzens, Peter. *No Better Place to Die: The Battle of Stones River* (1990).
Johns, John E. *Florida during the Civil War* (1963).

SLIDELL, JOHN
(1793–1871)
Confederate envoy to France

John Slidell was born in 1793 in New York City. In 1819, he moved to New Orleans and established a successful law practice. He ran unsuccessfully for Congress as a Democrat in 1828 and launched losing campaigns for the U.S. Senate in 1834 and 1836; however, the political connections he made in those races eventually secured him a congressional seat in 1843. He found enough time between elections to marry Marie Mathilde Deslonde, of a prominent Creole family, in 1835.

In September 1845, President James K. Polk appointed Slidell minister to Mexico and gave him the mission of purchasing California and New Mexico from that country for $25 million. When he arrived in Mexico City on 6 December 1845, Slidell learned that

John Slidell (*Library of Congress*)

the Mexican government, which had broken relations with the United States when the latter annexed Texas, refused to receive him. He left Mexico City in protest, but remained in the country while Polk moved U.S. troops toward the Rio Grande. By April 1846 it was apparent that the Mexicans were never going to meet with him, so Slidell left the country and was back in the United States by the time war broke out at the end of the month.

Although his diplomatic mission had failed, Slidell, who American expansionist newspapers portrayed as the aggrieved peacemaker, saw his political influence grow upon his return home. The Democratic Party rewarded his loyalty in 1853, when Louisiana Democrats chose him to replace the deceased Senator Alexander Barrow in Washington. Senator Slidell supported the Pierce administration's efforts to gain Cuba from Spain, argued for the Kansas-Nebraska Act, and avidly defended the Southern cause in the face of rising Northern power. After Louisiana's secession on 26 January 1861, he left Washington and returned home.

Convinced that Slidell's political prominence, diplomatic experience, and Creole connections made him the right man to represent the Confederacy in France,

President Jefferson Davis appointed him "special commissioner" to that country in August 1861. In November, the USS *San Jacinto* captured Slidell and James M. Mason, the Confederate envoy to England, as they steamed to Europe on board the *Trent*, a British mail ship. After vigorous British protests, which the French supported, the Federals released the two diplomats, and Slidell finally arrived in Paris on 30 January 1862.

A week later, Slidell had his first meeting with French foreign minister Edward Antoine Thouvenel, during which he protested France's acceptance of the Union's naval blockade of the South, which the Confederacy considered to be an illegal "paper" blockade as defined by the Declaration of Paris of 1856. Thouvenel insisted that the blockade must be an "effective" one, given that little Southern cotton had made its way to French ports since the blockade's inception in April of the previous year. Slidell could hardly counter this logic, as he knew the Confederacy was withholding cotton exports in the hope that such an embargo would ultimately force the French and British to break the blockade to prevent economic disaster and social unrest in their textile-dependent, industrial nations. In fact, Slidell's arguments were bound to fail. Thouvenel and his emperor, Napoleon III, who actually favored the Southern cause, had already decided that they, at least for the time, could not afford to upset French relations with England by pursuing a unilateral abrogation of the Union blockade or a unilateral recognition of Confederate independence.

Nevertheless, just two months after his meeting with Thouvenel, Slidell renewed his faith in French intervention. He received news that Napoleon, increasingly worried about the negative economic effects of the cotton shortage, had told the British that he was willing to send a blockade-breaking fleet to the South if they followed suit. Slidell's optimism quickly deflated, however, when it became clear that the British refused to support such a risky French move, and that Napoleon had backed down once Thouvenel voiced his opposition. His hopes revived in the summer of 1862 as news of Confederate victories in Virginia and his first private audience with Napoleon III on 16 July seemed to augur well for French intervention. Unfortunately, the British, whose policies toward the war guided French actions, counseled caution—their advice seemed justified after France heard of the Union's victory at Antietam. Napoleon, however, seemed undeterred; he met with Slidell again on 28 October and suggested a joint mediation of the war by France, England, and Russia; two days later, the emperor's new foreign minister, Edouard Drouyn de Lhuys, sent the proposal to England and Russia, but those nations rejected the offer.

While Slidell's main task in Paris was to secure French recognition of Southern independence, he tried to help the Confederacy's prospects in other ways as well. In

March 1863, he successfully concluded a deal with Erlanger & Company, a powerful French banking concern, for a loan of $15 million, which would be secured by sales of Confederate cotton bonds. Slidell used funds from the loan to pay for the construction of six warships (four wooden cruisers and two ironclads) in French ports, but after months of frustrating negotiations, the French, under heavy diplomatic pressure from the United States, refused to arm the vessels and release them to Confederate agents. More importantly, the French decision to block Slidell's naval contract was based on their assessment of the Confederacy's military prospects, which by the spring of 1864—the period when the ships were ready for delivery—seemed limited indeed. Slidell had long since realized that the French would never recognize his nation: their diplomacy toward the American war was too dependent on England; they were often distracted from American events by European crises, such as the Polish uprising of 1863; and they were increasingly preoccupied with Napoleon's imperial adventure in Mexico. Nevertheless, Slidell remained at his post in Paris until the Confederate collapse in 1865. Now an exile, Slidell never returned to the United States; he died in England on 2 July 1871.

—*R. Boyd Murphree*

See also Diplomacy, C.S.A.; Mason, James Murray; *Trent Affair.*

For further reading:

Case, Lynn M., and Warren F. Spencer. *The United States and France: Civil War Diplomacy* (1970).

Owsley, Frank L. *King Cotton Diplomacy: Foreign Relations of the Confederate States of America* (1959).

Sears, Louis Martin. *John Slidell* (1925).

SLOCUM, HENRY WARNER
(1827–1894)
Union general

Henry Warner Slocum was born at Delphi, New York, on 24 September 1827. He later attended Cazenovia Academy and taught school for several years.

In 1848, Slocum received an appointment to the U.S. Military Academy. He graduated seventh of forty-three cadets in the class of 1852. He soon received a commission of second lieutenant in the First U.S. Artillery. His military service carried him to Florida, and later to Fort Moultrie, South Carolina. He married Clara Rice in 1854, and soon he was promoted to first lieutenant. On 31 October 1856, Lieutenant Slocum resigned his commission in the army to pursue a career in law.

Henry Slocum returned to his native New York and was admitted to the New York bar in 1858. He established a law practice in Syracuse and later became a member of the state assembly. In 1860, Slocum was appointed artillery instructor and colonel in the New York State Militia.

In May 1861, Henry Slocum was appointed colonel of the 27th New York Volunteers. The regiment participated in the battle of First Bull Run with Porter's brigade of Hunter's division and suffered 130 casualties in the engagement. While serving with his regiment, Colonel Slocum was wounded in the fighting. Upon his return, Slocum was promoted to brigadier general and was assigned to command of brigade in VI Army Corps. Several months later, General Slocum received command of 1st Division, VI Army Corps during the midst of the Peninsula campaign. By July 1862, Slocum was promoted to major general and continued to lead his division through the Peninsula, Second Manassas, and Maryland campaigns of 1862.

In October 1862, General Slocum was tapped to command XII Army Corps. His corps remained in reserve until the battle of Chancellorsville, Virginia, in May 1863. His corps was instrumental in stopping the Confederate assault of 3 May 1863. Disgusted with Major General Joseph Hooker, General Slocum was a member of the cabal that worked to have him removed from command. During the battle of Gettysburg, General Slocum played a vital role in securing the Federal right flank, despite a lack of initiative displayed on 1 July 1863.

With the Federal loss at Chickamauga, Georgia, both the XI and XII Corps were transferred west to Tennessee under the command of General Hooker. General Slocum submitted his resignation upon learning of his assignment under Hooker. His resignation was not accepted, yet efforts were made to separate Slocum from Hooker. From late 1863 until the summer of 1864, General Slocum would command a variety of posts, such as Vicksburg, Mississippi, or command troops protecting the Nashville Railroad. With Hooker's resignation, Slocum returned to his old corps, which was now XX Corps, on 26 August 1864. On 2 September 1864, General Slocum's corps was the first Federal unit to enter Atlanta, Georgia.

For upcoming campaigns in the Georgia countryside, Major General William T. Sherman created an army consisting of the XIV and XX Corps to add another wing to his army. This detachment (the Army of Georgia, or left wing) was assigned to the command of General Slocum due to his seniority. Slocum commanded this ad hoc force of six infantry divisions and eight artillery batteries throughout the Savannah campaign (the March to the Sea) and the Carolinas campaign.

In March 1865, General Slocum led his army through a series of engagements that would mark the end of the Carolinas campaign. On 16 March 1865, General Slocum faced a Confederate rear-guard action at Averasboro, North Carolina. Later, on 19 March 1865,

Slocum's force was assaulted along the Goldsboro Road by Confederate general Joseph E. Johnston. After a day of severe fighting, General Slocum's veterans were able to secure their front to await the arrival of reinforcements from General Sherman. After two days, General Johnston withdrew his army, and Slocum was able to move his army into Goldsboro, North Carolina. General Slocum participated with final military campaigns in North Carolina and resigned his commission in September 1865.

Slocum returned to Syracuse, New York, and attempted to run as the Democratic candidate for secretary of state, but was defeated in the election. In 1866, Slocum moved to Brooklyn, New York to continue his law practice. He served in the U.S. House of Representatives from 1868 to 1873 and from 1883 to 1885. Representative Slocum was a strong supporter of Fitz John Porter during his efforts to clear his name. Slocum later served on the board of the Gettysburg Monument Commissioners. He died on 14 April 1894 in Brooklyn, New York.

—*William H. Brown*

For further reading:
Heitman, Francis B. *Historical Register and Dictionary of the United States Army* (1903).
Krick, Robert K. "'A Step All-Important and Essential to Victory': Henry W. Slocum and the Twelfth Corps on July 1–2, 1863," in Gary W. Gallagher, ed., *The Second Day at Gettysburg: Essays on Confederate and Union Leadership* (1993).
Slocum, Charles Elihu. *The Life and Services of Major General Henry Warner Slocum* (1913).

SMALL ARMS

During the American Civil War, small arms included muskets, rifles, carbines, and pistols—the firearms of the individual combatants. Although there was only marginal consistency in both Northern and Southern small arms issues, some general trends evolved as the war progressed. In 1861 both the Union and Confederacy lacked sufficient modern weapons to arm the flood of recruits mobbing their enlistment depots. As a result, they armed their fledgling armies with whatever arms were available, including sporting weapons and obsolete smoothbores of various calibers and origin.

Within months, however, the federal arsenal at Springfield, Massachusetts, and various private contractors began producing thousands of well-made modern weapons. Although the less industrialized South did establish arsenals, their products were often of inferior quality, and production was only a fraction of the North's. Consequently, Southern troops generally fielded captured Federal or imported weapons.

By 1863 the Union and Confederacy had retired or relegated to rear-echelon use most of their smoothbore weapons. Most front-line troops thus entered battle with modern percussion rifled small arms. The specific type of these weapons was further dictated by the branch of service, rank, and often personal preference of the individual soldier.

The infantryman's percussion rifle-musket was the most ubiquitous—and deadly—small arm used in the war. Fully 90 percent of all combat casualties were inflicted by rifled muskets. The two most common types of percussion rifle-muskets were the caliber .58 U.S. Models 1861 and 1863 Springfield and the caliber .577 Models 1853 and 1856 British Enfield. Some 800,000 Models 1861 and 1863 weapons were produced at the Springfield Arsenal with more than 670,000 additional rifles manufactured by private contractors. Both the North and the South imported a combined total of more than 800,000 Enfields. The Springfield and Enfield accepted a triangular-bladed socket bayonet and had similar effective ranges of roughly 500 yards.

The caliber .45, telescopically sighted Whitworth sniper rifle was the most accurate Civil War small arm. Imported in limited numbers from Britain by the Confederacy, the hexagonal-bored Whitworth was capable of hitting targets at ranges in excess of 1,200 yards.

Other infantry longarms used in significant numbers included the caliber .54 U.S. Model 1841 "Mississippi Rifle," caliber .69 Model 1842 U.S. Percussion Musket, caliber .58 Model 1855 U.S. Percussion Rifle-Musket, and the imported calibers .54 and .58 Austrian Lorenz rifles.

For their long-range weapon, most cavalrymen preferred the shorter and lighter carbine to the infantryman's rifle-musket. Northern inventors took the lead in carbine development, and numerous models entered Union and, through capture, Confederate service.

Most of the new carbines were breechloaders while some were also repeating weapons. Many were chambered for the new self-contained metallic cartridges. Carbines designed for the metallic cartridges also benefited the North in that the South had no facilities to manufacture their ammunition. Such captured weapons were thus useless to Confederate cavalrymen once they had expended their special cartridges. For this reason, many Southern horsemen retained their older shotguns and muzzle-loading carbines throughout the war.

The caliber .52, seven-shot Spencer Repeating Carbine was probably the most popular cavalry arm of the war. The Spencer chambered a rimfire, copper cartridge fed through a tubular magazine in its buttstock. The caliber .44 lever-action Henry Rifle was also a popular repeater, but more prone to breakage than the Spencer. Although a single-shot weapon, the caliber .52 Sharps was an immensely popular carbine as well.

Other widely used carbines included the caliber .54 Burnside, caliber .50 Gallager, caliber .52 Joslyn, calibers .35 and .50 Maynard, caliber .54 Merrill, caliber .50 Smith, and the calibers .52 and .54 Starr.

Cavalry troopers and officers received most pistol issues. Although many infantrymen privately purchased handguns early in the war, most found that their firepower hardly justified their weight and thus discarded them. Cavalrymen, however, found pistols useful in close-range combat, and officers found them more effective than their traditional swords.

The most popular handguns of combatants in both armies were the caliber .36 Colt Navy and caliber .44 Colt Army revolvers. Both models were reliable, six-shot, rifled, percussion weapons. The rugged calibers .36 and .44 Remington revolvers also saw extensive use, as did arms produced by Savage Revolving Fire-Arms Co. and the Starr Arms Co. Several Northern companies also manufactured copies of Colt's revolvers as did a number of Confederate concerns.

The LeMat two-barrel "Grape-Shot Revolver" was the most exotic Civil War handgun. Designed by Dr. Jean Alexandre Francois LeMat of New Orleans and manufactured in France and England, the LeMat was a favorite among several prominent Confederate generals. The LeMat featured a caliber .42, nine-shot cylinder that revolved around a caliber .63 shotgun barrel. A device on the LeMat's hammer allowed selection of either the conventional cylinder chambers or the single shotgun barrel designed for buckshot.

—*Jeff Kinard*

See also Rifles; Smoothbores.

For further reading:

Edwards, William B. *Civil War Guns: The Complete Story of Federal and Confederate Small Arms: Design, Manufacture, Identification, Procurement, Issue, Employment, Effectiveness, and Postwar Disposal* (1962; reprint, 1997).
Lord, Francis A. *Civil War Collector's Encyclopedia* (1995).
McWhiney, Grady, and Perry Jamieson. *Attack and Die: Civil War Military Tactics and the Southern Heritage* (1982).

SMALLEY, GEORGE WASHBURN
(1833–1916)

New York Tribune *war correspondent*

The most intellectual of the Civil War newspaper correspondents, George W. Smalley was regarded as a Boston aristocrat, if not a snob, by his more Bohemian counterparts in the field. Still, his account of the battle of Antietam, obtained and delivered under the most difficult of circumstances, was the best piece of reporting to come out of the American Civil War.

Smalley was born in Franklin, Massachusetts, on 2 June 1833. With Puritan ancestry on both sides of his family, he graduated from Yale in 1853. He completed a law degree at Harvard in 1856, but instead of pursuing a career in law he became involved in the New England abolitionist movement, serving as a bodyguard for Wendell Phillips in 1860. When money troubles threatened to delay his wedding, Phillips helped get Smalley a position on the *New York Tribune*, considered one the most influential newspapers in the United States.

Smalley expected a desk job, but he was dispatched to Port Royal, South Carolina, to cover the war instead. In his dismay he neglected to cover a skirmish a hundred miles away at Williamstown, North Carolina, evoking a sharp reprimand from *Tribune* publisher Horace Greeley. It was a lesson the cub reporter never forgot. Smalley employed an informal, first-person-singular narrative writing style in his dispatches. In a letter to a friend in 1862, he observed that the voice and tone of traditional personal letter-writing best duplicated the realities of war for his Northern newspaper readers, situated far from the battle lines.

Smalley petitioned for a vacation in the spring of 1862, but he was assigned to cover General John C. Frémont in Virginia instead. Smalley became friendly with Frémont and used some of his reports to petition Washington for better support for the general. When General John Pope replaced Frémont in June 1862, Smalley and other reporters had to resort to subterfuge after Union general-in-chief Henry W. Halleck ordered them to leave the field of battle. Smalley eventually obtained an appointment as an aide to General John Sedgwick, with the rank of captain. He had no specific duties and apparently wore his uniform or civilian clothes as the circumstances of the moment dictated. The only known time he preformed any direct military service was when General Joseph Hooker asked him to carry a message during the battle of Antietam in September 1862.

Smalley's account of Antietam, published in the *Tribune* on 19 September 1862, was the best battle report of the war, according to fellow correspondents Henry Villard and A. D. Richardson, and has been labeled the "greatest scoop" of the Civil War by historians. It was acclaimed by eyewitness military and journalistic observers at the time and reprinted in some 1,400 newspapers around the country. The competing *New York Evening Post* observed that it "ranks for clearness, animation and apparent accuracy with the best battle pieces in literature." The athletic Smalley, who had once stroked crew for Yale, got his material by dashing about on horseback observing the fighting from the front line, at times ahead of the Union line. Flying shrapnel once tore his blue jacket, and his horse was hit twice. Hooker's aides proclaimed him "bravest of the brave" and Hooker later recalled that he had never seen even a veteran soldier "exhibit more tranquil fortitude and unshaken valor than was exhibited by that young man."

Smalley's report, written beginning on the evening of 17 September, began with a reference that his educated readers would understand: "Fierce and desperate battle between 200,000 men has raged since daylight, yet night closes on an uncertain field. It is the greatest fight since Waterloo—all over the field contested with an obstinacy equal even to Waterloo." It contained detailed strategic information gathered from Union commanders such as Generals George McClellan, Ambrose E. Burnside, and Hooker, and firsthand accounts of desperate fighting and bravery. An accompanying map showed the positions of Union and Confederate forces and sites of the most vicious battles. In particular, Smalley complimented Hooker for his bravery and tactical ability. Using the first person, he wrote, "I have no personal relations whatever with him, never saw him till the day before the fight, and don't like his politics or opinions in general. But what are politics in such a battle?"

In keeping with early Civil War battlefield reports, Smalley waited until the last of sixty-eight paragraphs before reporting his estimate of casualties in what turned out to be stalemate for both sides. The beginning of the story was transmitted by telegraph, but an operator diverted it to the War Department, which was desperate for any news of the fighting. That account was read personally by President Lincoln. Meanwhile, Smalley hopped trains to Baltimore and Washington, scribbling the story throughout the night while standing beneath a dimly burning oil lamp in a boxcar. Compositors deciphered the nearly unreadable manuscript, and an extra edition hit the streets of New York early the following morning, producing a "masterpiece" of Civil War reporting, according to historian Louis M. Starr. Most significantly, Smalley's account failed to employ the unrestrained boosterism of previous Northern battlefield reports. Smalley was graphic yet restrained in his appraisal of the fighting instead, explaining the battle plan and observing that poor coordination hampered the fighting efforts of the North.

Smalley returned to the battlefield the next day, but he contracted camp fever and was relieved of his reporting duties a few weeks later. He made a tour of various army headquarters in the East in early 1863 but was otherwise relegated to editorial writing for the duration of the Civil War. From 1867 to 1906, Smalley was a pioneer foreign correspondent, reporting for the *Tribune* in London and later covering the United States for the London *Times*. He died in Washington D.C., on 4 April 1916.

—*Richard Digby-Junger*

See also Greeley, Horace; *New York Tribune*; War Correspondents.

For further reading:

Andrews, J. Cutler. *The North Reports the Civil War* (1955).
Bullard, F. Lewiston. *Famous War Correspondents* (1914).
Mathews, Joseph J. *George W. Smalley: Forty Years a Foreign Correspondent* (1973).
Starr, Louis M. *Bohemian Brigade: Civil War Newsmen in Action* (1954; reprint, 1987).
Weeks, James. "The Civil War's Greatest Scoop." *American Heritage* (1989).

SMALLS, ROBERT
(1839–1915)
Escaped slave and Union pilot

Robert Smalls was born 5 April 1839 in Beaufort, South Carolina, to a house slave, Lydia Smalls. His father was unknown, although there was speculation that he was either the offspring of Moses Goldsmith, a wealthy Jewish merchant of Charleston, or a product of an illicit affair between Lydia and her owner, John McKee, who died in 1848. Upon McKee's death, his son Henry McKee inherited Lydia and her son Robert. Although the younger McKee treated Robert and his mother well, Robert, because he saw the inequities and cruelties suffered by slaves around him, longed for freedom.

In 1851, Smalls moved with his owner to Charleston, where his owner hired him out in various occupations, including waiter, lamplighter, cotton stevedore, cotton foreman, horse driver on the Charleston wharves, sailmaker, rigger, and sailor. In 1857, Henry McKee permitted Smalls to hire himself out with the stipulation that Smalls would pay him $15 per month. In the same year, Smalls married Hannah Jones, the slave of Samuel Kingman. When the couple's first child, Elizabeth, was born on 12 February 1858, Smalls offered to purchase his wife and daughter from Kingman for $800. By 1861 Smalls had saved $700.00 for the purchase, but the Civil War provided him an opportunity to escape with his family without having to pay for their freedom.

By the time of the war, Smalls had become a skilled seaman with extensive knowledge of the waterways of South Carolina and Georgia. In 1861 he earned $16 a month as a sailor on the *Planter*, a cotton steamer that had been built in Charleston in 1860. It was 150 feet long, 7 feet 10 inches deep, and had a 10-foot beam. It could carry 1,400 bales of cotton or 1,000 men.

In late 1861, the Confederate government chartered the privately owned *Planter* and converted it to a dispatch vessel for General Roswell Ripley, who was second in command of Charleston's defenses. Under the Confederate government's control of the *Planter*, Smalls was elevated to wheelman. Though in fact he performed the role of a pilot, the title was not bestowed on Smalls because he was a slave. Working in such an important capacity, Smalls learned the signals that were given to clear passage through Confederate forts and batteries in Charleston harbor. He also knew the locations of hidden Confederate mines because he had helped to place them. Armed with this knowledge, Smalls and the black crew aboard the *Planter* developed an escape plan in April 1862. On 13 May, Smalls seized the opportunity to steal the ship when all the whites, including the captain, went into town, leaving only the eight black crewmen aboard. The black crewmen took the vessel to the North Atlantic wharf, where Smalls's family of three and five others were waiting to be picked up.

The previous night, 200 pounds of ammunition and four guns had been loaded on the ship for transport to Fort Riley and Fort Sumter. With this arsenal, Smalls and the others vowed to blow up the ship and themselves if they were caught.

Because Smalls knew the appropriate signals, he and his party of 15 were able to pass safely through the Confederate forts and batteries that defended Charleston harbor. Wearing the captain's hat and jacket, Smalls mimicked his gait and gestures to deceive the Confederate guards as the *Planter* passed through each checkpoint. After getting through Fort Jackson and beyond the guns of Fort Sumter, the last obstacle was to reach the Union fleet that blockaded the harbor without drawing fire from Union forces.

The *Planter*'s crewmen lowered their guns and raised a white sheet of surrender as they approached the closest Union ship, *Onward*. The Union commander held his fire when he saw the white sheet and heard Smalls's shouts of surrender. The *Onward*'s captain boarded the *Planter* and took possession of it. The incident was reported in newspapers around the world. Union supporters hailed Robert Smalls as a genuine war hero because of his courage. Confederates were not so impressed, and a $4,000 reward was offered for his capture.

Although the value of the *Planter* and its cargo was estimated as being anywhere from $30,000 to $70,000, the prize money given to Smalls and his crewmen was based on a much lower estimate. Nevertheless, Smalls's remarkable feat greatly influenced the 1862 debates over slavery and the Union's use of black soldiers. General David Hunter, commander of the Union's Department of the South, sent Smalls to Washington, D.C., to confer with President Abraham Lincoln and Secretary of State Edwin Stanton about the organization of black regiments. Smalls returned with Stanton's letter that authorized Hunter to recruit 5,000 black volunteers in South Carolina.

The intelligence and courage demonstrated by Smalls and his crew on the *Planter* also served to refute the proslavery argument that blacks were inferior to whites. Smalls's example provided evidence for abolitionists who wanted to end slavery in the South and for integrationists who wanted to abolish Jim Crow laws in the North.

During the first year that Smalls worked as a pilot for the Union, he did so without pay. He was placed on the *Crusader* and saw action at Simon's Bluff, South Carolina (June 1862); at Fort Sumter while aboard the

ironclad *Keokuk* (7 April 1863); and at Folly Island Creek, South Carolina, while serving on the *Planter* (May 1863). In the spring of 1863, Smalls was finally placed on the payroll with a pilot's salary of $50 per month.

While patrolling Folly Island Creek in May 1863, the *Planter* came under heavy Confederate attack. The *Planter*'s captain ordered Smalls to beach the vessel and surrender, but Smalls, knowing what would happen to him if he were captured, continued to steer the *Planter* out of the enemy's reach. The Confederates' relentless bombardment caused the *Planter*'s captain to panic and leave the pilot house to take cover below. Smalls then took command of the vessel and successfully steered it to safe waters. For this act of bravery under fire, Smalls was promoted to captain of the *Planter* in December 1863. He remained the ship's captain for the duration of the war, with a salary of $150 per month. From May to December 1864, the *Planter* was under repair in Philadelphia, where Smalls had taken it, even though he had never before navigated that part of the Atlantic coast.

Near the end of the war, the *Planter* was used for transporting General William T. Sherman's troops into South Carolina and ex-slaves to homesteads granted to them by Sherman. In June 1865, Smalls was ordered to Baltimore to be discharged. The *Planter* was put out of commission in 1866.

After the war, Smalls became a landowner and a prominent South Carolina politician. For $700 he bought the house of his former owner, Henry McKee, on Prince Street in Beaufort, South Carolina. He served as a delegate to the South Carolina constitutional convention in January 1868. In the same year, he was elected for one term to the lower house of the state legislature. Then he was elected to the state senate in 1870; and in 1872 he served as a delegate to the Republican National Convention.

Smalls served several terms in the U.S. House of Representatives between 1875 and 1887. When the Democrats regained political control of South Carolina in 1877, the Republicans who served in the state legislature during Reconstruction were targeted for investigation. Smalls got caught up in the investigations and was indicted on the charge of accepting a $5,000 bribe from the Republican Printing Company. Although Smalls was convicted by a jury and sentenced to three years in jail, the governor pardoned him. Reportedly, a deal had been struck between the federal government and the state whereby federal suits against white South Carolinians who had been charged with violating federal election laws would be dropped if the state dismissed charges against Reconstruction legislators. During the latter years of his political life, Smalls again served as a delegate to the state's constitutional convention in 1895 and was appointed customs collector for Beaufort in

1899 at a salary of $1,000 per year, plus 3 percent commission fees. With an interruption from 15 February 1894 to 22 June 1898, Smalls held the customs position until 1913.

On 22 February 1915, Smalls died in his sleep at the house where he and his mother had been a slave. His first wife, Hannah Jones, who died in 1883, bore him three children: Elizabeth (born 12 February 1858); Robert, Jr. (born 1861 and died in his third year); and Sarah (born 1 December 1863). Smalls married a second time in 1890 or 1891 to Annie Wigg, a teacher. This union produced one child, William Robert, who was born in 1892.

—Dorothy L. Drinkard

See also *Planter*.

For further reading:

Christopher, Maurine. *America's Black Congressmen* (1971).

Sterling, Dorothy. *Captain of the Planter* (1958).

Tindall, George Brown. *South Carolina Negroes 1877–1900* (1952).

Uya, Okon Edet. *From Slavery to Public Service: Robert Smalls, 1830–1915* (1971).

SMITH, ANDREW JACKSON
(1815–1897)
Union general

Born the son of Revolutionary War and War of 1812 veteran Samuel Smith in Bucks County, Pennsylvania, Andrew Jackson Smith was named after the Hero of New Orleans. Educated locally, Smith received an appointment to the U.S. Military Academy in 1834. He graduated thirty-sixth of forty-five in the class of 1838.

Upon graduation, Smith served with the 1st Dragoons on the western frontier. During the Mexican-American War, Smith served primarily in California and would remain in the far West for much of his pre–Civil War military career.

A major in the 1st Dragoons stationed in California at the commencement of the Civil War, Smith briefly held the volunteer commission of colonel of the 2d California Cavalry. Since this unit was not designated to leave the state, Smith resigned that commission and was transferred by the army to Missouri, where he came under the command of Henry Halleck. Promoted to colonel of the 2d Cavalry, Smith became Halleck's chief of cavalry in early 1862 and was promoted to brigadier general of volunteers in March 1862.

Smith continued to serve under Halleck through the advance on Corinth, Mississippi. In late summer 1862, he was sent to command at Covington, Kentucky, and through the fall commanded a division under Gordon Granger in the Army of Kentucky. In December he was given command of a division under William T. Sherman and led his men at Chickasaw Bluffs. Continuing under Sherman in John A. McClernand's Arkansas Post campaign in January 1863, Smith next commanded his division in the operations against Vicksburg.

He fought at Champion's Hill on 16 May 1863 and at Big Black River the following day commanding the 10th Division of XIII Corps. He continued in this command through the siege of Vicksburg and, after the city's capitulation, commanded his division in the Jackson, Mississippi, campaign of 5–25 July.

In August 1863, Smith was placed in command of the District of Columbus, Kentucky. He remained in that command until he was called on to command a division in Sherman's Meridian campaign in early 1864. After this expedition, he was transferred to Nathaniel P. Banks's Department of the Gulf and commanded detachments of XVI and XVII Corps of the Army of the Tennessee in the Red River campaign. Smith assumed the advance at the beginning of this campaign, moving what was generally referred to as his corps into Alexandria, Louisiana, on 18 March 1864. Smith fought in all the major engagements of the campaign and was promoted to major general of volunteers in May 1864.

During the summer of 1864, Smith commanded his corps out of LaGrange, Tennessee, leading them on an expedition to Tupelo, Mississippi, in July. Smith occupied Tupelo on 13 July and was attacked there by Nathan Bedford Forrest's cavalry the following day. Smith repulsed the attack, inflicting approximately 40 percent casualties on Forrest's force.

Later in the summer, Smith was sent with the 1st and 3d Divisions of XVI Corps to Missouri to aid with the repulse of Sterling Price's Missouri raid. He was summoned quickly east with his command to Nashville in early December 1864 to augment George H. Thomas's forces defending the city against John Bell Hood. He was commended for his actions at Nashville and was later given a brevet promotion in the regular army to major general for his performance there. In February 1865 he was given command of the entire XVI Corps, Army of the Tennessee. He led his corps in the spring to Mobile, where they fought in that campaign.

Although he was very well thought of by his commanders, Smith spent most of his Civil War career moving from army to army filling gaps and meeting emergencies. As a result he did not become as well known as some less talented officers.

After the war, Smith chose to remain in the army, becoming the colonel of the 7th Cavalry in 1866. When President Ulysses S. Grant offered him the postmaster's position in St. Louis, Missouri, in 1869, he resigned his commission to accept. During the next few decades he occupied a number of positions in St. Louis and was active in the state militia. As a reward for his wartime services, the U.S. Congress passed an act at the end of 1888 reinstating Smith in the army at the rank of colonel of cavalry so that he could retire at that rank. When the act took effect in January 1889, Smith was officially part of the army for a day before retiring later in the day. He lived the remainder of his life quietly in St. Louis, where he died on 30 January 1897.

—*David S. Heidler and Jeanne T. Heidler*

See also Red River Campaign; Tupelo, Battle of.

For further reading:

Hollings, Celestine Caldwell. *Our Ancestors: Daughters of Union Veterans of the Civil War, 1861–1865* (1996).

SMITH, CALEB BLOOD
(1808–1864)
United States secretary of the interior

Born in Boston, Massachusetts, Caleb Blood Smith moved with his family to Cincinnati, Ohio, when he was a small child. He was educated in local schools before attending the College of Cincinnati and Miami University. After leaving college, he studied law and began his practice in 1828 in Indiana. Along with his successful career as an Indiana attorney, Smith also became involved in state politics.

Smith was a strong supporter of the Whig Party, and when he failed to gain election to the state legislature, he bought a newspaper that he named the *Indiana Sentinel* and campaigned on its pages until he was successful. He rose to various leadership positions within the state legislature and used his position to advocate various internal improvements for the state of Indiana.

In 1842 Smith was elected to the United States House of Representatives, beginning his congressional career. During the 1840s Smith generally sided with his fellow Whigs, particularly in his opposition to the expansion of slavery. For that reason he strongly opposed the annexation of Texas and the subsequent hostilities with Mexico. In 1848 Smith campaigned for Zachary Taylor and was rewarded with appointment to the United States–Mexico Boundary Commission. Once that mission had been accomplished, Smith returned to private legal practice, now in Cincinnati, Ohio.

Besides his practice, Smith became involved in various business pursuits, including Ohio's growing railroad industry. After suffering business reverses, Smith returned to Indiana, where he again assumed a leadership role in the state's political scene—now as a Republican. He served as a delegate to the Republican National Convention in Chicago in 1860, where he supported the nomination of Abraham Lincoln. Following Lincoln's nomination, Smith was one of the ticket's most enthusiastic campaigners.

When Lincoln was elected in November 1860, Smith was selected as secretary of the interior. One of his primary duties during his short time in office was to supervise the various Indian agents in their attempts to keep the Native American population out of the Civil War. Because this activity was closely related to issues of national defense, Smith attempted to work closely with both Lincoln's secretaries of war, first Simon Cameron and then Edwin Stanton. Both men seemed somewhat impatient with what they perhaps saw as Smith's interference in their spheres and generally dealt with Smith through their underlings.

Still, Smith worked tirelessly to ensure the safety of the frontier, warning both Cameron and Stanton about the danger to the Southwest of Confederate activities and the need for more soldiers to guard against hostile Indian actions, particularly by the Sioux. In September 1862 Smith wrote to Stanton suggesting that, because the Sioux were attacking white settlers and Pawnee allied with the United States in Nebraska Territory, it might be wise to raise volunteers in that territory and to arm the Pawnee. Stanton, through one of his assistant secretaries, authorized more volunteers, but refused to arm the Pawnee. Smith must have felt some vindication later in the year when he was allowed to authorize his agents in the Indian Territory to muster into service Native Americans who wanted to fight for the United States so that they could be used against Indians attacking settlements in Kansas and Nebraska.

By that time Smith, whose health had never been strong, began to suffer the effects of overwork and asked the president if he might resign his position. Lincoln consented and appointed Smith a United States district judge in Indianapolis so that he could be near his home. For the remainder of the year Smith spent much of his time dealing with Copperhead activities in Indiana, particularly with those people who sought to obstruct the enrollment of recruits and draftees.

Still working entirely too hard, given what was probably a failing heart, Smith died suddenly on 7 January 1864 while attending to his duties in the Indianapolis federal courthouse.

—*David S. Heidler and Jeanne T. Heidler*

See also Copperheads; Sioux Indians.

For further reading:

Thomas, Richard J. "Caleb Blood Smith: Whig Orator and Politician—Lincoln's Secretary of Interior" (Ph.D. dissertation, 1969).

SMITH, CHARLES FERGUSON
(1807–1862)
Union general

Born to Samuel Blair Smith, a U.S. Army surgeon, and Mary Ferguson Smith in Philadelphia, Pennsylvania, Charles Ferguson received an appointment to the U.S. Military Academy in 1820 at age fourteen and graduated nineteenth of thirty-seven in

the class of 1825. Commissioned a second lieutenant at age eighteen, Ferguson saw duty as a part of the 2d Artillery on the frontier before becoming an instructor at West Point in 1829. While at West Point he rose to the position of commandant of cadets, a billet he occupied during the cadet years of his future commander, Ulysses S. Grant. Leaving West Point in 1842, Smith served at a variety of posts in the Northeast, including Governors Island, New York, before being sent to join Zachary Taylor's Army of Observation in Texas in 1845.

During the Mexican-American War, Smith participated in all the early battles in northern Mexico under Taylor before being moved to the army of Winfield Scott in preparation for the Mexico City campaign. He fought in that entire campaign. At the end of the war he had earned three brevet promotions.

After the war, Smith engaged in a variety of duties. He served on several boards dealing with reform of military training for the army, conducted topographical surveys, and participated in Albert Sidney Johnston's Utah expedition. After the conclusion of that campaign, he remained behind to command the Department of Utah. As civil war threatened in the East in early 1861, Smith was still in command in Utah but was promptly summoned to Washington.

Upon his arrival in the capital in the early spring of 1861, Smith, at the rank of brevet colonel, was placed in command of all the troops in Washington, D.C. At the end of April 1861 he was sent to Fort Columbus, New York, to head the recruiting efforts there. In August he was promoted to brigadier general of volunteers and was dispatched to Kentucky, where he was given command of the Department of Western Kentucky. The following month he was promoted to colonel in the regular army.

Throughout the fall of 1861, Smith operated out of Paducah, Kentucky, where he primarily dealt with Southern sympathizers, before joining Ulysses S. Grant in the campaign against Fort Henry and Fort Donelson in Tennessee. As a preliminary to this campaign, Smith led an expedition into western Kentucky in January 1862 to determine the transportation network in that area and in northern Tennessee. Commanding one of Grant's two divisions, Smith led his men in the investing of Fort Henry before moving overland to Fort Donelson.

At Fort Donelson, Smith commanded the Federal left and distinguished himself with one of the pivotal charges of the siege. On 15 February, Smith commanded an attack on some of the Confederate outworks, successfully occupying them by the afternoon. When the Confederate commander, Simon Bolivar Buckner, asked for surrender terms, his emissaries reached Smith's lines first and were taken to the general. After hearing their request for the appointment of commissioners to determine terms, Smith replied that if it were up to him he would grant no surrender terms. He later advised Grant

to accept nothing but unconditional surrender; Grant accepted this advice, which gained him one of his first Civil War nicknames: "Unconditional Surrender" Grant. Both Grant and theater commander Henry Halleck praised Smith in extravagant terms for his performance at Fort Donelson. Halleck recommended his promotion to major general, a promotion that was forthcoming in March 1862.

After the fall of Fort Donelson, Grant sent Smith to occupy Clarksville, Tennessee, and then Nashville. In the middle of March, Smith received command of the advance of the Union movement toward Albert Sidney Johnston's position at Corinth, Mississippi. Smith established the staging area at Savannah, Tennessee, near Pittsburg Landing to await the remainder of the army. While preparing this position, Smith injured his shin when he fell trying to get into a rowboat. The wound became infected and he was forced to relinquish his command to Lewis Wallace before Grant arrived. He was unable to participate in the two-day battle of Shiloh.

After Shiloh, Smith's infection steadily grew worse. Grant kept his former commandant at his headquarters, but the doctors' efforts proved futile. On the afternoon of 25 April 1862, Smith died. Grant personally wrote to Smith's widow informing her of his death.

—*David S. Heidler and Jeanne T. Heidler*

See also Fort Donelson, Battle of.

For further reading:
Cooling, Benjamin Franklin. *Forts Henry and Donelson: The Key to the Confederate Heartland* (1987).
Dubelier, Eric Alan. "Charles F. Smith: The Forgotten Soldier" (Honors thesis, 1977).

SMITH, CHARLES HENRY
(1826–1903)
Confederate officer, author

Born to Asahel Reid Smith and Caroline Ann Maguire Smith in Lawrenceville, Georgia, Charles Henry Smith attended the University of Georgia and studied law. After admission to the Georgia bar, he practiced around Rome, Georgia. Upon Georgia's secession and the formation of the Confederacy, Smith enlisted in the Confederate army. He rose to the rank of major and served primarily as a staff officer to fellow Georgians generals Francis S. Bartow and George Thomas Anderson. Late in the war he also served as a judge advocate.

While performing his various staff duties, Smith wrote letters home to the *Southern Confederacy* of Rome, Georgia, under the pseudonym "Bill Arp." Using an uneducated dialect, Smith initially criticized the war. The character, however, evolved over the years into more of a rural philosopher. The letters became popular on the home front and among soldiers in the field and are still valuable for their insights into the views of the common soldier.

After the war, while resuming his law practice in Rome and brief involvement in politics, Smith parlayed the success of the "Bill Arp" character into a writing career. He wrote a weekly "Bill Arp" letter to the Atlanta *Constitution* for twenty-five years. The letters were syndicated in various Southern newspapers, and Smith published several "Bill Arp" books. His clever use of satire and his biting social commentary are still studied today as windows on the Southern mind of the Civil War and post–Civil War period. Smith died in Cartersville, Georgia.

—*David S. Heidler and Jeanne T. Heidler*

See also Newspapers.
For further reading:
Brantley, Rabun Lee. *Georgia Journalism of the Civil War Period* (1929).
Parker, David B. *Alias Bill Arp: Charles Henry Smith and the South's "Godly Heritage"* (1991).

SMITH, CHARLES HENRY
(1827–1902)
Union general

Born to Aaron Smith and Sally Gile Smith in Hollis, Maine, Charles Henry Smith was educated at Waterville College (later Colby College). After graduation, he served as principal of a Maine secondary school and studied law. The outbreak of the Civil War interrupted those studies.

With the beginning of hostilities, Smith immediately volunteered for duty with a volunteer cavalry regiment being raised in Maine. He was soon elected captain of his company in what became the 1st Maine Cavalry. After training, the regiment was sent to the Army of the Potomac and was attached to Irvin McDowell's corps campaign. In May 1862 he and his regiment conducted a reconnaissance toward the Shenandoah Valley, but otherwise did not see any serious action.

Smith and the 1st Maine saw their first serious action at Cedar Mountain on 9 August 1862 and then at Second Bull Run. Following Bull Run, Smith was assigned to duty at Frederick, Maryland, as provost marshal. He remained there during Robert E. Lee's first invasion of Maryland through January 1863. After leaving Frederick, Smith returned to the 1st Maine and shortly thereafter was promoted to the rank of major and in March to lieutenant colonel.

In the Chancellorsville campaign Smith commanded the 1st Maine during George Stoneman's raid toward Richmond. Returning to the Army of the Potomac in late May 1863, he fought in all the engagements of the Gettysburg campaign, beginning with Brandy Station on 9 June. He continued to command the regiment at Aldie

and Middleburg before leading his men into Pennsylvania where they fought at Gettysburg. In the midst of this campaign, Smith was promoted to colonel. On the third day of the battle of Gettysburg, Smith and the 1st Maine occupied much of their time protecting infantry and artillery flanks on the right of the Union line.

Following Gettysburg, Smith participated in the pursuit of Lee's army and then at the end of the year in the Mine Run campaign. Toward the end of that campaign, he temporarily commanded the brigade. From 21–22 December 1863 Smith led his men on an expedition toward Luray, Virginia. By the spring of 1864 at the commencement of Ulysses S. Grant's campaign against Lee, Smith was back in command of the 1st Maine. He commanded the regiment through the early phases of that campaign under Philip Sheridan. He fought in the engagements at Todd's Tavern, the crossing at the South Anna, Trevilian Station, and at St. Mary's Church near Charles City Court House on 24 June. In that engagement Smith was seriously wounded in the thigh and commended for his bravery for refusing to leave the field until the battle was over. Thirty years later he received the Medal of Honor for his actions that day.

After recovering from his wounds Smith, returned to the regiment and on 27 August was made commander of the brigade again. Shortly after his return he fought at Ream's Station and then along the Weldon Railroad. For Smith's actions during these campaign's, George Gordon Meade, the commander of the Army of the Potomac, recommended that Smith be given a brevet promotion to brigadier general in November 1864. Meade's recommendation was accepted, and Smith was brevetted brigadier general of volunteers for his actions at St. Mary's Church.

Smith continued to command his brigade through the end of the Appomattox campaign in April 1865, particularly distinguishing himself at Sayler's Creek. He continued in the army until August 1865, when he was mustered out with the 1st Maine and returned to his home state to practice law. Smith, however, missed the military life and when in 1866 he was offered a regular colonel's commission (he was later brevetted brigadier general in the regular army for his actions at Sayler's Creek and major general for his service during the war), he accepted.

As colonel of the 28th United States Infantry, Smith served at a variety of western posts over the next twenty-five years. He retired to a home he had acquired in Washington, D.C., in 1891. He lived there quietly until his death on 17 July 1902.

—*David S. Heidler and Jeanne T. Heidler*

See also Aldie, Virginia, Battle of; Brandy Station, Battle of; Sayler's Creek / Harper's Farm, Battle of.
For further reading:
Holmes, Torlief S. *Horse Soldiers in Blue* (1985).

SMITH, EDMUND KIRBY
(1824–1893)
Confederate general

Edmund Kirby Smith was born 16 May 1824 in Saint Augustine, Florida. To prepare him for a military career, Smith's family sent him to a strict preparatory school in Virginia designed for those who aspired to a West Point education. At West Point, Smith turned in a mediocre scholastic performance and briefly considered resignation. In 1845 he graduated twenty-fifth in a class of forty-one. Smith secured his commission only after testimony by several West Point instructors that his myopia would not hamper his army career. Thus, the bespectacled and prematurely balding young officer joined the 5th U.S. Infantry in Texas as a second lieutenant under Zachary Taylor. Although Smith served with gallantry during the Mexican-American War, he complained of Taylor's failure to adhere to textbook military strategy. When passed over for promotion, Smith filed a protest and eventually received an elevation in rank to first lieutenant. After the war, Smith worked on behalf of a soldier's lobby representing the interests of war orphans and widows. After brief service in Missouri,

Edmund Kirby Smith (*Library of Congress*)

Smith received a promotion to captain and an assignment to West Point as a professor of mathematics. In 1852 Smith returned to active duty and in 1855 began service in the elite 2d Cavalry, organized by Secretary of War Jefferson Davis.

While stationed in Texas, Smith received news of Abraham Lincoln's election, which prompted him to write that he would rather shoulder a musket for the Confederacy than serve as commander in chief under Lincoln. Following the first wave of state secessions, Smith resigned his commission and offered his services to the Confederacy. Smith received the assignment to coordinate the vital defenses around New Orleans. Rather than report directly to Louisiana, however, Smith first visited family in Florida. This prompted his reassignment to the less appealing duty of organizing recruits in Virginia.

Smith was pessimistic about Southern enlistees and was critical of officers. He maintained that the army's position at Harper's Ferry was untenable and, along with his commanding officer Joseph E. Johnston, succeeded in having the Army of the Shenandoah moved to Winchester, Virginia. This change of base helped Confederate forces to concentrate rapidly against the Federals at First Bull Run. During the battle, Smith, by that time a brigadier, suffered what appeared to be a mortal wound. Although the wound proved comparatively minor and his participation in the fighting was minimal, Southern papers portrayed him as a hero. During his convalescence Smith courted and married a Virginian, whom the press christened the "Bride of the Confederacy." On 11 October 1861, Smith received a promotion to major general, and in March 1862 he took command of the Department of East Tennessee. Jefferson Davis believed that Smith's status as a Southern hero would help strengthen the Confederate presence there. Upon his arrival, Smith found the department in complete chaos and accused Davis of misrepresenting the assignment.

In July, Smith and Braxton Bragg, whose district bordered Smith's, initiated plans to combine forces at Chattanooga and use Tennessee as a staging ground for a raid into Kentucky. Although Smith offered to place his command under Bragg, Richmond's failure to consolidate the two armies under one general allowed Smith to operate independently. Smith took advantage of the loophole in command structure and unilaterally moved into Kentucky with plans to seize Cincinnati. Despite early victories, however, rumors of a Federal army on the march from Ohio compelled Smith to seek concentration with Bragg, by then also in Kentucky. Before the armies could concentrate, however, the Federals struck Bragg at Perryville, Kentucky, forcing his retreat. Bragg's retreat forced Smith to return to Tennessee. Smith blamed Bragg for the campaign's failure and considered resignation from the army. Instead, he accepted a promotion to lieutenant general and, in January 1863, reassignment to command of the Southwestern Army. Before he crossed the Mississippi, Richmond expanded his command to the Department of the Trans-Mississippi.

Smith's orders were to keep the river open and to defend the lower Mississippi Valley. He felt beholden, however, to the Arkansans in the Confederate Congress, who were instrumental in securing his appointment as commander of the Trans-Mississippi. Subsequently, Smith focused on the recapture of Arkansas and an invasion of Missouri, often at the expense of the rest of his department. He frequently withheld reinforcements from Louisianian Richard Taylor, commander of the District of Western Louisiana, and ordered him to abandon rather than to contest territory. This approach sparked a vitriolic relationship between the two generals that hampered operations. In the summer of 1863, Joseph E. Johnston and John C. Pemberton also criticized Smith for his failure to provide sufficient relief to Vicksburg. The fall of Vicksburg essentially cut off the Trans-Mississippi from the rest of the Confederacy. Smith's department became known as the "Kirby Smithdom" and functioned with a tremendous degree of autonomy. Davis granted Smith a wide range of civilian as well as military powers and elevated him to the rank of permanent general.

In March 1864, the Federals launched a pincer movement toward Shreveport, Louisiana, moving north along the Red River and south from Arkansas. Smith's strategy during the Red River campaign was to use interior lines and trade territory for time. Disgusted with the surrender of his territory, Richard Taylor unilaterally halted his retreat just forty miles south of Shreveport and dealt the advancing Federal column under Nathaniel P. Banks twin defeats at Mansfield and Pleasant Hill (8 and 9 April). Rather than allow pursuit of the retreating Federals in Louisiana, however, Smith detached the majority of Taylor's army and led them into Arkansas in pursuit of the Federal column under Frederick Steele. On 30 April, Smith caught up with Steele's retreat at Jenkins' Ferry, where, despite a tactical Confederate victory, the Federals continued their withdrawal to Little Rock. Smith's strategy stopped both Federal columns but destroyed neither. Taylor openly attacked Smith's strategy, and the resulting war of words led to Taylor's transfer. Yet much of the Southern press praised Taylor's efforts and castigated Smith's strategy as a blunder. In January 1865, rumors in the Confederate Congress alleged that Smith intentionally ordered Taylor's retreat to allow cotton speculators access to Louisiana's interior. Although they were never proved, the allegations damaged Smith's reputation.

With the surrender of Confederate armies in the East, Smith considered Lee and Davis prisoners of war and criticized Confederate deserters as unpatriotic. On 2 June, in Galveston, Texas, Smith reluctantly surrendered the last major Confederate command in the field to Edward R. S. Canby. On 26 June, Smith fled to Mexico and one month later to Cuba. In November he returned to Virginia and signed an amnesty oath. After several failed business attempts, Smith found employment in the academic world and from 1870 to 1875 worked as president at the University of Nashville. For the next eighteen years he taught mathematics at the University of the South in Sewanee, Tennessee. The last surviving full Confederate general, Smith died from a lingering respiratory ailment on 28 March 1893. He was laid to rest at the university in Sewanee.

—*Jeffery S. Prushankin*

See also Bull Run, First Battle of; Jenkins's Ferry, Battle of; Perryville, Battle of; Vicksburg Campaign.

For further reading:

Connelly, Thomas L. *Army of the Heartland: The Army of Tennessee, 1861–1861* (1967).

Johnson, Ludwell. *The Red River Campaign: Politics and Cotton in the Civil War* (1958).

Kerby, Robert L. *Kirby Smith's Confederacy: The Trans-Mississippi South, 1863–1865* (1972).

Parks, Joseph H. *General Edmund Kirby Smith, C.S.A.* (1954).

Parrish, T. Michael. *Richard Taylor: Soldier Prince of Dixie* (1992).

SMITH, GERRIT
(1797–1874)
Abolitionist and reformer

Gerrit Smith was born on 6 March 1797 in Utica, New York, the son of Peter Smith, Sr., whose brief partnership with John Jacob Astor in the fur trade had made him wealthy. Landed wealth came to the family both through Gerrit's mother, who was a Livingston, and from the shrewd purchases that his father made from Indians in Oneida and Onondaga counties, New York. Eventually the family's real estate holdings would stretch into Pennsylvania and Virginia to create an estate valued at $400,000 and generating an annual income of some $60,000. Yet disturbing incidents of mental and physical illness troubled the family. Gerrit's older brother, Peter, Jr., died after a brief life plagued by alcoholism and mental illness. A younger brother was declared clinically insane and eventually was lodged in an asylum. Gerrit, apparently the most stable of the siblings, nonetheless wrestled with hypochondria and depression his entire life. After he was implicated in the planning of John Brown's raid at Harper's Ferry in 1859, Smith became mentally ill and required confinement in an insane asylum in Utica. It was within this context of eccentricity occasionally edging toward mental illness that Gerrit Smith made his way through life as a philanthropist who embraced an extraordinary assortment of nineteenth-century reform movements.

Smith attended Hamilton College, graduating in 1818 and thereafter helping his father manage the family

fortune. Eventually Smith exercised exclusive control over these vast assets, and under his direction they prospered further to give him both the time and the money for good works. His family home at Peterboro, New York, became a center of reform activity. He was an advocate for temperance, dress reform, women's suffrage, and vegetarianism, frequently serving these movements as a generous benefactor. It was inevitable that he would espouse abolitionism, and his service in that cause is frequently cited as his most lasting legacy.

He initially supported the colonization of emancipated slaves, but by the 1830s he had adopted abolitionism and soon became a leader in the cause, persuading other influential figures, such as his cousin Elizabeth Cady Stanton, to take it up as well. Smith was vice president of the American Anti-Slavery Society and became the president of the New York Anti-Slavery Society in 1836. In 1839, he donated an extensive tract of 21,000 wilderness acres in western Virginia to the abolitionist Oberlin College of which Owen Brown, father of John, was a trustee.

In the 1840s, Smith helped to found the Liberty Party and unsuccessfully sought the governorship of New York on its ticket in 1840. He declined the party's nomination for the presidency in 1848. Instead, he joined disaffected Democrats and Whigs in the more expansive free-soil movement. This was the first widespread political consequence of the possibility that the western territories gained in the war with Mexico might become slave states. These men were the nucleus of the Free Soil Party, and Smith's association with them marked a growing militancy in his opposition to slavery. He promoted obstruction of the Fugitive Slave Act of 1850 by abetting slave escapes to Canada. Smith won a seat in Congress in 1852 as an independent, but his tendency to whimsy again surfaced when he ended his term with a resignation. He had recently been admitted to the bar, so he opened a law practice in Peterboro.

The Kansas-Nebraska Act of 1854 revived his activist impulses, and he was soon backing antislavery elements in Kansas, especially through generous donations to the New England Emigrant Aid Company, an organization that sponsored the migration of eastern abolitionists to the contested territory. Moreover, he began advocating violent resistance both to federal authority in Kansas and the proslavery settlers that he thought the national government sustained. Such a stance brought him into association with the radical abolitionist John Brown. According to witnesses and substantial documentation, by 1859 Smith was Brown's benefactor. He was also a member of a group of five other Northern abolitionists, dubbed the "Secret Six," who actively supported Brown's plans for the raid on Harper's Ferry. The existence of this band was disclosed by incriminating documents discovered in Maryland shortly after Brown's raid had failed. Apparently

the realization that Brown's violent plans would in fact lead to violence threw Smith into the throes of a mental breakdown. After his discharge from the mental institution, he undertook a life-long quest to distance himself from the raid and its consequences. Thomas Wentworth Higginson, another member of the Secret Six and in his own way equally troubled by his involvement in Brown's scheme, would years later characterize Smith as a cowardly romantic. Higginson scornfully noted that Smith had approached the idea of a raid with enthusiasm, but had balked at the reality of the actual event.

Smith ran for the presidency in 1860 as a radical abolitionist, representing a small and loosely organized remnant of the old Liberty Party. During the Civil War, however, he joined the Republican Party and devoted considerable energy to writing and speaking on behalf of the Union cause, especially working for Abraham Lincoln's reelection in 1864. By the end of the war, Smith was sickened by the violence and discord, and hence favored a lenient Reconstruction policy toward the South even as he pressed for African-American suffrage. He also joined Horace Greeley and Cornelius Vanderbilt in an offer to guarantee a million-dollar bond for the release of Jefferson Davis. To his chagrin, though, the ghosts of the turbulent prewar past continued to bedevil him. In 1867 the *Chicago Tribune* described Smith as deeply involved in the 1859 Harper's Ferry raid, and when Smith sued the paper for libel, he lost. Yet nothing could dim the altruism that had been the one constant in the varying resolve of his reformist impulses. An enigma to the end, he died in New York City on 28 December 1874 at the age of seventy-seven.

—*David S. Heidler and Jeanne T. Heidler*

See also Abolitionists; Brown, John.

For further reading:

Frothingham, Octavius Brooks. *Gerrit Smith: A Biography* (1878).

Hammond, Charles Addison. *Gerrit Smith: The Story of a Noble Life* (1908).

Harlow, Ralph Volney. *Gerrit Smith, Philanthropist and Reformer* (1939).

Hearn, Chester G. *Companions in Conspiracy: John Brown and Gerrit Smith* (1996).

Renehan, Edward J., Jr. *The Secret Six: The True Tale of the Men Who Conspired with John Brown* (1995).

Tatom, E. Lynn. "The Secret Six and Their Theory of Autonomous Individualism" (M.A. thesis, 1973).

Taylor, Edward Livingston. *Gerrit Smith* (1909).

SMITH, GILES ALEXANDER
(1829–1876)
Union general

Born to Cyrus Smith and Laura Wales Smith in Jefferson County, New York, Giles Alexander Smith moved as a young man to Ohio. First in London, Ohio, and then in Cincinnati, he became

involved in a dry-goods business, an occupation he would continue after moving to Illinois. Settling in Bloomington, Illinois, Smith used the profits from earlier business ventures to buy a hotel that he managed himself. Smith was living in Bloomington at the outbreak of the Civil War.

With the commencement of hostilities, Smith accepted a captain's commission in the 8th Missouri Volunteers, commanded by his older brother, Colonel Morgan Lewis Smith. The younger Smith commanded his company at Fort Henry and then at Fort Donelson in February 1862. Superiors commended him for his coolness under fire at Fort Donelson. Smith also fought at Shiloh and in the advance on Corinth, Mississippi, for which he was again commended for his bravery. In June 1862, when his brother was promoted to brigadier general, Smith succeeded to command of the 8th Missouri and was promoted first to lieutenant colonel and then to colonel of volunteers.

At the end of 1862, Smith led his regiment in William T. Sherman's Chickasaw Bluffs campaign and succeeded to command his brother's brigade when Morgan Lewis Smith was promoted to division commander. Morgan Lewis was seriously wounded in the campaign. The younger Smith continued to command the brigade in the Arkansas Post campaign of January 1863.

During the Vicksburg campaign, Smith displayed conspicuous courage and initiative in the Steele's Bayou expedition of 14–27 March 1863. His promotion to brigadier later in the summer of 1863 was partially as a result of his actions there. For the remainder of the Vicksburg campaign, Smith commanded 1st Brigade in Frank Blair's division, fighting at Jackson, Mississippi, on 14 May and in the siege operations of June and early July.

In August 1863, Smith temporarily commanded a convalescent camp at Murfreesboro, Tennessee. In October he was sent to command at Corinth, Mississippi. He remained there only a short time before being called back to Tennessee.

Smith led his brigade to Tennessee, where he participated in the defense of Chattanooga. He particularly distinguished himself on 24 November, first by using his brigade to cover the crossing of the Tennessee River by William T. Sherman's corps and then in an attack on Missionary Ridge in which he was severely wounded. Smith was unable to return to duty until the following March and was rumored killed by Confederate reports.

In early March 1864 Smith commanded his brigade in northern Alabama before joining William T. Sherman's Atlanta campaign in the late spring. Initially Smith commanded a brigade in Morgan Lewis Smith's division. The younger Smith was commended for his actions at Resaca and on 21 July 1864 was given command of a division of XVII Corps. A day later,

Smith's division was especially conspicuous in the battle of Atlanta when his flank was nearly overwhelmed during the midafternoon fighting. Smith was able to rally his men and prevent the turning of the Union flank. Again Confederate rumors had Smith killed in this engagement. He was recommended for promotion to major general of volunteers for his actions in the campaign thus far. Smith continued to lead his division through the capture of Atlanta and the subsequent March to the Sea.

Smith fought in Sherman's Carolina campaign for its duration. After Joseph E. Johnston's surrender, Smith was sent to the Department of Texas, where he served out his remaining months of military service. In November 1865 he was promoted to major general of volunteers, reputedly the last such promotion to that rank. After being mustered out of volunteer service in 1866, Smith was offered a regular colonel's commission but declined. His health had never fully recovered from his wound on Missionary Ridge, and he preferred to return home to Bloomington.

In 1869, President Ulysses S. Grant appointed Smith second assistant postmaster general, a position he held until 1872, when his poor health forced his resignation. Shortly thereafter, Smith moved to California in the hopes that the climate would bring about his recovery. It did not, and in September 1876 he returned to Bloomington. He died two months later, on 5 November 1876.

—*David S. Heidler and Jeanne T. Heidler*

See also Atlanta Campaign; Vicksburg Campaign.
For further reading:
Castel, Albert. *Decision in the West: The Atlanta Campaign of 1864* (1992).

SMITH, GUSTAVUS WOODSON
(1822–1896)
Confederate general

Gustavus Woodson Smith was born on 1 January 1822 in Georgetown, Kentucky, to Byrd and Sarah Woodson Smith, both of whom could trace their lineage back to Great Britain. In 1838 Smith enrolled at West Point. After graduating in 1842, he worked on fortifications in the port town of New London, Connecticut, as an engineer. There he met Lucretia Bassett, whom he would marry in 1844. Smith returned to West Point as assistant professor of engineering, after having spent two years in Connecticut.

During the Mexican-American War, Smith joined the only company of engineer soldiers in the United States Army as the second ranking officer. He assumed command of the small unit upon the death of its leader, Captain Alexander J. Swift in April 1847. As commander of the engineer company, he received two brevets for meritorious service at the battles of Cerro Gordo and Contreras. Smith resigned his commission in the army in December 1854 to participate in John A. Quitman's filibuster expedition against Cuba.

In the 1850s Smith found work as the superintendent of construction for several government projects, including the extension to the Treasury Building in Washington and repairs to the Branch Mint in New Orleans. Smith left the Crescent City to become the chief engineer of the Cooper and Hewitt Iron Company in Trenton, New Jersey. In 1857 his election to the board of directors of the Illinois Central Railroad pleased him very much. In April 1858 Mayor Daniel F. Tiemann appointed the industrialist Edward Cooper as street commissioner of New York City with Smith as his deputy. Smith succeeded Cooper as street commissioner seven months later, a position he held for nearly three years.

An influential leader of pro-Southern Democrats in his adopted city, Smith supported the Breckinridge-Lane ticket in the presidential election of 1860. As the nation stood on the brink of disintegration, Smith assumed an active role in the famous Pine Street meeting, one of the last attempts at averting civil war. While a cadet at West Point, Smith had predicted that the country would eventually split over slavery. Five months after the attack on Fort Sumter, he resigned from his New York City post.

On 19 September 1861, Jefferson Davis commissioned Smith a major general in the Confederate army and assigned him to command the 2d Corps of the Army of the Potomac. Doubtless, Smith's outstanding pre–Civil War reputation caused the Davis government to embrace him. Because of Smith's ill health and lack of skill at handling large armies, he did not meet the expectations of his superiors.

Smith got the chance to show what he could do at the battle of Seven Pines. With the wounding of Joseph E. Johnston on 31 May 1862, command of the Army of the Potomac devolved upon Smith. Smith's lack of endurance, combined with his inability to formulate a solid battle plan for the next day's fight, was his undoing. Davis's decision to replace Smith with Robert E. Lee as commander of the Army of Northern Virginia angered the proud Kentuckian. Because of illness, Smith did not return to active duty until August 1862. The next month, the Confederate War Department ordered him to take command of the state of North Carolina and the southern part of Virginia. In November Smith became the fourth secretary of war of the Confederacy, when Davis appointed him to that office ad interim. Smith commanded the Confederate forces at the battle of Goldsboro in North Carolina on 17 December 1862. This engagement represented another lost opportunity for Smith to prove his mettle as a field general. Although Smith's battlefield exploits were not impressive, he was nonetheless extremely vexed when Davis passed him over for promotion to lieutenant general. Unable to persuade his chief to elevate him in rank, Smith resigned his commission in the Confederate army in February 1863. The embittered general then departed from Richmond for Georgia, where he accepted the presidency of the Etowah Manufacturing & Mining Company. In June 1864 Governor Joseph E. Brown appointed Smith to command the Georgia state militia. Smith's motley unit provided valuable service to the Army of Tennessee during the Atlanta campaign. Smith's greatest victory as commander of the Georgia militia came at the battle of Honey Hill in South Carolina in November 1864. During the Savannah campaign, he constructed a pontoon bridge over the Savannah River, thereby giving William J. Hardee's army an avenue of retreat. Smith surrendered on 20 April to James H. Wilson at Macon, ending a checkered and controversial Civil War career.

During the postwar period, Smith worked as the general manager of the Southwestern Iron Company in Chattanooga. While in Tennessee, he received a presidential pardon. In 1870 he relocated to Frankfort to assume the office of insurance commissioner of Kentucky. Smith was one of the nation's leading insurance reformers.

Smith spent the last twenty years of his life in New York City, where he made good use of the publishing houses there. During that time he wrote several articles and books, including his memoir in 1884. In the memoir he criticized Davis, with whom he had feuded frequently during the war. Smith's wife died in 1881, ending a thirty-seven-year union that had not produced any offspring. Smith died of heart failure on 23 June 1896, at the age of seventy-four. Four days later he was buried in the Cedar Grove cemetery next to his wife in New London, Connecticut.

—*Leonne M. Hudson*

See also Fair Oaks/Seven Pines; Honey Hill, South Carolina, Battle of.
For further reading:
Bragg, William Harris. *Joe Brown's Army: The Georgia State Line, 1862–1865* (1987).
Freeman, Douglas Southall. *Lee's Lieutenants: A Study in Command* (1942–1944).
Hudson, Leonne M. *The Odyssey of a Southerner: The Life and Times of Gustavus Woodson Smith* (1998).
Smith, Gustavus W. *Confederate War Papers* (1884).

SMITH, JAMES YOUNGS
(1809–1876)
Governor of Rhode Island

Born to Amos Denison Smith and Priscilla Mitchell Smith in Groton, Connecticut, James Youngs Smith was educated in local schools before accepting a clerk's position in a Groton mercantile establishment. At age seventeen he moved to Providence, Rhode Island, where he worked as a clerk in a lumber business. Within eleven years he owned the business. He used the profits he gained from the business to invest and then become an active participant in Providence's cotton textile industry. At the outbreak of the Civil War he was one of the most important textile manufacturers in the state of Rhode Island.

Along with his business activities, Smith was very active in the Providence community and in state Republican politics. He served as the city's mayor in the mid-1850s, served in the state legislature, and then stood for governor in 1860 but lost the election. Smith was the Republican candidate again in 1862 and won the governorship. He served as governor for the remainder of the Civil War and worked tirelessly to raise money and troops for a Union victory.

The eccentricities of Rhode Island handicapped Smith somewhat in his endeavors to aid the war effort. The legislature refused to institute a draft to fill the state's troop quotas, and as a result, extra money and the appointment of numerous recruiting officials were necessary if the state was to supply the troops demanded by the federal government. When the U.S. Congress instituted conscription in 1863 there was considerable fear that Rhode Island would resist efforts to draft its citizens. As a result, Smith's relations with the U.S. provost marshal's office were strained from the time he took office until the end of the war.

To prevent resistance to the draft in Rhode Island, Smith worked diligently in the spring and early summer of 1863 to raise Rhode Island's quota so that conscription would not have to be used in the state. However, in June 1863 he complained to the provost marshal that he had not been given enough time to raise the troops before the institution of the draft. When the draft was used just a few weeks later, though, he reported to Secretary of War Edwin Stanton that it had gone very smoothly and that draftees were happily and patriotically accepting their fate.

During the next year, Smith was also active in raising African-American troops within the state. In August 1863 the War Department authorized him to raise a battalion of African-American artillery and cautioned him that the federal government would not allow a bounty to be paid to these troops as it would if it were a white battalion. Early the next year, Smith wrote to the War Department asking permission to raise more African-American units for federal service.

As governor, Smith also believed it to be his duty to protect the integrity and prestige of Rhode Island units serving in the war. For that reason he wrote angrily to the War Department in September 1863 when he learned that the 2d Rhode Island Cavalry was to be merged into the 1st Louisiana Cavalry and that its offi-

cers were to be mustered out of service. He argued that the men would lose all identity with their state and complained that even if the officers secured commissions in other units, they would lose their seniority. He also cautioned the War Department that recruiting in Rhode Island would certainly suffer, as men considering enlistment in Rhode Island units would fear that the same fate might befall them once they were in the army.

The only serious criticism leveled at Smith during his governorship came when some of the money allocated for recruitment bounties disappeared. Although no one believed that Smith had anything to do with the apparent corruption involved in the money's disappearance, his administration suffered under the criticism of the political opposition. The failure of the efforts to discredit him were evidenced, however, in the results of the next election, when Smith won every election district in the state.

Toward the end of the war, Smith demonstrated the state's patriotism and dedication to the war effort by encouraging shows of support from the legislature and the state military forces. He sent a congratulatory proclamation to William Tecumseh Sherman and the men of his army after their victory at Savannah, Georgia, in December 1864. When word reached Rhode Island regarding the fall of Richmond, Virginia, in April 1865, he ordered the firing of a 100-gun salute in Providence celebrating the news.

Smith remained governor until 1866, after which he returned to his business pursuits. He continued to be active in civic activities, serving on a variety of boards and committees. He became famous throughout the state in his later years for his generous acts of charity. He died in Providence on 26 March 1876.

—David S. Heidler and Jeanne T. Heidler

See also Conscription, U.S.A.
For further reading:
Dyer, Elisha, ed. *Annual Report of the Adjutant General of the State of Rhode Island and Providence Plantations for the Year 1865* (1893–1895).

SMITH, JOHN EUGENE
(1816–1897)
Union general

Born in Berne, Switzerland, on 3 August 1816, Smith has the distinction of being the only general officer in the Civil War to have been born in Switzerland. His father, John Banler Smith, was a former Napoleonic army officer, who, after fighting as a member of the Grande Armee from Moscow to Waterloo, immigrated with his family to Philadelphia, Pennsylvania. Smith spent his formative years in Philadelphia, where he received a basic education and became a jeweler and goldsmith by trade. After first moving to St. Louis, Missouri, he eventually settled in Galena, Illinois, in 1836. In Galena, Smith practiced his trade and became active in local politics. In 1860 he was elected the Jo Daviess County treasurer. In 1861 Smith was responsible for rescuing Captain Ulysses S. Grant from obscurity when he recommended Grant to the Illinois governor Richard Yates, describing Grant as someone who would be knowledgeable enough to organize an infantry regiment. Smith served briefly on Governor Yates's staff before resigning to recruit and organize the 45th Illinois Infantry Regiment, which he commanded with the rank of colonel from 23 July 1861.

Smith commanded the 45th Illinois Infantry Regiment during the capture of Forts Henry and Donelson and at the battles of Shiloh and Corinth. He was promoted to brigadier general of volunteers on 29 November 1862, and briefly, in December 1862, commanded the 1st Brigade, 3d Division (Right Wing), XIII Corps. After the reorganization and expansion of the U.S. Army in the Western theater, Smith commanded the 8th Division, XVI Corps, Army of the Tennessee, from 26 December 1862 to 3 April 1863, followed by the 1st Brigade, 3d Division, XVII Corps, Army of the Tennessee, from 23 April 1863 to 3 June 1863. During the latter part of the Vicksburg campaign in 1863, Smith commanded the 7th Division, XVII Corps, Army of the Tennessee, and then led the 2d Division of that corps at Missionary Ridge. Smith's division was the only division of XVII Corps to be involved in the defeat of Confederate general Braxton Bragg's Army of Tennessee. During the Atlanta campaign, throughout Major General William T. Sherman's March to the Sea, and during most of the Army of the Tennessee's campaigning in the Carolinas, Smith commanded the 3d Division, XV Corps. After distinguishing himself at the capture of Savannah, he was given command of the District of Western Tennessee during the final months of 1865.

In April 1866, Smith, who had been brevetted major general in the regular army, was mustered out of the volunteer service. Rather than return to civilian life, however, he accepted a regular army commission as a full colonel and an appointment as the commanding officer of the 14th Infantry Regiment. Smith served at various posts on the frontier until his retirement on 19 May 1881, after which he returned to his home state of Illinois and resided in Chicago. He died there on 29 January 1897 and was buried in the Greenwood Cemetery in Galena, Illinois.

—*Louis Bielakowski*

For further reading:
Smith, John E. Personal Papers. Kirby Smith, Barrington, Illinois.
———. Personal Papers. Galena/Jo Daviess County Historical Society, Galena, Illinois.

SMITH, MARTIN LUTHER
(1819–1866)
Confederate general

Born in Tomkins County, New York, Martin Luther Smith graduated sixteenth of fifty-six in the U.S. Military Academy class of 1842. He served in the topographical engineers primarily in the Southern states until the outbreak of the Civil War. Besides his duties with the army, he also served as an engineer for the Fernandina & Cedar Keys Railroad while stationed in Florida.

In spite of his Northern birth and upbringing, Smith wrestled with the issue of secession as the lower South, including his wife's home state of Georgia, left the Union in the early months of 1861. Finally deciding he could not bear arms against the South, he resigned his commission on 1 April 1861. A few days later he was commissioned a major in the Confederate army with a date of rank of 16 March 1861.

Sent to New Orleans as a member of the Confederate Corps of Engineers in May 1861, Smith spent the next year trying with limited resources to strengthen the defenses of that city. During that time he was promoted to colonel in February 1862 and to brigadier general in April 1862.

Upon the fall of New Orleans, Smith took command of a district of southern Mississippi. After his promotion to major general in November 1862, he became commander of Vicksburg. When William T. Sherman attacked Vicksburg in December 1862, Smith led the repulse of the Union offensive. When department commander Lieutenant General John C. Pemberton arrived to take personal command at Vicksburg, Smith was given command of a division in the city's defense. He was captured with the rest of the army upon the surrender of the city on 4 July 1863. Though soon paroled, Smith was not officially exchanged for seven months and was therefore out of action during that time.

Upon his exchange, Smith was assigned as chief engineer to the Army of Northern Virginia. He served in Virginia through the early spring and summer of 1864 before being transferred to the Army of Tennessee in July 1864. From July 1864 during the Atlanta campaign through October 1864, Smith served as John Bell Hood's chief engineer. After leaving Hood's command, Smith was sent to strengthen the defenses of Mobile, Alabama, following David Glasgow Farragut's smashing Union naval victory in Mobile Bay. He was captured at Mobile at the end of the war and soon paroled.

Smith's health was broken. He moved to his wife's home of Athens, Georgia, where he worked briefly as an engineer before dying in 1866.

—*David S. Heidler and Jeanne T. Heidler*

See also New Orleans, Capture of; Vicksburg Campaign.
For further reading:
Nichols, James L. *Confederate Engineers* (1957; reprint 1987).

SMITH, MORGAN LEWIS
(1821–1874)
Union general

Born to Cyrus Lewis Smith and Laura Wales Smith in Oswego County, New York, Morgan Lewis Smith moved to Pennsylvania as a young man and then to Indiana. After trying several different jobs, Smith enlisted in the army under an assumed name. There is no record indicating why he did not use his own name. He rose to the rank of sergeant and served as a drill instructor for new recruits at Newport, Kentucky. He left the army in 1850 and, for the years before the Civil War, worked on steamboats primarily out of St. Louis on the Mississippi River. At the outbreak of the Civil War, Smith raised a regiment of rivermen and in June 1861 became its commander as colonel of the 8th Missouri Volunteer Infantry. His younger brother, Giles Alexander Smith, served as one of the regiment's company commanders at the rank of captain. The two brothers would serve together for much of the war.

During the summer of 1861, Smith and his regiment operated primarily in Missouri before being sent to Paducah, Kentucky, in September 1861. After the fall of Fort Henry in early February 1862, Smith was given command of a brigade under Ulysses S. Grant in the attempt to take Fort Donelson. In leading an assault on the Confederate outworks, Smith was conspicuous for his bravery and coolness under fire. His division commander, Lewis Wallace, was effusive in his praise of Smith's actions, and Grant recommended that Smith be promoted to brigadier general.

Smith continued to command his brigade under Wallace in April 1862 at Shiloh, where the tremendous number of casualties suffered by his brigade demonstrated Smith's insistence on iron discipline. Smith served under William T. Sherman in the subsequent advance on Corinth, Mississippi. In heavy fighting on 17 May 1862 at Russell's house, Smith again demonstrated the almost reckless bravery for which he was becoming known and was commended in very strong terms by Sherman. In July, Smith was promoted to brigadier general.

During the summer and fall of 1862, Smith operated out of Memphis, Tennessee, into Mississippi primarily against Confederate guerrilla groups. His actions during that time caused Major General John A. McClernand to recommend Smith for promotion to major general of volunteers. In December, Smith was given command of a division as part of William T. Sherman's Yazoo campaign. In heavy fighting on 28 December, Smith's bravery finally caught up with him when he was severely wounded at Chickasaw Bluffs. He was unable to return to duty until August 1863, when he was given command of a division, again under Sherman. Two months later he would lead his division in the defense of Chattanooga.

In the Chattanooga campaign, Smith fought on Missionary Ridge in November 1863, after which his division was detailed to aid in the relief of Knoxville, Tennessee. From 25 January to 5 February 1864, Smith commanded an expedition from Scottsborough, Alabama, to Rome, Georgia, the purpose of which was to determine the extent of Unionism in the area and to scout transportation routes. In the spring, he and his division joined Sherman's army in preparation for the upcoming Atlanta campaign. Smith's division was a part of John A. Logan's XV Corps.

Smith fought in all the early battles of the Atlanta campaign and was especially conspicuous at Resaca and Kennesaw Mountain, where he commanded the attack on the southwestern side of the mountain. At the battle of Atlanta on 22 July 1864 he again recklessly exposed himself to enemy fire to rally his troops. The following day, Smith was temporarily placed in command of XV Corps when John Logan began his brief tenure as commander of the Army of the Tennessee. Upon Logan's return to XV Corps, Smith asked to be relieved of command of his division. His wound from Chickasaw Bluffs had never healed properly, and his health was failing quickly. He tried to resign his commission, but Sherman insisted that he was too valuable for the army to lose and persuaded Smith to take a sick leave instead.

After returning from his leave of absence at the end of September, Smith found that he was still unable to take a field command. Sherman, to keep him in the army, arranged for Smith to receive command of Vicksburg. After briefly commanding the District of Memphis in October 1864, Smith assumed command of the defenses of Vicksburg in November. He held that command until 27 February 1865, when he was given command of the District of Vicksburg, encompassing the area surrounding the city. His primary duty in both positions was to restrain the civilian population from acts of sabotage. He accomplished this task through very strict enforcement of martial law.

After the end of hostilities, Smith remained in command at Vicksburg until arrangements could be made for a successor. He resigned his commission in July 1865 and briefly returned to St. Louis. At the end of 1866, President Andrew Johnson appointed Smith consul to Hawaii, a position he held for two years. He lived the remainder of his life in Washington D.C., engaging in a variety of business activities, including government mail contracts. He died 28 December 1874 while on a trip to Jersey City, New Jersey. His remains were taken to Washington, where he was buried at Arlington National Cemetery.

—*David S. Heidler and Jeanne T. Heidler*

See also Atlanta Campaign; Chickasaw Bluffs, Battle of; Fort Donelson, Battle of.
For further reading:
Bearss, Edwin Cole. *The Campaign for Vicksburg* (1985–1986).

SMITH, THOMAS KILBY
(1820–1887)
Union general

Born in Dorchester, Massachusetts, Thomas Kilby Smith moved with his family to Ohio when he was a small child. He was educated at Cincinnati College, after which he studied law under Salmon P. Chase. Before the outbreak of the Civil War, Smith never actually practiced law, preferring instead to accept a variety of federal jobs, including serving as southern Ohio's U.S. marshal. After the commencement of hostilities, Smith helped to recruit a regiment for federal service and became the lieutenant colonel of the 54th Ohio in September 1861. In October 1861 he became the regiment's colonel.

Smith commanded his regiment at Shiloh in April 1862 and in the advance on Corinth, Mississippi. When the town was occupied, Smith and the 54th made up the original occupational garrison, assigned to that task by William T. Sherman. At the end of 1862, Smith commanded a brigade in Sherman's Yazoo expedition, fighting in the battle of Chickasaw Bluffs during that campaign. Smith fought in the Arkansas Post expedition in early 1863 and was commended by Sherman for his actions there. The following spring he distinguished himself under Sherman at Steele's Bayou.

During the Vicksburg campaign, Smith was sent to Milliken's Bend in May; during the subsequent siege of Vicksburg, he served on Ulysses S. Grant's staff. After the capitulation of Vicksburg, Grant recommended that Smith be promoted. In August 1863, Smith was promoted to brigadier general of volunteers. During the fall of 1863, he commanded a brigade of XVII Corps. Throughout that time he operated first out of Vicksburg and then out of Natchez trying to neutralize mobile Confederate units and guerrilla groups.

In early 1864, a provisional division was created out of XVII Corps to participate in Nathaniel P. Banks's Red River campaign. Smith was given command of the provisional division. The primary function of this division was to move along the river banks to protect the naval component of the campaign from Confederate attack. As a result, Smith was present at and participated in most of the major engagements of the campaign, including the seizing of Fort De Russy. After the end of the campaign, Smith and his provisional division were sent to Memphis, Tennessee.

Smith had been dispatched to Memphis to help with the efforts to combat Nathan Bedford Forrest. However, upon the arrival of the division, it was discovered that the division had suffered such hardship and deprivation on the Red River campaign that fewer than half the men were fit for immediate duty. Nevertheless, during the next several months, Smith and his men were very active against Forrest and his cavalry.

Smith had suffered as well on the arduous Red River campaign, and by the fall of 1864 his health was nearly shattered. He was forced to relinquish command of his division and accept less arduous duty in an effort to recover. His efforts partially successful, Smith was sent to the Department of the Gulf in early 1865 and then to Mobile in March 1865. Although he was still unable to accept a field command, Smith was made commander of the District of South Alabama on 19 March 1865. He held that position through the end of hostilities, after which he was made commander of the District of Mobile in June 1865.

After being mustered out of the army in 1866, Smith was appointed U.S. consul to Panama by President Andrew Johnson. Not caring for foreign duty, he resigned the position and retired to a home outside Philadelphia, Pennsylvania. He lived quietly there, still not in very good health, for twenty years. He moved to New York City shortly before his death, which occurred on 14 December 1887. His body was returned to Pennsylvania, where it was buried near his home in Torresdale.

—*David S. Heidler and Jeanne T. Heidler*

See also Red River Campaign.
For further reading:
Smith, Walter George. *Life and Letters of Thomas Kilby Smith, Brevet Major-General, United States Volunteers, 1820–1887* (1898).

SMITH, TRUMAN
(1791–1884)
U.S. congressman and judge

Born to Phineas Smith and Deborah Ann Judson Smith in Roxbury, Connecticut, Truman Smith was educated locally before enrolling at Yale. After graduation, he studied law at Litchfield Law School. He began practicing in 1818. After over a decade gaining a wide reputation as a very talented attorney, Smith became increasingly interested in Connecticut politics. He served in the state legislature in the early 1830s before being elected to the U.S. House of Representatives in 1838 as a Whig.

Smith served four terms in Congress in the late 1830s and through the 1840s, having one interruption in service in the mid-1840s. During that time he gained a reputation as a moderate on sectional issues, preferring to let nature take its course in the territories rather than have Congress address the question.

Following the Mexican-American War, however, Smith became increasingly disillusioned with what he viewed as fanatics in the South and their desire to expand slavery into all the territories. He strongly supported the Whig candidacy of Zachary Taylor for president in 1848 at the same time Smith was standing for election as one of Connecticut's senators. He was successful and entered

the Senate in 1849. Taylor attempted to reward him for his support with a cabinet post, but Smith refused.

Smith continued his efforts to serve as a voice of moderation throughout Taylor's presidency and during the first year of Franklin Pierce's term in office, but the support of Southern Whigs for the Kansas-Nebraska Act caused him to break off all contact with fellow Whigs from that region. He predicted that the act would in effect destroy the party and gave weight to that decision by resigning his Senate seat.

Smith's time in the House of Representatives and the Senate had hurt him financially, and upon his resignation he attempted to build up his resources by opening a law practice in New York City. Over the next few years, while not losing his interest in politics, he dedicated himself to the law. He became a member of the Republican Party and in 1860 again became active in state party circles. As preparations were made for the Republican National Convention in Chicago in the spring of 1860, Smith became convinced that Edward Bates of Missouri was the best possible presidential candidate for the party. He thought that a man from a border state would appeal more to western Republicans and if elected would be more likely to prevent a secession crisis. Even though his candidate was rejected, Smith strongly supported the efforts of the Abraham Lincoln administration to preserve the Union at the outbreak of the Civil War.

During the first year of the war, Smith continued his law practice. He took an interest in the progress of the war, and corresponded with acquaintances within the government regarding legal issues involved in its prosecution. Certain issues especially interested him, such as the imprisonment of civilians for political reasons and the emancipation of slaves in war zones.

By 1862 he came to the conclusion that the war should ultimately bring about the extinction of slavery within the United States. For that reason perhaps, the president in that year appointed him a judge on the British-American court that was created to handle ships taken by either navy suspected of engaging in the international slave trade. He remained a judge on the court until its abolition in 1870.

After leaving that tribunal, Smith, now quite elderly, returned only briefly to his private law practice before retiring. He maintained until his death, however, a strong interest in the affairs of the nation, particularly the issue of civil service reform and wrote extensively urging such reform on the national government. He died in retirement in Connecticut on 3 May 1884.

—*David S. Heidler and Jeanne T. Heidler*

See also Congress, U.S.A.; Republican Party.
For further reading:
Smith, Truman. *Considerations on the Slavery Question, Addressed to the President of the United States* (1862).

———. *The Spoils System, the Offspring of Modern Democracy, and the Source of Numberless Evils to the Country: Crush it Out!* (1876).

SMITH, WILLIAM
(1797–1887)
Confederate general; governor of Virginia

Born to Caleb Smith and Mary Waugh Smith at the family plantation, Marengo, in King George County, Virginia, William Smith was educated locally and at a private academy in Connecticut. He studied law in Fredericksburg and then opened his first practice in Culpeper County, Virginia. In 1827 he opened a private mail delivery service that soon expanded to deliveries as far south as Georgia. He held a number of contracts with the U.S. Postal Service, receiving extra payments from that quarter. From these payments he received the nickname that would be with him for the rest of his life, "Extra Billy" Smith.

Along with his legal practice and business activities, Smith also became involved in Virginia politics. He served in the state senate and served one term, from 1841 to 1843, in the U.S. House of Representatives. During the Mexican-American War he served as Virginia's governor. After the war, he moved to the new U.S. territory of California and lived in San Francisco during the territory's preparation for statehood. He chaired the state's first Democratic Convention but refused to become a citizen of the state and thus had to refuse the offer of that convention to run for the U.S. Senate from California.

In 1852, Smith returned to Virginia and won election to the U.S. House of Representatives in that year's election. He remained in that body until 1861. Upon Virginia's secession, Governor John Letcher offered Smith a brigadier general's commission in the state's forces, but Smith did not believe that he was qualified for a command position at that rank and offered his services to the Confederate army. He was commissioned colonel of the 49th Virginia volunteers.

Smith commanded his regiment at First Bull Run and was commended for bravery by P. G. T. Beauregard for his actions there. In the fall of 1861 he was elected to the Confederate House of Representatives, and until the spring of 1862 he divided his time between his regiment and his legislative duties in Richmond. This proved not to be too burdensome during the winter of 1861–1862, and Smith was a very active legislator, particularly in his support of the actions taken by Jefferson Davis to improve the military of the Confederacy. At the beginning of Union general George B. McClellan's Peninsula campaign in the spring of 1862, however, Smith could no longer serve both professions, and he resigned his seat in the Confederate Congress.

Smith fought with distinction during the Peninsula campaign and briefly commanded his brigade during the battle of Seven Pines due to the illness of his commander. D. H. Hill commended him for his actions there. During the Seven Days' he was back in command of the 49th and was again commended, this time by Brigadier General William Mahone, for his bravery during the battles.

When Robert E. Lee organized his army into two corps after the Peninsula campaign, Smith and the 49th became a part of the corps commanded by Thomas J. "Stonewall" Jackson. He and his men fought during the Second Bull Run campaign as part of Jubal Early's brigade. When Early was elevated to divisional command at Antietam, Smith assumed command of the brigade, and even though he was wounded three times during the battle, he remained on the field in command of the brigade until the fighting ended. After the battle, however, he faced a lengthy convalescence and was not able to return to his command until the battle of Fredericksburg in December 1862.

The following spring, Smith was promoted to brigadier general with a date of rank of January 1863. He commanded a brigade in Jackson's corps at Chancellorsville and, following the reorganization of the Army of Northern Virginia after Jackson's death, commanded his brigade in Early's division of Richard Ewell's corps at Gettysburg. Smith had been elected governor of Virginia before the Gettysburg campaign and was to assume office at the beginning of 1864. After the Gettysburg campaign, therefore, he determined to resign his commission to prepare for his new office. He was promoted to major general in August, however, and was persuaded to remain in the army until he became governor. His primary duty until he assumed office would be to travel throughout Virginia and neighboring states to encourage recruiting and the accumulation of supplies for the Confederate army.

Smith was inaugurated Virginia's governor in January 1864, and he used his position during the trying next year to encourage greater support for the military effort. In the fall of 1864 he presided over a meeting of the governors of North Carolina, South Carolina, Georgia, Alabama, and Mississippi in Augusta, Georgia. Out of this meeting came a series of resolutions, including one that pledged support for the war, another for increased efforts by state governments to apprehend deserters, and finally one for greater efforts to prevent Northern confiscation of slaves. Back home, Smith worked tirelessly to procure supplies for the Army of Northern Virginia and to provide slave labor for the trenches of Petersburg.

In the spring of 1865, with the state government in a precarious position in Richmond, Smith relocated it to Lynchburg. From there he fled to Danville, but news of the Confederacy's collapse brought him back to Richmond. For a time the federal government offered a bounty of $25,000 for his capture. After hiding with friends for several weeks, Smith surrendered to federal authorities.

After his parole, Smith went to his farm in Fauquier County, where he spent much of the rest of his life. He served one term in state legislature in the late 1870s, but for the most part he devoted his time to farming. He died at his home, Monterosa, on 18 May 1887 and was taken to Richmond for burial.

—*David S. Heidler and Jeanne T. Heidler*

See also Antietam, Battle of; Virginia.
For further reading:
Thomas, Emory M. *The Confederate State of Richmond: A Biography of the Capital* (1971; reprint 1998).

SMITH, WILLIAM FARRAR
(1824–1903)
Union general

Born in St. Albans, Vermont, to Ashbel Smith and Sarah Butler Smith, William Farrar Smith was educated locally before accepting an appointment to the U.S. Military Academy. He graduated fourth of forty-one in the class of 1845. Upon graduation, Smith was commissioned second lieutenant of topographical engineers. He spent most of his first decade and a half in the army as a member of the faculty at West Point. He did serve briefly in Florida during the early phases of the Third Seminole War, where he contracted a case of malaria that would plague him periodically for the remainder of his life.

With the outbreak of the Civil War, Smith was made colonel of the 3d Vermont Volunteers. He led his regiment at First Bull Run, after which he was promoted to brigadier general of volunteers. In the fall of 1861 he served at Chain Bridge, Virginia, commanding a brigade of the Army of the Potomac conducting reconnaissance missions of Confederate positions. In the spring he was given command of a division of IV Corps during the Peninsula campaign.

On the peninsula, Smith led his division at the siege of Yorktown, at the battle of Williamsburg, and during the Seven Days'. During that last series of battles, he especially distinguished himself at the battle of White Oak Swamp by preventing the flanking maneuver of "Stonewall" Jackson and D. H. Hill's divisions. For his actions during the campaign he was promoted to major general of volunteers, although later the Senate would refuse to confirm the promotion.

Commanding the 2d Division of William B. Franklin's VI Corps at Crampton's Gap on 14 September and at Antietam, Smith saw heavy action in the former engagement, but only saw action late in the day at Antietam. With Franklin's elevation to command of the

Left Grand Division before Fredericksburg, Smith became commander of VI Corps on 16 November 1862.

During the battle of Fredericksburg, his corps was only lightly engaged. After the battle, however, Smith made one of the first of his several political blunders during the war. He and Franklin wrote directly to President Abraham Lincoln criticizing Ambrose Burnside. Smith's sin of going behind his commander's back was compounded by his known affection for George B. McClellan. McClellan's enemies in Congress urged Lincoln to remove Smith from the army. Not wanting to take that drastic a step, the president relieved Smith from command of VI Corps, giving him instead IX Corps and banishing him from the Army of the Potomac to Newport News, Virginia. The Senate had its own revenge by refusing to confirm Smith's promotion to major general, causing him to revert to his former rank of brigadier general of volunteers.

Smith took his disgrace in stride, assuming command of IX Corps on 5 February 1863. When the Senate refused to confirm his promotion in March 1863, however, he lost his corps command as well. He was sent instead to command a division in the Department of the Susquehanna made up largely of militia and 90-day recruits. He did as he was told, however, traveling to Pennsylvania to take his command just as Robert E. Lee was preparing to invade the state. Rather than a backwater, Smith found himself in the middle of a major campaign with the duty of preparing local defense for a number of small Pennsylvania towns and hamlets. His main concern was the transportation network south of the Susquehanna, which he guarded tenaciously until after the battle of Gettysburg. Immediately after the battle, Smith brought his division to Gettysburg to guard the hospitals, following which he led his division as part of the pursuit of the Army of Northern Virginia. George Gordon Meade commended him for his actions during the campaign.

From the end of July through August 1863 Smith commanded at Hagerstown, Maryland. He yearned, however, for a more active command and requested a transfer at the end of the summer. The War Department, perhaps believing he had done enough penance, sent Smith west to Chattanooga, then being threatened by a Confederate attack. Named chief engineer of the Army of the Cumberland, Smith was charged with opening up a part of the Tennessee River out of the town to bring in much-needed supplies. On 27 October 1863, Smith floated pontoon bridges down the river, routing Confederates and opening a supply line to Bridgeport. William Rosecrans, who had been relieved as commander of the Army of the Cumberland by George H. Thomas, later claimed that the idea of using the pontoon bridges had been his, and the ever-testy Smith spent much of the remainder of his life fighting to gain credit for the scheme.

Later during the campaign, Smith again earned notice with his placement of batteries and building of temporary bridges to speed troop movement during the fight at Missionary Ridge. By that time, Smith had thoroughly impressed Ulysses S. Grant, who had come to Chattanooga to take personal command of the campaign. Grant wrote personally to Secretary of War Edwin Stanton urging Smith's promotion to major general, praising him in the highest terms as one of the most talented generals in the army. For the next several months Grant continued to press his case to the commanding general of the army, Henry Halleck, with the promotion finally being reaccomplished on 9 March 1864.

In the spring of 1864, Smith was transferred east to the Army of Virginia under Benjamin F. Butler. On 19 April 1864 he was given command of all troops at Yorktown and Gloucester Point across the York River. By the end of the month, however, he was up to his old tricks, writing directly to Grant criticizing Butler's management of his army. Grant ignored him, perhaps hoping that the talent he had seen earlier in Chattanooga would contribute to Union victory in the upcoming campaign against Lee. On 2 May Smith was given command of XVIII Corps, Army of Virginia. By the end of the month, however, the corps was moved to the Army of the Potomac, where it fought at Cold Harbor. After this debacle, Smith began to criticize the decisions of George Gordon Meade, the army's commander, again trying the patience of Grant.

In the middle of June, Smith and XVIII Corps were given the lead in the proposed assault against Petersburg. Smith delayed long enough to allow the Confederates to strengthen their position, ending the Federal offensive. Some reports had Smith debilitated with a bout of malaria at the critical time. Whatever the case, Grant could no longer protect Smith from his political and military enemies. On 19 July 1864, Smith was relieved of command of XVIII Corps and sent to New York City to await orders.

For the remainder of the war, Smith served on a variety of boards and other noncombat duties, the last of which was an inspection of the military situation west of the Mississippi conducted in early 1865. After the war, he remained in the army for two years, reverting in 1866 to the rank of major. He resigned in 1867 to accept the presidency of the International Ocean Telegraph Company. After leaving that position, he traveled for a while before returning to the United States. He lived for a number of years in New York City, where he put to work his engineering skills on harbor projects. He also spent much of his spare time writing about his Civil War experiences, primarily to defend himself against his many attackers. In 1893 he retired to Philadelphia, where he died on 28 February 1903.

—*David S. Heidler and Jeanne T. Heidler*

See also Burnside, Ambrose; Chattanooga Campaign; Petersburg Campaign.
For further reading:
Smith, William Farrar. *Autobiography of Major General William F. Smith, 1861–1864* (1990).
———. *From Chattanooga to Petersburg under Generals Grant and Butler: A Contribution to the History of the War and a Personal Vindication* (1893; reprint, 1975).

SMITH, WILLIAM SOOY
(1830–1916)
Union general

Born to Sooy Smith and Ann Hedges Smith in Tarlton, Ohio, William Sooy Smith was educated at Ohio University, graduating at age eighteen. Upon graduation he sought and received an appointment to the U.S. Military Academy. He graduated sixth of fifty-two in the class of 1853. He remained in the army for only one year, however, resigning to begin a career in engineering. Though he was never in particularly good health, Smith became very prominent in the engineering field, working on projects from Niagara Falls to the Savannah River.

At the outbreak of the Civil War, Smith left his engineering firm to volunteer for military service. He raised a regiment in Ohio and became its commander in June 1861 as colonel of the 13th Ohio. In the late summer and fall of 1861, Smith commanded his regiment in western Virginia, fighting most notably under William S. Rosecrans at Carnifex Ferry on 10 September. He was commended for his actions there.

At the end of the year, Smith was given command of a brigade of which the 13th was a part in the Army of the Ohio. He commanded that brigade at Shiloh in April 1862 and in the subsequent advance on Corinth, Mississippi. He was promoted to brigadier general of volunteers in April. After the occupation of Corinth, Smith's engineering skills were put to work when he was put on special duty of working on the railroad network in southern Tennessee. His work there completed, he was given command of a division in Tullahoma, Tennessee, in July 1862. He remained in command there until August, when he and his division went north into Kentucky as part of Don Carlos Buell's attempt to repulse the invasion of Braxton Bragg.

Smith fought at Perryville, although his division was not heavily engaged, and participated in the subsequent pursuit of Bragg out of Kentucky. For the remainder of the year, Smith commanded a division of XIV Corps in the Army of the Cumberland before being transferred to a division command in XVI Corps, Army of the Tennessee, in early 1863. He commanded that division through the Vicksburg campaign, operating primarily out of LaGrange, Tennessee, through June 1863.

After the fall of Vicksburg, Smith participated briefly in the Jackson, Mississippi, campaign but a severe attack of the arthritis that would plague him for the remainder of his life forced his withdrawal. Still his actions during the Vicksburg and Jackson campaigns earned him a recommendation from Ulysses S. Grant for a promotion to major general of volunteers.

Upon his recovery, Smith was made chief of cavalry in the Army of the Mississippi, headquartered at Nashville. Upon his arrival there to take command in November 1863, Smith was appalled at the condition and number of horses at his disposal. He worked for the next two months to improve the situation of his command.

In February 1864, he was directed to bring 7,000 troopers from Memphis into Mississippi to cooperate with William T. Sherman's Meridian campaign. Smith started late for his rendezvous with Sherman at Meridian and moved slowly, although he encountered little Confederate resistance until he ran into Nathan Bedford Forrest at West Point, Mississippi. Even though he outnumbered Forrest more than two to one, Smith retreated from West Point after skirmishing with Forrest. The forces fought again the next day at Okolona with similar results. Sherman was livid, not only that Smith had not followed instructions, but also that he had not taken the opportunity to use his superior numbers to deal Forrest a decisive defeat. Smith tried to defend himself and insisted in heated letters that Sherman change the wording in his official report. After the war Smith also insisted, with the same result, that Sherman change the offending passages of his memoirs.

Smith remained in his command until the summer of 1864, when his arthritis and perhaps humiliation caused his resignation from the army. He returned to his engineering career after two years of recuperation, and during the next few decades became one of the most sought-after engineers in the country. In his most important work of constructing railroad bridges, he was a pioneer in the use of a pneumatic pile driving process and in the use of steel. He also constructed lighthouses and some of the country's early skyscrapers. Even in retirement in Medford, Oregon, Smith continued to design buildings for the nation's major cities. He also wrote a vindication of his performance in the Meridian campaign that he did not publish until after Sherman's death. Smith died in Medford on 4 March 1916.

—*David S. Heidler and Jeanne T. Heidler*

See also Meridian Campaign; West Point, Battle of.
For further reading:
Smith, William Sooy. *The Mississippi Raid* (1907).

SMOOTHBORES

Smoothbores are firearms, both handguns and longarms, obsolete at the outbreak of hostilities and manufactured with smooth rather than rifled (spiral-grooved) barrels. Although modern rifled

weapons (notably the Model 1841 "Mississippi Rifle" and Colt Walker Model Revolver) had proven themselves in the Mexican-American War, neither Union nor Confederate arsenals held enough in stock to arm the recruits of 1861. Expediency thus dictated the issue of thousands of smoothbores, many converted from the flintlock to the percussion ignition system.

The smoothbore's greatest liability lay in its lack of range and accuracy owing to the loose fit of the projectile in its smooth-sided bore. This defect was somewhat alleviated by the use of buck-and-ball ammunition—cartridges consisting of one standard-sized ball and three buckshot. The scatter effect of buck-and-ball somewhat extended the killing range of the smoothbore, but never enough to rival that of rifled weapons. Still, albeit in steadily decreasing numbers, smoothbores saw service until the war's end.

The most common smoothbore pistols were the caliber .54 Model 1836, originally a flintlock weapon, and the caliber .54 Model 1842 Percussion Pistol. Smoothbore muskets included the caliber .69, originally flintlock, Models 1816 and 1840 Muskets and the caliber .69 Model 1842 U.S. Percussion Musket.

—Jeff Kinard

See also Rifles; Small Arms.
For further reading:
Evans, William B. *Civil War Guns* (1962).
Flayderman, E. Norman. *Flayderman's Guide to Antique American Firearms* (1987).
Lord, Francis A. *Civil War Collector's Encyclopedia* (1965).

SOLDIERS' VOTES

As soon as it was clear that the war would be more than a ninety-day fight, there was pressure on Northern state legislatures to enable enlisted men to vote in the field. Initially, Republicans opposed such moves, but by the spring of 1864, with the rising profile of generals who seemed likely to support Abraham Lincoln, and with political debate polarizing around the question of a negotiated peace, Republican politicians rushed to amend state legislation to give soldiers the ballot. By the time of the November election, eleven states had made such provisions. In the others, party campaigners were reliant on persuading the relevant authorities to furlough troops home on election day.

On polling day, 8 November 1864, 150,000 soldiers' ballots were cast, about 78 percent of them for Lincoln (as compared with 53 percent of the civilian vote). Evidence indicates that the total number of absentee ballots received from soldiers was much lower than some Union Party officials had hoped for. In several close states (New York and Connecticut in particular), the soldier's vote may have been crucial to Lincoln's victory.

More than anything else, soldiers voting dramatized the idea of the "citizen army." One Union Party pamphlet distributed both at the front and back home took the form of a discussion among the soldiers from various states about their right to vote. "In becoming soldiers we certainly did not cease to be men, nor any less citizens than before we put on our uniforms, drew our swords and shouldered our guns," explained a fictional captain in a Pennsylvania regiment, expressing a powerful theme in Union propaganda. The political sympathies of soldiers acquired a significance that went far beyond their mere capacity to influence the election results. The citizen army played a crucial role in the 1864 election as a symbol of the issues before the wider electorate. Voting in the field affirmed the army's status as a deliberative body that was actively participating in political life; it was not a passive instrument of the government, like the old professional army. Many soldiers consciously regarded elections as solemn political festivals that affirmed republican government. This belief in the affirming power of the voting ritual was illustrated by the many occasions, recorded in soldiers' letters and diaries (and later in newspaper reports), in which voting took place even when it was clear that it could have no impact on who was elected. Prisoners of war held in Confederate jails rigged up polling booths on election day and solemnly cast their ballots. Soldiers reported how keenly their units had supported the cause by voting for Lincoln with as much zeal as if reporting the outcome of a battle.

Enormous efforts were made by the private organizations and by the government and its agencies to get propaganda to soldiers in the field. The Post Office, under the instructions of Postmaster General Montgomery Blair, carried newspapers and Union pamphlets to the army for free, and special agents were appointed by Blair to ensure that the documents were distributed effectively to the troops. Both parties were publicly confident that they had the support of the army. Union Party leaders were sure that soldiers would support the vigorous prosecution of the war and the reelection of "Old Abe." Democrats claimed to be equally confident that their candidate, General George B. McClellan, would have the support of his former men in the Army of the Potomac. Both sides set up organizations specifically aimed at influencing the political opinions of the men. The McClellan Legion was a national network of current and former soldiers. On the other side, Simon Cameron, Union Party committee chairman in Pennsylvania, wrote to party workers reminding them that it was of the "utmost importance to get a full vote of our gallant soldiers in the army for our tickets at the November election." He assured them that the state government would provide the "requisite machinery" for carrying out that election, but that the work of "enabling soldiers to vote" would devolve upon the "friends of Lincoln and Johnson."

Studies of the correspondence of Civil War soldiers make clear that political feeling in the army ran strongly against the Democratic Party by the summer of 1864. Soldiers were impatient with those back home who seemed to be undermining their efforts, whose political success seemed to depend on Union military misfortune. McClellan, popular as he had been as a commander, was fatally tainted by association with the Copperhead wing of the party, and in particular by the nomination of George H. Pendleton as his running mate.

Democrats feared that their supporters in the army would not be allowed to express their preferences freely. General McClellan's brother reported that "nothing is seen by the troops but Republican papers and the Democrats seem to be afraid to open their mouth or do anything." One Democratic soldier reported that his company had been compelled to vote for Lincoln. He reported that when the men were in rank there was an order that all who wished to vote for McClellan should take a step back; "all those who favor the re-election of Lincoln will stand fast." Assistant Secretary of War Charles Dana later recalled that "all the power and influence of the War Department, then something enormous from the vast expenditure and extensive relations of the war, was employed to secure the re-election of Mr. Lincoln." There were many ways in which the Union Party's control of the apparatus of state governments over most of the North pushed up their majorities among Union troops. In Connecticut, for example, a state that had passed a constitutional amendment to allow soldier voting, local Union Party officials were quite open about the fact that they exercised partisan discretion when drawing up lists of registered soldiers. Soldiers' letters indicate that communal sentiment and the shared experience of combat were perhaps the strongest factors framing a soldier's political choices. Excessive pressure from above merely reinforced the immense pressure that was exerted by active partisans in the ranks to conform politically.

Voting for Lincoln was a highly important symbol of the connectedness of the political and the military campaign. Many soldiers concurred with the sentiments of an infantryman from Connecticut who declared that he felt as if he was using the bayonet against the enemy on the field and the ballot against the traitors in the rear. After casting his ballot for Lincoln, another soldier wrote: "The day of the greatest battle & I believe the greatest victory…has been fought and I know won today." But whether they were able to vote in the field or not, soldiers exercised a significant political influence over their home communities. Letters home urged families and neighbors to wage war on political opponents and dissidents. The military dimension also helped to transform the language of politics, giving concrete meaning to descriptions of the opposing party as traitors or the enemy. Union Party newspapers urged voters at home to support their soldiers by using their ballots "as our husbands and brothers have used their bullets."

—*Adam I.P. Smith*

See also Election of 1864.
For further reading:
Long, David E. *The Jewel of Liberty; Abraham Lincoln's Re-election and the End of Slavery* (1994).

SONS OF CONFEDERATE VETERANS

The South's celebration of the Confederacy and its heroes in what is commonly known as the "Lost Cause" resulted in the formation of several Confederate organizations. The first of these were the ladies' memorial associations (LMAs), which were formed at the end of the Civil War. Groups of former veterans formed into camps in the 1870s and 1880s, and in 1889 the United Confederate Veterans (UCV) was formed. Members of the LMAs and the UCV were the first generation of white Southerners to participate in the Lost Cause. In the 1890s, a second generation of men and women joined in the movement to commemorate the Confederacy—the United Daughters of the Confederacy in 1894 and, in 1896, the United Sons of Confederate Veterans.

The sons of veterans began creating their own auxiliaries to veterans' organizations as early as 1889, the year the UCV was formed. The movement to form a regional organization began in 1890 when a group of sons attempted to establish itself as a formal branch of the UCV. Their bid was unsuccessful, but six years later, in Richmond, Virginia, the United Sons of Confederate Veterans was inaugurated. The group eventually dropped "United" from its name in 1908 fearing that its abbreviation, USCV, might cause the group to be confused with the U.S. Colored Volunteers.

The SCV, like the UCV, was organized into local groups or camps, whose chief officer served as the commander. In its early history, the SCV drew most of its members from the middle and upper classes. Similar to the membership of the UCV and UDC, the SCV was organized in Southern towns and cities. Moreover, the first men to join the SCV were, literally, sons of Confederate veterans.

By the time the SCV was organized, the Lost Cause was taking new shape. The UDC, formed only two years earlier, experienced phenomenal growth and was well positioned to determine what direction the Lost Cause would take in the twentieth century. Building on the thirty-year tradition of the LMAs, the Daughters had established a broader set of objectives for honoring the Confederacy. The SCV, however, whose members were

primarily white-collar, urban, and essentially New South businessmen, showed little interest in continuing the Confederate tradition. They did not have the emotional enthusiasm of either their fathers in the UCV or their female contemporaries in the UDC. Indeed, the SCV never attracted a large membership and was often criticized by members of the UDC and the UCV for its apathetic response to Lost Cause projects.

The Sons of Confederate Veterans did join other Confederate organizations in promoting what they called "true" history. Like the UCV, the Sons formed committees to discuss the importance of promoting the use of "unbiased" texts in public schools so that students learned the "correct version" of the history of the War between the States—the official term for the Civil War within Confederate organizations. Aside from making official statements about "true" history, however, the SCV rarely became involved in the region's public schools in the same way as the UDC. SCV members did help raise money for building Confederate monuments, although generally they preferred to make donations and left the fundraising to the UDC.

Members of the modern SCV are noticeably different from the group's original membership. While the modern organization continues to promote what the founders called "true" history, its membership is more likely to include working-class men. According to contemporary accounts, the early SCV appeared disinterested in continuing the Confederate tradition. With Jim Crow on its side and widespread support of the Lost Cause among middle-class and upper-class whites, the early SCV membership was not consumed with its Confederate heritage.

The modern SCV, to the contrary, has taken responsibility for "protecting" Confederate heritage, making it a political issue. The modern SCV also operates under a different set of conditions. Civil rights transformed Southern race relations in the twentieth century, and support for the Confederate tradition has dwindled among most Southern whites. These very conditions have emboldened the SCV, although its message of "heritage, not hate" is clear evidence of an organization on the defensive. Indeed, the SCV has become an organization that must answer its critics as it attempts to preserve the history and symbols of the Confederacy in a world markedly different than the one in which the organization was founded.

—*Karen L. Cox*

See also Ladies Memorial Associations; Lost Cause; Memorials, C.S.A.; United Daughters of the Confederacy; Veterans' Organizations.
For further reading:
Foster, Gaines M. *Ghosts of the Confederacy: Defeat, The Lost Cause, and The Emergence of The New South, 1865–1913.* (1987)

SONS OF LIBERTY, ORDER OF
(1863–1864)

The Order of Sons of Liberty was a secret fraternal society organized across the Midwest in 1863 and 1864. Leaders of the order planned an uprising on 16 August 1864 to overthrow the governments of four Midwestern states and withdraw these states from the Union. The order was founded by New Orleans Unionist Phineas G. Wright as the Order of American Knights (O.A.K.). The O.A.K. took root in Illinois in the spring of 1863. Amos Green of Paris, Illinois, served as Illinois grand commander until March 1864, when S. Corning Judd of Lewistown, Illinois, replaced him. In the fall of 1863 the order spread into Indiana. Wright organized the first Indiana temple at the end of August in Terre Haute. Two weeks later, a second temple was organized in Indianapolis. Harrison H. Dodd, an Indianapolis printer and itinerant Democratic orator, was elected Indiana grand commander. At its peak, in the spring of 1864, the order probably numbered between 10,000 and 20,000 members in each state. Prominent temples were organized in Evansville, Fort Wayne, New Albany, Sullivan, Salem, Peru, Logansport, Laporte, and Huntington, Indiana, and in Quincy, Peoria, and Springfield, Illinois. Smaller organizations existed in Missouri and Kentucky. In February 1864, the order changed its name to the Sons of Liberty. Clement L. Vallandigham, an Ohio congressman banished by President Lincoln for his opposition to the war, accepted the nominal position as the order's supreme grand commander while in exile in Canada.

The order's membership consisted of two distinct groups. Lawyers, professional men, and Democratic Party leaders joined temples in major cities and county seats scattered across Indiana and Illinois. In the rural areas of southern Indiana and the Illinois and Wabash river valleys of Illinois, large numbers of farmers and laborers joined local associations for mutual protection. In late 1863 and early 1864, the order began to establish ties with these mutual protection associations and incorporate their members into its ranks. Urban and rural members often disagreed about the purposes of the order, however. Politicians and professionals in urban areas saw the order as a means to organize the Democratic Party for victory in the elections of 1864. They also saw the order as a potential military force to preserve Democratic access to the polls, access often blocked by mobs of Republicans and soldiers. Rural members, on the other hand, used their mutual protection associations to organize resistance to military arrests and the Conscription Act of 1863. They saw the order as an opportunity to coordinate resistance across the state and region. In late 1863 the order divided Indiana and Illinois into military

districts and appointed a "major general" to organize forces in each district.

In the spring of 1864, Harrison Dodd and several other leaders of the order, now reorganized as the Sons of Liberty, began to plan an uprising to forestall the draft due to take place on 5 September. Dodd had a small group of co-conspirators, including William A. Bowles, William Harrison, Horace Heffren, James B. Wilson, and John C. Walker from Indiana; Joshua Bullitt, W. R. Thomas, Mr. Williams, and Dr. Kalfus from Kentucky; and James Barrett, Charles Walsh, Robert Holloway, and B. B. Piper from Illinois. The plan called for the simultaneous release of Confederate prisoners at Camp Morton in Indianapolis, Camp Douglas in Chicago, and Rock Island in Illinois on 16 August 1864. The order would arm these prisoners by seizing arsenals in Indianapolis and Chicago. The combined military force of prisoners and members of the order would seize control of the state governments of Indiana, Illinois, Missouri, and Kentucky and withdraw these states from the Union. The conspirators attempted to coordinate their rising with the Confederate army through Confederate agents operating from Canada. Dodd and Walker purchased 2,500 revolvers and over 100,000 rounds of ammunition with Confederate funds advanced for this purpose.

When the Democratic leadership of Indiana learned of Dodd's plot, they demanded he cease all preparations. Dodd agreed, but Felix G. Stidger, a government detective, had already infiltrated the conspiracy. The Republican authorities of Indiana publicized details of the plot and arrested Dodd, Bowles, Harrison, and Heffren, as well as Stephen Horsey, Andrew Humphreys, and Lambdin P. Milligan. Horsey, Humphreys, and Milligan were never part of the conspiracy, but Humphreys and Milligan had been appointed major generals within the order's military structure. Even though William Harrison and Horace Heffren turned state's evidence, the evidence against the other conspirators was not sufficient to try them for treason in civil court. Consequently, Republican authorities chose to try Dodd, Bowles, Horsey, Humphreys, and Milligan before a military commission on charges of conspiracy, inciting insurrection, and offering aid and comfort to the Confederacy. The commission convicted all five defendants and sentenced all but Humphreys to die on the scaffold. In 1866, however, the Supreme Court heard Lambdin Milligan's appeal of the jurisdiction of the commission. In the decision *Ex parte Milligan*, the Court overturned the verdicts and set the defendants free, ruling that a military commission had no jurisdiction over civilians in areas where the civil courts were operating normally.

—*Robert H. Churchill*

See also *Ex parte Milligan*; Humphreys, Andrew Atkinson; Milligan, Lambdin P.; Vallandigham, Clement Laird.

For further reading:
Churchill, Robert H. "Liberty, Conscription, and Delusions of Grandeur: The Sons of Liberty Conspiracy of 1863–64." *Prologue Quarterly* (1998).
Klaus, Samuel, ed. *The Milligan Case* (1970).
Klement, Frank L. *Dark Lanterns: Secret Political Societies, Conspiracies, and Treason Trials in the Civil War* (1984).
Tredway, G. R., *Democratic Opposition to the Lincoln Administration during the Civil War* (1973).

SORREL, GILBERT MOXLEY
(1838–1901)
Confederate general

Born to Francis Sorrel and Matilda Moxley Sorrel in Savannah, Georgia, Gilbert Moxley Sorrel was educated locally before working for a regional railroad. As the sectional crisis heated up in 1860, Sorrel joined a local Savannah militia company, his only military experience before the war.

At the advent of the Confederacy, Sorrel enlisted in the Confederate army and offered his services as a voluntary aide to Brigadier General James Longstreet. Sorrel served in that capacity at First Bull Run and remained on Longstreet's staff, receiving the appointment as brigade acting adjutant general in the fall of 1861 with the rank of captain.

Sorrel continued to serve in that position through the Peninsula campaign. Promoted to major after that campaign, he served as acting adjutant general of Longstreet's division. Sorrel was in the thick of the fighting at Antietam and received a wound there. In the spring of 1863, he was promoted to lieutenant colonel and continued on Longstreet's staff at Gettysburg.

In the late summer of 1863, Sorrel accompanied Longstreet to Tennessee and Georgia, where he served as his adjutant during the Chickamauga and Knoxville campaigns. Returning with Longstreet to Virginia at the rank of colonel, Sorrel had so gained his commander's trust in the preceding campaigns that at the battle of the Wilderness Longstreet gave him command of the corps' right wing. Impressed with his actions in this battle and the succeeding campaign, Confederate authorities promoted Sorrel to brigadier general in the fall of 1864 and gave him a field command. He fought in the Petersburg campaign, and at the battle of Hatcher's Run in February 1865 he received a severe chest wound. He was unable to return to his command in the last months of the war.

After the war, Sorrel worked as a businessman in Savannah, Georgia. In his spare time he worked on his memoirs, which were published after his death. This effort, which provides an intimate view of the Army of Northern Virginia, is Sorrel's primary Civil War legacy.

—*David S. Heidler and Jeanne T. Heidler*

See also Longstreet, James.
For further reading:
Sorrel, Gilbert Moxley. *Recollections of a Confederate Staff Officer* (1959).

SOULÉ, PIERRE
(1801–1870)
Confederate politician and general

Born in France to Joseph Soulé, an officer under Napoleon, and Jeanne Lacroix Soulé, Pierre Soulé studied for the Jesuit priesthood before rejecting that calling to agitate for republican government in France. His political activities ultimately gained him exile from France. After a brief time in Great Britain, Soulé made his way to Baltimore, Maryland, and ultimately to New Orleans. He traveled around the southwest to Tennessee and Kentucky, learning fluent English in his travels before returning to New Orleans.

Having practiced law in France, Soulé had little work to do to prepare himself for that profession in Louisiana. Within a short time he became a prominent New Orleans attorney, married into a prominent family, and entered Louisiana Democratic politics. In addition to serving in the convention to revise the state constitution, Soulé was elected to the state legislature in 1844. In 1846 he was selected to fill a short unexpired U.S. Senate term, and in 1848 he thwarted his Louisiana rival, John Slidell, by being elected to a full Senate term. In the Senate he became known as an ardent advocate of states' rights.

With the advent of a Democratic administration in the election of Franklin Pierce in 1852, Soulé hoped for a diplomatic appointment. In spite of his ardent expansionism and stated desire for the United States to annex Spanish Cuba, Pierce appointed Soulé minister to Spain. He resigned his senate seat in April 1853 and accepted the appointment. While the Pierce administration was all too willing to acquire Cuba, Soulé's heavy-handed methods while serving as minister, and especially his authorship of the Ostend Manifesto publicly calling for annexation, put him in disfavor, and he resigned his post in December 1854. For the next several years, Soulé devoted himself to his law practice in New Orleans.

Chosen as one of Louisiana's delegates to the Democratic National Convention in Charleston, South Carolina, in 1860, Soulé illustrated his movement away from the extreme states' rights stance of his earlier career (and perhaps his renewed political ambition) by supporting the nomination of Stephen A. Douglas rather than one of the many Southern possibilities. When Douglas (and the other candidates) lost the election to Abraham Lincoln in the fall of 1860, Soulé opposed the immediate secession of Louisiana. When the state seceded, however, he followed the state into the Confederacy.

Having long engaged in a feud with Jefferson Davis, who by this time was president of the Confederacy, Soulé could not expect an appointment in the new Confederate government. Instead, he remained in New Orleans continuing his legal practice until the city was threatened in early 1862 with a Union attack. As one of the more prominent citizens of the city, he accepted appointment by the city government as a provost marshal, overseeing the mobilization of the civilian sector of the city for its defense. When the city was abandoned in May 1862 by most of its military forces, he wrote to the War Department bemoaning the government's neglect of the city. When New Orleans was occupied by the Federal troops of General Benjamin F. Butler shortly thereafter, Soulé wrote to the Confederate military forces outside of the city that for the good of the citizenry, there should be no attempt to retake New Orleans.

Shortly after writing this letter, Soulé was arrested for treason by order of Butler. He was sent to Fort Lafayette in New York to be held for trial. While in Fort Lafayette, Soulé's health began to suffer. A number of his former colleagues and the French minister to Washington urged his release on humanitarian grounds. In November 1862 his release was authorized on the condition that he be paroled to Boston. Once in Boston, however, Soulé escaped to the Bahamas. Making his way through the blockade back to the Confederacy, Soulé sought a military appointment from the Confederate government. Eventually he was granted an honorary rank of brigadier general and became a voluntary aide-de-camp to P. G. T. Beauregard in Charleston, South Carolina.

After the war, Soulé engaged in a number of schemes, including an attempt to establish a Confederate colony in Mexico. Ultimately his physical and mental health deteriorated and he died a broken man in New Orleans.

—*David S. Heidler and Jeanne T. Heidler*

See also Butler, Benjamin Franklin; Louisiana; New Orleans, Capture of.
For further reading:
Moore, John Preston. "Pierre Soulé: Southern Expansionist and Promoter." *Journal of Southern History* (1955).
Reinecke, Joseph Alfred. "Diplomatic Career of Pierre Soulé" (M.A. thesis, 1914).

SOUTH CAROLINA

No state so embodied the tragic meaning of the Confederate South as did the first state to shatter the bonds of union, South Carolina. Deeply entangled in the "peculiar institution" since the early colonial period, the Palmetto State developed an extreme attachment to the notion of states' rights as a means of protecting pride, profits, and their slaveholding social order.

Scholars long viewed South Carolina's "Hotspur"

Point Battery at Charleston, South Carolina, April 1865 (*Library of Congress*)

radicalism as a result of its domination by a pseudoaristo-cratic oligarchy made up of the cotton planters of the Up Country and the rice lords of the Low Country coast united under the political leadership of John C. Calhoun. In this version of South Carolina's peculiarity, the long shadow of Calhoun brooded over the state even after his death, sending it on its catastrophic career of political radicalism and neofeudal pretensions.

A more nuanced explanation recognizes the powerful influence of Calhoun and the planter class while also taking into account the widespread fear of the abolitionist North among slaveholding and non-slaveholding farmers. Unnerved by decades of assaults by abolitionists, terrified by John Brown's October 1859 raid on Harper's Ferry, and made fearfully resolute by the election of Abraham Lincoln in 1860, the yeomen of the northwestern hill country joined the Charleston

elite in electing a secession convention that unanimously voted to take the state out of the Union on 20 December 1860.

White South Carolinians believed that they had solved the question of sovereignty, but the federal government took a quite different view. The most immediate question concerned the fate of federal military installations, in particular Fort Sumter in Charleston harbor. On 26 December 1860, the fort's commander, Major Robert Anderson, had moved his men to Sumter from the land-bound Fort Moultrie under the cover of night, hoping that this would at least enable him to make a limited defense. Lame-duck President James Buchanan attempted to resupply the fort on 9 January 1861. The supply ship, *Star of the West*, found itself rattled by cannon fire and turned back. This situation, gallingly unsatisfactory to both sides, continued until

Ex-governor William Aiken's house at Charleston, 1865
(*Library of Congress*)

March, when the Confederate government took command of the Charleston batteries and demanded Sumter's surrender. When Anderson and the newly inaugurated Lincoln administration refused, bombardment of Sumter began on 12 April. Federal forces yielded on 14 April.

The bombardment of the harbor fort proved prophetic in that much of the fighting of the Civil War in South Carolina centered on the city of Charleston and its coastal environs. In November 1861, Union forces struck just south of Charleston at Port Royal, seeking a base for their tightening blockade of the South. Union commander Samuel F. Dupont's seventy-four-vessel fleet attacked the two Confederate redoubts guarding Port Royal, styled "Fort Beauregard" and "Fort Walker," shelling them into submission and quickly occupying both Port Royal and Beaufort. In 1862, a concentration of Confederate troops at Charleston led to the relinquishment of Georgetown, the fall of which opened almost thirty-five miles of the Waccamaw River to Union gunboats. Federal troops threatened Charleston itself in June 1862 by landing a large force on James Island. Outnumbered Confederate forces turned back this attempt to seize their "holy city" at the battle of Secessionville, though not without heavy casualties. The following spring, a massive bombardment of Fort Sumter failed to wrest away the strong point from the Confederacy. July 1863 would see yet another attempt at the Charleston defenses as Union ground troops attacked Morris Island's Battery Wagner, an attack led by

the scion of Boston abolitionists, Robert Gould Shaw, and his famous African-American regiment, the 54th Massachusetts. Failing to take the battery and suffering heavy casualties, Union forces besieged the position until it fell in September.

Union triumphs along the coast had the effect of bringing de facto freedom to a number of black South Carolinians months before Lincoln's call for emancipation. Northern missionaries, and entrepreneurs eager to apply free-labor principles to cotton culture, followed Federal troops into this region, most famously in the "Port Royal Experiment." The outcome of such experiments included a return to plantation agriculture and contractual and wage labor instead of the autonomous, subsistence farming to which many Sea Island freedpeople aspired.

War in South Carolina became more than a series of coastal pinpricks in February 1865 as William Tecumseh Sherman's veteran army, fresh from their famed "March to the Sea," crossed the Savannah River into the beleaguered state. Fragments of a Confederate force assembled by P. G. T. Beauregard fell back grudgingly before the blue flood tide, surrendering Columbia on 17 February. Federal troops (allegedly made especially enthusiastic for the Union cause by their discovery of a cache of abandoned Confederate whiskey) entered the statehouse and held a mock session of the recently fled South Carolina legislature, passing a resolution of censure against John C. Calhoun and jovially repealing the Ordinance of Secession. This bit of rowdy levity preceded the burning of Columbia, still controversial in its origins but apparently due in part to Confederate ineptitude in destroying stored cotton. Sherman's forces marched out of Columbia, which was then a smoldering ruin, on 20 February. Charleston had surrendered on 17 February, and the remainder of the Confederate forces either returned to their homes or made their way to

The Citadel and Marion Square, Charleston, 1865
(*Library of Congress*)

Ruins of the Western Depot at Charleston, 1865 (*National Archives*)

North Carolina for a final stand with the shattered remnants of the Army of Tennessee. The war in South Carolina was over.

The first state to secede paid a horrific cost for its precipitous decision. Historian Walter Edgar estimates that 30 to 35 percent of South Carolina's white men of military age did not return from the war. About a half of the state's total wealth disappeared, much of it in the form of emancipated slaves. White South Carolinians would soon find their "property" acting as a voting bloc that would ensure Republican ascendancy in the statehouse until 1876.

—*W. Scott Poole*

See also Calhoun, John Caldwell; Class Conflict, C.S.A.; Columbia, South Carolina, Burning of; Fort Sumter, Bombardment of; Fort Wagner, Battle of; Port Royal Sound, Battle of; Secession; Shaw, Robert Gould; *Star of the West.*

For further reading:

Barrett, John G. *Sherman's March through the Carolinas* (1956; reprint 1996).

Channing, Steven A. *Crisis of Fear: Secession in South Carolina* (1974).

Edgar, Walter. *South Carolina: A History* (1998).

Ford, Lacy K. *Origins of Southern Radicalism: The South Carolina Upcountry, 1800–1860* (1988).

Rose, Willie Lee. *Rehearsal for Reconstruction: The Port Royal Experiment* (1964).

SOUTH MOUNTAIN, MARYLAND, BATTLE OF
(14 September 1862)

A fifty-mile-long, 1,300-foot-high ridge between Catoctin Mountain to the east and Elk Mountain to the west, South Mountain was the site of the opening engagements between Robert E. Lee's Army of Northern Virginia and George B. McClellan's Army of the Potomac in what would become the Antietam campaign. South Mountain was cut from east to west by several passes, including Turner's Gap (through which ran the National Road to Hagerstown, Maryland, and beyond) and Crampton's Gap to the south (connecting western Maryland to Harper's Ferry).

The Confederate army began entering Frederick, Maryland, east of South Mountain and from where the National Road ran to Turner's Gap, on 6 September 1862. There Lee devised the plan embodied in his Order 191 that divided his army, sending more than half by different routes to take the Federal garrison at Harper's Ferry and sending the remainder to Boonsboro and then Hagerstown. On 10 September, Brigadier General John Walker left Frederick to approach Harper's Ferry from the south to take Loudoun Heights; Major General

Lafayette McLaws with Major General Richard Heron Anderson left to travel through Crampton's Gap to come at Harper's Ferry at Maryland Heights; and Thomas J. "Stonewall" Jackson departed with three divisions to travel through Turner's Gap, cross the Potomac River at Williamsport, and approach Harper's Ferry from Martinsburg, Virginia. The remainder of the army followed the same day through Turner's Gap and stopped briefly at Boonsboro. Major General D. H. Hill and his division remained there, and Lee moved with the remainder of Lieutenant General James Longstreet's corps to Hagerstown on 11 September. Major General J. E. B. Stuart and his cavalry were charged with watching the passes across South Mountain.

Meanwhile, McClellan was moving slowly toward Frederick. After arriving on the morning of 13 September in an encampment outside of town, Corporal Barton W. Mitchell found a copy of Lee's Order 191 wrapped around three cigars. The paper was passed up to McClellan's headquarters. Once McClellan realized that Lee's army was divided, he sent cavalry toward Turner's Gap to determine if it was being held. He planned to move the remainder of his army forward at dawn on 14 September.

D. H. Hill had brought part of his division back to Turner's Gap because of reports of Federal preparations. On the morning of 14 September he was there with a small part of Stuart's cavalry when the Union cavalry approached. Hill had sent word to Lee on the night of the 13th about the apparent Union activity. As a result Lee sent word to Hill to hold on as long as possible and sent Longstreet back toward South Mountain to lend assistance with the remainder of his corps. In the meantime, McClellan had sent Major General William Franklin and his VI Corps toward Crampton's Gap to push through to stop Jackson from taking Harper's Ferry. Franklin had about 20,000 men. Suspecting such a move on McClellan's part, Lee had sent word to Jackson to hurry with his operation and to McLaws and Anderson to watch their rear.

Hill did not have enough men to protect Turner's Gap and Fox's Gap, about a mile to the south. As he had only 2,300 men on the morning of 14 September, there is little doubt he would have been totally overwhelmed if McClellan had moved with any dispatch. Only Major General Jesse Reno's IX Corps was close enough to attack, and it proved very slow moving into position. Brigadier General Jacob Cox with his division was in the lead. He decided to move around Hill's right flank at Fox's Gap and, at about 9:00 A.M., sent 3,000 men against 1,000 defenders. Confederate brigadier general Samuel Garland was killed in the fierce fighting there that morning.

While the fighting went back and forth at Fox's Gap, Hill was desperately working to bring up the remainder

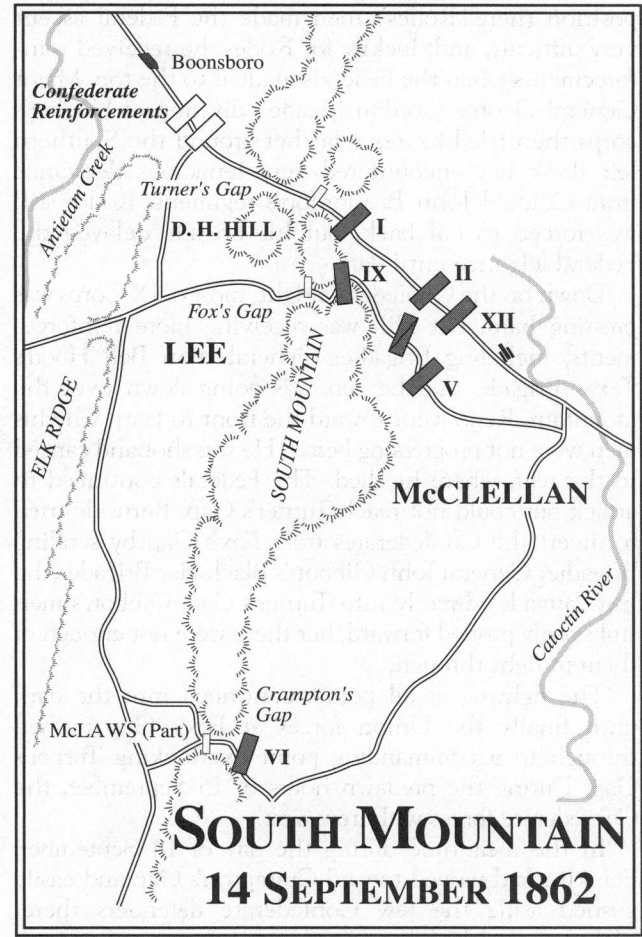

SOUTH MOUNTAIN
14 SEPTEMBER 1862

of his division. Luckily for Hill, McClellan was not hurrying the rest of his army up to South Mountain. Reno was still managing the fight there but was sending his divisions in piecemeal.

In early afternoon, Union major general Ambrose Burnside arrived and took command. He decided, however, to wait until Major General Joseph Hooker with his I Corps arrived before sending anyone else in to continue the assault on the Confederate flanks. As a result, Cox's efforts at Fox's Gap, while successful, had not been followed up with any further offensive.

Hill was now being reinforced. With these fresh troops he tried and failed in a counterattack against Cox. The two sides continued to fight throughout the afternoon.

In the afternoon, Lee arrived on the west side of the mountain and took command of the defenses. At about the same time, more of the Union army was finally arriving from the east. Hooker's I Corps was sent to the Confederate left at about 4:00 P.M. to flank the Southerners from the north. Hill had anticipated such a move and had placed Brigadier General Robert Rodes's brigade of about 1,200 in a fairly defensible

position there. Rodes's men made the Federal ascent very difficult, and, luckily for Rodes, he received reinforcements when the Federals made it to the top. Major General George Gordon Meade's division of Hooker's corps then tried to move farther around the Southern left flank but encountered very tenacious resistance from Colonel John B. Gordon's regiment. Rodes still was forced to fall back, but his brigade delayed the Federal advance until dark.

Down on the Confederate right, most of IX Corps was pressing hard, but Hill was receiving more reinforcements, including Brigadier General John Bell Hood's Texas Brigade. As the sun was going down over the mountain, Reno went toward the front to learn why his men were not progressing better. He was shot and carried to the rear, where he died. The Federals continued to attack but could not reach Turner's Gap. Burnside tried to divert the Confederates from Fox's Gap by sending Brigadier General John Gibbon's Black Hat Brigade (the Iron Brigade) directly into Turner's Gap. Gibbon's men stubbornly pushed forward, but there were not enough of them to fight through.

The fighting at all points continued into the dark until finally the Union forces at Fox's Gap pushed through to a commanding point overlooking Turner's Gap. During the predawn hours of 15 September, the Confederate forces withdrew west.

In the meantime during the day of 14 September, Franklin had moved toward Crampton's Gap and easily pushed aside the few Confederate defenders there. McLaws started back to repulse this threat to Jackson's operation against Harper's Ferry. Franklin delayed moving against McLaws until Jackson was able to secure Harper's Ferry the next day. As a result, most of the Confederate force assaulting Harper's Ferry was able to join Lee at Sharpsburg, Maryland, before McClellan attacked across Antietam Creek on 17 September.

—*David S. Heidler and Jeanne T. Heidler*

See also Antietam, Battle of; Burnside, Ambrose; Cox, Jacob; Crampton's Gap, Battle of; Franklin, William; Hill, Daniel Harvey; Iron Brigade; Reno, Jesse.

For further reading:

Priest, John M. *Antietam: Before Antietam: The Battle for South Mountain* (1992).

Sears, Stephen W. *Landscape Turned Red: The Battle of Antietam* (1983).

SOUTHERN ILLUSTRATED NEWS

Modeled on the London weekly of the same name, the *Southern Illustrated News* was founded in Richmond in September 1862 and was intended to give Southern audiences an alternative to the fiercely Republican and abolitionist *Harper's Weekly*, which, in addition to its unpopular politics, was no longer available in the South.

But while the magazine flourished, despite subscription prices that at one point reached $20, and published until the very last weeks of the war, it never achieved the influence of its Northern counterpart; despite its name, the *Illustrated News* had very few illustrations and, most importantly, lacked an artist with the talent and political zeal of *Harper's* Thomas Nast.

The magazine is best known for its literary offerings: it was edited for a time by John Reuben Thompson, who after the war became literary editor of the poet William Cullen Bryant's *New York Evening Post*; and its contributors included the novelist William Gilmore Simms and the poet James R. Randall, author of the song, "Maryland, My Maryland." Its principal correspondent was John Esten Cooke, who also served as a staff officer for both J. E. B. Stuart and "Stonewall" Jackson.

The *Illustrated News* was remarkably similar from issue to issue. The front page invariably featured a woodcut illustration and biography of a Confederate general; similar profiles appeared inside the paper, surrounded by fictional stories and poetry. Unlike *Harper's,* the *Illustrated News* contained no emotional and inspiring centerfold drawings; its scenes of camp life were humdrum and unlikely to rally the populace as did Nast's evocative illustrations.

Still, the magazine enjoyed tremendous popularity. Within a few weeks, it achieved a circulation of more than 20,000 and held it for the remainder of the war, despite a lack of competent engravers and a constant shortage of newsprint. Cooke in particular did his best to inspire his readers; his eulogy of William D. Farley, one of J. E. B. Stuart's most able scouts, who was killed at Fleetwood, made its subject—hailed by Cooke as "a man so notable for daring, skill and efficiency as a partisan, that all who valued those great qualities honored him as their chiefest exemplar"—a legend throughout the South.

Politically, it reflected orthodox Confederate thought. It labeled the Emancipation Proclamation a sign of Lincoln's desperation, claiming it was intended to stifle the resurgent War Democrats, who had begun to threaten Lincoln's presidency: "This proclamation is intended to keep them quiet, or to dispose of them in the most summary manner, if they should succeed in their ticket." As for the Lincoln administration itself, the *Illustrated News* opined that the government in Washington "is a military despotism, as absolute as that of Russia."

Gettysburg, the magazine maintained, was a victory for the South; Lee had retreated only to secure the many thousands of prisoners he had taken. But when Lee fell back, the *Illustrated News* wrote, "The most astounding lies were telegraphed to the [Northern] cities and spread over the country by means of the press. Lee's army, according to them, had been completely routed and disor-

ganized.... Before the end of the week, the truth with regard to Lee began to come out. He had gained a great victory and captured thousands of prisoners." Even at the end of 1863, when the tide of battle had clearly turned, the *Illustrated News* stubbornly insisted that it found "nothing in any part of [the year's events] which, for a moment, should stimulate gloom or relax our energy."

Inevitably, with Lee's army on the brink of defeat and the Confederacy collapsing, there was little use for the *Southern Illustrated News*. It published its final issue just two weeks before the surrender at Appomattox.

—Eric Fettmann

See also Cooke, John Esten; *Harper's Weekly*; Newspapers; Simms, William Gilmore.

For further reading:

Andrews, J. Cutler. *The South Reports the Civil War* (1970).
Harwell, Richard B., ed. *The Civil War Reader* (1957).
Lomazow, Steven. *American Periodicals: A Collector's Manual and Reference Guide* (1996).
Mott, Frank Luther: *A History of American Magazines* (1938).

SOUTHERN LITERARY MESSENGER

The most famous of Southern magazines enjoyed its heyday a quarter-century before the onset of the Civil War, when Edgar Allan Poe, who also served as a frequent contributor, edited it. Founded in 1834 by T. W. White and editor James Heath, it was meant to be the showcase of Southern culture and to foment the spread of a distinctively Southern literary style, but ultimately it fell victim to the economic devastation that accompanied the Civil War.

Despite its professed ambition to rally "Southern talents and Southern public spirit around the drooping and well-nigh prostrate banner of Southern literature," the *Messenger* never did seem to catch on among Southern readers, although it was widely read and respected by Northern writers. Washington Irving, James Fenimore Cooper, and John Quincy Adams offered early encouragement, but after only several issues, Heath complained that "from our Northern and Eastern friends we have received more complimentary notices than from any of our southern brethren without the limits of our own State." More than two decades later, one of Heath's successors, John Reuben Thompson, lamented that "*Harper's Magazine* has probably five times as many subscribers south of the Potomac... and even *Putnam's Monthly*, which has recently outraged the entire slave-holding portion of the Union by lending itself to the extremist views of the abolitionists, has a larger circulation among slave-holders."

Part of the problem may have been that there was not general agreement on just what constituted genuine Southern literature. "There is much senseless clamour over Southern books," the magazine wrote late in its life. "Many weak and trashy productions receive undue praise at the hands of Southern critics, merely because they are written and published south of the Potomac."

For the first two decades of its life, the *Messenger* largely eschewed politics, although it consistently defended slavery; early on, however, responding to a series of articles by Judge Beverly Tucker of the College of William and Mary praising the advantages of slavery, Heath openly branded slavery "a great evil, which society sooner or later will find not only to its interest to remove or mitigate, but will seek its gradual abolition, or amelioration...."

Under George William Bagby, a frequent contributor who became editor in June 1860, the magazine switched its primary emphasis to politics. "Some northern magazines could go through the years 1861–1865 without mentioning the war," wrote historian Frank Luther Mott. "Not so the *Messenger* with a Bagby at the helm." In December, Bagby vehemently called for Southern secession and demanded that Virginia take the lead: "Let us tear from the national flag the fifteen stars which the despots of the North have attempted to sully with the imputation of barbarism," he wrote. "Let us give these stars a double brilliance by forming them into a cross— the Southern Cross—emblem of that pure and holy religion which has been reviled, trampled, and spit upon in the interest of Abolitionism."

Throughout the war, Bagby aimed his pen not only at Lincoln and the North but at the South's leadership as well. Though initially supportive of Jefferson Davis, whom he had suggested for the Confederate presidency, Bagby became an outspoken critic of his prosecution of the war. "From the Chief Magistrate on down," he wrote in the summer of 1862, "none of us have got any common sense, any real energy, and certainly not any forecast."

But Bagby's fierce Southern patriotism proved to be the beginning of the end for the *Messenger*, which had never established a firm financial footing (as early as 1851, editor Thompson lamented that "The *Messenger* is almost 'gone.' I look into the future to see nothing but diseases.") Bagby's call for secession lost the magazine its substantial Northern readership and, surprisingly, much of its Southern readership as well. With its circulation decimated, the *Messenger* was in no position to cope with the drastically mounting costs of wartime publication; like other Southern journals, the magazine had gotten its ink and paper from Northern sources, which were now cut off. Adding to the problems was the *Messenger's* inability to get its equally impoverished readers to pay for their subscriptions. In 1862, Bagby struck hundreds of delinquents from the circulation list, admonishing them in print to "find someone else simple and rich enough to furnish you with reading matter free of cost." After publishing the June 1864 issue, the *Messenger's* printers were drafted to defend Richmond

against Union attack and it was decided to suspend publication for good.

—*Eric Fettmann*

See also Bagby, George W.
For further reading:
Minor, Benjamin B. *The Southern Literary Messenger, 1834–1864* (1905).
Mott, Frank Luther. *American Journalism* (1962).
———. *A History of American Magazines* (1938).

SOUTHERN UNIONISM

Southern support for the Union expressed itself in a variety of ways during the Civil War and was surprisingly strong from its outset. During the secession crisis of 1860–1861, most Southerners opposed leaving the Union. Many whites, three-fourths of whom owned no slaves, feared secession would bring on a rich man's war in which they had little stake. As for the South's enslaved blacks, they generally believed Abraham Lincoln was their best hope for freedom and looked on secession as a bar to that goal. Even some wealthy planters, many of them old-line Whigs, advised against secession. Such a move, they argued, might result in a civil war that a divided South could hardly survive. Ignoring the majority's will and the dangers inherent in the South's social divisions, state conventions and legislatures across the region, all of them dominated by slaveholders, pushed their states out of the Union. One Texas politician conceded that ambitious colleagues had engineered secession without strong backing from "the mass of the people."

Still, there was some general enthusiasm for the war among whites in the wake of Lincoln's call for volunteers to invade the South. But Southern enlistments declined rapidly after First Bull Run. Farmers were reluctant to leave their families in the winter of 1861–1862, and many of those already in the army deserted to help their own families. The Confederacy's response served only to weaken its support at home. In April 1862, it enacted a military draft that wealthy men could avoid by hiring a substitute or paying an exemption fee. Later that year, Congress made slaveholders with twenty or more slaves automatically exempt from the draft. Said Private Sam Watkins of this twenty-slave law: "It gave us the blues … and there was raised the howl of 'rich man's war, poor man's fight.'"

Another practice that helped turn many Southerners against the Richmond government was confiscation of private property, or impressment. Many impressment agents took whatever they wanted, and some even sold produce on the black market. On 22 August 1862, a writer for the *Richmond Enquirer* wrote, "We often hear persons say, 'The *Yankees cannot do us any more harm than our own soldiers have done.*'" When an impressment agent took two cows from a South Carolina farmer, the man swore that "the sooner this damned Government fell to pieces the better it would be for us."

Plain folk bore the brunt of impressment, since they were easier targets than the more influential planters. And small farmers were more likely to grow food products, which was what the impressment agents most often wanted. For the planters, old habits were hard to break. They continued to devote much of their land to cotton production while soldiers and their families went hungry. Although logistical problems contributed to hunger, most of the blame lay with the planters. They regularly smuggled cotton to Europe and even the North, some openly bragging that the longer the war went on, the more money they made. The resulting food shortage led to riots—with women as the main participants—throughout the South and increasing desertion rates in the army.

Desertion became so serious by the summer of 1863 that Jefferson Davis was begging absentees to return. If only they would, he insisted, the Confederacy could match Union armies man for man. But they did not return. A year later, Davis publicly admitted that two-thirds of Confederate soldiers were absent—most of them without leave. Many of these men became involved with the numerous Unionist organizations that had been active in the South since 1861. Some held secretive nighttime meetings at which they swore allegiance to the Union. The Peace and Constitutional Society worked to undermine Confederate authority in Arkansas, as did the Order of the Heroes of America in the southern Appalachians. Perhaps the largest Unionist organization in the South was the Peace Society, which counted membership in Mississippi, Tennessee, Alabama, Georgia, and Florida. Historian Walter Fleming estimated that by 1863 at least half of Alabama's males were associated with the Peace Society. Unionist influence and sentiment made itself felt at the polls that fall all across the South. Two-thirds of the Second Confederate Congress's newly elected members had opposed secession.

Some deserters joined with draft dodgers and other anti-Confederates to form guerrilla bands, sometimes called "tory" or "layout" gangs. They attacked government supply trains, burned bridges, raided local plantations, and harassed impressment agents and conscript officers. So violent did this internal civil war become that on 24 November 1863, a writer for the *Confederate Union* of Milledgeville, Georgia, wrote, "We are fighting each other harder than we ever fought the enemy." Tory gangs were most numerous in the Southern hill country and pine barrens, where they all but eliminated Confederate control by 1864. The Red River Valley of Texas and Louisiana served as a haven for those resisting the Confederacy, as did the Okefenokee Swamp in south Georgia. So too did Jackson County, Alabama, which

seceded from the Confederacy and rejoined the Union in March 1864.

Certainly among the most enthusiastic Unionists were Southern African-Americans. The Confederacy's vice president, Alexander H. Stephens, had said in 1861 that slavery was their natural condition and the cornerstone on which the Confederacy was founded. With the Union's Emancipation Proclamation came a promise of freedom that enslaved blacks eagerly embraced. In fact, they were taking freedom for themselves long before the proclamation took effect in 1863. From the war's outset, they began to travel at will, gather freely, refuse instruction, and resist punishment. In so doing they undermined both slavery and the Confederate war effort. Many fled North and joined Union forces. Of nearly 200,000 blacks under federal arms, three-fourths were native Southerners. Together with 100,000 Southern whites, a quarter of a million Southerners served in the Union military.

On 25 October 1862, Atlanta's *Southern Confederacy* warned its readers that "if we are defeated, it will be by the people at home." The strength of Southern Unionism, in all its degrees and expressions, helped make that prediction a reality.

—*David Williams*

See also Conscription, C.S.A.; Peace Movements.
For further reading:

Current, Richard N. *Lincoln's Loyalists: Union Soldiers from the Confederacy* (1992).
Degler, Carl N. *The Other South: Southern Dissenters in the Nineteenth Century* (1974).
Escott, Paul D. *After Secession: Jefferson Davis and the Failure of Confederate Nationalism* (1977).
Quarles, Benjamin. *The Negro in the Civil War* (1953; reprint, 1989).
Tatum, Georgia Lee. *Disloyalty in the Confederacy* (1934; reprint, 1970).
Watkins, Sam. *Co. Aytch: A Side Show of the Big Show* (1882; reprint 1997).
Williams, David. *Rich Man's War: Class, Caste, and Confederate Defeat in the Lower Chattahoochee Valley* (1998).

SPANISH FORT, BATTLE OF
(27 March–8 April 1865)

During their occupation of the Mobile area in the eighteenth century, the Spanish built a fortification located on the entrance to Bay Minette in southern Alabama. The Confederates used this ancient fort to guard the city of Mobile, a prime target for Union action and invasion. The battle of Spanish Fort, though a minor engagement, was part of the larger Mobile campaign undertaken after the successful actions of Admiral David Farragut in Mobile Bay during August 1864. Despite the capture of Forts Morgan and Gaines in the bay, the city of Mobile remained in Confederate hands and heavily fortified. The Union army lacked sufficient troops to move on the city, but its capture remained a priority.

In the spring of 1865, General Ulysses S. Grant made available troops to commence the Mobile campaign under the direction of West Point graduate Major General Edward Richard Sprigg Canby, then commander of the Federal forces in New Orleans. The strategy called for an attack on the city from the east, avoiding the heavily fortified western lines, and the capture of Spanish Fort, Fort Blakely, and two battery positions known as Battery Tracy and Battery Huger. To accomplish this goal, Canby devised a two-pronged attack with one column advancing from the lower part of Mobile Bay to invest Spanish Fort, while the second column was to progress from Pensacola and attack Fort Blakely. Unfortunately for Canby, terrible weather delayed the start of the operations until March.

Forces under the direction of General Dabney H. Maury, the commander of the Confederate District of the Gulf, opposed Canby. His troops, seasoned veterans of the Army of Tennessee, were deployed under fort commanders. Brigadier General Randall L. Gibson, who after the war became a United States senator from Louisiana, commanded the Spanish Fort garrison of approximately 2,000 men.

Union troops numbering some 32,000 were responsible for the first phase of the plan. They assembled at Fort Gaines and moved inland beginning on 17 March. Soldiers on foot were accompanied by a naval detachment of ironclad monitors that moved along the river systems and waterways. Men of the XIII and XVI Corps labored intensively building corduroy roads or rescuing teams, wagons, and artillery pieces from quicksand. On 27 March the column took up positions near Spanish Fort, complete with over fifty siege guns and over thirty field pieces.

To avoid a frontal assault against the heavy fortifications, Canby began a thirteen-day siege operation. General Gibson, in his account, told of intensive Union artillery fire directed on the fort, which was returned with equal energy by his artillery. However, his supplies were limited against an overwhelming Union force, and by 8 April Gibson realized that the situation was hopeless. General Maury had ordered him to give up the fort if the capture of the garrison was imminent, so Gibson spiked his guns, gathered the sick and wounded, and retreated from the fort along a hidden walkway into the marshes. Casualty estimates from this action vary, but one source puts Confederate losses at Spanish Fort at ninety-three killed and 350 wounded. Federal losses for the Mobile campaign were 230 killed and 1,400 wounded.

After the fall of Spanish Fort, the Mobile campaign continued against Fort Blakely and Batteries Huger and Tracy. All were defeated by 11 April, and Mobile stood

open. Maury ordered the evacuation of the remaining Confederate troops from Mobile, and on 12 April declared the city open. The evacuated Confederate garrison surrendered on 5 May 1865.

—*Eric L. Bobo*

See also Blakely, Alabama, Battle of; Mobile Campaign.

For further reading:
Hearn, Chester G. *Mobile Bay and the Mobile Campaign: The Last Great Battles of the Civil War* (1993).
Heyman, Max L. *Prudent Soldier: A Biography of Major General E. R. S. Canby 1817–1873* (1959).
Maury, Dabney H. *Recollections of a Virginian in the Mexican, Indian, and Civil Wars* (1894).
Owen, William Miller. *In Camp and Battle with the Washington Artillery of New Orleans: A Narrative of Events During the Late Civil War from Bull Run to Appomattox and Spanish Fort* (1885).
Parker, Prescott A. *Story of the Tensaw: Blakely, Spanish Fort, Jackson Oaks, Fort Mims* (1922).

SPARROW, EDWARD
(1810–1882)
Confederate congressman

Born in Dublin, Ireland, Edward Sparrow moved as a child with his parents to Columbus, Ohio. He may have attended Kenyon College. Afterward he studied law and briefly practiced in Ohio before moving to Louisiana. He served as a court clerk and soon opened his own law practice. In the early 1850s he became a planter in Carroll Parish, building a beautiful home on Lake Providence that he named Arlington. During these years, Sparrow also plunged into Louisiana politics.

In 1861 he was a member of the Louisiana secession convention; he supported and voted for withdrawal. He was sent from that body as a delegate to the Confederate Provisional Congress and was active in the drafting of the Confederate Constitution. He served on a number of important committees of the Provisional Congress, including the committee on military affairs.

In the first regular Confederate elections, held in the fall of 1861, Sparrow was chosen as one of Louisiana's Confederate senators. He served in that office until the end of the war. In the Confederate Senate, Sparrow chaired the Military Affairs Committee, from whence he strongly urged a centralized military. During the early years of the war, he quietly pressed for greater defensive measures for his home area of the trans-Mississippi. He also increasingly questioned President Jefferson Davis's choice of military commanders. Especially critical of Braxton Bragg, Sparrow urged that his personal friend P. G. T. Beauregard be given a greater role. Sparrow also believed that Congress should have a greater say in military decisions.

In the last months of the war, Sparrow urged that virtually dictatorial measures be adopted to save the military situation. In spite of his loyalty to Louisiana, he supported the consolidation of Confederate military power in the East and greater flexibility for procurement of supplies and equipment. His suggestions came too late to have an impact on the war.

After the war, Sparrow returned to his home of Arlington, where he resumed his law practice and tried to rebuild his plantation. He died at home.

—*David S. Heidler and Jeanne T. Heidler*

See also Congress, C.S.A..

For further reading:
Davis, William C. *"A Government of Our Own": The Making of the Confederacy* (1994).
Yearns, W. Buck. *The Confederate Congress* (1960).

SPAULDING, ELBRIDGE GERRY
(1809–1897)
Congressman, "Father of the Greenbacks"

Elbridge Spaulding remains a rarity among the Civil War personalities. Although he left an indelible mark on history, he is an obscure figure, and little has been written about him.

Spaulding was born in Cayuga County, New York. In 1836 he was admitted to the bar and began his law practice in Buffalo. He married the daughter of a banker and soon established the Farmers' and Mechanics' Bank in Buffalo. In 1845 he built "The Exchange" in downtown Buffalo to house his bank. He was elected mayor of Buffalo in 1847, then served as a New York state assemblyman in 1848 and as the treasurer of New York in 1854 and 1855.

Spaulding was elected to the House of Representatives as a Whig in the Thirty-first Congress (1849–1850). He declined to run for reelection, instead concentrating on his legal and business ventures. His success enabled him to accumulate a substantial fortune. He returned to Washington in 1859 as a Republican, winning elections to the Thirty-sixth and Thirty-seventh Congresses.

Spaulding's financial acumen helped him gain a seat on the House Ways and Means Committee. At the outbreak of the Civil War, Spaulding joined the subcommittee responsible for war loans. On 31 December 1861, when the major East Coast banks announced a suspension of specie payments, Spaulding responded. Having anticipated this event because of the hoarding of specie and the prickly relationship between the banks and Secretary of the Treasury Salmon P. Chase, Spaulding had secluded himself in the National Hotel for three days, preparing a bill to allow the secretary to request the issuance of $50 million in treasury notes that would be redeemable as legal tender. These notes became known as the greenbacks.

Spaulding's bill raised a firestorm in the House, as the federal government had never before used fiat money. "It was never intended by the originators of the legal tenders

act that the issue of an irredeemable paper currency should ever become the permanent policy of the government," he later wrote. Whether or not to employ the greenbacks created a bitter division within the Ways and Means Committee as well as in the Republican Party at large. Necessity overruled the principles of those who opposed greenbacks; with the expenses of the war mounting and specie frozen in the banks, Spaulding's paper currency became the only means for meeting the requisitions and keeping the Union's treasury afloat.

The greenbacks proved to be Spaulding's singular contribution to the Union's Civil War legislation. He returned to Buffalo at the end of his term in 1863 and resumed his career. He moved his bank into the national system in 1864 and continued to manage its operations until the 1890s.

In 1869 he compiled the documents relating to the passage of the greenback legislation and published an invaluable volume (*A Resource of War*, 1869). He advocated "a prompt redemption of the national currency … to insure success and permanency in the system," thus adding his voice to the controversy over what to do with the floating greenbacks once the war ended. He never held public office again, contenting himself with local philanthropy and the knowledge of being "a somewhat prominent though humble actor in originating and maturing …" a dramatic fiscal experiment.

—*Jane Flaherty*

See also Greenbacks.
For further reading:
Gresham, Otto. *The Greenbacks; or The Money that Won the Civil War and the World War* (1927).
Spaulding, Elbridge G. *A Resource of War: The Credit of the Government Made Immediately Available: A History of Legal Tender Paper Money Issue during the Great Rebellion* (1869; reprint 1971).

SPEED, JOSHUA
(1814–1882)
Friend of Abraham Lincoln

When Abraham Lincoln and Joshua Speed first met on 15 April 1837, they had much in common. Both were Whigs, born in modest circumstances in Kentucky, who had relocated to Springfield, Illinois. Speed came to Springfield first, becoming a partner in a successful general store. He was working in that capacity when Lincoln arrived in Springfield seeking lodging. Speed offered to share his room, and for four years the two men shared the same bed, a common arrangement at the time for single men who were just getting their start in the world. They became great friends. In fact, many historians consider Speed to be the only truly close friend Lincoln ever had.

Speed moved back to Kentucky in 1841 to try his hand at farming, around the same time that Lincoln temporarily broke his engagement to Mary Todd. Lincoln wrote many letters over the course of his life, but those he wrote to his only friend at that vulnerable point in his life are unique. They are undoubtedly the most personal and intimate items in his vast correspondence, and they give the modern reader the clearest insight into Lincoln's personality that is available. The content of Speed's and Lincoln's correspondence came to focus increasingly on their impending marriages, Speed's to Fanny Henning on 15 February 1842, and Lincoln's to Mary Todd on 2 November 1842.

After several years of married life, Lincoln and Speed began to grow apart. In a letter written in 1846, Lincoln expressed concern about "the suspension of our correspondence" and cautioned against "allowing a friendship, such as ours, to die by degrees." In 1851, Speed moved to Louisville and entered the real estate business, which made him wealthy. He served in the Kentucky legislature at the same time that Lincoln was in the U.S. House of Representatives, and the two men began to diverge politically. Like many people in the border state of Kentucky, Speed took a very conservative view of race questions, and he came to believe that the government should protect slavery. When Lincoln was nominated for the presidency in 1860, Speed noted that he could congratulate Lincoln only as a "warm personal friend," for he was an "avowed political opponent."

When war came, Speed remained loyal to the Union, and he played an important role in smuggling arms to pro-Union forces in Kentucky. Nonetheless, he remained conservative on issues related to slavery. He vigorously protested John C. Frémont's order emancipating slaves in Missouri, and when Lincoln issued the Emancipation Proclamation, Speed wrote that he was "so much distressed" that he was "unable to eat or sleep." Despite the proclamation, Speed continued to assist the Union cause in Kentucky, acting as a liaison between his state and the Lincoln administration.

After the war, Speed led a retired life. Shortly before his death in 1882, he delivered a speech, his "Reminiscences of Abraham Lincoln." The best-known passage from the speech deals with religion and indicates the extent to which the two men had grown apart. After finding Lincoln reading a Bible in 1864, Speed noted that he never read the book because he had never gotten over the religious skepticism of his youth. The president responded, "You are wrong Speed, take all of this book upon reason that you can, and the balance on faith, and you will live and die a happier and better man."

—*Christopher Bates*

See also Lincoln, Abraham.
For further reading:
Kincaid, Robert L. "Joshua Fry Speed—1814–1882." *Filson Club Historical Quarterly* (1943).

SPINNER, FRANCIS ELIAS
(1802–1890)
U.S. treasurer

Born to John Peter Spinner and Mary Magdalene Fidelis Brument Spinner in Herkimer County, New York, Francis Elias Spinner was educated in local schools before being apprenticed to a confectioner and then a saddler. Not caring for either trade, the younger Spinner entered the mercantile business and then became a cashier of the Mohawk Valley Bank. He rose to be president of that institution.

Along with his many business interests, Spinner became involved in New York philanthropic activities and state politics as a Democrat. His politics gained him the lucrative appointment of New York Port Collector in the James K. Polk administration. In 1854 he was elected to the United States House of Representatives.

Spinner entered Congress in the heat of the sectional controversy over Kansas. Though a Democrat, he opposed the expansion of slavery and increasingly became associated with the Republican Party during his first term. In the House he served on the committee that disciplined Preston Brooks for his caning of Senator Charles Sumner. When he stood for reelection later that year, he ran as a Republican. He was reelected again as a Republican in 1858. Besides his political activities, Spinner became very active in the New York state militia and rose to the rank of major general. For the remainder of his life he was referred to as "General" in official correspondence.

During the election of 1860, Spinner campaigned for Abraham Lincoln and was rewarded for his loyalty with appointment to the position of treasurer of the United States by the new president. He held that position from 1861 until he resigned in 1875.

As treasurer, Spinner presided over the tremendous expansion of his office and the issuing of paper currency. In July 1861 Congress authorized the first issuance of the demand notes that would become known as "greenbacks." When the notes were printed in August of that year, the plan was for Spinner, as treasurer, to sign each note in the same way that high-ranking officers of banks signed all bank notes. Spinner made a valiant effort to do so, but found he could not even make a dent in the several hundred thousand greenbacks that were a part of the first issue. He assigned the task to his clerks, requiring them to print the words "For the" in front of the word "Treasurer" before affixing his name. Eventually the printers were able to place a facsimile of his signature on the notes. Spinner's picture even appeared on one issue of fifty-cent notes.

The issuance of the greenbacks, as well as the tremendous increase in the outlay of money from the treasury, meant a proportionate increase in the staff of the treasurer's office. Congress, however, proved stingy in allocating the necessary money for more clerks and other staff. What small increases Spinner did receive did not come close to meeting the demands of his office. To handle the workload, Spinner resorted to hiring women for his office, an almost unprecedented move that opened the way for women in other government offices. While Spinner has been credited with pioneering the practice of equal pay for equal work for female employees, he lamented in his report of 1864 that the only way he could meet the demands of his office was to hire women workers at lower wages than male employees. By the end of the war, he was employing over four hundred women. While most of these women lost their jobs at the end of the war, the precedent had been set for using women in government clerical positions.

Throughout the war Spinner gained the reputation as a diligent, efficient treasurer and was retained in that position by both Andrew Johnson and Ulysses S. Grant. His lengthy service gave him a proprietary feeling about his department that sometimes put him at odds with whoever occupied the position of secretary of the treasury. When his authority over his office was challenged in 1875, he promptly resigned.

Following his resignation, Spinner retired to Jacksonville, Florida, where he became somewhat of a beachcomber. He read extensively and enjoyed the Florida sunshine until skin cancer took his life on 31 December 1890.

—David S. Heidler and Jeanne T. Heidler

See also Financing, U.S.A; Greenbacks.
For further reading:
Drew, John G. The Absorbing Power of Usury; or, Every Man His Own Actuary Prefaced by a Biographical Sketch of the Hon. F. E. Spinner (1876).

SPOTSYLVANIA COURT HOUSE, BATTLE OF
(8 May –19 May 1864)

The Army of the Potomac found it slow going as they moved out of the Wilderness on 7 May. The Brock Road, which led out of the Wilderness to Spotsylvania Court House, was blocked by Confederate Cavalry who were screening the Army of Northern Virginia's maneuver south to defend the crossroads there. Major General Philip H. Sheridan's Federal Cavalry had been tasked with clearing the Brock Road but had disengaged after pushing the rebels a couple of miles south of the crossroads at Todd's Tavern. Beating Grant to Spotsylvania gave Lee ample time to prepare his defenses. The extensive field works constructed by the Army of Northern Virginia were unparalleled in the Civil War and contributed to the intensity and the

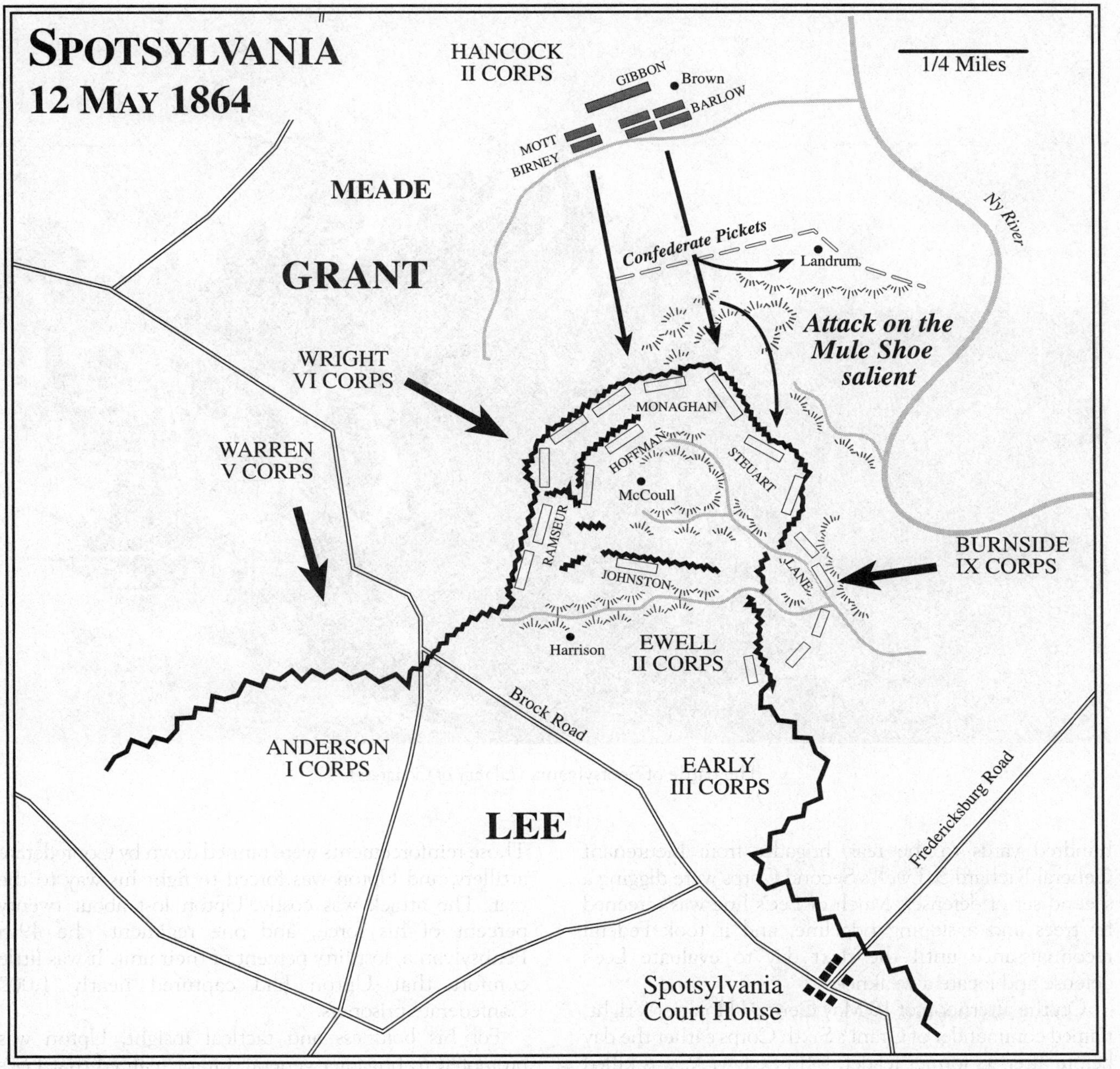

SPOTSYLVANIA 12 MAY 1864

HANCOCK II CORPS

GIBBON Brown

BARLOW

MOTT
BIRNEY

MEADE

GRANT

Confederate Pickets

Landrum

Ny River

WRIGHT VI CORPS

Attack on the Mule Shoe salient

MONAGHAN

WARREN V CORPS

HOFFMAN

STEUART

McCoull

RAMSEUR

JOHNSTON

LANE

BURNSIDE IX CORPS

Harrison

EWELL II CORPS

Brock Road

ANDERSON I CORPS

EARLY III CORPS

LEE

Fredericksburg Road

Spotsylvania Court House

1/4 Miles

---

brutality of the battle that followed. According to historian Robert Krick, the battle for Spotsylvania Court House "would establish a new standard for intense, short-range savagery. The twenty-hour hand-to-hand fight at Spotsylvania's 'Bloody Angle' was never matched during the Civil War, and rarely if ever anywhere else in the annals of military history."

The science of field fortification was still evolving in May 1864, and Lee pushed his engineers to the limits to design effective earth and log works. The base consisted of small trees that were cut down and laid lengthwise. A ditch was dug behind the trees and the dirt was piled on top resulting in a wall four to six feet thick and chest

high. On top of this, head logs were added leaving only narrow crevices to fire through.

While the Confederates continued to strengthen their defenses, they expected an attack at every moment. By the afternoon of 9 May, their earthworks roughly resembled an inverted V, with the tip pointed north and the sides swept back to defend against flanking attacks. By the 10th, the Army of Northern Virginia had constructed a formidable defensive barrier. An abatis of sharpened trees had been added to the exterior from the scrub pines that were cut to clear the fields of fire. Also added to the trenches were traverses of mounded earth to protect the defenders against enfilade fire, and one

The battle of Spotsylvania (*Library of Congress*)

hundred yards to the rear, brigades from Lieutenant General Richard S. Ewell's Second Corps were digging a second set of defenses. Much of Lee's line was screened by trees and a sloping ridgeline, and it took Federal reconnaissance until the next day to evaluate Lee's defense and locate a weakness.

On the afternoon of 10 May General Horatio Wright, named commander of Grant's Sixth Corps earlier the day before after its former leader, John Sedgwick, was killed by a Confederate sniper, made a reconnaissance of the Rebels' eastern defenses and decided that the Mule Shoe salient was the most vulnerable. To plan the assault, Wright turned to Colonel Emory Upton, a West Point graduate who had been promoting a new style of offensive warfare that relied on speed and concentrated force. Upton was given twelve regiments, or nearly 5,000 men, and the plan was laid. Advancing from the northeast, Upton planned to use the forest to screen his approach. At two hundred yards from Ewell's defenses, Upton would fix bayonets and charge the works.

About 6:00 P.M., the attack was on. The immediate Federal success sent the Georgian defenders scrambling, but Upton needed reinforcements to secure his gains.

Those reinforcements were pinned down by Confederate artillery, and Upton was forced to fight his way to the rear. The attack was costly. Upton lost about twenty percent of his force, and one regiment, the 49th Pennsylvania, lost fifty percent of their unit. It was little comfort that Upton had captured nearly 1,000 Confederate prisoners.

For his boldness and tactical insight, Upton was promoted to brigadier general. Grant realized that Lee's defenses could be beaten, and he was overheard saying, "A brigade today—we'll try a corps tomorrow." Later, in a message to General Halleck in Washington, Grant made his often quoted statement that he would "fight it out on this line if it takes all summer." On 11 May, a nor'easter blew in a cold rain, with wind, fog, and hail. The moisture dampened everyone's cartridges.

Throughout the day, Lee received reports that suggested that Grant was pulling out of Spotsylvania and moving east toward Fredericksburg, in search of another route to Richmond. Lee felt that this was his moment to attack. He had been held in his defenses since the beginning of May. He wanted to avoid a protracted Union siege declaring that "We must end this business on the battlefield, not in a fortified place." Immediately, he ordered Ewell to limber up twenty-two of his thirty field-pieces and move them to the rear in preparation for an eastward assault on Grant. This placed the Confederates defending the Mule Shoe in a vulnerable position. After midnight on 12 May, tensions grew within the works as a distant thunder was heard coming from the Union line. At 2:00 A.M., the order went out for the Confederate artillery to return, but an hour and a half later none of it had returned.

The Federals were using Upton's lightning assault tactics again; however, this time 15,000 infantrymen from Hancock's Second Corps—not the 5,000 from two days before—were massed with bayonets fixed in ranks fifty deep. At 4:30 A.M., the men moved out of the woodline and across the fog-shrouded field taking Confederate pickets by complete surprise. In less than an hour, thousands of Hancock's men had overrun the Mule Shoe. The heaviest damage was inflicted just east of the shoe's apex, an area known as the "Bloody Angle" where Hancock's Second Corps held over thirty strands of enemy colors. The failure of Confederate musketry in the wet environs combined with the absence of supporting artillery cost Lee a half mile of critical terrain in the center of his line.

At 5:30 A.M., Brigadier General John B. Gordon rushed three Confederate brigades toward the oncoming Federals driving them back to the trenches just inside the Bloody Angle. Once again, the Federal assault had been too successful, this time outrunning its own support. Order dissolved on both sides. The attacks and counterattacks continued unabated until early the next morning, some twenty hours later.

In places, the dead lay five deep; at times, the fighting would stop long enough to clear the dead from the trenches so that the living could take cover. The fighting extended out to either side of the defensive works. Brigadier General Louis Grant, commander of the Vermont Brigade, remembered that "many were shot and stabbed through crevices and holes between the logs; men mounted the works, and with muskets rapidly handed them, kept up a continuous fire until they were shot down, when others would take their place and continue the deadly work." In other places, soldiers had to fire their muskets from the hip because the combatants were too close to put the gun up to their shoulders. The battle continued throughout the day and into the evening, the Confederate defenders holding out while Ewell's men completed a second line of defense.

About midnight, a twenty-two inch oak near the center of the Bloody Angle came crashing down, severed completely by musket balls. By most accounts the battle ended "shortly before dawn," on 13 May around 4:00 A.M.

The experiences of both Union and Confederate combatants convey the horror of Spotsylvania. At one point during the fight a Mississippi soldier observed that the field between the Bloody Angle works and the advancing Union line "presented one vast Golgotha in immensity of the number of dead.... [Behind the Federal front line] the ground was almost covered with the dead and wounded, while between the lines they were literally piled." Robert Krick has condensed some of the Federal reactions to the spectacle: "Horse and men chopped into hash by the bullets ... appearing ... like piles of jelly." "The logs in the breastworks were shattered into splinters.... We had not only shot down an army, but also a forest.... Below the mass of fast-decaying corpses, the convulsive twitching of limbs and the writhing of bodies [revealed] wounded men ... struggling to extricate themselves from their horrid entombment."

The nightmare of the Bloody Angle did not end the battle of Spotsylvania. Fighting would continue along Lee's line for another week (until 19 May), although nothing would compare to the events of 12 May. Confederate losses at Spotsylvania—killed, wounded, and captured—were about 12,000; roughly eighty-five percent of those losses were in the Mule Shoe on 10 and 12 May. Union losses for the entire battle were about 18,000, with about sixty percent occurring in the Mule Shoe. After eleven days of near continuous fighting, Grant withdrew the Army of the Potomac eastward toward Fredericksburg before turning south along the Richmond, Fredericksburg & Potomac Railroad trying to turn Lee's right flank in search of an open road to the Confederate capital at Richmond.

—*Edward Ragan*

See also Ewell, Richard Stoddert; Hancock, Winfield Scott; Richmond Campaign; Sedgwick, John; Sheridan, Philip Henry.

For further reading:
Gallagher, Gary W., ed. *The Spotsylvania Campaign* (1998).
Matter, William D. *If It Takes All Summer: The Battle of Spotsylvania* (1988).
Power, J. Tracy. *Lee's Miserables: Life in the Army of Northern Virginia from the Wilderness to Appomattox* (1998).
Rhea, Gordon C. *The Battles for Spotsylvania Court House and the Road to Yellow Tavern, May 7–12, 1864* (1997).
Trudeau, Noah Andre. *Bloody Roads South: The Wilderness to Cold Harbor, May-June 1864* (1989).

SPRAGUE, KATE CHASE
(1840–1899)

Washington political hostess

Born in Cincinnati to Salmon Chase and his second wife, Eliza, Catherine Jane "Kate" Chase was the first of their three children and the only one to survive infancy. Her mother died when she was five years old, and Salmon Chase, a lawyer and abolitionist with growing political ambitions, married again.

Subsequently he enrolled Kate in an exclusive private school in New York.

Although her father wrote to her weekly and visited her occasionally, her childhood must have been lonely. Salmon Chase's letters often contained exhortations about "duty," especially the need to improve her handwriting and learn French, skills he thought befitting an accomplished woman. At school, Kate Chase thrived academically and matured socially, mingling with girls from the very best of New York families. She acquired a fine sense of fashion and taste, social graces she would cultivate for the rest of her life. More importantly, she developed the ability to move easily in any social situation.

At age fifteen she returned home to Ohio after her father's election as governor. His third wife having died in 1852, Chase made his daughter his unofficial hostess. She moved into the role with apparent ease, showing considerable talent for entertaining. During these years, Kate Chase also developed a strong sense of identification with her father's political aspirations and no doubt shared his disappointment when the Republican Party rejected him as presidential nominee in favor of Abraham Lincoln in 1860.

With Salmon Chase's appointment as treasury secretary, Kate Chase moved to Washington along with her younger half-sister, Nettie. She assisted her father by selecting and furnishing a house at Sixth and E streets in Washington, managing his household, and organizing informal breakfasts, tea parties, and formal dinners and receptions. Chase quickly found herself the center of much attention. Tall, shapely, with distinctive hazel eyes, beautiful fair skin, and golden-reddish hair, she was considered a belle in an era when youth, beauty, social ease, wealth, and family connections defined femininity. In 1862, with the president's wife in mourning for her son's death and the secretary of state's wife an invalid, lively and intelligent Kate Chase, daughter of the next-ranking cabinet member, became the most important hostess in Washington.

She relished the role both for herself and for the opportunity to further her father's political career. During a time when women could not exercise direct political influence, she became a masterful behind-the-scenes politician, courting members of Congress, military officers, editors, and businessmen. The *New York Times* wrote, "She wielded her power and the influence of her high social station as no other woman in this country had ever wielded such forces."

Although numerous men sought her attention, she decided to marry Governor (and later U.S. senator) William Sprague of Rhode Island, a Republican whose early support for the Union war effort and whose considerable family wealth made him appear a dashing figure. Salmon Chase encouraged the match. Their wedding on

12 November 1863 was a social high point in the Civil War capital and was widely reported nationally. The bride wore white velvet and a tiara estimated to be worth $50,000. Military officers, members of the cabinet, and President Lincoln attended the ceremony in the bride's home. Mrs. Lincoln did not appear, ostensibly because she was still in mourning, but perhaps also because she disliked Kate Chase as a rival hostess determined to promote her father at Lincoln's expense. Kate and William Sprague allegedly supported the "Pomeroy Circular," which promoted Chase as Republican presidential nominee over Abraham Lincoln in 1864.

The Sprague marriage, although it produced four children, was tempestuous from the beginning. With tendencies toward excessive drinking and womanizing, William Sprague quarreled often with his wife, whose forceful personality clashed with his own. As a senator, William Sprague voted in favor of conviction during Andrew Johnson's impeachment trial, angering his wife, who attended the proceedings, and disappointing his father-in-law, who presided as chief justice of the Supreme Court. Love for her father and his career remained the focal point of Kate Sprague's life. She actively supported his presidential candidacy in 1868 as a Democrat, was deeply disappointed when he was passed over for a major party nomination yet again, and was devastated when he died in 1873. Unsubstantiated public and newspaper gossip of an alleged affair between Kate Sprague and Republican senator Roscoe Conkling led to a divorce from William Sprague in 1882 and the adoption of her father's last name again. Her final years were marked by poverty and by the tragic death by suicide of her son William.

—*Wendy Hamand Venet*

See also Chase, Salmon Portland.; Pomeroy, Samuel Clarke; Sprague, William.
For further reading:
Niven, John. *Salmon P. Chase:* A (1995).
Sokoloff, Alice Hunt. *Kate Chase for the Defense* (1971).

SPRAGUE, WILLIAM
(1830–1915)
Governor of Rhode Island, U.S. senator

William Sprague was born on 12 September 1830, the heir to a Rhode Island textile empire. Any desire the young Sprague may have possessed for a formal education abruptly vanished in 1843 when his father was murdered. His mother insisted that William continue his education, but his indifference to learning soon convinced her of the futility of her efforts. By age fifteen his formal education ended and he joined the family business, which was being run by his uncle. Upon the death of his uncle, William, then twenty-six, his brother, and his cousin assumed control of the business. William possessed the

entrepreneurial urbanity of the trio and soon became its dominant member. By 1860, he had greatly increased the family holdings; with a net worth of $25 million, he was one of the richest men in the country.

While vacationing in Europe that year, his wealth and his mother's persuasion won him the Democratic nomination for governor, an office he captured at a cost of over $100,000, amid allegations of bribery. As Rhode Island's chief executive, Sprague personally financed the militia that he led to Washington, D.C., after the firing on Fort Sumter and Lincoln's call for volunteers. In full-dress military uniform topped with a yellow-plumed hat and astride his white horse, Sprague cut a figure of romance and gallantry at a time when Washingtonians believed war was romantic and gallant. The thirty-year-old governor offered his services to the government in exchange for a commission as a major general. However, Lincoln had already made another New Englander, Benjamin Butler, a major general and two New Englanders holding such a rank was politically unacceptable. Sprague was offered a brigadier generalship, which he declined.

The battle of First Bull Run in July 1861 dispelled any romantic notions about the war; the Rhode Islanders retreated from the field with the rest of the Union's defenders. Sprague had, however, acquitted himself well during the battle. He fought with his troops again, particularly during the Peninsula campaign in 1862, but his inability to secure a commission as a major general and the indifference with which the Lincoln administration met his suggestions on a strategy to win the war dampened Sprague's military ardor. He proved to be more successful in the political arena.

After winning the gubernatorial election in 1860 as a Democrat, Sprague successfully ran for reelection in 1861 and 1862 as a Republican. Also in 1862, the Rhode Island legislature elected him to the U.S. Senate. He took his seat on 4 March 1863 and held it until 3 March 1875.

Despite Sprague's dabbling in military and political affairs, he never lost sight of the cotton mills, the source of his wealth. During the war, Lincoln's naval blockade of the cotton-producing states threatened his empire. Conspiring with like-minded mill owners and entrepreneurs, Sprague helped finance a web of treason, called the Texas Adventure, connecting the New York Customs House with Matamoros, Mexico, and Texas. Over this web flowed guns, ammunition, and other war materiel to Confederate officials in exchange for cotton to supply New England's mills. Only the personal intervention of Secretary of War Edwin M. Stanton (for reasons that can only be speculated) saved Senator Sprague and his co-conspirators from a humiliating public trial.

Sprague's performance as a senator was undistin-guished, with the exception that he was the one lawmaker married to Kate Chase, daughter of Lincoln's secretary of the treasury (and, later, chief justice of the Supreme Court), Salmon P. Chase. Catherine Jane Chase (1840–1899) became her thrice-widowed father's closest female ally at age fifteen. At their home in Ohio and, later, Washington, D.C., Kate served as hostess at his lavish, politically motivated parties. She inherited his political ambitions and his penchant for living well above his means. The magnetism of young Senator Sprague's $25 million inexorably pulled the beautiful and much sought-after Kate into his orbit. In November 1863, Lincoln, his cabinet, and other powerful Washingtonians attended their marriage ceremony. Despite this auspicious beginning, marital bliss never graced their union. Rumors of infidelities by both, her extravagant spending, his legendary intemperance, and her continued obsession with her father's political ambitions doomed them to unhappiness. When the Panic of 1873 robbed him of his financial independence, Kate moved into the orbit of other powerful men. In 1882 she was granted a divorce, charging him with nonsupport.

The next year, Sprague married Dora Inez Calvert, and the happy couple retired to his country estate, Canonchet. When their home burned down after the turn of the century, they moved to Paris, France, where he died on 11 September 1915, one day before his eighty-fifth birthday. His remains were returned to Rhode Island, where the last of the war governors was honored with a state funeral.

—*Larry C. Skogen*

See also Sprague, Kate Chase.
For further reading:
Belden, Thomas Graham, and Marva Robins Belden. *So Fell the Angels* (1956).
D'Amato, Donald A. "William Sprague: Rhode Island's Enigmatic Governor and Senator" (M.A. thesis, 1956).
Shoemaker, Henry W. *The Last of the War Governors* (1916).

SPRINGFIELD ARMORY

The Springfield Armory was the primary rifled musket manufacturing facility of the Union. Immortalized in Henry Wadsworth Longfellow's poem, "The Armory at Springfield," the name of the home of the Springfield Rifle is something of a misnomer. Strictly speaking, an armory is a place where weapons and armaments are stored and maintained. An arsenal, on the other hand, is an installation where weapons are manufactured. Despite its primary manufacturing mission, its official name during the Civil War period was the National Armory at Springfield. From 1892 until its closing in 1968, its official name was Springfield Armory.

The Springfield Armory took its name from the city of Springfield, Massachusetts, first settled by William

Pynchon in 1636 on the banks of the Connecticut River. By the time of the American Revolution, the Springfield area was one of the centers of the western New England arms industry. In the summer of 1776, Colonel Henry Knox proposed to a committee of the Continental Congress "that there be one or more capital laboratories erected at a distance from the seat of the war in which shall be prepared large quantities of ordnance stores of every species and denomination." One of those installations was a depot established the following year in Springfield, which became the forerunner of the Springfield Armory.

After the Revolution, Congress in 1782 converted the Springfield depot into a storage magazine for ordnance materiel. This installation was the main target of Shay's Rebellion in 1787. George Washington personally inspected the Springfield facilities in 1789. On 2 April 1794, Congress authorized the establishment of a national system of arsenals, with the United States Armory at Springfield (its original name) becoming the first of America's manufacturing arsenals. It was followed in 1795 by the Harper's Ferry Arsenal. During the War of 1812, Springfield and Harper's Ferry furnished all of America's military small arms. Springfield tended to concentrate on muskets, while Harper's Ferry generally (but not exclusively) concentrated on pistols.

The building and expansion of the Springfield Armory continued throughout the first half of the nineteenth century and through the period of the Civil War. By 1860 the two main sections of the installation were known as the Hill Shops and the Water Shops. One of the most striking architectural features of the Hill Shops was a massive cast-iron outer fence, made from melted-down cannon from the Revolution.

With the abandonment of Harper's Ferry, Springfield became the North's major source of military muskets. The civilian arms industry of New England, most notably Colt and Remington, became the major suppliers of pistols. In 1862 Springfield was the target of a bizarre sabotage plot, when two Confederate sympathizers from Canada attempted to blow up one of the buildings with a crude homemade bomb. That plot failed, but on the night of 2 July 1864 a spark from a polishing wheel set off a fire that destroyed a 280-foot section of one shop building before it was brought under control.

In 1861 Springfield had a work force of 3,400. When Fort Sumter was fired upon, the monthly rate of production was about 1,000 muskets. Three months later that rate had tripled. With manufacturing operations running twenty hours a day, the output progressively increased until it hit the 1,000-per-day mark in 1864. Production focused on the Model 1861, caliber 0.58, rifled musket, and its two minor variants, the Model 1863 and Model 1864. Between 1861 and 1865 Springfield produced more than 1.5 million rifled muskets. The commanding officers during the Civil War were Colonel I. H. Wright (27 June 1860–25 April 1861); Captain George Dwight (25 April 1861–21 August 1861); Captain Alexander B. Dyer (25 August 1861–27 October 1864); and Major T. T. S. Laidley (27 October 1864–14 May 1866).

In the century following the Civil War, the Springfield Armory was one of the greatest military small arms design and manufacturing facilities in the world. In 1873 it introduced caliber 0.45 breech-loading rifles and carbines, known as Trap Door Springfields. In 1903 it started producing the caliber 0.30-06, bolt-action rifle that remains to this day one of the most accurate rifles ever made. And in 1939 Springfield introduced the U.S. Rifle, M-1, caliber 0.30, a semiautomatic, clip-fed rifle, known as the Garand after its designer, John Garand. It was the best infantry rifle of World War II.

Following World War II the Springfield Armory was the epicenter of military small arms research and development. Inexplicably, however, the Springfield Armory fell victim in the mid-1960s to the short-sighted efficiency purges of then Secretary of Defense Robert McNamara. On 30 April 1968 the Springfield Armory closed its doors after 174 years of continuous service. A part of its small arms manufacturing and design mission and a tiny fraction of its skilled work force were transferred to the Rock Island Arsenal in Illinois.

After its closure, most of the Springfield Armory's buildings and grounds were transferred to the city of Springfield and converted into a technical college. The old Main Arsenal building (built in 1807) was retained by the federal government to house the Springfield Armory's magnificent collection of small arms, which includes one of the stacked double racks of Model 1861 muskets (the "Organ of Muskets") that inspired Longfellow to write his poem. The National Park Service today administers the Springfield Armory Museum.

—*David T. Zabecki*

See also Armories, Arsenals, and Founderies; Springfield Rifle.
For further reading:
Dvarecka, Christopher L. *Springfield Armory—Pointless Sacrifice* (1968).
Miller, Clifford A. "Springfield Arms, 1794–1939: Milestones of a Great National Armory." *Army Ordnance* (1939).

SPRINGFIELD RIFLE

In its three basic types—the Models 1855, 1861, and 1863—the caliber 0.58 Springfield U.S. Rifle-Musket was the most common long arm used by either side during the war. The Springfield series owed its development to the success in the Mexican-American War of the caliber 0.54 Model 1841 Mississippi Rifle, the first percussion rifle adopted by the government.

The Springfield series introduced the "minié bullet,"

the revolutionary invention of a French army officer, Captain Claude Étienne Minié. Cylindro-conoidal in shape, much like a modern bullet, Minié's invention solved the long-standing dilemma of mating a quickly loaded bullet with a rifled barrel. To facilitate loading, Minié designed his bullet to be slightly smaller than the rifle's bore. He then introduced a cone-shaped cavity in the bullet's base. The resultant gasses from the weapon's discharge would then expand the thin walls of the cone into the rifling for a snug fit. A trained rifleman could thus fire three aimed shots per minute and easily hit a man-size target at 100 yards. With more time to aim he could be deadly at ranges up to 500 yards, and, in extreme cases, hit large targets at up to 1,000 yards.

The new caliber 0.58 bullet weighed nearly one ounce and was propelled by sixty grains of black powder. Both bullet and powder were contained in a paper cartridge that eliminated the separate powder and patched ball of earlier rifles. Tests proved that when fired from the Springfield, the minié bullet could penetrate eleven inches of pine boards at 100 yards and nearly six inches of pine at 500 yards. The minié's effect on the human body was predictably devastating. The soft lead bullet's slow velocity coupled with its tendency to distort upon impact, pulverized tissue and shattered bones. Most body and head wounds thus usually resulted in death and, if not fatal, wounds to the extremities typically resulted in amputation. Postwar studies showed that rifle bullets inflicted fully ninety percent of all Civil War casualties.

Military theory of the time also contributed to the percussion rifle-musket's lethality. Civil War officers adhered to Napoleonic tactics based on the capabilities of the earlier, inaccurate, smoothbore muskets. To maximize their firepower, troops thus fought in tight formations at ranges of approximately 100 yards. Schooled in a strict belief in offensive tactics, they were at first slow to grasp the deadly potential of entrenched troops armed with rifle-muskets. By late war, however, the combination of the new minié bullet with the rifle-musket proved a significant factor in revolutionizing warfare by shifting emphasis to defensive tactics.

The Model 1855 U.S. Percussion Rifle-Musket introduced the caliber 0.58 "minié bullet" as well as the Maynard tape priming ignition system. Weighing slightly over nine pounds, the Model 1855 is four feet, eight inches in overall length with a 40-inch barrel secured to its walnut stock by three barrel bands. The Model 1855, as well as the Models 1861 and 1863, accepts a standard 13-inch socket bayonet with a triangular blade. Manufactured between 1857 and 1861, 47,115 Model 1855s were manufactured at the Springfield Armory in Massachusetts with an additional 12,158 weapons produced at the Harper's Ferry Armory in Virginia.

The Model 1861 U.S. Rifle-Musket was a simplified Model 1855, discarding the complicated Maynard tape device for the more conventional percussion cap ignition system. The Model 1861 was thus cheaper to produce than the Model 1855 and less prone to breakage. The armory at Springfield, the only federal arms-making facility following the loss of Harper's Ferry, produced 265,129 Model 1861s during 1861 and 1862. Private contractors supplemented the government's output by manufacturing over 900,000 Model 1861s by war's end at a cost of between $18 and $25 per weapon.

The Model 1863 U.S. Rifle-Musket, in turn, was a refinement of the Model 1861. It differed only in minor details, such as the shape of its hammer, the elimination of the bolster clean-out screw, and its barrel bands' contours. Owing to further slight modifications, Model 1863s manufactured in 1863 are often designated as the Model 1863 Type I whereas weapons manufactured in 1864 and 1865 are designated as the Type II. The main differences between the two types are the simplified sights of the Type II and the elimination of the barrel-band retaining springs on the Type I—a component restored on the Type II. Springfield manufactured 273,265 Type I and 255,040 Type II Model 1863 rifle-muskets, the last muzzle-loading percussion arms produced by the United States government.

—*Jeff Kinard*

See also Minié Ball; Rifles; Tactics.
For further reading:
Evans, William B. *Civil War Guns* (1962).
Flayderman, E. Norman. *Flayderman's Guide to Antique American Firearms* (1987).
Lord, Francis A. *Civil War Collector's Encyclopedia* (1995).

ST. ALBANS, VERMONT, RAID
October 1864

The long border between the British North American provinces and the northern tier of United States still in the Union had the potential to cause Anglo-American friction, and even rupture, many times during the Civil War. Many Confederates made their way to the provinces as agents, schemers, sojourners, and escapees from Northern prison camps seeking passage back to the South. By the fall of 1864 Confederate leaders, facing defeat, grew less concerned about honoring neutrality than using the provinces as a base to mount raids into Northern territory.

These might generate an Anglo-American war, or at least influence the presidential election among the war-weary North. British and Union agents prowled the borderlands for rumors of plots and to forestall incidents, but as with all such intelligence work, it was poorly managed and difficult to sort imminent dangers from the welter of rumors that swirled in frontier towns and cities.

On 19 October 1864, a group of Kentuckians rode into St. Albans, Vermont, and registered at hotels as members of a Montreal hunting and fishing club. They scouted the town and midafternoon transformed into raiders commanded by Lieutenant Bennett Young, CSA. They robbed banks, stole wagons and horses, failed at arson, and fled in a running firefight. A Union officer organized a posse as news of the raid spread over telegraph lines. Vermont's governor sent troops to the border while, in hot pursuit, the posse arrested some raiders on British soil, but handed them to Canadian militiamen for examination by Charles Coursel, a Montreal police magistrate. Confederate and Union agents hired local lawyers, and a protracted, convoluted legal process ensued that threatened Anglo-American peace.

Conflicting legislation on extradition led Justice Coursel to deny jurisdiction and release the prisoners on 13 December. They promptly fled before Vermont attorneys could obtain new arrest warrants, although both the Canadian government and William Henry Seward, the American secretary of state, offered rewards for information leading to their capture. By February 1865 nine of the fugitives, including Young, were recaptured along with much of the stolen money. Other raiders bought a ship with their loot and sailed to Newfoundland to sit the war out.

Throughout December, Northern newspapers denounced Britain for connivance with the raiders and mishandling the case. Congressmen and senators demanded garrisons on the border, cancellation of the 1854 Reciprocity Treaty, and an end to the Rush-Bagot Agreement to limit armed vessels on the Great Lakes. Seward responded with a new passport order, watched the Senate vote to abrogate Rush-Bagot, then gave Britain the required six-months notice. This alarmed the British. The colonial secretary instructed Canadian officials to move against Confederate cabals wherever found. Minister John A. Macdonald called up militia and expanded his force of detectives in Canada West to penetrate Confederate groups along the Niagara and Detroit frontiers. In Canada East, he established a similar force. British authorities termed the raid an abuse of hospitality. Canadian newspapers lamented Coursel's decision, Montreal businessmen publicly called for an inquiry into the release of the raiders, and a formal investigation got underway. Even journalists with Southern sympathies denounced the affair. In March 1864, Canada's parliament voted $50,000 to reimburse the St. Albans banks.

At this point, Seward withdrew notice on the Rush-Bagot cancellation. And President Abraham Lincoln acted on his advice when he cancelled an order issued by the Union commander in the northern district, General John Dix, to pursue any future raiders onto British soil if necessary and refuse to turn any captives over to British authorities. The turmoil in border towns over fear of future raids and retaliation subsided. Robert E. Lee's surrender at Appomattox in April effectively ended the war and only the residue from four years of a conflict that challenged British neutrality and abraded American sensibilities remained to be dealt with. Both governments had successfully managed domestic politics and prevented a rupture.

—*Reginald C. Stuart*

See also Covert Action, Confederate.
For further reading:
Heath, Gary Earl. "The St. Albans Raid: Vermont Viewpoint." *Vermont History* (1965)
Kinchen, Oscar. *Daredevils of the Confederate Army: The Story of the St. Albans Raiders* (1959).
Snell, J. G. "H. H. Emmon, Detroit's Agent in Canadian-American Relations, 1864–1866." *Michigan History* (1972).
"The St. Albans Raid—A Bibliography." *Vermont History* (1958 and 1959).
Winks, Robin. *Canada and the United States: The Civil War Years* (1960; reprint, 1988).

ST. JOHN, ISAAC MUNROE
(1827–1880)

Confederate general and bureaucrat

Born to Isaac Richards St. John and Abigail Richardson Munroe St. John in Augusta, Georgia, Isaac Munroe St. John moved as a child with his family to New York City. He graduated from Yale College at the age of eighteen and briefly assumed the legal profession, before changing to journalism when offered the position of editor of the *Baltimore Patriot*. Not finding this calling any more to his liking, St. John studied civil engineering. Before the outbreak of the Civil War he worked in this capacity for several railroad companies in the Middle Atlantic and Southern states.

At the outbreak of the war, St. John enlisted in the Confederate army as a private. His engineering skills, however, soon earned him a transfer to the Corps of Engineers. He was sent to the York Peninsula in late 1861 to serve in the army of John Magruder. In February 1862 he became a captain of engineers and spent the next several months supervising the construction of works and inspecting others on the York Peninsula and along the Rappahannock River.

Promoted to major in April 1862, St. John was moved to Richmond, where he was appointed the acting chief of the Nitre and Mining Bureau. He became the permanent chief in January 1863. In this position, his primary duty was to procure the supplies necessary for the manufacture of weapons and gunpowder. In spite of the tightening Federal blockade, St. John proved amazingly resourceful in locating these essential supplies. His success earned him promotion to lieutenant colonel on 28 May 1863 and to colonel during the summer of 1864.

In the last months of the war, as disruption of the South's transportation system grew, the Confederate bureaucracy was having increasing difficulties supplying food to its scattered armies. St. John's skills in procurement, therefore, earned him the appointment as Confederate commissary general in February 1865. He was also promoted on 16 February to the rank of brigadier general. In spite of the Confederacy's ever-increasing chaotic condition, and the difficulties of dealing with intractable Confederate governors like Zebulon Vance, St. John designed a system of direct acquisition from producers that eased some of the army's supply problems. St. John was captured with the fall of Richmond, although his incarceration was brief.

After the war, St. John returned to civil engineering, this time in Kentucky. He continued with railroad work and for a time served as city engineer in Louisville. He died in White Sulphur Springs, West Virginia.

—*David S. Heidler and Jeanne T. Heidler*

See also Artillery; Ordnance, Naval; Small Arms.
For further reading:
Goff, Richard D. *Confederate Supply* (1969).
Jones, John William. *General Isaac Munroe St. John* (1881).

STAHEL-SZAMVALD, JULIUS
(1825–1912)
Union general

Born in Szeged, Hungary, Julius Stahel exhibited little military promise when young. He received a classical education at the University of Budapest and operated a small bookstore in the city after graduation. Frustrated with his future prospects, Stahel decided to join the Austrian army as a private and discovered a hidden talent for martial affairs. He rose quickly through the ranks, becoming a commissioned officer by the time the Hungarian revolution of 1848 broke out. Sympathizing completely with his rebel countrymen, he served on the staffs of the two primary Hungarian generals, and was awarded the Cross of Bravery for his efforts. The revolution was crushed in 1849, obliging Stahel to flee his beloved homeland. He spent the next seven years in exile, working as a teacher and journalist in Berlin and London.

In 1856 Stahel immigrated to the United States, settled in New York City, and served on the editorial staff of the *New York Illustrated News*. Incensed at the Confederate attack on Fort Sumter, he volunteered his services to Louis Blenker, then recruiting the 8th New York Infantry from the city's German and European immigrant population. The Germans in his regiment quickly came to admire Stahel, and the wider German-American community considered him one of their own. Elected lieutenant colonel by his men, Stahel commanded the 8th New York at First Bull Run,

assisting Blenker in covering the retreat of the Union army. For this action Stahel came to the attention of Abraham Lincoln, who praised him for his coolness under fire.

When Blenker was promoted to command of the German division in August 1861, Stahel succeeded him as colonel of his old regiment and in November was appointed brigadier general. He commanded four strongly German regiments from New York and Pennsylvania in John C. Frémont's small army as it moved against Stonewall Jackson in the Shenandoah Valley in the late spring of 1862. At the battle of Cross Keys, Stahel again received commendation for bravery by leading the chief Union attack, which fell apart from lack of support. At Second Bull Run he won further acclamation for coolness under fire from Brigadier General Robert C. Schenck, whose division Stahel commanded during the battle. After the Union reversal at Second Bull Run, Stahel led several daring and highly successful cavalry raids throughout fall 1862 and spring 1863 from his base at Fairfax Court House. In September he captured a thousand Confederates at Warrenton and in November raided one of Stonewall Jackson's supply depots near Sperryville, capturing several hundred prisoners and large numbers of horses and cattle.

As a result of his numerous citations for bravery and energetic pursuit of his missions, Stahel was first rewarded with command of XI Corps of the Army of the Potomac in January and later promotion to major general in March 1863. He yielded command of XI Corps to Carl Schurz, a personal friend, possibly in order to block Louis Blenker's promotion to major general. Blenker probably would have received command of the corps without Stahel's political maneuvering. The reaction of the German-American community to this action was mixed: New York Germans never forgave what they regarded as Stahel's treachery, while those from other states praised Stahel for chivalrously yielding the higher command to a better-qualified and deserving man. Having declined corps command, Stahel was entrusted with leadership of all Union cavalry in Major General Samuel P. Heintzelman's Department of Washington.

Stahel's glistening record became smudged after his intrigue against Blenker. Whether it was politically motivated is unknown, but Stahel's enemies began to complain about him. Instead of the dashing cavalry leader of the first two years of the war, he was described as lazy, inexcusably slow, and inefficient. Major General John F. Reynolds, to whom Stahel's cavalry command was attached during the Gettysburg campaign, lodged complaints against him, as did Major General David Hunter during his operations in the Shenandoah Valley in the summer of 1864. Even Franz Sigel, a constant Stahel supporter, berated him for his performance at New Market in May 1864. Some authors have contended that antiforeign prejudice contributed strongly to Stahel's poor image. Yet too many of his superior officers complained about his battlefield performance in the last two years of the war for nativism to be the sole factor.

Despite the barbs thrown at him by superiors, Stahel retained Lincoln's confidence and served as commander of the honor guard during the Gettysburg Address. He helped vindicate his damaged reputation by leading a brilliant cavalry charge at the battle of Piedmont in June 1864 while suffering from a severe wound in the arm. He was awarded the Medal of Honor in 1893 for this action.

As he recovered from his wound, Stahel was assigned recruiting duty in the Harper's Ferry region and served on several courts-martial in Washington and Baltimore. He resigned from active duty in February 1865 to embark on a celebrated career in diplomacy. He served in the American consulates in Osaka, Japan, and Shanghai, China, for more than ten years. After returning to the United States in October 1885, he invested in western mines and founded the Equitable Life Insurance Company in New York. Julius Stahel died in New York City in 1912 and was buried in Arlington National Cemetery.

—*Christian B. Keller*

See also Cavalry, U.S.A.; German-Americans.
For further reading:
Kaufmann, Wilhelm. *Die Deutschen im Amerikanischen Buergerkriege* (1911).
Lonn, Ella. *Foreigners in the Union Army and Navy* (1969).

STANLEY, DAVID SLOANE
(1828–1902)
Union general

Born to John Bratton Stanley and Sarah Peterson Stanley in Cedar Valley, Ohio, David Sloane Stanley was educated locally before beginning the study of medicine with a local physician. Abandoning that career goal, Stanley accepted an appointment to the U.S. Military Academy in 1848. He graduated ninth of forty-three in the class of 1852. Upon graduation, he served at frontier posts in Texas, California, and Kansas. At the outbreak of the Civil War, Stanley was offered a commission in the Confederate army while he was at Fort Smith, Arkansas. He refused the offer and took his garrison to Fort Leavenworth.

During the summer of 1861, Stanley fought in Missouri. After the battle of Wilson's Creek, he was promoted to brigadier general of volunteers. Stanley saw no further action that year due to a fractured leg suffered in a riding accident in November.

Under the command of John Pope in the early months of 1862, Stanley commanded a division at New Madrid and Island No. 10. He continued in command of his division in Henry Halleck's advance on Corinth in the spring of 1862. In September 1862, William Rosecrans commended him for his actions in the battle of Iuka. The following month he fought at the battle of Corinth.

In early November 1862, Stanley was named chief of cavalry, Army of the Cumberland. From 11 to 12 December 1862, he led his cavalry in a reconnaissance from Nashville to Franklin, Tennessee, and in the following weeks fought a number of skirmishes with Confederate cavalry as a prelude to the battle of Stones River at the end of the month. The skirmishing near Murfreesboro continued into the early months of 1863. In April 1863, Stanley was promoted to major general of volunteers with a date of rank of 29 November 1862.

To clear the area of Confederate guerrilla groups, Stanley led a number of missions from Murfreesboro through the spring of 1863. He then accompanied the Army of the Cumberland under Rosecrans on the Tullahoma campaign. Upon the completion of that campaign, Stanley led an expedition to Huntsville, Alabama, from 13 to 22 July 1863.

In September 1863, as a preliminary to the Chickamauga campaign, Stanley used his cavalry to protect William Rosecrans's communications back to Tennessee. Stanley was ill during the actual campaign, however, and did not participate in the battle.

In the fall of 1863, Stanley was relieved as cavalry chief of the Army of the Cumberland and was given command of a division in IV Corps. He fought at Chattanooga and in the Knoxville campaign. In the late spring of 1864, Stanley and his division joined William T. Sherman's Atlanta campaign.

Stanley fought in all the early engagements of the Atlanta campaign, especially distinguishing himself at Resaca. As the army closed in around Atlanta on 27 July, Stanley was named commander of IV Corps. He led his corps through the remainder of the campaign and the war. At the end of the Atlanta campaign, Stanley fought at Jonesboro on 1 September, but arrived too late in the day to have decisive impact on the battle. Although Sherman did not officially reprimand him for being late, "Uncle Billy" privately criticized Stanley for his tardiness.

After the Atlanta campaign, Stanley was sent with IV Corps back to Tennessee. He fought bravely at Franklin, receiving a severe wound while trying to rally some of his men when they threatened to fall back. The wound disabled him for several months, and he saw no more combat for the remainder of the war.

At the end of the war, Stanley and IV Corps were sent to New Orleans in June 1865 in preparation for assignment in Texas. He served there until being mustered out of volunteer service in 1866. Reverting to colonel of the 22d U.S. Infantry, for the next eighteen years Stanley served primarily on the western frontier in Texas and Montana. He was promoted to brigadier general in 1884. For the last part of his career he commanded the Department of Texas. Stanley retired in 1892. For five years after his retirement, Stanley oversaw the Washington, D.C., Soldier's Home. Following retirement from that position in 1898, he lived quietly in Washington, D.C., dying there on 13 March 1902.

—*David S. Heidler and Jeanne T. Heidler*

See also Atlanta Campaign; Franklin, Battle of; Island No. 10, Battle of; Stones River, Battle of.

For further reading:
Castel, Albert E. *Decision in the West: The Atlanta Campaign of 1864* (1992).
Daniel, Larry J., and Lynn N. Bock. *Island No. 10: Struggle for the Mississippi Valley* (1996).
Stanley, David Sloane. *Personal Memoirs of Major-General D. S. Stanley, U. S. A.* (1917).

STANLY, EDWARD
(1810–1872)
Union military governor of North Carolina

Born in New Bern, North Carolina, in 1810, Edward Stanly received his early education at the local academy, then attended what later became Norwich University in Middletown, Connecticut. Stanly then took up the study of law and in 1832 was admitted to the North Carolina bar. He married, then moved to Washington, North Carolina, where he established a law practice.

Stanly entered politics as a member of the Whig Party. He served in the U.S. House of Representatives from 1837 to 1843, when he was defeated for reelection after his district was gerrymandered. Returning to North Carolina, Stanly represented Beaufort County in the state assembly from 1844 to 1847, then became the state attorney general before resigning to return to the assembly in 1848. He again served in Congress from 1849 to 1853, during which time he fought against secession and earned the wrath of Southern Whigs. In 1851, Stanly and Samuel W. Inge of Alabama took part in the last duel fought by congressmen.

Weary of such struggles, Stanly did not seek reelection and went to California, where he started a law practice and was the state's Republican gubernatorial candidate in 1857. After serving as the city and county attorney at San Francisco, Stanly was surprised to receive a telegram from Secretary of War Edwin Stanton in April 1862, announcing that the Lincoln administration had just appointed him military governor of North Carolina.

Stanton advised Stanly that he was to act as governor of the state until the loyal citizens of North Carolina would organize a civil government that conformed to the Constitution of the United States. The new governor was instructed to uphold the existing laws of the state and strive to maintain peace and security for the inhabitants, all the while endeavoring to support Unionists wherever they might be found. Stanly accepted the post, for, like Lincoln, he believed that the war was being waged to restore the Union, and he wished to help the cause.

Stanly arrived in New Bern on 26 May 1862 and quickly became embroiled in controversy with Vincent Colyer, a New Yorker whose service in the Young Men's Christian Association led to involvement in the U.S. Christian Commission. Colyer had come to North Carolina and become "Superintendent of the Poor" under General Ambrose Burnside's direction. Colyer became especially interested in the plight of black contrabands and opened two schools for them in New Bern.

State law forbade the education of blacks, and Stanly expressed his concerns to Colyer. Stanly seems to have asked Colyer to suspend the schools until the Lincoln administration could develop a coherent policy toward contrabands, but Colyer overreacted and closed the schools. He then resigned his position and left the state. In Washington, Colyer complained to Senator Charles Sumner about Stanly. Other Northern abolitionists used the incident to flay Stanly in the newspapers and embarrass the administration.

Stanly also attempted to enforce the law that required runaway slaves to be returned to their owners. The new governor interpreted this law as pertaining to residents who had taken the oath of allegiance to the government. Stanly's efforts in this area, coupled with Colyer's outbursts in Washington, hampered his mission in North Carolina.

Confederate officials ignored Stanly and sent messages through the lines directly to Burnside. North Carolinians generally thought of Stanly as a traitor to his state. Stanly also found that the suspected widespread Union sentiment in North Carolina simply did not exist. If it did, misbehavior by Union soldiers, as well as the geographical limitations of Union occupation, contributed to the lack of Unionism in coastal North Carolina.

The Lincoln administration's lack of a policy toward both contrabands and reconstruction of the seceded states doomed Stanly's effectiveness as a wartime governor. When Lincoln issued the Emancipation Proclamation, Stanly offered his resignation, which Lincoln initially refused. Stanly continued to insist, and he served until 2 March 1863. He returned to California and resumed his law practice. He died on 12 July 1872 and was buried in the Mountain View Cemetery in Oakland.

—*Richard A. Sauers*

See also North Carolina.
For further reading:
Brown, Norman D. *Edward Stanly: Whiggery's Tarheel*

"Conqueror" (1974).

Harris, William C. "Lincoln and Wartime Reconstruction in North Carolina." *North Carolina Historical Review* (1986).

Sauers, Richard A. *"A Succession of Honorable Victories": The Burnside Expedition in North Carolina* (1996).

Stanly, Edward. *A Military Governor among Abolitionists. A Letter from Edward Stanly to Charles Sumner* (1865).

STANNARD, GEORGE JERRISON
(1820–1886)
Union general

Born in Georgia, Vermont, George Jerrison Stannard was educated locally and taught school part time as a young man. At age twenty-five he entered a local foundry enterprise as a clerk and eventually became a part owner of the company. Along with his business activities, Stannard was active in the Vermont militia and at the outbreak of the Civil War helped to organize the 2d Vermont Volunteers. In June 1861 he was named the regiment's lieutenant colonel.

Stannard and the 2d Vermont fought at First Bull Run in July 1861. Stannard was commended for his bravery in this battle. Later that summer Stannard and his regiment were stationed at Chain Bridge, Virginia, where they were engaged in reconnaissance actions against Confederate positions. In spring 1862, as part of the Army of the Potomac, Stannard and the 2d Vermont fought in the Peninsula campaign. Stannard was commended for his part in the battle of Williamsburg, especially in his efforts to extinguish a fire on a bridge. His actions prevented the severing of communications between different parts of the army. In July 1862 Stannard was promoted to colonel of volunteers and given command of the 9th Vermont.

In September 1862 Stannard and the 9th Vermont were stationed at Harper's Ferry. They were captured, along with the rest of the garrison, by Stonewall Jackson before he moved to join Robert E. Lee at Sharpsburg, Maryland. Stannard was not exchanged until the following spring. He was promoted to brigadier general of volunteers in March 1863 and sent to command a brigade under J. J. Abercrombie in the Department of Washington. In June 1863 he was given command of a brigade of I Corps, Army of the Potomac.

In the subsequent battle of Gettysburg, Stannard and his brigade were engaged late in the day on 2 July, but saw their greatest action the following day during the latter part of Pickett's Charge. As the Confederate forces began to withdraw after failing seriously to penetrate the Union line, Stannard and his largely Vermont brigade counterattacked the fleeing Southerners. Stannard was seriously wounded in the action.

By the end of the year Stannard was able to return to light duty, and from December 1863 through January 1864 he commanded troops in New York Harbor. In April 1864, now able to resume field service, Stannard reported to Benjamin F. Butler at Fort Monroe. The following month he was given command of a division in the Army of Virginia and detached for duty to the Army of the Potomac. He commanded his division at Cold Harbor, where he was again wounded on 3 June.

Upon his return to duty, Stannard was given command of a division in XVIII Corps and fought through July in the siege of Petersburg, when he was again wounded and forced temporarily to leave active service. Upon return to duty, Stannard commanded his division of XVIII Corps in its attack on the Richmond defensive work of Fort Harrison. When the attack was made on 30 September, Stannard led his men forward, but suffered a severe wound to his right arm. Later that day surgeons amputated the arm. Benjamin Butler commended Stannard for his gallantry in the attack, and he was given a brevet promotion to major general of volunteers for his part in the battle.

Stannard's recuperation was slow, and he was unable to return to combat duty for the remainder of the war. At the end of 1864, however, he reported for light duty and was assigned to the Department of the East. Sent to his home state of Vermont, Stannard spent the rest of the war supervising the border between Vermont and Canada.

Following the end of the war, Stannard was sent to Baltimore, Maryland, where he worked in the Freedmen's Bureau of that city. He remained there until he was mustered out of the army in 1866. He returned home to Vermont, where he became the collector of customs for the state. He left that position in 1872. In 1881 Stannard moved to Washington, D.C., to accept the position as the United States House of Representatives doorkeeper. In spite of declining health, Stannard remained as doorkeeper until he died on 1 June 1886. His remains were returned to Vermont for burial.

—*David S. Heidler and Jeanne T. Heidler*

See also Cold Harbor, Battle of; Gettysburg, Battle of; New Market Heights, Battle of; Petersburg, Campaign.

For further reading:

Sommers, Richard J. *Richmond Redeemed: The Siege of Petersburg* (1981).

Trudeau, Noah Andre. *The Last Citadel: Petersburg, Virginia, June 1864–April 1865* (1991).

STANTON, EDWIN McMASTERS
(1814–1869)
U.S. secretary of war

Born in Steubenville, Ohio, Edwin Stanton was the son of Lucy Norman and David Stanton, a physician. As a child, Stanton developed a chronic asthmatic condition that plagued him for the rest of his life and probably contributed to his somewhat hot temper. Young Stanton attended various schools until 1827, when his father's death compelled him to take a job in a local bookstore. He alternated between work and school for the next five years, finally entering the legal profession in 1836. In that year he also married Mary A. Lamson, with whom he had two children.

In 1837 Stanton formed a partnership with Judge Benjamin Tappan, an old family friend. Tappan, a Democrat with antislavery inclinations, had a great impact on Stanton's developing political philosophy. In that same year, Stanton was elected prosecuting attorney of Harrison County, Ohio. During the following year he played a major role in Tappan's successful campaign for a U.S. Senate seat, and he also campaigned actively for Martin Van Buren in the 1840 presidential election and for James K. Polk in the 1844 contest.

In 1844 Stanton's wife died, sending him into a deep depression. He plunged into his work, and his law practice began to blossom. He parted ways with Tappan in 1845, and in 1847 he formed a partnership with Charles Shaler. Their practice grew quickly, and they soon had clients throughout Ohio and Pennsylvania. Stanton was a shrewd and aggressive lawyer, given to browbeating witnesses and treating opposing lawyers with contempt. He soon came to be regarded as one of the finest lawyers in the country.

In 1856 Stanton married again, this time to Ellen Hutchinson, with whom he had four more children. In the same year, he also moved to Washington, D.C., in hopes of trying cases before the U.S. Supreme Court. Stanton quickly formed a close friendship with Jeremiah S. Black, attorney general for President James Buchanan. In the election of 1860, Stanton followed the lead of Buchanan and Black, supporting Southern Democrat John C. Breckinridge, because Stanton believed that only Breckinridge could save the Union. Shortly after Lincoln was elected, Black was elevated to secretary of state, and Stanton was named his successor as attorney general. Stanton did everything within his power to save the Union. He and Black pressured Buchanan to take strong action against secessionist elements in the South, and they did much to stiffen the president's resolve. Stanton also secretly funneled information about cabinet deliberations to incoming Secretary of State William Seward.

After the inauguration of President Lincoln, Stanton remained in Washington, D.C., where he occasionally served as a consultant to Secretary of War Simon Cameron. Stanton was becoming increasingly anti-slavery at this time, and in December 1861 he helped Cameron draft a report that called for the enlistment of African-American troops. Shortly thereafter, Cameron was compelled to resign due to mismanagement and corruption in the awarding of War Department contracts, and Lincoln named Stanton as his replace-

Edwin Stanton (*Library of Congress*)

ment. Why Lincoln made this choice is not entirely clear, but it seems likely that he was influenced by Seward (who thought of Stanton as a moderate), and Secretary of Treasury Salmon P. Chase (who was impressed with Stanton's antislavery views).

While Simon Cameron had been overwhelmed by the demands of leading the War Department, Stanton was more than up to the task. He worked well with leaders of both parties, and he made an effort to cultivate relationships with the leaders of committees that decided on military appropriations bills. He reorganized the War Department bureaucracy and reformed the guidelines by which the department did business, establishing a system of open, competitive bidding for contracts. He also instituted regulation of the Union's railroad system, and he placed telegraphs under War Department control.

Before assuming the post of secretary of war, Stanton had been a friend of Union commander George McClellan, but he quickly became disillusioned with the general after McClellan's repeated failures to take action. Stanton asked Lincoln to remove McClellan from command of all Union armies, and Lincoln complied, leaving the general in command of only the Army of the Potomac. Eventually, Stanton and the president

compelled McClellan to undertake the Peninsula campaign, which was unsuccessful. McClellan, who was angered by Stanton's actions, blamed the failure in part on the secretary. Henceforth they were bitter enemies, and each repeatedly called for the other's removal until Lincoln finally relieved McClellan of command in late 1862.

For much of the next year and a half, Stanton played a central role in the appointment and removal of military commanders. He also oversaw all military operations, and along with Lincoln he played a role in shaping Union strategy. He was a firm advocate of total war, and he supported the confiscation of slaves and other property of secessionists. He pressured Lincoln to issue the Emancipation Proclamation and to enlist black troops. His loyalties by this time were fully with the Republican Party, and he did not hesitate to use his power to advance the Republican cause, which he saw as synonymous with union. In particular, his handling of soldier voting helped the Republicans achieve victory in the 1864 elections.

In 1864, with the appointment of Ulysses S. Grant as commanding general, the Union finally found an effective command structure. Grant, assisted by Army Chief of Staff Henry Halleck, oversaw strategy. Stanton handled logistics and support, supplying the armies with what they needed to wage war. Lincoln provided overall direction and took care of the political maneuvering necessary to keep things running smoothly. Stanton liked Grant and got along well with him. Stanton's relations with William T. Sherman, whom he considered to be unfriendly to the freedmen, were less cordial. When Sherman extended generous terms to Joseph Johnston's surrendered army after Appomattox, mirroring what Grant had done for Lee's army, Stanton canceled the order. Sherman felt he was following Grant's lead, and Stanton's action infuriated him. For the rest of their lives, the two men were enemies.

Lincoln's assassination shortly after the end of the war shocked Stanton. He had initially disdained the president, but as the two men worked together, they had come to hold each other in high esteem. Stanton essentially assumed control of the government in the hours after the assassination, and he used all of his resources to hunt down the individuals who had played a part in the crime.

Stanton remained in control of the War Department as Reconstruction began, overseeing the demobilization of the Union armies. He initially supported Johnson's lenient Reconstruction policy, but reports of violence against freedmen caused Stanton to conclude that stronger measures were needed. He worked with Grant in an effort to convince the president to accept Congress' Reconstruction, while trying to avoid an alliance with the Radical Republicans. Stanton even supported the president's veto of the Tenure of Office Act, despite the fact that the bill was designed to protect Republicans in the cabinet, which included Stanton.

The president's intransigence on Reconstruction issues eventually forced Stanton's hand, and he and Grant began to move toward an alliance with Congress. Stanton supported the First and Second Reconstruction Acts, despite the president's opposition. This essentially ended Stanton's hopes for compromise, and he became an increasingly vocal supporter of radical policies. He and Grant drafted the Third Reconstruction Act that effectively removed the armies in the South from the president's control. His secretary of war's actions outraged Johnson, and he demanded Stanton's resignation. Stanton refused, and on 11 August 1867 Johnson suspended him and named Grant as his replacement. When Congress reconvened in January 1868, they ordered Stanton restored to his office under the terms of the Tenure of Office Act. Grant immediately stepped down, and Stanton resumed his duties. In February, Johnson again tried to replace Stanton, this time with General Lorenzo Thomas. Stanton refused to acknowledge the appointment and blockaded himself in his office. On 22 February, the House of Representatives voted to impeach Johnson on charges largely stemming from his violation of the Tenure of Office Act. Johnson was acquitted in the Senate.

Stanton remained in his post throughout the impeachment proceedings. He was disappointed that the Senate did not convict Johnson, and on 26 May he resigned and was replaced by General John M. Schofield. Stanton returned to life as a private citizen exhausted, in ill health, and virtually bankrupt from years of working for a modest government salary. After several months' rest, he recovered sufficiently to undertake a speaking tour supporting Grant's presidential bid. The tour triggered more health problems, however, and left Stanton a semi-invalid, financially dependent on his friends. When a seat on the Supreme Court became available, Grant appointed Stanton as a measure of his gratitude for years of friendship and service, but before Stanton could assume his new post the asthma that had dogged him since childhood took his life at the relatively young age of 55.

—Christopher Bates

See also Election of 1860; Lincoln, Abraham; McClellan, George Brinton.
For further reading:
Thomas, Benjamin P., and Harold M. Hyman. *Stanton: The Life and Times of Lincoln's Secretary of War* (1962).

STANTON, ELIZABETH CADY
(1815–1902)
Abolitionist and suffragist

Elizabeth Cady Stanton was born in Johnstown, New York, the daughter of Daniel and Margaret Cady. Stanton studied Greek, Latin, and mathematics as a girl and graduated from Emma Willard's Troy

Female Seminary in 1832. Through her cousin Gerrit Smith, an abolitionist, Stanton became interested in the antislavery movement. She met her future husband, Henry Brewster Stanton, when he lectured at a local antislavery meeting, and the two were married on 10 May 1840. Already interested in women's rights, Stanton demanded that the word "obey" not be used in their wedding ceremony.

Stanton's public career began after her marriage to Henry. For their honeymoon, the couple went to the World's Anti-Slavery Convention in London. Women delegates from the Philadelphia and Boston Female Anti-Slavery Societies were excluded from participating in the convention by more conservative British abolitionists. With the support of American male abolitionists, female delegates protested their exclusion. In London, Stanton met delegate Lucretia Mott, and the two resolved to hold a women's rights convention in the United States.

Upon her return to New York, Stanton petitioned state legislators to pass a women's property bill, which would allow married women to retain ownership of property they brought into the marriage. This bill passed the New York Legislature early in 1848. Stanton's victory encouraged her, and when she learned that Mott was to be in nearby Waterloo, New York, she, Mott, Jane Hunt, Mary Ann McClintock, and Martha Coffin Wright planned the first women's rights convention to be held in Stanton's hometown of Seneca Falls on 19 July. At the convention, Stanton submitted a radical resolution calling for women's right to vote. Stanton and other women continued to hold women's rights conventions throughout the 1850s. Stanton met her friend and ally, Susan B. Anthony, in 1851 and convinced her to join the women's rights movement.

As the conflict over slavery grew worse, Stanton and Anthony increased their efforts on behalf of the anti-slavery movement. Both women were victims of mobs in upstate New York in January 1861, when they lectured in support of abolition and disunion. When the Civil War began, Stanton and Anthony decided to temporarily put aside women's rights conventions. Abolitionists believed President Lincoln's Emancipation Proclamation to be insufficient, as it only abolished slavery in Confederate states. Stanton concluded that the best way to serve the Union and the cause of abolition was to advocate the emancipation of all enslaved African-Americans. She subsequently founded the Women's National Loyal League, which held its first meeting on 14 May 1863 in New York City. Stanton's goal was to obtain 1 million signatures on a petition to end slavery. The Loyal League's petition also called for an amendment to the Constitution abolishing slavery throughout the United States. Stanton urged women to use the only political right granted to them by the Constitution, that of petition: "Go to the rich, the poor, the high, the low, the soldier, the civilian, the white, the black—gather up the names of all who hate slavery—all who love LIBERTY, and would have it the LAW of the land—and lay them at the feet of Congress, your silent but potent vote for human freedom guarded by law." By the summer of 1864, the women of the Loyal League had collected 400,000 signatures. This was the largest petition drive in the history of the antislavery movement, and the Loyal League was the first national organization to support women's rights. Stanton continued to criticize Lincoln's antislavery policies and supported General John C. Frémont as the Republican candidate for president in 1864.

After the war, Stanton joined other abolitionists and supporters of women's rights in the American Equal Rights Association (AERA), which supported the vote for African-Americans and white women. When the association endorsed the Fifteenth Amendment even though it did not include women's right to vote, Stanton and Anthony left the AERA to form the National Woman Suffrage Association in 1869. Stanton devoted the rest of her career to the organized women's suffrage movement and lecturing and writing on behalf of women's rights. After the two women's suffrage associations united in 1890 as the National American Woman Suffrage Association, Stanton served as president for two years. She remained one of the most radical and outspoken supporters of women's rights until the day she died.

—*Carol Faulkner*

See also Abolitionists; Anthony, Susan Brownell; Mott, Lucretia.

For further reading:
Gordon, Ann D. *The Selected Papers of Elizabeth Cady Stanton and Susan B. Anthony: In the School of Anti-Slavery 1840–1866* (1997).
Griffith, Elisabeth. *In Her Own Right: The Life of Elizabeth Cady Stanton* (1984).
Stanton, Elizabeth Cady. *Eighty Years and More: Reminiscences 1815–1897* (1992).
Stanton, Elizabeth Cady, et al. *History of Woman Suffrage* (1970).
Venet, Wendy Hamand. *Neither Ballots nor Bullets: Women Abolitionists and the Civil War* (1991).

STAR OF THE WEST

The dispatch ship *Star of the West* earned national fame after an aborted attempt to resupply the besieged Union garrison at Fort Sumter, South Carolina. In January 1861 President James Buchanan secretly chartered the vessel to resupply Sumter's garrison with food and reinforcements. Although Buchanan initially favored sending the warship USS *Brooklyn*, Lieutenant General Winfield Scott believed that dispatching an armed vessel would only inflame the situation in Charleston. He convinced the president to send the civilian steamer *Star of the West* instead.

Built in 1852, the vessel became the pride of Commodore Cornelius Vanderbilt's Atlantic fleet. With its white oak hull and sculptured mahogany interior, the *Star of the West* exemplified the luxury to which Vanderbilt was accustomed. Vanderbilt used the 1,172-ton sidewheel steamer along the Atlantic and Gulf coasts between New York and Nicaragua before selling it to Marshall O. Roberts of New York in 1856. The *Star of the West* eventually became one of three ships owned by Roberts, who chartered his vessels to the U.S. government during the war. The government contracted the ship to resupply Sumter at a rate of $1,250 per day. The ship left New York harbor on 5 January 1861 on what was manifested as a routine run to New Orleans, but in fact was a "secret" mission to Charleston. The vessel detoured long enough for army officials to load ammunition, 300 stands of arms, 200 troops, and three months' provisions. Before the *Star of the West* arrived at Charleston harbor, however, Secretary of the Interior Jacob Thompson of Mississippi telegraphed South Carolina governor Francis Pickens a warning that a relief expedition was under way.

The ship arrived in the early hours of 9 January and waited for first light before crossing the sandbar. The *Star of the West* slowly steamed its way toward the fort when Confederate batteries on Morris Island suddenly opened fire, striking the vessel at least once, but causing no serious damage. After ten minutes of steaming under hostile fire and several near misses, the ship's captain, John McGowan, decided self-preservation to be the better part of valor and promptly returned to New York City. The affair marked one of the earliest hostilities of the Civil War, and symbolized Buchanan's failed policy of maintaining the status quo with the South.

The Federal government rechartered the *Star of the West* in March to repatriate paroled Federal troops near Indianola, Texas. At daybreak on 17 April 1861, Texas troops under the immediate command of Colonel (later Major General) Earl Van Dorn, boarded the vessel and captured it. Van Dorn sent the vessel to New Orleans before officially turning it over to the Confederacy. The Confederate navy subsequently rechristened the vessel the CSS *Saint Philip* and pressed it into service from April 1861 until April 1862 as a receiving vessel and a part-time hospital.

When Admiral David G. Farragut ran his ships past Forts Jackson and St. Philip below New Orleans, the vessel sailed up the Mississippi to Vicksburg to prevent capture, taking with it Confederate gold and specie. After unloading its cargo at Vicksburg, the craft found shelter on the Yazoo River at the Yazoo City shipyards.

Beginning in February 1863 Rear Admiral David D. Porter led an expedition via Yazoo Pass in an attempt to approach Vicksburg from the rear. Confederate forces quickly assembled near the convergence of the Tallahatchie and Yalobusha rivers to build Fort Pemberton, a makeshift earthen and cotton-bale fort just outside Greenwood, Mississippi. Unfortunately for the *Saint Philip*, fate determined that the ship would meet its demise at the hands of the Confederates. As part of assembling Pemberton's defenses, Confederate troops piloted the vessel downstream from Fort Pemberton and prepared to scuttle it by drilling and plugging 250 holes into the hull. They then tethered both ends of the craft to opposite shores, making the *Saint Philip* obstruct the Tallahatchie. When Porter's fleet finally arrived in March, Confederate forces scuttled the vessel to prevent Federal passage. Thus ended the interesting, yet inconsequential, career of the *Star of the West*.

As recently as the 1930s, visitors could still see remnants of the wrecked ship when the Tallahatchie River's levels dropped during the dry season. The ship's original flag and an ensign are currently on display at Cottonlandia Museum in Greenwood, Mississippi, as is a small display explaining Fort Pemberton and the vessel.

—*David P. Eldridge*

See also Fort Sumter, Bombardment of.

For further reading:

Bearss, Edwin C. *The Campaign for Vicksburg* (1985–1986).

Gibson, Charles Dana, and E. Kay Gibson. *Assault and Logistics: Union Army Coastal and River Operations, 1861–1866* (1995).

Miller, M. C. "Elegant, Luxurious *Star of the West* met a decidedly unromantic fate in the Mississippi Delta." *Ordnance* (date unknown).

Scharf, Thomas J. *The History of the Confederate States Navy: From Its Organization to the Surrender of Its Last Vessel* (1887; reprint, 1996).

STEARNS, GEORGE LUTHER
(1838–1867)
Abolitionist, military recruiter, and capitalist

George Luther Stearns secured his reputation as recruiter of former slaves and freedmen to serve in the Union military. The Massachusetts 54th and 55th army regiments were comprised of some two-thirds of Stearns's recruits. Stearns came to resent slavery as a result of both Southern resistance to tariff protection and the passage of the Fugitive Slave Act. He lent encouragement and comfort, and more importantly money, to the radical abolitionist John Brown. Stearns was one of the "Secret Six" implicated in Brown's Harper's Ferry raid.

Stearns was a principal in raising funds and equipment for the Emigrant Aid Company, which staked antislavery settlers from the North to occupy Kansas Territory. Stearns had become wealthy in the pipe manufacturing business, and his business instincts were never completely subservient to his bent for radical social reform. He supported runaways to Canada, settlements in Kansas, and John Brown. He also devoted immense

amounts of time and energy to the recruitment of runaways and freedmen for the military. He kept accounts of his loans and expenditures for land titles in Kansas, for purchase of Sharps rifles for John Brown, and of his personal speculations in plantations in Tennessee during the war.

He also pressed the federal War Department for fair treatment of the troops that he had enlisted. Many of these soldiers were the result of the subscription drafts of 1863. The purchase of substitutes, many of them freedmen, allowed whites to escape the draft; however, the use of these new soldiers posed a problem. The answer was the creation of African-American regiments to be led by white officers, many of whom came from the same classes who had sought to avoid military action. The Massachusetts 54th Regiment was led by Robert Gould Shaw, the ill-fated commander who was to lead his unit in a doomed mission at Battery Wagner, South Carolina, where he was unceremoniously buried in a mass grave with many of his command. The valor of the 54th validated Stearns's faith in the courage of black soldiers. By the end of the war, 10 percent of Union troops were African-Americans.

Stearns first came to his duty as recruiter at the request of Massachusetts governor John Andrew. But there were too few freedmen in Massachusetts for a unit of any size. Stearns was commissioned to go into New York State, especially into western New York, which was an avenue for runaways to Canada. Stearns established headquarters in the Buffalo and Rochester area and enjoyed immediate success. The War Department took notice and bestowed the rank and title of colonel on Stearns and extended his assignment throughout the North and to Tennessee, which was being liberated from Confederate control, thereby freeing many ex-slaves who were likely prospects for enlistment. Stearns enjoyed great success, but he also found himself at odds with the government as he pressed for equal pay and equal treatment of the new soldiers. Much to the embarrassment of the War Department, he made no secret of his outrage at the bigotry inherent in the failure of the government to provide better treatment for the black soldiers.

Stearns was discouraged and furious at the bureaucratic delays. He was also concerned that his long absences had caused both his family and his business to suffer. He resigned his commission and returned to Massachusetts to resume a normal life. When the war ended, Stearns continued to work to make reforms permanent. He backed the creation of *The Nation*, a journal under the editorship of Edwin L. Godkin, but soon retreated from sponsorship when the journal mocked abolitionist reformers who worked to ensure civil rights for the freedmen. Stearns then funded a newspaper, *The Right Way*, which failed for lack of subscribers.

Stearns was an uncommon and unique man who was always interested in personal economic success, but never ignored the basic principle of a free society meaning freedom for all persons. He joined his humanity to his purse. It was Stearns who paid for the return of the bodies of John Brown and his sons after the Harper's Ferry raid. It was he who financed Brown's purchase of his North Elba farm; and it was Stearns who provided the financial support for Brown's widow and the education of his daughters.

A proud and belligerent man, Stearns finally appeared before the congressional committees that investigated the Brown conspiracy, and he lied often and well. He had little regard for the right of Congress to question him about what he perceived to be a legitimate action against slavery. Both his health and his business interests deteriorated, and he died of pneumonia in New York City at the age of fifty-eight. His legacy remains as that of a true believer in the cause that John Brown represented: that the struggle against slavery in America had to be shared by the subjects of slavery. A memorial tablet commemorating his life is in the State House in Boston.

—*Jack J. Cardoso*

See also Brown, John; United States Colored Troops.
For further reading:
Cornish, Dudley Taylor. *The Sable Arm: Negro Troops in the Union Army, 1861–1865* (1966).
Heller, Charles E. *Portrait of an Abolitionist: A Biography of George Luther Stearns, 1809–1867* (1996).
Oates, Stephen B. *To Purge This Land with Blood: A Biography of John Brown* (1970).
Renehan, Edward J., Jr. *The Secret Six: The True Tales of the Men Who Conspired with John Brown* (1995).
Stearns, Frank Preston. *The Life and Public Services of George Luther Stearns* (1907).
Stearns, George Luther. *A Few Facts Pertaining to Our Currency and Banking Adapted to the Present Position of Our Finances* (1864).
———. *Universal Suffrage and Complete Equality in Citizenship: The Safeguard of Democratic Institutions* (1865).
Villard, Oswald Garrison. *John Brown 1800–1859: A Biography Fifty Years After* (1910; reprint, 1966).

STEEDMAN, JAMES BLAIR
(1818–1883)
Union general, editor, and politician

James Blair Steedman was born 30 July 1818 in Northumberland County, Pennsylvania, the son of Mellum and Margaret Blair Steedman, both of Scottish descent. Orphaned at age 13, he apprenticed himself to a printer but had little formal education. His lifelong affiliation with the Democratic Party began at the presses of the Lewisburg *Democrat*, where he also learned the rudiments of a common school education and business skills. Still a teenager, he organized a group

of laborers to build a portion of the state canal in Pennsylvania. Politics, patronage, and printing were life-long passions he acquired early on. Steedman moved to northwest Ohio in the 1830s, where he published *The Northwestern Democrat* in Defiance. He built a portion of the Wabash and Erie Canal and, later, the Toledo, Wabash & Western Railroad. In Ohio he married Miranda Stiles, who bore him three children. Always a local Democratic Party stalwart, he secured election for two terms in the Ohio House of Representatives and served on the State Board of Public Works. Thanks to his political connections, he served as public printer in Washington in the late 1850s.

Steedman was a partisan of Stephen Douglas and a delegate to the Democratic Party convention in Charleston and to the Baltimore convention that nominated Douglas for the presidency in 1860. Steedman lost a race for Congress that year from the Ninth District of Ohio and vowed to resist secession. A colonel in the Ohio militia, within days of the firing on Fort Sumter he was commissioned as a colonel of the Ohio Volunteers and raised an infantry regiment, the 14th Ohio. Steedman and the 14th served under George McClellan in early Union victories in the summer of 1861 in what is now West Virginia at Phillippi, Laurel Hill, and Carrick's Ford on the Cheat River. The regiment then took part in the campaign to secure Kentucky during the fall and winter of 1861–1862 and saw action at Wildcat and Logan's Cross Roads. There Steedman became friends with loyalist Senator Andrew Johnson when Johnson fled Tennessee and found refuge in the camp of the 14th.

Promoted to brigadier general in July 1862, Steedman played an important role in the Union victory at Perryville, Kentucky, saw limited action at Stones River, and fought at Hoover's Gap and in skirmishes around Tullahoma. The high point of Steedman's career came in the campaign around Chattanooga and the battle of Chickamauga. On the second day of the battle of Chickamauga, 20 September 1863, Steedman and his superior, Gordon Granger, left their reserve positions in the rear and rushed troops and ammunition to General George Thomas, thereby preventing a rout of the Union army. Steedman personally rallied his inexperienced troops by seizing a regimental standard and attacking an enemy-held ridge. His actions provided the most dramatic counterattack of the entire battle and secured his reputation for bravery and decisive action.

Promoted to major general after Chickamauga, Steedman was placed in charge of the District of Etowah in northern Georgia and Alabama behind Sherman's line when Sherman began his Atlanta campaign. He rescued besieged Union troops at Dalton in June 1864 and rushed his army to Nashville to defend the city from attack by General John Bell Hood in December 1864.

His troops occupied the far left of the Union line and attacked the enemy on two days of fighting.

After the surrender in April 1865, Steedman was named military commander of Georgia, a post he filled until the summer of 1866. Still loyal to Andrew Johnson and the Democratic Party, Steedman and General Joseph Fullerton wrote a critical assessment of Freedmen's Bureau operations, a report Johnson hoped would justify his veto of the bureau. Steedman then assumed the post of collector of internal revenue at New Orleans and helped secure the electoral votes of Louisiana for 1868 Democratic Party presidential nominee, Horatio Seymour. Steedman returned to Toledo in 1869, where he resumed his career in journalism. He was elected to the Ohio Senate in 1878, and he served briefly as police commissioner in Toledo before his death in 1883.

Steedman was a figure of controversy throughout his military career. Regular army officers regarded him as the worst kind of political general, and his fondness for gambling, alcohol, and women of easy virtue was widely known and disapproved. On the other hand, no one could deny his bravery and physical courage nor his ability to lead men into battle.

—*Gregory R. Zieren*

See also Chickamauga, Battle of; Nashville, Battle of.

For further reading:
Cimbala, Paul. *Under the Guardianship of the Nation: The Freedman's Bureau and the Reconstruction of Georgia, 1865-1870* (1997).
Cozzens, Peter. *This Terrible Sound: The Battle of Chickamauga* (1992).
Morgan, John M., "Old Steady: The Role of General James Blair Steedman at the Battle of Chickamauga." *Northwest Ohio Quarterly* (1950).
———. "Steedman's Action at Dalton, 1864." *Northwest Ohio Quarterly* (1981).
Reid, Whitelaw. *Ohio in the War: Her Statesmen, Generals and Soldiers* (1868).

STEELE, FREDERICK
(1819–1868)
Union general

Frederick Steele was an enigma who figured prominently in the Civil War in the Mississippi Valley. Although he occasionally displayed flashes of brilliance, his political conservatism, fondness for fine living, and strategic limitations kept him from dealing any decisive blows against the Confederacy.

Steele was born on 14 January 1819, in Delhi, New York. He entered the U.S. Military Academy in 1839 and graduated thirtieth in the Class of 1843, nine places behind his friend Ulysses S. Grant. Steele fought as a second lieutenant with the 2d U.S. Infantry in the Mexican-American War, winning a promotion to first

lieutenant on 6 June 1848, as well as two earlier brevets for gallantry. Serving at various posts in California, Minnesota, Nebraska, and Kansas during the next thirteen years, he made captain in 1855.

The outbreak of the Civil War found Captain Steele at Fort Leavenworth on the troubled Kansas-Missouri border. He received a promotion to major and led a composite battalion of regulars at Wilson's Creek, 10 August 1861. On 23 September, Steele joined the volunteer service as colonel of the 8th Iowa Volunteer Infantry, and he was upgraded to brigadier general on 29 January 1862. He headed the District of Southeast Missouri for several months until being transferred to Major General Samuel R. Curtis's Army of the Southwest. Steele commanded a division in Curtis's second invasion of Arkansas, assisting in the capture of Helena on 12 July 1862.

During a brief stint as commander of the Army of the Southwest beginning in September 1862, Steele reversed Curtis's policy of humane treatment for the thousands of runaway slaves who took refuge at Helena. He also turned a blind eye to the excesses of dishonest Northern cotton traders who flocked to the occupied river port.

Steele reported to the Army of the Tennessee in December 1862 and took charge of another division. He served under Major General William T. Sherman at Chickasaw Bluffs and Arkansas Post. On 17 March 1863, he was promoted to major general and proceeded to lead a division of the XV Army Corps through the Vicksburg campaign.

After Vicksburg's surrender, Steele returned to Helena on 31 July 1863 and assumed command of Union forces in Arkansas. In August, he set out with a 12,000-man army to capture Little Rock. Despite stifling heat and rampant sickness in his ranks, Steele maneuvered his foes into abandoning Little Rock on 10 September. The ease of his victory convinced him that he had virtually broken Confederate resistance in Arkansas. A conservative Democrat with little enthusiasm for the Lincoln administration's racial policies, Steele treated Confederate civilians with such laxity that many of his officers and men branded him a Copperhead.

In late March 1864, Steele, now the commander of the VII Army Corps and Department of Arkansas, marched into southwest Arkansas with 14,000 men to support Major General Nathaniel Banks's ill-fated thrust up the Red River toward Texas. Steele's campaign went well at first, as he outsmarted his outnumbered opponents and took the fortified city of Camden without undue difficulty on 15 April. In the next ten days, however, Confederate cavalry captured Union supply trains at Poison Spring and Marks' Mills, throwing Steele's logistics into disarray. The approach of three enemy infantry divisions from Louisiana forced Steele to abandon Camden on 26 April, and he herded his battered army back to the safety of Little Rock only after his subordinates fought a stubborn rear-guard action at Jenkins' Ferry on 30 April.

During the next few months, Steele seemed to stagnate while many of his soldiers debauched themselves in the bars and brothels of Little Rock. Relieved as departmental commander by Major General Joseph J. Reynolds on 29 November 1864, Steele transferred to the Department of the Gulf. He commanded the "Column from Pensacola" during the Mobile campaign in March and April 1865. Ironically, Steele's best unit was a division of black troops, which gave him a final taste of glory by precipitating the capture of Fort Blakely on 9 April. He finished the war as commander of the District of West Florida.

Steele resumed his career in the regular army, securing the colonelcy of the 20th U.S. Infantry on 28 July 1866. He was stationed on the West Coast and given command of the Department of the Columbia. While on leave in San Mateo, California, Steele suffered an apoplectic fit as he was driving a carriage and took a bad fall. He died as a result of his injuries on 12 January 1868.

—*Gregory J. W. Urwin*

See also Arkansas; Blakely, Alabama, Battle of; Helena, Battle of; Jenkins' Ferry, Battle of; Marks' Mills, Battle of; Poison Spring, Battle of; Red River Campaign.

For further reading:
Bearss, Edwin C. *Steele's Retreat from Camden and the Battle of Jenkins' Ferry* (1967).
Christ, Mark K., ed. *Rugged and Sublime: The Civil War in Arkansas* (1994).
Moneyhon, Carl H. *The Impact of the Civil War and Reconstruction on Arkansas: Persistence in the Midst of Ruin* (1994).
Shea, William L., and Earl J. Hess. *Pea Ridge: Civil War Campaign in the West* (1992).
Sperry, A. F. *History of the 33d Iowa Infantry Volunteer Regiment, 1863–6* (1999).

STEPHENS, ALEXANDER HAMILTON
(1812–1883)
Confederate vice president

Stephens was named for his grandfather, Alexander Stephens, a native of Scotland and veteran of the Revolutionary War who settled in Georgia in the early 1790s. Andrew Stephens, the only son of the elder Alexander to remain in Georgia, was a successful farmer and educator. He married Margaret Grier in 1806. Within months of young Alexander's birth in 1812, his mother died as the result of pneumonia. His father quickly remarried Matilda Lindsey, the daughter of a local war hero. Matilda had great influence upon her stepson's life, but the greatest inspiration to the young

Alexander Stephens (*Library of Congress*)

"Aleck" was his father. While not exhibiting any initial fondness for academic study, by 1824 Alexander was consumed with an interest in biblical narrative and history and he began to read widely. In 1826 Andrew Stephens died from pneumonia, and Alexander's stepmother soon followed from the same affliction. Alexander was overcome by grief. He became disconsolate and fell into a state of melancholy. Alexander and his brother Aaron were then taken in by their uncle, Aaron Grier. While living with his uncle, Alexander was befriended by two Presbyterian ministers, the Reverends Williams and Alexander Hamilton Webster. These men greatly aided Alexander's personal and intellectual development. Out of his respect and devotion to Reverend Webster, Stephens eventually changed his middle name to Hamilton. As the result of the encouragement offered by these clerics and others, the young Alexander Stephens entered Franklin College, which later became the University of Georgia. At Franklin, Stephens was guided in his studies by the eminent educator, Reverend Moses Waddel, the brother-in-law and teacher of John C. Calhoun and many of the emerging leaders of South Carolina.

Graduating first in his class at Franklin in 1832, Stephens had distinguished himself as a scholar and capable debater. He accepted a position as a tutor and began an independent study of the law. After passing the bar examination, Stephens was elected to the state legislature, spending six years in the statehouse and senate. It was becoming apparent that Stephens possessed the qualities necessary for political success.

When his political coalition merged with the Whig Party, Stephens decided to run for the U.S. Congress in 1843. As a candidate, he defended the Whig Party's positions on the national bank and tariffs. Stephens was elected, but within a short time he received news that his brother Aaron had died. Stephens was again stricken with a profound sense of loss. After arriving in Washington to assume his congressional seat, he was so sick that he was unable to the attend legislative sessions. On 9 February 1844, in his first speech as a member of Congress, he challenged his own election! Stephens eventually became a Whig stalwart, campaigning for various Whig candidates and related causes, including Henry Clay's unsuccessful presidential bid in 1844. The major issue before Congress at that time was the annexation of Texas. In opposition to many Southern congressmen, who viewed the annexation of Texas as essential to the preservation of a political equilibrium that protected slavery, Stephens opposed expansion. Eventually, though, Stephens was forced to see the benefits of annexation for the South and the Whig Party, but he opposed the measure if based solely on the extension of slavery.

Troubled by what he believed to be President Polk's bad management, including exacerbating tensions with England regarding Oregon and the situation in Mexico, Stephens became an outspoken critic of the administration. Polk ordered General Zachary Taylor to the Rio Grande and a conflict transpired, prompting Polk to state that a war had been initiated. While Congress provided a declaration of war, Stephens agreed with Calhoun that the war could escalate into a greater conflict. In conjunction with other Whigs, Stephens tried to limit his support of the war and to prevent Congress from acquiring territory as the spoils of the contest. He introduced legislation aimed at limiting the aggrandizing policies of the Polk administration. By 1847 Stephens had become a central figure in the Young Indians Club, a group of congressmen supporting the presidential candidacy of General Zachary Taylor, who they believed shared the worldview of Southern Whigs.

After Taylor's election, Stephens was forced to reconsider his support of "Old Zack." Stephens supported the doctrine of popular sovereignty because he believed it to be a countervailing force against the Northern Whigs who wanted to admit California and New Mexico as free states. Working with his fellow Georgian and friend Robert Toombs, Stephens challenged his Whig colleagues to adopt resolutions forbidding Congress from

ending the slave trade in the territories, but the effort failed. Within a short period of time, Stephens had moved from being a valued supporter of the administration to a critic and congressional opponent. He was forced to leave the Whig Party, but he maintained his legislative base of support in Georgia. In joining forces against the Whigs during a period of electoral realignment, he assisted in the formation of the Constitutional Union Party in Georgia.

In the midst of the turmoil, Stephens eventually joined the Democratic Party. He supported the Compromise of 1850 and was instrumental in the adoption of the Kansas-Nebraska Act of 1854. Stephens thought the acceptance of the Kansas-Nebraska Act was the "mission" of his life, and that "his cup of ambition was full."After unsuccessfully supporting various measures designed to secure the position of the South, Stephens announced that he was retiring from Congress. He was weary and tired of confronting "restless, captious, and fault-finding people." He did not support extremist measures offered by his colleagues from the South, but remained an advocate of states' rights nevertheless. Even as Southern radicals encouraged secession after the election of Lincoln in 1860, Stephens urged restraint, pleading with his follow Georgians to evince "good judgment," and arguing that the ascendancy of Lincoln did not merit secession. In a celebrated exchange with the new president, he reminded Lincoln that "Independent, sovereign states" had formed the Union and that these states could reassert their sovereignty. When Georgia convened a convention in January 1861 Stephens voted against secession, but when secession was approved by a vote of 166 to 130, he was part of the committee that drafted the secession ordinance.

As the Confederacy evolved, Stephens was selected as a delegate and to many he appeared to be a good candidate for the vice presidency. He assumed an important role in the drafting of the Confederate constitution and in other affairs, eventually accepting the vice presidency. Early in his tenure as vice president, on 21 March 1861, he gave his politically damaging "Cornerstone" address in Savannah, extolling the superiority of whites. President Jefferson Davis was greatly disturbed, as Stephens had shifted the basis of the political debate from states' rights to slavery. Stephens was convinced that slavery was a necessity. The estrangement between Davis and Stephens increased, and by early 1862 the vice president was not intimately involved in the affairs of state. Accordingly, he returned to his home in Crawfordville. Pursuing actions he thought might assist in the denouement of the conflict, Stephens attempted several assignments, including a diplomatic sojourn to Washington. In July 1863 President Abraham Lincoln refused Stephens permission to come to the federal capital. In February 1865 Stephens participated in the failed Hampton Roads Peace Conference.

At the conclusion of the war, Stephens was arrested and imprisoned at Fort Warren, Massachusetts. After his release, he devoted the remainder of his life to composing *A Constitutional View of the Late War Between the States*, a two-volume defense of Southern constitutionalism, which appeared in 1868 and 1870. According to Stephens, the foremost theoretical and practical distillation of authority and liberty was found within the American political tradition. The original system was predicated upon reserving the states' sphere of authority. For Stephens, this original diffusion, buttressed by a prudent mode of popular rule, was the primary achievement of American politics.

—*H. Lee Cheek, Jr.*

See also Davis, Jefferson; Georgia; Hampton Roads Peace Conference; Toombs, Robert Augustus.
For further reading:
Brumgardt, John R. "The Confederate Career of Alexander Stephens." *Civil War History* (1981).
Rabun, James Z. "Alexander Stephens and the Confederacy." *Emory University Quarterly* (1950).
Schott, Thomas E. *Alexander H. Stephens of Georgia: A Biography* (1988).
Stephens, Alexander H. *A Constitutional View of the Late War Between the States* (1868 and 1870; reprint, 1994).

STEUART, GEORGE HUME
(1828–1903)
Confederate general

Born the son of George Hume Steuart in Baltimore, Maryland, the younger Steuart was educated locally before receiving an appointment to the U.S. Military Academy in 1844. He graduated thirty-seventh of thirty-eight in the class of 1848 and was commissioned into the dragoons. Upon graduation he was sent to Texas, where he served for seven years. As a captain of cavalry after 1855 he served at a variety of frontier posts in Kansas and Nebraska. He fought in several Indian conflicts before being detailed to participate in Albert Sidney Johnston's Utah expedition. In 1860 he returned to Texas, where he fought in campaigns against the Comanche.

During the secession crisis of early 1861, Steuart returned to Maryland to await his state's decision regarding disunion. After the firing on Fort Sumter and Abraham Lincoln's call for volunteers, he assumed that Maryland would follow its neighbor Virginia out of the Union. In anticipation of that event, he resigned his commission and accepted the position of major general of the Maryland volunteers who supported secession. He worked through the remaining days of April into May procuring weapons from Virginia to arm these troops so that they would be prepared to defend the state once

Maryland seceded. That event never occurred, and Steuart as a result traveled with his men to Virginia, where he accepted a lieutenant colonel's commission in the Confederate army.

Serving under Colonel Arnold Elzey of the 1st Maryland for the first months of the war, Steuart and the regiment spent that time in the Shenandoah Valley under Joseph E. Johnston. Because of his close association with Maryland troops during the early phases of the war, he became known as "Maryland" Steuart during this time. In June 1861 he was sent with part of the regiment to Harper's Ferry to take possession of anything of value left at the armory there. He succeeded to command of the regiment at First Bull Run when Elzey was promoted to brigade command. Johnston commended Steuart for his actions at Bull Run and secured his promotion to colonel.

During the fall and winter of 1861–1862 he commanded his regiment under Thomas J. "Stonewall" Jackson in the Shenandoah Valley. In March 1862 he was promoted to brigadier general to serve under Major General Richard Ewell in the valley. In April, Steuart wrote personally to the Confederate secretary of war, George W. Randolph, urging the creation of the Maryland Line. While Steuart commanded the Maryland Brigade, he strongly believed that the creation of an entire Maryland division would greatly facilitate recruiting of Confederate forces in Maryland. This particular project, however, would have to wait, as Steuart and his men were by then heavily engaged in Jackson's famous Shenandoah Valley campaign.

Steuart fought in all the major engagements of that campaign. He created a considerable controversy on 25 May following the Confederate victory at Winchester, when he refused to follow Jackson's order to pursue some of the retreating Union forces because Jackson had not sent the order through Ewell. Two weeks later, on 8 June, he was severely wounded in the shoulder at Cross Keys. After a lengthy convalescence, Steuart assumed command of the Confederate forces around Winchester in September 1862. He remained in the Shenandoah Valley until the following spring, when, toward the end of May, he was ordered to report to Robert E. Lee at Fredericksburg.

Placed in command of a brigade of Edward Johnson's division in Ewell's corps, Steuart led his men (mostly Virginia and North Carolina units) north in Lee's invasion of the North. He participated in Ewell's victory at Winchester in mid-June 1863 before moving with his men into Pennsylvania. On the first day of the battle of Gettysburg, Steuart and his men were part of Ewell's attack against Union forces north of town. For the remainder of the battle he and his brigade concentrated their attention against the Union position on Culp's Hill.

In the fall of 1863, still in command of the same brigade Steuart fought in the Bristoe Station and Mine Run campaigns. In the latter campaign, his brigade was almost overrun by the attacking Federals before he was reinforced. In the spring he fought during the opening phases of Ulysses S. Grant's campaign against Lee, commanding his brigade at the Wilderness and then at the Bloody Angle at Spotsylvania. During that engagement on 12 May, Federal forces captured him and his entire brigade. Ironically, this event occurred almost at the same time that Union major general Lewis Wallace was confiscating Steuart's estate on the South River in Maryland.

Steuart endured only a brief imprisonment before being exchanged in August 1864. Upon his return to the Army of Northern Virginia on 11 August 1864, he was placed in command of a brigade in George Pickett's division of James Longstreet's corps. He remained with this brigade for the remainder of the war, although briefly in February and March, in Pickett's absence, he commanded the entire division. Toward the end of the war, he fought in the last phases of the siege of Petersburg, and on 30 March and 1 April he participated in Pickett's attack and the defense at Five Forks. He fought at Sayler's Creek on 6 April before retreating with what was left of Lee's army. He surrendered with that force at Appomattox Court House.

After being paroled, Steuart returned to Maryland. He farmed for the remainder of his life in Anne Arundel County and became very active in Confederate veterans groups. He died on his farm on 22 November 1903.

—*David S. Heidler and Jeanne T. Heidler*

See also Cross Keys, Battle of; Shenandoah Valley Campaign (1862); Spotsylvania Court House, Battle of; Winchester, First Battle of; Winchester, Second Battle of.

For further reading:
Matter, William D. *If It Takes All Summer: The Battle of Spotsylvania* (1988).
Tanner, Robert G. *Stonewall in the Valley: Thomas J. "Stonewall" Jackson's Shenandoah Valley Campaign, Spring 1862* (1976; reprint, 1996).

STEVENS, ISAAC INGALLS
(1818–1862)
Union general

A native of North Andover, Massachusetts, Isaac Stevens secured an appointment to the U.S. Military Academy, from which he graduated at the head of his class in 1839. After supervising construction at a number of East Coast fortifications, he served as an engineer officer on General Winfield Scott's staff during the Mexican-American War. Although Stevens led a number of important topographical reconnaissances and performed valiantly in the campaign from Vera Cruz to Mexico City, his efforts were overshadowed by those of his

fellow officer, Robert E. Lee. Stevens returned from Mexico with the brevet rank of major and a foot shattered by a ball taken during the attack on the Mexican capital.

After a stint as second-in-command of the U.S. Coast Survey, in 1853 Stevens obtained the positions of governor and superintendent of Indian affairs for the newly created Washington Territory as well as leading the northern transcontinental railway survey. Stevens negotiated ten Indian treaties in the Pacific Northwest, the action for which he is best remembered, and commanded the territorial militia in the conflict that followed. During the Indian war he came into sharp conflict with General John E. Wool, who advocated a conciliatory approach as opposed to Stevens's aggressive stance. Stevens obtained notoriety by declaring martial law in two Washington counties, an action that later earned him a presidential reprimand.

Stevens's four years as governor won him the support of the great majority of his constituency, who elected him to two terms as territory delegate to the U.S. House of Representatives. A Northern Democrat who sympathized with the South's constitutional arguments, Stevens achieved national prominence in 1860 by vigorously opposing the nomination of Stephen A. Douglas and then becoming the national campaign manager for the Breckinridge-Lane ticket. Although Stevens strongly repudiated secession and immediately offered his services to the Union after Fort Sumter, his political affiliations in the prewar period did not serve him well. Despite a military record equaled by few of his generation, Stevens managed to secure only a colonelcy with the 79th New York Highlanders.

Stevens's Civil War career reflected the characteristics he had amply displayed before the war. Extremely intelligent, energetic, aggressive, even pugnacious, Stevens did not readily tolerate dissent from his plans or opinions, and, like many of his peers, was not averse to voicing dissent to policies he deemed wrong-headed. Promoted to brigadier general in September 1861, Stevens and the Highlanders sailed to Port Royal in November as part of the military expedition that seized and occupied the Sea Islands. He remained during the winter and spring with headquarters at Beaufort, South Carolina, wrestling with primarily political problems related to thousands of freedmen who had come under the army's control and cotton agents and abolitionists who flocked to the area, which served, as one historian has suggested, as a rehearsal for Reconstruction.

Although eager for military action, Stevens disapproved of General Henry W. Benham's plan to move against Charleston in 1862. The campaign resulted in defeat on 16 June at Secessionville, where Stevens' division took heavy losses in attacks against a fortified Confederate position. Subsequently, Benham was arrested and relieved of command.

Isaac Stevens (*Library of Congress*)

In July, Stevens moved to the center of the conflict with assignment to the Army of the Potomac to command the 1st Division, IX Corps, under General Ambrose Burnside. At Second Bull Run, Stevens's division participated in the fierce piecemeal attacks of 29 August against Stonewall Jackson's forces, who were protected by a railroad cut. Early the next day, Stevens and other generals advised the optimistic John Pope of their tenuous position. Pope ordered Stevens to make a reconnaissance but rejected his report that the Confederates remained strongly entrenched. During the attack of the second day, Stevens helped hold the right flank and then protected the army's retreat toward Washington, D.C.

On 1 September, Stevens, with his division and a portion of a second, moved north to meet elements of Jackson's corps, whom General Lee had ordered to cut off Pope's retreat. Stevens's forces intercepted the Confederates at Chantilly, where a sharp engagement during a driving rainstorm frustrated Lee's plan. Heroically, but rashly, Stevens seized the Highlander's colors and led a charge just as thunder and lightning

crashed across the battlefield. At this dramatic moment, he was fatally struck by a minié ball in the head.

Stevens received posthumous promotion to major general. At the time of his death, his intelligence combined with his fearless, aggressive tactics were beginning to attract attention. Some even suggested that he was in line to lead the Army of the Potomac. This was probably premature speculation. One thing, as President Lincoln remarked, was certain—Stevens and other political opponents of the Republicans had proven with their blood that their devotion to the Union was second to none.

—*Kent D. Richards*

See also Breckinridge, John Cabell; Bull Run, Second Battle of; Chantilly, Battle of; Election of 1860; Port Royal Sound/Hilton Head, Battle of; Secessionville, Battle of.

For further reading:
Richards, Kent D. *Isaac I. Stevens* (1993).
Rose, Willie Lee. *Rehearsal for Reconstruction* (1964).
Stevens, Hazard. *Life of Isaac Ingalls Stevens* (1900).

STEVENS, THADDEUS
(1792–1868)
Radical Republican

Born in Danville, Vermont, on 4 April 1792 to Baptist parents, Thaddeus Stevens had a clubfoot. A later childhood disease made him bald, and he wore a red wig, which matched his fiery temper. After graduating from Dartmouth in 1814, Stevens moved to York, Pennsylvania, where he studied law. Practicing law in Gettysburg, he soon became a leading attorney in the state with a strong reputation as a defense lawyer for fugitive slaves. He entered the iron works business and met with considerable success.

Stevens's lifestyle always caused talk among his friends and enemies. He never married; he enjoyed gambling, and his political oration displayed a no-holds-barred approach. Politics would be the perfect outlet for his talents and temperament. Elected on the Anti-Masonic ticket to the

Thaddeus Steven lying in state in the Capitol, Washington, D.C. (*National Archives*)

Pennsylvania House of Representatives (1833–1835, 1837, and 1841), he also served as a delegate to the state constitutional convention in 1838. Stevens played a key role in the establishment and defense of the public education system in the Keystone State.

By 1842 he had moved to Lancaster, where, six years later, he was elected as a Whig to the U.S. House of Representatives. He soon was a leading spokesman for the antislavery cause. A significant contributor to the creation of the Republican Party in Pennsylvania, he served in the House for four succeeding Congresses, from 1859 until his death.

During the Civil War he opposed any concession to the Rebel states. As chairman of the powerful Ways and Means Committee, he urged a vigorous campaign against the Confederacy. Later, after Lincoln's death, as chairman of the House group of the Joint Committee on Reconstruction, he rejected the policies of President Andrew Johnson and supported the Freedmen's Bureau Bill in 1866 and the military reconstruction of the rebel states the next year. He guided the Civil Rights Act of 1866 through Congress as well as the Fourteenth Amendment, the key to a significant reordering of the American polity. By 1868 Stevens was chairman of the managers appointed by the House to conduct impeachment proceedings against President Johnson. His failing health prevented him from an active role in presenting the case against President Johnson. He died on 11 August 1868 and was buried in a Negro cemetery in Lancaster.

The traditional interpretation of Stevens's achievements is the claim that he was interested only in punishment of the wayward South and for strengthening of the Republican Party in the South and the entire country. Such a reading is wrong. His life clearly expressed the free labor and the upward social mobility of the expanding economy. The Radicals and Stevens attracted labor reformers during Reconstruction with their free-labor ideology and antimonopolist and antiaristocratic rhetoric. They combined the Jacksonian Democratic belief in the unlimited rule of the majority with the Whigs' conception of an activist state. As an heir of New England abolitionism and cultural Puritanism, Stevens's ideas and program of forty acres and a mule for the former slaves placed him on the forefront of the modernization of both the South and the entire nation.

Stevens supported the egalitarian ideal. He fought racism during his entire public career. He rejected the very popular notion of a Herrenvolk democracy, the equality of all men within a master race. He combined his disdain for racism with a commitment for land reform, homesteads for the freedpeople that anticipated the welfare state of the twentieth century. His burial in the all-black graveyard was a testament to his egalitarianism to his contemporaries and to later generations.

Stevens's historical reputation has improved in the last half century as a more critical and realistic evaluation of the Civil War and Reconstruction has emerged. In the 1930s, when the needless war doctrine had both popular and scholarly support, people rejected Stevens as a vindictive politician. Abolitionists and nationalists, however, are now counted among positive elements in the American story.

—*Donald K. Pickens*

See also Lincoln's Reconstruction Policy; Radical Republicans; Republican Party.

For further reading:
Belz, Herman. *Emancipation and Equal Rights, Politics and Constitutionalism in the Civil War Era* (1978).
Brodie, Fawn N. *Thaddeus Stevens, Scourge of the South* (1966).
Cortner, Richard C. *The Supreme Court and the Second Bill of Rights, The Fourteenth Amendment and the Nationalization of Civil Liberties* (1981).
Cox, LaWanda. "Negro Suffrage and Republican Politics: The Problem of Motivation in Reconstruction Historiography." *Journal of Southern History* (1967).
———. "The Promise of Land for the Freedmen." *Mississippi Valley Historical Review* (1958).
Current, Richard N. *Old Thad Stevens* (1942).
Foner, Eric. *Free Soil, Free Labor, Free Men: The Ideology of the Republican Party before the Civil War* (1970).
Pickens, Donald K. "The Republican Synthesis and Thaddeus Stevens." *Civil War History* (1985).
Trefousse, Hans Louis. *The Radical Republicans, Lincoln's Vanguard for Racial Justice* (1968).
Williams, T. Harry. *Lincoln and the Radicals* (1941).

STEVENSON, CARTER LITTLEPAGE
(1817–1888)
Confederate general

Born to Carter Littlepage Stevenson and Jane Herndon Stevenson at the family home outside Fredericksburg, Virginia, the younger Stevenson was educated locally before receiving an appointment to the U.S. Military Academy in 1834. He graduated forty-second of forty-five in the class of 1838 and was commissioned into the infantry. He fought in the Second Seminole War, after which he served on frontier posts in Wisconsin and Michigan. In 1846 he was sent to Texas, and during the next year served in northern Mexico during the Mexican-American War. After the war, he served at a variety of frontier posts, returned to Florida during the Third Seminole War, and participated in Albert Sidney Johnston's Utah expedition. While on duty in Utah, he learned of the secession of Virginia and in early June 1861 submitted his resignation from the army, requested and was granted a leave until the resignation was accepted in Washington, and returned to Virginia. His commander, however, neglected to forward the resignation, and when officials in Washington learned of Stevenson's return to Virginia and that he intended to enter Confederate service, he was dismissed from the U.S. Army.

In early July 1861, Stevenson received a lieutenant colonel's commission in the Confederate army and a few weeks later was promoted to colonel and given command of the 53d Virginia Infantry. He and his regiment were sent to the Department of Northwestern Virginia in the Shenandoah Valley. Stevenson's extensive military experience gained him the appointment as the department's adjutant, a position he held through the fall of 1861. In early 1862 he was promoted to brigadier general and was sent briefly to the Department of Norfolk with command of the garrison at Suffolk.

In March 1862 he was ordered to the Department of East Tennessee to serve under Major General E. Kirby Smith. In the spring of 1862 he commanded the Confederate occupation force at Cumberland Gap. After the Confederate evacuation of the gap in early summer, he commanded his division at Bean's Station, Tennessee, before joining the invasion of Kentucky. In September 1862 he was moved temporarily from Kirby Smith's command to that of Braxton Bragg. During the battle of Perryville, Stevenson protected Bragg's communication line to the north at Versailles and then led his men in Bragg's retreat south. Shortly after the campaign, Stevenson was promoted to major general with a date of rank of 10 October 1862.

Stevenson remained in Tennessee until December 1862, when he was transferred to Vicksburg, Mississippi, to serve in the defenses there. In March 1863 he commanded a division in the repulse of William T. Sherman's Steele's Bayou campaign and fought in the action at Champion's Hill on 16 May and the following day at the battle of Big Black River. He commanded John C. Pemberton's right in the subsequent siege. By the time of the surrender on 4 July, Stevenson's men were reduced to skeletons.

Stevenson was paroled soon after the surrender, but a controversy soon ensued between the Federal and Confederate officials about when he could return to duty. The Confederate exchange officials claimed that Stevenson had been exchanged soon after his parole and therefore could return to active duty. Federal prisoner exchange officers denied such an exchange had been made and that Stevenson should be treated as a paroled prisoner of war and hence was ineligible for active service in the Confederate army. Stevenson chose the Confederate interpretation and returned to active duty in September, although he performed desk duties as early as late July while stationed at Demopolis, Alabama.

When Stevenson returned to command of his division in the fall, he and his men served in Tennessee fighting a series of skirmishes around Philadelphia, Tennessee, in October before serving in William Hardee's corps in the Confederate attack on Chattanooga. In the middle of November he commanded a Confederate position on Lookout Mountain, and a little over a week later he participated in the defense of Missionary Ridge.

With the Confederate withdrawal from Tennessee, Stevenson commanded his division at Dalton, Georgia, in early 1864. During the early stages of the Atlanta campaign in late spring, Stevenson and his division were placed in John Bell Hood's corps. Stevenson fought in all the early engagements of that campaign and was commended for bravery for his actions at Resaca and Kennesaw Mountain. When Hood assumed command of the army defending Atlanta against William T. Sherman, Stevenson briefly commanded Hood's corps until Stephen Dill Lee was given permanent command. Stevenson served under Lee until the end of the year.

Stevenson, back in command of his division, fought in the remaining actions of the Atlanta campaign and then headed into Alabama and then Tennessee with Hood's army. He fought at Nashville in December. When Lee was wounded in that engagement, Stevenson assumed command of what was left of Lee's corps. Back in command of his division in early 1865, he took his men to Augusta, Georgia, in January and then the following month into South Carolina. Coming under command of Joseph E. Johnston in the Carolinas, Stevenson participated in the Carolina campaign against Sherman, fought at Bentonville, and surrendered with Johnston's army in April 1865.

After his parole, Stevenson returned to Virginia, where he worked as an engineer. He worked both in the mining industry and as a civil engineer until his death on 15 August 1888 in Caroline County, Virginia.

—*David S. Heidler and Jeanne T. Heidler*

See also Atlanta Campaign; Champion's Hill, Battle of; Nashville, Battle of; Vicksburg Campaign.

For further reading:

Bearss, Edwin C. *The Campaign for Vicksburg* (1985–1986).

Castel, Albert E. *Decision in the West: The Atlanta Campaign of 1864* (1992).

Cozzens, Peter. *The Shipwreck of Their Hopes: The Battles for Chattanooga* (1994).

STEWART, ALEXANDER PETER
(1821–1908)
Confederate general

Alexander P. Stewart became one of the highest-ranking Confederate generals in the Civil War. He was the ranking Tennesseean in the war, and at the time of his death in 1908 was the highest-ranking Confederate survivor. Stewart was known for his quiet temperament in political and personal affairs and for his very solid and dedicated performance in battle.

Stewart was born on 2 October 1821, in Rogersville, Tennessee. Spending his boyhood years in Winchester, Stewart attained a modest education that led to his

appointment to the U.S. Military Academy, where he graduated in 1842 as a second lieutenant. In that capacity, he served several years in the regular army before his resignation in 1845. In that year, Stewart entered education and taught at Cumberland University in Lebanon, Tennessee, and at Nashville University in Nashville.

Stewart vehemently opposed secession, but he remained loyal to his state when it seceded from the Union in June 1861. He quickly became a major in the Confederate army and served in various capacities, such as troop training and artillery defense. In this last capacity, he saw action at the battle of Belmont, across the Mississippi River from Columbus, Kentucky, in November 1861.

Stewart was then appointed brigadier general and took command of several regiments at New Madrid, Missouri. Withdrawing in the face of overwhelming enemy numbers, Stewart then worked to fortify Fort Pillow. Soon afterward, he transferred to Corinth, Mississippi, in the great Confederate concentration before Shiloh.

In the battle of Shiloh, 6–7 April 1862, Stewart received his first taste of actual combat. His efforts were dedicated, but the result was less than spectacular. He lost the majority of his brigade and fought with odd units for the remainder of the battle. Stewart performed with more skill in later battles at Perryville and Stones River. At Perryville, Kentucky, in October 1862, Stewart helped drive back the Union line, as he similarly did at Stones River, Tennessee, in December 1862. As a new brigade commander, Stewart drilled his men rigorously, which elicited grumbling. Stewart's performance in battle, as well as that of his trained men, soon silenced his detractors, however.

Because of his dedicated and solid service, Stewart was promoted to major general in the summer of 1863. He took command of a division and, after initial confusion in the Tullahoma campaign of June 1863, led it with great skill at Chickamauga in September 1863, where he split the Union line on the first day. At Chattanooga in November, Stewart held a line equal in length to that held by some six divisions on the opposing side. Federals under Ulysses S. Grant relentlessly attacked the Confederate army on top of Missionary Ridge, and Stewart's thin line, at some places with soldiers only feet apart, retreated in rout. Stewart then competently led his division throughout the first portions of the Atlanta campaign.

With the death of Lieutenant General Leonidas Polk in June 1864, Stewart took command of the Army of Tennessee's third corps. He fought well in the battles around Atlanta, but he ultimately failed to retain possession of the city. With the flurry of command changes after the Atlanta campaign, Stewart became the ranking corps commander on John Bell Hood's ill-fated Tennessee campaign. Stewart later led his corps to North Carolina and fought with Joseph E. Johnston at Bentonville in March 1865, even commanding the remnants of the Army of Tennessee.

After the war, Stewart returned to his first vocation, education. After serving as president of a St. Louis insurance company, Stewart became chancellor of the University of Mississippi. He held that position longer than any other former leader in that institution's history, but he resigned after clashing with the board of trustees over ideology.

After several years of travel, Stewart became the Southern member of the commission that established the Chickamauga-Chattanooga National Military Park. Stewart served as head of construction and was resident commissioner for several years. However, his health soon failed, and he was forced to turn over most of his duties to others. Stewart died in Biloxi, Mississippi, on 21 October 1908. He was buried beside his wife of over fifty years in Bellefontaine Cemetery in St. Louis.

Alexander P. Stewart was one of the few competent high-ranking Confederate officers in the Army of Tennessee. Making his contribution greater, Stewart refrained from the politics within the army, most often remaining neutral in the famous controversies revolving around Braxton Bragg. Stewart's life as a whole displayed just such commitment and restraint.

—*Timothy B. Smith*

See also Chattanooga Campaign; Chickamauga, Battle of; Perryville, Battle of; Shiloh, Battle of; Stones River, Battle of; Tullahoma Campaign.
For further reading:
Elliott, Sam Davis. *Soldier Of Tennessee and the Civil War in the West* (1999).

STOECKL, EDOUARD DE
(1808–?)
Russian minister to the United States

Born in Russia to a middle-class family, Stoeckl adopted the title "baron" once he arrived in the United States, though he was never a member of the Russian nobility. As a young man, he became a minor functionary in Russia's diplomatic service and first came to the United States in 1841 as a secretary to the Russian legation. Over the next decade he rose in influence in the United States Russian ministry and in 1854 was appointed the Russian chargé d'affaires in Washington. In that position during the latter phases of the Crimean War, Stoeckl tried to keep the rivalry between the United States and Great Britain alive so that he could persuade the United States openly to side with Russia. While he was unable to sway the United States to take that step, unofficially the United States remained on friendly terms with Russia during that conflict.

Shortly after the war in 1857, Stoeckl was promoted

to Russian minister plenipotentiary to the United States. Stoeckl was more than willing to extend his term of residence in the United States, having married an American the year before.

In his capacity as Russian minister to the United States, Stoeckl reported directly to Czar Alexander II's foreign minister, Prince Gorchakov. During the years before the outbreak of the Civil War, Stoeckl wrote long, detailed letters regarding the sectional conflict and his belief that the conflict would eventually result in disunion. Besides the apparently unsolvable issue of slavery, Stoeckl, a strong opponent of democratic government, believed that the American form of government was responsible for most of the country's problems. During the early phases of the 1860 presidential campaign, Stoeckl believed that William Henry Seward's winning the Republican nomination would best promote sectional harmony. Stoeckl had gained a great admiration for Seward during the New Yorker's service in the Senate. When Abraham Lincoln received the nomination, the minister predicted that Lincoln's election would mean the end of the Union.

During the secession winter of 1860–1861, Stoeckl sent Prince Gorchakov detailed reports on each of the Southern states' secession conventions and expressed his believe that the breakup of the Union was irreparable. Following Lincoln's inauguration, Stoeckl's opinion only intensified as the minister formed a low opinion of the new president's abilities. On the other hand, Stoeckl regarded Jefferson Davis highly. He had known Davis when the latter was serving in the United States Senate.

Shortly after the new administration took office in Washington, Stoeckl approached Seward with an offer to mediate the conflict. He suggested that he act as an intermediary between the Confederate commissioners sent by Jefferson Davis and the Lincoln administration. Seward's rebuff to this suggestion temporarily dimmed Stoeckl's admiration for the secretary of state.

From then on Stoeckl conferred frequently with the French minister, Henri Mercier, and the British minister, Lord Lyon, though he did not tie himself to their official stances on the war. Early in the war Stoeckl believed it only a matter of time before the shortage of cotton would require British recognition of the Confederacy and that the French would probably follow the British lead. He held that such an event would prove the deciding blow in the destruction of the Union.

Even though Stoeckl persisted in his doubt that the United States could restore the Union, he was obliged by his government instructions, as well as his own ties to the United States, to refrain from expressing any open support for the Confederacy. Consequently, he and his country were viewed as the United States' staunchest friends among the major powers. Yet similar to France and Great Britain, in the summer of 1862 he saw Lincoln's situation as virtually hopeless. Even after the Union victory at Antietam and Lincoln's announcement of the preliminary Emancipation Proclamation, he viewed the president's actions as desperate. He wrote to Prince Gorchakov that Lincoln had issued the Emancipation Proclamation to provoke a massive slave uprising in the South. Even after the war, when emancipation was an accomplished fact, Stoeckl pointed to the passage in the South of the various Black Codes as a clear indication that freeing the slaves had been an impulsive act bereft of effective protections for its supposed beneficiaries.

During the summer of 1863, Stoeckl reconciled with Seward when the secretary of state took the diplomatic corps on a tour of New York to escape Washington's frightful heat. During the trip, word reached the travelers of the impending arrival of the Russian Atlantic fleet in New York City and the Russian Pacific fleet in San Francisco. The czar's sending of these fleets to the United States was seen by the world as a goodwill gesture that established Russian support for the United States during this crisis. Others have argued that the czar was more interested in demonstrating to the British and the French that he would tolerate no interference with Russian trade. Whatever his motives, the czar's gesture was looked on favorably by the United States government. Stoeckl's standing with the Lincoln administration was correspondingly enhanced.

Until the end of the war, Stoeckl continued to send detailed reports to Prince Gorchakov about the military and political events of the day. No one could have been more surprised at the ultimate outcome. Stoeckl, trying to explain how his predictions of Union defeat had been so wrong, held that the triumph of the United States was due to the perseverance of the American people, for whom he had developed great admiration over the previous two decades.

After the war, Stoeckl remained in the United States as Russian minister and continued his good rapport with Secretary of State Seward. In the fall of 1866 he paid a visit home to confer with Prince Gorchakov about the possibility of selling Alaska to the United States. Stoeckl returned to the United States to begin negotiations on a treaty that was completed in 1867. It was later alleged that Stoeckl resorted to bribery to achieve the votes in the House of Representatives necessary for the funding of the Alaska purchase. Whatever the case, an embittered Stoeckl asked to be relieved as minister in 1868, apparently disgusted with the democratic political process in the United States and clearly disillusioned over what he gauged as the czar's paltry reward for his services in securing the Alaska treaty. His request was granted and he returned home permanently after twenty-seven years of service in the United States.

—*David S. Heidler and Jeanne T. Heidler*

See also Diplomacy, U.S.A.; Russian-American Relations.
For further reading:
Woldman, Albert A. *Lincoln and the Russians* (1952).

STONE, CHARLES POMEROY
(1824–1887)
Union general

Charles Pomeroy Stone was born on 30 September 1824 in Greenfield, Massachusetts. The son of Dr. Alpheus Fletcher Stone and Fanny Cushing Stone, he attended the U.S. Military Academy, graduating in 1845. He then served with the U.S. Army in the Mexican-American War, where he accompanied the siege train of General Winfield Scott. Advancing to the rank of first lieutenant, Stone was eventually stationed on the West Coast as chief of ordnance. His duties took him to California, Oregon, and Washington territory. In 1856, Stone left the army and accepted a position supervising the exploration of the Mexican province of Sonora. As a result of this work, Stone published *Notes on the State of Sonora* in 1861.

Stone returned to Washington, D.C., in 1861. At the request of General-in-Chief Winfield Scott, Stone was appointed colonel and inspector general of the District of Columbia. It was Stone's job to make sure the local militia was loyal so that President-elect Abraham Lincoln's inauguration was not disrupted. After the firing on Fort Sumter, Stone was promoted to the rank of brigadier general (U.S. Volunteers) and moved on to the Department of Pennsylvania and then the Department of the Shenandoah; in the fall of 1861, he commanded a division in the Army of the Potomac under George B. McClellan.

The pivotal event of Stone's life occurred on 21 October 1861 when Union forces under his command suffered a disastrous, humiliating defeat by Confederate forces at Ball's Bluff, near Leesburg, Virginia. The troops directly involved in battle were led by Edward D. Baker, a Republican senator from Oregon and a personal friend of President Lincoln. Stone had been ordered by McClellan to make a demonstration against Leesburg on the Maryland side of the Potomac River. Stone had not ordered Baker to cross the river, but to use his own judgment. Baker, inexperienced and reckless, crossed the river and deployed his troops in an amateurish military formation near the top of the Ball's Bluff. When Union forces were attacked by superior forces and tried to retreat across the Potomac, Baker's failure to provide adequate transportation resulted in a humiliating slaughter. Since Baker was an extremely popular figure, the public believed that he had been needlessly sacrificed. Stone proved to be a convenient scapegoat. Numerous papers demanded that he be removed from command, charging that Stone had deliberately sacrificed Baker's command. With the appointment of the Joint Committee on the Conduct of the War in December 1861, the Ball's Bluff disaster came under close scrutiny.

In January 1862, Stone appeared before the Committee on the Conduct of the War, where he was forced to answer all sorts of charges that touched on his loyalty to the Union. Had he engaged in irregular correspondence with Rebel officers on the other side of the Potomac? Had he allowed Confederate civilians to cross and recross the Potomac unimpeded? Despite Stone's persistent denials that he had done anything wrong, he was eventually arrested. Secretary of War Edwin Stanton had ordered the arrest in late January, and on 8 February 1862, Major General George McClellan had Stone arrested and incarcerated at Fort Lafayette. He was later transferred to Fort Hamilton. Stone was given no information as to the reason for his arrest. Despite the efforts of his attorneys and Democratic senator James McDougall, no charges were ever preferred against him. Nevertheless, Stone was imprisoned for 189 days and was released only after he made a personal appeal to the president in July 1862. His confinement was one of the most egregious examples of arbitrary authority in the entire American Civil War.

Once released from imprisonment, Stone returned to active duty, serving as chief of staff to Nathaniel Banks in the Department of the Gulf from May 1863. In April 1864, without any apparent reason, Stone was removed from this position and his volunteer's commission was taken away. While he used his regular army commission briefly to command a brigade with the Army of the Potomac during the siege of Petersburg, Stone eventually resigned from the army in September 1864. Undoubtedly, Stone's principal reason for resignation was the constant distrust and suspicion that seemed to surround him. Stone lived the rest of his life without finding out why he had been imprisoned or who ultimately was responsible for his long imprisonment.

After Stone left the army, he had a varied and successful career. After working as a mining engineer and superintendent for the Dover Mining Company in Virginia, in 1870 Stone left for Egypt, where he served the Khedive as chief of staff and then a lieutenant-general in the Egyptian army. Stone remained in Egypt until 1883, when he returned to the United States, where he worked as an engineer for the Florida Ship Canal Company and later supervised the construction of the foundation for the Statue of Liberty. Stone died in New York City on 24 January 1887. Stone was married twice. His first wife was Maria Louisa Clary and his second, Annie Jeannie Stone.

—Bruce Tap

See also Baker, Edward Dickinson; Ball's Bluff, Battle of; Joint Committee on the Conduct of the War.

For further reading:
Blaine, James Gillespie. *Twenty Years of Congress* (1884–1886).
Hesseltine, William B., and Hazel C. Wolf. *The Blue and Gray on the Nile* (1961).
Tap, Bruce. *Over Lincoln's Shoulder: The Committee on the Conduct of the War* (1998).

STONE, SARAH KATHERINE, "KATE"
(1841–1907)
Southern diarist

Kate Stone had just turned twenty years old when the Civil War broke out and prompted her to start keeping a diary. Her journal, which contains regular entries from May 1861 to November 1865 and summary entries for 1867 and 1868, is one of the finest examples of the genre. Stone's diary both tells the story of one young woman's experiences during the Civil War and chronicles her coming of age, as she moves from innocence to understanding. In *Patriotic Gore*, his classic study of the literature of the Civil War, Edmund Wilson called Stone "the typical Dixie heroine, as approved by the Southern tradition" and ranked *Brokenburn*, the published version of her journal, alongside two classics: Mary Boykin Chesnut's *Diary From Dixie* and Sarah Morgan Dawson's *Confederate Girl's Diary*.

Sarah Katherine Stone was born in Hinds County, Mississippi, on 8 January 1841 to William Patrick and Amanda Susan Ragan Stone. In 1861 Kate was living with her thirty-seven-year-old widowed mother, her older brother, four younger brothers, and a younger sister at Brokenburn Plantation, located in what is now Madison Parish, Louisiana, some thirty miles northwest of Vicksburg. Kate Stone was a daughter of great privilege, as her mother was managing an estate of 1,260 acres and owned approximately 150 slaves. An avid reader and student of French and Spanish, Kate described herself as "tall, not quite five foot six, and thin" with "an irregular face, a quantity of brown hair, a shy, quiet manner and talk but little."

Like many women of her age and class, Stone was prompted by the tumultuous events of 1861 to keep a journal, and into its pages she poured not only war news and her daily routine, but vibrant social commentary and vivid expressions of her own emotions and patriotism. Stone was initially seduced by the romantic flurry of excitement surrounding the outbreak of the war, and she lamented being left behind when her brothers went off to fight. Stone believed wholeheartedly in Confederate calls for independence, and discussions of the political and military situation are intermingled with reports of books read, games played, and sewing done. As the harsher realities of war intruded on Kate's life, she remained deeply committed to the Confederacy and grew frustrated with those around her whose own enthusiasm flagged.

At Brokenburn, Stone and her family were relatively insulated during the first months of the war, with complaints largely limited to shortages of food, clothing, and reading materials. This quiet was shattered in early 1862 when Union gunboats appeared on the Mississippi River, leading to the capture of New Orleans, Baton Rouge, and Natchez. Until early 1863 Stone had been spared any direct contact with Federal troops, but that winter Union forces under the commands of both Ulysses S. Grant and William Tecumseh Sherman appeared in the neighborhood. Their advance and foraging parties struck fear into the Stones, prompting Kate to comment anxiously in March that "the country seems possessed by demons, black and white." It was the former that would eventually prompt the Stones to abandon their plantation and head to Texas.

While frightened by the prospects of a slave uprising, Stone had few delusions about the tensions inherent in a slave society. She was annoyed when slaves ran away, resentful of what she perceived to be an increased burden on her, but she both understood and acknowledged the powerful pull that freedom and Union lines had on slaves. Unlike many of her class, she appeared not to believe that slaves were content with their lot, but rather remarked that "when told to run away from the soldiers, they go right to them and I cannot say I blame them."

In late March 1863, a few days after Federal soldiers arrived at Brokenburn and seized Kate's favorite horse, Kate and her sister, along with several neighboring women, were held at gunpoint while slaves ransacked a neighbor's home. That was the last straw for Stone's mother, who had already begun making arrangements for the family to head west. They left Brokenburn that night with little more than the clothes on their backs, and over the course of several weeks made their way first to Monroe, Louisiana, and then to Lamar County, Texas, where they were met by their overseer and 130 of their slaves. Stone disliked Lamar County intensely, finding the people coarse and the surroundings dismal, a contempt mirrored by the Texans' animosity towards the newcomers. Her situation and circumstances improved when the Stones moved to Tyler, Texas, at the end of 1863; they would remain there until the end of the war. Stone would look back on her time in Tyler, which was marked by considerable socializing and gaiety even as her beloved Confederacy was collapsing, as among the most pleasant of her life.

The end of the war, and with it the end of the Confederacy, thrust Stone into depression, briefly lifted by the assassination of Abraham Lincoln. Within a few months, however, her spirits had returned, and in the fall of 1865 she and the family, accompanied by a number of their former slaves, returned to Brokenburn and set about the task of rebuilding. The Stones struggled with crop failures, flooding, and a rocky adjustment to free labor over the next few years, but Stone ended her

journal in 1868 on an optimistic note. The following year she married Henry Bry Holmes, a young lieutenant she had met in Tyler, and subsequently had four children (only two of whom survived past childhood). Her love of the Confederacy was channeled in later life into Lost Cause activism, as she both founded a chapter of the United Daughters of the Confederacy and worked to erect a Confederate memorial in the town of Tallulah, Louisiana. She died in Tallulah on 28 December 1907.

—*Anne Sarah Rubin*

See also Chesnut, Mary Boykin.

For further reading:

Anderson, John Q., ed. *Brokenburn: The Journal of Kate Stone, 1861–1868* (1995).

Wilson, Edmund. *Patriotic Gore: Studies in the Literature of the American Civil War* (1962).

STONE, WILLIAM MILO
(1827–1893)
Union officer, governor of Iowa

Stone was born of old Yankee stock on a farm in Jefferson County, New York, on 14 October 1827. At age six he accompanied his parents to Coshocton County, Ohio. After two winter terms at a country school, he became a wage-earner at age thirteen, first as a hired farmhand, then as a team driver on the Ohio Canal, then as an apprenticed chairmaker, a calling that employed him until his mid-twenties. Meanwhile, a local ex-congressman, James Matthews, had encouraged Stone to read for the law in his spare time. In 1851 Stone was admitted to the bar, and for three years practiced with Matthews, later marrying Matthews's daughter Caroline.

In 1854 Stone removed to the frontier, settling at Knoxville, Iowa, where, eschewing the law for political journalism, he purchased a newspaper. This he edited as a nativist, anti-Catholic journal associated with the short-lived Know-Nothing Party in Iowa, until that movement's ultraconservative stance on slavery caused Stone—like thousands of others—to abandon it and urge formation of a Republican Party to oppose the westward spread of slavery. Stone claimed to be Iowa's first editor to suggest a state convention for that purpose.

At the historic gathering in February 1856, the delegates named Stone as one of the new party's four presidential electors. During the ensuing campaign he earned a reputation as an extemporaneous public speaker of rare vernacular eloquence. "On the hustings," testified a fellow lawyer, "he was one of the most effective political orators that the State [of Iowa] has ever seen." A handsome, slender man, Stone stood six feet tall, with intense grey eyes and copious dark hair and beard. He was down-to-earth and full of nervous energy, and he loved a good debate.

In 1857, Stone successfully ran for the office of district judge and was literally on the bench when word arrived of the Fort Sumter surrender. He immediately adjourned court, resigned his office, and raised a company of the 3d Iowa Infantry. After he was promoted to major, his and the regiment's baptism of fire came in September 1861 at Blue Mills, Missouri, where he suffered a bloody scalp wound. He was regimental commander in April 1862 on the first day of the great battle of Shiloh, where his wounded horse pinned him to the ground, allowing his capture. A few months later, Stone's fellow prisoners of war (POWs) elected him to a three-officer panel formed by the Confederates to negotiate a prisoner exchange. Stone twice shuttled between Richmond and Washington, and conferred with President Lincoln. Although the exchange was delayed until autumn 1862, Stone arranged a personal release that had him home by late summer.

His fame as a celebrity POW led to promotion. In August 1862 he accepted the colonelcy of the new 22d Iowa Infantry. In 1863, the regiment participated, as part of John A. McClernand's corps, in Ulysses S. Grant's Vicksburg campaign. At Port Gibson, Stone aggressively, if briefly, commanded a brigade. In the grand frontal assault on Vicksburg of 22 May—in which a dozen of Stone's men were the only Union soldiers to enter the Confederate earthworks—a bullet tore through his left forearm.

Sent home to recuperate, his arm in a sling, Stone attended Iowa's Republican nominating convention in June. Treated as a hero, Stone captivated the delegates with a rousing speech. The convention being deadlocked between two gubernatorial hopefuls, Stone's friends successfully touted him as a compromise candidate. In August he resigned his commission and undertook a vigorous campaign, defeating another popular army officer (a Democrat) in a landslide. He assumed office in January 1864 and was retroactively breveted a brigadier general for gallantry.

Stone's administration continued its predecessor's strong commitment to the Union. Militarily, the only threat to the state took the form of guerrilla incursions from Missouri, including one twelve-hour foray that involved the assassination of three Iowans. Stone redoubled efforts to maintain an effective civil defense border brigade and encouraged the organization of militias in every county. Some of these units became vehicles for draft resistance, which in one instance claimed the lives of two deputy U.S. marshals. Stone himself believed exaggerated reports that 33,000 secret Copperheads were active within the state. Eventually, his hard-line policy toward dissent, suspected subversion, and draft evasion alienated large numbers of even normally Republican voters.

But the divided Democrats, split by war and peace

factions, posed little political threat—until Appomattox. Nominated for reelection in June 1865, Stone found himself handicapped by his party's having endorsed voting rights for African-American Iowans. Rather than evading the proposition, however, he embraced it and explained in some detail his intellectual journey from racial conservative to progressive. Straightforwardly defying the openly racist, ostensibly nonpartisan "Union Anti-Negro Suffrage Party," he gained reelection with a margin only slightly diminished from 1863. His politically heroic defense of African-American equality paved the way for Iowa's uniquely successful black-suffrage referendum of 1868—the nation's only referendum victory for civil rights in which voters knew unequivocally what they were voting for and against.

Leaving office at age forty, Stone seemed destined for higher things. He sought the nomination for Congress from his district and even aspired to the Senate, but he was a would-be career politician without honor in his own country. To the jealous, he had come too far too quickly. Local immigrants from Holland remembered his Know-Nothing past. And Stone evidently paid a price for his racial progressivism in his southern Iowa district: voter majorities in half its eight counties—including his home county—had voted Republican in 1868 but rejected black suffrage. The best Stone could do among these conservative Republicans was a term in the Iowa legislature.

Stone moved to Colorado, where he practiced law and pursued unsuccessful mining enterprises before returning to Iowa. In 1889, on the advent of Benjamin Harrison's presidential administration, he was appointed assistant commissioner of the General Land Office, eventually becoming commissioner. But that job ended with Harrison's defeat in 1892.

In poor health, Stone retired to a farm in Oklahoma. He died in Oklahoma City on 18 July 1893.

—*Robert R. Dykstra and Jo Ann Manfra*

For further reading:
Dykstra, Robert. *Bright Radical Star: Black Freedom and White Supremacy on the Hawkeye Frontier* (1993).
Lathrop, Henry W. "The Late Governor Wm. M. Stone." *Iowa Historical Record* (1894).
Stiles, Edward H. "William M. Stone." In *Recollections and Sketches of Notable Lawyers and Public Men of Early Iowa* (1916).
Stuart, A. A. "William Milo Stone: Governor of Iowa." In *Iowa Colonels and Regiments* (1865).
Wubben, Hubert H. *Civil War Iowa and the Copperhead Movement* (1980).

STONEMAN'S RAID
(29 April–8 May 1863)

In February 1863, Army of the Potomac commander Joseph Hooker consolidated his dispersed cavalry forces into a united corps numbering 11,402 men commanded by Major General George Stoneman.

Hooker planned an important role for his cavalry in the upcoming spring campaign against Robert E. Lee by launching it on a massive raid behind rebel lines to disrupt communications and destroy the Army of Northern Virginia's vital railroad connections.

Stoneman left Falmouth, Virginia, on 13 April with 7,400 men in six brigades including four horse batteries, leaving only one brigade under Alfred Pleasonton with the main army. Severe rainstorms flooded the Rappahannock River and its tributaries, which prevented the cavalry from crossing immediately according to Hooker's intended timetable. For two weeks Stoneman delayed, finally getting his troopers across the stream on 29 April, the same day that Union infantry advanced.

The cavalry marched divided in two roughly equal columns. William W. Averell and some 3,500 troopers rode toward Gordonsville to decoy the Rebel cavalry. The other column, composed of David McMurtrie Gregg's division and John Buford's reserve brigade and horse artillery, marched to break the Virginia Central Railroad at Louisa Court House, then cut the Richmond & Fredericksburg's tracks at Hanover Junction. Averell's forces encountered and pushed W. H. F. Lee's Rebel brigade over the Rapidan River, but then vacillated and advanced no farther. Having lost contact with Stoneman's main column, Averell timidly idled near Rapidan Station until ordered on 2 May to rejoin Hooker's army engaged near Chancellorsville.

As Stoneman advanced into the Virginia countryside, he periodically divided his forces, intending each to inflict extensive damage on a wide front. One detachment, led by Colonel Percy Wyndham, attacked Columbia and destroyed a portion of the James River Canal. Another, under 12th Illinois Lieutenant Colonel Hasbrouck Davis, ripped up portions of the Virginia Central Railroad near Atlee's Station and Ashland, while a third segment, commanded by Colonel Judson Kilpatrick, advanced to Hungary Station outside Richmond, tore up rail lines and alarmed the Confederate capital. Kilpatrick next crossed the Chickahominy River and reached Federal lines at Gloucester on 7 May, joined shortly after by Hasbrouck Davis's detachment. Stoneman meanwhile reassembled his remaining forces on 5 May and withdrew toward Union lines along a route similar to that of his advance. His command, slowed by exhaustion and rain, safely recrossed the Rappahannock on 8 May.

The raid did not live up to its expected outcome. Except for assigning small forces to observe Federal movements, Stuart virtually ignored Stoneman's presence from the outset and joined Lee's army facing Hooker with the bulk of his cavalry. While Stoneman claimed to have inflicted considerable damage on the enemy at the cost of only 6 killed and an aggregate 189 total casualties, the

defeat of the Army of the Potomac at Chancellorsville nullified any of the raid's positive effects.

Hooker charged both Stoneman and Averell with lackluster performance and relieved them of their commands as partial scapegoats for the Chancellorsville defeat. While some Union cavalry troopers believed Stoneman's raid was a failure, others argued it was an important effort that illustrated the Union cavalry's rising offensive spirit destined to affect the course of the war.

—*David J. Gerleman*

See also Chancellorsville, Battle of; Stoneman, George.

For further reading:

Davis, George B. "The Stoneman Raid." *Journal of the United States Cavalry Association* (1914).

Greene, A. Wilson. "Stoneman's Raid." In *Chancellorsville: The Battle and its Aftermath*. Edited by Gary W. Gallagher (1996).

Longacre, Edward G. *Mounted Raids of the Civil War* (1975; reprint, 1994).

Sears, Stephen W. *Chancellorsville* (1996).

Starr, Stephen Z. *The Union Cavalry in the Civil War* (1979–1985).

STONEMAN'S RAID
(26 July–31 July 1864)

For Major General George Stoneman, the Atlanta campaign represented an opportunity to redeem what many perceived—in large part unjustly—to be his failure during Joseph Hooker's ill-fated encounter with Robert E. Lee at Chancellorsville in May 1863 that cost him the command of the cavalry corps of the Army of the Potomac. At the head of one of Sherman's four cavalry divisions, from the outset of the Atlanta campaign Stoneman constantly sought to deliver a brilliant stroke that would restore his reputation. Yet in spite of his best efforts, he met with equally constant frustration, and by late July it seemed as if he would never achieve the great success that he craved.

But then Sherman, whose army by now was pounding at Atlanta's formidable fortifications, decided to employ his mounted forces to cut the Macon Railroad, the sole remaining supply line of General John B. Hood's army defending the city. His plan, embodied in orders issued on 25 July, called for Stoneman's division, after feinting an eastward thrust toward Augusta, Georgia, to swing to the southwest and link up with Brigadier General Edward McCook's division in the vicinity of Lovejoy's Station, there to destroy two to five miles of track before returning to Union lines.

After receiving this order, Stoneman on 26 July wrote Sherman requesting permission to continue southward after wrecking the railroad at Lovejoy's Station, for the purpose of liberating Union officer prisoners at Macon and enlisted men held at Andersonville. On the same date Sherman granted his request. So, at least, states the official record. There are strong reasons, though, to believe that Stoneman informally asked Sherman to allow him to head straight for Macon and Andersonville without meeting McCook at Lovejoy's Station and that Sherman informally, perhaps verbally, authorized him to do this. If Stoneman succeeded, it would be the most sensational feat of the war, and make both him and Sherman heroes in the North. Should he, on the other hand, fail, then Sherman's formal orders and official correspondence would protect him from blame, while placing it solely on Stoneman.

On 27 July Stoneman, with 2,000 horsemen and two cannons, marched northeast to Covington, accompanied by Brigadier General Kenner Garrard's mounted division. According to his ostensible orders, he then was to proceed southwest to McDonough and from there to Lovejoy's Station. Instead, on 28 July he headed due south, leaving behind Garrard's division at Flat Rock, where it was to decoy the Confederates into concentrating against it and thus prevent them from pursuing Stoneman. This stratagem served its purpose, as it caused the Confederate cavalry commander, Major General Joseph Wheeler, first to go to Flat Rock, where he nearly captured Garrard's entire force, and then to send three brigades under Brigadier General Alfred Iverson to McDonough in the belief that Stoneman was heading there, while he with the rest of his force set forth to deal with McCook.

Believing correctly that he was not being pursued, Stoneman halted for the night at Monticello, then on 29 July continued toward Macon, his troopers often tarrying along the way to fill their saddlebags with plunder and themselves with whiskey. They did rip up some portions of the Macon Railroad, but the Confederates quickly repaired the damage, as they did that inflicted by McCook's men around Lovejoy's Station. Not until the afternoon of 30 July did Stoneman and his men approach Macon. Though in sight of the town, they found themselves faced by two obstacles: the Ocmulgee River, which could be crossed on a railroad bridge and a pontoon bridge, and 2,500 Rebel defenders. Although the latter consisted mostly of underage and overage home guards and some convalescent Confederate soldiers, they were posted behind barricades covering the bridges and supported by artillery.

Stoneman's two cannons bombarded a stockade that anchored the enemy line, then he ordered Colonel Silas Adams's Kentucky brigade to charge it on foot and take it. They advanced, but as soon as they came under fire they fell back. Not only did they detest Stoneman (his West Point notions of discipline offended them), but their enlistments were about to expire and they were more interested in preserving their lives than in fighting. Disgusted, Stoneman abandoned all notion of liberating the prisoners at Macon and Andersonville and ordered his reluctant warriors to head south for Union-held Pensacola.

Hardly had they started when a scout brought word—erroneous, as it later turned out—that a large Confederate cavalry column had entered Macon. Stoneman, fearing interception by this force, thereupon reversed course and marched northward along the same route by which he had come. At nightfall he reached Clinton, where a road branched off that led to Union lines. Initially, he had planned to take this road, but now he changed his mind and, over the protest of his brigade commanders, continued north toward Hillsboro where, so he declared, there would be a choice of three roads by which, come daylight, they could return to Sherman's army.

This proved to be Stoneman's final and fatal blunder. Two miles from Hillsboro he began encountering such stiff enemy resistance that he halted for the night. In the morning (31 July) he resumed his march, only to come upon a sizeable Confederate force posted near Sunshine Church, behind a log barricade in the shape of an inverted "V." It consisted of Iverson's three brigades, who, on discovering Stoneman's true destination, had set out in his wake. Stoneman promptly ordered a breakthrough attack. It failed, and for the rest of the morning and on into the afternoon both sides engaged in futile charges and countercharges. Finally the Kentuckians and a large number of other Union troopers managed to escape through a weak spot in Iverson's line, but Stoneman and about 700 of his men continued to hold out atop a hill until his cannons fired their last shells, whereupon he surrendered. He then sat down on a log and buried his tear-streaked face in his hands. Rather than glory, he had gained only grief.

Stoneman's—and Sherman's—attempt to free the prisoners at Macon and Andersonville probably would have failed even had Stoneman succeeded in seizing those places. The Confederates were very much on the alert for such an attempt. Thus, before Stoneman reached Macon, they had sent away nearly all of the officers being held there. At Andersonville the guards had posted cannons in position to sweep the prison stockade with canister, which would have mowed down hundreds—if not thousands—of the inmates. And, as Sherman himself later admitted, it would have been impossible for most of the prisoners at Andersonville, half-starved and weakened by disease, to have made it alive to Union lines if they had been freed. As McCook's division also was smashed, all that the raids by him and Stoneman accomplished was the greatest cavalry fiasco of the Civil War.

—*Albert Castel*

See also Iverson, Alfred; McCook, Edward; Stoneman, George.

For further reading:

Castel, Albert E. *Decision in the West: The Atlanta Campaign of 1864* (1992).
Evans, David. *Sherman's Horsemen: Union Cavalry Operations in the Atlanta Campaign* (1996).
Matthews, Byron H., Sr. *The McCook-Stoneman Raid* (1976).
Simpson, Brooks D., and Jean V. Berlin, eds. *Sherman's Civil War: Selected Correspondence of William T. Sherman, 1860–1865* (1999).

STONEMAN'S RAID
(December 1864–January 1865)

During the middle of November 1864, General George Stoneman, recently exchanged as a prisoner of war, assumed command of Union cavalry in east Tennessee. In an attempt to redeem himself after the humiliation of his Georgia raid, Stoneman quickly began planning a cavalry raid through east Tennessee and southwest Virginia to restore order, while depleting the Confederacy of much needed resources. Stoneman's prize objective was the salt works in Saltville, Virginia, a major source of salt for military and civilian needs throughout the South. Stoneman also planned to continue farther north to destroy the mines near Wytheville, Virginia. These mines provided roughly one-quarter of the lead used by the Confederate army, as well as serving as a major supplier of zinc. Along with wreaking havoc in the mines, Stoneman sought to disrupt the railroad, to shut down Rebel printing presses, and, hopefully, to drive the Confederate troops into North Carolina. At the end of November, General John M. Schofield approved only the portion of Stoneman's plan that involved moving into southwestern Virginia and destroying the salt works.

Stoneman quickly massed a force of 5,500 men. On 10 December, he left Knoxville with 1,500 Tennessee troops under command of General Alvan Gillem. Two days later, 4,500 Kentucky troops under command of General Richard Burbridge linked up with his command at Bean's Station, Tennessee. Stoneman faced an estimated 1,200 Confederate troops, under the command of General John C. Breckinridge, with the majority of these troops stationed near Saltville.

On 13 December, Stoneman easily routed an understrength Confederate cavalry brigade near Kingsport, Tennessee. The next day he marched twenty miles to the east to Bristol, where he dispersed a Confederate cavalry force under General John C. Vaughn. While in Bristol, Stoneman captured sixty civilian prisoners, a trainload of Confederate reinforcements destined for Vaughn, and five trains full of supplies. On 15 December, the Federal troopers crossed into Virginia and moved fifteen miles to the north of Bristol to Abingdon. While in Abingdon, they set fire to a number of buildings, including the courthouse. General Vaughn had anticipated rejoining Breckinridge, but with the Federals in control of Abingdon, he continued north, awaiting an opportunity to flank Stoneman's troops.

As Stoneman moved closer to Saltville, he had to

make a decision: should he move on the salt works first, or bypass them and attempt to capture Vaughn, destroy the railroad and the lead works at Wytheville, and then return to take the salt works at his leisure. Stoneman chose the latter course, ordering Gillem's men to Marion, where they encountered Vaughn. During the brief engagement that followed, Gillem forced Vaughn to retreat, capturing the Confederates' wagons, 200 prisoners, and eight pieces of artillery. Gillem continued north, taking Wytheville with little resistance and destroying the nearby lead mines before returning to Stoneman.

Realizing Stoneman's intentions, General Breckinridge left a detachment of about 400 home guards and reserves to guard the salt works, as he moved east to encounter Stoneman. On the night of 18 December, Breckinridge's forces met Stoneman at Marion. During the brief engagement, Stoneman's forces flanked Breckinridge, placing themselves between him and the salt works. After the battle, the remnants of Breckinridge's force headed east toward the mountains of North Carolina. Three months earlier, General Burbridge had been repulsed in his attempt to take the salt works; this time, with the resistance removed, Stoneman easily captured the salt works on 20 December. He spent the next two days burning all the buildings and destroying all the equipment associated with the salt works.

On 22 December, Stoneman left Saltville to return to Knoxville. In the previous twelve days he had traveled 461 miles over rough terrain and through poor weather, while capturing almost 900 prisoners and 19 cannons. In addition, Stoneman's raid successfully laid waste to the valuable mineral resources of southwest Virginia—the lead and salt mines. The loss of salt production not only hurt the Confederate military effort but also the civilian populace. The lead mines at Wytheville were out of production for more than three months. Thus, at little loss to himself, Stoneman's raid achieved much success, crippling the Confederacy while redeeming his reputation.

—*William T. Hartley*

See also Saltville, Battle of; Stoneman, George; Stoneman's Raid (July 1864).

For further reading:
Donelly, Ralph W. "The Confederate Lead Mines of Wythe County, Va." *Civil War History* (1959).
Ramsey, Thomas R., Jr. *The Raid* (1973).
U.S. War Department. *War of the Rebellion: A Compilation of the Official Records of the Union and Confederate Armies* (1880–1901).

STONEMAN'S RAID
(March–April 1865)

In February 1865, following the success of his raid through east Tennessee and southwest Virginia, Union general George Stoneman was promoted to commander of the District of East Tennessee. Stoneman immediately began planning for a second raid to continue where the first left off. Stoneman hoped to penetrate into the Carolinas, destroying the railroads and military resources of the Confederacy, while freeing Federal prisoners of war held at Salisbury, North Carolina. By mid-March, the rapid advance of General William T. Sherman through the Carolinas and the deteriorating Confederate situation around Richmond forced Stoneman to modify his plan of attack. Stoneman prepared to destroy the Tennessee & Virginia Railroad in southwest Virginia to cut General Robert E. Lee's line of supply and best route of retreat should he evacuate from Richmond. After accomplishing this objective, Stoneman would move into the piedmont of North Carolina to destroy Lee's lines of supply from the south.

On 23 March at Morristown, Tennessee, Stoneman assembled a force of nine cavalry regiments, including three regiments from Tennessee and three from Kentucky that had participated in his December raid, for a total of 6,000 men. To inflict the most damage possible and retain mobility, Stoneman gave his troops orders to destroy the enemy's resources but not fight battles. As Stoneman moved across the mountains from east Tennessee into western North Carolina, he fought skirmishes, destroyed buildings, and seized supplies at Boone, Wilkesboro, and Mount Airy. On 2 April, Stoneman crossed into Virginia, where he divided his command into three separate raiding parties of three regiments each. One party destroyed the bridges and supplies in Wytheville, another destroyed the railroad bridges in the New River Valley, while the last destroyed the bridges in the Roanoke River Valley and moved as far east as Lynchburg.

On 9 April, Stoneman reunited his command and the next day moved on Winston-Salem, North Carolina. To prevent the destruction of their town, the citizens of Winston-Salem sent out a party of prominent citizens to negotiate with the Federal troops, while the remaining citizens hid all the town's valuables. After occupying the town, Stoneman then rode eastward toward the Greensboro-Danville railroad line.

With Confederate concern and resources focused around Greensboro, Stoneman was free to turn his attention to Salisbury, which was the site of a Confederate prisoner-of-war camp and a major supply depot. On 12 April, as Stoneman moved on Salisbury, the Confederate officials scraped together a force of unlikely defenders, including clerks, junior reserves, elderly members of the Home Guard, and two hundred "Galvanized Irishmen" who had been Southern prisoners of war but swore allegiance to the Confederacy to leave the prison camps. Stoneman took the town easily after a small skirmish, but he found that the Confederates had already moved more than 500 prisoners to Charlotte. Before leaving, Stoneman methodi-

cally burned the town's government buildings, stores, prison, and foundry. Observers as far away as fifteen miles reported seeing the flames.

After leaving Salisbury, Stoneman felt he had accomplished all he could and began to retire to Tennessee. Stoneman took his prisoners back to Tennessee, leaving his cavalry to operate east of the mountains to prevent the rebels from using the valleys and passes for guerrilla raids. With Stoneman gone, it opened the opportunity for the loyal mountaineers within his command to wreak vengeance on the traitorous Southerners. At Lenoir, Morganton, and Asheville, the forces led by General Alvan Gillem burned, pillaged, and looted the possessions of those who had staunchly supported the Confederacy, particularly the Southern gentry.

Stoneman's raid was very successful, as he had accomplished everything he had set out to do except to liberate the Confederate prisoners at Salisbury. He had effectively laid waste to large parts of western North Carolina and southwestern Virginia, limiting the ability of the Southerners in these areas to wage war. By destroying the Tennessee & Virginia Railroad, his raiders had cut off supplies and avenues of escape open to Robert E. Lee's troops around Richmond, helping to contribute to the Confederate surrender at Appomattox. The destruction of the railroad between Greensboro and Danville had prevented the armies of General Lee in Virginia and General Joseph E. Johnston in North Carolina from possibly combining forces. Despite Stoneman's apparent success, some historians have questioned the value of the raid, claiming that it came too late in the war to be of any significance and that it was accompanied by excessive waste and needless destruction.

—*William Hartley*

See also Cavalry, U.S.A.; Stoneman, George; Stoneman's Raid (December 1864–January 1865).

For further reading:

Starr, Stephen Z. *The Union Cavalry in the Civil War* (1979–1985).

Trotter, William T. *Bushwhackers: The Civil War in the North Carolina Mountains* (1988).

U.S. War Department. *The War of the Rebellion: A Compilation of the Official Records of the Union and Confederate Armies* (1880–1901).

Van Noppen, Ina Woestemeyer. *Stoneman's Last Raid* (1961).

STONEMAN, GEORGE H., JR.
(1822–1894)
Union general

Born the eldest son of George and Catherine Cheney Stoneman on 8 August 1822 in Busti, Chatauqua County, New York, Stoneman attended nearby Jamestown Academy before appointment to West Point in 1842. Graduated thirty-third out of fifty-nine cadets in 1846, he was commissioned in the 1st Dragoons and served as quartermaster of the "Mormon Battalion" that marched from Fort Leavenworth, Kansas, to San Diego, California. He remained active on the Pacific Coast for eight years. After promotion to captain in the 2d Cavalry in 1855, he served mainly in Texas until 1861.

As commander of Fort Brown, he refused to surrender the post to secessionist General David E. Twiggs and evacuated his command by steamer to New York. Named major in the 1st Cavalry, Stoneman transferred to the 4th Cavalry on 3 August 1861 and ten days later was appointed brigadier general of volunteers. He took part in George B. McClellan's operations in western Virginia and then served as the Army of the Potomac's chief of cavalry, a largely administrative and advisory position. During the Peninsula campaign, Stoneman commanded the reserve cavalry division at Yorktown, Williamsburg, and operations before Richmond, but was on sick leave during the battles of the Seven Days'. He replaced slain General Philip Kearny as leader of the 1st Division, II Corps (17 July–15 August 1862) and then led the 1st Division, III Corps (13 September–30 October 1862) before superseding General Samuel P. Heintzelman as III Corps commander and directing the corps at Fredericksburg.

Stoneman, promoted major general of volunteers, was selected by Joseph Hooker in February 1863 to head the consolidated three-division cavalry corps. In late April he led some 7,400 troopers on a Virginia raid intended to sever General Robert E. Lee's communications with Richmond. Divided into two roughly equal columns, half the raiding force led by cautious General William W. Averell stalled at Rapidan Station, while Stoneman accompanied the other portion of the command deep into Virginia, destroying military supplies, bridges, cutting several railroads, and alarming the Confederate capital.

While a daring enterprise, the operation was tactically sterile and exerted little favorable impact on the outcome of the Chancellorsville campaign. As a result, Stoneman and Averell were both relieved of command by Hooker as partial scapegoats for defeat. Repeatedly troubled by chronic hemorrhoids exacerbated by cavalry service, Stoneman went on sick leave until 18 July 1863, when he was appointed chief of the newly created Cavalry Bureau headquartered in Washington, D.C.

On 29 January 1864 Stoneman transferred back to field service, commanding the Army of the Ohio's XXIII Corps before reassignment to lead that army's three-brigade cavalry division. Stoneman led a raid during General William T. Sherman's siege of Atlanta from east of the city designed to rendezvous with another force at Lovejoy's Station before advancing to free Union prisoners held in Macon and Andersonville. Stoneman failed to link up with General Edward M. McCook's forces and his poor tactical judgment, hindered by waning

General George Stoneman (*seated, right*) and General Henry M. Naglee (*seated, third from left*) with members of their staffs near Fair Oaks, Virginia, June 1862 (Photograph by James F. Gibson / *Library of Congress*)

health, resulted in his capture, along with part of his command, on 31 July at Clinton, Georgia.

Exchanged in October 1864, Stoneman commanded the Department of the Ohio (17 November 1864–17 January 1865) and undertook a December raid from East Tennessee into southwestern Virginia, destroying rail lines, lead mines, and important Confederate salt works. Commanding the District of East Tennessee, Department of the Cumberland, Stoneman conducted a final raid into North Carolina (20 March–23 April 1865) that destroyed large quantities of supplies and wrecked the Virginia Central Railroad between Wytheville and Lynchburg, although the action was mounted too late to assist Sherman's northward advance materially. Stoneman was mustered out of volunteer service in July 1866 and then commanded for four years at Richmond-Petersburg, before his appointment as colonel of the 21st Infantry.

Assigned commander of the Department of Arizona in 1870, Stoneman retired the following year due to poor health and resided with his wife, Mary Oliver Hardisty, with whom he had four children, at his estate, Los Robles, near Los Angeles. He was appointed California railroad commissioner in 1879 and actively opposed the growing political power of the Pacific railroads in state affairs. Stoneman served as Democratic governor of California from 1883 until 1887, before being reinstated as a colonel on the army retired list by a special act of Congress in 1891. He died in Buffalo, New York, on 5 September 1894 and was interred at Lakewood, New York, a few miles from his birthplace.

—*David J. Gerleman*

See also Stoneman's Raid (April–May 1863); Stoneman's Raid (July 1864); Stoneman's Raid (December 1864–January 1865); Stoneman's Raid (March–April 1865)

For further reading:
Evans, David. *Sherman's Horsemen: Union Cavalry Operations in the Atlanta Campaign* (1996).
Greene, A. Wilson. *"Stoneman's Raid," Chancellorsville: The Battle and its Aftermath* (1996).
Starr, Stephen Z. *The Union Cavalry in the Civil War* (1979–1985).
Van Noppen, Ina Woestemeyer. *Stoneman's Last Raid* (1961).

STONES RIVER, BATTLE OF
(31 December 1862–2 January 1963)

The big, confused battle of Stones River (or Murfreesboro, as the Confederates named it) began early in the morning of the last day of 1862. Major General William S. Rosecrans commanded the Union's Army of the Cumberland, some 44,000 strong, which had marched about 30 miles to the southeast of Nashville, intending to attack Braxton Bragg's 38,000-man Army of Tennessee. The Confederate force was drawn up along the banks of the west fork of Stones River, just a short distance from the little town of Murfreesboro. Both armies were astride the Nashville Turnpike and the Nashville & Chattanooga Railroad.

Rosecrans's advance had come at a good time for the Federals. A Southern division under Carter Stevenson had left to reinforce John Pemberton's army in Mississippi. Further weakening the Confederates at Murfreesboro was the absence of both Nathan Bedford Forrest and John Hunt Morgan, who had left on cavalry raids into west Tennessee and Kentucky, respectively. The troopers left to Bragg, under Joseph Wheeler, were stretched thin—although Wheeler would perform well in the campaign. Also, it was difficult to find a good defensive position at Murfreesboro. A number of roads radiated from the village, by which the enemy might outflank Bragg. Also, the Confederate line, as finally drawn up, was divided by the river, which flowed north and then northwest on the west side of the town.

But Bragg was not thinking primarily of defense. Like Rosecrans, he planned to attack. In fact, each general intended to strike his enemy's right flank early on the morning of 31 December. On the night before the battle, as the men in both armies sought warmth around their campfires, one of the unique happenings of the war

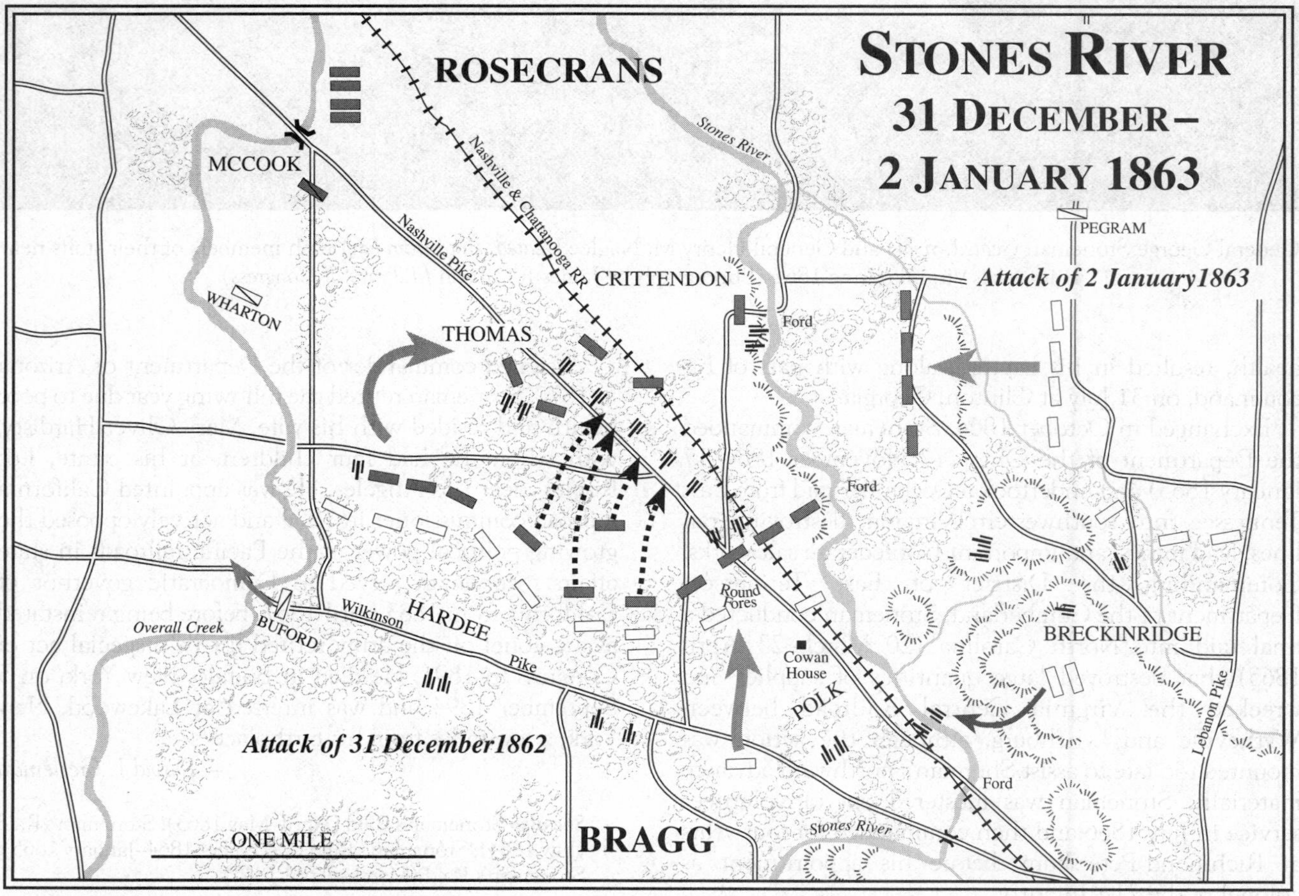

STONES RIVER
31 DECEMBER–
2 JANUARY 1863

Attack of 2 January 1863

Attack of 31 December 1862

ONE MILE

The battle of Stones River, 31 December 1862 (*Library of Congress*)

occurred. The military bands of both armies engaged in a type of competition, as a favorite selection of the Federals would be countered by a Southern piece. "Hail Columbia" might trigger a Confederate rejoinder of "The Bonnie Blue Flag." After this had gone on for some time, one of the bands began to play "Home Sweet Home," a tune well known and appreciated by both sides. Thus, one after another, Union and Confederate bands struck up the piece until all the bands in both armies were playing "Home Sweet Home." It was an unusual, and for many an unforgettable, prelude to one of the war's bloodiest engagements.

Early on the morning of Wednesday, 31 December, a cold and wet dawn, the Confederates struck first. Bragg's attack caught Rosecrans, who was concentrating on his own attack plans, unprepared and almost wrecked the Union army. Confederate soldiers from William J. Hardee's corps streamed out of the clumps of black-looking cedars, in the dim morning light, and smashed into the Yankee right flank, held by Major General Alexander M. McCook's soldiers, many of whom were still eating breakfast. Rosecrans had thought his planned attack against the Rebel right would relieve any potential danger to McCook's corps, but he had not anticipated the enemy striking first. Ironically, the Federal commander actually enhanced the Southern assault by deceiving the Confederates into believing the Union right flank was stronger than it was. Ordering campfires built for some distance beyond McCook's right, Rosecrans fooled Bragg, and the Confederate commander instructed his assaulting columns to move more widely to the Federal flank. As a result, the Southerners, when they struck, came in at a better angle than otherwise would have occurred. The attack was devastating. By midmorning McCook could do little but watch as his corps was routed and driven back almost three miles to a position near the Nashville Turnpike. Only Brigadier General Philip H. Sheridan of McCook's Corps was able to make a fighting retreat with his division.

Once Rosecrans realized the gravity of the situation (initially hesitating to believe a major enemy attack was under way), he called off his planned offensive and worked to build a defensive line along the turnpike and the railroad. It was paramount to protect his line of supply and reinforcement from Nashville. By noon the Federal line was at right angles. Thomas Crittenden's corps, with

Repairing rail near Murfreesboro following the battle of Stones River (*Library of Congress*)

whom Rosecrans had intended to launch an attack, still faced east, opposite John C. Breckinridge's Confederates on the far bank of the river. The Union corps of Major General George H. Thomas held the critical sector, where the Yankee line bent back to the west, just south of the turnpike and railroad. The remnants of McCook's corps were rallied and placed to the west of Thomas, extending the line along the pike toward Nashville.

Bragg then decided to break the Federal center under Thomas. He ordered Breckinridge's division, the largest

in the army, to cross Stones River and reinforce the effort west of the river. If Bragg had reinforced and extended his left flank, he would have had a good chance of seizing the Nashville Turnpike, cutting the Federals off from their Nashville base, and perhaps gaining a great triumph. Instead, Bragg and General Leonidas Polk concentrated against Thomas's men.

Again and again, Polk's soldiers charged against the angle where the Union line bent back toward Nashville; so also did Breckinridge's troops. The heart of the Federal position was a dense, four-acre thicket of cedars, known locally as the Round Forest, but afterward called "Hell's Half-Acre" by the soldiers who fiercely fought there. The Confederates tried desperately and suffered heavy casualties. Nevertheless, Thomas's men succeeded in holding that key ground that covered both the turnpike and the railroad, and the Southerners lost the opportunity for victory.

On the night of 31 December, Rosecrans and his corps commanders seriously considered a retreat to Nashville, although they ultimately elected to remain on the field. Both armies spent New Year's Day reorganizing and preparing to renew the battle. The Union sent a force across the river and occupied a ridge north of the rebel right flank from which enfilading fire could threaten the Confederate position. On 2 January, Bragg ordered Breckinridge to recross Stones River, attack and drive the Union troops from the high ground. Launched in the late afternoon, Breckinridge's assault drove the enemy from the hill, but as the Confederates pursued the Federals toward the river they were overwhelmed by massed Union artillery fire from high ground on the opposite side of the stream. With a third of the division numbered as casualties, the Rebels fell back. Soon the Federals recrossed the river and once more occupied the ridge. General Rosecrans held his position on 3 January and received reinforcements from Nashville. Bragg decided to retreat and began withdrawing during the night, pulling back along the Nashville & Chattanooga Railroad for about 30 miles to Tullahoma, Tennessee.

Total casualties for both sides numbered an estimated 24,645. Strategically, Stones River was a significant triumph for the Federals. While Rosecrans's army had been roughly handled on the first day of the battle, it had recovered and held its ground and, reinforced, was poised to advance against the major Confederate rail center of Chattanooga. The victory was also important to Federal morale, for after the recent defeats at Fredericksburg and Chickasaw Bluffs, the cause of the Union needed a triumph.

—*James L. McDonough*

See also Bragg, Braxton; Breckinridge, John Cabell; Crittenden, Thomas Leonidas; Polk, Leonidas; Rosecrans, William Starke; Thomas, George Henry; Tullahoma Campaign; Wheeler, Joseph.

For further reading:

Cozzens, Peter. *No Better Place to Die: The Battle of Stones River* (1990).

McDonough, James Lee. *Stones River—Bloody Winter in Tennessee* (1980).

STONEWALL BRIGADE

One of the most famous and embattled units to come out of the Civil War, the Confederate army's Stonewall Brigade was comprised of regiments recruited from the Shenandoah Valley and its immediate environs. Originally designated as the 1st Brigade, Virginia Volunteers, it consisted of the 2d, 4th, 5th, 27th, and 33d regiments of Virginia Infantry, commanded by Brigadier General Thomas J. Jackson. For the first year of the war the Rockbridge Artillery was associated with the brigade, but it was not assigned to it. On 21 July 1861 during the battle of First Bull Run, both Jackson and his command earned their immortal nicknames when Brigadier General Bernard Bee, attempting to rally his own troops, exclaimed, "Look! There is Jackson standing like a stone wall! Rally behind the Virginians!" During this Confederate victory, in which Jackson and his Virginians played a pivotal role, the brigade suffered 111 dead and 373 wounded and missing out of 2,600 engaged.

With Jackson's promotion to major general and transfer to a higher command—the so-called Valley District of the Department of Northern Virginia, a regional command—Brigadier General Richard Garnett took over the brigade in December 1861. The Stonewall Brigade, however, still would report to Jackson, as it also was assigned to the Valley District. Garnett's tenure as brigade commander would last only four months; he was relieved by General Jackson in the wake of the Confederate defeat at Kernstown in March 1862. During this battle (one of the few military defeats Stonewall Jackson ever would suffer) the Stonewall Brigade took heavy casualties: 343 killed, wounded, and missing out of 1,418 engaged. Jackson unfairly blamed Garnett for the Confederate defeat, and subsequently assigned Brigadier General Charles S. Winder to replace him.

During the Shenandoah Valley campaign in May and June 1862, Jackson's command—including the Stonewall Brigade—fought in the battles of McDowell, Front Royal, Winchester, Cross Keys, and Port Republic, marched over 350 miles in that time, and defeated three separate Union armies. After this important strategic success, Jackson's command was sent to reinforce the Army of Northern Virginia in the defense of Richmond. During the ensuing Seven Days' battles from 25 June to 1 July, the Stonewall Brigade fought in the bloody battles of Gaines' Mill and Malvern Hill.

After the Seven Days' battles, the brigade moved northward with the rest of Jackson's command to stem the advance of yet another Union army. General Winder took over command of the division to which the Stonewall Brigade was assigned, passing temporary command of his brigade to the 4th Virginia's Colonel Charles Ronald. The Stonewall Brigade was heavily engaged in the battle of Cedar Mountain on 9 August 1862, during which General Winder received a mortal wound. Replacing Winder as permanent brigade commander was the colonel of the 5th Virginia, William S. H. Baylor.

On 28 August during the battle of Groveton, the

Stonewall Brigade took on a Union brigade that also would be renowned for its fighting prowess: Brigadier General John Gibbon's brigade of Wisconsin and Indiana soldiers, soon to be nicknamed the Iron Brigade. Fighting in Napoleonic fashion less than seventy yards apart, the two brigades blasted away at each other for over two hours. The Stonewall Brigade stood its ground at Groveton, but at a severe price: over 200 casualties, not counting the 33d Virginia, whose records were lost. Two days later the Stonewall Brigade was once again involved in terrible combat, this time defending a railroad cut during the battle of Second Bull Run. At one point the Shenandoah Valley men ran so low on ammunition that they hurled rocks at the advancing Union soldiers, but their line held. Colonel Baylor's tenure as brigade commander ended on 30 August, when he fell to several Union bullets that killed him instantly.

The Army of Northern Virginia capitalized on its victory at Second Bull Run by embarking on its first invasion of the North. During the Maryland campaign that followed, the Stonewall Brigade participated in the capture of Harper's Ferry on 15 September and helped to defend the Confederate left flank at the bloody battle of Antietam on 17 September. The 2d Virginia Infantry had been detached as a provost guard at Martinsburg, Virginia, during the battle, reducing the already depleted brigade to approximately 250 men. Antietam thinned the brigade ranks by another eleven killed and seventy-seven wounded. During the Maryland campaign the brigade was under the temporary command of Colonel Andrew Grigsby of the 27th Virginia.

The next commander of the Stonewall Brigade was Stonewall Jackson's chief of staff, Elisha F. Paxton. Like Jackson a resident of Lexington, Virginia, Paxton took command of the brigade on 20 October and led it during the Fredericksburg campaign and through the spring of the following year, until his death on 3 May 1863 at Chancellorsville. Paxton was just one of 494 casualties that the brigade suffered at Chancellorsville, making that engagement its bloodiest battle. The most famous casualty of Chancellorsville, however, was the brigade's first commander, Thomas J. Jackson, old "Stonewall" himself.

Paxton was replaced on 19 May 1863 by James A. Walker, a former student of Jackson's at the Virginia Military Institute who was expelled from that college for challenging his professor to a duel. Shortly after taking command, Walker led the brigade during the Army of Northern Virginia's second Northern invasion, participating in the battles of Second Winchester and Gettysburg. At the latter battle the Stonewall Brigade assaulted Culp's Hill, named for a relative of one of the 2d Virginia's soldiers, former Gettysburg resident Wesley Culp, who was killed there on 3 July. In addition to Culp, the battle of Gettysburg cost the brigade an additional 34 dead, 208 wounded, and 87 missing.

The Stonewall Brigade saw action during the Mine Run campaign in November 1863, losing an additional 20 killed, 124 wounded, and 10 missing. Its final battles were the Wilderness and Spotsylvania Court House, the latter fight decimating the brigade, reducing its strength to less than 200. One of the wounded at Spotsylvania was James Walker, thus removing him from command. On 14 May the Stonewall Brigade was consolidated with three other brigades, with command going to the 4th Virginia's Colonel William Terry. The remnants of the Stonewall Brigade fought on to the very end and surrendered at Appomattox Court House on 12 April 1865.

—*Mark Snell*

See also Garnett, Richard Brooke; Jackson, Thomas Johnathan; Walker, James Alexander; Winder, Charles Sidney.
For further reading:
Robertson, James I., Jr. *The Stonewall Brigade* (1963).

STONEWALL, CSS

The CSS *Stonewall* holds an unusual position in naval history. In its twenty-seven-year career, this ironclad flew the flags of six different nations, precipitated international crises and courtroom battles, and yet never fulfilled the original purpose for which its revolutionary design was intended.

The Confederacy's success in its war for independence depended in a large part on military supplies from Europe. As the Union blockade deprived the Confederacy of more and more material, the Southern government attempted to obtain warships from Europe to break the blockade.

Captain James D. Bulloch, chief naval agent for the Confederacy in Europe, managed to get several wooden warships in England, but his attempts to obtain ironclads were blocked by Union diplomatic efforts. A similar attempt in France was eventually more successful. Lucien Arman, a shipbuilder in Bordeaux, met with Bulloch on 6 May 1863. A contract signed in July 1863 called for Arman to deliver two ironclad rams in June 1864 at a price of two million francs each, one-fifth down and the remainder payable in installments.

The specifications for the rams called for them to be small and maneuverable enough to operate in the Mississippi River. They were also to be armored to withstand 11- and 15-inch shells from Union guns. The compact ships measured 172 feet in length, 33 feet in width, and displaced 900 tons. Construction was of teak covering an iron frame. Armor consisted of 3.5 inches of iron, backed with 3 inches of teak, and lined with 1 inch of iron. Armament was concentrated in "turrets," actually armored casements. One was located at the front of the ship, where the forecastle would normally be. The second was just after the main mast. Each turret had five ports, so the pivot guns inside could fire in all directions. Constructed of only 18 inches of teak and 1.75 inches of

iron, the turrets were less well protected than the hull. On the *Stonewall*, one 11-inch gun was mounted forward, while two 5.5-inch guns were mounted in the after turret. A 20-foot ram completed the armament.

The engines generated 300 horsepower, capable of driving the rams at 12 knots. Unusual features included two wheels and twin screws, capable of counterrotation, which provided extraordinary maneuverability. Like many other ships of the time, the ironclads were rigged for sails to supplement their steam propulsion.

When the American minister to France became aware of Arman's dealings with the Confederacy, he complained to Napoleon III. Napoleon, no longer certain of Southern independence, and eager to protect his project in Mexico, blocked the sale of the ships to the Confederacy. Instead, the two rams, named the *Sphinx* and the *Cheops*, were offered for sale to Denmark and Prussia respectively. A ready market existed, because the two countries were at war. Renamed the *Staerkodder*, the Danish ironclad sailed for Copenhagen on 15 October 1864.

By that time, however, the war had ended badly for Denmark, and the need for an ironclad was over. The *Staerkodder* was a bad sailor, as well, plunging into waves instead of riding over them. The purchase was canceled, and Arman could again negotiate with Bulloch, because the ship was no longer in France. On 16 December 1864

the sale was finalized. Renamed the *Olinde*, the ship left Copenhagen on 7 January 1865, carrying a "Mr. Brown" as passenger. Mr. Brown was, in fact, Captain Thomas Jefferson Page of the Confederate Navy, destined to command the ship.

The *Olinde* rendezvoused with the blockade runner *City of Richmond* on 24 January off the island of Houat, near Bordeaux. A Confederate crew composed of survivors of the CSS *Florida* replaced the Danish crew. By 28 January supplies had been transshipped from the *City of Richmond* and the CSS *Stonewall* was commissioned under Page's command. The two ships then left French territorial waters.

Union agents became aware of the sale and were on the watch for the *Stonewall*. The ram was badly damaged by storms crossing the Bay of Biscay and was forced to put in at the Spanish naval base of Ferrol on 3 February. The Spanish allowed Page to take on stores and make repairs, but word of the *Stonewall*'s whereabouts was telegraphed all over Europe. The modern steam frigate *Niagara* and the sloop *Sacramento*, under Commodore Thomas T. Craven were quickly ordered to Corunna, across from Ferrol. Both ships were believed faster than the *Stonewall* and mounted more guns, but both were built of wood. Page believed that the *Stonewall* would be at a disadvantage in a fight, but Craven held the same belief about his own ships and hesitated to challenge the *Stonewall*.

The *Stonewall* at anchor off Washington, D.C., June 1865 (*Library of Congress*)

When repairs were completed, Page readied the *Stonewall* for a fight. On 21 March and again on 23 March, he sailed from Ferrol, but quickly returned when the seas proved too rough for his ship. Commodore Craven displayed no desire to fight on either occasion. On 24 March, Page sailed again. As the *Stonewall* left Spanish territorial waters, Craven's ships stayed at anchor in neighboring Corunna, watching but not offering a fight. The *Stonewall* was forced to put into Lisbon on 27 March for coal. Again Craven's ships followed, but did not attempt to stop the Confederate ironclad when it sailed for open waters. Craven was later court-martialled and found guilty twice for his failure to act.

After coaling at Tenerife, the *Stonewall* crossed the Atlantic using both steam and sail. A single merchantman was encountered and captured during the crossing. While the *Stonewall*'s location was unknown, newspapers and commanders in the United States fretted over its eventual landfall. The unknown quality of the *Stonewall* produced more panic and fear that events warranted.

Page and his command arrived at Nassau in the Bahamas on 6 May 1865. Page received enough coal to reach Havana, and there he learned that the Confederacy was no more. He sold the *Stonewall* to the Spanish authorities for $16,000, which he used to pay off his crew. Eventually, the United States acquired the *Stonewall* by reimbursing Spain the $16,000 they had paid for it.

The *Stonewall*'s story was far from over. The Japanese government, interested in modernizing their forces, purchased the *Stonewall* in 1867 for $400,000. The American crew that delivered the ship to Japan, however, arrived as civil war broke out between the forces of the shogun and the emperor. For months the Americans were forced to stay in Yokohama, while they determined which side actually owned the ironclad. Finally, early in 1869 the ship became the flagship of the emperor's navy, renamed *Kotetsu*. As such, it fought for the new government, destroying a rebel fleet and laying waste to the rebel strongholds. She remained in service in Japan as the *Azuma* until 1888, training a new generation of sailors who shaped the Japanese fleet of the twentieth century.

—*Tim J. Watts*

See also Bulloch, James Dunwody; Ironclads; Navy, C.S.A.
For further reading:
Kennett, Lee. "The Strange Career of the '*Stonewall*'." *U.S. Naval Institute Proceedings* (1968).
Miller, Edward Stokes. "The Dilemma of Commodore Craven." *Civil War Times Illustrated* (1994).
Orth, Michael. "The CSS *Stonewall*." *Civil War Times Illustrated* (1966).
Spencer, Warren F. *The Confederate Navy in Europe* (1983).
Strong, Edwin, Thomas Buckley, and Annetta St. Clair. "The Odyssey of the CSS *Stonewall*." *Civil War History* (1984).

STOWE, HARRIETT BEECHER
(1811–1896)
Abolitionist author and activist

Female authors during the nineteenth century were a product of the social and cultural mores of the time, as well as a force in shaping social history. History seems to have recognized Stowe based on the success of *Uncle Tom's Cabin*, leaving out her roles as wife and mother of seven children, champion of woman's suffrage, and author of numerous magazine articles. Consequently, Stowe's life represented the essence of paradox; she was raised by the fiery abolitionist minister Lyman Beecher, yet she herself disavowed her father's religion. She disliked slavery, yet she never fully became an abolitionist, and she supported women's rights, but her novels and articles championed the traditional history of women. Nevertheless, Stowe, referred to by Lincoln as the "little woman who wrote the book that started this great war," made an astounding contribution to the literary and historical worlds of her time. Both her Puritan heritage and revolutionary ideology enhanced her commitment to the fight for the betterment of her country, particularly in the tension-filled antebellum period and during the Civil War. Born in Litchfield, Connecticut, on 14 June 1811, the seventh child of the evangelist Lyman Beecher, Harriet Beecher learned from childhood about the connection between religion and politics. Well educated at both the Litchfield Female Academy and the Hartford Female Seminary, she discovered early on that education was the key to success.

It is arguable that Stowe's upbringing in a household dominated by her father allowed her to create her role as a facilitator of character as well as literary genius. She worked closely with her sister Catherine Beecher on her many ventures in the development of schools for girls, and later with her husband, Calvin Stowe, in his teaching experiences at Lane Seminary and Andover, among others. Throughout her life, educational development was a constant thread, as well as reading. Stowe helped popularize parlor literature, the nineteenth-century practice of reading works aloud within a family setting. Even as the era faded in which parlor literature had been fashionable, Stowe continued to practice this philosophy. Her family-centered tendencies would continue throughout her life, and her early formation of a literary circle, the Semi-Colon Club, set the tone for her future. It was during these sessions that she cemented her beliefs on abolitionism, women's rights, and education for women. She used her fiction, beginning with pieces published in periodicals such as *Godey's Lady's Book*, and later the *Atlantic Monthly*, as a vehicle to effect moral and cultural reformation.

That desire to effect change led to the publication of *Uncle Tom's Cabin* in serial form, beginning in 1851 and

ending in 1852. Prompted by the growing agitation over the Fugitive Slave Law, Stowe may have penned *Uncle Tom's Cabin* as an expression of her feelings. Nevertheless, although Stowe hoped that her readers would see African-Americans as fellow human beings, she also shared many of the misconceptions about race common during the nineteenth century. However unprepared Stowe may have been for the success of her novel, she was less prepared for the transitional period that followed. But, owing to her savvy business sense, Stowe became the sole financial provider in the family. Stowe may have been criticized for having cast herself on domestic subjects too small to catch the public's attention, but her shift after the Civil War to publishing in the fledgling magazine, the *Atlantic Monthly*, spotlighted a shift not only in Stowe's literary career, but also in the literary genre of the nineteenth century.

The events of the Civil War also paralleled events in Stowe's own life. Just as the nation entered its most tumultuous period, the Stowe family entered its own period of trials. Stowe's son Fred immediately responded to President Lincoln's call for 75,000 troops following the attack on Fort Sumter. Although Stowe publicly supported the young soldiers who "embrace [the cause] as a bride, and are ready to die [for it]," she privately prepared herself for the worst. She foresaw the war as continuing for several years, in contrast to the many who thought it would be over quickly. She saw it as "a long, grave period of severe self-denial which will task the resources, physical, mental and moral, of our Northern states." She could not, however, ignore the problem of slavery. Where she had once used the character of Topsy to provide a sense of comic relief in *Uncle Tom's Cabin*, demonstrating that white Southerners were faced with problems that white Northerners were not, she could no longer keep a sense of humor. In an article published in January 1863 in the *Atlantic Monthly*, she urged the immediate emancipation of slaves, and it is probable that she knew of Lincoln's Emancipation Proclamation when she wrote the article in 1862. In the article, she noted that it was time for the president to take a stance on the issue of slavery. Her chief concern was that political leaders might forget that human liberty was the chief aim of the war. Nevertheless, she simultaneously supported General William T. Sherman's march of destruction across Georgia.

After the end of the war and the assassination of Lincoln, Stowe still harbored resentment towards the South. Nevertheless, her desire to help the freedmen took precedence. In 1867 she traveled to Florida. Still a firm believer that education was the key to social change, she used her experience as a teacher in New England to assist the newly freed blacks. This cause, as well as that of women's rights, would occupy Harriet Beecher Stowe until her death in 1896. However, she

suffered a debilitating stroke in 1889 that left her with diminished faculties for the last seven years of her life, so her professional career all but ended with this setback. Nevertheless, through both her literature and her reform efforts, her voice reached a broad audience of concerned middle-class Americans.

—*Jennifer Harrison*

See also Abolitionists; *Uncle Tom's Cabin*.

For further reading:

Gossett, Thomas F. *Uncle Tom's Cabin and American Culture*. (1985).

Graham, Thomas. "Harriet Beecher Stowe and the Question of Race." *New England Quarterly* (1973).

Hedrick, Joan. *Harriet Beecher Stowe: A Life* (1994).

Hedrick, Joan, ed. *The Oxford Harriet Beecher Stowe Reader* (1999).

Tang, Edward. "Making Declarations of Her Own: Harriet Beecher Stowe as New England Historian." *New England Quarterly* (1998).

STRADER V. GRAHAM, 10 HOW. 82 (1851)

Slavery was a complex political, social, and moral issue in America in the generations preceding the Civil War. Increasingly, slavery also became the issue in litigation in the decade before that conflict. Some jurists believed that the courts might succeed in resolving the slavery question where legislative compromise and moral suasion had failed. They believed that judicial fiat might mandate an equitable disposition of the South's "peculiar institution" and the myriad concerns it engendered. The U.S. Supreme Court's decision in *Strader v. Graham*, 10 How. 82 (1851), established a short-lived precedent on the issue. However, it soon ignored its own ruling in that case when considering the infamous case of *Dred Scott v. San[d]ford* in 1857.

Dr. Christopher Graham was a Kentucky slaveowner who regularly hired out his slaves as professional musicians for performances in Ohio and Indiana minstrel shows. Trained as performers by a freedman and recognizing their potential social and economic value in the free states, some of these bonded artists grew disenchanted with their status as chattel property in Kentucky. In 1841 three of Graham's slaves escaped from Kentucky by crossing the Ohio River and seeking asylum as free men in Cincinnati. Because Kentucky law allowed the prosecution of anyone who aided or abetted the escape of slaves, Graham filed a lawsuit against Jacob Strader, who owned the steamboat *Pike* that had ferried the fugitives across the river.

The case involved several crucial legal questions that were yet unreconciled and untested in the national debate over a slaveowner's property rights in human capital. State law in Ohio recognized the fugitives as freedmen. Moreover, the language of the Northwest Ordinance (1787), a law of national scope, had explicitly prohibited slavery in the region where the musicians

performed and where they eventually sought their freedom. This was not merely a question of whether Ohio's laws could supersede the judicial prerogatives of Kentucky, but rather it called into question the validity of the U.S. government's assertion in the Northwest Ordinance that lands north of the Ohio River were free of slavery. While Graham only sought compensatory damages for the value of the slaves that he had lost, the case that he filed against Strader was fraught with more potent implications, as the repercussions from the decision would influence the national debate on slavery.

Kentucky courts had established a precedent in *Rankin v. Lydia* (1820) that authorized emancipation for those slaves taken by their owners into free states or territories and made permanent residents there. The Kentucky Court of Appeals did not find that precedent applicable in *Strader v. Graham* because the circumstances of the case were quite different. The court held that Graham's slaves were merely sojourners who visited free states while in temporary employment and that they were not taken into these regions to establish permanent residency outside of Kentucky. Accordingly, the Kentucky courts held Strader liable for the escape of Graham's slaves and ordered him to pay damages to Graham equivalent to the value of the three fugitives. Strader appealed the decision to the U.S. Supreme Court.

On 6 January 1851 Chief Justice Roger B. Taney announced the Supreme Court's unanimous decision to dismiss the case for lack of jurisdiction. In Taney's opinion, it was the exclusive right of each state "to determine the status, or domestic or social condition, of the persons domiciled within its territory." In what was largely viewed as a proslavery decision, the Supreme Court had implicitly promised noninterference by federal courts with decisions that state courts had reached on slavery-related questions.

Chief Justice Taney's ruling also included other controversial statements. Taney believed that the Northwest Ordinance (1787) had been superseded by the adoption of the U.S. Constitution (1789), which provided a sense of equality (comity) to all states. Specifically, Taney held that the prohibition against slavery in the Northwest Territory ceased to exist once a territory became a state, but that states did have the right to determine the status of individuals within their respective jurisdictions. Justices John McLean and John Catron each filed separate opinions in which they challenged Taney's statements on the Northwest Ordinance and on the free navigation of rivers.

Had the U.S. Supreme Court followed its own decision in *Strader v. Graham* (1851) as a precedent, it might have similarly dismissed the case of *Dred Scott v. San[d]ford* (1857), but that did not happen. Apparently the ensuing crisis fomented by the expansion of slavery into the western territories and the abject failure of popular sovereignty to remedy the situation had changed the judicial landscape by 1857.

—*Junius P. Rodriguez*

See also Catron, John; Curtis, Benjamin Robbins; *Dred Scott Case*; McLean John; Popular Sovereignty; Supreme Court, U.S.; Taney, Roger Brooke.

For further reading:

Finkelman, Paul. "Slavery." In *The Oxford Companion to the Supreme Court of the United States*. Edited by Kermit L. Hall (1992).

Rodriguez, Junius P. *Chronology of World Slavery* (1999).

Siegel, Martin. *The United States Supreme Court: Volume 3, The Taney Court, 1836–1864* (1995).

Witt, Elder, ed. *Congressional Quarterly's Guide to the U.S. Supreme Court* (1990).

STRATEGY, C.S.A.

Initial Confederate strategy was influenced by the political goal for which the government was fighting: political independence for the Confederate States of America. As a result, the initial strategy was primarily a defensive one that aimed to protect the borders of the seceded states. Complicating this defensive strategy were Missouri and Kentucky, two of the slave states that had not seceded. Both states had a substantial number of Confederate sympathizers who called for military action on the part of the Confederacy to bring them out of the Union. To ignore the call of those pro-Confederates might lose the Confederacy valuable resources, manpower, and a buffer for the Deep South. Therefore, Confederate strategy evolved quickly into primarily a defensive strategy, with the seemingly paradoxical goal of adding two states to its territory.

In the relatively compact Virginia theater, the Confederates learned early during the First Bull Run campaign the value of the telegraph and the railroad in offsetting their smaller numbers. As a result, they were able to exploit the use of their interior lines to move Joseph Johnston's men from the Shenandoah Valley to Manassas Junction in time to defeat Irvin McDowell at First Bull Run.

In the West, with a vast front to protect, less adequate railroads, and poorer roads, using the telegraph and the railroad to maintain that long front was less effective. General Albert Sidney Johnston, in command of the Confederate West, approached the defense of what amounted to the northern Tennessee state line by protecting the easiest approaches into Tennessee at Columbus, Missouri, on the Mississippi River, Fort Henry on the Tennessee River, Fort Donelson on the Cumberland River, and Bowling Green, Kentucky.

Ulysses S. Grant, breaking that line of defenses at Forts Henry and Donelson in February 1862, demonstrated the weakness of such a cordon strategy. Johnston had been unable or unwilling to concentrate his numbers

against a single threat like Grant. The result was that remaining Confederate forces had to fall back from that defensive line. The entire experience caused the Confederacy to change its western strategy and concentrate its forces to attack Grant at Shiloh on 6 April 1862. However, P. G. T. Beauregard later learned during the Federal advance on Corinth, Mississippi, that concentration did little good against a numerically superior, careful opponent.

Back in the East, the initial Confederate strategy regarding George McClellan's Peninsula campaign was to return to the defensive. Not dealing with an aggressive opponent in McClellan, Joseph Johnston was able to delay the Union army's arrival outside Richmond until the end of May 1862 and then to throw his opponent off guard by attacking an isolated part of the Union army at Seven Pines on 31 May. Although not a Confederate victory, the battle had the strategic result of delaying Federal offensive action even more. A serious injury suffered by Johnston in the battle brought Robert E. Lee to the command of the Confederate army at Richmond.

Lee had been looking at the strategic picture in Virginia for some weeks and knew that George McClellan was not the state's only problem. As Jefferson Davis's chief of staff, Lee had been following the movements of two smaller Union armies in western Virginia under John C. Frémont and Nathaniel P. Banks. Further, Irvin McDowell had moved out of Washington with 30,000 men and could easily move toward Richmond. Maintaining a strictly defensive strategy would allow these three forces to act with impunity, while the army at Richmond watched McClellan. That is why, even before Seven Pines, Lee had secured reinforcements for Stonewall Jackson in the Shenandoah Valley. The result was Jackson's masterful campaign that effectively neutralized Frémont, Banks, and McDowell. Jackson's campaign prevented any further Union gains in Virginia and prevented any of those forces from aiding McClellan. That task completed, Lee could then concentrate his forces at Richmond and go on the offensive against McClellan.

While the resulting campaign, called the Seven Days' battles, did not succeed in Lee's objective of destroying a large part of McClellan's army, with the Union withdrawal to the James River it did effectively end McClellan's Peninsula campaign. The offensive repulse of McClellan's threat, however, had produced high Southern casualties, something Confederate strategy would unsuccessfully try to avoid in the future.

The new threat of John Pope in northern Virginia, with much of McClellan's army still on the James River, forced Lee and Jefferson Davis once again to decide whether to remain in a strictly defensive posture or to meet the threat through an offensive strategy. Lee decided on a wide turning movement using Jackson to bring Pope into an advantageous position and then concentrating his forces against Pope's army. While offensive in nature, Lee's victory at Second Bull Run, by forcing Pope's retreat, had the effect of defending Virginia territory.

Perhaps learning from the success of smaller cavalry and guerrilla units operating behind Union lines destroying railroads and capturing supplies, both the Confederate commander in the West in 1862, Braxton Bragg, and Lee in Virginia saw the value of the raid in force as a viable strategy. Such an offensive action could have the benefit of drawing the enemy out of Southern territory, damaging Union war-making capability, and allowing the Confederacy to feed its soldiers at Northern expense. While Bragg's invasion of Kentucky in August 1862 also had the goal of recruiting Southern sympathizers and perhaps causing a popular uprising for the Confederacy in that state, the objective of pulling Union forces under General Don Carlos Buell out of Tennessee was paramount and temporarily successful. However, while some of the purposes of Bragg's invasion were realized, what some viewed as his premature retreat damaged Confederate morale.

In some ways Lee's raid into Maryland in September 1862 had similar purposes. While there was far less hope of a general popular uprising for the Confederacy in western Maryland, Lee hoped to draw Union forces out of Confederate territory and provide Northern food for his army. What Lee did not count on was McClellan, back in command, moving faster than usual. Demonstrating those incalculable elements in any strategy, McClellan also had the luck of finding Lee's lost Order 191 telling him exactly where Lee's divided army was. The resulting battle of Antietam meant that Lee had to retreat before the mission of the raid had been accomplished and that he did so after suffering severe casualties. Lee was forced to return to a defensive strategy for the winter and used it very successfully to repulse Ambrose Burnside at Fredericksburg in December 1862.

Confederate forces in the West during the winter of 1862 employed the raid on a smaller scale to delay Grant's advance on Vicksburg and William Rosecrans's advance on Murfreesboro, Tennessee. John Hunt Morgan's raid preceding the Murfreesboro (Stones River) campaign failed to stop Rosecrans. As a result, Bragg attacked Rosecrans as he moved on Bragg's position defending Murfreesboro. Although the attack surprised Rosecrans, it did not stop him, and Bragg retreated. At Vicksburg, while the raids on Grant's supply lines forced him to take another approach to Vicksburg, like Rosecrans he was undeterred. After Grant crossed the Mississippi south of Vicksburg and began moving on the town, Confederate commander John C. Pemberton made an unsuccessful attempt to attack Grant in the open at Champion's Hill and then

withdrew to his defenses at Vicksburg. The result was his surrender of the city on 4 July 1863 and Union control of the Mississippi River.

The effort to place the West under the overall command of Joseph E. Johnston in order to facilitate an overall western strategy came too late to help Bragg at Stones River and proved ineffective at saving Pemberton at Vicksburg. Including the trans-Mississippi in this vast area, the west proved not only strategically unmanageable for one man, but also an impossible theater in which to coordinate a concentrated defense. As a result, Johnston turned to cavalry raids as the best method to bring about the withdrawal of Union forces.

In the meantime, back in the East Lee resisted sending reinforcements to the dispersed, outnumbered western armies and maintained his defensive position on the Rappahannock River. Increasingly, because of Confederate casualties and supply difficulties, Lee began to view military action as a means to force the Union to the peace table. In order for this to happen, the Northern public would have to become so sick of the war that the current government would be turned out in the elections of 1864. For that reason Lee chose once again in May 1863 to go on the offensive, rather than adopt a defensive posture when Joseph Hooker attempted to flank Lee's position at Fredericksburg. Once again exploiting interior lines and using Stonewall Jackson to turn Hooker's position, Lee defeated a much larger army at Chancellorsville. Lee had been bold at Chancellorsville because of the importance of defending Confederate territory, but it had been done at some risk. As a result, for political reasons, as well as a need to preserve his supplies at home, Lee determined to return to the raiding strategy by moving north. The resulting invasion, while it allowed Lee to live off of Northern supplies for a brief period, resulted in the disastrous Confederate defeat at Gettysburg.

In the West Bragg, too, was planning an offensive against Rosecrans, but before he could effect such a move, Rosecrans advanced on Bragg at Chattanooga. Bragg fell back into north Georgia, intending to effect his concentration there. He succeeded well enough to defeat Rosecrans at Chickamauga and followed up the victory by besieging Chattanooga. By not moving faster to strike before Grant assumed command at Chattanooga and a supply line was opened, Bragg lost the opportunity to defeat Federal forces at Chattanooga and was himself driven back.

For the most part, beginning in the fall of 1863, strategic initiative passed to the Union army. Lee and the various western commanders, while occasionally developing effective defensive strategies, never held the initiative again. They merely reacted to what Northern commanders did. While various offensive strategies were proposed and even considered, when spring campaigning began in 1864, the Confederates found themselves on the defensive.

Lee in the Overland campaign and Johnston—and eventually Hood—in the Atlanta campaign increasingly found their flanks turned and ultimately their positions besieged. Although Hood escaped Atlanta with much of his army, Lee had the political necessity of defending Richmond and therefore had no choice but to dig in at Petersburg. First Lee in the summer of 1864, and then Hood in the fall, attempted to return to the raid as a means of drawing the Federals away from their offensive goals. Jubal Early's operations in the Shenandoah Valley and his raid on Washington, Hood's pitiable attempt to draw Sherman out of Georgia, and the disasters at Franklin and Nashville demonstrated that Union numerical and logistical superiority had reached a point that made such a Confederate strategy ineffective.

In the last months of the war Lee continued to react to Grant's efforts to extend the siege lines at Petersburg by extending the ever-thinning Confederate lines. At the same time, all Joseph Johnston could hope to do was delay Sherman's march through the Carolinas. As an act of desperation, Lee finally tried to concentrate the two forces by moving out of his lines at Petersburg and heading west. The result, of course, was his surrender at Appomattox Court House.

For the most part, high-ranking Confederate generals and President Jefferson Davis had a good understanding of the strategic situation during the war. It could be argued that their efforts to make the war unpopular in the North through the use of the strategic defensive and the opportune raid could have borne considerable fruit, had it not been for the strong strategic sense of Abraham Lincoln, Ulysses S. Grant, and William T. Sherman. In the end, the logistical difficulties and desertion rate doomed any Confederate strategy to certain defeat.

—*David S. Heidler and Jeanne T. Heidler*

See also Antietam, Battle of; Bragg, Braxton; Gettysburg, Battle of; Johnston, Albert Sidney; Johnston, Joseph Eggleston; Kentucky; Lee, Robert Edward; Missouri; Peninsula Campaign; Shenandoah Valley Campaign (1862).

For further reading:

Gallagher, Gary W. *The Confederate War: How Popular Will, Nationalism, and Military Strategy Could Not Stave Off Defeat* (1997).

Harsh, Joseph L. *Confederate Tide Rising: Robert E. Lee and the Making of Southern Strategy, 1861–1862* (1998).

Jones, Archer. *Civil War Command and Strategy: The Process of Victory and Defeat* (1992).

Woodworth, Steven E. *No Band of Brothers: Problems in the Rebel High Command* (1999).

STRATEGY, U.S.A.

Although the North possessed overwhelming superiority in human and material resources over the South, formulating a strategy for crushing the rebellion and restoring the Union proved to be no easy task. Because of the massive size and maneuverability of

Civil War armies and innovations in weapons technology that gave overwhelming advantages to armies operating on the tactical defensive, achieving decisive victories on the battlefield would prove exceedingly difficult, and the destruction of armies in battle virtually impossible. The Union task was further complicated by the absolute size and geography of the Confederacy, and the fact that the North's goal was to regain the loyalty of the South to the Union. Consequently, logistics and the state of civilian morale on both sides would play a much larger role in shaping the actions of the generals and statesmen upon whose shoulders fell the responsibility of formulating and implementing Union strategy than most Americans expected when the war began.

In the Virginia theater, the North had essentially two strategic options. It could operate along the overland route from Washington to Richmond, the Confederate capital, via Fredericksburg. However, logistics, in particular the dependency of the Union army on lines of communication that were vulnerable to cavalry raids and strategic turning movements, and the strength of the tactical defensive made a decisive victory on this line of operations difficult to achieve. Alternatively, the Union could operate against Richmond from the lower Chesapeake Bay. There, rivers reached deep into the Virginia heartland and the North's overwhelming naval superiority offered secure logistics and unmatched mobility, making this a very favorable area for conducting operations. But if the lower Chesapeake offered great operational advantages, it entailed considerable risks. To undertake operations on the rivers in sufficient force to be successful, it would be necessary to take the politically, if not militarily, hazardous step of significantly diminishing the forces that protected Washington, D.C.

In the West, the region between the Mississippi River and the Appalachian Mountains, the Ohio, Mississippi, Cumberland, and Tennessee rivers provided the Union with ideal lines of operation. Beyond a certain point, however, Union armies would have to operate away from the rivers and rely on railroads for logistical support. Railroads made it possible to support large armies deep in enemy territory, but they were highly vulnerable to cavalry raids. They also limited strategic flexibility, for no significant force could operate in hostile territory for an extended time without convenient access to a railroad or river.

The first effort to formulate strategy was undertaken by commanding General Winfield Scott in the aftermath of Fort Sumter. Scott's strategy, dubbed the Anaconda Plan by the press, reflected his desire to restore the Union with as little bloodshed as possible. He called for the Union navy to establish a blockade of the Atlantic and Gulf coasts, and for a thoroughly trained and disciplined army to seize the Mississippi River in cooperation with the navy. Conquering the South through invasion, he believed, would require large, costly armies, and, in the end, be counterproductive. The challenge to Southern honor, the destruction of property, and the bloodshed of a major invasion would, Scott feared, only inflame Southern hostility toward the Federal government. The Anaconda Plan would coerce the South in a much less provocative way. Once passions had cooled and the Southern people were deprived of the luxury items that they were dependent upon trade to provide, Scott believed they would realize that their best interests would be served by ceasing resistance and returning to the Union.

Although President Abraham Lincoln shared Scott's desire to avoid a bloody and destructive war, he rejected the Anaconda Plan, which would take months to implement and perhaps years to work, in favor of seeking a quick victory in battle. (He did, however, direct that a blockade be imposed on the South and recognized the importance of the Mississippi River.) A decisive, immediate display of Northern military power through a quick victory in battle, Lincoln believed, would discourage Southerners by impressing upon them the futility of resisting the authority of the Union. And so, over the protests of his military advisors, Lincoln ordered Irvin McDowell to attack Confederate forces at Manassas Junction. A humiliating defeat at Bull Run in July 1861, however, eliminated whatever chance there was for a quick victory and induced Lincoln to call George B. McClellan to Washington.

In November 1861 McClellan replaced Scott as general-in-chief and developed a strategy that combined political and military objectives. McClellan's goal, like Scott's and Lincoln's, was to facilitate sectional reconciliation by avoiding a long and bloody war. He recognized, however, that a major military effort would be required. With an eye on winning a short war, McClellan made operations in Virginia the Union's chief priority. To achieve victory there, he planned to take the time to raise and thoroughly train a massive army capable of making Southern resistance futile. To support operations in Virginia, McClellan sent Don Carlos Buell to Kentucky with orders to operate against east Tennessee to cut the railroad that linked the Old Dominion to the western Confederacy and rescue the Unionist residents of the region. McClellan also called for having the navy establish posts at various points along the Southern coastline to seize important logistical objectives and encourage the South to disperse its forces. Finally, McClellan sent Henry W. Halleck to Missouri to organize an expedition down the Mississippi River. To avoid inspiring Southern resistance, McClellan also advocated a policy of conciliation that rigidly respected slavery, while assuring Southerners that there would be no penalty for laying down their arms. In sum, he sought

to bring the South to reason by making resistance both futile and pointless.

To give Halleck and Buell time to organize their forces, McClellan decided to delay the commencement of operations until the spring of 1862. During the winter of 1861–1862, he also conceived a plan for operating against Richmond from the lower Chesapeake Bay. But by the time spring arrived, frustration with military delays, pressure from the Radical Republicans, and an intense aversion to the risks that operating from the lower Chesapeake entailed had dramatically eroded Lincoln's faith in McClellan. In March he let McClellan undertake his Peninsula campaign, but removed him as general-in-chief just before it began.

The failure of McClellan's approach to achieve victory by the summer of 1862 produced a dramatic shift in Union strategy. In July Lincoln brought Halleck to Washington and made him general-in-chief. He also decided to make the emancipation of Southern slaves a Northern war aim. The latter action had two important implications for Union strategy. First, the issuance of the Emancipation Proclamation ended whatever chance there was for shortening the war through a conciliatory policy. The South would have to be conquered. Second, Union armies were now free to make war on Southern resources.

In collaboration with Halleck, Lincoln also reworked the Union's operational priorities. First, they eliminated basing the Army of the Potomac's main operations on the peninsula as a strategic option. Although they recognized the advantages of operating from the peninsula and the significant obstacles to achieving a decisive victory on the overland route, Lincoln and Halleck concluded that the most important thing was to keep Union forces in Virginia concentrated and in a position that would keep Washington completely secure. They wanted the Army of the Potomac to seek out the Rebel army aggressively and hoped its brilliant commander, Robert E. Lee, might make a mistake, but they accepted the prospect of a stalemate in Virginia. At the same time, Lincoln and Halleck were becoming increasingly concerned that, if the Mississippi River remained in Rebel control, support for the war in the Old Northwest might slacken. This, and a pessimistic assessment of the possibility of achieving decisive success in Virginia, led Lincoln and Halleck to reverse McClellan's priorities. Virginia became secondary to operations in the west, where territorial objectives—control of the Mississippi River and the liberation of east Tennessee—became the Union's first priorities in 1863.

Working within the Lincoln-Halleck strategy, the Union was unable to break the stalemate in Virginia in 1863, although it did win a victory at Gettysburg and inflict substantial casualties on Lee's army. In the West, however, the North achieved both of its objectives in 1863. In July Ulysses S. Grant captured Vicksburg,

securing the Mississippi for the Union. Shortly thereafter, William S. Rosecrans, through a series of skillful turning movements, managed to maneuver Braxton Bragg's army out of middle and eastern Tennessee. Then, however, the Rebels took advantage of their interior lines to shift a large contingent of forces from Virginia to Bragg by rail, which helped him defeat Rosecrans at Chickamauga in September. The Lincoln administration responded by carrying out a rail transfer of its own, sending forces from the Army of the Potomac and Grant's army in Mississippi to Chattanooga, where Rosecrans's army was under siege. With Grant in command, in November the Union broke the siege at Chattanooga and ended the struggle for east Tennessee conclusively.

In March 1864 Grant replaced Halleck as general-in-chief. Once in his new post, Grant formulated a strategy that sought to employ simultaneous advances to prevent the Rebels from taking advantage of their interior lines as they had at Chickamauga. Grant recognized, however, that Civil War armies were too large and powerful to be destroyed in combat, so he also sought to make war on Southern logistics and war resources through a strategy of army-size raids. Rather than simply conquering and occupying territory, which was costly in resources and manpower, Grant would have armies march through the South, living off the land and ruthlessly destroying Southern crops, factories, railroads, and other war resources—and with them, Southern morale.

The summer of 1864 was, however, primarily a season of conventional campaigns by Grant against Lee's army in Virginia, and William T. Sherman against Joseph E. Johnston's army in Georgia, both of which were distinguished by tactical stalemates and the extensive use of turning movements and field fortifications. Not until the fall of 1864, when Sherman defeated the Rebel army in Georgia and captured Atlanta, and Philip Sheridan thrashed Confederate forces in the Shenandoah Valley, was the North able to carry out Grant's raiding strategy in earnest. By the time 1864 was over, Sherman had cut a fifty-mile-wide swath of destruction through Georgia and Sheridan had put the valley to the torch with devastating effect on the South's ability and will to continue the war. Sherman's and Sheridan's operations also ensured Lincoln's reelection and thus ended whatever hopes the Rebels had for achieving victory by political means.

For his part, Grant kept Lee occupied and unable to detach forces to resist Sherman's or Sheridan's operations, first in a series of bloody battles from the Wilderness to Petersburg in the summer of 1864 and then through a siege of Richmond and Petersburg that lasted until April 1865, when Lee abandoned his capital in a desperate attempt to join forces in North Carolina. Grant was able to prevent this, and on 9 April 1865

accepted Lee's surrender at Appomattox Court House. Within weeks after Appomattox, every other Confederate army had laid down its arms. Although the South still had considerable manpower available, Grant's strategy had so decimated its industrial and agricultural resources that further conventional resistance was impossible. The option of resorting to guerrilla warfare remained open, but the will to fight on for the Confederacy was no longer there. Grant's strategy had crushed it.

—*Ethan S. Rafuse*

See also Anaconda Plan; Strategy C.S.A., Tactics.

For further reading:

Basler, Roy P., ed. *The Collected Works of Abraham Lincoln* (1953–1955).

Grant, Ulysses S. *Personal Memoirs of U. S. Grant* (1885).

Grimsley, Mark. *The Hard Hand of War: Union Military Policy Toward Southern Civilians, 1861–1865* (1995).

Hattaway, Herman. *Shades of Blue and Gray: An Introductory Military History of the Civil War* (1997).

———, and Archer Jones. *How the North Won: A Military History of the Civil War* (1997).

Jones, Archer. *Civil War Command and Strategy: The Process of Victory and Defeat* (1992).

McClellan, George B. *McClellan's Own Story: The War for the Union, the Soldiers Who Fought It, the Civilians Who Directed It, and His Relations to It and to Them* (1887).

U.S. War Department. *The War of the Rebellion: A Compilation of the Official Records of the Union and Confederate Armies* (1880–1901).

STREIGHT'S RAID
(April–May 1863)

In spring 1863, Union colonel Abel D. Streight planned to lead an expedition of mounted infantry across northern Alabama into Georgia to strike the Western & Atlantic Railroad between Atlanta and Chattanooga. To accomplish this task, Streight chose a select body of men, who were to be mounted on mules—animals seemingly well adapted to the difficult terrain over which they would be traveling. The Federals would be moving across a lightly inhabited region whose few residents were mostly pro-Union. Brigadier General Grenville M. Dodge was to lead a diversionary attack on Tuscumbia, Alabama, as well, to draw attention away from the raiders.

Unfortunately for Streight, his meticulous planning went awry almost immediately. Many of the animals upon which the raid depended arrived from Nashville in poor condition or unbroken for riding. Complicating matters, Confederates under Colonel Philip D. Roddey stampeded the animals Streight had gathered. The expedition lost two days rounding up the loose mules.

On 21 April Streight and Dodge set out. Their combined forces easily drove Roddey's troopers toward Tuscumbia, which the Federals reached on the twenty-fourth. In the meantime, Brigadier General Nathan Bedford Forrest received orders to proceed to Alabama. Forrest joined Roddey, but initially failed to detect the detachment of the 1,500 to 2,000 men of the "mule brigade" from the main body of Union troops. On the twenty-eighth, Forrest began tracking Streight, having left part of his command with Roddey to watch Dodge.

Rainy conditions and an insufficient number of animals hampered the raiders. Impressing animals as they went, the column reached Moulton on the night of 28 April, having come an incredible thirty-five miles. Streight camped his men at Day's Gap at the foot of Sand Mountain. The progress, with no sign of enemy pursuit as yet, a break in the weather, and the requisition of enough animals to mount the entire command, seemed to bode well for the operation's success.

Early on 29 April, the Confederates shook Streight and his men out of their complacency. As the Federals were breaking camp, Captain William Forrest, the general's brother, hit them. General Forrest wanted to maintain the pressure, while resting the remainder of his command, a tactic he would repeat with success throughout the pursuit. He also planned to use flanking forces to head off the raiders.

However, Abel Streight proved a worthy opponent. He established a blocking force on the high, narrow roadway and waited for the Southerners to enter the trap he had set for them. Without scouting properly, Captain Forrest pressed the Union rear guard. Suddenly, volleys emptied Southern saddles, including Forrest's when a minié ball smashed into his leg, disabling him. A counterthrust netted the Federals two artillery pieces (which they later spiked) and forty prisoners. It was an embarrassing reversal for the Confederates.

By the morning of 1 May, Streight's men had put another forty-three miles behind them. They paused briefly to rest, eat, and replenish ammunition. Then their antagonists continued their counterpunching. The Confederates caught up with the raiders at Black Creek, where the Federals finally seemed secure, with the bridge over the steep-banked stream in flames. Yet sixteen-year-old Emma Sansom offered to show the Confederate general a ford by which cattle crossed the stream at low water. Forrest quickly had his men plunging across it.

By now the Federals were straggling badly. A brief respite twelve miles beyond Gadsden ended in a sharp firefight in which Streight lost his best lieutenant, Colonel Gilbert Hathaway. He was beginning to realize that, unless he put a significant barrier between himself and Forrest, the raid was doomed. To that end, he detached a squad to seize the bridge at Rome, Georgia. But the efforts of a local mail carrier, John Wisdom, to warn the people in Rome thwarted Streight's plan.

Finally, at 9 A.M. on 3 May, not far from the Alabama-

Georgia border, Streight halted his 1,466 men. Many of them fell asleep as they lay in the line of battle, despite bullets from Southern skirmishers passing overhead. Forrest arrived on the scene with two artillery pieces and approximately 600 men. Whatever their condition, he knew that the Federals outnumbered him. Rather than risk defeat with an assault, he decided to try another method to capture the raiders.

Under a flag of truce, the Confederate commander met with Streight to demand his surrender. His counterpart, still personally full of fight, agreed to listen. As they negotiated, Forrest engaged in a tour-de-force of bluff. He moved the two pieces of artillery and the men he had on hand so that Streight thought he was seeing a much larger command. Couriers from phantom units added to the deceit.

Streight became so convinced that he faced an overwhelmingly superior force that he finally agreed to surrender. The Federals stacked their arms and the Confederates came forward to receive them. When the Union colonel saw that he had been tricked, he demanded that his weapons be returned, a demand with which Forrest understandably refused to comply.

—Brian S. Wills

See also Cavalry, U.S.A.; Forrest, Nathan Bedford.

For further reading:

Henry, Robert Selph. *"First With the Most" Forrest* (1944).

Longacre, Edward G. "All is Fair in Love and War." *Civil War Times Illustrated* (1969).

Wills, Brian Steel. *A Battle from the Start: The Life of Nathan Bedford Forrest* (1992).

Wyeth, John A. *Life of General Nathan Bedford Forrest* (1899; reprint, 1989).

STRINGHAM, SILAS HORTON
(1798–1876)
Rear admiral, U.S. Navy

Although he was a seasoned officer with many years of valuable experience, Silas Stringham played only a small role in the American Civil War. Stringham pioneered many of the battle tactics for which many later Civil War naval officers were to receive fame. Stringham initiated aggressive steaming tactics, demonstrated that ships could reduce coastal fortifications, and established the pattern of coastal blockade emulated throughout the war. Stringham was also an early advocate of employing African-Americans in the Union Navy, leading to an eventual acceptance of African-Americans in the American naval service. His advanced age prevented him from more fully applying his accumulated skill in the naval war against the Confederacy, but Stringham's early impression earned him a well-deserved mention in the history of the Civil War.

Enlisting in the U.S. Navy at age eleven, Silas Stringham enjoyed a successful career before the Civil War. After serving as a midshipman under Commodore John Rodgers aboard the USS *President* during the War of 1812, Stringham was promoted to second lieutenant and served in the wars against the Barbary pirates. The seizure of several slave vessels off the African coast brought Stringham a promotion to lieutenant and duty in the West Indies Squadron. After a stint of shore duty at the Brooklyn Navy Yard, Stringham was promoted to commander and served in the Mediterranean Squadron. Between 1837 and 1841, Stringham commanded the Brooklyn Navy Yard with the rank of captain. In 1842, Stringham left the Navy Yard to take command of the USS *Independence*, but he returned to command the Navy Yard a year later. In 1846, Captain Stringham commanded the USS *Ohio* and led that vessel during the bombardment of Vera Cruz during the Mexican-American War. Serving with distinction in that conflict brought Stringham command of the South American Squadron from 1848 until 1851, when he commanded the Gosport Navy Yard. Temporarily promoted to commodore, Stringham commanded the Mediterranean Squadron until 1856, observing many modern naval tactics and technologies during the Crimean War.

Stringham was in the United States on a well-deserved leave of absence when the Fort Sumter crisis began. As the senior officer available for duty, Stringham served as a naval advisor to President James Buchanan and was a vocal proponent of any plan to relieve the Federal position by force. When Abraham Lincoln assumed the presidency, Stringham was named to command the fledgling Atlantic Blockading Squadron and was tasked with blockading the extensive Confederate coast. Faced with chronic manpower shortages, Stringham was an early advocate of employing contrabands in the navy, granting them freedom in exchange for accepting the risk of military service.

In August 1861, Stringham led the first major combined arms operations of the Civil War. Transporting 1,000 army troops under the command of General Benjamin F. Butler, Stringham assaulted and captured the Confederate fortifications at the Hatteras Inlet, North Carolina. The seizure of the inlet denied the area to Confederate privateers preying on Union commerce and gave the Union virtual control of North Carolina's inner coastal waters, although the original plan called for the sinking of block ships to close the inlet. Besides pioneering combined arms operations, during the attack Stringham employed several new tactics that he borrowed from the British and French experience during the Crimean War. Instead of dropping anchor and shooting from stationary positions, Stringham steamed his vessels in a circle to present a more difficult target. Stringham also employed high-angle plunging fire to destroy hardened targets and dismount Confederate guns hidden behind earthen ramparts. Unable to resist the fierce Union bombardment, the Confederates surrendered more than 700 men to General Butler, whose force suffered not a single fatality.

Despite his victory, which greatly boosted morale in the aftermath of the embarrassing Union defeat at Bull Run, Stringham was unjustly criticized by the Northern media for not immediately following up his triumph and seizing more North Carolina territory. Stung by the public criticism, the elderly Stringham asked to be relieved of command and was replaced by Rear Admiral Louis Goldsborough. While requesting retirement, Stringham was instead granted an extended leave of absence. In July 1862, Stringham was promoted to rear admiral and served the remainder of the war on various panels advising Secretary of the Navy Gideon Welles and commanding the Boston Navy Yard. He served at Boston until 1871, when he became the port admiral at New York until his death in 1876.

—Steven J. Ramold

See also African-American Sailors; Hatteras Inlet, Capture of.

For further reading:

Anderson, Bern. *By Sea and By River: The Naval History of the Civil War* (1962).

Fowler, William M., Jr. *Under Two Flags: The American Navy in the Civil War* (1990).

Mallison, Fred M. *The Civil War on the Outer Banks* (1997).

Trotter, William R. *The Civil War in North Carolina. Volume 3: Ironclads and Columbiads* (1989).

STRONG, GEORGE TEMPLETON
(1820–1875)

Diarist and treasurer of the U.S. Sanitary Commission

George Templeton Strong was born to attorney George Washington Strong and his wife, Eliza Catherine Templeton, in New York City. As a student at Columbia College, Strong excelled in music, literature, and classical languages. At this time he began his famous diary and aspired to a career in either journalism or teaching. His father, however, convinced Strong to study law at the family firm of Strong & Bidwell, in spite of the younger Strong's disinterest and self-doubt. "I've bent on making myself thorough in the law," Strong wrote in 1838. "But really and truly, I don't think I've one lawyerlike faculty." Nevertheless, he passed the New York Bar examination in 1844 and became a partner in the firm, where he handled realty and probate cases. Although Strong admired legal argument and took interest in constitutional issues, he found the practice of law "a kind of snowbank of mortgages, subpoenas, depositions, and polyonymous botherations" from which he escaped into music and general reading.

In 1848 Strong married Ellen Ruggles, the daughter of capitalist Samuel Bulkley Ruggles. Strong's diary suggests that he was extremely happy in this marriage, which produced three sons—John Ruggles (1851), George Templeton, Jr. (1856), and Lewis Barton (1860)—and widened Strong's social circle to include such New York elite as the Astor, Stuyvesant, and Brevoort families. Though naturally introverted, Strong came to enjoy the Sunday night receptions in which he and Ellen entertained a select circle of scholars, scientists, musicians, and prominent New York professionals. His election to the Columbia College Board of Trustees in 1853 deepened his influence as, in company with Senator Hamilton Fish and New York governor Morris Ogden, Strong campaigned to expand his alma mater into a modern university comprising schools of law and mining, as well as the humanities. He was among the founders of Columbia's School of Law, established in 1856.

From 1861 to 1865 Strong served without compensation as treasurer of the United States Sanitary Commission, a civilian agency empowered by President Abraham Lincoln and Secretary of War Simon Cameron to modernize and finance the medical care of Union soldiers. The Sanitary Commission was founded in 1861 by Dr. William H. Van Buren and Reverend Henry Whiting Bellows in response to reports of the Army Medical Bureau's poor organization, outdated practices, and inadequate supplies. Strong joined the commission as treasurer at its second meeting in June 1861. His "peculiar, anxious, and persistent" duties (as he termed them) included the raising and allocation of donated money, materials, and labor; visits to army camps and battlefields; and negotiations with President Lincoln, Secretary of War Edwin M. Stanton, General Ulysses S. Grant, and General George B. McClellan. Strong and other commissioners often worked against intense opposition from Stanton, who disagreed with the Sanitary Commission's decisions regarding personnel and bureaucratic reforms. Over the course of four years, Strong raised and allocated for the commission nearly $5 million in monetary donations from transportation, banking, mining, and insurance corporations across the North. His other patriotic activities included the founding of the Union League Club of New York, an organization intended to increase "love and respect for the Union," counteracting the Southern sympathies that he perceived among New York City's elite. Additionally, Strong, a devout Episcopalian, worked to persuade his church to publicize its pro-Union stance in 1862.

However, Strong is best known for his diary, which he began at Columbia in 1835 and continued until shortly before his death in 1875. The entries are rich in historically valuable observations on the culture, thought, and leadership of his times, given from the perspective of a

highly educated, financially secure, and respected New Yorker. Significantly, Strong's diary illustrates the Northern cause's intellectual shift from Unionism to abolitionism over the course of the war. Strong initially objected to slavery "on grounds of political economy, not of ethics" and agreed that the North had no constitutional right to outlaw slavery in the established states. His ardent support for the North sprang from national pride rather than principle: "We are a weak, divided, disgraced people, unable to maintain our national existence," he wrote in March of 1860, adding that "I shall never go abroad. ... I should be ashamed to show my face in the meanest corner of Europe." By 1864, however, Strong and his colleagues supported abolition and described the widespread change of opinion on that subject as a "great and blessed revolution." "God pardon our blindness of three years ago!" Strong continued, declaring that but "for our want of eyes to see and of courage to say what we saw, the South would never have ventured on rebellion." The diary also offers Strong's reactions to other issues—such as John Brown's hanging, Lincoln's inaugural speeches, New York City draft riots, and Irish immigration—as well as New York's musical performances, popular culture, and the current literature.

In addition, Strong's diary provides lively firsthand portraits of the contemporary leaders. For example, Strong described Lincoln as "lank and hard-featured, among the ugliest white men I have seen," having "the laugh of a yahoo, with a wrinkling of the nose that suggests affinity with the tapir and other pachyderms." However, Strong added, he "seems to me clear-headed and sound-hearted." Stanton, McClellan, Grant, and the influential poetess Julia Ward Howe also are characterized in Strong's expansive and witty record.

From 1865 until his death in 1875 Strong suffered from poor health, depression, and a diminishing income. Although he argued before the U.S. Supreme Court in 1866, he became increasingly dissatisfied with the legal profession, and in 1872 he retired from his practice. For the next three years Strong served as comptroller of Trinity Episcopal Church (New York City), managing the investments and real estate of that affluent parish. Meanwhile he presided over the New York Philharmonic Society and founded a Church Music Association to arrange ecclesiastical concerts in the city. Strong died on 21 July 1875 at his home in Manhattan. The funeral, attended by President Grant and former New York governor John A. Dix, took place at Trinity Church.

—*Rae Sikula*

See also Medicine; United States Sanitary Commission.
For further reading:
Auchincloss, Louis, ed. *The Hone and Strong Diaries of Old Manhattan* (1989).
Maxwell, William Quentin. *Lincoln's Fifth Wheel: The Political History of the United States Sanitary Commission* (1956).
Nevins, Allan, and Milton Halsey Thomas, eds. *The Diary of George Templeton Strong* (1952).
United States Sanitary Commission. *The Sanitary Commission of the United States Army: A Succinct Narrative of its Works and Purposes* (1972).

STUART, JAMES EWELL BROWN
(1833–1864)
Confederate general

James Ewell Brown "Jeb" Stuart was born at Laurel Hill, Patrick County, Virginia, on 6 February 1833. He studied for two years at Emory and Heath College before entering West Point in 1850, from which he graduated a respectable thirteenth in a class of forty-six in 1854. Commissioned a second lieutenant, Stuart was initially assigned to the Regiment of Mounted Rifles and saw considerable service along the Texas frontier. In March 1853 he transferred to the 1st U.S. Cavalry Regiment at Fort Leavenworth and partook of peace-keeping activities throughout the "Bleeding Kansas" struggle between proslavery and abolitionist factions. In this capacity Stuart had several encounters with the notorious John Brown, whom he would meet again. He also fought in several skirmishes against the Cheyenne and at the 1857 battle of Solomon's Fork sustained a point-blank chest wound that fortunately proved superficial. In 1855 Stuart had met and married Flora Cooke, the daughter of his superior and fellow Virginian, Colonel Philip St. George Cooke. This happy event did little to ameliorate the meager existence of a junior frontier officer and Stuart, ever the opportunist, invented a device for fixing swords to belts. He was in Washington, D.C., en route to the U.S. Patent Office with this invention in October 1859, when abolitionist Brown made his famous raid on Harper's Ferry. Stuart was then dispatched to find Colonel Robert E. Lee, his former superintendent at West Point, and assisted him in suppressing the disturbance.

Returning west, Stuart advanced to captain in April 1861, just as the Civil War commenced. Unflinchingly loyal to Virginia, he quickly resigned from the army and tendered his services to the Confederacy.

Over the next three years, Stuart acquired the well-deserved reputation of a flamboyant, dashing cavalry leader, and one of the finest exponents of mounted reconnaissance in American history. In July 1861 he gained appointment as colonel of the 1st Virginia Cavalry, then attached to the army of General Joseph E. Johnston in the Shenandoah Valley. He made indelible contributions in the ensuing Bull Run campaign by carefully screening Johnston's departure from the valley and his arrival on the battlefield. During the engagement of 21 July 1861, Stuart conducted a dramatic, saber-in-hand charge that scattered some New York infantry and aided the Confederate victory. In consequence of this sterling performance, and in recognition of his ability as a cavalry drill master, he gained promotion to brigadier general in September 1861. A Confederate star was on the ascent.

Stuart spent the ensuing winter drilling and honing his troopers to a fine edge, impressing upon them his personal stamp of confidence and leadership. In the late spring and summer of 1862 he again rendered useful service throughout the Peninsula campaign against General George B. McClellan. He fought well in a succession of battles from Yorktown to Seven Pines, which culminated in the slow advance of Union forces to the very outskirts of Richmond. Robert E. Lee, who succeeded Johnston, desired to attack immediately and requested Stuart to scout McClellan's lines and report on the disposition of their right wing. Departing 12 June 1862, Stuart accomplished his mission by ascertaining that Union troops had not yet occupied the region between the Chickahominy and Totopotomoy rivers. But rather than retrace his steps, Stuart boldly exceeded orders by taking 1,200 troopers completely around McClellan's army of 105,000, completing a circuit of over 100 miles. All the while, Stuart was pursued by his father-in-law, General Cooke, but the ineptly led, indifferently mounted Union cavalry could not corner him. For the loss of one man, the Confederates took 165 prisoners, along with numerous wagons and horses. More importantly, the intelligence conveyed to Lee enabled him to attack at Mechanicsville and commence hammering the Army of the Potomac away from Richmond.

McClellan's timid performance resulted in his replacement by General John Pope. Stuart, now a twenty-eight-year-old major general commanding all the cavalry in the Army of Northern Virginia, was tasked with harassing Pope's lines of communication and possibly raiding his headquarters at Catlett's Station. This he accomplished with great dash on 22 August 1862, capturing both Pope's uniform and his dispatch book. Moreover, the Confederates now possessed positive intelligence regarding Union troop dispositions. Thus informed, Lee subsequently ordered General Thomas J. "Stonewall" Jackson's II Corps on a pincers movement that routed Pope's beleaguered forces at Second Bull Run. Stuart's startling success, the result of headstrong audacity and meticulous planning, rendered him a legendary figure in both armies.

Having driven the enemy from Virginia, Lee took the war into Northern territory by invading Maryland that September. Stuart's cavalry did invaluable service screening the army's advance at South Mountain and Antietam, where he conducted another spectacular end run around McClellan's forces. The Confederates were eventually forced back, but on 8 October 1862, Lee authorized another raid to cut McClellan's supply line at

J. E. B. Stuart (*Library of Congress*)

the Conococheage Bridge near Chambersburg, Pennsylvania. Stuart clattered off at dawn, covered forty miles without encountering opposition, and occupied the town. His men failed to destroy the iron bridge in question, but they did torch numerous machine shops and other valuable property. Three days later the Confederates trotted back to camp, after traversing nearly 200 miles and with 280 prisoners and 1,200 horses in tow.

In December 1862 Stuart formed on the flank of the Confederate line at Fredericksburg, and performed creditably in repulsing Federal attacks. On Christmas Day he departed on another raid to disrupt the supply lines of General Ambrose Burnside. His sudden descent upon Greenwood Church netted another 100 prisoners and captured the telegraph office intact. Stuart then audaciously wired Union quartermaster Montgomery C. Meigs and complained about the poor quality of Federal mules. He returned safely to camp on New Years Day, 1863, having seized 200 prisoners and twenty-five wagons, for a loss of one killed and six wounded.

Throughout the spring of 1863, Stuart performed some of the most effective scouting and reconnaissance of the Civil War. A large Union force under General Joseph Hooker had outflanked Lee at Fredericksburg by marching through a heavily forested region known as the Wilderness. Stuart was accordingly sent to appraise

the situation in the vicinity of Chancellorsville. There a brigade under General Fitzhugh Lee discovered that the right flank of the Union XI Corps was totally "in the air." This information induced Lee to order Jackson's corps again on another dangerous flank attack that succeeded brilliantly. Moreover, when Jackson and his successor, A. P. Hill, were wounded, Stuart succeeded to the command of II Corps. His handling of mixed infantry, artillery, and cavalry units was sound, and a contributing factor in the impressive Confederate victory.

Stuart had made and sustained his reputation as a dashing cavalier, and cultivated that image by sporting a flamboyant, flowing beard and a plumed hat. However, at this critical juncture supreme self-confidence clouded his better judgment. As Lee began his second invasion of the North, Stuart's cavalry was carelessly encamped in the vicinity of Brandy Station, and preoccupied with their commander's numerous and showy reviews. On 9 June 1863, a Union cavalry division under General Alfred Pleasonton surprised the Confederates in their camp and nearly drove them off. Stuart quickly rallied

Stuart's grave in Hollywood Cemetery at Richmond, Virginia, 1865 (*Library of Congress*)

his men and charged full-tilt into the fray, which developed into the largest cavalry encounter of the war. For the first time, Northern cavalry gave a competent showing, and the heretofore unbeatable gray troopers were hard pressed to keep the field. Stuart eventually prevailed and inflicted twice as many casualties as he suffered, but the deceptively easy days of 1861 and 1862 were behind him. Moreover, the former beau sabre of the South found himself roundly criticized in the press for being surprised. Stung by these remarks, Stuart determined to redeem his reputation by some kind of grand gesture in the upcoming campaign.

In late June 1863 Lee sent Stuart northward into Pennsylvania with discretionary orders to raid, provided that he relay any information as to the location of Union forces with all dispatch. Stuart, however, either deliberately or unintentionally misunderstood his instructions, and commenced another one of his publicity-oriented "rides" around the enemy. He thus remained out of touch with headquarters for several days as the Army of Northern Virginia collided with forces under General George G. Meade at Gettysburg on 1 July 1863. Stuart's indiscretion cost the Confederates dearly as Lee fought blindly, uninformed as to Union strength or dispositions. Stuart finally arrived at headquarters on the evening of 2 July, having ridden as far north as Carlisle and having accomplished little of military value. On the climactic third day of the battle, he launched several unsuccessful attacks as a diversion for the main assault on the Union center, but was repulsed by Union cavalry under George Armstrong Custer. Once Lee retreated in good order back to Virginia, Stuart skillfully covered the Confederates' withdrawal. Contemporaries and historians alike, then and now, blame the Gettysburg debacle on Lee's lack of intelligence. Only Stuart could have addressed this deficiency, and in this critical assignment he was remiss.

Throughout the fall of 1863, Stuart's cavalry was closely, but indecisively, engaged with their Union counterparts at Liberty Mills, Brandy Station, and Buckland Mills, all of which served to wear down the Confederate cavalry even further. But after Gettysburg and the harsh criticism it engendered, Stuart dutifully resolved to maintain close contact with Lee's headquarters. Throughout the opening phases of General Ulysses S. Grant's Overland campaign of 1864, Stuart's troopers functioned capably as a screening, scouting, and delaying force, sending valuable streams of information back to the commanding general. At length, an exasperated Grant directed General Philip H. Sheridan from Spotsylvania with 10,000 veteran troopers on a raid. His orders were explicit: lure Stuart out into the open and destroy him. An indecisive skirmish occurred at Todd's Tavern on 9 May 1864, but two days later Stuart confronted Sheridan's legions with half his number at Yellow Tavern. A confused fight ensued less than six miles from Richmond. The veteran Confederates were holding their own, when Stuart was mortally shot. He was painfully conveyed back to the Confederate capital that evening, where he died one day later on 12 May 1864. Lee particularly lamented the passing of this bright blade, for in his own words, Stuart "never brought me a piece of false information."

—*John C. Fredriksen*

See also Brandy Station, Battle of; Gettysburg, Battle of; Stuart's Ride Around McClellan; Yellow Tavern, Battle of.

For further reading:

Brewer, James D. *The Raiders of 1862* (1997).

Nesbitt, Mark. *Saber and Scapegoat: J. E. B. Stuart and the Gettysburg Controversy* (1994).

Rhea, Gordon C. *The Battles for Spotsylvania Court House and the Road to Yellow Tavern, May 7–12, 1864* (1997).

Thomas, Emory A. *Bold Dragoon: The Life of J. E. B. Stuart* (1988).

Trout, Robert J. *They Followed the Plume: The Story of J. E. B. Stuart and His Staff* (1993).

STUART'S DUMFRIES (VIRGINIA) RAID
(26–31 December 1862)

After the disaster to Federal arms known as the battle of Fredericksburg (11–13 December 1862) concluded, the Army of the Potomac and its commander, Ambrose E. Burnside, went into winter quarters on the north side of the Rappahannock River above Stafford, Virginia. There the Federals hoped to recover from the brutal defeat inflicted upon them just to the south of the river. The army was to be replenished and rebuilt from its supply bases situated at Aquia Creek Landing on the Potomac River. But from Aquia Creek to the army encamped in Stafford County, Virginia, lay vulnerable lines of communication that would be easy prey to Confederate disruption.

General Wade Hampton, of J. E. B. Stuart's cavalry of the Army of Northern Virginia, had proved how tenuous Union supply routes were by successfully striking them in late November and twice more in December 1862. Captured enemy horses, wagons, and prisoners were the trophies garnered from Hampton's bold, quick thrusts into the heart of the Union army's rear areas.

Stuart proposed his plan for a winter raid to General Robert E. Lee after the latter expressed interest in discovering the dispositions of Burnside's army and what that army's future intent might be—that is, was it to remain on the defensive, or once more go on the attack? Lee gave his assent to his cavalry chief's plan to use a force of 1,800 troopers and four guns to conduct a sweep of the area between Dumfries and Occoquan (about a ten-mile radius) in order to collect supplies, gather up prisoners, and generally disrupt the enemy's communica-tions between the Potomac and its army across from Fredericksburg.

Starting the raid on 26 December, Stuart and his force crossed the Rappahannock at Kelly's Ford. Camping that evening at the town of Bristersburg, Stuart divided his command into three parts and announced his plans: Fitzhugh Lee would strike eastward and capture the village of Dumfries; Wade Hampton's 600-man group was ordered to go north to Occoquan; and William Henry "Rooney" Lee's brigade of 600 troopers, accompanied by Stuart, was to head for the valley of Quantico Creek and join Fitzhugh Lee's drive into Dumfries. Stuart hoped that by his traversing and plundering this fifteen-mile area of Federal communica-tions between the Army of the Potomac and Washington, D.C., Burnside might be compelled to decamp further north and thus free northern Virginia from the Yankees.

Next day the raiders mounted up early and started on their missions. Most of 27 December was spent moving toward their objectives. It was only late in the day that Fitzhugh Lee's men encountered and took captive nine sutler's wagons and their owners. Meanwhile, Rooney Lee's column came within a mile south of Dumfries, when it collided with a small mixed force of Union infantry and cavalry. Closer to the hamlet the Confederates discovered that two Federal infantry regi-ments held the place and were ready to receive the gray visitors. Then occurred a chase and counterchase between the opposing cavalry. This ended when Stuart ordered up some of his artillery, which promptly commenced firing at, and receiving fire in return from, an enemy battery.

Late in the day Fitzhugh and his men joined Stuart before the defenses at Dumfries. The cavalry leader wanted to carry out a grand assault against the town, but was persuaded not to do so after information reached him that the garrison outnumbered his own force, and substantial stores had already been removed from the place.

The twenty-seventh also saw Wade Hampton and his men cross swords with Union forces at Occoquan. While his 2d South Carolina Regiment rushed at the enemy frontally, Hampton brought the rest of his brigade around to the southern end of the town to bag any retreating Federals. The plan failed, in part because the object of the South Carolina regiment's charge, the 17th Pennsylvania Cavalry Regiment, bolted as soon as it encountered the South Carolina troopers in the town, and thus raced past the encircling Confederates to the south before the latter could take up an interception position. For Hampton's trouble he captured a few horses, some feed, nineteen prisoners, and eight wagons. He pulled out that night in order to link up with Stuart at Cole's Store.

On 28 December, cold, frustrated, and almost empty-handed Confederate raiders rode back to Occoquan. On route, near Greenwood Church, they tangled with two regiments of Yankee cavalry out looking for Stuart. After a brief, but sharp, running fight in which the saber and revolver were freely used, the gray-jackets were able to rout the enemy and take 100 Federals captive. Occoquan was also occupied by the Rebels; the enemy camps were destroyed and much booty in the form of horses and equipage was seized. After burning what could not be carried along, Stuart's column, rejuvenated by its recent success, struck out to the north in the dark windy night.

Hitting the Orange & Alexandria Railroad at Burke's Station, Stuart sent a message to Washington, D.C., addressed to Union quartermaster general Montgomery Meigs. In this missive the Southerner complained to the Union officer that the mules the former had recently captured were of poor quality, and this made moving the captured wagons much more difficult!

From Burke's Station Stuart's raiders moved west to Fairfax Court House, Virginia. Stuart wished to take the Union garrison posted there, but realized that the strong presence of Federal troops and fortifications in the area made that project impracticable. During the twenty-ninth the gray riders moved on to Middleburg, and then, after another uneventful day, to Culpepper Court House on the thirty-first.

Major General Stuart's latest raid netted him 200 prisoners, about the same number of serviceable horses, and twenty wagonloads of equipment. The cost to his command totaled one killed, thirteen wounded, and thirteen missing. The Dumfries Raid added additional luster to "Jeb" Stuart's already considerable reputation as a consummate mounted raider, as well as a brilliant intelligence gatherer. It would also be the last such successful operation that the beau sabre of the South would engage in during the war.

—*Arnold D. Blumberg*

See also Fredericksburg, First Battle of; Hampton, Wade; Stuart, James Ewell Brown.

For further reading:
Bushong, Millard K., and M. Dean. *Fightin' Tom Rosser, C.S.A.* (1983).
McClellan, Henry B. *The Campaigns of Stuart's Cavalry* (1993).
Thomas, Emory M. *Bold Dragoon: The Life of J. E. B. Stuart* (1988).
Thomason, John. W., Jr. *Jeb Stuart* (1930).
Von Borcke, Heros. *Memoirs of the Confederate War for Independence* (1938; reprint, 1985).

STUART'S RIDE AROUND MCCLELLAN
(12–15 June 1862)

In the late spring of 1862, General George B. McClellan's enormous Union army of more than 100,000 men landed in Virginia and plodded slowly but inexorably towards the Confederate capital of Richmond. The local Southern commander, General Joseph E. Johnston, fought several defensive battles with the invaders and repeatedly gave ground, until being wounded at Seven Pines. His successor, the redoubtable Robert Edward Lee, bore a much more aggressive stamp and resolved to attack what he deemed as a cautious, hesitant McClellan. However, this action required current and accurate intelligence regarding the Union dispositions.

Before striking, Lee wished to know specifically if McClellan's forces occupied valuable ground between the Chickahominy and Totopotomoy rivers. It so happened that several days previously, and on his own initiative, Brigadier General J. E. B. Stuart dispatched his best scout, the future guerilla John S. Mosby, on a scouting mission along the south bank of the Pamunkey River. Mosby returned with information suggesting that the Union right flank was unsecured and vulnerable to attack. Lee wanted solid confirmation of such tantalizing rumors, so on 12 June 1862 he dispatched Stuart on a daring reconnaissance behind enemy lines to ascertain these facts. He also directed him to raid and disrupt Union supplies and communications, if practicable, thereby heightening McClellan's perceived insecurities. But, knowing the temperament of his youthful charge, Lee insisted that he proceed with caution. To this end, Lee also granted Stuart discretionary powers to ride around any obstacle threatening the success of his mission.

In fact, Stuart, an old acquaintance of Lee, had suggested such a move several days before and had studiously prepared himself should the contingency arrive. At two o'clock in the morning of 12 June he aroused his startled staff, declaring, "Gentlemen, in ten minutes every man must be in the saddle." Accordingly, 1,200 troopers (drawn from the 1st, 4th, and 9th Virginia Cavalry and the Jeff Davis Legion) clattered out of camp into the predawn darkness, and rode northwest from Richmond towards the North Anna River, twenty-two miles distant. The column was particularly large and well armed for a reconnaissance mission, for Stuart intended to overwhelm any rear-area detachments that he might likely encounter. The first day's movement proved uneventful, as Stuart anticipated, so before daybreak on the thirteenth his column swung eastward around McClellan's left flank. The Confederates encountered no resistance as they jogged along the Union rear area and into Hanover Court House and Haw's Shop. Passing on through Old Church, Stuart was alerted that a Union cavalry division under his father-in-law and fellow Virginian, General Philip St. George Cooke, was hot on his heels. Stuart would have liked nothing better than to try conclusions with Cooke, whom he regarded as a traitor,

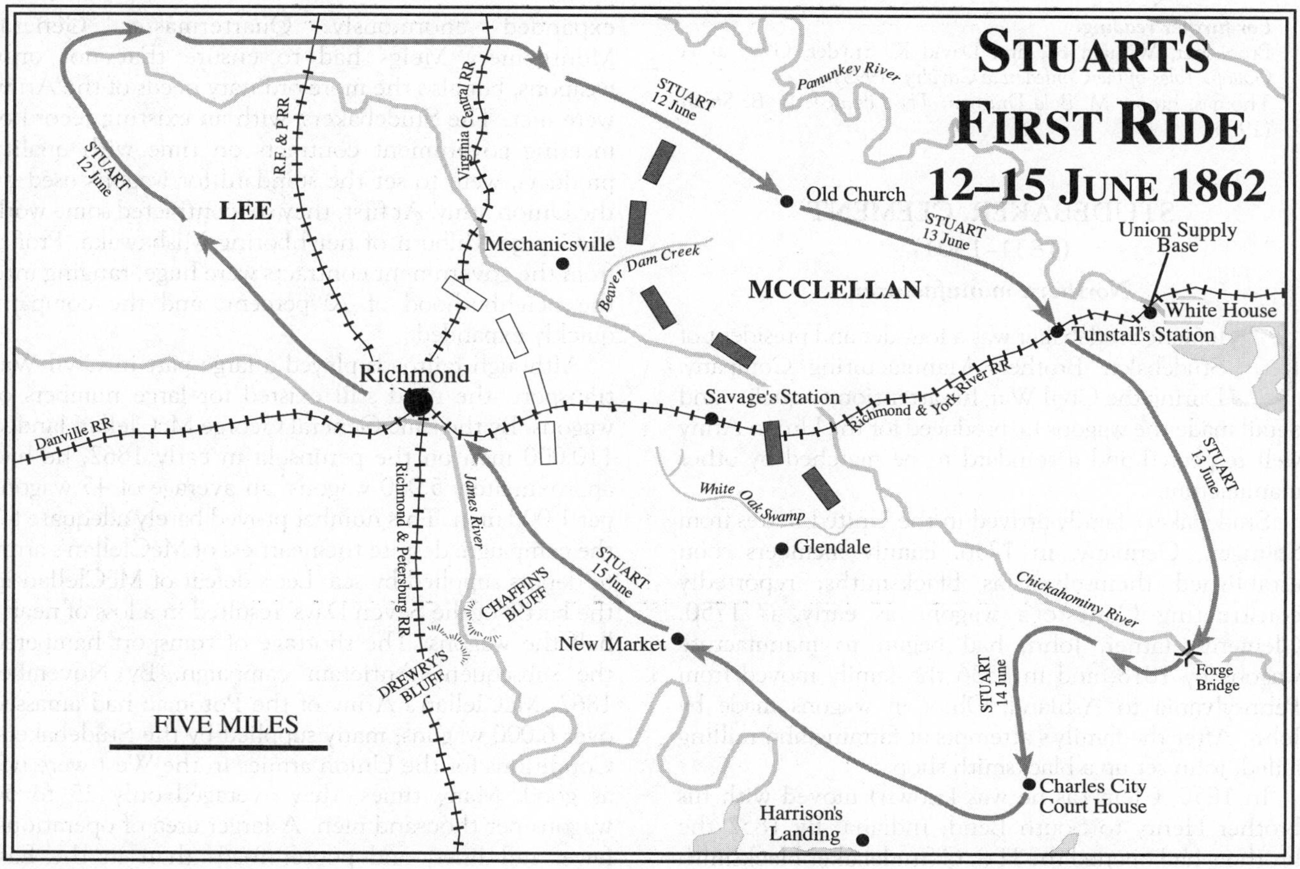

STUART'S FIRST RIDE 12–15 JUNE 1862

Map showing Stuart's route and locations including Lee, Richmond, Mechanicsville, Old Church, Union Supply Base, White House, Tunstall's Station, McClellan, Savage's Station, Glendale, Chaffin's Bluff, Drewry's Bluff, New Market, Charles City Court House, Harrison's Landing, Forge Bridge, and various railroads and rivers.

FIVE MILES

but the urgency of his mission prompted him to move on. En route there was a brief flurry of activity as the Confederates brushed aside a small detachment of the U.S. 5th Cavalry. The only fatality of this encounter, Captain William Latane of the 9th Virginia Cavalry, was subsequently enshrined in art and verse as a Southern martyr.

By the evening of the thirteenth, Stuart had reasonably concluded that McClellan's right flank was "in the air" and vulnerable to a Southern counterstroke. He urgently wished to relay this intelligence back to Lee as quickly as possible, but was loath to retrace his steps for fear of running headlong into Cooke's division. He therefore boldly—and typically for him—chose to press on and completely circle the Union army. Mosby was first ordered to scout the terrain ahead, and he reported the route clear. Stuart then galloped on to Tunstall's Station, capturing and burning numerous wagons and supply ships. His men, eager for action, even shot up a passing supply train. Alert for pursuers, Stuart then halted at Chickahominy Creek as planned, only to learn that it was flooded and impassable. Some anxious moments ensued as Stuart ordered his men to rebuild a nearby bridge, while lookouts scanned the horizon for signs of Union cavalry. These eventually appeared in

driblets, but then stood idle and watched as the gray-clad column wound its way across the Chickahominy and to safety. Under Stuart's dynamic leadership, the Confederates had spent three days behind enemy lines and covered over 100 miles without incident. Furthermore, the raiders had captured 165 prisoners and absconded with 260 mules, while completing one of the most celebrated reconnaissance raids in military history. On the morning of 15 June Stuart charged into Richmond alone, ahead of his column, and reported to Lee. The intelligence he presented allowed the Confederates to attack at Mechanicsville, the first of the Seven Days' battles, which marked the beginning of the end for McClellan's ill-fated Peninsula campaign. In retrospect, Stuart's penchant for meticulous planning and audacious execution was never more evident. His ride around the Army of the Potomac was a daring, imaginative affair, although it was greatly abetted by the timid and inept nature of Union cavalry leadership. Nonetheless, it catapulted Stuart into the pantheon of Confederate heroes, and assured his place as America's greatest cavalry leader.

—*John C. Fredriksen*

See also Mosby, John Singleton; Peninsula Campaign; Stuart, James Ewell Brown.

For further reading:
Brooksher, William R., and David K. Snyder. *Glory at A Gallop: Tales of the Confederate Cavalry* (1993).
Thomas, Emory M. *Bold Dragoon: The Life of J. E. B. Stuart* (1988).

STUDEBAKER, CLEMENT
(1831–1901)
Northern manufacturer

Clement Studebaker was a founder and president of Studebaker Brothers Manufacturing Company. During the Civil War, his attention to quality and detail made the wagons he produced for the Union Army well respected and a standard to be matched by other manufacturers.

Studebaker's family arrived in the United States from Solingen, Germany, in 1736. Family members soon established themselves as blacksmiths, reportedly constructing Conestoga wagons as early as 1750. Clement's father, John, had begun to manufacture wagons by 1818, and in 1836 the family moved from Pennsylvania to Ashland, Ohio, in wagons made by John. After the family's attempts at farming and milling failed, John set up a blacksmith shop.

In 1850, Clem (as he was known) moved with his brother Henry to South Bend, Indiana. By 1852 the brothers had opened the H & C Studebaker blacksmith shop there with capital of $68 and two sets of blacksmith tools. Henry and Clem (joined over time by their three brothers) built wagons, and when John Mohler Studebaker decided to seek his fortune in California in 1853, he and his brothers built the wagon in which John traveled. Specially designed for the trip, with extra large wheels and smaller body, the wagon exhibited a strength that became obvious as John went west. The hundreds of broken-down and abandoned wagons John saw impressed him with the need for quality and excellence in production, a lesson he brought back to South Bend in 1858.

In 1857 Henry withdrew from the partnership with Clem. The brothers had received contracts from the U.S. Army for wagons to be used to support units fighting the Mormon War of 1857–1858 in Utah. Henry was raised a devout member of the Church of the Brethren and opposed military activities. His moral position was made more difficult because the Studebakers were also selling wagons to Mormon settlers. Henry was replaced by his brother John, who had made considerable money building wheelbarrows for gold prospectors in California. He bought out Henry's share for $3,000 in 1858. With John supervising manufacturing, the Studebakers continued to build a fine reputation.

When the Civil War broke out, the Union army expanded enormously. Quartermaster General Montgomery Meigs had to ensure that not only weapons, but also the more ordinary needs of the Army were met. The Studebakers, with an existing record of meeting government contracts on time with quality products, were to set the standard for wagons used by the Union army. At first, they subcontracted some work to George Milburn of neighboring Mishawaka. Profits from the government contracts were huge, ranging into the neighborhood of 20 percent, and the company quickly expanded.

Although railroads played a large part in Civil War transport, the need still existed for large numbers of wagons. By the time General George McClellan landed 110,000 men on the peninsula in early 1862, he had approximately 5,000 wagons, an average of 45 wagons per 1,000 men. This number proved barely adequate for the campaign, despite the nearness of McClellan's army to depots supplied by sea. Lee's defeat of McClellan in the battle of the Seven Days' resulted in a loss of nearly half the wagons. The shortage of transport hampered the subsequent Antietam campaign. By November 1862, McClellan's Army of the Potomac had amassed over 6,000 wagons, many supplied by the Studebakers. Conditions for the Union armies in the West were not as good. Many times, they averaged only 25 to 30 wagons per thousand men. A larger area of operations, fewer rail lines, and poorer roads than in the East hampered logistics. Campaigns in the West were often marked by lengthy halts to build up supplies, resulting in constant demand for Studebaker wagons.

The typical Studebaker wagon, drawn by six mules, was versatile and sturdy. Many wagons first used at the battle of Bull Run in July 1861 were available for the Grand Review at the war's end. Portable forges, tools, and spare parts were often carried for field repairs. A typical load for one of Studebaker's wagons was 1,400 short rations and eight days' rations of short forage for the mules; an alternative load might be 25 boxes of small-arms ammunition. Pack mules were sometimes used to supplement the wagons for short hauls in rough country, but they could not replace the wagons.

By the end of the nineteenth century, Studebaker was the world's largest wagon manufacturer, turning out 250 wagons a day. Clement Studebaker continued as president of the corporation until his death in 1901. The first tentative moves into automobile manufacturing were taking place at Studebaker, a change that was complete by 1920. During World War I, the Studebakers again manufactured wagons, supplying thousands to the U.S. Army and Allied nations. While Studebaker did not fight on the battlefield, his wagons played a large part in the Union victory.

—*Tim J. Watts*

See also Logistics.

For further reading:
Critchlow, Donald T. "Studebaker: Wagonmaker/Automaker" (1987).
Durnbaugh, Donald F. "Studebaker and Stutz: The Evolution of Dunker Entrepreneurs" (1992).
Fox, Fred K. "John Mohler Studebaker's 1853 Overland Journal from Indiana to California" (1990).
Hagerman, Edward. "Field Transportation and Strategic Mobility in the Union Armies" (1988).

STURGIS, SAMUEL DAVIS
(1822–1889)
Union general

Samuel Davis Sturgis was born at Shippensburg, Pennsylvania, on 11 June 1822. In July 1842 he entered West Point and graduated thirty-second in his class of 1846.

Sturgis's first appointment was with the Second Dragoons as a second lieutenant. He was transferred to the First Dragoons and was captured while performing a reconnaissance near Buena Vista during the Mexican-American War. After the war, he continued his career in the West and was promoted to first lieutenant. In March of 1855 he was promoted to captain and was transferred to the 1st Cavalry. While on assignment in Fort Smith, Arkansas, in April 1861, Captain Sturgis received orders to evacuate the post and take the two companies under his command to Indian Territory. From intelligence reports, Sturgis learned that state troops were advancing on Fort Smith from Little Rock. In a letter to the assistant adjutant general of the Department of the West, Sturgis described the situation at Fort Smith: "After supplies were cut off by the State of Arkansas, the post of course became untenable and we could have occupied it in any case but a few more days. One hour after we left, two boats arrived with three hundred men and ten pieces of artillery. To have contended against this force with two companies of cavalry, and that too while the entire population of the surrounding country were ready at a moments notice to take up arms against us, could only have resulted eventually in our being taken prisoners and the loss to the government of all the arms, horses, means of transportation &c, at the post."

A month later, in May, Arkansas officially joined the Confederate States of America and Sturgis accepted a promotion to major. In August of 1861, he was reassigned to the 4th U.S. Cavalry and was cited for gallant and meritorious service after the battle of Wilson's Creek. Sturgis received the brevet rank of lieutenant colonel after he took command of Federal forces after the death of General Nathaniel Lyon.

Sturgis went to Washington, D.C., and served in the defense of the city until he was sent to support General John Pope in the battle of Second Bull Run in August 1862. He received a citation for gallant and meritorious service and the brevet rank of colonel. He suffered a delay in reaching the action at Second Bull Run and made his now-famous remark, "I don't care for John Pope one pinch of owl dung."

He fought with distinction in the Maryland campaign in the fall of 1862, received a citation for gallant and meritorious service, and was brevetted to brigadier general for his participation at South Mountain. He commanded a division at Antietam, where one of his brigades carried the famous Burnside's Bridge. Sturgis again proved himself in December 1862 at Fredericksburg, where he received a citation and was brevetted to major general.

In 1863 he went west and served as chief of cavalry of the Department of the Ohio. In June of 1864, his good fortune changed. General William T. Sherman ordered Sturgis to protect his vulnerable line of supply while he concentrated his efforts on Atlanta. In addition, Sturgis had orders to seek out and destroy the command of Confederate general Nathan Bedford Forrest, who had been causing Sherman many problems. The two commanders met at Brice's Cross Roads in Mississippi on 10 June 1864. Sturgis had 8,500 men to Forrest's 3,500. Forrest engaged Sturgis's cavalry before infantry could be brought up in support. The infantry made a forced march but arrived exhausted and failed to advance.

An orderly withdrawal soon became a confused rout, with Forrest pursuing Sturgis for twenty-five miles, inflicting 2,612 casualties while sustaining only 493. The tragic defeat for Sturgis haunted him for the rest of the Civil War, while it solidified the reputation of Forrest as a tactical genius.

After the war, Sturgis went back to his regular rank of lieutenant colonel. He was promoted to colonel and was transferred to the 7th Cavalry in 1869. As colonel of the 7th, his lieutenant colonel was George Custer. Sturgis and Custer shared a mutual disdain for each other. Sturgis's oldest son, James, was a second lieutenant in the 7th Cavalry and died in battle with Custer at the Little Big Horn.

Sturgis retired in 1886 and died 28 September 1889 in St. Paul, Minnesota. He is buried in Arlington National Cemetery.

—*Thomas A. Wing*

See also Antietam, Battle of; Brice's Cross Roads, Battle of; Bull Run, Second Battle of; Forrest, Nathan Bedford; Fort Smith, Arkansas; South Mountain, Battle of; Wilson's Creek, Missouri.

For further reading:
Eisenhower, John S. D. *So Far from God: The U.S. War with Mexico 1846–1848* (1989).
Heitman, Francis B. *Historical Register and Dictionary of the U.S. Army* (1903).
Sears, Stephen W. *Landscape Turned Red: The Battle of Antietam* (1983).

SUFFOLK, VIRGINIA, SIEGE OF
(April–May 1863)

By the spring of 1863, the supply problems faced by the Confederate armed forces in Virginia had reached critical proportions. General Robert E. Lee faced enormous shortages that would have to be addressed before the 1863 campaign season opened. President Jefferson Davis and Secretary of War James Seddon also worried that Petersburg and Richmond lay open to attack from the southeast, particularly once Union major general Ambrose Burnside brought the IX Corps to Newport News in March. Southeastern Virginia's largely untapped resources would provide the supplies Lee's army desperately needed, while the Confederate capture or containment of the Union garrisons in the region would protect Richmond from threats from that quarter.

With these missions in mind, General Lee agreed to detach the divisions of Major Generals John Bell Hood and George E. Pickett from the Army of Northern Virginia. Subsequently, Lee reassigned the corps commander, Lieutenant General James Longstreet, putting him in charge of the Department of Virginia and North Carolina.

Throughout March and early April, Longstreet, Lee's "Old War Horse" watched developments in North Carolina with a keen interest. Major General Daniel H. Hill struck the Union garrisons at Washington and New Bern, drawing substantial supplies from the nearby farms. Longstreet contemplated a similar move of his own against the Union-held town of Suffolk, Virginia. By 10 April he was prepared to march with some 20,000 battle-hardened veterans.

The Federals in Suffolk had constructed elaborate defenses that were well covered by artillery and manned by a similar number of troops under Brigadier General John James Peck. Longstreet hoped to move swiftly enough to capture the town, but the Federals remained alert. This state of readiness and a lack of assistance from the Confederate naval department encouraged Longstreet to content himself with holding the Union garrison at bay while his wagons scoured the region for supplies.

By 11 April, Longstreet had his command before Suffolk. He rested the right flank of his command under Pickett on the Dismal Swamp and the left under Hood and Major General Samuel French on the Nansemond River. The latter, whom Longstreet had ordered to accompany him to Suffolk, was to serve as the commander and coordinator for the Confederate artillery. French employed artillery along the Nansemond River in an effort to blockade that avenue of communication and reinforcement. However, at no time were the Confederates able to close the rail lines from Suffolk into Portsmouth and Norfolk. Although the operation would come to be known as the "Siege of Suffolk," it was not a siege in the strictest sense of the word.

Nevertheless, the Confederate batteries on the Nansemond proved more than a nuisance for the Federals. Peck hoped to supplement his defense of the town with lightly armed converted steamers. These vessels were capable of moving into the narrow upper Nansemond, but they were vulnerable to artillery and small arms fire. Proof of this came on 16 April, when the Confederates severely disabled the Union gunboat *Mount Washington*. Southern artillery fire severely damaged the small flotilla and prompted acting Rear Admiral Samuel P. Lee to be more wary of using the craft in the river.

Countermoves by Union brigadier general George W. Getty helped to secure the river flank and silence the pesky Confederate batteries. Getty ordered the construction of masked batteries across the river from the Norfleet House battery, which had pulverized the tiny Union fleet on the 16th. Employing one of these batteries as bait to convince the Confederates to expose their positions, he used the other to silence the Southern artillery position. Then, in a cooperative venture with the navy, he helped to mastermind a successful assault against the Confederate earthwork known as Fort Huger. Carried out on 19 April, the surprise assault led to the capture of Captain Robert M. Stribling's Fauquier Artillery. The loss of five artillery pieces and 130 prisoners embarrassed the Confederates and led to recriminations among the infantry units that were supposed to be supporting the positions.

Much of the fighting that followed amounted to probes, sharpshooting, and shelling. Both sides constructed or improved elaborate defenses that made frontal assaults unlikely. Reconnaissances in force characterized the heaviest fighting between the antagonists, with Union brigadier general Michael Corcoran surprising the troops on Pickett's front on the 26th. At the very least, Pickett's mind was with his sweetheart, LaSalle Corbell, who was staying with family on the opposite side of the Confederate line. But, the Southerners rallied and succeeded in driving the Federals back.

The situation changed when Union general Joseph Hooker shook the Army of the Potomac into motion. General Lee immediately ordered Longstreet to disengage at Suffolk and return to central Virginia, but Longstreet's wagons were scattered widely throughout the region. It would take time for him to bring them back and put them on the road to Petersburg safely. Despite the odds against him, Lee authorized "Old Peter" to do so and return as quickly as circumstances would permit.

On 1 May, Union probes increased as Peck sought to detect evidence of a Confederate retreat. This assault, and a subsequent three-pronged operation on 3 May, demonstrated that a strong Confederate presence still existed at Suffolk. But that presence ended on the 4th with a phased withdrawal of Longstreet's forces. Despite Union efforts to detect a retreat, the Southerners covered their movements well, getting across the Blackwater River with only minimal harassment.

Longstreet hastened to Richmond, while his troops marched to the railroad and boarded trains for the remainder of their journey. However, these exertions were not enough for Longstreet's veterans to reach the Army of Northern Virginia and the battle of Chancellorsville, but the supplies the men had gathered enabled Lee to launch a second invasion of the North.

Casualties in Longstreet's Suffolk campaign were approximately 900 for the Confederates and 260 for the Federals. In the end, the lesser-known Union generals acquitted themselves better than their more popularly regarded opponents. Ironically, within two months after Longstreet's withdrawal, the Federals pulled up the rails, pulled down their defenses, and pulled back to positions nearer Portsmouth and Norfolk. Suffolk would remain a no-man's land subject to raids and expeditions from both sides for the remainder of the war.

—Brian S. Wills

See also Fort Huger/Hill's Point.
For further reading:

Cormier, Steven A. *The Siege of Suffolk* (1989).
Hobbs, O. Kermit, Jr. *Storm over Suffolk* (1979).
U.S. Naval War Records Department. *Official Records of the Union and Confederate Navies in the War of the Rebellion* (1894–1922).
U.S. War Department. *The War of the Rebellion: A Compilation of the Official Records of the Union and Confederate Armies* (1880–1901).

SULTANA

On 27 April 1865, the steamboat *Sultana* exploded and sank in the Mississippi River near Memphis, Tennessee, causing the greatest marine disaster in U.S. history. Approximately 1,700 people, mostly discharged Union soldiers, lost their lives on a frigid spring night when boilers aboard the overcrowded steamer exploded. April 1865 brought turmoil in America with General Lee's surrender, President Lincoln's assassination, and John Wilkes Booth's death. As a result, the *Sultana* tragedy was given few headlines in America's influential newspapers.

Launched from Cincinnati, Ohio, in January 1863, the side-wheeled steamer was named *Sultana* meaning a sultan's wife, sister, or mother. It was considered one of the best steamers of its time with its new lightweight tubular boilers. The boat measured 260 feet in length and had the capacity to carry 1,000 tons while trimming only 34 inches of water; thus making it ideal for travel on the Mississippi, Ohio, and Tennessee rivers. It provided accommodations for 376 passengers including crew, which was the *Sultana*'s legal capacity.

Like many boats during the Civil War, the *Sultana* came under fire. Twice in 1863, Rebel forces fired at the boat, causing heavy damage to its upper works. The Union ironclad *Eastport* also fired upon the *Sultana* later that year on the Mississippi River. As the Union began to seize more of the Mississippi River Valley, the *Sultana* began to carry troops, supplies, and cargo for the Federals.

On 21 April 1865, the *Sultana* departed from New Orleans with 100 passengers and headed north on the Mississippi River. As the boat steadily moved upriver, a *Sultana* engineer noticed a leaking boiler and sought out a boilermaker in Vicksburg, Mississippi, to repair the problem on 23 April. The boilermaker, R. G. Taylor, told Captain J. Cass Mason that two sheets on the boiler had to be replaced. Concerned about time and money, Captain Mason told Taylor to patch the boiler and promised to finish the repairs once he reached St. Louis. Taylor disagreed with Mason, but made the patch for the *Sultana* anyway.

Owners of the *Sultana*, which included Captain Mason, anxiously awaited the layover in Vicksburg. In Vicksburg, they hoped to find former Union prisoners of war from Cahaba and Andersonville prisons because a government contract offered boats five dollars per enlisted soldier and ten dollars per officer to take them back north. Even though there were two steamboats docked at Vicksburg, Captain Mason and other *Sultana* officers lobbied prison officials to let their steamboat take all the soldiers. The tactic worked. The *Sultana* left the dock on the evening of 24 April 1865 with approximately 2,100 troops, 200 civilians, and cargo, more than six times its legal carrying capacity. The former prisoners, weakened from disease, dysentery, and malnutrition, were cramped together but in good spirits because the war had ended, and they were only a few days from reaching their homes.

On the evening of 26 April, the *Sultana* reached Memphis, Tennessee, to unload cargo, and then crossed the river to Arkansas to buy coal. Soon afterward, the boat slowly moved against the stream at 1:00 A.M. despite continued boiler problems and a strong current. Meanwhile, the Mississippi River rose to flood stage from spring rain and levees and dikes ruined by the war.

Seven miles north of Memphis at 2:00 A.M., the *Sultana* swung around a bend and began to labor through Paddy's Hen and Chicken Islands. An explosion instantly tore through the decks above the boilers. Red-hot shrapnel and steam from the boilers killed or maimed scores of passengers instantly. The eruption hurled many people into the air and out into the frigid river. Passengers threw doors, shutters, mattresses, bales of hay, and anything else buoyant overboard. Few life preservers, only one lifeboat, the flood conditions, dark-

The *Sultana* (*Library of Congress*)

ness, and weakened passengers made the chances of survival slim.

The explosion was audible in Memphis, but it took two hours for help to arrive. A steamboat heading downriver and boats from Memphis went to help after hearing the screams and seeing the flames. But for most, it was too late. While rescuers attempted to save people still clinging to makeshift rafts or treetops, they saw the river full of dead bodies floating downstream. Boats searched for survivors all morning but stopped looking by midday. Of the estimated 2,300 passengers, only 600 survived. The rest died in the explosion, drowned in the dangerous currents, or died soon after their rescue.

On 30 April 1865, Secretary of War Edwin Stanton created a board of inquiry to investigate the *Sultana* disaster. Rumors circulated that a Confederate had placed a torpedo in a lump of coal during the refueling in Arkansas, but nothing was proved. The board received testimony from surviving crew, passengers, and steamboat experts, but their reports only shifted blame from one person to another. Without conclusive evidence, the board decided that insufficient water in the boilers created the explosion, and that overcrowding did not cause the catastrophe. No individual was blamed for the tragedy, and no one knew definitively what caused the boiler malfunction.

With the nation's mind focused on the closing scenes of the Civil War, little attention was given to the *Sultana* tragedy. The passengers who were lucky enough to survive formed the *Sultana* Survivor Association, which met every 27 April. More people died in the *Sultana* disaster than did on the *Titanic* 47 years later, yet the tragic story remains largely overlooked due to the dramatic events at the end of the war.

—*Nathan R. Meyer*

See also Prisoners of War.
For further reading:
Elliott, James W. *Transport to Disaster* (1962).
Potter, Jerry O. *The Sultana Tragedy: America's Greatest Maritime Disaster* (1992).
Salecker, Gene Eric. *Disaster on the Mississippi: The Sultana Explosion, April 27, 1865* (1996).
Walker, John L. *Cahaba Prison and the Sultana Disaster* (1910).

SUMNER, CHARLES
(1811–1874)
U.S. senator

Charles Sumner was born to Charles Pinckney Sumner, a lawyer and Harvard graduate, and Relief Jacob Sumner on 6 January 1811 in Boston, Massachusetts. Attending the elite Boston Latin School

(1821–1826), Sumner was influenced in his abolitionist views by classmates such as Wendell Phillips. At age fifteen, failing to receive an appointment to West Point, which accounted for his antimilitarist sentiments, he entered Harvard College. At Harvard, he developed a strong interest in subjects like literature, law, debating, and history. On 25 August 1830 he received his B.A. In 1831 he entered Harvard Law School, where he came under the influence of the noted jurist Joseph Story. Upon graduation in January 1834, he entered into private practice. Finding it not to his liking, he devoted himself to the academic side of law. He regularly lectured at Harvard Law, wrote frequently for the *American Jurist,* and reviewed and revised numerous legal texts. During the flowering of New England Transcendentalism, he developed close relationships with Francis Lieber and William Ellery Channing. From 1837 to 1840 he decided to leave his practice and travel in Europe. He visited France, Great Britain, Italy, and Germany.

Time away from home permitted Sumner the opportunity to consider entering reform causes. When he returned to the United States in 1844 he spoke out against the manufacturing Whig lobby. He allied himself with a young faction, the Conscience Whigs. He also engaged in school and prison reform. Sumner's political prominence took shape when he delivered a stirring speech, "True Grandeur of Nations" during Boston's Independence Day celebration in 1845. In this speech he criticized war as degrading and wasteful of resources. He insisted that West Point should be abolished, nations should cease their military spending, and all funds should be diverted to educational and charitable causes. As a member of the Conscience Whigs, he openly criticized the Mexican-American War as a plot to promote the extension of slavery into the Western territories. His antiwar sentiments strengthened in this decade. In 1849 he addressed the annual meeting of the American Peace Society, making a vigorous plea for a "Congress of Nations" to adjudicate international disputes.

It was his criticisms of the Mexican-American War that led to his cooperation with nonresistant abolitionists like fellow New Englander William Lloyd Garrison. As the traditional party affiliations split over the slavery issue, dissident Whigs formed a Free-Soil coalition and elected Sumner to the U.S. Senate in 1851. In the Senate, Sumner's electrifying speeches against the evils of slavery such as "Freedom National" (26 August 1852), "Appeal of the Independent Democrats" (22 January 1854), and "Crime Against Kansas" (19–20 May 1856) netted him a supportive Northern audience. At the same time, these speeches angered his Southern colleagues. His 1856 speech so infuriated South Carolina congressman Preston Brooks that he attacked Sumner with a cane. Sumner spent the next three years recuperating away from the Senate.

Returning in 1859 Sumner resumed his attacks on slavery. On 4 June 1860 he delivered "The Barbarism of Slavery" and on 6 October 1862 he publicly supported the Civil War as a noble cause in his speech, "The Proclamation of Emancipation: Its Policy and Necessity as a War Measure for the Suppression of the Rebellion." Throughout the war Sumner insisted that it was being fought to abolish slavery, not to preserve the Union. He continually urged Abraham Lincoln to emancipate slaves in all states, not just in the seceded states, and called for stiff readmission requirements for the former Confederate states.

During the early years of Reconstruction, Sumner sought to secure the equality of civil rights for the former slaves. It was Sumner who led the Senate to include the requirements for "readmission" of the seceded states as a constitutional guarantee for equal suffrage for whites and blacks. Sumner was also largely responsible for Andrew Johnson's impeachment trial. Sumner regarded impeachment as a political rather than judicial proceeding. He voted for conviction, and his opinion was the longest and most bitter of those presented. During the heated Congressional debates on Reconstruction, at age fifty-five, he married a young widow, Mrs. Alice Mason Hooper, on 17 October 1866. The marriage failed, and they were divorced on 10 May 1873.

During the Civil War, Sumner had been appointed chairman of the Senate Foreign Relations Committee. He took his job seriously and served until 1871. Throughout the war years he kept a cautious eye on Louis Napoleon's expansionist aims in Mexico and criticized British neutrality ("Our Foreign Relations," 10 September 1863). After the war he delivered a speech, "Claims on England—Individual and National" (13 April 1869) in executive session in which he advocated rejection of the Johnson-Clarendon Treaty aimed at settling the *Alabama* claims. In 1871 he suffered his greatest political defeat. On 23 December, he delivered a speech entitled, "Naboth's Vineyard," opposing the annexation of Santo Domingo. His blocking the treaty in the Foreign Relations Committee so angered President Ulysses S. Grant that he indirectly engineered his removal as chairman by a vote of 26 to 21.

Sumner continued his senatorial duties despite this setback. He devoted his remaining years to championing civil rights for the freedmen and calling for the establishment of an academy of arts and letters. Learned, independent in thought and action, meticulous in work habits, and committed to peace and justice, Sumner worked in the Senate until the last day of his life. After returning home on 10 March 1874, he was felled by a heart attack. He died the next day. His body lay in state in the Capitol's rotunda and later was removed for burial in Cambridge, Massachusetts.

—*Charles F. Howlett*

See also Brooks, Preston Smith; Congress, U.S.; Emancipation Proclamation; Garrison, William Lloyd; Kansas.

For further reading:
Donald, David Herbert. *Charles Sumner and the Coming of the Civil War* (1960).
———. *Charles Sumner and the Rights of Man* (1970).
Edward, Gambill. "Who Were the Senate Radicals?" *Civil War History* (1965).
Pierce, Edward L., ed. *Memoir and Letters of Charles Sumner* (1877–1894).
Williams, T. Harry. *Lincoln and the Radicals* (1941).

SUMNER, EDWIN VOSE
(1797–1863)
Union general

A veteran of forty-one years when the Civil War erupted, Edwin Sumner brought ample experience to the Union army. Born in Boston, Massachusetts, he joined the U.S. Army in 1819 and held a variety of postings in the Louisiana Purchase prior to duty in the Mexican-American War in 1846. He served under Stephen W. Kearny in the capture of Santa Fe and under Winfield Scott in the conquest of Mexico City. During the latter campaign, he earned his nickname "bull head" after a musket ball bounced off his skull during the battle of Cerro Gordo.

During the 1850s, he policed the tense situation between proslavery and antislavery forces in the Territory of Kansas, at one point dismissing the Free Soil legislature in Lawrence at the point of the bayonet. He also directed raids against the Cheyenne into the plains of Colorado, then part of the Territory of Kansas. He also survived a court-martial, which culminated a ten-year-long feud with William S. Harney, in no small part because of the intervention of Winfield Scott for Sumner.

In 1861, Sumner escorted President-elect Lincoln from Springfield, Illinois, to Harrisburg, Pennsylvania, and was chagrined that he was not allowed to ensure Lincoln's safe arrival into Washington, D.C. Lincoln was persuaded that a surreptitious entry was safer. To assuage this affront to Sumner's honor, Lincoln had him promoted to brigadier general and made commander of the Department of the Pacific. In that capacity, he helped hold California and the Nevada Territory for the Union.

In the fall of 1861, Scott and Sumner made plans for an invasion of Texas by landing in Mazatlán, Mexico, and marching toward San Antonio. Sumner preferred to invade through Guaymas, basing his preference on better roads and a shorter distance. Military exigencies in the East led to Sumner's being reassigned and the aborting of the Texas invasion.

In March 1862, Sumner assumed command of II Corps of the Army of the Potomac, then commanded by George B. McClellan. McClellan had not wanted this configuration of his army, which was forced upon him by Lincoln. McClellan preferred to reward his generals with positions based on their battlefield performance.

Sumner's first combat duty as a corps commander came during the Peninsula campaign at the battle of Williamsburg on 5 May 1862. New to directing large numbers of troops, he was slow in reinforcing Joseph Hooker. But unlike his commanding general, Sumner was a fighter. At the battle of Fair Oaks, he ordered his division across the swollen Chickahominy River to aid troops under Samuel P. Heintzelman and Erasmus D. Keyes. Told by an engineer that crossing the two flooded bridges was impossible, he responded, "Impossible? Sir, I tell you I can cross." His courage and fighting spirit led him to oppose McClellan's withdrawal from the gates of Richmond to the James River. His fortitude won him promotion to brevet major general and then to major general of volunteers.

Construing battle in the East as a cavalry charge against nomadic Indians, Sumner often led his troops into battle, which he did at the Peach Orchard during the Seven Days' battles and again at Antietam. There he led John Sedgwick's division deep into Thomas J. "Stonewall" Jackson's line until it was exposed to enfilading fire. Indeed, Sumner's bull-headed determination to engage the enemy resulted in his corps' sustaining 5,138 of the 11,657 total casualties suffered by the Union in that battle.

After Lincoln's removal of McClellan, Sumner became commander of the Right Grand Division of the Army of the Potomac under Ambrose E. Burnside. He directed the assault across the Rappahannock River against James Longstreet's corps, which was defending Marye's Heights behind Fredericksburg. Sumner's Right Grand Division absorbed 5,444 of the 12,653 Union casualties. Although other general officers considered mutiny, Sumner remained loyal to his commander, even after the disastrous "Mud March."

In this turbulent atmosphere, Sumner asked to be relieved and was reassigned to the Department of the West. He died in Syracuse, New York, on 21 March 1863, before he could assume his new command.

The prewar army had not prepared Sumner for combat on a large scale, and his career in the Army of the Potomac reflects some of his limitations. Yet, at a time when President Lincoln was desperate for fighting generals, no one could find fault with Sumner's courage. If he waged war in the East in the manner of a dragoon captain on the frontier, one could not fault his fighting zeal, and, as Bruce Catton noted, "Worse men have worn a Major General's stars."

—*Edward R. Crowther*

See also Antietam, Battle of; Fair Oaks/Seven Pines, Battle of; Fredericksburg, First Battle of; Seven Days, Battle of the.

General Edwin V. Sumner (*fourth from left*) and staff at Warrenton, Virginia, 13 November 1862 (*Library of Congress*)

For further reading:
Catton, Bruce. *The Army of the Potomac: Glory Road* (1952).
Stanley, F. E. V. *Sumner: Major General United States Army (1797–1863)* (1969).
Utley, Robert M. *Frontiersmen in Blue: The United States Army and the Indian, 1848–1865* (1967).

SUMTER, CSS

Originally intending to outfit a small fleet of privateers to seize Union merchant ships, the Confederacy had its plans thwarted when Great Britain closed its ports to prize cases for the duration of the Civil War. With other European nations following suit and the Union blockade guarding Southern ports, the Confederacy was forced to destroy all captured Union merchant vessels, and the commerce-raider became the South's primary economic weapon.

The first Confederate raider to take to the seas in June 1861 was the CSS *Sumter*, commanded by Commander Raphael Semmes. Originally constructed as a fast passenger/cargo ship named *Habana*, the *Sumter* was not an ideal commerce, raider. Its armament of an eight-inch pivot gun in its bow and four thirty-pounders on the broadsides was enough to subdue unarmed merchant ships but was inadequate against virtually any Union warship it was likely to meet. Also, having been designed to run between Havana and New Orleans, the *Sumter* could carry only enough coal to steam for eight days, making the ship dangerously reliant on friendly or neutral ports for fuel.

Despite the ship's shortcomings, Semmes was determined to try to use it as a raider. Slipping out of New Orleans when the Union blockading ship *Brooklyn* was away investigating potential blockade runners, Semmes headed for the southern coast of Cuba, seizing six Union merchant vessels along the way (another was destroyed and another was used to dispatch messages to the Confederate government). Towed into the prize court at Cienfuegos, Cuba, the Union prizes were soon returned to their crews after Spain asserted its neutrality and refused to permit adjudication of the prizes. Denied a friendly reception in Cuba, *Sumter* headed for the coast of Brazil, coaling at Curaçao, Suriname, and Trinidad along the way. U.S. diplomatic missions at every location attempted to deny coal to the *Sumter*, delaying its progress. Also, the Union warship *Powhatan* under the command of Captain David D. Porter had intercepted Semmes's dispatch ship, knew of his whereabouts, and was soon in pursuit.

Tipped off to the presence of the *Powhatan*, Semmes fled from Brazil and made for European waters, destroying several Union merchantmen in the process. Unfortunately, the arduous journey had nearly wrecked the *Sumter*'s machinery. The *Sumter* had not been built for extended cruising, and it required extensive repairs. Semmes sailed for Cadiz, Spain, hoping to mend his ship in a neutral port. The Spanish denied Semmes docking rights, however, and Semmes had to flee to the only friendly port in the area, the British enclave at Gibraltar. Not long after *Sumter* sailed into Gibraltar in January 1862, the Union warships *Kearsarge* and *St. Louis* arrived to take up monitoring positions.

Semmes realized he was in an impossible position. Gibraltar did not have the facilities to repair his ship; parts and supplies from the Confederacy were a faint hope; he could not hope to fight the Union warships that were watching his every move; and his restive and

unpaid crew was on the verge of mutiny. Balanced against the destruction of eighteen Union merchant vessels, Semmes decided to abandon the *Sumter*. The crewmen were paid their back wages and prize money, the ship was put up for sale, and Semmes and his officers booked passage on a British ship for the trip back to the South.

Although it was not the most successful Confederate raider, the *Sumter* was important for several reasons. First, the ship was the Confederate test case to determine what rights and privileges the Europeans would grant to Southern raiders. Second, the *Sumter* demonstrated that a relatively inexpensive commerce-raider could reap huge advantages by destroying Union commerce valued at several times its own worth. Next, the *Sumter* showed that commerce-raiders were extremely difficult to find and were therefore survivable. Lastly, the cruise of the *Sumter* demonstrated that Raphael Semmes was an outstanding officer well suited to the task of hunting Union merchantmen. Promoted to captain, Semmes was given command of a new raider, the *Alabama*, which would plague the Union economy to a much greater extent than the *Sumter* until it was eventually destroyed in 1864.

—*Steven J. Ramold*

See also *Alabama*, CSS; *Kearsarge*, USS; Porter, David Dixon; Semmes, Raphael.

For further reading:

Fowler, William M., Jr. *Under Two Flags: The American Navy in the Civil War* (1990).

Semmes, Raphael. *Memoirs of Service Afloat* (1869; reprint, 1987).

Spencer, Warren F. *Raphael Semmes: The Philosophical Mariner* (1997).

Summersell, Charles G. *The Cruise of the C.S.S. Sumter* (1965).

SUPREME COURT, U.S.

Beginning with Chief Justice John Marshall's contention that the power to determine constitutionality "is the very essence of judicial duty," the new U.S. Supreme Court established the concept that the American government is one of laws, not of men. In his seminal 1803 *Marbury v. Madison* decision, Marshall defined the power of the Court to declare not only the acts of Congress unconstitutional but the acts of the various state legislatures as well. But the ultimate power of the Court remained untested. Could it survive an extralegal emergency like the Civil War, one that it helped to create with the incendiary 1857 *Dred Scott v. John F. A. San[d]ford* decision? The Civil War proved to be such a test. The Court demonstrated that it could survive as an equal of the other two branches of government and that the United States was a nation based on laws and not personalities. Even during the darkest hours of the war, during the time of mass suspensions of indi-

vidual rights, as exemplified in *Ex parte Merryman* and *Ex parte Milligan*, the Supreme Court continued to advocate the preeminence of the rule of law and the prerogative of judges to "do that which shall be fit for a judge to do," as legal scholar Edward Coke later explained, in checking the ambitions, vagaries, and excesses of politicians.

The independent tone and direction of the early Supreme Court, established during Chief Justice Marshall's tenure between 1801 and 1835, proved more elusive in the years between 1836 and 1864. Marshall's successor, Maryland native Roger B. Taney, had a less secure intellectual grasp on constitutional intent. At the same time, the growth in male suffrage, as evidenced by the extension of voting rights to all white adult males, the development of sectionalism, the split between the various regions of the country, the festering controversy over federalism and states' rights as evidenced by the nullification controversy, and even the increase in industrialization and the growing gap between rich and poor proved to be difficult issues for the Court to assimilate. As a result, the Taney Court drifted into politics in the years before the Civil War, at times dangerously so. In response to the rise of egalitarianism, antebellum judicial theorists developed formalism, the concept that judicial decisions should be based on abstract, general rules of law rather than an evaluation of fairness in individual cases. The Marshall Supreme Court demonstrated formalism in many of its decisions, but the Taney Court was less rigid and became more involved in judicial intervention, legislating from the bench.

The most notorious example of the Taney Court's drift was a case that future Chief Justice Charles Evans Hughes called one of the two most grievous "self-inflicted wounds" in the history of the Supreme Court. It was also a deciding factor in the Civil War, the nudge that pushed many Northerners from dislike toward disgust of slavery. The 1857 *Scott v. San[d]ford* decision involved a Missouri slave named Dred Scott, whose owner, a U.S. Army surgeon, had taken him to live in nonslave Illinois and the free territory of Wisconsin. Scott filed suit in federal court claiming he was entitled to freedom because he had lived in a free state and territory. The Court's 7–2 decision, written by Chief Justice Taney, held that the federal court system did not have jurisdiction to hear the case because African-Americans, free or not, were not citizens of the United States. Blacks, the former slave owner Taney wrote, had been "regarded as beings of an inferior order, so far inferior that they had no rights which the white man was bound to respect" at the time of the adoption of the Constitution.

The decision also held that Scott's residence in what had originally been part of the Louisiana Territory did not entitle him to freedom because the Missouri Compromise of 1820, which had banned slavery in the Louisiana Purchase north of latitude 36° 30', was unconstitutional.

The latter ruling became the second time the Court declared an act of Congress unconstitutional, but it involved a critical and carefully crafted piece of legislation on national policy, a major public issue in contrast to *Marbury*. Taney's legal rationale involved an important constitutional principle, due process, which guaranteed that no citizen should be denied his or her legal rights. "An act of Congress which deprives a citizen of the United States of his liberty or property," Taney wrote, the latter in reference to the slave owner, not Scott, "who had committed no offence against the laws, could hardly be dignified with the name of due process of law." The effect was that Congress had no power to ban slavery from any territory because it would deny slave owners their rights. Subsequent legal scholars have determined that the Court could have taken a more narrow view of the case, leaving determinations about slaves to the individual states. But Taney, who was then nearing the end of his life, and the majority Southern contingent on the Court, saw *Scott v. San[d]ford* as an opportunity to strike a blow for the South and their Democratic Party by invalidating the detested Missouri Compromise.

While Southerners rejoiced at the unexpected outcome of the case, the North was dumbfounded. Abolitionist and *New York Tribune* editor Horace Greeley declared that the decision was "entitled to just so much moral weight as it would be the judgment of a majority of those congregated in any Washington barroom." New Hampshire senator John Parker Hale, the first abolitionist elected to Congress, declared that "If the opinion of the Supreme Court be true, it makes the immortal authors of the Declaration of Independence liars before God and hypocrites before the world." U.S. Senate candidate Abraham Lincoln promised that "we shall do what we can to have [the Supreme Court] overrule this." Lincoln was half right. Congress and President Lincoln, not the Supreme Court, ignored *Scott v. San[d]ford* in 1861 when they banned slavery from all territories and freed some 2,000 slaves living in the District of Columbia, and Lincoln eventually extended freedom to all slaves in areas under rebellion in his Emancipation Proclamation. Instead of enhancing the public perception of the Supreme Court, *Scott v. San[d]ford* heightened the sense of crisis in the years before the Civil War and strengthened the forces of extremism in American politics.

The most serious threat to the Constitution came during the early days of the Civil War. President Lincoln assumed a number of unprecedented presidential powers in the wake of Fort Sumter, involving wholesale arrests without warrants, detentions without trial, imprisonments without convictions, and the suppression of newspapers. But his most serious breach of the Constitution was to suspend the writ of habeas corpus, the obligation of the government to produce a suspect in open court. He and Chief Justice Taney clashed over the issue in *Ex parte Merryman*, decided in 1861. The case involved a civilian secessionist who was arrested and held without trial by the Union army. Taney's decision, sharply condemning the suspension of Merryman's right of habeas corpus, was largely ignored by the military during the war. Yet Merryman was freed a year later, and Taney's condemnation of arbitrary military power in the face of individual liberties was a remarkable restatement of the principles of the Declaration of Independence. Lincoln did not relish the powers he had seized. "I am a patient man," he wrote in an 1862 letter, "always willing to forgive on the Christian terms of repentance; and also give ample time for repentance. Still I must save this government if possible." *Merryman* was a check created to deal with a future president who might not be so repentant.

The Supreme Court also decided the "Prize Cases" during the Civil War. In the immediate wake of Fort Sumter, President Lincoln ordered a naval blockade of Southern ports, and four ships were seized and brought into ports to be sold as prizes. The Supreme Court eventually recognized Lincoln's act as the de facto start of the Civil War, but it came before Congress had made its judgment known on the matter. Could a president begin a war without violating the claimed "inexorable rule" that the country could be involved in war legally only by declaration of Congress? In the Prize Cases, the Court sidestepped the direct question but maintained that Lincoln did not, by his blockade proclamation or any other act, initiate the conflict. A president could deal with a potential situation as war and employ what belligerent measures he deemed necessary without a congressional declaration. The decision was an important precedent in the quest to define the limits of presidential powers, but, more importantly, it discarded the notion that only Congress could wage war. Today, in an age when wars can be commenced in twenty minutes, delays can mean annihilation. The Civil War–era Supreme Court held wisely that a constitution that does not permit a president to defend his country's interests is little more than a suicide pact.

The issue of military versus civilian authority during wartime came before the Supreme Court one more time, a year after the Civil War ended and civilian control had been reinstated. Chief Justice Taney died in 1864 and Lincoln replaced him with Salmon P. Chase, who had been his secretary of the treasury. It was a radically different Court that heard *Ex parte Milligan* in 1866, but the verdict was remarkably similar to *Ex parte Merryman*. Union army general Alvin Hovey seized a suspected Confederate spy named Lambdin Milligan. He was tried before a military commission near Indianapolis, Indiana, in late 1864 and was sentenced to be executed. Milligan maintained that he was a civilian and was therefore not subject to military rule. As he awaited his fate in prison, the Supreme Court heard the case and ruled that the

military commission that had tried Milligan was illegal. "Martial rule can never exist where the courts are open," Justice David Davis wrote in the Court's opinion. As long as courts can operate in the United States, the laws of the Constitution and Bill of Rights should prevail. The *Milligan* decision reiterated Justice Taney in *Ex parte Merryman* and ensured the continued role of the judiciary in American government.

The Supreme Court continued to reassert itself in the immediate years following the Civil War, in cases such as *Cummings v. Missouri* and *Ex parte Garland*, which had been brought by individuals wishing to limit Reconstruction in the South. Both decisions angered as they controlled Radical Republican legislators. The court set back its efforts in 1870, however, in *Hepburn v. Griswold*. In that case the Court ruled that the greenback laws, passed during the Civil War to create a paper currency not backed by gold or silver, were unconstitutional. The decision threatened the nation's entire postwar recovery and economic system. President Ulysses S. Grant responded by appointing two new justices who were known to support the constitutionality of the greenback laws, and the Court reversed itself a year later. Subsequent chief justice Charles Evans Hughes considered *Hepburn* the second of the two most grievous "self-inflicted wounds" in the history of the Supreme Court, after *Scott v. San[d]ford*.

—*Richard Digby-Junger*

See also Civil Liberties, U.S.A.; *Dred Scott* Case; *Ex parte Merryman*; *Ex parte Milligan*; Habeas Corpus, Writ of (U.S.A.); McLean, John; Merryman, John; Milligan, Lambdin P.; *Prigg v Pennsylvania*; Prize Cases; Taney, Roger Brooke.

For further reading:
Fribourg, Marjorie G. *The Supreme Court in American History* (1965).
Friedman, Lawrence M. *A History of American Law* (1985).
Horowitz, Morton J. *The Transformation of American Law* (1977).
Kutler, Stanley I. *Judicial Power and Reconstruction Politics* (1968).
Lively, Donald E. *Foreshadows of the Law: Supreme Court Dissents and Constitutional Development* (1992).
McCloskey, Robert G., and Sanford Levinson. *The American Supreme Court*, 2d ed. (1994).
Schwartz, Bernard. *A History of the Supreme Court* (1993).
Steamer, Robert J. *The Supreme Court in Crisis: A History of Conflict* (1971).
Stern, Robert L. "Chief Justice Taney and the Shadow of *Dred Scott*." *Journal of Supreme Court History* (1992).

SURRATT, JOHN HARRISION, JR.
(1844–1916)

Alleged Lincoln conspirator

John Surratt was born on 13 April 1844 in Prince Georges County, Maryland, as the youngest child of John Surratt and Mary E. Jenkins. The community where they lived was named Surrattsville in 1854 when a post office opened at the tavern owned by John, Sr., who was also appointed its postmaster. In the fall of 1859 John Surratt, Jr., enrolled in Saint Charles College in rural Howard County, Maryland, to begin preliminary study for the priesthood. However, at the end of June 1862 John left school and returned home. After his father died on the night of 25 August 1862, John, Jr., took over duties as postmaster, effective 1 September 1862. At about this time, Surratt was recruited by the Confederacy as a courier to deliver mail and messages for the State Department.

The Surratt's tavern was well known as a "safe house" for Confederate agents operating in southern Maryland. John's work consisted mostly of carrying dispatches from Washington through the Union lines to boats on the Potomac River or to contacts in Richmond, Virginia. He was also known to have traveled as far as New York City and Montreal, Canada. In the fall of 1864, Mary Surratt rented out the tavern and moved with John and his sister to a house her husband had acquired years before in Washington, D.C. There she opened a boardinghouse.

It was in Washington that John Surratt's life took a sudden turn on 23 December 1864. On that date he ran into an acquaintance, Dr. Samuel Mudd. Mudd was with John Wilkes Booth, who had known of Surratt's work for the Confederacy and was eager to enlist his help in a plan to capture President Lincoln. Surratt agreed to do so and arranged Confederate connections on Booth's behalf. After the capture operation failed, Surratt continued to work as an agent for the Confederate State Department. Surratt's connection with Booth, however, would later implicate him in the assassination conspiracy. Surratt's actual role in the plot to kill President Lincoln has been a source of controversy. He claimed that on the night of 14 April 1865 he was in Elmira, New York, and fled across the border to Canada after hearing of the president's murder.

Surratt was concealed by two Catholic priests in Canada until 15 September 1865, when he left for Europe. First spending a short period in England, he then moved on to Sezze, Italy, a small town near Rome. While in this city, he joined the Papal Zouaves and changed his name to Watson. Ironically, another member of the unit, Henri Beaumont de Saint Marie, had known Surratt in Maryland and instantly recognized him. He contacted the American consulate, but Surratt's immediate capture was impossible because the United States did not have an extradition treaty with the Pope. The State Department negotiated through the American minister to the Papal States for six months before securing permission to extradite John Surratt to the United States to stand trial. Efforts to arrest Surratt proved difficult, as he escaped from his first captors before finally being apprehended in Alexandria, Egypt.

While Surratt had hidden in Canada, a military trial in Washington, D.C., convicted eight persons as conspirators in the death of President Lincoln. Four of those convicted were hanged for their role in the assassination, including Mary Surratt. On 10 June 1867, Surratt's civilian trial began in the Criminal Court of the District of Columbia on the charge of complicity in the assassination of Abraham Lincoln. The trial lasted two months, with eighty witnesses called for the United States government and ninety witnesses for the defense. A principal witness for the prosecution was Louis Weichmann, who had shared a room with Surratt at his mother's boardinghouse. After three days of deliberation, the trial ended with the jury deadlocked eight to four for acquittal. Surratt was sent back to jail to wait for a new trial, which never materialized. Surratt was finally set free after spending more than a year in jail.

After his release from prison, Surratt became a teacher in Rockville, Maryland. Embittered by the death of his mother, Surratt went on the lecture circuit to tell his version of events. On 6 August 1870 Surratt delivered a seventy-five-minute lecture at the Montgomery County, Maryland, courthouse. During his talk he admitted his role in the abduction plot, but denied having a part in the assassination. He also claimed that the Confederate government was not involved in the plot. Another lecture by Surratt was scheduled for 30 December 1870 in Washington, D.C., but enraged citizens forced its cancellation. In 1872 Surratt settled in Baltimore and took work with a Chesapeake Bay waterborne freight company, Old Bay Line. Retiring in August 1915, Surratt died a year later on 2 April 1916 in Baltimore.

—Mitchell Yockelson

See also Booth, John Wilkes; Lincoln Assassination; Mudd, Samuel; Surratt, Mary E.

For further reading:

Bryan, George S. *The Great American Myth: The True Story of Lincoln's Murder* (1990).

The Trial of John H. Surratt (1867).

Tidwell, William A., and James O. Hall, and David Winfred Gaddy. *Come Retribution: The Confederate Secret Service and the Assassination of Abraham Lincoln* (1988).

Weichmann, Louis, Jr. *A True History of the Assassination of Abraham Lincoln and of the Confederacy of 1865* (1975).

SURRATT, MARY EUGENIA
(1823–1865)
Convicted Lincoln assassination conspirator

Mary Eugenia Jenkins was born in Maryland in 1823. As an adolescent she attended a Catholic seminary for girls in Virginia, but at sixteen she married John Surratt, at least ten years her senior, and in 1840 settled with him in Prince George's County, Maryland. In the early years of their marriage the Surratts prospered as a result of John's success as a planter, which allowed him to expand his land holdings

and open a general store and tavern, making up the core of the community that came to be known as Surrattsville (now Clinton). In 1854, a post office was even established in town, with John as its first postmaster. John's earlier achievements were undermined, however, by his excessive drinking, which led to neglect of his farm and crops and a steady decline in his fortunes. In August 1862, John died. The Surratts' eldest son Isaac (b. 1841), having taken a job as a pony-express rider in Mexico, left Mary Surratt alone to care for her two younger children, Anna (b. 1843) and John, Jr. (b. 1844).

Surratt struggled to manage what remained of the family's holdings in Surrattsville, but she found it increasingly difficult, not least of all because John, Jr. showed so little interest in helping on the farm. By fall 1864, Mary Surratt had moved with John, Jr. and Anna to a house on H Street in Washington, D.C., which her husband had purchased in 1853 and which she converted into a boardinghouse. Happily for the Surratts, the boardinghouse did quite well, with a small number of steady boarders and the constant flow of more transient traffic through the federal capital during the war.

As early as 1863, John Surratt, Jr.—a loyal Southerner like his late father—began serving the Confederacy as a courier. In connection with this work, and with his college studies, John brought a number of people home to H Street, some of whom would later become entangled in the assassination conspiracy. In the spring of 1863, John introduced his mother to a school chum named Louis Weichmann, who took up residence in the Surratt boardinghouse in November 1864. By January 1865, John had met and become good friends with the ardent secessionist and actor John Wilkes Booth. Subsequently Booth was a regular visitor to H Street as well. German immigrant and assassination co-conspirator George Atzerodt also stayed at the boardinghouse for a few days in February 1865, until Mary Surratt evicted him for excessive drinking. Posing as a Baptist preacher, Lewis Powell—later found guilty of the 14 April attack on Secretary of State William H. Seward—lodged at the Surratt boardinghouse for three days in March.

It was not long after the shooting at Ford's Theater that government investigators first descended on the boardinghouse. At approximately 2:30 on the morning of 15 April, several officials arrived and demanded to search the house in connection with the murder of the President. It appears that these men were looking for John, Jr., whom they believed at the time to have been the one to assault Seward. On the evening of the 17th, two detectives and two army officers returned, this time to arrest Mary Surratt and the rest of the people remaining in the house (Weichmann had slipped out on the 15th and was arrested that day; other boarders, disturbed by the crowds gathering around the house, had moved out on the 16th). Of the five who were arrested, all were women, with the exception of Lewis Powell, who

arrived in disguise at the last, and for him most inopportune, moment. John Surratt, Jr., was nowhere to be found, and Booth had already escaped across the Potomac.

Mary Surratt and the others were questioned intensively at the headquarters of General Christopher Augur, commander of the Union troops in the capital, and the women were then taken to the Old Capitol Prison, where they were incarcerated. Although the other women arrested with her (including Anna Surratt) were subsequently released, Mary Surratt was not. Instead, along with Atzerodt, Powell, and five others (Samuel Arnold, David Herold, Dr. Samuel A. Mudd, Michael O'Laughlin, and Edward Spangler) Mary Surratt was charged in the conspiracy to assassinate the president and subjected to trial by a military commission. The trial began on 11 May and ended on 28 June. All eight were found guilty in varying degrees, and on 5 July, when President Andrew Johnson issued his orders in connection with the commission's verdict, four were sentenced to hang, Mary Surratt among them. Gallows for Surratt, Herold, Atzerodt, and Powell were swiftly constructed, and on 7 July 1865, despite all expectations that her sentence would be converted, Mary Surratt was executed.

The legitimacy of a military commission trying a case involving civilians, and the quality of both the investigation and the evidence supplied during the trial (particularly in her case) have continued to be matters of steady debate for well over a century. Doubts about Mary Surratt's guilt were from the start exacerbated by her own unwavering claims—even to her priest—about her innocence. It does not help the cause of the prosecutors, or the commission with its guilty verdict, or President Johnson with his determination to execute Surratt and the others as quickly as possible, that John Surratt, Jr., though finally captured and brought to trial in 1867, walked away free and lived until 1916.

—*Elizabeth D. Leonard*

See also Lincoln Assassination; Surratt, John Harrison Jr.
For further reading:
Bryan, George S. *The Great American Myth: The True Story of Lincoln's Murder* (1990).
Busch, Francis X. *Enemies of the State* (1954).
DeWitt, David M. *The Judicial Murder of Mary E. Surratt* (1895; reprint, 1970).
Eisenschiml, Otto. *Why Was Lincoln Murdered?* (1937).
Moore, Guy W. *The Case of Mrs. Surratt: Her Controversial Trial and Execution* (1954).
Trindal, Mary E., and Elizabeth S. *Mary Surratt: An American Tragedy* (1996).
Turner, Thomas Reed. *Beware the People Weeping; Public Opinion and the Assassination of Abraham Lincoln* (1982).

SUTLERS

Sutlers were merchants who were officially permitted to sell goods not provided by the government to soldiers of a particular military unit or post. Army regiments or posts were each allowed one sutler. There were also dozens of brigade, division, and corps sutlers in the Union army. As they were civilians, sutlers had no claim for government pay, quarters, uniforms, transportation, or other privileges. They were not exempt from conscription on either side, and they could be taken and held as prisoners of war. Sutlers were appointed by the secretary of war, by regimental officers, or by state governors. Most soldiers considered sutlers (sometimes with justification) to be greedy swindlers who sold shoddy or overpriced goods. The army slang term for a cluster of sutler shops was "Robbers' Row."

Sutlers usually accompanied their regiments, although they were ordered away when battle was imminent and many voluntarily left when the soldiers' pay ran out. While on the move, they sold goods from their wagons. In camp, they usually set up tents, although in permanent camps many built stores with log walls and canvas roofs, or even sawed lumber buildings. To protect their goods, sutlers often slept in their stores or wagons.

Technically, sutlers were allowed to sell only certain enumerated items, at prescribed prices set by boards of brigade officers. Most of the permitted items were edibles, and much of the sutler's profit came from selling a variety of foods to supplement the monotonous army rations. Popular foods included fresh and dried fruit, butter, cheese, milk, eggs, syrup, molasses, candy, crackers, fresh meat, canned meat and oysters, pepper, mustard, pickles, sardines, and self-rising flour. Baked goods sold well, despite their often dubious quality. John D. Billings remembered his sutler selling molasses cookies, a reasonably palatable dessert, at the price of six for a quarter. Billings was less fond of his sutler's pies, which he described as "moist and indigestible below, tough and indestructible above, with untold horrors within." Although sutler pies were often fried in condemned lard, or sold after going rancid, they still found ready buyers.

Sales of liquor by sutlers were prohibited, but many if not most seemed to have ignored the restrictions. There were many "dodges" used to sell liquor. Sutlers could drop peaches in whiskey and sell "pickled peaches," or they could sell would-be drinkers bay rum hair tonic or alcohol-laden patent medicines. Liquor was hidden in kegs and barrels of innocent-sounding goods. A navy guardboat once seized a sutler's schooner loaded with thousands of cans, marked "milk drink," that contained "a villainous eggnog."

Other popular sutler merchandise included chewing and pipe tobacco, cigars, razors, toothbrushes, combs, soap, needles and thread, stamps, stationery, pens and ink, reading material, patent medicines, officers' uniforms, pistols, and cartridges.

Sutlers could sell to the men on credit, although the credit was not to exceed one-third of a man's monthly pay without the permission of the soldier's commanding officer. Three days before the end of each month, the sutler was to present a written account of the debts owed him, which would be added to the muster rolls. When a paymaster arrived, debts owed to the government and to the laundresses were paid first, then the sutler's accounts. Sutlers were allowed to sit at the pay table with their account books while the men were being paid.

Soldiers resented the high profits made by sutlers, who often charged several times normal retail prices for their stock. Many sutlers increased their profits by giving change in scrip or tokens redeemable only in their own establishments. Peddlers were barred from many camps, giving the sutlers a virtual monopoly.

Sutlers could reap great profits, but they also took great risks. Travel expenses and losses from spoilage or damage from the weather cut into their profits. They might lose money from goods sold on credit when soldiers deserted or died, or if the amounts were not properly entered on the muster rolls. Many sutlers lost everything when army camps or wagon trains were overrun by enemy troops.

Besides enemy action, the sutler also faced the danger of being "cleaned out," or raided by men from his own side. Many soldiers felt justified in "going through" a sutler, a phrase that meant completely plundering his establishment. A common method was for a crowd of soldiers to gather around the sutler's tent after dark, cut or pull down the tent's guy ropes, and help themselves to whatever they could get. Another way was to stage a brawl and use the ensuing confusion as cover for looting. Sutlers' wagons could be plundered by a crowd of "customers" picking up merchandise as if to buy, then stampeding the sutler's horse and disappearing. Many officers covered for their men in such cases if they felt that the sutler had been cheating them.

Some Civil War prisons had sutlers. In the North, regulations on prison sutlers and what they could sell changed frequently; sutler sales were at times forbidden or curtailed to retaliate for poor conditions in prisons in the South. Goods were not sold directly to prisoners; their money was deposited with the camp commander, who paid the sutler.

Most Confederate regiments did not have sutlers, due to the scarcity of goods and high prices in the South, and widespread conscription. Three rebel sutlers surrendered at Appomattox.

Sutlers had served American military units since the French and Indian War. The origin of the word goes back to the obsolete Dutch word "settler," which meant to perform mean duties or to follow a low trade. Sutlers were abolished in the postwar U.S. Army, largely because of the abuses of the Civil War era. The post trader first replaced the sutler, then the army canteen, which evolved into today's post exchange, or PX.

—*David A. Norris*

For further reading:
Billings, John D. *Hardtack and Coffee: The Unwritten Story of Army Life* (1887; reprint, 1990).
Delo, David Michael. *Peddlers and Post Traders: The Army Sutler on the Frontier* (1992).
Lord, Francis A. *Civil War Sutlers and Their Wares* (1969).
Spear, Donald P. "The Sutler in the Union Army." *Civil War History* (1970).

SWEENY, THOMAS WILLIAM
(1820–1892)
Union general

Thomas Sweeny was born on 25 December 1820 in County Cork, Ireland. After the death of his father, he joined his mother, Honora Sweeny, in New York City in 1836. Employed in a law publishing business, he joined a local militia unit, the Baxter Blues, in 1843. When war broke out with Mexico in 1846, the unit became Company A, First New York Volunteers.

As a lieutenant, Sweeny fought from Vera Cruz to Churubusco, where he suffered a serious wound that necessitated the amputation of his right arm. Distinguished by his courageous aggression, Sweeny emerged from the Mexican-American War with the nickname "Fighting Tom" and a regular commission as lieutenant in the Second U.S. Infantry. He served in western posts until 1858, after which he undertook general recruitment duties in New York City. Promoted to captain in January 1861, he was posted to the St. Louis arsenal, which he successfully defended against pro-Confederate state troops until Captain (later Brigadier General) Nathaniel Lyon assumed command in February 1861.

Serving under Lyon, Sweeny played a prominent role in securing Missouri for the Union. Commissioned brigadier general of ninety-day pro-Union state volunteers, Sweeny fought at Wilson's Creek, 10 August 1861, where he was wounded in the thigh. Mustered out of service with his command that month, Sweeny briefly served as acting adjutant general to Major General John C. Frémont. Appointed colonel of the 52d Illinois Infantry in January 1862, he served under Ulysses S. Grant at Fort Donelson. He played a crucial role in saving the Union line at the "Hornet's Nest" at Shiloh, 6 April 1862, where he was again badly wounded. Sweeny led his regiment at the battles of Iuka (September 1862) and Corinth (October 1862) and was promoted to brigadier general of volunteers on 16 March 1863, to rank from 29 November 1862. Returning to New York City to recover from his wounds, Sweeny spent most of 1863 in garrison duty in Mississippi and Tennessee.

During the Atlanta campaign, Sweeny returned to active field duty as the commander of the 2d Division, XVI Corps, Army of the Tennessee. He fought at Resaca (14 May 1864), Dallas (28 May 1864), and Kennesaw Mountain (27 June 1864). On 22 July 1864, Sweeny distinguished himself during the battle of Atlanta, where his command helped defeat General William Hardee's attempt to outflank and destroy the Army of the Tennessee. A hot-tempered Irishman known for his profane language, Sweeny disliked service under his corps commander, General Grenville M. Dodge, a political general. Sweeny thought Dodge an amateur soldier, and he was probably annoyed at Dodge's promotion to major general on 7 June 1864. Their long-standing feud came to a head on 25 July 1864 in an incident that ended Sweeny's active field command.

Furious that Dodge had directly issued orders to regiments under his command, Sweeny confronted Dodge and Brigadier General John W. Fuller, another political general whom Sweeny disliked even more for being an Englishman. He accused Fuller of cowardice, and when Dodge came to Fuller's defense, a heated verbal argument became a brawl. Sweeny struck Dodge, though who threw the first punch remains debatable. Arrested, Sweeny was sent to Nashville for court-martial, but he was honorably acquitted in December 1864. Sweeny spent the rest of the war in garrison duty in Nashville and was mustered out of volunteer service in August 1865 and was dismissed from regular service in December 1865 for being absent without leave.

A dedicated Fenian, an organization founded to overthrow British rule in Ireland, Sweeny had actually invited Confederate general Patrick R. Cleburne, who was also born in Cork, to join the organization during the Atlanta campaign. Cleburne declined, but Sweeny became a leading advocate for a Fenian invasion of Canada. Appointed by the organization as the secretary of war for the "Irish republic," Sweeny organized and led such an invasion in June 1866. The invasion was a fiasco, and Sweeny was arrested. Yet because of his standing in the Irish-American community, he was released without trial, and political considerations led to his reappointment to regular service.

Finally retiring from the U.S. Army with the rank of brigadier general on 11 May 1870, Sweeny spent the rest of his life in Astoria, New York, with his second wife, Eugenia Reagan of Augusta, Georgia. She and his three sons and a daughter survived him after his death on 10 April 1892. Buried in Greenwood Cemetery, New York, he is remembered by the General Sweeny Civil War Museum in Republic, Missouri.

—*Rory T. Cornish*

See also Atlanta Campaign; Dodge, Grenville Mellen; Irish-Americans; Lyon, Nathaniel.
For further reading:
Anders, Leslie. "Fisticuffs at Headquarters: Sweeny vs. Dodge." *Civil War Times Illustrated* (1977).
Brooksher, William R. *Bloody Hill: The Civil War Battle of Wilson's Creek* (1995).

Cannan, John. *The Atlanta Campaign, May–November, 1864* (1991).

Castel, Albert E. *Decision in the West: The Atlanta Campaign of 1864* (1992).

Crompton, James. "The Second Division of the 16th Corps in the Atlanta Campaign." In *The Atlanta Papers* (1980).

Dodge, Grenville M. *The Battle of Atlanta and Other Campaigns* (1911).

SWINTON, WILLIAM
(1833–1892)
Northern journalist

Swinton was one of the most prolific and high-profile of the team of Northern journalists who covered the war from the front lines. Born in Scotland, Swinton emigrated to Canada with his family when he was a child and was educated at a Presbyterian school in Toronto. During the 1850s he taught in North Carolina and then New York City, while training to enter the Presbyterian ministry. But in 1858 he secured a job on the staff of the *New York Times*, where his brother (who was later to become notable as a campaigner for the rights of organized labor) was chief of the editorial staff. Swinton abandoned his religious calling in favor of journalism, and in 1861 was sent to the Virginia front as a special correspondent.

His reports, although appearing in a newspaper that was always supportive of the administration, were often scathingly critical of Union generals. Swinton quickly gained a reputation among the public as a result of the practice—highly unusual in newspapers at this time—of signing his name to his dispatches. He was never popular with the military authorities, however, not only because of the tone of his articles, but because of the unscrupulousness with which he conducted his research. In 1864 Swinton crept into a hiding place during a conference between General Grant and General Meade in order to eavesdrop. He was noticed by a junior officer who hauled him out and threatened to shoot him as a spy. Instead, an order was issued forbidding him to remain with the army.

Undaunted, Swinton turned to producing pamphlets in support of Lincoln's reelection in 1864. His contribution to the Union Party election campaign in 1864 was considerable, as he constructed pithy formulations of the essential nature of the political and military contest and how they were related. In a peroration he wrote for a Loyal Publication Society pamphlet, he contrasted the glorious and honorable peace promised by the Union Party with the base surrender offered by the Democrats, who would project the war into history as a monument of a nation's folly. His argument, which was characteristic of the Union Party campaign, was that it was the duty, rather than merely in the interest, of all patriotic and honest citizens to vote for Lincoln. Swinton claimed that the Democratic Party had the entire sympathy and moral support of the leaders of the rebellion. Swinton wrote a pamphlet attacking McClellan for having wasted the North's military strength, blamed the administration for his failures, and then for endorsing the spirit of faction by entering politics. During the summer of 1864, Swinton was commissioned by the Union Congressional Committee to write a pamphlet specifically designed to appeal to soldiers. Drawing on his genuine knowledge of the experience and attitudes of the rank and file, Swinton's appeal was one of the most widely distributed pieces of pro-Lincoln propaganda.

After the war, Swinton was for a few years a professor of English at the University of California before developing a successful and lucrative career as a school textbook writer.

—*Adam I. P. Smith*

See also Newspapers; War Correspondents.
For further reading:

Grant, Ulysses S. *Personal Memoirs of U. S. Grant* (1885).

"Obituary of William Swinton." *New York Times* (1892).

Swinton, William. *A Few Plain Words with the Rank and File of the Union Armies* (1864).

———. *The 'Times' Review of McClellan. His Military Career Reviewed and Exposed* (1864).

———. *The War for the Union: The First, Second, Third, and Fourth Years of the War* (1864).

SYKES, GEORGE
(1822–1880)
Union general

Born the son of William Sykes in Dover, Delaware, George Sykes was the grandson of a former governor of the state. He was educated locally before receiving an appointment to the U.S. Military Academy. Upon graduating thirty-ninth of fifty-six in the class of 1842, he was sent to fight in the last phases of the Second Seminole War in Florida. After the end of that conflict, Sykes was stationed at a variety of posts in the South and on the Western frontier. During the Mexican-American War, Sykes served in Winfield Scott's Mexico City campaign and received a brevet promotion to captain for his actions. After the war, he continued to serve on the frontier and by the outbreak of the Civil War was a major in the 14th U.S. Infantry.

Sykes commanded a battalion of regulars at the battle of First Bull Run, where he distinguished himself guarding the retreat of the inexperienced Union army. In September he was promoted to brigadier general of volunteers and was given command of a regular brigade stationed in Washington, D.C. On 8 February 1862, he had the unpleasant duty of commanding the detachment sent to arrest Charles P. Stone, the unfortunate scapegoat for the debacle at Ball's Bluff.

In the spring of 1862, Sykes was given command of a division in the Peninsula campaign. He commanded his men at the siege of Yorktown and the subsequent battle of Williamsburg. Shortly after that battle, his division of largely regular troops was made a part of Fitz John Porter's V Corps. He continued to command his division during the Seven Days'.

In August, along with the rest of V Corps, Sykes and his division became a part of John Pope's Army of Virginia. His division was perhaps the most heavily engaged of V Corps at Second Bull Run on 30 August. Later that year, he testified for his commander Fitz John Porter at Porter's court-martial for disobedience of orders at Second Bull Run.

Sykes's division was not heavily engaged at Antietam on 17 September, but three days later he commanded part of the pursuit of Robert E. Lee's Army of Northern Virginia in the engagement at Blackford's Ford. He commanded his division of regulars at Fredericksburg in December 1862 but again was not heavily engaged. During the infamous "Mud March" the following month, however, he commanded V Corps.

Back in command of his division at Chancellorsville, Sykes fought on the Union left and center at different times in the battle. After the elevation of the corps' commander, George Gordon Meade, to command of the Army of the Potomac at the end of June 1863, Sykes was made the commander of V Corps. In the spring he had been promoted to major general of volunteers with a date of rank of 29 November 1862.

During the battle of Gettysburg, Sykes and V Corps were not engaged until 2 July. On that day, Sykes was sent to anchor the Union left on the Round Tops south of town. As a result, he and his corps saw some of the heaviest fighting of the battle holding the Union flank against James Longstreet's offensive. During Meade's council of war on the evening of 2 July, Sykes counseled holding their ground. For his actions on 2 July, Sykes received a brevet promotion to brigadier general in the regular army. Shortly after the battle, however, Sykes and Meade entered a dispute regarding whether Meade had instructed Sykes to pursue Lee's retreating army. Sykes claimed to have received no such instructions, whereas Meade claimed to have given them. The relationship between the two would remain strained until Meade finally relieved Sykes from command of V Corps in early 1864.

In the meantime, Sykes led his corps in the battle at Rappahannock Station, 7–8 November 1863 and in the Mine Run campaign. Again Meade criticized Sykes in the latter campaign for his lack of aggression, and it was this incident that ostensibly led to Sykes's removal from command. The reorganization of the Army of the Potomac left Sykes without a unit, and on 23 March 1864 he was detached from the Army of the Potomac and sent to the Department of Kansas headquartered at Fort Leavenworth.

After reporting to Fort Leavenworth in April 1864, Sykes was given command of the District of South Kansas. He spent most of the summer and early fall of that year operating against guerrillas in the Cherokee Nation. In the fall he was occupied combating Sterling Price's Missouri Raid. Sykes remained on duty in Kansas and the Indian Territory until the end of the war.

Following the war and the reorganization of the army in 1866, Sykes became a lieutenant colonel of the 5th U.S. Infantry. In 1868 he was promoted to colonel of the 20th Infantry. He remained in command of that unit until he died at Fort Brown, Texas, on 8 February 1880.

—*David S. Heidler and Jeanne T. Heidler*

See also Gettysburg, Battle of.
For further reading:
Gross, George J. *The Battlefield of Gettysburg* (1866).

Strategic planning for battle was the responsibility of the field army's commanding general, while movement of troops to the battlefield and leadership of troops in battle were the responsibilities of subordinate officers. Entire field armies, even individual corps, were simply too large for one person to command in battle. Corps commanders were responsible for moving their corps to the battlefield and for positioning and maintaining tactical direction over their corps's divisions. Division, brigade, and regimental commanders led infantry into battle and were responsible for execution of tactical maneuvers.

Civil War armies employed Napoleonic tactical formations of line, column, mixed order (line and column), and square, although these formations were not identical in every detail to Napoleon's, and their use was considerably modified in the Civil War by new developments in weaponry.

The line was the basic formation for attack and defense. Although it was difficult to maneuver and required highly trained and disciplined soldiers, officers could advance the line close to the enemy, while controlling the direction and rate of fire. The line could deliver devastating firepower to its front at close range, but was vulnerable on its flanks. Lines consisted of two or three ranks, each rank of soldiers standing side by side facing the enemy. Each rank would alternately fire and load. This concentration produced a high density of fire and compensated for the inherent defects of smoothbore muskets, the standard infantry weapon in Napoleon's time, which had not been completely superseded by the time of the Civil War.

The musket's bore, the inner surface of the barrel, was a simple smooth tube, and the weapon fired a round ball slightly smaller than the diameter of the bore. The standard U.S. smoothbore musket fired a 0.69 caliber ball. The smoothbore was loaded at the muzzle (the front end of the barrel) by first pouring a measure of gunpowder down the barrel and then driving the ball down with a ramrod. The musket was loaded while standing to employ the assistance of gravity. The smooth inner surface permitted infantrymen to load and fire two to three rounds a minute, a rapid rate for firearms before the Civil War. However, the smoothbore also imparted no spin to the ball and allowed part of the force from the powder ignition to be dissipated around the ball. These factors combined to produce the smoothbore's short range and inaccuracy. A ball fired from a smoothbore musket might carry well beyond 300 yards, but field tests revealed its effective range, at which an infantryman might score more hits than misses, to be roughly seventy-five yards, and under battle conditions this distance could be considerably less.

An attacking army could advance to the smoothbore's effective range with few casualties, exchange

TACTICS

Henry Halleck defined tactics as the "art of bringing troops into action, or of moving them in the presence of an enemy, that is, within his view, and within the reach of his artillery."

Typical of Civil War era generals, Halleck equated tactics with the maneuver of troops on the battlefield preparatory to and in battle. By contrast, Halleck defined *strategy* as "the art of directing masses on decisive points, or the hostile movements of armies beyond the range of each other's cannon"; that is, maneuvering an army to the battlefield and positioning its units to maximize the potential for victory. Responsibility for execution of strategic and tactical maneuvers was distributed throughout the command structure of a field army.

Civil War field armies (such as the Union Army of the Potomac and the Confederate Army of Northern Virginia in the East, or the Union Army of the Cumberland and the Confederate Army of Tennessee in the West) were organized by 1862 into corps, large unit formations that had their own infantry, artillery, engineers, and logistical support. Union corps were commanded by major generals, Confederate corps by lieutenant generals. Corps were subdivided into divisions, usually two to five, commanded by general officers. Divisions were divided into two or more brigades commanded by brigadier generals. Brigades were usually composed of two to five regiments commanded by colonels. Regiments of volunteers were divided into ten companies, each ideally of 100 officers and men, commanded by captains. Regular army regiments were divided into at least two battalions of eight companies. Battlefield attrition often resulted in command by officers of lower rank and in much-diminished troop strength in regiments by midwar.

volleys with the defending army, and complete the attack with a frontal assault, the bayonet charge. The defending army attempted to disrupt the attackers with their volleys. If enough attackers survived the frontal assault to close effectively with the defender's line, the defenders often broke and ran rather than face the bayonet charge.

Column formations massed the ranks and files (rows of soldiers standing front to rear) of infantry in depth. Columns preferably were formations of maneuver rather than attack. Able to move faster than line formations, columns could advance rapidly across a battlefield and deploy into lines to engage the enemy with firepower. Infantry required less training and discipline to fight in column formations than they did in line, but the column's narrow frontage relative to the enemy's line rendered the column unable to match the line's volume of fire, while making the column an easy target for artillery and infantry fire on its front and flanks. Thus, deep columns, which were also unwieldy to move, were avoided. Combining column and line formations produced the mixed order. This allowed commanders to employ the firepower of line with the mobility of columns. Squares were closely compacted formations of infantry facing outward on all four sides to protect against cavalry attacks. Smoothbore artillery and cavalry supported infantry actions. Artillery was used effectively both offensively to degrade enemy forces and defensively to protect infantry from attack. The short range and inaccuracy of the smoothbore enabled cavalry armed with edged weapons—the saber being the most prominent—to close effectively with infantry. Offensively, cavalry was used for shock actions and to help pursue a defeated enemy from the battlefield. Defensively, cavalry protected the vulnerable flanks of the line and guarded against enemy cavalry. Two important prebattle functions of cavalry were scouting and screening their own army's movements from the enemy.

Napoleon had been able on occasion to win decisive battles, victories so complete that defeated armies could not continue the war. Part of Napoleon's legacy was the general perception that strategic objectives and even entire wars could be won by a battle and that successful commanders ought to seize the initiative and fight offensively. American strategic thinking before the war was closely associated with French theorists, especially the influential interpreter of Napoleon, Antoine Henri de Jomini. Jomini wrote extensively about both offensive and defensive movements, but it was his offensive writings that received the most attention. These emphasized massed frontal assaults against weak points in the enemy defenses to gain interior lines. (A force possesses interior lines when it can concentrate troops more quickly on a position than can its enemy, which is then said to be on exterior lines.)

The degree to which Jomini influenced West Point's graduates is debated. Professor Dennis Hart Mahan, the nation's leading military theorist in the era before the Civil War, could devote only a few course hours to formal instruction on strategy and tactics, but he did provide supplemental instruction for his best students through discussion and study in West Point's Napoleon Club.

The lessons of the Mexican-American War (1846–1848), which served as a training ground for many Civil War soldiers may well have exerted more influence than Napoleon or Jomini in shaping American thinking about strategy and tactics. In a war in which infantry still fought mainly with smoothbore muskets and bayonets, success was possible using frontal assaults in line, light columns, and the mixed order of line and column, even against entrenchments (although the entrenchments were not always well constructed). The reputation of Napoleon, the offensive strategy of Jomini, and the experience of the Mexican-American War all combined to reinforce belief in the primacy of offensive actions. When the Civil War began, therefore, the general expectation was that the war could be won or lost with a single battle, that victory would go to those who seized the initiative and implemented offensive strategies and tactics, and that battles would be won with frontal assaults culminating in bayonet charges. It was also assumed that superiority in troop strength, even a modest one, would be sufficient to assure that an able aggressive commander achieved victory. In practice, however, the progression and outcome of battles was not at all what had been anticipated, largely because of new weaponry. In the 1850s armies began replacing their smoothbore muskets with rifled muskets, a change made possible by technological developments.

Rifled muskets required a close fit of ball to barrel so that the rifling, curved grooves cut into the barrel, scored the ball's surface. The tight fit helped to contain the force of the powder upon ignition and the rifling, which imparted a spin to the ball, produced accuracy at long range. Early rifles were slow to load and black powder residue quickly fouled the barrels. Their rate of fire was about half that of the smoothbore, sufficiently slow that positions defended by rifles could be overrun during loading.

Towards the middle of the nineteenth century, the development of the so-called minié ball allowed the rifled musket to be loaded and fired as quickly as the smoothbore. Sufficiently smaller than the caliber of the rifle musket to permit easy loading, the Civil War version of the minié ball was a pointed bullet with a hollow base that, upon the force of the black power ignition, expanded to fit the rifling. The industrial revolution made possible the economical mass supply of rifled muskets of standardized caliber, and the U.S. Army adopted the rifled musket for its infantry in 1855. The most widely used models in the Civil War were the 0.58 caliber Springfield Model 1861 and the British 0.577

caliber Enfield. The range of these weapons was three to four times that of the smoothbore. A round might carry over a thousand yards, but the rifled musket could be effective in the hands of infantry at 600 yards, with its most effective range in the hands of Civil War infantry extending 200 to 300 yards.

In spite of the prevailing emphasis on offensive strategy, Mahan and other military professionals in the decades before the war anticipated the increasing advantage to defense and considered the impact of both entrenchments and the rifled musket on offensive movements. Mahan advocated maneuver as an alternative to the frontal assault. An enemy could be forced to withdraw from an entrenched position if a force moved around the enemy's flank to threaten a vital point, such as its line of communications (the route connecting an army to its base of operations, its line of supply and reinforcement). Such a threat could force an enemy to move from its prepared position to retreat or fight the turning force at a disadvantage. The turning movement was used by Winfield Scott in the Mexican-American War, for example at Cerro Gordo, and by Civil War commanding generals on both sides, such as George B. McClellan and Robert E. Lee, who sought to avoid direct attacks and gain advantage by maneuver. That commanders were not always successful and resorted to frontal engagements was due in part to the difficulties of maneuvering large untrained armies.

It does not appear, however, that anyone anticipated the degree to which the rifle would change warfare, and Mahan's ideas did not permeate throughout the army. William J. Hardee's *Rifle and Light Infantry Tactics*, the army's tactical manual written to accompany the introduction of the rifled musket, principally responded to the new weapon by providing for more rapid deployments and increasing the length of the stride and the rate of steps per minute. Such disparate responses as Mahan's and Hardee's reveal that the army was not of one mind about the potential of its new weapon.

The rifle combined with other factors to make conduct of successful offensive actions extremely difficult in the Civil War. Napoleonic formations required training and discipline of large numbers of troops on a scale that was nonexistent, and not needed, in North America before 1860. Furthermore, officers were not experienced in the command and maneuver of large units, a point Irvin McDowell tried to make to Abraham Lincoln before First Bull Run. There were no maneuvers to train officers and men to anticipate the unexpected and react to the increased strength of the defense. For example, a problem inherent in Civil War battles was the inability or failure to exploit a successful assault. Assaults, in line or column, that managed to close with the defending line usually created a breach. Successful completion of the attack required that enough troops be available in support to exploit the opening, but typically adequate support was not provided. This was often due to communication failures and unity of command problems, but sometimes those in the chain of command did not think or know to anticipate the need for additional troops to support an action. The breach of the Confederate right at Fredericksburg by George Gordon Meade's division and the breach of the Confederate line at Spotsylvania by Emory Upton's column are just two examples of attacks that were forced to withdraw because of insufficient support.

Civil War assaults usually failed, and even when successful, accomplished little. A successful assault in which the attacking line would close with, and overwhelm the length of, the defending line was a rare occurrence in the Civil War. The Union attacks on Matthew's Hill at First Bull Run, Missionary Ridge at Chattanooga, and against the Army of Tennessee at Nashville are examples of attackers overwhelming and taking enemy positions. In each case, the assaulting army had strength enough to move against the defender's front and flanks, forcing retreat, but the defenders did escape. John Bell Hood's brigade, assaulting without stopping to fire, successfully breached the Union line at Gaines' Mill and won the battle by forcing the Union from the field, but the Union was able to retreat. The victor might hold the battlefield, but even in defeat an army could use the advantage of defense to retreat from the battlefield to fight another day, and the war continued.

The rifled musket further hampered offensive operations by denying commanders the full use of all arms: artillery and cavalry were reduced to subordinate roles on the battlefield. The rifled musket drove artillery from the front lines in early battles to rear positions beyond the weapon's range, and, as artillery was not yet adept at supporting infantry attacks at long range, batteries became less useful in support of offensive actions (Union artillery at Antietam being an exception). Artillery was, however, quite valuable in support of defense using rifled cannon at long range and the smoothbore Napoleons to fire canister at short range. The long-range fire of rifled muskets also took heavy tolls against the large targets of horses and men, limiting cavalry's battlefield actions against infantry for much of the war. The carbine, however, enabled cavalry to augment their traditional roles of scouting and screening with dismounted skirmishing and delaying actions. With shorter barrels and lighter charges than the infantry's rifles, the range of the carbine could not match the rifled musket's range, but Union cavalry in particular, armed with breechloading and repeating carbines, could conduct effective fire actions against infantry. Civil War armies advanced to the battlefield in march columns four miles wide, called columns of fours, from which they deployed their brigades into battle formations. Reserves would be held

back, typically in column for rapid deployment. An army preparing to attack would send out one or two companies from each regiment, or sometimes whole regiments, as skirmishers. Skirmishers advanced several hundred yards ahead of the line of battle strung out in loose or open order, using terrain as cover when possible, to probe enemy positions and disrupt or delay enemy advances. As the battle developed, skirmishers could fall back or be incorporated into the line as it advanced.

The remaining companies, whole regiments, brigades, or divisions would deploy into battle formations of line, column, or line and column. The line was the most common formation for both offense and defense because it delivered the greatest volume of fire across the widest front. Civil War armies typically attacked in the two-line formation, each line composed of two ranks. Troops advanced in close order, elbow to elbow. Silas Casey's *Infantry Tactics* (1862) set thirteen inches from the backs or knapsacks of the front ranks to the breasts of the rear rank as the distance between ranks, but did not set a distance between lines. That was to be determined by battlefield conditions, but second lines would generally deploy for battle 150 to 200 yards or more behind the first.

If the attack of the two lines was spaced too far apart, the firepower of the defense would likely defeat each line individually. If the distance between the lines was reduced so that the second line might better support the first, the second line, instead of being able to carry the attack forward, would intermingle with the first. This compromised command and control of units and contributed confusion instead of strength to the attack.

Attack columns were used, sometimes in combination with lines as at Second Fredericksburg, to penetrate on a narrow front. The companies of a regiment would form in depth in two-company fronts called columns of divisions (not to be confused with the large unit formation, the division) or in columns doubled in the center (which had a different positioning of companies and deployment). Each pair of companies would form a line of two ranks so that a regiment of ten companies at full strength would be five lines or ten ranks deep. Like the line, the column was a close-order formation. The distance between ranks remained at thirteen inches, but the distance between lines when closed in mass, from front rank to front rank of successive company lines, was six paces, about five yards. Columns normally advanced behind skirmishers and tried to advance rapidly without halting fire. Columns were increased in depth by having additional regiments form to the rear as at Kennesaw Mountain and Spotsylvania. Such deep columns were probably the most ineffective of all offensive formations and almost assured heavy casualties for the attackers. As the war progressed, armies made tactical changes in an effort to improve offensive actions. Attackers began to employ heavier skirmish lines, using open order and the cover of terrain to advance against enemy defenses. Supported by cover fire from the skirmishers, attackers might also advance lines in rushes, also called Indian tactics or Zouave rushes. Infantry would run forward in line, lay down and fire, then rush forward again and repeat the process until the lines were close enough to attack the defenses in a heavy skirmish line. Loose-order formations were, however, difficult for officers to control, and, though used, did not replace close-order formations.

Armies also attacked behind heavy skirmish lines using a succession of two-line formations to support and sustain the assault. Divisions would typically deploy each of their brigades into a long line of two ranks, with each brigade separated from the brigade to its front by perhaps 150 yards. These formations had difficulty carrying the attack forward and their lines tended to intermingle well short of the defense's line. Attacking in succession of lines continued to be widely used throughout the war, but did not solve the problems of the two-line formation.

Another tactical development of the war was the increased reliance on field fortifications and use of hasty entrenchments. Armies did not always entrench in early battles. At First Bull Run and Antietam, soldiers on both sides engaged in standing fire fights, but after the failed Union assaults at Fredericksburg, entrenchment became common. Trench warfare developed as armies constructed extensive field works, and on offense attackers began entrenching as well to help hold the ground they had taken.

In 1864 the war's tactical stalemate was broken as the Union was able to undertake a war of maneuver. The Union field armies consisted of experienced officers and men able to conduct large unit maneuvers. Union infantry was now able to coordinate operations effectively with Union cavalry, many of whom were now armed with repeating breechloading carbines. Sherman advanced to Atlanta and Grant advanced to Petersburg by maneuver, using turning movements to dislodge Confederate armies when frontal assaults, such as those at Kennesaw Mountain and Cold Harbor, failed. Lee, too, maneuvered exceeding well to delay Grant's progress, but the Union was using infantry to seize vital points or attack the flanks of the enemy, a far more effective use of manpower than attacking in frontal assaults. This process reached its apex in the Appomattox campaign. As Grant's forces advanced westward around Lee's right flank, Sheridan's cavalry moved quickly ahead seizing important road and rail centers, forcing Lee to keep falling back with no chance to consolidate a position. With veteran armies Union strategy and tactics merged.

—*Sharon S. MacDonald and W. Robert Beckman*

For further reading:
Casey, Silas. *Infantry Tactics, for the Instruction, Exercise, and Manoeuvers of the Soldier, a Company, Line of Skirmishers, Battalion, Brigade, or Corps d' Armee* (1862; reprint, 1985).

Dal Bello, Dominic J. *Parade, Inspection, and Basic Evolutions of the Infantry Battalion* (1988).

Hagerman, Edward. *The American Civil War and the Origins of Modern Warfare: Ideas, Organization, and Field Command* (1988).

Halleck, Henry Wager. *Elements of Military Art and Science* (1846; reprint, 1971).

Mahon, John K. "Civil War Infantry Assault Tactics." *Military Affairs* (1961).

McWhiney, Grady, and Perry D. Jamieson. *Attack and Die: Civil War Military Tactics and the Southern Heritage* (1982).

Wagner, Arthur L. *Organization and Tactics* (1894).

TALIAFERRO, WILLIAM BOOTH
(1822–1898)
Confederate general

The son of Warner T. Taliaferro and Frances Booth Taliaferro, William Booth Taliaferro was born in Gloucester County, Virginia. Educated at the College of William and Mary and Harvard Law School, Taliaferro's early practice of law was interrupted when he accepted a commission as a captain in the 11th U.S. Infantry during the Mexican-American War. During that conflict he reached the rank of major.

Returning home after the war, Taliaferro resumed his law practice and became interested in state politics. He served in the Virginia House of Delegates from 1850 to 1853, and in 1856 he was a presidential elector for James Buchanan. Taliaferro's military experience during the Mexican-American War caused him to be sought out as a state militia officer, and during John Brown's raid on Harper's Ferry in the fall of 1859, Taliaferro commanded the state forces there.

Immediately after Virginia's secession in April 1861, Taliaferro was major general and commander of Virginia's militia. When Virginia officially became a part of the Confederacy, Taliaferro accepted the colonelcy and command of the 23d Virginia Infantry. In the spring of 1861 he and his regiment were stationed on Gloucester Point opposite Yorktown on the York River guarding the approaches up that river from Chesapeake Bay.

In the summer of 1861, Taliaferro and his regiment were transferred to western Virginia under the command of Brigadier General Robert S. Garnett. Taliaferro was with that officer when he was killed at Carrick's Ford in July 1861. Taliaferro remained in western Virginia (what is now West Virginia) until December 1861, when he was sent to the Shenandoah Valley to serve under Stonewall Jackson.

Taliaferro did not get off to a good start with his new commander, becoming involved in early 1862 with the feud between Jackson and William Wing Loring. Taliaferro signed the petition arranged by Loring protesting Jackson's placement of troops at Romney, Virginia. In spite of this indiscretion, however, Taliaferro was promoted to major general in March 1862.

In the spring of 1862, Taliaferro participated with distinction in Jackson's Shenandoah Valley campaign. The following August at Cedar Mountain, Taliaferro gained temporary command of Jackson's old division and fought so well in that engagement that Jackson gave him permanent command of the unit. He led that division north in Jackson's move on Manassas Junction a few weeks later, but was seriously wounded in one of the battles preliminary to Second Bull Run at Groveton. Taliaferro was unable to resume command of his division until December 1862 at Fredericksburg. In that battle he repulsed the attack of George Gordon Meade's division.

In early 1863, Taliaferro was transferred to the defenses of Savannah, Georgia, although by February 1863 he had moved again to Charleston, South Carolina, under the direct command of P. G. T. Beauregard. Taliaferro aided his new commander in preparing the coastal fortifications guarding the approaches to Charleston. In July 1863 he earned Beauregard's enthusiastic commendation with his defense of Fort Wagner on Morris Island against a numerically superior Union attack. In August 1863, Beauregard moved him to the defense of James Island, where he remained for the next year except for a brief trip to inspect the defenses of eastern Florida in early 1864.

As William T. Sherman neared Savannah, Georgia, in December 1864, Taliaferro was sent to that city to supervise the evacuation of the city's Confederate troops. Over the next few months he would do the same along the South Carolina coast, taking his men to join Joseph Johnston's retreating army in the Carolinas. He fought with Johnston's army at Bentonville in March 1865 and surrendered with that army in April 1865.

After the war, Taliaferro returned to his law practice. After Reconstruction, he served for five years in the Virginia legislature, and in the 1890s he served as a county judge. He died at his family home, Dunham Massie.

—*David S. Heidler and Jeanne T. Heidler*

See also Carrick's Ford; Fort Wagner, Battle of; Loring, William Wing.

For further reading:
Bolander, Robert Charles. "The Military Career of William Booth Taliaferro, April 1861–February 1863" (Thesis, 1964).

Sibley, Martha Arle. "William Booth Taliaferro: A Biography" (Thesis, 1973).

TANEY, ROGER BROOKE
(1777–1864)
U.S. attorney general, secretary of the treasury, and chief justice of the Supreme Court

Roger Brooke Taney was largely responsible for the 1857 *Dred Scott* decision, which hardened the sectional divide in the years preceding the Civil War. Taney was born in Calvert County, Maryland, to a family of planters descended from Michael Taney, an

Roger Brooke Taney (*Library of Congress*)

indentured servant who had arrived in America circa 1660. Taney graduated from Dickinson College in 1795, read law in Annapolis, and was called to the bar in 1799. He briefly served in the Maryland state legislature from 1799 to 1800 as a Federalist. In 1806, he married Anne Key, the sister of Francis Scott Key. Breaking with the Federalists in 1812, Taney became something of a political maverick within Maryland state politics and, although somewhat aristocratic and a Catholic, he supported Andrew Jackson in 1824. Becoming a Democrat, Taney was quickly recognized by Jackson as a clever legal talent and effective political organizer.

In 1831, Jackson appointed Taney attorney general. As a loyal member of Jackson's "Kitchen Cabinet," Taney fully supported the war against the Bank of the United States. When William J. Duanne, the secretary of the treasury, refused Jackson's order in September 1833 to remove the government's deposits from the bank, Jackson replaced him with Taney, who carried out the removal. The Whigs came to hate Taney, whom they saw, because of his own interests in Maryland state banking, as a corrupt tool of the president, and they held up his appointment in March 1835 as an associate justice of the Supreme Court. After the death of John Marshall in 1835, however, Jackson successfully secured Taney the appointment of chief justice in March 1836.

Taney's appointment coincided with an almost total turnover in the personnel of the Court, due to death or retirement. His difficulty in maintaining unity in the Court was hampered also by a congressional decision to increase the number of justices to nine in 1837. Taney proved to be less dictatorial than Marshall and, perhaps due to his own weak powers of persuasion, he often found himself in the minority. Not surprisingly, however, the Court increasingly reflected the Jacksonian notion of "Dual Sovereignty" between the states and the federal government. In a series of early decisions—*New York v. Miln, Briscoe v. the Bank of Kentucky*, and *Charles River Bridge v. Warren Bridge*—all in 1837, the Court reversed the drift to economic centralization long evident in the Marshall Court. As the growing expansion and complexity of American society greatly strained and tested sectional interests, no other issue except that of slavery would threaten the actual Union itself; it was a topic the Court hoped it could avoid by keeping the question on the state level where the Constitution had put it. Taney was personally antislavery. He had freed his own slaves, but was increasingly concerned that abolitionist demands threatened the power of the South within the Union. The new president, James Buchanan, hoped that the Court's involvement, however, could finally end the dispute over the question of the extension of slavery in the territories, and in 1857 Taney handed down his decision in *Dred Scott v. San[d]ford.*

The nominal issue in the case was whether a black slave named Scott, who had resided in the free state of Illinois and the free territory of Minnesota (made free by the Missouri Compromise of 1820), was made free by his residence and whether, upon his return to the slave state of Missouri, he could sue in federal court for this freedom. He had won his case in a lower court, but the decision was overturned by the Missouri Supreme Court, hence Scott's appeal. The Missouri Supreme Court had followed the precedent laid down by *Prigg v. Pennsylvania* (1842) and the later decision of *Strader v. Graham* (1850), which had ruled that Kentuckian slave minstrels who had been taken into Ohio by their owner were still slaves upon their return to Kentucky. The *Dred Scott* case became an important one within the Court because two ardent abolitionists, Justices John McLean of Ohio and Benjamin Curtis of Massachusetts, were determined to write dissenting opinions, which prompted the five Southern justices on the Court, led by Taney, to write a decision upon the controversial question of whether federal power could limit slavery in the territories. So controversial was the question that, when it was rendered, all nine justices presented separate opinions.

Taney's majority decision was brutal. All slaves and their descendants, whether free or not, could not be considered citizens of the United States, though they could become citizens of particular states, and could not, consequently, use the federal court system. Scott remained a slave, Taney ordered, as his residence in a free

state did not alone establish his freedom. The Court's decision should have ended there, but Taney went on to render on the issue of congressional power to restrict the expansion of slavery in the territories.

This part of the ruling, it seems mainly Taney's, was a bombshell, for he ruled that the Fifth Amendment barred Congress from depriving people of their property without due process, and, consequently, any citizen could take his or her property (slaves) into any territory of the United States. The Missouri Compromise of 1820 was thus unconstitutional. Rather than quieting the agitation over slavery and the Fugitive Slave Act of 1850, Taney's decision not only provoked a storm of protest in the North, it also undercut Southern moderate voices, now drowned by Southern extremist demands that their constitutional right to take their slaves anywhere be upheld. In an equally controversial ruling in 1859, *Ableman v. Booth*, the Taney court did just that by declaring that all Northern state liberty laws were unconstitutional. These decisions would help fracture the national Democratic Party and make possible the election of Abraham Lincoln in 1860, an event that triggered the secession of the lower Southern states.

Horrified by the secession of the South and the Northern attempt to coerce the South after the attack on Fort Sumter in April 1861, Taney considered Lincoln's call for volunteers and the blockade of Southern ports clearly unconstitutional. As his own reputation was now ruined and as the make-up of the Court was changed by Southern Justices going south and by Lincoln appointees taking their place, Taney was powerless. Whether Lincoln overstepped his constitutional authority is still a matter for debate, but when Taney, concerned at the suspension of habeas corpus, ignored Lincoln's order and issued a writ to free a suspected Maryland saboteur in *Ex parte Merryman* (1862), Lincoln ordered the army not to obey Taney's ruling. Taney's able constitutional reasoning during the first years of the war, paradoxically upheld by the Chase court after the war, and now respectfully studied by law students, only tended to make him again the object of bitter denunciation in the North. So hated was the chief justice that, after his death in Washington, D.C., on 12 October 1864, his funeral cortege was insulted by hostile onlookers.

Taney's name is now forever linked with the *Dred Scott* decision and a prewar Southern racist attitude. That he was a creature of his time is, perhaps, no excuse, but his other careful and judicious decisions should not be ignored. A deeply religious and modest man, his court's renderings on important economic questions before the Civil War, as well as his rather reserved handling of the Court as chief justice, are now increasingly appreciated. The longevity of his tenure alone, second only to Marshall himself, has made him, as a successor Charles E. Hughes declared, a great chief justice.

—*Rory T. Cornish*

See also Dred Scott Case; *Ex parte Merryman*; Scott, Dred; Supreme Court, U.S.
For further reading:
Corwin, Edwin S. "National Power and State Interposition, 1787–1861." *Michigan Law Review* (1912).
Cover, Robert M. *Justice Accused: Antislavery and the Judicial Process* (1975).
Fehrenbacher, Don E. *The Dred Scott Case: Its Significance in American Law and Politics* (1978).
Lewis, Walker. *Without Fear or Favor: A Biography of Chief Justice Roger Brooke Taney* (1965).
McDonald, Forrest. *A Constitutional History of the United States* (1982).
Randall, James G. *Constitutional Problems under Lincoln* (1951).
Swisher, Carl B. *History of the Supreme Court of the United States: The Taney Period, 1836–1864* (1974).

TAPPAN, LEWIS
(1788–1873)
Abolitionist

On the eve of the Civil War, Lewis Tappan was one of the nation's foremost abolitionists. Tappan was born on 23 May 1788, in Northampton, Massachusetts, into a devoutly Calvinist family. Throughout his life, he combined business acumen with a fervent devotion to social reform and especially the abolition of slavery. Tappan's experience as the credit manager for his brother Arthur Tappan's silk jobbing firm gave him the insight to create the Mercantile Agency in 1841, the first firm to specialize in providing commercial credit ratings to prospective investors and lenders. The firm later became Dun & Bradstreet, Inc.

Both Lewis and Arthur Tappan supported the American Board of Commissioners of Foreign Missions and the American Bible Society; together they helped to finance the construction of the Broadway Tabernacle in New York City for Charles Grandison Finney. Both were founding members of the New York Anti-Slavery Society and the American Anti-Slavery Society in 1833. One biographer noted that through these activities, Tappan brought upon himself both "hate and obloquy." In July 1834, Tappan's New York home was ransacked and its contents consigned to a bonfire on the street. Tappan's activities continued nonetheless: his ransacked home served, in his words, as a "silent Anti-Slavery preacher" to passersby. Between 1839 and 1841, he advocated forcefully to free the *Amistad* captives and return them to Africa. After the passage of the Fugitive Slave Act in 1850, Tappan funded activists in the Underground Railroad. John Brown's raid on Harper's Ferry in 1859, however, foretold a violent end to slavery, one that Tappan dreaded even though he saw Brown as a martyr to the cause.

For Tappan, the sin of slavery was the cause of the Civil War, and "immediate emancipation" was its only

remedy. In May 1861, Tappan published two pamphlets, *The War: Its Cause and Remedy* and *Immediate Emancipation: The Only Wise and Safe Mode.* He argued that the scourge of slavery affected all citizens, both North and South: "It is not the South alone that is guilty. The North has participated in the guilt. Judged by divine rule, 'For unto whomsoever much is given, of him much shall be required,' we may be more guilty than the people of the Southern States." Thus the Civil War was God's judgment against the entire nation. If slavery was the cause of the war, then there could be but one remedy: "IMMEDIATE AND UNIVERSAL EMANCIPATION." To justify this argument, Tappan cited the comments of John Quincy Adams during an 1842 congressional debate to the effect that, during a war, "whether servile, civil or foreign, not only the President of the United States, but the commander of the army, has power to order the universal emancipation of the slaves."

Tappan had not supported Abraham Lincoln in 1860, considering him too conservative to press the abolitionist case. After the Emancipation Proclamation, Tappan softened his views on Lincoln, even casting a ballot for him in 1864, but he still chafed at the hesitancy with which many Republicans endorsed civil rights for African-Americans. In February 1865, Tappan wrote his friend Charles Sumner, "When will the poor negro have his rights? Never, I believe, until he has a musket in one hand and a ballot in the other." Nevertheless, Tappan continued to view the world in evangelical terms, demonstrating through his acts a devotion to what his biographer Bertram Wyatt-Brown called "an outworn time." Through the American Missionary Association, Tappan helped to send numerous missionaries, including his own brother Charles, throughout the South to assist former slaves in making lives of their own. In a pamphlet entitled *Is It Right to Be Rich?* (1869), Tappan chided those blinded by the allure of earthly gain to the needs of those less fortunate. In the following year, Tappan completed *The Life of Arthur Tappan,* a biography of his brother that extolled above all else the "evangelical faith" that was woven amongst Arthur's other traits of "truthfulness,…integrity,…industry," "perseverance, stewardship," and "unselfishness." In 1873, having outlived almost all of his compatriots in the antebellum abolition movements, Tappan died at age eighty-five.

—*Robert S. Wolff*

See also Abolitionist Movement; Abolitionists; Underground Railroad.

For further reading:

Freidel, Frank, ed. *Union Pamphlets of the Civil War, 1861–1865* (1967).
Jones, Howard. *Mutiny on the Amistad* (1987).
Tappan, Lewis. *The Life of Arthur Tappan* (1870).
Wyatt-Brown, Bertram. *Lewis Tappan and the Evangelical War on Slavery* (1969; reprint, 1997).

TATTNALL, JOSIAH
(1795–1871)
Confederate naval officer

Born to Josiah Tattnall, the governor of Georgia, and Harriet Fenwick Tattnall at the family home outside Savannah, Georgia, the younger Tattnall traveled to Great Britain at age nine for his education after the death of both of his parents. Upon his return to the United States in 1812, he accepted appointment as a midshipman in the U.S. Navy. During the War of 1812 he served aboard the USS *Constellation,* which never saw action; he also fought at the engagements of Craney Island and Bladensburg.

After the war, Tattnall served under Stephen Decatur against Algiers and then in the 1820s served tours in the West Indies, in the Mediterranean, and along the Florida coast. During the 1830s he served primarily in the Gulf of Mexico before being appointed the commandant of the Boston Navy Yard. After this tour, Tattnall served in the Mediterranean and off the coast of Africa before coming back to participate in the Mexican-American War. In that conflict he commanded the Mosquito Division off the eastern coast of Mexico. This division's most important action came during the landings and subsequent siege of Vera Cruz in Winfield Scott's Mexico City campaign. Tattnall's bombardment of Vera Cruz was instrumental in the quick capitulation of that city.

After the Mexican-American War, Tattnall was promoted to captain and served in the West Indies and the Pacific during the 1850s. Upon his return to the United States in 1860 from an Asian cruise, Tattnall was given command at Sacketts Harbor, New York. He was there when he received word of the secession of Georgia. Though he did not agree with secession, he resigned his commission and returned home, where he became the commander of the Georgia state navy before accepting a captain's commission in the Confederate States Navy.

Commanding the waters off Georgia and South Carolina, Tattnall in November 1861 unsuccessfully tried to dislodge the Federals from Port Royal Sound. During the next few months he also cooperated with commanders of coastal fortifications like Fort Pulaski on the Georgia coast in defending their positions. In March 1862 he was ordered to take command of the defense of the waters around Norfolk and Hampton Roads.

Upon his arrival in Norfolk, Tattnall took command of the CSS *Virginia* after its inconclusive duel with the USS *Monitor.* He was forced to burn the ship in May 1862, however, to prevent it from falling into Union hands. He was later censured for this action, but a court-martial, convened at his insistence, exonerated him.

With Union naval forces in command of the waters of Hampton Roads, Tattnall was sent back to protect Georgia waters. For the remainder of the war he tena-

ciously tried to keep the Savannah River open to blockade runners. In December 1864 he aided in the evacuation of movable Confederate property from Savannah before the city was occupied by William T. Sherman. A month later, he made a successful attack on Union naval forces in the Savannah River.

In the spring of 1865, Tattnall and many of his men joined the retreating army of Joseph Johnston. In April 1865, Tattnall surrendered with that army to William Sherman.

After the war, Tattnall lived for several years in Nova Scotia. He returned to live out his life in Savannah when offered the position of port inspector. He died in that position.

—*David S. Heidler and Jeanne T. Heidler*

See also Navy, C.S.A.; Port Royal Sound/Hilton Head, Battle of; Savannah, Siege of; *Virginia*, CSS.

For further reading:
Jones, Charles Colcock, Jr. *The Life and Services of Commodore Josiah Tattnall* (1878).

TAX-IN-KIND

The Confederate problem of financing both a new government and the war it had to prosecute was intensified by a multitude of difficulties. One of the most formidable was the predisposition of Southerners to limit their government's powers, especially in regard to the intrusive authority to tax. Secretary of the Treasury Christopher Memminger labored under the heavy burden of empty coffers, coupled with the politically charged issue of how to fill them.

Early in the life of the Confederacy, direct taxation was possible because the Provisional Constitution, adopted in February 1861, did not specifically bar such levies. Consequently, a 19 August 1861 measure directly taxed property, including slaves. Even so, revenues from this tax proved disappointing, likely because states could shield their citizens from its terms by assuming the burden themselves. States most often did this with bond issues that were simply transferred to the Confederacy. As the financial situation worsened, foreign loans and Confederate bond issues were combined with taxes as ways to raise revenue. All three methods fell short of the mark, but taxation was especially unsatisfactory as a way to garner funds.

On 24 April 1863, the Confederate Congress passed new tax legislation to address the heightening crisis. This complicated measure included, in part, a graduated income tax, but it could not impose direct taxes, made illegitimate under the Permanent Constitution unless apportioned to the population. A way around the restriction was found in establishing a tax-in-kind. Derived from the ancient church practice of the tithe, the Confederate policy was levied against agricultural produce and livestock. Farmers from all economic groups, ranging from the lowliest yeomen to the wealthiest planters, would set aside for their own subsistence a portion of their foodstuffs. The remainder of their harvests—commodities such as wheat, rye, oats, corn, rice, potatoes, fodder, sugar, wool, tobacco, legumes, bacon, and, of course, cotton—would be subject to a 10 percent appropriation by the Confederate government. The plan was to provide both a source of revenue for the treasury and supplies to be directly transported to armies in the field.

The tax-in-kind was extraordinarily unpopular in many areas of the Confederacy. It ranked with impressment and conscription as a cause of disaffection and occasionally resulted in outright defiance. The method of collection by Confederate agents was frequently inefficient and sometimes corrupt. Small farmers regarded the tax-in-kind as especially obnoxious because it was regressive: the yeomen's 10 percent contribution was a much greater sacrifice for him than was the same rate when applied to the wealthy planter. Amendments to the law in December 1863 and the following February tried to address the more objectionable imperfections with cash payment alternatives and exemptions for certain groups, such as the families of soldiers.

Although some parts of the Confederacy, such as the trans-Mississippi area, stoically accepted the policy, poorer areas condemned it as archaic and despotic. The tax-in-kind became, with conscription, another source of class resentment and corresponding alienation from the Confederate cause. Benefits from the policy were both monetary and material, the one in about $40 million in revenue for the treasury and the other in supplies for the Confederate armies. Yet these compensations were often outweighed by the negative attitudes the tax-in-kind animated.

—*David S. Heidler and Jeanne T. Heidler*

See also Class Conflict, C.S.A.; Financing, C.S.A.; Impressment; Memminger, Christopher.

For further reading:
Ball, Douglas B. *Financial Failure and Confederate Defeat* (1991).
Black, Dan Anderson. "Financing the Confederacy" (M.B.A. thesis, 1981).
Todd, Richard Cecil. *Confederate Finance* (1954).

TAYLOR, RICHARD
(1826–1879)
Confederate general

Born near Louisville, Kentucky, son of Colonel (later general and president) Zachary Taylor, "Dick" Taylor lived on diverse military posts, and before age ten briefly had Lieutenant (later Confederate president) Jefferson Davis as his brother-in-law. Taylor graduated from Yale in 1845. During the Mexican-

Richard Taylor (*Library of Congress*)

American War, he spent a month in the field with his father, his only military experience before 1861.

Zachary Taylor was elected president as a Whig in 1848, putting the younger Taylor in prominent circles during his father's short presidency. President Taylor's 1850 death left Dick wealthy, and he bought the sugar plantation Fashion near New Orleans, eventually owning nearly 200 slaves.

In the 1850s, Taylor evolved from Whig to Know-Nothing to Democrat and was first elected to the Louisiana state senate in 1855 and would serve there until 1861. Moderate on slavery and secession, Taylor attended the Democratic Convention in Charleston in 1860, hoping for party unity, but when Lincoln's victory brought secession, Taylor advocated military preparedness.

Although he had had no formal military training, Taylor had a reputation as a student of military history, having read virtually all the great captains. Taylor's prodigious memory and ability to synthesize voluminous information proved key to his military career, for, he noted, "The cardinal principles [of] war … are few and unchangeable, resembling the code of morality." The 9th Louisiana Infantry Regiment elected Taylor its colonel in June 1861 and set out for Virginia, joining the main Confederate army just after First Bull Run.

The 9th along with the 6th, 7th, and 8th Louisiana Infantries formed a brigade, and in October 1861, Taylor's connection to Jefferson Davis surfaced when the Confederate president, over Taylor's protests, bypassed the brigade's three more experienced colonels to promote Taylor to brigadier general and brigade command. The embarrassed Taylor burned for action, which came when the Louisiana Brigade (Ewell's Division) joined Thomas J. "Stonewall" Jackson in the Shenandoah Valley in late April 1862.

The well-disciplined brigade and its young general soon won Jackson's respect, for Taylor skillfully demonstrated initiative and personal courage, as the Louisiana Brigade determined the outcome of at least two critical victories in the remainder of Jackson's renowned Shenandoah Valley campaign in May and June. With Jackson, Taylor's brigade then joined Lee's army for the Seven Days' battles. Taylor's lifelong rheumatoid arthritis then flared, and he directed his men from an ambulance before temporarily yielding field command.

Nonetheless, in two months, Taylor had gone from being considered the beneficiary of presidential nepotism to being a respected combat leader, well regarded by both his men and his superiors. Jackson recommended Taylor for promotion to major general, which came quickly, with orders to report to Louisiana. Taylor's reputation had so grown that a distinguished historian later wrote that Lee's "Army was the poorer for Taylor's departure."

In mid-August 1862, Taylor arrived to command the District of West Louisiana, but circumstances were dire. The Federals had captured New Orleans in April, and Taylor found few troops or supplies, while his own "Fashion" had been looted by Union troops. Initial hopes of recapturing New Orleans quickly faded to marginal hopes of stopping further Federal advances as Taylor struggled to field an effective force. Recruits frequently deserted, and organized units sent to Taylor often proved to be ill disciplined or poorly led. Topography worsened Taylor's difficulties, as the Union navy roamed many bayous with impunity, penetrating Louisiana's heartland.

In April 1863, the Federals launched the first Red River campaign, with General Nathaniel Banks leading 16,000 men against Taylor's 4,000 via Bayou Teche. On 12–14 April, Taylor engaged the Federals near Fort Bisland and Irish Bend, but hopes of victory collapsed under the intoxicated ineptitude of Brigadier General Henry Sibley. Skillfully extricating his men from a closing trap, Taylor retreated up the Red River Valley, but preservation of his force allowed him to threaten southern Louisiana as Banks veered toward Vicksburg.

Hoping to disrupt the Federals near Vicksburg as Jackson's Valley campaign had distracted McClellan in 1862, Taylor launched daring forays into lower Louisiana, in June 1863 capturing Brashear City and over $2 million in supplies, and advancing on lightly

defended New Orleans. Unfortunately, the fall of Vicksburg freed Union troops to move against Taylor, who abandoned his plan.

The Union triumphs at Vicksburg and Gettysburg devastated morale in Louisiana, and thousands of men deserted as Taylor ceaselessly shifted small detachments to meet Federal raiders in lower Louisiana. Such actions, coupled with his own harassment of Union units, forestalled further Federal activity until the spring of 1864.

The second Red River campaign entailed a fleet of transports and ironclads under Admiral David D. Porter and 25,000 men under Banks. Throughout March 1864, the Federals moved up the Red River, threatening Shreveport, an indispensable Confederate nerve center. Taylor retreated, hoping for an opportune moment, and on 8 April, near Mansfield, he seized it. Taylor threw 9,000 men against Banks in a furious assault that broke and panicked the bluecoats. Taylor's pursuit netted copious supplies and prisoners, and he renewed battle on 9 April at Pleasant Hill. Though suffering greater casualties and tactically defeated on that day, Taylor's intrepidity so demoralized the Federals that they retreated to the Mississippi River. In a brilliant campaign, Taylor, badly outnumbered, saved the Trans-Mississippi Department and became a Southern hero. Tendered the thanks of the Confederate Congress and promoted to lieutenant general on 18 July, Taylor took command of the Department of Alabama, Mississippi, and East Louisiana on 6 September.

Although he considered the defeat of the South inevitable, Taylor performed resolutely, directing harassment of Federal forces and the skillful defense of Mobile with little manpower or supplies. The inevitable came at Appomattox in April 1865, and on 4 May Taylor became the last major Confederate commander east of the Mississippi to surrender.

After the war, Taylor used his connections in both the North and South to rebuild his financial base and to plead for the South. He published *Destruction and Reconstruction*, perhaps the most literate war memoir, just before his death on 12 April 1879. Though without military training, Taylor demonstrated skill and achieved success in every command he held, one of the few citizen-soldiers on either side to do so.

—*Broeck N. Oder*

See also Irish Bend/Bayou Teche; Mansfield, Louisiana, Battle of; Pleasant Hill, Louisiana, Battle of; Shenandoah Valley Campaign (1862).

For further reading:

Freeman, Douglas Southall. *Lee's Lieutenants: A Study in Command* (1942–1944).
Josephy, Alvin M. *The Civil War in the American West* (1991).
Parrish, T. Michael. *Richard Taylor: Soldier Prince of Dixie* (1992).
Porter, David D. *Naval History of the Civil War* (1886; reprint, 1984).

Taylor, Richard. *Destruction and Reconstruction: Personal Experiences of the Late War* (1879; reprint, 1983).

TAYLOR, SUSIE KING
(1848–?)
African-American army woman

Of the hundreds, or perhaps thousands, of African-American women to serve with the Union army's "colored" regiments during the second half of the war, Susie King Taylor is the only one to have left a published memoir of her experiences. This unique memoir provides readers with a good look at the workings of the first African-American regiment formed during the war, and it demonstrates that military service for African-American army women was quite similar to what it was for white women. Like her white counterparts in other regiments, Taylor spent her time in the army doing a range of tasks to support the common soldiers, some of which occasionally bordered on the paramilitary.

Susie Baker was born a slave in Georgia in 1848. She became a freedwoman at age fourteen, after first becoming contraband of war when her uncle in April 1862 did what so many slaves had already begun to do across the South. He sought liberation behind Union lines (in his case, boarding a Federal gunboat that was passing near Fort Pulaski). Susie Baker's uncle took as many members of his extended family with him as he could. She was one of these escapees, many of whom later found themselves associated with a newly formed regiment of black soldiers, the 1st South Carolina Infantry Volunteers (later renamed the 33d Regiment, U.S. Colored Troops) organized by Major General David Hunter of the Union's Department of the South and commanded by Colonel Thomas Wentworth Higginson of Massachusetts.

Initially assigned the position of a regimental laundress, Susie Baker's ready demonstration of her many skills—not the least of which was her ability to read and write—soon resulted in the expansion of her responsibilities. During the course of her time with the regiment, Baker continued to do washing and cooking for the men, but she also served as a regimental nurse, making use of both conventional and folk techniques when tending to the sick and wounded and to sustain her own good health. "I was not in the least afraid of the small-pox," she later wrote, "and I drank sassafras tea constantly, which kept my blood purged and prevented me from contracting this dread scourge."

Baker also functioned as the regiment's reading and writing instructor, sharing with the other former slaves the lessons she had learned secretly as a child. As for her own learning of new things while in the regiment, Baker rejoiced at the opportunity to master the inner workings

of a musket and to develop considerable skill in shooting at a target. At some point during her first year, Susie Baker married a sergeant in the regiment named Edward King. Together they served until the 33d's mustering out in February 1866.

After the war, Susie Baker King and her husband moved to Savannah, Georgia, where she opened a private school for black children. Edward King died suddenly in September 1866, leaving his wife to fend for herself, a task made more difficult by the opening of a free school for blacks in town. By 1868 Susie King was reduced to employment as a domestic servant, the waged job most readily available to African-American women in the postwar period (and into the twentieth century). Although she continued in domestic service, she did not remain in the South, instead heading north in 1874 and settling in Boston, a city she praised for being a far more just environment for blacks than any to be found in her native South.

In 1879 Susie Baker married again, this time to one Russell Taylor. She dedicated much of her later life to the Woman's Relief Corps, a national organization for female Civil War veterans established in 1873. "All this time," she wrote in her 1902 memoir, "my interest in the boys in blue has not abated. My hands have never left undone anything they could do toward their aid and comfort in the twilight of their lives." Susie Baker King Taylor's date of death is unknown.

—*Elizabeth D. Leonard*

See also Contrabands; Nurses; Women.

For further reading:
Leonard, Elizabeth D. *All the Daring of the Soldier: Women of the Civil War Armies* (1999).
Taylor, Susie King. *A Black Woman's Civil War Memoirs: Reminiscences of My Life in Camp with the 33d U.S. Colored Troops, Late 1st South Carolina Volunteers* (1988).

TECUMSEH, USS

The USS *Tecumseh* was a Civil War Union monitor, a warship completely armored above the waterline (a waterline very close to the upper deck indeed), that carried no masts or sails and that mounted its heavy guns in a revolving, armored turret. This ironclad was a unit in the Canonicus class, which were improved Passaic-class monitors. The ships of the Canonicus class were the first monitors to incorporate into their design the battle and day-to-day operational experience of two years of naval warfare. The objectionable "overhang" between the upper deck and the lower hulls of the original *Monitor* and the Passaics, which had caused serious leakage, was eliminated. An armored "glacis," 15 inches high and 5 inches thick, protected the base of the Canonicus class's single turrets and thus diminished the possibility of jamming by enemy projectiles. More significantly, armament was increased from the Passaics'

awkward arrangement of one 15-inch and one 11-inch Dahlgren smoothbore, to a pair of 15-inch Dahlgrens. The *Tecumseh* was 223 feet long, with an extreme beam of 43.3 feet, and a draft of 11.5 feet. (Its freeboard was so low that a long-armed man could dip his hand into the water from the upper deck.) It displaced 2,100 tons and had a designed speed of 13 knots from two Ericsson vibrating engines of 320 indicated horsepower. All Canonicus monitors were to have been fitted with a wooden upper deck laid over the upper deck's iron plates (another wartime lesson), but in the rush to put the class into service the wooden decking was never installed. In the warm southern climates in which these ironclads operated, this omission resulted in below-decks temperatures that, despite a much improved artificial ventilation system, ranged into the low one hundreds, while conditions in the engine rooms could beggar description.

The *Tecumseh* was launched on 1 August 1863 and commissioned on 19 April 1864. Her primary contractor was Secor & Company of New York City, whose allowable *Tecumseh* billings totaled $460,000.

The *Tecumseh* was dispatched to Admiral David Glasgow Farragut's fleet, then preparing to fight its way into Mobile Bay, Alabama. There Farragut aimed to destroy the two Confederate armorclads, the *Tennessee* and the almost-completed *Nashville*, and thus to eliminate Mobile as a blockade-running port.

Early on the morning of 5 August, Farragut's fleet, with its four new monitors (the *Tecumseh*, *Manhattan*, *Winnebago*, and *Chickasaw*, in that order) stationed between the wooden ships of the squadron, made its way toward the mouth of the bay and its main Confederate guardian, Fort Morgan. In his eagerness to come to grips with the looming *Tennessee*, the *Tecumseh*'s captain, Tunis A. M. Craven, ordered his warship straight through, rather than around a line of "torpedoes" (anchored mines). Almost immediately a large explosion tore a hole in the *Tecumseh*. The giant monitor heeled to starboard and plunged to the bottom in about twenty-five seconds. Only three officers and seventeen seamen somehow clambered out of the sealed ironclad and survived. Captain Craven was not among them. The pilot did escape and reported that as he and Craven simultaneously leapt for the ladder leading up from the hull into the turret and possible escape through the gun ports, the *Tecumseh*'s captain stepped back courteously and said, "After you, pilot," and went down with his ship.

Farragut was not shaken by this disaster to his lead warship, and his reaction to the hesitation he detected on the part of the *Brooklyn*'s captain has gone down in American history: "Damn the torpedoes! Jouett, full speed!" and a few other choice words to similar effect. The media soon enough shortened this to "Damn the torpedoes! Full speed ahead!"

Under such leadership, the Confederate forts were run,

the *Tennessee* was battered into surrender, and Mobile ceased to function as a major blockade-running port.

The USS *Tecumseh* is noteworthy as the first warship in history to have been suddenly destroyed in battle, a harbinger of a fate all too common in future naval battles. Today the *Tecumseh* lies half covered in the mud on the bottom of Mobile Bay. Periodically, interest revives in her salvage, but such a project would cost in the tens of millions of dollars and would not likely prove successful at any rate, considering her wood and iron construction.

—Stanley Sandler

See also Ironclads; Mobile Bay; *Tennessee*, CSS.

For further reading:

Bennett, Frank M. *The Monitor and the Navy Under Steam* (1900).

Bergeron, Arthur W. *Confederate Mobile* (1991).

Cracknell, William H. *United States Monitors of the Civil War* (1973).

Eskew, G. L. "Our Navy's Ships and Their Builders, 1775–1883" (1962).

Greene, Jack, and Alessandro Massignani. *Ironclads at War: The Origin and Development of the Armored Warship, 1854–1891* (1998).

Parker, Foxhall. *The Battle of Mobile Bay , and the Capture of Forts Powell, Gaines, and Morgan by the Combined Sea and Land Forces of the United States under the Command of Rear-Admiral David Glasgow Farragut, and Major-General Gordon Granger, August, 1864* (1878).

Sandler, Stanley. *The Emergence of the Modern Capital Ship* (1979).

Shapack, Arnold. "Oak to Iron—Monitors in United States Naval History" (M.A thesis, 1973).

U.S. National Archives. Bureau of Construction and Repair, Plans of Ships and stations, with related records (1794–1910).

U.S. Navy Department. Naval History Division. *Monitors of the U.S. Navy, 1861–1937* (1969).

———. *Report of the Secretary of the Navy in Relation to Armored Vessels 1864* (1864).

TELEGRAPH

The telegraph was used extensively during the Civil War. There were primarily three telegraph entities: commercial telegraph companies, the Military Telegraph Service, and the Signal Corps Field Telegraph. All three services played an important part in providing tactical and strategic communications.

At the outbreak of the war, several commercial companies were providing telegraph service to the Union. The American Telegraph Company was the principal company to the north of Washington, and in early 1861 the company extended its wires to Washington and the War Department. Secretary of War Simeon Cameron solicited the aid of several telegraph

The military telegraph to Ackworth, Georgia (*Harper's Weekly / Library of Congress*)

Union telegraphers at the battle of Fredericksburg, 13 December 1862 (*Library of Congress*)

executives and enlisted the services of Thomas S. Scott of the Pennsylvania Railroad who was made general manager of all lines in and around Washington. The American Telegraph Company was requested to install telegraph lines and facilities necessary to support the war. Anson Stager from the Western Union recommended that the government take control of existing commercial telegraph facilities, and in October 1861 the U.S. Military Telegraph Service was formed. The government assumed control of all telegraphic facilities for use by the Military Telegraph Service, and Stager became its chief with the eventual rank of colonel.

The Military Telegraph Service was in reality a civilian bureau attached to the Quartermaster's Department. The supervisors were granted commissions in the Quartermaster's Department, but the operators remained civilians throughout the war. Cameron's replacement, Secretary of War Edwin Stanton, a former telegraph executive, assumed effective control of the

service and championed it throughout the war. Stager was stationed in Cleveland, Ohio, and his principle subordinate, Major Thomas Eckert, assumed tactical control of the service in the east and accompanied the Army of the Potomac during its various campaigns. Of the approximately 2,000 telegraph operators working in the country during the war, more than half, including some women, eventually worked for the Military Telegraph Service. Mary E. Smith, Louisa E. Volker, and Ann Marean all served in the Military Telegraph Service, and numerous other women served as operators in private telegraph companies, thus replacing men that had joined the Military Telegraph Service.

The Military Telegraph Service used the commercial equipment of the day and concentrated on the strategic use of the system. Wiretapping became a problem on long lines and several cipher systems were used, which on occasion caused difficulties in being read by the operators. The Military Telegraph Service became the

Field telegraph station at Wilcox's Landing, Virginia, 1864 (*Library of Congress*)

primary means of strategic communications, and President Abraham Lincoln spent many evenings in the cipher room at the War Department's Telegraph Office waiting for news from his battlefield commanders.

Both sides obtained intelligence by tapping the enemy's lines, and the operators of the Military Telegraph Service were often employed in that role. Confederate telegraph wires were frequently tapped during Sherman's March and provided important information on Confederate movements.

The principle problem with the Military Telegraph Service was the autonomy of its civilian operators. Although Stanton believed that if the operators were soldiers they would be subject to the whims of field commanders, on numerous occasions, the operators made their own decisions as to their deployment, causing difficulties in command and control. A typical example is reflected in Major General Daniel Butterfield's message to Major Eckert: "General Meade desires to know under whose orders and authority the telegraph operators possessing the cipher are appointed and controlled. The operator, Mr. Caldwell, at these headquarters presumes to act in an independent manner, and has left headquarters for Westminster, selecting his own location, without authority or permission. The commanding general is unable to send dispatches from these headquarters in cipher...."

Concurrent with the formation of the Military

Telegraph Service, the Field Telegraph Service was formed as a part of the Union Army's Signal Corps. Unlike the operators of the Military Telegraph Service, the Signal Corps Field Telegraph operators were soldiers who had been detailed from various regiments and trained by the army. The Field Telegraph Service did not use commercial equipment. They employed the Beardslee telegraph device that operated with the use of a magneto generator instead of the heavy wet cells of the conventional telegraph. The device worked by moving a handle on a dial instead of the usual key. When the handle was moved to a particular letter on the sending machine dial, an index on the dial of the receiving machine was moved to the corresponding letter. The Beardslee telegraph device was designed to be used by soldiers who did not have the extensive training that the Military Telegraph Service operators received. The Beardslee device was employed during the Peninsula campaign and used extensively at Chancellorsville. It had severe limitations and at times would produce garbled messages. Colonel Albert Myer, the founder of the Signal Corps, on several occasions attempted to take control of all telegraphic operations. When he attempted to remove the less than dependable Beardslee device and recruit trained telegraphers, Colonel Stager objected and wrote Stanton. Stanton removed Myer from his position as chief signal officer and gave the responsibility for field telegraph service to the Military Telegraph Service.

The Military Telegraph Service discarded the Beardslee device and maintained field telegraph service with conventional commercial equipment after Myer was removed as chief signal officer. During the campaigns of 1864 and 1865, the Military Telegraph Service typically connected the major headquarters with telegraph lines and earned kudos from General Ulysses S. Grant who wrote that "…telegraph wagons would take their positions near where the head-quarters they belonged to were to be established, and would connect with the wire. Thus, in a few minutes longer time than it took a mule to walk the length of its coil, telegraphic communications would be effected between all the head-quarters of the army. No orders ever had to be given to establish the telegraph."

Colonel Myer continued an acrimonious relationship with Stanton and worked with various political contacts to regain his original position. On 30 October 1866, due to the influence of Grant and President Andrew Johnson, Myer was reinstated as chief signal officer, whose duties encompassed control of the field telegraph. After the war, the Military Telegraph Service ceased to exist, and by 1873 Myer began to recognize his dream of controlling military telegraphy as the Signal Corps constructed an extensive telegraph network.

—*Bill Cameron*

See also Myer, Albert James; Signal Corps.

For further reading:

Bates, David Homer. *Lincoln in the Telegraph Office: Recollections of the United States Military Telegraph Corps during the Civil War* (1907).

Brown, J. Willard. *The Signal Corps, U.S.A. in the War of the Rebellion* (1896).

Coker, Kathy R., and Carol E. Rios. *A Concise History of the U.S. Army Signal Corps* (1988).

Greely, A. W. *The Military-Telegraph Service.* Vol. 4 of *The Photographic History of the Civil War* (reprint, 1987).

Plum, William R. *The Military Telegraph during the Civil War in the United States* (1882).

Raines, Rebecca Robbins. *Getting the Message Through, A Branch History of the U.S. Army Signal Corps* (1996).

Scheips, Paul J. "Union Signal Communications: Innovation and Conflict." *Civil War History* (1963).

TENNESSEE

Tennessee was the location of more than 200 engagements during the American Civil War. Only Virginia had a higher total. Furthermore, Tennessee enlisted men for both sides: more than 185,000 for the Confederacy and an additional 31,000, mostly former slaves, for the Union army. Both sides coveted the state for its strategic significance. Tennessee borders eight states (more than any other state in the Union) and stretches from the Mississippi River to the Appalachian Mountains, dividing the Midwest from the Lower South. Internally, the state has three major geographic regions, commonly referred to as "Grand Divisions."

The eastern part of the state, encompassing rocky portions of the Cumberland and Great Smoky Mountain ranges, boasted the South's second-largest wheat production region and 90 percent of the South's copper deposits. Because the land was unfavorable to plantation agriculture, east Tennesseans had little need for slaves. Two vital railroad lines converged in east Tennessee at Chattanooga. The Atlanta-Richmond line connected the Lower South with Virginia and the Northeast, and the Nashville-Chattanooga line linked Southern iron and mineral mines with the manufacturing regions in middle Tennessee and northern Alabama.

Middle Tennessee had abundant acreage suitable for cotton, corn, or livestock and possessed large quantities of mineral resources, especially those needed for gunpowder production. Furthermore, the Tennessee and Cumberland river systems flowed across large areas of this region, providing numerous transportation and economic advantages. Nashville, straddling the Cumberland River and the Louisville-Atlanta railroad, was one of the South's leading agricultural and industrial centers by 1860.

West Tennessee, located in the alluvial valley between the Tennessee and Mississippi rivers, had relatively level ground and had excellent soil for cotton production. West Tennessee raised more cotton in 1860 than east and middle Tennessee combined and was also the state leader in tobacco production. The majority of the state's slaves were also found in west Tennessee. River tributaries and a well-maintained system of macadamized turnpikes provided west Tennessee with excellent avenues of transportation and communication connecting the North and South. Memphis, in the southwest corner of the state, was a key port on the Mississippi River, linking the Midwest and Upper South with New Orleans.

Not surprisingly, each Grand Division developed its own distinctive political culture and zealously guarded its individual interests within state government. Consequently, the 1850s Tennessee railroad boom connected each region to the nation along a north-south axis, but not one line ran across the state joining Memphis, Nashville, and Knoxville. In the antebellum era, Whigs in west and east Tennessee usually prevailed over the Democratic strongholds of middle Tennessee.

As the issue of slavery, the South's "peculiar institution," divided the nation and destroyed the Whig Party, west Tennesseans shifted their loyalties to the Democrats. Ironically, state Democratic leader and two-term governor Andrew Johnson of east Tennessee was influential in strengthening the Democratic Party in the West. Johnson, who had declined a third term as governor in 1857 to accept a U.S. Senate seat in 1859,

Railroad trestle built by Union engineers at Whiteside, Tennessee (*Photography by George N. Barnard/Library of Congress*)

selected his occasional party rival, Isham G. Harris of Memphis, to succeed him as governor. This choice was pivotal in Tennessee's future. With slavery at the forefront of American politics and a candidate with connections to Memphis on the ballot, west Tennesseans cemented their alliance with fellow planters in middle Tennessee by easily electing Harris governor in 1857 and again in 1859. After Lincoln's election in 1860, an outraged Harris began ardently campaigning for secession. He called for a statewide referendum on the issue to be held in February. To Harris's dismay, Tennesseans overwhelmingly rejected secession; many considered themselves "conditional Unionists" who would support the government as long as it continued a "hands-off" policy toward the seceded states.

After Fort Sumter, a new wave of secessionist support swept over the state, turning many "conditional Unionists" into "reluctant Confederates." Harris took maximum advantage of Tennesseans' outrage over the incident by persuading the state legislature to issue a "declaration of independence" and entering the state into a "military league" with the Confederacy. The state was soon teeming with Southern troops constructing fortifications and Confederate officers recruiting Tennesseans for a provisional army. In June 1861,

Tennessee held another special election on a new secessionist constitution. This time the secessionists won, partially because of the violent intimidation of Unionists at the polls. Thus, Tennessee officially became the last state to join the Confederacy on 22 July 1861.

The vast majority of east Tennesseans, however, were yeoman farmers who had come to resent the political and economic power of the "slaveocracies" in middle and west Tennessee. As a result, many east Tennesseans identified themselves with the Union cause. Pro-Union men met at the Greenville Convention in June 1861 and adopted a resolution asking the state legislature to declare east Tennessee an independent state. Their demands were simply ignored in Nashville. Harris hoped that over time the majority of east Tennesseans would join the Confederate cause, but opinions in the East remained decidedly pro-Union. President Lincoln made the "redemption" of Unionist east Tennessee a major military and political objective. Throughout the war, east Tennessee Unionists would carry out both guerrilla and conventional military operations against Confederate targets. Their actions forced the Confederacy to declare martial law and allocate precious manpower and material resources to secure the area.

The Confederacy recognized early the importance of

protecting the river networks in Tennessee against Union assault. To that end, they constructed several large fortifications along the Mississippi, Tennessee, and Cumberland rivers. Lincoln and his military advisors also realized the value of the rivers to the Confederate war effort and adopted the "Anaconda" plan to seal off the Confederate economy, especially on the Mississippi and other major rivers. In February 1862, Union troops under General Ulysses S. Grant, assisted by gunboats, captured Fort Henry on the Tennessee and Fort Donelson on the Cumberland. In panic, the Confederates abandoned Nashville on 25 February, surrendering a major logistical hub to the enemy and leaving behind many of their supplies stored there. Governor Harris and the state legislature fled Union-occupied Nashville to reestablish the state capital at Memphis. By June 1862, Union forces had destroyed the Confederate river defenses at Island No. 10 and Fort Pillow and occupied Memphis. Without a home, the state legislature went into exile in Mississippi, while Harris attached himself to the Army of Tennessee as a staff officer.

In April 1862, the 40,000 Confederates led by General Albert Sidney Johnston surprised Grant's Army of the Tennessee along the banks of the Tennessee River near Shiloh Church. In two days of the bloodiest fighting in American history to that date, Union forces, reinforced by General Don Carlos Buell's Army of the Cumberland, fought off numerous Confederate assaults. During the battle, the Union suffered over 13,000 casualties and the Confederates 11,000, including Johnston, who was mortally wounded. Reeling from their losses at Shiloh, the Confederates fell back to Corinth just inside Mississippi.

President Lincoln moved quickly to restore federal government to Tennessee. He appointed former governor and U.S. senator Andrew Johnson as military governor in March 1862. An east Tennessee Unionist, Johnson had resented the planters' domination of state government and their declaration of secession. Furthermore, he had been the only Democrat to remain in the Senate after Fort Sumter and seemed an ideal choice to begin the process of reconstructing Tennessee under Lincoln's conciliatory policy. But Johnson's Unionist supporters in east Tennessee were still under Confederate control. Johnson was forced to depend upon a small minority of Unionists and converted Democrats in the middle and west, who as Whigs had been opposed to his previous gubernatorial administrations. Therefore, Johnson relied heavily on the military to maintain order and enforce his decisions.

The practices of foraging and confiscation by the Union armies, which were closely associated with Johnson's military regime, created resentment among Tennessee's citizens. Frequently, the state erupted into widespread violence and open defiance of federal authority. Confederate cavalry, taking advantage of the widely dispersed Union garrisons protecting the railroads and rivers, conducted raids into the state throughout the war, causing nervousness and embarrassment in both Nashville and Washington. Due to the increasing losses resulting from these raids and escalated guerrilla activities, federal authorities gradually abandoned their conciliatory approach to restoring Tennessee to the Union. Johnson and the local military commanders increasingly responded to such attacks with harsh, punitive measures against known and suspected secessionists.

Confederate forces invaded Kentucky in the fall of 1862 from bases located in east Tennessee in hopes of converting the border state. The attack failed miserably at Perryville, and the Army of Tennessee retreated back into middle Tennessee. At the battle of Stones River (Murfreesboro) in December 1862, the Army of the Cumberland again pushed the Confederates back toward Chattanooga. The two armies remained in place without a major engagement for the next six months. Then, in June 1863, Union general William Rosecrans began a campaign that would ultimately end in November with the Federal occupation of Chattanooga. Simultaneously, Lincoln ordered General Ambrose Burnside to take his army and liberate Knoxville. Knoxville was occupied in August 1863, although the Confederates did conduct a failed counterattack to retake the city in November. By the beginning of 1864, Tennessee had become the first and only state to be completely occupied by Union forces during the war.

The Confederacy made one last desperate attempt to seize Tennessee in the summer of 1864. The fatigued and battle-weary Army of Tennessee under their new commander, John Bell Hood, marched northward from Georgia into Tennessee. In two engagements, Franklin and Nashville, Union troops, many former slaves, decisively defeated the Confederate invaders and eliminated the Army of Tennessee as an effective fighting unit for the rest of the war.

Reconstruction of the state had begun as early as December 1863 with the announcement of Lincoln's Ten Percent Plan. This plan called for the restoration of any state in which 10 percent of its citizens took an oath of allegiance. Johnson worried that Lincoln's plan was too lenient and might allow former secessionists to regain control of the state. Therefore, he instituted his own plan with more stringent requirements, which also meant that even some Unionists, mostly Johnson's former opponents, were also denied citizenship.

Tennessee held elections during the 1864 presidential election, but the returns were rejected because Congress still considered Tennessee in rebellion. Even without Tennessee's votes, Lincoln and his new vice president, Andrew Johnson, won the election. The ascension of Johnson to the ticket bolstered the remaining Tennessee

Unionists, who began at once to restore civil authority. A convention of Unionists met in Nashville in early 1865 to repeal all acts under the secessionist constitution and replace it with a new constitution that abolished slavery (Tennessee had been exempted from the Emancipation Proclamation). A new state government was inaugurated on 5 April 1865 with outspoken Unionist and newspaper editor Willam G. Brownlow as governor. Just ten days later, Lincoln was assassinated, and Andrew Johnson stepped into the presidency. Johnson favored the rapid readmission of states to the Union but was challenged by the Radical Republicans in Congress. Brownlow, Johnson's successor as governor, aligned himself with the Congress and succeeded in pushing the Fourteenth Amendment through the state legislature in 1866. The amendment's ratification allowed Tennessee to become the first state readmitted after the war. As such, the state was exempted from the congressionally mandated military occupation of the South that would remain in place until 1877.

—*Derek W. Frisby*

See also Brownlow, William G.; Chattanooga Campaign; Chattanooga, Tennessee; Fort Donelson, Battle of; Fort Henry, Battle of; Fort Pillow; Franklin, Battle of; Harris, Isham; Island No. 10, Battle of; Johnson, Andrew; Knoxville Campaign; Lincoln's Reconstruction Policy; Nashville, Battle of; Shiloh, Battle of; Stones River, Battle of.

For further reading:

Ash, Steven V. *Middle Tennessee Society Transformed: War and Peace in the Upper South* (1988).

Bergeron, Paul, Stephen Ash, and Jeanette Keith. *Tennesseans and Their History* (1999).

Connelly, Thomas L. *Civil War Tennessee: Battles and Leaders* (1979).

Crofts, Daniel W. *Reluctant Confederates: Upper South Unionists in the Secession Crisis* (1989).

Fisher, Noel. *War at Every Door: Partisan Politics and Guerilla Violence in East Tennessee, 1860–1869* (1998).

Horn, Stanley, ed. *Tennessee's War, 1861–1865: Described by Participants* (1965).

TENNESSEE, CSS

Two Confederate ironclads bore the name *Tennessee*. The first was a ram begun by John Shirley of Memphis in October 1861. A sister of the famous *Arkansas*, the first *Tennessee* was designed to carry eight guns (two 9-inch, two 8-inch, two 6-inch, and two 32-pounders). However, the warship had not been launched when Federal forces approached Memphis, and on 5 June 1862 she was burned on the slipway the night before the city fell.

The second *Tennessee* proved to be one of the most formidable warships constructed by the Confederate States Navy, and because of her capture and incorporation into the United States Navy, the one for which the most precise details survive. Laid down by Harry D. Bassett at Selma, Alabama, the ram was launched in February 1863 and towed down the Alabama River in an incomplete state. Under the direction of Admiral Franklin Buchanan, the ironclad was fitted out at Mobile and finally commissioned on 16 February 1864 with Captain James D. Johnston her commanding officer. Her 13-foot draft kept her out of the lower Mobile Bay until specially built "camels," or caissons, allowed her to be towed over the 9.5-foot Dog River Bar on 18 May. Four days later Buchanan hoisted his admiral's pennant on her as flagship of the Mobile Squadron.

The *Tennessee* measured 209 feet in length with a beam of 48 feet and a displacement of 1,273 tons. Her machinery, taken from a riverboat, consisted of four boilers providing steam for two engines. At full power, her single propeller could drive her to a speed of 6 knots. Her protection consisted of heavy armor plating made by Shelby Iron Company of Columbiana, Alabama, and rolled by the Atlanta Rolling Mill. Backed by 18.5 inches of yellow pine and 4 inches of oak, her casemate armor was 4 to 6 inches thick, with the plates being sloped to enhance their powers of resistance. Her 4-inch side armor extended about 6 feet below the waterline.

For offensive punch, the *Tennessee* carried six heavy Brooke rifled cannon, probably made by the Selma Naval Foundry—two of 7-inch caliber mounted fore and aft, and four of 6.4-inch caliber, two along each side. The larger guns could swivel to add to the broadside fire. Surprisingly, she mounted no spar torpedo, and her value as a ram was largely negated by her slow speed and unresponsiveness. When operational, the ship's crew numbered 133. The noted naval historian and theorist Alfred Thayer Mahan would later describe the *Tennessee* as the most powerful ironclad built, from the keel up, by the Confederacy.

Yet certain defects in her design would become apparent in battle. For example, hinged shutters that slammed closed if their chains were cut by enemy gunfire protected her gunports. Worse, by some oversight the chains controlling her tiller ran exposed on the quarterdeck.

In the summer of 1864, the *Tennessee* was the linchpin of the Confederate force defending Mobile Bay, and during the engagement on 5 August she put up a terrific fight. Flying Buchanan's flag, the ram, assisted by three small gunboats, challenged the entire fleet of Rear Admiral David Glasgow Farragut, which consisted of fourteen wooden ships and four ironclad monitors. While doing considerable damage to the Union flotilla, the unwieldy Confederate was rammed repeatedly and hit by dozens of major caliber projectiles. She was finally brought to bay by two of the monitors. The *Manhattan*, firing 428-pound 15-inch projectiles made the only penetration of the Confederate vessel's armor. At point blank range, the *Chickasaw* with her 11-inch projectiles

The CSS *Tennessee* (*Library of Congress*)

cut the chains to the ram's port gun shutters and her rudder chains.

With her armament useless, her smokestack and rudder chains shot away, and almost out of ammunition, the *Tennessee* had to surrender. Her protection with its sloping armor had shown to good effect, and her personnel losses totaled only twelve killed and twenty wounded. A Union survey board concluded within the week that the ram was suitable for Union service despite her battle damage. She was commissioned into the U.S. Navy on 19 August and took part in the assault four days later on Fort Morgan at the mouth of Mobile Bay.

Decommissioned on 19 August 1865, the ram was sold for scrap on 27 November 1867. Although broken up, four of her rifles (one 7-inch and three 6.4-inch) survive on display in Willard Park at the Washington Navy Yard.

—*Malcolm Muir, Jr.*

See also Buchanan, Franklin; Mobile Bay; Navy, C.S.A.

For further reading:

Durkin, Joseph T. *Confederate Navy Chief: Stephen R. Mallory* (1954).

Luraghi, Raimondo. *A History of the Confederate Navy.* Translated by Paolo E. Coletta (1996).

Silverstone, Paul H. *Warships of the Civil War Navies* (1989).

Still, William N., Jr. *Iron Afloat: The Story of the Confederate Armorclads* (1985).

TERRY, ALFRED HOWE
(1827–1890)
Union general

Born to Alfred Terry and Clarissa Howe Terry in Hartford, Connecticut, Alfred Howe Terry attended Yale Law School but chose not to complete his course of study there after his early admission to the Connecticut bar. In the years before the Civil War, Terry served as a clerk of the New Haven Superior Court. Upon the outbreak of the war he raised a ninety-day regiment known as the 2d Connecticut and led it to Washington as its colonel.

Terry and the 2d fought in the battle of First Bull Run, after which he and the regiment were mustered out of federal service. He returned to Connecticut to raise a long-term regiment, which, when brought into federal service, became the 9th Connecticut Volunteers with Terry as its colonel. In the fall of 1861, the 9th participated in the Port Royal expedition, which secured that position on the South Carolina coast for the Union. For the next two and a half years Terry fought along that coast.

In April 1862, Terry commanded his regiment in the attack and capture of Fort Pulaski, Georgia. After the fall of the fort, Terry was placed in temporary command of the garrison there. In the same month he was promoted to brigadier general of volunteers.

In June 1862, Terry went back to South Carolina to participate in the attempt on Charleston via James Island. At the battle of Secessionville on 16 June 1862 he commanded a brigade in the Union defeat. For the remainder of the year he and his brigade were at Hilton Head, although in October they did participate in the fight at Pocotaligo Bridge. After this engagement Terry assumed command of Hilton Head.

The following year, Terry spent much of the first months operating along the South Carolina coast. During the summer of 1863 he led his brigade to James Island, where he attempted to divert Confederate forces away from Morris Island in preparation for the Federal assault on Fort Wagner. Terry and his men repulsed a Confederate attack on their position at Grimball's Landing on 16 July 1863 and then moved to Morris Island, where they joined the siege of Fort Wagner. Terry served on Morris Island for the remainder of the year.

At the end of 1863, Terry learned that he was being transferred to Benjamin F. Butler's Army of the James. After leaving South Carolina in March 1864, Terry assumed command of 1st Division, X Corps stationed at Gloucester Point across from Yorktown, Virginia. Through the summer and into the fall of 1864 Terry led his division in the assaults against the defenses of Petersburg, Virginia. In October 1864, on the death of the corps' commander David Bell Birney, Terry assumed temporary command of X Corps.

At the end of the year Terry led what was by then being called Terry's provisional corps in Butler's aborted campaign against Fort Fisher at Wilmington, North Carolina. Butler's poor performance led Ulysses S. Grant to place Terry in direct command of the next attempt on Fort Fisher in January 1865. With David D. Porter commanding the naval force, Terry sailed from Virginia on 4 January. He landed on 13 January after a naval bombardment of the fort of over twelve hours' duration. Terry spent the next day and a half deploying his men to strike the fort from several different directions. After about seven hours of assaults, the fort surrendered to Union forces on the night of 15 January. A damper was put on the celebrations the next day when two of Porter's sailors, looking for loot, entered the powder magazine with lit torches. The resulting explosion killed twenty-five Union soldiers and injured many more. The accident, however, did not dampen the enthusiasm of Congress, which celebrated the closing of Wilmington—the last open Confederate port—by voting its thanks to Terry. For his achievement, Terry also received a promotion to brigadier general in the regular army.

Terry remained in North Carolina, with his command falling under the authority of John M. Schofield and the Army of the Ohio. At the end of March 1865, Terry was given command of the newly reorganized X Corps. He moved to cooperate with William T. Sherman as Sherman moved up through the Carolinas. He joined with Sherman in the latter part of the campaign against Joseph Johnston.

After Johnston's surrender, Terry was promoted to major general of volunteers dating back to the Fort Fisher campaign. After enjoying a brief leave in Connecticut, he was named commander of the Department of Virginia at the end of June 1865. After being mustered out of the volunteer army in 1866, Terry retained his regular commission and was given command of the Department of Dakota. After three years in that command he became commander of the Department of the South during the height of Reconstruction. He returned to command the Department of Dakota in 1872 and remained in that command through the George A. Custer fiasco at the Little Bighorn. In overall command of the expedition, Terry was criticized by some for Custer's fate. He never publicly commented on the controversy regarding whether Custer disobeyed his orders. During the Rutherford B. Hayes administration he had sat on the board that reviewed the Fitz John Porter court-martial of 1862–1863.

Terry remained in the army, largely commanding on the frontier, until his promotion to major general in 1886. He was one of only a few non–West Point graduates in the post–Civil War 19th-century army to reach that rank. In 1888 he retired to New Haven, Connecticut, where he died on 16 December 1890.

—*David S. Heidler and Jeanne T. Heidler*

See also Fort Fisher; Fort Wagner, Battle of.

For further reading:

Finan, William J. *Major General Alfred Howe Terry (1827–1890), Hero of Fort Fisher* (1965).

Marino, Carl W. "General Alfred Howe Terry: Soldier From Connecticut" (Ph.D. dissertation, 1968).

Osborne, Arthur Dimon. *Capture of Fort Fisher by Major General Alfred H. Terry and What It Accomplished* (1911).

TEXAS

At the western limits of the Confederate nation, Texas was the only Southern state to border on a foreign nation (Mexico), the only Confederate state with an active Indian frontier, and the threshold to a possible Confederate empire in the West. When Texans seceded on 1 February 1861, the state's population of 604,215 included more than 182,000 slaves. Germans living in central Texas and Hispanics in south Texas made a small contribution to the total number. The census indicated 92,145 white males of military age, and a significant percentage of these men served in Confederate armies.

Only 8 of 174 delegates to the Secession Convention

opposed the decision to leave the Union, and the Ordinance of Secession, which was subject to the approval of voters, received an overwhelming majority in a general election in February. Unionist governor Sam Houston, realizing he had failed to prevent the state from seceding, refused to take the oath of loyalty to the new government and was removed from office. Lieutenant Governor Edward Clark completed the term.

In early 1861, Texans enthusiastically joined the Confederate army. The best known unit, Hood's Texas brigade, composed of the 1st, 4th, and 5th Texas, fought with the Army of Northern Virginia under Robert E. Lee. First under Louis T. Wigfall and later under John Bell Hood, the brigade gained fame in battles from Virginia to Georgia. Granbury's Texas brigade of Cleburne's division, Army of Tennessee, earned acclaim in the Western theater, while the 8th Texas Cavalry or Terry's Texas Rangers was the state's most famous cavalry regiment. Texans also participated in the invasion of New Mexico late in 1861 and early 1862. Still, the majority of Texans wanted to protect their homes and fought in the Trans-Mississippi states of Louisiana and Arkansas and in the Indian Territory.

Although Texans never permitted invading armies to move inland, the 400 miles of unprotected coastline concerned both state and Confederate officials. The first Federal vessels arrived off Galveston Island in the summer of 1862; in September of that year, Federal soldiers landed at Sabine Pass, inflicting minor damage, but they soon retreated without capitalizing on their momentary success. Galveston surrendered to Federal forces in October but was recaptured by Confederates on 1 January 1863.

Two motives prompted the Union desire to occupy key regions of Texas. The border with Mexico was one concern, while the desire to control east Texas cotton fields was a second. One result of Abraham Lincoln's interest in the state was the battle of Sabine Pass in September 1863. Lincoln hoped Union armies could plant the U.S. flag on the coast as well as gain access to cotton for New England mills. Although Federal troops never succeeded in taking either Texas or its cotton, there were numerous incursions along the Gulf Coast throughout the war.

The final Federal attempt to invade Texas came in the spring of 1864. Union major general Nathaniel P. Banks moved up the Red River toward Shreveport, Louisiana, while Major General Frederick Steele pushed through Arkansas toward the same objective. Texas soldiers rallied to the defense of their state, and again Lincoln saw his hope of a Federal presence in Texas thwarted. Throughout the war, Lincoln never completely forgot Texas, while the Confederate president, Jefferson Davis, seldom gave the state much thought.

One frustration for Lincoln was that the flourishing trade between Texas and Mexico brought supplies into the Confederacy in exchange for cotton. Mexico served as a vital conduit to foreign markets for Confederate agents and speculators. In April 1863, cotton crossing the border brought a good price. Bales that went for six cents a pound in Galveston sold for thirty-six cents at Matamoros, and by December the price was as high as seventy to ninety cents. Ironically, cotton going through Mexico often provided New England mills with the cotton Lincoln was unable to obtain by military means.

While cotton heading illegally for Mexico annoyed both the Confederate and state governments, another problem was of more immediate concern. Unique to Texas was an active Indian frontier, for a significant percentage of the state's 267,339 square miles was unoccupied. Kiowas, Comanches, and occasionally Apaches preyed on isolated settlements. Before the war, the frontier line ran west of San Antonio, Austin, and Fort Worth, but as the Indians learned that men had left, they became increasingly bold. Governors Francis R. Lubbock (from 1861 to 1863) and Pendleton Murrah (from 1863 to 1865) guarded the frontier with state units, but this continued to be a problem throughout the war and one that kept state officials at odds with the Confederate government and in the constant turmoil over states' rights. Since the Confederate government had done no better in protecting settlers from the Indians than the old U.S. government (the state had listed that as a grievance in the ordinance of secession), many Texans questioned the wisdom of trading one ineffectual government for another. Moreover, an increasing number of deserters recognized the safety of the Texas frontier, and they became a growing problem after 1864.

Texas also had a significant number of Unionists, and some even joined one of the two Federal cavalry units raised along the Rio Grande. There were Unionists throughout the state from the Red River to the Mexican border, particularly in the German settlements in the Hill Country and in north Texas, where many settlers had migrated from the Midwest. After the passage of the conscription act in 1862, Confederates arrested Unionists in north Texas who protested the draft. Of the men incarcerated in Wise, Denton, and Grayson Counties, several were executed. In August 1863, German Unionists fleeing for Mexico were stopped at the Nueces River, and more than twenty were killed by Confederate cavalry, many after they had surrendered.

The final battle of the Civil War came at Palmito (Palmetto) Ranch, between Brazos Santiago and Brownsville, Texas, on 13 May 1865. Confederate cavalry charged a detachment that included Texas Unionists, Mexicans, and members of the 62d U.S. Colored Infantry. The battle was nothing more than a skirmish, but Texas Confederates routed the Federals and proudly proclaimed that they had won the last battle of the Civil War.

—*Anne J. Bailey*

See also Cotton; Galveston, Texas; Houston, Sam; Lubbock, Francis Richard; Matamoros, Mexico; Mexico; Murrah, Pendleton; Palmito Ranch, Battle of; Red River Campaign; Rio Grande Campaign; Sabine Pass, First Battle of; Sabine Pass, Second Battle of.

For further reading:

Buenger, Walter L. *Secession and the Union in Texas* (1984).

Frazier, Donald S. *Blood & Treasure: Confederate Empire in the Southwest* (1995).

Marten, James. *Texas Divided: Loyalty and Dissent in the Lone Star State, 1856–1874* (1990).

McCaslin, Richard B. *Tainted Breeze: The Great Hanging at Gainesville, Texas* (1994).

Smith, David P. *Frontier Defense in the Civil War: Texas' Rangers and Rebels* (1992).

Wooster, Ralph A., ed. *Lone Star Blue and Gray: Essays on Texas in the Civil War* (1995).

———. *Texas and Texans in the Civil War* (1995).

TEXAS RANGERS
(1861–1865)

The 8th Texas Cavalry Regiment (styled "Terry's Texas Rangers" and unaffiliated with the celebrated paramilitary Texas Rangers of the Republic of Texas), was organized by wealthy Houston sugar planter Benjamin F. Terry in 1861. Although intended for the Virginia theater of the war, the Rangers spent the war fighting in the West. Among their most significant battles were Chickamauga, Chattanooga, the Atlanta campaign, and efforts to delay William Tecumseh Sherman's march through Georgia. The regiment disbanded at the end of the war.

After the first battle of Bull Run in July 1861, Benjamin F. Terry and Thomas S. Lubbock returned to Texas from Virginia with orders to raise a regiment of cavalry. Their cavalry regiment was to return and fight as part of the Army of Northern Virginia. Upon reaching Houston, Texas, Terry and Lubbock began recruiting. They dispatched ten captains to recruit units of 100 volunteers each from the counties of south Texas. Although the Confederate States Army would provide them with horses, each trooper was required to supply his own rifle or shotgun, two revolvers, and a Bowie knife, as well as his own saddlery and tack. Within a month, Terry's captains had raised a regiment of 1,170 men, which was sworn into Confederate service on 9 September 1861. When given the choice to enlist for a period of one year, three years, or the duration of the war, the Rangers enthusiastically signed up for the duration.

It should be pointed out that neither Terry nor Lubbock—nor the vast majority of their regiment, for that matter—had any official affiliation with the original and celebrated Texas Rangers. They were "Rangers" in name only and took their name to signify a tribute to the original Rangers and their defense of Texas during the days of the Republic of Texas and the Mexican-American War. Terry's men were conscious of this symbolic connection and strove in their actions to give an account of themselves of which the old Rangers would approve.

Terry's Texas Rangers departed Houston for New Orleans on 10 September 1861, en route to the war. Instead of Virginia, however, the Confederate army dispatched them to Bowling Green, Kentucky, where they came under the command of General Albert Sidney Johnston. They would spend the remainder of the war campaigning in the West with the Army of Tennessee. In December 1861, Colonel Terry was killed in battle during the regiment's first engagement, at Woodsonville, Kentucky. Sent to draw Federal troops into the range of Confederate infantry and artillery, Terry instead ordered his regiment to charge. The Rangers broke the Union line, but at the cost of high casualties to themselves and the loss of their commander. After Terry's death, Lieutenant Colonel Lubbock assumed command, only to die of disease shortly thereafter. John A. Wharton replaced Lubbock as colonel of the 8th Texas Cavalry. When he was later promoted and transferred, the regiment's Major Thomas Harrison took over and led the Rangers for the remainder of the war.

After the fall of Fort Henry and Fort Donelson in February 1862 and the battle of Shiloh in April 1862, Ulysses S. Grant's Union army pushed the Confederates out of eastern Kentucky and penetrated northern Tennessee, seizing Nashville. As the Confederate forces fell back toward Mississippi, Terry's Texas Rangers defended the retreating columns.

In August 1862, the Rangers participated in General Braxton Bragg's attempted reconquest of Kentucky, but again served as a rear guard when the Confederates abandoned the field and retreated. In December 1862 and January 1863, the Rangers fought at the battle of Murfreesboro (Stones River), Tennessee. There, the Rangers infiltrated the Union lines and attacked the Federal supply columns.

Autumn of 1863 found the Rangers defending the Confederate railroad center at Chattanooga, Tennessee, where they fought at Chickamauga in September and the battle of Chattanooga in November. As Union forces gained momentum in 1864, Terry's Texas Rangers played a defensive role. They served as raiders of Union supply lines in the West, riding with Lieutenant General Nathan Bedford Forrest. During the summer of 1864, they served under General Joseph E. Johnston, resisting the Federal attempt to seize Atlanta, Georgia. That autumn, the Rangers rode hard to harass and delay (without much success) Sherman's troops marching through Georgia toward Savannah. At the battle of Bentonville in March 1865, Terry's Texas Rangers made the Army of Tennessee's final cavalry charge. When

Johnston surrendered his army in April 1865, most of the Rangers headed south to join other Confederate units still fighting. But before they could reach those forces, news arrived that the war had ended. Defeated, the Rangers trickled home to Texas.

—*Alicia E. Rodriquez*

See also Lubbock, Francis Richard; Terry, Benjamin F; Texas.
For further reading:
Blackburn, James Knox Polk. *Reminiscences of Terry's Texas Rangers* (1919; reprint, 1979).
Cutrer, Thomas W., ed. "'We Are Stern and Resolved': The Civil War Letters of John Wesley Rabb, Terry's Texas Rangers." *Southwestern Historical Quarterly* (1987).
Giles, Leonidas B. *Terry's Texas Rangers* (1911).
Jeffries, C. C. "The Character of Terry's Texas Rangers." *Southwestern Historical Quarterly* (1961).
Oates, Stephen B. "Recruiting Confederate Cavalry in Texas." *Southwestern Historical Quarterly* (1961).

THAYER, JOHN MILTON
(1820–1906)
Union general

Born to Elias Thayer and Ruthe Staples Thayer in Bellingham, Massachusetts, John Milton Thayer was educated locally before attending and graduating from Brown University. Upon graduation, Thayer studied law and practiced in Worcester County, Massachusetts, for about twelve years. In the mid-1850s he acquired land in Nebraska and moved there with his family. In Nebraska, Thayer farmed, practiced law, and was very active in the territorial militia. He rose to the rank of brigadier general in the militia and gained considerable fighting experience against the Indian tribes of the territory.

At the outbreak of the Civil War, Thayer was made major general of the Nebraska militia. His primary concern initially was the removal of many Federal troops from posts in Nebraska so that they would be available to fight in the East. He wrote to the War Department expressing his anxiety and offering to replace the exiting soldiers with Nebraska militia if the federal government would pay for such a step.

Shortly thereafter, Thayer decided to join the fray himself by raising a regiment for Federal service. On 21 July 1861 he was commissioned the colonel of the 1st Nebraska Volunteers. He would serve the entire war in the Western theater and trans-Mississippi West.

In February 1862, Thayer was given command of a brigade in Lew Wallace's division during Ulysses S. Grant's Fort Donelson campaign. He commanded the same brigade in April at the battle of Shiloh. In October of that year he was promoted to brigadier general of volunteers. The promotion expired without Senate approval the following March, but he was immediately reappointed and confirmed by the Senate. In November 1862, he was sent to assume temporary command at Helena, Arkansas. In December he commanded a brigade in Frederick Steele's division in William T. Sherman's Yazoo expedition, fighting at Chickasaw Bluffs. A month later he commanded his brigade in the Arkansas Post campaign, although he saw little action, and upon his return he commanded the same brigade in the operations outside Vicksburg and in the siege of the city.

After his participation in the Jackson, Mississippi, campaign of July 1863, Thayer was given command of 1st Division in XV Corps at the end of July 1863 when the division's commander, Frederick Steele, was placed in charge of an expedition into Arkansas. Thayer led the 1st Division in that campaign, which commenced in August 1863. The expedition moved toward Little Rock, which the Federals occupied on 10 September 1863.

In January 1864, when Steele was given command of VII Corps, Thayer was given command of the District of the Frontier, headquartered at Fort Smith, Arkansas, within Steele's command. In March 1864, he led his men in Steele's Camden, Arkansas, campaign. The campaign started too late to be of any help to Nathaniel P. Banks in his Red River campaign as it was intended. By early May, Steele had returned to Little Rock, and Thayer went with his division back to Fort Smith.

Thayer remained at Fort Smith through 1864. His main concern while there were attacks against his outlying works by Confederate guerrilla groups and cavalry units. During the summer of 1864 he saw the greatest threats to his position when Confederates operating out of the Indian Territory made periodic raids on the outskirts of town. Things remained fairly quiet for the remainder of the year.

In February 1865, Thayer was moved to command the Union position at Saint Charles, Arkansas. In May he was given command of the District of Eastern Arkansas, headquartered at Helena, Arkansas. He remained there until receiving a brevet promotion to major general of volunteers in July 1865, at which time he resigned his volunteer commission to return to Nebraska.

The following year, Nebraska having become a state, Thayer was elected one of its first senators. In the Senate, Thayer was firmly in the Radical Republican camp. Having drawn the short term, Thayer failed to be reelected in 1870. His strong support of the Grant administration, however, earned him an appointment as territorial governor of Wyoming in 1875. He served in that position until 1879, when he returned to his home in Nebraska. While still remaining active in state politics, Thayer also became the state commander of the Grand Army of the Republic. In the late 1880s he served two terms as governor of Nebraska, after which he retired to Lincoln, Nebraska. He died in Lincoln on 19 March 1906.

—*David S. Heidler and Jeanne T. Heidler*

For further reading:
Curtis, Earl Guy. "Biography of John Milton Thayer" (M.A. thesis, 1933).

THAYER, SYLVANUS
(1785–1872)
Union general and "Father of the Military Academy"

Sylvanus Thayer, who was born on 9 June 1785 in Braintree, Massachusetts, was descended from seventeenth-century Puritan immigrants. He attended Dartmouth College for three years and then received an appointment to the U.S. Military Academy. After graduating from the military academy in February 1808 (he was only the thirty-third graduate in its history), he was commissioned a second lieutenant in the Corps of Engineers.

In the four years that followed his graduation from West Point, Thayer divided his time between supervising the construction of coastal fortifications and serving as an instructor at the Military Academy. The War of 1812 proved a crucial career event for him, as it provided both quick promotion and battlefield experience. During the battle of Chateauguay in October 1813, Thayer, who was by now both a captain and the aide-de-camp to Major General Wade Hampton, had the first and, as it would turn out, only combat experience of his military career. The battle, which was part of a disastrously unsuccessful attempt to invade Canada, left an indelible impression on Thayer. The incompetence or outright cowardice of many of the officers involved in the battle convinced him that it would be necessary to properly train officers in order for them to competently lead troops in combat.

After spending the last year of the war improving fortifications along the Atlantic coast, brevet Major Thayer was sent to France in 1815 to study European engineering, fortification, and instructional techniques. Upon his return from Europe in 1817, he was appointed the superintendent of the Military Academy and initiated a series of reforms in the curriculum of instruction at West Point that would remain basically unchanged for more than a century. Between 1817 and 1833, the course of study at the Military Academy was formalized, the four-class system was established, and a more professional sense of both instruction and military discipline was created. With the addition of both better educated instructors and more diverse subjects of study, Thayer was able to convert West Point from a rather academically undisciplined environment into the first true engineering school in the United States.

After the election of President Andrew Jackson in 1828, Thayer found both the Military Academy and his administration of the superintendent's office under attack. "Jacksonian Democracy" had little love for professional soldiers, and West Point seemed to be an obvious symbol of the "elitist" professional military. The strict discipline with which Thayer had overseen the Military Academy did little to help matters. Many graduates and ex-cadets had a genuine dislike for what they perceived as Thayer's cold indifference and harshness. Though President Jackson did not, himself, ever make any negative statements regarding either West Point or Thayer, it seemed clear that the concept of a "military aristocracy" did not sit well with his concept of a democratic society. After several years of defending both himself and the Military Academy against the political machinations of the Jacksonian Democrats in Congress, Thayer decided to resign as superintendent in the hope that it would divert some of the Democrats' rage away from West Point.

After leaving the Military Academy in 1833, Thayer became responsible for the design and construction of the coastal fortifications at Boston harbor. Despite being promoted to lieutenant colonel in 1838 and regularly working twelve-hour days, Thayer found his new position rather mentally unchallenging when compared with his superintendency at West Point. After serving briefly as the acting chief of the Army Corps of Engineers (which he should rightly have been appointed to permanently), Thayer asked to be put on sick leave in 1858. Promoted to colonel on 3 March 1863 and brevetted brigadier general in the regular army on 31 May 1863, Thayer retired, after more than fifty years on active duty, on 1 June 1863. A bachelor all his life, Thayer died at the home of his niece in Braintree, Massachusetts, on 7 September 1872 and was eventually buried at the Military Academy. Thayer was also responsible for endowing and founding the Thayer School of Engineering at Dartmouth College and was highly influential in the development of engineering schools throughout America.

—*Alexander M. Bielakowski*

For further reading:
Dupuy, R. Ernest. *Sylvanus Thayer: Father of Technology in the United States* (1958).
Kershner, James W. *Sylvanus Thayer: A Biography* (1982).

THIRTEENTH AMENDMENT
(1865)

The wording of the Thirteenth Amendment to the U.S. Constitution is simple and straightforward: "Neither slavery nor involuntary servitude… shall exist within the United States, or any place subject to their jurisdiction." Its passage ended debate about the status of slavery in the United States that was "somehow

...the cause of the [Civil] war." Because it lacked the grandeur of President Abraham Lincoln's Emancipation Proclamation and because it was ratified after Lincoln's assassination, the Thirteenth Amendment often receives short shrift. But Lincoln recognized its importance. The validity of his Emancipation Proclamation rested on his powers as commander in chief. Whether his wartime measure would have permanence after the war was an open question. Second, his Emancipation Proclamation excluded portions of the seceding states that were already in Union hands. And although these states, taking advantage of Lincoln's Proclamation of Amnesty and Reconstruction, had crafted state constitutions that abolished slavery, nothing prevented these states from resurrecting their barbarous and peculiar institutions in the future. Finally, the border slave states had not acted on proposals for compensated emancipation, and their domestic institutions lay wholly outside the scope of Lincoln's executive authority. Without a constitutional amendment, the surety of slavery's demise at war's end remained uncertain.

Such an amendment traveled an uncertain road. In January 1864, a draft proposal for an antislavery amendment came from John Henderson, a congressman from Missouri, likely at Lincoln's prodding. Abolitionists, acting through Senator Charles Sumner, submitted their version too, which included broad language banning insidious discrimination. The Senate Judiciary Committee, though, provided the eventual language of the amendment by borrowing the spare phrases from the Northwest Ordinance of 1787, which had banned slavery from federal territories north of the Ohio River. This version passed the Senate but died in the House in June 1864, as Democrats rallied in the name of states' rights to kill the measure, despite Lincoln's championing of the proposal.

Politically, the fate of the amendment rode on the 1864 presidential election. The platform of the Democratic Party pledged recognition to states' rights, which was understood to refer to the right of states to authorize and maintain slavery if they so chose. Lincoln's Republican Party platform called for the "utter and complete extirpation" of slavery, which was understood to include the passage of the Thirteenth Amendment.

Reelected by a wide margin in 1864, Lincoln lent his personal prestige and employed his vast patronage and political powers to prod the House into passing the amendment. Lincoln believed in the morality of the proposed amendment and thought its passage by the Congress would further erode the Confederate war effort. Although the 1864 election gave his party a sufficient majority to break the deadlock in the House, he wanted the sitting Congress to approve the proposal. Should Democrats generally, and especially those from the border states, reverse their votes, it would dash the hopes of the Confederacy that the border states might come to its rescue.

To that end, Lincoln authorized and supported Secretary of State William Henry Seward's massive lobbying effort in New York, whose large congressional delegation was critical to the fate of the amendment and whose borders contained many Democrats. Lincoln's influence, in addition to the Democrats' recognition that opposition to the amendment cost them votes, led to its passing the House on 31 January 1865, whereupon it was submitted to the states.

Ratification by the states followed quickly, with only New Jersey failing to vote for it among the free states. The border states of Maryland and Missouri followed suit. Under President Andrew Johnson's plan of restoration, the seceding states had to ratify the amendment as a condition of their readmission to the Union. Although neither Congress, the president, nor the several states agreed on whether the Thirteenth Amendment implied any further rights, such as federally guaranteed civil rights, it settled one thing for certain: the Union would no longer be half slave and half free, for slavery was now unconstitutional.

In recent years, it is fashionable to denigrate the Thirteenth Amendment because it did not give former slaves equality before the law and it did not compensate them for the travail of slavery. It simply freed them from chattel bondage but left former slaves prisoners in the emerging state of Jim Crow. This present-minded view misses how radical the Thirteenth Amendment really was. If the Constitution was, as William Lloyd Garrison insisted, "a covenant with death and an agreement with Hell" because it explicitly protected slavery, reversing that recognition was mightily important.

—*Edward R. Crowther*

See also Emancipation Proclamation; Freedmen's Bureau; Lincoln's Reconstruction Policy; Slaves.

For further reading:
Cox, LaWanda. *Lincoln and Black Freedom: A Study in Presidential Leadership* (1981).
Hyman, Harold. *"A More Perfect Union": The Impact of the Civil War and Reconstruction on the Constitution* (1973).
Paludan, Phillip S. *A Covenant with Death: The Constitution, Law and Equality in the Civil War Era* (1975).

THOMAS, GEORGE HENRY
(1816–1870)
Union general

George H. Thomas was born on 31 July 1816 in Southampton County, Virginia. He was nearly twenty years old when he entered West Point, a little older than the typical cadet. Thomas graduated in 1840, ranking twelfth in his class of forty-two, six behind William T. Sherman. He accepted the commission of

George H. Thomas at a council of war near Ringgold, Georgia, 5 May 1864 (*National Archives*)

second lieutenant of artillery in the U.S. Army. He was soon sent to Florida, where he participated in the Second Seminole War. For his performance in action, Thomas was breveted first lieutenant. In 1844 he officially obtained the rank of first lieutenant in the regular army.

Thomas also served with distinction during the Mexican-American War. In the expedition led by General Zachary Taylor, Thomas took part in the battles of Resaca de la Palma, Monterey, and Buena Vista. For each of the latter battles, Thomas received a brevet, ending his service in the war as a brevet major. Within a span of seven years, Thomas had been recognized for meritorious conduct three times.

In the years between the Mexican-American War and the American Civil War, Thomas held numerous posts. The more notable assignments included a return to West Point (1851–1854), where he instructed cadets in artillery and cavalry tactics. In December 1853 Thomas was promoted to captain. After serving a year at Fort Yuma in California, in 1855 Thomas attained the rank of major in the regular army and was ordered to serve with the elite 2d Cavalry, which later reported to Texas. This assignment was due to Thomas's fine mili-

tary record. The officers of this elite corps of mounted troops read like a list of prominent Confederates. Officers in the 2d Cavalry included Colonel Albert S. Johnston, Lieutenant Colonel Robert E. Lee, Major William J. Hardee, Captains Earl Van Dorn and E. Kirby Smith, and Lieutenants John Bell Hood, Fitzhugh Lee, and J. E. B. Stuart.

While in the 2d Cavalry Thomas occasionally led expeditions that surveyed the geography of the region and patrolled against the Indians. It was on one such patrol in August 1860 that Thomas was severely injured, when an arrow lodged in his chest after piercing his chin. Although painful, this injury was not ultimately debilitating. A more serious injury occurred on his trip home during his one-year leave of absence from the military, which began in November 1860. While disembarking from a train in Virginia, Thomas fell into a deep ravine, permanently injuring his back. Much of his abbreviated leave was spent trying to recuperate.

It was during this time that Thomas chose to stay loyal to the country to which he had been in service over the last twenty years. Even if his home state of Virginia seceded, he was determined to remain loyal to the

Union. He made significant sacrifices in choosing this allegiance. He was disowned by most of his family and deemed a traitor by Virginia. Also, most of the officers who served with Thomas and knew his abilities would be wearing gray. On the other hand, while Thomas's Southern birth may not have caused his Northern superiors to doubt his loyalty, it did cause them to pass Thomas over for promotions and assignments. Thus, Thomas frequently served as a subordinate to many less capable but Northern-born political generals.

As tensions increased between the seceded states and the United States, the War Department canceled the rest of Thomas's leave (10 April), promoted him to lieutenant colonel (25 April), and ordered him to report to Carlisle Barracks, Pennsylvania. There Thomas was in command of the 2d Cavalry, due to the resignations of its more senior officers. His assignment was to reorganize and reequip the remnants of the 2d Cavalry arriving from Texas. On 3 May Thomas received his second promotion in as many months, becoming colonel of the 2d Cavalry.

Over the next three months Thomas commanded the 1st Brigade in the 1st Division in the Department of Pennsylvania (29 May–25 July), in the Department of the Shenandoah (25 July–17 August), and in Banks's Division, Army of the Potomac (17–26 August). On 17 August 1861, Thomas was promoted to brigadier general of volunteers with orders to report to Cincinnati, the headquarters of the Department of the Cumberland.

On 10 September 1861 Thomas assumed command of Camp Dick Robinson in Kentucky. Thomas spent the rest of the war in the Western theater and began his association with what would eventually become the Army of the Cumberland. While at Camp Dick Robinson, Thomas organized three brigades that would eventually become part of the 1st Division in Don Carlos Buell's Army of the Ohio. Thomas assumed command of this 5,000-man, five-brigade division on 6 December 1861.

As a commander—whether of a division, a corps, or an army—Thomas always had an efficient and highly capable staff. When at all possible, Thomas went into battle with troops who were well trained, armed, fed, and supplied. He served near the front lines with his troops, provided them with clear and concise orders, and was careful about their safety. These qualities endeared him to his officers and soldiers. Thomas was meticulous in his preparation for battle, often receiving the unjust criticism of being slow or sluggish. He wanted everything in order before a battle to minimize surprises. Because of this fastidiousness, Thomas never lost a battle he commanded.

Buell assigned Thomas to eastern Kentucky with the goal of finding the Confederate force operating in this area. On 17 January 1862 Thomas received reports that the Rebels had their backs up against the Cumberland River. They would not be able to use the river to escape, as it was too deep and the current too strong. Thomas waited to attack, spending the time consolidating his forces along a defensive line. To minimize the chances of being caught by a surprise Rebel attack, Thomas had a number of pickets and mounted sentinels patrolling ahead of his force. The new Confederate commander, realizing his vulnerable position, ordered an attack.

Elements of the Confederate force ran into Thomas's pickets on the morning of 19 January 1862. The battle of Logan's Cross Roads would be the first major engagement since Bull Run. Thomas managed his forces with acumen and brought up his reserves at the right moment. As their left began to crumble, the entire Rebel line broke. That evening the Confederates were able to escape across the river using boats, but their heavier equipment had to be left behind. Thomas's planning allowed his force to completely rout the enemy, inflicting 529 casualties while sustaining 246.

The battle of Logan's Cross Roads was significant because it opened a gap in the Confederate defensive line in the west. This victory, coupled with Grant's victories in February 1862 at Forts Henry and Donelson and in April at Shiloh, helped to keep Kentucky in the Union and provided a forward base from which to carry out future operations in the west. For his service, Thomas was promoted to major general of volunteers in April 1862.

General Henry W. Halleck, unhappy with Grant's performance in the Federal near-disaster at Shiloh, chose to take command personally of the Union forces in the west, which were undergoing reorganization. This left Grant with the powerless position of second-in-command of Halleck's army (the Army of the Department of the Mississippi).

Under orders from Halleck, Thomas assumed command of Grant's Army of the Tennessee, redesignated the right wing of Halleck's army. This contributed to Grant's growing animosity towards Thomas.

On 10 June 1862 Thomas returned again to Buell's Army of the Ohio as a division commander, after Halleck was promoted to general-in-chief. Command of the Army of the Tennessee was returned to Grant. By September 1862 Buell's forces were spread throughout Kentucky, garrisoning critical points, including railroads and telegraph lines.

In the meantime Thomas had given up his plan for taking Chattanooga and soon found the Confederates launching an invasion into Kentucky. To meet this threat, Buell and Thomas arrived in Louisville and began gathering their troops. Buell's inaction caused many western politicians to call for his replacement. On 29 September, Lincoln ordered Halleck to replace Buell with Thomas. Thomas did not want, nor think it appropriate, to replace Buell on the eve of an upcoming battle with Confederate forces under Braxton Bragg. The orders were temporarily suspended, as Halleck agreed to give Buell a second chance. A portion of Buell's Army of the Ohio defeated Bragg in the battle of Perryville (8 October), causing Bragg to retreat from Kentucky.

By late October Buell's pursuit proved half-hearted and Lincoln again sought a replacement for him. Thomas, who would not be given a second chance to turn down the promotion, was passed over in favor of an officer his junior, Major General William S. Rosecrans. This angered Thomas immensely, but when informed by Halleck that Rosecrans's date of rank had been pushed back (by Lincoln) making Rosecrans senior to Thomas, Thomas dropped the matter. Rosecrans proved to be as inept as Buell, delaying his departure from Nashville and constantly requesting more supplies and men.

Thomas spent the next year laying the foundation of a modern army. Again he appointed his own staff of nineteen capable officers, large for a Civil War army. He organized an efficient way to keep the railroads operating in western Tennessee and Kentucky through the use of repair crews. He set up a reliable and quick communication system so he could keep in touch with his forces. He had accurate maps drawn up of the areas in which he planned to operate, giving him vital information of the terrain of future battlefields. All these efforts helped Thomas to establish command and control. Thomas also set up a mobile field army system that saved many lives in the Army of the Ohio, redesignated the Army of the Cumberland. Thomas took charge of the center wing of the army.

The forces of Bragg and Rosecrans finally met at the end of the year during the battle of Stones River, a three-day engagement (31 December 1862–2 January 1863). The Union forces numbered about 45,000 and the Rebels around 38,000. Each side came up with a similar strategy: each wanted to hold with their right and attack the enemy flank with their left. The Confederates began their attack first, which rolled up the right wing of the Army of the Cumberland.

In the meantime Rosecrans had called off the Union attack. The first day of fighting was a Confederate victory. At the war council held that night, Thomas convinced Rosecrans not to retreat to Nashville, but to remain in position and continue the fight. During the first day, Thomas's center wing was occupied with reinforcing and halting the retreat of the right wing. The second day saw no significant action. On the third day, Bragg attempted to dislodge the Union troops and Thomas again used his central position to reinforce and support the advancing right and left wings of the Union army. Bragg retreated during the night, leaving the battlefield in Union hands. The Union claimed this battle as a victory, which helped Northern morale recover from the tremendous casualties suffered by the Army of the Potomac at Fredericksburg (13 December).

The next eight months were spent maneuvering the Confederates out of Tennessee and into northern Georgia. The armies next met again in the two-day battle of Chickamauga on 19 and 20 September 1863. The first day ended as a stalemate, but the second day would prove more significant. Union divisions were shifted around to shore up weakened areas. A hole in the Union line opened when Rosecrans, who was not sure of the locations of his forces, mistakenly ordered a division to relocate, leaving an unintentional gap in the Union line at the precise spot where Bragg ordered Longstreet's attack.

General Rosecrans and two corps commanders could not rally their troops and proceeded to retreat in panic towards Chattanooga with about a third of the Union army. Thomas, on the Union left, had his XIV Corps and elements of the two other corps, leaving him with 40,000 troops. Thomas's actions, along with the arrival of reinforcements at opportune times, allowed the Union defenders to repulse attack after attack by the numerically superior Confederate forces. Although a Confederate victory, Thomas's actions prevented a total rout of the Union Army. His stance on Horseshoe Ridge allowed Rosecrans and his retreating forces to safely enter Chattanooga and man its defenses, giving Thomas the nickname "Rock of Chickamauga." By nightfall, Thomas retreated into the city. Bragg moved north to surround Chattanooga.

After this defeat Grant was given overall command in the west. Grant removed Rosecrans as commander of the Army of the Cumberland and replaced him with Thomas on 28 October. The day before Thomas had been promoted to brigadier general in the regular army. He received orders from Grant to hold Chattanooga at all costs and word that relief was on its way, including Grant. Thomas still did not have a completely independent command. Grant, arriving as commander of the newly created District of the Mississippi, exerted command over the Armies of the Ohio, the Tennessee, and the Cumberland.

Thomas's first task, which he accomplished by the end of October, was to open up a supply route to the besieged city. This allowed vital supplies and reinforcements to arrive in Chattanooga, dramatically increasing the morale of the beaten Army of the Cumberland and restoring combat effectiveness. When Grant arrived, he wanted to remove the Confederate Army of Tennessee from Missionary Ridge. While planning the battle of Chattanooga, Grant had little faith in the Army of the Cumberland, because of their defeat at Chickamauga.

Thus, the main part of the attack involved Sherman's Army of the Tennessee. Sherman attacked the right flank of the Rebel position, while Burnside, with a reinforced corps, flanked the Confederates on their left. The flank attacks stalled and Thomas's army was committed in the center to draw Confederate troops away from Sherman's front. Instead of halting at the base of Missionary Ridge, the Army of the Cumberland, without

orders, proceeded to charge to the top. The onrushing Yankees surprised the Confederates, who believed their center to be impregnable. The Army of the Cumberland succeeded in chasing the Confederates off of Missionary Ridge (25 November) and achieved one of the few successful frontal assaults of the Civil War.

Thomas's next campaign was as the commander of the Army of the Cumberland in Sherman's march on Atlanta (1 May–8 September 1864). The Army of the Cumberland was left intact and Thomas commanded about two-thirds (65,000) of Sherman's entire force. The Army of the Ohio under General John A. Schofield, and the Army of the Tennessee under General James M. McPherson, rounded out the rest of Sherman's force. Thomas's army had the center position, often sending troops to either Schofield or McPherson, depending on who was engaged with the enemy. Sherman criticized Thomas for being slow in the advance on Atlanta, while Thomas recommended against Sherman's ill-conceived frontal assault on Kennesaw Mountain. A few days later the Rebel position was taken by maneuver, proving that the heavy Union casualties suffered in that action could have been avoided. Atlanta eventually fell to Sherman's forces on 2 September 1864. On 8 September Union forces returned to Atlanta after chasing Hood to a highly defensible position. Thomas's command occupied Atlanta.

The last of Thomas's campaigns began when Confederate General John B. Hood moved his Army of Tennessee behind Sherman's army to disrupt his lines of communication. Hood hoped that this action would force Sherman to evacuate Atlanta. Instead, Sherman entrusted Thomas with the task of preventing Hood from threatening Tennessee and the Union supply lines. As Sherman headed for Savannah, Georgia, Thomas headed to Nashville to organize a force with which to repel Hood. At the core of Thomas's force were the IV and XXIII Corps, but he would later be reinforced with a detachment from the Army of the Tennessee.

Sherman left Thomas to deal comfortably with Hood's Army of Tennessee. Luckily, Hood delayed his advance into Tennessee by three weeks, which allowed Thomas to organize the defense of his department. At this point the Confederate forces numbered 40,000, while Thomas's 30,000 troops were scattered throughout Tennessee. Union troops were arriving into Nashville by rail, water, and road in order to concentrate a force powerful enough to match the strength of Hood's force. When Hood resumed his thrust into Tennessee, Thomas was better prepared to check his advance.

The IV and XXIII Corps under Schofield defeated Hood at Franklin on 30 November 1864. Schofield placed his forces in the well-entrenched positions surrounding the city. Hood, without artillery to soften up the Union positions, ordered an unsupported frontal assault. This reduced Hood's fighting strength by nearly 25 percent. Thirteen of the Army of Tennessee's twenty-eight generals were either killed, wounded, or captured. After the battle the Union troops retreated to Nashville and deployed in its defensive positions.

Thomas knew that the Army of Tennessee could not replace its losses, while his army was growing stronger by the day. Thomas bided his time until his cavalry was ready. He then deployed General James A. Wilson's cavalry in a unique fashion, using the cavalry as the major striking force to demolish Hood's army. In the meantime, Thomas's superiors in Washington were growing concerned at what they perceived as inaction or lack of aggression. They did not understand how much Thomas was actually in control of the situation. Grant almost had Thomas relieved for not attacking. A severe ice and snowstorm also delayed Thomas. With the warming of the weather, Thomas began his attack on 15 December, which proved to be an astounding success.

The Federal left wing launched a diversionary attack, while the right wing, containing nearly 80 percent of the Union army's strength, crushed Hood's left. The Army of Tennessee held its lines until dark, then retreated to the rear and took up other entrenched positions. On 16 December Thomas followed the battle plan of the previous day. This time the Union army broke through the depleted Confederate lines. Now it was time for the Union army to pursue Hood's surviving army relentlessly. Thomas's victory at Nashville inflicted the worst defeat on an army during the entire war. After the battle, the Army of Tennessee retreated south and was no longer an effective fighting force. For his victory, Thomas was promoted in December 1864 to the rank of major general in the regular army.

Thomas's forces were now sent off to other commands, and he spent the rest of the war in Tennessee, effectively removed from any more fighting. He maintained his position as commander of the western departments until 1867. Next he was transferred to the Military Division of the Pacific, where he died of a stroke in 1870.

—*James L. Isemann*

See also Army of the Cumberland; Atlanta Campaign; Chickamauga, Battle of; Logan's Cross Roads, Battle of; Missionary Ridge, Battle of; Nashville, Battle of; Stones River, Battle of.

For further reading:

Andrews, Peter. "The Rock of Chickamauga." *American Heritage* (1990).

Buell, Thomas B. *The Warrior Generals: Combat Leadership in the Civil War* (1997).

Cleaves, Freeman. *Rock of Chickamauga: The Life of General George H. Thomas* (1948; reprint, 1974).

Macartney, Clarence Edward. *Grant and His Generals* (1953).

McKinney, Francis F. *Education in Violence: The Life of George H. Thomas and the History of the Army of the Cumberland* (1961).

Thomas, Wilbur. *General George H. Thomas: The Indomitable Warrior* (1964).

Welcher, Frank J. *The Union Army, 1861–1865: Organization and Operations*, vol. 2 (1989).

THOMAS, LORENZO
(1804–1875)
Union general

Born in New Castle, Delaware, to Evan Thomas and Elizabeth Sherer Thomas, Lorenzo Thomas accepted an appointment to the U.S. Military Academy in 1819. He graduated seventeenth of thirty-five in the class of 1823. Commissioned into the 4th Infantry, Thomas occupied a number of staff positions over the next thirty-five years. He served in the Second Seminole War as a quartermaster and then in Washington, D.C., as an assistant adjutant general. During the Mexican-American War he served as chief of staff to Major General William O. Butler during Zachary Taylor's campaign in northern Mexico. He received a brevet promotion to lieutenant colonel for his actions at Monterey.

After the war, Thomas returned to the adjutant general's office until he became Winfield Scott's chief of staff in 1853. Though technically still attached to the adjutant general's office, he remained Scott's chief of staff until the outbreak of the Civil War. The beginning of that conflict brought about the resignation of Adjutant General of the Army Samuel Cooper. Thomas was promoted to colonel in April and was made acting adjutant general. In August the position became permanent, and he was promoted to brigadier general.

At the beginning of the war, Thomas's office was entirely too small and understaffed to handle the sudden demand on its resources. Thomas was never able to bring the office to the level of efficiency expected by some, and some people even speculated that he intentionally maintained a sloppy operation because of his lack of support for the war. There is no evidence to support such an accusation.

On the contrary, the evidence from the myriad correspondence that came from his office to officers all over the country indicates that he was trying but was simply unable to keep up with the monumental task before him. Along with the usual duties of his office, such as sending directives to all the military departments of the War Department, Thomas also sat on boards and handled some of the details of prisoner exchanges. Perhaps the criticism of his office would never have amounted to anything serious, however, had he not offended Secretary of War Edwin Stanton with his independent attitude. His years of working for the commanding general of the army, Winfield Scott, no doubt had given him a certain arrogance when dealing with others in the government.

Stanton finally tired of Thomas, however, and in March 1863 sent him on an inspection tour of Ulysses S. Grant's operation against Vicksburg and on a mission to recruit African-American soldiers for the Union army. If Stanton thought such duty would bring about Thomas's resignation, he was to be disappointed. Not only did Thomas accept the duty, he kept his adjutant general's position, though many of the day-to-day duties were carried out by E. D. Townsend in Washington. Despite becoming ill on the trip west, Thomas carried out his instructions within a few weeks and returned to the East.

Perhaps to prove his vigilance and dedication to duty, in late June 1863 he traveled to Harrisburg, Pennsylvania, to be near the scene of the action during the Gettysburg campaign. He remained there until after the battle. Stanton was not satisfied and continued to send Thomas on special missions, primarily concerning the recruitment of African-American troops. Thomas traveled back to Vicksburg, to Louisiana, and to Louisville, Kentucky, spending very little time in Washington during the last year of the war. Despite his difficulties with the secretary, in March 1865, like so many others, he received a brevet promotion to major general for his service during the war.

After the war was over, Thomas and Stanton finally made a permanent break, and Thomas found an ally in new president Andrew Johnson. When Johnson fired Stanton in February 1868, he appointed Thomas interim secretary. Since Stanton refused to leave his office, Thomas boasted that he would force the recalcitrant secretary out of the War Department. Stanton responded by ordering Thomas's arrest, although Thomas was soon released on bail. In his testimony during President Johnson's impeachment trial, Thomas convinced most senators that he alone was responsible for the attempt to force Stanton out of his office. He also convinced most observers that he was not fit to hold the adjutant general's office, and in February 1869 he was forced to retire from the army. For the remainder of his life, Thomas lived quietly in Washington, D.C., where he died on 2 March 1875.

—*David S. Heidler and Jeanne T. Heidler*

See also African-American Soldiers U.S.A.; Stanton, Edwin.
For further reading:
Townsend, E. D. *Memoir of Lorenzo Thomas* (n.d.).
Trudeau, Noah Andre. *Like Men of War: Black Troops in the Civil War, 1862–1865* (1998).

THOMAS, WILLIAM HOLLAND
(1805–1893)
Confederate officer

Born on 5 February 1805, William Holland Thomas was raised fatherless in Waynesville, North Carolina, and was adopted in his early teenage years by Cherokee chief Yonaguska (Drowning Bear). By his late teens, Thomas had opened one of several stores that served the Cherokees in western North Carolina. Since many of Thomas's Cherokee neighbors had legally

avoided removal, he became their representative and purchased land for them. This land eventually comprised the modern-day Qualla Boundary Reservation. In 1839, shortly before Yonaguska's death, the Cherokees accepted their ailing chief's request that Thomas succeed him, thus he became the only white man to become chief of the Eastern Band of Cherokees. Thomas lobbied for the rights of the Qualla Cherokees in Washington. Elected to the North Carolina Senate in 1848, he pushed for Cherokee citizenship and recognition as permanent state residents. As chairman of the Committee on Internal Improvements, he also championed the construction of roads and railroads in western North Carolina.

With the Civil War approaching, Senator Thomas favored secession, but—like his Western counterpart, Chief John Ross—Thomas wanted his Cherokees to remain neutral. Realizing this would be impossible, Thomas and his company of Indians were mustered into Confederate service in April 1862 by Major George Washington Morgan, a mixed-blood Cherokee who had fought at First Bull Run. Thomas was chosen as captain, and the company was stationed at Strawberry Plains near Knoxville, Tennessee, attached to Colonel John C. Vaughn's 3d Tennessee Regiment. There they guarded the railroad bridge across the Holston River. By July Thomas's command had reached battalion strength, with two companies of Indians and six of whites.

Thomas and his men first saw action at Baptist Gap near the Virginia border on 13 September, where an Indiana regiment attacked them. Artoogatogeh, the grandson of Junaluska, was killed during the battle, which inflamed the Cherokees to drive the Indiana regiment out of the valley. The victors took several scalps but later returned them to be buried with the soldiers.

By late September, Thomas was commanding more than 2,000 soldiers. He was named colonel of a legion (often mistakenly called the 69th North Carolina Regiment), which became known as Thomas's Legion of Indian and Highlanders or simply the Thomas Legion. In January 1863, Thomas was ordered to North Carolina and north Georgia to round up deserters. When he returned to Tennessee in March, he found that his legion had been placed under Brigadier General Alfred E. Jackson, stripping Thomas of much of his authority. Hostility arose between the ill-humored Jackson and Thomas, which lasted throughout the war. The feud resulted in three courts-martial for Thomas but the charges were dismissed. His accuser, General Jackson, was eventually found unfit for field duty.

In early December 1862, some of Thomas's men were captured while on a scouting mission near Sevierville, Tennessee, and thrown into jail. With about 200 men Thomas stormed the jail, released his men, and captured 60 Unionists and 6 soldiers.

In February 1864, Thomas and his men were surprised at the mouth of Deep Creek about ten miles west of Quallatown, losing between 20 and 30 Indians and whites. The Cherokees were taken back to Knoxville, where they were wined and dined and promised $5,000 in gold for the scalp of Thomas. Some Cherokees pretended to agree, returned to tell Thomas "his worth," and then continued to serve under him. Nevertheless, more than thirty Cherokees did fight under Colonel George W. Kirk and other Union leaders.

In early May 1865, shortly after Appomattox, Thomas's legion and some Union troops traded what are considered to have been the final shots of the Civil War in North Carolina. On the night of 6 May, Thomas positioned his Cherokees on mountains above Waynesville, where they lit large bonfires and punctuated the night with blood-chilling war whoops. The following day, Thomas, dressed and painted like an Indian, demanded unsuccessfully that the Federals surrender.

In 1867, Thomas resigned as chief. Like many others, he was financially ruined by the Civil War. He lost most of his holdings, including Cherokee land in his name. Depression and old age contributed to senility, and the death of his wife greatly aggravated his frame of mind. Eventually he was committed to Broughton Hospital, probably because of something resembling Alzheimer's disease. Ruled competent on affairs of the past, Thomas made one last act of kindness toward the Cherokees. He testified on behalf of the Indians and against himself, in a case concerning the Indian lands in his name. He died on 10 May 1893. A marker, later erected, proclaimed Thomas to be "the best friend the Cherokees ever had."

—*William L. Anderson*

See also Cherokee Indians.
For further reading:
Crow, Vernon H. *Storm in the Mountains: Thomas' Confederate Legion of Cherokee Indians and Mountaineers* (1982).
Finger, John R. *The Eastern Band of Cherokees* (1984).
Godbold, E. Stanly, and Mattie U. Russell. *Confederate Colonel and Cherokee Chief: The Life of William Holland Thomas* (1990).

THOMPSON, JACOB
(1810–1885)
Confederate officer and agent

The son of Nicholas Thompson and Lucretia Van Hook Thompson, born in Caswell County, North Carolina, Jacob Thompson was educated locally before he was admitted to the University of North Carolina. After graduation from that institution, Thompson studied law and then emigrated with his older brother to Mississippi. He first settled in Natchez, then moved to Pontotoc, and finally to Oxford.

In Mississippi, Thompson practiced law and quickly became active in Mississippi politics. In 1838 he was elected to the U.S. House of Representatives and served six consecutive terms. He was defeated by Jefferson Davis for the U.S. Senate in 1854. In 1856, Thompson actively supported James Buchanan's presidential candidacy, and as a reward he received appointment as Buchanan's secretary of the interior. He occupied this position until January 1861. During his tenure, Thompson endured a scandal regarding corruption within the department but at the same time was responsible for an increase in efficiency. The corruption, for which he was completely exonerated, was used to discredit him politically after the war.

In January 1861, Thompson differed with Buchanan over the sending of the relief ship *Star of the West* to Fort Sumter and resigned his post. Returning to Mississippi, he offered his services to the Confederate army and received a commission as a lieutenant colonel. He served as a voluntary aide-de-camp to P. G. T. Beauregard at Shiloh and, after the battle, managed the paroling of some of the Union prisoners. In early 1863, he joined the staff of John Pemberton at Vicksburg, serving as the department's inspector general. In that capacity he fulfilled many different duties, including procuring supplies for the increasingly beleaguered army. He was captured with Pemberton's army at Vicksburg but was soon paroled.

After Thompson's parole, he served in the Mississippi legislature until the spring of 1864, when he was contacted directly by President Jefferson Davis to conduct a secret mission to Canada. Sent with Clement C. Clay, Thompson's mission was several fold. Both men were to attempt to arrange for a raid on Camp Douglas, a federal prisoner-of-war facility near Chicago, to secure the release of Confederate prisoners there. In addition they were to cooperate with Southern sympathizers and antiwar leaders in the upper Midwest to encourage more antiwar feeling in the North. Working with such people as Clement Vallandigham and such organizations as the Sons of Liberty and the Knights of the Golden Circle, the Confederate agents hoped to disrupt the Union's ability to make war on the South. They also worked with other Confederate agents in Canada to help repatriate Confederate soldiers who had escaped into Canada from Northern prisons. Thompson was accused, though he denied involvement, of helping to plan the Confederate raid on St. Albans, Vermont.

In April 1865, because of his secret service activities in Canada, Thompson came under suspicion for complicity in the assassination of Abraham Lincoln. A $25,000 reward that was later increased to $100,000 was offered for his capture. For that reason he did not return to the United States, remaining in Canada for a time and then traveling to Europe. Even though the reward was dropped in November 1865, Thompson did not return to the United States until 1868.

Upon his return to the United States, Thompson worked to rebuild his fortunes. His home in Mississippi had been burned by Union troops in August 1864. Thompson moved to Memphis, where he became a wealthy businessman. He was only briefly distracted in 1876 when the old charges regarding corruption in the Interior Department surfaced, primarily a distraction manufactured by the Grant administration to draw attention away from corruption in its own departments. The matter soon dropped, and Thompson lived out the remainder of his life happily removed from public life, dying in Memphis.

—*David S. Heidler and Jeanne T. Heidler*

See also Clay, Clement Claiborne; Covert Action, Confederate; Knights of the Golden Circle; Order of American Knights; Secret Service, C.S.A.; Sons of Liberty; St. Albans, Vermont, Raid; Vallandigham, Clement.

For further reading:
Bivins, Joseph Francis. *The Life and Character of Jacob Thompson* (1898; reprint, 1970).

THOMPSON, MERIWETHER JEFF
(1826–1876)
Confederate general

Born in Virginia, Meriwether Jeff Thompson moved to Missouri as a young man. Settling in St. Joseph, Missouri, Thompson was the mayor of that city in 1860. Known for his Southern sympathies, he worked in the early months of 1861 to bring about the secession of the state. As colonel and inspector of the 4th Military District of the Missouri militia, Thompson stockpiled arms and ammunition in the St. Joseph area. In April he wrote to Confederate president Jefferson Davis asking for the procedure for providing volunteers for the Confederate army from a state that had not seceded. When he learned of the Union attack on the pro-Confederate position at Camp Jackson outside of St. Louis, he tried to persuade Missouri governor Claiborne Jackson to allow him to raise a military force to retaliate. When the governor refused, Thompson took the men who had already agreed to follow him and went into southeastern Missouri to recruit more.

Thompson designated the battalion he raised as the Missouri State Guard and he its brigadier general. Most people began referring to his men as the Swamp Rats because of their ability to disappear into the swamps of the borderlands. Thompson wrote to Jefferson Davis again on 2 July 1861 from Pocahontas, Arkansas, offering the services of his Swamp Rats to the Confederacy.

During the next few months, Thompson and his men made raids against Federal positions in Missouri. By late summer he had been placed under the command of

Major General Leonidas Polk and had established his headquarters at Camp Belmont, Missouri. When Major General John C. Frémont, in command of U.S. troops in Missouri, issued a proclamation declaring martial law, emancipating Missouri's slaves, and threatening to execute any Missourians found in arms against the United States, Thompson issued his own proclamation threatening to kill a Union man for every man Frémont killed. He followed up his threat by riding into Charleston, Missouri, and robbing the bank there of $56,000 to buy supplies for the Swamp Rats.

Throughout the fall of 1861, Thompson continued to make raids in southeastern Missouri, taking what he needed to continue his fighting from merchants of known Northern sympathies. By early 1862 he had moved his base of operations to New Madrid, Missouri, but Federal pressure on the area following the fall of Forts Henry and Donelson caused him to fall back to Pocahontas, Arkansas. From there he wrote to Confederate major general Earl Van Dorn to exert pressure to have Thompson's unit recognized as a legitimate brigade.

In the meantime, Thompson and the Swamp Rats, living up to their name, sought to lend assistance to the Confederate gunboat flotilla protecting Memphis, Tennessee, in early June 1862. They manned guns aboard some of the gunboats in the battle off the city on 6 June but were forced to retreat when they were overwhelmed by the Union flotilla. Thompson led his men back into northern Arkansas until being summoned by Van Dorn to Vicksburg in August. Throughout the remainder of the summer, Thompson and his men conducted scouting missions for Van Dorn and John C. Breckinridge in northern Louisiana in an effort to anticipate any threats to Port Hudson on the Mississippi.

In early 1863, Thompson and his guerrillas were allowed to move back into northern Arkansas to resume raids into Missouri and to prevent Federal movements into southeastern Arkansas. In May 1863, Thompson went with only a few of his men into Missouri to try to determine the political climate there. In friendly areas, he even made speeches urging the people to join the Confederate war effort. He returned to his base in Pocahontas and resumed his military efforts. By August 1863 his activities had become quite vexing to Federal officials in Missouri, and a military raid was sent down to break up his activities. Thompson's camp was caught by surprise, and he and many of his men were captured.

Thompson was imprisoned at Johnson's Island Prison near Sandusky, Ohio, a prison camp reserved primarily for Confederate officers. Union major general Benjamin Butler tried to secure his parole because Thompson had treated some Union prisoners who fell into his hands with great kindness. Butler succeeded in having Thompson moved to Fort Delaware in February 1864

and shortly thereafter secured his release to Confederate authorities at City Point, Virginia.

As soon as he was free, Thompson made his way back west, where he was given command of a brigade under Major General Sterling Price. Thompson led his brigade in Price's Missouri Raid in the late summer and fall of 1864. Upon his return from this expedition, Thompson was given command of the Northern Sub-District of Arkansas. His activities in this command primarily involved hiding in the bayous from large Federal patrols. At the end of the war, a detachment of Union soldiers was sent into the area at the end of April 1865 to negotiate his surrender. After a lengthy exchange of correspondence, the Union detachment finally secured Thompson's surrender on 9 May 1865. His men were sent home as paroled prisoners of war, but Thompson was taken to St. Louis, where he was briefly imprisoned. After his release, he lived in Missouri until his death in 1876.

—*David S. Heidler and Jeanne T. Heidler*

See also Guerrilla Warfare; Missouri; Price's Missouri Raid.
For further reading:
Monaghan, Jay. *Civil War on the Western Border, 1854–1865* (1955).
———. *Swamp Fox of the Confederacy: The Life and Military Services of M. Jeff Thompson* (1956).

THOMPSON'S STATION/SPRING HILL
(4–5 March 1863)

This was the scene of one of Confederate brigadier general Nathan Bedford Forrest's earliest successes and helped to confirm his reputation as an outstanding fighter. Located below Nashville on the Franklin-Columbia Turnpike and the Central Alabama Railroad, Thompson's Station was in an area that saw extensive activity by both sides following the fall of the state capital in February 1862.

In the spring of 1863, Forrest had just returned to middle Tennessee from an unsuccessful attack against the small Union garrison at Dover under the command of Major General Joseph Wheeler. He reorganized his command by consolidating several units with diminished numbers due to combat casualties. Forrest smarted from the Dover defeat and was extremely anxious for another encounter with the Federals to demonstrate the worth of his command and avenge the earlier loss.

That opportunity came in early March, when a Federal force under Colonel John Coburn marched southward from Franklin toward Spring Hill. Confederates under the overall command of Major General Earl Van Dorn approached the area of Thompson's Station in response. The Union command consisted of 2,857 infantry and cavalry, and six artillery pieces. Their immediate opponents were cavalry under

Brigadier General William H. "Red" Jackson. To these would be added the remainder of Van Dorn's force, which would swell the Confederate total on the field to some 6,000 men and twelve guns.

A long-range artillery duel ensued between the opposing forces on 4 March, with the Confederates dropping below Thompson's Station. At nightfall both sides camped in close proximity to each other. In the meantime, Van Dorn brought up the remainder of his troops. Despite his numerical superiority, the Confederate commander decided to remain on the defensive, inviting a Union attack against his line. For his part, Colonel Coburn was convinced that Southern numbers were even greater than they were, but saw no alternative but to give battle. Although reluctant to oblige Van Dorn, Coburn nevertheless ordered his men forward about midmorning on the fifth.

Forrest held a position on the Confederate right with some 2,000 men and artillery of his own. He watched as the Union lines advanced. When they began to recoil from the Confederate fire, he saw his opportunity. Forrest advanced his artillery to gain a more favorable position and sent his dismounted cavalrymen against the Union left flank. The fire of Captain Samuel Freeman's battery drove the Federal artillery from its position. Soon, both the artillery and the cavalry were hastening back toward Nashville.

Van Dorn then ordered Forrest to find the Union rear, an order the cavalry commander was quite pleased to obey. To that end, he sent Colonel James W. Starnes to his right and led another force even farther to the right, hoping to gain the Union flank and rear and block the Union retreat route. Thus, while the main Confederate force kept the Union infantry occupied, Forrest worked his way around the Union left flank. Resistance proved stubborn, but the Southerners pressed on, hoping to capture the remainder of Coburn's force on the field.

Even with their artillery and cavalry gone, Coburn's infantry fought valiantly. They held stubbornly to the summit of one of the two hills that bordered the road and held off repeated Confederate assaults. Finally, a bold charge in the face of a galling fire, led by Forrest in person, carried his men to the top and convinced the exhausted and outnumbered Federals to surrender.

In the heat of this combat, Forrest, who would have twenty-nine horses killed from beneath him by the time the war had ended, lost his favorite charger, Roderick. He had sent the horse to the rear with several wounds, when the animal bounded away and returned to his master. This act of loyalty ended in a fourth and fatal wound for the animal.

In the fighting at Thompson's Station, Van Dorn's Confederates captured 1,221 men, while losing 357 casualties of all kinds. Among those captured was Major

William R. Shafter, future commander of American forces in the Spanish-American War. Forrest, whose final assault by all accounts, including Van Dorn's, had carried the day, listed nine killed, fifty-eight wounded, and two missing.

Two additional incidents served as postscripts for the fighting at Thompson's Station. One was Forrest's subsequent capture of a Union garrison at Brentwood and another force guarding a bridge on the road from Nashville to Franklin. Both forces, numbering 529 and 230 men respectively, were composed of soldiers who had escaped his grip before at Thompson's Station. They would not escape a second time.

The other incident arose from a disagreement over the disposition of captured materiel and the publicity that followed the combat of 4–5 March. General Van Dorn accused Forrest of keeping captured Union supplies for himself and his command. He also expressed his belief that Forrest's staff members had manipulated news reports so as to receive the lion's share of praise for the Confederate victory from the press. Forrest vehemently denied both allegations, pointing out on the latter charge that he had done nothing except see that his command received the credit they deserved for the victory. The two hotheaded generals confronted each other on these matters and very nearly came to blows. Fortunately for the two men, their tempers cooled before either could harm the other.

—*Brian S. Wills*

See also Forrest, Nathan Bedford; Van Dorn, Earl.
For further reading:
Hartje, Robert G. *Van Dorn: The Life and Times of A Confederate General* (1967).
Henry, Robert Selph. *"First With the Most." Forrest* (1944).
Wills, Brian Steel. *A Battle from the Start: The Life of Nathan Bedford Forrest* (1992).
Wyeth, John Allen. *Life of General Nathan Bedford Forrest* (1899; reprint 1989).

THOREAU, HENRY DAVID
(1817–1862)
Author

Born in Concord, Massachusetts, on 12 July 1817, Henry David Thoreau attended the Concord Academy, entered Harvard College in 1833, and was graduated in 1837. Family members influenced his vehement stance against the institution of slavery— most importantly his mother, Cynthia Dunbar, who subscribed to antislavery literature. Household members also belonged to Concord's antislavery society, one of the most energetic in the nation. Thoreau met the foremost New England abolitionists when they were lodged in his mother's Concord boardinghouse. The transcendentalist Thoreau's deep conviction in individual reformation, however, was a major factor in his unwillingness to join abolitionist organizations. Still, they affected him: his important friendships were with abolitionists Ralph Waldo Emerson and Charles Sumner.

Thoreau lived courageously beside Walden Pond from July 1845 to September 1847. This act of personal freedom presaged his growing involvement in the antislavery movement. As curator of the Concord Lyceum, the naturalist and socially conscious Thoreau, a continual reader, encouraged the presentation of controversial topics. In 1845, for example, he defended Wendell Phillips's right to speak on the abolitionist movement.

Thoreau was imprisoned overnight in the Concord jail in July 1846, for refusing to pay his poll tax—chiefly as a protest against government-sanctioned slavery. This experience moved the strong-minded moralist to publish "Resistance to Civil Government" (1849). (The previous year, he had delivered a lecture before the Concord Lyceum on this topic, entitled "The Right and Duties of the Individual in Relation to Government.") Abolitionists had adopted nonviolent resistance, but it was Thoreau's exceptional efforts that spread the principle. Purposeful and determined (Puritan traits), he enunciated his basic premise in this celebrated essay (popularly known as "Civil Disobedience"): the transcendentalist doctrine that there was a higher law; that is, a citizen had the responsibility and right to act according to his conscience when it conflicted with civil authority. Thoreau conceded that government had legitimate functions; his quarrel was with unjust laws that aroused in him active resistance, not passivity. In this essay, he derided the Mexican-American War of 1846, which he believed was waged for the extension of slavery. (In an important sense, the Civil War had begun then.)

With the passage of the Fugitive Slave Act in 1850, Thoreau became even more distressed over the slavery controversy. His resistance to the political state became bolder, as he was now defying a specific law by aiding runaway slaves sheltered in Concord in their escape to freedom, as he wrote in *Walden* (1854). On 24 May 1854, Anthony Burns, a fugitive slave, was arrested in Boston and sent back to Virginia by federal and local authorities. (Thoreau had earlier become agitated when, in 1851, a similar incident happened in Boston to the fugitive slave Thomas Sims.) Thoreau, plagued by this incident, made it the focus of his essay, "Slavery in Massachusetts" (1854), which he presented as a speech on 4 July of the same year before an antislavery convention in Framingham. In this powerful address calling for disobedience to a law that he believed to be wrong, he assailed coercive government for excusing slavery, attacking also the press and the church for their acceptance of it. Angered by his own state's complicity, he stated explicitly: "My thoughts are murder to the State; I endeavor in vain to observe nature, my thoughts involuntarily go

plotting against the state." At the convention, Thoreau thoroughly approved the action of William Lloyd Garrison when the defiant abolitionist publicly burned a copy of the Constitution of the United States. Thoreau also agreed with the Northern opposition to the Kansas-Nebraska Act of 1854. Enacted one day after Anthony Burns had been apprehended, it authorized the expansion of slavery west of Missouri and north of latitude 36° 30′, thereby heightening sectional conflict.

For several years, beginning in 1855, Thoreau's interest in abolitionist John Brown was nourished by Brown's loyal supporter Franklin Benjamin Sanborn, who had come to live in Concord. In 1857 and 1859, Thoreau heard Brown speak at the Concord Town Hall on his activism in Kansas between 1855 and 1858, the period when "civil war" broke out between antislavery supporters and Southern sympathizers along the Kansas-Missouri border. (Brown's second talk in particular swayed him.) When on 19 October 1859, Thoreau learned of Brown's doomed raid at Harper's Ferry (Virginia), his immediate response was to embrace him as a considerable hero for his idealism and moralism. He acclaimed Brown as a true transcendentalist—a man of principles whose goal was to liberate slaves.

Thoreau now advocated forceful resistance to the federal government. In his genuinely enthusiastic and well-received speech, "A Plea for Captain John Brown," at the Concord Town Hall—a meeting he had called for 30 October—Thoreau almost singly defended Brown unequivocally, interceding entreatingly for one individual who had the courage to heed his own conscience. On 2 December 1859, the day Brown was hanged, Thoreau spoke in Concord again at the memorial service for Brown on the "Martyrdom of John Brown" (also known as "After the Death of John Brown"), expressing contempt for and wrath at those who misunderstood and maligned Brown. His third defense of Brown, "The Last Days of John Brown," was read for him at the John Brown memorial celebration in North Elba, New York, on 4 July 1860, at the time of Brown's burial there. The address tracked the shift in popular opinion of Brown's raid from one of hostility to one of developing awareness of his motives.

Essentially apolitical, Thoreau supported the Civil War after all. The Union army defeats in the spring of 1861 had a marked effect on him. In ill health, he remarked that he "could never recover while the war lasted." He died in Concord on 6 May 1862.

—*Bernard Hirschhorn*

See also Brown, John; Burns, Anthony; Emerson, Ralph Waldo; Kansas-Nebraska Act; Phillips, Wendell.
For further reading:
Harding, Walter. *The Days of Henry Thoreau: A Biography* (1982).
———, and Carl Bode, eds. *The Correspondence of Henry David Thoreau* (1958).

Paul, Sherman. *The Shores of America: Thoreau's Inward Exploration* (1958).
Richardson, Robert D., Jr. *Henry Thoreau: A Life of the Mind* (1986).
Salt, Henry Stephens. *Life of Henry David Thoreau* (1896).

THORNWELL, JAMES HENLEY
(1812–1862)
Presbyterian clergyman and proslavery theorist

Born into humble circumstances in Marlboro District, South Carolina, James H. Thornwell became an orphan at age eight. Kind benefactors nurtured him and funded his efforts to acquire a superior education at South Carolina College. He served as pastor for a number of Presbyterian churches in the Palmetto State and eventually held a chair at the Columbia Theological Seminary in South Carolina's capital city. His profound disquisitions on religious, ecclesiastical, and political affairs earned him the sobriquet "Calhoun of the Southern Church."

Active as an educator and in ecclesiastical politics, Thornwell earned and then wielded a powerful influence in Southern society. He corresponded with other Southern intellectuals and political leaders. Like many clergymen, he wrote, delivered, and had printed a number of sermons that upheld Southern society, especially slaveholding, against the caprice of Northern economics and social values. He especially emphasized the social compact between superior and inferior, between master and slave, which obliged the inferior to labor and the superior to care for the inferior both in material and spiritual matters.

Like most proslavery preachers, Thornwell took quite literally biblical injunctions for slaves to obey masters as proof that God Almighty did not consider slaveholding a sin. Furthermore, he found nothing in the abstract concept of slavery to prohibit a slave from converting to Christianity and pursuing a Christian life, a standard by which he judged all institutions. However, he differed from many proslavery theorists, because he took the whole Bible seriously. Although slavery might enjoy God's blessing in the abstract, God's word also commanded slave owners to treat slaves humanely.

For most of his ministerial career, Thornwell supported and directed efforts to obtain legal recognition by slave states of slave marriages and to garner legal restrictions on slave owners' power to separate slave families by sale. Although he considered that Southern society treated its slaves better than Northern society treated its laborers, he was never entirely sure that slavery as practiced in the South enjoyed God's blessing. His position underscored the tension between evangelical values and slaveholding values in antebellum Southern society.

Indeed, Thornwell challenged many of the legal assumptions implicit in antebellum slavery. Thornwell held that slave owners owned only the labor of the slave, as opposed to owning the slave body and soul. This limitation on the power of the master created the legal loophole through which the state might compel slave owners to allow the Christian gospel to be brought to the slaves. For slavery to enjoy God's blessing, Thornwell believed, the institution had to effect the spiritual conversion of Africans held in bondage. To bring about conversion in slavery, Thornwell chaired a committee of South Carolina Presbyterians that petitioned the state legislature to repeal laws forbidding slaves to be taught to read. In this way, they might have direct access to the Bible. This extreme position rooted itself in Thornwell's religious views, not his social attitudes.

Unlike some other proslavery preachers, Thornwell supported the Union until South Carolina seceded. His position grew from a pronounced social conservatism that made him quite reluctant to support efforts to create a new nation that might easily be swayed by chaotic social and political doctrines. However, he believed that Northern antislavery was likely a greater threat to godly values of stability, order, and hierarchy than Southern separatism, a position he made clear in his widely published Fast Day sermon, "Our National Sins," delivered in 1860.

When Northern Presbyterians required the General Assembly of the Presbyterian Church to pass a resolution in support of the Union, Thornwell supported the secession of Southern Presbyterians from that body in January 1861. Eleven months later, Thornwell helped constitute the Presbyterian Church of the Confederate States of American and drafted "An Address to All the Churches of Jesus Christ Throughout the Earth." In this he argued that a Presbyterian General Assembly made up of Southerners made sense because of secession. He also held that the church was not a tool of the state and existed in a different moral orbit. The will of the people bound the state, but the will of God governed the church.

He noted that Southerners in an ecclesiastical league with Northerners would subject Southern religious values to "foreign culture" and "foreign domination," illustrating rhetorically how religious ideas, if holding many distinctions from notions of secular politics, moved in a parallel direction with and provided moral support for Southern nationalism. His ideas illustrated, too, that Southern evangelicalism supported Southern nationalism to further a religious agenda.

—*Edward R. Crowther*

See also Churches.
For further reading:
Farmer, James Oscar, Jr. *The Metaphysical Confederacy: James Henley Thornwell and the Synthesis of Southern Values* (1986).
Freehling, William W. "James Henley Thornwell's Mysterious Antislavery Moment." *Journal of Southern History* (1991).
Palmer, Benjamin M. *The Life and Letters of James Henley*

Thornwell, D.D., LL.D.: Ex–President of the South Carolina College: Late Professor of Theology in the Theological Seminary at Columbia, South Carolina (1875).

TIDBALL, JOHN CALDWELL
(1825–1906)
Union general

The descendent of Scotch-Irish and Welsh ancestors, John Tidball was born to William and Maria Caldwell Tidball in Ohio County, Virginia (now West Virginia), on 25 January 1825. Following the death of his mother when he was nine years old, and after several family moves, John completed his education at a local common school. At age seventeen, he made application to the secretary of war for an appointment to West Point.

Tidball entered the U.S. Military Academy in June 1844, struggled academically throughout his four years, but through hard effort graduated eleventh in a class of thirty-eight. Upon graduation in 1848, he was appointed a brevet second lieutenant in the 3d Artillery. A prolific writer, his earliest memoirs recount his service against the Seminole Indians in Florida in 1849–1850, performing frontier duty at Fort Defiance, New Mexico, finding various routes to California, surveying the Pacific and Atlantic coasts, and quelling John Brown's raid at Harper's Ferry in 1859.

Tidball was present at some of the most important campaigns and battles of the Civil War. Shortly after the cannons were silenced at Fort Sumter, he took part in an expedition to Fort Pickens, Florida, from April to July 1861. Promoted captain in May, he returned to Washington in command of Battery A, 2d Artillery. He fought at First Bull Run, and his battery, with that of Henry Jackson Hunt, covered the retreat of the Union forces back to the defenses of Washington. In September Tidball successfully integrated his battery with that of the cavalry by mounting his cannoneers.

Tidball and his newly formed horse artillery battery fought in all the battles of the Peninsula campaign from March to August 1862. At the battle of Mechanicsville on 26 June 1862, Tidball's battery supported General Fitz John Porter's withdrawal to Gaines' Mill. Upon reaching Gaines' Mill, Tidball checked the Confederate envelopment and again assisted the Union withdrawal. According to Tidball's memoirs, it was during this campaign that he initiated the custom of having "Taps" sounded at a soldier's burial, instead of firing volleys, to avoid causing an alarm.

In the Maryland campaign of 1862 Tidball served with the cavalry. At Boonsboro, and repeatedly at Antietam, the fire of his battery was decisive. He participated in Stoneman's Raid on Richmond (13 April–2 May 1863) and in the operations in northern Virginia that culminated in the battle of Chancellorsville (2–4 May). Becoming an expert in the massed employment of field artillery, Tidball was assigned to command a brigade of horse artillery in June 1863. His battery fired the opening salvo at Gettysburg and continued to support the cavalry throughout the campaign. In August, after President Lincoln personally cited him for his efforts in Pennsylvania, Tidball was appointed colonel of the 4th New York Volunteer Artillery (foot) and assigned to the defenses of Washington.

Reassigned to the Army of the Potomac in March 1864, Colonel Tidball commanded the artillery of II Corps. He was cited for conspicuous gallantry at the battle of Spotsylvania and the North Anna (May 1864). While recovering from a wound, he was appointed commandant of cadets at the Military Academy in July, but in October rejoined the Army of the Potomac as chief of artillery, IX Corps. On 25 March 1865, when a Confederate force surprised and captured Fort Stedman, a key point in the Union lines near Petersburg, Tidball concentrated his artillery fire and paralyzed the Rebel army. This allowed the Union forces to recapture the position. A week later he helped plan and commanded the final artillery assault on Petersburg, which resulted in its evacuation.

Having received brevets of major general of volunteers and brigadier general, United States Army, for gallantry during the war, Tidball reverted to his regular army rank of captain after the South's surrender. He then served on the West Coast and as commandant of the District of Alaska. He was promoted to major in 1867 and was superintendent of artillery instruction at Fort Monroe from 1874 to 1881. It was during this period that he made a significant contribution to the professionalization of the artillery branch when he wrote *The Manual of Heavy Artillery Service* (1880). Other of his writings included "The Artillery Service in the War of the Rebellion" published in the *Journal of the Military Service Institution* (1891–1892) and various official reports included in the *Annual Report of the Secretary of War*. Tidball was promoted to lieutenant colonel in 1882 and to colonel in 1885. From 1881 to 1884 he served as aide-de-camp and confidant to the commanding general of the army, William Tecumseh Sherman, and from 1883 to 1888, he served as commandant of the Artillery School. He was retired for age on 25 January 1889 and died on 15 May 1906.

—*Mark R. Grandstaff*

See also Fort Stedman, Battle of.
For further reading:
Jamieson, Perry D. *Crossing the Deadly Ground: United States Army Tactics, 1865–1899* (1994).
Morrison, James L., Jr., ed. "Getting Through West Point: The Cadet Memoirs of John C. Tidball, Class of 1848." *Civil War History* (1980).

Tidball, Eugene C. "The Fort Pickens Relief Expedition of 1861: Lieutenant John C. Tidball's Journals." *Civil War History* (1996).

———. "John C. Tidball: Soldier-Artist of the Great Reconnaissance." *Journal of Arizona History* (1996).

———. "The View From The Top of the Knoll: Capt. John C. Tidball's Memoir of the First Battle of Bull Run." *Civil War History* (1998).

TILDEN, SAMUEL JONES
(1814–1886)
New York Democrat and governor of New York

Samuel Jones Tilden's chief fame as a national figure rests in his defeat by Republican Rutherford B. Hayes in the presidential election of 1876, the most disputed election in U.S. history. Yet Tilden had achieved a significant measure of celebrity in New York politics before and during the Civil War, and after it he had become renowned in the Democratic Party and beyond as a dedicated reformer and enemy of governmental corruption.

Born in New Lebanon, New York, on 9 February 1814, Tilden was assailed in his youth by chronic illness, a condition that hampered his education. Whether because of his health or his personality, Tilden developed habits of procrastination that bordered on the laggardly, but he also exhibited a natural intellectual talent and occasional flashes of concentration. He attended Yale in 1834, but he left after a term. After a stint of writing political essays supporting Martin Van Buren, Tilden attended and graduated from the law school at the University of the City of New York (now New York University). This education and his time spent working in John W. Edmonds's law office facilitated his admission to the New York bar in 1841

He remained active in politics. Tilden had been a fervent Jacksonian and supporter of Martin Van Buren in the 1830s, and he continued to work for the Democratic Party in the 1840s. He supported James K. Polk's candidacy in the election of 1844 and soon afterward became a principal among the Barnburner faction, New York Democrats who followed Van Buren's antislavery principles. The fissuring of the state party over the slavery issue diminished his influence, however, and he went so far as to attend the Free Soil Party's national convention in 1848 as a delegate. Subsequently distanced from the New York Democratic leadership, he focused on his career as a lawyer. He exhibited a special understanding of the intricacies of railroad organization and finance and built a flourishing practice as a corporation lawyer, making a great deal of money in the process and increasing it with astute investments. In spite of his antislavery sentiments, which were at some variance with much of the state Democratic Party's leadership, he

remained a member and eschewed any thought of joining the Republicans.

Consequently, Tilden opposed Abraham Lincoln's election to the presidency in 1860. Yet, like many Democrats, his views on the Civil War and its impact on American politics and culture were riddled by ambiguities. Although initially opposed to the idea of coercing secessionists to remain in the Union, he found despicable the armed rebellion that ensued and encouraged the government to suppress it quickly with force. At the same time, he was wary of the growing centralization of federal authority that the war encouraged. He could never be counted, though, among the so-called Peace Democrats, whose activities were motivated variously by defeatism and sometimes took on the trappings of sedition. Tilden, in fact, was one of the impediments to the Peace Democrats' ascendancy in the eastern wing of the party. He joined with other figures associated with the New York Central Railroad, sometimes described as the heirs to the old Albany Regency, in an occasional alliance with Tammany Hall to obstruct the plans of Clement Vallandigham's backers.

Tilden found President Andrew Johnson's accommodating Reconstruction policy far more agreeable than the stringent methods advocated by the Radical Republicans. Meanwhile, while he served as New York's chairman of the Democratic Committee from 1866 to 1874 he took on and brought about the removal of the notorious William M. Tweed whose ring of dishonest politicians had long preyed upon New York City. Tilden also improved the state's government and judiciary as a whole. Such service brought him considerable prestige, and he was elected governor in 1874. From Albany he worked to make more efficient the state's budget and to reduce taxes. He crushed the Canal Ring, whose members had enriched themselves by skimming money from allocations for canal construction and improvements. With such a glowing reputation for honesty and integrity, Tilden greatly appealed to Americans weary of the scandals of Ulysses S. Grant's administration, so the Democratic Party nominated him for the presidency in 1876. In the confusion and controversy generated by that disputed contest, he agreed to accept Rutherford Hayes's election to prevent the possible outbreak of another civil war. He rebuffed overtures inviting him to run in 1880 and 1884, though he continued his prominent activities as a national political leader. When Tilden died on 4 August 1886 in Yonkers, New York, he bequeathed most of his estate of more than $3 million to help found the New York Public Library.

—*David S. Heidler and Jeanne T. Heidler*

See also Democratic Party.

For further reading:
Bigelow, John. *The Life of Samuel J. Tilden* (1895).
Flick, Alexander C., and Gustav S. Lobrano. *Samuel Jones Tilden: A Study in Political Sagacity* (1939).
Kelley, Robert L. "Samuel J. Tilden." *Historian* (1963).

TILGHMAN, LLOYD
(1816–1863)
Confederate general

Born near Claiborne, Maryland, on 18 January 1816, Lloyd Tilghman graduated from West Point in 1836. He decided not to become a professional soldier and resigned from the service. His only active military duty came during the Mexican War (1846–1848), when he served as a volunteer aid to General David E. Twiggs. Tilghman then worked as a construction engineer for various railroads. He entered Confederate service as a volunteer from Kentucky, which state he had adopted in 1852. In October 1861 Tilghman secured a commission as a brigadier general and was originally appointed to inspect Fort Henry on the Tennessee River and Fort Donelson on the Cumberland. In December 1861 he assumed command of the two forts.

Tilghman and others who served at Fort Henry consistently criticized its location, and Tilghman later called it "a wretched military position." Located on low ground close to the river, Fort Henry could easily be commanded by high ground on the opposite (west) bank. Yet Tilghman, while complaining, was also dilatory in efforts to rectify the situation. By January 1862 he had barely started to fortify the heights on the west bank, named Fort Heiman after Fort Henry's second in command. Having ordered the work done months before, theater commander General Albert Sidney Johnston was not pleased. Although he telegraphed Tilghman to push efforts to entrench Heiman, work there remained unfinished when the Union expedition under General Ulysses S. Grant and Commodore Andrew H. Foote arrived.

At Fort Henry, Tilghman had only 2,610 men in two brigades under Colonels Adolphus Heiman and Joseph Drake. Many of the defenders were raw recruits who had only shotguns or hunting rifles. Some even had flintlocks.

Tilghman was at Fort Donelson when late on 4 February he received word of the arrival above Henry of the Union flotilla. Tilghman immediately left Donelson to take up the direction of Fort Henry's defense. He telegraphed General Leonidas Polk for reinforcements and on the next day optimistically stated "there was a glorious chance to overwhelm the enemy." But no reinforcements arrived.

On the night of the fifth, realizing the strength of the opposing forces, Tilghman called together his principal officers. All were pessimistic, believing they could not withstand attack by an enemy they estimated to number at least 25,000 men. Tilghman then asked his artillery commander if his guns could hold out for an hour against a determined Union attack. When this officer replied in the affirmative, Tilghman ordered his commanders to have their men ready to move at a "moment's notice."

At ten o'clock on the morning of the sixth, just before the Union attack began, Tilghman ordered all but the artillery company manning the batteries to go to Fort Donelson. This left only about a hundred men at Henry, including those too sick to move. Tilghman saw the rest of the men on their way to safety and then returned to the fort to share its fate. His intention was to delay the attackers long enough for most of his command to escape, and in this he was successful.

The Confederate gunners grew dispirited during the gunboat attack and Tilghman tried unsuccessfully to encourage them by working one of the guns himself. Finally, with only four guns able to return fire, at about 2 P.M., Tilghman surrendered to Union flotilla commander Flag Officer Andrew H. Foote. Later, at Foote's request, Tilghman went aboard the flagship.

Made a prisoner of war, Tilghman was exchanged in the fall of 1862. He then took command of the 1st Brigade in Major General William Wing Loring's Army of the West and led that unit in the battle of Corinth, in the rear guard after Holly Springs, and in the Vicksburg campaign. He was struck by a shell fragment and killed while directing artillery fire on 16 May 1863, during the battle of Champion's Hill.

—*Spencer C. Tucker*

See also Foote, Andrew H.; Fort Donelson, Battle of; Fort Henry, Battle of; Grant, Ulysses S.; Johnston, Albert Sidney.

For further reading:

Cooling, Benjamin Franklin. *Forts Henry and Donelson: The Key to the Confederate Heartland* (1987).

Milligan, John D. *Gunboats Down the Mississippi* (1965).

Tucker, Spencer C. *Andrew Hull Foote* (1999).

TIMROD, HENRY
(1828–1867)
Southern poet

Casual strollers through the graveyard of Trinity Episcopal Cathedral in Columbia, South Carolina, might easily overlook the modest tomb of one of the Confederacy's greatest literary figures. Henry Timrod, who is buried beneath the stone monument, was known as the unofficial poet laureate of the Confederacy, and during his short life he was widely acclaimed as a writer of fine lyrical verse.

Born in Charleston, South Carolina, of German ancestry, Timrod attended that city's Coates School, where he befriended Paul Hamilton Hayne. Timrod attended the University of Georgia to study classics, but ill health and financial difficulties prevented him from graduating. Briefly he entertained the idea of entering law practice, but he felt called to write instead. To support himself, he taught in rural schools and served as a private tutor.

Timrod's readings in classical literature are evident in

his early poetry. A small collection of his nature poems appeared in 1860, and between 1857 and 1860 he contributed literary essays to *Russell's Magazine*, a distinguished periodical of its day, published in Charleston.

Timrod enlisted in the Confederate army as a clerk on 1 March 1862 but was reassigned to the Army of the West as a war correspondent for the *Charleston Mercury*. Leaving the Shiloh battlefield, Timrod, according to Hayne, "staggered home, half-blinded, bewildered with a dull red mist before his eyes, and a shuddering horror at heart." Timrod soon became assistant editor of the *Charleston Courier*. Late in 1862, several backers of Timrod invested their money and used their influence to see another volume of his poetry published. Corrected proofs were shipped to England but were apparently lost in the blockade. Of this episode, Jay Hubbell writes poignantly, "Thus vanished Timrod's last chance of seeing his best poems appear in book form. To the end of his life he hoped in vain to see a [new] collection of his poems."

In 1864 Timrod was named associate editor of the *Columbia South Carolinian*. He married Kate S. Goodwin, a young Englishwoman, in February of the same year. His married bliss, however, was short-lived.

When General W. T. Sherman entered Columbia on 17 February 1865, Timrod was left destitute. Ill with tuberculosis, he sold his own furniture and silver for food and medicine. Seeking a healthier climate, Timrod borrowed money to travel to Copse Hill, Georgia, to visit Hayne, but found only temporary relief there. His fragile health deteriorated further, and he died in Columbia on 7 October 1867.

In death, however, came the recognition he had always sought. Hayne issued *The Poems of Henry Timrod* in 1873; a volume of uncollected verse, edited by Guy A. Cardwell, Jr., was published in 1942. Edd Winfield Parks edited *The Essays of Henry Timrod* (1942). George A. Wauchope (1915), Henry T. Thompson (1928), and Jay Broadus Hubbell (1941) wrote biographies.

Best known are Timrod's wartime poems. "Ethnogenesis" is an ecstatic celebration of the Confederacy. Timrod predicts the South's victory in the war and its greatness in peacetime. He extols cotton, the backbone of the South's economy, as the "snow of Southern summers" and makes boastful claims about the righteousness of the Confederate cause in its crusade against the satanic North. Another poem, "Charleston," reflects the writer's deep affection for his native city and his concerns for its security.

Timrod's "Ode," composed for the first Confederate memorial observance in Charleston's picturesque Magnolia Cemetery on 16 June 1866, is a sad, dirge-like tribute to the Confederate dead. He notes that no monument has yet been erected to the memory of the fallen: "The shaft is in the stone." This poem is as reflective of Timrod's reduced circumstances as it is revelatory about the defeated Confederacy.

—*Harry M. Bayne*

See also Hayne, Paul Hamilton.
For further reading:
Hubbell, Jay B. *The Last Years of Henry Timrod* (1941).

TOD, DAVID
(1805–1868)
Governor of Ohio

Born to George Tod and Sarah Isaacs Tod outside of Youngstown, Ohio, David Tod was educated locally and at Burton Academy before beginning the study of law. He began his practice at age twenty-two in Warren, Ohio, and became active in the state Democratic Party. His political connections gained him an appointment as postmaster in Warren in 1830. Later in the decade he served one term in the state senate. He tried to use the latter position as a stepping-stone to the governorship of Ohio but lost both of his bids during the 1840s. In 1847, President Martin Van Buren appointed Tod U.S. Minister to Brazil, a position in which he remained during the Whig presidency of Zachary Taylor.

During Tod's long and varied political career he also was an active businessman, especially in the burgeoning coal and iron industry in Youngstown and the railroad business throughout the state. From 1859 until his death in 1868 Tod served as the president of the Cleveland & Mahoning Valley Railroad.

Still, Tod's first love was politics, and he was determined in 1860 to have his favorite, Stephen Douglas, gain the Democratic nomination for president and to win the election. He was selected one of Ohio's delegates to the Democratic National Convention in Charleston, South Carolina, where he was chosen first vice president of the convention. When the convention, unable to nominate a candidate, adjourned to reconvene in Baltimore in June 1860, Tod remained in the same position during the subsequent convention. When Caleb Cushing, the chair of the convention, withdrew in protest for what he perceived to be rule violations, Tod assumed the chair of the convention and engineered a Douglas nomination.

As a strong Union Democrat at the outbreak of the Civil War, Tod seemed a logical choice for governor by the coalition party known as the Union Party. He was elected and served for the first half of the war. Although no one questioned his loyalty to the Union, his rather dictatorial methods as governor rankled some people and prevented his renomination in 1863.

During Tod's one term as governor of Ohio he dealt with a number of crises and important issues regarding the defense of the state and the prosecution of the war.

While Tod's primary concern during his two years in office was recruiting soldiers for Federal service—and he devoted considerable amounts of time to that task—other matters constantly intruded on his time. The loyalty of many Ohio citizens became a major problem for Tod early on. Not only did he have to worry about housing political prisoners, but the Clement Vallandigham faction in Ohio politics presented Tod with the issue of how to deal with a superficially loyal opposition. Tod was very supportive of Vallandigham's exile to the Confederacy and worked to neutralize Vallandigham's followers who remained in the state.

During July 1862, Tod received frantic calls from Don Carlos Buell for short-term reinforcements to deal with John Hunt Morgan's first raid into neighboring Kentucky. Tod did what he could to meet the call, but it was followed by additional calls in August and September to meet Braxton Bragg's invasion of Kentucky. Not only was Kentucky's security a concern, but also rumors abounded that the Confederate invasion force intended to move into Ohio. Again Tod worked around the clock to meet the demand in this emergency, but he became increasingly concerned that the men he was sending to Kentucky were not properly equipped and supplied by the Federal authorities. His protectiveness toward Ohio citizens in Federal service became one of the hallmarks of his administration and extended to his efforts to secure the rapid exchange of Ohio soldiers in Confederate hands.

Morgan's periodic raids continued to be a problem when the intrepid Southerner moved back into Kentucky at the end of the year. Tod again mobilized militia forces to guard against a move into Ohio, but Morgan turned back in the face of strong Union opposition.

The threat became far more serious the following summer, when in July Morgan moved north into Kentucky with the intention of crossing the Ohio River into Northern territory. Tod had had to make so many previous calls for militia forces and short-term enlistments that this time when the threat to the state was genuine, he had a great deal of difficulty raising the needed troops. The institution of conscription by the North at that time made men reluctant to join for a short time when they would still be subject to the draft later. As Tod frantically tried to prepare his state for invasion, he urged the War Department to give men credit for service if they met this temporary emergency. In the meantime, Morgan was closing in on Cincinnati. Luckily for Tod and the state, enough regulars and militia were organized to meet Morgan's men and ultimately bring about the capture of Morgan and most of his troopers.

Tod was determined that a Confederate as slippery as Morgan be detained someplace more secure than Ohio's prisoner-of-war camps. Therefore he agreed with the suggestion made by Henry Halleck that Morgan and his officers be imprisoned at the Ohio Penitentiary. Morgan was taken there soon after his capture, but, much to Tod's chagrin, managed to escape on 26 November 1863, just four months after his capture. Tod offered a $1,000 reward for Morgan's capture, to no effect.

Shortly before leaving office, Tod made a request to the War Department that he found very distasteful. The state had supplied more than its quota of volunteers and short-term enlistees since the beginning of the war, and when a call for more soldiers was made, Tod requested that for the good of the morale of the state, the number be reduced. His protectiveness toward the citizens of the state extended even to this time when he knew he had been defeated for reelection to the governor's chair.

After leaving office, Tod returned to his many business interests. He turned down an offer from Abraham Lincoln to be secretary of the treasury in 1864, preferring instead to remain in Ohio for the duration of the war. He remained active in Ohio politics after the war, having switched to the Republican Party. He died of a stroke on 13 November 1868.

—*David S. Heidler and Jeanne T. Heidler*

See also Morgan's Raids.
For further reading:
Abbott, Richard H. *Ohio's War Governors* (1962).
Wright, George Bohan. *Hon. David Tod. Biography and Personal Recollections* (1900).

TODD, GEORGE
(1841–1864)
Confederate guerrilla

Information about George Todd's prewar career is scanty and contradictory. He was purportedly born in Canada, came to Missouri in 1859 with his parents and some brothers, and worked in the Kansas City area as a stonemason. Some sources claim that he turned guerrilla in order to escape arrest for alleged crimes, others because of Unionist persecution of his family, but neither explanation is supported by hard evidence. All that is known for certain is that in the late fall of 1861 he joined a small band of pro-Confederate guerrillas operating around Blue Springs in Jackson County, Missouri, and headed by William Clarke Quantrill. Although illiterate, Todd was cunning, utterly fearless, a crack shot, and in time became viciously brutal. Thanks to these attributes, he soon became Quantrill's right-hand man, the one who did the executing—often literally—of Quantrill's plans.

For this reason the story of Todd's career is inseparable from that of Quantrill's until the spring of 1864, when a drastic change took place in their relationship. Prior to then Todd participated in virtually all of Quantrill's raids into Kansas and against Missouri Unionists and his ambushes of and fights with Union troops. Moreover, he inherited Quantrill's mistress when that chieftain entered into a different liaison; accompanied Quantrill to Hannibal, Missouri, where they acquired a large reserve supply of ammunition; and, as commander of Quantrill's rear guard, fended off the Federal pursuit following the August 1863 raid on Lawrence, Kansas, in which the guerrillas massacred nearly 200 men and boys. Quantrill expressed his appreciation for this last service—and also sought to appease Todd's growing ambition—by giving him and his cronies a greater share of the plunder from Lawrence than any of the other guerrillas. This, though, merely whetted Todd's desire to be more than Quantrill's top subordinate, a desire that manifested itself at the Baxter Springs, Kansas, massacre (6 October 1863) when Todd—not Quantrill—gave the order to charge Major General James G. Blunt's escort, nearly all of whom were killed.

During the winter of 1863–1864, which he and his band spent in northern Texas, Quantrill came under strong pressure from the Confederate military authorities to provide men for the regular service. As a result, Quantrill reduced his force to 100 men, Todd became the captain, and Quantrill assumed the essentially mean-ingless title of "colonel." Furthermore, many of the older members left, and most of those who remained were younger, wilder types who looked to Todd as their true leader. Consequently, on returning to Missouri in the spring of 1864, Todd took control in name, as well as fact, by forcing Quantrill at gunpoint to admit that he was afraid of him. No member of the band came to Quantrill's support and only a few accompanied him as he left to spend the summer and fall with his mistress in a hideout in north-central Missouri.

Todd celebrated his ascendancy by carrying out a successful ambush of a Union patrol in Jackson County, but then passed the summer lying low in the guerrillas' favorite refuge, the Sni-A-Bar hills in the eastern part of that county. Not until September did he resume active operations by raiding, in conjunction with another bush-whacker band, Keytesville, Missouri, capturing its garrison, and then joining with William "Bloody Bill" Anderson's gang in an unsuccessful attack on Fayette, Missouri. This setback, however, was more than made up on 27 September 1864, when Todd, combining forces with several other bushwhacker bands, including Anderson's, lured a Union battalion into an ambush near Centralia and slaughtered some 125 of its men.

Todd's return to the warpath was inspired by a desire to facilitate the invasion of Missouri by a Confederate army under Major General Sterling Price, who was making a last, desperate attempt to "liberate" the state from Unionist domination. When that army reached Jackson County on the way to Kansas City, Todd's men joined it as scouts. On 21 October Todd rode to the top

of a hill west of Independence to survey the countryside. A Union picket saw him, fired, and a rifle bullet tore through Todd's throat, killing him—he who had survived scores of bloody encounters unscathed. His grieving followers buried him in Independence's Woodlawn Cemetery where, presumably, whatever is left of him still remains. Todd himself pronounced his most fitting epitaph when he told a captured Union officer at Keytesville: "I am the bushwhacker Todd. You need not consider me a Confederate officer. I intend to follow bushwhacking as long as I live." That he did.

—*Albert Castel*

See also Anderson, William, Battle of "Bloody Bill"; Baxter Springs Massacre; Centralia Massacre; Lawrence, Kansas; Quantrill, William Clarke.

For further reading:

Barton, O. S. *Three Years with Quantrill: A True Story Told by His Scout John McCorkle* (1992).

Castel, Albert. *William Clarke Quantrill: His Life and Times* (1962; reprint, 1998).

Connelley, William E. *Quantrill and the Border Wars* (1910).

Leslie, Edward E. *The Devil Knows How to Ride: The True Story of William Clarke Quantrill and His Confederate Raiders* (1996).

TODD'S TAVERN, BATTLE OF
(7 May 1864)

On the morning of 7 May 1864, Major General Ulysses S. Grant pondered his next move. For the past two days, the Army of the Potomac had been engaged with Robert E. Lee's Army of Northern Virginia at the Wilderness in some of the heaviest, most brutal combat of the war. Despite the high casualties in the Wilderness, Grant had not wavered from his two principle objectives: the destruction of the Army of Northern Virginia and the capture of the Confederate capital at Richmond. Lee was equally pensive as he considered the various moves that Grant could make.

During May 1864 Lee masterfully waged a series of defensive battles. Given the reality of his situation, Lee had no other alternative, as Grant's offensive presented a number of problems for Lee to overcome. The Army of Northern Virginia was outnumbered two to one, with heavy casualties from the previous two days of fighting in the Wilderness, and it was faced with keeping itself between the Army of the Potomac and Richmond. Added to this was the loss of Lee's Corps commanders: Lieutenant Generals James Longstreet, Richard S. Ewell, and Ambrose P. Hill. Ewell and Hill were too ill to fight, and Longstreet had been shot accidentally by one of his own men. Since the war began, Lee had not faced a more severe manpower crisis, both in terms of officers and soldiers. For his next move, then, he turned to his cavalry, led by his most dependable junior officer, Major General James Ewell Brown "Jeb" Stuart.

Lee sent Stuart south out of the Wilderness to probe Grant's line and discover his intentions. Once Stuart confirmed that Grant was moving toward Spotsylvania Court House, Lee moved the remaining elements of his cavalry into position to screen Major General Richard Anderson (now commanding Longstreet's First Corps) as he shifted south to the crossroads at Spotsylvania. For this screening operation, Lee selected his nephew and cavalry division commander, Major General Fitzhugh Lee. Joining the younger Lee was a second division commanded by Major General Wade Hampton of South Carolina. Their plan was to establish defensive positions near Todd's Tavern, where the Brock and Catharpin Roads intersected. Fitzhugh Lee set his defensive perimeter one mile north of the tavern across Brock Road; Hampton dug in west of the tavern across the Catharpin. The Federal cavalry, then, was tasked with clearing the Brock Road so that Grant could continue his push southward and closer to Richmond.

The Federal calvary was led by Major General Philip H. Sheridan. Sheridan had fought with Grant in the west. However, he had limited cavalry experience, and he argued openly with General Meade about the cavalry's role. According to historian Gordon Rhea, Meade "wanted Sheridan to screen his [Meade's] advance, locate the enemy, and protect the supply chain. Sheridan . . . insisted on using the cavalry aggressively, like infantry." Sheridan had not fought effectively in the Wilderness and had allowed Lee to move undetected. The skirmish that erupted at Todd's Tavern on 7 May highlighted the command and communication problems that existed in Grant's command early in the 1864 campaign.

Sheridan's objectives for the day were to protect the Union supply train and open the Brock Road south of Todd's Tavern, giving Grant unfettered access to Spotsylvania. For the second task, Sheridan could only spare one division. He selected Brigadier General Wesley Merritt, who was encamped east of Todd's Tavern along Furnace Road. On point that morning was Brigadier General George A. Custer. His Michigan Wolverines were the first to encounter Fitzhugh Lee's advance patrols. Custer's 1st Michigan dismounted and moved into the trees along Brock Road, while his main force continued to press ahead. What they encountered were Fitzhugh Lee's cavalrymen fighting dismounted behind makeshift barricades. Without reinforcements, Merritt's advance ground to a halt in less than an hour.

At 10 A.M., Sheridan received word that he could detach a portion of his cavalry from guarding the supply train and redirect them toward offensive operations. Immediately, Sheridan sent reinforcements to bring Merritt's division to full strength. Then he deployed a second division under Brigadier General David Gregg, who approached Todd's Tavern from the east along the Catharpin Road. Gregg split his force, sending one

brigade straight ahead to confront Fitzhugh Lee's right flank at the crossroads, while a second brigade shifted south in an effort to come up Brock Road from Fitzhugh Lee's rear and close the pincers. Shortly after noon, however, Lee had decided to shift south to take advantage of the better defenses south of the tavern. Gregg's brigades met at the crossroads around 3 P.M., where they realized that Lee had escaped and that they now faced two Confederate fronts. Merritt turned his attentions to Hampton, who was still in his defenses west of the tavern on Catharpin Road, while Gregg charged back down the Brock after Fitzhugh Lee.

The battle raged for the remainder of the day with heavy casualties on both sides. A soldier in the 4th Virginia Cavalry remembered that for "a half hour there was one of the hottest fights between opposing brigades of dismounted cavalry that occurred during the war. Every tree, every sapling was marked by the flying lead, and a steady stream of wounded were going back." When darkness came, the Confederate lines were in disarray, but once again they had held. The Union held the crossroads at Todd's Tavern and Sheridan, deeming the day a success, ordered his cavalry to disengage. In doing so he gave up over a mile of Brock Road south of the tavern and failed to accomplish his larger objective of clearing the Brock Road for Grant's infantry. In this sense, Lee's bold move at Todd's Tavern had worked. The Confederate cavalry had stalled the Union advance and provided precious time for Anderson as he made his way toward Spotsylvania.

—*Edward Ragan*

See also Custer, George Armstrong; Hampton, Wade; Lee, William Henry Fitzhugh; Sheridan, Philip Henry; Spotsylvania Court House, Battle of; Stuart, James Ewell Brown; Wilderness, Battle of the.
For further reading:
Power, J. Tracy. *Lee's Miserables: Life in the Army of Northern Virginia from the Wilderness to Appomattox* (1998).
Rhea, Gordon C. *The Battles for Spotsylvania Court House and the Road to Yellow Tavern, May 7–12, 1864* (1997).
Trudeau, Noah Andre. *Bloody Roads South: The Wilderness to Cold Harbor, May–June 1864* (1989).

TOMPKINS, SALLY LOUISA
(1833–1916)
Confederate nurse

Sally Tompkins devoted the war years to running a small hospital in the home of Judge John Robertson, situated at Main and Third Streets in Richmond. So superior was the rate of recovery there that when the Confederate government closed many of Richmond's private homes to centralize relief efforts in larger general hospitals late in 1861, it allowed Tompkins to keep her facility open by granting her a captain's commission. Outfitting the hospital with her own funds, Tompkins opened Robertson Hospital after First Manassas and did not disband it until June 1865.

Robertson's staff consisted of white female volunteers and four slaves—including the Tompkins's family cook—who prepared food and medical supplies and brought them to the hospital. Among the Confederate surgeons assigned to Robertson were John Spottswood Wellford, A. Y. P. Garnett, and Thomas S. Latimer. With a bed capacity of twenty-five, Robertson Hospital cared for over 1,300 patients in four years and lost only 73, achieving the lowest mortality rate of any Confederate medical establishment. Tompkins's dedication to sanitary procedures made for a miraculously low rate of dysentery cases, a notable achievement in the era before antisepsis was widely practiced.

Born among the first families of Virginia, Tompkins spent the first five years of her life at Poplar Grove, a plantation in Mathews County that had belonged to her maternal grandfather. Tompkins's father, Christopher, was a sea merchant, state legislator, and militia officer before his death in 1838 occasioned the family's move to Richmond. There Tompkins spent the remainder of her childhood with siblings and stepsiblings, and absorbed the Christian devotion that she would take into her hospital work. Living modestly, she used her abundant resources, including her captain's salary, to procure high-quality food for patients, even when scarcity and runaway inflation made the cost of the raw materials exorbitant.

Tompkins was only five feet tall, but what she lacked in stature, she made up for in presence. Soldiers feared her temperance lectures and genuflected with her in prayer regardless of their own religious customs. She never married, though she received numerous proposals. Like many of her Confederate peers, she spent the postwar years in semireclusion, using the Episcopal Church as the locus of her charitable endeavors. She also took pleasure in Confederate veterans' activities, attending reunions and contributing generously to United Daughters of the Confederacy (UDC) memorial initiatives. Ultimately, four UDC chapters were named in honor of Tompkins's service. By the turn of the century, with her fortune on the wane, Tompkins went to live in the Richmond Home for Confederate Women, where she died penniless at age 82.

—*Jane E. Schultz*

See also Nurses; Women.
For further reading:
Andrews, Matthew Page. *Women of the South in War Times* (1920).
Marshall, Mary Louise. "Nurse Heroines of the Confederacy." *Bulletin of the Medical Librarians' Association* (1957).
Paquette, Patricia. "A Bandage in One Hand and a Bible in the Other: The Story of Captain Sally L. Tompkins (C.S.A.)." *Minerva Quarterly* (1990).
Robertson Hospital Morning Reports of Patients and Attendants. Record Group 109. National Archives, Washington, D.C.
Tompkins, Sally. Letters. Virginia State Library Archives, Richmond.

TOM'S BROOK, BATTLE OF
(9 October 1864)

Tom's Brook ranks as the most complete and humiliating reverse suffered by the Confederate cavalry in the Eastern theater. In an open, set-piece battle, two Union cavalry divisions outmaneuvered, outfought, and stampeded two divisions of Confederate horsemen. The exultant Federals chased their gray-clad foes twenty or more miles up Virginia's Shenandoah Valley in a wild rout that was known ever after as the "Woodstock Races."

After the smashing Union victories at Winchester and Fisher's Hill in September 1864, Major General Philip H. Sheridan's Army of the Shenandoah advanced up the valley to Harrisonburg, while the remnants of Lieutenant General Jubal A. Early's Confederate Army of the Valley sought refuge near Brown's Gap in the Blue Ridge Mountains. Deciding that the campaign had ended, Sheridan instructed his command to retire down the valley beginning on 6 October 1864. Sheridan was determined that the Shenandoah Valley should no longer serve as a granary for enemy forces. While his infantry trudged north, he had his three cavalry divisions trail behind to burn any crops and slaughter any livestock that might feed Early's troops. Soon the wake of Sheridan's host could be traced by the smoke of burning barns, mills, and haystacks.

Early reacted to Sheridan's retrograde movement by dispatching his newly appointed cavalry commander, Brigadier General Thomas L. Rosser, to pursue and harass the Federals. As the self-proclaimed "Savior of the Valley," Rosser executed his mission with ferocious enthusiasm. Many of his 4,000 to 5,000 riders were natives of the region, and they had a score to settle with the men who were devastating their homes and impoverishing their families. On 6, 7, and 8 October, Rosser repeatedly lashed at the rear guards of two of Sheridan's cavalry divisions, the 1st under Brigadier General Wesley Merritt and the 3d under Brigadier General George A. Custer.

Much to the disgust of Merritt and Custer, Sheridan's chief of cavalry, Brigadier General Alfred T. A. Torbert, refused to let them interrupt their withdrawal and strike back at Rosser. After Sheridan learned of this, however, his famous temper exploded. On the evening of 8 October, he told Torbert to "start out at daylight and whip the Rebel cavalry or get whipped." Sheridan added that he intended to watch the engagement from Round Top Mountain.

At 6:00 A.M. on 9 October, Custer led his 2,500 Union troopers south along the Back Road to confront

Brigadier General George A. Custer bowing to Brigadier General Thomas L. Rosser before starting the Battle of Tom's Brook, from an eyewitness sketch by Alfred R. Waud (*Library of Congress*)

the 3,000 to 3,500 Confederates in a division under Rosser's personal command. Custer and Rosser had been close friends at West Point before the war. Once the young Union general's two brigades had deployed, he rode close enough to Rosser's lines to be recognized, doffed his hat, bowed, and shouted: "Let's have a fair fight boys! No malice!"

To the east of Custer on the Valley Pike, Merritt's 3,500 Yankee cavalry wheeled into battle formation facing the 1,000 to 1,500 Confederates in Brigadier General Lunsford L. Lomax's division. Commanding three brigades, Merritt was able to extend his right far enough to establish contact with Custer's left.

Thanks to a comfortable superiority in numbers, Merritt easily turned Lomax's right flank and put the Rebel division to flight. Lomax's troopers were further handicapped by the fact that they carried only single-shot Enfield infantry rifles, which made it impossible for them to engage in any horseback melees.

Custer encountered stiffer resistance along Rosser's front. Not only was Rosser's division larger, but it stood

on a steep ridge south of Tom's Brook, where stone walls and other barricades provided ample cover for dismounted marksmen and a six-gun battery.

Initially, Rosser's artillery gained an advantage over Custer's two batteries. Rather than sacrifice lives in a useless frontal attack, Custer slipped three regiments around Rosser's left flank, forcing the Rebels to abandon their strong position. Rosser managed to rally his division and turned on the Federals two miles beyond Tom's Brook, but Custer regrouped his regiments and led them forward in a mounted charge that threw Rosser into an irreversible rout.

Custer chased Rosser for twenty miles, taking six cannon. Lomax left five guns in Merritt's hands and fled for twenty-six miles up the Valley Pike, passing Woodstock and not halting until he reached the protection of Early's infantry. Custer and Merritt also took 350 prisoners and every wagon and ambulance assigned to Early's cavalry. Union losses numbered only nine killed and forty-eight wounded.

In the months following Tom's Brook, Sheridan's

cavalry enjoyed an almost unassailable superiority in the Shenandoah Valley.

—*Gregory J. W. Urwin*

See also Custer, George Armstrong; Fisher's Hill, Battle of; Lomax, Lunsford Lindsay; Merritt, Wesley; Rosser, Thomas Lafayette; Sheridan, Philip Henry; Torbert, Alfred Thomas Archimedes; Winchester, Third Battle of (Opequon).

For further reading:
Bushong, Millard K., and Dean M. Bushong. *Fightin' Tom Rosser, C.S.A.* (1983).
Lewis, Thomas A. *The Guns of Cedar Creek* (1988).
Starr, Stephen Z. *The Union Cavalry in the Civil War* (1979–1985).
Urwin, Gregory J. W. *Custer Victorious: The Civil War Battles of General George Armstrong Custer* (1990).
Wert, Jeffry D. *From Winchester to Cedar Creek: The Shenandoah Campaign of 1864* (1987; reprint, 1997).

TOOMBS, ROBERT AUGUSTUS
(1810–1885)
Confederate secretary of state and general

Born in Wilkes County, Georgia, on 2 July 1810, Robert Toombs served as the first secretary of state of the Confederate States of America and later become a brigadier general in the Confederate army. Before the Civil War, Toombs was a member of the Georgia legislature from 1836 to 1843, secured election to the United States House of Representatives in 1844, and in 1850 took a seat in the United States Senate. As a senator throughout the 1850s he played an important role in national politics.

His parents were Robert, a Revolutionary War soldier, and Catharine Huling Toombs. The family was relatively wealthy, owning 2,200 acres of land and forty-five slaves. Shortly after his fourteenth birthday, young Robert, the fourth of five children, entered Franklin College (today's University of Georgia), but was expelled for unruly behavior during his senior year. He subsequently enrolled at Union College in Schenectady, New York, where he received his bachelor's degree. The following fall he matriculated at the University of Virginia law school, completing only one year of a two-year law program. Upon his return to Georgia in 1830 he was admitted to the Georgia bar. By all accounts a skilled lawyer, Robert A. Toombs was endowed with a brilliant intellect and was regarded by contemporaries as a great orator. However, in spite of his talents in the political arena, he had a tendency to be erratic and inconsistent in the policies he pursued. Commenting on his national congressional service, one of his biographers noted that he possessed a "fatal flaw in his political character which denied him the stature of greatness—a tendency under pressure and commotion to slide into the role of extremist."

Although he was often categorized as a Southern zealot, during the 1850 crisis over the admission of California to the Union, Toombs actively campaigned to preserve the Union. After the election of President Abraham Lincoln a decade later, he was one of five Southerners appointed to the Senate Committee of Thirteen to contrive a compromise. When Republicans rejected the Crittenden Compromise, Toombs concluded that immediate secession was the only course of action. Resigning from the Senate in early January 1861, he later that month attended the Georgia secession convention as a strong proponent for withdrawing from the Union. After secession was an accomplished fact, Toombs was one of ten Georgians representing the state at the Montgomery, Alabama, convention (February 1861) that established the Confederate States of America.

Many considered Toombs to be the leading contender for the Confederate presidency, but several states came out in support of Jefferson Davis. Perhaps old political animosities or Toombs's drunkenness at a dinner party persuaded the delegates to bypass the Georgian. Toombs was appointed to a committee to produce the Confederate constitution and was eventually chosen by President Davis to become secretary of state. In the cabinet meetings preceding the attack upon Fort Sumter in April 1861, Toombs advised against such a course of action stating that "[i]t is unnecessary; it puts us in the wrong; it is fatal." Temperamentally unsuited to playing a secondary role and frustrated by his relations with President Davis, Toombs became increasingly unhappy as secretary of state and hence resigned after only five months.

Toombs then entered the Confederate army as a brigadier general and began advocating a Confederate invasion of Maryland a year before it happened. As permitted by the Confederate constitution, Toombs also kept a seat in the Confederate Congress and frequently attended legislative sessions in Richmond. Such absences from the army were likely fortunate, for Toombs's performance as a Confederate officer reportedly verged on disastrous. Having no formal military training and accustomed to a leading role in political affairs, he found military discipline and subordination irritating. Also, according to fellow Georgian Thomas R. R. Cobb, Toombs frequently drank too much. Cobb wrote to his wife that Toombs was "drunk almost every afternoon and makes himself most ridiculous." His involvement in several controversies saw Toombs at one point under military arrest. Of special note was a verbal confrontation with D. H. Hill during the battle of Malvern Hill (1 July 1862). Toombs's brigade, fighting under General John B. Magruder on the Confederate right, became disorganized during the course of battle. General Hill, whose men were located in the Confederate center, believed Magruder's forces were not fully engaged in the battle. Hill commanded Toombs's men to move forward in support of his position, which

they did, although the two commanders exchanged insults. Soon afterwards, Toombs's men retreated. The animosity continued after the battle, with Hill implying that Toombs had acted in a cowardly manner. Toombs issued a challenge to a duel, which Hill refused.

During the battle of Antietam, Toombs partially redeemed himself with a courageous performance defending the Stone Bridge from Ambrose Burnside's relentless assaults. Shot through his hand at Antietam, he returned home for recovery, but in March 1863 resigned from the army, probably because his heroic deeds at Antietam had not earned him a promotion. Doubtless his departure from the army was a relief to it.

Toombs, already an avowed critic of President Davis and his policies, returned to Georgia in 1863 and joined his long-time friend Alexander H. Stephens, vice president of the Confederacy, Alexander's brother Linton, and Georgia governor Joseph E. Brown as a vocal opponent of the Davis government. These prominent Georgians could not understand why the principles of states' rights had to be set aside to conduct the war effectively. They opposed conscription, impressment of supplies, the tax-in-kind, and the suspension of the writ of habeas corpus, along with other policies emanating from Richmond. In November 1863 Toombs made a bid for the Confederate Senate but, much to his chagrin, was rejected by the Georgia General Assembly in favor of Herschel V. Johnson.

By August 1863, Toombs was a colonel in the state guard formed to defend Georgia, but his cavalry regiment disbanded after six months. When Union general William T. Sherman invaded Georgia, Toombs reentered the Georgia militia, serving as chief of staff and inspector general for General Gustavus Woodson Smith. As such, Toombs was in the midst of the forty-day siege of Atlanta and found himself in Savannah as General Sherman approached that city. As the Confederacy collapsed, Toombs returned to his residence in Washington, Georgia. In early May 1865 President Davis and his party of fugitives spent the night in Toombs's hometown, but Toombs made no effort to meet him. On 11 May 1865, as Union soldiers approached his house to arrest him, Toombs escaped through the back door. Hiding in various parts of the state for several months, he eventually made his way to New Orleans and boarded a passenger ship to Havana, Cuba. Later travelling to Paris, he was joined by his wife. After more than a year of exile in Europe, he returned to Georgia during the spring of 1867. He never made any effort to take an oath of loyalty to the United States government and died on 15 December 1885, an unreconstructed and unrepentant Rebel.

—*Mary Ellen Wilson*

See also Antietam, Battle of; Congress, C.S.A.; Georgia; Malvern Hill, Battle of.
For further reading:
Phillips, Ulrich B. *The Life of Robert Toombs* (1913).
Phillips, Ulrich B., ed. *The Correspondence of Robert Toombs, Alexander H. Stephens, and Howell Cobb* (1913).
Stovall, Pleasant A. *Robert Toombs: Statesman, Speaker, Soldier, Sage* (1892).
Thompson, William Y. *Robert Toombs of Georgia* (1966).

TORBERT, ALFRED THOMAS ARCHIMEDES
(1833–1880)
Union general

Born to Jonathan R. Torbert and Catharine Milby Torbert in Georgetown, Delaware, Alfred T. A. Torbert was educated locally before receiving an appointment in 1851 to the U.S. Military Academy. He graduated twenty-first of thirty-four in the class of 1855. After graduation, Torbert was stationed on the western frontier in Texas and New Mexico before being sent to Florida to fight in the Third Seminole War. After that duty he participated in Albert Sidney Johnston's Utah expedition. At the outbreak of the Civil War, Torbert was a first lieutenant in the 5th U.S. Infantry on leave at home. During that time, an apparent misunderstanding occurred with the Confederate army, when someone mistook Torbert's Southern background to indicate a desire to serve the Confederacy. Briefly, Torbert was listed on the Confederate army rolls as an artillery first lieutenant. He quickly disabused everyone of the notion that he was leaving the U.S. Army by traveling to New Jersey to recruit a regiment for Federal service.

In September 1861, Torbert was commissioned colonel of the 1st New Jersey Volunteers, and that unit became a part of the Army of the Potomac. On 7 March 1862, Torbert led his regiment in the advance from Washington to the then-abandoned Confederate works at Manassas Junction. That mission accomplished, the regiment became a part of VI Corps during the Peninsula campaign. Torbert commanded the regiment in all the early engagements of that campaign and in the Seven Days', though he was ill and unable to take the field during the battle of Gaines' Mill.

When VI Corps became a part of the Army of Virginia in August 1862, Torbert was given command of a brigade. He led his men at Second Bull Run and in the early phases of the Maryland campaign before falling wounded at Crampton's Gap. The injury proved not to be serious, and he returned to duty to lead his brigade at Antietam.

Torbert remained in command of his brigade through the fall of 1862, leading them in the battle of Fredericksburg. Although they were not a part of the actual offensive conducted by VI Corps against the Confederate right, Torbert and his brigade guarded the retreat of the corps when it moved back across the Rappahannock. In early 1863, Torbert was promoted to brigadier general of volunteers with a date of rank of 29 November 1862.

In one of the few cases of command continuity during the war, Torbert retained command of the same brigade of which he had assumed leadership in August 1862 until March 1864. They fought together at Chancellorsville, marched north into Pennsylvania (Torbert's brigade was never actually engaged in the battle of Gettysburg), and then went south again in pursuit of Robert E. Lee. After Gettysburg, Torbert fought at Rappahannock Station and in the Mine Run campaign. In the spring of 1864, however, the direction of Torbert's Civil War career changed.

The Army of the Potomac underwent a major reorganization in preparation for Ulysses S. Grant's campaign against Lee. On 27 March 1864, Torbert was given command of the 1st Division of Philip Sheridan's cavalry corps. The primary job of this corps in the initial phases of the campaign beginning in April was to guard the left flank of Grant's army as it moved south. With George Armstrong Custer commanding his first brigade, Torbert had a very aggressive division that never wasted an opportunity to skirmish with Confederate cavalry units.

Bringing up the rear of Sheridan's cavalry during Grant's turning movement at the end of May, Torbert's men fought Confederate cavalry at Hanover Court House on 27 May. Beginning on 7 June to distract Lee from Grant's movement across the James River toward Petersburg, Sheridan led an expedition toward Trevilian Station. On 11 June Torbert encountered a Confederate cavalry force under Wade Hampton near Trevilian Station, and by maneuvering Custer's brigade to the Confederates' rear he was able to defeat the Southern force. The following day, however, the Confederates were reinforced, and Torbert and ultimately the entire cavalry corps were forced to retreat.

At the end of July, again in an attempt to distract the Confederates from what would be the disastrous Crater explosion, Torbert accompanied Sheridan on a raid toward Richmond that was ultimately repulsed at Deep Bottom Run. Shortly thereafter, Torbert was given command of all cavalry in the Middle Military District in Sheridan's Army of the Shenandoah. Through the remainder of the summer through the fall of 1864, Torbert led his cavalry in every major engagement of Sheridan's Shenandoah Valley campaign. He particularly distinguished himself at Winchester, where he moved around the Confederate left flank, forcing the retreat. At Tom's Brook on 9 October 1864, Torbert was acting under an ultimatum from Sheridan that if he lost to Confederate cavalry he would be removed. Torbert completely routed a Confederate cavalry force there commanded by Thomas L. Rosser and Lunsford Lomax.

When he was not fighting, Torbert led his men throughout the valley destroying anything that could be of use to Confederate forces. From 19 to 28 December he led one such raid from Winchester to Gordonsville in a failed attempt to destroy most of the railroads in the area.

Torbert remained in the Shenandoah Valley until the end of the war, and in March 1865 received a brevet promotion to major general in the regular army. In July 1865 he was assigned to the Department of Virginia under Alfred Terry. After being mustered out of the volunteer service in 1866, Torbert resigned his regular commission. In 1869 he began a diplomatic career as U.S. minister to El Salvador. From 1871 until 1878 he served successively as consul to Havana, Cuba, and to Paris. In 1878 he went into business in Mexico, but he died on 29 August 1880 when the ship on which he was a passenger went down en route from New York to Mexico.

—*David S. Heidler and Jeanne T. Heidler*

See also Cedar Creek, Battle of; Hanover Court House, Battle of; Tom's Brook, Battle of; Trevilian Station, Battle of.

For further reading:

Slade, A. D. A. T. A. *Torbert: Southern Gentleman in Union Blue* (1992).

Townsend, George Alfred. *Major General Alfred Thomas Archimedes Torbert: Delaware's Most Famous Civil War Hero* (1993).

TORPEDOES

Because mines (called torpedoes in the nineteenth century) are principally defensive weapons, it was perhaps inevitable that the Confederate side made the most use of them during the Civil War. Land mines were first used in the Civil War during the 1862 Peninsula campaign. When the Confederates withdrew from Yorktown in May, they left behind artillery shells in the roads to explode if stepped on. At the time, this was considered a controversial practice and outside the bounds of civilized warfare. But as the war increased in destructiveness, such prohibitions were ignored.

Naval mines (torpedoes) date back to the War of 1812, when the inventor Robert Fulton (known for inventing a profitable steamboat) conducted experiments with them, although nothing came of these. Naval mines were first used effectively in war by the Russians during the Crimean War of 1854. There were those who believed that mines could be a major factor in helping to reduce the Union naval advantage during the war. Matthew Fontaine Maury was an early proponent of their use and conducted experiments with them.

Civil War naval mines (torpedoes) were of a variety of types, either built from scratch or constructed from barrels as casings. They were essentially stationary weapons, positioned in Southern rivers or harbors to explode against the hulls of Union warships. Two basic types of detonation were used: by contact or by electrical connections from batteries on shore. The first type was more certain to explode but was also dangerous to friendly vessels. The second type could be used only close to shore.

More often than not, such early mines failed to explode as a result of faulty detonating equipment or

Confederate torpedoes, shot, and shell in the Arsenal yard (Charleston, South Carolina), 1865 (*Library of Congress*)

becoming waterlogged, or they were swept away by the current. Even so, they had a profound psychological effect on sailors aboard ship, producing what was called "torpedo fever" among Union crews.

One of the first uses of mines during the Civil War came during the February 1862 Union assault on Fort Henry on the Tennessee River. The wife of a

Confederate captain at the fort inadvertently revealed their presence in a conversation with some of Brigadier General Ulysses S. Grant's scouts. Flag Officer Andrew H. Foote then immediately set the crews of some of his lighter gunboats to sweeping for them. The mines, sheet-iron cylinders some five and a half feet long, pointed at each end and containing about seventy-five pounds of

A Union station on the James River, Virginia, established for extracting gunpowder from Confederate torpedoes, 1864 (Photograph by Egbert Guy Fox/*National Archives*)

gunpowder each, were fired by contact-type detonators. They were known to be located near Panther Island several miles downriver from Fort Henry, and the Union sailors used cutters to bring eight of them to the surface. All those recovered were soaked and harmless.

Civil War mine powder charges ranged from approximately fifty pounds to large mines of up to a ton of powder. One of the latter type, detonated electronically, sank the 542-ton Union gunboat *Commodore Jones* in the James River on 6 May 1864. She and two other Union vessels were sweeping for mines when she was sunk. Her captain said the mine exploded directly under the converted ferryboat, "absolutely blowing the ship to smithers." It also claimed some forty lives. A landing party went ashore immediately and captured two of the Confederate torpedomen and the galvanic batteries that had detonated the mine. Jeffries Johnson, one of the Confederates, refused to divulge information on the location of other torpedoes until he was placed in the bow of the forward Union ship.

Mines were also used offensively. Spar torpedoes were mines placed at the end of a spar or pole. The semisubmersible Confederate vessel *David* had a spar torpedo fixed to her bow. The most famous of spar torpedoes during the war was the one on board the Union Picket Boat No. 1, which on 28 October 1864 sank the 376-ton Confederate ironclad ram *Albermarle*. This mine was affixed to the end of a 14-foot spar lowered by a windless. Once the mine was in position under the enemy vessel's hull, a tug on a line released the mine, which floated up under the bottom of the ship. A second line activated the firing mechanism. The Confederates also used spar torpedoes and equipped small boats, as well as ironclad rams, with them.

Mines proved quite effective during the war. On 12 December 1862, the 512-ton Union ironclad *Cairo* struck a mine while in the Yazoo River and sank. The wreck was raised in 1965 and is today exhibited at the Vicksburg battlefield site. On 15 January 1865, despite precautionary sweeps by boats with drags and the fact that she had torpedo netting out, the 1,335-ton Union monitor *Patapsco* was sunk by a large mine or mines in the channel off Fort Sumter. She went down so rapidly that she took with her sixty-four men, more than half her crew. The largest ship sunk by a mine during the war, however, was the 1,934-ton Union steam sloop *Housatonic*. On 17 February 1864 she sank off Charleston, the victim of a ninety-pound spar torpedo on the partially submerged Confederate submarine *H. L. Hunley*, which, however, went down with her. The *Housatonic* was also the first ship sunk by a submarine in the history of warfare. In all, Confederate torpedoes sank

Another view of the Charleston Arsenal, 1865 (Photograph by Selmar Rush Seibert/*National Archives*)

seven Union ironclads and twenty-two wooden gunboats; fourteen other Union ships were damaged.

One of the most famous quotations of the war relates to mines: Flag Officer David Farragut's instruction at Mobile Bay of "Damn the torpedoes. Full speed ahead!"

—*Spencer C. Tucker*

See also Farragut, David G.; Fort Henry; *Housatonic*; *Hunley*; Maury, Matthew Fontaine.

For further reading:
Civil War Naval Chronology, 1861–1865 (1971).
Lord, Francis A. *Civil War Collector's Encyclopedia* (1995).
Silverstone, Paul H. *Warships of the Civil War Navies* (1989).
Slagle, Jay. *Ironclad Captain. Seth Ledyard Phelps and the U.S. Navy, 1841–1864* (1996).
Still, William N., Jr. *The Confederate Navy. The Ships, Men and Organization, 1861–1865* (1997).

TOTOPOTOMY CREEK, BATTLE OF
(28–30 May 1864)

After withdrawing back across the North Anna, the Army of the Potomac continued its movement southeast along the north bank of the Pamunkey River as Ulysses S. Grant searched for the next location to try and break through Robert E. Lee's defenses. Ill and barely able to keep his saddle, Lee moved his headquarters closer to Richmond near Atlee's Station on the morning of 28 May. From here, Lee considered Grant's options. Grant might continue his southeasterly movement as he had previously in an effort to turn Lee's right flank. Or, he might make a sudden move to the west, cross the Pamunkey, and drive on Richmond. Lee could not second-guess Grant's intent and had to wait for the Union commander to make the first move. That was just as well for Lee, who was preoccupied with his own army.

Illness, injury, and a lack of seasoned leadership continued to plague the Army of Northern Virginia. Two of Lee's corps commanders were out: 1st Corps commander Lieutenant General James Longstreet had been wounded at the Wilderness by one of his own men, and 2d Corps commander Lieutenant General Richard Ewell suffered dysentery and was too sick to command. Lee himself was still recovering from an illness that had incapacitated him at a critical moment four days earlier along the North Anna. After reviewing the order of battle for the Army of Northern Virginia, Civil War historian Noah Trudeau found that in addition to Lee, Longstreet, and Ewell, "three new major generals now commanded divisions, the leadership of fourteen brigades had changed, and no overall cavalry commander had yet been appointed by Lee to replace 'Jeb' Stuart," who had been killed on 11 May. These manpower concerns extended beyond the officer corps to the rank and file soldiers as well.

Reinforcements were not available to Lee from the west. As Grant disengaged along the North Anna three days earlier, he ordered the Army of the Potomac to destroy several miles of the Virginia Central Railroad to the northwest of Lee's current position. This deprived Lee of much-needed reinforcements and food supplies from the Shenandoah Valley. So Lee turned to his south, where General P. G. T. Beauregard, commander of the district south of Richmond, was stationed. Beauregard had opposed the Federal advance up the James River and had effectively halted Benjamin Butler's forces at the Bermuda Hundred. Given this, Lee felt that Beaureguard could spare a portion of his 12,000-man army to reinforce the Army of Northern Virginia. But Beaureguard refused Lee's request, citing the threat that Butler posed. The continued drain on manpower limited Lee's tactical options, hence Lee's wait-and-see attitude on the morning of 28 May, when Grant moved the Army of the Potomac across the Pamunkey River.

Lee pondered Grant's options and allocated his resources accordingly. A. P. Hill's 3d Corps was kept along the Virginia Central Railroad to guard it in case Grant tried to move to the northwest along Lee's left. Meanwhile, Major General Richard Anderson's 1st Corps and Early's 2d extended eastward, using the marshland of Totopotomy Creek as a defensive barrier.

While Hancock's II Corps pushed toward Totopotomy Creek, fighting their way through the tangled bottomlands, Grant sent Wright's VI Corps to the northwest toward Hanover Court House.

On 30 May Grant set both flanks in motion. Hancock's II Corps began moving south across the Totopotomy bottomlands to begin its push westward. Grant ordered Warren's V Corps to push south across the Totopotomy and then turn west, following the Shady Grove Church Road to its intersection with the east-west Mechanicsville Pike.

Jubal Early, Ewell's replacement as commander of the Confederate 2d Corps, anticipated Warren's maneuver and had previously instructed his cavalry to cut paths through the underbrush from the Shady Grove Church Road to the Old Church Road, which ran parallel and one mile south. Warren's left did not extend far enough south to see that it was exposed to a flanking maneuver by Early. Early planned to march east along the Old Church Road until he reached Bethesda Church, then turn north, following his precut traces to smash Warren's line.

For Warren's part, he had been nervous about his left flank all day. The initial accounts of Early's offensive conveyed confusion in the Union line. Taking the brunt of the assault were the Pennsylvania reserves, whose three-year enlistments were up at the end of the day. The Pennsylvanians were overrun in their slender breastworks, but Early was unable to control the attack. In the excitement, some Confederates ran beyond their objectives and became lost in the confusion. Moreover, the follow-up attack came late, giving Warren's Federals a chance to reform and throw up hasty breastworks. Warren's line held, and the Confederate follow-up, led by the impetuous Stephen Ramseur, failed miserably.

Early's failure mattered little when Lee found out that the Army of the Potomac was receiving massive reinforcements from Butler's army on the James River. Even more alarming, Butler's troops were not joining Grant at Totopotomy Creek. Instead, they were landing at White House, some fifteen miles down the Pamunkey River. From there, Grant would have an opening around Lee's right flank through the crossroads at Cold Harbor. Lee had no infantry to spare, so he sent Fitzhugh Lee's cavalry to hold the critical crossroads. Finally, at 10:15 P.M. on 30 May, Beauregard released a division from his command and sent them racing for the crossroads.

—*Edward Ragan*

See also Anderson, Richard Heron; Early, Jubal Anderson; Richmond Campaign.

For further reading:

Power, J. Tracy. *Lee's Miserables: Life in the Army of Northern Virginia from the Wilderness to Appomattox* (1998).
Trudeau, Noah Andre. *Bloody Roads South: The Wilderness to Cold Harbor, May–June 1864* (1989).

TOTTEN, JOSEPH GILBERT
(1788–1864)
Union general

Born to Peter Totten and Grace Mansfield Totten in New Haven, Connecticut, Joseph Gilbert Totten was brought up largely by his maternal uncle due to the early death of Totten's mother and the diplomatic career of his father. Totten's uncle was one of the first professors named to teach at the newly created U.S. Military Academy in 1802 and as a result was able to secure an appointment for his nephew in that first year. Therefore, Totten entered the academy at age 14. He graduated three years later, receiving his second lieutenant's commission at age 17. He left the army briefly a year later to serve as his uncle's secretary on a surveying mission to the Northwest Territory but returned in 1808.

At the beginning of the War of 1812, Totten was made a captain of engineers and won two brevet promotions for his conduct during that war. After the war he worked on a variety of engineering projects for the army, rapidly rising in the esteem of his superior officers. By 1838 he had risen to the rank of colonel and in that year was made chief engineer of the army. He also began to serve as inspector of the U.S. Military Academy. He would hold both positions until he died in 1864.

During the Mexican-American War, Totten served on Winfield Scott's staff during the Mexico City campaign. After that conflict he continued in his role as chief engineer and in that capacity served on a variety of boards, most notably the Lighthouse Board and harbor commissions from the East Coast to the West Coast. Along with these activities he wrote and studied extensively on various scientific and engineering subjects and was active in scientific organizations.

During the secession crisis of 1860–1861, Totten maintained very close contact with his engineering officers stationed throughout the South, consulting with them on the defensibility of the Federal installations in those states. When the secession of Southern states began, he received regular notifications about the various places seized by Southern forces. Once Abraham Lincoln assumed office, he consulted Totten regarding the fortifications that were still in Federal hands, most importantly Fort Sumter. At the end of March 1861, Totten made a report to the entire cabinet regarding the difficulty of relieving Fort Sumter.

Besides this concern regarding the various Federal installations around the country, Totten also busily worked to strengthen those around the national capital, especially those that bordered on potentially hostile Virginia. Once Virginia seceded at the end of April, this work accelerated. Along with performing these duties during the war, Totten also sat on a number of boards, some related to his primary duty such as ordnance boards, and others not, like retirement boards. He received regular reports from engineering officers attached to various units on all major and many minor engagements fought by the Union army and advised those officers on difficult engineering problems they might encounter in the field.

In March 1863, Totten was promoted to brigadier general in the regular army. At the same time he was supervising a renewed look at Washington's defenses that would intensify after the Union defeat at the battle of Chancellorsville in May. This activity would mortgage much of his time through the Gettysburg campaign in July.

In early 1864, the elderly Totten's health began to decline. In April, he contracted pneumonia and died on 22 April 1864. To honor him for his 62 years of service to the country, the War Department awarded him a brevet promotion to major general retroactive to the day before he died.

—*David S. Heidler and Jeanne T. Heidler*

See also Fortifications; Ordnance, Naval.
  For further reading:
  Barnard, John Gross. *Memoir of Joseph Gilbert Totten: 1788–1864* (1979).

TOWN CREEK, BATTLE OF
See Wilmington, North Carolina

TOWNSEND, GEORGE ALFRED
(1841–1914)
Union journalist

Born in Georgetown, Delaware, on 30 January 1841, George A. Townsend is best remembered for building a memorial arch on the site of the battlefield at Crampton's Gap, Maryland, to honor Civil War newspaper correspondents, himself included.

Townsend began his journalism career with the Philadelphia *Inquirer* and continued with the Philadelphia *Press*. During the Civil War he worked as a battlefield correspondent, first for the *New York Herald* and later for the *New York World*. His coverage of the Peninsula campaign, Cedar Mountain, the final days of the war in Virginia, as well as Lincoln's assassination, gained Townsend national recognition, even though he was only twenty-four years old in the spring of 1865.

When the Civil War ended, Townsend married Bessie Rhodes, a Philadelphia woman, and the couple then traveled to Europe so that he might cover the Austro-Prussian War. While in Europe he published his Civil War memoirs under the title *Campaigns of a Non-Combatant*, probably his most well-know work among modern-day Civil War enthusiasts. Upon their return to the United States the Townsends, with their new baby born in Paris, moved to Washington, D.C. From there, Townsend wrote for several important newspapers, including the Chicago *Tribune*, using the pseudonym "GAT" (his initials). He later added an "H" to his pen name, thus becoming known as "Gath" in reference to the biblical city in Philistine.

In addition to writing his newspaper columns, Townsend turned to lecturing, composing poetry, and writing books, including historical novels. While on an 1884 trip to research the 1862 Maryland campaign, he visited the battlefield of Crampton's Gap and subsequently became enamored with the mountaintop vistas that the battlefield provided. He purchased land on the summit of the South Mountain range where Crampton's Gap cuts through it and commenced building a house and outbuildings to serve as a retreat where he could write his books and newspaper columns. He soon made it his permanent home and named the estate Gapland. His 1886 book, *Katy of Catoctin or the Chain Breakers*, A *National Romance*, was a Civil War novel that included an inaccurate depiction of the battle of Crampton's Gap.

By 1892 Townsend had purchased 110 acres around Crampton's Gap. He attempted to have a memorial erected to the Army of the Potomac's Sixth Corps, the victors of the battle fought on his land, but the veterans of that unit were not interested. Undismayed, Townsend instead decided to erect a monument to honor men like himself who had reported the events of the war, even though there were no war correspondents at the battle of Crampton's Gap. Soliciting donations from other veteran war correspondents as well as the great philanthropers of the age, Townsend designed and oversaw the construction of a masonry arch measuring forty feet wide and fifty feet high. Two tablets on its wall list the names of 157 correspondents and war artists. Built on the summit of the mountain at the intersection of two roads leading from the valley below, the War Correspondents Memorial Arch was dedicated on 16 October 16 1896.

The death of Townsend's wife in 1903 left him a broken man, and his writing career suffered as well. Townsend gave his memorial arch to the federal government in 1904, and he began to sell off his assets in the following years. Suffering from diabetes, he moved from Gapland in 1911 and died on 15 April 1914 at his daughter's home in New York City. He is buried in Laurel Hill Cemetery in Philadelphia.

Deserted since Townsend's departure in 1911, Gapland was sold for payment of back taxes. Abandoned and overgrown, the estate was deeded in 1949 to Maryland, but the arch remained the property of the U.S. government. It eventually became a small state park with the bastardized name of "Gathland."

—*Mark Snell*

See also Crampton's Gap, Battle of; Newspapers; War Correspondents.

For further reading:
Reese, Timothy J. *Sealed with Their Lives: The Battle for Crampton's Gap* (1998).
Townsend, George Alfred. *Campaigns of a Non-Combatant* (1866; reprint 1982).
Weisberger, Bernard A. *Reporters for the Union* (1953).

TREDEGAR IRON WORKS

When the Civil War began, the Confederacy's lack of industry weakened its military efforts. The Tredegar Iron Works, located on land between the James River and Kanawha Canal in Richmond, Virginia, was the largest industrial site in the South in 1861. The only Southern ordnance producer capable of making cannon and rails when fighting began, Tredegar supplied necessary artillery throughout the war. The Confederacy struggled to procure sufficient weaponry of a high quality, relying on the Tredegar Iron Works to innovate and produce ordnance according to demand. Tredegar also fulfilled orders for iron plating for naval vessels. Although there were smaller ironworks in the lower South, Tredegar led Confederate ordnance production and served as the model for efficiency and quality.

Entrepreneur Francis B. Deane created the Tredegar Iron Works in the mid-1830s. Consisting of a forge, rolling mill, and foundry, the Tredegar Iron Works, the namesake of a Welsh ironworks, was incorporated by the Virginia legislature on 27 February 1837. Within four years, Tredegar suffered from poor sales and was indebted to creditors. Joseph Reid Anderson, a West Point graduate, submitted a proposal to the ironworks' directors that he serve as its commercial agent to salvage financial matters. He secured new investors and managed sales so that Tredegar thrived monetarily. By 1843, Anderson held Tredegar's lease and five years later bought the company from its stockholders for $125,000. His use of slave laborers caused friction with white wage-earning workers, who struck in 1847 complaining about the competition posed by blacks. Labor strife plagued Tredegar throughout the 1840s as Anderson introduced more African-Americans, both slaves and freedmen, into the ironworks. He commented that he used slaves because of the quality of their work, noting that production costs were lessened by costs he incurred to feed, clothe, and house slaves. Despite these problems, the Tredegar Iron Works expanded in the 1850s. Tredegar's reputation for high-quality products resulted in government contracts, and Tredegar increased the type and quantity of products. Anderson secured professional partnerships to attain expertise for processes new to the ironworks. In 1859, under Anderson's direction Tredegar merged with its neighboring munitions works owned by the Archer family, Anderson's in-laws, buying the shares of some partners and consolidating with others to form Joseph R. Anderson & Company.

Although Tredegar provided bridge materials throughout the United States, as sectional tensions heightened, Anderson sought business deals with more Southern markets. When states began seceding, Tredegar supported the Confederacy and ceased sales to the North. Anderson attempted to fill individual orders from seceding states for ordnance and munitions such as cannons ordered in January 1861 to guard Alabama's Mobile Bay. Anderson offered to lease or sell the ironworks to the Confederate government, but the Confederate War and Navy Departments preferred signing long-term contracts and promising financial support. Tredegar also produced wartime supplies for private railroads used by the Confederacy and had a tannery, shoemaking shop, and brick factory. On 16 April 1861, President Abraham Lincoln banned Northern states from trading with Southern businesses, affecting Tredegar economically within weeks. This loss was offset by the largest order ever received by Tredegar. Confederate chief of ordnance Josiah Gorgas requested several hundred weapons, necessitating expansion of the ironworks' rolling mill. Tredegar was limited only by the lack of sufficient pig iron and coal.

A year later, in April 1862, the Confederate Congress approved loans to Tredegar to procure pig iron and fuel sources and to build new blast furnaces. With this limited

The Tredegar Iron Works at Richmond, Virginia, April 1865 (Photograph by Alexander Gardner / *Library of Congress*)

assistance, Tredegar grew during the Civil War but only achieved one-third of its full operation capacity. The scarcity of raw materials impeded Tredegar's production, and the ironworks competed for resources with similar industries in the South, especially manufacturers at Selma, Alabama. Distribution was disrupted by incompatible rail systems, requiring raw resources to be shipped by time-consuming routes to Richmond. Anderson and his partners complained that government price controls for war goods limited Tredegar's profits. He hired more blacks, justifying his decision by the fact that foreign and Northern employees had left to serve in the Union army. He asked the Confederate War Department to assign skilled ironworkers to Tredegar. By 1863, half of Tredegar's 2,000 laborers were African-Americans, an increase from 100 slaves among 1,000 employees in 1861.

Anderson was distracted by other matters. In September 1861, he raised a battalion of Tredegar workers and served in North Carolina and Virginia before he resigned in July 1862, returning to Tredegar. Anderson was not always receptive to new technology such as the Rodman method of casting heavy ordnance. This method was safer, minimizing explosion risks. As a result, he lost some Confederate contracts. Anderson believed such changes meant costly retooling and only agreed to do this in 1864 when Gorgas demanded that Tredegar manufacture crucial heavy ordnance as specified. Gorgas confidently relied on

Tredegar to supply cannon, armor plating, siege and field artillery, seacoast ordnance, and rails, spikes, axles, and bolts for trains. He defended Tredegar's manufacturing of heavy ordnance and machinery for their quality, noting that Tredegar consistently produced large quantities of these goods complementing other arsenals that concentrated on making small arms. The increased demands on Tredegar sometimes resulted in inferior workmanship. On 1 May 1862, Gorgas wrote his friend, Confederate secretary of war George Randolph, regarding General Daniel H. Hill's complaint about the quality of ordnance. Hill suggested that laborers might have purposefully sabotaged weapons. "As to the worthlessness of many of the Tredegar guns I full[y] agree with Genl. Hill. That establishment has not sustained its old reputation," Gorgas admitted. "Yet I shall ever be slow to attach bad motives to those who carry it on; or attribute to 'treachery' what is in great measure due to our failing resources."

On 5 December 1862, General Robert E. Lee requested longer-range guns, and Gorgas ordered Anderson to meet Lee's demands. Tredegar operated twenty-four hours daily, its furnace fires blazing at night in the Richmond sky. The ironworks made a variety of ammunition to be used in the differing types of artillery used by Confederate forces. Tredegar also made iron plate for ironclads, including the CSS *Virginia*, and records indicate that an experimental submersible boat was built and launched, but it did not enter active service. Tredegar manufactured torpedoes and mines for use in river warfare and innovated a wrought iron mountain howitzer for use in the hills of eastern Tennessee and western Virginia. The rifled and banded Brooke guns were considered one of Tredegar's best weapons.

A fire in May 1863 destroyed portions of the Tredegar Iron Works, which were not rebuilt during the war. In addition to the perpetual struggle to secure ample raw goods, Anderson also could not procure enough grain to feed the draft animals required to move tons of metal within Tredegar. Also, during the winter of 1864–1865, the James River and Kanawha Canal froze, restricting transportation of materials. Tredegar's reduced capabilities proved disastrous for the Confederacy, which was overmatched by better-supplied Union troops. By April 1865, when victorious Union forces approached, Tredegar's managers debated whether to destroy the ironworks. As the Tredegar Battalion, an employee militia in force since 1861, guarded the ironworks, Union troops occupied the ironworks. Major General Henry Halleck approved the repair of damages. Meeting with President Andrew Johnson, Anderson and his partners received pardons in September 1865. Two years later the company reorganized, with Anderson serving as president. Tredegar made the transition from wartime ordnance production to peacetime industry, regaining antebellum customers. Having peaked during the Civil War, Tredegar had to meet employees' demands because it could no longer rely on slave labor. The company suffered financial woes during the Panic of 1873, going into receivership. As steel production replaced iron goods, Tredegar was unable to compete in the market, closing in 1958.

—*Elizabeth D. Schafer*

See also Anderson, Joseph Reid; Armories, Arsenals, and Foundries; Artillery; Gorgas, Josiah; Ordnance, Naval.

For further reading:

Beringer, Richard E., Herman Hattaway, Archer Jones, and William N. Still, Jr. *Why The South Lost the Civil War* (1986).

Bruce, Kathleen. *Virginia Iron Manufacture in the Slave Era* (1930; reprint, 1968).

Daniel, Larry J. "Manufacturing Cannon in the Confederacy." *Civil War Times Illustrated* (1973).

Dew, Charles B. *Ironmaker to the Confederacy: Joseph R. Anderson and the Tredegar Iron Works* (1966).

Vandiver, Frank E., ed. *Ploughshares into Swords: Josiah Gorgas and Confederate Ordnance* (1952; reprint, 1994).

TRENHOLM, GEORGE ALFRED
(1807–1876)

Confederate secretary of the treasury

The son of William Trenholm and Irena de Greffin Trenholm, George Alfred Trenholm was born in Charleston, South Carolina. He was educated locally and went into business as a cotton merchant. By the 1850s he was a very wealthy man and very prominent in South Carolina politics.

In the early years of the Civil War, Trenholm financed the construction of blockade runners and, through his offices in England, facilitated Confederate purchases abroad. Informally, Trenholm acted as an adviser to the Confederate government.

Along with his activities to aid the Confederate supply problem and to make the Confederate government more fiscally sound, Trenholm also took an active interest in the defense of his native Charleston. He served as a commissioner for the defense of the city beginning in 1862. When the city was threatened with Union invasion in 1863, Trenholm's committee supervised the evaluation of those too weak or infirm to aid in the city's defense and aided in the evacuation of those people.

It was to the solvency of the Confederacy and its credit abroad that Trenholm lent his greatest efforts. His sound advice and obvious concern for the Confederacy's well-being finally led to his appointment in July 1864 as the nation's secretary of the treasury. He served in that position until the collapse of the Confederate government in April 1865. Trenholm's sound though conservative financial policy came too late to help the already desperate Confederate economy. The Confederacy was too far gone for any foreign government or financial house to take the chance by granting the country a loan, and the state of Confederate currency made taxes virtually worthless. To make matters worse, Trenholm had the job of trying to convert Confederate staples like cotton, rice, and tobacco into hard money, a nearly impossible task by that point in the war. In the last months of the conflict Trenholm also had to deal with complaints from officers as high ranking as Robert E. Lee regarding the lack of regular pay for the men in the Confederate army. Trenholm blamed the Confederate Congress and it likewise blamed the executive branch.

At the end of the war, Trenholm was arrested and imprisoned in Fort Pulaski, Georgia, with other members and former members of the Confederate government. He remained there until his release in October 1865. He then returned to Charleston and worked for the next several years rebuilding his business. He briefly became involved in South Carolina politics near the end of Reconstruction. He died in Charleston.

—*David S. Heidler and Jeanne T. Heidler*

See also Blockade Runners; Financing, C.S.A.

For further reading:

Smith, Lawrence A. "A Confederate Gentleman: George Alfred Trenholm of Charleston, South Carolina" (Thesis, 1989).

TRENT AFFAIR
(8 November 1861–10 January 1862)

When Lieutenant Donald Fairfax of the USS *San Jacinto* removed Confederate envoys James Mason and John Slidell from the British mail steamer *Trent*, he precipitated an international incident that brought the United States to the brink of war with Britain. The most serious diplomatic crisis associated with the Civil War, the *Trent* Affair symbolized the tension in Anglo-American relations produced by the Federal blockade of the South.

Accredited in August 1861 as the Confederacy's envoys to Britain and France respectively, James Mason and John Slidell received orders from Confederate president Jefferson Davis to proceed to Europe and obtain official recognition of the South's independence. Running the blockade at Charleston aboard the *Theodora* on 12 October 1861, Mason and Slidell (with their secretaries, James Macfarland and George Eustis, and Slidell's family) reached Nassau two days later and proceeded to Cuba. On 7 November, they left Havana on the *Trent*, bound for the Danish island of St. Thomas, where they hoped to catch a British steamer for Southampton. Evidence suggests that the federal government hoped to intercept the Confederate envoys. Unable to contact its naval units in the West Indies, however, it would have to rely on the individual initiative of its officers in the region.

This hope was not misplaced, for having just left the African squadron, the twelve-gun sloop-of-war USS *San Jacinto* under Captain Charles Wilkes reached the Caribbean in mid-October with orders to join the Federal expedition against Port Royal, South Carolina. While engaged in an unauthorized hunt for the Confederate raider *Sumter* in Cuban waters, Wilkes found out about the Confederate commissioners' plans to leave Havana aboard the *Trent*. Entertaining the idea of capturing Mason and Slidell, Wilkes consulted various works about international law in his cabin but had difficulty finding precedents for his contemplated action. Although empowered to seize enemy dispatches, he could not legally justify capturing the Confederate envoys. Eventually, he decided to arrest the commissioners as the "embodiment of dispatches." Wilkes discussed the matter with Fairfax, his first officer. Fairfax apparently protested that such an act would lead to war between Britain and the United States. Brushing aside his subordinate's fears and taking his position on questionable legal ground, Wilkes went ahead with his plan and awaited the *Trent* in the Old Bahama Channel.

Shortly after noon on 8 November, the *San Jacinto* encountered and stopped the *Trent*. Wilkes sent Fairfax to the British vessel in a cutter, instructing the lieutenant to demand the ship's papers, arrest the Confederate envoys, and seize the *Trent* as a prize of war. As Mason saw the cutter approaching, he asked Commander Richard Williams, the British mail agent, to conceal Confederate dispatches and forward them to London, a task to which Williams readily assented. Upon boarding the British steamer, Fairfax encountered its uncooperative commander, Captain James Moir, who protested the manner in which the *San Jacinto* had stopped his vessel, refused to permit the Americans to conduct a search, refused to produce the ship's papers, and announced that it would require force to remove Mason and Slidell from the *Trent*. After some confusion (as well as melodramatics provided by Slidell's daughter), Fairfax's men succeeded in seizing the Confederate envoys, their secretaries, and their baggage, transferring all to the *San Jacinto*. Fairfax then disobeyed his orders by allowing the *Trent* to proceed on its course. Fairfax successfully justified his actions to Wilkes with several arguments: putting a prize crew aboard the *Trent* would hamper the *San Jacinto*'s effectiveness should it participate in operations against Port Royal; taking the *Trent* to a prize court would inconvenience the passengers; and most important of all, seizure of the *Trent* would provide a great insult to Britain. Satisfied that Fairfax had acted judiciously, Wilkes proceeded to Fortress Monroe, where he put in for coal on 15 November and informed his superiors of what had transpired. Continuing northward, Wilkes delivered his charges to Fort Warren in Boston harbor on 24 November.

In the encounter between the *Trent* and the *San Jacinto*, neither side displayed a good grasp of international law. The Americans had no right to arrest the Confederate commissioners aboard a neutral vessel on a voyage between two neutral ports.

Moreover, as civilian representatives of a belligerent power engaged in a civil war, Mason and Slidell possessed the diplomatic immunity bestowed by international custom upon such envoys. The Britons involved in the incident proved equally ignorant. Contrary to Moir's contention, the Americans had every right to stop and search the *Trent*. By refusing to show the passenger, crew, and cargo lists to Fairfax, Moir provided the Americans with justification to seize the *Trent* (although not the Confederate commissioners) as a prize. Williams compounded this error by committing an "unneutral act" when he hid Mason's dispatch bag and promised to deliver it to Confederate agents in London. On these grounds, a federal prize court could have condemned the *Trent* and its valuable cargo, which included $1,500,000 in specie. Since a prize court could only proceed against property and not persons, however, Mason and Slidell would have gone free whatever the circumstances.

Such legal niceties escaped most Northerners, who greeted news of Wilkes's actions with great enthusiasm. Overnight, Wilkes became a great hero. The Federal navy's successful interception of the Rebel commissioners provided the Northern public with its first good news in quite some time. The North also admired Wilkes's display of boldness and initiative against Britain, America's traditional enemy at sea. Moreover, the capture proved particularly welcome, since the Confederate envoys were universally detested in the North. Before the war, Mason had won notoriety as a prominent advocate of the hated Fugitive Slave Law and the Kansas-Nebraska Act. Slidell had an undeserved reputation as the most dedicated and devious of the Southern secessionists. Both President Abraham Lincoln and Secretary of State William Seward, along with the rest of the federal cabinet, adopted a wait-and-see policy, hoping they could hold onto the prisoners without risking war. Although Wilkes had acted on his own initiative, the federal government would not disavow the popular captain's actions unless it felt substantial pressure from Britain.

News of the seizure reached Britain on 27 November and provoked much hostility toward the United States. Many Britons viewed the incident as the culmination of an American foreign policy that sought to compensate for defeats at home with bullying abroad. Even pro-Northern Britons believed Wilkes had blundered. News of the North's rapturous reaction to the seizure of the Confederate commissioners irritated British feeling still further. Despite public confusion regarding the application of international law in this matter, the British cabinet instantly grasped the nature of the Americans' trespass. In mid-November, foreseeing that an incident of this sort might happen, the cabinet had asked Britain's leading jurists—the lord chancellor, the judge of the High Court of Admiralty, along with the three chief law officers of the Crown—what rights the Americans could exercise against a British vessel carrying the Confederate commissioners. The first two authorities clashed with the latter three, but Lord Palmerston, the prime minister, properly sided with the Crown's law officers, whose opinion proved correct.

Accordingly, after news of Wilkes's actions reached Britain, Earl Russell, the foreign secretary, prepared two dispatches for Lord Lyons, the British minister in Washington, D.C. Approved by the cabinet and redrafted by the prince consort, who softened its tone, the first dispatch demanded the United States give up the Confederate envoys and apologize for its breach of international law. The second dispatch provided Seward with seven days to respond to the British note and gave Lyons the authority to determine if Seward's answer was satisfactory. Should Lyons find the Americans' response inadequate, he was to leave the United States, along with the legation's staff and archives.

Having sent these dispatches on 1 December, the British cabinet prepared for war. It banned the export of saltpeter, weapons, and ammunition to the United States.

More than 11,000 British regulars left for Canada, bringing the garrison to 18,000 men. The admiralty sent fifteen ships to Rear Admiral Sir Alexander Milne, commander of the North American station, giving him a force of forty steam vessels mounting 1,273 guns. Although the British government hoped to slow down any American advance in Canada, it had reconciled itself to losing the colony. It hoped, however, to recoup its fortunes with a quick and massive blow against the Americans at sea. Milne planned to destroy the Federal blockading squadrons along the Southern coast before implementing a blockade of his own against the major Northern ports. In the meantime, British naval units throughout the world would hunt down American commerce.

Lyons, who had hitherto acted with great discretion, finally received Russell's dispatches on 18 December. On the next day, he informed Seward unofficially of their contents. After various delays at Seward's request, Lyons finally made an official presentation of British demands on 23 December, giving the Americans until noon on 30 December to comply. Having received news of the British public's reaction to the *Trent* Affair only a few days earlier, the federal government had just begun to appreciate the seriousness of its predicament. Seward favored releasing the captives, but Lincoln proved reluctant. Prompted by Charles Sumner and others, the president toyed with the idea of submitting the dispute to arbitration by a collection of neutral countries. Cabinet meetings on 25 and 26 December, however, persuaded Lincoln to surrender the Confederate envoys. Several considerations proved decisive. Letters from pro-Northern British radicals such as John Bright and Richard Cobden urging that America avoid a catastrophic war with Britain brought home the gravity of the situation. A French note supporting the British position indicated that America would not fare well in arbitration. Perhaps most important of all, the Federal cabinet realized the North could not fight both the Confederacy and Britain at once.

On 27 December, Seward informed the House Foreign Affairs Committee and the Senate Foreign Relations Committee of Lincoln's decision. Although they received the news without enthusiasm, they—like most Americans—had reconciled themselves to surrendering the captives. On the same day, Seward presented Lyons with his official response, a long, badly written note intended primarily for domestic consumption. Although it was no apology, Lyons deemed the American note satisfactory. Lyons's report reached Earl Russell on 8 January. Russell accepted Seward's note and on 10 January wrote to Lyons that he considered the case closed.

On 1 January 1862, Mason and Slidell left Fort Warren for Provincetown, where federal authorities sent them aboard the British vessel HMS *Rinaldo*. Eventually reaching Southampton on 29 January, the two

Confederate envoys immediately sought to obtain European recognition of Southern independence.

Although the crisis passed without bloodshed, it embittered British opinion against the United States and vindicated Britons who sought to pursue a hard line against the federal government. Never again, however, would the British come so close to intervening in the Civil War. By preventing British involvement, the North avoided what would have been a grievous blow to the Federal war effort and thus greatly diminished the Confederacy's chances of survival.

—*Hubert F. Dubrulle*

See also Diplomacy, C.S.A.; Diplomacy, U.S.A.; Great Britain; Lyons, Lord Richard; Mason, James Murray; Russell, Lord John; Seward, William Henry; Slidell, John; Wilkes, Charles.
For further reading:

Adams, Ephraim D. *Great Britain and the American Civil War* (1925).
Crook, D. P. *The North, the South, and the Powers 1861–1865* (1974).
Ferris, Norman B. *The Trent Affair: A Diplomatic Crisis* (1977).
Jenkins, Brian. *Britain and the War for the Union* (1974).
Jones, Howard. *Union in Peril: The Crisis over British Intervention in the Civil War* (1992).
Warren, Gordon H. *Fountain of Discontent: The* Trent *Affair and Freedom of the Seas* (1981).

TREVILIAN STATION, BATTLE OF
(11–12 June 1864)

Trevilian Station was one of the most confusing and ferocious cavalry fights to occur in the Eastern theater. At a heavy cost to themselves, two Confederate divisions compelled a slightly larger Union force to abort its raid toward Charlottesville and saved much of Virginia's railroad network.

On 5 June 1864, Union lieutenant general Ulysses S. Grant directed Major General Philip H. Sheridan, commander of the Army of the Potomac's Cavalry Corps, to take two divisions and conduct a raid along the Virginia Central Railroad as far west as Charlottesville. Grant hoped that Sheridan's marauding would distract the enemy's cavalry and allow the Army of the Potomac to slip south of the James River to continue the Richmond campaign.

Sheridan massed 6,000 troopers from Brigadier General Alfred T. A. Torbert's 1st Division and David McMurtrie Gregg's 2d Division at New Castle Ferry on 6 June. To facilitate rapid movement, the raiding force took along only four artillery batteries. Brigadier General James H. Wilson's 3d Division remained behind to provide reconnaissance and security for Grant's advance across the James.

Sheridan left New Castle Ferry early on 7 June and headed northwest toward Trevilian Station, a stop on the Virginia Central. Alert Confederate scouts apprised

Major General Wade Hampton, "Jeb" Stuart's successor as chief of the Army of Northern Virginia's Cavalry Corps, of Sheridan's sortie within twenty-four hours of the latter's departure. Guessing the enemy's intentions, Hampton rode to intercept Sheridan with 4,700 troopers and three batteries.

On the evening of 10 June, Hampton and his own division reached the Virginia Central at a point three miles west of Trevilian Station. His second division, under Major General Fitzhugh Lee, bivouacked six miles south of Trevilian, while Sheridan halted his command at Clayton's Store, three miles north of the station.

At daylight on 11 June, Sheridan marched south along the Carpenter's Ford–Trevilian Station road to engage Hampton's division, which was moving north to meet him. Discovering a wooded road that paralleled his route a mile to the left, Sheridan detached Brigadier General George A. Custer's Michigan Cavalry Brigade to pass Hampton's right flank and strike the enemy's rear.

Custer moved with his usual speed. By 8:00 A.M., his advance guard could see Hampton's baggage train parked near Trevilian Station. Custer ordered an immediate charge by the 5th Michigan Cavalry, which captured six caissons, forty ambulances, fifty wagons, one flag, 800 prisoners, and 1,500 horses left behind by rebel troopers who had dismounted to fight Sheridan.

As Custer counted his trophies, a tardy Fitzhugh Lee entered the battlefield from the southeast and threw his division at the Michigan Brigade's rear. At the same time, Hampton sent Brigadier General Thomas L. Rosser's brigade back to the station to attack Custer. The Confederates recaptured their lost personnel and property, scattering the 5th Michigan Cavalry and a third of the 6th Michigan Cavalry. Then they closed in to destroy the rest of Custer's brigade. Surrounded and outnumbered, Custer formed the 1st and 7th Michigan Cavalry and the remainder of the 6th into a triangular perimeter. Leading repeated counterattacks, he endeavored to hold the Rebels at bay until help arrived. One of Custer's "Wolverines" later recalled, "It was 'cut and slash,' we being outnumbered four to one, … charging back and forth three or four times before relief came by our…making connections with the balance of the Corps."

Delayed by Hampton's stubborn resistance, Sheridan's main force did not reach Custer until late afternoon. The final Union breakthrough drove 500 Confederate troopers into Custer's position, where they were taken prisoner.

The next day, 12 June, Sheridan sent Torbert's division two miles north to confront Hampton's regrouped command at Mallory's Cross Roads. While Hampton repulsed at least seven Union attacks, Gregg's division tore up the Virginia Central's tracks between Trevilian Station and Louisa Court House. With ammunition running low and Hampton still a potent threat, Sheridan cut his raid short and ordered a return to Grant. Shadowed by Hampton, Sheridan led his divisions east at a leisurely pace, finally rejoining the Army of the Potomac near Petersburg on 25 June.

It cost Sheridan 735 killed, wounded, and captured to destroy five miles of railroad track below Trevilian Station. Custer's Michigan Brigade alone sustained 416 losses, including 41 dead and 242 taken prisoner. Custer saw half his staff and escort shot down and experienced a near miss from a sharpshooter's bullet as he carried a dying trooper to safety. Confederate casualties numbered roughly 1,000, but Hampton had subjected his opponents to rough handling and spoiled Sheridan's plans.

—*Gregory J. W. Urwin*

See also Custer, George Armstrong; Gregg, David McMurtrie; Hampton, Wade; Lee, Fitzhugh; Rosser, Thomas Lafayette; Sheridan, Philip Henry; Torbert, Alfred Thomas Archimedes.

For further reading:

Kidd, J. H. *Riding with Custer: Recollections of a Cavalryman in the Civil War* (1997).

Longacre, Edward G. *Custer and His Wolverines: The Michigan Cavalry Brigade, 1861–1865* (1997).

Starr, Stephen Z. *The Union Cavalry in the Civil War* (1979–1985).

Swank, Walbrook Davis. *Battle of Trevilian Station: The Civil War's Greatest and Bloodiest All Cavalry Battle* (1994).

Urwin, Gregory J. W. *Custer Victorious: The Civil War Battles of General George Armstrong Custer* (1990).

TRIMBLE, ISAAC RIDGEWAY
(1802–1888)
Confederate general

Born in Culpeper County, Virginia, the son of John Trimble, Isaac Trimble moved as a child to Kentucky with his family. He was educated locally before receiving an appointment at age 16 to the U.S. Military Academy. He graduated seventeenth of twenty in the class of 1822. For the next ten years Trimble served at a variety of posts, primarily surveying military roads. He resigned his commission in 1832 to accept a position as an engineer for the Boston & Providence Railroad. During the next few decades, he worked as an engineer for a variety of railroads, primarily in the Middle Atlantic states.

At the outbreak of the Civil War, Trimble lived in Baltimore. Upon the secession of Virginia, he offered his services to that state and was given a colonel's commission as a Virginia engineering officer. His first duty was to prevent as many Union volunteers as possible from reaching Washington, D.C. He did so by destroying railroad track into Baltimore. He was then sent to Norfolk briefly to survey the defenses there. In August 1861 he was taken into Confederate service as a brigadier general, and he was assigned in this capacity as an engi-

neer to locate likely places for shore batteries on the Virginia side of the Potomac to disrupt Union naval traffic up the river.

In early 1862, Trimble was given command of his own brigade as part of the division commanded by Richard Ewell in Joseph Johnston's command. On 3 March 1862, in the wake of the Confederate withdrawal below the Rappahannock River, Johnston sent Trimble and his brigade to Manassas Junction to remove any Confederate property of value. After the successful execution of this mission, Trimble's brigade was sent to Stonewall Jackson's command in the Shenandoah Valley, where it participated in the Valley campaign of the spring of 1862.

Trimble fought at the Seven Days' and at Cedar Mountain on 9 August 1862. He led his brigade north with Jackson a few weeks later and led the advance party that captured the Union stores at Manassas Junction. In the ensuing battle of Second Bull Run, Trimble was seriously injured and would not be fit for command until the following year. During his convalescence, Trimble was recommended for promotion to major general by Robert E. Lee. The promotion was approved in April 1863 to date from January, and upon his return to duty in May 1863 Trimble was given command of the Shenandoah Valley District to guard the Confederate rear as it moved north in Lee's second invasion. Once the Army of Northern Virginia cleared the valley, Trimble traveled quickly north to catch Lee's army, and since he yet had no command, he accompanied Lee for a while. From this trip, we have some of the best accounts of Lee's intentions as he moved into Northern territory.

Once the army began moving into Pennsylvania, Trimble moved north with Richard Ewell's corps. Trimble made it as far north as Carlisle, Pennsylvania, before being ordered to move south toward Gettysburg. During the first day of the battle of Gettysburg when Ewell was given discretionary orders by Lee about dislodging the Union troops from Cemetery Hill, Trimble argued with Ewell when the corps commander chose not to attack the Federal position. Given troops to command, Trimble offered to lead the attack himself, but Ewell refused.

On the second day of the battle, Trimble finally received a command when Confederate major general Dorsey Pender was injured. This division was part of A. P. Hill's corps, which undoubtedly relieved Trimble given his now low opinion of Ewell. The following day Trimble and his new division took part in what would become known as Pickett's Charge, even though George Pickett shared command with Trimble and James Johnston Pettigrew. In the attack, Trimble was severely wounded in the leg and left on the field during the retreat. He was taken prisoner by Union forces, and Federal doctors amputated his leg.

After his recovery, Trimble was imprisoned at Fort Warren in Boston harbor. He was not exchanged until February 1865 and did not see active service for the remainder of the war.

After the war, Trimble returned to his home in Baltimore. He lived there for the remainder of his life, working primarily as an engineer.

—David S. Heidler and Jeanne T. Heidler

See also Bull Run, Second Battle of; Gettysburg, Battle of.
For further reading:
Grace, William M. "Isaac Ridgeway Trimble, the Indefatigable and Courageous" (M.A. thesis, 1986).

TRUMBULL, LYMAN
(1813–1896)
Chairman, Senate Committee on the Judiciary

Born in Colchester, Connecticut, Lyman Trumbull was educated at nearby Bacon Academy. For a time, he taught school in neighboring Portland, but he became dissatisfied with teaching while he was principal of Greenville Academy in Greenville, Georgia.

Trumbull passed the bar in 1836 and moved to Belleville, Illinois, to open a law office. He was elected to the legislature as a Jacksonian Democrat in 1840. Resigning before he could complete his term to become Illinois secretary of state, he ran for Congress unsuccessfully in 1846. But this setback would not fetter the rise of Trumbull's star.

Although he spent little time in Belleville after his first marriage in 1843, he maintained ties with the area's German-Americans. While "riding the circuit," he also became familiar with the state's top lawyers, including rival Abraham Lincoln, against whom he never won a case. With links to politicos in Belleville and at the bar, it was not surprising that Trumbull was considered for the Senate in 1855. The surprise was the manner in which Trumbull won election; after Lincoln failed to garner enough votes for his candidacy, he threw his support behind his competitor.

As a senator, Trumbull's professorial manner curried additional favor, particularly in Chicago, where his backers included Horace White of the Chicago Tribune. White quickly became one of Trumbull's staunchest supporters; he even harbored presidential aspirations for his friend. But once Trumbull and his allies became convinced of Lincoln's intention to run in 1860, Trumbull set his ambitions aside and supported Lincoln's campaign, returning the favor from 1855. Trumbull acted as Lincoln's unofficial spokesman after the election.

Before Lincoln could even be inaugurated, however, the Trumbull-Lincoln relationship reverted to form. Differences first developed over patronage appointments. Lincoln was less receptive to Trumbull's recommendations than Trumbull expected, while Trumbull disdained Lincoln's decision to appoint Simon Cameron secretary of war. Trumbull later forestalled Cameron's consideration as minister to Russia in January 1862—after the former secretary had been ousted from the cabinet amidst charges of gross inefficiency and corruption—in a pique–filled but futile attempt to prevent his confirmation.

Trumbull and Lincoln also differed on how to prosecute the war. At first, Trumbull pushed Lincoln to take stronger measures. Convinced of the necessity of stepping up the Union war effort after observing (and being forced to flee from) Bull Run, Trumbull decided to strike at slavery, the bulwark of the Confederate war effort. He authored an amendment to what would become the Confiscation Act of 6 August 1861—a measure designed to appropriate Confederate property—to free slaves used "in aid of this rebellion, in digging ditches or intrenchments [sic], or in any other way." Though the vague act was not vigorously enforced, Trumbull's legislation prodded Lincoln to consider emancipation.

Trumbull encouraged forceful prosecution of the war in other ways as well. As one of three Radical Republicans dubbed the "Jacobin Club" by Lincoln secretary John Hay—Benjamin Wade of Ohio and Zachariah Chandler of Michigan were the others—Trumbull roused the president to accept Winfield Scott's retirement as general-in-chief in favor of George McClellan. Unfortunately, after Lincoln promoted McClellan, the younger man prosecuted the war with as little vigor as Scott, proving to be a disappointment to Trumbull and Lincoln.

In later years, Trumbull reversed his ground and opposed Lincoln for prosecuting the war too fully. Though he tried to stitch together a habeas corpus measure that Lincoln and Congress could support in 1861, it was not until 3 March 1863 that an act was signed. In the interim, Trumbull protested the number of arbitrary arrests by calling for a Senate inquiry on 12 December 1861. Similarly, after General Ambrose Burnside suppressed the Chicago Times, a Democratic paper, on 1 June 1863, Trumbull sent a telegram to Lincoln demanding the order's rescission (even though White, of the competing Tribune, favored Burnside's move). Convinced by Trumbull's constitutional concerns, Lincoln revoked the order.

The Trumbull-Lincoln relationship was unquestionably rocky. But in the war's last years, both men found policies they could agree with, particularly the Thirteenth Amendment, which ended slavery, and Lincoln's ten-percent plan to reconstruct Louisiana. Nevertheless, Trumbull's independence was typical of the problems Lincoln faced with Radicals in his party; it also foreshadowed differences within the Republican cause after Ulysses S. Grant became president. During Grant's first term, Trumbull would leave the party over

similar questions of patronage and policy. Trumbull died on 25 June 1896.

—*Robert W. Burg*

See also Congress, U.S.A.; Lincoln's Reconstruction Policy; Radical Republicans; Republican Party.

For further reading:
Krug, Mark M. *Lyman Trumbull: Conservative Radical* (1965).
Richardson, Heather Cox. *The Greatest Nation of the Earth: Republican Economic Policies during the Civil War* (1997).
Roske, Ralph J. *His Own Counsel: The Life and Times of Lyman Trumbull* (1979).
White, Horace. *The Life of Lyman Trumbull* (1913).

TRUTH, SOJOURNER
(ca. 1797–1883)
Freed slave and abolitionist

Sojourner Truth was the most famous African-American woman in the nineteenth century. A slave for nearly thirty years, the illiterate Truth gained fame as an itinerant minister and outspoken advocate for African-Americans and women.

Truth's origins hardly suggested that she would become a national icon. Born Isabella Baumfree around 1797 in New York State, Truth was born a slave and remained so until 1826. She experienced firsthand the brutality of slavery as told in her autobiography, *Narrative of Sojourner Truth*, first published in 1850. Along with enduring harsh physical punishments, the slave Isabella was sold several times during her life, as were her siblings and children. After gaining her freedom, Truth labored as a domestic servant but remained poor despite her diligence and strong moral beliefs.

Truth might have faded into obscurity as an illiterate and anonymous black woman, but she had a knack for pursuing a cause until it became a *cause célèbre*. For example, in 1828 Truth became the first black woman to take a white man to court in New York State—and won. Her young son, Peter, had been illegally sold to a plantation owner in Alabama, and Truth secured a lawyer and prevailed in court to gain her son's freedom. In the mid-1830s, Truth lived and worked within a religious cult, the Kingdom of Matthias, led by the self-styled prophet Robert Matthews. When the cult imploded over charges of sexual promiscuity and murder, Truth was falsely accused by one white couple of trying to poison them. To clear her name, Truth again went to court in 1835 and sued for slander, winning damages of $125.

Truth's subsequent fame grew out of intense religiosity following her "rebirth" in June 1827. A practicing Methodist, Truth joined thousands of other Americans who found religion during a wave of revivals known as the Second Great Awakening. Yet Isabella would not become "Sojourner Truth" until 1843 while living in New York City. Feeling called by the Holy Spirit on 1 June, the day of Pentecost, she adopted a new name and identity as "Sojourner Truth," becoming an itinerant preacher who exhorted others to embrace Jesus and avoid sin.

Upon departing from New York City in 1843, Truth made her way to Northampton, Massachusetts, where she mingled with other social reformers and antislavery activists, including the ex-slave Frederick Douglass. Continuing to preach at prayer meetings in exchange for food and shelter, Truth became known for her heartfelt testimonials about her religious faith and her life in bondage. Her fame increased with the publication in 1850 of her autobiography, written with the aid of a white friend and sold by Truth at public events, including the women's rights convention in Akron, Ohio, in 1851.

Truth made her mark in these and other public gatherings. A tall woman with an earnest air, Truth spoke forcefully and with conviction, often leaving her audience spellbound. Some of Truth's speeches became legendary, as was true of her talk at the Akron women's rights convention. Writing twelve years later in 1863, Frances Dana Gage provided an embellished account of Truth's speech, which she claimed included the following refrain: "I have plowed, and planted, and gathered into barns, and no man could head me—and ar'n't I a woman? I could work as much and eat as much as a man (when I could get it), and bear de lash as well—and ar'n't I a woman?" Although this publication added to Truth's growing fame during the Civil War, recent scholarship has questioned the authenticity of Gage's account.

Sojourner Truth remained prominent and active during the Civil War. Besides actively aiding the enlistment of African-American troops for the Union army, Truth spent much of the war's final two years in the nation's capital, where she met with President Lincoln, administered to wounded African-American soldiers in hospitals, and battled segregation in the city's public conveyances. After the war, Truth crisscrossed the country to call for the distribution of western lands to former slaves. In her public addresses, Truth called for economic justice and greater educational opportunities for freed men and women. Truth continued to speak out about equal rights for blacks and women until her death in Battle Creek, Michigan, on 26 November 1883.

—*Earl F. Mulderink III*

See also Abolitionists; Women.
For further reading:
Mabee, Carleton, and Susan Mabee Newhouse. *Sojourner Truth: Slave, Prophet, Legend* (1993).
Painter, Nell Irvin. *Sojourner Truth: A Life, a Symbol* (1996).
Truth, Sojourner, and Olive Gilbert. *Narrative of Sojourner Truth; A Bondswoman of Olden Time, With a History of Her Labors and Correspondence, Drawn from her "Book of Life"* (1998).

TUBMAN, HARRIET
(c. 1821–1913)
Union spy, scout, and nurse

Most people know of Harriet Tubman as the conductor of the Underground Railroad, a woman who shepherded, at great personal risk, perhaps as many as 300 former slaves to freedom in the antebellum North. Less well known are Tubman's contributions to the Union cause as a wartime nurse, and as a spy and scout for the Union army. When she died in 1913, however, a *New York Times* obituary ranked these less familiar accomplishments favorably, among the many reasons for celebrating Tubman's long and arduous life. In 1868, Frederick Douglass honored Tubman with the words: "Excepting John Brown... I know of no one who has willingly encountered more perils and hardships to serve our enslaved people than you have."

The woman who came to be nicknamed "Moses" was born a slave in Maryland about forty years before the Civil War began. One of eleven children, young Araminta Ross—who later adopted her mother's name, Harriet—early on experienced all the brutality of the "peculiar institution," including the harsh demands of fieldwork and the intense scrutiny of domestic service. Moreover, Harriet was unable to avoid the personal violence that permeated the master-slave relationship: when she was still an adolescent her master (or possibly one of his overseers) hit her in the head with a heavy object, perhaps by accident but nevertheless with serious consequences for her long-term health. For the rest of her life, Harriet Tubman suffered from periodic seizures that resulted from this blow.

In 1849 Harriet, who had married a free black named John Tubman in 1844, decided to break the slavery chain that bound her. Having learned that she was about to be forcibly separated from her family members after the death of her owner, she determined to take matters into her own hands. Traveling to Philadelphia without her husband, Tubman soon began the work of rescuing not only her relatives, but other slaves as well. As early as 1851, Maryland planters were offering a reward of $40,000 for her capture. Undeterred, Tubman continued her rescue work through the last decade before the war, in 1857 liberating—among others—her own parents, who eventually settled in Auburn, New York. Throughout these years leading up to the war, Tubman developed a network of friends and supporters and made numerous speeches on behalf of the abolitionist cause. When the Civil War began, Tubman looked eagerly for a Union victory and the end of slavery.

Neither one of these anticipated goals came quickly, and in 1862 Harriet Tubman continued her activism by traveling to Port Royal, South Carolina, where she turned her hand not only to hospital work on behalf of the soldiers black and white, but also to serving as a spy and scout for the Union army. Employed by early 1863 by General David Hunter (then commander of the Department of the South), she was granted free passage on all federal government transports and access to provisions from Union army commissaries. Tubman proved to be a uniquely appropriate choice for the job. Because of her many prewar trips though the South, she was quite familiar with the region in which she operated, which included South Carolina, Georgia, and Florida. Unlike most white spies and scouts, too, Tubman found it easy to secure the confidence of slaves and free blacks in the area who could then provide information, shelter, and supplies. "She gained the confidence of the slaves by her cheery words, and songs, and sacred hymns," wrote one biographer. Despite the lingering disability that stemmed from the childhood blow to her head, Tubman repeatedly demonstrated that she was a highly skilled organizer and a crafty operative. She was also apparently fearless even in the midst of battle, "when the shot was falling like hail, and the bodies of dead and wounded men were dropping around her like leaves in autumn."

Despite her courage and her hard labor for the Union and the cause of freedom, Tubman found herself struggling after the war to persuade the federal government to allocate her a pension. Success came only after three decades of regular petitioning, at which point she was granted $20 per month for life, the same amount received by most former army nurses. Tubman died in 1913, having continued throughout her later years to dedicate herself to social reform projects aimed at the relief and welfare of those whose freedom from slavery had been the dominant theme of her early life.

—*Elizabeth D. Leonard*

See also Abolitionist Movement; Abolitionists; Espionage; Nurses; Women.

For further reading:

Bradford, Sarah E. *Harriet Tubman: The Moses of her People* (1869; reprint, 1981).

Conrad, Earl. *Harriet Tubman* (1943).

Leonard, Elizabeth D. *All the Daring of the Soldier: Women of the Civil War Armies* (1999).

TUCKER, JOHN RANDOLPH
(1812–1883)
Confederate naval officer

Born at Alexandria, Virginia, on 31 January 1812, John Randolph "Handsome Jack" Tucker entered the United States Navy as a midshipman at age fourteen. He fashioned an exemplary, thirty-five-year career that included extended sea duty with all the principal U.S. squadrons, command of the bomb brig *Stromboli* during the Mexican-American War, and several important assignments ashore. Commander Tucker was

ordnance officer at the Norfolk Navy Yard when the Civil War began. With the secession of Virginia, Tucker submitted his resignation on 18 April 1861, and entered the service of his home state and, later, the Confederacy, carrying with him his U.S. Navy rank.

As skipper of the CSS *Patrick Henry* he commanded a squadron of makeshift gunboats that defended the James River approach to Richmond. On 8–9 March 1862 Tucker's James River Squadron rendezvoused with the ironclad CSS *Virginia* at the battle of Hampton Roads. Thereafter, Tucker's squadron supported the Confederate withdrawal from Norfolk and the army's defense of the Virginia Peninsula against General George B. McClellan's Army of the Potomac. With guns removed from the *Patrick Henry* and remounted on shore, Tucker and his sailors joined army artillerymen in turning back a Union navy flotilla at Drewry's Bluff just below Richmond on 15 May 1862.

In September 1862 Commander Tucker took charge of the ironclad ram *Chicora* at Charleston, South Carolina. Under the direction of Commodore Duncan N. Ingraham, the *Chicora* and her sister ship *Palmetto State* on 30 January 1862 left the safety of the inner harbor—guarded by Fort Sumter—and attacked the Union blockading squadron. Tucker's aggressiveness during this raid, combined with the aged Ingraham's indecision, prompted Navy Secretary Stephen R. Mallory at the end of March to give Tucker command of the squadron. Promoted to the rank of captain in January 1864 Flag Officer Tucker was addressed with the courtesy title "commodore."

Under Tucker's command, the Charleston Squadron became a showcase for Confederate contributions to naval technology, including defensive mines, torpedo boats (most notably the CSS *David*), and the submarine *H. L. Hunley*, the first undersea craft to sink a ship in combat. In his defense of the city, Tucker cooperated closely with the Confederate army commander, General Pierre G. T. Beauregard. In April and September 1863 Tucker's squadron assisted in turning back concerted attacks on Fort Sumter by the Union navy under Admirals Samuel F. Du Pont and John A. B. Dahlgren. The commodore's sailors also supported the army's defense of Morris Island, at the southern shore of the harbor's entrance. But the Union's capture of this place (with its stronghold, Battery Wagner) in September 1863 exposed lower Charleston and the squadron's anchorage to almost constant bombardment by the enemy's long-range guns.

On 18 February 1865, as the army of General William T. Sherman approached Charleston from the rear, Commodore Tucker's sailors destroyed their ships and evacuated the city. After a brief assignment protecting the arsenal at Fayetteville, North Carolina, Tucker and his men were ordered to Richmond where, in early

March, Tucker became flag officer commanding ashore. While some of his sailors manned artillery positions overlooking the James River east of the beleaguered Confederate capital, Tucker drilled the others as infantry, a role they had often played during the final months in Charleston.

Commodore Tucker's Naval Brigade—as his force of some 400 sailors and marines came to be called—evacuated Richmond on 3 April (a day after the army), and became part of the rear guard for General Robert E. Lee's Army of Northern Virginia as it retreated toward Appomattox. On 6 April, three days before Lee's surrender to General Ulysses S. Grant, the Naval Brigade distinguished itself at the battle of Sayler's Creek (or "Sailor's Creek" as it was often appropriately mislabeled). Suffering heavy casualties while stopping several determined Union assaults, the Naval Brigade was acknowledged by Federal commanders to have fought harder and longer than any of the other Southern units. In this battle, the final major field engagement of the Civil War, Commodore Tucker was the last of Lee's "generals" to surrender. Excluded from the parole provided in the terms of Lee's surrender to Grant, Tucker was imprisoned at Fort Warren in Boston Harbor until 24 July 1865, when he returned home to Virginia.

In May 1866 Peru's minister to the United States recruited Tucker for service in South America. Assisted by a personal staff of two former Confederate naval officers, *Contra Almirante* (Rear Admiral) John Randolph Tucker assumed command of the combined fleet of Peru and Chile in their war against Spain. Notwithstanding the hostility of nationalistic Peruvian officers (and even a brief mutiny), Tucker prepared his force of a half-dozen major warships, including two formidable new ironclads, for an attack against the Spanish Pacific Squadron anchored at Manila in the Philippine Islands. In consultation with Hunter Davidson, the former commander of the Confederate Submarine Battery Service, Admiral Tucker's tactical plans emphasized the offensive use of torpedoes. As at Charleston, his major warships mounted spar torpedoes. In addition, they carried small, steam torpedo boats that could be launched at sea.

Admiral Tucker resigned from the Peruvian navy in March 1867, due to continued opposition from the Latin American officers, the postponement of his proposed cruise against the Spaniards, and a "war of salutes" that threatened a diplomatic rupture with the United States. The vindictive Admiral Dahlgren, Tucker's Union navy opponent at Charleston who now commanded the United States South Pacific Squadron, ordered his officers to deny traditional naval courtesies to "ex-Commander Tucker," whose Peruvian commission he would not recognize.

In May 1867 Tucker was named president of Peru's new Hydrographic Commission of the Amazon. Based at

the remote river port of Iquitos, some 2,300 miles upstream from the mouth of the Amazon, Admiral Tucker and his expanded team of former Confederates spent seven years in the jungles of eastern Peru, exploring and mapping the headwaters of the world's mightiest river for steam navigation. Returning to the United States in 1874, Admiral Tucker died at his home in Petersburg, Virginia, on 12 June 1883.

—*David P. Werlich*

See also Dahlgren, John Aldoph; Drewry's Bluff, Battle of; *Hunley*; Sayler's Creek / Harper's Farm, Battle of.

For further reading:

Rochelle, James Henry. *Life of Rear Admiral John Randolph Tucker* (1903).

Werlich, David P. *Admiral of the Amazon: John Randolph Tucker, His Confederate Colleagues, and Peru* (1990).

TULLAHOMA CAMPAIGN
(January–August 1863)

After the battle of Stones River (Murfreesboro), Confederate general Braxton Bragg's Army of Tennessee retreated on 2 January 1863 approximately thirty-five miles southeast along the Nashville & Chattanooga Railroad. At Tullahoma, Bragg began to regroup and establish a new defensive line. To block any advance by William Rosecrans's Army of the Cumberland toward Chattanooga, the Confederate army deployed along a fifteen-mile line south of a ridge known as the Highland Rim.

The largest of Bragg's corps under General Leonidas Polk took position on the Confederate left flank around Shelbyville about twenty miles northwest of Tullahoma. From Shelbyville, Polk could protect the turnpike that ran along the western edge of the Highland Rim through Guy's Gap, the widest and most accessible of the ridge's four passes. Bragg placed General William Hardee's corps at Wartrace, eight miles to Polk's east, to defend the remaining three passes at Bell Buckle, Liberty, and Hoover's gaps. The Bell Buckle Gap contained the railroad, while Liberty and Hoover's gaps had turnpikes. The road through Hoover's Gap was particularly important because it was in the best condition and ran through Manchester, a town straddling a branch line of the Nashville & Chattanooga Railroad. Bragg hoped that by strongly fortifying Shelbyville, Rosecrans would be lured into the three eastern gaps, where, once engaged by Hardee, Polk would move out and smash into the Union right flank. Rosecrans, however, was in no hurry to advance during the wet months of 1863 and paused to consolidate his position at Murfreesboro. The two opposing armies, separated by only thirty miles, remained motionless for the next six months: the cautious Bragg believing in the superiority of his defensive position, and the perfectionist Rosecrans methodically preparing for a campaign to take Chattanooga.

The delay was disastrous for the Confederates. During the six months spent at Tullahoma, troop morale gradually deteriorated from a combination of hunger, leadership quarrels, and inactivity. The defensive advantages inherent in Bragg's geographical location imposed a few significant handicaps. Located in an area aptly referred to as "the Barrens," the Tullahoma-Shelbyville-Wartrace-Manchester perimeter encompassed a zone of poor, rocky soil that was incapable of supporting an entrenched army with food. Confederate logistical inefficiency and the supply demands placed on the South's agricultural resources by the Army of Northern Virginia exacerbated Bragg's predicament. The Army of Tennessee thus found itself in the ironic situation of facing starvation while protecting the South's primary agricultural region so that Lee's men could eat. Between January and June 1863, the Atlanta supply depot shipped almost 100 times more salted meat every week to Lee than to Bragg, leaving the Army of Tennessee stocked with only three days' rations. The shortage of rations compelled Bragg to extend his lines and forage on the countryside. Bragg's army of about 40,000 men quickly depleted the area of all foodstuffs and forced the creation of a supply network that reached north far behind enemy lines from Franklin, Tennessee, into central Kentucky. Furthermore, the same Highland Rim protecting Bragg also afforded Rosecrans concealment. To conduct reconnaissance, escort supply trains, and raid Federal supply lines, the Army of Tennessee reorganized its cavalry arm into two large corps commanded by Generals Earl Van Dorn and Joseph Wheeler. Despite some notable successes by Nathan Bedford Forrest and John Hunt Morgan, these cavalry raids did little to improve Bragg's situation.

Perhaps most devastating to the army's condition was the politics of command. The army's subordinate officers had lost confidence in their commander, especially after the debacles of the October 1862 Perryville campaign. Bragg earned even more criticism after the fiasco at Murfreesboro. Staff infighting and public recriminations of Bragg's performance had become so prominent by the end of January 1863 that Confederate president Jefferson Davis dispatched General Joseph Johnston to Tullahoma. Davis hoped that by sending his senior western commander to the area that Bragg would be outranked and defer to Johnston, who would stay permanently as the overall army commander. However, Johnston arrived in Tullahoma at a time when troop morale was high and reported back to Davis that any internal staff problems were the rumblings of a few malcontents. Fearing the perception that he had advanced his own career at Bragg's expense, Johnston departed Tullahoma, leaving Bragg firmly in charge.

During the ensuing months, infighting among the key general officers intensified and provoked Davis to order Johnston back to Tullahoma with explicit instructions to remove Bragg. Upon his arrival, Johnston found Bragg on

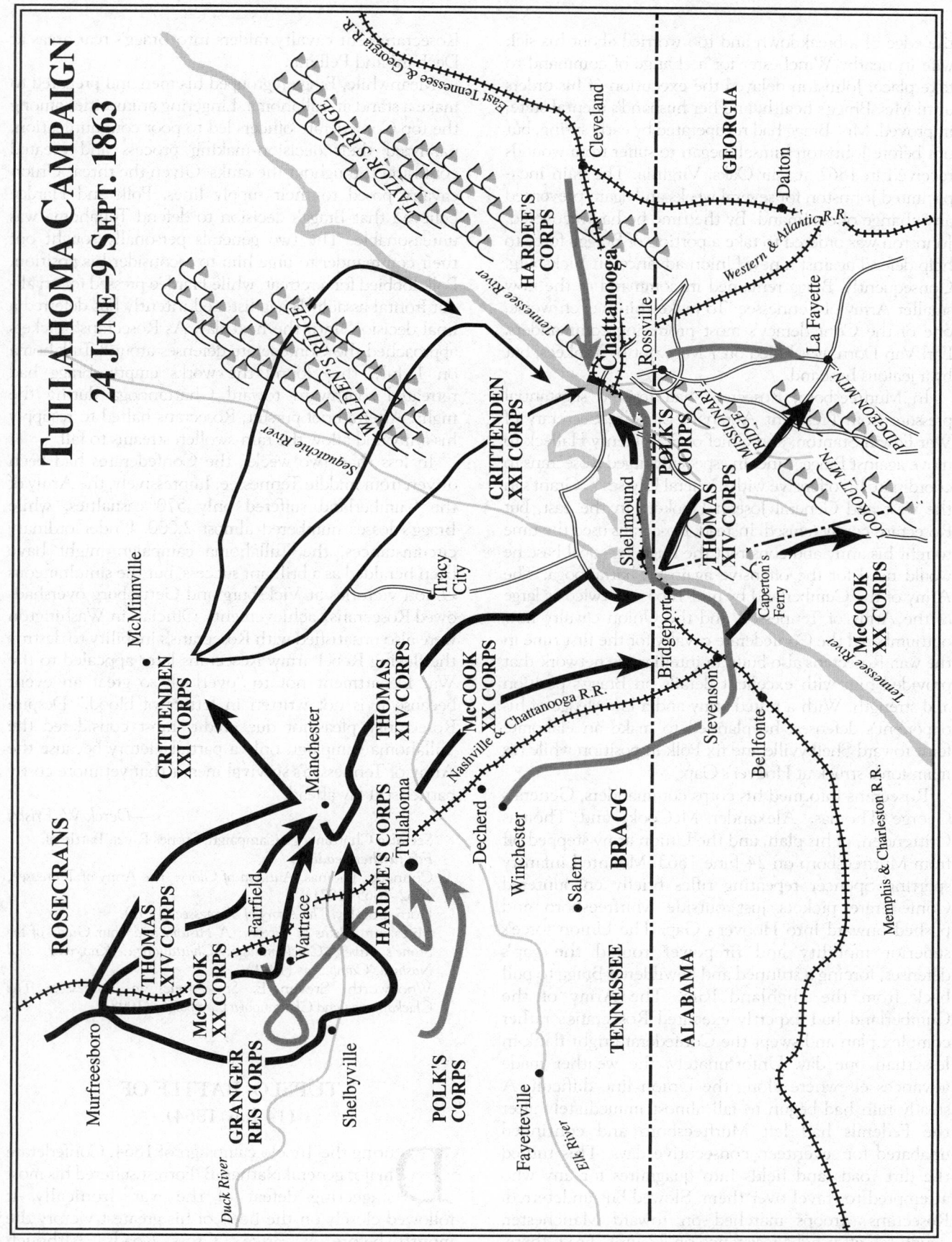

TULLAHOMA CAMPAIGN
24 June–9 Sept. 1863

GEORGIA

Cleveland

Dalton

HARDEE'S CORPS

East Tennessee & Georgia R.R.

Western & Atlantic R.R.

Chattanooga

Rossville

La Fayette

TAYLOR'S RIDGE

Tennessee River

WALDEN'S RIDGE

Sequatchie River

CRITTENDEN
XXI CORPS

POLK'S
CORPS

MISSIONARY RIDGE

PIGEON MTN.

LOOKOUT MTN.

Shellmound

THOMAS
XIV CORPS

McMinnville

Tracy
City

Caperton's
Ferry

Bridgeport

McCOOK
XX CORPS

Tennessee River

Stevenson

McCOOK
XX CORPS

Nashville & Chattanooga R.R.

Bellfonte

CRITTENDEN
XXI CORPS

THOMAS
XIV CORPS

Manchester

Decherd

Salem

Memphis & Charleston R.R.

ROSECRANS

THOMAS
XIV CORPS

McCOOK
XX CORPS

Tullahoma

Winchester

BRAGG

Fairfield

Wartrace

HARDEE'S CORPS

TENNESSEE

ALABAMA

Murfreesboro

Duck River

Shelbyville

GRANGER
RES CORPS

POLK'S
CORPS

Fayetteville

Elk River

the edge of a breakdown and too worried about his sick wife in nearby Winchester for a change of command to take place. Johnston delayed the execution of his orders until Mrs. Bragg's health, and her husband's mental state, improved. Mrs. Bragg had recuperated by early spring, but not before Johnston himself began to suffer from wounds received in 1862 at Fair Oaks, Virginia. The pain incapacitated Johnston for several weeks and again prevented any change of command. By the time he had recovered, Johnston was ordered to take a portion of Bragg's force to help defend against a new Union advance on Vicksburg. Consequently, Bragg remained in command of the now smaller Army of Tennessee. To make things even worse, one of the Confederacy's most promising commanders, Earl Van Dorn, was killed on 7 May, not by Yankees, but by a jealous husband.

In Murfreesboro, Rosecrans had resisted substantial pressure from President Abraham Lincoln, Secretary of War Edwin Stanton, and Chief of Staff Henry Halleck to move against Bragg. Lincoln especially urged Rosecrans to coordinate his offensive with General Ulysses S. Grant's in the west and General Joseph Hooker's in the east, but Rosecrans coolly refused. Instead, Rosecrans used the time to refit his army and construct the huge logistical base he would need for the offensive against Chattanooga. The Army of the Cumberland by mid-1863 was twice as large as the Army of Tennessee, and the Union cavalry now outnumbered the Confederate cavalry for the first time in the war. Rosecrans also built an intelligence network that provided him with excellent details on Bragg's position and strength. With a rested army and a knowledge of his opponent's defenses, he planned to make an elaborate feint toward Shelbyville and fix Polk in position while his main force struck at Hoover's Gap.

Rosecrans informed his corps commanders, Generals George Thomas, Alexander McCook, and Thomas Crittenden, of his plan, and the Union army stepped off from Murfreesboro on 24 June 1863. Mounted infantry sporting Spencer repeating rifles briefly encountered Confederate pickets just outside Murfreesboro and pushed onward into Hoover's Gap. The Union force's superior mobility and firepower routed the gap's defenses, forcing a stunned and bewildered Bragg to pull back from the Highland Rim. The Army of the Cumberland had expertly executed Rosecrans's rather complex plan and swept the Confederate right flank in less than one day. Unfortunately, the weather made advances elsewhere along the Union line difficult. A steady rain had begun to fall almost immediately after the Federals had left Murfreesboro and continued unabated for seventeen consecutive days. This turned the dirt roads and fields into quagmires for any who attempted to travel over them. Slowed but undeterred, Rosecrans's troops marched on toward Manchester, which fell after light resistance on 27 June. From there,

Rosecrans sent cavalry raiders into Bragg's rear areas at Dechard and Pelham.

Meanwhile, Bragg regrouped his men and prepared to make a stand at Tullahoma. Lingering animosities among the top Confederate officers led to poor communication, paralyzed their decision-making process and created confusion throughout the ranks. Given the threat Union cavalry posed to their supply lines, Polk and Hardee believed that Bragg's decision to defend Tullahoma was unreasonable. The two generals personally sought out their commander to urge him to reconsider his position. Polk lobbied for a retreat, while Hardee pressed for an all-out frontal assault. Bragg listened intently but deferred a final decision until the next day. As Rosecrans's pickets approached the Confederate defenses around Tullahoma on 1 July, they found the works empty. Bragg had retreated southward toward Chattanooga during the night. After a brief pursuit, Rosecrans halted to resupply his army and allow the rain-swollen streams to fall.

In less than two weeks, the Confederates had been driven from middle Tennessee. Impressively, the Army of the Cumberland suffered only 570 casualties, while Bragg's losses numbered almost 2,000. Under ordinary circumstances, the Tullahoma campaign might have been heralded as a brilliant success, but the simultaneous Union victories at Vicksburg and Gettysburg overshadowed Rosecrans's achievements. Officials in Washington were also unsatisfied with Rosecrans's inability to destroy the fleeing Rebel army. Rosecrans later appealed to the War Department not to "overlook so great an event because it is not written in letters of blood." Despite Rosecrans's pleas for due credit, most considered the Tullahoma campaign only a partial victory because the Army of Tennessee's survival meant that yet more costly battles still lay ahead.

—Derek W. Frisby

See also Chattanooga Campaign; Stones River, Battle of.
For further reading:
Connelly, Thomas. *Autumn of Glory: The Army of Tennessee, 1862–1865* (1971).
Horn, Stanley. *The Army of Tennessee* (1952).
Miles, Jim. *Paths to Victory: A History and Tour Guide of the Stone's River, Chickamauga, Chattanooga, Knoxville, and Nashville Campaigns* (1991).
Woodworth, Steven E. *Six Armies in Tennessee: The Chickamauga and Chattanooga Campaigns* (1998).

TUPELO, BATTLE OF
(14 July 1864)

During the Tupelo campaign of 1864, Confederate major general Nathan B. Forrest suffered his most staggering defeat of the war. Ironically, it followed closely on the heels of his greatest victory the month before at Brice's Cross Roads. Although

command of the Confederate force rested with the senior officer present, Lieutenant General Stephen D. Lee, most of the troops were part of Forrest's immediate command. Their defeat by Union major general Andrew J. Smith ensured that Forrest never had the strength to threaten Federal infantry again.

The Tupelo campaign began on 22 June when Smith departed La Grange, Tennessee. It ended on 23 July with his return to Memphis via La Grange. Smith marched into Mississippi with 14,200 effectives supported by twenty-four field guns. Confederate opposition included 7,500 cavalrymen and 2,100 dismounted troopers supported by twenty cannons. Major General William T. Sherman ordered Smith to pursue and shatter Forrest's command to protect Federal logistical lines during the Atlanta campaign; Sherman also expected Smith to destroy supply depots and apply pressure against Lee's already beleaguered Department of Alabama, Mississippi, and East Louisiana. The critical areas in this department were Mobile and the vicinity of Jackson. The U.S. Navy, working with Brigadier General E. R. S. Canby and his 20,000 men at Pascagoula, Mississippi, threatened Mobile. Union brigadier general Henry W. Slocum advanced from Vicksburg against Brigadier General Wirt Adams encamped near the Big Black River and Bayou Pierre. Lee knew he had to disband the force in north Mississippi to reinforce Mobile and Jackson, but he felt compelled to engage the enemy while he still had the manpower available.

Following a strategy similar to that used at the battle of West Point, Forrest tried to lure Smith into a trap around the prairie country of Okolona. The prudent Smith, not wanting to repeat the Union disaster at Brice's Cross Roads, turned instead toward Tupelo and entrenched. Neither Lee nor Forrest liked the tactical situation and even discussed postponing the attack. In the end, neither had the courage to suggest withdrawing, and both allowed the impending battle to gain a life of its own. Lee offered Forrest command of the battle, which the latter declined in part because of protocol, and perhaps out of a sense of foreboding. Forrest commanded the right wing of the attack, while Lee commanded the center and left wings.

The battle of Tupelo (also known as the battle of Harrisburg) started at 7:00 A.M. on 14 July 1864 and was in full force by 8:00. Smith formed his battle line on the crest of a low ridge overlooking a creek near Harrisburg, a small community west of Tupelo that is now part of the city. Smith chose his terrain well. The surrounding woods had little undergrowth, exposing potential attackers for up to three-quarters of a mile. Communications quickly deteriorated once the battle began; the Confederate strike was neither coordinated nor unified. Lee either prematurely committed a Kentucky brigade assigned to lead the center charge, or

Forrest delayed in deploying his troops in support of the charge. This piecemeal attack allowed the entrenched Federals to destroy one brigade after another. During the two-and-a-half-hour fight, Federal troops withstood the onslaught of several determined attacks. In the end, Southern forces withdrew from the field with irreplaceable losses. Confederate brigades engaged in the center attack suffered 34 percent casualty rates and would never again regain their combat effectiveness.

Smith won a tactical victory but failed to launch a counterattack that could have routed the only significant opposition in north Mississippi and west Alabama. Smith suffered 77 killed, 559 wounded, and 38 captured for a total of 674, compared to Forrest's 210 killed and 1,116 wounded for a total of 1,326. Forrest's losses are even more staggering when one considers that one out of five mounted troopers did not participate in the battle due to "horse-holding" duty.

Federal troops withdrew from Harrisburg toward Tupelo on the evening of the 14th, while Forrest and Lee waited nervously for an attack that never came. On the 15th, Federal troops retreated through Tupelo along Ellistown road, with Confederate patrols in pursuit. The Southerners first gained the initiative during brisk skirmishes near Oldtown Creek, but lost it and retired. Lee called off the pursuit and ordered Forrest's patrols to harass the Union withdrawal. Smith's official reason for returning to Memphis was his limited supply of rations and ammunition (one day of rations and one hundred rounds per gun). Rather than risk his gains by forcing another engagement, Smith returned to Memphis. His force arrived at La Grange on 20 July, where it boarded boxcars and traveled to Memphis. The sudden withdrawal by Smith disgruntled Sherman; Smith, however, did accomplish his main objective of keeping Sherman's supply lines intact.

Controversy arose over which Southern general had lost the battle, with supporters of each general blaming the other. Forrest's defenders claimed that the general did not want to attack and only followed the orders of his superior. Defenders of Lee countered that Forrest had pressured for an attack and then did not support it with his wing. It remains unclear whether Forrest agreed with the decision to fight. His official report, written seventeen days after the battle, did not address this issue. Lee never wrote an after-action report due to his immediate transfer to the Army of Tennessee, fighting near Atlanta, Georgia. Despite the controversy, both men remained friends. Thirty-seven years later, Lee wrote, "I am sure he [Forrest] did the best as he saw it. I am sure I did my best as I saw it."

—*David P. Eldridge*

See also Brice's Cross Roads, Battle of; Forrest, Nathan Bedford; Smith, Andrew Jackson; West Point, Battle of.
For further reading:
Bearss, Edwin C. *Forrest at Brice's Cross Roads and in North Mississippi in 1864* (1979).
Jordan, Thomas, and J. P. Pryor. *The Campaigns of Lieutenant*

General Nathan Bedford Forrest, and of Forrest's Cavalry (1868; reprint, 1988).

Lee, Stephen D. "The Battle of Tupelo or Harrisburg, July 14, 1864." *Mississippi Valley Historical Society, Publications* (1902).

Maness, Lonnie E. *An Untutored Genius: The Military Career of General Nathan Bedford Forrest* (1990).

TURCHIN, JOHN BASIL
(1822–1901)
Union general

The only Russian immigrant to serve as a senior officer in the Civil War, John Basil Turchin was born Ivan Vasilovich Turchinov on 30 January 1822 in the Province of the Don. He began his military career at the prestigious St. Petersburg Imperial Military School, graduating with honors in 1841. Turchin saw his first military action as an ensign in the tsar's artillery when Russian troops were sent to help the Austrians put down the Hungarian revolt of 1848–1849. During the Crimean War, Turchin served in the elite Imperial Guards, rising to the rank of colonel. During this period, Turchin designed and supervised the construction of the excellent coastal defenses between St. Petersburg and Narva, as well as serving on the personal staff of the crown prince, who would become Tsar Alexander II in 1855. Leaving his promising career in the Russian Empire, Turchin immigrated with his wife to the United States in 1856, anglicized his name, and found work as an engineer in Chicago with the Illinois Central Railroad.

After the outbreak of the Civil War, John Basil Turchin accepted a commission as a colonel in command of the 19th Illinois Infantry Regiment on 17 June 1861. He brought with him Russian notions of precision in drill and strict discipline, which he laid out in his widely read pamphlet, "Brigade Drill." Along with his reputation as a drillmaster, Turchin proved to be an aggressive and effective battlefield commander. And yet his most significant military legacy did not come from any of his several important victories, but rather from his willingness to let his soldiers pillage in occupied territory. Russian officers routinely allowed their men to loot conquered civilians as a reward for victory. Initially, Turchin tried to justify the illegal actions by his troops as being necessary for basic provisioning to supplement inadequate army rations. Although he was ordered to discontinue the practice, evidence suggests that he did not. For example, after taking Bowling Green, Kentucky, Turchin's men looted and gutted a large number of houses. Another such incident in Alabama led to his court-martial.

In April 1862, Colonel Turchin led an attack against Hunstville and Athens, Alabama, to seize from the Confederacy a vital east-west rail line. On 1 May, Confederate cavalry forced Turchin's 18th Ohio into retreat and took the town of Athens with the active support of about 100 civilians. When Turchin arrived the following day with the 8th Brigade, the Rebel regulars had vanished, leaving the civilians to bear the brunt of the Russian colonel's rage. According to Steven Kellmeyer, Turchin told his troops, "I shut mine eyes for two hours. I see nothing." The Union troops ransacked the town, pillaging and raping in the process. When news of this brutal behavior reached General Don Carlos Buell in June, Buell launched an investigation and relieved Turchin of command on 2 July. The charges stemmed not only from the looting but also from the fact that Turchin, in the European tradition, allowed his wife to accompany him in the field (she reportedly commanded his regiment during a minor skirmish when he was ill). This practice was in violation of direct orders. Turchin was court-martialed, found guilty, and sentenced to dismissal from the army in August 1862.

President Abraham Lincoln, after a meeting with Mrs. Turchin, set the verdict aside and promoted Turchin to brigadier general, retroactive to 17 July. Lincoln apparently was swayed by two factors. First, the Russian was a successful combat commander at a time when the Union had very few. Second, Lincoln was beginning to accept that reprisals might be an occasionally necessary evil to tame rebellious civilians. For his part, General Turchin avoided similar controversies for the rest of the war and continued to serve with distinction. At the battle of Chickamauga he earned the nickname "The Russian Thunderbolt" for the precision lightning charges by his troops. Near Chattanooga, one of Turchin's regiments was the first to scale the enemy works at Missionary Ridge. Finally, he served effectively under General William Sherman during his famed march to Atlanta. Turchin relinquished his command after falling ill in July 1864, and he eventually resigned on 4 October 1864 due to continuing health problems.

After the war, Turchin moved back to Chicago, wrote a book about the battle of Chickamauga, and worked as a solicitor of patents. In 1873 he founded the Polish community of Radom in southern Illinois. Late in his life, Turchin was institutionalized and then died in the Southern Hospital for the Insane in Anna, Illinois, on 19 June 1901. He was buried in the National Soldiers' Cemetery in Mound City, Illinois.

John Basil Turchin was a stern drillmaster and a highly effective field commander, but he will probably be remembered more for condoning looting and brutal reprisals against civilians. These "Russian" practices may even have been the start of a trend in which some Union officers began to treat rebellious civilians almost as if they were enemy combatants.

—*Edward Sharp*

See also Turchin, Nadine.
For further reading:
Haynie, J. Henry. The Nineteenth Illinois (1912).
Kellmeyer, Steven. "A Union Colonel Was the Russian Connection in the American Civil War." Military History (1993).
Leonard, Elizabeth D. All the Daring of the Soldier: Women of the Civil War Armies (1999).
Livermore, Mary A. My Story of the War (1887; reprint, 1974).
McElligott, Ellen, ed. "'A Monotony Full of Sadness': The Diary of Nadine Turchin, May, 1863–April, 1864." Journal of the Illinois State Historical Society (1977).

TURCHIN, NADINE
(1826–1904)
Army woman

Born Nedeshda Lvova in 1826, the woman who came to be known during the Civil War as Nadine Turchin grew up in the Russian army as the daughter of an officer. In 1856 she married a military man named Ivan Vasilovitch Turchinov, with whom she immigrated to the United States, settling by 1858 in Mattoon, Illinois. In 1861 Turchenov (who had anglicized his name to John Basil Turchin) was working as an engineer for the Illinois Central Railroad, one of whose vice presidents was George B. McClellan. When the Civil War broke out, McClellan might have been instrumental in arranging for Turchin's appointment as colonel in command of the 19th Illinois Infantry Volunteers.

Because Nadine was without children of her own to tie her to the home front, and no doubt also because of her own long association with military life, Nadine followed the European custom of accompanying her husband's regiment whenever and wherever she could. Reasonably, her initial concern seems to have been simply to be close to her husband and to attend to his needs. Testimony given after the war by the men of the 19th Illinois, however, indicates that Mrs. Turchin soon dedicated herself to the care of the common soldiers as well. "Dear Madame Turchin!" recalled one former member of the regiment; "how we all respected, believed in, and came to love her for her bravery, gentleness and constant care of the sick and wounded in the Regiment."

Some accounts of Nadine Turchin's Civil War service with the 19th Illinois suggest that her military upbringing and her perhaps unusually bold and fearless temperament may have led her occasionally to adopt a role with her regiment that greatly exceeded that of the typical army woman. In 1889, Civil War nurse and sanitary aid worker Mary Livermore claimed in her memoir that Nadine Turchin was "not one whit behind her husband in courage or military skill," and that on at least one occasion, when her husband was too ill to take command of the men, Nadine "led the troops into action, facing the hottest fire, and fought bravely at their head." Despite the fact that some women during the war disguised themselves as men and fought as soldiers, and despite the fact that many army women served in paramilitary capacities—without disguising their true identities—when circumstances demanded that they do so, it seems unlikely that Nadine Turchin actually led her husband's regiment in battle in quite the manner Livermore describes.

However, it is clear from the historical record that Nadine's unwillingness to remain in the rear at all times, at least during the first year of the war, got her and her husband into trouble. In July 1862 John Turchin underwent a court-martial in connection with a series of charges relating to his conduct as an officer, including the charge of violating general orders forbidding officers to allow their wives to follow them into the field. Turchin did not deny the charge, and a dishonorable dismissal seemed imminent. John Turchin's career was saved, however, by none other than President Abraham Lincoln, who intervened in the proceedings, unwilling at this time to dispense with such an effective and beloved officer.

Nevertheless, the diary Nadine began to keep almost a year after the court-martial clearly indicates that she was trying very hard to restrict herself to her caretaking responsibilities and to steer away from combat situations as much as possible, if only to protect her husband's reputation and his position as a commanding officer. Nadine's diary also clearly indicates that the earlier challenge to her husband's integrity deeply embittered her. Moreover, the required shift in her understanding of her role with the army left her bored, frustrated, and yearning for more excitement. "I would rather live a few years of life exuberant, full, brilliant, than a long existence of dull inertia," she wrote. Weary of military life and constantly annoyed at the army high brass for their insufficient respect for her husband's obviously superior talents, Nadine surely welcomed their joint release from service when it came in the fall of 1864. The Turchins returned to Illinois, where they struggled to make ends meet, dependent in part on army pensions. Nadine Turchin died three years after her husband, in 1904.

—Elizabeth D. Leonard

See also Turchin, John Basil.
For further reading:
Brockett, Linus P., and Mary C. Vaughan. Woman's Work in the Civil War (1867).
Haynie, J. Henry. The Nineteenth Illinois (1912).
Leonard, Elizabeth D. All the Daring of the Soldier: Women of the Civil War Armies (1999).
Livermore, Mary A. My Story of the War (1887; reprint, 1995).
McElligott, Ellen, ed. "'A Monotony Full of Sadness': The Diary of Nadine Turchin, May, 1863–April, 1864." Journal of the Illinois State Historical Society (1977).

TURNER, JOHN WESLEY
(1833–1899)
Union general

Born to John Bice Turner and Martha Voluntine Turner outside Saratoga, New York, John Wesley Turner moved with his family to Chicago when he was ten years old. In 1851 he received an appointment to the U.S. Military Academy and graduated fourteenth of thirty-four in the class of 1855. After graduation he served as a lieutenant of artillery in the Third Seminole War and in the Pacific Northwest in Oregon.

At the outbreak of the Civil War, Turner changed from infantry to the Commissary Department and served as chief commissary of subsistence, Army of Western Missouri, in the fall of 1861. In November he took over the same responsibility for David Hunter's Department of Kansas, headquartered in St. Louis. He moved to the Department of the South in March 1862 and, as commissary of subsistence, accompanied the force that took Fort Pulaski, Georgia, in April 1862. When the attackers ran short of artillerymen, Turner volunteered to help man some of the guns. His commander, Quincy A. Gillmore, commended him for his actions there. Within a week of that engagement Turner was transferred to the Department of the Gulf under Benjamin F. Butler.

Upon arrival in New Orleans, Turner was made Butler's aide-de-camp as well as commissary of subsistence for the department. He was promoted to colonel of volunteers. Turner would be associated with Butler off and on for the remainder of the war.

The following spring, Turner returned to the Department of the South, where his efforts on behalf of Gillmore's force the year before had so impressed his commander that he sought Turner's assignment there. Turner became Gillmore's chief of staff in June 1863 and in July was also made the department's chief of artillery in the midst of the campaign against Charleston. He remained in that position through April 1864 and in September 1863 was promoted to brigadier general of volunteers. Turner directed much of the artillery efforts against Fort Wagner on Morris Island and the bombardment of Fort Sumter.

When Gillmore was transferred north to Benjamin Butler's Army of the James to command X Corps, Turner accompanied him to command the 2d Division of that corps. Turner fought at Drewry's Bluff and then, along with much of Butler's force, moved to Bermuda Hundred. Turner fought in the opening stages of the Petersburg campaign and at the end of July 1864 led his division in support of Ambrose Burnside's corps at the disaster of the Crater.

In the fall of 1864, Turner became the chief of staff for Butler and the Army of the James. He remained in that position until March 1865, even after Butler's removal in January. In March, as the war wound to a close, he longed for a combat command and was given the Independent Division of XXIV Corps. Turner commanded that division in the last phases of the siege of Petersburg at Fort Gregg and in the pursuit of Lee in the Appomattox campaign. For Fort Gregg he received a brevet promotion to colonel in the regular army. After the war he would receive succeeding brevets to brigadier general and major general. He was commended by Major General John Gibbon for his part in the Appomattox campaign.

On 9 June 1865, Turner was given command of the District of Henrico. He held that command, which included the city of Richmond, until April 1866. Upon being mustered out of the volunteer army in 1866, Turner reverted to the commissary department at the rank of colonel. He was stationed as commissary in St. Louis until 1871, when he resigned his commission.

After leaving the army, Turner engaged in various business activities, including banking and serving as president of a lead mine company. He also served for over a decade as the street commissioner for St. Louis. He lived in St. Louis for much of the rest of life, and died there on 8 April 1899.

—*David S. Heidler and Jeanne T. Heidler*

See also Butler, Benjamin Franklin; Crater, Battle of the; Petersburg Campaign.

For further reading:

Hearn, Chester G. *When the Devil Came Down to Dixie: Ben Butler in New Orleans* (1997).

Longacre, Edward G. *Army of Amateurs: General Benjamin F. Butler and the Army of the James, 1863–1865* (1997).

TWIGGS, DAVID EMANUEL
(1790–1862)
Confederate general

David E. Twiggs was born to John Twiggs, a Revolutionary War hero, and Ruth Emanuel Twiggs at the family home outside Augusta, Georgia. As a young man, Twiggs studied law and was about to begin the practice of that profession at the outbreak of the War of 1812. Twiggs accepted a captain's commission in the 8th Infantry, thus beginning a lifelong military career.

He served in the Southeast during the War of 1812 and chose to remain in the army after the war. In the coming years he would participate in virtually every armed conflict of the U.S. government. In 1818 he accompanied Andrew Jackson in the general's invasion of Spanish Florida in what would become known as the First Seminole War. After that conflict, he served in frontier posts, including a stint in what would become Wisconsin. The mid-1830s found him transferred to New Orleans and the command of Edmund Pendleton Gaines. When the Second Seminole War erupted in

1835, Twiggs accompanied Gaines to Florida. He would serve several tours of duty in Florida during that war.

Twiggs was attached to Zachary Taylor's Army of Observation at the commencement of hostilities with Mexico in 1846 and would serve with Taylor in his campaign in northern Mexico before being transferred to Winfield Scott's command for the Mexico City campaign. Twiggs distinguished himself in this conflict, winning the thanks of Congress and the Georgia legislature.

After the Mexican-American War, Twiggs, who by then had achieved the rank of brigadier general, served in a variety of frontier posts and in New Orleans, where he had made his permanent home. In 1857, he received the assignment that would bring an ignominious end to his career in the U.S. Army; he became the commander of the Department of Texas.

Twiggs's first three years in command of the department were relatively uneventful. He expanded the network of fortifications, particularly in the thinly populated parts of the state, seeking to protect frontier settlers from Comanches and bandits raiding from Mexico. By this point in his career, Twiggs, now in his late sixties, suffered from increasingly declining health. He took numerous sick leaves home, including one for almost the entire year of 1860.

The growing sectional problems in the country had deeply troubled Twiggs. A native Georgian, he intended to resign from the army if Georgia seceded. In the meantime, he knew when he resumed command in Texas in December 1860, he would have his hands full keeping the situation calm in that quarter. Over the next two months he wrote numerous letters to the War Department and to the commanding general of the army, Winfield Scott, asking for instructions on what to do in the event of hostilities in Texas.

Secessionist feeling was growing in Texas with armed bands, some Texas Rangers, supporting the secession of the state and threatening to attack U.S. posts once the state left the Union. Twiggs, along with his repeated pleas to Washington for guidance, took precautions to protect public property, putting his garrison at his headquarters in San Antonio on alert and bringing in soldiers from some outlying posts. He ordered his men to protect the public property at all costs.

In early February, the War Department, though it did not inform Twiggs, issued orders that Twiggs would be relieved of command and replaced by Colonel Carlos Waite. In the meantime, on 1 February the Texas convention voted to secede but also decided to put the question to the people in the form of a referendum to be held on 23 February. The convention decided, however, to try to secure the surrender of the public property to the state before that referendum was held. For that reason a committee was appointed to negotiate with General Twiggs.

Over the next two weeks, sometimes heated negotiations were held between Twiggs and the committee. The general insisted that, in the event of a surrender of property, all U.S. soldiers should be allowed to keep their small arms and leave the state. The committee, however, wanted to keep these valuable weapons in the state, and it was on this point that the negotiations stalled. To encourage Twiggs to resume the talks, over 1,000 state troops were brought into San Antonio to face Twiggs's 160 men. The arrival of these forces certainly contributed to the tensions in the town, but when the commissioners learned that the arrival of Twiggs's successor, Waite, was imminent and that he was unlikely to negotiate any surrender, the committee agreed to Twiggs's conditions. The agreement was signed on 18 February 1861.

Waite arrived the following day and assumed command of the evacuation of U.S. forces from Texas. Twiggs, after seeing to personal affairs, left for his home in New Orleans, where he received word that on 1 March 1861 he had been dismissed from the army for treachery. While Twiggs had never made any secret of his intention to surrender property in Texas once the state seceded and that he would not be responsible for starting a war in Texas, the government in Washington needed a scapegoat to blame for the surrender, and Twiggs, an avowed Southern sympathizer, was the obvious choice.

Many people in the Confederate government did not want to waste Twiggs's many years of military experience. He was mentioned for several commands, but his failing health would not allow him to accept a combat role in the coming conflict. His son-in-law Abraham Myers (married to Twiggs's only daughter, Marion), acting Confederate quartermaster general, lobbied the Confederate government for Twiggs to receive command of New Orleans. At the end of May 1861, President Jefferson Davis made the offer to Twiggs of the command of Department Number One with headquarters in New Orleans, and Twiggs accepted.

For the next four and a half months, with the help of engineering officer Paul O. Hébert, Twiggs worked to shore up the defenses of the Gulf Coast and New Orleans. His age and failing health convinced him by fall 1861 that he could not continue in the active service. He requested to be relieved of command, and on 18 October 1861 he was replaced by Mansfield Lovell. Twiggs remained in New Orleans until the Federal occupation in April 1862 and would not hold another command during the war.

Once it became apparent that Federals would occupy the city, Twiggs, after seeing to the safekeeping of some of his valuables, fled his home for Georgia. The commander of occupation forces, Major General Benjamin Butler, used Twiggs's home for his headquarters. Years later, long after Twiggs's death, his family waged a legal battle with the federal government for the return of some of Twiggs's property confiscated by Butler.

Twiggs would not live to hear of these confiscations. The events of the previous months had broken his already fragile health, and he died at his family's home outside Augusta, Georgia, on 15 July 1862.

Although he was certainly not a great general, Twiggs's long years of service to the U.S. Army were obscured by these last two years of his life.

—David S. Heidler and Jeanne T. Heidler

See also Butler, Benjamin Franklin; Hébert, Paul Octave; Lovell, Mansfield; New Orleans; Texas.

For further reading:
Heidler, Jeanne T. "The Military Career of David Emanuel Twiggs" (Ph.D. dissertation, 1988).

TYLER, JOHN
(1790–1862)
Tenth president of the United States

The namesake son of a Virginia governor, John Tyler was born on 29 March 1790 at Greenway, Charles City County, Virginia. In a long and varied career, Tyler was a chancellor of the College of William and Mary, president of the Virginia Colonization Society, peace commissioner to President James Buchanan in 1861, Peace Convention president in 1861, member of the Virginia Secession Convention of 1861, member of the Virginia Constitutional Convention of 1829–1830, member of the Virginia Council of State, speaker of the Virginia House of Delegates, member of the U.S. House of Representatives, member of the Provisional Congress of the Confederate States of America, member of the U.S. Senate, governor of Virginia, vice-president of the United States, and the tenth president of the United States.

Born into Tidewater Virginia's social and political aristocracy (though not into great wealth), Tyler came by his political opinions honestly. His father, an admirer of Patrick Henry and a good friend of Thomas Jefferson, had been a prominent opponent of the federal Constitution in the Richmond Convention of 1788, and young Tyler early imbibed the overwhelming particularism that marked Tidewater Virginia's variant of the Commonwealth's dominant Jeffersonianism. Throughout his life, the younger Tyler insisted that Jefferson's political example was his guiding star. His education at the College of William and Mary, Jefferson's alma mater in nearby Williamsburg, reinforced the future president's sense of the great weight of the political legacy his father's generation had left him. Tyler remained a stalwart political defender of his college (of which his son eventually would be president) for the remainder of his life.

Tyler's first participation in politics came in the Virginia House of Delegates in the period 1811 to 1815. In recompense for his service, his constituents elected him to the U.S. House of Representatives. Almost alone among Southerners there, he saw that the Missouri Compromise doomed his state's system of chattel slavery to eventual extinction. His opposition to the compromise was unsuccessful.

Western Virginia reformers finally succeeded in bringing about a constitutional convention in 1829. Tyler, who as an incumbent senator had no desire to rile either the western or eastern parts of the state, endeavored to avoid election. When his constituents selected him anyway, he kept a low profile throughout the proceedings; however, when votes were taken, Tyler consistently supported the reactionary position of his home county. His lack of statesmanship on this occasion marked the low point of Tyler's otherwise consistently principled public career.

In the Senate, Tyler played a leading role in the adoption of the Compromise of 1833, which averted the potentially violent showdown between President Andrew Jackson and South Carolina Nullifiers. Henry Clay, the senator usually credited with the measures that prevented bloodshed in this political impasse, was perfectly happy to rely on the advice of his personal and political friend from Virginia on this occasion; Tyler's drafting of the legislation Clay eventually sponsored is often overlooked. Clay would resent Tyler's insistence that the Compromise live out its appointed life span when the latter became president. Alone among senators, Tyler voted "nay" to the president's "force bill," which authorized use of the military against anti-tariff Carolinians. This move marked the break between the onetime Jackson supporter and the administration he had helped to elect.

Tyler supported Henry Clay for the 1840 Whig presidential nomination. His candidate was defeated, but Tyler found himself nominated for the largely ceremonial second spot on the Whig ticket. Party leaders hoped that Tyler's candidacy would help it to cultivate favor with states' rights advocates who, in common with the Virginia senator, thought that Jackson had been too high-handed toward the sovereign units of the federal republic. Not once during the campaign did Tyler, who had always consistently and vocally opposed national banks, federal infrastructure programs, and protective tariffs, give any indication that he had sold his political soul for the nomination.

The death of President William Henry Harrison within days of his inauguration made Tyler the tenth president of the United States. Tyler insisted that he was president, not acting president, and other leading political actors eventually agreed. Clay saw "his man's" elevation as an opportunity, and he undertook to have the Whig majorities in both houses of Congress enact all the favorite proposals of the party's ultranationalist wing.

Despite Tyler's warnings that only a bank bill specifically tailored to meet his constitutional qualms—that is, without power to erect branches in states that had not consented to their establishment—would escape a veto, Clay and the Whigs passed a bill to which Tyler objected. Tyler vetoed it, repeated his warnings, and was forced by Clay's supporters to veto a similar bill again. The nationalist Whigs who dominated the party's caucus then assembled on the Capitol steps and read Tyler out of their party. They had decided that they would rather forfeit any chance of progress toward their policy goals for four years in hopes of electing Clay president than cooperate with Tyler. For the remainder of his term, Tyler was subjected to vituperation of the kind in which nineteenth-century newspaper editors specialized. However, he had the last laugh, because no national bank bill ever again passed, and Clay never became president.

Besides the defeat of the main items on the Whig nationalist agenda—an achievement greater than Andrew Jackson's victory in the "Bank War"—President Tyler secured several significant foreign policy triumphs. Among other things, his administration formalized the eastern boundary with Canada, established favorable relations with China, extended the Monroe Doctrine to Hawaii, and, most importantly (and one might say unconstitutionally), arranged to bring the Republic of Texas into the federal Union. Both a sense of national destiny and a desire to provide new territory for the slave system animated Tyler's and his advisors' behavior.

At his presidency's end in 1845, Tyler moved to a Tidewater estate that he dubbed Sherwood Forest, which he thought a fit name for a political outlaw's home. When war seemed in the offing in 1860 and 1861, Tyler's fellow Virginians sent him to negotiate with President James Buchanan and President-elect Abraham Lincoln. Tyler tried as president of the Peace Convention to secure endorsement of a program for constitutional change the South would accept, but when he failed, Virginia agreed with him that the time for secession had arrived.

Fully expecting Confederate military defeat, Tyler served in the Provisional Congress of the Confederate States of America. He proposed, among other things, that a body of cavalry be sent immediately to seize Washington. Had his advice been heeded when offered, matters might have turned out differently. Tyler was elected to the first Congress under the Confederate Constitution, but he died at the capital, Richmond, on 18 January 1862 before he could take his seat. His second wife, the former Julia Gardiner, and eleven of his fifteen children survived him.

—*K.R. Constantine Gutzman*

See also Congress, C.S.A.; Washington Peace Conference.
For further reading:
Chitwood, Oliver Perry. *John Tyler: Champion of the Old South* (1996).
Crapol, Edward P. "John Tyler and the Pursuit of National Destiny." *Journal of the Early Republic* (1997).

TYLER, ROBERT OGDEN
(1831–1874)
Union general

Born to Frederick Tyler and Sophia Sharp Tyler in Hunter, New York, Robert Ogden Tyler received an appointment to the U.S. Military Academy in 1849. He graduated twenty-second of fifty-two in the class of 1853. Upon being commissioned as an artillery officer, Tyler served primarily in the west in Utah, California, and Washington. He also served briefly in Minnesota before being sent to New York during the secession crisis for recruiting duty. In early April 1861, Tyler was sent with the relief expedition to Fort Sumter and watched from his ship as the fort was bombarded into submission.

After returning north with the relief expedition, Tyler served briefly in Baltimore, Maryland, before being transferred to the quartermaster's corps. For several months he managed the supply depot at Alexandria, Virginia, before accepting the difficult task of commanding the 4th Connecticut Volunteer Infantry. This unit had suffered several defeats at the hands of the Confederates in the Shenandoah Valley and was suffering from very low morale. Tyler had as his charge not only to reinvigorate the unit but also to convert them to a heavy artillery regiment. He succeeded on both counts, and the new regiment became the 1st Connecticut Heavy Artillery.

During the early months of 1862, Tyler and his regiment operated within the defenses of Washington, but in the spring they were attached to Fitz John Porter's V Corps in the Peninsula campaign. Tyler commanded the siege train during that campaign and was particularly active in arranging the guns for the siege of Yorktown, although they were never put into operation. His greatest difficulty during the entire movement up the York Peninsula was the wet and sometimes boggy terrain, but he managed to move his guns quickly and efficiently and earned the praise of his superior officers. Tyler was engaged in most of the battles of the Seven Days, most notably at Gaines' Mill and Malvern Hill. He lost only one artillery piece during the entire Peninsula campaign.

Back in the defenses of Washington, Tyler did not see any major action again until Fredericksburg in December 1862. In the meantime he had been promoted to brigadier general of volunteers for his services on the peninsula. At Fredericksburg, Tyler commanded the artillery of the Center Grand Division and bombarded the town in preparation for the Union crossing of the

Rappahannock River. After Fredericksburg, Tyler returned to Washington for two months to command the defenses at Alexandria. Back with the Army of the Potomac at Chancellorsville in May 1863, Tyler commanded the reserve artillery.

Still in command of the reserve artillery at Gettysburg, Tyler did not see significant action until the third day. It became his charge in the afternoon of 3 July to bring his guns to bear on the Confederate infantry in what became known as Pickett's Charge. Tyler did so with devastating efficiency.

At the end of 1863, Tyler was sent back to Washington, where he remained in the defenses there commanding the heavy artillery until the opening of Ulysses S. Grant's campaign against Robert E. Lee in the spring of 1864. At the time, Grant had plenty of artillerymen and not enough infantry. Therefore Tyler and his men were sent to Virginia to serve as infantry. Tyler commanded a brigade in II Corps at the battles of the Wilderness, Spotsylvania, North Anna, and Cold Harbor. At one of the early charges in the latter battle, Tyler was struck in the ankle by a Confederate musket ball. He was unable to return to active duty until December 1864 and was permanently affected by the injury.

Upon his return, Tyler could perform nothing but desk and board duty. In January, after seeing several specialists about his ankle, he requested and received a transfer to Philadelphia, where a surgeon hoped to restore some of the use of his foot. After the surgery, which was not entirely successful, Tyler was sent to New York on recruiting duty. After the end of the war, he was assigned to the Middle Department under Winfield Scott Hancock. He had been given a brevet promotion in both the volunteer and regular service to major general for Cold Harbor and war service.

With the reorganization of the army and his mustering out of volunteer service in 1866, Tyler reverted to lieutenant colonel in the Quartermaster Department. In the early 1870s, his health began a steady decline, something he hoped travel abroad would cure. It did not. He died on 1 December 1874 in Boston, Massachusetts. His memoirs were published posthumously.

—*David S. Heidler and Jeanne T. Heidler*

See also Artillery; Cold Harbor, Battle of; Peninsula Campaign.

For further reading:

Tyler, Robert Ogden. *Memoir of Brevet Major-General Robert Ogden Tyler, U.S. Army, Together with His Journal of Two Months Travels in British and Farther India* (1878).

U

ULLMANN, DANIEL
(1810–1892)
Union general

Daniel Ullmann, born 28 April 1810, charted a course that embodied the radicalization of the Union on issues of slavery and race. A native of Wilmington, Delaware, he graduated from Yale in 1829 and entered the practice of law in New York City. There he established a large practice and served as a master in chancery.

Ullmann remained a respectable critic of the Democratic Party in the city for many years. He ran for New York attorney general in 1851 as a Whig and for governor on the American or Know-Nothing ticket in 1854. According to the New York City newspapers, he enjoyed the support of many antislavery voters and the National Reformers of George Henry Evans, but he seems to have avoided an explicit embrace of any radical proposals. Rather, his course represented the shifts that marked the collapse of the old party system pitting Democrats against Whigs.

So, too, Ullmann's military career after 1861 would mirror broader shifts in the politics of warmaking. As a colonel, he took charge of the 78th New York (the "Highlanders") in April 1862. Performing mostly garrison duty in the Shenandoah Valley, he assumed command of a brigade in the Army of Virginia defending Washington in July and, while down with typhoid, was captured and sent to Libby Prison until his parole in October. By his release, the nature of the war had changed radically.

Ullmann contributed directly to that change. After promotion to a brigadier generalship in January 1863, he went to New Orleans to raise black troops for the Corps d'Afrique. However, shortly afterward, the radical administration of General Benjamin F. Butler had given way to that of General Nathaniel Banks. Under the latter, Federal officers actively sabotaged the efforts of Ullmann, who complained of their "implacable prejudice which led them to say and do many foolish things." Most obviously, he complained that the high command kept his men employed in manual labor rather than using them to break the military stalemate in Louisiana.

Nevertheless, by May 1863, Ullmann's men had entered the fighting along the lower Mississippi valley at places like Milliken's Bend. Most importantly, part of Ullmann's new brigade participated in the siege of Port Hudson. Ullmann commented that their conspicuous roles in several ill-fated but valiant assaults on the Confederate works had "silenced cavilers and changed sneers into eulogizers," but black achievements on the battlefield inspired fear as well as admiration among white superiors. One officer told an astonished Ullmann that the black soldiers fought too well: "We must not discipline them, for if we do, we will have to fight them some day ourselves."

Certainly, the U.S. Army never fully cultivated the potential of neither Ullmann's troops nor their commander. He remained at Port Hudson until November 1864, when he took command of the post at Morganza until he was relieved in February 1865.

After the war, Ullmann returned to New York. However, his wartime experience clearly dampened his zeal for politics. Instead, Ullmann traveled extensively and devoted much time to literary and scientific studies. He died on 20 September 1892.

—*Mark A. Lause*

See also Army of Virginia; Banks, Nathaniel P.; Butler, Benjamin F.; Evans, George Henry; Libby Prison; Milliken's Bend, Battle of; Port Hudson Campaign.

For further reading:
Glatthaar, Joseph T. *Forged in Battle: the Civil War Alliance of Black Soldiers and White Officers* (1990).
Trudeau, Noah Andre. *Like Men of War: Black Troops in the Civil War, 1862–1865* (1998).

UNCLE TOM'S CABIN

The decades before the publication of *Uncle Tom's Cabin* in 1852 were full of political and social agitation and afforded perfect subject matter for Harriet Beecher Stowe's novel. Often classified as sentimental fiction, *Uncle Tom's Cabin* is much more; some critics have even gone so far as to contend that the novel had something to do with furthering racial tensions just before the Civil War. However, once the war ceased, the value of Stowe's novel seemed to disappear as well. Nevertheless, in recent years, it has become a favorite sounding board for historians and literary scholars alike and has become part of the American literary canon. By

UNCLE TOM'S CABIN;

OR,

LIFE AMONG THE LOWLY.

BY

HARRIET BEECHER STOWE.

VOL. I.

BOSTON:
JOHN P. JEWETT & COMPANY.
CLEVELAND, OHIO:
JEWETT, PROCTOR & WORTHINGTON.
1852.

Uncle Tom's Cabin: Title page from the first edition in book form, 1852 (*Library of Congress*)

the time of the novel's publication in serial format from 1851 to 1852 in *The National Era*, the United States was embroiled in an intense debate over slavery. The anti-slavery forces suffered a setback with the 1850 Fugitive Slave Law, which required federal assistance in the capture and return of escaped slaves; in many ways, Stowe's outrage over this law precipitated *Uncle Tom's Cabin.* Her objective, as she stated in a letter to the editor of the *Era,* was "to hold up in the most lifelike and graphic manner possible Slavery, its reverses, changes, and the Negro character, which I have had ample opportunities for studying. There is no arguing with *pictures,* and everybody is impressed by them, whether they mean to be or not." *Uncle Tom's Cabin* was an overnight success, and 50,000 copies were sold within eight weeks after its publication in book form in 1852.

Extremely thematic, *Uncle Tom's Cabin* focuses on universal themes. Its central issue is slavery and Stowe's interpretations of slavery as a manifestation of evil. Consequently, the novel retains its centrality today because of Stowe's emphasis on the centrality of politics

and the universal human dilemma of suffering. Through her characters, Stowe presents various responses to evil. George Harris, an escaped slave, questions how a benevolent God could have allowed slavery to exist. Uncle Tom argues that atonement for evil will be achieved and suffering leads to redemption. According to the kindly plantation owner St. Clare, there is nothing that can be done to end suffering and oppression. Each of these responses to evil is part of Stowe's construction of *Uncle Tom's Cabin* as an argument against slavery. Stowe includes the representation of the Christ figure, typical of this type of novel, in the form of Tom, but also with Evangeline (or Eva), the daughter of St. Clare, whose very name implies an evangelical bent. Eva and Tom represent one of two key stories in *Uncle Tom's Cabin,* one the tale of slaves and whites and the other the tale of miscegenation.

At the beginning of the novel, Tom submits without protest to being sold in New Orleans, even though he has a wife and children in Kentucky. On the way to New Orleans, he saves Eva St. Clare from drowning. In gratitude her father, Augustine St. Clare, purchases Tom, who is well treated by the family. But after the deaths of St. Clare and Eva, his life takes a turn for the worse, and he becomes the property of Simon Legree, who savagely mistreats his slaves, and it is Legree who ultimately causes Tom's death. A simultaneous tale is that of George and Eliza Harris and their son, Harry, mulatto characters who could almost pass for white, but who encounter their own forms of prejudice. By using two plots, Stowe was able to examine black and white relations in both the South and the North. Tom's three masters represent the extremes; St. Clare represents the kindly master, with Legree at the opposite end, and his first master, Shelby, in the middle. The plot of the Harris family allowed Stowe to involve the North since their tale centers on the family's flight to Canada.

Yet *Uncle Tom's Cabin* is not without stereotypes, which is still one of its strongest criticisms today. To represent the dangers of "undomesticated" slaves, Stowe includes the figure of Topsy, an intelligent, but hyperactive child who refuses to accept the rules of white society. In contrast to Topsy's devilish nature and "black, keen, subtle, cringing" nature, Stowe uses Eva as the "fair, high-bred child, with golden eyes." Where one is completely innocent, the other embodies a lack of self-control stereotypically ascribed to the slave. Stowe also does not neglect the subject of miscegenation. The character of the quadroon Eliza Harris, George's wife, represents one of the dangers of slavery, essentially that female slaves could be used to gratify the sexual passions of their white masters. And, even though the marriage between George and Eliza was not recognized as legal by nineteenth-century law, Eliza tried to fulfill the traditional Southern role of wife and mother.

CHAPTER XL.

THE MARTYR.

"Deem not the just by Heaven forgot!
Though life its common gifts deny,—
Though, with a crushed and bleeding heart,
And spurned of man, he goes to die!
For God hath marked each sorrowing day,
And numbered every bitter tear;
And heaven's long years of bliss shall pay
For all his children suffer here."

BRYANT.

HE longest way must have its close,— the gloomiest night will wear on to a morning. An eternal, inexorable lapse of moments is ever hurrying the day of the evil to an eternal night, and the night of the just to an eternal day. We have walked with our humble friend thus far in the valley of slavery; first through flowery fields of

Uncle Tom's Cabin: From the first edition in book form, 1852 (*Library of Congress*)

Stowe uses her characters to express her views, and the most genuine indictment of slavery comes from Augustine St. Clare. Although not publicly an abolitionist for fear of the trouble it would bring him, he dismissed all arguments that slavery was reasonable since it was described in the Bible. He argued that white Northerners were not superior to white Southerners, and Stowe perceived the gulf correctly when she argued that the difference between Northern and Southern whites lay in slavery as an economic institution. By effectively using St. Clare as the expression of antislavery sentiment, Stowe had set the stage for the martyrdom of Uncle Tom.

The New Orleans descriptions of slavery demonstrate some of the less negative aspects of slavery, but they further serve to demonstrate that the institution of slavery made slaves completely dependent upon their masters for support. When the tale takes a negative turn with the Legree plantation, the only working plantation described in detail by Stowe, Stowe depicts Legree as typical of an entire class of slaveholders, thus

contributing to further stereotypes. Yet, Stowe did not lose sight of the fact that her mission was to create a fictional world, yet one based on reality, and one that could be believable.

—*Jennifer Harrison*

See also Abolitionist Movement; Abolitionists; Slaves; Stowe, Harriet Beecher.

For further reading:

Donovan, Josephine. *Uncle Tom's Cabin: Evil, Affliction, and Redemptive Love* (1991).

Gossett, Thomas F. *Uncle Tom's Cabin and American Culture* (1985).

Stowe, Harriet Beecher. *A Key to Uncle Tom's Cabin: Presenting the Original Facts and Documents upon Which the Story Is Founded* (1853; reprint, 1968).

Yarborough, Richard. "Strategies of Black Characterization in *Uncle Tom's Cabin* and the Early Afro-American Novel." In *New Essays on* Uncle Tom's Cabin (1986).

UNDERGROUND RAILROAD

The Underground Railroad was a loosely organized system that aided fugitive slaves escaping from Southern bondage in the decades before the Civil War. Although a few runaways reached Mexico, Spanish Florida (until 1819), or the Caribbean, the vast majority headed northward after the Northern states abandoned slavery in the wake of the American Revolution. Some continued on to the safety of Canada, especially after passage of the Fugitive Slave Act of 1850, which created a federal apparatus for capturing and returning runaways. Census figures suggest that about 1,000 slaves escaped from the South each year; the actual figure may have been twice that number. When trains first came into widespread use in the 1830s, the term "underground railroad" and other railroad nomenclature began to be applied to this system. Americans spoke of hiding places as "stations"; those who aided runaways as "conductors"; escaping slaves as "passengers," "packages," or "cargoes"; and the paths traveled by the runaways as "routes." Although it was rarely as highly organized as this terminology suggests, the system increasingly angered Southern slaveholders and their political allies and contributed to the growing sectional division between the North and South that culminated in the Civil War.

Little organized Underground Railroad activity existed in the South. Slaves usually escaped on their own initiative. Most came northward on foot, traveling by night to avoid detection and hiding out in woods, swamps, or caves by day. Some avoided any human contact until they crossed the Mason-Dixon Line. Others obtained informal assistance from fellow slaves, free blacks, or a few intrepid Southern Quakers. Along the Atlantic coast, runaways often stowed away on northbound vessels, occasionally with the aid of African-American seamen. A few slaves employed particularly creative forms of escape. William Craft and his light-skinned wife, Ellen, traveled by sea and rail from Macon, Georgia, to Philadelphia disguised as a young planter and his black servant. Henry "Box" Brown of Richmond, Virginia, was shipped to Philadelphia in a wooden crate via Adams Express. Although few fugitive slaves found organized assistance in the South, there were exceptions. Northern abolitionists such as John P. Parker of Ohio and Charles T. Torrey of Massachusetts made occasional forays into the region to help liberate groups of slaves. Former slave Harriet Tubman returned to Maryland nineteen times and led some 300 slaves northward to freedom. Beginning in the mid-1830s and continuing through most of the following decade, free blacks in Washington, D.C., operated a covert network that freed thousands of slaves from plantations in nearby Virginia and Maryland.

Upon reaching the free states, fugitive slaves usually found individuals and groups willing to provide them with food, clothing, shelter, medical care, information, and transportation farther northward. Aiding runaways was often clandestine work. But at certain times and in certain places, it was conducted openly and even publicized in antislavery journals. Quaker Levi Coffin of Indiana and black abolitionist William Still of Philadelphia gained notoriety for personally assisting thousands of fugitives. The best-organized efforts occurred in the urban North. In New York, Boston, Philadelphia, Detroit, and dozens of other cities, interracial or all-black networks known as vigilance committees aggressively aided fugitive slaves, providing them with material assistance, physical protection, and legal counsel. On occasion, they rescued fugitives from the custody of federal authorities. These efforts became even more substantial after 1850. Runaways were forwarded to Canada via the Detroit or Niagara frontiers, up the Hudson or Connecticut river valleys, or even by sea to the Maritime Provinces. Such efforts involved Quakers and other white abolitionists of a variety of religious affiliations, but the most direct and sustained involvement came from free blacks. Speaking of the Underground Railroad in 1837, abolitionist James G. Birney reported that "such matters are almost uniformly managed by the colored people."

After the Civil War, the Underground Railroad became the basis of a popular legend constructed by former abolitionists, a few sensationalizing journalists, and local historians. Stories of hairsbreadth escapes, secret tunnels, heroic white conductors (nearly always Quakers or New England Yankees), villainous slave catchers, and terrified and pathetic fugitives were at the center of this mythology. In this version, the system was a highly organized national network with coded messages, prearranged secret signals, a carefully structured hierarchy (including several "presidents of the underground railroad"), and well-defined routes running from the deep South to Canada. Free blacks and the slaves themselves rarely figured as more than passive participants in these tales. More than a century later, few Americans question the veracity of this legendary Underground Railroad.

—*Roy E. Finkenbine*

See also Abolitionist Movement; Abolitionists; Fugitive Slave Act; Slaves; Tubman, Harriet.

For further reading:

Blockson, Charles L., ed. *The Underground Railroad* (1987).
Gara, Larry. *The Liberty Line: The Legend of the Underground Railroad* (1967).
Horton, James O. "Links to Bondage: Free Blacks and the Underground Railroad." In *Free People of Color: Inside the African American Community* (1993).
Ripley, C. Peter. "The Underground Railroad." In *Underground Railroad: Official National Park Handbook* (1998).
Siebert, Wilbur H. *The Underground Railroad: From Slavery to Freedom* (1898).

UNDERWOOD, ADIN BALLOU
(1828–1888)
Union general

Born in Milford, Massachusetts, Adin Ballou Underwood was educated at Brown University. After graduation he enrolled in Harvard Law School. He was admitted to the Massachusetts bar in 1853 and eventually began his practice of law in Boston. At the outbreak of the Civil War, Underwood helped recruit for what would become the 2d Massachusetts Volunteer Infantry and was commissioned a captain of one of the regiment's companies.

The regiment saw little action during the first year of the war, but in the spring of 1862 it was in the Shenandoah Valley under Nathaniel P. Banks fighting Thomas J. "Stonewall" Jackson. After Banks's defeat at the battle of Winchester on 25 May, Underwood's men made up the rear guard of Banks's retreating force. The following August, Underwood was promoted to lieutenant colonel of volunteers in the 33d Massachusetts.

The 33d became part of the Army of the Potomac, and Underwood fought with them at the battle of Fredericksburg. He was promoted to colonel of the regiment in April 1863. As part of XI Corps under Oliver O. Howard, Underwood and his regiment saw a great deal of action in the battle of Chancellorsville in May 1863 as part of the Federal right flank that bore the brunt of Stonewall Jackson's attack on the evening of 2 May. Underwood was able to rally his men and keep them together, thereby avoiding the high casualty rates experienced by other regiments.

Underwood continued to command the 33d at the battle of Gettysburg. Arriving on the field during the first day of the battle, he saw his largest amount of action on 1 July when his regiment was driven back to Cemetery

Hill. He and his men fought very little for the remainder of the battle, but Underwood was commended for the bravery he exhibited on that first day.

In the early fall of 1863, Underwood and the 33d were attached to the command of Joseph Hooker when Hooker was sent with XI and XII Corps in relief of Chattanooga. At the end of October, Hooker's command was part of the effort to reopen the Tennessee River to bring in supplies to the army. In the night attack of Wauhatchie, 28–29 October 1863, Underwood led his regiment forward. During the attack, he was struck in the side of his upper thigh with a Confederate bullet. The bullet traveled through his thighbone upward, exiting through the lower part of his penis, carrying with it a piece of his thighbone, which had been shattered. Though after a considerable convalescence, Underwood recovered somewhat from the wound, the affected leg was four inches shorter than the other, giving him a permanent limp.

Hooker commended Underwood in very strong terms for the extreme bravery he displayed that night and recommended that, at the very least, Underwood should be given a promotion to brigadier general of volunteers for his gallantry. The promotion was made on 19 November 1863 with a date of rank of 6 November. After the war he was given a brevet promotion to major general for his conduct in the war.

Underwood was unable to take any active part for the remainder of the war. After receiving his brevet promotion, he was mustered out of the volunteer army and returned to his home in Boston. For most of the rest of his life he served as the surveyor of Boston's port. He died in Newton, Massachusetts, on 28 January 1888.

—David S. Heidler and Jeanne T. Heidler

See also Wauhatchie, Battle at (Brown's Ferry); Winchester, First Battle of.

For further reading:
Bates, William Carver. *Adin Ballou Underwood* (1888).

UNIFORMS, INSIGNIA, AND EQUIPMENT

When the Civil War began, both Union and Confederate forces were uniformed and equipped in a wide variety of styles, colors, and fashions. The standard uniform of the U.S. Army before the war had been a dark blue wool jacket that extended to the midthigh and a pair of sky blue wool pants with a colored stripe alongside the outside of each leg. The color of the stripe represented the branch of service: Red indicated artillery; yellow indicated cavalry; and blue indicated infantry. A black "Hardee" hat—a tall hat with a round crown and a wide brim, which was usually rolled up on the right side and fastened with a brass eagle—was the headgear. Cavalrymen and light artillerymen wore high knee-length boots, while all others wore ankle-length "Jefferson" boots. In contrast to the conformity of the regular army, the volunteer and militia regiments that mustered for service during the war displayed a wide diversity of uniform styles.

Union volunteer and militia regiments often had distinctive uniforms for regional or ethnic reasons. The Zouave uniform of the French army in North Africa was particularly popular and a great number of regiments were initially attired as such. The Zouave uniform consisted of white leggings, baggy red pants, a dark blue jacket, and a red fez. Other eccentrically clad regiments were also mustered into Union service. The 79th New York Infantry Regiment (Highlanders) was attired in Scottish kilts. The 39th New York Infantry Regiment (Garibaldi Guard) wore a uniform that was almost identical to the sharpshooters of the Italian Bersaglieri Light Infantry. The 3d New Jersey Cavalry Regiment (1st U.S. Hussars) wore European hussar-style uniforms, and the 6th Pennsylvania Cavalry Regiment (Rush's Lancers) was attired in a uniform similar to European lancers, and was initially armed with lances rather than with pistols or rifles.

By 1862 the Union took steps to bring some level of standardization to the uniforms of the army. This desire for standardization was based on two principles. First, the distinctive uniforms tended to be both expensive and highly impractical in the field. Second, the lack of conformity among uniforms often made it difficult to determine friend from foe on the battlefield. By 1863 the standard Union uniform had been largely established throughout the army. This uniform was almost identical to the prewar uniform with the exception of the Hardee hat, which was replaced by a French-style *kepi*, a military cap with a short, round, flat crown and a leather visor. Nonetheless, headgear seems to have been one of the least important aspects of the uniform as far as the U.S. Army was concerned. The wide variation in hats seems to have been predominantly a regimental decision, rather than a regional or state issue. More western regiments seem to have been equipped with the Hardee hat or other forms of headgear.

In the Confederate army, distinctive uniforms were also very popular, particularly the Zouave uniform. The supply shortage that existed in the Confederacy, however, caused most regiments to choose a much more practical uniform. The Confederate army did attempt to establish a standard uniform, which was almost identical to the standard Union uniform, but was "cadet" gray rather than dark blue. In practice, however, the shortage of material with which to produce the uniforms caused even that much standardization to be impossible. During the final years of the war in particular, Confederate soldiers were wearing completely nonstandard uniforms that had been pieced together from any possible sources, including both Union and Confederate dead. The

One variation of the Zouave uniform (Ellsworth's Zouaves) (*National Archives*)

appearance of so-called butternut uniforms was the result of dying homespun clothes in the oil of walnut or butternut trees, a consequence of the Confederate army's inability to provide standardized uniforms.

The insignia of rank used during the Civil War differed somewhat between the Union and the Confederacy. In the Union army, insignia of rank for officers was carried on shoulder straps on each shoulder. The ranks were represented as follows: the shoulder strap of a 2d lieutenant was empty; 1st lieutenant contained a silver bar; captain contained a pair of silver bars; major contained a gold oak leaf; lieutenant colonel contained a silver oak leaf; colonel contained a silver eagle; brigadier general contained a silver star; major general contained two silver stars; and lieutenant general contained three silver stars.

In the Confederate army, insignia of rank for officers was carried on the uniform collar on each side of the throat. The ranks were represented as follows: the collar of a 2d lieutenant contained a single bar; 1st lieutenant contained two bars; captain contained three bars; major contained a single star; lieutenant colonel contained two stars; colonel contained three stars; and all general officers, regardless of exact rank, contained one large star

between two smaller stars surrounded by a wreath. The noncommissioned officer insignia of rank were identical for both the Union and the Confederacy. The noncommissioned officer insignia was as follows: corporal was represented by two chevrons; sergeant was represented by three chevrons; first sergeant was represented by three chevrons topped by a diamond; ordnance sergeant was represented by three chevrons topped by a five-pointed star; quartermaster sergeant was represented by three chevrons topped by three bars; and sergeant major was represented by three chevrons topped by three rockers.

In the area of equipment, the Union and Confederate forces officially differed very little, though in practice the Confederate forces were always subject to severe shortages. An infantryman would ideally be equipped with a rifled musket, bayonet, knapsack and blanket roll, haversack, canteen, tin cup, and leather belt with percussion cap pouch and cartridge box. The equipment of a cavalryman would differ from an infantryman in that a carbine, a revolver, and a saber would replace the rifled musket and bayonet. Officers would generally be equipped with only a leather belt with a revolver, a saber, a percussion cap pouch, and a cartridge box.

—*Alexander M. Bielakowski*

For further reading:
Katcher, Philip R. N. *American Civil War Armies: Confederate Artillery, Cavalry, and Infantry* (1986).
———. *American Civil War Armies: Confederate Artillery, Cavalry, and Infantry*(1987).
Lloyd, Mark. *Combat Uniforms of the Civil War* (1990).

UNION LEAGUES

Union leagues (also called the loyal leagues or Lincoln leagues) played a sometimes vital political role in the Civil War period. These evolved through three distinct stages, originating and ending in the Southern states.

Various associations of Southern Unionists appeared with secession. By May 1861, antisecessionist clubs and associations began to take form in eastern Tennessee and western Virginia as well as in cities like Louisville, Kentucky, and St. Louis, Missouri. In the latter three of these areas, these clubs played sometimes important roles in thwarting secessionist plans. Where secession triumphed, such organizations continued as small underground cells of resistance whose destinies rose and fell counter to the prospects of the Confederacy. In eastern Tennessee, a strong Unionist underground sought to actively participate in the war through sabotage of the trans-mountain railroad, and the Confederate suppression of "bridge burners" drove large numbers of Southern whites north.

The Union leagues appeared in the North in 1862. A Unionist refugee from Tennessee participated with a handful of local men at Pekin, Illinois, in organizing what became a Republican political club. A state structure followed in Illinois and the organization spread through the Northern states by 1863. Patriotic businessmen dominated the local organizations in Chicago, Philadelphia, and other major cities and survived into the next century. However, the national Union League represented a mass of organizations based on many smaller communities where clubs espoused a particularly radical Republicanism. Within the party, the leagues constituted a coherent force for emancipation, an aggressive war policy, and other radical reform measures with regard to Reconstruction. Their power partly inspired the short-lived 1864 effort to seek a more radical Republican candidate than President Lincoln. Nevertheless, the leagues provided the shock troops for his reelection that year.

The final phase brought the flowering of these clubs in the South. The advance of Federal forces into the South created a large number of political associations among Unionists, but the character of Southern Unionism had changed with emancipation. Blacks formed a new core constituency of the loyal organizations both within and outside of Confederate lines. These new kinds of loyal leagues provided the foundations for the postwar Reconstruction governments and Republican Parties.

Generally, recent scholarship on the importance of the Union leagues has been divided. Some tend to ascribe greater importance to official responses to alleged secret societies than to the orders themselves, ascribing much to a "paranoid style" evident in American politics. Others, more unwilling to discard all such evidence, respond that erroneous assumptions about secret societies and conspiracies in one time and place hardly disprove their existence elsewhere. Insofar as the leagues expressed legitimate local concerns for the nation's survival as a republic, they had a pervasive importance on the war and its course.

—*Mark A. Lause*

See also Southern Unionism.
For further reading:
Klement, Frank L. *Dark Lanterns: Secret Political Societies, Conspiracies, and Treason Trials in the Civil War* (1984).
Silvestro, Clement M. *Rally Round the Flag: the Union Leagues in the Civil War* (1966).

UNIONISTS, SOUTHERN

Although most Southerners who opposed the Confederacy did so for reasons related to social class, Southern Unionists came from across the social spectrum and expressed themselves in a variety of ways. Many conditional Unionists, like Alexander Stephens of Georgia, opposed secession but cast their lots with the Confederacy when their states left the Union. Others, like Sam Houston and Benjamin Perry, were reluctant Confederates at best. Only when Lincoln called for 75,000 volunteers to invade the South did Houston finally decide that "the time has come when a man's section is his country." After thirty years of trying to save them from "the horrors of disunion," Perry wrote of his fellow South Carolinians, "They are now going to the devil, and I will go with them." But many Unionists were more steadfast in their opposition to the Confederacy. Andrew Johnson of Tennessee refused to give up his U.S. Senate seat after his state seceded. Francis H. Pierpont led the effort to hold Virginia's western counties for the Union and became West Virginia's first governor.

Among the most assertive of Southern Unionists was William G. "Parson" Brownlow of Tennessee. As editor of the Knoxville *Whig*, Brownlow constantly antagonized the Davis administration with his writings against the Confederacy. He was finally jailed, then banished to the North, where he continued to speak out against the legitimacy of secession and wrote *Sketches of the Rise, Progress, and Decline of Secession* (1862). When the Federals occupied Knoxville, Brownlow reopened his newspaper offices, calling his new periodical the *Whig and Rebel Ventilator*. The paper became a leading pro-Union organ for the rest of the war.

Thomas A. Watson, a Southern Unionist
(*Georgia Department of Archives and History*)

Like Brownlow, William Woods Holden ran what became one of the South's most ardent Unionist newspapers, the *North Carolina Standard,* in Raleigh. Initially more anti-Davis than pro-Union, Holden organized and led the Conservative Party that swept Zebulon Vance into the governor's office in 1862. But relations between the two men were increasingly strained as Holden became more pro-Union. Holden's efforts resulted in a series of "peace meetings" throughout the state by 1863, and Holden even threatened to lead North Carolina out of the Confederacy. So inflammatory was Holden's language that a band of Rebel soldiers sacked his newspaper office while passing through Raleigh.

As the war dragged on, more and more Southerners, particularly the common folk, turned against the Confederacy. Speculation, conscription, the "Twenty Slave Law," cotton overproduction, widespread hunger, government corruption, and impressment all undermined domestic support. When an impressment agent took two cows from a South Carolina farmer, the man swore that "the sooner this damned Government fell to pieces the better it would be for us." Nancy Mann of Harris County, Georgia, encouraged her brother to desert. "There is so much rascality carried on in this confedracy," she complained, "untill I think some times I do not no what will be come of the people and nor the confedracy and I do not care much." Mrs. T. J. Jarrell of Alabama threatened suicide unless her husband returned. Many Southern women, left with farms to run and children to raise, simply could not cope. Thousands sent letters to their absent husbands begging for help. One woman wrote of her children crying from hunger and closed her letter with, "before God, Edward, unless you come home, we must die." Such letters were among the leading causes of desertion and created, in effect, de facto Unionists.

Some of the South's most enthusiastic Unionists were blacks, both slave and free. Like most held in bondage, Louis Meadows of Alabama knew that as long as the Confederacy survived he would never be free. "That was why," Meadows said, "everybody hoped Master Lincoln would conquer." Robert Smalls, a South Carolina slave employed as wheelman on the steam ship *Planter,* led several of his fellow slaves in taking the vessel out of Charleston harbor under cover of darkness. He presented it to the Union blockade fleet, saying, "I thought the *Planter* might be of some use to Uncle Abe." Elizabeth Geary and her husband, a free black couple in Darien, Georgia, were forced to flee the town because of their candid Unionism. Several of their sons served in the Union navy. Many blacks expressed their violent opposition to the Confederacy and slavery without ever leaving home. A group of slaves in Brooks County, Georgia, conspired with a local white man, John Vickery, to take control of the county, hold it for the Union, and kill all who stood in their way. Two southeast Alabama slaves helped John Ward, leader of a local gang of white anti-Confederates, in killing their owner.

Anti-Confederate guerrilla bands composed mainly of deserters and draft dodgers were common in many parts of the South by 1864, especially the hill country and pine barrens. Though some had little ideological commitment to the Union, their anti-Confederate sentiments and marauding activities aided the Union war effort. And many were very much pro-Union. James Madison Wells of Louisiana, though a man of some wealth, denounced the Confederate cause as a rich man's war. An unreserved opponent of secession, Wells organized a guerrilla campaign against Confederate authority in Louisiana. From his "Bear Wallow" stronghold, he repeatedly led poor whites and deserters in raids against Confederate supply lines. Joseph G. Sanders, leader of a Unionist gang in southern Alabama, made his anti-Confederate status official by accepting a lieutenant's commission in the Union army.

Many others did likewise. From general officers like Winfield Scott of Virginia and Montgomery Meigs of Georgia to enlisted men like John Fuller of Russell County, Alabama, and Thomas A. Watson of Fannin County, Georgia, at least 100,000 Southern whites joined the Union military. Together with 150,000 Southern blacks who did the same, Southerners who served in uniform against the Confederacy totaled a quarter of a million.

As early as 19 July 1861, the *Richmond Examiner* warned that the South was "more rife with treason to her own independence and honour than any community that ever engaged before in a struggle with an adversary." The numbers of Southern Unionists only became greater as the war continued, ensuring that the Confederacy's collapse would be as much for internal as external reasons.

—*David Williams*

See also Brownlow, William Gannaway; Holden, William Woods; Johnson, Andrew; Peace Movements; Pierpont, Francis Harrison.

For further reading:

Current, Richard N. *Lincoln's Loyalists: Union Soldiers from the Confederacy* (1992).

Degler, Carl N. *The Other South: Southern Dissenters in the Nineteenth Century* (1974).

Meyers, Christopher C. "'The Wretch Vickery' and the Brooks County Civil War Slave Conspiracy." *Journal of Southwest Georgia History* (1997).

Quarles, Benjamin. *The Negro in the Civil War* (1953; reprint, 1989).

Tatum, Georgia Lee. *Disloyalty in the Confederacy* (1934; reprint, 1970).

Thomas, Henry W. *History of the Doles-Cook Brigade Army of Northern Virginia, C.S.A.* (1903; reprint, 1988).

Williams, David. *Rich Man's War: Class, Caste, and Confederate Defeat in the Lower Chattahoochee Valley* (1998).

UNITED DAUGHTERS OF THE CONFEDERACY

Beginning almost immediately after the war, Confederate memorial associations began commemorating the Southern war effort and the South's fallen soldiers. Devoted, and seemingly not defeated, Confederate women decorated soldiers' graves and erected monuments throughout the country in honor of the "Lost Cause." In the 1890s a group of these women formed the United Daughters of the Confederacy (UDC) in an attempt to consolidate the South's many women's commemorative groups and their activities. Only five years later, the Daughters were flourishing in every Southern state, eclipsing other Confederate organizations, including male groups like the United Confederate Veterans and the Sons of Confederate Veterans. By World War I, the UDC claimed almost 100,000 members in chapters across the nation.

When it began on 10 September 1894, the UDC built on a limited but firm foundation of women's activism established by wartime organizations like sewing clubs and soldiers' aid societies as well as postwar groups, including ladies' auxiliaries to various veterans groups and memorial, cemetery, monument, and Confederate home associations. Although in later years there was some dispute over which woman could claim the most credit for the origin of the UDC, Anna Davenport Raines of Savannah, Georgia, and Caroline M. Goodlett of Nashville, Tennessee, were indisputably at the center of discussions that led to the creation of the Daughters. The UDC arose, both Raines and Goodlett agreed, out of a fear that the rapid passing away of many of the war's veterans would result in the "passing away" of the ladies' activism as well. The best solution, as these two women saw it, was to unite Southern women under one banner (the "Cause"); one mission (the celebration of the "Old South" and the Confederacy); and the official name—The United Daughters of the Confederacy.

Basing their constitution and governmental structure on that of the United Confederate Veterans, Southern women began organizing local chapters and state divisions of the UDC. Their professed purposes were social, literary, historical, monumental, benevolent, and, above all else, honorable. Although much of the early work focused on the founding of the organization, beginning as early as 1895, the Daughters turned their attention to their "real" work: constructing countless monuments and memorials, publishing pamphlets, essays, and books written from the Southern point of view to "correct" history, establishing numerous educational scholarships for children of Confederate veterans, male and female, and distributing aid to Confederate veterans and their families. Eventually, the UDC's activism expanded beyond the cause as the Daughters contributed to U.S. war efforts during the Spanish-American and First and Second World Wars. With as much zeal as they had dedicated to the cause, the women of the UDC collected money, rolled bandages, and provided other relief services to U.S. servicemen.

Although their constitution and rhetoric claimed an allegiance to notions of proper womanhood in which women were supposed to be confined within the home, the very foundation and scope of the UDC, like other women's organizations of the nineteenth and early twentieth centuries, required members to participate in such "unwomanly endeavors" and serious activities as the process of incorporation, the maintenance of a budget, parliamentary procedure, constitution making, and public speaking. Moreover, women, who previously had operated only within the private sphere, petitioned and appeared before state legislatures, lobbied city councils and other government committees in their individual communities, and wrote to various governors and state congressmen to accomplish the UDC's goals.

Membership in women's associations in the South from the Civil War period up through the birth of the UDC provided women with administrative and organizational experience and created an autonomous space for them in which they wielded total power, independent of male control. And while some women who joined the UDC were motivated solely by their love of the Confederacy and avowed hatred of the Yankees, "who

had exposed their vulnerability and denied them respect," others joined because they enjoyed being part of a community of women and relished the responsibilities and autonomy that it afforded. When viewed by today's standards, the UDC seems a very conservative organization. However, during its heyday it contributed to an increase in women's sphere of activities and the arrival of feminism in the South, a region long known for its traditional gender prescriptions.

—*Jennifer L. Gross*

See also Ladies Memorial Associations; Memorials, C.S.A.; Sons of Confederate Veterans; Women.

For further reading:

Bailey, Fred. "The Textbooks of the Lost Cause: Censorship and the Creation of Southern State Histories." *The Georgia Historical Quarterly* (1991).

Cox, Karen Lynne. "Women, the Lost Cause, and the New South: The United Daughters of the Confederacy and the Transmission of Confederate Culture, 1894–1919" (Ph.D. dissertation, 1997).

Foster, Gaines M. *Ghosts of the Confederacy: Defeat, the Lost Cause, and the Emergence of the New South, 1865–1913* (1987).

Gulley, H. E. "Women and the Lost Cause: Preserving a Confederate Identity in the American Deep South." *Journal of Historical Geography* (1993).

LaCavera, Tommie Phillips. *History of the Georgia Division, of the United Daughters of the Confederacy, 1895–1995* (1995).

Parrott, Angie. "'Love Makes Memory Eternal': The United Daughters of the Confederacy in Richmond, Virginia, 1897–1920," in Edward L. Ayers and John C. Willis (eds.), *The Edge of the South: Life in Nineteenth-Century Virginia* (1991).

Poppenheim, Mary B., et al. *The History of the United Daughters of the Confederacy* (1938).

Wilson, Charles Reagan. *Baptized in Blood: The Religion of the Lost Cause, 1865–1920* (1980).

UNITED STATES CHRISTIAN COMMISSION
(1861–1865)

In the autumn of 1861, the New York Young Men's Christian Association issued a call to all evangelical groups to form an umbrella organization in which the Union soldiers could receive pastoral care. At a conference held in Philadelphia in November of that year, the participants formed the United States Christian Commission and elected as its first and only president, George H. Stuart, a wealthy Philadelphia merchant and Presbyterian layman.

Maimed soldiers and others at the U.S. Christian Commission, Washington, D.C., April 1865 (*Library of Congress*)

U.S. Christian Commission field headquarters near Germantown, Maryland, September 1863
(Photograph by Alexander Gardner / *Library of Congress*)

The commission later established its national headquarters in Stuart's business establishment.

The Christian Commission organized on eight foundational principles: catholicity, nationality, voluntarism, benefits for the body and soul, reliance upon unpaid delegates, personal distribution and personal ministrations, cooperation (especially with chaplains and surgeons), and a respect for authority.

The structure of the Christian Commission grew out of its experience in the field. The administration consisted of a general commission, an executive committee, home secretary, field secretary, permanent field agents, branch commissions, ladies commissions, and short-term missionaries or delegates.

The ideal of personal accountability dominated the governance and discipline of the Christian Commission's representatives. The field personnel received instructions not to interfere with military authorities and they were warned of dismissal for either personal or private misbehavior. Upon acceptance of a commission, the delegates agreed to report to an agent in charge of a geographical area, to go where assigned, and to continue in the work until relieved by another delegate.

Throughout the war, an executive committee ran the daily affairs of the commission. As the war dragged on and the size of the armies grew, the Christian Commission increased in size to keep pace with demand. The executive committee also expanded from twelve to fifty-five members.

Below the executive committee served ministers, called station agents. Some station agents ministered to army corps, and others served in larger cities or near theaters of operations. Station agents monitored the activities of the delegates.

Several auxiliary groups, such as branch commissions and ladies commissions, also served. Branch commissions served as the public relations and fund-raising arm of the Christian Commission. Though the branch commissions remained largely autonomous, they labored under the authority of the national group and functioned within its organizational structure. Ladies' commissions also raised funds for the war effort, but their support came in more direct ways, such as preparing clothes, foods, and gifts for distribution by the field workers, known as the delegates.

An example of the ladies' commission contributions can be seen in the work of Mrs. Annie Wittenmyer. Wittenmyer became concerned about the soldiers' diets after witnessing the wretched conditions and fare of the soldiers in Missouri. The Lincoln administration approved her work and, with the help of Reverend E. P. Smith, agent for the commission in the west, the first kitchen was established in Cumberland Hospital in Nashville, Tennessee. In a short time the army consumed a healthier diet and those who had special dietary needs were able to receive the fare they required.

According to the final report of the Christian Commission issued in 1866, the ladies' commissions numbered 266, were located in seventeen states of the Union, and raised over $200,000 in funds.

Armed with a memo book, instructions, food, bedding, utensils, and publications of various genres, the delegates or field representatives of the commission labored for an average of thirty-eight days. Official

enlistment required membership in an evangelical church and the endorsement of a clergyman. Delegates traveled wherever needed, took charge of all supplies sent, and aided the surgeons and chaplains as requested. The tasks of delegates were twofold: to aid the chaplains in their direct pastoral and evangelistic work and to perform acts of mercy in Christ's name. President Stuart noted that "there is a good deal of religion in a warm shirt and a good beefsteak." Delegates acted as nurses, social workers, librarians, postmen, worship leaders, lay ministers, and directors of burial details. By the end of hostilities, more than 5,000 delegates—all of them unpaid volunteers—had provided selfless service in the Union army's camps. The delegates remained the backbone of the Christian Commission's ministry.

The Christian Commission leadership cultivated the support of the Lincoln administration, which in turn recognized the commission's positive impact on troop morale. General Grant, while campaigning in the Western theater, gave the Christian commission free access to his men. When Grant came east, the Christian Commission found even greater access to the men of his new command. A few generals, notably William T. Sherman, did not approve of civilians traveling with his army; Sherman believed the civilians hampered military operations.

The Christian Commission drew on the financial resources of every element in Northern society, both religious and secular. By the war's end, the commission's leaders spent over $6 million—more than $2.5 million in cash and more than $3 million in supplies.

The commission's original mission was to aid the chaplains in their daily work. Early in the war the Union armies suffered from a shortage of available and qualified chaplains. In units without chaplains, the delegates stepped up and served as quasi-military pastors. Where chaplains did serve, the commission kept them supplied in tracts and Bibles. The delegates succeeded in distributing 1.5 million Bibles, 1 million hymnals, and 39 million tracts. They also preached over 58,000 sermons, led 77,000 prayer meetings, and wrote over 92,000 letters on behalf of the soldiers. The Christian Commission's personal service to the sick, dying, and bereaved cannot be measured.

—*James S. Baugess*

See also Chaplains; Churches; Religion; United States Sanitary Commission; Wittenmyer, Annie.

For further reading:

Henry, Joseph O. "The United States Christian Commission in the Civil War." *Civil War History* (1960).

Moss, Lemuel. *Annals of the United States Christian Commission* (1868).

Shattuck, Gardiner H., Jr. *A Shield and Hiding Place: The Religious Life of the Civil War Armies* (1985).

United States Christian Commission. *Address of the Christian Commission* (1862).

———. *Christian Commission for the Army and Navy of the United States of America* (1862).

UNITED STATES COLORED TROOPS

By incorporating the United States Colored Troops (USCT) into the Union army, the Lincoln administration bolstered its war effort with additional manpower. This revolutionary move strengthened African-American demands for equal rights by giving blacks a chance to prove their courage and patriotism. It also inflamed Confederate racial fears, inspiring a string of atrocities and reprisals that intensified the savagery exhibited by both sides.

When the Civil War began, Abraham Lincoln rejected any thought of abolishing slavery or tapping black military assistance. He feared that such policies would alienate the border states, arouse the prejudices of Northern whites, and stiffen Confederate resistance. By the summer of 1862, however, Lincoln had come to realize that one way to weaken an unexpectedly resilient Confederacy was to undermine slavery. He also looked the other way as isolated Union commanders started forming black units to augment their forces in Kansas and occupied portions of Louisiana and South Carolina.

Lincoln inserted a guarded endorsement for arming African-Americans in his Emancipation Proclamation, which was promulgated on 1 January 1863. The Union army soon launched a vigorous recruitment drive that ultimately raised 166 black regiments, 145 of infantry, 7 of cavalry, 12 of heavy artillery, 1 of light artillery, and 1 of engineers. A total of 7,122 officers and 178,895 enlisted men served in the USCT. More than 80 percent of the rank and file came from Confederate states, and most were former slaves.

On 22 May 1863, the Union War Department established the Bureau of Colored Troops to oversee black recruitment and assemble examining boards to screen applicants for commissions in black regiments. The vast majority of USCT officers were white. Only about 110 African-Americans obtained commissions, and more than 70 of them were harassed by their own superiors until they resigned. This surrender to racial prejudice sprang from the recognition that few white Union soldiers would willingly take orders from black officers. Ironically, racially biased officer procurement provided black regiments with a higher quality of leadership than that originally enjoyed by their white counterparts. Ninety percent of the USCT's white officers were combat veterans, and most obtained their commissions after passing rigorous examinations. Because the creation of black regiments increased the likelihood of promotion, white junior officers and enlisted men throughout the Union army came to accept the experiment as a sensible war measure.

Even so, black soldiers encountered discrimination in various forms from the very government they sought to preserve. All black enlisted men, including noncommissioned officers, were paid $10.00 a month, $3.00 less than white privates. As a further insult, black soldiers

The 26th U.S. Colored Volunteer Infantry on parade at Camp William Penn, Pennsylvania, 1865 (*National Archives*)

had $3.00 deducted from their monthly pay to cover the cost of their clothing. Congress voted equal pay for the USCT on 15 June 1864, but the pay increase applied only to men who had been free at the war's start. This petty restriction remained in force until 3 March 1865.

In addition to discrepancies in pay, black soldiers usually had to perform a greater share of fatigue duty than their white comrades. Many Union generals thought USCT units should be used exclusively as labor and garrison battalions. When African-American troops were finally thrust into combat, they often carried inferior weapons. Furthermore, black regiments lost 29,000 dead to disease, nine times as many as perished from wounds and a much higher proportion than the number of white troops who died in Union hospitals. Part of the problem was that Federal commanders tended to assign USCT units to their most unhealthy posts. Regardless of where they served, African-American soldiers had to put up with inferior medical facilities and care.

As if the USCT did not suffer enough slights at the hands of the Union army, they faced extra peril whenever they met the enemy on the battlefield. Confederate officials warned that captured black soldiers would be reenslaved or executed and that USCT officers could expect treatment as war criminals for allegedly fomenting servile insurrection. President Lincoln threatened to retaliate against Confederate prisoners of war, which caused authorities at Richmond to back away from their draconian policy. Nevertheless, nothing could stop some Confederate commands from murdering any black Federals who fell into their hands. Atrocities bred reprisals as some USCT regiments refused to spare captured Confederates.

By the end of the Civil War, African-Americans composed 12 percent of the Union army. They had participated in 41 major battles and 449 smaller actions. Thirty-seven thousand black soldiers died in service. Sixteen received the Medal of Honor, and many others performed unrecognized feats of valor and endurance that contributed materially to the destruction of the Confederacy.

—*Gregory J. W. Urwin*

See also Emancipation Proclamation.

For further reading:
Cornish, Dudley Taylor. *The Sable Arm: Negro Troops in the Union Army, 1861–1865* (1966).

Gladstone, William A. *Men of Color* (1993).

Glatthaar, Joseph T. *Forged in Battle: The Civil War Alliance of Black Soldiers and White Officers* (1990).

Hollandsworth, James G. *The Louisiana Native Guards: The Black Military Experience during the Civil War* (1995).

Miller, Edward A., Jr. *The Black Civil War Soldiers of Illinois: The Story of the Twenty-ninth U.S. Colored Infantry* (1998).

UNITED STATES SANITARY COMMISSION

The explosive growth of the United States Army during the summer of 1861 inspired a small group of Northern civilians to develop an organization dedicated to providing medical care, supplies, and other comforts and necessities to soldiers in the field. During the next four years, the United States Sanitary Commission (USSC) raised at least $7 million and distributed supplies worth $15 million. Combining the antebellum reform spirit with a wartime emphasis on centralization and professionalization, the USSC built and administered hospitals and soldiers' lodging houses; recruited nurses, doctors, and ambulance drivers; and provided blankets and stationery, delivered telegrams and letters, and helped soldiers apply for disability pensions. To do this, the commission formed 7,000 aid societies, organized branches in ten cities—including the Northwestern Branch, located in Chicago—and employed hundreds of paid agents.

Although tens of thousands of women performed the bulk of the commission's work at the local level, it was led at the national level by men from the highest ranks of society. Its president was Henry W. Bellows, a Unitarian minister, while the conservative New York lawyer George Templeton Strong served as treasurer, and Frederick Law Olmsted was secretary. Rejecting the idealism of antebellum reformers, the men who set commission policy insisted on practical reform, on administering an organization that paid its own way, on setting measurable, hard-headed goals. Bellows condemned Northerners whose "ideal or abstract aspirations," while sometimes concealed in religious or philanthropic terms, were "nevertheless revolutionary and anarchical." More specifically, one supporter claimed that the purpose of the commission was "neither humanity nor charity," but "to economize for the National service the life and strength of the National soldier." As a large, centrally administered organization dedicated to practical objects, the commission was seen at least by some of its leaders apparently as a way to educate Americans about the value of order, of the importance of sacrifice as a moral lesson, and of the necessity of discipline in modern society.

Not all volunteers in the thousands of local branches

Sanitary Commission Home Lodge for Invalid Soldiers, Washington, D.C., April 1865 (*Library of Congress*)

Nurses and officers of the United States Sanitary Commission at Fredericksburg, Virgina, during the Wilderness Campaign
(Photograph by Alexander Gardner/ *Library of Congress*)

who performed the bulk of the work for the commission necessarily agreed with their leaders. Dorothea Dix squabbled constantly with the administrators in New York, who held her empathetic approach to wartime volunteerism in contempt. Also erupting were controversies over the increasing bureaucratization of the commission's operations, the high overhead that ate up precious dollars, and the seemingly mercenary attitudes displayed by the agents sent out by the central office to raise funds and to buy and distribute supplies. Walt Whitman, for one, believed that they undermined the

spirit of philanthropy required by the national emergency. "They seem to me always a set of foxes & wolves," wrote the sometime volunteer in army hospitals. That was, of course, the point: the men of the USSC's central office believed they did know better than most Americans about how to face the great challenge of civil war. They also felt free to advise the government on a wide range of matters, involving themselves in discussions of the plight of Union and Confederate prisoners of war and the postwar treatment of disabled soldiers.

Despite the distrust of the tiny elite controlling the

commission's policies for the spontaneous benevolence of the general public, most of the men, women, and children who pitched in as volunteers were, indeed, acting out of unabashed compassion and enthusiasm. Local women's organizations and soldiers' aid societies eagerly attached their own work to the commission's. Building on long-time Northern traditions of church, school, and community "fairs" to raise money for benevolent projects, the commission staged giant "Sanitary Fairs" in cities large and small, from Damariscotta, Maine, to Dubuque, Iowa, and from New York City and Brooklyn to Cincinnati and St. Louis. The Northwestern Branch held the first fair in the fall of 1863—it held another in May 1865—and provided the model for the fairs organized over the next two years. Schools and businesses closed for the day, allowing tens of thousands of people, young and old, to elbow their way into the dozens of displays, exhibits, and shops. The fairs, which generally lasted ten days to two weeks, raised money in several ways: by charging admission; by soliciting cash donations; by selling a huge range of crafts, toys, and baked goods and other food products; and by sponsoring amateur theatricals and tableaux, and singing and gymnastics demonstrations by schoolchildren. Regular features at the fairs included tables or booths displaying and selling arts, crafts, and snacks peculiar to individual Northern states. Many had "New England Kitchens," while most included displays of little girls dressed as "The Old Lady Who Lived in a Shoe" surrounded by dolls that were, of course for sale. Rooms were packed with Union and Confederate flags; battlefield artifacts such as captured guns, swords, and splinters from famous ships; and famous documents—a draft of President Lincoln's Emancipation Proclamation was auctioned off for $3,000 at the Chicago fair in 1863. Many fairs published their own newspapers, like Albany's *Canteen* and Brooklyn's *Drumbeat*, which listed hundreds of contributors, ranging from the economic and political elite to lowly residents of orphanages and members of Sabbath school classes. All told, the fairs raised more than $4 million and provided a significant percentage of the commission's budget.

One of the long-term effects of the USSC was to cast philanthropy as a business proposition administered increasingly by professional fund raisers and case workers. Yet it was probably better known as the most recognizable charitable organization devoted to the welfare of the soldiers saving the Union.

—*James Marten*

See also Bellows, Henry W.; Dix, Dorothea; Olmsted, Frederick Law; Strong, George Templeton.

For further reading

Frederickson, George M. *The Inner Civil War: Northern Intellectuals and the Crisis of the Union* (1965).

Gordon, Beverly. "A Furor of Benevolence." *Chicago History* (1986–1987).

Maxwell, William Quentin. *Lincoln's Fifth Wheel: The Political History of the United States Sanitary Commission* (1956).

Paludan, Phillip. "*A People's Contest": The Union and Civil War, 1861–1865* (1988).

Thompson, William Y. "Sanitary Fairs of the Civil War." *Civil War History* (1958).

UPTON, EMORY
(1839–1881)
Union officer and army reformer

Emory Upton was born on 27 August 1839 on a farm near Batavia, New York. The sixth son of Daniel and Electra Randall Upton, he imbibed a strong moral sense from his parents, a tendency strengthened when he attended abolitionist Oberlin College in 1855–1856. In 1856 he accepted an appointment to the United States Military Academy at West Point, where he proved to be an excellent student. While at the academy he maintained his strong moral sentiments, including loyalty to the Union and the contentious cause of abolitionism.

Graduating eighth in his class of forty-five on 6 May 1861, he was commissioned second lieutenant of artillery and sent to the nation's capital to drill Federal volunteers pouring into the city. Shortly thereafter, he was appointed first lieutenant with the 5th Artillery Regiment, until ordered to active service in the field as part of General Irvin McDowell's army in northern Virginia.

Advancing in rank to brevet major general for outstanding service through numerous battles in the Eastern theater of war, Upton proved his battlefield merit in all three branches of the army (artillery, infantry, and cavalry): at First Bull Run (July 1861); during the Peninsula campaign (March–August 1862); at Crampton's Gap and Antietam (September 1862); at Fredericksburg (December 1862); at Gettysburg (July 1863), there leading a thirty-five-mile march to Little Round Top from Manchester, Maryland, on the night of 1–2 July; at Rappahannock Station (November 1863) as a brigade commander; at Spotsylvania Court House (May 1864), where he was promoted to brigadier general by General Ulysses S. Grant for his tactical brilliance at the Mule Shoe, the "Bloody Angle," by launching an attack by a three-regiment successive column, rather than by accepted linear movement; at Cold Harbor (June 1864); at Winchester in the Shenandoah Valley (September 1864), after which he was given command of the First Division, VI Army Corps as breveted major general; and, under Major General James H. Wilson, at Selma, Alabama, and Columbus, Georgia, (April 1865) in command of the 4th Cavalry Division.

Reduced to the regular rank of captain after Appomattox, after short assignments in Tennessee and the District of Colorado, Upton was assigned to West Point as a member of a board to consider his new system of infantry tactics, approved in 1867. Securing a leave of

Upton's Brigade at the Bloody Angle during the battle of Spotsylvania, May 1864 (*Library of Congress*)

absence, he spent some months in Europe before returning to regular army duty. From July 1870 through June 1875, he served as commandant of cadets at West Point, as well as instructor in infantry, artillery, and cavalry tactics.

In 1875 he was assigned by General William T. Sherman, the commanding general of the U.S. Army, to tour Europe and Asia to study military organizations in these parts of the world. He did so, and while in Shanghai in 1876 constructed a plan for a military academy in China. Returning to the United States, Upton was appointed superintendent of theoretical instruction at the Artillery School of Practice located at Fort Monroe, Virginia. Here he emphasized combined arms tactics. In 1880 he was transferred to the Presidio of San Francisco to command the 4th Artillery Regiment. There, on 15 March 1881, this model soldier and influential army reformer took his own life—probably while mentally deranged from extreme pain caused by "chronic catarrh"—after writing out his resignation as

colonel the day before. He was buried at Auburn, New York, on 29 March 1881.

Often considered the U.S. Army's counterpart to the U.S. Navy reformer Alfred Thayer Mahan, the abstemious and single-minded Upton published two books on tactics and military history during his brief lifetime: *A New System of Infantry Tactics, Double and Single Rank, Adapted to American Topography and Improved Firearms* (1867, revised 1874) and *The Armies of Asia and Europe* (1878), the latter ending with fifty-four pages of recommendations as to how the United States Army and the nation's military policies should be changed.

Of greatest impact, however, was his "The Military Policy of the United States from 1775," over which he had labored for years and had completed through the second year of the Civil War. Widely circulated among military circles in manuscript form, in 1903–1904 it was read by Secretary of War Elihu Root. Root ordered it printed in 1904 under the title *The Military Policy of the United States*. This measured analysis of American military policies and practices and first systematic examination of the nation's military history had a tremendous impact upon the army. In the book Upton advocated such reforms as maneuvering by groups of four three-battalion infantry regiments, the adoption of a general staff system on the Prussian model, compulsory retirement of officers at a certain age, examinations to determine promotion, advanced military education, the end of paying bounties for enlistment, and the expansible army concept of regular cadres supplemented by volunteers or conscripts in time of war.

Emory Upton's battlefield deeds during the Civil War and his cogent analysis of needed changes in army policies and practices remain as monuments to him as a model officer and reformer.

—James M. Morris

See also Spotsylvania.

For further reading:

Ambrose, Stephen E. *Upton and the Army* (1964).

Brown, Richard C. "Emory Upton, The Army's Mahan." *Military Affairs* (1953).

Michie, Peter Smith. *Life and Letters of General Emory Upton* (1885).

Upton, Emory. *The Military Policy of the United States* (1904).

———. *A New System of Infantry Tactics: Double and Single Ranks* (1867).

Walker, Wallace E. "Emory Upton and the Army's Officer's Creed." *Military Review* (1981)

UTOY CREEK, BATTLE OF
(6–7 August 1864)

After the battle of Bald Hill (also called the battle of Atlanta) on 22 July, Major General William T. Sherman ordered his Union troops to shift counterclockwise and west of Atlanta. His objective was to capture the last railroad junction held by the Confederate forces and thereby cut the last supply line into the beleaguered city. Southern forces under the command of General John Bell Hood had temporarily checked this federal westward movement at the battle of Ezra Church on 28 July but, in doing so, incurred heavy causalities. In early August, Sherman ordered the Army of the Ohio, under the command of General John M. Schofield, to continue the Federal flanking movement to the west and south in a second attempt to capture the railroad junction at East Point, Georgia, five miles south and west of Atlanta.

Hood, aware of the continued Union effort, reinforced his earthworks around the railroad junction and prepared for a Union assault. On 4 August, Sherman directed the Army of the Ohio, reinforced with General John M. Palmer's XIV Corps from the Army of the Cumberland, to breakthrough the Confederate earthworks near the junction of the Sandtown Road and Utoy Creek, two miles west of the East Point railway junction. The remaining Union forces, the Army of the Tennessee and Army of the Cumberland, would demonstrate up and down Federal lines in support of Schofield's attack. The attack was to commence on 5 August, but a dispute erupted between Generals Schofield and Palmer over the command structure of the joint attacking force, thereby delaying the assault by one day. On the night of 5 August, Confederate forces were heard chopping trees and strengthening their fortifications near Sandtown Road and Utoy Creek.

The command dispute finally resolved, Federal forces attacked early on 6 August. General Schofield sent Jacob D. Cox's division southward toward Hood's left near the Sandtown Road. Milo Hascall's division was to support Cox on his right, while two divisions from Palmer's XIV Corps were to occupy the rebel right with skirmish and artillery fire. At 10:00 A.M., Union forces under Cox had pushed back Confederate pickets near the Sandtown Road and were beginning to come up against the first line of Confederate entrenchments. The Southern soldiers had entrenched along a ridge east of Utoy Creek near the Sandtown Road. The defenders, William B. Bate's division of Stephen D. Lee's corps, had erected a web of abatis and earthworks. The Confederates were aided by a tangle of thick underbrush that made the slow-moving Northern attackers easy targets. The Federals fell back with heavy losses. Units regrouped, attacked again, and once more were repulsed. A third time the Northern soldiers advanced into the buzz saw of canister and minié balls. Their advance came to a halt twenty-five yards from the Confederate trenches and was again repelled. Cox informed Schofield that a successful assault across this portion of the creek was impossible due to enemy forces and terrain. In late afternoon, after the Confederate right had repulsed the Union troops under Cox, the extreme left of the rebel line came under assault by Union forces led by Hascall. Union troops gained an initial advantage, pushing back Southern cavalry and one artillery battery, but as the Federals attempted to turn the Confederate southern flank, darkness and a rainstorm brought the advance to a halt.

During the night of 6 August, Southern forces retreated into the main line of trenches just west of the railroad connecting Atlanta and East Point. The next morning, hoping to continue the flanking movement of the previous day, Hascall's division again attempted to move west and south, but he and his men came upon the main Confederate fortifications. Hascall informed Schofield that the enemy's obstacles extended southwest as far as the eye could see and success could not be expected. By late afternoon of the 7th, Sherman ordered Schofield to break off the attack and dig in just west of the Sandtown Road and Utoy Creek.

The battle of Utoy Creek caused the Union 306 casualties. Confederate losses were less than 100. Sherman's failure to out flank the Southern forces at Ezra Church and Utoy Creek and capture the only supply line into the city brought an alteration in his strategy. He informed General Henry W. Halleck in Washington, that in the future he would press the Rebels along their entire line, each day pounding the enemy with artillery and pressing them with infantry assault.

—*Franklin Forts*

See also Atlanta Campaign; Ezra Church, Battle of.
For further reading:
Castel, Albert E. *Decision in the West: The Atlanta Campaign of 1864* (1992).

Connelly, Thomas L. *Autumn of Glory: The Army of Tennessee, 1862–1865* (1971).
McDonough, James L., and James Pickett Jones. *War So Terrible: Sherman and Atlanta* (1987).
McMurry, Richard M. *John Bell Hood and the War for Southern Independence* (1982).
Savas, Theodore P., and David A. Woodbury, eds. *The Campaign for Atlanta & Sherman's March to the Sea: Essays on the American Civil War in Georgia, 1864* (1994).

VAL VERDE, NEW MEXICO, BATTLE OF
(21 February 1862)

The small engagement at Val Verde, New Mexico, occurred five miles north of Fort Craig, New Mexico, and was the first major encounter between U.S. and Confederate troops in the Far West.

The previous summer and fall, Confederate forces had been heading west out of San Antonio, Texas, intent upon seizing all of New Mexico Territory, preparatory to a larger-scale invasion of the western portions of the United States. Ultimately, Confederate forces hope to capture Colorado and California. When Texan soldiers under the command of Lieutenant Colonel John Robert Baylor rode into the southern New Mexico towns of Mesilla, Doña Ana, and Tucson, the residents proclaimed the Confederate Territory of Arizona and moved to attach themselves politically to that nation. In early February 1862, a heavily reinforced Southern force, some 3,000 men under the command of Brigadier General Henry Hopkins Sibley, pushed north from encampments around Mesilla intent on capturing the key Union position at Fort Craig. Once this point had been taken, Confederates planned to move on and take the cities of Albuquerque and Santa Fe.

Defending this gateway to New Mexico were just over 1,000 U.S. regulars, supported by an equal number of volunteers and militia under Colonel Edward R. S. Canby. After strengthening the defenses of Fort Craig, Canby laid in a large quantity of supplies, determined to outlast his Rebel opponents, whom he knew would not have artillery capable of breaching the post's adobe walls. His strategy was simply to force the Confederates to fritter away time and supplies that they could not replace. Meanwhile, Canby sent for reinforcements from Colorado, California, and Kansas.

The Confederates began their approaches to Fort Craig on 15 February, but they soon realized that they could not force the Federals into the decisive engagement that Sibley needed. Frustrated, the Texans decided to swing east of the post, across the difficult Rio Grande and through a trackless area of sandy ravines, and to threaten Canby's communications with the rest of the territory by seizing the Val Verde fords above the looming Mesa de la Contadera.

Canby ordered his men to observe the Texans, but made no major moves to keep them from their task. On 21 February, some of his subordinates precipitated the battle by attacking the vanguard of the Texan force as it reached the fords. Both sides reinforced until both Sibley and Canby had committed their troops to a decisive showdown. The Federals pushed their troops across the river, pinned the Texans in a shallow ravine, and appeared ready to carry the day. Sibley, incapacitated due to a chronic illness, turned over command to his senior colonel, Tom Green.

Seeing that his position was about to be flanked, Green decided upon a bold strategy. Abandoning his threatened left to its fate, he massed his forces on the right and charged what he correctly identified as the key to the Union line, Captain Alexander McCrae's five-gun battery. After a brief struggle, the Confederates prevailed, driving the Federals from the field and into the defenses of Fort Craig.

The Confederates had forced battle upon their enemy, but the results were indecisive. Both sides were bloodied—each lost between 10 and 15 percent of those engaged—but neither had gained an advantage. Canby and his men remained snug inside their fort, while Sibley's men, with only three days' rations left, faced the hard choices of either retreat or continuing the campaign but leaving a potent enemy between them and Texas. Sibley decided on the latter course, and within weeks the Texans had captured Albuquerque and Santa Fe.

—*Donald S. Frazier*

See also Canby, Edward R. S.; Fort Craig; New Mexico; Sibley, Henry Hopkins.

For further reading:
Alberts, Don E. *Rebels on the Rio Grande* (1985).
Frazier, Donald S. *Blood and Treasure: Confederate Empire in the Southwest* (1995).
Taylor, John. *Bloody Valverde: A Civil War Battle on the Rio Grande, February 21, 1862* (1995).

VALLANDIGHAM, CLEMENT LAIRD
(1820–1871)

Peace Democrat and Copperhead

Clement Vallandigham was born on 29 July 1820 in New Lisbon, Ohio, the son of Presbyterian minister Clement Vallandigham and a Scottish-Irish mother, Rebecca Laird. Described as a "high-spir-

ited" and "self-willed" individual, the younger Vallandigham attended the New Lisbon Academy established by his father. In 1837 he entered Jefferson College (now Washington and Jefferson College), Cannonsburg, Pennsylvania. His strong academic skills and persistence enabled him to enter as a junior. In 1838, seeking a new challenge, he left to teach school at Snow Hill, Maryland. Two years later, he returned to Jefferson. He engaged in a heated argument with the college president over matters involving constitutional law and left without his degree. In 1842, after studying law on his own for two years, he was admitted to the Ohio bar.

A skilled lawyer and effective orator, Vallandigham became the youngest member elected to the Ohio legislature in 1845. Upon reelection the following year, he was chosen speaker of the house. In 1847 he formed a law partnership with Thomas J. S. Smith at Dayton, Ohio. On 27 August of that year he married Louisa A. McMahon. They had two sons. For two years he was also part owner and editor of the Dayton *Empire*.

Although he disapproved of slavery on moral and political grounds, Vallandigham was enamored of Southern society, home of his paternal ancestors. Opposed to a strong national army and centralized government, he volunteered his services as an officer in the Ohio militia and rose to the rank of brigadier general in 1857. Before the Civil War, he addressed a number of politically explosive issues: support for the Mexican-American War, opposition to the Wilmot Proviso, and praise for the Compromise of 1850. First and foremost, he was a strict constructionist and longed for a return to Jeffersonian states' rights. He was highly critical of abolitionists, whom he charged were the real forces behind disunion.

His entry on the national political level was rocky. In 1852 his run for U.S. Congress was sidetracked by the abolitionists and the Liberty Party. In 1854 he again met defeat at the hand of the Know-Nothings. However, after accusing the Republicans of being instigators of sectionalism and leading the nation toward civil war, he was elected to the House of Representatives in 1858. From 1858 to 1862 he spoke out against war and the disruption of the Union. In 1859 he criticized the tariff of 1857 as a means to placate manufacturing interests and condemned John Brown's raid at Harper's Ferry, Virginia, calling it a conspiracy to destroy the peace and stability of the nation. He criticized both sectionalists and ultraists. In 1860, as secretary of the Democratic National Committee, he supported Stephen A. Douglas's presidential bid despite his own personal opposition to popular sovereignty. Despised by Republican colleagues in the House, Vallandigham's 1862 call for the restoration of peace, no matter what the terms, led to charges of suspected treason. He was defeated in the fall elections that year.

Many Northerners tired of war considered Vallandigham "the true apostle of liberty." By Ohioans, as well as peace supporters in the Northwest, he was anointed leader of the Peace Democrats, or Copperheads. Although derivation of the name "Copperheads" remains uncertain—either from a snake or from buttons cut from copper coins depicting the god of liberty—Peace Democrats advocated a compromise with the Confederacy. Vallandigham's forces objected to the North's vigorous prosecution of the war on the belief that a conquest of the Confederacy was illegal or impossible. In a speech delivered before the House on 14 January 1863, Vallandigham warned that a prolonged war would cause the Northwest to join forces with the South and that the time had now arrived for a negotiated peace. His influence grew as pro-Southern elements, numbering between 200,000 and 300,000 and calling themselves the Sons of Liberty, would later appoint him supreme commander in 1864.

In the spring of 1863, General Ambrose E. Burnside issued General Order No. 38. The order warned Peace Democrats that sympathy for the enemy would no longer be permitted in the Military District of Ohio. Vallandigham defied the order in speeches delivered at Columbus and Mount Vernon, and on 5 May 1863 he was arrested. He was tried and convicted by a military tribunal in Cincinnati. The charge was "expressing treasonable sympathy." He was sentenced to Federal imprisonment at Fort Warren for the duration of the war, but President Lincoln banished him to the Confederacy on 25 May. He went South, but soon relocated to Windsor, Ontario, in August.

In February 1864 Vallandigham appealed his conviction to the U.S. Supreme Court. His petition was denied for lack of jurisdiction. The Court ruled (later challenged in *Ex Parte Milligan*, 1866) that it had no authority to issue a writ of habeas corpus to a military commission. Support for Vallandigham remained strong, especially in Ohio and the border states. Backed by the Sons of Liberty, he returned to the United States that year. He gave speeches in Hamilton and Dayton, Ohio, and conducted a speaking tour in Chicago. While in the North, he criticized "King Lincoln" and publicly spat upon General Order No. 38. Lincoln chose to ignore his return in order not to focus further attention on his actions. In 1864 Vallandigham helped write the Democratic Party National Platform. However, his resolution arguing that war was a failure and calling for an immediate end to hostilities spelled defeat for the party.

Union military victories and opposition by Northern governors ended Vallandigham's and the Peace Democrats' influence. In 1867 Vallandigham entered the Ohio state elections, but Democratic leaders refused to select him as a senatorial candidate. The next year, he played a minor role in writing the party's national platform. During Reconstruction he finally accepted the outcome of the war. Passionate about political realities, he now sought to bridge differences between Democrats and Republicans. He did not live to see the movement that he helped spawn take shape in 1872 as the Liberal Republican Party. On 17 June 1871, while defending the accused in an Ohio murder case, he accidentally killed himself attempting to show a friend how the victim had been shot.

—*Charles F. Howlett*

See also Copperheads; Peace Democrats.
For further reading:
Benton, Elbert J. *The Movement for Peace without Victory during the Civil War* (1918).
Hubbart, Henry Clyde. "'Pro-Southern' Influences in the Free West, 1840–1865." *Mississippi Valley Historical Review* (1933).
Kirkland, Edward Chase. *The Peacemakers of 1864* (1927).
Klement, Frank L. *The Limits of Dissent: Clement L. Vallandigham and the Civil War* (1970).
Long, Roger. "Copperhead Clement Vallandigham." *Civil War Times Illustrated* (1981).

VAN CLEVE, HORATIO PHILLIPS
(1809–1891)
Union general

Horatio Van Cleve served in the Western theater with the Army of the Cumberland before his disgrace at the battle of Chickamauga. That battle effectively ended his military career.

Born in New Jersey, Van Cleve attended West Point and graduated in the class of 1831, ranking twenty-fourth of thirty-three cadets. He received his commission in the infantry and served on the western frontier until he resigned in 1836. He farmed in Michigan and Minnesota and served at various times as a teacher, civil engineer, and surveyor.

Van Cleve volunteered his services to the federal government when the war came. Because of his West Point education, he received a commission as colonel of the 2d Minnesota Regiment in July 1861. The 2d Minnesota participated in the battle of Logan's Cross Roads.

Promoted to brigadier general in March 1862, Van Cleve assumed command of the 14th Brigade of the 5th (Thomas L. Crittenden's) Division of the Army of the Ohio in July 1862. Van Cleve and Crittenden would stand and fall together in the coming months. The new commander participated in Henry Halleck's advance on Corinth and Don Carlos Buell's later advance toward Chattanooga.

Promoted to divisional command under Crittenden in September 1862, Van Cleve did not participate in the battle of Perryville. Van Cleve held this command through the Perryville, Stones River, Tullahoma, and Chickamauga campaigns. The division originally consisted of the brigades of Samuel Beatty, James P. Fyffe, and Samuel W. Price. Later, George Dick and Sidney Barnes replaced Fyffe and Price as brigade commanders.

The apex of Van Cleve's Civil War career was the battle of Stones River. Van Cleve's division was poised on the Union left to deliver a powerful flanking attack when the Confederates struck the Union right first. Van Cleve's division had to redeploy and sustained heavy casualties during the battle. Van Cleve completed a difficult maneuver in the midst of battle. He fought well and suffered a serious wound. For his reputation, however, it would have been better for him to have retired after this battle as a Union war hero.

Van Cleve recovered from his wounds in time to participate in the Tullahoma campaign. During the Chickamauga campaign, he performed miserably. After James Longstreet's breakthrough of the Federal line, the Federal troops panicked. The strain of trying to restore the line was more than Van Cleve could handle. His troops ran, literally taking Van Cleve and other officers with them. They did not stop until they reached Chattanooga. Chickamauga was the nadir of Van Cleve's career.

After the battle, the recriminations among the officers began. Van Cleve had done poorly and there were calls for his removal. A report concerning his crying about his retreating troops did not help his public image. As a result, Van Cleve was relieved and an investigation followed. Although he was cleared of any wrongdoing, his usefulness in active command ended.

Van Cleve served the remainder of the war in minor positions. He commanded the post of Murfreesboro from November 1863 to January 1864 and the post of Nashville from January to July 1864. The last year of the war, Van Cleve oversaw the defenses of the Nashville & Chattanooga Railroad, thereby contributing to the supply of William Tecumseh Sherman's forces in Georgia and George Henry Thomas's later defense of Nashville. The Union government used Van Cleve's administrative skills and avoided placing him under the stress of active command.

Van Cleve retired from the army after the war and returned to private life in Minnesota. He held the office of postmaster and eventually became state adjutant general. He died in 1891. Unfortunately, Van Cleve never published his memoirs.

Van Cleve never should have been assigned combat commander. He needed talented subordinates but he did not have them. A talented superior officer could have recognized Van Cleve's shortcomings and planned accordingly, but Crittenden had as many weaknesses as Van Cleve did. The Minnesotan was an officer of mediocre skills surrounded by others of likewise meager ability but who had to perform superbly at Chickamauga

to avoid disaster. Unfortunately for Van Cleve, this did not happen.

—*Damon R. Eubank*

See also Chickamauga, Battle of; Stones River, Battle of.

For further reading:

Cozzens, Peter. *The Civil War in the West: From Stones River to Chattanooga* (1996).

Lamers, William M. *The Edge of Glory: A Biography of William S. Rosecrans* (1999).

McKinney, Francis F. *Education in Violence: The Life of George H. Thomas and the History of the Army of the Cumberland* (1961).

Van Horne, Thomas B. *History of the Army of the Cumberland: Its Organization, Campaigns, and Battles, Written at the Request of Major-General George H. Thomas Chiefly from His Private Military Journal and Official and Other Documents Furnished by Him*(1875).

VAN DORN, EARL
(1820–1863)
Confederate general

Earl Van Dorn (*Library of Congress*)

Born on 17 September 1820 in Port Gibson, Mississippi, to Peter Aaron and Sophia Ponelson Van Dorn, Earl Van Dorn graduated fifty-second of fifty-six in the West Point class of 1842. There, Professor Dennis H. Mahan taught Van Dorn Jomini's combat tactics that dealt with swift and precise movements. This type of warfare served Van Dorn well in the cavalry; yet when he overemphasized speed with his infantry, disaster resulted. Therefore, Van Dorn's greatest success came while in command of mounted troops.

Van Dorn's first taste of battle came during the Mexican-American War, where as a lieutenant he participated in nearly all the major battles, including those at Fort Brown, Monterrey, Vera Cruz, Cerro Gordo, and Mexico City. Serving with distinction, he gained the brevet rank of major and personal recognition from General Winfield Scott.

At the war's end, army officials promoted Van Dorn to captain and placed him in command of Company A in the 2d Cavalry under Lieutenant Colonel Joseph E. Johnston. Soon transferred to Texas, Van Dorn fought in several engagements against the Native Americans across the frontier, quelling uprisings and dealing with raiding parties. Primarily fighting Comanches and briefly Seminoles in Florida, Van Dorn received national recognition as well as several wounds during his campaigns from 1855 to 1861.

Van Dorn resigned his U.S. Army commission in January 1861 to join his native state of Mississippi in the approaching rebellion. After a brief period serving in the Mississippi volunteers (January–February 1861), he joined the Confederate States of America in March 1861, and, because of his experience in the region, returned to Texas.

Shortly after his arrival, Van Dorn, by then a colonel, seized the Union ship *Star of the West* near Galveston. While continuing to clear Texas of Federal forces, he captured 350 Union troops under the command of Colonel Isaac V. D. Reeve near San Antonio. With no official policy yet in place for dealing with such prisoners, Van Dorn created the first prisoner-of-war camp of the American Civil War. Little more than a designated plot of land with Confederate guards placed around the perimeter, Camp Van Dorn was a temporary holding area for Union captives.

On 5 June 1861, Confederate officials promoted Van Dorn to brigadier general and, on 19 September 1861, to major general. Moving to the Eastern theater, he served under Major General Joseph E. Johnston as commander of the 18th Division in the Confederate Army of the Potomac, and when Johnston transferred to the Department of Northern Virginia at the end of 1861, Van Dorn followed. Although he constantly anticipated Union attack in Virginia, Van Dorn never saw combat there. Instead, his combat action would occur west of the Mississippi River.

Major General Sterling Price and Brigadier General Ben McCulloch, both in the Trans-Mississippi theater, constantly bickered with one another and remained thorns in President Jefferson Davis's side. Hoping to find a competent leader to unite the two, Davis gave

Van Dorn command of the newly formed Trans-Mississippi Department on 10 January 1862.

In March 1862, Van Dorn planned to drive Union forces out of Missouri from a base in northern Arkansas. As he moved northward, Van Dorn encountered Federal forces under the command of General Samuel Curtis at Pea Ridge, Arkansas. Poor communication, lack of proper planning and supplies, and bad weather crippled the motley Southern army. After two days of battle, the defeated Confederate troops retreated eastward.

Ordered east of the Mississippi River to link with General P. G. T. Beauregard's men to form the Army of the West, Van Dorn moved across Arkansas toward Memphis, Tennessee. To resupply his soldiers, Van Dorn took every piece of military equipment available, leaving the northern half of Arkansas unprotected. This action, coupled with the loss at Pea Ridge, caused many Southerners to despise the Mississippian. Arriving too late to participate in the battle of Shiloh, Van Dorn's men did join Beauregard in the unsuccessful defense of Corinth, Mississippi, in May 1862.

In June 1862, Van Dorn relinquished control of the Army of the West and assumed command of Department of Southern Mississippi and East Louisiana, which included Vicksburg. In June and July 1862, he successfully defended Vicksburg against Union admiral David G. Farragut's gunboats and infantry under the control of Brigadier General Thomas Williams.

In the fall of 1862, Van Dorn tried unsuccessfully to recapture Corinth. Allegations of misconduct and drunkenness in the field produced an investigation of Van Dorn. Although the probe vindicated him for the loss and subsequent retreat at Corinth, he was transferred to cavalry operations under Major General John Pemberton.

Commanding cavalry provided Van Dorn's best results. In December 1862, he raided the Union-held position at Holly Springs, Mississippi, destroying $500,000 in Federal supplies. Continuing his advance, Van Dorn traveled 500 miles in two weeks, burning provisions and causing confusion. This operation induced Major General Ulysses S. Grant to postpone his move farther south. In early 1863, Van Dorn again illustrated his ability as a cavalryman in Tennessee and northern Alabama.

By the spring of 1863, many considered him one of the greatest Southern cavalrymen. Unfortunately for the South, Van Dorn died too prematurely to exploit his newly found success. On 7 May 1863, in Spring Hill, Tennessee, Dr. George B. Peters shot and killed Van Dorn for having an affair with his wife.

Van Dorn achieved what he had always desired—fame and recognition. Contemporaries described him as handsome, quick-witted, and dapper. Friends knew him as a ladies' man, despite his marriage to Caroline Godbold in 1843. Although it came late in his career, Van Dorn did find his calling in the cavalry corps and distinguished himself in his commands.

—*Buck T. Foster*

See also Cavalry, C.S.A.; Holly Springs Raid; Pea Ridge, Battle of.

For further reading:
Hartje, Robert G. *Van Dorn: The Life and Times of a Confederate General* (1967; reprint, 1994).
Miller, Emily Van Dorn. *A Soldier's Honor with Reminiscences of Major-General Earl Van Dorn* (1902).

VAN LEW, ELIZABETH
(1818–1900)
Unionist resistance leader

It is impossible to know whether Elizabeth Van Lew's wealthy parents foresaw the results of sending their young daughter north to Philadelphia during the 1830s for her education. By the time she returned home to Richmond, Van Lew had made a lasting personal commitment to abolitionism. Her strong antislavery sentiment caused Van Lew, once she was able, to free her own family's slaves and to participate as actively as she could in the Underground Railroad. When the war began, Van Lew's hatred of slavery became the underpinning of her support for the Union cause.

It is not clear precisely when Van Lew began serving as the key player among Unionists in Richmond, but not long after the war, General George H. Sharpe, the chief of the Union's Bureau of Military Intelligence, recalled Van Lew as having come to represent "all that was left of the power of the U.S. Government in the city of Richmond." Evidence suggests that from early in the war Van Lew had been surreptitiously providing information to Union army officials elsewhere regarding the situation in Richmond. But the peak of her activity came during General Ulysses S. Grant's siege of the city in 1864–1865. During this period, Van Lew transformed her elegant family home into a hub of resistance, entertaining unsuspecting Confederates there and plying them for information. She also spent substantial time visiting Union prisoners of war incarcerated in Richmond's jails. She and her mother were among the few female Richmonders who voiced any interest in the well-being of the captured Union soldiers. Devoting much time to the infamous Libby Prison, located at the foot of the hill on which her family home perched, Van Lew tended the prisoners when they were ill; stored up whatever confidences they could offer her for later transmission to the Federal authorities; and on occasion provided safe haven for escapees or materiel in the secret rooms and passageways of her home. She also devised and oversaw a complicated relay system for the information she was receiving and sending, in which a number of trusted associates also took part, including Mary Elizabeth Bowser, a former Van Lew family slave whom Van Lew managed to have placed as a domestic servant in the Confederate White House, and who gave regular reports to a Unionist baker in town when he made his deliveries.

A significant aspect of Van Lew's career as a resistance activist in Richmond was her adoption of a persona clearly designed to make her appear daft before those who might otherwise suspect her of hard-nosed duplicity. Like other women engaged in espionage and resistance, Van Lew openly expressed her political sentiments. At the same time, however, she undercut the seriousness with which those sentiments would be heard by simultaneously presenting herself as an individual whose mental stability was worth questioning. Known to wander through town wearing unconventional clothing and singing nonsense songs to herself, Van Lew provoked some of her townsfolk to nickname her "Crazy Bet." Others refused to be taken in by what they rightly perceived as a clever ruse, but even these opponents failed to obstruct Van Lew's activities on behalf of the Union cause.

During 1864 and 1865, Van Lew provided crucially important service to the Union in the business of gathering strategic and other information and transmitting it out of the Confederate capital. She also provided a different sort of service to the Union, and to the family of a fallen Union officer, when she personally saw to the exhumation and reburial of Colonel Ulrich Dahlgren, who had been killed while participating in a surprise raid on Richmond, possibly prompted by information from Van Lew herself. Thanks to the cooperation of Van Lew and a man who had witnessed enraged Confederates tossing Dahlgren's body into an unmarked grave, the colonel's body was reinterred beneath a peach tree on friendlier soil.

Van Lew's work on behalf of the Union brought her to the attention of key figures in the Federal army, not least of all General Ulysses S. Grant, who reportedly sent a special guard to her house (where they found a huge Union flag flying) as soon as he and his troops occupied the city in April 1865. Predictably, the respect and gratitude that Grant and his men displayed was matched measure for measure by hostility and resentment on the part of the bulk of her townsfolk, who saw Van Lew only as a traitor to the cause of the fallen South. In the remaining decades of her life Van Lew—who served as the city's postmaster during the Grant administration—endured a good deal of malicious behavior by those who continued to blame her for the Confederacy's demise. When she died in September 1900, Van Lew was poor and alone, having been celebrated by some, but despised by most, in her community.

—Elizabeth D. Leonard

See also Espionage; Women.

For further reading:
Beymer, William Gilmore. On Hazardous Service: Scouts and Spies of the North and South (1912).
Kane, Harnett T. Spies for the Blue and Gray (1954).
Leonard, Elizabeth D. All the Daring of the Soldier: Women of the Civil War Armies (1999).
Ryan, David D. A Yankee Spy in Richmond: The Civil War Diary of "Crazy Bet" Van Lew (1996).

VANCE, ZEBULON BAIRD
(1830–1894)
Governor of North Carolina

Zebulon Baird Vance, governor of North Carolina from the fall of 1862 through the end of the Civil War, was an immensely talented politician who encountered some of the most painful dilemmas faced by any Southern state leader. A Unionist in the secession crisis, Zeb Vance led a state whose strong pro-Union sympathies could not prevent it from becoming a mainstay of the Confederacy. Although reluctant to secede, North Carolinians found themselves called upon to make disproportionately great sacrifices for the Confederate cause. As their burdens increased, their complaints swelled in volume, and Governor Vance struggled to defend his constituents while remaining loyal to the new Southern nation. His trials highlighted the rapidly growing disaffection of those eastern states that remained within the Confederacy's control throughout the war.

Zeb Vance began his career as an attorney from Buncombe County, in the western part of North Carolina. He entered politics in the 1850s as a Whig, serving first in the state legislature. Shunning the Democrats, he later became a Know-Nothing, triumphed in a special election to the U.S. House of Representatives in 1858, and won reelection a year later. As secession approached, Vance defended the Union and supported measures of compromise proposed in Congress. After campaigning for John Bell and the Constitutional Union Party, he urged voters in North Carolina's referendum on secession to defend the Union. Only when he learned that war had begun did Vance surrender his Unionism to become a supporter of the Confederacy.

After loyal but undistinguished service in the army, Vance became the Conservative Party's nominee for governor in the summer of 1862. Thus he led former Whigs and Unionists in opposition to the Democrats and secessionists, who called themselves Confederates but were soon derided in the state as Destructives. Winning handily, he took office in September 1862. Vance's background and sentiments were in tune with popular feeling in North Carolina, and his brilliance in political rhetoric and ability to communicate with the voters equipped him well to express the frustrations of a hard-pressed, suffering citizenry.

Because it lay within Confederate lines and remained almost entirely under control of the Richmond administration throughout the war, North Carolina made unusually large contributions to the war effort. Approximately 120,000 men from the state served in the Confederate military (a number larger than the population of white males aged eighteen to forty-five), and 40,000 died. Although the state had only one-ninth of the Confederacy's white population, it furnished one-sixth of its soldiers and nearly one-fourth of all Confederate conscripts. Likewise, impressments, taxes, and collections of foodstuffs under the tax-in-kind came disproportionately from North Carolina.

As the weight of these burdens began to be felt, Vance sprang to the defense of his constituents' interests. Repeatedly clashing with President Jefferson Davis, Vance urged that conscription be suspended and furloughs given in counties whose white families had no slaves to cultivate the fields. With a sharp tongue and rapier wit he denounced impressments and the depredations of undisciplined Confederate cavalry units. Vance also deplored Confederate distilleries, demanded more promotions of North Carolina troops, and kept almost 15,000 men out of the army because they held some post in the state government. At the same time, Vance energetically launched initiatives to provide relief for the people of his state. His manufacturing operations produced an abundance of uniforms and blankets that he kept under his control and supplied only to troops from North Carolina. He provided salt for the poor and supported large appropriations for relief by the state legislature. A state blockade-running operation, featuring a British-built steamer dubbed the *Ad-Vance*, brought tons of provisions that were in short supply into the state.

Although Jefferson Davis sometimes despaired at the acrimonious exchanges he had with the Tar Heel governor, Zeb Vance remained loyal to the Confederacy. After protesting administration policies, he always gave in and cooperated with Confederate laws and measures. In fact, his protests made the enforcement of unpopular policies possible, because Vance gave voice to his constituents' grievances and provided an outlet for their frustrations. Vance's skill in keeping a suffering, unhappy state within the Confederate nation was never more evident than in his 1864 campaign for reelection.

That year Vance faced a strong challenge from William W. Holden, editor of the *Raleigh Standard* and a former Democratic leader and secessionist. By 1864 Holden's disaffection had grown to the point that he led a well-organized movement openly committed to taking North Carolina out of the war. Vance decided to run as a supporter of peace also. He emphasized the advice he had given Jefferson Davis to seek a negotiated settlement after Southern victories, and he warned North Carolinians that Holden's tactics would only embroil the state in a new war with its Confederate neighbors. Although war-weariness was very great, Tar Heel voters chose to stay with their popular, hardworking governor, believing that somehow he would find a way to ease their burdens.

As the war's end approached in North Carolina, Zeb Vance concluded that Southern independence would require more "blood and misery, ... *and our people will not pay this price.*" Convinced that "the great *popular heart* is not now & never has been in this war," Vance nevertheless found ways to carry out his "duty" and keep North Carolina loyal to the Confederacy. His political skills and energetic efforts won him immense popularity and gratitude from the citizens of his state. In the postwar period he enjoyed a long political career, first as governor and then as U.S. senator, but he was primarily remembered for his leadership during the Civil War.

—*Paul D. Escott*

See also Holden, William W.; Impressment; North Carolina; Tax-in-Kind.

For further reading:

Barrett, John G. *The Civil War in North Carolina* (1963).

Escott, Paul D. *Many Excellent People: Power and Privilege in North Carolina, 1850–1900* (1985).

Tucker, Glenn. *Zeb Vance: Champion of Personal Freedom* (1966).

Yates, Richard E. *The Confederacy and Zeb Vance* (1958).

Yearns, W. Buck, ed. *The Confederate Governors* (1985).

VANDERBILT, CORNELIUS
(1794-1877)
Businessman

Born to Cornelius Vander Bilt and Phebe Hand Vander Bilt on Staten Island, New York, Cornelius Vanderbilt received only a rudimentary local education before entering into a business ferrying passengers to Manhattan. (His children adopted the modern spelling of his name.) The younger Vanderbilt's business expanded with the shipping contracts he was able to obtain during the War of 1812, a lesson he would take to that larger American conflict, the Civil War. With the profits made during the War of 1812, he was able to buy more ships and begin hauling cargo.

In 1818 Vanderbilt went to work for Thomas Gibbons and set about to destroy the New York steamship monopoly of Robert Fulton. Vanderbilt successfully competed and ultimately pushed to have the monopoly overturned in the case of *Gibbons v. Ogden*. In 1829 Vanderbilt went back into business on his own.

Entering the passenger trade on the Hudson and other New York waters, Vanderbilt began the practice of drastically cutting prices to force the competition to either sell him their businesses or pay him to take his business elsewhere. He also damaged the competition by building elegant ships that were far more comfortable for the passengers.

In the early 1850s Vanderbilt added to his growing fortune by creating a combined land-sea route to the West Coast via Nicaragua. When filibusterer William Walker, who had taken over the government of Nicaragua, threatened Vanderbilt's business interests there, the "Commodore," as he was known, orchestrated Walker's overthrow. Shortly thereafter, in return for a yearly payment from the Pacific Mail Steamship Company and the United States Mail Steamship Company, which sent contracted United States mail through Panama to the West Coast and back, Vanderbilt agreed to abandon his Nicaraguan route. Because the United States government paid those two companies to carry the mail from coast to coast, the United States Senate investigated the payments the companies made to Vanderbilt. United States senators Jefferson Davis of Mississippi and Robert Toombs of Georgia protested—to no effect—that government funds were surely being used to bribe Vanderbilt not to transport cargo through Nicaragua.

At the beginning of the Civil War, Vanderbilt expressed strong support for the Union cause and demonstrated that support by donating one of his luxury steamships, the *Vanderbilt*, to the United States Navy. For this act he received the thanks of the United States Congress. Vanderbilt no doubt hoped to receive consideration when it came to awarding shipping contracts during the war, and he was not disappointed.

In the fall of 1862, Vanderbilt's company received the contract to transport Major General Nathaniel Prentiss Banks's army from New York to New Orleans. Not only did the company charge the government exorbitant rates for the expedition, but many of the ships were rotten, and there were not enough of them. Consequently, the men were crowded onto old, decrepit vessels, in very unsanitary conditions. Disease was rampant. A subsequent congressional investigation resulted in a Senate resolution of censure, but Vanderbilt's influence arranged that the actual resolution not mention him by name.

During the war Vanderbilt came to the realization that more money could be made in railroads than steamships. He began his foray into this new business by buying as much stock as possible in New York City railroads and eventually, through clever stock manipulation, he cornered the market in that area. He next turned to some of the New York state lines and managed to take control of them as well shortly after the war. Like many Northern businessmen, he profited handsomely from the increased business activities during the war.

After the war, with the help of his son William, Vanderbilt expanded his railroad holdings outside of the state. Vanderbilt continued to remain active in his business affairs until he neared death. He died at his New York home on 4 January 1877.

—*David S. Heidler and Jeanne T. Heidler*

See also Banks, Nathaniel Prentiss; Walker, William.
For further reading:
Lane, Wheaton Joshua. *Commodore Vanderbilt: An Epic of the Steam Age* (1942).
Smith, Arthur D. Howden. *Commodore Vanderbilt: An Epic of American Achievement* (1927).

VELAZQUEZ, LORETA JANETA
(? – ?)
Author

Few if any stories of women's Civil War service as soldiers or as spies are as difficult to sort out and verify as the one contained in *The Woman in Battle*, published in 1876 by Loreta Janeta Velazquez. Velazquez's "memoir" represents one of only two such works written by women who claimed to have served in the army during the Civil War. The other is Sarah Emma Edmonds's *Nurse and Spy in the Union Army*, published in 1864. Although, like *The Woman in Battle*, *Nurse and Spy* contains much material that is romanticized and even fully fictionalized, nevertheless the author's two years of military service (as Private Franklin Thompson of the 2d Michigan Infantry Volunteers) and many of the events described in *Nurse and Spy* are fully established in the historical record. Such is not the case with Velazquez or her work, however. But it is also true that substantial evidence indicates that *The Woman in Battle* is not wholly the product of its author's imagination.

According to *The Woman in Battle*, Loreta Velazquez was born in Cuba (her year of birth is not known) to a Spanish father and a Franco-American mother. When her father inherited a large estate in Texas, the family immigrated to the United States, and Velazquez herself spent time in Texas and then in New Orleans, where her family sent her to complete her education. In 1856, contrary to her parents' plans that she marry a Spaniard, young Velazquez fell in love and eloped with an officer in the U.S. Army, whom she identifies only as "William." The two had three children over the next four years, all of whom had died by 1860.

When the Civil War broke out, William was not the only one who saw it as an opportunity for adventure and service. "As for me," Velazquez claims, "I was perfectly wild on the subject of war." After William's enlistment and departure in June 1861, Velazquez chose to disregard his orders to abandon all hope of following him. Instead, she cut her hair, donned a soldier's uniform and a false mustache, assumed the pseudonym Harry T. Buford, and began to gather troops to form her own regiment, the "Arkansas Grays," for Confederate army service.

Velazquez then traveled with her recruits to her husband's encampment in Pensacola, Florida, where, as it turns out, William had only a short time to express displeasure over Velazquez's disobedience before being killed in a freak accident. Delivering the Grays into someone else's command, Velazquez soon left Pensacola in search of the war.

The bulk of *The Woman in Battle* details Velazquez's experiences as Harry Buford, and readers find her over the course of the war participating in a number of battles (including First Bull Run, Ball's Bluff, and Shiloh) and operating as a spy for the Confederacy. Periodically arrested, Velazquez always finds her way back to the safety of the Confederate lines. In short, the book is full of the sort of adventure and excitement that lead one to assume its fundamental implausibility. *The Woman in Battle* is also, however, replete with details that can be corroborated elsewhere. For example, we know that on 27 July 1863, the Confederate secretary of war received a request for an officer's commission signed by a soldier named H. T. Buford. We also know that as early as October 1861, at least one newspaper reported the arrest in Richmond of a woman soldier who had registered as "Lieutenant Buford" at a hotel in Lynchburg, Virginia. Furthermore, in 1863 another newspaper published the story of one Laura J. Williams (note the similarity to the name Loreta Janeta Velazquez), who had disguised herself as a soldier named Henry Benford (cf. "Harry Buford") and whose experiences in the ranks very much resembled those later recorded by Velazquez in *The Woman in Battle*.

One could point out a number of other instances of links between material contained in Velazquez's "memoir" and the actual experiences and activities of a woman soldier (or perhaps several women soldiers) recorded elsewhere during the war. In the end, while clearly *The Woman in Battle* is hardly a work of pure nonfiction, the book and its author have considerable significance for the study of women's involvement in Civil War military life. If the story contained in the book is not entirely an accurate representation of its author's own wartime experiences, it is clear—especially based on what we know indisputably about other women's wartime activities as soldiers and spies—that much, if not all, of it could have been.

—*Elizabeth D. Leonard*

See also Edmonds, Sarah Emma; Hodgers, Jennie; Wakeman, Sarah Rosetta; Women Soldiers.

For further reading:

Hoffert, Sylvia. "Madame Loretta [sic] Velazquez: Heroine or Hoaxer?" *Civil War Times Illustrated* (1978).

Leonard, Elizabeth D. *All the Daring of the Soldier: Women of the Civil War Armies* (1999).

Velazquez, Loreta Janeta. *The Woman in Battle* (1876).

Wheelwright, Julie. *Amazons and Military Maids: Women Who Dressed as Men in the Pursuit of Life, Liberty and Happiness* (1989).

Young, Elizabeth. "Confederate Counterfeit." In *Passing and the Fictions of Identity*. Elaine K. Ginsberg, ed. (1996).

VERMONT BRIGADE

The Vermont Brigade lost more men than any other Union brigade organization during the Civil War. It was also the only brigade that remained intact; the five regiments that constituted its original formation served together throughout the entire war. In 1864, upon the expiration of their original enlistments, the men of the Vermont Brigade reenlisted and thus sustained its existence. Consequently, the only organizational change came when the 11th Regiment was placed in the brigade in May 1864 as the 1st Vermont Heavy Artillery. Yet even in this, the brigade was unique because its regiments were all originally from the same state and continued to be so. Unlike their Confederate counterparts, Federal armies usually constituted their brigades with regiments from different states as a matter of policy.

The Vermont Brigade was composed of the 2d, 3d, 4th, 5th, and 6th Vermont Infantry when it became part of Union forces performing picket duty at Chain Bridge, Virginia, in September 1861. (The 1st Vermont Infantry was a ninety-day regiment that saw action at Big Bethel and was then mustered out.) As part of the 2d Division, VI Corps, Army of the Potomac, the brigade took part in the Peninsula campaign and fought at Antietam and Fredericksburg. After Gettysburg, the Vermont Brigade was part of the pursuit of Lee's army. Alone it held a strong position more than a mile long at Funkstown, Maryland, against repeated charges by a larger Confederate force. Yet the brigade's most arduous service was at the beginning of Grant's Overland campaign in May 1864. In the space of a week at the Wilderness and Spotsylvania, the brigade lost 1,645 out of the 2,800 effective men who had crossed the Rapidan, a figure that accounted for 58 percent of its strength.

The Vermont Brigade's commanders were General William F. "Baldy" Smith, once of the 3d Vermont, General William T. Brooks, Colonel Henry Whiting of the 2d Vermont, and General Lewis Addison Grant of the 5th Vermont. The same regiments that had constituted the brigade in 1861 marched together in the Grand Review in 1865.

This Vermont Brigade is occasionally referred to as the "old" Vermont Brigade to distinguish it from Brigadier General George J. Stannard's Vermont Brigade that helped repulse Pickett's Charge at Gettysburg. Part of I Corps, Stannard's brigade was composed of the 12th, 13th, 14th, 15th, and 16th Vermont Infantry. Its troops were under a nine-month enlistment, and Gettysburg was their only battle.

—*David S. Heidler and Jeanne T. Heidler*

See also Fairbanks, Erastus; Grant, Lewis Addison; Stannard, George Jerrison.
For further reading:
Benedict, George Grenville. *Vermont in the Civil War* (1889).
Coffin, Howard. *Full Duty: Vermonters in the Civil War* (1993).
———. *Nine Months to Gettysburg: Stannard's Vermonters and the Repulse of Pickett's Charge* (1997).
Gallagher, Gary W., ed. *The Wilderness Campaign* (1997).
Parsons, George W. *Put the Vermonters Ahead: The First Vermont Brigade in the Civil War* (1996).

VEROT, JEAN PIERRE AUGUSTIN
(1805–1876)
Catholic bishop

Born to Jean-Pierre Augustin Marcellin Verot and Magdeleine Marcet Verot in LePuy, France, Augustin Verot studied for the priesthood and was ordained in the Sulpician Order in 1828. Two years later he was sent to Baltimore, Maryland, where he worked as a teacher and pastor before being sent to Florida in 1858 as vicar apostolic of Florida.

Florida was still a thinly populated, poor state when Verot arrived in 1858. He worked diligently to repair and rebuild churches, including the Spanish cathedral in St. Augustine and to minister to the Indian and African-American slave population. Verot did not disapprove of the institution of slavery, though he did encourage Catholic slaveholders to treat their slaves with compassion.

At the outbreak of the Civil War, Verot wrote and published "A Tract for the Times: Slavery and Abolition." In this tract, while condemning the slave trade, Verot affirmed the rights of slave owners. This and other writings he would produce during the war proved an encouragement to Southern Catholics to support the Confederacy. Verot was in Baltimore on a visit when this publication was first circulated, and he was arrested for disloyalty. Realizing the public relations problem of imprisoning a high-ranking Catholic clergyman in the North, the U.S. War Department released Verot in September 1861.

In 1861 Verot was made bishop of Savannah. He served there, still with jurisdiction over Florida, for the remainder of the war. While he strongly supported the Confederacy and urged Catholics to do likewise, he also used the resources of the church to ease the suffering of Union prisoners.

During the Union occupation of Savannah beginning in December 1864, Verot was horrified by the desecration of church property by the Northern soldiers. Not only were the churches themselves used for storage and barracks, but the Catholic cemetery in Savannah was vandalized and used as a Federal encampment. After gaining no satisfaction from the Union officers in Savannah, Verot wrote directly to Union secretary of war Edwin Stanton urging him to right this wrong.

After the war, Verot sought to rebuild war-damaged church property. He also dedicated new efforts to Catholic education in Georgia and Florida, bringing in nuns to establish schools in the poverty-stricken region. In 1870, Verot traveled to Rome as a member of the Vatican Council. He returned to the United States as the newly created bishop of St. Augustine, Florida. He died in that city.

—David S. Heidler and Jeanne T. Heidler

See also Catholics; Savannah, Georgia.
For further reading:
Gannon, Michael. *Rebel Bishop: Augustin Verot, Florida's Civil War Prelate* (1997).

VETERANS' ORGANIZATIONS

The American Civil War spawned a plethora of organizations catering to veterans of both sides. The largest and most important was the Grand Army of the Republic (GAR), the brainchild of former Union generals John A. Logan and Richard J. Oglesby, and surgeon Benjamin F. Stephenson. Scholars do not agree on which of these three first divulged the plan for the GAR. The first post appeared in Illinois in 1866, and the organization then spread rapidly throughout states in which Union veterans resided. Each state numbered its own posts as part of its own department and elected its own state commander. Delegates to a national convention then elected national officers. Members had to be honorably discharged veterans. Although the GAR espoused racial equality, the social mores of the late nineteenth century meant that blacks generally formed their own separate posts.

The GAR's membership peaked at more than 409,000 in 1890. During the decades following the war, the GAR's political power was a force to be reckoned with. Every presidential candidate from Ulysses S. Grant to William McKinley had to court the GAR to ensure success. When Grover Cleveland vetoed a key pension bill and supported returning captured Confederate flags to the Southern states during his first term in office, veterans turned against him and were instrumental in defeating Cleveland for a second term. Cleveland came back four years later, after having mended relations with the GAR.

The GAR aimed to promote fraternal feeling among veterans, aid needy or disabled comrades and their families, encourage public allegiance to the government, and facilitate the passage of pension laws and other benefits. Among its many accomplishments were the establishment of Decoration Day (Memorial Day) as a national holiday, the recitation of the pledge of allegiance in schools, the establishment of liberal pension benefits, and the teaching of "loyal" history in the public schools.

Many other veterans' groups were associated with the

GAR. Chief among these was the Sons of Union Veterans, which was open to descendants of Union soldiers and is still in existence. The Sons was followed by the Woman's Relief Corps (established in 1883), which was the official auxiliary to the GAR, and by the Ladies of the GAR (established in 1886). The Daughters of Veterans was formed in 1885.

Soon after Lincoln's assassination, several veteran officers gathered in Philadelphia to form the Military Order of the Loyal Legion of the United States, better known as MOLLUS. Membership was restricted to Union officers and their eldest male sons. With such restrictions, MOLLUS never became as politically powerful as the GAR, but it continues to function by accepting descendants of Union officers. The original MOLLUS library continues today as the Civil War Library and Museum, located at 1805 Pine Street in Philadelphia. The Dames of the Loyal Legion was formed in 1899 and also still continues.

Other Union veterans' organizations included the Union Veteran Legion, formed in Pittsburgh in 1884. Membership was limited to veterans who had enlisted before 1 July 1863 and had either served two years or had been discharged because of wounds received in battle. Its peak year was 1894, with 9,256 members. In 1886, the Union Veterans' Union was organized in Washington, to consist of men who had served at least six months, with at least part of this time spent on active duty. In 1892, the Veteran Nurses of the Civil War organized; three years later it changed its name to the National Association of Nurses of the Civil War.

The primary Confederate veterans' organization was the United Confederate Veterans (UCV), created in New Orleans in 1889 by the union of several independent state organizations. General John B. Gordon was chosen as its first commander. Each post was called a camp, each of which was numbered in the order it was accepted into membership. At its peak, the UCV included 1,855 camps. National conventions began in 1890 and ended in 1951, when only three members attended. Along with aiding disabled and needy veterans and their families, the UCV lobbied for state pensions for Southern veterans, raised funds for monuments, established homes for aged veterans, and worked to keep the memory of the war alive. The magazine *Confederate Veteran* became the official organ of the UCV, which also underwrote the publication of the 12-volume *Confederate Military History* in 1899.

In 1894, Mrs. C. H. Goodlett of Nashville gathered friends about her and formed the United Daughters of the Confederacy, which remained completely independent of the UCV. Two years later, the United Sons of Confederate Veterans was formed; this organization is still functioning today.

—*Richard A. Sauers*

See also Lost Cause; Memorials, C.S.A.; Memorials, U.S.A.; Pensions; Sons of Confederate Veterans; United Daughters of the Confederacy.
For further reading:
Davies, Wallace E. *Patriotism on Parade: The Story of Veterans' and Hereditary Organizations in America, 1783–1900* (1955).
Dearing, Mary R. *Veterans in Politics: The Story of the G.A.R.* (1952).
McConnell, Stuart. *Glorious Contentment: The Grand Army of the Republic, 1865–1900* (1992).
White, William W. *The Confederate Veteran* (1962).

VICKSBURG CAMPAIGN
(May–July 1863)

During the winter of 1862–1863, Union major general Ulysses S. Grant made several unsuccessful forays to capture the strategic fortress city of Vicksburg, Mississippi. A combination of swampy bogs along the Yazoo River north of the city, the 200-foot-high bluffs fringing the river west of the city, determined Confederate resistance, and rebel cavalry raids along his lines of communication thwarted Grant's every attempt to seize the "Gibraltar of the Confederacy."

In March 1863, Grant proposed a bold stroke to circumvent Vicksburg's natural obstacles and Confederate fortifications. He ordered his army to march south of Vicksburg on the west side of the Mississippi and sent Rear Admiral David D. Porter's supporting flotilla past the citadel's batteries to rendezvous with his forces south of Vicksburg. To disrupt rebel communications east of Vicksburg, he sent Colonel Benjamin H. Grierson's 1,700 cavalrymen on a lengthy raid from La Grange to Baton Rouge, Louisiana.

Lieutenant General John C. Pemberton, Confederate commander of Mississippi and Eastern Louisiana, on the other hand, found himself bereft of cavalry, "deprived of his eyes" and a "blinded leader dangerously in the dark." That situation had resulted because Lieutenant General Joseph E. Johnston had reassigned most of Pemberton's cavalry to the Army of Tennessee, rendering Pemberton's intelligence slow and ineffectual.

Consolidating at Hard Times, Louisiana, Grant prepared to launch Major General John McClernand's XIII Corps and Major General James B. McPherson's XVII Corps across the Mississippi. He had left Major General William T. Sherman's XV Corps to demonstrate along the Yazoo to divert Pemberton's attention from the Union crossing. When Grant discovered Confederate defenses at Grand Gulf, twenty-five miles south of Vicksburg, to be too imposing, he selected a landing site farther downriver. From 30 April through 1 May, Grant hurled 24,000 men across the Mississippi at undefended Bruinsburg in America's largest amphibious operation up to that time.

Throughout 1 May, Brigadier General John S. Bowen

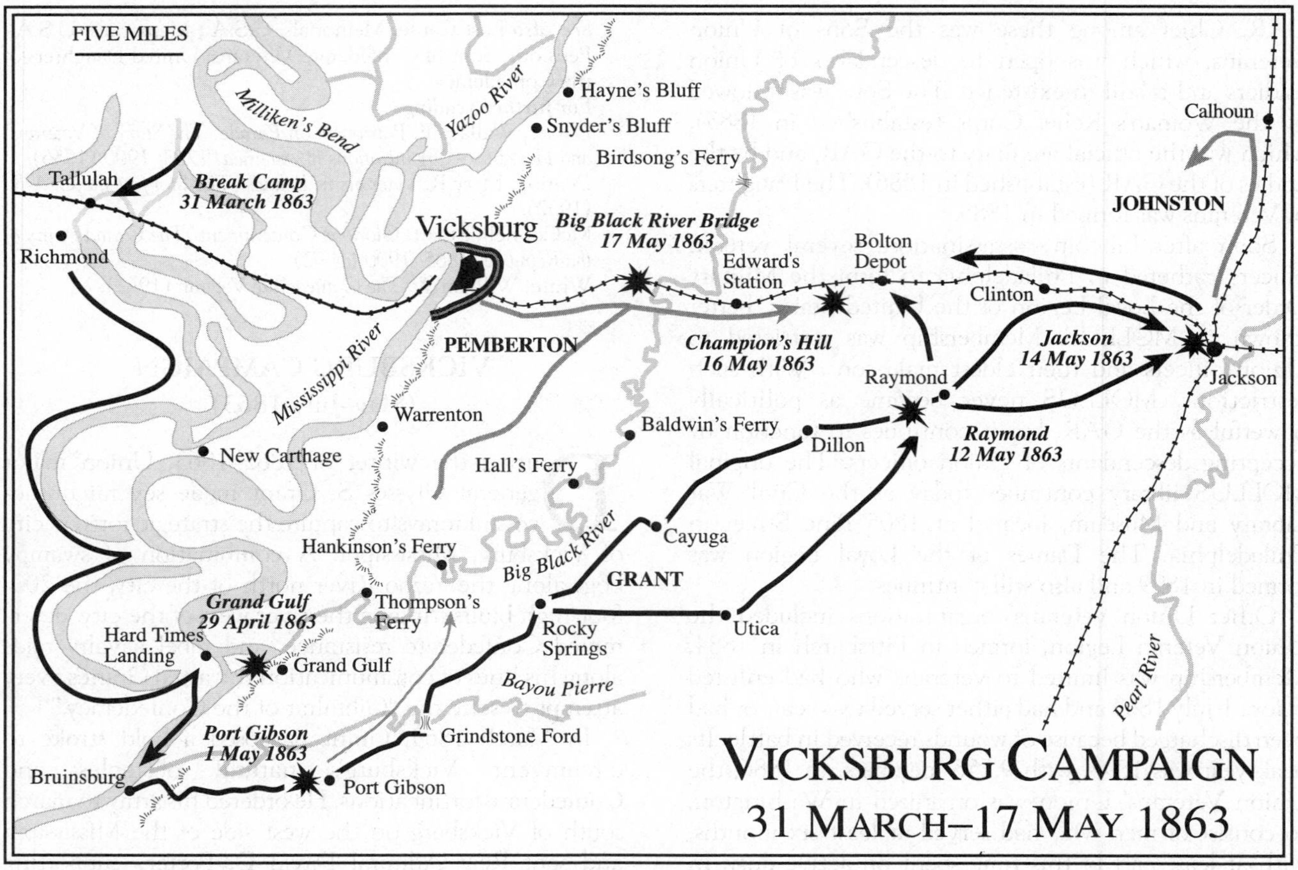

FIVE MILES

Milliken's Bend

Yazoo River

Tallulah

*Break Camp
31 March 1863*

Richmond

Hayne's Bluff

Snyder's Bluff

Birdsong's Ferry

Calhoun

JOHNSTON

Vicksburg

*Big Black River Bridge
17 May 1863*

Edward's
Station

Bolton
Depot

Clinton

PEMBERTON

*Champion's Hill
16 May 1863*

Raymond

*Jackson
14 May 1863*

Jackson

Mississippi River

Warrenton

Baldwin's Ferry

Dillon

*Raymond
12 May 1863*

New Carthage

Hall's Ferry

Big Black River

Cayuga

GRANT

Hankinson's Ferry

*Grand Gulf
29 April 1863*

Thompson's
Ferry

Rocky
Springs

Utica

Hard Times
Landing

Grand Gulf

Bayou Pierre

Pearl River

*Port Gibson
1 May 1863*

Grindstone Ford

Bruinsburg

Port Gibson

VICKSBURG CAMPAIGN
31 MARCH–17 MAY 1863

furiously counterattacked with his 8,000 troops but failed to push the Union invaders back into the river. On 3 May, Grant dislodged the remaining defenders of Port Gibson, securing his beachhead and forcing Bowen to abandon Grand Gulf. Grant then continued his overland campaign to capture Vicksburg.

Pemberton found himself in a dilemma. Johnston directed Pemberton to link up with him to defeat Grant in open battle. Convoluting the issue, President Jefferson Davis ordered Pemberton to "hold the city at all cost." Pemberton followed his president's instructions and his own inclination to defend the fortified city. Confederate indecision allowed Grant to proceed with his revised plan to cross the Big Black River and advance northeast to threaten both Jackson and Vicksburg.

Grant organized his 41,000 infantry into three columns. McClernand advanced on the left with instructions to hug the river. Sherman arrived at Grand Gulf with his corps to fill Grant's center, while McPherson marched on the right.

On 12 May near Raymond, fourteen miles southwest of Jackson, Grant encountered the first major Confederate resistance. Brigadier General John Gregg advanced out of Jackson with his brigade and confronted McPherson's advance guard, led by Major General John A. Logan. In a heated battle, Gregg's 5,000 men held

their line for six hours before superior numbers forced them to retreat. Reports listed Union losses as 66 killed, 339 wounded, and 37 missing, while Gregg reportedly lost 100 killed, 305 wounded, and 415 taken prisoner.

Grant seized an opportunity to drive a wedge between two Confederate forces and occupy Jackson. He directed McPherson northeast to Clinton to destroy the railroad and then to move on to Jackson, while Sherman moved straight through Raymond toward the capital. McClernand's orders included being in position to support the other two corps and guard against any attack by Pemberton from the west.

On the night of 13 May, as Grant made his dispositions, Johnston arrived in Jackson to take command of all Confederate forces in Mississippi. Piqued to discover Grant's force between Jackson and Vicksburg, Johnston abandoned his initial plan for a consolidated attack against Grant. Union troops cut both the rail and telegraph lines, making any coordination between the separate Confederate armies slow and unreliable at best.

The same day that Gregg confronted the advancing Yankees at Raymond, Pemberton sallied out of Vicksburg with 18,500 men, crossed the Big Black River, and marched about halfway to Jackson. Advised of Pemberton's actions, Johnston recognized an opportunity to strike Grant's divided forces. He sent three

The siege of Vicksburg (*Library of Congress*)

couriers to convey his instructions to Pemberton to descend on the Federals' rear at Clinton. In the meantime, on 14 May, with only 6,000 troops to defend the incomplete earthworks at Jackson, Johnston decided to abandon the city and reconsolidate near Calhoun. This action actually took Johnston farther from Pemberton. By the end of the 14th, Sherman's troops had fought their way through the thin Confederate rear guard and occupied Jackson, capturing three artillery batteries and 200 prisoners in the process.

After a council of war with his subordinate commanders, Pemberton took their advice and chose not to join Johnston. Instead he would march southeast with his outnumbered force to cut Grant's lines to the Mississippi. He remained unaware that Grant had departed Grand Gulf with all the ammunition his army could transport in confiscated wagons, carts, and fancy carriages. (Grant had, however, issued only five days' rations for his troops, planning to forage freely from local farms and plantations. His men ate so much poultry during their march that the mere mention of chickens or turkeys spoiled their appetite.) With this shrewd maneuver, Grant negated Pemberton's threat by intentionally cutting himself off from a long supply trail to the Mississippi.

When Johnston learned of Pemberton's plans he hurriedly sent additional dispatches urging Pemberton's compliance with his initial guidance to consolidate their forces. By then it was too late. One of Johnston's original couriers, secretly a Northern sympathizer, informed Grant of Johnston's plans, and on 16 May the Union commander thrust most of his army westward from Jackson to engage Pemberton. Grant left Sherman in Jackson with orders to destroy anything of military value within the city. Sherman's men reacted with alacrity, ransacking and burning much of the city before departing.

On 16 May, eighteen miles west of the capital, the two forces collided at Champion's Hill. Pemberton chose the best defensible terrain in the area and deployed his divisions with William W. Loring situated on the right, Bowen covering the center, and Major General Carter L. Stevenson on the left. McPherson's corps attacked the main Confederate positions across the road over Champion's Hill, and the concentrated Union pressure forced Pemberton to shift Bowen to support Stevenson. Determined Confederate counterattacks initially drove McPherson's men back, but the Rebels soon recoiled before superior numbers. McClernand initially failed to follow Grant's orders to advance, and XIII Corps did not strike the depleted Confederate line until late afternoon. Unable to arrest the Union advance, portions of Pemberton's line broke, forcing him to withdraw to prepared positions along the Big Black River.

The levee at Vicksburg, February 1864 (Photograph by William R. Pywell / *Library of Congress*)

Confederate losses were 3,624, while Grant reported total losses of 2,441.

The next day at the Big Black River, Pemberton displayed tactical ineptness by misusing the natural obstacle of the river. High bluffs bordered the west side of the river crossing but, unaccountably, Pemberton chose to defend on the comparatively level terrain east of the river. He arrayed his artillery in a mile-long series of strong points, connected by infantry breastworks, along the east side of the river and west of a small waterway that made the Confederate positions an island. Perhaps he believed he could halt Grant on the level ground that fronted his main positions.

The initial Federal advance, however, did not come over this flat land. Under cover of darkness Sherman came around on the north and crossed some of his troops on a pontoon bridge. At daylight, Union infantry advanced to the river concealed by a copse of woods north of the Rebel defenses. Outflanked and with his men retreating in disorder, Pemberton ordered a total withdrawal. Grant lost fewer than 300 men, and Pemberton listed 1,024 casualties. When the Rebel line collapsed, Yankee infantrymen leaped on the stringers of the railroad bridge and "ran across them like squirrels."

At other points the Federals charged across the river on trees felled as footbridges.

After the fiasco at the river crossing, Pemberton rushed back to Vicksburg, with the Union army in hot pursuit. He wrote Johnston that his position was untenable and he felt compelled to return to Vicksburg's defenses. Cut off east of the river, Loring marched his division on a circuitous route to join Johnston.

Johnston again ordered Pemberton to evacuate Vicksburg and march northeast to join him in a coordinated attack on Grant. In response to Johnston's message, Pemberton held a council of war and his officers unanimously elected to remain within the confines of the city's substantial defenses. Boasting more than 100 field pieces, the Confederate emplacements ran along the crest of a wooded ridge north of the city, thence south and westward to the river. Numerous deep ravines and streams, favoring the defender, cut the rugged, brush-covered terrain. Pemberton wrote Johnston that "I still conceive it [Vicksburg] to be the most important point in the Confederacy."

By this time, however, the retention of Vicksburg was only a symbolic, political, and psychological gesture. The city had lost its strategic significance when Porter's gunboats successfully ran the batteries in April. With Union vessels both north and south of the city, steamboats could no longer reach the railhead in Vicksburg. Thus, along with Memphis and New Orleans, the Confederacy had lost its last rail link to the Trans-Mississippi Department.

Grant, apprehensive about an extended siege, made two costly frontal assaults on Vicksburg. At 2:00 P.M. on 19 May, he ordered an attack along the main roads leading into the Rebel bastion. Although several Union companies advanced to the outer parapets, the defenders drove them back with heavy casualties.

During the next few days, Grant's engineers alleviated his supply problems somewhat. North of Vicksburg the engineers constructed a pontoon bridge that allowed supplies to be unloaded at the landing near Haynes's Bluff on the Yazoo River. From there and from Chickasaw Bayou, wagon trains transported vital rations, medical supplies, clothing, and ammunition around enemy positions to Grant's three corps investing Vicksburg.

On the 22d, under cover of a thunderous bombardment, Grant launched another frontal assault on the Confederate earthworks. By midafternoon Grant determined that the attack had failed, but he received a note from McClernand claiming that he had taken three of the enemies' outer parapets and that "the flag of our beloved country floated over the stronghold of Vicksburg." McClernand asked for reinforcements and for Grant to press his attack so that McClernand could consolidate his gains. Grant passed the note to Sherman, commenting, "If only I could believe it." Grant hesitantly renewed the attack.

Unfortunately for the Federals, McClernand was wrong, and Grant's infantry fell back with bloody losses of over 3,000. The dead lay decomposing in the sun for three days before the stench prompted both sides to agree on a cease-fire to bury the rotting corpses. The only thing McClernand had captured were a few advanced picket posts outside the Confederate defenses.

Shortly, copies of the *St. Louis Democrat* arrived with a vainglorious account of the battle, along with a congratulatory order from McClernand to his corps. In the most laudatory terms he congratulated his troops and asserted that if at Champion's Hill and Vicksburg the other corps "had only done their duty, the stronghold would now be ours." Infuriated by McClernand's misrepresentations, Sherman and McPherson sent heated letters to Grant. Grant, also outraged at McClernand's blatant attempt to further his political career at the expense of others, queried McClernand concerning the accuracy of the report. Grant also asked why he had not received a copy of the order, as regulations required. McClernand affirmed the accuracy of the article and blamed his adjutant for not forwarding a copy of the order to Grant. Grant relieved this disloyal officer and

appointed Major General Edward O. C. Ord to command XIII Corps. The entire army rejoiced at McClernand's departure, while Ord's appointment greatly improved the efficacy of the XIII Corps.

In twenty days, Grant's army marched over 180 miles from Bruinsburg to invest Vicksburg. Along the way it captured Jackson and destroyed the city's arsenal and burned anything of military value. During the march, Grant's troops fought five major engagements and captured over 6,000 prisoners and 88 artillery pieces.

Forced into siege warfare, Grant ordered his engineers to dig a series of trenches along the seven miles of Confederate earthworks. When completed, the Union entrenchments measured almost fifteen miles. Sherman occupied the right, McPherson the center, and McClernand, who would remain in command until 19 June, the left; both Sherman and McClernand extended their lines to the Mississippi north and south of Vicksburg. Initially the trenches were about 600 yards away from the Confederate outer defenses, but Union soldiers dug a series of zigzag saps and parallels that approached to within a few feet of the Rebel positions. At night soldiers from both sides left their trenches to swap tobacco, coffee, and newspapers. By the end of May, 50,000 Union soldiers occupied the trenches, and two weeks later 21,000 more joined the Federal army surrounding Vicksburg.

Grant commanded a large infantry force but suffered a paucity of artillery, especially heavy siege guns. He had to depend on six thirty-two-pounders and a battery of heavy cannon borrowed from Porter's gunboats. Porter's boats also mounted several large mortars, and Grant's men fabricated several more by boring out large logs and reinforcing them with iron bands. Although they were not designed for the task, Grant employed his field artillery as his major weapon to breach the formidable Rebel earthworks. By the end of June, the Federal army trained 220 guns on Vicksburg. Unlike the Confederates, the Union artillerymen drew upon "an inexhaustible supply of ammunition" and "used it freely."

Beginning on 23 May, Grant's pioneers, infantrymen, and hired black laborers dug a series of trenches containing numerous rifle pits with overhead cover of timber and sandbags. At many points the opposing fighting positions were close enough for the Rebels and Yankees to banter back and forth. The Union soldiers threw hardtack over to the defenders, while the Confederates responded with twists of tobacco. Often, however, the exchanges were hand grenades.

Grant's men also dug a series of mines, or tunnels, under the Confederate lines and packed them with black powder to blow gaps in the Confederate defenses. At 3:00 P.M. on 25 June the Federals exploded the first of these mines. When the mine detonated, it blew tons of earth and several Confederate workers into the air, some

of the men landing relatively unhurt in the Union lines. Two regiments charged into the breach, but the Confederates repulsed the Union infantry with hand grenades and short-fused artillery shells rolled into the crater. Confederate losses numbered eighty-eight, while Grant reported about thirty of his men killed or wounded during the combat. On 1 July the Federals detonated another mine, killing and wounding several Confederates, but they did not rush into the huge chasm, fearing another loss of men in an abortive charge. Confederate countermines failed to block any of the Union tunnels.

Forced to change his plans, Johnston concentrated on raising an army large enough to lift the siege, or at least open a gap in the Union lines long enough for Vicksburg's defenders to escape. Through May and part of June, he repeatedly requested reinforcements, but few were forthcoming. He managed to build an army of 31,000, but, considering Grant's overwhelming numbers, Johnston needed more men. Johnston, along with Lieutenant General James Longstreet and P. G. T. Beauregard proposed that reinforcements from the Army of Northern Virginia join General Braxton Bragg, who planned to open an offensive against Major General William Rosecrans in Tennessee. Robert E. Lee's opposition to depleting his forces east of the Appalachians scuttled their plans. Lee averred that his planned campaign into Pennsylvania would relieve the pressure on Vicksburg.

Pemberton could expect little relief from the Trans-Mississippi either. Johnston had scoured the department and gathered all the troops available. Across the river on 7 June, Major General John G. Walker attempted to destroy Grant's supply depot at Milliken's Bend, but his attack came too late to help Pemberton. (Milliken's Bend was the first major engagement of the war in which black combat troops participated.) Therefore, on 15 June, Johnston informed the War Department that saving Vicksburg was "hopeless."

Grant realized that Johnston still posed a considerable threat to his rear and took measures to prevent the Confederate general from disrupting his siege. Union troops had already destroyed most of the rail lines around Jackson and burned the majority of the rolling stock. Grant dispatched a division to destroy all the remaining bridges between the opposing armies and to make the roads as impassable as possible. This forced Johnston to rely on an insufficient number of wagons and carts to bring supplies to his army. Grant's foraging parties also thoroughly scavenged the countryside for horses, mules, and all victuals. Without adequate supplies and rations, Johnston's troops found it almost impossible to sustain themselves within striking distance of Grant.

Concerned nevertheless about his position between two enemy forces, Grant placed Sherman in command of all troops from Haynes' Bluff to the Big Black River and directed him to deploy some of his 34,000 men along a defensive line about fifteen miles east of Vicksburg. Grant believed Vicksburg to be so important to the South that the Confederates "would make the most strenuous efforts to raise the siege." He also ordered his cavalry to guard the fords on the Big Black River and monitor Johnston's movements. The Union army now faced both west and east, prepared both to besiege Vicksburg and defend itself from any Rebel attack.

Although Pemberton had begun stockpiling provisions in March, conditions inside Vicksburg rapidly deteriorated. Both citizens and soldiers sought shelter from incessant bombardments in cellars or caves dug into the city's numerous hillsides, often discovering large rattlesnakes sharing their beds in these caves. Drinking water became scarce, and the food supply dwindled. Mule meat replaced beef and pork, and the bread ration was halved, then halved again. The Confederates experimented with a mixture of ground peas and corn meal, but this concoction "had the properties of Indian rubber and was worse than leather to digest."

Johnston held few options for extricating Pemberton's trapped men. He considered the possibility that a coordinated assault on both Grant and Sherman might prevent either Union force from coming to the aid of the other and open a way out for Pemberton. Outnumbered, the Confederates would have to rely on a Union blunder to open a path for escape. This option required precise timing and organization, and with the uncertain communications between himself and Pemberton, Johnston abandoned this plan.

On 28 June, Johnston sent a courier to Pemberton with a message describing a final plan to break the siege. Operating on Pemberton's assumption that he could hold Vicksburg until 10 July, Johnston would initiate a diversionary attack on 7 July. He believed such an attack would disrupt Grant's attention long enough for Pemberton to fight his way out of the encircled city. Johnston's message never reached Pemberton.

On 3 July, after a forty-six-day siege, Pemberton concluded that his beleaguered men could no longer stand the rigors of sustained combat and starvation. Consequently, at about 10:00 A.M., under flags of truce, he arranged a meeting with Grant between the lines. On Independence Day 1863, Pemberton surrendered 2,166 officers, 27,230 enlisted men, 172 cannon, and 60,000 long arms. Many of the long arms were modern Enfield rifles, smuggled in from England, which Grant used to reequip his volunteers, who had been carrying older smoothbore muskets.

The entire Union force, both soldiers and sailors, celebrated the Fourth of July with the ceremony of surrender. The army marched into the city "with colors flying and bands playing." On the river vessels, "decorated with flags and sailors in holiday dress, and guns

firing" joined in the victory jubilation. Among the gutted houses and debris of war, magnanimous Union infantrymen shared their bacon and hardtack with the ravenous occupants of Vicksburg, but Independence Day was not celebrated in Vicksburg again until World War II, eighty-one years later. The National Cemetery at Vicksburg contains the graves of 16,822 Union soldiers killed near the city.

The capture of Vicksburg solidified Grant's reputation as a fighting general, prepared to win the war despite the casualties. Along with his later victories near Chattanooga, Vicksburg guaranteed his spectacular rise to lieutenant general and commander of all Union armies.

The loss of Vicksburg cut off the Confederacy from replacements, horses, cattle, pigs, sugar, and salt available from Arkansas, Louisiana, and Texas. When Port Hudson fell a few days later, President Abraham Lincoln commented that the Mississippi River "again goes unvexed to the sea."

—*Stanley S. McGowen*

See also Big Black River, First Battle of; Bowen, John Stevens; Champion's Hill, Battle of; Grant, Ulysses S.; Grierson's Raid; Johnston, Joseph E.; Loring, William Wing; McClernand, John A.; McPherson, James B.; Milliken's Bend, Battle of; Pemberton, John C.; Port Hudson, Louisiana Campaign; Porter, David Dixon; Sherman, William Tecumseh; Smith, Martin Luther.

For further reading:

Bearss, Edwin C. *The Campaign for Vicksburg* (1985–1986).

Cannan, John, ed. *War in the West: Shiloh to Vicksburg, 1862–1863: Eyewitness History of the Civil War* (1990).

Carter, Samuel, III. *The Final Fortress: The Campaign for Vicksburg, 1862–1863* (1980).

Johnson, Robert Underwood, and Clarence Clough Buel, eds. *Battles and Leaders of the Civil War: Being for the Most Part Contributions by Union and Confederate Officers* (1887–1888).

Pemberton, John C. *Pemberton, Defender of Vicksburg* (1987).

Woodworth, Steven E. *Jefferson Davis and His Generals: The Failure of Confederate Command in the West* (1990).

Miers, Earl Schenck. *The Web of Victory: Grant at Vicksburg* (1955; reprint, 1983).

VICTOR, ORVILLE JAMES
(1827–1910)
Editor and early Civil War historian

Though best remembered today—when he is remembered at all—as the longtime editor of the Beadle Dime Novels, Orville Victor was a passionate pro-Union writer and historian who in the years before and during the Civil War brought his perspective to the public using both his own writings and his position as editor for Erastus Beadle's many series of cheap books.

Born in Sandusky, Ohio, Victor spent a short time studying law there but quickly found his real career in editing. He held a variety of positions as a writer and editor in Ohio, including five years at the *Sandusky Daily Register*. Like his future wife, Metta Victoria Fuller, Victor was befriended by prominent editor Rufus Griswold, who was instrumental in introducing many "western" writers to East Coast readers. Victor married Metta Fuller in 1856, and the couple moved to New York, where Victor edited both the *Cosmopolitan Art Journal* and the *United States Journal*.

Sometime early in 1861 Victor went to work for Erastus Beadle and served as editor for various Beadle publications. He also continued to write, focusing on political and historical topics, including slavery and, eventually, the Civil War. Victor's first major statement on the war was published in London by Beadle's London branch. *The American Rebellion, Some Facts and Reflections for the Consideration of the English People* was published as by "An American Citizen," but the attribution to Victor is sure, beginning with the preface, which is signed "V." Victor also gave a hand-signed copy to the Library of Congress. *The American Rebellion* is only forty-eight pages long, but in the essay Victor manages to discuss nine different topics, including "The Immediate Cause of the Rebellion," "The Religious Sentiment of the Country on the Rebellion," "Purposes of the Federal Authorities in Waging a Contest with the 'Southern Confederacy,'" and "Confederate Dishonor." He ends with an appeal to commercial interests, arguing that the English public would be economically unwise to cast their fate with that of the slaveholding South.

Around the same time, Victor also produced a series of essays on "American Conspiracies," including discussions of the Denmark Vesey and Nat Turner rebellions. These essays were published first in 1861 in the June and August issues of the *Atlantic Monthly* and were republished by the firm of J. D. Torrey in 1863 as part of the volume *History of American Conspiracies*. In this volume, Victor also included a sketch of John Brown's conspiracy, though he feared that so much of a partisan nature had been written about Brown that it was perhaps premature to hope for accuracy. Victor wrote, however, that his sketch "was as complete as it is possible at this time to make it."

Victor also promoted his views through the production, promotion, and sale of his wife's antislavery novel, *Maum Guinea*. He had even more direct responsibility for Beadle productions such as the three *Men of the Time* pamphlets. These three small (99- to 100-page) booklets each profiled a number of Civil War generals. Halleck, Pope, Siegel, Corcoran, Prentiss, Kearny, Hatch, and Augur were the subjects of the first booklet, which was published in September 1862. In October, a second volume profiled Butler, Banks, Burnside, Baker, Stevens, Wilcox, and Weber. Finally, in November, Generals Hooker, Rosecrans, Grant, Mitchell, and McClernand were profiled. Each booklet included four or five portraits, as well as the biographical sketches.

Also in 1862, Victor (under his frequent pen name, "Louis LeGrand, M.D."); wrote a full-length biography of Major General George B. McClellan, which ended with a chapter on the western Virginia campaign and McClellan's appointment as "General-in-Chief." Victor also wrote a biography, *The Private and Public Life of Abraham Lincoln* (1864), for Beadle. In the Lincoln volume (which was first published just before the assassination and was reprinted with extra material just after), Victor wrote that he was writing despite the plethora of other Lincoln biographies, because those books were "prepared for partisan purposes chiefly" and did not include "the material which we most desired—the facts of his boyhood and student days, and the narrative of his first steps in public life." Despite this claim, and Victor's use of half of the volume's pages to describe Lincoln's life before his first election, the biography is primarily a political document, with no details of Lincoln's marriage or his children and fully half of the pages devoted to the Civil War. Victor (who also edited the Beadle books of classic speeches) included a complete transcription of Lincoln's Gettysburg Address, which he introduced as "this beautiful address."

Victor was also involved in other Beadle publications published about the war, ranging from *Victor Hugo's Letter on John Brown with Mrs. Ann S. Stephens' Reply* (1860) to *The Soldiers' Directory to Pensions and Bounties* (1862) and *Report of Lieut.-General Ulyssus [sic] S. Grant on the Operations of the Union Army from March, 1862 to the Close of the Rebellion* (1865, with a fifth edition published in 1866). (Johannsen notes that on the title page, if not the cover, "Ulysses" is spelled correctly.)

Beginning in 1861, Victor began work with J. D. Torrey on a compendium history of the war. The work was originally sold by canvassers through subscription and published in sections with "thirty-two octavo letterpress pages being demanded weekly" according to the preface that Victor wrote later for the complete series. Victor compiled his information by collating the information published in the New York newspapers and adding to that government documents and private correspondence from various actors in the war. Eventually, the project grew to four volumes that covered the war and ended with an account of Lincoln's assassination and the death of John Wilkes Booth. Included in each volume are maps, documents, and some illustrations. One interesting and modern feature is a nearly day-by-day chronology at the beginning of each volume that briefly recounts the major events of each month of the war.

Victor's advice was crucial to the many authors who wrote for the publishing house of Beadle & Adams, and his influence over what was printed by the firm was enormous. With few exceptions (for example, *The Unionist's Daughter* in 1864), Victor did not encourage fiction about the war. His devotion to the Union, and his serious and deep concern about slavery and the horrors of the Civil War led him to separate his own historical work from the entertainments produced by the firm of Beadle & Adams. He would have been pleased to note that his obituaries included admiring mention of his early historical work on the war, even if his long relationship with the dime novel has since overshadowed his scholarly efforts.

—JoAnn E. Castagna

See also Maum Guinea.
For further reading:
Derby, J. C. *Fifty Years among Authors, Readers, and Publishers* (1884).
Johannsen, Albert. *The House of Beadle and Adams* (1950).
Pearson, Edmund. *Dime Novels* (1929).

VILLARD, HENRY
(1835–1900)
Journalist

Born Ferdinand Heinrich Gustave Hilgard in the Bavarian region of Germany in 1835, the young immigrant renamed himself Henry Villard upon arrival in the United States in 1853. Like many German immigrants of this period, he had links to the abortive Revolution of 1848. Villard was the university-educated son of a judge who arrived in America with no knowledge of English, yet within six years he became a primary reporter for several of the most influential English-language newspapers during one of the most critical periods of American history.

After trying several careers, including the study of law, Villard became a reporter for the German-language newspaper the *Staats-Zeitung* in 1858. His quick progress in learning English and recognition of the importance of the story of the discovery of gold at Pike's Peak, Colorado, led to a position as a correspondent for the English-language *Cincinnati Commercial* in 1859. He quickly exploited that experience and produced a popular guidebook, *The Past and Present of the Pike's Peak Gold Regions*. He covered the Lincoln-Douglas debates in Illinois for the *Commercial*. As a result of the experience, Villard became an early admirer of Abraham Lincoln, with whom he would have an enduring friendship. Villard thus displayed in his early years in America the talent, drive, and versatility that would mark his entire career and bring him in contact with some of the most important men and events of Civil War–era America.

As a correspondent for the Cincinnati paper, he covered the 1860 Republican National Convention in Chicago. During the presidential campaign season he also supplied copy for the *St. Louis Daily Missouri Democrat* and the *New York Tribune*. After the election of Lincoln, the *New York Herald* appointed him to a correspondent's position to cover Lincoln in his home town of Springfield, Illinois, and Lincoln's departure for Washington D.C. Villard concurrently supplied western dailies and other East Coast newspapers with news of the new administration's plans. This series made the twenty-five-year-old German immigrant, in the country only seven years, the primary reporter of political news in the United States.

Following his own political inclinations and the influence of Lincoln and the Republicans he covered in the late 1850s and early 1860s, Villard unsurprisingly became an ardent supporter of the Union. When the war broke out, he became a correspondent alternately for the *New York Herald* and the *New York Tribune*. During the war years, his byline was seen in numerous American newspapers through reprints of his stories for the New York papers and his continuing relationship with western newspapers. Villard reported on the war first-hand from the lines of the Union army in the Virginia and western campaigns until poor health forced him temporarily to give up his job in 1863.

In 1864, Henry Villard was back on the front lines with the Army of the Potomac in Virginia for the news agency he formed with reporters from a Chicago daily. After the war ended he served as a reporter for American and European newspapers, and in 1866 he married Helen Frances Garrison, daughter of editor and abolitionist Henry Lloyd Garrison. Henry Villard's active career as a journalist ended by 1868, when he accepted the secretaryship of the American Social Science Association, which involved him in a number of govern-mental reform efforts. This position served as a transition to the career in finance that would occupy him for the remainder of his life.

In the 1870s he turned to financing transportation corporations and gained control of various steamship and rail companies on the Pacific coast. Villard had great confidence in the future of the region and became an early benefactor of the University of Oregon. By 1881 he managed to gain control of the Northern Pacific Railroad and was considered the most powerful man in the industry. His investments from 1870 to 1890 included Thomas Edison's General Electric Company (in which he served as president from 1889 to 1893) and controlling shares of *The New York Evening Post* and *The Nation* in 1881.

Henry Villard could serve as an example of an immigrant who, in the dynamic culture and economy of mid-nineteenth-century America, arrived with nothing and rose to the top of society. He arrived in America at a critical moment in history with the intelligence, talents, and good fortune that placed him among important events and people. But ultimately it was his ability to shift from reporting to creating events that marked not only the man, but also this volatile period of history.

—*Gretchen A. Adams*

See also New York Tribune; Newspapers; War Correspondents.
For further reading:
Hedges, James Blaine. *Henry Villard and the Railways of the Northwest* (1930).
Villard, Henry. *Memoirs of Henry Villard* (1904; reprint, 1969).

A Federal cavalry column along the Rappahannock River, Virginia, 1862 (*National Archives*)

VIRGINIA

No state experienced the Civil War more completely than Virginia. Its geographical location, its industries, its food production, and the presence of the Confederate capital at Richmond made it a logical battleground for most of the fighting in the Eastern theater of the war. As a result, the civilian population saw and felt the results of war almost from the very beginning of the conflict.

Like all states of the Confederacy, the civilian population was divided in its loyalties. Many Virginians opposed secession, and many others came to embrace secession very reluctantly. Therefore, one of the last of the Southern states to secede became one of the most hotly contested battlegrounds of the war.

Before the start of the Civil War, and even before the election of 1860 and the secession crisis it triggered, Virginia was home to supporters of disunion. Radical secessionists, or "Fire-eaters" such as Edmund Ruffin, had been urging disunion for years and were given added ammunition in the fall of 1859 when abolitionist John Brown led his raid on Harper's Ferry, Virginia. The elec-

tion of Republican Abraham Lincoln the following fall further excited passions in Virginia and throughout the South. As the Gulf States made their exit, however, most Virginians preferred to wait and see what the new president planned.

Governor John Letcher, who like many in the state during the early stages of the crisis preferred to remain in the Union, called for the election of a convention to decide the matter for the state. Meanwhile, Virginia also sponsored the convening of the Washington Peace Conference in order to arrive at a compromise.

While the actions of the Peace Conference came to nothing, the Virginia convention that gathered had no intention of taking Virginia out of the Union, unless the Federal government attempted to use force against the seceded states. Both the Confederate States of America—as those seceded states were now known—and the United States anxiously watched to see what Virginia would do.

The crisis in Charleston Harbor spurred Virginia to make a choice. When Lincoln on 15 April 1861 called for 75,000 militiamen to suppress the rebellion, the

Barricades on Duke Street in Alexandria, Virginia, built to protect the Orange & Alexandria Railroad from Confederate cavalry, 1861. (*National Archives*)

Pontoon bridge across the James River at Richmond, Virginia, 1865 (*National Archives*)

Virginia convention voted two days later by a vote of 88 to 55 to secede. Military expeditions were launched to seize the Federal arsenal at Harper's Ferry and the Gosport Navy Yard in Norfolk. One of the partially destroyed ships captured there, the USS *Merrimack*, was salvaged and converted into the CSS *Virginia*, the Confederacy's first ironclad. By the end of April Virginia had joined the Confederacy, and Richmond became the capital of the Confederate States of America.

Virginia added a large population and considerable industrial and natural resources to the Confederacy. The Tredegar Iron Works in Richmond alone proved invaluable to the Confederacy's warmaking capacity. These resources, along with Virginia's location, meant that when fighting began, much of it would be in the Old Dominion. Knowing this as well, many sons of Virginia left the officer ranks of the United States Army and offered their services to the state. One of them, Robert E. Lee, assumed command of state forces at the end of April 1861. In June the force he organized entered the Confederate army.

In spite of this apparent show of unity and strength, Virginia was a divided state. The people of the western mountains had opposed secession and now opposed supplying troops to the Confederacy. The United States hoped to take advantage of this disaffection by opening military operations in western Virginia in June 1861. This Federal presence would eventually result in the secession of West Virginia from Virginia.

In the meantime, fighting had started on the York Peninsula at Big Bethel on 10 June and in the lower Shenandoah Valley. The early military confrontations in Virginia were capped by the first major battle of the war near Bull Run Creek at Manassas Junction on 21 July 1861. The Federal attempt to take this important rail junction failed.

Militarily, while the Confederacy still suffered reverses in western Virginia, the other Federal attempts to gain significant territory in the state had failed by the end of 1861. During the early months of 1862 it appeared that the state would remain relatively untouched. Finally, under orders from President Lincoln, Major General George McClellan undertook the operation that would become known as his Peninsula campaign. In April and May 1862 McClellan moved his large army up the York Peninsula toward Richmond causing civilians in his path and in Richmond to flee in panic. After fighting at Seven Pines just outside of Richmond on 31 May resulted in the serious wounding of Confederate field commander General Joseph E. Johnston of Virginia, command of the army was given to General Robert E. Lee, who dubbed his force the Army of Northern Virginia.

Street scene in Warrenton, Virginia, ca. 1862 (*National Archives*)

During these early stages of the Peninsula campaign, the brilliant campaign of Confederate major general Thomas Jonathan "Stonewall" Jackson in what would become his famous Shenandoah Valley campaign, effectively neutralized over twice his numbers in Federal troops. Through the first weeks of June, while Jackson completed his work in the valley, Lee strengthened his defenses at Richmond and prepared to attack. Lee intended to destroy the Union army in the series of battles that became known as the Seven Days', but he was able to push McClellan back only to the James River.

In August Lee moved north of Richmond to counter the threat posed by Major General John Pope's Army of Virginia. At the battle of Second Bull Run, Lee dealt the Union general a decisive defeat. By then Virginia had been experiencing the war firsthand for over a year, and some areas had suffered terrible devastation. As a result, Lee determined to take the fighting out of the state during the crucial harvest season. This decision resulted in Lee's Maryland invasion of September 1862 and his retreat back to Virginia following the battle of Antietam.

McClellan's failure to pursue Lee's army after Antietam resulted in his replacement by Major General

Ambrose Burnside. While Burnside moved toward Richmond from the north, Lee collected his army on the heights overlooking Fredericksburg, Virginia. Burnside's ill-fated attack there on 13 December 1862 resulted in a miserable Union defeat. In early 1863 Joseph Hooker replaced Burnside.

Even with Burnside's defeat, Union forces still operated widely throughout western Virginia and throughout the area north of the Rappahannock River, making life unpleasant for the civilian population of the state. Confederate soldiers in Lee's army fared even worse. Chronic shortages of everything from shoes to food to medical supplies plagued the Army of Northern Virginia. Virginia and most people in it were suffering.

Neither the Confederate nor the state government seemed equipped to deal with the suffering and poverty brought by the war. Virginia was hardly unique in this, and like the other Confederate states was unable to cope with the misery the war brought to so many. By 1863 shortages of every sort plagued the common people. Even when necessities were available, growing inflation put most prices out of range for the average person. On 2 April 1863 the first of the Richmond Bread Riots occurred. Hungry women and their children first

Digging the Durch Gap Canal on the James River, Virginia, 1864 (*National Archives*)

protested the high prices and shortages and then stormed Richmond stores and took what they needed.

Far more dangerous lawlessness threatened more remote parts of the state, as criminals took advantage of the breakdown in law and order to prey on the helpless or isolated areas of the state. Richmond did not escape this criminal element as the increased population of the capital drew in those who saw an opportunity to make a quick buck. Prostitutes, gamblers, and petty thieves all flocked to the city.

The spring of 1863 brought more fighting, while throughout Virginia women and children alone on many farms struggled to plant crops and feed themselves. The plantations of the Tidewater and Piedmont also tried to put in crops, in spite of an ever-dwindling slave population brought on by the African-American exodus to Union lines. Those slaves found near combat areas often were pressed into labor by both armies.

While the cavalry of both sides tested each other's weaknesses, Joseph Hooker planned to flank Lee's position at Fredericksburg. This maneuver resulted in the battle of Chancellorsville in May 1863, some would argue Lee's greatest victory. The victory was not without cost because it resulted in the death of one of Virginia's

greatest heroes, Stonewall Jackson. Following the battle, Lee determined once again to take the war to the North in an attempt to draw the Union armies out of Virginia.

Lee's second invasion resulted in his defeat at Gettysburg, Pennsylvania, and the return of his army and the Union army to Virginia in the fall of 1863. The two armies maneuvered throughout the fall and then watched each other through the winter months. The suffering among civilians and soldiers brought on by shortages of every kind increased.

In March 1864 Ulysses S. Grant assumed command of all Union armies and joined the Army of the Potomac in a crushing campaign against the Army of Northern Virginia. While Union forces were turned loose in the Shenandoah Valley to prevent that fertile area from supplying Lee's army, Grant, beginning at the Wilderness in early May 1864, hammered away at Lee's depleted force. From the Wilderness to Spotsylvania to the North Anna Crossing to Cold Harbor, Grant pounded and flanked. While Lee's army did not break, it suffered horrific casualties. Although these losses were not as great as Grant's, Lee's could not be replaced. Unable to push through Lee's defenses, Grant in the middle of June 1864 crossed the James River and

Loading supplies at City Point, Virginia, 1864 (*National Archives*)

attempted to move on Richmond from the south, via Petersburg. Lee shifted his forces just in time to meet the threat, and the siege of Petersburg began. During the nine months of the siege the people of southern Virginia suffered as they had never suffered before. Now added to their hunger and disease was the bombardment by Federal artillery.

Southern Virginia was not the only area of the state feeling the effects of combat. During the late spring and early summer of 1864 the army of Major General David Hunter devastated the Shenandoah Valley. In the fall another Federal army commanded by Major General Philip Sheridan, in pursuit of Major General Jubal Early's force, completed the work of destruction.

Meanwhile Grant continued to extend his lines at Petersburg, forcing Lee to do the same, until finally at the end of March 1865 Lee knew he would be trapped if he did not leave his trenches. He made a run west, was defeated in several rear-guard actions and finally was forced to surrender at Appomattox Court House. While Lee tried to escape, Richmond was occupied by Federal troops. The war in Virginia was over.

During that war, more than 200 battles and skirmishes were fought in Virginia. In the process, countless millions of dollars' worth of property was destroyed, and thousands of lives were lost. The economy was wrecked for a generation. One need only travel the roads of Virginia today and observe the monuments and historical markers to see that there was hardly a place in the state not touched by the war.

—*David S. Heidler and Jeanne T. Heidler*

See also Army of Northern Virginia; Big Bethel, Battle of; Bull Run, First Battle of; Chancellorsville, Battle of; Fredericksburg, First Battle of; Lee, Robert Edward; Peninsula Campaign; Petersburg Campaign; Seven Days', Battles; Tredegar Iron Works; West Virginia.

For further reading:

Blair, William. *Virginia's Private War: Feeding Body and Soul in the Confederacy, 1861–1865* (1998).

Robertson, James I., Jr. *Civil War Virginia: Battleground for a Nation* (1991).

VIRGINIA, CSS
Confederate ironclad

The CSS *Virginia* fought in the March 1862 battle at Hampton Roads against the Union ironclad *Monitor*. The *Virginia* was originally the USS *Merrimack*, an auxiliary steam-powered forty-gun frigate of 3,500 tons. It was launched from the Boston Navy

Ruins of the Navy Yard at Norfolk, Virginia, December 1864 (*National Archives*)

Yard at Charlestown, Massachusetts in June 1855, and although in its best days it never exceeded seven knots, it was for several years the pride of the U.S. Navy. Immediately after its completion, the *Merrimack* served with the West Indian Squadron for a year before being decommissioned for engine repairs in 1857. In September 1857 the frigate returned to service as the flagship of the Pacific Squadron and remained with that station until it was again decommissioned for an extensive equipment overhaul at Norfolk in February 1860.

The *Merrimack* fell into Confederate hands when the Norfolk Gosport Navy Yard was captured from the Union at the outset of the Civil War. During the morning of 20 April 1861, the commander of the navy yard, Commodore C. S. McCauley, ordered his forces to spike the yard's guns and scuttle the ships rather than allow them to be captured. Three hours later, Captain Charles Wilkes arrived to evacuate the beleaguered Union force, but he did not perceive the immediate danger; Wilkes instead tried to save the doomed vessels. But failing to salvage them, he ordered the ships completely destroyed to prevent their use by the Confederates. Union troops fired the seven ships present, including the *Merrimack*.

Forty days later, a salvage company raised the *Merrimack* and towed it into dry dock. Confederate secretary of the navy Stephen Russell Mallory convinced Congress to appropriate the $172,523 needed to convert the 275-foot burned-out hull into an ironclad; Lieutenant John M. Brooke prepared the drawings and calculations necessary for the transformation. By mid-July, carpenters had stripped the charred timbers from the hull and eliminated all timbers above the berth deck (three feet above the ship's unladen waterline). Workers laid a new gun deck from bow to stern. By the end of July, carpenters prepared to attach the casemated, or bombproof, iron exterior.

Procuring iron for the *Merrimack* soon became the greatest obstacle. The Tredegar Iron Works at Richmond was the only plant in the South capable of supplying the necessary metal for the project, yet the company was not initially prepared to roll iron for plating. It took weeks to transform its operations, train its workers, and create tools to produce the required material. Additionally, the iron itself had to be found to create the two-inch-thick, eight-inch-wide plating. Ultimately, more than 300 tons of scrap iron was gathered from the ruins of the Gosport

The beached smokestack of the CSS *Virginia* (*Library of Congress*)

Navy Yard, scavenged from captured Union railroad lines, and purchased from Confederate railroad companies whose tracks were too close to the front to operate.

At the beginning of 1862, the ship's stern remained unarmored. By mid-January, machinists, blacksmiths, and bolt drivers agreed to work until 8:00 P.M. seven days a week until they had finished the project. The ship was completely armored by 27 January 1862. Three weeks later, on 17 February 1862, the rechristened CSS *Virginia* slid out of dry dock into the Elizabeth River.

With a hull measuring almost 263 feet from bow to stern, the rebuilt *Virginia* had a 178-foot, 3-inch iron casemated base atop its hull sloping upward at a 36-degree angle. The casemated sides, 24 feet from waterline to top, consisted of an outer shell of two 2-inch layers of iron plate fastened horizontally by metal bolts to a 2-foot-thick solid pine and 4-inch-thick oak backing. The ship had four gun ports on each side of the casemate and three 7-inch rifle ports at each end. The main deck, also covered with iron plating, stretched 29 feet 6 inches in front of the casemate and 55 feet to the rear. Just below the waterline on the bow, the ship had a 1,500-pound cast-iron ram.

On 8 March 1862, the *Virginia* confronted the Union blockading force in Chesapeake Bay. The ironclad sank two Union frigates, drove three steam frigates aground, and exchanged fire with several small armed steamers and shore batteries. The following day the *Virginia* fought its duel against the *Monitor*, the Union ironclad. Beginning at about 8:45 A.M., the two ships began circling one another while trying to gain an advantageous position. The two ironclads battled furiously at close range for the next four hours, but they did minimal damage to each other. Neither vessel could claim a clear victory.

Because Union forces had gained control over Norfolk and the Gosport Navy Yard, Confederates destroyed the *Virginia* on the morning of 12 May 1862 to prevent it from being captured

—*Gene A. Smith*

See also Brooke, John Mercer; Gosport Navy Yard; *Monitor*; *Monitor* versus *Virginia*.

For further reading:

Brooke, John M. "The Virginia or Merrimac: Her Real Projector." Southern Historical Society Papers (1891).

Cline, William R. "The Ironclad Ram Virginia." Southern Historical Society Papers (1904).

Davis, William C. Duel between the First Ironclads (1975).

Smith, Gene A. Iron and Heavy Guns: Duel between the Monitor and Merrimac (1996).

Still, William N. Iron Afloat: The Story of the Confederate Armorclads (1985).

Trexler, Harrison A. The Confederate Ironclad Virginia (Merrimac) (1938).

VIRGINIA MILITARY INSTITUTE

Founded in 1839, the Virginia Military Institute (VMI) was established on the site of a Virginia state arsenal at Lexington. The guard there disturbed the life of the small community, and Lexington's leading citizens sought to change the arsenal into a military college whereby the students would protect the arms stored there, but also pursue an education. The Virginia legislature agreed, and on its establishment VMI was only the second governmental military academy in America after the United States Military Academy was established at West Point in 1802. One of its founders, Colonel J. T. L. Preston, designed the name: "Virginia" to designate its nature as a state institution, "Military" for its salient feature, and "Institute" to indicate that it differed from either a college or university.

VMI was a leader in providing scientific education (in 1846 it offered the first course in industrial chemistry in the South), and it had the special mission of providing teachers for the commonwealth. In addition to Preston, its early leaders included Claudius Crozet and Francis H. Smith. State Engineer of Virginia Colonel Crozet was a graduate from the École Polytechnique in France and had served as an officer under Napoleon and a professor of engineering at West Point. He headed the Board of Visitors. Smith, a distinguished graduate of West Point, was VMI's superintendent during its first half-century and became a leader in education in the South. Among VMI's instructors at the start of the Civil War was Thomas J. "Stonewall" Jackson, who joined the faculty in 1851 and taught natural philosophy (physics), but was disliked by the cadets for his inflexible manner of teaching.

When Virginia joined the Confederacy, the VMI Cadet Corps was called out under the command of Jackson to train recruits for the Confederate army at Richmond. After serving as drill instructors for eight months, the cadets returned to Lexington to further their education and prepare to be Confederate officers. During the next three years, the Corps was called into active duty on a number of occasions for service in the Shenandoah Valley. The cadets played a key role in the 15 May 1864 battle of New Market; 279 of them were at New Market, where the result temporarily saved the Shenandoah Valley from Union occupation. Five died, five were mortally wounded, and forty-seven were wounded, for a 20 percent casualty rate. It is the only instance in United States history in which students from an educational institution fought as a unit in battle.

Numerous VMI graduates served in the Confederate army during the war. Confederate officers from VMI included three major generals, seventeen brigadier generals, ninety-two colonels, sixty-four lieutenant colonels, 107 majors, 306 captains, and 221 lieutenants. Just before the May 1863 battle of Chancellorsville, Lieutenant General Jackson saw so many VMI men around him that he remarked, "The Institute will be heard from today." A total of 249 VMI alumni and cadets died in the Civil War on the Confederate side.

In retaliation for the role of the cadets in the battle of New Market, on 12 June 1864 Union major general David Hunter ordered the destruction of the Institute, despite pleas by some of his subordinate officers. Only two buildings were spared. The Corps relocated to Richmond, where it spent the remainder of the war helping to defend the Confederate capital.

Following the Civil War, VMI was rebuilt and continued its mission of educating "citizen soldiers." Immediately after the war, VMI included among its faculty such well-known Confederate figures as John Mercer Brooke and Matthew Fontaine Maury. It also continued to contribute outstanding leaders both to civilian pursuits and the military, and it had a direct impact as a model for the creation of other educational institutions in the South, such as Louisiana State University and Texas A&M.

Today VMI prepares men and women for civilian and military life in a variety of educational pursuits. Among its distinguished graduates have been two commandants of the U.S. Marine Corps, but its most illustrious graduate was General of the Army George C. Marshall, chief of staff of the United States Army during the Second World War. One of this nation's greatest soldiers and the consummate national servant, Marshall was the only professional soldier ever awarded the Nobel Prize for peace.

—Spencer C. Tucker

See also Brooke, John Mercer; Hunter, David; Jackson, Thomas J.; Maury, Matthew Fontaine; New Market, Battle of.

For further reading:

Conrad, James Lee. The Young Lions. Confederate Cadets at War (1997).

Wise, Jennings C. The Military History of the Virginia Military Institute from 1839 to 1865 (1915).

VON STEINWEHR, BARON ADOLF WILHELM AUGUST FRIEDRICH
(1822–1877)
Union general

Born into an aristocratic family of military leaders in Blankenburg, Brunswick, Adolf von Steinwehr had martial blood in his veins. His grandfather had served as a lieutenant general in the Prussian army against Napoleon, and his father was a major in the ducal army. Adolf von Steinwehr studied at the Brunswick military academy and entered the service of the duke as a lieutenant. He missed the turmoil of the 1848 revolution by requesting a leave of absence in 1847, coming to the United States, and serving as an officer in a volunteer Alabama regiment. After the Mexican-American War, he served with the Engineer Corps surveying Southern ports. During this time he married an Alabamian, but he failed to receive a regular army commission. Discouraged, he returned to Germany with his new family, and then he resigned his commission in the Brunswick army and resettled in Connecticut in 1854 as a farmer.

After the attack on Fort Sumter, von Steinwehr recruited a regiment of German volunteers in New York. His regiment, the 29th New York, was attached to Louis Blenker's all-German brigade, and as such was held in reserve during the battle of First Bull Run. Holding its ground at the stone bridge, the 29th New York was instrumental in covering the retreat of Irvin McDowell's army to Washington. Awarded a brigadier generalship for his foresight and bravery, von Steinwehr was assigned command of the second brigade of Blenker's division and took part in John C. Frémont's ill-fated Shenandoah campaign of 1862. He served in Franz Sigel's headquarters during Second Bull Run and commanded the 2d Division of XI Corps at Chancellorsville, where he used his engineering background effectively, building defensive ramparts in expectation of the Confederate flank attack that crashed into his corps. Unlike many of his German compatriots, von Steinwehr escaped much of the negative publicity surrounding Chancellorsville and retained command of his division at Gettysburg.

The nobleman's greatest day was 1 July 1863. Steinwehr's military experience helped him recognize the strategic value of Cemetery Hill for the Union. After arriving on the field, he pleaded with Major General Winfield Scott Hancock, temporarily commanding XI Corps, to allow his division to occupy a defensive position on the hill, rather than plunging directly into the battle with the rest of the corps. The Federal situation was deteriorating rapidly, and again XI Corps took the brunt of the Rebel assault. Looking through his binoculars, von Steinwehr could see that his corps was hard pressed north of town and needed the reinforcement his division could provide. Yet he also weighed the value of a solid, prepared defensive position for the corps to rally around, and he wisely chose the safer course of action, with Hancock's consent. Had von Steinwehr's division not occupied Cemetery Hill, as he had insisted, it is highly possible that the Confederates would have swept over the crest of the hill, occupied it, and taken the high ground at Gettysburg. Both Major General Oliver Otis Howard, commander of XI Corps, and Hancock later commended von Steinwehr for his foresight at Gettysburg, crediting him with saving the high ground for the Union. Congress, however, disagreed: its vote of thanks went to Howard.

Steinwehr accompanied XI Corps when it was transferred to Tennessee in late July 1863 to relieve besieged Chattanooga. His troops were integral in the famous Union night victory at Wauhatchie, but again von Steinwehr failed to receive his due credit. Unlike other German leaders such as Franz Sigel and Carl Schurz, von Steinwehr did not seek the glory of rank; instead, he comforted himself on duty well served. Especially gifted in matters relating to the general staff, von Steinwehr was nonetheless a talented field commander. He won the respect of many West Point officers for the performance of his men at Lookout Mountain and Missionary Ridge. He also was well known as an effective antiguerrilla leader: in the Shenandoah Valley he took civilian hostages as security against bushwhackers, earning the enmity of the Confederate government. Richmond declared that if he were captured, von Steinwehr would never be paroled.

"If knowledge, experience, and military ability had determined the selection of a supreme commander of the German troops in the East," Ella Lonn writes, "[von Steinwehr] would have probably received the distinction." Yet this German refused to play the political games of other German and ethnic leaders and did not complain when passed over for promotion. He was a true soldier, whose greatest assets were his European military training and background coupled with an astute eye, which allowed him to scan battlefields and instantly recognize the strategic pressure points. His detailed knowledge of military history, experience in the Mexican-American War, engineering ability, and organizational skills combined to make him one of the most gifted ethnic commanders of the war.

After the war, von Steinwehr belatedly received recognition for his talents as a professor of military science at Yale. He soon left academia and became an engineer for the federal government, inculcating a higher standard of accuracy, beauty, and professionalism in postwar American cartography. He died on 25 February 1877 in Buffalo, New York.

—*Christian B. Keller*

See also German-Americans.

For further reading:
Burton, William L. *Melting Pot Soldiers: The Union's Ethnic Regiments* (1988; reprint, 1998).

Kaufmann, Wilhelm. *Die Deutschen im Amerikanischen Buergerkriege* (1911).
Lonn, Ella. *Foreigners in the Union Army and Navy* (1951).

For further reading:
Barrow, William L. Suckow, For Suckow, The Emigrant Bauer.
Agawam (Wisc.), reprint 1996.

Kirchhoff, Wilhelm. Die Deutschen im Amerikanischen
Haupttreffen (1911).
Diehm, Das Programm zum Union Army of 1862-1863.

WADDELL, JAMES IREDELL
(1824–1886)
Confederate naval officer

Born in Pittsboro, North Carolina, on 13 July 1824 and reared by his parental grandparents, James Waddell was educated at the Bingham's School in Hillsboro. He received an appointment as a midshipman in the U.S. Navy on 10 September 1841. His first assignment was aboard the USS *Vandalia*. A duel with another midshipman in 1842 left Waddell with a permanent limp and cost him eleven months of active duty. During the Mexican War from February to October 1846 he served aboard the brig USS *Somers*. He then reported to the Naval Academy at Annapolis, where he remained for two years. In August 1847 he became a passed midshipman.

Waddell then briefly served at the Naval Observatory, Washington, D.C., followed by assignments in the Mediterranean and at the Naval Academy. He then served three years on the USS *Germantown* off Brazil, during which cruise in September 1855 he was promoted to lieutenant. For a time he taught navigation at the Naval Academy. Ordered to the steamer *Saginaw* in July 1859, he sailed with her to the Pacific. Later transferred to the sloop of war USS *John Adams*, he was at St. Helena in November 1861 when he first learned of the actual start of the Civil War. He immediately wrote to Secretary of the Navy Gideon Welles to resign his commission, which Welles accepted in January 1862 when the *John Adams* arrived at New York. Two months later, on 27 March 1862, Waddell was commissioned a lieutenant in the Confederate navy.

Waddell's first assignment was to the ram CSS *Mississippi*, then under construction at New Orleans, but she had to be destroyed to prevent capture by Flag Officer David Farragut's Federal squadron. Waddell returned to Richmond and was then assigned to naval batteries ashore, first at Drewry's Bluff, Virginia, and then at Charleston, South Carolina.

In March 1863 Confederate secretary of the navy Stephen Mallory ordered Waddell to Europe, where he was to be assigned to one of the Laird Rams then nearing completion in England. When Union protests caused the British government to block the transfer of these ships to the Confederacy, Waddell was told he would be assigned to a commerce raider or blockade runner.

On 5 September 1863 Flag Officer Samuel Barron, the ranking Confederate officer in Europe, promoted Waddell to lieutenant commander. Confederate naval agent in Britain James D. Bulloch had secured the fast merchant ship *Sea King*, the last Confederate cruiser he was able to get to sea. Waddell was named her commander, and Barron instructed him to locate and destroy the Union whaling fleet.

Her ownership concealed, the *Sea King* slipped out of the Thames estuary on what appeared to be a merchant voyage, but then proceeded to Funchal on the Island of Madeira where she rendezvoused with the supply ship *Laurel* carrying the remainder of her crew and her armament. On 19 October 1864 Waddell officially commissioned the *Sea King* a Confederate warship under the name *Shenandoah* and began his cruise for Union vessels.

The *Shenandoah* took six Union vessels as prizes in the Atlantic. During January and early February 1865 Waddell was at Melbourne, Australia, where the ship was drydocked to repair a defective propeller shaft and bearing. She sailed again on 18 February. Although the *Shenandoah* took Union ships in four oceans, most of the damage she effected was in the Bering Sea and the Arctic Ocean, where Waddell located and destroyed much of the Union whaling fleet. Seamen from his prizes even enlisted in the Confederate navy. Refusing to believe reports of the end of the war, Waddell even planned a descent on San Francisco to destroy Union shipping there. Despite the discovery aboard Union vessels of newspapers carrying news of Lee's surrender, not until 2 August, after he had left Northern waters, was Waddell convinced by news from a British ship that the war was over.

The strain of the long cruise and threat of possible encounter with Union warships took a toll on the crew. Journals by crew members tell of drunkenness and occasional fights aboard the ship, and one of his officers charged that Waddell turned into a vicious, unreasonable tyrant. Like Raphael Semmes of the CSS *Alabama*, Waddell held himself aloof from his officers and men and was considered humorless and single-minded.

Believing that the destruction of so many Union merchant ships after the official end of the war would

lead the United States to accuse him of piracy, Waddell disguised his ship and sailed her 17,000 miles to Britain without stopping at any port or communicating with any other ship. In the process, the *Shenandoah* became the only Confederate warship to sail around the world. Reaching Liverpool on 6 November 1865, Waddell surrendered to British authorities. In all, the *Shenandoah* had traveled some 58,000 miles, during which journey she had put into port only once. Waddell had taken in all 38 prizes. He burned 32 of them and commandeered the remainder; damage to Union shipping was estimated at more than $1.36 million.

Confined to his ship for a few days by British authorities, Waddell was soon released. He remained in Britain until he was certain he would not be prosecuted by U.S. authorities. In 1875, he returned to the United States and became a captain for the Pacific Mail Company. Waddell was captain of the 4,000-ton liner *San Francisco* when, on 16 May 1877, during her maiden voyage to the United States from Melbourne, she struck an unmarked reef fourteen miles off the coast of Mexico. Waddell brought the ship to within three miles of shore before she went down, and all hands survived. The company directors did not blame Waddell, and he continued as a captain with that firm for several years before becoming commander of the Maryland State Fishery Force. Waddell wrote an account of the *Shenandoah*'s cruise, probably for his family. He died at Annapolis on 15 March 1886.

—Spencer C. Tucker

See also Bulloch, James D.; Mallory, Stephen R.; Navy, C.S.A.; *Shenandoah*, CSS.

For further reading:
Hearn, Chester G. *Gray Raiders of the Sea. How Eight Confederate Warships Destroyed the Union's High Sea Commerce* (1992).
Horn, Stanley F. *Gallant Rebel: The Fabulous Cruise of the C.S.S. Shenandoah* (1947).
Morgan, Murray. *Dixie Raider: The Saga of the C.S.S. Shenandoah* (1948).
Waddell, James T. *C.S.S. Shenandoah: The Memoirs of Lieutenant Commander James I. Waddell.* James D. Horan, ed. (1960).

WADE, BENJAMIN FRANKLIN
(1800–1878)
U.S. senator

Born on 27 October 1800 in Feeding Hills, Massachusetts, Benjamin Franklin Wade spent his formative years on his family's modest farm. At twenty-one, Wade followed his older siblings to Ohio, where in 1826 he entered upon a legal career. In 1831 he formed a law partnership with Joshua Giddings in the town of Jefferson; soon they both were converted to the antislavery cause. Wade was voted to Ohio's senate in 1837 as a Whig, but his early dedication to the rights of African-Americans contributed largely to preventing his being reelected two years later.

Wade married the former Caroline M. Rosecrans in 1841 and the next year served his second term in the Ohio senate. From 1847 to 1850, he served as the presiding judge of the Third Ohio Circuit Court, a forum from which he forcefully expressed his maturing antislavery sentiments. Wade was elected to the U.S. Senate in 1850, where his outspoken criticism of both Democrats and conservative members of his own Whig Party over the slavery question gained him notoriety. After the passage of the Kansas-Nebraska Act in 1854, Wade, disgusted by his party's acquiescence to Southern slaveholders, proclaimed himself an abolitionist and joined the new Republican organization.

Wade quickly established himself as a leader of the nascent party. His oratory was volatile as he battled congressional Democrats during the Kansas crisis. So too were his actions: after the notorious Preston Brooks–Charles Sumner caning incident, Wade attempted to bait Georgia senator Robert A. Toombs into fighting a duel. Along with other senators Zachariah Chandler and Simon Cameron, Wade swore to defend Northern honor, even to the extent of "carry[ing] the quarrel into the coffin."

After the outbreak of hostilities, Wade assumed the militant stance of most Radical Republicans in their desire to punish the Confederacy. His own thirst for war was unquenchable. For example, the Ohioan was present at the battle of First Bull Run as a civilian spectator, where he unsuccessfully attempted to stem the Federal rout. Wade's fanatical zeal—on and off the battlefield—earned him appointment as chair of the Joint Committee on the Conduct of the War in December 1861.

The committee, dominated by Wade and Chandler, became a persistent opponent to President Abraham Lincoln as the latter supervised the nation's military policy. Rather than attacking the president directly, however, Wade focused much of the committee's attention to the Union's politically conservative, West Point–trained officer cadre, whose members he considered inept at best, and treasonous at worst. Loyal soldiers emerged from committee investigations with damaged reputations. The tribunal in turn endorsed officers who supported the Radical program, regardless of their performance. In the end, the committee's actions did much to provoke distrust between the nation's army officers and political leadership.

Nonetheless, by 1864 the "Wade Committee" had become the leading mouthpiece for Radical Republicanism throughout the North. Indeed, its propaganda efforts condemning Rebel treatment of Federal prisoners at Fort Pillow, Tennessee, and elsewhere were widely successful and solidified Wade's reputation as a party principal. It was

in this background that the Ohioan made a desperate attempt to wrest party control away from Lincoln.

Wade, along with most congressional Radical Republicans, reacted negatively to the president's 1863 Proclamation of Amnesty and Reconstruction, believing it to be not only unconstitutional, but also unacceptably lenient toward former Confederate officials. Fighting for congressional control over Reconstruction, Wade and Maryland representative Henry W. Davis steered their more severe Reconstruction plan through Congress in July 1864. Lincoln then pocket vetoed the Wade-Davis Bill, thus incurring the fiery senator's wrath. In August, Davis and Wade took their case to the people, publishing the strident "Wade-Davis Manifesto" in the *New York Tribune*. The ploy backfired, creating deeper fissures within the Republican Party, and hurt Wade's own standing.

After Lincoln's assassination, Wade, like most Radical Republicans, hoped that Andrew Johnson would pursue a punitive Reconstruction policy, but Johnson did not live up to expectations. The president offered wholesale pardons to former Confederate officials and vetoed the Freedman's Bureau and civil rights bills. In 1868, Congress began impeachment proceedings against Johnson, charging executive usurpation. All present knew that Wade, as president pro tem of the Senate, would succeed Johnson as chief magistrate. The impeachment effort, a referendum on not only Johnson's leadership but also the eventuality of a Wade presidency, failed by one vote. His power broken, Wade retired at the close of the Fortieth Congress that December.

The former senator spent his remaining years engaged in various reform movements, including women's and worker's rights. Wade died at his Jefferson, Ohio, home on 2 March 1878.

—*Christopher S. Stowe*

See also Davis, Henry Winter; Joint Committee on the Conduct of the War; Radical Republicans; Republican Party; Wade-Davis Bill.

For further reading:

Land, Mary. "Ben Wade." In *For the Union: Ohio Leaders in the Civil War* (1968).

Riddle, A. G. *The Life of Benjamin F. Wade* (1886).

Tap, Bruce. *Over Lincoln's Shoulder: The Committee on the Conduct of the War* (1998).

Trefouse, Hans Louis. *Benjamin Franklin Wade: Radical Republican from Ohio* (1963).

Williams, T. Harry. *Lincoln and the Radicals* (1941).

WADE-DAVIS BILL
(July 1864)

In December 1863, Abraham Lincoln addressed Congress and announced a Proclamation of Amnesty and Reconstruction. His plan included a full pardon to all Rebels who had not held high Confederate office, accompanied by a full restoration of property rights in everything but slaves. To take advantage of the pardon, and to ensure full political participation in the future, a loyalty oath pledging to obey the laws of the U.S. Congress and the Constitution would have to be taken. Oath takers would also have to pledge to obey future presidential proclamations regarding slavery. The rebellious states would be granted political recognition when they called constitutional conventions and reestablished loyal state governments supported by at least one-tenth of the voters who had registered for the presidential election of 1860.

Lincoln's plan was well received by the majority of Republicans in Congress. His insistence on obedience to antislavery edicts made emancipation a cornerstone of the plan and won Lincoln many friends among the antislavery radicals in his party. Lincoln also acknowledged the integral role of Congress in the reconstruction process, particularly in the acceptance and readmission of those states that had been in a state of rebellion.

Discord between the executive and legislative branches of the Union government came about as a result of Lincoln's policies for the reestablishment of civil government in the occupied areas of Arkansas and Louisiana. Ongoing attempts to reorganize Louisiana's government were being obstructed by Unionist planters who claimed that the Emancipation Proclamation had been a wartime measure and that slavery, as under the former state constitution, could be reinstated after the war. By December 1863, Lincoln had decided to exert closer administrative control over the reconstruction process. The president turned control of Louisiana affairs to General Nathaniel Banks with instructions to expedite a free-state reorganization of the area. To comply with the president's wishes, Banks rejected recommendations for a state constitutional convention and called for an election of state officers in accordance with the old state constitution. The general also promised a state constitutional convention after the government was formed, but the plan aroused suspicion in Congress.

As events in Louisiana and Arkansas continued to unfold, congressional opposition to executive control of Reconstruction mounted for a number of reasons. Many members of Congress felt that the military involvement in the political reorganization of those areas usurped legislative authority. Many others felt that the president's policies would not be comprehensive enough to exclude former Rebels from government nor to ensure the rights of emancipated slaves. Some members of Lincoln's own party had political reasons; they sought to replace the president with Secretary of the Treasury Salmon Chase in the upcoming presidential election. On 2 July 1864, as the Thirty-eighth Congress drew to a close, a bill was passed that confronted executive policy and embodied many of the concerns and intentions of Congress. Named for Senator Benjamin Wade of Ohio and Representative Henry Winter Davis of Maryland, the Wade-Davis Bill made the abolition of slavery a first step in the political reorganization of any Southern state. To ensure republican government elected by the majority of voters, the bill also required that 50 percent, rather than 10 percent, of 1860 voters participate in the elections to reconstitute state governments. In addition, any electors to the state constitutional conventions were required to swear an "ironclad oath" of loyalty stating that they had never taken up arms against the United States.

Confronted with rebellion in his own party, Lincoln opposed the measure on the grounds that it promoted the abolition of slavery as the privilege of the legislature, rather than as a constitutional process. In addition, the president had previously stated his objections to being bound to a single set of inflexible guidelines for Reconstruction. Lincoln came under considerable party pressure to sign the bill, but because it had been passed at the very end of the congressional session, he was able to kill the legislation with a pocket veto. That Congress had adjourned shielded Lincoln from much criticism and debate over his failure to sign the measure. However, in August 1864, Wade and Davis collaborated to produce a manifesto denouncing the president's action. Printed in the *New York Tribune*, the Wade-Davis Manifesto blasted Lincoln for blocking congressional reconstruction. The two legislators charged that the president's actions constituted a "studied outrage" and that it was the place of the executive to obey and execute the laws, not make them.

Some Republicans criticized the Wade-Davis Bill as being too similar to the administration plan, so the bill was not symbolic of insurmountable philosophical differences between executive and legislature over the ultimate course of Reconstruction. Both sides envisioned the process of political reorganization within the regions as being the privilege of white voters. Lincoln, however, saw his plan as being implemented during the war, whereas the Wade-Davis plan saw Reconstruction as a postwar event. The bill revealed the congressional concern for the reestablishment of representative "republican" government through its imposition of the 50 percent requirement. The "ironclad oath" was also more stringent than the presidential oath because it made loyalty to the Union a matter of past, as opposed to current, behavior. The actions of Wade and Davis did reflect the fears shared by some within the Republican ranks that Lincoln was not firmly committed to the cause of emancipation. But regardless of loyalty percentages and oath refinements, both sides were firmly committed to the elimination of slavery and, in 1864, the majority of party members had no desire to repudiate the president.

—Stephen P. Budney

See also Congress, U.S.A.; Davis, Henry Winter; Election of 1864; Lincoln's Reconstruction Policy; Louisiana; Radical Republicans; Wade, Benjamin.

For further reading:
Belz, Herman. *Reconstructing the Union: Theory and Policy During the Civil War* (1969).
Cox, LaWanda. *Lincoln and Black Freedom: A Study in Presidential Leadership* (1981).
Donald, David Herbert. *Lincoln* (1995).
———. *Lincoln Reconsidered: Essays on the Civil War Era* (1956).

WADLEY, WILLIAM MORRILL
(1812–1882)
Confederate bureaucrat

William Morrill Wadley was born in Brentwood, New Hampshire, and immigrated to the South as a young man seeking his fortune. He settled in Savannah, Georgia, where he began working in the railroad industry. Over the years, he worked for a number of companies, gaining a reputation as one of the most knowledgeable railroad men in the South. As a result, when the Civil War began, he was in much demand by the Confederacy to help bring some order to its transportation system.

Although popular with the military and the Confederacy's executive branch, Wadley earned the everlasting enmity of Southern railroad owners, and hence their congressional representatives, by advocating the commandeering of all Southern railroads by the government for military use. In the fall of 1862, Jefferson Davis placed Wadley in charge of railroad transportation for the Army of Northern Virginia. When Davis named him superintendent of railroad transportation for all Confederate armies, however, the Confederate Congress refused to confirm the appointment. Davis then appointed him to head the Confederate Iron Commission, but even though Wadley held that position for the remainder of the war, he remained active in helping the armies manage their railroad transportation.

While working with the railroads, Wadley held what amounted to the honorary rank of colonel. However, without the authority of railroad superintendent, he had a great deal of trouble forcing states to comply with his directives. Even so, he was in much demand. In early 1863, Lieutenant General John C. Pemberton begged the War Department to send Wadley to Mississippi to help with the railroad transportation in the defense of Vicksburg.

Wadley's failure to bring any sort of coherence to the South's railroad transportation system illustrated the difficulties of fighting a war for survival in a country dedicated to the principles of private property and states' rights. Wadley's early call for central government management of the disorganized Southern railroads presented one of the few hopes the Confederacy had of truly capitalizing on its railroads.

After the war, Wadley moved to New Orleans. Returning to the work he knew best, he became the president of several Southern railroads in succession. He died in Saratoga Springs, New York.

—*David S. Heidler and Jeanne T. Heidler*

See also Railroads, C.S.A.

For further reading:
Wadley, Sarah Lois. *A Brief Record of the Life of William M. Wadley* (1884).

WADSWORTH, JAMES SAMUEL
(1807–1864)
Union general

Brevet Major General James S. Wadsworth inherited and built upon a sizable fortune, and by the onset of the Civil War he enjoyed an influence that extended well beyond his beloved Genesee Valley in western New York.

James Samuel Wadsworth was born 30 October 1807, the second child of five and the first son, to James Wadsworth and Naomi Wolcott Wadsworth, the latter a member of a prominent Connecticut family. In 1824, after less than a year at Havard College, young Wadsworth was dismissed. After studying law with Daniel Webster and others, and admission to the bar, Wadsworth began speculating in land in a manner rivaling that of his father. The result was his ownership of more than 70,000 acres in four states and a commodious house lavishly decorated for his six children and his wife, Mary Craig Wharton, one of the Philadelphia Whartons. Wadsworth was increasingly drawn into politics, and by 1858 he had shifted his allegiance from the Democratic Party to the Republicans.

By 1861, the ardor that characterized his life had induced the future general to conclude that "the time has come to strike [slavery] down for ever." This verdict led to his appointment to the ill-fated Washington Peace Conference in February 1861 and less than two months later motivated the 53-year-old Wadsworth to offer his services to the Union.

Initially Wadsworth bankrolled ferries to transport the 7th New York Volunteers to Washington after the rails between Washington and Baltimore were severed by secessionists. Shortly thereafter, when his appointment as a major general by New York State's governor was disallowed, Wadsworth became an unpaid aide to Major General Irvin McDowell at First Bull Run in July 1861. In turn, this led to Wadsworth's appointment as a brigade commander and military governor of the District of Columbia, where he commanded troops defending the capital or awaiting assignment. There his antislavery practices incurred the wrath of Marylanders and Virginians who demanded his compliance with the Fugitive Slave Law. However, he enjoyed the support of congressional Republicans and the administration.

In 1862, Military Governor Wadsworth played a role—possibly at Secretary of War Edwin Stanton's urging—in the administration's retention of McDowell's 25,000-man corps to defend Washington. Wadsworth thereby incurred the wrath of Major General George B. McClellan, who blamed the Army of the Potomac's failure to capture Richmond during the 1862 Peninsula campaign on the machinations of Wadsworth and other "Black Republicans." During the remainder of 1862, Wadsworth continued to receive and train incoming troops, provide refuge for freed people, and direct foraging expeditions. He was also a reluctant (and unsuccessful) candidate for governor of New York State.

Duty in Washington, however demanding, proved too inactive for General Wadsworth. Repeated requests for active duty resulted in his appointment as 1st Division commander in Major General John F. Reynolds's I Corps in 1863 just before Chancellorsville, in which he played a small role. By contrast, Wadsworth's small division was the first on the field in relief of Major General John Buford's beleaguered cavalry on 1 July 1863 at Gettysburg. Until late afternoon, his Iron Brigade staved off attacks by Major General A. P. Hill's Corps south of the Cashtown (Chambersburg) Road, while the 6th Wisconsin and regiments from Brigadier General Lyman Curler's brigade raced to the unfinished railroad, where they grabbed prisoners and momentarily helped check attacks by Lieutenant General Richard Ewell's Corps.

General Wadsworth's impetuousness led him to protest General George Meade's unwillingness to pursue more vigorously the Army of Northern Virginia. It also prompted him to resign his commission shortly after Gettysburg. Secretary Stanton instead sent him to determine the status of freed blacks in the Mississippi Valley, including their enlistment in the Union army. Wadsworth's report lent support to the Freedmen's Bureau, which was created later.

The reorganization of the Army of the Potomac in March 1864 led to Wadsworth's assignment as 4th Division commander in Major General Gouverneur K. Warren's redesignated V Corps. On 5 May 1864, Wadsworth's division faced the same confusion as others along the Orange Turnpike in the battle of the Wilderness and was beaten back. Early the next morning, his men assisted Major General Winfield Scott Hancock's II Corps in driving Hill's corps back down the Orange Plank Road. However, when Lieutenant General James Longstreet's corps came to Hill's relief, despite confessing fatigue, Wadsworth personally led a suicidal charge by the 20th Massachusetts against troops from Major General Richard Anderson's division. In that charge, the New Yorker was mortally wounded in the head by a minié ball and succumbed on 8 May 1864. After negotiations, Wadsworth's remains were recovered and escorted to Washington and then to New York City before being returned to Genesee, New York. There the 56-year-old civilian soldier was laid to rest in the large, fenced family plot.

—*Wayne Mahood*

See also Gettysburg, Battle of; Peninsula Campaign; Wilderness, Battle of the.
For further reading:
New York Monuments Commission. *Major General James S. Wadsworth at Gettysburg and Other Fields* (1916).
Pearson, Henry G. *James S. Wadsworth of Geneseo, Brevet Major General (U.S.V.)* (1913).
Wadsworth Family Papers. Library of Congress, Washington, D.C..

WAKEMAN, SARAH ROSETTA
(1843–1864)
Woman soldier

A farm girl from central New York State, Sarah Rosetta Wakeman made an astonishing contribution to American history when her Civil War–era letters to her family were discovered and published in 1994. For reasons that are only glimpsed in the collection, Rosetta Wakeman at age nineteen decided to leave her home in Afton, New York, and disguise herself as a man. In her travels, she encountered recruiters for the 153d New York State Volunteers, and she enlisted for three years or the duration of the war. For the next two years she served as a private in the Union army, using the name Lyons Wakeman.

Only two of approximately 400 women soldiers who took part in the Civil War wrote published memoirs of their army service, and only one of these memoirs, that of Sarah Emma E. Edmonds, has been confirmed as a substantially true account through biographical research. Viewed in this perspective, the Wakeman letters are all the more valuable. They represent the only unvarnished, contemporary account of a woman's experiences as a soldier during the Civil War to come to light.

Few clues are available as to why Wakeman left home in early August 1862, dressed as a man, and signed on as a Chenango Canal boatman. At the end of the month she reported her name as Lyons Wakeman to army recruiters, inflated her age to twenty-one, and enrolled in the 153d New York State Volunteers. The regiment was mustered into U.S. service in October 1862 and embarked for Washington, D.C., the next day. Private Lyons Wakeman's army career had begun.

On arriving in Washington on 22 October, the 153d Regiment was sent to perform provost marshal and guard duty in Alexandria, Virginia, as part of the extensive defenses of Washington City. While posted there for nine months, the 153d was often roused from sleep and formed in line of battle across the approaches to Washington to repel expected attacks.

Wakeman's letters home began during this period. Like most soldiers, she focused mainly on family and practical matters. But her situation as a soldier did not escape comment. "I don't fear the rebel bullets nor I don't fear the cannon," she wrote. She also assured her family that "For my part I am ready at a minute's warning to go into the field of battle and take my stand with the rest."

In July 1863, the 153d was transferred to Washington to guard against expected draft riots similar to those that had occurred in New York City. The 153d guarded the train depot, patrolled the city, and performed guard duty at several installations, including the Carroll and Old Capitol Prisons. Without irony, Wakeman reported home that one of the prisoners she guarded had served in the Union army as a major. "When the Rebels bullets was acoming like a hail storm she rode her horse and gave orders to her men," Wakeman related, and "Now She is in Prison for not doing aCordingly to the regulation of war."

In February 1864, the 153d was transferred to the field to take part in Major General Nathaniel P. Banks's ill-fated Red River campaign in Louisiana. The campaign commenced in March. Bad water, bad army diet, and almost 700 miles of hard marching and fighting in hot, humid Louisiana bayou and hill country wreaked havoc on unacclimated troops such as those of the 153d, who were said by one veteran of the campaign to sicken and die by the thousands.

Private Wakeman finally met the enemy on the field of battle at Pleasant Hill in early April, the second major engagement of the Red River campaign. She stood to her task with her comrades throughout many hours of artillery bombardment and in the front ranks throughout the day, repulsing six Confederate charges. Although the 153d's first battle successfully checked Confederate forces, Banks's army was forced to retreat down the Red River to Alexandria, Louisiana.

With the end of the campaign almost in sight, Wakeman came down with dysentery. She reported to the regimental hospital on 3 May and was transferred to Marine U.S.A. General Hospital in New Orleans, where she arrived in late May. After a month of hospitalization, she died with her secret undiscovered on 19 June 1864. She is buried in Chalmette National Cemetery in New Orleans under a headstone bearing her male enlisted name, Lyons Wakeman.

—*Lauren Cook Burgess*

See also Edmonds, Sarah Emma; Women Soldiers.
For further reading:
Blanton, DeAnne. "Women Soldiers of the Civil War." *Prologue* (1993).
Burgess, Lauren Cook, ed. *An Uncommon Soldier: The Civil War Letters of Sarah Rosetta Wakeman, Alias Private Lyons*

Wakeman, Co. H, 153d New York State Volunteers, 1862–1864 (1994).

Dannett, Sylvia G. L. *She Rode with the Generals* (1960).

Edmonds, Sarah Emma. *Nurse and Spy in the Union Army: Comprising the Adventures and Experiences of a Woman in Hospitals, Camps, Battle-Fields* (1865).

Leonard, Elizabeth D. *All the Daring of the Soldier: Women of the Civil War Armies* (1999).

Velazquez, Loreta Janeta. *The Woman in Battle* (1876).

WALKER, JAMES ALEXANDER
(1832–1901)
Confederate general

James Alexander Walker was born to Alexander Walker and Hannah Hinton Walker in Augusta County, Virginia. Walker attended Virginia Military Institute but did not graduate because of his dismissal in his senior year. Charges concerning Walker's angry and inappropriate behavior during a class were brought by one of his instructors, Thomas Jonathan Jackson, resulting in the dismissal. After this event, Walker tried several different career paths. He studied law and began a practice and served briefly as an engineer for a Virginia railroad.

At the outbreak of the Civil War, Walker accepted a captain's commission in the Pulaski Guards that ironically became a part of the brigade commanded by Thomas Jonathan Jackson. In the fall of 1861, Walker was at Harper's Ferry. His service during the fall earned him a promotion to colonel and command of the 13th Virginia Infantry. He led the regiment in Jackson's Shenandoah Valley campaign, during which he temporarily commanded a brigade in Richard Ewell's division. Walker returned to command the 13th during the Seven Days' and at Cedar Mountain and Second Bull Run, where he was seriously wounded. He returned in time to command the wounded Isaac Trimble's brigade at Antietam. At Fredericksburg he commanded Jubal Early's brigade while that general temporarily held a divisional command.

Walker was finally promoted to brigadier general on 15 May 1863 reputedly at the insistence of the dying Stonewall Jackson, though he had been recommended for promotion to that rank in October 1862. Ironically the new brigadier general was given command of the Stonewall Brigade, which he led into Pennsylvania in June 1863 as part of Richard Ewell's corps. Walker commanded the brigade at Gettysburg, where he fought on the second and third day at Culp's Hill, and in the Virginia campaigns of the fall of 1863.

In the spring of 1864, Walker commanded his brigade at the Wilderness and Spotsylvania, where he was again wounded in defense of the "Bloody Angle." The brigade had suffered such heavy casualties by then that it ceased to exist as a brigade after Spotsylvania. Back in the field by July, Walker protected the Danville Railroad through the fall of 1864. Walker fought in the siege of Petersburg, and, during the Appomattox campaign, he temporally commanded Early's division. He surrendered at Appomattox and was paroled with the rest of the army.

After the war, Walker returned to his law practice and became active in Virginia politics. He served a term in the Virginia lower house and was elected lieutenant governor in 1877. During the 1890s Walker became a Republican and served in the U.S. House of Representatives as a member of that party. He died in Wytheville, Virginia.

—David S. Heidler and Jeanne T. Heidler

See also Spotsylvania, Battle of; Stonewall Brigade.
For further reading:
Caldwell, Willie Walker. *Stonewall Jim: A Biography of General James A. Walker, C.S.A.* (1990).

Campbell, Edward Christian. "James Alexander Walker: A Biography" (M.A. thesis, 1972).

WALKER, JOHN GEORGE
(1822–1893)
Confederate general

John George Walker was born on 22 July 1822 in Cole County, Missouri, to state treasurer John G. Walker and the former Sarah Caffery. After graduating from Jesuit College (now St. Louis University), he was commissioned in May 1846 as a first lieutenant in Company K of Persifor F. Smith's Mounted Rifle Regiment. In the Mexican-American War he fought at Contreras, Churubusco, Molino del Rey (where he was severely wounded), and San Juan de los Llanos (after which he was brevetted to captain). After the war he served in Arizona, California, Oregon, and New Mexico (becoming captain on 30 June 1851) and then on the Texas frontier from 1854 to 1856. After a possible previous marriage to Melissa Smith on 6 July 1856, Walker married Sophie M. Baylor in New Orleans on 10 April 1858. In 1859 he went exploring through Navajo territory.

After his resignation from the United States Army at Fort Union, New Mexico (31 July 1861), Walker became a Confederate cavalry major (21 December 1861 with rank from 16 March) and then lieutenant colonel and colonel of the 8th Texas Cavalry. On 9 January 1862 he was promoted to brigadier general. Walker served in the Aquia District of Virginia and commanded a brigade in the North Carolina Department and then a division in the Army of Northern Virginia, taking Loudoun Heights at Harper's Ferry (12–15 September 1862) and fighting at Antietam (17 September 1862).

Promoted to major general on 8 November 1862, Walker was ordered to report for duty to the elderly

Theophilus H. Holmes at Little Rock, Arkansas, in the Trans-Mississippi Department, soon to be commanded by E. Kirby Smith.

On New Year's Day 1863 the energetic Walker assumed command of Henry E. McCulloch's Texas Division. The previous October McCulloch had organized Texas infantry volunteers (camped at Camp Nelson near Little Rock) into a division consisting of four brigades, with a battery of light artillery attached to each. Designated the 1st Division of II Corps, it left Camp Nelson in late November for Little Rock and then Pine Bluff. By the end of December it was marching back and forth every few days between Camp Nelson and Pine Bluff for training.

The Missourian continued to command this backbone of the Trans-Mississippi Department until June 1864. The largest Confederate unit composed of soldiers from a single state, Union soldiers called the Texas Division "Walker's Greyhounds" because Walker's rapid marches over muddy roads put his men wherever needed in Arkansas or Louisiana.

Fifteen hundred men died of disease before they had a chance to see action. Despite this problem, Richard Taylor, who commanded the West Louisiana District, wrote of Walker: "Seconded by good brigade and regimental officers, he had thoroughly disciplined his men, and made them in every sense soldiers; and their efficiency in action was soon established."

One of Walker's best officers, Elijah P. Petty, wrote to his daughter (15 March 1863) that Walker "has made a universally favourable impression here and is very much respected and I may almost say loved." To his wife (24 September 1863) Petty said simply, "He is a glorious General."

Douglas French Forrest wrote in his diary (15 May 1865) that Walker was "the most popular General in the Trans Mississippi & has acquired his popularity by gallant service in the field & an equal & regular, but very rigid discipline." Newly appointed to Walker's staff, Forrest described him as "a small spare man, very quiet, courteous in his deportment to all, of great force of character & great capacity."

One of Walker's privates described his general as "a man of slight frame, and apparently delicate constitution; of a grave, pleasing demeanor, and of most affable and courteous manner." He was "kind and courteous to all, without compromising his dignity. He was beloved by his officers, almost adored by his men." Walker did "everything by rule" and left "nothing to chance." He made "arrangements for battle with caution and foresight, ... sure to have every brigade of his division move with clock-work regularity, and strike at the proper time and place. Nothing disturbs or unnerves him."

On 11 January 1863 Smith ordered Walker's division to Fort Hindman, at Arkansas Post, unaware that it had surrendered that very day. In April Smith ordered the division to Monroe in the mudflats opposite Vicksburg. The division went into in action at Perkins' Landing (31 May 1863) and at both Milliken's Bend and Young's Point (7 June 1863). With one-third of his division down with Mississippi bottomlands sickness, Walker tried to convince Smith of the impossibility of defending Vicksburg.

After the fall of that strategic city, Walker moved to Alexandria to await Taylor's orders. He spent the rest of the year marching, fighting, and dueling with Federal gunboats in the south Louisiana bayou country, especially at Bayou Bourbeau (3 November 1863). Walker also began fortifying the upper Teche and lower Red River area.

Although an invasion had been expected for more than a year, the Confederates remained almost unprepared while Nathaniel P. Banks readied a force of 40,000 to march up the Red River to capture Shreveport, secure cotton for Northern textile mills, and end possible French intervention from Mexico through Texas. On 10 March 1864, when David D. Porter's flotilla proceeded up the Red River with Banks's forces following along a river road, Taylor had barely 7,000 men under his command. Although Taylor was finally able to muster 25,000, in the meantime Walker was forced to fall back, fighting small skirmishes against overwhelming odds. On 8 April 1864 Taylor, who had pulled together every available unit from three states, decided to make a stand three miles south of Mansfield at Sabine Crossroads, a strategic communications center, and organized a defensive position with Walker's and Alexander Mouton's infantry divisions and Hamilton P. Bee's cavalry. Walker's division consisted of Thomas N. Waul's, William R. Scurry's, and Horace Randal's brigades and an artillery battery. As the gallant Mouton's Charge began to cave the Union line, Taylor ordered a general advance. About 3,000 Federals were killed, wounded, captured, or missing; about 1,500, almost all killed or wounded, were missing from the Confederate ranks.

That night, when the defeated Banks withdrew, Taylor, wanting to complete the destruction of the Federal army, sent his outnumbered men in pursuit. The tired soldiers resumed a long and bloody fight the next day at Pleasant Hill (9 April 1864). Walker's division, deployed in the center to pin down the Union defenders, had its assault repulsed with heavy losses. Walker was taken from the field severely wounded, begging to continue in command.

As Banks now could neither capture Shreveport nor conquer part of Texas, Smith put Walker's men on the road to Camden, Arkansas, to face Frederick Steele, who was moving on Shreveport from Little Rock. On 30 April 1864 they collided west of Jenkins' Ferry on the Saline River. Before the fight Walker's men gave repeated cheers to their general, still feeble from his wound. According to one of his men, "They had implicit confidence in his judgment, and that he would not tolerate any useless sacrifice of life in the forthcoming battle." In repeated assaults with many casualties, Scurry and Randal were both killed and Waul was wounded. In the resulting confusion Steele was able to continue crossing the swollen river, but his return to Little Rock ended the last real Union threat to western Louisiana and Texas during the war.

Wanting to be relieved of command, the angry Taylor criticized Smith in several letters, calling this long battle a badly bungled affair, not building on the success of Mansfield. Walker agreed with Taylor about Smith's decision to face Steele. Now he was again ordered to Alexandria, but Banks successfully evacuated it before his arrival. With Banks no longer a threat, Walker marched to the Mississippi, but found it impractical to cross over the river, although Taylor, despite Smith's objections, wanted that done.

In June 1864 Kirby Smith ordered Walker to relieve the short-tempered Taylor of his command of the Army of Western Louisiana. (Eventually command of his old division went to the unpopular martinet, John H. Forney.) In early August 1864, after Smith placed Simon Bolivar Buckner in command of the Western Louisiana District, Walker replaced John B. Magruder as commander of the District of Texas, New Mexico, and Arizona. There he faced great financial difficulties as the war was winding down. In January 1865 he kept the Confederate cause alive west of the Mississippi by his stirring rejection of surrender to Lew Wallace. When Magruder resumed command of his old district in May of 1865, Walker, rather than taking over the Arkansas District, chose to command a cavalry unit and then his old division. Although they had been clamoring loudly for his return, Walker was unable to hold his men together at Camp Groce near Hempstead, Texas, during the breakup at the end of the war. On 21 May most of his soldiers mutinied and began leaving for home. Recently paid from secret service gold, Walker fled to Mexico as part of his unsuccessful scheme to resettle his officers and men there.

He then proceeded to England, working for a Virginia-based Venezuelan company seeking to promote Confederate settlement in Venezuela and planning mining operations in that country. He was also a partner in the New York firm of Walker & Hoffman, supplying railroad iron and machinery to Southern states and Southern staples to England. By the late 1860s he returned to the United States, working for the Mound City Mutual Life Insurance Company of St. Louis and the Houston & Texas Central Railway. In the early 1870s he lived in Texas, where he helped establish and edit newspapers and promoted European immigration to

Texas for the Texas & Pacific Railway. In the late 1870s he settled in the vicinity of Winchester, Virginia. During Grover Cleveland's first term, Walker served as United States consul general in Bogota, Colombia, and as a special commissioner for the Pan American Convention in 1889. Walker died of a stroke on 20 July 1893 in Washington, D.C., and was buried in Winchester, Virginia. His wife, four daughters, and a son survived him.

—*Charles Ellis Dickson*

See also Red River Campaign; Taylor, Richard.
For further reading:
Bearss, Edwin C. *Steele's Retreat from Camden and the Battle of Jenkins' Ferry* (1967).
Blessington, Joseph P. *The Campaigns of Walker's Texas Division* (1875).
Brown, Norman D., ed. *Journey to Pleasant Hill: The Civil War Letters of Captain Elijah P. Petty, Walker's Texas Division, C.S.A.* (1982).
Forrest, Douglas French. *Odyssey in Gray: A Diary of Confederate Service, 1863–1865* (1979).
Kerby, Robert L. *Kirby Smith's Confederacy: The Trans-Mississippi South, 1863–1865* (1972).
Parks, Joseph H. *General Edmund Kirby Smith, C.S.A.* (1954).
Parrish, T. Michael. *Richard Taylor: Soldier Prince of Dixie* (1992).
Taylor, Richard. *Destruction and Reconstruction: Personal Experiences of the Late War* (1879; reprint 1983).

WALKER, LEROY POPE
(1817–1884)
Confederate secretary of war and general

Born to John Williams Walker and Maria Pope Walker in Huntsville, Alabama, Leroy Pope Walker was educated at the University of Alabama and the University of Virginia before studying law in Huntsville. He opened his practice in Mississippi in 1837 but remained there only a short time before returning to practice in Alabama. Soon Walker had built a prominent practice and become active in Alabama Democratic politics. Following in the footsteps of his politically active father, the younger Walker became a powerful force in Alabama politics by the time he was thirty.

During the 1840s, Walker served in the lower house of the Alabama legislature and was elected that body's speaker in 1847. During his time in the legislature, he became increasingly a supporter of states' rights and for that reason was selected to represent the state at the Nashville Convention in 1850. After a brief stint as a state circuit judge, Walker returned to the state legislature. He also served three stints from 1848 through 1856 as a presidential elector from the state of Alabama.

In 1860 Walker was selected as the chair of the Alabama delegation to the Democratic National Convention in Charleston, South Carolina. He was given instructions by the state party that, if the convention did not adopt the Alabama Platform guaranteeing the protection of slavery in the territories, he was to lead his delegation out of the convention. He did so, triggering a large Southern exodus from the convention that resulted in a split in the Democratic Party for the election of 1860. Walker also represented the state in the walkouts' convention in Richmond and supported the candidacy of John C. Breckinridge in the election of 1860.

Upon the secession of Alabama after Abraham Lincoln's election, Walker was sent by Alabama governor Andrew B. Moore to Tennessee as an emissary to encourage secession. While there in January 1861, Walker addressed the state legislature and, after talking with a few influential Tennessee politicians, came to the mistaken conclusion that Tennessee would secede in January 1861.

His mission to Tennessee completed though unsuccessful, Walker on 16 February 1861 received the appointment of secretary of war of the Confederacy from the new provisional president of the Confederacy, Jefferson Davis. Davis's motivation in appointing Walker was to balance his appointments among the states and to appease the strong states' rights element within the new Confederacy. Walker's governmental experience, however, was limited to the state legislature. His lack of administrative experience was going to be a serious detriment to the new Confederate War Department during this organizational phase of its development.

Still, in spite of his lack of experience, Walker worked hard to organize a Confederate army, to procure supplies and arms for that army, and to establish a bureaucratic mechanism to fight a war if necessary. One of his earliest concerns was the presence of Federal troops in Federal forts within the borders of the new Confederacy. Increasingly, as was the case with everyone else, Walker's main focus became Fort Sumter in Charleston harbor.

He communicated regularly with P. G. T. Beauregard, Confederate commander in Charleston, encouraging him to do everything possible to secure the surrender of the fort from Major Robert Anderson, without a fight if possible. Walker was hopeful that the fort could be secure with as little damage as possible so that it could then be used to protect the harbor from possible Union attack.

In addition to his strong interest in Fort Sumter, Walker also concerned himself with the security of the Confederacy's borders. He communicated with those border slave states that had yet to secede, trying to determine how they would react to Union troops marching through those states to reach the Confederacy. As soon as the states of Virginia, North Carolina, Tennessee, and Arkansas seceded after Lincoln's call for volunteers, Walker worked not only to muster into Confederate service those states' troops but also to supply troops to those key border areas. He also encouraged the negotiation of alliances with the Indians in Indian Territory. In addition to these immediate concerns for the Confederacy's security, Walker also handled the more mundane duties of mustering in state troops and commissioning Confederate officers.

In spite of Walker's hard work, as the war intensified in the summer of 1861, it became apparent to him, Davis, and the Confederate Congress that Walker's lack of administrative skills was causing the Confederate military to suffer. After considerable criticism from Congress, and with his health declining from overwork, Walker resigned his post on 16 September 1861 with the understanding that Davis would then give him a military appointment. Davis complied the following day with a brigadier general's commission and assignment to the Department of Alabama and West Florida.

From the fall of 1861 through January 1862, Walker served in Mobile. In January 1862 he was ordered to Montgomery to construct an army training depot. The following month he was again transferred to north Alabama to command the guard at the Florence, Alabama, bridge over the Tennessee River. Not finding the active command he sought, however, Walker resigned his commission in March 1862 and served the remainder of the war as a military court judge. In May 1865 he handled some of the negotiations for the surrender of the remaining Confederate and state troops in Alabama.

After the war, Walker returned to his home in Huntsville, Alabama, where he resumed his law practice. Though an interested observer, Walker did not resume an active political career, though in 1875 he was the presiding member over the Alabama Constitutional Convention. He died at his home in Huntsville.

—*David S. Heidler and Jeanne T. Heidler*

See also Alabama; Davis, Jefferson.
For further reading:
Halperin, Rick. "Leroy Pope Walker and the Problems of the Confederate War Department" (Ph.D. dissertation, 1978).
Harris, William C. *Leroy Pope Walker, Confederate Secretary of War* (1962).

WALKER, MARY EDWARDS
(1832–1919)
Civil War surgeon

Born into a progressive farming family in Oswego, New York, Mary Edwards Walker was one of the first women to take advantage of Syracuse Medical College's willingness in the middle of the nineteenth century to admit women. Having received her M.D. degree in 1855, Walker did not hesitate, when the Civil War broke out, to offer her services to the United States Army's Medical Department. The fall of 1861 found her in Washington, D.C., seeking a formal commission as a

Dr. Mary Walker (*Library of Congress*)

military surgeon. Always a maverick as well as a patriot, Walker refused to accept an appointment as a nurse, believing that her skills and training could be more wisely utilized if she were employed as a physician. When the Federal government turned her down, Walker volunteered her services instead, exchanging them for rations and a place to stay.

As a volunteer physician and surgeon, Walker tended to the sick and wounded first at the so-called Indiana Hospital, housed in the United States Patent Office, and later in the field at Warrenton, Virginia, where a typhoid fever epidemic raged during the fall of 1862. Late in December 1862, Walker went from Warrenton to Fredericksburg, where she cared for the survivors of that brutal battle, still without formal appointment or pay. In all of the situations in which she placed herself, Walker earned the respect and admiration of key male medical personnel and military officers who observed her work. The surgeon in charge of the Indiana Hospital, Dr. J. N. Green, offered to give her a part of his own salary in the absence of her own, but she refused. At Warrenton, General Ambrose Burnside honored her with permission to escort the sickest and most gravely wounded soldiers back to Washington on a train chartered for that purpose, and in January 1863 Dr. Preston King, who had served with Walker at Fredericksburg, penned a letter to

Secretary of War Edwin M. Stanton requesting that she receive government compensation for her labors. Walker also earned the respect and the gratitude of countless soldiers who benefitted from her talents and her dedication, among them a number of men whose limbs were slated for amputation and on whose behalf the homeopathically oriented Walker argued successfully with her allopathic colleagues against such unnecessary sacrifice. Walker earned praise from many, but her unconventional and persistent demand for a surgeon's commission, her forthright personality, her distaste for surgical heroics, and perhaps most notably her insistence on wearing a modified version of the popular women's reform dress (which included trousers beneath a knee-length skirt), led others to urge her removal from action.

The exigencies of war worked against such critics. In January 1864 the 52d Ohio Infantry's assistant surgeon died unexpectedly, and the Medical Department, on the recommendation of General George H. Thomas, assigned Walker to the regiment as a noncommissioned civilian contract surgeon, paying her a standard salary of $80 per month. Within a few weeks, however, while riding about the Tennessee countryside where the 52d was bivouacked and tending to the desperate civilian population she found beyond the Union lines, Walker came upon a Confederate sentry who took her into custody. Walker spent four months at Castle Thunder prison in Richmond, then was reassigned to the Female Military Prison at Louisville, Kentucky, as the surgeon in charge. There she endured the hostility of her proudly secessionist inmates, as well as the disdain of her male counterparts in the nearby prison for men, none of whom cared to countenance the idea of an outspoken woman doctor in their midst.

When the war ended, Walker hoped to parlay her years of dedicated military service into a career with the army, seeking first an appointment as a medical inspector for the Freedmen's Bureau under the assumption that the government's significantly lower standards for the medical treatment of African-Americans might offer her an opening. She was mistaken. In the fall of 1865, after reviewing a lengthy dissertation by the army's Judge Advocate Joseph Holt, in which he argued that there was no precedent in the army's medical department for employing a woman doctor, President Andrew Johnson refused Walker's request, granting her the Medal of Honor instead.

Permanently weakened by her months at Castle Thunder, Walker finally turned her attention to other things, notably the dress reform and women's suffrage movements. But she continued throughout her life to wear the Medal of Honor, symbol of the army's appreciation—and, in her case, rejection—with pride. In 1918, a year before she died, Walker and more than 900 other recipients suffered a humiliating revocation of the Medal

of Honor when Congress redefined the terms under which it was to be presented. In 1977, thanks to the efforts of her posthumous supporters, Walker's medal was reinstated.

—*Elizabeth D. Leonard*

See also Medicine; Women.
For further reading:
Leonard, Elizabeth D. *Yankee Women: Gender Battles in the Civil War* (1994).
Poynter, Lida. "Dr. Mary Walker, M.D.: Pioneer Woman Physician." *Medical Woman's Journal* (1946).
Snyder, Charles McCool. *Dr. Mary Walker: The Little Lady in Pants* (1974).
Walker, Mary Edwards. *Hit* (1871).

WALKER, ROBERT JOHN
(1801–1869)
Governor of Kansas Territory, publisher, Union financial minister to Europe

Walker embodied many of the virtues and questionable ethics of politicians of the Civil War era. He was a short, sickly man, but he was indefatigable when healthy and intellectually formidable. His "driving quest for the acquisition of material wealth" and insatiable "desire to be in the limelight politically" propelled him to the center of the tumultuous stage of this period.

Born in 1801 in northwestern Pennsylvania, he attended the University of Pennsylvania, graduating *magna cum laude* in 1819. Walker surprised his Federalist and Whig relatives by joining the Democratic Party. Through his new political friends he met Mary Bache, a granddaughter of Benjamin Franklin and a member of the influential Dallas and Bache families. They married in 1825.

Walker relocated to Natchez, Mississippi, in 1826 to save the foundering law practice his brother Duncan had established in the midst of the Southwest cotton boom. Walker plunged into the swirl of land speculation and loose finance. Shortly he owned thousands of acres of plantation land and inculcated himself into the "Mississippi Regency," the circle of political leaders in the state.

Walker supported Andrew Jackson's bid for the presidency in 1828. He parlayed his loyalty to Jackson into a run for the Senate and presented his credentials to the chamber in 1836. He made a name for himself nationally through the publication of his well-crafted essay, *A Letter on the Annexation of Texas*, advocating statehood and displaying his unrelenting belief in Manifest Destiny. Walker supported James K. Polk's bid for the presidency in 1844; the grateful president-elect named Walker secretary of the treasury.

His "Walker tariff" of 1846 lowered overall tariff rates

and established a "free trade" doctrine that lasted until the Civil War. Walker claimed, and received, credit for ushering the nation into a period of growth and prosperity. Ill health and rumors of his graft prevented him from considering a run for the presidency in 1848.

With the Whig victory that year, Walker resumed his private law practice, milking as much as possible from the contacts he made while in the Senate and cabinet. Walker joined the political fray again in 1856 in support of James Buchanan's presidential campaign. Buchanan offered Walker the governorship of Kansas Territory; Walker accepted, confident that with Buchanan's unqualified support he could bring order to the territory and reoccupy his place in the national spotlight.

Walker and Buchanan had agreed that true residents of the territory would determine the fate of Kansas. Upon his arrival in May 1857 Walker was greeted cautiously. Not until his inaugural address, in which he expressed his belief that Kansas would enter the United States a free state, since "there is a law more powerful than the legislation of man ... that must ultimately determine the location of slavery in this country," did the proslavery faction react vehemently. One detractor called Walker a "miserable pygmy," threatening, "we have unmade governors before, and by God I'll tell you sir, we can unmake them again!" As Walker mustered troops to suppress the proslavery reactions, Buchanan's support wavered. When Walker returned to Washington to renounce the Lecompton Constitution, Buchanan and the cabinet disavowed him. Walker was absolved from blame in the resulting political fiasco when he revealed to the Covode Commission in 1860 the initial letter Buchanan had sent him endorsing his position on Popular Sovereignty. Again, Walker returned to private law practice, gloomily predicting the nation was on the verge of dissolution.

During the Lincoln administration, Walker emerged as a leading War Democrat, publishing the *Continental Monthly*. Secretary of the Treasury Salmon P. Chase appointed his friend as a financial minister to England in 1863. This proved to be a brilliant selection; Walker's free-trade, hard-money policies had endeared him to many influential Britons. Walker sold $250 million of Union bonds to European investors. Equally important, he launched an effective propaganda campaign against the Confederacy, claiming President Jefferson Davis had been involved in the repudiation of Mississippi bonds in which British investors had lost millions during the 1840s. Subsequently, Confederate bonds lost their value on European markets.

When Walker returned to Washington, his precarious health deteriorated rapidly. He supported President Andrew Johnson, often offering advice on patronage. After a lifetime of financial scheming, Walker found himself deeply in debt as he neared death. He was forced

to sell most of his personal property to provide his wife with an inheritance. Walker died on 11 November 1869.

—*Jane Flaherty*

See also Kansas; War Democrats.
For further reading:
Brown, George W. *Reminiscences of Governor R. J. Walker; With the True Story of the Rescue of Kansas from Slavery* (1902).
Dodd, William Edward. *Robert J. Walker, Imperialist* (1914).
Shenton, James P. *Robert John Walker: A Politician from Jackson to Lincoln* (1961).

WALKER, WILLIAM
(1824–1860)
Filibuster

William Walker's exploits in Nicaragua made him the most famous filibuster of the 1850s. He was born on 8 May 1824 in Nashville, Tennessee, where he graduated from college at age fourteen before going on to complete medical school in Pennsylvania by age nineteen. He soon grew bored with medicine, however, and in 1845 he moved from Nashville to New Orleans to study law. There he met and fell deeply in love with Ellen Galt Martin and made friends with leading New Orleans newspapermen, who convinced the diminutive, grey-eyed Tennessean to leave the law in 1848 to write for the *Daily Crescent*. He penned editorials denouncing the Southern slave economy and attacked filibusterism as an inept way to fulfill the desire for American hemispheric expansion.

When Ellen died of cholera in the spring of 1849, Walker, who was shattered by her loss, decided to leave New Orleans for California to find a new life in the booming gold-rush port of San Francisco, where he again edited a newspaper and briefly practiced law. He could not remain satisfied with a conventional occupation, however; since Ellen's death he had come to believe that the only thing that would give his life meaning was to perform great deeds on a world stage, or to die a Byronic death in the attempt.

Walker's first opportunity to fulfill this ambition came in 1853. He led a filibuster force of forty-five men into Mexico in an attempt to seize control of the sparsely populated, mineral-rich province of Sonora. After first landing in Baja California, he moved north to invade Sonora, but his campaign ended at the Colorado River when his exhausted and starving men refused to go on. Walker surrendered himself to American troops at San Diego on 8 May 1854 and stood trial five months later in San Francisco for violating United States neutrality laws. A friendly jury took only eight minutes to render a verdict of not guilty.

Even before his trial began, Walker had become interested in a new filibustering scheme aimed against Nicaragua that proposed to take over that country's substantial mineral resources and its profitable interoceanic transit route, which was then being served by the vessels of Cornelius Vanderbilt's Accessory Transit Company. He offered his services to the Nicaraguan Democrats, the insurrectionist party in control of the northern half of the country, as opposed to the Legitimists, the traditional pro-British ruling party that maintained power in the south. On 4 May 1855, he and fifty-eight soldiers of fortune, whom Walker would dub the "Immortals," sailed for the Nicaraguan coast, where they landed at Realejo on 16 June.

After losing his first battle, Walker beat the Legitimist army and captured their capital of Granada on 11 October. The Democrats and Legitimists then agreed to suspend hostilities and establish a coalition government, which included Walker as commander in chief of the Nicaraguan army. Walker's success allowed him to recruit new men from the United States and found *El Nicaraguense,* a newspaper he created to promote his cause both back in the United States and in Nicaragua, where he now proclaimed himself to be the "Grey-Eyed Man" of Indian legend who had come to liberate the common people.

Despite these efforts, Walker's regime faced serious, long-term opposition from Commodore Vanderbilt, who transferred his shipping routes to Panama in retaliation for Walker's revocation of the Accessory Transit Company's transport concession. The British believed the new Anglo-Nicaraguan government threatened their hold on the Mosquito Coast, so they as well as Vanderbilt provided support to the Legitimist, anti-Walker regimes in Honduras, Costa Rica, and Guatemala.

These threats encouraged an increasingly isolated Walker to have himself "elected" president in June 1856 and to seek recognition of his government from the administration of Franklin Pierce. He also sought financial aid from proslavery Southern investors, whom the previously antislavery editorialist sought to appease by ordering the reintroduction of African slavery into Nicaragua. By the end of 1856, however, Nicaragua was under attack by an alliance of Central American nations. These enemies eventually defeated Walker's army and convinced him to leave Nicaragua for the United States, where he returned aboard an American warship on 27 May 1857.

Acclaimed a hero by many Americans, especially Southerners, Walker made three more failed attempts (1857, 1858, and 1860) to reestablish his rule in Central America. In August 1860, he launched a last, fatal invasion in Honduras, where after landing with some 100 men, he was surrounded by a combination of British and Honduran forces and forced to surrender. The British, who had long resented his interference in their Central American empire, turned Walker over to the

Hondurans, who executed him at Trujillo on the morning of 12 September 1860.

—*R. Boyd Murphree*

See also Vanderbilt, Cornelius.
For further reading:
Brown, Charles H. *Agents of Manifest Destiny: The Lives and Times of the Filibusters* (1980).
Carr, Albert Z. *The World and William Walker* (1963).
Geyer, Alejandro Bolanos. *William Walker: El Predestinado de los Ojos Grises* (1995).

WALKER, WILLIAM HENRY TALBOT
(1816-1864)
Confederate general

Known to some as the "Georgia Firebrand," William Henry Talbot Walker was born in Augusta, Georgia, 26 November 1816, the son of Freeman Walker and Mary Garlington Cresswell Walker. His father was a lawyer by profession and at different times state legislator, mayor of Augusta, and United States senator.

William graduated from West Point in 1837. He fought in the Seminole and Mexican Wars, being critically wounded at Lake Okeechobee in 1837 and Molino del Rey in 1847. He won brevet promotions to major and lieutenant colonel in Mexico for his valor at Churubusco and Molino del Rey. Chronic asthma since his youth and the effects of his wounds rendered him unfit for field duty after 1848. He served mainly on recruiting duty and was deputy governor of the soldiers' asylum in Mississippi (1852–1854). From 1854 to 1856 he was commandant of cadets at West Point, serving the first nine months under Superintendent Robert E. Lee. His tenure at the military academy ended on a sour note when he became embroiled in a seniority controversy with another officer and he resigned his position. Walker was on extended leave of absence until 1860 and farmed in Georgia.

With the impending secession of South Carolina, Walker resigned his U.S. Army commission in December 1860 and later claimed to be the first officer of the "old army" to do so. He spent the first few months of 1861 organizing and training Georgia's volunteer forces, first as a colonel in the Georgia Army, then as major general of Georgia volunteers, a state commission. In May 1861 he was commissioned brigadier general in the Provisional Army of the Confederate States. He served two months at Pensacola, Florida, as Braxton Bragg's second-in-command, and then two months in Virginia commanding the Louisiana Brigade. Walker resigned his Confederate commission in a fit of temper in October 1861 because he felt he had been "overslaughed" by junior officers. He had been recommended by Generals J. E. Johnston, P. G. T. Beauregard, and G. W. Smith to be the senior of the new major generals in the Confederate Army of the Potomac, but he was not so promoted. His intemperate correspondence with President Jefferson Davis and Secretary of War Judah P. Benjamin, whom he blamed for the slight, made scandalous reading in newspapers all over the South.

Walker next served at Savannah with the Georgia State Troops from December 1861 to April 1862. He was out of service until he was restored to his former Confederate rank in February 1863 after having apologized to the War Department for his disrespectful correspondence in 1861. He commanded a brigade on the Georgia and South Carolina coast at the time of the Union naval attack on Charleston in April 1863. That May his was one of two brigades sent to Mississippi during the Vicksburg campaign. While in Mississippi, Walker was promoted to major general on the recommendation of Joseph E. Johnston, who termed him "indispensable" and "the only officer competent to command" a division.

In August 1863 Walker's division was sent to Bragg's Army of Tennessee. For the battle of Chickamauga (19–20 September 1863), Bragg made Walker commander of his Reserve Corps, a small force of five brigades. Walker performed noteworthy service on the first day of the battle, supporting Forrest's dismounted cavalry on the extreme right of the Confederate line. On the second day, as part of Leonidas Polk's right wing, Walker played little part, except to provide troops to shore up holes in the line. After the battle he returned to command of his division. He was home on leave during the battle at Chattanooga in November where S. R. Gist commanded his division.

Walker took little part in the political wrangling in the Army of Tennessee in the fall of 1863. His correspondence with his wife indicates he was friendly to and supportive of Bragg, but there is no evidence of any outward manifestation of such support. When Bragg was relieved and J. E. Johnston took command of the army in December, Walker was pleased with the change.

The proposal by Patrick Cleburne in January 1864 to arm slaves caused Walker great outrage. Despite Johnston's admonition to his officers to keep the proposal within their own circles, Walker wrote about it to Jefferson Davis, and maintained a correspondence with Bragg, now Davis's military adviser, on the names of those involved. Walker's action drew the ire of William J. Hardee, his corps commander, B. F. Cheatham, and others.

For the opening of the spring campaign of 1864 Walker's division served as a mobile reserve. During the battle at Resaca on 13–14 May, he was sent to guard crossings of the Oostanaula River to prevent Johnston's left flank from being turned. In a mismanaged attack at Lay's Ferry on 14 May, one of Walker's brigades failed in an attempt to dislodge a Union force that had crossed. Walker seems to have been unaware of or unable to control the action. Johnston's line of communication to Atlanta was threatened, and he withdrew from the field at Resaca.

Walker's division played a role in the battles at Dallas and Kennesaw Mountain during the withdrawal to Atlanta, and suffered heavy casualties in the attack on entrenched Union defenses at Peachtree Creek on 20 July. On 22 July 1864, at the battle of Atlanta, Walker's division formed part of Hardee's flanking movement. At the beginning of the battle, Walker was killed by a sniper as his men approached the Union line. His body was carried by train to Augusta and interred in the family burial ground.

Walker's greatest contribution to the Southern cause was in training, disciplining, and organizing troops. His reputation as a young soldier and his long experience as a regular officer made him the ideal commander and model for the volunteer troops he led. As a senior battlefield commander he played only secondary roles. His dedication, personal bravery, and integrity won the respect of his superiors and contemporaries, but his pride, his bad temper, and his intemperate language negated his better qualities. On the day Walker died, a rebuke from Hardee over the positioning of his troops left him in a black mood and vowing vengeance. It can fairly be said that W. H. T. Walker never realized his full potential as a soldier.

Walker married Mary "Molly" Townsend of Albany, New York, on 9 May 1846. There were eight children from the marriage, of whom four died in early childhood.

—*Russell K. Brown*

See also Chickamauga, Battle of; Cleburne, Patrick; Dallas, Georgia, Battle of; Kennesaw Mountain, Battle of; Peachtree Creek, Battle of; Resaca, Battle of; Vicksburg Campaign.

For further reading:

Brown, Russell K. *To the Manner Born: The Life of General William H. T. Walker* (1994).

Davis, Stephen. "A Georgia Firebrand: Major General William H. T. Walker, C.S.A." *Georgia Historical Quarterly* (1979).

———. "That Extraordinary Document: W. H. T. Walker and Patrick Cleburne's Emancipation Proposal." *Civil War Times Illustrated* (1977).

Kurtz, Wilbur G. "The Death of Major General William H. T. Walker, July 22, 1864." *Civil War History* (1960).

Mosser, Jeffrey S. "I Shall Make Him Remember This Insult." *Civil War Times Illustrated* (1993).

WALLACE, LEWIS (LEW)
(1827–1905)
Union general

Born in Brookville, Indiana, Lewis Wallace was one of four sons raised by David and Esther Test Wallace. In 1837, after his election as Indiana governor, the senior Wallace moved his family to Indianapolis. As a young man, Lew Wallace was uninterested in school, even briefly running away from home

in an unsuccessful attempt to join the Texas navy during Texas's struggle for independence from Mexico. Thereafter, he worked for the Marion County clerk's office and reported on the legislature for the *Indianapolis Daily Journal*. In 1846, after failing to pass the bar examination, he volunteered for service in the army during the Mexican-American War. Wallace rose to the rank of second lieutenant in the First Indiana Infantry, but saw no battle action.

Upon his return to Indiana, Wallace was admitted to the bar in 1849 and opened a law practice in Covington, where he served two terms as prosecuting attorney. He moved to Crawfordsville in 1853, where he was elected to the state senate in 1856. Also that year he put together a military group called the Montgomery (County) Guards. After learning about the French Algerian Zouaves, Wallace converted his company to their system, emulating their colorful uniforms, theatrical drill, and commando tactics.

Wallace was ready when hostilities commenced between the North and South with the firing on Fort Sumter on 12 April 1861. In his autobiography, Wallace said he believed that the "conflict would be long and great, but that it would also be crowded with opportunities for distinction not in the least inconsistent with patriotism." The day after the war's outbreak, Wallace visited the offices of Indiana governor Oliver P. Morton, who asked him to become the state's adjutant general. Wallace agreed and became responsible for organizing the state's quota of six regiments (4,683 men) for the Union cause. Wallace had managed to raise more than twice the number called for by President Abraham Lincoln.

His task complete, Wallace resigned as adjutant general and received command of the 11th Indiana (Zouave) regiment as its colonel. Before they left Indianapolis, Wallace had his men march to the state house, where he made them kneel and swear an oath to avenge their comrades who they felt had been unjustly accused of cowardice by General Zachary Taylor at the battle of Buena Vista. The stirring scene and oath to "Remember Buena Vista!" was captured for the country to see in the pages of *Harper's Weekly*.

In June 1861, Wallace and his men surprised Confederate forces in Romney, Virginia, driving them from the town. Moving back to the Western theater of war, the regiment participated in the successful campaigns under Ulysses S. Grant to capture Forts Henry and Donelson. In March 1862, at age thirty-four, Wallace received promotion to major general (the youngest person to hold that rank in the Union army) and was given command of a division. Wallace's career received a major blow, however, at the battle of Shiloh. Several miles to the north of the battlefield, Wallace received what were, to him, unclear orders from Grant. He took his command on a confusing march that essen-

tially put his force out of action on the battle's first day. Although Wallace and his men, combined with reinforcements brought by Major General Don Carlos Buell, did join other Union soldiers to drive the Rebels from the field on the second day, the Hoosier general received heavy criticism from his superiors for his tardiness and was eventually stripped of his command.

In the late summer of 1862, Wallace was called back into action to help bolster defenses around Cincinnati to thwart an unexpected Confederate attack. On 12 March 1864 he received orders to take command of the Eighth Army Corps and of the Middle Department, headquartered in Baltimore. On 9 July, Wallace led Union soldiers against a superior Confederate force under Jubal Early that threatened Washington, D.C. Wallace's troops withstood five attacks in what came to be known as the battle of Monocacy before retreating toward Baltimore. Although they were defeated, Wallace's troops delayed Early's advance on the Union capital by one day, giving Grant enough time to rush reinforcements to the capital to beat back the Confederate invasion.

After the war, Wallace served on the court-martial that tried the conspirators in the Lincoln assassination, and he was president of the commission that tried and convicted Henry Wirz, commander of Andersonville Prison. Later serving as governor of the New Mexico Territory and U.S. minister to Turkey, Wallace achieved his greatest fame as author of the best-selling novel *Ben-Hur*.

—*Ray E. Boomhower*

See also Zouaves.
For further reading:
McKee, Irving. *"Ben-Hur" Wallace: The Life of General Lew Wallace* (1947).
Morsberger, Robert E., and Katharine M. Morsberger. *Lew Wallace: Militant Romantic* (1980).
Wallace, Lew. *Lew Wallace: An Autobiography* (1906).

WALLACE, WILLIAM HENRY
(1827–1905)
Confederate general

Born in Laurens District, South Carolina, William Henry Wallace was educated at South Carolina College. Upon graduation he studied law. After admission to the South Carolina bar, he opened a practice, but he also became interested in politics and became involved in a brief career as a journalist. Before the outbreak of the Civil War, Wallace served in the South Carolina legislature, where in 1860 he strongly supported the call for a secession convention.

When war commenced in April 1861, Wallace enlisted as a private in the 18th South Carolina Infantry. His education quickly gained him the appointment as the regiment's adjutant and a promotion to lieutenant colonel. Wallace and the 18th were sent to Virginia in the summer of 1861 and the following spring distinguished themselves in the Peninsula campaign, during which Wallace served as the regiment's lieutenant colonel.

On 5 August 1862, Wallace led his men on a reconnaissance toward Malvern Hill to dislodge the Union forces that had moved out of their position at Harrison's Landing to reoccupy that position. He fought a sharp skirmish there that perhaps had some influence on the Federals' ultimate decision to withdraw back to Harrison's Landing. During the last week of the month, Wallace and his men skirmished with Federal troops along the Rappahannock River before moving forward to participate in the Confederate victory at Second Bull Run. After the battle of Second Bull Run, Wallace was promoted to colonel and commander of the regiment then serving in Nathan "Shanks" Evans's "Tramp Brigade." Shortly afterward, Wallace commanded the 18th at South Mountain and Antietam.

The 18th and the "Tramp Brigade" were sent to South Carolina shortly after the Maryland campaign to aid in the defense of Charleston. Wallace and his men served in the defenses of the city and on James Island through the late spring of 1863, when the brigade was sent to Mississippi to serve under Joseph E. Johnston. In June 1863 the brigade was in the division of John C. Breckinridge at Jackson, Mississippi, and then after the fall of Vicksburg was placed under William Hardee in the Department of Mississippi and Eastern Louisiana.

At the end of the summer, Wallace and the 18th were sent back to South Carolina, where they remained through the spring of 1864. At the end of the spring, Wallace and his men became a part of the Department of North Carolina and Southern Virginia under P. G. T. Beauregard. By the end of June, he and the 18th were part of the defenses of Petersburg. He fought in defense of the Confederate position that became the focus of the Union offensive known as the Crater, suffering heavy losses to the regiment.

For the remainder of the summer, Wallace and the 18th served in Bushrod Johnson's division. In September, Johnson recommended that Wallace be promoted to brigadier general and that he be given command of the brigade of Stephen Elliott, Jr. Elliott had been wounded at the Crater, and since no one expected him to recover from his wounds (he eventually succumbed to them, but not until 1866), Johnson needed a permanent replacement. Johnson's recommendation was acted on, and at the end of the month, Wallace was promoted and accepted his new brigade command (which included the 18th South Carolina).

For the remainder of the year, Wallace and his brigade held the Confederate position at the Crater, skirmishing frequently with Union forces probing for weaknesses. The following spring he moved out of the defenses of Petersburg with the remainder of the army and led his

brigade in the fighting retreat that followed. He fought at Five Forks on 1 April and then skirmished with Federal forces at Amelia Court House on 3 April. He and his men skirmished with Union troops all the way to Appomattox Court House, where Wallace temporarily assumed command of the division just before the surrender.

After his parole, Wallace made his way home to South Carolina. For a time he lived quietly on his plantation, where he worked to rebuild his property and to reestablish his legal practice. Once his political disabilities were removed, he reentered South Carolina politics and returned to the South Carolina legislature in 1872. In 1877 he began service as a state circuit judge, retiring in 1893. He died in retirement in Union, South Carolina.

—*David S. Heidler and Jeanne T. Heidler*

See also Crater, Battle of the; Evans, Nathan George; Johnson, Bushrod Rust.

For further reading:
Wallace, Margaret L. *William Henry Wallace* (1930).

WALTHALL, EDWARD CARY
(1831–1898)
Confederate general

Confederate officer and politician Edward Cary Walthall successfully weathered Mississippi's difficult transition from the antebellum to the postbellum period. An up-and-coming lawyer before the Civil War, Walthall entered Confederate service in 1861 as a lieutenant, and by 1865 he had risen to the rank of major general. After the war, he returned to Mississippi a hero. He reestablished his law practice representing railroads and other corporate interests, and he parlayed his wealth and military notoriety into a successful political career. During the last quarter of the nineteenth century, the former Confederate general was one of Mississippi's most influential political figures. He served the state's Democratic Party in various capacities, culminating in his appointment as a U.S. senator.

Walthall was born in Richmond, Virginia, on 4 April 1831 and as a child moved with his family to Holly Springs, in Marshall County, Mississippi. He received his education at St. Thomas Hall military school in Holly Springs and afterward studied law in the office of his brother-in-law, George R. Freeman. Walthall was admitted to the bar in 1852, at which time he moved to Coffeeville, Yalobusha County, Mississippi, and established his own practice. In 1856 he won election as district attorney for the 10th Judicial District of Mississippi and was reelected in 1859.

At the outbreak of the Civil War, Walthall resigned his civil post and enlisted in the Yalobusha Rifles, a volunteer company raised in Coffeeville. His prominence in the community led to his election to lieu-

tenant. As Mississippi organized for war in late May 1861, the Yalobusha Rifles became Company H of the 15th Mississippi Infantry. A few weeks after the organization of the 15th Mississippi, Walthall won election as the regiment's lieutenant colonel and was second in command under Colonel Walter Scott Statham.

By late 1861, the 15th Mississippi was part of Brigadier General Felix Kirk Zollicoffer's brigade under Major General George Bibb Crittenden in eastern Kentucky. With Statham absent on a medical furlough, Walthall led the regiment during its first major engagement at Mill Springs, Kentucky, in January 1862. The result was a major Confederate defeat. Despite the setback, Crittenden's report of the battle praised the 15th Mississippi for its conduct under fire and Walthall in particular for his leadership. The report circulated widely in Confederate command circles, and Walthall received permission to raise his own regiment. In April of 1862 he organized the 29th Mississippi Infantry and took command as the regiment's colonel.

Walthall led the 29th Mississippi during the siege of Corinth in May 1862. Later that year the regiment moved to Chattanooga and into Kentucky as part of General Braxton Bragg's Army of Mississippi. The regiment became part of the newly organized Army of Tennessee in December. On Bragg's recommendation, Walthall received a brigade command with promotion to brigadier general. During 1863 he led a brigade during the Tullahoma campaign and at Chickamauga. He helped defend Lookout Mountain at Chattanooga and on 25 November was wounded at Missionary Ridge. After his recovery he led a brigade during the Atlanta campaign, during which his men were heavily engaged at Kennesaw Mountain, Peachtree Creek, and Ezra Church. During the campaign he was elevated to division commander with a promotion to major general. After the surrender of Atlanta, Walthall accompanied John Bell Hood on his ill-fated invasion of Tennessee. He commanded a division during the army's disastrous charge at Franklin, where two horses were shot out from under him, and during the battle of Nashville. Walthall's career as a Confederate soldier ended in North Carolina, where he commanded a division under General Joseph Eggleston Johnston. He was among the troops surrendered by Johnston at Durham Station, North Carolina, on 26 April 1865.

At the war's conclusion, Walthall returned to Coffeeville and reestablished his law practice. In 1871 he moved to Grenada, Mississippi, where he became one of the state's most successful corporate lawyers. His reputation enhanced by his status as an ex-Confederate general, he was heavily involved in the state's Democratic Party as one of the self-styled "Redeemers" who helped broker the end of Reconstruction. Walthall served as chairman of the Mississippi delegation to the Democratic National

Conventions of 1868, 1876, 1880, and 1884. When Lucius Quintus Cincinnatus Lamar resigned his seat in the U.S. Senate in 1885 to become secretary of the interior under President Grover Cleveland, Mississippi governor Robert Lowry appointed Walthall to fill the vacancy. He subsequently was elected in his own right by the legislature and held the office at the time of his death in Washington, D.C., on 21 April 1898.

—Ben Wynne

See also Atlanta Campaign.
For further reading:
Rowland, Dunbar, ed. *Mississippi: Comprising Sketches of Counties, Towns, Events, Institutions, and Persons, Arranged in Cyclopedic Form* (1907; reprint, 1972).
Sword, Wiley. *Embrace an Angry Wind: The Confederacy's Last Hurrah: Spring Hill, Franklin, and Nashville* (1992).
Sykes, E. T. "Walthall's Brigade—A Cursory Sketch with Personal Experiences of Walthall's Brigade, Army of Tennessee, C.S.A., 1862–1865." In *Publications of the Mississippi Historical Society* (1917).

WAR CORRESPONDENTS

Journalists had covered wars before—an American newsman was killed by a mob during the War of 1812, and English correspondents reported from the Crimean War during the 1850s—but the Civil War created an unprecedented demand for war coverage because Americans were fighting Americans. Dozens of correspondents responded, reporting for both sides and creating names and careers for themselves. The first American war correspondents were killed during the Civil War as well.

B. S. Osbon, a minister's son making $9 a week for the *New York World,* proved the adage about being in the right place at the right time when he watched the bombardment of Fort Sumter on 12 April 1861. "The ball is opened," he reported. "War is inaugurated." He was quickly hired by the *New York Herald,* which featured the most aggressive war coverage, for $25 a week. Dozens of correspondents watched the confusion of the battle of First Bull Run three months later. A reporter for the *Memphis Appeal* became the first journalist prisoner of war when he found himself behind Union lines. *Herald* correspondent and German immigrant Henry Villard "scooped" his competition with the first complete account of the battle. Villard went on to provide an exclusive account of the battle of Fredericksburg in 1862. His report was partially censored by his paper but was provided in person to President Lincoln.

Many Northern newspapers devoted as much as one-third of their news space to war accounts. George W. Smalley's sixty-nine-paragraph account of Antietam, published in the *New York Tribune* on 19 September 1862, was considered the best battlefield account of the war. Written at night in a railroad boxcar, it was

War correspondents lunching in the Bull Run area, Virginia, 1862 (*National Archives*)

acclaimed by eyewitness military and journalistic observers alike and was reprinted in 1,400 newspapers around the country. Albert D. Richardson of the *Chicago Tribune* reported extensively from the South with coded transmissions by way of New York banks. He ran the blockade of Vicksburg, was knocked from the deck of a ship by the shock of a cannonball, and was picked up in the water by the Confederates.

Censorship was a particular problem. In the North, the military controlled telegraph lines and severely restricted anything but military transmissions. The government's official censor, H. E. Thayer, prohibited dispatches related even to civil operations of the government. Correspondents were forced to gather news as best they could. Many wrote under pen names to facilitate their behind-the-scene efforts. *Cincinnati Gazette* correspondent Whitelaw Reid, writing as "Agate," filled fourteen columns with an account of the first day of fighting at Gettysburg in 1863, noting, "Right on came the Rebels. They were upon the guns, were bayoneting the gunners, were waving their flags over our pieces. But they had penetrated to the fatal

point...." Southern correspondents were constantly reminded that their reports needed to meet "public interests," but General P. G. T. Beauregard was chided for holding up telegraphic news dispatches.

Southern editors got most of their news from the Press Association of the Confederate States, known as PA, the reverse of the northern Associated Press, or AP. PA dispatches were permitted on military telegraph lines because accurate, militarily "secure" news was considered good for morale. Among the best-known Southern reporters was Felix Gregory de Fontaine, known as "Personne" in dispatches to the *Charleston Courier*. His 8,000-word account of Antietam was the best piece of Southern war reporting. Peter W. Alexander, identified in the *Savannah Republican* and other newspapers as "P. W. A.," gained fame for his account of Gettysburg that questioned General Robert E. Lee's full-scale assault strategy. They were joined by Samuel C. Reid, Jr., of the *New Orleans Picayune*, Albert J. Street of the *Mobile Register*, and a number of others, including unidentified reporters such as "Shadow," who may have been a young Henry Watterson of the *Louisville Courier-Journal*.

Eight correspondents lost their lives reporting the Civil War. The *Chicago Tribune*'s Irving Carson was decapitated by a six-pound cannonball while covering Shiloh with General Ulysses S. Grant in April 1862. The *New York Herald* lost three of its correspondents, including Lynde Buckingham, who was thrown from his horse during an ambush by John Mosby's Confederate troops near Aldie, Virginia, in 1863. John Linebaugh of the *Memphis Daily Appeal* drowned in October 1864 when he swam from a grounded steamboat. Coverage became more restricted later in the war.

The PA collapsed with the fall of the South, and paper shortages reduced the number of Southern newspapers. Union general William Tecumseh Sherman ignored the press during his March to the Sea, and other Northern correspondents had learned to be cooperative with the military by war's end. The South had no counterparts, but Northern war correspondents who styled themselves the "Bohemian Brigade" basked in the glory of their efforts long after the war had ended.

—*Richard Digby-Junger*

See also Newspapers; Reid, Whitelaw; Richardson, Albert Deane; Smalley, George W.; Villard, Henry; Watterson, Henry.
For further reading:
Andrews, J. Cutler. *The North Reports the Civil War* (1955).
———. *The South Reports the Civil War* (1970).
Bullard, F. Lewiston. *Famous War Correspondents* (1914).
Goldsmith, Adoph O. "Reporting the Civil War: Union Army Press Relations." *Journalism Quarterly* (1956).
Mathews, Joseph J. *Reporting the Wars* (1957).
Reynolds, Donald E. *Editors Make War* (1966).
Starr, Louis M. *Bohemian Brigade: Civil War Newsmen in Action* (1954; reprint, 1987).

WAR DEMOCRATS

The term *War Democrats* refers to a group of Democrats that supported Abraham Lincoln's administration during the Civil War. Although primarily from Northern states, these men were not from similar socioeconomic backgrounds, nor were they from the same faction of the Democratic Party or the same geographic region. Democrats that supported the war originated from every state loyal to the Union. Also, a number of important figures came from the South. Most notable among them were Andrew Johnson of Tennessee, John B. Henderson of Missouri, and Joseph Holt of Kentucky. The reasons these men aligned themselves with the Union Party are difficult to discern. However, one idea held these diverse individuals together—the belief that the federal government should forcibly preserve the Union. For this reason, they broke with the position of the Peace Democrats, who supported a national peace conference or a negotiated peace to end the crisis, and favored the wartime policies of Abraham Lincoln. Before his death in 1861, Stephen A. Douglas was the most prominent of the group.

Douglas supported the peace program espoused by many Democrats during the secession crisis, but with the outbreak of hostilities, he fervently supported the war until his death on 3 June 1861. In a speaking tour that shortly followed the shelling of Fort Sumter, Douglas roused support for the war effort and called for a nonpartisan commitment to preserving the Union. Although his commitment to the war was short lived, Douglas's conversion is considered by many to be the origin of the war faction of the Democratic Party. His incredible political influence and national stature caused many likeminded Democrats to support the cause. In their support, however, many War Democrats still differed with the Lincoln administration on the conduct of the war and its goals.

The conflict between the president and some War Democrats over certain issues shows that this faction was not monolithic. The most controversial measures were the suspension of habeas corpus and the confiscation of the slaves. Many believed that these measures violated both personal rights of free speech and assembly and the property rights of Southern slaveholders. This is represented by the arguments that surrounded the Second Confiscation Act of 1862. War Democrats opposed the measure as too harsh and designed to punish all Southerners, and not just those in rebellion. This issue represented the fact that, as a group, War Democrats were hesitant to support all policies of the Lincoln administration. However, as the war progressed, the loyalty of War Democrats to Lincoln grew, and a number of them changed positions and favored the antislavery policies of the Radical Republicans. One such person was John B. Henderson, the pro-Union and proslavery

Southerner who eventually wrote the Thirteenth Amendment.

Some greatly supported the administration from the beginning, whereas others even joined the cabinet. John A. McClernand, a little-known congressman from Illinois, supported peace measures until provoked by Southern obstinacy. James A. McDougall, a senator from California, supported Lincoln's actions in response to the outbreak of war. Although both men were Unionists and supported the war effort, they also represented the dichotomy of the War Democrats. Each hoped for the destruction of the Confederacy, but they wished that slavery would not become an issue of the war. John A. Dix became Buchanan's secretary of the treasury. In January of 1861, Dix urged customs officers in Southern ports to shoot secessionists actively engaged in pulling down the American flag. In 1861, Joseph Holt became Buchanan's secretary of war. Holt was influential in preventing Kentucky from joining the Confederacy. Another War Democrat, Edwin M. Stanton, became Lincoln's secretary of war in 1862 and held the post until 1866. Also, Andrew Johnson became vice president in 1865. Johnson fought desperately to keep Tennessee in the Union. Many high-ranking military officers, including Benjamin F. Butler and Daniel E. Sickles, were War Democrats as well.

The importance of this political group is debatable. Lincoln certainly believed that they played an important role in holding his war coalition together, and the Republicans certainly used this small but very vocal faction of Democrats as a political tool to discredit their opposition in Congress and also during elections. Some believe that War Democrats played an important role in the congressional elections of 1862 by solidifying the war coalition in Congress. They were essential to stemming the growing peace movement in the elections of 1862 and in reelecting Lincoln in 1864. It is believed that Lincoln presented the Emancipation Proclamation only when a number of War Democrats assumed an anti-slavery stance as well. In addition, the location of many War Democrats in upper-echelon positions in government and the military suggests a crucial role in supporting the war until its end. These politicians also enabled the Lincoln administration to create the illusion to the South that the war effort was a united and bipartisan endeavor. However, as the burden of fighting the war continued and a sense of gloom overcame the North, the number of identifiable War Democrats diminished and the group, as a political faction, began to dissolve. Many rejoined with mainline Democrats and supported a peace platform, while others were absorbed into the ranks of the Republican Party.

Another view is that the War Democrats crippled the effectiveness of the Democratic Party's opposition to the Lincoln administration. Others refute this position and identify War Democrats more as a nuance than as a hindrance to the party's capabilities. Many voters still supported the Democratic Party in the North and did not vote for War Democrats. Also, the War Democrats constituted only a small fraction of the party. This enabled the Democrats to remain a potent political force and a real threat to the administration. In addition, by increasingly working with other members of the war coalition, the War Democrats removed themselves from the daily operations of the Democratic Party and did not affect political decisions or party strategies. Regardless of their effectiveness as a tool in mass politics, the War Democrats are an interesting group of politicians, and their historical importance is open to interpretation.

—*Peter S. Genovese*

See also Democratic Party; Douglas, Stephen Arnold; Johnson, Andrew.

For further reading:
Dell, Christopher. *Lincoln and the War Democrats: The Grand Erosion of Conservative Tradition* (1975).
Silbey, Joel H. *"A Respectable Minority": The Democratic Party in the Civil War Era, 1860–1868* (1977).

THE WAR OF THE REBELLION (OFFICIAL RECORDS)

Beginning in 1864, the federal government contemplated publishing the most important documents and reports associated with the Civil War. After two projects were stopped for lack of funds and a more serious lack of organization, in 1877 the secretary of war appointed Captain Robert N. Scott as director of the Publications Office, War Records.

Under Scott's demanding influence, the first volume of records appeared in 1881. Entitled *The War of the Rebellion: A Compilation of the Official Records of the Union and Confederate Armies*, this important documentary publication is generally known simply as the *Official Records*. The entire series contained 128 volumes and was finished in 1901. After Scott's death in 1887, seven successive editors saw the project to completion.

Scott ensured that the records selected for inclusion in the set were authentic, contemporary records, not postwar corrected reports that many officers asked to include in lieu of their original reports. He included what were deemed significant orders, telegrams, and other correspondence to further enhance the military reports of officers. Research and copying documents took up much time during the long course of this project.

The *Official Records* included both Union and Confederate reports, since Scott believed that both sides must be included to ensure accuracy and fairness. Former Confederate general Marcus J. Wright assisted Scott and others in obtaining documents from former comrades for inclusion in the set, as well as loans of other documents for copying.

The 128 volumes are divided into four series of books.

Series I (111 volumes) contains reports of military operations, organized chronologically by campaign and place. Union reports are followed by Confederate reports, with associated correspondence and telegrams in the same order following the reports. Series II (8 volumes) contains Union and Confederate documents concerning prisoners of war and political prisoners. Series III (5 volumes) includes miscellaneous Union correspondence pertaining to the war effort, while Series IV (3 volumes) has Confederate documents about its war effort. The last volume (Number 130) is an abridged general index to the entire set. Volumes 112 and 113 were reserved for a more extensive index that was never published.

In 1895, the *Atlas to Accompany the Official Records of the Union and Confederate Armies* was published. This oversized volume contains 175 plates, primarily maps concerning military operations. Also printed was a general topographic map of the entire area of operations (in 26 plates) as well as maps illustrating the military divisions and departments of both sides, and some drawings of weapons, uniforms, insignia, and flags.

Between 1894 and 1927, the U.S. Navy Department published the 31-volume *Official Records of the Union and Confederate Navies in the War of the Rebellion*. Series I (27 volumes) contains the reports and correspondence pertaining to naval operations, while the three volumes of Series II includes statistical data on warships and a number of Confederate-related documents. The last volume is the general index to the set.

From 1995 to 1999, Broadfoot Publishing Company of Wilmington, North Carolina, published the *Supplement to the Official Records of the Union and Confederate Armies*, an additional 100 volumes of reports and correspondence either unavailable to or omitted by the original editors. Broadfoot has also issued a CD-ROM version of the army *Official Records*, as has Guild Press of Indiana. Both versions allow users to search for any name, phrase, or date mentioned in the entire set of books.

—*Richard A. Sauers*

See also "Annals of the War."
For further reading:
Aimone, Alan C., and Barbara A. Aimone *A User's Guide to the Official Records of the American Civil War* (1993).
Mahan, Harold E. "Arsenal of History: The Official Records of the Rebellion." *Civil War History* (1983).
United States National Archives and Records Service. *Military Operations of the Civil War: A Guide-Index to the Official Records, 1861–1865* (1961–1978).

WARE BOTTOM CHURCH, VIRGINIA
(20 May 1864)

An engagement in the Bermuda Hundred campaign, the battle of Ware Bottom Church occurred after Benjamin Butler and his Army of the James failed in their offensive at Drewry's Bluff on 14–16 May, and withdrew to their defensive line at Bermuda Hundred, between the James and Appomattox rivers. Confederate commander P. G. T. Beauregard determined to follow up his success at Drewry's Bluff by bottling up Butler on the Bermuda Hundred Peninsula.

Following Drewry's Bluff Beauregard had established a thin line in front of Butler's positions at Bermuda Hundred, but knew he would have to push into a narrower part of the peninsula if he was to hold his line against Union counterattacks. Therefore, he ordered attacks to commence against the Union positions near Ware Bottom Church by the James River on the morning of 20 May.

The Confederates chose as their targets the X Corps divisions of Alfred Howe Terry to the north and, immediately to Terry's south, the division of Adelbert Ames. The Confederate attacks against Terry were moderately successful, but only against the southern part of his picket line that abutted Ames. The attacks against the rifle pits of Ames's pickets, however, were successful all along the line and in some places pushed forward as much as three quarters of a mile. The brigades of Henry Alexander Wise and James Green Martin achieved the greatest Confederate gains.

In the early afternoon, X Corps commander Major General Quincy A. Gillmore directed a series of counterattacks beginning with the 97th Pennsylvania and 13th Indiana of Ames's division. The two regiments were unsuccessful in regaining their former lines and had to establish a new picket line farther back on the peninsula. At about 2 P.M. Colonel Joshua Howell led three regiments in an attack to retake the southern part of Terry's line. After heavy fighting, he and his men succeeded in driving the Confederates back to their original positions. The Confederates attempted a counterattack at this position with a newly arrived brigade under the command of William S. Walker. The offensive was very uncoordinated and resulted in very heavy Confederate casualties. One of the casualties was Walker, who accidentally rode into the Union lines. He refused to surrender and tried to flee, only to be shot from his horse. A serious wound in the ankle forced the amputation of his lower leg by Union surgeons.

Even with the setback on Terry's front, Beauregard was able to shorten his line in what became known as the Howlett Line, named after the home of a local physician. Beauregard thus even more effectively bottled up Butler on the Bermuda Hundred Peninsula, reducing Butler's usefulness to Ulysses S. Grant in fighting Robert E. Lee north of Richmond. The day's casualties were approximately 800 for the Confederates and 702 for the Union.

—*David S. Heidler and Jeanne T. Heidler*

See also Bermuda Hundred Campaign; Drewry's Bluff, Battle of.

For further reading:
Robertson, William Glenn. *Back Door to Richmond: The Bermuda Hundred Campaign, April–June 1864* (1987).

WARREN, GOUVERNEUR KEMBLE
(1830–1882)
Union general

Born the son of Sylvanus Warren in Cold Spring, New York, Gouverneur Kemble Warren was educated locally before receiving an appointment to the U.S. Military Academy at age sixteen. He graduated second of forty-four in the class of 1850. After graduation, Warren was commissioned into the Topographical Engineers and served on a variety of surveys throughout the country. He also served as an engineer during the Sioux Expedition of 1855 and had his first combat experience during that mission. Along with the river surveys and various engineering boards, Warren also spent a brief time before the Civil War as an instructor at West Point.

As an instructor at West Point at the outbreak of the war, living near his hometown, it became relatively easy for Warren to help raise a local regiment for service in the Union army. In May 1861 he was commissioned lieutenant colonel of the 5th New York Volunteers. He and the regiment saw their first action at Big Bethel in Virginia on 10 June 1861. In September, Warren was promoted to colonel of volunteers and commander of the 5th New York as well as captain in the regular army.

As part of the Army of the Potomac, Warren and the 5th participated in the Peninsula campaign in the spring of 1862. Warren commanded the regiment at the siege of Yorktown. Besides his regimental responsibilities, Warren also worked closely with Andrew A. Humphreys, chief topographical engineer for the Army of the Potomac. Warren led several reconnaissance missions at the end of May up the York Peninsula, drawing maps of the best routes the army should take. For these actions he was commended by Humphreys.

After the battle of Seven Pines, Warren was given command of a brigade in V Corps. He commanded this brigade during the Seven Days', where he was especially conspicuous at the battle of Gaines' Mill. Warren was wounded in the battle but refused to leave the field. A few days later, he again distinguished himself in the repulse of the Confederate attack at Malvern Hill.

Warren continued in command of the same brigade during the Second Bull Run campaign and at Antietam. After the latter battle he was promoted to brigadier general of volunteers. Warren fought at Fredericksburg and then, in the reorganization of the Army of the Potomac by Joseph Hooker in February 1863, he was made chief topographical engineer of the army. He was commended for his actions at the battle of Chancellorsville.

When Confederate general Robert E. Lee began his movement north in June 1863, Hooker consulted with Warren regarding the best route for the Army of the Potomac to use to block Lee's campaign. Warren advised Hooker that the best place for the army to prevent Lee from moving into Pennsylvania and to protect Washington was Harper's Ferry. Hooker feared moving that far west, and as a result, Lee moved into Pennsylvania unmolested.

Warren remained in the same position under Hooker's successor, George Gordon Meade, during the Gettysburg campaign. At Gettysburg, though he had no formal command over any troops, Warren moved over the terrain continually, trying to find weakness in the Federal line that needed strengthening. On 2 July about midday he noticed the potential for a Confederate turning movement on the Union left at the area of Big and Little Round Top. Only signaling crews occupied the position, and Warren realized that if Confederate forces were to occupy one or both of those hills, the Federal position would be untenable. Therefore he frantically gathered whatever troops he could near the hills and placed them on Little Round Top. In the ensuing Confederate attack, his makeshift defensive force held, although Warren was wounded in the assault. A memorial statue of Warren was placed on Little Round Top twenty years later to commemorate his bravery and foresight.

On 8 August 1863, Warren was promoted to major general of volunteers with a date of rank of 3 May. At that time, Warren, still chief topographical engineer, was in charge of laying temporary bridges against streams and rivers during the pursuit of the Army of Northern Virginia from Gettysburg. This duty completed, in September 1863 Warren was given temporary command of II Corps because of an injury to Winfield Scott Hancock. Warren commanded the corps through March 1864, during which time he distinguished himself at Bristoe Station.

Upon the return of Hancock, Warren was given command of V Corps. In Ulysses S. Grant's campaign against Robert E. Lee in the spring of 1864, Warren fought at the Wilderness, Spotsylvania, and Cold Harbor. During the initial assaults on Petersburg in June 1864, Warren and V Corps occupied the Union left. In the siege of Petersburg that followed, Warren and V Corps participated in the Crater disaster; Warren testified in the court of inquiry that followed that he never thought the plan would work. In other operations during the next year, Warren commanded his corps against the Weldon Railroad, at Hatcher's Run, and on 5 April 1865 at Five Forks.

In the latter battle, Warren was ordered to bring his corps up in an attack on the Confederate flank. He did so with what was generally seen as a great deal of skill. Despite the Union success, however, Warren was immediately

relieved of command of V Corps by Philip Sheridan, who had received authorization to do so in writing from Grant. Even though no one at the time believed that such actions were warranted by anything Warren had or had not done, there had apparently been some bad feeling between Warren and Sheridan, and perhaps Grant as well, that had caused the action. No doubt Sheridan had heard about occasions when Warren had criticized Sheridan's cavalry in earlier engagements; when given command of the proposed attack at Five Forks, Sheridan had complained to Grant about what he believed to be Warren's methodical approach to battle. To reassure Sheridan regarding his authority, Grant had armed him with the power to dismiss Warren if the hero of Little Round Top did not live up to Sheridan's expectations. The following day, Warren was placed in command of the defenses of Petersburg at City Point and the Southside Railroad. His request after Lee's surrender at Appomattox for a court of inquiry to investigate his relief from command of his corps was refused by Grant on 6 May.

After the war, Warren briefly commanded the Department of Mississippi before resigning his volunteer commission and reverting to major of topographical engineers. For the next seventeen years he worked on river and harbor improvements, bridge surveys, and railroad surveys. He frequently made requests that his dismissal at Five Forks be investigated, but he was always refused until 1879. The lengthy investigation that followed produced a report that exonerated Warren of the gravest charges brought by Sheridan and praised his performance during the battle. Although he knew of the board's findings, they were not published until after his premature death. He died while still on active duty on 8 August 1882 at Newport, Rhode Island, at the rank of lieutenant colonel. In making arrangements for his funeral, Warren had insisted that he not be buried in his army uniform.

—*David S. Heidler and Jeanne T. Heidler*

See also Five Forks, Battle of; Gettysburg, Battle of.
For further reading:
Flanagan, Vincent J. "The Life of Gouverneur Kemble Warren" (Ph.D. dissertation, 1969).
Kelly, Michael T. *"I Will Have Justice Done": General Gouverneur K. Warren, U.S.A.* (1997).
Taylor, Emerson Gifford. *Gouverneur Kemble Warren; The Life and Letters of an American Soldier, 1830–1882* (1900).

WASHBURN, CADWALLADER COLDER
(1818–1882)
Union general

Third in a trio of brothers from Maine who served simultaneously in Congress, Cadwallader Washburn was a lawyer turned businessman who made his fortune in Wisconsin. As a land agent in the newly opened territories, he purchased timberlands and

Cadwallader Washburn
(*Wahburn-Norlands Foundation Archives*)

mineral rights that, by the 1850s, made him the richest man in the state.

Elected to Congress in 1854 as a Whig, he joined his brothers Israel (Maine) and Elihu (Illinois) in supporting the formation of the Republican Party and its antislavery position. In 1858, during a heated debate over Kansas's admission into the Union, Washburn attempted to restrain two colleagues from coming to blows by grabbing one, William Barksdale of Mississippi, by his hair, which turned out to be a hairpiece. Further violence was averted as the House dissolved into laughter. While in Congress, he served on the Committee of Thirty-Three, Congress's last attempt to find a legislative compromise to avert secession and war.

When war broke out, Washburn resigned his seat to raise and outfit the 2d Wisconsin Cavalry and was commissioned in October 1861 as its colonel. Early in 1862 the regiment was ordered to Benton Barracks, Missouri, as part of the Army of the Southwest. A politician turned soldier with no military training, Washburn used his connections and organizational skills to gain a position as Grant's aide-de-camp at Fort Donelson. He kept his brother Elihu informed about affairs in the west, calling Grant "the only regular Army General worth a cuss."

Promoted to brigadier general in July 1862, then to major general in November, Washburn was posted to the District of West Tennessee, where he led 2,000

cavalry troops on a raid to Granada, Mississippi, defeating Confederate forces at the Yazoo Pass. At Haynes Bluff during the Vicksburg campaign, he commanded a detachment of Memphis-based troops from XVI Corps. After the fall of Vicksburg, he was sent to Louisiana to command the 1st Division, XIII Corps, in General Edward Ord's absence. He participated in the ill-fated Teche Bayou and Red River campaigns, making a notable contribution at the battle of Grand Coteau when his forces saved Stephen Burbridge's 4th Division.

In April 1864, after several months leave to attend to his business affairs in Wisconsin, Washburn received the most challenging assignment of his army career when Grant ordered him to relieve Stephen Hurlburt as commander of the District of West Tennessee in the aftermath of the Union defeat at Fort Pillow. Not only did Washburn have to deal with Hurlburt's initial refusal to resign his post, he also faced the issues relating to reports of the massacre of African-American troops garrisoned at the Fort by forces commanded by Confederate general Nathan Bedford Forrest.

In a remarkable series of official correspondences, Washburn placed the blame for the incident squarely on Forrest's shoulders and challenged him to clarify his government's position regarding the treatment of captured colored troops. Forrest found Washburn's accusation as "grossly insulting to myself. You assume the privilege of denouncing me as a murderer and as guilty of the wholesale slaughter of the garrison at Fort Pillow." Forrest, in turn, accused Washburn of fostering revenge in the hearts of the colored troops, which jeopardized the treatment of Confederate forces captured at Brice's Crossroads (Tishomingo Creek). Washburn responded, "The desperate fortunes of a bad cause excuse much irritation of temper, and I pass it by. Indeed, I receive it as a favorable augury and as evidence that you are not indifferent to the opinions of the civilized world."

It is little wonder that when Forrest staged a daring cavalry raid on Memphis the morning of 21 August 1864 to relieve pressure on northern Mississippi, Washburn's capture was the main objective. Alerted to the attack, Washburn fled in his nightclothes to safety at Fort Pickering, leaving his uniform and sword to the Confederate raiders. Forrest gallantly returned his prize under a flag of truce, and Washburn responded by having a uniform made for Forrest by his prewar tailor. Washburn's dignity was thus sacrificed to the higher cause of keeping Forrest busy, while Sherman progressed through Tennessee enroute to Georgia. A better administrator than field commander, Washburn enjoyed greater success in his efforts at fighting corruption and illicit trade in occupied Memphis.

After the war, Washburn served two more terms in Congress and one as governor of Wisconsin. His greatest fame came in business, as founder of the Gold Medal Flour Company. Upon his death in 1882, he willed much of his fortune to charity.

—*Judith Bielecki*

See also Forrest's Raids; Fort Pillow Massacre; Washburne, Elihu; Washburne, Cadwallader.
For further reading:
Bicha, Karel D. C. C. *Washburn and the Upper Mississippi Valley* (1995).
Cadwallader C. Washburn Collection. Washburn-Norlands Foundation Archives, Livermore, Maine.
Hunt, Gaillard. *Israel, Elihu and Cadwallader Washburn: A Chapter in American Biography* (1925).
Wyeth, John Allen. *Life of General Nathan Bedford Forrest* (1899; reprint, 1989).

WASHBURN, FRANCIS
(1838–1865)
Union officer

Francis Washburn was born in Lancaster, Massachusetts, the son of John Marshall and Harriet Washburn, a family involved in the abolitionist movement. He attended the Lawrence Scientific School at Harvard and the University of Freiberg, Germany, studying engineering.

Washburn sailed home in 1861 to join the army, only to find his father gravely ill. He received his commission as a second lieutenant in the First Massachusetts Cavalry the day after Christmas, the same day his father died. Washburn's older brother Edward had already volunteered, while another brother, John Washburn, remained in Massachusetts.

Washburn was first stationed at Port Royal, South Carolina, in the company of his tentmate, Charles Francis Adams, Jr., where his duty consisted of occupying abandoned plantations.

An adventurous, bold spirit marked Washburn's career. He had a bizarre brush with disaster early in his career when the commander of his unit ordered Washburn to go forward alone and determine whether any Confederates waited in ambush in a grove. Washburn approached the woods, found himself faced by a force of Confederates, yet drew his revolver, fired twice and attempted to withdraw with a prisoner. His superior observed Washburn's perilous position, then hurried with the larger force to his assistance, placing all in a perilous position. Decades later, Adams observed, "mature military experience had come to neither side.... Our audacity, paralyzing them, saved us." Both Washburn and Adams had difficulty with their commander, which may have prompted Washburn to join the Second Massachusetts Cavalry.

In 1864, Washburn joined the new Fourth Massachusetts Cavalry. In the same year, his older

brother, Edward R. Washburn, died of injuries received earlier at Port Hudson, Louisiana.

By the spring of 1865, the commander of the Fourth Massachusetts Cavalry resigned and Washburn become colonel. The regiment had been dispersed a year earlier, and Washburn wanted to reunite the original companies. Instead, elements of the First and Fourth Massachusetts Cavalry were combined but the manpower of the regiment remained greatly reduced. Washburn appealed personally to General Ulysses S. Grant, but even the endorsement of Generals Edward Ord and Grant failed to obtain the return of the companies by April.

With his reduced command, Washburn pursued Confederates across central Virginia in the opening days of April 1865. Confederate general Robert E. Lee's forces moved rapidly, making good use of the bridges to cross and recross the rivers as all raced westward. This strategy raised the issue of where and when to destroy the bridges, since the location of enemy troops would determine whether the destruction of any bridge might strand the enemy or cut off the Union pursuit.

On the night of 5 April, Washburn received verbal orders to take his cavalry and some infantry to the High Bridge near Farmville, Virginia, "and there be governed by circumstances." He was also under instructions to confront any rebel force he encountered, since they would give way. The vagueness of these orders reflected the chaotic nature of what were, literally, the closing hours of the war. Ord later realized that the situation had changed, and countermanded; but the messenger never reached Washburn. He was already far afield amidst Confederate forces that were in a far more confrontational mood than Union commanders realized.

Confederate general Thomas Rosser was en route to the High Bridge with orders to destroy it at any cost. Both Union and Confederates were on a collision course to a bridge, which was a formidable objective either to destroy or defend.

Upon their arrival, Washburn and the Fourth Massachusetts Cavalry drove off or captured a small force of the defenders and commenced the destruction of the bridge. In the midst of rounding up prisoners they were suddenly confronted by a large Confederate cavalry force, which Washburn aggressively charged. The result left every officer of the Massachusetts force either shot dead or wounded.

Yet the Confederate army stopped in its tracks when the decision was made to halt and entrench. In the aftermath of the battle, Washburn was struck across the head by a Confederate when he protested the removal of his sword and personal effects. The blow resulted in a deep wound and a fractured skull.

Days later, Washburn was breveted to brigadier general for gallantry. General Ord later praised Washburn for having forced the Confederate column to halt. Ulysses S. Grant wrote in his *Memoirs* that it was Washburn's bold attack on the head of the Confederate column that had enabled the Union to capture the forces behind Rosser. In other words, the Fourth Massachusetts under Washburn's command had slowed the Confederate forces long enough for the Union to head them off the next morning at Appomattox.

Washburn was evacuated home, but he died as a result of his head injuries two weeks later on 22 April 1865.

—*Teresa A. Thomas*

See also Adams, Charles Francis, Jr.; Farmville/High Bridge, Battle of; Rosser, Thomas.

For further reading:

Adams, Charles Francis, Jr. "Address Delivered at the Dedication of Memorial Hall, Lancaster, Mass., June 17 1868" (1868).

Calkins, Chris. *Thirty-Six Hours before Appomattox* (1980).

Crowninshield, Benjamin W. A *History of the First Regiment of Massachusetts Cavalry Volunteers* (1891).

Thomas, Teresa A. "For Union, Not For Glory: Memory and the Civil War Volunteers of Lancaster, Massachusetts." In *Civil War History* (1994).

———. "For Union, Not For Glory: Memory and the Civil War Volunteers of Lancaster, Massachusetts" (M. A. thesis, n.d.).

WASHBURN, ISRAEL, JR.
(1813–1883)
Governor of Maine

The eldest in a remarkable family of seven brothers who rose from humble beginnings in rural Maine to positions of national prominence in politics and business, Israel Washburn, Jr., was influenced from an early age by the values of his native New England. Born before Maine entered the Union as part of the Missouri Compromise of 1820, he was imbued with the history of his state's role in the great debate over slavery that gripped the nation in the first half of the nineteenth century.

A lawyer by profession, Washburn was elected to the U.S. House of Representatives in 1851 as a member of the Whig Party. His passionate support for the Missouri Compromise, by which Maine had become a state, led him to assume a central role in the congressional battle to limit the extension of slavery. His opposition to the 1850 Fugitive Slave Law caused him to advocate preventing slavery's extension into the territories. His growing dissatisfaction with what he saw as the Whig Party's surrender to the slave interests reached a breaking point in 1854 with the passage of the Kansas-Nebraska Act, which Washburn saw as a nullification of the Missouri Compromise. He convened a meeting of antislavery Whigs, Democrats, and Free-Soilers to consider the formation of a new national party, whose express purpose would be to oppose slavery. Israel Washburn proposed that the new alliance be known as the Republican Party. Dedicated to stopping the spread of

Israel Washburn
(*Washburn-Norlands Foundation Archives*)

slavery into the western territories, the new party was formally organized as the Republican Party at its first national convention in Pittsburgh in 1856.

As one of the leaders of the Republicans, Washburn was an eloquent spokesman for the party's political and moral philosophy. Although not an abolitionist, he nevertheless believed that the extension of slavery was contrary to the intent of the Founding Fathers and a threat to the principle of free labor in the existing states and the territories. A supporter of Lincoln's views on slavery, Washburn came to support its abolition only because of the act of secession.

During nine years in Congress, Washburn served as chair of the Committee on Elections and, in his last term, as chair of the powerful Ways and Means Committee. For five of these years, he served alongside his younger brothers Elihu and Cadwallader, who represented districts in Illinois and Wisconsin, a record for simultaneous service by siblings unequalled in American politics.

In 1860 Israel Washburn was elected to the first of two one-year terms as governor of Maine. With Lincoln's call for 75,000 volunteers in April 1861, Washburn became one of the war governors responsible for raising and outfitting the volunteer regiments needed for the Union army. This he did with notable skill and organization, exceeding Maine's initial quota of 17,124 recruits by 578. A hands-on administrator, by the end of his second term,

he had overseen the recruitment, equipping, and commissioning of all of his state's three-year regiments, including the last, the famous 20th Maine.

Declining to run for a third term, Washburn also chose not to run for the Senate. Instead, he accepted President Lincoln's appointment as collector of customs of the port of Portland, a pleasant and lucrative Federal position that he held from 1863 to 1878. After the war, he remained faithful to the party he helped to found, supporting the Radical Republican position on African-American suffrage and congressional Reconstruction policies. In his later years, he criticized the excesses that he saw in public life, calling the federal treasury a "reservoir of corruption" and urging a return to smaller and more economical government.

Along with his public service, Israel Washburn Jr. was a prominent and devout Universalist. He served on the Board of Trustees of Tufts College in Medford, Massachusetts, from 1852 to 1883, the longest term of service in the school's history. He died in Philadelphia in May 1883 and is buried in Mount Hope Cemetery in Bangor, Maine.

—*Judith Bielecki*

See also Republican Party; Washburn, Cadwallader; Washburne, Elihu.
For further reading:
Annual Report of the Adjutant General of the State of Maine, 1862 (1863).
Hunt, Gaillard. Israel, Elihu and Cadwallader Washburn: A Chapter in American Biography (1925).
Israel Washburn, Jr. Collection. Washburn-Norlands Foundation Archives, Livermore, Maine.

WASHBURNE, ELIHU BENJAMIN
(1816–1887)
United States congressman

Raised with the Yankee values of industriousness and optimistic energy, Elihu, the third son in a poor, but close-knit Maine family, became the most politically prominent and influential of the Washburn brothers.

After studying law at Harvard and adding an ancestral *e* to his surname, Elihu followed the example of his younger brother, Cadwallader, and sought his fortune in the west, settling in Galena, Illinois, in 1840. Unlike his brothers, who tended to be stiff and blunt, Elihu was sociable and charming, qualities that served him well throughout his long career. His marriage to Adele Gratiot, daughter of a prominent Midwest family of French Huguenot descent, provided both social access and lifelong happiness, and formed the emotional underpinnings for his years of public service.

Washburne's passion for politics, instilled by his parents, led him to involvement in the affairs of his adopted state.

Elihu Washurne
(*Washburn-Norlands Foundation Archives*)

He quickly became known for his tireless energy, and upstanding and unambiguous character. He described his approach to politics by stating, "It is generally known where I am. If I am for a man, I am for him, and if I am against him, I am against him." One man he was for was a young lawyer from Springfield named Abraham Lincoln.

Elected to his first of nine terms in Congress in 1852, Washburne broke with the Whigs over the slavery issue. He opposed the 1854 Kansas-Nebraska Act because it violated the Missouri Compromise and the treaty rights of Native Americans in those territories. Washburne joined the Republican Party upon its formation and became chair of the powerful Committee on Commerce, a position he held for ten years. In the 1860 presidential campaign, Washburne's support for Lincoln increased the candidate's credibility among eastern Republicans in the House. When assassination threats forced the newly elected president to arrive secretly in Washington for his first inauguration, Washburne met Lincoln's train at Union Station and escorted him to the Willard Hotel.

Elihu Washburne was physically unfit for military service during the Civil War, yet he influenced the outcome of the conflict through his friendship with a fellow citizen of Galena, Ulysses S. Grant. They first met in May 1861 and, learning of Grant's military background, Washburne requested that he be appointed colonel of the 21st Illinois Volunteers. The regiment had its first drills on the front lawn of the congressman's home in Galena. In August of that year, he arranged Grant's promotion to brigadier general of volunteers and in 1864 introduced the bill that restored the rank of lieutenant general of the army, a position created specifically for Grant.

Throughout the war, Washburne served as a close advisor to both Lincoln and Grant, and enjoyed great political prestige as a result. He often was the president's personal observer at the front, reporting directly back to the White House upon his return. He was present during First Bull Run and the chaotic stampede back to Washington. He also served the president by keeping him politically informed about Congress, in particular about the controversial Committee on the Conduct of the War.

Always an advocate for Grant, Washburne described his friend as the "great head and soul of the Army," without whom the North would have lost the war. As Grant's guest during the Wilderness and Spotsylvania campaigns, Washburne's unidentified presence in dark civilian clothes prompted comments among the troops that "the Old Man had brought along his private undertaker."

Washburne was on a steamship near Richmond when he learned of Lincoln's assassination. He accompanied the president's body on the train to Illinois and served as a pallbearer at his funeral.

After the war, Washburne's senior status as the House of Representative's longest-serving member gained him the title, "Father of the House." Washburne headed the congressional investigation of the 1866 riots and massacres in Memphis. He served on the Joint Committee on Reconstruction and as chair of the House Committee on Appropriations during his last term. Initially opposed to Johnson's impeachment, he eventually adopted the position of the Radical Republicans, serving as chair of the Committee of the Whole.

Upon Grant's election as president, Washburne was appointed secretary of state, a position he immediately resigned, serving instead as United States minister to France from 1869 to 1877. In 1880, his name was placed in nomination at the Republican Convention by forces opposed to Grant's bid for a third term. Grant blamed Washburne, and the two men never spoke again. Grant's memoirs, published shortly before his death in 1885, make scant reference to Washburne, who died two years later.

—*Judith Bielecki*

See also Congress, U.S.A.; Joint Committee on the Conduct of the War; Washburn, Cadwallader; Washburn, Israel.

For further reading:

Catton, Bruce. *A Stillness at Appomattox* (1953).

Elihu B. Washburne Collection. Washburn-Norlands Foundation Archives, Livermore, Maine.

Grant, Ulysses S., and E. B. Washburne. *General Grant's Letters to a Friend, 1861–1880* (1997).

Hunt, Gaillard. *Israel, Elihu and Cadwallader Washburn: A Chapter in American Biography* (1925).

Tap, Bruce. *Over Lincoln's Shoulder: The Committee on the Conduct of the War* (1998).

WASHINGTON, D.C.

At the outbreak of the American Civil War, the United States government faced many daunting problems, but the one closest to home was the situation and character of the national capital. Maryland had donated the ten-square-mile tract designated as the District of Columbia in the 1790s, when plans were made to move the capital to a Southern location. Still new and raw when the government moved operations there at the turn of the century, it remained more a plan than a realization even at mid-century. Aside from its unfinished appearance, the most striking feature about the city was its Southern character. Some feared, and others hoped, that the characteristic would translate into Southern sympathies.

Within the city, several small, distinct communities clustered in what was essentially a rural setting. City government was based on the ward system and was conducted from the city hall complex on Judiciary Square. It was inefficient and in terms of law enforcement only erratically effective, making many areas of the district unsafe, especially at night. Actually, just as the federal government's activities coincided with and frequently overshadowed the administration of the city, its buildings were the most dominant feature of the southern third of the district along the line of Pennsylvania Avenue, a broad but untidy thoroughfare running diagonally from the southeast to the northwest. On the southeastern end on a promontory sat the Capitol, still undergoing a major renovation that was, in fact, a significant restructuring. It was being enlarged both outward and upward with new northern and southern wings sprawling out from the original sandstone center. A cast-iron dome was under construction to replace the wooden one. This work would occupy a considerable amount of Quartermaster General Montgomery Meigs's time, an indication of the importance placed on some activities proceeding in spite of the war, in fact proceeding as though nothing unusual at all was occurring. The work on the Capitol probably advanced with greater fervor than it would have in peacetime.

The Capitol sat at the hub of Delaware, Maryland, New Jersey, and Pennsylvania Avenues. Along the length of Pennsylvania Avenue a study in contrasts and variety was presented. The southern side was a hurly-burly of vending and seediness, while the northern side functioned as an unofficial promenade for Washington society and politicians. Brown's and the National Hotel occupied prominent spots on the street, as did Willard's, the preferred gathering place for the fashionable and

The U.S. Capitol with dome under construction, 1860 (*Library of Congress*)

Company M, 9th New York Heavy Artillery, manning Union defenses on the outskirts of Washington, D.C. (*Library of Congress*)

celebrated to take meals and be seen. The eccentric architecture of the Smithsonian Institution rose up to the south, but the most dominant feature on the northwestern end of Pennsylvania Avenue was the massive Treasury Building, large enough also to house the State Department. The treasury was planted conspicuously on the northeastern corner of Executive Square. Here the cluster of buildings included the Executive Mansion in the center with the Navy and War Departments housed in modest structures just to the west.

The southern portion of Executive Square was called President's Park, but it was actually a marshy expanse bordered by the old City Canal. This watercourse had once connected the Potomac and the Eastern Branch, but it had fallen into disuse and consequent disrepair, a fetid receptacle that in summer months became a malodorous breeder of disease. Washington's social season capitulated to the climate and marshy terrain, emptying the city in the late spring and filling it back up in the fall for the rounds of banquets, entertainments, and balls.

The presidential residence, or Executive Mansion, was only informally known as the White House. (Not until Theodore Roosevelt's administration would it gain that designation officially.) Here the Lincoln family took up residence in the spring of 1861, just before the annual exodus from the heat should have been occurring. Yet office seekers always swamped new administrations, and Lincoln's was no exception. What was different was that just when this activity should have relented, the outbreak of the war invigorated the mad rush for positions, and it would continue unabated for the length of

the conflict. The Lincolns consequently enjoyed little privacy and probably less than previous presidential families. Lincoln refused to close the White House because he felt that to make the residence inaccessible to the public would break with the tradition of the place at the very worst time to do so. The Lincolns had private quarters that amounted to nine rooms on the western end of the second floor. The main corridor, at the east end of which were the president's and his secretaries' offices, was frequently trafficked by both official operatives and office seekers, many of the latter being strangers. Once Lincoln's call to arms had been answered, the soldiers who crowded into the city to encamp in such varied places as the Capitol Rotunda also slept in the hallways and carpeted East Room of the White House.

Yet for all the legend about the president's residence being as open to the public as a general store or museum gallery, guards did patrol the halls. They dressed as civilians and worked under the euphemistic designation of "doormen," but they were armed and vigilant. Only the north door was really open and unguarded, and though visitors could enter it without passing a sentry, they were watched and directed to destinations. Except for the cavernous East Room, the main floor was closed to the public. Lincoln usually used the service stairs to move around the house because they allowed him to do so unseen. He also could depart the building without being seen, as he frequently did through the west wing's colonnade to cross the wooded grounds to the telegraph room in the War Department.

The war filled Washington with equal parts of oppor-

tunity, excitement, and fear. The British had proven in 1814 just how assailable the city was to a determined foe, and now geography posed itself as an even greater ally of a potential attacker. Washington was as strategically exposed as it was politically vulnerable. Encircled by Virginia and Maryland, the city would have become an isolated island in a sea of secession had both states withdrawn from the Union. Ensuring Maryland's loyalty was paramount, and the harsh policy directed toward that state's government and citizens was compelled by the necessity of keeping Washington tenable. Virginia's secession complicated matters, but nobody ever seriously contemplated abandoning Washington for a more removed and safer location. The capital was a symbol of the Union, and its role as the seat of government had to be sustained, bolstering Northern confidence and making the rebellion at least seem less dire. A government put to flight might not be worth defending.

Washington was naked to threats from within as well. When Colonel Charles P. Stone first organized the capital's defenses, he was alarmed to discover serious evidence of disloyalty among local militia organizations. Most of the National Rifles were unabashed Southern sympathizers, and eventually many of them would head South to serve the Confederacy. Stone diligently undertook to weed out dubious elements and strengthen the discipline and effectiveness of the militia, but even at the time of Lincoln's inauguration, the capital's defenses were woefully undermanned and remained vulnerable to internal subversion. The atmosphere of an armed camp darkened the Lincoln inauguration, but people were meant to know that sharpshooters stood ready in windows along the parade route.

After the attack on Fort Sumter and Lincoln had called for volunteers, local militia was bolstered by the arrival of the 6th Massachusetts Infantry—the same regiment harassed by a Baltimore mob while changing trains in that city—but effectiveness was still low considering the capital's defensive requirements. Stone proposed to Scott that if Washington were invaded he would defend the Capitol, the Patent Office, Post Office, and the Executive buildings, including the president's house. Scott insisted that the plan was too ambitious for the numbers at Stone's disposal. They could defend only Executive Square, said Scott, and they could only do that from the Treasury Building where a reliable water supply and stored food would allow the president and his cabinet to hole up indefinitely.

Scott had a point. The city spanned a broad front across the point of the "V" formed by the Potomac and Anacostia rivers, the latter sometimes called the Eastern Branch, and was easily approachable from a variety of directions. On the southwest, Long Bridge crossed the Potomac linking the Alexandria Road to Maryland Avenue; on the southeast, the Navy Yard Bridge crossed

the Eastern Branch from Maryland. True, these could be defended with relative ease and even destroyed if necessary, but the wide arc of northern approaches was another matter. The railroad from Baltimore entered the city from the northeast, crossing the city limits at Boundary Street (currently Florida Avenue) to the railroad station three blocks north of the Capitol. The 7th Street Road headed straight north toward the Soldiers' Home (a favorite retreat for Lincoln) and Silver Spring. Bridges across Rock Creek west of town linked the capital with Georgetown. Also above Georgetown there was Chain Bridge, which spanned the Potomac on the road from Harper's Ferry and Leesburg.

When additional troops finally began arriving in Washington in late spring, the increasing numbers were not that encouraging to professional military men. The recruits were untrained, of course, and the capital could not accommodate their increasing numbers. Suddenly a city whose prewar population had hovered around 50,000 at the peak of its season found itself coping with not only a horde of office seekers, but also a growing legion of raucous and occasionally unruly soldiers. Not until George B. McClellan cleaned up the camps and established a systematic discipline did this military presence pose as much more than a nuisance. And with the soldiers came associated ills. Enterprising madams from all over the country simply moved the denizens of their bawdy houses to Washington. The burgeoning population of prostitutes was remarkable even for a city whose character had always encouraged such a trade. Petty and major crimes also increased as pickpockets and felons joined the stream of humanity flooding the capital. Some parts of the city never slept, and because other offenses were so prevalent, that of prostitution receded to minor importance. Neither the District's constables and courts, nor the army's provost officers could do much, and the flouting of laws continued to reach such a crescendo that by 1863 a crackdown was necessary to suppress the most unabashed "houses of ill-fame."

Actually, the army was more concerned about protecting the capital from Confederates than from sneak thieves and harlots. Colonel Joseph Mansfield, commanding the Department of Washington, urged that fortifications be erected on the Virginia side of Long and Chain Bridges and the Aqueduct west of town. Federal troops also occupied Alexandria—an action that cost young Elmer Ellsworth his life in a famous early incident of the war. Yet defensive works were still in their infancy when Federal forces were defeated at First Bull Run in July 1861, and considerable alarm spread among citizens fearing a Confederate invasion. The disorganized Southern army, however, was in no better shape to assail Washington than was the beaten Northern one to defend it. The memory of a Confederate menace hung heavy, though, and Lincoln with Secretary of War Edwin

Stanton insisted that offensive operations in Virginia always include resources for Washington's protection. According to George B. McClellan, his Peninsula campaign in the spring of 1862 was hopelessly hobbled by such a requirement.

Those in charge of defending Washington fretted, nonetheless. Even though an extensive series of batteries and fortifications eventually ringed the city, manpower shortages were a constant concern. When John Pope's Army of Virginia was reinforced from the city's garrisons, Joseph Barnard complained that he had less than 6,000 men and fully two-thirds of these were either ending their terms of service or were still being detached for offensive operations in Virginia.

The Confederate strategy of seeming to threaten Washington and thus relieve pressure on Richmond was an effective ploy, but fears of a Confederate assault on the capital remained largely unfounded until the summer of 1864. A raid mounted by Jubal Early reached the northern environs of the city on 11 July. By then extensive reinforcements had moved into the works at Fort Stevens guarding the 7th Street Road. Early probed the fort, was dissuaded from mounting an attack, and withdrew, although not before giving Lincoln his only firsthand look at combat during the war. Visiting Fort Stevens during Early's demonstrations against it, the president stubbornly remained on the ramparts oblivious to both the bullets and the warnings being shouted at him. Horatio Wright's entreaties proved fruitless, but Lieutenant Colonel Oliver Wendell Holmes finally got the commander in chief's attention when he shouted, "Get down, you fool!"

Washington, both symbol of the Union and seat of the central government, eventually became the nexus of a thousand tendrils of command and the place where weighty decisions determined the fate of thousands of people. The city was both changed by the war and remained stubbornly the same as before it. To the south of the White House across the City Canal's Potomac inlet sat what there was of the Washington Monument. Rising above random rubble and scattered construction materials, the obelisk was only a third completed, its funding dependent on private subscriptions that had dried up. Lincoln could see the jagged top of this abandoned needle from his office and from the family's library in the Oval Room. Some regarded it an apt metaphor for the Union, unfinished and now probably undone. If Lincoln ever despaired over such allusions, he kept it to himself, likely believing that for both the Union and the monument to the father of it, the country would find a way.

—*David S. Heidler and Jeanne T. Heidler*

See also Congress, U.S.A; Lincoln, Abraham Assassination; Lincoln; Old Capitol Prison; Peninsula Campaign; Scott, Winfield; Stone, Charles P.

For further reading:
Leech, Margaret. *Reveille in Washington: 1860–1865* (1941).

Stoddard, William Osborn. *Inside the White House in War Times: Memoirs and Reports of Lincoln's Secretary* (2000).

WASHINGTON PEACE CONFERENCE
(4 February–27 February 1861)

Upon the failure of John J. Crittenden's compromise efforts and as the Virginia secession convention awaited possible conciliatory developments, on 19 January 1861 the Virginia legislature issued a call for a convention of the states. Delegates to this meeting would renew compromise efforts with the object of restoring the Union. The Conference Convention accordingly met on 4 February in Washington, D.C., commencing deliberations in what had been a Presbyterian church but had since been incorporated into Willard's Hotel. The 131 delegates would soon be referred to as the Peace Conference or, less optimistically, the "Old Gentlemen's Convention."

The venture from the start was not promising. A feeling prevailed that its efforts, even if meaningful, would be too late. As if to underscore that sentiment, on the same day that the Peace Conference assembled in Washington, the Confederate government was gathering in Montgomery, Alabama. The Conference's attendance also revealed a certain hopelessness. Standing on the reality, as well as the principal, of secession, not one of the seven Deep South states sent delegates. Arkansas was also absent, as were California and Oregon, likely because they were too far away to respond to Virginia's call. Michigan, Wisconsin, and Minnesota resolutely opposed the meeting, however, and the Michigan legislature went on record to proclaim that secession was treason with which there could be no compromise and from whence there could be no negotiation.

Any optimism about the Conference stemmed from a realization that the meeting was likely the last hope for restoring the Union peacefully. And those who did attend from twenty-one states included some distinguished public figures. The Virginia delegation was headed by former president John Tyler, who presided over the meeting, and included James A. Seddon and William Cabell Rives. Pennsylvania sent David Wilmot; Maryland, Reverdy Johnson; Maine, William P. Fessenden; and Ohio, Salmon P. Chase. The Illinois representatives included Stephen T. Logan, who was well acquainted with President-elect Abraham Lincoln. Yet, the age of many delegates—Tyler, for instance, was seventy-one—prompted the label "Old Gentlemen's Convention," a sign that contemporary feeling viewed it as an exercise in futility.

Both the Northern and Southern press derided the enterprise, and radicals from both sections scoffed at its deliberations. The press was especially annoyed that the

conference conducted secret proceedings, but the delegates had concluded that the heat of the crisis required their candor without the glare of daily publicity. It was a wise decision—perhaps the meeting's only one—because the sessions were turbulent. Acrimony marked deliberations more than conciliation, and the oratory, long and impassioned, staked out positions for inflexible defense rather than possible compromise. Republicans, under instructions from party leaders, were obviously present to squelch pro-Southern initiatives, and even the Virginians began to exhibit resignation and fatigue. When Tyler and Rives vividly envisioned the horrible likelihood of civil war should the conference fail, sadly it seemed that either most delegates did not care or they were ready to accept the consequences as inevitable.

Three weeks of debate could only produce a slightly altered version of the Crittenden Compromise, and even that achievement had been close run. On 26 February delegates defeated the recommendation to revive 36 degrees 30 minutes of latitude (the Missouri Compromise Line) as the dividing line between slave states and free states with a constitutional amendment extending it to the Pacific. That evening members of the Virginia delegation called on the recently arrived president-elect at his rooms in Willard's. In what would become a widely circulated exchange between Lincoln and Rives, it seemed that the crisis over Fort Sumter would be averted to keep Virginia in the Union. On the following day, the Illinois delegation promptly changed its position on the extension of the border of 36 degrees 30 minutes, and the measure passed. Speculation followed that Lincoln was responsible for the change in the Illinois delegation's sentiments, and for the first time in months there was a small sense that a positive breakthrough was at hand.

The hopefulness was short lived. On 27 February, the conference adopted the Missouri Compromise resolution as well as one assuring that slavery would be forever secure south of 36 degrees 30 minutes of latitude. In addition to proposing that the nation be forever made half-slave and half-free, the delegates also proposed restricting the acquisition of additional territory (to do so would require a majority of Southern and Northern senators' consent). Also, a complicated bolstering of the Fugitive Slave Law included compensating slaveowners frustrated by Northern obstructions to the law's enforcement. Finally, the conference recommended the adoption of an ironclad constitutional amendment to protect slavery in perpetuity. This warmed-over restatement of the Crittenden proposals landed in Congress to a response that was as lukewarm there as it was everywhere else. Even Virginia would not support the measures, and the Senate on 2 March followed the lead of Republicans in defeating the conference's recommendations by an overwhelming majority.

Thus ended the last systematic attempt for reconciliation before the firing on Fort Sumter further divided the Republic and opened the Civil War. The Washington Peace Conference's chances for success were never much in question. At once bombastic and careworn, the conference mainly revealed the persistence of Border State Unionism. The 26 February meeting between some Virginia delegates and Lincoln also had the effect of disclosing the president-elect's mood just days away from his inauguration. In spite of his remarks to Rives about Fort Sumter's status and Virginia's loyalty, Lincoln had resolutely declared that he would do whatever was necessary to enforce the laws and protect the Constitution. Southern secession and Lincoln's adamant stance regarding disunion placed the Washington Peace Conference in an impossible position and gave it a hopeless task. Consequently, the gathering was only a symptom of quiet desperation and never a conceivable way to solve the crisis of the Union.

—*David S. Heidler and Jeanne T. Heidler*

See also Peace Democrats; Peace Movements.

For further reading:

Chittenden, L. E. *A Report of the Debates and Proceedings in the Secret Session of the Conference Convention* (1864).

Gunderson, Robert G. *Old Gentlemen's Convention: The Washington Peace Conference of 1861* (1961).

Keene, Jesse L. *The Peace Convention of 1861* (1961).

Matlock, Joseph Dixon. "The Peace Conference of 1861 in Washington, D.C." (M.A. thesis, 1931).

Wright, Crafts J. *Official Journal of the Conference Convention Held at Washington City, February 1861* (1861).

WATIE, STAND
(1806–1871)
Confederate brigadier general

Born into an affluent Cherokee family in the town of Oothcaloga (near present-day Rome, Georgia) on 12 December 1806, Degadoga, or "He Stands," was given the name Isaac S. Watie by his Moravian parents. After dropping his Christian first name, Degadoga became known as Stand Watie. As large landowners, Watie's family had the necessary status to help Watie procure a job as clerk of the Cherokee Supreme Court at the age of twenty-two and ultimately acquire a license to practice law within the Cherokee Nation. His older brother, Kilakeena (better known as Buck Watie or Elias Boudinot), was editor of the *Cherokee Phoenix*. Watie's uncle, Major Ridge, played a prominent role in Cherokee politics during the removal crisis of the 1820s and 1830s, ultimately defying the wishes of the Cherokee Council by advocating removal and signing the Treaty of New Echota in 1835. Watie's own support of this treaty placed him in direct conflict with Cherokee principal chief John Ross, who was a staunch opponent of removal. This animosity between Watie and Ross heightened after their move to Indian Territory when Watie's uncle, two brothers, and a cousin were assassinated by Ross supporters for their compliance with the removal policy. Watie was fortunate to escape attempts on his own life ultimately to become the lone survivor of those Cherokee leaders who formally supported removal.

During the secession crisis, Watie organized in Indian Territory a secret organization of supporters of Southern rights known as the Knights of the Golden Circle. At the outbreak of the Civil War, his followers actively worked to bring the Cherokee into the Confederate fold. Another secret society called the Keetowahs (or Pins) opposed the efforts of the Knights and endorsed John Ross in his efforts to maintain the established treaties with the United States. Violence first broke out between the two groups at Webbers Falls in the summer of 1861 over the raising of a Confederate flag.

On 12 July 1861, Stand Watie received a colonel's commission in the Confederate military. He raised a regiment of 300 mixed-bloods and headed toward the northeastern border with Kansas to guard against a possible Federal invasion. Watie's increasing authority served to persuade John Ross to support a formal treaty of recognition and association with the Confederacy. The principal chief was also aware of a rumor that Watie was going to establish a separate Cherokee government and ally with the Confederacy if Ross continued on his path of neutrality. Ross signed the treaty of alliance on 7 October 1861 with Special Commissioner Albert Pike of the Confederate Bureau of Indian Affairs. Accordingly, Watie's regiment was mustered into Confederate military service as the Cherokee Mounted Volunteers.

One of the first objectives of the Cherokee Mounted Volunteers was to participate in the pursuit of Opethyelahola's band of loyal Creeks, who were attempting to flee northward to Kansas. Colonel James McIntosh, commanding 2,000 troops from Arkansas, chose to engage Opethyelahola's numerically superior forces on 26 December 1861 at Chustenahlah. Warriors mixed with men, women, and children fled the field in panic pursued by white Confederate cavalrymen and Stand Watie's mixed-blood Cherokee regiment. Watie's 300 men killed or captured many of the stragglers who were too weak to flee.

As Federal military operations increased in the region, Indian regiments were being pressed for service in Arkansas, outside the bounds of Indian Territory and in violation of the treaties. Special Commissioner Pike (who had held the military rank of brigadier general) reluctantly led his force of 1,000 Choctaws, Chickasaws, and Stand Watie's Cherokees into Arkansas, where they participated in the battle of Pea Ridge on 7–8 March 1862. Although the battle was a Confederate defeat,

Watie's regiment performed relatively well, capturing a Federal battery in the process.

By the summer of 1862, many disenchanted and embittered Indian refugees in Kansas joined Union forces and returned to Indian Territory determined to take revenge upon the Confederate Cherokees, Creeks, and their allies. Federal troops marched on the Cherokee capital at Tahlequah, captured John Ross, and returned to Kansas. Ross went to Washington, where he argued that he had no choice but to sign a treaty with the Confederates. The exiled principal chief of the Cherokee Nation then issued a proclamation of Cherokee loyalty to the Union.

With Ross in Washington, Stand Watie used the opportunity to declare himself the new principal chief of the Cherokee Nation and proceeded to consolidate his power. Thus the division of the Cherokees in Indian Territory was complete. Although Watie and his regiment participated in numerous conventional battles and smaller skirmishes with Federal troops, for the remainder of the war supporters of each faction still living in the territory staged hit-and-run campaigns against the other. Families were murdered, homes vandalized, crops burned, and livestock butchered.

By the summer of 1863, Confederate hopes for retaining control of Indian Territory vanished. Northwestern Arkansas was in the hands of Federal forces after their strategic victory at Prairie Grove the previous December. United States troops and loyal Indians invaded Indian Territory once again, forcing many pro-Confederate Cherokee, Creek, and Seminole Indians to flee south to the Red River Valley to become refugees among the Chickasaw and Choctaw Nations. The Confederate defeats at Gettysburg and Vicksburg in July dampened hopes for ultimate triumph. Even ardent Confederates like Stand Watie recognized the unlikeliness of a Southern victory in the war. Nevertheless, Watie remained true to the alliance for the remainder of the conflict, motivated primarily by the desire to maintain his power within the Cherokee Nation over the supporters of John Ross. On 6 May 1864, in return for his loyalty, Watie was promoted to brigadier general, the only Indian to hold this rank in the Civil War.

Perhaps Watie's greatest military accomplishments occurred in the summer and fall of 1864. On 15 June, Watie captured the Federal steamboat *J. R. Williams* on the Arkansas River with its $100,000's worth of supplies, including 150 barrels of flour and 16,000 pounds of bacon. Three months later, in what has been called "the biggest Confederate victory in the Indian Territory," Watie and his men captured a 300-wagon Federal supply train and its $1.5 million's worth of supplies at the second battle of Cabin Creek on 19 September 1864. He finally surrendered his command on 23 June 1865, the last Confederate general to capitulate. After a brief venture in the tobacco

business, Watie retired from public life and died at his home along Honey Creek on 9 September 1871.

—*Alan C. Downs*

See also Cherokee Indians; Pea Ridge, Battle of; Pike, Albert; Ross, John.

For further reading:
Franks, Kenny. *Stand Watie and the Agony of the Cherokee Nation* (1979).
Hauptman, Laurence M. *Between Two Fires: American Indians in the Civil War* (1995).
Josephy, Alvin M. *The Civil War in the American West* (1991).

WATTERSON, HENRY
(1840–1921)
Confederate journalist

Born to Harvey Magee Watterson and Talitha Black Watterson in Washington, D.C., Henry Watterson spent some of his childhood in Washington, where his father was a member of the U.S. House of Representatives, and some at the family homes in Tennessee. Watterson was educated primarily by tutors until 1858, when he traveled to New York City to accept a position as a reporter for the *New York Times*.

Watterson did not remain in New York long. After accepting a position with the *Washington Daily States*, Watterson also performed clerk duties for the Interior Department. Though he considered himself a strong Democrat and loyal Southerner, Watterson opposed secession upon the election of Abraham Lincoln and was even given the assignment of reporting on Lincoln's inauguration by the *Daily States*. Though he would soon change his position regarding secession, Watterson developed a life-long admiration for Lincoln during this early period of Lincoln's administration.

When offered a commission in the Union army, Watterson returned to Tennessee, where he not only came to support secession but the war effort as well. He enlisted in the Confederate army and, because of his writing skills, for much of the war served on the staffs of various high-ranking Confederate officers. Early in the conflict, he served on Leonidas Polk's staff, but illness forced him to leave that job. For a short time he worked on a Nashville propaganda newspaper, but the fall of that city to the Union caused him to move to Chattanooga, where he edited the Tennessee state newspaper the *Rebel*. The paper's stories, many written by Watterson, sought to increase the state's morale in the face of increasing Union occupation.

In the face of the growing threat to Chattanooga, Watterson had to abandon the state himself, accepting a job on the *Atlanta Southern Confederacy* at the end of 1863. In the face of Union general William T. Sherman's Atlanta campaign, however, Watterson again left the newspaper business to accept a position on the staff of Joseph E. Johnston. He served as Johnston's chief of scouts and continued on the staff of Johnston's successor John Bell Hood until Atlanta fell in September 1864. After that event, Watterson traveled to Montgomery, Alabama, where he worked for a short time as editor of the *Montgomery Mail*.

In a desperate attempt to raise funds in the last few months of the war, Watterson was recruited by the Confederate government to try to reach Great Britain with a cargo of cotton. He was unable to get out of the country and, after a brief time in Union hands, he returned to the newspaper business.

After the war, Watterson moved briefly to Cincinnati, where he edited the *Evening Times*. He returned to Nashville a year later and then traveled for a few months in Great Britain. Watterson returned to accept a position with the *Louisville Daily Journal* in 1867, which merged the following year with the other Louisville daily, becoming the *Louisville Courier-Journal*. Watterson remained the editor of the *Courier-Journal* with a partial ownership of the paper until 1918.

During that fifty-year period, Watterson became one of the most influential newspaper editors in the country. With the advent of Congressional Reconstruction, Watterson's editorials urged the return of home rule (with the caveat that African-Americans should be enfranchised) to Southern whites. He also became involved in national Democratic politics to achieve that goal, serving one year of an uncompleted term in the U.S. House of Representatives to help with the presidential campaign of Samuel J. Tilden in 1876.

Over the next decades, using his "Marse Robert" editorials, Watterson influenced the politics of several generations. His influence gained him entry into the highest political circles and allowed him to meet every president who served during his lifetime and several future presidents as well. After his retirement in 1918, he traveled but took little official interest in public life. He died in Jacksonville, Florida, and was buried in Louisville.

—*David S. Heidler and Jeanne T. Heidler*

See also Newspapers.
For further reading:
Wall Joseph Frazier. *Henry Watterson, Reconstructed Rebel* (1956).
Watterson, Henry. *The Editorials of Henry Watterson; Compiled with an Introduction and Notes by Arthur Krock* (1923).

WATTS, THOMAS HILL
(1819–1892)
Confederate attorney general and governor of Alabama

Thomas Hill Watts was born in Butler County, Alabama, the son of John Hughes Watts and Prudence Hill Watts. He was educated locally and at the University of Virginia. He studied law and prac-

ticed in Greenville, Alabama, before seeing the benefits in 1847 of moving to Montgomery, the new state capital. Except for service in various places during the Civil War, he lived in Montgomery for the remainder of his life.

Even before relocating his practice, Watts had been active in state politics. He was a Whig member of the state legislature for many years, serving in both the lower and upper houses. With the death of the Whig Party, Watts briefly became a member of the American (Know-Nothing) Party.

As the sectional crisis worsened in the late 1850s, Watts strongly supported remaining in the Union. In the election of 1860 he worked for the election of John Bell of the Constitutional Union Party. Like so many other Southerners, however, Watts saw the election of Abraham Lincoln as a reason to shift rapidly to the secessionist camp. Watts served as a member of the Alabama secession convention in January 1861 and voted for secession. In the same year, he ran for governor of Alabama, but lost to John Gill Shorter.

After his defeat for elective office, Watts raised a regiment of infantry and became the colonel of the 17th Alabama Infantry. Upon being mustered into Confederate service, Watts took his regiment to Pensacola, where he served under Braxton Bragg in the fall of 1861. He went with Bragg to Corinth, Mississippi, but, before seeing action, he was offered by Jefferson Davis the position of attorney general of the Confederacy. He served in that position from 17 March 1862 until 1 October 1863. During that time, Watts provided cabinet members and government agencies with opinions regarding the legality and/or constitutionality of their actions. With the passage of the first and subsequent Confederate Conscription Acts, Confederate secretaries of war George W. Randolph and James Seddon kept Watts busy interpreting those laws, particularly as they affected exemptions.

In the autumn of 1863, Watts resigned his post to run for governor of Alabama. He won this contest and served as governor for the remainder of the war. Watts's less than two years as governor were characterized by increasingly futile attempts to prevent the Federal invasions of the state and fights with the Confederate government over state prerogative regarding property and troops.

Watts worked closely with Confederate commanders in the state and, because of frequent Federal raids in 1864, did everything he could to raise as many able-bodied males for military service as possible. He still fought tenaciously, however, to prevent state militia officers from being impressed into Confederate service, though he insisted that he be able to use men exempted from the Confederate draft in the state militia. As the military situation deteriorated in the spring of 1865, Watts begged for military assistance to maintain order in the state.

After the war, Watts was briefly imprisoned. Upon his release, he returned home to find his personal property destroyed. Using his legal practice to rebuild his fortunes, Watts also became a powerful member of the Alabama Democratic Party. He served in the state legislature and as a president of the state bar association. He died on 16 September 1892 in Montgomery.

—*David S. Heidler and Jeanne T. Heidler*

See also Alabama.
For further reading:
Fleming, Walter Lynwood. *Civil War and Reconstruction in Alabama* (1905).
Lynch, Jeanne Hall. "Thomas Hill Watts, Civil War Governor of Alabama, 1863–1865" (M.A. thesis, 1957).

WAUD, ALFRED RUDOLPH
(1828–1891)
Sketch artist

Alfred Rudolph Waud was the most prolific, and arguably the most important, combat artist of the American Civil War. Although his work spanned the second half of the nineteenth century, the war was its primary focus. His pencil and ink sketches and engravings captured the nature of the conflict and its impact on soldiers and civilians.

An Englishman, Alfred Rudolph Waud was born 2 October 1828 in London. At an early age he cultivated his interest and skills in art. He apprenticed as a decorator, graduated from the School of Design at Somerset House in London, and found work painting scenes for English theaters. In 1850 Waud moved to the United States, initially to New York and then to Boston.

By the eve of the American Civil War, Waud had established both a family and career. He married Mary Gertrude Jewett and together they had four children: Mary, Selina, Alfred, and Edith. As his family grew, so did Waud's career in art. His sketches appeared as engravings in American periodicals and books and they reveal his early affinity for, and skill in, nautical subjects. In 1860 Waud earned a position as an illustrator at the *New York Illustrated News*. The Civil War began a year later.

The Civil War wrought horrible death and destruction, but it also afforded considerable opportunities for advancement, even in the world of art and literature. Developments in transportation, communication, and publication made this war more accessible to the public than any previous one. Americans wanted information from the battlefield, and several publications sought to provide it. The *New York Illustrated News*, *Harper's Weekly*, and *Frank Leslie's Illustrated Newspaper* promptly hired "special artists" and "special correspondents" to bring battlefield images and experiences to a hungry readership. The *Illustrated News* assigned Alfred Waud to serve as one of their "specials"—a position he held until

Alfred Waud sketching at Gettysburg, July 1863
(Photograph by Timothy H. O'Sullivan
/ Library of Congress)

joining *Harper's Weekly* in late 1861—and *Leslie's Illustrated Newspaper* hired Waud's brother, William, who also proved to be an accomplished artist.

"Specials" often saw the Civil War from the same perspective as its soldiers. Alfred Waud suffered the discomforts of camp life, found himself the target of enemy fire, and witnessed the brutality of war. He followed Union forces—primarily the Army of the Potomac—onto virtually all of the Eastern theater's major battlefields, including First and Second Bull Run, the Peninsula campaign, Antietam, Fredericksburg, Chancellorsville, Gettysburg, the Wilderness, Cold Harbor, and Petersburg. According to one British observer, Waud "probably knew more about the several campaigns, the rights and wrongs of the several fights, the merits and demerits of the commanders, than two out of three wearers of generals' shoulder-straps." Consequently, Waud's sketches often chronicled the action, offered a keen observer's perspective, and captured the intensity and emotions of combat in many of the most significant engagements.

Waud's work was not limited to the clash of arms. He brought to the public's view a broad spectrum of wartime experiences and images: a grand vista of Maryland Heights, a slave family entering a Union camp, Abraham Lincoln attending a military review, and the wounded receiving treatment, among other things. As Waud completed each sketch, it was sent to the publisher's offices in New York, copied to wood blocks (and occasionally edited), carved by engravers, and printed in the

weekly issues. By war's end, 344 Waud drawings had appeared in the *Illustrated News* or *Harper's Weekly*, a total considerably larger than any other "special." Waud was even more prolific than that total suggests. The Library of Congress holds more than 1,100 Waud sketches.

Waud's art career did not end with the coming of peace. *Harper's* sent him, along with Theodore R. Davis, on a tour of the postwar South to produce illustrations for issues in 1866 and 1867. In succeeding years Waud found additional outlets for his art, including periodicals and books. He also broadened the subject matter of his later work, returning to nautical themes but also drawing sketches for historical publications and travel books.

In the early 1890s Waud toured the Southern battlefields to sketch illustrations for a Civil War volume. On 6 April 1891, while in Marietta, Georgia, he died from what the *Atlanta Constitution* identified as heart disease. His reputation subsequently faded until his work received renewed attention a half century later.

—*J. Mark Thompson*

See also Art; *Frank Leslie's Illustrated Newspaper; Harper's Weekly.*

For further reading:
Ray, Frederic E. *Alfred R. Waud: Civil War Artist* (1974).

WAUHATCHIE, BATTLE AT (BROWN'S FERRY)
(28–29 October 1863)

After the battle of Chickamauga on 19–20 September 1863, the Union Army of the Cumberland under William S. Rosecrans withdrew into Chattanooga. Confederate general Braxton Bragg's Army of Tennessee took up commanding positions above the city on Lookout Mountain and Missionary Ridge, effectively interdicting the Union supply line along the Tennessee River. All materials coming to the army in Chattanooga had to negotiate a tortuous route across the mountains from the West.

Ulysses S. Grant came to Chattanooga on 23 October and made opening the supply line one of his first priorities. He approved the plan of his chief engineer, General William F. "Baldy" Smith, to drive the Confederate forces from their westernmost position at Raccoon Mountain so that supplies could begin to come in by way of the river.

In a hazardous operation in the early morning of 27 October, two brigades of IV Corps secured a base on the south side of the Tennessee River at Brown's Ferry. The brigade of William B. Hazen floated down river from Chattanooga in the dark and made an assault landing against the Confederate pickets while the brigade of John Turchin marched overland to support Hazen and then threw a pontoon bridge across the river. Despite a determined counterattack on the bridgehead by the 15th

Alabama, the Confederates were compelled to withdraw their left, thereby opening up the river.

Meanwhile, Major General Joseph Hooker's XI and XII Corps, brought by rail from Virginia, were waiting at Bridgeport, Alabama, to join the army in Chattanooga. On Grant's order, Hooker left one division at Bridgeport and began to march forward toward Brown's Ferry with the two divisions of Oliver O. Howard's XI Corps and John Geary's division of XII Corps. Hooker's movement was clearly visible from the Confederate positions on Lookout Mountain and both Bragg and James Longstreet, commanding on the Rebel left, observed his advance. Hooker left Geary's division at Wauhatchie to protect his flank and moved to Brown's Ferry with Howard's corps, the divisions of Adolph von Steinwehr and Carl Schurz, arriving at his destination on 28 October.

Bragg had been expecting an attempt to open the river and had warned Longstreet several times. At first Longstreet ignored him. He believed that Hooker's real intention at Bridgeport was to come up the southern end of Lookout Mountain and attack the Confederate rear. Even after Brown's Ferry was taken, he thought it was only a feint to mask Hooker's move. However, on 27 October Bragg directed Longstreet to recover Brown's Ferry. Longstreet was dilatory and still wished to send a brigade to the south end of Lookout Mountain. At length, on Bragg's insistence, he agreed to take action. Bragg put at his disposal the divisions of Micah Jenkins (Hood's) and Lafayette McLaws, that had come from Virginia, plus the division of W. H. T. Walker.

Rather than taking advantage of all these troops, in a remarkable display of truculence, Longstreet finally, on the night of 28 October, launched an attack with the single division of Micah Jenkins, not on Brown's Ferry, but on Geary's isolated division at Wauhatchie. The brigades of E. M. Law and Jerome Robertson were to block the Brown's Ferry road to prevent Hooker from coming to Geary's aid. The lone brigade of Colonel John Bratton, nominally Jenkins's own, was to attack Wauhatchie with Henry L. Benning's brigade in support. George T. Anderson's brigade was left on Lookout Mountain.

The ensuing action was so confused that many of the participants were unaware of what was happening. First, Longstreet and Jenkins could not find Geary's position in the dark. Longstreet, perhaps deciding to abandon the attack, returned to camp. Jenkins, on his own initiative, or not understanding Longstreet's probable cancellation, launched the attack himself in the early hours of 29 October.

Geary had arranged his two small brigades, Colonel George A. Cobham's and General George S. Greene's, in a right angle formation and had a four-gun battery in support. The attacking and defending forces were about equal in strength. Jenkins began his assault on the Federal left, then the fighting spread gradually all along

the line. The combat was heavy and confused, but Geary beat off all attacks. In the darkness the opponents could not see each other, so they fired at the enemy's musket flashes. By 3:00 A.M. Geary's men had nearly exhausted their ammunition and were preparing to defend with the bayonet when the Rebel attacks suddenly ended. Jenkins probably thought that the defenders outnumbered him. In any case, he was not in control of the fighting, and the noise of battle from Law's position made him concerned for his rear. A myth persisted afterward that a stampede of Yankee mules into Bratton's position occurred and the Confederates, taking it for a cavalry attack, withdrew. Even Grant wrote of the event, but there is no truth to it. Geary was left in command of the field.

Meanwhile, Hooker at Brown's Ferry heard the sounds of the firing and sent the divisions of Schurz and Steinwehr, the latter under Colonel Orland Smith, to Geary's relief. As they marched toward the battle, they were fired on by Law's force and diverted from their primary mission. They spent several hours fighting in the dark before driving Law away and never made it to Wauhatchie. Benning's brigade was drawn into this action.

Casualties were about equal on both sides. Combined Union losses at Brown's Ferry and Wauhatchie were roughly 400 killed, wounded, and missing. General Greene was wounded so severely in the face that he was away from duty for over a year. Lieutenant Edward Geary, son of the general, was killed while serving with the artillery. Total Confederate casualties were slightly more than 400; Bratton's brigade, which bore the brunt of the fighting at Wauhatchie, reported losses of 356.

Longstreet blamed the failure on everyone but himself. He faulted his brigade commanders; he blamed jealousy among the generals for their lack of cooperation; he thought the cavalry had failed by providing insufficient reconnaissance; he later stated he felt that Bragg's order for a corps attack was discretionary. In self-justification, he wrote in his report that the failure to retake Brown's Ferry was not significant because the Union army had been supplying itself over the mountains for six weeks before the river line was reopened. The whole episode reflected poorly on leadership and morale in the Army of Tennessee. On the Union side, Hooker threatened Schurz and one of his brigadiers with charges of inefficiency for failing to come to Geary's aid, but both men were exonerated by a court of inquiry.

The importance of the Brown's Ferry–Wauhatchie battles was the opening of Grant's river supply line, the so-called cracker line. The first boatload of rations from downriver arrived in Chattanooga the day after the battle. W. T. Sherman's four divisions from Mississippi, along with Hooker's two corps, came by the same route. Grant had the supplies and troops to fight the successful battle of Chattanooga the next month.

—Russell K. Brown

See also Chattanooga Campaign; Chickamauga, Battle of.
For further reading:
Alexander, Edward Porter. Military Memoirs of a Confederate: A Critical Narrative (1907).
Connelly, Thomas L. Autumn of Glory: The Army of Tennessee, 1862–1865 (1971).
Hallock, Judith Lee. Braxton Bragg and Confederate Defeat (1991).
Longstreet, James. From Manassas to Appomattox: Memoirs of the Civil War in America (1896; reprint, 1960).
McDonough, James L. Chattanooga: A Death Grip on the Confederacy (1984).
U.S. War Department. The War of the Rebellion: A Compilation of the Official Records of the Union and Confederate Armies (1880–1901).

WAYNE, JAMES MOORE
(1790–1867)
U.S. Supreme Court justice

Born to Richard Wayne and Elizabeth Clifford Wayne in Savannah, Georgia, James Moore Wayne was educated locally before gaining admission to the College of New Jersey (later Princeton). He graduated at the age of eighteen. Following graduation from college he studied law in Savannah and New Haven, Connecticut. He began practicing in Savannah in 1810.

During the War of 1812, Wayne received a commission in a Georgia volunteer unit. After the war he served in the state legislature for one term and then a stint as mayor of Savannah. Following his service as mayor, he resumed private law practice, but remained intensely interested in Georgia politics. During the 1820s he served five years as a state superior court judge, but was drawn back into electoral politics in 1828, when he ran for a seat in the United States House of Representatives as a staunch supporter of Andrew Jackson.

In Congress Wayne remained a strong supporter of Andrew Jackson's administration and policies. Though he did not disagree with such things as a national bank and internal improvements on constitutional grounds, he sided with Jackson on these issues because it best served the interests of the Democratic Party. With his support for Jackson's actions, he also sought and gained Jackson's aid for Georgia's efforts to remove the Cherokee and Creek Indians from its borders.

Wayne's loyalty did not go unrewarded. In early 1835 Jackson appointed Wayne to the United States Supreme Court, and he was quickly confirmed. During Wayne's thirty-two years on the bench, his opinions were judged logical and based on sound legal reasoning. The one exception came in 1857 when he sided with the majority in the Dred Scott case (Scott v. San[d]ford).

During the 1850s Wayne had come to the opinion that Congress had no power to prohibit slavery in the territories, and like many Southerners, he hoped that the Dred Scott case could be used to settle that issue conclusively. During the deliberations on the case, he corresponded with other Southerners, most notably fellow Georgian, Congressman Alexander Stephens. Stephens urged Wayne to use influence on his fellow justices to bring about a resolution in favor of the South. When it appeared that Justice Samuel Nelson, originally slated to write the majority opinion, would offer up a very narrow view that would not address the territory issue, Wayne suggested that Chief Justice Roger B. Taney speak for the majority instead. Wayne, who had been working on a more comprehensive opinion himself, may have even supplied what he had written so far to Taney to help the chief justice produce his opinion more quickly. Whatever the case, because he agreed with Taney's opinion in every particular, Wayne did not offer an official opinion, writing instead that he concurred with the chief justice.

Like all the seven justices who ruled against Scott and especially those who also held that slavery could not be prohibited in the territories, Wayne was attacked in the North. Misguided though it may have been, however, Wayne's opinion was based not just on his Southern partisanship, but also on his belief that such a decision would quiet the sectional animosities over slavery in the territories. He, of course, was ultimately proved wrong, but Chief Justice Taney bore the brunt of the criticism.

Upon the election of Abraham Lincoln to the presidency in the fall of 1860, Justice Wayne urged caution to his fellow Southerners. He opposed secession and believed that Lincoln would not prove the danger to the Southern way of life that many predicted. When Georgia seceded, Wayne decided to remain on the Court rather than follow his state out of the Union.

During the war Wayne proved to true to his Unionist beliefs. While he did spend much of his time trying to extricate political prisoners from their difficulties, he also tended to side with the administration on such controversial issues as the use of military courts in cases of suspected disloyalty. While at times he believed the administration went too far in some of its actions regarding political prisoners, he offered the opinion that in the case of a civil war, the powers of the executive in this regard were expanded.

Wayne remained on the bench throughout the war and the early days of Reconstruction. He died on 5 July 1867 of typhoid fever during an outbreak in Washington, D.C. His body was returned to his home in Savannah for burial.

—David S. Heidler and Jeanne T. Heidler

See also Dred Scott Case.
For further reading:
Fehrenbacher, Don E. The Dred Scott Case: Its Significance in American Law and Politics (1978).
Lawrence, Alexander A. James Moore Wayne, Southern Unionist (1943; reprint, 1970).
O'Connor, Sandra Day. "Supreme Court Justices from Georgia." The Georgia Journal of Southern Legal History (1991).

WAYNESBORO, GEORGIA
(27 November–4 December 1864)

Cavalries clashed for eight days between General Judson Kilpatrick's Union troopers and the Confederates under General Joseph Wheeler in and around Waynesboro, Georgia. When General William T. Sherman left Milledgeville, Georgia, on 24 November, he sent his cavalry under Kilpatrick to Waynesboro, Georgia, to threaten Augusta thirty miles away by cutting the Augusta & Savannah Railroad. Strategically, this action would also divert Confederate attention away from Sherman's real objective: to march with the bulk of his army to Savannah, bypassing heavily reinforced and fortified Augusta.

Leaving Waynesboro, Kilpatrick was to proceed south thirty miles to liberate the Federal prisoners of war at Camp Lawton prison near Millen, Georgia. Ever vigilant and with a genius for cavalry tactics, General Wheeler pursued his adversary relentlessly over the nine days that Kilpatrick was in the vicinity of Waynesboro. On one occasion, the Confederates very nearly captured the Federal cavalry chief in a morning raid. Wheeler also burned bridges to impede the enemy's progress and constantly harassed the foe. The following list of engagements compose the Waynesboro campaign:

27 November—skirmish at Brier Creek Swamp
27 and 28 November—skirmish at Waynesboro
28 November—skirmish at Buckhead Church; skirmish near Waynesboro; skirmish at Reynolds Farm
2 December—skirmish near Buckhead Creek; skirmish at Rock Creek Church
3 December—skirmish at Thomas Station
4 December—engagement at Waynesboro

In these clashes, the action was spirited and bloody, as the Confederates fought with unwonted desperation to block the Union cavalry and protect the civilian population. Confederate losses were approximately 240, Union losses 830. The Southern units were helped with information from the populace and thus had the advantage of knowing the terrain. In addition, the prisoners of war at Camp Lawton were evacuated before Kilpatrick arrived. Still, the Federals were strategically victorious because Kilpatrick kept Sherman's main force unmolested all the way to the coast of Georgia.

—*Gerald J. Smith*

See also Kilpatrick, Hugh Judson; Wheeler, Joseph.

For further reading:

Lee, Angela. "Tangling with 'Kilcavalry.'" *Civil War Times Illustrated* (1998).

U.S. War Department. *The War of the Rebellion: A Compilation of the Official Records of the Union and Confederate Armies* (1880–1901).

WAYNESBORO, VIRGINIA, BATTLE OF
(2 March 1865)

The Union victory at Waynesboro, Virginia, closed Major General Philip H. Sheridan's Shenandoah Valley campaign. A single Union cavalry division required only three hours to destroy the last Confederate army to operate in the valley.

In the four months after Sheridan's triumph at Cedar Creek, 19 October 1864, most of his Army of the Shenandoah was reassigned to the Army of the Potomac and other Union commands. By late February 1865, Sheridan's force had been reduced to a cavalry corps of two divisions under Major General Wesley Merritt. A recent infusion of remounted troopers made that corps a strong one, totaling 10,000 officers and troopers, with Major General George A. Custer's 3d Division and Brigadier General Thomas C. Devin's 1st Division.

On 27 February, Sheridan and his cavalry left Winchester and headed south. Orders from Lieutenant General Ulysses S. Grant directed Sheridan to proceed to Lynchburg, wreck the Virginia Central Railroad and the James River Canal, and then join Major General William T. Sherman's Union army, which was rampaging through the Carolinas. These instructions did not please Sheridan, however; he wanted to reunite with Grant at Petersburg to assist in the destruction of General Robert E. Lee's Army of Northern Virginia. Unfolding circumstances soon furnished Sheridan with an excuse to do as he wished.

Lieutenant General Jubal A. Early, the commander of the shrunken Confederate Army of the Valley, sent his chief of cavalry, Brigadier General Thomas L. Rosser, to block Sheridan's march, but Rosser could scrape together only a few hundred men. Nevertheless, Rosser attempted to obstruct Sheridan on 1 March by setting fire to the covered bridge spanning the Middle Fork of the Shenandoah River at Mount Crawford. Sheridan's vanguard, Custer's 240 officers and 4,600 troopers, arrived on the scene minutes later. Sending two regiments a mile upstream to swim the river and hit Rosser's flank, Custer charged across the burning structure, scattered his opponents, and extinguished the fire before the bridge suffered serious damage.

Pushing on, the Federal column reached Staunton, the site of Early's winter camps, on the morning of 2 March. Townsfolk informed Sheridan that Early had retreated with 2,000 soldiers to Waynesboro, a town sitting in a bend of the South River near Rockfish Gap in the Blue Ridge Mountains. Sheridan interrupted his southward trek and directed Custer to lead the way to Waynesboro. Sheridan later argued that continuing to Lynchburg would have invited an attack on his rear or freed the Confederates to move down the Shenandoah Valley, but Early's badly depleted ranks could not have done much damage in either case.

Custer arrived outside Waynesboro after 2:00 P.M. to find Early's army entrenched atop a ridge west of town. Most of the Confederates belonged to Brigadier General Gabriel C. Wharton's two tiny infantry brigades, but Rosser guarded Early's right with his cavalry, and enough gunners were on hand to operate eleven field pieces. At first glance, Early's position seemed formidable, but he had placed his line too far forward to anchor its flanks on the South River.

After testing Early's strength with a reconnaissance in force, Custer personally scouted the enemy's dispositions and discovered a gap an eighth of a mile wide between the Confederate left and the South River. This area was wooded, allowing Custer to slip three dismounted regiments armed with Spencer repeating carbines around the open flank undetected. As the flanking force moved into position, Custer shelled the Confederates with his horse artillery and sent mounted skirmishers to menace their front.

When all was ready, Custer had a bugler sound the "Charge." The Union flankers burst from cover and surged forward, firing into Early's left and rear, while Custer led two mounted brigades up the face of the ridge. At that, the Confederate line simply dissolved. Two Union regiments galloped through the fleeing Confederates, cleared Waynesboro, and crossed the South River. Then the Federals turned around and formed a cordon that cut off any further retreat.

Spurring their horses, Early and a small group of generals, aides, and orderlies barely escaped Custer's trap and disappeared east of the Blue Ridge. Rosser's cavalry also rode clear and fled into the upper valley. The rest of the Confederate army and its baggage, a total of 1,600 men, seventeen colors, eleven cannon, and 200 wagons and ambulances, fell into Custer's hands. These prizes cost the Federals nine killed and wounded.

Waynesboro marked the end of organized Confederate resistance in the Shenandoah Valley. Sheridan would continue to "pursue" Early until he rendezvoused with Grant on 27 March.

—*Gregory J. W. Urwin*

See also Custer, George Armstrong; Devin, Thomas Casimer; Early, Jubal Anderson; Merritt, Wesley; Rosser, Thomas Lafayette; Shenandoah Valley Campaign (August 1864–March 1865).

For further reading:

Alberts, Don E. *Brandy Station to Manila Bay: A Biography of General Wesley Merritt* (1980).

Bushong, Millard K. *Old Jube: A Biography of General Jubal A. Early* (1988).

Stackpole, Edward J. *Sheridan in the Shenandoah: Jubal Early's Nemesis* (1992).

Starr, Stephen Z. *The Union Cavalry in the Civil War* (1979–1985).

Urwin, Gregory J. W. *Custer Victorious: The Civil War Battles of General George Armstrong Custer* (1990).

WEAVER, JAMES BAIRD
(1833–1912)
Union officer and populist politician

Born on 12 June 1833, James Baird Weaver became for half a century the country's foremost proponent of what he called the genuinely Democratic principles of Thomas Jefferson and Andrew Jackson and the true Republican principles of Abraham Lincoln and Thaddeus Stevens. The descendant of Revolutionary patriots, Weaver's family had crossed into the Ohio valley near the turn of the century and James Baird was born near Dayton. With his family he moved into Michigan and then the backwoods of the Iowa Territory. They remained there until the family's 1847 move to the newly built town of Bloomfield. As a young adult, James became interested in law after a trip to the California gold fields. He studied law under Samuel G. McAchran, a supporter of the land reform goals of George Henry Evans. Weaver gained admission to the bar in the spring of 1856 and two years later married a local schoolteacher.

In the ardently Jacksonian politics of the frontier, Weaver tirelessly promoted Democratic politics until passage of the Kansas-Nebraska Act led to his passionate advocacy of the new Republican cause. A pioneer of the new party in Davis County and southeastern Iowa, he attended the 1860 national convention that nominated Lincoln.

Weaver enlisted in May 1861 as a private in a Bloomfield company that elected him first lieutenant. He mustered into the 2d Iowa Regiment, one of the earliest units devastated in the war. After helping to garrison Missouri, the 2d Iowa joined the army of General Ulysses S. Grant on the Tennessee River, and participated in the February 1862 storming of the first line of Confederate works at Fort Donelson. Two months later, the 2d Iowa was nearly lost in the Hornet's Nest at Shiloh. Six months later, the Confederate attack on Corinth took a further toll and left the regiment's command in the hands of Major Weaver. His advancement represented both the good fortune of his survival and a fearlessness under fire. From the fall of 1862 into the spring of 1864, the remnants of the 2d under Weaver served on garrison duty at various points in Tennessee, Alabama, and Georgia, until it joined General William T. Sherman's advance into Georgia. In March 1865, Weaver received a brevet brigadier generalship.

After the war Weaver returned to an ambivalent relationship with the Republican Party. Like other pioneering insurgents, he balked at abandoning a party that had well served the purposes of change. Although he received appointments to various local Iowa offices, Weaver failed to secure the Republican nomination for lieutenant governor in 1865, for Congress in 1874, or for governor in 1875. Weaver's persistent Republican loyalty

was evident in his declining the 1876 congressional nomination by the new Greenback Party, launched locally by Captain Horace A. Spencer, one of McAchron's old cothinkers. As late as June 1877 Weaver planned to remain in the Republican camp.

Nevertheless, Weaver joined the insurgents anyway by August 1877. In the intervening weeks, Republicans had sent federal troops against American citizens guilty only of having gone on strike against the railroads, and Weaver also shared the general suspicion about the official abandonment of wartime paper currency, the "greenbacks" that seemed to have fueled the prosperity of the farmers. Weaver won a congressional seat in 1878. "Men die," Weaver once said, "but principles live forever and are lasting." His national status made him the most important national critic of government complicity in the rise of monopolistic control over essentials like currency, transportation, industry, and land. With socialist support, Weaver made an 1880 presidential bid on the Greenback-Labor platform, from which he bitterly denounced the Republican abandonment of the freed people and poor whites of the South in the Reconstruction as a betrayal of wartime Unionism. He also defended the right of workers to organize for better wages and conditions and of women to participate equally in civic life. He reprised these themes in his 1892 campaign on the Peoples' or Populist ticket. Long after Weaver's death at Des Moines on 6 February 1912, the issues he believed implicit in Civil War–era Unionism remained just beneath the surface of political business as usual.

—*Mark A. Lause*

See also Corinth, Battle of; Evans, George Henry; Fort Donelson; Greenbacks; Shiloh, Battle of.

For further reading:
Haynes, Fred E. *James Baird Weaver* (1919).
Lause, Mark. "Voting Yourself a Farm in Antebellum Iowa: Towards an Urban Working Class Prehistory of the Post Civil-War Agrarian Insurgency." *The Annals of Iowa* (1988).

WEBB, ALEXANDER STEWART
(1835–1911)
Union general

On the verge of resigning from the army in 1863 when others had been promoted ahead of him, "Andy" Webb, as his friends and family knew him, unexpectedly received his commission as brigadier general, U.S. volunteers, on 28 June 1863. It was the turning point of a remarkable career for a soldier and educator who is best remembered for his distinguished service at Gettysburg. Born 15 February 1835, Alexander Stewart Webb was of a prominent military lineage. His grandfather, Samuel Blatchley Webb, had been wounded at Bunker Hill, and later served as lieutenant colonel and military secretary to George

Washington. His father, James Watson Webb, was a former regular army officer and owner of the *New York Morning Courier and Enquirer* who became minister to Brazil in 1861. Andy Webb graduated from West Point thirteenth of thirty-four in the class of 1855.

After serving as a mathematics instructor at West Point, and in Florida during the Third Seminole War, Lieutenant Webb began the Civil War at Fort Pickens, Florida, but was recalled to Washington, D.C., in July 1861. Promoted to captain retroactive to 14 May 1861, Webb began a long tenure on staff duty, serving as assistant to the chief of artillery, Major William F. Barry, at First Bull Run. Politically aligned with the McClellan faction, Webb became assistant inspector general and chief of staff of V Corps, earning promotion to major (of volunteers) 14 September 1861, and lieutenant colonel 20 August 1862. Webb participated in the 1862 Peninsula campaign and was highly commended for aiding in the formation of the final artillery line at Malvern Hill that Brigadier Daniel Butterfield said saved the army from destruction. Webb fought with distinction at Antietam and Fredericksburg. At Chancellorsville, Lieutenant Colonel Webb earned high praise for leading Brigadier General Erastus B. Tyler's brigade forward at a critical point.

A seasoned veteran of nearly all the battles of the Army of the Potomac, Webb was thus highly regarded, yet seemed to be in limbo following McClellan's departure from the army. During the early days of the Gettysburg campaign, Webb, then twenty-eight, became so discouraged as to write to his wife on 24 June that he might resign; even some of his West Point pupils had been given brigadier general's commissions. Ironically, Major General Joseph Hooker had requested Webb's promotion on 8 June, and his brigadier's commission was signed 23 June. Only three days prior to Gettysburg, Webb received this commission, and was quickly assigned to command the often unruly Philadelphia Brigade in II Corps.

By chance, Webb's brigade was at the center of the action on Cemetery Ridge at Gettysburg during the main attack on 3 July. Posted at the landmark clump of umbrella shaped trees, Webb's men defended the famous angle in the stone wall that became the focal point of the Pickett-Pettigrew-Trimble Charge. Webb remained on foot among his men, and was so courageous in leading the defenders there that he was later awarded the Medal of Honor. Webb's opposite number, Brigadier General Lewis A. Armistead was mortally injured within forty paces of Webb, who was only slightly wounded in the right leg during the bloody fray.

Later assuming temporary command of a division in II Corps, Andy Webb fought with distinguished valor at Bristoe Station, Virginia, in 1863, and during Grant's Overland Virginia campaign in 1864. During an attack

on the Bloody Angle at Spotsylvania on 11 May, Webb was shot severely in the head. A minié ball entered near the corner of his right eye, ranged along the skull, and passed out behind his ear. Only prompt medical care enabled Webb to survive.

Following an absence of eight months, he returned to duty in January 1865, and became Major General George G. Meade's chief of staff. Following the war, Webb reverted to the rank of lieutenant colonel and remained in the regular army until discharged at his own request in December 1870.

Having been appointed in 1869 as president of the City College of New York, Webb served in this capacity until 1902. Breveted numerous times (lieutenant colonel through major general) for distinguished military service (Gettysburg, Bristoe Station, Spotsylvania, and the Appomattox campaign), Andy Webb received the Medal of Honor on 28 September 1891 for his actions at Gettysburg. An articulate and graphic writer, Andy Webb wrote extensively about the Civil War, including his book published by Charles Scribner's Sons in 1881, *The Peninsula: McClellan's Campaign of 1862*. Alexander Webb died three days before his seventy-sixth birthday on 12 February 1911 in Riverdale, New York. He was much honored and admired as a leader, and today his full-length bronze statue stands at Gettysburg overlooking the scene of Pickett's Charge.

—*Wiley Sword*

See also Gettysburg, Battle of; Webb, James Watson.
For further reading:
In Memoriam, Alexander Stewart Webb 1835–1911 (1916).
Sword, Wiley. "Facing the Gray Wave, Alexander Webb at Gettysburg." *Civil War Times Illustrated* (1981).
Webb, Alexander S. *The Peninsula: McClellan's Campaign of 1862* (1881).

WEBB, JAMES WATSON
(1802–1884)
U.S. minister to Brazil

Stirred by his family's distinguished military service during the Revolutionary War and the War of 1812, James Watson Webb ran away from home as a youth and joined the army. His career there was brief, however, and he soon embarked on a two-decade-long career in journalism, publishing a paper, the *New York Courier and Enquirer*, that was as influential as it was controversial and lively. He pioneered new innovative ways of procuring the news, helping to develop the use of pony expresses and newsboats—devices that would be used to greater effectiveness by one of his employees and future enemies, James Gordon Bennett, founder of the *New York Herald*.

At the age of twenty-five Webb purchased the *Morning Courier* shortly after its founding and merged it

with Mordecai M. Noah's *New York Enquirer*, giving it one of New York's largest circulations. Catering principally to the city's business interests, its main rival was the *Journal of Commerce*. Politically, it began as a Jacksonian organ but turned Whig over the issue of the Bank of the United States. (Word had it that the bank gave Webb a $52,000 loan.) In 1848 Webb and Henry Raymond, founder of the *New York Times*, jointly published a Whig campaign paper, the *Grape-Shot*.

Personally, Webb was belligerent; he twice horsewhipped his rival Bennett in the streets. The latter belittled Webb as "a bully, a brawler, a blackguard and a bankrupt" and claimed that "his indolence, carelessness and recklessness are so notorious that he cannot be trusted with the business affairs of his own paper."

Webb also fought duels with several members of Congress. For one of them, he was sentenced to two years in Sing-Sing Prison but was pardoned by Governor William Seward before beginning his term. Webb returned the favor by pushing Seward's nomination for president in 1860 by the Republican Party, whose ranks Webb had joined despite his lukewarm feelings on the slavery issue. When Lincoln emerged victorious, Webb urged the South to support him, insisting that he would protect the region's constitutional rights and would strictly enforce the Fugitive Slave Law. So little did Webb understand the South's antipathy to Lincoln that he actually hailed the Republican's victory as "the harbinger of peace to the union and prosperity to all of its great interests." Following secession, however, Webb was adamant about Lincoln's obligation to "put down Rebellion, crush out Treason, and hang the Traitors."

Prosperity at this point was much on Webb's mind. The *Courier and Enquirer* was in serious trouble, its mercantile coverage having been overtaken by that of the widely read "cheap" papers such as Bennett's *Herald* and the *New York Sun*. At the beginning of Lincoln's term, Webb's paper stood on the edge of bankruptcy and the editor had mounting personal debts. He prevailed on his old ally, William Seward—now Lincoln's secretary of state—for a diplomatic assignment. With the help of Vice-president Hannibal Hamlin, Webb was named U.S. minister to Brazil in May 1861. One month later, he sold his paper to the fledgling *New York World*.

Although he considered this assignment beneath his talents (he refused to learn the Portuguese language spoken in Brazil and took along 150 novels to occupy his time), Webb proved to be an effective, if rash, diplomat. His most effective service to the Union cause came about because of his association with the French emperor Napoleon III, with whom he had forged a lifelong friendship during the then-Prince Louis Napoleon's political exile in New York during the 1830s. Webb used his influence to forestall what he feared was a bid by England and France to pressure Lincoln into negotiating a peace agreement with the Confederacy. Believing that Britain would enlist France to break the Northern blockade of Southern ports, Webb traveled to Brazil by way of Paris at the urging of American minister William Dayton, who persuaded him to speak with his many friends in the French government. Webb persuaded Napoleon and Lord John Russell that such a move would not give Europe a supply of Southern cotton. Before leaving for Rio de Janeiro, he wrote Seward a twenty-five-page memorandum with suggestions for prosecuting what he predicted would be a short war, including the immediate execution of all Southern leaders.

In Brazil Webb was forced to deal with a nation that, save for the Confederacy, was the only large nation where slavery was both legal and an integral economic factor. His predecessor as minister, R. K. Meade, was a Southern sympathizer who had stressed the two nations' common interest in perpetuating slavery. Webb's goal was to correct those sentiments and to ensure that Brazil would launch no interference in American affairs. His insistence on criticizing Meade in his presentation speech was vetoed by the Brazilians and led to tense relations with the nation's leaders. Webb's efforts to stop the use of Brazilian ports as refueling points by Confederate privateers were similarly disapproved. Webb labeled this a blatant "breach of neutrality."

Webb won a significant victory, however, in the summer of 1862, when he successfully blocked the sale of four Confederate ships to a British firm, which was planning to sail them in safety under the Union Jack to England and there resell them to the South. But tensions over private Southern ships—which undercut U.S. commercial interests in South America—continued until the end of the war.

Another of Webb's eventual successes almost never happened because of his efforts to profit personally from the scheme. He persuaded Lincoln and Seward to press Congress to set up a route of mail steamers between the United States and Brazil as a way to break Britain's commercial monopoly in South America that required even the United States to buy goods through London. But the president blocked the plan when he learned that Webb, claiming that only he could win Brazil's approval, insisted that he be given the lucrative concession. Further, Webb claimed that Brazil would only accept the plan if he were given long-term involvement. Lincoln and Seward agreed that this was "entirely indefensible" and a flagrant violation of U.S. law. Eventually, Webb relented: the plan was approved, but without his involvement.

Webb's other ambitious proposal was to colonize emancipated American slaves in Brazil, a move he predicted would simultaneously solve Brazil's labor problem and rid the United States "of a curse which has well nigh destroyed her." Lincoln and Seward, who favored colonization, were receptive, but the plan came

to naught on two counts: First, Brazilian law banned the entry of free blacks; and second, Seward soon realized that under Webb's proposal, the ex-slaves would not be true freedmen but rather indentured servants.

Webb at first tried to push Seward as the Republican presidential candidate in 1864, but eventually he supported Lincoln. After the election, he pressed for a post in Europe but was flatly rejected and spent four more years in Brazil. His heavy-handed efforts to mediate a settlement in the Paraguayan War almost disrupted U.S.-Brazilian relations and tarnished America's diplomatic reputation in South America. His biographer, James Crouthamel, wrote that Webb's "conduct in Brazil would comprise a handy 'How not to do' manual for American diplomats today," noting that "the United States was decidedly less popular there when Webb left Brazil in 1869 than it had been when he arrived."

—*Eric Fettmann*

See also Diplomacy, U.S.A.; Great Britain; Newspapers; Webb, Alexander Stewart.

For further reading:
Crouthamel, James L. *James Watson Webb: A Biography* (1969).
Hudson, Frederic. *Journalism in the United States from 1690 to 1872* (1873; reprint, 1968).
Mott, Frank Luther. *American Journalism* (1962).

WEBSTER, DANIEL
(1782–1852)
Nationalist and American statesman

Born on 18 January 1782 in Salisbury, New Hampshire, in the hill country of the upper Merrimack River, to Ebenezer Webster and his second wife, Abigail Eastman, Daniel was the youngest son in a family of ten children. Although raised in a farming environment, the young Daniel preferred working in his father's tavern and conversing with the establishment's visitors. The integrity, devotion to union, and political acumen of Ebenezer Webster would soon be evident in his son. As the boy became well known among the tavern patrons, he was given the nickname "Black Dan," owing to his dark hair and skin complexion.

Following his early education at local schools and through his voracious reading of great works, Webster was able to attend Phillips Exeter Academy and Dartmouth College. At Dartmouth, he was an active student who was elected to Phi Beta Kappa. Webster proceeded to study law under Federalist teachers and to practice law in his native New Hampshire. After marrying Grace Fletcher in 1808, Webster became more interested in politics. After several unsuccessful campaigns, Webster was elected to the U.S. House of Representatives in 1812. Establishing himself as a critic of the Madison administration, he believed the country should practice self-restraint while maintaining national integrity. In approving the Hartford Convention's listing of complaints against the Federal government, he did not endorse the secessionist elements within the gathering.

After moving to Boston and acquiring the reputation as an orator and defender of the nationalist tradition, Webster spent a great deal of time practicing law and presenting cases before the Supreme Court, including *McCulloch v. Maryland* and *Gibbons v. Ogden*. He was elected to the U.S. Senate in 1827. In 1828 he supported the prevailing tariff proposal, and this endorsement led to a famous debate with Senator Robert Y. Hayne of South Carolina. In the course of the debate, Webster declared: "Liberty and Union, now and forever, one and inseparable!" These sentiments would embody his devotion to the importance of union for the remainder of his political career.

In 1836 and 1840 Webster unsuccessfully attempted to obtain the Whig Party's presidential nomination; he nevertheless served as secretary of state under presidents Harrison, Tyler, and Fillmore. Webster returned to the Senate from 1844 until 1850. He supported the Compromise of 1850 in a famous speech on 7 March 1850, criticizing secessionists and abolitionists as not possessing enough devotion to the Union. It was a remarkable performance that had the effect of moderating sectional discord, even as it inflamed Massachusetts abolitionists. Webster remained unforgiven by them when he died two years later on 24 October 1852.

—*H. Lee Cheek, Jr.*

For further reading:
Peterson, Merrill D. *The Great Triumvirate: Webster, Clay, and Calhoun* (1987).
Remini, Robert V. *Daniel Webster: The Man and His Time* (1997).

WEED, THURLOW
(1797–1882)
Journalist and political advisor

Few subjects present a more apt personification of the era in American history when mass-based political parties developed and matured than Thurlow Weed. His political career spanned six decades; he was running election campaigns throughout the rise and the fall of the second party system and still exercising his mastery of the "black arts" of political fixing after the Civil War. The grandfather of modern "spin-doctors," Weed was so successful at controlling the party machine, through bribery and blatant cronyism if necessary, that he was known as "the Dictator."

Weed was born in Greene County, New York, the son of a farmer and failed carter, and received little formal schooling. At the age of eighteen he had his first taste of politics while working for two printers in Albany during the legislative session. The young Weed soon demonstrated an unusual aptitude for deal making and partisanship, finding ways of mobilizing coalitions of support behind particular projects. He edited the *Albany Evening Journal* for over thirty years, making it a leading advocate for business interests and the state's promotion of economic development. It was also famous for attacks on "licentiousness": drinking, gambling, and prostitution. Weed had always disliked slavery and, when sectional conflict exploded into the political arena in the 1850s, he saw the partisan advantages of tarring Democrats by associating them with the "Slavepower."

Although he was instantly recognizable to his contemporaries—in the form of caricatures in the weekly press, and because of the attention paid by his fellow newspaper editors to his political pronouncements—Weed never held or sought elected public office for himself. Much of his public influence was due to his close connection with William H. Seward. The two became close allies in the 1830s when Seward first entered anti-Masonic, then Whig, party politics. The partnership of Seward and Weed was a gift to satirists: with his beaked nose, short spindly legs, and puffed chest, Seward resembled a well-fed parrot, while the spidery Weed was tall with a protruding nose. Weed advised Seward against seeking the Republican nomination in 1856, but he energetically promoted his candidacy in 1860 and was deeply frustrated by the outcome at the nominating convention.

During the secession crisis Weed was among those Republicans who advocated compromise, at least in order to prevent the secession of the upper South. He travelled to Springfield after the election to discuss the policy and composition of the new cabinet with Lincoln, acting as a spokesman for Seward, who remained in Washington expecting to be the controlling figure in the new administration. Weed was deeply concerned about Lincoln's enthusiastic embrace of old Democrats in his new cabinet—especially the appointment of Salmon P. Chase and Montgomery Blair to head the two departments that dispensed the bulk of federal government patronage, the Treasury and the Post Office. Once war broke out, however, Weed was an advocate of a "prompt and stringent blockade," and he fully supported the administration throughout the first year of the war. Weed persuaded James Gordon Bennett, editor of the *New York Herald*, to dampen down his opposition to the administration, and in November 1861 Weed embarked on a trip to England to encourage support for the Union cause. From London, he warned Seward that the British government was prepared to go to war with the United States over the *Trent* crisis, advising his friend that it would be best to "turn the other cheek" and release the two Confederate emissaries who had been illegally seized by the United States from a British ship.

During 1862 Weed became increasingly concerned about the influence of radicals within the administration. He was pleased by Lincoln's reply to Greeley's "Prayer of Twenty Millions," fearing that a policy of emancipation would turn the Democrats against the war. Within New York, Weed felt that the president was preferring radicals for plum patronage posts. The nomination of James S. Wadsworth for governor in 1862 seemed to confirm this radical shift. He and Seward withheld their support, which partly accounted for the victory of the Democratic candidate, Horatio Seymour. Weed sold the *Albany Evening Journal* in early 1863 and spent more of his time on his highly lucrative business interests.

Weed's disillusionment with the administration was such that in 1863 he flirted with the idea of forming a third party. He never entirely despaired of Lincoln, though, and Seward worked hard to persuade him that radical influence within the party could be effectively contained. Indeed, bringing conservatives like Weed back in line was a major objective of the administration as it prepared for the 1864 election. The emancipation policy was played down and a strong appeal made to the former Whig and Know-Nothing vote. By 1864 Weed was back in his more familiar role of party insider, helping to ensure the renomination of the president. Weed complained that Lincoln's main party rival, Treasury Secretary Chase "had a small army traversing the…country under pay from the treasury," and he was delighted when it became clear that Chase's candidacy was failing at the first hurdle. During the hot and frustrating summer of 1864, however, Weed again became anxious that Lincoln's public commitment to emancipation as a war aim would cost him the presidency. In August he reported that there had been a sharp reaction against the administration and that Lincoln's reelection had become an impossibility.

Weed supported Lincoln's renomination and reelection because, like many other conservative Republicans, he recognized that Lincoln's moderation and political acumen was the most effective bulwark against radicalism. In any case Weed was, like many other conservatives, appalled by the Democrat's Chicago platform (which called for a cessation of hostilities and an armistice) and by the nomination of a Copperhead as George B. McClellan's running mate. He observed that the "objections to the election of General McClellan are found less in himself than in his political surroundings. These are largely disloyal, and it requires a higher degree of moral courage than he possesses to shake them off." Like his alter ego Seward, Weed supported Andrew Johnson's Reconstruction policy, further widening his break with much of his own party.

By the end of the war, the aging Weed lacked much of the political influence on which he had thrived for so long. But he remained active for many years, giving advice on patronage matters and commenting on public issues. He was an extraordinary man, whose energy, tactical judgment, and understanding of the workings of the political process provides a fascinating insight into the way in which mid-nineteenth-century politicians harnessed popular energies and conflicting interests for partisan ends.

—*Adam I. P. Smith*

See also Republican Party; Seward, William Henry.

For further reading:
David Davis Papers, Illinois State Historical Library.
Gienapp, William. *The Origins of the Republican Party, 1852–1856* (1987).
Lincoln, Abraham. Papers. Library of Congress, Washington D.C.
Rawley, James A. *Turning Points of the Civil War* (1966).
Van Deusen, Glyndon. *Thurlow Weed: Wizard of the Lobby* (1947).
Weed, Harriet A., ed. *Life of Thurlow Weed* (1883).
Weed, Thurlow. Papers. University of Rochester, New York; and Library of Congress, Washington, D.C.
William H. Seward Papers, University of Rochester.

WEITZEL, GODFREY
(1835–1884)
Union general

Born to Louis Weitzel and Susan Weitzel in Cincinnati, Ohio, Godfrey Weitzel received an appointment to the U.S. Military Academy at age 15 and graduated second of thirty-four in the class of 1855. For his first four years after graduation, Weitzel served as an engineering officer in New Orleans and was then transferred back to West Point to teach engineering.

With hostilities between North and South appearing likely in early 1861, Weitzel was sent to Washington, D.C., to aid in preparing the defenses there. After the commencement of the war with the taking of Fort Sumter, he was detailed to Fort Pickens in Pensacola, Florida, to strengthen the defenses of that fort. For the remainder of the year Weitzel was sent to a variety of sites, shoring up the defenses of Cincinnati and Washington. At the end of the year he was selected to accompany the combined naval and army expedition to take New Orleans, his-four years there before the war being considered a major asset to the campaign.

Benjamin F. Butler made Weitzel chief engineer for the Department of the Gulf. Weitzel quickly gained the trust of his commander, who made him the acting mayor (essentially military governor) of New Orleans after the fall of the city. In July and August 1862 he helped prepare the defenses of Federally occupied Baton Rouge. In August he was promoted to brigadier general of volunteers.

For the remainder of the year through 1863, Weitzel operated in Louisiana commanding first a brigade and then a division of XIX Corps. At the end of October

1862 he commanded the expedition to La Fourche, Louisiana, and commanded the land forces at Irish Bend (Bayou Teche) on 14 January 1863. He commanded a division in all of the preliminary engagements around Port Hudson, skirmishing at Cotile's Bayou and Cheneyville and the subsequent siege and assaults on the Confederate works there. In September 1863 he commanded the same division during the Sabine Pass expedition. In early 1864, Weitzel was temporarily assigned to New Orleans before being transferred east to Benjamin F. Butler's Army of the James.

Upon arrival in Virginia, Weitzel was temporarily placed in command of a division of XVIII Corps operating south of the James River. On 20 May, however, Butler made Weitzel chief engineer of the Army of the James. He held that position until the end of September 1864, during which time he was heavily relied on by Butler for advice on where and when to strike Confederate positions.

With the wounding of Edward Ord at the attack on Fort Harrison at the end of September, Weitzel was given temporary command of Ord's XVIII Corps. Weitzel had been at Fort Harrison as well and was commended for gallantry for his part in the battle. He also received a brevet promotion to colonel in the regular army for his actions there.

Weitzel was promoted to major general of volunteers in November 1864. In December 1864 he was given command of XXV Corps. The infantry component of the corps consisted entirely of African-American troops. By this time in his career, Weitzel was known for his ability to command such men.

He commanded his corps at the first attempt on Fort Fisher, North Carolina, in the same month, serving as Butler's second-in-command. Although the expedition failed, largely due to the timidity of Butler, Weitzel was not blamed and remained in command of XXV Corps for the remainder of the war.

During the final push against Robert E. Lee's lines, Weitzel operated with his corps between the James River and the Appomattox River. When Lee evacuated his positions, leaving Richmond vulnerable, Weitzel and his men were the first to enter the city on 3 April. He received a brevet promotion to brigadier general and major general in the regular army for his actions in the last weeks of the war.

With the end of hostilities, Weitzel and XXV Corps were sent immediately to Fort Monroe to prepare for embarkation to Texas to aid in the handling of the French threat there. He was mustered out of the volunteer army the following year and reverted to major of engineers. During the next eighteen years Weitzel remained in the Corps of Engineers working on a variety of important projects, including ship canals, Stannard's Rock Lighthouse, and the large lock at Sault Sainte Marie. His

declining health forced his transfer to Philadelphia in 1882. He died in that city on 19 March 1884.

—*David S. Heidler and Jeanne T. Heidler*

See also Fort Fisher; Irish Bend/Bayou Teche; New Orleans, Capture of; Port Hudson, Louisisana Campaign; Richmond, Virginia, Surrender of.

For further reading:

Weitzel, Godfrey. *Richmond Occupied: Entry of the United States Forces into Richmond, Va., April 3, 1865* (1965).

WELD, THEODORE DWIGHT
(1803–1895)
Reformer

Born the son of a socially prominent Congregational minister in Connecticut on 23 November 1803, Theodore Dwight Weld as an adult shunned offices, honors, and the public spotlight, often preferring to wield his pen anonymously. In the three decades before the Civil War, Weld's commitment to the antislavery cause resulted not only in influential publications of his own, but also inspired Harriet Beecher Stowe's *Uncle Tom's Cabin*. If Stowe and others were the public faces and voices of the abolitionist movement, Weld was in many ways its philosopher and moral center.

In 1825 the Weld family moved New York, where Theodore attended Hamilton College and Oneida Institute to prepare for the ministry. There the evangelical preaching of Charles Grandison Finney influenced him. He formed an influential friendship with well-traveled local educator Charles Stuart, with whom he committed himself to advancing Finney's evangelistic crusade. Stuart induced Weld to join the antislavery movement, and Weld in turn recruited New York merchant-philanthropists Arthur and Lewis Tappan. Weld convinced the Tappan brothers to fund Lane Theological Seminary in Cincinnati, Ohio, in 1831 to prepare ministers in the Finney and Oneida mold. The famed and strong-minded Lyman Beecher was recruited as the first president of Lane.

By 1834, Weld's abolitionist militancy had spawned a debate series at Lane about the morality of slavery, which resulted in the radicalization of much of the student body. The debates themselves focused on the sin of slavery and its corrosive effects on both the slaves and American society in general. The students became involved in creating schools for Cincinnati African-Americans, and their boarding and socializing with them caused difficulties between the community and the seminary. Lyman Beecher and the board favored a moderate course on abolition and expelled Weld and the other militants. Weld then entered full-time work with the American Anti-Slavery Society in New York. By 1836, Weld's energies were increasingly devoted to behind-the-scenes work, as he recruited agents for the society and wrote detailed rebuttals of proslavery arguments. Many of these publications, including *The Power of Congress over Slavery in the District of Columbia* (1836), *The Bible Against Slavery* (1837), and *American Slavery As It Is* (1839) became central sources for antislavery oratory and writings for the next two decades.

In 1838, Theodore Dwight Weld married fellow abolitionist and feminist Angelina Grimké, who, with her sister Sarah, joined him on his project to research *American Slavery As It Is; Testimony of a Thousand Witnesses*. The Grimké sisters provided their own firsthand testimony as daughters of a South Carolina slaveholder, and Weld provided analysis of the material the trio culled from thousands of Southern newspapers and publications. The emphasis of the pamphlet was on the physical cruelty and moral depravity of slavery. Weld thus challenged the benign face of slavery with evidence that contradicted the claim of family bonds with slaves. Although the book had a large and enthusiastic audience among abolitionists, Lyman Beecher's daughter Harriet Beecher Stowe made Weld's material the source for *Uncle Tom's Cabin* (1851), which became the single most important influence on Northern white public opinion regarding slavery.

When Stowe's novel was attacked by Southern critics as a fantasy, she produced a 262-page rebuttal entitled *A Key to Uncle Tom's Cabin*, within which she credited *American Slavery As It Is* and other Weld books as both the inspiration for and source of her novel. By distilling Weld's research into a dramatic fictional treatment, Stowe was able to reach people who might not have read tract literature, but whose emotional reaction to Weld's research was crucial to Northern white support for abolition.

Weld became alienated by the schisms in the antislavery movement, and he complained as early as 1840 that most involved cared little for the hard work of abolition but much for the public platform and offices in the organizations. His interests turned to personal piety as the first step in reform, so that by 1844 both he and Angelina had retired from public battles and lecture platforms to make only occasional appearances. From 1848 onward, he was involved with a number of progressive educational initiatives, including a coeducational school he and his wife founded in 1848. After the Civil War, Weld became an advocate for equal rights of freedpeople and became increasingly interested in the women's rights movement. He avoided public arguments among former abolitionists, preferring anonymity to mention in histories of the movement. When he died in 1895 at age ninety-one, he had outlived both Angelina and most of his fellow reformers.

—*Gretchen A. Adams*

See also Abolitionist Movement; Abolitionists; Grimké, Angelina; Grimké, Sarah Moore; Stowe, Harriet Beecher; Tappan, Lewis; *Uncle Tom's Cabin*.

For further reading:
Abzug, Robert H. *Passionate Liberator: Theodore Dwight Weld and the Dilemma of Reform* (1980).
Thomas, Benjamin P. *Theodore Weld: Crusader for Freedom* (1950).

WELDON & PETERSBURG RAILROAD

During the spring of 1864, General Ulysses S. Grant began his campaign to take the Confederate capital of Richmond. But by mid-June 1864, the Federal commander had abandoned his direct assault against the city and moved the bulk of his army across the James River to Petersburg, twenty miles to the south of Richmond. In Grant's opinion, capturing Petersburg (or at least the railroads that ran into the city) would force the Confederates to abandon Richmond. The reason for this belief was that the main transportation and supply routes that linked the Confederate capital to the rest of the South first went through Petersburg.

Grant's troops captured the Norfolk & Petersburg Railroad (the easternmost of the three major lines running from the South into the city) very quickly. The Federal commander then turned his attention to the Weldon & Petersburg Railroad (commonly called the Weldon line). This line ran almost due south from Petersburg to Weldon, North Carolina. From there it was linked to other lines that brought in supplies from the Carolinas and Georgia. Cutting this line would create major difficulties in supplying the Confederate troops defending Petersburg and Richmond.

Grant launched his first offensive against the Weldon Railroad on 22 June, sending 5,000 cavalrymen under General James H. Wilson and General August V. Kautz to damage that line and any others they could safely reach. The Federal troopers inflicted minor damage on the Weldon Road in the vicinity of Reams' Station (fifteen miles south of Petersburg) before moving westward. Union infantry from the II and VI Corps were supposed to follow the cavalry and make a permanent lodgment across the line. However, alerted by the earlier activity of the horsemen, General Robert E. Lee sent a corps led by General A. P. Hill to the area. Hill prevented the Federal infantry from reaching the railroad and doing further damage. Following the raid, the railroad was quickly repaired.

The second Northern attempt to break the Weldon line came two months later. On 18 August General George G. Meade sent General Gouvernor K. Warren's V Corps to destroy the railroad around Globe Tavern, about five miles south of Petersburg. General P. G. T. Beauregard (commanding the Confederate forces at Petersburg in Lee's absence) quickly sent a division toward the tavern in an effort to repulse Warren's men. For the next three days Meade and Beauregard sent rein-

forcements into the fighting. When the battle ended on 22 August, the Federal forces had a firm grip on the portion of the Weldon Railroad around Globe Tavern.

However, the Confederates found this break in their supply line to be mostly an inconvenience. They simply stopped trains travelling on the Weldon line a day's ride south of Petersburg and transported the supplies into the city by wagon. Realizing this, Grant ordered his troops to continue destroying the line southward. Two days after the fighting ended at Globe Tavern, Grant ordered General Winfield S. Hancock to take two divisions from the II Corps and continue the demolition of the railroad around Reams' Station. On 25 August, after destroying eight more miles of track, Hancock's men found themselves under a full-scale attack from Confederate infantry from Hill's corps and cavalrymen commanded by General Wade Hampton. This assault succeeded in driving the Federal force from the railroad, inflicting heavy casualties on Hancock's troops in the process. For the time being, the Weldon Railroad south of Reams' Station remained securely in Confederate hands.

Grant refused to be content with the damage his troops had so far inflicted on the line. In early December 1864, he sent Warren's V Corps, reinforced by General David Gregg's cavalry division and a division of infantry from the II Corps, to destroy the Weldon road as far south as Hicksford, Virginia, forty miles below Petersburg. A patchwork force of Confederate troops prevented the Federal troops from burning the vital railroad bridge across the Meherrin River at Hicksford, but Warren's men destroyed most of the track between there and the Union lines at Globe Tavern. Although Lee dispatched A. P. Hill's corps to destroy the raiders, Warren and his men completed their work and escaped with only minor losses.

The damage to the Weldon Railroad from this final assault proved so severe that it would be March 1865 before it would once again be able to transport cargo north of Hicksford. During this period, only the overtaxed Southside Railroad remained as the main supply line for the Confederates defending Petersburg. The destruction of the Weldon line inflicted severe hardships on Lee's army, reducing its effectiveness and contributing to the rapidly rising number of desertions that occurred during the last months of the war.

—David McGee

See also Globe Tavern, Virginia; Petersburg Campaign; Railroads, Confederate; Reams' Station, Virginia.

For further reading:

Davis, William C. *Death in the Trenches: Grant at Petersburg* (1986).

Horn, John. *The Destruction of the Weldon Railroad: Deep Bottom, Globe Tavern, and Reams Station* (1991).

———. *The Petersburg Campaign, June 1864–April 1865* (1993).

Trudeau, Noah Andre. *The Last Citadel: Petersburg, Virginia, June 1864–April 1865* (1991).

WELLES, GIDEON
(1802–1878)
U.S. secretary of the navy

Born on 1 July 1802 in Glastonbury, Connecticut, Welles came from a prosperous family (his father being a shipbuilder and West Indies merchant) with a tradition of public service. Welles received an excellent education, first at the Episcopal Academy at Cheshire (where one of his classmates was Andrew H. Foote) and then at Captain Alden Partridge's military institute at Norwich, Vermont (which later became Norwich University). He then became interested in journalism and politics.

Welles associated himself with John M. Niles in publishing the *Hartford Times and Weekly Advertizer*, the only Jeffersonian newspaper in Connecticut. He took a leading role in organizing the Democratic Party in Connecticut and was an ardent supporter of Andrew Jackson for the presidency in the election of 1828. When Jackson won, Welles helped advise him on political patronage in Connecticut. In 1835 Welles became comptroller of Connecticut, a post he again held in the 1840s. In 1836 he was postmaster of Hartford and the next year he was elected to the state legislature. He backed Martin Van Buren for the presidency in 1844, but when James K. Polk won the nomination, Welles shifted his support to him. Polk won the election, and at the end of 1845, he offered Welles the post of chief of the naval Bureau of Provisions and Clothing. There was some opposition among naval officers to a civilian in this position, but Polk persisted and Welles quieted concerns by doing an admirable job. He held the position during the Mexican War, from April 1846 until the new Whig president, Zachary Taylor, removed him in 1849.

Welles returned to Connecticut that fall and wrote for a number of Democratic journals. He opposed the Fugitive Slave Law and broke with the Democratic Party over the Kansas-Nebraska Act. Welles opposed fellow Democrat Franklin Pierce's ambiguous stance on slavery, and when the new Republican Party formed in 1855, Welles became the first Republican candidate for governor of Connecticut. Although he failed to win the 1856 election, in May 1860 he was a member of the Connecticut delegation to the Republican national convention and contributed significantly to the nomination of Abraham Lincoln for the presidency.

Certainly Welles was one of Lincoln's top choices for his cabinet and, shortly after becoming president, Lincoln appointed him secretary of the navy. This proved a very astute choice, and not only because Welles had more experience with the department than any of his predecessors.

Welles took over a department in disarray. Morale was quite low throughout the navy. Many of the department's

Gideon Welles (*Library of Congress*)

clerks were openly hostile to the government, and Welles's predecessor, Isaac Toucey, had allowed many officers from the South to resign. Others had been dismissed, so that the officer corps was at about only half strength. Some of those remaining in key posts were of uncertain loyalty, including chief of the Bureau of Ordnance, Captain George Magruder, and commander of the Washington Navy Yard, Captain Franklin Buchanan. Also, the navy was far from ready for war. In early 1861 it had about ninety ships, designed to carry a total of 2,415 guns, but only forty-two of them were in commission, and Toucey had scattered most on foreign station. At the start of the war, the home squadron numbered only twelve vessels with a total of 187 guns.

The navy clearly needed a strong hand and effective leadership, and it required these immediately. Welles had these qualities in ample measure and was certainly one of the great secretaries of the navy in U.S. history. A capable administrator, he was not afraid to experiment with new ideas. Direct in his dealings with others, he was also a good judge of people. He appointed such capable individuals as Assistant Secretary of the Navy Gustavus Vasa Fox and Chief Clerk William Faxon. Welles also had to oversee the development of naval strategy and direction of operations. He seems to have had the respect and loyalty of the officers in the navy.

The first major problem Welles faced was securing ships. To enforce the blockade of the Confederate coast (proclaimed by Lincoln on 19 April 1861), the Navy Department had to convert its small, and for the most part, obsolete collection of ships into an effective force. Welles immediately launched a large naval construction program. This included building seven ironclads, but for immediate use the navy purchased ships of all types and assigned them to blockade duty. By midsummer, the Union blockade of some 3,500 miles of the South Atlantic and Gulf coasts was well under way. By 1865 the U.S. Navy, with 700 vessels of all types, including sixty ironclads, was the second largest in the world, behind only Great Britain.

Another problem was manning the ships. For this, Welles recruited a large number of black seamen. Ultimately African-Americans made up about a quarter of U.S. Navy personnel. Under Welles, the number of seamen and officers went from 7,600 men to 51,500.

Welles served until the end of the administration of Lincoln's successor, Andrew Johnson, and he oversaw the shrinkage of the navy back to peacetime size. He left office on 4 March 1869. His tenure as secretary is the longest in the history of the Navy Department.

Welles remained active in retirement. He spent part of his time editing the detailed diary he kept while in office; this work sheds much light on the inner workings of the federal government under Lincoln and Johnson as well as the navy during the Civil War. It was published after his death, which occurred at Hartford, Connecticut on 11 February 1878.

—*Spencer C. Tucker*

See also African-American Sailors; Buchanan, Franklin; Fox, Gustavus Vasa; Lincoln, Abraham; Navy, U.S.A.; Republican Party.

For further reading:
Niven, John. "Gideon Welles." In *American Secretaries of the Navy. Volume 1: 1775–1913.* Edited by Paolo Coletta (1980).
———. *Gideon Welles, Lincoln's Secretary of the Navy* (1973).
Welles, Gideon. *Diary of Gideon Welles, Secretary of the Navy Under Lincoln and Johnson* (1911).
West, Richard S., Jr. *Gideon Welles. Lincoln's Navy Department* (1943).

WEST POINT, MISSISSIPPI, BATTLE OF
(21–22 February 1864)

The battle of West Point, Mississippi, was a series of skirmishes on the outskirts of Union major general William T. Sherman's Meridian expedition, albeit with important consequences. West Point, the political seat for Clay County, is located 48 miles south of Tupelo, Mississippi, and 142 miles northeast of Jackson, the state capital. The skirmishes took place near West Point on 20 and 21 February 1863, followed by a bloody engage-

ment the next day around the town of Okalona, Mississippi. Approximately 2,500 Confederates turned back a Union force of 7,600, composed primarily of cavalry. Although this Confederate victory did little to alter the Civil War in the West, it did give a significant boost to the morale of Major General Nathan Bedford Forrest's green troops, recently recruited from western Tennessee. The victory also checked Union advances in the northern portion of the state, saving the arsenal and supply depots at Columbus, Mississippi, and discouraged Sherman from continuing his expedition to Selma, Alabama, an important town for the manufacturing and storing of war materials.

Sherman explained in his memoirs the reasons for the expedition. First, he wanted to paralyze Confederate troop movements by destroying the railroad system. Second, he needed to reduce the enemy threat, which would allow the Union to withdraw 20,000 troops from the area for use in the upcoming Georgia campaign. Third, he sought to neutralize Forrest as a threat to Union-held territory and supply lines. On 3 February, Sherman departed Vicksburg with the XVI and XVII Corps, approximately 26,800 troops. Sherman's force arrived in Meridian, Mississippi, on 15 February and stayed in the area five days before returning to Vicksburg via Canton, Mississippi, on 21 February 1864.

As a key part of the expedition, Sherman ordered Brigadier General William Sooy Smith (chief of cavalry for the Military Division of the Mississippi) to Meridian by 10 February 1864. Smith, however, waited at Collierville, Tennessee, for Colonel George E. Waring, Jr.'s cavalry brigade en route from Kentucky before proceeding. Waring finally rendezvoused with Smith on 8 February, and the combined force departed Collierville on 11 February, one day after its scheduled arrival in Meridian.

On 20 February, Union skirmishers contacted Confederate vedettes approximately fifteen miles north of West Point, at Prairie Station. These mounted pickets, under the leadership of Forrest's younger brother Jeffrey, fought a delaying action toward the town of West Point. A sizable skirmish occurred about a mile north of West Point, at which point Confederate troopers fell back though the town, allowing it to fall into Union hands.

The following morning, Union forces headed south only to fight another series of small skirmishes against troops led again by Jeffrey E. Forrest. Although the skirmishes were heavy at times, Jeff Forrest deliberately avoided a major engagement, trying to pull Smith's command into a trap set by his older brother. The elder Forrest planned to lure Smith into a swampy cul-de-sac where the Sakatonchee (now called the Chuquatonchee) and the Oktibbeha (now called Tibbee) Creeks met, approximately three miles south of West Point, and then surround the force.

The heaviest skirmishing lasted two hours and caused

Smith to stop and reevaluate his situation before Forrest could spring his trap. Smith then ordered a withdrawal through West Point for two reasons. First, thousands of slaves weighted Union field trains, thus increasing the demands for guard and work details. Second, heavy losses, coupled with reports of Forrest having 8,000 to 9,000 troops, convinced Smith that he faced a superior foe. As Federal troops withdrew, Forrest seized the initiative and ordered an advance across his front, albeit a cautious one. He managed to punch his way through Smith's rear guard, creating havoc with the Union rear.

Federal forces regrouped the next day to make a determined stand four miles south of Okalona, situated north of West Point. The heaviest engagement took place at Ivey's Hill, where Federal troops killed the younger Forrest as he rallied his troops. Rather than risk the previous two days' gains, the elder Forrest broke off the attack due to lack of ammunition, exhaustion, and inferior numbers. He allowed the enemy to withdraw across the Tallahatchie River on the night of the 23d, burning the bridge behind them. Smith promptly returned to the safety of Memphis.

Smith's official report lists his expedition as responsible for damaging thirty miles of track, capturing 200 prisoners, liberating 3,000 slaves, and confiscating 3,000 horses and mules (many were brought by the slaves). In addition, Smith claimed to have burned two million bushels of corn and 2,000 bales of cotton. His casualties totaled 324 (forty-seven killed, 157 wounded, and 120 missing). Forrest's small band captured six pieces of artillery, three stands of colors, and 162 prisoners. Confederate losses consisted of twenty-seven killed, ninety-seven wounded, and twenty missing, for a total of 144 troops.

—David P. Eldridge

See also Meridian Campaign.
For further reading:
Bearss, Margie Riddle. *Sherman's Forgotten Campaign: The Meridian Expedition* (1987).
Henry, Robert Selph. *"The First with the Most." Forrest* (1944).
Jordan, Thomas, and J. P. Pryor. *The Campaigns of Lieutenant General Nathan Bedford Forrest, and of Forrest's Cavalry* (1868; reprint, 1988).

WEST VIRGINIA

West Virginia was a creature of the Civil War, being admitted to the Union in 1863. For decades, settlers in the Virginia counties west of the Front Ridge of the Alleghenies found themselves in an uneasily unequal relationship with the established society in the Tidewater to the east. The terrain precluded the prominence of planters and plantation slavery in the west, and the small farmers and townsmen of the region complained of a state government that overtaxed and underrepresented them. While the

Alleghenies separated them from the rest of the Virginians, they shared similar terrain and extensive frontiers with Pennsylvania (for 120 miles) and Ohio (250 miles).

The flow of population and commerce along the river systems also connected them to Pennsylvanians and Ohioans more immediately than to eastern Virginians. The Ohio River not only divided but united the peoples along the banks, while the Little Kanawha and Kanawha rivers flowed into the Ohio from the interior.

Every step toward Virginia's secession expanded the opposition in these western counties. The legislature's January call for a state convention brushed aside the precedent of requiring a popular vote to sanction such a call. The convention deliberated from February into April with emissaries from the new Confederacy, whose supporters packed the galleries and threatened delegates by hanging nooses from lampposts; delegates from the western counties voted disproportionately with the majority, which repudiated secession on 4 April by 89 to 45. Western Virginians also suspected that the coincidence of Fort Sumter with the long-scheduled 16 April secessionist gathering at Richmond created an atmosphere that pushed the convention to a 17 April vote of 81 to 51 for secession.

The secessionist effort to impose virtual martial law through the state, despite the narrowness of their victory, faced serious problems in the western counties, where local opinion clearly opposed it. Within hours of secession, officials in Wheeling and other communities received orders from the state to seize Federal property, leading to their direct rejection of the state's authority. During the next few weeks, Unionists sponsored public meetings at Wheeling, Parkersburg, and other Ohio River communities, as well as at Clarksburg and other interior towns. County conventions followed, leading to a loyalist state convention at Wheeling on 13 May. As elsewhere in border states, recruiters for both sides periodically worked in the same community. At a second convention on 11 June, fifty-seven delegates established the Unionist "Restored Government of Virginia," which subsequently sanctioned the course of the western counties toward independence from Virginia.

Geography meant the war would come first to western Virginia and shaped its course there. Railroads crossed the northern corner of the region. The Baltimore & Ohio Railroad ran up the Potomac River from Harper's Ferry to Grafton, then swung north to Wheeling before entering the valley, and the Northwestern Railroad went from Parkersburg on the Ohio River to Grafton. Three east-west roads connected the region to the Shenandoah Valley of Virginia. The Northwestern Turnpike ran along the rails from Parkersburg through Grafton before crossing into Winchester; the Parkersburg & Staunton Turnpike went southeast from Parkersburg through Beverly before continuing east into Staunton; and the James River & Kanawha Turnpike ran from Guyandotte through Charleston, then through Gauley Bridge and White Sulphur Springs on the border. So, too, a network of roads formed a north-south route from Grafton down to Gauley Bridge, linking the three turnpikes. The war was fought primarily along these routes through the state.

Loyal Virginians, aided by troops from Ohio and elsewhere, occupied Unionist communities like Wheeling and Parkersburg. However, the Confederate occupation of Grafton forced the Federals either to move into the interior or to accept the loss of the B & O linking Washington to the Ohio Valley. After their occupation of Grafton in late May, Union victories at Phillippi (3 June 1861) and Rich Mountain (10 June) secured the area near the railroad. As these forces pushed south, another Federal column battled up the Kanawha River, the two converging at Gauley Bridge late in the summer.

Fearing that this might be the prelude to a Union drive across the mountains into the Shenandoah, the Confederates secured the area around Sewell Mountain. Although small armies clashed at the top of Alleghany Mountain (13 December), neither side could overcome the logistical problems of movement and supply that plagued the operations of large numbers in the mountains.

As the war progressed, the Federals sought to hold the region with the least possible numbers, which invited repeated Confederate incursions, which, in turn, could not remain long. William E. Jones, John D. Imoden, and Albert Jenkins led such raids in 1863. Some towns changed hands frequently. Romney did so fifty-three times in the course of the war.

Something of such tactics in the political sphere also failed to forestall the formal creation of West Virginia as a separate state. Local politicians opposed to the move sought to prevent it by expanding the proposed boundaries to include more pro-secessionist counties in the south that were expected to vote against independence. Predictably, though, the turnout was so low in those counties that the plan backfired, leaving the new state with a number of counties that might well have preferred remaining with Virginia.

Persistent military efforts to negotiate large columns through the mountains failed. Federal attempts to push east into the Shenandoah Valley ended at White Sulphur Springs (26–27 August 1863). Similar drives to the south against the Virginia & Tennessee Railroad ended at Droop Mountain (6 November). Through 1864, Federals made several additional raids against the railroad, and Confederates continued their incursions into the region. However, that year's Union victories in the Shenandoah Valley left the war in West Virginia to sputter into guerrilla fighting.

As internal dissenters within the United States,

Virginia secessionists appealed to the ideals of self-determination implicit in the Declaration of Independence only to find its own internal dissenters eager to do the same against the authority of the state. However, West Virginia's secessionist minority found themselves hostages to geography, their own ill-fated attempt to thwart the new state, and the fortunes of war. In the end, West Virginia became a standing monument to the role of power rather than ideals in the Civil War era.

—*Mark A. Lause*

See also Alleghany Mountain, [West] Virginia, Battle of; Averell's Raids; Border States; Philippi, Battle of; Rich Mountain, Battle of.

For further reading:

Andre, Richard, Stan Cohen, and Bill Wintz. *Bullets & Steel: The Fight for the Great Kanawha Valley, 1861–1865* (1995).

Cohen, Stan B. *The Civil War in West Virginia, a Pictorial History* (1976).

———. *A Pictorial Guide to West Virginia's Civil War Sites and Related Information* (1990).

Lang, Theodore F. *Loyal West Virginia, from 1861 to 1865* (1895).

WESTERN SANITARY COMMISSION

On 5 September 1861, Reverend William Greenleaf Eliot submitted a formal suggestion to Major General John C. Frémont requesting authority to establish and operate a public relief agency in St. Louis, Missouri. Jessie Benton Frémont, the general's wife, also endorsed the need for such an organization in the Trans-Mississippi and Western theaters. On 10 September, therefore, General Frémont issued Special Order No. 159, establishing the Western Sanitary Commission (WSC). Its five-member executive committee consisted of Reverend Eliot, James E. Yeatman, Carlos S. Greeley, Dr. John B. Johnson, and George Partridge. Yeatman served as the organization's president, working in close tandem with Reverend Eliot.

As with the New York–based U.S. Sanitary Commission (USSC), the WSC functioned as a voluntary civilian relief agency. Intended as a supplemental agency to the U.S. Army Medical Bureau, the WSC was authorized to collect and distribute food, clothing, and medical supplies; select and furnish buildings for use as army and brigade hospitals; and appoint female nurses according to the guidelines established by General Superintendent of Nurses Dorothea L. Dix.

The WSC managed thirteen hospitals throughout Missouri, with accommodations for approximately 8,000 patients. The WSC also experimented with hospital specialization, establishing an ear and eye infirmary as well as a smallpox hospital. In addition, in Missouri, Tennessee, and Kentucky the WSC managed at least four soldiers' homes, which served as temporary shelters for soldiers traveling to and from their regiments.

The WSC adopted several innovations to improve the quality and quantity of medical care in the Trans-Mississippi and Western theaters. For example, the WSC converted Mississippi River steamboats for use as floating hospitals as early as 1862; once converted, vessels such as the *R. C. Wood* and the *D. A. January* allowed the WSC to transport supplies and medical personnel wherever needed along the Mississippi River and its tributaries. The WSC maintained a detailed registry of patients; this registry recorded each patient's name, regiment, and medical condition, as well as their hospital or place of burial. By establishing agencies specifically designed to meet the needs of freed people throughout the Trans-Mississippi and Western theaters, the WSC helped reform ideas concerning who could properly receive public aid. In conjunction with his work for the WSC, for example, James E. Yeatman wrote one of the first published reports to address the need for employment opportunities for freed people. As a result of this report, Yeatman was offered the position of head of the Freedmen's Bureau, but turned the offer down. One of the WSC's most noteworthy operations was its supervision of the Mississippi Valley Sanitary Fair, held in St. Louis between 17 May and 18 June 1864. This event proved a great financial success, raising $554,591 for the WSC treasury.

Throughout the war, the WSC received the public and private praise of such western military commanders as Ulysses S. Grant, William T. Sherman, and John M. Schofield. Despite the WSC's many achievements, the WSC and USSC developed a rivalry that lasted the length of the war. In 1861, the USSC attempted through political pressure from Washington, D.C., to force the WSC to accept branch office status within the USSC. This effort backfired, however, when Secretary of War Edwin M. Stanton issued Special Order No. 397. Stanton's order confirmed Frémont's previous order. Nonetheless, the USSC consistently portrayed the WSC as a decentralized local effort narrowly focused on helping only those soldiers from specific states. In truth, however, the WSC worked on behalf of all Union soldiers and civilians in the Trans-Mississippi and Western theaters, regardless of their state of origin; the WSC also worked to improve the care received by Confederate prisoners of war.

Between September 1861 and the war's end, the WSC distributed 4,218,922 articles with an approximate value of $3,500,000. During that same period, the WSC also distributed 433,764 articles to freed people and refugees. Through arrangements with numerous rail and express companies, who provided the WSC with free transportation for its goods and agents, the commission's expenses amounted to less than 1.5 percent of the value of its distributions.

With the end of hostilities, the WSC effectively ceased its daily operations, although it continued to exercise considerable influence over the direction of philanthropic practices in St. Louis. For the next twenty years, the WSC donated its remaining funds to a variety of St. Louis relief and educational agencies. With the 1886 death of Reverend Eliot, the spiritual force behind the organization, the WSC finally disbanded.

—*Robert Patrick Bender*

See also United States Sanitary Commission.

For further reading:
Eliot, William Greenleaf. Papers. Missouri Historical Society, St. Louis.
———. Papers. Washington University, St. Louis.
Final Report of the Western Sanitary Commission (1866).
Forman, Jacob G. *The Western Sanitary Commission: A Sketch* (1864).
Parrish, William E. "The Western Sanitary Commission." *Civil War History* (1990).

WESTPORT, BATTLE OF
(23 October 1864)

The battle of Westport resulted from the convergence of three armies in the largest battle of the Civil War in the upper Trans-Mississippi. The poorly equipped and chaotically organized Confederate Army of Missouri under General Sterling Price had between 10,000 and 14,000 men wedged between two Union armies with a combined total of about 25,000. Price hoped to seize the forage and military stores in Kansas by defeating the Federals in detail, while the Unionists sought to destroy his army or push it back south. The poorly reported casualties over the three days of fighting probably ran as high as 10 percent of the Federal troops engaged and 20 percent of the Confederates.

Since mid-September, Price's Missouri Raid had generally moved through the state with minimal opposition. By mid-October, General William S. Rosecrans had placed 8,000 to 10,000 cavalry under General Alfred Pleasonton west of Jefferson City in pursuit, while General Samuel R. Curtis assembled at the Kansas state line about 10,000 men, whose mounted advance under General James G. Blunt probed east into Missouri. On 21 October westbound Confederates pushed Blunt's advance back through Independence to Curtis's main defenses along the Big Blue River. The next day, 22 October, the Rebels breached those defenses at Byram's Ford, driving Curtis back to the area around Westport, while Pleasonton's Federals simultaneously pushed the Confederate rear guard through Independence and advanced on the Big Blue.

On 23 October, Price's Confederates held both the heights south of Brush Creek overlooking Curtis at Westport and the eastern defenses along the Big Blue against Pleasonton. Starting early, Blunt advanced beyond Brush Creek in a preemptive attack to thwart a Confederate drive into Kansas and to allow Pleasonton's attack to begin. Price's men pushed the Federals back across Brush Creek, but had no reserve to pursue their success, owing to the need to hold the river line against Pleasonton's cavalry.

During the late morning, the tide turned. Guided by a German farmer, Curtis took his own escort with artillery up the defile formed by Swan's Creek onto the heights against the Confederate left, while the rest of the line under Blunt pressed back south beyond Brush Creek. As the battle raged, more Federal troops entered the field, particularly members of the Kansas state militia, alerted to the threat to their communities. They eventually had about thirty cannons in operation.

Meanwhile, after two hours of hard fighting, Pleasonton's men made their way across the Big Blue and pushed the Confederate defenders on the bluffs back. Curtis's men had made slow, but definite, progress to the south when Pleasonton arrived from the Big Blue, placing a battery at Hinkle's Grove on the enemy right and rear.

With this, the Confederate line faltered, then broke in flight to the southwest. The remnants of one brigade rallied briefly along a stone wall, buying time for the bulk of Price's army and its supply train to escape.

However, lack of coordination between the two Federal armies crippled pursuit far more effectively. Although Curtis, Pleasant, Blunt, and others of the Union high command made it to Indian Creek by 3 P.M., their brief meeting to plan the continued destruction of Price's army led to little coordination over the next two weeks. Price's movement south, initially through Kansas, weakened the interests of Pleasonton and his column from the Department of Missouri, while the pressures of the upcoming election led to the rapid dispersal of the Kansas state militia.

Indirectly, this division of the Union forces contributed to making the battlefield itself a casualty. Early in the twentieth century, the growth of Kansas City threatened efforts by veterans and others to protect it. The U.S. Congress considered federal legislation to help. However, not only were rival cities unenthusiastic about a federally subsidized park in Kansas City, but the project divided proponents of a site on the Big Blue from those of Westport with allied real estate interests, effectively undercutting each other's claims. Most importantly, the city fathers had little interest in sacrificing their plans for development. Almost inadvertently, Loose and Swope Parks are located on parts of the respective battlefields, although few landmarks of the once rural landscape have survived within the now very urbanized neighborhoods.

—*Mark A. Lause*

See also Army of Missouri; Price, Sterling; Price's Missouri Raid.

For further reading:
Brown, D. Alexander "The Battle of Westport." *Civil War Times Illustrated* (1966).
Crittenden, H. H. *The Battle of Westport and National Military Park* (1938).
Jenkins, Paul B. *The Battle of Westport* (1906).
Monnett, Howard N. *Action Before Westport 1864* (1995).

WHEAT, CHATHAM ROBERDEAU
(1826–1862)
Confederate officer

Born to John Thomas Wheat, an Episcopal minister, and Selina Blair Patten Wheat in Alexandria, Virginia, Chatham Roberdeau Wheat, known as "Rob" to his friends and family, moved frequently with his family as a child as his father was transferred from parish to parish. When he was ten years old, Wheat went with his family to New Orleans, the city that would eventually be his home. At this time, however, he and his family remained in New Orleans for only a year before moving to a parish in Nashville, Tennessee. When he was fifteen, Wheat was sent to Alexandria, Virginia, to attend an Episcopal school. He returned to Nashville, where he enrolled in the University of Nashville, graduating in 1845 at the age of nineteen.

Upon graduation, Wheat moved to New Orleans to study law, but his studies were interrupted by the outbreak of the Mexican-American War. He immediately joined a volunteer unit, but illness kept him out of the war until the commencement of Winfield Scott's Mexico City campaign in March 1847. Wheat was elected lieutenant of his company and then captain on the march to Mexico City. En route, however, he contracted yellow fever and was taken back to Vera Cruz to recuperate. He joined his men during the last push against Mexico City in August 1847. With the fall of the capital, Wheat was sent to Tennessee to recruit and by the time he returned, the war was over.

After being mustered out of the volunteer service, Wheat lived briefly in Nashville, but soon returned to New Orleans to complete his law studies. He began his practice in 1849 and became involved in Louisiana Whig politics. Wheat's Mexican-American War experience, however, had whet his appetite for military adventure, and the talk in New Orleans of various filibustering expeditions to Latin America increased his desire to resume the military life.

In 1850 Wheat joined the expedition to Cuba organized by Narciso Lopez. He was wounded early in the expedition, but escaped capture by the Spanish authorities. He was indicted for violating United States neutrality upon his return, but the case was dismissed before coming to trial. The following year he participated in the organization of a second invasion and was slated to bring in the second wave of the foray when the first met with disaster. Though he never made it to Cuba, in 1851 he made numerous speeches throughout New Orleans trying to stir up crowds against the Spanish government.

Later in 1851 and into 1852, Wheat joined Mexican revolutionaries operating just south of Texas. Upon his return to New Orleans in 1852 he spent much of his time campaigning for Winfield Scott for president and conducting his own campaign for the state legislature. Scott lost his bid, but Wheat won and traveled to Baton Rouge in early 1853 to take his seat.

After his various military adventures, Wheat found the life of a state legislator boring, and he rarely attended legislative sessions. Soon he involved himself in the filibustering plans of adventurer William Walker. In 1854 he joined Walker in an expedition into northwestern Mexico and then in 1856 took reinforcements to Walker in Nicaragua. Wheat returned to the United States in 1857.

Wheat took the next couple of years off from military adventures, spending much of his time trying to recover his legal practice and promoting to the War Department an accelerating cannon invented by James Haskell. By 1859, however, the wanderlust overcame him again, and he returned to Mexico to fight in another revolution there. He returned to New Orleans in July 1860, in time to campaign briefly for the presidential candidacy of John C. Breckinridge. He left the country before the campaign was over, however, making his way to London in September 1860 to join a group of British soldiers of fortune heading for Italy to fight with Garibaldi.

Wheat went to Italy and fought briefly with the Italians before hearing of the election of Abraham Lincoln. It is unclear whether the election of a Republican angered him or he simply believed that such an event would start a war in the United States and he wanted to be a part of it. Whatever the case, he started back to the United States immediately. After visiting his family in North Carolina, Wheat made his way to New Orleans, where he began raising a battalion for service to the Confederacy.

Wheat's unit was designated the 1st Special Battalion and eventually consisted of six companies. It quickly became more popularly known as the Louisiana Tigers. Wheat was commissioned major of the battalion on 25 May 1861 and immediately began preparations to take his men to the scene of action in Virginia. They all departed in mid-June and upon arrival in the Old Dominion were sent to Centreville, where they were placed under the command of Colonel Philip St. George Cocke.

At the end of June, Wheat and his men saw their first action when they skirmished with Federal probes. On 17 July, Wheat was moved back with the Tigers to Manassas Junction. On 21 July, the day of the battle of First Bull Run, Wheat and his men were stationed at the Stone Bridge over Bull Run Creek. When he detected Union movement farther up the creek at Sudley Ford, he shifted his men in that direction. In his effort to delay a much larger Union force, Wheat was shot in the side. The bullet traveled through his chest and exited his other side, puncturing one of his lungs in its transit. His men carried him from the field in their retreat.

Wheat was immediately taken to a field hospital, where the surgeons pronounced his case hopeless. He was made as comfortable as possible, and his family was summoned to what was supposed to be his deathbed. Much to everyone's surprise, he soon began a miraculous recovery, after telling the doctors he was not ready to die. In the meantime, Wheat was commended by several of his superior officers for his bravery at Bull Run and was credited with delaying the Federal forces long enough for Confederates to counter the flanking maneuver.

Wheat returned to duty in mid-September 1861. By the time of his return, his Tigers were gaining a reputation as the wildest unit in the army. Wheat, while somewhat calmer than many of his men, also had a reputation as someone who loved the finer things in life, and his cooking skills and hospitality (including his uncanny ability to procure fine spirits) made an invitation to his mess one of the most sought-after in northern Virginia.

By early 1862 Wheat and his Tigers, bored with inactivity, were delighted by the news that they would soon be sent to join Stonewall Jackson in the Shenandoah Valley. En route they fought a brief action with Union forces at Somerville Heights, Virginia, on 7 May 1862. Their first real action under Jackson, however, did not come until 23 May at Front Royal, where Wheat was commended for his bravery. At Cross Keys two weeks later, the Louisiana Tigers were part of the reserve. The following day at Port Republic, Wheat again distinguished himself by moving in among the Union artillery horses and killing many of them with his knife so that retreating Federals would have to leave behind many of their guns. For Wheat's actions in the valley his brigade commander Richard Taylor recommended him for promotion.

The promotion never happened. Wheat and the Tigers traveled as part of Jackson's army to Richmond in late June and saw their first action at Gaines' Mill on 27 June 1862. Wheat led his men into the heaviest fighting and early in the fray was shot in the head. According to some accounts, his last words were a request to be buried on the battlefield, an entreaty that was carried out by his men later that evening. His father moved Wheat's remains in 1863 to Hollywood Cemetery in Richmond. The Louisiana Tigers, their numbers tremendously depleted by the heavy actions of the first year of the war, were dissolved later that summer.

—*David S. Heidler and Jeanne T. Heidler*

See also Bull Run, First Battle of; Gaines' Mill, Battle of; Port Republic, Battle of.

For further reading:

Dufour, Charles L. *Gentle Tiger: The Gallant Life of Roberdeau Wheat* (1957).
Moore, Alison. *He Died Furious* (1983).

WHEATON, FRANK
(1833–1903)
Union general

Born to Francis Levison Wheaton and Amelia Burrill Wheaton in Providence, Rhode Island, Frank Wheaton was educated locally and attended, but did not graduate from, Brown University. After the Civil War he was given an honorary degree from that institution. Wheaton left Brown to become a part of the United States–Mexico Boundary Commission in 1850. After leaving that position five years later, he received a lieutenant's commission in the 1st U.S. Cavalry. Stationed primarily on the western frontier before the Civil War, Wheaton participated in Albert Sidney Johnston's Utah expedition. In early 1861 he was promoted to captain of the 4th U.S. Cavalry.

At the outbreak of the Civil War, Wheaton went home to Rhode Island to help raise a regiment of volunteers for Federal service. In July 1861 he was made lieutenant colonel of the 2d Rhode Island volunteers. He fought with the regiment at First Bull Run, where the regiment incurred very heavy casualties, including the death of Colonel John Slocum. As a result of Slocum's death, Wheaton became the colonel of the regiment. Wheaton was commended for his conduct during the battle.

As part of the Army of the Potomac, the 2d Rhode Island participated in the Peninsula campaign in 1862. Wheaton was commended for his actions at the battle of Williamsburg on 5 May. He continued in command of the 5th until late fall, when he was promoted to brigadier general of volunteers.

Wheaton commanded a brigade of VI Corps at Fredericksburg. He would remain a part of VI Corps for the rest of the war. During the Chancellorsville campaign the following May, Wheaton, as part of VI Corps, remained opposite Fredericksburg while the rest of the Army of the Potomac tried to flank Robert E. Lee's position. Wheaton participated in the subsequent taking of Fredericksburg and Marye's Heights and then fought in the battle of Salem Church.

At the battle of Gettysburg on 2 July, Wheaton temporarily succeeded to the command of the 3d Division when the division's commander, John Newton, became the commander of I Corps. After the battle Wheaton returned to his old brigade. He led his men at Bristoe Station and the Mine Run campaign before being transferred temporarily to the Department of West Virginia in early 1864.

Back with the Army of the Potomac in March 1864, Wheaton commanded his brigade with distinction at the Wilderness and again temporarily took command of the division on 6 May with the injury of the division's commander, George Washington Getty. Wheaton commanded his brigade again at Spotsylvania, Cold Harbor, and the 18 June assault on Petersburg's defenses.

In early July, Wheaton was sent with his brigade to Washington to help meet the threat posed by Jubal Early. He fought at Fort Stevens on 11 and 12 July 1864. After the repulse of Early, Wheaton received a brevet promotion to major general for his actions in defense of the capital.

In early August, Wheaton and VI Corps were sent to the Shenandoah Valley to fight Early. They became a part of Philip Sheridan's Army of the Shenandoah. Wheaton commanded his brigade in all the early engagements of that campaign, including Winchester on 19 September. He was commended by Horatio G. Wright for his part in that battle and was recommended for promotion to brevet major general. After the battle, Wheaton was given command of a division in VI Corps.

Wheaton returned with his division to the Army of the Potomac in December 1865 and fought in the siege of Petersburg for the remainder of the war. On 2 April he fought at the final assault on Petersburg's defenses at Fort Fisher. In June, George Gordon Meade, commander of the Army of the Potomac, recommended Wheaton for promotion to major general of volunteers for his actions in the last months of the war.

Wheaton remained in the army after the war, reverting to lieutenant colonel of the 39th Infantry during the reorganization of the army in 1866. During the next thirty years he served primarily on the western frontier, fighting in the Modoc War of 1872 and eventually becoming commander of the Department of Texas. Wheaton reached the rank of major general in 1897, immediately before his retirement from active duty. He lived quietly in Washington, D.C., after his retirement and died there on 18 June 1903. Wheaton was married to a daughter of Samuel Cooper, former adjutant general of the U.S. Army and adjutant general of the Confederate army during the Civil War.

—*David S. Heidler and Jeanne T. Heidler*

See also Petersburg Campaign; Shenandoah Valley Campaign (1864–1865).
For further reading:
Wheaton, Frank. *Civil and Military Record of Frank Wheaton, Brevet Major General U.S. Army, Colonel Second U.S. Infantry* (1888).

WHEELER, JOSEPH
(1836–1906)
Confederate general

Joseph Wheeler was born in Augusta, Georgia, on 10 September 1836 and was educated in Connecticut at the Cheshire Academy. He gained appointment to West Point in 1854 and graduated five years later, a mediocre eighteenth in a class of twenty-two. As a cadet, Wheeler was demonstrably deficient in cavalry tactics, but the young second lieutenant nonetheless found himself assigned to the cavalry school at Carlisle

Joseph Wheeler (*Library of Congress*)

Barracks, Pennsylvania, for further instruction. At length he billeted with the Regiment of Mounted Riflemen, and joined this rough-riding unit at Fort Craig, New Mexico. Wheeler distinguished himself in several skirmishes against the Apache, displaying such aplomb under fire that he gained the sobriquet "Fightin' Joe."

Despite his Northern upbringing, Wheeler resigned his commission on 27 February 1861, in anticipation of civil war. That April he joined the Confederate army as a first lieutenant of artillery and performed garrison service along the Florida coast. Wheeler's commander, General Braxton Bragg, was favorably impressed by his performance and arranged for his promotion to colonel of the 19th Alabama Infantry. In this capacity Wheeler joined the Army of Mississippi under Bragg and fought well at the bloody 6–7 April battle of Shiloh. He garnered additional praise by covering the Confederate withdrawal, a feat he would perform continually and admirably over the next three years.

In July 1862 Wheeler rejoined the mounted arm when Bragg appointed him cavalry commander in the Army of Mississippi. The appointment proved fortunate for Southern arms as "Fightin' Joe" proved himself one of the hardest-riding and most tactically astute troopers of

the war. He spearheaded Bragg's drive into Kentucky in August 1862 and subsequently fought well at Perryville the following October. For effectively covering another retreat, Wheeler gained promotion to brigadier general. He then skillfully contested the advance of General William S. Rosecrans at Murfreesboro (Stones River) before rising to major general in January 1863. In consequence of another fine performance, Bragg appointed him commander of all cavalry in his newly organized Army of Tennessee with a rank of major general. Wheeler also found time to author a manual entitled *Cavalry Tactics* (1863), which became standard issue for Confederate mounted units.

Throughout most of 1863, Wheeler rendered useful service during maneuvers associated with the Tullahoma campaign in central Tennessee. He was next closely engaged at the furious engagement at Chickamauga on 18–20 September 1863, before launching one of the most devastating cavalry raids of the Civil War. With Rosecrans's defeated Union forces besieged at Chattanooga, Bragg ordered Wheeler to cut off his supply lines and possibly prompt his surrender. On 1 October 1863 Wheeler's division splashed across the Tennessee River in full view of Union cavalry under General George Crook, brushed them aside, and made for the interior. Over the next week his gray-clad troopers ran roughshod throughout the Sequatchie Valley, capturing 1,000 supply wagons and inflicting an estimated 1,000 casualties for the loss of 212. It was a masterstroke against Rosecrans's lines of communication and nearly destroyed his ability to resist. Bragg then dispatched Wheeler to cooperate with forces under General James Longstreet at the siege of Knoxville. In his absence, the Army of Tennessee was heavily defeated by General Ulysses S. Grant at Chattanooga in November 1863, and Wheeler's cavalry once again covered a Confederate retreat into Georgia.

Throughout the ensuing 1864 Atlanta campaign, Wheeler provided the most obstinate resistance to the advancing columns of General William T. Sherman. He clashed repeatedly with the Union advance guard, giving General Joseph E. Johnston sufficient time to withdraw his forces intact. Following the death of J. E. B. Stuart that May, Wheeler also became the Confederacy's senior cavalry officer. Outnumbered but never outfought, he enjoyed his greatest battlefield success in July 1864, when he thwarted the so-called Stoneman's Raid. This victory culminated in the capture of Generals George Stoneman, Kenner Garrard, and Edward M. McCook, along with 3,200 Union cavalrymen. However, Sherman inexorably advanced against Atlanta and a new general, John Bell Hood, dispatched Wheeler on a protracted raid against his supply lines.

Wheeler departed Atlanta on 10 August 1864 and made directly for the tracks of the Western & Atlantic Railway. His men tore up nearly thirty miles of rail near

Marietta and Dalton, before pursing Union forces drove them off. Wheeler then committed a desperate gambit by riding into Tennessee to strike at the heart of Sherman's supply system. The raiders ripped up tracks and burned wagons within sight of Nashville, before Wheeler judged the operation ineffective and withdrew into Alabama. Once Hood had himself marched into Tennessee, Wheeler rode east and rejoined Johnston in Georgia to contest Sherman's ongoing March to the Sea.

As Confederate fortunes ebbed, Wheeler was advanced to lieutenant general in February 1865. The appointment rang hollow, given the dilapidated state of Southern forces, but Wheeler scored numerous small-scale successes against pursuing Union cavalry. However, when his troopers were criticized for ostensible lack of discipline, Wheeler was placed under the command of General Wade Hampton for the remainder of the war. Shortly after Johnston's surrender, Wheeler was captured in Georgia in May 1865. At that time he was the veteran of 200 major engagements, had lost sixteen horses in combat, and witnessed thirty-six staff officers fall by his side. His reputation as "Fightin' Joe" was well deserved.

Wheeler was briefly confined after the war, before relocating to Alabama to practice law. From there he was reelected to Congress as a Democrat over the next fifteen years. Moreover, he served as a symbol of national reconciliation in 1898 when President William McKinley appointed him brigadier general of volunteers during the war with Spain. Wheeler had lost none of his dash as a soldier and played a conspicuous role in the victory at Las Guasimas on 24 June 1898. Two years later he served as brigadier in the regular army and commanded the Department of the Lakes. Wheeler died in Brooklyn, New York, on 25 January 1906, becoming one of few ex-Confederates to be buried at Arlington National Cemetery. Civil War historians generally agree that, in terms of screening an advance and covering a withdrawal, he was unsurpassed by any trooper in either army.

—*John C. Fredriksen*

See also Atlanta Campaign; Stones River, Battle of; Wheeler's Middle Tennessee Raid; Wheeler's Raid.

For further reading:

Dyer, John P. *"Fightin' Joe" Wheeler* (1941).

Fisher, John E. *They Rode with Wheeler: A Chronicle of Five Tennessee Brothers' Service in the Western Confederate Cavalry* (1995).

Lawson, Lewis A. *Wheeler's Last Raid* (1986).

WHEELER'S MIDDLE TENNESSEE RAID
(30 September–9 October 1863)

After the climatic battle of Chickamauga (19–20 September 1863) was fought in northern Georgia, the Confederate advantage in the West was allowed to slip away by the timidity of Braxton

Bragg, the commander of the Army of Tennessee. Instead of pressing the confused and routing Union Army of the Cumberland with a determined pursuit off the battlefield, Bragg had allowed the stricken enemy army to take hurried refuge after Chickamauga in the fortified western Tennessee city of Chattanooga.

With a costly and time-consuming siege facing him, Bragg looked around for a better way to dislodge the Federal army at Chattanooga under General William Rosecrans. He finally decided to drive the enemy out of the city by crossing to the north of the Tennessee River to break up his opponent's tenuous supply lines to Nashville. Although some of his subordinates insisted that the entire army pass over the Tennessee, thus more completely cutting the Army of the Cumberland's communications with the North, Bragg opted to send only a part of his cavalry to perform this huge and vital job. Regardless of the number or type of forces that were to carry out the assignment, if successful, Rosecrans would have to stay in his entrenchments or make a run north, thus allowing Bragg's army another chance of destroying it in battle.

Major General "Fighting Joe" Joseph Wheeler, chief of Bragg's cavalry, was given the operation. His target would be the sixty-mile stretch of territory, from the Seuatchie Valley and Walden's Ridge, that separated Chattanooga from its closest supply base at Stevenson, Alabama. Upon orders from the army commander, Wheeler was to move his cavalry to Decatur, cross the Tennessee near there, then go thirty-five miles northeast of the Federal occupied city, then turn west into the Sequatchie Valley. While in the valley, he was to capture or destroy all enemy supplies and transports found and move toward Nashville, eliminating track and rail stations as he went.

Wheeler started on his expedition on the morning of 30 September. He rode along the south bank of the Tennessee, shadowed by Federal cavalry on the opposite bank. At Cottonport he joined with reinforcements from Nathan Bedford Forrest's mounted command. (Forrest was not with them, since he refused to serve under Bragg.) The Confederate raiding group now numbered a little under 4,000, supported by a six-gun horse artillery company. They crossed the Tennessee with virtually no opposition from the enemy cavalry that had been tailing them.

It took a day (1 October) for Wheeler to sort out his command once across the river. That evening he headed for Walden's Ridge, beyond which lay the Sequatchie Valley. On the next day Wheeler spilt his command. He would lead a portion of it six miles into the valley to capture a reported large Federal supply train making its way to Chattanooga; the other part of the Confederate raiding force would strike the enemy supply base at McMinnville.

Once in the valley, Wheeler quickly captured thirty-two wagons. Riding on, he fell upon a huge supply train containing hundreds of mule-drawn vehicles guarded by infantry and cavalry. A first attack on the protected wagons was thrown back. A second more concentrated mounted attack succeeded in capturing the train's 1,200 enemy soldiers, 800 wagons, and 4,000 mules. It took eight hours for Wheeler's men to lay waste to the ten-mile-long Yankee supply train.

Meanwhile, Wheeler's McMinnville raiding party of 2,500 troopers under General Wharton captured the Federal supply depot there from 585 man Union garrison. The next day, 4 October, Wharton destroyed the place and all the goods he could not carry away. That day the two Rebel forces were reunited and left McMinnville on the 5th. The combined column headed for Murfreesboro, but made no attempt to attack the town. On 6 October the gray troopers engaged in ripping up track and bridges between Murfreesboro and the Duck River.

While Wheeler was destroying millions of dollars' worth of Union supplies and equipment, the Federal command had been organizing a pursuit of the raiders. Taking charge of this effort was General Robert B. Mitchell, cavalry corps leader of the Army of the Cumberland. By 5 October, Michell's 2d Cavalry Division under Brigadier Crook caught up with Wheeler's rear guard near Murfreesboro. A spirited charge by the Federals scattered the Rebel battleline but nevertheless could not prevent the Confederates from withdrawing as dark fell.

That same day saw Mitchell's 1st Cavalry Division join his 2d in the valley. On the 6th the Union 2d Division attacked part of Wheeler's command near Farmington, driving the graycoats three miles along the north shore of the Duck River. Only darkness and the lack of reinforcements prevented the Confederates from being pushed into the Duck.

By 8 October Wheeler could only think about eluding his pursuers and recrossing to the south side of the Tennessee River. While holding off the rapidly following enemy, he crossed most of his command over the Tennessee at Muscle Shoals. This was completed on the 9th with little interference from his Union opponents.

Wheeler's Sequatchie Valley Raid was a tremendous success when the cost to the Union in lost supplies and hardship suffered by the beleaguered Federal troops in Chattanooga is counted. But on the Confederate side, Wheeler's performance—especially his delay in getting back to the Tennessee after the destruction his men wrought in the valley and at McMinnville—nearly caused his command to be destroyed. It certainly cost Wheeler himself much prestige and raised questions as to his true ability to competently lead independent strike forces in the future.

—*Arnold D. Blumberg*

See also Wheeler, Joesph.
For further reading:
Dodson, W. C., ed. *Campaigns of Wheeler and His Cavalry, 1862–1865* (1901).
Dubose, John W. *General Joseph Wheeler and the Army of Tennessee* (1912).

Dyer, John P. *From Shiloh to San Juan: The Life of "Fightin Joe" Wheeler*(1941).

Fisher, John E. *They Rode With Forrest and Wheeler* (1995).

Longacre, Edward G. *Mounted Raids of the Civil War* (1975).

Wilson, George S. "Wilder's Brigade of Mounted Infantry in the Tullahoma-Chickamauga Campaigns." In *The Military Order of the Loyal Legion of the United States*, vol. 15 (1992).

WHEELER'S RAID
(10 August–10 September 1864)

By early August 1864, John Bell Hood's offensives against William T. Sherman's army outside Atlanta had proved to be miserable failures, and President Jefferson Davis had instructed Hood not to waste manpower on any more attacks while the Union forces were entrenched. As a result, Hood decided to try to force Sherman from his entrenchments and out of the state by having Confederate cavalry commander Joseph Wheeler raid the rail lines into Tennessee, cutting off Sherman's supplies.

Hood instructed Wheeler to cut the Western & Atlantic Railroad to the north of Atlanta, move into Tennessee and damage the Nashville & Chattanooga line, leave about 1,200 men in Tennessee to continue to keep the Nashville & Chattanooga disrupted, and then bring the remainder of his troopers back to Hood. Wheeler, with these instructions, moved out of Covington, Georgia, on 10 August 1864 with about 4,500 men in eight cavalry brigades. He left behind approximately the same number with Hood's army.

Wheeler struck the Western & Atlantic first at Marietta, and then Cassville, Calhoun, and Resaca. During the ride his men destroyed tracks, captured Union prisoners at several points, and confiscated Union cattle. At Calhoun, Wheeler sent most of the cattle back to Hood's army. From Resaca, Wheeler moved to Dalton and on 14 August destroyed much of the track south of the town. For the next two days he probed the Federal defenses of the town, intending to capture the Federal garrison there, but when the Union forces received reinforcements, Wheeler moved north again.

Wheeler entered Tennessee east of Chattanooga and moved east to Loudon and then toward Knoxville. He then turned around, heading southwest, and destroyed some of the track of the Nashville & Chattanooga Railroad. Wheeler then rode toward Franklin, where he damaged the Nashville & Decatur track. He moved south from there and crossed the Tennessee River on 10 September into Alabama at Tuscumbia.

While Wheeler was gone Sherman used his cavalry—now opposed by only half the number of Confederate cavalry as before—to cut the railroads south of Atlanta, thus making Hood's position in the city untenable.

When Wheeler completed his raid, Sherman already had possession of Atlanta.

Wheeler's raid had been a wasted effort. Hood's orders had Wheeler going too far north to cripple Sherman's supply lines permanently, and Wheeler compounded this circumstance by moving farther away than Hood had authorized. He also failed to leave behind men on the Nashville & Chattanooga Railroad. Because Sherman had well-defended fortifications at all the major bridges and tunnels, Wheeler was able to destroy only track. Sherman had repair crews that moved out at a moment's notice with all the men, equipment, and materials necessary to make very rapid repairs. Supplies continued to roll in to Sherman's army throughout Wheeler's raid. Sherman had been prepared for the raid for some time and only used it to his own advantage. Neither Hood nor Wheeler, however, ever admitted that it had been a mistake.

—*David S. Heidler and Jeanne T. Heidler*

See also Atlanta Campaign; Hood, John Bell; Wheeler, Joseph.

For further reading:

Castel, Albert E. *Decision in the West: The Atlanta Campaign of 1864* (1992).

Dyer, John P. *From Shiloh to San Juan* (1961).

WHITING, WILLIAM HENRY CHASE
(1824–1865)
Confederate general

Born to Levi Whiting and Mary Whiting in Biloxi, Mississippi, William Henry Chase Whiting was educated in Boston, Massachusetts, near his parents' original home and was then enrolled in Georgetown College in the District of Columbia. After graduating from Georgetown first in his class at age sixteen, Whiting sought admission to the U.S. Military Academy. Whiting entered the academy in 1841 and graduated first of forty-one in the class of 1845. Commissioned into the Corps of Engineers, Whiting for the most part worked on coastal fortifications in the South and the West Coast for the next sixteen years. In 1850, Whiting also made a survey of defensive needs along the frontier of Texas, during which time he produced a diary that was published long after his death. The project for which he would be most remembered was the defenses he designed for the Cape Fear River. While working there, he married a local woman and considered the Wilmington, North Carolina, area his home for the remainder of his life.

On 20 February 1861, Whiting resigned his captain's commission and offered his services to the newly formed Confederate States of America in Montgomery, Alabama. He was immediately commissioned a major in the Confederate engineers. On 23 February 1861,

Confederate president Jefferson Davis sent Whiting to Charleston, South Carolina, to confer with Governor Francis Pickens and to inspect the fortifications there.

Whiting remained in Charleston through the reduction of Fort Sumter, primarily working under the direction of Brigadier General P. G. T. Beauregard in the construction of batteries guarding the entrance to the harbor and pointing at Fort Sumter. When news arrived of the impending appearance of a Federal relief expedition, Whiting went to Morris Island to arrange for the defense of that place against the landing of Federal troops. After the surrender of Fort Sumter, Whiting supervised the evacuation of the surrendered Federal troops.

From Charleston, Whiting went to his home in Wilmington, North Carolina, to supervise the defenses of that area and in June was transferred to the command of Brigadier General Joseph E. Johnston, commander of the Army of the Shenandoah. Upon arrival in the Shenandoah Valley, Whiting became the chief engineer of the army. In mid-July 1861, Whiting had the unenviable task of moving most of Johnston's army from the Shenandoah to Manassas Junction by rail. He accomplished this job with amazing speed, and as a result, the Confederate army defeated the Union force under Brigadier General Irvin McDowell on 21 July 1861. He was commended by Johnston for his actions before and during the battle and was given a field promotion to brigadier general by President Davis.

In late August 1861 Whiting was given command of a division and was sent to command near Dumfries, Virginia. In the spring of 1862 he joined the defenses of Richmond in preparation for Union major general George B. McClellan's Peninsula campaign. Whiting led his division at the battle of Seven Pines and then in early June took his division to the Shenandoah Valley, where it was temporarily attached to the command of Thomas J. "Stonewall" Jackson. He and his men returned to the Richmond area with Jackson's force and fought in the Seven Days'. Whiting especially distinguished himself at the battle of Gaines' Mill on 27 June when he led his men in a charge that forced Brigadier General Fitz John Porter's corps to retreat across the Chickahominy River. Whiting was commended by both Jackson and Major General James Longstreet for his actions that day. Whiting and his division also fought in the concluding battle of the Seven Days' at Malvern Hill.

In November 1862, Whiting was given command of the District of Wilmington, North Carolina. During the next few months he strengthened the defenses of Wilmington and the Cape Fear River. As a result of his efforts, particularly with Fort Fisher at the river's mouth, Confederate blockade runners were able to use the port of Wilmington almost until the end of the war. For his efforts he was promoted to major general in February 1863.

In July 1863, Whiting was given command of the Department of North Carolina. With his efforts concentrated primarily on protecting the southern coast of the state, this new responsibility stretched his already thin resources. As a result, in November 1863, the North Carolina military situation was reorganized by the Confederate War Department, and Whiting was given command of the District of Cape Fear and Wilmington Defenses.

Whiting still found his resources strained, and throughout the end of 1863 and the early months of 1864 he repeatedly asked for reinforcements. He continued to try to make his position stronger with what he had, when to his dismay he was summoned to Petersburg, Virginia, in May 1864 to help with the defenses there. During the campaign against Major General Benjamin Butler that resulted in the battle of Drewry's Bluff and the neutralizing of Butler's force at Bermuda Hundred, Whiting was ill and unable to carry out his part of the campaign. After it was over he requested and received a transfer back to Wilmington.

Back where he wanted to be, all Whiting could do was wait and hope that the Union did not attack his well-built but undermanned defenses. With Wilmington being one of the only ports left to blockade runners and the only port of entry left for supplies destined for Robert E. Lee's Army of Northern Virginia, it was inevitable that the area would become a target. At the end of 1864, Benjamin Butler organized a combined navy-army expedition that attacked Fort Fisher at the end of December. The badly managed assault failed, and Butler returned to Virginia. A more capably led expedition was sent in January, however, and, after a brutal naval bombardment destroyed much of the fort, an assault carried the fort on 15 January 1865. During the bombardment, Whiting came to the fort to help with the defense and was there when the fort fell. He was badly wounded in the attack and was captured by the Union troops. At first his wounds were not considered fatal, and three days after the fall of the fort he was even able to write his report of the battle as a prisoner of war. He was taken to New York City, where he was confined on Governor's Island, and died there of complications from his injuries on 10 March 1865.

—*David S. Heidler and Jeanne T. Heidler*

See also Bermuda Hundred Campaign; Drewry's Bluff, Battle of; Fort Fisher; Gaines' Mill, Battle of.

For further reading:

Gragg, Rod. *Confederate Goliath: The Battle of Fort Fisher* (1991).

Robinson, Charles M. *Hurricane of Fire: The Union Assault on Fort Fisher* (1998).

Whiting, William Henry Chase. *Diary of a March from El Paso to San Antonio* (1902).

———. *Whiting Diary, March from Fredericksburg to El Paso del Norte* (1906).

WHITMAN, WALT[ER]
(1819–1892)
Poet, journalist, essayist

Walt Whitman's *Leaves of Grass* (1855–1892), his collection of poems *Drum-Taps* (1865), and his autobiographical prose *Specimen Days and Collect* (1882) are among the most celebrated literary works inspired by the American Civil War. Born in Huntington, New York, Whitman received only a few years of education in public schools. He went to work as a printer's devil for the *Long Island Patriot* in 1832 and after a time occasionally contributed stories to newspapers. His work in journalism was mixed with teaching stints in various Long Island schools. For an interval he lived in New Orleans while working for the *New Orleans Crescent*, but by the end of the 1850s he was back in New York City, editing and working for various newspapers. By then he had embarked upon a career as a poet, publishing *Leaves of Grass* in 1855, but he enjoyed such little success at it that he made ends meet by working with his father in construction.

The Civil War profoundly changed Walt Whitman. Seeking to embody the ideal American in his poetry, Whitman in the poem "To Thee Old Cause" claimed, "my book and the war are one." He was not an abolitionist, and he did not view the North and South as irreconcilable. Nevertheless, Whitman initially embraced the war as a rite of national purification in a time of materialism and political corruption.

In "Beat! Beat! Drums!", which Whitman wrote shortly after the battle of First Bull Run, the poet sounds a call to arms. Whitman, however, avoided military service; he continued to lead a bohemian life as a writer in New York. On 16 December 1862, however, Whitman learned that his brother George had been wounded at Fredericksburg. He immediately went to Virginia to find George already recovered from his injuries. Excited and moved by his experiences in the camps and hospitals, Whitman found a part-time job as a copyist in the Army Paymaster's Office to remain in Washington. He volunteered as a nurse's assistant in the hospitals, doing small acts of kindness for the men, writing letters for them, reading to them, and bringing them small gifts. Meanwhile, he made observations for the New York newspapers and kept an extensive diary.

Although not literally autobiographical, Whitman's experiences in Washington from 1862 to 1865 provided much of the material for *Drum-Taps*. Attempting to encapsulate the emotional experience of the war, the sequence of forty-three poems depicts several themes in particular: routine military activity ("Cavalry Crossing a Ford," "Bivouac on a Mountain Side," "An Army Corps on the March"), the comradeship of soldiers ("O Tan-Faced Prairie-Boy," "As I Lay With My Head in Your Lap Camerado"), and the human costs of war ("Vigil Strange I Kept on the Field One Night," "The Wound-Dresser").

Overall, *Drum-Taps* presents the transformation of patriotic militarism (both the poet's and the nation's) into a sense of grief for the wounded and dying. The central poem, "The Wound Dresser," marks this point of transformation: "Arous'd and angry, I'd thought to beat the alarum, and urge relentless war, But soon my fingers fail'd me, my face droop'd and I resign'd myself, To sit by the wounded and soothe them, or silently watch the dead." Patriotism and grief are united near the conclusion of the sequence, which seeks to reconcile the North and South: "my enemy is dead, a man divine as myself is dead, I look where he lies white-faced and still in the coffin—I draw near, Bend down and touch lightly with my lips the white face in the coffin."

Drum-Taps was published in a small edition by Whitman on 1 April 1865. After the assassination of Lincoln on 14 April, Whitman felt his poetic summing up of the war would be incomplete without some tribute to the Union's fallen helmsman. He soon added an appendix called *Sequel to Drum-Taps*, which contained several tributes to Lincoln, including "O Captain! My Captain!" and "When Lilacs Last in the Dooryard Bloom'd." To Whitman, the death of Lincoln was the final redemptive sacrifice of the war that enabled a rebirth of the nation and his own poetic voice.

Whitman was never again so inspired as a poet. He saw Gilded Age America as hopelessly corrupt, and he turned with nostalgia to the heroism and sacrifice of the Civil War years. Whitman increasingly regarded the Civil War as the central event in the unfolding of America's destiny, and he integrated *Drum-Taps* into *Leaves*. He eventually published his war diaries as *Memoranda During the War* and *Specimen Days and Collect*. As in *Drum-Taps*, Whitman's firsthand reflections in these works most often focus on everyday events, particularly the sufferings of common soldiers: "A New York Soldier," "A Secesh Brave," and "Ambulance Processions." They also include numerous sketches of subjects of historical interest: "Hospital Scenes," "Deserters," "Army Surgeons," "Female Nurses"; Whitman's descriptions of Lincoln are incomparably perceptive.

By the 1880s, commemoration of the Civil War became the central theme in Whitman's poetry and his public persona. In the 1870s and 1880s, on the anniversary of Lincoln's murder, he gave public readings of "The Death of Abraham Lincoln," an account of the assassination, which he usually followed with what became his most popular poem: "O Captain!" Although Whitman had been fired from a clerkship in the Department of the Interior in 1865 for being the author of an obscene book (*Leaves*), by 1886 Congress considered granting "the Good Gray Poet" a pension. By the time of his death in 1892, Whitman was regarded by many as the poet laureate of the Civil War.

—*William A. Pannapacker*

See also Cooke, John Esten; Emerson, Ralph Waldo; Longfellow, Henry Wadsworth; Thoreau, Henry David; Whittier, John Greenleaf.

For further reading:

Aaron, Daniel. *The Unwritten War: American Writers and the Civil War* (1973).

Allen, Gay Wilson. *The Solitary Singer: A Critical Biography of Walt Whitman* (1955; reprint, 1985).

Erkkila, Betsy. *Whitman the Political Poet* (1989).

Whitman, Walt. *Poetry and Prose* (1982).

———. *Walt Whitman's Civil War* (1960).

WHITTIER, JOHN GREENLEAF
(1807–1892)
Poet

John Greenleaf Whittier was considered by many of his contemporaries to be more of a versifying anti-slavery activist and editor than a significant literary figure. His position as an assistant editor with the anti-slavery newspaper the *National Era* provided him with an important role in the publication of *Uncle Tom's Cabin*. In his antislavery poems, his moral passion and familiar meters uniquely suited him to the important purpose of moving the public's emotions on the slavery question.

One of the most important relationships of Whittier's career was a result of his sister Mary's submission of one of his poems to the *Massachusetts Free Press* without his knowledge. The editor, abolitionist William Lloyd Garrison, was impressed with the young man's intellect and visited the Whittier farm in early 1827. During his visit, Garrison pleaded with the senior Whittier to send his son for more schooling. The additional urgings of editor Abijah W. Thayer of the local *Essex Gazette* (then the *Haverhill Gazette*) resulted in young Whittier's enrollment in the newly established Haverhill Academy in May 1827. He attended for roughly one year broken by stints teaching in local schools.

By January 1829, Whittier, with the assistance of Garrison, began the first of a career series of editorships with *The American Manufacturer* in Boston. From 1829 to 1860 he was employed in an editorial capacity by a variety of local and national periodicals that ranged from *The Emancipator and Anti-Slavery Record* in New York to the *National Era*. The *Pennsylvania Freeman* was burned in 1838 by a mob infuriated in part by his antislavery editorials. Harriet Beecher Stowe's *Uncle Tom's Cabin* was serialized in 1851–1852 under the editorship of

Whittier in the *National Era* published by the Foreign and American Anti-Slavery Society in Washington, D.C. Along with his editorials, he continued to produce poems on slavery and general topics for newspapers and periodicals.

His popular literary fame began with the newspaper poems and was extended by the publication of *Legends of New England* in 1831. His use of his farm boyhood and native region in such poems as "Barefoot Boy" and "Snow-Bound" made him a cultural force in nineteenth-century America. Whittier's audience was more often the newspaper reader than the elite educated reader of a Longfellow or Hawthorne, but his popularity in the public press and in the schoolroom provided him with broad influence that he used to good effect in his abolitionist work.

Whittier's own writings to promote the abolition of slavery began with the publication in 1833 of his *Justice and Expediency*. When Daniel Webster supported the 1850 Compromise and the hated Fugitive Slave Law, Whittier aimed a poetic blast at him in "Ichabod" that is a full measure of the heat that the normally calm Quaker could summon when he felt condemnation was justified. His equally strong "Massachusetts to Virginia"—written in 1843 in response to Whittier's reading of the case of George Latimer, an escaped slave captured in the North and returned to Virginia—aroused public opinion on the issue. In 1846 his antislavery poems were collected and published as *Voices of Freedom*.

Whittier also was involved in politics, successfully seeking elective office as a member of the Massachusetts House of Representatives in 1835–1836, serving as a lobbyist, and helping to found the Liberty Party in 1839. He was an early member of the Free-Soil Party and finally joined the newly formed Republican Party in 1856. He convinced Charles Sumner to stand for election as U.S. senator from Massachusetts. He often remarked that his duties as a presidential elector from Massachusetts in 1860 and 1864 allowed him the unique experience of voting four times for Lincoln as a citizen and as an elector. His attitude toward the Civil War was conflicted. He broke with old friend Garrison when the sectional crisis grew violent and offended his Quaker values. When war was declared, Whittier firmly supported a Union victory and the freedom it would bring to the enslaved while expressing real torment over warfare itself.

Whittier's health was often poor, and he remained a bachelor all his life. A devout Quaker involved in a number of moral reform movements, he shunned social events that involved alcohol or tobacco and theatrical plays. After the war, with the abolitionists' task done and his own literary reputation established, Whittier devoted his last two decades to a quiet life of writing in the homes of various family members and friends. He died on 7

September 1892 at the home of his niece in Hampton Falls, New Hampshire.

—*Gretchen A. Adams*

See also Abolitionist Movement; Abolitionists; *Uncle Tom's Cabin.*

For further reading:
Wagenknecht, Edward. *John Greenleaf Whittier: A Portrait in Paradox* (1967).
Woodwell, Roland H. *John Greenleaf Whittier: A Biography* (1985).

WICKHAM, WILLIAMS CARTER
(1820–1888)

Confederate general and congressman

Born to William Fanning Wickham and Ann Carter Wickham in Richmond, Virginia, Williams Carter Wickham was educated at the University of Virginia, where he studied law. Along with his law practice in Hanover County, Virginia, Wickham also became involved in Virginia Whig politics. He served several terms in the Virginia legislature before becoming a Hanover County judge and then returning to the state senate on the eve of the Civil War.

Wickham opposed secession and, as a member of the Virginia Convention called to consider the issue, voted against the secession of the state. After Abraham Lincoln's call for volunteers, the measure carried in spite of the opposition of Unionists such as Wickham. He accepted the vote and immediately raised a cavalry company to aid in the defense of the state. Called the Hanover Dragoons, Wickham's unit fought at First Bull Run. Two months later, Wickham was promoted to lieutenant colonel of the 4th Virginia Cavalry.

Wickham fought in only the first stages of the Peninsula campaign. He received a severe wound at Williamsburg and was sent home to recuperate. While at home, a Union patrol entered his home and made him a prisoner. He was soon exchanged and in August promoted to colonel of the 4th Virginia, serving in the brigade of Brigadier General Fitzhugh Lee. Wickham led his regiment in the Second Bull Run campaign and at Antietam, but was wounded again in the fall of 1862. He returned to duty in time for the battle of Fredericksburg that December. He also fought at Chancellorsville, where the 4th guarded Lee's right flank, and at Brandy Station, where Wickham's command was cut in two and almost defeated in detail. Wickham led his men north with Jeb Stuart shortly afterward and took little part in the battle of Gettysburg. In September 1863, Wickham was promoted to brigadier general.

Wickham commanded his brigade during the Bristoe Station and Mine Run campaigns. In February and March 1864, his brigade participated in the defeat of the Judson Kilpatrick–Ulric Dahlgren raid on Richmond. In the spring of 1864, Wickham fought in the battles of the Wilderness, Spotsylvania, Yellow Tavern, and Cold Harbor before accompanying Jubal Early on his Shenandoah Valley campaign in the late summer of 1864.

Wickham had been elected to the Second Confederate Congress, defeating a former strong secessionist for the seat. Though he seldom attended congressional sessions, he was considered a member of the conservative faction in Congress and generally opposed the measures proposed by Jefferson Davis. He served on the Military Affairs Committee and tried to use his influence to bring about a stronger military policy for the Confederacy. Believing by the fall of 1864 that he could do more good in the Confederate Congress than in the army, he resigned his commission and became more active in legislative affairs.

By the first of the year, Wickham had come to the conclusion that the Confederacy could not win the war and that therefore the best course was to try to negotiate a favorable peace. For that reason, he supported the initiative that resulted in the Hampton Roads Peace Conference. At the end of the war, Wickham believed that reconciliation could best be achieved through complete cooperation. To that end, he joined the Republican Party in 1865, one of the first former Confederates to do so. The result, however, was to anger his former colleagues.

In the postwar years, Wickham became prominent in business, primarily as a railroad executive. He retained his interest in politics and in the last years of his life returned to the Virginia Senate. He died on 23 June 1888 in Richmond.

—*David S. Heidler and Jeanne T. Heidler*

See also Brandy Station, Battle of; Kilpatrick-Dahlgren Raid; Virginia; Williamsburg, Battle of.

For further reading:
Alexander, Thomas Benjamin, and Richard E. Beringer. *The Anatomy of the Confederate Congress: A Study of the Influences of Member Characteristics on Legislative Voting Behavior, 1861–1865* (1972).

WIGFALL, LOUIS TREZEVANT
(1816–1874)

Confederate senator and general

The son of Levi Durand Wigfall and Eliza Thompson Wigfall, Louis Wigfall was born in Edgefield District, South Carolina. He was educated at the University of Virginia and South Carolina College. Upon his graduation from the latter institution, Wigfall studied law and opened a practice in Edgefield. Taking a keen interest in politics, Wigfall from the beginning of his political career became a strong proponent of disunion as the best way to protect Southern rights. He served briefly in the Second Seminole War and gained a small amount of military experience whose importance he would later exaggerate. Upon his return from Florida, he became a colonel in the South Carolina militia. Wigfall's political career also took a controversial turn that cast him in several duels, including one with Preston Brooks that left both men wounded.

In 1848 Wigfall moved to Marshall, Texas, where he continued his crusade for Southern independence. During the crisis that resulted in the Compromise of 1850, Wigfall served in the Texas legislature. He urged that the state secede rather than accept the compromise measures. In 1859 he took his crusade for Southern rights to the U.S. Senate.

After the election of Abraham Lincoln in the fall of 1860, Wigfall helped write the "Southern Address," calling for the unity and secession of the South. Against the strong opposition of Sam Houston, Wigfall worked hard to secure the secession of Texas. To advance his secessionist cause, in early 1861 he helped to block the Crittenden Compromise. He also wrote to South Carolina officials, strongly urging them to take Fort Sumter by force if necessary.

Even after the secession of Texas, Wigfall remained briefly in the U.S. Senate to report to the Confederacy on the Senate's actions. He resigned his seat on 23 March 1861 and immediately traveled to Baltimore, Maryland, where he recruited soldiers for the Confederate army, urging General P. G. T. Beauregard in Charleston to take the men he had recruited. In early April, Wigfall himself traveled to Charleston to offer his services to the Confederate military.

During the Confederate bombardment of Fort Sumter, Wigfall impetuously—though some labeled it bravery—rowed out to the fort to demand Major Robert Anderson's surrender. Wigfall gained a national reputation throughout the Confederacy for this bit of bravado. Soon he was made lieutenant colonel of the Texas Battalion, and later that fall he became the colonel and commander of the 1st Texas Infantry. He participated in an action against Union gunboats at Dumfries, Virginia, in September 1861. In October 1861, he was promoted to brigadier general and became the commander of the Texas Brigade. Throughout the remainder of 1861, Wigfall served between Richmond and Washington, though he did not see much action. While serving in the army, Wigfall also held a seat in the Provisional Confederate Congress, where he initially developed a close relationship with Confederate president Jefferson Davis.

During the fall of 1861, Wigfall was elected as one of Texas's Confederate senators, and in February 1862 he resigned his commission to take his seat. He served in the Confederate Senate for the remainder of the war.

Once permanently ensconced in the legislature, Wigfall quickly joined the opposition to the Davis administration. Davis was not prosecuting the war with sufficient vigor, Wigfall complained. He also believed that Davis did not adequately support his most competent officers, particularly Joseph E. Johnston and P. G. T. Beauregard. That Wigfall supported these two contentious officers fueled a growing animosity with the president.

Wigfall did support such Davis measures, however, as conscription, impressment, and the suspension of the writ of habeas corpus. Anything that would strengthen the military Wigfall believed was necessary for the survival of the Confederacy. Yet he opposed such measures that he believed would permanently strengthen the Confederate central government at the expense of the states. For example, he successfully opposed the creation of a Confederate supreme court.

By the summer of 1863, Wigfall became so disillusioned with Davis's management of the war that his opposition became strident. Blaming Davis for the loss of Vicksburg, Wigfall worked in the Confederate Congress to limit the president's war-making power. As a member of the Senate's Military Affairs and Foreign Affairs Committees, Wigfall also exerted considerable influence over Confederate policy. His growing power in the senate was revealed by the direct communication Robert E. Lee maintained with him, particularly on the issue of recruiting within Texas. Wigfall in turn supported a more important role for Lee in directing Confederate strategy and was partially responsible for Lee's elevation to overall Confederate commander in early 1865.

After the war, Wigfall fled to Texas and from Galveston to Great Britain rather than submit to Federal imprisonment. He lived there for seven years, returning to the United States in 1872. He lived briefly in Baltimore before returning to Texas. He died in Galveston on 18 February 1874.

—*David S. Heidler and Jeanne T. Heidler*

See also Congress, C.S.A.; Fire-eaters; Texas.
For further reading:
King, Alvy L. *Louis T. Wigfall, Southern Fire-eater* (1970).

WILCOX, CADMUS MARCELLUS
(1825–1890)
Confederate general

Cadmus Wilcox was born on 29 May 1825 in North Carolina. Two years later his family moved to Tennessee. Wilcox entered West Point in 1842, joining the famed class of 1846 and finishing fifty-fourth among fifty-nine. Like his classmates, Wilcox immediately went to the just-declared Mexican-American War. He fought with the 4th and 7th Infantry Regiments at Vera Cruz, Cerro Gordo, Chapultepec, and Mexico City, winning commission as second lieutenant of infantry and a brevet to first lieutenant for bravery. Routine assignments in Missouri, Florida, and Texas preceded Wilcox's 1852 return to West Point as instructor of infantry tactics. During a two-year medical leave from 1857 to 1859, Wilcox wrote *Rifles and Rifle Practice* (1859), the first such American opus, and enthusiastic reviews led West Point to adopt it as a textbook.

When Tennessee seceded in June 1861, Captain Wilcox was in New Mexico Territory with the 7th Infantry. He resigned his commission, became colonel of the 9th Alabama, and led it at First Bull Run in July 1861. Promotion to brigadier general in October 1861 brought command of an Alabama brigade, which Wilcox led successfully through the Peninsula campaign and the Seven Days' battles of the spring and summer of 1862. Holding interim division command at the triumph of Second Bull Run in August 1862, Wilcox earned praise from both Robert E. Lee and James Longstreet in their official reports.

Wilcox missed Antietam as a result of illness and held Lee's unengaged flank at Fredericksburg, thus losing those opportunities for advancement. At Chancellorsville in May 1863, while others swept down on the Federals in Jackson's slashing attack, Wilcox's brigade was well to Lee's rear, surveilling Banks' Ford on the Rappahannock River. Despite the tedium of his post, Wilcox, early on 3 May, observed Northern sentries opposite him carrying haversacks, suggesting future enemy movement. On his own initiative, Wilcox shifted his brigade to meet the Union advance at Salem Church. With a textbook demonstration of a holding action, Wilcox stalled superior Northern forces for hours while Lee concluded the engagement with Hooker's Army of the Potomac before coming to relieve Wilcox. Anything less than the perfection that Wilcox demonstrated at Salem Church would likely have resulted in the destruction of the Army of Northern Virginia. The normally reserved Lee heaped praise on Wilcox in his official report, and a prominent historian later asserted that Wilcox's performance was "a model of what an observant commander of a detached Brigade [sic] can...accomplish."

Two months later at Gettysburg on 2 July 1863, Wilcox again distinguished himself as his brigade led an assault that penetrated the center of the Union lines, but, faced with overpowering numbers in a Federal counterattack, he had to withdraw. On 3 July, Wilcox's brigade, though bloodied the day before, supported the climactic, unsuccessful charge led by his classmate George Pickett.

Finally winning well-deserved promotion to major general in August 1863, Wilcox proved himself a capable division commander through the hideously bloody Wilderness, Spotsylvania, and Petersburg campaigns of 1864 as Union forces under Ulysses S. Grant and George Gordon Meade relentlessly bludgeoned Lee's army. Despite heavy casualties in his divi-

sion, Wilcox sustained the morale of his men and had a relatively low desertion rate right up to Lee's surrender at Appomattox in April 1865.

Wilcox then escaped to Mexico with "Jo" Shelby and others but quickly came back to Washington, D.C., where, unmarried himself, he cared for the family of his late older brother. This responsibility caused Wilcox to refuse offers from foreign armies (Korea, Egypt), but fortunately, his friendships and popularity both North and South increased his employment prospects. Wilcox, who was a friend of Grant's and an attendant at Grant's wedding, held increasingly important positions in the federal government, finally being tapped by President Grover Cleveland in 1888 to lead the railroad division of the General Land Office, a position that Wilcox took after urgings from his friend Philip Sheridan.

"Beloved by all who came in contact with him [and a] good man of integrity...and truthfulness and always charitable in his speech," Wilcox, who died from injuries in a fall, went to the grave borne by both Union and Confederate friends. In 1892, his family published his *History of the Mexican War*, on which he was working when he died on 2 December 1890.

Frequently overshadowed by others, Wilcox nonetheless consistently demonstrated dependable skill in brigade and division command. The reputations of military geniuses from Alexander the Great to Douglas MacArthur rest in part on men such as Cadmus Wilcox.

—*Broeck N. Oder*

See also Gettysburg, Battle of; Salem Church, Battle of.

For further reading:

Couch, Darius N. "Obituary of Cadmus Wilcox." In *Twenty-Second Annual Reunion of the Association of the Graduates of the United States Military Academy* (1891).

Freeman, Douglas Southall. *Lee's Lieutenants: A Study in Command* (1942–1944).

Porter, James D. *Tennessee*. Vol. 8 of *Confederate Military History* (n.d.).

Sears, Stephen W. *Chancellorsville* (1996).

WILD, EDWARD AUGUSTUS
(1825–1891)

Physician, Union general

Edward Augustus Wild was born on 25 November 1825 in Brookline, Massachusetts. After taking his Harvard University degree in 1844, he attended Philadelphia's Jefferson Medical College, completing his studies there in 1847. He continued his education in Paris and served as a surgeon in the Turkish army during the Crimean War. He returned to a medical practice in Brookline, only to be drawn back to the military when the Civil War began. At the commencement of the war, he chose to serve his country in the infantry rather than the medical corps, and on 23 May 1861 he received a captain's

Edward Augustus Wild (*Library of Congress*)

commission in the 1st Massachusetts Volunteer Infantry. At the battle of Seven Pines, Wild's right hand was seriously wounded, leaving him the use of only two fingers and the thumb. Afterward, he helped recruit troops in his home state. On 21 August 1862, he received a colonel's commission to command the 35th Massachusetts Volunteer Infantry Regiment. On 14 September 1862, at the battle of South Mountain, he was wounded again, this time losing his left arm as a consequence.

On 13 April 1863, the War Department authorized Wild to recruit a brigade of ex-slaves in North Carolina, and on 24 April 1863 he was commissioned brigadier general of volunteers. He commanded his African Brigade on Folly Island near Charleston, South Carolina, from 11 August 1863 to 2 October 1863. He returned to North Carolina to complete the organization of his brigade and served in the Department of Virginia and North Carolina under Benjamin F. Butler from November 1863 into January 1864. During December, he led a raid into North Carolina that provoked contro-

versy and hatred among Confederates. Wild and his men foraged, assisted runaway slaves, and skirmished with guerrillas, hanging one of them. Wild burned not only guerrilla camps but also the houses and barns of individuals he believed were in some way connected with the guerrillas. Furthermore, to ensure the proper treatment of captured African-American troops, he made hostages of some female relatives of the guerrillas.

Wild understood the nature of guerrilla warfare. He later explained that to end partisan warfare, one had to make war so distasteful to civilians that they would turn away guerrillas from their doors, thus depriving those "pirates" of the resources they needed to conduct their campaigns. Butler, responding to negative reaction to the raid, transferred Wild to command troops at Norfolk and Portsmouth, Virginia. In May 1864 Wild was back in the field commanding an African-American brigade in the Army of the James. During the spring 1864 drive on Richmond, Wild continued to treat Rebels with a degree of harshness that almost resulted in a court-martial. At the same time, on 24 May at Wilson's Wharf, he earned praise for stubbornly resisting an attack by superior forces commanded by Major General Fitzhugh Lee. Shortly thereafter, he was court-martialed and in July 1864 convicted for refusing to obey an order to replace his brigade quartermaster. Butler set aside that verdict on a technicality, but Wild lost his field command and did duty as a recruiter at Newport News. At the end of December 1864 Butler made him commander of an African-American division, and he continued as such until he became subject of another court-martial in February 1865 for a disruption caused by his conflict with another officer. He was acquitted, but on 27 March 1865 he was removed from divisional command and placed in charge of a brigade of African-American troops. In that capacity, Wild accompanied his men into Richmond on 3 April, being among the first Union troops to enter the city.

Wild's experiences during the war revealed a man who was brave and intelligent but at times imprudent, being quick to criticize fellow officers who held views different from his own. Furthermore, they show that he was committed not only to the Union cause but also to the cause of the freedpeople. In September 1863, while stationed at Folly Island, one of his African-American regiments was ordered to set up camp for a white regiment. The black regiment's officer objected through Wild, who endorsed the protest letter, noting that he had ordered his subordinates to disregard all such orders in the future. A few months later, in December, Wild warned an officer that "severe punishment" would be the consequence if anyone obstructed the flow of freedpeople into Union lines. On 31 January 1865, J. M. Mickly, a chaplain of a Pennsylvania regiment of African-American troops stationed near Richmond, wrote to the adjutant general of the Army expressing his thanks for the kindness of Wild, among other officers, in helping to facilitate his educational and missionary work.

On 31 May 1865 Wild was appointed to the Freedmen's Bureau to serve under Brigadier General Rufus Saxton, the assistant commissioner for South Carolina, Georgia, and, temporarily, Florida. On 16 June 1865, Saxton put him in charge of bureau operations on most of the Georgia mainland as his acting assistant commissioner. Wild arrived in Augusta, Georgia on 30 June 1865, with the charge to expand the presence of the bureau into the interior of the state.

Wild approached his duties ever suspicious that the erstwhile Confederates were only allowing their treasonous plans to lie dormant, awaiting the proper moment to obstruct the nation's new course. They required a firm if not harsh hand, Wild reasoned, or else peace would not be lasting. This assumption, reinforced by the inability of white Georgians to accept the full consequences of emancipation, guided Wild's brief tenure in the bureau. But Wild, one of the most radical of bureau officers, also had constructive ideas for guiding his actions. He hoped to eliminate all discriminatory treatment of the freedpeople. To that end, he attempted to end the use of the word *colored* in copies of bureau documents and in newspaper reports of bureau claims proceedings because he believed that such distinctions were the cause of more serious acts of discrimination. Furthermore, he was committed to seeing the freedpeople established as landholders and he understood the importance of the bureau's charge to facilitate their education. To further these ends, Wild expected to confiscate all state and county property. He believed such property was made subject to confiscation by Georgia's participation in the rebellion. Wild even planned to confiscate the state's rail system. In Wilkes County, a place where he believed ex-slaveholders still tried to deprive their former slaves of their freedom, he attempted to put his plans into action with disastrous consequences for his own military career. In mid-July 1865, he arrived at the county seat, Washington, and seized several buildings, among them the county courthouse, which he turned over to the American Missionary Association for use as a schoolhouse. He evicted the wife of Confederate politician-soldier Robert Toombs from her property, expecting to divide the land into homesteads for the freedpeople. And he roughly treated a Wilkes County family to try to obtain information about some gold that had been stolen from the Confederate government. Unsurprisingly, before the end of Wild's tenure in Georgia, someone made an attempt on his life.

Wild's efforts at establishing the Georgia bureau failed primarily because of the agency's lack of resources.

But Wild's lack of subtlety and tact in his dealings with white Georgians and the officers of the military jurisdiction that overlapped his own also significantly contributed to his lack of success. By the end of the summer, white Georgians had made their complaints to the military, which was inclined to listen. Wild had already clashed with Major General James B. Steedman, the commander of the Department of Georgia, and his subordinates over the extent of the jurisdiction of the Freedmen's Bureau. Clearly, personal ideology determined how one judged Wild. Earlier in June 1863, one reporter noted that freedpeople in North Carolina "look upon General Wilde [sic] as the Moses sent by God to be their deliverer."

But in August 1865, after Wild had had time to make an impression in Georgia, Lieutenant Colonel Joseph S. Fullerton informed Freedmen's Bureau commissioner Oliver Otis Howard that Wild was an unpredictable character, concluding, "I really believe that he is a little crazy." Even after Wild had alienated the military, Saxton, an officer close to Wild in his beliefs about the freedpeople's needs and the bureau's duties, continued to defend his subordinate as being a man with "many redeeming traits of character & is earnest and energetic but lacking somewhat in system."

Nevertheless, Saxton finally removed Wild on or shortly after 12 September 1865. With a less radical bureau administration in place in Georgia after that date, Wild's activities continued to be remembered as dangerous and extraordinary. In June 1866, a reporter wrote that Wild was "not a bad man at heart, not a negro swindler...but a raving fanatic, who sought to elevate the black man to the same footing with intelligent and educated whites by a mere say-so."

After his bureau service, Wild found new opportunities for making a living by becoming a superintendent of the Diana mine in Austin, Nevada. He later became involved in mining enterprises in South America. He died on 28 August 1891 in Medellín, Colombia.

—*Paul A. Cimbala*

See also Freedmen's Bureau; Guerrilla Warfare; Saxton, Rufus; Steedman, James B.; United States Colored Troops.

For further reading:

Berlin, Ira, Joseph P. Reidy, and Leslie S. Rowland, eds. *Freedom: A Documentary History of Emancipation, 1861–1867. Series 2: The Black Military Experience* (1982).

Cimbala, Paul A. *Under the Guardianship of the Nation: The Freedmen's Bureau and the Reconstruction of Georgia, 1865–1870* (1997).

Glatthaar, Joseph T. *Forged in Battle: The Civil War Alliance of Black Soldiers and White Officers* (1990).

Longacre, Edward G. "Brave, Radical, Wild: The Contentious Career of Brigadier General Edward A. Wild." In *Civil War Times Illustrated* (June 1980).

U.S. War Department. *The War of the Rebellion: A Compilation of the Official Records of the Union and Confederate Armies* (1880–1901).

WILDER, JOHN THOMAS
(1830–1917)
Union general

Born to Reuben Wilder and Mary Merritt Wilder in Hunter Village, New York, John Thomas Wilder moved to Ohio and then Indiana as a young man and became a millwright in an iron foundry. At the outbreak of the Civil War he was living in Indiana and there enlisted in an artillery battery as a private but was elected the unit's captain on 22 April 1861. Less than two months later, the governor of Indiana made Wilder lieutenant colonel of the 17th Indiana Infantry.

Wilder saw his first action in the campaign in western Virginia in the fall of 1861. At the end of the year, Wilder and the 17th came under Don Carlos Buell and the Army of the Ohio. As a result, Wilder fought on the second day of the battle of Shiloh. He continued in command of the 17th during the advance on Corinth, for which he was commended for his zealousness in the performance of his duty.

During the summer of 1862, Wilder was given command of a mounted brigade. Wilder was able to secure Spencer repeating rifles for his mounted troops, thus forever distinguishing his men from other mounted infantry. In September 1862 during Braxton Bragg's invasion of Kentucky, Wilder found himself in command of the defenses of Munfordville, Kentucky, on the Green River. When initially attacked by a Confederate force commanded by Brigadier General James R. Chalmers, Wilder held on. Chalmers, however, knew that a much larger force under Simon Bolivar Buckner would arrive soon and suggested to Wilder that in order to avoid further bloodshed he should surrender. Wilder replied to Chalmers that if the Confederate general was so interested in preventing further bloodshed, he should not come within range of Wilder's guns. Unfortunately for Wilder, Buckner arrived soon after and demanded the Union force surrender. Wilder did not want to comply, but he also was uncertain as to the size of the Confederate force. He requested a meeting with Buckner and took the Confederate commander aback by asking his advice about whether or not Buckner would surrender under similar circumstances. Buckner refused to say, but did allow Wilder an opportunity to see the number of Confederates and their artillery, after which Wilder surrendered.

After his exchange, Wilder was back in command of his reconstituted mounted brigade in Tennessee. In the early months of 1863 he operated out of Murfreesboro. He skirmished with Confederates at Woodbury, Tennessee, on 24 January and from 1 to 8 April led an expedition from Murfreesboro to Lebanon, Carthage, and Liberty, Tennessee, looking for horses. His mission accomplished, the brigade returned to Murfreesboro.

During the Tullahoma campaign of June 1863, Wilder and his brigade gained their greatest notoriety. At Hoover's Gap on 24 June Wilder and his men drove a Confederate force out of their positions and into full retreat. During the engagement, Wilder's brigade gained its nickname of "Wilder's Lightning Brigade." Wilder continued to command the brigade in the subsequent occupation of Chattanooga, leading the advance into the town. At Chickamauga, Wilder and the brigade acquitted themselves so well that George H. Thomas recommended Wilder for promotion to brigadier general of volunteers for his performance. The following summer, in August 1864, while leading his men during the Atlanta campaign, Wilder received a brevet promotion to brigadier general.

By that time, Wilder's business interests were suffering and it did not appear that his advancement in the army would occur at the rate he desired. As a result, in October 1864, Wilder resigned his commission. He returned home briefly but had come to see the area around Chattanooga as an industrial gold mine. He moved there and took advantage of the Union occupation to advance his business interests.

After the war, Wilder took advantage of the demand for iron and rails to establish an iron works and rail mill outside the town. As a natural offshoot of these activities, Wilder became very active in the railroad business in the South and Midwest. In addition to these business activities, Wilder was also very involved in civic affairs and held several positions in Chattanooga government, including mayor. In his later years, Wilder spent part of his time in semiretirement in Florida and died in the city of Jacksonville on 20 October 1917. His remains were returned to Chattanooga for burial.

—*David S. Heidler and Jeanne T. Heidler*

See also Munfordville, Battle of; Tullahoma Campaign.
For further reading:
Sunderland, Glenn W. *Lightning at Hoover's Gap: The Story of Wilder's Brigade* (1969).
———. *Wilder's Lightning Brigade…and Its Spencer Repeaters* (1984).
Williams, Samuel Cole. *General John T. Wilder, Commander of the Lightning Brigade* (1936).

WILDERNESS, BATTLE OF THE
(4–6 May 1864)

Major General Ulysses S. Grant took command of the Union army in March 1864. Immediately he set in motion a strategy designed not to occupy territory but to destroy the two remaining Confederate armies: Robert E. Lee's Army of Northern Virginia and the consolidated Western army under Joseph Johnston. To accomplish this, Grant sent William Sherman into Georgia after Johnston. Grant

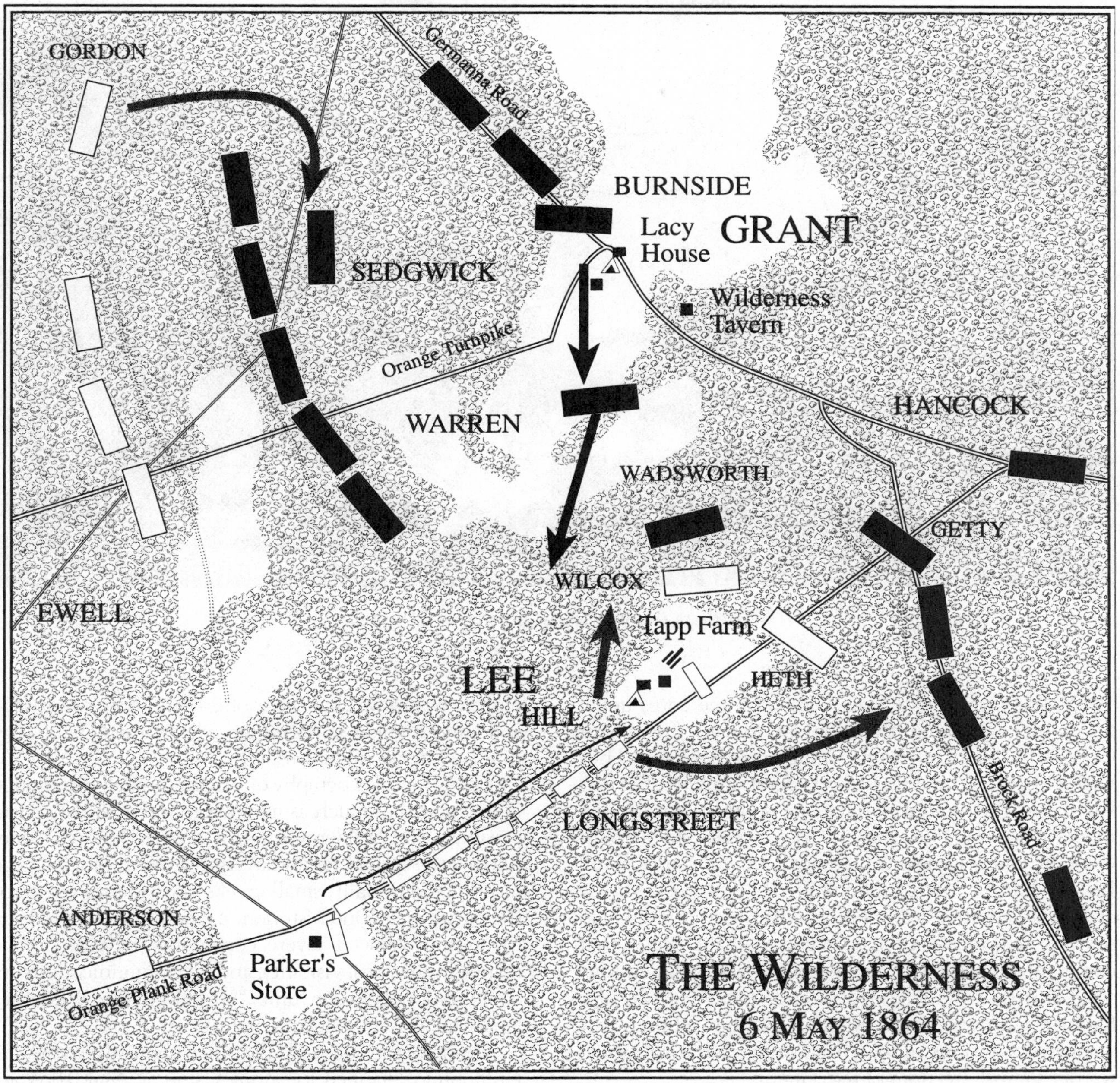

GORDON

Germanna Road

BURNSIDE

Lacy House

GRANT

SEDGWICK

Wilderness Tavern

Orange Turnpike

WARREN

HANCOCK

WADSWORTH

GETTY

EWELL

WILCOX

Tapp Farm

HETH

LEE

HILL

Brock Road

LONGSTREET

ANDERSON

Parker's Store

Orange Plank Road

THE WILDERNESS
6 MAY 1864

attached his own command to George Meade's Army of the Potomac and planned his concerted attack on Lee. Grant understood the importance of taking the Confederate capital at Richmond, but he was reminded that the Army of the Potomac had been unable to force Lee's Army of Northern Virginia out of its defensive position. As part of a more aggressive strategy, Grant put two additional Federal armies on the move in Virginia. Major General Franz Sigel was ordered to move south, up the Shenandoah Valley, to deprive Lee of much-needed food and rail support from the west. Major General Benjamin Butler was to move up the James

River to deny Lee support from the east and to look for an opportunity to join Meade.

As it prepared for the 1864 Overland campaign, Grant had four corps and Philip Sheridan's 12,000-horse cavalry at his disposal. All told, Grant had some 118,000 men available to him. Grant's II Corps was commanded by Major General Winfield Scott Hancock; V Corps was commanded by General Gouverneur Warren; and VI Corps was commanded by Major General John Sedgwick. The IX Corps, commanded by Major General Ambrose E. Burnside, was held back to protect the rebuilt Orange & Alexandria Railroad, which ran from Manassas Junction to Rappahannock Station.

Battle of the Wilderness (*Library of Congress*)

On the Confederate side, Lee had three corps under his command along the Rapidan River. Lieutenant General Richard S. Ewell commanded II Corps. They were closest to the advancing Federal army. A. P. Hill's III Corps was located upriver and south of Ewell. Ten miles south of Hill was I Corps under Lieutenant General James Longstreet. Major General James Ewell Brown "Jeb" Stuart commanded Lee's 8,000-horse cavalry. In all, the Army of Northern Virginia could field some 61,000 men—a force roughly half the size of that commanded by Grant. Lee's principal advantage in May 1864 was that he defended interior lines. He was also familiar with the territory, and Lee had chosen key defensive positions along rivers and roads that would restrict Grant's freedom of movement.

Roads were necessary to put men and materiel where they were needed. As such, the transportation network of Virginia's upper middle peninsula directed the course of battle. Two primary roads ran easterly from Orange Court House through Lee's winter encampment in the Wilderness to Fredericksburg. The more northerly of the two, the Orange-Fredericksburg Turnpike, passed through Chancellorsville. Two miles to the south, the Orange Plank Road passed through Spotsylvania. A third road, the Carpathian, also led eastward from south of Orange Court House, at Gordonsville, toward Spotsylvania. Each of these intersected with the Brock Road that the southbound federal army traveled. Hence, combat in the Wilderness was forced in defense of

narrow roadways that were often less than twenty feet wide and blanketed on either side by thickets of scrub pine and dense underbrush.

The physical geography of Virginia guided the conduct of operations as much as manpower and political considerations. The Wilderness was a heavily forested region filled with scrub pines and overgrown with tangled vegetation. Additionally, small creeks and swamps cut across the entire area. One historian, J. Tracy Power, noted that the terrain "placed severe constraints on troop movements, formations, visibility, and on communications and coordination between units." In short, the Wilderness landscape was a tactician's nightmare.

Meade's chief of staff, Brigadier General Andrew A. Humphreys, planned for a quick start in May 1864 and summed up the Union's tactical perspective: "By setting the whole army in motion at midnight, it might move so far beyond the Rapidan the first day that it would be able to pass out of the Wilderness and turn, or partially turn, the right flank of Lee before a general engagement took place." Grant moved southeasterly toward the Wilderness both to screen Washington, D.C., from a Confederate advance and to force Lee out of his winter quarters south of the Rapidan. Lee, on the other hand, chose the Wilderness as an area where the Army of the Potomac's superior numbers and artillery would be least effective.

On the morning of 4 May 1864, the Army of the Potomac moved south out of its winter encampment and crossed the Rapidan River. Warren and Sedgwick crossed

Evacuation of Point Royal, Virginia, May 1864 (Photograph by Timothy O'Sullivan / *Library of Congress*)

first with their V and VI Corps at Germanna Ford. Hancock's II Corps crossed six miles to the east at Ely's Ford. Each moved southward toward Germanna Plank Road, with Hancock making the farthest advance south to the Brock Road where it intersected with the Orange Plank Road. By 9 A.M., Lee's scouts confirmed that Grant's Federals were crossing the Rapidan on the Confederate right. The Army of Northern Virginia left its encampment at Orange and headed east to intercept Grant's army at the Wilderness.

Lee ordered Ewell to move out along the more northerly Orange Turnpike. Hill sent two divisions of his III Corps forward along the Orange Plank Road. Longstreet, returning from winter operations in Tennessee, was still some thirty miles west of the Wilderness. His instructions were to move along the Carpathian Road toward Spotsylvania.

Grant crossed the Rapidan around noon. He established a temporary headquarters at an abandoned farmhouse and, after receiving an intelligence report of Confederate movement, sent for Burnside's IX Corps, which had remained at Culpeper to protect the railroad. By leaving the rail relatively unprotected, Grant opened Confederate access to Washington. However, Grant

planned to apply considerable pressure to Lee's right flank to keep Confederate attentions focused eastward and diverted from the rail lines to the west. More significantly, Grant's push toward the southeast meant that his Federals would have access to Virginia's tidal rivers to maintain vital supply lines. The vast wagon train that kept Grant supplied over land slowed the army's movement south, and by early afternoon on 4 May, the Army of the Potomac had to stop. The Confederate and Union armies bivouacked within five miles of each other. Neither side realized how close the other was.

Grant understood the tactical disadvantage of confronting Lee in the Wilderness. Grant hoped to avoid a major encounter until he moved into open country, so he ordered his army to begin moving southward at 5:00 A.M. on 5 May. Grant instructed Warren to create a diversion along the Orange Turnpike to screen the Federals' push south. Warren deployed a division under Brigadier General Charles Griffin along the turnpike as Warren's V Corps continued south. Given the physical constraints of the countryside, Griffin's infantrymen had little room for maneuver within their lines. Likewise, artillery and cavalry units were of limited value in the dense underbrush and constricted roadways

Burial of soldiers near Fredericksburg, Virginia, May 1864 (*Library of Congress*)

of the Wilderness. Instead, sharpshooters, or skirmishers, proved the most valuable asset. Along the turnpike, Griffin's initial assault focused on the Confederate left.

Lee had kept Ewell and Hill on the defensive as he awaited the arrival of Longstreet. On the evening of 4 May, Lee had ordered Ewell to advance along the turnpike and engage the enemy, cautioning Ewell to limit his opening attack. Confederate and Federal forces formed up in a bramble-covered clearing known as Sanders's Field. When Griffin attacked, with the 140th and 146th New York Zouaves leading the charge across gullies and through matted brambles and tangled brush, three brigades from Ewell's II Corps opened fire. The New Yorkers pressed on, were reinforced, and drove the Confederates back.

Within minutes, the battlefield had erupted in fire, which compounded the terror and confusion. Captain H. W. S. Sweet of the 146th New York remembered that, "through the trees rolled dense clouds of battle smoke, circling about the green of the pines and mingling with the white of the flowering dogwoods. Underneath, men ran to and fro, firing, shouting, stabbing each other with bayonets, beating each other with the butts of their guns. Each man fought on his own resources, grimly and

desperately." The battlefield artist Alfred Waud sketched the grisly scene. He remembered that the "fire advanced on all sides through the tall grass, and taking the dry pines, raged up to their tops."

Finally, Brigadier General John B. Gordon's Georgia troops arrived to reinforce the Confederate right, and Ewell counterattacked. His advance stalled, and both sides spent the remainder of the day trying to restore order to their disintegrated lines.

Farther south, along the Orange Plank Road, the grisly battle was reenacted with different players. That afternoon, Federals advanced on the Confederate right, attacking Hill's III Corps. Lee had sent Hill to take and hold the junction of Orange Plank and Brock Roads. If Hill could accomplish this objective, he would cut the Army of the Potomac in half and close their only north-south route. Meade, fearful that Lee would succeed, sent a division from Sedgwick's VI commanded by Brigadier General Richard Getty to guard the intersection until Hancock could move north along the Brock Road from his position at Todd's Tavern.

The ensuing battle closely mirrored what Ewell and Warren had experienced earlier that day along the Orange Turnpike. The roadways, cramped with ordnance wagons and artillery pieces, made troop movement slow. The open fields were too overgrown to make effective use of either artillery or cavalry, and infantry lines were severely limited in their fire and maneuver. By the end of the day, Lee's lines were still intact but there was a considerable gap between Ewell and Hill.

Grant's primary objective on the second day of fighting was to exploit the opening in the Confederate line between the II and III Corps. Early in the morning, Warren repulsed a second counterattack by Ewell. To the south, Hancock moved on Hill's weakened position. Longstreet arrived to support Hill, pushed the Federals back, and began a major assault of his own in an effort to turn the exposed Federal left flank. The plan stalled when Longstreet was wounded by his own men. Fighting throughout the day was characterized by frontal assaults that achieved little, and darkness fell without either side gaining a tactical victory.

At the end of the day, casualty figures were high. In two days of fighting, Lee had lost some 10,000 to Grant's 18,000 killed, wounded, and captured. That evening, Grant sent word to President Lincoln "that whatever happens, there will be no turning back." He also dispatched a corps ten miles to the southeast to guard the critical junction at Spotsylvania Court House. On the Confederate side, spirits remained high, with the troops convinced that two days of hard fighting would send the Army of the Potomac back to Washington. Lee knew better, and he ordered I Corps, commanded by Major General Richard H. Anderson in Longstreet's absence, to Spotsylvania. Once again, the two armies made their way toward a new battlefield unaware of the other's presence.

—*Edward Ragan*

See also Richmond Campaign.

For further reading:

Gallagher, Gary W., ed. *The Wilderness Campaign* (1997).
Power, J. Tracy. *Lee's Miserables: Life in the Army of Northern Virginia from the Wilderness to Appomattox* (1998).
Rhea, Gordon C. *The Battle of the Wilderness, May 5–6 1864* (1994).
Scott, Robert Garth, ed. *Into the Wilderness with the Army of the Potomac* (1985).
Trudeau, Noah Andre. *Bloody Roads South: The Wilderness to Cold Harbor, May–June 1864* (1989).

WILKES, CHARLES
(1798–1877)
Naval officer and explorer

Born in New York City, Charles Wilkes began his naval service as a midshipman in 1818. His early career consisted of routine duty in various squadrons, survey work, and four years as superintendent of the Depot of Charts and Instruments. He first came to prominence as commander of the U.S. Surveying and Exploring Expedition of 1838–1842. This mission completed surveys of the Northwest Coast, Pacific islands, and Antarctica, which Wilkes was credited with being the first to identify as a continent. Despite being court-martialed over his treatment of the expedition's officers and men and receiving a reprimand, Wilkes was promoted to commander shortly after returning to the United States.

Wilkes spent the next eighteen years on special duty preparing the expedition's reports and received promotion to captain in 1855 even as many other officers were being dismissed from the navy due to lack of sea duty. Upon the outbreak of war, Wilkes was assigned to help destroy the Norfolk Navy Yard before it was abandoned to the Confederates and was one of the last Union officers to leave that facility. Shortly afterward, he received orders to return to sea in command of the screw frigate *San Jacinto*, then assigned to the anti–slave trade patrol with the Africa Squadron.

Wilkes took command of the *San Jacinto* in August 1861 in Monrovia, Liberia, and immediately sailed for the West Indies to search for Confederate raiders, particularly the CSS *Sumter*, commanded by Raphael Semmes. Unable to locate the *Sumter*, in early November Wilkes put into Cienfuegos, Cuba, for coal. While there, he learned that Confederate diplomats James Mason and John Slidell were en route to Europe in an attempt to open relations with Great Britain. Unable to capture the blockade-runner *Theodora* on which they traveled to Cuba, Wilkes discovered that the two would be traveling on the British mail steamer *Trent* for the next stage of their voyage. Determined to capture the pair and convinced of the legality of his action, Wilkes positioned his vessel in Old Bahama Channel. There, on 8 November, he stopped the British ship and forcibly removed the Confederate envoys and their secretaries before allowing the steamer and its enraged passengers to continue on their voyage.

This action led to Wilkes's being acclaimed a hero and receiving a vote of thanks from Congress as well as an official commendation from Secretary of the Navy Gideon Welles. Nevertheless, it was in fact a serious violation of Britain's rights as a neutral country and raised tensions between the United States and Great Britain. To appease the infuriated British, whose initial response included preliminary war preparations, the U.S. government formally disavowed the action, and both Mason and Slidell were released. Wilkes again had to face a court-martial to account for his actions. While he was officially reprimanded as a result of his actions, Wilkes's career seemed to suffer no direct harm from the incident.

Detached from his command when *San Jacinto* underwent a long overdue refit in late November, Wilkes served on the Board of Examiners until July 1862, when he received command of the James River Flotilla with the rank of commodore. On 29 August he transferred to command the Potomac River Flotilla, but just ten days

later he received orders to take command of the West Indies Squadron with the rank of acting rear admiral. In this assignment he led meager forces that unsuccessfully sought out blockade runners and Confederate raiders in the Caribbean region. His constant requests for reinforcements were ignored by the Navy Department.

Wilkes remained on duty even after being placed on the retired list for age in November 1862. At this time, his promotion to commodore was also rescinded, though he remained an acting rear admiral until detached on 1 June 1863. His replacement came about in part because of his failure to capture Confederate raiders and in part because he detained vessels for service in his squadron despite their orders to patrol in other areas.

In Welles's Annual Report for 1863, the secretary made disparaging remarks about Wilkes's conduct of the *Trent* Affair. Wilkes responded by publicly castigating Welles and as a result was again court-martialed in April 1864. Found guilty of disobedience of orders, insubordination, and other charges, Wilkes was sentenced to a public reprimand and a three-year suspension from duty. Although President Abraham Lincoln later reduced the suspension to one year, Wilkes never again saw active service at sea.

After the war, Wilkes twice served briefly on active duty in connection with the reports of the Exploring Expedition, receiving promotion to rear admiral on the retired list in July 1866. He died 8 February 1877 and in 1920 was reburied in Arlington National Cemetery.

—Stephen C. Svonavec

See also Great Britain; *Trent* Affair.

For further reading:
Anderson, Bern. *By Sea and by River: The Naval History of the Civil War* (1962).
Fowler, William M., Jr. *Under Two Flags: The American Navy in the Civil War* (1990).
Warren, Gordon H. *Fountain of Discontent: The* Trent *Affair and Freedom of the Seas* (1981).

WILLCOX, ORLANDO BOLIVAR
(1823–1907)
Union general

Born to Charles Willcox and Almira Rood Powers Willcox in Detroit, Michigan, Orlando Bolivar Willcox was educated locally before receiving an appointment to the U.S. Military Academy in 1843. He graduated eighth of thirty-eight in the class of 1847. After graduation and commissioning into the artillery, Willcox was sent immediately to Mexico, where he arrived too late to fight in the Mexican-American War. Over the next ten years, Willcox served at a variety of posts in New Mexico and Massachusetts as well as fighting in the Third Seminole War. He resigned his commission in 1857 to begin the practice of law in Detroit.

At the outbreak of the Civil War, Willcox accepted a volunteer commission as the colonel of the 1st Michigan. He led his regiment to Washington, D.C., where they participated in the expedition to take control of Alexandria, Virginia, at the end of May 1861. They then became a part of Irvin McDowell's campaign against the Confederate position at Manassas Junction. Before the commencement of the march toward Manassas, because of his previous military experience, Willcox was given command of 2d Brigade, 3d Division. In the attack on Henry House Hill, Willcox was wounded and captured. Thirty-four years later Willcox was awarded the Medal of Honor for his actions on 21 July 1861.

Unfortunately for Willcox, he was one of only a few high-ranking prisoners in the early months of the war. Just a day after the battle of First Bull Run, the merchant vessel *Enchantress* was captured with its Confederate prize crew aboard. The CSS *Jeff Davis* had taken the ship. The Federal government threatened to hang the crew as pirates rather than treat them as prisoners of war. The Confederate government then removed from the status of prisoners of war the six Federal colonels in its possession, including Willcox, and seven other officers and threatened to execute them if the Federals executed the Confederate crew. Federal courts eventually ruled that the Confederates were prisoners of war, but the delay in the decision prevented Willcox from being exchanged for more than a year.

Upon his release from Confederate custody on 19 August 1862, Willcox was promoted to brigadier general with a date of rank of 21 July 1861. Given command of a division of IX Corps under Ambrose Burnside, Willcox fought at South Mountain and then at Antietam at the bridge that would later bear his corps commander's name. At Fredericksburg, Willcox commanded IX Corps. When Burnside was made the commander of the Army of the Ohio in early 1863 and IX Corps was transferred to that theater, Willcox was transferred as well.

Over the next few months, Willcox occupied several positions within the Army of the Ohio. In April he took command of the District of Central Kentucky, headquartered at Lexington. During the summer he was sent to Indianapolis to command the District of Indiana and Michigan. This command allowed him to make several short visits home to Detroit. By September he was back with the Army of the Ohio and in command of the left wing later in the year in the Knoxville campaign.

In early 1864 Willcox assumed temporary command of IX Corps. When Burnside and IX Corps were summoned east to participate in Ulysses S. Grant's Virginia campaign against Robert E. Lee, Willcox assumed command of a division of IX Corps. He led his division at the Wilderness, Spotsylvania, and Cold Harbor. Though he and his division fought in IX Corps's debacle at the Crater, Willcox did not receive the condemnation received by a lot of many high-ranking officers in the corps. He remained in command of his division upon the removal of Burnside as commander, and he remained a division commander in IX Corps for the remainder of the war.

Willcox fought in many of the major engagements during the siege of Petersburg, distinguishing himself at Poplar Springs Church in the fall of 1864. He also led his division in the final attack against Lee's positions at Petersburg on 2 April 1865.

After Lee's surrender, Willcox was placed in command of the District of Washington. In June the commander of the Army of the Potomac, George Gordon Meade, recommended Willcox for promotion to major general of volunteers. He received brevet promotions to that rank in both the volunteer and regular army. In July 1865 he was sent to the Department of the Ohio.

Willcox left the army in 1866 with the mustering out of the volunteer force. He practiced law in Detroit for several months before being offered an appointment as the colonel of the 29th Infantry. After serving briefly in Virginia during Reconstruction, Willcox was sent to California as the colonel of the 12th Infantry. After that assignment, he served as the commander of the Department of Arizona in a campaign against the Apache. In 1886 Willcox was promoted to brigadier general, and he retired the following year as the commander of the Department of the Missouri. After his retirement, Willcox lived for a while in Washington, D.C., before moving to Ontario, Canada. He lived there from 1905 until his death on 10 May 1907 in Coburg, Ontario.

—*David S. Heidler and Jeanne T. Heidler*

See also Bull Run, First Battle of; *Enchantress* Affair; Petersburg Campaign; Poplar Springs Church.
For further reading:
Davis, William C. *Battle of Bull Run: A History of the First Major Campaign of the Civil War* (1977).
Trudeau, Noah Andre. *Bloody Roads South: The Wilderness to Cold Harbor, May–June 1864* (1989).

WILLIAMS, ALPHESUS STARKEY
(1810–1878)
Union general

Alphesus S. Williams was born in Deep River, Connecticut, on 20 September 1810. His father died when Alphesus was eight years old, so the boy was raised by relatives. Williams attended Yale College and graduated from the school in 1831. After traveling in Europe, Williams went to New York for legal studies in 1836. Williams moved to Detroit, Michigan, which would become his home for the rest of his life. He entered into a law practice and married Jane Pierson in 1839. During the period 1840–1847, Williams was involved in several business ventures and was elected a county probate judge.

During the Mexican-American War, Williams found a position in the 1st Michigan Volunteers. He was appointed lieutenant colonel, but his unit arrived on the scene too late to see any major combat. Instead, it guarded supply lines from guerrillas. In 1848 Williams's regiment returned home. Soon thereafter Williams's wife died in Detroit. As before the war, Williams again became involved in several business ventures, such as the Michigan Oil Company. In addition, Williams served in several elected positions within Detroit and Wayne County, Michigan. His military experience led to his attainment of the rank of major of the Detroit Light Guard and the appointment as president of the State Military Board.

In August 1861 President Abraham Lincoln appointed Williams brigadier general of volunteers. He was sent to Washington, D.C., in October 1861 and was assigned a brigade. General Williams was soon given command of a division in the Shenandoah Valley of Virginia. He performed creditable service as a divisional commander during the Shenandoah campaign of 1862, especially at the battle of Winchester, Virginia, on 25 May 1862. Later, on 9 August 1862, during the battle of Cedar Mountain, Virginia, Williams's division routed the Stonewall Brigade. By the time of the Second Bull Run campaign, Williams's division had become a part of II Corps, Major General John Pope's Army of the Rappahannock. When this army was disbanded, Williams's division found itself assigned to XII Corps commanded by Major General J. K. F. Mansfield.

During the Antietam campaign, it was General Williams's troops who found the famous Lost Order. During the battle of Sharpsburg, Maryland, on 17 September 1862, Mansfield was killed, and Williams moved up to corps commander, holding that position until Major General Henry Slocum replaced him. Missing the fighting at Fredericksburg, Williams and his division performed excellent service at the battle of Chancellorsville in May 1863 by stopping Lieutenant General Thomas "Stonewall" Jackson's flank attack. Later, at the battle of Gettysburg, General Williams (as acting corps commander) was responsible for the excellent defense of Culp's Hill and for securing the Federal right flank.

With the transfer of XI and XII Corps to the West, Williams and his division spent the next six months guarding the supply lines of the Army of the Cumberland. Soon Williams's division became a part of XX Corps, which was created by consolidation of both eastern corps. Williams and his division drew the lion's share of the fighting during the early stages of the Atlanta campaign starting in May 1864. By the fall of Atlanta in September 1864, Williams had been elevated

to command of the corps due to Major General Henry Slocum's promotion. Williams led this corps through the Savannah campaign (the March to the Sea) and the Carolinas campaign. At the battles of Averasboro (16 March 1865) and Bentonville (19–21 March 1865), Williams's corps performed excellent service in defeating deployed Confederate brigades at Averasboro and in beating back Confederate assaults at Bentonville. Unfortunately, Williams was soon relieved of command by Major General Joseph Mower and was returned to divisional command. He finally received a brevet promotion to major general on 12 January 1866, before being mustered out of service.

In 1866 Williams was appointed to a three-year term as minister to San Salvador. After returning to the United States, he ran unsuccessfully for governor of Michigan. However, he was elected to the U.S. House of Representatives in 1874 and again in 1876. In 1873 Williams married Martha Tillman, the widow of James Tillman. Williams died on 21 December 1878, while serving in the U.S. Congress. He was laid to rest in Elmwood Cemetery in Detroit, Michigan.

—*William H. Brown*

See also Antietam, Battle of; Atlanta Campaign.
For further reading:
American Council of Learned Societies, ed. *Concise Dictionary of American Biography* (1964).
Faust, Patricia. *Historical Times Illustrated Encyclopedia of the Civil War* (1986).
Malone, Dumas, ed. *Dictionary of American Biography*, vol. 20 (1936).

Quaife, Milo M., ed. *From the Cannon's Mouth: The Wartime Letters of Alphesus S. Williams* (1959).
Warner, Ezra J. *Generals in Blue, Lives of Confederate Generals* (1959; reprint, 1987).

WILLIAMSBURG, BATTLE OF
(4–5 May 1862)

In the spring of 1862, Major General George B. McClellan, commander of the Army of the Potomac, decided on a campaign up the Virginia Peninsula to capture the Confederate capital of Richmond. This major offensive, known as the Peninsula campaign, was designed to bring the Civil War to a close by means of a quick and decisive Union victory.

The Peninsula campaign began in earnest on 2 April 1862, with the arrival of McClellan at Fort Monroe, Virginia. This position, located at the confluence of the James and York rivers, served as the base of operations for the assault on Richmond. Fort Monroe afforded McClellan the ability to guard his flanks by gunboat as the Army of the Potomac moved up the peninsula. Only two towns, Williamsburg and Yorktown, and two lines of defensive works stood between this starting point and the Confederate capital, located approximately seventy-five miles to the northwest. At the time of McClellan's arrival, there was only one Confederate army between the Army of the Potomac and Richmond, the Army of the Peninsula commanded by Major General John B.

The battle of Williamsburg (*Library of Congress*)

General Kearny at the battle of Williamsburg (*Library of Congress*)

Magruder. This force of 19,000 Confederate troops was all that initially protected Richmond from McClellan and more than 100,000 Union troops.

On 12 April, Confederate general Joseph Johnston was recalled to Richmond and then ordered by President Jefferson Davis to the peninsula with his entire army to support Magruder in his effort to halt the coming Union assault. Johnston assumed command of the combined Confederate forces upon his arrival in Yorktown and initiated plans for a retreat up the peninsula to the defenses surrounding Richmond.

On 4 April, General McClellan and the Army of the Potomac set out for Yorktown, the anchor of the Warwick River Line on the York River. Upon their arrival, Union troops immediately began preparations for a siege of the town. The Army of the Potomac laboriously constructed entrenchments and bombarded Yorktown for several weeks. An attempt to break the Warwick River Line was carried out at Damn No. 1 near Lee's Mill, south of Yorktown. Confederate forces held off an assault by the 3d, 4th, and 6th Vermont Regiments lead by Brigadier General William "Baldy" Smith at the battle of Burnt Chimneys on 16 April 1862. McClellan resumed plans for the siege of Yorktown. On the morning of 4 May, he found that Johnston had evacuated Yorktown the previous evening and had begun his retreat to the Richmond defenses.

Due to heavy rains, Johnston's withdrawal from Yorktown was extremely slow. The roads were a muddy quagmire from the downpour and flooded with troops, supplies, horses, and artillery pieces. The Confederate retreat by way of the Yorktown and Hampton Roads made the Union advance over these same routes an even more arduous task. However, on 4 May, Brigadier General George Stoneman, commanding an advanced guard of Union cavalry, threatened Johnston's rear guard. The rear-guard troops were forced to defend the Confederate retreat at the Williamsburg Line, just outside of the town of Williamsburg. This defensive line of redoubts was oriented around a central bastion, Fort Magruder, at the junction of the Yorktown and Hampton Roads.

The engagements of 4 May 1862 consisted mainly of cavalry clashes on the roads leading to Williamsburg and several small artillery duels. The heaviest fighting of the day took place when Brigadier General Lafayette McLaws, in command of the Confederate rear guard, ordered a charge and successfully overwhelmed the Union cavalry and accompanying artillery under Brigadier General Philip St. George Cooke.

On the morning of 5 May 1862, Union brigadier general Joseph Hooker, commanding the 2d Division of Brigadier General Samuel Heintzelman's 3d Corps, attacked Fort Magruder. Hooker was repulsed with heavy casualties, but he was remembered for his inspired attacks. Major General James Longstreet assumed command of the Confederate rear guard on 5 May, because General Johnston sent McLaws up the peninsula to West Point in anticipation of a pincer movement by McClellan. Longstreet ordered a counterattack on Hooker's retreating forces; however, Brigadier General

Philip Kearny's division arrived to reinforce and stabilize the Union line.

The battle of Williamsburg is best remembered for the fighting that took place on the Confederate left flank at the redoubts near the York River. Brigadier General Winfield Scott Hancock, commanding a brigade of Brigadier General Erasmus Keyes's IV Corps, crossed Cub Dam Creek and occupied two redoubts. From this position, Hancock's artillery assaulted the Confederate rear and flank. To silence Hancock, Longstreet authorized the 24th and 38th Virginia and the 23d and 5th North Carolina of Brigadier General Jubal Early's brigade to flank Hancock's position. The Confederate charge, lead by Early and Major General D. H. Hill, was a complete failure. The lines of the 24th Virginia and 5th North Carolina were ripped apart by Union fire during the initial charge, as well as the retreat that followed. Numerous officers were among the wounded, including Jubal Early.

During the night of 5 May, Longstreet withdrew the Confederate rear guard and joined Johnston's retreat up the Virginia Peninsula. The battle of Williamsburg was the first major engagement of the Peninsula campaign of 1862, and both sides were quick to claim victory. Johnston, with casualties totaling 1,560 men, achieved his goal of a Confederate withdrawal. Although Union casualties totaled 2,239, McClellan claimed victory and continued the Peninsula campaign toward the Southern capital. However, General McClellan had once again failed to engage the Confederate army in a decisive battle.

—*Brock A. Magoon*

See also Longstreet, James; McLaws, Lafayette; Peninsula Campaign; Yorktown.

For further reading:
Hastings, Earl C., Jr., and David S. Hastings. *A Pitiless Rain: The Battle of Williamsburg, 1862* (1997).
Longstreet, James. *From Manassas to Appomattox: Memoirs of the Civil War in America* (1896; reprint, 1960).
Sears, Stephen W. *To the Gates of Richmond: The Peninsula Campaign* (1992).
Wheeler, Richard. *Sword over Richmond: An Eyewitness History of McClellan's Peninsula Campaign* (1986).

WILLICH, AUGUST (VON)
(1810–1878)
Union officer

Born in Braunsberg (Gorzyn) Prussia, August von Willich grew up in the house of the noted theologian Friedrich Schleiermacher. Willich relinquished his Prussian Army career (he was a Premierleutnant; that is, a first lieutenant) and his noble title to become a freethinker and a communist. In the German revolutions of 1848–1849, Willich was a leading figure, commanding the pan-European Besancon Workers' Legion in the last campaign for the democratic constitution in May–July 1849. His aide-de-camp was Friedrich Engels. After the defeat, Willich's unit was the last to leave the country.

Exiled to London, Willich tried to raise a new army before ideological differences led to a split with Marx and Engels. They accused Willich of "social romanticism," spread rumors that he was an illegitimate offspring of the German royal family, and alternately claimed that Willich was a philanderer and a homosexual. There is no evidence for either claim.

Willich emigrated to the United States and worked in a Brooklyn shipyard and the U.S. Coastal Survey Bureau before becoming editor of the radical Cincinnati *Republikaner*. He was an influential socialist speaker, labor organizer, and Turnerbund activist. His prominence as a "Forty-eighter" made him a key figure during the secession crisis, rallying immigrants and political refugees to defend the principles of democracy, union, and equal human rights. His knowledge of tactics and his military skills stood him in good service during the Civil War. Willich served as adjutant and drillmaster for the 9th Ohio Infantry until he was appointed colonel of the 32d Indiana. Both regiments were raised among the immigrants and "Turnvereine" of Indiana, Kentucky, and Ohio. The 32d Indiana drilled in German according to the Prussian manual of arms.

At Rowlett's Station on 17 December 1861, the regiment held against superior numbers, and at Shiloh, where it had begun to waver under fire, Colonel Willich rode around its front and began drilling it in the manual of arms. The 32d rallied and charged successfully. Willich was brevetted brigadier general.

Captured at Stones River, Willich spent months in Libby Prison before he was exchanged. The reception given him by his brigade upon his return was triumphal. During the Tullahoma campaign his brigade took Liberty Gap. At Chickamauga, his units remained intact, and there is evidence that Willich was the first commanding officer to order his brigade forward in the charge up Missionary Ridge on 25 November 1863 during the battle of Chattanooga. In May 1864, a bullet at Resaca paralyzed his right arm, ending his career in the field. Willich became commander of the District of Cincinnati, rejoining his corps only briefly in Texas before being mustered out as a brevet major general of volunteers in October 1865.

A stern disciplinarian in the field, Willich was a warm-hearted humanitarian. He always saw to it that his soldiers were not only well equipped but also adequately fed and rested. Willich was loved as much by his men—who affectionately called him "Papa Willich"—as he was sometimes eyed suspiciously by other officers. His suggestion to mobilize infantry units by transporting them on wagons went unheeded by military authorities; nor was

his system of a rolling advance in four ranks adopted. His English was the result of reading Shakespeare and educating himself, and he could be as temperamental as he was energetic. Some of his colleagues and even a few of his friends thought the avowed Communist a little crazy ("*naerrisch*"). Off duty, he would address his men as "citizen" (in the tradition of the French Revolution), and in winter camp he organized a series of educational lectures. The regimental hymn of the 32d Indiana was the "Marseillaise," with the German text by Freiligrath

After the war, Willich moved to St. Marys, Ohio. Politically he moved further in the direction of labor unionism and syndicalism and again became a noted speaker at workers' rallies, Turnfeste, and Fourth of July celebrations. Still, in 1870 Willich offered his services when the Franco-Prussian War started, even though William I had commanded the forces opposite Willich in 1849. When his offer was refused, he enrolled briefly at the University in Berlin.

In his later years, Willich devoted much time to cultural affairs, becoming one of the first members of the Hegel Society of the United States. Locally, he founded a Shakespeare Society and the "Schlabberhannes Clubb" [sic], a political discussion circle, and sponsored Schubert evenings. Willich never raised a family but spent much of his invalid's pension on candy for the local children. "Old General Willich" was a well-known figure in his adoptive home town and much mourned when he died unexpectedly on 23 January 1878.

—*Wolfgang Hochbruck*

See also German-Americans.
For further reading:
Diesbach, Alfred. "August von Willich." In *Badische Heimat* (1978).
Easton, Loyd. *Hegel's First American Followers: The Ohio Hegelians* (1966).
Rattermann, H. "General August Willich." *Der Deutsche Pionier* (1878–1879).
Stewart, Charles D. "A Bachelor General." In *Wisconsin Magazine of History* (1933).

WILMINGTON, NORTH CAROLINA

Wilmington, North Carolina, was the principal port of entry for blockade-running ships carrying supplies essential to the Confederacy's war effort. By the summer of 1864, Wilmington ranked second only to the capital of Richmond, Virginia, in importance to the South. The city's fall the following winter sealed the fate of the Confederacy.

Wilmington is located on the east bank of the Cape Fear River, about 26 miles from where the waterway empties into the Atlantic Ocean in southeastern North Carolina. Founded in 1732, Wilmington is one of the Tar Heel State's oldest communities and the seat of New Hanover County. In 1860, the "city by the sea" boasted a population of 9,552 people, one-third of whom were slaves and free blacks, making it the most populated city in North Carolina at the time. Wilmington grew from a small colonial trading post, at the point where the Cape Fear River and the Northeast Cape Fear River meet, to a bustling seaport with an active mercantile trade and an impressive array of industry.

Until the Civil War, the Lower Cape Fear's main industry was in naval stores—tar, pitch, and turpentine made from pine rosin—for the construction and maintenance of wooden-hulled vessels. Turpentine distilleries and tar kilns dotted the area's forested landscape. During the war cotton eclipsed naval stores as the region's major export.

Two ironworks thrived in wartime Wilmington—the Wilmington Iron and Copper Works and Clarendon Iron Works. Another metal fabricating shop appeared in the city by late September 1861. Established by Louis L. Froelich, the Wilmington Sword Factory (renamed the Confederate Arms Factory) produced swords, sabers, bayonets, lances, buttons, and accouterments for Southern forces. A destructive fire at the Wilmington plant in February 1863 compelled Froelich to move his arsenal to Kenansville, North Carolina.

Two commercial shipbuilding yards at Wilmington constructed vessels for the Confederate navy and repaired blockade runners. Beery Brothers Shipyard (designated the Confederate Navy Yard), owned and operated by Benjamin W. and William L. Beery, built small gunboats, floating batteries, torpedo launches, a submarine, and a Richmond-class ironclad—the CSS *North Carolina*. James Cassidey & Sons constructed a similar iron titan named the CSS *Raleigh*.

Confederate vessels helped defend Wilmington's harbor and interior lines of communication, which served as pipelines for forwarding reinforcements and imported goods and receiving food for Wilmington's residents and cotton for export to Europe. The Cape Fear River was navigable to Fayetteville, North Carolina, 100 miles northwest of Wilmington.

As important as the river were Wilmington's railroads. The Wilmington & Manchester indirectly linked the seaport to Charleston, South Carolina. The Wilmington, Charlotte & Rutherford Railroad traversed the Tar Heel State's piedmont to Charlotte and Rutherfordton. The Wilmington & Weldon Railroad ran northward to Weldon, North Carolina, where it connected to the Petersburg & Weldon Railroad into southeastern Virginia. By 1864 the Wilmington & Weldon Railroad served as the main supply route for General Robert E. Lee's Army of Northern Virginia.

Most of the supplies imported for Lee's army—firearms, artillery, ammunition and provisions—came in through Wilmington. More than a hundred sleek, stealthy

steamers operated in and out of the seaport during the war, excluding the sailing vessels employed as blockade runners early on. The success rate for runners at Wilmington was about 75 percent. The blockade runner *Hansa* made twenty runs through the Cape Fear blockade, making her the most successful blockade runner at the Carolina seaport. More blockade runners entered the Confederacy by way of Wilmington than all other Southern seaports combined. Yet little of the supplies remained in the Cape Fear area, as most were forwarded to factories and distribution centers in Virginia and Georgia.

Blockade runners also brought in coveted civilian goods, the sale or auction of which often made huge profits for investors. Traders, speculators, and entrepreneurs spent enormous amounts of money purchasing imported items in Wilmington, but few citizens profited from the business. In fact, critics claimed that the trade caused more problems—inflation, crime and disease—than benefits for the region. Residents blamed the blockade-runner *Kate* for bringing in yellow fever when she berthed at Wilmington's docks on 6 August 1862. By mid-September a full-blown epidemic gripped the town. When cold weather finally ended the pestilence in late November, at least 654 residents were dead of the infectious disease. City officials, headed by Mayor John Dawson, worked with the Cape Fear District military commander, Major General W.H.C. Whiting, to combat the growing problems. Even so, many families sought refuge elsewhere from the bawdy, frontierlike atmosphere of wartime Wilmington. Local residents recognized that blockade running was both life-saving and death-dealing to the Confederacy.

Blockade runners preferred trading at Wilmington because it was located near the British transshipment points of Bermuda and Nassau and because the Federal blockade of the Cape Fear was largely ineffectual. The Cape Fear River could be accessed by one of two passageways—Old Inlet (also called the Western Bar), the main entrance; and New Inlet, a shallow strait five miles to the northeast at the tip of a narrow sand peninsula called Federal Point. Bald Head Island and Frying Pan Shoals separated Old and New inlets, offering blockade runners a choice of entrance and exit from the harbor. The dual passageways made it virtually impossible for Union gunboats of the Cape Fear squadron to halt the clandestine maritime trade at Wilmington. Making it even more difficult for the U.S. Navy, Wilmington was located far upriver and out of range of naval bombardment.

To protect the Confederacy's most important blockade-running port at Wilmington, the blockade runners, the inlets, and the railroads, engineers built a vast network of forts, batteries, and fieldworks throughout southeastern North Carolina. Next to Charleston, Wilmington was the most heavily fortified city along the Atlantic seaboard, and it soon took on the appearance of an armed camp. Artillery emplacements ringed the city, while outer defenses guarded the environs against an overland attack from Union-occupied New Bern, North Carolina, only ninety miles to the north, or from an enemy invasion along the ocean shoreline. A series of gun batteries along the east side of the Cape Fear River three miles south of Wilmington guarded the water approaches to the city. On the river's west bank fifteen miles below the city loomed Fort Anderson, the area's largest interior fortification. Anderson protected the river channel and the western land approaches to Wilmington.

The strongest and best-armed forts in the Lower Cape Fear were built to guard the harbor's inlets for incoming and outgoing blockade runners. Forts Caswell and Campbell and Battery Shaw on Oak Island, and Fort Holmes on Bald Head Island, defended Old Inlet. To safeguard New Inlet, Engineers constructed Fort Fisher, the largest and strongest seacoast fortification in the Confederacy, and the key to the Cape Fear defense system.

By the summer of 1864, the ultimate fate of the Confederacy appeared to rest on the survival of Wilmington. With blockade running uncertain at best at the besieged city of Charleston, and the close of Mobile Bay by Admiral David G. Farragut in August 1864, Wilmington remained the only major seaport open to trade with the outside world. General Robert E. Lee sent word to the Cape Fear District military high command that if Wilmington fell, "he could not maintain his army" entrenched along the Richmond and Petersburg line.

Determined to sever Lee's lifeline through Wilmington, the Union high command made plans to attack Fort Fisher, the main guardian of the Carolina seaport. A two-day battle, 23–24 December 1864, to close the harbor to blockade running resulted in the heaviest Union naval bombardment of the Civil War. Despite the action of Rear Admiral David D. Porter's armada, the U.S. Army's expeditionary force withdrew when the warships' fire failed to damage Fort Fisher enough to warrant a ground assault.

The Federals renewed their attack on Fort Fisher just two-and-a-half weeks after the ill-fated December expedition. The main objective of the second strike was to capture Wilmington itself, thereby gaining control of the Cape Fear River and the city's railroads. These routes of supply were needed to support General William T. Sherman's proposed advance through the Carolinas en route to Virginia to attack Lee's Confederate army, already embattled by General U.S. Grant's operational forces.

After a continuous two-and-a-half-day naval bombardment, 13–15 January 1865, Brigadier General Alfred H. Terry's Provisional Corps, comprising 9,600 soldiers of the 24th and 25th Army Corps, assaulted and captured Fort Fisher. Among the prisoners were Colonel William Lamb, Fort Fisher's commander, and Major General W.H.C. Whiting. With the harbor now closed

to blockade running, the Federals turned their sites on Wilmington. Admiral Porter pushed a flotilla of light-draft gunboats through the inlets and onto the Cape Fear River to support an army advance.

General Grant traveled to the Cape Fear on 28 January to finalize plans for the Wilmington campaign. Porter and Terry recommended moving against the city by way of Fort Anderson on the mainland across the river from Federal Point, where the army would have more room to maneuver. To reinforce Terry's bloodied and exhausted troops, Grant dispatched reinforcements from the XXXIII Army Corps, commanded by Major General John M. Schofield. The corps 3d Division, led by Major General Jacob D. Cox, reached the Cape Fear in early February.

While Schofield and Cox advanced on Fort Anderson to the west, General Terry's corps moved against 4,500 strongly entrenched Confederates, commanded by General Braxton Bragg and Major General Robert F. Hoke, at Sugar Loaf Hill, on the east side of the river directly opposite Anderson and four-and-one-half miles north of Fort Fisher. Porter's flotilla supported both Union wings with covering fire.

Pressed by Cox's ground forces and Porter's warships, Brigadier General Johnson Hagood withdrew his garrison from Fort Anderson before dawn on 19 February. The evacuation of Fort Anderson compelled General Hoke to retreat from Sugar Loaf toward Wilmington. Hagood fought a delaying action against Cox's pursuing force at Town Creek on 19–20 February, while Hoke attempted to impede Terry's corps at Forks Road, three miles south of Wilmington, on 20 February. Hagood's rapid withdrawal into the city's defenses late on 20 February enabled General Cox to advance within artillery range of Wilmington the following day. Outnumbered and over-whelmed, Bragg's Confederates evacuated Wilmington before sunrise on 22 February. Federal forces occupied the city later that morning. On 11 March, a Union navy vessel from Wilmington made contact with General Sherman's vanguard by way of the Cape Fear River and opened up a line of supply for Sherman's rapidly advancing legion.

The loss of the Confederacy's lifeline through Wilmington, and a renewal of offenses by Grant's Army of the Potomac and Army of the James in late March 1865, forced Robert E. Lee to withdraw from the Petersburg-Richmond lines. Grant chased Lee to Appomattox Court House, where Lee surrendered on 9 April. As Lee had predicted, if Wilmington fell, he could not maintain his army. As one Southern soldier observed, Wilmington was "the last rays of departing hope" for the Confederacy.

—*Chris E. Fonvielle, Jr.*

See also Blockade Runners; Fort Fisher.
For further reading:
Fonvielle, Chris E., Jr. *The Wilmington Campaign: Last Rays of Departing Hope* (1997).
Gragg, Rod. *Confederate Goliath: The Battle of Fort Fisher* (1991).

WILMOT, DAVID
(1814–1868)
U.S. representative and senator

Born on 20 January 1814 in Bethany, Pennsylvania, to Daniel Wilmot, a local merchant, and Mary Grant Wilmot, who died in 1820, David Wilmot enjoyed a comfortable childhood. His father's fortunes rose throughout David's early life, allowing the family to build a large house and David to gain an education. He received his early education at the local Beech Woods Academy and later enrolled in Cayuga Lake Academy at Aurora, New York. Upon moving to Wilkes-Barre in 1832, he began to read law at the office of George W. Woodward and was admitted to the Pennsylvania bar in August 1834. On 28 November 1836, Wilmot married Anna Morgan of Bethlehem, Pennsylvania, with whom he would have three children, all destined to die young.

Active in politics at all levels, Wilmot soon made a name for himself as a staunch Jacksonian. By the middle 1840s, he had moved from supporting others to promoting himself as a congressional candidate. In 1845, he won a seat in the U.S. House of Representatives, where he would serve until 1851.

In his first term, Wilmot surprisingly supported the administration of President James K. Polk. Throughout his presidency, Polk alienated many Northerners as a result of his pro-Southern agenda. Because of his largely agrarian constituency, Wilmot voted for the Tariff of 1846 and was the only Pennsylvania congressman to do so. Into his second term, Wilmot began to fear the Southern abuse of political power. Feeling that the South was on its way to becoming the dominant region of the nation, Wilmot, like many other Northern politicians, searched for a way to slow Southern advances. He saw an opportunity in the Mexican-American War.

Wilmot and many of his Northern colleagues believed that the result of a U.S. victory would be the annexation of more territory and the subsequent expansion of slavery. On 8 August 1846, President Polk asked for a $2 million appropriation to use in negotiations for peace with Mexico. Sensing his chance, Wilmot attached a proviso to the bill. Wilmot's amendment, carefully worded to resemble the Northwest Ordinance, stipulated that slavery would be prohibited in any territory purchased with the money. Jacob Brinkerhoff of Ohio offered a similar plan, but because of Brinkerhoff's public antislavery record the House Democrats agreed to support Wilmot's carefully worded proposal. The House accepted the Wilmot Proviso, but it failed to pass in the Senate. While the legislative effects of the proviso are insignificant, it did arouse feelings of sectionalism and mistrust between Northern and Southern states. In many circles, the Wilmot Proviso is considered to have been the first step down the path toward Civil War.

Wilmot would serve two more terms in the House of Representatives but would gain little more notoriety. Although a moderate for much of his early congressional career, he broke with the mainstream of the Democratic Party in 1848 and became a staunch Free Soiler. These moves placed him at odds with the Pennsylvania Democrats, who were at this time led by future president James Buchanan, and culminated in his withdrawal from the 1850 congressional race in favor of more moderate Galusha Grow. After Wilmot's departure from the House, he was elected president judge of the 13th Judicial District, a position he would hold for a decade. With the Free-Soil faction splintering, Wilmot helped to found the Republican Party in Pennsylvania, where he chaired the state committee on the Republican platform and worked diligently for John C. Frémont's failed run at the presidency.

By 1857, Wilmot was again growing bored with supporting others for public office and became the Republican Party's first gubernatorial candidate in Pennsylvania. His run, although strong, was unsuccessful. Wilmot again returned to play the role of king-maker in Pennsylvania and was instrumental in securing Abraham Lincoln's nomination for president. In return for his support, Lincoln was prepared to offer Wilmot a position in his cabinet, but Wilmot deferred to run for a possible seat in the Senate. In March 1861, Wilmot returned to national politics as a U.S. senator. He was chosen to serve out the remaining two years of the term of recently appointed Secretary of War Simon Cameron, but this would prove to be the extent of his senatorial service. Cameron lasted only a short time in Lincoln's cabinet and was readying for political exile as minister to Russia when he found that he could be reelected to his old Senate seat. To reward Wilmot's faithful service, Lincoln appointed him to the bench of the newly reorganized Court of Claims on 7 March 1863, a position he held until his death on 16 March 1868.

—*Brian D. McKnight*

See also Grow, Galusha; Wilmot Proviso.
For further reading:
Going, Charles Buxton. *David Wilmot: Free Soiler* (1924).
Stenberg, Richard R. "The Motivation of the Wilmot Proviso." *The Mississippi Valley Historical Review* (1932).

WILMOT PROVISO
(1846)

The brainchild of Pennsylvania Democrat David Wilmot, the Wilmot Proviso was presented as a rider to a $2 million appropriations bill intended for use by President James K. Polk in negotiations to end the Mexican-American War. Wilmot's proviso stipulated that slavery must be prohibited in any territory acquired in a treaty to end the war.

Wilmot, much wanting to take a stand against the institution of slavery, attached his proviso to the $2 Million Bill. The proviso itself was safely worded, recalling the Northwest Ordinance, but the difficulty lay with the method of its introduction. President Polk eagerly sought to bring the war with Mexico to a close and, when he requested the appropriation on 8 August 1846, Congress knew that his intention was to purchase the land in question. Wilmot seized the opportunity and attached his amendment to the bill. With the close of the session looming in less than two days, the House wasted little time in dealing with the bill. It was debated hotly, but only briefly, and was passed along strictly sectional lines. The bill was then sent to the Senate, arriving within one hour of the adjournment of the session. With little time available, Senator John Davis of Massachusetts took the floor in defense of the bill and refused to yield. His plan was to occupy so much of the remaining hour that argument against the bill would be minute, but he overshot his mark and Congress was adjourned without considering the bill. Although Davis was one of the bill's most ardent supporters, it was he who had inadvertently killed the Wilmot Proviso. At the next session, after much time for conference and debate, political forces were aligned sufficiently to strike down the proviso with a vote.

Even though the proviso was officially dead, it still had a great impact on the nation. Feelings of sectionalism grew as Southerners viewed the proviso as an attempt to undermine the institution of slavery by trickery. Northerners, however, saw the proviso's demise as a result of the ignorance of Davis and feared the expansion of the perceived political dominance of the South. Many historians consider the Wilmot Proviso to be the catalyst that began the slide of the United States through the 1850s toward civil war.

—*Brian D. McKnight*

See also Wilmot, David.
For further reading:
Going, Charles Buxton. *David Wilmot: Free Soiler* (1924).
Stenberg, Richard R. "The Motivation of the Wilmot Proviso." *The Mississippi Valley Historical Review* (1932).

WILSON, HENRY
(1812–1875)
United States senator

Born to Winthrop Colbath and Abigail Witham Colbath in Farmington, New Hampshire, the man who would become Henry Wilson was originally named Jeremiah Jones Colbath. His family was very poor, and as a result Jeremiah was indentured to a local farmer. During the ten years of his indenture he became largely self-educated and extremely well read. When he

left his master's employ, he was given some livestock, which he sold, and changed his name to Henry Wilson. With the money from his livestock he paid for instruction in the cobbler's trade, after which he set up shop in Natick, Massachusetts, making shoes. He became moderately prosperous.

On a holiday to Virginia in the 1830s, he had his first experience with slavery when he saw slave markets in operation in Washington, D.C. He returned to Natick determined to work for abolition. Once home, Wilson saved money from school teaching and shoe making to open a shoe factory. This objective accomplished, he quickly became known as a model employer to his workers by treating them as equals.

His business interests also led him to involvement in politics, particularly after the panic of 1837 damaged Northern business interests. He became an avowed Whig and successfully stood for election to the Massachusetts legislature in 1840. In over a decade's service to the state legislature, Wilson became increasingly vocal in his antislavery views. As a Massachusetts delegate to the Whig National Convention in 1848, he withdrew from the convention when the party refused to endorse the Wilmot Proviso and was part of the group that formed the Free Soil Party that year. His primary activity as a member of the new party over the next few years was editing the party newspaper, the *Boston Republican.*

In 1854 Wilson made a blunder that almost cost him his political career. Believing that the American (Know-Nothing) Party appealed to a wider constituency than the Free Soil Party or the new group calling themselves Republicans, he joined the American Party. He quickly learned that he would be unable to sway the leadership of the party toward abolition, and he objected to the antiforeigner element within the party. As a result he left in 1855, the same year he took his seat in the United States Senate, filling the unexpired term of Edward Everett.

In the United States Senate Wilson quickly became one of the loudest of the antislavery voices. When he denounced the caning of fellow Massachusetts senator Charles Sumner by Congressman Preston Brooks, Brooks challenged Wilson to a duel, which Wilson refused.

By 1860 Wilson had joined the ranks of the Republican Party. When Abraham Lincoln was elected president in the fall of that year, Wilson urged his party to avoid compromise with the slaveholders of the South. While certainly not wanting a war, Wilson believed that further compromise on the issue of slavery only postponed an inevitable conflict. When that conflict finally erupted in April 1861, Wilson found himself in the thick of the military preparations for prolonged conflict.

Wilson had been interested in military affairs for a number of years. As a brigadier general in the Massachusetts militia, he had some experience in the bureaucracy involved in managing a military force. In the Senate he had served on the Committee on Military Affairs, and in the new Congress he became the committee's chair. During the four years of the war Wilson worked tirelessly to maintain the fighting capability of all the country's armed services. He wanted preparedness, but also efficiency, and as a result was always looking for ways to save money.

Unlike many of his fellow Radical Republicans, Wilson believed that one way to strengthen the United States Army was to increase the numbers of regulars and the allotment of slots to the United States Military Academy. Like other radicals, he doubted the loyalty of many of the officers in the Army of the Potomac, but believed that the best way to dilute such disloyalty was to increase the number of loyal, Republican officers.

As a senator in a very powerful position in wartime, Wilson also found himself the magnet for all manner of requests from officers and civilians alike. For example, William Rosecrans wrote to Wilson in early 1863 asking for greater authority from Congress to discipline recalcitrant or negligent officers without having to go to the trouble of military trials. Perennial political general Benjamin Butler urged fellow Massachusetts man Wilson in the spring of 1864 to speed the confirmation process for one of his corps commanders, Quincy Gillmore, to major general. However, once Butler came to know Gillmore and did not like him, he wrote again to Wilson asking that the confirmation be denied. It was. Ironically, in early 1865 it was Wilson who called for an investigation by the Committee on the Conduct of the War of Butler's failed Fort Fisher expedition.

While not immune to the political finagling in Congress, Wilson ended the war with a reputation as a strong and efficient chairman of the Senate Military Affairs Committee. During the postwar years he proved a loyal radical and strongly supported congressional control of Reconstruction. His primary concern during those years was to ensure the political rights and economic well-being of the former slaves. In 1872 he received the party's nomination for vice president and was elected to serve during Ulysses S. Grant's second term. At the end of 1875, however, he suffered a stroke in the Capitol. It was not deemed safe to move him from the building, and he died in his offices twelve days later on 22 November 1875.

—*David S. Heidler and Jeanne T. Heidler*

See also Congress, U. S.A.; Joint Committee on the Conduct of the War.

For further reading:

Abbott, Richard H. "Cobbler in Congress; Life of Henry Wilson, 1812–1875" (Ph.D. dissertation, 1965).

McKay, Ernest A. *Henry Wilson: Practical Radical; A Portrait of a Politician* (1971).

WILSON, JAMES HARRISON
(1837–1925)
Union general

One of the boy generals forged in the fierce crucible of the Civil War, James Harrison Wilson was born on a farm near Shawneetown, Illinois, on 2 September 1837 to Harrison Wilson and Katharine Schneyder Wilson. The family traced its origins to ancient Northumberland. In the seventeenth century, Wilson's ancestors migrated to Virginia and later followed the typical westward flow of settlers across the mountains to Kentucky and eventually Illinois. Military service was not unknown in the Wilson family. Harrison Wilson had served as an officer in both the War of 1812 and the Blackhawk War, whereas Wilson's maternal grandfather was a veteran of Napoleon's army. Following a year of preparation at McKendree College, near St. Louis, "Harry" Wilson, as James was known to family and friends, entered West Point in 1855. Classmates included Thomas Rosser, George Custer, and Wesley Merritt.

In physical appearance, Wilson stood five feet ten inches tall with a medium build, though one contemporary suggested that his straight bearing made him appear somewhat taller. He possessed a superior intellect and boundless self-confidence. His blunt, outspoken manner, and policy of never backing away from a fight, were traits that earned him enough demerits to affect his West Point class standing, despite his academic excellence. Despite this, he managed to rank sixth in a class of forty-one at graduation on 1 July 1860.

Following graduation, Wilson was assigned to the elite Topographical Engineers and sent out to the Pacific Northwest. With the firing on Fort Sumter, he wasted no time successfully importuning headquarters and influential contacts for a transfer back east.

Wilson reached the East Coast during the summer of 1861, but shortly thereafter he was struck down by cholera and laid up for several weeks. That fall he was appointed chief topographical engineer for the upcoming Front Royal, Virginia, expedition and subsequently played an important role in the successful siege of Fort Pulaski in April 1862.

Recalled to Washington, Wilson was assigned to General George McClellan's staff early in September, arriving just in time to participate in the battle of Antietam.

Following Antietam, Wilson again returned to Washington, where, after a brief stint on a court-martial board, he was transferred to the Western theater as chief topographical engineer in General Ulysses Grant's Army of the Tennessee.

The transfer to Grant's command proved to be a turning point in Wilson's career. Here, in Grant's official family, he found kindred spirits among the likes of John

James Wilson (*Library of Congress*)

A. Rawlins, Adam Badeau, and a bit later, the War Department observer, Charles A. Dana. If Wilson did not find Grant a physically imposing figure, he nevertheless soon developed a deep-seated respect for Grant's determination and business-like approach to winning this war. And in time, Grant also came to appreciate Wilson's soldierly skills.

Just how much Grant appreciated Wilson was made clear in February 1863. As Wilson was about to be promoted to lieutenant colonel and transferred back east, Grant appointed him assistant inspector general, Army of the Tennessee, with the rank of lieutenant colonel.

Grant's triumph at Vicksburg won him a promotion to major general in the regular army and that fall of 1863 he was ordered to Chattanooga, Tennessee, to replace General William S. Rosecrans, whose Army of the Cumberland was then under siege by Braxton Bragg's Confederate Army of Tennessee. Wilson accompanied his chief and in December 1863, at Grant's urging, Wilson was promoted to brigadier general of volunteers.

Grant had also been impressed with the way Wilson attended to the needs of the mounted units while serving as inspector general. Accordingly, in mid-January, upon Grant's recommendation, Wilson was appointed chief of the recently created Cavalry Bureau in Washington, with orders to clean up what had turned into a first-class mess.

Many unscrupulous contractors had been getting rich at the government's expense, selling broken down, unfit horses at scandalous profits. With his characteristic vigor and no-nonsense approach, Wilson waded into the mess and soon revamped the bureau. In addition to cleaning up the system of purchasing horses, Wilson initiated a program to have all mounted regiments equipped with repeating carbines, a program from which he himself would benefit before the war's end.

In the spring of 1864 Wilson was assigned to command General Phil Sheridan's 3d Cavalry Division, despite the fact that he was junior to several other officers, including George Custer, who were not pleased with this development. Custer, in fact, regarded him as an "imbecile." Once again, however, the impetus for the appointment had come from Grant, who did not feel obligated always to honor seniority when making such appointments.

Wilson was delighted for the opportunity to have a field command. During that spring and summer of 1864, the 3d Cavalry Division played an active role in Union operations in Virginia. Wilson made some costly mistakes, but he also learned his lessons well and by summer's end had developed into a promising leader of mounted troops.

That fall, William T. Sherman asked Grant to send a capable officer to command his cavalry. Never one with any faith in the mounted arm, Sherman had decided to take only one division of cavalry with him on his March to the Sea. The rest of the horsemen in his military jurisdiction would remain behind under the command of whomever Grant sent and that turned out to be Wilson. "I believe Wilson will add fifty per cent to the effectiveness of your cavalry," Grant told Sherman. It was a high tribute and one that Wilson never forgot.

Taking command in October 1864, Wilson proceeded to completely reorganize Sherman's horsemen, creating a new organization named the Cavalry Corps Military Division of the Mississippi, with headquarters in Nashville, where he operated under the immediate command of Major General George H. Thomas.

In the autumn of 1864 General John Bell Hood's Confederate Army of Tennessee launched an invasion of middle Tennessee, driving back Federal forces in the area, including Wilson's freshly organized brigades. For a time there was fear that the Confederates might slip around Nashville and reach the Ohio River. The Confederate invasion, however, was blunted at Franklin, Tennessee, on 30 November and then, two weeks later,

in what has been called the "decisive" battle of Nashville, Wilson's cavalry played a key role in the destruction of Hood's army.

In the spring of 1865, Wilson led three divisions of his Cavalry Corps, nearly 14,000 men armed with Spencer carbines, on a full-scale expedition through Alabama and Georgia. The campaign, which has been called the most successful of its kind during the war, resulted in the defeat of Nathan Bedford Forrest, the capture of Selma, Montgomery, Columbus, and Macon, as well as the ex-president of the Confederacy, Jefferson Davis. It was a significant achievement, even considering that it occurred during the waning days of war.

After the war, Wilson, like many other officers, was forced to take a substantial reduction in grade to remain in the rapidly shrinking peacetime army. His postwar military career had been jeopardized, however, as the result of a rift with the then vice president-elect, Andrew Johnson. During the Nashville campaign, Wilson had clashed with the vice president and military governor of Tennessee over the creation and employment of volunteer cavalry regiments from that state. Though Wilson's position was fully justified, his upbraiding of Johnson was not a tactful way of dealing with the problem, and he would later pay the price for his lack of prudence. Johnson called him a "bumptious puppy," and never forgave him.

Wilson's postwar career was effectively stifled by Johnson, in spite of Grant's intercession. Yet Wilson elected to remain in the army and was eventually appointed lieutenant colonel of the 35th Infantry. He spent the next five years on various engineering assignments in the Midwest. By 1870, now a married man and father, he had concluded that better opportunities existed in civilian life and resigned his commission.

During the next three decades, Wilson engaged in various business enterprises, often connected with railroading. An unfortunate aspect of this period in Wilson's life was the breakup of his friendship with Ulysses Grant over a division of political loyalties stemming from the Whiskey Ring Scandal of 1875. Afterward, the two men who had been friends for twenty years refused to speak to each other.

In 1885 Wilson made an extended visit to China and had also begun to turn his hand to writing. He would eventually write a number of books, including his own two-volume memoirs, *Under The Old Flag*, published in 1912. An unswerving advocate of Manifest Destiny, he was an unabashed proponent of U.S. expansion into Canada and the Caribbean.

With the outbreak of the Spanish-American War in 1898, Wilson returned to the army, as major general of volunteers, serving under General Nelson A. Miles in the Puerto Rican campaign. Later he was appointed military governor of Matanzas District, Cuba, and

proved an effective administrator, despite some conflicts with President William McKinley's policies. Following the tragic death of his wife, Ella, who died from burns when her clothing caught fire in a freak accident, Wilson resigned his post and returned to the United States.

During the Boxer Rebellion of 1900, Wilson served under General Adna R. Chaffee as second-in-command of the U.S. column sent to the relief of the besieged diplomatic community in Beijing, China. Returning home, Wilson retired from public life, only to be called out in 1902 to represent the U.S. Army at the coronation of Edward, Prince of Wales.

During the remaining twenty-three years of his life, Wilson continued traveling, writing, and speaking to various groups. In 1915 he was promoted to the rank of major general in the regular army and placed on the retired list. With the entrance of the U.S. into World War I, he pressed for an active duty assignment but was politely rejected.

On 23 February 1925, at age eighty-seven, Wilson suffered a fatal heart attack while shaving. He was the last surviving member of his West Point class.

—*Jerry Keenan*

See also Army of the Tennessee; Cavalry, U.S.A.; Fort Pulaski, Reduction of; Front Royal, Battle of; Nashville, Tennessee; Thomas, George H.; Wilson's Selma Raid.

For further reading:

Jones, James Pickett. *Yankee Blitzkrieg: Wilson's Raid through Alabama and Georgia* (1976).

Keenan, Jerry. *Wilson's Cavalry: Union Campaigns in the Western Theatre, October 1864 through Spring 1865* (1998).

Longacre, Edward G. *From Union Stars to Top Hat: A Biography of the Extraordinary General James Harrison Wilson* (1972).

Wilson, James H. *Under the Old Flag: Recollections of Military Operations in the War for the Union, the Spanish War, the Boxer Rebellion, etc.* (1912; reprint 1971).

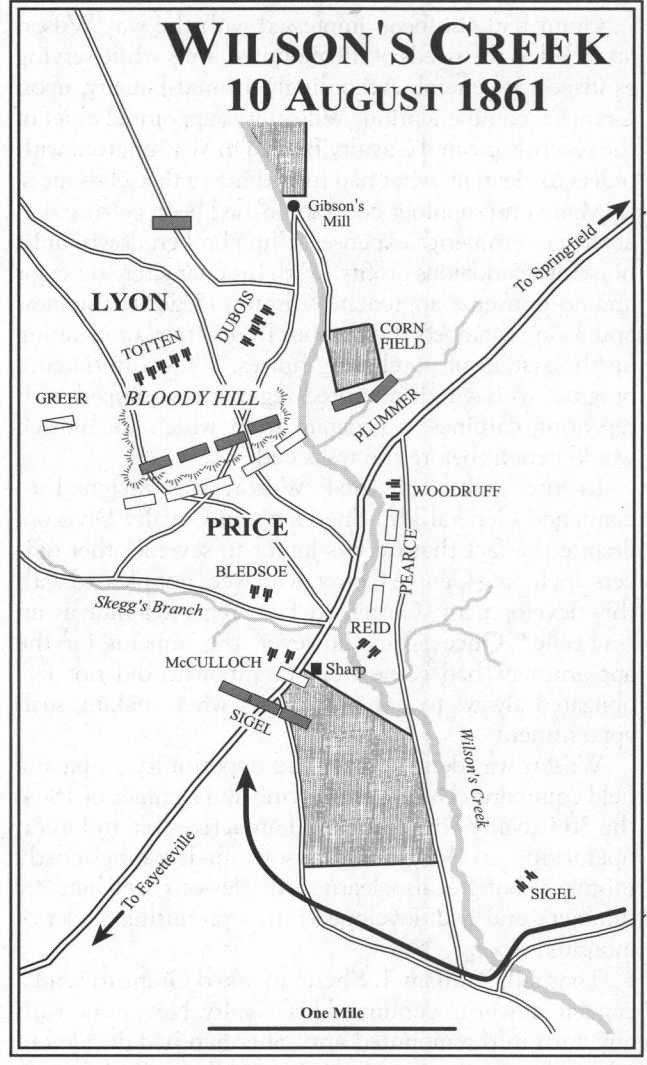

WILSON'S CREEK
10 AUGUST 1861

WILSON'S CREEK, MISSOURI
(10 August 1861)

In early August 1861, Union brigadier general Nathaniel Lyon, with a few regulars and volunteers from Kansas, Iowa, and Missouri, and with the help of Brigadier General Franz Sigel and his German Brigade, determined to push the Confederate forces gathering in southwestern Missouri out of the state. Those Confederates already there were camped near Wilson's Creek. They consisted of the Texas Brigade of Brigadier General Ben McCulloch, the Missouri State Guard under Major General Sterling Price, and Arkansas state troopers under Brigadier General Nicholas Pearce. With the exception of McCulloch's brigade, the roughly 11,000 men were generally disorganized, ill equipped, and undisciplined.

The Wilson's Creek camp was located ten miles southwest of Springfield, Missouri, which was Lyon's headquarters. The Confederate commanders knew that they outnumbered Lyon by as much as two to one and considered attacking his position at Springfield on the night of 9 August. Because of a steady rain, they decided against it. However, Lyon was making plans of his own. He intended to leave Springfield the night of 9 August. Sigel with about 1,200 men was to move out at the same time and approach the Southern camps at Wilson's Creek from the south, while Lyon took most of the army—about 3,600 men—and moved in from the north.

Both Union forces left Springfield before midnight on the ninth and marched through most of the night. Sigel was to move into position to begin his attack but was not to reveal his presence until he heard Lyon attack. After resting his men for a couple of hours, Lyon moved into position to attack at about 5 A.M. Shortly after beginning the march, Lyon's men encountered their first Confederate pickets. Lyon tried to speed the march so that they could attack before too many people in the

Death of General Lyon at the battle of Wilson's Creek (*Library of Congress*)

Confederate camps knew what was happening. Lyon began his attack shortly after 5 A.M. When Sigel heard the firing to the north, he manned his artillery, which was already in position overlooking the encampment of most of the Southern cavalry. He ordered the guns to fire, causing most of the just-waking men below to run from their camps.

At the same time, the entrance of Lyon to the north also caused the camps of Price's State Guard to erupt in panic, and the men began moving south toward Skegg's Branch. Price quickly assessed the situation and had his officers start organizing the men. The State Guard, having realized that they were not in imminent danger, allowed themselves to be formed up and moved toward Lyon's column. Lyon was already in a strong defensive position on high ground that would after this day be called Bloody Hill.

McCulloch, who had moved to the south end of the Confederate encampments, was doing the same thing as Price with the men who had fled before Sigel's guns. McCulloch rushed his artillery up to either side of the Springfield road north of Skegg's Branch, putting Pearce in command of the dismounted forces at the road. Now that he had Price's rear protected, McCulloch moved

south to organize the cavalrymen who had been run out of their camps.

To the north, Price was moving his men toward Bloody Hill. Lyon prepared his troops for the inevitable attack as Price moved his men rapidly up the slope, both sides firing furiously at one another at close range. The men fought frantically for about an hour until Union major James Totten's battery firing canister into the Confederates finally brought about their withdrawal.

The lull was short-lived. Price determined to knock out Totten's battery and sent the Missouri State Guard in with a vengeance. Lyon moved his men around quickly, trying to meet this new threat. When the Southerners failed to reach the battery, they pulled back again, only to attack after half an hour's rest.

The next attack by Price was made primarily at the Union left, but Lyon was able to turn some of his artillery to strike the attacking Missourians squarely in their left flank, forcing them to fall back with heavy losses. Lyon, in the meantime, waited impatiently for Sigel to appear to Price's rear.

Sigel, after putting the Confederate cavalry to flight on the south end of the battlefield, moved onto the field and pushed another Confederate force back toward

Skegg's Branch. His men then started moving through the first Confederate encampment they had routed, looking for anything of value. While the looting was going on, the Confederate battery that had been placed by McCulloch opened on the Sigel's men, sending them into the woods. Sigel at that point decided against any further offensive action and instead determined to wait where he was to cutoff the Confederate retreat that he assumed would result from Lyon's attack.

McCulloch then moved around with artillery east of Wilson's Creek to the position that Sigel had occupied before the battle began. As a result, he could do to Sigel what the Union officer had done to the Confederate cavalry earlier in the morning. The surprise worked, and the attacking Confederates were able to move very close to Sigel's position, helped somewhat by the fact that some of their uniforms resembled those of the state units that were with Lyon. The Confederate attack brought about a precipitous, disorganized Union retreat of Sigel's forces. Sigel with his staff withdrew all the way back to Springfield.

The Confederates who had routed Sigel now moved to join the fight against Lyon. Price, with these added troops, prepared to send more infantry against Bloody Hill, while also sending 800 mounted troops, screened by the hills, around Lyon's right to attack the Union rear. The cavalry attack distracted the Union forces somewhat, but did not do irreparable damage.

At about 9 A.M. the Confederate frontal offensive began. Confederate artillery, including some of Sigel's captured guns, signaled the beginning of the offensive by pounding the Union position. As the Confederate soldiers then poured up the hill at about 10 A.M., Lyon was forced to put in all of his reserves. The Union forces on the hill still had no idea that Sigel had retreated.

In the furious fighting of the next half hour Lyon was hit twice, once in the leg and a graze wound on his head. He continued to exercise command, trying to shift his small numbers back and forth to meet the Confederate waves. At about 10:30 A.M. Lyon, while on the left of the Union line, was struck in the heart by a Confederate bullet and died within minutes. In spite of this heavy blow, the Union lines held. At about 11:30 A.M. the Confederates withdrew.

Major Sam Sturgis, who had succeeded Lyon in command, made the controversial decision to withdraw the Union forces as well. Some of his officers argued for pursuit of the Confederates, but Sturgis knew that his force was low on ammunition and that the men were exhausted. In fact, the depleted Union forces evacuated Springfield, and it was occupied by McCulloch. Each side suffered about 1,200 casualties on 10 August. The war for control of southern Missouri continued.

—*David S. Heidler and Jeanne T. Heidler*

See also Lyon, Nathaniel; McCulloch, Ben; Missouri; Price, Sterling; Sigel, Franz.

For further reading:
Adamson, Hans Christian. *Rebellion in Missouri: 1861, Nathaniel Lyon and His Army of the West* (1961).
Bearss, Edwin C. *The Battle of Wilson's Creek* (1992).
Piston, William Garrett, and Richard W. Hatcher. *Wilson's Creek: The Second Battle of the Civil War and the Men Who Fought It* (2000).

WILSON'S SELMA RAID
(March–April 1865)

In the autumn of 1864, Major General William T. Sherman, commanding the Military Division of the Mississippi, despaired of finding any commander for his cavalry worthy of the title. To solve Sherman's dilemma, Lieutenant General Ulysses S. Grant appointed twenty-seven-year-old Brigadier General James H. Wilson as chief of cavalry to Sherman on 30 September 1864. By November, Wilson, promoted to major general of volunteers, had assumed his duties and secured Sherman's approval to reorganize the cavalry command into a corps of eight divisions with two brigades apiece. Sherman, preoccupied with his March to the Sea, told Wilson he expected little from the effort, but whatever Wilson could accomplish, the credit would be his own.

Grant's plan for the spring of 1865 envisioned Major General George Meade's Army of the Potomac continuing to pressure General Lee, while Sherman attacked north through the Carolinas into Virginia. As part of his plan, Grant ordered Major General Edward R. S. Canby, commanding the Military Division of West Mississippi, to launch an expedition to Mobile and central Alabama. Wilson was ordered to demonstrate with 5,000 cavalry in the direction of Selma, Alabama, to draw attention away from Canby. Wilson demurred. He felt that if he attacked with all his available troops instead, he might destroy Lieutenant General Nathan Bedford Forrest's cavalry command in Alabama, seize the cities of Tuscaloosa, Selma, and Montgomery in Alabama, and Columbus in Georgia, and destroy agricultural and military supplies and rail communications as he found them. This would deny the last vital source of supplies and manufactures to the Confederacy, and might forestall any attempt to defend the Deep South as a final bastion of resistance. With the aid of Major General George H. Thomas, Wilson persuaded Grant and Wilson's orders were changed accordingly.

Several of Wilson's divisions were detached before he could act. For example, the 3d Division was with Sherman in the Carolinas, and the 7th had gone to support Canby. Wilson would therefore have three effective divisions, the 1st, 2d, and 4th, under Brigadier Generals Edward M. McCook, Eli Long, and Emory Upton, comprising roughly 13,500 men in all. Wilson

had planned to begin as early as 3 March, but heavy rains and high water made the roads impassable and rivers and streams unfordable for several weeks. He finally began to cross to the south bank of the Tennessee River on 18 March, completed the move on the twenty-first, and began the march south towards Selma on the twenty-second. To deceive the Confederates about his true objective as long as possible, the divisions marched as three columns. Upton took the eastern route through Barton's Station, Russellville, and Mount Hope. Long marched in the center to Cherokee Station, Frankfort, and Bear Creek. McCook initially followed Long, but then struck west toward Tuscaloosa as far as Eldridge. All three divisions were then to converge on Jasper for the final march on Selma. On 29 March, McCook's 1st Brigade under Brigadier John T. Croxton was detached at Elyton to destroy facilities at Tuscaloosa. It then operated independently until 1 May, when it rejoined the corps at Macon, Georgia. McCook and his 2d Brigade were shortly detached to secure and bring up the corps wagon train.

Up to 31 March there had been no effective opposition to the corps's march, although Forrest had begun concentrating his forces in and around Selma as early as the twenty-third. On the afternoon of 31 March, Upton encountered Confederate cavalry and militia two miles south of Montevallo, which he overpowered and then pursued with his 1st Brigade until nightfall. Forrest had parts of two cavalry divisions concentrated near Ebenezer Church on 1 April. With only two divisions available, Wilson skillfully maneuvered Long onto Forrest's front and then attacked Forrest's flank and rear with Upton's division, defeating Forrest in a running battle. Forrest fell back on Selma, well defended by entrenched infantry and artillery. Wilson followed him and, after securing a plan of the city defenses from the British civil engineer who had helped build them, attacked late in the afternoon of 2 April 1865.

Long's and Upton's divisions carried the outer line of Confederate works by dismounted assault near dusk. Wilson, now within the works and attempting to reorganize Long's troops after Long was wounded, hoped to carry the second line and so end the affair quickly, before the Confederates could recover. Therefore, he led his escort, a battalion of the 4th U.S. Cavalry, in a mounted assault upon the entrenchments. Wilson's own horse was shot out from under him and the assault faltered. However, reinforced by the 17th Indiana (Mounted) Infantry and the 3d Ohio Volunteer Cavalry, and supported by the fire of a section of the Chicago Board of Trade Battery that Wilson had brought within the outer works, a second, dismounted charge, carried. The Confederates then abandoned the city. The militia was dispersed or captured, along with many artillery pieces, but Forrest escaped with his cavalry. Selma demon-

strated, however, that even Nathan Bedford Forrest could not stop the unrelenting Union forces at this stage in the war. The same day that Selma fell, Jefferson Davis and his government abandoned Richmond.

Wilson destroyed considerable Confederate property at Selma, sent Upton to clear any Confederate forces from west of the Cahaba River, and constructed a pontoon bridge over the Alabama River. McCook and his 2d Brigade, escorting the corps wagon train, meanwhile rejoined the corps at Selma on 6 April. Wilson completed the crossing of the Alabama on 11 April and marched on Montgomery, seizing it on the twelfth and destroying all Confederate public stores. On the morning of 14 April the corps resumed the march east towards Tuskegee. There, McCook's 2d Brigade was again detached and directed toward Macon, Georgia, while Upton, followed by Colonel Robert H. G. Minty, now commanding Long's division, marched directly on Columbus, Georgia. Upton reached Columbus on 16 April. He assaulted and carried its forward works on the west bank of the Chattahoochee River that night, and pursued the retreating Confederates so closely that he seized the bridges before they could be destroyed. His division captured 1,200 prisoners and fifty-two cannon. The corps then destroyed considerable Confederate property, including a navy yard and arsenal, the ironclad CSS *Jackson* (with 6 x 7-inch rifled guns), a foundry, armory, and weapons factory, four cotton factories and 100,000 cotton bales, a mass of ammunition, and fifteen locomotive engines and 200 freight cars. They also destroyed all the bridges on the Chattahoochee. The same day McCook's 2d Brigade had treated West Point similarly, capturing Fort Tyler, and destroying nineteen more locomotive engines and 200 additional railroad cars. On 17 April, the corps resumed its march, with Minty's 2d Division now leading. Minty reached Macon on 20 April, and the remainder of the corps, less McCook's still-wandering 1st Brigade, closed in the next day. On 22 April Wilson received a telegram from Sherman announcing the general armistice.

Since it had been detached on 29 March, Croxton's 1st Brigade, 1st Division, only 1,100 men in all, had led a chase of over 650 miles in thirty days through the South as it eluded various parts of Forrest's command. Croxton successfully took Tuscaloosa, Alabama, on 4 April, capturing three cannon and burning substantial Confederate public stores and buildings, including the military school there. Unable to rejoin Wilson by a direct route, Croxton both evaded the enemy and skirmished with him, making his way east. His rear guard lost two officers, thirty-two men, and two broken-down ambulances to the Confederate Wirt Adams's 2,600-man cavalry division near Eutaw on 6 April. The brigade then moved from Eutaw via Hanby's Mills on 18

April to cross the Coosa River at Talladega on 22 April. They then defeated and dispersed the Confederate brigadier general Hill's brigade of 500 "conscripts and deserters" near Blue Mountain and burned a number of factories and the last ironworks in Alabama. Finally, the brigade marched through Carrollton on 26 April, Newman the next day, and Forsyth on the twenty-ninth to rejoin the corps at Macon on 1 May.

Wilson's Corps contributed largely to ripping the heart out of the Confederacy. His brigades traveled an average of 525 miles in twenty-eight days. In that time they captured "five fortified cities, 23 stand of colors, 288 pieces of artillery, and 6,820 prisoners including 5 generals." They also "captured or destroyed 2 gun-boats, 99,000 stand of small arms, 7 iron-works, 7 foundries, 7 machine-shops, 2 rolling-mills, 5 collieries, 13 factories, 4 niter works, 1 military university, 3 C. S. arsenals and contents, 1 naval yard and contents, 5 steam-boats, 35 engines and 565 cars." In accomplishing this feat of arms, Wilson's Corps lost only thirteen officers and eighty-six men killed, thirty-nine officers and 559 men wounded, and seven officers and twenty-one men missing. The corps conclusively demonstrated to Sherman and others what Union cavalry, properly equipped and led, could accomplish.

Following up on its success the corps performed one last fateful mission. The 4th Michigan Volunteer Cavalry of Minty's (Long's) division captured Jefferson Davis near Irwinville, Georgia, on the morning of 10 May 1865. Upton's division had in the meantime detained Confederate vice president Alexander Stephens, Secretary of the Navy Mallory, and Georgia senator Benjamin H. Hill.

—*Duane C. Young*

See also Cavalry, C.S.A.; Mobile Campaign; Wilson, James H.
For further reading:

Jones, James Pickett. *Yankee Blitzkrieg: Wilson's Raid through Alabama and Georgia* (1976).

Keenan, Jerry. *Wilson's Cavalry Corps: Union Campaigns in the Western Theatre, October 1864 through Spring 1865* (1998).

Longacre, Edward G. *Mounted Raids of the Civil War* (1975; reprint, 1994).

Sunderland, Glenn W. *Wilder's Lightening Brigade and its Spencer Repeaters* (1984).

U.S. War Department. *The War of the Rebellion: A Compilation of the Official Records of the Union and Confederate Armies* (1880–1901).

WINCHESTER, FIRST BATTLE OF
(25 May 1862)

In early May 1862, Major General Thomas J. "Stonewall" Jackson was the Confederate commander in the Shenandoah Valley. His single division was reinforced by Major General Richard S. Ewell's troops,

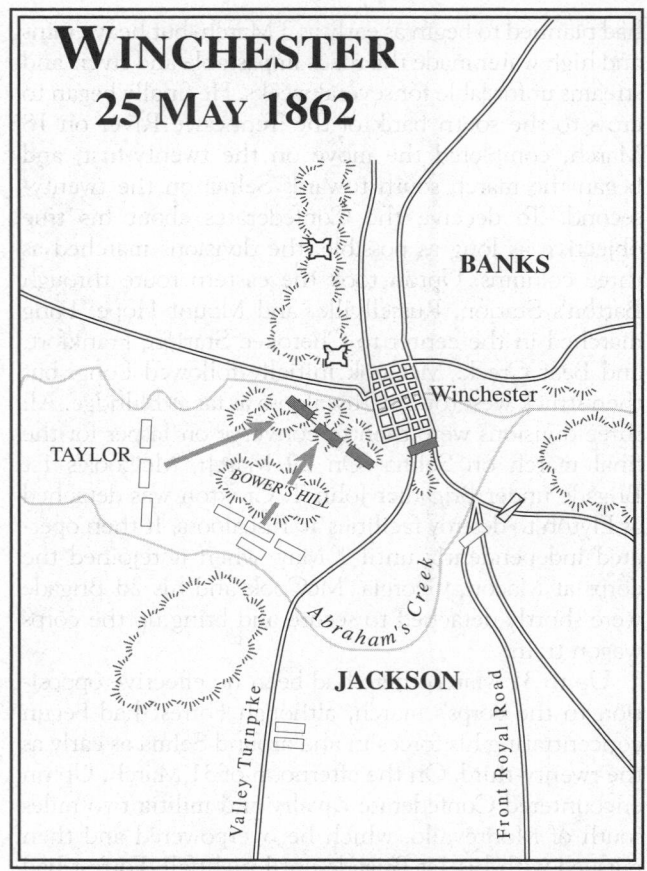

bringing Jackson's command to approximately 17,000 men with forty-eight cannon. To relieve pressure on Richmond, Jackson decided to attack the Federals in the area before they could combine their forces against him.

Jackson first struck on 8 May at a detachment of Major General John C. Frémont's troops at McDowell, in western Virginia, forcing a Union retreat into the western Virginia mountains. Then, Jackson decided to march north down the valley toward Winchester. Major General Nathaniel P. Banks was in command of Union troops in the valley. Most of his troops—two brigades of infantry led by Brigadier General Alpheus S. Williams— were in the vicinity of Strasburg, where they were erecting strong fortifications. A small garrison occupied Front Royal. Banks's force had been reduced when James Shields's division had departed to join Major General Irvin McDowell at Fredericksburg, preparatory to that general's southward advance toward Richmond. Banks was left with fewer than 10,000 men to watch the valley.

Jackson began a northward march from Harrisonburg toward New Market, where his division veered eastward across the Massanutten Mountain. Once across, Jackson and Ewell joined forces and headed north along the Shenandoah River. On 23 May, Jackson's troops attacked Colonel John R. Kenly's 1,100-man garrison at

Front Royal. Heavily outnumbered, most of Kenly's troops were captured; fewer than 200 escaped to bring word to Banks about the battle.

Once Front Royal had been captured, Jackson continued north, his own division moving northwest toward the Valley Turnpike, while Ewell moved up the main Winchester–Front Royal Road. Jackson hoped to move his troops between Banks and his line of retreat. Banks almost fell for this maneuver. Although he learned of the fighting at Front Royal, he did not order a retreat until mid-morning on 24 May. Slowed by elements of Brigadier General John P. Hatch's Union cavalry, Jackson's division finally reached the turnpike in time to assail Banks's rear guard in the vicinity of Newtown, capturing many supply wagons and a few prisoners. Banks's troops fell back to a range of hills just south of Winchester and deployed to allow the baggage trains time to roll north toward the Potomac River. Colonel Dudley Donnelly's 1st Brigade held the Union left, with Colonel George H. Gordon's 3d Brigade deployed on the right.

Jackson's division advanced against Gordon's line early on the morning of 25 May. His three brigades, led by Brigadier Generals Charles S. Winder and William B. Taliaferro, and Colonel John A. Campbell, were effectively halted by fierce Union resistance, especially the fire of Union batteries supporting the infantry. Brigadier General Isaac R. Trimble's brigade of Ewell's division, supported by Maryland troops, engaged Donnelly's brigade, pushing back advanced elements to the hills south of Winchester.

Jackson then sent Brigadier General Richard Taylor's Louisiana brigade of Ewell's division to the left with orders to flank the Yankee right. Taylor's men charged, and after a stubborn resistance, the men in blue broke and retreated. Ewell's troops simultaneously forced the Union left back, and in a moment the entire Union line gave way and began a hurried withdrawal through Winchester. Pandemonium ensued as units became mixed. Some civilians fired from their homes upon the hated bluecoats fleeing through the streets.

Banks's defeated troops continued their retreat more than 35 miles and crossed the Potomac into Maryland before halting to reorganize. Including the fighting at Front Royal, Banks sustained a loss of 62 killed, 243 wounded, and 1,714 captured or missing; Jackson reported that prisoners numbered 3,050, which included sick and wounded men. Confederate losses totaled 400 (68 killed, 329 wounded, 3 missing). Jackson was unable to capitalize on this victory because Shields was sent back toward the valley from the east, while Frémont's troops appeared from the west, threatening the Confederates with capture if they did not retreat from Winchester.

—*Richard A. Sauers*

See also Shenandoah Valley Campaign (1862).

For further reading:
Allan, William. *History of the Campaign of General T. J. (Stonewall) Jackson in the Shenandoah Valley of Virginia, from November 4, 1861, to June 17, 1862* (1880).
Beck, Brandon H., and Charles S. Grunder. *Three Battles of Winchester: A History and Guided Tour* (1988).
Tanner, Robert G. *Stonewall in the Valley: Thomas J. "Stonewall" Jackson's Shenandoah Valley Campaign, Spring, 1862* (1976; reprint, 1996).

WINCHESTER, SECOND BATTLE OF
(14 June 1863)

Robert E. Lee's second invasion of the North that would culminate in the battle of Gettysburg began in June 1863 when he shifted the Army of Northern Virginia west of the Blue Ridge Mountains and toward the Potomac River. As the vanguard of the Rebel army moved into the area, it bore down upon the relatively meager Federal presence consisting of the 2d Division, VIII Corps, commanded by Major General Robert Milroy headquartered at Winchester.

In the days before the battle at Winchester, there was confusion about what to do with the Federal deployments in the region. General-in-Chief Henry Wager Halleck had observed weeks before that Winchester was "no place to fight a battle." He iterated the observation on 11 June that the place should be only an outpost, so Lieutenant Colonel Donn Piatt, chief of staff for VIII Corps, telegraphed Milroy instructions to call in Colonel Andrew T. McReynolds from Berryville and pull the entire division back to Harper's Ferry. Milroy objected and claimed that he could hold Winchester against all comers, so within an hour the corps commander Major General Robert C. Schenck essentially countermanded the withdrawal order. Schenck told Milroy merely to be ready to move if necessary.

To be fair to Milroy, he did not know that Winchester would be the target of the Army of Northern Virginia. If Lee was coming Milroy's way, someone would surely tell him, he thought. When, on the night of 12 June, Milroy did detect something large moving toward him from the southeast, he asked Schenck if he should abandon Winchester. Only later would Milroy learn that a coded telegram was sent to him the next day ordering his immediate withdrawal to Harper's Ferry. Confederate cavalry had cut the wires at Martinsburg, however; so, as Lee's army bore down on him, Milroy was not only isolated, he was locked in silence.

Lieutenant General Richard Ewell's II Corps led the Rebel advance. Some of these men had been in the recently deceased Stonewall Jackson's command, so they knew the valley and had experience in moving rapidly on the difficult roads through its mountainous terrain. Ewell planned to descend on Winchester while detachments

assailed garrisons at Berryville and Martinsburg. He also knew that Winchester's fortifications were vulnerable only from the west and northwest, where high ground could match their elevation. So, on 13 June he sent Jubal Early's division ahead on the Valley Pike toward Newtown, while Edward Johnson's division moved north on the Front Royal Road. Johnson fought a small skirmish before forming a line of battle a couple of miles from Winchester. Confederate and Federal artillery were exchanging fire when Early arrived about 5:00 P.M. and brushed up against a Federal brigade near Kernstown. It rained that night as the garrison from Milroy's outpost at Berryville arrived with the news that a large force—it had been Rodes's division—had moved on them that afternoon. Alarmed, Milroy arranged to send out scouts to discover enemy strength. He meanwhile put his forces into the forts west of town. It is exactly what Ewell had expected would happen.

Ewell did not expect, however, to see Federal works on Flint Ridge, the very ground he had planned to occupy and from which he wanted to launch his attack. Yet first thing on 14 June, Milroy had placed the 110th and 116th Ohio Volunteer Infantry and a battery of the 5th U.S. Artillery on the ridge. Ewell sent Johnson to demonstrate against this force and distract attention from Jubal Early, who proceeded undetected to a position west of town that placed his artillery at close range to Milroy's southern fortifications. Johnson not only entertained the small force on Flint Ridge, he drove it back into the main bastion. At about 6:00 P.M., when Early's artillery opened close in with twenty guns, Milroy soon saw this withering fire and his own dwindling ammunition silence the Federal batteries. Worse, the rebel maneuvers had restricted his position to the main fort and the star fort just north of it.

It was now obvious that this was not a mere raiding party of rebels from the valley. It was not even a larger force such as Jeb Stuart's cavalry. Something with a lot of artillery and many men was out there in the darkness, moving on him from different directions, and his earlier claim that he could hold Winchester against any Rebel force now collapsed under the weight of those numbers. He simply had not calculated on that Rebel force being the Army of Northern Virginia. Surrender was out of the question, but he could not stay in the cramped forts with only a day's rations and no operative artillery. At 9:00 P.M. a glum council of war in the main fort concluded that the garrison would spike its guns, abandon its wagons, and make a run for it—the sooner the better.

Ewell had prepared for such a decision by sending most of Johnson's division supported by artillery north on the Martinsburg Road. At 1:00 A.M., Milroy pulled out of his forts, avoided Winchester by sliding through a ravine for about a mile, and reached the road to Martinsburg. But he had not moved more than five miles north when he ran into Johnson at Stephenson's Depot. Between 3:00 and 4:00 A.M., a furious fight developed as the Federals tried to cut through and outflank the rebel wall between them and safety. As word reached him that the enemy was moving up from Winchester on his rear, Milroy elected to break off the engagement and slip his forces away. Confusion over his orders, however, made elements of the force more vulnerable in the face of the Confederates. Milroy's horse was shot from under him, and by the time he had remounted, his people were hopelessly divided into two columns. Many became trapped. Milroy and fragments of his shattered division (about 2,700 men) finally made their way by various routes to Bloody Run.

Ewell had captured Winchester and considerably more. At a cost of 269 casualties, he had taken about 4,000 prisoners, 23 artillery pieces (most of them rifled), 300 wagons, as many horses, and abundant provisions. Moreover, any doubts about "Old Baldy" leading Jackson's men with less élan than Stonewall were at least temporarily dispelled. With the scattering of the Federal garrison at Martinsburg that same day, the Confederate advance down the valley to the Potomac could continue at a quick and unimpeded pace.

Milroy was relieved of command and sent to Baltimore, where he was placed under arrest pending an inquiry. A court examined the affair at Winchester, including the skirmish at Berryville, and resolved that the luckless commander was essentially blameless for a disaster that had resulted more from circumstance than any dereliction on his part. It was small comfort for the smashed 2d Division.

—*David S. Heidler and Jeanne T. Heidler*

See also Berryville, Virginia; Martinsburg, Virginia; Milroy, Robert H.

For further reading:

Colt, Margaretta Barton. *Defend the Valley: A Shenandoah Family in the Civil War* (1999).

Hurst, Lora Ruth. "The Effect of Military Operations upon Civilian Life in Winchester, Virginia, during the Civil War" (Thesis, 1953).

Lopp, Larry G. "The Campaigns of General Robert H. Milroy, 1862–1863" (M.A. thesis, 1970).

Paulus, Margaret Babcock, comp. *Papers of General Robert Huston Milroy* (1965).

WINCHESTER, VIRGINIA, THIRD BATTLE OF (OPEQUON)
(19 September 1864)

The third battle of Winchester was the first real battle of Philip Sheridan's Shenandoah Valley campaign against Jubal Early. In early August an infantry division and a cavalry division under the overall command of Richard Anderson had reinforced Early. As a result, Ulysses S. Grant had instructed Sheridan to remain on the defensive. This defensive posture convinced Early that Sheridan was timid and disorgan-

ized and that he never had any intention of going on the offensive. The two spent over a month maneuvering.

Early's conviction that Sheridan did not intend to attack his position at Winchester east of Opequon Creek led Early on 14 September to send Anderson's infantry back to Lee. This diminution in Early's forces was exactly what Sheridan had been waiting for.

In Winchester lived a Quaker woman named Rebecca Wright who regularly supplied Sheridan with information regarding Early's movements. On 16 September she sent word regarding the infantry division's departure. On 17 September Grant came to Charlestown, West Virginia, to confer with Sheridan and approved Sheridan's plan to go on the offensive.

Early, still convinced of Sheridan's timidity, sent Robert Emmett Rodes's division and John Brown Gordon's division thirteen miles north of Winchester to Bunker Hill on 17 September. On 18 September, Early went with Gordon to Martinsburg, where he learned of Grant's presence at Charlestown and the meeting with Sheridan. He immediately surmised that something was afoot and turned around with Gordon and returned to Bunker Hill. There he sent Rodes and his division on a night march to Stephenson's Depot, five miles north of

Winchester, and instructed Gordon to rest for a few hours and to be at the same place by dawn on the nineteenth. John C. Breckinridge's division was already at Stephenson's Depot. Early's other remaining infantry division, commanded by Stephen Dodson Ramseur, was east of Winchester guarding the Berryville Pike approach to the town. Early placed Lunsford Lindsay Lomax's cavalry division to the southeast of town and Fitzhugh Lee's cavalry division to the north guarding the Confederate right and left flanks. In all Early had about 17,000 men to face Sheridan's 37,000.

Sheridan's plan was to send William Woods Averell's and Wesley Merritt's cavalry divisions toward Winchester from the north along the Martinsburg Pike, and cavalry brigades under Thomas Casimer Devin and Charles Russell Lowell in from the northeast along the Charlestown Road. James Harrison Wilson's cavalry division, in the meantime, would come from the east along the Berryville Pike, which after crossing Opequon Creek cut through a canyon before reaching the outskirts of Winchester. Wilson was to take possession of the canyon before the Confederates knew about the attack. In this way he would prevent Confederate guns from being placed atop the canyon walls and therefore allow the Federal infantry to reach Ramseur's defensive

The Battle of Opequan, 19 September 1864 (*Library of Congress*)

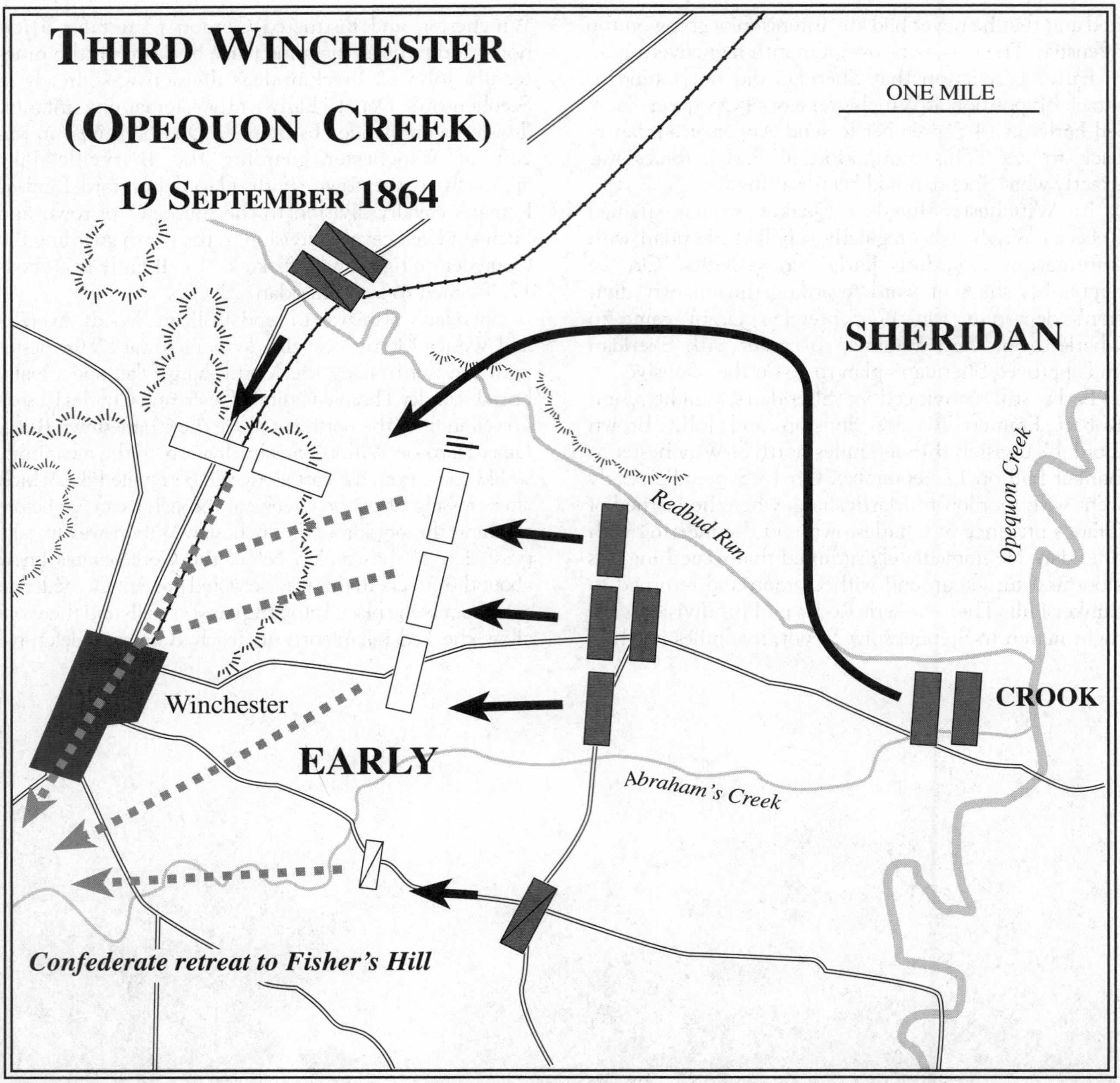

THIRD WINCHESTER (OPEQUON CREEK)

19 SEPTEMBER 1864

ONE MILE

SHERIDAN

Redbud Run

Opequon Creek

CROOK

Winchester

EARLY

Abraham's Creek

Confederate retreat to Fisher's Hill

positions east of Winchester. Wilson was to be followed quickly by the VI Corps under Horatio Gouverneur Wright and the XIX Corps under William Hemsley Emory. George Crook's VIII Corps would be kept in reserve behind the VI and XIX Corps. Wilson's mission accomplished, he was to move south of Winchester to prevent Early's retreat along the Valley Pike.

Wilson started out at about 2 A.M., crossed the Opequon, and made it through the canyon and to Ramseur's picket's before encountering opposition. Wilson pressed Ramseur's position, while waiting for Wright's and Emory's corps. In the meantime, Early had sent word to Rodes and Gordon at Stephenson's Depot to move south

to reinforce Ramseur's left flank, with Gordon arriving first. Breckinridge remained at Stephenson's Depot, and then moved east to oppose the movement down the Charlestown Road by Devin and Lowell.

Gordon's arrival did a great deal to shore up the Confederate lines, as the Federal infantry—particularly Emory's corps—was slow to move into position. Emory's tardiness was due to Wright, who, contrary to Sheridan's instructions, brought his wagon train, which temporarily blocked Emory's route of march through Berryville Pike canyon. When Emory did not appear as scheduled, Sheridan rode back to determine the reason for the delay. He ordered the wagons off the road so that XIX

Corps could march to the battlefield. Still, the delay resulted in a gap between VI and XIX Corps that at about 11 A.M. Gordon and Rodes determined to exploit. Both commanders saw that the bulk of the Union effort was directed against Ramseur's division on the Confederate right. Ramseur's men had been fighting all morning and were quite fatigued. This situation fit nicely into Sheridan's plan because, if he succeeded in turning the Confederate right with the Union cavalry coming down on the Confederate left, he would be able to envelop Early's entire army. Rodes and Gordon, seeing what was happening and seeing the gap in the Union line decided to turn Sheridan's right.

The two divisions attacked, resulting immediately in heavy casualties, including the death of Rodes. The Union forces tried to counterattack, but were pushed back by Confederate artillery. Supported by the same artillery, part of Rodes's division attacked toward the gap at the Berryville Pike and came close to bringing about the collapse of Sheridan's right, but a timely move into the gap by a Federal brigade and the arrival of fresh artillery broke the Confederate advance. The Confederates were driven back again with heavy losses on both sides. At that point Sheridan sent Crook, whom he had been hoping to send with Wilson's cavalry to prevent a retreat, in to reinforce the right of the Union advance.

By now it was early afternoon and the outnumbered Confederates, threatened now from the east and the north, had begun to form at a right angle facing both directions. Breckinridge arrived at about 2 P.M., having withdrawn in the face of the Union cavalry moves to the north, and now formed the extreme left of the Confederate lines. Early pulled back slowly, establishing new defensive lines as he went, still facing east and north. At about 5 P.M. he was positioned just northeast of town and realized if he was not to be overwhelmed or have his retreat options completely cut, he would have to order a retreat. Being pressed by Union cavalry from the north and infantry from the east, Early's army was near panic when orders were finally issued to begin moving up the Valley Pike. The withdrawal commenced before dark up the Valley Pike south to Strasburg, where he found a defensible position at Fisher's Hill. The retreat was chaotic and threatened to disintegrate completely when a pursuit was organized by Crook. Darkness saved Early's army, however, and it moved quickly south. Total casualties for the day were 5,018 for Sheridan and 1,818 for Early.

—David S. Heidler and Jeanne T. Heidler

See also Early, Jubal A.; Fisher's Hill, Battle of; Shenandoah Valley Campaign (August 1864–March 1865); Sheridan, Philip Henry.

For further reading:

Stackpole, Edward J. *Sheridan in the Shenandoah; Jubal Early's Nemesis* (1992).

Wert, Jeffry D. *From Winchester to Cedar Creek: The Shenandoah Campaign of 1864* (1987; reprint 1997).

WINDER, CHARLES SIDNEY
(1829–1862)
Confederate general

Born in Talbot County on Maryland's Eastern Shore, Charles Sidney Winder was educated locally before receiving an appointment to the U.S. Military Academy in 1846. He graduated twenty-second of forty-four in the class of 1850. For the first four years of his service, he was stationed at a variety of frontier posts. In 1854 he was transferred to the West Coast. En route to California his ship was caught in a hurricane. He was credited with saving many of the soldiers on the ship and promoted to captain for his heroism. While serving in the Pacific Northwest, Winder distinguished himself in combat against the Spokane Indians.

A strong proponent of Southern rights, Winder resigned his commission in March 1861, deciding not to wait to see if his native Maryland would secede from the Union. He immediately offered his services to the Confederate States Army and was commissioned a major in the Confederate artillery. Sent to South Carolina as part of the Confederate force watching Major Robert Anderson's garrison at Fort Sumter, Winder participated in the artillery bombardment of the fort that resulted in its surrender in April 1861. He remained in South Carolina after the surrender of the fort and in early July was made the colonel of the 6th South Carolina Infantry.

Sent to Virginia after the mustering in of the regiment, Winder and his men arrived at Manassas Junction immediately after the fighting ended in the battle of First Bull Run. Winder and his men served near Manassas Junction under Joseph E. Johnston for the remainder of the year. During that time Johnston became impressed with Winder's military bearing. In February 1862 Johnston recommended Winder's promotion to brigadier general. The promotion occurred during the first week of March with a date of rank of 1 March 1862. For the next few weeks, Winder commanded the troops around Manassas Junction. Later in March he received a transfer to command the Stonewall Brigade then serving in the Shenandoah Valley.

Winder was to replace Richard Garnett who had been arrested by Jackson for withdrawing the brigade at Kernstown. Garnett was popular with the brigade, and when Winder arrived to take command he was greeted with sullen stares and occasional jeers. Because he was a stern disciplinarian and rather cold in his personal demeanor, Winder would never be popular with the brigade, but he won the grudging respect of the men with his thorough professionalism and his obvious courage and cool-headedness in battle.

Winder commanded the Stonewall Brigade and served as Jackson's second-in-command through the remainder of Jackson's Shenandoah Valley campaign.

During the battles of the campaign, Winder increasingly came to the attention of Jackson as a brave and energetic commander whom Jackson could depend on during the constant marching throughout the valley. Winder especially distinguished himself at Winchester and at Port Republic. In the latter battle, he charged the Federal forces in his front because he knew that he was outnumbered and might not be able to withstand an attack by the other side. His attack caught his enemy off guard long enough for Winder to receive reinforcements.

Winder and the Stonewall Brigade, along with most of Jackson's army, went with Jackson to the environs of Richmond in the fourth week of June. Winder and his brigade distinguished themselves at Gaines' Mill and Malvern Hill during the Seven Days' battles.

When Jackson moved toward part of John Pope's advancing army near Cedar Mountain in early August 1862, Winder was in bed with a severe fever. He followed the army in an ambulance, and, though still quite unwell, insisted on the night of 8 August that he could resume command. The following morning Winder was given command of the division (Jackson having been elevated to corps command). Later that day, Jackson's corps encountered Nathaniel P. Banks's force at Cedar Mountain. In the midst of an artillery duel as a preliminary to the battle, Winder, while giving instructions to his own gunners, was struck in the left side by a Union artillery shell. His side, arm, and back were horribly mangled though he did not lose consciousness. After being quickly examined by a surgeon, he was carried to the rear on a stretcher to die. He lingered for two hours before succumbing to his wounds. His remains were returned to his home outside Easton, Maryland, for burial. Both Jackson and Robert E. Lee, who saw great promise in Winder's Confederate military career, lamented his loss.

—*David S. Heidler and Jeanne T. Heidler*

See also Cedar Mountain, Battle of; Stonewall Brigade.
For further reading:
Robertson, James I., Jr. *The Stonewall Brigade* (1963).

WINDER, JOHN HENRY
(1800–1865)
Confederate general

John Henry Winder was born in Somerset County, Maryland, the son of War of 1812 veteran William H. Winder and Gertrude Polk Winder. He was educated at the U.S. Military Academy, where he graduated eleventh of thirty in the class of 1820. He was commissioned a second lieutenant of artillery and served in Florida and at Fort McHenry in Baltimore harbor. He resigned his commission in 1823, but decided to return to the army in 1827. He served in Florida again and on the Maine frontier

John H. Winder (*Library of Congess*)

before returning for a time as an instructor at West Point. While Winder was there, future Confederate president Jefferson Davis matriculated as a cadet.

Winder fought in the Mexican-American War, where he received two brevet promotions. At the time of his resignation to accept a commission in the Confederate army, Winder had achieved the regular rank of major.

Winder's extensive military experience gained him a Confederate commission as a brigadier general in June 1861. His first assignment, which would set the tone for his entire Civil War career, was commander of military prisons in Richmond, including Libby Prison and Belle Isle, and as provost marshal for the city of Richmond. In both jobs he received criticism. As commander of numerous prisons throughout the war, Winder was criticized by Northerners and Southerners for the dirty conditions and the deprivation suffered by the Union soldiers. As provost marshal in Richmond, he was criticized for the high prices and lawless element that seemed drawn to the wartime city. Given the command of the Department of Henrico (Richmond and surrounding area) later in 1861, Winder used his new power to fix prices, stop the distillation of alcoholic beverages, and restore some semblance of order to the town by the spring, just in time for George McClellan's Peninsula campaign.

Along with his duties of overseeing prisons and maintaining order in Richmond during the first two years of the war, Winder also dealt with prisoner exchanges, supervised instruction of new recruits, and during combat around the city, moved troops through the city as quickly as possible toward the front.

In May 1864 Winder was sent to the 2d Military District of North Carolina and Southern Virginia, but in June he was transferred again to assume command of Andersonville Prison in Georgia. A month later he was made commander of all prisons in Georgia and Alabama. In August of that year, one prison inspector recommended that someone with more energy and humanity replace Winder. Instead, in November 1864 Winder was made commissary general of all Confederate prisons east of the Mississippi.

Winder's new duties came at a particularly stressful time for prisons in the Deep South. With William T. Sherman beginning his march through Georgia and subsequently conducting the Carolina campaign, Winder and other prison officials struggled to keep Union prisoners from being liberated by Union soldiers. Winder supervised the attempt to move some of the prisoners out of Andersonville and was still working frantically to deal with the prisoner situation in the Carolinas when he died of apparent exhaustion in February 1865. Some speculated that had he not died during the war, Winder would have been tried for war crimes along with Henry Wirz, the commander at Andersonville at the end of the war, and possibly executed.

—*David S. Heidler and Jeanne T. Heidler*

See also Andersonville; Prisons, C.S.A.; Wirz, Henry.
For further reading:
Blakey, Arch Fredric. *General John H. Winder, C.S.A.* (1990).

WINSLOW, JOHN ANCRUM
(1811–1873)
U.S. Navy rear admiral

A relatively unknown officer before the war, John Winslow overcame a relatively lackluster antebellum career to become one of the Union's most prominent naval heroes of the Civil War. Moving only slowly through the ranks before the war, Winslow took advantage of the situations the war presented him and ended his career at the highest commands.

Born to a prestigious family in Wilmington, North Carolina, John Winslow defied his parent's expectations of his pursuing a college education and enlisted as a U.S. Navy midshipman at the age of sixteen in 1827. Serving on various vessels in home waters, Winslow did not advance to the rank of second lieutenant until 1839, when he transferred to the South American Squadron. In 1842, Winslow was to accompany the USS *Missouri* to China, but the unfortunate vessel was destroyed by fire at Gibraltar. Returned to duty in home waters, second lieutenant Winslow's career lagged until notable service during the Mexican-American War earned him temporary command of a captured vessel, the USS *Morris*, until the end of the war. Between 1849 and 1855, Winslow, promoted to lieutenant, acted as ordnance officer at the Boston Navy Yard and aboard the USS *St. Lawrence* of the Pacific Squadron. Promoted to commander in 1855, Winslow supervised naval recruiting in Boston for three years, followed by a two-year stint as a lighthouse inspector.

The outbreak of the Civil War found the U.S. Navy in need of experienced officers to construct and supervise its forces on the Mississippi River, and Commander Winslow found himself supervising the construction of gunboats far from the ocean. Commanding the new gunboats in support of General Ulysses S. Grant's advance into Tennessee, Winslow's ability to organize effective crews attracted the navy's attention, although his career was nearly cut short. Leading a section of gunboats from the ironclad *St. Louis* in 1862, Winslow suffered a horrible injury when an anchor chain broke, and flying fragments nearly severed his left arm. Refusing to relinquish his command, Winslow accepted only a brief medical leave and was back in action in only a few weeks.

Winslow's aggressiveness earned him a promotion to captain in July 1862, and command of the USS *Kearsarge* in European waters. The navy had lost confidence in *Kearsarge*'s commanding officer, Captain Charles W. Pickering, who was accused of not vigorously pursuing Confederate commerce-raiders destroying Union merchant vessels. The *Kearsarge* spent most of the next two years carefully observing the Confederate raiders CSS *Florida* and *Rappahannock* refitting in French ports, but could not engage the vessels without violating France's nominal neutrality. In June 1864, however, Winslow and the *Kearsarge* were offered battle by the CSS *Alabama*, under the command of Captain Raphael Semmes, off the French port of Cherbourg. Although eager to dispose of the Confederate raider, Winslow carefully positioned his ship well outside French territorial waters to ensure that *Alabama* did not escape. In the only major high-seas encounter of the Civil War, Winslow adroitly directed the *Kearsarge*'s fire until, riddled below the waterline, the *Alabama* sank. Semmes and most of his officers, however, escaped to Great Britain.

Winslow was promoted to commodore upon his triumphal return to the United States. Granted an extended leave, Winslow did not see any more action before the end of the war. In 1866, he was given command of the Gulf Squadron. In 1870, he received the rank of rear admiral and command of the Pacific Squadron. Due to ill health, Winslow retired from the navy in 1872 and moved to Boston, where he died in 1873.

—*Steven J. Ramold*

See also *Alabama*, CSS; *Kearsarge*, USS; Navy, U.S.A.; Riverine Warfare, U.S.N.

For further reading:

Anderson, Bern. *By Sea and by River: The Naval History of the Civil War* (1962).

Ellicott, John M. *The Life of John Ancrum Winslow, Rear Admiral, United States Navy* (1902).

Fowler, William M., Jr. *Under Two Flags: The American Navy in the Civil War* (1990).

Marvel, William. *The Alabama and the Kearsarge: The Sailor's Civil War* (1996).

WIRZ, HENRY
(1823–1865)
Commander of Andersonville Prison

Hartman Heinrich Wirz, the only Confederate soldier tried and executed for war crimes, was born in Zurich, Switzerland, on 25 November 1823. He probably arrived in New York in the spring of 1849 and resided in New Orleans a year later. In 1854 Wirz moved to Hopkinsville, Kentucky, and then Louisville, where he apprenticed with several physicians. He settled in Madison Parish, Louisiana, in 1856 to become a homeopathic physician and a physician to slaves. In May 1861, Wirz joined the Madison Infantry of the 4th Louisiana Battalion as a private.

While the battalion guarded Union prisoners in Richmond after Bull Run, Wirz came to the notice of Inspector General John H. Winder. Transferred to Winder's command on 26 August 1861 and promoted to sergeant, Wirz served as a clerk and supervised prisoners. In December, Wirz was assigned to the prison in Tuscaloosa, Alabama. When Captain Elias Griswold received another posting the following April, residents there successfully petitioned that Wirz take command. In early June, however, Winder recalled Wirz to Richmond. Promoted to captain, Wirz enforced martial law and later commanded all the prisons in Richmond, which were

The execution of Captain Henry Wirz, Washington, D.C., 10 November 1865 (*Library of Congress*)

rapidly emptying as a result of prisoner exchanges with the North. Beginning in September 1862, Wirz escorted Union soldiers from prisons across the Confederacy to Richmond and Vicksburg for exchange. His travels extended from Richmond to Houston, Texas, and probably at this time Wirz suffered severe injuries to his right wrist and shoulders in a stagecoach accident. (His later claim of being wounded at Seven Pines is contradicted by the evidence.) From late December 1862 until March, Wirz was on a medical furlough at his Louisiana home.

Upon his return to active duty, Wirz traveled to Europe. His business there is shrouded in mystery, but aside from visiting Parisian doctors, Wirz probably delivered messages to Confederate emissaries. In late January 1864, a blockade runner brought Wirz to the port of Wilmington. No sooner had Wirz returned to Richmond than Winder assigned him to take charge of the new prison camp near Andersonville, Georgia.

The horrors at Andersonville are well documented, but scholars disagree over Wirz's responsibility for them. The Union ceased prisoner exchanges, and the deteriorating conditions in the Confederacy by 1864 hindered the acquisition of proper food, medicine, and other supplies. Wirz tried to alleviate some of the conditions, but he grew frustrated and generally interpreted his orders strictly. Approximately 30 percent of the 46,000 prisoners perished at Andersonville, and the remainder suffered from scurvy, exposure, dysentery, and other diseases. "There are deeds, crimes that may be forgiven," Walt Whitman wrote after seeing many of the survivors of Andersonville, "but this is not among them."

The government and the Northern public agreed. On 7 May 1865, Wirz was arrested. After a harrowing journey in which camp survivors tried to seize and kill him, Wirz was incarcerated in the Old Capitol Prison in Washington, D.C. Colonel Norton Parker Chipman of the Bureau of Military Justice presented a military commission two charges: conspiracy "to injure the health and destroy the lives of soldiers in the military service of the United States" and murder.

Wirz was doomed. Judge Advocate Chipman aspired to establish a conspiracy involving Jefferson Davis and other high Confederate authorities, "and not simply to submit evidence to convict Wirz, which was of comparatively small consequence and the work of only a few days." The trial began on 23 August and ultimately involved 160 witnesses. On 24 October, the court found Wirz guilty of conspiracy and the murder of eleven individuals despite many procedural irregularities and flagrant perjury on the murder charges. On the morning of 10 November 1865, in the yard of the Old Capitol Prison (present site of the Supreme Court), Wirz was hanged as four companies of soldiers chanted, "Wirz—remember—Andersonville."

In many respects, Wirz was an ill-starred individual, a victim of superiors and forces totally beyond his control. No amount of training could have prepared him for the supervision of the largest prison population in the war. Whatever compassion he had was overwhelmed by the conditions that grew more hideous through the spring and summer of 1864. Ultimately the ignominious demise of 13,000 soldiers was too much to ignore, and Wirz became the last victim of Andersonville.

—M. *Philip Lucas*

See also Andersonville; Prisoners of War; Prisons, C.S.A.; Winder, John Henry.

For further reading:

Chipman, Norton Parker. *The Tragedy of Andersonville* (1911).

LaForce, Glen W. "The Trial of Major Henry Wirz—A National Disgrace." *The Army Lawyer* (1988).

Marvel, William. *Andersonville: The Last Depot* (1994).

Morsberger, Robert E., and Katharine M. Morsberger. "After Andersonville: The First War Crimes Trial." *Civil War Times Illustrated* (1974).

U.S. Congress. House. *Trial of Henry Wirz* (1868).

WISE, HENRY ALEXANDER
(1806–1876)
Governor of Virginia and Confederate general

Born the son of John Wise and Sarah Corbin Cropper Wise in Accomac County on Virginia's Eastern Shore, Henry Alexander Wise was orphaned by the age of six and reared by relatives. He was educated locally before being sent to Washington College in Washington, Pennsylvania. Upon his return, he studied law under Henry St. George Tucker. After completing his studies, Wise moved briefly to Nashville, Tennessee, where he practiced law before returning home to Accomac County to open a practice there.

A successful local attorney, Wise also became active in Virginia politics as a strong supporter of Andrew Jackson. Wise served in the U.S. House of Representatives from 1833 until 1844. A supporter of the Second Bank of the United States, Wise broke with Jackson over the president's removal of the federal deposits from the bank, and for a few years Wise became a Whig. During the presidency of Virginian friend John Tyler, Wise gained the appointment of U.S. minister to Brazil, a post he continued to occupy under the presidency of Tyler's successor, Democrat James K. Polk.

Upon his return to the United States in 1847, Wise return to law, though he remained interested in Virginia state politics, serving in the state constitutional convention and in 1855 running and winning election as the governor of the state. Though Wise had been a fairly active proponent of states' rights before becoming governor, in his new office he became much more national in his interest. As a strong supporter of James Buchanan's candidacy for the presidency in 1856, Wise

apparently had hopes of winning the nomination himself four years later. The John Brown raid of the fall of 1859, however, pushed Wise back into the states' rights camp, and his insistence on a vigorous prosecution of Brown earned him many friends in the Deep South.

Having left office in 1860, Wise was eligible to serve in the Virginia secession convention in 1861. In that body, Wise initially opposed secession, believing that Virginia could defend its rights within the Union. However, he opposed the use of force to coerce those states that had already seceded and, when Abraham Lincoln called for volunteers to suppress those states' attempt at separation, Wise joined the majority of delegates to the Virginia convention in voting for secession.

Upon Virginia's joining of the Confederacy, Wise offered his military services to the Confederate army and was commissioned a brigadier general. Serving initially in western Virginia in the Kanawha Valley, where he had raised a legion, Wise was commanded by Robert E. Lee. Wise fought a skirmish at Scarey Creek in western Virginia in July 1861 and continued to patrol the region until September 1861, when he was relieved of command and sent to North Carolina.

In January 1862 he was given command of the District of Albemarle, headquartered on Roanoke Island. Defeated there the following month in Ambrose Burnside's campaign against coastal North Carolina, Wise lost his son O. Jennings Wise who was mortally wounded in the attack.

In June 1862 Wise fought in the Seven Days' battles and was commended for his actions in the engagements that immediately preceded Malvern Hill. After the Peninsula campaign, he remained in southern Virginia and North Carolina, guarding against Union raids while the Army of Northern Virginia operated north of Richmond. In the spring and summer of 1863 while serving under Major General Arnold Elzey on the James River, Wise watched Federal troops on the tip of the York Peninsula.

At the end of the summer of 1863, Wise was transferred to Charleston to aid General P. G. T. Beauregard in the defense of the South Carolina coast. Wise served there until the spring of 1864, when he moved north with Beauregard to take command of the First Military District, Department of North Carolina and Southern Virginia. In May 1864, Wise fought in the repulse of Benjamin Butler at Drewry's Bluff and for the next ten months in the trenches of Petersburg. In the breakout from Petersburg, Wise fought bravely at Sayler's Creek and, according to one report, received a battlefield promotion from Lee to major general there. He surrendered with Lee's army three days later at Appomattox Court House.

After the war, Wise refused to ask for a pardon from the federal government. He did resume his law practice, however, working with one of his sons, John. Wise died in Richmond in September 1876.

Not considered a great commander during the war, Wise nevertheless demonstrated tremendous courage in battle and won the respect of everyone who fought beside him.

—*David S. Heidler and Jeanne T. Heidler*

See also Drewry's Bluff, Battle of; Roanoke Island, North Carolina; Virginia.
For further reading:
Simpson, Craig M. *A Good Southerner: The Life of Henry A. Wise of Virginia* (1985).

WITHERS, JONES MITCHELL
(1814–1890)
Confederate general

Born the son of John Wright Withers and Mary Herbert Jones Withers in Huntsville, Alabama, Jones Mitchell Withers was educated locally before accepting an appointment to the U.S. Military Academy, where he graduated forty-fourth of fifty-six in the class of 1835. Withers quickly determined, however, that he did not enjoy the military life and resigned his commission to study law. He served briefly in the Creek War of 1836. Eventually opening a practice in Mobile, Alabama, Withers interrupted his career to serve as a lieutenant colonel and colonel in the Mexican-American War.

After his service in Mexico, Withers became active in politics. As a member of the American, or Know-Nothing, Party, he was elected to the U.S. House of Representatives and served one term from 1855 to 1857. Immediately before the Civil War, he served as the mayor of Mobile. The secession of Alabama and formation of the Confederacy brought about his resignation as mayor and his entrance into the Confederate army.

Given a commission as the colonel of the 3d Alabama Infantry, Withers took his regiment to Virginia, where he served at Norfolk until July 1861, when he was promoted to brigadier general and given command of the Department of Alabama and Eastern Mississippi. In December he was given command of the District of Alabama, headquartered at Mobile. His command was changed to the Army of Mobile in January 1862.

In March 1862, Withers commanded Fort Pillow and then commanded a division of Braxton Bragg's corps at Shiloh. He was commended by Bragg for his actions at Shiloh. In August 1862, Withers was promoted to major general and led his division in Bragg's Kentucky campaign of the fall of 1862. He fought at Stones River, where he once again was commended for his bravery.

After Stones River, Withers went on extended sick leave. By late spring he was back in command to lead his division in the Tullahoma campaign. That summer saw his health again force him to relinquish command, but by

early 1864 he was sufficiently recovered to take command of the Northern District of Alabama. Two months later in April 1864, Withers assumed command of the Reserve Forces of the state of Alabama. His primary duty through the summer of 1864 was to recruit and organize men for Confederate service. Initially headquartered at Montgomery, Withers moved his recruiting operation to Mobile after the battle of Mobile Bay. He was there at the end of the war and surrendered his command.

After his parole, Withers remained in Mobile. He practiced law and renewed his interest in politics. He was elected mayor in 1867. Along with his law practice and political activities, Withers owned a cotton brokerage and briefly served as editor of the *Mobile Tribune*. He died in Mobile on 13 March 1890.

—*David S. Heidler and Jeanne T. Heidler*

See also Alabama; Shiloh, Battle of; Stones River, Battle of.
For further reading:
McMillan, Malcolm C. *The Alabama Confederate Reader* (1963).

WITTENMYER, ANNIE TURNER
(1827–1900)
Civilian aid organizer

At the time the Civil War broke out, widow Annie Turner Wittenmyer of Iowa had already established herself as a force for benevolence in what would quickly become the strategically important town of Keokuk, at the southeastern corner of the state on the Mississippi River. Wittenmyer was among those who joined in the work of organizing the Keokuk Ladies' Soldiers' Aid Society just over a month after the fall of Fort Sumter. As the society's corresponding secretary and later its general agent, Wittenmyer strove with great success to generate interest among her townsfolk, and across her state, for the massive labor of supplying Iowa's soldiers with the material goods that the United States government was unprepared to provide. Like its sister societies in Iowa and elsewhere across both the Union and the Confederacy, the Keokuk Society, with Wittenmyer at the helm, coordinated the production and distribution of a wide range of goods—uniforms, bandages, bedding, food—necessary for the soldiers' effective performance on the battlefield, as well as for their care and survival off of it. Within months of its founding, the Keokuk Society became the premier soldiers' aid organization in Iowa. Wittenmyer, who traveled widely to assess and report on the needs of Union soldiers in general, and Iowa soldiers in particular, became known across much of the North and among the Union army's leadership.

In the fall of 1861, Annie Wittenmyer's Keokuk Ladies' Soldiers' Aid Society suffered a temporary setback to its dominance of Iowa's civilian aid to the Union soldiers. In October Governor Samuel J. Kirkwood established the Iowa State Army Sanitary Commission as the state's official branch of the United States Sanitary Commission (USSC), founded in June to provide a national umbrella for the thousands of aid organizations that were cropping up across the Union. Some women active in soldiers' aid enjoyed the centralizing influence and the national status that submission to the control of the USSC offered. Wittenmyer and most of her colleagues in the Keokuk Society did not, and they resented perhaps most deeply the implication that the men who dominated the leadership of the USSC (and those who led the Iowa State Army Sanitary Commission) knew more than they about the work they had taken up on behalf of the soldiers. With an unswerving determination to complete the work she and her townswomen had begun in the aftermath of Sumter, Wittenmyer led an ultimately successful struggle for the society's right to maintain control over Iowa's civilian aid to the soldiers. Finally, after two confusing years, in the fall of 1863 Governor Kirkwood conceded to Wittenmyer's demands, merging the two organizations and naming Wittenmyer the corresponding secretary and general agent of the newly reorganized Iowa Sanitary Commission. With this victory under her belt, and having significantly honed her political skills, Wittenmyer turned the leadership of the new organization over to others and moved on.

In the last year and a half of the war, Wittenmyer undertook the establishment of a series of institutions in Iowa dedicated to the care of the orphans of deceased Union soldiers. The most famous was the home in Davenport, which could house as many as 600 children and for which Wittenmyer persuaded the United States Congress to donate an initial $6,000 worth of hospital supplies. Wittenmyer's best known Civil War work, however, was her creation of a system of special-diet kitchens in hospitals across the theater of war to provide for the dietary requirements of the most gravely wounded and sick soldiers. These kitchens were staffed by a hand-selected group of white, middle-class women of irreproachable reputation and dedication to the cause. Through their diligence, competence, and good will, Wittenmyer's salaried kitchen managers earned the often reluctant respect of the male hospital staff with whom they worked. Wittenmyer herself earned a national reputation for her material role in saving the lives of thousands of sick and wounded soldiers of both the North and the South. After the war, Wittenmyer wrote extensively and published her memoir of her war years, *Under the Guns*, in 1895. She also continued her work in benevolence, becoming, among other things, the founding president of the Woman's Christian Temperance Union in 1874. Until her death in 1900,

Wittenmyer remained in the public eye as a reformer. In one of her last campaigns she lobbied for the passage of a bill granting Civil War nurses a monthly pension. With her help, the bill passed in 1892.

—*Elizabeth D. Leonard*

See also United States Sanitary Commission; Women.

For further reading:

Brockett, Linus P., and Mary C. Vaughan. *Woman's Work in the Civil War* (1867).

Fulbrook, Earl. "Relief Work in Iowa during the Civil War." *Iowa Journal of History and Politics* (1918).

Gallaher, Ruth A. "Annie Turner Wittenmyer." *Iowa Journal of History and Politics* (1931).

Leonard, Elizabeth. *Yankee Women: Gender Battles in the Civil War* (1994).

Wittenmyer, Annie. *Under the Guns: A Woman's Reminiscences of the Civil War* (1895).

WOFFORD, WILLIAM TATUM
(1823–1884)
Confederate general

Born in Habersham County, Georgia, on 28 June 1823, William Tatum Wofford was raised in Cassville, in the northwestern part of the state. He attended the Gwinnett Manual Labor Institute at Lawrenceville, Georgia, and Franklin College (University of Georgia) at Athens. Admitted to the Georgia bar in 1844, he practiced law in his hometown. After service in the Mexican-American War as a captain of mounted volunteers, Wofford in 1849 was elected to the Georgia House of Representatives, where he served two consecutive terms. As a Jackson Union Democrat, he was active in the Wilmot Proviso discussions and the Georgia Platform that upheld the Compromise of 1850.

Wofford served as clerk of the Lower House during the 1853–1854 session and then returned to his law practice in Cassville. He owned and edited *The Cassville Standard* for three years; his editorials therein were politically conservative and consistent in his call for good sense and leadership in government. In 1859, he married Julia Dwight of Spring Place, Murray County, Georgia, and they had four daughters, three of whom died in early childhood.

A delegate to the Georgia Secession Convention, 16 January 1861, Wofford voted against secession, but after the state seceded he raised at his own expense the 18th Georgia Infantry Regiment and became its colonel. In late 1861, the regiment was brigaded with three Texas regiments in Virginia and with them became the Texas Brigade of General John Bell Hood. After the Peninsula campaign of 1862, Hood was elevated to divisional command; Wofford, as senior colonel, was given command of the brigade and led it at Second Bull Run on 29–30 August 1862 and at Antietam on 17 September 1862. In November, the 18th Georgia was transferred to Brigadier General Thomas R. R. Cobb's Georgia brigade and served at Fredericksburg on 13 December 1862. Upon Cobb's death in the latter battle, Wofford was promoted to brigadier general and given command of the brigade. As such, he had conspicuous roles in the great battles of 1863 and 1864, particularly at Gettysburg and the Wilderness. In the latter, he suggested General James Longstreet's flank attack upon the Federal left wing on 6 May 1864.

In January 1865, Wofford was given command of the Department of North Georgia. In that command he sought to restore law and order and alleviate the civilian destitution wrought by the Dalton-to-Atlanta campaign of the previous year. On 2 May 1865, he surrendered his forces at Kingston, Georgia. Wofford was elected to the U.S. Congress later that year, but, along with other Southern congressmen, was not seated. While in Washington, however, he sought and procured aid for his region from Congressman William Darrah Kelley and the Freedmen's Bureau.

After the war, Wofford practiced law in Cassville and was active in the Democratic Party. As a delegate to the Georgia Constitutional Convention of 1877, he argued eloquently for the repeal of convict leasing, for Confederate veterans' benefits, for African-American education, and for good sense in state government. Many of his ideas were echoed in the platform of the Populist Party a decade later. He died in Cassville on 22 May 1884 and was buried in the Cassville cemetery.

—*Gerald J. Smith*

See also Wilderness, Battle of the.

For further reading:

Smith, Gerald J. *"One of the Most Daring of Men": The Life of Confederate General William Tatum Wofford* (1997).

WOMAN ORDER
See Butler's Proclamation

WOMEN

After touring America during the Civil War, Englishman George A. Sala questioned "whether either ancient or modern history can furnish an example of a conflict which was so much of a 'woman's war' as this." Sala perceptively drew attention to women's active participation and unprecedented sacrifice during the war. The Civil War forced women to take on new roles in support of their nations and families. In many ways, women made the Civil War their war.

Interest in the sectional crisis began before the outbreak of hostilities. In the South, many white women pushed their husbands toward secession. By appealing to their husbands' sense of familial duty, Southern women encouraged men to echo their political sentiments.

A daughter of the regiment (*National Archives*)

Other white women applauded their states' decisions to secede. South Carolinian Emma Holmes, for example, wrote that she was "doubly proud . . . of [her] native state, that she should be the first to arise and shake off the hated chain which linked us with Black Republicans and Abolitionists."

Northern women also voiced political opinions on secession. In a letter to President James Buchanan, one Minnesota woman urged action: "Are these Free States going to sit down quietly and let those Southern lunatics have their own way?"

When the hostilities began, white women made themselves essential to the war effort by encouraging men to enlist. They appealed to the manhood and honor of men and urged them to fill the ranks of the military. Men who refused often found themselves snubbed by the ladies. Emma Edmonds, a Union spy, noted that Southern women were "the best recruiting officers," refusing "to tolerate, or admit to their society any young man who refuses to enlist." Southern women's actions confirmed this observation. A woman in Selma, Alabama, broke off her engagement to a man who did not enlist. Instead, she sent him a petticoat, a skirt, and a note reading "wear these, or volunteer." Such sentiments were not restricted to the South. In 1861 one Northern woman proclaimed "I wouldn't look at a nonresistant" to secession.

By encouraging men to enlist, white women revealed their confidence in their own abilities. They understood that sending their men to battle meant that they would have to take on new responsibilities at home. One popular Northern song made this clear: "Take your gun and go, John / Take your gun and go / For Ruth can drive the oxen, John / And I can use the hoe."

With their husbands, sons, fathers, brothers, and overseers off fighting, white women remained at home to manage their homes, farms, stores, and plantations. The actions of women on the home front proved vital to the Confederate and Union war efforts. Through work in aid societies, factories, and farms, white women became major suppliers of food, uniforms, and other goods. Only weeks after the war began, women had already formed 20,000 aid societies. Most towns had their own female aid societies that provided soldiers with countless socks, undergarments, shirts, gloves, blankets, shoes, comforters, handkerchiefs, scarves, bandages, and food. Other women worked as individuals to send supplies to the soldiers. In the South, white women tried to supply the dietary needs of the nation and their families by joining their slaves in the fields.

Women also planned and attended bazaars, fairs, concerts, raffles, and dances to raise money for army supplies. These events, although invaluable to the causes they supported, faced resistance from some men. Union general William Tecumseh Sherman, for example, admonished his wife in 1865 for working at a bazaar: "I notice that you propose to take part in a Sanitary Fair at Chicago. I don't much approve of ladies selling things at a table. ... [I]t merely looks unbecoming for a lady to stand behind a table to sell things." Despite this attitude, one that was shared by men of both regions, women ran public fundraisers throughout the war.

Thousands of white women took on the traditionally male occupation of nurse during the Civil War. Approximately 20,000 women served as Union nurses. In the North, the Women's Central Relief Association (WCRA) and the United States Sanitary Commission (USSC) coordinated and enlisted white women's relief work. Both of these organizations restricted women's participation to the domestic spheres. Female volunteers aboard Union army hospital transport ships were recruited primarily for their organizational skill, an ability that was believed to be acquired through years of household management. These women assisted soldiers, but remained a safe distance from the battlefield. Other Northern women refused to conform to such restrictions. Clara Barton, for example, worked directly on the battlefields. Barton received special permission to supply and nurse Union troops in Fredericksburg, Virginia. She continued her battlefront efforts throughout the Civil War.

Without a centralized organization, relief work and nursing in the Confederacy remained localized.

Southern women took on the care of the wounded as best they could. One nurse, Kate Cumming, encouraged other women to care for the sick and wounded. She asked young girls to "do what, in all ages, has been the special duty of woman—to relieve suffering." In addition, because many Confederate towns became battlefields during the Civil War, many women unintentionally became frontline nurses. Hospitals were set up anywhere—homes, churches, town halls, and streets.

Some women crossed the boundaries of womanhood by dressing as men and enlisting as soldiers. Scholars have documented at least 400 women who donned military uniforms to fight for their nation. One woman, Mrs. L. M. Blalock, enlisted as Samuel Blalock to fight alongside her husband for the Confederacy. Others either fought with husbands or as individuals for their nation. These disguised women were rarely exposed by their fellow soldiers. Only when they were injured or killed did their identities become known.

Other women worked as spies during the Civil War. Because white women were rarely searched when they passed through enemy lines, they smuggled information, guns, medicine, and other items to troops under their skirts. Because of the secretive and dangerous nature of the work, it is impossible to determine an accurate count of female spies. However, some female spies left written accounts of their wartime work. Confederate Belle Boyd, for example, left letters that chronicled how she smuggled quinine and information to help Thomas "Stonewall" Jackson. Similarly, Sarah Emma Edmonds wrote about her experiences as a Union spy. She dressed as a man, nursed wounded soldiers, and fought on the battlefield. Harriet Tubman—the renowned "conductor" of the Underground Railroad—also spied during the war. Tubman, who had escaped from slavery in the 1840s, continued to lead slaves to freedom during the war. Tubman also alerted slaves to the location of Union troops and convinced slaves to trust the Northern men.

For many white women, war demanded that they find work outside the home. Some found work in occupations that had been open to them in antebellum America; they worked as maids, laundresses, seamstresses, and boardinghouse keepers. Those who lived in towns and cities also found work in factories. Some worked in ordnance plants, where they made minié balls, paper cartridges, percussion caps, fuses, and shells. Other white women became teachers when men left the home front. Union and Confederate women also found positions as nurses and government workers. By 1865, the United States Treasury Department employed 447 female copyists, clerks, and currency counters. Southern women also took government positions in the Confederate Post Office and Treasury Departments. The Treasury Note Bureau in Columbia, South Carolina, employed 200 female workers in 1864. Finally, the Civil War promoted

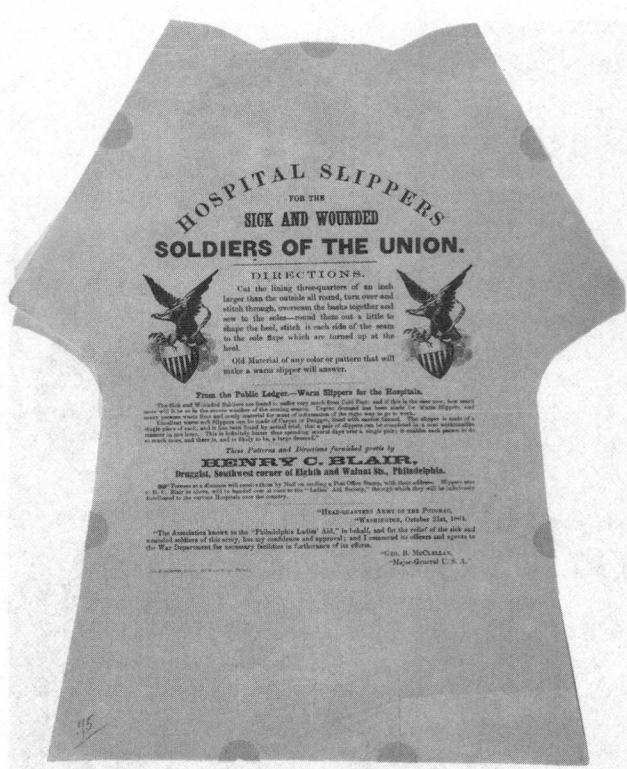

A flyer printed by a Pennsylvania druggist gives instructions for making slippers to assist the women's war effort. (*National Archives*)

the growth of prostitution in America's cities. Women in both regions turned to this trade to support themselves.

Southern women in occupied territories found countless ways to demonstrate their Confederate loyalty and displeasure with the Union invaders. In New Orleans, one Rebel woman dumped the contents of a chamber pot on Admiral David Farragut's head. This, combined with outward expressions of Confederate sentiments and a refusal to walk on the same side of the street as the Union soldiers, provoked General Benjamin Butler's infamous "Woman Order." With General Order No. 28, Butler asserted that any woman who refused to treat the soldiers with respect would be "treated as a woman of the town plying her avocation." This order intensified the hatred of "Beast Butler" among the women of New Orleans and the people of the Confederacy.

Not all white women supported the war. By 1863 food shortages, inflation, and government policies provoked riots. Bread riots disrupted life in Southern cities, where the influx of female refugees resulted in severe food shortages. The best-known food riot occurred in 1863 in Richmond, where over 1,000 women looted shops for bacon, flour, sugar, coffee, candles, cloth, and shoes, among other things. The Northern home front experienced similar problems. In New York City lower-class men and women protested the 1863 Draft Law because its loopholes allowed wealthy men to "buy out" or hire a substitute to escape conscription. Although the riot began as a call to end draft exemptions, the rioters eventually turned their anger toward free blacks. After six days of rioting, hundreds of women were arrested and convicted for their role in the racial violence.

The American Civil War created opportunities that allowed slave women to make the Civil War their war, too. For most slaves, this meant escaping from slavery, protecting children, and reuniting with family members. Shortly after the arrival of Union troops, one slave woman escaped to the Sea Islands with two of her children because her master "had just 'licked' her eldest son almost to death because he was suspected of wanting to join the Yankees." Some slave women rejected opportunities for personal freedom when it did not include freedom for their children. The arrival of Union troops provided black women, especially those in the Upper South, the opportunity to run towards freedom with their children and reunite with their husbands. As Union troops approached, one Southern mistress despaired that "Dinah has gone, and Daphne and herself busied themselves in packing up and carrying off everything out of Papa's house." So many slave women escaped to Union lines that soldiers complained of the "helpless women and children" who followed them and ate their rations.

Women of both the Union and the Confederacy took active roles in the war. They shaped the decisions that led to war, encouraged men to enlist, organized aid societies, spied on the enemy, worked as nurses, ran households, and fought as soldiers. Margaret Mitchell's narrator in *Gone with the Wind* asserted that war "is men's business, not ladies'." The American Civil War proved otherwise.

—Lisa Tendrich Frank

See also Nurses; Women Soldiers.

For further reading:

Attie, Jeanie. *Patriotic Toil: Northern Women and the American Civil War* (1998).

Edmonds, Sarah Emma. *Nurse and Spy in the Union Army: Comprising the Adventures and Experiences of a Woman in Hospitals, Camps, Battle-Fields* (1865).

Faust, Drew Gilpin. *Mothers of Invention: Women of the Slaveholding South in the American Civil War* (1996).

Frank, Lisa Tendrich. "'To Cure Her of Her Pride and Boasting': The Gendered Implications of Sherman's March" (Ph.D. dissertation, forthcoming).

Harwell, Richard Barksdale, ed. *Kate: The Journal of a Confederate Nurse* (1959).

Howe, M. A. DeWolfe, ed. *Home Letters of General Sherman* (1909).

Marszalek, John F., ed. *The Diary of Miss Emma Holmes, 1861–1866* (1979).

Massey, Mary Elizabeth. *Women in the Civil War* (1994).

Mitchell, Margaret. *Gone With the Wind* (1973).

Rable, George C. *Civil Wars: Women and the Crisis of Southern Nationalism* (1991).

Sala, George Augustus. *My Diary in America in the Midst of the War* (1865).

Sewell, Richard H. *A House Divided: Sectionalism and Civil War, 1848–1865* (1988).

Stevenson, William. *Thirteen Months in the Rebel Army: Being a Narrative of Personal Adventures in the Infantry, Ordnance, Cavalry, Courier, and Hospital Services; With an Exhibition of the Power, Purposes, Earnestness, Military Despotism, and Demoralization of the South* (1862).

Williamson, Joel. *After Slavery: The Negro in South Carolina During Reconstruction, 1861–1877* (1965).

WOMEN SOLDIERS

It comes as no surprise that women across the United States valiantly served the causes of the Union and the Confederacy both on the home front and in Civil War hospitals. That a great number of women traveled with the armies as support staff and as "daughters of the regiment" is a considerably more striking and less familiar detail of the military history of the war. Perhaps least well known, however, is that several hundred women and perhaps as many as a thousand masqueraded as men and enlisted as common soldiers between the years 1861 and 1865. In so doing, they upheld a tradition of women disguising themselves in men's clothes and assuming men's identities to serve their country. This tradition, which had European roots, dates back in America at least as far as the Revolution, when, for example, Deborah Sampson served as a soldier in the Continental army under the alias Robert Shurtliff of the 4th Massachusetts Regiment.

The best-known woman to serve as a soldier in the Civil War was Sarah Emma Edmonds, who in May 1861 enlisted as a private in Company F of the 2d Michigan Infantry Regiment. Edmonds served with the 2d Michigan until the spring of 1863, when a combination of complex factors—including increased fear of discovery—drove her to desert. Edmonds is well known to history because in 1864 she wrote a widely read, if curiously veiled, memoir of her Civil War army service and because later in her life she chose to apply for a veteran's pension. To do so (having resumed her own female identity in 1863), she was forced to make known the details of her wartime imposture, all of which are gathered in her lengthy pension record in the National Archives. Edmonds was joined, however, by hundreds of other women who, like her, were driven into military service for the Union and for the Confederacy by one or more impulses: their own fervent patriotism; their yearning for adventure; their devotion to a husband, brother, or other enlisted man; or—like so many men as well—their simple need of a job.

The duration of women soldiers' service to the armies varied considerably. Some aspiring women soldiers were discovered by observant recruiters at the moment they tried to enlist and were sent packing before they could ever muster in officially. Others successfully avoided

disclosure for a few weeks or a few months. Still others served for years or for the duration of the war. When they left the service, women soldiers—as far as we know—commonly resumed their former identities and lives, but some continued to live and work as men. At least one soldier, Jennie Hodgers (who enlisted in the 95th Illinois Infantry as Albert D. J. Cashier) maintained her masquerade late into her life. She even applied for and received a pension under the assumed name that she had adopted before the war and under which she had served.

Because discovery by the officials generally resulted in immediate dismissal, women struggled against great odds to sustain their impostures, undoubtedly assisted in some cases by male comrades who knew their secret, but who helped them continue to "pass." After all, from the perspective of most common soldiers, one more capable fighter on the line was always welcome. A woman soldier's true identity was most likely to become known when she fell ill or was wounded in battle, when subsequent hospitalization included the sort of careful physical examination that most Civil War soldiers avoided at the point of enlistment. Of course, Civil War medicine being what it was, the identities of some women soldiers, such as Rosetta Wakeman (alias Private Lyons Wakeman, 153d New York Infantry), remained undetected despite lengthy and ultimately fatal hospitalizations. Like their male comrades-in-arms, many women soldiers died unknown on the battlefield.

—Elizabeth D. Leonard

See also Daughters of the Regiment; Edmonds, Sarah Emma; Hodgers, Jennie; Wakeman, Sarah Rosetta; Women.

For further reading:

Blanton, DeAnne. "Women Soldiers of the Civil War." *Prologue* (1993).

Burgess, Lauren Cook, ed. *An Uncommon Soldier: The Civil War Letters of Sarah Rosetta Wakeman, Alias Private Lyons Wakeman, 153d Regiment, New York State Volunteers, 1862–1864* (1994).

Edmonds, Sarah Emma. *The Memoirs of a Soldier, Nurse, and Spy* (1999).

Leonard, Elizabeth D. *All the Daring of the Soldier: Women of the Civil War Armies* (1999).

Massey, Mary Elizabeth. *Bonnet Brigades* (1966).

WOOD, FERNANDO
(1812–1881)

Mayor of New York and United States congressman

Born in Philadelphia, Pennsylvania, to Benjamin Wood and Rebecca Lehman Wood, a couple of modest means, Fernando Wood moved to a variety of places with his family before settling with them in New York City. He was educated in local schools for a few years, but the poverty of his family forced him to go to work when he was thirteen. Over the next few years, the youth worked in a variety of mercantile enterprises

and became interested in New York politics at an early age. In the late 1820s and early 1830s he became a strong supporter of Andrew Jackson. In 1836 he joined the Tammany Society, a major step toward establishing a place in the New York City Democratic Party. In that year he became a member of the Young Men's Democratic-Republican General Committee and the Democratic Vigilance Committee.

Wood began these political activities by generally associating himself with the party's more conservative wing, believing that to be the best way to advance in the party. He quickly learned, however, to shift with the political winds and turned on those conservative elements to gain support from the party's younger members.

Wood continued to gain influence in city party circles, intending by the end of the 1830s to translate his influence into a run for political office. The scandal of his wife's adultery and his subsequent divorce suit threatened these ambitions. He recovered enough by 1840 to run for the United States House of Representatives. He overcame accusations (probably true) of financial impropriety and won the election, partly because of his efforts to appeal to immigrant voters, primarily among the Irish.

In Congress, Wood served on the Public Buildings and Grounds Committee. He also quickly associated himself with Southern Democrats in Congress and generally voted with that group. This voting pattern and association hurt him with the Martin Van Buren wing of the Democratic Party in New York. Along with these activities, Wood worked hard to procure as many federal appropriations for New York City as possible, especially for new customs facilities and harbor improvements. He also had the foresight to push for funding for Samuel F. B. Morse's new invention, the telegraph, and to increase his support at home by dismantling restrictions on Irish immigration.

Hoping to expand his power base in New York City, Wood moved to a new district in the city for the election of 1842. The scheme may have made him known to a wider group of New Yorkers, but it cost him the election. Business failures also complicated his life by putting him in danger of bankruptcy. He responded to these financial reverses by using his connections in Washington to gain a federal appointment in New York City. His close connections to Southerners reaped benefits in May 1844 when he prevailed upon new Secretary of State John C. Calhoun to appoint him New York's dispatch agent. He held that position until 1847 and in the meantime rebuilt his business interests. Building a solid base in various mercantile interests, by 1847 Wood was able to purchase a ship chandlery business. While he became involved in shipping throughout many parts of the country, Wood found his most lucrative markets to be in the South, tying him permanently to that region.

Wood's business interests continued to expand in 1849 when he and a group of partners took advantage of the population boom in California by sending a vessel laden with trade goods to San Francisco. They realized a very large profit from the venture. In addition, in the early 1850s Wood began investing in large tracts of real estate in New York and California.

As Wood's financial standing increased, so did his political fortunes. Increasingly prominent in the Tammany Society, he was selected to run for mayor in 1850. Accusations (again probably true) that he had cheated some of his partners out of part of the profits in the California shipping venture, however, cost him the election. He did not begin to recover his political influence until 1854, when the Kansas-Nebraska Act effectively killed the New York Whig Party.

In that year he again ran for mayor and, in spite of repeated attacks on his character and financial dealings, he was elected. He assumed office on 1 January 1855. In constant battle with the Republican–controlled state legislature, Wood spent much of his time trying to boost New York City's economy. He was reelected in 1856 amidst growing accusations of corruption within his government. These accusations, and what Republicans viewed as Wood's dictatorial ways, caused Republican legislators to renew their efforts to limit his power. In 1857 measures were passed in Albany that limited Wood's appointment power within the city, took control of many public works, and created a Metropolitan Police Force to remove his patronage and control over the powerful New York constabulary. All of these actions resulted in a decisive collision between Wood and his enemies that brought about his arrest when he defied the new laws. The powerful Tammany Society now regarded Wood as a liability and abandoned him, so he was defeated for reelection in 1858.

Most New Yorkers saw Wood's defeat as the end of his political career, but they had misjudged this savvy political survivor. He spent the next two years rebuilding his power base in New York by creating his own organization headquartered at Mozart Hall and courting the national party. In 1859 he was again elected mayor.

In April 1860 Wood took a delegation to the Democratic National Convention in Charleston, South Carolina, but his credentials were challenged by a rival delegation, and he and his men were not seated. He gained much attention on this trip, however, and became increasingly associated with the Southern wing of the Democratic Party. Meanwhile, Wood's political fortunes at home were helped by his brother Benjamin Wood's purchase of the *New York Daily News*.

After Abraham Lincoln's election to the presidency in November 1860 and the subsequent calls for secession in the Gulf States, Wood began to worry about his own business interests and New York City's prosperity should there be a Southern exodus from the Union. These worries led Wood to deliver perhaps the most famous speech of his political career. On 7 January 1861 his annual address to the city suggested that New York City consider breaking its ties to the state and become what he termed a "free city." The suggestion was met with little enthusiasm. Always one to change with the prevailing political winds, Wood altered his position as soon as Fort Sumter was fired upon in April 1861. He then called for New Yorkers to answer enthusiastically the call for volunteers to fight for the Union. In spite of this newly found patriotism, Wood's earlier inconstancy probably cost him reelection in the fall of 1861.

Ever the survivor, Wood gained the nomination from his district for the United States House of Representatives in the fall of 1862 and was elected. In Congress he was generally critical of the prosecution of the war and quickly became associated with the small Peace Democrat faction. His constant calls for a negotiated peace were blamed by many for the draft riots that occurred in New York City in the summer of 1863. These accusations did not discourage him. If anything, Wood became bolder, as evidenced by his visit to President Lincoln at the end of 1863. At this meeting he urged the president to appoint a commission, with Wood as a member, to travel to the South to treat with the Confederate government.

In 1864 Wood and many other Democrats had hopes that the appropriate candidate could thwart Abraham Lincoln's reelection. As early as 1862, Wood had voiced the opinion that George McClellan might be the ideal candidate for the 1864 contest. Yet, by the spring of 1864 Wood was not so sure, fearing that McClellan's commitment to peace was not strong enough. Nonetheless, when McClellan received the nomination, Wood worked for him. Both McClellan and Wood were defeated in 1864, and again the New Yorker was pronounced politically dead.

After leaving Congress in early 1865, Wood took his family on a tour of Europe. Upon his return he reentered the political fray and in 1866 was again a candidate for Congress. He won the election and remained in office until his death. During those fourteen years, he fought against Congressional Reconstruction in the South and against protective tariffs. As majority leader and chairman of the House Ways and Means Committee, toward the end of his life he finally became a political force to be reckoned with on the national stage. He died while on vacation in Hot Springs, Arkansas, on 14 February 1881.

—*David S. Heidler and Jeanne T. Heidler*

See also Peace Democrats.

For further reading:
Anbinder, Tyler G. "Fernando Wood and New York City's Secession from the Union: A Political Reappraisal." *New York History* (1987).
Mushkat, Jerome. *Fernando Wood; A Political Biography* (1990).

WOOD, JOHN TAYLOR
(1830–1904)
Confederate naval officer

John Taylor Wood was born at Fort Snelling, in what would become the state of Minnesota, to U.S. Army surgeon Robert Crooks Wood and Anne Marshall Taylor Wood, the daughter of future president Zachary Taylor. Wood decided early against an army career, choosing the navy instead. After receiving appointment as a midshipman in 1847, Wood served in the Pacific and along the African coast before accepting an appointment to the U.S. Naval Academy from which he graduated in 1853. He served in various posts, including the Mediterranean Squadron and as an instructor at the academy, achieving the rank of lieutenant before the outbreak of the Civil War.

The firing on Fort Sumter saw Wood an instructor at the academy. His Southern roots caused him to agonize over what his role should be in the coming conflict. On 21 April 1861, he resigned his commission and retired briefly to a small farm he owned outside Annapolis, Maryland. Several months of inactivity, however, proved very trying for the energetic Wood, and in October 1861 he offered his services to the Confederacy. He was given a lieutenant's commission and for the first few months of his service worked to improve the batteries along the Virginia shore of the Potomac.

With the refitting of the *Merrimack* and its recommissioning as the ironclad CSS *Virginia*, Wood served as one of that vessel's officers, fighting in the famous engagement with the USS *Monitor* on 9 March 1862 after having taken the surrender of the USS *Congress* the previous day.

The forced destruction of the *Virginia* in May 1862 again left Wood without a ship. He commanded a group of naval sharpshooters at Drewry's Bluff and successfully repulsed a force of Federals on 15 May 1862. Later that fall, he conducted a series of night raids against Union vessels moored in the Potomac River and Chesapeake Bay. A few months later he was called to Richmond by President Jefferson Davis (Wood was Davis's first wife's nephew) to serve as the president's naval aide. In this position he was given the honorary rank of colonel of cavalry and the salary of that rank.

Chafing under the tedious restrictions of his new job inspecting harbor defenses and ship construction, Wood requested and was given permission to continue the raiding activities that had been so successful in the fall of 1862. In August, while still in the rank of colonel of cavalry, he led a naval raid against two Federal gunboats in the Rappahannock River near Chesapeake Bay. The capture of the *Satellite* and the *Reliance* earned Wood the thanks of the Confederate Congress. Retaining his colonel's commission, he was also promoted to commander in the Confederate navy for this exploit.

In early 1864, Wood fought in the unsuccessful Confederate attempt to retake New Bern, North Carolina. Wood, however, in command of a flotilla of small boats, slipped by the Federal gunboats in the Neuse River and destroyed the U.S. gunboat *Underwriter*.

In the summer of 1864, Wood was given command of the CSS *Tallahassee*, a steam commerce raider. Operating from Wilmington, North Carolina, to Halifax, Nova Scotia, Wood captured 33 Union coastal vessels and 190 Union prisoners. His success earned him promotion to captain.

Wood returned to Richmond in the last weeks of the war to aid President Davis in his attempted flight to safety. He traveled with the Davis party for part of its trip south, but was no longer with Davis when the president was captured in Georgia. Wood made it to Florida, where he was able to gain passage to Cuba. From there he traveled to Halifax, where he had spent much of the last part of the war disposing of his prizes. He lived there with his family for the remainder of his life. A successful businessman involved in shipping and commercial naval insurance, Wood died in Halifax on 19 July 1904.

—*David S. Heidler and Jeanne T. Heidler*

See also Monitor versus *Virginia*; Navy, C.S.A.

For further reading:

Shingleton, Royce. *John Taylor Wood, Sea Ghost of the Confederacy* (1979).
Wood, John Taylor. "Escape of General Breckinridge." In *Famous Adventures and Prison Escapes of the Civil War* (1893).

WOOD, THOMAS JOHN
(1823–1906)
Union general

Born to George T. Wood and Elizabeth Helm Wood in Munfordville, Kentucky, Thomas John Wood was educated locally before receiving an appointment to the U.S. Military Academy in 1841. He graduated fifth of forty-one in the class of 1845. One of his roommates while at the academy was Ulysses S. Grant. Upon graduation Wood was sent to Texas to join Zachary Taylor's Army of Observation. He fought under Taylor in that general's campaign in northern Mexico and received one brevet promotion for his actions during the battle of Buena Vista.

During the Mexican-American War, Wood had transferred from the Topographical Engineers to the Dragoons (what would later be the Cavalry). He served with 2d Dragoons and then with several cavalry regiments in Kansas and on Albert Sidney Johnston's Utah expedition. Wood took a leave of absence in 1859 to tour Europe and returned just in time for the start of the Civil War.

In March 1861 Wood was promoted to major in the

1st Cavalry and two months later to lieutenant colonel. He spent the summer of 1861 recruiting in Indiana. Some estimates have him raising as many as 40,000 troops during those months. For his efforts he was promoted to brigadier general of volunteers in the fall of 1861. For the remainder of 1861, Wood commanded a brigade of Indiana troops in the Army of the Ohio. He commanded his brigade in command at Bardstown, Kentucky, at the end of 1861, and in early 1862 he was given command of a division.

At Shiloh in April 1862 he commanded his division on the second day of the battle. In May he commanded the same division in the advance on Corinth, Mississippi. In the late summer and fall of 1862, Wood led his division in the repulse of Braxton Bragg from Kentucky. Late in the year, while commanding a division in the Army of the Cumberland, Wood fought at Stones River and managed, in spite of a painful wound, to shore up the crumbling Union right on 31 December. He would not leave the field until he was certain that the right would hold.

In early 1863 after returning to duty, Wood was given command of a division of XXI Corps, Army of the Cumberland. He briefly commanded the entire corps in March and then through the summer of that year commanded his division during the Tullahoma campaign and then at Chickamauga in September. During the latter battle, William Rosecrans ordered Wood to move his division into a position already occupied by another division. Confused by the order, Wood tried to move his men into some semblance of the position Rosecrans wanted, inadvertently leaving a dangerous gap that was exploited by the Confederates. After the battle, Wood entered into a dispute with his commanding general over the nature and results of Rosecrans's order. Ultimately Wood was vindicated by events when Rosecrans was removed and Wood retained command of his division.

During the Chattanooga campaign, Wood again distinguished himself, particularly in the attack on Missionary Ridge. He also commanded his division in the Knoxville campaign later in the year. The following spring and summer, Wood continued to command his division of XXI Corps in the Atlanta campaign. He fought in all the early engagements of the campaign, including Resaca and Kennesaw Mountain. In the battles around Atlanta from July to September 1864 he fought at Peachtree Creek, Jonesboro, and Lovejoy. In the latter battle on 2 September he broke his leg, but rather than leave the field, he had it wrapped tightly so he could continue to command his troops. He did not leave the field until the end of the day and was commended in strong terms by William T. Sherman, who also recommended that he be promoted to major general of volunteers. Wood never fully recovered from this injury, though he remained on active duty for the remainder of the war.

After the end of the Atlanta campaign, Wood went back to Tennessee with much of the Army of the Cumberland. In early November he commanded at Pulaski, Tennessee. Wood commanded his division at Franklin and took command of IV Corps when David Stanley was wounded there. Wood continued to command IV Corps in the repulse of John Bell Hood from Nashville and led the pursuit of Hood after the battle. In February 1865 Wood was promoted to major general of volunteers with a date of rank of 27 January 1865.

After the end of the war, Wood was sent to the Department of Arkansas and then in August 1865 to the Department of Texas. In November 1865 he was placed in command of the Department of Mississippi, where he served for the next several years. Wood was one of the few military commanders in the South during Reconstruction who became somewhat popular with the inhabitants. In 1868 his war injuries forced his retirement from the army at the rank of major general.

In retirement Wood worked tirelessly for various veterans organizations and for battlefield conservation. He also served on the board of visitors for the U.S. Military Academy. Most of the time he lived in Dayton, Ohio, where he died on 25 February 1906.

—*David S. Heidler and Jeanne T. Heidler*

See also Chickamauga, Battle of; Franklin, Battle of; Lovejoy, Georgia, Battle of; Nashville, Tennessee; Stones River, Battle of.

For further reading:

Bowers, John. *Chickamauga and Chattanooga: The Battles That Doomed the Confederacy* (1994).
McDonough, James L., and Thomas L. Connelly. *Five Tragic Hours: The Battle of Franklin* (1983).
Sword, Wiley. *Embrace an Angry Wind: The Confederacy's Last Hurrah—Spring Hill, Franklin, and Nashville* (1992).

WOODS, CHARLES ROBERT
(1827–1885)
Union general

Born to Ezekiel S. Woods and Sarah Judith Burnham Woods in Newark, Ohio, Charles Robert Woods was educated locally before receiving an appointment to the U.S. Military Academy in 1848. He graduated twentieth of forty-three in the class of 1852. Commissioned an infantry officer, Woods served in Texas and the Pacific Northwest before the outbreak of the Civil War. As a lieutenant of the 9th Infantry he commanded the army component of the *Star of the West* expedition that attempted and failed to relieve Fort Sumter in January 1861.

In the early stages of the war, Woods served in western Virginia before returning to Ohio to raise a regi-

ment for federal service. In November 1861 he was commissioned colonel of the 76th Ohio Infantry. Woods and his regiment fought at Fort Donelson under Lew Wallace and again under Wallace at Shiloh in April 1862. After the advance on Corinth in May 1862, Woods was temporarily placed in command of a brigade. He commanded this brigade in an expedition from Helena, Arkansas, from 16 to 27 August 1862. Woods returned to command of his regiment in the fall.

Woods and the 76th participated in William T. Sherman's Yazoo campaign at the end of 1862 and fought at Chickasaw Bluffs. In January 1863 they went on the Arkansas Post expedition. During the Vicksburg campaign in the spring of 1863, Woods was given command of a brigade in Sherman's corps on the Union right. He would serve under Sherman in one capacity or another for the remainder of the war. After the surrender of Vicksburg, Woods led his brigade in the campaign against Jackson, Mississippi.

In August 1863 Woods was promoted to brigadier general of volunteers and began operating with his brigade along the Memphis & Charleston Railroad, skirmishing frequently with Confederate forces. In November 1863 he went in relief to Chattanooga, where he distinguished himself at Lookout Mountain. He received a brevet promotion to colonel in the regular army for his actions at Chattanooga.

In February 1864 Woods was given command of 1st Division, XV Corps. He commanded that division in north Alabama in early 1864 and through the Atlanta campaign. In that campaign, Woods was especially conspicuous for his actions at Resaca, Kennesaw Mountain, and the battle of Atlanta on 22 July. In the latter battle he fought on the Union right and managed to turn his division around in a very short time to face a Confederate flanking maneuver.

After the fall of Atlanta and after the pursuit of John Bell Hood north, Woods fought in Sherman's March to the Sea and in the Carolinas campaign. He was commended for gallantry for his part in the battle of Bentonville. He received a brevet promotion to major general of volunteers for his part in the Atlanta campaign and was breveted to major general in the regular army for his participation in the Carolinas. His corps commander, John A. Logan, recommended him for promotion to major general of volunteers.

After the war, Woods remained in the army, reverting to lieutenant colonel of the 33d Infantry with the mustering out of the volunteers in 1866. He served in Kansas, primarily on the Indian frontier and in 1874 was promoted to colonel of the 2d Infantry. His health forced his retirement at the rank of colonel that same year. Woods lived his last years on his farm outside Dayton. He died there on 26 February 1885.

—*David S. Heidler and Jeanne T. Heidler*

See also Atlanta Campaign; Lookout Mountain, Battle of; *Star of the West*.

For further reading:

Castel, Albert E. *Decision in the West: The Atlanta Campaign of 1864* (1992).

Glatthaar, Joseph T. *The March to the Sea and Beyond: Sherman's Troops in the Savannah and Carolinas Campaigns* (1985).

McDonough, James L. *Chattanooga—A Death Grip on the Confederacy* (1984).

WOODSON'S CAVALRY

Woodson's Cavalry was the only Confederate Missouri unit to serve in Virginia during the Civil War. Charles Hugh Woodson raised the group of eight to one hundred men from a larger group of prisoners sent from the Alton Prison to Virginia for exchange in April and May 1863. All the men had served in other Missouri regiments before being captured. A resident of Chariton County, Missouri, Woodson may have been a member of John Porter's 1st Northeast Missouri Cavalry. During late 1864 and 1865, Woodson also recruited a number of native Virginians, particularly from the Harrisonburg area.

The Confederate War Department formally named the unit Company A, 1st Missouri Cavalry, even though a 1st Missouri Cavalry with its own Company A had been serving in the West since the first year of the war. During the first year of its existence, it was cavalry in name only. The Missourians spent the summer and fall of 1863 and the winter of 1864 on garrison duty or attached to the 62d Virginia Mounted Infantry. The battle of New Market on 15 May 1864 presented the westerners with an opportunity to distinguish themselves. At one point early in the confrontation, Woodson's men used their sharpshooting skills to silence a battery of cannon that had pinned down the 62d and the 51st Virginia Infantry. Later the cadets of the Virginia Military Institute captured one of those guns after it was abandoned on the field during the rout of the Federals.

The engagement proved costly for the "Missouri exiles." Five men died, and of the rest who participated, most were wounded. Only five men were fit for duty on the following day. Of all the Confederate units engaged at New Market, Woodson's Cavalry suffered the highest casualty rate. Today, one of only two markers on the battle site honors the men of Woodson's Cavalry who fell there. Four days after the battle, eighteen of the Missourians traveled with Major General John C. Breckinridge and 2,500 other Confederates to join Lee's army in defending Richmond.

On 7 June, four days after Grant's ill-fated assault at Cold Harbor, Breckinridge and his forces left the Richmond defenses to return to the Shenandoah Valley to face a new threat there from a new Union assault.

After the Federals were turned back at Lynchburg, ending the assault into the valley, Woodson received orders to obtain horses for his men from those recently captured by partisan commander John McNeill and his rangers.

Woodson's Cavalry helped to scout Jubal Early's advance across the Potomac River into Maryland during Early's 1864 Washington campaign and also took part in the battle of Monocacy on 9 July. For most of the rest of the war, Woodson's Cavalry operated as an independent unit of cavalry in Hardy and Hampshire counties, West Virginia. On several occasions the Missourians performed in cooperation with McNeill's Rangers, harassing Union supply and communications lines, gathering cattle, and skirmishing with Federals.

After John McNeill died in November 1864, his men seriously considered casting their lot with Woodson and his men before they finally decided to accept his son Jesse as their new commander. The incident strained the relationship between Woodson and the younger McNeill, but their two groups on a few occasions did work together during the last months of the war. For instance, they guarded Brigadier General Thomas Rosser's rear and supply lines, fending off an assault at Moorefield, West Virginia, while Rosser besieged the Federal garrison at New Creek, causing extensive damage.

In March 1865, Woodson received orders to unite with a force led by Thomas Rosser farther south in the Shenandoah Valley, but before they could make the rendezvous, word came of Lee's surrender at Appomattox. Unsure of what to do, Woodson's men scattered. Some went south in a vain attempt to reach Joseph Johnston's forces in North Carolina. Others turned themselves over to Union officials at various places in the Shenandoah to make their parole. Others just struck out on the long trip back to Missouri.

—*Thomas F. Curran*

See also McNeill, John Hanson and Jesse; New Market, Battle of; Rosser, Thomas Lafayette.

For further reading:
Curran, Thomas F. "Memory, Myth, and Musty Records: Charles Woodson's Missouri Cavalry in the Army of Northern Virginia." *Missouri Historical Review* (1999–2000).
Davis, William C. *The Battle of New Market* (1976).

WOODWARD, GEORGE WASHINGTON
(1809–1875)
Pennsylvania judge

Born into a family of lawyers in Bethany, Pennsylvania, George Washington Woodward was educated locally before attending Hobart College. After graduating from that institution he began his own legal studies. He opened a practice in Bethany and became active in Pennsylvania Democratic politics. Woodward quickly gained the reputation as one of the best legal minds

in the state and for that reason was chosen in 1837 as a member of the Pennsylvania constitutional convention. In 1841 he left his practice to accept appointment as a judge on the Pennsylvania Fourth Judicial District Court. He served in that position until 1852 when he was chosen to be a justice on the Pennsylvania Supreme Court, where he remained until 1868.

Even while on the bench, Woodward was associated with the more conservative wing of the Pennsylvania Democratic Party. As the sectional crisis worsened in the late 1850s through 1860, he privately criticized abolitionists and antislavery Democrats for exacerbating the tensions between the sections. In the election of 1860 he supported the candidacy of John C. Breckinridge. When Abraham Lincoln was elected president, Woodward privately speculated about the feasibility of Pennsylvania joining a Southern union. At a rally supporting the preservation of the Union held in Philadelphia on 13 December 1860, Woodward was among a number of speakers who urged conciliation of the South. In his speech he stated that slavery was a legal right and a positive good for both master and slave and urged strict enforcement of the Fugitive Slave Act.

Once the war began Woodward raised money to outfit Union units and publicly supported his two sons' decisions to fight with the Union army. Privately he opposed coercion of the South, believing that such military force was unconstitutional. Unlike many Northerners with Southern sympathies during the war, Woodward had no family ties to the South and no financial interests there. In his private correspondence, however, he became increasingly critical of the Lincoln administration's growing power, believing that the growing power of the executive branch would lead to a dictatorship. Publicly, he remained silent on these issues, though some of his judicial decisions give a hint of his true feelings. In 1862 he ruled with the majority of the court that soldiers' votes could not be counted in state elections, interpreting narrowly a Pennsylvania law that a voter must currently reside in the district in which he voted. His 13 December 1860 speech also gave his critics ammunition to use against him in the press, including accusations that he had sympathy with the Peace Democrats in Congress and even the Copperhead movement.

Still Woodward's reputation for personal integrity led the Democrats in 1863 to nominate him for governor. By 1863 the Republican governor, Andrew Curtin, was not very popular, and the Democrats saw an opportunity to regain control of the state. The Republicans capitalized on some of Woodward's earlier statements, particularly his 13 December speech, and apparently manufactured additional remarks, making his loyalty to the Union the primary issue of the campaign. He lost to Curtin in a very narrow election. Shortly after the election results were in, Woodward ruled with the majority of the state

supreme court that the Federal conscription act of the previous spring was unconstitutional and should not be enforced within the state of Pennsylvania. Shortly after the new year, with a change in the membership of the court, that decision was overturned. By that time Woodward had become the chief justice of the court.

Woodward remained on the court until after the war. When his term expired, he was elected to the United States House of Representatives. He served two terms, during which time as a member of the Reconstruction Committee he opposed the military occupation of the South. He also served on the Committee on the Revision of the Laws, his expertise in that area serving the committee well. After leaving Congress he returned to live quietly in Bethany for a brief time and then took a holiday to Europe. He died suddenly in Rome on 10 May 1875.

—*David S. Heidler and Jeanne T. Heidler*

See also Peace Democrats; Pennsylvania.

For further reading:
A Picture of Slavery Drawn from the Decisions of Southern Courts (1863; reprint, 1972).
Shankman, Arnold M. *The Pennsylvania Antiwar Movement, 1861–1865* (1980).

WOOL, JOHN ELLIS
(1784–1869)
Union general

John E. Wool's not entirely satisfactory Civil War service came as something of an anticlimax to one of the longest, most distinguished military careers in U.S. history. A native of Newburgh, New York, Wool became an orphan at the age of four. After studying law in Troy, New York, Wool volunteered for service after the outbreak of the War of 1812. Commissioned a captain in the regular army, Wool displayed great courage and ability at the battle of Queenston Heights in October 1812. Although shot through both legs, Wool led his forces in seizing and holding a vital position. Subsequently promoted to major, Wool also distinguished himself in September 1814 at the battle of Plattsburgh, for which he received a brevet of lieutenant colonel in the regular army.

Having earned a reputation as one of the army's strictest and most capable officers, Wool found himself marked for increased responsibilities, even after the close of hostilities with Great Britain in 1815. In 1816 he was assigned to duty as the army's inspector general, and in 1818 the War Department promoted him to the rank of lieutenant colonel. Thereafter he performed mostly routine frontier service, although he did participate in the ruthless campaign to remove the Cherokee Indians from Georgia in 1836. In 1841 Wool was promoted to brigadier general, a rank he would retain for more than two decades.

With the outbreak of war with Mexico in 1846, President James K. Polk quickly decided that Wool, one of only three officers in the regular army with the permanent rank of general, should be given an important assignment. In June, Polk ordered the general to report to San Antonio and take command of the various forces assembling there—two regiments of Illinois volunteers, a regiment of Arkansas volunteer cavalry, several hundred regular cavalry, a battalion from the 6th Infantry, an artillery battery, and a few Texas Ranger "scouts." With this motley force of some 3,400 men, mostly composed of nearly undisciplined citizen soldiers, Wool crossed the Rio Grande in September 1846 and marched 900 punishing miles. Wool rendezvoused with Zachary Taylor's forces at Saltillo in December just before the War Department stripped Taylor of most of his forces to reinforce Winfield Scott's amphibious operation against Vera Cruz.

Realizing that his forces now far outnumbered Taylor's, Mexican leader Santa Anna was determined to crush the U.S. forces remaining in the north and then turn and deal with Scott. This bold move nearly succeeded; that it did not was largely because of John Wool's skill and foresight. Although Taylor considered retreat in the face of the enemy to be humiliating, Wool convinced Taylor to abandon his exposed position and withdraw to an excellent defensive line at Buena Vista. Wool carefully supervised the positioning of the U.S. forces there, and the successful U.S. repulse of the Mexican attack in February 1847 justified Taylor's confidence in his subordinate. The New York legislature voted its thanks to Wool and bestowed upon him a ceremonial sword for his role in this battle. He was honored also with a brevet promotion to major general. In November 1847 Wool succeeded Taylor (who had received a leave of absence) in command of the Army of Occupation at Monterrey, where Wool employed stern retaliatory tactics to halt the activities of local guerrillas.

In the years between the Mexican-American War and the Civil War, Wool commanded in turn the Eastern Military District, the Department of the Pacific, and the Department of the East. In February 1861 Wool served as a delegate to the Washington Peace Conference, which attempted to craft a compromise to avert the impending sectional conflict. This "old gentlemen's convention" did not succeed and, with the onset of hostilities in April, Wool assumed that he would play a leading role in the conflict. Abraham Lincoln's administration, however, had other plans. Wool, the army's senior brigadier general, was slighted by the promotion of three other men (George B. McClellan, Henry W. Halleck, and John C. Frémont) over his head to the rank of major general in the regular army. Although Lincoln considered the septuagenarian Wool too old for effective field service, he recognized the value of Wool's experience—and the political benefits of assigning one of the most respected citizens of the crucial state of New York to a prominent (if comparatively unimportant) position. Wool was relegated to a minor assignment commanding the Department of Virginia, which essentially consisted of only the small Federal garrison at Fort Monroe.

Wool swiftly ran into problems with his new command. When McClellan initiated his Peninsula campaign in April 1862, he insisted on having control of Wool's garrison by virtue of his seniority as a regular major general. The old general, however, claimed independence as the commander of a separate department. Secretary of War Edwin Stanton and President Lincoln essentially sided with McClellan, advising Wool to cooperate with the commander of the Army of the Potomac regardless of the technical geographical boundaries of his command.

In May, Wool suffered further embarrassment during a visit from Lincoln and Secretary of the Treasury Salmon P. Chase. The president and Chase tried to convince Wool to move against Norfolk, which they believed to be lightly defended. While Wool and his staff pondered the feasibility of such a move, an impatient Chase personally led Union troops against the town and forced its surrender. Although Wool received a promotion to major general in the regular army in the wake of this action, he had hardly earned the confidence of the administration. In June, he was transferred away from Virginia.

Wool next took command of the rear-area Middle Department, consisting of the states of New Jersey, Delaware, Pennsylvania, and eastern portions of Maryland and Virginia. When Robert E. Lee's Confederates invaded Maryland in September 1862, Wool again found himself embroiled in a controversy with McClellan, who arrived to organize the Union opposition to Lee's movement. McClellan charged Wool with responsibility for the encirclement and surrender of the Union garrison at Harper's Ferry and had Wool censured by a board of inquiry. In December Wool was again relieved of command, and the next month the War Department assigned him to another position even farther behind the lines—his old Department of the East, now consisting of New York, New Jersey, and the New England states.

Six months after Wool took command of this seemingly quiet department, the New York City draft riots broke out. With a limited number of troops at his command, and hesitant to employ deadly force against civilians, Wool was unable to deal with the crisis. Elements of the Army of the Potomac arrived to restore order, and General John A. Dix superseded Wool on 18 July. Two weeks later, on 1 August, Wool resigned. At age seventy-nine, the general, although he had valiantly attempted to carry out his duties, was simply no longer equal to the stress and rigor of wartime service. He spent his remaining years in Troy, having richly earned the right to a comfortable retirement after more than fifty years of active service.

—*Michael Thomas Smith*

See also New York Draft Riots; Washington Peace Conference.

For further reading:

Baylies, Francis. *A Narrative of Major General Wool's Campaign in Mexico in the Years 1846, 1847 and 1848* (1851).

Eisenhower, John S. D. *So Far from God: The U.S. War with Mexico, 1846–1848* (1989).

Hinton, Perry. "The Military Career of John Ellis Wool, 1812–1863" (Ph.D. dissertation, 1960).

Rezneck, Samuel. "The Civil War Role, 1861–1863, of a Veteran New York Officer, Major General John E. Wool." *New York History* (1963).

WORDEN, JOHN LORIMER
(1818–1897)
Naval officer

Born in Westchester County, New York, John Lorimer Worden by the start of the Civil War had served in the U.S. Navy for twenty-seven years, with varied sea duty interspersed with three tours at the Naval Observatory in Washington, D.C. Because of the glacial pace of promotion in the antebellum navy, in early 1861 Worden was still only a lieutenant and relatively far down the promotion list. Shortly before the outbreak of hostilities he was selected by Secretary of the Navy Gideon Welles to carry secret dispatches to the forces at Fort Pickens, near Pensacola, Florida, ordering the landing of additional troops to protect the fort. Memorizing his orders and barely evading capture by Confederate troops under the command of Brigadier General Braxton Bragg on his way south, Worden successfully completed this duty, helping to keep Fort Pickens one of the few Federal installations in the South to stay out of Confederate hands.

On his return north Worden was taken into custody and remained a prisoner of war until being released in poor health in November 1861. After a period of sick leave, in January 1862 Worden received as his first command the experimental ironclad *Monitor*, then being built by John Ericsson in New York. That a junior officer received the posting indicates that the *Monitor* was not viewed as a prestigious command. Worden nonetheless took up his new duties with confidence in the ship's potential. The ship was commissioned in late February, and in early March Worden took the vessel, under tow, to Hampton Roads with orders to proceed to the defense of Washington.

When the *Monitor* arrived at Hampton Roads on the evening of 8 March, it was to witness the aftermath of that day's attack by the CSS *Virginia* on the blockading Union squadron. Worden, after consulting with Captain John Marston of the USS *Roanoke*, chose to remain at

John Worden (*Library of Congress*)

Hampton Roads to counter the anticipated sortie of the *Virginia* the next morning. When the *Virginia* appeared early on 9 March, Worden interposed the *Monitor* between the Confederate vessel and the remaining Union ships, particularly the steam frigate *Minnesota*, which had run aground during the previous day's action. In the ensuing four-hour battle, the two ironclads fought to a tactical draw, with the *Virginia* unable to inflict further harm on the blockaders and the *Monitor* unable to damage the Confederate ship seriously. During the fight, Worden became the only Union casualty when he was temporarily blinded as a shell exploded near the tiny slit in the pilothouse armor through which he observed the action. He then turned command over to his executive officer, Lieutenant Samuel Dana Greene, for the rest of the battle. In spite of the inconclusive tactical outcome, the engagement proved the usefulness of armored vessels.

After recovering from his wounds in December, the newly promoted Commander Worden took command of the single-turret ironclad *Montauk*, an Ericsson-built "improved" monitor, which he led in actions off Charleston, South Carolina, and Savannah, Georgia. In January and February 1863, he conducted a pair of bombardments against Fort McAllister, just south of Savannah. *Montauk* took thirteen hits in the first engagement and forty-eight in the second, but suffered no serious damage. However, Worden was unable to

destroy or capture the fort in spite of expending nearly all his ammunition. Later in February, Worden destroyed the blockade-runner *Rattlesnake* (formerly CSS *Nashville*), which had run aground near Fort McAllister. While returning from this engagement, *Montauk* struck a torpedo, keeping it out of action for a month.

Worden's final assignment in the *Montauk* came on 7 and 8 April 1863, when he led his ship in the squadron's unsuccessful attack on Charleston Harbor. Worden was among the officers who advised Rear Admiral Samuel Du Pont against continuing the attack after the flotilla took much more damage than it inflicted on the city's defenses. Later that month, Worden was transferred to New York where, by now promoted to captain, he spent the rest of the war overseeing ironclad construction.

Worden remained in the navy after the war, receiving promotions to commodore in 1868 and rear admiral in 1872. He served as superintendent of the Naval Academy from 1869 to 1874, as commander of the European Squadron from 1874 to 1877, and finally as a member and later president of the Naval Examining and Retiring Board. Upon his own retirement in 1886, a grateful Congress voted to award him full sea pay for life in his permanent rank of rear admiral. John Worden died in October 1897 and is buried in Pauling, New York.

—*Stephen C. Svonavec*

See also Fort Pickens; Ironclads; *Monitor*; *Monitor versus Virginia*.

For further reading:
Anderson, Bern. *By Sea and by River: The Naval History of the Civil War* (1962).
Fowler, William M., Jr. *Under Two Flags: The American Navy in the Civil War* (1990).

WRIGHT, AMBROSE RANSOM
(1826–1872)
Confederate general

Born the son of Ambrose Wright and Sarah Hammond Wright in Louisville, Georgia, the younger Wright was educated locally and studied law under prominent Georgia lawyer and politician Herschel V. Johnson. Wright practiced law and became active in Georgia politics first as a Democrat and then as a member of the American Party (Know-Nothings). As the sectional crisis intensified, Wright opposed secession and supported the Constitutional Union candidacy of John Bell in the election of 1860. Abraham Lincoln's election, however, changed Wright from a Unionist to a secessionist. After Georgia's secession in January 1861, Wright accepted appointment by the Georgia secession convention as an emissary to Maryland to urge that state's secession.

The commencement of hostilities in April 1861 caused Wright to enlist in the Confederate army. While initially a private, Wright was soon elected the colonel of the 3d

Georgia Infantry. In September 1861, Wright's regiment served in the brigade of Benjamin Huger near Roanoke, North Carolina. In November 1861, he was sent to Savannah to strengthen the coastal defenses there.

In the spring of 1862, he took the 3d north to Virginia to participate in the upcoming Peninsula campaign. Wright led the 3d Georgia Regiment at the battle of Seven Pines on 31 May 1862. For his actions in that battle, Wright was promoted to brigadier general on 3 June 1862. He commanded a brigade of Huger's division during the Seven Days' battles and was commended for his actions at Mechanicsville and Malvern Hill.

In September 1862, Wright led his brigade in the invasion of Maryland, where he was seriously wounded at the battle of Antietam. Still recovering from his wounds in December 1862, Wright and his brigade were held in reserve at the battle of Fredericksburg. Wright returned to action at Chancellorsville and led his brigade north in Lee's second invasion in June 1863. He fought on the second day of the battle of Gettysburg and was part of the guard for the retreat south after the Southern defeat. He fought in the Bristoe Station and Mine Run campaigns and in the first stages of the campaign the following spring that resulted in the siege of Petersburg.

In August 1864 Wright was sent south to join John Bell Hood's Army of Tennessee. En route, he received orders to take command at Augusta, Georgia, to prepare that city's defenses. After supervising the construction of defenses at Augusta, Wright joined Hood and commanded a division under that general in the late fall of 1864 after being promoted major general in November 1864. In 1865 he participated in Joseph E. Johnston's retreat through North Carolina and surrendered with Johnston there. Wright's popularity in Georgia had gained him election to the Georgia Senate late in the war, though he never left the army to take his seat.

After the war, Wright practiced law in Augusta and edited a local newspaper. He died in Augusta on 21 December 1872.

—David S. Heidler and Jeanne T. Heidler

See also Malvern Hill, Battle of; Mechanicsville, Battle of.
For further reading:
Snead, Claiborne. *Address by Colonel Claiborne Snead at the Reunion of the Third Georgia Regiment at Union Point, on the 31st July, 1874. History of the Third Georgia Regiment, and the Career of Its First Commander, General Ambrose R. Wright* (1874).

WRIGHT, HORATIO GOUVERNEUR
(1820–1899)
Union general

Born to Edward Wright and Nancy Wright in Clinton, Connecticut, Horatio Gouverneur Wright was educated locally before accepting an appointment to the U.S. Military Academy in 1837. He graduated second of fifty-two in the class of 1841. Commissioned into the Corps of Engineers, Wright occupied several staff positions for his first five years of service. In 1846 he was sent to Florida, where he spent ten years working on the harbor of St. Augustine and strengthening the defenses of Key West. In the years immediately preceding the Civil War, Wright served as an assistant to the army's chief engineer. In that capacity, Wright corresponded frequently with the federal garrison in Charleston harbor regarding the defensibility of its positions.

With the threat of Virginia's secession in April 1861, Wright was sent to the Norfolk Navy Yard to assess its situation. When the state seceded, Wright attempted to destroy the yard's dry dock but was captured by state forces before he could complete the task. They released him shortly thereafter.

Wright returned to Washington where he busily worked to strengthen the capital's defenses. For Irvin

General Horatio Wright's VI fighting at Spotsylvania, sketched by Alfred R. Waud (*Library of Congress*)

McDowell's campaign against Manassas Junction, Virginia, he was made chief engineer for the division commanded by Samuel P. Heintzelman. In September 1861, he was given the same position in Thomas W. Sherman's Port Royal expedition and promoted to brigadier general of volunteers. Over the next ten months, Wright distinguished himself along the southern coastline as both an engineer officer and combat commander.

Commanding a brigade, Wright took possession of Fort Walker in early November 1861. He commanded his force at Hilton Head for the remainder of the year and then in early 1862 was dispatched to Florida, where he took St. Augustine, with whose defenses he was intimately familiar, Jacksonville, and Amelia Island. Back outside Charleston by early summer, Wright commanded a division at the Union defeat at Secessionville on James Island on 16 June 1862. Wright suffered heavy casualties in the attack that he had advised his commander, Henry W. Benham, not to make.

In July 1862 Wright was promoted to major general of volunteers and the following month given command of the Department of the Ohio headquartered at Lexington, Kentucky. In this capacity Wright lent logistical support to the campaign against Braxton Bragg in the late summer and fall of 1862. In the spring of 1863, however, the U.S. Senate refused to confirm Wright's promotion to major general and he reverted to brigadier general. In that rank it was not deemed appropriate for him to command a department, and Ambrose Burnside was sent to relieve him. Upon Burnside's arrival in March 1863, Wright remained briefly as the commander of the District of Western Kentucky under Burnside before being summoned east to assume a command in the Army of the Potomac.

In May 1863 Wright took command of 1st Division, John Sedgwick's VI Corps. He participated in the Gettysburg campaign, though his men played only a nominal part in the battle. In the campaign against Robert E. Lee in the fall of 1863, Wright, in command of his division, distinguished himself in the attack at Rappahannock Station in November. He also fought in the Mine Run campaign the following month.

In early 1864 Wright was detached from the Army of the Potomac to serve on an engineering board in Washington, D.C., but in February he was sent back to command his division in Sedgwick's corps. He fought in the Wilderness campaign in early May 1864 and at Spotsylvania a few days later. When Sedgwick was killed at Spotsylvania on 9 May, Wright assumed command of VI Corps, a position he would hold for the remainder of the war. For the rest of the battle at Spotsylvania, Wright and VI Corps assailed the Confederate position at the Bloody Angle, suffering heavy casualties. Wright was slightly wounded in the engagement. After the battle, he was reappointed major general of volunteers and this time confirmed by the Senate with a date of rank of 12 May 1864.

In early July, Wright and VI Corps were sent to Washington in response to Jubal Early's raid toward the capital. They fought in the repulse of Early, and on 13 July Wright and his corps led the pursuit of Early out of the environs of Washington. Shortly thereafter, Wright and VI Corps were made a part of Philip Sheridan's Army of the Shenandoah, organized to continue the campaign against Early in the valley.

Wright fought in all the major engagements of Sheridan's Shenandoah Valley campaign. At Cedar Creek on 19 October, Wright commanded the Union forces. He did not demonstrate a great deal of talent for independent command in this engagement, and probably only the timely arrival of Sheridan saved the day. Wright was wounded in the battle.

Returning to the Army of the Potomac in early 1865, Wright led the VI Corps in the final stages of the siege of Petersburg. He fought in the final assault on the Petersburg lines on 2 April and at Sayler's Creek on 6 April. Wright was present at Lee's surrender at Appomattox Court House.

After the war Wright chose to stay in the army. From the summer of 1865 to August 1866 he commanded the Department of Texas. Upon being mustered out of the volunteer service in 1866, he reverted to lieutenant colonel of engineers. He worked on a variety of harbor and river projects over the next few years and was the engineer on the final phases of the building of the Washington Monument. He was promoted to brigadier general and chief engineer in 1879. He retired at that rank in 1884. In retirement, he lived quietly in Washington, D.C., where he died on 2 July 1899.

—*David S. Heidler and Jeanne T. Heidler*

See also Cedar Creek; Rappahannock Station; Shenandoah Valley Campaign (1864–1865); Virginia, Third Battle of; Spotsylvania; Winchester.

For further reading:

Lewis, Thomas A. *The Guns of Cedar Creek* (1988).

Stackpole, Edward J. *Sheridan in the Shenandoah: Jubal Early's Nemesis* (1992).

Wert, Jeffrey D. From Winchester to Cedar Creek: The Shenandoah Campaign of 1864 (1987; reprint, 1997).

YANCEY, WILLIAM LOWNDES
(1814–1863)
Secessionist; C.S.A. senator and diplomat

William Lowndes Yancey was born at his mother's family plantation on the Shoals of the Ogeechee River in Hancock County, Georgia. His father, Benjamin Cudworth Yancey, was a rising young lawyer from South Carolina and ventured into politics as a foe of the already powerful John C. Calhoun. The senior Yancey died from malaria in 1817; four years later, Yancey's mother, Caroline Bird, married Reverend Nathan S. S. Beman, a Presbyterian minister from New York. Beman's evangelical zeal, his growing condemnation of slavery, and the verbal and physical clashes with Caroline and their children led young Yancey to consider many men like Beman cruel and hypocritical. When Beman sold his wife's slaves before the family's removal to Troy, New York, in 1823, Yancey's suspicions gained confirmation.

In the North, Yancey received a superior education at private academies and at Williams College. The tensions between his mother and stepfather increased, though, with their marriage and separation spilling into public discourse in Troy. Yancey left college in his junior year and moved back south, living with various relatives in Georgia and South Carolina. By 1834 he settled in Greenville, South Carolina. There, his uncle Robert Cunningham and law teacher Benjamin F. Perry imbued Yancey with staunchly Unionist ideals at the end of the nullification crisis. As a nineteen-year-old editor of the *Greenville Mountaineer*, Yancey savagely attacked his father's old enemy, Calhoun, who Yancey considered a plotter of secession.

In 1835 Yancey married Sarah Caroline Earle. She owned thirty-five slaves; the next year, Yancey purchased land near Cahaba, Alabama, near another relative, a states' rights leader, Jesse Beene. A bizarre series of events drew Yancey away from absolute Unionism. The Panic of 1837 hit Yancey hard, and the next year his infant son died. Before Yancey could deal with either blow, an argument and street fight in Greenville led to Yancey's killing his wife's uncle, Dr. Robinson Earle. Convicted of manslaughter and released after a few months, Yancey returned to his plantation in 1839. That summer an angry neighbor tried to murder Yancey's overseer by poisoning a well; instead, most of Yancey's slaves died. Throughout his personal traumas and with Beman rising to prominence as an abolitionist, Yancey felt under siege by a growing antislavery North and suddenly found wisdom and greatness in Calhoun's staunch defense of the South.

Simultaneous with his changing political philosophy, Yancey entered public office. He won election to Alabama's lower house in 1841, did not seek reelection in 1842, but sought and won a state senate seat in 1843. The next year, at age 30, he was elected to his first of two terms in Congress. Already renowned back home for his fiery oratory, Yancey in his first major speech in Congress so antagonized North Carolina representative Thomas Clingman that the two met in a duel, a bloodless one. Yancey railed against mighty Whigs Henry Clay, Daniel Webster, and John Quincy Adams, and even fellow Democrat Stephen A. Douglas. Finally disgusted with compromises and party politics, he resigned in 1846.

As a young man, Yancey always sought father figures. During the 1840s, Dixon Hall Lewis emerged as his last and most important. A powerful Alabama politician, Lewis completed Yancey's conversion to states' rights. But Yancey went further than this mentor in 1848 by bolting from the Democratic National Convention upon the failure of the Alabama platform, that state's demand for federal protection of slavery in the national territories. When Lewis died suddenly later that year, Yancey fully embraced Calhoun as a replacement. But Calhoun died in the midst of mounting sectional tensions two years later, conflict that resulted in the Compromise of 1850. Standing finally on his own, Yancey refused to accept the deal and henceforth fought for secession.

Over the next decade, Yancey moved in and out of Democratic Party activities, but always disdained elective office. Freeing himself to organize behind the scenes, Yancey remained focused on his goal: absolute protection of Southern rights and interests, in the Union or out of it. With the rise of the Republican Party, the bloodshed and chaos in Kansas, the failure of efforts to expand slavery to Latin America, and John Brown's raid south, the South was finally poised to listen to Yancey. At the National Democratic Convention of 1860 in Charleston, South

Carolina, Yancey again demanded essentially the Alabama platform. Northern delegates defeated it again, but this time when Yancey bolted so too did most delegates from slave states. The split among Democrats did not heal; it helped ensure the victory of Abraham Lincoln, an event so frightening to slaveholders that seven states seceded before Lincoln's inauguration.

Yancey's hometown, Montgomery, served as the first capital of the Confederate States of America. Yancey had the honor of introducing the first president, Jefferson Davis, with the proclamation, "The man and the hour have met." Davis selected Yancey to head a diplomatic mission to England and France to gain official recognition and material aid. Yancey failed, not, as critics have maintained, because of his hot-headedness, but instead because an interested England watched to see if the Confederacy could deliver a fatal blow to Union forces (France determined to follow England). Early in 1862 Yancey returned home, only to leave again for the new capital at Richmond, Virginia, as a senator. There with all his might he supported the country he helped create, but insisted that war not compromise states' rights. That position led him into conflict with Davis, but one that most have exaggerated in its scale and disruptiveness. Just as the two settled one dispute in July 1863, Yancey suddenly fell ill and died of kidney disease in his home in Montgomery, just shy of his forty-ninth birthday.

—*Eric H. Walther*

See also Alabama; Congress, C.S.A.; Diplomacy, C.S.A.; Fire-eaters; Great Britain; Secession.

For further reading:

Draughon, Ralph Brown, Jr. "William Lowndes Yancey: From Unionist to Secessionist, 1814–1852" (Ph.D. dissertation, 1968).

DuBose, John Witherspoon. *The Life and Times of William Lowndes Yancey: A History of Political Parties in the United States from 1834 to 1864; Especially As to the Origins of the Confederate States* (1892).

Heidler, David S. *Pulling the Temple Down: The Fire-eaters and the Destruction of the Union* (1994).

Walther, Eric H. *The Fire-eaters* (1992).

YATES, RICHARD
(1815–1873)
Governor of Illinois

As the governor of Illinois during the war, Richard Yates was a staunch Unionist in a state where antiwar feeling and obstructionism among Democrats was strong. He was born in Kentucky and moved to Illinois as a young man, setting up a law practice in Jacksonville. In the 1840s he served as a Whig in the state legislature, where he met Abraham Lincoln, followed by two terms in the U.S. Congress between 1850 and 1854. He was a vocal opponent of the Kansas-Nebraska Act and a key organizer of the

Republican Party in Illinois in 1856. He was elected governor of the state in 1860, taking office in January 1861. Yates was a ferocious opponent of compromise with the secessionists, warning that "our people will wade through seas of blood before they will see a single star or a solitary stripe erased from the glorious flag of our Union." When an American flag was burned outside a recruiting station in Illinois in 1861, the governor put this declaration into practice by ordering that anyone found desecrating the stars and stripes should be shot. He was an energetic war leader, visiting hospitals and recruitment stations, and making as many speeches as he could to departing Illinois regiments.

Relations between Yates and President Lincoln were sometimes strained by the constant demands Yates made on the president for more patronage posts and because of differences over the conduct of the war. Yates was an early advocate of emancipation and in July 1862 he publicly criticized generals who "fritter away the sinews of our brave men in guarding the property of traitors and in driving back into their hands loyal blacks who offer us their labour and seek shelter with the federal flag." He was also a supporter of African-American troops and of penalties for traitors when their states were returned to the Union.

The tone of Yates's private correspondence indicates that he was a man who was inclined to fear the worst in any situation and to search nervously for conspiracies and treason at every turn. The result was that he never gave the impression of being entirely in control. Yates exemplified the difficulty of distinguishing between patriotism and partisanship in a highly competitive party system. A dramatic confrontation in the summer of 1862 ensued when the state constitutional convention, which was dominated by Peace Democrats, sought to go beyond its stipulated powers and set about trying to find ways of removing the governor from office. The convention passed a resolution absolving the South of all responsibility for the condition of the country and blaming the Republicans instead. The governor feared civil war. In 1863 the Democratic-controlled Illinois House of Representatives passed a resolution favoring an armistice with a view to negotiating with the Rebels. In response, Yates prorogued the legislature on a technicality and governed alone, until a solid Republican majority was returned in 1864.

Yates played a key role in encouraging the growth of secret societies called Union Leagues. Although the leagues performed electioneering roles, such as canvassing, holding public meetings, and distributing documents, they fervently disclaimed a partisan character. In the spring of 1864, the 140,000 Union League members in Illinois were organized into militia, which acted as vigilante groups reporting the names of suspected disloyalists to the War Department. Leagues

were even involved in mobbing the offices of several small-town newspapers, the editors of which had expressed support for the election of Democratic candidates or had attacked the administration. With the enthusiastic support of Yates, the leagues became the self-appointed arbiters of patriotism. They aggressively blurred the line between political opposition to the Republican Party and disloyalty to the United States and, in doing so, challenged the legitimacy of party politics in wartime.

As the 1864 election campaign approached, Yates remained loyal to Lincoln even as many other radicals were searching for another candidate. Yet he continued to worry that the president would not be reelected, convincing himself in the late summer of 1864 that the draft would hand Illinois to the Democrats. Governor Yates and *Chicago Times* editor Joseph Medill vigorously urged the president to furlough Illinois troops home for the election to shore up the Unionist vote.

As governor, Yates was never calm in the face of the tumultuous events around him, but he had a disarming capacity to recognize his own mistakes. Even before Lincoln's assassination, Yates confessed that he had been wrong and the president right about the timing of emancipation. After the war he served a term in the U.S. Senate, where he was regarded as a radical who supported the impeachment of Andrew Johnson. In these later years his long-standing drinking problem worsened and in 1873 he died suddenly of a heart attack. His was the voice of impassioned Unionism (albeit flawed by frustration and impatience) and in the volatile world of the Midwest during the war, he provided a necessary counterblast to the internal threat posed by Copperheads.

—*Adam I. P. Smith*

See also Peace Democrats; Union Leagues.
For further reading
Hesseltine, William B. *Lincoln and the War Governors* (1955).
Klement, Frank L. *The Copperheads in the Middle West* (1972).
Krenkel, John H. *Richard Yates: Civil War Governor* (1966).
Yates, Richard. Papers. Illinois State Historical Library, Springfield.

YAZOO EXPEDITION

(December 1862)

Ulysses S. Grant, the commanding general of the Army of the Tennessee, formed the Yazoo expedition to help facilitate the capture of the Confederate stronghold on the Mississippi River, Vicksburg. This expedition would be the first in a series of attempts by Grant to capture or bypass this strategically important location. Grant's plan called for a 40,000-man force under him to move overland, roughly following the Mississippi Central Railroad, and move onto Vicksburg from the north and east. The second force, the Yazoo expedition, Department of the Tennessee, under General William T. Sherman, would use a water route in an effort to land troops north of Vicksburg by surprise. Sherman's Yazoo expedition would be the westernmost part of a projected two-pronged attack on Vicksburg. The plan called for Grant to keep the large part of Confederate forces in the area occupied, while the Yazoo expedition would encounter only a small garrison in Vicksburg. Sherman's force would ultimately be made up of 32,000 men divided into four divisions.

After conferring with Grant in northern Mississippi, Sherman returned to Memphis, Tennessee, on 13 December 1862, with one division ordered to amass an expeditionary force. This would have to be done hastily if surprise was to be achieved. In Memphis, Sherman incorporated into his force two divisions that had recently arrived there from the North. One of the newly arrived divisions was the 7th Division of Don Carlos Buell's Army of the Ohio; the other was 1st Division, Army of Kentucky. The former division under George W. Morgan was redesignated as 3d Division, XIII Corps; the latter division under Andrew J. Smith was renamed 1st Division, XIII Corps. Sherman's original division, commanded by Morgan L. Smith, became the 2d Division, XIII Corps. Frederick Steele's division in Helena, Arkansas, became the final division to constitute Sherman's Yazoo expedition. This force was redesignated 4th Division, XIII Corps.

The move on Vicksburg had significant political overtones. While organizing his forces, Sherman realized that the divisions under Morgan and Smith were understaffed. To bring these forces up to strength, Sherman turned to the forces being gathered in Memphis by the political general, John A. McClernand. McClernand, a War Democrat, was a political appointee from President Abraham Lincoln's state of Illinois. He had petitioned Lincoln to acquire an independent command for the purposes of capturing Vicksburg by way of the Mississippi River.

Lincoln did not see a move on Vicksburg by Grant in the immediate future. He had to appease the powerful Democrats in his home state, and he believed that a proactive move needed to occur to bring about a needed Union victory, or some combination of the above wrongly influenced Lincoln's decision. When General Henry W. Halleck, overall commander in the West, and Ulysses S. Grant heard about McClernand's independent command, they were furious.

While the situation was being worked out between Halleck and Lincoln, Sherman used the forces from Illinois, Indiana, and Iowa, gathered by McClernand for his Army of the Mississippi, to reinforce the understaffed 1st and 3d Divisions. McClernand was still in the North on his honeymoon when the Yazoo expedition was forming. He was surprised on his arrival in Memphis to discover that the forces he had been accumulating left in the direction of Vicksburg without him. Through the pressure exerted on Lincoln by Halleck, McClernand would lose his independent command and he and his forces would be incorporated into Grant's Army of the Tennessee. McClernand became a corps commander.

By 19 December 1862, Sherman's three divisions of 23,000 men were ready to move. Sherman's force would be accompanied by parts of the U.S. Navy's Mississippi Squadron commanded by Admiral David D. Porter. Steamboats and rams made up this force, which assembled in St. Louis, Missouri, and Cairo, Illinois, and was sent to Memphis. The force left on 20 December and picked up Steele's 4th Division of 9,000 men the following day. On 26 December, the transports turned up the Yazoo River, where the troops disembarked about ten miles up the river. In the end, the Yazoo expedition was a failure: Sherman's troops were repulsed by the Confederates at the battle of Chickasaw Bluffs.

—*James L. Isemann*

See also Chickasaw Bluffs, Battle of; McClernand, John Alexander; Sherman, William Tecumseh.
For further reading:
Lloyd, Lewis. *Sherman: Fighting Prophet* (1960).
Welcher, Frank J. *The Union Army, 1861–1865: Organization and Operations* (1989).

YAZOO PASS EXPEDITION
(February–April 1863)

The Yazoo Pass expedition was one of several failed attempts by Major General Ulysses S. Grant to reach high, dry ground north of Vicksburg, Mississippi. Taking place in early 1863 in the context of other endeavors such as the Chickasaw Bayou expedition, Grant's Canal, and the Steele's Bayou expedition, the Yazoo Pass expedition showed the extent to which Grant, confounded by Vicksburg's defensibility, would go to reduce the Confederate garrison.

The entire operation hinged on traversing a series of little-used water routes through the Mississippi Delta. Yazoo Pass itself led from Moon Lake, which connected with the Mississippi River near Helena, Arkansas, to the Coldwater River. The Coldwater then flowed into the Tallahatchie River, combining with the Yalobusha River to form the Yazoo River, which emptied into the Mississippi River just north of Vicksburg. A Union force could sail the bayous and small rivers and ultimately reach high ground north of Vicksburg and the Confederate batteries that closed the Yazoo River to Union traffic. Originally used by Delta farmers and planters to trade with Memphis, the Yazoo Pass route was closed when the state of Mississippi erected a levee that

deprived access to the Mississippi River and lowered water levels in the delta.

Grant, through subordinates, learned of the pass and ordered testing done to determine the feasibility of such a route. Engineering officer Lieutenant Colonel James Harrison Wilson reported that cutting the levee would raise the water level and allow transports and ironclads into the tricky Delta waterways. With Grant's approval, Wilson cut the levee on 2 February 1863 and raised the water level just as Grant had hoped. Exploration, however, found that trees obstructed Yazoo Pass itself. Entire regiments worked in the harsh surroundings, but cleared the pass by 24 February.

With an open path, Federal infantry aboard transports, commanded by Brigadier General Leonard F. Ross, began making their way southward. Two ironclads, the *Chillicothe* and *Baron De Kalb*, led the transports as they entered enemy country. The expedition encountered all types of wildlife, from snakes to bears to bobcats, a number of which fell to the decks as the tall smokestacks slammed against tree limbs. A novelty to Northern soldiers was the native alligator, which became a favorite target for Union soldiers. The Federals saw few Confederates, however, until they reached Greenwood, which lay at the confluence of the Tallahatchie and Yalobusha rivers.

At Greenwood, the Confederates made a stand. Under Major General William W. Loring, the Southerners established Fort Pemberton in a bend of the Tallahatchie River, just west of the mouth of the Yalobusha. The Confederates mounted several guns, including a powerful rifle, and even sunk the famed *Star of the West* in the channel to block Federal vessels. As time passed, more guns and men arrived to garrison the earth and cotton-bale fort.

Stopped by the Confederate fort, the Federals landed artillery and infantry, but primarily tried to reduce the garrison with the two ironclads. The Union vessels attacked on 13 and 16 March, each time receiving the worst of the fight. The gunboats were obviously useless, and because of high water, the infantry could not reach the fort. Ross had to reboard and retreat on 20 March.

Soon, Ross met Brigadier General Isaac F. Quinby steaming southward with reinforcements. Quinby, the ranking officer, took charge and ordered a return to Fort Pemberton. Several days of skirmishing developed, but Quinby soon realized the futility of remaining near Greenwood. On 4 April, Quinby likewise turned his force northward for the arduous journey to the Mississippi River.

The Federals arrived safely but were defeated in their attempt to reach Vicksburg. The Confederates had managed to defend the heart of Mississippi again, but the operation caused some damage in the relationship between Loring and his commanding officer, Lieutenant

General John C. Pemberton. Loring requested more material and men, which Pemberton refused. The two exchanged heated words that no doubt soured the relationship, causing much more damage in May when Pemberton relied heavily on Loring at the critical battle of Champion's Hill.

—*Timothy B. Smith*

See also Vicksburg Campaign.
For further reading:
Bearss, Edwin C. *The Campaign for Vicksburg* (1985–1986).

YELLOW BAYOU (BAYOU DE GLAIZE), LOUISIANA
(18 May 1864)

During David Dixon Porter's and Nathaniel Banks's retreat from Alexandria, Louisiana, at the close of the Red River campaign in 1864, Banks fought skirmishes with Confederates from 13 May until the army crossed the Atchafalaya River on 19 May. During the first engagement on 14 May, Banks's men easily drove back the outnumbered Confederates. On 15 May, however, the Confederate cavalry brigades of Arthur Pendleton Bagby and James Patrick Major sharply engaged Banks's rear guard at Avoyelles. The Confederates were again driven back, and the Union forces spent an uneasy night at Marksville.

The following day, the sixteenth, Banks's forces ran into Confederates at Mansura. Bagby and Major had been reinforced by an infantry division under Brigadier General Camille Armand Polignac and a cavalry brigade under Brigadier General Xavier Blanchard De Bray, two Frenchmen who had immigrated to the South. Bagby and Major occupied the ground right of town, and Polignac and De Bray deployed to the left. The Confederates also possessed batteries totaling thirty-two guns. The engagement began with both forces' artillery exchanging rounds for a few hours. Then, because they were still outnumbered, the Confederates withdrew when the Union infantry and cavalry advanced. The Federals then spent the rest of the day and evening plundering the town of Mansura.

As the Federals moved on their way the following day, Confederate sharpshooters harried their advance. At Bayou de Glaize on 17 May the Federals moved across the wetlands along the only bridge and then destroyed it. The following day as the Union forces trudged their way toward Simmesport near Yellow Bayou, the Confederates closed in again on the Federal rear guard. Federal major general Andrew Jackson Smith sent Brigadier General Joseph Anthony Mower with 4,500 men to push the Confederates back.

Mower had three brigades commanded by Colonel Sylvester Hill, Colonel William Shaw, and Colonel William Francis Lynch, and two batteries. The initial Federal assault succeeded in pushing the Confederates back across Yellow Bayou. At that point the Union troops ran into an area of very thick undergrowth. After hacking their way into a very wide clearing, they looked out at about 5,000 Confederates facing their position.

Confederate cavalryman John Wharton commanded a mixed force of infantry, cavalry, and artillery. When it appeared that the discovery of the Confederates was causing the Union forces to withdraw, Wharton ordered Colonel William Parsons with his 12th Texas Cavalry to charge the Union infantry. Parsons sent word back to Wharton objecting to the order. He claimed that if Union forces were retreating, it would be a needless expenditure of his men's lives to charge. Wharton repeated the order, threatening to arrest Parsons if it were not carried out. Parsons charged and quickly met with Federal cavalry outnumbering his own. There was a sharp cavalry engagement, during which the Federal infantry, supported by their artillery, began moving forward. They succeeded in pushing the Confederates back a short distance.

By that time everyone was suffering from the oppressive heat and the lack of available water in the area. The Confederates countercharged into the undergrowth where the Federals had taken refuge from the sun. Some hand to hand fighting ensued, during which the undergrowth caught fire, worsening the situation for everyone. The Union troops succeeded in pushing the Confederates back out into the open but were too exhausted to pursue. By that time it was getting dark, and both sides simply withdrew. Casualties for the Confederates were 608 and for the Union 350. By the end of the battle the Federal engineers had succeeded in creating a makeshift bridge of boats over the Atchafalaya River, and the next day the Union army crossed. Yellow Bayou was the last engagement of the Red River campaign.

—*David S. Heidler and Jeanne T. Heidler*

See also Mower, Joseph Anthony; Polignac, Camille Armand; Red River Campaign; Smith, Andrew Jackson.
For further reading:
Brooksher, William R. *War along the Bayous: The 1864 Red River Campaign in Louisiana* (1998).
Johnson, Ludwell H. *Red River Campaign: Politics and Cotton in the Civil War* (1958).

YELLOW TAVERN, BATTLE OF
(11 May 1864)

Yellow Tavern was the first major cavalry fight in the Eastern theater to end in an unqualified victory. In a single stroke, Major General Philip H. Sheridan established the superiority of his Union cavalry and caused the death of Major General James E. B. "Jeb" Stuart, General Robert E. Lee's flamboyant chief of

cavalry. Nevertheless, Sheridan erred by leading almost all his cavalry on a distant raid while the Army of the Potomac was warmly engaged at Spotsylvania Court House. Robbed of his reconnaissance capacity, Lieutenant General Ulysses S. Grant found himself badly handicapped as he tried to fight his way through Lee's entrenched lines.

On the morning of 8 May 1864, Major General George G. Meade, the commander of the Army of the Potomac, had a stormy meeting with Sheridan, the newly appointed head of his Cavalry Corps. Angry because Union troopers had been relegated to supporting Meade's infantry and guarding supply trains during the battle of the Wilderness, Sheridan demanded leave to act independently, promising to neutralize the Army of Northern Virginia's troublesome cavalry. As Sheridan later recalled: "I told him I could whip Stuart if he (Meade) would only let me." When Meade reported Sheridan's boast to Grant, the latter replied: "Let him start right out and do it."

The appropriate orders were issued and Sheridan cut loose from the Army of the Potomac with virtually his entire corps, three divisions and six artillery batteries. Riding four abreast, the 10,000 blue troopers made an impressive sight in a column measuring thirteen miles long.

Sheridan planned to draw Stuart into a showdown by swinging around Lee's left and raiding toward Richmond, Virginia. Rebel scouts informed Stuart of Sheridan's movement shortly after it began, and the Southern cavalier took half of his own corps, roughly 4,000 to 5,000 troopers in three brigades, to counter this latest threat to the Confederate capital. Hoping to buy time, Stuart dispatched Brigadier General James B. Gordon's brigade to harass Sheridan's rear, and then he plunged south with the brigades of Brigadier Generals Lunsford L. Lomax and William C. Wickham to intercept the head of Sheridan's expedition.

Stuart attained his objective sometime between 8:00 and 10:00 A.M. on 11 May by beating Sheridan to Yellow Tavern, a strategic crossroads six miles north of Richmond. Intent on blocking Sheridan's progress long enough for reinforcements to reach him, Stuart deployed his 3,000 weary troopers in a V-shaped line. Lomax's brigade formed along the Telegraph Road facing west toward the Mountain Road, the route down which Sheridan was marching. Wickham aligned his brigade to the west of the Telegraph Road on a ridge overlooking Lomax's position. Wickham's four regiments faced south to enfilade any Federals who might assail Lomax's front.

Sheridan came in sight of Yellow Tavern about an hour after Stuart. Finding his prey in battle array, Sheridan brought up Brigadier General Wesley Merritt's 1st Division to engage the enemy. Posted at the left end of Merritt's line, Brigadier General George A. Custer's Michigan Brigade came under a vicious crossfire as it edged toward the apex of Stuart's line. Merritt's two other brigades drew some pressure off Custer by working around Lomax's left. With his flank turned, Lomax withdrew to the high ground east of the Telegraph Road. In effect, Lomax simply extended Wickham's southward-facing line by falling in on the latter's left.

It was now 2:00 P.M., and a two-hour lull fell over the battlefield. Sheridan used that time to place Brigadier General James H. Wilson's 3d Division on Merritt's left. As the Federals redeployed, Custer's brigade moved from the left of Sheridan's line to nearer the center. From there, Custer spotted a Confederate battery in an exposed position beside the Telegraph Road. Determined to take those guns, Custer dismounted two of his regiments, the 5th and 6th Michigan Cavalry, and instructed them to distract the Confederates with a rapid fire from their Spencer carbines. Then he massed the 1st Michigan Cavalry in a column of squadrons to swamp the guns with a mounted charge from the flank. Custer ordered his fourth regiment, the 7th Michigan Cavalry, to support the 1st Michigan's charge. He also borrowed the 1st Vermont Cavalry from Wilson's division to fill any break that might appear in the 1st Michigan's line.

Custer completed his dispositions by 4:00 P.M. As bugles sounded, Custer motioned his reinforced brigade forward. With Wilson's and Merritt's other brigades advancing simultaneously on his flanks, Custer's charge assumed an irresistible momentum, and the "Wolverines" soon had possession of two Confederate guns. The charge also threw Lomax's brigade into disorder, and the Confederate left wing began to waver.

Jeb Stuart dashed bravely to the front to rally his men, but a dismounted Michigander spotted the enemy officer in the conspicuous plumed hat and shot him in the abdomen. Mortally wounded, Stuart shouted to some retreating Confederates as he was conducted to the rear: "Go back! Go back! I had rather die than be whipped!"

Major General Fitzhugh Lee, Stuart's second-in-command, tried to stabilize the Confederate position, but there were too many Federals and they were pressing too hard. Despite a desperate counterattack by the 1st Virginia Cavalry, the gray line soon disintegrated. Fitzhugh Lee's battered units streamed away to the north, east, or south as darkness fell to cover their flight.

Sheridan reported 704 of his corps killed, wounded, and missing at Yellow Tavern. Confederate casualties were closer to 300, but there was no doubting that the Federals won the fight. Victory at Yellow Tavern made Sheridan the idol of the Army of the Potomac's cavalry. It infused his troopers with immense pride and confidence, qualities sadly lacking in the Union cavalry earlier in the war. History has recognized these achievements, but Sheridan should be faulted for leaving Grant with only three cavalry regiments at Spotsylvania Court House, greatly reducing his commander's ability to

gather intelligence and read events. And although the death of Jeb Stuart saddened Lee and lowered Confederate morale, the Army of Northern Virginia's cavalry would receive a more mature brand of leadership from Stuart's successor, Major General Wade Hampton.

—*Gregory J. W. Urwin*

See also Cavalry, C.S.A.; Cavalry, U.S.A.; Custer, George Armstrong; Lee, Fitzhugh; Lomax, Lunsford Lindsay; Merritt, Wesley; Sheridan, Philip Henry; Spotsylvania Court House, Battle of; Stuart, James Ewell Brown; Wickham, Williams Carter; Wilson, James Harrison.

For further reading:

Morris, Roy, Jr. *Sheridan: The Life and Wars of General Phil Sheridan* (1992).

Rhea, Gordon C. *The Battles for Spotsylvania Court House and the Road to Yellow Tavern, May 7–12, 1864* (1997).

Starr, Stephen Z. *The Union Cavalry in the Civil War* (1979–1985).

Thomas, Emory M. *Bold Dragoon: The Life of J. E. B. Stuart* (1986).

Urwin, Gregory J. W. *Custer Victorious: The Civil War Battles of General George Armstrong Custer* (1990).

YORKTOWN
(April–May 1862)

Located near the end of the peninsula formed by the York and James rivers in southeastern Virginia, Yorktown held some distinction in U.S. history as the location of the British surrender to Franco-American forces in 1781. Following Virginia's secession from the Union in April 1861, the area was largely under the control of state and Confederate forces, with the exception of Federal retention of Fort Monroe at the tip of the peninsula, seventy miles from the Confederate capital.

On 24 March 1862, messages arrived in Richmond from Major General John B. Magruder, in command of the 11,000 Confederate soldiers at Yorktown, announcing the arrival of Federal troops in his vicinity. The Federal force of over 100,000 was under the command of Major General George B. McClellan, who planned to move

Federal artillery park at Yorktown, Virginia, 1862 (*Library of Congress*)

Confederate fortifications at Yorktown reinforced with cotton bales, June 1862 (*Library of Congress*)

rapidly up the peninsula and threaten the Confederate capital. McClellan's intentions became clear to the Confederates in early April as his army began a general advance toward Yorktown. After inspecting Magruder's positions around Yorktown, General Joseph E. Johnston, commander of the Confederate army in Virginia, emphasized to President Jefferson Davis and members of his cabinet his belief that a major attempt to defend the peninsula around Yorktown could be successful only temporarily because of the vulnerability any defensive line would have to flank attack from the rivers. Therefore, if the Confederates could keep McClellan at bay for only a few weeks at most, it was not worth the detrimental effect

the tidal swamps and bad water would have upon the men. Furthermore, any victory on the peninsula (if indeed it was possible) would necessarily be incomplete, due to the proximity of Fort Monroe. The latter would provide a haven for McClellan's retreating army and prevent its complete annihilation.

Johnston believed a withdrawal was necessary, but Davis and his secretary of war opposed the plan because it meant the abandonment of the navy yard at Norfolk, the forfeiture of valuable machinery located therein, and the loss of the base for the CSS *Virginia*. Their desire was to see Confederate forces hold the peninsula in a defensive designed to prevent the loss of geographic points.

Federal wagon park at Yorktown, 1862 (*Library of Congress*)

Consequently, Johnston, along with the divisions of Gustavus W. Smith and James Longstreet, received orders to depart for the peninsula, where the former assumed command of over 53,000 troops on 17 April.

McClellan, meanwhile, was surprised to find what he interpreted to be an elaborate and well-manned defensive position stretching across his projected route to the Confederate capital. This inaccurate impression was the result of an elaborate ruse contrived by Magruder, combined with faulty Federal intelligence reports originating in part from Allan Pinkerton. The Federal general had expected to outflank Yorktown and press on. However, without making a major effort to test the enemy's defenses, he decided to commence siege operations. McClellan clearly wanted to avoid the massive bloodletting associated with frontal assaults against prepared positions. Accordingly, his engineers constructed impressive field works and prepared for the arrival of heavy artillery from Fort Monroe.

Upon his return to Yorktown, Johnston was confronted with a plethora of problems. The men of Magruder's command were tired from the continuous efforts to construct and improve their lines. Food was of poor quality and insufficient in quantity. Both health and morale were in a state of decline, due to the frequently heavy rains, lack of adequate shelter, and harassing small-arms fire from Federal sharpshooters. Johnston's main concern, however, focused on indications that McClellan was preparing to bombard the Yorktown position and the York River water batteries with thirty mortars and one hundred rifled cannon from a distance greater than the Confederates could adequately respond with their primarily antiquated smoothbore artillery. This information, combined with word on 22 April that Federal major general William Buel Franklin had arrived with his division of approximately 11,000 men and was still on board ship, indicated an impending turning movement up the York River. The general informed Richmond that a withdrawal might be necessary and requested that bridges to his rear be repaired in the event such a move was required.

On 27 April Johnston sent word to the War Department that he intended to evacuate the Yorktown–Warwick River line before the Federals began their bombardment. A retrograde movement prior to McClellan's assault was preferable to one attempted during an attack in which soldiers could succumb to artillery fire and confusion. Major General Benjamin Huger was directed to prepare to evacuate Norfolk, removing as much property from the navy yard as possible. Flag Officer Josiah Tattnall, of the James River Squadron, was queried on the possibility of taking the CSS *Virginia* to the York River to destroy the Federal transports. Tattnall responded that the operation could not be done safely. Lastly, Johnston reiterated an earlier suggestion that a large army be concentrated in Richmond for a strike against McClellan.

On 29 April word reached Yorktown from forward observers that the Federal batteries were almost all in place, and the cannonading would surely begin soon. The general wrote Robert E. Lee: "The fight for Yorktown, as I said in Richmond, must be one of artillery, in which we cannot win. The result is certain; the time only doubtful. Should the attack upon Yorktown be made earnestly, we cannot prevent its fall; nor can it hold out more than a few hours. We must abandon the Peninsula soon." At midnight on 4–5 May, concealed by heavy artillery fire, Confederate forces withdrew from their position astride the peninsula and fell back toward the old colonial capital of Williamsburg. The opportunity for a decisive battle on the peninsula would have to be postponed.

—*Alan C. Downs*

See also Magruder, John Bankhead; Peninsula Campaign.
For further reading:
Sears, Stephen W. *To the Gates of Richmond, The Peninsula Campaign* (1992).

YOUNG, BRIGHAM
(1801–1877)
Leader of the Mormon Church

Born in Vermont to religious parents, Young grew to adulthood in western New York, where he was swept up in the enthusiasm of the Second Great Awakening, joining the Methodist Church before coming under the influence of Joseph Smith and the Mormons in 1832. Having desired upward mobility and self-improvement, and having failed to enjoy great success in secular vocations such as carpentry and furnituremaking, Young rose quickly in the Mormon Church, becoming a member of the Twelve Apostles in 1835 and succeeding Prophet Joseph Smith in 1844.

Seeking refuge from persecution faced in Illinois by the Mormons, Young orchestrated their trek to Deseret, land that was subsequently incorporated into the Territory of Utah, with Young serving as territorial governor. Anti-Mormon sentiment led to Young's removal as governor, and in 1857 the U.S. government actually contemplated war with Young and the Mormons to bring them to heel after the Mountain Meadows Massacre, in which travelers in a wagon train were slain by Mormons near Cedar City, Utah.

Although Young and the Mormon Church pledged fealty to the Union when the Civil War erupted, the U.S. government considered them suspect and wanted to secure the Utah Territory because the route of the Butterfield Overland Express passed through Mormon land. Furthermore, a few Mormons practiced slavery, and commissioners from the Confederacy offered Young statehood for Utah should the Mormons join with the secessionists. Although most Mormons hailed from the free states or from northern Europe, considered slavery a blight to prosperity, and did not believe support of the Confederate States of America a fit course of action, the Union sent a volunteer regiment from California to Utah to ensure its loyalty.

During the war, relations between Young and the U.S. government proved stormy. Territorial governor John Dawson demanded that the Mormons pay a large sum of taxes that he claimed they owed the federal government, and he vetoed a bill to petition Congress to admit Utah as a state. Then Congress reduced the size of Utah, placing it in adjacent territories that became the states of Nevada, Colorado, and Wyoming. Congress also passed the Morrill Anti-Bigamy Act, which made illegal the Mormon practice of plural marriage and limited the amount of property owned by the Mormon Church.

Complicating the tense relations with federal authority, Colonel Patrick Connor marched his troops through Salt Lake City and camped them near the town at hastily erected Fort Douglas, named for the late, anti-Mormon senator from Illinois. Only a perceived menace by the Shoshone Indians along the Bear River in lower Idaho averted crisis. Connor's troops left Fort Douglas, temporarily ending the day-to-day confrontations between the Mormons and the army. Then the army massacred the Shoshone in January 1863, which caused the Mormons to perceive the army in a more favorable light. Mormon farmers also recognized that the fort served as a good market for their crops.

The respite was short-lived, as Connor and Governor Stephen Harding made plans to declare martial law and arrest Young in the spring of 1863. Abraham Lincoln himself averted further conflict by removing the governor, replacing him with the more congenial J. Duane Doty, and adopting a policy of leaving the Mormons alone unless they directly provoked the government. General Irwin

McDowell, Connor's superior, ordered the fiery Irishmen to do the same thing. Relations had improved significantly by 1865. Young and the Mormons joined with the army in celebrating Lincoln's second inauguration and commiserated with them in mourning Lincoln's assassination the following month.

After the Civil War, Young confronted three public challenges: renewed conflict with Native Americans, congressional attempts to limit plural marriage and to punish those who practiced it, and the influx of Gentiles (non-Mormons) into the territory, a circumstance exacerbated by the completion of the Transcontinental Railroad in 1869. There were other personal problems. Young faced competition from within the ranks of Mormonism for control over the church, and he had to spend a night in jail during divorce proceedings from one of his many wives, Anne Eliza Webb. The deaths of Joseph A. Young, a favored son and possible successor, and George A. Smith, a close friend and advisor, grieved him greatly. John D. Lee, a former follower who had led the Mormons at Mountain Meadows, and who would be executed for his part in the massacre, accused Young in the pages of the *New York Herald* of ordering the Mountain Meadows Massacre, which fanned the flames of anti-Mormon sentiment in the United States. Growing increasingly weary of such obstacles, Young died at age 76, likely from appendicitis.

—*Edward R. Crowther*

See also Churches; Connor, Patrick; Mormons.

For further reading:
Bringhurst, Newell G. *Brigham Young and the Expanding American Frontier* (1986).
Josephy, Alvin M. *The Civil War in the American West* (1991).
Long, E. B. *The Saints and the Union: Utah Territory during the Civil War* (1981).

YOUNG, JOHN RUSSELL
(1840–1899)
Union journalist

Born in Tyrone County, Ireland, to George Young and Rebecca Rankin Young, John Russell Young immigrated to the United States with his parents when he was an infant. He spent much of his childhood in Philadelphia but moved to New Orleans when he was eleven to live with an uncle. He moved back to Philadelphia four years later as an apprentice to his cousin, a publisher named William Young. At sixteen, Young went to work for the *Philadelphia Press* as a copy messenger, but quickly came to the attention of the editor of the paper, John W. Forney, who promoted him to reporter.

At the outbreak of the Civil War, Young was a correspondent for the newspaper in Washington and traveled with Irvin McDowell's army to Manassas Junction in July 1861 to cover the expected battle there. During the conflict, Young stayed close to the action and followed the battle closely until it became apparent to him that the Union forces had the Confederates on the run at Henry House Hill. Because of his desire to file his story before other reporters, Young did not remain to see the outcome; he left before observing the subsequent turn in the battle and resulting retreat of the Federal forces. He rode through the afternoon to Fairfax Court House to wire his story to the paper only to learn just before sending his report that the Union army was in retreat. After gaining access to some of the early official dispatches and talking to Union troops who had made their way to the town, he was able to send in the heavily revised story and still beat most of the other reporters to print. At age twenty-one, Young quickly became one of the most widely read war correspondents.

While still serving as a war correspondent for the *Philadelphia Press* in Washington, Young was also made managing editor of the *Washington Chronicle*, also edited by Forney. At the beginning of George B. McClellan's Peninsula campaign, Young was arrested by the military for printing a story in the *Chronicle* that mentioned some of McClellan's troop movements in preparation for the upcoming campaign. Receiving a stiff lecture on the importance of secrecy regarding such movements, Young was released after he promised never to let it happen again. During the campaign, Young served as a correspondent for both the *Chronicle* and the *Press*.

In 1863 Young assumed duties as managing editor of the *Press*, but he missed the exciting life of a war correspondent and asked Forney's permission to accompany the army of Nathaniel P. Banks on the upcoming Red River campaign in Louisiana. In early 1864, Young returned to his childhood home of New Orleans and sent colorful dispatches back to Philadelphia and Washington about the impact of the war on the largest of Southern cities.

From New Orleans, Young traveled to join Banks's army and quickly developed a friendly relationship with the Union commander. Along with frequently filing stories on the campaign, Young volunteered to serve on Banks's staff, a request Banks granted, allowing Young an even closer look at the inner workings of the failed campaign. After the army's rather ignominious return from the campaign when Banks came in for rather heavy criticism, Young was one of his staunchest defenders in the press.

Upon his return from Louisiana, Young returned to his duties with the *Philadelphia Press*. Throughout the war, Young had maintained a fairly close relationship with the Republican government in Washington (with the exception of the little misunderstanding before the Peninsula campaign), and those ties became even closer in the later part of the war. He ran pieces in the *Press* and

wrote others for newspapers such as the *New York Tribune* encouraging support for the war and the purchase of war bonds. After the war, this support gained him several government appointments and the attention of other influential newspaper people.

In 1866, Horace Greeley named Young managing editor of the *New York Tribune*. He remained in that position until 1871, when the call of war correspondent led him to accept the position of European correspondent for the *New York Herald* during the Franco-Prussian War. He arrived too late to cover the war, but did send back articles on the destruction of the Paris Commune.

Young remained in Europe until 1877, when he accompanied Ulysses S. Grant on the ex-president's world tour. During the Asian phase of this journey, Young developed an appreciation for the Chinese, which led to his appointment in 1882 as U.S. minister to that country. He remained in that position until 1885, when he returned to the *New York Herald* as European correspondent. In 1890 he returned to the United States for good, and in his last years he served as Librarian of Congress from 1897 until his death on 17 January 1899.

Besides his extensive writing for a variety of newspapers, Young also wrote memoirs of his many adventures, including an account of his journey with President Grant and a memoir of his entire life published after his death.

—*David S. Heidler and Jeanne T. Heidler*

See also Newspapers.
For further reading:
Andrews, J. Cutler. *The North Reports the Civil War* (1955).
Young, John Russell. *Men and Memories: Personal Reminiscences* (1901).

YOUNG, PIERCE MANNING BUTLER
(1836–1896)
Confederate general

Born to Robert Maxwell Young, a physician, and Elizabeth Caroline Jones Young in Spartanburg, South Carolina, Young moved as a child with his family to Cartersville, Georgia. He received his early education at home and graduated from the Georgia Military Academy in 1856. After graduation, he accepted an appointment to the U.S. Military Academy. He was in his final year there when the secession crisis compelled his resignation in March 1861. Young then accepted a commission as a second lieutenant of artillery in the Confederate army.

Young served first in Pensacola before being promoted to first lieutenant and accepting the position of aide-de-camp to Brigadier General W. H. T. Walker. Soon Young became adjutant in Cobb's Legion. By the time of the Peninsula campaign, Young was a lieutenant colonel and briefly commanded the Legion at Malvern Hill during the Seven Days' battles.

During the Maryland campaign of September 1862, Young again commanded the Legion as part of J. E. B. Stuart's cavalry. Young was commended by Stuart for his actions near Crampton's Gap on 14 September. Young fought at Fredericksburg and was promoted to colonel and command of the Legion in early 1863.

At Brandy Station in June 1863, Young and Cobb's Legion fought as part of Wade Hampton's brigade. They earned distinction as part of the force that held Fleetwood Hill, a feat that won Stuart's accolades. Fighting only in the latter stages of the Gettysburg campaign, Young was again commended for his courage.

In September 1863, Young was promoted to brigadier general and command of Hampton's Legion. During the Bristoe Station and Mine Run campaigns of the fall of 1863, he temporarily commanded Hampton's division and was slightly wounded leading his men in the latter campaign.

Like most of the soldiers in the Army of Northern Virginia, Young saw little action until Grant's move south in the spring of 1864. While most of the army fought around Spotsylvania in the middle of May 1864, Young was ordered to Richmond to round up dispersed cavalry units and bring them to Lee's army. In November 1864, he was sent with what was left of Hampton's division to Georgia to attempt to raise reinforcements and find horses for the cavalry in Virginia.

While in Georgia, Young argued with General Joseph Wheeler, who threatened to have Young removed from command. Doubtless because of Young's recruiting and horse procurement as a threat to his own command, Wheeler tried unsuccessfully to prevent Young's promotion to major general in December 1864.

In the early months of 1865, Young operated out of Augusta, Georgia, briefly directing that town's defenses in February 1865. Technically he was part of Joseph E. Johnston's command in the Carolinas, so Young and his legion came under the terms of Johnston's surrender to William T. Sherman in April 1865. When he received instructions from Johnston in May to surrender his force, he did so.

After the war, Young returned to his home in Cartersville, Georgia. He became involved in politics and served several terms in the U.S. House of Representatives before entering the diplomatic service as consul general to St. Petersburg and minister to Guatemala and Honduras. He was valued for his diplomatic skills in dealing with several Latin American disputes, but bad health forced him cut his diplomatic career short. He returned to the United States and died in New York City before he could return home to Georgia. He was buried in Cartersville after a military funeral conducted by the United Confederate Veterans.

—*David S. Heidler and Jeanne T. Heidler*

See also Brandy Station; Crampton's Gap; Malvern Hill.

For further reading:
Holland, Lynwood Mathis. *Pierce M. B. Young: The Warwick of the South* (1964).

YULEE, DAVID LEVY
(1810–1886)
U.S. senator

David Levy Yulee, best known as the first Jewish senator and a leading firebrand for secession, was also one of the most enigmatic men ever to hold high office. His parentage and early faith were Jewish, yet he allegedly converted to Christianity to gain social acceptance and win the hand of Nancy C. Wickliffe, the daughter of the former governor of Kentucky, Charles A. Wickliffe, who also served as postmaster general under President John Tyler. Yulee was supposed to be a firebrand for secession and a strong supporter of the Confederate government, but he strongly resisted that same government when it had a direct impact on his economic interests. His resignation from the U.S. Senate engendered no real conflict, as he had already announced his determination to retire from public life in mid-1860. The reality of the war for David Levy Yulee was one of split loyalties and ambivalence.

Yulee's early life was spent in the West Indies, where he had been born in 1810, and on the frontier of Florida. His father was the strong-willed and capable Moses Levy, a merchant of vast connections and a speculator in Florida lands. Moses's plan for a Jewish colony in the wilderness of Florida, centering on the outpost of Micanopy, raised many an eyebrow within and without the small group of Jewish settlers in the South. Moses Levy's claim to citizenship in the U.S. territory of Florida raised many questions that later haunted his son's political future.

An unusual divorce by his parents left David in the care of his mother while the older siblings were sent to England for an education. During his growing years, young David seldom saw his father. In 1819, David and his brother, Elias, were reunited with their father, who brought them to the United States. David was placed with a friend of the family, Moses Myers, in Norfolk, Virginia, where he attended the Norfolk Academy. At the academy, he is supposed to have fallen under the influence of the school's principal, a devout Presbyterian cleric, who began David's slow conversion to Christianity. David's Virginia education came to a halt in 1827 when his father stopped funding his educational advancement and David was ordered to his father's plantation three miles west of the outpost of Micanopy. There he spent nearly three years working on the plantation and as a part-time deputy clerk in the office of the Clerk of the Court for the Alachua Circuit. Here David found a way to advance far differently from that envisioned by his father. By 1832 he had settled in St. Augustine and begun working in the law offices of Judge Robert Raymond Reid and was admitted to practice later in the same year. Reid, a powerful political influence throughout Florida, became both model and mentor to the young man.

David Levy's rise in Florida politics was brilliant and rapid. Within seven years of his being admitted to practice law, he had been elected an officer in the militia (actually leading scouting parties during the Second Seminole War), elected to the Legislative Council, and became a deputy at the St. Joseph's Constitutional Convention, which paved the way to statehood in 1845. Levy became the leading speaker for statehood and a major voice in the politics of the Democratic Party of Florida. He was rewarded for his efforts by being elected as one of the first two U.S. senators from Florida in 1845. In every campaign, however, he faced the negative sentiments of anti-Semitism and the constant questioning of his U.S. citizenship. His marriage to Nancy Wickliffe in the following year did little to reduce the feelings of his opposition.

At the same time that David Levy Yulee (he had his name legally changed in 1845) was leading the Democratic Party in Florida, he was developing his plans to construct a railroad across the peninsula of Florida. He had already backed many earlier internal improvement schemes, but this one was his dream and passion. Using his political position to its best advantage for the railroad, Yulee was able to receive important assistance in making the road a success. His ambition also cost him political support, many doubting his ability to complete the line and others jealous of the land grants that the road received from the state and federal governments. One of his closest associates in the building of the Florida Railroad was Joseph Finegan, later Confederate general and leader of the Confederate forces at the battle of Olustee. Some of Yulee's other associates were George W. Call, Judge Isaac Bronson, Judge Augustus Steele, and A. H. Cole. Yet, Florida was a cash-starved frontier state, and Yulee had to look to the North for financing and steel. This put him greatly in debt to New York financier Edward Dickerson and the firm of Vose & Livingston for the rails. Although the war would cripple the railroad, it did not end it, and Yulee spent most of his remaining years in making the road profitable and as an officer in the firm.

Yulee's senatorial career, which ended with his resignation, was marked by his promoting internal improvements, voting against anything smacking of abolitionist sentiment, and uniting with many of the leading secessionists. Yet, Yulee was shrewd enough to realize that secession would mean disaster for his economic interests, especially the Florida Railroad. After helping to lead Florida out of the Union and retiring to his plantation

on the Homosassa River, Yulee spent immense energy fighting the Confederate government and that of the state of Florida. He opposed any confiscation of his property or crops for the benefit of the cause and brought many law suits against both entities. Many began to doubt the sincerity of Yulee as a Confederate. This did not prevent his arrest at the end of the war, and he spent ten months in confinement at Fort Pulaski. He was released in March 1866.

The remainder of this active man's life was spent in revitalizing the railroad and developing the towns of Fernandina and Cedar Key, the termini of his railroad. In getting the railroad back on its feet and paying, through many transformations, he was successful. At his wife's request, however, Yulee left Florida in 1881 and resided

in Washington, D.C., until his death in October 1886, a little over a year after his wife's death. He is buried at Oak Hill Cemetery in Washington.

—*Joe Knetsch*

See also Florida.
For further reading:

Adler, Joseph Gary. "The Public Career of Senator David Levy Yulee" (Ph.D. dissertation, 1973).
Kavanaugh, Celeste H. *David Levy Yulee: A Man and His Vision* (1995).
Knetsch, Joe. "Madison Starke Perry vs. David Levy Yulee: The Fight for the Tampa Bay Route." *Sunland Tribune* (1997).
Thompson, Arthur W. "David Yulee: A Study of Nineteenth Century American Thought and Enterprise" (Ph.D. dissertation, 1954).
Yulee, C. Wickliffe. "Senator Yulee." *Florida Historical Quarterly* (1909).

Z

ZOLLICOFFER, FELIX
(1812–1862)
Confederate general

Born in Maury County, Tennessee, on 19 May 1812, Felix Kirk Zollicoffer was of Swiss ancestry. He received some formal educational training before entering the newspaper business at age sixteen, and later rose to state prominence as editor of several influential newspapers, including the *Nashville Republican Banner*. His only military experience before the Civil War was a brief and undistinguished stint as lieutenant in the Second Seminole War in 1836. He served Tennessee as comptroller of the state treasury (1845–1849), state senator (1849–1852), and member of the U.S. Congress (1853–1859). Politically, Zollicoffer was a Unionist and member of the Whig Party until its demise in the mid-1850s. His moderate political stance led to his selection as a member of the ill-fated Washington Peace Conference in 1861.

With the firing on Fort Sumter, Zollicoffer faced the dilemma of maintaining his Union allegiance or supporting his state. He went the way of many others and declared his allegiance to the Confederacy and Tennessee. He was appointed brigadier general in the Confederate army on 9 July 1861 and was assigned to command the east Tennessee district. His specific purpose was to counter the 4,000 Unionist "Home Guards" at Camp Dick Robinson in central Kentucky, whom Confederate authorities believed could at any moment invade eastern Tennessee and control the strategic Cumberland Gap.

In early September, Confederate major general Leonidas Polk violated Kentucky's neutrality, which prompted Zollicoffer to send several hundred men through Cumberland Gap into southeastern Kentucky. His command consisted of seven infantry regiments and four cavalry battalions, the majority of whom were Tennesseans. Throughout the next several months, Zollicoffer probed southeastern Kentucky, skirmishing with Union troops on occasion, but never seriously threatening Camp Dick Robinson. General Albert Sidney Johnston, Confederate commanding general in the West, even advised Zollicoffer against making any further offensive movements, only later to recant and allow Zollicoffer discretion in attacking the enemy.

In November 1861, Zollicoffer sent word to Johnston that he was leaving troops at Cumberland Gap and preparing to advance toward central Kentucky. But Confederate president Jefferson Davis, unhappy with Zollicoffer's performance thus far, appointed a native Kentuckian, Major General George B. Crittenden, to supersede Zollicoffer, the latter remaining with the army. Unfortunately, word of Crittenden's appointment arrived after Johnston had approved Zollicoffer's plan to establish a camp at Mill Springs, Kentucky, and, if not threatened by the enemy during the winter months ahead, launch a spring offensive into the central part of the state. On 29 November, Zollicoffer arrived at Mill Springs, a small community on the southern bank of the Cumberland River. With formidable bluffs edging the river, Zollicoffer had an excellent location for establishing winter quarters for his troops, while also presenting the Union command with an offensive threat to central Kentucky.

But less than two weeks later, Zollicoffer sent five infantry regiments, seven cavalry companies, and four pieces of artillery directly across the river to Beech Grove. In a letter to Johnston, Zollicoffer argued that his new position, with both flanks protected by a bend in the river, was a strong one that provided him an excellent opportunity to strike scattered Union troops, something that could not be accomplished from south of the river. When Crittenden arrived at Knoxville to assume command, he immediately ordered Zollicoffer to recross the Cumberland, but Zollicoffer chose to remain at Beech Grove, hopeful of convincing Crittenden of the wisdom of the move when he arrived in person in early January 1862. Such was not the case. In fact, the Confederate army was endangered by the presence of Union general George Thomas and 4,000 troops who had advanced to Logan's Cross Roads, ten miles north of Beech Grove.

Faced with a Union force in front and river behind, on 19 January 1862, Crittenden ordered an advance on Union troops, hopeful of catching them by surprise. But a steady rain and muddy roads prevented rapid movement. During the ensuing battle, Zollicoffer, clad in a raincoat, decided to ride over to the Confederate left. With limited visibility due to smoke, fog, and rain, he

Felix Zollicoffer (*Library of Congress*)

unknowingly rode into Union ranks and engaged Union colonel Speed Fry in a conversation. Zollicoffer mistakenly believed that Fry's 4th Kentucky regiment was part of his command and firing on fellow Confederate troops. As Fry returned to his men, another mounted officer emerged from the trees where the brief conversation had just taken place, firing his pistol into Union ranks and striking Fry's horse. Somewhat confused but acting on instinct, Fry returned the fire, as did his men. The second unidentified officer fled, but the one with whom Fry had just spoken fell from his mount, killed instantly. Upon viewing the body, there was no doubt as to the identity: It was General Felix Zollicoffer.

Like many other Southerners, Felix K. Zollicoffer was a citizen-soldier, thrust into war only after his state withdrew from the Union. His occupation of Beech Grove has remained an object of controversy and no real assessment of his military ability can be deduced from his brief service. Following the battle of Logan's Cross Roads, Thomas sent Zollicoffer's body into Confederate ranks for proper burial. His remains lie in the Old City Cemetery in Nashville.

—*C. David Dalton*

See also Logan's Cross Roads, Battle of.
For further reading
Dalton, C. David. "Zollicoffer, Crittenden, and the Mill Springs Campaign: Some Persistent Questions." *The Filson Club History Quarterly* (1986).
McMurtry, Gerald. "Zollicoffer and the Battle of Mill Springs." *The Filson Club History Quarterly* (1955).
Myers, Raymond. *The Zollie Tree* (1964).
Wright, Marcus J. "Sketch of General Felix K. Zollicoffer." *The Southern Bivouac* (1884).

ZOOK, SAMUEL KOSCIUSZKO
(1821–1863)
Union general

Born in Chester County, Pennsylvania, Samuel Kosciuszko Zook spent most of his childhood near Valley Forge. He was active in the local militia until moving to New York City to become the superintendent of the Washington & New York Telegraph Company. There he joined a local militia regiment, rising to the rank of lieutenant colonel. His regiment was brought into Federal service for ninety days at the beginning of the Civil War. One of its duties was to garrison Annapolis, Maryland, and while there, Zook served as the military governor of the town.

At the end of the regiment's ninety days, Zook returned to New York to recruit a regiment for the duration of the war. His task completed in the early fall, he was commissioned the colonel of the 57th New York, and the regiment became a part of the Army of the Potomac. In March 1862 Zook and the 57th participated in a reconnaissance mission to Cedar Mountain, Virginia.

Zook and the 57th served in II Corps during the Peninsula campaign. He and the regiment particularly distinguished themselves at Seven Pines, for which Zook was commended by the regiment's brigade commander William French. In the fall of 1862 after the battle of Antietam, Zook commanded a brigade at Harper's Ferry and from there conducted reconnaissance missions nearby. During one such mission from 16 to 17 October, Zook and his brigade skirmished with Confederates outside Charlestown, Virginia (now West Virginia).

In the Fredericksburg campaign, Zook continued to command his brigade in the division of Winfield Scott Hancock. Zook led his men in the assault upon Marye's Heights and bravely held his position until nightfall, in spite of having his horse shot from under him and the brigade's having suffered 35 percent casualties. Hancock commended Zook in very strong terms for his gallantry.

After the Fredericksburg campaign, Zook briefly commanded a division of II Corps, but reverted to the command of his brigade in time for the Chancellorsville campaign. On 23 March 1863, Zook was promoted to brigadier general of volunteers with a date of rank of 29

November 1862. At Chancellorsville he commanded the 3d Brigade, 1st Division, II Corps under Hancock.

Zook commanded the same brigade at Gettysburg, with Hancock in command of II Corps. In the midst of James Longstreet's attack on the Union left on 2 July, Zook's brigade was sent forward to try to prevent a break in the Union line. He led his brigade forward through the ranks of a retreating brigade, maintaining order and unit cohesion in the process. At the front of his troops, Zook fell from a Confederate bullet in his abdomen. He was carried to the rear, and before dawn on 3 July he died of his wound.

—*David S. Heidler and Jeanne T. Heidler*

See also Fredericksburg, First Battle of; Gettysburg, Battle of.

For further reading:

Gambone, Albert M. *The Life of Samuel K. Zook: Another Forgotten Union Hero* (1996).

ZOUAVES

A flamboyant deviation from traditional U.S. military garb, the Zouave style of uniform was adopted by dozens of Civil War volunteer units, the majority of them Northern companies and regiments. Produced in a variety of colorful patterns, Zouave uniforms were the ultimate expression of the prevailing influence of French military fashion in the mid-nineteenth century.

The origins of the Zouaves can be traced to the *Zouaoua*, Berbers inhabiting the rocky foothills of Algeria who tendered their services to the French colonial forces in 1830. Although the Zouave units were increasingly comprised of Frenchmen, and by the 1850s entirely so, their distinctive attire remained a derivation of traditional North African dress: a short, dark-blue collarless jacket with red trim; sleeveless vest; baggy red trousers and long woolen sash; white canvas leggings; a tasseled red fez; and turban.

The army of Emperor Napoleon III included four regiments of Zouaves as well as several battalions of Tirailleurs Algeriens (*Turcos*), native North Africans serving under French officers and wearing a light-blue version of the Zouave uniform. The Crimean War (1854–1855) and the Franco-Austrian War of 1859 confirmed the fighting reputation of the Zouaves, whose exploits were widely publicized in European and North American journals. Reporting at the conclusion of his official tour of foreign armies, U.S. Captain George B. McClellan characterized the Zouaves as "the most reckless, self-reliant, and complete infantry that Europe can produce…the beau-ideal of a soldier."

Charge of the New York 9th Hawkins Zouaves at Roanoke Island, 8 February 1862 (*Library of Congress*)

A company of Zouaves, unknown location (*National Archives*)

Inspired by the fighting prowess and exotic uniforms of the French Zouaves, in 1859 a charismatic twenty-two-year-old Illinois militiaman named Elmer Ephraim Ellsworth organized the United States Zouave Cadets of Chicago. Clad in a Zouave style of Ellsworth's design, and brought to a state of clockwork-like perfection in drill, in the summer of 1860 the Zouave Cadets displayed their prowess to admiring audiences in twenty cities across the Midwest and Northeast. The resulting "Zouave craze" encouraged numerous militia units to adopt varying styles of Zouave attire virtually on the eve of Civil War.

Within days of the capitulation of Fort Sumter, Ellsworth became colonel of the 11th New York Infantry, a regiment recruited from the ranks of Manhattan's Volunteer Fire Department and popularly known as Ellsworth's Fire Zouaves. On 24 May 1861, Alexandria, Virginia, innkeeper James W. Jackson killed Ellsworth after he had removed a large secessionist banner from atop Jackson's Marshall House hotel. Jackson was promptly shot and bayoneted by Zouave Corporal Francis Brownell. The two fatalities were among the first of the conflict, and Ellsworth's status as martyr for the Northern war effort spawned even more Zouave regiments, including one New York unit (the 44th Volunteer Infantry) dubbed Ellsworth's Avengers.

Many Zouave organizations were popularly known by the name of their respective commanders, officers who tended to adopt a swashbuckling bravado befitting their military finery. Examples include the 23d Pennsylvania (Birney's Zouaves), 72d Pennsylvania (Baxter's Fire Zouaves), 95th Pennsylvania (Gosline's Zouaves), 114th Pennsylvania (Collis's Zouaves), 9th New York (Hawkins's Zouaves), 34th Ohio (Piatt's Zouaves), and 11th Indiana (Wallace's Zouaves). Despite their colorful attire, which at times more closely resembled the uniforms of the French *Chasseur* units rather than the true Zouave outfit, in general the military abilities of these units were no better or worse than those of their less sartorially embellished comrades. The 5th New York (Duryée's Zouaves) was widely considered the best-disciplined volunteer regiment in the Army of the Potomac, whereas the 11th New York (First Fire Zouaves) and 53d New York (d'Epineuil's Zouaves) were among the most disruptive and lackluster organizations in Federal service.

Compared with their Northern opponents, only a relative handful of Confederate units adopted the Zouave uniform. This was due in large part to the difficulty of resupply, but also to the fact that Elmer Ellsworth's prewar tour had bypassed the Southern states. The notable exception was Louisiana, which furnished the Confederacy two of its most colorful and free-spirited units, Major Roberdeau Wheat's 1st Louisiana Special Battalion and Lieutenant Colonel Gaston Coppens's 1st Louisiana Zouave Battalion. But neither "Wheat's Tigers" nor Coppens's Zouaves were able to maintain their distinctive garb beyond the first year of their wartime service.

Federal armies, however, continued to field Zouave units throughout the war and, although some commands did away with their early war finery, others exchanged their regulation blue uniforms for Zouave regalia. These included the 146th New York, which in June 1863 adopted a uniform modeled on that of the French *Turcos*, and the 140th New York and 155th Pennsylvania, both of which received their Zouave attire in January 1864. Along with the 5th New York Veteran Volunteers, those units comprised a Zouave Brigade that served with the V Corps through the Wilderness, Petersburg, and Appomattox campaigns.

The 10th New York (National Zouaves) and 164th New York (McMahon's Zouaves) likewise saw considerable action with the Army of the Potomac in the final year of the war, whereas the 114th Pennsylvania (Collis's Zouaves) functioned as Headquarters' Guard for Union army commander George Meade.

Though Zouave dress was less common in Federal armies of the Western theater, the 33d New Jersey and 17th New York Veteran Volunteers both sported Zouave outfits during William T. Sherman's campaigns, and the latter unit fought at Bentonville, North Carolina, in one of the war's final battles. The 165th New York (2d Battalion, Duryée's Zouaves) spearheaded one of the Union assaults on Port Hudson, Louisiana, and later accompanied the XIX Corps in Philip Sheridan's Shenandoah Valley campaign, while the 76th Pennsylvania (Keystone Zouaves) took part in the siege of Charleston and the attack on Fort Wagner.

From the first weeks to the last days of the conflict, Zouave regiments were a conspicuous evocation of European influence on the American way of war.

—Brian C. Pohanka

For further reading:
Bennett, Brian A. *Sons of Old Monroe: A Regimental History of Patrick O'Rorke's 140th New York Volunteer Infantry* (1992).
DuFour, Charles L. *Gentle Tiger: The Gallant Life of Roberdeau Wheat* (1957).
Graham, Matthew J. *The Ninth Regiment New York Volunteers (Hawkins' Zouaves)* (1900; reprint, 1998).
Hagerty, Edward J. *Collis' Zouaves: The 114th Pennsylvania Volunteers in the Civil War* (1997).
Ingraham, Charles A. *Elmer E. Ellsworth and the Zouaves of '61* (1925).
Livingstone, Charles B. *Charlie's Civil War: A Private's Trial by Fire in the 5th and 146th New York Zouaves* (1997).
McAfee, Michael J. *Zouaves: The First and the Bravest* (1991).
Randall, Ruth Painter. *Colonel Elmer Ellsworth* (1960).
Smith, Robin. *American Civil War Zouaves* (1996).
Southwick, Thomas P. *A Duryee Zouave* (1930; reprint, 1995).

DOCUMENTS

DOCUMENT LIST

THE POLITICAL CRISIS

THE MILITARY CRISIS

IX. Federal Property in the Confederacy

A. FORT PULASKI AND FORT CLINCH

B. FORT PICKENS

C. FORT SUMTER

D. HARPER'S FERRY

THE WAR

X. The Union Responds

XI. Secession—The Second Wave

A. VIRGINIA

B. TENNESSEE

C. ARKANSAS

D. NORTH CAROLINA

XII. Lee Goes With Virginia

XIX. The Peninsula Campaign

XX. Benjamin Butler in New Orleans

XXI. Second Battle of Bull Run

XXII. The Antietam Campaign

XXIII. Fredericksburg

XXIV. Stones River

XXV. Chancellorsville

XXVI. The Vicksburg Campaign

XXVII. Gettysburg

A. THE BATTLE

XXXIX. Balloons
1. Letter to Secretary of War Cameron Regarding Lowe's Balloon (21 June 1861), 2414
2. Lowe's Balloon Contract (2 August 1861), 2414

XL. Civil Liberties
1. Lincoln's Suspension of the Writ of Habeas Corpus (1861), 2415
2. Chief Justice Taney's Opinion in *Ex Parte Merryman* (1861), 2415
3. An Act to Suppress Insurrection, to Punish Treason and Rebellion, to Seize and Confiscate the Property of Rebels, and for Other Purposes (1862), 2416
4. An Act of the U.S. Congress Approved March 3, 1863, Relating to Habeas Corpus, &c., 2418
5. Proclamation of Martial Law in Baltimore and the Western Counties of Maryland (30 June 1863), 2420
6. Justice Davis's Opinion in *Ex Parte Milligan* (1866), 2420

XLI. Emancipation
1. John C. Frémont's Proclamation on Slaves (30 August 1861), 2424
2. Letter from a Maryland Fugitive Slave to his Wife (12 January 1862), 2424
3. David Hunter's Emancipation Order (General Orders, No. 7) (13 April 1862), 2425
4. The District of Columbia Emancipation Act (16 April 1862), 2425
5. Horace Greeley's "The Prayer of the Twenty Millions" (19 August 1862), 2426
6. Lincoln's Reply to Greeley (22 August 1862), 2429
7. Testimony of Capt. C. B. Wilder before the American Freedmen's Inquiry Commission [Excerpts] (9 May 1863), 2429
8. The Emancipation Proclamation (1 January 1863), 2430
9. Lincoln to General Hurlbut Regarding the Emancipation Proclamation [Excerpt] (31 July 1863), 2431
10. Lincoln to James C. Conkling Regarding the Emancipation Proclamation [Excerpt] (26 August 1863), 2431
11. Amendment XIII to the United States Constitution (1865), 2432
12. Amendment XIV to the United States Constitution (1868), 2432
13. Amendment XV to the United States Constitution (1870), 2433

XLII. Guerrilla Warfare
1. Thomas Ewing's "Banishment Order" (25 August 1863), 2433
2. Instruction to General Merritt Regarding Guerrillas in Northern Virginia (27 November 1864), 2433

XLIII. Immigrants
1. Lincoln to Halleck Regarding German Soldiers (15 January 1862), 2434
2. Halleck to Lincoln Regarding German Soldiers (21 January 1862), 2434

XLIV. Medicine
1. General Orders, No. 9 [Excerpts] (9 September 1861), 2435
2. General Orders, No. 20 (3 October 1861), 2435
3. Confederate Surgeon General's Letter in Regard to Indigenous Botanical Remedies (22 July 1862), 2436
4. Report of Surgeon Charles S. Tripler, Medical Director of the Army of the Potomac, of the Operations of the Medical Department of that Army from August 12, 1861, to March 17, 1862 [Excerpts], 2436

XLV. Music
1. "Dixie's Land," by Daniel Decatur Emmett (1860), 2438
2. "Battle Hymn of the Republic," by Julia Ward Howe (1863), 2439
3. "The Bonnie Blue Flag," by Harry McCarthy (1861), 2439
4. "Maryland! My Maryland!" by James Ryder Randall (1861), 2440
5. "Richmond is a Hard Road to Travel," attr. to John R. Thompson (1863), 2440
6. "The Battle-Cry of Freedom," by George F. Root (1865), 2441
7. "Marching Through Georgia," by Henry Clay Work (1865), 2442
8. "Lorena," by Rev. H. D. L. Webster (1857), 2442

XLVI: Prisoners of War

1. An Act Relating to Prisoners of War, Approved May 21, 1861; 2444
2. Major General Hunter's Orders Regarding Confederate Prisoners (20 June 1862); 2447
3. Evidence Taken before the Committee of the House of Representatives of the Committee once Appointed to Inquire into the Treatment of Prisoners at Castle Morris, Belle Isle (17 April 1864); 2447
4. Report on the Exchange of Warnings of Prisoners (9 November 1864); 2448
5. Prison Inspection Report (9 December 1864); 2448
6. Ration for Each Prisoner Retained at Andersonville to May 1864; 2449
7. War to Major General E. O. C. Ord, U.S. Army (7 May 1865); 2449
8. General Orders No. 607 (3 November 1863; 2454

XLVII: Religion

1. General Order Respecting the Observance of the Sabbath Day in the Army and Navy (15 November 1862); 2455
2. Memorial from ... (13 April 1861); 2455
3. Christians in the Conference of the Border, by Samuel J. May (Philadelphia, 1860); 2455
4. Grant's Order to General W. Tecumseh (1862); 2456
5. General Orders No. 11 (1862); 2456
6. Letter to Lincoln from [Reprint] from Lincoln (29 December 1862); 2457
7. Revolution in Session Order No. 11 (January 1863); 2457
8. Halleck to Grant in Regard to General Order No. 11 (Reprint) (21 January 1863); 2457
9. Robert E. Lee, the Reverend Max Michelbacher of Richmond, Virginia Congregation Beth Ahabah (29 September 1861); 2457
10. "Prayers—A Reminiscence of the War" (1862); 2458

XLVIII: Telegraph

1. Report of Operations of the Signal Corps, U.S. Army, for the Year Commencing November 1, 1863, and Ending October 31, 1864 [Excerpt]; 2458

XLIX: United States Sanitary Commission

1. Bulletin to Subject of Report from the Sanitary Commission [Excerpt] (27 May 1862); 2459
2. Special Orders No. 85 (29 March 1861); 2460

DOCUMENTS

THE POLITICAL CRISIS

I. Abraham Lincoln and the 1858 Illinois Senate Contest

In 1858, the Illinois Republican state convention nominated Abraham Lincoln for the United States Senate to challenge incumbent Stephen A. Douglas. The campaign set the stage for the famous Lincoln-Douglas debates. Lincoln would lose the election, but the campaign, beginning with this speech accepting the nomination, would make Lincoln a national figure. It was to become one of his most famous addresses and was especially notable for the biblical paraphrase adapted to the sectional controversy of the time: "A house divided against itself cannot stand." [See Douglas, Stephen A.; Elections of 1858; Lincoln, Abraham; Republican Party]

1. "A House Divided against Itself Cannot Stand" (17 June 1858)

MR. PRESIDENT AND GENTLEMEN OF THE CONVENTION:

If we could first know where we are, and whither we are tending, we could better judge what to do, and how to do it. We are now far into the fifth year since a policy was initiated with the avowed object and confident promise of putting an end to slavery agitation. Under the operation of that policy, that agitation has not only not ceased, but has constantly augmented. In my opinion, it will not cease until a crisis shall have been reached and passed. "A house divided against itself cannot stand." I believe this government cannot endure permanently half slave and half free. I do not expect the Union to be dissolved; I do not expect the house to fall; but I do expect it will cease to be divided. It will become all one thing, or all the other. Either the opponents of slavery will arrest the further spread of it, and place it where the public mind shall rest in the belief that it is in the course of ultimate extinction, or its advocates will push it forward till it shall become alike lawful in all the States, old as well as new, North as well as South.

Have we no tendency to the latter condition?

Let any one who doubts, carefully contemplate that now almost complete legal combination—piece of machinery, so to speak—compounded of the Nebraska doctrine and the Dred Scott decision. Let him consider, not only what work the machinery is adapted to do, and how well adapted, but also let him study the histo-

ry of its construction, and trace, if he can, or rather fail, if he can, to trace the evidences of design, and concert of action, among its chief architects, from the beginning.

The new year of 1854 found slavery excluded from more than half the states by State Constitutions, and from most of the National territory by Congressional prohibition. Four days later, commenced the struggle which ended in repealing that Congressional prohibition. This opened all the National territory to slavery, and was the first point gained.

But, so far, Congress only had acted, and an indorsement by the people, real or apparent, was indispensable to save the point already gained, and give chance for more.

This necessity had not been overlooked, but had been provided for, as well as might be, in the notable argument of "squatter sovereignty," otherwise called sacred right of self-government, which latter phrase, though expressive of the only rightful basis of any government, was so perverted in this attempted use of it as to amount to just this: That if any one man choose to enslave another, no third man shall be allowed to object. That argument was incorporated into the Nebraska Bill itself, in the language which follows: "It being the true intent and meaning of this Act not to legislate slavery into any Territory or State, nor to exclude it therefrom, but to leave the people thereof perfectly free to form and regulate their domestic institutions in their own way, subject only to the Constitution of the United States." Then opened the roar of loose declamation in favor of "squatter sovereignty," and "sacred right of self-government." "But," said opposition members, "let us amend the bill so as to expressly declare that the people of the Territory may exclude slavery." "Not we," said the friends of the measure, and down they voted the amendment.

While the Nebraska Bill was passing through Congress, a law case, involving the question of a Negro's freedom, by reason of his owner having voluntarily taken him first into a free State, and then into a territory covered by the Congressional prohibition, and held him as a slave for a long time in each, was passing through the United States Circuit Court for the District of Missouri; and both Nebraska Bill and lawsuit were brought to a decision in the same month of May, 1854. The Negro's name was "Dred Scott," which name now designates the decision finally made in the

case. Before the then next Presidential election, the law case came to, and was argued in, the Supreme Court of the United States; but the decision of it was deferred until after the election. Still, before the election, Senator Trumbull, on the floor of the Senate, requested the leading advocate of the Nebraska Bill to state his opinion whether the people of a Territory can constitutionally exclude slavery from their limits; and the latter answers: "That is a question for the Supreme Court."

The election came. Mr. Buchanan was elected, and the indorsement, such as it was, secured. That was the second point gained. The endorsement, however, fell short of a clear popular majority by nearly four hundred thousand votes, and so, perhaps, was not overwhelmingly reliable and satisfactory. The outgoing President, in his last annual message, as impressively as possible echoed back upon the people the weight and authority of the endorsement. The Supreme Court met again, did not announce their decision, but ordered a reargument. The Presidential inauguration came, and still no decision of the court; but the incoming President, in his inaugural address, fervently exhorted the people to abide by the forthcoming decisions whatever it might be. Then, in a few days, came the decision.

The reputed author of the Nebraska Bill finds an early occasion to make a speech at this capital indorsing the Dred Scott decision, and vehemently denouncing all opposition to it. The new President, too, seizes the early occasion of the Silliman letter to indorse and strongly construe that decision, and to express his astonishment that any different view had ever been entertained!

At length a squabble springs up between the President and the author of the Nebraska Bill, on the mere question of fact, whether the Lecompton Constitution was or was not in any just sense made by the people of Kansas; and in that quarrel the latter declares that all he wants is a fair vote for the people, and that he cares not whether slavery be voted down or voted up. I do not understand his declaration, that he cares not whether slavery be voted down or voted up, to be intended by him other than as an apt definition of the policy he would impress upon the public mind,— the principle for which he declares he has suffered so much, and is ready to suffer to the end. And well may he cling to that principle! If he has any parental feeling, well may he cling to it. That principle is the only shred left of his original Nebraska doctrine. Under the Dred Scott decision "squatter sovereignty" squatted out of existence, tumbled down like temporary scaffolding; like the mould at the foundry, served through one blast, and fell back into loose sand; helped to carry an election, and then was kicked to the winds. His late joint struggle with the Republicans, against the Lecompton Constitution, involves nothing of the original Nebraska doctrine. That struggle was made on a point—the right

of a people to make their own constitution—upon which he and the Republicans have never differed.

The several points of the Dred Scott decision, in connection with Senator Douglas's "care not" policy, constitute the piece of machinery, in its present state of advancement. This was the third point gained. The working points of that machinery are:

Firstly, That no Negro slave, imported as such from Africa, and no descendant of such slave, can ever be a citizen of any State, in the sense of that term as used in the Constitution of the United States. This point is made in order to deprive the Negro, in every possible event, of the benefit of that provision of the United States Constitution which declares that "The citizens of each State shall be entitled to all privileges and immunities of citizens in the several States."

Secondly, That, "subject to the Constitution of the United States," neither Congress nor a Territorial Legislature can exclude slavery from any United States Territory. This point is made in order that individual men may fill up the Territories with slaves, without danger of losing them as property, and thus to enhance the chances of permanency to the institution through all the future.

Thirdly, That whether the holding a Negro in actual slavery in a free State makes him free, as against the holder, the United States courts will not decide, but will leave to be decided by the courts of any slave State the Negro may be forced into by the master. This point is made, not to be pressed, immediately; but, if acquiesced in for a while, and apparently indorsed by the people at an election, then to sustain the logical conclusion that what Dred Scott's master might lawfully do with Dred Scott, in the free State of Illinois, every other master may lawfully do with any other one, or one thousand slaves, in Illinois, or in any other free State.

Auxiliary to all this, and working hand in hand with it, the Nebraska doctrine, or what is left of it, is to educate and mould public opinion, at least Northern public opinion, not to care whether slavery is voted down or voted up. This shows exactly where we now are; and partially, also, whither we are tending.

It will throw additional light on the latter, to go back and run the mind over the string of historical facts already stated. Several things will now appear less dark and mysterious than they did when they were transpiring. The people were to be left "perfectly free," "subject only to the Constitution." What the Constitution had to do with it, outsiders could not then see. Plainly enough now,—it was an exactly fitted niche, for the Dred Scott decision to afterward come in, and declare the perfect freedom of the people to be just no freedom at all. Why was the amendment, expressly declaring the right of the people, voted down? Plainly enough now,— the adoption of it would have spoiled the niche for the

Dred Scott decision. Why was the court decision held up? Why even a Senator's individual opinion withheld, till after the Presidential election? Plainly enough now,—the speaking out then would have damaged the "perfectly free" argument upon which the election was to be carried. Why the outgoing President's felicitation on the indorsement? Why the delay of a reargument? Why the incoming President's advance exhortation in favor of the decision? These things look like the cautious patting and petting of a spirited horse preparatory to mounting him, when it is dreaded that he may give the rider a fall. And why the hasty after-indorsement of the decision by the President and others?

We cannot absolutely know that all these exact adaptations are the result of preconcert. But when we see a lot of framed timbers, different portions of which we know have been gotten out at different times and places and by different workmen,—Stephen, Franklin, Roger, and James, for instance,—and when we see these timbers joined together, and see they exactly make the frame of a house or a mill, all the tenons and mortises exactly fitting, and all the lengths and proportions of the different pieces exactly adapted to their respective places, and not a piece too many or too few,-not omitting even scaffolding,—or, if a single piece be lacking, we see the place in the frame exactly fitted and prepared yet to bring such piece in,—in such a case, we find it impossible not to believe that Stephen and Franklin and Roger and James all understood one another from the beginning, and all worked upon a common plan or draft drawn up before the first blow was struck.

It should not be overlooked that by the Nebraska Bill the people of a State as well as Territory were to be left "perfectly free," "subject only to the Constitution." Why mention a State? They were legislating for Territories, and not for or about Sates. Certainly the people of a State are and ought to be subject to the Constitution of the United States; but why is mention of this lugged into this merely Territorial law? Why are the people of a Territory and the people of a State therein lumped together, and their relation to the Constitution therein treated as being precisely the same? While opinion of the court, by Chief Justice Taney, in the Dred Scott case, and the separate opinions of all the concurring judges, expressly declare that the Constitution of the United States neither permits Congress nor a Territorial Legislature to exclude slavery from any United States Territory, they all omit to declare whether or not the same Constitution permits a State, or the people of a State, to exclude it. Possibly, this is a mere omission; but who can be quite sure, if McLean or Curtis had sought to get into the opinion a declaration of unlimited power in the people of a State to exclude slavery from their limits, just as Chase and Mace sought to get such declaration, in behalf of the

people of a Territory, into the Nebraska Bill,—I ask, who can be quite sure that it would not have been voted down in the one case as it had been in the other? The nearest approach to the point of declaring the power of a State over slavery is made by Judge Nelson. He approaches it more than once, using the precise idea, and almost the language, too, of the Nebraska Act. On one occasion, his exact language is, "Except in cases where the power is restrained by the Constitution of the United States, the law of the State is supreme over the subject of slavery within its jurisdiction." In what cases the power of the States is so restrained by the United States Constitution, is left an open question, precisely as the same question, as to the restraint on the power of the Territories, was left open in the Nebraska Act. Put this and that together, and we have another nice little niche, which we may, ere long, see filled with another Supreme Court decision, declaring that the Constitution of the United States does not permit a State to exclude slavery from its limits. And this may especially be expected if the doctrine of "care not whether slavery be voted down or voted up" shall gain upon the public mind sufficiently to give promise that such a decision can be maintained when made.

Such a decision is all that slavery now lacks of being alike lawful in all the States. Welcome or unwelcome, such decision is probably coming, and will soon be upon us, unless the power of the present political dynasty shall be met and overthrown. We shall lie down pleasantly dreaming that the people of Missouri are on the verge of making their State free, and we shall awake to the reality instead that the Supreme Court has made Illinois a slave State. To meet and overthrow the power of that dynasty is the work now before all those who would prevent that consummation. That is what we have to do. How can we best do it?

There are those who denounce us openly to their n friends, and yet whisper us softly that Senator Douglas is the aptest instrument there is with which to effect that object. They wish us to infer all, from the fact that he now has a little quarrel with the present head of the dynasty, and that he has regularly voted with us on a single point, upon which he and we have never differed. They remind us that he is great man, and that the largest of us are very small ones. Let this be granted. But "a living dog is better than a dead lion." Judge Douglas, if not a dead lion, for this work is at least a caged and toothless one. How can he oppose the advances of slavery? He don't care anything about it. His avowed mission is impressing the "public heart" to care nothing about it. A leading Douglas Democratic newspaper thinks Douglas's superior talent will be needed to resist the revival of the African slave trade. Does Douglas believe an effort to revive that trade is approaching? He has not said so. Does he really think

so? But if it is, how can he resist it? For years he has labored to prove it a sacred right of white men to take Negro slaves into the new Territories. Can he possibly show that it is less a sacred right to buy them where they can be bought cheapest? And unquestionably they can be bought cheaper in Africa than in Virginia. He has done all in his power to reduce the whole question of slavery to one of a mere right of property; and, as such, how can he oppose the foreign slave trade,—how can he refuse that trade in that "property" shall be "perfectly free,"—unless he does it as a protection to the home production? And as the home producers will probably not ask the protection, he will be wholly without a ground of opposition.

Senator Douglas holds, we know, that a man may rightfully be wiser to-day than he was yesterday; that he may rightfully change when he finds himself wrong. But can we for that reason, run ahead, and infer that he will make any particular change, of which he himself has given no intimation? Can we safely base our action upon any such vague inference? Now, as ever, I wish not to misrepresent judge Douglas's position, question his motives, or do aught that can be personally offensive to him. Whenever, if ever, he and we can come together on principle so that our cause may have assistance from his great ability, I hope to have interposed no adventitious obstacles. But clearly he is not now with us; he does not pretend to be,—he does not promise ever to be.

Our cause, then, must be intrusted to, and conducted by, its own undoubted friends,—those whose hands are free, whose hearts are in the work, who do care for the result. Two years ago the Republicans of the nation mustered over thirteen hundred thousand strong. We did this under the single impulse of resistance to a common danger, with every external circumstance against us. Of strange, discordant, and even hostile elements we gathered from the four winds, and armed and fought the battle through, under the constant hot fire of a disciplined, proud, and pampered enemy. Did we brave all then to falter now,—now, when that same enemy is wavering, dissevered, and belligerent? The result is not doubtful. We shall not fail; if we stand firm, we shall not fail. Wise counsels may accelerate, or mistakes delay it, but, sooner or later, the victory is sure to come.

(Source: Lapsley, Arthur Brooks, ed. *The Writings of Abraham Lincoln.* Vol. 5. New York: G. P. Putnam's Sons, 1906.)

II. The Bane of Slavery

A. THE THIRST FOR FREEDOM

Frederick Douglass was born into slavery as Frederick Augustus Washington Bailey on 7 February 1817 in Tuckahoe, Maryland. After fleeing to the North in 1838, he adopted the last name Douglass and eventually came to the attention of prominent Northern abolitionists. Soon he was one of abolitionism's most renowned spokesmen. He traveled extensively in the North to speak before large audiences. In 1845 he published a memoir entitled Narrative of the Life of Frederick Douglass *that would form the basis for other works that included* My Bondage and My Freedom *in 1855 and* The Life and Times of Frederick Douglass *in 1881, from which the following excerpt is drawn. His work is regarded as including the best accounts of slavery while providing matchless autobiography.* [See Douglass, Frederick]

1. Excerpts from "My Escape from Slavery" (1881)

It was the custom in the State of Maryland to require the free colored people to have what were called free papers. These instruments they were required to renew very often, and by charging a fee for this writing, considerable sums from time to time were collected by the State. In these papers the name, age, color, height, and form of the freeman were described, together with any scars or other marks upon his person which could assist in his identification. This device in some measure defeated itself—since more than one man could be found to answer the same general description. Hence many slaves could escape by personating the owner of one set of papers; and this was often done as follows: A slave, nearly or sufficiently answering the description set forth in the papers, would borrow or hire them till by means of them he could escape to a free State, and then, by mail or otherwise, would return them to the owner. The operation was a hazardous one for the lender as well as for the borrower. A failure on the part of the fugitive to send back the papers would imperil his benefactor, and the discovery of the papers in possession of the wrong man would imperil both the fugitive and his friend. It was, therefore, an act of supreme trust on the part of a freeman of color thus to put in jeopardy his own liberty that another might be free. It was, however, not unfrequently bravely done, and was seldom discovered. I was not so fortunate as to resemble any of my free acquaintances sufficiently to answer the description of their papers. But I had a friend—a sailor—who owned a sailor's protection, which answered somewhat the purpose of free papers—describing his person, and certifying to the fact that he was a free American sailor. The instrument had at its head the American eagle, which gave it the appearance at once of an authorized document. This protection, when in my hands, did not describe its bearer very accurately. Indeed, it called for a man much darker than myself, and close examination of it would have caused my arrest at the start.

In order to avoid this fatal scrutiny on the part of railroad officials, I arranged with Isaac Rolls, a Baltimore hackman, to bring my baggage to the Philadelphia train just on the moment of starting, and jumped upon the car myself when the train was in motion. Had I gone into the station and offered to purchase a ticket, I should have been instantly and carefully examined, and undoubtedly arrested. In choosing this plan I considered the jostle of the train, and the natural haste of the conductor, in a train crowded with passengers, and relied upon my skill and address in playing the sailor, as described in my protection, to do the rest. One element in my favor was the kind feeling which prevailed in Baltimore and other sea-ports at the time, toward "those who go down to the sea in ships." "Free trade and sailors' rights" just then expressed the sentiment of the country. In my clothing I was rigged out in sailor style. I had on a red shirt and a tarpaulin hat, and a black cravat tied in sailor fashion carelessly and loosely about my neck. My knowledge of ships and sailor's talk came much to my assistance, for I knew a ship from stem to stern, and from keelson to cross-trees, and could talk sailor like an "old salt." I was well on the way to Havre de Grace before the conductor came into the negro car to collect tickets and examine the papers of his black passengers. This was a critical moment in the drama. My whole future depended upon the decision of this conductor. Agitated though I was while this ceremony was proceeding, still, externally, at least, I was apparently calm and self-possessed. He went on with his duty—examining several colored passengers before reaching me. He was somewhat harsh in tone and peremptory in manner until he reached me, when, strange enough, and to my surprise and relief, his whole manner changed. Seeing that I did not readily produce my free papers, as the other colored persons in the car had done, he said to me, in friendly contrast with his bearing toward the others:

"I suppose you have your free papers?"

To which I answered:

"No sir; I never carry my free papers to sea with me."

"But you have something to show that you are a freeman, haven't you?"

"Yes, sir," I answered; "I have a paper with the American Eagle on it, and that will carry me around the world."

With this I drew from my deep sailor's pocket my seaman's protection, as before described. The merest glance at the paper satisfied him, and he took my fare and went on about his business. This moment of time was one of the most anxious I ever experienced. Had the conductor looked closely at the paper, he could not have failed to discover that it called for a very different-looking person from myself, and in that case it would have been his duty to arrest me on the instant, and send me back to Baltimore from the first station. When he left me with the assurance that I was all right, though much relieved, I realized that I was still in great danger: I was still in Maryland, and subject to arrest at any moment. I saw on the train several persons who would have known me in any other clothes, and I feared they might recognize me, even in my sailor "rig," and report me to the conductor, who would then subject me to a closer examination, which I knew well would be fatal to me.

Though I was not a murderer fleeing from justice, I felt perhaps quite as miserable as such a criminal. The train was moving at a very high rate of speed for that epoch of railroad travel, but to my anxious mind it was moving far too slowly. Minutes were hours, and hours were days during this part of my flight. After Maryland, I was to pass through Delaware—another slave State, where slave-catchers generally awaited their prey, for it was not in the interior of the State, but on its borders, that these human hounds were most vigilant and active. The border lines between slavery and freedom were the dangerous ones for the fugitives. The heart of no fox or deer, with hungry hounds on his trail in full chase, could have beaten more anxiously or noisily than did mine from the time I left Baltimore till I reached Philadelphia. The passage of the Susquehanna River at Havre de Grace was at that time made by ferry-boat, on board of which I met a young colored man by the name of Nichols, who came very near betraying me. He was a "hand" on the boat, but, instead of minding his business, he insisted upon knowing me, and asking me dangerous questions as to where I was going, when I was coming back, etc. I got away from my old and inconvenient acquaintance as soon as I could decently do so, and went to another part of the boat. Once across the river, I encountered a new danger. Only a few days before, I had been at work on a revenue cutter, in Mr. Price's ship-yard in Baltimore, under the care of Captain McGowan. On the meeting at this point of the two trains, the one going south stopped on the track just opposite to the one going north, and it so happened that this Captain McGowan sat at a window where he could see me very distinctly, and would certainly have recognized me had he looked at me but for a second. Fortunately, in the hurry of the moment, he did not see me; and the trains soon passed each other on their respective ways. But this was not my only hair- breadth escape. A German blacksmith whom I knew well was on the train with me, and looked at me very intently, as if he thought he had seen me somewhere before in his travels. I really believe he knew me, but had no heart to betray me. At any rate, he saw me escaping and held his peace.

The last point of imminent danger, and the one I dreaded most, was Wilmington. Here we left the train and took the steam-boat for Philadelphia. In making the change here I again apprehended arrest, but no one disturbed me, and I was soon on the broad and beautiful Delaware, speeding away to the Quaker City. On reaching Philadelphia in the afternoon, I inquired of a

colored man how I could get on to New York. He directed me to the William-street depot, and thither I went, taking the train that night. I reached New York Tuesday morning, having completed the journey in less than twenty-four hours.

My free life began on the third of September, 1838. On the morning of the fourth of that month, after an anxious and most perilous but safe journey, I found myself in the big city of New York, a FREE MAN—one more added to the mighty throng which, like the confused waves of the troubled sea, surged to and fro between the lofty walls of Broadway. Though dazzled with the wonders which met me on every hand, my thoughts could not be much withdrawn from my strange situation. For the moment, the dreams of my youth and the hopes of my manhood were completely fulfilled. The bonds that had held me to "old master" were broken. No man now had a right to call me his slave or assert mastery over me. . . .

(Source: Douglass, Frederick. "My Escape from Slavery." *The Century Illustrated Magazine*, November 1881, pp. 125–131.)

B. THE JUDICIARY

Dred Scott, a litigant in the famous 1857 United States Supreme Court case Scott v. San[d]ford, *was born to slave parents in Virginia sometime between the years 1795 and 1809. Beginning in 1846 upon the death of his owner, Scott began a legal quest for his freedom. After years in state and federal courts, in February 1856, his case reached the United States Supreme Court and in March 1857 the Court handed down a majority decision that denied Scott his freedom. Chief Justice Roger Taney drafted the majority opinion and Associate Justice Benjamin Curtis wrote an eloquent dissent.*

1. Chief Justice Taney's Opinion in *Dred Scott* (1857)

Taney, C. J. . . . There are two leading questions presented by the record:

1. Had the Circuit Court of the United States jurisdiction to hear and determine the case between these parties? And,

2. If it had jurisdiction, is the judgment it has given erroneous or not?

The plaintiff in error, who was also the plaintiff in the court below, was, with his wife and children, held as slaves by the defendant, in the State of Missouri, and he brought this action in the Circuit Court of the United States for that district, to assert the title of himself and his family to freedom.

The declaration is... that he and the defendant are citizens of different States; that is, that he is a citizen of Missouri, and the defendant a citizen of New York.

The defendant pleaded in abatement to the jurisdiction of the court, that the plaintiff was not a citizen of the State of Missouri, as alleged in his declaration, being a negro of African descent whose ancestors were of pure African blood, and who were brought into this country and sold as slaves.

To this plea the plaintiff demurred, and the defendant joined in demurrer. . . .

Before we speak of the pleas in bar, it will be proper to disposd of the questions which have arisen on the plea in abatement.

That plea denies the right of the plaintiff to sue in a court of the United States, for the reasons therein stated.

If the question raised by it is legally before us, and the court should be of opinion that the facts stated in it disqualify the plaintiff from becoming a citizen, in the sense in which that word is used in the Constitution of the United States, then the judgment of the Circuit Court is erroneous, and must be reversed. . . .

The question to be decided is, whether the facts stated in the plea are sufficient to show that the plaintiff is not entitled to sue as a citizen in a court of the United States.

This is certainly a very serious question, and one that now for the first time has been brought for decision before this court. But it is brought here by those who have a right to bring it, and it is our duty to meet it and decide it.

The question is simply this: Can a negro, whose ancestors were imported into this country, and sold as slaves, become a member of the political community formed and brought into existence by the Constitution of the United States, and as such become entitled to all the rights, and privileges, and immunities, guarantied by that instrument to the citizen? One of which rights is the privilege of suing in a court of the United States in the cases specified in the Constitution.

It will be observed, that the plea applies to that class of persons only whose ancestors were negroes of the African race, and imported into this country, and sold and held as slaves. The only matter in issue before the court, therefore, is, whether the descendants of such slaves, when they shall be emancipated, or who are born of parents who had become free before their birth, are citizens of a State, in the sense in which the word citizen is used in the Constitution of the United States. And this being the only matter in dispute on the pleadings, the court must be understood as speaking in this opinion of that class only, that is of persons who are the descendants of Africans who were imported into this country and sold as slaves. . . .

We proceed to examine the case as presented by the pleadings.

The words "people of the United States" and "citizens" are synonymous terms, and mean the same thing. They both describe the political body who, according to our republican institutions, form the sovereignty, and who hold the power and conduct the government through their representatives. They are what we familiarly call the "sovereign people," and every citizen is one of this people, and a constituent member of this sovereignty. The question before us is, whether the class persons described in the plea in abatement compose a portion of this people, and constituent members of this sovereignty? We think they are not, and that they are not included, and were not intended to be included, under the word "citizens" in the Constitution, and can, therefore, claim none of the rights and privileges which that instrument provides for and secures to citizens the United States. On the contrary, they were at that time considered as a subordinate and inferior class of beings, who had been subjugated by the dominant race, and whether emancipated or not, yet remained subject to their authority, and had no rights or privileges but such as those who held the power and the government might choose to grant them. . . .

In discussing this question, we must not confound the rights of citizenship which a state may confer within its own limits, and the rights of citizenship as a member of the Union. It does not by any means follow, because he has all the rights and privileges of a citizen of a State, that he must be a citizen of the United States. He may have all of the rights and privileges of the citizen of a State, and yet not be entitled to the rights and privileges of a citizen in any other State. For, previous to the adoption of the Constitution of the United States, every State had the undoubted right to confer on whomsoever it pleased the character of a citizen, and to endow him with all its rights. But this character, of course, was confined to the boundaries of the State, and gave him no rights or privileges in other States beyond those secured to him by the laws of nations and the comity of States. Nor have the several States surrendered the power of conferring these rights and privileges by adopting the Constitution of the United States. Each State may still confer them upon an alien, or any one it thinks proper, or upon any class or description of persons; yet he would not be a citizen in the sense in which that word is used in the Constitution of the United States, nor entitled to sue as such in one of its courts, nor to the privileges and immunities of a citizen in the other States. The rights which he would acquire would be restricted to the State which gave them. . . .

It is very clear, therefore, that no State can, by any Act or law of its own, passed since the adoption of the Constitution, introduce a new member into the political community created by the Constitution of the United States. It cannot make him a member this community by making him a member its own. And for the same reason it cannot introduce any person, or descrip-

tion of persons, who were not intended to be embraced this new political family, which the Constitution brought into existence, but were intended to be excluded from it.

The question then arises, whether the provisions of the Constitution, in relation to the personal rights and privileges to which the citizen of a State should be entitled, embraced the negro African race, at that time in this country, or who might afterwards be imported, who had then or should afterwards be made free in any State; and to put it in the power of a single State to make him a citizen the United States, and endue him with the full rights of citizenship in every other State without their consent. Does the Constitution of the United States act upon him whenever he shall be made free under the laws of a State, and raised there to the rank of a citizen, and immediately clothe him with all the privileges of a citizen in every other State, and in its own courts?

The court think the affirmative of these propositions cannot be maintained. And if it cannot, the plaintiff in error could not be a citizen of the State of Missouri, within the meaning of the Constitution of the United States, and, consequently, was not entitled to sue in its courts.

It is true, every person, and every class and description of persons, who were at the time of the adoption of the Constitution recognized as citizens in the several States, became also citizens of this new political body; but none other; it was formed by them, and for them and their posterity, but for no one else. And the personal rights and privileges guarantied to citizens of this new sovereignty were intended to embrace those only who were then members of the several state communities, or who should afterwards, by birthright or otherwise, become members, according to the provisions of the Constitution and the principles on which it was founded. . . .

It becomes necessary, therefore, to determine who were citizens of the several States when the Constitution was adopted. And in order to do this, we must recur to the governments and institutions of the thirteen Colonies, when they separated from Great Britain and formed new sovereignties.... We must inquire who, at that time, were recognized as the people or citizens of a State. . . .

In the opinion of the court, the legislation and histories of the times, and the language used in the Declaration of Independence, show that neither the class of persons who had been imported as slaves, nor their descendants, whether they had become free or not, were then acknowledged as a part of the people, nor intended to be included in the general words used in that memorable instrument.

It is difficult at this day to realize the state of public opinion in relation to that unfortunate race, which prevailed in the civilized and enlightened portions of the world at the time of the Declaration of Independence, and when the Constitution of the United States was framed and adopted. . . .

They had for more than a century before been regarded as beings of an inferior order; and altogether unfit to associate with the white race, either in social or political relations; and so far inferior that they had no rights which the white man was bound to respect; and that the negro might justly and lawfully be reduced to slavery for his benefit.

This opinion was at that time fixed and universal in the civilized portion of the white race. It was regarded as an axiom in morals as well as in politics, which no one thought of disputing, or supposed to be open to dispute; and men in every grade and position in society daily and habitually acted upon it in their private pursuits, as well as in matters of public concern, without doubting for a moment the correctness of this opinion. . . .

The legislation of the different Colonies furnishes positive and undisputable proof of this fact. . . .

The language of the Declaration of Independence is equally conclusive. . . .

This state of public opinion had undergone no change when the Constitution was adopted, as is equally evident from its provisions and language. . . .

But there are two clauses in the Constitution which point directly and specifically to the negro race as a separate class of persons, and show clearly that they were not regarded as a portion of the people or citizens of the Government then formed.

One of these clauses reserves to each of the thirteen States the right to import slaves until the year 1808, if he thinks it proper. And the importation which it thus sanctions was unquestionably of persons of the race of which we are speaking, as the traffic in slaves in the United States had always been confined to them. And by the other provision the States pledge themselves to each other to maintain the right of property of the master, by delivering up to him any slave who may have escaped from his service, and be found within their respective territories. . . . And these two provisions show, conclusively, that neither the description of persons therein referred to, nor their descendants, were embraced in any of the other provisions of the Constitution; for certainly these two clauses were not intended to confer on them or their posterity the blessings of liberty, or any of the personal rights so carefully provided for the citizen. . . .

Indeed, when we look to the condition of this race in the several States at the time, it is impossible to believe that these rights and privileges were intended to be extended to them. . . .

The legislation of the States therefore shows, in a manner not to be mistaken, the inferior and subject

condition of that race at the time the Constitution was adopted, and long afterwards, throughout the thirteen States by which that instrument was framed; and it is hardly consistent with the respect due to these States, to suppose that they regarded at that time, as fellow-citizens and members of the sovereignty, a class of beings whom they had thus stigmatized; . . . More especially, it cannot be believed that the large slave-holding States regarded them as included in the word "citizens," or would have consented to a constitution which might compel them to receive them in that character from another State. For if they were so received, and entitled to the privileges and immunities of citizens, it would exempt them from the operation of the special laws and from the police regulations which they considered to be necessary for their own safety. . . .

And all of this would be done in the face of the subject race of the same color, both free and slaves, inevitably producing discontent and insubordination among them, and endangering the peace and safety of the State. . . .

But it is said that a person may be a citizen, and entitled to that character, although he does not possess all the rights which may belong to other citizens; as, for example, the right to vote, or to hold particular offices; and that yet, when he goes into another State, he is entitled to be recognized there as a citizen, although the State may measure his rights by the rights which it allows to persons of a like character or class, resident in the State, and refuse to him the full rights of citizenship.

This argument overlooks the language of the provision in the Constitution of which we are speaking.

Undoubtedly, a person may be a citizen, that is, a member of the community who form the sovereignty, although he exercises no share of the political power, and is incapacitated from holding particular offices. . . .

So, too, a person may be entitled to vote by the law of the State, who is not a citizen even of the State itself. And in some of the States of the Union foreigners not naturalized are allowed to vote. And the State may give the right to free negroes and mulattoes, but that does not make them citizens of the State, and still less of the United States. And the provision in the Constitution giving privileges and immunities in other States, does not apply to them.

Neither does it apply to a person who, being the citizen of a State, migrates to another State. For then he becomes subject to the laws of the State in which he lives, and he is no longer a citizen of the State from which he removed. And the State in which he resides may then, unquestionably, determine his status or condition, and place him among the class of persons who are not recognized as citizens, but belong to an inferior and subject race; and may deny him the privileges and immunities enjoyed by its citizens. . . .

. . . But if he ranks as a citizen of the State to which he belongs, within the meaning of the Constitution of the United States, then, whenever he goes into another State, the Constitution clothes him, as to the rights of person, with all the privileges and immunities which belong to citizens of the State. And if persons of the African race are citizens of a state, and of the United States, they would be entitled to all of these privileges and immunities in every State, and the State could not restrict them; for they would hold these privileges and immunities, under the paramount authority of the Federal Government, and its courts would be bound to maintain and enforce them, the Constitution and laws of the State to the contrary notwithstanding. . . .

And upon a full and careful consideration of the subject, the court is of opinion that, upon the facts stated in the plea in abatement, Dred Scott was not a citizen of Missouri within the meaning of the Constitution of the United States, and not entitled as such to sue in its courts; and, consequently, that the Circuit Court had no jurisdiction of the case, and that the judgment on the plea in abatement is erroneous. . . .

We proceed, therefore, to inquire whether the facts relied on by the plaintiff entitled him to his freedom. . . .

In considering this part of the controversy, two questions arise: 1st. Was he, together with his family, free in Missouri by reason of the stay in the territory of the United States hereinbefore mentioned? And 2d, If they were not, is Scott himself free by reason of his removal to Rock Island, in the State of Illinois, as stated in the above admissions?

We proceed to examine the first question. The Act of Congress, upon which the plaintiff relies, declares that slavery and involuntary servitude, except as a punishment for crime, shall be forever prohibited in all that part of the territory ceded by France, under the name of Louisiana, which lies north of thirty-six degrees thirty minutes north latitude, and not included within the limits of Missouri. And the difficulty which meets us at the threshold of this part of the inquiry is, whether Congress was authorized to pass this law under any of the powers granted to it by the Constitution; for if the authority is not given by that instrument, it is the duty of this court to declare it void and inoperative, and incapable of conferring freedom upon any one who is held as a slave under the laws of any one of the States.

The counsel for the plaintiff has laid much stress upon that article in the Constitution which confers on Congress the power "to dispose of and make all needful rules and regulations respecting the territory or other property belonging to the United States"; but, in the judgment of the court, that provision has no bearing on the present controversy, and the power there given, whatever it may be, is confined, and was intended to be confined, to the territory which at that time belonged to, or was claimed by, the United States, and was within their boundaries as settled by the treaty with Great Britain, and can have no influence upon a territory afterwards acquired from a foreign Government. It was a special provision for a known and particular territory, and to meet a present emergency, and nothing more. . . .

If this clause is construed to extend to territory acquired by the present Government from a foreign nation, outside of the limits of any charter from the British Government to a colony, it would be difficult to say, why it was deemed necessary to give the Government the power to sell any vacant lands belonging to the sovereignty which might be found within it; and if this was necessary, why the grant of this power should precede the power to legislate over it and establish a Government there; and still more difficult to say, why it was deemed necessary so specially and particularly to grant the power to make needful rules and regulations in relation to any personal or movable property it might acquire there. For the words, other property necessarily, by every known rule of interpretation, must mean property of a different description from territory or land. And the difficulty would perhaps be insurmountable in endeavoring to account for the last member of the sentence, which provides that "nothing in this Constitution shall be so construed as to prejudice any claims of the United States or any particular State," or to say how any particular State could have claims in or to a territory ceded by a foreign Government, or to account for associating this provision with the preceding provisions of the clause, with which it would appear to have no connection. . . .

But the power of Congress over the person or property of a citizen can never be a mere discretionary power under our Constitution and form of Government. The powers of the Government and the rights and privileges of the citizen are regulated and plainly defined by the Constitution itself. And when the Territory becomes a part of the United States, the Federal Government enters into possession in the character impressed upon it by those who created it. It enters upon it with its powers over the citizen strictly defined, and limited by the Constitution, from which it derives its own existence, and by virtue of which alone it continues to exist and act as a Government and sovereignty. It has no power of any kind beyond it; and it cannot, when it enters a Territory of the United States, put off its character, and assume discretionary or despotic powers which the Constitution has denied to it. It cannot create for itself a new character separated from the citizens of the United States, and the duties it owes them under the provisions of the Constitution. The Territory being a part of the United States, the Government and the citizen both enter it under the authority of the Constitution, with their respective

rights defined and marked out; and the Federal Government can exercise no power over his person or property, beyond what that instrument confers, nor lawfully deny any right which it has reserved. . . .

The rights of private property have been guarded with equal care. Thus the rights of property are united with the rights of person, and placed on the same ground by the fifth amendment to the Constitution ... An Act of Congress which deprives a person of the United States of his liberty or property merely because he came himself or brought his property into a particular Territory of the United States, and who had committed no offense against the laws, could hardly be dignified with the name of due process of law. . . .

And this prohibition is not confined to the States, but the words are general, and extend to the whole territory over which the Constitution gives it power to legislate, including those portions of it remaining under territorial government, as well as that covered by States. It is a total absence of power everywhere within the dominion of the United States, and places the citizens of a territory, so far as these rights are concerned, on the same footing with citizens of the States, and guards them as firmly and plainly against any inroads which the general government might attempt, under the plea of implied or incidental powers. And if Congress itself cannot do this—if it is beyond the powers conferred on the Federal Government—it will be admitted, we presume, that it could not authorize a territorial government to exercise them. It could confer no power on any local government, established by its authority, to violate the provisions of the Constitution.

It seems, however, to be supposed, that there is a difference between property in a slave and other property, and that different rules may be applied to it in expounding the Constitution of the United States. And the laws and usages of nations, and the writings of eminent jurists upon the relation of master and slave and their mutual rights and duties, and the powers which governments may exercise over it, have been dwelt upon in the argument.

But . . . if the Constitution recognizes the right of property of the master in a slave, and makes no distinction between that description of property and other property owned by a citizen, no tribunal, acting under the authority of the United States, whether it be legislative, executive, or judicial, has a right to draw such a distinction, or deny to it the benefit of the provisions and guarantees which have been provided for the protection of private property against the encroachments of the Government.

Now . . . the right of property in a slave is distinctly and expressly affirmed in the Constitution. The right to traffic in it, like an ordinary article of merchandise and property, was guaranteed to the citizens of the United States, in every State that might desire it, for twenty years. And the Government in express terms is pledged to protect it in all future time, if the slave escapes from his owner. . . . And no word can be found in the Constitution which gives Congress a greater power over slave property, or which entitles property of that kind to less protection than property of any other description. The only power conferred is the power coupled with the duty of guarding and protecting the owner in his rights.

Upon these considerations, it is the opinion of the court that the Act of Congress which prohibited a citizen from holding and owning property of this kind in the territory of the United States north of the line therein mentioned, is not warranted by the Constitution, and is therefore void; and that neither Dred Scott himself, nor any of his family, were made free by being carried into this territory; even if they had been carried there by the owner, with the intention of becoming a permanent resident. . . .

Upon the whole, therefore, it is the judgment of this court, that it appears by the record before us that the plaintiff in error is not a citizen of Missouri, in the sense in which that word is used in the Constitution; and that the Circuit Court of the United States, for that reason, had no jurisdiction in the case, and could give no judgment in it.

Its judgment for the defendant must, consequently, be reversed, and a mandate issued directing the suit to be dismissed for want of jurisdiction.

Wayne, J., Nelson, J., Grier, J., Daniel, J., and Catron, J., filed separate concurring opinions. McLean, J., and Curtis, J., dissented.

(Source: *Scott v. San[d]ford*, 19 Howard, 393 1857.)

2. Justice Curtis's Dissent in *Dred Scott* (1857)

I dissent from the opinion pronounced by the Chief Justice, and from the judgment which the majority of the court think it proper to render in this case. The plaintiff alleged, in his declaration, that he was a citizen of the State of Missouri, and that the defendant was a citizen of the State of New York. It is not doubted that it was necessary to make each of these allegations, to sustain the jurisdiction of the Circuit Court. The defendant denied, by a plea to the jurisdiction, either sufficient or insufficient, that the plaintiff was a citizen of the State of Missouri. The plaintiff demurred to that plea. The Circuit Court adjudged the plea insufficient, and the first question for our consideration is, whether the sufficiency of that plea is before this court for judgment, upon this writ of error. The part of the judicial power of the United States, conferred by Congress on the Circuit Courts, being limited to certain described cases and controversies, the question whether a particular case is within the cognizance of a Circuit Court, may be raised by a plea to the jurisdiction of such court. When that question has been raised, the Circuit Court must, in the first instance, pass upon and determine it. Whether its determination be final, or subject to review by this appellate court, must depend upon the will of Congress; upon which body the Constitution has conferred the power, with certain restrictions, to establish inferior courts, to determine their jurisdiction, and to regulate the appellate power of this court. The twenty-second section of the judiciary act of 1789, which allows a writ of error from final judgments of Circuit Courts, provides that there shall be no reversal in this court, on such writ of error, for error in ruling any plea in abatement, other than a plea to the jurisdiction of the court.

Accordingly it has been held, from the origin of the court to the present day, that Circuit Courts have not been made by Congress the final judges of their own jurisdiction in civil cases. And that when a record comes here upon a writ of error or appeal, and, on its inspection, it appears to this court that the Circuit Court had not jurisdiction, its judgment must be reversed, and the cause remanded, to be dismissed for want of jurisdiction.

It is alleged by the defendant in error, in this case, that the plea to the jurisdiction was a sufficient plea; that it shows, on inspection of its allegations, confessed by the demurrer, that the plaintiff was not a citizen of the State of Missouri; that upon this record, it must appear to this court that the case was not within the judicial power of the United States, as defined and granted by the Constitution, because it was not a suit by a citizen of one State against a citizen of another State.

To this it is answered, first, that the defendant, by pleading over, after the plea to the jurisdiction was adjudged insufficient, finally waived all benefit of that plea.

When that plea was adjudged insufficient, the defendant was obliged to answer over. He held no alternative. He could not stop the further progress of the case in the Circuit Court by a writ of error, on which the sufficiency of his plea to the jurisdiction could be tried in this court, because the judgment on that plea was not final, and no writ of error would lie. He was forced to plead to the merits. It cannot be true, then, that he waived the benefit of his plea to the jurisdiction by answering over. Waiver includes consent. Here, there was no consent. And if the benefit of the plea was finally lost, it must be, not by any waiver, but because the laws of the United States have not provided any mode of reviewing the decision of the Circuit Court on such a plea, when that decision is against the defen-

dant. This is not the law. Whether the decision of the Circuit Court on a plea to the jurisdiction be against the plaintiff, or against the defendant, the losing party may have any alleged error in law, in ruling such a plea, examined in this court on a writ of error, when the matter in controversy exceeds the sum or value of two thousand dollars. If the decision be against the plaintiff, and his suit dismissed for want of jurisdiction, the judgment is technically final, and he may at once sue out his writ of error. (Mollan v. Torrance, 9 Wheat., 537.) If the decision be against the defendant, though he must answer over, and wait for a final judgment in the cause, he may then have his writ of error, and upon it obtain the judgment of this court on any question of law apparent on the record, touching the jurisdiction. The fact that he pleaded over to the merits, under compulsion, can have no effect on his right to object to the jurisdiction. If this were not so, the condition of the two parties would be grossly unequal. For if a plea to the jurisdiction were ruled against the plaintiff, he could at once take his writ of error, and have the ruling reviewed here; while, if the same plea were ruled against the defendant, he must not only wait for a final judgment, but could in no event have the ruling of the Circuit Court upon the plea reviewed by this court. I know of no ground for saying that the laws of the United States have thus discriminated between the parties to a suit in its courts.

It is further objected, that as the judgment of the Circuit Court was in favor of the defendant, and the writ of error in this cause was sued out by the plaintiff, the defendant is not in a condition to assign any error in the record, and therefore this court is precluded from considering the question whether the Circuit Court had jurisdiction.

The practice of this court does not require a technical assignment of errors. (See the rule.) Upon a writ of error, the whole record is open for inspection; and if any error be found in it, the judgment is reversed. (Bank of U.S. v. Smith, 11 Wheat., 171.)

It is true, as a general rule, that the court will not allow a party to rely on anything as cause for reversing a judgment, which was for his advantage. In this, we follow an ancient rule of the common law. But so careful was that law of the preservation of the course of its courts, that it made an exception out of that general rule, and allowed a party to assign for error that which was for his advantage, if it were a departure by the court itself from its settled course of procedure. The cases on this subject are collected in Bac. Ab., Error H. 4. And this court followed this practice in Capron v. Van Noorden, (2 Cranch, 126,) where the plaintiff below procured the reversal of a judgment for the defendant, on the ground that the plaintiff's allegations of citizenship had not shown jurisdiction.

But it is not necessary to determine whether the defendant can be allowed to assign want of jurisdiction as an error in a judgment in his own favor. The true question is, not what either of the parties may be allowed to do, but whether this court will affirm or reverse a judgment of the Circuit Court on the merits, when it appears on the record, by a plea to the jurisdiction, that it is a case to which the judicial power of the United States does not extend. The course of the court is, where no motion is made by either party, on its own motion, to reverse such a judgment for want of jurisdiction, not only in cases where it is shown, negatively, by a plea to the jurisdiction, that jurisdiction does not exist, but ever where it does not appear, affirmatively, that it does exist. (Pequignot v. The Pennsylvania R.R. Co., 16 How., 104.) It acts upon the principle that the judicial power of the United States must not be exerted in a case to which it does not extend, even if both parties desire to have it exerted. (Cutler v. Rae, 7 How., 729.) I consider, therefore, that when there was a plea to the jurisdiction of the Circuit Court in a case brought here by a writ of error, the first duty of this court is, sua sponte, if not moved to it by either party, to examine the sufficiency of that plea; and thus to take care that neither the Circuit Court nor this court shall use the judicial power of the United States in a case to which the Constitution and laws of the United States have not extended that power.

I proceed, therefore, to examine the plea to the jurisdiction.

I do not perceive any sound reason why it is not to be judged by the rules of the common law applicable to such pleas. It is true, where the jurisdiction of the Circuit Court depends on the citizenship of the parties, it is incumbent on the plaintiff to allege on the record the necessary citizenship; but when he has done so, the defendant must interpose a plea in abatement, the allegations whereof show that the court has not jurisdiction; and it is incumbent on him to prove the truth of his plea.

In Sheppard v. Graves, (14 How., 27,) the rules on this subject are thus stated in the opinion of the court: *"That although, in the courts of the United States, it is necessary to set forth the grounds of their cognizance as courts of limited jurisdiction, yet wherever jurisdiction shall be averred in the pleadings, in conformity with the laws creating those courts, it must be taken, prima facic, as existing; and it is incumbent on him who would impeach that jurisdiction for causes dehors the pleading, to allege and prove such causes; that the necessity for the allegation, and the burden of sustaining it by proof, both rest upon the party taking the exception."* These positions are sustained by the authorities there cited, as well as by Wickliffe v. Owings, (17 How., 47.)

When, therefore, as in this case, the necessary averments as to citizenship are made on the record, and

jurisdiction is assumed to exist, and the defendant comes by a plea to the jurisdiction to displace that presumption, he occupies, in my judgment, precisely the position described in Bacon Ab., Abatement: *"Abatement, in the general acceptation of the word, signifies a plea, put in by the defendant, in which he shows cause to the court why he should not be impleaded; or, if at all, not in the manner and form he now is."*

This being, then, a plea in abatement, to the jurisdiction of the court, I must judge of its sufficiency by those rules of the common law applicable to such pleas.

The plea was as follows:

"And the said John F. A. Sandford, in his own proper person, comes and says that this court ought not to have or take further cognizance of the action aforesaid, because he says that said cause of action, and each and every of them, (if any such have accrued to the said Dred Scott,) accrued to the said Dred Scott out of the jurisdiction of this court, and exclusively within the jurisdiction of the courts of the State of Missouri; for that, to wit, the said plaintiff, Dred Scott, is not a citizen of the State of Missouri, as alleged in his declaration, because he is a negro of African descent; his ancestors were of pure African blood, and were brought into this country and sold as negro slaves, and this the said Sandford is ready to verify. Wherefore, he prays judgment whether this court can or will take further cognizance of the action aforesaid."

The plaintiff demurred, and the judgment of the Circuit Court was, that the plea was insufficient.

I cannot treat this plea as a general traverse of the citizenship alleged by the plaintiff. Indeed, if it were so treated, the plea was clearly bad, for it concludes with a verification, and not to the country, as a general traverse should. And though this defect in a plea in bar must be pointed out by a special demurrer, it is never necessary to demur specially to a plea in abatement; all matters, though of form only, may be taken advantage of upon a general demurrer to such a plea. (Chitty on Pl., 465.)

The truth is, that though not drawn with the utmost technical accuracy, it is a special traverse of the plaintiff's allegation of citizenship, and was a suitable and proper mode of traverse under the circumstances. By reference to Mr. Stephen's description of the uses of such a traverse, contained in his excellent analysis of pleadings, (Steph. on Pl., 176,) it will be seen how precisely this plea meets one of his descriptions. No doubt the defendant might have traversed, by a common or general traverse, the plaintiff's allegation that he was a citizen of the State of Missouri, concluding to the country. The issue thus presented being joined, would have involved matter of law, on which the jury must have passed, under the direction of the court. But by traversing the plaintiffs citizenship specially—that is, averring those facts on which the defendant relied to show that in point of law the plaintiff was not a citizen, and basing the traverse on those facts as a deduction therefrom—opportunity was given to do, what was done; that is, to present directly to the court, by a demurrer, the sufficiency of those facts to negative, in point of law, the plaintiff's allegation of citizenship. This, then, being a special, and not a general or common traverse, the rule is settled, that the facts thus set out in the plea, as the reason or ground of the traverse, must of themselves constitute, in point of law, a negative of the allegation thus traversed. (Stephen on Pl., 183; Ch. on Pl., 620.) And upon a demurrer to this plea, the question which arises is, whether the facts, that the plaintiff is a negro, of African descent, whose ancestors were of pure African blood, and were brought into this country and sold as negro slaves, may all be true, and yet the plaintiff be a citizen of the State of Missouri, within the meaning of the Constitution and laws of the United States, which confer on citizens of one State the right to sue citizens of another State in the Circuit Courts. Undoubtedly, if these facts, taken together, amount to an allegation that, at the time of action brought, the plaintiff was himself a slave, the plea is sufficient. It has been suggested that the plea, in legal effect, does so aver, because, if his ancestors were sold as slaves, the presumption is they continued slaves; and if so, the presumption is, the plaintiff was born a slave; and if so, the presumption is, he continued to be a slave to the time of action brought.

I cannot think such presumptions can be resorted to, to help out defective averments in pleading; especially, in pleading in abatement, where the utmost certainty and precision are required. (Chitty on Pl., 457.) That the plaintiff himself was a slave at the time of action brought, is a substantive fact, having no necessary connection with the fact that his parents were sold as slaves. For they might have been sold after he was born; or the plaintiff himself, if once a slave, might have became a freeman before action brought. To aver that his ancestors were sold as slaves, is not equivalent, in point of law, to an averment that he was a slave. If it were, he could not even confess and avoid the averment of the slavery of his ancestors, which would be monstrous; and if it be not equivalent in point of law, it cannot be treated as amounting thereto when demurred to; for a demurrer confesses only those substantive facts which are well pleaded, and not other distinct substantive facts which might be inferred therefrom by a jury. To treat an averment that the plaintiff's ancestors were Africans, brought to this country and sold as slaves, as amounting to an averment on the record that he was a slave, because it may lay some foundation for presuming so, is to hold that the facts actually alleged may be treated as intended as evidence of another distinct fact not alleged. But it is a

cardinal rule of pleading, laid down in Dowman's case, (9 Rep., 9 b,) and in even earlier authorities therein referred to, "*that evidence shall never be pleaded, for it only tends to prove matter of fact; and therefore the matter of fact shall be pleaded.*" Or, as the rule is sometimes stated, pleadings must not be argumentative. (Stephen on Pleading, 384, and, authorities cited by him.) In Com. Dig., Pleader E. 3, and Bac. Abridgement, Pleas I, 5, and Stephen on Pl., many decisions under this rule are collected. In trover, for an indenture whereby A granted a manor, it is no plea that A did not grant the manor, for it does not answer the declaration except by argument. (Yelv., 223.).

So in trespass for taking and carrying away the plaintiff's goods, the defendant pleaded that the plaintiff never had any goods. The court said, "*this is an infallible argument that the defendant is not guilty, but it is no plea.*" (Dyer, a 43.)

In ejectment, the defendant pleaded a surrender of a copyhold by the hand of Fosset, the steward. The plaintiff replied, that Fosset was not steward. The court held this no issue, for it traversed the surrender only argumentatively. (Cro. Elis., 260.)

In these cases, and many others reported in the books, the inferences from the facts stated were irresistible. But the court held they did not, when demurred to, amount to such inferable facts. In the case at bar, the inference that the defendant was a slave at the time of action brought, even if it can be made at all, from the fact that his parents were slaves, is certainly not a necessary inference. This case, therefore, is like that of Digby v. Alexander, (8 Bing., 116.) In that case, the defendant pleaded many facts strongly tending to show that he was once Earl of Stirling; but as there was no positive allegation that he was so at the time of action brought, and as every fact averred might be true, and yet the defendant not have been Earl of Stirling at the time of action brought, the plea was held to be insufficient.

A lawful seizing of land is presumed to continue. But if, in an action of trespass quare clausum, the defendant were to plead that he was lawfully seized of the locus in quo, one month before the time of the alleged trespass, I should have no doubt it would be a bad plea. (See Mollan v. Torrance, 9 Wheat., 537.) So if a plea to the jurisdiction, instead of alleging that the plaintiff was a citizen of the same State as the defendant, were to allege that the plaintiff's ancestors were citizens of that State, I think the plea could not be supported. My judgment would be, as it is in this case, that if the defendant meant to aver a particular substantive fact, as existing at the time of action brought, he must do it directly and explicitly, and not by way of inference from certain other averments, which are quite consistent with the contrary hypothesis. I cannot, therefore, treat this plea as containing an averment that the plaintiff himself was a slave at the time of action brought; and the inquiry recurs, whether the facts, that he is of African descent, and that his parents were once slaves, are necessarily inconsistent with his own citizenship in the State of Missouri, within the meaning of the Constitution and laws of the United States.

In Gassies v. Ballon, (6 Pet., 761,) the defendant was described on the record as a naturalized citizen of the United States, residing in Louisiana. The court held this equivalent to an averment that the defendant was a citizen of Louisiana; because a citizen of the United States, residing in any State of the Union, is, for purposes of jurisdiction, a citizen of that State. Now, the plea to the jurisdiction in this case does not controvert the fact that the plaintiff resided in Missouri at the date of the writ. If he did then reside there, and was also a citizen of the United States, no provisions contained in the Constitution or laws of Missouri can deprive the plaintiff of his right to sue citizens of States other than Missouri, in the courts of the United States.

So that, under the allegations contained in this plea, and admitted by the demurrer, the question is, whether any person of African descent, whose ancestors were sold as slaves in the United States, can be a citizen of the United States. If any such person can be a citizen, this plaintiff has the right to the judgment of the court that he is so; for no cause is shown by the plea why he is not so, except his descent and the slavery of his ancestors.

The first section of the second article of the Constitution uses the language, "*a citizen of the United States at the time of the adoption of the Constitution.*" One mode of approaching this question is, to inquire who were citizens of the United States at the time of the adoption of the Constitution.

Citizens of the United States at the time of the adoption of the Constitution can have been no other than citizens of the United States under the Confederation. By the Articles of Confederation, a Government was organized, the style whereof was, "The United States of America." This Government was in existence when the Constitution was framed and proposed for adoption, and was to be superseded by the new Government of the United States of America, organized under the Constitution. When, therefore, the Constitution speaks of citizenship of the United States, existing at the time of the adoption of the Constitution, it must necessarily refer to citizenship under the Government which existed prior to and at the time of such adoption.

Without going into any question concerning the powers of the Confederation to govern the territory of the United States out of the limits of the States, and consequently to sustain the relation of Government and citizen in respect to the inhabitants of such territory, it may safely be said that the citizens of the several States were citizens of the United States under the Confederation.

That Government was simply a confederacy of the several States, possessing a few defined powers over subjects of general concern, each State retaining every power, jurisdiction, and right, not expressly delegated to the United States in Congress assembled. And no power was thus delegated to the Governement of the Confederation, to act on any question of citizenship, or to make any rules in respect thereto. The whole matter was left to stand upon the action of the several States, and to the natural consequence of such action, that the citizens of each State should be citizens of that Confederacy into which that State had entered, the style whereof was, "The United States of America."

To determine whether any free persons, descended from Africans held in slavery, were citizens of the United States under the Confederation, and consequently at the time of the adoption of the Constitution of the United States, it is only necessary to know whether any such persons were citizens of either of the States under the Confederation, at the time of the adoption of the Constitution.

Of this there can be no doubt. At the time of the ratification of the Articles of Confederation, all free native-born inhabitants of the States of New Hampshire, Massachusetts, New York, New Jersey, and North Carolina, though descended from African slaves, were not only citizens of those States, but such of them as had the other necessary qualifications possessed the franchise of electors, on equal terms with other citizens.

The Supreme Court of North Carolina, in the case of the State v. Manuel, (4 Dev. and Bat., 20,) has declared the law of that State on this subject, in terms which I believe to be as sound law in the other States I have enumerated, as it was in North Carolina.

"*According to the laws of this State,*" says Judge Gaston, in delivering the opinion of the court, "*all human beings within it, who are not slaves, fall within one of two classes. Whatever distinctions may have existed in the Roman laws between citizens and free inhabitants, they are unknown to our institutions. Before our Revolution, all free persons born within the dominions of the King of Great Britain, whatever their color or complexion, were native-born British subjects—those born out of his allegiance were aliens. Slavery did not exist in England, but it did in the British colonies. Slaves were not in legal parlance persons, but property. The moment the incapacity, the disqualification of slavery, was removed, they became persons, and were then either British subjects, or not British subjects, according as they were or were not born within the allegiance of the British King. Upon the Revolution, no other change took place in the laws of North Carolina than was*"

consequent on the transition from a colony dependent on a European King, to a free and sovereign State. Slaves remained slaves. British subjects in North Carolina became North Carolina freemen. Foreigners, until made members of the State, remained aliens. Slaves, manumitted here, became freemen, and therefore, if born within North Carolina, are citizens of North Carolina, and all free persons born within the State are born citizens of the State. The Constitution extended the elective franchise to every freeman who had arrived at the age of twenty-one, and paid a public tax; and it is a matter of universal notoriety, that, under it, free persons, without regard to color, claimed and exercised the franchise, until it was taken from free men of color a few years since by our amended Constitution."

In the State v. Newcomb, (5 Iredell's R., 253,) decided in 1844, the same court referred to this case of the State v. Manuel, and said: *"That case underwent a very laborious investigation, both by the bar and the bench. The case was brought here by appeal, and was felt to be one of great importance in principle. It was considered with an anxiety and care worthy of the principle involved, and which give it a controlling influence and authority on all questions of a similar character."*

An argument from speculative premises, however well chosen, that the then state of opinion in the Commonwealth of Massachusetts was not consistent with the natural rights of people of color who were born on that soil, and that they were not, by the Constitution of 1780 of that State, admitted to the condition of citizens, would be received with surprise by the people of that State, who know their own political history. It is true, beyond all controversy, that persons of color, descended from African slaves, were by that Constitution made citizens of the State; and such of them as have had the necessary qualifications, have held and exercised the elective franchise, as citizens, from that time to the present. (See Com. v. Aves, 18 Pick. R., 210.)

The Constitution of New Hampshire conferred the elective franchise upon *"every inhabitant of the State having the necessary qualifications,"* of which color or descent was not one.

The Constitution of New York gave the right to vote to *"every male inhabitant, who shall have resided,"* &c.; making no discrimination between free colored persons and others. (See Con. of N.Y., Art. 2, Rev. Stats. of N.Y., vol. 1, p. 126.)

That of New Jersey, to *"all inhabitants of this colony, of full age, who are worth $50 proclamation money, clear estate."*

New York, by its Constitution of 1820, required colored persons to have some qualifications as prerequisites for voting, which white persons need not possess. And New Jersey, by its present Constitution, restricts the right to vote to white male citizens. But these changes can have no other effect upon the present inquiry, except to show, that before they were made, no such restrictions existed; and colored in common with white persons, were not only citizens of those States, but entitled to the elective franchise on the same qualifications as white persons, as they now are in New Hampshire and Massachusetts. I shall not enter into an examination of the existing opinions of that period respecting the African race, nor into any discussion concerning the meaning of those who asserted, in the Declaration of Independence, that all men are created equal; that they are endowed by their Creator with certain inalienable rights; that among these are life, liberty, and the pursuit of happiness. My own opinion is, that a calm comparison of these assertions of universal abstract truths, and of their own individual opinions and acts, would not leave these men under any reproach of inconsistency; that the great truths they asserted on that solemn occasion, they were ready and anxious to make effectual, wherever a necessary regard to circumstances, which no statesman can disregard without producing more evil than good, would allow; and that it would not be just to them, nor true in itself, to allege that they intended to say that the Creator of all men had endowed the white race, exclusively, with the great natural rights which the Declaration of Independence asserts. But this is not the place to vindicate their memory. As I conceive, we should deal here, not with such disputes, if there can be a dispute concerning this subject, but with those substantial facts evinced by the written Constitutions of States, and by the notorious practice under them. And they show, in a manner which no argument can obscure, that in some of the original thirteen States, free colored persons, before and at the time of the formation of the Constitution, were citizens of those States.

The fourth of the fundamental articles of the Confederation was as follows: *"The free inhabitants of each of these States, paupers, vagabonds, and fugitives from justice, excepted, shall be entitled to all the privileges and immunities of free citizens in the several States."*

The fact that free persons of color were citizens of some of the several States, and the consequence, that this fourth article of the Confederation would have the effect to confer on such persons the privileges and immunities of general citizenship, were not only known to those who framed and adopted those articles, but the evidence is decisive, that the fourth article was intended to have that effect, and that more restricted language, which would have excluded such persons, was deliberately and purposely rejected.

On the 25th of June, 1778, the Articles of Confederation being under consideration by the Congress, the delegates from South Carolina moved to amend this fourth article, by inserting after the word

"*free,*" and before the word "*inhabitants,*" the word "*white,*" so that the privileges and immunities of general citizenship would be secured only to white persons. Two States voted for the amendment, eight States against it, and the vote of one State was divided. The language of the article stood unchanged, and both by its terms of inclusion, "*free inhabitants,*" and the strong implication from its terms of exclusion, "*paupers, vagabonds, and fugitives from justice,*" who alone were excepted, it is clear, that under the Confederation, and at the time of the adoption of the Constitution, free colored persons of African descent might be, and, by reason of their citizenship in certain States, were entitled to the privileges and immunities of general citizenship of the United States.

Did the Constitution of the United States deprive them or their descendants of citizenship?

That Constitution was ordained and established by the people of the United States, through the action, in each State, of those persons who were qualified by its laws to act thereon, in behalf of themselves and all other citizens of that State. In some of the States, as we have seen, colored persons were among those qualified by law to act on this subject. These colored persons were not only included in the body of "*the people of the United States,*" by whom the Constitution was ordained and established, but in at least five of the States they had the power to act, and doubtless did act, by their suffrages, upon the question of its adoption. It would be strange, if we were to find in that instrument anything which deprived of their citizenship any part of the people of the United States who were among those by whom it was established.

I can find nothing in the Constitution which, proprio vigore, deprives of their citizenship any class of persons who were citizens of the United States at the time of its adoption, or who should be native-born citizens of any State after its adoption; nor any power enabling Congress to disfranchise persons born on the soil of any State, and entitled to citizenship of such State by its Constitution and laws. And my opinion is, that, under the Constitution of the United States, every free person born on the soil of a State, who is a citizen of that State by force of its Constitution or laws, is also a citizen of the United States.

I will proceed to state the grounds of that opinion.

The first section of the second article of the Constitution uses the language, "*a natural-born citizen.*" It thus assumes that citizenship may be acquired by birth. Undoubtedly, this language of the Constitution was used in reference to that principle of public law, well understood in this country at the time of the adoption of the Constitution, which referred citizenship to the place of birth. At the Declaration of Independence, and ever since, the received general doctrine has been,

in conformity with the common law, that free persons born within either of the colonies were subjects of the King; that by the Declaration of Independence, and the consequent acquisition of sovereignty by the several States. All such persons ceased to be subjects, and became citizens of the several States, except so far as some of them were disfranchised by the legislative power of the States, or availed themselves, seasonably, of the right to adhere to the British Crown in the civil contest, and thus to continue British subjects. (McIlvain v. Coxe's Lessee, 4 Cranch, 209; Inglis v. Sailors' Snug Harbor, 3 Peters, p. 99; Shanks v. Dupont, Ibid, p. 242.)

The Constitution having recognized the rule that persons born within the several States are citizens of the United States, one of four things must be true:

First.

That the Constitution itself has described what native-born persons shall or shall not be citizens of the United States; or,

Second.

That it has empowered Congress to do so; or,

Third.

That all free persons, born within the several States, are citizens of the United States; or,

Fourth.

That it is left to each State to determine what free persons, born within its limits, shall be citizens of such State, and thereby be citizens of the United States.

If there be such a thing as citizenship of the United States acquired by birth within the States, which the Constitution expressly recognizes, and no one denies, then these four alternatives embrace the entire subject, and it only remains to select that one which is true.

That the Constitution itself has defined citizenship of the United States by declaring what persons, born within the several States, shall or shall not be citizens of the United States, will not be pretended. It contains no such declaration. We may dismiss the first alternative, as without doubt unfounded.

Has it empowered Congress to enact what free persons, born within the several States, shall or shall not be citizens of the United States?

Before examining the various provisions of the Constitution which may relate to this question, it is important to consider for a moment the substantial nature of this inquiry. It is, in effect, whether the Constitution has empowered Congress to create privileged classes within the States, who alone can be entitled to the franchises and powers of citizenship of the United States. If it be admitted that the Constitution has enabled Congress to declare what free persons, born within the several States, shall be citizens of the United States, it must at the same time be admitted that it is an unlimited power. If this subject is within the control of

Congress, it must depend wholly on its discretion. For, certainly, on limits of that discretion can be found in the Constitution, which is wholly silent concerning it; and the necessary consequence is, that the Federal Government may select classes of persons within the several States who alone can be entitled to the political privileges of citizenship of the United States. If this power exists, what persons born within the States may be President or Vice President of the United States, or members of either House of Congress, or hold any office or enjoy any privilege whereof citizenship of the United States is a necessary qualification, must depend solely on the will of Congress. By virtue of it, though Congress can grant no title of nobility, they may create an oligarchy, in whose hands would be concentrated the entire power of the Federal Government.

It is a substantive power, distinct in its nature from all others; capable of affecting not only the relations of the States to the General Government, but of controlling the political condition of the people of the United States. Certainly we ought to find this power granted by the Constitution, at least by some necessary inference, before we can say it does not remain to the States or the people. I proceed therefore to examine all the provisions of the Constitution which may have some bearing on this subject.

Among the powers expressly granted to Congress is *"the power to establish a uniform rule of naturalization."* It is not doubted that this is a power to prescribe a rule for the removal of the disabilities consequent on foreign birth. To hold that it extends further than this, would do violence to the meaning of the term naturalization, fixed in the common law, (Co. Lit., 8 a, 129 a; 2 Ves., sen., 286; 2 Bl. Com., 293,) and in the minds of those who concurred in framing and adopting the Constitution. It was in this sense of conferring on an alien and his issue the rights and powers of a native-born citizen, that it was employed in the Declaration of Independence. It was in this sense it was expounded in the *Federalist,* (No. 42,) has been understood by Congress, by the Judiciary, (2 Wheat., 259, 269; 3 Wash. R., 313, 322; 12 Wheat., 277,) and by commentators on the Constitution. (3 Story's Com. on Con., 1—3; 1 Rawle on Con., 84—88; 1 Tucker's Bl. Com. App., 255—259.) It appears, then, that the only power expressly granted to Congress to legislate concerning citizenship, is confined to the removal of the disabilities of foreign birth.

Whether there be anything in the Constitution from which a broader power may be implied, will best be seen when we come to examine the two other alternatives, which are, whether all free persons, born on the soil of the several States, or only such of them as may be citizens of each State, respectively, are thereby citizens of the United States. The last of these alternatives, in my judgment, contains the truth.

Undoubtedly, as has already been said, it is a principle of public law, recognized by the Constitution itself, that birth on the soil of a country both creates the duties and confers the rights of citizenship. But it must be remembered, that though the Constitution was to form a Government, and under it the United States of America were to be one united sovereign nation, to which loyalty and obedience on the one side, and from which protection and privileges on the other, would be due, yet the several sovereign States, whose people were then citizens, were not only to continue in existence, but with powers unimpaired, except so far as they were granted by the people to the National Government.

Among the powers unquestionably possessed by the several States, was that of determining what persons should and what persons should not be citizens. It was practicable to confer on the Government of the Union this entire power. It embraced what may, well enough for the purpose now in view, be divided into three parts.

First: The power to remove the disabilities of alienage, either by special acts in reference to each individual case, or by establishing a rule of naturalization to be administered and applied by the courts.

Second: Determining what persons should enjoy the privileges of citizenship, in respect to the internal affairs of the several States.

Third: What native-born persons should be citizens of the United States.

The first-named power, that of establishing a uniform rule of naturalization, was granted; and here the grant, according to its terms, stopped. Construing a Constitution containing only limited and defined powers of government, the argument derived from this definite and restricted power to establish a rule of naturalization, must be admitted to be exceedingly strong. I do not say it is necessarily decisive. It might be controlled by other parts of the Constitution. But when this particular subject of citizenship was under consideration, and, in the clause specially intended to define the extent of power concerning it, we find a particular part of this entire power separated from the residue, and conferred on the General Government, there arises a strong presumption that this is all which is granted, and that the residue is left to the States and to the people. And this presumption is, in my opinion, converted into a certainty, by an examination of all such other clauses of the Constitution as touch this subject.

I will examine each which can have any possible bearing on this question.

The first clause of the second section of the third article of the Constitution is, *"The judicial power shall extend to controversies between a State and citizens of another State; between citizens of different States; between*

citizens of the same State, claiming lands under grants of different States; and between States, or the citizens thereof, and foreign States, citizens, or subjects." I do not think this clause has any considerable bearing upon the particular inquiry now under consideration. Its purpose was, to extend the judicial power to those controversies into which local feelings or interests might so enter as to disturb the course of justice, or give rise to suspicions that they had done so, and thus possibly give occasion to jealousy or ill will between different States, or a particular State and a foreign nation. At the same time, I would remark, in passing, that it has never been held, I do not know that it has ever been supposed, that any citizen of a State could bring himself under this clause and the eleventh and twelfth sections of the judiciary act of 1789, passed in pursuance of it, who was not a citizen of the United States. But I have referred to the clause, only because it is one of the places where citizenship is mentioned by the Constitution. Whether it is entitled to any weight in this inquiry or not, it refers only to citizenship of the several States; it recognizes that; but it does not recognize citizenship of the United States as something distinct therefrom.

As has been said, the purpose of this clause did not necessarily connect it with citizenship of the United States, even if that were something distinct from citizenship of the several States, in the contemplation of the Constitution. This cannot be said of other clauses of the Constitution, which I now proceed to refer to.

"The citizens of each State shall be entitled to all the privileges and immunities of citizens of the several States." Nowhere else in the Constitution is there anything concerning a general citizenship; but here, privileges and immunities to be enjoyed throughout the United States, under and by force of the national compact, are granted and secured. In selecting those who are to enjoy these national rights of citizenship, how are they described? As citizens of each State. It is to them these national rights are secured. The qualification for them is not to be looked for in any provision of the Constitution or laws of the United States. They are to be citizens of the several States, and, as such, the privileges and immunities of general citizenship, derived from and guaranteed by the Constitution, are to be enjoyed by them. It would seem that if it had been intended to constitute a class of native-born persons within the States, who should derive their citizenship of the United States from the action of the Federal Government, this was an occasion for referring to them. It cannot be supposed that it was the purpose of this article to confer the privileges and immunities of citizens in all the States upon persons not citizens of the United States.

And if it was intended to secure these rights only to citizens of the United States, how has the Constitution

here described such persons? Simply as citizens of each State.

But, further: though, as I shall presently more fully state, I do not think the enjoyment of the elective franchise essential to citizenship, there can be no doubt it is one of the chiefest attributes of citizenship under the American Constitutions; and the just and constitutional possession of this right is decisive evidence of citizenship. The provisions made by a Constitution on this subject must therefore be looked to as bearing directly on the question what persons are citizens under that Constitution; and as being decisive, to this extent, that all such persons as are allowed by the Constitution to exercise the elective franchise, and thus, to participate in the Government of the United States, must be deemed citizens of the United States.

Here, again, the consideration presses itself upon us, that if there was designed to be a particular class of native-born persons within the States, deriving their citizenship from the Constitution and laws of the United States, they should at least have been referred to as those by whom the President and House of Representatives were to be elected, and to whom they should be responsible.

Instead of that, we again find this subject referred to the laws of the several States. The electors of President are to be appointed in such manner as the Legislature of each State may direct, and the qualifications of electors of members of the House of Representatives shall be the same as for electors of the most numerous branch of the State Legislature.

Laying aside, then, the case of aliens, concerning which the Constitution of the United States has provided, and confining our view to free persons born within the several States, we find that the Constitution has recognized the general principle of public law, that allegiance and citizenship depend on the place of birth; that it has not attempted practically to apply this principle by designating the particular classes of persons who should or should not come under it; that when we turn to the Constitution for an answer to the question, what free persons, born within the several States, are citizens of the United States, the only answer we can receive from any of its express provisions is, the citizens of the several States are to enjoy the privileges and immunities of citizens in every State, and their franchise as electors under the Constitution depends on their citizenship in the several States. Add to this, that the Constitution was ordained by the citizens of the several States; that they were "the people of the United States," for whom and whose posterity the Government was declared in the preamble of the Constitution to be made; that each of them was a citizen of the United States at the time of the adoption of the Constitution," within the meaning of those words in that instrument;

that by them the Government was to be and was in fact organized; and that no power is conferred on the Government of the Union to discriminate between them, or to disfranchise any of them—the necessary conclusion is, that those persons born within the several States, who, by force of their respective Constitutions and laws, are citizens of the State, are thereby citizens of the United States.

It may be proper here to notice some supposed objections to this view of the subject.

It has been often asserted that the Constitution was made exclusively by and for the white race. It has already been shown that in five of the thirteen original States, colored persons then possessed the elective franchise, and were among those by whom the Constitution was ordained and established. If so, it is not true, in point of fact, that the Constitution was made exclusively by the white race. And that it was made exclusively for the white race is, in my opinion, not only an assumption not warranted by anything in the Constitution, but contradicted by its opening declaration, that it was ordained and established by the people of the United States, for themselves and their posterity. And as free colored persons were then citizens of at least five States, and so in every sense part of the people of the United States, they were among those for whom and whose posterity the Constitution was ordained and established.

Again, it has been objected, that if the Constitution has left to the several States the rightful power to determine who of their inhabitants shall be citizens of the United States, the States may make aliens citizens.

The answer is obvious. The Constitution has left to the States the determination what persons, born within their respective limits, shall acquire by birth citizenship of the United States; it has not left to them any power to prescribe any rule for the removal of the disabilities of alienage. This power is exclusively in Congress.

It has been further objected, that if free colored persons, born within a particular State, and made citizens of that State by its Constitution and laws, are thereby made citizens of the United States, then, under the second section of the fourth article of the Constitution, such persons would be entitled to all the privileges and immunities of citizens in the several States; and if so, then colored persons could vote, and be eligible to not only Federal offices, but offices even in those States whose Constitutions and laws disqualify colored persons from voting or being elected to office.

But this position rests upon an assumption which I deem untenable. Its basis is, that no one can be deemed a citizen of the United States who is not entitled to enjoy all the privileges and franchises which are conferred on any citizen. (See 1 Lit. Kentucky R., 326.)

That this is not true, under the Constitution of the United States, seems to me clear.

A naturalized citizen cannot be President of the United States, nor a Senator till after the lapse of nine years, nor a Representative till after the lapse of seven years, from his naturalization. Yet, as soon as naturalized, he is certainly a citizen of the United States. Nor is any inhabitant of the District of Columbia, or of either of the Territories, eligible to the office of Senator or Representative in Congress, though they may be citizens of the United States. So, in all the States, numerous persons, though citizens, cannot vote, or cannot hold office, either on account of their age, or sex, or the want of the necessary legal qualifications. The truth is, that citizenship, under the Constitution of the United States, is not dependent on the possession of any particular political or even of all civil rights; and any attempt so to define it must lead to error. To what citizens the elective franchise shall be confided, is a question to be determined by each State, in accordance with its own views of the necessities or expediencies of its condition. What civil rights shall be enjoyed by its citizens, and whether all shall enjoy the same, or how they may be gained or lost, are to be determined in the same way.

One may confine the right or suffrage to white male citizens; another may extend it to colored persons and females; one may allow all persons above a prescribed age to convey property and transact business; another may exclude married women. But whether native-born women, or persons under age, or under guardianship because insane or spendthrifts, be excluded from voting or holding office, or allowed to do so, I apprehend no one will deny that they are citizens of the United States. Besides, this clause of the Constitution does not confer on the citizens of one State, in all other States, specific and enumerated privileges and immunities. They are entitled to such as belong to citizenship, but not to such as belong to particular citizens attended by other qualifications. Privileges and immunities which belong to certain citizens of a State, by reason of the operation of causes other than mere citizenship, are not conferred. Thus, if the laws of a State require, in addition to citizenship of the State, some qualification for office, or the exercise of the elective franchise, citizens of all other States, coming thither to reside, and not possessing those qualifications, cannot enjoy those privileges, not because they are not to be deemed entitled to the privileges of citizens of the State in which they reside, but because they, in common with the native-born citizens of that State, must have the qualifications prescribed by law for the enjoyment of such privileges, under its Constitution and laws. It rests with the States themselves so to frame their Constitutions and laws as not to attach a particular privilege or immunity to mere naked citizenship. If one of the States will not deny to any of its own citizens a particular privilege or immunity, if it confer it on all of them by reason of mere naked citizenship, then it may be claimed by every citizen of each State by force of the Constitution; and it must be borne in mind, that the difficulties which attend the allowance of the claims of colored persons to be citizens of the United States are not avoided by saying that, though each State may make them its citizens, they are not thereby made citizens of the United States, because the privileges of general citizenship are secured to the citizens of each State. The language of the Constitution is, *"The citizens of each State shall be entitled to all privileges and immunities of citizens in the several States."* If each State may make such persons its citizens, they become, as such, entitled to the benefits of this article, if there be a native-born citizenship of the United States distinct from a native-born citizenship of the several States.

There is one view of this article entitled to consideration in this connection. It is manifestly copied from the fourth of the Articles of Confederation, with only slight changes of phraseology, which render its meaning more precise, and dropping the clause which excluded paupers, vagabonds, and fugitives from justice, probably because these cases could be dealt with under the police powers of the States, and a special provision therefor was not necessary. It has been suggested, that in adopting it into the Constitution, the words *"free inhabitants"* were changed for the word *"citizens."* An examination of the forms of expression commonly used in the State papers of that day, and an attention to the substance of this article of the Confederation, will show that the words *"free inhabitants,"* as then used, were synonymous with citizens. When the Articles of Confederation were adopted, we were in the midst of the war of the Revolution, and there were very few persons then embraced in the words *"free inhabitants,"* who were not born on our soil. It was not a time when many, save the children of the soil, were willing to embark their fortunes in our cause; and though there might be an inaccuracy in the uses of words to call free inhabitants citizens, it was then a technical rather than a substantial difference. If we look into the Constitutions and State papers of that period, we find the inhabitants or people of these colonies, or the inhabitants of this State, or Commonwealth, employed to designate those whom we should now denominate citizens. The substance and purpose of the article prove it was in this sense it used these words: it secures to the free inhabitants of each State the privileges and immunities of free citizens in every State. It is not conceivable that the States should have agreed to extend the privileges of citizenship to persons not entitled to enjoy the privileges of citizens in the States where they dwelt; that under this article

there was a class of persons in some of the States, not citizens, to whom were secured all the privileges and immunities of citizens when they went into other States; and the just conclusion is, that though the Constitution cured an inaccuracy of language, it left the substance of this article in the National Constitution the same as it was in the Articles of Confederation.

The history of this fourth article, respecting the attempt to exclude free persons of color from its operation, has been already stated. It is reasonable to conclude that this history was known to those who framed and adopted the Constitution. That under this fourth article of the Confederation, free persons of color might be entitled to the privileges of general citizenship, if otherwise entitled thereto, is clear. When this article was, in substance, placed in and made part of the Constitution of the United States, with no change in its language calculated to exclude free colored persons from the benefit of its provisions, the presumption is, to say the least, strong, that the practical effect which it was designed to have, and did have, under the former Government, it was designed to have, and should be further objected, that if free colored persons may be citizens of the United States, it depends only on the will of a master whether he will emancipate his slave, and thereby make him a citizen. Not so. The master is subject to the will of the State. Whether he shall be allowed to emancipate his slave at all; if so, on what conditions; and what is to be the political status of the freed man, depend, not on the will of the master, but on the will of the State, upon which the political status of all its native-born inhabitants depends. Under the Constitution of the United States, each State has retained this power of determining the political status of its native-born inhabitants, and no exception thereto can be found in the Constitution. And if a master in a slaveholding State should carry his slave into a free State, and there emancipate him, he would not thereby make him a native-born citizen of that State, and consequently no privileges could be claimed by such emancipated slave as a citizen of the United States. For, whatever powers the States may exercise to confer privileges of citizenship on persons not born on their soil, the Constitution of the United States does not recognize such citizens. As has already been said, it recognizes the great principle of public law, that allegiance and citizenship spring from the place of birth. It leaves to the States the application of that principle to individual cases. It secured to the citizens of each State the privileges and immunities of citizens in every other State. But it does not allow to the States the power to make aliens citizens, or permit one State to take persons born on the soil of another State, and, contrary to the laws and policy of the State where they were born, make them its citizens, and so citizens of the United States. No such deviation from the great rule of public law was contemplated by the Constitution; and when any such attempt shall be actually made, it is to be met by applying to it those rules of law and those principles of good faith which will be sufficient to decide it, and not, in my judgment, by denying that all the free native-born inhabitants of a State, who are its citizens under its Constitution and laws, are also citizens of the United States. It has sometimes been urged that colored persons are shown not to be citizens of the United States by the fact that the naturalization laws apply only to white persons. But whether a person born in the United States be or be not a citizen, cannot depend on laws which refer only to aliens, and do not affect the status of persons born in the United States. The utmost effect which can be attributed to them is, to show that Congress has not deemed it expedient generally to apply the rule to colored aliens. That they might do so, if thought fit, is clear. The Constitution has not excluded them. And since that has conferred the power on Congress to naturalize colored aliens, it certainly shows color is not a necessary qualification for citizenship under the Constitution of the United States. It may be added, that the power to make colored persons citizens of the United States, under the Constitution, has been actually exercised in repeated and important instances. (See the Treaties with the Choctaws, of September 27, 1830, art. 14; with the Cherokees, of May 23, 1836, art 12 Treaty of Guadalupe Hidalgo, February 2, 1848, art. 8.)

I do not deem it necessary to review at length the legislation of Congress having more or less bearing on the citizenship of colored persons. It does not seem to me to have any considerable tendency to prove that it has been considered by the legislative department of the Government, that no such persons are citizens of the United States. Undoubtedly they have been debarred from the exercise of particular rights or privileges extended to white persons, but, I believe, always in terms which, by implication, admit they may be citizens. Thus the act of May 17, 1792, for the organization of the militia, directs the enrolment of *"every free, able-bodied, white male citizen."* An assumption that none but white persons are citizens, would be as inconsistent with the just import of this language, as that all citizens are able-bodied, or males.

So the act of February 28, 1803, (2 Stat. at Large, 205,) to prevent the importation of certain persons into States, when by the laws thereof admission is prohibited, in its first section forbids all masters of vessels to import or bring *"any negro, mulatto, or other person of color, not being a native, a citizen, or registered seaman of the United States,"* &c.

The acts of March 3, 1813, section 1, (2 Stat. at Large, 809,) and March 1, 1817, section 3, (3 Stat. at Large, 351,) concerning seamen, certainly imply there

may be persons of color, natives of the United States, who are not citizens of the United States. This implication is undoubtedly in accordance with the fact. For not only slaves, but free persons of color, born in some of the States, are not citizens. But there is nothing in these laws inconsistent with the citizenship of persons of color in others of the States, nor with their being citizens of the United States.

Whether much or little weight should be attached to the particular phraseology of these and other laws, which were not passed with any direct reference to this subject, I consider their tendency to be, as already indicated, to show that, in the apprehension of their framers, color was not a necessary qualification of citizenship. It would be strange, if laws were found on our statute book to that effect, when, by solemn treaties, large bodies of Mexican and North American Indians as well as free colored inhabitants of Louisiana have been admitted to citizenship of the United States.

In the legislative debates which preceded the admission of the State of Missouri into the Union, this question was agitated. Its result is found in the resolution of Congress, of March 5, 1821, for the admission of that State into the Union. The Constitution of Missouri, under which that State applied for admission into the Union, provided, that it should be the duty of the Legislature *"to pass laws to prevent free negroes and mulattoes from coming to and settling in the State, under any pretext whatever."* One ground of objection to the admission of the State under this Constitution was, that it would require the Legislature to exclude free persons of color, who would be entitled, under the second section of the fourth article of the Constitution, not only to come within the State, but to enjoy there the privileges and immunities of citizens. The resolution of Congress admitting the State was upon the fundamental condition, *"that the Constitution of Missouri shall never be construed to authorize the passage of any law, and that no law shall be passed in conformity thereto, by which any citizen of either of the States of this Union shall be excluded from the enjoyment of any of the privileges and immunities to which such citizen is entitled under the Constitution of the United States."* It is true, that neither this legislative declaration, nor anything in the Constitution or laws of Missouri, could confer or take away any privilege or immunity granted by the Constitution. But it is also true, that it expresses the then conviction of the legislative power of the United States, that free negroes, as citizens of some of the States, might be entitled to the privileges and immunities of citizens in all the States.

The conclusions at which I have arrived on this part of the case are:

First.

That the free native-born citizens of each State are citizens of the United States.

Second.

That as free colored persons born within some of the States are citizens of those States, such persons are also citizens of the United States.

Third.

That every such citizen, residing in any State, has the right to sue and is liable to be used in the Federal courts, as a citizen of that State in which he resides.

Fourth.

That as the plea to the jurisdiction in this case shows no facts, except that the plaintiff was of African descent, and his ancestors were sold as slaves, and as these facts are not inconsistent with his citizenship of the United States, and his residence in the State of Missouri, the plea to the jurisdiction was bad, and judgment of the Circuit Court overruling it was correct.

I dissent, therefore, from that part of the opinion of the majority of the court, in which it is held that a person of African descent cannot be a citizen of the United States; and I regret I must go further, and dissent both from what I deem their assumption of authority to examine the constitutionality of the act of Congress commonly called the Missouri compromise act, and the grounds and conclusions announced in their opinion.

Having first decided that they were bound to consider the sufficiency of the plea to the jurisdiction of the Circuit Court, and having decided that this plea showed that the Circuit Court had not jurisdiction, and consequently that this is a case to which the judicial power of the United States does not extend, they have gone on to examine the merits of the case as they appeared on the trial before the court and jury, on the issues joined on the pleas in bar, and so have reached the question of the power of Congress to pass the act of 1820. On so grave a subject as this, I feel obliged to say that, in my opinion, such an exertion of judicial power transcends the limits of the authority of the court, as described by its repeated decisions, and, as I understand, acknowledged in this opinion of the majority of the court.

In the course of that opinion, it became necessary to comment on the case of Legrand v. Darnall, (reported in 2 Peters's R., 664.) In that case, a bill was filed, by one alleged to be a citizen of Maryland, against one alleged to be a citizen of Pennsylvania. The bill stated that the defendant was the son of a white man by one of his slaves; and that the defendant's father devised to him certain lands, the title to which was put in controversy by the bill. These facts were admitted in the answer, and upon these and other facts the court made its decree, founded on the principle that a devise of land by a master to a slave was by implication also a bequest of his freedom. The facts that the defendant was of African descent, and was born a slave, were not only before the court, but entered into the entire substance of its inquires. The opinion of the majority of my brethren in this case disposes of the case of Legrand v. Darnall, by saying, among other things, that as the fact that the defendant was born a slave only came before this court on the bill and answer, it was then too late to raise the question of the personal disability of the party, and therefore that decision is altogether inapplicable in this case.

In this I concur. Since the decision of this court in Livingston v. Story, (11 Pet., 351,) the law has been settled, that when the declaration or bill contains the necessary averments of citizenship, this court cannot look at the record, to see whether those averments are true, except so far as they are put in issue by a plea to the jurisdiction. In that case, the defendant denied by his answer that Mr. Livingston was a citizen of New York, as he had alleged in the bill. Both parties went into proofs. The court refused to examine those proofs, with reference to the personal disability of the plaintiff. This is the settled law of the court, affirmed so lately as Shepherd v. Graves, (14 How., 27,) and Wickliff v. Owings, (17 How., 51.) (See also De Wolf v. Rabaud, 1 Pet., 476.) But I do not understand this to be a rule which the court may depart from at its pleasure. If it be a rule, it is as binding on the court as on the suitors. If it removes from the latter the power to take any objection to the personal disability of a party alleged by the record to be competent, which is not shown by a plea to the jurisdiction, it is because the court are forbidden by law to consider and decide on objections so taken. I do not consider it to be within the scope of the judicial power of the majority of the court to pass upon any question respecting the plaintiff's citizenship in Missouri, save that raised by the plea to the jurisdiction; and I do not hold any opinion of this court, or any court, binding, when expressed on a question not legitimately before it. (Carroll v. Carroll, 16 How., 275.) The judgment of this court is, that the case is to be dismissed for want of jurisdiction, because the plaintiff was not a citizen of Missouri, as he alleged in his declaration. Into that judgment, according to the settled course of this court, nothing appearing after a plea to the merits can enter. A great question of constitutional law, deeply affecting the peace and welfare of the country, is not, in my opinion, a fit subject to be thus reached.

But as, in my opinion, the Circuit Court had jurisdiction, I am obliged to consider the question whether its judgment on the merits of the case should stand or be reversed.

The residence of the plaintiff in the State of Illinois, and the residence of himself and his wife in the territory acquired from France lying north of latitude thirty-six degrees thirty minutes, and other of the State of Missouri, are each relied on by the plaintiff in error. As

the residence in the territory affects the plaintiff's wife and children as well as himself, I must inquire what was its effect.

The general question may be stated to be, whether the plaintiff's status, as a slave, was so changed by his residence within that territory, that he was not a slave in the State of Missouri, at the time this action was brought.

In such cases, two inquiries arise, which may be confounded, but should be kept distinct.

The first is, what was the law of the Territory into which the master and slave went, respecting the relation between them?

The second is, whether the State of Missouri recognizes and allows the effect of that law of the Territory, on the status of the slave, on his return within its jurisdiction.

As to the first of these questions, the will of States and nations, by whose municipal law slavery is not recognized, has been manifested in three different ways.

One is, absolutely to dissolve the relation, and terminate the rights of the master existing under the law of the country whence the parties came. This is said by Lord Stowell, in the case of the slave Grace, (2 Hag. Ad. R., 94,) and by the Supreme Court of Louisiana in the case of Maria Louise v. Marot, (9 Louis, R., 473,) to be the law of France; and it has been the law of several States of this Union, in respect to slaves introduced under certain conditions. (Wilson v. Isabel, 5 Call's R., 430; Hunter v. Hulcher, 1 Leigh, 172; Stewart v. Oaks, 5 Har. and John., 107.)

The second is, where the municipal law of a country not recognizing slavery, it is the will of the State to refuse the master all aid to exercise any control over his slave; and if he attempt to do so, in a manner justifiable only by that relation, to prevent the exercise of that control. But no law exists, designed to operate directly on the relation of master and slave, and put an end to that relation. This is said by Lord Stowell, in the case above mentioned, to be the law of England, and by Mr. Chief Justice Shaw, in the case of the Commonwealth v. Aves, (18 Pick., 193,) to be the law of Massachusetts.

The third is, to make a distinction between the case of a master and his slave only temporarily in the country, animo non manendi, and those who are there to reside for permanent or indefinite purposes. This is said by Mr. Wheaton to be the law of Prussia, and was formerly the statute law of several States of our Union. It is necessary in this case to keep in view this distinction between those countries whose laws are designed to act directly on the status of a slave, and make him a freeman, and those where his master can obtain no aid from the laws to enforce his rights.

It is to the last case only that the authorities, out of Missouri, relied on by defendant, apply, when the residence in the non-slaveholding Territory was permanent. In the Commonwealth v. Aves, (18 Pick., 218,) Mr. Chief Justice Shaw said: *"From the principle above stated, on which a slave brought here becomes free, to wit: that he becomes entitled to the protection of our laws, it would seem to follow, as a necessary conclusion, that if the slave waives the protection of those laws, and returns to the State where he is held as a slave, his condition is not changed."* It was upon this ground, as is apparent from his whole reasoning, that Sir William Scott rests his opinion in the case of the slave Grace. To use one of his expressions, the effect of the law of England was to put the liberty of the slave into a parenthesis. If there had been an act of Parliament declaring that a slave coming to England with his master should thereby be deemed no longer to be a slave, it is easy to see that the learned judge could not have arrived at the same conclusion. This distinction is very clearly stated and shown by President Tucker, in his opinion in the case of Betty v. Horton, (5 Leigh's Virginia R., 615) (See also Hunter v. Fletcher, 1 Leigh's Va. R., 172; Maria Louise v. Marot, 9 Louisiana R.; Smith v. Smith, 13 Ib., 441; Thomas v. Genevieve, 16 Ib., 483; Rankin v. Lydia, 2 A.K. Marshall, 467; Davies v. Tingle, 8 B. Munroe, 539; Griffeth v. Fanny, Gilm. Va. R., 143; Lumford v. Coquillon, 14 Martin's La. R., 405; Josephine v. Poultney, 1 Louis. Ann. R., 329.)

But if the acts of Congress on this subject are valid, the law of the Territory of Wisconsin, within whose limits the residence of the plaintiff and his wife, and their marriage and the birth of one or both of their children, took place, falls under the first category, and is a law operating directly on the status of the slave. By the eighth section of the act of March 6, 1820, (3 Stat. at Large, 548,) it was enacted that, within this Territory, *"slavery and involuntary servitude, otherwise than in the punishment of crimes, whereof the parties shall have been duly convicted, shall be, and is hereby, forever prohibited: Provided, always, that any person escaping into the same, from whom labor or service is lawfully claimed in any State or Territory of the United States, such fugitive may be lawfully reclaimed, and conveyed to the person claiming his or her labor or service, as aforesaid."*

By the act of April 20, 1836, (4 Stat. at Large, 10,) passed in the same month and year of the removal of the plaintiff to Fort Snelling, this part of the territory ceded by France, where Fort Snelling is, together with so much of the territory of the United States east of the Mississippi as now constitutes the State of Wisconsin, was brought under a Territorial Government, under the name of the Territory of Wisconsin. By the eighteenth section of this act, it was enacted, *"That the inhabitants of this Territory shall be entitled to and enjoy all and singular the rights, privileges, and advantages, granted and secured to the people of the Territory of the United States*

northwest of the river Ohio, by the articles of compact contained in the ordinance for the government of said Territory, passed on the 13th day of July, 1787; and shall be subject to all the restriction and prohibitions in said articles of compact imposed upon the people of the said Territory." The sixth article of that compact is, *"there shall be neither slavery nor involuntary servitude in the said Territory, otherwise than in the punishment of crimes, whereof the party shall have been duly convicted. Provided, always, that any person escaping into the same, from whom labor or service is lawfully claimed in any one of the original States, such fugitive may be lawfully reclaimed, and conveyed to the person claiming his or her labor or service, as aforesaid."* By other provisions of this act establishing the Territory of Wisconsin, the laws of the United States, and the then existing laws of the State of Michigan, are extended over the Territory; the latter being subject to alteration and repeal by the legislative power of the Territory created by the act.

Fort Snelling was within the Territory of Wisconsin, and these laws were extended over it. The Indian title to that site for a military post had been acquired from the Sioux nation as early as September 23, 1805, (Am State Papers, Indian Affaires, vol. 1, p. 744,) and until the erection of the Territorial Government, the persons at that post were governed by the rules and articles of war, and such laws of the United States, including the eighth section of the act of March 6, 1820, prohibiting slavery, as were applicable to their condition; but after the erection of the Territory, and the extension of the laws of the United States and the laws of Michigan over the whole of the Territory, including this military post, the persons residing there were under the dominion of those laws in all particulars to which the rules and articles of war did not apply.

It thus appears that, by these acts of Congress, not only was a general system of municipal law borrowed from the State of Michigan, which did not tolerate slavery, but it was positively enacted that slavery and involuntary servitude, with only one exception, specifically described, should not exist there. It is not simply that slavery is not recognized and cannot be aided by the municipal law. It is recognised for the purpose of being absolutely prohibited, and declared incapable of existing within the Territory, save in the instance of a fugitive slave.

It would not be easy for the Legislature to employ more explicit language to signify its will that the status of slavery should not exist within the Territory, than the words found in the act of 1820, and in the ordinance of 1787; and if any doubt could exist concerning their application to cases of masters coming into the Territory with their slaves to reside, that doubt must yield to the inference required by the words of exception. That exception is, of cases of fugitive slaves. An

exception from a prohibition marks the extent of the prohibition; for it would be absurd, as well as useless, to except from a prohibition a case not contained within it. (9 Wheat., 200.) I must conclude, therefore, that it was the will of Congress that the state of involuntary servitude of a slave, coming into the Territory with his master, should cease to exist. The Supreme Court of Missouri so held in Rachel v. Walker, (4 Misso. R., 350,) which was the case of a military officer going into the Territory with two slaves.

But it is a distinct question, whether the law of Missouri recognised and allowed effect to the change wrought in the status of the plaintiff, by force of the laws of the Territory of Wisconsin. I say the law of Missouri, because a judicial tribunal, in one State or nation, can recognise personal rights acquired by force of the law of any other State or nation, only so far as it is the law of the former State that those rights should be recognised. But, in the absence of positive law to the contrary, the will of every civilized State must be presumed to be to allow such effect to foreign laws as is in accordance with the settled rules of international law. And legal tribunals are bound to act on this presumption. It may be assumed that the motive of the State in allowing such operation to foreign laws is what has been termed comity. But, as has justly been said, (per Chief Justice Taney, 13 Pet., 589,) it is the comity of the State, not of the court. The judges have nothing to do with the motive of the State. Their duty is simply to ascertain and give effect to its will. And when it is found by them that its will to depart from a rule of international law has not been manifested by the State, they are bound to assume that its will is to give effect to it. Undoubtedly, every sovereign State may refuse to recognise a change, wrought by the law of a foreign State, on the status of a person, while within such foreign State, even in cases where the rules of international law require that recognition. Its will to refuse such recognition may be manifested by what we term statute law, or by the customary law of the State. It is within the province of its judicial tribunals to inquire and adjudge whether it appears, from the statute or customary law of the State, to be the will of the State to refuse to recognise such changes of status by force of foreign law, as the rules of the law of nations require to be recognised. But, in my opinion, it is not within the province of any judicial tribunal to refuse such recognition from any political considerations, or any view it may take of the exterior political relations between the State and one or more foreign States, or any impressions it may have that a change of foreign opinion and action on the subject of slavery may afford a reason why the State should change its own action. To understand and give just effect to such considerations, and to change the action of the State in consequence of them, are functions of diplomatists and legislators, not of judges.

The inquiry to be made on this part of the case is, therefore, whether the State of Missouri has, by its statute, or its customary law, manifested its will to displace any rule of international law, applicable to a change of the status of a slave, by foreign law.

I have not heard it suggested that there was any statute of the State of Missouri bearing on this question. The customary law of Missouri is the common law, introduced by statute in 1816. (1 Ter. Laws, 436.) And the common law, as Blackstone says, (4 Com., 67,) adopts, in its full extent, the law of nations, and holds it to be a part of the law of the land.

I know of no sufficient warrant for declaring that any rule of international law, concerning the recognition, in that State, of a change of status, wrought by an extra-territorial law, has been displaced or varied by the will of the State of Missouri.

I proceed then to inquire what the rules of international law prescribe concerning the change of status of the plaintiff wrought by the law of the Territory of Wisconsin.

It is generally agreed by writers upon international law, and the rule has been judicially applied in a great number of cases, that wherever any question may arise concerning the status of a person, it must be determined according to that law which has next previously rightfully operated on and fixed that status. And, further, that the laws of a country do not rightfully operate upon and fix the status of persons who are within its limits in itinere, or who are abiding there for definite temporary purposes, as for health, curiosity, or occasional business; that these laws, known to writers on public and private international law as personal statutes, operate only on the inhabitants of the country. Not that it is or can be denied that each independent nation may, if it thinks fit, apply them to all persons within their limits. But when this is done, not in conformity with the principles of international law, other States are not understood to be willing to recognise or allow effect to such applications of personal statutes.

It becomes necessary, therefore, to inquire whether the operation of the laws of the Territory of Wisconsin upon the status of the plaintiff was or was not such an operation as these principles of international law require other States to recognise and allow effect to.

And this renders it needful to attend to the particular facts and circumstances of this case.

It appears that this case came on for trial before the Circuit Court and a jury, upon an issue, in substance, whether the plaintiff, together with his wife and children, were the slaves of the defendant.

The court instructed the jury that, *"upon the facts in this case, the law is with the defendant."* This withdrew from the jury the consideration and decision of every matter of fact. The evidence in the case consisted of written admissions, signed by the counsel of the parties. If the case had been submitted to the judgment of the court, upon an agreed statement of facts, entered of record, in place of a special verdict, it would have been necessary for the court below, and for this court, to pronounce its judgment solely on those facts, thus agreed, without inferring any other facts therefrom. By the rules of the common law applicable to such a case, and by force of the seventh article of the amendments of the Constitution, this court is precluded from finding any fact not agreed to by the parties on the record. No submission to the court on a statement of facts was made. It was a trial by jury, in which certain admissions, made by the parties, were the evidence. The jury were not only competent, but were bound to draw from that evidence every inference which, in their judgment, exercised according to the rules of law, it would warrant. The Circuit Court took from the jury the power to draw any inferences from the admissions made by the parties, and decided the case for the defendant. This course can be justified here, if at all, only by its appearing that upon the facts agreed, and all such inferences of fact favorable to the plaintiff's case, as the jury might have been warranted in drawing from those admissions, the law was with the defendant. Otherwise, the plaintiff would be deprived of the benefit of his trial by jury, by whom, for aught we can know, those inferences favorable to his case would have been drawn.

The material facts agreed, bearing on this part of the case, are, that Dr. Emerson, the plaintiff's master, resided about two years at the military post of Fort Snelling, being a surgeon in the army of the United States, his domicil of origin being unknown; and what, if anything, he had done, to preserve or change his domicil prior to his residence at Rock Island, being also unknown.

Now, it is true, that under some circumstances the residence of a military officer at a particular place, in the discharge of his official duties, does not amount to the acquisition of a technical domicil. But it cannot be affirmed, with correctness, that it never does. There being actual residence, and this being presumptive evidence of domicil, all the circumstances of the case must be considered, before a legal conclusion can be reached, that his place of residence is not his domicil. If a military officer stationed at a particular post should entertain an expectation that his residence there would be indefinitely protracted, and in consequence should remove his family to the place where his duties were to be discharged, from a permanent domestic establishment there, exercise there the civil rights and discharge the civil duties of an inhabitant, while he did no act and manifested no intent to have a domicil elsewhere,

I think no one would say that the mere fact that he was himself liable to be called away by the orders of the Government would prevent his acquisition of a technical domicil at the place of the residence of himself and his family. In other words, I do not think a military officer incapable of acquiring a domicil. (Bruce v. Bruce, 2 Bos. and Pul., 230; Munroe v. Douglass, 5 Mad. Ch. R., 232.) This being so, this case stands thus: there was evidence before the jury that Emerson resided about two years at Fort Snelling, in the Territory of Wisconsin. This may or may not have been with such intent as to make it his technical domicil. The presumption is that it was. It is so laid down by this court, in Ennis v. Smith, (14 How.,) and the authorities in support of the position are there referred to. His intent was a question of fact for the jury. (Fitchburg v. Winchendon, 4 Cush., 190.)

The case was taken from the jury. If they had power to find that the presumption of the necessary intent had not been rebutted, we cannot say, on this record, that Emerson had not his technical domicil at Fort Snelling. But, for reasons which I shall now proceed to give, I do not deem it necessary in this case to determine the question of the technical domicil of Dr. Emerson.

It must be admitted that the inquiry whether the law of a particular country has rightfully fixed the status of a person, so that in accordance with the principles of international law that status should be recognised in other jurisdictions, ordinarily depends on the question whether the person was domiciled in the country whose laws are asserted to have fixed his status. But, in the United States, questions of this kind may arise, where an attempt to decide solely with reference to technical domicil, tested by the rules which are applicable to changes of places of abode from one country to another, would not be consistent with sound principles. And, in my judgment, thus is one of those cases.

The residence of the plaintiff, who was taken by his master, Dr. Emerson, as a slave, from Missouri to the State of Illinois, and thence to the Territory of Wisconsin, must be deemed to have been for the time being, and until he asserted his own separate intention, the same as the residence of his master; and the inquiry, whether the personal statutes of the Territory were rightfully extended over the plaintiff, and ought, in accordance with the rules of international law, to be allowed to fix has status, must depend upon the circumstances under which Dr. Emerson went into that Territory, and remained there; and upon the further question, whether anything was there rightfully done by the plaintiff to cause those personal statutes to operate on him.

Dr. Emerson was an officer in the army of the United States. He went into the Territory to discharge his duty to the United States. The place was out of the jurisdiction of any particular State, and within the exclusive jurisdiction of the United States. It does not appear where the domicil of origin of Dr. Emerson was, nor whether or not he had lost it, and gained another domicil, nor of what particular State, if any, he was a citizen.

On what ground can it be denied that all valid laws of the United States, constitutionally enacted by Congress for the government of the Territory, rightfully extended over an officer of the United States and his servant who went into the Territory to remain there for an indefinite length of time, to take part in its civil or military affairs? They were not foreigners, coming from abroad. Dr. Emerson was a citizen of the country which had exclusive jurisdiction over the Territory; and not only a citizen, but he went there in a public capacity, in the service of the same sovereignty which made the laws. Whatever those laws might be, whether, of the kind denominated personal statutes, or not, so far as they were intended by the legislative will, constitutionally expressed, to operate on him and his servant, and on the relations between them, they had a rightful operation, and no other State or country can refuse to allow that those laws might rightfully operate on the plaintiff and his servant, because such a refusal would be a denial that the United States could, by laws constitutionally enacted, govern their own servants, residing on their own Territory, over which the United States had the exclusive control, and in respect to which they are an independent sovereign power. Whether the laws now in question were constitutionally enacted, I repeat once more, is a separate question. But, assuming that they were, and that they operated directly on the status of the plaintiff, I consider that no other State or country could question the rightful power of the United States so to legislate, or, consistently with the settled rules of international law, could refuse to recognise the effects of such legislation upon the status of their officers and servants, as valid everywhere.

This alone would, in my apprehension, be sufficient to decide this question.

But there are other facts stated on the record which should not be passed over. It is agreed that, in the year 1836, the plaintiff, while residing in the Territory, was married, with the consent of Dr. Emerson, to Harriet, named in the declaration as his wife, and that Eliza and Lizzie were the children of that marriage, the first named having been born on the Mississippi river, north of the line of Missouri, and the other having been born after their return to Missouri. And the inquiry is, whether, after the marriage of the plaintiff in the Territory, with the consent of Dr. Emerson, any other State or Country can, consistently with the settled rules of international law, refuse to recognise and treat him as a free man, when suing for the liberty of himself, his wife, and the children of that marriage. It is in reference to his status, as viewed in other States and countries, that the contract of marriage and the birth of children becomes strictly material. At the same time, it is proper to observe that the female to whom he was married having been taken to the same military post of Fort Snelling as a slave, and Dr. Emerson claiming also to be her master at the time of her marriage, her status, and that of the children of the marriage, are also affected by the same considerations.

If the laws of Congress governing the Territory of Wisconsin were constitutional and valid laws, there can be no doubt these parties were capable of contracting a lawful marriage, attended with all the usual civil rights and obligations of that condition. In that Territory they were absolutely free persons, having full capacity to enter into the civil contract of marriage.

It is a principle of international law, settled beyond controversy in England and America, that a marriage, valid by the law of the place where it was contracted, and not in fraud of the law of any other place, is valid everywhere; and that no technical domicil at the place of the contract is necessary to make it so. (See Bishop on Mar. and Div., 125-129, where the cases are collected.)

If, in Missouri, the plaintiff were held to be a slave, the validity and operation of his contract of marriage must be denied. He can have no legal rights; of course, not those of a husband and father. And the same is true of his wife and children. The denial of his rights is the denial of theirs. So that, though lawfully married in the Territory, when they came out of it, into the State of Missouri, they were no longer husband and wife; and a child of that lawful marriage, though born under the same dominion where its parents contracted a lawful marriage, is not the fruit of that marriage, nor the child of its father, but subject to the maxim, partus sequitur ventrem.

It must be borne in mind that in this case there is no ground for the inquiry, whether it be the will of the State of Missouri not to recognise the validity of the marriage of a fugitive slave, who escapes into a State or country where slavery is not allowed, and there contracts a marriage; or the validity of such a marriage, where the master, being a citizen of the State of Missouri, voluntarily goes with his slave, in itinere, into a State or country which does not permit slavery to exist, and the slave there contracts marriage without the consent of his master; for in this case, it is agreed, Dr. Emerson did consent; and no further question can arise concerning his rights, so far as their assertion is inconsistent with the validity of the marriage. Nor do I know of any ground for the assertion that this marriage was in fraud of any law of Missouri. It has been held by this court, that a bequest of property by a master to his slave, by necessary implication entitles the slave to his freedom; because, only as a freeman could he take and hold the bequest. (Legrand v. Darnall, 2 Pet. R., 664.) It has also been held, that when a master goes with his

slave to reside for an indefinite period in a State where slavery is not tolerated, this operates as an act of manumission; because it is sufficiently expressive of the consent of the master that the slave should be free. (2 Marshall's Ken. R., 470; 14 Martin's Louis. R., 401.)

What, then, shall we say of the consent of the master, that the slave may contract a lawful marriage, attended with all the civil rights and duties which belong to that relation; that he may enter into a relation which none but a free man can assume—a relation which involves not only the rights and duties of the slave, but those of the other party to the contract, and of their descendants to the remotest generation? In my judgment, there can be no more effectual abandonment of the legal rights of a master over his slave, than by the consent of the master that the slave should enter into a contract of marriage, in a free State, attended by all the civil rights and obligations which belong to that condition.

And any claim by Dr. Emerson, or any one claiming under him, the effect of which is to deny the validity of this marriage, and the lawful paternity of the children born from it, wherever asserted, is, in my judgment, a claim inconsistent with good faith and sound reason, as well as with the rules of international law. And I go further: in my opinion, a law of the State of Missouri, which should thus annul a marriage, lawfully contracted by these parties while resident in Wisconsin, not in fraud of any law of Missouri, or of any right of Dr. Emerson, who consented thereto, would be a law impairing the obligation of a contract, and within the prohibition of the Constitution of the United States. (See 4 Wheat., 629, 695, 696.)

To avoid misapprehension on this important and difficult subject, I will state, distinctly, the conclusions at which I have arrived. They are:

First.

The rules of international law respecting the emancipation of slaves, by the rightful operation of the laws of another State or country upon the status of the slave, while resident in such foreign State or country, are part of the common law of Missouri, and have not been abrogated by any statute law of that State.

Second.

The laws of the United States, constitutionally enacted, which operated directly on and changed the status of a slave coming into the Territory of Wisconsin with his master, who went thither to reside for an indefinite length of time, in the performance of his duties as an officer of the United States, had a rightful operation on the status of the slave, and it is in conformity with the rules of international law that this change of status should be recognised everywhere.

Third.

The laws of the United States, in operation in the Territory of Wisconsin at the time of the plaintiff's residence there, did act directly on the status of the plaintiff, and change his status to that of a free man.

Fourth.

The plaintiff and his wife were capable of contracting, and, with the consent of Dr. Emerson, did contract a marriage in that Territory, valid its laws; and the validity of this marriage cannot be questioned in Missouri, save by showing that it was in fraud of the laws of that State, or of some right derived from them; which cannot be shown in this case, because the master consented to it.

Fifth.

That the consent of the master that his slave, residing in a country which does not tolerate slavery, may enter into a lawful contract of marriage, attended with the civil rights and duties which belong to that condition, is an effectual act of emancipation. And the law does not enable Dr. Emerson, or any one claiming under him, to assert a title to the married persons as slaves, and thus destroy the obligation of the contract of marriage, and bastardize their issue, and reduce them to slavery.

But it is insisted that the Supreme Court of Missouri has settled this case by its decision in Scott v. Emerson, (15 Missouri Reports, 576;) and that this decision is in conformity with the weight of authority elsewhere, and with sound principles. If the Supreme Court of Missouri had placed its decision on the ground that it appeared Dr. Emerson never became domiciled in the Territory, and so its laws could not rightfully operate on him and his slave; and the facts that he went there to reside indefinitely, as an officer of the United States, and that the plaintiff was lawfully married there, with Dr. Emerson's consent, were left out of view, the decision would find support in other cases, and I might not be prepared to deny its correctness. But the decision is not rested on this ground. The domicil of Dr. Emerson in that Territory is not questioned in that decision; and it is placed on a broad denial of the operation, in Missouri, of the law of any foreign State or country upon the status of a slave, going with his master from Missouri into foreign State or country, even though they went thither to become, and actually became, permanent inhabitants of such foreign State or country, the laws whereof acted directly on the status of the slave, and changed his status to that of a freeman.

To the correctness of such a decision I cannot assent. In my judgment, the opinion of the majority of the court in that case is in conflict with its previous decisions, with a great weight of judicial authority in other slaveholding States, and with fundamental principles of private international law. Mr. Chief Justice Gamble, in his dissenting opinion in that case, said:

"I regard the question as conclusively settled by repeated adjudications of this court; and if I doubted or denied the propriety of those decisions, I would not feel myself any more at liberty to overturn them, than I would any other series of decisions by which the law upon any other question had been settled. There is with me nothing in the law of slavery which distinguishes it from the law on any other subject, or allows any more accommodation to the temporary excitements which have gathered around it. But in the midst of all such excitement, it is proper that the judicial mind, calm and self-balanced, should adhere to principles established when there was no feeling to disturb the view of the legal questions upon which the rights of parties depend."

"In this State, it has been recognised from the beginning of the Government as a correct position in law, that the master who takes his slave to reside in a State or Territory where slavery is prohibited, thereby emancipates his slave." (Winney v. Whitesides, 1 Mo., 743; Le Grange v. Chouteau, 2 Mo., 20; Milley v. Smith, Ib., 36; Ralph v. Duncan, 3 Mo., 194; Julia v. McKinney, Ib., 270; Nat v. Ruddle, Ib., 400; Rachel v. Walker, 4 Mo., 350; Wilson v. Melvin, 592.)

Chief Justice Gamble has also examined the decisions of the courts of other States in which slavery is established, and finds them in accordance with these preceding decisions of the Supreme Court of Missouri to which he refers.

It would be a useless parade of learning for me to go over the ground which he has so fully and ably occupied.

But it is further insisted we are bound to follow this decision. I do not think so. In this case, it is to be determined what laws of the United States were in operation in the Territory of Wisconsin, and what was their effect on the status of the plaintiff. Could the plaintiff contract a lawful marriage there? Does any law of the State of Missouri impair the obligation of that contract of marriage, destroy his rights as a husband, bastardize the issue of the marriage, and reduce them to a state of slavery?

These questions, which arise exclusively under the Constitution and laws of the United States, this court, under the Constitution and laws of the United States, has the rightful authority finally to decide. And if we look beyond these questions, we come to the consideration whether the rules of international law, which are part of the laws of Missouri until displaced by some statute not alleged to exist, do or do not require the status of the plaintiff, as fixed by the laws of the Territory of Wisconsin, to be recognised in Missouri. Upon such a question, not depending on any statute or local usage, but on principles of universal jurisprudence, this court has repeatedly asserted it could not hold itself bound by the decisions of State courts, however great respect might be felt for their learning, ability, and impartiality. (See Swift v. Tyson, 16 Peters's R., 1; Carpenter v. Whe Providence Ins. Co., Ib., 495; Foxcroft v. Mallet, 4 How., 353; Rowan v. Runnels, 5 How., 134.)

Some reliance has been placed on the fact that the decision in the Supreme Court of Missouri was between these parties, and the suit there was abandoned to obtain another trial in the courts of the United States.

In Homer v. Brown, (16 How., 354) this court made a decision upon the construction of a devise of lands, in direct opposition to the unanimous opinion of the Supreme Court of Massachusetts, between the same parties, respecting the same subject-matter—the claimant having become nonsuit in the State court, in order to bring his action in the Circuit Court of the United States. I did not sit in that case, having been of counsel for one of the parties while at the bar; but, on examining the report of the argument of the counsel for the plaintiff in error, I find they made the point, that this court ought to give effect to the construction put upon the will by the State court, to the end that rights respecting lands may be governed by one law, and that the law of the place where the lands are situated; that they referred to the State decision of the case, reported in 3 Cushing, 390, and to many decisions of this court. But this court does not seem to have considered the point of sufficient importance to notice it in their opinions. In Millar v. Austin, (13 How., 218,) an action was brought by the endorsee of a written promise. The question was, whether it was negotiable under a statute of Ohio. The Supreme Court of that State having decided it was not negotiable, the plaintiff became nonsuit, and brought his action in the Circuit Court of the United States. The decision of the Supreme Court of the State, reported in 4 Ves., L.J., 527, was relied on. This court unanimously held the paper to be negotiable.

When the decisions of the highest court of a State are directly in conflict with each other, it has been repeatedly held, here, that the last decision is not necessarily to be taken as the rule. (State Bank v. Knoop, 16 How., 369; Pease v. Peck, 18 How., 599.)

To these considerations I desire to add, that it was not made known to the Supreme Court of Missouri, so far as appears, that the plaintiff was married in Wisconsin with the consent of Dr. Emerson, and it is not made known to us that Dr. Emerson was a citizen of Missouri, a fact to which that court seem to have attached much importance.

Sitting here to administer the law between these parties, I do not feel at liberty to surrender my own convictions of what the law requires, to the authority of the decision in 15 Missouri Reports.

I have thus far assumed, merely for the purpose of the argument, that the laws of the United States,

respecting slavery in this Territory, were constitutionally enacted by Congress. It remains to inquire whether they are constitutional and binding laws.

In the argument of this part of the case at bar, it was justly considered by all the counsel to be necessary to ascertain the source of the power of Congress over the territory belonging to the United States. Until this is ascertained, it is not possible to determine the extent of that power. On the one side it was maintained that the Constitution contains no express grant of power to organize and govern what is now known to the laws of the United States as a Territory. That whatever power of this kind exists, is derived by implication from the capacity of the United States to hold and acquire territory out of the limits of any State, and the necessity for its having some government

On the other side, it was insisted that the Constitution has not failed to make an express provision for this end, and that it is found in the third section of the fourth article of the Constitution.

To determine which of these is the correct view, it is needful to advert to some facts respecting this subject, which existed when the Constitution was framed and adopted. It will be found that these facts not only shed much light on the question, whether the framers of the Constitution omitted to make a provision concerning the power of Congress to organize and govern Territories, but they will also aid in the construction of any provision which may have been made respecting this subject.

Under the Confederation, the unsettled territory within the limits of the United States had been a subject of deep interest. Some of the States insisted that these lands were within their chartered boundaries, and that they had succeeded to the title of the Crown to the soil. On the other hand, it was argued that the vacant lands had been acquired by the United States, by the war carried on by them under a common Government and for the common interest.

This dispute was further complicated by unsettled questions of boundary among several States. It not only delayed the accession of Maryland to the Confederation, but at one time seriously threatened its existence. (5 Jour. of Cong., 208, 442.) Under the pressure of these circumstances, Congress earnestly recommended to the several States a cession of their claims and rights to the United States. (5 Jour. of Cong., 442.) And before the Constitution was framed, it had been begun. That by New York had been made on the 1st day of March, 1781; that of Virginia on the 1st day of March, 1784; that of Massachusetts on the 19th day of April, 1785; that of Connecticut on the 14th day of September, 1786; that of South Carolina on the 8th day of August, 1787, while the Convention for framing the Constitution was in session.

It is very material to observe, in this connection, that each of these acts cedes, in terms, to the United States, as well the jurisdiction as the soil.

It is also equally important to note that, when the Constitution was framed and adopted, this plan of vesting in the United States, for the common good, the great tracts of ungranted lands claimed by the several States, in which so deep an interest was felt, was yet incomplete. It remained for North Carolina and Georgia to cede their extensive and valuable claims. These were made, by North Carolina on the 25th day of February, 1790, and by Georgia on the 24th day of April, 1802. The terms of these last-mentioned cessions will hereafter be noticed in another connection; but I observe here that each of them distinctly shows, upon its face, that they were not only in execution of the general plan proposed by the Congress of the Confederation, but of a formed purpose of each of these States, existing when the assent of their respective people was given to the Constitution of the United States.

It appears, then, that when the Federal Constitution was framed, and presented to the people of the several States for their consideration, the unsettled territory was viewed as justly applicable to the common benefit, so far as it then had or might attain thereafter a pecuniary value; and so far as it might become the seat of new States, to be admitted into the Union upon an equal footing with the original States. And also that the relations of the United States to that unsettled territory were of different kinds. The titles of the States of New York, Virginia, Massachusetts, Connecticut, and South Carolina, as well of soil as of jurisdiction, had been transferred to the United States. North Carolina and Georgia had not actually made transfers, but a confident expectation, founded on their appreciation of the justice of the general claim, and fully justified by the results, was entertained, that these cessions would be made. The ordinance of 1787 had made provision for the temporary government of so much of the territory actually ceded as lay northwest of the river Ohio.

But it must have been apparent, both to the framers of the Constitution and the people of the several States who were to act upon it, that the Government thus provided for could not continue, unless the Constitution should confer on the United States the necessary powers to continue it. That temporary Government, under the ordinance was to consist of certain officers, to be appointed by and responsible to the Congress of the Confederation; their powers had been conferred and defined by the ordinance. So far as it provided for the temporary government of the Territory, it was an ordinary act of legislation, deriving its force from the legislative power of Congress, and depending for its vitality upon the continuance of that legislative power. But the officers to be appointed for the Northwestern Territory, after the adoption of the Constitution, must necessarily be officers of the United States, and not of the Congress of the Confederation; appointed and commissioned by the President, and exercising powers derived from the United States under the Constitution.

Such was the relation between the United States and the Northwestern Territory, which all reflecting men must have foreseen would exist, when the Government created by the Constitution should supersede that of the Confederation. That if the new Government should be without power to govern this Territory, it could not appoint and commission officers, and send them into the Territory, to exercise there legislative, judicial, and executive power; and that this Territory, which was even then foreseen to be so important, both politically and financially, to all the existing States, must be left not only without the control of the General Government, in respect to its future political relations to the rest of the States, but absolutely without any Government, save what its inhabitants, acting in their primary capacity, might from time to time create for themselves.

But this Northwestern Territory was not the only territory, the soil and jurisdiction whereof were then understood to have been ceded to the United States. The cession by South Carolina, made in August, 1787, was of *"all the territory included within the river Mississippi, and a line beginning at that part of the said river which is intersected by the southern boundary of North Carolina, and continuing along the said boundary line until it intersects the ridge or chain of mountains which divides the Eastern from the Western waters; then to be continued along the top of the said ridge of mountains, until it intersects a line to be drawn due west from the head of the southern branch of the Tugaloo river, to the said mountains; and thence to run a due west course to the river Mississippi."*

It is true that by subsequent explorations it was ascertained that the source of the Tugaloo river, upon which the title of South Carolina depended, was so far to the northward, that the transfer conveyed only a narrow slip of land, about twelve miles wide, lying on the top of the ridge of mountains, and extending from the northern boundary of Georgia to the southern boundary of North Carolina. But this was a discovery made long after the cession, and there can be no doubt that the State of South Carolina, in making the cession, and the Congress in accepting it, viewed it as a transfer to the United States of the soil and jurisdiction of an extensive and important part of the unsettled territory ceded by the Crown of Great Britain by the treaty of peace, though its quantity or extent then remained to be ascertained.

[Note by Mr. Justice Curtis. This statement that some territory did actually pass by this cession, is taken from the opinion of the court, delivered by Mr. Justice Wayne, in the case of Howard v. Ingersoll, reported in 13 How., 405. It is an obscure matter, and, on some examination of it, I have been led to doubt whether any territory actually passed by this cession. But as the fact is not important to the argument, I have not thought it necessary further to investigate it.]

It must be remembered also, as has been already stated, that not only was there a confident expectation entertained by the other States, that North Carolina and Georgia would complete the plan already so far executed by New York, Virginia, Massachusetts, Connecticut, and South Carolina, but that the opinion was in no small degree prevalent, that the just title to this "back country,"as it was termed, had vested in the United States by the treaty of peace, and could not rightfully be claimed by any individual State.

There is another consideration applicable to this part of the subject, and entitled, in my judgment, to great weight.

The Congress of the Confederation had assumed the power not only to dispose of the lands ceded, but to institute Governments and make laws for their inhabitants. In other words, they had proceeded to act under the cession, which, as we have seen, was as well of the jurisdiction as of the soil. This ordinance was passed on the 13th of July, 1787. The Convention for framing the Constitution was then in session at Philadelphia. The proof is direct and decisive, that it was known to the Convention. It is equally clear that it was admitted and understood not to be within the legitimate powers of the Confederation to pass this ordinance. (Jefferson's Works, vol. 9, pp. 251, 276; Federalist, Nos. 38, 43.)

The importance of conferring on the new Government regular powers commensurate with the objects to be attained, and thus avoiding the alternative of a failure to execute the trust assumed by the acceptance of the cessions made and expected, or its execution by usurpation, could scarcely fail to be perceived. That it was in fact perceived, is clearly shown by the *Federalist*, (No. 38,) where this very argument is made use of in commendation of the Constitution. Keeping these facts in view, it may confidently be asserted that there is very strong reason to believe, before we examine the Constitution itself, that the necessity for a competent grant of power to hold, dispose of, and govern territory, ceded and expected to be ceded, could not have escaped the attention of those who framed or adopted the Constitution; and that if it did not escape their attention, it could not fail to be adequately provided for.

Any other conclusion would involve the assumption that a subject of the gravest national concern, respecting which the small States felt so much jealousy that it had been almost an insurmountable obstacle to the for-mation of the Confederation, and as to which all the States had deep pecuniary and political interests, and which had been so recently and constantly agitated, was nevertheless overlooked; or that such a subject was not overlooked, but designedly left unprovided for, though it was manifestly a subject of common concern, which belonged to the care of the General Government, and adequate provision for which could not fail to be deemed necessary and proper.

The admission of new States, to be framed out of the ceded territory, early attracted the attention of the Convention. Among the resolutions introduced by Mr. Randolph, on the 29th of May, was one on this subject, (Res. No. 10, 5 Elliot, 128,) which, having been affirmed in Committee of the Whole, on the 5th of June, (5 Elliot, 156,) and reported to the Convention on the 13th of June, (5 Elliot, 190,) was referred to the Committee of Detail, to prepare the Constitution, on the 26th of July, (5 Elliot, 376.) This committee reported an article for the admission of new States *"lawfully constituted or established."* Nothing was said concerning the power of Congress to prepare or form such States. This omission struck Mr. Madison, who, on the 18th of August, (5 Elliot, 439,) moved for the insertion of power to dispose of the unappropriated lands of the United States, and to institute temporary Governments for new States arising therein.

On the 29th of August, (5 Elliot, 492,) the report of the committee was taken up, and after debate, which exhibited great diversity of views concerning the proper mode of providing for the subject, arising out of the supposed diversity of interests of the large and small States, and between those which had and those which had not unsettled territory, but no difference of opinion respecting the propriety and necessity of some adequate provision for the subject, Gouverneur Morris moved the clause as it stands in the Constitution. This met with general approbation, and was at once adopted. The whole section is as follows:

"New States may be admitted by the Congress into this Union; but no new State shall be formed or erected within the jurisdiction of any other State, nor any State be formed by the junction of two or more States, or parts of States, without the consent of the Legislatures of the States concerned, as well as of Congress.

"The Congress shall have power to dispose of and make all needful rules and regulations respecting the territory or other property belonging to the United States; and nothing in this Constitution shall be so construed as to prejudice any claims of the United States or any particular State."

That Congress has some power to institute temporary Governments over the territory, I believe all agree; and, if it be admitted that the necessity of some power to govern the territory of the United States could not and did not escape the attention of the Convention and the people, and that the necessity is so great, that, in the absence of any express grant, it is strong enough to raise an implication of the existence of that power, it would seem to follow that it is also strong enough to afford material aid in construing an express grant of power respecting that territory; and that they who maintain the existence of the power, without finding any words at all in which it is conveyed, should be willing to receive a reasonable interpretation of language of the Constitution, manifestly intended to relate to the territory, and to convey to Congress some authority concerning it.

It would seem, also, that when we find the subject-matter of the growth and formation and admission of new States, and the disposal of the territory for these ends, were under consideration, and that some provision therefor was expressly made, it is improbable that it would be, in its terms, a grossly inadequate provision; and that an indispensably necessary power to institute temporary Governments, and to legislate for the inhabitants of the territory, was passed silently by, and left to be deduced from the necessity of the case.

In the argument at the bar, great attention has been paid to the meaning of the word "*territory*." Ordinarily, when the territory of a sovereign power is spoken of, it refers to that tract of country which is under the political jurisdiction of that sovereign power. Thus Chief Justice Marshall (in United States v. Bevans, 3 Wheat., 386) says: "*What, then, is the extent of jurisdiction which a State possesses? We answer, without hesitation, the jurisdiction of a State is coextensive with its territory.*" Examples might easily be multiplies of this use of the word, but they are unnecessary, because it is familiar. But the word "*territory*" is not used in this broad and general sense in this clause of the Constitution.

At the time of the adoption of the Constitution, the United States held a great tract of country northwest of the Ohio; another tract, then of unknown extent, ceded by South Carolina; and a confident expectation was then entertained and afterwards realized, that they then were or would become the owners of other great tracts, claimed by North Carolina and Georgia. These ceded tracts lay within the limits of the United States, and out of the limits of any particular State; and the cessions embraced the civil and political jurisdiction, and so much of the soil as had not previously been granted to individuals.

These words, "*territory belonging to the United States,*" were not used in the Constitution to describe and abstraction, but to identify and apply to these actual subjects matter then existing and belonging to the United States, and other similar subjects which might afterwards be acquired; and this being so, all the essential qualities and incidents attending such actual sub-

jects are embraced within the words "*territory belonging to the United States,*" as fully as if each of those essential qualities and incidents had been specifically described.

I say, the essential qualities and incidents. But in determining what were the essential qualities and incidents of the subject with which they were dealing, we must take into consideration not only all the particular facts which were immediately before them, but the great consideration, ever present to the minds of those who framed and adopted the Constitution, that they were making a frame of government for the people of the United States and their posterity, under which they hoped the United States might be, what they have now become, a great and powerful nation, possessing the power to make war and to conclude treaties, and thus to acquire territory. (See Cerre v. Pitot, 6 Cr., 336; Am. Ins. Co. v. Canter, 1 Pet., 542.) With these in view, I turn to examine the clause of the article now in question.

It is said this provision has no application to any territory save that then belonging to the United States. I have already shown that, when the Constitution was framed, a confident expectation was entertained, which was speedily realized, that North Carolina and Georgia would cede their claims to that great territory which lay west of those States. No doubt has been suggested that the first clause of this same article, which enabled Congress to admit new States, refers to and includes new States to be formed out of this territory, expected to be thereafter ceded by North Carolina and Georgia, as well as new States to be formed out of territory northwest of the Ohio, which then had been ceded by Virginia. It must have been seen, therefore, that the same necessity would exist for an authority to dispose of and make all needful regulations respecting this territory, when ceded, as existed for a like authority respecting territory which had been ceded.

No reason has been suggested why any reluctance should have been felt, by the framers of the Constitution, to apply this provision to all the territory which might belong to the United States, or why any distinction should have been made, founded on the accidental circumstance of the dates of the cessions; a circumstance in no way material as respects the necessity for rules and regulations, or the propriety of conferring on the Congress power to make them. And if we look at the course of the debates in the Convention on this article, we shall find that the then unceded lands, so far from having been left out of view in adopting this article, constituted, in the minds of members, a subject of even paramount importance.

Again, in what an extraordinary position would the limitation of this clause to territory then belonging to the United States, place the territory which lay within the chartered limits of North Carolina and Georgia. The title to that territory was then claimed by those

States, and by the United States; their respective claims are purposely left unsettled by the express words of this clause; and when cessions were made by those States, they were merely of their claims to this territory, the United States neither admitting nor denying the validity of those claims; so that it was impossible then, and has ever since remained impossible, to know whether this territory did or did not then belong to the United States; and, consequently, to know whether it was within or without the authority conferred by this clause, to dispose of and make rules and regulations respecting the territory of the United States. This attributes to the eminent men who acted on this subject a want of ability and forecast, or a want of attention to the known facts upon which they were acting, in which I cannot concur.

There is not, in my judgment, anything in the language, the history, or the subject-matter of this article, which restricts its operation to territory owned by the United States when the Constitution was adopted.

But it is also insisted that provisions of the Constitution respecting territory belonging to the United States do not apply to territory acquired by treaty from a foreign nation. This objection must rest upon the position that the Constitution did not authorize the Federal Government to acquire foreign territory, and consequently has made no provision for its government when acquired; or, that though the acquisition of foreign territory was contemplated by the Constitution, its provisions concerning the admission of new States, and the making of all needful rules and regulations respecting territory belonging to the United States, were not designed to be applicable to territory acquired from foreign nations.

It is undoubtedly true, that at the date of the treaty of 1803, between the United States and France, for the cession of Louisiana, it was made a question, whether the Constitution had conferred on the executive department of the Government of the United States power to acquire foreign territory by a treaty.

There is evidence that very grave doubts were then entertained concerning the existence of this power. But that there was then a settled opinion in the executive and legislative branches of the Government, that this power did not exist, cannot be admitted, without at the same time imputing to those who negotiated and ratified the treaty, and passed the laws necessary to carry it into execution, a deliberate and known violation of their oaths to support the Constitution; and whatever doubts may then have existed, the question must now be taken to have been settled. Four distinct acquisitions of foreign territory have been made by as many different treaties, under as many different Administrations. Six States, formed on such territory, are now in the Union. Every branch of this Government, during a period of more than fifty years, has participated in these transactions. To question their validity now, is vain. As was said by Mr. Chief Justice Marshall, in the American Insurance Company v. Canter, (1 Peters, 542,) *"the Constitution confers absolutely on the Government of the Union the powers of making war and or making treaties; consequently, that Government possesses the power of acquiring territory, either by conquest or treaty."* (See Cerre v. Pitot, 6 Cr., 336.) And I add, it also possesses the power of governing it, when acquired, not by resorting to supposititious powers, nowhere found described in the Constitution, but expressly granted in the authority to make all needful rules and regulations respecting the territory of the United States.

There was to be established by the Constitution a frame of government, under which the people of the United States and their posterity were to continue indefinitely. To take one of its provisions, the language of which is broad enough to extend throughout the existence of the Government, and embrace all territory belonging to the United States throughout all time, and the purposes and objects of which apply to all territory of the United States, and narrow it down to territory belonging to the United States when the Constitution was framed, while at the same time it is admitted that the Constitution contemplated and authorized the acquisition, from time to time, of other and foreign territory, seems to me to be an interpretation as inconsistent with the nature and purposes of the instrument, as it is with its language, and I can have no hesitation in rejecting it.

I construe this clause, therefore, as if it had read, Congress shall have power to make all needful rules and regulations respecting those tracts of country, out of the limits of the several States, which the United States have acquired, or may hereafter acquire, by cessions, as well of the jurisdiction as of the soil, so far as the soil may be the property of the party making the cession, at the time of making it.

It has been urged that the words *"rules and regulations"* are not appropriate terms in which to convey authority to make laws for the government of the territory. But it must be remembered that this is a grant of power to the Congress—that it is therefore necessarily a grant of power to legislate—and, certainly, rules and regulation respecting a particular subject, made by the legislative power of a country, can be nothing but laws. Nor do the particular terms employed, in my judgment, tend in any degree to restrict this legislative power. Power granted to a Legislature to make all needful rules and regulations respecting the territory, is a power to pass all needful laws respecting it.

The word regulate, or regulation, is several times used in the Constitution. It is used in the fourth section of the first article to describe those laws of the States which prescribe the times, places, and manner, of choosing Senators and Representatives; in the second section of the fourth article, to designate the legislative action of a State on the subject of fugitives from service, having a very close relation to the matter of our present inquiry; in the second section of the third article, to empower Congress to fix the extent of the appellate jurisdiction of this court; and, finally, in the eighth section of the first article are the words, "*Congress shall have power to regulate commerce.*"

It is unnecessary to describe the body of legislation which has been enacted under this grant of power; its variety and extent are well known. But it may be mentioned, in passing, that under this power to regulate commerce, Congress has enacted a great system of municipal laws, and extended it over the vessels and crews of the United States on the high seas and in foreign ports, and even over citizens of the United States resident in China; and has established judicatures, with power to inflict even capital punishment within that country.

If, then, this clause does contain a power to legislate respecting the territory, what art the limits of that power?

To this I answer, that, in common with all the other legislative powers of Congress, it finds limits in the express prohibitions on Congress not to do certain things; that, in the exercise of the legislative power, Congress cannot pass an ex post facto law or bill of attainder; and so in respect to each of the other prohibitions contained in the Constitution.

Besides this, the rules and regulations must be needful. But undoubtedly the question whether a particular rule or regulation be needful, must be finally determined by Congress itself. Whether a law be needful, is a legislative or political, not a judicial, question. Whatever Congress deems needful is so, under the grant of power.

Nor am I aware that it has ever been questioned that laws providing for the temporary government of the settlers on the public lands are needful, not only to prepare them for admission to the Union as States, but even to enable the United States to dispose of the lands.

Without government and social order, there can be no property; for without law, its ownership, its use, and the power of disposing of it, cease to exist, in the sense in which those words are used and understood in all civilized States.

Since, then, this power was manifestly conferred to enable the United States to dispose of its public lands to settlers, and to admit them into the Union as States, when in the judgment of Congress they should be fitted therefor, since these were the needs provided for, since it is confessed that Government is indispensable to provide for those needs, and the power is, to make all need-

ful rules and regulations respecting the territory, I cannot doubt that this is a power to govern the inhabitants of the territory, by such laws as Congress deems needful, until they obtain admission as States. Whether they should be thus governed solely by laws enacted by Congress, or partly by laws enacted by legislative power conferred by Congress, is one of those questions which depend on the judgment of Congress—a question which of these is needful.

But it is insisted, that whatever other powers Congress may have respecting the territory of the United States, the subject of negro slavery forms an exception.

The Constitution declares that Congress shall have power to make "*all needful rules and regulations*" respecting the territory belonging to the United States.

The assertion is, though the Constitution says all, it does not mean all—though it says all, without qualification, it means all except such as allow or prohibit slavery. It cannot be doubted that it is incumbent on those who would thus introduce an exception not found in the language of the instrument, to exhibit some solid and satisfactory reason, drawn from the subject-matter or the purposes and objects of the clause, the context, or from other provisions of the Constitution, showing that the words employed in this clause are not to be understood according to their clear, plain, and natural signification.

The subject-matter is the territory of the United States out of the limits of every State, and consequently under the exclusive power of the people of the United States. Their will respecting it, manifested in the Constitution, can be subject to no restriction. The purposes and objects of the clause were the enactment of laws concerning the disposal of the public lands, and temporary government of the settlers thereon until new States should be formed. It will not be questioned that, when the Constitution of the United States was framed and adopted, the allowance and the prohibition of negro slavery were recognised subjects of municipal legislation; every State had in some measure acted thereon; and the only legislative act concerning the territory—the ordinance of 1787, which had then so recently been passed—contained a prohibition of slavery. The purpose and object of the clause being to enable Congress to provide a body of municipal law for the government of the settlers, the allowance or the prohibition of slavery comes within the known and recognised scope of that purpose and object.

There is nothing in the context which qualifies the grant of power. The regulations must be "*respecting the territory.*" An enactment that slavery may or may not exist there, is a regulation respecting the territory. Regulations must be needful; but it is necessarily left to the legislative discretion to determine whether a law be needful. No other clause of the Constitution has been referred to at the bar, or has been seen by me, which imposes any restriction or makes any exception concerning the power of Congress to allow or prohibit slavery in the territory belonging to the United States.

A practical construction, nearly contemporaneous with the adoption of the Constitution, and continued by repeated instances through a long series of years, may always influence, and in doubtful cases should determine, the judicial mind, on a question of the interpretation of the Constitution. (Stuart v. Laird, 1 Cranch, 269; Martin v. Hunter, 1 Wheat., 304; Cohens v. Virginia, 6 Wheat., 264; Prigg v. Pennsylvania, 16 Pet., 621; Cooley v. Port Wardens, 12 How., 315.)

It this view, I proceed briefly to examine the practical construction placed on the clause now in question, so far as it respects the inclusion therein of power to permit or prohibit slavery in the Territories.

It has already been stated, that after the Government of the United States was organized under the Constitution, the temporary Government of the Territory northwest of the river Ohio could no longer exist, save under the powers conferred on Congress by the Constitution. Whatever legislative, judicial, or executive authority should be exercised therein could be derived only from the people of the United States under the Constitution. And, accordingly, an act was passed on the 7th day of August, 1789, (1 Stat. at Large, 50,) which recites: It then provides for the appointment by the President of all officers, who, by force of the ordinance, were to have been appointed by the Congress of the Confederation, and their commission in the manner required by the Constitution; and empowers the Secretary of the Territory to exercise the powers of the Governor in case of the death or necessary absence of the latter.

Here is an explicit declaration of the will of the first Congress, of which fourteen members, including Mr. Madison, had been members of the Convention which framed the Constitution, that the ordinance, one article of which prohibited slavery, "should continue to have full effect." Gen. Washington, who signed this bill, as President, was the President of that Convention.

It does not appear to me to be important, in this connection, that that clause in the ordinance which prohibited slavery was one of a series of articles of what is therein termed a compact. The Congress of the Confederation had no power to make such a compact, nor to act at all on the subject; and after what had been so recently said by Mr. Madison on this subject, in the thirty-eighth number of the Federalist, I cannot suppose that he, or any others who voted for this bill, attributed any intrinsic effect to what was denominated in the ordinance a compact between "the original States and the people and States in the new territory;" there being no new States then in existence in the territory,

with whom a compact could be made, and the few scattered inhabitants, unorganized into a political body, not being capable of becoming a party to a treaty, even if the Congress of the Confederation had power to make one touching the government of that territory.

I consider the passage of this law to have been an assertion by the first Congress of the power of the United States to prohibit slavery within this part of the territory of the United States; for it clearly shows that slavery was thereafter to be prohibited there, and it could be prohibited only by an exertion of the power of the United States, under the Constitution; no other power being capable of operating within that territory after the Constitution took effect.

On the 2d of April, 1790, (1 Stat. at Large, 106,) the first Congress passed an act accepting a deed of cession by North Carolina of that territory afterwards erected into the State of Tennessee. The fourth express condition contained in this deed of cession, after providing that the inhabitants of the Territory shall be temporarily governed in the same manner as those beyond the Ohio, is followed by these words: "*Provided, always, that no regulations made or to be made by Congress shall tend to emancipate slaves.*"

This provision shows that it was then understood Congress might make a regulation prohibiting slavery, and that Congress might also allow it to continue to exist in the Territory; and accordingly, when, a few days later, Congress passed the act of May 20th, 1790, (1 Stat. at Large, 123,) for the government of the Territory south of the river Ohio, it provided, "*and the Government of the Territory south of the Ohio shall be similar to that now exercised in the Territory northwest of the Ohio, except so far as is otherwise provided in the conditions expressed in an act of Congress of the present session, entitled, 'An act to accept a cession of the claims of the State of North Carolina to a certain district of western territory.'*" Under the Government thus established, slavery existed until the Territory became the State of Tennessee.

On the 7th of April, 1798, (1 Stat. at Large, 649,) an act was passed to establish a Government in the Mississippi Territory in all respects like that exercised in the Territory northwest of the Ohio, "*excepting and excluding the last article of the ordinance made for the government thereof by the late Congress, on the 13th day of July, 1787.*" When the limits of this Territory had been amicably settled with Georgia, and the latter ceded all its claim thereto, it was one stipulation in the compact of cession, that the ordinance of July 13th, 1787, "*shall in all its parts extend to the Territory contained in the present act of cession, that article only excepted which forbids slavery.*" The Government of this Territory was subsequently established and organized under the act of May 10th, 1800; but so much of the ordinance as prohibited slavery was not put in operation there.

Without going minutely into the details of each case, I will now give reference to two classes of acts, in one of which Congress has extended the ordinance of 1787, including the article prohibiting slavery, over different Territories, and thus exerted its power to prohibit it; in the other, Congress has erected Governments over Territories acquired from France and Spain, in which slavery already existed, but refused to apply to them that part of the Government under the ordinance which excluded slavery.

Of the first class are the act of May 7th, 1800, (2 Stat. at Large, 58,) for the government of the Indiana Territory; the act of January 11th, 1805, (2 Stat. at Large, 309,) for the government of Michigan Territory; the act of May 3d, 1809, (2 Stat. at Large, 514,) for the government of the Illinois Territory; the act of April 20th, 1836, (5 Stat. at Large, 10,) for the government of the Territory of Wisconsin; the act of June 12th, 1838, for the government of the Territory of Iowa; the act of August 14th, 1848, for the government of the Territory of Oregon. To these instances should be added the act of March 6th, 1820, (3 Stat. at Large, 548,) prohibiting slavery in the territory acquired from France, being northwest of Missouri, and north of thirty-six degrees thirty minutes north latitude.

Of the second class, in which Congress refused to interfere with slavery already existing under the municipal law of France or Spain, and established Governments by which slavery was recognised and allowed, are: the act of March 26th, 1804, (2 Stat. at Large, 283,) for the government of Louisiana; the act of March 2d, 1805, (2 Stat. at Large, 322,) for the government of the Territory of Orleans; the act of June 4th, 1812, (2 Stat. at Large, 743,) for the government of the Missouri Territory; the act of March 30th, 1822, (3 Stat. at Large, 654,) for the government of the Territory of Florida. Here are eight distinct instances, beginning with the first Congress, and coming down to the year 1848, in which Congress has excluded slavery from the territory of the United States; and six distinct instances in which Congress organized Governments of Territories by which slavery was recognised and continued, beginning also with the first Congress, and coming down to the year 1822. These acts were severally signed by seven Presidents of the United States, beginning with General Washington, and coming regularly down as far as Mr. John Quincy Adams, thus including all who were in public life when the Constitution was adopted.

If the practical construction of the Constitution contemporaneously with its going into effect, by men intimately acquainted with its history from their personal participation in framing and adopting it, and continued by them through a long series of acts of the gravest importance, be entitled to weight in the judicial mind on a question of construction, it would seem to be difficult to resist the force of the acts above adverted to.

It appears, however, from what has taken place at the bar, that notwithstanding the language of the Constitution, and the long line of legislative and executive precedents under it, three different and opposite views are taken of the power of Congress respecting slavery in the Territories.

One is, that though Congress can make a regulation prohibiting slavery in a Territory, they cannot make a regulation allowing it; another is, that it can neither be established nor prohibited by Congress, but that the people of a Territory, when organized by Congress, can establish or prohibit slavery; while the third is, that the Constitution itself secures to every citizen who holds slaves, under the laws of any State, the indefeasible right to carry them into any Territory, and there hold them as property.

No particular clause of the Constitution has been referred to at the bar in support of either of these views. The first seems to be rested upon general considerations concerning the social and moral evils of slavery, its relations to republican Governments, its inconsistency with the Declaration of Independence and with natural right.

The second is drawn from considerations equally general, concerning the right of self-government, and the nature of the political institutions which have been established by the people of the United States.

While the third is said to rest upon the equal right of all citizens to go with their property upon the public domain, and the inequality of a regulation which would admit the property of some and exclude the property of other citizens; and, inasmuch as slaves are chiefly held by citizens of those particular States where slavery is established, it is insisted that a regulation excluding slavery from a Territory operates, practically, to make an unjust discrimination between citizens of different States, in respect to their use and enjoyment of the territory of the United States.

With the weight of either of these considerations, when presented to Congress to influence its action, this court has no concern. One or the other may be justly entitled to guide or control the legislative judgment upon what is a needful regulation. The question here is, whether they are sufficient to authorize this court to insert into this clause of the Constitution an exception of the exclusion or allowance of slavery, not found therein, nor in any other part of that instrument. To engraft on any instrument a substantive exception not found in it, must be admitted to be a matter attended with great difficulty. And the difficulty increases with the importance of the instrument, and the magnitude and complexity of the interests involved in its construction. To allow this to be done with the

Constitution, upon reasons purely political, renders its judicial interpretation impossible—because judicial tribunals, as such, cannot decide upon political considerations. Political reasons have not the requisite certainty to afford rules of juridical interpretation. They are different in different men. They are different in the same men at different times. And when a strict interpretation of the Constitution, according to the fixed rules which govern the interpretation of laws, is abandoned, and the theoretical opinions of individuals are allowed to control its meaning, we have no longer a Constitution; we are under the government of individual men, who for the time being have power to declare what the Constitution is, according to their own views of what it ought to mean. When such a method of interpretation of the Constitution obtains, in place of a republican Government, with limited and defined powers, we have a Government which is merely an exponent of the will of Congress; in my opinion, would not be preferable, an exponent of the individual political opinions of the members of this court.

If it can be shown, by anything in the Constitution itself, that when it confers on Congress the power to make all needful rules and regulations respecting the territory belonging to the United States, the exclusion or the allowance of slavery was excepted; or if anything in the history of this provision tends to show that such an exception was intended by those who framed and adopted the Constitution to be introduced into it, I hold it to be my duty carefully to consider, and to allow just weight to such considerations in interpreting the positive text of the Constitution. But where the Constitution has said all needful rules and regulations, I must find something more than theoretical reasoning to induce me to say it did not mean all.

There have been eminent instances in this court closely analogous to this one, in which such an attempt to introduce an exception, not found in the Constitution itself, has failed of success. By the eighth section of the first article, Congress has the power of exclusive legislation in all cases whatsoever within this District.

In the case of Loughborough v. Blake, (5 Whea., 324,) the question arose, whether Congress has power to impose direct taxes on persons and property in this District. It was insisted, that though the grant of power was in its terms broad enough to include direct taxation, it must be limited by the principle, that taxation and representation are inseparable. It would not be easy to fix on any political truth, better established or more fully admitted in our country, than that taxation and representation must exist together. We went into the war of the Revolution to assert it, and it is incorporated as fundamental into all American Governments. But however true and important this maxim may be, it

is not necessarily of universal application. It was for the people of the United States, who ordained the Constitution, to decide whether it should or should not be permitted to operate within this District. Their decision was embodied in the words of the Constitution; and as that contained no such exception as would permit the maxim to operate in this District, this court, interpreting that language, held that the exception did not exist.

Again, the Constitution confers on Congress power to regulate commerce with foreign nations. Under this, Congress passed an act on the 22d of December, 1807, unlimited in duration, laying an embargo on all ships and vessels in the ports or within the limits and jurisdiction of the United States. No law of the United States ever pressed so severely upon particular States. Though the constitutionality of the law was contested with an earnestness and zeal proportioned to the ruinous effects which were felt from it, and though, as Mr. Chief Justice Marshall has said, (9 Wheat., 192,) "*a want of acuteness in discovering objections to a measure to which they felt the most deep-rooted hostility will not be imputed to those who were arrayed in opposition to this,*" I am not aware that the fact that it prohibited the use of a particular species of property, belonging almost exclusively to citizens of a few States, and this indefinitely, was ever supposed to show that it was unconstitutional. Something much more stringent, as a ground of legal judgment, was relied on—that the power to regulate commerce did not include the power to annihilate commerce.

But the decision was, that under the power to regulate commerce, the power of Congress over the subject was restricted only by those exceptions and limitations contained in the Constitution; and as neither the clause in question, which was a general grant of power to regulate commerce, nor any other clause of the Constitution, imposed any restrictions as to the duration of an embargo, an unlimited prohibition of the use of the shipping of the country was within the power of Congress. On this subject, Mr. Justice Daniel, speaking for the court in the case of United States v. Marigold, (9 How., 560,) says: "*Congress are, by the Constitution, vested with the power to regulate commerce with foreign nations; and however, at periods of high excitement, an application of the terms 'to regulate commerce,' such as would embrace absolute prohibition, may have been questioned, yet, since the passage of the embargo and non-intercourse laws, and the repeated judicial sanctions these statutes have received, it can scarcely at this day be open to doubt, that every subject falling legitimately within the sphere of commercial regulation may be partially or wholly excluded, when either measure shall be demanded by the safety or the important interests of the entire nation. The power once conceded, it may operate on any and every sub-*"

ject of commerce to which the legislative discretion may apply it."

If power to regulate commerce extends to an indefinite prohibition of the use of all vessels belonging to citizens of the several States, and may operate, without exception, upon every subject of commerce to which the legislative discretion may apply it, upon what grounds can I say that power to make all needful rules and regulations respecting the territory of the United States is subject to an exception of the allowance or prohibition of slavery therein?

While the regulation is one *"respecting the territory,"* while it is, in the judgment of Congress, *"a needful regulation,"* and is thus completely within the words of the grant, while no other clause of the Constitution can be shown, which requires the insertion of an exception respecting slavery, and while the practical construction for a period of upwards of fifty years forbids such an exception, it would, in my opinion, violate every sound rule of interpretation to force that exception into the Constitution upon the strength of abstract political reasoning, which we are bound to believe the people of the United States thought insufficient to induce them to limit the power of Congress, because what they have said contains no such limitation.

Before I proceed further to notice some other grounds of supposed objection to this power of Congress, I desire to say, that if it were not for my anxiety to insist upon what I deem a correct exposition of the Constitution, if I looked only to the purposes of the argument, the source of the power of Congress asserted in the opinion of the majority of the court would answer those purposes equally well. For they admit that Congress has power to organize and govern the Territories until they arrive at a suitable condition for admission to the Union; they admit, also, that the kind of Government which shall thus exist should be regulated by the condition and wants of each Territory, and that it is necessarily committed to the discretion of Congress to enact such laws for that purpose as that discretion may dictate; and no limit to that discretion has been shown, or even suggested, save those positive prohibitions to legislate, which are found in the Constitution.

I confess myself unable to perceive any difference whatever between my own opinion of the general extent of the power of Congress and the opinion of the majority of the court, save that I consider it derivable from the express language of the Constitution, while they hold it to be silently implied from the power to acquire territory. Looking at the power of Congress over the Territories as of the extent just described, what positive prohibition exists in the Constitution, which restrained Congress from enacting a law in 1820 to prohibit slavery north of thirty-six degrees thirty minutes north latitude?

The only one suggested is that clause in the fifth article of the amendments of the Constitution which declares that no person shall be deprived of his life, liberty, or property, without due process of law. I will now proceed to examine the question, whether this clause is entitled to the effect thus attributed to it. It is necessary, first, to have a clear view of the nature and incidents of that particular species of property which is now in question.

Slavery, being contrary to natural right, is created only by municipal law. This is not only plain in itself, and agreed by all writers on the subject, but is inferable from the Constitution, and has been explicitly declared by this court. The Constitution refers to slaves as *"persons held to service in one State, under the laws thereof."* Nothing can more clearly describe a status created by municipal law. In Prigg v. Pennsylvania, (10 Pet., 611,) this court said: *"The state of slavery is deemed to be a mere municipal regulation, founded on and limited to the range of territorial laws."* In Rankin v. Lydia, (2 Marsh., 12, 470,) the Supreme Court of Appeals of Kentucky said: *"Slavery is sanctioned by the laws of this State, and the right to hold them under our municipal regulations is unquestionable. But we view this as a right existing by positive law of a municipal character, without foundation in the law of nature or the unwritten common law."* I am not acquainted with any case or writer questioning the correctness of this doctrine. (See also 1 Burge, Col. and For. Laws, 738—741, where the authorities are collected.)

The status of slavery is not necessarily always attended with the same powers on the part of the master. The master is subject to the supreme power of the State, whose will controls his action towards his slave, and this control must be defined and regulated by the municipal law. In one State, as at one period of the Roman law, it may put the life of the slave into the hand of the master; others, as those of the United States, which tolerate slavery, may treat the slave as a person, when the master takes his life; while in others, the law may recognise a right of the slave to be protected from cruel treatment. In other words, the status of slavery embraces every condition, from that in which the slave is known to the law simply as a chattel, with no civil rights, to that in which he is recognised as a person for all purposes, save the compulsory power of directing and receiving the fruits of his labor. Which of these conditions shall attend the status of slavery, must depend on the municipal law which creates and upholds it.

And not only must the status of slavery be created and measured by municipal law, but the rights, powers, and obligations, which grow out of that status, must be defined, protected, and enforced, by such laws. The liability of the master for the torts and crimes of his slave, and of third persons for assaulting or injuring or harboring or kidnapping him, the forms and modes of emancipation and sale, their subjection to the debts of the master, succession by death of the master, suits for freedom, the capacity of the slave to be party to a suit, or to be a witness, with such police regulations as have existed in all civilized States where slavery has been tolerated, are among the subjects upon which municipal legislation becomes necessary when slavery is introduced.

Is it conceivable that the Constitution has conferred the right on every citizen to become a resident on the territory of the United States with his slaves, and there to hold them as such, but has neither made nor provided for any municipal regulations which are essential to the existence of slavery?

Is it not more rational to conclude that they who framed and adopted the Constitution were aware that persons held to service under the laws of a State are property only to the extent and under the conditions fixed by those laws; that they must cease to be available as property, when their owners voluntarily place them permanently within another jurisdiction, where no municipal laws on the subject of slavery exist; and that, being aware of these principles, and having said nothing to interfere with or displace them, or to compel Congress to legislate in any particular manner on the subject, and having empowered Congress to make all needful rules and regulations respecting the territory of the United States, it was their intention to leave to the discretion of Congress what regulations, if any, should be made concerning slavery therein? Moreover, if the right exists, what are its limits, and what are its conditions? If citizens of the United States have the right to take their slaves to a Territory, and hold them there as slaves, without regard to the laws of the Territory, I suppose this right is not to be restricted to the citizens of slaveholding States. A citizen of a State which does not tolerate slavery can hardly be denied the power of doing the same thing. And what law of slavery does either take with him to the Territory? If it be said to be those laws respecting slavery which existed in the particular State from which each slave last came, what an anomaly is this? Where else can we find, under the law of any civilized country, the power to introduce and permanently continue diverse systems of foreign municipal law, for holding persons in slavery? I say, not merely to introduce, but permanently to continue, these anomalies. For the offspring of the female must be governed by the foreign municipal laws to which the mother was subject; and when any slave is sold or passes by succession on the death of the owner, there must pass with him, by a species of subrogation, and as a kind of unknown jus in re, the foreign municipal laws which constituted, regulated, and preserved, the status of the slave before his exportation. Whatever theoretical importance may be now supposed to belong to the maintenance of such a right, I feel a perfect conviction that it would, if ever tried, prove to be as impracticable in fact, as it is, in my judgment, monstrous in theory.

I consider the assumption which lies at the basis of this theory to be unsound; not in its just sense, and when properly understood, but in the sense which has been attached to it. That assumption is, that the territory ceded by France was acquired for the equal benefit of all the citizens of the United States. I agree to the position. But it was acquired for their benefit in their collective, not their individual, capacities. It was acquired for their benefit, as an organized political society, subsisting as *the people of the United States,*" under the Constitution of the United States; to be administered justly and impartially, and as nearly as possible for the equal benefit of every individual citizen, according to the best judgment and discretion of the Congress; to whose power, as the Legislature of the nation which acquired it, the people of the United States have committed its administration. Whatever individual claims may be founded on local circumstances, or sectional differences of condition, cannot, in my opinion, be recognised in this court, without arrogating to the judicial branch of the Government powers not committed to it; and which, with all the unaffected respect I feel for it, when acting in its proper sphere, I do not think it fitted to wield.

Nor, in my judgment, will the position, that a prohibition to bring slaves into a Territory deprives any one of his property without due process of law, bear examination.

It must be remembered that this restriction on the legislative power is not peculiar to the Constitution of the United States; it was borrowed from Magna Charta; was brought to America by our ancestors, as part of their inherited liberties, and has existed in all the States, usually in the very words of the great charter. It existed in every political community in America in 1787, when the ordinance prohibiting slavery north and west of the Ohio was passed.

And if a prohibition of slavery in a Territory in 1820 violated this principle of Magna Charta, the ordinance of 1787 also violated it; and what power had, I do not say the Congress of the Confederation alone, but the Legislature of Virginia, or the Legislature of any or all the States of the Confederacy, to consent to such a violation? The people of the States had conferred no such power. I think I may at least say, if the Congress did then violate Magna Charta by the ordinance, no one discovered that violation. Besides, if the prohibition upon all persons, citizens as well as others, to bring slaves into a Territory, and a declaration that if brought they shall be free, deprives citizens of their property without due process of law, what shall we say of the legislation of many of the slaveholding States which have enacted the same prohibition? As early as October, 1778, a law was passed in Virginia, that thereafter no slave should be imported into that Commonwealth by sea or by land, and that every slave who should be imported should become free. A citizen of Virginia purchased in Maryland a slave who belonged to another citizen of Virginia, and removed with the slave to Virginia. The slave sued for her freedom, and recovered it; as may be seen in Wilson v. Isabel, (5 Call's R., 425.) See also Hunter v. Hulsher, (1 Leigh, 172;) and a similar law has been recognised as valid in Maryland, in Stewart v. Oaks, (5 Har. and John., 107.) I am not aware that such laws, though they exist in many States, were ever supposed to be in conflict with the principle of Magna Charta incorporated into the State Constitutions. It was certainly understood by the Convention which framed the Constitution, and has been so understood ever since, that, under the power to regulate commerce, Congress could prohibit the importation of slaves; and the exercise of the power was restrained till 1808. A citizen of the United States owns slaves in Cuba, and brings them to the United States, where they are set free by the legislation of Congress. Does this legislation deprive him of his property without due process of law? If so, what becomes of the laws prohibiting the slave trade? If not, how can a similar regulation respecting a Territory violate the fifth amendment of the Constitution?

Some reliance was placed by the defendant's counsel upon the fact that the prohibition of slavery in this territory was in the words, *"that slavery, &c., shall be and is hereby forever prohibited."* But the insertion of the word forever can have no legal effect. Every enactment not expressly limited it its duration continues in force until repealed or abrogated by some competent power, and the use of the word *"forever"* can give to the law no more durable operation. The argument is, that Congress cannot so legislate as to bind the future States formed out of the territory, and that in this instance it has attempted to do so. Of the political reasons which may have induced the Congress to use these words, and which caused them to expect that subsequent Legislatures would conform their action to the then general opinion of the country that it ought to be permanent, this court can take no cognizance.

However fit such considerations are to control the action of Congress, and however reluctant a statesman may be to disturb what has been settled, every law made by Congress may be repealed, and, saving private rights, and public rights gained by States, its repeal is subject to absolute will of the same power which enacted it. If Congress had enacted that the crime of murder, committed in this Indian Territory, north of thirty-six degrees thirty minutes, by or on any white man, should forever be punishable with death, it would seem to me

an insufficient objection to an indictment, found while it was a Territory, that at some future day States might exist there, and so the law was invalid, because, by its terms, it was to continue in force forever. Such an objection rests upon a misapprehension of the province and power of courts respecting the constitutionality of laws enacted by the Legislature.

If the Constitution prescribe one rule, and the law another and different rule, it is the duty of courts to declare that the Constitution, and not the law, governs the case before them for judgment. If the law include no case save those for which the Constitution has furnished a different rule, or no case which the Legislature has the power to govern, then the law can have no operation. If it includes cases which the Legislature has power to govern, and concerning which the Constitution does not prescribe a different rule, the law governs those cases, though it may, in its terms, attempt to include others, on which it cannot operate. In other words, this court cannot declare void an act of Congress which constitutionally embraces some cases, though other cases, within its terms, are beyond the control of Congress, or beyond the reach of that particular law. If, therefore, Congress had power to make a law excluding slavery from this territory while under the exclusive power of the United States, the use of the word "forever" does not invalidate the law, so long as Congress has the exclusive legislative power in the territory.

But it is further insisted that the treaty of 1803, between the United States and France, by which this territory was acquired, has so restrained the constitutional powers of Congress, that it cannot, by law, prohibit the introduction of slavery into that part of this territory north and west of Missouri, and north of thirty-six degrees thirty minutes north latitude.

By a treaty with a foreign nation, the United States may rightfully stipulate that the Congress will or will not exercise its legislative power in some particular manner, on some particular subject. Such promises, when made, should be voluntarily kept, with the most scrupulous good faith. But that a treaty with a foreign nation can deprive the Congress of any part of the legislative power conferred by the people, so that in no longer can legislate as it was empowered by the Constitution to do, I more than doubt.

The powers of the Government do and must remain unimpaired. The responsibility of the Government to a foreign nation, for the exercise of those powers, is quite another matter. That responsibility is to be met, and justified to the foreign nation, according to the requirements of the rules of public law; but never upon the assumption that the United States had parted with or restricted any power of acting according to its own free will, governed solely by its own appreciation of its duty. The second section of the fourth article is, *"This*

Constitution, and the laws of the United States which shall be made in pursuance thereof, and all treaties made or which shall be made under the authority of the United States, shall be the supreme law of the land." This has made treaties part of our municipal law; but it has not assigned to them any particular degree of authority, nor declared that laws so enacted shall be irrepealable. No supremacy is assigned to treaties over acts of Congress. That they are not perpetual, and must be in some way repealable, all will agree.

If the President and the Senate alone possess the power to repeal or modify a law found in a treaty, inasmuch as they can change or abrogate one treaty only by making another inconsistent with the first, the Government of the United States could not act at all, to that effect, without the consent of some foreign Government. I do not consider, I am not aware it has ever been considered, that the Constitution has placed our country in this helpless condition. The action of Congress in repealing the treaties with France by the act of July 7th, 1798, (1 Stat. at Large, 578,) was in conformity with these views. In the case of Taylor et al. v. Morton, (2 Curtis's Cir. Ct. R., 454,) I had occasion to consider this subject, and I adhere to the views there expressed.

If, therefore, it were admitted that the treaty between the United States and France did contain an express stipulation that the United States would not exclude slavery from so much of the ceded territory as is now in question, this court could not declare that an act of Congress excluding it was void by force of the treaty. Whether or no a case existed sufficient to justify a refusal to execute such a stipulation, would not be a judicial, but a political and legislative question, wholly beyond the authority of this court to try and determine. It would belong to diplomacy and legislation, and not to the administration of existing laws. Such a stipulation in a treaty, to legislate or not to legislate in a particular way, has been repeatedly held in this court to address itself to the political or the legislative power, by whose action thereon this court is bound. (Foster v. Nicolson, 2 Peters, 314; Garcia v. Lee, 12 Peters, 519.)

But, in my judgment, this treaty contains no stipulation in any manner affecting the action of the United States respecting the territory in question. Before examining the language of the treaty, it is material to bear in mine that the part of the ceded territory lying north of thirty-six degrees thirty minutes, and west and north of the present State of Missouri, was then a wilderness, uninhabited save by savages, whose possessory title had not then been extinguished.

It is impossible for me to conceive on what ground France could have advanced a claim, or could have desired to advance a claim, to restrain the United States from making any rules and regulations respecting this territory, which the United States might think fit to make; and still less can I conceive of any reason which would have induced, the United States to yield to such a claim. It was to be expected that France would desire to make the change of sovereignty and jurisdiction as little burdensome as possible to the then inhabitants of Louisiana, and might well exhibit even an anxious solicitude to protect their property and persons, and secure to them and their posterity their religious and political rights; and the United States, as a just Government, might readily accede to all proper stipulations respecting those who were about to have their allegiance transferred. But what interest France could have in uninhabited territory, which, in the language of the treaty, was to be transferred *"forever, and in full sovereignty,"* to the United States, or how the United States could consent to allow a foreign nation to interfere in its purely internal affairs, in which that foreign nation had no concern whatever, is difficult for me to conjecture. In my judgment, this treaty contains nothing of the kind.

The third article is supposed to have a bearing on the question. It is as follows: *"The inhabitants of the ceded territory shall be incorporated in the Union of the United States, and admitted as soon as possible, according to the principles of the Federal Constitution, to the enjoyment of all the rights, advantages, and immunities, of citizens of the United States; and in the mean time they shall be maintained and protected in the enjoyment of their liberty, property, and the religion they profess."*

There are two views of this article, each of which, I think, decisively shows that it was intended to restrain the Congress from excluding slavery from that part of the ceded territory then uninhabited. The first is, that, manifestly, its sole object was to protect individual rights of the then inhabitants of the territory. They are to be *"maintained and protected in the free enjoyment of their liberty, property, and the religion they profess."* But this article does not secure to them the right to go upon the public domain ceded by the treaty, either with or without their slaves. The right or power of doing this did not exist before or at the time the treaty was made. The French and Spanish Governments while they held the country, as well as the united States when they acquired it, always exercised the undoubted right of excluding inhabitants from the Indian country, and of determining when and on what conditions it should be opened to settlers. And a stipulation, that the then inhabitants of Louisiana should be protected in their property, can have no reference to their use of that property, where they had no right, under the treaty, to go with it, save at the will of the United States. If one who was an inhabitant of Louisiana at the time of the treaty had afterwards taken property then owned by him, consisting of fire-arms, ammunition, and spirits, and had gone into the Indian country north of thirty-six degrees thirty minutes, to sell them to the Indians, all must agree the third article of the treaty would not have protected him from indictment under the act of Congress of March 30, 1802, (2 Stat. at Large, 139,) adopted and extended to this territory by the act of March 26, 1804, (2 Stat. at Large, 283.)

Besides, whatever rights were secured were individual rights. If Congress should pass any law which violated such rights of any individual, and those rights were of such a character as not to be within the lawful control of Congress under the Constitution, that individual could complain, and the act of Congress, as to such rights of his, would be inoperative; but it would be valid and operative as to all other persons, whose individual rights did not come under the protection of the treaty. And inasmuch as it does not appear that any inhabitant of Louisiana, whose rights were secured by treaty, had been injured, it would be wholly inadmissible for this court to assume, first, that one or more such cases may have existed; and, second, that if any did exist, the entire law was void—not only as to those cases, if any, in which it could not rightfully operate, but as to all others, wholly unconnected with the treaty, in which such law could rightfully operate.

But it is quite unnecessary, in my opinion, to pursue this inquiry further, because it clearly appears from the language of the article, and it has been decided by this court, that the stipulation was temporary, and ceased to have any effect when the then inhabitants of the Territory of Louisiana, in whose behalf the stipulation was made, were incorporated into the Union.

In the cases of New Orleans v. De Armas et al., (9 Peters, 223,) the question was, whether a title to property, which existed at the date of the treaty, continued to be protected by the treaty after the State of Louisiana was admitted to the Union. The third article of the treaty was relied on. Mr. Chief Justice Marshall said: "This article obviously contemplates two objects. One, that Louisiana shall be admitted into the Union as soon as possible, on an equal footing with the other States; and the other, that, till such admission, the inhabitants of the ceded territory shall be protected in the free enjoyment of their liberty, property, and religion. Had any one of these rights been violated while these stipulations continued in force, the individual supposing himself to be injured might have brought his case into this court, under the twenty-fifth section of the judicial act. But this stipulation ceased to operate when Louisiana became a member of the Union, and its inhabitants were "admitted to the enjoyment of all the rights, advantages, and immunities, of citizens of the United States."

The cases of Chouteau v. Marguerita, (12 Peters, 507,) and Permoli v. New Orleans, (3 How., 589,) are in conformity with this view of the treaty.

To convert this temporary stipulation of the treaty, in behalf of French subjects who then inhabited a small portion of Louisiana, into a permanent restriction upon the power of Congress to regulate territory then uninhabited, and to assert that it not only restrains Congress from affecting the rights of property of the then inhabitants, but enabled them and all other citizens of the United States to go into any part of the ceded territory with their slaves, and hold them there, is a construction of this treaty so opposed to its natural meaning, and so far beyond its subject-matter and the evident design of the parties, that I cannot assent to it. In my opinion, this treaty has no bearing on the present question.

For these reasons, I am of opinion that so much of the several acts of Congress as prohibited slavery and involuntary servitude within that part of the Territory of Wisconsin lying north of thirty-six degrees thirty minutes north latitude, and west of the river Mississippi, were constitutional and valid laws.

I have expressed my opinion, and the reasons therefor, at far greater length than I could have wished, upon the different questions on which I have found it necessary to pass, to arrive at a judgment on the case at bar. These questions are numerous, and the grave importance of some of them required me to exhibit fully the grounds of my opinion. I have touched no question which, in the view I have taken, it was not absolutely necessary for me to pass upon, to ascertain whether the judgment of the Circuit Court should stand or be reversed. I have avoided no question on which the validity of that judgment depends. To have done either more or less, would have been inconsistent with my views of my duty.

In my opinion, the judgment of the Circuit Court should be reversed, and the cause remanded for a new trial.

(Source: *Scott v. San[d]ford*, 19 Howard, 393 1857.)

The South won another important judicial victory in the case of Ableman v. Booth. *As a part of the Compromise of 1850, the Fugitive Slave Act of 1850 specifically forbade states from interfering with the apprehension and return of fugitive slaves. Many Northern states nonetheless maintained or passed new Personal Liberty Laws that required noncompliance with the Federal statute. Federal efforts to uphold the slaveholders' property rights frequently met with outright obstruction. In 1859, the Supreme Court delivered a stinging rebuke to Personal Liberty Laws in* Ableman v. Booth. [See *Dred Scott* Case; Personal Liberty Laws]

3. Majority Decision in *Ableman v. Booth* (1859)
TANEY, C. J. . . . It will be seen, from the foregoing statement of facts, that a judge of the supreme court of the State of Wisconsin, in the first of these cases, claimed and exercised the right to supervise and annul the proceedings of a commissioner of the United States,

and to discharge a prisoner who had been committed by the commissioner for an offense against the laws of this government, and that this exercise of power by the judge was afterwards sanctioned and affirmed by the supreme court of the State.

In the second case, the state court has gone a step further, and claimed and exercised this jurisdiction, but have also determined that their decision is final and conclusive upon all the courts of the United States, and ordered their clerk to disregard and refuse obedience to the writ of error issued by this court, pursuant to the act of Congress of 1789, to bring here for examination and revision the judgment of the state court.

These propositions are new in the jurisprudence of the United States, as well as of the States; and the supremacy of the state courts over the courts of the United States, in cases arising under the Constitution and laws of the United States, is now for the first time asserted and acted upon in the supreme court of a State. . . .

If the judicial power exercised in this instance has been reserved to the States, no offence against the laws of the United States can be punished by their own courts, without the permission and according to the judgement of the courts of the State in which the party happens to be imprisoned; for if the Supreme Court of Wisconsin possessed the power it has exercised in relation to offences against the act of Congress in question, it necessarily follows that they must have the same judicial authority in relation to any other law of the United States; and, consequently, their supervising and controlling power would embrace the whole criminal code of the United States, and extend to offences against our revenue laws, or any other law, intended to guard the different departments of the General Government from fraud or violence. And it would embrace all crimes, from the highest to the lowest; including felonies which are punished with death, as well as misdemeanours, which are punished by imprisonment. . . .

It would seem to be hardly necessary to do more than state the result to which these decisions of the State courts must inevitably lead. It is, of itself, a sufficient and conclusive answer; for no one will suppose that a Government which has now lasted nearly seventy years, enforcing its laws by its own tribunals, and preserving the union of the States could have lasted a single year, or fulfilled the high trusts committed to it, if offences against its laws could not have been punished without the consent of the State in which the culprit was found.

The judges of the supreme court of Wisconsin do not distinctly state from what source they suppose they have derived this judicial power. There can be no such thing as judicial authority, unless it is conferred by a government or sovereignty; and if the judges and courts of Wisconsin possess the jurisdiction they claim, they must derive it either from the United States or the State. It certainly has not been conferred on them by the United States; and it is equally clear that it was not in the power of the State to confer it, even if it had attempted to do so; for no State can authorize one of its judges or courts to exercise judicial power, by habeas corpus or otherwise, within the jurisdiction of another and independent government. And although the State of Wisconsin is sovereign within its territorial limits to a certain extent, yet that sovereignty is limited and restricted by the Constitution of the United States.

And the State of Wisconsin had no more power to authorize these proceedings of its judges and courts, than it would have had if the prisoner had been confined in Michigan, or in any other State of the Union, for an offense against the laws of the State in which he was imprisoned. . . .

But, as we have already said, questions of this kind must always depend upon the Constitution and laws of the United States, and not of a State. The Constitution was not formed merely to guard the States against danger from foreign nations, but mainly to secure union and harmony at home; for if this object could be attained, there would be but little danger from abroad; and to accomplish this purpose, it was felt by the statesmen who framed the Constitution, and by the people who adopted it, that it was necessary that many of the rights of sovereignty which the States then possessed should be ceded to the general government; and that, in the sphere of action assigned to it, it should be supreme, and strong enough to execute its own laws by its own tribunals, without interruption from a State or from state authorities. And it was evident that anything short of this would be inadequate to the main object for which the government was established; and that local interests, local passions or prejudices, incited and fostered by individuals for sinister purposes, would lead to acts of aggression and injustice by one State upon the rights of another, which would ultimately terminate in violence and force, unless there was a common arbiter between them, armed with power enough to protect and guard the rights of all, by appropriate laws, to be carried into execution peaceably by its judicial tribunals.

The language of the Constitution, by which this power is granted is too plain to admit of doubt or to need comment. It declares that "this Constitution, and the laws of the United States which shall be passed in pursuance thereof, and all treaties made, or which shall be made, under the authority of the United States, shall be the supreme law of the land, and the judges in every State shall be bound thereby, anything in the constitution or laws of any State to the contrary notwithstanding."

But the supremacy thus conferred on this government could not peaceably be maintained, unless it was clothed with judicial power, equally paramount in authority to carry it into execution; for if left to the courts of justice of the several States, conflicting decisions would unavoidably take place, and the local tribunals could hardly be expected to be always free from the local influences of which we have spoken. And the Constitution and laws and treaties of the United States, and the powers granted to the federal government, would soon receive different interpretations in different States, and the government of the United States would soon become one thing in one State and another thing in another. It was essential, therefore, to its very existence as a government, that it should have the power of establishing courts of justice, altogether independent of state power, to carry into effect its own laws; and that a tribunal should be established in which all cases which might arise under the Constitution and laws and treaties of the United States, whether in a state court or in a court of the United States, should be finally and conclusively decided. Without such a tribunal, it is obvious that there would be no uniformity of judicial decision; and that the supremacy (which is but another name for independence), so carefully provided in the clause of the Constitution above referred to, could not possibly be maintained peaceably, unless it was associated with this paramount judicial authority.

Accordingly, it was conferred on the general government, in clear, precise, and comprehensive terms. . . .

The importance which the framers of the Constitution attached to such a tribunal for the purpose of preserving internal tranquillity, is strikingly manifested by the clause which gives this court jurisdiction over the sovereign States which compose this Union, when a controversy arises between them. Experience has demonstrated that this power was not unwisely surrendered by the States; for in the time that has already elapsed since this government came into existence, several irritating and angry controversies have taken place between adjoining States, in relation to their respective boundaries, and which have sometimes threatened to end in force and violence, but for the power vested in this court to hear them and decide between them.

The same purposes are clearly indicated by the different language employed when conferring supremacy upon the laws of the United States, and jurisdiction upon its courts. In the first case, it provides that "this Constitution, and the laws of the United States *which shall be made in pursuance thereof*, shall be the supreme law of the land, and obligatory upon the judges in every State." The words in italics show the precision and forethought which marks every clause in the instrument. The sovereignty to be created was to be limited in its powers of legislation, and it passed a law not authorized by its enumerated powers, it was not to be regarded as the supreme law of the land, nor were the state judges bound to carry it into execution. And as the courts of a State, and the courts of the United States, might, and indeed certainly would, often differ as to the extent of the powers conferred by the general government, it was manifested that serious controversies would arise between the authorities of the United States and of the States, which must be settled by force of arms, unless some tribunal was created to decide between them finally and without appeal.

The Constitution has accordingly provided, as far as human foresight could provide, against this danger. And in conferring judicial power upon the federal government, it declares that the jurisdiction of its courts shall extend to all cases arising under "this constitution" and the laws of the United States—leaving out the words of restriction contained in the grant of legislative power which we have above noticed. The judicial power covers every legislative act of Congress, whether it be made within the limits of its delegated powers, or be an assumption of power beyond the grants in the Constitution.

This judicial power was justly regarded as indispensable, not merely to maintain the supremacy of the laws of the United States, but also to guard the States from any encroachment upon their reserved rights by the general government. And as the Constitution is the fundamental and supreme law, if it appears that an act of Congress is not pursuant to and within the limits of the power assigned to the federal government, it is the duty of the courts of the United States to declare it unconstitutional and void. . . .

We do not question the authority of a state court, or judge, who is authorized by the laws of the State to issue the writ of habeas corpus, to issue it in any case where the party is imprisoned within its territorial limits, provided it does not appear, when the application is made, that the person imprisoned is in custody under the authority of the United States. But, after the return is made, and the state judge or court judicially apprized that the party is in custody under the authority of the United States, they can proceed no further. No State judge or Court after they are judicially informed that the party is imprisoned under the authority of the United States, has any right to interfere with him, or to require him to be brought before them. And if the authority of a State, in the form of judicial process or otherwise, should attempt to control the marshal or other authorized officer or agent of the United States, in any respect, in the custody of his prisoner, it would be his duty to resist it, and to call to his aid any force that might be necessary to maintain the authority of law against illegal interference. No judicial process, whatever form it may assume, can have any lawful authority outside of the limits of the jurisdiction of the court or judge by whom it is issued; and an attempt to enforce it beyond these boundaries is nothing less than lawless violence.

And no power is more clearly conferred by the Constitution and the laws of the United States, than the power of this court to decide ultimately and finally, all cases arising under such Constitution and laws; and for that purpose to bring here for revision, by writ of error, the judgement of a state court, where such questions have arisen, and the right claimed under them is denied by the highest judicial tribunal in the State....

If there was any defect of power in the commissioner, or in his mode of proceeding, it was for the tribunals of the United States to revise and correct it, and not for a state court....

But although we think it unnecessary to discuss these questions, yet, as they have been decided by the state court, and are before us on the record, and we are not willing to be misunderstood, it is proper to say that, in the judgement of this court, the act of Congress commonly called the fugitive slave law is, in all of its provisions, fully authorized by the Constitution of the United States; that the commissioner had lawful authority to issue the warrant and commit the party, and that his proceedings were regular and conformable to law....

Judgement of the state court reversed.

(Source: *Ableman v. Booth*, 21 Howard, 506 1859.)

C. SOUTHERN SLAVERY ON THE EVE OF THE CRISIS

The South became increasingly protective of slavery as the sectional crisis intensified in the years before the Civil War. Laws prohibited slave literacy, slave gatherings were viewed with suspicion and occasionally banned altogether, and abolitionist propaganda was forbidden. Although only one-quarter of all Southern whites owned slaves in 1860, and only 10,000 families owned at least 50 slaves, there were powerful cultural as well as economic forces compelling the Southern maintenance of the "peculiar institution." The following selections demonstrate the tangible dehumanization of slavery as well as the attempted intellectualization of racism that guided Southern thought in the antebellum period. [See Slaves]

1. "Great Auction Sale of Slaves, at Savannah, Georgia, March 2d & 3d, 1859," by Q. K. Philander Doesticks [Excerpts]
SALE OF SLAVES.
The largest sale of human chattels that has been made in Star-Spangled America for several years, took place on Wednesday and Thursday of last week, at the Race-

course near the City of Savannah, Georgia. The lot consisted of four hundred and thirty-six men, women, children and infants, being that half of the negro stock remaining on the old Major Butler plantations which fell to one of the two heirs to that estate. Major Butler, dying, left a property valued at more than a million of dollars, the major part of which was invested in rice and cotton plantations, and the slaves thereon, all of which immense fortune descended to two heirs, his sons, Mr. John A. Butler, sometime deceased, and Mr. Pierce M. Butler, still living, and resident in the City of Philadelphia, in the free State of Pennsylvania. Losses in the great crash of 1857–8, and other exigencies of business, have compelled the latter gentleman to realize on his Southern investments, that he may satisfy his pressing creditors. This necessity led to a partition of the negro stock on the Georgia plantations ...

For several days before the sale every hotel in Savannah was crowded with negro speculators from North and South Carolina, Virginia, Georgia, Alabama, and Louisiana, who had been attracted hither by the prospects of making good bargains. Nothing was heard for days, in the bar-rooms and public rooms, but talk of the great sale; criticisms of the business affairs of Mr. Butler, and speculations as to the probable prices the stock would bring. The office of Joseph Bryan, the Negro Broker, who had the management of the sale, was thronged every day by eager inquirers in search of information, and by some who were anxious to buy, but were uncertain as to whether their securities would prove acceptable. Little parties were made up from the various hotels every day to visit the Race-course, distant some three miles from the city, to look over the chattels, discuss their points, and make memoranda for guidance on the day of sale. The buyers were generally of a rough breed, slangy, profane and bearish, being for the most part from the back river and swamp plantations, where the elegancies of polite life are not, perhaps, developed to their fullest extent. In fact, the humanities are sadly neglected by the petty tyrants of the rice-fields that border the great Dismal Swamp, their knowledge of the luxuries of our best society comprehending only revolvers and kindred delicacies.

WHERE THE NEGROES CAME FROM.
The negroes came from two plantations, the one a rice plantation near Darien, in the State of Georgia, not far from the great Okefonokee Swamp, and the other a cotton plantation on the extreme northern point of St. Simon's Island.... There were among them a number of very passable mechanics, who had been taught to do all the rougher sorts of mechanical work on the plantations. There were coopers, carpenters, shoemakers and blacksmiths, each one equal, in his various craft, to the ordinary requirements of a plantation... Though prob-

ably no one of all these would be called a superior, or even an average workman, among the masters of the craft, their knowledge of these various trades sold in some cases for nearly as much as the man—that is, a man without a trade, who would be valued at $900, would readily bring $1,600 or $1,700 if he was a passable blacksmith or cooper.

HOW THEY WERE TREATED IN SAVANNAH.

The negroes were brought to Savannah in small lots, as many at a time as could be conveniently taken care of, the last of them reaching the city the Friday before the sale. They were consigned to the care of Mr. J. Bryan, Auctioneer and Negro Broker, who was to feed and keep them in condition until disposed of. Immediately on their arrival they were taken to the Race-course, and there quartered in the sheds erected for the accommodation of the horses and carriages of gentlemen attending the races. Into these sheds they were huddled pell-mell, without any more attention to their comfort than was necessary to prevent their becoming ill and unsaleable. Each "family" had one or more boxes or bundles, in which were stowed such scanty articles of their clothing as were not brought into immediate requisition, and their tin dishes and gourds for their food and drink.

In these sheds were the chattels huddled together on the floor, there being no sign of bench or table. They eat and slept on the bare boards, their food being rice and beans, with occasionally a bit of bacon and corn bread. Their huge bundles were scattered over the floor, and thereon the slaves sat or reclined, when not restlessly moving about, or gathered into sorrowful groups, discussing the chances of their future fate.

For these preliminary days their shed was constantly visited by speculators. The negroes were examined with as little consideration as if they had been brutes indeed; the buyers pulling their mouths open to see their teeth, pinching their limbs to find how muscular they were, walking them up and down to detect any signs of lameness, making them stoop and bend in different ways that they might be certain there was no concealed rupture or wound; and in addition to all this treatment, asking them scores of questions relative to their qualifications and accomplishments. All these humiliations were submitted to without a murmur, and in some instances with good-natured cheerfulness—where the slave liked the appearance of the proposed buyer, and fancied that he might prove a kind "Mas'r."

THE SALE.

At about 11 o'clock the business men took their places, and announced that the sale would begin. Mr. Bryan, the Negro Broker, is a dapper little man, wearing spectacles and a yachting hat, sharp and sudden in his movements, and perhaps the least bit in the world obtrusively officious—as earnest in his language as he could be without actual swearing. The auctioneer proper was a Mr. Walsh, … a rollicking old boy, with an eye ever on the look-out, and that never lets a bidding nod escape him; a hearty word for every bidder who cares for it, and plenty of jokes to let off when the business gets a little slack.

Mr. Walsh mounted the stand and announced the terms of the sale, "one-third cash, the remainder payable in two equal annual instalments, bearing interest from the day of sale, to be secured by approved mortgage and personal security, or approved acceptances in Savannah, Ga., or Charleston, S. C. Purchasers to pay for papers." The buyers, who were present to the number of about two hundred, clustered around the platform; while the negroes, who were not likely to be immediately wanted, gathered into sad groups in the back-ground, to watch the progress of the selling in which they were so sorrowfully interested. The wind howled outside, and through the open side of the building the driving rain came pouring in; the bar down stairs ceased for a short time its brisk trade; the buyers lit fresh cigars, got ready their catalogues and pencils, and the first lot of human chattels was led upon the stand, not by a white man, but by a sleek mulatto, himself a slave, and who seems to regard the selling of his brethren, in which he so glibly assists, as a capital joke. It had been announced that the negroes would be sold in "families," that is to say, a man would not be parted from his wife, or a mother from a very young child. There is perhaps as much policy as humanity in this arrangement, for thereby many aged and unserviceable people are disposed of, who otherwise would not find a ready sale.

It seems as if every shade of character capable of being implicated in the sale of human flesh and blood was represented among the buyers. There was the Georgia fast young man, with his pantaloons tucked into his boots, his velvet cap jauntily dragged over to one side, his cheek full of tobacco… White-neckclothed, gold-spectacled, and silver-haired old men were there, resembling in appearance that noxious breed of sanctimonious deacons we have at the North. These gentry, with quiet step and subdued voice, moved carefully about among the live stock, ignoring, as a general rule, the men, but tormenting the women with questions which, when accidentally overheard by the disinterested spectator, bred in that spectator's mind an almost irresistible desire to knock somebody down. And then, all imaginable varieties of rough, backwoods rowdies, who began the day in a spirited manner, but who, as its hours progressed, and their practice at the bar became more prolific in results, waxed louder and talkier and more violent, were present, and added a characteristic feature to the assemblage. Those of your readers who have read "Uncle Tom,"—and who has not?—will remember, with peculiar feelings, Legree, the slave-driver and woman-whipper. That that character is not been overdrawn, or too highly colored, there is abundant testimony.

The expression on the faces of all who stepped on the block was always the same, and told of more anguish than it is in the power of words to express. Blighted homes, crushed hopes and broken hearts, was the sad story to be read in all the anxious faces. Some of them regarded the sale with perfect indifference, never making a motion, save to turn from one side to the other at the word of the dapper Mr. Bryan, that all the crowd might have a fair view of their proportions, and then, when the sale was accomplished, stepped down from the block without caring to cast even a look at the buyer, who now held all their happiness in his hands. Others, again, strained their eyes with eager glances from one buyer to another as the bidding went on, trying with earnest attention to follow the rapid voice of the auctioneer. Sometimes, two persons only would be bidding for the same chattel, all the others having resigned the contest, and then the poor creature on the block, conceiving an instantaneous preference for one of the buyers over the other, would regard the rivalry with the intensest interest, the expression of his face changing with every bid, settling into a half smile of joy if the favorite buyer persevered unto the end and secured the property, and settling down into a look of hopeless despair if the other won the victory.

DAPHNEY'S BABY.

The family of Primus, plantation carpenter, consisting of Daphney his wife, with her young babe, and Dido, a girl of three years old, were reached in due course of time. Daphney had a large shawl, which she kept carefully wrapped round her infant and herself. This unusual proceeding attracted much attention, and provoked many remarks, such as these:

"What do you keep your nigger covered up for? Pull off her blanket."

"What's the matter with the gal? Has she got the headache?"

"What's the fault of the gal? Ain't she sound? Pull off her rags and let us see her."

"Who's going to bid on that nigger, if you keep her covered up. Let's see her face."

And a loud chorus of similar remarks, emphasized with profanity, and mingled with sayings too indecent and obscene to be even hinted at here, went up from the crowd of chivalrous Southern gentlemen.

At last the auctioneer obtained a hearing long enough to explain that there was no attempt to practise any deception in the case—the parties were not to be wronged in any way; he had no desire to palm off on them an inferior article; but the truth of the matter was that Daphney had been confined only fifteen days ago, and he thought that on that account she was entitled to the slight indulgence of a blanket, to keep from herself and child the chill air and the driving rain.

Many other babies, of all ages of baby-hood, were sold, but there was nothing particularly interesting about them. There were some thirty babies in the lot; they are esteemed worth to the master a hundred dollars the day they are born, and to increase in value at the rate of a hundred dollars a year till they are sixteen or seventeen years old, at which age they bring the best prices.

THE LOVE STORY OF JEFFREY AND DORCAS.

Jeffrey, chattel No. 319, marked as a "prime cotton hand," aged 23 years, was put up. Jeffrey being a likely lad, the competition was high. The first bid was $1,100, and he was finally sold for $1,310. Jeffrey was sold alone; he had no incumbrance in the shape of an aged father or mother, who must necessarily be sold with him; nor had he any children, for Jeffrey was not married. But Jeffrey, chattel No. 319, being human in his affections, had dared to cherish a love for Dorcas, chattel No. 278; and Dorcas, not having the fear of her master before her eyes, had given her heart to Jeffrey. …Be that as it may, Jeffrey was sold. He finds out his new master; and hat in hand, the big tears standing in his eyes, and his voice trembling with emotion, he stands before that master and tells his simple story, praying that his betrothed may be bought with him. Though his voice trembles, there is no embarrassment in his manner; his fears have killed all the bashfulness that would naturally attend such a recital to a stranger, and before unsympathizing witnesses; he feels that he is pleading for the happiness of her he loves, as well as for his own, and his tale is told in a frank and manly way.

The man seems touched by Jeffrey's last remarks, and bids him fetch out his "gal, and let's see what she looks like." Jeffrey goes into the long room, and presently returns with Dorcas, looking very sad and self-possessed, without a particle of embarrassment at the trying position in which she is placed. She makes the accustomed curtsy, and stands meekly with her hands clasped across her bosom, waiting the result. The buyer regards her with a critical eye, and growls in a low voice that the "gal has good p'ints." Then he goes on to a more minute and careful examination of her working abilities. He turns her around, makes her stoop, and walk; and then he takes off her turban to look at her head that no wound or disease be concealed by the gay handkerchief; he looks at her teeth, and feels of her arms, and at last announces himself pleased with the

result of his observations, whereat Jeffrey, who has stood near, trembling with eager hope, is overjoyed, and he smiles for the first time. The buyer then crowns Jeffrey's happiness by making a promise that he will buy her, if the price isn't run up too high. And the two lovers step aside and congratulate each other on their good fortune. But Dorcas is not to be sold till the next day, and there are twenty-four long hours of feverish expectation.

At last comes the trying moment, and Dorcas steps up on the stand. But now a most unexpected feature in the drama is for the first time unmasked: *Dorcas is not to be sold alone*, but with a family of four others. Full of dismay, Jeffrey looks to his master, who shakes his head, for, although he might be induced to buy Dorcas alone, he has no use for the rest of the family. Jeffrey reads his doom in his master's look, and turns away, the tears streaming down his honest face. So Dorcas is sold, and her toiling life is to be spent in the cotton fields of South Carolina, while Jeffrey goes to the rice plantation of the Great Swamp. . . .

MR. PIERCE BUTLER GIVES
HIS PEOPLE A DOLLAR A-PIECE.
Leaving the Race buildings, where the scenes we have described took place, a crowd of negroes were seen gathered eagerly about a white man. That man was Pierce M. Butler, of the free City of Philadelphia, who was solacing the wounded hearts of the people he had sold from their firesides and their homes, by doling out to them small change at the rate of a dollar a head. To every negro he had sold, who presented his claim for the paltry pittance, he gave the munificent stipend of one whole dollar, in specie; he being provided with two canvas bags of 25 cent pieces, fresh from the mint, to give an additional glitter to his generosity.

As the last family stepped down the block, the rain ceased, for the first time in four days the clouds broke away, and the soft sunlight fell on the scene. The unhappy slaves had many of them been already removed, and others were now departing with their new masters.

That night, not a steamer left that Southern port, not a train of cars sped away from that cruel city, that did not bear each its own sad burden of those unhappy ones, whose only crime is that they are not strong and wise. Some of them maimed and wounded, some scarred and gashed, by accident, or by the hand of ruthless drivers—all sad and sorrowful as human hearts can be.

(Source: Doesticks, Q. K. Philander. *Great Auction Sale of Slaves, at Savannah, Georgia, March 2d & 3d, 1859*. n.p., 1863. Daniel A. P. Murray Pamphlet Collection, Library of Congress, Washington, D.C.)

2. "Characteristics and Capabilities of the Negro Race," by William H. Holcombe, M.D. [Excerpt] (December 1861)

The negro is easily mesmerized, very easily impressed by the superior volitional energy of the white man. This is indeed the secret of their obedience and subservience in the South; the whip has very little to do with their subjugation, and is used quite as often to protect them from each other as to render them dutiful to their masters. There is in the negro an instinctive sense of his own hopeless inferiority to the white man, and a strong natural feeling of the perfect propriety of a reasonable and just subordination. This may be claimed as a relic of his barbarism—a servile nature generated by submission for ages to despotic power; but even if this were so, it has at least blunted the sensibilities and ameliorated the cares of his present transitional state of bondage. It is a pity to mar the beautiful and heroic pictures of abolition novelists and poets, but science and fact are both unimaginative and inexorable, and a negro animated by the spirit of Hampden, or Tell, or Hancock, is a monstrosity which nature has never yet produced. This apathy or feebleness of will makes them easily managed; they are readily subdued by corporeal punishment, and, as is generally the case with white children, the chastisement, instead of leaving them sulky and revengeful, puts them into the best imaginable humor both with themselves and master. Very few Northern people know this, or understand the reason of it.

(Source: *Southern Literary Messenger*, December 1861, p. 404.)

III. The Harper's Ferry Raid

On Sunday, 16 October 1859, radical abolitionist John Brown led a small band of raiders to capture the federal arsenal at Harper's Ferry. A company of United States Marines under the leadership of Colonel Robert E. Lee stormed the engine house where Brown had holed up and killed ten of Brown's men, including two of his sons. Seriously wounded himself, Brown was captured. On 2 November, Brown was convicted of treason, murder, and insurrection and was sentenced to death. His final address to the court appears below. On 2 December 1859, he was hanged in Charles Town, Virginia, and instantly became a martyr for the abolitionist cause. [See Brown, John]

1. John Brown's Final Address to the Court (2 November 1859)

I have, may it please the court, a few words to say.

In the first place, I deny everything but what I have all along admitted: of a design on my part to free slaves. I intended certainly to have made a clean thing of that matter, as I did last winter, when I went into Missouri and there took slaves without the snapping of a gun on either side, moving them through the country, and

finally leaving them in Canada. I designed to have done the same thing again on a larger scale. That was all I intended. I never did intend murder, or treason, or the destruction of property, or to excite or incite slaves to rebellion, or to make insurrection.

I have another objection, and that is that it is unjust that I should suffer such a penalty. Had I interfered in the manner which I admit, and which I admit has been fairly proved—for I admire the truthfulness and candor of the greater portion of the witnesses who have testified in this case—had I so interfered in behalf of the rich, the powerful, the intelligent, the so called great, or in the behalf of any of their friends, either father, mother, brother, sister, wife, or children, or any of that class, and suffered and sacrificed what I have in this interference, it would have been all right. Every man in this court would have deemed it an act worthy of reward rather than punishment.

This court acknowledges, too, as I suppose, the validity of the law of God. I see a book kissed, which I suppose to be the Bible, or at least the New Testament, which teaches me that all things whatsoever I would that men should do to me, I should do even so to them. It teaches me, further, to remember them that are in bonds as bound with them. I endeavored to act up to the instruction. I say I am yet too young to understand that God is any respecter of persons. I believe that to have interfered as I have done, as I have always freely admitted I have done, in behalf of his despised poor, I did not wrong but right. Now, if it is deemed necessary that I should forfeit my life for the furtherance of the ends of justice, and mingle my blood further with the blood of my children and with the blood of millions in this slave country whose rights are disregarded by wicked, cruel, and unjust enactments, I say let it be done.

Let me say one word further. I feel entirely satisfied with the treatment I have received on my trial. Considering all the circumstances, it has been more generous than I expected. But I feel no consciousness of guilt. I have stated from the first what was my intention, and what was not. I never had any design against the liberty of any person, nor any disposition to commit treason or incite slaves to rebel or make any general insurrection. I never encouraged any man to do so, but always discouraged any idea of that kind.

Let me say, also, in regard to the statements made by some of those who were connected with me, I hear it has been stated by some of them that I have induced them to join me. But the contrary is true. I do not say this to injure them, but as regretting their weakness. Not one but joined me of his own accord, and the greater part at his own expense. A number of them I never saw, and never had a word of conversation with, till the day they came to me, and that was for the purpose I have stated.

Now I have done.

(Source: National Archives, Washington, DC.)

IV. The Election of 1860

The election of 1860 marked a major watershed in American politics. The Democratic Party divided over the issue of slavery, and other disaffected voters tried to find a political home in the hastily created Constitutional Union Party. Meanwhile, the Republican Party mounted its second presidential campaign, an endeavor that would elect Abraham Lincoln and impel the secession crisis. The platforms of the two Democratic Party factions, of the Republicans, and of the Constitutional Union Party follow. [See Constitutional Union Party; Democratic Party; Election of 1860; Republican Party]

1. The Democratic Party Platform of 1860
June 18, 1860

1. Resolved, That we, the Democracy of the Union in Convention assembled, hereby declare our affirmance of the resolutions unanimously adopted and declared as a platform of principles by the Democratic Convention at Cincinnati, in the year 1856, believing that Democratic principles are unchangeable in their nature, when applied to the same subject matters; and we recommend, as the only further resolutions, the following:

2. Inasmuch as difference of opinion exists in the Democratic party as to the nature and extent of the powers of a Territorial Legislature, and as to the powers and duties of Congress, under the Constitution of the United States, over the institution of slavery within the Territories,

Resolved, That the Democratic party will abide by the decision of the Supreme Court of the United States upon these questions of Constitutional law.

3. Resolved, That it is the duty of the United States to afford ample and complete protection to all its citizens, whether at home or abroad, and whether native or foreign born.

4. Resolved, That one of the necessities of the age, in a military, commercial, and postal point of view, is speedy communication between the Atlantic and Pacific States; and the Democratic party pledge such Constitutional Government aid as will insure the construction of a Railroad to the Pacific coast, at the earliest practicable period.

5. Resolved, That the Democratic party are in favor of the acquisition of the Island of Cuba on such terms as shall be honorable to ourselves and just to Spain.

6. Resolved, That the enactments of the State Legislatures to defeat the faithful execution of the Fugitive Slave Law, are hostile in character, subversive of the Constitution, and revolutionary in their effect.

7. *Resolved,* That it is in accordance with the interpretation of the Cincinnati platform, that during the existence of the Territorial Governments the measure of restriction, whatever it may be, imposed by the Federal Constitution on the power of the Territorial Legislature over the subject, of the domestic relations, as the same has been, or shall hereafter be finally determined by the Supreme Court of the United States, should be respected by all good citizens, and enforced with promptness and fidelity by every branch of the general government.

(Source: Porter, Kirk H., and Donald Bruce Johnson. *National Party Platforms 1840–1960.* Urbana: University of Illinois Press, 1961.)

2. The Democratic (Breckinridge Faction) Platform of 1860

June, 1860

Resolved, That the platform adopted by the Democratic party at Cincinnati be affirmed, with the following explanatory resolutions:

1. That the Government of a Territory organized by an act of Congress is provisional and temporary, and during its existence all citizens of the United States have an equal right to settle with their property in the Territory, without their rights, either of person or property being destroyed or impaired by Congressional or Territorial legislation.

2. That it is the duty of the Federal Government, in all its departments, to protect, when necessary, the rights of persons and property in the Territories, and wherever else its constitutional authority extends.

3. That when the settlers in a Territory, having an adequate population, form a State Constitution, the right of sovereignty commences, and being consummated by admission into the Union, they stand on an equal footing with the people of other States, and the State thus organized ought to be admitted into the Federal Union, whether its Constitution prohibits or recognizes the institution of slavery.

Resolved, That the Democratic party are in favor of the acquisition of the Island of Cuba, on such terms as shall be honorable to ourselves and just to Spain, at the earliest practicable moment.

Resolved, That the enactments of State Legislatures to defeat the faithful execution of the Fugitive Slave Law are hostile in character, subversive of the Constitution, and revolutionary in their effect.

Resolved, That the Democracy of the United States recognize it as the imperative duty of this Government to protect the naturalized citizen in all his rights, whether at home or in foreign lands, to the same extent as its native-born citizens.

WHEREAS, One of the greatest necessities of the age, in a political, commercial, postal and military point of view, is a speedy communication between the Pacific and Atlantic coasts, Therefore be it

Resolved, That the National Democratic party do hereby pledge themselves to use every means in their power to secure the passage of some bills, to the extent of the constitutional authority of Congress for the construction of a Pacific Railroad from the Mississippi River to the Pacific Ocean, at the earliest practicable moment.

(Source: Porter, Kirk H., and Donald Bruce Johnson. *National Party Platforms 1840–1960.* Urbana: University of Illinois Press, 1961.)

3. Platform of the Republican Party (1860)

Chicago, Illinois, May 16, 1860

Resolved, That we, the delegated representatives of the Republican electors of the United States, in Convention assembled, in discharge of the duty we owe to our constituents and our country, unite in the following declarations:

1. That the history of the nation, during the last four years, has fully established the propriety and necessity of the organization and perpetuation of the Republican party, and that the causes which called it into existence are permanent in their nature, and now, more than ever before, demand its peaceful and constitutional triumph.

2. That the maintenance of the principles promulgated in the Declaration of Independence and embodied in the Federal Constitution, "That all men are created equal; that they are endowed by their Creator with certain inalienable rights; that among these are life, liberty and the pursuit of happiness; that, to secure these rights, governments are instituted among men, deriving their just powers from the consent of the governed," is essential to the preservation of our Republican institutions; and that the Federal Constitution, the Rights of the States, and the Union of the States, must and shall be preserved.

3. That to the Union of the States this nation owes its unprecedented increase in population, its surprising development of material resources, its rapid augmentation of wealth, its happiness at home and its honor abroad; and we hold in abhorrence all schemes for Disunion, come from whatever source they may; And we congratulate the country that no Republican member of Congress has uttered or countenanced the threats of Disunion so often made by Democratic members, without rebuke and with applause from their political associates; and we denounce those threats of Disunion, in case of a popular overthrow of their ascendency, as denying the vital principles of a free government, and as an avowal of contemplated treason, which it is the imperative duty of an indignant People sternly to rebuke and forever silence.

4. That the maintenance inviolate of the rights of the States, and especially the right of each State to order and control its own domestic institutions according to its own judgment exclusively, is essential to that balance of powers on which the perfection and endurance of our political fabric depends; and we denounce the lawless invasion by armed force of the soil of any State or Territory, no matter under what pretext, as among the gravest of crimes.

5. That the present Democratic Administration has far exceeded our worst apprehensions, in its measureless subserviency to the exactions of a sectional interest, as especially evinced in its desperate exertions to force the infamous Lecompton constitution upon the protesting people of Kansas; in construing the personal relation between master and servant to involve an unqualified property in persons; in its attempted enforcement, everywhere, on land and sea, through the intervention of Congress and of the Federal Courts of the extreme pretensions of a purely local interest; and in its general and unvarying abuse of the power intrusted to it by a confiding people. . . .

7. That the new dogma that the Constitution, of its own force, carries Slavery into any or all of the Territories of the United States, is a dangerous political heresy, at variance with the explicit provisions of that instrument itself, with contemporaneous exposition, and with legislative and judicial precedent; is revolutionary in its tendency, and subversive of the peace and harmony of the country.

8. That the normal condition of all the territory of the United States is that of freedom; That as our Republican fathers, when they had abolished slavery in all our national territory, ordained that "*no* person should be deprived of life, liberty, or property, without due process of law," it becomes our duty, by legislation, whenever such legislation is necessary, to maintain this provision of the Constitution against all attempts to violate it; and we deny the authority of Congress, of a territorial legislature, or of any individuals, to give legal existence to Slavery in any Territory of the United States.

9. That we brand the recent reopening of the African slave-trade, under the cover of our national flag, aided by perversions of judicial power, as a crime against humanity and a burning shame to our country and age; and we call upon Congress to take prompt and efficient measures for the total and final suppression of that execrable traffic.

10. That in the recent vetoes, by their Federal Governors, of the acts of the Legislatures of Kansas and Nebraska, prohibiting Slavery in those Territories, we find a practical illustration of the boasted Democratic principle of Non-Intervention and Popular Sovereignty embodied in the Kansas-Nebraska bill, and a demonstration of the deception and fraud involved therein.

11. That Kansas should, of right, be immediately admitted as a State under the Constitution recently formed and adopted by her people, and accepted by the House of Representatives.

12. That, while providing revenue for the support of the General Government by duties upon imports, sound policy requires such an adjustment of these imposts as to encourage the development of the industrial interests of the whole country; and we commend that policy of national exchanges which secures to the working men liberal wages, to agriculture remunerating prices, to mechanics and manufacturers an adequate reward for their skill, labor and enterprise, and to the nation commercial prosperity and independence.

13. That we protest against any sale or alienation to others of the Public Lands held by actual settlers, and against any view of the Homestead policy which regards the settlers as paupers or supplicants for public bounty; and we demand the passage by Congress of the complete and satisfactory Homestead measure which has already passed the house.

14. That the Republican Party is opposed to any change in our Naturalization Laws or any State legislation by which the rights of our citizenship hitherto accorded to immigrants from foreign lands shall be abridged or impaired; and in favor of giving a full and efficient protection to the rights of all classes of citizens, whether native or naturalized, both at home and abroad.

15. That appropriations by Congress for River and Harbor improvements of a National character, required for the accommodation and security of an existing commerce, are authorized by the Constitution, and justified by the obligations of Government to protect the lives and property of its citizens.

16. That a Railroad to the Pacific Ocean is imperatively demanded by the interests of the whole country; that the Federal Government ought to render immediate and efficient aid in its construction; and that, as preliminary thereto, a daily Overland Mail should be promptly established. . . .

(Source: Porter, Kirk H., and Donald Bruce Johnson. *National Party Platforms 1840–1960.* Urbana: University of Illinois Press, 1961.)

4. The Constitutional Union Party (1860)

Whereas, experience has demonstrated that platforms adopted by the partisan conventions of the country have had the effect to mislead and deceive the people, and at the same time to widen the political divisions of the country, by the creation and encouragement of geographical and sectional parties; therefore,

Resolved, that it is both the part of patriotism and of duty to *recognize* no political principles other than the CONSTITUTION OF THE COUNTRY, THE UNION OF THE STATES, AND THE ENFORCE-MENT OF THE LAWS; and that, as representatives of the Constitutional Union men of the country in national convention assembled, we hereby pledge our-selves to maintain, protect, and defend, separately and unitedly, these great principles of public liberty and national safety against all enemies, at home and abroad, believing that thereby peace may once more be restored to the country, the rights of the people and of the states reestablished, and the government again placed in that condition of justice, fraternity, and equality which, under the example and Constitution of our fathers, has solemnly bound every citizen of the United States to maintain a more perfect Union, establish justice, insure domestic tranquillity, provide for the common defense, promote the general welfare and secure the blessings of liberty to ourselves and our posterity.

(Source: Thomas H. McKee, ed. *The National Convention and Platforms of the Political Parties, 1789–1905* [1906].)

V. Secession—The First Wave

Abraham Lincoln's election caused seven southern states to secede during the winter of 1860–1861. As this crisis was about to evolve, President James Buchanan's annual message blamed the predicament on the North, but he denounced secession as unconstitutional. He also announced his aversion to coercing seceding states and strongly supported efforts to frame a compromise. Tennessee's Andrew Johnson had always supported home-stead legislation and public education, while opposing radical states' rights doctrines. Although Johnson endorsed John C. Breckinridge in the 1860 presidential contest, he fiercely condemned secession after Lincoln's election. Johnson's sup-port of the Union was unique in its vehemence, especially among Southern Unionists. [See Buchanan, James; Johnson, Andrew]

1. James Buchanan's Annual Message (3 December 1860)

Throughout the year since our last meeting, the coun-try has been eminently prosperous in all its material interests. The general health has been excellent, our harvests have been abundant, and plenty smiles throughout the land. Our commerce and manufactures have been prosecuted with energy and industry, and have yielded fair and ample returns. In short, no nation in the tide of time has ever presented a spectacle of greater material prosperity than we have done until within a very recent period.

Why is it, then, that discontent now so extensively prevails, and the Union of the States, which is the source of all these blessings, is threatened with destruc-tion? The long-continued and intemperate interference of the Northern people with the question of slavery in the Southern States has at length produced its natural effects. The different sections of the Union are now arrayed against each other, and the time has arrived, so much dreaded by the Father of his Country, when hos-tile geographical parties have been formed. I have long foreseen and often forewarned my countrymen of the now impending danger.

This does not proceed solely from the claim on the part of Congress or the territorial legislatures to exclude slavery from the Territories, or from the efforts of differ-ent States to defeat the execution of the Fugitive Slave Law. All or any of these evils might have been endured by the South without danger to the Union—as others have been—in the hope that time and reflection might apply the remedy. The immediate peril arises, not so much from these causes, as from the fact that the inces-sant and violent agitation of the slavery question throughout the North for the last quarter of a century has at length produced its malign influence on the slaves, and inspired them with vague notions of freedom.

Hence a sense of security no longer exists around the family altar. This feeling of peace at home has given place to apprehensions of servile insurrection. Many a matron throughout the South retires at night in dread of what may befall herself and her children before the morning. Should this apprehension of domestic danger, whether real or imaginary, extend and intensify itself until it shall prevade the masses of the Southern peo-ple, then disunion will become inevitable.

Self-preservation is the first law of nature, and has been implanted in the heart of man by his Creator for the wisest purpose; and no political union, however fraught with blessings and benefits in all other respects, can long continue, if the necessary consequence be to render the homes and firesides of nearly half the parties to it habitually and hopelessly insecure. Sooner or later the bonds of such a union must be severed. It is my con-viction that this fatal period has not yet arrived; and my prayer to God is that He will preserve the Constitution and the Union throughout all generations.

But let us take warning in time, and remove the cause of danger. It cannot be denied that, for five and twenty years, the agitation at the North against slavery in the South has been incessant. In 1835 pictorial handbills and inflammatory appeals were circulated extensively throughout the South, of a character to excite the passions of the slaves; and in the language of General Jackson, "to stimulate them to insurrection, and produce all the horrors of a servile war." This agi-tation has ever since been continued by the public press, by the proceedings of State and county conven-tions, and by abolition sermons and lectures. The time of Congress has been occupied in violent speeches on this never-ending subject; and appeals in pamphlet and other forms, indorsed by distinguished names, have been sent forth from this central point, and spread broadcast over the Union.

How easy would it be for the American people to settle the slavery question forever, and to restore peace and harmony to this distracted country!

They, and they alone, can do it. All that is necessary to accomplish the object, and all for which the slave States have ever contended, is to be let alone, and permitted to manage their domestic institutions in their own way. As sovereign States, they, and they alone, are responsible before God and the world for the slavery existing among them. For this, the people of the North are not more responsible, and have no more right to interfere, than with similar institutions in Russia or in Brazil. Upon their good sense and patriotic forbearance I confess I still greatly rely. Without their aid, it is beyond the power of any President, no matter what may be his own political proclivities, to restore peace and harmony among the States. Wisely limited and restrained as is his power, under our Constitution and laws, he alone can accomplish but little, for good or for evil, on such a momentous question.

(*Source:* National Archives, Washington, DC)

2. "Not a Southern or Any Other Confederacy" (18 December 1860)
Andrew Johnson of Tennessee Senate, December 18 1860

We are told that certain States will go out and tear this accursed Constitution into fragments, and drag the pillars of this mighty edifice down upon us and involve us all in one common ruin. Will the border States submit to such a threat? No. If they do not come into the movement the pillars of this stupendous fabric of human freedom and greatness and goodness are to be pulled down, and all will be involved in one common ruin. Such is the threatening language used. "You shall come into our confederacy, or we will coerce you to the emancipation of your slaves." That is the language which is held toward us.

We in the South have complained of and condemned the position assumed by the Abolitionists. We have complained that their intention was to hem slavery in, so that, like the scorpion when surrounded by fire, if it did not die from the intense heat of the scorching flames, it would perish in its own poisonous skin. Now, our sister, without consulting her sisters, without caring for their interest or their consent, says that she will move forward; that she will destroy the Government under which we have lived, and that hereafter, when she forms a government or a constitu-

tion, unless the border States come in, she will pass laws prohibiting the importation of slaves into her State from those States, and thereby obstruct the slave trade among the States, and throw the institution back upon the border States, so that they will be compelled to emancipate their slaves upon the principle laid down by the Abolition party. That is the rod held over us!

I tell our sisters in the South that so far as Tennessee is concerned she will not be dragged into a Southern or any other confederacy until she has had time to consider; and then she will go when she believes it to be her interest, and not before. I tell our Northern friends, who are resisting the execution of the laws made in conformity with the Constitution, that we will not be driven on the other hand into their confederacy, and we will not go into it unless it suits us, and they give us such guaranties as we deem right and proper. We say to you of the South we are not to be frightened and coerced. Oh, when one talks about coercing a State, how maddening and insulting to the State; but, when you want to bring the other States to terms, how easy to point out a means by which to coerce them! But, sir, we do not intend to be coerced.

There are many ideas afloat about this threatened dissolution, and it is time to speak out. The question arises in reference to the protection and preservation of the institution of slavery, whether dissolution is a remedy or will give to it protection. I avow here, to-day, that if I were an Abolitionist, and wanted to accomplish the overthrow and abolition of the institution of slavery in the Southern States, the first step that I would take would be to break the bonds of this Union, and dissolve this Government. I believe the continuance of slavery depends upon the preservation of this Union and a compliance with all the guaranties of the Constitution. I believe an interference with it will break up the Union; and I believe a dissolution of the Union will, in the end, though it may be some time to come, overthrow the institution of slavery. Hence we find so many in the North who desire the dissolution of these States as the most certain and direct and effectual means of overthrowing the institution of slavery.

What protection would it be to dissolve this Union? What protection would it be to us to convert this nation into two hostile powers, the one warring with the other? Whose property is at stake? Whose interest is endangered? Is it not the property of the border States? Yes; slavery would commence to retreat southward the very moment this Government was converted into hostile powers, and you made the line between the slaveholding and non-slaveholding States the line of division. Then what remedy do we get for the institution of slavery? Must we keep up a standing army? Must we keep up forts bristling with arms along the whole border? This is a question to be considered, one that involves the future; and no step should be taken without mature reflection.

Again: if there is one division of the states, will there not be more than one? I heard a Senator say the other day that he would rather see this Government separated into thirty-three fractional parts than to see it consolidated. I am opposed to the consolidation of Government, and I am as much for the reserved rights of States as any one; but, rather than see this Union divided into thirty-three petty governments, with a little prince in one, a potentate in another, a little aristocracy in a third, a little democracy in a fourth, and a republic somewhere else; a citizen not being able to pass from one State to another without a passport or a commission from his government; with quarreling and warring among the little petty powers, which would result in anarchy; I would rather see this Government to-day converted into a consolidated government. It would be better for the American people; it would be better for our kind; it would be better for humanity; better for Christianity; better for all that tends to elevate and ennoble man, than breaking up this splendid, this magnificent, this stupendous fabric of human government, the most perfect that the world ever saw, and which has succeeded thus far without a parallel in the history of the world.

I tell our Northern friends that the constitutional guaranties must be carried out; for the time may come when, after we have exhausted all honorable and fair means, if this Government still fails to execute the laws, and protect us in our rights, it will be at an end. Gentlemen of the North need not deceive themselves in that particular; but we intend to act in the Union and under the Constitution, and not out of it. We do not intend that you shall drive us out of this house that was reared by the hands of our fathers. It is our house. We have a right here; and because you come forward and violate the ordinances of this house I do not intend to go out; and if you persist in the violation of the ordinances of the house we intend to eject you from the building and retain the possession ourselves.

(Source: *Great Debates in American History*. Vol. 5. New York: Current Literature Publishing Co., 1913.)

South Carolina led the wave of secession that swept through the Gulf states after Lincoln's election. By early February six other states had joined South Carolina in withdrawing from the Union. The instruments that each used to accomplish this, and occasionally to offer even more elaborate justifications for disunion, are reproduced below in the order of their passage. By the time Texas had seceded, the Confederate States of America was on the verge of being formed in Montgomery, Alabama, and Texas was duly admitted to the Confederacy, establishing a pattern that
would be followed in the second wave of secession after the firing on Fort Sumter. [See Secession]

A. SOUTH CAROLINA

1. Secession Ordinance (20 December 1860)

AN ORDINANCE to dissolve the union between the State of South Carolina and other States united with her under the compact entitled "The Constitution of the United States of America."

We, the people of the State of South Carolina, in convention assembled, do declare and ordain, and it is hereby declared and ordained, That the ordinance adopted by us in convention on the twenty-third day of May, in the year of our Lord one thousand seven hundred and eighty-eight, whereby the Constitution of the United States of America was ratified, and also all acts and parts of acts of the General Assembly of this State ratifying amendments of the said Constitution, are hereby repealed; and that the union now subsisting between South Carolina and other States, under the name of the "United States of America," is hereby dissolved.

Done at Charleston the twentieth day of December, in the year of our Lord one thousand eight hundred and sixty.

(Source: U.S. War Department. *War of the Rebellion: A Compilation of the Official Records of the Union and Confederate Armies*. Ser. IV, Vol. I [S# 127].)

2. Declaration of the Immediate Causes which Induce and Justify the Secession of South Carolina from the Federal Union (24 December 1860)

The people of the State of South Carolina, in Convention assembled, on the 26th day of April, A.D., 1852, declared that the frequent violations of the Constitution of the United States, by the Federal Government, and its encroachments upon the reserved rights of the States, fully justified this State in then withdrawing from the Federal Union; but in deference to the opinions and wishes of the other slaveholding States, she forbore at that time to exercise this right. Since that time, these encroachments have continued to increase, and further forbearance ceases to be a virtue.

And now the State of South Carolina having resumed her separate and equal place among nations, deems it due to herself, to the remaining United States of America, and to the nations of the world, that she should declare the immediate causes which have led to this act.

In the year 1765, that portion of the British Empire embracing Great Britain, undertook to make laws for the government of that portion composed of the thirteen American Colonies. A struggle for the right of self-government ensued, which resulted, on the 4th of

July, 1776, in a Declaration, by the Colonies, "that they are, and of right ought to be, FREE AND INDEPENDENT STATES; and that, as free and independent States, they have full power to levy war, conclude peace, contract alliances, establish commerce, and to do all other acts and things which independent States may of right do."

They further solemnly declared that whenever any "form of government becomes destructive of the ends for which it was established, it is the right of the people to alter or abolish it, and to institute a new government." Deeming the Government of Great Britain to have become destructive of these ends, they declared that the Colonies "are absolved from all allegiance to the British Crown, and that all political connection between them and the State of Great Britain is, and ought to be, totally dissolved."

In pursuance of this Declaration of Independence, each of the thirteen States proceeded to exercise its separate sovereignty; adopted for itself a Constitution, and appointed officers for the administration of government in all its departments—Legislative, Executive and Judicial. For purposes of defense, they united their arms and their counsels; and, in 1778, they entered into a League known as the Articles of Confederation, whereby they agreed to entrust the administration of their external relations to a common agent, known as the Congress of the United States, expressly declaring, in the first Article "that each State retains its sovereignty, freedom and independence, and every power, jurisdiction and right which is not, by this Confederation, expressly delegated to the United States in Congress assembled."

Under this Confederation the war of the Revolution was carried on, and on the 3rd of September, 1783, the contest ended, and a definite Treaty was signed by Great Britain, in which she acknowledged the independence of the Colonies in the following terms: "ARTICLE 1—His Britannic Majesty acknowledges the said United States, viz: New Hampshire, Massachusetts Bay, Rhode Island and Providence Plantations, Connecticut, New York, New Jersey, Pennsylvania, Delaware, Maryland, Virginia, North Carolina, South Carolina and Georgia, to be FREE, SOVEREIGN AND INDEPENDENT STATES; that he treats with them as such; and for himself, his heirs and successors, relinquishes all claims to the government, propriety and territorial rights of the same and every part thereof."

Thus were established the two great principles asserted by the Colonies, namely: the right of a State to govern itself; and the right of a people to abolish a Government when it becomes destructive of the ends for which it was instituted. And concurrent with the establishment of these principles, was the fact, that each Colony became and was recognized by the mother Country a FREE, SOVEREIGN AND INDEPENDENT STATE.

In 1787, Deputies were appointed by the States to revise the Articles of Confederation, and on 17th September, 1787, these Deputies recommended for the adoption of the States, the Articles of Union, known as the Constitution of the United States.

The parties to whom this Constitution was submitted, were the several sovereign States; they were to agree or disagree, and when nine of them agreed the compact was to take effect among those concurring; and the General Government, as the common agent, was then invested with their authority.

If only nine of the thirteen States had concurred, the other four would have remained as they then were—separate, sovereign States, independent of any of the provisions of the Constitution. In fact, two of the States did not accede to the Constitution until long after it had gone into operation among the other eleven; and during that interval, they each exercised the functions of an independent nation.

By this Constitution, certain duties were imposed upon the several States, and the exercise of certain of their powers was restrained, which necessarily implied their continued existence as sovereign States. But to remove all doubt, an amendment was added, which declared that the powers not delegated to the United States by the Constitution, nor prohibited by it to the States, are reserved to the States, respectively, or to the people. On the 23d May, 1788, South Carolina, by a Convention of her People, passed an Ordinance assenting to this Constitution, and afterwards altered her own Constitution, to conform herself to the obligations she had undertaken.

Thus was established, by compact between the States, a Government with definite objects and powers, limited to the express words of the grant. This limitation left the whole remaining mass of power subject to the clause reserving it to the States or to the people, and rendered unnecessary any specification of reserved rights.

We hold that the Government thus established is subject to the two great principles asserted in the Declaration of Independence; and we hold further, that the mode of its formation subjects it to a third fundamental principle, namely: the law of compact. We maintain that in every compact between two or more parties, the obligation is mutual; that the failure of one of the contracting parties to perform a material part of the agreement, entirely releases the obligation of the other; and that where no arbiter is provided, each party is remitted to his own judgment to determine the fact of failure, with all its consequences.

In the present case, that fact is established with certainty. We assert that fourteen of the States have deliberately refused, for years past, to fulfill their constitutional obligations, and we refer to their own Statutes for the proof.

The Constitution of the United States, in its fourth Article, provides as follows: "No person held to service or labor in one State, under the laws thereof, escaping into another, shall, in consequence of any law or regulation therein, be discharged from such service or labor, but shall be delivered up, on claim of the party to whom such service or labor may be due."

This stipulation was so material to the compact, that without it that compact would not have been made. The greater number of the contracting parties held slaves, and they had previously evinced their estimate of the value of such a stipulation by making it a condition in the Ordinance for the government of the territory ceded by Virginia, which now composes the States north of the Ohio River.

The same article of the Constitution stipulates also for rendition by the several States of fugitives from justice from the other States.

The General Government, as the common agent, passed laws to carry into effect these stipulations of the States. For many years these laws were executed. But an increasing hostility on the part of the non-slaveholding States to the institution of slavery, has led to a disregard of their obligations, and the laws of the General Government have ceased to effect the objects of the Constitution. The States of Maine, New Hampshire, Vermont, Massachusetts, Connecticut, Rhode Island, New York, Pennsylvania, Illinois, Indiana, Michigan, Wisconsin and Iowa, have enacted laws which either nullify the Acts of Congress or render useless any attempt to execute them. In many of these States the fugitive is discharged from service or labor claimed, and in none of them has the State Government complied with the stipulation made in the Constitution. The State of New Jersey, at an early day, passed a law in conformity with her constitutional obligation; but the current of anti-slavery feeling has led her more recently to enact laws which render inoperative the remedies provided by her own law and by the laws of Congress. In the State of New York even the right of transit for a slave has been denied by her tribunals; and the States of Ohio and Iowa have refused to surrender to justice fugitives charged with murder, and with inciting servile insurrection in the State of Virginia. Thus the constituted compact has been deliberately broken and disregarded by the non-slaveholding States, and the consequence follows that South Carolina is released from her obligation.

The ends for which the Constitution was framed are declared by itself to be "to form a more perfect union, establish justice, insure domestic tranquility, provide for the common defence, promote the general welfare, and secure the blessings of liberty to ourselves and our posterity."

These ends it endeavored to accomplish by a Federal Government, in which each State was recognized as an equal, and had separate control over its own institutions. The right of property in slaves was recognized by giving to free persons distinct political rights, by giving them the right to represent, and burthening them with direct taxes for three-fifths of their slaves; by authorizing the importation of slaves for twenty years; and by stipulating for the rendition of fugitives from labor.

We affirm that these ends for which this Government was instituted have been defeated, and the Government itself has been made destructive of them by the action of the non-slaveholding States. Those States have assume the right of deciding upon the propriety of our domestic institutions; and have denied the rights of property established in fifteen of the States and recognized by the Constitution; they have denounced as sinful the institution of slavery; they have permitted open establishment among them of societies, whose avowed object is to disturb the peace and to eloign the property of the citizens of other States. They have encouraged and assisted thousands of our slaves to leave their homes; and those who remain, have been incited by emissaries, books and pictures to servile insurrection.

For twenty-five years this agitation has been steadily increasing, until it has now secured to its aid the power of the common Government. Observing the *forms* of the Constitution, a sectional party has found within that Article establishing the Executive Department, the means of subverting the Constitution itself. A geographical line has been drawn across the Union, and all the States north of that line have united in the election of a man to the high office of President of the United States, whose opinions and purposes are hostile to slavery. He is to be entrusted with the administration of the common Government, because he has declared that that "Government cannot endure permanently half slave, half free," and that the public mind must rest in the belief that slavery is in the course of ultimate extinction.

This sectional combination for the submersion of the Constitution, has been aided in some of the States by elevating to citizenship, persons who, by the supreme law of the land, are incapable of becoming citizens; and their votes have been used to inaugurate a new policy, hostile to the South, and destructive of its beliefs and safety.

On the 4th day of March next, this party will take possession of the Government. It has announced that the South shall be excluded from the common territory, that the judicial tribunals shall be made sectional, and that a war must be waged against slavery until it shall cease throughout the United States.

The guaranties of the Constitution will then no longer exist; the equal rights of the States will be lost. The slaveholding States will no longer have the power of self-government, or self-protection, and the Federal Government will have become their enemy.

Sectional interest and animosity will deepen the irritation, and all hope of remedy is rendered vain, by the fact that public opinion at the North has invested a great political error with the sanction of more erroneous religious belief.

We, therefore, the People of South Carolina, by our delegates in Convention assembled, appealing to the Supreme Judge of the world for the rectitude of our intentions, have solemnly declared that the Union heretofore existing between this State and the other States of North America, is dissolved, and that the State of South Carolina has resumed her position among the nations of the world, as a separate and independent State; with full power to levy war, conclude peace, contract alliances, establish commerce, and to do all other acts and things which independent States may of right do.

Adopted December 24, 1860

[Committee signatures]

(Source: May, J. A., and J. R. Faunt. *South Carolina Secedes*. Columbia: University of South Carolina Press, 1960.)

B. MISSISSIPPI

1. Secession Ordinance (9 January 1861)

AN ORDINANCE to dissolve the union between the State of Mississippi and other States united with her under the compact entitled "The Constitution of the United States of America."

The people of the State of Mississippi, in convention assembled, do ordain and declare, and it is hereby ordained and declared, as follows, to wit:

SECTION 1. That all the laws and ordinances by which the said State of Mississippi became a member of the Federal Union of the United States of America be, and the same are hereby, repealed, and that all obligations on the part of the said State or the people thereof to observe the same be withdrawn, and that the said State doth hereby resume all the rights, functions, and powers which by any of said laws or ordinances were conveyed to the Government of the said United States, and is absolved from all the obligations, restraints, and duties incurred to the said Federal Union, and shall from henceforth be a free, sovereign, and independent State.

SEC. 2. That so much of the first section of the seventh article of the constitution of this State as requires members of the Legislature and all officers, executive and judicial, to take an oath or affirmation to support the Constitution of the United States be, and the same is hereby, abrogated and annulled.

SEC. 3. That all rights acquired and vested under the Constitution of the United States, or under any act of Congress passed, or treaty made, in pursuance thereof, or under any law of this State, and not incompatible with this ordinance, shall remain in force and have the same effect as if this ordinance had not been passed.

SEC. 4. That the people of the State of Mississippi hereby consent to form a federal union with such of the States as may have seceded or may secede from the Union of the United States of America, upon the basis of the present Constitution of the said United States, except such parts thereof as embrace other portions than such seceding States.

Thus ordained and declared in convention the 9th day of January, in the year of our Lord 1861.

WILLIAM S. BARRY, *President*.

F. A. POPE, *Secretary*.

(Source: U.S. War Department. *War of the Rebellion: A Compilation of the Official Records of the Union and Confederate Armies*. Ser. IV, Vol. I.)

2. A Declaration of the Immediate Causes which Induce and Justify the Secession of the State of Mississippi from the Federal Union (1861)

In the momentous step which our State has taken of dissolving its connection with the government of which we so long formed a part, it is but just that we should declare the prominent reasons which have induced our course.

Our position is thoroughly identified with the institution of slavery—the greatest material interest of the world. Its labor supplies the product which constitutes by far the largest and most important portions of commerce of the earth. These products are peculiar to the climate verging on the tropical regions, and by an imperious law of nature, none but the black race can bear exposure to the tropical sun. These products have become necessities of the world, and a blow at slavery is a blow at commerce and civilization. That blow has been long aimed at the institution, and was at the point of reaching its consummation. There was no choice left us but submission to the mandates of abolition, or a dissolution of the Union, whose principles had been subverted to work out our ruin.

That we do not overstate the dangers to our institution, a reference to a few facts will sufficiently prove.

The hostility to this institution commenced before the adoption of the Constitution, and was manifested in the well-known Ordinance of 1787, in regard to the Northwestern Territory.

The feeling increased, until, in 1819–20, it deprived the South of more than half the vast territory acquired from France.

The same hostility dismembered Texas and seized upon all the territory acquired from Mexico.

It has grown until it denies the right of property in slaves, and refuses protection to that right on the high seas, in the Territories, and wherever the government of the United States had jurisdiction.

It refuses the admission of new slave States into the Union, and seeks to extinguish it by confining it within its present limits, denying the power of expansion.

It tramples the original equality of the South under foot.

It has nullified the Fugitive Slave Law in almost every free State in the Union, and has utterly broken the compact which our fathers pledged their faith to maintain.

It advocates negro equality, socially and politically, and promotes insurrection and incendiarism in our midst.

It has enlisted its press, its pulpit and its schools against us, until the whole popular mind of the North is excited and inflamed with prejudice.

It has made combinations and formed associations to carry out its schemes of emancipation in the States and wherever else slavery exists.

It seeks not to elevate or to support the slave, but to destroy his present condition without providing a better.

It has invaded a State, and invested with the honors of martyrdom the wretch whose purpose was to apply flames to our dwellings, and the weapons of destruction to our lives.

It has broken every compact into which it has entered for our security.

It has given indubitable evidence of its design to ruin our agriculture, to prostrate our industrial pursuits and to destroy our social system.

It knows no relenting or hesitation in its purposes; it stops not in its march of aggression, and leaves us no room to hope for cessation or for pause.

It has recently obtained control of the Government, by the prosecution of its unhallowed schemes, and destroyed the last expectation of living together in friendship and brotherhood.

Utter subjugation awaits us in the Union, if we should consent longer to remain in it. It is not a matter of choice, but of necessity. We must either submit to degradation, and to the loss of property worth four billions of money, or we must secede from the Union framed by our fathers, to secure this as well as every other species of property. For far less cause than this, our fathers separated from the Crown of England.

Our decision is made. We follow their footsteps. We embrace the alternative of separation; and for the reasons here stated, we resolve to maintain our rights with the full consciousness of the justice of our course, and the undoubting belief of our ability to maintain it.

(Source: *Journal of the State Convention.* Jackson, MS: E. Barksdale, State Printer, 1861.)

C. FLORIDA

1. Secession Ordinance (10 January 1861)

We, the people of the State of Florida, in convention assembled, do solemnly ordain, publish, and declare, That the State of Florida hereby withdraws herself from the confederacy of States existing under the name of the United States of America and from the existing Government of the said States; and that all political connection between her and the Government of said States ought to be, and the same is hereby, totally annulled, and said Union of States dissolved; and the State of Florida is hereby declared a sovereign and independent nation; and that all ordinances heretofore adopted, in so far as they create or recognize said Union, are rescinded; and all laws or parts of laws in force in this State, in so far as they recognize or assent to said Union, be, and they are hereby, repealed.

(Source: U.S. War Department. *War of the Rebellion: A Compilation of the Official Records of the Union and Confederate Armies.* Ser. IV, Vol. I.)

D. ALABAMA

1. Secession Ordinance (11 January 1861)

AN ORDINANCE to dissolve the union between the State of Alabama and other States united under the compact styled "The Constitution of the United States of America."

Whereas, the election of Abraham Lincoln and Hannibal Hamlin to the offices of President and Vice-President of the United States of America by a sectional party avowedly hostile to the domestic institutions and to the peace and security of the people of the State of Alabama, preceded by many and dangerous infractions of the Constitution of the United States by many of the States and people of the Northern section, is a political wrong of so insulting and menacing a character as to justify the people of the State of Alabama in the adoption of prompt and decided measures for their future peace and security: Therefore,

Be it declared and ordained by the people of the State of Alabama in convention assembled, That the State of Alabama now withdraws, and is hereby withdrawn, from the Union known as "the United States of America," and henceforth ceases to be one of said United States, and is, and of right ought to be, a sovereign and independent State.

SEC. 2. *Be it further declared and ordained by the people of the State of Alabama in convention assembled,* That all the powers over the territory of said State and over the people thereof heretofore delegated to the Government of the United States of America be, and they are hereby, withdrawn from said Government, and are hereby resumed and vested in the people of the State of Alabama.

Be it resolved by the people of Alabama in convention assembled, That the people of the States of Delaware, Maryland, Virginia, North Carolina, South Carolina, Florida, Georgia, Mississippi, Louisiana, Texas, Arkansas, Tennessee, Kentucky, and Missouri be, and are hereby, invited to meet the people of the State of Alabama, by their delegates in convention, on the 4th day of February, A. D. 1861, at the city of Montgomery, in the State of Alabama, for the purpose of consulting with each other as to the most effectual mode of securing concerted and harmonious action in whatever measures may be deemed most desirable for our common peace and security.

And be it further resolved, That the president of this convention be, and is hereby, instructed to transmit forthwith a copy of the foregoing preamble, ordinance, and resolutions to the Governors of the several States named in said resolutions.

Done by the people of the State of Alabama, in convention assembled, at Montgomery, on this the 11th day of January, A. D. 1861.

(Source: U.S. War Department. *War of the Rebellion: A Compilation of the Official Records of the Union and Confederate Armies.* Ser. IV, Vol. I.)

2. Letter from the Governor of Alabama to President Buchanan (January 1861)

EXECUTIVE DEPARTMENT,
Montgomery, Ala., January 4 [?], 1861.

To his Excellency JAMES BUCHANAN,
President of the United States:
SIR: In a spirit of frankness I hasten to inform you by letter that by my order Fort Morgan and Fort Gaines, and the United States Arsenal at Mount Vernon were on yesterday peacefully occupied, and are now held by the troops of the State of Alabama. That this act on my part may not be misunderstood by the Government of the United States, I proceed to state the motives which have induced it, and the reasons which justify it, and also the course of conduct with which I design to follow that act.

A convention of the people of this State will, in pursuance of a previously-enacted law, assemble on the 7th instant. I was fully convinced by the evidences which I had that that convention would at an early day, in the exercise of an authority which in my judgment of right belongs to it, withdraw the State of Alabama from the Government of the United States and place it in the attitude of a separate and independent power. Being thus convinced I deemed it my duty to take every precautionary step to make the secession of the State peaceful, and prevent detriment to her people.

While entertaining such a conviction as to my duty, I received such information as left but little, if any, room to doubt that the Government of the United States, anticipating the secession of Alabama, and preparing to maintain its authority within this State by force, even to the shedding of the blood and the sacrifice of the lives of the people, was about to re-enforce those forts and put a guard over the arsenal. Having that information, it was but an act of self-defense, and the plainest dictate of prudence, to anticipate and guard against the contemplated movement of the authorities of the General Government. Appreciating, as I am sure you do, the courage and spirit of our people, you must be sensible that no attempt at the coercion of the State, or at the enforcement by military power of the authority of the United States within its jurisdiction in contravention of the ordinance of secession can be effectual, unless our utmost capacity for resistance can be exhausted. It would have been an unwise policy, suicidal in its character, to have permitted the Government of the United States to have made undisturbed preparations within this State to enforce by war and bloodshed an authority which it is the fixed purpose of the people of the State to resist to the uttermost of their power. A policy so manifestly unwise would probably have been overruled by an excited and discontented people, and popular violence might have accomplished that which has been done by the State much more appropriately and much more consistently with the prospect of peace and the interests of the parties concerned.

The purpose with which my order was given and has been executed was to avoid and not to provoke hostilities between the State and Federal Government. There is no object, save the honor and independence of my State, which is by me so ardently desired as the preservation of amicable relations between this State and the Government of the United States. That the secession of the State, made necessary by the conduct of others, may be peaceful is my prayer as well as the prayer of every patriotic man in the State.

An inventory of the property in the forts and arsenal has been ordered, and the strictest care will be taken to prevent the injury or destruction of it while peaceable relations continue to subsist, as I trust they will. The forts and arsenal will be held by my order only for the precautionary purpose for which they were taken, and subject to the control of the convention of the people to assemble on the 7th instant.

With distinguished consideration, I am your obedient servant,
A. B. MOORE.

(Source: U.S. War Department. *War of the Rebellion: A Compilation of the Official Records of the Union and Confederate Armies.* Ser. I, Vol. 1, Chapter III.)

E. GEORGIA

1. Secession Ordinance (19 January 1861)

AN ORDINANCE to dissolve the union between the State of Georgia and other States united with her under a compact of government entitled "The Constitution of the United States of America."

We, the people of the State of Georgia, in convention assembled, do declare and ordain, and it is hereby declared and ordained, That the ordinance adopted by the people of the State of Georgia, in convention, on the 2d day of January, in the year of our Lord seventeen hundred and eighty-eight, whereby the Constitution of the United States of America was assented to, ratified, and adopted, and also all acts and parts of acts of the General Assembly of this State ratifying and adopting amendments of the said Constitution, are hereby repealed, rescinded, and abrogated.

We do further declare and ordain, That the union now subsisting between the State of Georgia and other States, under the name of the "United States of America," is hereby dissolved, and that the State of Georgia is in the full possession and exercise of all those rights of sovereignty which belong and appertain to a free and independent State.

Passed January 19, 1861.
GEO. W. CRAWFORD, *President.*
Attest.
A. R. LAMAR, *Secretary.*

(Source: U.S. War Department. *War of the Rebellion: A Compilation of the Official Records of the Union and Confederate Armies.* Ser. IV, Vol. I.)

2. Declaration of Causes of Seceding States: Georgia

The people of Georgia having dissolved their political connection with the Government of the United States of America, present to their confederates and the world the causes which have led to the separation. For the last ten years we have had numerous and serious causes of complaint against our non-slave-holding confederate States with reference to the subject of African slavery. They have endeavored to weaken our security, to disturb our domestic peace and tranquility, and persistently refused to comply with their express constitutional obligations to us in reference to that property, and by the use of their power in the Federal Government have striven to deprive us of an equal enjoyment of the common Territories of the Republic. This hostile policy of our confederates has been pursued with every circumstance of aggravation which could arouse the passions and excite the hatred of our people, and has placed the two sections of the Union for many years past in the condition of virtual civil war. Our people, still attached to the Union from habit and national traditions, and averse to change, hoped that time, reason, and argument would bring, if not redress, at least exemption from further insults, injuries, and dangers. Recent events have fully dissipated all such hopes and demonstrated the necessity of separation. Our Northern confederates, after a full and calm hearing of all the facts, after a fair warning of our purpose not to submit to the rule of the authors of all these wrongs and injuries, have by a large majority committed the Government of the United States into their hands. The people of Georgia, after an equally full and fair and deliberate hearing of the case, have declared with equal firmness that they shall not rule over them. A brief history of the rise, progress, and policy of anti-slavery and the political organization into whose hands the administration of the Federal Government has been committed will fully justify the pronounced verdict of the people of Georgia. The party of Lincoln, called the Republican party, under its present name and organization, is of recent origin. It is admitted to be an anti-slavery party. While it attracts to itself by its creed the scattered advocates of exploded political heresies, of condemned theories in political economy, the advocates of commercial restrictions, of protection, of special privileges, of waste and corruption in the administration of Government, anti-slavery is its mission and its purpose. By anti-slavery it is made a power in the state. The question of slavery was the great difficulty in the way of the formation of the Constitution. While the subordination and the political and social inequality of the African race was fully conceded by all, it was plainly apparent that slavery would soon disappear from what are now the non-slave-holding States of the original thirteen. The opposition to slavery was then, as now, general in those States and the Constitution was made with direct reference to that fact. But a distinct abolition party was not formed in the United States for more than half a century after the Government went into operation. The main reason was that the North, even if united, could not control both branches of the Legislature during any portion of that time. Therefore such an organization must have resulted either in utter failure or in the total overthrow of the Government. The material prosperity of the North was greatly dependent on the Federal Government; that of the the South not at all. In the first years of the Republic the navigating, commercial, and manufacturing interests of the North began to seek profit and aggrandizement at the expense of the agricultural interests. Even the owners of fishing smacks sought and obtained bounties for pursuing their own business (which yet continue), and $500,000 is now paid them annually out of the Treasury. The navigating interests begged for protection against foreign shipbuilders and against competition in the coasting trade. Congress granted both requests, and by prohibitory acts gave an absolute monopoly of this business to each of their interests, which they enjoy without diminution to this day. Not content with these great and unjust advantages, they have sought to throw the legitimate burden of their business as much as possible upon the public; they have succeeded in throwing the cost of light-houses, buoys, and the maintenance of their seamen upon the Treasury, and the Government now pays above $2,000,000 annually for the support of these objects. These interests, in connection with the commercial and manufacturing classes, have also succeeded, by means of subventions to mail steamers and the reduction in postage, in relieving their business from the payment of about $7,000,000 annually, throwing it upon the public Treasury under the name of postal deficiency. The manufacturing interests entered into the same struggle early, and has clamored steadily for Government bounties and special favors. This interest was confined mainly to the Eastern and Middle non-slave-holding States. Wielding these great States it held great power and influence, and its demands were in full proportion to its power. The manufacturers and miners wisely based their demands upon special facts and reasons rather than upon general principles, and thereby mollified much of the opposition of the opposing interest. They pleaded in their favor the infancy of their business in this country, the scarcity of labor and capital, the hostile legislation of other countries toward them, the great necessity of their fabrics in the time of war, and the necessity of high duties to pay the debt incurred in our war for independence. These reasons prevailed, and they received for many years enormous bounties by the general acquiescence of the whole country.

But when these reasons ceased they were no less clamorous for Government protection, but their clamors were less heeded—the country had put the principle of protection upon trial and condemned it. After having enjoyed protection to the extent of from 15 to 200 per cent. upon their entire business for above thirty years, the act of 1846 was passed. It avoided sudden change, but the principle was settled, and free trade, low duties, and economy in public expenditures was the verdict of the American people. The South and the Northwestern States sustained this policy. There was but small hope of its reversal; upon the direct issue, none at all.

All these classes saw this and felt it and cast about for new allies. The anti-slavery sentiment of the North offered the best chance for success. An anti-slavery party must necessarily look to the North alone for support, but a united North was now strong enough to control the Government in all of its departments, and a sectional party was therefore determined upon. Time and issues upon slavery were necessary to its completion and final triumph. The feeling of anti-slavery, which it was well known was very general among the people of the North, had been long dormant or passive; it needed only a question to arouse it into aggressive activity. This question was before us. We had acquired a large territory by successful war with Mexico; Congress had to govern it; how, in relation to slavery, was the question then demanding solution. This state of facts gave form and shape to the anti-slavery sentiment throughout the North and the conflict began. Northern anti-slavery men of all parties asserted the right to exclude slavery from the territory by Congressional legislation and demanded the prompt and efficient exercise of this power to that end. This insulting and unconstitutional demand was met with great moderation and firmness by the South. We had shed our blood and paid our money for its acquisition; we demanded a division of it on the line of the Missouri restriction or an equal participation in the whole of it. These propositions were refused, the agitation became general, and the public danger was great. The case of the South was impregnable. The price of the acquisition was the blood and treasure of both sections—of all, and, therefore, it belonged to all upon the principles of equity and justice.

The Constitution delegated no power to Congress to excluded either party from its free enjoyment; therefore our right was good under the Constitution. Our rights were further fortified by the practice of the Government from the beginning. Slavery was forbidden in the country northwest of the Ohio River by what is called the ordinance of 1787. That ordinance was adopted under the old confederation and by the assent of Virginia, who owned and ceded the country, and therefore this case must stand on its own special circumstances. The Government of the United States claimed territory by virtue of the treaty of 1783 with Great Britain, acquired territory by cession from Georgia and North Carolina, by treaty from France, and by treaty from Spain. These acquisitions largely exceeded the original limits of the Republic. In all of these acquisitions the policy of the Government was uniform. It opened them to the settlement of all the citizens of all the States of the Union. They emigrated thither with their property of every kind (including slaves). All were equally protected by public authority in their persons and property until the inhabitants became sufficiently numerous and otherwise capable of bearing the burdens and performing the duties of self-government, when they were admitted into the Union upon equal terms with the other States, with whatever republican constitution they might adopt for themselves.

Under this equally just and beneficent policy law and order, stability and progress, peace and prosperity marked every step of the progress of these new communities until they entered as great and prosperous commonwealths into the sisterhood of American States. In 1820 the North endeavored to overturn this wise and successful policy and demanded that the State of Missouri should not be admitted into the Union unless she first prohibited slavery within her limits by her constitution. After a bitter and protracted struggle the North was defeated in her special object, but her policy and position led to the adoption of a section in the law for the admission of Missouri, prohibiting slavery in all that portion of the territory acquired from France lying North of 36 [degrees] 30 [minutes] north latitude and outside of Missouri. The venerable Madison at the time of its adoption declared it unconstitutional. Mr. Jefferson condemned the restriction and foresaw its consequences and predicted that it would result in the dissolution of the Union. His prediction is now history. The North demanded the application of the principle of prohibition of slavery to all of the territory acquired from Mexico and all other parts of the public domain then and in all future time. It was the announcement of her purpose to appropriate to herself all the public domain then owned and thereafter to be acquired by the United States. The claim itself was less arrogant and insulting than the reason with which she supported it. That reason was her fixed purpose to limit, restrain, and finally abolish slavery in the States where it exists. The South with great unanimity declared her purpose to resist the principle of prohibition to the last extremity. This particular question, in connection with a series of questions affecting the same subject, was finally disposed of by the defeat of prohibitory legislation.

The Presidential election of 1852 resulted in the total overthrow of the advocates of restriction and their party friends. Immediately after this result the anti-slavery portion of the defeated party resolved to unite all the elements in the North opposed to slavery and to stake their future political fortunes upon their hostility to slavery everywhere. This is the party two whom the people of the North have committed the Government. They raised their standard in 1856 and were barely defeated. They entered the Presidential contest again in 1860 and succeeded.

The prohibition of slavery in the Territories, hostility to it everywhere, the equality of the black and white races, disregard of all constitutional guarantees in its favor, were boldly proclaimed by its leaders and applauded by its followers.

With these principles on their banners and these utterances on their lips the majority of the people of the North demand that we shall receive them as our rulers.

The prohibition of slavery in the Territories is the cardinal principle of this organization.

For forty years this question has been considered and debated in the halls of Congress, before the people, by the press, and before the tribunals of justice. The majority of the people of the North in 1860 decided it in their own favor. We refuse to submit to that judgment, and in vindication of our refusal we offer the Constitution of our country and point to the total absence of any express power to exclude us. We offer the practice of our Government for the first thirty years of its existence in complete refutation of the position that any such power is either necessary or proper to the execution of any other power in relation to the Territories. We offer the judgment of a large minority of the people of the North, amounting to more than one-third, who united with the unanimous voice of the South against this usurpation; and, finally, we offer the judgment of the Supreme Court of the United States, the highest judicial tribunal of our country, in our favor. This evidence ought to be conclusive that we have never surrendered this right. The conduct of our adversaries admonishes us that if we had surrendered it, it is time to resume it.

The faithless conduct of our adversaries is not confined to such acts as might aggrandize themselves or their section of the Union. They are content if they can only injure us. The Constitution declares that persons charged with crimes in one State and fleeing to another shall be delivered up on the demand of the executive authority of the State from which they may flee, to be tried in the jurisdiction where the crime was committed. It would appear difficult to employ language freer from ambiguity, yet for above twenty years the non-slave-holding States generally have wholly refused to deliver up to us persons charged with crimes affecting slave property. Our confederates, with punic faith, shield and give sanctuary to all criminals who seek to deprive us of this property or who use it to destroy us. This clause of the Constitution has no other sanction than their good faith; that is withheld from us; we are remediless in the Union; out of it we are remitted to the laws of nations.

A similar provision of the Constitution requires them to surrender fugitives from labor. This provision and the one last referred to were our main inducements for confederating with the Northern States. Without them it is historically true that we would have rejected the Constitution. In the fourth year of the Republic Congress passed a law to give full vigor and efficiency to this important provision. This act depended to a considerable degree upon the local magistrates in the several States for its efficiency. The non-slave-holding States generally repealed all laws intended to aid the execution of that act, and imposed penalties upon those citizens whose loyalty to the Constitution and their oaths might induce them to discharge their duty. Congress then passed the act of 1850, providing for the complete execution of this duty by Federal officers. This law, which their own bad faith rendered absolutely indispensible for the protection of constitutional rights, was instantly met with ferocious revilings and all conceivable modes of hostility. The Supreme Court unanimously, and their own local courts with equal unanimity (with the single and temporary exception of the supreme court of Wisconsin), sustained its constitutionality in all of its provisions. Yet it stands to-day a dead letter for all practicable purposes in every non-slave-holding State in the Union. We have their convenants, we have their oaths to keep and observe it, but the unfortunate claimant, even accompanied by a Federal officer with the mandate of the highest judicial authority in his hands, is everywhere met with fraud, with force, and with legislative enactments to elude, to resist, and defeat him. Claimants are murdered with impunity; officers of the law are beaten by frantic mobs instigated by inflammatory appeals from persons holding the highest public employment in these States, and supported by legislation in conflict with the clearest provisions of the Constitution, and even the ordinary principles of humanity. In several of our confederate States a citizen cannot travel the highway with his servant who may voluntarily accompany him, without being declared by law a felon and being subjected to infamous punishments. It is difficult to perceive how we could suffer more by the hostility than by the fraternity of such brethren.

The public law of civilized nations requires every State to restrain its citizens or subjects from committing acts injurious to the peace and security of any other State and from attempting to excite insurrection, or to lessen the security, or to disturb the tranquillity of their neighbors, and our Constitution wisely gives Congress the power to punish all offenses against the laws of nations.

These are sound and just principles which have received the approbation of just men in all countries and all centuries; but they are wholly disregarded by the people of the Northern States, and the Federal Government is impotent to maintain them. For twenty years past the abolitionists and their allies in the Northern States have been engaged in constant efforts to subvert our institutions and to excite insurrection and servile war among us. They have sent emissaries among us for the accomplishment of these purposes. Some of these efforts have received the public sanction of a majority of the leading men of the Republican party in the national councils, the same men who are now proposed as our rulers. These efforts have in one instance led to the actual invasion of one of the slave-holding States, and those of the murderers and incendiaries who escaped public justice by flight have found fraternal protection among our Northern confederates.

These are the same men who say the Union shall be preserved.

Such are the opinions and such are the practices of the Republican party, who have been called by their own votes to administer the Federal Government under the Constitution of the United States. We know their treachery; we know the shallow pretenses under which they daily disregard its plainest obligations. If we submit to them it will be our fault and not theirs. The people of Georgia have ever been willing to stand by this bargain, this contract; they have never sought to evade any of its obligations; they have never hitherto sought to establish any new government; they have struggled to maintain the ancient right of themselves and the human race through and by that Constitution. But they know the value of parchment rights in treacherous hands, and therefore they refuse to commit their own to the rulers whom the North offers us. Why? Because by their declared principles and policy they have outlawed $3,000,000,000 of our property in the common territories of the Union; put it under the ban of the Republic in the States where it exists and out of the protection of Federal law everywhere; because they give sanctuary to thieves and incendiaries who assail it to the whole extent of their power, in spite of their most solemn obligations and covenants; because their avowed purpose is to subvert our society and subject us not only to the loss of our property but the destruction of ourselves, our wives, and our children, and the desolation of our homes, our altars, and our firesides. To avoid these evils we resume the powers which our fathers delegated to the Government of the United States, and henceforth will seek new safeguards for our liberty, equality, security, and tranquillity.

[Approved, Tuesday, January 29, 1861]

(Source: U.S. War Department. *War of the Rebellion: A Compilation of the Official Records of the Union and Confederate Armies.* Ser. IV, Vol. I.)

F. LOUISIANA

1. Secession Ordinance (26 January 1861)

AN ORDINANCE to dissolve the union between the State of Louisiana and other States united with her under the compact entitled "The Constitution of the United States of America."

We, the people of the State of Louisiana, in convention assembled, do declare and ordain, and it is hereby declared

and ordained, That the ordinance passed by us in convention on the 22d day of November, in the year eighteen hundred and eleven, whereby the Constitution of the United States of America and the amendments of the said Constitution were adopted, and all laws and ordinances by which the State of Louisiana became a member of the Federal Union, be, and the same are hereby, repealed and abrogated; and that the union now subsisting between Louisiana and other States under the name of "The United States of America" is hereby dissolved.

We do further declare and ordain, That the State of Louisiana hereby resumes all rights and powers heretofore delegated to the Government of the United States of America; that her citizens are absolved from all allegiance to said Government, and that she is in full possession and exercise of all those rights of sovereignty which appertain to a free and independent State.

We do further declare and ordain, That all rights acquired and vested under the Constitution of the United States, or any act of Congress, or treaty, or under any law of this State, and not incompatible with this ordinance, shall remain in force and have the same effect as if this ordinance had not been passed.

Adopted in convention at Baton Rouge this 26th day of January, 1861.

A. MOUTON, *President of the Convention.*

Attest.

J. THOS. WHEAT, *Secretary of the Convention.*

Resolution relative to the navigation of the Mississippi River.

Resolved, That we, the people of the State of Louisiana, recognize the right of the free navigation of the Mississippi River and its tributaries by all friendly States bordering thereon; and we also recognize the right of egress and ingress of the mouths of the Mississippi by all friendly States and Powers; and we do hereby declare our willingness to enter into any stipulations to guarantee the exercise of said rights.

(Source: U.S. War Department. *War of the Rebellion: A Compilation of the Official Records of the Union and Confederate Armies.* Ser. IV, Vol. I.)

G. TEXAS

1. A Declaration of the Causes which Impel the State of Texas to Secede from the Federal Union (2 February 1861)

The government of the United States, by certain joint resolutions, bearing date the 1st day of March, in the year A.D. 1845, proposed to the Republic of Texas, then a free, sovereign and independent nation, the annexation of the latter to the former, as one of the co-equal states thereof,

The people of Texas, by deputies in convention assembled, on the fourth day of July of the same year, assented to and accepted said proposals and formed a constitution for the proposed State, upon which on the 29th day of December in the same year, said State was formally admitted into the Confederated Union.

Texas abandoned her separate national existence and consented to become one of the Confederated Union to promote her welfare, insure domestic tranquility and secure more substantially the blessings of peace and liberty to her people. She was received into the confederacy with her own constitution, under the guarantee of the federal constitution and the compact of annexation, that she should enjoy these blessings. She was received as a commonwealth holding, maintaining and protecting the institution known as negro slavery—the servitude of the African to the white race within her limits—a relation that had existed from the first settlement of her wilderness by the white race, and which her people intended should exist in all future time. Her institutions and geographical position established the strongest ties between her and other slaveholding States of the confederacy. Those ties have been strengthened by association. But what has been the course of the government of the United States, and of the people and authorities of the non-slave-holding States, since our connection with them?

The controlling majority of the Federal Government, under various pretences and disguises, has so administered the same as to exclude the citizens of the Southern States, unless under odious and unconstitutional restrictions, from all the immense territory owned in common by all the States on the Pacific Ocean, for the avowed purpose of acquiring sufficient power in the common government to use it as a means of destroying the institutions of Texas and her sister slaveholding States.

By the disloyalty of the Northern States and their citizens and the imbecility of the Federal Government, infamous combinations of incendiaries and outlaws have been permitted in those States and the common territory of Kansas to trample upon the federal laws, to war upon the lives and property of Southern citizens in that territory, and finally, by violence and mob law, to usurp the possession of the same as exclusively the property of the Northern States.

The Federal Government, while but partially under the control of these our unnatural and sectional enemies, has for years almost entirely failed to protect the lives and property of the people of Texas against the Indian savages on our border, and more recently against the murderous forays of banditti from the neighboring territory of Mexico; and when our State government has expended large amounts for such purpose, the Federal Government has refuse reimbursement therefor, thus rendering our condition more insecure and harassing than it was during the existence of the Republic of Texas.

These and other wrongs we have patiently borne in the vain hope that a returning sense of justice and humanity would induce a different course of administration.

When we advert to the course of individual non-slave-holding States, and that a majority of their citizens, our grievances assume far greater magnitude.

The States of Maine, Vermont, New Hampshire, Connecticut, Rhode Island, Massachusetts, New York, Pennsylvania, Ohio, Wisconsin, Michigan and Iowa, by solemn legislative enactments, have deliberately, directly or indirectly violated the 3rd clause of the 2nd section of the 4th article [the fugitive slave clause] of the federal constitution, and laws passed in pursuance thereof; thereby annulling a material provision of the compact, designed by its framers to perpetuate the amity between the members of the confederacy and to secure the rights of the slave-holding States in their domestic institutions—a provision founded in justice and wisdom, and without the enforcement of which the compact fails to accomplish the object of its creation. Some of those States have imposed high fines and degrading penalties upon any of their citizens or officers who may carry out in good faith that provision of the compact, or the federal laws enacted in accordance therewith.

In all the non-slave-holding States, in violation of that good faith and comity which should exist between entirely distinct nations, the people have formed themselves into a great sectional party, now strong enough in numbers to control the affairs of each of those States, based upon an unnatural feeling of hostility to these Southern States and their beneficent and patriarchal system of African slavery, proclaiming the debasing doctrine of equality of all men, irrespective of race or color—a doctrine at war with nature, in opposition to the experience of mankind, and in violation of the plainest revelations of Divine Law. They demand the abolition of negro slavery throughout the confederacy, the recognition of political equality between the white and negro races, and avow their determination to press on their crusade against us, so long as a negro slave remains in these States.

For years past this abolition organization has been actively sowing the seeds of discord through the Union, and has rendered the federal congress the arena for spreading firebrands and hatred between the slave-holding and non-slave-holding States.

By consolidating their strength, they have placed the slave-holding States in a hopeless minority in the federal congress, and rendered representation of no avail in protecting Southern rights against their exactions and encroachments.

They have proclaimed, and at the ballot box sustained, the revolutionary doctrine that there is a 'higher law' than the constitution and laws of our Federal Union, and virtually that they will disregard their oaths and trample upon our rights.

They have for years past encouraged and sustained lawless organizations to steal our slaves and prevent their recapture, and have repeatedly murdered Southern citizens while lawfully seeking their rendition.

They have invaded Southern soil and murdered unoffending citizens, and through the press their leading men and a fanatical pulpit have bestowed praise upon the actors and assassins in these crimes, while the governors of several of their States have refused to deliver parties implicated and indicted for participation in such offenses, upon the legal demands of the States aggrieved.

They have, through the mails and hired emissaries, sent seditious pamphlets and papers among us to stir up servile insurrection and bring blood and carnage to our firesides.

They have sent hired emissaries among us to burn our towns and distribute arms and poison to our slaves for the same purpose.

They have impoverished the slave-holding States by unequal and partial legislation, thereby enriching themselves by draining our substance.

They have refused to vote appropriations for protecting Texas against ruthless savages, for the sole reason that she is a slave-holding State.

And, finally, by the combined sectional vote of the seventeen non-slave-holding States, they have elected as president and vice-president of the whole confederacy two men whose chief claims to such high positions are their approval of these long continued wrongs, and their pledges to continue them to the final consummation of these schemes for the ruin of the slave-holding States.

In view of these and many other facts, it is meet that our own views should be distinctly proclaimed.

We hold as undeniable truths that the governments of the various States, and of the confederacy itself, were established exclusively by the white race, for themselves and their posterity; that the African race had no agency in their establishment; that they were rightfully held and regarded as an inferior and dependent race, and in that condition only could their existence in this country be rendered beneficial or tolerable.

That in this free government all white men are and of right ought to be entitled to equal civil and political rights; that the servitude of the African race, as existing in these States, is mutually beneficial to both bond and free, and is abundantly authorized and justified by the experience of mankind, and the revealed will of the Almighty Creator, as recognized by all Christian

nations; while the destruction of the existing relations between the two races, as advocated by our sectional enemies, would bring inevitable calamities upon both and desolation upon the fifteen slave-holding states.

By the secession of six of the slave-holding States, and the certainty that others will speedily do likewise, Texas has no alternative but to remain in an isolated connection with the North, or unite her destinies with the South.

For these and other reasons, solemnly asserting that the federal constitution has been violated and virtually abrogated by the several States named, seeing that the federal government is now passing under the control of our enemies to be diverted from the exalted objects of its creation to those of oppression and wrong, and realizing that our own State can no longer look for protection, but to God and her own sons—We the delegates of the people of Texas, in Convention assembled, have passed an ordinance dissolving all political connection with the government of the United States of America and the people thereof and confidently appeal to the intelligence and patriotism of the freemen of Texas to ratify the same at the ballot box, on the 23rd day of the present month.

Adopted in Convention on the 2nd day of Feby, in the year of our Lord one thousand eight hundred and sixty-one and of the independence of Texas the twenty-fifth.

[Delegates' signatures]

(Source: *Journal of the Secession Convention of Texas*. n.p., 1861.)

2. An Act to Admit Texas as a Member of the Confederate States of America (2 March 1861)
The Congress of the Confederate States of America do enact, That the State of Texas be and is hereby admitted as a member of this Confederacy, upon an equal footing with the other Confederate States.

APPROVED March 2, 1861.

(Source: *Acts and Resolutions of the First Session of the Provisional Congress of the Confederate States, Held at Montgomery, Ala.* Richmond, VA: Enquirer Book & Job Press, 1861.)

VI. The Quest for Compromise
Even as the secession crisis was unfolding, effecting reconciliation through compromise became paramount. The specter of possible civil war cast an ominous shadow, as the editorial below laments. Meanwhile, Senator John J. Crittenden's attempt to fashion a compromise was to prove fruitless. [See Crittenden Compromise; Washington Peace Conference]

1. "Northern Citizens at the South" (Editorial, 7 January 1861)
It is computed that at least one million of the citizens of the South are natives of the Northern States, who have settled in the South, and in many instances intermarried with Southern families, and are among the most loyal and public spirited of the population. This is especially true of Georgia, South Carolina, and Louisiana. We ever find the adopted citizens of the South the foremost in loyalty and devotion to the land that they have chosen as home. The number of citizens in the North of Southern birth is also very large. There are more natives of Virginia now resident in New York than of New Yorkers resident in Virginia. They have too intermarried. Thus linked together by the most sacred ties, what new and unspeakable horrors are involved in the idea of civil war! Does it not become all good men, all men who have humanity, to besiege the throne of Heaven with their supplications, that this hitherto the happiest of all nations may be saved from such an unnatural collision and fearful catastrophe?

(Source: Baltimore *American*, 7 January 1861, p. 2.)

2. Amendments Proposed in Congress by Senator John J. Crittenden (18 December 1860)
Whereas, serious and alarming dissensions have arisen between the Northern and Southern States, concerning the rights and security of the rights of the slave-holding States, and especially their rights in the common territory of the United States; and whereas it is eminently desirable and proper that these dissensions, which now threaten the very existence of this Union, should be permanently quieted and settled by constitutional provisions, which shall do equal justice to all sections, and thereby restore to the people that peace and good will which ought to prevail between all the citizens of the United States: Therefore,

Resolved by the Senate and House of Representatives of the United States of America in Congress assembled (two-thirds of both Houses concurring), That the following articles be, and are hereby, proposed and submitted as amendments to the Constitution of the United States, which shall be valid to all intents and purposes, as part of said Constitution, when ratified by conventions of three-fourths of the several States:

ARTICLE I.

In all the territory of the United States now held, or hereafter acquired, situated north of latitude 36 30', slavery or involuntary servitude, except as a punishment for crime, is prohibited while such territory shall remain under territorial government. In all the territory south of said line of latitude, slavery of the African race is hereby recognized as existing, and shall not be interfered with by Congress, but shall be protected as property by all the departments of the territorial government during its continuance. And when any Territory, north or south of said line, within such boundaries as Congress may prescribe, shall contain the population requisite for a member of Congress according to the then Federal ratio of representation of the people of the United States, it shall, if its form of government be republican, be admitted into the Union, on an equal footing with the original States, with or without slavery, as the constitution of such new State may provide.

ARTICLE II.

Congress shall have no power to abolish slavery in places under its exclusive jurisdiction, and situate within the limits of States that permit the holding of slaves.

ARTICLE III.

Congress shall have no power to abolish slavery within the District of Columbia, so long as it exists in the adjoining States of Virginia and Maryland, or either, nor without the consent of the inhabitants, nor without just compensation first made to such owners of slaves as do not consent to such abolishment. Nor shall Congress at any time prohibit officers of the Federal Government, or members of Congress, whose duties require them to be in said District, from bringing with them their slaves, and holding them as such, during the time their duties may require them to remain there, and afterward taking them from the District.

ARTICLE IV.

Congress shall have no power to prohibit or hinder the transportation of slaves from one State to another, or to a Territory in which slaves are by law permitted to be held, whether that transportation be by land, navigable rivers, or by the sea.

ARTICLE V.

That in addition to the provisions of the third paragraph of the second section of the fourth article of the Constitution of the United States, Congress shall have power to provide by law, and it shall be its duty so to provide, that the United States shall pay to the owner who shall apply for it, the full value of his fugitive slave in all cases when the marshal or other officer whose duty it was to arrest said fugitive was prevented from so doing by violence or intimidation, or when, after arrest, said fugitive was rescued by force, the owner thereby prevented and obstructed in the pursuit of his remedy for the recovery of his fugitive slave under the said clause of the Constitution and the laws made in pursuance thereof. And in all such cases, when the United States shall pay for such fugitive, they shall have the right, in their own name, to sue the county in which said violence, intimidation, or rescue was committed, and to recover from it, with interest and damages, the amount paid by them for said fugitive slave. And the said county, after it has paid said amount to the United States may, for its indemnity, sue and recover from the wrongdoers or rescuers by whom the owner was prevented from the recovery of his fugitive slave, in like manner as the owner himself might have sued and recovered.

ARTICLE VI.

No future amendment of the Constitution shall affect the five preceding articles; nor the third paragraph of the second section of the first article of the Constitution, nor the third paragraph of the second section of the fourth article of said Constitution and no amendment shall be made to the Constitution which shall authorize or give to Congress any power to abolish or interfere with slavery in any of the States by whose laws it is, or may be allowed or permitted.

And whereas, also, besides these causes of dissension embraced in the foregoing amendments proposed to the Constitution of the United States, there are others which come within the jurisdiction of Congress, as far as its power will extend, to remove all just cause for the popular discontent and agitation which now disturb the peace of the country, and threaten the stability of its institutions: Therefore,

1. Resolved by the Senate and House of Representatives of the United States of America in Congress assembled That the laws now in force for the recovery of fugitive slaves are in strict pursuance of the plain and mandatory provisions of the Constitution, and have been sanctioned as valid and constitutional by the judgment of the Supreme Court of the United States, that the slaveholding States are entitled to the faithful observance and execution of those laws, and that they ought not to be repealed, or so modified or changed as to impair their efficiency; and that laws ought to be made for the punishment of those who attempt by rescue of the slave, or other illegal means, to hinder or defeat the clue execution of said laws,

2. That all State laws which conflict with the fugitive slave acts of Congress, or any other constitutional acts of Congress, or which, in their operation, impede, hinder, or delay the free course and due execution of any of said acts, are null and void by the plain provisions of the Constitution of the United States; yet those State laws, void as they are, have given color to practice, and led to consequences which have obstructed the due administration and execution of acts of Congress, and especially the acts for the delivery of fugitive slaves, and have thereby contributed much to the discord and commotion now prevailing. Congress, therefore, in the present perilous juncture, does not deem it improper respectfully and earnestly to recommend the repeal of those laws to the several States

which have enacted them, or such legislative corrections or explanations of them as may prevent their being used or perverted to such mischievous purposes.

3. That the act of the 18th of September, 1850, commonly called the fugitive slave law, ought to be so amended as to make the fee of the commissioner, mentioned in the eighth section of the act equal in amount, in the cases decided by claimant. And to avoid misconstruction, the last clause of the fifth section of said act which authorizes the person holding a warrant for the arrest or detention of a fugitive slave, to summon to his aid the posse comitatus, and which declares it to be the duty of all good citizens to assist hen in its execution, ought to be so amended as to expressly limit the authority and duty to cases in which there shall be resistance or danger of resistance or rescue.

4. That the laws for the suppression of the African slave-trade and especially those prohibiting the importation of slaves in the United States, ought to be made effectual, and ought to be thoroughly executed; and all further enactments necessary to those ends ought to be promptly made.

(Source: McPherson, Edward. *The Political History of the United States of America during the Great Rebellion.* Washington DC: Philp & Solomons, 1865.)

VII. The Confederate States of America

A. THE STATE

Following the first wave of secession, a convention met in Montgomery, Alabama, to establish a Southern government. Convening on 4 February 1861 and calling themselves the Provisional Congress of the Confederate States of America, the delegates four days later unanimously adopted a Provisional Constitution almost exactly replicating that of the United States and then commenced to conceive a permanent document. The convention regarded as urgent the need to write a permanent instrument of government, establish an executive, and provide the provisional legislature with authority until regular congressional elections could be held. The permanent Constitution that was adopted on 11 March closely resembled the United States Constitution, even in its wording. Differences were in its emphasis on states' rights, protecting slavery, and correcting what were regarded as defects in the processes of government. [See Constitution, C.S.A]

1. Constitution of the Confederate States of America (1861)

We, the people of the Confederate States, each State acting in its sovereign and independent character, in order to form a permanent federal government, estab-

lish justice, insure domestic tranquility and secure the blessings of liberty to ourselves and our posterity— invoking the favor and guidance of Almighty God—do ordain and establish this Constitution for the Confederate States of America.

ARTICLE I.
SECTION 1.
All legislative powers herein delegated shall be vested in Congress of the Confederate States, which shall consist of a Senate and House of Representatives.

SECTION 2.
1. The House of Representatives shall be composed of members chosen every second year by the people of the several States; and the electors in each State shall be citizens of the Confederate States, and have the qualifications requisite for electors of the most numerous branch of the State Legislature; but no person of foreign birth, not a citizen of the Confederate States, shall be allowed to vote for any officer, civil or political, State or Federal.

2. No person shall be a representative, who shall not have attained the age of twenty-five years, and be a citizen of the Confederate States, and who shall not, when elected, be an inhabitant of that State in which he shall be chosen.

3. Representatives and Direct Taxes shall be apportioned among the several States which may be included within this Confederacy, according to their respective numbers, which shall be determined by adding to the whole number of free persons, including those bound to service for a term of years and excluding Indians not taxed, three-fifths of all slaves. The actual enumeration shall be made within three years after the first meeting of the Congress of the Confederate States, and within every subsequent term of ten years, in such manner as they shall, by law, direct. The number of Representatives shall not exceed one for every fifty thousand, but each State shall have at least one Representative; and until such enumeration shall be made, the State of South Carolina shall be entitled to choose six; the State of Georgia ten; the State of Alabama nine; the State of Florida two; the State of Mississippi seven; the State of Louisiana six; and the State of Texas six.

4. When vacancies happen in the representation from any State, the Executive authority thereof shall issue writs of election to fill such vacancies.

5. The House of Representatives shall choose their speaker and other officers, and shall have the sole power of impeachment; except that any judicial or other federal officer, resident and acting solely within the limits of any State, may be impeached by a vote of two-thirds of both branches of the Legislature thereof.

SECTION 3.

1. The Senate of the Confederate States shall be composed of two Senators from each State, chosen for six years by the legislature thereof, at the regular session next immediately preceding the commencement of the term of service; and each Senator shall have one vote.

2. Immediately after they shall be assembled, in consequence of the first election, they shall be divided as equally as may be into three classes. The seats of the Senators of the first class shall be vacated at the expiration of the second year; of the second class at the expiration of the fourth year, and of the third class at the expiration of the sixth year; so that one-third may be chosen every second year; and if vacancies happen by resignation, or otherwise, during the recess of the Legislature of any State, the Executive thereof may make temporary appointments until the next meeting of the Legislature, which shall then fill such vacancies.

3. No person shall be a Senator who shall not have attained the age of thirty years, and be a citizen of the Confederate States; and who shall not, when elected, be an inhabitant of the State for which he shall be chosen.

4. The Vice-President of the Confederate States shall be President of the Senate, but shall have no vote, unless they be equally divided.

5. The Senate shall choose their other officers; and also a President pro tempore in the absence of the Vice-President, or when he shall exercise the office of President of the Confederate States.

6. The Senate shall have the sole power to try all impeachments. When sitting for that purpose, they shall be on oath or affirmation. When the President of the Confederate States is tried, the Chief Justice shall preside; and no person shall be convicted without the concurrence of two-thirds of the members present.

7. Judgment in cases of impeachment shall not extend further than to removal from office, and disqualification to hold and enjoy any office of honor, trust or profit, under the Confederate States; but the party convicted shall, nevertheless, be liable and subject to indictment, trial, judgment and punishment according to law.

SECTION 4.

1. The times, places and manner of holding elections for Senators and Representatives shall be prescribed in each State by the Legislature thereof, subject to the provisions of this Constitution; but the Congress may, at any time, by law, make or alter such regulations, except as to the times and places of choosing Senators.

2. The Congress shall assemble at least once in every year; and such meeting shall be on the first Monday in December, unless they shall, by law, appoint a different day.

SECTION 5.

1. Each House shall be the judge of the elections, returns and qualifications of its own members, and a majority of each shall constitute a quorum to do business; but a smaller number may adjourn from day to day, and may be authorized to compel the attendance of absent members, in such manner and tinder such penalties as each House may provide.

2. Each House may determine the rules of its proceedings, punish its members for disorderly behavior, and, with the concurrence of two-thirds of the whole number, expel a member.

3. Each House shall keep a journal of its proceedings, and from time to time publish the same, excepting such parts as may, in their judgment, require secrecy; and the yeas and nays of the members of either House, on any question, shall, at the desire of one-fifth of those present, be entered on the journal.

4. Neither House, during the session of Congress, shall without the consent of the other, adjourn for more than three days, nor to any other place than that in which the two Houses shall be sitting.

SECTION 6.

1. The Senators and Representatives shall receive a compensation for their services to be ascertained by law, and paid out of the treasury of the Confederate States. They shall, in all cases, except treason, felony, and breach of the peace, be privileged from arrest during their attendance at the session of their respective Houses, and in going to and returning from the same; and for any speech or debate in either House, they shall not be questioned in any other place.

2. No Senator or Representative shall, during the time for which he was elected, be appointed to any civil office under the authority of the Confederate States, which shall have been created, or the emoluments whereof shall have been increased during such time; and no person holding any office under the Confederate States shall be a member of either House during his continuance in office. But Congress may, by law, grant to the principal officers in each of the Executive Departments a seat upon the floor of either House, with the privilege of discussing any measures appertaining to his department.

SECTION 7.

1. All bills for raising revenue shall originate in the House of Representatives; but the Senate may propose or concur with amendments as on other bills.

2. Every bill which shall have passed both Houses, shall before it becomes a law, be presented to the President of the Confederate States; if he approve, he shall sign it; but if not, he shall return it with hit; objections to that House in which it shall have originated,

who shall enter the objections at large on their journal, and proceed to reconsider it. If, after such reconsideration, two-thirds of that House shall agree to pass the bill, it shall be sent, together with the objections, to the other House, by which it shall likewise he reconsidered, and if approved by two-thirds of that House, it shall become a law. But in all such cases, the votes of both Houses shall be determined by yeas and nays, and the names of the persons voting for and against the bill, shall be entered on the journal of each House respectively. If any bill shall not be returned by the President within ten days (Sundays excepted) after it shall have been presented to him, the same shall be a law, in like manner as if he had signed it, unless the Congress, by their adjournment, prevent its return; in which case it shall not be a law. The President may approve any appropriation and disapprove any other appropriation in the same bill. In such case he shall, in signing the bill, designate the appropriations disapproved; and shall return a copy of such appropriations, with his objections, to the House in which the bill shall have originated; and the same proceedings shall then be had as in case of other bills disapproved by the President.

3. Every order, resolution or vote, to which the concurrence of both Houses may be necessary (except on a question of adjournment) shall be presented to the President of the Confederate States; and before the same shall take effect, shall be approved by him; or being disapproved by him, shall be re-passed by two-thirds of both Houses according to the rules and limitations prescribed in case of a bill.

SECTION 8.
The Congress shall have power—

1. To lay and collect taxes, duties, imposts and excises, for revenue necessary to pay the debts, provide for the common defense, and carry on the Government of the Confederate States; but no bounties shall be granted from the treasury, nor shall an duties or taxes on importations from foreign nations be laid to promote or foster any branch of industry; and all duties, imposts and excises shall be uniform throughout the Confederate States:

2. To borrow money on the credit of the Confederate States:

3. To regulate commerce with foreign nations, and among the several States, and with the Indian tribes; but neither this, nor any other clause contained in the constitution, shall ever be construed to delegate the power to Congress to appropriate money for any internal improvement intended to facilitate commerce; except for the purpose of furnishing lights, beacon, and buoys, and other aids to navigation upon the coasts, and the improvement of harbors, all the removing of obstructions in river navigation, in all which cases, such duties shall be laid on the navigation facilitated thereby, as may be necessary to pay the Costs, and expenses thereof:

4. To establish uniform laws of naturalization, and uniform laws on the subject of bankruptcies throughout the Confederate States; but no law of Congress shall discharge any debt contracted before the passage of the same:

5. To coin money, regulate the value thereof and, of foreign coin, and fix the standard of weights and measures:

6. To provide for the punishment of counterfeiting the securities—and current coin of the Confederate States:

7. To establish post offices and post routes; but the expenses of the Post Office Department, after the first day of March, in the year of our Lord eighteen hundred and sixty-three, shall be paid out of its own revenues:

8. To promote the progress of science and useful arts, by securing for limited times, to authors and inventors, the exclusive right to their respective writings and discoveries:

9. To constitute tribunals inferior to the Supreme Court:

10. To define and punish piracies and felonies committed on the high seas, and offenses against the law of nations:

11. To declare war, grant letters of marque and reprisal, and make rules concerning captures on land and water:

12. To raise and support armies; but no appropriation of money to that use shall be for a longer term than two years:

13. To provide and maintain a navy:

14. To make rules for the government and regulation of the land and naval forces:

15. To provide for calling forth the militia to execute the laws of the Confederate States, suppress insurrections, and repel invasions:

16. To provide for organizing, arming and disciplining the militia, and for governing such part of them as may be employed in the service of the Confederate States; reserving to the States, respectively, the appointment of the officers, and the authority of training the militia according to the discipline prescribed by Congress:

17. To exercise exclusive legislation, in all cases whatsoever, over such district (not exceeding ten miles square) as may, by cession of one or more States, and the acceptance of Congress, become the seat of the Government of the Confederate States; and to exercise like authority over all places purchased by the consent of the Legislature of the State in which the same shall be, for the erection of forts, magazines, arsenals, dockyards, and other needful buildings: and

18. To make all laws which shall be necessary and proper for carrying into execution the foregoing powers, and all other powers vested by this Constitution in the government of the Confederate States, or in any department or officer thereof.

SECTION 9.

1. The importation of negroes of the African race, from any foreign country, other than the slaveholding States or Territories of the United States of America, is hereby forbidden; and Congress is required to pass such laws as shall effectually prevent the same.

2. Congress shall also have power to prohibit the introduction of slaves from any State not a member of, or Territory not belonging to, this Confederacy.

3. The privilege of the writ of habeas corpus shall not be suspended, unless when in cases of rebellion or invasion, the public safety may require it.

4. No bill of attainder, ex post facto law, or law denying or impairing the right of property in negro slaves, shall be passed.

5. No capitation or other direct tax shall be laid, unless in proportion to the census or enumeration hereinbefore directed to be taken.

6. No tax or duty shall be laid on articles exported from any State, except by a vote of two-thirds of both Houses.

7. No preference shall be given by any regulation of commerce or revenue to the ports of one State over those of another.

8. No money shall be drawn from the treasury, but in consequence of appropriations made by law; and a regular statement arid account of the receipts arid expenditures of all public money shall be published front time to time.

9. Congress shall appropriate no money front the treasury except by a vote of two-thirds of both Houses, taken by yeas and nays, unless it be asked and estimate for by some one of the heads of Department, and submitted to Congress by the President; or for the purpose of paying its own expenses and contingencies; or for the payment of claims against the Confederate States, the justice of which shall have been judicially declared by a tribunal for the investigation of claims against the government, which it is hereby made the duty of Congress to establish.

10. All bills appropriating money shall specify in federal currency, the exact amount of each appropriation, and the purposes for which it is made; and Congress shall grant no extra compensation to any public contractor, officer, agent or servant, after such contract shall have been made or such service rendered.

11. No title of nobility shall be granted by the Confederate States; and no person holding any office of profit or trust under them, shall, without the consent of the Congress, accept of any present, emolument, office or title of any kind whatever from any king, prince or foreign State.

12. Congress shall make no law respecting an establishment of religion, or prohibiting the free exercise thereof, or abridging the freedom of speech, or of the press; or the right of the people peaceably to assemble and petition the government for a redress of grievances.

13. A well regulated militia being necessary to the security of a free State, the right of the people to keep and bear arms shall not be infringed.

14. No soldier shall, in time of peace, be quartered in any house without the consent of the owner; nor in time of war, but in a manner to be prescribed by law.

15. The right of the people to be secure in their persons, houses, papers and effects against unreasonable searches and seizures, shall not be violated; and no warrants shall issue but upon probable cause, supported by oath or affirmation, and particularly describing the place to be searched, and the persons or things to be seized.

16. No person shall be held to answer for a capital or otherwise infamous crime, unless on a presentment or indictment of a grand jury, except in cases arising in the land or naval forces, or in the militia, when in actual service, in time of war or public danger; nor shall any person be subject for the same offence, to be twice put in jeopardy of life or limb; nor be compelled, in any criminal case, to be a witness against himself; nor be deprived of life, liberty, or property, without due process of law; nor shall private property to be taken for public use, without just compensation.

17. In all criminal prosecution the accused shall enjoy the right to a speedy and public trial, by an impartial jury of the State and district wherein the crime shall have been committed, which district shall have been previously ascertained by law, and to be informed of the nature and cause of the accusation; to be confronted with the witnesses against him; to have compulsory process for obtaining witnesses in his favor; arid to have the assistance of counsel for his defense.

18. In suits at common law, where the value in controversy shall exceed twenty dollars, the right of trial by jury shall be preserved; and no fact so tried by a jury shall be otherwise re-examined in any court of the Confederacy, than according to the rules of the common law.

19. Excessive bail shall not be required, nor excessive fines imposed, nor cruel and unusual punishments inflicted.

20. Every law, or resolution having the force of law, shall relate to but one subject, and that shall be expressed in the title.

SECTION 10.

1. No State shall enter into any treaty, alliance, or confederation; grant letters of marque and reprisal; coin money; make anything but gold and silver coin a tender in payment of debts; pass any bill of attainder, or ex post facto law, or law impairing the obligation of contracts; or grant any title of nobility.

2. No State shall, without the consent of the Congress; lay any imposts or duties on imports or exports, except what may be absolutely necessary for executing its inspection laws; and the net produce of all duties and imposts, laid by any State on imports or exports, shall be for the use of the treasury of the Confederate States; and all such laws shall be subject to the revision and control of Congress.

3. No State shall, without the consent of Congress, lay any duty on tonnage, except on sea-going vessels, for the improvement of its rivers and harbors navigated by the said vessels, but such duties shall not conflict with any treaties of the Confederate States with foreign nations; and any surplus revenue thus derived, shall, after making such improvement, be paid into the common treasury. Nor shall any State keep troops or ships of war in time of peace, enter into any agreement or compact with another State, or with a foreign power, or engage in war, unless actually invaded, or in such imminent danger as will not admit of delay. But when any river divides or flows through two or more States, they may enter into compacts with each other to improve the navigation thereof.

ARTICLE II.
SECTION 1.

1. The executive power shall be vested in a President of the Confederate States of America. He and the Vice-President shall hold their offices for the term of six years: but the President shall not be re-eligible. The President and Vice-President shall be elected as follows:

2. Each State shall appoint, in such manner as the legislature thereof may direct, a number of electors equal to the whole number of Senators and Representatives to which the State may be entitled in the Congress; but no Senator or Representative, or person holding an office of trust or profit under the Confederate States, shall be appointed an elector.

3. The electors shall meet in their respective States and vote by ballot for President and Vice-President, one of whom, at least, shall not be an inhabitant of the same State with themselves; they shall name in their ballots the person voted for as President, and in distinct ballots the person voted for as Vice-President, and they shall make distinct lists of all persons voted for as President, and of all persons voted for as Vice-President, and of the number of votes for each, which lists they shall sign and certify, and transmit, sealed, to the seat of the government of the Confederate States, directed to the President of the Senate; the President of the Senate shall, in the presence of the Senate and House of Representatives, open all the certificates, and the votes shall then be counted, the person having the greatest number of votes for President shall be the President, if such number be a majority of the whole number of electors appointed; and if no person have such majority, then, from the persons having the highest numbers, not exceeding three, on the list of those voted for as President, the House of Representatives shall choose immediately, by ballot, the President. But in choosing the President, the votes shall be taken by States, the representation from each State having one vote; a quorum for this purpose shall consist of a member or members from two-thirds of the States, and a majority of all the States shall be necessary to a choice. And if the House of Representatives shall not choose a President, whenever the right of choice shall devolve upon them, before the fourth day of March next following, then the Vice-President shall act as President, as in case of the death, or other constitutional disability of the President.

4. The person having the greatest number of votes, as Vice-President shall be the Vice-President, if such number be a majority of the whole number of electors appointed and if no person have a majority, then from the two highest numbers on the list the Senate shall choose the Vice-President; a quorum for the purpose shall consist of two-thirds of the whole number of Senators, and a majority of the whole number shall be necessary to a choice.

5. But no person constitutionally ineligible to the office of President shall be eligible to that of Vice-President of the Confederate States.

6. The Congress may determine the time of choosing the electors, and the day on which they shall give their votes; which day shall be the same throughout the Confederate States.

7. No person except natural born citizen of the Confederate States, or at citizen thereof at the time of the adoption of this Constitution, or a citizen thereof born in the United States prior to the 20th of December, 1860, shall be eligible to the office of President; neither shall any person be eligible to that office who shall not have attained the age of thirty-five years, and been fourteen years a resident within the limits of the Confederate States, as they may exist at the time of his election.

8. In case of the removal of the President from office, or of his death, resignation, or inability to discharge the powers and duties of said office, the same shall devolve on the Vice-President; and the Congress may, by law, provide for the case of removal, death, resignation or inability both of the President and Vice President,

declaring what officer shall then act as President, and such officer shall act accordingly until the disability be removed or a President shall be elected.

9. The President shall, at stated times, receive for his services a compensation, which shall neither be increased nor diminished during the period for which he shall have been elected; and he shall not receive within that period any other emolument from the Confederate States, or any of them.

10. Before he enters on the execution of his office, he shall take the following oath or affirmation:

"I do solemnly swear (or affirm) that I will faithfully execute the office of President of the Confederate States, and will, to the best of my ability, preserve, protect, and defend the Constitution thereof."

SECTION 2.

1. The President shall be commander-in-chief of the army and navy of the Confederate States, and of the militia of the several States, when called into the actual service of the Confederate States; he may require the opinion, in writing, of the principal officer in each of the Executive Departments, upon any subject relating to the duties of their respective offices; and he shall have power to grant reprieves and pardons for offences against the Confederate States, except in cases of impeachment.

2. He shall have power, by and with the advice and consent of the Senate, to make treaties, provided two-thirds of the Senators present concur; and he shall nominate, and by and with the advice and consent of the Senate, shall appoint ambassadors, other public ministers and consuls, Judges of the Supreme Court, and all other officers of the Confederate States, whose appointments are not herein otherwise provided for, and which shall be established by law; but the Congress may, by law, vest the appointment of such inferior officers, as they think proper, in the President alone, in courts of law or in the heads of Departments.

3. The principal officer in each of the Executive Departments, and all persons connected with the diplomatic service, may be removed from office at the pleasure of the President. All other civil officers of the Executive Department may be removed at any time by the President, or other appointing power, when their services are unnecessary, or for dishonesty, incapacity, inefficiency, misconduct or neglect of duty; and when so removed, the removal shall be reported to the Senate, together with the reasons therefore.

4. The President shall have power to fill vacancies that may happen during the recess of the Senate, by granting commissions which shall expire at the end of their next session; but no person rejected by the Senate shall be reappointed to the same office during their ensuing recess.

SECTION 3.

1. The President shall from time to time, give to the Congress information of the state of the Confederacy, and recommend to their confederation such measures as he shall judge necessary and expedient; he may, on extraordinary occasions, convene both Houses, or either of them: and in case of disagreement between them, with respect to the time of adjournment, he may adjourn them to such time as he shall think proper; he shall receive ambassadors and other public ministers; he shall take care that the laws be faithfully executed, and shall commission all the officers of the Confederate States.

SECTION 4.

1. The President, Vice-President, and all civil officers of the Confederate States, shall be removed from office on impeachment for, and conviction of treason, bribery, or other high crimes and misdemeanors.

ARTICLE III.
SECTION 1.

1. The judicial power of the Confederate States shall be vested in one Supreme Court, and in such Inferior Courts as the Congress may from time to time ordain and establish. The judges, both of the Supreme and Inferior Courts, shall hold their offices during good behavior, and shall, at stated times receive for their services a compensation which shall not be diminished during their continuance in office.

SECTION 2.

1. The judicial power shall extend to all cases arising under this Constitution, the laws of the Confederate States, and treaties made or which shall be made under their authority; to all cases affecting ambassadors, other public ministers and consuls; to all cases of admiralty and maritime jurisdiction; to controversies to which the Confederate States shall be a party; to controversies between two or more States; between a State and citizens of another State where the State is plaintiff, between citizens claiming lands under grants of different States, and between a State or the citizens thereof, and foreign States, citizens or subjects; but no State shall be sued by a citizen or subject of any foreign State.

2. In all cases affecting ambassadors, other public ministers and consuls, and those in which a State shall be a party, the Supreme Court shall have original jurisdiction. In all the other cases before mentioned, the Supreme Court shall have appellate jurisdiction, both as to law and fact, with such exceptions, and under such regulations, as the Congress shall make.

3. The trial of all crimes, except in cases of impeachment, shall be by jury, and such trial shall be held in the State where the said crimes shall have been committed;

but when not committed within any State, the trial shall be at such place or places as the Congress may by law have directed.

SECTION 3.

1. Treason against the Confederate States shall consist only in levying war against them, or in adhering to their enemies, giving them aid and comfort. No person shall be convicted of treason unless on the testimony of two witnesses to the same overt act, or on confession in open court.

2. The Congress shall have power to declare the punishment of treason, but no attainder of treason shall work corruption of blood, or forfeiture, except during the life of the person attainted.

ARTICLE IV.
SECTION 1.

1. Full faith and credit shall be given in each State to the public acts, records and judicial proceedings of every other State. And the Congress may, by general laws, prescribe the manner in which such acts, records, and proceedings shall be proved, and the effect thereof.

SECTION 2.

1. The citizens of each State shall be entitled to all the privileges and immunities of citizens in the several States, and shall have the right of transit and sojourn in any State of this Confederacy, with their slaves and other property; and the right of property in said slaves shall not be thereby impaired.

2. A person charged in any State with treason, felony, or other crime against the laws of such State, who shall flee from justice, and be found in another State, shall, on demand of the Executive authority of the State from which he fled, be delivered up, to be removed to the State having jurisdiction of the crime.

3. No slave or other person held to service or labor in any State or Territory of the Confederate States, under the laws thereof, escaping or lawfully carried into another, shall, in consequence of any law or regulation therein, be discharged from such service or labor; but shall be delivered up on claim of the party to whom such slave belongs, or to whom such service or labor may be due.

SECTION 3.

1. Other States may be admitted into this Confederacy by a vote of two-thirds of the whole House of Representatives, and two-thirds of the Senate, the Senate voting by States; but no new State shall be formed or erected within the jurisdiction of any other State; nor any State be formed by the junction of two or more States, or parts of States, without the consent of the Legislatures of the States concerned as well as of the Congress.

2. The Congress shall have power to dispose of and make all needful rules and regulations concerning the property of the Confederate States, including the lands thereof.

3. The Confederate States may acquire new territory, and Congress shall have power to legislate and provide government for the inhabitants of all territory belonging to the Confederate States, lying without the limits of the several States; and may permit them, at such times, and in such manner as it may by law provide, to form states to be admitted into the Confederacy. In all such territory, the institution of negro slavery as it now exists in the Confederate States, shall be recognized and protected by Congress, and by the territorial government; and the inhabitants of the several Confederate States and Territories, shall have the right to take to such territory any slaves, lawfully held by them in any of the States or Territories of the Confederate States.

4. The Confederate States shall guaranty to every State that now is or hereafter may become a member of this Confederacy, a republican form of government, and shall protect each of them against invasion; and on application of the Legislature (or of the Executive when the legislature is not in session) against domestic violence.

ARTICLE V.
SECTION 1.

1. Upon the demand of any three States, legally assembled in their several conventions, the Congress shall summon a convention of all the States, to take into consideration such amendments to the Constitution as the said States shall concur in suggesting at the time when the said demand is made; and should any of the proposed amendments to the Constitution be agreed on by the said convention—voting by States—and the same be ratified by the Legislatures of two-thirds of the several States, or by conventions in two-thirds thereof—as the one or the other mode of ratification may be proposed by the general convention—they shall thenceforward form a part of this Constitution. But no State shall, without its consent, be deprived of its equal representation in the Senate.

ARTICLE VI.

1. The government established by this Constitution is successor of the Provisional Government of the Confederate States of America; and all the laws passed by the latter shall continue in force until the same shall be repealed or modified; and all the officers appointed by the same shall remain in office until their successors are appointed and qualified, or the offices abolished.

2. All debts contracted and engagements entered into before the adoption of this Constitution shall be as

valid against the Confederate States under this Constitution as under the Provisional Government.

3. This Constitution, and the laws of the Confederate States, made in pursuance thereof, and all treaties made, or which shall be made, under the authority of the Confederate States, shall be the supreme law of the land; and the judges in every State shall be bound thereby, anything in the constitution or laws of any State to the contrary notwithstanding.

4. The Senators and Representatives before mentioned, and the members of the several State Legislatures, and all executive and judicial officers, both of the Confederate States and of the several States, shall be bound by oath or affirmation, to support this Constitution; but no religious test shall ever be required as a qualification to any office or public trust under the Confederate States.

5. The enumeration, in the Constitution, of certain rights shall not be construed to deny or disparage others retained by the people of the several States.

6. The powers not delegated to the Confederate States by the Constitution, nor prohibited by it to the States, are reserved to the States, respectively, or the people thereof.

ARTICLE VII.

1. The ratification of the conventions of five States shall be sufficient for the establishment of this Constitution between the States so ratifying the same.

2. When five States shall have ratified this Constitution, in the manner before specified, the Congress under the Provisional Constitution, shall prescribe the time for holding the election of President and Vice-President; and for the meeting of the Electoral College; and for counting the votes, and inaugurating the President. They shall also prescribe the time for holding the first election of members of Congress under this Constitution, and the time for assembling the same. Until the assembling of such Congress, the Congress under the Provisional Constitution shall continue to exercise the legislative powers granted them; not extending beyond the time limited by the Constitution of the Provisional Government.

B. THE CONGRESS

The Provisional Congress remained in session until early 1862. The task of organizing the new Confederate government took most of its attention during these first months in office. Once the permanent constitution had been adopted, the provisional Congress adopted all U.S. laws consistent with the Confederate Constitution, elected Jefferson Davis as president and Alexander Stephens as vice president, and established a bureaucracy, including a postal system and judiciary that emulated those of the United States. The

Congress arranged to have its laws published both in book form and in the largest newspaper in each Confederate state. [See Congress, C.S.A.]

1. Selected Acts and Resolutions of the First Provisional Congress of the Confederate States (1861)

No. 17.] A RESOLUTION

For the appointment of Commissioners to the Government of the United States of America.

Resolved by the Confederate States of America in Congress assembled, That it is the sense of this Congress, that a commission of three persons be appointed by the President elect as early as may be convenient after his inauguration, and sent to the Government of the United States of America, for the purpose of negotiating friendly relations between that Government and the Confederate States of America, and for the settlement of all questions of disagreement between the two Governments upon principles of right, justice, equity, and good faith.

ADOPTED February 15, 1861.

No. 18.] A RESOLUTION

For the Enforcement of the Revenue Laws.

Resolved by the Confederate States of America in Congress assembled, That the President of Congress instruct the collectors of the several ports of this Confederacy to enforce the existing revenue laws against all foreign countries, except the State of Texas.

ADOPTED February 16, 1861.

No. 21.] AN ACT

To Provide Munitions of War and for other purposes.

SECTION 1. *Be it enacted by the Confederate States of America in Congress assembled,* That the President or Secretary of War, under his direction, is hereby authorized and empowered to make contracts for the purchase and manufacture of heavy ordnance and small arms; and of machinery for the manufacture or alteration of small arms and munitions of war; and to employ the necessary agents and artisans for these purposes; and to make contracts for the establishment of powder mills and the manufacture of powder; and the President is authorized to make contracts provided for in this act, in such manner and on such terms as in his judgment the public exigencies may require.

APPROVED February 20, 1861.

No. 24.] AN ACT

To organize the Department of State.

SECTION 1. The Congress of the Confederate States of America do enact, That there shall be an Executive Department to be denominated the Department of State; and there shall be a principal offi-

cer therein to be called the Secretary of State, who shall perform and execute such duties as shall, from time to time, be enjoined on or entrusted to him by the President of the Confederate States, agreeably to the Constitution, relative to correspondences, commissions or instructions to or with public ministers or consuls from the Confederate States, or to negotiations with public ministers from Foreign States, or princes, or to memorials or other applications from foreign public ministers, and other foreigners, or to such other matters respecting foreign affairs as the President of the Confederate States shall assign to the said department; and furthermore the said principal officer shall conduct the business of the said department in such manner as the President of the Confederate States shall from time to time order or instruct. Said Secretary shall be appointed by the President, by and with the advice and consent of the Congress, and shall receive a compensation to be ascertained and regulated by law.

SEC. 2. Be it further enacted, It shall be the duty of the Secretary of State to keep and preserve all bills and resolutions of the Congress having been approved or signed by the President or otherwise become laws, and he shall carefully preserve the originals, and shall, as soon as conveniently may be after he shall receive the same, cause every such law, order and resolution to be published in at least three public newspapers, published within the Confederate States, and shall also cause two printed copies, duly authenticated, to be sent to the executive authority of each State. It shall be the duty of the Secretary to keep the great seal of the Confederate States, and to make out and record and affix said seal to all civil commissions to officers of the Confederate States, to be appointed by the President, by and with the advice of the Congress, or by the President alone: Provided, That said seal shall not be affixed to any commission before it is signed by the President, nor to any other instrument or act without the special warrant of the President, therefor. The said Secretary shall also cause a seal of office to be made for said department, of such device as the President shall approve, and all copies of records and papers in said office, authenticated under the said seal, shall be evidence equally as the original record or paper.

SEC. 3. Be it further enacted, That there shall be in the said department a chief clerk to be appointed by the Secretary, and such other clerks as from time to time may be found necessary, and authorized by the Congress, who shall receive a compensation for their services to be fixed by law; and the Secretary of State and every other person to be appointed or employed in said department shall, before he enters on the execution of his office or employment, take an oath or affirmation well and faithfully to execute the trust committed to him.

SEC. 4. Be it further enacted, There shall be paid to the Secretary, for the use of the Confederate States, the following fees of office by the persons requiring the services to be performed, except when they are performed for any officer of the Confederate States in a matter relating to the duties of his office, to wit: for making out and authenticating copies of records, ten cents for each hundred words; for authenticating a copy of a record or paper, under the seal of office, one dollar.

SEC. 5. And be it further enacted, This act shall be in force and take effect from and after its passage.

APPROVED February 21, 1861.

No. 25.] AN ACT
To establish the Treasury Department.

SECTION 1. The Congress of the Confederate States of America do enact, That there shall be an executive department known as the Department of Treasury, in which shall be the following officers, namely: A Secretary of the Treasury, to be deemed the head of the department; a Comptroller, an Auditor, a Register, a Treasurer, and an Assistant to the Secretary of the Treasury, which assistant shall be appointed by the said Secretary; all of which officers shall receive such salaries respectively as may be provided by law.

SEC. 2. And be it further enacted, That it shall be the duty of the Secretary of the Treasury to superintend the collection of the public revenue; to digest and prepare plans for the improvement and management thereof, and for the support of the public credit; to prepare and report estimates of the public revenue and the public expenditures; to decide on the forms of keeping and stating accounts and making returns, and to grant, under the limitations herein established or to be hereafter provided, all warrants for moneys to be paid into the Treasury, and all warrants for moneys to be issued from the Treasury in pursuance of appropriations by law: to execute such services relative to the sale of the public property belonging to the Confederate States as by law may be required of him; to make reports and give information to the Congress or the President—in person or in writing, as may be required—concerning all matters referred to him by the Congress or the President respectively, and which shall appertain to his office; and generally to perform all such services relative to the finances, and all such other duties, as he may by law be directed to perform.

SEC. 3. And be it further enacted, That the Secretary of the Treasury shall have power to appoint a chief clerk, and also such other clerks, from time to time, as he may deem necessary, and Congress may authorize by law, which officers shall respectively receive such compensation as may be provided by law.

SEC. 4. And be it further enacted, That the Secretary of the Treasury shall cause to be procured an official seal for the Department of Treasury, to be approved by the President; and copies of all official papers or records in said department, certified under the seal thereof, shall be received in evidence in all the courts of the Confederate States, in lieu of such original papers or records.

SEC. 5. And be it further enacted, That it shall be the duty of the Assistant Secretary of the Treasury to examine all letters, contracts and warrants prepared for the signatures of the Secretary of the Treasury, and perform all such other duties as may be devolved on him by law or by the Secretary of the Treasury.

SEC. 6. And be it further enacted, That it shall be the duty of the Comptroller to superintend the adjustment and preservation of the public accounts; to examine all accounts settled by the Auditor, and certify the balances arising thereon to the Register; to countersign all warrants drawn by the Secretary of the Treasury which shall be authorized by law; to report to the Secretary the official forms of all papers to be issued in the different offices for collecting the public revenue, and the manner and form of keeping and stating the accounts of the several persons employed therein. He shall moreover provide for the regular and punctual payment of all moneys which may be collected, and shall direct prosecutions for all delinquencies of officers of the revenue, and for debts that are or shall be due to the Confederate States.

SEC. 7. And be it further enacted, That it shall be the duty of the Auditor to receive all public accounts, and after examination to certify the balance and transmit the accounts, with the vouchers and certificate, to the comptroller for his decision thereon: Provided, That if any person whose account shall be so audited be dissatisfied therewith, he may appeal to the comptroller against such settlement.

SEC. 8. And be it further enacted, That the Auditor of the public accounts shall be empowered to administer oaths or affirmations to witnesses in any case in which he may deem it necessary or proper for the due examination of the accounts with which he may be charged.

SEC. 9. And be it further enacted, That it shall be the duty of the Register to keep all accounts of the receipts and expenditures of the public money, and of all debts due to or from the Confederate States; to receive from the comptroller the accounts which shall have been finally adjusted, and to preserve such accounts, with their vouchers and certificates; to record all warrants for the receipt or payment of moneys at the treasury, certify the same thereon, and to transmit to the Secretary of the Treasury copies of the certificates of balances of accounts adjusted as herein directed.

SEC. 10. And be it further enacted, That it shall be the duty of the treasurer to receive and keep the moneys of the Confederate States, and to disburse the same upon warrants drawn by the secretary of the treasury, countersigned by the comptroller, and recorded by the register, and not otherwise; he shall take receipts for all moneys paid by him, and all receipts for moneys received by him shall be endorsed upon warrants signed by the secretary of the treasury, without which warrant, so signed, no acknowledgment for money received into the public treasury shall be valid. And the said treasurer shall render his accounts to the comptroller quarterly, or oftener if required, and shall transmit a copy thereof, when settled, to the secretary of the treasury. He shall, at all times, submit to the Secretary of the Treasury and the Comptroller, or either of them, the inspection of the books and records in his office, and of all moneys in his hands; and shall, prior to entering upon the duties of his office, give bond, with good and sufficient sureties, to be approved by the Secretary of the Treasury and Comptroller, in the sum of one hundred and fifty thousand dollars, payable to the Confederate States of America, with condition for the faithful performance of the duties of his office, and for the fidelity of the persons to be by him employed, which bond shall be lodged in the office of the Comptroller.

SEC. 11. And be it further enacted, That no person appointed to any office instituted by this act, shall directly or indirectly be concerned or interested as owner in whole or in part of any sea vessel, or purchase by himself, or another in trust for him, any public property or forfeited goods, or be concerned in the purchase by himself, or another in trust for him, any public property or forfeited goods, or be concerned in the purchase or disposal of any public securities of any State or of the Confederate States, or take or apply to his own use any emolument or gain for negotiating or transacting any business in the said department, other than what shall be allowed by law; and if any person shall offend against any of the prohibitions of this act, he shall be guilty of a high misdemeanor, and forfeit to the Confederate States the penalty of three thousand dollars, and shall upon conviction be removed from office, and forever thereafter be incapable of holding any office under the Confederate States: Provided, That if any other person than a public prosecutor shall give information of any such offence, upon which a prosecution and conviction shall be had, one-half of the aforesaid penalty of three thousand dollars, when recovered shall be for the use of the person giving such information.

APPROVED February 21, 1861.

No. 26.] AN ACT
To establish the War Department.

SECTION 1. The Congress of the Confederate States of America do enact, That an Executive

Department be and the same is hereby established, under the name of the War Department, the chief officer of which shall be called the Secretary of War.

SEC. 2. Be it further enacted, That said Secretary shall, under the direction and control of the President, have charge of all matters and things connected with the army, and with the Indian tribes within the limits of the Confederacy, and shall perform such duties appertaining to the army, and to said Indian tribes, as may from time to time be assigned to him by the President.

SEC. 3. And be it further enacted, That the Secretary of said department is hereby authorized to appoint a chief clerk thereof, and as many inferior clerks as may be found necessary, and may be authorized by law.

APPROVED February 21, 1861.

No. 27.] AN ACT
To establish the Navy Department.

SECTION 1. The Congress of the Confederate States of America do enact, That an Executive Department be and the same is hereby established to be called the Navy Department.

SEC. 2. Be it further enacted, That the chief officer of said department shall be called the Secretary of the Navy, and shall, under the direction and control of the President, have charge of all matters and things connected with the Navy of the Confederacy, and shall perform all such duties appertaining to the Navy as shall from time to time be assigned to him by the President.

SEC. 3. Be it further enacted, That said Secretary shall be authorized to appoint a chief clerk, and such other clerks as may be found necessary, and be authorized by law.

APPROVED February 21, 1861.

No. 28.] AN ACT
To establish the Post Office Department.

The Congress of the Confederate States of America do enact, That there shall be an executive department, to be denominated the Post Office Department, and there shall be a principal officer therein, to be called the Postmaster General, who shall perform such duties in relation to post offices and post routes, as shall be enjoined on him by the President of the Confederate States, agreeably to the Constitution and the laws of the land, who shall be paid an annual salary to be fixed by law, and have power to appoint a chief clerk, and such inferior clerks as may be found necessary, who shall receive such compensation as may be fixed by law.

APPROVED February 21, 1861.

No 29.] AN ACT
To organize and establish an Executive Department, to be known as the Department of Justice.

SECTION 1. The Congress of the Confederate States of America do enact, That from and after the passage of this act, there shall be an executive department to be known as the Department of Justice. The principal officer at the head of said department shall be denominated the Attorney General, who shall be paid an annual salary to be fixed by law, and who shall have the power to appoint a clerk, at such compensation as may be fixed by law.

SEC. 2. It shall be the duty of the Attorney General to prosecute and conduct all suits in the Supreme Court, in which the Confederate States shall be concerned, and to give his advice and opinion upon questions of law, when required by the President of the Confederate States, or when requested by any of the heads of departments, touching any matters that may concern their departments on subjects before them. He shall also have supervisory power over the accounts of the marshals, clerks, and officers of all the courts of the Confederate States, and all claims against the Confederate States.

APPROVED February 21, 1861.

No. 34.] AN ACT
To declare and establish the Free Navigation of the Mississippi River.

SECTION 1. The Congress of the Confederate States of America do enact, That the peaceful navigation of the Mississippi River is hereby declared free to the citizens of any of the States upon its borders, or upon the borders of its navigable tributaries; and all ships, boats, rafts or vessels may navigate the same, under such regulations as may be established by authority of law, or under such police regulations as may be established by the States within their several jurisdictions.

SEC. 2. Be it further enacted, All ships, boats or vessels which may enter the waters of the said river within the limits of this Confederacy, from any port or place beyond the said limits, may freely pass with their cargoes to any other port or place beyond the limits of this Confederacy without any duty or hindrance, except light-money, pilotage, and other like charges: but it shall not be lawful for any such ship, boat or vessel to sell, deliver, or in any way dispose of any part of her cargo, or land any portion thereof for the purpose of sale and delivery within the limits of this Confederacy; and in case any portion of such cargo shall be sold or delivered, or landed for that purpose in violation of the provisions of this act, the same shall be forfeited, and shall be seized and condemned by a proceeding in admiralty, before the court having jurisdiction of the same in the district in which the same may be found; and the ship, boat or vessel shall forfeit four times the amount of the value of the duties chargeable on the said goods, wares or merchandise so landed, sold or disposed of in violation of the provisions of this act, to be recovered by a proper proceeding in admiralty before the said court, in the district in which such ship, boat, or vessel may be found, one-half for the use of the collector of the district, who shall institute and conduct such proceeding, the other half for the use of the Government of the Confederate States: Provided, That if any such ship, boat or vessel shall be stranded, or front any cause become unable to proceed on its voyage, the cargo thereof may be landed and the same be entered at the nearest port of entry, in the same manner as goods, wares and merchandise regularly consigned to said port; and the person so entering the same shall be entitled to the benefit of drawback of duties or of warehousing said goods, wares and merchandise as provided by law in other cases.

SEC. 3. And be it further enacted, If any person having the charge of or being concerned in the transportation of any goods, wares or merchandize upon the said river, shall, with intent to defraud the revenue, break open or unpack, within the limits of the Confederate States, any part of the merchandize entered for transportation beyond the said limits, or shall exchange or consume the same, or with like intent shall break or deface any seal or fastening placed thereon by any officer of the revenue, or if any person shall deface, alter or forge any certificate granted for the protection of merchandize transported as aforesaid, each and every person so offending shall forfeit and pay five hundred dollars, and shall be imprisoned not less than one or more than six months, at the discretion of the court before which such person shall be convicted.

SEC. 4. Be it further enacted, In case any ship, boat or vessel shall enter the waters of the said river within the limits of the Confederate States, having on board any goods, wares or merchandize subject to the payment of duties, and the master, consignee or owner shall desire to land the same for sale or otherwise, it shall be lawful to enter said goods, wares and merchandize at any port of entry, in the same manner as goods, wares or merchandize regularly consigned to the said port, or to forward them under bond or seal, according to the regulations customary in such cases, when consigned to any port or place beyond the limits of this Confederacy, and on payment of the duties on said goods, to obtain from the collector a license to land the same at any point on the river; and when goods, wares or merchandize shall be entered as aforesaid, the owner, importer or consignee shall be entitled to the benefit of drawback of duties or of warehousing the said goods, wares and merchandise, as is provided by law, upon complying with all the laws and regulations which apply to cases of entry for drawback or warehousing respectively.

SEC. 5. Be it further enacted, When any such ship, boat or vessel, having on board goods, wares and merchandize subject to the payment of duties, as set forth in the fourth section, shall arrive at the first port of her entry of Confederate States, the master or person in command of such ship, boat or vessel shall, before he pass the said port, and immediately after his arrival, deposit with the collector a manifest of the cargo on board subject to the payment of duties, and the said collector shall, after registering the same, transmit it, duly certified to have been deposited, to the officers with whom the entries are to be made, and the said collector may, if he judge it necessary for the security of the revenue, put an inspector of the customs on board any such ship, boat or vessel, to accompany the same until her arrival at the first port of entry to which her cargo may be consigned; and if the master or person in command shall omit to deposit a manifest as aforesaid, or refuse to receive such inspector on board, he shall forfeit and pay five hundred dollars, with costs of suit, one-half to the use of the officer with whom the manifest should have been deposited, and the other half to the use of the collector of the district to which the vessel was bound: Provided, however, That until ports of entry shall be established above the city of Vicksburg, on the Mississippi River, the penalties of this act shall not extend to the delivery of goods above that port by vessels or boats descending said river.

APPROVED February 25, 1861.

No. 43.] AN ACT
To raise Provisional Forces for the Confederate States of America, and for other purposes.

SECTION 1. The Congress of the Confederate States of America do enact, That to enable the Government of the Confederate States to maintain its jurisdiction over all questions of peace and war, and to provide for the public defence, the President be and he is hereby authorized and directed to assume control of all military operations in every State, having reference to or connection with questions between said States, or any of them, and powers foreign to them.

SEC. 2. Be it further enacted, That the President is hereby authorized to receive from the several States the arms and munitions of war which have been acquired from the United States, and which are now in the forts, arsenals and navy yards of said States, and all other arms and munitions which they may desire to turn over and make chargeable to this government.

SEC. 3. And be it further enacted, That the President be authorized to receive into the service of this Government such forces now in the service of said States as may be tendered, or who may volunteer, by consent of their State, in such numbers as he may require, for any time not less than twelve months, unless sooner discharged.

SEC. 4. Be it further enacted, That such forces may be received, with their officers, by companies, battal-

ions or regiments, and when so received shall form a part of the Provisional Army of the Confederate States, according to the terms of their enlistment; and the President shall appoint, by and with the advice and consent of Congress, such general officer or officers for said forces as may be necessary for the service.

SEC. 5. Be it further enacted, That said forces, when received into the service of this Government, shall have the same pay and allowances as may be provided by law for volunteers entering the service, or for the army of the Confederate States, and shall be subject to the same rules and government.

APPROVED February 28, 1861.

No. 48.] AN ACT
To provide for the Public Defence.

SECTION 1. The Congress of the Confederate States of America do enact, That in order to provide speedily forces to repel invasion, maintain the rightful possession of the Confederate States of America in every portion of territory belonging to each State, and to secure the public tranquility and independence against threatened assault, the President be and he is hereby authorized to employ the militia, military and naval forces of the Confederate States of America, and to ask for and accept the services of any number of volunteers, not exceeding one hundred thousand, who may offer their services, either as cavalry, mounted riflemen, artillery or infantry, in such proportion of these several arms as he may deem expedient, to serve for twelve months after they shall be mustered into service, unless sooner discharged.

SEC. 2. And be it further enacted, That the militia, when called into service by virtue of this act or any other act, if in the opinion of the President the public interest requires, may be compelled to serve for a term not exceeding six months after they shall be mustered into service, unless sooner discharged.

SEC. 3. And be it further enacted, That said volunteers shall furnish their own clothes, and, if mounted men, their own horses and horse equipments; and when mustered into service, shall be armed by the States from which they come, or by the Confederate States of America.

SEC. 4. And be it further enacted, That said volunteers shall, when called into actual service, and while remaining therein, be subject to the rules and articles of war, and instead of clothing, every non-commissioned officer and private in any company shall be entitled, when called into actual service, to money in a sum equal to the cost of clothing of a non-commissioned officer or private in the regular army of the Confederate States of America.

SEC. 5. And be it further enacted, That the said volunteers so offering their services may be accepted by the President in companies, squadrons, battalions and regiments, whose officers shall be appointed in the manner prescribed by law in the several States to which they shall respectively belong; but when inspected, mustered, and received into the service of the Confederate States, said troops shall be regarded in all respects as a part of the army of said Confederate States, according to the terms of their respective enlistments.

SEC. 6. And be it further enacted, That the President is hereby authorized to organize companies so tendering their services into battalions or squadrons, battalions or squadrons into regiments, regiments into brigades, and brigades into divisions, whenever in his judgment such organization may be expedient; and whenever brigades or divisions shall be organized, the President shall appoint the commanding officers for such brigades and divisions, subject to the confirmation of Congress, who shall hold their offices only while such brigades and divisions are in service; and the President shall, if necessary, apportion the staff and general officers among the respective States from which the volunteers shall tender their services, as he may deem proper.

SEC. 7. And be it further enacted, That whenever the militia or volunteers are called and received into the service of the Confederate States, under the provisions of this act, they shall have the same organization, and shall have the same pay and allowances as may be provided for the regular army; and all mounted non-commissioned officers, privates, musicians and artificers, shall be allowed forty cents per day for the use and risk of their horses; and if any volunteer shall not keep himself provided with a serviceable horse, such volunteer shall serve on foot. For horses killed in action, volunteers shall be allowed compensation according to their appraised value at the date of muster into service.

SEC. 8. And be it further enacted, That the field and staff officers of a separate battalion of volunteers shall be one lieutenant colonel or major, one adjutant with the rank of lieutenant, one sergeant-major, one quartermaster- sergeant, and a chief bugler or principal musician, according to corps; and that each company shall be entitled to an additional 2d lieutenant; and that the President may limit the privates in any volunteer company, according to his discretion, at from sixty-four to one hundred.

SEC. 9. And be it further enacted, That when volunteers or militia are called into the service of the Confederate States in such numbers that the officers of the quartermaster, commissary, and medical departments, which may be authorized by law for the regular service, are not sufficient to provide for the supplying, quartering, transporting, and furnishing them with the requisite medical attendance, it shall be lawful for the President to appoint, with the advice and consent of the

Congress, as many additional officers of said departments as the service may require, not exceeding one commissary and one quartermaster for each brigade, with the rank of major, and one assistant quartermaster with the rank of captain, one assistant commissary with the rank of captain, one surgeon and one assistant surgeon for each regiment; the said quartermasters and commissaries, assistant quartermasters and commissaries, to give bonds with good sureties for the faithful performance of their duties, the said officers to be allowed the same pay and emoluments as shall be allowed to officers of the same grade in the regular service, and to be subject to the rules and articles of war, and to continue in service only so long as their services may be required in connection with the militia or volunteers.

SEC. 10. And be it further enacted, That the President be and he is hereby authorized to purchase or charter, arm, equip and man such merchant vessels and steamships or boats as may be found fit or easily converted into armed vessels, and in such number as he may deem necessary for the protection of the seaboard and the general defence of the country.

APPROVED March 6, 1861.

No. 61.] AN ACT
To fix the pay of Members of the Congress of the Confederate States of America.

SECTION 1. The Congress of the Confederate States of America do enact, That the pay of the members of Congress shall be eight dollars per day during the session, and that each member shall be allowed ten cents per mile for coming to, and ten cents per mile for returning from, the place where Congress may assemble for each session, to be computed by the usual mail route from his residence to the seat of government.

SEC. 2. Be it further enacted, That the pay of the President of Congress shall be sixteen dollars per day, and the same mileage as the members.

APPROVED March 11, 1861.

No. 72.] RESOLUTIONS
In reference to Forts, Dock-yards, Reservations, and Property ceded to the Confederate States.

Resolved by the Congress of the Confederate States, That the Congress do recommend to the respective states to cede the forts, arsenals, navy-yards, dock-yards and other public establishments within their respective limits to the Confederate States, and moreover, to cede so much of the lands reserved heretofore by the government of the United States, or other public vacant lands in their respective limits as may be necessary for timber or lumber for naval or other purposes of public concern; and that the President of Congress be requested to communicate these resolutions and the accompanying report to the governors of the respective states.

Resolved further, That in case of such cession, the President be and be is hereby authorized and empowered to take charge of any such property ceded.

APPROVED March 15, 1861.

No. 86.] AN ACT
To establish the Bureau of Indian Affairs.

SECTION 1. The Congress of the Confederate States of America do enact, That an additional bureau in the War Department be and the same is hereby established, to be known as the Bureau of Indian Affairs, and charged with the management of our relations with the Indian tribes.

SEC. 2. Be it further enacted, That the President, by and with the advice and consent of the Congress, may appoint a Commissioner of Indian Affairs and one clerk, to take charge of the business of the bureau hereby established, the salary of the Commissioner to be twenty-five hundred dollars per annum, and the salary of the clerk fifteen hundred dollars per annum.

APPROVED March 15, 1861.
CONFEDERATE STATES OF AMERICA,
DEPARTMENT OF STATE.

I certify that the foregoing Laws and Resolutions have been carefully compared with the original copies on file in the office of the Secretary of State.
WM. F. ALEXANDER,
Chief Clerk.
MONTGOMERY, 18th April, 1861.

(Source: *Acts and Resolutions of the First Session of the Provisional Congress of the Confederate States, Held at Montgomery, Ala.* Richmond, VA: Enquirer Book & Job Press, 1861.)

C. THE EXECUTIVE

U.S. senator Jefferson Davis was the last of the Mississippi delegation to leave Washington after the state's secession. On 21 January 1861, he delivered a farewell address to a crowded Senate chamber. After returning to his home in Mississippi, he was informed on 9 February of his election as provisional president of the Confederacy. His inaugural address was both an exhortation and a warning, and he lost no time in trying to set his new country on an equal diplomatic footing with the United States. [See Davis, Jefferson]

1. Jefferson Davis's Farewell to the U.S. Senate (21 January 1861)

I rise, Mr. President, for the purpose of announcing to the Senate that I have satisfactory evidence that the State of Mississippi, by a solemn ordinance of her people, in convention assembled, has declared her separation from the United States. Under these circumstances, of course, my functions are terminated here. It has seemed to me proper, however, that I should appear in the Senate to announce that fact to my associates, and I will say but very little more. The occasion does not invite me to go into argument; and my physical condition would not permit me to do so, if it were otherwise; and yet it seems to become me to say something on the part of the State I here represent on an occasion as solemn as this.

It is known to Senators who have served with me here that I have for many years advocated, as an essential attribute of State sovereignty, the right of a State to secede from the Union. Therefore, if I had thought that Mississippi was acting without sufficient provocation, or without an existing necessity, I should still, under my theory of the Government, because of my allegiance to the State of which I am a citizen, have been bound by her action. I, however, may be permitted to say that I do think she has justifiable cause, and I approve of her act. I conferred with her people before that act was taken, counseled them then that, if the state of things which they apprehended should exist when their Convention met, they should take the action which they have now adopted.

I hope none who hear me will confound this expression of mine with the advocacy of the right of a State to remain in the Union, and to disregard its constitutional obligation by the nullification of the law. Such is not my theory. Nullification and secession, so often confounded, are, indeed, antagonistic principles. Nullification is a remedy which it is sought to apply within the Union, against the agent of the States. It is only to be justified when the agent has violated his constitutional obligations, and a State, assuming to judge for itself, denies the right of the agent thus to act, and appeals to the other states of the Union for a decision; but, when the States themselves and when the people of the States have so acted as to convince us that they will not regard our constitutional rights, then, and then for the first time, arises the doctrine of secession in its practical application.

A great man who now reposes with his fathers, and who has often been arraigned for want of fealty to the Union, advocated the doctrine of nullification because it preserved the Union. It was because of his deep-seated attachment to the Union—his determination to find some remedy for existing ills short of a severance of the ties which bound South Carolina to the other States—that Mr. Calhoun advocated the doctrine of nullification, which he proclaimed to be peaceful, to be within the limits of State power, not to disturb the Union, but only to be a means of bringing the agent before the tribunal of the States for their judgement.

Secession belongs to a different class of remedies. It is to be justified upon the basis that the states are sovereign. There was a time when none denied it. I hope the time may come again when a better comprehension of the theory of our Government, and the inalienable rights of the people of the States, will prevent any one from denying that each State is a sovereign, and thus may reclaim the grants which it has made to any agent whomsoever.

I, therefore, say I concur in the action of the people of Mississippi, believing it to be necessary and proper, and should have been bound by their action if my belief had been otherwise; and this brings me to the important point which I wish, on this last occasion, to present to the Senate. It is by this confounding of nullification and secession that the name of a great man whose ashes now mingle with his mother earth has been invoked to justify coercion against a seceded State. The phrase, "to execute the laws," was an expression which General Jackson applied to the case of a State refusing to obey the laws while yet a member of the Union. That is not the case which is now presented. The laws are to be executed over the United States, and upon the people of the United States. They have no relation to any foreign country. It is a perversion of terms—at least, it is a great mis-apprehension of the case—which cites that expression for application to a State which has withdrawn from the Union. You may make war on a foreign state. If it be the purpose of gentlemen, they may make war against a State which has withdrawn from the Union; but there are no laws of the United States to be executed within the limits of a seceded State. A State, finding herself in the condition in which Mississippi has judged she is—in which her safety requires that she should provide for the maintenance of her rights out of the Union—surrenders all the benefits (and they are known to be many), deprives herself of the advantages (and they are known to be great), severs all the ties of affection (and they are close and enduring), which have bound her to the Union; and thus divesting herself of every benefit—taking upon herself every burden—she claims to be exempt from any power to execute the laws of the United States within her limits.

I well remember an occasion when Massachusetts was arraigned before the bar of the Senate, and when the doctrine of coercion was rife, and to be applied against her, because of the rescue of a fugitive slave in Boston. My opinion then was the same that it is now. Not in a spirit of egotism, but to show that I am not influenced in my opinions because the case is my own, I refer to that time and that occasion as containing the opinion which I then entertained, and on which my present conduct is based. I then said that if Massachusetts—following her purpose through a stated line of conduct—chose to take the last step, which separates her from the Union, it is her right to go, and I will neither vote one dollar nor one man to coerce her back; but I will say to her, Godspeed, in memory of the kind associations which once existed between her and the other States.

It has been a conviction of pressing necessity—it has been a belief that we are to be deprived in the Union of the rights which our fathers bequeathed to us—which has brought Mississippi to her present decision. She has heard proclaimed the theory that all men are created free and equal, and this made the basis of an attack upon her social institutions; and the sacred Declaration of Independence has been invoked to maintain the position of the equality of the races. That Declaration is to be construed by the circumstances and purposes for which it was made. The communities were declaring their independence; the people of those communities were asserting that no man was born—to use the language of Mr. Jefferson—booted and spurred, to ride over the rest of mankind; that men were created equal— meaning the men of the political community; that there was no divine right to rule; that no man inherited the right to govern; that there were no classes by which power and place descended to families; but that all stations were equally within the grasp of each member of the body politic. These were the great principles they announced; these were the purposes for which they made their declaration; these were the ends to which their enunciation was directed. They have no reference to the slave; else, how happened it that among the items of arraignment against George III was that he endeavored to do just what the North has been endeavoring of late to do, to stir up insurrection among our slaves? Had the Declaration announced that the negroes were free and equal, how was the prince to be arraigned for raising up insurrection among them? And how was this to be enumerated among the high crimes which caused the colonies to sever their connection with the mother-country? When our Constitution was formed, the same idea was rendered more palpable; for there we find provision made for that very class of persons as property; they were not put upon the equality of footing with white men—not even upon that of paupers and convicts; but, so far as representation was concerned, were discriminated against as a lower caste, only to be represented in the numerical proportion of three-fifths. So stands the compact which binds us together.

Then, Senators, we recur to the principles upon which our Government was founded; and when you deny them, and when you deny us the right to withdraw from a Government which, thus perverted, threatens to be destructive of our rights, we but tread in the path of our fathers when we proclaim our independence and take the hazard. This is done, not in hostility to others, not to injure any section of the country, not even for our own pecuniary benefit, but from the high and solemn motive of defending and protecting the rights we inherited, and which it is our duty to transmit unshorn to our children.

I find in myself perhaps a type of the general feeling of my constituents towards yours. I am sure I feel no hostility toward you, Senators from the North. I am sure there is not one of you, whatever sharp discussion there may have been between us, to whom I cannot now say, in the presence of my God, I wish you well; and such, I feel, is the feeling of the people whom I represent toward those whom you represent. I, therefore, feel that I but express their desire when I say I hope, and they hope, for peaceable relations with you, though we must part. They may be mutually beneficial to us in the future, as they have been in the past, if you so will it. The reverse may bring disaster on every portion of the country, and, if you will have it thus, we will invoke the God of our fathers, who delivered them from the power of the lion, to protect us from the ravages of the bear; and thus, putting our trust in God and in our firm hearts and strong arms, we will vindicate the right as best we may.

In the course of my service here, associated at different times with a variety of Senators, I see now around me some with whom I have served long; there have been points of collision, but, whatever of offense there has been to me, I leave here. I carry with me no hostile remembrance. Whatever offense I have given which has not been redressed, or for which satisfaction has not been demanded, I have, Senators, in this hour of our parting, to offer you my apology for any pain which, in the heat of discussion, I have inflicted. I go hence unencumbered by the remembrance of any injury received, and having discharged the duty of making the only reparation in my power for any injury offered.

Mr. President and Senators, having made the announcement which the occasion seemed to me to require, it only remains for me to bid you a final adieu.

(Source: Davis, Jefferson. *The Rise and Fall of the Confederate Government*. Vol. 1. New York: D. Appleton, 1881.)

2. Inaugural Address of Jefferson Davis as Provisional President of the Confederacy
[Montgomery, February 18, 1861]

Gentlemen Of The Congress Of The Confederate States Of America, Friends And Fellow-Citizens:
Called to the difficult and responsible station of Chief Executive of the Provisional Government which you have instituted, I approach the discharge of the duties assigned to me with an humble distrust of my abilities, but with a sustaining confidence in the wisdom of those who are to guide and to aid me in the administration of public affairs, and an abiding faith in the virtue and patriotism of the people.

Looking forward to the speedy establishment of a permanent government to take the place of this, and which by its greater moral and physical power will be better able to combat with the many difficulties which arise from the conflicting interests of separate nations, I enter upon the duties of the office to which I have been chosen with the hope that the beginning of our career as a Confederacy may not be obstructed by hostile opposition to our enjoyment of the separate existence and independence which we have asserted, and, with the blessing of Providence, intend to maintain. Our present condition, achieved in a manner unprecedented in the history of nations, illustrates the American idea that governments rest upon the consent of the governed, and that it is the right of the people to alter or abolish governments whenever they become destructive of the ends for which they were established.

The declared purpose of the compact of Union from which we have withdrawn was "to establish justice, insure domestic tranquillity, provide for the common defense, promote the general welfare, and secure the blessings of liberty to ourselves and our posterity;" and when, in the judgment of the sovereign States now composing this Confederacy, it had been perverted from the purposes for which it was ordained, and had ceased to answer the ends for which it was established, a peaceful appeal to the ballot-box declared that so far as they were concerned, the government created by that compact should cease to exist. In this they merely asserted a right which the Declaration of Independence of 1776 had defined to be inalienable; of the time and occasion for its exercise, they, as sovereigns, were the final judges, each for itself. The impartial and enlightened verdict of mankind will vindicate the rectitude of our conduct, and He who knows the hearts of men will judge of the sincerity with which we labored to preserve the Government of our fathers in its spirit. The right solemnly proclaimed at the birth of the States, and which has been affirmed and reaffirmed in the bills of rights of States subsequently admitted into the Union of 1789, undeniably recognize in the people the power to resume the authority delegated for the purposes of government. Thus the sovereign States here represented proceeded to form this Confederacy, and it is by abuse of language that their act has been denominated a revolution. They formed a new alliance, but within each State its government has remained, the rights of person and property have not been disturbed. The agent through whom they communicated with foreign nations is changed, but this does not necessarily interrupt their international relations.

Sustained by the consciousness that the transition from the former Union to the present Confederacy has not proceeded from a disregard on our part of just obligations, or any failure to perform every constitutional duty, moved b! no interest or passion to invade the rights of others, anxious to cultivate peace and commerce with all nations, if we may not hope to avoid war, we may at least expect that posterity will acquit us of having needlessly engaged in it. Doubly justified by the absence of wrong on our part, and by wanton aggression on the part of others, there can be no cause to doubt that the courage and patriotism of the people of the Confederate States will be found equal to any measures of defense which honor and security may require.

An agricultural people, whose chief interest is the export of a commodity required in every manufacturing country, our true policy is peace, and the freest trade which our necessities will permit. It is alike our interest, and that of all those to whom we would sell and from whom we would buy, that there should be the fewest practicable restrictions upon the interchange of commodities. There can be but little rivalry between ours and any manufacturing or navigating community, such as the Northeastern States of the American Union. It must follow, therefore, that a mutual interest would invite good will and kind offices. If, however, passion or the lust of dominion should cloud the judgment or inflame the ambition of those States, we must prepare to meet the emergency and to maintain, by the final arbitrament of the sword, the position which we have assumed among the nations of the earth. We have entered upon the career of independence, and it must be inflexibly pursued. Through many years of controversy with our late associates, the Northern States, we have vainly endeavored to secure tranquillity, and to obtain respect for the rights to which we were entitled. As a necessity, not a choice, we have resorted to the remedy of separation; and henceforth our energies must he directed to the conduct of our own affairs, and the perpetuity of the Confederacy which we have formed. If a just perception of mutual interest shall permit us peaceably to pursue our separate political career, my most earnest desire will have been fulfilled. But, if this be denied to us, and the integrity of our territory and jurisdiction be assailed, it will but remain for us, with firm resolve, to appeal to arms and invoke the blessings of Providence on a just cause.

As a consequence of our new condition and with a view to meet anticipated wants, it will be necessary to provide for the speedy and efficient organization of branches of the executive department, having special charge of foreign intercourse, finance, military affairs, and the postal service.

For purposes of defense, the Confederate States may, under ordinary circumstances, rely mainly upon their militia, but it is deemed advisable, in the present condition of affairs, that there should be a well-instructed and disciplined army, more numerous than would usually be required on a peace establishment. I also suggest that for the protection of our harbors and commerce on the high seas a navy adapted to those objects will be required. These necessities have doubtless engaged the attention of Congress.

With a Constitution differing only from that of our fathers in so far as it is explanatory of their well-known intent, freed from the sectional conflicts which have interfered with the pursuit of the general welfare it is not unreasonable to expect that States from which we have recently parted may seek to unite their fortunes with ours under the government which we have instituted. For this your Constitution makes adequate provision; but beyond this, if I mistake not the judgment and will of the people, a reunion with the States from which we have separated is neither practicable nor desirable. To increase the power, develop the resources, and promote the happiness of a confederacy, it is requisite that there should be so much of homogeneity that the welfare of every portion shall be the aim of the whole. Where this does not exist, antagonisms are engendered which must and should result in separation.

Actuated solely by the desire to preserve our own rights and promote our own welfare, the separation of the Confederate States has been marked by no aggression upon others and followed by no domestic convulsion. Our industrial pursuits have received no check. The cultivation of our fields has progressed as heretofore, and even should we be involved in war there would be no considerable diminution in the production of the staples which have constituted our exports and in which the commercial world has an interest scarcely less than our own. This common interest of the producer and consumer can only be interrupted by an exterior force which should obstruct its transmission to foreign markets—a course of conduct which would be as unjust toward us as it would be detrimental to manufacturing and commercial interests abroad. Should reason guide the action of the Government from which we have separated, a policy so detrimental to the civilized world, the Northern States included, could not be dictated by even the strongest desire to inflict injury upon us; but otherwise a terrible responsibility will rest upon it, and the suffering of millions will bear testimony to the folly and wickedness of our aggressors. In the meantime there will remain to us, besides the ordinary means before suggested, the well-known resources for retaliation upon the commerce of an enemy.

Experience in public stations, of subordinate grade to this which your kindness has conferred, has taught me that care and toil and disappointment are the price of official elevation. You will see many errors to forgive, many deficiencies to tolerate, but you shall not find in me either a want of zeal or fidelity to the cause that is to me highest in hope and of most enduring affection. Your generosity has bestowed upon me an undeserved distinction, one which I neither sought nor desired. Upon the continuance of that sentiment and upon your wisdom and patriotism I rely to direct and support me in the performance of the duty required at my hands.

We have changed the constituent parts, but not the system of our Government. The Constitution formed by our fathers is that of these Confederate States, in their exposition of it, and in the judicial construction it has received, we have a light which reveals its true meaning.

Thus instructed as to the just interpretation of the instrument, and ever remembering that all offices are but trusts held for the people, and that delegated powers are to be strictly construed, I will hope, by due diligence in the performance of my duties, though I may disappoint your expectations, yet to retain, when retiring, something of the good will and confidence which welcome my entrance into office.

It is joyous, in the midst of perilous times, to look around upon a people united in heart, where one purpose of high resolve animates and actuates the whole—where the sacrifices to be made are not weighed in the balance against honor and right and liberty and equality. Obstacles may retard, they cannot long prevent the progress of a movement sanctified by its justice, and sustained by a virtuous people. Reverently let us invoke the God of our fathers to guide and protect us in our efforts to perpetuate the principles which, by his blessing, they were able to vindicate, establish and transmit to their posterity, and with a continuance of His favor, ever gratefully acknowledged, we may hopefully look forward to success, to peace, and to prosperity.

(Source: Confederate States of America. *Congressional Journal* 1: 64–66, 1861.)

3. Jefferson Davis to Abraham Lincoln (27 February 1861)
MONTGOMERY, February 27, 1861.

The President of the United States:
Being animated by an earnest desire to unite and bind together our respective countries by friendly ties, I have appointed M. J. Crawford, one of our most settled and trustworthy citizens, as special commissioner of the Confederate States of America to the Government of the United States; and I have now the honor to introduce him to you, and to ask for him a reception and treatment corresponding to his station and to the purpose for which he is sent. Those purposes he will more particularly explain to you. Hoping that through his agency. &c. [sic.]
JEFF'N DAVIS.

For the purpose of establishing friendly relations between the Confederate States and the United States,

and reposing special trust, &c., Martin J. Crawford, John Forsyth, and A. B. Roman are appointed special commissioners of the Confederate States to the United States. I have invested them with full and all manner of power and authority for and in the name of the Confederate States to meet and confer with any person or persons duly authorized by the Government of the United States being furnished with like powers and authority, and with them to agree, treat, consult, and negotiate of and concerning all matters and subjects interesting to both nations, and to conclude and sign a treaty or treaties, convention or conventions, touching the premises, transmitting the same to the President of the Confederate States for his final ratification by and with the consent of the Congress of the Confederate States.

Given under my hand at the city of Montgomery this 27th day of February, A.D. 1861, and of the Independence of the Confederate States the eighty-fifth.
JEFF N DAVIS.
ROBERT TOOMBS, Secretary of State.

(Source: Richardson, James D., ed. *A Compilation of the Messages and Papers of the Confederacy, including the Diplomatic Correspondence, 1861–1865.* Nashville, TN: United States Publishing Co., 1905.)

D. THE COURTS

Article III of the Confederate Constitution established the nation's judicial system, which, like that of the United States, would function within a prescribed jurisdiction along with extant state courts. Created by Congress in the Judiciary Act of 16 March 1861, the Confederacy's court system was manifest at the district level, with each state constituting one or more districts. A Confederate Supreme Court was authorized by both the Provisional and Permanent Constitutions and was created by Congress in this legislation of 16 March 1861, yet the Court never physically existed. [See Courts, C.S.A.]

1. An Act to Establish the Judicial Courts of the Confederate States of America (1861)

SECTION 1. *The Congress of the Confederate States of America do enact,* That the Supreme Court of the Confederate States shall hold annually, at the seat of government, one session, commencing the first Monday of January, and continue until the business of said court is disposed of.

SEC. 2. That each of the Confederate States shall constitute one district, in which there shall be a court called a District Court, to consist of one judge, who shall reside in the state for which he is appointed, and shall receive a salary equal to that paid to a judge of the court of the highest jurisdiction in the state where he resides, payable quarterly.

SEC. 3. *And be it further enacted,* That the Supreme Court may, by any one or more of its judges being present, be adjourned from day to day until a quorum be convened; and that a district court, in case of the inability of the judge to attend at the commencement of a session, may be adjourned by the marshal of the district from day to day for three successive days, and at the close of the third day the same shall stand adjourned to the next regular term, if the judge do not appear; and in all cases of failure to hold the court, all process, pleadings and proceedings, of what nature soever, pending before the said court, shall be continued of course.

SEC. 4. There shall be a marshal and one or more clerks appointed for each court—the marshal by the President of the Confederate States, and the clerks by the judge of said court—and said clerks shall not be connected with the said judge by blood or marriage, who shall hold their offices during the provisional government, subject to removal by the said judge. They shall each take the oath or affirmation prescribed in the constitution, and for the faithful discharge of the duties of their respective offices. They shall each give bond with sureties, to be approved by the judge, for the faithful discharge of their respective duties, in the penalty and for the amount which may be prescribed by the judge; but that of the marshal in no instance shall be less than twenty thousand dollars. The marshal may appoint as many deputies as may be necessary, for whose acts he and his sureties shall be bound as for his own.

SEC. 5. It shall be the duty of the marshal to attend the court when sitting in his district; and the marshal of the district in which the Supreme Court shall be held, shall attend the sessions of said court. He shall by himself or his deputy execute throughout his district all lawful precepts directed to him, and issued under the authority of the Confederate States, and he shall have power to command a *posse comitatus* in the execution of his duty.

SEC. 6. *And be it further enacted,* That in all cases in which the marshal or his deputy shall be a party, the writs and precepts therein shall be directed to some disinterested person, to be appointed by the court or judge thereof, and such person is hereby authorized to execute and return the same. And in case of the death, resignation or removal of any marshal, his deputy or deputies shall continue in office, unless otherwise removed, and shall execute the same in the name of the deceased, resigned or removed marshal, until another marshal shall be appointed and qualified; and the defaults or misfeasances in office of such deputy or deputies in the meantime, as well as before, shall be adjudged a breach of the condition of the bond given as before directed by the marshal who appointed them; and the executor or administrator of the deceased marshal shall have like remedy for the defaults and misfeasances in office of such deputy or deputies, during such interval is the marshal would be entitled to if he had continued in life or in office and in the exercise of his said office until his successor was appointed and qualified; and every marshal or deputy, when removed from office, or when the term for which the marshal is appointed shall expire, shall have power, notwithstanding, to execute all such precepts and process as may be in their hand respectively at the time of such removal or expiration of office, until the next term of the court; and the marshal shall be held answerable for the delivery to his successor of all prisoners which may be in his custody at the time of his removal or resignation, or when the term for which he is appointed shall expire, and for that purpose may retain such prisoners in his custody until his successor shall be appointed and qualified as the law directs; or he may deliver his prisoners to the keeper of one of the jails of the state in which he is marshal in cases where by law of such state it is made the duty of jailors to receive them.

SEC. 7. All writs and process, either mesne or final, which shall issue from the Supreme Court, shall bear test in the name of either of the judges thereof; and all issued from the district court shall bear test of the judge of such court, and shall be under the seal of the court from whence they issue, and be signed by the clerk thereof. The seals of the Supreme and district courts to be provided by the respective judges of the same.

SEC. 8. The judge of each district shall appoint the times and places of holding the courts in his district, and where, under the laws of the United States, his state was divided into two or more districts, he shall annually hold not less than two terms of his court in each of these districts, as they existed on the first day of November, 1860. But in Louisiana he shall only be required to hold his court out of New Orleans at such time or times as he may consider the public interest requires him to do, and the counties, districts or parishes which constitute the divisions of his district, shall be the same as those which constituted the different districts under the laws aforesaid.

SEC. 9. The said judges, before they proceed to execute the duties of their respective offices, shall take the oath or affirmation prescribed in the constitution, and shall also swear or affirm to administer justice without respect to persons, and to do equal right to the poor and to the rich, and faithfully and impartially to perform and discharge all the duties of his office agreeably to the constitution and laws of the Confederate States, to the best of his ability.

SEC. 10. The district courts shall have jurisdiction, concurrent with the courts of the several States, of all civil suits at common law or in equity, where the matter in dispute, exclusive of costs, exceeds the sum or value of five thousand dollars, and where the character of the parties is such as by the Constitution to authorize said court to entertain jurisdiction. But no person shall be arrested or summoned in any such suit in one division of district for trial in another; and no civil suit shall be brought before any of said courts against an inhabitant of the Confederate States by any original process in any other district than that of which he is an inhabitant, nor shall any district court have cognizance of any suit to recover the contents of any promissory note or other chose in action in favor of an assignee or transferee, unless a suit might have been prosecuted in such court to recover such contents if no assignment or transfer had been made, except in cases of foreign bills of exchange.

SEC. 11. Upon joint bills, bonds, notes or obligations, suits may be brought against any one or more of the parties, except that separate suits shall not be brought against joint parties thereto residing in the same district; and when several actions shall be brought against persons who might be legally joined in one action, the plaintiff, if judgment be given in his favor, shall not recover the costs of more than one action.

SEC. 12. Suits in equity shall not be sustained in any of the courts of the Confederate States in any case where plain, adequate remedy may be had at law. And in any State in which there is or may be no separate court of equity, the district court shall administer and decide on matters of equity, according to the course of practice in the courts of such State.

SEC. 13. The laws of the several States, except where the Constitution, treaties or statutes of the Confederate States shall otherwise require or provide, shall be regarded as rules of decision in the courts of the Confederate States, in cases where they apply. And where the decision of the highest court in a State has become a rule of property, the same shall be adopted as a rule in the courts of the Confederate States, in cases in which the laws of such State apply.

SEC. 14. Except the style, the forms of writs and executions and other process, and the forms and modes of proceeding in the progress and trial of suits, and in enforcing the judgments in the district courts of the Confederate States in cases at law, shall be the same in each of said States, respectively, as are now in use in the highest court of original general jurisdiction of the same; and in proceedings in equity, according to the principles, laws and rules which govern courts of equity in such State. And whenever any State shall, by law, change such forms or modes of proceeding, in its own courts, such change shall be applicable to the forms and modes of proceeding in the said district courts held in such State, unless Congress shall otherwise provide by law. And the said district courts shall likewise have power to grant new trials.

SEC. 15. The costs and fees of clerks and marshals in the said district courts shall be the same in all cases, both civil and criminal, as are allowed by the law of the State in which such court is held, for similar services, to the officers of such State in the highest court of original jurisdiction therein, except that the marshal shall be entitled to mileage at the rate of five cents per mile for the service of process on persons residing out of the county, district or parish in which the court is holden, such mileage to be computed for the distance travelled in the service of such process, upon the most direct route, computed from the place of holding such court; and if there be more than one defendant in the same case in one county, but one charge for mileage shall be made.

SEC. 16. Both the district and supreme courts, and the judges thereof, out of term shall have power to issue writs of injunction, *scire facias* and *habeas corpus*, and all other writs not specially provided for by statute which may be necessary for the exercise of their respective jurisdictions and agreeable to the principles and usages of law: *Provided*, That writs of *habeas corpus* shall in no case extend to prisoners, unless when they are in custody under or by virtue of the authority of the Confederate States.

SEC. 17. The rules for taking the deposition of any witnesses in a case at law whose attendance cannot be procured, shall be the same as are in force by law in the highest court of original jurisdiction in the State in which such depositions are to be used; and they shall be read in evidence upon the trial of the cause, subject to all legal exceptions to which they would be liable in the said court of the State. No witness, under any circumstances, shall be compelled to attend a court in a civil cause in any other district or division than that in which he resides. And where his attendance cannot be procured, his deposition may be taken. In suits in equity, deposition shall be taken under a commission issued under the seal of the court, in the same manner and under the same rules and regulations in and by which depositions may be taken in the highest court of original equity jurisdiction in the State in which such depositions are to be used, and when so taken they shall be read upon the hearing of the cause, if subject to no legal exception; and the said district courts may also, on application thereof as a court of equity, direct depositions to be taken to perpetuate testimony relating to matters cognizable in any court of the Confederate States, such depositions to be taken according to the law and practice in the state in which the order is made: *Provided*, That in Louisiana and Texas depositions may in all cases be taken according to the laws regulating the practice of the highest courts of original jurisdiction in these States.

SEC. 18. The judges of the several district courts may, each for his own district, appoint as many commissioners as he may deem necessary, to administer oaths and take acknowledgments of deeds or other papers and take depositions, which acts of such commissioner shall have the same force and effect in all the Confederate States and the courts thereof, as if done by a judge of such court. And any person swearing falsely in any oath or matter before such commissioner shall, upon conviction, be liable to the same punishment as if the oath had been made before such judge. And the same fees shall be allowed such commissioner as are allowed for similar services by the laws of the State in which they are performed. All the powers and authority conferred on commissioners in and by the preceding clause are hereby vested in and may be exercised by any legally appointed notary public in any of the Confederate States.

SEC. 19. In all the courts of the Confederate States the parties shall have a right to be heard either by themselves or counsel.

SEC. 20. Where judgments are a mortgage or lien upon the property of a defendant in any of the States, they shall have the same effect or lien when rendered in one of the district courts of the Confederate States as if rendered in a State court, and be subject to the same rules as to enrollment, or recording of judgments or abstracts of judgments. And the lien of executions shall be the same as in the courts of the State where such district court sits. But in all cases of conflict between levies of process from the State and Federal courts, the first levy shall have priority.

SEC. 21. The mode of proof by oral testimony and examination of witnesses in open court, in trials at law, shall be the same in the said district courts as in the court of the highest original jurisdiction in the State in which such trial takes place; and the compensation of witnesses shall likewise be the same. The rules to determine the competency of witnesses shall also be the same.

SEC. 22. In any suit depending in any of the courts of the Confederate States, if either of the parties should die and the cause of action should survive, such suit may be revived in the same manner as in similar cases in the courts of the highest original jurisdiction in the State in which the cause is pending, and when there are two or more plaintiffs and defendants, and one or more of them should die, the suits shall not be thereby abated, but such death being suggested on the record, the suit may then proceed in the name of the survivor or survivors; or where the law of any State permits the representative of the deceased to be joined in such suit, the same may be done in the district court; or if the cause should be pending in the Supreme Court, then it may be revived by *scire facias* against the executor or administrator, issued from the office of the clerk of such court, returnable to the next term thereof, and duly served by the marshal twenty days before the sitting of such court.

SEC. 23. The said district court shall have power in the trial of actions at law, on motion and due notice thereof, to require the parties to produce books or writings in their possession or power which contain evidence pertinent to the issue; and if the plaintiff shall fail to comply with such order, judgment of non-suit may be given against him; and if the defendant shall so fail, then judgment by default may be rendered against him.

SEC. 24. The courts of the Confederate States shall have power to inflict punishment for contempts of court, but such power shall not be construed to extend to any cases except misbehavior in the presence of the court, or so near thereto as to obstruct the administration of justice, the misbehavior of any of the officers of said court in their official transactions, and the disobedience, resistance or obstruction by any person whatsoever of the process, order, rule, decree or command of said courts; but such punishment shall not exceed the imposition of a fine of one hundred dollars and imprisonment during the term of the court.

SEC. 25. Jurors, in all cases, to serve in the courts of the Confederate States, shall have the like qualifications, and be entitled to the like exemptions, as jurors in the highest court of original jurisdiction of the State in which the district court is held, and shall be selected by lot or otherwise, according to the form and mode of forming such juries in the courts of the State, in so far as such mode may be practicable; and for this purpose, the district courts shall have power to make all rules and regulations necessary to conform to the selection and empanneling of juries to the laws of the State, so as to secure an impartial trial, without needless expense, and without undue burden to the citizens of any part of the district. And when from any cause there shall not be a jury to determine any criminal or civil case the court may direct a jury to be summoned of the bystanders to complete the panel. And it shall be the duty of the judge, thirty days before the holding of the first court in his district under this law, to direct the marshal in what manner and to what extent to summon jurors for such court.

The compensation to jurors in both civil and criminal cases shall be the same as is allowed to jurors in courts of the highest original jurisdiction in the State in which such court is held; and if in such State court there be no allowance for mileage, the jurors shall be allowed five cents per mile for travelling from their respective places of abode to the place where the court is holden, and the same for returning.

SEC. 26. In all suits on bonds, agreements, or specialities for penalties, or breach of covenant, the amount recovered by the default or confession of the defendant or upon demurrer, shall be the sum actually due; and when the sum for which judgment is rendered is uncertain, the same shall be assessed by a jury. On all judgments in civil cases for the payment of money, interest shall be allowed at such rate as is allowed upon judgments tendered in the highest court of original jurisdiction in the State in which such district court sits.

SEC. 27. Every mistake, omission, defect or imperfection in the process, declaration, pleading, or any of the proceedings in any cause, or in the judgment, shall be amended from time to time, at the instance of either party, according to the several statutes of amendments or jeofails in the State in which the court sits, so as to secure a trial upon the merits, and that justice may be done, subject to any rule for the costs of amendment which the judge may impose.

SEC. 28. Where, in any State, there are two or more divisions of the district court, all writs of execution upon any judgment rendered in the court of either division may run and be executed in any part of such State, but shall be issued and made returnable to the court in which the judgment was rendered.

SEC. 29. A writ of error, when authorized by law to operate as a supersedes and stay of execution, shall only have that effect when a copy thereof and a citation have been served on the adverse party or his counsel of record; but no execution shall issue in less than ten days from the rendition of the judgment or decree, unless upon affidavit made, showing a necessity therefor.

SEC. 30. Should the marshal or clerk fail to pay over to the party entitled thereto, or to his attorney of record, upon demand made, any money which may have come to his hands by virtue of any order or process of the court, such money, with legal interest and ten per cent. damages, may be recovered from him and his sureties in his official bond, upon motion and three days' notice in the court of which he is marshal or clerk.

SEC. 31. There shall be appointed in each of the districts by the President, a meet person, learned in the law, to act as attorney for the Confederate States in such district, who shall be sworn or affirmed to the faithful performance of his duty in office, and to support the Constitution; and it shall be his duty to prosecute, in such district, all delinquents for crimes and offences cognizable in such court under the laws of the Confederate States, and to prosecute or defend all civil actions in which the Confederate States shall be concerned, except before the Supreme Court, in the district in which that court shall be holden. And he shall receive as compensation for his services a salary of two hundred dollars per annum, payable quarterly, and ten dollars per diem for every day that he is engaged in attending said court, together with such fees as shall hereafter be prescribed by law. And where there are three divisions in the district for which he is appointed, he shall be allowed mileage, at the rate of ten cents per mile, for going to and returning from the court which is most distant from his place of residence, to be computed on the most usual line of travel; and in case of the absence of such attorney from any term of the court, the presiding judge may appoint a fit person to act for him for the term.

SEC. 32. Whenever a marshal shall sell any lands or tenements by virtue of any process in his hands, and shall die, or in any manner go out of office before making a deed to the same, the court to which the process is returnable may, upon written application and notice thereof to the plaintiff and defendant, or their counsel, and upon a statement and proof of the facts, direct his successor to make the necessary deed therefor upon the payment of any purchase money or costs remaining unpaid.

SEC. 33. In any civil case in any of the courts of the Confederate States, the plaintiff may, upon motion, be required to give security for the costs, upon such terms as the court by its rules may prescribe; and if he should fail to comply within the time allowed, the suit shall be dismissed at the next term, unless good cause be shown against it. And the said district courts shall have power, from time to time, to make all needful rules for the conduct and dispatch of business therein, not inconsistent with the Constitution and laws of the Confederate States, or with the provisions of this act.

SEC. 34. The laws of the several States abolishing imprisonment for debt, and providing relief for debtors held in custody, shall take effect in favor of all persons held in custody for debt under the process of the federal courts of the Confederacy.

SEC. 35. *And be it further enacted,* That the said district courts shall have exclusive cognizance of all crimes and offences cognizable under the authority of the Confederate States, except where the laws of said Confederate States shall otherwise provide.

SEC. 36. The said courts, in term, shall have power to direct a grand jury to be summoned and empannelled, whenever in its judgment it may be proper to do so, and at such time as it may direct. After such jury is empannelled the proceedings shall conform, as nearly as may be, to the law and practice of the court of the highest original criminal jurisdiction in the State where such district court is held. But no grand jury shall be summoned unless upon the order of the judge or court, and if made by the judge out of term, shall be in writing under his hand and seal.

SEC. 37. Until otherwise provided by law of Congress, the laws of the United States in regard to crimes and offences, and to the mode of procedure, practice and trial in all criminal cases shall be in force, and form the rule of practice and decision in the district courts of the Confederate States, and where there is no such law governing the practice, then the rule and course shall conform as nearly as practicable to the practice established by law of the State court of highest original jurisdiction in which the said district court sits. And this provision shall extend to the rules of evidence and mode of examining witnesses in such cases.

SEC. 38. Writs of error or appeals to the Supreme Court of the Confederate States shall be allowed the accused in all cases in which the punishment or penalty upon conviction is death or imprisonment in the penitentiary, in the same manner and upon the same terms as are allowed in courts of highest original criminal jurisdiction in the State in which such district court is holden; and the remedy upon any bond given in such case, shall be the same as in the courts of the State from which such appeal or writ of error is taken. Such writ of error shall operate as a stay to the execution of the sentence or judgment, upon the execution of such bond as may be required by the State law in similar cases; and if such sentence or judgment shall be affirmed, and the time for executing the same shall have passed, the Supreme Court shall give such judgment or pronounce such sentence as the law prescribes, and appoint the time and place for carrying the same into effect by the marshal of the court from which said writ of error emanated.

SEC. 39. The said district courts shall have original cognizance of all civil causes of admiralty and maritime jurisdiction, including all seizures under the revenue laws or laws of navigation and trade of the Confederate States, which are navigable from the sea by vessels of one hundred or more tons burden, within the respective districts as well as upon the high seas; saving to suitors in all cases the right of a common law remedy, where the remedy at common law is ample and complete. And said district courts, as courts of admiralty, shall be deemed always open for the purpose of filing libels, petitions, answers and other pleadings, for issuing and returning mesne and final process and commissions, and for making all interlocutory orders or rules which may be necessary.

And the laws of the United States and the rules of court in reference to admiralty proceedings in force in the admiralty courts of the United States of America, on the twentieth day of December, one thousand eight hundred and sixty, so far as the same may be applicable, and are not inconsistent with the Constitution and laws of the Confederate States, are hereby continued in full force and effect in the courts of the Confederate States, until altered or repealed by law.

SEC. 40. Final judgments and decrees in civil actions, and final decrees in equity in a district court, where the matter in dispute exceeds in value the sum of five thousand dollars, exclusive of costs, may be re-examined, and reversed or affirmed upon a writ of error in the Supreme Court, the citation in such case being signed by a judge of the district court or of the Supreme

Court, and the adverse party having at least thirty days' notice. Writs of error, shall not be brought but within two years after rendering or passing the judgment or decree complained of, or in case the person entitled to such writ of [error] be an infant, femme covert, non compos mentis or imprisoned, then within two years, as aforesaid, exclusive of the time of such disability. And every judge signing a citation or any writ of error, as aforesaid, shall take bond, and good and sufficient sureties, that the plaintiff shall prosecute his writ with effect, and answer all costs if he fail to make good his plea; and no writ of error shall operate as a supersedeas and stay of execution, unless such bond be with sureties and of sufficient amount to secure the whole judgment, if it be affirmed, in addition to the costs.

And the said court or the judges thereof, shall have power to appoint a clerk, who shall take the oath prescribed for the clerks of the district courts, and give bond for the faithful discharge of his duty, in such amount as said court may direct, whose fees shall be the same as those now allowed to the clerks of the Supreme Courts of the United States.

SEC. 41. Where, upon such writ of error, the Supreme Court shall affirm a judgment or decree, they may adjudge or decree to the defendant in error just damages for his delay not exceeding ten per cent. per annum, but such damages shall only be given when it is manifest to the court that the appeal or writ of error was taken for delay, and all costs. The Supreme Courts shall not issue executions in causes that are removed before them by writs of error, but shall send a special mandate to the district court to award execution thereupon, including lawful costs accruing upon such appeal.

SEC. 42. From all final judgments or decrees which may be rendered in any district court in any cases of equity, of admiralty and maritime jurisdiction, and of prize or no prize, an appeal, where the matter in dispute, exclusive of costs, exceeds the sum or value of five thousand dollars in equity, or of five hundred dollars in courts of admiralty and maritime jurisdiction, shall be allowed to the Supreme Court, and upon such appeal, a transcript of the libel, bill, answer, depositions and all other proceedings of what kind soever in the cause, shall be transmitted to the said Supreme Court; and no new evidence shall be received in the said court on the hearing of such appeal; and such appeals shall be subject to the same rules, regulations, and restrictions as are prescribed in law in case of writs of error; and the said Supreme Court shall be and hereby is authorized and required to receive, hear and determine such appeal: *Provided always*, That appeals or writs of error in any case to the Supreme Court of this Confederacy from existing judgments or decrees, may be taken under the same rules and regulations required by the laws of the United States for appeals or writs of error to the

Supreme Court of the United States existing at the time the said judgment or decrees were rendered.

SEC. 43. The Supreme Court shall have power from time to time to make all such rules and regulations as it may deem needful for the orderly and correct dispatch of cases not inconsistent with the rules of law, and this power shall extend both to original and appellate causes therein. In all cases in the Supreme Court where there is an equal division of opinion among the judges thereof, and the court is not full, there shall be awarded a re-argument before a full court. If there be such division when the court is full, then the judgment of the court below shall be affirmed.

SEC. 44. The Supreme Court shall have original jurisdiction of all controversies of a civil nature where a State is a party, except between a State and its citizens, or citizens of any other State or nation. It shall also have exclusively all such jurisdiction of suits or proceedings against ambassadors or other public ministers, or their servants, as a court of law can have or exercise consistently with the law of nations, and original, but not exclusive jurisdiction, of all suits brought by ambassadors or other public ministers, or in which a consul or vice-consul shall be a party. And the trial of issues in fact in the Supreme Court, in all actions at law against citizens of the Confederate States shall be by jury, and it shall have power to issue writs of prohibition to the district courts, when proceeding as courts of admiralty and maritime jurisdiction, and writs of mandamus, in cases warranted by the principles and usages of law, to any courts appointed under the authority of the Confederate States.

SEC. 45. *Be it further enacted*, That a final judgment or decree in any suit, in the highest court of law or equity of a State in which a decision in the suit could be had, where is drawn in question the validity of a treaty or statute of, or an authority exercised under the Confederate States:

Or where is drawn in question the validity of a statute of, or an authority exercised under any State, on the ground of their being repugnant to the Constitution, treaty or laws of the Confederate States:

Or where is drawn in question the construction of any clause of the Constitution, or of a treaty, or statute or commission held under the Confederate States:

In each of these causes the decision may be re-examined, and reversed or affirmed in the Supreme Court of the Confederate States, upon a writ of error, the citation being signed by any judge of the said Supreme Court, in the same manner and under the same regulations, and with the like effect as if the judgment or decree complained of had been rendered or passed in a district court of the Confederate States; and the proceeding upon reversal shall be the same, except that the Supreme Court, instead of remanding the cause for a final decision, may at their discretion, if the cause shall have once been remanded before, proceed to a final decision of the same and award execution. But no other error shall be assigned or regarded as a ground of reversal in any such case as aforesaid than such as appears in the face of the record, and immediately respects the beforementioned questions of validity or construction of the said Constitution, treaties, statute, commissions or authorities in dispute.

SEC. 46. All judgments, orders and decrees made by any State court since the date of the secession of such State, upon any subject or matter which before such secession was within the jurisdiction of the courts of the United States, shall have the force and effect of judgments, orders and decrees of the courts herein established, with the privilege of either party to appeal or sue out a writ of error.

SEC. 47. *And be it further enacted,* That all the records, papers, dockets, depositions and judicial proceedings of every kind appertaining to any suit now pending in the circuit or district courts of the United States, within any of the States of the Confederacy, shall be transferred to the District Court of the Confederate States of America in the same State and district in which the same was pending; and the late clerk of said court or district courts, or other persons in whose custody said records, papers, dockets, depositions and judicial proceedings may be, shall deliver the same to the clerk of the district court to which they may be transferred under the provisions of this act, and the same shall stand in the same plight and condition in which they were in said circuit and district courts respectively, and all previous orders therein made shall have the same effect. And the court to which said causes are hereby transferred shall proceed to hear and determine the same according to law, and all dockets, books, records, documents and papers of every kind pertaining to judicial proceedings in any of said courts, and to suits heretofore decided therein, and all patents, deeds, records, books and papers pertaining to any land office which may be law have been deposited with the clerk of any of said courts or transferred to his office for safe keeping, shall be delivered to the clerk of the district court for the district in which such court is situated, and the same shall be safely kept and preserved by said clerk until otherwise provided by law. And copies of any such records or other papers made out by said clerk of the district court and authenticated according to law, shall have the force and effect given to copies of other instruments of like character in such State, and be admissable in evidence in all cases in which copies are admitted as evidence in the courts of the Confederate States: *Provided,* That all suits which shall have been pending in any of said courts for the space of five years without prosecution shall be considered as abandoned, unless prosecuted within six months from the time of such transfer.

And the judgments in all civil cases heretofore rendered in said circuit and district courts of the United States remaining unsatisfied, shall have the same force and effect which they had before the secession of the state in which said court is situated, and the same proceedings may be had thereon in the district court of the Confederate States, by execution or otherwise, which might have been taken in the court in which they were rendered at the time of their rendition. And where, under any such judgment of the circuit courts of the United States, any execution may have been in part executed by levy on property or otherwise, it shall be the duty of the marshal or officer in whose hands such execution and property may be, to turn over the same to the marshal of the Confederate States for the district in which such judgment was rendered, and to take his receipt therefor; and thereupon the said marshal shall proceed to dispose of the same according to the laws in force at the time such judgment was rendered, and pay over the proceeds to the party entitled. And new process shall be issued in such district courts when requisite; but all suits pending in said courts in which the United States are plaintiffs shall remain suspended, and no further proceedings shall be had therein until the independence of this Confederacy shall be recognized by the United States; and execution of all judgments rendered in favor of said United States is hereby suspended, and all seizures on executions heretofore made in behalf of the said United States are hereby declared to be inoperative and void, and shall not be renewed until recognition be made of the independence of this Confederacy as aforesaid. But this section shall be subject to such disposition of the causes therein provided for as has been made by the several states before the adoption of the Provisional Constitution, unless said states shall conform their legislation to the provisions in this act contained.

SEC. 48. Where cases are now pending in the Supreme Court of the United States upon appeal or writ of error, from any court of the states now forming the Confederate States, it shall be lawful for the appellant or plaintiff in error, at any time within twelve months from the date, to dismiss such appeal or writ of error, and file a transcript of the record and a copy of the bond for the appeal or writ of error in the Supreme Court of the Confederate States, and thereupon the same shall be considered in all respects as if it had been originally filed in the said Supreme Court of the Confederate States, and shall be heard and determined in said court according to the laws in force at the time said cause was determined in the court below, and the rights of the respective parties shall be the same as when said cause was taken up to the Supreme Court of the United

States. And if such cause shall not be transferred in twelve months as aforesaid, then the judgment of the court from which the appeal or writ of error was taken shall be deemed final and in all things affirmed. And in case of such transfer, the bond given for the appeal or writ of error shall be and remain in full force in the court of the Confederate States; and in cases where the transcripts of the records have already been printed in the Supreme Court of the United States under the rules thereof, such printed copy duly certified by the clerk of that court may be filed in the Supreme Court of these Confederate States, and it shall not be necessary to have a new transcript made by the clerk of the court from which the appeal or writ of error was prosecuted.

SEC. 49. And where there shall heretofore have been any judgment or decree in the Supreme Court of the United States in a case from any of the district or circuit courts of the United States for any one of the states now forming a part of the Confederate States, and which remains in force and unexecuted, it shall be and it is hereby made the duty of the district court of such Confederate State and its officers to carry into effect and to execute such judgment or decree according to the mandate of the Supreme Court of the United States, as if there had been no dissolution of the Union: *Provided*, That such judgment or decree was rendered before the secession of the state from which such cause went to the Supreme Court.

When any cause is transferred under the provisions of this law, notice of such transfer shall be given to the adverse party or his counsel thirty days before the term of the court at which such cause is to be tried.

SEC. 50. In all cases where persons are under judgment or sentence, or are imprisoned upon conviction of any crime or offence, before any court of the United States, in any of the states now forming a part of the Confederate States of America, such judgment or sentence shall continue in full force and effect until the same has been executed and carried out, and the said district courts of the Confederate States are hereby clothed with all necessary powers to have such judgment or sentence executed.

And no person now under arrest or in custody upon any criminal charge or offence, on process issued from the courts of the United States, shall be released by reason of the dissolution of the Union, but he shall continue under arrest or in custody until discharged by due course of law. And any bail bond given by any party to answer any charge under process from any of said courts shall be obligatory upon such party and his sureties, and bind him to appear at the first term of the Confederate States to be held for the district in which he was arrested.

And all indictments heretofore found in any of the said courts and not yet disposed of shall continue in full force and virtue until heard and determined in the dis-

trict court of the Confederate States for the district in which the same was found. And all warrants or other process issuing on any criminal charge from any of said courts shall continue in force and be made returnable to the court of the district in the Confederate States in which the offence therein charged is alleged to have been committed. And to these ends full authority is hereby granted to said district courts.

SEC. 51. Where, by the laws of any state, its penitentiary or jails may be used by the courts or marshals of the Confederate States, the same shall be so used whenever necessary; but if in any state there be no law authorizing their use, then it shall be the duty of the marshal to provide a suitable place or places for the custody and confinement of all prisoners or convicts who may be committed to his custody by competent legal authority.

SEC. 52. Where any forfeiture or penalty is by law prescribed against misfeasance or malfeasance in office by any of the officers of the Confederate States residing at the seat of government, or where crimes or offences are committed by any of said officers in their respective offices, which are or may be punishable by indictment, or where suits may become necessary upon the official bonds of any such officers, made payable to the Confederate States of America, the jurisdiction in all such cases shall pertain to and be exercised by the district court of the Confederate States which shall be held at the seat of government.

SEC. 53. From all judgments or decrees which shall be rendered in causes pending in the courts of the United States at the time of the secession of the states in which the same were, and which causes shall be transferred to and decided by the courts of this Confederacy, writs of error or appeal may lie to the Supreme Court of this Confederacy, when the sum or matter in controversy exceeds the sum of two thousand dollars.

SEC. 54. This act shall be in force and have effect from and after the passage thereof, and all laws and parts of laws, coming within the purview of this act shall be and the same are hereby repealed.

APPROVED March 16, 1861.

(Source: *Acts and Resolutions of the First Session of the Provisional Congress of the Confederate States, Held at Montgomery, Ala.* Richmond, VA: Enquirer Book & Job Press, 1861.)

E. FINANCES

The Confederacy from its inception labored under severe financial limitations, especially in supporting an economy strained by the rigors of war. Yet it tried. Economic circumstances forced the adoption of a policy for printing treasury notes, paper money unbacked by specie. More than $1.5 billion worth of treasury notes were printed over the four years of the conflict. [See Financing, C.S.A.]

1. An Act to Raise Money for the Support of the Government, and to Provide for the Defence of the Confederate States of America (1861)

SECTION 1. *The Congress of the Confederate States of America do enact*, That the President of the Confederate States be and he is hereby authorized, at any time within twelve months after the passage of this act, to borrow, on the credit of the Confederate States, a sum not exceeding fifteen millions of dollars, or so much thereof as in his opinion the exigencies of the public service may require, to be applied to the payment of appropriations made by law for the support of the Government and for the defences of the Confederate States.

SEC. 2. The Secretary of the Treasury is hereby authorized, by the consent of the President of the Confederate States, to cause to be prepared certificates of stock or bonds, in such sums as are hereinafter mentioned, for the amount to be borrowed as aforesaid, to be signed by the Register of the Treasury and sealed with the seal of the Treasury; and the said certificates of stock or bonds shall be made payable at the expiration of ten years from the first day of September next; and the interest thereon shall be paid semi-annually, at the rate of eight per cent. per annum, at the Treasury and such other place as the Secretary of the Treasury may designate. And to the bonds which shall be issued as aforesaid shall be attached coupons for the semi-annual interest which shall accrue, which coupons may be signed by officers to be appointed for the purpose by the Secretary of the Treasury. And the faith of the Confederate States is hereby pledged for the due payment of the principal and interest of the said stock and bonds.

SEC. 3. At the expiration of five years from the first day of September next, the Confederate States may pay up any portion of the bonds or stocks, upon giving three months *previous public* notice, at the seat of Government, of the particular stocks or bonds to be paid, and the time and place of payment; and from and after the time so appointed, no further interest shall be paid on said stock or bonds.

SEC. 4. The certificates of stock and bonds shall be issued in such form and for such amounts as may be determined by the Secretary of the Treasury, and may be assigned or delivered under such regulations as he may establish. But none of them shall be for a less sum than fifty dollars, and he shall report to Congress, at its next session, a statement in detail of his proceedings, and the rate at which the loans may have been made, and all the expenses attending the same.

SEC. 5. From and after the first day of August 1861, there shall be levied and collected and paid a duty of one-eighth of one cent. per pound on all cotton in the raw state exported from the Confederate States, which duty is hereby specially pledged to the due payment of interest and principal of the loan provided for in this act; and the Secretary of the Treasury is hereby authorized and required to establish a sinking fund to carry into effect the provisions of this section: *Provided, however*, That the interest coupons, issued under the second section of this act, when due, shall be receivable in payment of the export duty on cotton: *Provided, also*, That when the debt and interest thereon herein authorized to be contracted shall be extinguished, or the sinking fund provided for that purpose shall be adequate to that end, the said export duty shall cease and determine.

APPROVED February 28, 1861.

(Source: *Acts and Resolutions of the First Session of the Provisional Congress of the Confederate States, Held at Montgomery, Ala.* Richmond, VA: Enquirer Book & Job Press, 1861.)

2. An Act to Authorize the Issue of Treasury Notes, and to Prescribe the Punishment for Forging the Same, and for Forging Certificates of Stock, Bonds, or Coupons (1861)

SECTION 1. *The Congress of the Confederate States of America do enact*, That the President of the Confederate States of America is hereby authorized to cause Treasury notes to be issued for such sum or sums as the exigencies of the public service may require, but not to exceed at any time one million of dollars, and of denominations not less than fifty dollars for any such note, to be prepared, signed and issued in the manner hereinafter provided.

SEC. 2. *And be it further enacted*, That such Treasury notes shall be paid and redeemed by the Confederate States at the Treasury thereof, after the expiration of one year from the dates of said notes, from which dates they shall bear interest at the rate of one cent per day for every hundred dollars issued: *Provided*, That after the maturity of any of said notes, interest thereon shall cease at the expiration of sixty days' notice of readiness to pay and redeem the same, which may at any time or times be given by the Secretary of the Treasury, in one or more newspapers published at the seat of Government. The payment or redemption of said notes herein provided shall be made to the lawful holders thereof respectively, upon presentment at the Treasury, and shall include the principal of each note and the interest which shall be due thereon. And for such payment and redemption, at the time or times herein specified, the faith of the Confederate States of America is hereby pledged.

SEC. 3. *And be it further enacted*, That such Treasury notes shall be prepared under the direction of the Secretary of the Treasury, and shall be signed, in behalf of the Confederate States of America, by the Treasurer thereof, and countersigned by the Register of the Treasury. Each of these officers shall keep in a book or books provided for that purpose, separate, full and accurate accounts showing the number, date, amount and rate of interest of each Treasury note signed and countersigned by them respectively; and also similar accounts showing all such notes as may be paid, redeemed and cancelled, as the same may be returned, all which accounts shall be carefully preserved in the Treasury Department. And the Treasurer shall account quarterly for all such Treasury notes as shall have been countersigned by the Register, and delivered to the Treasurer for issue.

SEC. 4. *And be it further enacted*, That the Secretary of the Treasury is hereby authorized, with the approbation of the President, to cause such portion of said Treasury notes as may be deemed expedient to be issued by the Treasurer in payment of warrants in favor of public creditors or other persons lawfully entitled to such payment who may choose to receive such notes in payment at par. And the Secretary of the Treasury is further authorized, with the approbation of the President, to borrow from time to time such sums of money, upon the credit of such notes, as the President may deem expedient: *Provided*, That no Treasury notes shall be pledged, hypothecated, sold or disposed of in any way, for any purpose whatever, either directly or indirectly, for any sum less than the amount of such notes, including the principal and interest thereof.

SEC. 5. *And be it further enacted*, That said Treasury notes shall be transferable, by assignment endorsed thereon by the person to whose order the same shall be made payable, accompanied together with the delivery of notes so assigned.

SEC. 6. *And be it further enacted*, That said Treasury notes shall be received by the proper officers in payment of all duties and taxes laid by the authority of the Confederate States of America, of all public lands sold by said authority, and of all debts to the Confederate States of America, of any character whatever, which may be due and payable at the time when said Treasury notes may be offered in payment thereof, except the export duty on cotton; and upon every such payment credit shall be given for the amount of principal and interest, if any, due on the note or notes received in payment on the day when the same shall have been received by such officer.

SEC. 7. *And be it further enacted*, That every collector of the customs, receiver of public moneys, or other officer or agent of the Confederate States of America, who shall receive any Treasury note or notes in payment on account of the Confederate States of America, shall take from the holder of such note or notes a receipt upon the back of each, stating distinctly the date of such payment and the amount allowed upon such note; and every such officer or agent shall keep regular and specific entries of all Treasury notes received in payment showing the person from whom received, the number, date and amount of principal and interest, if any, allowed on each and every Treasury note received in payment, which entries shall be delivered to the Treasury, with the Treasury note or notes mentioned therein, and if found correct such officer or agent shall receive credit for the amount.

SEC. 8. *And be it further enacted*, That the Secretary of the Treasury be and he is hereby authorized to make and issue from time to time such instructions, rules and regulations to the several collectors, receivers, depositaries and all others who may be required to receive such treasury notes in behalf of and as agents in any capacity for the Confederate States of America, as to the custody, disposal, canceling and return of any such notes as may be paid to and received by them respectively, and as to the accounts and returns to be made to the Treasury Department of such receipts, as he shall deem best calculated to promote the public convenience and security and to protect the Confederate States of America, as well as individuals, from frauds and loss.

SEC. 9. *And be it further enacted*, That the Secretary of the Treasury be and he is hereby authorized and directed to cause to be paid the principal and interest of such treasury notes as may be issued under this act, at the time and times when, according to its provisions, the same should be paid. And the said secretary is further authorized to purchase said notes at par, for the amount of principal and interest due at the time of the purchase of such notes. And so much of any unappropriated money in the treasury as may be necessary for the purpose is hereby appropriated to the payment of the principal and interest of said notes.

SEC. 10. *And be it further enacted*, That in place of such treasury notes as may have been paid and redeemed, other treasury notes to the same amount may be issued: *Provided*, That the aggregate sum outstanding under the authority of this act shall at not time exceed one million of dollars: *And provided further*, That the power to issue and re-issue treasury notes conferred on the President by this act shall cease and determine on the first day of March, eighteen hundred and sixty-two.

SEC. 11. *And be it further enacted*, That if any person shall falsely make, forge or counterfeit, or cause or procure to be falsely made, forged or counterfeited, or willingly aid or assist in falsely making, forging or counterfeiting any note in imitation of or purporting to be a treasury note, issued as aforesaid, or shall pass, utter or publish, or attempt to pass, utter or publish as true any false, forged or counterfeited note, purporting to be a treasury note as aforesaid, knowing the same to be falsely made, forged or counterfeited, or shall falsely alter, or cause or procure to be falsely altered, or willingly aid and assist in falsely altering any treasury note, issued as aforesaid, knowing the same to be falsely altered, every such person shall be deemed and adjudged guilty of felony, and being thereof convicted by due course of law, shall be sentenced to be imprisoned and kept at hard labor for a period not less than three years nor more than ten years, and to be fined in a sum not exceeding five thousand dollars.

SEC. 12. *And be it further enacted,* That if any person shall make or engrave, or cause or procure to be made or engraved, shall have in his possession any metallic plate engraved after the similitude of any plate from which any notes issued as aforesaid shall have been printed, with intent to use such plate, or cause or suffer the same to be used in forging or counterfeiting any of the notes issued as aforesaid, or shall have in his custody or possession any blank note or notes engraved and printed after the similitude of any notes issued as aforesaid, with intent to use such blanks, or cause or suffer the same to be used in forging or counterfeiting any of the notes issued as aforesaid, or shall have in his custody or possession any paper adapted to the making of such notes, and similar to the paper upon which any such notes shall have been issued, with intent to use such paper or cause or suffer the same to be used in forging or counterfeiting any of the notes issued as aforesaid, every such person, being thereof convicted by due course of law, shall be sentenced to be imprisoned and kept at hard labor for a term not less than three nor more than ten years, and fined in a sum not exceeding five thousand dollars.

SEC. 13. *And be it further enacted,* That if any person shall falsely make, forge or counterfeit, or cause or procure to be falsely made, forged or counterfeited, or willingly aid or assist in falsely making or forging, or counterfeiting any certificate of stock or bond, or coupon, in imitation of or purporting to be certificate of stock or bond, or coupon, issued in accordance with the provisions of the act entitled an act to raise money for the support of the government, and to provide for the defence of the Confederate States of America, approved the 28th day of February, eighteen hundred and sixty-one, or shall pass, utter or publish, or attempt to pass, utter or publish as true any false, forged or counterfeited certificate of stock or bond, or coupon, purporting to be a certificate of stock or bond, or coupon, as aforesaid, knowing the same to be falsely made, forged or counterfeited, or shall falsely alter or cause, or procure to be falsely altered, or willingly aid or assist in falsely altering any certificate of stock or bond, or coupon, issued as aforesaid, or shall pass, utter or publish, or attempt to pass, utter or publish as true any falsely altered certificate of stock or bond, or coupon,

issued as aforesaid, knowing the same to be falsely altered, every such person shall be deemed and adjudged guilty of a felony, and being thereof convicted by due course of law, shall be sentenced to be imprisoned and kept at labor for a period not less than three years nor more than ten years, and be fined in a sum not exceeding five thousand dollars.

APPROVED March 9, 1861.

(Source: *Acts and Resolutions of the First Session of the Provisional Congress of the Confederate States, Held at Montgomery, Ala.* Richmond, VA: Enquirer Book & Job Press, 1861.)

F. NATIONAL DEFENSE
Within weeks of its creation, the Confederacy entered the crucible of war. Although its efforts to establish a means of national defense preceded the outbreak of hostilities, they only barely did so, and they were therefore accompanied by some sense of gravity. [See Army Organization, C.S.A.; Navy, C.S.A.]

1. An Act for the Establishment and Organization of a General Staff for the Army of the Confederate States of America (1861)

SECTION 1. *The Congress of the Confederate States of America do enact,* That from and after the passage of this act, the general staff of the army of the Confederate States shall consist of an Adjutant and Inspector General's Department, Quartermaster General's Department, Subsistence Department, and the Medical Department.

SEC. 2. *Be it further enacted,* That the Adjutant and Inspector General's Department shall consist of one Adjutant and Inspector General with the rank of Colonel, four Assistant Adjutants General with the rank of Major, and four Assistant Adjutants General with the rank of Captain.

SEC. 3. *Be it further enacted,* That the Quartermaster General's Department shall consist of one Quartermaster General with the rank of Colonel, six Quartermasters with the rank of major; and as many Assistant Quartermasters as may from time to time be required by the service may be detailed by the War Department from the subalterns of the line, who, in addition to their pay in the line, shall receive twenty dollars per month while engaged in that service. The Quartermasters herein provided for shall also discharge the duties of Paymasters, under such regulations as may be prescribed by the Secretary of War.

SEC. 4. *Be it further enacted,* That the Commissary General's Department shall consist of one Commissary General with the rank of Colonel, four Commissaries with the rank of Captain; and as many Assistant Commissaries as may from time to time be required by the service may be detailed by the War Department from the subalterns of the line, who, in addition to their pay in the line, shall receive twenty dollars per month while engaged in that service. The Assistant Quartermasters and Assistant Commissaries shall be subject to duties in both departments at the same time, but shall not receive the additional compensation but in one department.

SEC. 5. *And be it further enacted,* That the Medical Department shall consist of one Surgeon General with the rank of Colonel, four Surgeons with the rank of Major, and six Assistant Surgeons with the rank of Captain; and as many Assistant Surgeons as the service may require may be employed by the Department of War, and receive the pay of Assistant Surgeons.

SEC. 6. *Be it further enacted,* That the officers of the Adjutant General's, Quartermaster General's and Commissary General's Department, though eligible to command, according to the rank they hold in the army of the Confederate States of America, shall not assume command of troops, unless put on duty under orders which specially so direct by authority of the President. The officers of the Medical Department shall not exercise command except in their own department.

SEC. 7. *Be it further enacted,* That the staff officers herein provided for shall be appointed by the President, by and with the advice and consent of the Congress, and shall receive such pay and allowances as shall be hereafter established by law.

APPROVED February 26, 1861.

(Source: *Acts and Resolutions of the First Session of the Provisional Congress of the Confederate States, Held at Montgomery, Ala.* Richmond, VA: Enquirer Book & Job Press, 1861.)

2. An Act for the Establishment and Organization of the Army of the Confederate States of America (1861)

SECTION 1. *The Congress of the Confederate States of America do enact,* That from and after the passage of this act the military establishment of the Confederate States shall be composed of one corps of engineers, one corps of artillery, six regiments of infantry, one regiment of cavalry, and of the staff departments already established by law.

SEC. 2. The Corps of Engineers shall consist of one Colonel, four Majors, five Captains, and one company of sappers, miners and pontoniers, which shall consist of ten sergeants or master workmen, ten corporals or overseers, two musicians, and thirty-nine privates of the first class, or artificers, and thirty-nine privates of the second class, or laborers, making in all one hundred.

SEC. 3. The said company shall be officered by one captain of the corps of engineers, and as many lieutenants, to be selected by the President from the line of

the army, as he may deem necessary for the service, and shall be instructed in and perform all the duties of sappers, miners and pontoniers, and shall, moreover, under the orders of the chief engineer, be liable to serve by detachments in overseeing and aiding laborers upon fortifications or other works, under the engineer department, and in supervising finished fortifications, as fortkeepers, preventing injury and making repairs.

SEC. 4. It shall be the duty of the colonel of the engineer corps, subject to the approval of the Secretary of War, to prescribe the number, quantity, form, dimensions, &c., of the necessary vehicles, arms, pontons, tools, implements, and other supplies for the service of the said company as a body of sappers, miners and pontoniers.

SEC. 5. The Corps of Artillery, which shall also be charged with ordnance duties, shall consist of one colonel, one lieutenant colonel, ten majors, and forty companies of artillerists and artificers, and each company shall consist of one captain, two first lieutenants, one second lieutenant, four sergeants, four corporals, two musicians and seventy privates. There shall also be one adjutant, to be selected by the colonel from the first lieutenants, and one sergeant-major, to be selected from the enlisted men of the corps.

The President may equip as light batteries, of six pieces each, such of these companies as he may deem expedient, not exceeding four in time of peace.

SEC. 6. Each regiment of infantry shall consist of one colonel, one lieutenant colonel, one major and ten companies; each company shall consist of one captain, one first lieutenant, two second lieutenants, four sergeants, four corporals, two musicians and ninety privates; and to each regiment there shall be attached one adjutant, to be selected from the lieutenants, and one sergeant major, to be selected from the enlisted men of the regiment.

SEC. 7. The regiment of cavalry shall consist of one colonel, one lieutenant colonel, one major and ten companies, each of which shall consist of one captain, one first lieutenant, two second lieutenants, four sergeants, four corporals, one farrier, one blacksmith, two musicians and sixty privates. There shall also be one adjutant and one sergeant major, to be selected as aforesaid.

SEC. 8. There shall be four brigadier generals, who shall be assigned to such commands and duties as the President may specially direct, and shall be entitled to one aid-de-camp, each, to be selected from the subalterns of the line of the army, who, in addition to their duties as aid-de-camp, may perform the duties of assistants adjutant general.

SEC. 9. All officers of the army shall be appointed by the President, by and with the advice and consent of the Congress, and the rank and file shall be enlisted for

a term not less than three nor more than five years, under such regulations as may be established.

SEC. 10. No officer shall be appointed in the army until he shall have passed an examination satisfactory to the President, and in such manner as he may prescribe, as to his character and fitness for the service. The President, however, shall have power to postpone this examination for one year after appointment, if in his judgment necessary for the public interest.

SEC. 11. All vacancies in established regiments and corps, to and including the rank of colonel, shall be filled by promotion according to seniority, except in case of disability or other incompetency. Promotions to and including the rank of colonel shall be made regimentally in the infantry and cavalry, in the staff departments, and in the engineers and artillery, according to corps. Appointments to the rank of brigadier general, after the army is organized, shall be made by selection from the army.

SEC. 12. The President of the Confederate States is hereby authorized to appoint to the lowest grade of subaltern officers such meritorious non-commissioned officers as may, upon the recommendation of their colonels and company officers, be brought before an army board, specially convened for the purpose, and found qualified for the duties of commissioned officers, and to attach them to regiments or corps, as supernumerary officers, if there be no vacancies: *Provided*, There shall not be more than one so attached to any one company at the same time.

SEC. 13. The pay of a brigadier general shall be three hundred and one dollars per month. The aid-de-camp of a brigadier general, in addition to his pay as lieutenant, shall receive thirty-five dollars per month.

SEC. 14. The monthly pay of the officers of the corps of engineers shall be as follows: of the colonel, two hundred and ten dollars; of a major, one hundred and sixty-two dollars; of a captain, one hundred and forty dollars; lieutenants serving with the company of sappers and miners, shall receive the pay of cavalry officers of the same grade.

SEC. 15. The monthly pay of the colonel of the corps of artillery shall be two hundred and ten dollars; of a lieutenant-colonel, one hundred and eighty-five dollars; of a major, one hundred and fifty dollars, and when serving on ordnance duty, one hundred and sixty-two dollars; of a captain, one hundred and thirty dollars; of a first lieutenant, ninety dollars; of a second lieutenant, eighty dollars; and the adjutant shall receive, in addition to his pay as lieutenant, ten dollars per month. Officers of artillery serving in the light artillery, or performing ordnance duty, shall receive the same pay as officers of cavalry of the same grade.

SEC. 16. The monthly pay of the officers of the infantry shall be as follows: of a colonel, one hundred

and ninety-five dollars; of a lieutenant-colonel, one hundred and seventy dollars; of a major, one hundred and fifty dollars; of a captain, one hundred and thirty dollars; of a first lieutenant, ninety dollars; of a second lieutenant, eighty dollars; the adjutant, in addition to his pay as lieutenant, ten dollars.

SEC. 17. The monthly pay of the officers of the cavalry shall be as follows: of a colonel, two hundred and ten dollars; of a lieutenant- colonel, one hundred and eighty-five dollars; a major, one hundred and sixty-two dollars; a captain, one hundred and forty dollars, a first lieutenant, one hundred dollars; a second lieutenant, ninety dollars; the adjutant, ten dollars per month, in addition to his pay as lieutenant.

SEC. 18. The pay of the officers of the general staff, except those of the medical department, shall be the same as that of officers of cavalry of the same grade. The surgeon-general shall receive an annual salary of three thousand dollars, which shall be in full of all pay and allowances, except fuel and quarters. The monthly pay of a surgeon, of ten years' service in that grade, shall be two hundred dollars; a surgeon of less than ten years' service in that grade, one hundred and sixty-two dollars; an assistant surgeon of ten years' service in that grade, one hundred and fifty dollars; an assistant surgeon of five years' service in that grade, one hundred and thirty dollars; and an assistant surgeon of less than five years' service, one hundred and ten dollars.

SEC. 19. There shall be allowed, in addition to the pay hereinbefore provided, to every commissioned officer, except the surgeon-general, nine dollars per month for every five years' service; and to the officers of the army of the United States, who have resigned or may resign to be received into the service of the Confederate States, this additional pay shall be allowed from the date of their entrance into the former service. There shall also be an additional monthly allowance to every general officer commanding in chief a separate army actually in the field, of one hundred dollars.

SEC. 20. The pay of officers as hereinbefore established shall be in full of all allowances, except forage, fuel, quarters and travelling expenses while travelling under orders. The allowance of forage, fuel and quarters shall be fixed by regulations and shall be furnished in kind, except when officers are serving at stations without troops where public quarters cannot be had, in which case they may be allowed, in lieu of forage, eight dollars per month for each horse to which they may be entitled, provided they are actually kept in service and mustered, and quarters may be commuted at a rate to be fixed by the Secretary of War, and fuel at the market price delivered. An officer when travelling under orders shall be allowed mileage at the rate of ten cents per mile.

SEC. 21. In time of war, officers of the army shall be entitled to draw forage for horses, according to grade, as follows: A brigadier- general, four; the adjutant and inspector-general, quartermaster-general, commissary-general, and the colonels of engineers, artillery, infantry and cavalry, three each; all lieutenant-colonels and majors, and captains of the general staff, engineer corps, light artillery and cavalry, three each; lieutenants serving in the corps of engineers, lieutenants of light artillery and of cavalry, two each. In time of peace: general and field officers, three; officers below the rank of field officers, in the general staff, corps of engineers, light artillery and cavalry, two; *Provided*, in all cases that the horses are actually kept in service and mustered. No enlisted man in the service of the Confederate States shall be employed as a servant by any officer of the army.

SEC. 22. The monthly pay of the enlisted men of the army of the Confederate States shall be as follows: That of a sergeant or master workman of the engineer corps, thirty-four dollars; that of a corporal or overseer, twenty dollars; privates of the first class, or artificers, seventeen dollars; and privates of the second class, or laborers, and musicians, thirteen dollars. The sergeant-major of cavalry, twenty-one dollars; first sergeants, twenty dollars; sergeants, seventeen dollars; corporals, farriers and blacksmiths, thirteen dollars; musicians, thirteen dollars; and privates, twelve dollars. Sergeants-major of artillery and infantry, twenty-one dollars; first sergeants, twenty dollars each; sergeants, seventeen dollars; corporals and artificers, thirteen dollars; musicians, twelve dollars; and privates eleven dollars each. The non-commissioned officers, artificers, musicians and privates serving in light batteries shall receive the same pay as those of cavalry.

SEC. 23. The President shall be authorized to enlist as many master armorers, master carriage-makers, master blacksmiths, armorers, carriage-makers, blacksmiths, artificers, and laborers, for ordnance service, as he may deem necessary, not exceeding in all one hundred men, who shall be attached to the corps of artillery. The pay of a master armorer, master carriage-maker, master blacksmith, shall be thirty-four dollars per month; armorers, carriage-makers and blacksmiths, twenty dollars per month; artificers, seventeen dollars, and laborers, thirteen dollars per month.

SEC. 24. Each enlisted man of the army of the Confederate States shall receive one ration per day, and a yearly allowance of clothing, the quantity and kind of each to be established by regulations from the War Department, to be approved by the President.

SEC. 25. Rations shall generally be issued in kind, but under circumstances rendering a commutation necessary. The commutation value of the ration shall be fixed by regulations of the War Department, to be approved by the President.

SEC. 26. The officers appointed in the army of the Confederate States by virtue of this act, shall perform all military duties to which they may be severally assigned by authority of the President, and it shall be the duty of the Secretary of War to prepare and publish regulations, prescribing the details of every department in the service, for the general government of the army, which regulations shall be approved by the President, and when so approved shall be binding.

SEC. 27. All officers of the quartermaster's and commissary departments shall, previous to entering on the duties of their respective offices, give bonds with good and sufficient sureties to the Confederate States, in such sum as the Secretary of War shall direct, fully to account for all moneys and public property which they may receive.

SEC. 28. Neither the quartermaster-general, the commissary-general, nor any or either of their assistants, shall be concerned, directly or indirectly, in the purchase or sale of any articles intended for, making a part of, or appertaining to public supplies, except for and on account of the Confederate States; nor shall they, or either of them, take or apply to his or their own use any gain or emolument for negotiating any business in their respective departments, other than what is or may be allowed by law.

SEC. 29. The Rules and Articles of War established by the laws of the United States of America for the government of the army are hereby declared to be of force, except that wherever the words "United States" occur, the words "Confederate States" shall be substituted therefor; and except that the articles of war numbers sixty-one and sixty-two are hereby abrogated, and the following articles substituted therefor:

ARTICLE 61. Officers having brevets or commissions of a prior date to those of the corps in which they serve will take place on courts martial or of inquiry, and on boards detailed for military purposes, when composed of different corps, according to the ranks given them in their brevet or former commissions, but in the regiment, corps, or company to which such officers belong, they shall do duty and take rank, both in courts and on boards as aforesaid, which shall be composed of their own corps, according to the commission by which they are there mustered.

ARTICLE 62. If upon marches, guards, or in quarters, different corps shall happen to join or do duty together, the officer highest in rank, according to the commission by which he is mustered in the army, navy, marine corps, or militia, there on duty by orders from competent authority, shall command the whole and give orders for what is needful for the service, unless otherwise directed by the President of the Confederate States in orders of special assignment providing for the case.

SEC. 30. The President shall call into the service of the Confederate States only so many of the troops herein provided for as he may deem the safety of the

Confederacy may require.

SEC. 31. All laws or parts of laws of the United States, which have been adopted by the Congress of the Confederate States, repugnant to or inconsistent with this act, are hereby repealed.

APPROVED March 6, 1861.

(Source: *Acts and Resolutions of the First Session of the Provisional Congress of the Confederate States, Held at Montgomery, Ala.* Richmond, VA: Enquirer Book & Job Press, 1861.)

3. An Act to Provide for the Organization of the Navy [Excerpts] (1861)

SECTION 1. *The Congress of the Confederate States of America do enact*, That the President be authorized to appoint, in the manner prescribed by law, the following commissioned officers of the navy, viz: four captains, four commanders, thirty lieutenants, five surgeons, five assistant surgeons, six paymasters and two chief engineers, and to employ as masters, midshipmen, engineers, naval constructors, boatswains, gunners, carpenters, sailmakers and other warrant and petty officers and seamen as he may deem necessary, not to exceed in the aggregate three thousand.

SEC. 4. The pay of seamen of the navy shall be determined by the President, and may be altered by him from time to time as circumstances may require.

SEC. 5. There shall be a corps of marines, to consist of one major, one quartermaster, one paymaster, one adjutant, one sergeant-major, one quartermaster-sergeant, and six companies, each company to consist of one captain, one first and one second lieutenant, four sergeants, four corporals, one hundred men and two musicians; and the pay and allowances of the officers and enlisted men shall be the same as that of the officers and enlisted men of like grade in the infantry of the army, except that the ration of the enlisted marines shall be the ration allowed by law to seamen.

SEC. 6. The following officers shall be attached to the Navy Department, to wit: An officer, not below the grade of commander, who shall be charged with the purchase or preparation of ordnance, ordnance stores and supplies and equipments, and with hydrography, and with such other duties as the Secretary of the Navy may from time to time assign to him; an officer not below the grade of lieutenant, to be designated as the officer of orders and detail, who shall, under the orders of the Secretary of the Navy, prepare and issue all orders and details for service, and who shall also, under the direction of the Secretary of the Navy, have charge of all matters and things connected with courts martial and courts of inquiry, and with the custody of all records and papers thereunto appertaining, and perform such other duties relating to the personnel of the navy, as the secretary may from time to time direct; a surgeon

or an assistant Surgeon, who shall, under the direction of the Secretary of the Navy, make all purchases of medicines and medical supplies for the navy, and perform such other duties appertaining to the medical department as the secretary may from time to time direct; a paymaster, who shall, under the direction of the Secretary of the Navy, make all contracts for or purchases of provisions, clothing and coal for the use of the navy, and perform such other duties as the secretary may direct. The Secretary of the Navy is authorized to appoint one clerk to aid each of the above officers in the discharge of his duties, whose annual salary shall not exceed fifteen hundred dollars each; but the officers therein detailed for duty, shall receive no compensation for their services beyond their regular pay as on other duty.

SEC. 7. It shall be the duty of the quartermaster of the marine corps to visit the different posts where portions of the corps may be stationed, as often as may be necessary for the proper discharge of his duties.

SEC. 8. It shall be the duty of the Secretary of the Navy to prepare and publish regulations for the general government of all persons connected with or employed in the naval service, which regulations shall take effect as soon as they shall be approved by the President and published.

SEC. 9. All laws of the United States heretofore enacted for the government of the officers, seamen and marines of the navy of the United States, that are not inconsistent with the provisions of this act, are hereby adopted and applied to the officers, seamen and marines of the navy of the Confederate States.

SEC. 10. The President may determine the relative and assimilated rank which officers of the navy shall hold toward those of the army.

APPROVED March 16, 1861.

(Source: *Acts and Resolutions of the First Session of the Provisional Congress of the Confederate States, Held at Montgomery, Ala.* Richmond, VA: Enquirer Book & Job Press, 1861.)

G. THE CONFEDERATE DOMINION

Expansionism was an American habit of the nineteenth century, and once hostilities had broken out, there were empire builders in the Confederate States who, as the following report shows, wasted no time in advocating the augmentation of the Confederate dominion. [See Kansas]

1. Report to Jefferson Davis Regarding the Western States and Territories (20 May 1861)

MARYSVILLE, *KANS.*, *May 20, 1861.*

His Excellency JEFFERSON DAVIS, *President of Confederate States of America:*

SIR: I addressed you on the 16th instant a brief communication in reference to the propriety and importance of taking possession of the forts and property of the United States Government in the Northwest, and now avail myself of an opportunity of going more fully into detail on the subject. I refer to all that portion of country west of the Mississippi River to the summit of the Rocky Mountains and south of the Platte River, in Nebraska, and northern line of Missouri to the northern line of Arkansas and Texas, almost all of which is rich in agricultural and mineral resources....

Within the boundaries of this great country are the States of Missouri and Kansas. The former, being surrounded on three sides by free States, although identified in sympathy and interest with the Southern Confederacy, scarcely dare make a move toward secession in the present state of affairs. Kansas is controlled by a majority of poor, worthless, starving abolitionists, who receive their support from donations of provisions from the Northern States, which are transported through Missouri and delivered to them on the banks of the Missouri River. There is still in Kansas a strong pro-slavery element, kept in subjection to this dominant party, that will gladly unite with any movement made by the Confederate States to throw off the yoke, and will fly to arms at a moment's warning. The question now presents itself whether all this valuable territory shall go with the North or the South. The answer depends upon the prompt action of your Government. Missouri cannot be secured to the South unless the country west of it is taken possession of and held by the Confederate States. With six regiments of cavalry from Arkansas and Texas and the forces that can be obtained from the Indian Territory, I can seize and hold Forts Laramie and Wise, and Fort Union, if necessary, and take possession of all military stores and munitions of war at the other forts in Kansas and Colorado, and will destroy what will be of no utility, establish headquarters near the Cheyenne Pass, and with the possession of Forts Laramie and Wise, cut off all communication between the Northern States and the Pacific coast; and at the same time, acting in conjunction with Missouri, can seize Forts Leavenworth and Riley, and expel from Kansas the horde of Northern vandals that now infests it, opposed to your Government, and declare Missouri, Kansas, and Colorado a part of the Confederate States of America. Also seize the daily overland express mail to California, and appropriate it to the transportation of mail and express matter to and from the Southern States only. A majority of the owners of the capital stock of this company entertain warm Southern views, and would willingly acquiesce therein.

Hoping these suggestions will meet with your approbation, I have the honor to be, your most obedient servant,

F. J. MARSHALL.

I have carefully read the foregoing, and heartily indorse the suggestions therein politically and in a

military point of view.
R. H. WEIGHTMAN,
Col., Comdg. Camp Holloway, Missouri State Guard.

(Source: U.S. War Department. *War of the Rebellion: A Compilation of the Official Records of the Union and Confederate Armies.* Ser. 1, Vol. III.)

VIII. The Lincoln Administration
In an inaugural address that labored to be obliging, Abraham Lincoln nonetheless made plain that the government would sustain its authority. In spite of the attempt, many Southerners saw the inaugural as the Richmond Enquirer did, as a declaration of war pronounced by a "fanatic."

1. Lincoln's First Inaugural Address
(4 March 1861)
Fellow citizens of the United States: In compliance with a custom as old as the government itself, I appear before you to address you briefly and to take, in your presence, the oath prescribed by the Constitution of the United States, to be taken by the President "before he enters on the execution of his office."

I do not consider it necessary, at present, for me to discuss those matters of administration about which there is no special anxiety, or excitement.

Apprehension seems to exist among the people of the Southern States that by the accession of a Republican administration their property and their peace and personal security are to be endangered. There has never been any reasonable cause for such apprehension. Indeed, the most ample evidence to the contrary has all the while existed and been open to their inspection. It is found in nearly all the published speeches of him who now addresses you. I do but quote from one of those speeches when I declare that "I have no purpose, directly or indirectly, to interfere with the institution of slavery where it exists. I believe I have no lawful right to do so, and I have no inclination to do so." Those who nominated and elected me did so with full knowledge that I had made this and many similar declarations, and had never recanted them. And, more than this, they placed in the platform for my acceptance, and as a law to themselves and to me, the clear and emphatic resolution which I now read:

"Resolved: that the maintenance inviolate of the rights of the States, and especially the right of each State to order and control its own domestic institutions according to its own judgment exclusively, is essential to that balance of power on which the perfection and endurance of our political fabric depend, and we denounce the lawless invasion by armed force of the soil of any State or Territory, no matter under what pretext, as among the gravest of crimes."

I now reiterate these sentiments; and, in doing so, I only press upon the public attention the most conclu-

sive evidence of which the case is susceptible, that the property, peace, and security of no section are to be in any wise endangered by the now incoming administration. I add, too, that all the protection which, consistently with the Constitution and the laws, can be given, will be cheerfully given to all the States when lawfully demanded, for whatever cause—as cheerfully to one section as to another.

There is much controversy about the delivering up of fugitives from service or labor. The clause I now read is as plainly written in the Constitution as any other of its provisions:

"No person held to service or labor in one State, under the laws thereof, escaping into another, shall in consequence of any law or regulation therein be discharged from such service or labor, but shall be delivered up on claim of the party to whom such service or labor may be due."

It is scarcely questioned that this provision was intended by those who made it for the reclaiming of what we call fugitive slaves; and the intention of the lawgiver is the law. All members of Congress swear their support to the whole Constitution—to this provision as much as to any other. To the proposition, then, that slaves whose cases come within the terms of this clause "shall be delivered up", their oaths are unanimous. Now, if they would make the effort in good temper, could they not with nearly equal unanimity frame and pass a law by means of which to keep good that unanimous oath?

There is some difference of opinion whether this clause should be enforced by national or by State authority; but surely that difference is not a very material one. If the slave is to be surrendered, it can be of but little consequence to him or to others by which authority it is done. And should any one in any case be content that his oath shall go unkept on a merely unsubstantial controversy as to HOW it shall be kept?

Again, in any law upon this subject, ought not all the safeguards of liberty known in civilized and humane jurisprudence to be introduced, so that a free man be not, in any case, surrendered as a slave? And might it not be well at the same time to provide by law for the enforcement of that clause in the Constitution which guarantees that "the citizen of each State shall be entitled to all privileged and immunities of citizens in the several States?"

I take the official oath today with no mental reservations, and with no purpose to construe the Constitution or laws by any hypercritical rules. And while I do not choose now to specify particular acts of Congress as proper to be enforced, I do suggest that it will be much safer for all, both in official and private stations, to conform to and abide by all those acts which stand unrepealed, than to violate any of them,

trusting to find impunity in having them held to be unconstitutional.

It is seventy-two years since the first inauguration of a President under our national Constitution. During that period fifteen different and greatly distinguished citizens have, in succession, administered the executive branch of the government. They have conducted it through many perils, and generally with great success. Yet, with all this scope of precedent, I now enter upon the same task for the brief Constitutional term of four years under great and peculiar difficulty. A disruption of the Federal Union, heretofore only menaced, is now formidably attempted.

I hold that, in contemplation of universal law and of the Constitution, the Union of these States is perpetual. Perpetuity is implied, if not expressed, in the fundamental law of all national governments. It is safe to assert that no government proper ever had a provision in its organic law for its own termination. Continue to execute all the express provisions of our National Constitution, and the Union will endure forever—it being impossible to destroy it except by some action not provided for in the instrument itself.

Again, if the United States be not a government proper, but an association of States in the nature of contract merely, can it, as a contract, be peaceably unmade by less than all the parties who made it? One party to a contract may violate it—break it, so to speak; but does it not require all to lawfully rescind it?

Descending from these general principles, we find the proposition that in legal contemplation the Union is perpetual confirmed by the history of the Union itself. The Union is much older than the Constitution. It was formed, in fact, by the Articles of Association in 1774. It was matured and continued by the Declaration of Independence in 1776. It was further matured, and the faith of all the then thirteen States expressly plighted and engaged that it should be perpetual, by the Articles of Confederation in 1778. And, finally, in 1787 one of the declared objects for ordaining and establishing the Constitution was "TO FORM A MORE PERFECT UNION."

But if the destruction of the Union by one or by a part only of the States be lawfully possible, the Union is LESS perfect than before the Constitution, having lost the vital element of perpetuity.

It follows from these views that no State upon its own mere motion can lawfully get out of the Union; that Resolves and Ordinances to that effect are legally void; and that acts of violence, within any State or States, against the authority of the United States, are insurrectionary or revolutionary, according to circumstances.

I therefore consider that, in view of the Constitution and the laws, the Union is unbroken; and to the extent of my ability I shall take care, as the Constitution itself expressly enjoins upon me, that the laws of the Union be faithfully executed in all the States. Doing this I deem to be only a simple duty on my part; and I shall perform it so far as practicable, unless my rightful masters, the American people, shall withhold the requisite means, or in some authoritative manner direct the contrary. I trust this will not be regarded as a menace, but only as the declared purpose of the Union that it WILL Constitutionally defend and maintain itself.

In doing this there needs to be no bloodshed or violence; and there shall be none, unless it be forced upon the national authority. The power confided to me will be used to hold, occupy, and possess the property and places belonging to the government, and to collect the duties and imposts; but beyond what may be necessary for these objects, there will be no invasion, no using of force against or among the people anywhere. Where hostility to the United States, in any interior locality, shall be so great and universal as to prevent competent resident citizens from holding the Federal offices, there will be no attempt to force obnoxious strangers among the people for that object. While the strict legal right may exist in the government to enforce the exercise of these offices, the attempt to do so would be so irritating, and so nearly impracticable withal, that I deem it better to forego for the time the uses of such offices.

The mails, unless repelled, will continue to be furnished in all parts of the Union. So far as possible, the people everywhere shall have that sense of perfect security which is most favorable to calm thought and reflection. The course here indicated will be followed unless current events and experience shall show a modification or change to be proper, and in every case and exigency my best discretion will be exercised according to circumstances actually existing, and with a view and a hope of a peaceful solution of the national troubles and the restoration of fraternal sympathies and affections.

That there are persons in one section or another who seek to destroy the Union at all events, and are glad of any pretext to do it, I will neither affirm nor deny; but if there be such, I need address no word to them. To those, however, who really love the Union may I not speak?

Before entering upon so grave a matter as the destruction of our national fabric, with all its benefits, its memories, and its hopes, would it not be wise to ascertain precisely why we do it? Will you hazard so desperate a step while there is any possibility that any portion of the ills you fly from have no real existence? Will you, while the certain ills you fly to are greater than all the real ones you fly from—will you risk the commission of so fearful a mistake?

All profess to be content in the Union if all Constitutional rights can be maintained. Is it true, then, that any right, plainly written in the Constitu-

tion, has been denied? I think not. Happily the human mind is so constituted that no party can reach to the audacity of doing this. Think, if you can, of a single instance in which a plainly written provision of the Constitution has ever been denied. If by the mere force of numbers a majority should deprive a minority of any clearly written Constitutional right, it might, in a moral point of view, justify revolution—certainly would if such a right were a vital one. But such is not our case. All the vital rights of minorities and of individuals are so plainly assured to them by affirmations and negations, guaranties and prohibitions, in the Constitution, that controversies never arise concerning them. But no organic law can ever be framed with a provision specifically applicable to every question which may occur in practical administration. No foresight can anticipate, nor any document of reasonable length contain, express provisions for all possible questions. Shall fugitives from labor be surrendered by national or State authority? The Constitution does not expressly say. May Congress prohibit slavery in the Territories? The Constitution does not expressly say. MUST Congress protect slavery in the Territories? The Constitution does not expressly say.

From questions of this class spring all our constitutional controversies, and we divide upon them into majorities and minorities. If the minority will not acquiesce, the majority must, or the government must cease. There is no other alternative; for continuing the government is acquiescence on one side or the other.

If a minority in such case will secede rather than acquiesce, they make a precedent which in turn will divide and ruin them; for a minority of their own will secede from them whenever a majority refuses to be controlled by such minority. For instance, why may not any portion of a new confederacy a year or two hence arbitrarily secede again, precisely as portions of the present Union now claim to secede from it? All who cherish disunion sentiments are now being educated to the exact temper of doing this.

Is there such perfect identity of interests among the States to compose a new Union, as to produce harmony only, and prevent renewed secession?

Plainly, the central idea of secession is the essence of anarchy. A majority held in restraint by constitutional checks and limitations, and always changing easily with deliberate changes of popular opinions and sentiments, is the only true sovereign of a free people. Whoever rejects it does, of necessity, fly to anarchy or to despotism. Unanimity is impossible; the rule of a minority, as a permanent arrangement, is wholly inadmissible; so that, rejecting the majority principle, anarchy or despotism in some form is all that is left.

I do not forget the position, assumed by some, that Constitutional questions are to be decided by the

Supreme Court; nor do I deny that such decisions must be binding, in any case, upon the parties to a suit, as to the object of that suit, while they are also entitled to very high respect and consideration in all parallel cases by all other departments of the government. And while it is obviously possible that such decision may be erroneous in any given case, still the evil effect following it, being limited to that particular case, with the chance that it may be overruled and never become a precedent for other cases, can better be borne than could the evils of a different practice. At the same time, the candid citizen must confess that if the policy of the government, upon vital questions affecting the whole people, is to be irrevocably fixed by decisions of the Supreme Court, the instant they are made, in ordinary litigation between parties in personal actions, the people will have ceased to be their own rulers, having to that extent practically resigned their government into the hands of that eminent tribunal. Nor is there in this view any assault upon the court or the judges. It is a duty from which they may not shrink to decide cases properly brought before them, and it is no fault of theirs if others seek to turn their decisions to political purposes.

One section of our country believes slavery is RIGHT, and ought to be extended, while the other believes it is WRONG, and ought not to be extended. This is the only substantial dispute. The fugitive-slave clause of the Constitution, and the law for the suppression of the foreign slave-trade, are each as well enforced, perhaps, as any law can ever be in a community where the moral sense of the people imperfectly supports the law itself. The great body of the people abide by the dry legal obligation in both cases, and a few break over in each. This, I think, cannot be perfectly cured; and it would be worse in both cases AFTER the separation of the sections than BEFORE. The foreign slave-trade, now imperfectly suppressed, would be ultimately revived, without restriction, in one section, while fugitive slaves, now only partially surrendered, would not be surrendered at all by the other.

Physically speaking, we cannot separate. We cannot remove our respective sections from each other, nor build an impassable wall between them. A husband and wife may be divorced, and go out of the presence and beyond the reach of each other; but the different parts of our country cannot do this. They cannot but remain face to face, and intercourse, either amicable or hostile, must continue between them. Is it possible, then, to make that intercourse more advantageous or more satisfactory after separation than before? Can aliens make treaties easier than friends can make laws? Can treaties be more faithfully enforced between aliens than laws can among friends? Suppose you go to war, you cannot fight always; and when, after much loss on both sides, an no gain on either, you cease fighting, the

identical old questions as to terms of intercourse are again upon you.

This country, with its institutions, belongs to the people who inhabit it. Whenever they shall grow weary of the existing government, they can exercise their CONSTITUTIONAL right of amending it, or their REVOLUTIONARY right to dismember or overthrow it. I cannot be ignorant of the fact that many worthy and patriotic citizens are desirous of having the national Constitution amended. While I make no recommendation of amendments, I fully recognize the rightful authority of the people over the whole subject, to be exercised in either of the modes prescribed in the instrument itself; and I should, under existing circumstances, favor rather than oppose a fair opportunity being afforded the people to act upon it. I will venture to add that to me the convention mode seems preferable, in that it allows amendments to originate with the people themselves, instead of only permitting them to take or reject propositions originated by others not especially chosen for the purpose, and which might not be precisely such as they would wish to either accept or refuse. I understand a proposed amendment to the Constitution—which amendment, however, I have not seen—has passed Congress, to the effect that the Federal Government shall never interfere with the domestic institutions of the States, including that of persons held to service. To avoid misconstruction of what I have said, I depart from my purpose not to speak of particular amendments so far as to say that, holding such a provision to now be implied Constitutional law, I have no objection to its being made express and irrevocable.

The chief magistrate derives all his authority from the people, and they have conferred none upon him to fix terms for the separation of the states. The people themselves can do this also if they choose; but the executive, as such, has nothing to do with it. His duty is to administer the present government, as it came to his hands, and to transmit it, unimpaired by him, to his successor.

Why should there not be a patient confidence in the ultimate justice of the people? Is there any better or equal hope in the world? In our present differences is either party without faith of being in the right? If the Almighty Ruler of Nations, with his eternal truth and justice, be on your side of the North, or on yours of the South, that truth and that justice will surely prevail, by the judgment of this great tribunal, the American people.

By the frame of the government under which we live, this same people have wisely given their public servants but little power for mischief; and have, with equal wisdom, provided for the return of that little to their own hands at very short intervals. While the people retain their virtue and vigilance, no administration, by any extreme of wickedness or folly, can very seriously injure the government in the short space of four years.

My countrymen, one and all, think calmly and WELL upon this whole subject. Nothing valuable can be lost by taking time. If there be an object to HURRY any of you in hot haste to a step which you would never take DELIBERATELY, that object will be frustrated by taking time; but no good object can be frustrated by it. Such of you as are now dissatisfied, still have the old Constitution unimpaired, and, on the sensitive point, the laws of your own framing under it; while the new administration will have no immediate power, if it would, to change either. If it were admitted that you who are dissatisfied hold the right side in the dispute, there still is no single good reason for precipitate action. Intelligence, patriotism, Christianity, and a firm reliance on him who has never yet forsaken this favored land, are still competent to adjust in the best way all our present difficulty.

In YOUR hands, my dissatisfied fellow-countrymen, and not in MINE, is the momentous issue of civil war. The government will not assail YOU. You can have no conflict without being yourselves the aggressors. YOU have no oath registered in heaven to destroy the government, while I shall have the most solemn one to "preserve, protect, and defend it."

I am loathe to close. We are not enemies, but friends. We must not be enemies. Though passion may have strained, it must not break our bonds of affection. The mystic chords of memory, stretching from every battlefield and patriot grave to every living heart and hearthstone all over this broad land, will yet swell the chorus of the Union when again touched, as surely they will be, by the better angels of our nature.

(Source: Lapsley, Arthur Brooks, ed. *The Writings of Abraham Lincoln.* Vol. 5. New York: G. P. Putnam's Sons, 1906.)

2. "The Declaration of War" (Editorial, 5 March 1861)

Mr. Lincoln's Inaugural Address is before our readers—couched in the cool, unimpassioned, deliberate language of the fanatic, with the purpose of pursuing the promptings of fanaticism even to the dismemberment of the Government with the horrors of civil war. Virginia has long looked for and promised peace offering before her—and she has more, she has the denial of all hope of peace. Civil war must now come. Sectional war, declared by Mr. Lincoln, awaits only this signal gun from the insulted Southern Confederacy, to light its horrid fires all along the borders of Virginia. No action of our Convention can now maintain the peace. *She must fight!* The liberty of choice is yet hers. She may march to the contest with her sister States of the South, or *she must* march to the conflict *against* them. There is left no middle course; There is left no peace; we must settle the conflict, and the God of battle give victory to the right!

We must be invaded by Davis or by Lincoln. The former can rally fifty thousand of the best and bravest sons of Virginia, who will rush with willing hearts and ready hands to the standard that protects the rights and defends the honor of the South—for every traitor heart that offers aid to Lincoln there will be *many, many* who will glory in the opportunity to avenge the treason by a sharp and certain death. Let not Virginians be arrayed against each other, and since we cannot avoid war, let us determine that together, as people of the same State, we will defend each other, and preserve the soil of the State from the polluting foot of the Black Republican invader.

The question, "where shall Virginia go?" is answered by Mr. Lincoln, She must go *to war*—and she must decide with whom she wars—whether with those who have suffered her wrongs, or with those who have inflicted her injuries.

Our ultimate destruction pales before the present emergency. To war! to arms! is now the cry, and when peace is declared, if ever, in our day, Virginia may decide where she will finally rest. But for the present she has no choice left; war with Lincoln or with Davis is the choice left us. Read the inaugural carefully, and then let every reader demand of his delegate in the Convention the prompt measures of defense which it is now apparent we must make.

(Source: Richmond *Enquirer,* 5 March 1861: p. 2.)

In less than a month, the Lincoln administration faced a grave crisis over Fort Sumter in Charleston, South Carolina. In cabinet discussions, Secretary of State William H. Seward opposed reinforcing Fort Sumter because he believed that time would bring Southerners to their senses. At this early point in the administration, Seward underrated Lincoln's political judgment and skill, so on 1 April 1861, he dispatched an audacious memorandum to Lincoln. Lincoln's response was firm, and Seward immediately reassessed his chief. After that, the two men worked well together. [See Lincoln, Abraham; Seward, William Henry]

3. Seward's Suggestions to the President on Domestic and Foreign Policy (1 April 1861)

Some thoughts for the President's consideration, April 1, 1861:

First. We are at the end of a month's administration and yet without a policy, either domestic or foreign.

Second. This, however, is not culpable, and it has even been unavoidable. The presence of the Senate, with the need to meet applications for patronage, has prevented tention to other and more grave matters.

Third. But further delay to adopt and prosecute our policies for both domestic and foreign affairs would not

only bring scandal on the administration but danger upon the country.

Fourth. To do this we must dismiss the applicants for office. But how? I suggest that we make the local appointments forthwith, leaving foreign or general ones for ulterior and occasional action.

Fifth. The policy at home. I am aware that my views are singular and perhaps not sufficiently explained. My system is built upon this idea as a ruling one, namely, that we must CHANGE THE QUESTION BEFORE THE PUBLIC FROM ONE UPON SLAVERY, OR ABOUT SLAVERY, for a question upon UNION OR DISUNION. In other words, from what would be regarded as a party question to one of patriotism or union.

The occupation or evacuation of Fort Sumter, although not in fact a slavery or a party question, is so regarded. Witness the temper manifested by the Republicans in the free states, and even by the Union men in the South.

I would therefore terminate it as a safe means for changing the issue. I deem it fortunate that the last administration created the necessity.

For the rest, I would simultaneously defend and reinforce all the ports in the Gulf and have the Navy recalled from foreign stations to be prepared for a blockade. Put the island of Key West under martial law.

This will raise distinctly the question of union or disunion. I would maintain every fort and possession in the South.

For foreign nations, I would demand explanations from Spain and France, categorically, at once. I would seek explanations from Great Britain and Russia, and send agents into Canada, Mexico, and Central America to rouse a vigorous continental spirit of independence on this continent against European intervention. And, if satisfactory explanations are not received from Spain and France, would convene Congress and declare war against them.

But whatever policy we adopt, there must be an energetic prosecution of it.

For this purpose it must be somebody's business to pursue and direct it incessantly. Either the President must do it himself, and be all the while active in it, or devolve it on some member of his Cabinet. Once adopted, debates on it must end, and all agree and abide.

It is not in my especial province; but I neither seek to evade nor assume responsibility.

(Source: Nicolay, John G., and John Hay, John. *Abraham Lincoln: A History.* Vol. 7. New York: The Century Co., 1890.)

4. Lincoln's Reply to Seward (April 1861)

Since parting with you, I have been considering your paper dated this day, and entitled "Some Thoughts for the President's Consideration." The first proposition in it is: "*First.* We are at the end of a month's administration and yet without a policy, either domestic or foreign."

At the beginning of that month, in the inaugural, I said: "The power confided to me will be used to hold, occupy, and possess the property and places belonging to the government, and to collect the duties and imposts." This had your distinct approval at the time; and, taken in connection with the order I immediately gave General Scott directing him to employ every means in his power to strengthen and hold the forts, comprises the exact domestic policy you now urge, with the single exception that it does not propose to abandon Fort Sumter.

Again, I do not perceive how the reinforcement of Fort Sumter would be done on a slavery or a party issue, while that of Fort Pickens would be on a more national and patriotic one.

The news received yesterday in regard to Santo Domingo certainly brings a new item within the range of our foreign policy; but up to that time we have been preparing circulars and instructions to ministers and the like, all in perfect harmony, without even a suggestion that we had no foreign policy.

Upon your closing propositions—that "whatever policy we adopt, there must be an energetic prosecution of it. For this purpose it must be somebody's business to pursue and direct it incessantly. Either the President must do it himself, and be all the while active in it, or devolve it on some member of his Cabinet. Once adopted, debates on it must end, and all agree and abide"—I remark that if this must be done, I must do it. When a general line of policy is adopted, I apprehend there is no danger of its being changed without good reason, or continuing to be a subject of unnecessary debate; still, upon points arising in its progress, I wish, and suppose I am entitled to have, the advice of all the Cabinet.

(Source: Nicolay, John G., and John Hay, John. *Abraham Lincoln: A History*, Vol. 7. New York: The Century Co., 1890.)

THE MILITARY CRISIS

IX. Federal Property in the Confederacy

Federal properties within the newly formed Confederacy were the greatest source of friction with the United States, especially when those properties were military posts. Southern state forces quickly occupied various forts after secession. The following selections reveal the uncertainties and dilemmas caused by this unprecedented series of events.

A. FORT PULASKI AND FORT CLINCH

Fort Pulaski was at Savannah, Georgia; Fort Marion was the old Castillo de San Marcos in St. Augustine, Florida;

while Fort Clinch was at Fernandina, Florida, on Amelia Island. [See Fort Pulaski]

1. Captain Whiting to General Totten
(7 January 1861)

U.S. ENGINEER OFFICE,*Savannah, January 7, 1861.*

GENERAL: I have to report that on the 3d instant, being at Fort Clinch, I received a telegram from my clerk informing me that troops of the State of Georgia were moving to occupy Fort Pulaski, by order of the governor. I replied by telegraph, directing Mr. Hirsch to inform the commandant of Engineers of the fact. I took the first opportunity to reach Savannah on the 6th, and arrived last night. This morning I proceeded to Fort Pulaski, which I found occupied by Georgia troops, commanded by Colonel Lawton. I was received with great civility, and informed by him that he held possession of all the Government property for the present, by order of the governor of the State, and intended to preserve it from loss or damage. He requested a return of the public property, both Ordnance and Engineer, which I have given as existing January 1. Those returns for the fourth quarter, 1860, will be forwarded with my quarterly papers, signed as usual up to the commencement of the present quarter. I can sign no more, however, for I cannot be responsible for property of the charge of which I have been forcibly deprived. I have directed Ordnance Sergeant Walker to report at Oglethorpe Barracks until further orders. The fort keeper I have discharged.

On Saturday, 3d instant, the regular mail-boat from Fernandina to this place, by which I intended to travel, was taken off the line by the governor of Florida and ordered, as I was informed, to Saint Augustine, with a force to seize the ordnance mounted in the water battery of Fort Marion for the purpose of arming Fort Clinch.

It is, perhaps, unnecessary for me to say to the Department that in the present condition of Fort Clinch the idea of arming it either for offense or defense is simply absurd. My presence, however, is necessary there, for I know that I have sufficient influence in the community to prevent anything like spoliation or plunder of the public property by lawless individuals. I shall, therefore, return there on Wednesday, the 9th instant. Previous to leaving that post, I received assurances from the principal citizens to the effect that they would promptly put down anything like an attempt on the part of unauthorized mobs to take a dime's worth of the large amount of valuable material and property at the fort. They manifest a desire that the work shall continue without molestation, and this I believe to be the desire also of the members of the State Convention. I have a force of sixty men at work pushing the masonry as rapidly as possible. On the authority of Department letter of 9th ultimo, I have continued the work with the funds in my hands. The payments for December, which will be immediately made, will exhaust all funds in my hands belonging to Fort Clinch, and perhaps exceed a little. I have, as will be seen by the monthly statement, enough of other funds to continue for the present; but unless a portion at least of my last estimates is sent to me, I shall be compelled to close my operations. I respectfully request instructions. It is necessary to inform you that the telegraph is in the hands of the State authorities, and no message of a military or political character is allowed to be sent or delivered except by permission of the governor. The telegram of Mr. Hirsch to Colonel De Russy was refused until countersigned by Governor Brown.

As to the Savannah River improvement, no interference with the property belonging to the appropriation has been attempted, nor is any at present anticipated. I have, however, directed the discharge of all employes except a watchman. Fort Jackson remains as heretofore. The mail between Charleston and Fernandina having been discontinued, I request that communications be addressed to me via Savannah.
Very respectfully,
WM. H. C. WHITING,
Captain of Engineers.
General J. G. TOTTEN,
Chief Engineer, Washington.

(Source: U.S. War Department. *War of the Rebellion: A Compilation of the Official Records of the Union and Confederate Armies.* Ser. I, Vol. 1, Chapter II.)

B. FORT PICKENS

Fort Pickens in Pensacola could have been the place where the Civil War began had it not been for an uneasy truce between Florida authorities and the federal garrison there. Early attitudes about this installation range from the assertive one of Southern state authorities to the sadly defiant stance of federal forces. Finally there was the unvarnished caution and perspective of those, including one who had entertained second thoughts, who ironically pointed to Fort Sumter in Charleston as an example to follow. [See Fort Pickens]

1. Confederate Correspondence
Regarding Pensacola (1861)

WASHINGTON, *January 5, 1861.*

JOSEPH FINEGAN, *Esq.,*
or Col. GEO. W. CALL [*Tallahassee, Fla.*]:
MY DEAR SIR: The *immediately* important thing to be done is the occupation of the forts and arsenal in Florida. The naval station and forts at Pensacola are *first* in consequence. For this a force is necessary. I have

conversed with Mr. Toombs upon the subject. He will start this week for Georgia, and says if the convention of sov'y [sovereignty] will ask Governor Brown, of Georgia, for a force he will immediately send on sufficient force and take the navy-yard and forts. The occupation of the navy-yard will give us a good supply of ordnance and make the capture of the forts easier. Major Chase built the forts and will know all about them. Lose no time, for, my opinion is, troops will be very soon dispatched to re-enforce and strengthen the forts in Florida. The arsenal at Chattahoochee should be looked to, and that at once, to prevent removal of arms.

I shall give the enemy a shot next week before retiring. I say *enemy!* Yes, I am theirs, and they are mine. I am willing to be their masters, but not their brothers.
Yours, in haste,
D. L. YULEE.

Lose no time about the navy-yard and forts at Pensacola.

* * *

[STATE OF ALABAMA,] EXECUTIVE DEPARTMENT, January 8, 1861.

Hon. WILLIAM M. BROOKS, President of the Convention of the State of Alabama:
In reply to a verbal communication from the body over which you preside, made by one of its members, I make the following statement:

My information in regard to Pensacola is that Governor Perry, of Florida, has informed me by dispatch that he has ordered the forts to be occupied by the troops of Florida and asks aid from Alabama.

The force at his command in West Florida is small and not sufficient to take and maintain the forts. Troops from Alabama could reach that point before the troops of East and Middle Florida. This fact, with the importance of the position to Alabama as well as to Florida, induces him to make the request, as I am informed. It is believed at Washington, in South Carolina, and Georgia, as I am advised from high sources, that it is not only the policy of the Federal Government to coerce the seceding States, but as soon as possible to put herself in position by re-enforcing all the forts in the States where secession is expected. I need not suggest the danger to Florida and Alabama that must result from permitting a strong force to get possession of these forts.
With sentiments of high consideration and respect,
A. B. MOORE.

(Source: U.S. War Department. *War of the Rebellion: A Compilation of the Official Records of the Union and Confederate Armies.* Ser. I, Vol. 1, Chapter IV)

2. Colonel William H. Chase to Lieutenant A. J. Slemmer (15 January 1861)

HEADQUARTERS PENSACOLA DISTRICT, *January* 15, 1861.

Lieut. A. J. SLEMMER, *U.S. Army, Commanding Fort Pickens, Harbor of Pensacola:*
SIR: I have full powers from the governor of Florida to take possession of the forts and navy-yard, &c., &c., in this harbor. I desire to perform this duty without the effusion of blood. You can contribute toward this desirable result, and, in my judgment, without sacrifice of the honor of yourself or your gallant officers and men. Now, as commissioner on the part of the governor of the State of Florida, I request the surrender of Fort Pickens and the public property it contains into my hands, to be held subject to any agreement that may be entered into between the commissioners of the State of Florida and the Federal Government at Washington. I would not counsel you to do aught that was dishonorable; On the contrary, to do that which will secure for you the commendation of all Christian gentlemen; and if you refuse and hold out, for whom do you consent that blood shall flow—the blood of brethren? Certainly not for the deadly enemies to the assaulters, for they are not such, but brethren of the same race. If the Union now broken should be reconstructed Fort Pickens and all the public property passes peacefully under Federal authority. If a Southern Confederacy separates itself from the Union would it not be worse than folly to attempt the maintenance of Fort Pickens or any other fortified place within its limits!

Listen to me, then, I beg of you, and act with me in preventing the shedding the blood of your brethren. Surrender the fort. You and your command may reoccupy the barracks and quarters at Barrancas on your simple parole to remain there quietly until ordered away, or to resume the command of the harbor should an adjustment of present difficulties in the Union be arrived at.

All the baggage and private property of any kind belonging to yourself, officers, men, and their families shall be preserved to you. Consider this well, and take care that you will so act as to have no fearful recollections of a tragedy that you might have averted, but rather to make the present moment one of the most glorious, because christianlike, of your life.

I beg of you to receive this communication in the same spirit in which it is offered.

I have the honor to be, sir, very respectfully, your obedient servant,
WM. H. CHASE.

(Source: U.S. War Department. *War of the Rebellion: A Compilation of the Official Records of the Union and Confederate Armies.* Ser. I, Vol. 1, Chapter IV.)

3. Lieutenant J. H. Gilman to Colonel Chase (16 January 1861)

FORT PICKENS, FLA., *Pensacola Harbor,*
January 16, 1861.

Col. W. H. Chase, *Commissioner for the State of Florida:*
SIR: Under the orders we now have from the War Department, we have decided, after consultation with the Government officers in the harbor, that it is our duty to hold our position until such a force is brought against us as to render it impossible to defend it, or until the political condition of the country is such as to induce us to surrender the public property in our keeping to such authorities as may be delegated *legally to* receive it.

We deprecate as much as you or any individual can the present condition of affairs, or the shedding of the blood of our brethren. In regard to this matter, however, we must consider you the aggressors, and if blood is shed that you are responsible therefor.

By order of A. J. Slemmer, first lieutenant, First Artillery, commanding:
J. H. GILMAN,
Second Lieutenant, First Artillery, Act. Post Adjt.

(Source: U.S. War Department. *War of the Rebellion: A Compilation of the Official Records of the Union and Confederate Armies.* Ser. I, Vol. 1, Chapter IV.)

4. Senators Mallory and Yulee to Governor Perry (20 January 1861)

WASHINGTON, January 20, 1861.

Gov. M. S. PERRY, Tallahassee, Fla.:
The Southern Senators all agree that no assault on Fort Pickens should be made; that the fort is not worth one drop of blood at this time, and desire us to invoke you to prevent bloodshed. First get the Southern Government in operation. The same advice has been given as to Charleston, and will no doubt be adopted there.
S. R. MALLORY.
D. L. YULEE.

(Source: U.S. War Department. *War of the Rebellion: A Compilation of the Official Records of the Union and Confederate Armies.* Ser. I, Vol. 1, Chapter IV)

C. FORT SUMTER

The example of Fort Sumter would finally prove wanting, for the firing on that fort in Charleston harbor would begin the Civil War. Planning for the inevitable while trying to resist an irresistible momentum, making irreversible decisions while striving to save the chance for retraction, and finally succumbing to the inescapable clash—all that was part of the education of this war about to happen that spring in Charleston. [See Fort Sumter, Bombardment of]

1. Major Anderson to Governor Pickens (11 January 1861)

SIR: Two of your batteries fired this morning on an unarmed vessel bearing the flag of my Government. I am not notified that war has been declared by South Carolina against the United States—and I cannot but think that this hostile act has been committed without your sanction or authority. Under that hope I refrain from opening fire on your batteries.

I have the honor, therefore, respectfully to ask whether the abovementioned act, one I believe without a parallel in the history of our country or any other civilized government, was committed in obedience to your instructions? And I notify you, if the act is not disclaimed, that I shall regard it as an act of war, and shall not, after a reasonable time allowed for the return of my messenger, permit any vessel to pass within range of the guns of my fort. In order to save, as far as is in my power, the shedding of blood, I beg you will have due notification of my decision given to all concerned.

Hoping, however, that your answer may justify a further continuance of forbearance on my part, I am
Yours respectfully,
Robert Anderson

(Source: Reprinted in the Baltimore *American,* 11 January 1861, p. 1.)

2. Report of Brig. Gen. G. T. Beauregard, C.S. Army, of Operations against Fort Sumter (6 March 1861)

HEADQUARTERS C. S. ARMY, Charleston, S. C., March 6, 1861.

General L. P. WALKER, Secretary of War, Montgomery, Ala.
SIR: In obedience to War Department orders of the 1st instant I arrived at this place on the 3d instant, and immediately reported to Governor Pickens for military duty. That day we inspected the floating battery now being constructed here. On the 4th instant we inspected the works on the southern portion of the harbor (Morris Island and Fort Johnson) and yesterday those on the north (Fort Moultrie, &c., including Castle Pinckney).

I have now the honor to state that I coincide fully in the opinion and views contained in Maj. W. H. C. Whiting's letter preceding his full report, and that, as I have not time to write more fully on the subject, I desire that portion of his letter referring to the above works should be annexed to this report, and a copy thereof sent to me for my files.

On Morris Island the flanking defects are being remedied, and will probably soon be completed, as well as the position, &c., of said works will permit. I have ordered that only six mortars, instead of twelve, intended for that point, should be put in position there. I have ordered the construction of a series of small batteries of heavy guns, two in each, and twenty in all, well protected by traverses along the channel shore of that island, said batteries to be about fifty or one hundred yards apart (according to the nature of the ground), to prevent the broadsides of a vessel, from silencing them in a few minutes. When those batteries shall be ready, I will remove into them all the heavy guns I can dispose of. I have ordered to that island the whole of Colonel Gregg's regiment, with two short 12-pounders and one light battery, for the protection of said works, selecting a strong natural position to protect their right flank from a land attack.

I have ordered an additional battery (for two mortars) to be constructed near Fort Johnson, to receive half of those intended for a defectively-placed mortar battery, to the south of said work, the latter not being in itself of much importance, containing only an open battery of four 24-pounders bearing on the inner harbor. At Fort Moultrie, towards the north of Fort Sumter, I have ordered additional traverses to be thrown up, of a better construction than those already there, for the protection of the channel guns against enfilade from Fort Sumter. Between Moultrie and the western extremity of Sullivan's Island I have ordered the construction of a four-gun concealed battery, to enfilade the channel face of Sumter, having nine or ten guns (en barbette) bearing on the Morris Island works. I have ordered two more 32-pounders to be added to the extreme five-gun battery, commanding the Maffitt or northern shore channel into the harbor, and I have selected the site of two more mortar batteries, of two each, to take in reverse the casemate and barbette guns of Fort Sumter bearing on Morris Island.

I have fortunately found that we would soon have mortars enough for all our present wants; but, generally, the carriages and chassis of nearly all the guns, especially those on the Morris Island works, are either defective or not of the proper kind. I am going to remedy this defect as soon as practicable.

I find that the gorge of Fort Sumter is too much inclined to the guns on Morris Island to be breached by them at this distance (thirteen hundred yards); and, moreover, they have double the number of guns bearing on them, reversing thereby the advantages of the attack over the defense. If we succeed in constructing my enfilading battery on Sullivan's Island we will then have a preponderating fire against said gorge wall (four feet six inches thick); but, as already stated, at about thirteen hundred yards, and at an angle of about fifty degrees.

I find that the battery of heavy guns (10-inch columbiads), which I proposed putting up in the vicinity of Fort Johnson, would be impracticable (if we had said guns), the grounds being too low and marshy.

I have now given you a general view of the condition of the offensive works of this harbor, and I am of the opinion that, if Sumter was properly garrisoned and armed, it would be a perfect Gibraltar to anything but constant shelling, night and day, from the four points of the compass. As it is, the weakness of the garrison constitutes our greatest advantage, and we must, for the present, turn our attention to preventing it front being re-enforced. This idea I am gradually and cautiously infusing into the minds of all here; but, should we have to open our batteries upon it, I hope to be able to do so with all the advantages the condition of things here will permit. All that I ask is time for completing my batteries and preparing and organizing properly my command, which is still in a more or less confused state, not having yet my general staff officers around me. So soon as I shall have here a competent engineer officer (Major Whiting arrived here on the 4th, and will probably leave again for Savannah to day, where his presence is required), I will send to the department a plan of this harbor, with the position, &c., of all the works marked thereon. Those Drummond lights, ordered from New York, will be here in about ten days.

I remain, sir, very respectfully,

G. T. BEAUREGARD, Brigadier-General, Commanding.

(Source: U.S. War Department. *War of the Rebellion: A Compilation of the Official Records of the Union and Confederate Armies.* Ser. I, Vol. 1, Chapter I.)

3. Opinions Written by Members of the Cabinet at the Verbal Request of the President, at a Cabinet Meeting Held to Determine the Question of Sending an Expedition to Relieve Fort Sumter (29 March 1861)

Mr. Seward, Secretary of State, wrote:

First. The dispatch of an expedition to supply or reinforce Sumter would provoke an attack, and so involve a war at that point.

The fact of preparation for such an expedition would inevitably transpire, and would therefore precipitate the war, and probably defeat the object. I do not think it wise to provoke a civil war beginning at Charleston, and in rescue of an untenable position.

Therefore I advise against the expedition in every view.

Second. I would call in Captain M. C. Meigs forthwith. Aided by his counsel, I would at once, and at every cost, prepare for a war at Pensacola and Texas: to be taken, however, only as a consequence of maintaining the possessions and authority of the United States.

Third. I would instruct Major Anderson to retire from Sumter forthwith.

Mr. Blair, Postmaster-General, wrote:
First. As regards General Scott, I have no confidence in his judgment on the questions of the day. His political views control his judgment, and his course as remarked on by the President shows that whilst no one will question his patriotism, the results are the same as if he was in fact traitorous.

Second. It is acknowledged to be possible to relieve Fort Sumter. It ought to be relieved without reference to Pickens or any other possession. South Carolina is the head and front of this rebellion, and when that State is safely delivered from the authority of the United Stares it will strike a blow against our authority from which it will take us years of bloody strife to recover.

Third. For my own part, I am unwilling to share in the responsibility of such a policy.

Mr. Welles, Secretary of the Navy wrote:
I concur in the proposition to send an armed force off Charleston with supplies of provisions and reinforcements for the garrison at Fort Sumter, and of communicating at the proper time the intentions of the government to provision the fort peaceably if unmolested. There is little probability that this will be permitted if the opposing forces can prevent it. An attempt to force in provisions without reinforcing the garrison at the same time might not be advisable; but armed resistance to a peaceable attempt to send provisions to one of our own forts will justify the government in using all the power at its command to reinforce the garrison and furnish the necessary supplies.

Fort Pickens and other places retained should be strengthened by additional troops, and, if possible, made impregnable.

The naval force in the gulf and on the southern coast should be increased. Accounts are published that vessels having on board marketable products for the crews of the squadron at Pensacola are seized—the inhabitants we know are prohibited from furnishing the ships with provisions or water; and the time has arrived when it is the duty of the government to assert and maintain its authority.

(Source: National Archives, Washington, D.C.)

1. Correspondence and Orders Relating to Operations in Charleston Harbor, 1861.
March 8, 1861.

To the CHIEF OF STAFF OF BRIGADIER-GENERAL BEAUREGARD:

SIR: I am informed by Major Stevens that a shot was accidentally fired from the iron battery this morning, which struck Fort Sumter. Major Stevens was practicing with blank cartridges, and does not know how a shot got in. He does not suspect that it was put in by any man intentionally. Major Stevens is about to go with a flag to Fort Sumter to explain the accident.

I have to request that General Beauregard will forward this note for the information of the commander-in-chief.

I have the honor to be, your obedient servant,
MAXCY GREGG,
Colonel First Regiment South Carolina Volunteers,
Commanding on Morris Island.

* * *

CHARLESTON, *April 8, 1861.*

L. P. WALKER:
Authorized messenger from Lincoln just informed Governor Pickens and myself that provisions would be sent to Sumter peaceably, otherwise by force.
G. T. BEAUREGARD.

* * *

MONTGOMERY, *April 8, 1861.*

General BEAUREGARD, *Charleston:*
Under no circumstances are you to allow provisions to be sent to Fort Sumter.
L. P. WALKER.

* * *

HEADQUARTERS PROVISIONAL ARMY, C. S. A.,
Charleston, S. C., April 11, 1861.

SIR: The Government of the Confederate States has hitherto forborne from any hostile demonstration against Fort Sumter, in the hope that the Government of the United States, with a view to the amicable adjustment of all questions between the two Governments, and to avert the calamities of war, would voluntarily evacuate it.

There was reason at one time to believe that such would be the course pursued by the Government of the United States, and under that impression my Government has refrained from making any demand for the surrender of the fort. But the Confederate States can no longer delay assuming actual possession of a fortification commanding the entrance of one of their harbors, and necessary to its defense and security.

I am ordered by the Government of the Confederate States to demand the evacuation of Fort Sumter. My aides, Colonel Chesnut and Captain Lee, are authorized to make such demand of you. All proper facilities will be afforded for the removal of yourself and command, together with company arms and property, and all private property, to any post in the United States which you may select. The flag which you have upheld so long and with so much fortitude, under the most trying circumstances, may be saluted by you on taking it down.

Colonel Chesnut and Captain Lee will, for a reasonable time, await your answer.

I am, sir, very respectfully, your obedient servant,

G. T. BEAUREGARD,
Brigadier-General, Commanding.
Maj. ROBERT ANDERSON,
Commanding at Fort Sumter, Charleston Harbor, S.C.

* * *

FORT SUMTER, S. C., *April 11, 1861.*

GENERAL: I have the honor to acknowledge the receipt of your communication demanding the evacuation of this fort, and to say, in reply thereto, that it is a demand with which I regret that my sense of honor, and of my obligations to my Government, prevent my compliance. Thanking you for the fair, manly, and courteous terms proposed, and for the high compliment paid me,

I am, general, very respectfully, your obedient servant,

ROBERT ANDERSON,
Major, First Artillery, Commanding.
Brig. Gen. BEAUREGARD,
Commanding Provisional Army.

* * * *

HEADQUARTERS PROVISIONAL ARMY,
C. S. A.,
Charleston, S.C., April 11, 1861.

MAJOR: In consequence of the verbal observation made by you to my aides, Messrs. Chesnut and Lee, in relation to the condition of your supplies, and that you would in a few days be starved out if our guns did not batter you to pieces, or words to that effect, and desiring no useless effusion of blood, I communicated both the verbal observations and your written answer to my communications to my Government.

If you will state the time at which you will evacuate Fort Sumter, and agree that in the mean time you will not use your guns against us unless ours shall be employed against Fort Sumter, we will abstain from opening fire upon you. Colonel Chesnut and Captain

Lee are authorized by me to enter into such an agreement with you. You are, therefore, requested to communicate to them an open answer.

I remain, major, very respectfully, your obedient servant,

G. T. BEAUREGARD,
Brigadier-General, Commanding.
Maj. ROBERT ANDERSON,
Commanding Fort Sumter, Charleston Harbor, S.C.

* * *

Fort SUMTER, S.C., *April 12, 1861.*

GENERAL: I have the honor to acknowledge the receipt by Colonel Chesnut of your second communication of the 11th instant, and to state in reply that, cordially uniting with you in the desire to avoid the useless effusion of blood, I will, if provided with the proper and necessary means of transportation, evacuate Fort Sumter by noon on the 15th instant, and that I will not in the mean time open my fires upon your forces unless compelled to do so by some hostile act against this fort or the flag of my Government by the forces under your command, or by some portion of them, or by the perpetration of some act showing a hostile intention on your part against this fort or the flag it bears, should I not receive prior to that time controlling instructions from my Government or additional supplies.

I am, general, very respectfully, your obedient servant,

ROBERT ANDERSON,
Major, First Artillery, Commanding.
Brig. Gen. BEAUREGARD,
Commanding.

* * *

FORT SUMTER, S.C., *April 12, 1861—3.20 a.m.*

SIR: By authority of Brigadier-General Beauregard, commanding the Provisional Forces of the Confederate States, we have the honor to notify you that he will open the fire of his batteries on Fort Sumter in one hour from this time.

We have the honor to be, very respectfully, your obedient servants,

JAMES CHESNUT, JR.,
Aide-de-Camp.
STEPHEN D. LEE,
Captain, C. S. Army, Aide-de-Camp.
Maj. ROBERT ANDERSON,
U. S. Army, Commanding Fort Sumter.

* * *

CHARLESTON, S.C., *April* 13, 1861—2 *p.m.*

President JEFF. DAVIS, *Montgomery, Ala.:*
Quarters in Sumter all burned down. White flag up.
Have sent a boat to receive surrender. But half an hour
before had sent a boat to stop our firing and offer assis-
tance.
G. T. BEAUREGARD.

* * *

CHARLESTON, S.C., *April* 13, 1861.

Gov. F. W. PICKENS, *Present:*
DEAR GOVERNOR: I have sent Major Jones,
Captain Hartstene, and Colonels Miles and Pryor to
Major Anderson to tell him that I offer him the same
terms that I did on the 11th, and that a vessel or steamer would be sent to him in the morning to take him to
the steamer outside, and that he must be responsible in
the mean time for the fort; otherwise, I would put four
companies of artillery in there to-night. I also told
Captain Hartstene to go out to the fleet and tell them
that the fort was now ours, but under the safe-keeping
of Major Anderson, and that no attack could be made
upon it by them.

In the morning I will order two of Colonel Ripley's
companies and two of De Saussure's to take possession
of Fort Sumter.
Respectfully, your obedient servant,
G. T. BEAUREGARD.

* * *

CHARLESTON, April 13, 1861.
Hon. L. P. WALKER:
Fort Sumter has unconditionally surrendered to the
Confederate States, represented by General Beaure-
gard, Colonel Wigfall, his aide, receiving the surrender.
The same terms just offered will be granted. Engines are
about to go down to put out the fire. Fight expected on
Morris Island to-night.
R. B. RHETT, JR.

(Source: U.S. War Department. *War of the Rebellion: A
Compilation of the Official Records of the Union and Confederate
Armies.* Ser. I, Vol. 1, Chapter I.)

D. HARPER'S FERRY
*After the firing on Fort Sumter, all eyes looked toward
Virginia. The armory at Harper's Ferry would be a major
prize for the Confederacy, but federal authorities on the site
were determined not to let that happen. [See Harper's
Ferry, (West) Virginia]*

1. Confederate Correspondence Relating to the Armory at Harper's Ferry (April 1861)
RICHMOND, VA., *April 17, 1861.*

His Excellency JEFFERSON DAVIS, President of the
Confederate States of America:
I came here last night. You may rely now that
Virginia will secede, and promptly. Vessels sunk last
night in the harbor at Norfolk to cut off the navy-yard,
and troops ordered there to sustain the movement.
Harper's Ferry Arsenal to be seized at once. You shall
hear as things advance. If you have anything to reply,
telegraph to me here.
J. M. MASON.
WAR DEPARTMENT, C. S. A., *Montgomery,*
April 18, 1861.

(Source: U.S. War Department. *War of the Rebellion: A
Compilation of the Official Records of the Union and Confederate
Armies.* Ser. I, Vol. LI/2.)

* * *

RICHMOND, *April 22, 1861.*

President DAVIS:
Arrived here this morning. Shall meet the convention
in closed doors to-morrow at 1 o'clock. Harper's Ferry
in our own hands. Arsenal, containing 16,000 arms,
blown up by U.S. forces; 4,000 or 5,000 saved. Best
guns, all machinery of value, estimated at $2,000,000,
saved. . . . Col. Robert E. Lee is expected to-day, and is
looked to as the commander. . . .
ALEX. H. STEPHENS.

2. Union Correspondence Relating to the Armory at Harper's Ferry (April 1861)
HEADQUARTERS UNITED STATES ARMORY,
Harper's Ferry, Va., April 18, 1861—9 p.m.

SIR: Up to the present time no assault or attempt to
seize the Government property here has been made,
but there is decided evidence that the subject is in contemplation, and has been all day, by a large number of
people living in the direction of Charlestown; and at
sundown this evening several companies of troops had
assembled at Halltown, about three or four miles from
here on the road to Charlestown, with the intention of
seizing the Government property, and the last report is
that the attack will be made to-night. I telegraphed this
evening to General Scott that I had received information confirming his dispatch of this morning, and later
to the Adjutant-General that I expected an attack to-
night. I have taken steps which ought to insure my
receiving early intelligence of the advance of any

forces, and my determination is to *destroy* what I cannot defend, and if the forces sent against me are clearly overwhelming, my present intention is to retreat into Pennsylvania.

The steps I have taken to destroy the arsenal, which contains nearly 15,000 stand of arms, are so complete that I can conceive of nothing that will prevent their entire destruction.

If the Government purposes maintaining its authority here, no time should be lost in sending large bodies of troops to my assistance, and as many of them as possible should be regulars.

A courier has just reported the advance of the troops from Halltown. Respectfully, I am, sir, your obedient servant,

R. JONES,

First Lieutenant, Mounted Riflemen, Commanding.

(Source: U.S. War Department. *War of the Rebellion: A Compilation of the Official Records of the Union and Confederate Armies.* Ser. I, Vol. LI/2 [S# 108].)

* * *

CARLISLE BARRACKS, PA., *April 20, 1861.*

SIR: Immediately after finishing my dispatch of the night of the 18th instant, I received positive and reliable information that 2,500 or 3,000 State troops would reach Harper's Ferry in two hours, from Winchester, and that the troops from Halltown, increased to 300 men, were advancing, and were at that time (few minutes after 10 o'clock) within twenty minutes' march of the Ferry. Under these circumstances I decided the time had arrived to carry out my determination, as expressed in the dispatch above referred to, and accordingly gave the order to apply the torch. In three minutes, or less, both of the arsenal buildings, containing nearly 15,000 arms, together with the carpenter's shop, which was at the upper end of a long and connected series of workshops of the armory proper, were in a complete blaze.

There is every reason for believing the destruction was complete. After firing the buildings I withdrew my command, marching all night, and arrived here at 2_ p.m. yesterday, where I shall await orders. Four men were missing on leaving the armory, and two deserted during the night.

Respectfully, I am, sir, your obedient servant,

R. JONES,

First Lieut. Mounted Riflemen, Comdg.

Detachment Recruits.

To the ASSISTANT ADJUTANT-GENERAL,

Headquarters of the Army, Washington, D.C.

(Source: U.S. War Department. *War of the Rebellion: A Compilation of the Official Records of the Union and Confederate Armies.* Ser. I, Vol. LI/2 [S# 108].)

THE WAR

X. The Union Responds

Lincoln called for 75,000 volunteers to suppress the rebellion and shortly afterward initiated a blockade of Southern ports. As the government anxiously awaited the arrival of the first volunteers to protect the national capital, an ugly incident in Baltimore set already frayed Northern nerves on edge. By July, however, a coalescing support for the Union cause was manifest, as indicated by resolutions put forward by the erstwhile compromiser John J. Crittenden and the fiery Tennessee Unionist Andrew Johnson. [See Lincoln, Abraham; Baltimore Riots; Crittenden, John J.; Johnson, Andrew]

1. Lincoln's Proclamation Calling Militia and Convening Congress (15 April 1861)

April 15, 1861

BY THE PRESIDENT OF THE UNITED STATES
A PROCLAMATION.

Whereas the laws of the United States have been for some time past, and now are opposed, and the execution thereof obstructed, in the States of South Carolina, Georgia, Alabama, Florida, Mississippi, Louisiana and Texas, by combinations too powerful to be suppressed by the ordinary course of judicial proceedings, or by the powers vested in the Marshals by law,

Now therefore, I, Abraham Lincoln, President of the United States, in virtue of the power in me vested by the Constitution, and the laws, have thought fit to call forth, and hereby do call forth, the militia of the several States of the Union, to the aggregate number of seventy-five thousand, in order to suppress said combinations, and to cause the laws to be duly executed. The details, for this object, will be immediately communicated to the State authorities through the War Department.

I appeal to all loyal citizens to favor, facilitate and aid this effort to maintain the honor, the integrity, and the existence of our National Union, and the perpetuity of popular government; and to redress wrongs already long enough endured.

I deem it proper to say that the first service assigned to the forces hereby called forth will probably be to repossess the forts, places, and property which have been seized from the Union; and in every event, the utmost care will be observed, consistently with the objects aforesaid, to avoid any devastation, any destruction of, or interference with, property, or any disturbance of peaceful citizens in any part of the country.

And I hereby command the persons composing the combinations aforesaid to disperse, and retire peaceably to their respective abodes within twenty days from this date.

Deeming that the present condition of public affairs presents an extraordinary occasion, I do hereby, in virtue of the power in me vested by the Constitution, convene both Houses of Congress. Senators and Representatives are therefore summoned to assemble at their respective chambers, at 12 o'clock, noon, on Thursday, the fourth day of July, next, then and there to consider and determine, such measures, as, in their wisdom, the public safety, and interest may seem to demand.

In Witness Whereof I have hereunto set my hand, and caused the Seal of the United States to be affixed.

Done at the city of Washington this fifteenth day of April in the year of our Lord One thousand, Eight hundred and Sixty one, and of the Independence the United States the Eighty-fifth.

ABRAHAM LINCOLN

By the President:

WILLIAM H. SEWARD, Secretary of State.

(Source: National Archives, Washington, DC.)

2. Lincoln's Proclamation of a Blockade (29 April 1861)

April 29, 1861

By the President of the United States of America:
A Proclamation.

Whereas an insurrection against the Government of the United States has broken out in the States of South Carolina, Georgia, Alabama, Florida, Mississippi, Louisiana, and Texas, and the laws of the United States for the collection of the revenue cannot be effectually executed therein conformably to that provision of the Constitution which requires duties to be uniform throughout the United States:

And whereas a combination of persons engaged in such insurrection, have threatened to grant pretended letters of marque to authorize the bearers thereof to commit assaults on the lives, vessels, and property of good citizens of the country lawfully engaged in commerce on the high seas, and in waters of the United States: And whereas an Executive Proclamation has been already issued, requiring the persons engaged in these disorderly proceedings to desist therefrom, calling out a militia force for the purpose of repressing the same, and convening Congress in extraordinary session, to deliberate and determine thereon:

Now, therefore, I, Abraham Lincoln, President of the United States, with a view to the same purposes before mentioned, and to the protection of the public peace, and the lives and property of quiet and orderly citizens pursuing their lawful occupations, until Congress shall have assembled and deliberated on the said unlawful proceedings, or until the same shall have ceased, have further deemed it advisable to set on foot a blockade of the ports within the States aforesaid, in pursuance of the laws of the United States, and of the law of Nations, in such case provided. For this purpose a competent force will be posted so as to prevent entrance and exit of vessels from the ports aforesaid. If, therefore, with a view to violate such blockade, a vessel shall approach or shall attempt to leave either of the said ports, she will he duly warned by the Commander of one of the blockading vessels, who will endorse on her register the fact and date of such warning, and if the same vessel shall again attempt to enter or leave the blockaded port, she will be captured and sent to the nearest convenient port, for such proceedings against her and her cargo as prize, as may be deemed advisable.

And I hereby proclaim and declare that if any person, under the pretended authority of the said States, or under any other pretense, shall molest a vessel of the United States, or the persons or cargo on board of her, such person will be held amenable to the laws of the United States for the prevention and punishment of piracy,

In witness whereof, I have hereunto set my hand, and caused the seal of the United States to be affixed. Done at the City of Washington, this nineteenth day of April, in the year of our Lord one thousand eight hundred and sixty-one, and of the Independence of the United States the eighty-fifth.

ABRAHAM LINCOLN

By the President:

WILLIAM H. SEWARD, Secretary of State

3. Report of the Baltimore Police Commissioners [Excerpts] (May 1861)

OFFICE BOARD OF POLICE COMMISSIONERS, Baltimore, May 3, 1861.

To the honorable the General Assembly of Maryland: The board of police of the city of Baltimore, created and appointed by your honorable body by the provisions of the fourth article of the Code of Public Local Laws, section 806, &c., deem it their duty respectfully to report:

The board continued from the date of their above report to exercise their regular functions until Friday, the 19th April. On that day a large detachment of, it is understood, about 1,800 men of the Massachusetts and Pennsylvania Militia arrived in the forenoon in the city via the Philadelphia, Wilmington and Baltimore Railroad. No member of the board of police had any information that these troops were expected on that day until from half an hour to one hour of the time at which they were to arrive. The marshal of police was immediately notified, and called out at once a large portion of his force to preserve order during their transit through the city. When they arrived, there were manifestations to interfere with their passage; and after some had been transported by cars through the streets to the Washington depot obstructions were placed on the track in the city which stopped the progress of the remainder. These alighted to march to the depot, and to prevent any difficulty the mayor placed himself at their head, and they thus proceeded on their route. Missiles were, notwithstanding, thrown at the troops, and some of them were injured. Their assailants were fired upon, and in some instances with fatal effect. An intense and irrepressible feeling appeared to be at once aroused, and repeated conflicts between parties of citizens and the Massachusetts troops took place, several being killed on both sides.

The marshal, who had been on active duty at the Camden-street depot, and did not know that these troops were on their route or expected, hearing of this, hastened to meet them with a force of the police, and under their escort they reached the Washington depot, and after some delay the train finally started for Washington. Attempts were made to hinder it by placing obstructions on the track of the railroad, but by the interference of the police these were soon removed.

The city authorities were meanwhile informed that there had been another arrival of military, who were then at the Philadelphia depot. The marshal of police hastened to that point, and as it was impossible for them at that time to be taken through the streets without a general and bloody conflict, he protected them with a party of his police until they were sent back by the railroad company in the cars to Havre de Grace.

During the afternoon and night a large number of stragglers from some of the above detachments of troops sought the aid and protection of the police; they were safely cared for at the several station-houses, and were sent off in security by the earliest opportunity to Havre de Grace or Philadelphia in the cars. The same night the board had a meeting, when the opinion was unanimously expressed that it was utterly impossible from the state of the public mind that any more forces from other States could, by any probability, then pass through the city to Washington without a fierce and bloody conflict at every step of their progress, and that whatever might be the result, great loss of life and imminent danger to the safety of the city would necessarily ensue. The board were equally unanimous in their judgment that, as good citizens, it was their duty to the city, and to the State of Maryland, to adopt any measures whatsoever that might be necessary at such a juncture to prevent the immediate arrival in the city of further bodies of troops from the Eastern or Northern States, though the object of the latter might be solely to pass through the city. It was suggested that the most feasible, if not the most practicable, mode of thus stopping for a time the approach of such troops would be to obstruct the Philadelphia, Wilmington and Baltimore, and the Northern Central Railroads by disabling some of the bridges on both roads. His honor the mayor stated to the board that his excellency the governor, with whom he had a few minutes before been in consultation in the presence of several citizens, concurred in these views; they were likewise those of the board, and instructions were given for carrying them into effect. This was accordingly done. The injury thus done on the railroads amounted to but a few thousand dollars on each; subsequently, as has been stated, further and greater damage was done to other structures on the roads by parties in the country or others, but this was without the sanction or authority of the board, and they have no accurate information on the subject.

The absolute necessity of the measures thus determined upon by the governor, mayor, and police board is fully illustrated by the fact that early on Sunday morning reliable information reached the city of the presence of a large body of Pennsylvania troops, amounting to about twenty-four hundred men, [who] had reached Ashland, near Cockeysville, by the way of the Northern Central Railroad, and were stopped in their progress toward Baltimore by the partial destruction of the Ashland Bridge. Every intelligent citizen at all acquainted with the state of feeling then existing must be satisfied that if these troops had attempted to march through the city an immense loss of life would have ensued in the conflict which would necessarily have taken place. The bitter feelings already engendered would have been intensely increased by such a conflict; all attempts at conciliation would have been vain, and terrible destruction would have been the consequence, if, as is certain, other bodies of troops had insisted upon forcing their way through the city.

The tone of the whole of the Northern press and of the mass of the population was violent in the extreme. Incursions upon our city were daily threatened, not only by troops in the service of the Federal Government, but by the vilest and most reckless desperadoes, acting independently, and, as they threatened, in despite of the Government, backed by well-known, influential citizens, and sworn to the commission of all kinds of excesses. In short, every possible effort was made to alarm this community. In this condition of things the board felt it to be their solemn duty to continue the organization which had already been commenced for the purpose of assuring the people of Baltimore that no effort would be spared to protect all within its borders to the full extent of their ability. All the means employed were devoted to this end, and with no view of producing a collision with the General Government, which the board were particularly anxious to avoid, and an arrangement was happily effected by the mayor with the General Government that no troops should be passed through the city. As an evidence of the determination of the board to prevent such collision, a sufficient guard was sent in the neighborhood of Fort McHenry several nights to arrest all parties who might be engaged in a threatened attack upon it, and a steam-tug was employed, properly manned, to prevent any hostile demonstration upon the receiving ship *Allegheny*, lying at anchor in the harbor, of all which the United States officers in command were duly notified.

Property of various descriptions, belonging to the Government and individuals, was taken possession of by the police force with a view to its security. The best care has been taken of it. Every effort has been made to discover the rightful owners, and a portion of it has already been forwarded to order. Arrangements have been made with the Government agents satisfactory to them for the portion belonging to it, and the balance is held subject to the order of its owners. Amidst all the excitement and confusion which has since prevailed, the board take great pleasure in stating that the good order and peace of the city have been preserved to an extraordinary degree. Indeed to judge from the accounts given by the press of other cities of what has been the state of things in their own communities, Baltimore, during the whole of the past week and up to this date, will compare favorably, as to the protection which persons and property have enjoyed, with any other large city in the United States.

All of which is respectfully submitted.

By order of the board: CHARLES HOWARD.

(Source: U.S. War Department. *War of the Rebellion: A Compilation of the Official Records of the Union and Confederate Armies*. Ser. I, Vol. 2, Chapter IX)

4. Dispatch from General Scott to General Butler, 14 May 1861

WASHINGTON, D.C., May 14, 1861.

Brig. Gen. BENJAMIN F. BUTLER, Commanding Department of Annapolis, Md.:

SIR: Your hazardous occupation of Baltimore was made without my knowledge, and of course without my approbation. It is a God-send that it was without conflict of arms. It is also reported that you have sent a detachment to Frederick, but this is impossible. Not a word have I received from you as to either movement. Let me hear from you.

Very respectfully, yours,

WINFIELD SCOTT.

(Source: U.S. War Department. *War of the Rebellion: A Compilation of the Official Records of the Union and Confederate Armies*. Ser. I, Vol. 2, Chapter IX.)

5. The Crittenden-Johnson Resolutions on the Objects of the War (July 1861)

THE CRITTENDEN RESOLUTIONS

Resolved by the House of Representatives of the Congress of the United States, That the present deplorable civil war has been forced upon the country by the disunionists of the Southern States now in revolt against the constitutional Government and in arms around the capital; that in this national emergency Congress, banishing all feelings of mere passion or resentment, will recollect only its duty to the whole country; that this war is not waged upon our part in any spirit of oppression, nor for any purpose of conquest or subjugation, nor purpose of overthrowing or interfering with the rights or established institutions of those States, but to defend and maintain the supremacy of the Constitution and to preserve the Union, with all the dignity, equality, and rights of the several States unimpaired; and that as soon as these objects are accomplished the war ought to cease.

THE JOHNSON RESOLUTIONS

Resolved, That the present deplorable civil war has been forced upon the country by the disunionists of the Southern States now in revolt against the constitutional Government and in arms around the capital; that in this national emergency Congress, banishing all feeling of mere passion or resentment, will recollect only its duty to the whole country; that this war is not prosecuted upon our part in any spirit of oppression, nor for any purpose of conquest or subjugation, nor purpose of overthrowing or interfering with the rights or established institutions of those States, but to defend and maintain the supremacy of the Constitution and all laws made in pursuance thereof and to preserve the Union, with all the dignity, equality, and rights of the several States unimpaired; that as soon as these objects are accomplished the war ought to cease.

(Source: Richardson, James D., comp. *A Compilation of Messages and Papers of the Presidents*. Vol. VI. Washington, DC: Bureau of National Literature and Art, 1910.)

XI. Secession—The Second Wave

Lincoln's call for volunteers finally forced the Upper South to the difficult decision of disunion. Four additional states, important among them Virginia, quit the United States. Significantly absent from this second wave, however, would be the crucial border states of Maryland, Kentucky, and Missouri. Thus North Carolina would be the last state to join the Confederacy and would have the grisly distinction of losing more of her sons in the coming war than any other Southern state.

A. VIRGINIA

1. Secession Ordinance (17 April 1861)

AN ORDINANCE to repeal the ratification of the Constitution of the United States of America by the State of Virginia, and to resume all the rights and powers granted under said Constitution.

The people of Virginia in their ratification of the Constitution of the United States of America, adopted by them in convention on the twenty-fifth day of June, in the year of our Lord one thousand seven hundred and eighty-eight, having declared that the powers granted under said Constitution were derived from the people of the United States and might be resumed whensoever the same should be perverted to their injury and oppression, and the Federal Government having perverted said powers not only to the injury of the people of Virginia, but to the oppression of the Southern slave-holding States:

Now, therefore, we, the people of Virginia, do declare and ordain, That the ordinance adopted by the people of this State in convention on the twenty-fifth day of June, in the year of our Lord one thousand seven hundred and eighty-eight, whereby the Constitution of the United States of America was ratified, and all acts of the General Assembly of this State ratifying and adopting amendments to said Constitution, are hereby repealed and abrogated; that the union between the State of Virginia and the other States under the Constitution aforesaid is hereby dissolved, and that the State of Virginia is in the full possession and exercise of all the rights of sovereignty which belong and appertain to a free and independent State.

And they do further declare, That said Constitution of the United States of America is no longer binding on any of the citizens of this State.

This ordinance shall take effect and be an act of this day, when ratified by a majority of the votes of the people of this State cast at a poll to be taken thereon on the fourth Thursday in May next, in pursuance of a schedule hereafter to be enacted.

Adopted by the convention of Virginia April 17, 1861.

JOHN JANNEY,
President.

JOHN L. EUBANK,
Secretary.

(Source: U.S. War Department. War of the Rebellion: A Compilation of the Official Records of the Union and Confederate Armies. Ser. IV, Vol. I.)

2. Jefferson Davis's Proclamation (19 April 1861)

JEFFERSON DAVIS, PRESIDENT OF THE CONFEDERATE STATES OF AMERICA, TO ALL WHOM THESE PRESENTS SHALL CONCERN, GREETING:

Know ye, that for the purpose of establishing friendly relations between the Confederate States of America and the Commonwealth of Virginia, and reposing special trust and confidence in the integrity, prudence, and ability of Alexander H. Stephens, Vice President of the Confederate States of America, appointed special commissioner of the Confederate States to the Commonwealth of Virginia, I have invested him with full and all manner of power and authority, for and in the name of the Confederate States, to meet and confer with any person or persons authorized by the Government of Virginia, being furnished with like power and authority, and with him or them to agree, treat, consult, and negotiate of and concerning all matters and subjects interesting to both Republics; and to conclude and sign a treaty or treaties, convention or conventions, touching the premises, transmitting the same to the President of the Confederate States for his final ratification, by and with the advice and consent of the Congress of the Confederate States.

In testimony whereof I have caused the seal of the Confederate States to be hereunto affixed.

Given under my hand at the city of Montgomery this 19th day of April, A.D. 1861.

JEFF'N DAVIS.

By the President: ROBERT TOOMBS, Secretary of State.

(Source: Richardson, James D. A Compilation of the Messages and Papers of the Confederacy, including the Diplomatic Correspondence, 1861–1865. Nashville, TN: United States Publishing Co., 1905.)

B. TENNESSEE

1. Secession Ordinance (6 May 1861)

AN ACT to submit to a vote of the people a declaration of independence, and for other purposes.

SECTION 1. Be it enacted by the General Assembly of the State of Tennessee, That immediately after the passage of this act the Governor of this State shall, by proclamation, direct the sheriffs of the several counties in this State to open and hold an election at the various voting precincts in their respective counties on the 8th day of June, 1861; that said sheriffs, or in the absence of the sheriffs the coroner of the county, shall immediately advertise the election contemplated by this act; that said sheriffs appoint a deputy to hold said election for each voting precinct, and that said deputy appoint three judges and two clerks for each precinct. And if no officer shall, from any cause, attend any voting precinct to open and hold said election, then any justice of the peace, or in the absence of a justice of the peace any respectable freeholder, may appoint an officer, judges, and clerks to open and hold said election. Said officers, judges, and clerks shall be sworn as now required by law, and who after being so sworn shall open and hold an election, open and close at the time of day and in the manner now required by law in elections for members to the General Assembly.

SEC. 2. Be it further enacted, That at said election the following declaration shall be submitted to a vote of the qualified voters of the State of Tennessee for their ratification or rejection:

DECLARATION OF INDEPENDENCE AND ORDINANCE dissolving the federal relations between the State of Tennessee and the United States of America.

First. We, the people of the State of Tennessee, waiving any expression of opinion as to the abstract doctrine of secession, but asserting the right, as a free and independent people, to alter, reform, or abolish our form of government in such manner as we think proper, do ordain and declare that all the laws and ordinances by which the State of Tennessee became a member of the Federal Union of the United States of America are hereby abrogated and annulled, and that all obligations on our part be withdrawn therefrom; and we do hereby resume all the rights, functions, and powers which by any of said laws and ordinances were conveyed to the Government of the United States, and absolve ourselves from all the obligations, restraints, and duties incurred thereto; and do hereby henceforth become a free, sovereign, and independent State.

Second. We furthermore declare and ordain that article 10, sections 1 and 2, of the constitution of the State of Tennessee, which requires members of the General Assembly and all officers, civil and military, to take an oath to support the Constitution of the United States be, and the same are hereby, abrogated and annulled, and all parts of the constitution of the State of Tennessee making citizenship of the United States a qualification for office and recognizing the Constitution of the United States as the supreme law of this State are in like manner abrogated and annulled.

Third. We furthermore ordain and declare that all rights acquired and vested under the Constitution of the United States, or under any act of Congress passed in pursuance thereof, or under any laws of this State, and not incompatible with this ordinance, shall remain in force and have the same effect as if this ordinance had not been passed.

SEC. 3. Be it further enacted, That said election shall be by ballot; that those voting for the declaration and ordinance shall have written or printed on their ballots "Separation," and those voting against it shall have written or printed on their ballots "No separation;" that the clerks holding said election shall keep regular scrolls of the voters as now required by law in the election of members to the General Assembly; that the clerks and judges shall certify the same, with the number of votes for "Separation" and the number of votes "No separation." The officer holding the election shall return the same to the sheriff of the county, at the county seat, on the Monday next after the election. The sheriff shall immediately make out, certify, and send to the Governor the number of votes polled, and the number of votes for "Separation" and the number "No separation," and file one of the original scrolls with the clerk of the county court; that upon comparing the vote by the Governor, in the office of the secretary of state, which shall be at least by the 24th day of June, 1861, and may be sooner if the returns are all received by the Governor, if a majority of the votes polled shall be for "Separation," the Governor shall by his proclamation make it known and declare all connection by the State of Tennessee with the Federal Union dissolved, and that Tennessee is a free, independent Government—free from all obligations to or connection with the Federal Government. And that the Governor shall cause the vote by counties to be published, the number for "Separation" and the number "No separation," whether a majority votes for "Separation" or "No separation."

SEC. 4. Be it further enacted, That, in the election to be held under the provisions of this act, upon the declaration submitted to the people, all volunteers and other persons connected with the service of this State, qualified to vote for members of the Legislature in the counties where they reside, shall be entitled to vote in any county in the State where they may be in active service, or under orders, or on parole, at the time of said election, and all other voters shall vote in the county where they reside, as now required by law in voting for members to the General Assembly.

SEC. 5. Be it further enacted, That at the same time and under the rules and regulations prescribed for the election hereinbefore ordered, the following ordinance shall be submitted to the popular vote, to wit:

AN ORDINANCE for the adoption of the Constitution of the Provisional Government of the Confederate States of America.

We, the people of Tennessee, solemnly impressed by the perils which surround us, do hereby adopt and ratify the Constitution of the Provisional Government of the Confederate States of America, ordained and established at Montgomery, Ala., on the 8th day of February, 1861, to be in force during the existence thereof or until such time as we may supersede it by the adoption of a permanent constitution.

SEC. 6. Be it further enacted, That those in favor of the adoption of said Provisional Constitution, and thereby securing to Tennessee equal representation in the deliberations and councils of the Confederate

States, shall have written or printed on their ballots the word "Representation;" those opposed, the words "No representation."

SEC. 7. Be it further enacted, That in the event the people shall adopt the Constitution of the Provisional Government of the Confederate States at the election herein ordered, it shall be the duty of the Governor forthwith to issue writs of election for delegates to represent the State of Tennessee in the said Provisional Government; that the State shall be represented by as many delegates as it was entitled to members of Congress to the recent Congress of the United States of America, who shall be elected from the several Congressional districts as now established by law, in the mode and manner now prescribed for the election of members of the Congress of the United States.

SEC. 8. Be it further enacted, That this act take effect from and after its passage.

W. C. WHITTHORNE,
Speaker of the House of Representatives.

B. L. STOVALL,
Speaker of the Senate.

Passed May 6, 1861.

(Source: U.S. War Department. *War of the Rebellion: A Compilation of the Official Records of the Union and Confederate Armies.* Ser. IV, Vol. I.)

C. ARKANSAS

1. Secession Ordinance (6 May 1861)

AN ORDINANCE to dissolve the union now existing between the State of Arkansas and the other States united with her under the compact entitled "The Constitution of the United States of America."

Whereas, in addition to the well-founded causes of complaint set forth by this convention, in resolutions adopted on the 11th of March, A.D. 1861, against the sectional party now in power at Washington City, headed by Abraham Lincoln, he has, in the face of resolutions passed by this convention pledging the State of Arkansas to resist to the last extremity any attempt on the part of such power to coerce any State that had seceded from the old Union, proclaimed to the world that war should be waged against such States until they should be compelled to submit to their rule, and large forces to accomplish this have by this same power been called out, and are now being marshaled to carry out this inhuman design; and to longer submit to such rule, or remain in the old Union of the United States, would be disgraceful and ruinous to the State of Arkansas:

Therefore we, the people of the State of Arkansas, in convention assembled, do hereby declare and ordain, and it is hereby declared and ordained, That the "ordinance and acceptance of compact" passed and approved by the General Assembly of the State of Arkansas on the 18th day of October, A.D. 1836, whereby it was by said General Assembly ordained that by virtue of the authority vested in said General Assembly by the provisions of the ordinance adopted by the convention of delegates assembled at Little Rock for the purpose of forming a constitution and system of government for said State, the propositions set forth in "An act supplementary to an act entitled An act for the admission of the State of Arkansas into the Union, and to provide for the due execution of the laws of the United States within the same, and for other purposes, were freely accepted, ratified, and irrevocably confirmed, articles of compact and union between the State of Arkansas and the United States," and all other laws and every other law and ordinance, whereby the State of Arkansas became a member of the Federal Union, be, and the same are hereby, in all respects and for every purpose herewith consistent, repealed, abrogated, and fully set aside; and the union now subsisting between the State of Arkansas and the other States, under the name of the United States of America, is hereby forever dissolved.

And we do further hereby declare and ordain, That the State of Arkansas hereby resumes to herself all rights and powers heretofore delegated to the Government of the United States of America; that her citizens are absolved from all allegiance to said Government of the United States, and that she is in full possession and exercise of all the rights and sovereignty which appertain to a free and independent State.

We do further ordain and declare, That all rights acquired and vested under the Constitution of the United States of America, or of any act or acts of Congress, or treaty, or under any law of this State, and not incompatible with this ordinance, shall remain in full force and effect, in nowise altered or impaired, and have the same effect as if this ordinance had not been passed.

Adopted and passed in open convention on the 6th day of May, A.D. 1861.

DAVID WALKER,
President of the Convention and Delegate from the County of Washington.

JAMES L. TOTTEN,
Arkansas County.

MARCUS L. HAWKINS,
Ashley County.

[AND SIXTY-EIGHT OTHERS.]

Attest.

ELIAS C. BOUDINOT,
Secretary of the Arkansas State Convention.

(Source: U.S. War Department. *War of the Rebellion: A Compilation of the Official Records of the Union and Confederate Armies.* Ser. IV, Vol. I.)

D. NORTH CAROLINA

1. Secession Ordinance (20 May 1861)

AN ORDINANCE to dissolve the union between the State of North Carolina and the other States united with her, under the compact of government entitled "The Constitution of the United States."

We, the people of the State of North Carolina in convention assembled, do declare and ordain, and it is hereby declared and ordained, That the ordinance adopted by the State of North Carolina in the convention of 1789, whereby the Constitution of the United States was ratified and adopted, and also all acts and parts of acts of the General Assembly ratifying and adopting amendments to the said Constitution, are hereby repealed, rescinded, and abrogated.

We do further declare and ordain, That the union now subsisting between the State of North Carolina and the other States, under the title of the United States of America, is hereby dissolved, and that the State of North Carolina is in full possession and exercise of all those rights of sovereignty which belong and appertain to a free and independent State.

Done in convention at the city of Raleigh this the 20th day of May, in the year of our Lord 1861, and in the eighty-fifth year of the independence of said State.
W. N. EDWARDS, *President of the Convention.*
Teste.
WALTER L. STEELE, *Secretary of Convention.*

(Source: U.S. War Department. *War of the Rebellion: A Compilation of the Official Records of the Union and Confederate Armies.* Ser. IV, Vol. I.)

XII. Lee Goes with Virginia

On 18 April 1861, Robert E. Lee was offered command of the federal army being raised to put down the rebellion, but he refused it. Lee opposed secession, but he would not fight against his native Virginia. On 20 April, Lee's one-sentence resignation from the United States Army belied his anguish over the decision. His longer letter of explanation to his superior, friend, and mentor Winfield Scott, written on the same day, revealed his distress, however. Lee's resignation became official on 25 April. By then command of Virginia's military forces had been offered to him, and he had accepted the rank of major general in the state's service. [See Lee, Robert Edward]

1. Robert E. Lee to Winfield Scott (20 April 1861)

ARLINGTON, VA, April 20, 1861.

GENERAL: Since my interview with you on the 18th inst. I have felt that I ought not longer to retain my commission in the army. I therefore tender my resignation, which I request you will recommend for acceptance. It would have been presented at once, but for the struggle it has cost me to separate myself from a service to which I have devoted the best years of my life and all the ability I possessed. During the whole of that time—more than a quarter of a century—I have experienced nothing but kindness from my superiors and a most cordial friendship from my comrades. To no one, general, have I been as much indebted as to yourself for uniform kindness and consideration, and it has always been my ardent desire to merit your approbation. I shall carry to the grave the most grateful recollections of your kind consideration, and your name and fame will always be dear to me.

Save in the defence of my native State, I never desire again to draw my sword. Be pleased to accept my most earnest wishes for the continuance of your happiness and prosperity, and believe me most truly yours,
R. E. LEE

(Source: Long, A. L. *Memoirs of Robert E. Lee: His Military and Personal History* [1983], p. 94.)

2. Secretary of State Munford to President Davis (22 April 1861)

RICHMOND, *VA., April 22, 1861.*

His Excellency JEFFERSON DAVIS, *President of the Confederate States of America:*
I am directed by the Governor to inform you that Colonel Lee is here. The Governor has sent in his nomination as commander of the land and naval forces of Virginia, with rank of major-general. Nomination will be confirmed....
GEORGE W. MUNFORD,
Secretary of State.

(Source: U.S. War Department. *War of the Rebellion: A Compilation of the Official Records of the Union and Confederate Armies.* Ser. I, Vol. LI/2.)

3. General Orders, No. 1 (23 April 1861)

HEADQUARTERS, *Richmond, Va., April 23, 1861.*

In obedience to orders from his excellency John Letcher, governor of the State, Maj. Gen. Robert E. Lee assumes command of the military and naval forces of Virginia.
R. E. LEE,
Major-General.

(Source: U.S. War Department. *War of the Rebellion: A Compilation of the Official Records of the Union and Confederate Armies.* Ser. I, Vol. 2.)

XIII. First Battle of Bull Run

The belief that one big battle would decide the war guided much thinking in the early days. Lincoln felt compelled to bring on that battle in spite of warnings that the hastily assembled volunteers were not yet ready. Nonetheless, the railroads at Manassas Junction drew the Union and Confederate armies to the banks of a creek called Bull Run in July 1861. The Manassas Gap Railroad was especially important because Confederate forces in northern Virginia were scattered between the Shenandoah Valley to the west and Manassas, Centreville, and Fairfax Court House to the east. The Manassas Gap made it possible for the South to concentrate its forces, and upon that logistical reality, as well as upon the inexperience of the rank and file on both sides, the fate of this first major battle in the East would hinge. The Union disaster left the North stunned. A day of fasting and humiliation seemed most appropriate. [See Bull Run, First Battle of]

1. Letter from General Beauregard to President Davis (17 July 1861)

MANASSAS, *July 17, 1861.*

JEFFERSON DAVIS, President of the Confederate States:

The enemy has assailed my outposts in heavy force. I have fallen back on the line of Bull Run, and will make a stand at Mitchell's Ford.

If his force is overwhelming I shall retire to the Rappahannock Railroad Bridge, saving my command for defense there and future operations. Please inform Johnston of this, via Staunton, and also Holmes. Send forward any re-enforcements at the earliest possible instant and by every possible means.

G. T. BEAUREGARD.

(Source: U.S. War Department. *War of the Rebellion: A Compilation of the Official Records of the Union and Confederate Armies.* Ser. I, Vol. 2, Chapter IX.)

2. General Orders I (20 July 1861)

HDQRS. DEP'T NORTHEASTERN VIRGINIA, *Centreville, July 20, 1861.*

The enemy has planted a battery on the Warrenton turnpike to defend the passage of Bull Run, has mined the stone bridge, and made a heavy abatis on the right bank to oppose our advance in that direction. The ford above the bridge is also guarded, whether with artillery or not is not positively known, but every indication favors the belief that he purposes defending the passage of the stream.

It is intended to turn the position, force the enemy from the road, that it may be reopened, and, if possible, destroy the railroad leading from Manassas to the valley of Virginia, where the enemy has a large force. As this may be resisted by all the force of the enemy, the troops will be disposed of as follows:

The First Division (General Tyler's), with the exception of Richardson's brigade, will move at 2.30 a.m. precisely, on the Warrenton turnpike, to threaten the passage of the bridge, but will not open fire until full daybreak.

The Second Division Hunter's will move from its camp at 2 a.m. precisely, and, led by Captain Woodbury, of the Engineers, will, after passing Cub Run, turn to the right and pass the Bull Run stream above the lower ford at Sudley Springs, and then, turning down to the left descend the stream and clear away the enemy who may be guarding the lower ford and bridge. It will then bear off to the right, to make room for the succeeding division.

The Third Division (Heintzelman's) will march at 2.30 a.m. and follow the road taken by the Second Division (Hunter's), but will cross at the lower ford after it has been turned as above, and then, going to the left, take place between the stream and Second Division.

The Fifth Division (Miles') will take position on the Centreville heights. (Richardson's brigade will for the time form part of his division, and will continue in its present position.) One brigade will be in the village and one near the present station of Richardson's brigade. This division will threaten Blackburn's Ford and remain in reserve at Centreville.

The commander will open fire with artillery only, and will bear in mind that it is a demonstration only he is to make. He will cause such defensive works, abatis, earthworks, &c., to be thrown up as will strengthen his position. Lieutenant Prime, of the Engineers, will be charged with this duty.

These movements may lead to the gravest results, and commanders of divisions and brigades should bear in mind the immense consequences involved. There must be no failure, and every effort must be made to prevent straggling. No one must be allowed to leave the ranks without special authority. After completing the movements ordered the troops must be held in order of battle, as they may be attacked at any moment.

By command of Brigadier-General McDowell:

JAMES B. FRY,
Assistant Adjutant-General.

(Source: U.S. War Department. *War of the Rebellion: A Compilation of the Official Records of the Union and Confederate Armies.* Ser. I, Vol. 2, Chapter IX.)

3. Reports of Brigadier General Irvin McDowell

CENTREVILLE, *July 21, 1861—5.45 p.m.*

We passed Bull Run. Engaged the enemy, who, it seems,

had just been re-enforced by General Johnston. We drove them for several hours, and finally routed them.

They rallied and repulsed us, but only to give us again the victory, which seemed complete. But our men, exhausted with fatigue and thirst and confused by firing into each other, were attacked by the enemy's reserves, and driven from the position we had gained, overlooking Manassas. After this the men could not be rallied, but slowly left the field. In the mean time the enemy outflanked Richardson at Blackburn's Ford, and we have now to hold Centreville till our men can get behind it. Miles' division is holding the town. It is reported Colonel Cameron is killed, Hunter and Heintzelman wounded, neither dangerously.

* * *

FAIRFAX COURT-HOUSE, *July 21, 1861*:
The men having thrown away their haversacks in the battle and left them behind, they are without food; have eaten nothing since breakfast. We are without artillery ammunition. The larger part of the men are a confused mob, entirely demoralized. It was the opinion of all the commanders that no stand could be made this side of the Potomac. We will, however, make the attempt at Fairfax Court-House. From a prisoner we learn that 20,000 from Johnston joined last night, and they march on us to-night.

* * *

FAIRFAX COURT-HOUSE, *[July]* 22, 1861.
Many of the volunteers did not wait for authority to proceed to the Potomac, but left on their own decision. They are now pouring through this place in a state of utter disorganization. They could not be prepared for action by to-morrow morning even were they willing. I learn from prisoners that we are to be pressed here to-night and to-morrow morning, as the enemy's force is very large and they are elated. I think we heard cannon on our rear guard. I think now, as all of my commanders thought at Centreville, there is no alternative but to fall back to the Potomac, and I shall proceed to do so with as much regularity as possible.
IRVIN McDOWELL.
Colonel TOWNSEND.

(Source: U.S. War Department. *War of the Rebellion: A Compilation of the Official Records of the Union and Confederate Armies.* Ser. I, Vol. 2, Chapter IX.)

4. Jefferson Davis's Telegram to Samuel Cooper (21 July 1861)
Received at [Richmond] July 21 1861
By Telegraph from Manassas July 21

Night has closed upon a hard fought field—Our forces have won a glorious victory The Enemy was routed & fled precipatately abandoning a very large amount of arms munitions Knapsacks and Baggige—The Ground was strewn for miles with those Killed & the farm houses and Grounds around were filled with his wounded—The Pursuit was continued along several routes towards Leesburg & Centerville until darkness covered the fugitives—We have captured several field Batteries & Regimental Standards & one US Flag Many prisoners have been taken—Too high praise cannot be bestowed whether for the skill of the principal officers or for the Gallantry of all the Troops—The Battle was mainly fought on our left, several miles from our field works;—our force engaged there not Exceeding Fifteen thousand (15,000) that of the Enemy Estimated at Thirty five thousand (35,000).
Jeff Davis

(Source: U.S. War Department. *War of the Rebellion: A Compilation of the Official Records of the Union and Confederate Armies.* Ser. I, Vol. II.)

5. Lincoln's Proclamation of a Day of Fasting (12 August 1861)
BY THE PRESIDENT OF THE UNITED STATES OF AMERICA: A PROCLAMATION.
Whereas a joint Committee of both Houses of Congress has waited on the President of the United States, and requested him to "recommend a day of public humiliation, prayer and fasting, to be observed by the people of the United States with religious solemnities, and the offering of fervent supplications to Almighty God for the safety and welfare of these States, His blessings on their arms, and a speedy restoration of peace:"—

And whereas it is fit and becoming in all people, at all times, to acknowledge and revere the Supreme Government of God; to bow in humble submission to his chastisements; to confess and deplore their sins and transgressions in the full conviction that the fear of the Lord is the beginning of wisdom; and to pray, with all fervency and contrition, for the pardon of their past offences, and for a blessing upon their present and prospective action:

And whereas, when our own beloved Country, once, by the blessing of God, united, prosperous and happy, is now afflicted with faction and civil war, it is peculiarly fit for us to recognize the hand of God in this terrible visitation, and in sorrowful remembrance of our own faults and crimes as a nation and as individuals, to humble ourselves before Him, and to pray for His mercy,—to pray that we may be spared further punishment, though most justly deserved; that our arms may be blessed and made effectual for the re-establishment

of law, order and peace, throughout the wide extent of our country; and that the inestimable boon of civil and religious liberty, earned under His guidance and blessing, by the labors and sufferings of our fathers, may be restored in all its original excellence:—

Therefore, I, Abraham Lincoln, President of the United States, do appoint the last Thursday in September next, as a day of humiliation, prayer and fasting for all the people of the nation. And I do earnestly recommend to all the People, and especially to all ministers and teachers of religion of all denominations, and to all heads of families, to observe and keep that day according to their several creeds and modes of worship, in all humility and with all religious solemnity, to the end that the united prayer of the nation may ascend to the Throne of Grace and bring down plentiful blessings upon our Country.

In testimony whereof, I have hereunto set my hand, and caused the Seal of the United States to be affixed, this 12th, day of August A.D. 1861, and of the Independence of the United States of America the 86th. ABRAHAM LINCOLN.
By the President:
WILLIAM H. SEWARD, Secretary of State.

(Source: Lapsley, Arthur Brooks, ed. *The Writings of Abraham Lincoln*. Vol. 7. New York: G. P. Putnam's Sons, 1906.)

XIV. The *Trent* Affair

The United States Navy's removal of Confederate envoys James Mason and John Slidell from the British mail steamer Trent *caused an international incident of the first order. It was, in fact, the Union's most serious diplomatic crisis of the Civil War. The* Trent *Affair would heighten the strain in Anglo-American relations caused by the Union's blockade of the South, and though the crisis would end peacefully, it rankled British feeling. The courtesies extended to Mason and Slidell and the deft handling of the matter by the Lincoln administration resolved matters as positively as possible. The response was favorable throughout Europe, as evidenced by the Russian attitude, reinforcing sympathy for the Union that sustained the genial dealings between the two nations for the entire war. In any event, as Charles Francis Adams, the American minister to Great Britain, observed, improvement in the North's military fortunes would have the most telling and felicitous diplomatic effect. [See Adams, Charles Francis; Diplomacy, U.S.A.; Great Britain; Mason, James Murray; Russian-American Relations; Slidell, John;* Trent *Affair]*

1. Protest by Master of the *Trent*
(14 November 1861)

PROTEST.
HER BRITANNIC MAJESTY'S CONSULATE,
Saint Thomas, West Indies.
Be it known that on this 14th of November, 1861,

before me, Robert Boyd Lamb, esq., Her Britannic Majesty's consul in the Island of Saint Thomas, personally appeared James Moir, master of the steamship *Trent,* of London, of the burden of 1,856 tons or thereabouts, and entered a protest declaring as follows:

That he sailed in the said steamship *Trent* from Havana under contract with Her Britannic Majesty's Government as a mail packet bound for Saint Thomas with Her Majesty's mails under charge of Commander Richard Williams, of Her Majesty's navy, sixty-odd passengers, $1,500,000 in specie and a valuable cargo, on the 7th instant, at 8 a.m.; that nothing particular occurred till the succeeding day, 8th instant, at about meridian, when the ship was in the narrow part of the Bahama Channel approaching the Paredon Grande Light-House, the coast of Cuba distant about 4 miles, a steamer having the appearance of a man-of-war but not showing any colors was observed ahead hove to; that the British ensign was immediately hoisted on board the *Trent* with the Royal Mail Company's distinguishing flag at the main, and on approaching the vessel ahead, which still showed no colors, at 1.05 p.m. she fired a round shot across the *Trent's* bows and then hoisted American colors, when the *Trent's* engines were immediately slowed, and while she was approaching the American vessel a shell was discharged from the latter's pivot gun across the *Trent's* bows which burst half a cable's length ahead of her. The *Trent's* engines were then stopped, when she was hailed by an officer from the American vessel and ordered to heave to.

A boat from her then came on board with armed boat's crew and an armed guard of marines accompanied by an officer in uniform of the U.S. Navy, who stated that the ship was the U.S. war steamer the San Jacinto, commanded by Captain Wilkes, and demanded a list of the passengers on board, which demand the master of the *Trent* refused to comply with, on which refusal a further force was sent for from the San Jacinto and two more boats with armed marines and armed boat's crews came on board the *Trent;* that the same officer then stated that he had orders whatever might be the consequence to arrest Messrs. Slidell, Mason, Macfarland and Eustis whom he knew were on board the ship. He was then asked by the master of the *Trent* what would be his course in case of a refusal to give up these parties, to which he replied that his orders were to take the ship in case of necessity. He was then informed by the master of the *Trent* that the passengers would not be given up unless such force was used as could not be resisted, on which Mr. Slidell stepped forward and informed the officer of the San Jacinto that the parties he demanded were before him under the protection of the British flag, and claiming same they would not consent to be taken out of the ship except by force of arms. They were then seized by order of the U.S. officers and after being allowed a short time to collect some necessaries and separate themselves from their families they were forcibly dragged out of the ship by the armed force, notwithstanding the strong and repeated protest by master of the *Trent* and Commander Williams against an act of hostility and violence committed on a vessel carrying the British flag by a ship of war of a nation on terms of peace and amity with Her Britannia Majesty's Government, to which protest the officer of the San Jacinto replied that he was obeying his orders to effect the arrest at all hazards.

That from the time the first boat was sent to the *Trent* the San Jacinto lay on the port beam about 200 yards off with her ports open, her guns (seven broadside iron-pivot) run out, tompions out and crew at quarters; that the American officer before leaving the *Trent* made a further demand that the commander of the *Trent* should proceed on board the San Jacinto, to which the reply was made that he would not leave the ship unless taken out by force of arms. Against all of which illegal, hostile and piratical acts as before detailed the said James Moir, on his own behalf as a British subject commanding a British ship engaged in the postal service of Her Majesty and on behalf of all others whom it may concern, did declare to protest as by these presents he doth solemnly protest against all and every person and persons, officers and governments directly or indirectly concerned in said illegal and hostile acts, holding them liable for all losses, damages and consequences of the same. And I, the said consul, at the request of the said James Moir, master of the said ship *Trent*, do hereby solemnly protest against the same, manner and form aforesaid.

This done, &c., at the port of Saint Thomas.
JAMES MOIR,
Master of H. M. S. Trent.

(Source: U.S. War Department. *War of the Rebellion: A Compilation of the Official Records of the Union and Confederate Armies.* Ser. II, Vol. II.)

2. Letter from James Mason to His Wife (15 November 1861)
U.S. SHIP SAN JACINTO,
Off the Capes of Virginia, November 15, 1861.

MY VERY DEAR WIFE: The date of this will show you that we have been captured, and on the way to New York the ship will put in for coal into Hampton Roads. Captain Wilkes has been good enough to say that he would give this to the officer at Fort Monroe to take its chance of being sent to Norfolk by any flag of truce that may offer. We left Havana on the 7th instant on board a British mail steamer bound for England, and on

the next day this ship fell in with us at sea and Captain Wilkes, the commander, it seems felt himself authorized to demand us from the English captain and here we are.

As to all questions arising from the circumstances attending the capture it would not become me to discuss them here as my letter will of course pass under inspection. Messrs. Eustis, Slidell, Macfarland and myself were taken. The ladies proceeded on the voyage to England. Of course there will be all sorts of speculations in the newspapers concerning our capture and its consequences but I have only to say, my dear wife, that you should not permit your mind to be affected by them, and draw no other inference from my silence concerning them except that I of necessity write under constraint…. We have been treated with every possible courtesy and respect by Captain Wilkes and his officers and are guests in the cabin….
From yours, most affectionately, forever,
J. M. MASON.

(Source: U.S. War Department. *War of the Rebellion: A Compilation of the Official Records of the Union and Confederate Armies.* Suspected and Disloyal Persons. Case of Mason, Slidell, Macfarland and Eustis. Confederate Reports. Ser. II, Vol. II.)

3. Instruction from Prince Gortchakoff to Eduard de Stoeckl (9 January 1862)
Saint Petersburg, *January 9*, 1862.
M. De Stoeckl, *&C.*

SIR: The Federal Government cannot doubt the lively interest with which we have followed the diverse phases of the incident which has lately held in suspense the anxious attention of both worlds.

His Majesty the Emperor has not presumed too much upon the wisdom of the cabinet of Washington in resting convinced that it would consult only in these grave conjunctures sentiments of justice and of conciliation and the important interests of the country.

It is with the highest satisfaction that his Imperial Majesty has found his foresight confirmed by the determination which the Federal Government has just taken.

Although it has not yet come to our knowledge except through the channel of the newspapers our august master has been unwilling to delay transmitting to the President the sentiments with which his Imperial Majesty has appreciated this proof of moderation and equity so much the more meritorious because it was rendered the more difficult by national impulses.

I have no need to add, sir, that by remaining faithful to the political principles which she has always maintained even when those principles were turned against her and by abstaining from invoking in her turn the

benefit of doctrines which she has always repudiated the American nation has given a proof of political integrity which gives her incontestable titles to the esteem and gratitude of all governments interested in seeing the peace of the seas maintained, and the principles of right pervading over those of force in international relations, for the repose of the world, the progress of civilization and the welfare of humanity.

His Majesty the Emperor is gratified in the hope that the same wisdom and the same moderation which dictated to the Federal Government its late decision will alike preside over its steps amid the internal difficulties with which it finds itself at this moment striving.

The event must have shown to it how much these difficulties affect its political standing; how much they are of a nature to encourage aspirations connected with a diminution of the power of the United States, and how much consequently it is for its interest to get through with them at the earliest day.

The Emperor is persuaded that the statesmen who have understood how to appreciate from a point of view so exalted the external political interests of their country will understand equally well how to ground their internal policy above popular passions.

Please to convey to the Federal Government these hopes of our august master; and reiterate the assurance of the satisfaction with which his Imperial Majesty would see the American Union again regain strength through measures of conciliation which may regulate the present without bequeathing to the future any seeds of discord, and again enter upon the condition of power and prosperity which we desire for it not only because of the cordial sympathy which unites the two countries but moreover because the maintenance of its power interests in the highest degree the general political equilibrium.

Receive, sir, the assurance of my very distinguished consideration.
GORTCHAKOFF.

(Source: U.S. War Department. *War of the Rebellion: A Compilation of the Official Records of the Union and Confederate Armies.* Ser. II, Vol. II.)

4. Charles Francis Adams in Regard to the *Trent* Affair (10 January 1862)

LEGATION OF THE UNITED STATES, London, January 10, 1862.

Hon. WILLIAM H. SEWARD, Secretary of State, Washington.

SIR: Though not yet favored with any information from the Department respecting the course of the proceedings between the two Governments in regard to the case of the Trent at Washington I am bound to believe from what I see in the newspapers that the difference has been settled by the release of the captives.

It is with great satisfaction that I gather from the abstract of the correspondence which has been communicated by telegraph that the Government has adhered to the principle for which it has so long contended and in the recognition of which the whole civilized world will now concur. Considering the remarkable unanimity which has been shown in the judgment of the merits of this case throughout Europe the step that has been taken will meet with very general approbation. The satisfaction expressed in this city everywhere, excepting among the small society of the Confederate emissaries and the party which habitually looks to war as an attractive pastime, stands in remarkable contrast with the feelings which animated almost everybody only six weeks ago. Not many, however, have yet opened their eyes to the conviction of the fact that the apparent victory of Great Britain involves in reality the necessary surrender of one of her most odious assumptions of power over the ocean. In this light it is not difficult to comprehend the policy of France which sacrifices no consistency whilst it more surely places a new ligature around the maritime supremacy of its great rival.

A consequence of this result is probably a continuance of the mission with which the Government has honored me for some time longer. But the questions immediately arise how long and under what promise of future usefulness? In order to answer these it is necessary to take a brief survey of the ground we occupy. Parliament is summoned to assemble for the dispatch of business on the 6th of February. I have reason to believe that arrangements predicated upon a particular contingency had been made to bring on an early discussion of the American difficulty with a view to press a direct interference with the blockade and a recognition of the Confederate States. I regret to learn that the first of these measures has found favor in some quarters from which I had hoped better things. The only question to consider is whether the settlement of the case of the Trent will have much effect in altering the presentation of the programme or in preventing its adoption.

It is too early to determine what may be the degree of the reaction in popular opinion but there is no reason to doubt it will be considerable. Besides which the position of the ministry has been so much fortified by its success as to place its continuance at least for another year almost beyond doubt. It will therefore be in a situation to act with firmness and independence should it be inclined to resist any hasty movements. Whether that inclination does or does not exist is the problem. If I were to judge from the temper shown in certain presses believed to be prompted by the prime minister I should augur a very unfavorable result. On the other

hand I think I had a right to infer from the language of Lord Russell in our very latest conference that there was no disposition to embarrass us so long as there was a reasonable prospect of our success. Besides this so marked has been the late development of a disinclination to a war with the United States among the quiet and religious citizens of the middle classes, and particularly when its practical effect would be the establishment of a slave-holding oligarchy with which they have no sympathy whatever, that any policy entered into with an apparent desire to revive that measure for the benefit of the latter would scarcely meet with a second response like the last. From all these considerations I am inclined to conclude that without the occurrence of any new disturbing matter the probabilities are rather in favor of the continuance of diplomatic relations for some time to come.

Yet so doubtful do I regard it that I cannot help wishing for the occurrence of some decisive event in the war which would completely turn the current of opinion in our favor. It is not for me to interfere in any manner with the course of the operations in the field. I am well aware of the difficulties in the way of action and entertain too lively a recollection of the consequences of the disaster at Bull Run to favor precipitation anywhere. At the same time I cannot fail to perceive the force of the argument constantly pressed here in a community which measures military results by the sole standard of success of the apparent inability to command it. I feel that one clear victory at home might perhaps save us a foreign war, and so feeling it can scarcely be wondered at if I look forward to it with more than ordinary anxiety. An advance into the rebellious States would be as productive of sensible results in Parliament here as on the spot itself, whilst a decided triumph would put a more effective stop to Confederate operations in England than all the labors of orators and statesmen and philosophers of both countries combined.

I have the honor to be, sir, your obedient servant, CHARLES FRANCIS ADAMS.

(Source: U.S. War Department. *War of the Rebellion: A Compilation of the Official Records of the Union and Confederate Armies*. Ser. II, Vol. II.)

XV. George B. McClellan Takes Command

The days after the Union calamity at First Bull Run were desperate ones. It was in this fretful atmosphere that George B. McClellan appeared as the Union's savior. Summoned from a successful campaign in the mountains of western Virginia, McClellan arrived in Washington on 26 July 1861 to take command of a demoralized army. Tirelessly working to replenish ranks and boost morale, he created the famous Army of the Potomac. Yet an overarching ego and a tendency to clash with superiors flawed McClellan. He

was candidly immodest with his wife and openly contemptuous of General-in-Chief Winfield Scott, eventually to the point of forcing the latter's retirement in November 1861. [See McClellan, George Brinton; Scott, Winfield]

1. Lorenzo Thomas to George B. McClellan (22 July 1861)

ADJUTANT-GENERAL OFFICE, *Washington, D.C., July 22, 1861.*

General GEORGE B. McCLELLAN, *Beverly, Va.:*
Circumstances make your presence here necessary. Charge Rosecrans or some other general with your present department and come hither without delay.
L. THOMAS.
Adjutant-General.

(Source: U.S. War Department. *War of the Rebellion: A Compilation of the Official Records of the Union and Confederate Armies*. Ser. I, Vol. II.)

2. George B. McClellan to Mary Ellen McClellan (27 July 1861)

July 27/61 Washington D.C. Saturday

I have been assigned to the command of a Division—composed of Depts of N.E. Va (that under McDowell) & that of Washington (now under Mansfield)—neither of them like it much—especially Mansfield, but I think they must ere long become accustomed to it, as there is no help for it. . . .

I find myself in a new & strange position here—Presdt, Cabinet, Genl Scott & all deferring to me—by some strange operation of magic I seem to have become *the* power of the land. I almost think that were I to win some small success now I could become Dictator or anything else that might please me—but nothing of that kind would please me—*therefore I won't* be Dictator. Admirable self denial! I see already the main causes of our recent failure—I am *sure* that I can remedy these & am confident that I can lead these armies of men to victory once more. I start tomorrow very early on a tour through the lines on the other side of the river—it will occupy me all day long & a rather fatiguing ride it will be—but I will be able to make up my mind as to the state of things. Refused invitations to dine today from Genl Scott & four Secy's—had too many things to attend to. . . .

I will endeavor to enclose with this the "thanks of Congress" which please preserve. I feel very proud of it. Genl Scott objected to it on the ground that it ought to be accompanied by a gold medal. I cheerfully acquiesce in the Thanks by themselves, hoping to win the medal by some other action, & the sword by some other fait d' éclat.

(Source: Stephen W. Sears, ed., *The Civil War Papers of George B. McClellan: Selected Correspondence, 1860–1865* [1989], p. 70.)

3. Winfield Scott to Simon Cameron (4 October 1861)

HEADQUARTERS OF THE ARMY,
Washington, D.C., October 4, 1861.

Hon. SIMON CAMERON, *Secretary of War:*
SIR: You are, I believe, aware that I hailed the arrival here of Major-General McClellan as an event of happy consequence to the country and the Army. Indeed, if I did not call for him, I heartily approved of the suggestion, and gave him the most cordial reception and support.

He, however, had hardly entered upon his new duties when, encouraged to communicate directly with the President and certain members of the cabinet, he in a few days forgot that he had any intermediate commander, and has now long prided himself in treating me with uniform neglect, running into disobedience of orders.

Of the smaller matters—neglects—though in themselves grave military offenses, I need not speak in the face of the following:

First. To suppress an irregularity more conspicuous in Major-General McClellan than in any other officer I published the following:

GENERAL ORDERS No. 17.
HEADQUARTERS OF THE ARMY,
Washington, D.C., September 16, 1861.
There are irregularities in the correspondence of the Army which need prompt correction. It is highly important that junior officers on duty be not permitted to correspond with the General-in-Chief or other commander on current official business except through intermediate commanders; and the same rule applies to correspondence with the President direct or with him through the Secretary of War, unless it be by the special invitation or request of the President.
By command of Lieutenant-General Scott:
E. D. TOWNSEND,
Assistant Adjutant-General.

With this order fresh in his memory, Major-General McClellan addressed two important communications to the Secretary of War on, respectively, the 19th and 20th of the same month, over my head, and how many since to the Secretary, and even to the President direct, I have not inquired, but many, I have no doubt, besides daily oral communications with the same high functionaries—all without my knowledge.

Second. To correct another case of gross neglect I

the same day caused to be addressed to Major-General McClellan the following order:

HEADQUARTERS OF THE ARMY,
Washington, D.C., September 26, 1861.

Major-General MCCLELLAN, *U.S. Army,*
Commanding Department of the Potomac:
The commanding general of the Army of the Potomac will cause the positions, State, and numbers of troops under him to be reported at once to general headquarters, by divisions, brigades, and independent regiments or detachments, which General report will be followed by reports of new troops as they arrive, with the dispositions made of them, together with all material changes which may take place in the same army.
By command of General Scott:
E. D. TOWNSEND,
Assistant Adjutant-General.

Eighteen days have now elapsed and not the slightest respect has been shown to either of those orders by Major-General McClellan. Perhaps he will say, in respect to the latter, it has been difficult for him to procure exact returns of divisions, brigades, &c. No doubt; but why not have given me proximate returns; such as he so eagerly furnishes the President and certain Secretaries?

Has, then, a senior no corrective power over a junior officer in case of such persistent neglect and disobedience? The remedy by arrest and trial before a court-martial would probably soon cure the evil. But it has been feared that a conflict of authority near the head of the Army would be highly encouraging to the enemies and depressing to the friends of the Union; hence my long forbearance; and, continuing (though but nominally) on duty, I shall try to hold out till the arrival of Major-General Halleck, when, as his presence will give me increased confidence in the safety of the Union—and being as I am unable to ride in the saddle or to walk by reason of dropsy in my feet and legs and paralysis in the small of my back—I shall definitively retire from the Army.

I have the honor to be, with high respect, your most obedient servant,
WINFIELD SCOTT.

(Source: U.S. War Department. *War of the Rebellion: A Compilation of the Official Records of the Union and Confederate Armies.* Ser. I, Vol. LI/1.)

XVI. Disaster at Ball's Bluff

Ball's Bluff was a small battle, but as only the second consequential clash in the East, it accordingly received considerable notice in both North and South. The tragedy directly touched

the Lincoln family. Oregon senator Edward Baker, a close friend of Lincoln and his deceased son Eddie's namesake, was killed at Ball's Bluff. The defeat at Ball's Bluff also tarnished the McClellan mystique. In the battle's wake, Congress created the Joint Committee on the Conduct of the War, which often badgered and sometimes persecuted those it perceived as sympathetic to the Confederacy and slavery. The ordeal of General Charles P. Stone, who became the scapegoat for the debacle, was one of the first results of the committee's labor. [See Ball's Bluff, Battle of; Joint Committee on the Conduct of the War; Stone, Charles P.]

1. Special Orders (20 October 1861)
HEADQUARTERS CORPS OF OBSERVATION,
Poolesville, October 20, 1861—10.30 p.m.

Colonel Devens will land opposite Harrison's Island with five companies of his regiment, and proceed to surprise the camp of the enemy discovered by Captain Philbrick in the direction of Leesburg. The landing and march will be effected with silence and rapidity.

Colonel Lee, Twentieth Massachusetts Volunteers, will immediately after Colonel Devens' departure occupy Harrison's Island with four companies of his regiment, and will cause the four-oared boat to be taken across the island to the point of departure of Colonel Deven.

One company will be thrown across to occupy the heights on the Virginia shore after Colonel Devens' departure to cover his return.

Two mountain howitzers will be taken silently up the tow-path, and carried to the opposite side of the island under the orders of Colonel Lee.

Colonel Devens will attack the camp of the enemy at daybreak, and, having routed them, will pursue them as far as he deems prudent, and will destroy the camp, if practicable, before returning. He will make all the observations possible on the country; will, under all circumstances, keep his command well in hand, and not sacrifice them to any supposed advantage of rapid pursuit.

Having accomplished this duty, Colonel Devens will return to his present position: unless he shall see one on the Virginia side, near the river, which he can undoubtedly hold until re-enforced, and one which can be successfully held against largely superior numbers. In such case he will hold on and report.
CHAS. P. STONE,
Brigadier General.

2. General Orders, No. 32 (25 October 1861)
HDQRS. ARMY OF THE POTOMAC,
Washington, October 25, 1861.

The major-general commanding the Army of the Potomac desires to offer his thanks, and to express his admiration of their conduct, to the officers and men of the detachments of the Fifteenth and Twentieth Massachusetts, First California, and Tammany Regiments, the First U.S. Artillery, and Rhode Island Battery, engaged in the affair of Monday last near Harrison's Island. The gallantry and discipline there displayed deserved a more fortunate result; but situated as these troops were—cut off alike from retreat and re-enforcements, and attacked by an overwhelming force, 500 against 1,700—it was not possible that the issue could have been successful. Under happier auspices such devotion will insure victory. The general commanding feels increased confidence in General Stoners division, and is sure that when they next meet the enemy they will fully retrieve this check, for which they are not accountable.
By command of Major-General McClellan:
S. WILLIAMS,
Assistant Adjutant-General.

3. Charles P. Stone to Benjamin F. Wade (6 March 1863)
WASHINGTON, *D.C., March 6, 1863.*

SIR: During my recent examination (27th ultimo) you asked me the question, "Who arrested you?" My answer was long, and referred to a number of papers which I had not with me. As my answer indicated, I am yet in doubt as to whom the responsibility of the arrest attaches; but I inclose copies of such papers (ten in number) as are now in my possession, and respectfully place them at the disposition of the honorable the committee.

Very respectfully, I am, sir, your most obedient servant,
CHAS. P. STONE,
Brigadier-General.
[Inclosures.]
ORDER, No.——

Washington City, D.C., January 28, 1862.
Ordered, That the general commanding be, and is hereby, directed to relieve Brig. Gen. C. P. Stone from command of his division in the Army of the Potomac forthwith, and that he be placed in arrest and kept in close custody until further orders.
EDWIN M. STANTON,
Secretary of War.

HEADQUARTERS OF THE ARMY,
Washington, February 8, 1862.
GENERAL: You will please at once arrest Brig. Gen. Charles P. Stone, U.S. volunteers, and retain him in close custody, sending him under suitable escort by the first train to Fort Lafayette, where he will be placed in

charge of the commanding officer. See that he has no communication with any one from the time of his arrest.

Very respectfully, yours,
 GEO. B. McCLELLAN,
Major-General.
 Brig. Gen. ANDREW PORTER,
Provost-Marshal.

HEADQUARTERS OF THE ARMY,
Washington, February 8, 1862.
SIR: This will be handed to you by the officer sent in charge of Brig. Gen. Charles P. Stone, who is under close arrest.

You will please confine General Stone in Fort Lafayette, allowing him the comforts due his rank, and allowing him no communication with any one by letter or otherwise, except under the usual supervision.
 GEO. B. McCLELLAN,
Major-General.

WASHINGTON, *D.C., February 9, 1862.*
GENERAL: This morning about 1 o'clock I was arrested by Brigadier-General Sykes, commanding city guard, and made a close prisoner by order, as I was informed, of the Major-General Commanding-in-Chief.

Conscious of being and having been at all times a faithful soldier of the United States, I most respectfully request that I may be furnished, at as early a moment as practicable, with a copy of whatever charges may have been preferred against me and the opportunity of promptly meeting them.

Very respectfully, I am, general, your most obedient servant,
 CHAS. P. STONE,
Brigadier-General.
 Brig. Gen. S. WILLIAMAS,
Assistant Adjutant-General General, Hdqrs. Army of the Potomac.

FORT HAMILTON, *BAY OF NEW YORK,*
April 5, 1862.
COLONEL: I respectfully request of you a copy of the order by authority of which, on the 10th of February last, I was confined in Fort Lafayette.

Very respectfully, I am, colonel, your most obedient servant,
 CHAS. P. STONE,
Brigadier-General.
 Lieut. Col. MARTIN BURKE,
Fort Hamilton.
P. S.—I would also request copies of any letters which have passed between any authority in Washington and yourself relating to the nature and place of my confinement since that date.

HEADQUARTERS ARMY OF THE POTOMAC,
September 7, 1862.
SIR: I have been applied to by General Stone for permission to serve with the Army during the impending movements, even if only as a spectator.

I have no doubt as to the loyalty and devotion of General Stone, but am unwilling to use his services unless I know that it meets the approval of Government.

I not only have no objection to his employment in this army, but, more than that, would be glad to avail myself of his services as soon as circumstances permit.

Very truly, yours,
 GEO. B. McCLELLAN,
Major-General.
 Hon. E. M. STANTON,
Secretary of War.

WASHINGTON, *D.C., September 25, 1862.*
GENERAL: I have the honor to submit the following for the consideration of the General-in-Chief:

On the 8th February, 1862, about the hour of midnight, I was arrested by an armed guard, commanded by Brig. Gen. George Sykes, and placed in close confinement, under guard, in the quarters of the officers of the provost-marshal's guard.

At the time of the arrest I asked of General Sykes the cause, but were informed that he was perfectly ignorant of it.

Early on the morning of the 9th February I addressed the following letter to the headquarters of the Army of the Potomac, viz:

WASHINGTON, *D.C., February 9, 1862.*
GENERAL: This morning, about 1 o'clock, I was arrested by Brigadier-General Sykes, commanding City Guard, and made a close prisoner, by order, as I was informed, of the Major-General Commanding-in-Chief. Conscious of being and having been at all times a faithful soldier of the United States, I most respectfully request that I may be furnished, at as early a moment as practicable, with a copy of whatever charges may have been preferred against me, and the opportunity of promptly meeting them.

Very respectfully, I am, general, your most obedient servant,
 CHAS. P. STONE,
Brigadier-General Volunteers.
 Brig. Gen. S. WILLIAMS,
Assistant Adjutant-General, Headquarters Army of the Potomac.

The above letter was carried by General Sykes to General Williams early in the morning of the 9th February. No answer has ever been received by me.

During the night of February 9 I was conveyed, in charge of a lieutenant and two police officers, to Fort Hamilton, New York Harbor, and turned over to the custody of Lieut. Col. Martin Burke, Third Artillery, who immediately sent me in charge of a guard to Fort Lafayette, where I was delivered to Lieutenant Wood, Ninth Infantry.

At Fort Lafayette the money was taken from my pockets, and I was placed in solitary confinement in a room ordinarily used as enlisted-men's quarters, where I was kept forty-nine days, no letter being allowed to reach or to leave me without inspection.

During this confinement I applied at different times, through the proper channels, for speedy trial, for charges, for change of locality, and access to the records of my office and headquarters to enable me to prepare for trial, &c., but never received any response to any of my communications.

After forty-nine days I was transferred to Fort Hamilton, and allowed opportunities of obtaining air and exercise, but the same restrictions were continued on my correspondence.

I applied for a copy of the order placing me in confinement, but could not obtain it, I applied to my custodian to learn what crime was alleged against me, and he informed me that he knew nothing of it.

After thus awaiting charges more than two months, I applied for suspension of arrest and opportunity to serve before Yorktown, but received no reply.

Again, on the occasion of the retreat of our forces from the Shenandoah Valley, I applied for suspension of arrest and opportunity to serve, but received no reply.

On the 4th of July I again applied, but received no reply.

I applied for an extension of limits, but received only the reply that the Secretary of War was absent, and no extension could be given until his return.

Finally, on the 16th August, 1862, after one hundred and eighty-nine days of confinement, I was fully released from arrest, without any order what to do.

I immediately reported myself for duty.

I would respectfully represent that the law requires, peremptorily, that when an officer is placed in arrest, it shall be the duty of the officer who orders the arrest to see that the officer arrested is furnished within eight days with a copy of the charges against him. Two hundred and twenty-eight days have now elapsed since my arrest, and not only have no charges been furnished me, but no allegation of crime to justify arrest has been made to me or to those who had me in custody.

I now respectfully apply again to the General-in-Chief for a copy of any charges or allegations which may have been made against me and the opportunity of promptly meeting them, and in case trial cannot be

had, I would respectfully ask that at least the charges may be furnished, so that I may know what falsehoods require refutation and witnesses I shall require to accomplish the refutation.

It is perhaps superfluous for me to call attention to the fact that those who have, served under my orders, and therefore must be the witnesses of my conduct in service, have been falling in battle and by disease by hundreds and thousands since the date of my arrest. So great have been the casualties, that the command from which I was taken is now reduced more than one-half.

Very respectfully, I am, general, your most obedient servant,
CHAS. P. STONE,
Brigadier-General.
Brig. Gen. L. THOMAS,
Adjutant-General General U. S. Army.

HEADQUARTERS OF THE ARMY, *Washington,*
September 30, 1862.
GENERAL: Your letter of the 25th to the Adjutant-General of the Army has been referred to me for reply.

I learn from the Secretary of War that the order releasing you from Fort Hamilton also released you from arrest. You therefore are no longer under arrest, but as you have not been assigned to me for duty, I can give you no orders.

I have no official information of the cause of your arrest, but I understood that it was made by the orders of the President. No charges or specifications are, so far as I can ascertain, on file against you.

The matter, I learn, is to be immediately investigated, and copies of charges, when preferred, will be furnished you by the Judge-Advocate-General.
Very respectfully, your obedient servant,
H. W. HALLECK,
General-in-Chief.
Brig. Gen. CHARLES P. STONE,
Washington.

WASHINGTON, *D.C., December* 1, 1862.
GENERAL: At the time of my arrest and imprisonment, in February last, the officer who effected it (Brigadier-General Sykes) claimed to act under your order, although he exhibited no other authority than an armed force.

Under the eleventh section of the act of Congress approved July 17, 1862, it is made the duty of any officer who shall order the arrest of another to see that a copy of the charges be furnished to the arrested officer within eight days of the date of the arrest; and by proviso the requirements of the section were made applicable to all officers under arrest at the date of the passage of the act.

Under this law I respectfully request that you will cause me to be furnished with a copy of the charges which led to my arrest, and which I have repeatedly asked for, through the ordinary channels of official communication, without success.

I have the honor to remain, general, with much respect, your most obedient servant,

CHAS. P. STONE,
Brigadier-General.

Maj. Gen. GEORGE B. McCLELLAN,
U. S. Army, New York.

NEW YORK, December 5, 1862.
GENERAL: I have the honor to acknowledge the receipt of your letter of the 1st instant.

The order for your arrest in February last was given by the Secretary of War. I had the order in his handwriting several days before it was finally carried into effect.

When the order was first given by the Secretary, he informed me that it was at the solicitation of the Congressional Committee on the Conduct of the War and based upon testimony taken by them.

On the evening when you were arrested I submitted to the Secretary the written result of the examination of a refugee from Leesburg. This information, to a certain extent, agreed with the evidence stated to have been taken by the committee, and upon its being imparted to the Secretary he again instructed me to cause you to be arrested, which I at once did.

At the time I stated to the Secretary that I could not from the information in my possession understand how charges could be framed against you; that the case was too indefinite.

On several occasions after your arrest I called the attention of the Secretary to the propriety of giving you a prompt trial, but the reply always was either that there was no time to attend to the case or that the Congressional committee were still engaged in collecting additional evidence in your' case, and were not yet fully prepared to frame the charges.

I am, general, very respectfully, your obedient servant,

GEO. B. McCLELLAN,
Major-General, U. S. Army.

Brig. Gen. CHARLES P. STONE,
U. S. Volunteers, Washington, D.C.

[NOTE.]—On the receipt of General McClellan's letter of December 5, 1862, General Stone addressed a letter to him, asking that he might be furnished with the name of the Leesburg refugee referred to and a copy of his statement. The following reply was received:

WILLARD'S HOTEL, *Washington, D.C.,*
December 10, 1862.

GENERAL: I am directed by General McClellan to acknowledge the receipt of your note of December 8, 1862.

The name of the refugee he does not recollect, and the last time he recollects seeing the statement was at the War Department, immediately previous to your arrest. If he has a copy, it is among his official papers, which papers are *en route* for New York, and will be examined on his return, and if the paper referred to be found among them, he will furnish you with a copy.

I am, general, very respectfully, your obedient servant,

N. B. SWEITZER,
Lieutenant-Colonel and Aide-de-Camp.

Brig. Gen. CHARLES P. STONE,
U.S. Volunteers.

[NOTE.]—The statement referred to within has not up to this date been furnished me.

CHAS. P. STONE,
Brigadier-General General.

MARCH 6, 1863.

(Source: U.S. War Department. *War of the Rebellion: A Compilation of the Official Records of the Union and Confederate Armies.* Ser. I, Vol. V [S# 5].)

XVII. To Shiloh and Beyond

A. FORTS HENRY AND DONELSON FALL

By the spring of 1862, the Confederacy had stretched its resources beyond their limits in trying to place a cordon against Northern invasion across its vast western expanse. Albert Sidney Johnston's "Long Kentucky Line" was actually a makeshift dispersal of forces that extended from eastern Tennessee to western Arkansas. Breaking this line as a prelude to controlling the Mississippi River became the main thrust of Union strategy in the region, and Ulysses S. Grant came to prominence by successfully advancing the plan with his capture of two key Confederate forts on the Tennessee and Cumberland rivers. His terms for capitulation at Fort Donelson against his old friend Simon Bolivar Buckner would make him a Northern hero when they were in exceedingly short supply. [See Fort Donelson; Fort Henry; Grant, Ulysses Simpson]

1. Foote's Report of the Capture of Fort Henry [Excerpts] (6 February 1862)

CAIRO, Ill., February 7, 1862.

SIR: I have the honor to report that on the 6th instant, at 12.30 o'clock p.m., I made an attack on Fort Henry, on the Tennessee River, with the iron-clad gunboats *Cincinnati,* Commander Stembel; the flagship *Essex,* Commander Porter; *Carondelet,* Commander Walker, and *St. Louis,* Lieutenant-Commander Paulding; also taking with me the three old gunboats, *Conestoga*, Lieutenant-Commander Phelps; the *Tyler*, Lieutenant-Commander Gwin, and the *Lexington*, Lieutenant-Commander Shirk, as a second division, in charge or Lieutenant-Commander Phelps, which took position astern and inshore of the armed boats, doing good execution there during the action, while the armed boats were placed in the first order of steaming, approaching the fort in a parallel line.

The fire was opened at 1,700 yards' distance from the flag-ship, which was followed by the other gunboats, and responded to by the fort. As we approached the fort under slow steaming till we reached within 600 yards of the rebel batteries the fire both from the gunboats and fort increased in rapidity and accuracy of range. At twenty minutes before the rebel flag was struck the *Essex* unfortunately received a shot in her boilers, which resulted in wounding, by scalding, 29 officers and men, including Commander Porter, as will be seen in the inclosed list of casualties. The *Essex* then necessarily dropped out of line astern, entirely disabled, and unable to continue the fight, in which she had so gallantly participated until the sad catastrophe. The firing continued with unabated rapidity and effect upon the three gunboats as they continued still to approach the fort with their destructive fire until the rebel flag was hauled down, after a very severe and closely-contested action of one hour and fifteen minutes.

The plan of the attack, so far as the Army reaching the rear of the fort to make a demonstration simultaneously with the Navy, was prevented by the excessively muddy roads and high stage of water, preventing the arrival of our troops until some time after I had taken possession of the fort. . . .

The armed gunboats resisted effectually the shot of the enemy when striking the casemate. The *Cincinnati* (flag-ship) received 31 shots, the *Essex* 15, the *St. Louis* 7, and the *Carondelet* 6, killing 1 and wounding 9 in the *Cincinnati* and killing 1 in the *Essex,* while the casualties in the latter from steam amounted to 28 in number. The *Carondelet* and *St. Louis* met with no casualties. The steamers were admirably handled by their commanders and officers, presenting only their bow guns to the enemy, to avoid exposure of the vulnerable parts of their vessels. . . .

Very respectfully, your obedient servant,
A. H. FOOTE,
Flag-Officer, Commanding U. S. Naval Forces
Western Waters.
Major-General HALLECK,
Commanding Department of the Missouri.

(Source: U.S. War Department. *War of the Rebellion: A Compilation of the Official Records of the Union and Confederate Armies.* Ser. I, Vol. 7.)

2. Grant's Unconditional Surrender Demand at Fort Donelson (16 February 1862)

HEADQUARTERS, *Fort Donelson, February* 16, 1862.

SIR: In consideration of all the circumstances governing the present situation of affairs at this station I propose to the commanding officers of the Federal forces the appointment of commissioners to agree upon terms of capitulation of the forces and post under my command, and in that view suggest an armistice until 12 o'clock to-day.
I am, sir, very respectfully, your obedient servant,
S. B. BUCKNER,
Brigadier-General, C. S. Army.
Brig. Gen. U.S. GRANT,
Commanding U.S. Forces near Fort Donelson.

* * *

HEADQUARTERS ARMY IN THE FIELD,
Camp near Fort Donelson, February 16, 1862.

SIR: Yours of this date, proposing armistice and appointment of commissioners to settle terms of capitulation, is just received. No terms except unconditional and immediate surrender can be accepted. I propose to move immediately upon your works.
I am, sir, very respectfully, your obedient servant,
U.S. GRANT,
Brigadier-General, Commanding.
General S. B. BUCKNER,
Confederate Army.

* * *

H E A D Q U A R T E R S ,
Dover, Tenn., February 16, 1862.

SIR: The distribution of the forces under my command incident to an unexpected change of commanders and the overwhelming force under your command compel me, notwithstanding the brilliant success of the Confederate arms yesterday, to accept the ungenerous and unchivalrous terms which you propose.
I am, sir, your very obedient servant,
S. B. BUCKNER,
Brigadier-General, C. S. Army.
Brig. Gen. U.S. GRANT,
U. S. A.

(Source: U.S. War Department. *War of the Rebellion: A Compilation of the Official Records of the Union and Confederate Armies.* Ser. I, Vol. VII.)

B. BATTLE OF SHILOH

After the fall of Forts Henry and Donelson, the federal Army of the Tennessee moved south toward Corinth, Mississippi, pausing to encamp on the west bank of the Tennessee River just north of the Mississippi state line. At Corinth, Confederate forces that had fallen back from Memphis and Nashville concentrated with other units brought from places as diverse as Mobile, Pensacola, and New Orleans. Under Albert Sidney Johnston with P. G. T. Beauregard as second-in-command, this Confederate army marched north and surprised Grant's forces at Shiloh. It was, up to that time, the biggest battle fought on American soil. For two days in April, 100,000 soldiers in all fought near a steamboat docking point called Pittsburg Landing. The defeat for the Confederacy was compounded by the death on the first day of Johnston, a loss that many regarded as irreplaceable. [See Shiloh, Battle of]

1. P. G. T. Beauregard Describes the First Day

At 5.30 a.m. our lines and columns were in motion, all animated, evidently, by a promising spirit. The front line was engaged at once but advanced steadily, followed in due order, with equal resolution and steadiness, by the other lines, which were brought successively into action with rare skill, judgment, and gallantry by the several corps commanders as the enemy made a stand, with his masses rallied for the struggle for his encampments.

Like an Alpine avalanche our troops moved forward, despite the determined resistance of the enemy, until after 6 p.m., when we were in possession of all his encampments between Owl and Lick Creeks but one; nearly all of his field artillery; about 30 flags, colors, and standards; over 3,000 prisoners, including a division commander (General Prentiss), and several brigade commanders; thousands of small-arms; an immense supply of subsistence, forage, and munitions of war, and a large amount of means of transportation—all the substantial fruits of a complete victory, such, indeed, as rarely have followed the most successful battles; for never was an army so well provided as that of our enemy.

The remnant of his army had been driven in utter disorder to the immediate vicinity of Pittsburg, under the shelter of the heavy guns of his ironclad gunboats, and we remained undisputed masters of his well-selected, admirably-provided cantonments, after ever twelve hours of obstinate conflict with his forces, who had been beaten from them and the contiguous covert, but only by a sustained onset of all the men we could bring into action.

Our loss was heavy, as will appear from the accompanying return, marked B. Our commander-in-chief, General A. S. Johnston, fell mortally wounded, and died on the field at 2.30 p.m., after having shown the highest qualities of the commander and a personal intrepidity that inspired all around him and gave resistless impulsion to his columns at critical moments.

The chief command then devolved upon me, though at the time I was greatly prostrated and suffering from the prolonged sickness with which I had been afflicted since early in February. The responsibility was one which in my physical condition I would have gladly avoided, though cast upon me when our forces were successfully pushing the enemy back upon the Tennessee River, and though supported on the immediate field by such corps commanders as Major-Generals Polk, Bragg, and Hardee, and Brigadier-General Breckinridge, commanding the reserve.

It was after 6 p.m., as before said, when the enemy's last position was carried, and his forces finally broke and sought refuge behind a commanding eminence covering the Pittsburg Landing, not more than half a mile distant, and under the guns of the gunboats, which opened on our eager columns a fierce and annoying fire with shot and shell of the heaviest description.

Darkness was close at hand. Officers and men were exhausted by a combat of over twelve hours without food, and jaded by the march of the preceding day through mud and water. It was, therefore, impossible to collect the rich and opportune spoils of war scattered broadcast on the field left in our possession, and impracticable to make any effective dispositions for their removal to the rear.

I accordingly established my headquarters at the church of Shiloh, in the enemy's encampments, with Major-General Bragg, and directed our troops to sleep on their arms in such positions in advance and rear as corps commanders should determine, hoping, from news received by a special dispatch, that delays had been encountered by General Buell in his march from Columbia, and that his main force, therefore, could not reach the field of battle in time to save General Grant's shattered fugitive forces from capture or destruction on the following day.

During the night the rain fell in torrents, adding to the discomforts and harassed condition of the men. The enemy, moreover, had broken their rest by a discharge at measured intervals of heavy shells thrown from the gunboats; therefore on the following morning the troops under my command were not in condition to cope with an equal force of fresh troops, armed and equipped like our adversary, in the immediate possession of his depots and sheltered by such an auxiliary as the enemy's gunboats.

(Source: U.S. War Department. *War of the Rebellion: A Compilation of the Official Records of the Union and Confederate Armies.* Ser. I, Vol. X/1.)

2. Ulysses S. Grant Describes the Battle

It becomes my duty again to report another battle fought between two great armies, one contending for the maintenance of the best government ever devised, the other for its destruction. It is pleasant to record the success of the army contending for the former principle.

On Sunday morning our pickets were attacked and driven in by the enemy. Immediately the five divisions stationed at this place were drawn up in line of battle, ready to meet them. The battle soon waxed warm on the left and center, varying at times to all parts of the line. The most continuous firing of musketry and artillery ever heard on this continent was kept up until nightfall, the enemy having forced the entire line to fall back nearly half way from their camps to the Landing.

At a late hour in the afternoon a desperate effort was made by the enemy to turn our left and get possession of the Landing, transports, &c. This point was guarded by the gunboats Tyler and Lexington, Captains Gwin and Shirk, U.S. Navy, commanding, four 20-pounder Parrott guns and a battery of rifled guns. As there is a deep and impassable ravine for artillery or cavalry, and very difficult for infantry, at this point, no troops were stationed here, except the necessary artillerists and a small infantry force for their support. Just at this moment the advance of Major-General Buell's column (a part of the division under General Nelson) arrived, the two generals named both being present. An advance was immediately made upon the point of attack and the enemy soon driven back. In this repulse much is due to the presence of the gunboats Tyler and Lexington, and their able commanders, Captains Gwin and Shirk.

During the night the divisions under Generals Crittenden and McCook arrived. General Lewis Wallace, at Crump's Landing, 6 miles below, was ordered at an early hour in the morning to hold his division in readiness to be moved in any direction to which it might be ordered. At about 11 o'clock the order was delivered to move it up to Pittsburg, but owing to its being led by a circuitous route did not arrive in time to take part in Sunday's action.

During the night all was quiet, and feeling that a great moral advantage would be gained by becoming the attacking party, an advance was ordered as soon as day dawned. The result was a gradual repulse of the enemy at all parts of the line from morning until probably 5 o'clock in the afternoon, when it became evident the enemy was retreating. Before the close of the action the advance of General T. J. Wood's division arrived in time to take part in the action.

My force was too much fatigued from two days' hard fighting and exposure in the open air to a drenching rain during the intervening night to pursue immediately.

Night closed in cloudy and with heavy rain, making the roads impracticable for artillery by the next morn-ing. General Sherman, however, followed the enemy, finding that the main part of the army had retreated in good order.

(Source: U.S. War Department. *War of the Rebellion: A Compilation of the Official Records of the Union and Confederate Armies.* Ser. I, Vol. X.)

3. Beauregard to Grant (8 April 1862)

HEADQUARTERS ARMY OF THE MISSISSIPPI,
Monterey, April 8, 1862.

SIR: At the close of the conflict of yesterday, my forces being exhausted by the extraordinary length of time during which they were engaged with yours on that and the preceding day, and it being apparent that you had received and were still receiving re-enforcements, I felt it my duty to withdraw my troops from the immediate scene of conflict.

Under these circumstances, in accordance with usages of war, I shall transmit this under a flag of truce, to ask permission to send a mounted party to the battle-field of Shiloh for the purpose of giving decent interment to my dead.

Certain gentlemen wishing to avail themselves of this opportunity to remove the remains of their sons and friends, I must request for them the privilege of accompanying the burial party, and in this connection I deem it proper to say I am asking only what I have extended to your own countrymen under similar circumstances.
Respectfully, general, your obedient servant,
 G. T. BEAUREGARD,
 General, Commanding.
Maj. Gen. U.S. GRANT. U.S.A.,
Commanding U. S. Forces near Pittsburg, Tenn.

(Source: U.S. War Department. *War of the Rebellion: A Compilation of the Official Records of the Union and Confederate Armies.* Ser. I, Vol. X/1.)

4. Grant to Beauregard (8 April 1862)

HEADQUARTERS ARMY IN THE FIELD,
Pittsburg, April 9, 1862.

Your dispatch of yesterday is just received. Owing to the warmth of the weather I deemed it advisable to have all the dead of both parties buried immediately. Heavy details were made for this purpose, and now it is accomplished. There cannot, therefore, be any necessity of admitting within our lines the parties you desire to send on the grounds asked.

I shall always be glad to extend any courtesy consistent with duty, and especially so when dictated by humanity.

I am, general, very respectfully, your obedient servant,

U.S. GRANT,
Major-General, Commanding.
General G. T. BEAUREGARD,
Comdg. Confederate Army of the Mississippi,
Monterey, Tenn.

(Source: U.S. War Department. *War of the Rebellion: A Compilation of the Official Records of the Union and Confederate Armies.* Ser. I, Vol. X/1.)

C. SIEGE OF CORINTH

After Shiloh, General P. G. T. Beauregard took his battered Confederate army back to Corinth, Mississippi. Holding Corinth's railroad crossing was imperative for it could furnish supplies and reinforcements. Beauregard constructed fortifications. At Pittsburg Landing, Henry Wager Halleck had arrived to assume command of the federal advance, which began on 30 April 1862. Greatly outnumbered, Beauregard elected to save his army rather than risk losing it by defending Corinth. He employed clever ruses to stall Halleck while masking the Confederate evacuation. On 30 May, Halleck's army occupied Corinth, but Beauregard had escaped. [See Corinth, Siege of]

1. Halleck to Stanton (22 May 1862)
CAMP, *CORINTH ROAD, May 22, 1862.*

Daily skirmishing between our reconnoitering parties and the enemy. General Buell lost 25 men killed and wounded yesterday. Country in our front marshy and densely wooded. I hear nothing of the Kansas troops. Have they been ordered here? All my re-enforcements will be here in about four days. Beyond that I have nothing to expect from this department, and if none from other sources, there will be no use in further delaying an attack. The Sanitary Commission and State Governors carry away troops faster than I can recruit. Men only slightly unwell or feigning sickness are carried away without any authority.
H. W. HALLECK, *Major-General.*
Hon. E. M. STANTON, *Secretary of War.*

2. Lincoln to Halleck (24 May 1862)
WAR DEPARTMENT, *May 24, 1862.*

Major-General HALLECK, *Near Corinth, Miss.:*
Several dispatches from Assistant Secretary Scott and one from Governor Morton, asking re-enforcements for you, have been received. I beg you to be assured we do the best we can. I mean to cast no blame when I tell you each of our commanders along our line from Richmond to Corinth supposes himself to be confronted by numbers superior to his own. Under this pressure we thinned the line on the Upper Potomac, until yesterday it was broken at heavy loss to us, and General Banks

put in great peril, out of which he is not yet extricated, and may be actually captured. We need men to repair this breach, and have them not at hand. My dear general, I feel justified to rely very much on you. I believe you and the brave officers and men with you can and will get the victory at Corinth.
A. LINCOLN.

3. Halleck's Reports to Stanton (28 May–4 June 1862)
HEADQUARTERS DEPARTMENT OF MISSISSIPPI,
Camp on Corinth Road, May 28, 1862.

Three strong reconnoitering columns advanced this morning on the right center and left, to feel the enemy and unmask his batteries. Enemy hotly contested his ground at each point, but was driven back with considerable loss. The column on the left encountered the strongest opposition. Our loss there 25 killed and wounded. The enemy left 30 dead on the field. Losses at other points not yet ascertained. Some 5 or 6 officers and a number of privates captured. The fighting will probably be renewed to-morrow morning at daybreak. The whole country is so thickly wooded that we are compelled to feel our way.

* * *

H E A D Q U A R T E R S ,
Camp near Corinth, May 30, 1862.

Enemy's positions and works in front of Corinth were exceedingly strong. He cannot occupy stronger positions. In his flight this morning he destroyed an immense amount of public and private property— stores, provisions, wagons, tents, &c. For miles out of the town the roads are filled with arms, haversacks, &c., thrown away by his flying troops. A large number of prisoners and deserters have been captured, and estimated by General Pope at 2,000. General Beauregard evidently distrusts his army, or he would have defended so strong a position. His troops are generally much discouraged and demoralized. In all their engagements the last few days their resistance has been weak.

* * *

HALLECK'S HEADQUARTERS,
Corinth, May 31, 1862.

Main body of the enemy has moved south toward Okolona. General Pope, with 50,000, men is following him. I do not, however, propose to pursue him far into Mississippi. Having no baggage trains except railroad trains, he can move much faster than we can pursue. I propose to immediately open the railroad to Decatur, Ala., and to Columbus, Ky. The fall of the Tennessee River will soon render the use of this road necessary to us for supplies. The destruction of the Decatur Bridge by General Mitchel was a most foolish operation. If that had not been done we could have had a connection with him in one week. As it is, we must receive our locomotives and cars from the Ohio River. I have ordered an examination of the road toward Florence, and I think a couple of locomotives landing at that place with cars could be immediately brought here, and be of great assistance to us in repairing the road to Columbus, Ky. Please inform me immediately if an agent of the War Department will act in this matter of procuring locomotives and cars or if I shall detail a quartermaster for that duty. There is no time to be lost in this matter.

* * *

HALLECK'S HEADQUARTERS, *Corinth,*
June 1, 1862.

A brigade of cavalry, under Colonel Elliott, cut the enemy's line of retreat at Booneville, 20 miles south of Corinth, captured three pieces of artillery, 600 infantry, and a squadron of cavalry, and destroyed a large quantity of quartermaster's and commissary stores and a part of the railroad. The enemy is hard pressed for food, and has released all prisoners, rank and file, taken at Pittsburg.

* * *

HALLECK'S HEADQUARTERS, *June 4, 1862.*

General Pope, with 40,000, is 30 miles south of Corinth, pushing the enemy hard. He already reports 10,000 prisoners and deserters from the enemy and 15,000 stand of arms captured. Thousands of the enemy are throwing away their arms. A farmer says that when Beauregard learned that Colonel Elliott had cut the railroad on his line of retreat he became frantic, and told his men to save themselves the best they could. We have captured nine locomotives and a number of cars. One is already repaired and is running today. Several more will be in running order in two or three days. The result is all I could possibly desire.

(Source: U.S. War Department. *War of the Rebellion: A Compilation of the Official Records of the Union and Confederate Armies.* Ser. I, Vol. X/1.)

D. BATTLE OF IUKA

In September 1862, General Braxton Bragg, commander of the Army of Mississippi, ordered General Sterling Price's Army of the West to prevent the federal army in Corinth from reinforcing General Don Carlos Buell in middle Tennessee. Thus was set in motion the circumstance wherein Iuka, a small town thirty miles east of Corinth and near the Tennessee River, became the site of a battle between Price's Confederates and federal forces under William S. Rosecrans. After initial success, Price became convinced that he was about to be attacked by a combined force led by Ulysses S. Grant, so he broke off and evacuated Iuka. [See Iuka, Battle of]

1. Union Correspondence and Reports (September 1862)

ARMY OF THE MISSISSIPPI, TWO MILES
SOUTH OF IUKA, Miss.,
September 19, 1862—10.30 p.m.

GENERAL [GRANT]:
We met the enemy in force just above this point. The engagement lasted several hours. We have lost two or three pieces of artillery. Firing was very heavy. You must attack in the morning and in force. The ground is horrid, unknown to us, and no room for development. Could not use our artillery at all. Fired but few shots. Push in onto them until we can have time to do something. We will try to get a position on our right which will take Iuka.
W. S. ROSECRANS,
Brigadier-General, U. S. Army.

(Source: U.S. War Department. *War of the Rebellion: A Compilation of the Official Records of the Union and Confederate Armies.* Ser. I, Vol. XVII/1.)

* * *

BURNSVILLE, September 20, 1862—8.35 a.m.

General ORD:
Get your troops up and attack as soon as possible. Rosecrans had two hours' fighting last night and now this morning again, and unless you can create a diversion in his favor he may find his hands full. Hurry your troops all possible.
U. S. GRANT,
Major-General.

(Source: U.S. War Department. *War of the Rebellion: A Compilation of the Official Records of the Union and Confederate Armies.* Ser. I, Vol. XVII/1.)

* * *

REPORT OF MAJ. GEN. ULYSSES S. GRANT
IUKA, *Miss., September 20, 1862.*

General Rosecrans, with Stanley's and Hamilton's divisions and Mizner's cavalry, attacked Price, south of this village, about two hours before dark yesterday, and had a sharp fight, until night closed in. General Ord was to the north, with a mixed force of about 5,000 men. Had some skirmishing with rebel pickets. This morning the fight was renewed by General Rosecrans, who was nearest the town, but it was found that the enemy had been evacuating during the night, going south. Hamilton and Stanley, with the cavalry, are in full pursuit, and will no doubt break up the enemy badly, and possibly force them to abandon much of their artillery....

I cannot speak too highly of the energy and skill displayed by General Rosecrans in this attack and of the endurance of the troops under him. General Ord's command showed untiring zeal, but the direction taken by the enemy prevented them taking the active part they desired.

Among the enemy's loss are General Little killed, and General Whitfield, wounded. I have reliable information that it was Price's intention to move over east of the Tennessee. In this he has been thwarted. Price's force consisted of about 18,000 men.

U.S. GRANT, *Major-General.*
Maj. Gen. H. W. HALLECK, *Washington, D.C.*

(Source: U.S. War Department. *War of the Rebellion: A Compilation of the Official Records of the Union and Confederate Armies.* Ser. I, Vol. XVII/1.)

E. BATTLE OF CORINTH
Shortly after the Battle of Iuka, Confederate generals Earl Van Dorn and Sterling Price combined to attack federal forces at Corinth under William S. Rosecrans. The result was a two-day clash that ended in Confederate failure to retake the town. [See Corinth, Battle of]

1. Union Reports and Correspondence (October 1862)
Grant's Headquarters,
Jackson, Tenn., *October 5, 1862.*

Yesterday the rebels, under Van Dorn, Price, and Lovell, were repulsed from their attack on Corinth with great slaughter. The enemy are in full retreat, leaving their dead and wounded on the field. Rosecrans telegraphs that the loss is serious on our side, particularly in officers, but bears no comparison with that of the enemy. General Hackleman fell while gallantly leading his brigade. General Oglesby is dangerously wounded. McPherson reached Corinth with his command yesterday. Rosecrans pursued the retreating

enemy this morning, and should he attempt to reach Bolivar will follow him to that place. Hurlbut is at the Hatchie with 5,000 or 6,000 men, and is no doubt with the pursuing column. From 700 to 1,000 prisoners, besides wounded, are left in our hands.

U.S. Grant, Major-General, Commanding.
Major-General Halleck.

* * *

Jackson, Tenn., *October 8, 1862.*

Before telegraphing you this morning for re-enforcements to follow up our victories I ordered General Rosecrans to return. He showed such reluctance that I consented to allow him to remain until you could be heard from if further re-enforcements could be had. On reflection I deem it idle to pursue farther without more preparation, and have for the third time ordered his return.

U. S. Grant, Major-General.
Major-General HALLECK, Commander-in-Chief.

* * *

War Department, Washington, *October 8, 1862.*

Why order a return of our troops? Why not re-enforce Rosecrans and pursue the enemy into Mississippi, supporting your army on the country?

H. W. Halleck, General-in-Chief.
Major-General GRANT, Jackson, Tenn.

* * *

JACKSON, TENN., October 8, 1862—7.30 p.m.

An army cannot subsist itself on the country except in forage. They did not start out to follow for more than a few days, and are much worn out, and I have information not only that the enemy have reserves that are on their way to join their retreating columns, but they have fortifications to return to in case of need. The Mobile road is also open to the enemy to near Rienzi, and Corinth would be exposed by the advance. Although partial success might result from farther pursuit disaster would follow in the end. If you say so, however, it is not too late yet to go on, and I will join the moving column and go to the farthest extent possible. Rosecrans has been re-enforced with everything at hand, even at the risk of this road against raids.

U. S. GRANT, Major-general.
Major-General HALLECK, General-in-Chief.

(Source: U.S. War Department. *War of the Rebellion: A Compilation of the Official Records of the Union and Confederate Armies.* Ser. I, Vol. XVII/1.)

XVIII. The First Clash of Ironclads

The American Civil War saw the first broad employment of ironclad warships in battle. The Virginia was constructed on the hull of the sunken Union steam frigate Merrimack, *and with it, the Confederacy set the design for many of its ironclads: a sloping armored casemate with openings for broadside guns, the superstructure resting on a low-riding hull. John Ericsson's unique USS Monitor, was a single-turret, low-lying, vessel, a flawed design especially because of its extremely low freeboard. Most unfavorable was the* Monitor's *upper body connection with its underwater hull, a frailty that allowed in water and that would sink the original* Monitor *in a moderately heavy sea. On 8 March 1862 off Norfolk, Virginia, at Hampton Roads, the two ships exchanged blows for almost four hours and did insignificant damage to each other. Yet, the battle forced General George B. McClellan to adjust his spring 1862 campaign against Richmond, and though neither side could claim total triumph, no one doubted that naval warfare had been transformed.* [See Ironclads; *Monitor, U.S.S.; Monitor v. Virginia; Virginia, C.S.S.*]

1. Report of Flag-Officer Goldsborough, U.S. Navy, Regarding the Preparation of the CSS *Virginia* (17 October 1861)

Confidential.] U.S. FLAGSHIP MINNESOTA,
Hampton Roads, October 17, 1861.

SIR: I have received further minute reliable information with regard to the preparation of the *Merrimack* for an attack on Newport News and these roads, and I am now quite satisfied that unless her stability be compromitted by her heavy top works of wood and iron and her weight of batteries, she will, in all probability, prove to be exceedingly formidable.

The supposition of the insurgents is that she will be impregnable, and a trial of her sufficiently to resist shot of the heaviest caliber, at a short range, is to take place before she is sent out to engage us.

She is still in the dry dock at Norfolk, and yet needs a goodly quantity of iron to complete her casing, all of which is furnished from Richmond. She has her old engines on board, and they have been made to work tolerably well. They are not expected, however, I understand, to afford anything more than a moderate velocity.

On coming out, she must necessarily, proceed as low down as about Sewell's Point before she can shape her course to the westward for Newport News, and this will bring her within 3_ miles of us. My present purpose is to let her get well over toward the *Congress* and *Cumberland*, off Newport News, and then to put at her with this ship and everything else that may be on hand at the time, with the view of bringing her between the fire of those ships and these, and cutting off all retreat on her part. It is understood that she is to be assisted by the two steamers now up the James River, but as they can not be made very powerful I attach no very great consequences to this intention.

Nothing, I think, but very close work can possibly be of service in accomplishing the destruction of the *Merrimack*, and even of that a great deal may be necessary. From what I gather, boarding is impracticable, as she can only be assailed in that way through her ports, of which she has, in all, but fourteen.

If I could be furnished with a couple of tugs, or small steamers, to attend upon the *Congress* and *Cumberland* in season, so as to tow them promptly into position in case of necessity, they might prove of very great service. It will be, I infer, at least a fortnight before the *Merrimack* will make her attempt, but in the meantime I could employ those tugs or steamers very advantageously in the way of guard vessels at night, dispatch and tow vessels by day, etc. On the 9th instant all attempt, no doubt, was made by the insurgents to get an infernal machine among our shipping here, but it was happily foiled by the alertness of the Lockwood, which they tried to cut off with their two tugs engaged in the nefarious business. The night was dark and boisterous. Since then, they dispatched a tug with six armed boats in tow, toward Newport News, during the night; but, after proceeding a considerable way in that direction, concluded that it was too light for their purposes. I only mention these things to show the utility of active guard steamers.
Your most obedient servant,
L. M. GOLDSBOROUGH,
Flag-Officer.

(Source: *Official Records of the Union and Confederate Navy in the War of the Rebellion.* Washington, D.C.: Government Printing Office, 1897.)

2. Letter from the Secretary of the Navy of the Confederate States Suggesting an Attack by the CSS *Virginia* upon New York City (7 March 1862)

Confidential.] C. S. NAVY DEPARTMENT,
Richmond, March 7, 1862.

SIR: I submit for your consideration the attack of New York by the *Virginia*. Can the *Virginia* steam to New York and attack and burn the city? She can, I doubt not, pass Old Point safely, and, in good weather and a smooth sea, could doubtless go to New York. Once in the bay, she could shell and burn the city and the shipping. Such an event would eclipse all the glories of the combats of the sea, would place every man in it preeminently high, and would strike a blow from which the enemy could never recover. Peace would inevitably follow. Bankers would withdraw their capital from the city. The Brooklyn, [New York] navy yard and its magazines and all the lower part of the city would be destroyed, and such an event, by a single ship, would do more to achieve our immediate independence than would the results of many campaigns.

Can the ship go there? Please give me your views. Very respectfully, your obedient servant,
S. R. MALLORY, Secretary of the Navy.

(Source: *Official Records of the Union and Confederate Navy in the War of the Rebellion*. Washington, D.C.: Government Printing Office, 1897.)

3. Union Correspondence Regarding the CSS *Virginia*
HEADQUARTERS ARMY OF THE POTOMAC, *Washington, March 9, 1862.*

COMMANDING OFFICERS *Fort Delaware;
Fort Mifflin; New York Harbor, N. Y.; Newport, R. I;
Fort Trumbull, New London; Boston Harbor;
Portland, Me.:*
The rebel iron-clad steamer *Merrimac* has destroyed two of our frigates near Fort Monroe and finally retired last night to Craney Island. She may succeed in passing the batteries and go to sea. It is necessary that you at once place your post in the best possible condition for defense, and do your best to stop her should she endeavor to run by. Anything that can be effected in the way of temporary batteries should be done at once.
GEO. B. McCLELLAN,
Major-General, U. S. A

(Source: U.S. War Department. *War of the Rebellion: A Compilation of the Official Records of the Union and Confederate Armies.* Ser. I, Vol. IX.)

* * *

WAR DEPARTMENT,
Washington, March 9, 1862.

To the GOVERNOR OF *NEW YORK, Albany;* MASS-ACHUSETTS, *Boston;* MAINE, *Portland:*
The opinion of the naval commanders here is that the *Merrimac* will not venture to sea, but they advise that immediate preparations be made to guard against the danger to our ports by large timber rafts, protected by batteries. They regard timber rafts, guarded by batteries, as the best protection for temporary purposes.
General Totten says do not neglect the batteries.
EDWIN M. STANTON,
Secretary of War.

(Source: U.S. War Department. *War of the Rebellion: A Compilation of the Official Records of the Union and Confederate Armies.* Ser. I, Vol. IX.)

* * *

EXECUTIVE MANSION, *Washington, March 9, 1862.*

Colonel INGALLS, *Quartermaster, Annapolis:*
Should the *Merrimac*, which did so much damage at Newport News, attempt anything at Annapolis, it is believed that the best defense would be an attack by a number of swift steamers, full of men, who should board her by a sudden rush, fire down through her hatches or grated deck, and throw cartridges, grenades, or shells down her smoke-pipes; sacrifice the steamers in order to take the *Merrimac*.

If an overwhelming force can be thus thrown on board there will be little loss of life, though the steam transports may be destroyed. Of course the steamers should be provided with ladders, planks, grapplers, and other means to board with. The *Merrimac* has iron sides, sloping above water to a deck about 9 feet wide. Said to be an iron-grated deck.

Promotion, ample reward, awaits whoever takes or destroys her.
By order of the Secretary of War:
M. C. MEIGS,
Quartermaster-General.
You, of course, have a swift steamer outside on the look out.

(Source: U.S. War Department. *War of the Rebellion: A Compilation of the Official Records of the Union and Confederate Armies.* Ser. I, Vol. IX.)

4. Union Correspondence and Reports on *Monitor* vs. *Virginia*
FORT MONROE, VA.,
March 9, 1862—10.45 p.m.

Major-General McCLELLAN,
Washington, D.C.:
Your telegram to Major-General Wool received. The performance of the *Monitor* to-day against the *Merrimac* shows a slight superiority in favor of the *Monitor*, as the *Merrimac* was forced to retreat to Norfolk after a four hour's engagement, at times the vessels touching each other. The damage to the *Merrimac* cannot be ascertained. She retreated under steam without assistance.

The *Monitor* is all ready for her to-morrow, but I think the *Merrimac* may be obliged to lay up for a few days. She is an ugly customer, and it is too good luck to believe we are yet clear of her. Our hopes are upon the *Monitor*, and this days' work shows that the *Merrimac* must attend to her alone. Have ordered the large frigates to leave.
G. V. FOX,
Assistant Secretary.

(Source: U.S. War Department. *War of the Rebellion: A Compilation of the Official Records of the Union and Confederate Armies.* Ser. I, Vol. IX.)

* * *

FAIRFAX COURT-HOUSE,
March 12, 1862.

G. V. Fox,
Assistant Secretary of the Navy:
The possibility of the *Merrimac* appearing again paralyzes the movements of this army by whatever route is adopted. How long a time would it require to complete the vessel built at Mystic River, working night and day? How long would Stevens require to finish his vessel, so far as to enable her to contend with the *Merrimac?* If she is uninjured, of course no precaution would avail, and the *Monitor* must be the sole reliance. But if injured so as to require considerable repairs, these things are important to be considered. The General would desire any suggestion of your own on this subject.
By order of Major-General McClellan:
J. G. BARNARD,
Chief Engineer.

(Source: U.S. War Department. *War of the Rebellion: A Compilation of the Official Records of the Union and Confederate Armies.* Ser. I, Vol. IX.)

* * *

NAVY DEPARTMENT, March 13, 1862.

Maj. Gen. GEORGE B. MCCLELLAN,
Fairfax Court-House:
The *Monitor* is more than a match for the *Merrimac,* but she might be disabled in the next encounter. I cannot advise so great dependence upon her. Burnside and Goldsborough are very strong for the Chowan River route to Norfolk, and I brought up maps, explanations, &c., to show you. It turns everything, and is only 27 miles to Norfolk by two good roads. Burnside will have New Berne this week. The *Monitor* may, and I think will, destroy the *Merrimac* in the next fight, but this is hope, not certainty. The *Merrimac* must dock for repairs.
G. V. FOX.

(Source: U.S. War Department. *War of the Rebellion: A Compilation of the Official Records of the Union and Confederate Armies.* Ser. I, Vol. V.)

* * *

FORT MONROE, May 11, 1862.

P. H. WATSON,
Assistant Secretary of War:
The *Merrimac* was blown up by the rebels at two minutes before 5 o'clock this morning. She was set fire to about 3 o'clock, and the explosion took place at the time stated. It is said to have been a grand sight by those who saw it. The *Monitor,* Stevens, and the gunboats have gone up toward Norfolk.
EDWIN M. STANTON,
Secretary of War.
[Similar dispatch to McClellan.]

(Source: U.S. War Department. *War of the Rebellion: A Compilation of the Official Records of the Union and Confederate Armies.* Ser. I, Vol. 14 [S# 14].)

XIX. The Peninsula Campaign

McClellan's affable relationship with Secretary of War Edwin Stanton and Congress became bitter after Ball's Bluff and the prolonged inactivity of the Army of the Potomac. Lincoln remained supportive, but McClellan's plan for assaulting Richmond—formulated only after Lincoln insisted the army do something—worried him. Others were adamantly opposed. Finally, however, McClellan received approval for his Peninsula campaign, which got underway in March 1862. Nearly 400 vessels transported 121,500 Union troops and their supplies from the area around Washington, D.C., to Fort Monroe on the Virginia peninsula. From the start, McClellan claimed that administration meddling, bad weather, and superior Confederate numbers hobbled him. Moving with cautious deliberation, the Army of the Potomac reached Richmond's environs at the end of May and began siege preparations. On 31 May 1862, Joseph Johnston attacked elements of McClellan's army near Fair Oaks Station, but the Confederate attack went adrift, and Johnston himself was seriously wounded. Johnston's replacement, Robert E. Lee, went on the offensive in late June in a series of battles known as the Seven Days' that forced McClellan from the gates of Richmond. The battle of Malvern Hill on 1 July, however, was a bloody end to a disappointing campaign for Lee as well as McClellan, for the Confederate army had missed several opportunities to shatter its foe. For McClellan, the failure of his Peninsula campaign exhausted Lincoln's patience. McClellan did not help his cause by blaming the administration for the campaign's misadventures, and after the Seven Days' he drafted a letter of high presumption that lectured Lincoln on the aims of the war and how best to secure them. It was the last straw. McClellan was ordered to support Pope's newly created Army of Virginia that was planning to mount an overland campaign against Richmond. [See Fair Oaks, Battle of; Gaines' Mill, Battle of; Lee, Robert Edward; Magruder, John Bankhead; Malvern Hill, Battle of; McClellan,

George Brinton; Peninsula Campaign; Seven Days' Battles; White Oak Swamp, Battle of]

1. President's General War Order, No. 1 (27 January 1862)

EXECUTIVE MANSION,
Washington, January 27, 1862.

Ordered, That the 22d day of February, 1862, be the day for a general movement of the land and naval forces of the United States against the insurgent forces. That especially the army at and about Fortress Monroe; the Army of the Potomac; the Army of Western Virginia; the army near Munfordville, Ky.; the army and flotilla at Cairo, and a naval force in the Gulf of Mexico, be ready to move on that day.

That all other forces, both land and naval, with their respective commanders, obey existing orders for the time, and be reply to obey additional orders when duly given.

That the heads of Departments, and especially the Secretaries of War and of the Navy, with all their subordinates, and the General-in-Chief, with all other commanders and subordinates of land and naval forces, will severally be held to their strict and full responsibilities for prompt execution of this order.
ABRAHAM LINCOLN.

(Source: U.S. War Department. *War of the Rebellion: A Compilation of the Official Records of the Union and Confederate Armies.* Ser. I, Vol. V.)

2. President's Special War Order, No. 1 (31 January 1862)

EXECUTIVE MANSION,
Washington, January 31, 1862.

Ordered, That all the disposable force of the Army of the Potomac, after providing safely for the defense of Washington, be formed into an expedition for the immediate object of seizing and occupying a point upon the railroad southwestward of what is known as Manassas Junction, all details to be in the discretion of the Commander-in-Chief, and the expedition to move before or on the 22d day of February next.
ABRAHAM LINCOLN.

(Source: U.S. War Department. *War of the Rebellion: A Compilation of the Official Records of the Union and Confederate Armies.* Ser. I, Vol. V.)

3. Lincoln to McClellan (3 February 1862)

EXECUTIVE MANSION,
Washington, February 3, 1862.

Major-General *McCLELLAN:*
My DEAR SIR: You and I have distinct and different plans for a movement of the Army of the Potomac: Yours to be down the Chesapeake, up the Rappahannock to Urbana, and across land to the terminus of the railroad on the York River; mine, to move directly to a point on the railroad southwest of Manassas.

If you will give me satisfactory answers to the following questions I shall gladly yield my plan to yours:

1st Does not your plan involve a greatly larger expenditure of time and money than mine?

2d. Wherein is a victory more certain by your plan than mine?

3d. Wherein is a victory more valuable by your plan than mine?

4th. In fact would it not be less valuable in this, that it would break no great line of the enemy's communication, while mine would?

5th. In case of disaster would not a safe retreat be more difficult by your plan than by mine?
Yours, truly,
A. LINCOLN.

(Source: U.S. War Department. *War of the Rebellion: A Compilation of the Official Records of the Union and Confederate Armies.* Ser. I, Vol. XV.)

4. McClellan to Lincoln (3 February 1862)

HEADQUARTERS OF THE ARMY,
Washington, February 3, 1862.

SIR: I ask your indulgence for the following paper, rendered necessary by circumstances.

I assumed command of the troops in the vicinity of Washington on Saturday, July 27, 1861, six days after the battle of Bull Run.

I found no army to command—a mere collection of regiments cowering on the banks of the Potomac, some perfectly raw, others dispirited by the recent defeat.

Nothing of any consequence had been done to secure the southern approaches to the capital by means of defensive works; nothing whatever had been undertaken to defend the avenues to the city on the northern side of the Potomac. The troops were not only undisciplined, undrilled, and dispirited; they were not even placed in military positions. The city was almost in a condition to have been taken by a dash of a regiment of cavalry.

Without one day's delay I undertook the difficult task assigned to me; that task the honorable Secretary knows was given to me without my solicitation or foreknowledge. How far I have accomplished it will best be shown by the past and the present.

The capital is secure against attack, the extensive fortifications erected by the labor of our troops enable a small garrison to hold it against a numerous army, the enemy have been held in check, the State of Maryland is securely in our possession, the detached counties of Virginia are again within the pale of our laws, and all apprehension of trouble in Delaware is at an end; the enemy are confined to the positions they occupied before the disaster of the 21st July. More than all this, I have now under my command a well-drilled and reliable army, to which the destinies of the country may be confidently committed. This army is young and untried in battle, but it is animated by the highest spirit and is capable of great deeds.

That so much has been accomplished, and such an army created in so short a time from nothing, will hereafter be regarded as one of the highest glories of the administration and the nation.

Many weeks, I may say many months, ago, this Army of the Potomac was fully in condition to repel any attack; but there is a vast difference between that and the efficiency required to enable troops to attack successfully an army elated by victory and intrenched in a position long since selected, studied, and fortified.

In the earliest papers I submitted to the President I asked for an effective and movable force far exceeding the aggregate now on the banks of the Potomac. I have not the force I asked for....

Two bases of operation seem to present themselves for the advance of the Army of the Potomac:

I. That of Washington—its present position—involving a direct attack upon the intrenched positions of the enemy at Centreville, Manassas, &c., or else a movement to turn one or both flanks of those positions, or a combination of the two plans.

The relative force of the two armies will not justify an attack on both flanks; an attack on his left flank alone involves a long line of wagon communication, and cannot prevent him from collecting for the decisive battle all the detachments now on his extreme right and left.

Should we attack his right flank by the line of the Occoquan, and a crossing of the Potomac below that river, and near his batteries, we could perhaps prevent the junction of the enemy's right with his center (we might destroy the former); we would remove the obstructions to the navigation of the Potomac, reduce the length of wagon transportation by establishing new depots at the nearest points of the Potomac, and strike more directly his main railway communication.

The fords of the Occoquan below the mouth of the Bull Run are watched by the rebels; batteries are said to be placed on the heights in the rear (concealed by the woods), and the arrangement of his troops is such that he can oppose some considerable resistance to a passage of that stream. Information has just been received to the effect that the enemy are intrenching a line of heights extending from the vicinity of Sangster's (Union Mills) towards Evansport. Early in January Spriggs' Ford was occupied by General Redes with 3,600 men and eight guns. There are strong reasons for believing that Davis' Ford is occupied. These circumstances indicate or prove that the enemy anticipates the movement in question and is prepared to resist, it. Assuming for the present that this operation is determined upon, it may be well to examine briefly its probable progress. In the present state of affairs our column (for the movement of so large a force must be made in several columns, at, least five or six) can reach the Accotink without danger. During the march thence to the Occoquan our right flank becomes exposed to an attack from Fairfax Station, Sangster's, and Union Mills. This danger must be met by occupying in some force either the two first-named places, or, better, the point of junction of the roads leading thence to the village of Occoquan. This occupation must be continued so long as we continue to draw supplies by the roads from this city or until a battle is won.

The crossing of the Occoquan should be made at all the fords from Wolf Run to the mouth, the points of crossing not being necessarily confined to the fords themselves. Should the enemy occupy this line in force, we must, with what assistance the flotilla can afford, endeavor to three the passage near the mouth, thus forcing the enemy to abandon the whole line, or be taken in flank himself.

Having gained the line of the Occoquan, it would be necessary to throw a column by the shortest route to Dumfries, partly to force the enemy to abandon his batteries on the Potomac, partly to cover our left flank against an attack front the direction of Aquia, and lastly, to establish our communications with the river by the best roads, and thus give us new depots. The enemy would by this time have occupied the line of the Occoquan above Bull Run, holding Brentsville in force, and perhaps extending his lines somewhat farther to the southwest.

Our next step would then be to prevent the enemy from crossing the Occoquan between Bull Run and Broad Run, to fall upon our right flank while moving on Brentsville. This might be effected by occupying Bacon Race Church and the cross-roads near the mouth of Bull Run, or still more effectually by moving to the fords themselves, and preventing hint front debouching on our side.

These operations would possibly be resisted, and it would require some time to effect them, as nearly at the same time as possible we should gain the fords neces-

sary to our purposes above Broad Run. Having secured our right flank, it would become necessary to carry Brentsville at any cost; for we could not leave it between our right flank and the main body. The final movement on the railroad must be determined by circumstances existing at the time.

This brief sketch brings out in bold relief the great advantage possessed by the enemy in the strong central position he occupies, with roads diverging in every direction, and a strong line of defense enabling him to remain on the defensive, with a small force on one flank, while he concentrates everything on the other for a decisive action.

Should we place a portion of our force in front of Centreville, while the rest crosses the Occoquan, we commit the error of dividing our army by a very difficult obstacle, and by a distance too great to enable the two parts to support each other, should either be attacked by the masses of the enemy while the other is held in check.

I should perhaps have dwelt more decidedly on the fact that the force left near Sangster's must be allowed to remain somewhere on that side of the Occoquan until the decisive battle is over, so as to cover our retreat in the event of disaster, unless it should be decided to select and intrench a new base somewhere near Dumfries, a proceeding involving much time.

After the passage of the Occoquan by the main army, this covering force could be drawn into a more central and less exposed position—say Brimstone Hill or nearer the Occoquan. In this latitude the weather will for a considerable period be very uncertain, and a movement commenced in force on roads in tolerably firm condition will be liable, almost certain, to be much delayed by rains and snow. It will therefore be next to impossible to surprise the enemy or take him at a disadvantage by rapid maneuvers. Our slow progress will enable him to divine our purposes and take his measures accordingly. The probability is, from the best information we possess, that the enemy has improved the roads leading to his lines of defense, while we will have to work as we advance.

Bearing in mind what has been said, and the present unprecedented and impassable condition of the roads, it will be evident that no precise period can be fixed upon for the movement on this line, nor can its duration be closely calculated; it seems certain that many weeks may elapse before it is possible to commence the march. Assuming the success of this operation, and the defeat of the enemy as certain, the question at once arises as to the importance of the results gained. I think these results would be confined to the possession of the field of battle, the evacuation of the line of the Upper Potomac by the enemy, and the moral effect of the victory—important results, it is true, but not decisive of the war, nor securing the destruction of the enemy's main army; for he could fall back upon other positions and fight us again and again, should the condition of his troops permit. If he is in no condition to fight us again out of the range of the intrenchments at Richmond, we would find it a very difficult and tedious matter to follow him up there, for he would destroy his railroad bridges and otherwise impede our progress through a region where the roads are as bad as they well can be, and we would probably find ourselves forced at last to change the whole theater of war, or to seek a shorter land route to Richmond, with a smaller available force, and at an expenditure of much more time than were we to adopt the short line at once. We would also have forced the enemy to concentrate his forces and perfect his defensive measures at the very points where it is desirable to strike him when least prepared.

II. The second base of operations available for the Army of the Potomac is that of the Lower Chesapeake Bay, which affords the shortest possible land route to Richmond, and strikes directly at the heart of the enemy's power in the east.

The roads in that region are passable at all seasons of the year. The country now alluded to is much more favorable for offensive operations than that in front of Washington (which is very unfavorable), much more level, more cleared land, the woods less dense, the soil more sandy, and the spring some two or three weeks earlier. A movement in force on that line obliges the enemy to abandon his intrenched position at Manassas, in order to hasten to cover Richmond and Norfolk. He must do this; for should he permit us to occupy Richmond, his destruction can be averted only by entirely defeating us in battle, in which he must be the assailant. This movement, if successful, gives us the capital, the communications, the supplies of the rebels. Norfolk would fall, all the waters of the Chesapeake would be ours, all Virginia would be in our power, and the enemy forced to abandon Tennessee and North Carolina. The alternative presented to the enemy would be to beat us in a position selected by ourselves, disperse, or pass beneath the Candine Forks.

Should we be beaten in battle, we have a perfectly secure retreat down the Peninsula upon Fort Monroe, with our flanks perfectly covered by the fleet. During the whole movement our left flank is covered by the water. Our right is secure, for the reason that the enemy is too distant to reach us in time. He can only oppose us in front. We bring our fleet into full play.

After a successful battle our position would be: Burnside forming our left, Norfolk held securely; our center connecting Burnside with Buell, both by Raleigh and Lynchburg; Buell in Eastern Tennessee and North Alabama; Halleck at Nashville and Memphis. The next movement would be to connect with Sherman on the left, by reducing Wilmington and Charleston; to advance our center into South Carolina and Georgia; to push Buell either towards Montgomery or to unite with the main army in Georgia; to throw Halleck southward to meet the naval expedition from New Orleans. We should then be in a condition to reduce at our leisure all the Southern sea ports; to occupy all the avenues of communication; to use the great outlet of the Mississippi; to re-establish our Government and arms in Arkansas, Louisiana, and Texas; to force the slaves to labor for our subsistence instead of that of the rebels; to bid defiance to all foreign interference. Such is the object I have ever had in view; this is the general plan which I hope to accomplish....

Should it be determined to operate from the Lower Chesapeake, the point of landing which promises the most brilliant result is Urbana, on the Lower Rappahannock. This point is easily reached by vessels of heavy draught; it is neither occupied nor observed by the enemy; it is but one march from West Point, the key of that region, and thence but two marches to Richmond. A rapid movement from Urbana would probably cut off Magruder in the Peninsula, and enable us to occupy Richmond before it could be strongly re-enforced. Should we fail in that, we could, with the co-operation of the Navy, cross the James and throw ourselves in the rear of Richmond, thus forcing the enemy to come out and attack us, for his position would be untenable with us on the southern bank of the river. Should circumstances render it not advisable to land at Urbana, we can use Mob Jack Bay; or, the worst coming to 1he worst, we can take Fort Monroe as a base, and operate with complete security, although with less celerity and brilliancy of results, up the Peninsula.

To reach whatever point may be selected as a base a large amount of cheap water transportation must be collected, consisting mainly of canal-boats, barges, wood boats, schooners, &c., towed by small steamers, all of a very different character from those required for all previous expeditions. This can certainly be accomplished within thirty days from the time the order is given. I propose, as the best possible plan that can, in my judgment, be adopted, to select Urbana as a landing place for the first detachments; to transport by water four divisions of infantry with their batteries, the regular infantry, a few wagons, one bridge train, and a few squadrons of cavalry, making the vicinity of Hooker's position the place of embarkation for as many as possible; to move the regular cavalry and reserve artillery, the remaining bridge trains and wagons, to a point somewhere near Cape Lookout; then ferry them over the river by means of North River ferry-boats, march them over to the Rappahannock (covering the movement by an infantry force near Heathsville), and to cross the Rappahannock in a similar way. The expense

and difficulty of the movement will then be very much diminished (a saving of transportation of about 10,000 horses), and the result none the less certain.

The concentration of the cavalry, &c., on the lower counties of Maryland can be effected without exciting suspicion, and the movement made without delay from that cause.

This movement, if adopted, will not at all expose the city of Washington to danger. The total force to be thrown upon the new line would be, according to circumstances, from 110,000 to 140,000. I hope to use the latter number by bringing fresh troops into Washington, and still leaving it quite safe. I fully realize that in all projects offered time will probably be the most valuable consideration. It is my decided opinion that, in that point of view, the second plan should be adopted. It is possible, nay, highly probable, that the weather and state of the roads may be such as to delay the direct movement from Washington, with its unsatisfactory results and great risks, far beyond the time required to complete the second plan. In the first case we can fix no definite time for an advance. The roads have gone from bad to worse. Nothing like their present condition was ever known here before; they are impassable at present. We are entirely at the mercy of the weather. It is by no means certain that we can beat them at Manassas. On the other line I regard success as certain by all the chances of war. We demoralize the enemy by forcing him to abandon his prepared position for one which we have chosen, in which all in our favor, and where success must produce immense results.

My judgment as a general is clearly in favor of this project. Nothing is certain in war, but all the chances are in favor of this movement. So much am I in favor of the southern line of operations, that I would prefer the move from Fortress Monroe as a base as a certain though less brilliant movement than that from Urbana to an attack upon Manassas.

I know that his excellency the President, you, and I all agree in our wishes, and that these wishes are to bring this war to a close as promptly as the means in our possession will permit. I believe that the mass of the people have entire confidence in us. I am sure of it. Let us then look only to the great result to be accomplished and disregard everything else.

I am, very respectfully, your obedient servant,
GEORGE McCLELLAN,
Major-General.

(Source: U.S. War Department. *War of the Rebellion: A Compilation of the Official Records of the Union and Confederate Armies*. Ser. I, Vol. V.)

5. President's General War Order, No. 3 (8 March 1862)

EXECUTIVE MANSION,
Washington, March 8, 1862.

Ordered, That no change of the base of operations of the Army of the Potomac shall be made without leaving in and about Washington such a force as in the opinion of the General-in-Chief and the commanders of all the army corps shall leave said city entirely secure.

That no more than two army corps (about 50,000 troops) of said Army of the Potomac shall be moved *en route* for a new base of operations until the navigation of the Potomac from Washington to the Chesapeake Bay shall be freed from enemy's batteries and other obstructions, or until the President shall hereafter give express permission.

That any movement as aforesaid *en route* for a new base of operations which may be ordered by the General-in-Chief, and which may be intended to move upon the Chesapeake Bay, shall begin to move upon the bay as early as the 18th day of March instant, and the General-in-Chief shall be responsible that it so move as early as that day.

Ordered, That the Army and Navy co-operate in an immediate effort to capture the enemy's batteries upon the Potomac between Washington and the Chesapeake Bay.

A. LINCOLN.

(Source: U.S. War Department. *War of the Rebellion: A Compilation of the Official Records of the Union and Confederate Armies.* Ser. I, Vol. XIV.)

6. Lincoln to McClellan (9 April 1862)

WASHINGTON, *April 9, 1862.*

Major-General McClellan:

MY DEAR SIR: Your dispatches complaining that you are not properly sustained, while they do not offend me, do pain me very much.

Blenker's division was withdrawn from you before you left here, and you knew the pressure under which I did it, and, as I thought, acquiesced in it—certainly not without reluctance.

After you left I ascertained that less than 20,000 unorganized men, without a single field battery, were all you designed to be left for the defense of Washington and Manassas Junction, and part of this even was to go to General Hooker's old position. General Banks' corps, once designed for Manassas Junction, was divided and tied up on the line of Winchester and Strasburg, and could not leave it without again exposing the Upper Potomac and the Baltimore and Ohio Railroad. This presented (or would present, when McDowell and Sumner should be gone) a great temptation to the enemy to turn back from the Rappahannock and sack Washington. My explicit order that Washington should, by the judgment of all the commanders of corps, be left entirely secure had been neglected. It was precisely this that drove me to detain McDowell.

I do not forget that I was satisfied with your arrangements to leave Banks at Manassas Junction, but when that arrangement was broken up and nothing was substituted for it of course I was not satisfied. I was constrained to substitute something for it myself.

And now allow me to ask, "Do you really think I should permit the line from Richmond via Manassas Junction to this city to be entirely open, except what resistance could be presented by less than 20,000 unorganized troops?" This is a question which the country will not allow me to evade.

There is a curious mystery about the number of the troops now with you. When I telegraphed you on the 6th, saying you had over 100,000 with you, I had just obtained from the Secretary of War a statement, taken as he said from your own returns, making 108,000 then with you and *en route* to you. You now say you will have but 85,000 when all *en route* to you shall have reached you. How can this discrepancy of 35,000 be accounted for?

As to General Wool's command, I understand it is doing for you precisely what a like number of your own would have to do if that command was away. I suppose the whole force which has gone forward to you is with you by this time, and, if so, I think it is the precise time for you to strike a blow. By delay the enemy will relatively gain upon you; that is, he will gain faster by fortifications and re-enforcements than you can by re-enforcements alone.

And once more let me tell you it is indispensable to you that you strike a blow. I am powerless to help this. You will do me the justice to remember I always insisted that going down the bay in search of a field instead of fighting at or near Manassas was only shifting and not surmounting a difficulty; that we would find the same enemy and the same or equal intrenchments at either place. The country will not fail to note—is noting now—that the present hesitation to move upon an intrenched enemy is but the story of Manassas repeated.

I beg to assure you that I have never written you or spoken to you in greater kindness of feeling than now, nor with a fuller purpose to sustain you, so far as in my most anxious judgment I consistently can; but you must act.

Yours, very truly,

A. LINCOLN.

(Source: U.S. War Department. *War of the Rebellion: A Compilation of the Official Records of the Union and Confederate Armies.* Ser. I, Vol. XV.)

7. Robert E. Lee Describes the Battle of Malvern Hill

Early on July 1 Jackson reached the battle-field of the previous day, having succeeded in crossing White Oak Swamp, where he captured a part of the enemy's artillery and a number of prisoners. He was directed to continue the pursuit down the Willis Church road, and soon found the enemy occupying a high range, extending obliquely across the road, in front of Malvern Hill. On this position of great natural strength he had concentrated his powerful artillery, supported by masses of infantry, partially protected by earthworks. His left rested near Crew's house and his right near Binford's. Immediately in his front the ground was open, varying in width from a quarter to half a mile, and, sloping gradually from the crest, was completely swept by the fire of his infantry and artillery. To reach this open ground our troops had to advance through a broken and thickly-wooded country, traversed nearly throughout its whole extent by a swamp passable at but few places and difficult at those. The whole was within range of the batteries on the heights and the gunboats in the river, under whose incessant fire our movements had to be executed.

Jackson formed his line with Whiting's division on his left and D. H. Hill's on his right, one of Ewell's brigades occupying the interval. The rest of Ewell's and Jackson's own divisions were held in reserve. Magruder was directed to take position on Jackson's right, but before his arrival two of Huger's brigades came up and were placed next to Hill. Magruder subsequently formed on the right of these brigades, which, with a third of Huger's, were placed under his command. Longstreet and A. P. Hill were held in reserve and took no part in the engagement. Owing to ignorance of the country, the dense forests impeding necessary communication, and the extreme difficulty of the ground, the whole line was not formed until a late hour in the afternoon. The obstacles presented by the woods and swamp made it impracticable to bring up a sufficient amount of artillery to oppose successfully the extraordinary force of that arm employed by the enemy, while the field itself afforded us few positions favorable for its use and none for its proper concentration. Orders were issued for a general advance at a given signal, but the causes referred to prevented a proper concert of action among the troops. D.H. Hill pressed forward across the open field and engaged the enemy gallantly, breaking and driving back his first line; but a simultaneous advance of the other troops not taking place, he found himself unable to maintain the ground he had gained against the overwhelming numbers and numerous batteries of the enemy. Jackson sent to his support his own division and that part of Ewell's which was in reserve, but owing to the increasing darkness and intricacy of the forest and swamp they did not arrive in time to ren-

der the desired assistance. Hill was therefore compelled to abandon part of the ground he had gained after suffering severe loss and inflicting heavy damage upon the enemy. On the right the attack was gallantly made by Huger's and Magruder's commands. Two brigades of the former commenced the action; the other two were subsequently sent to the support of Magruder and Hill. Several determined efforts were made to storm the hill at Crew's house. The brigades advanced bravely across the open field, raked by the fire of a hundred cannon and the musketry of large bodies of infantry. Some were broken and gave way, others approached close to the guns, driving back the infantry, compelling the advanced batteries to retire to escape capture, and mingling their dead with those of the enemy. For want of concert among the attacking columns their assaults were too weak to break the Federal line, and after struggling gallantly, sustaining and inflicting great loss, they were compelled successively to retire. Night was approaching when the attack began, and it soon became difficult to distinguish friend from foe. The firing continued until after 9 p.m., but no decided result was gained. Part of the troops were withdrawn to their original positions, others remained on the open field, and some rested within a hundred yards of the batteries that had been so bravely but vainly assailed. The general conduct of the troops was excellent.—in some instances heroic. The lateness of the hour at which the attack necessarily began gave the enemy the full advantage of his superior position and augmented the natural difficulties of our own.

After seizing the York River Railroad on June 28 and driving the enemy across the Chickahominy, as already narrated, the cavalry under General Stuart proceeded down the railroad to ascertain if there was any movement of the enemy in that direction.

He encountered but little opposition, and reached the vicinity of the White House on the 29th. At his approach the enemy destroyed the greater part of the immense stores accumulated at that depot and retreated toward Fort Monroe. With one gun and some dismounted men General Stuart drove off a gunboat which lay near the White House and rescued a large amount of property, including more than 10,000 stands of small-arms partially burned. Leaving one squadron at the White House, in compliance with his orders, he returned to guard the lower bridges of the Chickahominy.

On the 30th he was directed to recross and co-operate with General Jackson. After a long march he reached the rear of the enemy at Mal-vern Hill on the night of July 1 at the close of the engagement.

On July 2 it was discovered that the enemy had withdrawn during the night, leaving the ground covered with his dead and wounded, and his route exhibiting abundant evidence of precipitate retreat. The pursuit was commenced, General Stuart with his cavalry in the advance, but a violent storm, which prevailed throughout the day, greatly retarded our progress. The enemy, harassed and closely followed by the cavalry, succeeded in gaining Westover, on James River, and the protection of his gunboats. He immediately began to fortify his position, which was one of great natural strength, flanked on each side by a creek, and the approach to his front commanded by the heavy guns of his shipping, in addition to those mounted in his intrenchments. It was deemed inexpedient to attack him, and in view of the condition of our troops, who had been marching and fighting almost incessantly for seven days under the most trying circumstances, it was determined to withdraw, in order to afford them the repose of which they stood so much in need.

(Source: U.S. War Department. *War of the Rebellion: A Compilation of the Official Records of the Union and Confederate Armies.* Ser. I, Vol. XI.)

8. McClellan to Lincoln (7 July 1862)
HEADQUARTERS ARMY OF THE POTOMAC,
Camp near Harrison's Landing, Va., July 7, 1862.

Mr. PRESIDENT: You have been fully informed that the rebel army is in our front with the purpose of overwhelming us by attacking our positions or reducing us by blocking our river communications. I cannot but regard our condition as critical, and I earnestly desire, in view of possible contingencies, to lay before Your Excellency for your private consideration my general views concerning the existing state of the rebellion, although they do not strictly relate to the situation of this army or strictly come within the scope of my official duties. These views amount to convictions, and are deeply impressed upon my mind and heart. Our cause must never be abandoned; it is the cause of free institutions and self-government. The Constitution and the Union must be preserved, whatever may be the cost in time, treasure, and blood. If secession is successful, other dissolution's are clearly to be seen in the future. Let neither military disaster, political faction, nor foreign war shake your settled purpose to enforce the equal operation of the laws of the United States upon the people of every State.

The time has come when the Government must determine upon a civil and military policy covering the whole ground of our national trouble. The responsibility of determining, declaring, and supporting such civil and military policy, and of directing the whole course of national affairs in regard to the rebellion, must now be assumed and exercised by you, or our cause will be lost. The Constitution gives you power sufficient even for the present terrible exigency.

This rebellion has assumed the character of a war. As such it should be regarded, and it should be conducted upon the highest principles known to Christian civilization. It should not be a war looking to the subjugation of the people of any State in any event. It should not be at all a war upon population, but against armed forces and political organizations. Neither confiscation of property, political executions of persons, territorial organization of States, or forcible abolition of slavery should be contemplated for a moment.

In prosecuting the war all private property and unarmed persons should be strictly protected, subject only to the necessity of military operations; all private property taken for military use should be paid or receipted for; pillage and waste should be treated as high crimes, all unnecessary trespass sternly prohibited, and offensive demeanor by the military toward citizens promptly rebuked. Military arrests should not be tolerated, except in places where active hostilities exist, and oaths not required by enactment's constitutionally made should be neither demanded nor received. Military government should be confined to the preservation of public order and the protection of political rights. Military power should not be allowed to interfere with the relations of servitude, either by supporting or impairing the authority of the master, except for repressing disorder, as in other cases. Slaves, contraband under the act of Congress, seeking military protection, should receive it. The right of the Government to appropriate permanently to its own service claims to slave labor should be asserted, and the right of the owner to compensation therefor should be recognized. This principle might be extended, upon grounds of military necessity and security, to all the slaves of a particular State, thus working manumission in such State; and in Missouri, perhaps in Western Virginia also, and possibly even in Maryland, the expediency of such a measure is only a question of time. A system of policy thus constitutional, and pervaded by the influences of Christianity and freedom, would receive the support of almost all truly loyal men, would deeply impress the rebel masses and all foreign nations, and it might be humbly hoped that it would commend itself to the favor of the Almighty.

Unless the principles governing the future conduct of our struggle shall be made known and approved the effort to obtain requisite forces will be almost hopeless. A declaration of radical views, especially upon slavery, will rapidly disintegrate our present armies. The policy of the Government must be supported by concentrations of military power. The national forces should not be dispersed in expeditions, posts of occupation, and numerous armies, but should be mainly collected into masses, and brought to bear upon the armies of the Confederate States. Those armies thoroughly defeated, the political structure which they support would soon cease to exist.

In carrying out any system of policy which you may form you will require a Commander-in-Chief of the Army-one who possesses your confidence, understands your views, and who is competent to execute your orders by directing the military forces of the nation to the accomplishment of the objects by you proposed. I do not ask that place for myself. I am willing to serve you in such position as you may assign me, and I will do so as faithfully as ever subordinate served superior.

I may be on the brink of eternity, and as I hope forgiveness from my Maker I have written this letter with sincerity toward you and from love for my country.

Very respectfully, your obedient servant,
GEO. B. McCLELLAN,
Major-General, Commanding.
His Excellency ABRAHAM LINCOLN,
President.

(Source: U.S. War Department. *War of the Rebellion: A Compilation of the Official Records of the Union and Confederate Armies.* Ser. I, Vol. XI.)

XX. Benjamin Butler in New Orleans

Brigadier General Benjamin F. Butler took command of the recently captured city of New Orleans on 1 May 1862. Butler's grating manner irritated the population, and the women of New Orleans were resolved to ostracize the Northern invaders. Butler ironically had always esteemed women, but in the feverish atmosphere of New Orleans he could not abide their behavior. The result was the infamous "Woman Order" (officially, Order Number 28), issued on 15 May. The Confederate reaction reflected a general outrage over the order that was not limited to the South. [See Butler's Proclamation]

1. General Orders No. 28 (15 May 1862)

Headquarters Department of the Gulf,
New Orleans, May 15, 1862.

As the officers and soldiers of the United States have been subject to repeated insults from the women (calling themselves ladies) of New Orleans, in return for the most scrupulous non-interference and courtesy on our part, it is ordered that hereafter when any female shall, by word, gesture, or movement, insult or show contempt for any officer or soldier of the United States, she shall be regarded and held liable to be treated as a woman of the town plying her avocation.
By command of Major-General Butler:
Geo. C. Strong.
Assistant Adjutant-General, Chief of Staff.

(Source: U.S. War Department. *War of the Rebellion: A Compilation of the Official Records of the Union and Confederate Armies.* Ser. I, Vol. X/2.)

2. Confederate Response to General Orders No. 28

PROCLAMATION.
EXECUTIVE OFFICE,
Opelousas, La., May 24, 1862.

To the People of Louisiana:
The general commanding the troops of the United States now holding possession of New Orleans issued the following order on the 15th instant:

As the officers and soldiers of the United States have been subject to repeated insults from the women (calling themselves ladies) of New Orleans, in return for the most scrupulous non-interference and courtesy on our part, it is ordered that hereafter, when any female shall, by word, gesture, or movement, insult or show contempt for any officer or soldier of the United States, she shall be regarded and held liable to be treated as a woman of the town plying her avocation.

By command of Major-General Butler.

The annals of warfare between civilized nations afford no similar instance of infamy to this order. It is thus proclaimed to the world that the exhibition of any disgust or repulsiveness by the women of New Orleans to the hated invaders of their home and the slayers of their fathers, brothers, and husbands shall constitute a justification to a brutal soldiery for the indulgence of their lust. The commanding general, from his headquarters, announces to his insolent followers that they are at liberty to treat as women of the town the wives, the mothers, the daughters of our citizens, if by word, gesture, or movement any contempt is indicated for their persons or insult offered to their presence. Of the nature of the movement and the meaning of the look these vagabond refuse of the Northern States are to be the judges.

What else than contempt and abhorrence can the women of New Orleans feel or exhibit for these officers and soldiers of the United States? The spontaneous impulse of their hearts must appear involuntary upon their countenances and thus constitute the crime for which the general of those soldiers adjudges the punishment of rape and brutalized passion.

History records instances of cities sacked and inhuman atrocities committed upon the women of a conquered town, but in no instance in modern times, at least without the brutal ravishers suffering condign punishment from the hands of their own commanders. It was reserved for a Federal general to invite his soldiers to the perpetration of outrages at the mention of which the blood recoils in horror—to quicken the impulses of their sensual instincts by the suggestion of transparent excuses for their gratification, and to add to an infamy already well merited these crowning titles of a panderer to lust and a desecrator of virtue.

Maddened by the noble loyalty of our people to the Government of their affections, and at their disgust and execration of their invaders; stung into obliviousness of the world's censure by the grand offering made of our property upon the altar of our liberties; his passions inflamed by the sight of burning cotton illumining the river upon whose waters floats the powerful fleet that effected the downfall of our chief city; disappointed, chafed, and chagrined that our people, unlike his own, do not measure liberty, truth, or honor by a pecuniary standard, he sees the fruits of a victory he did not help to win eluding his grasp, and nothing left upon which to gloat his vengeance but unarmed men and helpless women.

Louisianians! will you suffer such foul conduct of your oppressors to pass unpunished? Will you permit such indignities to remain unavenged? A mind so debased as to be capable of conceiving the alternative presented in this order must be fruitful of inventions wherewith to pollute humanity. Shameless enough to allow their publication in the city, by the countenance of such atrocities they will be multiplied in the country. Its inhabitants must arm and strike, or the insolent victors will offer this outrage to your wives, your sisters, and your daughters. Possessed of New Orleans by means of his superior naval force, he cannot penetrate the interior if you resolve to prevent it. It does not require a force of imposing magnitude to impede his progress. Companies of experienced woodsmen in every exposed locality, with their trusty rifles and shot-guns, will harass his invading columns, deprive him of his pilots, and assure him he is in the country of an enemy. At proper points larger forces will be collected, but every man can be soldier to guard the approaches to his home. Organize, then, quickly and efficiently. If your enemy attempt to proceed into the interior let his pathway be marked by his blood. It is your homes that you have to defend. It is the jewel of your hearths—the chastity of your women—you have to guard. Let that thought animate your breasts, nerve your arms, quicken your energies, and inspire your resolution. Strike home to the heart of your foe the blow that rids your country of his presence. If need be let his blood moisten your own grave. It will rise up before your children as a perpetual memento of a race whom it will teach to hate now and evermore.
THOS. O. MOORE.

(Source: U.S. War Department. *War of the Rebellion: A Compilation of the Official Records of the Union and Confederate Armies.* Ser. I, Vol. X/2.)

XXI. Second Battle of Bull Run

John Pope's success in taking the Confederate bastion of Island No. 10 on the Mississippi River caused Lincoln to summon him to the Eastern theater. Pope began badly by adopting a swaggering manner, but in the wake of McClellan's failure on the peninsula, Pope's newly created Army of Virginia became the North's main hope for taking Richmond. Pope direly misjudged Robert E. Lee, though. The Confederate commander audaciously split his army to send Thomas "Stonewall" Jackson to Cedar Mountain as a diversion while Lee advanced upon Pope with his main force. When Jackson then circled to the north, Pope was lured into a trap. On the same battlefield as first Bull Run, Pope on 29 August 1862 did not press his advantage against Jackson and Lee, and the following day James Longstreet's flanking attack shattered Pope's Army of Virginia. In the wake of the battle, there were considerable efforts to place blame, and for his part, Pope uncharitably pointed to Fitz John Porter as especially culpable for the defeat. [See Bull Run, Second Battle of; Pope, John; Porter, Fitz John]

1. John Pope's Address to His Troops (14 July 1862)
HEADQUARTERS ARMY OF VIRGINIA,
Washington, D.C., July 14, 1862.

To the Officers and Soldiers of the Army of Virginia:
By special assignment of the President of the United States I have assumed the command of this army. I have spent two weeks in learning your whereabouts, your condition, and your wants, in preparing you for active operations, and in placing you in positions from which you can act promptly and to the purpose. These labors are nearly completed, and I am about to join you in the field.

Let us understand each other. I have come to you from the West, where we have always seen the backs of our enemies; from an army whose business it has been to seek the adversary and to beat him when he was found; whose policy has been attack and not defense. In but one instance has the enemy been able to place our Western armies in defensive attitude. I presume that I have been called here to pursue the same system and to lead you against the enemy. It is my purpose to do so, and that speedily. I am sure you long for an opportunity to win the distinction you are capable of achieving. That opportunity I shall endeavor to give you. Meantime I desire you to dismiss from your minds certain phrases, which I am sorry to find so much in vogue amongst you. I hear constantly of "taking strong positions and holding them," of "lines of retreat," and of "bases of supplies." Let us discard such ideas. The strongest position a soldier should desire to occupy is one from which he can most easily advance against the enemy. Let us study the probable lines of retreat of our opponents, and leave our own to take care of themselves. Let us look before us, and not behind. Success and glory are in the advance, disaster and shame lurk in the rear. Let us act on this understanding, and it is safe to predict that your banners shall be inscribed with many a glorious deed and that your names will be dear to your countrymen forever.

JNO. POPE,
Major-General, Commanding.

(Source: U.S. War Department. *War of the Rebellion: A Compilation of the Official Records of the Union and Confederate Armies.* Ser. I, Vol. XII/3.)

2. Charges and Specifications Exhibited against Maj. Gen. Fitz John Porter

CHARGE 1st.—Violation of the Ninth Article of War.

Specification 1st.—In this, that the said Maj. Gen. Fitz John Porter, of the volunteers of the United States, having received a lawful order, on or about the 27th August, 1862, while at or near Warrenton Junction, in Virginia, from Maj. Gen. John Pope, his superior and commanding officer, in the following figures and letters, to wit:

HEADQUARTERS ARMY OF VIRGINIA,
Bristoe Station, August 27, 1862—6.30 p.m.
Maj. Gen. F. J. PORTER, *Warrenton Junction:*
GENERAL: The major-general commanding directs that you start at 1 o'clock to-night, and come forward with your whole corps, or such part of it as is with you, so as to be here by daylight to-morrow morning. Hooker has had very severe action with the enemy, with a loss of about 300 killed and wounded. The enemy has been driven back, but is retiring along the railroad. We must drive him from Manassas, and clear the country between that place and Gainesville, where McDowell is. If Morell has not joined you, send word to him to push forward immediately; also send word to Banks to hurry forward with all speed, to take your place at Warrenton Junction. It is necessary, on all accounts, that you should be here by daylight. I send an officer with this dispatch, who will conduct you to this place. Be sure to send word to Banks, who is on the road from Fayetteville, probably in the direction of Bealeton. Say to Banks, also, that he had best run back the railroad trains to this side of Cedar Run. If he is not with you, write him to that effect.
By command of Major-General Pope:
GEO. D. RUGGLES,
Colonel and Chief of Staff.
P. S.—If Banks is not at Warrenton Junction, leave a regiment of infantry and two pieces of artillery as a guard till he comes up, with instructions to follow you immediately. If Banks is not at the junction, instruct Colonel Clary to run the train back to this side of Cedar Run, and post a regiment and section of artillery with it.

By command of Major-General Pope:
GEO. D. RUGGLES,
Colonel and Chief of Staff—

Did then and there disobey the said order, being at the time in the face of the enemy. This at or near Warrenton, in the State of Virginia, on or about the 28th of August, 1862.

Specification 2d.—In this, that the said Maj. Gen. Fitz John Porter, being in front of the enemy, at Manassas, Va., on or about the morning of August 29, 1862, did receive from Maj. Gen. John Pope, his superior and commanding officer, a lawful order, in the following letters and figures, to wit:

HEADQUARTERS ARMY OF VIRGINIA,
Centreville, August 29, 1862.
Generals McDOWELL and PORTER:
You will please move forward with your joint commands toward Gainesville. I sent General Porter written orders to that effect an hour and a half ago. Heintzelman, Sigel, and Reno are moving on the Warrenton turnpike, and must now be not far from Gainesville. I desire that, as soon as communication is established between this force and your own, the whole command shall halt. It may be necessary to fall back behind Bull Run, at Centreville, to-night. I presume it will be so on account of our supplies. I have sent no orders of any description to Ricketts, and none to interfere in any way with the movements of McDowell's troops, except what I sent by his aide-de-camp last night, which were to hold his position on the Warrenton pike until the troops from here should fall on the enemy's flank and rear. I do not even know Ricketts' position, as I have not been able to find out where General McDowell was until a late hour this morning. General McDowell will take immediate steps to communicate with General Ricketts, and instruct him to join the other divisions of his corps as soon as practicable. If any considerable advantages are to be gained by departing from this order, it will not be strictly carried out. One thing must be held in view: that the troops must occupy a position from which they can reach Bull Run to-night or by morning. The indications are that the whole force of the enemy is moving in this direction at a pace that will bring them here by to-morrow night or the next day. My own headquarters will for the present be with Heintzelman's corps, or at this place.
JOHN POPE,
Major-General, Commanding—

Which order the said Major-General Porter did then and there disobey. This at or near Manassas, in the State of Virginia, on or about the 29th of August, 1862.
Specification 3d.—In this, that the said Maj. Gen. Fitz

John Porter, having been in front of the enemy during the battle of Manassas, on Friday, the 29th of August, 1862, did on that day receive from Maj. Gen. John Pope, his superior and commanding officer, a lawful order, in the following letters and figures, to wit:

HEADQUARTERS IN THE FIELD,
August 29, 1862—4.30 p.m.
Major-General PORTER:
Your line of march brings you in on the enemy's right flank. I desire you to push forward into action at once on the enemy's flank, and, if possible, on his rear, keeping your right in communication with General Reynolds. The enemy is massed in the woods in front of us, but can be shelled out as soon as you engage their flank. Keep heavy reserves, and use your batteries, keeping well closed to your right all the time. In case you are obliged to fall back, do so to your right and rear, so as to keep you in close communication with the right wing.
JOHN POPE,
Major-General, Commanding—

Which said order the said Major-General Porter did then and there disobey, and did fail to push forward his forces into action either on the enemy's flank or rear, and in all other respects did fail to obey said order. This at or near Manassas, in the State of Virginia, on or about the 29th of August, 1862.

Specification 4th.—In that the said Maj. Gen. Fitz John Porter, being at or near Manassas Junction, on the night of the 29th August, 1862, did receive from Maj. Gen. John Pope, his superior and commanding officer, a lawful order, in figures and words as follows, to wit:

HEADQUARTERS ARMY OF VIRGINIA,.
In the Field, near Bull Run, August 29, 1862—8.50 p.m.
Maj. Gen. F. J. PORTER:
GENERAL: Immediately upon receipt of this order, the precise hour of receiving which you will acknowledge, you will march your command to the field of battle of to-day, and report to me in person for orders. You are to understand that you are expected to comply strictly with this order, and to be present on the field within three hours after its reception, or after daybreak to-morrow morning.
JOHN POPE,
Major-General, Commanding—

And the said Maj. Gen. Fitz John Porter did then and there disobey the said order, and did permit one of the brigades of his command to march to Centreville—out of the way of the field of battle—and there to remain during the entire day of Saturday, the 30th of August. This at or near Manassas Station, in the State of Virginia, on the 29th and 30th days of August, 1862.

Specification 5th.—In this, that the said Maj. Gen. Fitz John Porter, being at or near Manassas Station, in the State of Virginia., on the night of the 29th August, 1862, and having received from his superior commanding officer, Maj. Gen. John Pope, the lawful order set forth in specification fourth to this charge, did then and there disobey the same, and did permit one other brigade attached to his command—being the brigade commanded by Brig. Gen. A. S. Piatt—to march to Centreville, and did thereby greatly delay the arrival of the said General Piatt's brigade on the field of battle of Manassas, on Saturday, the 30th August, 1862. This at or near Manassas, in the State of Virginia, on or about the 29th day of August, 1862.
B. S. ROBERTS,
Brigadier-General of Volunteers and Inspector-General of Pope's Army.

CHARGE 2d.—Violation of the Fifty-second Article of War.
Specification 1st.—In this, that the said Maj. Gen. Fitz John Porter, during the battle of Manassas, on Friday, the 29th August, 1862, and while within sight of the field and in full hearing of its artillery, did receive from Maj. Gen. John Pope, his superior and commanding officer, a lawful order to attack the enemy, in the following figures and letters, to wit:

HEADQUARTERS IN THE FIELD,
August 29, 1862—4.30 p.m.
Major-General PORTER:
Your line of march brings you in on the enemy's right flank. I desire you to push forward into action at once on the enemy's flank, and, if possible, on his rear, keeping your right in communication with General Reynolds. The enemy is massed in the woods in front of us, but can be shelled out as soon as you engage their flank. Keep heavy reserves, and use your batteries, keeping well closed to your right all the time. In case you are obliged to fall back, do so to your right and rear, so as to keep you in close communication with the right wing.
JOHN POPE,
Major-General, Commanding—

Which said order the said Major-General Porter did then and there shamefully disobey, and did retreat from advancing forces of the enemy without any attempt to engage them, or to aid the troops who were already fighting greatly superior numbers, and were relying on the flank attack he was thus ordered to make to secure a decisive victory, and to capture the enemy's army, a result which must have followed from said flank attack, had it been made by the said General Porter in compliance with the said order, which he so shamefully disobeyed. This at or near Manassas, in the State of Virginia, on or about the 29th of August, 1862.

Specification 2d.—In this, that the said Maj. Gen. Fitz John Porter, being with his army corps, on Friday, the 29th August, 1862, between Manassas Station and the field of a battle then pending between the forces of the United States and those of the rebels, and within sound of the guns and in the presence of the enemy, and knowing that a severe action of great consequence was being fought, and that the aid of his corps was greatly needed, did fail all day to bring it on to the field, and did shamefully fall back and retreat from the advance of the enemy, without any attempt to give them battle, and without knowing the forces from which he shamefully retreated. This near Manassas Station, in the State of Virginia, on the 29th of August, 1862.

Specification 3d.—In that the said Maj. Gen. Fitz John Porter, being with his army corps near the field of battle of Manassas, on the 29th August, 1862, while a severe action was being fought by the troops of Major-General Pope's command, and being in the belief that the troops of the said General Pope were sustaining defeat and retiring from the field, did shamefully fail to go to the aid of the said troops and general, and did shamefully retreat away and fall back with his army to the Manassas Junction, and leave to the disasters of a presumed defeat the said army, and did fail, by any attempt, to attack the enemy, to aid in averting the misfortunes of a disaster that would have endangered the safety of the capital of the country. This at or near Manassas Station, in the State of Virginia, on the 29th day of August, 1862.

Specification 4th.—In this, that the said Maj. Gen. Fitz John Porter, on the field of battle of Manassas, on Saturday, the 30th August, 1862, having received a lawful order from his superior officer and commanding general, Maj. Gen. John Pope, to engage the enemy's lines and to carry a position near their center, and to take an annoying battery there posted did proceed in the execution of that order with unnecessary slowness, and, by delays, give the enemy opportunities to watch and know his movements and to prepare to meet his attack; and did finally so feebly fall upon the enemy's lines as to make little or no impression on the same, and did fall back and draw away his forces unnecessarily, and without making any of the great personal efforts to rally his troops or to keep their lines, or to inspire his troops to meet the sacrifices and to make the resistance demanded by the importance of his position, and the momentous consequences and disasters of a retreat at so critical a juncture of the day. [NOTE: THIS LAST SPECIFICATION WAS WITHDRAWN BUT REMAINED IN THE RECORD.]
B. S. ROBERTS,
*Brigadier-General Volunteers and Inspector-General
Pope's Army*

(Source: U.S. War Department. *War of the Rebellion: A Compilation of the Official Records of the Union and Confederate Armies.* Ser. I, Vol. XII. Supplement.)

XXII. The Antietam Campaign

After his victory at Second Bull Run, Lee thought that by taking the fight to the North he would be able to provision his troops from a region untouched by the war. Lee weighed the considerable risks in the move but persuaded President Davis of its necessity. The resulting Maryland campaign caused the bloodiest single day of the American Civil War near the banks of Antietam Creek when the Army of the Potomac clashed with the Army of Northern Virginia on 17 September 1862. In the opening hours of the battle, Union major general Joseph Hooker was wounded during his assault on the soon famous cornfield north of Sharpsburg, Maryland. His report details maneuvers prior to and during the first stage of the battle of Antietam. McClellan, restored to command following Pope's performance, was obviously impressed. His recommendation that Hooker be made a brigadier general in the regular army was made to General Henry Wager Halleck in a telegram on 19 September, and Hooker's appointment would date from that day.

1. Robert E. Lee to Jefferson Davis in Regard to Entering Maryland (3 September 1862)

Head Qurs Alex: & Leesburg Road near
Drainsville [Va.] 3d September 1862

Mr. President—
The present seems to be the most propitious time, since the commencement of the war, for the Confederate Army to enter Maryland. The two grand armies of the U. S. that have been operating in Virginia, though now united, are much weakened and demoralized. Their new levees, of which, I understand, sixty thousand men have already been posted in Washington, are not yet organized, and will take some time to prepare for the field. If it is ever desired to give material aid to Maryland, and afford her an opportunity of throwing off the oppression to which she is now subject, this would seem the most favorable. After the enemy had disappeared from the vicinity of Fairfax C. H. and taken the road to Alexandri[a] & Washington, I did not think it would be advantageous to follow him further. I had no intention of attacking him in his fortifications, and am not prepared to invest them. If I possessed the necessary munitions, I should be unable to supply provisions for the troops. I therefore determined while threatening the approaches to Washington to draw the troops into Loudon, where forage and some provisions can be obtained, menace their possession of the Shenandoah Valley, and if found practicable, to cross into Maryland.

The purpose, if discovered, will have the effect of carrying the enemy north of the Potomac, and if prevented, will not result in much evil. The army is not properly equipped for an invasion of an enemy's territory. It lacks much of the material of war, is feeble in transportation, the animals being much reduced, and the men are poorly provided with clothes, and in thousands of instances, are destitute of shoes. Still we cannot afford to be idle, and though weaker than our opponents in men and military equipments, must endeavor to harass, if we cannot destroy them. I am aware that the movement is attended with much risk, yet I do not consider success impossible, and shall endeavor to guard it from loss. As long as the army of the enemy are employed on this frontier, I have no fears for the safety of Richmond, yet I earnestly recommend that advantage be taken of this period of comparative safety, to place its defence, both by land and water, in the most, perfect condition. A respectable force can be collected to defend its approaches by land, and the steamer Richmond I hope is now ready to clear the river of hostile vessels. Should Genl [Braxton] Bragg find it impracticable to operate to advantage on his present frontier, his army, after leaving sufficient garrisons, could be advantageously employed in opposing the overwhelming numbers which it seems to be the intention of the enemy now to concentrate in Virginia. I have already been told by prisoners that some of [Don Carlos] Buell's Cavalry have been joined to Gen'l. [John] Pope's Army, and have reason to beleive that the whole of [George B.] McClellan's, the larger portions of [Ambrose E.] Burnside's & [Jacob D.] Coxe's, and a portion of [David] Hunter's, are united to it, what occasions me most concern is the fear of getting out of ammunition. I beg you will instruct the Ordnance Dept: to spare no pains in manufacturing a sufficient amount of the best kind, & to be particular in preparing that for the Artillery, to provide three times as much of the long range ammunition, as of that for smooth bore or short range guns.

The points to which I desire the ammunition to be forwarded, will be made known to the Department in time. If the Qur. Master's Department—in time—can furnish any shoes, it would be the greatest releif.

We have entered upon September, and the nights are becoming cool. I have the honor to be with high respect
Your Ob't Servant,
R.E. Lee, General.

(Source: *The Papers of Jefferson Davis*. Vol. 8. Baton Rouge: Louisiana State University Press, 1994.)

2. Hooker's Unfinished Antietam Report (8 November 1862)

HEADQUARTERS FIRST CORPS, *ARMY OF THE POTOMAC*,
Washington, D.C., November 8, 1862.

GENERAL: At dawn the morning following the battle of South Mountain, September 15, Hartsuff's skirmishers, supported by his brigade, were thrown forward, when it was ascertained that the enemy had fallen back from our front, leaving his dead and wounded in our hands, toward Boonsborough, and from thence had taken the road to Sharpsburg.

Soon after Hartsuff's advance, General Richardson, with his brigade of Sumner's corps, was ordered to take the place of Hartsuff, and to proceed in vigorous pursuit, with no other instructions than not to engage the enemy if he overtook him, but await my arrival. Mean time my corps were ordered to make a little coffee and eat their breakfasts, which they had not been able to do since the beginning of their march from the Monocacy, the morning previous. Pleasanton's cavalry followed in the footsteps of Richardson's brigade, and soon after the First Corps resumed its march in pursuit of the enemy.

About 10 o'clock a.m. word was received that he had made a stand a mile or more in front of Sharpsburg, and about that distance from Richardson's command. As General Richardson was without artillery, he had borrowed a section from Pleasonton, and had already opened on the enemy when I reached the field. The rebels appeared to be ostentatiously deployed in two lines, perpendicular to the road leading to Sharpsburg, with his batteries posted to resist the passage of our forces over the bridge which crosses that stream. All of his troops appeared exposed to view, and numbered, as nearly as I could estimate, about 30,000 men. Fully conscious of my weakness in number and *morale*, I did not feel strong enough to attack him in front, even after the arrival of the First Corps, and it was only after the left of the enemy was observed to break into column and march to the rear, behind a forest, on which appeared to be the Williamsport road, that Maj. D.C. Houston, of the Engineers, was dispatched up the river to find practicable fords, by the means of which my troops might be thrown across the Antietam River to attack the enemy, and perhaps cut off his artillery, as soon as his numbers were sufficiently reduced to justify the movement. A bridge was found, and also two fords, which with little labor on the banks were rendered practicable for the passage of infantry and artillery. At 5 o'clock p.m. about one-half of the enemy's infantry force had passed to the rear, when I deemed it too late to make the detour, in order to come up with the enemy, without a night march through a country of which we were profoundly ignorant.

Meanwhile the bulk of the army was arriving in the valley of Antietam, and all the enemy's artillery, with a considerable portion of his infantry, remained in the position in which we had found them in the morning.

Between 1 and 2 o'clock the day following, I received instructions from the major-general commanding the Army of the Potomac to cross the river with the First Corps, and attack the enemy on his left flank, Meade's and Ricketts' divisions crossing the bridge near Keedysville, and Doubleday's division at the ford just below it.

As soon as I saw my command under way, I rode to the headquarters of the commanding general for any further orders he might have to give me, when I was informed that I was at liberty to call for re-enforcements if I should need them, and that on their arrival they would be placed under my command, and I returned find joined my troops on their march. Our direction was nearly perpendicular to the river we had crossed, my object being to gain the high ground or divide between the Potomac and Antietam Rivers, and then incline to the left, following the elevation toward the left of the rebel army. Two regiments of Meade's division were thrown forward as skirmishers, followed by a squadron of Owen's cavalry, and all supported by Meade's division. We had not proceeded over a half a mile before the commanding general with his staff joined me, apparently to see how we were progressing. Among other subjects of conversation, I said to the general that he had ordered my small corps, now numbering between 12,000 and 13,000 (as I had just lost nearly 1,000 men in the battle of South Mountain), across the river to attack the whole rebel army, and that if re-enforcements were not forwarded promptly, or if another attack was not made on the enemy's right, the rebels would eat me up. Pretty soon after this interview, my skirmishers became engaged with the enemy's advanced post, and the firing was continued incessantly until dark, we advancing slowly, and the enemy retiring before us. During the last part of the time the resistance became formidable, and we all slept on our arms that night. The cleared space between the forests necessitated a change in my front from a division to a brigade, and Seymour's command held the advance when night overtook us, and bivouacked in advance of my corps when operations were suspended.

The night becoming dark and drizzly, I sought shelter in Miller's barn, a few yards to the left of the Hagerstown pike (facing the south), and directly in the rear of Seymour's brigade. Desultory firing was kept up between the pickets almost throughout the night, and about 9 o'clock p.m. I visited them in order to satisfy myself concerning this firing, and found that the lines of pickets of the two armies were so near each other as to be able to hear each other walk, but were not visible to each other. I found Seymour's officers and men keenly alive to their proximity to our enemy, and seemed to realize the responsible character of their services for the night. Indeed, their conduct inspired me with the fullest confidence, and on returning to the barn I immediately dispatched a courier informing the com-

manding general of my surroundings, and assuring him that the battle would be renewed at the earliest dawn, and that re-enforcements should be ordered forward in season to reach me before that moment.

General Mansfield, with his corps, did cross the creek that night, and encamped his command about 1 mile in rear of my own, and in the morning participated actively in the battle. We were now 3 or 4 miles in advance of where we had crossed the Antietam Bridge. At daylight we were fully prepared to renew our march, which lay through orchards, corn-fields, and over plowed ground, skirted on either side by forests, the cleared space between which averaging not more than 400 or 500 yards in width, the field and the object in view narrowing my front to quite a limited degree. Doubleday's division was posted on the right, Ricketts' on the left, and Meade's in reserve. At daylight Gibbon's and Hartsuff's brigades were thrown forward, supported with the brigades of their respective divisions, while Meade followed them up in the center, instructed to spring to the assistance of either, as circumstances might require. Seymour continued to hold the advance, with the utmost firmness and resolution, until our troops had passed him. With these dispositions completed, the battle was soon renewed on the morning of the 17th. My object was to gain the high ground nearly three-quarters of a mile in advance of me, and which commanded the position taken by the enemy on his retreat from South Mountain; to prevent which he had been re enforced by Jackson's corps during the night, and at the same time had planted field batteries on high ground on our right and rear, to enfilade our lines when exposed during the advance.

We had not proceeded far before I discovered that a heavy force of the enemy had taken possession of a corn-field (I have since learned about a thirty-acre field) in my immediate front, and from the sun's rays falling on their bayonets projecting above the corn could see that the field was filled with the enemy, with arms in their hands, standing apparently at "support arms." Instructions were immediately given for the assemblage of all of my spare batteries, near at hand, of which I think there were five or six, to spring into battery, on the right of this field, and to open with canister at once. In the time I am writing every stalk of corn in the northern and greater part of the field was cut as closely as could have been done with a knife, and the slain lay in rows precisely as they had stood in their ranks a few moments before. It was never my fortune to witness a more bloody, dismal battle-field. Those that escaped fled in the opposite direction from our advance, and sought refuge behind the trees, fences, and stone ledges nearly on a line with the Dunker Church, &c., as there was no resisting this torrent of death-dealing missiles. I have since been informed by

a division commander of Jackson's corps that the latter was waiting for some stragglers to arrive which had been left during his night march from Harper's Ferry, in anticipation of delivering an attack on my command.

The whole morning had been one of unusual animation to me and fraught with the grandest events. The conduct of my troops was sublime, and the occasion almost lifted me to the skies, and its memories will ever remain near me. My command followed the fugitives closely until we had passed the corn-field a quarter of a mile or more, when I was removed from my saddle in the act of falling out of it from loss of blood, having previously been struck without my knowledge. While my wound was being examined by the surgeons, Sumner's corps appeared upon the field on my immediate right, and I have an indistinct recollection of having seen Sedgwick's division pass to the front. I do not think that I examined my watch that morning, but feel confident as to the time—10 o'clock a.m. I was carried to the rear at once, to the house of Mr. Pry, on the left bank of Antietam Creek.

Throughout the foregoing operations all of my officers and men of all arms, as well as the officers composing my staff, without a solitary exception, seemed to be emulous of each other in their eagerness to learn my wishes and execute my orders.
[HOOKER.]
Brig. Gen. S. WILLIAMS,
Assistant Adjutant-General, Army of the Potomac.

(Source: U.S. War Department. *War of the Rebellion: A Compilation of the Official Records of the Union and Confederate Armies.* Ser. I, Vol. XXIX/1 [S# 27].)

3. McClellan to Hooker (20 September 1862)
HEADQUARTERS ARMY OF THE POTOMAC,
Sharpsburg, September 20, 1862.

Maj. Gen. JOSEPH HOOKER, *Commanding Corps:*
MY DEAR HOOKER: I have been very sick the last few days, and just able to go where my presence was absolutely necessary, so I could not come to see you and thank you for what you did the other day, and express my intense regret and sympathy for your unfortunate wound. Had you not been wounded when you were, I believe the result of the battle would have been the entire destruction of the rebel army, for I know that, with you at its head, your corps would have kept on until it gained the main road. As a slight expression of what I think you merit, I have requested that the brigadier-general's commission rendered vacant by Mansfield's death may be given to you. I will this evening write a private note to the President on the subject, and I am glad to assure you that, so far as I can learn, it is the universal feeling of the army that you are the most deserving in it.

With the sincere hope that your health may soon be restored, so that you may again be with us in the field, I am, my dear general, your sincere friend,
GEO. B. McCLELLAN, *Major-general.*

(Source: U.S. War Department. *War of the Rebellion: A Compilation of the Official Records of the Union and Confederate Armies.* Ser. I, Vol. XXIX/1 [S# 27].)

At Antietam, McClellan had done little more than fight Lee to a draw, and he rejected a pursuit of the Army of Northern Virginia into Virginia. Lincoln nudged him to action, but McClellan hesitated and lodged now familiar complaints about equipment shortages and undermanned forces. Meanwhile, in early October Lee authorized "Jeb" Stuart to conduct another raid to cut McClellan's supply line near Chambersburg, Pennsylvania, an operation that destroyed much valuable property while capturing almost 300 prisoners and about 1,200 horses. In addition to everything else, this intrepid act, in contrast to McClellan's torpor, was too much. In November, McClellan was relieved of command to be replaced by Ambrose Burnside. [See Antietam, Battle of; Burnside, Ambrose; McCellan, George Brinton; Chambersburg Raid]

4. Orders and Correspondence in Regard to Stuart's Expedition into Maryland (October 1862)
HEADQUARTERS ARMY OF NORTHERN VIRGINIA,
Camp near Winchester, Va., October 8, 1862.

Maj. Gen. J. E. B. STUART,
Commanding Cavalry, &c.:
GENERAL: An expedition into Maryland with a detachment of cavalry, if it can be successfully executed, is at this time desirable, You will, therefore, form a detachment of from 1,200 to 1,500 well-mounted men, suitable for such an expedition, and, should the information from your scouts lead you to suppose that your movement can be concealed from bodies of the enemy that would be able to resist it, you are desired to cross the Potomac above Williamsport, leave Hagerstown and Green-castle on your right, and proceed to the rear of Chambersburg and endeavor to destroy the railroad bridge over the branch of the Conococheague. Any other damage that you can inflict upon the enemy or his means of transportation you will also execute. You are desired to gain all information of the position, force, and probable intention of the enemy which you can, and in your progress into Pennsylvania you will take measures to inform yourself of the various routes that you may take on your return to Virginia.

To keep your movement secret, it will be necessary for you to arrest all citizens that may give information to the enemy, and should you meet with citizens of

Pennsylvania holding State or Government offices, it will be desirable, if convenient, to bring them with you, that they may be used as hostages, or the means of exchanges, for our own citizens that have been carried off by the enemy. Such persons will, of course, be treated with all the respect and consideration that circumstances will admit. Should it be in your power to supply yourself with horses or other necessary articles on the list of legal captures, you are authorized to do so.

Having accomplished your errand, you will rejoin this army as soon as practicable. Reliance is placed upon your skill and judgment in the successful execution of this plan, and it is not intended or desired that you should jeopardize the safety of your command, or go farther than your good judgment and prudence may dictate.

Colonel Imboden has been desired to attract the attention of the enemy toward Cumberland, so that the river between that point and where you may recross may be less guarded. You will, of course, keep out your scouts to give you information, and take every other precaution to secure the success and safety of the expedition. Should you be led so far east as to make it better, in your opinion, to continue around to the Potomac, you will have to cross the river in the vicinity of Leesburg.
I am, with great respect, your obedient servant,
R. E. LEE,
General.

* * *

HEADQUARTERS CAVALRY DIVISION,
October 9, 1862.

SOLDIERS: You are about to engage in an enterprise which, to insure success, imperatively demands at your hands coolness, decision, and bravery; implicit obedience to orders without question or cavil, and the strictest order and sobriety on the march and in bivouac. The destination and extent of this expedition had better be kept to myself than known to you. Suffice it to say, that with the hearty cooperation of officers and men I have not a doubt of its success—a success which will reflect credit in the highest degree upon your arms. The orders which are herewith published for your government are absolutely necessary, and must be rigidly enforced.
J. E. B. STUART,
Major-General, Commanding.

* * *

ORDERS No. 13.
HEADQUARTERS CAVALRY DIVISION,
October 9, 1862.

During the expedition into the enemy's country on which this command is about to engage, brigade commanders will make arrangements for seizing horses, the property of citizens of the United States, and all other property subject to legal capture, provided, that in no case will any species of property be taken except by authority, given in person or in writing, of the commander of brigade, regiment, or captain of company in the absence of his superior officers. In all cases, a simple receipt will be given to the effect that the article is seized for the use of the Confederate States, giving place, date, and name of owner, in order to enable the individual to have recourse upon his Government for damage. Individual plunder for private use is positively forbidden, and every instance must be punished in the severest manner, for an army of plunderers consummates its own destruction. The capture of anything will not give the captor any individual claim, and all horses and equipments will be kept to be apportioned, upon the return of the expedition, through the entire divisions.

Brigade commanders will arrange to have one-third of their respective commands engaged in leading horses, provided enough can be procured, each man linking, so as to lead three horses, the led horses being habitually in the center of the brigade, and the remaining two-thirds will keep at all times prepared for action.

The attack, when made, must be vigorous and overwhelming, giving the enemy no time to collect, reconnoiter, or consider anything except his best means of flight. All persons found in transit must be detained, subject to the orders of division provost-marshal, to prevent information reaching the enemy.

As a measure of justice to our many good citizens who, without crime, have been taken from their homes and kept by the enemy in prison, all public functionaries, such as magistrates, postmasters, sheriffs, &c., will be seized as prisoners. They will be kindly treated and kept as hostages for our own.

No straggling from the route of march or bivouac for the purpose of obtaining provisions, &c., will be permitted in any case, the commissaries and quartermasters being required to obtain and furnish all such supplies in bulk as may be necessary.

So much of this order as authorizes seizures of persons and property will not take effect until the command crosses the Pennsylvania line.

The utmost activity is enjoined upon the detachments procuring horses, and unceasing vigilance upon the entire command.

Maj. J. T. W. Hairston is hereby appointed division provost-marshal. By command of Maj. Gen. J. E. B. Stuart:
R. CHANNING PRICE,
First Lieutenant and Aide-de-Camp.

(Source: U.S. War Department. *War of the Rebellion: A Compilation of the Official Records of the Union and Confederate Armies.* Ser. I, Vol. XIX/2.)

5. Lincoln to McClellan
(24 October 1862)

WAR DEPARTMENT,
Washington City, October 24, 1862.

Major-General McCLELLAN:
I have just read your dispatch about sore-tongued and fatigued horses. Will you pardon me for asking what the horses of your army have done since the battle of Antietam that fatigues anything?
A. LINCOLN.

(Source: U.S. War Department. *War of the Rebellion: A Compilation of the Official Records of the Union and Confederate Armies.* Ser. I, Vol. XIX/2.)

6. Lincoln Relieves McClellan of Command
(5 November 1862)

EXECUTIVE MANSION,
Washington, November 5, 1862.

By direction of the President, it is ordered that Major-General McClellan be relieved from the command of the Army of the Potomac, and that Major-General Burnside take the command of that army. Also that Major-General Hunter take command of the corps in said army which is now commanded by General Burnside. That Major-General Fitz John Porter be relieved from the command of the corps he now commands in said army, and that Major-General Hooker take command of said corps.

The General-in-Chief is authorized, in discretion, to issue an order substantially as the above, forthwith, or so soon as he may deem proper.
A. LINCOLN.

(Source: U.S. War Department. *War of the Rebellion: A Compilation of the Official Records of the Union and Confederate Armies.* Ser. I, Vol. XIX/2.)

XXIII. Fredericksburg

When Burnside replaced McClellan, he planned to move quickly to Fredericksburg to outflank Lee, but the Army of the Potomac was delayed while waiting for pontoon bridges to be built across the Rappahannock River. Lee meanwhile had time to entrench his army behind Fredericksburg in a formidable position on Marye's Heights. Burnside persisted in his original plan, however, crossing the river and fighting a battle on 13 December. The main effort saw wave after wave of vulnerable bluecoats moving toward the Confederates arrayed at Marye's Heights, a gesture that Joseph Hooker objected to in both its planning and execution. From the Confederate perspective, it was a significant victo-

ry, with Burnside suffering more than 12,000 casualties in these failed assaults. Then in January Burnside's hapless attempt to flank Lee out of Fredericksburg seemed to establish of pattern of incompetence. Undertaken in inclement weather that worsened already marginal roads, the "Mud March" was Burnside's undoing. His relief brought Joseph Hooker to command, although Hooker had spoken and behaved in such way as to raise the administration's concerns over his relations in the army and his attitude toward the government. Lincoln's addressing of those concerns was a masterpiece of tactful firmness and careful admonishment. [See Burnside, Ambrose; Fredericksburg, Battle of Hooker, Joseph; Longstreet, James; Mud March]

1. Joseph Hooker Objects to the Attack on Marye's Heights

The grand division commanders were assembled to discuss and determine the place and method of crossing the river. It was proposed by the major-general commanding that a portion of the army should cross at Falmouth and a portion 12 miles below. To this I objected by my vote, and proposed a crossing above. It was finally determined by General Burnside to cross at Falmouth and 12 miles below. This plan was afterward changed, and three bridges thrown across the river at Fredericksburg and two about 4 miles below, my orders being to hold my troops in hand, and, in event of a successful crossing, to spring upon the enemy's line of retreat with my whole force. My corps were moved to the three upper bridges to carry out the proposed plans, General Stoneman's corps in advance, followed by General Butterfield's corps.

The night previous to the attack (December 12), I was ordered to send two divisions (Sickles' and Birney's) of General Stoneman's corps to the bridges, 4 miles below, to support General Franklin.

On December 13, during the attack of General Franklin, without any knowledge or information on my part, these two divisions were ordered forward with Franklin. Subsequently I was ordered to send the remaining division (Whipple's) of the Third Corps to relieve the division of General Howard, in Fredericksburg. The corps of General Butterfield was left intact up to this time, ready to cross the bridges.

At 1.30 o'clock, or thereabouts, I received orders to cross this corps and attack. Before the corps had fully crossed, I was directed to send one division to support General Sturgis. General Griffin's division, the largest of the three, being nearest in position, for the purpose, was assigned to this duty. General Butterfield was then left with the two smallest divisions of his corps to make an attack upon the right, where General Sumner's (Second) and a portion of the Ninth Corps, greatly outnumbering this force, had been at work all day without making any impression.

A prisoner in the morning had given to General Burnside, General Sumner, and myself full information of the position and defenses of the enemy, stating that it was their desire that we should attack at that point, in rear of Fredericksburg, on the Telegraph road; that it was perfectly impossible for any troops to carry the position; that, if the first line was carried, a second line of batteries commanded it.

The result of the operations of General Sumner's corps, which had made a determined, spirited attack, without success, fully confirmed the statements of this prisoner. I carefully surveyed the point of attack, and, after conversation with several of the general officers of Sumner's and my own command, I was convinced that it would be a useless waste of life to attack with the force at my disposal. I dispatched an aide to General Burnside, to say that I advised him not to attack. The reply came that the attack must be made.

Under ordinary circumstances I should have complied at once, but so impressed was I with the conviction heretofore stated, that I determined it to be my duty to the troops under my command to give General Burnside a fuller explanation, and dissuade him, if possible, from what I considered a hopeless attack, especially as the few moments it would take for this purpose could not possibly affect the result of the attack in the slightest degree. Accordingly I did so. The general insisted upon the attack being made.

I returned and brought up every available battery, with the intention of breaking their barriers, to enable Butterfield's attacking column to carry the crest. This artillery fire was continued with great vigor until near sunset, when the attack with bayonet was made by Humphreys' division, General Sykes' division moving on its right, to assault *en echelon* and support. This attack was made with a spirit and determination seldom, if ever, equaled in war. The impregnable position of the enemy had given them so strong an advantage that the attack was almost immediately repulsed, and Sykes' division was recalled, without having fully assaulted, to cover the withdrawal of Humphreys'. This movement was a necessity, for the loss and repulse of the attacking columns had been so severe that, should the enemy have followed up their advantage, without this precaution, the result could not have failed to be of the most disastrous character.

(Source: U.S. War Department. *War of the Rebellion: A Compilation of the Official Records of the Union and Confederate Armies*. Ser. I, Vol. XXI [S# 31].)

2. James Longstreet Describes the Attack on Marye's Heights

Early on the morning of the 13th I rode to the right of my position (Hood's division). The dense fog in the early twilight concealed the enemy from view, but his commands, "Forward, guide center, march!" were distinctly heard at different points near my right. From the direction of the sound and the position of his troops the day before, I concluded that his attack would be upon General Jackson at some point beyond my right. I therefore rode back to a point near the center of my forces, giving notice to General Hood that the enemy would attack General Jackson beyond his right; that he should watch carefully the movements, and when an opportunity offered he should move forward and attack the enemy's flank. Similar instructions were given to General Pickett, with orders to co-operate with General Hood. The attack was made as had been anticipated. It did not appear to have all the force of a real attack, however, and General Hood did not feel authorized to make more than a partial advance. When he did move out, he drove the enemy back in handsome style. About 11 a.m. I sent orders for the batteries to play upon the streets and bridges beyond the city, by way of diversion in favor of our right. The batteries had hardly opened when the enemy's infantry began to move out toward my line. Our pickets in front of the Marye house were soon driven in, and the enemy began to deploy his forces in front of that point. Our artillery, being in position, opened fire as soon as the masses became dense enough to warrant it. This fire was very destructive and demoralizing in its effects, and frequently made gaps in the enemy's ranks that could be seen at the distance of a mile. The enemy continued his advance and made his attack at the Marye Hill in handsome style. He did not meet the fire of our infantry with any heart, however, and was therefore readily repulsed. Another effort was speedily made, but with little more success. The attack was again renewed, and again repulsed. Other forces were seen preparing for another attack, when I suggested to General McLaws the propriety of re-enforcing his advanced line by a brigade. He had previously re-enforced with part of General Kershaw's brigade and ordered forward the balance. About this time Brig. Gen. T. R. R. Cobb fell, mortally wounded, and almost simultaneously Brig. Gen. J. R. Cooke was severely wounded. General Kershaw dashed to the front to take the command.

General Ransom, on the Marye Hill, was charged with the immediate care of the point attacked, with orders to send forward additional re-enforcements if it should become necessary, and to use Featherston's brigade, Anderson' division, if he should require it.

The attack upon our right seemed to subside about 2 o'clock, when I directed Major-General-Pickett to send me two of his brigades. One (Kemper's) was sent to General Ransom, to be placed in some secure position, to be ready in case it should be wanted. The other (Jenkins') was ordered to General McLaws, to replace

that of Kershaw in his line. The enemy soon completed his arrangements for a renewed attack, and moved forward with much determination. He met with no better success than he had on the previous occasions. These efforts were repeated and continued from time to time until after night: when he left, the field literally strewn with his dead and wounded.

(Source: U.S. War Department. *War of the Rebellion: A Compilation of the Official Records of the Union and Confederate Armies.* Ser. I, Vol. XXI.)

3. Lincoln Relieves Ambrose Burnside, General Orders, No. 20 (25 January 1863)
WAR DEPARTMENT, ADJT. GEN.'S OFFICE, Washington, D.C., January 25, 1863.

I. The President of the United States has directed:

1st. That Maj. Gen. A. E. Burnside, at his own request, be relieved from the command of the Army of the Potomac.

2d. That Maj. Gen. E. V. Sumner, at his own request, be relieved from duty in the Army of the Potomac.

3d. That Maj. Gen. W. B. Franklin be relieved from duty in the Army of the Potomac.

4th. That Maj. Gen. J. Hooker be assigned to the command of the Army of the Potomac.

II. The officers relieved as above will report in person to the Adjutant-General of the Army.

By order of the Secretary of War:
E. D. TOWNSEND,
Assistant Adjutant-General.

(Source: U.S. War Department. *War of the Rebellion: A Compilation of the Official Records of the Union and Confederate Armies.* Ser. I, Vol. XXI.)

4. Lincoln to Joseph Hooker (26 January 1863)
Executive Mansion,
Washington, January 26, 1863.

Major General Hooker:
General.

I have placed you at the head of the Army of the Potomac. Of course I have done this upon what appear to me to be sufficient reasons. And yet I think it best for you to know that there are some things in regard to which, I am not quite satisfied with you. I believe you to be a brave and skillful soldier, which, of course, I like. I also believe you do not mix politics with your profession, in which you are right. You have confidence in yourself, which is a valuable, if not an indispensable quality. You are ambitious, which, within reasonable bounds, does good rather than harm. But I think that during Gen. Burnside's command of the Army, you

have taken counsel of your ambition, and thwarted him as much as you could, in which you did a great wrong to the country, and to a most meritorious and honorable brother officer. I have heard, in such a way as to believe it, of your recently saying that both the Army and the Government needed a Dictator. Of course it was not for this, but in spite of it, that I have given you the command. Only those generals who gain successes, can set up dictators. What I now ask of you is military success, and I will risk the dictatorship. The government will support you to the utmost of it's ability, which is neither more nor less than it has done and will do for all commanders. I much fear that the spirit which you have aided to infuse into the Army, of criticizing their Commander, and withholding confidence from him, will now turn upon you. I shall assist you as far as I can, to put it down. Neither you, nor Napoleon, if he were alive again, could get any good out of an army, while such a spirit prevails in it.

And now, beware of rashness. Beware of rashness, but with energy, and sleepless vigilance, go forward, and give us victories.
Yours very truly
A. Lincoln.

(Source: Basler, Roy P., ed. *Abraham Lincoln: His Speeches and Writings* [1946].)

XXIV. Stones River
When Major General William S. Rosecrans's Army of the Cumberland marched about thirty miles southeast of Nashville to attack Braxton Bragg's Army of Tennessee on Stones River, he started a fierce battle on 31 December 1862 near Murfreesboro, Tennessee. After a confused day of severe fighting, Rosecrans and his subordinates contemplated a retreat to Nashville, but they ultimately remained on the field where both armies spent 1 January 1863 preparing to resume the fray. Late in the afternoon of 2 January, a Confederate attack enjoyed initial success but was soon forced back. When Rosecrans received reinforcements from Nashville on 3 January, Bragg began a retreat that night along the Nashville & Chattanooga Railroad toward Tullahoma. The Union rejoiced over a hard-won victory, while Bragg tried to claim a victory of sorts in the gallant comportment of his soldiers. [See Stones River, Battle of]

1. William S. Rosecrans Exhorts His Troops (31 December 1862)
GENERAL ORDERS No.—.
HDQRS. DEPT. OF THE CUMBERLAND,
In front of Murfreesborough, December 31, 1862.

The general commanding desires to say to the soldiers of the Army of the Cumberland that he was well pleased with their conduct yesterday; it is all he could

have wished for; he neither saw nor heard of any skulking; they behaved with the coolness and gallantry of veterans. He now feels perfectly confident, with God's grace and their help, of striking this day a blow for the country the most crushing, perhaps, which the rebellion has yet sustained.

Soldiers, the eyes of the whole nation are upon you; the very fate of the nation may be said to hang on the issue of this day's battle. Be true, then, to yourselves, true to your own manly character and soldierly reputation, true to the love of your dear ones at home, whose prayers ascend to God this day for your success.

Be cool? I need not ask you to be brave. Keep ranks. Do not throw away your fire. Fire slowly, deliberately; above all, fire low, and be always sure of your aim. Close steadily in upon the enemy, and, when you get within charging distance, rush on him with the bayonet. Do this, and the victory will certainly be yours. Recollect that there are hardly any troops in the world that will stand a bayonet charge, and that those who make it, therefore, are sure to win.

By command of Maj. Gen. W. S. Rosecrans:

J. P. GARESCHE,
Assistant Adjutant-General and Chief of Staff.

(Source: U.S. War Department. *War of the Rebellion: A Compilation of the Official Records of the Union and Confederate Armies.* Ser. I, Vol. XX/1.)

2. Rosecrans to Halleck (5 January 1863)
HEADQUARTERS DEPARTMENT OF THE CUMBERLAND,
Via Nashville, Tenn., January 5, 1863.

We have fought one of the greatest battles of the war, and are victorious. Our entire success on the 31st was prevented by a surprise of the right flank; but have, nevertheless, beaten the enemy, after a three-days' battle. They fled with great precipitancy on Saturday night. The last of their columns of cavalry left this morning. Their loss has been very heavy. Generals Rains and Hanson killed. Chalmers, Adams, and Breckinridge are wounded.

W. S. ROSECRANS, *Major-General.*
H. W. HALLECK, *General-in-Chief.*

(Source: U.S. War Department. *War of the Rebellion: A Compilation of the Official Records of the Union and Confederate Armies.* Ser. I, Vol. XX/1.)

3. Lincoln to Rosecrans (5 January 1863)
EXECUTIVE MANSION,
Washington, January 5, 1863.

Maj. Gen. W. S. ROSECRANS,
Murfreesborough, Tenn.:

Your dispatch announcing retreat of enemy has just reached here. God bless you, and all with you! Please tender to all, and accept for yourself, the nation's gratitude for your and their skill, endurance, and dauntless courage.
A. LINCOLN.

(Source: U.S. War Department. *War of the Rebellion: A Compilation of the Official Records of the Union and Confederate Armies.* Ser. I, Vol. XX.)

4. Braxton Bragg Congratulates His Army
HEADQUARTERS ARMY OF TENNESSEE,
Winchester, [Tenn.], January 8, 1863.

SOLDIERS OF THE ARMY OF TENNESSEE! Your gallant deeds have won the admiration of your general, your Government, and your country. For myself, I thank you, and am proud of you; for them, I tender you the gratitude and praise you have so nobly won.

In a campaign of less than one month, in the face of winter, your achievements have been unparalleled. You have captured more than 10,000 prisoners, taken and preserved 30 pieces of artillery and 7,000 small-arms, in addition to many thousands destroyed. You have, besides, captured 800 wagons, loaded chiefly with supplies, which have been destroyed or brought safely to your lines; and in pitched battles you have driven the enemy before you, inflicting a loss at least three to one greater than you have sustained.

In retiring to a stronger position, without molestation from a superior force, you have left him a barren field in which to bury his hosts of slain, and to rally and recuperate his shattered ranks. Cut off from his Government, both by rail and telegraph, and deprived of supplies by the interruption of his communications, we shall yet teach him a severe lesson for the rashness of penetrating a country so hostile to his cause. Whilst the infantry and artillery defy him in front, our invincible cavalry will assail him in flank and rear, until we goad him to another advance, only to meet another signal defeat.

Your general deplores, in common with you, the loss of your gallant comrades, who have fallen in our recent conflicts. Let their memories be enshrined in your hearts, as they will ever be tenderly cherished by their countrymen. Let it be yours to avenge their fate, and proudly to emulate their deeds. Remember that your face is to the foe, and that on you rests the defense of all that is dear to freemen. Soldiers, the proudest reflection of your general's life is to be known as the commander of an army so brave and invincible as you have proven. He asks no higher boon than to lead such men to victory. To share their trials, and to stand or fall with them, will be the crown of his ambition.

BRAXTON BRAGG,
General, Commanding.

(Source: U.S. War Department. *War of the Rebellion: A Compilation of the Official Records of the Union and Confederate Armies.* Ser. I, Vol. XX/1.)

XXV. Chancellorsville

After the battle of Fredericksburg, the Army of Northern Virginia enjoyed four months of inactivity. Then came the news that the Union army under Joseph Hooker again was on the offensive. Lee sent "Stonewall" Jackson westward into the Wilderness, where he slowed Hooker's advance near Chancellorsville. After Lee and Jackson consulted, Jackson set out on another sweeping maneuver that took the bulk of Lee's army on a twelve-mile march around the Federals' exposed right flank. Late in the afternoon of 2 May, Jackson hit Oliver O. Howard's XI Corps in a surprise assault that drove the shocked Yankees for more than two miles before darkness, confusion, and federal resistance finally halted the flight. It was the beginning of Lee's greatest victory, but its cost would eventually be incalculable. Jackson was scouting ahead of his disordered units when he was wounded by "friendly fire." Later his left arm was amputated, but pneumonia killed him on 10 May. Neither Lee nor the Confederacy would ever recover from the loss. [See Chancellorsville, Battle of; Jackson, Thomas Jonathan]

1. J. E. B. Stuart Describes Jackson's Surprise Attack

This corps, under its immortal leader, Lieutenant-General [T. J.] Jackson, attacked the enemy on his right, turning his right flank by the Turnpike road at Melzi Chancellor's, 2 miles above Chancellorsville, making the attack late in the evening, after an arduous and necessarily circuitous march from the Plank road, 2 miles below Chancellorsville. The enemy had a fine position, and, if time had been given him to recover from his first surprise and mass troops on that front, it would have been a difficult task to dislodge them; but Jackson's entire corps, both when marching and when in position, had been purposely screened from view by the cavalry of Fitzhugh Lee's brigade, an important duty which he performed with great skill and address. The attack was thus in a measure a surprise. The enemy's line of intrenchments was carried, and his legions driven in confusion from the field.

It was already dark when I sought General Jackson, and proposed, as there appeared nothing else for me to do, to take some cavalry and infantry over and hold the Ely's Ford road. He approved the proposition, and I had already gained the heights overlooking the ford, where was a large number of camp-fires, when Captain [R. H. T.] Adams, of General A. P. Hill's staff, reached me post-haste, and informed me of the sad calamities which for the time deprived the troops of the leadership of both Jackson and Hill, and the urgent demand for me to come and take command as quickly as possible. I

rode with rapidity back 5 miles, determined to press the pursuit already so gloriously begun. General Jackson had gone to the rear, but General A. P. Hill was still on the ground, and formally turned over the command to me. I sent also a staff officer to General Jackson to inform him that I would cheerfully carry out any instructions he would give, and proceeded immediately to the front, which I reached at 10 p.m.

I found, upon reaching it, A. P. Hill's division in front, under Heth, with Lane's, McGowan's, Archer's, and Heth's brigades on the right of the road, within half a mile of Chancellorsville, near the apex of the ridge, and Pender's and Thomas' on the left. I found that the enemy had made an attack on our right flank, but were repulsed. The fact, however, that the attack was made, and at night, made the apprehensive of a repetition of it, and necessitated throwing back the right wing, so as to meet it. I was also informed that there was much confusion on the right, owing to the fact that some troops mistook friends for the enemy and fired upon them. Knowing that an advance under such circumstances would be extremely hazardous, much against my inclination, I felt bound to wait for daylight. General Jackson had also sent me word to use my own discretion. The commanding general was with the right wing of the army, with which I had no communication except by a very circuitous and uncertain route. I nevertheless sent a dispatch to inform him of the state of affairs, and rode around the lines restoring order, imposing silence, and making arrangements for the attack early next day. I sent Col. E. P. Alexander, senior officer of artillery, to select and occupy with artillery positions along the line bearing upon the enemy's position, with which duty he was engaged all night.

(Source: U.S. War Department. *War of the Rebellion: A Compilation of the Official Records of the Union and Confederate Armies.* Ser. I, Vol. XXV/2.)

2. O. O. Howard Describes the Confederate Assault

At about 6 p.m. I was at my headquarters, at Dowdall's Tavern, when the attack commenced. I sent my chief of staff to the front when firing was heard. General Schurz, who was with me, left at once to take command of his line. It was not three minutes before I followed. When I reached General Schurz's command, I saw that the enemy had enveloped my right, and that the First Division was giving way. I first tried to change the front of the deployed regiments. I next directed the artillery where to go; then formed a line by deploying some of the reserve regiments near the church. By this time the whole front on the north of the Plank road had given way. Colonel Buschbeck's brigade was faced about, and, lying on the other side of the rifle-pit embankment, held on with praiseworthy firmness. A part of General Schimmelfennig's and a part of General Krzyzanowski's brigades moved gradually back to the north of the Plank road and kept up their fire. At the center and near the Plank road there was a blind panic and great confusion. By the assistance of my staff and some other officers, one of whom was Colonel Dickinson, of General Hooker's staff, the rout was considerably checked, and all the artillery, except eight pieces, withdrawn. Some of the artillery was well served, and told effectively on the advancing enemy. Captain Dilger kept up a continuous fire until we reached General Betty's position.

Now as to the causes of this disaster to my corps:

1. Though constantly threatened and apprised of the moving of the enemy, yet the woods was so dense that he was able to mass a large force, whose exact whereabouts neither patrols, reconnaissances, nor scouts ascertained. He succeeded in forming a column opposite to and outflanking my right.

2. By the panic produced by the enemy's reverse fire, regiments and artillery were thrown suddenly upon those in position.

3. The absence of General Barlow's brigade, which I had previously located in reserve and *en echelon* with Colonel von Gilsa's, so as to cover his right flank. This was the only general reserve I had. My corps was very soon reorganized near Chancellorsville, and relieved General Meade's corps, on the left of the general line. Here it remained until Wednesday morning, when it resumed its position, as ordered, at the old camp.

The division and brigade commanders showed the greatest attention to duty and a hearty co-operation with me at all times.

(Source: U.S. War Department. *War of the Rebellion: A Compilation of the Official Records of the Union and Confederate Armies.* Ser. I, Vol. XV/1.)

3. Robert E. Lee to Jefferson Davis (3 May 1863)
MILFORD, May 3, 1863.

President DAVIS:
Yesterday General Jackson, with three of his divisions, penetrated to the rear of the enemy, and drove him from all his positions from the Wilderness to within 1 mile of Chancellorsville. He was engaged at the same time in front by two of Longstreet's divisions. This morning the battle was renewed. He was dislodged from all his positions around Chancellorsville and driven back toward the Rappahannock, over which he is now retreating. Many prisoners were taken, and the enemy's loss in killed and wounded large.

We have again to thank Almighty God for a great victory. I regret to state that General [E. F.] Paxton was

killed, General Jackson severely, and Generals [Henry] Heth and A. P. Hill slightly, wounded.
R. E. LEE,
General, Commanding

(Source: U.S. War Department. *War of the Rebellion: A Compilation of the Official Records of the Union and Confederate Armies.* Ser. I, Vol. XXV/2.)

4. Stonewall Jackson's Death, General Orders, No. 61 (11 May 1863)
HDQRS. ARMY OF NORTHERN VIRGINIA,
May 11, 1863.

With deep grief the commanding general announces to the army the death of Lieut. Gen. T. J. Jackson, who expired on the 10th instant, at 3.15 p.m. The daring, skill, and energy of this great and good soldier, by the decree of an all-wise Providence, are now lost to us. But while we mourn his death, we feel that his spirit still lives, and will inspire the whole army with his indomitable courage and unshaken confidence in God as our hope and our strength. Let his name be a watchword to his corps, who have followed him to victory on so many fields. Let officers and soldiers emulate his invincible determination to do everything in the defense of our beloved country.
R. E. LEE,
General.

(Source: U.S. War Department. *War of the Rebellion: A Compilation of the Official Records of the Union and Confederate Armies.* Ser. I, Vol. XXV/2.)

XXVI. The Vicksburg Campaign
In early 1863, Ulysses S. Grant made no less than four abortive attempts to crack the conundrum of how to assail the "Confederate Gibraltar" of Vicksburg. At the end, however, his campaign would be a strategic and tactical masterpiece, demonstrating a careful, deliberate approach to a military problem of the first order. Meanwhile Grant's rising star was illustrated by a growing interest in his appearance and habits. One of those habits was a straightforward insistence on subordination that brought him into conflict with political general and would-be rival John McClernand. Throughout the Vicksburg campaign McClernand and Grant's relations degenerated until Grant relieved McClernand on 18 June 1863. The immediate and ostensible reason was McClernand's publication of a self-congratulatory order, but there was more to it than that, as Lincoln uncomfortably knew. McClernand was politically influential, but the time for making that kind of influence a paramount consideration was passing; hence, Lincoln's gentle, consoling tone was nonetheless firm in its conviction to support Grant. [See Grant, Ulysses Simpson; McClernand, John Alexander; Vicksburg Campaign]

1. Grant to Halleck (25 May 1863)

NEAR VICKSBURG, May 22, 1863,
VIA MEMPHIS, May 25.

General H. W. HALLECK,
Washington, D.C.:

Vicksburg is now completely invested. I have possession of Haynes' Bluff and the Yazoo; consequently have supplies. To-day an attempt was made to carry the city by assault, but was not entirely successful. We hold possession, however, of two of the enemy's forts, and have skirmishers close under all of them. Our loss was not severe. The nature of the ground about Vicksburg is such that it can only be taken by a siege. It is entirely safe to us in time, I would say one week, if the enemy do not send a large army upon my rear. With the railroad destroyed to beyond Pearl River, I do not see the hope that the enemy can entertain of such relief.

I learn that Jeff Davis has promised that if the garrison can hold out for fifteen days he will send 100,000 men, if he has to evacuate Tennessee to do it.
U. S. GRANT,
Major-General.

(Source: U.S. War Department. *War of the Rebellion: A Compilation of the Official Records of the Union and Confederate Armies.* Ser. I, Vol. XXIV/1.)

2. "General Grant in the Field," by a *New York Times* Correspondent (1863)

Almost at any time one can see a small but compactly-build man of about forty-five years of age walking through the camps. He moves with his shoulders thrown a little forward of the perpendicular, his left hand in the pocket of his pantaloons, an unlighted cigar in his mouth, his eyes thrown straight forward, which, from the haze of abstraction that veils them, and a countenance drawn into furrows of thought, would seem to indicate that he is intensely preoccupied. The soldiers observe him coming, and rising to their feet, gather on each side of the way to see him pass—they do not salute him, they only watch him curiously, with a certain sort of familiar reverence. His abstract air is not so great, while he thus moves along, as to prevent his seeing everything without apparently looking at it; you will see this in the fact, that however dense the crowd in which you stand, if you are an acquaintance, his eye will for an instant rest on yours with a glance of recollection, and with it a grave nod of recognition. A plain blue suit, without scarf, sword, or trappings of any sort, save the double-starred shoulder strap—an indifferently good "Kossuth" hat, with the top battered in close to his head; full beard, of a cross between "light" and "sandy;" a square cut face, whose lines and contour indicate extreme endurance and determination, complete the external appearance of this small man, as one sees him passing along, turning and chewing restlessly the end of his unlighted cigar.

His countenance, in rest, has the rigid immobility of cast iron; and, while this indicates the unyielding tenacity of a bulldog, one finds only in his gray eyes the smiles and other evidences of the possession of those softer traits seen upon the lips and over the entire faces of ordinary people. On horseback he loses all the awkwardness which distinguishes him as he moves about on foot. Erect and graceful, he seems a portion of his steed, without which the full effect would be incomplete. He held in early days the reputation of being the best rider in the Academy, and he seems to have lost none of his excellence in this respect.

Of Gen. Grant's ability I need say nothing—he has been so long before the public that all can judge for themselves. The South calls his successes "luck;" we in the West believe that he owes them mostly to the possession of a cautious military judgment, assisted by good advisers, and backed by invincible perseverance, endurance and determination.

(Source: Wilkie, Franc. "General Grant in the Field." *New York Times*, 12 June 1863.)

3. McClernand to Grant Regarding His Actions at Vicksburg (4 June 1863)

HEADQUARTERS THIRTEENTH ARMY CORPS,
Battle-field near Vicksburg, Miss., June 4, 1863.

[Maj. Gen. U. S. GRANT:]
GENERAL: What appears to be a systematic effort to destroy my usefulness and character as a commander makes it proper that I should address you this note. It is reported, among other things, as I understand, that I attacked on the 22d ultimo without authority; again, that I attacked too late; again, that I am responsible for your failure and losses; again, that I am arrested and being sent North; again, that my command is turned over to another officer, and, again, that you have personally assumed command of it. These reports are finding their way from the landings up the river. I hardly need say to you that all these reports are false; that I obeyed orders in attacking; that my attack was prompt and in a larger measure more successful than any other; that the ultimate failure of the general attack and the losses attending it were, under the circumstances, unavoidable consequences of obstacles found to be unsurmountable, and [notwithstanding] a determined effort, at least on my part, to carry and hold the works in obedience to your express and peremptory order. You know that I am not yet under arrest, or being sent away, or superseded in my command. All these things being known to you, and these false reports being brought to

your notice, it remains for you to determine whether truth, justice, and generosity do not call on you for such a declaration as will be conclusive on the matter.
Your obedient servant,
JOHN A. McCLERNAND,
Major-general, Commanding.

(Source: U.S. War Department. *War of the Rebellion: A Compilation of the Official Records of the Union and Confederate Armies*. Ser. I, Vol. XXIV/1.)

4. Grant Relieves McClernand (19 June 1863)
NEAR VICKSBURG, MISS., June 19, 1863,
VIA CAIRO, ILL., June 23.

Maj. Gen. H. W. HALLECK,
General-in-Chief:
I have found it necessary to relieve Major-General McClernand, particularly at this time, for his publication of a congratulatory address calculated to create dissension and ill-feeling in the army. I should have relieved him long since for general unfitness for his position. Major-General Ord is appointed to his place, subject to the approval of the President.
U. S. GRANT,
Major-General, Commanding.

(Source: U.S. War Department. *War of the Rebellion: A Compilation of the Official Records of the Union and Confederate Armies*. Ser. I, Vol. XXIV/1.)

5. Lincoln to McClernand (12 August 1863)
Executive Mansion,
Washington, August 12, 1863.

Major-General McClernand:
My Dear Sir: Our friend William G. Greene has just presented a kind letter in regard to yourself, addressed to me by our other friends, Yates, Hatch, and Dubois.

I doubt whether your present position is more painful to you than to myself. Grateful for the patriotic stand so early taken by you in this life-and-death struggle of the nation, I have done whatever has appeared practicable to advance you and the public interest together. No charges with a view to a trial have been preferred against you by any one, nor do I suppose any will be. All there is, so far as I have heard, is General Grant's statement of his reasons for relieving you. And even this I have not seen or sought to see, because it is a case, as appears to me, in which I could do nothing without doing harm. General Grant and yourself have been conspicuous in our most important successes, and for me to interfere and thus magnify a breach between you could not but be of evil effect. Better leave it where the law of the case has placed it. For me to force you back upon General Grant would be forcing him to resign. I cannot

give you a new command, because we have no forces except such as already have commanders.

I am constantly pressed by those who scold before they think, or without thinking at all, to give commands respectively to Frémont, McClellan, Butler, Sigel, Curtis, Hunter, Hooker, and perhaps others, when, all else out of the way, I have no commands to give them. This is now your case, which, as I have said, pains me not less than it does you. My belief is that the permanent estimate of what a general does in the field is fixed by the "cloud of witnesses" who have been with him in the field, and that, relying on these, he who has the right needs not to fear.
Your friend, as ever,
A. LINCOLN.

(Source: U.S. War Department. *War of the Rebellion: A Compilation of the Official Records of the Union and Confederate Armies*. Ser. I, Vol. LII/1.)

XXVII. Gettysburg

A. THE BATTLE
The Gettysburg campaign began on 3 June 1863 when parts of General Robert E. Lee's Army of Northern Virginia began leaving their positions near Fredericksburg and heading for the Shenandoah Valley. Lee planned a raid into Pennsylvania to alleviate pressure on the bruised Virginia countryside and perhaps bring foreign recognition to the Confederacy. The result was the titanic three-day clash at Gettysburg on 1–3 July 1863. Later contemplating his error in ordering the final assault on 3 July, Lee was especially disturbed by the censure that appeared in some Southern newspapers. He offered to resign as commander of the Army of Northern Virginia, but Jefferson Davis would not hear of it. [See Gettysburg, Battle of]

1. Official Reports of Robert E. Lee (4–16 July, 1863)
HEADQUARTERS ARMY OF NORTHERN VIRGINIA,
Near Gettysburg, Pa., July 4, 1863.

Mr. PRESIDENT:
After the rear of the army had crossed the Potomac, leading corps, under General Ewell, pushed on to Carlisle and York, passing through Chambersburg. The other two corps closed up at the latter place, and soon afterward intelligence was received that the army of General Hooker was advancing. Our whole force was directed to concentrate at Gettysburg, and the corps of Generals Ewell and A. P. Hill reached that place on the 1st July the former advancing from Carlisle and the latter from Chambersburg. The two leading divisions of these corps, upon reaching the vicinity of Gettysburg,

found the enemy, and attacked him, driving him from the town, which was occupied by our troops. The enemy's loss was heavy, including more, than 4,000 prisoners. He took up a strong position in rear of the town, which he immediately began to fortify, and where his re-enforcements joined him.

On the 2nd July, Longstreet's corps, with the exception of one division, having arrived, we attempted to dislodge the enemy, and, though we gained some ground, we were unable to get possession of his position. The next day, the third division of General Longstreet having come up, a more extensive attack was made. The works on the enemy's extreme right and left were taken, but his numbers were so great and his position so commanding, that our troops were compelled to relinquish their advantage and retire.

It is believed that the enemy suffered severely in these operations, but our own loss has not bee light. General Barksdale is killed. Generals Garnett and Armistead are missing a prisoner. Generals Pender and Trimble are wounded in the leg, General Hood in the arm, and General Heth slightly in the head. General Kemper, it is feared, is mortally wounded. Our losses embrace many other valuable officers and men. General Wade Hampton was severely wounded in a different action in which the cavalry was engaged yesterday. Very respectfully, your obedient servant,

R. E. LEE,
General.

* * *

His Excellency President DAVIS, Richmond.
HAGERSTOWN, July 7, 1863.

Mr. PRESIDENT:

My letter of the 4th instant will have informed you of the unsuccessful issue of our final attack on the enemy in the rear of Gettysburg. Finding the position too strong to be carried, and, being much hindered in collecting necessary supplies for the army, by the numerous bodies of local and other troops which watched the passes, I determined to withdraw to the west side of the mountains. This has been safely accomplished with great labor, and the army is now in the vicinity of this place.

One of my reason for moving in this direction, after crossing the mountains, was to protect our trains with the sick and wounded, which had been sent back to Williamsport, and which were threatened by the enemy's cavalry. Our advance reached here yesterday afternoon in time to support our cavalry in repulsing an attempt of the enemy to reach our trains. Before leaving Gettysburg, such of the sick and wounded as could be removed were sent back to Williamsport, but the

trains that have interfered so much with our general movements have so swollen the Potomac as to render it unfordable, and they are still on the north side. Arrangements are being made to ferry them across today. We captured at Gettysburg about 6, 000 prisoners, besides the wounded that remained in our hands after the engagements of the 1st and 2d. Fifteen hundred of these prisoners and the wounded were paroled, but I suppose that under the late arrangements these paroles will not be regarded. The rest have been sent to Williamsport, where they will cross. We were obliged to leave a large number of our wounded who were unable to travel, and many arms that had been collected on the field at Gettysburg.

In addition to the general officers killed or wounded, of whom I sent you a list in my former letter, I have to mention General Semmes, General G. T. Anderson, Pettigrew, and General J. M. Jones, wounded; General Archer was made prisoner. General Heth is again in command. In sending back our trains in advance, that of General Ewell was cut the enemy's cavalry, and a number of wagon, said to be about 40 were captured. The enemy's cavalry force, which attempt to reach our cavalry trains yesterday afternoon, was a large one. They came as far as Hagerstown, where they were attacked by General Stuart, and driven back rapidly toward Sharpsburg.
Very respectfully, your obedient servant,

R. E. LEE, General.

* * *

His Excellency JEFFERSON DAVIS,
President Confederate States
HEADQUARTERS ARMY OF NORTHERN VIRGINIA,
Near Hagerstown, Md., July 8, 1863.

MR PRESIDENT:

My letter of yesterday will have informed you of the position of this army. Though reduced in numbers by the hardships and battles through which it has passed since leaving the Rappahannock, its condition is good, and its confidence unimpaired. Upon crossing the Potomac into Maryland, I had calculated upon the river remaining fordable during the summer, so as to enable me to recross at my pleasure, but a series of storms, commencing the day after our entrance into Maryland, has placed the river beyond fording stage, and the present storm will keep it so for at least week. I shall, therefore, have to accept battle if the enemy offers it, whether I wish to or not, and as the result is in the hands of the Sovereign Ruler of the Universe, and known to Him only, I deem it prudent to make every arrangement in our power to meet any emergency that may arise.

From information gathered from the papers, I believe that the troops from North Carolina and the coast of Virginia, under Generals Foster and Dix, have been ordered to the Potomac, and that recently additional re-enforcement have been sent from the coast of South Carolina Banks. If I am correct in my opinion, this will liberate most of the troops in those regions, and should Your Excellency have not already done so, I earnestly that all that can be spared be concentrated on the Upper Rappahannock, under General Beauregard, with directions to cross that river and make a demonstration upon Washington. This command will answer the double purpose of affording protection to the capital at Richmond and relieving the pressure upon this army.

I hope Your Excellency will understand that I am not in the least discouraged, or that my faith in the protection of an all-merciful Providence, or in the fortitude of this army is at all shaken. But, though conscious that the enemy has been much shattered in the recent battle, I am aware that he can be easily re-enforced, while no addition can be made to our numbers. The measure, therefore, that I have recommended is altogether one of a prudential nature.
I am, most respectfully, your obedient servant,
R. E. LEE,
General.

P. S.—I see it stated in a letter from the special correspondent of the New York Times that a bearer of dispatches from Your Excellency to myself was captured at Hagerstown on the 2nd July, and the dispatched are said to be of the greatest importance, and to have a great bearing on coming events. I have thought proper to mention this, that you may know whether it is so.

* * *

HEADQUARTERS ARMY OF NORTHERN VIRGINIA
July 10, 1863.

Mr. PRESIDENT:
Since my letter of the 8th instant, nothing of importance, in a military point of view, has transpired. The Potomac continues to be past fording, and, owing to the rapidity of the stream, and the limited we have for crossing, the prisoners and wounded are not yet over. I hope they will be able to cross to-day. I have not received any definite intelligence of the movements or designs of the enemy. A scout that a column which followed us across the mountain has reached Waynesborough, Pa., and other bodies are reported as moving by way of Fredericksburg from Emmitsburg, as if approaching in this direction. If these reports be correct, it would appear to be intention of the enemy to

deliver battle, and we have no alternative but to accept it if offered. The army is in good condition, and we have a good supply of ammunition, The supply of flour is affected by the highs waters, which interfere with the working of the mills.

With the blessing of Heaven, I trust that the courage and fortitude of the army will be found sufficient to relieve us from the embarrassment caused by the unlooked-for natural difficulties of our situation, if not to secure valuable and substantial results.
Very respectfully, your obedient servant,
R. E. LEE,
General.

* * *

HEADQUARTERS ARMY OF NORTHERN VIRGINIA,
July 12, 1863.

Mr. PRESIDENT:
I have nothing of moment to add to what I have said in my letter of the 10th. So far, everything goes well. The army is in good condition, and occupies a strong position, covering the Potomac from Williamsport to Falling Waters. The enemy seems to be collecting his forces in the Valley of the Antietam, his main body from Boonsborough to Sharpsburg. But for the power he possesses of accumulating troops, I should be willing to await his attack, excepting that in our restricted limits the means of obtaining subsistence are becoming precarious.

The river has now fallen to 4 feet, and a bridge, which is being constructed, I hope will be passable by to-morrow. Should the river continue to subside, our communication with the south bank will be open to-morrow. Had the late unexpected rise not occured, there would have been no cause for anxiety, as it would have been in my power to recross the Potomac on my first reaching it without molestation. Everything would have been accomplished that could have been reasonably expected—the Army of the Potomac would have been thrown north of that river, the forces invading the coast of North Carolina and Virginia diminished, their plan of the present campaign broken up, and, before new arrangements could have been made for its resumption, the summer would have been ended.

I still trust that a kind Providence will cause all things work together for our good. Very respectfully, your obedient servant,
R. E. LEE,
General

* * *

HEADQUARTERS ARMY OF NORTHERN VIRGINIA
Bunker Hill, Va., July 16, 1863.

His Excellency JEFFERSON DAVIS,
President Confederate States.
Mr. PRESIDENT:
I have received your letter of the 12th instant, and thank you for the kind terms you speak of the army, and for your consideration of myself. I inclose a copy of my letter of the 7th instant, which failed to reach you. The army is encamped around this place, where we shall rest today. The men are in good health and spirits, but want shoes and clothing badly. I have sent back to endeavor to procure a supply of both, and also horseshoes, for want of which nearly our cavalry is unserviceable. As soon as these articles are obtained, we shall be prepared to resume operations.

I shall not need the pontoon train now, as the boats used at Falling Waters have been brought away, excepting the new ones constructed by us, which were too heavy and too large for transportation. I have accordingly ordered the train of which you speak to come no farther. The attack on the coast may have been caused by the information contained in the captured letter. I think that all these demonstrations of the enemy are designed to retain troops from the field, and while he must be resisted and a force kept at threatened points sufficient to secure them, we should endeavor to avoid being misled as to his numbers and real intentions, and thus enable him to accomplish his purpose I do not know that I shall need any more troops here, and they had better be kept in front of Richmond, to secure it from attack and protect our railroads.

I learn that the enemy has thrown a pontoon bridge over the Potomac at Harper's Ferry. Should he follow us in this direction, I shall lead him up the Valley, and endeavor to attack him as far from his base as possible. I share in Your Excellency's regret for the fall of Vicksburg. It will be necessary for us to endeavor to select some point on the Mississippi, and fortify it strongly, so that it may be held by a small garrison, which could be supplied with ammunition and provisions, to enable it to stand a siege, thus leaving as many troops as possible free to operate against the enemy. I think that in this way a land attack against such position as we may select can be prevented.

I am, with great respect, Your Excellency's obedient servant,
R. E. LEE,
General

(Source: U.S. War Department. *War of the Rebellion: A Compilation of the Official Records of the Union and Confederate Armies*. Ser. I, Vol. XXVII/2.)

2. Lee's General Orders, No. 76 (11 July 1863)
GENERAL ORDERS, No. 76.
HDQRS. ARMY OF NORTHERN VIRGINIA,
July 11, 1863.

After along and trying marches, endured with the fortitude that has ever characterized the soldiers of the Army of Northern Virginia, you have penetrated the country of our enemies, and recalled to the defense of their own soil those who were engaged in the invasion of ours. You have fought a fierce and sanguinary battle, which, if not attended with the success that has hitherto crowned your efforts, was marked by the same heroic spirit that has commanded the respect of your enemies, the gratitude of your country, and the admiration of mankind.

Once more you are called to meet the army from which you have won on so many fields a mane that will never die. Once more the eyes of your countrymen, are turned upon you, and again do wives and sisters, fathers, mothers, and helpless children lean for defense on your strong arms and brave hearts. Let every soldier remember that on his courage and fidelity depends all that makes life worth having-the freedom of his country, the honor of his people, and the security of his home.

Let each heart grown strong in the remembrance of your glorious past, and in the thought of the inestimable blessing for which we contend, and invoking the assistance of that Divine Power which has so signally blessed our former efforts let us go forth in confidence to secure the peace and safety of your country. Soldiers! your old enemy is before you! Win from him honors worthy of your righteous cause—worthy of your comrades dead on so many illustrious fields.
R. E. LEE,
General

3. Report of Medical Inspector Edward P. Vollum, U.S. Army (25 July 1863)
WASHINGTON, *D.C., July 25,* 1863.

GENERAL: I have the honor to report that, pursuant to your orders of the 7th July, I proceeded on the same day to Gettysburg, Pa., for the purpose of reporting to Medical Inspector Cuyler, U.S. Army, for duty in connection with the transportation of the wounded at that place. I was detained a few hours, on the 8th, at Hanover, Pa., where I found about 150 wounded, chiefly from Kilpatrick's cavalry, under charge of Assistant Surgeon Gardner, First [West] Virginia Cavalry. They were comfortably situated in a school-house and in dwellings. The inhabitants had furnished them with bunks, bedding, dressings, utensils, and food in sufficient quantity, the people in each street in the town furnishing food, delicacies, nurses, &c., two days at a time.

I arrived at Gettysburg about 7 p.m. on the 8th, and in consequence of some irregularity or delay in the railroad trains, there were about 2,000 slightly wounded men collected at a point a mile from town, where the trains stopped, without food, shelter, or attendance for the night. Fortunately, through the agents of the Sanitary Commission, these men were all fed, and some 300 sheltered that night. No system had as yet been adopted for the transportation of the wounded, nor had this been possible in the deranged condition of the railroad, though Surg. J. D. Osborne, Fourth New Jersey, detailed for this purpose by Surg. H. Janes, U.S. Volunteers, in charge of the hospitals at Gettysburg, was using his best endeavors to work through the confusion and crowds of wounded with which he was surrounded, and I have to acknowledge the important services of this gentleman until the time of my departure. The railroad authorities were perplexed, and deficient in motive power and rolling stock. The bridges put up since the rebel raids proved too weak excepting for the lightest engines, and for a second time some were carried away by the floods. The telegraph wires were down, and the obstruction to transportation seemed insurmountable until General Haupt arrived and assumed military control of the road to Hanover Junction. We then experienced no further delays till the 18th, when an important bridge on the road to Harrisburg gave way under a cattle train, thus diverting, for the following five days, the trains that were intended for New York to Baltimore and York, Pa.

Medical Inspector Cuyler arrived on the 11th, when I reported to him for duty, and, by mutual arrangement, I continued in immediate charge of the transportation of the wounded, which confined me to the railroad depot and city of Gettysburg. Every train of wounded was placed in charge of a medical officer detailed by Surg. H. Janes. Instruments, dressings, stimulants, &c., were furnished him, and he was instructed to announce his coming by telegraph, if possible, and to report in person to the medical director at the place of his destination. Each car was filled with a sufficient quantity of hay, and, on the longer routes, water-coolers, tin cups, bed-pans, and urinals were placed in them, and guarded on the route by some agents of the Sanitary Commission. In some instances, these conveniencies were furnished by the medical department, but the demand for them by the hospitals often exhausted the supplies at the purveyors. Before leaving, the wounded were fed and watered by the Sanitary Commission, and often hundreds of wounded, laid over for a night or a part of a day, were attended and fed by the Commission, whose agents placed them in the cars. At Hanover Junction they were again refreshed and fed by the Christian Commission. At Baltimore, the agents of several benevolent societies distributed food bountifully to the wounded in the cars immediately on their arrival; and at Harrisburg the Commissary Department had made arrangements for feeding any number likely to pass that way. . . .

Before the arrival of Medical Inspector Cuyler, as far as my time and opportunities admitted, I endeavored to make up the deficiencies in medical supplies at Gettysburg by telegraphing to Surgeon [Josiah] Simpson, U.S. Army, at Baltimore. In reply, he ordered liberal supplies of alcohol, solution chloride of soda, tincture of iron, creosote, nitric acid, permanganate of potassa, buckets, tin cups, stretchers, bed-sacks, and stationery of all kinds for 10,000 men in field hospitals. On the day after my arrival, the demand for stationery, disinfectants, iodine, tincture of iron, and some other articles was so great and immediate, that I purchased them in Gettysburg, and sent the bills to the quartermaster there for payment.

Very respectfully, your obedient servant,

EDW. P. VOLLUM,

Medical Inspector, U.S. Army.

The SURGEON-GENERAL U.S. ARMY.

P. S.—I neglected to comment in the proper place upon the utter indifference manifested by the railroad companies toward the sufferings and wants of our wounded at Gettysburg, Pa. I allude to those over whose roads our mangled soldiers traveled to various points from Gettysburg. The period of ten days following the battle of Gettysburg was the occasion of the greatest amount of human suffering known to this nation since its birth, and, as was natural and unavoidable among a Christian people, benevolent societies, Sanitary and Christian Commissions, express companies, fire organizations, bands of generous people of all denominations, and individuals from great distances, all came forward with their offerings, sympathy, and personal services, forming a spectacle at once touching and magnificent, exceeding any similar outburst of sympathy and sacrifice ever witnessed. The railroad companies, who got the only profit of the battle, and who had the greatest opportunities of ameliorating the sufferings of the wounded, alone stood aloof and rendered no aid. Their trains were allowed to go off without a single individual attached to them in any way authorized to minister to the wounded.

There was no check-line or means of stopping the train in case of necessity; no way provided for passing from car to car. The cars—ordinary stock and freight cars—were always unclean; no one connected with the companies to clean them; the dung of cattle and litter from freight often remaining to be removed by any extemporized means at hand. There was no water, or vessels to contain it, no lanterns, no straw—absolutely nothing but the bare cars, filthy from the business of

transporting freight and cattle. The only agents of the railroad companies that appeared upon this memorable scene were those sent especially to look after their pecuniary interests, and I can testify to their zeal in getting the actual numbers transported and securing the proper certificates therefor, but beyond this they did nothing.

(Source: U.S. War Department. *War of the Rebellion: A Compilation of the Official Records of the Union and Confederate Armies*. Ser. I, Vol. XXVII/1.)

4. Excerpts from the Diary of Private Louis Leon, Company B, 53rd Regiment N.C. Troops (1–6 July 1863)

July 1: We left camp at 6 A.M., passed through Heidelsburg and Middleton. At the latter place we heard firing in the direction of Gettysburg. We were pushed forward after letting the wagon trains get in our rear. We got to Gettysburg at 1 P.M., 15 miles. We were drawn up in line of battle about one mile south of town, and a little to the left of the Lutheran Seminary. We then advanced to the enemy's line of battle in double quick time. We had not gotten more than 50 paces when Norman of our company fell dead by my side. Katz was going to pick him up. I stopped him, as it is strictly forbidden for anyone to help take the dead or wounded off the field except the ambulance corps. We then crossed over a rail fence, where our Lieutenant McMathews and Lieutenant Alexander were both wounded. That left us with a captain and one lieutenant. After this we got into battle in earnest, and lost in our company very heavily, both killed and wounded. This fight lasted four hours and a half, when at last we drove them clear out of town, and took at least 3,000 prisoners. They also lost very heavily in killed and wounded, which all fell into our hands. After the fight our company was ordered to pick up all straggling Yankees in town, and bring them together to be brought to the rear as prisoners. One fellow I took up could not speak one word of English, and the first thing he asked me in German was "Will I get my pay in prison?" After we had them all put up in a pen we went to our regiment and rested. Major Iredell, of our regiment, came to me and shook my hand, and also complimented me for action in the fight. At dusk I was about going to hunt up my brother Morris, when he came to me. Thank God, we are both safe as yet. We laid all night about the dead Yankees, but they did not disturb our peaceful slumbers.

July 2: Our division was in reserve until dark, but our regiment was supporting a battery all day. We lost several killed and wounded, although we had no chance to fire—only lay by a battery of artillery and be shot at. The caisson of the batter we were supporting

was blown up and we got a big good sprinkling of the wood from it. Just at dark we were sent to the front under terrible cannonading. Still, it was certainly a beautiful sight. It being dark, we could see the cannon vomit forth fire. Our company had to cross a rail fence. It gave way and several of our boys were hurt by others walking over them. We laid down here a short time, in fact no longer than 10 minutes, when I positively fell asleep. The cannonading did not disturb me. One of the boys shook me and told me Katz was wounded by a piece of a shell striking him on the side, and he was sent to the rear. We went on to the Baltimore Turnpike until 3 in the morning of the 3d.

July 3: When under a very heavy fire, we were ordered on Culps Hill, to the support of Gen. A. Johnson. Here we stayed all day—no, here, I may say, we melted away. We were on the brow of one hill, the enemy on the brow of another. We charged on them several times, but of course, running down our hill, and then to get them was impossible, and every time we attempted it we came back leaving some of our comrades behind. Here our Lieutenant Belt lost his arm. We have now in our company a captain. All of our lieutenants are wounded. We fought here until 7 P.M., when what was left of us was withdrawn and taken to the first day's battlefield. At the commencement of this fight our Brigade was the strongest in our division, but she is not now. We lost the most men, for we were in the fight all the time, and I have it from Colonel Owens, that our regiment lost the most in the Brigade. I know that our company went in the fight with 60 men. When we left Culps Hill there were 16 of us that answered to the roll call. The balance were all killed and wounded. There were 12 sharpshooters in our company and now John Cochran and myself are the only ones that are left. This day none will forget, that participated in the fight. It was truly awful how fast, how very fast, did our poor boys fall by our sides—almost as fast as the leaves that fell as cannon and musket balls hit them, as they flew on their deadly errand. You could see one with his head shot off, others cut in two, then one with his brain oozing out, one with his leg off, others shot through the heart. They you would hear some poor friend or foe crying for water, or for "God's sake" to kill him. You would see some of your comrades, shot through the leg, lying between the lines, asking his friends to take him out, but no one could get to this relief, and you would have to leave him there, perhaps to die, or, at best, to become a prisoner. Our brigade was the only one sent to Culps Hill to support General Johnson. In our rapid firing today my gun became so hot that the ramrod would not come out, so I shot it at the Yankees, and picked up a gun from the ground, a gun that some poor comrade dropped after being shot. I wonder if it hit a Yankee; if so, I pity him. Our regiment was in a very exposed position at one time to-day, and our General Daniels ordered a courier of his to bring us from the hill. He was killed before he got to us. The General sent another. He was also killed before he reached us. Then General Daniels would not order any one, but called for volunteers. Capt. Ed. Stitt, of Charlotte, one of his aides, responded, and he took us out of the exposed position.

July 4: We laid on the battlefield of the first day, this the fourth day of July. No fighting to-day, but we are burying the dead. They have been lying on the field in the sun since the first day's fight; it being dusty and hot, the dead smell terribly. The funny part of it is, the Yankees have all turned black. Several of our company, wounded, have died. Katz is getting along all right. The battle is over, and although we did not succeed in pushing the enemy out of their strong position, I am sure they have not anything to boast about. They have lost at least as many in killed and wounded as we have. We have taken more prisoners from them than they have from us. If that is not the case, why did they lay still all to-day and see our army going to the rear? An army that has gained a great victory follows it up while the enemy is badly crippled; but Meade, their commander, knows he has had as much as he gave, at least, if not more. As yet I have not heard a word from my brother Morris since the first day's fight.

July 5: Left this morning at 5 o'clock. Only marched ten miles to-day. The enemy being in our rear, and skirmishing very strong.

July 6: Our company was ordered out as skirmishers today, as our regular skirmish corps was broken up during the fight. We were the rear of the army, and therefore had a very hard job before us. Fighting all day in falling back we certainly had fun. We were close enough to the enemy to hear their commands. We would hold them in check and give them a few rounds, then fall back again. They would advance until we would make a stand, fight again, and so it was until we reached Fairfield, six miles from Gettysburg. I don't think there were many lost on either side in this skirmish. We crossed South Mountain at Monteray Gap. When we came to the above town I pressed into service a citizen's coat, in this way: We were ordered to rest, and, as usual, we would sit on fences and lay about on the road. Some of the boys jumped on an old hog pen. It broke through. They fell in, and, lo and behold, there were boxes of clothing, dresses, shawls, blankets, and, in fact, everything in the line of wearing apparel. I, being a little fellow, crawled through some of the boys' legs and captured the coat. If the fool citizen would have left his things in his house they would have been safe, but to put it in our way was too much for us to leave behind.

(Source: *Diary of A Tar Heel Confederate Soldier.* Charlotte, NC: Stone Publishing, 1913.)

5. Lee's Offer to Resign (8 August 1863)

CAMP ORANGE, *August* 8, 1863.

His Excellency JEFFERSON DAVIS,
President of the Confederate States:
Mr. PRESIDENT: Your letters of July 28 and August 2 have been received, and I have waited for a leisure hour to reply, but I fear that will never come. I am extremely obliged to you for the attention given to the wants of this army, and the efforts made to supply them. Our absentees are returning, and I hope the earnest and beautiful appeal made to the country in your proclamation may stir up the virtue of the whole people, and that they may see their duty and perform it. Nothing is wanted but that their fortitude should equal their bravery to insure the success of our cause. We must expect reverses, even defeats. They are sent to teach us wisdom and prudence, to call forth greater energies, and to prevent our falling into greater disasters. Our people have only to be true and united, to bear manfully the misfortunes incident to war, and all will come right in the end.

I know how prone we are to censure and how ready to blame others for the non-fulfillment of our expectations. This is unbecoming in a generous people, and I grieve to see its expression. The general remedy for the want of success in a military commander is his removal. This is natural, and, in many instances, proper. For, no matter what may be the ability of the officer, if he loses the confidence of his troops disaster must sooner or later ensue.

I have been prompted by these reflections more than once since my return from Pennsylvania to propose to Your Excellency the propriety of selecting another commander for this army. I have seen and heard of expression of discontent in the public journals at the result of the expedition. I do not know how far this feeling extends in the army. My brother officers have been too kind to report it, and so far the troops have been too generous to exhibit it. It is fair, however, to suppose that it does exist, and success is so necessary to us that nothing should be risked to secure it. I therefore, in all sincerity, request Your Excellency to take measures to supply my place. I do this with the more earnestness because no one is more aware than myself of my inability for the duties of my position. I cannot even accomplish what I myself desire. How can I fulfill the expectations of others? In addition I sensibly feel the growing failure of my bodily strength. I have not yet recovered from the attack I experienced the past spring. I am becoming more and more incapable of exertion, and am thus prevented from making the personal examinations and giving the personal supervision to the operations in the field which I feel to be necessary. I am so dull that in making use of the eyes of oth-

ers I am frequently misled. Everything, therefore, points to the advantages to be derived from a new commander, and I the more anxiously urge the matter upon Your Excellency from my belief that a younger and abler man than myself can readily be attained. I know that he will have as gallant and brave an army as ever existed to second his efforts, and it would be the happiest day of my life to see at its head a worthy leader—one that would accomplish more than I could perform and all that I have wished. I hope Your Excellency will attribute my request to the true reason, the desire to serve my country, and to do all in my power to insure the success of her righteous cause.

I have no complaints to make of any one but myself. I have received nothing but kindness from those above me, and the most considerate attention from my comrades and companions in arms. To Your Excellency I am specially indebted for uniform kindness and consideration. You have done everything in your power to aid me in the work committed to my charge, without omitting anything to promote the general welfare. I pray that your efforts may at length be crowned with success, and that you may long live to enjoy the thanks of a grateful people.

With sentiments of great esteem, I am, very respectfully and truly, yours,

R. E. LEE,
General.

(Source: U.S. War Department. *War of the Rebellion: A Compilation of the Official Records of the Union and Confederate Armies.* Ser. I, Vol. LI/2.)

* * *

Jefferson Davis to Robert E. Lee (11 August 1863)
RICHMOND, VA.,
August 11, 1863.

General R. E. LEE,
Commanding Army of Northern Virginia:
Yours of 8th instant has been received. I am glad that you concur so entirely with me as to the want of our country in this trying hour, and am happy to add that after the first depression consequent upon our disaster in the west, indications have appeared that our people will exhibit that fortitude which we agree in believing is alone needful to secure ultimate success.

It well became Sidney Johnston, when overwhelmed by a senseless clamor, to admit the rule that success is the test of merit; and yet there has been nothing which I have found to require a greater effort of patience than to bear the criticisms of the ignorant, who pronounce everything a failure which does not equal their expectations or desires, and can see no good result which is

not in the line of their own imaginings. I admit the propriety of your conclusions, that an officer who loses the confidence of his troops should have his position changed, whatever may be his ability, but when I read the sentence I was not at all prepared for the application you were about to make. Expressions of discontent in the public journals furnish but little evidence of the sentiment of an army. I wish it were otherwise, even though all the abuse of myself should be accepted as the results of honest observation. I say I wish I could feel that the public journals were not generally partisan nor venal.

Were you capable of stooping to it, you could easily surround yourself with those who would fill the press with your laudations, and seek to exalt you for what you had not done, rather than detract from the achievements which will make you and your army the subject of history and object of the world's admiration for generations to come.

I am truly sorry to know that you still feel the effects of the illness you suffered last spring, and can readily understand the embarrassments you experience in using the eyes of others, having been so much accustomed to make your own reconnaissances. Practice will, however, do much to relieve that embarrassment, and the minute knowledge of the country which you have acquired will render you less dependent for topographical information.

But suppose, my dear friend, that I were to admit, with all their implications, the points which you present, where am I to find that new commander who is to possess the greater ability which you believe to be required? I do not doubt the readiness with which you would give way to one who could accomplish all that you have wished, and you will do me the justice to believe that if Providence should kindly offer such a person for our use, I would not hesitate to avail of his services.

My sight is not sufficiently penetrating to discover such hidden merit, if it exists, and I have but used to you the language of sober earnestness when I have impressed upon you the propriety of avoiding all unnecessary exposure to danger, because I felt our country could not bear to lose you. To ask me to substitute you by some one in my judgment more fit to command, or who would possess more of the confidence of the army, or of the reflecting men of the country, is to demand an impossibility.

It only remains for me to hope that you will take all possible care of yourself, that your health and strength may be entirely restored, and that the Lord will preserve you for the important duties devolved upon you in the struggle of our suffering country for the independence which we have engaged in war to maintain.
As ever, very respectfully and truly, yours,
JEFFERSON DAVIS.

(Source: U.S. War Department. *War of the Rebellion: A Compilation of the Official Records of the Union and Confederate Armies.* Ser. I, Vol. XXIX, Pt. 2 [S# 49].)

B. THE ADDRESS

Even before he was invited to participate in the dedication of the cemetery at Gettysburg, Abraham Lincoln apparently had decided that the time had come for a public statement that would expound upon the purposes and consequences of the war. On 19 November 1863 at the ceremony in Gettysburg, he delivered the most famous utterance of the Civil War and one of the great speeches of American history. There are five extant manuscript copies of the Gettysburg Address. The first two of the three versions produced below bear the distinction of being either the first or second draft of the address—historians differ regarding the chronology. Lincoln penned the third—the "Bliss Copy"— for Colonel Alexander Bliss to include as a facsimile in an 1864 book entitled Leaves of Our Country's Authors. *Although the other versions contain only minor differences, the Bliss Copy has become the standard rendition of the Address.* [See Gettysburg Address]

1. Transcript of the Nicolay Copy of the Gettysburg Address

Four score and seven years ago our fathers brought forth, upon this continent, a new nation, conceived in liberty, and dedicated to the proposition that "all men are created equal"

Now we are engaged in a great civil war, testing whether that nation, or any nation so conceived, and so dedicated, can long endure. We are met on a great battle field of that war. We come to dedicate a portion of it, as a final resting place for those who died here, that the nation might live. This we may, in all propriety do. But, in a larger sense, we can not dedicate—we can not consecrate—we can not hallow, this ground— The brave men, living and dead, who struggled here, have hallowed it, far above our poor power to add or detract. The world will little note, nor long remember what we say here; while it can never forget what they did here.

It is rather for us, the living, we here be dedicated to the great task remaining before us—that, from these honored dead we take increased devotion to that cause for which they here, gave the last full measure of devotion—that we here highly resolve these dead shall not have died in vain; that the nation, shall have a new birth of freedom, and that government of the people by the people for the people, shall not perish from the earth.

(Source: National Archives, Washington, D.C.)

2. Transcript of the Hay Draft of the Gettysburg Address

Four score and seven years ago our fathers brought forth, upon this continent, a new nation, conceived in Liberty, and dedicated to the proposition that all men are created equal.

Now we are engaged in a great civil war, testing whether that nation, or any nation so conceived, and so dedicated, can long endure. We are met here on a great battlefield of that war. We have come to dedicate a portion of it as a final resting place for those who here gave their lives that that nation might live. It is altogether fitting and proper that we should do this.

But in a larger sense we can not dedicate—we can not consecrate—we can not hallow this ground. The brave men, living and dead, who struggled, here, have consecrated it far above our poor power to add or detract. The world will little note, nor long remember, what we say here, but can never forget what they did here. It is for us, the living, rather to be dedicated here to the unfinished work which they have, thus far, so nobly carried on. It is rather for us to be here dedicated to the great task remaining before us—that from these honored dead we take increased devotion to that cause for which they here gave the last full measure of devotion—that we here highly resolve that these dead shall not have died in vain; that this nation shall have a new birth of freedom; and that this government of the people, by the people, for the people, shall not perish from the earth.

(Source: National Archives, Washington, D.C.)

3. Transcript of the Bliss Copy of the Gettysburg Address ("Standard" Version)

Fourscore and seven years ago our fathers brought forth on this continent a new nation, conceived in liberty and dedicated to the proposition that all men are created equal. Now we are engaged in a great civil war, testing whether that nation or any nation so conceived and so dedicated can long endure. We are met on a great battlefield of that war. We have come to dedicate a portion of that field as a final resting-place for those who here gave their lives that that nation might live. It is altogether fitting and proper that we should do this. But in a larger sense, we cannot dedicate, we cannot consecrate, we cannot hallow this ground. The brave men, living and dead who struggled here have consecrated it far above our poor power to add or detract. The world will little note nor long remember what we say here, but it can never forget what they did here.

It is for us the living rather to be dedicated here to the unfinished work which they who fought here have thus far so nobly advanced. It is rather for us to be here dedicated to the great task remaining before us—that

from these honored dead we take increased devotion to that cause for which they gave the last full measure of devotion—that we here highly resolve that these dead shall not have died in vain, that this nation under God shall have a new birth of freedom, and that government of the people, by the people, for the people shall not perish from the earth.

(Source: National Archives, Washington, D.C.)

XXVII. Chickamauga

The battle of Chickamauga was the climax of a month-long series of maneuvers by Major General William S. Rosecrans's Army of the Cumberland and General Braxton Bragg's Confederate Army of Tennessee. When a Confederate assault by James Longstreet caused the right side of the Union line to dissolve into chaos, much of Rosecrans's army was soon in full retreat toward Chattanooga. Rosecrans himself accompanied the withdrawal, so George H. Thomas remained on the field as the ranking commander, his lone corps about to be enveloped by Longstreet's unchecked assault. Federal forces rallied on Snodgrass Hill and were reinforced by the arrival of General Gordon Granger's Reserve Corps. Longstreet could not break this line, and George H. Thomas became the "Rock of Chickamauga." Thus shielded, the balance of the Union army managed to withdraw successfully, and that night Thomas pulled away to join the retreat to Chattanooga. On the Confederate side, Bragg's subordinates were incensed that he did not order an aggressive pursuit. When some openly demanded Bragg's ouster, Jefferson Davis personally visited Bragg's headquarters, but in ultimately sustaining Bragg the president only worsened the situation. [See Bragg, Braxton; Chickamauga, Battle of; Granger, Gordon; Thomas, George Henry]

1. Gordon Granger Goes to Thomas's Aid on Snodgrass Hill

The enemy did not make his appearance in our immediate front during the morning, but large clouds of dust could be seen beyond our position arising from the La Fayette and Harrison roads, moving in the direction of the sound of battle.

At 10.30 a.m. I heard heavy firing, which was momentarily increasing in volume and intensity on our right, in the direction of General Thomas position. Soon afterward, being well convinced, judging from the sound of battle, that the enemy were pushing him hard, and fearing that he would not be able to resist their combined attack, I determined to go to his assistance at once. It was now about 11 a.m. I started with General Whitaker's and Colonel Mitchell's brigades, under the immediate command of General Steedman, and left Colonel McCook's brigade at the McAfee Church in position to cover the Ringgold road.

General Thomas was at this time engaging the enemy at a point between the La Fayette and Dry Valley roads, in the vicinity of —— house, about 3-1/2 miles from our place of starting. We had not proceeded more than 2 miles when the enemy made his appearance in the woods on the left of our advancing column, about three-fourths of a mile from the road.

They opened upon us quite briskly with their skirmishers and a section of artillery. I then made a short halt to feel them, and becoming convinced that they constituted only a party of observation, I again rapidly pushed forward my troops.

At this juncture, I sent back and ordered up Colonel McCook's brigade to watch the movements of the enemy at this point, to keep open the La Fayette road, and to cover the open fields on the right of the road, and those that intervened between this point and the position held by General Thomas. As rapidly as possible, Colonel McCook brought up his brigade, took the position assigned to him, and held it until he marched to Rossville from the field of battle at 10 p.m. At 6 p.m. the enemy opened an artillery fire upon Colonel McCook, but he soon silenced their battery, which had done little or no damage to his troops. At about 1 p.m. I reported to General Thomas. His forces were at that time stationed upon the brow of and holding a "horseshoe ridge." The enemy were pressing him hard in front and endeavoring to turn both of his flanks.

To the right of this position was a ridge running east and west, and nearly at right angles therewith. Upon this the enemy were just forming. They also had possession of a gorge in the same, through which they were rapidly moving in large masses, with the design of falling upon the right flank and rear of the forces upon the Horseshoe Ridge. General Thomas had not the troops to oppose this movement of the enemy, and in fifteen minutes from the time when we appeared on the field, had it not been for our fortunate arrival, his forces would have been terribly cut up and captured.

As rapidly as possible I formed General Whitaker's and Colonel Mitchell's brigades, to hurl them against this threatening force of the enemy, which afterward proved to be General Hindman's division.

The gallant Steedman, seizing the colors of a regiment, led his men to the attack. With loud cheers they rushed upon the enemy, and, after a terrific conflict lasting but twenty minutes, drove them from their ground, and occupied the ridge and gorge. The slaughter of both friend and foe was frightful. General Whitaker, while rushing forward at the head of his brigade, was knocked from his horse by a musket-ball, and was for a short time rendered unfit for duty; while 2 of his staff officers were killed, and 2 mortally wounded.

General Steedman's horse was killed, and he was severely bruised, yet he was able to remain on duty dur-

ing the day. This attack was made by our troops, very few of whom had ever been in an action before, against a division of old soldiers, who largely outnumbered them; yet with resolution and energy they drove the enemy from his strong position, occupied it themselves, and afterward held the ground they had gained with such terrible losses. The victory was dearly won, but to this army it was a priceless one.

There was now a lull in the battle. It was of short duration, however, for within thirty minutes after we had gained possession of the ridge, we were impetuously attacked by two divisions of Longstreet's veterans.

Again the enemy was driven back, and from this time until dark the battle between these two opposing forces raged furiously.

Our whole line was continually enveloped in smoke and fire. The assaults of the enemy were now made with that energy which was inspired by the bright prospect of a speedy victory, and by a consciousness that it was only necessary to carry this position and crush our forces to enable him to overthrow our army and drive it across the Tennessee River. Their forces were massed and hurled upon us for the purpose of terminating at once this great and bloody battle. But the stout hearts of the handful of men who stood before them as a wall of fire quailed not. They understood our perilous position and held their ground, determined to perish rather than yield it. Never had a commander such just cause for congratulation over the action of his troops.

The ammunition which was brought in our train to this part of the field was divided with Generals Brannan's and Wood's divisions early in the afternoon, and we soon exhausted the remainder. All that we could then procure was taken from the cartridge boxes of our own and the enemy's dead and wounded. Even this supply was exhausted before the battle was over, and while the enemy was still in our front, hurling fresh troops against us. It was almost dark; the enemy had been driven back, but we had not a round of ammunition left. All now seemed to be lost if he should return to the contest. Anticipating another attack, I ordered the command to be given to the men to stand firm, and to use the cold steel. After an ominous silence of a few minutes, the enemy came rushing upon us again. With fixed bayonets our troops gallantly charged them and drove them back in confusion, Twice more were these charges repeated and the enemy driven back before darkness brought an end to the battle. Night came, and the enemy fell back whipped and discomfited.

(Source: U.S. War Department. *War of the Rebellion: A Compilation of the Official Records of the Union and Confederate Armies*. Ser. I, Vol. XXX/1.)

2. James Longstreet Describes Jefferson Davis's Visit

The President came to us on the 9th of October and called the commanders of the army to meet him at General Bragg's office. After some talk, in the presence of General Bragg, he made known the object of the call, and asked the generals, in turn, their opinion of their commanding officer, beginning with myself. It seemed rather a stretch of authority, even with a President, and I gave an evasive answer and made an effort to turn the channel of thought, but he would not be satisfied, and got back to his question. The condition of the army was briefly referred to, and the failure to make an effort to get the fruits of our success, when the opinion was given, in substance, that our commander could be of greater service elsewhere than at the head of the Army of Tennessee. Major-General Buckner was called, and gave opinion somewhat similar. So did Major-General Cheatham, who was then commanding the corps recently commanded by Lieutenant-General Polk, and General D. H. Hill, who was called last, agreed with emphasis to the views expressed by others.

The next morning the President called me to private conference, and had an all day talk. He thought to assign me to command, but the time had passed for handling that army as an independent force. Regarding this question, as considered in Virginia, it was understood that the assignment would be made at once, and in time for opportunity to handle the army sufficiently to gain the confidence of the officers and soldiers before offering or accepting battle. The action was not taken, a battle had been made and won, the army was then seriously entangled in a *quasi* siege, the officers and soldiers were disappointed, and disaffected in *morale*. General Grant was moving his army to reinforce against us, and an important part of the Union army of Virginia was moving to the same purpose.

In my judgment our last opportunity was lost when we failed to follow the success at Chickamauga, and capture or disperse the Union army, and it could not be just to the service or myself to call me to a position of such responsibility. The army was part of General Joseph E. Johnston's department, and could only be used in strong organization by him in combining its operations with his other forces in Alabama and Mississippi. I said that under him I could cheerfully work in any position. The suggestion of that name only served to increase his displeasure, and his severe rebuke.

(Source: Longstreet, James. *From Manassas To Appomattox: Memoirs of the Civil War in America*, p. 466.)

XXIX. Chattanooga

After Chickamauga, Bragg besieged the Union army in Chattanooga for a month, a siege finally raised after the

arrival of Ulysses S. Grant and reinforcements. On 23 November 1863, as part of a coordinated attack, George H. Thomas stormed Missionary Ridge while William T. Sherman attacked Bragg's right, and Joseph Hooker assailed Confederates on Lookout Mountain. Union soldiers impulsively charged up Missionary Ridge and routed the Confederates there, forcing Bragg to flee Chattanooga. Bragg was understandably appalled by the irrational panic that put Confederates to flight off Missionary Ridge, but his remarks about veteran soldiers whose resolve had been shaken by, for one thing, Bragg's failure at Chickamauga were ungenerous. [See Bragg, Braxton; Chattanooga, Battle of]

1. Grant to Halleck (23 November 1863)

CHATTANOOGA, *TENN., November 23,*
1863—3 p.m.
(Received 6.40 p.m.)

General Thomas' troops attacked the enemy's left at 2 p.m. to-day, carried the first line of rifle-pits running over the knoll, 1,200 yards in front of Fort Wood, and low ridge to the right of it, taking about 200 prisoners, besides killed and wounded. Our loss small. The troops moved under fire with all the precision of veterans on parade. Thomas' troops will intrench themselves, and hold their position until daylight, when Sherman will join the attack from the mouth of the Chickamauga, and a decisive battle will be fought.

U. S. GRANT,
Major-General.

Maj. Gen. H. W. HALLECK,
General-in- Chief.

(Source: U.S. War Department. *War of the Rebellion: A Compilation of the Official Records of the Union and Confederate Armies.* Ser. I.)

2. Bragg Deplores the Panic on Missionary Ridge

No satisfactory excuse can possibly be given for the shameful conduct of our troops on the left in allowing their line to be penetrated. The position was one which ought to have been held by a line of skirmishers against any assaulting column, and wherever resistance was made the enemy fled in disorder after suffering heavy loss. Those who reached the ridge did so in a condition of exhaustion from the great physical exertion in climbing, which rendered them powerless, and the slightest effort would have destroyed them. Having secured much of our artillery, they soon availed themselves of our panic, and, turning our guns upon us, enfiladed the lines, both right and left, rendering them entirely untenable.

Had all parts of the line been maintained with equal gallantry and persistence no enemy could ever have dislodged us, and but one possible reason presents itself to my mind in explanation of this bad conduct in veteran troops who had never before failed in any duty assigned them, however difficult and hazardous. They had for two days confronted the enemy, marshaling his immense forces in plain view, and exhibiting to their sight such a superiority in numbers as may have intimidated weak-minded and untried soldiers; but our veterans had so often encountered similar hosts when the strength of position was against us, and with perfect success, that not a doubt crossed my mind. As yet I am not fully informed as to the commands which first fled and brought this great disaster and disgrace upon our arms. Investigation will bring out the truth, however, and full justice shall be done to the good and the bad.

(Source: U.S. War Department. *War of the Rebellion: A Compilation of the Official Records of the Union and Confederate Armies.* Ser. I, Vol. XXXI.)

XXX. The Richmond Campaign

Promoted to lieutenant general and given overall command of federal armies in the spring of 1864, Ulysses S. Grant planned a vast and coordinated military endeavor against several key points of the Confederacy. The centerpiece was the May–June 1864 Overland campaign against Richmond. It would produce the fiercest carnage of the entire Civil War. Fighting in the Wilderness on 5–6 May continued through Spotsylvania, Trevilian Station, North Anna, Totopotomoy Creek, Bethesda Church, Cold Harbor, and the onset of the Siege of Petersburg in mid-June. The casualties were staggering, but the campaign ended Robert E. Lee's war of maneuver and forced the Army of Northern Virginia into defensive siege lines around Richmond and Petersburg that would collapse in the spring of 1865, ushering in the final days of the war. [See Grant, Ulysses Simpson; Lee, Robert Edward; Petersburg Campaign; Richmond Campaign]

1. Report of Lieutenant General U. S. Grant, U.S. Army (June 1864)

CITY POINT, *VA., June 23, 1864—9 a.m.*

Yesterday and this morning have been consumed in extending our lines to the left to envelop Petersburg. The Second and Sixth Corps are now west of the Jerusalem plank road. Yesterday, in moving to this position, the two corps became separated. The enemy pushed out between them and caused some confusion in the left of the Second Corps, and captured 4 pieces of artillery. Order was soon restored and the enemy pushed back. This morning no enemy is found on the left. This will be pushed forward until the enemy is found. The Petersburg papers of yesterday state that Hunter has been routed and already 3,000 of his men have been captured.

U. S. GRANT, *Lieutenant-General.*

Major-General HALLECK, *Washington, D. C.*

(Source: U.S. War Department. *War of the Rebellion: A Compilation of the Official Records of the Union and Confederate Armies.* Ser. I, Vol. XL/1.)

XXXI. Atlanta and the March to the Sea

In the early spring of 1864, Atlanta, Georgia, was a key to ending the war. As part of Grant's grand coordinated strategy of pressing the Confederacy on as many salients as possible, William T. Sherman began pushing south from Chattanooga in a campaign of maneuver against Braxton Bragg's replacement, Joseph E. Johnston. The Atlanta campaign would see almost five months of violent contact between the two forces. At a decisive point in the campaign, Jefferson Davis relieved Johnston of command and replaced him with John Bell Hood, who challenged Sherman's advance in a costly battle that assured the loss of Atlanta. Sherman's bombardment of the city had begun on 20 July, and on 2 September 1864, Mayor James Calhoun surrendered it to him. Sherman left Atlanta after systematically wrecking its railroads and war industries; the resultant blaze gutted almost 5,000 buildings, including many residences. Sherman then commenced his "March to the Sea," a sixty-mile-wide journey of devastation that he carved across Georgia to Savannah. When Sherman occupied Savannah on 21 December, he had effectively separated the upper South from the lower South with a crippling blow to the Confederacy. [See Atlanta; Atlanta Campaign; Sherman, William Tecumseh; Sherman's March to the Sea]

1. Sherman-Hood Correspondence
(September 1864)

HDQRS. MILITARY DIVISION OF THE MISSISSIPPI,
In the Field, Atlanta, Ga., September 10, 1864.

General J. B. HOOD, *C. S. Army, Comdg.*
Army of Tennessee:
GENERAL: I have the honor to acknowledge the receipt of your letter of this date [9th], at the hands of Messrs. Ball and Crew, consenting to the arrangements I had proposed to facilitate the removal south of the people of Atlanta who prefer to go in that direction. I inclose you a copy of my orders, which will, I am satisfied, accomplish my purpose perfectly. You style the measure proposed "unprecedented," and appeal to the dark history of war for a parallel as an act of "studied and ingenious cruelty." It is not unprecedented, for General Johnston himself, very wisely and properly, removed the families all the way from Dalton down, and I see no reason why Atlanta should be excepted. Nor is it necessary to appeal to the dark history of war when recent and modern examples are so handy. You, yourself, burned dwelling-houses along your parapet, and I have seen to-day fifty houses that you have rendered uninhabitable because they stood in the way of your forts and men. You defended Atlanta on a line so close to town that every cannon shot and many musket shots from our line of investment that overshot their mark went into the habitations of women and children. General Hardee did the same at Jonesborough, and General Johnston did the same last summer at Jackson, Miss. I have not accused you of heartless cruelty, but merely instance these cases of very recent occurrence, and could go on and enumerate hundreds of others and challenge any fair man to judge which of us has the heart of pity for the families of a "brave people." I say that it is kindness to these families of Atlanta to remove them now at once from scenes that women and children should not be exposed to, and the "brave people" should scorn to commit their wives and children to the rude barbarians who thus, as you say, violate the laws of war, as illustrated in the pages of its dark history. In the name of common sense I ask you not to appeal to a just God in such a sacrilegious manner; you who, in the midst of peace and prosperity, have plunged a nation into war, dark and cruel war; who dared and badgered us to battle, insulted our flag, seized our arsenals and forts that were left in the honorable custody of peaceful ordnance sergeants; seized and made "prisoners of war" the very garrisons sent to protect your people against negroes and Indians long before any overt act was committed by the, to you, hated Lincoln Government; tried to force Kentucky and Missouri into rebellion, spite of themselves; falsified the vote of Louisiana, turned loose your privateers to plunder unarmed ships; expelled Union families by the thousands; burned their houses and declared by an act of your Congress the confiscation of all debts due Northern men for goods had and received. Talk thus to the marines, but not to me, who have seen these things, and who will this day make as much sacrifice for the peace and honor of the South as the best born Southerner among you. If we must be enemies, let us be men and fight it out, as we propose to do, and not deal in such hypocritical appeals to God and humanity. God will judge us in due time, and He will pronounce whether it be more humane to fight with a town full of women, and the families of "a brave people" at our back, or to remove them in time to places of safety among their own friends and people.
W. T. SHERMAN

* * *

HEADQUARTERS ARMY OF TENNESSEE,
September 12, 1864.

Maj. Gen. W. T. SHERMAN,
Commanding Military Division of the Mississippi:
GENERAL; I have the honor to acknowledge the receipt of your letter of the 9th [10th] instant, with its

inclosure, in reference to the women, children, and others whom you have thought proper to expel from their homes in the city of Atlanta. Had you seen proper to let the matter rest there, I would gladly have allowed your letter to close this correspondence, and without your expressing it in words would have been willing to believe that whilst "the interests of the United States," in your opinion, compelled you to an act of barbarous cruelty, you regretted the necessity, and we would have dropped the subject. But you have chosen to indulge in statements which I feel compelled to notice, at least so far as to signify my dissent and not allow silence in regard to them to be construed as acquiescence. I see nothing in your communication which induces me to modify the language of condemnation with which I characterized your order. It but strengthens me in the opinion that it stands "pre-eminent in the dark history of war, for studied and ingenious cruelty." Your original order was stripped of all pretenses; you announced the edict for the sole reason that it was "to the interest of the United States." This alone you offered to us and the civilized world as an all-sufficient reason for disregarding the laws of God and man. You say that "General Johnston himself, very wisely and properly, removed the families all the way from Dalton down," It is due to that gallant soldier and gentleman to say that no act of his distinguished career gives the least color to your unfounded aspersions upon his conduct. He depopulated no villages nor towns nor cities, either friendly or hostile. He offered and extended friendly aid to his unfortunate fellow-citizens who desired to flee from your fraternal embraces. You are equally unfortunate in your attempt to find a justification for this act of cruelty either in the defense of Jonesborough, by General Hardee, or of Atlanta by myself. General Hardee defended his position in front of Jonesborough at the expense of injury to the houses, an ordinary, proper, and justifiable act of war. I defended Atlanta at the same risk and cost. If there was any fault in either case, it was your own, in not giving notice, especially in the case of Atlanta, of your purpose to shell the town, which is usual in war among civilized nations. No inhabitant was expelled from his home and fireside by the orders of General Hardee or myself, and therefore your recent order can find no support from the conduct of either of us. I feel no other emotion than pain in reading that portion of your letter which attempts to justify your shelling Atlanta without notice under pretense that I defended Atlanta upon a line so close to town that every cannon shot, and many musket balls from your line of investment, that over-shot their mark went into the habitations of women and children. I made no complaint of your firing into Atlanta in any way you thought proper. I make none now, but there are a hundred thousand witnesses that you fired into the habitations of women and children for weeks, firing far above and miles beyond my line of defense. I have too good an opinion, founded both upon observation and experience, of the skill of your artillerists to credit the insinuation that they for several weeks unintentionally fired too high for my modest field-works, and slaughtered women and children by accident and want of skill.

The residue of your letter is rather discussion. It opens a wide field for the discussion of questions which I do not feel are committed to me. I am only a general of one of the armies of the Confederate States, charged with military operations in the field, under the direction of my superior officers, and I am not called upon to discuss with you the causes of the present war, or the political questions which led to or resulted from it. These grave and important questions have been committed to far abler hands than mine, and I shall only refer to them so far as to repel any unjust conclusion which might be drawn from my silence. You charge my country with "daring and badgering you to battle." The truth is, we sent commissioners to you respectfully offering a peaceful separation before the first gun was fired on either side. You say we insulted your flag. The truth is we fired upon it and those who fought under it when you came to our doors upon the mission of subjugation. You say we seized upon your forts and arsenals and made prisoners of the garrisons sent to protect us against negroes and Indians. The truth is, we, by force of arms, drove out insolent intruders, and took possession of our own forts and arsenals to resist your claims to dominion over masters, slaves, and Indians, all of whom are to this day, with a unanimity unexampled in the history of the world, warring against your attempts to become their masters. You say that we tried to force Missouri and Kentucky into rebellion in spite of themselves. The truth is my Government, from the beginning of this struggle to this hour, has again and again offered, before the whole world to leave it to the unbiased will of these States and all others to determine for themselves whether they will cast their destiny with your Government or ours? and your Government has resisted this fundamental principle of free institutions with the bayonet, and labors daily by force and fraud to fasten its hateful tyranny upon the unfortunate freemen of these States. You say we falsified the vote of Louisiana. The truth is, Louisiana not only separated herself from your Government by nearly a unanimous vote of her people, but has vindicated the act upon every battle-field from Gettysburg to the Sabine, and has exhibited an heroic devotion to her decision which challenges the admiration and respect of every man capable of feeling sympathy for the oppressed or admiration for heroic valor. You say that we turned loose pirates to plunder your unarmed ships. The truth is, when you robbed us of our part of the navy, we built and bought a few vessels, hoisted the flag of our country, and swept the seas, in defiance of your navy, around the whole circumference of the globe. You say we have expelled Union families by thousands. The truth is not a single family has been expelled from the Confederate States, that I am aware of, but, on the contrary, the moderation of our Government toward traitors has been a fruitful theme of denunciation by its enemies and many well-meaning friends of our cause. You say my Government, by acts of Congress, has "confiscated all debts due Northern men for goods sold and delivered." The truth is our Congress gave due and ample time to your merchants and traders to depart from our shores with their ships, goods, and effects, and only sequestrated the property of our enemies in retaliation for their acts, declaring us traitors and confiscating our property wherever their power extended, either in their country or our own. Such are your accusations, and such are the facts known of all men to be true.

You order into exile the whole population of a city, drive men, women, and children from their homes at the point of the bayonet, under the plea that it is to the interest of your Government, and on the claim that it is an act of "kindness to these families of Atlanta." Butler only banished from New Orleans the registered enemies of his Government, and acknowledged that he did it as a punishment. You issue a sweeping edict covering all the inhabitants of a city and add insult to the injury heaped upon the defenseless by assuming that you have done them a kindness. This you follow by the assertion that you will "make as much sacrifice for the peace and honor of the South as the best born Southerner." And because I characterized what you call a kindness as being real cruelty you presume to sit in judgment between me and my God and you decide that my earnest prayer to the Almighty Father to save our women and children from what you call kindness is a "sacrilegious, hypocritical appeal." You came into our country with your army avowedly for the purpose of subjugating free white men, women, and children, and not only intend to rule over them, but you make negroes your allies and desire to place over us an inferior race, which we have raised from barbarism to its present position, which is the highest ever attained by that race in any country in all time. I must, therefore, decline to accept your statements in reference to your kindness toward the people of Atlanta, and your willingness to sacrifice everything for the peace and honor of the South, and refuse to be governed by your decision in regard to matters between myself, my country, and my God. You say, "let us fight it out like men." To this my reply is, for myself, and, I believe, for all the true men, aye, and women and children, in my country, we will fight you to the death. Better die a thousand deaths than submit to live under you or your Government and your negro allies.

Having answered the points forced upon me by your letter of the 9th [10th] of September, I close this correspondence with you, and notwithstanding your comments upon my appeal to God in the cause of humanity, I again humbly and reverently invoke His Almighty aid in defense of justice and right.

Respectfully, your obedient servant,

J. B. HOOD, *General.*

* * *

HDQRS. MILITARY DIVISION OF THE MISSISSIPPI,
In the Field, Atlanta, Ga., September 14, 1864.

General J. B. HOOD, *C. S. Army,*
Commanding Army of Tennessee:

GENERAL: Yours of September 12 is received and has been carefully perused. I agree with you that this discussion by two soldiers is out of place and profitless, but you must admit that you began the controversy by characterizing an official act of mine in unfair and improper terms. I reiterate my former answer, and to the only new matter contained in your rejoinder I add, we have no negro "allies" in this army; not a single negro soldier left Chattanooga with this army or is with it now. There are a few guarding Chattanooga, which General Steedman sent to drive Wheeler out of Dalton. I was not bound by the laws of war to give notice of the shelling of Atlanta, a "fortified town" with magazines, arsenals, foundries, and public stores. You were bound to take notice. See the books. This is the conclusion of our correspondence, which I did not begin, and terminate with satisfaction.

I am, with respect, your obedient servant,

W. T. SHERMAN,

Major-General, Commanding.

(Source: U.S. War Department. *War of the Rebellion: A Compilation of the Official Records of the Union and Confederate Armies.* Ser. I, Vol. XXXIX/2 [S# 78].)

2. Sherman's Orders (8–9 November 1864)
Headquarters Military Division of the Mississippi
In the Field, Kingston, Georgia, *November* 8, 1864.

The general commanding deems it proper at this time to inform the officers and men of the Fourteenth, Fifteenth, Seventeenth, and Twentieth Corps, that he has organized them into an army for a special purpose, well known to the War Department from our present base, and a long and difficult march to a new one. All the chances of war have been considered and provided for, as far as human sagacity can. All he asks of you is to maintain that discipline, patience, and courage,

which have characterized you in the past; and he hopes, through you, to strike a blow at our enemy that will have a material effect in producing what we all so much desire, his complete overthrow. Of all things, the most important is, that the men, during marches and in camp, keep their places and do not scatter about as stragglers or foragers, to be picked up by a hostile people in detail. It is also of the utmost importance that our wagons should not be loaded with any thing but provisions and ammunition. All surplus servants, non-combatants, and refugees, should now go to the rear, and none should be encouraged to encumber us on the march. At some future time we will be able to provide for the poor whites and blacks who seek to escape the bondage under which they are now suffering. With these few simple cautions, he hopes to lead you to achievements equal in importance to those of the past.
By order of Major-General W. T. Sherman,
L. M. Dayton, *Aide-de-Camp.*

* * *

Headquarters Military Division of the Mississippi
In the Field, Kingston, Georgia, November 9, 1864

1. For the purpose of military operations, this army is divided into two wings, viz.:

The right wing, Major-General O. O. Howard, commanding, composed of the Fifteenth and Seventeenth Corps; the left wing, major-General H. W. Slocum commanding, composed of the Fourteenth and Twentieth Corps.

2. The habitual order of march will be, wherever practicable, by four roads, as nearly parallel as possible, and converging at points hereafter to be indicated in orders. The cavalry, Brigadier-General Kilpatrick commanding, will receive special orders from the commander-in-chief.

3. There will be no general train of supplies, but each corps will have its ammunition-train and provision-train, distributed habitually as follows: Behind each regiment should follow one wagon and one ambulance; behind each brigade should follow a due proportion of ammunition-wagons, provision-wagons, and ambulances. In case of danger, each corps commander should change this order of march, by having his advance and rear brigades unencumbered by wheels. The separate columns will start habitually at 7 a.m., and make about fifteen miles per day, unless otherwise fixed in orders.

4. The army will forage liberally on the country during the march. To this end, each brigade commander will organize a good and sufficient foraging party, under the command of one or more discreet officers, who will gather, near the route traveled, corn or forage of any kind, meat of any kind, vegetables, corn-meal, or whatever is needed by the command, aiming at all times to keep in the wagons at least ten days' provisions for his command, and three days' forage. Soldiers must not enter the dwellings of the inhabitants, or commit any trespass; but, during a halt or camp, they may be permitted to gather turnips, potatoes, and other vegetables, and to drive in stock in sight of their camp. To regular foraging-parties must be intrusted the gathering of provisions and forage, at any distance from the road traveled.

5. To corps commanders alone is intrusted the power to destroy mills, houses, cotton-gins, etc.; and for them this general principle is laid down: In districts and neighborhoods where the army is unmolested, no destruction of such property should be permitted; but should guerrillas or bushwhackers molest our march, or should the inhabitants burn bridges, obstruct roads, or otherwise manifest local hostility, then army commanders should order and enforce a devastation more or less relentless, according to the measure of such hostility.

6. As for horses, mules, wagons, etc., belonging to the inhabitants, the cavalry and artillery may appropriate freely and without limit; discriminating, however, between the rich, who are usually hostile, and the poor and industrious, usually neutral or friendly. Foraging-parties may also take mules or horses, to replace the jaded animals of their trains, or to serve as pack-mules for the regiments of brigades. In all foraging, of whatever kind, the parties engaged will refrain abusive or threatening language, and may, where the officer in command thinks proper, given written certificates of the facts, but no receipts; and they will endeavor to leave with each family a reasonable portion for their maintenance.

7. Negroes who are able-bodied and can be of service to the several columns may be taken along; but each army commander will bear in mind that the question of supplies is a very important one, and this his first duty is to see to those who bear arms.

8. The organization, at once, of a good pioneer battalion for each army corps, composed if possible of Negroes, should be attended to. This battalion should follow the advance-guard, repair roads and double them if possible, so that the columns will not be delayed after reaching bad places. Also, army commanders should practise the habit of giving the artillery and wagons the road, marching their troops on one side, and instruct their troops to assist wagons at steep hills or bad crossings of streams.

9. Captain O. M. Poe, chief-engineer, will assign to each wing of the army a pontoon-train, fully equipped and organized; and the commanders thereof will see to their being properly protected at all times.
By order of Major-General W. T. Sherman,
L. M. Dayton, *Aide-de-Camp.*

(Source: U.S. War Department. *The War of the Rebellion: A Compilation of the Official Records of the Union and Confederate Armies.* Ser. I, Vol. XLIV.)

3. Sherman's Report to Grant
(16 December 1864)

Headquarters Military Division of the Mississippi
In the Field, near Savannah
December 16, 1864.

Lieutenant-General U. S. Grant,
Commander-in-Chief, City Point, Virginia.
GENERAL: I received, day before yesterday, at the hands of Lieutenant Dunn, your letter of December 3, and last night, at the hands of Colonel Babcock, that of December 6. I had previously made you a hasty scrawl from the tug-boat *Dandelion,* in Ogeechee River, advising you that the army had reached the sea-coast, destroying all railroads across the State of Georgia and investing closely the city of Savannah, and had made connection with the fleet. Since writing that note I have in person met and conferred with General Foster and Admiral Dahlgren, and made all the arrangements which I deemed essential to reducing the city of Savannah to our possession. But since the receipt of yours of the 6th I have initiated measures looking principally to coming to you with 50,000 or 60,000 infantry, and, incidentally, to take Savannah, if time will allow. At the time we carried Fort McAllister by assault so handsomely, with its 22 guns and entire garrison, I was hardly aware of its importance; but since passing down the river with General Foster and up with Admiral Dahlgren I realize how admirably adapted are Ossabaw Sound and Ogeechee River to supply an army operating against Savannah. Sea-going vessels can easily come to King's Bridge, a point on Ogeechee River, fourteen and a half miles due west of Savannah, from which point we have roads leading to all our camps. The country is low and sandy, and cut up with marshes, which, in wet weather, will be very bad; but we have been so favored with weather that they are all now comparatively good, and heavy details are constantly employed in double corduroying the marshes, so that I have no fears even of bad weather. Fortunately, also, by liberal and judicious foraging, we reached the sea-coast abundantly supplied with forage and provisions, needing nothing on arrival except bread; of this we started from Atlanta provided with from eight to twenty days' supply per corps, and some of the troops only had one days' issue of bread during the trip of thirty days; and yet they did not want, for sweet potatoes were very abundant, as well as corn meal, and our soldiers took to them naturally.

We started with about 5,000 head of cattle, and arrived with over 10,000; of course, consuming mostly turkeys, chickens, sheep, hogs, and the cattle of the country. As to our mules and horses, we left Atlanta with about 2,500 wagons, many of which were drawn by mules which had not recovered from the Chattanooga starvation, all of which were replaced, the poor mules shot, and our transportation is now in superb condition. I have no doubt the State of Georgia has lost by our operation, 15,000 first-rate mules. As to horses, Kilpatrick collected all his remounts, and it looks to me, in riding along our columns, as though every officer had three or four led horses, and each regiment seems to be followed by at least fifty negroes and foot-sore soldiers riding on horses and mules. The custom was for each brigade to send out daily a foraging-party of about fifty men, on foot, who invariably returned mounted, with several wagons loaded with poultry, potatoes, &c.; and as the army is composed of about forty brigades you can estimate approximately the number of horses collected. Great numbers of these were shot by my order, because of the disorganizing effect on our infantry of having too many idlers mounted. General Easton is now engaged in collecting statistics in this line; but I know the Government will never receive full accounts of our captures, although the result aimed at was fully attained, viz., to deprive our enemy of them. All these animals I will have sent to Port Royal, or collected behind Fort McAllister, to be used by General Saxton in his farming operations, or by the quartermaster's department, after they are systematically accounted for. While General Easton is collecting transportation for my troops to James River I will throw to Port Royal Island all our means of transportation I can, and collect the balance near Fort McAllister, covered by the Ogeechee River and intrenchments [sic] to be erected, and for which Captain Poe, my chief engineer, is now reconnoitering the ground; but in the meantime will act as I have begun, as though Savannah City was my objective, namely: the troops will continue to invest Savannah closely, making attacks and feints wherever we have fair ground to stand upon; and I will place some 30-pound Parrotts, which I have got from General Foster, in position near enough to reach the center of the city, and then will demand its surrender. If General Hardee is alarmed or fears starvation he may surrender; otherwise, I will bombard the city, but not risk the lives of our men by assaults across the narrow causeways by which alone I can now reach it. If I had time, Savannah, with all its dependent fortifications, is already in our possession, for we hold all its avenues of supply. The enemy has made two desperate efforts to get boats from above to the city, in both of which he has been foiled—General Slocum, whose left flank rests on the river, capturing and burning the first boat, and in the second instance driving back two gun-boats and capturing the steamer *Resolute,* with seven naval officers and a crew of twenty-five seamen.

General Slocum occupies Argyle Island and the upper end of Hutchinson's Island, and has a brigade on the South Carolina shore opposite, and he is very urgent to pass one of his corps over to that shore; but, in view of the change of plan made necessary by your order of the 6th, I will maintain things in *statu quo* till I have got all my transportation to the rear and out of the way, and until I have sea transportation for the troops you require at James River, which I will accompany and command in person. Of course I will leave Kilpatrick, with his cavalry, say 5,300, and it may be a division of the Fifteenth Corps; but before determining this I must see General Foster, and may arrange to shift his force (now over above the Charleston railroad, at the head of Broad River) to the Ogeechee, where, in co-operation with Kilpatrick's cavalry, he can better threaten the State of Georgia than from the direction of Port Royal. Besides, I would much prefer not to detach from my regular corps any of its veteran divisions, and would even prefer that other less valuable troops should be sent to reenforce Foster from some other quarter. My four corps, full of experience and full of ardor, coming to you *en masse*, equal to 60,000 fighting-men, will be a re-enforcement that Lee cannot disregard. Indeed, with my present command, I had expected upon reducing Savannah instantly to march to Columbia, S.C., thence to Raleigh, and thence to report to you; but this would consume, it may be, six weeks time after the fall of Savannah, whereas by sea I can probably reach you with my men and arms before the middle of January.

I myself am somewhat astonished at the attitude of things in Tennessee. I purposely delayed at Kingston until General Thomas assured me that he was "all ready," and my last dispatch from him, of the 12th of November, was full of confidence, in which he promised me that he would "ruin Hood" if he dared to advance from Florence, urging me to go ahead and give myself no concern about Hood's army in Tennessee. Why he did not turn on Hood at Franklin, after checking and discomfiting him, surpasses my understanding. Indeed, I do not approve of his evacuating Decatur, but think he should have assumed the offensive against Hood from Pulaski in the direction of Waynesburg [Waynesboro]. I know full well that General Thomas is slow in mind and in action, but he is judicious and brave, and the troops feel great confidence in him. I still hope he will out-maneuver and destroy Hood.

As to matters in the Southeast, I think Hardee, in Savannah, has good artillerists, some 5,000 or 6,000 infantry, and it may be a mongrel mass of 8,000 to 10,000 militia. In all our marching through Georgia he has not forced us to use anything but a skirmish line, though at several points he had erected fortifications and tried to alarm us by bombastic threats. In Savannah he has taken refuge in a line constructed behind swamps and overflowed rice fields, extending from a point on the Savannah River about three miles above the city around by a branch of the Little Ogeechee, which stream is impassable from its salt marshes and boggy swamps, crossed only by narrow causeways or common corduroy roads. There must be 25,000 citizens—men, women, and children—in Savannah that must also be fed, and how he is to feed them beyond a few days I cannot imagine, as I know that his requisitions for corn on the interior counties were not filled, and we are in possession of the rice fields and mills which could alone be of service to him in this neighborhood. He can draw nothing from South Carolina, save from a small corner down in the southeast, and that by a disused wagon road. I could easily get possession of this, but hardly deem it worth the risk of making a detachment, which would be in danger by its isolation from the main army.

Our whole army is in fine condition as to health, and the weather is splendid; for that reason alone, I feel a personal dislike to turning northward. I will keep Lieutenant Dunn here until I know the result of my demand for the surrender of Savannah; but, whether successful or not, shall not delay my execution of your order of the 6th, which will depend alone upon the time it will require to obtain transportation by sea.

I am, with respect, &c., your obedient servant,

W. T. Sherman, *Major-General, U.S. Army*

(Source: U.S. War Department. *War of the Rebellion: A Compilation of the Official Records of the Union and Confederate Armies.* Ser. I, Vol. XLIV.)

4. Sherman to Hardee Regarding the Reduction of Savannah (17 December 1864)

Headquarters Military Division of the Mississippi
In the Field, near Savannah, Ga., December 17, 1864.

General William J. Hardee,
Commanding Confederate Forces in Savannah:
GENERAL: You have doubtless observed from your station at Rosedew that sea-going vessels now come through Ossabaw Sound and up Ogeechee to the rear of my army, giving me abundant supplies of all kinds, and more especially heavy ordnance necessary to the reduction of Savannah. I have already received guns that can cast heavy and destructive shot as far as the heart of your city; also, I have for some days held and controlled every avenue by which the people and garrison of Savannah can be supplied; and I am therefore justified in demanding the surrender of the city of Savannah and its dependent forts, and shall await a reasonable time your answer before opening with heavy ordnance. Should you entertain the proposition I am prepared to grant liberal terms to the inhabitants and garrison; but

should I be forced to resort to assault, or the slower and surer process of starvation, I shall then feel justified in resorting to the harshest measures, and shall make little effort to restrain my army—burning to avenge a great national wrong they attach to Savannah and other large cities which have been so prominent in dragging our country into civil war. I inclose you a copy of General Hood's demand for the surrender of the town of Resaca, to be used by you for what it is worth. I have the honor to be your obedient servant,

W. T. Sherman, *Major-General*

(Source: U.S. War Department. *War of the Rebellion: A Compilation of the Official Records of the Union and Confederate Armies* Ser. I, Vol. XLIV.)

XXXII. Sheridan in the Valley

Operating out of the Shenandoah Valley in the summer of 1864, Confederate lieutenant general Jubal Early led a raid on Washington, D.C., that not only embarrassed the Union forces, but revealed another reason to close down the Shenandoah Valley. It was both a breadbasket for the Army of Northern Virginia and a refuge for ranging Rebel forces. Accordingly, on 6 August, Grant gave Philip Sheridan orders for a campaign to remove Early's army as a factor in the war and to despoil the valley of everything that could contribute to the Confederate war effort. The result was the application of the hard war policy in the Shenandoah—similar to that of Sherman in Georgia and the Carolinas—that would be remembered there for generations. [See Shenandoah Valley Campaign, 1864–1865]

1. General Sheridan's Reports (October 1864)
HARRISONBURG, *October 1, 1864—10 a.m.*
(Received 3d.)

Lieutenant-General GRANT:
I have ordered General Wilson to report to Sherman. He is the best man for the position. I have devastated the Valley from Staunton down to Mount Crawford, and will continue. The destruction of mills, grain, forage, foundries, &c., is very great. The cavalry report to me that they have collected 3,000 head of cattle and sheep between Staunton and Mount Crawford. The difficulty of transporting this army through the mountain passes onto the railroad at Charlottesville is such that I regard it as impracticable, with my present means of transportation. The rebels have given up the Valley, excepting Waynesborough, which has been occupied by them since my cavalry was there. I think that the best policy will be to let the burning of the crops of the Valley be the end of this campaign, and let some of this army go somewhere else.

P. H. SHERIDAN, *Major-General.*

(Source: U.S. War Department. *War of the Rebellion: A Compilation of the Official Records of the Union and Confederate Armies.* Ser. I, Vol. XLIII/1.)

* * *

WOODSTOCK, October 7, 1864—9 p.m.
(Received 9th.)

I have the honor to report my command at this point to-night. I commenced moving back from Port Republic, Mount Crawford, Bridgewater, and Harrisonburg yesterday morning. The grain and forage in advance of these points up to Staunton had previously been destroyed. In moving back to this point the whole country from the Blue Ridge to the North Mountains has been made untenable for a rebel army. I have destroyed over 2,000 barns filled with wheat, hay, and farming implements; over seventy mills filled with flour and wheat; have driven in front of the army over 4[,000] head of stock, and have killed and issued to the troops not less than 3,000 sheep. This destruction embraces the Luray Valley and Little Fort Valley, as well as the main valley. A large number of horses have been obtained, a proper estimate of which I cannot now make. Lieut. John R. Meigs, my engineer officer, was murdered beyond Harrisonburg, near Dayton. For this atrocious act all the houses within an area of five miles were burned. Since I came into the Valley, from Harper's Ferry up to Harrisonburg, every train, every small party, and every straggler has been bushwhacked by people, many of whom have protection papers from commanders who have been hitherto in this valley. From the vicinity of Harrisonburg over 400 wagonloads of refugees have been sent back to Martinsburg; most of these people were Dunkers and had been conscripted. The people here are getting sick of the war; heretofore they have had no reason to complain, because they have been living in great abundance. I have not been followed by the enemy up to this point, with the exception of a small force of rebel cavalry that showed themselves some distance behind my rear guard to-day. A party of 100 of the Eighth Ohio Cavalry, which I had stationed at the bridge over the North Shenandoah, near Mount Jackson, was attacked by McNeill, with seventeen men; report they were asleep, and the whole party dispersed or captured. I think that they will all turn up; I learn that fifty-six of them have reached Winchester. McNeill was mortally wounded and fell into our hands. This was fortunate, as he was the most daring and dangerous of all the bushwhackers in this section of the country. I would have preferred sending troops to you by the Baltimore and Ohio Railroad; it would have been the quickest and most concealed way of sending them. The keeping open of

the road to Front Royal will require large guards to protect it against a very small number of partisan troops. It also obliges me to have a pontoon train, if it is to be kept open, to bridge the Shenandoah and keep up communication with Winchester. However, in a day or two I can tell better. I sent a party of cavalry through Thornton's Gap, and directed the balance of the division of cavalry which I have left in the Valley to take position at Millwood, occupying Chester Gap and Front Royal. Thornton's Gap I have given up, as of no value. With this disposition of forces, I will move infantry round the mountains, via Strasburg, as soon as possible. To-morrow I will continue the destruction of wheat, forage, &c., down to Fisher's Hill. When this is completed the Valley, from Winchester up to Staunton, ninety-two miles, will have but little in it for man or beast. In previous dispatches I have used "lower Valley" when I should have said "upper Valley," or, in other words, in my last dispatch I intended to say that the grain and forage from Staunton up to Lexington had been sent to Richmond, and that the grain and forage from Staunton to Strasburg had been left for the wintering of Early's army. Yesterday Colonel Powell captured a guerrilla camp on the mountains, with ten wagons and teams.

P. H. SHERIDAN, Major-General.

(Source: U.S. War Department. *War of the Rebellion: A Compilation of the Official Records of the Union and Confederate Armies*. Ser. I, Vol. XLIII/1.)

XXXIII. The Early Struggle over Reconstruction

Arguments over Reconstruction began as early as when Abraham Lincoln delivered his first inaugural address in March 1861. His intention to preserve the Union was based on his belief that secession did not exist and that it was his constitutional duty to restore legitimate governments in states that ostensibly had been misguided by usurpers. In Lincoln's view, a core of Unionists would enlarge as federal forces quelled the insurrection. Such a process would promote a kind of self-reconstruction. Even his emancipation policy was aimed at an early reunion of the seceded South with the Union. Though Lincoln never doubted that Reconstruction should be a limited process, he nonetheless became impatient with its postponed realization. On 8 December 1863, he announced a new plan in his Proclamation of Amnesty and Reconstruction. Under its provisions, Southerners could take a simple loyalty oath that pledged them to obey all federal laws and presidential proclamations regarding slavery. On 2 July 1864, congressional Radical Republicans led by Henry Winter Davis and Benjamin Wade proclaimed a plan of Reconstruction that would ensure black freedom as well as dictate harsher terms for resolution of the Southern rebellion. Lincoln's pocket veto of this bill allowed the work of his plan already under way in Louisiana, Arkansas, and Tennessee

to proceed. Yet the veto provoked Wade and Davis to draft a scalding rebuke of Lincoln's policy. It boded ill for the entire process of Reconstruction, and only Lincoln's reelection in November postponed the argument that would erupt anew upon the end of the war and take a decidedly bitter turn after Lincoln's assassination. [See Lincoln's Reconstruction Policy; Wade-Davis Bill]

1. Lincoln's Proclamation of Amnesty (8 December 1863)

December 8, 1863

BY THE PRESIDENT OF THE UNITED STATES OF AMERICA:

A PROCLAMATION.

WHEREAS, in and by the Constitution of the United States, it is provided that the President "shall have power to grant reprieves and pardons for offences against the United States, except in cases of impeachment;" and

Whereas, a rebellion now exists whereby the loyal state governments of several states have for a long time been subverted, and many persons have committed, and are now guilty of, treason against the United States; and

Whereas, with reference to said rebellion and treason, laws have been enacted by congress, declaring forfeitures and confiscation of property and liberation of slaves, all upon terms and conditions therein stated, and also declaring that the President was thereby authorized at any time thereafter, by proclamation, to extend to persons who may have participated in the existing rebellion, in any state or part thereof, pardon and amnesty, with such exceptions and at such times and on such conditions as he may deem expedient for the public welfare; and

Whereas, the congressional declaration for limited and conditional pardon accords with well-established judicial exposition of the pardoning power; and

Whereas, with reference to said rebellion, the President of the United States has issued several proclamations, with provisions in regard to the liberation of slaves; and

Whereas, it is now desired by some persons heretofore engaged in said rebellion to resume their allegiance to the United States, and to reinaugurate loyal state governments within and for their respective states: Therefore—

I, ABRAHAM LINCOLN, President of the United States, do proclaim, declare, and make known to all persons who have, directly or by implication, participated in the existing rebellion, except as hereinafter excepted, that a full pardon is hereby granted to them and each of them, with restoration of all rights of property, except as to slaves, and in property cases where rights of third parties shall have intervened, and upon the condition that every such person shall take and subscribe an oath, and thenceforward keep and maintain said oath inviolate; and which oath shall be registered for permanent preservation, and shall be of the tenor and effect following, to wit:—

"I do solemnly swear, in presence of Almighty God, that I will henceforth faithfully support, protect, and defend the Constitution of the United States and the Union of the States thereunder; and that I will, in like manner, abide by and faithfully support all acts of congress passed during the existing rebellion with reference to slaves, so long and so far as not repealed, modified, or held void by congress, or by decision of the supreme court; and that I will, in like manner, abide by and faithfully support all proclamations of the President made during the existing rebellion having reference to slaves, so long and so far as not modified or declared void by decision of the supreme court. So help me God."

The persons excepted from the benefits of the foregoing provisions are all who are, or shall have been, civil or diplomatic officers or agents of the so-called Confederate government; all who have left judicial stations under the United States to aid the rebellion; all who are, or shall have been, military or naval officers of said so-called Confederate government above the rank of colonel in the army or of lieutenant in the navy; all who left seats in the United States congress to aid the rebellion; all who resigned commissions in the army or navy of the United States and afterwards aided the rebellion; and all who have engaged in any way in treating colored persons, or white persons in charge of such, otherwise than lawfully as prisoners of war, and which persons may have been found in the United States service as soldiers, seamen, or in any other capacity.

And I do further proclaim, declare, and make known that whenever, in any of the States of Arkansas, Texas, Louisiana, Mississippi, Tennessee, Alabama, Georgia, Florida, South Carolina, and North Carolina, a number of persons, not less than one tenth in number of the votes cast in such state at the presidential election of the year of our Lord one thousand eight hundred and sixty, each having taken the oath aforesaid, and not having since violated it, and being a qualified voter by the election law of the state existing immediately before the so-called act of secession, and excluding all others, shall reestablish a state government which shall be republican, and in nowise contravening said oath, such shall be recognized as the true government of the state, and the state shall receive thereunder the benefits of the constitutional provision which declares that "the United States shall guaranty to every state in this Union a republican form of government, and shall protect each of them against invasion; and on application of the legislature, or the executive, (when the legislature cannot be convened,) against domestic violence."

And I do further proclaim, declare, and make known that any provision which may be adopted by such state government in relation to the freed people of such state, which shall recognize and declare their permanent freedom, provide for their education, and which may yet be consistent as a temporary arrangement with their present condition as a laboring, landless, and homeless class, will not be objected to by the National Executive.

And it is suggested as not improper that, in constructing a loyal state government in any state, the name of the state, the boundary, the subdivisions, the constitution, and the general code of laws, as before the rebellion, be maintained, subject only to the modifications made necessary by the conditions hereinbefore stated, and such others, if any, not contravening said conditions, and which may be deemed expedient by those framing the new state government.

To avoid misunderstanding, it may be proper to say that this proclamation, so far as it relates to state governments, has no reference to states wherein loyal state governments have all the while been maintained. And, for the same reason, it may be proper to further say, that whether members sent to congress from any state shall be admitted to seats constitutionally rests exclusively with the respective houses, and not to any extent with the Executive. And still further, that this proclamation is intended to present the people of the states wherein the national authority has been suspended, and loyal state governments have been subverted, a mode in and by which the national authority and loyal state governments may be reestablished within said states, or in any of them; and while the mode presented is the best the Executive can suggest, with his present impressions, it must not be understood that no other possible mode would be acceptable.

Given under my hand at the city of Washington the eighth day of December, A.D. one thousand eight hundred and sixty-three, and of the Independence of the United States of America the eighty-eighth.
ABRAHAM LINCOLN.
By the President:
WILLIAM H. SEWARD, *Secretary of State.*

(Source: *Statutes at Large, Treaties, and Proclamations of the United States of America.* Vol. 13. Boston: n.p., 1866.)

2. An Act to Guarantee to Certain States Whose Governments Have Been Usurped or Overthrown a Republican Form of Government (8 July 1864)

Be it enacted, That in the states declared in rebellion against the United States, the President shall, by and with the advice and consent of the Senate, appoint for each a provisional governor, . . . who shall be charged with the civil administration of such state until a state

government therein shall be recognized as hereinafter provided.

Sec. 2. That so soon as the military resistance to the United States shall have been suppressed in any such state, and the people thereof shall have sufficiently returned to their obedience to the constitution and the laws of the United States, the provisional governor shall direct the marshal of the United States, as speedily as may be, to name a sufficient number of deputies, and to enroll all white male citizens of the United States, resident in the state in their respective counties, and to request each one to take the oath to support the constitution of the United States, and in his enrolment to designate those who take and those who refuse to take that oath, which rolls shall be forthwith returned to the provisional governor; and if the persons taking that oath shall amount to a majority of the persons enrolled in the state, he shall, by proclamation, invite the loyal people of the state to elect delegates to a convention charged to declare the will of the people of the state relative to the reestablishment of a state government subject to, and in conformity with, the constitution of the United States.

Sec. 3. That the convention shall consist of as many members as both houses of the last constitutional state legislature, apportioned by the provisional governor among the counties, parishes, or districts of the state, in proportion to the white population, returned as electors, by the marshal, in compliance with the provisions of this act. The provisional governor shall provide an adequate force to keep the peace during the election.

Sec. 4. That the delegates shall be elected by the loyal white male citizens of the United States of the age of twenty-one years, and resident at the time in the county, parish, or district in which they shall offer to vote, and enrolled as aforesaid, or absent in the military service of the United States, and who shall take and subscribe the oath of allegiance to the United States in the form contained in the act of July 2, 1862; and all such citizens of the United States who are in the military service of the United States shall vote at the headquarters of their respective commands, under such regulations as may be prescribed by the provisional governor for the taking and return of their votes; but no person who has held or exercised any office, civil or military, state or confederate, under the rebel usurpation, or who has voluntarily borne arms against the United States, shall vote, or be eligible to be elected as delegate, at such election.

Sec. 5. That the said commissioners,... shall hold the election in conformity with this act and.... shall proceed in the manner used in the state prior to the rebellion. The oath of allegiance shall be taken and subscribed on the poll-book by every voter in the form above prescribed, but every person known by, or proved to, the commissioners to have held or exercised any office, civil or military, state or confederate, under the rebel usurpation, or to have voluntarily borne arms against the United States, shall be excluded, though he offer to take the oath; and in case any person who shall have borne arms against the United States shall offer to vote he shall be deemed to have borne arms voluntarily unless he shall prove the contrary by the testimony of a qualified voter. . . .

Sec. 6. That the provisional governor shall, by proclamation, convene the delegates elected as aforesaid, at the capital of the state, on a day not more than three months after the election, giving at least thirty days' notice of such day. In case the said capital shall in his judgment be unfit, he shall in his proclamation appoint another place. He shall preside over the deliberations of the convention, and administer to each delegate, before taking his seat in the convention, the oath of allegiance to the United States in the form above prescribed.

Sec. 7. That the convention shall declare, on behalf of the people of the state, their submission to the constitution and laws of the United States, and shall adopt the following provisions, hereby prescribed by the United States in the execution of the constitutional duty to guarantee a republican form of government to every state, and incorporate them in the constitution of the state, that is to say:

First. No person who has held or exercised any office, civil or military, except offices merely ministerial, and military offices below the grade of colonel, state or confederate, under the usurping power, shall vote for or be a member of the legislature, or governor.

Second. Involuntary servitude is forever prohibited, and the freedom of all persons is guaranteed in said state.

Third. No debt, state or confederate, created by or under the sanction of the usurping power, shall be recognized or paid by the state.

Sec. 8. That when the convention shall have adopted those provisions, it shall proceed to reestablish a republican form of government, and ordain a constitution containing those provisions, which, when adopted, the convention shall by ordinance provide for submitting to the people of the state, entitled to vote under this law, at an election to be held in the manner prescribed by the act for the election of delegates; but at a time and place named by the convention, at which election the said electors, and none others, shall vote directly for or against such constitution and form of state government, and the returns of said election shall be made to the provisional governor, who shall canvass the same in the presence of the electors, and if a majority of the votes cast shall be for the constitution and form of government, he shall certify the same, with a copy thereof, to the President of the United States, who, after obtaining the assent of congress, shall, by proclamation, recognize the government so established, and none other, as the constitutional government of the state, and from the date of such recognition, and not before, Senators and Representatives, and electors for President and Vice-President may be elected in such state, according to the laws of the state and of the United States.

Sec. 9. That if the convention shall refuse to reestablish the state government on the conditions aforesaid, the provisional governor shall declare it dissolved; but it shall be the duty of the President, whenever he shall have reason to believe that a sufficient number of the people of the state entitled to vote under this act, in number not less than a majority of those enrolled, as aforesaid, are willing to reestablish a state government on the conditions aforesaid, to direct the provisional governor to order another election of delegates to a convention for the purpose....

Sec. 10. That, until the United States shall have recognized a republican form of state government, the provisional governor in each of said states shall see that this act, and the laws of the United States, and the laws of the state in force when the state government was overthrown by the rebellion, are faithfully executed within the state; but no law or usage whereby any person was heretofore held in involuntary servitude shall be recognized or enforced by any court or officer in such state, and the laws for the trial and punishment of white persons shall extend to all persons, and jurors shall have the qualifications of voters under this law for delegates to the convention....

Sec. 11. That until the recognition of a state government as aforesaid, the provisional governor shall, under such regulations as he may prescribe, cause to be assessed, levied, and collected, for the year eighteen hundred and sixty-four, and every year thereafter, the taxes provided by the laws of such state to be levied during the fiscal year preceding the overthrow of the state government thereof, in the manner prescribed by the laws of the state, as nearly as may be;... The proceeds of such taxes shall be accounted for to the provisional governor, and be by him applied to the expenses of the administration of the laws in such state, subject to the direction of the President, and the surplus shall be deposited in the treasury of the United States to the credit of such. state, to be paid to the state upon an appropriation therefor, to be made when a republican form of government shall be recognized therein by the United States.

Sec. 12. That all persons held to involuntary servitude or labor in the states aforesaid are hereby emancipated and discharged therefrom, and they and their posterity shall be forever free. And if any such persons or their posterity shall be restrained of liberty, under pretence of any claim to such service or labor, the courts of the United States shall, on habeas corpus, discharge them.

Sec. 13. That if any person declared free by this act, or any law of the United States, or any proclamation of the President, be restrained of liberty, with intent to be held in or reduced to involuntary servitude or labor, the person convicted before a court of competent jurisdiction of such act shall be punished by fine of not less than fifteen hundred dollars, and be imprisoned not less than five nor more than twenty years.

Sec. 14. That every person who shall hereafter hold or exercise any office, civil or military, except offices merely ministerial, and military offices below the grade of colonel, in the rebel service, state or confederate, is hereby declared not to be a citizen of the United States shall, on habeas corpus, discharge them.

(Source: Richardson, James, ed. *A Compilation of the Message and Papers of the Presidents 1789–1902.* Vol. VI. Washington, DC: Bureau of National Literature and Art, 1904.)

3. Lincoln's Proclamation on the Wade-Davis Bill (8 July 1864)

BY THE PRESIDENT OF THE UNITED STATES:
A Proclamation.
Whereas at the late session Congress passed a bill "to guarantee to certain States whose governments have been usurped or overthrown a republican form of government," a copy of which is hereunto annexed; and

Whereas the said bill was presented to the President of the United States for his approval less than one hour before the *sine die* adjournment of said session, and was not signed by him and

Whereas the said bill contains, among other things, a plan for restoring the States in rebellion to their proper practical relation in the Union, which plan expresses the sense of Congress upon that subject, and which plan it is now thought fit to lay before the people for their consideration:

Now, therefore, I, Abraham Lincoln, President of the United States, do proclaim, declare, and make known that while I am (as I was in December last, when, by proclamation, I propounded a plan for restoration) unprepared by a formal approval of this bill to be inflexibly committed to any single plan of restoration, and while I am also unprepared to declare that the free State constitutions and governments already adopted and installed in Arkansas and Louisiana shall be set aside and held for naught, thereby repelling and discouraging the loyal citizens who have set up the same as to further effort, or to declare a constitutional competency in Congress to abolish slavery in States, but am at the same time sincerely hoping and expecting that a constitutional amendment abolishing slavery throughout the nation may be adopted, nevertheless I am fully satisfied with the system for restoration contained in the bill as one very proper plan for the loyal people of any State choosing to adopt it, and that I am and at all times shall be prepared to give the Executive aid and assistance to any such people so soon as the military resistance to the United States shall have been suppressed in any such State and the people thereof shall have sufficiently returned to their obedience to the Constitution and the laws of the United States, in which cases military governors will be appointed with directions to proceed according to the bill. . . .

ABRAHAM LINCOLN.

(Source: Richardson, James, ed. *A Compilation of the Message and Papers of the Presidents 1789–1902.* Vol. VI. Washington, DC: Bureau of National Literature and Art, 1904.)

4. The Wade-Davis Manifesto (5 August 1864)

We have read without surprise, but not without indignation, the proclamation of the President of the 8th of July....

The President, by preventing this bill from becoming a law, holds the electoral votes of the rebel States at the dictation of his personal ambition.

If those votes turn the balance in his favor, is it to be supposed that his competitor, defeated by such means, will acquiesce?

If the rebel majority assert their supremacy in those States, and send votes which elect an enemy of the Government, will we not repel his claims?

And is not that civil war for the Presidency inaugurated by the votes of rebel States?

Seriously impressed with these dangers, Congress, *"the proper constituted authority,* "formally declared that there are no State governments in the rebel States, and provided for their erection at a proper time; and both the Senate and the House of Representatives rejected the Senators and Representatives chosen under the authority of what the President calls the free constitution and government of Arkansas.

The President's proclamation *"holds for naught"* this judgment, and discards the authority of the Supreme Court, and strides headlong toward the anarchy his proclamation 6f the 8th of December inaugurated.

If electors for President be allowed to be chosen in either of those States, a sinister light will be cast on the motives which induced the President to "hold for naught" the will of Congress rather than his government in Louisiana and Arkansas.

That judgment of Congress which the President defies was the exercise of an authority exclusively vested in Congress by the Constitution to determine what is the established government in a State, and in its own nature and by the highest judicial authority binding on all other departments of the Government. . . .

A more studied outrage on the legislative authority of the people has never been perpetrated.

Congress passed a bill; the President refused to approve it, and then by proclamation puts as much of it in force as he sees fit, and proposes to execute those parts by officers unknown to the laws of the United States and not subject to the confirmation of the Senate!

The bill directed the appointment of Provisional Governors by and with the advice and consent of the Senate.

The President, after defeating the law, proposes to appoint without law, and without the advice and consent of the Senate, *Military* Governors for the rebel States!

He has already exercised this dictatorial usurpation in Louisiana, and he defeated the bill to prevent its limitation. . . .

The President has greatly presumed on the forbearance which the supporters of his Administration have so long practiced, in view of the arduous conflict in which we are engaged, and the reckless ferocity of our political opponents.

But he must understand that our support is of a cause and not of a man; that the authority of Congress is paramount and must be respected; that the whole body of the Union men of Congress will not submit to be impeached by him of rash and unconstitutional legislation; and if he wishes our support, he must confine himself to his executive duties—to obey and execute, not make the laws—to suppress by arms armed rebellion, and leave political reorganization to Congress.

If the supporters of the Government fail to insist on this, they become responsible for the usurpations which they fail to rebuke, and are justly liable to the indignation of the people whose rights and security, committed to their keeping, they sacrifice.

Let them consider the remedy for these usurpations, and, having found it, fearlessly execute it.

(Source: McPherson, Edward, ed. *The Political History of the United States of America during the Great Rebellion.* 2nd ed. Washington, DC: Philip & Solomons, 1865.)

XXXIV. The Election of 1864

The election of 1864 was a testament that even civil war would not interrupt the democratic process in the United States. Laboring under the stigma that it was the party of treason, the Democratic Party nominated George B. McClellan. Lincoln, meanwhile, had overcome several challenges within the Republican Party (styling itself now the National Union Party to emphasize its patriotic loyalty)

to secure the nomination and enter the contest with what he regarded as a reasonable platform. His reelection in November, assisted by soldiers voting in the field by absentee ballot, was a vote of confidence in his administration and a mandate that the war should continue to victory. [See Election of 1864]

1. The Democratic National Platform of 1864 (August 29 1864)

Resolved, That this Convention does explicitly declare, as the sense of the American people, that after four years of failure to retore the Union by the experiment of war, during which, under the pretence of a military necessity, or war power higher than the Constitution, the Constitution itself has been disregarded in every part, and public liberty and private right alike trodden down and the material prosperity of the country essentially impaired—justice, humanity, liberty, and the public welfare demand that immediate efforts be made for a cessation of hostilities, with a view to an ultimate Convention of the States, or other peaceable means, to the end that at the earliest practicable moment peace may be retored on the basis of the Federal Union of the States.

Resolved, That the direct interference of the military authorities of the United States in the recent elections held in Kentucky, Maryland, Missouri, and Delaware, was a shameful violation of the Constitution; and a repetition of such acts in the approaching election will be held as revolutionary, and will be resisted with all the means and power under our control.

Resolved, That the aim and object of the Democratic Party is to preserve the Federal Union and the rights of the States unimpaired; and they hereby declare that they consider that the administrative usurpation of extraordinary and dangerous powers not granted by the Constitution; the subversion of the civil by the military law in States not in insurrection; the arbitrary arrest, imprisonment, trial, and sentence of American citizens in States where civil law exists in full force; the suppression of freedom of speech and of the press; the denial of the right of asylum; the open and avowed disregard of State rights; the employment of unusual testoaths, and the interference with and denial of the right of the people to bear arms in their defence, is calculated to prevent a restoration of the Union and the perpetuation of a Government deriving its just powers from the consent of the governed.

(Source: Birley, Robert. *Speeches and Documents in American History.* London: Oxford University Press, 1962.)

2. Platform of the National Union Convention (7 June 1864)

Baltimore, Maryland
June 7, 1864

1. Resolved, That it is the highest duty of every American citizen to maintain against all their enemies the integrity of the Union and the paramount authority of the Constitution and laws of the United States; and that, laying aside all differences of political opinion, we pledge ourselves, as Union men, animated by a common sentiment and aiming at a common object, to do everything in our power to aid the Government in quelling by force of arms the rebellion now raging against its authority, and in bringing to the punishment due to their crimes the rebels and traitors arrayed against it.

2. Resolved, That we approve the determination of the Government of the United States not to compromise with rebels, or to offer them any terms of peace, except such as may be based upon an unconditional surrender of their hostility and a return to their just allegiance to the Constitution and laws of the United States, and that we call upon the Government to maintain this position, and to prosecute the war with the utmost possible vigor to the complete suppression of the rebellion, in full reliance upon the self-sacrificing patriotism, the heroic valor, and the undying devotion of the American people to their country and its free institutions.

3. Resolved, That as slavery was the cause, and now constitutes the strength, of this rebellion, and as it must be, always and everywhere, hostile to the principles of publican government, justice and the national safety demand its utter and complete extirpation from the soil of the republic; and that while we uphold and maintain the acts, and proclamations by which the Government, in its own defense, has aimed a deathblow at this gigantic evil, we are in favor, furthermore, of such an amendment to the Constitution, to be made by the people in conformity with its provisions, as shall terminate and forever prohibit the existence of slavery within the limits or the jurisdiction of the United States.

4. Resolved, That the thanks of the American people are due to the soldiers and sailors of the Army and Navy, who have periled their lives in defense of their country and in vindication of the honor of its flag; that the nation owes to them some permanent recognition of their patriotism and their valor, and ample and permanent provision for those of their survivors who have received disabling and honorable wounds in the service of the country; and that the memories of those who have fallen in its defense shall be held in grateful and everlasting remembrance.

5. Resolved, That we approve and applaud the practical wisdom, the unselfish patriotism, and the unswerving fidelity to the Constitution and the principles of American liberty, with which Abraham Lincoln has discharged under circumstances of unparalleled difficulty the great duties and responsibilities of the Presidential office; that he approve and indorse as demanded by the emergency and essential to the preservation of the nation, and as within the provisions of the Constitution, the measures and acts which he has adopted to defend the nation against its open and secret foes; that we approve, especially, the Proclamation

Emancipation, and the employment as Union soldiers of men heretofore held in slavery; and that we have full confidence in his determination to carry these and all other constitutional measures essential to the salvation of the country into full and complete effect.

6. *Resolved,* That we deem it essential to the general welfare that harmony should prevail in the national councils, and we regard as worthy of public confidence and official trust those only who cordially indorse the principles proclaimed in these resolutions, and which should characterize the administration of the Government.

7. *Resolved,* That the Government owes to all men employed in its armies, without regard to distinction of color, the full protection of the laws of war, and that any violation of these laws, or of the usages of civilized nations in time of war, by the rebels now in arms, should be made the subject of prompt and full redress.

8. *Resolved,* That foreign immigration, which in the past has added so much to the wealth, development of resources, and increase of power to this nation, the asylum of the oppressed of all nations, should be fostered and encouraged by a liberal and just policy.

9. *Resolved,* That we are in favor of the speedy construction of the railroad to the Pacific coast.

10. *Resolved,* That the national faith, pledged for the redemption of the public debt, must be kept inviolate, and that for this purpose we recommend economy and rigid responsibility in the public expenditures, and a vigorous and just system of taxation: and that it is the duty of every loyal State to sustain the credit and promote the use of the national currency.

11. *Resolved,* That we approve the position taken by the Government that the people of the United States can never regard with indifference the attempt of any European power to overthrow by force or to supplant by fraud the institutions of any republican government on the Western Continent, and that they will view with extreme jealousy, as menacing to the peace and independence of their own country, the efforts of any such power to obtain new footholds for monarchical governments, sustained by foreign military force, in near proximity to the United States.

(Source: Porter, Kirk H., and Donald Bruce Johnson. *National Party Platforms 1840–1960.* Urbana: University of Illinois Press, 1961.)

XXXV. The End of the War

A. THE HOPE FOR A NEW BEGINNING
Lincoln's second inaugural addressed the war on several levels: its cause, its justification, and its impending conclusion. The president's Old Testament reference to a vengeful God exacting careful payment for the sin of slavery was, at the close, balanced by a New Testament exhortation of charity that began with the ringing admonition to hold malice toward none. Like the Gettysburg Address of fifteen months earlier, it held out the challenge of hard work with the promise of hope. [See Lincoln, Abraham; Lincoln's Reconstruction Policy]

1. Lincoln's Second Inaugural Address
(4 March 1865)

FELLOW-COUNTRYMEN:—At this second appearing to take the oath of the presidential office there is less occasion for an extended address than there was at the first. Then a statement somewhat in detail of a course to be pursued seemed fitting and proper. Now, at the expiration of four years, during which public declarations have been constantly called forth on every point and phase of the great contest which still absorbs the attention and engrosses the energies of the nation, little that is new could be presented. The progress of our arms, upon which all else chiefly depends, is as well known to the public as to myself, and it is, I trust, reasonably satisfactory and encouraging to all. With high hope for the future, no prediction in regard to it is ventured.

On the occasion corresponding to this four years ago all thoughts were anxiously directed to an impending civil war. All dreaded it, all sought to avert it. While the inaugural address was being delivered from this place, devoted altogether to saving the Union without war, insurgent agents were in the city seeking to destroy it without war—seeking to dissolve the Union and divide effects by negotiation. Both parties deprecated war, but one of them would make war rather than let the nation survive, and the other would accept war rather than let it perish, and the war came.

One eighth of the whole population was colored slaves, not distributed generally over the Union, but localized in the southern part of it. These slaves constituted a peculiar and powerful interest. All knew that this interest was somehow the cause of the war. To strengthen, perpetuate, and extend this interest was the object for which the insurgents would rend the Union even by war, while the Government claimed no right to do more than to restrict the territorial enlargement of it. Neither party expected for the war the magnitude or the duration which it has already attained. Neither anticipated that the cause of the conflict might cease with or even before the conflict itself should cease. Each looked for an easier triumph, and a result less fundamental and astounding. Both read the same Bible and pray to the same God, and each invokes His aid against the other. It may seem strange that any men should dare to ask a just God's assistance in wringing their bread from the sweat of other men's faces, but let us judge not, that we be not judged. The prayers of both could not be answered. That of neither has been answered fully. The Almighty has His own purposes. "Woe unto the world because of offenses; for it must needs be that offenses come, but woe to that man by whom the offense cometh." If we shall suppose that American slavery is one of those offenses which, in the providence of God, must needs come, but which, having continued through His appointed time, He now wills to remove, and that He gives to both North and South this terrible war as the woe due to those by whom the offense came, shall we discern therein any departure from those divine attributes which the believers in a living God always ascribe to Him? Fondly do we hope, fervently do we pray, that this mighty scourge of war may speedily pass away. Yet, if God wills that it continue until all the wealth piled by the bondsman's two hundred and fifty years of unrequited toil shall be sunk, and until every drop of blood drawn with the lash shall be paid by another drawn with the sword, as was said three thousand years ago, so still it must be said, "The judgments of the Lord are true and righteous altogether."

With malice toward none, with charity for all, with firmness in the right as God gives us to see the right, let us strive on to finish the work we are in, to bind up the nation's wounds, to care for him who shall have borne the battle and for his widow and his orphan, to do all which may achieve and cherish a just and lasting peace among ourselves and with all nations.

(Source: Lapsley, Arthur Brooks, ed. *The Writings of Abraham Lincoln.* Vol. 7. New York: G. P. Putnam's Sons, 1906.)

B. THE DEVASTATED SOUTH

William T. Sherman's progress through South Carolina was even more devastating for that state than his March to the Sea had been for Georgia. From Orangeburg, South Carolina, the army headed for the South Carolina capital of Columbia, stopping south of the city on 15 February. Many officers and men viewed South Carolina as the fomenter of the war, and some now pledged to burn Columbia as a continuation of the retribution they had exacted on the Carolina countryside. When Columbia went up in flames during the federal occupation on 17 February, it apparently was the result of willful arson on the part of some Union soldiers—some of them inebriated—combining with the efforts of evacuating Confederates to destroy property of military value. When Sherman left the city to head north, Columbia was a smoldering landscape of ruins. [See Columbia, South Carolina, Burning of]

1. Report on the Burning of Columbia, S.C., of Bvt. Brig. Gen. Orlando M. Poe, Corps of Engineers, U. S. Army, Chief Engineer (February 1865)

On the 17th a pontoon bridge was built just above the ruins of the former bridge over Broad River, three miles above Columbia, and the Right Wing crossed to the north bank and occupied the city, the greater part of which was burned during the night. Many reasons are given for this flagrant violation of General Sherman's orders, but, as far as I could judge, it was principally due to the fact that the citizens gave liquor to the troops until they were crazily drunk and beyond the control of their officers. The burning cotton, fired by retreating rebels, and the presence of a large number of escaped prisoners, excited the intoxicated soldiers to the first acts of violence, after which they could not be restrained.

I don't know that I am called upon to give an opinion respecting this matter, but I volunteer the above. One thing is certain, the burning houses, lighting up the faces of shrieking women, terrified children, and frantic, raving, drunken men, formed a scene which no man of the slightest sensibility wants to witness a second time.

(Source: U.S. War Department. *War of the Rebellion: A Compilation of the Official Records of the Union and Confederate Armies.* Ser. I, Vol. XLVII/1.)

As Sherman moved north, Grant at Petersburg stretched the entrenched Army of Northern Virginia beyond its breaking point. By March 1865, the prospect of abandoning Richmond loomed as an imminent probability. The deliberate destruction of important property to keep it out of the invaders' hands became a grim but routine topic of contemplation. It was a subtle but telling indication of Confederate hopelessness that someone at last announced that destroying property was useless spoliation; such an announcement amounted to an unspoken reminder that some places and things would be needed to put things together again after the struggle was lost. [See Armories, Arsenals, and Foundries; Fayetteville Arsenal; Tredegar Iron Works]

2. Confederate Correspondence Regarding Disposition of the Tredegar Iron Works (March 1865)

CONFIDENTIAL.] TREDEGAR IRON-WORKS, *Richmond, March 7, 1865.*

Hon. JOHN C. BRECKINRIDGE, *Secretary of War:*

SIR: We regret to see by the removal of Government supplies from this city that its evacuation must be a contingency which the Government feels it necessary or prudent to provide for. Under these circumstances we trust you will pardon us for asking that the Government will inform us (in confidence) what disposition in such an event will be made of these works. Since the war began they have been placed at the disposal of the Government, but it is presumed that it will not be considered proper that our forces should destroy them, unless they may be of considerable use to the enemy, as it would involve a loss of a large sum to the Government.

On this point our judgment is convinced. The enemy have more iron-works than are necessary to supply their munitions of war, and they could more cheaply and expeditiously manufacture them in their own works and bring them here than transport the material and make them in these works.

In view also of danger of forced evacuation, we ask that we may be paid upon the work in progress for the Government as much as we have expended upon it. This is necessary to discharge the obligations we have contracted for the Government work, as in consequence of the rapid depreciation in the currency it has cost us much more than we have received for it in the past two years.

As our contract is jointly with the War and Navy Departments, may we ask the favor of you to confer with the honorable Secretary of the Navy and give us the result of your joint decision.

We have the honor to be, your most obedient servant,
JOSEPH R. ANDERSON & CO.

* * *

[Second indorsement.]
MARCH—, 1865.
Respectfully returned to the honorable
 Secretary of War.

If we abandon Richmond it will be done, I presume, without hope of recovery; and in doing so we should, in my judgment, see that these works are not left to do the enemy service. Without some preparation in advance of an abandonment they could not and would not be destroyed; and any such preparation should be made and would be best made with the aid and advice of the company owning them. My suggestion, then, is that preparations be made to destroy these works, in which preparations the aid of the company will be looked to, that the Government assume to pay for them.
S. R. MALLORY, *Secretary of the Navy.*

* * *

[Fourth indorsement.]
MARCH 11, 1865.

I have considered this question of burning already in reference to our establishments at Fayetteville, N.C., and decided that everything should be removed and concealed as far as possible, but nothing burned or destroyed. I earnestly recommend the same policy here. The resources of the enemy are so great in machinery and manufactures that no addition the Confederacy can make will increase their power to do us harm or to do harm to others; and any unnecessary or objectless destruction of private property, or even public, ought to be avoided. I see no adequate result in the case from the destruction of this establishment. The unfinished work must be left to future adjustment, and will be covered by advances made heretofore—$500,000 from War and Navy, and $150,000 from Nitre and Mining Bureau, I learn.
J. GORGAS, *Chief of Ordnance.*

(Source: U.S. War Department. *War of the Rebellion: A Compilation of the Official Records of the Union and Confederate Armies.* Ser. I, Vol. XLVI/2.)

C. GRANT AND LEE

At Appomattox Court House, ninety miles east of Richmond, Lee's surrender of the Army of Northern Virginia to federal forces on 9 April 1865 ended a twelve-day campaign that had begun when Grant began breaking Lee's lines around Petersburg. Lee finally gave in to greater Union numbers and resources. Adhering to Lincoln's instructions, Grant was benevolent in victory. A desolate Lee was characteristically stoic in defeat. The surrender ended the Civil War in Virginia and marked the beginning of the end of the war everywhere else. [See Appomattox Court House]

1. Grant-Lee Correspondence Regarding Surrender (April 1865)

Appomattox Court-House, Va.,
7 April 1865

General R. E. LEE:
GENERAL: The result of the last week must convince you of the hopelessness of further resistance on the part

of the Army of Northern Virginia in this struggle. I feel that it is so, and regard it as my duty to shift from myself the responsibility of any further effusion of blood by asking of you the surrender of that portion of the C. S. army known as the Army of Northern Virginia.
U. S. Grant, *Lieutenant-General.*

* * *

Headquarters Army of Northern Virginia,
7 April 1865

Lieut. Gen. U. S. Grant:
General: I have received your note of this date. Though not entertaining the opinion you express on the hope-lessness of further resistance on the part of the Army of Northern Virginia, I reciprocate your desire to avoid useless effusion of blood, and therefore, before consid-ering your proposition, ask the terms you will offer on condition of its surrender.
R. E. Lee, *General.*

* * *

Appomattox Court-House, Va.,
8 April 1865

General R. E. Lee:
General: Your note of last evening, in reply to mine of same date, asking the condition on which I will accept the surrender of the Army of Northern Virginia, is just received. In reply I would say that, peace being my great desire, there is but one condition I would insist upon, namely, that the men and officers surrendered shall be disqualified for taking up arms again against the Government of the United States until properly exchanged. I will meet you, or will designate officers to meet any officers you may name for the same purpose, at any point agreeable to you, for the purpose of arrang-ing definitely the terms upon which the surrender of the Army of Northern Virginia will be received.
U. S. Grant, *Lieutenant-General.*

* * *

Headquarters Army of Northern Virginia,
8 April 1865

Lieut. Gen. U. S. Grant:
General: I received at a late hour your note of to-day. In mine of yesterday I did not intend to propose the surrender of the Army of Northern Virginia, but to ask the terms of your proposition. To be frank, I do not think the emergency has arisen to call for the surrender of this army, but as the restoration of peace should be

the sole object of all, I desired to know whether your proposals would lead to that end. I cannot, therefore, meet you with a view to surrender the Army of Northern Virginia, but as far as your proposal may affect the C. S. forces under my command, and tend to the restoration of peace, I should be pleased to meet you at 10 a.m., to-morrow, on the old stage road to Richmond, between the picket-lines of the two armies.
R. E. Lee, *General.*

* * *

Appomattox Court-House, Va.,
April 9, 1865.

General R. E. Lee:
General: In accordance with the substance of my letter to you of the 8th instant, I propose to receive the sur-render of the Army of Northern Virginia on the fol-lowing terms, to wit: Rolls of all the officers and men to be made in duplicate, one copy to be given to an offi-cer to be designated by me, the other to be retained by such officer or officers as you may designate. The offi-cers to give their individual paroles not to take up arms against the Government of the United States until properly exchanged; and each company or regimental commander sign a like parole for the; men of their commands. The arms, artillery, and public property to be parked and stacked, and turned over to the officers appointed by me to receive them. This will not embrace the side-arms of the officers nor their private horses or baggage. This done, each officer and man will be allowed to return to his home, not to be disturbed by U.S. authority so long as they observe their paroles and the laws in force where they may reside.
U. S. Grant, *Lieutenant-General.*

* * *

Headquarters Army of Northern Virginia,
April 9, 1865.

Lieut. Gen. U. S. Grant:
General: I received your letter of this date containing the terms of surrender of the Army of Northern Virginia as proposed by you. As they are substantially the same as those expressed in your letter of the 8th instant, they are accepted. I will proceed to designate the proper officers to carry the stipulations into effect.
R. E. Lee, *General.*

(Source: U.S. War Department. *War of the Rebellion: A Compilation of the Official Records of the Union and Confederate Armies.* Ser. I, Vol. XXXIV/1 [S# 61].)

2. Terms of Surrender (9 April 1865)

Head Quarters of the Armies of the United States
Appomattox C.H. Va. Apl 9th 1865

Gen. R. E. Lee
Comd'g C.S.A.
General,
In accordance with the substance of my letter to you of the 8th inst., I propose to receive the surrender of the Army of N. Va. on the following terms to wit;

Rolls of all the officers and men be made in duplicate, one copy to be given to an officer to be designated by me, the other to be retained by such officer or officers as you may designate. The officers to give their individual paroles not to take up arms against the Government of the United States until properly exchanged, and each company or regimental commander to sign a like parole for the men of their commands -

The arms, artillery and public property to be parked and stacked and turned over to the officer appointed by me to receive them. This will not embrace the side arms of the officers nor their private horses or baggage. This done each officer and man will be allowed to return to their homes, not to be disturbed by United States authority as long as they observe their parole and the laws in force where they may reside—
Very Respectfully
U. S. Grant, *Lt. Gen.*

(Source: National Archives, Washington, DC.)

3. Parole of General Robert E. Lee and Staff (9 April 1865)

We, the undersigned prisoners of war belonging to the Army of Northern Virginia, having been this day surrendered by General Robert E. Lee, C. S. Army, commanding said army, to Lieut. Gen. U. S. Grant, commanding Armies of the United States, do hereby give our solemn parole of honor that we will not hereafter serve in the armies of the Confederate States, or in any military capacity whatever, against the United States of America, or render aid to the enemies of the latter, until properly exchanged, in such manner as shall be mutually approved by the respective authorities.

Done at Appomattox Court House, Va., this 9th day of April, 1865
R. E. LEE,
General
W. H. TAYLOR,
Lieutenant-Colonel and Assistant Adjutant-General.
CHARLES S. VENABLE,
Lieutenant-Colonel and Assistant Adjutant-General.
CHARLES MARSHALL,
Lieutenant-Colonel and Assistant Adjutant-General.
H. E. PEYTON,
Lieutenant-Colonel, Adjutant and Inspector General.
GILES B. COOKE,
Major and Assistant Adjutant and Inspector General.
H. E. YOUNG,
Major, Assistant Adjutant-General, and Judge.
Advocate-General.

(Source: U.S. War Department. *War of the Rebellion: A Compilation of the Official Records of the Union and Confederate Armies.* Ser. I, Vol. XLVI/3 [S#2].)

4. Lee's General Order No. 9 (10 April 1865)

HDQRS. ARMY OF NORTHERN VIRGINIA,
April 10, 1865.

After four years of arduous service, marked by unsurpassed courage and fortitude, the Army of Northern Virginia has been compelled to yield to overwhelming numbers and resources. I need not tell the brave survivors of so many hard-fought battles, who have remained steadfast to the last, that I have consented to the result from no distrust of them. But, feeling that valor and devotion could accomplish nothing that could compensate for the loss that must have attended the continuance of the contest, I determined to avoid the useless sacrifice of those whose past services have endeared them to their countrymen.

By the terms of the agreement officers and men can return to their homes and remain until exchanged. You will take with you the satisfaction that proceeds from the consciousness of duty faithfully performed; and I earnestly pray that a merciful God will extend to you his blessing and protection.

With an increasing admiration of your constancy and devotion to your country, and a grateful remembrance of your kind and generous considerations for myself, I bid you all an affectionate farewell.
R. E. LEE, *General.*

(Source: U.S. War Department. *War of the Rebellion: A Compilation of the Official Records of the Union and Confederate Armies.* Ser. I, Vol. XLVI/1.)

5. Report of General Robert E. Lee, C.S. Army, Commanding Army of Northern Virginia. Surrender at Appomattox (12 April 1865)

NEAR APPOMATTOX COURT-HOUSE, VA.,
April 12, 1865.

His Excellency JEFFERSON DAVIS.
Mr. PRESIDENT: It is with pain that I announce to Your Excellency the surrender of the Army of Northern Virginia. The operations which preceded this result will be reported in full. I will therefore only now state that, upon arriving at Amelia Court-House on the morning

of the 4th with the advance of the army, on the retreat from the lines in front of Richmond and Petersburg, and not finding the supplies ordered to be placed there, nearly twenty-four hours were lost in endeavoring to collect in the country subsistence for men and horses. This delay was fatal, and could not be retrieved. The troops, wearied by continual fighting and marching for several days and nights, obtained neither rest nor refreshment; and on moving, on the 5th, on the Richmond and Danville Railroad, I found at Jetersville the enemy's cavalry, and learned the approach of his infantry and the general advance of his army toward Burkeville. This deprived us of the use of the railroad, and rendered it impracticable to procure from Danville the supplies ordered to meet us at points of our march. Nothing could be obtained from the adjacent country. Our route to the Roanoke was therefore changed, and the march directed upon Farmville, where supplies were ordered from Lynchburg. The change of route threw the troops over the roads pursued by the artillery and wagon trains west of the railroad, which impeded our advance and embarrassed our movements. On the morning of the 6th General Longstreet's corps reached Rice's Station, on the Lynchburg railroad. It was followed by the commands of Generals R. H. Anderson, Ewell, and Gordon, with orders to close upon it as fast as the progress of the trains would permit or as they could be directed on roads farther west. General Anderson, commanding Pickett's and B. R. Johnson's divisions, became disconnected with Mahone's division, forming the rear of Longstreet. The enemy's cavalry penetrated the line of march through the interval thus left and attacked the wagon train moving toward Farmville. This caused serious delay in the march of the center and rear of the column, and enabled the enemy to mass upon their flank. After successive attacks Anderson's and Ewell's corps were captured or driven from their position. The latter general, with both of his division commanders, Kershaw and Custis Lee, and his brigadiers, were taken prisoners. Gordon, who all the morning, aided by General W. H. F. Lee's cavalry, had checked the advance of the enemy on the road from Amelia Springs and protected the trains, became exposed to his combined assaults, which he bravely resisted and twice repulsed; but the cavalry having been withdrawn to another part of the line of march, and the enemy massing heavily on his front and both flanks, renewed the attack about 6 p.m., and drove him from the field in much confusion.

The army continued its march during the night, and every effort was made to reorganize the divisions which had been shattered by the day's operations; but the men being depressed by fatigue and hunger, many threw away their arms, while others followed the wagon trains and embarrassed their progress. On the morning of the

7th rations were issued to the troops as they passed Farmville, but the safety of the trains requiring their removal upon the approach of the enemy all could not be supplied. The army, reduced to two corps, under Longstreet and Gordon, moved steadily on the road to Appomattox Court-House; thence its march was ordered by Campbell Court-House, through Pittsylvania, toward Danville. The roads were wretched and the progress slow. By great efforts the head of the column reached Appomattox Court-House on the evening of the 8th, and the troops were halted for rest. The march was ordered to be resumed at 1 a.m. on the 9th. Fitz Lee, with the cavalry, supported by Gordon, was ordered to drive the enemy from his front, wheel to the left, and cover the passage of the trains; while Longstreet, who from Rice's Station had formed the rear guard, should close up and hold the position. Two battalions of artillery and the ammunition wagons were directed to accompany the army, the rest of the artillery and wagons to move toward Lynchburg. In the early part of the night the enemy attacked Walker's artillery train near Appomattox Station, on the Lynchburg railroad, and were repelled. Shortly afterward their cavalry dashed toward the Court-House, till halted by our line. During the night there were indications of a large force massing on our left and front. Fitz Lee was directed to ascertain its strength, and to suspend his advance till daylight if necessary. About 5 a.m. on the 9th, with Gordon on his left, he moved forward and opened the way. A heavy force of the enemy was discovered opposite Gordon's right, which, moving in the direction of Appomattox Court-House, drove back the left of the cavalry and threatened to cut off Gordon from Longstreet, his cavalry at the same time threatening to envelop his left flank. Gordon withdrew across the Appomattox River, and the cavalry advanced on the Lynchburg road and became separated from the army.

Learning the condition of affairs on the lines, where I had gone under the expectation of meeting General Grant to learn definitely the terms he proposed in a communication received from him on the 8th, in the event of the surrender of the army, I requested a suspension of hostilities until these terms could be arranged. In the interview which occurred with General Grant in compliance with my request, terms having been agreed on, I surrendered that portion of the Army of Northern Virginia which was on the field, with its arms, artillery, and wagon trains, the officers and men to be paroled, retaining their sidearms and private effects. I deemed this course the best under all the circumstances by which we were surrounded. On the morning of the 9th, according to the reports of the ordnance officers, there were 7,892 organized infantry with arms, with an average of seventy-five rounds of ammunition per man. The artillery, though reduced to sixty-three pieces, with ninety-three rounds of ammunition, was sufficient. These comprised all the supplies of ordnance that could be relied on in the State of Virginia. I have no accurate report of the cavalry, but believe it did not exceed 2,100 effective men. The enemy were more than five times our numbers. If we could have forced our way one day longer it would have been at a great sacrifice of life, and at its end I did not see how a surrender could have been avoided. We had no subsistence for man or horse, and it could not be gathered in the country. The supplies ordered to Pamplin's Station from Lynchburg could not reach us, and the men, deprived of food and sleep for many days, were worn out and exhausted.

With great respect, your obedient servant,

R. E. LEE, General.

(Source: U.S. War Department. *War of the Rebellion: A Compilation of the Official Records of the Union and Confederate Armies.* Ser. I, Vol. XLVI/1.)

D. SHERMAN AND JOHNSTON

Rumors of Lee's surrender soon filtered into Joseph E. Johnston's camp in North Carolina. For the Confederate commander, it was chilling news. Now the huge Army of the Potomac was free to range out of Virginia and could join Sherman's army that was marching north through North Carolina. Johnston advised Jefferson Davis of the situation's hopelessness and on 14 April wrote to Sherman asking for an armistice. The two generals held meetings that produced a peace agreement so broad and lenient that federal authorities rejected it. Sherman was required to adhere to the terms established at Appomattox Court House. On 26 April, Johnston and Sherman met for a third time to sign a surrender that conformed to those specifications and ended the war in the Carolinas, Georgia, and Florida. [See Bennett House]

1. Union Correspondence Regarding General Johnston's Surrender (April 1865)

HEADQUARTERS ARMY OF GEORGIA,
Raleigh, N. C., April 17, 1865—9 a.m.

Bvt. Maj. Gen. J. C. DAVIS,
Commanding Fourteenth Corps:
GENERAL: I am directed by the major-general commanding to say that a few days ago a communication was received from General Johnston, broaching the matter of a surrender, and that in consequence General Sherman has appointed a meeting with him to-day at 12 o'clock m. General Slocum wishes you to remain quietly in your present camp until further orders.

Very respectfully, your obedient servant,

ROBT. P. DECHERT,
Acting Assistant Adjutant-General.

* * *

RALEIGH, N. C., *April 26, 1865—7.30 p.m*
(Received 10 a.m. 28th.)

Hon. E. M. STANTON:
Sherman and Johnston had another interview to-day, and Johnston has surrendered on same terms as Lee accepted. I think the great bulk of the army will start for Washington overland in a few days. I will be guided by circumstances in the absence of any instructions from you. I think we will hold on here for some time.

U. S. GRANT,
Lieutenant-General.

(Source: U.S. War Department. *War of the Rebellion: A Compilation of the Official Records of the Union and Confederate Armies.* Ser. I, Vol. XLVII/3.)

* * *

2. Surrender Terms of 26 April 1864

Terms of a Military Convention Held this Twenty-sixth (26th) Day of April, 1865, at Bennett's House, near Durham's Station, N.C., between Gen. Joseph E. Johnston, Commanding the Confederate Army, and Major-General W. T. Sherman, Commanding the United States Army in North Carolina.

All acts of War on the part of the troops under Gen. Johnston's command to cease from this date.

All arms and public property to be deposited at Greensboro, to be delivered to an Ordnance officer of the United States Army.

Rolls of all the officers and men to be made in duplicate-one copy to be retained by the Commander of the troops, and the other to be given to an officer to be designated by Gen. Sherman.

Each officer and man to give his individual obligation in writing, not to take up arms against the Government of the United States until properly released from this obligation.

The side-arms of officers and their private horses and baggage to be retained by them.

This being done, all the officers and men will be permitted to return to their homes, not to be disturbed by the United States authority so long as they observe their obligation and the laws in force where they may reside.

W. T. SHERMAN, *Major General,*
Commanding Forces in North Carolina.
J. E. JOHNSTON, *General,*
Commanding C. S. Forces in North Carolina.
Approved:
U. S. Grant, *Lt.-Gen.,*
Raleigh, N. C., *April 26, 1865.*

(Source: U.S. War Department. *War of the Rebellion: A Compilation of the Official Records of the Union and Confederate Armies.* Ser. I, Vol. XLVII/3.)

*   *   *

General Order No. 8 (27 April 1865)
GENERAL ORDER No. 8

Headquarters, Army of Tennessee, near
Greensboro, N.C.,
April 27, 1865.
By the terms of a Military Convention, made on the 26th inst., by Major-General W. T. Sherman, U.S. Army, and General J. E. Johnston, C. S. Army, the officers and men of this army are to bind themselves not to take up arms against the United States until properly relieved from this obligation, and shall receive guaranties from the United States officers against molestation by the United States authorities so long as they observe that obligation, and the laws in force where they reside.

For these objects, duplicate muster-rolls will be made immediately, and after the distribution of the necessary papers, the troops will march under their officers to their respective States, and there be disbanded, all retaining personal property.

The object of this Convention is Pacification, to the extent of the Commanders who made it.

Events in Virginia, which broke every hope of success by war, imposed on its Generals the duty of sparing the blood of this gallant army, and saving our country from further devastation, and our people from ruin.
J. E. JOHNSTON, *General.*

(Source: U.S. War Department. *War of the Rebellion: A Compilation of the Official Records of the Union and Confederate Armies.* Ser. I, Vol. XLVII/3.)

XXXVI. The Two Presidents

A. THE ASSASSINATION
As all of Washington celebrated the victorious end of the war, just two days after Lee's surrender, Abraham Lincoln made his last public address, delivering it to an impromptu crowd gathered at the Executive Mansion. In it, he addressed the problems facing the reunited nation over Reconstruction. He would never have the chance to elaborate on or even alter his ideas. On 14 April 1865, the president and Mrs. Lincoln were attending a performance of Our American Cousin *at Ford's Theater when the actor John Wilkes Booth, a fanatical Confederate sympathizer, mortally wounded Lincoln with a derringer shot to his head. Another assassin attempted but failed to kill Secretary of State William H. Seward in his home. Although it would be difficult to see otherwise in the immediate term, not all former Confederates took comfort in this vile deed. As a stunned nation buried its slain chieftain,*

the shadowy contours of a conspiracy induced a military tribunal to prosecute a handful of Booth's accomplices; four of them—Mary Surratt, George Atzerodt, Lewis Powell (a.k.a. Paine), and David Herold—would hang. Prison awaited the others. [See Lincoln Assassination]

1. Lincoln's Last Public Address (11 April 1865)
We meet this evening, not in sorrow, but in gladness of heart. The evacuation of Petersburg and Richmond, and the surrender of the principal insurgent army, give hope of a righteous and speedy peace whose joyous expression can not be restrained. In the midst of this, however, He, from Whom all blessings flow, must not be forgotten. A call for a national thanksgiving is being prepared, and will be duly promulgated. Nor must those whose harder part gives us the cause of rejoicing, be overlooked. Their honors must not be parcelled out with others. I myself, was near the front, and had the high pleasure of transmitting much of the good news to you; but no part of the honor, for plan or execution, is mine. To Gen. Grant, his skilful officers, and brave men, all belongs. The gallant Navy stood ready, but was not in reach to take active part.

By these recent successes the re-inauguration of the national authority—reconstruction—which has had a large share thought from the first, is pressed much more closely upon our attention. It is fraught with great difficulty. Unlike the case of a war between independent nations, there is no authorized organ for us to treat with. No one man has authority to give up the rebellion for any other man. We simply must begin with, and mould from, disorganized and discordant elements. Nor is it a small additional embarrassment that we, the loyal people, differ among ourselves as to the mode, manner, and means of reconstruction.

As a general rule, I abstain from reading the reports of attacks upon myself, wishing not to be provoked by that to which I can not properly offer an answer. In spite of this precaution, however, it comes to my knowledge that I am much censured for some supposed agency in setting up, and seeking to sustain, the new State Government of Louisiana. In this I have done just so much as, and no more than, the public knows. In the Annual Message of Dec. 1863 and accompanying Proclamation, I presented a plan of re-construction (as the phrase goes) which, I promised, if adopted by any State, should be acceptable to, and sustained by, the Executive government of the nation. I distinctly stated that this was not the only plan which might possibly be acceptable; and I also distinctly protested that the Executive claimed no right to say when, or whether members should be admitted to seats in Congress from such States. This plan was, in advance, submitted to the then Cabinet, and distinctly approved by every

member of it. One of them suggested that I should then, and in that connection, apply the Emancipation Proclamation to the theretofore excepted parts of Virginia and Louisiana; that I should drop the suggestion about apprenticeship for freed-people, and that I should omit the protest against my own power, in regard to the admission of members to Congress; but even he approved every part and parcel of the plan which has since been employed or touched by the action of Louisiana. The new constitution of Louisiana, declaring emancipation for the whole State, practically applies the Proclamation to the part previously excepted. It does not adopt apprenticeship for freed-people; and it is silent, as it could not well be otherwise, about the admission of members to Congress. So that, as it applies to Louisiana, every member of the Cabinet fully approved the plan. The Message went to Congress, and I received many commendations of the plan, written and verbal; and not a single objection to it, from any professed emancipationist, came to my knowledge, until after the news reached Washington that the people of Louisiana had begun to move in accordance with it. From about July 1862, I had corresponded with different persons, supposed to be interested, seeking a reconstruction of a State government for Louisiana. When the Message of 1863, with the plan before mentioned, reached New-Orleans, Gen. Banks wrote me that he was confident the people, with his military co-operation, would reconstruct, substantially on that plan. I wrote him, and some of them to try it; they tried it, and the result is known. Such only has been my agency in getting up the Louisiana government. As to sustaining it, my promise is out, as before stated. But, as bad promises are better broken than kept, I shall treat this as a bad promise, and break it, whenever I shall be convinced that keeping it is adverse to the public interest. But I have not yet been so convinced.

I have been shown a letter on this subject, supposed to be an able one, in which the writer expresses regret that my mind has not seemed to be definitely fixed on the question whether the seceded States, so called, are in the Union or out of it. It would perhaps, add astonishment to his regret, were he to learn that since I have found professed Union men endeavoring to make that question, I have *purposely* forborne any public expression upon it. As appears to me that question has not been, nor yet is, a practically material one, and that any discussion of it, while it thus remains practically immaterial, could have no effect other than the mischievous one of dividing our friends. As yet, whatever it may hereafter become, that question is bad, as the basis of a controversy, and good for nothing at all—a merely pernicious abstraction.

We all agree that the seceded States, so called, are out of their proper practical relation with the Union; and that the sole object of the government, civil and military, in regard to those States is to again get them into that proper practical relation. I believe it is not only possible, but in fact, easier, to do this, without deciding, or even considering, whether these states have even been out of the Union, than with it. Finding themselves safely at home, it would be utterly immaterial whether they had ever been abroad. Let us all join in doing the acts necessary to restoring the proper practical relations between these states and the Union; and each forever after, innocently indulge his own opinion whether, in doing the acts, he brought the States from without, into the Union, or only gave them proper assistance, they never having been out of it.

The amount of constituency, so to speak, on which the new Louisiana government rests, would be more satisfactory to all, if it contained fifty, thirty, or even twenty thousand, instead of only about twelve thousand, as it does. It is also unsatisfactory to some that the elective franchise is not given to the colored man. I would myself prefer that it were now conferred on the very intelligent, and on those who serve our cause as soldiers. Still the question is not whether the Louisiana government, as it stands, is quite all that is desirable. The question is "Will it be wiser to take it as it is, and help to improve it; or to reject, and disperse it?…. Can Louisiana be brought into proper practical relation with the Union *sooner* by *sustaining*, or by *discarding* her new State Government?"

Some twelve thousand voters in the heretofore slave-state of Louisiana have sworn allegiance to the Union, assumed to be the rightful political power of the State, held elections, organized a State government, adopted a free-state constitution, giving the benefit of public schools equally to black and white, and empowering the Legislature to confer the elective franchise upon the colored man. Their Legislature has already voted to ratify the constitutional amendment recently passed by Congress, abolishing slavery throughout the nation. These twelve thousand persons are thus fully committed to the Union, and to perpetual freedom in the state—committed to the very things, and nearly all the things the nation wants—and they ask the nations recognition, and it's assistance to make good their committal. Now, if we reject, and spurn them, we do our utmost to disorganize and disperse them. We in effect say to the white men "You are worthless, or worse—we will neither help you, nor be helped by you." To the blacks we say "This cup of liberty which these, your old masters, hold to your lips, we will dash from you, and leave you to the chances of gathering the spilled and scattered contents in some vague and undefined when, where, and how." If this course, discouraging and paralyzing both white and black, has any tendency to bring Louisiana into proper practical relations with the Union, I have, so far, been unable to perceive it. If, on the contrary, we recognize, and sustain the new government of Louisiana the converse of all this is made true. We encourage the hearts, and nerve the arms of the twelve thousand to adhere to their work, and argue for it, and proselyte for it, and fight for it, and feed it, and grow it, and ripen it to a complete success. The colored man too, in seeing all united for him, is inspired with vigilance, and energy, and daring, to the same end. Grant that he desires the elective franchise, will he not attain it sooner by saving the already advanced steps toward it, than by running backward over them? Concede that the new government of Louisiana is only to what it should be as the egg is to the fowl, we shall sooner have the fowl by hatching the egg than by smashing it? Again, if we reject Louisiana, we also reject one vote in favor of the proposed amendment to the national constitution. To meet this proposition, it has been argued that no more than three fourths of those States which have not attempted secession are necessary to validly ratify the amendment. I do not commit myself against this, further than to say that such a ratification would be questionable, and sure to be persistently questioned; while a ratification by three fourths of all the States would be unquestioned and unquestionable.

I repeat the question. Can Louisiana be brought into proper practical relation with the Union *sooner* by *sustaining* or by *discarding* her new State Government?

What has been said of Louisiana will apply generally to other States. And yet so great peculiarities pertain to each state; and such important and sudden changes occur in the same state; and, withal, so new and unprecedented is the whole case, that no exclusive, and inflexible plan can safely be prescribed as to details and colatterals. Such exclusive, and inflexible plan, would surely become a new entanglement. Important principles may, and must, be inflexible.

In the present "*situation*" as the phrase goes, it may be my duty to make some new announcement to the people of the South. I am considering, and shall not fail to act, when satisfied that action will be proper.

(Source: Lapsley, Arthur Brooks, ed. *The Writings of Abraham Lincoln.* Vol. 7. New York: G. P. Putnam's Sons, 1906.)

2. Orders and Correspondence Regarding the Lincoln Assassination
WASHINGTON CITY,
No. 458 Tenth Street, April 15, 1865
3 a.m. (Sent 3.20 a.m.)

Major-General Dix:
(Care Horner, New York.)
The President still breathes, but is quite insensible, as he has been ever since he was shot. He evidently did not see the person who shot him, but was looking on

the stage as he was approached behind.

Mr. Seward has rallied, and it is hoped he may live. Frederick Seward's condition is very critical. The attendant who was present was stabbed through the lungs, and is not expected to live. The wounds of Major Seward are not serious. Investigation strongly indicates J. Wilkes Booth as the assassin of the President. Whether it was the same or a different person that attempted to murder Mr. Seward remains in doubt. Chief Justice Cartter is engaged in taking the evidence. Every exertion has been made to prevent the escape of the murderer. His horse has been found on the road, near Washington.
EDWIN M. STANTON,
Secretary of War.

(Source: U.S. War Department. *War of the Rebellion: A Compilation of the Official Records of the Union and Confederate Armies.* Ser. I, Vol. XLVI/3.)

* * *

HEADQUARTERS DEPARTMENT
OF WASHINGTON,
TWENTY-SECOND ARMY CORPS,
Washington, D.C., April 15, 1865—4 a.m.

General SLOUGH, Military Governor:
The murderer of the President is undoubtedly J. Wilkes Booth, the actor. The other party is a smooth-faced man, quite stout. You had better have a squad of cavalry sent down toward the Occoquan to intercept anything crossing the river. The fishermen along the river should be notified and kept on the lookout.
C. C. AUGUR,
Major-General.

(Source: U.S. War Department. *War of the Rebellion: A Compilation of the Official Records of the Union and Confederate Armies.* Ser. I, Vol. XLVI/3.)

* * *

BALTIMORE, MD., April 15, 1865—4.20 a.m.

Brig. Gen. J. R. KENLY,
Commanding Officer, Wilmington, Del.:
In consequence of the assassination of the President and Secretary of State the most vigorous measures will be taken in this department to suppress any outbreak. J. Wilkes Booth, tragedian, is the murderer of Mr. Lincoln. No trains will be permitted to leave this city. Do your utmost to preserve order and keep a sharp lookout for Booth. Report your action.
By order:
SAML. B. LAWRENCE,
Assistant Adjutant-General.

(Source: U.S. War Department. *War of the Rebellion: A Compilation of the Official Records of the Union and Confederate Armies.* Ser. I, Vol. XLVI/3.)

* * *

WASHINGTON, *April 16, 1865.*

Major-General MEADE:
The President died at 7.22 yesterday morning. J. Wilkes Booth was the assassin of the President. Secretary Seward passed a bad night, but is much better this morning and probably out of danger. His son Frederick will not live, although he still lingers with wonderful tenacity.
THOS. T. ECKERT.
(Same to General Sheridan.)

(Source: U.S. War Department. *War of the Rebellion: A Compilation of the Official Records of the Union and Confederate Armies.* Ser. I, Vol. XLVI/3.)

* * *

WAR DEPARTMENT,
Washington, April 27, 1865—9.35 a.m.

Major-General DIX,
New York:
J. Wilkes Booth and Herold were chased from the swamp in Saint Mary's County, Md.; pursued yesterday morning to Garrett's farm, near Port Royal, on the Rappahannock, by Colonel Baker's force. The barn in which they took refuge was fired. Booth, in making his escape, was shot through the head and killed, lingering about three hours, and Herold captured. Booth's body and Herold are now here.
EDWIN M. STANTON, *Secretary of War.*

(Source: U.S. War Department. *War of the Rebellion: A Compilation of the Official Records of the Union and Confederate Armies.* Ser. I, Vol. XLVI/3.)

* * *

General Ewell's Letter of Condolence
(16 April 1865)
FORT WARREN, *April 16, 1865.*

Lieut. Gen. U.S. GRANT,
Commanding U.S. Army:
GENERAL: You will appreciate, I am sure, the sentiment which prompts me to drop you these lines. Of all the misfortunes which could befall the Southern people, or any Southern man, by far the greatest, in my judgement, would be the prevalence of the idea that

they could entertain any other feelings of unqualified abhorrence and indignation for the assassination of the President of the United States, and the attempt to assassinate the Secretary of State. No language can adequately express the shock produced upon myself, in common with all the other general officers confined here with me, by the occurrence of this appalling crime, and by the seeming tendency in the publc mind to connect the South and Southern men with it. Need we say that we are not assassins, nor the allies of assassins, be they from the North or the South, and that coming as we do from most of the States of the South we would be ashamed of our own people, were we not assured that they will reprobate this crime. Under the circumstances I could not refrain from some expression of my feelings. I thus utter them to a soldier who will comprehend them. The following officers, Maj. Gens. Ed. Johnson, of Virginia, and Kershaw, of South Carolina; Brigadier-Generals Barton, Corse, Hunton, and Jones, of Virginia; Du Bose, Simms, and H. R. Jackson, of Georgia; Frazer, of Alabama; Smith and Gordon, of Tennessee; Cabell, of Arkansas, and Marmaduke, of Missouri, and Commodore Tucker, of Virginia, all heartily concur with me in what I have said.
Respectfully, general,
R. S. EWELL,
Lieutenant-General, C.S. Army.

(Source: U.S. War Department. *War of the Rebellion: A Compilation of the Official Records of the Union and Confederate Armies of the Union and Confederate Armies.* Vol. XLVI/3.)

General Court-Martial Orders No. 356
(5 July 1865)
WAR DEPARTMENT,
ADJUTANT-GENERAL'S OFFICE,
Washington, July 5, 1865.

I. Before a military commission which convened at Washington, D. C., May 9, 1865, pursuant to paragraph 4 of Special Orders, No. 211, dated May 6, 1865, and paragraph 91 of Special Orders, No. 216, dated May 9, 1865, War Department, Adjutant General's Office, Washington, and of which Maj. Gen. David Hunter, U.S. Volunteers, is president, were arraigned and tried—
David E. Herold, G. A. Atzerodt, Lewis Payne, Mary E. Surratt, Michael O'Laughlin, Edward Spangler, Samuel Arnold, and Samuel A. Mudd.

CHARGE I: For maliciously, unlawfully, and traitorously, and in aid of the existing armed rebellion against the United States of America, on or before the 6th day of March, A.D. 1865, and on divers other days between that day and the 15th day of April, A.D. 1865, combining, confederating, and conspiring, together with one John H. Surratt, John Wilkes Booth, Jefferson Davis, George N. Sanders, Beverly Tucker, Jacob Thompson, William C. Cleary, Clement C. Clay, George Harper, George Young, and others unknown, to kill and murder, within the Military Department of Washington, and within the fortified and intrenched lines thereof, Abraham Lincoln, late, and at the time of said combining, confederating, and conspiring, President of the United States of America and Commander-in-Chief of the Army and Navy thereof; Andrew Johnson, now Vice-President of the United States aforesaid; William H. Seward, Secretary of State of the United States aforesaid, and Ulysses S. Grant, lieutenant-general of the Army of the United States aforesaid, then in command of the Armies of the United States, under the direction of the said Abraham Lincoln; and in pursuance of and in prosecuting said malicious, unlawful, and traitorous conspiracy afore-said, and in aid of said rebellion, afterward, to wit, on the 14th day of April, A.D. 1865, within the Military Department of Washington aforesaid, and within the fortified and intrenched lines of said military depart-ment, together with said John Wilkes Booth and John H. Surratt, maliciously, unlawfully, and traitorously murdering the said Abraham Lincoln, then President of the United States and Commander-in-Chief of the Army and Navy of the United States, as aforesaid; and maliciously, unlawfully, and traitorously asaaulting, with intent to kill and murder, the said William H. Seward, then Secretary of State of the United States, as aforesaid; and lying in wait, with intent maliciously, unlawfully, and traitorously, to kill and murder the said Andrew Johnson, then being Vice-President of the United States; and the said Ulysses S. Grant, then being lieutenant-general and in command of the Armies of the United States, as aforesaid.

Specification 1.—In this, that they, the said David E. Herold, Edward Spangler, Lewis Payne, Michael O'Laughlin, Samuel Arnold, Mary E. Surratt, George A. Atzerodt, and Samuel A. Mudd, together with the said John H. Surratt and John Wilkes Booth, incited and encouraged thereunto by Jefferson Davis, George N. Sanders, Beverly Tucker, Jacob Thompson, William C. Cleary, Clement C. Clay, George Harper, George Young, and others unknown, citizens of the United States aforesaid, and who were then engaged in armed rebellion against the United States of America, within the limits thereof, did, in aid of said armed rebellion, on or before the 6th day of March, A.D. 1865, and on divers other days and times between that day and the 15th day of April, A.D. 1865, combine, confederate, and conspire together at Washington City, within the Military Department of Washington, and within the intrenched fortifications and military lines of the said United States, there being, unlawfully, maliciously, and

traitorously to kill and murder Abraham Lincoln, then President of the United States aforesaid, and Commander-in-Chief of the Army and Navy thereof; and unlawfully, maliciously, and traitorously to kill and murder Andrew Johnson, now Vice-President of the said United States, upon whom, on the death of said Abraham Lincoln, after the 4th day of March, A.D. 1865, the office of President of the said United States and Commander-in-Chief of the Army and Navy thereof would devolve; and to unlawfully, maliciously, and traitorously kill and murder Ulysses S. Grant, then lieutenant-general, and, under the direction of the said Abraham Lincoln, in command of the Armies of the United States aforesaid; and unlawfully, maliciously, and traitorously to kill and murder William H. Seward, then Secretary of State of the United States aforesaid, whose duty it was by law, upon the death of said President and Vice-President of the United States aforesaid, to cause an election to be held for electors of President of the United States—the conspirators afore-said designing and intending by the killing and murder of the said Abraham Lincoln, Andrew Johnson, Ulysses S. Grant, and William H. Seward, as aforesaid, to deprive the Army and Navy of the said United States of a constitutional commander-in-chief; and to deprive the Armies of the United States of their lawful commander; and to prevent a lawful election of President and Vice-President of the United States aforesaid; and by the means aforesaid to aid and com-fort the insurgents engaged in armed rebellion against the said United States, as aforesaid, and thereby to aid in the subversion and overthrow of the Constitution and laws of the said United States.

And being so combined, confederated, and conspir-ing together in the prosecution of said unlawful and traitorous conspiracy on the night of the 14th day of April, A.D. 1865, at the hour of about 10 o'clock and 15 minutes p.m., at Ford's Theater, on Tenth street, in the city of Washington, and within the military depart-ment and military lines aforesaid, John Wilkes Booth, one of the conspirators aforesaid, in pursuance of said unlawful and traitorous conspiracy, did, then and there, unlawfully, maliciously, and traitorously, and with intent to kill and murder the said Abraham Lincoln, discharge a pistol, then held in the hands of him, the said Booth, the same being then loaded with powder and a leaden ball, against and upon the left and poste-rior side of the head of the said Abraham Lincoln; and did thereby, then and there, inflict upon him, the said Abraham Lincoln, then President of the said United States and Commander-in-Chief of the Army and Navy thereof, a mortal wound, whereof afterward, to wit, on the 15th day of April, A.D. 1865, at Washington City aforesaid, the said Abraham Lincoln died; and thereby, then and there, and in pursuance of

said conspiracy, the said defendants and the said John Wilkes Booth and John H. Surratt did, unlawfully, traitorously, and maliciously, and with the intent to aid the rebellion as aforesaid, kill and murder the said Abraham Lincoln, President of the United States, as aforesaid.

And in further prosecution of the unlawful and traitorous conspiracy aforesaid, and of the murderous and traitorous intent of said conspiracy, the said Edward Spangler, on said 14th day of April, A.D. 1865, at about the same hour of that day, as aforesaid, within said military department and the military lines aforesaid, did aid and assist the said John Wilkes Booth to obtain entrance to the box in said theater in which said Abraham Lincoln was sitting at the time he was assaulted and shot, as aforesaid, by John Wilkes Booth; and also did then and there aid said Booth in barring and obstructing the door of the box of said theater so as to hinder and prevent any assistance to or rescue of the said Abraham Lincoln against the murderous assault of the said John Wilkes Booth, and did aid and abet him in making his escape after the said Abraham Lincoln had been murdered in manner aforesaid.

And in further prosecution of said unlawful, murderous, and traitorous conspiracy, and in pursuance thereof and with the intent, as aforesaid, the said David E. Herold did, on the night of the 14th of April, A.D. 1865, within the military department and military lines aforesaid, aid, abet and assist the said John Wilkes Booth in the killing and murder of the said Abraham Lincoln, and did then and there aid and abet and assist him, the said John Wilkes Booth, in attempting to escape through the military lines aforesaid, and did accompany and assist the said John Wilkes Booth in attempting to conceal himself and escape from justice after killing and murdering said Abraham Lincoln, as aforesaid.

And in further prosecution of said unlawful and traitorous conspiracy, and of the intent thereof, as aforesaid, the said Lewis Payne did, on the same night of the 14th day of April, A.D. 1865, about the same hour of 10 o'clock and 15 minutes p.m., at the city of Washington, and within the military department and the military lines aforesaid, unlawfully and maliciously make an assault upon the said William H. Seward, Secretary of State, as aforesaid, in the dwelling-house and bedchamber of him, the said William H. Seward, and the said Payne did then and there, with a large knife, held in his hand, unlawfully, traitorously, and in pursuance of said conspiracy, strike, stab, cut, and attempt to kill and murder the said William H. Seward, and did thereby, then and there, and with the intent aforesaid, with said knife inflict upon the face and throat of the said William H. Seward divers grievous wounds. And the said Lewis Payne, in further prosecution of said conspiracy, at the same time and place last aforesaid, did attempt, with the knife aforesaid, and a pistol held in his hand, to kill and murder Frederick W. Seward, Augustus H. Seward, Emrick W. Hansell, and George F. Robinson, who were then striving to protect and rescue the said William H. Seward from murder by the said Lewis Payne, and did then and there, with said knife and pistol held in his hands, inflict upon the head of said Frederick W. Seward, and upon the persons of said Augustus H. Seward, Emrick W. Hansell, and George F. Robinson, divers grievous and dangerous wounds with intent, then and there, to kill and murder the said Frederick W. Seward, Augustus H. Seward, Emrick W. Hansell, and George F. Robinson.

And in further prosecution of said conspiracy and its traitorous and murderous designs, the said George A. Atzerodt did, on the night of the 14th of April, A.D. 1865, and about the same hour of the night aforesaid, within the military department and the military lines aforesaid, lie in wait for Andrew Johnson, then Vice-President of the United States aforesaid, with the intent unlawfully and maliciously to kill and murder him, the said Andrew Johnson.

And in the further prosecution of the conspiracy aforesaid, and of its murderous and treasonable purposes aforesaid, on the nights of the 13th and 14th of April, A.D. 1865, at Washington City, and within the military department and military lines aforesaid, the said Michael O'Laughlin did then and there lie in wait for Ulysses S. Grant, then lieutenant-general and commander of the Armies of the United States, as aforesaid, with intent then and there to kill and murder the said Ulysses S. Grant.

And in further prosecution of said conspiracy, the said Samuel Arnold did, within the military department and military lines aforesaid, on or before the 6th day of March, A.D. 1865, and on divers other days and times between that day and the 15th day of April, A.D. 1865, combine, conspire with, and aid, counsel, abet, comfort, and support, the said John Wilkes Booth, Lewis Payne, George A. Atzerodt, Michael O'Laughlin, and their confederates, in said unlawful, murderous, and traitorous conspiracy and in the execution thereof, as aforesaid.

And in further prosecution of the said conspiracy, Mary E. Surratt did, at Washington City, and within the military department and military lines aforesaid, on or before the 6th day of March, A.D. 1865, and on divers other days and times between that day and the 20th day of April, A.D. 1865. receive, entertain, harbor and conceal, aid and assist the said John Wilkes Booth, David E. Herold, Lewis Payne, John H. Surratt, Michael O'Langhlin, George A. Atzerodt, Samuel Arnold, and their confederates, with knowledge of the murderous and traitorous conspiracy aforesaid, and with intent to aid, abet, and assist them in the execution thereof, and in escaping from justice after the murder of the said Abraham Lincoln, as aforesaid.

And in further prosecution of said conspiracy, the said Samuel A. Mudd did, at Washington City, and within the military department and military lines aforesaid, on or before the 6th day of March, A.D. 1865, and on divers other days and times between that day and the 20th day of April, A.D. 1865, advise, encourage, receive, entertain, harbor and conceal, aid and assist the said John Wilkes Booth, David E. Herold, Lewis Payne, John H. Surratt, Michael O'Laughlin, George A. Atzerodt, Mary E. Surratt, and Samuel Arnold, and their confederates, with knowledge of the murderous and traitorous conspiracy aforesaid, and with intent to aid, abet, and assist them in the execution thereof, and in escaping from justice after the murder of said Abraham Lincoln, in pursuance of said conspiracy in manner aforesaid.

To which charge and specification the accused, David E. Herold, G. A. Atzerodt, Lewis Payne, Mary E. Surratt, Michael O'Laughlin, Edward Spangler, Samuel Arnold, and Samuel A. Mudd, pleaded not guilty.

(Source: U.S. War Department. *War of the Rebellion: A Compilation of the Official Records of the Union and Confederate Armies*. Ser. II, Vol. VIII.)

B. THE IMPRISONMENT

Jefferson Davis had become a fugitive upon the evacuation of Richmond in April 1865. When Union cavalrymen captured him on 10 May near Irwinville, Georgia, some Northerners believed that he was involved in the Lincoln assassination, though no credible evidence could link him to Lincoln's death. Charged with treason and imprisoned at Fort Monroe, Virginia, Davis endured harsh conditions that prohibited visitors and recreation. Insomnia further wrecked his already precarious health. As he mentally and physically declined, federal authorities finally softened from fear that his death would lead to his martyrdom. By 1866, upon giving the promise that he would not escape, Davis was moved to better lodgings on the fort's grounds and allowed to exercise. Best of all, he could visit with his wife and child. And though demands for his prosecution eventually receded and he might have been given amnesty, he consistently refused to pursue a pardon. Finally in 1867, Davis was released on bond when distinguished citizens in both the North and the South put up the money. In December 1868 the indictment against him was dropped, but the personal trials of Jefferson Davis, which included the specter of his failed cause and defeated country, would not end for him until his death in 1889. [See Davis, Jefferson]

1. Surgeon's Examination of Jefferson Davis (9 May 1866)

FORT MONROE, VA., *May 9, 1866.*

ADJUTANT-GENERAL U.S. ARMY,
Washington, D.C.:

SIR: In compliance with directions from the President of the United States to me, given through the office of the Adjutant-General, I have made a special examination of state prisoner Jefferson Davis, now in confinement at this post, and report the following to be the result of said examination:

He is considerably emaciated, the fatty tissue having almost disappeared leaving his skin much shriveled. His muscles are small, flaccid, and very soft, and he has but little muscular strength. He is quite weak and debilitated, consequently his gait is becoming uneven and irregular. His digestive organs at present are in comparatively good condition but become quickly deranged under anything but the most carefully prepared food. With a diet disagreeing with him dyspeptic symptoms promptly make their appearance, soon followed by vertigo, severe facial and cranial neuralgia, an erysipelatous inflammation of the posterior scalp and right side of nose, which quickly affects the right eye (the only sound one he now has) and extends through the nasal duct into the interior nose. His nervous system is greatly deranged, being much prostrated and excessively irritable. Slight noises, which are scarcely perceptible to a man in robust health cause him much pain, the description of the sensation being as of one flayed and having every sentient nerve exposed to the waves of sound. Want of sleep has been a great and almost the principal cause of his nervous excitability. This has been produced by the tramp of the creaking boots of the sentinels on post round the prison room and the relief of the guard at the expiration of every two hours which almost invariably wakens him.

Prisoner Davis states that he has scarcely enjoyed over two hours of sleep unbroken at one time since his confinement. Means have been taken by placing matting on the floors for the sentinels to walk on to alleviate this source of disturbance, but with only partial success. His vital condition is low and he has but little recuperative force. Should he be attacked by any of the severe forms of disease to which the tidewater region of Virginia is subject, I, with reason, fear for the result.

A copy of this report I have furnished to the headquarters of the Military District of Fort Monroe, in compliance with orders from the major-general commanding.

Respectfully, your obedient servant,
GEO. E. COOPER,
Surgeon, U.S. Army.

(Source: U.S. War Department. *War of the Rebellion: A Compilation of the Official Records of the Union and Confederate Armies*. Ser. II, Vol. VIII.)

2. Jefferson Davis's Pledge (25 May 1866)

FORT MONROE, *May 25, 1866.*

For the privilege of being allowed the liberty of the grounds inside the walls of Fort Monroe between the hours of sunrise and sunset I, Jefferson Davis, do hereby give my parole of honor that I will make no attempt to nor take any advantage of any opportunity that may be offered to effect my escape therefrom.

JEFFERSON DAVIS.

Witness:

J. A. FESSENDEN,

First Lieutenant, Fifth Artillery.

(Source: U.S. War Department. *War of the Rebellion: A Compilation of the Official Records of the Union and Confederate Armies.* Ser. II, Vol. VIII.)

SOCIETY, CULTURE, AND TECHNOLOGY

XXXVII. African-American Soldiers

A. UNITED STATES COLORED TROOPS

After Abraham Lincoln's Emancipation Proclamation, the Union army began recruiting black troops. In the end, 166 black regiments were raised, more than 80 percent of their numbers coming from Confederate states where they had been slaves. Designated as the United States Colored Troops (USCT), they provided another source of men for the Northern military, but moreover their use in this unprecedented fashion encouraged their appeals for treatment equal with that of whites. The valiant performance of African-American soldiers often earned the respect of their commanders, but racial prejudice just as frequently denied them commensurate rights and privileges. Also black soldiers dismayed Confederates who occasionally responded with ugly brutality. Nonetheless, the United States Colored Troops substantially assisted in defeating the Confederacy.
[See United States Colored Troops]

1. Confederate General Orders No. 60 (21 August 1862)

WAR DEPT., *ADJT. AND INSP. GENERAL'S OFFICE,*

Richmond, August 21, 1862.

I. Whereas, Major-General Hunter, recently in command of the enemy's forces on the coast of South Carolina, and Brigadier-General Phelps, a military commander of the enemy in the State of Louisiana, have organized and armed negro slaves for military service against their masters, citizens of this Confederacy; and whereas, the Government of the United States has refused to answer an inquiry whether said conduct of its officers meets its sanction, and has thus left to this Government no other means of repressing said crimes and outrages than the adoption of such measures of retaliation as shall serve to prevent their repetition:

Ordered, That Major-General Hunter and Brigadier-General Phelps be no longer held and treated as public enemies of the Confederate States, but as outlaws, and that in the event of the capture of either of them, or that of any other commissioned officer employed in drilling, organizing, or instructing slaves with a view to their armed service in this war, he shall not be regarded as a prisoner of war, but held in close confinement for execution as a felon, at such time and place as the President shall order.

By order:

S. COOPER,

Adjutant and Inspector General.

(Source: U.S. War Department. *War of the Rebellion: A Compilation of the Official Records of the Union and Confederate Armies.* Ser. III, Vol. V.)

2. Edwin M. Stanton to Brigadier General Saxton (25 August 1862)

WAR DEPARTMENT,

Washington City, D.C., August 25, 1862.

Brigadier-General SAXTON:

GENERAL: Your dispatch of the 16th has this moment been received. It is considered by the Department that the instructions given at the time of your appointment were sufficient to enable you to do what you have now requested authority for doing. But in order to place your authority beyond all doubt you are hereby authorized and instructed:

1st. To enroll and organize, in any convenient organization, by squads, companies, battalions, regiments, and brigades, or otherwise, colored persons of African descent for volunteer laborers to a number not exceeding 5,000, and muster them into the service of the United States for the term of the war, at a rate of compensation not exceeding $5 per month for common laborers and $8 per month for mechanical or skilled laborers, and assign them to the quartermaster's department, to do and perform such laborers' duty as may be required in the military service of the United States, and wherever the same may be required during the present war, and to be subject to the Rules and Articles of War.

2d. The laboring forces herein authorized shall, under the order of the general-in.-chief or of this Department, be detailed by the Quartermaster-General for laboring service with the armies of the United States, and they shall be clothed and subsisted after enrollment in the same manner as other persons in the Quartermaster's service.

3d. In view of the small force under your command and the inability of the Government at the present time to increase it, in order to guard the plantations and settlements occupied by the United States from invasion and protect the inhabitants thereof from captivity and murder by the enemy, you are also authorized to arm, uniform, equip, and receive into the service of the United States such number of volunteers of African descent as you may deem expedient, not exceeding 50,000, and may detail officers to instruct them in military drill, discipline, and duty, and to command them. The persons so received into service and their officers to be entitled to and receive the same pay and rations as are allowed by law to volunteers in the service.

4th. You will re-occupy, if possible, all the islands and plantations heretofore occupied by the Government, and secure and harvest the crops and cultivate and improve the plantations.

5th. The population of African descent that cultivate the lands and perform the labor of the rebels constitute a large share of their military strength, and enable the white masters to fill the rebel armies and wage a cruel and murderous war against the people of the Northern States. By reducing the laboring strength of the rebels their military power Will be reduced. You are therefore authorized by every means in your power to withdraw from the enemy their laboring force and population, and to spare no effort consistent with civilized warfare to weaken, harass, and annoy them, and to establish the authority of the Government of the United States within your department.

6th. You may turn over to the Navy any number of colored volunteers that may be required for the naval service.

7th. By recent act of Congress all men and boys received into the service of the United States who may have been the slaves of rebel masters are, with their wives, mothers and children, declared to be forever free. You and all in your command will so treat and regard them.

Yours, truly,

EDWIN M. STANTON,
Secretary of War.

(Source: U.S. War Department. *War of the Rebellion: A Compilation of the Official Records of the Union and Confederate Armies.* Ser. I, Vol. XIV.)

3. Letter from Lincoln to Grant [Excerpt] (9 August 1863)

EXECUTIVE MANSION,
Washington, D. C., August 9, 1863.

Maj. Gen. U. S. GRANT:
General Thomas has gone again to the Mississippi Valley, with the view of raising colored troops. I have no reason to doubt that you are doing what you reasonably can upon the same subject. I believe it is a resource which, if vigorously applied now, will soon close this contest. It works doubly—weakening the enemy and strengthening us. We were not fully ripe for it until the river was opened. Now I think at least 100,000 can and ought to be organized along its shores, relieving all the white troops to serve elsewhere.

Mr. Dana understands you as believing that the emancipation proclamation has helped some in your military operations. I am very glad if this is so.

A. LINCOLN.

(Source: U.S. War Department. *War of the Rebellion: A Compilation of the Official Records of the Union and Confederate Armies.* Ser. I, Vol. XXIV/3.)

4. Letter from an African-American Soldier to President Lincoln (28 September 1863)

Morris Island [S.C.]. Sept 28th 1863.

Your Excelency will pardon the presumtion of an humble individual like myself, in addressing you. but the earnest Solicitation of my Comrades in Arms, besides the genuine interest felt by myself in the matter is my excuse, for placing before the Executive head of the Nation our Common Grievance: On the 6th of the last Month, the Paymaster of the department, informed us, that if we would decide to recieve the sum of $10 (ten dollars) per month, he would come and pay us that sum, but, that, on the sitting of Congress, the Regt would, in his opinion, be *allowed* the other 3 (three.) He did not give us any guarantee that this would be, as he hoped, certainly *he* had no authority for making any such guarantee, and we can not supose him acting in any way interested. Now the main question is. Are we *Soldiers*, or are we LABOURERS. We are fully armed, and equipped, have done all the various Duties, pertaining to a Soldiers life, have conducted ourselves, to the complete satisfaction of General Officers, who, were if any, prejudiced *against* us, but who now accord us all the encouragement, and honour due us: have shared the perils, and Labour, of Reducing the first stronghold, that flaunted a Traitor Flag: and more, Mr President. Today, the Anglo Saxon Mother, Wife, or Sister, are not alone, in tears for departed Sons, Husbands, and Brothers. The patient Trusting Decendants of Africs Clime, have dyed the ground with blood, in defense of the Union, and Democracy. Men too your Excellency, who know in a measure, the cruelties of the Iron heel of oppression, which in years gone by, the very Power, their blood is now being spilled to maintain, ever ground them to the dust. But When the war trumpet sounded o'er the land, when men knew not the Friend from the Traitor, the Black

man laid his life at the Altar of the Nation,—and he was refused. When the arms of the Union, were beaten, in the first year of the War, And the Executive called more food. for its ravaging maw, again the black man begged, the privelege of Aiding his Country in her need, to be again refused, And now, he is in the War: and how has he conducted himself? Let their dusky forms, rise up, out the mires of James Island, and give the answer. Let the rich mould around Wagners parapets be upturned, and there will be found an Eloquent answer. Obedient and patient, and Solid as a wall are they. all we lack, is a paler hue, and a better acquaintance with the Alphabet. Now Your Excellency, We have done a Soldiers Duty. Why cant we have a Soldiers pay? You caution the Rebel Chieftain, that the United States, knows, no distinction, in her Soldiers: She insists on having all her Soldiers, of whatever, creed or Color, to be treated, according to the usages of War. Now if the United States exacts uniformity of treatment of her Soldiers, from the Insurgents, would it not be well, and consistent, to set the example herself, by paying all her *Soldiers* alike? We of this Regt. were not enlisted under any "contraband" act. But we do not wish to be understood, as rating our Service, of more Value to the Government, than the service of the exslave, Their Service *is* undoubtedly worth much to the Nation, but Congress made express, provision touching their case, as slaves freed by military necessity, and assuming the Government, to be their temporary Gaurdian:—Not so with us—Freemen by birth, and consequently, having the advantage of *thinking*, and acting for ourselves, so far as the Laws would allow us. We do not consider ourselves fit subjects for the Contraband act. We appeal to You, Sir: as the Executive of the Nation, to have us Justly Dealt with. The Regt, do pray, that they be assured their service will be fairly appreciated, by paying them as american SOLDIERS, not as menial hierlings. Black men You may well know, are poor, three dollars per month, for a year, will suply their needy Wives, and little ones, with fuel. If you, as chief Magistrate of the Nation, will assure us, of our whole pay. We are content, our Patriotism, our enthusiasm will have a new impetus, to exert our energy more and more to aid Our Country. Not that our hearts ever flagged, in Devotion, spite the evident apathy displayed in our behalf, but We feel as though, our Country spurned us, now we are sworn to serve her.

Please give this a moments attention

James Henry Gooding

(Source: Letters Received, Ser. 360, Colored Troops Division, Adjutant General's Office, Record Group 94. National Archives, Washington, DC.)

5. Benjamin Butler to Edwin M. Stanton (3 October 1864)

HEADQUARTERS ARMY OF THE JAMES,
Near Junction of Varina and New Market Roads,
October 3, 1864—7.45 p.m.

Hon. E. M. STANTON, *Secretary of War:*
Dispatch relative to the negro troops received. I told you they would do well in my department. My colored troops under General Paine, 2,500 strong, carried intrenchments at the point of the bayonet that in a former movement across the river stopped double their number. It was most gallantly done, with most severe loss. Their praises are in the mouth of every officer in this army. Treated fairly and disciplined, they have fought most heroically. …
BENJ. F. BUTLER,
Major-general, Commanding.

(Source: U.S. War Department. *War of the Rebellion: A Compilation of the Official Records of the Union and Confederate Armies.* Ser. I, Vol. XLII/3.)

6. Colored Men and Their Relation to the Military Service, as Established by Laws and Orders during the Late War, and Their Recruitment as Soldiers (17 March 1866)

WAR DEPT., *PROVOST-MARSHAL-GENERAL'S BUREAU,*
Washington, D.C., March 17, 1866.

At the commencement of the rebellion, April 15, 1861, the Army was composed exclusively of white troops. The regulations of the Army governing the recruiting service (par. 1299) provided that "any free white male person above the age of eighteen," &c., "might be enlisted." Negro slavery existed in fifteen States of the Union, and fugitive slaves escaping from one State to another were delivered up on claim of their owners.

The first legislation by Congress directly affecting colored persons was the act approved March 13, 1862. It prohibited all officers or persons in the military or naval service of the United States from employing any of the forces under their respective commands for the purpose of returning fugitives from service or labor who escaped from any persons to whom such service or labor was claimed to be duo, and provided that any officer found guilty by a court-martial of violating this article should be dismissed from the service.

This was followed by an act, a approved July 17, 1862, the twelfth section of which authorized the President to receive into the service of the United States, for the purpose of constructing intrenchments, or performing camp duty, or any other labor, or any military or naval service for which they were found competent, persons of African descent, and provided that such persons should be enrolled and organized, under such regulations, not inconsistent with the Constitution and laws, as the President might prescribe.

The thirteenth section of this act directs—

That when any man or boy of African descent, who by the laws of any State shall owe service or labor to any person who during the present rebellion has levied war, or has borne arms against the United States, or adhered to their enemies by giving them aid and comfort, shall render any such service as is provided for in this act, he, his mother, and his wife and children, shall forever thereafter be free, any law, usage, or custom whatsoever to the contrary notwithstanding: *Provided,* That the mother, wife, and children of such man or boy of African descent shall not be made free by the operation of this act, except where such mother, wife, or children owe service or labor to some person who during the present rebellion has borne arms against the United States, or adhered to their enemies by giving them aid and comfort.

The fourteenth section provides that "the expenses incurred to carry this act into effect shall be paid out of the general appropriation for the Army and volunteers."

The fifteenth section directs that—

All persons who have been or who shall be hereafter enrolled in the service of the United States under this act shall receive the pay and rations now allowed by law to soldiers, according to their respective grades: Provided, That persons of African descent, who under this law shall be employed, shall receive ten dollars per month and one ration, three dollars of which monthly pay may be in clothing.

The amount of pay allowed to infantry soldiers (white) at the passage of this act was $13 per month, and an allowance in clothing of $3.50 per month, and one ration each.

The act entitled "An act to suppress insurrection, to punish treason and rebellion, to seize and confiscate the property of rebels, and for other purposes," approved July 17, 1863, provides that whoever shall commit treason "shall suffer death" and all his slaves be "declared free."

Section 9 provides—

That all slaves of persons who shall hereafter be engaged in rebellion against the Government of the United States, or who shall in any way give aid or comfort thereto, escaping from such persons and taking refuge within the lines of the Army; and all slaves captured from such persons or deserted by them and coming under the control of the Government of the United States, and all slaves of such persons found on [or] being within any place occupied by rebel forces and afterward occupied by the forces of the United States

shall be deemed captives of war, and shall be forever free of their servitude, and not again held as slaves.

Section 10 provides—

That no slave escaping into any State, Territory, or the District of Columbia, from any other State, shall be delivered up, or in any way impeded or hindered of his liberty, except for crime, or some offense against the laws, unless the person claiming said fugitive shall first make oath that the person to whom the labor or service of such fugitive is alleged to be due is his lawful owner, and has not borne arms against the United States in the present rebellion, nor in any way given aid and comfort thereto; and no person engaged in the military or naval service of the United States shall, under any pretense whatever, assume to decide on the validity of the claim of any person to the service or labor of any other person, or surrender up any such person to the claimant, on pain of being dismissed from the service.

Section 11 declares—

That the President of the United States is authorized to employ as many persons of African descent as he may deem necessary and proper for the suppression of this rebellion, and for this purpose he may organize and use them in such manner as he may judge best for the public welfare.

And by the latter section the authority of the President to receive into the service persons of African descent is extended, giving him authority to employ as many of this class of persons as he might deem necessary for the suppression of the rebellion.

The pay of this class of persons, as fixed by the twelfth section of the preceding act, was not changed.

Section 12 declares—

That the President of the United States is hereby authorized to make provision for the transportation, colonization, and settlement, in some tropical country beyond the limits of the United States, of such persons of the African race, made free by the provisions of this act, as may be willing to emigrate, having first obtained the consent of the government of said country to their protection and settlement within the same, with all the rights and privileges of freemen.

Under the authority conferred by the two preceding acts of Congress the President, on the 22d day of July, issued the following order:

First. Ordered, "That military commanders within the States of Virginia, South Carolina, Georgia, Florida, Alabama, Mississippi, Louisiana, Texas, and Arkansas, in an orderly manner, seize and use any property, real or personal, which may be necessary or convenient for their several commands as supplies, or for other military purposes; and that while property may be destroyed for proper military objects, none shall be destroyed in wantonness or malice."

Second. "That military and naval commanders shall employ as laborers, within and from said States, so many persons of African descent as can be advantageously used for military and naval purposes, giving them reasonable wages for their labor."

Third. "That as to both property and persons of African descent, accounts shall be kept sufficiently accurate and in detail to show quantities and amounts, and from whom both property and such persons shall have come, as a basis upon which compensation can be made in proper cases; and the several departments of this government shall attend to and perform their appropriate parts toward the execution of these orders."

On the 22d day of September, 1862, the President issued a proclamation announcing:

First. "That it was his purpose, upon the next meeting of Congress, to again recommend the adoption of a practical measure tendering pecuniary aid to the free acceptance or rejection of all slave States, so called, the people whereof may not then be in rebellion against the United States, and which States may then have voluntarily adopted, or thereafter may voluntarily adopt, immediate or gradual abolishment of slavery within their respective limits."

Second. "That the effort to colonize persons of African descent, with their consent, upon this continent or elsewhere, with the previously obtained consent of the governments existing there, should be continued."

Third. "That on the first day of January following all persons held as slaves within any State or designated part of a State, the people whereof shall then be in rebellion against the United States, should be then, thenceforward, and forever free; and the Executive government of the United States, including the military and naval authority thereof, will recognize and maintain the freedom of such persons, and will do no act or acts to repress such persons, or any of them, in any efforts they may make for their actual freedom."

Fourth. "That the Executive would, on the first day of January aforesaid, by proclamation designate the States and parts of States, if any, in which the people thereof, respectively, should then be in rebellion against the United States; and the fact that any State, or the people thereof, should on that day be, in good faith, represented in the Congress of the United States by members chosen thereto at elections wherein a majority of the qualified voters of such State should have participated, should, in the absence of strong countervailing testimony, be deemed conclusive evidence that such State and the people thereof were not then in rebellion against the United States."

On the 1st day of January, 1863, the immortal decree of emancipation a proclaimed freedom to the blacks of all the States declared in rebellion, with the exception of certain parishes in Louisiana.

By an act approved March 3, 1863, it is provided as follows:

That cooks shall be detailed, in turn, from the privates of each company of troops in the service of the United States, at the rate of one cook for each company numbering less than thirty men, and two cooks for each company numbering over thirty men, who shall serve ten days each.

That the President of the United States be, and he is hereby, authorized to cause to be enlisted, for each cook, two under-cooks of African descent, who shall receive for their full compensation ten dollars per month and one ration per day, three dollars of said monthly pay being in clothing.

On the 30th of July, 1863, the President ordered as follows:

The act of February 24, 1864, amendatory of the enrollment act, section 24, provided—

That all able-bodied male colored persons between the ages of twenty and forty-five years, resident in the United States, shall be enrolled according to the provisions of this act, and of the act to which this is an amendment, and form part of the national forces; and when a slave of a loyal master shall be drafted and mustered into the service of the United States, his master shall have a certificate thereof, and thereupon such slave shall be free; and the bounty of one hundred dollars, now payable by law for each drafted man, shall be paid to the person to whom such drafted person was owing service or labor at the time of his muster into the service of the United States. The Secretary of War shall appoint a commission in each of the slave States represented in Congress, charged to award each loyal person to whom a colored volunteer may owe service a just compensation, not exceeding three hundred dollars, for each such colored volunteer, payable out of the fund derived from commutations, and every such colored volunteer on being mustered into service shall be free. And in all cases where men of color have been heretofore enlisted, or have volunteered in the military service of the United States, all the provisions of this act, so far as the payment of bounty and compensation are provided, shall be equally applicable as to those who may be hereafter recruited. But men of color, drafted or enlisted, or who may volunteer into the military service, while they shall be credited on the quotas of the several States, or subdivisions of States, wherein they are respectively drafted, enlisted, or shall volunteer, shall not be assigned as State troops, but shall be mustered into regiments or companies as United States colored troops.

It will be observed that the able-bodied male colored persons were thenceforward to form part of the national forces. But it was provided, in the case of a slave being drafted, that the $100 bounty then allowed to drafted men should be paid to his master; and where a slave entered the service as a volunteer, instead of receiving the bounty which was allowed to other recruits, the master was entitled to receive a compensation from the Government, not to exceed $300. It was further provided that men of color drafted or enlisted should "be credited upon the quotas of the several States or subdivisions of States."

A fair construction of this statute authorizes the payment of $100 bounty to free colored men who might be drafted; and in lieu of bounty to the slave it gave him his freedom, while his master, if loyal, received a compensation for the loss of his services.

Up to this time and until the passage of the act entitled "An act making appropriations for the support of the Army for the year ending the thirtieth day of June, eighteen hundred and sixty-five, and for other purposes," approved June 15, 1864, there was no law providing for the payment of bounty to colored volunteers, either free or slave, and the pay of colored troops still remained at $10 per month, as fixed by the act of July 17, 1862.

The act just cited provides—

That all persons of color who have been or may be mustered into the military service of the United States shall receive the same uniform, clothing, arms, equipments, camp equipage, rations, medical and hospital attendance, pay and emoluments, other than bounty, as other soldiers of the regular or volunteer forces of the United States of like arm of the service, from and after the first day of January, eighteen hundred and sixty-four; and that every person of color who shall hereafter be mustered into the service shall receive such sums in bounty as the President shall order in the different States and parts of the United States, not exceeding one hundred dollars.

This section placed colored troops on an equal footing with white troops in all respects touching pay and allowances, but withheld the bounty as hitherto, except in such amount as the President might order, not to exceed $100.

The third section provided—

That all persons enlisted and mustered into service as volunteers under the call, dated October seventeen, eighteen hundred and sixty-three, for three hundred thousand volunteers, who were at the time of enlistment actually enrolled and subject to draft in the State in which they volunteered, shall receive from the United States the same amount of bounty without regard to color.

This section was practically inoperative for the reason that but few colored persons were enrolled, drafted, or credited on the call of October 17, 1863. The law directing the enrollment of colored men was not passed until February 24, 1864, and the colored men raised by draft or voluntary enlistment prior to this date were credited to the call of February 1, 1864 (which was being filled when the law directing the enrollment and draft of colored men was passed), and to the subsequent calls.

The fourth section provided—

That all persons of color who were free on the nineteenth day of April, eighteen hundred and sixty-one, and who have been enlisted and mustered into the military service of the United States, shall, from the time of their enlistment, be entitled to receive the pay, bounty, and clothing allowed to such persons by the laws existing at the time of their enlistment. And the Attorney-General of the United States is hereby authorized to determine any question of law arising under this provision. And if the Attorney-General aforesaid shall determine that any of such enlisted persons are entitled to receive any pay, bounty, or clothing, in addition to what they have already received, the Secretary of War shall make all necessary regulations.

In conformity with this section the Secretary of War ordered as follows:

An act approved July 4, 1864, provided—

That the President of the United States may, at his discretion, at any time hereafter, call for any number of men as volunteers, for the respective terms of one, two, and three years, for military service; and any such volunteer, or, in case of draft, as hereinafter provided, any substitute, shall be credited to the town, township, ward of a city, precinct, or election district, or of a county not so subdivided, toward the quota of which he may have volunteered or engaged as a substitute; and every volunteer who is accepted and mustered into the service for a term of one year, unless sooner discharged, shall receive and be paid by the United States a bounty of one hundred dollars; and if for a term of two years, unless sooner discharged, a bounty of two hundred dollars; and if for a term of three years, unless sooner discharged, a bounty of three hundred dollars, one-third of which bounty shall be paid to the soldier at the time of his being mustered into the service, one-third at the expiration of one-half of his term of service, and one-third at the expiration of his term of service. And in case of his death while in service, the residue of his bounty unpaid shall be paid to his widow, if he shall have left a widow; if not, to his children; or if there be none, to his mother, if she be a widow.

This section authorized the payment of like bounty to all persons enlisting, omitting the distinction hitherto observed in regard to colored troops, and was evidently intended to allow the same amount to both classes, and bounties were paid accordingly.

Section 3 provides "That it shall be lawful for the Executive of any of the States to send recruiting agents into any of the States declared to be in rebellion, except the States of Arkansas, Tennessee, and Louisiana, to recruit volunteers under any call under the provisions of this act, who shall be credited to the

State and to the respective subdivisions thereof, which may procure the enlistment," but was repealed by the act of March 3, 1865.

Section 14 of an act approved July 4, 1864, provided—

That the widows and children of colored soldiers who have been, or who may be hereafter, killed, or who have died or may hereafter die of wounds received in battle, or who have died or may hereafter die of disease contracted in the military service of the United States, and in the line of duty, shall be entitled to receive the pensions now provided by law, without other proof of marriage than that the parties had habitually recognized each other as man and wife, and lived together as such for a definite period next preceding the soldier's enlistment, not less than two years, to be shown by the affidavits of credible witnesses: Provided, however, That such widow and children are free persons: Provided *further*, That if such parties resided in any State in which their marriage may have been legally solemnized the usual evidence shall be required.

Section 5 of an act approved March 3, 1865, provided—

That all persons of color who were enlisted and mustered into the military service of the United States in South Carolina, by and under the direction of Major-General Hunter and Brigadier-General Saxton, in pursuance of the authority from the Secretary of War, dated August twenty-fifth, eighteen hundred and sixty-two, "that the persons so received into service, and their officers, to be entitled to and receive the same pay and rations as are allowed by law to other volunteers in the service"—and in every case where it shall be made to appear to the satisfaction of the Secretary of War that any regiment of colored troops has been mustered into the service of the United States, under any assurance by the President or the Secretary of War, that the non-commissioned officers and privates of such regiment should be paid the same as other troops of the same arm of the service—shall from the date of their enlistment, receive the same pay and allowances as are allowed by law to other volunteers in the military service; and the Secretary of War shall make all necessary regulations to cause payment to be made in accordance herewith.

Section 22 provided—

That the third section of the act entitled "An act [further] to regulate and provide for the enrolling and calling out the national forces, and for other purposes," approved July fourth, eighteen hundred and sixty-four, be, and the same is hereby, repealed.

The foregoing embraces the entire legislation and the most important Executive orders touching the relation of colored men to the military service.

PAYMASTER-GENERAL'S OFFICE,
Washington, D.C., May 26, 1865.

The following brief outline of the recruitment of colored persons is taken mainly from the reports and records of the Bureau for Colored Troops, and is inserted here in connection with the foregoing recapitulation of the laws and orders on the subject.

The acceptance of colored men as soldiers in the service of the United States began in Louisiana by the muster in, on the 27th of September, 1862, of the First Louisiana Native Guards, subsequently designated Seventy-third Regiment U.S. Colored Troops.

Four other regiments were raised in that military department and mustered in prior to March 7, 1863, two of them before the 1st of January, 1863.

The efforts made in the early summer of 1862 to raise colored troops in South Carolina did not result in the muster of an organization until January 31, 1863, when the First South Carolina Volunteers, subsequently designated Thirty-third U.S. Colored Troops, was mustered into the service as soldiers. Three other regiments were mustered in that department prior to July 1, 1863.

In April, 1863, a regiment was completed in Kansas, called the First Kansas Volunteers, subsequently designated Seventy-ninth U.S. Colored Troops. Another regiment then in process of organization was some time after completed.

Early in the spring of 1863 the organization of colored troops was commenced in the Mississippi Valley under the personal supervision of the Adjutant-General of the Army. His first regiment was mustered into service on the 1st of May, 1863, as the First Arkansas Volunteers of African Descent, afterward designated Forty-sixth Regiment U.S. Colored Troops. Five other regiments raised in like manner were mustered in prior to June 30, 1863.

The Fifty-fourth and Fifty-fifth Regiments of Massachusetts Volunteers were colored troops. They were organized in Massachusetts, and were mustered into service between March 30 and June 22, 1863. They were organized, officered, &c., by the State authorities, like other regiments of volunteers, and so continued until mustered out.

The foregoing colored troops were raised prior to the commencement of the operations of the Bureau for Colored Troops, which was created by General Orders, No. 143, dated May 29, 1863.

Under the immediate supervision of that Bureau, a regiment designated the First U.S. Colored Troops was mustered into service in the District of Columbia on the 30th of June, 1863, and simultaneously with this a regiment was mustered in in North Carolina.

At this period, June, 1863, the recruitment of colored troops was going on all over the country, and so continued until stopped by orders on April 29, 1865, in consequence of no more troops being required.

With the exception of the two Massachusetts regiments above mentioned, the military organizations composed of colored men were mustered directly into the service of the United States, and were organized and officered by officers acting under the authority of the United States, and not of any particular State.

Since March 27, 1865, all appointments of officers for these troops have been made exclusively by the War Department, and after an examination by a board of officers. Prior to that time the Adjutant-General of the Army, in the Mississippi Valley, made appointments, in the name of the Secretary of War, to the regiments which he organized; and department commanders made, subject to the approval of the President, provisional appointments to the regiments organized by them.

The recruitment of men of color by draft and substitution was exclusively under the control of this Bureau, but their recruitment as volunteers was mainly under the Bureau for Colored Troops, especially established for that purpose. To present together the entire results of these operations, which, however, were produced in the main by the action of the Bureau for Colored Troops, the following extract is made from the report of the chief of that Bureau:

On the 15th of July, 1865, the date on which the last organization of colored troops was mustered in, there were—

In the service of the United States 120 regiments of infantry, numbering in the aggregate, 98,938

Twelve regiments of heavy artillery, 15,662
Ten companies of light artillery, 1,311
Seven regiments of cavalry, 7,245
Grand aggregate, 128,156

The foregoing is the largest number of colored troops in service at any one time during the war.

The entire number of troops commissioned and enlisted in this branch of the service during the war is 186,017.

The States in which this force was recruited or drafted are as follows, viz:

Maine	104
Vermont	120
Massachusetts	3,966
New York	4,125
Pennsylvania	8,612
Maryland	8,718
Virginia	5,723
West Virginia	196
Georgia	3,486
Alabama	4,969
Louisiana	24,052

Tennessee	20,133
Michigan	1,387
Indiana	1,537
Missouri	8,344
Iowa	440
Kansas	2,080
Colorado Territory	95
Not accounted for	5,083
New Hampshire	125
Rhode Island	1,837
Connecticut	1,764
New Jersey	1,185
Delaware	954
District of Columbia	3,269
North Carolina	5,035
South Carolina	5,462
Florida	1,044
Mississippi	17,869
Arkansas	5,526
Kentucky	28,703
Ohio	5,092
Illinois	1,811
Minnesota	104
Wisconsin	165
Texas	47
At large	783
Officers	7,122
Total	**186,017**

(Source: U.S. War Department. *War of the Rebellion: A Compilation of the Official Records of the Union and Confederate Armies.* Ser. III, Vol. V.)

B. THE CONFEDERACY

Why African-Americans would support the Confederate cause in any fashion is a riddle. For most of the war, the main role of African-Americans in the Confederate military was as support staff, where they served as servants, cooks, teamsters, and musicians. In January 1864, however, Major General Patrick Cleburne of the Army of Tennessee called for the enlistment of slaves in the Confederate military, stressing the need for more troops of any kind. The Confederate government resisted the idea until military necessity made imperative the replenishment of depleted Confederate ranks. In late 1864, Secretary of State Judah Benjamin also called for slave enlistment, and in January 1865, Robert E. Lee concurred. Consequently, on 13 March 1865 the Confederate Congress finally authorized the recruitment of "Negro Soldiers" in exchange for a loosely defined emancipation upon the defeat of the Union. Their newly defined status and presence was too late to assist the Southern war effort. [See African-American Soldiers, C.S.A.]

1. F. W. Hancock to R. S. Ewell
(14 February 1865)
HEADQUARTERS JACKSON HOSPITAL,
February 14, 1865.

Lieut. Gen. R. S. EWELL:
DEAR SIR: For my own gratification, as well as those who are taking great interest in the important question, with regard to the using of the slaves of the Confederacy as an assisting element to us in defending our homes, firesides, and country from those who would destroy us, I would respectfully say that this morning I caused the hired male slaves at this hospital to be convened, and after asking them the deliberate question, if they would be willing to take up arms to protect their masters' families, homes, and their own from an attacking foe, sixty out of seventy-two responded they would volunteer to go to the trenches and fight the enemy to the bitter end.
Very respectfully, your most obedient servant,
F. W. HANCOCK,
Surgeon in charge.

(Source: U.S. War Department. *War of the Rebellion: A Compilation of the Official Records of the Union and Confederate Armies.* Ser. III, Vol. V.)

2. Robert E. Lee to Jefferson Davis
(24 March 1865)
HEADQUARTERS C.S. ARMIES,
March 24, 1865.

His Excellency JEFFERSON DAVIS,
President of the Confederate States, Richmond:
Mr. PRESIDENT: I have the honor to ask that you will call upon the governor of the State of Virginia for the whole number of negroes, slave and free, between the ages of eighteen and forty-five, for services as soldiers authorized by the joint resolution adopted by the Senate and House of Delegates of the State [of Virginia] on the 4th of March. The services of these men are now necessary to enable us to oppose the enemy.
With great respect, your obedient servant,
R. E. LEE, *General.*

(Source: U.S. War Department. *War of the Rebellion: A Compilation of the Official Records of the Union and Confederate Armies.* Ser. I, Vol. XLVI/3.)

3. Theodor P. Turner to Lieutenant S. R. Shinn
(2 April 1865)
RICHMOND, VA., *April 2, 1865.*

Lieut. S. R. SHINN:
DEAR SHINN: I have delayed writing in order to be able to give you some definite information on the negro question. The Secretary of War day before yesterday directed that the authority asked for be given Colonel Otey, and I telegraphed you to that effect. I have no doubt the orders have reached him by this time. Go to work and work, work, work. If the people of Virginia only knew and appreciated General Lee's solicitude on this subject they would not longer hold back their slaves. Their wives and daughters and the negroes are the only elements left us to recruit from, and it does seem that our people would rather send the former even to face death and danger than give up the latter.
Let me hear from you at once.
Yours, truly,
TH. P. TURNER.

(Source: U.S. War Department. *War of the Rebellion: A Compilation of the Official Records of the Union and Confederate Armies.* Ser. III, Vol. V.)

XXXVIII. Armies

A. THE UNION
General Orders, No. 100, written primarily by Francis Lieber, is consequently also known as Lieber's Code. It was designed to guide the federal military's conduct toward the Confederate army and Southern civilians. Enduring into the twentieth century as the policy of American field soldiers during wartime, the code would continue its influence on military policy far beyond its original purpose. [See General Order, No. 100; Lieber, Francis]

1. Instructions for the Government of Armies of the United States in the Field

Prepared by Francis Lieber, Promulgated as General Orders No. 100 by President Lincoln, 24 April 1863.

SECTION I. Martial Law—Military jurisdiction—Military necessity—Retaliation.
    Article 1. A place, district, or country occupied by an enemy stands, in consequence of the occupation, under the Martial Law of the invading or occupying army, whether any proclamation declaring Martial Law, or any public warning to the inhabitants, has been issued or not. Martial Law is the immediate and direct effect and consequence of occupation or conquest. The presence of a hostile army proclaims its Martial Law.
    Article 2. Martial Law does not cease during the hostile occupation, except by special proclamation, ordered by the commander in chief; or by special mention in the treaty of peace concluding the war, when the occupation of a place or territory continues beyond the conclusion of peace as one of the conditions of the same.
    Article 3. Martial Law in a hostile country consists in the suspension, by the occupying military authority, of the criminal and civil law, and of the domestic adminis-

tration and government in the occupied place or territory, and in the substitution of military rule and force for the same, as well as in the dictation of general laws, as far as military necessity requires this suspension, substitution, or dictation. The commander of the forces may proclaim that the administration of all civil and penal law shall continue either wholly or in part, as in times of peace, unless otherwise ordered by the military authority.

Article 4. Martial Law is simply military authority exercised in accordance with the laws and usages of war. Military oppression is not Martial Law: it is the abuse of the power which that law confers. As Martial Law is executed by military force, it is incumbent upon those who administer it to be strictly guided by the principles of justice, honor, and humanity—virtues adorning a soldier even more than other men, for the very reason that he possesses the power of his arms against the unarmed.

Article 5. Martial Law should be less stringent in places and countries fully occupied and fairly conquered. Much greater severity may be exercised in places or regions where actual hostilities exist, or are expected and must be prepared for. Its most complete sway is allowed—even in the commander's own country—when face to face with the enemy, because of the absolute necessities of the case, and of the paramount duty to defend the country against invasion. To save the country is paramount to all other considerations.

Article 6. All civil and penal law shall continue to take its usual course in the enemy's places and territories under Martial Law, unless interrupted or stopped by order of the occupying military power; but all the functions of the hostile government—legislative executive, or administrative—whether of a general, provincial, or local character, cease under Martial Law, or continue only with the sanction, or, if deemed necessary, the participation of the occupier or invader.

Article 7. Martial Law extends to property, and to persons, whether they are subjects of the enemy or aliens to that government.

Article 8. Consuls, among American and European nations, are not diplomatic agents. Nevertheless, their offices and persons will be subjected to Martial Law in cases of urgent necessity only: their property and business are not exempted. Any delinquency they commit against the established military rule may be punished as in the case of any other inhabitant, and such punishment furnishes no reasonable ground for international complaint.

Article 9. The functions of Ambassadors, Ministers, or other diplomatic agents accredited by neutral powers to the hostile government, cease, so far as regards the displaced government; but the conquering or occupying power usually recognizes them as temporarily accredited to itself.

Article 10. Martial Law affects chiefly the police and collection of public revenue and taxes, whether imposed by the expelled government or by the invader, and refers mainly to the support and efficiency of the army, its safety, and the safety of its operations.

Article 11. The law of war does not only disclaim all cruelty and bad faith concerning engagements concluded with the enemy during the war, but also the breaking of stipulations solemnly contracted by the belligerents in time of peace, and avowedly intended to remain in force in case of war between the contracting powers. It disclaims all extortions and other transactions for individual gain; all acts of private revenge, or connivance at such acts. Offenses to the contrary shall be severely punished, and especially so if committed by officers.

Article 12. Whenever feasible, Martial Law is carried out in cases of individual offenders by Military Courts; but sentences of death shall be executed only with the approval of the chief executive, provided the urgency of the case does not require a speedier execution, and then only with the approval of the chief commander.

Article 13. Military jurisdiction is of two kinds: First, that which is conferred and defined by statute; second, that which is derived from the common law of war. Military offenses under the statute law must be tried in the manner therein directed; but military offenses which do not come within the statute must be tried and punished under the common law of war. The character of the courts which exercise these jurisdictions depends upon the local laws of each particular country. In the armies of the United States the first is exercised by courts-martial, while cases which do not come within the "Rules and Articles of War," or the jurisdiction conferred by statute on courts-martial, are tried by military commissions.

Article 14. Military necessity, as understood by modern civilized nations, consists in the necessity of those measures which are indispensable for securing the ends of the war, and which are lawful according to the modern law and usages of war.

Article 15. Military necessity admits of all direct destruction of life or limb of armed enemies, and of other persons whose destruction is incidentally unavoidable in the armed contests of the war; it allows of the capturing of every armed enemy, and every enemy of importance to the hostile government, or of peculiar danger to the captor; it allows of all destruction of property, and obstruction of the ways and channels of traffic, travel, or communication, and of all withholding of sustenance or means of life from the enemy; of the appropriation of whatever an enemy's country affords necessary for the subsistence and safety of the army, and of such deception as does not involve the breaking of good faith either positively pledged,

regarding agreements entered into during the war, or supposed by the modern law of war to exist. Men who take up arms against one another in public war do not cease on this account to be moral beings, responsible to one another and to God.

Article 16. Military necessity does not admit of cruelty—that is, the infliction of suffering for the sake of suffering or for revenge, nor of maiming or wounding except in fight, nor of torture to extort confessions. It does not admit of the use of poison in any way, nor of the wanton devastation of a district. It admits of deception, but disclaims acts of perfidy; and, in general, military necessity does not include any act of hostility which makes the return to peace unnecessarily difficult.

Article 17. War is not carried on by arms alone. It is lawful to starve the hostile belligerent, armed or unarmed, so that it leads to the speedier subjection of the enemy.

Article 18. When a commander of a besieged place expels the noncombatants, in order to lessen the number of those who consume his stock of provisions, it is lawful, though an extreme measure, to drive them back, so as to hasten on the surrender.

Article 19. Commanders, whenever admissible, inform the enemy of their intention to bombard a place, so that the noncombatants, and especially the women and children, may be removed before the bombardment commences. But it is no infraction of the common law of war to omit thus to inform the enemy. Surprise may be a necessity.

Article 20. Public war is a state of armed hostility between sovereign nations or governments. It is a law and requisite of civilized existence that men live in political, continuous societies, forming organized units, called states or nations, whose constituents bear, enjoy, suffer, advance and retrograde together, in peace and in war.

Article 21. The citizen or native of a hostile country is thus an enemy, as one of the constituents of the hostile state or nation, and as such is subjected to the hardships of the war.

Article 22. Nevertheless, as civilization has advanced during the last centuries, so has likewise steadily advanced, especially in war on land, the distinction between the private individual belonging to a hostile country and the hostile country itself, with its men in arms. The principle has been more and more acknowledged that the unarmed citizen is to be spared in person, property, and honor as much as the exigencies of war will admit.

Article 23. Private citizens are no longer murdered, enslaved, or carried off to distant parts, and the inoffensive individual is as little disturbed in his private relations as the commander of the hostile troops can afford to grant in the overruling demands of a vigorous war.

Article 24. The almost universal rule in remote times was, and continues to be with barbarous armies, that the private individual of the hostile country is destined to suffer every privation of liberty and protection, and every disruption of family ties. Protection was, and still is with uncivilized people, the exception.

Article 25. In modern regular wars of the Europeans, and their descendants in other portions of the globe, protection of the inoffensive citizen of the hostile country is the rule; privation and disturbance of private relations are the exceptions.

Article 26. Commanding generals may cause the magistrates and civil officers of the hostile country to take the oath of temporary allegiance or an oath of fidelity to their own victorious government or rulers, and they may expel everyone who declines to do so. But whether they do so or not, the people and their civil officers owe strict obedience to them as long as they hold sway over the district or country, at the peril of their lives.

Article 27. The law of war can no more wholly dispense with retaliation than can the law of nations, of which it is a branch. Yet civilized nations acknowledge retaliation as the sternest feature of war. A reckless enemy often leaves to his opponent no other means of securing himself against the repetition of barbarous outrage

Article 28. Retaliation will, therefore, never be resorted to as a measure of mere revenge, but only as a means of protective retribution, and moreover, cautiously and unavoidably; that is to say, retaliation shall only be resorted to after careful inquiry into the real occurrence, and the character of the misdeeds that may demand retribution. Unjust or inconsiderate retaliation removes the belligerents farther and farther from the mitigating rules of regular war, and by rapid steps leads them nearer to the internecine wars of savages.

Article 29. Modern times are distinguished from earlier ages by the existence, at one and the same time, of many nations and great governments related to one another in close intercourse. Peace is their normal condition; war is the exception. The ultimate object of all modern war is a renewed state of peace. The more vigorously wars are pursued, the better it is for humanity. Sharp wars are brief.

Article 30. Ever since the formation and coexistence of modern nations, and ever since wars have become great national wars, war has come to be acknowledged not to be its own end, but the means to obtain great ends of state, or to consist in defense against wrong; and no conventional restriction of the modes adopted to injure the enemy is any longer admitted; but the law of war imposes many limitations and restrictions on principles of justice, faith, and honor.

SECTION II. Public and private property of the enemy—Protection of persons, and especially of women, of religion, the arts and sciences—Punishment of crimes against the inhabitants of hostile countries.

Article 31. A victorious army appropriates all public money, seizes all public movable property until further direction by its government, and sequesters for its own benefit or of that of its government all the revenues of real property belonging to the hostile government or nation. The title to such real property remains in abeyance during military occupation, and until the conquest is made complete.

Article 32. A victorious army, by the martial power inherent in the same, may suspend, change, or abolish, as far as the martial power extends, the relations which arise from the services due, according to the existing laws of the invaded country, from one citizen, subject, or native of the same to another. The commander of the army must leave it to the ultimate treaty of peace to settle the permanency of this change.

Article 33. It is no longer considered lawful—on the contrary, it is held to be a serious breach of the law of war—to force the subjects of the enemy into the service of the victorious government, except the latter should proclaim, after a fair and complete conquest of the hostile country or district, that it is resolved to keep the country, district, or place permanently as its own and make it a portion of its own country.

Article 34. As a general rule, the property belonging to churches, to hospitals, or other establishments of an exclusively charitable character, to establishments of education, or foundations for the promotion of knowledge, whether public schools, universities, academies of learning or observatories, museums of the fine arts, or of a scientific character such property is not to be considered public property in the sense of paragraph 31; but it may be taxed or used when the public service may require it.

Article 35. Classical works of art, libraries, scientific collections, or precious instruments, such as astronomical telescopes, as well as hospitals, must be secured against all avoidable injury, even when they are contained in fortified places whilst besieged or bombarded.

Article 36. If such works of art, libraries, collections, or instruments belonging to a hostile nation or government, can be removed without injury, the ruler of the conquering state or nation may order them to be seized and removed for the benefit of the said nation. The ultimate ownership is to be settled by the ensuing treaty of peace. In no case shall they be sold or given away, if captured by the armies of the United States, nor shall they ever be privately appropriated, or wantonly destroyed or injured.

Article 37. The United States acknowledge and protect, in hostile countries occupied by them, religion and morality; strictly private property; the persons of the inhabitants, especially those of women: and the sacredness of domestic relations. Offenses to the contrary shall be rigorously punished. This rule does not interfere with the right of the victorious invader to tax the people or their property, to levy forced loans, to billet soldiers, or to appropriate property, especially houses, lands, boats or ships, and churches, for temporary and military uses

Article 38. Private property, unless forfeited by crimes or by offenses of the owner, can be seized only by way of military necessity, for the support or other benefit of the army or of the United States. If the owner has not fled, the commanding officer will cause receipts to be given, which may serve the spoliated owner to obtain indemnity.

Article 39. The salaries of civil officers of the hostile government who remain in the invaded territory, and continue the work of their office, and can continue it according to the circumstances arising out of the war— such as judges, administrative or police officers, officers of city or communal governments—are paid from the public revenue of the invaded territory, until the military government has reason wholly or partially to discontinue it. Salaries or incomes connected with purely honorary titles are always stopped.

Article 40. There exists no law or body of authoritative rules of action between hostile armies, except that branch of the law of nature and nations which is called the law and usages of war on land.

Article 41. All municipal law of the ground on which the armies stand, or of the countries to which they belong, is silent and of no effect between armies in the field.

Article 42. Slavery, complicating and confounding the ideas of property, (that is of a thing,) and of personality, (that is of humanity,) exists according to municipal or local law only. The law of nature and nations has never acknowledged it. The digest of the Roman law enacts the early dictum of the pagan jurist, that "so far as the law of nature is concerned, all men are equal." Fugitives escaping from a country in which they were slaves, villains, or serfs, into another country, have, for centuries past, been held free and acknowledged free by judicial decisions of European countries, even though the municipal law of the country in which the slave had taken refuge acknowledged slavery within its own dominions.

Article 43. Therefore, in a war between the United States and a belligerent which admits of slavery, if a person held in bondage by that belligerent be captured by or come as a fugitive under the protection of the military forces of the United States, such person is immediately entitled to the rights and privileges of a freeman To return such person into slavery would amount to

enslaving a free person, and neither the United States nor any officer under their authority can enslave any human being. Moreover, a person so made free by the law of war is under the shield of the law of nations, and the former owner or State can have, by the law of postliminy, no belligerent lien or claim of service.

Article 44. All wanton violence committed against persons in the invaded country, all destruction of property not commanded by the authorized officer, all robbery, all pillage or sacking, even after taking a place by main force, all rape, wounding, maiming, or killing of such inhabitants, are prohibited under the penalty of death, or such other severe punishment as may seem adequate for the gravity of the offense. A soldier, officer or private, in the act of committing such violence, and disobeying a superior ordering him to abstain from it, may be lawfully killed on the spot by such superior.

Article 45. All captures and booty belong, according to the modern law of war, primarily to the government of the captor. Prize money, whether on sea or land, can now only be claimed under local law.

Article 46. Neither officers nor soldiers are allowed to make use of their position or power in the hostile country for private gain, not even for commercial transactions otherwise legitimate. Offenses to the contrary committed by commissioned officers will be punished with cashiering or such other punishment as the nature of the offense may require; if by soldiers, they shall be punished according to the nature of the offense.

Article 47. Crimes punishable by all penal codes, such as arson, murder, maiming, assaults, highway robbery, theft, burglary, fraud, forgery, and rape, if committed by an American soldier in a hostile country against its inhabitants, are not only punishable as at home, but in all cases in which death is not inflicted, the severer punishment shall be preferred.

SECTION III. Deserters—Prisoners of war—Hostages—Booty on the battle-field.

Article 48. Deserters from the American Army, having entered the service of the enemy, suffer death if they fall again into the hands of the United States, whether by capture, or being delivered up to the American Army; and if a deserter from the enemy, having taken service in the Army of the United States, is captured by the enemy, and punished by them with death or otherwise, it is not a breach against the law and usages of war, requiring redress or retaliation.

Article 49. A prisoner of war is a public enemy armed or attached to the hostile army for active aid, who has fallen into the hands of the captor, either fighting or wounded, on the field or in the hospital, by individual surrender or by capitulation. All soldiers, of whatever species of arms; all men who belong to the rising en masse of the hostile country; all those who are attached to the army for its efficiency and promote directly the object of the war, except such as are hereinafter provided for; all disabled men or officers on the field or elsewhere, if captured; all enemies who have thrown away their arms and ask for quarter, are prisoners of war, and as such exposed to the inconveniences as well as entitled to the privileges of a prisoner of war.

Article 50. Moreover, citizens who accompany an army for whatever purpose, such as sutlers, editors, or reporters of journals, or contractors, if captured, may be made prisoners of war, and be detained as such. The monarch and members of the hostile reigning family, male or female, the chief, and chief officers of the hostile government, its diplomatic agents, and all persons who are of particular and singular use and benefit to the hostile army or its government, are, if captured on belligerent ground, and if unprovided with a safe conduct granted by the captor's government, prisoners of war.

Article 51. If the people of that portion of an invaded country which is not yet occupied by the enemy, or of the whole country, at the approach of a hostile army, rise, under a duly authorized levy en masse to resist the invader, they are now treated as public enemies, and, if captured, are prisoners of war.

Article 52. No belligerent has the right to declare that he will treat every captured man in arms of a levy en masse as a brigand or bandit. If, however, the people of a country, or any portion of the same, already occupied by an army, rise against it, they are violators of the laws of war, and are not entitled to their protection.

Article 53. The enemy's chaplains, officers of the medical staff, apothecaries, hospital nurses and servants, if they fall into the hands of the American Army, are not prisoners of war, unless the commander has reasons to retain them. In this latter case; or if, at their own desire, they are allowed to remain with their captured companions, they are treated as prisoners of war, and may be exchanged if the commander sees fit.

Article 54. A hostage is a person accepted as a pledge for the fulfillment of an agreement concluded between belligerents during the war, or in consequence of a war. Hostages are rare in the present age.

Article 55. If a hostage is accepted, he is treated like a prisoner of war, according to rank and condition, as circumstances may admit.

Article 56. A prisoner of war is subject to no punishment for being a public enemy, nor is any revenge wreaked upon him by the intentional infliction of any suffering, or disgrace, by cruel imprisonment, want of food, by mutilation, death, or any other barbarity.

Article 57. So soon as a man is armed by a sovereign government and takes the soldier's oath of fidelity, he is a belligerent; his killing, wounding, or other warlike acts are not individual crimes or offenses. No belligerent has a right to declare that enemies of a certain class, color, or condition, when properly organized as soldiers, will not be treated by him as public enemies.

Article 58. The law of nations knows of no distinction of color, and if an enemy of the United States should enslave and sell any captured persons of their army, it would be a case for the severest retaliation, if not redressed upon complaint. The United States cannot retaliate by enslavement; therefore death must be the retaliation for this crime against the law of nations.

Article 59. A prisoner of war remains answerable for his crimes committed against the captor's army or people, committed before he was captured, and for which he has not been punished by his own authorities. All prisoners of war are liable to the infliction of retaliatory measures.

Article 60. It is against the usage of modern war to resolve, in hatred and revenge, to give no quarter. No body of troops has the right to declare that it will not give, and therefore will not expect, quarter; but a commander is permitted to direct his troops to give no quarter, in great straits, when his own salvation makes it impossible to cumber himself with prisoners.

Article 61. Troops that give no quarter have no right to kill enemies already disabled on the ground, or prisoners captured by other troops.

Article 62. All troops of the enemy known or discovered to give no quarter in general, or to any portion of the army, receive none.

Article 63. Troops who fight in the uniform of their enemies, without any plain, striking, and uniform mark of distinction of their own, can expect no quarter.

Article 64. If American troops capture a train containing uniforms of the enemy, and the commander considers it advisable to distribute them for use among his men, some striking mark or sign must be adopted to distinguish the American soldier from the enemy.

Article 65. The use of the enemy's national standard, flag, or other emblem of nationality, for the purpose of deceiving the enemy in battle, is an act of perfidy by which they lose all claim to the protection of the laws of war.

Article 66. Quarter having been given to an enemy by American troops, under a misapprehension of his true character, he may, nevertheless, be ordered to suffer death if, within three days after the battle, it be discovered that he belongs to a corps which gives no quarter.

Article 67. The law of nations allows every sovereign government to make war upon another sovereign state, and, therefore, admits of no rules or laws different from those of regular warfare, regarding the treatment of prisoners of war, although they may belong to the army of a government which the captor may consider as a wanton and unjust assailant.

Article 68. Modern wars are not internecine wars, in which the killing of the enemy is the object. The destruction of the enemy in modern war, and, indeed, modern war itself, are means to obtain that object of the belligerent which lies beyond the war. Unnecessary or revengeful destruction of life is not lawful.

Article 69. Outposts, sentinels, or pickets are not to be fired upon, except to drive them in, or when a positive order, special or general, has been issued to that effect.

Article 70. The use of poison in any manner, be it to poison wells, or food, or arms, is wholly excluded from modern warfare. He that uses it puts himself out of the pale of the law and usages of war.

Article 71. Whoever intentionally inflicts additional wounds on an enemy already wholly disabled, or kills such an enemy, or who orders or encourages soldiers to do so, shall suffer death, if duly convicted, whether he belongs to the Army of the United States, or is an enemy captured after having committed his misdeed.

Article 72. Money and other valuables on the person of a prisoner, such as watches or jewelry, as well as extra clothing, are regarded by the American Army as the private property of the prisoner, and the appropriation of such valuables or money is considered dishonorable, and is prohibited. Nevertheless, if large sums are found upon the persons of prisoners, or in their possession, they shall be taken from them, and the surplus, after providing for their own support, appropriated for the use of the army, under the direction of the commander, unless otherwise ordered by the government. Nor can prisoners claim, as private property, large sums found and captured in their train, although they have been placed in the private luggage of the prisoners.

Article 73. All officers, when captured, must surrender their side arms to the captor. They may be restored to the prisoner in marked cases, by the commander, to signalize admiration of his distinguished bravery or approbation of his humane treatment of prisoners before his capture. The captured officer to whom they may be restored can not wear them during captivity.

Article 74. A prisoner of war, being a public enemy, is the prisoner of the government, and not of the captor. No ransom can be paid by a prisoner of war to his individual captor or to any officer in command. The government alone releases captives, according to rules prescribed by itself.

Article 75. Prisoners of war are subject to confinement or imprisonment such as may be deemed necessary on account of safety, but they are to be subjected to no other intentional suffering or indignity. The confinement and mode of treating a prisoner may be varied during his captivity according to the demands of safety.

Article 76. Prisoners of war shall be fed upon plain and wholesome food, whenever practicable, and treated with humanity. They may be required to work for the benefit of the captor's government, according to their rank and condition.

Article 77. A prisoner of war who escapes may be shot or otherwise killed in his flight; but neither death nor any other punishment shall be inflicted upon him simply for his attempt to escape, which the law of war does not consider a crime. Stricter means of security shall be used after an unsuccessful attempt at escape. If, however, a conspiracy is discovered, the purpose of which is a united or general escape, the conspirators may be rigorously punished, even with death; and capital punishment may also be inflicted upon prisoners of war discovered to have plotted rebellion against the authorities of the captors, whether in union with fellow prisoners or other persons.

Article 78. If prisoners of war, having given no pledge nor made any promise on their honor, forcibly or otherwise escape, and are captured again in battle after having rejoined their own army, they shall not be punished for their escape, but shall be treated as simple prisoners of war, although they will be subjected to stricter confinement.

Article 79. Every captured wounded enemy shall be medically treated, according to the ability of the medical staff.

Article 80. Honorable men, when captured, will abstain from giving to the enemy information concerning their own army, and the modern law of war permits no longer the use of any violence against prisoners in order to extort the desired information or to punish them for having given false information.

SECTION IV. Partisans—Armed enemies not belonging to the hostile army—Scouts—Armed prowlers—War-rebels.

Article 81. Partisans are soldiers armed and wearing the uniform of their army, but belonging to a corps which acts detached from the main body for the purpose of making inroads into the territory occupied by the enemy. If captured, they are entitled to all the privileges of the prisoner of war.

Article 82. Men, or squads of men, who commit hostilities, whether by fighting, or inroads for destruction or plunder, or by raids of any kind, without commission, without being part and portion of the organized hostile army, and without sharing continuously in the war, but who do so with intermitting returns to their homes and avocations, or with the occasional assumption of the semblance of peaceful pursuits, divesting themselves of the character or appearance of soldiers—such men, or squads of men, are not public enemies, and, therefore, if captured, are not entitled to the privileges of prisoners of war, but shall be treated summarily as highway robbers or pirates.

Article 83. Scouts, or single soldiers, if disguised in the dress of the country or in the uniform of the army hostile to their own, employed in obtaining information, if found within or lurking about the lines of the captor, are treated as spies, and suffer death.

Article 84. Armed prowlers, by whatever names they may be called, or persons of the enemy's territory, who steal within the lines of the hostile army for the purpose of robbing, killing, or of destroying bridges, roads or canals, or of robbing or destroying the mail, or of cutting the telegraph wires, are not entitled to the privileges of the prisoner of war.

Article 85. War-rebels are persons within an occupied territory who rise in arms against the occupying or conquering army, or against the authorities established by the same. If captured, they may suffer death, whether they rise singly, in small or large bands, and whether called upon to do so by their own, but expelled, government or not. They are not prisoners of war; nor are they if discovered and secured before their conspiracy has matured to an actual rising or armed violence.

SECTION V. Safe-conduct—Spies—War-traitors—Captured messengers—Abuse of the flag of truce.

Article 86. All intercourse between the territories occupied by belligerent armies, whether by traffic, by letter, by travel, or in any other way, ceases. This is the general rule, to be observed without special proclamation. Exceptions to this rule, whether by safe-conduct, or permission to trade on a small or large scale, or by exchanging mails, or by travel from one territory into the other, can take place only according to agreement approved by the government, or by the highest military authority. Contraventions of this rule are highly punishable.

Article 87. Ambassadors, and all other diplomatic agents of neutral powers, accredited to the enemy, may receive safe-conducts through the territories occupied by the belligerents, unless there are military reasons to the contrary, and unless they may reach the place of their destination conveniently by another route. It implies no international affront if the safe-conduct is declined. Such passes are usually given by the supreme authority of the State, and not by subordinate officers.

Article 88. A spy is a person who secretly, in disguise or under false pretense, seeks information with the intention of communicating it to the enemy. The spy is punishable with death by hanging by the neck, whether or not he succeed in obtaining the information or in conveying it to the enemy.

Article 89. If a citizen of the United States obtains information in a legitimate manner, and betrays it to the enemy, be he a military or civil officer, or a private citizen, he shall suffer death.

Article 90. A traitor under the law of war, or a war-traitor, is a person in a place or district under Martial Law who, unauthorized by the military commander, gives information of any kind to the enemy, or holds intercourse with him.

Article 91. The war-traitor is always severely punished. If his offense consists in betraying to the enemy anything concerning the condition, safety, operations, or plans of the troops holding or occupying the place or district, his punishment is death.

Article 92. If the citizen or subject of a country or place invaded or conquered gives information to his own government, from which he is separated by the hostile army, or to the army of his government, he is a war-traitor, and death is the penalty of his offense.

Article 93. All armies in the field stand in need of guides, and impress them if they cannot obtain them otherwise.

Article 94. No person having been forced by the enemy to serve as guide is punishable for having done so.

Article 95. If a citizen of a hostile and invaded district voluntarily serves as a guide to the enemy, or offers to do so, he is deemed a war-traitor, and shall suffer death.

Article 96. A citizen serving voluntarily as a guide against his own country commits treason, and will be dealt with according to the law of his country.

Article 97. Guides, when it is clearly proved that they have misled intentionally, may be put to death.

Article 98. AU unauthorized or secret communication with the enemy is considered treasonable by the law of war. Foreign residents in an invaded or occupied territory, or foreign visitors in the same, can claim no immunity from this law. They may communicate with foreign parts, or with the inhabitants of the hostile country, so far as the military authority permits, but no further. Instant expulsion from the occupied territory would be the very least punishment for the infraction of this rule.

Article 99. A messenger carrying written dispatches or verbal messages from one portion of the army, or from a besieged place, to another portion of the same army, or its government, if armed, and in the uniform of his army, and if captured, while doing so, in the territory occupied by the enemy, is treated by the captor as a prisoner of war. If not in uniform, nor a soldier, the circumstances connected with his capture must determine the disposition that shall be made of him.

Article 100. A messenger or agent who attempts to steal through the territory occupied by the enemy, to further, in any manner, the interests of the enemy, if captured, is not entitled to the privileges of the prisoner of war, and may be dealt with according to the circumstances of the case.

Article 101. While deception in war is admitted as a just and necessary means of hostility, and is consistent with honorable warfare, the common law of war allows even capital punishment for clandestine or treacherous attempts to injure an enemy, because they are so dangerous, and it is difficult to guard against them.

Article 102. The law of war, like the criminal law regarding other offenses, makes no difference on account of the difference of sexes, concerning the spy, the war-traitor, or the war-rebel.

Article 103. Spies, war-traitors, and war-rebels are not exchanged according to the common law of war. The exchange of such persons would require a special cartel, authorized by the government, or, at a great distance from it, by the chief commander of the army in the field.

Article 104. A successful spy or war-traitor, safely returned to his own army, and afterwards captured as an enemy, is not subject to punishment for his acts as a spy or war-traitor, but he may be held in closer custody as a person individually dangerous.

SECTION VI. Exchange of prisoners—Flags of truce—Flags of protection.

Article 105. Exchanges of prisoners take place—number for number—rank for rank wounded for wounded—with added condition for added condition—such, for instance, as not to serve for a certain period.

Article 106. In exchanging prisoners of war, such numbers of persons of inferior rank may be substituted as an equivalent for one of superior rank as may be agreed upon by cartel, which requires the sanction of the government, or of the commander of the army in the field.

Article 107. A prisoner of war is in honor bound truly to state to the captor his rank; and he is not to assume a lower rank than belongs to him, in order to cause a more advantageous exchange, nor a higher rank, for the purpose of obtaining better treatment. Offenses to the contrary have been justly punished by the commanders of released prisoners, and may be good cause for refusing to release such prisoners.

Article 108. The surplus number of prisoners of war remaining after an exchange has taken place is sometimes released either for the payment of a stipulated sum of money, or, in urgent cases, of provision, clothing, or other necessaries. Such arrangement, however, requires the sanction of the highest authority.

Article 109. The exchange of prisoners of war is an act of convenience to both belligerents. If no general cartel has been concluded, it cannot be demanded by either of them. No belligerent is obliged to exchange prisoners of war. A cartel is voidable as soon as either party has violated it.

Article 110. No exchange of prisoners shall be made

except after complete capture, and after an accurate account of them, and a list of the captured officers, has been taken.

Article 111. The bearer of a flag of truce cannot insist upon being admitted. He must always be admitted with great caution. Unnecessary frequency is carefully to be avoided.

Article 112. If the bearer of a flag of truce offer himself during an engagement, he can be admitted as a very rare exception only. It is no breach of good faith to retain such flag of truce, if admitted during the engagement. Firing is not required to cease on the appearance of a flag of truce in battle.

Article 113. If the bearer of a flag of truce, presenting himself during an engagement, is killed or wounded, it furnishes no ground of complaint whatever.

Article 114. If it be discovered, and fairly proved, that a flag of truce has been abused for surreptitiously obtaining military knowledge, the bearer of the flag thus abusing his sacred character is deemed a spy. So sacred is the character of a flag of truce, and so necessary is its sacredness, that while its abuse is an especially heinous offense, great caution is requisite, on the other hand, in convicting the bearer of a flag of truce as a spy.

Article 115. It is customary to designate by certain flags (usually yellow) the hospitals in places which are shelled, so that the besieging enemy may avoid firing on them. The same has been done in battles, when hospitals are situated within the field of the engagement.

Article 116. Honorable belligerents often request that the hospitals within the territory of the enemy may be designated, so that they may be spared. An honorable belligerent allows himself to be guided by flags or signals of protection as much as the contingencies and the necessities of the fight will permit.

Article 117. It is justly considered an act of bad faith, of infamy or fiendishness, to deceive the enemy by flags of protection. Such act of bad faith may be good cause for refusing to respect such flags.

Article 118. The besieging belligerent has sometimes requested the besieged to designate the buildings containing collections of works of art, scientific museums, astronomical observatories, or precious libraries, so that their destruction may be avoided as much as possible.

SECTION VII. Parole.

Article 119. Prisoners of war may be released from captivity by exchange, and, under certain circumstances, also by parole.

Article 120. The term Parole designates the pledge of individual good faith and honor to do, or to omit doing, certain acts after he who gives his parole shall have been dismissed, wholly or partially, from the power of the captor.

Article 121. The pledge of the parole is always an individual, but not a private act.

Article 122. The parole applies chiefly to prisoners of war whom the captor allows to return to their country, or to live in greater freedom within the captor's country or territory, on conditions stated in the parole.

Article 123. Release of prisoners of war by exchange is the general rule; release by parole is the exception.

Article 124. Breaking the parole is punished with death when the person breaking the parole is captured again. Accurate lists, therefore, of the paroled persons must be kept by the belligerents.

Article 125. When paroles are given and received there must be an exchange of two written documents, in which the name and rank of the paroled individuals are accurately and truthfully stated.

Article 126. Commissioned officers only are allowed to give their parole, and they can give it only with the permission of their superior, as long as a superior in rank is within reach.

Article 127. No noncommissioned officer or private can give his parole except through an officer. Individual paroles not given through an officer are not only void, but subject the individuals giving them to the punishment of death as deserters. The only admissible exception is where individuals, properly separated from their commands, have suffered long confinement without the possibility of being paroled through an officer.

Article 128. No paroling on the battlefield; no paroling of entire bodies of troops after a battle; and no dismissal of large numbers of prisoners, with a general declaration that they are paroled, is permitted, or of any value.

Article 129. In capitulations for the surrender of strong places or fortified camps the commanding officer, in cases of urgent necessity, may agree that the troops under his command shall not fight again during the war, unless exchanged.

Article 130. The usual pledge given in the parole is not to serve during the existing war, unless exchanged. This pledge refers only to the active service in the field, against the paroling belligerent or his allies actively engaged in the same war. These cases of breaking the parole are patent acts, and can be visited with the punishment of death; but the pledge does not refer to internal service, such as recruiting or drilling the recruits, fortifying places not besieged, quelling civil commotions, fighting against belligerents unconnected with the paroling belligerents, or to civil or diplomatic service for which the paroled officer may be employed.

Article 131. If the government does not approve of the parole, the paroled officer must return into captivity, and should the enemy refuse to receive him, he is free of his parole.

Article 132. A belligerent government may declare,

by a general order, whether it will allow paroling, and on what conditions it will allow it. Such order is communicated to the enemy.

Article 133. No prisoner of war can be forced by the hostile government to parole himself, and no government is obliged to parole prisoners of war, or to parole all captured officers, if it paroles any. As the pledging of the parole is an individual act, so is paroling, on the other hand, an act of choice on the part of the belligerent.

Article 134. The commander of an occupying army may require of the civil officers of the enemy, and of its citizens, any pledge he may consider necessary for the safety or security of his army, and upon their failure to give it he may arrest, confine, or detain them.

SECTION VIII. Armistice—Capitulation.

Article 135. An armistice is the cessation of active hostilities for a period agreed between belligerents. It must be agreed upon in writing, and duly ratified by the highest authorities of the contending parties.

Article 136. If an armistice be declared, without conditions, it extends no further than to require a total cessation of hostilities along the front of both belligerents. If conditions be agreed upon, they should be clearly expressed, and must be rigidly adhered to by both parties. If either party violates any express condition, the armistice may be declared null and void by the other.

Article 137. An armistice may be general, and valid for all points and lines of the belligerents, or special, that is, referring to certain troops or certain localities only. An armistice may be concluded for a definite time; or for an indefinite time, during which either belligerent may resume hostilities on giving the notice agreed upon to the other.

Article 138. The motives which induce the one or the other belligerent to conclude an armistice, whether it be expected to be preliminary to a treaty of peace, or to prepare during the armistice for a more vigorous prosecution of the war, does in no way affect the character of the armistice itself.

Article 139. An armistice is binding upon the belligerents from the day of the agreed commencement; but the officers of the armies are responsible from the day only when they receive official information of its existence.

Article 140. Commanding officers have the right to conclude armistices binding on the district over which their command extends, but such armistice is subject to the ratification of the superior authority, and ceases so soon as it is made known to the enemy that the armistice is not ratified, even if a certain time for the elapsing between giving notice of cessation and the resumption of hostilities should have been stipulated for.

Article 141. It is incumbent upon the contracting parties of an armistice to stipulate what intercourse of persons or traffic between the inhabitants of the territories occupied by the hostile armies shall be allowed, if any. If nothing is stipulated the intercourse remains suspended, as during actual hostilities.

Article 142. An armistice is not a partial or a temporary peace; it is only the suspension of military operations to the extent agreed upon by the parties.

Article 143. When an armistice is concluded between a fortified place and the army besieging it, it is agreed by all the authorities on this subject that the besieger must cease all extension, perfection, or advance of his attacking works as much so as from attacks by main force. But as there is a difference of opinion among martial jurists, whether the besieged have the right to repair breaches or to erect new works of defense within the place during an armistice, this point should be determined by express agreement between the parties.

Article 144. So soon as a capitulation is signed, the capitulator has no right to demolish, destroy, or injure the works, arms, stores, or ammunition, in his possession, during the time which elapses between the signing and the execution of the capitulation, unless otherwise stipulated in the same.

Article 145. When an armistice is clearly broken by one of the parties, the other party is released from all obligation to observe it.

Article 146. Prisoners taken in the act of breaking an armistice must be treated as prisoners of war, the officer alone being responsible who gives the order for such a violation of an armistice. The highest authority of the belligerent aggrieved may demand redress for the infraction of an armistice.

Article 147. Belligerents sometimes conclude an armistice while their plenipotentiaries are met to discuss the conditions of a treaty of peace; but plenipotentiaries may meet without a preliminary armistice; in the latter case, the war is carried on without any abatement.

SECTION IX. Assassination.

Article 148. The law of war does not allow proclaiming either an individual belonging to the hostile army, or a citizen, or a subject of the hostile government, an outlaw, who may be slain without trial by any captor, any more than the modern law of peace allows such intentional outlawry; on the contrary, it abhors such outrage. The sternest retaliation should follow the murder committed in consequence of such proclamation, made by whatever authority. Civilized nations look with horror upon offers of rewards for the assassination of enemies as relapses into barbarism.

SECTION X Insurrection—Civil War—Rebellion.

Article 149. Insurrection is the rising of people in arms against their government, or a portion of it, or against one or more of its laws, or against an officer or

officers of the government. It may be confined to mere armed resistance, or it may have greater ends in view.

Article 150. Civil war is war between two or more portions of a country or state, each contending for the mastery of the whole, and each claiming to be the legitimate government. The term is also sometimes applied to war of rebellion, when the rebellious provinces or portions of the state are contiguous to those containing the seat of government.

Article 151. The term rebellion is applied to an insurrection of large extent, and is usually a war between the legitimate government of a country and portions of provinces of the same who seek to throw off their allegiance to it and set up a government of their own.

Article 152. When humanity induces the adoption of the rules of regular war to ward rebels, whether the adoption is partial or entire, it does in no way whatever imply a partial or complete acknowledgement of their government, if they have set up one, or of them, as an independent and sovereign power. Neutrals have no right to make the adoption of the rules of war by the assailed government toward rebels the ground of their own acknowledgment of the revolted people as an independent power.

Article 153. Treating captured rebels as prisoners of war, exchanging them, concluding of cartels, capitulations, or other warlike agreements with them; addressing officers of a rebel army by the rank they may have in the same; accepting flags of truce; or, on the other hand, proclaiming Martial Law in their territory, or levying war-taxes or forced loans, or doing any other act sanctioned or demanded by the law and usages of public war between sovereign belligerents, neither proves nor establishes an acknowledgment of the rebellious people, or of the government which they may have erected, as a public or sovereign power. Nor does the adoption of the rules of war toward rebels imply an engagement with them extending beyond the limits of these rules. It is victory in the field that ends the strife and settles the future relations between the contending parties.

Article 154. Treating, in the field, the rebellious enemy according to the law and usages of war has never prevented the legitimate government from trying the leaders of the rebellion or chief rebels for high treason, and from treating them accordingly, unless they are included in a general amnesty.

Article 155. All enemies in regular war are divided into two general classes—that is to say, into combatants and noncombatants, or unarmed citizens of the hostile government. The military commander of the legitimate government, in a war of rebellion, distinguishes between the loyal citizen in the revolted portion of the country and the disloyal citizen. The disloyal citizens may further be classified into those citizens known to sympathize with the rebellion without positively aiding it, and those who, without taking up arms, give positive aid and comfort to the rebellious enemy without being bodily forced thereto.

Article 156. Common justice and plain expediency require that the military commander protect the manifestly loyal citizens, in revolted territories, against the hardships of the war as much as the common misfortune of all war admits. The commander will throw the burden of the war, as much as lies within his power, on the disloyal citizens, of the revolted portion or province, subjecting them to a stricter police than the noncombatant enemies have to suffer in regular war; and if he deems it appropriate, or if his government demands of him that every citizen shall, by an oath of allegiance, or by some other manifest act, declare his fidelity to the legitimate government, he may expel, transfer, imprison, or fine the revolted citizens who refuse to pledge themselves anew as citizens obedient to the law and loyal to the government. Whether it is expedient to do so, and whether reliance can be placed upon such oaths, the commander or his government have the right to decide.

Article 157. Armed or unarmed resistance by citizens of the United States against the lawful movements of their troops is levying war against the United States, and is therefore treason.

(Source: *General Orders No. 100, Adjutant General's Office, 1863.* Washington, D.C.: Government Printing Office, 1898.)

By the end of 1862, military volunteers in the North had decreased to the point that Union armies were facing a potentially dire manpower shortage. In response, the federal government passed "An Act for Enrolling and Calling Out the National Forces, and for Other Purposes" in March 1863, thus establishing a national draft. Under this legislation, Lincoln called for the first draft the following June. It was an unpopular measure from the start, and the administration was increasingly forced to deal with civil disturbances and military desertion. At the close of war, the War Department took stock of this last problem and came to some conclusions about who deserted and why. [See Conscription, U.S.A; Desertion]

2. Lincoln's Proclamation in Regard to Conscription (15 June 1863)

WAR DEPARTMENT,
June 15, 1863.

By the President of the United States of America.
A PROCLAMATION.
Whereas the armed insurrectionary combinations now existing in several of the States are threatening to make inroads into the States of Maryland, West Virginia, Pennsylvania, and Ohio, requiring immediately an additional force for the service of the United States:

Now, therefore, I, Abraham Lincoln, President of the United States, and Commander-in-Chief of the Army and Navy thereof, and of the militia of the several States when called into actual service, do hereby call into the service of the United States 100,000 militia from the States following, namely: From the State of Maryland, 10,000; from the State of Pennsylvania, 50,000; from the State of Ohio, 30,000; from the State of West Virginia, 10,000; to be mustered into the service of the United States forthwith, and to serve for the period of six months from the date of such muster into said service, unless sooner discharged; to be mustered in as infantry, artillery, and cavalry, in proportions which will be made known through the War Department, which Department will also designate the several places of rendezvous. These militia to be organized according to the rules and regulations of the volunteer service, and such orders as may hereafter be issued. The States aforesaid will be respectively under the enrollment act for the militia service rendered under this proclamation.

In testimony whereof, I have hereunto set my hand, and caused the seal of the United States to be affixed.

Done at the city of Washington, this fifteenth day of June, in the year of our Lord one thousand eight hundred and sixty-three, and of the Independence of the United States the eighty-seventh.

A. LINCOLN.

By the President:

WILLIAM H. SEWARD, *Secretary of State.*

(Source: U.S. War Department. *War of the Rebellion: A Compilation of the Official Records of the Union and Confederate Armies.* Ser. I, Vol. XXVII/3.)

3. By the President of the United States: A Proclamation. Respecting Soldiers Absent without Leave (10 March 1863)

EXECUTIVE MANSION,
March 10, 1863.

In pursuance of the twenty-sixth section of the act of Congress, entitled "An act for enrolling and calling out the national forces, and for other purposes," approved on the third day of March, in the year one thousand eight hundred and sixty-three, I, Abraham Lincoln, President and Commander-in-Chief of the Army and Navy of the United States, do hereby order and command that all soldiers enlisted or drafted in the service of the United States now absent from their regiments without leave shall forthwith return to their respective regiments.

And I do hereby declare and proclaim that all soldiers now absent from their respective regiments without leave, who shall, on or before the first day of April,

in the year one thousand eight hundred and sixty-three, report themselves at any rendezvous designated by the General Orders of the War Department, Number Fifty-eight, hereto annexed, may be restored to their respective regiments without punishment, except the forfeiture of pay and allowances during their absence; and all who do not return within the time above specified shall be arrested as deserters and punished as the law provides.

And whereas evil-disposed and disloyal persons at sundry places have enticed and procured soldiers to desert and absent themselves from their regiments, thereby weakening the strength of the armies and prolonging the war, giving aid and comfort to the enemy, and cruelly exposing the gallant and faithful soldiers remaining in the ranks to increased hardships and danger, I do therefore call upon all patriotic and faithful citizens to oppose and resist the aforementioned dangerous and treasonable crimes, and to aid in restoring to their regiments all soldiers absent without leave, and to assist in the execution of the act of Congress "for enrolling and calling out the national forces, and for other purposes," and to support the proper authorities in the prosecution and punishment of offenders against said act, and in suppressing the insurrection and rebellion.

In testimony whereof I have hereunto set my hand.

Done at the city of Washington this tenth day of March, in the year of our Lord one thousand eight hundred and sixty-three, and of the Independence of the United States the eighty-seventh.

ABRAHAM LINCOLN.

By the President:

EDWIN M. STANTON, *Secretary of War.*

(Source: U.S. War Department. *War of the Rebellion: A Compilation of the Official Records of the Union and Confederate Armies.* Ser. I, Vol. XXVII/3.)

4. U.S. Provost Marshall Report (17 March 1866)

WAR DEPT., *PROVOST-MARSHAL-GENERAL'S BUREAU,*
Washington, D.C., March 17, 1866.

Desertions.

It appears beyond dispute that the crime of desertion is especially characteristic of troops from large cities and of the districts which they supply with recruits. The ratio per thousand of desertions to credits throughout the loyal States is 62.51. In the State of New York it rises to 89.06, and in the small States near New York City it is still higher. In New Jersey it is 107.00; in Connecticut, 117.23; in New Hampshire, 112.22. Yet the general ratio of New England is but 74.24, the ratio

of Massachusetts being 66.68, that of Vermont 51.75, and that of Maine 43.90. In the West, where large cities are rare, the average ratio sinks to 45.51.

It is probable that a more minute examination of the statistics of the Army than has yet been made would' reveal the fact that desertion is a crime of foreign rather than native birth, and that but a small proportion of the men who forsook their colors were Americans. It is a notorious circumstance that the great mass of the professional bounty jumpers were Europeans. In general, the manufacturing States, as, for instance, Massachusetts, Connecticut, Rhode Island, New York, and New Jersey, rank high in the column of desertion; and this result is to be attributed not only to the fact that such States are dotted with towns and cities, but to the secondary fact that these towns and cities are crowded with foreigners. The respectable and industrious part of this population did, indeed, produce a mass of faithful troops; but with these were mixed a vast number of adventurers, unworthy of any country, who had no affection for the Republic, and who only enlisted for money.

In general, those States which gave the highest local bounties are marked by the largest proportion of deserters. The bounty was meant to be an inducement to enlistment; it became, in fact, an inducement to desertion and fraudulent re-enlistment.

It is a singular and at first sight a puzzling fact that two extreme Western States, Kansas and California, are distinguished, respectively, by the high ratios in desertion of 117.54 and 101.86. But it must be remembered that more than half the male population of Kansas entered the service, and that consequently its contingent contained an unusually large percentage of men whose presence was necessary to the subsistence and protection of their families. In further explanation of this fact something may be attributed to a lax state of discipline natural in border regiments serving for the most part in a somewhat irregular defense of their own frontiers. As for California, it is to be observed that a portion of the contingent of that State consisted of men levied in the large cities of the East or of adventurers from all quarters of the globe collected in the cosmopolitan thoroughfares of San Francisco.

(Source: U.S. War Department. *War of the Rebellion: A Compilation of the Official Records of the Union and Confederate Armies.* Ser. I, Vol. XXV/2.)

B. THE CONFEDERACY

Manpower shortages began to afflict the Confederacy after only a year into the war, when the spring of 1862 saw looming the expiration of twelve-month voluntary enlistments. Comprehending that dependence on volunteers would render insufficient forces, the Confederate Congress passed the first of three conscription acts on 16 April 1862, the first national military draft in American history. It was no more popular in the South than it would later be in the North, and the Confederacy soon was trying to cope with a serious problem of desertion, with both a stick and a carrot. [See Conscription, C.S.A.; Desertion]

1. CSA First Conscription Act
AN ACT TO FURTHER PROVIDE FOR THE PUBLIC DEFENCE
April 16, 1862.

Preamble.

In view of the exigencies of the country, and the absolute necessity of keeping in the service our gallant army, and of placing in the field a large additional force to meet the advancing columns of the enemy now invading our soil: Therefore

The Congress of the Confederate States of America do enact, That the President be, and he is hereby authorized to call out and place in the military service of the Confederate States, for three years, unless the war shall have been sooner ended, all white men who are residents of the Confederate States, between the ages of eighteen and thirty-five years at the time the call or calls may be made, who are not legally exempted from military service. All of the persons aforesaid who are now in the armies of the Confederacy, and whose term of service will expire before the end of the war, shall be continued in the service for three years from the date of their original enlistment, unless the war shall have been sooner ended: Provided, however, That all such companies, squadrons, battalions, and regiments, whose term of original enlistment was for twelve months, shall have the right, within forty days, on a day to be fixed by the Commander of the Brigade, to re-organize said companies, battalions, and regiments, by electing all their officers, which they had a right heretofore to elect, who shall be commissioned by the President: Provided further, That furloughs not exceeding sixty days, with transportation home and back, shall be granted to all those retained in the service by the provisions of this Act beyond the period of their original enlistment, and who have not heretofore received furloughs under the provisions of an Act entitled "An Act providing for the granting of bounty and furloughs to privates and non-commissioned officers in the Provisional Army," approved eleventh December, eighteen hundred and sixty-one, said furloughs to be granted at such times and in such numbers as the Secretary of War may deem most compatible with the public interest: and Provided, further, That in lieu of a furlough the commutation value in money of the transportation herein above granted, shall be paid to each private, musician, or non-commissioned officer who

may elect to receive it, at such time as the furlough would otherwise be granted: Provided further, That all persons under the age of eighteen years or over the age of thirty-five years, who are now enrolled in the military service of the Confederate States, in the regiments, squadrons, battalions, and companies hereafter to be re-organized, shall be required to remain in their respective companies, squadrons, battalions and regiments for ninety days, unless their places can be sooner supplied by other recruits not now in the service, who are between the ages of eighteen and thirty-five years; and all laws and parts of laws providing for the re-enlistment of volunteers and the organization thereof into companies, squadron, battalions, or regiments, shall be and the same are hereby repealed.

SEC. 2. Be it further enacted, That such companies, squadrons, battalions, or regiments organized, or in process of organization by authority from the Secretary of War, as may be within thirty days from the passage of this Act, so far completed as to have the whole number of men requisite for organization actually enrolled, not embracing in said organization any persons now in service, shall be mustered into the service of the Confederate States as part of the land forces of the same, to be received in that arm of the service in which they are authorized to organize, and shall elect their company, battalion, and regimental officers.

SEC. 3. Be it further enacted, That for the enrollment of all persons comprehended within the provisions of this Act, who are not already in service in the armies of the Confederate States, it shall be lawful for the President, with the consent of the Governors of the respective States, to employ State officers, and on failure to obtain such consent, he shall employ Confederate officers, charged with the duty of making such enrollment in accordance with rules and regulations to be prescribed by him.

SEC. 4. Be it further enacted, That persons enrolled under the provisions of the preceding Section, shall be assigned by the Secretary of War, to the different companies now in the service, until each company is filled to its maximum number, and the persons so enrolled shall be assigned to companies from the States from which they respectively come.

SEC. 5. Be it further enacted, That all Seamen and ordinary Seamen in the land forces of the Confederate States, enrolled under the provisions of this Act, may, on application of the Secretary of the Navy, be transferred from the land forces to the Naval service.

SEC. 6. Be it further enacted, That in all cases where a State may not have in the army a number of Regiments, Battalions, Squadrons or Companies, sufficient to absorb the number of persons subject to military service under this Act, belonging to such State, then the residue or excess thereof, shall be kept as a reserve, under such regulations as may be established by the Secretary of War, and that at stated periods of not greater than three months, details, determined by lot, shall be made from said reserve, so that each company shall, as nearly as practicable, be kept full: Provided, That the persons held in reserve may remain at home until called into service by the President: Provided, also, That during their stay at home, they shall not receive pay: Provided, further, That the persons comprehended in this Act, shall not be subject to the Rules and Articles of War, until mustered into the actual service of the Confederate States; except that said persons, when enrolled and liable to duty, if they shall wilfully refuse to obey said call, each of them shall be held to be a deserter, and punished as such, under said Articles: Provided, further, That whenever, in the opinion of the President, the exigencies of the public service may require it, he shall be authorized to call into actual service the entire reserve, or so much as may be necessary, not previously assigned to different companies in service under provision of section four of this Act; said reserve shall be organized under such rules as the Secretary of War may adopt: Provided, The company, battalion and regimental officers shall be elected by the troops composing the same: Provided, The troops raised in any one State shall not be combined in regimental, battalion, squadron or company organization with troops raised in any other States.

SEC. 7. Be it further enacted, That all soldiers now serving in the army or mustered in the military service of the Confederate States, or enrolled in said service under the authorizations heretofore issued by the Secretary of War, and who are continued in the service by virtue of this Act, who have not received the bounty of fifty dollars allowed by existing laws, shall be entitled to receive said bounty.

SEC. 8. Be it further enacted, That each man who may hereafter be mustered into service, and who shall arm himself with a musket, shot-gun, rifle or carbine, accepted as an efficient weapon, shall be paid the value thereof, to be ascertained by the mustering officer under such regulations as may be prescribed by the Secretary of War, if he is willing to sell the same, and if he is not, then he shall be entitled to receive one dollar a month for the use of said received and approved musket, rifle, shot-gun or carbine.

SEC. 9. Be it further enacted, That persons not liable for duty may be received as substitutes for those who are, under such regulations as may be prescribed by the Secretary of War.

SEC. 10. Be it further enacted, That all vacancies shall be filled by the President from the company, battalion, squadron, or regiment in which such vacancies shall occur, by promotion according to seniority, except in case of disability or other incompetency: Provided, however, That the President may, when in his opinion,

it may be proper, fill such vacancy or vacancies by the promotion of any officer or officers, or private or privates from such company, battalion, squadron or regiment who shall have been distinguished in the service by exhibition of valor and skill; and that whenever a vacancy shall occur in the lowest grade of the commissioned officers of a company, said vacancy shall be filled by election: Provided, That all appointments made by the President shall be by and with the advice and consent of the Senate.

SEC. 11. Be it further enacted, That the provisions of the first section of this Act, relating to the election of officers, shall apply to those regiments, battalions, and squadrons which are composed of twelve months and war companies combined in the same organization, without regard to the manner in which the officers thereof were originally appointed.

SEC. 12. Be it further enacted, That each company of infantry shall consist of one hundred and twenty-five, rank and file; each company of field artillery of one hundred and fifty, rank and file; each of cavalry, of eighty, rank and file.

SEC. 13. Be it further enacted, That all persons, subject to enrollment, who are not now in the service, under the provisions of this Act, shall be permitted, previous to such enrollment, to volunteer in companies now in the service.

APPROVED April 16, 1862.

(Source: *The Statutes at Large of the Confederate States of America, Commencing with the First Session of the First Congress; 1862. Public Laws of the Confederate States of America, Passed at the First Session of the First Congress; 1862.* Richmond: R.M. Smith, Printer to Congress, 1862.)

2. Confidential Circular, in Regard to CSA Desertion (17 July 1862)

CONFEDERATE STATES OF AMERICA,
WAR DEPARTMENT,
Richmond, July 17, 1862.

SIR: Our armies are so much weakened by desertions, and by the absence of officers and men without leave, that we are unable to reap the fruits of our victories and to invade the territory of the enemy. We have resorted to courts-martial and military executions, and we have ordered all officers employed in enrolling conscripts to arrest both deserters and absentees, and offered rewards for the former. In Virginia the sheriffs, constables, and jailers have also been employed by the permission of the Governor, but still the evil continues, and unless public opinion comes to our aid we shall fail to fill our ranks in time to avail ourselves of the weakness and disorganization of the enemy.

Their resources enable them to repair defeat with great rapidity, and they are more numerous now in Virginia than they were before the recent battles near Richmond.

I must therefore beg Your Excellency's aid in bringing back to our colors all deserters and absentees. If you will authorize their arrest by State officers, and bring to our assistance the powerful influence of public opinion in your State, we may yet cross the Potomac before a fresh army is raised to oppose us.

It is desirable that this cause of weakness should be concealed as much as possible from the enemy, but we cannot adopt measures to remove it without risking to some extent a disclosure of its existence.
Very respectfully,
GEO. W. RANDOLPH, *Secretary of War.*
(Sent to the Governors of States.)

(Source: U.S. War Department. *War of the Rebellion: A Compilation of the Official Records of the Union and Confederate Armies.* Ser. IV, Vol. II.)

3. General Orders No. 109 in Regard to CSA Desertion (11 August 1863)

ADJT. AND INSP. GENERAL'S OFFICE,
Richmond, August 11, 1863.

I. A general pardon is given to all officers and men within the Confederacy, now absent without leave from the army, who shall (within twenty days from the publication of the address of the President in the State in which the absentees may then be) return to their posts of duty.

II. All men who have been accused or convicted, and undergoing sentence for absence without leave, or desertion, except only those who have been twice convicted of desertion, will be returned to their respective commands for duty.
By order:
S. COOPER,
Adjutant and Inspector-General.

(Source: U.S. War Department. *War of the Rebellion: A Compilation of the Official Records of the Union and Confederate Armies.* Ser. I, Vol. XXX/4.)

4. Letter from Robert E. Lee to Jefferson Davis in re Conscription (27 July 1863)

HEADQUARTERS ARMY OF
NORTHERN VIRGINIA,
July 27, 1863.

His Excellency JEFFERSON DAVIS,
President of the Confederate States:
Mr. PRESIDENT: Feeling the importance of increasing the aggregate of our armies as rapidly and as much as possible, I beg leave to submit to Your Excellency a few considerations upon the subject.

It does not appear to me that the activity and efficiency of the conscription bureau is as great as it might be. From all that I can learn, the enrolling officers of the different districts and the medical examining officers are natives of the districts in which they operate. Besides this, the purchasing commissaries and quartermasters in the various counties, and at the posts in the interior, are usually assigned to duty in their own neighborhood. Thus the enrolling officer has every temptation to be careless and good-natured in the performance of his duty; the number of exemptions given by the medical officers is very great, and the number who are not exempted is again reduced in number by details for special duty with the assistant commissaries and quartermasters, who gather around them their friends and relatives, in order to keep them out of the army. A case has been reported to me of one captain and assistant commissary of subsistence, near Danville, who has 13 able-bodied conscripts in his employment, and I heard of others who have still more.

I would respectfully submit to Your Excellency whether, in the arrangements necessary under the late proclamation, something may not be done to remedy the defect of the former conscription, or whether an examination of former exemptions, and some diminution of the great number of details made from among the conscripts, might not materially promote the increase of the army.

There are many thousand men improperly absent from this army. I have caused to-day an appeal to be made to them to return at once to duty. I do not know whether it will have much effect, unless accompanied by the declaration of an amnesty. I doubted the policy of this, but I would respectfully submit that perhaps a general amnesty declared by Your Excellency might bring many delinquents back to the different armies of the Confederacy.

I am, with great respect, your obedient servant,

R. E. LEE, *General*.

(Source: U.S. War Department. *War of the Rebellion: A Compilation of the Official Records of the Union and Confederate Armies.* Ser. I, Vol. XXVII/3.)

5. An Act to Regulate the Business of Conscription, C.S.A. (1865)

The Congress of the Confederate States of America do enact, That the general officers commanding the reserves in each State shall be charged with the duty of directing and controlling the enforcement of the laws relating to conscription, exemption, and details therein; that the said officers shall report to the Secretary of War, through the Adjutant and Inspector General, who shall assign an assistant adjutant-general in his office to the special duty of receiving and arranging all

returns, and discharging such other duties as may be necessary in the enforcement of the conscription acts.

SEC. 2. That all applications for exemption and detail, except as hereinafter provided, shall be decided by the general officers having charge of the business of conscription in the several States. Appeals may be taken from their decisions to the Secretary of War, but during the pendency of such appeals the appellants shall be liable to military service.

SEC. 3. That there shall be assigned from the Invalid Corps, or from officers certified by the proper medical boards to be unfit for active service in the field, a sufficient number of enrolling officers, who shall report to and be under the immediate direction and control of the general officers conducting the business of conscription in the several States.

SEC. 4. That all conscripts shall be examined by the medical boards of the Army after joining the commands in the field to which they may be respectively assigned; and every discharge granted by an Army medical board shall be final, and shall relieve the party from all military service in the future, when the disability is permanent and the cause of it is set forth in the certificate of discharge.

SEC. 5. (a) That if any conscript shall furnish to the enrolling officer of his county a certificate, under oath, from a respectable physician or from any Army surgeon, that he is unable to travel to the command to which he may be assigned, without serious prejudice to his health, or that he is seriously maimed or manifestly unfit for field service, or shall present to such an enrolling officer a certificate of discharge on account of permanent disability heretofore granted, a furlough shall be granted to him until the next meeting of the medical board, hereinafter provided for.

SEC. 6. That there shall be assigned to each Congressional district a medical board, consisting of three surgeons, two of whom shall be Army surgeons, who, after due notice of the time and place of their meeting, shall visit each county of the district at least once in three months, and shall examine, for discharge or recommendation for light duty, all conscripts who have been furloughed under the provisions of the preceding section. Every discharge granted by the said medical board shall be final, and shall relieve the party from military service in the future, when the disability is permanent and the cause of it is set forth in the certificate.

SEC. 7. (b) It shall be the duty of all officers and others employed in the military service of the Confederate States, and not actually in the field nor attached to any army in the field, including quartermasters and commissaries, commanders of posts, provost-marshals, officers of the Ordnance, Niter and Mining, and Medical Bureaus, and others, to make certified returns under oath, every two months, to the

nearest conscript officer, of the names, ages, and physical condition of all persons employed in their service, which returns shall be forwarded to the general officer controlling conscription in the State.

SEC. 8. That for the enforcement of the duties imposed by this act upon the general officers controlling conscription in the several States, they may employ such detachments of the reserve forces as they may deem necessary.

SEC. 9. That the Bureau of Conscription and the camps of instruction are hereby abolished, and all rules and regulations of the War Department inconsistent with this act are hereby abrogated.

Approved March 7, 1865.

(Source: U.S. War Department. *War of the Rebellion: A Compilation of the Official Records of the Union and Confederate Armies*. Ser. IV, Vol. III.)

XXXIX. Balloons

Even before the shooting started, the U.S. War Department was hearing proposals that touted balloons as ideal for making battlefield observations. Among the most enthusiastic proponents was Thaddeus Lowe, who in June 1861 demonstrated his balloon in Washington. A report to Secretary of War Simon Cameron related the results. Eventually directed to construct a new balloon, Lowe on 29 August went aloft to observe Confederate activities just across the Potomac from Washington. Soon senior officers, including Major General George McClellan, were ascending to take in the view. [See Balloons]

1. Letter to Secretary of War Cameron Regarding Lowe's Balloon (21 June 1861)
SMITHSONIAN INSTITUTION, *June 21, 1861.*

Hon. SIMON CAMERON:
DEAR SIR: In accordance with your request, made to me orally on the morning of the 6th of June, I have examined the apparatus and witnessed the balloon experiments of Mr. Lowe, and have come to the following conclusions:

First. The balloon prepared by Mr. Lowe, inflated with ordinary street gas, will retain its charge for several days.

Second. In an inflated condition it can be towed by a few men along an ordinary road or over fields in ordinarily calm weather from the places where it is filled to another twenty or more miles distant.

Third. It can be let up into the air by means of a rope in a calm day to a height sufficient to observe the country for twenty miles around and more, according to the degree of clearness of the atmosphere. The ascent may also be made at night and the camp lights of the enemy observed.

Fourth. From experiments made here for the first time it is conclusively proved that telegrams can be sent with ease and certainty between the balloon and the quarters of the commanding officer.

Fifth. I feel assured, although I have not witnessed the experiment, that when the surface wind is from the east, as it was for several days last week, an observer in the balloon can be made to float nearly to the enemy's camp (as it is now situated, to the west of us), or even to float over it, and then return eastward by rising to a higher elevation. This assumption is based on the fact that the upper strata of wind in this latitude is always flowing eastward. Mr. Lowe informs me, and I do not doubt his statement, that he will on any day which is favorable make an excursion of the kind above mentioned.

Sixth. From all the facts I have observed and the information I have gathered I am sure that important information may be obtained in regard to the topography of the country and to the position and movements of an enemy by means of the balloon, and that Mr. Lowe is well qualified to render service in this way by the balloon now in his possession.

Seventh. The balloon which Mr. Lowe now has in Washington can only be inflated in a city where street gas is to be obtained. If an exploration is required at a point too distant for the transportation of the inflated balloon, an additional apparatus for the generation of hydrogen gas will be required. The necessity of generating the gas renders the use of the balloon more expensive, but this, where important results are required, is of comparatively small importance.

For these preliminary experiments, as you may recollect, a sum not to exceed $200 or $250 was to be appropriated, and in accordance with this Mr. Lowe has presented me with the inclosed statement of items, which I think are reasonable, since nothing is charged for labor and time of the aeronaut.

I have the honor to remain, very respectfully, your obedient servant,
JOSEPH HENRY,
Secretary Smithsonian Institution.

(Source: U.S. War Department. *War of the Rebellion: A Compilation of the Official Records of the Union and Confederate Armies*. Ser. III, Vol. I.)

2. Lowe's Balloon Contract (2 August 1861)
HEADQUARTERS DEPARTMENT OF NORTHEASTERN VIRGINIA,
Arlington, August 2, 1861.

Mr. T. S. C. LOWE, *Aeronaut:*
SIR: You are hereby employed to construct a balloon for military purposes capable of containing at least 25,000 cubic feet of gas, to be made of the best India silk, not inferior to the sample which is divided

between us, you retaining a part, with best linen network, and three guys of manilla cordage from 1,200 to 1,500 feet in length. The materials you will purchase immediately, the best the markets afford and at prices not exceeding ordinary rates; and the bills you will forward to me through Maj. Hartman Bache, chief of the Corps of Topographical Engineers. When these materials shall have been collected at Philadelphia, where the balloon is to be constructed, you will report to me, that I may send an officer of the corps to inspect them. You need not, however, wait for the inspecting officer, but go on rapidly with the work, with the understanding that it may be suspended, provided that upon examination the materials or work prove unsatisfactory.

Your compensation from the day of collecting the materials and during the time of making the balloon shall be $5 per day, provided that a reasonable time be allowed for the collection and ten days for making. From and after the day that the balloon shall be ready for inflation at Washington, D.C., your compensation will be $10 per day as long as the Government may require your services.

Inclosed herewith is an order authorizing the purchase of materials necessary for the operation with which you are charged.

Very respectfully,
A. W. WHIPPLE,
Captain, Topographical Engineers.

(Source: U.S. War Department. *War of the Rebellion: A Compilation of the Official Records of the Union and Confederate Armies.* Ser. III, Vol. I.)

XL. Civil Liberties

When the Lincoln administration suspended the writ of habeas corpus in the first weeks of the war, several pro-secessionist Marylanders, including John Merryman, were jailed without warrants. When Supreme Court Chief Justice Roger Taney declared that Lincoln had no authority to deprive citizens of this fundamental protection, Lincoln virtually ignored the decision. Although Congress would enlarge his power to suspend the writ, Lincoln was careful that arbitrary arrests did not become a wholesale event. The exigencies of the war (such as Lee's invasion of Pennsylvania in 1863) naturally impinged upon the administration's policy in regard to civil liberties, but at war's end the conundrum of balancing citizens' rights against the government's search for security again became the focus in the case of Lambdin Milligan. [See Civil Liberties, U.S.A; Ex parte Merryman; Ex parte Milligan]

1. Lincoln's Suspension of the Writ of Habeas Corpus (1861)

Maj. Gen. H. W. HALLECK,
Commanding in the Dept of Missouri:

GENERAL: As an insurrection exists in the United States and is in arms in the State of Missouri, you are hereby authorized and empowered to suspend the writ of habeas corpus within the limits of the military division under your command, and to exercise martial law as you find it necessary, in your discretion, to secure the public safety and the authority of the United States.

In witness whereof I have hereunto set my hand and caused the seal of the United States to be affixed, at Washington, this second day of December, A.D. 1861. ABRAHAM LINCOLN.
By the President:
WILLIAM H. SEWARD, *Secretary of State.*

(Source: U.S. War Department. *War of the Rebellion: A Compilation of the Official Records of the Union and Confederate Armies.* Ser. I, Vol. VIII.)

2. Chief Justice Taney's Opinion in *Ex Parte Merryman* (1861)

Circuit Court, District of Maryland. Petition for a writ of *habeas corpus.*

TANEY, C. J.: The application in this case for a writ of *habeas corpus* is made to me. under the 14th section of the Judiciary Act of 1789, which renders effectual for the citizen the constitutional privilege of the writ of *habeas corpus.* That act gives to the Courts of the United States, as well as to each justice of the Supreme Court, and to every District Judge, power to grant writs of *habeas corpus* for the purpose of an inquiry into the cause of commitment. The petition was presented to me at Washington, under the impression that I would order the prisoner to be brought before me there, but as he was confined in Fort McHenry, at the City of Baltimore, which is in my circuit, I resolved to hear it in the latter city, as obedience to the writ, under such circumstances, would not withdraw Gen. Cadwalader who had him in charge from the limits of his military command. . . .

A copy of the warrant or order, under which the prisoner was arrested, was demanded by his counsel, and refused. And it is not alleged in the return that any specific act, constituting an offence against the laws of the United States, has been charged against him upon oath; but he appears to have been arrested upon general charges of treason and rebellion, without proof, and without giving the names of the witnesses, or specifying the acts, which in the judgement of the military officer, constituted the crime. And having the prisoner thus in custody on these vague and unsupported accusations, he refuses to obey the writ of *habeas corpus,* upon the ground that he is duly authorized by the President to Suspend it.

The case, then, is simply this: A military officer residing in Pennsylvania issues an order to arrest a cit-

izen of Maryland, upon vague and indefinite charges, without any proof, so far as appears. Under this order his house is entered in the night; he is seized as a prisoner, and conveyed to Fort McHenry, and there kept in close confinement. And when a *habeas corpus* is served on the commanding officer, requiring him to produce the prisoner before a justice of the Supreme Court, in order that he may examine into the legality of the imprisonment, the answer of the officer is that he is authorized by the President to suspend the writ of *habeas corpus* at his discretion, and, in the exercise of that discretion, suspends it in this case, and on that ground refuses obedience to the writ.

As the case comes before me, therefore, I understand that the President not only claims the right to suspend the writ of *habeas corpus* himself, at his discretion, but to delegate that discretionary power to a military officer, and to leave it to him to determine whether he will or will not obey judicial process that may be served upon him.

No official notice has been given to the Courts of Justice, or to the public, by proclamation or otherwise, that the President claimed this power and had exercised it in the matter stated in the return. And I certainly listened to it with some surprise, for I had supposed it to be one of those points of constitutional law upon which there was no difference of opinion, and that it was admitted on all hands that the privilege of the writ could not be suspended except by act of Congress. . . .

The clause in the Constitution which authorizes the suspension of the privilege of the writ of *habeas corpus* is in the ninth section of the first article.

This article is devoted to the Legislative Department of the United States, and has not the slightest reference to the Executive Department. It begins by providing "that all legislative powers therein granted shall be vested in a Congress of the United States...." After prescribing the manner in which these two branches of the Legislative department shall be chosen, it proceeds to enumerate specifically the legislative powers which it thereby grants and legislative powers which it expressly prohibits, and at the conclusion of this specification, a clause is inserted giving Congress "the power to make all laws which may be necessary and proper for carrying into execution the foregoing powers, and all other powers vested by this Constitution in the Government of the United States or in any department or office thereof."

The power of legislation granted by this latter clause is by its word carefully confined to the specific objects before enumerated. But as this limitation was unavoidably somewhat indefinite, it was deemed necessary to guard more effectively certain great cardinal principles essential to the liberty of the citizen and to the rights and equality of the States by denying to Congress, in express terms, any power of legislation over them. It

was apprehended, it seems, that such legislation might be attempted under the pretext that it was necessary and proper to carry into execution the powers granted; and it was determined that there should be no room to doubt, where rights of such vital importance were concerned, and accordingly this clause is immediately followed by an enumeration of certain subjects to which the powers of legislation shall not extend; and the great importance which the framers of the Constitution attached to the privilege of the writ of *habeas corpus* to protect the liberty of the citizen, is proved by the fact that its suspension, except in cases of invasion and rebellion, is first in the list of prohibited power; and even in these cases the power is denied and its exercise prohibited unless the public safety shall require it. It is true that in the cases mentioned Congress is of necessity to judge whether the public safety does or does not require it; and its judgement is conclusive.

(Source: *Ex parte Merryman*, 17 Federal Cases, 144 1861.)

3. An Act to Suppress Insurrection, to Punish Treason and Rebellion, to Seize and Confiscate the Property of Rebels, and for Other Purposes (1862)

Be it enacted by the Senate and House of Representatives of the United States of America in Congress assembled, That every person who shall hereafter commit the crime of treason against the United States, and shall be adjudged guilty thereof, shall suffer death, and all his slaves, if any, shall be declared and made free; or, at the discretion of the court, he shall be imprisoned for not less than five years and fined not less than ten thousand dollars, and all his slaves, if any, shall be declared and made free; said fine shall be levied and collected on any or all of the property, real and personal, excluding slaves, of which the said person so convicted was the owner at the time of committing the said crime, any sale or conveyance to the contrary notwithstanding.

SEC. 2. *And be it further enacted*, That if any person shall hereafter incite, set on foot, assist, or engage in any rebellion or insurrection against the authority of the United States, or the laws thereof, or shall give aid or comfort thereto, or shall engage in, or give aid and comfort to, any such existing rebellion or insurrection, and be convicted thereof, such person shall be punished by imprisonment for a period not exceeding ten years, or by a fine not exceeding ten thousand dollars, and by the liberation of all his slaves, if any he have; or by both of said punishments, at the discretion of the court.

SEC. 3. *And be it further enacted*, That every person guilty of either of the offences described in this act shall be forever incapable and disqualified to hold any office under the United States.

SEC. 4. *And be it further enacted*, That this act shall

not be construed in any way to affect or alter the prosecution, conviction, or punishment of any person or persons guilty of treason against the United States before the passage of this act, unless such person is convicted under this act.

SEC. 5. *And be it further enacted,* That, to insure the speedy termination of the present rebellion, it shall be the duty of the President of the United States to cause the seizure of all the estate and property, money, stocks, credits, and effects of the persons hereinafter named in this section, and to apply and use the same and the proceeds thereof for the support of the army of the United States, that is to say:

First. Of any person hereafter acting as an officer of the army or navy of the rebels in arms against the government of the United States.

Secondly. Of any person hereafter acting as President, Vice-President, member of Congress, judge of any court, cabinet officer, foreign minister, commissioner or consul of the so-called confederate states of America.

Thirdly. Of any person acting as governor of a state, member of a convention or legislature, or judge of any court of any of the so-called confederate states of America.

Fourthly. Of any person who, having held an office of honor, trust, or profit in the United States, shall hereafter hold an office in the so-called confederate states of America.

Fifthly. Of any person hereafter holding any office or agency under the government of the so-called confederate states of America, or under any of the several states of the said confederacy, or the laws thereof, whether such office or agency be national, state, or municipal in its name or character: *Provided,* That the persons, thirdly, fourthly, and fifthly above described shall have accepted their appointment or election since the date of the pretended ordinance of secession of the state, or shall have taken an oath of allegiance to, or to support the constitution of the so-called confederate states.

Sixthly. Of any person who, owning property in any loyal State or Territory of the United States, or in the District of Columbia, shall hereafter assist and give aid and comfort to such rebellion; and all sales, transfers, or conveyances of any such property shall be null and void; and it shall be a sufficient bar to any suit brought by such person for the possession or the use of such property, or any of it, to allege and prove that he is one of the persons described in this section.

SEC. 6. *And be it further enacted,* That if any person within any State or Territory of the United States, other than those named as aforesaid, after the passage of this act, being engaged in armed rebellion against the government of the United States, or aiding or abetting such rebellion, shall not, within sixty days after public warning and proclamation duly given and made by the President of the United States, cease to aid, countenance, and abet such rebellion, and return to his allegiance to the United States, all the estate and property, moneys, stocks, and credits of such person shall be liable to seizure as aforesaid, and it shall be the duty of the President to seize and use them as aforesaid or the proceeds thereof. And all sales, transfers, or conveyances, of any such property after the expiration of the said sixty days from the date of such warning and proclamation shall be null and void; and it shall be a sufficient bar to any suit brought by such person for the possession or the use of such property, or any of it, to allege and prove that he is one of the persons described in this section.

SEC. 7. *And be it further enacted,* That to secure the condemnation and sale of any of such property, after the same shall have been seized, so that it may be made available for the purpose aforesaid, proceedings in rem shall be instituted in the name of the United States in any district court thereof, or in any territorial court, or in the United States district court for the District of Columbia, within which the property above described, or any part thereof, may be found, or into which the same, if movable, may first be brought, which proceedings shall conform as nearly as may be to proceedings in admiralty or revenue cases, and if said property, whether real or personal, shall be found to have belonged to a person engaged in rebellion, or who has given aid or comfort thereto, the same shall be condemned as enemies' property and become the property of the United States, and may be disposed of as the court shall decree and the proceeds thereof paid into the treasury of the United States for the purposes aforesaid.

SEC. 8. *And be it further enacted,* That the several courts aforesaid shall have power to make such orders, establish such forms of decree and sale, and direct such deeds and conveyances to be executed and delivered by the marshals thereof where real estate shall be the subject of sale, as shall fitly and efficiently effect the purposes of this act, and vest in the purchasers of such property good and valid titles thereto. And the said courts shall have power to allow such fees and charges of their officers as shall be reasonable and proper in the premises.

SEC. 9. *And be it further enacted,* That all slaves of persons who shall hereafter be engaged in rebellion against the government of the United States, or who shall in any way give aid or comfort thereto, escaping from such persons and taking refuge within the lines of the army; and all slaves captured from such persons or deserted by them and coming under the control of the government of the United States; and all slaves of such person found on [*or*] being within any place occupied by rebel forces and afterwards occupied by the forces of the United

States, shall be deemed captives of war, and shall be forever free of their servitude, and not again held as slaves.

SEC. 10. *And be it further enacted*, That no slave escaping into any State, Territory, or the District of Columbia, from any other State, shall be delivered up, or in any way impeded or hindered of his liberty, except for crime, or some offence against the laws, unless the person claiming said fugitive shall first make oath that the person to whom the labor or service of such fugitive is alleged to be due is his lawful owner, and has not borne arms against the United States in the present rebellion, nor in any way given aid and comfort thereto; and no person engaged in the military or naval service of the United States shall, under any pretence whatever, assume to decide on the validity of the claim of any person to the service or labor of any other person, or surrender up any such person to the claimant, on pain of being dismissed from the service.

SEC. 11. *And be it further enacted*, That the President of the United States is authorized to employ as many persons of African descent as he may deem necessary and proper for the suppression of this rebellion, and for this purpose he may organize and use them in such manner as he may judge best for the public welfare.

SEC. 12. *And be it further enacted*, That the President of the United States is hereby authorized to make provision for the transportation, colonization, and settlement, in some tropical country beyond the limits of the United States, of such persons of the African race, made free by the provisions of this act, as may be willing to emigrate, having first obtained the consent of the government of said country to their protection and settlement within the same, with all the rights and privileges of freemen.

SEC. 13. *And be it further enacted*, That the President is hereby authorized, at any time hereafter, by proclamation, to extend to persons who may have participated in the existing rebellion in any State or part thereof, pardon and amnesty, with such exceptions and at such time and on such conditions as he may deem expedient for the public welfare.

SEC. 14. *And be it further enacted*, That the courts of the United States shall have full power to institute proceedings, make orders and decrees, issue process, and do all other things necessary to carry this act into effect.

APPROVED, July 17, 1862.

(Source: *Statutes at Large, Treaties, and Proclamations of the United States of America*. Vol. 12. Washington, DC: 1863.)

4. An Act of the U.S. Congress Approved March 3, 1863, Relating to Habeas Corpus, &c.

Be it enacted by the Senate and House of Representatives of the United States of America in Congress assembled, That during the present rebellion the President of the United States whenever in his judgment the public safety may require it is authorized to suspend the privilege of the writ of *habeas corpus* in any case throughout the United States or any part thereof. And whenever and wherever the said privilege shall be suspended as aforesaid no military or other officer shall be compelled in answer to any writ of *habeas corpus to* return the body of any person or persons detained by him by authority of the President; but upon a certificate under oath of the officer having charge of any one so detained that such person is detained by him as a prisoner under authority of the President further proceedings under the writ of *habeas corpus* shall be suspended by the judge or court having issued the said writ so long as said suspension by the President shall remain in force and said rebellion continue.

SEC. 2. *And be it further enacted*, That the Secretary of State and the Secretary of War be and they are hereby directed as soon as may be practicable to furnish to the judges of the circuit and district courts of the United States and of the District of Columbia a list of the names of all persons, citizens of States in which the administration of the laws has continued unimpaired in the said Federal courts, who are now or may hereafter be held as prisoners of the United States by order or authority of the President of the United States or either of said Secretaries in any fort, arsenal or other place as State or political prisoners or otherwise than as prisoners of war; the said list to contain the names of all those who reside in the respective jurisdictions of said judges or who may be deemed by the said Secretaries or either of them to have violated any law of the United States in any of said jurisdictions, and also the date of each arrest—the Secretary of State to furnish a list of such persons as are imprisoned by the order or authority of the President acting through the State Department and the Secretary of War a list of such as are imprisoned by the order or authority of the President acting through the Department of War. And in all cases where a grand jury having attended any of said courts having jurisdiction in the premises after the passage of this act and after the furnishing of said list as aforesaid has terminated its session without finding an indictment or presentment or other proceeding against any such person, it shall be the duty of the judge of said court forthwith to make an order that any such prisoner desiring a discharge from said imprisonment be brought before him to be discharged; and every officer of the United States having custody of such prisoner is hereby directed immediately to obey and execute said judge's order; and in case he shall delay or refuse to do so he shall be subject to indictment for a misdemeanor, and be punished by a fine of not less than $500 and imprisonment in the common jail for a period not less than six months, in the discretion of the court: *Provided, however*, That no person

shall be discharged by virtue of the provisions of this act until after he or she shall have taken an oath of allegiance to the Government of the United States and to support the Constitution thereof, and that he or she will not hereafter in any way encourage or give aid and comfort to the present rebellion or the supporters thereof: *And provided, also,* That the judge or court before whom such person may be brought before discharging him or her from imprisonment shall have power on examination of the case and if the public safety shall require it shall be required to cause him or her to enter into recognizance with or without surety in a sum to be fixed by said judge or court to keep the peace and be of good behavior toward the United States and its citizens, and from time to time and at such times as such judge or court may direct appear before said judge or court to be further dealt with according to law as the circumstances may require. And it shall be the duty of the district attorney of the United States to attend such examination before the judge.

SEC. 3. *And be it further enacted,* That in case any such prisoners shall be under indictment or presentment for any offense against the laws of the United States and by existing laws bail or a recognizance be taken for the appearance for trial of such persons it shall be the duty of said judge at once to discharge such persons upon bail or recognizance for trial as aforesaid. And in case the said Secretaries of State and War shall for any reason refuse or omit to furnish the said list of persons held as prisoners as aforesaid at the time of the passage of this act within twenty days thereafter, and of such persons as hereafter may be arrested within twenty days from the time of the arrest, any citizen may after a grand jury shall have terminated its session without finding an indictment or presentment as provided in the second section of this act by a petition alleging the facts aforesaid touching any of the persons so as aforesaid imprisoned, supported by the oath of such petitioner or any other credible person, obtain and be entitled to have the said judge's order to discharge such prisoner on the same terms and conditions prescribed in the second section of this act: *Provided, however,* That the said judge shall be satisfied such allegations are true.

SEC. 4. *And be it further enacted,* That any order of the President or under his authority made at any time during the existence of the present rebellion shall be a defense in all courts to any action or prosecution, civil or criminal, pending or to be commenced for any search seizure, arrest or imprisonment made, done or committed or acts omitted to be done under or by virtue of such order, or under color of any law of Congress; and such defense may be made by special plea or under the general issue.

SEC. 5. *And be it further enacted,* That if any suit or prosecution, civil or criminal, has been or shall be commenced in any State court against any officer, civil or military, or against any other person for any arrest or imprisonment made or other trespasses or wrongs done or committed or any act omitted to be done at any time during the present rebellion by virtue or under color of any authority derived from or exercised by or under the President of the United States or any act of Congress, and the defendant shall at the time of entering his appearance in such court or if such appearance shall have been entered before the passage of this act, then at the next session of the court in which such suit or prosecution is pending file a petition stating the facts and verified by affidavit for the removal of the cause for trial at the next circuit court of the United States to be holden in the district where the suit is pending, and offer good and sufficient surety for his filing in such court on the first day of its session copies of such process and other proceedings against him, and also for his appearing in such court and entering special bail in the cause if special bail was originally required thereon, and it shall then be the duty of the State court to accept the surety and proceed no further in the cause or prosecution and the bail that shall have been originally taken shall be discharged. And such copies being filed as aforesaid in such court of the United States the cause shall proceed therein in the same manner as if it had been brought in said court by original process, whatever may be the amount in dispute or the damages claimed or whatever the citizenship of the parties, any former law to the contrary notwithstanding.

And any attachment of the goods or estate of the defendant by the original process shall hold the goods or estate so attached to answer the final judgment in the same manner as by the laws of such State they would have been holden to answer final judgment had it been rendered in the court in which the suit or prosecution was commenced. And it shall be lawful in any such action or prosecution which may be now pending or hereafter commenced before any State court whatever for any cause aforesaid after final judgment for either party to remove and transfer by appeal such case during the session or term of said court at which the same shall have taken place from such court to the next circuit court of the United States to be held in the district in which such appeal shall be taken in manner aforesaid. And it shall be the duty of the person taking such appeal to produce and file in the said circuit court attested copies of the process, proceedings and judgment in such cause; and it shall also be competent for either party within six months after the rendition of a judgment in any such cause by writ of error or other process to remove the same to the circuit court of the United States of that district in which such judgment shall have been rendered; and the said circuit court shall thereupon proceed to try and determine the facts and the law in

such action in the same manner as if the same had been there originally commenced, the judgment in such case notwithstanding. And any bail which may have been taken or property attached shall be holden on the final judgment of the said court in such action in the same manner as if no such removal and transfer had been made as aforesaid. And the State court from which any such action, civil or criminal, may be removed and transferred as aforesaid upon the parties giving good and sufficient security for the prosecution thereof shall allow the same to be removed and transferred, and proceed no further in the case: *Provided, however,* That if the party aforesaid shall fail duly to enter the removal and transfer as aforesaid in the circuit court of the United States agreeably to this act the State court by which judgment shall have been rendered and from which the transfer and removal shall have been made as aforesaid shall be authorized on motion for that purpose to issue execution and to carry into effect any such judgment the same as if no such removal and transfer had been made: *And provided also,* That no such appeal or writ of error shall be allowed in any criminal action or prosecution where final judgment shall have been rendered in favor of the defendant or respondent by the State court. And if in any suit hereafter commenced the plaintiff is non suited or judgment passed against him the defendant shall recover double costs.

SEC. 6. And be it further enacted, That any suit or prosecution described in this act in which final judgment may be rendered in the circuit court may be carried by writ of error to the Supreme Court whatever may be the amount of said judgment.

SEC. 7. *And be it further enacted,* That no suit or prosecution, civil or criminal, shall be maintained for any arrest or imprisonment made or other trespasses or wrongs done or committed or act omitted to be done at any time during the present rebellion by virtue or under color of any authority derived from or exercised by or under the President of the United States or by or under any act of Congress unless the same shall have been commenced within two years next after such arrest, imprisonment, trespass or wrong may have been done or committed or act may have been omitted to be done: *Provided,* That in no case shall the limitation herein provided commence to run until the passage of this act, so that no party shall by virtue of this act be debarred of his remedy by suit or prosecution until two years from and after the passage of this act.

(Source: U.S. War Department. *War of the Rebellion: A Compilation of the Official Records of the Union and Confederate Armies.* Ser. II, Vol. V.)

5. Proclamation of Martial Law in Baltimore and the Western Counties of Maryland (30 June 1863)

HEADQUARTERS EIGHTH ARMY CORPS, *Baltimore, Md., June 30, 1863.*

The immediate presence of a rebel army within this department and in the State of Maryland requires as a military necessity a resort to all the proper and usual means of defense and security.

This security is to be provided against known hostility and opposition to the lawful National Government from every quarter and in every form. Traitors and disaffected persons within must be restrained and made to contribute to the common safety, while the enemy in front is to be met and punished for his bold invasion.

Martial law is, therefore, declared and hereby established in the city and county of Baltimore, and in all the counties of the western shore of Maryland.

The general commanding gives assurance that this suspension of the civil government within the limits defined shall not extend beyond the necessities of the occasion. All the courts, tribunals, and political functionaries of State, county, and city authority are to continue in the discharge of their duties as in times of peace, only in no way interfering with the exercise of the predominant power assumed and asserted by the military authority. All peaceful citizens are required to remain quietly at their homes and in pursuit of their ordinary avocations, excepting as they may be possibly subject to call for personal service, or other necessary requisitions, for military purposes or uses hereafter. All seditious language or mischievous practices tending to the encouragement of the rebellion are especially prohibited, and will be promptly made the subject of observation and treatment.

Traitorous and dangerous persons must expect to be dealt with as the public safety may seem to require. "To save the country is paramount to all other considerations."

When the occasion for this proclamation passes by, no one will be more rejoiced than the commanding general that he can revoke his order, and return to the normal condition of a country at peace, and a Government sustained by a united and loyal people.

ROBT. C. SCHENCK, *Major-General.*

(Source: U.S. War Department. *War of the Rebellion: A Compilation of the Official Records of the Union and Confederate Armies.* Ser. I, Vol. XXVII/3.)

6. Justice Davis's Opinion in *Ex Parte Milligan* (1866)

DAVIS, J. . . . The importance of the main question presented by this record cannot be overstated; for it

involves the very framework of the government and the fundamental principles of American liberty.

During the late wicked rebellion, the temper of the times did not allow that calmness in deliberation and discussion so necessary to a correct conclusion of a purely judicial question. *Then,* considerations of safety were mingled with the exercise of power; and feelings and interests prevailed which are happily terminated. *Now,* that the public safety is assured, this question, as well as all others, can be discussed and decided without passion or the admixture of any element not required to form a legal judgment. We approach the investigation of this case, fully sensible of the magnitude of the inquiry and the necessity of full and cautious deliberation. . . .

The controlling question in the case is this: Upon the *facts* stated in Milligan's petition, and the exhibits filed, had the military commission mentioned in it *jurisdiction,* legally, to try and sentence him? Milligan, not a resident of one of the rebellious states, or a prisoner of war, but a citizen of Indiana for twenty years past, and never in the military or naval service, is, while at his home, arrested by the military power of the United States, imprisoned, and, on certain criminal charges preferred against him, tried, convicted, and sentenced to be hanged by a military commission, organized under the direction of the military commander of the military district of Indiana. Had this tribunal the legal power and authority to try and punish this man?

No graver question was ever considered by this court, nor one which more nearly concerns the rights of the whole people; for it is the birthright of every American citizen when charged with crime, to be tried and punished according to law. The power of punishment is alone through the means which the laws have provided for that purpose, and if they are ineffectual, there is an immunity from punishment no matter how great an offender the individual may be, or how much his crimes may have shocked the sense of justice of the country, or endangered its safety. By the protection of the law human rights are secured; withdraw that protection, and they are at the mercy of wicked rulers, or the clamor of an excited people. If there was law to justify this military trial, it is not our province to interfere; if there was not, it is our duty to declare the nullity of the whole proceedings. The decision of this question does not depend on argument or judicial precedents, numerous and highly illustrative as they are. These precedents inform us of the extent of the struggle to preserve liberty, and to relieve those in civil life from military trials. The founders of our government were familiar with the history of that struggle, and secured in a written Constitution every right which the people had wrested from power during a contest of ages. By that Constitution and the laws authorized by this question must be determined. The provisions of that instrument

on the administration of criminal justice are too plain and direct to leave room for misconstruction or doubt of their true meaning. Those applicable to this case are found in that clause of the original Constitution which says, "That the trial of all crimes, except in case of impeachment, shall be by jury" ; and in the fourth, fifth, and sixth articles of the amendments. . . .

Time has proven the discernment of our ancestors; for even these provisions, expressed in such plain English words, that it would seem the ingenuity of man could not evade them, are *now,* after the lapse of more than seventy years, sought to be avoided.

The Constitution of the United States is a law for rulers and people, equally in war and in peace, and covers with the shield of its protection all classes of men, at all times, and under all circumstances. No doctrine involving more pernicious consequences was; ever invented by the wit of man than that any of its provisions can be suspended during any of the great exigencies of government. Such a doctrine leads directly to anarchy or despotism, but the theory of necessity on which it is based is false; for the government, within the Constitution, has all the powers granted to it which are necessary to preserve its existence; as has been happily proved by the result of the great effort to throw off its just authority.

Have any of the rights guaranteed by the Constitution been violated in the case of Milligan? and if so, what are they?

Every trial involves the exercise of judicial power; and from what source did the military commission that tried him derive their authority? Certainly no part of the judicial power of the country was conferred on them; because the Constitution expressly vests it "in one Supreme Court and such inferior courts as the Congress may from time to time ordain and establish," and it is not pretended that the commission was a court ordained and established by Congress. They cannot justify on the mandate of the President, because he is controlled by law, and has his appropriate sphere of duty, which is to execute, not to make, the laws; and there is "no unwritten criminal code to which resort can be had as a source of jurisdiction."

But it is said that the jurisdiction is complete under the "laws and usages of war."

It can serve no useful purpose to inquire what those laws and usages are, whence they originated, where found, and on whom they operate; they can never be applied to citizens in states which have upheld the authority of the government, and where the courts are open and their process unobstructed. This court has judicial knowledge that in Indiana the federal authority was always unopposed, and its courts always open to hear criminal accusations and redress grievances; and no usage of war could sanction a military trial there for

any offense whatever of a citizen in civil life, in nowise connected with the military service. Congress could grant no such power; and to the honor of our national legislature be it said, it has never been provoked by the state of the country even to attempt its exercise. One of the plainest constitutional provisions was, therefore, infringed when Milligan was tried by a court not ordained and established by Congress, and not composed of judges appointed during good behavior.

Why was he not delivered to the circuit court of Indiana to be proceeded against according to law? No reason of necessity could be urged against it; because Congress had declared penalties against the offenses charged, provided for their punishment, and directed that court to hear and determine them. And soon after this military tribunal was ended, the circuit court met, peacefully transacted its business, and adjourned. It needed no bayonets to protect it, and required no military aid to execute its judgments. It was held in a state, eminently distinguished for patriotism, by judges commissioned during the rebellion who were provided with juries, upright, intelligent, and selected by a marshal appointed by the President. The government had no right to conclude that Milligan, if guilty, would not receive in that court merited punishment; for its records disclose that it was constantly engaged in the trial of similar offenses, and was never interrupted in its administration of criminal justice. If it was dangerous, in the distracted condition of affairs, to leave Milligan unrestrained of his liberty, because he "conspired against the government, afforded aid and comfort to rebels, and incited the people to insurrection," the *law* said, arrest him, confine him closely, render him powerless to do further mischief; and then present his case to the grand jury of the district, with proofs of his guilt, and, if indicted, try him according to the course of the common law. If this had been done, the Constitution would have been vindicated, the law of 1863 enforced, and the securities for personal liberty preserved and defended.

Another guarantee of freedom was broken when Milligan was denied a trial by jury. The great minds of the country have differed on the correct interpretation to be given to the various provisions of the federal Constitution; and judicial decision has been often invoked to settle their true meaning; but until recently no one ever doubted that the right of trial by jury was forfeited in the organic law against the power of attack. It is *now* assailed; but if ideas can be expressed in words, and language has any meaning, *this right*—one of the most valuable in a free country—is preserved to every one accused of crime who is not attached to the army, or navy, or militia in actual service. . . .

It is claimed that martial law covers with its broad mantle the proceedings of this military commission,

The proposition is this: that in a time of war the commander of an armed force (if, in his opinion, the exigencies of the country demand it, and of which he is to judge) has the power, within the lines of his military district, to suspend all civil rights and their remedies, and subject citizens as well as soldiers to the rule of *his will*; and in the exercise of his lawful authority cannot be restrained, except by his superior officer or the President of the United States.

If this position is sound to the extent claimed, then when war exists, foreign or domestic, and the country is subdivided into military departments for mere convenience, the commander of one of them can, if he chooses, within his limits, on the plea of necessity, with the approval of the Executive, substitute military force for, and to the exclusion of, the laws, and punish all persons, as he thinks right and proper, without fixed or certain rules.

The statement of this proposition shows its importance; for, if true, republican government is a failure, and there is an end of liberty regulated by law. Martial law, established on such a basis, destroys every guarantee of the Constitution, and effectually renders the "military independent of, and superior to, the civil power,"—the attempt to do which by the king of Great Britain was deemed by our fathers such an offense, that they assigned it to the world as one of the causes which impelled them to declare their independence. Civil liberty and this kind of martial law cannot endure together; the antagonism is irreconcilable; and, in the conflict, one or the other must perish.

This nation, as experience has proved, cannot always remain at peace, and has no right to expect that it will always have wise and humane rulers, sincerely attached to the principles of the Constitution. Wicked men, ambitious of power, with hatred of liberty and contempt of law, may fill the place once occupied by Washington and Lincoln; and if this right is conceded, and the calamities of war again befall us, the dangers to human liberty are frightful to contemplate. If our fathers had failed to provide for just such a contingency, they would have been false to the trust reposed in them. They knew—the history of the world told them—the nation they were founding, be its existence short or long, would be involved in war; how often or how long continued, human foresight could not tell; and that unlimited power, wherever lodged at such a time, was especially hazardous to freemen. For this, and other equally weighty reasons, they secured the inheritance they had fought to maintain, by incorporating in a written Constitution the safeguards which time had proved were essential to its preservation. Not one of these safeguards can the President, or Congress, or the judiciary disturb, except the one concerning the writ of habeas corpus.

It is essential to the safety of every government that, in a great crisis like the one we have just passed through, there should be a power somewhere of suspending the writ of habeas corpus. In every war, there are men of previously good character, wicked enough to counsel their fellow-citizens to resist the measures deemed necessary by a good government to sustain its just authority and overthrow its enemies; and their influence may lead to dangerous combinations. In the emergency of the times, an immediate public investigation according to law may not be possible; and yet the peril to the country may be too imminent to suffer such persons to go at large. Unquestionably, there is then an exigency which demands that the government, if it should see fit, in the exercise of a proper discretion, to make arrests, should not be required to produce the persons arrested in answer to a writ of habeas corpus. The Constitution goes no further. It does not say after a writ of habeas corpus is denied a citizen, that he shall be tried otherwise than by the course of the common law; if it had intended this result, it was easy by the use of direct words to have accomplished it. The illustrious men who framed that instrument were guarding the foundations of civil liberty against the abuses of unlimited power; they were full of wisdom, and the lessons of history informed them that a trial by an established court, assisted by an impartial jury, was the only sure way of protecting the citizen against oppression and wrong. Knowing this, they limited the suspension to one great right, and left the rest to remain forever inviolable. But, it is insisted that the safety of the country in time of war demands that this broad claim for martial law shall be sustained. If this were true, it could be well said that a country, preserved at the sacrifice of all the cardinal principles of liberty, is not worth the cost of preservation. Happily, it is not so.

It will be borne in mind that this is not a question of the power to proclaim martial law, when war exists in a community and the courts and civil authorities are overthrown. Nor is it a question what rule a military commander, at the head of his army, can impose on states in rebellion to cripple their resources and quell the insurrection. The jurisdiction claimed is much more extensive. The necessities of the service, during the late rebellion, required that the loyal states should be placed within the limits of certain military districts and commanders appointed in them; and, it is urged, that this, in a military sense, constituted them the theatre of military operations; and, as in this case, Indiana had been and was again threatened with invasion by the enemy, the occasion was furnished to establish martial law. The conclusion does not follow from the premises. If armies were collected in Indiana, they were to be employed in another locality, where the laws were obstructed and the national authority disputed. On *her* soil there was no hostile foot; if once invaded, that invasion was at an end, and with it all pretext for martial law. Martial law cannot arise from a *threatened* inva-

sion. The necessity must be actual and present; the invasion real, such as effectually closes the courts and deposes the civil administration.

It is difficult to see how the *safety* of the country required martial law in Indiana. If any of her citizens were plotting treason, the power of arrest could secure them, until the government was prepared for their trial, when the courts were open and ready to try them. It was as easy to protect witnesses before a civil as a military tribunal; and as there could be no wish to convict, except on sufficient legal evidence, surely an ordained and established court was better able to judge of this than a military tribunal composed of gentlemen not trained to the profession of the law.

It follows, from what has been said on this subject, that there are occasions when martial rule can be properly applied. If, in foreign invasion or civil war, the courts are actually closed, and it is impossible to administer criminal justice according to law, *then*, on the theatre of active military operations, where war really prevails, there is a necessity to furnish a substitute for the civil authority, thus overthrown, to preserve the safety of the army and society; and as no power is left but the military, it is allowed to govern by martial rule until the laws can have their free course. As necessity creates the rule, so it limits its duration; for, if this government is continued *after* the courts are reinstated, it is a gross usurpation of power. Martial rule can never exist where the courts are open, and in the proper and unobstructed exercise of their jurisdiction. It is also confined to the locality of actual war. Because, during the late rebellion it could have been enforced in Virginia, where the national authority was overturned and the courts driven out, it does not follow that it should obtain in Indiana, where that authority was never disputed, and justice was always administered. . . .

Mr. Chief Justice Chase, for himself and Mr. Justice Wayne, Mr. Justice Swayne, and Mr. Justice Miller, delivered an opinion in which he differed from the court in several important points, but concurred in the judgement in the case.

(Source: *Ex parte Milligan*, 4 Wallace, 2 1866.)

XLI. Emancipation

Emancipation was an incident of the American Civil War rather than a goal of it. Nevertheless, the existence of slavery in the South was plainly the main reason that the sectional conflict had become so politically unmanageable that secession and war had resulted. The following selections chart the sometimes eager, sometimes stumbling progress toward emancipation that began in the earliest months of the war, from John C. Frémont's proclamation (quickly rescinded by Lincoln) to the adoption of a confiscation policy, the budding

attempts at legislated emancipation, and the poignant account of a "contraband." At the center of this drama was the Emancipation Proclamation, which would not appear until the fall of 1862 and would not become official until 1 January 1863. Prior to its first issuance, Lincoln in the summer of 1862 was enjoined to the deed and was compelled to provide reasons for not achieving it. Even when the famous proclamation became official, it was controversial on both sides of the question. While abolitionists were disappointed that the emancipation policy would be only conditionally applied, others questioned its constitutionality to the point that Lincoln was forced to answer them. Unmistakable, however, was the thirst for freedom manifest in the continued influx of fugitives from bondage, a thirst that was impossible to ignore if the country was to have, as Lincoln had insisted at Gettysburg, "a new birth of freedom." The constitutional contemplation of slavery would be settled, at least, by the three constitutional amendments that followed the Civil War, although even these gestures would leave ambiguities regarding the rights and status of the freed people as citizens, questions that would remain for subsequent generations of Americans to try to resolve. [See Contrabands; Emancipation Proclamation]

1. John C. Frémont's Proclamation on Slaves (30 August 1861)

St. Louis, August 30, 1861
Headquarters Western Department.

Circumstances in my judgment are of sufficient urgency to render it necessary that the commanding General of this department should assume the administrative powers of the State. Its disorganized condition, helplessness of civil authority and the total insecurity of life, and devastation of property by bands of murderers and marauders, who infest nearly every county in the State, and avail themselves of public misfortunes, in the vicinity of a hostile force, to gratify private and neighborhood vengeance, and who find an enemy wherever they find plunder, finally demand the severest measures to repress the daily increasing crimes and outrages, which are driving off the inhabitants and ruining the State.

In this condition, the public safety and success of our arms require unity of purpose, without let or hindrance to the prompt administration of affairs. In order, therefore. to suppress disorders, maintain the public peace, and give security to the persons and property of loyal citizens, I do hereby extend and declare established martial law through out the State of Missouri. The lines of the army occupation in this State are for the present declared to extend from Leavenworth, by way of posts of Jefferson City, Rolla, and Ironton, to Cape Girardeau on the Mississippi River. All persons who shall be taken with arms in their hands within these lines shall be tried by court-martial, and if found guilty, will be shot. Real and personal property of those who shall take up arms against the United States, or who shall be directly proven to have taken an active part with their enemies in the field, is declared confiscated to public use, and their slaves, if any they have, are hereby declared free men.

All persons who shall be proven to have destroyed, after the publication of this order, railroad tracks, bridges, or telegraph lines, shall suffer the extreme penalty of the law. All persons engaged in treasonable correspondence, in giving or procuring aid to the enemy, in fermenting turmoil, and disturbing public tranquillity, by creating or circulating false reports, or incendiary documents, are warned that they are exposing themselves.

All persons who have been led away from *allegiance*, are *required* to return to their homes forthwith, Any such absence without sufficient cause, will be held to be presumptive evidence against them. The object of this declaration is to place in the hands of military authorities power to give instantaneous effect to the existing laws, and supply such deficiencies as the conditions of the war demand; but it is not intended to suspend the ordinary tribunals of the country, where law will be administered by civil officers in the usual manner, and with their customary authority, while the same can be peaceably administered.

The commanding General will labor vigilantly for the public welfare, and, by his efforts for their safety, hopes to obtain not only acquiescence, but the active support of the people of the country.

J. C. FREMONT,
Major-General Commanding.

(Source: Moore, Frank, ed. *The Rebellion Record: A Diary of American Events*, Vol. III. New York: G. P. Putnam, 1862.)

2. Letter from a Maryland Fugitive Slave to his Wife (12 January 1862)

Upton Hill [*Va.*] January the 12 1862

My Dear Wife it is with grate joy I take this time to let you know Whare I am i am now in Safety in the 14th Regiment of Brooklyn this Day i can Adress you thank god as a free man I had a little truble in giting away But as the lord led the Children of Isrel to the land of Canon So he led me to a land Whare fredom Will rain in spite Of earth and hell Dear you must make your Self content i am free from al the Slavers Lash and as you have chose the Wise plan Of Serving the lord i hope you Will pray Much and i Will try by the help of god To Serv him With all my hart I am With a very nice man and have All that hart Can Wish But My Dear I Cant express my grate desire that i Have to See you i trust the time Will Come When We Shal meet again And if We dont met on earth We Will Meet in heven Whare Jesas ranes Dear Elizabeth tell Mrs Own That i trust that She Will Continue Her kindness to you and that god Will Bless her on earth and Save her In grate eternity My

Acomplements To Mrs Owens and her Children may
They Prosper through life I never Shall forgit her kind-
ness to me Dear Wife i must Close rest yourself
Contented i am free i Want you to rite To me Soon as
you Can Without Delay Direct your letter to the 14th
Reigment New york State malitia Uptons Hill Virginea
In Care of Mr Cranford Comary Write my Dear Soon
As you C Your Affectionate Husban Kiss Daniel For me
John Boston
Give my love to Father and Mother

(Source: Letters Received, Ser. 12, Adjutant General's Office,
Record Group 94. National Archives, Washington, DC.)

3. David Hunter's Emancipation Order (General Orders, No. 7) (13 April 1862)

General Orders, No. 7.
Hdqrs. Department Of The South,
Fort Pulaski, Cockspur Island, April 13, 1862.

All persons of color lately held to involuntary service by
enemies of the United States in Fort Pulaski and on
Cockspur Island, Georgia, are hereby confiscated and
declared free, in conformity with law, and shall hereafter
receive the fruits of their own labor. Such of said persons
of color as are able-bodied and may be required shall be
employed in the quartermaster's department at the rates
heretofore established by Brig. Gen. T. W. Sherman.
By command of Maj. Gen. D. Hunter:

_____,
Assistant Adjutant-General.

(Source: U.S. War Department. *War of the Rebellion: A
Compilation of the Official Records of the Union and Confederate
Armies.* Ser. I, Vol. XIV [S# 20].)

4. The District of Columbia Emancipation Act (16 April 1862)

An Act for the Release of certain Persons held to
Service or Labor in the District of Columbia.

Be it enacted by the Senate and House of
Representatives of the United States of America in
Congress assembled, That all persons held to service or
labor within the District of Columbia by reason of
African descent are hereby discharged and freed of and
from all claim to such service or labor; and from and
after the passage of this act neither slavery nor involuntary servitude, except for crime, whereof the party
shall be duly convicted, shall hereafter exist in said
District.

Sec. 2. And be it further enacted, That all persons
loyal to the United States, holding claims to service or
labor against persons discharged therefrom by this act,
may, within ninety days from the passage thereof, but
not thereafter, present to the commissioners hereinafter mentioned their respective statements or petitions in writing, verified by oath or affirmation, setting
forth the names, ages, and personal description of such
persons, the manner in which said petitioners acquired
such claim, and any facts touching the value thereof,
and declaring his allegiance to the Government of the
United States, and that he has not borne arms against
the United States during the present rebellion, nor in
any way given aid or comfort thereto: Provided, That
the oath of the party to the petition shall not be evidence of the facts therein stated.

Sec. 3. And be it further enacted, That the President
of the United States, with the advice and consent of
the Senate, shall appoint three commissioners, residents of the District of Columbia, any two of whom
shall have power to act, who shall receive the petitions
above mentioned, and who shall investigate and determine the validity and value of the claims therein presented, as aforesaid, and appraise and apportion, under
the proviso hereto annexed, the value in money of the
several claims by them found to be valid: Provided,
however, That the entire sum so appraised and apportioned shall not exceed in the aggregate an amount
equal to three hundred dollars for each person shown to
have been so held by lawful claim: And provided, further, That no claim shall be allowed for any slave or
slaves brought into said District after the passage of this
act, nor for any slave claimed by any person who has
borne arms against the Government of the United
States in the present rebellion, or in any way given aid
or comfort thereto, or which originates in or by virtue
of any transfer heretofore made, or which shall hereafter be made by any person who has in any manner
aided or sustained the rebellion against the
Government of the United States.

Sec. 4. And be it further enacted, That said commissioners shall, within nine months from the passage
of this act, make a full and final report of their proceedings, findings, and appraisement, and shall deliver
the same to the Secretary of the Treasury, which report
shall be deemed and taken to be conclusive in all
respects, except as hereinafter provided; and the
Secretary of the Treasury shall, with like exception,
cause the amounts so apportioned to said claims to be
paid from the Treasury of the United States to the parties found by said report to be entitled thereto as aforesaid, and the same shall be received in full and complete compensation: Provided, That in cases where
petitions may be filed presenting conflicting claims, or
setting up liens, said commissioners shall so specify in
said report, and payment shall not be made according
to the award of said commissioners until a period of
sixty days shall have elapsed, during which time any
petitioner claiming an interest in the particular

amount may file a bill in equity in the Circuit Court of the District of Columbia, making all other claimants defendants thereto, setting forth the proceedings in such case before said commissioners and their actions therein, and praying that the party to whom payment has been awarded may be enjoined form receiving the same; and if said court shall grant such provisional order, a copy thereof may, on motion of said complainant, be served upon the Secretary of the Treasury, who shall thereupon cause the said amount of money to be paid into said court, subject to its orders and final decree, which payment shall be in full and complete compensation, as in other cases.

Sec. 5. And be it further enacted, That said commissioners shall hold their sessions in the city of Washington, at such place and times as the President of the United States may direct, of which they shall give due and public notice. They shall have power to subpoena and compel the attendance of witnesses, and to receive testimony and enforce its production, as in civil cases before courts of justice, without the exclusion of any witness on account of color; and they may summon before them the persons making claim to service or labor, and examine them under oath; and they may also, for purposes of identification and appraisement, call before them the persons so claimed. Said commissioners shall appoint a clerk, who shall keep files and [a] complete record of all proceedings before them, who shall have power to administer oaths and affirmations in said proceedings, and who shall issue all lawful process by them ordered. The Marshal of the District of Columbia shall personally, or by deputy, attend upon the sessions of said commissioners, and shall execute the process issued by said clerk.

Sec.6. And be it further enacted, That said commissioners shall receive in compensation for their services the sum of two thousand dollars each, to be paid upon the filing of their report; that said clerk shall receive for his services the sum of two hundred dollars per month; that said marshal shall receive such fees as are allowed by law for similar services performed by him in the Circuit Court of the District of Columbia; that the Secretary of the Treasury shall cause all other reasonable expenses of said commission to be audited and allowed, and that said compensation, fees, and expenses shall be paid from the Treasury of the United States.

Sec. 7. And be it further enacted, That for the purpose of carrying this act into effect there is hereby appropriated, out of any money in the Treasury not otherwise appropriated, a sum not exceeding one million of dollars.

Sec. 8. And be it further enacted, That any person or persons who shall kidnap, or in any manner transport or procure to be taken out of said District, any person or persons discharged and freed by the provisions of this act, or any free person or persons with intent to re-enslave or sell such person or person into slavery, or shall re-enslave

any of said freed persons, the person of persons so offending shall be deemed guilty of a felony, and on conviction thereof in any court of competent jurisdiction in said District, shall be imprisoned in the penitentiary not less than five nor more that twenty years.

Sec. 9. And be it further enacted, That within twenty days, or within such further time as the commissioners herein provided for shall limit, after the passage of this act, a statement in writing or schedule shall be filed with the clerk of the Circuit court for the District of Columbia, by the several owners or claimants to the services of the persons made free or manumitted by this act, setting forth the names, ages, sex, and particular description of such persons, severally; and the said clerk shall receive and record, in a book by him to be provided and kept for that purpose, the said statements or schedules on receiving fifty cents each therefor, and no claim shall be allowed to any claimant or owner who shall neglect this requirement.

Sec. 10. And be it further enacted, That the said clerk and his successors in office shall, from time to time, on demand, and on receiving twenty-five cents therefor, prepare, sign, and deliver to each person made free or manumitted by this act, a certificate under the seal of said court, setting out the name, age, and description of such person, and stating that such person was duly manumitted and set free by this act.

Sec. 11. And be it further enacted, That the sum of one hundred thousand dollars, out of any money in the Treasury not otherwise appropriated, is hereby appropriated, to be expended under the direction of the President of the United States, to aid in the colonization and settlement of such free persons of African descent now residing in said District, including those to be liberated by this act, as may desire to emigrate to the Republics of Hayti or Liberia, or such other country beyond the limits of the United States as the President may determine: Provided, The expenditure for this purpose shall not exceed one hundred dollars for each emigrant.

Sec. 12. And be it further enacted, That all acts of Congress and all laws of the State of Maryland in force in said District, and all ordinances of the cities of Washington and Georgetown, inconsistent with the provisions of this act, are hereby repealed.

Approved, April 16, 1862.

(Source: National Archives, Washington, D.C.)

5. Horace Greeley's "The Prayer of the Twenty Millions" (19 August 1862)

To ABRAHAM LINCOLN, president of the United States:

DEAR SIR: I do not intrude to tell you—for you must know already—that a great proportion of those who triumphed in your election, and of all who desire the unqualified suppression of the Rebellion now desolating our country, are sorely disappointed and deeply pained by the policy you seem to be pursuing with regard to the slaves of the Rebels. I write only to set succinctly and unmistakably before you what we require, what we think we have a right to expect, and of what we complain.

I. We require of you, as the first servant of the Republic, charged especially and preeminently with this duty, that you EXECUTE THE LAWS. Most emphatically do we demand that such laws as have been recently enacted, which therefore may fairly be presumed to embody the present will and to be dictated by the present needs of the Republic, and which, after due consideration have received your personal sanction, shall by you be carried into full effect, and that you publicly and decisively instruct your subordinates that such laws exist, that they are binding on all functionaries and citizens, and that they are to be obeyed to the letter.

II. We think you are strangely and disastrously remiss in the discharge of your official and imperative duty with regard to the emancipating provisions of the new Confiscation Act. Those provisions were designed to fight Slavery with Liberty. They prescribe that men loyal to the Union, and willing to shed their blood in her behalf, shall no longer be held, with the Nation's consent, in bondage to persistent, malignant traitors, who for twenty years have been plotting and for sixteen months have been fighting to divide and destroy our country. Why these traitors should be treated with tenderness by you, to the prejudice of the dearest rights of loyal men, We cannot conceive.

III. We think you are unduly influenced by the counsels, the representations, the menaces, of certain fossil politicians hailing from the Border Slave States. Knowing well that the heartily, unconditionally loyal portion of the White citizens of those States do not expect nor desire that Slavery shall be upheld to the prejudice of the Union—(for the truth of which we appeal not only to every Republican residing in those States, but to such eminent loyalists as H. Winter Davis, Parson Brownlow, the Union Central Committee of Baltimore, and to *The Nashville Union*)—we ask you to consider that Slavery is everywhere the inciting cause and sustaining base of treason: the most slaveholding sections of Maryland and Delaware being this day, though under the Union flag, in full sympathy with the Rebellion, while the Free-Labor portions of Tennessee and of Texas, though writhing under the bloody heel of Treason, are unconquerably loyal to the Union. So emphatically is this the case, that a most intelligent Union banker of Baltimore recently avowed his confident belief that a majority of the present Legislature of Maryland, though elected as and still professing to be Unionists, are at heart desirous of the triumph of the Jeff. Davis conspiracy;

and when asked how they could be won back to loyalty, replied "only by the complete Abolition of Slavery." It seems to us the most obvious truth, that whatever strengthens or fortifies Slavery in the Border States strengthens also Treason, and drives home the wedge intended to divide the Union. Had you from the first refused to recognize in those States, as here, any other than unconditional loyalty—that which stands for the Union, whatever may become of Slaver),those States would have been, and would be, far more helpful and less troublesome to the defenders of the Union than they have been, or now are.

IV. We think timid counsels in such a crisis calculated to prove perilous, and probably disastrous. It is the duty of a Government so wantonly, wickedly assailed by Rebellion as ours has been to oppose force to force in a defiant, dauntless spirit. It cannot afford to temporize with traitors nor with semi-traitors. It must not bribe them to behave themselves, nor make them fair promises in the hope of disarming their causeless hostility. Representing a brave and high-spirited people, it can afford to forfeit anything else better than its own self-respect, or their admiring confidence. For our Government even to seek, after war has been made on it, to dispel the affected apprehensions of armed traitors that their cherished privileges may be assailed by it, is to invite insult and encourage hopes of its own downfail. The rush to arms of Ohio, Indiana, Illinois, is the true answer at once to the Rebel raids of John Morgan and the traitorous sophistries of Beriah Magoffin.

V. We complain that the Union cause has suffered, and is now suffering immensely, from mistaken deference to Rebel Slavery. Had you, Sir, in your Inaugural Address, unmistakably given notice that, in case the Rebellion already commenced were persisted in, and your efforts to preserve the Union and enforce the laws should be resisted by armed force, you would recognize no loyal person as rightfully held in Slavery by a traitor, we believe the Rebellion would therein have received a staggering if not fatal blow. At that moment, according to the returns of the most recent elections, the Unionists were a large majority of the voters of the Slave States. But they were composed in good part of the aged, the feeble, the wealthy, the timid—the young, the reckless, the aspiring, the adventurous, had already been largely lured by the gamblers and negro-traders, the politicians by trade and the conspirators by instinct, into the toils of Treason. Had you then proclaimed that Rebellion would strike the shackles from the slaves of every traitor, the wealthy and the cautious would have been supplied with a powerful inducement to remain loyal. As it was, every coward in the South soon became a traitor from fear; for Loyalty was perilous, while Treason seemed comparatively safe. Hence the boasted unanimity of the South—a unanimity based on

Rebel terrorism and the fact that immunity and safety were found on that side, danger and probable death on ours. The Rebels from the first have been eager to confiscate, imprison, scourge and kill: we have fought wolves with the devices of sheep. The result is just what might have been expected. Tens of thousands are fighting in the Rebel ranks to-day whose, original bias and natural leanings would have led them into ours.

VI. We complain that the Confiscation Act which you approved is habitually disregarded by your Generals, and that no word of rebuke for them from you has yet reached the public ear. Fremont's Proclamation and Hunter's Order favoring Emancipation were promptly annulled by you; while Halleck's No. 3, forbidding fugitives from Slavery to Rebels to come within his lines— an order as unmilitary as inhuman, and which received the hearty approbation of every traitor in America— with scores of like tendency, have never provoked even your own remonstrance. We complain that the officers of your Armies have habitually repelled rather than invited approach of slaves who would have gladly taken the risks of escaping from their Rebel masters to our camps, bringing intelligence often of inestimable value to the Union cause. We complain that those who have thus escaped to us, avowing a willingness to do for us whatever might be required, have been brutally and madly repulsed, and often surrendered to be scourged, maimed and tortured by the ruffian traitors, who pretend to own them. We complain that a large proportion of our regular Army Officers, with many of the Volunteers, evince fat more solicitude to uphold Slavery than to put down the Rebellion. And finally, we complain that you, Mr. President, elected as a Republican, knowing well what an abomination Slavery is, and how emphatically it is the core and essence of this atrocious Rebellion, seem never to interfere with these atrocities, and never give a direction to your Military subordinates, which does not appear to have been conceived in the interest of Slavery rather than of Freedom.

VII. Let me call your attention to the recent tragedy in New-Orleans, whereof the facts are obtained entirely through Pro-Slavery channels. A considerable body of resolute, able-bodied men, held in Slavery by two Rebel sugar-planters in defiance of the Confiscation Act which you have approved, left plantations thirty miles distant and made their way to the great mart of the South-West, which they knew to be the indisputed possession of the Union forces. They made their way safely and quietly through thirty miles of Rebel territory, expecting to find freedom under the protection of our flag. Whether they had or had not heard of the passage of the Confiscation Act, they reasoned logically that we could not kill them for deserting the service of their lifelong oppressors, who had through treason become our implacable enemies. They came to us for

liberty and protection, for which they were willing to render their best service: they met with hostility, captivity, and murder. The barking o the base curs of Slavery in this quarter deceives no one—not even themselves. They say, indeed, that the negroes had no right to appear in New Orleans armed (with their implements of daily labor in the cane-field); but no one doubts that they would gladly have laid these down if assured that they should be free. They were set upon and maimed, captured and killed, because they sought the benefit of that act of Congress which they may not specifically have heard of, but which was none the less the law of the land which they had a clear right to the benefit of—which it was somebody's duty to publish far and wide, in order that so many as possible should be impelled to desist from serving Rebels and the Rebellion and come over to the side of the Union. They sought their liberty in strict accordance with the law of the land—they were butchered or re-enslaved for so doing by the help of Union soldiers enlisted to fight against slaveholding Treason. It was somebody's fault that they were so murdered—if others shall hereafter suffer in like manner, in default of explicit and public directions to your generals that they are to recognize and obey the Confiscation Act, the world will lay the blame on you. Whether you will choose to hear it through future History and 'at the bar of God, I will not judge. I can only hope.

VIII. On the face of this wide earth, Mr. President, there is not one disinterested, determined, intelligent champion of the Union cause who does not feel that all attempts to put down the Rebellion and at the same time uphold its inciting cause are preposterous and futile—that the Rebellion, if crushed out tomorrow, would be renewed within a year if Slavery were left in full vigor—that Army officers who remain to this day devoted to Slavery can at best be but half-way loyal to the Union—and that every hour of deference to Slavery is an hour of added and deepened peril to the Union. I appeal to the testimony of your Ambassadors in Europe. It is freely at your service, not at mine. Ask them to tell you candidly whether the seeming subserviency of your policy to the slaveholding, slavery-upholding interest, is not the perplexity, the despair of statesmen of all parties, and be admonished by the general answer.

IX. I close as I began with the statement that what an immense majority of the Loyal Millions of your countrymen require of you is a frank, declared, unqualified, ungrudging execution of the laws of the land, more especially of the Confiscation Act. That Act gives freedom to the slaves of Rebels coming within our lines, or whom those lines may at any time inclose—we ask you to render it due obedience by publicly requiring all your subordinates to recognize and obey it. The rebels are everywhere using the late anti-negro riots in the North, as they have long used your officers' treatment of negroes in the South, to convince the slaves that they have nothing to hope from a Union success—that we mean in that case to sell them into a bitter bondage to defray the cost of war. Let them impress this as a truth on the great mass of their ignorant and credulous bondsmen, and the Union will never be restored—never. We cannot conquer Ten Millions of People united in solid phalanx against us, powerfully aided by the Northern sympathizers and European allies. We must have scouts, guides, spies, cooks, teamsters, diggers and choppers from the Blacks of the South, whether we allow them to fight for us or not, or we shall be baffled and repelled. As one of the millions who would gladly have avoided this struggle at any sacrifice but that of Principle and Honor, but who now feel that the triumph of the Union is indispensable not only to the existence of our country but to the well-being of mankind, I entreat you to render a hearty and unequivocal obedience to the law of the land.

Yours,
Horace Greeley.
New York, August 19, 1862.

(Source: Hotner, Harlan Hoyt. *Lincoln and Greeley*. Urbana: University of Illinois Press, 1953.)

6. Lincoln's Reply to Greeley (22 August 1862)

Executive Mansion,
Washington, August 22, 1862.

Hon. Horace Greeley:

Dear Sir. I have just read yours of the 19th. addressed to myself through the New-York Tribune. If there be in it any statements, or assumptions of fact, which I may know to be erroneous, I do not, now and here, controvert them. If there be in it any inferences which I may believe to be falsely drawn, I do not now and here, argue against them. If there be perceptable in it an impatient and dictatorial tone, I waive it in deference to an old friend, whose heart I have always supposed to be right.

As to the policy I "seem to be pursuing" as you say, I have not meant to leave any one in doubt.

I would save the Union. I would save it the shortest way under the Constitution. The sooner the national authority can be restored; the nearer the Union will be "the Union as it was." If there be those who would not save the Union, unless they could at the same time *save* slavery, I do not agree with them. If there be those who would not save the Union unless they could at the same time *destroy* slavery, I do not agree with them. My paramount object in this struggle *is* to save the Union, and is *not* either to save or to destroy slavery. If I could save the Union without freeing *any* slave I would do it, and if I could save it by freeing *all* the slaves, I would do

it; and if I could save it by freeing some and leaving others alone I would also do that. What I do about slavery, and the colored race, I do because I believe it helps to save the Union; and what I forbear, I forbear because I do *not* believe it would help to save the Union. I shall do *less* whenever I shall believe what I am doing hurts the cause, and I shall do *more* whenever I shall believe doing more will help the cause. I shall try to correct errors when shown to be errors; and I shall adopt new views so fast as they shall appear to be true views.

I have here stated my purpose according to my view of *official* duty; and I intend no modification of my oft-expressed *personal* wish that all men everywhere could be free.

Yours,
A. Lincoln.

(Source: Basler, Roy P., ed. *Abraham Lincoln: His Speeches and Writings* [1946], pp. 651–652.)

7. Testimony of Capt. C. B. Wilder before the American Freedmen's Inquiry Commission [Excerpts] (9 May 1863)

[Fortress Monroe, Va.] May 9, 1863.

Question How many of the people called contrabands, have come under your observation?

Answer Some 10,000 have come under our control, to be fed in part, and clothed in part, but I cannot speak accurately in regard to the number. This is the rendezvous. They come here from all about, from Richmond and 200 miles off in North Carolina There was one gang that started from Richmond 23 strong and only 3 got through.

Q. In your opinion, is there any communication between the refugees and the black men still in slavery?

A. Yes Sir, we have had men here who have gone back 200 miles.

Q. In your opinion would a change in our policy which would cause them to be treated with fairness, their wages punctually paid and employment furnished them in the army, become known and would it have any effect upon others in slavery?

A. Yes—Thousands upon Thousands. I went to Suffolk a short time ago to enquire into the state of things there—for I found I could not get any foot hold to make things work there, through the Commanding General, and I went to the Provost Marshall and all hands—and the colored people actually sent a deputation to me one morning before I was up to know if we put black men in irons and sent them off to Cuba to be sold or set them at work and put balls on their legs and whipped them, just as in slavery; because that was the story up there, and they were

frightened and didn't know what to do. When I got at the feelings of these people I found they were not afraid of the slaveholders. They said there was nobody on the plantations but women and they were not afraid of them One woman came through 200 miles in Men's clothes. The most valuable information we received in regard to the Merrimack and the operations of the rebels came from the colored people and they got no credit for it. I found hundreds who had left their wives and families behind. I asked them "Why did you come away and leave them there?" and I found they had heard these stories, and wanted to come and see how it was. "I am going back again after my wife" some of them have said "When I have earned a little money" What as far as that?" "Yes" and I have had them come to me to borrow money, or to get their pay, if they had earned a months wages, and to get passes. "I am going for my family" they say." Are you not afraid to risk it?" "No I know the Way" Colored men will help colored men and they will work along the by paths and get through. In that way I have known quite a number who have gone up from time to time in the neighborhood of Richmond and several have brought back their families; some I have never heard from. As I was saying they do not feel afraid now. The white people have nearly all gone, the blood hounds are not there now to hunt them and they are not afraid, before they were afraid to stir. There are hundreds of negroes at Williamsburgh with their families working for nothing. They would not get pay here and they had rather stay where they are." "We are not afraid of being carried back," a great many have told us, and "if we are, we can get away again." Now that they are getting their eyes open they are coming in. Fifty came this morning from Yorktown who followed Stoneman's Cavalry when they returned from their raid. The officers reported to their Quartermaster that they had so many horses and fifty or sixty negroes. "What did you bring them for" "Why they followed us and we could not stop them." I asked one of the men about it and he said they would leave their work in the field as soon as they found the Soldiers were Union men and follow them sometimes without hat or coat. They would take best horse they could get and every where they rode they would take fresh horses, leave the old ones and follow on and so they came in. I have questioned a great many of them and they do not feel much afraid; and there are a great many courageous fellows who have come from long distances in rebeldom. Some men who came here from North Carolina, knew all about the [*Emancipation*] Proclamation and they started on the belief in it; but they had heard these stories and they wanted to know how it was. Well, I gave them the evidence and I have no doubt their friends will hear of it. Within the last two or three months the rebel guards have been doubled on the line and the officers and privates of the 99th New York between Norfolk and Suffolk have caught hundreds of fugitives and got pay for them.

Q. Do I understand you to say that a great many who have escaped have been sent back?

A. Yes Sir, The masters will come in to Suffolk in the day time and with the help of some of the 99th carry off their fugitives and by and by smuggle them across the lines and the soldier will get his $20. or $50.

(Source: Letters Received, Ser. 12, Record Group 94, Adjutant General's Office. National Archives, Washington, DC.)

8. The Emancipation Proclamation (1 January 1863)

By the President of the United States of America:
A Proclamation.

Whereas, on the twenty-second day of September, in the year of our Lord one thousand eight hundred and sixty-two, a proclamation was issued by the President of the United States, containing, among other things, the following, to wit: "That on the first day of January, in the year of our Lord one thousand eight hundred and sixty-three, all persons held as slaves within any State or designated part of a State, the people whereof shall then be in rebellion against the United States, shall be then, thenceforward, and forever free; and the Executive Government of the United States, including the military and naval authority thereof, will recognize and maintain the freedom of such persons, and will do no act or acts to repress such persons, or any of them, in any efforts they may make for their actual freedom.

"That the Executive will, on the first day of January aforesaid, by proclamation, designate the States and parts of States, if any, in which the people thereof, respectively, shall then be in rebellion against the United States; and the fact that any State, or the people thereof, shall on that day be, in good faith, represented in the Congress of the United States by members chosen thereto at elections wherein a majority of the qualified voters of such State shall have participated, shall, in the absence of strong countervailing testimony, be deemed conclusive evidence that such State, and the people thereof, are not then in rebellion against the United States."

Now, therefore I, Abraham Lincoln, President of the United States, by virtue of the power in me vested as Commander-in-Chief, of the Army and Navy of the United States in time of actual armed rebellion against the authority and government of the United States, and as a fit and necessary war measure for suppressing said rebellion, do, on this first day of January, in the year of our Lord one thousand eight hundred and sixty-three, and in accordance with my purpose so to do publicly proclaimed for the full period of one hundred days, from the day first above mentioned, order and designate as the States and parts of States wherein the people thereof respectively, are this day in rebellion against the United States, the following, to wit:

Arkansas, Texas, Louisiana, (except the Parishes of St. Bernard, Plaquemines, Jefferson, St. John, St. Charles, St. James Ascension, Assumption, Terrebonne, Lafourche, St. Mary, St. Martin, and Orleans, including the City of New Orleans) Mississippi, Alabama, Florida, Georgia, South Carolina, North Carolina, and Virginia, (except the forty-eight counties designated as West Virginia, and also the counties of Berkley, Accomac, Northampton, Elizabeth City, York, Princess Ann, and Norfolk, including the cities of Norfolk and Portsmouth), and which excepted parts, are for the present, left precisely as if this proclamation were not issued.

And by virtue of the power, and for the purpose aforesaid, I do order and declare that all persons held as slaves within said designated States, and parts of States, are, and henceforward shall be free; and that the Executive government of the United States, including the military and naval authorities thereof, will recognize and maintain the freedom of said persons.

And I hereby enjoin upon the people so declared to be free to abstain from all violence, unless in necessary self-defence; and I recommend to them that, in all cases when allowed, they labor faithfully for reasonable wages.

And I further declare and make known, that such persons of suitable condition, will be received into the armed service of the United States to garrison forts, positions, stations, and other places, and to man vessels of all sorts in said service.

And upon this act, sincerely believed to be an act of justice, warranted by the Constitution, upon military necessity, I invoke the considerate judgment of mankind, and the gracious favor of Almighty God.

In witness whereof, I have hereunto set my hand and caused the seal of the United States to be affixed.

Done at the City of Washington, this first day of January, in the year of our Lord one thousand eight hundred and sixty three, and of the Independence of the United States of America the eighty-seventh.

By the President: ABRAHAM LINCOLN.
WILLIAM H. SEWARD, Secretary of State.

(Source: National Archives, Washington, DC.)

9. Lincoln to General Hurlbut Regarding the Emancipation Proclamation [Excerpt] (31 July 1863)

EXECUTIVE MANSION,
Washington, July 31, 1863.

MY DEAR GENERAL HURLBUT: . . . I think it [the Emanicpation Proclamation] is valid in law, and will be so held by the courts. I think I shall not retract or repudiate it. Those who shall have tasted actual freedom I believe can never be slaves or *quasi* slaves again. For the rest, I believe some plan, substantially being gradual emancipation, would be better for both white and black. The Missouri plan, recently adopted, I do not object to on account of the time for ending the institution; but I am sorry the beginning should have been postponed for seven years, leaving all that time to agitate for the repeal of the whole thing. It should begin at once, giving at least the new-born a vested interest in freedom which could not be taken away. If Senator Sebastian could come with something of this sort from Arkansas, I, at least, should take great interest in his case; and I believe a single individual will have scarcely done the world so great a service. See him, if you can, and read this to him; but charge him to not make it public for the present. Write me again.
Yours, very truly,
A. LINCOLN.

(Source: U.S. War Department. *War of the Rebellion: A Compilation of the Official Records of the Union and Confederate Armies.* Ser. I, Vol. XXIV/3.)

10. Lincoln to James C. Conkling Regarding the Emancipation Proclamation [Excerpt] (26 August 1863)

EXECUTIVE MANSION,
Washington, August 26, 1863.

Hon. JAMES C. CONKLING:
MY DEAR SIR: . . . You dislike the emancipation proclamation; and perhaps would have it retracted. You say it is unconstitutional. I think differently. I think the Constitution invests its Commander-in-Chief with the law of war in the time of war. The most that can be said,—if so much,—is that slaves are property. Is there—has there ever been—any question that by the law of war, property, both of enemies and friends, may be taken when needed? And is it not needed whenever taking it, helps us, or hurts the enemy? Armies, the world over, destroy enemies' property when they cannot use it; and even destroy their own to keep it from the enemy. Civilized belligerents do all in their power to help themselves, or hurt the enemy, except a few things regarded as barbarous or cruel. Among the exceptions are the massacre of vanquished foes, and non-combatants, male and female.

But the proclamation, as law, either is valid, or is not valid. If it is not valid, it needs no retraction. If it is valid, it cannot be retracted, any more than the dead can be brought to life. Some of you profess to think its retraction would operate favorably for the Union. Why better *after* the retraction than *before* the issue? There was more than a year and a half of trial to suppress the rebellion before the proclamation issued, the last one

hundred days of which passed under an explicit notice that it was coming, unless averted by those in revolt, returning to their allegiance. The war has certainly progressed as favorably for us, since the issue of the proclamation as before. (I know, as fully as one can know the opinions of others, that some of the commanders of our armies in the field, who have given us our most important successes, believe the emancipation policy and the use of colored troops constitute the heaviest blow yet dealt to the rebellion, and that at least one of those important successes could not have been achieved when it was but for the aid of black soldiers. Among the commanders holding these views are some who have never had any affinity with what is called abolitionism, or with Republican party politics, but who hold them purely as military opinions. I submit these opinions as being entitled to some weight against the objections often urged that emancipation and arming the blacks are unwise as military measures, and were not adopted as such in good faith.) You say you will not fight to free negroes. Some of them seem willing to fight for you; but, no matter. Fight you, then, exclusively to save the Union. I issued the proclamation on purpose to aid you in saving the Union. Whenever you shall have conquered all resistance to the Union, if I shall urge you to continue fighting, it will be an apt time, then, for you to declare you will not fight to free negroes.

I thought that in your struggle for the Union, to whatever extent the negroes should cease helping the enemy, to that extent it weakened the enemy in his resistance to you. Do you think differently? I thought that whatever negroes can be got to do as soldiers, leaves just so much less for white soldiers to do, in saving the Union. Does it appear otherwise to you? But negroes, like other people, act upon motives. Why should they do anything for us, if we will do nothing for them? If they stake their lives for us, they must be prompted by the strongest motive—even the promise of freedom. And the promise being made, must be kept. . . .
Yours, very truly,
A. LINCOLN.

(Source: U.S. War Department. *War of the Rebellion: A Compilation of the Official Records of the Union and Confederate Armies.* Ser. III, Vol. III.)

11. Amendment XIII to the United States Constitution (1865)

Section 1. Neither slavery nor involuntary servitude, except as a punishment for crime whereof the party shall have been duly convicted, shall exist within the United States, or any place subject to their jurisdiction.

Section 2. Congress shall have power to enforce this article by appropriate legislation.

(Source: National Archives, Washington, DC.)

12. Amendment XIV to the United States Constitution (1868)

Section 1. All persons born or naturalized in the United States, and subject to the jurisdiction thereof, are citizens of the United States and of the state wherein they reside. No state shall make or enforce any law which shall abridge the privileges or immunities of citizens of the United States; nor shall any state deprive any person of life, liberty, or property, without due process of law; nor deny to any person within its jurisdiction the equal protection of the laws.

Section 2. Representatives shall be apportioned among the several states according to their respective numbers, counting the whole number of persons in each state, excluding Indians not taxed. But when the right to vote at any election for the choice of electors for President and Vice President of the United States, Representatives in Congress, the executive and judicial officers of a state, or the members of the legislature thereof, is denied to any of the male inhabitants of such state, being twenty-one years of age, and citizens of the United States, or in any way abridged, except for participation in rebellion, or other crime, the basis of representation therein shall be reduced in the proportion which the number of such male citizens shall bear to the whole number of male citizens twenty-one years of age in such state.

Section 3. No person shall be a Senator or Representative in Congress, or elector of President and Vice President, or hold any office, civil or military, under the United States, or under any state, who, having previously taken an oath, as a member of Congress, or as an officer of the United States, or as a member of any state legislature, or as an executive or judicial officer of any state, to support the Constitution of the United States, shall have engaged in insurrection or rebellion against the same, or given aid or comfort to the enemies thereof. But Congress may by a vote of two-thirds of each House, remove such disability.

Section 4. The validity of the public debt of the United States, authorized by law, including debts incurred for payment of pensions and bounties for services in suppressing insurrection or rebellion, shall not be questioned. But neither the United States nor any state shall assume or pay any debt or obligation incurred in aid of insurrection or rebellion against the United States, or any claim for the loss or emancipation of any slave; but all such debts, obligations and claims shall be held illegal and void.

Section 5. The Congress shall have power to

enforce, by appropriate legislation, the provisions of this article.

(Source: National Archives, Washington, DC.)

13. Amendment XV to the United States Constitution (1870)

Section 1. The right of citizens of the United States to vote shall not be denied or abridged by the United States or by any state on account of race, color, or previous condition of servitude.

Section 2. The Congress shall have power to enforce this article by appropriate legislation.

(Source: National Archives, Washington, DC.)

XLII. Guerrilla Warfare

Guerrilla warfare was conspicuous in several theaters of the Civil War, especially in Missouri and Kansas. Although irregular warriors had little impact on the operations of regular armies, they often perverted the war by inflicting terror and misery on noncombatants. Frustrated by guerrilla activity—such as the sack of Lawrence, Kansas, by the notorious William Clarke Quantrill's band—Union general Thomas Ewing, Jr., began the wholesale deportation of guerrilla families from border counties. Confederate partisans also operated east of the Mississippi River, and occasionally their depredations, like those of their western counterparts, were indistinguishable from simple lawlessness. [See Guerrilla Warfare]

1. Thomas Ewing's "Banishment Order" (25 August 1863)

GENERAL ORDERS, No. 11.
HDQRS. DISTRICT OF THE BORDER,
Kansas City, Mo., August 25, 1863.

I. All persons living in Jackson, Cuss, and Bates Counties, Missouri, and in that part of Vernon included in this district, except those living within 1 mile of the limits of Independence, Hickman Mills, Pleasant Hill, and Harrisonville, and except those in that part of Kaw Township, Jackson County, north of Brush Creek and west of the Big Blue, are hereby ordered to remove from their present places of residence within fifteen days from the date hereof. Those who, within that time, establish their loyalty to the satisfaction of the commanding officer of the military station nearest their present places of residence will receive from him certificates stating the fact of their loyalty, and the names of the witnesses by whom it can be shown. All who receive such certificates will be permitted to remove to any military station in this district, or to any part of the State of Kansas, except the counties on the eastern border of the State. All others shall remove out

of this district. Officers commanding companies and detachments serving in the counties named will see that this paragraph is promptly obeyed.

II. All grain and hay in the field or under shelter in the district from which the inhabitants are required to remove within reach of military stations after the 9th day of September next will be taken to such stations and turned over to the proper officers there, and report of the amount so turned over made to district headquarters, specifying the names of all loyal owners and the amount of such produce taken from them. All grain and hay found in such district after the 9th day of September next not convenient to such stations will be destroyed.

III. The provisions of General Orders, No. 10, from these headquarters will be at once vigorously executed by officers commanding in the parts of the district and at the stations not subject to the operation of Paragraph I of this order, and especially in the towns of Independence, Westport, and Kansas City.

IV. Paragraph III, General Orders, No. 10, is revoked as to all who have borne arms against the Government in this district since the 21st day of August, 1863.
By order of Brigadier-General Ewing:
 H. HANNAHS,
 Acting Assistant Adjutant-General

(Source: U.S. War Department. *War of the Rebellion: A Compilation of the Official Records of the Union and Confederate Armies.* Ser. I, Vol. XXII.)

2. Instruction to General Merritt Regarding Guerrillas in Northern Virginia (27 November 1864)

HEADQUARTERS MIDDLE MILITARY DIVISION,
November 27, 1864.

Bvt. Maj. Gen. WESLEY MERRITT,
Commanding First Cavalry Division:
GENERAL: You are hereby directed to proceed to-morrow morning at 7 o'clock, with the two brigades of your division now in camp, to the east side of the Blue Ridge, via Ashby's Gap, and operate against the guerrillas in the district of country bounded on the south by the line of the Manassas Gap Railroad as far east as White Plains, on the east by the Bull Run range, on the west by the Shenandoah River, and on the north by the Potomac. This section has been the hot-bed of lawless bands, who have from time to time depredated upon small parties on the line of army communications, on safeguards left at houses, and on troops. Their real object is plunder and highway robbery. To clear the country of these parties that are bringing destruction upon the innocent, as well as their guilty supporters, by

their cowardly acts, you will consume and destroy all forage and subsistence, burn all barns and mills and their contents, and drive off all stock in the region the boundaries of which are above described. This order must be literally executed, bearing in mind, however, that no dwellings are to be burned, and that no personal violence be offered the citizens. The ultimate results of the guerrilla system of warfare is the total destruction of all private rights in the country occupied by such parties. This destruction may as well commence at once, and the responsibility of it must rest upon the authorities at Richmond, who have acknowledged the legitimacy of guerrilla bands. The injury done this army by them is very slight. The injury they have inflicted upon the people, and upon the rebel army, may be counted by millions. The Reserve Brigade of your division will move to Snickersville on the 29th. Snickersville should be your point of concentration and the point from which you should operate in destroying toward the Potomac. Four days' subsistence will be taken by the command. Forage can be gathered from the country through which you pass. You will return to your present camp at Snickersville on the fifth day.

By command of Maj. Gen. P. H. Sheridan:

JAMES W. FORSYTH,
Lieutenant-Colonel and Chief of Staff.

(Source: U.S. War Department. *War of the Rebellion: A Compilation of the Official Records of the Union and Confederate Armies.* Ser. I, Vol. XLIII/1 [S# 90].)

XLIII. Immigrants

Foreign-born Americans served in the war for both sides as volunteers and draftees and thus took part in striving to protect their adoptive countries. In the North, German-American participation in the Civil War was a convincing example of immigrant patriotism. Their participation in the war gave Germans considerable visibility in American society and contributed both to their acceptance as a unique ethnic entity and to their assimilation in the American experience. [See German-Americans; Immigrants]

1. Lincoln to Halleck Regarding German Soldiers (15 January 1862)

EXECUTIVE MANSION,
Washington, January 15, 1862.

Major-General HALLECK:

MY DEAR SIR: The Germans are true and patriotic, and so far as they have got cross in Missouri it is upon mistake and misunderstanding. Without a knowledge of its contents Governor Koerner, of Illinois, will hand you this letter. He is an educated and talented German gentleman, as true a man as lives. With his assistance you can set everything right with the Germans. I write

this without his knowledge, asking him at the same time, by letter, to deliver it. My clear judgment is that, with reference to the German element in your command, you should have Governor Koerner with you; and if agreeable to you and him, I will make him a brigadier-general, so that he can afford to so give his time. He does not wish to command in the field, though he has more military knowledge than many who do. If he goes into the place he will simply be an efficient, zealous, and unselfish assistant to you. I say all this upon intimate personal acquaintance with Governor Koerner.

Yours, very truly,

A. LINCOLN.

(Source: U.S. War Department. *War of the Rebellion: A Compilation of the Official Records of the Union and Confederate Armies.* Ser. I, Vol. VIII.)

2. Halleck to Lincoln Regarding German Soldiers (21 January 1862)

SAINT LOUIS, *January 21, 1862.*

His Excellency ABRAHAM LINCOLN,
President of the United States:

Your Excellency's letter of the 15th, by Governor Koerner, is just received. I nominated Governor K. [Koerner] some time ago for appointment as aide-de-camp, with the rank of colonel, the highest authorized by law as a staff officer. Should Your Excellency see fit to make him a brigadier-general I will use my best endeavors to give him such employment as may best suit him.

The difficulty with the Germans results from two causes: 1st, the want of pay, the pay department here being out of funds, which fact it is very difficult to satisfactorily explain to them; 2d, they are continually tampered with by designing politicians in and out of service in order to serve particular ends. A part of the scheme is the story about the ill-treatment of General Sigel, which is without the slightest foundation.

All these difficulties are being satisfactorily arranged. A firm and decided course will end them forever. Any yielding on the part of the Government will only create new difficulties and give rise to new demands. Being a German myself by descent, I know something of the German character, and I am confident that in a few weeks, if the Government does not interfere, I can reduce these disaffected elements to order and discipline.

Very respectfully, your obedient servant,

H. W. HALLECK, *Major-General.*

(Source: U.S. War Department. *War of the Rebellion: A Compilation of the Official Records of the Union and Confederate Armies.* Ser. I, Vol. VIII.)

XLIV. Medicine

Medical art in the mid-nineteenth century was more primitive than modern, and soldiers understandably shied from physicians. A doctor's care could do as much harm as good, especially for the wounded who first came to surgeons of dubious proficiency and then were placed in often filthy convalescent wards to be treated with nostrums that hobbled healing. Yet talented and conscientious doctors accomplished good work, and medical advances, while not stunning, were occasionally notable. The hard task of coping with the butchery of war and the epidemic diseases of moving armies would have direly taxed a more modern medical establishment, so the accomplishments of the Civil War era physician should not be discounted. [See Medicine]

1. General Orders, No. 9 [Excerpts] (9 September 1861)
HDQRS. ARMY OF THE POTOMAC,
Washington, September 9, 1861.

III. Leaves of absence to medical officers are prohibited, unless granted at these headquarters.

VI. Male nurses and cooks for general hospitals are to be detailed from the privates of the army, regular and volunteer. The allowance will be 1 nurse to 10 patients, and 1 cook to 30. Where women are employed, the number of men to be called for will not exceed the number sufficient to make up the whole force to the allowance above authorized. Hired nurses and cooks will be forthwith discharged.

IX. Ambulances will not be used for any other than the specific purpose for which they are designed, viz, the transportation of the sick and wounded, except by the written authority of the brigade commander, the medical director of the army, and the quartermasters in charge of them in the city of Washington. The provost-marshal is directed to see that the provisions of this order are carried out, and will arrest every officer and confine every private and non-commissioned officer who is found violating it.

X. All Government ambulances now in possession of regiments or separate corps will be turned in to the chief quartermaster, with the exception of 1 two-wheeled ambulance to each regiment. One two-wheeled transport cart will be allowed to each general hospital for the conveyance of marketing and hospital stores.

XI. The reveille will not be beaten until after sunrise, and hot coffee will be issued to the troops immediately after reveille roll-call, as a preventive of the effects of malaria.
By command of Major-General McClellan:
S. WILLIAMS,
Assistant Adjutant-General

2. General Orders, No. 20 (3 October 1861)
HDQRS. ARMY OF THE POTOMAC,
Washington, October 3, 1861.

The following regulations respecting the duties of brigade surgeons are published for the government of all concerned:

I. The brigade surgeons will frequently inspect the police, cooking, clothing, and cleanliness of the camps and men in their respective brigades; the position and condition of the sinks, the drainage of the camp grounds, the ventilation of the tents, &c.; making written reports to the brigade commanders whenever, in their opinion, any errors in these respects require correction, and sending duplicates of these reports to the medical director of the army.

II. They will see that the medicines, hospital stores, instruments, and dressings of the several regimental surgeons are kept constantly sufficient in quantity in good order, and always ready for active service.

III. They will collect from the several regimental surgeons and transmit every Saturday morning to the medical director a copy of their morning report made to the commanding officer of their regiment, and will accompany these with remarks showing the character of the principal diseases prevailing.

IV. They will promptly report to the medical director all changes in station or location of themselves or of any of the medical officers in their brigades, with the number, date, and authority of the order by which such changes were made.

V. They will inspect carefully all men receiving certificates of disability for discharge, and if they approve, they will countersign such certificates.

VI. The hospital attendants, to the number of 10 men to a regiment, and the regimental bands, will be assembled under the supervision of the brigade surgeons, and will be drilled one hour each day, except Sunday, by the regimental medical officers, in setting up and dismantling the hand-stretchers, litters, and ambulances; in handling men carefully; placing them upon the litters and ambulance beds; putting them into the ambulances, taking them out, &c.; carrying men upon the hand-stretchers (observing that the leading bearer steps off with the *left* foot and the rear bearer with the *right*); in short, in everything that can render this service effective and the most comfortable for the wounded who are to be transported.

VII. Brigade surgeons will see that the orders of the commanding general in relation to the uses to which ambulances are to be applied are strictly obeyed, and they will report promptly to the brigade commanders all infractions of these orders.

VIII. Whenever a skirmish or affair of outposts occurs in which any portion of their brigades is

engaged, they will see that the ambulances and stretchers, properly manned with the drilled men, are in immediate attendance to bring off the wounded, and that the regimental medical officers are at their posts, with their instruments, dressings, and hospital knapsacks in complete order and ready for immediate use, so that no delay may occur in rendering the necessary surgical aid to the wounded.

IX. They will report in writing to the medical director, within twenty-four hours after any affair with the enemy, the name, rank, and regiment of each of the wounded, the nature and situation of the wound, and the surgical means adopted in the case.

X. Brigade surgeons will be held responsible that the hospital service in their brigades is kept constantly effective and in readiness for any emergency. No remissness in this respect will be tolerated or overlooked.

By command of Major-General McClellan:

S. WILLIAMS,
Assistant Adjutant-General.

NOTE.—The medical director desires that exsection of the shoulder and elbow joint shall be resorted to in preference to amputation in all cases offering a reasonable hope of success, and that Pirigoff's operation at the ankle should be preferred to Chopart's or to amputation above the ankle, in cases that might admit of a choice.

(Source: U.S. War Department. *War of the Rebellion: A Compilation of the Official Records of the Union and Confederate Armies.* Ser. I, Vol. V.)

3. Confederate Surgeon General's Letter in Regard to Indigenous Botanical Remedies (22 July 1862)

SURGEON-GENERAL'S OFFICE,
Richmond, July 22, 1862.

Surg. T. H. WILLIAMS,
Medical Director and Inspector, Danville, Va.:

SIR: The attention of medical directors is again called to pamphlet of March 21 and circular of April 2 from this office urging upon medical officers the necessity for collecting the indigenous botanical remedies of the South and employing them liberally in the treatment of the sick. Medical directors are now specially instructed to bring the subject promptly to the notice of the medical officers of their respective districts, and will be required to report to them what articles have been collected and in what quantities, in order that this office may be kept informed of the progress of this work.

The indigenous astringents, the crane's-bill, marsh rosemary, blackberry, sweet gum, &c., should be made available in the treatment of the bowel complaints of the warm season. In malarious districts the dogwood, tulip-bearing poplar, willow, boneset, centaury, and other indigenous tonics should be used as prophylactics as well as curatives. Especially should medical officers be instructed to procure an ample supply of articles of mucilaginous properties as the bene, the leaves of which are now about falling; the twigs, bark, and pith of sassafras; the bark of the elm, seed of the flax, or other accessible substances which might in a measure be substituted for the acacia or other imported articles of like character. Attention should also be particularly invited to a further investigation of the medicinal virtues of the Pinckneya pubens or calico bush (not the Kalmia latifolia or calico bush) frequenting South Carolina, Georgia, and more abundantly Middle Florida, it being closely allied in character to the cinchona, and having been used successfully in intermittent fever. Any interesting information elicited on this subject will be transmitted to this office.

With the ample supply of indigenous remedial agents afforded by the materia medica of the South and at their disposal in the vicinity of every camp and garrison, it is considered an injustice to their profession and to their corps that medical officers should complain of a want of means of treating the sick under their charge, and it is to be hoped that the example of some few regimental medical officers who have had collected and used and have reported upon the beneficial results derived from the use of these remedies will be generally emulated. The receipt of these circulars will be acknowledged.

S. P. MOORE,
Surgeon-General.

(Source: U.S. War Department. *War of the Rebellion: A Compilation of the Official Records of the Union and Confederate Armies.* Ser. IV, Vol. II.)

4. Report of Surgeon Charles S. Tripler, Medical Director of the Army of the Potomac, of the Operations of the Medical Department of that Army from August 12, 1861, to March 17, 1862 [Excerpts]

DETROIT, MICH., *February 7, 1863.*

GENERAL: In compliance with your instructions, I have the honor to submit the following report of the operations of the medical department of the Army of the Potomac during the time I was connected with it as medical director:

I joined the Army of the Potomac August 12, 1861, and was immediately charged with the organization of the medical department. At that time... [e]very regimental surgeon sent what men he pleased to the general hospitals, without knowing whether there was room

for them or not, and men were discharged from the hospitals with no means provided to insure their return to their regiments. It was not an unusual circumstance for sick men to pass the night in the ambulances, wandering about the streets from hospital to hospital seeking admission. . . .

On the 19th of August I directed all the prisoners at the Capitol Prison to be vaccinated, a bath to be fitted up for their use, and such outdoor exercise to be allowed them as was consistent with their safe-keeping. On the 22d of August I sent a surgeon to remedy the defects in the police of the camp of the Pennsylvania cavalry, on Seventh street. This camp at the time was a nuisance. On the same day I recommended the removal of the troops encamped upon the flats near Arlington to the higher grounds, if practicable. Thirty-three per cent. of some of the regiments there were reported sick with diarrhea, intermittent, and typhoid fevers. . . .

First among the causes assigned for the numbers on the sick report, and the one as to which there was a general concurrence of opinion, was the recklessness with which the men had been enlisted. General Orders, No. 51, War Department, August 3, 1861, commanded that when volunteers were mustered in they should be minutely examined by the surgeon and assistant surgeon of the regiment as to their physical qualifications. I doubt whether this most important order has ever received the slightest attention from the persons whose duty it was to execute it. . . . The surgeon of the Sixty-first New York reported to me as a reason for his large sick report that he had a large number of broken-down men—many 60 to 70 years old, many affected with hernia, old ulcers, epilepsy, and the like. . . .

During the months of October, November, and December 3,939 men were discharged from the Army of the Potomac upon certificates of disability. Of these 2,881 were for disabilities that existed at the time the men were enlisted. . . .

The general prevalence of the measles was another accident increasing the ratio of the sick. I know of no means of preventing the occurrence of this disease. . . . In many of our regiments it broke out before they left their homes. Some were more severely scourged than others, but nearly all suffered to some extent. . . .

Complaints were made to me in several instances of the inferior quality of the blankets issued to the men. This was perhaps to some degree a cause of disease, but I knew it to be irremediable. It was impossible for the clothing department to furnish the heavy army blankets instantaneously to 600,000 men. The same remarks apply to a considerable proportion of the tents in use. Some regiments suffered for want of good and sufficient clothing. A singular circumstance presents itself in this connection. On the 8th of November, 1861, the surgeon of the Eighth Illinois Cavalry report-

ed to me that 200 of the men had received no overalls from the United States. Many of them were reduced to their drawers. . . .

The principal causes of disease, however, in our camps were the same that we have always to deplore and find it so difficult to remedy, simply because citizens suddenly called to the field cannot comprehend that men in masses require the attention of their officers to enforce certain hygienic conditions without which health cannot be preserved. The individual man at home finds his meals well cooked and punctually served, his bed made, his quarters policed and ventilated, his clothing washed and kept in order without any agency of his own, and without his ever having bestowed a thought upon the matter. The officer in ninety-nine cases in a hundred has given no more reflection than the private to these important subjects. . . .

The prophylactic use of quinine and whisky having been suggested as a means of preventing malarial disease, I determined to try its efficacy. There being no warrant for such an issue in the Regulations of the Army, I procured a small quantity from the Sanitary Commission, and received favorable reports of its effects. Upon representing this to the Surgeon-General, I was authorized to issue it in reasonable quantities to regiments whose condition seemed most to demand it. I required reports as to the effect. These reports were generally favorable; so much so, that I was induced to keep it constantly on hand afterwards in the purveyor's store.... Much prejudice and aversion, however, had to be overcome in inducing the men to take it.

While the Army of the Potomac was in process of organization small-pox was prevailing rather extensively in several of the districts from which the troops were being drawn. It was unsafe to travel without protection over any railway in the country. The city of Washington was infected, as I knew from the number of applications made to me by the authorities for the use of our small-pox ambulances to convey city patients to the pest-house. . . . Orders were issued and reiterated for the vaccination of all volunteers unprotected.

The next subject I shall glance at is that of ambulance transportation. . . . A considerable number of the two-wheeled [carriages] had already been accumulated in Washington before my arrival and had been distributed to the several camps. I found them in general use as pleasure carriages for idlers and accommodation cabs for conveying officers and men from their camps to the city of Washington. A large number of them had already been broken down in this service. This was immediately stopped.

In estimating the number of ambulances required for the Army of the Potomac it was at once apparent that the army allowance was altogether in excess of what

could be obtained or what could be managed, even if it were to be had.... Here I estimated for 250 four-wheeled. I hoped this number might be obtained. It was, however, never reached, and I was obliged afterwards to contrive the best I could to make the number actually furnished go as far as possible.

During this period there were frequent skirmishes, giving a number of wounded men. Two affairs of importance took place: On the 21st of October, 1861, the battle of Ball's Bluff, and on the 20th of December, General Ord's affair at Dranesville. In the former, 280 men were reported wounded; in the latter, 34. Of the wounds at Ball's Bluff 93 were in the head and face—a very large proportion—showing the accuracy of fire of the enemy, as well as the skill with which they availed themselves of the advantage they possessed on that occasion. . . .
Very respectfully, your obedient servant,
CHAS. S. TRIPLER,
Surgeon, U.S. Army. *Maj. Gen.*
GEORGE B. McCLELLAN, U.S. Army.

(Source: U.S. War Department. *War of the Rebellion: A Compilation of the Official Records of the Union and Confederate Armies.* Ser. I, Vol. V.)

XLV. Music

Music is the universal balm of soldiers at war. It can inspire the weary and soothe the troubled, summon emotional memories of home and ridicule tribulations of martial custom. Perhaps the two most enduring songs of the war were the lively "Dixie" and the majestic "Battle Hymn of the Republic." Yet the generation of soldiers that went to war in 1861 would sing a variety of tunes that invoked a variety of emotions and satisfied a variety of needs. A selection of these songs appears below, beginning with the aforementioned "Dixie" and "Battle Hymn." Set to the tune of "The Irish Jaunting Car," Harry Macarthy's "Bonnie Blue Flag" was, after "Dixie," perhaps the most popular Confederate song. James R. Randall's "Maryland! My Maryland!" (to the tune of "Tannenbaum") was written in Louisiana to protest the violent passage of the 6th Massachusetts Infantry through Baltimore, while "Richmond is a Hard Road to Travel," to the tune of Daniel Emmett's "Jordan is a Hard Road to Travel," was an 1863 parody of Union offensives in Virginia attributed to John R. Thompson, editor of The Southern Literary Messenger. *George F. Root's "Battle-Cry of Freedom" was, according to many, the most inspiring camp song of the Union army and was always featured at patriotic rallies throughout the war. "Marching through Georgia," by talented and prolific Henry Clay Work, celebrated William T. Sherman's March to the Sea. J. P. Webster (who wrote the melody of the hymn "Sweet By and By") composed the tune of the sentimental "Lorena." The lyrics were by Reverend H. D. L. Webster, who was unrelated to the composer. The haunting refrains of "Lorena" could be heard around both Northern and Southern campfires, but some-*

thing about the ballad especially appealed to Confederates, possibly because their dreams of both sweethearts and causes endured even as they were slipping into the past. The reader should consult Irwin Silber, comp. and ed., The Songs of the Civil War *(1960; reprint ed., 1995) for a thorough discussion of the music of the period and its context. [See "Dixie"; "Battle Hymn of the Republic"; Music]*

1. "Dixie's Land,"
by Daniel Decatur Emmett (1860)

I wish I was in de land ob cotton
Old times dar am not forgotten
Look away! Look away!
Look away! Dixie Land.
In Dixie Land whar I was born in
Early on a frosty mornin'
Look away! Look away!
Look away! Dixie Land.

[Chorus] Den I wish I was in Dixie
Hooray! Hooray!
In Dixie Land I'll take my stand
To lib and die in Dixie,
Away, away, away down south in Dixie.
Away, away, away down south in Dixie.

Ole missus marry "Will de Weaber,"
William was a gay deceiber;
Look away! Look away!
Look away! Dixie Land.
But when he put his arm around'er,
He smiled as fierce as a forty pounder,
Look away! Look away!
Look away! Dixie Land.

His face was sharp as a butcher's cleaber,
But dat did not seem to greab' er;
Look away, etc.
Ole missus acted de foolish part,
And died for a man dat broke her heart,
Look away, etc.

Now here's a health to the next old Missus,
An' all de gals dat want to kiss us;
Look away, etc.
But if you want to drive'way sorrow,
Come and hear dis song tomorrow,
Look away, etc.

Dar's buck-wheat cakes and Ingen' batter,
Makes you fat or a little fatter;
Look away, etc.
Den hoe it down an' scratch your grabble,
To Dixie's Land I'm bound to trabble,
Look away, etc.

(Source: Emmett, Daniel Decatur. "Dixie's Land." New York: Firth, Pond & Co., 1860.)

2. "Battle Hymn of the Republic,"
by Julia Ward Howe (1863)

Mine eyes have seen the glory of the coming of the
Lord
He is trampling out the vintage where the grapes of
wrath are stored,
He has loosed the fateful lightening of His terrible
swift sword
His truth is marching on.

[Chorus:] Glory! Glory! Hallelujah!
Glory! Glory! Hallelujah!
Glory! Glory! Hallelujah!
His truth is marching on.

I have seen Him in the watch-fires of a hundred
circling camps
They have builded Him an altar in the evening
dews and damps
I can read His righteous sentence by the dim and
flaring lamps
His day is marching on.
[Chorus]

I have read a fiery gospel writ in burnish`d rows of
steel,
"As ye deal with my contemners, So with you my
grace shall deal;"
Let the Hero, born of woman, crush the serpent
with his heel
Since God is marching on.
[Chorus]

He has sounded form the trumpet that shall never
call retreat
He is sifting out the hearts of men before His judg-
ment-seat
Oh, be swift, my soul, to answer Him! be jubilant,
my feet!
Our God is marching on.
[Chorus]

He has sounded form the trumpet that shall never
call retreat
He is sifting out the hearts of men before His judg-
ment-seat
Oh, be swift, my soul, to answer Him! be jubilant,
my feet!
Our God is marching on.
[Chorus]

In the beauty of the lilies Christ was born across
the sea,
With a glory in His bosom that transfigures you
and me:

As He died to make men holy, let us die to make
men free,
While God is marching on.
[Chorus]

(Source: Howe, Julia Ward. "Battle Hymn of the Republic."
Philadelphia: Supervisory Committee for Recruiting Colored
Regiments, *ca.* 1863.)

3. "The Bonnie Blue Flag,"
by Harry McCarthy (1861)

We are a band of brothers, and native to the soil,
Fighting for the property we gained by honest toil;
And when our rights were threatened, the cry rose
near and far:
Hurrah for the bonnie Blue Flag that bears a single
star!
Hurrah! hurrah! for the bonnie Blue Flag
That bears a single star.

As long as the Union was faithful to her trust,
Like friends and like brothers, kind were we and just;
But now when Northern treachery attempts our
rights to mar,
We hoist on high the bonnie Blue Flag that bears a
single star.

First, gallant South Carolina nobly made the stand;
Then came Alabama, who took her by the hand;
Next, quickly Mississippi, Georgia, and Florida—
All raised the flag, the bonnie Blue Flag that bears
a single star.

Ye men of valor, gather round the banner of the
right;
Texas and fair Louisiana join us in the fight.
Davis, our loved President, and Stephens, statesmen are;
Now rally round the bonnie Blue Flag that bears a
single star.

And here's to brave Virginia! the Old Dominion
State
With the young Confederacy at length has linked
her fate.
Impelled by her example, now other States prepare
To hoist on high the bonnie Blue Flag that bears a
single star.
Then here's to our Confederacy; strong we are and
brave,
Like patriots of old we'll fight, our heritage to save;
And rather than submit to shame, to die we would
prefer;
So cheer for the bonnie Blue Flag that bears a sin-
gle star.

Then cheer, boys, cheer, raise the joyous shout,
For Arkansas and North Carolina now have both
   gone out;
And let another rousing cheer for Tennessee be
   given,
The single star of the bonnie Blue Flag has grown
   to be eleven!
Hurrah! hurrah! for the bonnie Blue Flag
That bears a single star.

(Source: Silber, Irwin. *Songs of the Civil War* [1995].)

4. "Maryland! My Maryland!"
by James Ryder Randall (1861)

The despot's heel is on thy shore,
Maryland!
His torch is at thy temple door,
Maryland!
Avenge the patriotic gore
That flecked the streets of Baltimore,
And be the battle queen of yore,
Maryland! My Maryland!

Hark to an exiled son's appeal,
Maryland!
My mother State! to thee I kneel,
Maryland!
For life and death, for woe and weal,
Thy peerless chivalry reveal,
And gird thy beauteous limbs with steel,
Maryland! My Maryland!

Thou wilt not cower in the dust,
Maryland!
Thy beaming sword shall never rust,
Maryland!
Remember Carroll's sacred trust,
Remember Howard's warlike thrust,-
And all thy slumberers with the just,
Maryland! My Maryland!

Come! for thy shield is bright and strong,
Maryland!
Come! for thy dalliance does thee wrong,
Maryland!
Come to thine own heroic throng,
Stalking with Liberty along,
And chaunt thy dauntless slogan song,
Maryland! My Maryland!

Dear Mother! burst the tyrant's chain,
Maryland!
Virginia should not call in vain,
Maryland!
She meets her sisters on the plain

"*Sic semper!*" 'tis the proud refrain
That baffles minions back again,
Maryland! My Maryland!

I hear the distant thunder-hum,
Maryland!
The Old Line's bugle, fife, and drum,
Maryland!
She is not dead, nor deaf, nor dumb—
Huzza! she spurns the Northern scum!
She breathes! she burns! she'll come! she'll come!
Maryland! My Maryland!

(Source: Silber, Irwin. *Songs of the Civil War* [1995].)

5. "Richmond is a Hard Road to Travel,"
attr. to John R. Thompson (1863)

Would you like to hear my song? I'm afraid it's
   rather long,
Of the famous "On to Richmond" double trouble;
Of the half a dozen trips and half a dozen slips
And the very latest bursting of the bubble.
'Tis pretty hard to sing and, like a round, round
   ring,
'Tis a dreadful knotty puzzle to unravel;
Though all the papers swore, when we touched
   Virginia's shore,
That Richmond was a hard road to travel.
Then pull off your coat and roll up your sleeve,
For Richmond is a hard road to travel.
Then pull off your coat and roll up your sleeve,
For Richmond is a hard road to travel, I believe.

First McDowell, bold and gay, set forth the shortest
   way
By Manassas in the pleasant summer weather
But unfortunately ran on a Stonewall (foolish
   man!)
And had a rocky journey altogether.
And he found it rather hard to ride over
   Beauregard
And Johnston proved a deuce of a bother.
'Twas clear beyond a doubt that he didn't like the
   route
And a second time would have to try another.
Then pull off your coat and roll up your sleeve,
For Manassas is a hard road to travel.
Manassas gave us fits, and Bull Run made us grieve,
For Richmond is a hard road to travel, I believe.

Next came the Wooly Horse with an overwhelming
   force
To march down to Richmond by the Valley,
But he couldn't find the road, and his onward
   movement showed

His campaigning was a mere shilly-shally.
Then Commissary Banks, with his motley foreign
    ranks
Kicking up a great noise, fuss, and flurry,
Lost the whole of his supplies and with tears in his
    eyes
From the Stonewall ran away in a hurry.
Then pull off your coat and roll up your sleeve,
For the Valley is a hard road to travel.
The Valley wouldn't do, and we all had to leave,
For Richmond is a hard road to travel, I believe.

Then the great Galena came, with her portholes all
    aflame,
And the Monitor, that famous naval wonder,
But the guns at Drury's Bluff gave them speedily
    enough
The loudest sort of reg'lar Rebel thunder.
The Galena was astonished and the Monitor
    admonished,
Our patent shot and shell were mocked at,
While the dreadful Naugatuck, by the hardest kind
    of luck,
Was knocked into an ugly cocked hat.
Then pull off your coat and roll up your sleeve,
For James River is a hard road to travel.
The gunboats gave up in terror and despair,
For Richmond is a hard road to travel, I declare.

Then McClellan followed soon, both with spade
    and balloon,
To try the Peninsular approaches,
But one and all agreed that his best rate of speed
Was no faster than the slowest of slow coaches.
Instead of easy ground, at Williamsburg he found
A Longstreet indeed and nothing shorter.
And it put him in the dumps that spades wasn't
    trumps
And the Hills he couldn't level "as he orter!"
Then pull off your coat and roll up your sleeve,
For Longstreet is a hard road to travel.
Lay down the shovel and throw away the spade,
For Richmond is a hard road to travel, I'm afraid.

Then said Lincoln unto Pope, "You can make the
    trip, I hope."
"I will save the universal Yankee nation!
"To make sure of no defeat, I'll leave no lines of
    retreat,
"And issue a famous proclamation!"
But that same dreaded Jackson, this fella laid his
    whacks on
And made him, by compulsion, a seceder.
Pope took rapid flight from Manassas' second fight,
'Twas his very last appearance as a leader.

Then pull off your coat and roll up your sleeve,
Stonewall is a hard road to travel.
Pope did his very best but was evidently sold,
For Richmond is a hard road to travel, I am told.

Last of all Burnside, with his pontoon bridges, tried
A road no one had thought of before him,
With two hundred thousand men for the Rebel
    slaughter pen
And the blessed Union flag waving o'er him.
He met a fire like hell of canister and shell
That mowed down his men with great slaughter.
'Twas a shocking sight to view, that second
    Waterloo,
And the river ran with more blood than water.
Then pull off your coat and roll up your sleeve,
Rappahannock is a hard road to travel.
Burnside got in a trap, which caused for him to
    grieve,
For Richmond is a hard road to travel, I believe.

We are very much perplexed to know who is the
    next
To command the new Richmond expedition,
For the capital must blaze, and that in ninety days,
And Jeff and his men be sent to perdition.
We'll take the cursed town, and then we'll burn it
    down
And plunder and hang each cursed Rebel.
Yet the contraband was right when he told us they
    would fight:
"Oh, yes, massa, dey will fight like the debil!"
Then pull off your coat and roll up your sleeve,
For Richmond is a hard road to travel.
Then pull off your coat and roll up your sleeves,
For Richmond is a hard road to travel, I believe.

(Source: Silber, Irwin. *Songs of the Civil War* [1995].)

6. "The Battle-Cry of Freedom," by George F. Root (1865)

Yes, we'll rally round the flag, boys, we'll rally once
    again,
Shouting the battle cry of Freedom,
We will rally from the hillside, we'll gather from
    the plain,
Shouting the battle cry of Freedom.

[Chorus]: The Union forever,
Hurrah! boys, hurrah!
Down with the traitors,
Up with the stars,
While we rally round the flag, boys,
Rally once again,
Shouting the battle cry of Freedom.

We are springing to the call of our brothers gone
   before,
Shouting the battle cry of Freedom,
And we'll fill our vacant ranks with a million
   freemen more,
Shouting the battle cry of Freedom.
[Chorus]

We will welcome to our numbers the loyal, true
   and brave,
Shouting the battle cry of Freedom,
And although they may be poor, not a man shall be
   a slave,
Shouting the battle cry of Freedom.
[Chorus]

So we're springing to the call from the East and
   from the West,
Shouting the battle cry of Freedom,
And we'll hurl the Rebel crew from the land that
   we love best,
Shouting the battle cry of Freedom.
[Chorus]

(Source: Silber, Irwin. *Songs of the Civil War* [1995].)

7. "Marching Through Georgia," by Henry Clay Work (1865)

Bring the good old bugle, boys, we'll sing another
   song;
Sing it with a spirit that will start the world along,
Sing it as we used to sing it, fifty thousand strong,
While we were marching through Georgia.

[Chorus:] Hurrah! Hurrah! We bring the jubilee!
Hurrah! Hurrah! The flag that makes you free!
So we sang the chorus from Atlanta to the sea,
While we were marching through Georgia.

How the darkeys shouted when they heard the joy-
   ful sound!
How the turkeys gobbled which our commissary
   found!
How the sweet potatoes even started from the
   ground,
While we were marching through Georgia.
[Chorus]

Yes, and there were Union men who wept with joyful tears,
When they saw the honored flag they had not seen
   for years;
Hardly could they be restrained from breaking forth
   in cheers,
While we were marching through Georgia.

[Chorus]

"Sherman's dashing Yankee boys will never reach
   the coast!"
So the saucy Rebels said, and 'twas a handsome
   boast;
Had they not forgot, alas! to reckon with the host,
While we were marching through Georgia.
[Chorus]

So we made a thoroughfare for Freedom and her
   train,
Sixty miles in latitude, three hundred to the main;
Treason fled before us, for resistance was in vain,
While we were marching through Georgia.
[Chorus]

(Source: Silber, Irwin. *Songs of the Civil War* [1995].)

8. "Lorena," by Rev. H. D. L. Webster (1857)

The years creep slowly by, Lorena,
The snow is on the grass again;
The sun's low down the sky Lorena,
The frost gleams where the flowers have been;
But the heart throbs on as lovely now,
As when the summer days were nigh;
Oh, the sun can never dip so low,
Adown affection's cloudless sky.

A hundred months have passed, Lorena,
Since last I held your hand in mine,
And felt that pulse beat fast, Lorena,
Though mine beat faster far than thine;
A hundred months—'twas flow'ry May,
When up the hilly slopes we climbed,
To watch the dying of the day,
And hear the distant church bells chimed.

We loved each other then, Lorena,
More than we ever dared to tell,
And what we might have been, Lorena,
Had but our loving prospered well—
But then, 'tis past, the years are gone,
I'll not call up their shadowy forms;
I'll say to them, "Lost years, sleep on,
Sleep on, nor heed life's pelting storms."

The story of the past, Lorena,
Alas, I care not to repeat,
The hopes that could not last, Lorena,
They lived, but only lived to cheat;
I would not cause e'en one regret,
To rankle in your bosom now;
For "if we try, we may forget,"
Were words of thine long years ago.

Yes, these were words of thine, Lorena,
They burn within my memory yet;
They touch some tender chords, Lorena,
Which thrill and tremble with regret;
'Twas not thy woman's heart that spoke;
Thy heart was always true to me—
A duty, stern and pressing, broke
The tie which linked my soul to thee.

It matters little now, Lorena,
The past—is in eternal past,
Our heads will soon lie down, Lorena,
Life's tide is ebbing out so fast;
There is a future—Oh, thank God—
Of life this is so small a part,
'Tis dust to dust beneath the sod,
But there, up there, 'tis heart to heart.

(Source: Silber, Irwin. *Songs of the Civil War* [1995].)

XLVI. Prisoners of War

Some of the most horrible conditions of the war occurred in prison camps in both the North and the South. Neither side was prepared to deal with thousands of long-term prisoners, and until mid-1863, many were exchanged immediately after capture or paroled fairly quickly. In July 1862 the Dix-Hill cartel began a standard process for prisoner exchanges. Yet the cartel broke down in 1863 coincidentally with a series of major battles that saw multitudes of soldiers on both sides falling prisoner. Both the Union and the Confederacy accordingly opened or expanded their prison camps where conditions were barely adequate and often were abysmal. The Confederacy's compound at Andersonville, Georgia, was to become the most notorious prison camp of the war. The treatment of Union prisoners at Andersonville led after the war to the military trial and conviction of Henry Wirz, who had commanded at Andersonville. He was hanged in November 1865. [See Andersonville; Castle Thunder; Prisoners of War; Prisons, C.S.A.; Prisons, U.S.A.; Wirz, Henry]

1. An Act Relative to Prisoners of War, Approved May 21, 1861

The Congress of the Confederate States of America do enact, That all prisoners of war taken whether on land or at sea during the pending hostilities with the United States shall be transferred by the captors from time to time and as often as convenient to the Department of War; and it shall be the duty of the Secretary of War with the approval of the President to issue such instructions to the Quartermaster-General and his subordinates as shall provide for the safe custody and sustenance of prisoners of war; and the rations furnished prisoners of war shall be the same in quantity and quality as those furnished to enlisted men in the Army of the Confederacy.

SEC. 2. That the eighth section of the act entitled "An act recognizing the existence of war between the United States and the Confederate States, and concerning letters of marque, prizes and prize goods," shall not be so construed as to authorize the holding as prisoners of war the officers or crew of any unarmed vessel, nor any passengers on such vessel, unless such passengers be persons employed in the public service of the enemy.

SEC. 3. That the tenth section of the above-recited act shall not be so construed as to allow a bounty for prisoners captured on vessels of the enemy and brought into port unless such prisoners were captured on board of an armed ship or vessel of the enemy of equal or superior force to that of the private armed vessel making the capture.

(Source: U.S. War Department. *War of the Rebellion: A Compilation of the Official Records of the Union and Confederate Armies.* Ser. II, Vol. II.)

2. Major-General Hunter's Orders Regarding Confederate Prisoners (10 June 1863)

HEADQUARTERS DEPARTMENT
OF THE SOUTH,
Hilton Head, Port Royal, S. C., June 10, 1863.

Col. JAMES MONTGOMERY, *Commanding Raids,
Georgia and Florida.*
COLONEL: Every rebel man you may capture, citizen or soldier, you will send in irons to this place to be kept as hostages for the proper treatment of any of your men who may accidentally fall into the hands of the enemy. Very respectfully, your most obedient servant,
D. HUNTER,
Major-General, Commanding.

(Source: U.S. War Department. *War of the Rebellion: A Compilation of the Official Records of the Union and Confederate Armies.* Ser. II, Vol. V.)

3. Evidence Taken before the Committee of the House of Representatives of the Confederate States Appointed to Inquire into the Treatment of Prisoners at Castle Thunder [Excerpts] (11 April 1863)

Saturday, *April 11, 1863.*

William Causey sworn: I have seen men severely whipped on the buttocks with straps; don't know how many lashes were laid on, but I should think about fifty. I only saw one whipping. On this occasion the officers were requested by Captain Alexander to go up into the prison room and see the men whipped. The whipping strap was secured onto wooden handles. They were made of harness leather or sole leather from eighteen

inches to two feet in length. The blows were laid on about as hard as a man could do it. I have seen prisoners wear the same clothes for months until they were ready to drop off in rags.

T. G. Bland sworn: I have seen on one or two occasions fifteen or twenty prisoners "bucked" and "gagged" at a time. The "gag" is effected by a stick inserted crosswise in the mouth, and the "buck" is to tie the arms at the elbows to a cross-piece beneath the thighs. They were generally ironed, wore ball and chain, and were charged with various offenses.

John Caphart, sworn: I have never seen a prisoner harshly treated except by orders. It was really dangerous at times for the officers to go among the prisoners, some of them were such desperate characters. A new prisoner sent in among them was usually knocked down, beat and robbed if he had anything about him.

(Source: U.S. War Department. *War of the Rebellion: A Compilation of the Official Records of the Union and Confederate Armies.* Ser. II, Vol. V.)

4. Inspection Report of Prisoners of War at Fort Delaware (3 September 1863)

Col. WILLIAM HOFFMAN,
Commissary. General of Prisoners, Washington, D.C.:
There are 8,000 prisoners of war at this point, and they have been much crowded together, sick and well, in the same barracks, which it has been impossible to keep clean. The opening of a new hospital at this post which contains 600 beds will improve the condition of affairs very much, and the separation of the sick will improve their sanitary condition immensely. ... I do not consider Fort Delaware a desirable location, in a sanitary point of view, for a large depot of prisoners. The ground is wet and marshy and the locality favorable for the development of malarious diseases. There have been many deaths at this place from typhoid fever, the result of their being crowded together in large numbers in a confined space.
C. H. CRANE.

(Source: U.S. War Department. *War of the Rebellion: A Compilation of the Official Records of the Union and Confederate Armies.* Ser. II, Vol. VI.)

5. Prison Inspection Report (7 December 1863)

WASHINGTON CITY, *D. C., December 7, 1863.*

Hon. EDWIN M. STANTON, *Secretary of War:*
SIR: In obedience to the order from you to make an inspection of the several places named where rebel prisoners of war are confined and report as to the supplies, means for guarding and keeping the prisoners, their sanitary condition, &c., I have the honor to submit the following report:

On the 12th day of November, A.D. 1863, I left the city of Washington and prior to my return on the 5th of December visited each of the places hereinafter named.

CAMP DOUGLAS, CHICAGO, ILL. There are here 5,964 rebel prisoners of war; too many for the capacity of the barracks, which are long, wooden, one-story buildings, with bunks on either side, and stoves in the passageway between the bunks. The prisoners are well supplied with food, the ration actually issued being three.quarters of a pound of bacon (1 pound of fresh beef three times a week), good, well-baked wheat bread, hominy, coffee, tea, sugar, vinegar, candles, soap, salt, pepper, potatoes, and molasses. These articles are all of good quality. There is no good system for cooking, each man being left to arrange for himself. The result is a great waste of food and fuel, the latter of which especially is a serious item of expense at this camp. There is a sutler's shop, containing nearly everything (except liquors), including cider, butter, eggs, milk, canned fruits, boots, &c., underclothing, and all the minor articles usually found in a sutler's stock, of which the prisoners are allowed to purchase. Money received for prisoners from their friends is retained by the commanding officer and issued to them in small amounts in sutler's checks. The sanitary condition of this camp is very good. The sinks are well arranged and kept clean and pure. During October there were eighty-two deaths. The prison hospital is clean, neat, well attended, and comfortable. The garrison is under command of Col. Charles V. De Land, who has his regiment of Michigan sharpshooters, 540 strong, two companies Eighth Regiment Invalid Corps, 336 strong. During the three months ending November 18, 1863, sixty one prisoners escaped. If this garrison were so increased as to throw around the camp on the outside of the prison fence a chain of sentries, it would prevent all escapes, especially by the new process of burrowing out.

CAMP MORTON, INDIANAPOLIS. There are 2,881 rebel prisoners of war here. They occupy long, wooden barracks, without floors, with bunks of all shapes and designs. Nearly every barrack was warmed by stoves, but there were some barracks which had no stove or other means of heating. The supplies here are the same as at Camp Douglas and the same want of system in cooking exists (see page 2). A sutler's shop is also allowed here, similar to the one at Camp Douglas. The sanitary condition of this camp has been much neglected, but under the present commander it is receiving proper attention. The deaths for thirty days ending November 18 were forty. The number of sick in hospital (which is very clean and comfortable) at that date was 200. The garrison is in command of Col. A. A. Stevens, Fifth [Regiment] Invalid Corps. He has twelve

companies, averaging about seventy-five men, for duty and four other companies now organizing. This camp is well and securely guarded. A new fence is badly needed around the prison inclosure.

JOHNSON'S ISLAND, NEAR SANDUSKY, OHIO. There are 2,381 rebel prisoners of war here, all of whom but 59 are officers. They occupy very comfortable barracks, which are two-story frame buildings, with floors and well ceiled up, and with good ventilation. The barracks were mostly very clean and neat, the extent of the cleanliness depending upon the taste of the occupants. These barracks are built in two rows, facing each other, with a wide street between. The supply of food is abundant and of good quality, the bread being good wheat bread of the same kind used by our own officers and men composing the garrison. The prisoners have arranged themselves into convenient messes and have cooking-stoves and other facilities for cooking, by means of which they get along comfortably. No sutler is allowed here. The sanitary condition of these prisoners is very good. The whole number of deaths among prisoners during the year 1863 up to November was only sixty-nine out of a total of 2,695 prisoners. During 1862 the deaths were only thirty-seven, most all of these cases resulting from diseases incurred before reaching this camp. The number of sick is forty-two. These prisoners look well and hearty. The garrison, under command of Lieutenant-Colonel Pierson, Hoffman's Battalion Ohio Infantry, 400 effective men, is ample for this post.

CAMP CHASE, NEAR COLUMBUS, OHIO. There are 2,448 rebel prisoners of war here who are quartered in wooden barracks, with floors, and bunks arranged on the sides. Some of these barracks are too much crowded. Each one is comfortably heated by stoves. The supply of food is abundant and good, as at Camp Douglas, and although their arrangements for cooking are somewhat better than at Camp Douglas, yet they are not what they should be. A sutler is permitted here, who furnishes a supply of articles as at the other camps. In the stock here I noticed several bottles of gin or schnapps, which were being sold to prisoners, to which I called the attention of the commanding officer. The sanitary condition of this camp is very good. The deaths for October were twenty-eight, and during the first twenty days of November were twelve. There are twenty-eight sick in hospital. The hospital is not as clean and neat as it should be. The garrison is under command of Col. William Wallace and is sufficient for the duty.

COLUMBUS PENITENTIARY, OHIO. There are seventy-nine rebel prisoners here, consisting of Gen. John Morgan and his subordinate officers, who are con-

fined in a portion of the building to themselves. They are quartered in the cells and have clean, comfortable beds and bedding. They have their washing done in the prison and their cells cleaned and swept by the convicts. They are supplied with prison fare (with the difference of coffee being allowed them), which is well cooked for them; a table set for them and cleaned away by convicts. These prisoners wear their own clothing and have no labor whatever imposed upon them. They are prohibited newspapers and intercourse with any person. They are in good health and condition, only six of them being slightly sick, but they are kindly and comfortably cared for in the hospital. Since my visit General Morgan and six of his officers escaped. In this prison I find a Doctor Brickley, a prisoner under military orders, but, as he affirms, he is a citizen of Cincinnati, and is ignorant of the reason of his detention.

LOUISVILLE AND NASHVILLE. The prisons at these points are principally used as depots for prisoners *en route* from the front to other points. At Louisville, November 22, there were 133 rebel prisoners; at Nashville, November 24, there were 315 rebel prisoners, who are well fed on regular rations. These prisons are kept clean and thoroughly policed.

WHEELING, W. VA. There were only thirty-two rebel prisoners of war. There are here seven citizens under military orders, and twelve citizens held as hostages by the Governor's order. This is principally a prison depot for passing prisoners. Those on hand are well fed and cared for. The prison is a building rented at $1,500 a year by the Government.

GRATIOT STREET PRISON, SAINT LOUIS, MO. There are 382 rebel prisoners of war and 114 citizens held under military orders at this prison. They are kept in a large building, which is well and conveniently arranged for the purpose. They receive an abundant supply of good food and have good facilities for cooking. There is an abundant supply of pure water at this prison. The prison building and yards are well policed and kept clean, but there is a great lack of personal cleanliness among the prisoners. The prisoners are generally in good health, though there are a large number on hand sick. The garrison is ample for the guard duty required.

ALTON PENITENTIARY, ILL. There are 1,550 rebel prisoners of war here, who are confined in this building, which was formerly used as the State penitentiary, but some years since abandoned. They are comfortably quartered and well supplied with good, warm bedding. This prison is too much crowded. It should be relieved

of 500 men. The prisoners are well supplied with an abundance of food, which is well prepared and cooked. A sutler is allowed to sell to them. The sanitary condition of this prison is very good. It is cleanly and well kept and under good discipline. There were, November 25, 119 sick in hospital. The deaths for October were thirty-five and for November twenty-nine. The garrison, commanded by Colonel Kincaid with his regiment, 450 strong, is sufficient. The wall surrounding this prison is in some places in bad condition and propped up, much facilitating chances for escape. It could be cheaply rebuilt by the labor of prisoners here under sentence. There are very many prisoners here under sentence, by court-martial or military commission, of hard labor, &c. Some 200 Federal soldiers are here under sentence, but there is no mode of executing the sentence at this place.

M'LEAN BARRACKS, CINCINNATI, OHIO. There are only twenty-six prisoners of war here; the other forty-three are citizens under military arrest. The prisoners here are well and abundantly fed and allowed to purchase articles under supervision of commanding officer. They are all in good health. The garrison of twenty-eight men is ample for the present duty.

ALLEGHENY CITY PENITENTIARY, PA. There are 112 rebel prisoners, subordinate officers of General Morgan's command. They are quartered in the cells, which are large and well ventilated. Each cell is supplied with water and gas. The former is used *ad libitum* and the latter until 10 p.m. Since the latter part of November they have been closely confined to their cells. Prior to that they were allowed the privilege of the prison yard at stated hours of the day, on their parole of honor that they would not escape nor attempt to do so. Two of them were caught on the roof in the act of escaping. For this breach of the parole by two of the prisoners they are all closely confined. They have their washing done at the prison, are allowed to purchase most anything they desire, and are very kindly and considerately treated. They are supplied with the prison fare; good wheat bread, soups, beef, and potatoes at stated times. There are about twelve of these prisoners who expressed a desire to take the oath of allegiance.

ROCK ISLAND, ILL. There were no prisoners at this point November 30, but arrangements were being rapidly perfected for their reception. The capacity of the barracks will be 10,000 men. The garrison here is under command of Colonel Rush and should be in my opinion at least fourteen full companies of the Invalid Corps, as the natural obstacles to an escape are very trivial around this island.

It gives me pleasure to report that at each post I visited the officers were active in the discharge of their duties. There is, however, a want of uniformity in the treatment of the prisoners at the different prisons, at some more privileges being allowed them than at others, while at all places, however, they are kindly treated and well supplied with food. The whole number of prisoners that I visited is about 16,300, and taking into consideration that these men have been gathered from all parts of the Southern States, have endured immense hardships and fatigue, and have been exposed to all kinds of weather and finally compelled to change climate by being removed as prisoners to the Northern States, the present sanitary condition of them is in my opinion very good. At all the prison camps the commandants have taken from the prisoners large amounts of Confederate money, which they hold without any special orders and seek instruction as to its disposition. At several of these camps I found large numbers of Union soldiers under sentence of courts-martial. Although not within the purview of this report, I cannot help from suggesting that there are many fine soldiers who have already been punished sufficiently and who would render good service if sent back to their commands. At Camp Chase, Columbus, Ohio, I found some 200 or 300 paroled Federal soldiers, without commander, discipline, or any kind of order. At the Columbus, Ohio, penitentiary, I found General John Morgan and seventy-eight of his officers. They were not shaved and dressed in convict clothes as alleged, but wore their own dress and were confined in a part of the building to themselves. The warden assured me that they were not shaved on the head on their entry into his prison, but that their hair was simply trimmed or cut off (but not short), as a necessary measure for personal cleanliness. I would suggest that at each camp where a large number of prisoners may be kept there should be as a part of the garrison defense two or more howitzers, which would be of great service in the event of trouble among the prisoners. Some good plan of cooking for the prisoners at all these large camps should be adopted, by means of which the Government could save very largely in expense, both in rations and fuel. By the present unorganized system at the larger camps every man takes care of himself, and thus wastes rations and uses as much fuel to cook his dinner as could otherwise be used to cook for twenty-five. If our brave soldiers whom the fortunes of war have thrown into the hands of the enemy as prisoners are as well treated as the rebel prisoners I have visited, then indeed might we rest comparatively easy while they are withheld from us. I have appended hereto on one sheet a brief synopsis of my report.

I have the honor to be, sir, your most obedient servant,

WM. W. ORME,
Brigadier-General, U.S. Volunteers.

(Source: U.S. War Department. *War of the Rebellion: A Compilation of the Official Records of the Union and Confederate Armies.* Ser. II, Vol. VI.)

6. Report of E. J. Eldridge in Regard to Andersonville (6 May 1864)

HEADQUARTERS GEORGIA RESERVES,
Macon, Ga., May 6, 1864.

Maj. LAMAR COBB,
Asst. Adjt. and Insp. Gen., Georgia Reserves,
Macon, Ga.:
MAJOR: In obedience to instructions from Maj. Gen. Howell Cobb, I have the honor to make the following report of my visit, in company with the general, to the prison camp at Andersonville:

I found the prisoners, in my opinion, too much crowded for the promotion or even continuance of their present health, particularly during the approaching summer months. The construction of properly arranged barracks would, of course, allow the same number of men to occupy the inclosures with material advantage to their comfort and health. At present their shelters consist of such as they can make of the boughs of trees, poles, &c., covered with dirt. The few tents they have are occupied as hospitals. I found the police of the camp throughout very good—as well arranged as their crowded condition and the limited number of shovels would allow. Since necessary tools have been received for ditching, &c., which has been very recently, it is proposed to arrange their sinks so that the fecal matter may be at once carried away by the stream running through the inclosure, which will at once materially improve the condition of the camp. I found the condition of a large number of the Belle Isle prisoners on their arrival to be such as to require more attention to their diet and cleanliness than to the actual administration of medicines, very many of them suffering from chronic diarrhea, combined with the scorbutic disposition, with extreme emaciation as the consequence. The hospital being within the inclosure, it has been found impracticable to administer such diet and give them such attention as they require, as unless constantly watched such diet as is prepared for them is stolen and eaten by the other prisoners. There is a fine stream within a few hundred yards of the present inclosure, across which, in my opinion, there should be made another inclosure, with sufficient hospital buildings, two stories high, to accommodate from 800 to 1,000 patients. Such an inclosure as I should suggest—a plank fence ten feet high—would require but very few additional guards, which guard appears to be the objection urged at Richmond to separate inclosure.

The patients upon their admission into the hospital should be well washed, and a pool arranged on the side of the stream, and furnished only with a clean shirt, with which dress they would hardly attempt to escape. The nurses could be detailed with such discretion that but few would attempt to escape, and with frequent roll-calls they would be absent but a few hours before detected, and would be readily caught by the dogs, always at hand for that purpose. I consider the establishment of a hospital outside of the present inclosure as essential to the proper treatment to the sick, and most urgently recommend its immediate construction. I would also recommend the construction of as many bathing-pools within the prison as the stream would warrant, feeling assured, from the appearance of the prisoners, that their use would contribute materially to the health of the bathers. Other improvements would be suggested but for the difficulty of obtaining labor, tools, and materials, but with those above mentioned the urgent necessities of the prison would be supplied.

The bakery just being completed will be the means of furnishing better prepared food, particularly bread, the half-cooked condition of which has doubtless contributed to the continuance of the bowel affections. I will add that as far as I have been able to judge from my short visit, the management of the medical department of the prison, under the direction of Chief Surg. I. H. White, reflects credit upon that officer, who seems well qualified for the position he occupies.

I have the honor to be, very respectfully, your obedient servant,
E. J. ELDRIDGE,
Chief Surgeon Georgia Reserves.

(Source: U.S. War Department. *War of the Rebellion: A Compilation of the Official Records of the Union and Confederate Armies.* Ser. II, Vol. VII.)

7. Wirz to Major General J. H. Wilson, U.S. Army (7 May 1865)

ANDERSONVILLE, GA., *May 7, 1865.*

Maj. Gen. J. H. WILSON, *U.S. Army,*
Commanding, Macon, Ga.:
GENERAL: It is with great reluctance that I address you these lines, being fully aware how little time is left you to attend to such matters as I now have the honor to lay before you; and if I could see any other way to accomplish my object I would not intrude upon you. I am a native of Switzerland, and was before the war a citizen of Louisiana, by profession a physician. Like hundreds and thousands of others I was carried away by the maelstrom of excitement and joined the Southern Army. I was very severely wounded at the battle of the Seven Pines, near Richmond, Va., and have nearly lost the use of my right arm. Unfit for field duty, I was ordered to report to Bvt. Brig. Gen. J. H. Winder, in

charge of Federal prisoners of war, who ordered me to take charge of a prison in Tuscaloosa, Ala. My health failing me, I applied for a furlough and went to Europe, from whence I returned in February, 1864. I was then ordered to report to the commandant of military prisons at Andersonville, Ga., who assigned me to the command of the interior of the prison. The duties I had to perform were arduous and unpleasant, and I am satisfied that no man can or will justly blame me for things that happened here and which were beyond my power to control. I do not think that I ought to be held responsible for the shortness of rations, for the overcrowded state of the prison (which was in itself a prolific source of the fearful mortality), for the inadequate supplies of clothing, want of shelters, &c. Still I now bear the odium, and men who were prisoners here seem disposed to wreak their vengeance upon me for what they have suffered, who was only the medium, or, I may better say, the tool in the hands of my superiors. This is my condition. I am a man with a family; I lost all my property when the Federal army besieged Vicksburg; I have no means at present to go any place, and even if I had I know of no place where I could go. My life is in danger, and I most respectfully ask of you help and relief. If you will be so generous as to give me some sort of a safe-conduct, or, what I should greatly prefer, a guard to protect myself and family against violence, I shall be thankful to you, and you may rest assured that your protection will not be given to one who is unworthy of it. My intention is to return with my family to Europe so soon as I can make the arrangements.

In the meantime I have the honor, general, to remain,

Very respectfully, your obedient servant,

HY. WIRZ,

Captain, C. S. Army.

(Source: U.S. War Department. *War of the Rebellion: A Compilation of the Official Records of the Union and Confederate Armies.* Ser. II, Vol. VIII.)

8. General Court Martial Orders No. 607 (6 November 1865)

WAR DEPARTMENT,
ADJUTANT-GENERAL'S OFFICE,
Washington, November 6, 1865.

I. Before a military commission which convened at Washington, D.C., August 23, 1865, pursuant to paragraph 3, Special Orders, No. 453, dated August 23, 1865, and paragraph 13, Special Orders, No. 524, dated October 2, 1865, War Department, Adjutant-General's Office, Washington, and of which Maj. Gen. Lewis Wallace, U.S. Volunteers, is president, was arraigned and tried—

Henry Wirz.

CHARGE I: Maliciously, willfully, and traitorously, and in aid of the then existing armed rebellion against the United States of America, on or before the let day of March, A.D. 1864, and on divers other days between that day and the 10th day of April, 1865, combining, confederating, and conspiring, together with John H. Winder, Richard B. Winder, Joseph [Isaiah H.] White, W. S. Winder, R. R. Stevenson, and others unknown, to injure the health and destroy the lives of soldiers in the military service of the United States, then held and being prisoners of war within the lines of the so-called Confederate States, and in the military prisons thereof, to the end that the armies of the United States might be weakened and impaired, in violation of the laws and customs of war.

Specification.—In this, that he, the said Henry Wirz, did combine, confederate, and conspire with them, the said John H. Winder, Richard B. Winder, Joseph [Isaiah H.] White, W. S. Winder, R. R. Stevenson, and others whose names are unknown, citizens of the United States aforesaid, and who were then engaged in armed rebellion against the United States, maliciously, traitorously, and in violation of the laws of war, to impair and injure the health and to destroy the lives—by subjecting to torture and great suffering; by confining in unhealthy and uuwholesome quarters; by exposing to the inclemency of winter and to the dews and burning sun of summer; by compelling the use of impure water; and by furnishing insufficient and unwholesome food— of large numbers of Federal prisoners, to wit, the number of 30,000 soldiers in the military service of the United States of America, held as prisoners of war at Andersonville, in the State of Georgia, within the lines of the so-called Confederate States, on or before the 1st day of March, A.D. 1864, and at divers times between that day and the 10th day of April, A.D. 1865, to the end that the armies of the United States might be weakened and impaired and the insurgents engaged in armed rebellion against the United States might be aided and comforted. And he, the said Henry Wirz, an officer in the military service of the so-called Confederate States, being then and there commandant of a military prison at Andersonville, in the State of Georgia, located, by authority of the so-called Confederate States, for the confinement of prisoners of war, and, as such commandant, fully clothed with authority, and in duty bound to treat, care, and provide for such prisoners held as aforesaid as were or might be placed in his custody according to the law of war, did, in furtherance of such combination, confederation, and conspiracy, and incited thereunto by them, the said John H. Winder, Richard B. Winder, Joseph [Isaiah H.] White, W. S. Winder, R. R. Stevenson, and others whose names are unknown, maliciously, wickedly, and traitorously confine a large number of such prisoners of

war, soldiers in the military service of the United States, to the amount of 30,000 men, in unhealthy and unwholesome quarters, in a close and small area of ground wholly inadequate to their wants and destructive to their health, which he well knew and intended; and, while there so confined during the time aforesaid, did, in furtherance of his evil design, and in aid of the said conspiracy, willfully and maliciously neglect to furnish tents, barracks, or other shelter sufficient for their protection from the inclemency of winter and the dews and burning sun of summer; and with such evil intent did take, and cause to be taken, from them their clothing, blankets, camp equipage, and other property of which they were possessed at the time of being placed in his custody; and, with like malice and evil intent, did refuse to furnish, or cause to be furnished, food either of a quality or quantity sufficient to preserve health and sustain life; and did refuse and neglect to furnish wood sufficient for cooking in summer and to keep the said prisoners warm in winter; and did compel the said prisoners to subsist upon unwholesome food, and that in limited quantities entirely inadequate to sustain health, which he well knew; and did compel the said prisoners to use unwholesome water, reeking with the filth and garbage of the prison and prison guard, and the offal and drainage of the cookhouse of said prison, whereby the prisoners became greatly reduced in their bodily strength, and emaciated and injured in their bodily health; their minds impaired and their intellects broken; and many of them, to wit, the number of 10,000, whose names are unknown, sickened and died by reason thereof, which he, the said Henry Wirz, then and there well knew and intended; and, so knowing and evilly intending, did refuse and neglect to provide proper lodgings, food, or nourishment for the sick, and necessary medicine and medical attendance for the restoration of their health; and did knowingly, willfully, and maliciously, in furtherance of his evil designs, permit them to languish and die from want of care and proper treatment. And the said Henry Wirz, still pursuing his evil purpose, did permit to remain in the said prison, among the emaciated sick and languishing living, the bodies of the dead, until they became corrupt and loathsome and filled the air with fetid and noxious exhalations, and thereby greatly increased the unwholesomeness of the prison, insomuch that great numbers of said prisoners, to wit, the number of 1,000. whose names are unknown, sickened and died by reason thereof. And the said Henry Wirz, still pursuing his wicked and cruel purpose, wholly disregarding the usages of civilized warfare, did, at the time and place aforesaid, maliciously and willfully subject the prisoners aforesaid to cruel, unusual, and infamous punishment upon slight, trivial, and fictitious pretenses, by fastening large balls of iron to their feet, and binding large numbers of the prisoners aforesaid closely together with large chains around their necks and feet, so that they walked with the greatest difficulty—and, being so confined, were subjected to the burning rays of the sun, often without food or drink for hours, and even days—from which said cruel treatment large numbers, to wit, the number of 100, whose names are unknown, sickened, fainted, and died. And he, the said Wirz, did further cruelly treat and injure said prisoners by maliciously confining them within an instrument of torture called the "stocks," thus depriving them of the use of their limbs, and forcing them to lie, sit, and stand for many hours without the power of changing position, and being without food or drink, in consequence of which many, to wit, the number of thirty, whose names are unknown, sickened and died. And he, the said Wirz, still wickedly pursuing his evil purpose, did establish and cause to be designated within the prison inclosure containing said prisoners, a "dead-line," being a line around the inner face of the stockade or wall inclosing said prison, and about twenty feet distant from and within said stockade; and having so established said dead-line, which was in many places an imaginary line, and in many other places marked by insecure and shifting strips of boards nailed upon the top of small and insecure stakes or posts, he, the said Wirz, instructed the prison guard stationed around the top of said stockade to fire upon and kill any of the prisoners aforesaid who might touch, fall upon, pass over or under or across the said "dead-line." Pursuant to which said orders and instructions, maliciously and needlessly given by said Wirz, the said prison guard did fire upon and kill a large number of said prisoners, to wit, the number of about 300. And the said Wirz, still pursuing his evil purpose, did keep and use ferocious and bloodthirsty beasts, dangerous to human life, called bloodhounds, to hunt down prisoners of war aforesaid who made their escape from his custody, and did then and there willfully and maliciously suffer, incite, and encourage the said beasts to seize, tear, mangle, and maim the bodies and limbs of said fugitive prisoners of war, which the said beasts, incited as aforesaid, then and there did, whereby a large number of said prisoners of war, who, during the time aforesaid, made their escape and were recaptured, and were, by the said beasts then and there cruelly and inhumanly injured, insomuch that many of said prisoners, to wit, the number of about fifty died. And the said Wirz, still pursuing his wicked purpose, and still aiding in carrying out said conspiracy, did use and cause to be used, for the pretended purposes of vaccination, impure and poisonous vaccine matter, which said impure and poisonous matter was then and there, by the direction and order of said Wirz, maliciously, cruelly, and wickedly deposited in the arms of many of said prisoners, by reason of

which large numbers of them, to wit, 100, lost the use of their arms, and many of them, to wit, about the number of 200, were so injured that they soon thereafter died. All of which he, the said Henry Wirz, well knew and maliciously intended, and in aid of the then existing rebellion against the United States, with the view to assist in weakening and impairing the armies of the United States, and in furtherance of the said conspiracy and with the full knowledge, consent, and connivance of his co-conspirators aforesaid, he, the said Wirz, then and there did.

CHARGE 2: Murder, in violation of the laws and customs of war.

Specification 1.—In this, that the said Henry Wirz, an officer in the military service of the so-called Confederate States of America, at Andersonville, in the State of Georgia, on or about the 8th day of July, A.D. 1864, then and there being commandant of a prison there located, by the authority of the said so-called Confederate States, for the confinement of prisoners of war taken and held as such from the armies of the United States of America, while acting as said commandant, feloniously, willfully, and of his malice aforethought, did make an assault, and he, the said Henry Wirz, a certain pistol called a revolver then and there loaded and charged with gunpowder and bullets, which said pistol the said Henry Wirz in his hand then and there had and held to, against, and upon a soldier belonging to the Army of the United States, in his, the said Henry Wirz's, custody, as a prisoner of war, whose name is unknown, then and there feloniously, and of his malice aforethought, did shoot and discharge, inflicting upon the body of the soldier aforesaid a mortal wound with the pistol aforesaid, in consequence of which said mortal wound, murderously inflicted by the said Henry Wirz, the said soldier thereafter, to wit, on the 9th day of July, A.D. 1864, died.

Specification 2.—In this, that the said Henry Wirz, an officer in the military service of the so-called Confederate States of America, at Andersonville, in the State of Georgia, on or about the 20th day of September, A.D. 1864, then and there being commandant of a prison there located, by the authority of the said so-called Confederate States, for the confinement of prisoners of war taken and held as such from the armies of the United States of America, while acting as said commandant, feloniously, willfully, and of his malice aforethought, did jump upon, stamp, kick, bruise, and otherwise injure with the heels of his boots, a soldier belonging to the Army of the United States, in his, the said Henry Wirz's, custody as a prisoner of war, whose name is unknown, of which said stamping, kicking, and bruising, maliciously done and inflicted by the said Wirz, he, the said soldier, soon thereafter, to wit,

on the 20th day of September, A. D. 1864, died.

Specification 3.—In this, that the said Henry Wirz, an officer in the military service of the so-called Confederate States of America, at Andersonville, in the State of Georgia, on or about the 13th day of June, A. D. 1864, then and there being commandant of a prison there located, by the authority of the said so-called Confederate States, for the confinement of prisoners of war, taken and held as such from the armies of the United States of America, while acting as said commandant, feloniously, and of his malice aforethought, did make an assault, and he, the said Henry Wirz, a certain pistol called a revolver then and there loaded and charged with gunpowder and bullets, which said pistol the said Henry Wirz, in his hand then and there had and held to, against, and upon a soldier belonging to the Army of the United States, in his, the said Henry Wirz's, custody as a prisoner of war, whose name is unknown, then and there feloniously, and of his malice aforethought, did shoot and discharge, inflicting upon the body of the soldier aforesaid a mortal wound with the pistol aforesaid, in consequence of which said mortal wound, murderously inflicted by the said Henry Wirz, the said soldier immediately, to wit, on the day aforesaid, died.

Specification 4.—In this, that the said Henry Wirz, an officer in the military service of the so-called Confederate States of America, at Andersonville, in the State of Georgia, on or about the 30th day of May, A.D. 1864, then and there being commandant of a prison there located, by the authority of the said so-called Confederate States, for the confinement of prisoners of war, taken and held as such from the armies of the United States of America, while acting as said commandant, feloniously, and of his malice aforethought, did make an assault, and he, the said Henry Wirz, a certain pistol called a revolver then and there loaded and charged with gunpowder and bullets, which said pistol the said Henry Wirz in his hand then and there had and held to, against, and upon a soldier belonging to the Army of the United States, in his, the said Henry Wirz's, custody as a prisoner of war, whose name is unknown, then and there feloniously, and of his malice aforethought, did shoot and discharge, inflicting upon the body of the soldier aforesaid a mortal wound with the pistol aforesaid, in consequence of which said mortal wound, murderously inflicted by the said Henry Wirz, the said soldier, on the 30th day of May, A.D. 1864, died.

Specification 5.—In this, that the said Henry Wirz, an officer in the military service of the so-called Confederate States of America, at Andersonville, in the State of Georgia, on or about the 20th day of August, A.D. 1864, then and there being commandant of a prison there located, by the authority of the said so-called Confederate States, for the confinement of prisoners of war, taken and held as such from the armies of the United States of America, while acting as said commandant, feloniously, and of his malice aforethought, did confine and bind with an instrument of torture called "the stocks," a soldier belonging to the Army of the United States, in his, the said Henry Wirz's, custody as a prisoner of war, whose name is unknown, in consequence of which such cruel treatment, maliciously and murderously inflicted as aforesaid, he, the said soldier, soon thereafter, to wit, on the 30th day of August, A.D. 1864, died.

Specification 6.—In this, that the said Henry Wirz, an officer in the military service of the so-called Confederate States of America, at Andersonville, in the State of Georgia, on or about the 1st day of February, 1865, then and there being commandant of a prison there located, by the authority of the said so-called Confederate States, for the confinement of prisoners of war, taken and held as such from the armies of the United States of America, while acting as said commandant, feloniously, and of his malice aforethought, did confine and bind within an instrument of torture called "the stocks," a soldier belonging to the Army of the United States, in his, the said Henry Wirz's, custody as a prisoner of war, whose name is unknown, in consequence of which said cruel treatment, maliciously and murderously inflicted as aforesaid, he, the said soldier, soon thereafter, to wit, on the 6th day of February, A.D. 1865, died.

Specification 7.—In this, that the said Henry Wirz, an officer in the military service of the so-called Confederate States of America, at Andersonville, in the State of Georgia, on or about the 20th day of July, A.D. 1864, then and there being commandant of a prison there located, by the authority of the said so-called Confederate States, for the confinement of prisoners of war, taken and held as such from the armies of the United States of America, while acting as said commandant, feloniously, and of his malice aforethought, did fasten and chain together several persons, soldiers, belonging to the Army of the United States, in his, the said Henry Wirz's, custody as prisoners of war, whose names are unknown, binding the necks and feet of said prisoners closely together, and compelling them to carry great burdens, to wit, large iron balls chained to their feet, so that, in consequence of the said cruel treatment inflicted upon them by the said Henry Wirz as aforesaid, one of said soldiers, a prisoner of war as aforesaid, whose name is unknown, on the 25th day of July, A.D. 1864, died.

Specification 8.—In this, that the said Henry Wirz, an officer in the military service of the so-called Confederate States of America, at Andersonville, in the State of Georgia, on or about the 15th day of May,

A.D. 1864, then and there being commandant of a prison there located, by the authority of the said so-called Confederate States, for the confinement of prisoners of war, taken and held as such from the armies of the United States of America, while acting as said commandant, feloniously, willfully, and of his malice aforethought, did order a rebel soldier, whose name is unknown, then on duty as a sentinel or guard to the prison of which said Henry Wirz was commandant as aforesaid, to fire upon a soldier belonging to the Army of the United States, in his, the said Henry Wirz's, custody as a prisoner of war, whose name is unknown; and in pursuance of said order, so as aforesaid maliciously and murderously given as aforesaid, he, the said rebel soldier, did, with a musket loaded with gunpowder and bullet, then and there fire at the said soldier so as aforesaid held as a prisoner of war, inflicting upon him a mortal wound with the musket aforesaid, of which he, the said prisoner, soon thereafter, to wit, on the day aforesaid, died.

Specification 9.—In this, that the said Henry Wirz, an officer in the military service of the so-called Confederate States of America, at Andersonville, in the State of Georgia, on or about the 1st day of July, A.D. 1864, then and there being commandant of a prison there located, by the authority of the said so-called Confederate States, for the confinement of prisoners of war, taken and held as such from the armies of the United States of America, while acting as said commandant, feloniously, and of his malice aforethought, did order a rebel soldier, whose name is unknown, then on duty as a sentinel or guard to the prison of which said Wirz was commandant as aforesaid, to fire upon a soldier belonging to the Army of the United States, in his, the said Henry Wirz's, custody as a prisoner of war, whose name is unknown; and in pursuance of said order, so as aforesaid maliciously and murderously given as aforesaid, he, the said rebel soldier, did, with a musket loaded with gunpowder and bullet, then and there fire at the said soldier so as aforesaid held as a prisoner of war, inflicting upon him a mortal wound with the said musket, of which he, the said prisoner, soon thereafter, to wit, on the day aforesaid, died.

Specification 10.—In this, that the said Henry Wirz, an officer in the military service of the so-called Confederate States of America, at Andersonville, in the State of Georgia, on or about the 20th day of August, A.D. 1864, then and there being commandant of a prison there located, by the authority of the said so-called Confederate States, for the confinement of prisoners of war, taken and held as such from the armies of the United States of America, while acting as said commandant, feloniously, and of his malice aforethought, did order a rebel soldier, whose name is unknown, then on duty as a sentinel or guard to the prison of which said Wirz was commandant as aforesaid, to fire upon a soldier belonging to the Army of the United States, in his, the said Henry Wirz's, custody as a prisoner of war, whose name is unknown; and in pursuance of said order, so as aforesaid maliciously and murderously given as aforesaid, he, the said rebel soldier, did, with a musket loaded with gunpowder and bullet, then and there fire at the said soldier so as aforesaid held as a prisoner of war, inflicting upon him a mortal wound with the said musket, of which he, the said prisoner, soon thereafter, to wit, on the day aforesaid, died.

Specification 11.—In this, that the said Henry Wirz, an officer in the military service of the so-called Confederate States of America, at Andersonville, in the State of Georgia, on or about the 1st day of July, A.D. 1864, then and there being commandant of a prison there located, by, the authority of the said so-called Confederate States, for the confinement of prisoners of war, taken and held as such from the armies of the United States of America, while acting as said commandant, feloniously, and of his malice aforethought, did cause, incite, and urge certain ferocious and blood-thirsty animals, called bloodhounds, to pursue, attack, wound, and tear in pieces a soldier belonging to the Army of the United States, in his, the said Henry Wirz's, custody as a prisoner of war, whose name is unknown; and in consequence thereof the said bloodhounds did then and there, with the knowledge, encouragement, and instigation of him, the said Wirz, maliciously and murderously given by him, attack and mortally wound the said soldier, in consequence of which said mortal wound he, the said prisoner, soon thereafter, to wit, on the 6th day of July, A. D. 1864, died.

Specification 12.—In this, that the said Henry Wirz, an officer in the military service of the so-called Confederate States of America, at Andersonville, in the State of Georgia, on or about the 27th day of July, A. D. 1864, then and there being commandant of a prison there located, by the authority of the said so-called Confederate States, for the confinement of prisoners of war, taken and held as such from the armies of the United States of America, while acting as said commandant, feloniously, and of his malice aforethought, did order a rebel soldier, whose name is unknown, then on duty as a sentinel or guard to the prison of which said Wirz was commandant as aforesaid, to fire upon a soldier belonging to the Army of the United States, in his, the said Henry Wirz's, custody as a prisoner of war, whose name is unknown; and in pursuance of said order, so as aforesaid maliciously and murderously given as aforesaid, he, the said rebel soldier, did, with a musket loaded with gunpowder and bullet, then and there fire at the said soldier so as

aforesaid held as a prisoner of war, inflicting upon him a mortal wound with the said musket of which said mortal wound he, the said prisoner, soon thereafter, to wit, on the day aforesaid, died.

Specification 13.—In this, that the said Henry Wirz, an officer in the military service of the so-called Confederate States of America, at Andersonville, in the State of Georgia, on or about the 3d day of August, 1864, then and there being commandant of a prison there located, by the authority of the said so-called Confederate States, for the confinement of prisoners of war, taken and held as such from the armies of the United States of America, while acting as said commandant, feloniously, and of his malice aforethought, did make an assault upon a soldier belonging to the Army of the United States, in his, the said Henry Wirz's, custody as a prisoner of war, whose name is unknown, and with a pistol called a revolver, then and there held in the hands of the said Wirz, did beat and bruise said soldier upon the head, shoulders, and breast, inflicting thereby mortal wounds, from which said beating and bruising aforesaid, and mortal wounds caused thereby, the said soldier soon thereafter, to wit, on the 4th day of August, A.D. 1864, died.

To which charges and specifications the accused, Henry Wirz, pleaded not guilty.

FINDING.

The court, having maturely considered the evidence adduced, finds the accused, Henry Wirz, as follows:

Charge I.

Of the specification, guilty, after amending said specification to read as follows:

In this, that he, the said Henry Wirz, did combine, confederate, and conspire with them, the said Jefferson Davis, James A. Seddon, Howell Cobb, John H. Winder, Richard B. Winder, Isaiah H. White, W. S. Winder, W. Shelby Reed, R. R. Stevenson, S. P. Moore, [W. J. W.] Kerr (late hospital steward at Andersonville), James W. Duncan. Wesley W. Turner, Benjamin Harris, and others whose names are unknown, citizens of the United States aforesaid, and who were then engaged in armed rebellion against the United States, maliciously, traitorously, and in violation of the laws of war, to impair and injure the health and to destroy the lives—by subjecting to torture and great suffering; by confining in unhealthy and unwholesome quarters; by exposing to the inclemency of winter and to the dews and burning sun of summer; by compelling the use of impure water, and by furnishing insufficient and unwholesome food—of large numbers of Federal prisoners, to wit, the number of about 45,000 soldiers in the military service of the United States of America, held as prisoners of war at Andersonville, in the State of Georgia, within the lines of the so-called Confederate States, on or before the 27th day of March,

A.D. 1864, and at divers times between that day and the 10th day of April, A.D. 1865, to the end that the armies of the United States might be weakened and impaired, and the insurgents engaged in armed rebellion against the United States might be aided and comforted. And he, the said Henry Wirz, an officer in the military service of the so-called Confederate States, being then and there commandant of a military prison at Andersonville, in the State of Georgia, located by authority of the so-called Confederate States for the confinement of prisoners of war, and as such commandant, fully clothed with authority, and in duty bound to treat, care, and provide for such prisoners, held as aforesaid, as were or might be placed in his custody, according to the law of war, did, in furtherance of such combination, confederation, and conspiracy, maliciously, wickedly, and traitorously confine a large number of prisoners of war, soldiers in the military service of the United States, to the number of about 45,000 men, in unhealthy and unwholesome quarters, in a close and small area of ground wholly inadequate to their wants and destructive to their health, which he well knew and intended; and, while there so confined during the time aforesaid, did, in furtherance of his evil design, and in aid of the said conspiracy, willfully and maliciously neglect to furnish tents, barracks, or other shelter sufficient for their protection from the inclemency of winter and the dews and burning sun of summer; and with such evil intent did take, and cause to be taken, from them, their clothing, blankets, camp equipage, and other property of which they were possessed at the time of being placed in his custody; and, with like malice and evil intent, did refuse to furnish, or cause to be furnished, food either of a quality or quantity sufficient to preserve health and sustain life; and did refuse and neglect to furnish wood sufficient for cooking in summer and to keep the said prisoners warm in winter; and did compel the said prisoners to subsist upon unwholesome food, and that in limited quantities, entirely inadequate to sustain health, which he well knew; and did compel the said prisoners to use unwholesome water, reeking with the filth and garbage of the prison and prison guard and the offal and drainage of the cook-house of said prison, whereby the prisoners became greatly reduced in their bodily strength, and emaciated and injured in their bodily health; their minds impaired and their intellects broken; and many of them, to wit, about the number of 10,000, whose names are unknown, sickened and died by reason thereof, which he, the said Henry Wirz, then and there well knew and intended; and, so knowing and evilly intending, did refuse and neglect to provide proper lodgings, food, or nourishment for the sick, and necessary medicine and medical attendance for the restoration of their health; and did knowingly, willfully, and maliciously, in furtherance of his evil designs, permit them to languish and die from want of care and proper treatment. And the said Henry Wirz, still pursuing his evil purposes,

did permit to remain in the said prison among the emaciated sick and languishing living, the bodies of the dead until they became corrupt and loathsome, and filled the air with fetid and noxious exhalations, and thereby greatly increased the unwholesomeness of the prison, insomuch that great numbers of said prisoners, whose names are unknown, sickened and died by reason thereof. And the said Henry Wirz, still pursuing his wicked and cruel purpose, wholly disregarding the usages of civilized warfare, did, at the time and place aforesaid, maliciously and willfully subject the prisoners aforesaid to cruel, unusual, and infamous punishment, upon slight trivial, and fictitious pretenses, by fastening large balls of iron to their feet, and binding numbers of the prisoners aforesaid closely together with large chains around their necks and feet, so that they walked with the greatest difficulty, and being so confined were subjected to the burning rays of the sun, often without food or drink for hours, and even days, from which said cruel treatment numbers, whose names are unknown, sickened, fainted, and died. And he, the said Wirz, did further cruelly treat and injure said prisoners by maliciously tying them up by the thumbs, and willfully confining them within an instrument of torture called "the stocks," thus depriving them of the use of their limbs, and forcing them to lie, sit, and stand for many hours without the power of changing position, and being without food or drink, in consequence of which many, whose names are unknown, sickened and died. And he, the said Wirz, still wickedly pursuing his evil purpose, did establish, and cause to be designated within the prison inclosure containing said prisoners, a "dead-line," being a line around the inner face of the stockade or wall inclosing said prison, and about twenty feet distant from and within said stockade; and having so established said deadline, which was in some places an imaginary line, and in other places marked by insecure and shifting strips of boards, nailed upon the top of small and insecure stakes or posts, he, the said Wirz, instructed the prison guard stationed around the top of said stockade to fire upon and kill any of the prisoners aforesaid who might fall upon, pass over or under or across the said dead-line; pursuant to which said orders and instructions, maliciously and needlessly given by said Wirz, the said prison guard did fire upon and kill a number of said prisoners. And the said Wirz, still pursuing his evil purpose, did keep and use ferocious and bloodthirsty dogs, dangerous to human life, to hunt down prisoners of war aforesaid who made their escape from his custody; and did then and there willfully and maliciously suffer, incite, and encourage the said dogs to seize, tear, mangle, and maim the bodies and limbs of said fugitive prisoners of war, which the said dogs, incited as aforesaid, then and there did, whereby a number of said prisoners of war, who, during the time aforesaid, made their escape and were recaptured, died. And the said Wirz, still pursuing his wicked purpose, and still aiding in

carrying out said conspiracy, did cause to be used for the pretended purposes of vaccination, impure and poisonous vaccine matter, which said impure and poisonous matter was then and there, by the direction and order of said Wirz, maliciously, cruelly, and wickedly deposited in the arms of many of said prisoners, by reason of which large numbers of them lost the use of their arms, and many of them were so injured that they soon thereafter died. All of which he, the said Henry Wirz, well knew and maliciously intended, and in aid of the then existing rebellion against the United States, with a view to assist in weakening and impairing the armies of the United States, and in furtherance of the said conspiracy, and with the full knowledge, consent, and connivance of his co-conspirators aforesaid, he, the said Wirz, then and there did,

Of the charge, guilty, after amending said charge to read as follows:

Maliciously, willfully, and traitorously, and in aid of the then existing armed rebellion against the United States of America, on or before the 27th day of March, A.D. 1864, and on divers other days between that day and the 10th day of April, A.D. 1865, combining, confederating, and conspiring, together with Jefferson Davis, James A. Seddon, Howell Cobb, John H. Winder, Richard B. Winder, Isaiah H. White, W. S. Winder, W. Shelby Reed, R.R. Stevenson, S. P. Moore, [W. J. W.] Kerr (late hospital steward at Andersonville), James W. Duncan, Wesley W. Turner, Benjamin Harris, and others unknown, to injure the health and destroy the lives of soldiers in the military service of the United States, then held and being prisoners of war within the lines of the so-called Confederate States, and in the military prisons thereof, to the end that the armies of the United States might be weakened and impaired, in violation of the laws and customs of war.

Charge II.

Of the first specification, guilty, adding the words "or about" immediately before the phrase "the 9th day of July."

Of the second specification, guilty.

Of the third specification, guilty, after striking out "June" and inserting instead "September."

Of the fourth specification, not guilty.

Of the 5th specification, guilty, after striking out the phrase "on the 30th day" and inserting instead the phrase "on or about the 25th day."

Of the sixth specification, guilty, after striking out the word "1st" and inserting "15th," and also striking out the phrase "on the 6th day" and inserting instead the phrase "on or about the 16th day.

Of the seventh specification, guilty, after striking out the word "20th" and inserting instead the word "1st," and also after inserting" or about "immediately before the phrase" the 25th day."

Of the eighth specification, guilty.

Of the ninth specification, guilty.

Of the tenth specification, not guilty.

Of the eleventh specification, guilty, after striking out the word "1st" and inserting instead the word "6th;" after striking out also the phrase "incite and urge" and the phrase "encouragement and instigation" and by adding the words "or about" after the word "on," where it occurs in the specification; and also after striking out the phrase "animals called bloodhounds" and inserting the word "dogs;" and also striking out the word "bloodhounds" where it afterward occurs and insert the word "dogs;" and also striking out the words "given by him."

Of the twelfth specification, guilty.

Of the thirteenth specification, not guilty.

Of the charge, guilty.

SENTENCE.

And the court does therefore sentence him, Henry Wirz, to be hanged by the neck till he be dead at such time and place as the President of the United States may direct, two-thirds of the members of the court concurring herein.

And the court also finds the prisoner, Henry Wirz, guilty of having caused the death, in manner as alleged in specification 11, to charge 2, by means of dogs, of three prisoners of war in his custody, and soldiers of the United States, one occurring on or about the 15th day of May, 1864; another occurring on or about the 11th day of July, 1864; another occurring on or about the 1st day of September, 1864; but which finding, as here expressed, has not and did not enter into the sentence of the court as before given.

II. The proceedings, finding, and sentence in the foregoing case having been submitted to the President of the United States, the following are his orders:

EXECUTIVE MANSION, *November 3, 1865.*

The proceedings, finding, and sentence of the court in the within case are approved, and it is ordered that the sentence be carried into execution by the officer commanding the Department of Washington on Friday the 10th day of November, 1865, between the hours of 6 o'clock a.m. and 12 o'clock noon.
ANDREW JOHNSON,
President.

(Source: U.S. War Department. *War of the Rebellion: A Compilation of the Official Records of the Union and Confederate Armies.* Ser. II, Vol. VIII.)

XLVII. Religion
Americans during the Civil War were a religious people. Piety was not unusual for a time that took its faith seriously and

saw the intervention of God as direct and likely. The institution of religious ritual, such as a presidential directive regarding the Sabbath, would not have struck anyone as peculiar or objectionable, and the role of chaplains in the maintenance of soldiers' spiritual health was regarded as so essential that particular protocols were fashioned to define their situation. And while keeping Christmas in the beleaguered Confederacy of 1864 was a challenge even for its First Family, the essence of faith was embodied in small pleasures ennobled by sacrifice and the timeless verities of simple gifts, handsome boys, and laughing girls. [See Catholics; Chaplains, African-American; Chaplains; Churches; Religion]

1. General Order Respecting the Observance of the Sabbath Day in the Army and Navy (15 November 1862)

EXECUTIVE MANSION,
Washington, November 15, 1862.

The President, Commander-in-Chief of the Army and Navy, desires and enjoins the orderly observance of the Sabbath by the officers and men in military and naval service. The importance for man and beast of the prescribed weekly rest, the sacred rights of Christian soldiers and sailors, a becoming deference to the best sentiment of a Christian people, and a due regard for the Divine will, demand that Sunday labor in the Army and Navy be reduced to the measure of strict necessity.

The discipline and character of the national forces should not suffer, nor the cause they defend be imperiled, by the profanation of the day or name of the Most High. At this time of public distress, adopting the words of Washington in 1776, "men may find enough to do in the service of God and their country without abandoning themselves to vice and immorality." The first general order issued by the Father of his Country after the Declaration of Independence indicates the spirit in which our institutions were founded and should ever be defended: "The general hopes and trusts that every officer and man will endeavor to live and act as becomes a Christian soldier, defending the dearest rights and liberties of his country."
ABRAHAM LINCOLN.

(Source: U.S. War Department. *War of the Rebellion: A Compilation of the Official Records of the Union and Confederate Armies.* Ser. III, Vol. II.)

2. General Orders No. 158 (13 April 1864)

WAR DEPT., ADJT. GENERAL'S OFFICE,
Washington, April 13, 1864.

The following act of Congress is published for the information of all concerned:
PUBLIC—No. 44.

AN ACT to amend section nine of the act approved July seventeenth, eighteen hundred and sixty-two, entitled "An act to define the pay and emoluments of certain officers of the Army, and for other purposes."

Be it enacted by the Senate and House of Representatives of the United States of America in Congress assembled, That the rank of chaplain, without command, in the regular and volunteer service of the United States, is hereby recognized. Chaplains shall be borne on the field and staff rolls next after the surgeons, and shall wear such uniform as is or may be prescribed by the Army Regulations, and shall be subject to the same rules and regulations as other officers of the Army....

SEC. 2. *And be it further enacted,* That the act approved July fourteenth, eighteen hundred and sixty-two entitled "An act to grant pensions," is hereby so amended as to include chaplains in the regular and volunteer forces of the Army...

SEC. 3. *And be it further enacted,* That it shall be the duty of chaplains in the military service of the United States to make monthly reports to the Adjutant-General of the Army, through the usual military channels, of the moral condition and general history of the regiments, hospitals, or posts to which they may be attached; and it shall be the duty of all commanders of regiments, hospitals, and posts, to render such facilities as will aid in the discharge of the duties assigned to them by the Government.

SEC 4. *And be it further enacted,* That all chaplains in the military service of the United States shall hold appropriate religious services at the burial of soldiers who may die in the command to which they are assigned to duty, and it shall be their duty to hold public religious services at least once each Sabbath, when practicable.
Approved April 9, 1864.
By order of the Secretary of War:
E. D. TOWNSEND,
Assistant Adjutant-General.

(Source: U.S. War Department. *War of the Rebellion: A Compilation of the Official Records of the Union and Confederate Armies.* Ser. III, Vol. IV.)

3. "Christmas in the Confederate White House," by Varina Davis [Excerpts] (1896)

On Christmas morning the children awoke early and came in to see their toys. They were followed by the negro women, who one after another "caught" us by wishing us a merry Christmas before we could say it to them, which gave them a right to a gift. Of course, there was a present for every one, small though it might be, and one who had been born and brought up at our plantation was vocal in her admiration of a gay handkerchief.

As she left the room she ejaculated: "Lord knows mistress knows our insides; she jest got the very thing I wanted."

For me there were six cakes of delicious soap, made from the grease of ham boiled for a family at Farmville, a skein of exquisitely fine gray linen thread spun at home, a pincushion of some plain brown cotton material made by some poor woman and stuffed with wool from her pet sheep, and a little baby hat plaited by the orphans and presented by the industrious little pain who sewed the straw together. They pushed each other silently to speak, and at last mutely offered the hat, and considered the kiss they gave the sleeping little one ample reward for the industry and far above the fruit with which they were laden. Another present was a fine, delicate little baby frock without an inch of lace or embroidery upon it, but the delicate fabric was set with fairy stitches by the dear invalid neighbor who made it, and it was very precious in my eyes. There were also a few of Swinburne's best songs bound in wall-paper and a chamois needlebook left for me by young Mr. P., now succeeded to his title in England. In it was a Brobdinagian thimble "for my own finger, you know," said the handsome, cheerful young fellow....

The night closed with a "starvation" party, where there were no refreshments, at a neighboring house. The rooms lighted as well as practicable, some one willing to play dance music on the piano and plenty of young men and girls comprised the entertainment. Sam Weller's soiry, consisting of boiled mutton and capers, would have been a royal feast in the Confederacy. The officers, who rode into town with their long cavalry boots pulled well up over their knees, but splashed up their waists, put up their horses and rushed to the places where their dress uniform suits had been left for safekeeping. They very soon emerged, however, in full toggery and entered into the pleasures of their dance with the bright-eyed girls, who many of them were fragile as fairies, but worked like peasants for their home and country. These young people are gray-haired now, but the lessons of self-denial, industry and frugality in which they became past mistresses then, have made of them the most dignified, self-reliant and tender women I have ever known—all honor to them.

So, in the interchange of the courtesies and charities of life, to which we could not add its comforts and pleasures, passed the last Christmas in the Confederate mansion.

(Source: Davis, Varina J. "Christmas in the Confederate White House." *New York World Sunday Magazine*, 13 December 1896, p. 26)

Jews in both the Union and the Confederacy were often discriminated against because of their faith. The most flagrant instance was Ulysses S. Grant's expulsion of "Jews, as a class" from the Department of Tennessee (including Kentucky, Mississippi and Tennessee), ostensibly to punish smugglers and charlatans. Made aware of the outrage, Lincoln revoked the order, perhaps the only time that he officially questioned Grant's judgment. More routinely, allowing furloughs for the observance of Jewish religious holidays was a predicament for commanders in both armies and was usually handled as it was by Robert E. Lee in September 1864. The resilience of the human spirit, whether Jew or gentile, was certainly illuminated in the makeshift Passover ceremony approved by a sympathetic officer and produced by a resourceful Yankee and his fellows more than accustomed to being strangers in a strange land. [See Jews]

4. Grant's Order to General Webster (1862)
LA GRANGE, *November 10, 1862.*

General WEBSTER, *Jackson, Tenn.:*
Give orders to all the conductors on the road that no Jews are to be permitted to travel on the railroad southward from any point. They may go north and be encouraged in it; but they are such an intolerable nuisance that the department must be purged of them.
U. S. GRANT, *Major-General.*

(Source: U.S. War Department. *War of the Rebellion: A Compilation of the Official Records of the Union and Confederate Armies.* Ser. I, Vol. XVII.)

5. Grant's General Orders No. 11 (1862)
GENERAL ORDERS No. 11.
HDQRS. 13TH A. C., *DEPT. OF THE TENN.,*
Holly Springs, December 17, 1862.

The Jews, as a class violating every regulation of trade established by the Treasury Department and also department orders, are hereby expelled from the department within twenty-four hours from the receipt of this order.

Post commanders will see that all of this class of people be furnished passes and required to leave, and any one returning after such notification will be arrested and held in confinement until an opportunity occurs of sending them out as prisoners, unless furnished with permit from headquarters.

No passes will be given these people to visit headquarters for the purpose of making personal application for trade permits.
By order of Maj. Gen. U.S. Grant:
JNO. A. RAWLINS,
Assistant Adjutant-General.

(Source: U.S. War Department. *War of the Rebellion: A Compilation of the Official Records of the Union and Confederate Armies.* Ser. I, Vol. XVII.)

6. Letter to Lincoln from Deported Jewish Citizens (29 December 1862)

PADUCAH, *KY., December 29, 1862.*

Hon. ABRAHAM LINCOLN,
President of the United States:
General Orders, No. 11, issued by General Grant at Oxford, Miss., December the 17th, commands all post commanders to expel all Jews, without distinction, within twenty-four hours, from his entire department. The undersigned, good and loyal citizens of the United States and residents of this town for many years, engaged in legitimate business as merchants, feel greatly insulted and outraged by this inhuman order, the carrying out of which would be the grossest violation of the Constitution and our rights as good citizens under it, and would place us, besides a large number of other Jewish families of this town, as outlaws before the whole world. We respectfully ask your immediate attention to this enormous outrage on all law and humanity, and pray for your effectual and immediate interposition. We would respectfully refer you to the post commander and post adjutant as to our loyalty, and to all respectable citizens of this community as to our standing as citizens and merchants. We respectfully ask for immediate instructions to be sent to the commander of this post.
D. WOLFF & BROS.
C. F. KASKELL.
J. W. KASWELL.

(Source: U.S. War Department. *War of the Rebellion: A Compilation of the Official Records of the Union and Confederate Armies.* Ser. I, Vol. XVII/2.)

7. Revocation of General Order No. 11 (January 1863)

WAR DEPARTMENT,
Washington, January 4, 1863.

Major-General GRANT,
Holly Springs, Miss.:
A paper purporting to be General Orders, No. 11, issued by you December 17, has been presented here. By its terms it expels all Jews from your department. If such an order has been issued, it will be immediately revoked.
H. W. HALLECK,
General-in-Chief.

* * *

[CIRCULAR.] HDQRS. 13TH ARMY CORPS, DEPT. OF THE TENN.,
Holly Springs, Miss., January 7, 1863.

By direction of General-in-Chief of the Army, at Washington, the general order from these headquarters expelling Jews from the department is hereby revoked. By order of Maj. Gen. U. S. Grant:

JNO. A. RAWLINS,
Assistant Adjutant-General.

(Source: U.S. War Department. *War of the Rebellion: A Compilation of the Official Records of the Union and Confederate Armies.* Ser. I, XVII/2.)

8. Halleck to Grant in Regard to General Orders No. 11 [Excerpt] (21 January 1863)

HEADQUARTERS OF THE ARMY,
Washington, January 21, 1863.
Major-General GRANT, *Memphis:*

. . . It may be proper to give you some explanation of the revocation of your order expelling all Jews from your department. The President has no objection to your expelling traitors and Jew peddlers, which, I suppose, was the object of your order; but, as it in terms proscribed an entire religious class, some of whom are fighting in our ranks, the President deemed it necessary to revoke it.
Very respectfully, your obedient servant,
H. W. HALLECK,
General-in-Chief.
WASHINGTON, *D.C., January 25, 1863.*

(Source: U.S. War Department. *War of the Rebellion: A Compilation of the Official Records of the Union and Confederate Armies.* Ser. I, Vol. XXIV/1.)

9. Robert E. Lee to Reverend Max Michelbacher of Richmond, Virginia, Congregation Beth Ahabah (20 September 1864)

Headquarters Army Northern Virginia
Sept. 20, 1864.

Rev. M.J. Michelbacher, Richmond, Va.
Sir:
I have received your letter of the 15th inst., asking that furloughs may be granted to the Israelites in the army, from September 30th to October 11th, to enable them to repair to Richmond to observe the holy days appointed by the Jewish religion.

It would afford me much pleasure to comply with your request did the interests of the service permit; but it is impossible to grant a general furlough to one class of our soldiers without recognizing the claims of others to a like indulgence. I can only grant furloughs on applications setting forth special grounds for them, or in accordance with the general orders on that subject applicable to all the army alike.

I will gladly do all in my power to facilitate the observance of the duties of their religion by the Israelites in the army, and will allow them every indulgence consistent with safety and discipline. If their applications be forwarded to me in the usual way, and it appears that they can be spared, I will be glad to approve as many of them as circumstances will permit. Accept my thanks for your kind wishes for myself, and believe me to be,

With great respect, your obedient servant,

R. E. Lee

(Source: Ezekiel, Herbert, and Gaston Lichtenstein. *The History of the Jews of Richmond from 1769 to 1917.* Richmond, VA: Herbert Ezekial, 1917)

10. "Passover—A Reminiscence of the War" (1866)

In the commencement of the war of 1861, I enlisted from Cleveland, Ohio, in the Union cause, to sustain intact the Government of the United States, and became attached to the 23rd Regiment, one of the first sent from the "Buckeye State." Our destination was West Virginia—a portion of the wildest and most mountainous region of that State, well adapted for the guerrillas who infested that part, and caused such trouble to our pickets all through the war. After an arduous march of several hundred miles through Clarksburgh, Weston, Sommerville, and several other places of less note, which have become famous during the war, we encountered on the 10th of September, 1861, at Carnifax Ferry, the forces under the rebel Gen. Floyd. After this, we were ordered to take up our position at the foot of Sewell Mountain, and we remained there until we marched to the village of Fayette, to take it, and to establish there our Winter-quarters, having again routed Gen. Floyd and his forces. While lying there, our camp duties were not of an arduous character, and being apprised of the approaching Feast of Passover, twenty of my comrades and co-religionists belonging to the Regiment, united in a request to our commanding officer for relief from duty, in order that we might keep the holydays, which he readily acceded to. The first point was gained, and, as the Paymaster had lately visited the Regiment, he had left us plenty of greenbacks. Our next business was to find some suitable person to proceed to Cincinnati, Ohio, to buy us [Matzos]. Our sutler being a co-religionist and going home to that city, readily undertook to send them. We were anxiously awaiting to receive our matzos and about the middle of the morning of [Eve of Passover] a supply train arrived in camp, and to our delight seven barrels of Matzos. On opening them, we were surprised and pleased to find that our thoughtful sutler had enclosed two Hagedahs and prayer-books. We were now able to keep the seder

nights, if we could only obtain the other requisites for that occasion. We held a consultation and decided to send parties to forage in the country while a party stayed to build a log hut for the services.

About the middle of the afternoon the foragers arrived, having been quite successful. We obtained two kegs of cider, a lamb, several chickens and some eggs. Horseradish or parsley we could not obtain, but in lieu we found a weed, whose bitterness, I apprehend, exceeded anything our forefathers "enjoyed." We were still in a great quandary; we were like the man who drew the elephant in the lottery. We had the lamb, but did not know what part was to represent it at the table; but Yankee ingenuity prevailed, and it was decided to cook the whole and put it on the table, then we could dine off it, and be sure we had the right part. The necessaries for the choroutzes we could not obtain, so we got a brick which, rather hard to digest, reminded us, by looking at it, for what purpose it was intended.

At dark we had all prepared, and were ready to commence the service. There being no [?] present, I was selected to read the services, which I commenced by asking the blessing of the Almighty on the food before us, and to preserve our lives from danger. The ceremonies were passing off very nicely, until we arrived at the part where the bitter herb was to be taken. We all had a large portion of the herb ready to eat at the moment I said the blessing; each eat his portion, when horrors! what a scene ensued in our little congregation, it is impossible for my pen to describe. The herb was very bitter and very fiery like Cayenne pepper, and excited our thirst to such a degree, that we forgot the law authorizing us to drink only four cups, and the consequence was we drank up all the cider. Those that drank the more freely became excited, and one thought he was Moses, another Aaron, and one had the audacity to call himself Pharaoh. The consequence was a skirmish, with nobody hurt, only Moses, Aaron and Pharaoh, had to be carried to the camp, and there left in the arms of Morpheus. This slight incident did not take away our appetite, and, after doing justice to our lamb, chickens and eggs, we resumed the second portion of the service without anything occurring worthy of note.

There, in the wild woods of West Virginia, away from home and friends, we consecrated and offered up to the ever-loving G_d of Israel our prayers and sacrifice. I doubt whether the spirits of our forefathers, had they been looking down on us, standing there with our arms by our side ready for an attack, faithful to our G_d and our cause, would have imagined themselves amongst mortals, enacting this commemoration of the scene that transpired in Egypt.

J. A. Joel

(Source: *The Jewish Messenger*, April 1866.)

XLVIII. Telegraph

Technological advances helped revolutionize warfare during the Civil War, and the indispensable field of communications was a particularly obvious instance of how this last of the old wars was also the first of the new ones. [See Telegraph]

1. Report of Operations of the Signal Corps, U.S. Army, for the Year Commencing November 1, 1863, and Ending October 31, 1864 [Excerpt]

The history of field telegraphs, as far as the Signal Corps is concerned, shows that as early as August 6, 1861, the Signal Officer of the Army proposed, with the permission of the Secretary of War, to organize a telegraphic or signal train to accompany the Army on the march, the wagons of this train to carry all articles needed for temporary telegraphic uses in the field; that is, apparatus and supplies for the use of both electric and aerial telegraphs, rockets, and composition night signals, carefully prepared, packed, numbered, and arranged for instant use. Four flying field telegraphs were to be carried in the train, which was to be accompanied by and be in charge of suitable officers and men, to each of whom his duties should be assigned, and of whom a proper proportion should be selected electric telegraphists, fully instructed in the use of the telescope and aerial signals, and who, employed for the war, should be sworn to the faithful discharge of their duties.

In the report of the Signal Officer of the Army and Chief Signal Officer, Army of the Potomac, rendered to the commanding general of that army October 21, 1862, is found the following allusion to this subject:

"It was from the beginning the intention to place in charge of this corps the flying or field electric telegraphs for use upon the field of battle, or in the immediate presence of the enemy. These were to be similar in their general construction to those telegraphic trains at a later day brought into use on the Peninsula.

"The efforts to procure these trains were thwarted, to some extent, by the action of persons who seemed to greatly desire that all the duties of electric telegraphy should be in the hands of civilians, and in part, perhaps, by the hesitation of officers in authority to become responsible, by favoring it, for the success of what was then an experiment in our service....

"One train was, however, partially completed, and the officers of the corps were familiarized with its use. This was the first movable telegraphic train of which there is record, as made for the United States."

The incomplete train referred to above was used by the Signal Corps with satisfactory results in the campaign upon the Peninsula in Virginia.

This induced the general commanding to order the purchase of three trains of improved construction, each bearing two instruments and five miles of insulated wire. These trains were equipped with instruments invented by Mr. G. W. Beardslee, of New York. They work without batteries, and can be used by any one who can read and write after a day's practice. This obviated the difficulties experienced in using the electric telegraphs, which required skilled operators and were difficult of transportation. During the year ending June, 1863, the field trains became generally introduced, and were acknowledged as a part of the corps equipment.

WM. J. L. NICODEMUS,
Lieut. Col. and Acting Signal Officer of the Army.

(Source: U.S. War Department. *War of the Rebellion: A Compilation of the Official Records of the Union and Confederate Armies.* Ser. III, Vol. IV.)

XLIX. United States Sanitary Commission

Formed by Northern civilians to provide medical care, supplies, and other necessities to soldiers in the field, the United States Sanitary Commission raised millions of dollars, built and supervised hospitals, and recruited medical personnel to staff them. The commission furnished soldiers everything from blankets to stationery and performed services that ranged from delivering letters to assisting in applications for disability pensions. Yet in its early days, the commission's activities were regarded with suspicion and caused complaint among some Union commanders. Gradually, however, the practical value of the commission's work was realized and its efforts abetted. [See United States Sanitary Commission]

1. Halleck to Stanton Regarding the Sanitary Commission [Excerpt] (22 May 1862)

CAMP, CORINTH ROAD, May 22, 1862.

Hon. E. M. STANTON,
Secretary of War.

The Sanitary Commission and State Governors carry away troops faster than I can recruit. Men only slightly unwell or feigning sickness are carried away without any authority.

H. W. HALLECK,
Major-General.

(Source: U.S. War Department. *War of the Rebellion: A Compilation of the Official Records of the Union and Confederate Armies.* Ser. I, Vol. X/1.)

2. Special Orders, No. 88 (29 March 1863)

HDQRS. DEPT. OF THE TENNESSEE,
Young's Point, La., March 29, 1863.

I. The quartermaster's department will furnish a suitable steamboat, to be called the "United States Sanitary Store-boat," and put the same in charge of the

United States Sanitary Commission, to be used exclusively for the conveyance of goods calculated to prevent disease, and supplement the Government supply of stores for the relief of the sick and wounded.

II. No persons will be permitted to travel on said boat except officers of the army and navy (and they only on permits from their proper commanding officers), discharged soldiers, and employes of the Sanitary Commission. No goods whatever for traveling or commercial purposes will be carried on said steamer, and no goods will be taken for individuals, or with any conditions which will prevent their being delivered to those most needing them in the army or navy.

III. The contents of all packages to be shipped on said United States Sanitary Store-boat will be inspected before shipment by an agent of said Sanitary Commission, at the point of shipment, unless an invoice of their contents shall have been received, the correctness of which is assured by the signature of some person of known loyalty and integrity. A statement showing what goods have been placed on board at each trip will be sent to the medical director of the department at these headquarters.

IV. A weekly statement will also be made by said Sanitary Commission to the department medical director, showing what sanitary supplies have been issued by said Sanitary Commission, and to whom issued.

V All orders from these headquarters authorizing the free transportation of sanitary stores from Cairo south on boats other than the one herein assigned for that exclusive purpose are hereby rescinded.

By order of Maj. Gen. U. S. Grant:

JNO. A. RAWLINS,

Assistant Adjutant-General.

(Source: U.S. War Department. *War of the Rebellion: A Compilation of the Official Records of the Union and Confederate Armies.* Ser. I, Vol. XXIV/3.)

Appendix I

CONFEDERATE STATES OF AMERICA—GENERAL OFFICERS

To be considered a Confederate general officially, an individual must have been appointed by President Jefferson Davis, had their name sent in nomination to the Confederate Senate, and then be confirmed by the Senate. Some presidential appointments, however, were rejected by the Senate; others were appointed by Davis without going through the nominating process; while still other nominations were either withdrawn by Davis or were never confirmed by the Senate because of the officer's death or the end of the war. An entirely separate class included state militia generals who may have commanded Confederate troops but who never held commissions issued by the Confederate government. Consequently, some officers have long been considered Confederate generals despite the fact that they did not complete the nomination and confirmation process. The following list includes generals nominated and confirmed, as well as those officers appointed or nominated by Davis but never confirmed. It does not include militia officers who held the rank of general in state forces but not in the armies of the Confederacy. For a more thorough discussion of who was or was not a Confederate general, see: Eicher, David. *The Civil War in Books: An Analytical Bibliography* (Urbana: University of Illinois Press, 1997); Warner, Ezra J. *Generals in Gray* (Baton Rouge: Louisiana State University Press, 1959); and Allardice, Bruce S. *More Generals in Gray* (Baton Rouge: Louisiana State University Press, 1995).

Brig. Gen. Daniel W. Adams
Brig. Gen. John Adams (killed at Franklin)
Brig. Gen. Wirt Adams
Brig. Gen. E. Porter Alexander
Brig. Gen. Henry W. Allen
Brig. Gen. William W. Allen
Brig. Gen. Charles D. Anderson
Brig. Gen. George B. Anderson (mortally wounded at Antietam)
Brig. Gen. George T. Anderson
Brig. Gen. J. Patton Anderson
Brig. Gen. Joseph R. Anderson
Maj. Gen. Richard H. Anderson
Brig. Gen. Robert H. Anderson
Brig. Gen. Samuel R. Anderson
Brig. Gen. James J. Archer
Brig. Gen. Lewis A. Armistead (killed at Gettysburg)
Brig. Gen. Frank C. Armstrong

Brig. Gen. Arthur P. Bagby
Brig. Gen. Alpheus Baker
Brig. Gen. Lawrence S. Baker
Brig. Gen. William E. Baldwin
Brig. Gen. William Barksdale (killed at Gettysburg)
Brig. Gen. Rufus Barringer
Brig. Gen. Seth M. Barton
Brig. Gen. John D. Barry
Maj. Gen. William B. Bate
Brig. Gen. Cullen A. Battle
Brig. Gen. Richard L. T. Beale
Brig. Gen. William N. R. Beall
Gen. P. G. T. Beauregard
Brig. Gen. Barnard E. Bee (killed at First Bull Run)
Brig. Gen. Hamilton P. Bee
Brig. Gen. Tyrell H. Bell
Brig. Gen. Henry L. Benning
Brig. Gen. Samuel Benton (killed at Ezra Church)
Brig. Gen. Albert G. Blanchard
Brig. Gen. William R. Boggs
Brig. Gen. Milledge L. Bonham
Maj. Gen. John S. Bowen
Brig. Gen. Pinckney D. Bowles
Gen. Braxton Bragg
Brig. Gen. Lawrence O'B. Branch (killed at Antietam)
Brig. Gen. William Brandon
Brig. Gen. William F. Brantly
Brig. Gen. John Bratton
Maj. Gen. John C. Breckinridge
Actg. Brig. Gen. Joseph L. Brent
Brig. Gen. Theodore W. Brevard
Brig. Gen. John C. Brown
Brig. Gen. William M. Browne
Brig. Gen. Goode Bryan
Lieut. Gen. Simon B. Buckner
Brig. Gen. Abraham Buford
Brig. Gen. Robert Bulloch
Maj. Gen. Matthew C. Butler
Brig. Gen. William L. Cabell
Brig. Gen. Alexander W. Cameron
Brig. Gen. James Cantey
Brig. Gen. Ellison Capers
Brig. Gen. John C. Carpenter
Brig. Gen. William H. Carroll
Brig. Gen. John C. Carter
Brig. Gen. James R. Chalmers
Brig. Gen. John R. Chambliss, Jr. (killed at Deep Bottom)

Maj. Gen. Benjamin F. Cheatham
Brig. Gen. James Chesnut, Jr.
Brig. Gen. Robert H. Chilton
Maj. Gen. Thomas J. Churchill
Brig. Gen. James H. Clanton
Brig. Gen. Charles Clark
Brig. Gen. John B. Clark, Jr.
Maj. Gen. Henry D. Clayton
Maj. Gen. Patrick R. Cleburne (killed at Franklin)
Brig. Gen. Thomas L. Clingman
Brig. Gen. Howell Cobb
Brig. Gen. Thomas R. R. Cobb (killed at Fredericksburg)
Brig. Gen. Philip St. George Cocke
Brig. Gen. Francis M. Cockrell
Brig. Gen. Alfred H. Colquitt
Brig. Gen. Raleigh E. Colston
Brig. Gen. James Conner
Brig. Gen. Philip Cook
Brig. Gen. John R. Cooke
Brig. Gen. Douglas H. Cooper
Gen. Samuel Cooper
Brig. Gen. Montgomery D. Corse
Brig. Gen. George B. Cosby
Brig. Gen. William R. Cox
Brig. Gen. Charles C. Crews
Brig. Gen. George B. Crittenden
Brig. Gen. Alfred Cumming
Brig. Gen. Junius Daniel
Brig. Gen. Henry B. Davidson
Brig. Gen. Joseph R. Davis
Brig. Gen. William G. Davis
Brig. Gen. James Dearing (mortally wounded at High Bridge)
Brig. Gen. Zachariah C. Deas
Actg. Brig. Gen. Xavier B. Debray
Brig. Gen. Junius A. De Lagnel
Brig. Gen. James Deshler (killed at Chickamauga)
Brig. Gen. George G. Dibrell
Brig. Gen. Thomas A. Dockery
Brig. Gen. George Doles (killed at Bethesda Church)
Maj. Gen. Daniel S. Donelson
Brig. Gen. Thomas F. Drayton
Brig. Gen. Dudley M. Du Bose
Brig. Gen. Basil W. Duke
Brig. Gen. Johnson K. Duncan
Brig. Gen. John Dunovant (killed at Fort Harrison)
Lieut. Gen. Jubal A. Early
Brig. Gen. John Echols
Brig. Gen. Matthew D. Ector
Brig. Gen. Stephen Elliott, Jr. (mortally wounded at Petersburg)
Maj. Gen. Arnold Elzey
Brig. Gen. Clement A. Evans
Brig. Gen. Nathan G. Evans

Lieut. Gen. Richard S. Ewell
Maj. Gen. James F. Fagan
Brig. Gen. Winfield S. Featherston
Brig. Gen. Samuel W. Ferguson
Maj. Gen. Charles W. Field
Brig. Gen. Joseph Finegan
Brig. Gen. Jesse J. Finley
Maj. Gen. John H. Forney
Brig. Gen. William H. Forney
Brig. Gen. Nathan B. Forrest
Brig. Gen. John W. Frazer
Maj. Gen. Samuel G. French
Brig. Gen. Daniel M. Frost
Brig. Gen. Birkett D. Fry
Brig. Gen. Richard M. Gano
Brig. Gen. Edward W. Gantt
Maj. Gen. Franklin Gardner
Brig. Gen. William M. Gardner
Brig. Gen. Samuel Garland, Jr. (killed at South Mountain)
Brig. Gen. Richard B. Garnett (killed at Gettysburg)
Brig. Gen. Robert S. Garnett (killed at Carrick's Ford)
Brig. Gen. Isham W. Garrott
Brig. Gen. Lucius J. Gartrell
Brig. Gen. Martin W. Gary
Brig. Gen. Richard C. Gatlin
Brig. Gen. Samuel J. Gholson
Brig. Gen. Randall L. Gibson
Maj. Gen. Jeremy F. Gilmer
Brig. Gen. Victor J. Girardey (killed at Deep Bottom)
Brig. Gen. States Rights Gist (killed at Franklin)
Brig. Gen. Adley H. Gladden (mortally wounded at Shiloh)
Brig. Gen. Archibald C. Godwin (killed at Opequon)
Brig. Gen. B. Frank Gordon
Brig. Gen. George W. Gordon
Brig. Gen. James B. Gordon (mortally wounded at Meadow Bridge)
Maj. Gen. John B. Gordon
Brig. Gen. Josiah Gorgas
Brig. Gen. Daniel C. Govan
Brig. Gen. Archibald Gracie, Jr. (killed at Petersburg)
Brig. Gen. Hiram B. Granbury (killed at Franklin)
Brig. Gen. Henry Gray
Brig. Gen. John B. Grayson
Brig. Gen. Colton Green
Brig. Gen. Martin E. Green (killed at Vicksburg)
Brig. Gen. Thomas Green (killed at Pleasant Hill)
Brig. Gen. John Gregg (killed at Darbytown Road)
Brig. Gen. Maxcy Gregg (killed at Fredericksburg)
Brig. Gen. Richard Griffith (mortally wounded at Savage's Station)
Brig. Gen. Bryan Grimes
Brig. Gen. James Hagan
Brig. Gen. Johnson Hagood

Lieut. Gen. Wade Hampton
Brig. Gen. Roger W. Hanson (killed at Stones River)
Lieut. Gen. William J. Hardee
Brig. Gen. William P. Hardeman
Brig. Gen. Nathaniel H. Harms
Brig. Gen. George P. J. Harrison
Brig. Gen. James E. Harrison
Brig. Gen. Thomas Harrison
Brig. Gen. Robert Hatton (killed at Fair Oaks)
Brig. Gen. James M. Hawes
Brig. Gen. Alexander T. Hawthorn
Brig. Gen. Harry T. Hays
Brig. Gen. Louis Hébert
Brig. Gen. Paul O. Hébert
Brig. Gen. Benjamin H. Helm (killed at
  Chickamauga)
Maj. Gen. Henry Heth
Brig. Gen. Edward Higgins
Lieut. Gen. Ambrose P. Hill (killed at Petersburg)
Lieut. Gen. Daniel H. Hill
Maj. Gen. Thomas C. Hindman
Brig. Gen. George B. Hodge
Brig. Gen. Joseph L. Hogg
Maj. Gen. Robert F. Hoke
Lieut. Gen. Theophilus Holmes
Brig. Gen. James T. Holtzclaw
Lieut. Gen. John B. Hood
Brig. Gen. William Y. C. Humes
Brig. Gen. Benjamin G. Humphreys
Brig. Gen. Eppa Hunton
Brig. Gen. John D. Imboden
Brig. Gen. Alfred Iverson
Brig. Gen. Sidney D. Jackman
Brig. Gen. A. E. Jackson
Brig. Gen. Henry R. Jackson
Brig. Gen. John K. Jackson
Lieut. Gen. Thomas J. Jackson (mortally wounded at
  Chancellorsville)
Brig. Gen. William H. Jackson
Brig. Gen. William L. Jackson
Brig. Gen. Albert G. Jenkins
Brig. Gen. Micah Jenkins (killed at the Wilderness)
Brig. Gen. Adam R. Johnson
Brig. Gen. Bradley T. Johnson
Maj. Gen. Bushrod R. Johnson
Maj. Gen. Edward Johnson
Gen. Albert Sidney Johnston (killed at Shiloh)
Brig. Gen. George D. Johnston
Gen. Joseph E. Johnston
Brig. Gen. Robert D. Johnston
Brig. Gen. David R. Jones
Brig. Gen. John M. Jones (killed at the Wilderness)
Brig. Gen. John R. Jones
Maj. Gen. Samuel Jones
Brig. Gen. Thomas M. Jones

Brig. Gen. William E. Jones (killed at Piedmont)
Brig. Gen. Thomas Jordan
Brig. Gen. John H. Kelly
Maj. Gen. James L. Kemper
Brig. Gen. John D. Kennedy
Maj. Gen. Joseph B. Kershaw
Brig. Gen. William H. King
Brig. Gen. William W. Kirkland
Brig. Gen. James H. Lane
Brig. Gen. Evander M. Law
Brig. Gen. Alexander R. Lawton
Brig. Gen. Danville Leadbetter
Brig. Gen. Edwin Lee
Maj. Gen. Fitzhugh Lee
Brig. Gen. George W. C. Lee
Gen. Robert E. Lee
Lieut. Gen. Stephen D. Lee
Maj. Gen. William H. F. Lee
Brig. Gen. Collett Leventhorpe
Brig. Gen. Joseph H. Lewis
Brig. Gen. Levin M. Lewis
Brig. Gen. William G. Lewis
Brig. Gen. St. John R. Liddell
Brig. Gen. Robert D. Lilley
Brig. Gen. Henry Little (killed at Iuka)
Brig. Gen. Thomas M. Logan
Maj. Gen. Lunsford L. Lomax
Brig. Gen. Armistead L. Long
Lieut. Gen. James Longstreet
Maj. Gen. William W. Loring
Brig. Gen. Mark P. Lowrey
Brig. Gen. Robert Lowry
Brig. Gen. Hylan B. Lyon
Brig. Gen. Hinchie P. Mabry
Brig. Gen. William W. Mackall
Brig. Gen. Robert P. Maclay
Maj. Gen. John Bankhead Magruder
Maj. Gen. William Mahone
Brig. Gen. James P. Major
Brig. Gen. George Maney
Brig. Gen. Arthur M. Manigault
Maj. Gen. John S. Marmaduke
Brig. Gen. Humphrey Marshall
Brig. Gen. James G. Martin
Maj. Gen. William T. Martin
Maj. Gen. Dabney H. Maury
Maj. Gen. Samuel B. Maxey
Brig. Gen. John McCausland
Maj. Gen. John P. McCown
Brig. Gen. William McCrae
Brig. Gen. Ben McCulloch (killed at Pea Ridge)
Brig. Gen. Henry E. McCulloch
Brig. Gen. Peter A. McGlashan
Brig. Gen. Samuel McGowan
Brig. Gen. James McIntosh (killed at Pea Ridge)

Maj. Gen. Lafayette McLaws
Brig. Gen. Evander McNair
Brig. Gen. Hugh W. Mercer
Brig. Gen. William Miller
Brig. Gen. Young M. Moody
Brig. Gen. John C. Moore
Brig. Gen. Patrick T. Moore
Brig. Gen. John Hunt Morgan (killed at Greenville, Tennessee)
Brig. Gen. John T. Morgan
Brig. Gen. Alfred Mouton (killed at Mansfield)
Brig. Gen. Thomas T. Munsford
Quartermaster Gen. Abraham C. Myers
Brig. Gen. Allison Nelson
Brig. Gen. F. T. Nicholls
Brig. Gen. Lucius B. Northrop
Brig. Gen. Edward A. O'Neal
Brig. Gen. Richard L. Page
Brig. Gen. Joseph B. Palmer
Maj. Gen. Mosby Monroe Parsons
Brig. Gen. Elisha F. Paxton (killed at Chancellorsville)
Brig. Gen. William H. Payne
Brig. Gen. Nicholas B. Pearce
Brig. Gen. John Pegram (killed at Hatcher's Run)
Maj. Gen. John C. Pemberton
Maj. Gen. William Dorsey Pender (mortally wounded at Gettysburg)
Brig. Gen. William N. Pendleton
Brig. Gen. Abner Perrin (killed at Spotsylvania)
Brig. Gen. Edward A. Perry
Brig. Gen. James J. Pettigrew (killed at Falling Waters)
Brig. Gen. Edmund W. Pettus
Maj. Gen. George E. Pickett
Brig. Gen. Albert Pike
Brig. Gen. Gideon J. Pillow
Maj. Gen. Camille J. Polignac
Lieut. Gen. Leonidas Polk (killed at Pine Mountain)
Brig. Gen. Lucius E. Polk
Brig. Gen. Carnot Posey (mortally wounded at Bristoe Station)
Brig. Gen. John S. Preston
Maj. Gen. William Preston
Maj. Gen. Sterling Price
Brig. Gen. Roger A. Pryor
Brig. Gen. William A. Quarles
Brig. Gen. Gabriel J. Rains
Brig. Gen. James E. Rains (killed at Stones River)
Maj. Gen. Stephen D. Ramseur (mortally wounded at Cedar Creek)
Brig. Gen. Horace Randall
Brig. Gen. George Wythe Randolph
Brig. Gen. Matthew W. Ransom
Maj. Gen. Robert Ransom, Jr.

Brig. Gen. Alexander W. Reynolds
Brig. Gen. Daniel H. Reynolds
Brig. Gen. Roswell S. Ripley
Brig. Gen. John Selden Roane
Brig. Gen. William P. Roberts
Brig. Gen. Beverly H. Robertson
Brig. Gen. Felix H. Robertson
Brig. Gen. Jerome B. Robertson
Brig. Gen. Philip D. Roddey
Maj. Gen. Robert E. Rodes (killed at Opequon)
Brig. Gen. Lawrence S. Ross
Brig. Gen. Thomas L. Rosser
Brig. Gen. Daniel Ruggles
Brig. Gen. Albert Rust
Brig. Gen. Isaac M. St. John
Brig. Gen. John C. Sanders (killed at Weldon Railroad)
Brig. Gen. Alfred M. Scales
Brig. Gen. Thomas M. Scott
Brig. Gen. William R. Scurry (killed at Jenkins' Ferry)
Brig. Gen. Claudius W. Sears
Brig. Gen. Paul J. Semmes (mortally wounded at Gettysburg)
Brig. Gen. Jacob H. Sharp
Brig. Gen. Joseph O. Shelby
Brig. Gen. Charles M. Shelley
Brig. Gen. Francis A. Shoup
Brig. Gen. Henry Hopkins Sibley
Brig. Gen. James P. Simms
Brig. Gen. William Y. Slack (mortally wounded at Pea Ridge)
Brig. Gen. James E. Slaughter
Lieut. Gen. Edmund Kirby Smith
Maj. Gen. Gustavus W. Smith
Brig. Gen. James A. Smith
Brig. Gen. Martin L. Smith
Brig. Gen. Preston Smith (killed at Chickamauga)
Brig. Gen. Thomas B. Smith
Maj. Gen. William Smith
Brig. Gen. G. Moxley Sorrel
Brig. Gen. Pierre Soulé
Brig. Gen. Leroy A. Stafford (killed at the Wilderness)
Brig. Gen. Peter B. Starke
Brig. Gen. William E. Starke (killed at Antietam)
Brig. Gen. William Steele
Brig. Gen. George H. Steuart
Brig. Gen. Clement H. Stevens (mortally wounded at Peachtree Creek)
Brig. Gen. Walter H. Stevens
Maj Gen. Carter L. Stevenson
Lieut. Gen. Alexander P. Stewart
Brig. Gen. Marcellus A. Stovall
Brig. Gen. Otho F. Strahl (killed at Franklin)
Maj. Gen. James E. B. Stuart (mortally wounded at Yellow Tavern)

Brig. Gen. William B. Taliaferro

Brig. Gen. James C. Tappan

Lieut. Gen. Richard Taylor

Brig. Gen. Alexander W. Terrell

Brig. Gen. James B. Terrill

Brig. Gen. William Terry

Brig. Gen. William R. Terry

Brig. Gen. Allen Thomas

Brig. Gen. Bryan M. Thomas

Brig. Gen. Edward L. Thomas

Brig. Gen. Lloyd Tilghman (killed at Champion's Hill)

Brig. Gen. Robert Toombs

Brig. Gen. Thomas T. Toon

Brig. Gen. Edward D. Tracy (killed at Port Gibson)

Brig. Gen. James H. Trapier

Brig. Gen. Isaac R. Trimble

Brig. Gen. William F. Tucker

Maj. Gen. David E. Twiggs

Brig. Gen. Robert C. Tyler

Maj. Gen. Earl Van Dorn

Brig. Gen. Robert B. Vance

Brig. Gen. Alfred J. Vaughan, Jr.

Brig. Gen. John C. Vaughn

Brig. Gen. John B. Villepigue

Brig. Gen. Henry H. Walker

Brig. Gen. James A. Walker

Maj. Gen. John G. Walker

Brig. Gen. Leroy Pope Walker

Brig. Gen. Lucius M. Walker

Brig. Gen. Reuben L. Walker

Maj. Gen. William H. T. Walker (killed at Atlanta)

Brig. Gen. William H. Wallace

Maj. Gen. Edward C. Walthall

Brig. Gen. Richard Waterhouse

Brig. Gen. Stand Watie

Brig. Gen. Thomas N. Waul

Brig. Gen. Henry C. Wayne

Brig. Gen. David A. Weisiger

Brig. Gen. Gabriel C. Wharton

Maj. Gen. John A. Wharton

Maj. Gen. Joseph Wheeler

Brig. Gen. John W. Whitfield

Maj. Gen. William H. C. Whiting

Brig. Gen. Williams C. Wickham

Brig. Gen. Louis T. Wigfall

Maj. Gen. Cadmus M. Wilcox

Brig. Gen. John S. Williams

Brig. Gen. Claudius C. Wilson

Brig. Gen. Charles S. Winder (killed at Cedar Mountain)

Brig. Gen. John H. Winder

Brig. Gen. Henry A. Wise

Maj. Gen. Jones M. Withers

Brig. Gen. Williams C. Wickham

Brig. Gen. William T. Wofford

Brig. Gen. Sterling A. M. Wood

Brig. Gen. Ambrose R. Wright

Brig. Gen. Marcus J. Wright

Brig. Gen. Zebulon York

Brig. Gen. Pierce M. B. Young

Brig. Gen. William H. Young

Brig. Gen. Felix K. Zollicoffer (killed at Logan's Cross Roads / Mill Springs)

Appendix II

THE CONFEDERATE STATES OF AMERICA—GOVERNMENT
(1861–1865)

Executive Officers

President: Jefferson Davis of Mississippi, Provisional, 18 February 1861; 22 February 1862

Vice-president: Alexander H. Stephens of Georgia, Provisional, 18 February 1861; 22 February 1862

Secretary of State: Robert Toombs of Georgia, 21 February 1861; Robert M. T. Hunter of Virginia, 25 July 1861; William M. Browne of Georgia (ad interim) to 18 March 1862; Judah P. Benjamin of Louisiana, 18 March 1862

Secretary of War: Leroy P. Walker of Alabama, 21 February 1861; Judah P. Benjamin, Acting 17 September 1861 to 21 November 1861; George W. Randolph of Virginia, 18 March 1862; Judah P. Benjamin, Acting 18 March 1862 to 23 March 1862; George W. Randolph, 23 March 1862; Gustavus W. Smith of Kentucky, 17 November 1862 to 21 November 1862; James A. Seddon of Virginia, 21 November 1862; John C. Breckinridge of Kentucky, 6 February 1865

Secretary of the Treasury: Christopher G. Memminger of South Carolina, 21 February 1861; George A. Trenholm of South Carolina, 18 July 1864

Secretary of the Navy: Stephen R. Mallory of Florida, 4 March 1861

Attorney General: Judah P. Benjamin, 25 February 1861; Thomas Bragg of North Carolina, 21 November 1861; Thomas H. Watts of Alabama, 18 March 1862; Wade Keyes of Alabama (ad interim); George Davis of North Carolina, 2 January 1864

Postmaster General: Henry T. Ellet of Virginia, 25 February 1861 (Ellet declined the appointment); John H. Reagan of Texas, 6 March 1861

Provisional Congress
(4 February 1861–17 March 1862)

The Provisional Congress of the Confederate States of America held five sessions.

- The first session assembled at Montgomery, Alabama, on 4 February 1861 and adjourned on 16 March 1861.
- The second session was called early to assemble in Montgomery on 29 April 1861 and adjourned on 21 May 1861.
- The third session assembled in Richmond, Virginia, on 20 July 1861 and adjourned on 31 August 1861.
- The fourth session was specially called in Richmond on 3 September 1861 and sat for only one day.
- The fifth session assembled in Richmond on 18 November 1861 and adjourned on 17 February 1862.

President of the Congress: Howell Cobb of Georgia

ALABAMA
Richard W. Walker
Robert H. Smith
Jabez L. M. Curry
William P. Chilton
Stephen F. Hale
Colin J. McRae
John Gill Shorter
Thomas Fearn, 8 February and resigned on 29 April
David P. Lewis, 8 February and resigned on 29 April
Nicholas Davis, 29 April
H. C. Jones, 29 April
Cornelius Robinson, 30 November 1861 and resigned on 24 January 1862

ARKANSAS
[Delegation was admitted on 18 May 1861]
Robert W. Johnson
Albert Rust
Hugh F. Thomason
W.W. Watkins
Augustus H. Garland

FLORIDA
J. Patton Anderson resigned on 2 May 1861
James B. Owens
Jackson Morton, 6 February 1861
George T. Ward, 2 May 1861 and resigned on 5 February 1862
John P. Sanderson, 5 February 1862

GEORGIA
Robert Toombs
Howell Cobb
Francis S. Bartow killed at Battle of First Bull Run, 21 July 1861
Martin J. Crawford
Eugenius A. Nisbet
Benjamin H. Hill
Augustus R. Wright
Thomas R. R. Cobb
Augustus H. Kenan
Alexander H. Stephens
Thomas M. Foreman, 7 August 1861
Nathan Bass, 14 January 1862

KENTUCKY
Thomas B. Monroe, 16 December 1861
Henry C. Burnett, 16 December 1861
Thomas Johnson, 18 December 1861
John J. Thomas, 30 December 1861
Theodore L. Burnett, 30 December 1861
Daniel P. White, 2 January 1862
L. H. Ford, 4 January 1862
George B. Hedge, 11 January 1862
John M. Elliott, 15 January 1862
George W. Ewing, 14 February 1862

LOUISIANA
John Perkins, Jr.
Alexander De Clouet
Duncan F. Kenner
Edward Sparrow
Henry Marshall
Charles M. Conrad, 7 February 1861

MISSISSIPPI
Wiley P. Harris
Walker Brooke
William S. Wilson resigned on 29 April 1861
William S. Barry
James T. Harrison
Alexander M. Clayton, 8 February 1861 and resigned on 11 May 1861
J. A. P. Campbell
Jehu A. Orr, seated 29 April 1861
Alexander B. Bradford, 5 December 1861

MISSOURI
George G. Vest, 2 December 1861
Caspar W. Bell, 2 December 1861
Aaron H. Conrow, 2 December 1861
Thomas A. Harris, 6 December 1861
John B. Clark, 6 December 1861
Robert L. Y. Peyton, 22 January 1862

NORTH CAROLINA
George Davis, 20 July 1861
W. W. Avery, 20 July 1861
W. N. H. Smith, 20 July 1861
Thomas D. McDowell, 22 July 1861
A. W. Venable, 20 July 1861
John M. Morehead, 20 July 1861
R. C. Puryear, 20 July 1861
A. T. Davidson, 20 July 1861
Burton Craige, 23 July 1861
Thomas Ruffin, 25 July 1861

SOUTH CAROLINA
Robert Barnwell Rhett, Sr.
Robert W. Barnwell
Lawrence M. Keitt
James Chesnut, Jr.
Christopher G. Memminger
William Porcher Miles
Thomas J. Withers
William W. Boyce
James L. Orr, 17 February 1862

TENNESSEE
Robert L. Caruthers, 12 August 1861
Thomas M. Jones, 12 August 1861
J. H. Thomas, 12 August 1861
John F. House, 12 August 1861
John D.C. Atkins, 13 August 1861
David M. Curtin, 16 August 1861
W. H. De Witt, 16 August 1861

TEXAS
John Gregg, 15 February 1861
Thomas N. Waul, 19 February 1861
William B. Ochiltree, 19 February 1861
John H. Reagan, 2 March 1861
Williamson S. Oldham, 2 March 1861
John Hemphill, 2 March 1861; died on 4 January 1862
Louis T. Wigfall, 29 April 1861

VIRGINIA
John W. Brockenbrough, 7 May 1861
Waller R. Staples, 7 May 1861
Robert M. T. Hunter, 10 May 1861
William C. Rives, 13 May 1861
James A. Seddon, 20 July 1861
William B. Preston, 20 July 1861
W. H. MacFarland, 20 July 1861
Charles W. Russell, 20 July 1861
Robert Johnston, 20 July 1861
Robert E. Scott, 22 July 1861
Walter Preston, 22 July 1861
Thomas S. Bocock, 23 July 1861
James M. Mason, 24 July 1861

Roger A. Pryor, 24 July 1861
Alexander R. Boteler, 27 November 1861
John Tyler, 1 August 1861; died on 18 January 1862

ARIZONA TERRITORY
Granville H. Oury, 18 January 1862

Under the Permanent Constitution of the Confederate States of America the Confederate Congress was a bicameral legislature consisting of a Senate and a House of Representatives. There were two Congresses from 18 February 1862 to 18 March 1865.

**First Congress
(18 February 1862–17 February 1864)**

The First Congress of the Confederate States of America held four sessions in Richmond, Virginia.
- The first session assembled on 18 February 1862 and adjourned on 21 April 1862.
- The second session assembled on 18 August 1862 and adjourned on 13 October 1862.
- The third session assembled on 12 January 1863 and adjourned on 1 May 1863.
- The fourth session assembled on 7 December 1863 and adjourned on 17 February 1864.

Senate

President of the Senate: Alexander H. Stephens of Georgia
President Pro Tempore of the Senate: Robert M. T. Hunter of Virginia

ALABAMA
Clement C. Clay, Jr., 19 February 1862
William Lowndes Yancey, 22 March 1862; died 28 July 1863
Robert Jemison, Jr., 28 December 1863

ARKANSAS
Robert W. Johnson
Charles B. Mitchel

FLORIDA
Augustus E. Maxwell
James M. Baker

GEORGIA
Benjamin H. Hill
John W. Lewis, 7 April 1863 by appointment of the governor
Herschel V. Johnson, 19 January 1863

KENTUCKY
William E. Simms
Henry C. Burnett, 26 February 1862

LOUISIANA
Edward Sparrow
Thomas J. Semmes, 22 February 1862

MISSISSIPPI
Albert G. Brown
James Phelan, 19 February 1862

MISSOURI
John B. Clark
Robert L. Y. Peyton died on 19 June 1863
Waldo P. Johnson, 24 December 1863 by appointment of the governor

NORTH CAROLINA
George Davis resigned 22 January 1864
William T. Dortch
Edwin G. Reade, 22 January 1864 by appointment of the governor

SOUTH CAROLINA
Robert W. Barnwell
James L. Orr

TENNESSEE
Landon C. Haynes
Gustavus A. Henry

TEXAS
Williamson S. Oldham
Louis T. Wigfall

VIRGINIA
Robert M. T. Hunter
William B. Preston died on 15 January 1863
Allen T. Caperton, 26 January 1863

House of Representatives

Speaker of the House of Representatives: Thomas S. Bocock of Virginia

ALABAMA
E. S. Dargan
William P. Chilton
James L. Pugh
Jabez L. M. Curry
John P. Ralls
David Clopton
Francis S. Lyon
Thomas J. Foster, 19 February 1862

William R. Smith, 21 February 1862

ARKANSAS
Felix I. Batson
Grandison D. Royston
Augustus H. Garland
Thomas B. Hanly

FLORIDA
James B. Dawkins, resigned 8 December 1862
Robert B. Hilton
John M. Martin, 25 March 1863

GEORGIA
Augustus H. Kenan
Hines Holt, resigned prior to 12 January 1864
Augustus R. Wright
Lucius J. Gartrell
William W. Clark
Robert P. Trippe
David W. Lewis
Hardy Strickland
Charles J. Munnerlyn, 22 February 1862
Julian Hartridge, 14 March 1862
Porter Ingram, 12 January 1864 to succeed Holt

KENTUCKY
Willis B. Machen
John W. Crockett
Henry E. Read
George W. Ewing
Horatio W. Bruce
James W. Moore
Robert J. Breckinridge, Jr.
John M. Elliott
Theodore L. Burnett, 19 February 1862
James S. Chrisman, 3 March 1862
Ely M. Bruce, 20 March 1862
George B. Hodge, 18 August 1862

LOUISIANA
Duncan F. Kenner
Charles J. Villeré
John Perkins, Jr.
Charles M. Conrad
Henry Marshall
Lucius J. Dupré

MISSISSIPPI
Ethelbert Barksdale
John J. McRae
J. W. Clapp
Israel Welsh
Otho R. Singleton
Reuben Davis

Henry C. Chambers, 19 February 1862
William D. Holder, 21 January 1864

MISSOURI
Caspar W. Bell
George G. Vest
Aaron H. Conrow
William M. Cooke
Thomas W. Freeman
Thomas A. Harris

NORTH CAROLINA
Robert R. Bridgers
Owen R. Kenan
Thomas D. McDowell
Thomas S. Ashe
J. R. McLean
William Lander
Burgess S. Gaither
A. T. Davidson
W. N. H. Smith, 19 February 1862
Archibald H. Arrington, 20 February 1862

SOUTH CAROLINA
William W. Boyce
William Porcher Miles
Milledge Luke Bonham, resigned 17 January 1863
John McQueen
James Farrow
Lewis M. Ayer, 6 March 1862
William D. Simpson, 5 February 1863

TENNESSEE
David M. Currin
Henry S. Foote
Thomas Menees
George W. Jones
William G. Swan
William H. Tibbs
E. L. Gardenhire
John V. Wright
Joseph B. Heiskell
John D. C. Atkins, 8 March 1862
Meredith P. Gentry, 17 March 1862

TEXAS
John A. Wilcox died 7 February 1864
Peter W. Gray
Caleb C. Herbert
William B. Wright
M. D. Graham
Frank B. Sexton

VIRGINIA
John R. Chambliss

James Lyons
Roger A. Pryor, resigned on 5 April 1862
Thomas S. Bocock
John Goode, Jr.
Daniel C. De Jarnette
William Smith, resigned on 6 April 1863
Alexander R. Boteler
Waller R. Staples
Walter Preston
Albert G. Jenkins, resigned 5 August 1862
Robert Johnston
Charles W. Russell
James P. Holcombe, 20 February 1862
John B. Baldwin, 27 February 1862
Charles F. Collier, 18 August 1862
Samuel A. Miller, 24 February 1863
David Funsten, 7 December 1863
Muscoe R. H. Garnett, 21 February 1862

ARIZONA TERRITORY
Marcus H. Macwillie, 11 March 1862

CHEROKEE NATION
Elias C. Boudinot, first appearance on 8 January 1864

CHOCTAW NATION
Robert M. Jones, 17 January 1863

Second Congress
(2 May 1864–18 March 1865)

The Second Congress of the Confederate States of America conducted two sessions in Richmond.
- The first session assembled on 2 May 1864 and adjourned on 14 June 1864.
- The second session assembled on 7 November 1864 and adjourned on 18 March 1865.

Senate

President of the Senate: Alexander H. Stephens of Georgia
President Pro Tempore of the Senate: Robert M. T. Hunter of Virginia

ALABAMA
Robert Jemison, Jr.
Richard W. Walker

ARKANSAS
Charles B. Mitchel, died before 8 November 1864
Robert W. Johnson
Augustus H. Garland, 8 November 1864 to succeed Mitchel

FLORIDA
Augustus E. Maxwell
James M. Baker

GEORGIA
Benjamin H. Hill
Herschel V. Johnson, 24 May 1864

KENTUCKY
Henry C. Burnett
William E. Simms

LOUISIANA
Thomas J. Semmes
Edward Sparrow

MISSISSIPPI
Albert G. Brown
John W. C. Watson

MISSOURI
Waldo P. Johnson
George G. Vest, 12 January 1865 by appointment of the governor

NORTH CAROLINA
William T. Dortch
William A. Graham

SOUTH CAROLINA
James L. Orr
Robert W. Barnwell

TENNESSEE
Landon C. Haynes
Gustavus A. Henry

TEXAS
Williamson S. Oldham
Louis T. Wigfall

VIRGINIA
Robert M. T. Hunter
Allen T. Caperton

House of Representatives

Speaker of the House of Representatives: Thomas S. Bocock of Virginia

ALABAMA
M. H. Cruikshank
William P. Chilton
David Clopton
James L. Pugh

James S. Dickinson
Francis S. Lyon, 4 May 1864
Thomas J. Foster, 6 May 1864
William R. Smith, 21 May 1864

ARKANSAS
Augustus H. Garland, elected to CSA Senate on 8
    November 1864
Thomas B. Hanly
Rufus K. Garland, 21 May 1864
Felix I. Batson, 8 November 1864
David W. Carroll, 11 January 1865

FLORIDA
Robert B. Hilton
S. St. George Rogers, 3 May 1864

GEORGIA
Julian Hartridge
William E. Smith
Mark H. Blandford
Clifford Anderson
John T. Shewmake
Joseph H. Echols
James M. Smith
George N. Lester
Hiram P. Bell
Warren Akin

KENTUCKY
Willis B. Machen
Henry E. Read
James S. Chrisman
Theodore L. Burnett
Horatio W. Bruce
Humphrey Marshall
Ely M. Bruce
James W. Moore
Benjamin F. Bradley
George W. Triplett
George W. Ewing, 24 May 1864
John M. Elliott, 24 May 1864

LOUISIANA
Charles J. Villeré
Charles M. Conrad
Lucius J. Dupré
John Perkins, Jr.
Benjamin L. Hodge, 25 May 1864
Duncan F. Kenner, 25 May 1864
Henry Gray, 28 December 1864 to succeed Hodge,
    deceased

MISSISSIPPI
Jehu A. Orr

Israel Welsh
Henry C. Chambers
Ethelbert Barksdale
John T. Lamkin
William D. Holder, 4 May 1864
Otho R. Singleton, 9 May 1864

MISSOURI
John B. Clark, 10 June 1864
Thomas L. Snead, 7 November 1864
 Aaron H. Conrow, 7 November 1864
George G. Vest, 7 November 1864, appointed to CSA
    Senate 12 January 1865
Robert A. Hatcher, 7 November 1864
Peter S. Wilkes, 8 November 1864
N. L. Norton, 21 November 1864

NORTH CAROLINA
W. N. H. Smith
James T. Leach
Josiah Turner, Jr.
John A. Gilmer
James M. Leach
Burgess S. Gaither
George W. Logan
James G. Ramsay
Thomas C. Fuller
Robert R. Bridgers, 24 May 1864

SOUTH CAROLINA
William Porcher Miles
William D. Simpson
James Farrow
William W. Boyce
Lewis M. Ayer
James H. Witherspoon, 5 May 1864

TENNESSEE
Joseph B. Heiskell
William G. Swan
Arthur S. Colyar
John P. Murray
Henry S. Foote
Edwin A. Keeble
Thomas Menees
John D. C. Atkins
John V. Wright, 25 May 1864
James McCallum, 3 May 1864
Michael W. Cluskey, 7 November 1864
David M. Currin, died 21 May 1864

TEXAS
A. M. Branch
Frank B. Sexton

Simpson H. Morgan, 21 May 1864; died on 16 January 1865
John R. Baylor, 25 May 1864
Stephen H. Darden, 21 November 1864
Caleb C. Herbert, 21 November 1864

VIRGINIA
Robert L. Montague
Robert H. Whitfield
Thomas S. Gholson
Thomas S. Bocock
John Goode, Jr.
William C. Rives, resigned on 1 March 1865
Daniel C. De Jarnette
John B. Baldwin
Waller R. Staples
Fayette McMullen
Robert Johnston

Charles W. Russell
David Funsten, 3 May 1864
Samuel A. Miller, 3 May 1864
Frederick W. M. Holliday, 4 Mary 1864
Williams C. Wickham, 7 November 1864

ARIZONA TERRITORY
Marcus H. Macwillie

CHEROKEE NATION
Elias C. Boudinot

CHOCTAW NATION
Robert M. Jones

CREEK AND SEMINOLE NATIONS
S. B. Callahan, 30 May 1864

Appendix III

UNITED STATES OF AMERICA—GENERAL OFFICERS

During the Civil War, Union generals were appointed by the War Department and confirmed by the U.S. Senate. Officers could hold commissions in the Regular Army as well as in volunteer service. Likewise, an individual could hold a brevet, or honorary rank, in both the regular and volunteer service. Nearly 600 individuals received substantive commissions as brigadier, major, or lieutenant generals, while some 1,400 others earned brevet promotions. The list below includes Union generals of substantive rank. Officers promoted to general officer rank by brevet only are not listed. For a more detailed discussion of the issue of Union generals' rankings, see Warner, Ezra J. *Generals in Blue* (Baton Rouge: Louisiana State University Press, 1964); Hunt, Roger D., and Jack R. Brown. *Brevet Brigadier Generals in Blue* (Gaithersburg, MD: Olde Soldier Books, 1990); and Eicher, David J. *The Civil War in Books: An Analytical Bibliography* (Urbana: University of Illinois Press, 1997).

Brig. Gen. John J. Abercrombie
Brig. Gen. Adelbert Ames
Brig. Gen. Robert Anderson
Brig. Gen. Christopher C. Andrews
Brig. Gen. George L. Andrews
Brig. Gen. Lewis G. Arnold
Brig. Gen. Richard Arnold
Brig. Gen. Alexander Asboth
Brig. Gen. William W. Averell
Maj. Gen. Romeyn B. Ayres
Brig. Gen. Absalom Baird
Brig. Gen. Edward D. Baker (killed at Ball's Bluff)
Brig. Gen. Lafayette C. Baker
Maj. Gen. Nathaniel P. Banks
Brig. Gen. Francis C. Barlow
Brig. Gen. James Barnes
Brig. Gen. Joseph Barnes (Surgeon General)
Brig. Gen. Henry Barnum
Brig. Gen. William F. Barry
Brig. Gen. Joseph J. Bartlett
Brig. Gen. Henry Baxter
Brig. Gen. George D. Bayard (mortally wounded at Fredericksburg)
Brig. Gen. George L. Beal
Brig. Gen. John Beatty
Brig. Gen. Samuel Beatty
Brig. Gen. William W. Belknap
Brig. Gen. Henry W. Benham

Brig. Gen. William Benton
Maj. Gen. Hiram G. Berry (killed at Chancellorsville)
Brig. Gen. Daniel D. Bidwell (killed at Cedar Creek)
Brig. Gen. Henry W. Birge
Maj. Gen. David B. Birney
Brig. Gen. William Birney
Maj. Gen. Frank P. Blair, Jr.
Brig. Gen. Louis Blenker
Maj. Gen. James Blunt
Brig. Gen. Henry Bohlen (killed at Freeman's Ford)
Brig. Gen. James Bowen
Brig. Gen. Jeremiah T. Boyle
Brig. Gen. Luther P. Bradley
Brig. Gen. Edward S. Bragg
Brig. Gen. John M. Brannan
Brig. Gen. Mason Brayman
Brig. Gen. Henry S. Briggs
Brig. Gen. Henry S. Brisbin
Brig. Gen. John R. Brooke
Brig. Gen. William T. H. Brooks
Brig. Gen. Egbert B. Brown
Brig. Gen. Robert C. Buchanan
Brig. Gen. Catharinus P. Buckingham
Brig. Gen. Ralph P. Buckland
Maj. Gen. Don Carlos Buell
Maj. Gen. John Buford
Brig. Gen. N. B. Buford
Brig. Gen. Stephen G. Burbridge
Brig. Gen. Hiram Burnham (killed at Fort Harrison)
Brig. Gen. William W. Burns
Maj. Gen. Ambrose E. Burnside
Brig. Gen. Cyrus Bussey
Maj. Gen. Benjamin F. Butler
Brig. Gen. Daniel Butterfield
Maj. Gen. George Cadwalader
Brig. Gen. John C. Caldwell
Brig. Gen. Robert A. Cameron
Brig. Gen. Charles T. Campbell
Brig. Gen. William B. Campbell
Maj. Gen. Edward R. S. Canby
Brig. Gen. Joseph B. Care
Brig. Gen. James H. Carleton
Brig. Gen. William P. Carlin
Brig. Gen. Eugene A. Carr
Brig. Gen. Joseph B. Carr
Brig. Gen. Henry B. Carrington
Brig. Gen. Samuel S. Carroll
Brig. Gen. Samuel P. Carter

Maj. Gen. Silas Casey
Brig. Gen. Robert F. Catterson
Brig. Gen. Joshua L. Chamberlain
Brig. Gen. Alexander Chambers
Brig. Gen. Stephen G. Champlin
Brig. Gen. Edward P. Chapin (killed at Port Hudson)
Brig. Gen. George H. Chapman
Brig. Gen. Augustus L. Chetlain
Brig. Gen. Morgan H. Chrysler
Brig. Gen. William T. Clark
Brig. Gen. Powell Clayton
Brig. Gen. Gustave P. Cluseret
Brig. Gen. John Cochrane
Brig. Gen. Charles H. T. Collis
Brig. Gen. Patrick E. Connor
Brig. Gen. Selden Connor
Brig. Gen. John Cook
Brig. Gen. P. St. George Cooke
Brig. Gen. James Cooper
Brig. Gen. Joseph H. Cooper
Brig. Gen. Joseph T. Copeland
Brig. Gen. Michael Corcoran
Brig. Gen. John Murry Corse
Maj. Gen. Darius N. Couch
Brig. Gen. R. Cowdin
Maj. Gen. Jacob D. Cox
Brig. Gen. Samuel W. Crawford
Maj. Gen. Thomas L. Crittenden
Brig. Gen. Thomas T. Crittenden
Brig. Gen. Marcellus M. Crocker
Maj. Gen. George Crook
Brig. Gen. John Thomas Croxton
Brig. Gen. Charles Cruft
Brig. Gen. George W. Cullum
Brig. Gen. N. Martin Curtis
Maj. Gen. Samuel R. Curtis
Brig. Gen. George A. Custer
Brig. Gen. Lysander Cutler
Maj. Gen. Napoleon Jackson Tecumseh Dana
Brig. Gen. John W. Davidson
Brig. Gen. Henry E. Davies, Jr.
Brig. Gen. Thomas A. Davies
Brig. Gen. Jefferson C. Davis
Brig. Gen. Gustave A. De Russy
Brig. Gen. P. Regis De Trobriand
Brig. Gen. Richard Delafield
Brig. Gen. Andrew W. Denison
Brig. Gen. Elias S. Dennis
Brig. Gen. Frederick T. Dent
Brig. Gen. James W. Denver
Brig. Gen. Charles Devens, Jr.
Brig. Gen. Thomas C. Devin
Brig. Gen. Joel A. Dewey
Brig. Gen. George W. Dietzler
Maj. Gen. John A. Dix

Brig. Gen. Charles C. Dodge
Maj. Gen. Grenville M. Dodge
Brig. Gen. Charles C. Doolittle
Maj. Gen. Abner Doubleday
Brig. Gen. Ulysses Doubleday
Brig. Gen. Neil Dow
Brig. Gen. Alfred Duffié
Brig. Gen. Ebenezer Dumont
Brig. Gen. Abram Duryée
Brig. Gen. Isaac H. Duval
Brig. Gen. William Dwight
Brig. Gen. John Edwards
Brig. Gen. Oliver Edwards
Brig. Gen. Thoms W. Egan
Brig. Gen. Alfred W. Ellet
Brig. Gen. Washington L. Elliott
Brig. Gen. William H. Emory
Brig. Gen. Henry L. Eustis
Brig. Gen. Charles Ewing
Brig. Gen. Hugh Ewing
Brig. Gen. Thomas Ewing
Brig. Gen. Lucius Fairchild
Brig. Gen. Elon J. Farnsworth (killed at Gettysburg)
Brig. Gen. John F. Farnsworth
Brig. Gen. Edward Ferrero
Brig. Gen. Orris S. Ferry
Maj. Gen. Francis Fessenden
Brig. Gen. James D. Fessenden
Brig. Gen. Clinton B. Fisk
Brig. Gen. Manning F. Force
Brig. Gen. James W. Forsyth
Brig. Gen. John G. Foster
Brig. Gen. Robert S. Foster
Maj. Gen. William B. Franklin
Maj. Gen. John C. Frémont
Brig. Gen. William H. French
Brig. Gen. James B. Fry
Brig. Gen. Speed S. Fry
Brig. Gen. John W. Fuller
Brig. Gen. William Gamble
Maj. Gen. James A. Garfield
Brig. Gen. Kenner Garrard
Brig. Gen. Theophilus T. Garrard
Brig. Gen. John W. Geary
Brig. Gen. George W. Getty
Maj. Gen. John Gibbon
Brig. Gen. Alfred Gibbs
Acting Maj. Gen. Charles C. Gilbert
Brig. Gen. James I. Gilbert
Brig. Gen. Alvan C. Gillem
Brig. Gen. Quincy A. Gillmore
Brig. Gen. George H. Gordon
Brig. Gen. Willis A. Gorman
Brig. Gen. Charles K. Graham
Brig. Gen. Lawrence P. Graham

Maj. Gen. Gordon Granger
Brig. Gen. Robert S. Granger
Brig. Gen. Lewis A. Grant
Lieut. Gen. U. S. Grant
Brig. Gen. George S. Greene
Brig. Gen. David McMurtrie Gregg
Brig. Gen. Walter Q. Gresham
Brig. Gen. Benjamin H. Grierson
Brig. Gen. Charles Griffin
Brig. Gen. Simon G. Griffin
Brig. Gen. William Gross
Brig. Gen. Cuvier Grover
Brig. Gen. Pleasant A. Hackleman (killed at Corinth)
Maj. Gen. Henry W. Halleck
Brig. Gen. Joseph E. Hamblin
Brig. Gen. Andrew J. Hamilton
Maj. Gen. Charles S. Hamilton
Brig. Gen. Schuyler Hamilton
Brig. Gen. Cyrus Hamlin
Brig. Gen. William A. Hammond
Maj. Gen. Winfield S. Hancock
Brig. Gen. Charles G. Harker (killed at Kennesaw Mountain)
Brig. Gen. Edward Harland
Brig. Gen. William A. Harney
Brig. Gen. Thomas M. Harris
Brig. Gen. William Harrow
Brig. Gen. John F. Hartranft
Maj. Gen. George L. Hartsuff
Brig. Gen. Milo S. Hascall
Brig. Gen. Joseph A. Haskin
Brig. Gen. Edward Hatch
Brig. Gen. John P. Hatch
Brig. Gen. Herman Haupt
Brig. Gen. John P. Hawkins
Brig. Gen. Joseph R. Hawley
Brig. Gen. Joseph Hayes
Brig. Gen. Rutherford B. Hayes
Brig. Gen. Isham N. Haynie
Brig. Gen. Alexander Hays (killed at the Wilderness)
Brig. Gen. William Hays
Brig. Gen. William B. Hazen
Brig. Gen. Charles A. Heckman
Brig. Gen. Samuel P. Heintzelman
Brig. Gen. Francis J. Herron
Brig. Gen. Edward W. Hinks
Maj. Gen. Ethan Allen Hitchcock
Brig. Gen. Edward H. Hobson
Brig. Gen. Joseph Holt
Maj. Gen. Joseph Hooker
Brig. Gen. Alvin P. Hovey
Brig. Gen. Charles E. Hovey
Brig. Gen. Oliver O. Howard
Brig. Gen. Albion P. Howe
Brig. Gen. Andrew A. Humphreys

Brig. Gen. Henry J. Hunt
Brig. Gen. Stephen A. Hurlbut
Brig. Gen. Rufus Infalls
Brig. Gen. Conrad F. Jackson (killed at Fredericksburg)
Brig. Gen. James S. Jackson (killed at Perryville)
Brig. Gen. Nathaniel J. Jackson
Brig. Gen. Richard H. Jackson
Brig. Gen. Charles D. Jameson
Brig. Gen. Andrew Johnson
Brig. Gen. Richard W. Johnson
Brig. Gen. Patrick H. Jones
Brig. Gen. Thomas L. Kane
Brig. Gen. August V. Kautz
Maj. Gen. Philip Kearny (killed at Chantilly)
Brig. Gen. William H. Keim
Brig. Gen. Benjamin F. Kelley
Brig. Gen. John R. Kenly
Brig. Gen. John H. Ketcham
Brig. Gen. William S. Ketchum
Maj. Gen. Erasmus D. Keyes
Maj. Gen. Judson Kilpatrick
Brig. Gen. Nathan Kimball
Brig. Gen. John H. King
Brig. Gen. Rufus King
Brig. Gen. Edmund Kirby
Brig. Gen. Edward N. Kirk
Brig. Gen. Joseph F. Knipe
Brig. Gen. Jacob G. Lauman
Brig. Gen. Michael K. Lawler
Brig. Gen. James H. Ledlie
Brig. Gen. Albert L. Lee
Brig. Gen. Mortimer D. Leggett
Brig. Gen. Joseph A. J. Lightburn
Brig. Gen. Henry H. Lockwood
Maj. Gen. John A. Logan
Brig. Gen. Eli Long
Maj. Gen. Mansfield Lovell
Brig. Gen. Charles R. Lowell (mortally wounded at Cedar Creek)
Brig. Gen. Thomas J. Lucas
Brig. Gen. Nathaniel Lyon (killed at Wilson's Creek)
Brig. Gen. William H. Lytle (killed at Chickamauga)
Brig. Gen. Ranald S. Mackenzie
Brig. Gen. Jasper A. Maltby
Maj. Gen. Joseph K. F. Mansfield (killed at Antietam)
Brig. Gen. Mahlon D. Manson
Brig. Gen. Randoph B. Marcy
Brig. Gen. Gilman Marston
Brig. Gen. John H. Martindale
Brig. Gen. Charles L. Matthias
Brig. Gen. John McArthur
Maj. Gen. George B. McClellan
Maj. Gen. John A. McClernand
Brig. Gen. Alexander McD. McCook

Brig. Gen. Daniel McCook (mortally wounded at Kennesaw Mountain)

Brig. Gen. Edward M. McCook

Brig. Gen. Robert L. McCook (murdered by Confederate guerrillas at Decherd, Tennessee)

Maj. Gen. Irvin McDowell

Brig. Gen. George F. McGinnis

Brig. Gen. John B. McIntosh

Brig. Gen. Thomas J. McKean

Brig. Gen. Justus McKinstry

Brig. Gen. Nathaniel C. McLean

Brig. Gen. James W. McMillan

Brig. Gen. John McNeil

Maj. Gen. James B. McPherson (killed at Atlanta)

Maj. Gen. George Gordon Meade

Brig. Gen. Thomas F. Meagher

Brig. Gen. Montgomery Meigs

Brig. Gen. Solomon Meredith

Brig. Gen. Sullivan Meredith

Maj. Gen. Wesley Merritt

Maj. Gen. Nelson A. Miles

Brig. Gen. John F. Miller

Brig. Gen. Stephen Miller

Brig. Gen. Robert H. Milroy

Maj. Gen. Ormsby M. Mitchel

Brig. Gen. John G. Mitchell

Brig. Gen. Robert B. Mitchell

Brig. Gen. William R. Montgomery

Maj. Gen. George W. Morell

Brig. Gen. Charles H. Morgan

Brig. Gen. George W. Morgan

Brig. Gen. James D. Morgan

Brig. Gen. Thomas A. Morris

Brig. Gen. William H. Morris

Brig. Gen. James St. Clair Morton (killed at Petersburg)

Brig. Gen. Gershom Mott

Brig. Gen. Joseph A. Mower

Brig. Gen. James Nagle

Brig. Gen. Henry M. Naglee

Maj. Gen. James S. Negley

Brig. Gen. Thomas H. Neill

Maj. Gen. William Nelson

Maj. Gen. John Newton

Brig. Gen. Franklin S. Nickerson

Brig. Gen. Richard J. Oglesby

Brig. Gen. John M. Oliver

Brig. Gen. Emerson Opdycke

Maj. Gen. Edward O. C. Ord

Brig. Gen. William W. Orme

Brig. Gen. Thomas O. Osborn

Maj. Gen. Peter J. Osterhaus

Brig. Gen. Joshua T. Owen

Brig. Gen. Charles J. Paine

Brig. Gen. Eleazar A. Paine

Brig. Gen. Halbert E. Paine

Brig. Gen. Innis N. Palmer

Maj. Gen. John M. Palmer

Maj. Gen. John G. Parke

Brig. Gen. Lewis B. Parsons

Brig. Gen. Marsena R. Patrick

Brig. Gen. Francis E. Patterson

Brig. Gen. Gabriel R. Paul

Maj. Gen. John J. Peck

Brig. Gen. Galusha Pennypacker

Brig. Gen. William H. Penrose

Brig. Gen. John S. Phelps

Brig. Gen. John W. Phelps

Brig. Gen. A. Sanders Piatt

Brig. Gen. Byron R. Pierce

Brig. Gen. William A. Pile

Brig. Gen. Thomas G. Pitcher

Maj. Gen. Alfred Pleasonton

Brig. Gen. J. B. Plummer

Brig. Gen. Orlando M. Poe

Maj. Gen. John Pope

Brig. Gen. Andrew Porter

Maj. Gen. Fitz John Porter

Brig. Gen. Edward E. Potter

Brig. Gen. Joseph H. Potter

Maj. Gen. Robert B. Potter

Brig. Gen. Benjamin F. Potts

Brig. Gen. William H. Powell

Brig. Gen. Calvin E. Pratt

Maj. Gen. Benjamin M. Prentiss

Brig. Gen. Henry Prince

Brig. Gen. Isaac F. Quinby

Brig. Gen. George D. Ramsey

Brig. Gen. Green B. Raum

Brig. Gen. John A. Rawlins

Brig. Gen. Hugh T. Reid

Brig. Gen. James W. Reilly

Maj. Gen. Jesse L. Reno (killed at South Mountain)

Brig. Gen. Joseph W. Revere

Maj. Gen. John F. Reynolds (killed at Gettysburg)

Maj. Gen. Joseph J. Reynolds

Brig. Gen. Americus V. Rice

Brig. Gen. Elliott W. Rice

Brig. Gen. James C. Rice (killed at Spotsylvania)

Brig. Gen. Samuel A. Rice (mortally wounded at Jenkins' Ferry)

Maj. Gen. Israel B. Richardson (mortally wounded at Antietam)

Brig. Gen. James B. Ricketts

Brig. Gen. James W. Ripley

Brig. Gen. Benjamin S. Roberts

Brig. Gen. James S. Robinson

Brig. Gen. John C. Robinson

Brig. Gen. Isaac P. Rodman (mortally wounded at Antietam)

Maj. Gen. William S. Rosecrans

Brig. Gen. Leonard F. Ross
Brig. Gen. Lovell H. Rousseau
Brig. Gen. Thomas A. Rowley
Brig. Gen. Daniel H. Rucker
Brig. Gen. Thomas H. Ruger
Brig. Gen. Theodore Runyon
Brig. Gen. David A. Russell (killed at Opequon)
Brig. Gen. Friend S. Rutherford
Brig. Gen. Frederick S. Salomon
Brig. Gen. John B. Sanborn
Brig. Gen. William P. Sanders (killed at Knoxville)
Brig. Gen. Rufus Saxton
Brig. Gen. Eliakim P. Scammon
Maj. Gen Robert C. Schenck
Brig. Gen. Alex. Schimmelfennig
Brig. Gen. Albin Schoepf
Maj. Gen. John M. Schofield
Brig. Gen. Carl Schurz
Brig. Gen. Robert K. Scott
Gen. Winfield Scott
Maj. Gen. John Sedgwick (killed at Spotsylvania)
Brig. Gen. William H. Seward, Jr.
Brig. Gen. Truman Seymour
Brig. Gen. James M. Shackleford
Brig. Gen. Alexander Shaler
Brig. Gen. Isaac F. Shepard
Brig. Gen. George F. Shepley
Maj. Gen. Philip H. Sheridan
Brig. Gen. Francis T. Sherman
Brig. Gen. Thomas W. Sherman
Maj. Gen. William T. Sherman
Brig. Gen. James Shields
Brig. Gen. Henry Hastings Sibley
Maj. Gen. Daniel E. Sickles
Maj. Gen. Franz Sigel
Brig. Gen. Joshua W. Sill (killed at Stones River)
Brig. Gen. James R. Slack
Brig. Gen. Adam J. Slemmer
Maj. Gen. Henry W. Slocum
Brig. Gen. John P. Slough
Maj. Gen. Andrew J. Smith
Maj. Gen. Charles F. Smith
Brig. Gen. Giles A. Smith
Brig. Gen. Green Clay Smith
Brig. Gen. Gustavus A. Smith
Brig. Gen. John E. Smith
Brig. Gen. Morgan L. Smith
Brig. Gen. Thomas Kilby Smith
Maj. Gen. William F. Smith
Brig. Gen. William Sooy Smith
Brig. Gen. Thomas A. Smyth (mortally wounded at
    Farmville)
Brig. Gen. James G. Spears
Brig. Gen. Francis B. Spinola
Brig. Gen. John W. Sprague

Maj. Gen. Julius Stahel
Brig. Gen. David S. Stanley
Brig. Gen. George J. Stannard
Brig. Gen. John C. Starkweather
Maj. Gen. James B. Steedman
Maj. Gen. Frederick Steele
Brig. Gen. Isaac L. Stevens (killed at Chantilly)
Brig. Gen. John D. Stevenson
Brig. Gen. Thomas G. Stevenson (killed at
    Spotsylvania)
Brig. Gen. James H. Stokes
Brig. Gen. Carlos J. M. Stolbrand
Brig. Gen. Charles P. Stone
Maj. Gen. George Stoneman
Brig. Gen. Edwin H. Stoughton
Maj. Gen. George C. Strong (mortally wounded at
    Fort Wagner)
Brig. Gen. William K. Strong
Brig. Gen. David Stuart
Brig. Gen. Samuel D. Sturgis
Brig. Gen. Jeremiah C. Sullivan
Brig. Gen. Alfred Sully
Maj. Gen. Edwin V. Sumner
Brig. Gen. Wager Swayne
Brig. Gen. Thomas W. Sweeny
Maj. Gen. George Sykes
Brig. Gen. George W. Taylor (mortally wounded dur-
    ing Second Bull Run campaign)
Brig. Gen. Joseph P. Taylor
Brig. Gen. Nelson Taylor
Brig. Gen. William R. Terrill (killed at Perryville)
Brig. Gen. Alfred H. Terry
Brig. Gen. Henry D. Terry
Brig. Gen. John M. Thayer
Maj. Gen. George H. Thomas
Brig. Gen. Henry G. Thomas
Brig. Gen. Lorenzo Thomas
Brig. Gen. Stephen Thomas
Brig. Gen. Charles M. Thruston
Brig. Gen. William B. Tibbits
Brig. Gen. Davis S. Tillson
Brig. Gen. John B. S. Todd
Brig. Gen. Alfred T. A. Torbert
Brig. Gen. Joseph G. Totten
Brig. Gen. Zealous B. Tower
Brig. Gen. John B. Turchin
Brig. Gen. John W. Turner
Brig. Gen. James M. Tuttle
Brig. Gen. Daniel Tyler
Brig. Gen. Erastus B. Tyler
Brig. Gen. Robert O. Tyler
Brig. Gen. Hector Tyndale
Brig. Gen. Daniel U. Ullman
Brig. Gen. Adin B. Underwood
Brig. Gen. Emory Upton

Brig. Gen. James H. Van Alen
Brig. Gen. Horatio P. Van Cleve
Brig. Gen. Ferdinand Van Derveer
Brig. Gen. Stewart Van Vliet
Brig. Gen. Charles H. Van Wyck
Brig. Gen. William Vandever
Brig. Gen. James C. Veatch
Brig. Gen. Egbert L. Viele
Brig. Gen. Strong Vincent (mortally wounded at Gettysburg)
Brig. Gen. Israel Vogdes
Brig. Gen. Adolph Von Steinwehr
Brig. Gen. Melancthon S. Wade
Brig. Gen. James S. Wadsworth (killed at the Wilderness)
Brig. Gen. George D. Wagner
Brig. Gen. Charles C. Walcutt
Maj. Gen. Lewis Wallace
Brig. Gen. W. H. L. Wallace (mortally wounded at Shiloh)
Brig. Gen. John H. Hobart Ward
Brig. Gen. William T. Ward
Brig. Gen. James M. Warner
Brig. Gen. Fitz Henry Warren
Maj. Gen. Gouverneur K. Warren
Brig. Gen. Cadwallader C. Washburn
Brig. Gen. Alexander S. Webb
Brig. Gen. Max Weber
Brig. Gen. Joseph D. Webster
Brig. Gen. Stephen H. Weed (killed at Gettysburg)

Maj. Gen. Godfrey Weitzel
Brig. Gen. William Wells
Brig. Gen. Thomas Welsh
Brig. Gen. Henry W. Wessells
Brig. Gen. Joseph R. West
Brig. Gen. Frank Wheaton
Maj. Gen. Amiel W. Whipple (mortally wounded at Chancellorsville)
Brig. Gen. William D. Whipple
Brig. Gen. Walter C. Whitaker
Brig. Gen. Julius White
Brig. Gen. Edward A. Wild
Brig. Gen. Orlando B. Willcox
Brig. Gen. Alpheus S. Williams
Brig. Gen. David H. Williams
Brig. Gen. Seth Williams
Brig. Gen. Thomas Williams (killed at Baton Rouge)
Brig. Gen. James A. Williamson
Brig. Gen. August Willich
Brig. Gen. James H. Wilson
Brig. Gen. Isaac J. Wistar
Brig. Gen. Thomas J. Wood
Brig. Gen. Daniel P. Woodbury
Brig. Gen. Charles R. Woods
Brig. Gen. William B. Woods
Maj. Gen. John E. Wool
Brig. Gen. George Wright
Maj. Gen. Horatio G. Wright
Brig. Gen. Samuel K. Zook (killed at Gettysburg)

THE UNITED STATES OF AMERICA—GOVERNMENT
(1857–1865)

Executive Officers
(4 March 1857–3 March 1861)

President of the United States: James Buchanan of Pennsylvania

Vice President of the United States: John C. Breckinridge of Kentucky

Secretary Of State: William L. Marcy of New York from preceding administration; Lewis Cass of Michigan, 6 March 1857; William Hunter (chief clerk), ad interim, 15 December 1860; Jeremiah S. Black of Pennsylvania, 17 December 1860

Secretary Of War: Samuel Cooper (Adjutant General, U.S. Army), ad interim, 4 March 1857; John B. Floyd of Virginia, 6 March 1857; Joseph Holt of Kentucky (Postmaster General), ad interim, 1 January 1861; Joseph Holt of Kentucky, 18 January 1861

Secretary Of The Treasury: James Guthrie, of Kentucky, continued from preceding administration. Howell Cobb of Georgia, 6 March 1857; Isaac Toucey of Connecticut (Secretary of the Navy), ad interim, 10 December 1860; Philip E Thomas of Maryland, 12 December 1860; John A. Dix of New York, 11 January 1861, assumed office on 15 January 1861.

Attorney General: Caleb Cushing of Massachusetts, continued from preceding administration; Jeremiah S. Black of Pennsylvania, 6 March 1857, assumed duties 11 Match 1857; Edwin M. Stanton of Pennsylvania, 20 December 1860, assumed duties 22 December 1860

Postmaster General: James Campbell of Pennsylvania, continued from preceding administration; Aaron V. Brown of Tennessee, 6 March 1857, died on 8 March 1859; Horatio King of Maine (First Assistant Postmaster General), ad interim, 9 March 1859; Joseph Holt of Kentucky, 14 March 1859; Horatio King (First Assistant Postmaster General), ad interim, 1 January 1861; Horatio King, 12 February 1861

Secretary Of The Navy: James C. Dorbin of North Carolina, continued from preceding administration; Isaac Toucey of Connecticut, 6 March 1857

Secretary Of The Interior: Robert McClelland of Michigan, continued from preceding administration; Jacob Thompson of Mississippi, 6 March 1857, assumed duties 10 March 1857; Moses Kelly (chief clerk), ad interim, 10 January 1861

Executive Officers
(4 March 1861–3 March 1865)

President of the United States: Abraham Lincoln of Illinois

Vice-president of the United States: Hannibal Hamlin of Maine

Secretary of State: Jeremiah S. Black of Pennsylvania, continued from preceding administration; William H. Seward of New York, 5 March 1861

Secretary of the Treasury: John A. Dix of New York, continued from preceding administration; Salmon P. Chase of Ohio, 5 March 1861, assumed duties 7 March 1861; George Harrington of the District of Columbia (Assistant Secretary), ad interim, 1 July 1864; William P. Fessenden of Maine, 1 July 1864, assumed duties 5 July 1864

Secretary of War: Joseph Holt of Kentucky, continued from preceding administration; Simon Cameron of Pennsylvania, 5 March 1861, assumed duties 11 March 1861; Edwin M. Stanton of Pennsylvania, 15 January 1862, assumed duties 20 January 1862

Attorney General: Edwin M. Stanton of Pennsylvania, continued from preceding administration; Edwin Bates of Missouri, 5 March 1861; James Speed of Kentucky, 2 December 1864 assumed duties 5 December 1864

Postmaster General: Horatio King of Maine, continued from preceding administration; Montgomery Blair of the District of Columbia, 5 March 1861, assumed duties 9 March 1861; William Dennison of Ohio, 24 September 1864, entered upon duties 1 October 1864

Secretary of the Navy: Isaac Toucey of Connecticut, continued from preceding administration; Gideon

Welles of Connecticut, 5 March 1861, assumed duties 7 March 1861

Secretary of the Interior: Moses Kelly (chief clerk), ad interim, 4 March 1861; Caleb B. Smith of Indiana, 5 March 1861; John P. Usher of Indiana (assistant secretary), ad interim, 1 January 1863; John P. Usher, 8 January 1863

Executive Officers
(4 March 1865–15 April 1865)

President of the United States: Abraham Lincoln of Illinois, died 15 April 1865

Vice President of the United States: Andrew Johnson of Tennessee

Secretary of State: William H. Seward of New York, continued from preceding administration.

Secretary of the Treasury: George Harrington of the District of Columbia (assistant secretary), ad interim, 4 March 1865, Hugh McCulloch of Indiana, 7 March 1865, assumed duties 9 March 1865

Secretary of War: Edwin M. Stanton of Pennsylvania, continued from preceding administration

Attorney General: James Speed of Kentucky, continued from preceding administration

Postmaster General: William Dennison of Ohio, continued from preceding administration

Secretary of the Navy: Gideon Welles of Connecticut, continued from preceding administration

Secretary of the Interior: John P. Usher of Indiana, continued from preceding administration

Legislature

Thirty-Sixth Congress
(4 March 1859–3 March 1861)

The Thirty-Sixth Congress held two sessions, and the Senate held two additional special sessions.
- The first session assembled on 5 December 1859 and adjourned on 25 June 1860.
- The second session assembled on 3 December 1860 and adjourned on 3 March 1861.
- The special sessions of the Senate were held from 4 March 1859 to 10 March 1859 and from 26 June 1860 to 28 June 1860.

Senate

President of the United States Senate: John C. Breckinridge of Kentucky

President pro tempore of the Senate: Benjamin Fitzpatrick of Alabama, 9 March 1859 (special session), 20 February 1860, 26 June 1860 (special session); Jesse D. Bright of Indiana, 12 June 1860; Solomon Foot of Vermont, 16 February 1861

ALABAMA
[Seceded from the Union on 11 January 1861]
Benjamin Fitzpatrick, withdrew on 21 January 1861
Clement C. Clay, withdrew on 21 January 1861

ARKANSAS
William K. Sebastian
Robert W. Johnson

CALIFORNIA
William M. Gwin
David C. Broderick, died 16 September 1859
Henry P. Haun, 5 December 1859 by appointment of governor to succeed Broderick
Milton S. Latham, 5 March 1860 to succeed Broderick permanently

CONNECTICUT
Lafayette S. Foster
James Dixon

DELAWARE
James A. Bayard
Willard Saulsbury

FLORIDA
[Seceded from the Union on 11 January 1861]
Stephen R. Mallory, withdrew on 21 January 1861
David Levy Yulee, withdrew on 21 January 1861

GEORGIA
[Seceded from the Union on 19 January 1861]
Robert Toombs, did not appear after 4 February 1861
Alfred Iverson, withdrew 28 January 1861

ILLINOIS
Stephen A. Douglas
Lyman Trumbull

INDIANA
Jesse D. Bright
Graham N. Fitch

IOWA
James Harlan
James W. Grimes

KANSAS
[Territory was admitted to the Union on 29 January 1861]

KENTUCKY
John J. Crittenden
Lazarus W. Powell

LOUISIANA
[Seceded from the Union on 26 January 1861]
Judah P. Benjamin, withdrew 4 February 1861
John Slidell, withdrew 4 February 1861

MAINE
William Pitt Fessenden
Hannibal Hamlin, resigned 17 January 1861
Lot M. Morrill, 17 January 1861 to succeed Hamlin

MARYLAND
James A. Pearce
Anthony Kennedy

MASSACHUSETTS
Charles Sumner
Henry Wilson

MICHIGAN
Zachariah Chandler
Kinsley S. Bingham

MINNESOTA
Henry M. Rice
Morton S. Wilkinson

MISSISSIPPI
[Seceded from the Union on 9 January 1861]
Albert G. Brown, withdrew 12 January 1861
Jefferson Davis, withdrew 21 January 1861

MISSOURI
James S. Green
Trusten Polk

NEW HAMPSHIRE
John P. Hale
Daniel Clark

NEW JERSEY
John R. Thomson
John C. Ten Eyek

NEW YORK
William H. Seward
Preston King

NORTH CAROLINA
Thomas L. Clingman
Thomas Bragg

OHIO
Benjamin F. Wade
George E. Pugh

OREGON
Joseph Lane
Edward D. Baker, 5 December 1860

PENNSYLVANIA
William Bigler
Simon Cameron

RHODE ISLAND
James F. Simmons
Henry B. Anthony

SOUTH CAROLINA
[Seceded from the Union on 20 December 1860]
James H. Hammond, withdrew on 11 November 1860
James Chesnut, Jr., withdrew on 10 November 1860

TENNESSEE
Andrew Johnson
Alfred O. P. Nicholson, withdrew on 3 March 1861

TEXAS
[Legislature voted to secede from the Union on 1 February 1861, confirmed by referendum on 1 March 1861]
Matthias Ward
Louis T. Wigfall, 4 January 1860, to succeed J. Pinckney Henderson, deceased
John Hemphill

VERMONT
Solomon Foot
Jacob Collamer

VIRGINIA
James M. Mason,
Robert M. T. Hunter

WISCONSIN
Charles Durkee
James R. Doolittle

House of Representatives
Speaker of the House of Representatives: William Pennington of New Jersey

ALABAMA
[Seceded from the Union on 11 January 1861, and entire delegation withdrew on 8 January 1861]
James A. Stallworth
James L. Pugh
David Clopton
Sydenham Moore
George S. Houston
Williamson R. W. Cobb
Jabez L. M. Curry

ARKANSAS
Thomas C. Hindman
Albert Rust

CALIFORNIA
Charles L. Scott, at large
John C. Burch, at large

CONNECTICUT
Dwight Loomis
John Woodruff
Alfred A, Burnham
Orris S. Ferry

DELAWARE
William G. Whiteley, at large

FLORIDA
[Seceded from the Union on 10 January 1861]
George S. Hawkins, at large, withdrew on 21 January 1861

GEORGIA
[Seceded from the Union on 19 January 1861 and the delegation, excepting Hill who resigned, withdrew on 23 January 1861]
Peter E. Love
Martin J. Crawford
Thomas Hardeman, Jr.
Lucius J. Gartrell
John W. H. Underwood
Rome James Jackson
Joshua Hill, resigned 23 January 1861
John J. Jones

ILLINOIS
Elihu B. Washburue
John F. Farusworth
Owen Lovejoy
William Kellogg
Isaac N. Morris

John A. McClernand, 5 December 1859, to succeed Thomas L. Harris, deceased
James C. Robinson
Philip B. Fouke
John A. Logan

INDIANA
William E. Niblack
Wllliam H. English
William McKee
William S. Holman
David Kilgore
Albert G. Porter
John G. Davis
James Wilson
Schuyler Coffax
Charles Case
John U. Pettit

IOWA
Samuel R. Curtis
William Vandever

KANSAS
[Territory was admitted to the Union on 29 January 1861]
Martin F. Conway, 30 January 1861

KENTUCKY
Henry C. Burnett
Samuel O. Peyton
Francis N. Bristow
William C. Anderson
John Young Brawn
Green Adams
Robert Mallory
William E. Simms
Laban T. Moore
John W. Stevenson

LOUISIANA
[Seceded from the Union on 26 January 1861]
John E. Bouligny
Miles Tyler, withdrew 5 February 1861
Thomas G. Davidson, did not appear after 5 February 1861
John M. Landrum

MAINE
Daniel E. Seines
John J. Perry
Ezra B. French
Freeman H. Morse
Israel Washburn, Jr., resigned 1 January 1861
Stephen Coburn, 2 January 1861, to succeed Washburn
Stephen C. Foster

MARYLAND
James A. Stewart
Edwin H. Webster
J. Morrison Harris,
Henry Winter Davis
Jacob M. Kunkel
George W. Hughes

MASSACHUSETTS
Thomas D. Eliot
James Buffington
Charles Francis Adams
Alexander H. Rice
Anson Burlingame
John B. Alley
Daniel W. Gooch
Charles R. Train
Eli Thayer
Charles Delano
Henry L. Dawes

MICHIGAN
George B. Cooper, election contested, replaced on 15
    May 1860 by Howard
William A. Howard, 15 May 1860
Henry Waldron
Francis W. Kellogg
De Witt C. Leach

MINNESOTA
Cyrus Aldrich, at large
William Windom, at large

MISSISSIPPI
[Seceded from the Union on 9 January 1861]
Lucius Q. C. Lamar, retired in December 1860
Reuben Davis
William Barksdale
Otho R. Singleton
John J. McRae

MISSOURI
John R. Barret, election contested, replaced on 8 June
    1860 by Blair; filled Blair's vacancy on 3 December
    1860
Francis P. Blair, Jr., 8 June 1860, resigned on 25 June
    1860
Thomas L. Anderson
John B. Clark
James Craig
Samuel H. Woodson
John S. Phelps
John W. Noell

NEW HAMPSHIRE
Gilman Marston
Mason W. Tappan
Thomas M. Edwards

NEW JERSEY
John T Nixon
John L. N. Stratton
Garnett B. Adrain
Jetur R. Riggs
William Pennington

NEW YORK
Luther C. Carter
James Humphrey
Daniel E. Sickles
Thomas J. Bert
William B. Maclay
John Cochrane
George Briggs
Horace F. Clark
John B. Haskin
Charles H. Van Wyck
William S. Kenyon
Charles L. Beale
Abram B. Olin
John H. Reynolds
James B. McKean
George W. Palmer
Francis E. Spinner
Clark B. Cochrane
James H. Graham
Roscoe Conkling
R. Holland Duell
M. Lindley Lee
Charles B. Hoard
Charles B. Sedgwick
Martin Butterfield
Emory B. Pottle
Alfred Wells
William Irvine
Alfred Ely
Augustus Frank
Silas M. Burroughs, died on 3 June 1860
Edwin R. Reynolds, 5 December 1860 to succeed
    Burroughs
Elbridge G. Spaulding
Reuben E. Fenton

NORTH CAROLINA
William N. H. Smith
Thomas Ruffin
Warren Winslow
Lawrence O'Bryan Branch

John A. Gilmer
James M. Leach
F. Burton Craige
Zebulon B. Vance

OHIO
George H. Pendleton
John A. Gurley
Clement L. Vallandigham
William Allen
James M. Ashley
William Howard
Thomas Corwin
Benjamin Stanton
John Carey
Carey A. Trimble
Charles D. Martin
Samuel S. Cox
John Sherman
Cyrus Spink, never seated, died on 31 May 1859
Harrison G. O. Blake, 5 December 1860, to succeed Spink
William Helmick
Cydnor B. Tompkins
Thomas C. Theaker
Sidney Edgerton
Edward Wade
John Hutchins
John A. Bingham

OREGON
Lansing Stout, at large

PENNSYLVANIA
Thomas B. Florence
Edward Joy Morris
John P. Verree
William Millward
John Wood
John Hickman
Henry C. Longnecker
John Schwartz, died on 20 June 1860
Jacob K. McKenty, 3 December 1860, to succeed Schwartz
Thaddeus Stevens
John W. Killinger
James H. Campbell
George W. Scranton
William H. Dimmick
Galusha A. Grow
James T. Hale
Benjamin F. Junkin
Edward McPherson
Samuel S. Blair
John Covode

William Montgomery
James K. Moorhead
Robert McKnight
William Stewart
Chapin Hall
Elijah Babbitt

RHODE ISLAND
Christopher Robinson
William D. Brayton

SOUTH CAROLINA
[Seceded from the Union on 20 December 1860]
John McQueen, withdrew on 21 December 1860
William Porcher Miles, did not appear after 13 December 1860
Laurence M. Keitt, did not appear after 10 December 1860
Milledge L. Bonham, withdrew on 21 December 1860
John D. Ashmore, withdrew on 21 December 1860
William W. Boyce, withdrew on 21 December 1860

TENNESSEE
Thomas A. R. Nelson
Horace Maynard
Reese B. Brabson
William B. Stokes
Robert H. Hatton
James H. Thomas
John V. Wright
James M. Quarles
Emerson Etheridge
William T. Avery

TEXAS
[Legislature voted to secede from the Union on 1 February 1861, confirmed by referendum on 1 March 1861]
John H. Reagan
Andrew J. Hamilton

VERMONT
Justin S. Morrill
Eliakim P. Walton
Homer E. Royce

VIRGINIA
Muscoe R. H. Garnett
John S. Millson
Daniel C. DeJarnette
William O. Goode, died on 3 July 1860
Roger A. Pryor, 7 December 1859, to succeed Goode
Thomas S. Bocock
Shelton F. Leake
William Smith

Alexander R. Boteler
John T. Harris
Sherrard Clemens
Albert G. Jenkins
Henry A. Edmundson
Elbert S. Martin

WISCONSIN
John F. Potter
Cadwallader C. Washburn
La Charles H. Larrabee

TERRITORY OF KANSAS DELEGATE
Marcus J. Parrott, seated until 29 January 1861 when Kansas became a state

TERRITORY OF NEBRASKA DELEGATE
Experience Estabrook, replaced on 18 May 1860 by Daily
Samuel G. Daily, 18 May 1860

TERRITORY OF NEW MEXICO DELEGATE
Miguel A. Otero

TERRITORY OF UTAH DELEGATE
William H. Hooper

TERRITORY OF WASHINGTON DELEGATE
Isaac I. Stevens

Thirty-Seventh Congress
(4 March 1861–3 March 1863)

The Thirty-Seventh Congress held three sessions, and the Senate held one additional special session.
- The first session assembled on 4 July 1861 and adjourned on 6 August 1861.
- The second session assembled on 2 December 1861 and adjourned on 17 July 1862.
- The third session assembled on 1 December 1862 and adjourned on 3 March 1863.
- The special session of the Senate was held from 4 March 1862 to 28 March 1862.

Senate

President of the Senate: Hannibal Hamlin of Maine
President Pro Tempore of the Senate: Solomon Foot of Vermont

ARKANSAS
[Seceded from the Union on 6 May 1861]
William K. Sebastian, expelled by resolution of 11 July 1861; expulsion later annulled by resolution of 3 March 1877

Charles B Mitchel, expelled by resolution of 11 July 1861

CALIFORNIA
Milton S. Latham
James A. McDougall

CONNECTICUT
Lafayette S. Foster
James Dixon

DELAWARE
James A. Bayard
Willard Saulsbury

ILLINOIS
Stephen A. Douglas, died on 3 June 1861
Orville H. Browning, 4 July 1861, appointed by the governor to succeed Douglas
William A. Richardson, 30 January 1863, elected to succeed Douglas
Lyman Trumbull

INDIANA
Jesse D. Bright, expelled on 5 February 1862
Joseph A. Wright, 3 March 1862, appointed by the governor to fill Bright's vacancy
David Turpie, 22 January 1863, elected to fill Bright's vacancy
Henry S. Lane

IOWA
James Harlan
James W. Grimes

KANSAS
Samuel C. Pomeroy, 4 July 1861, term to expire on 3 March 1867 by lot
James H. Lane, 4 July 1861, term to expire on 3 March 1865 by lot

KENTUCKY
Lazarus W. Powell
John J. Crittenden, expelled 4 December 1861
Garrett Davis, 23 December 1861, to fill Crittenden's vacancy

LOUISIANA
[Seceded from the Union on 26 January 1861]
Judah P. Benjamin, seat declared vacant 14 March 1861

MAINE
William Pitt Fessenden
Lot M. Morrill

MARYLAND
James A. Pearce, died on 20 December 1862
Thomas H. Hicks, 14 January 1863, by appointment of governor to succeed Pearce
Anthony Kennedy

MASSACHUSETTS
Charles Sumner
Henry Wilson

MICHIGAN
Zachariah Chandler
Kinsley S. Bingham, died on 5 October 1861
Jacob M. Howard, 17 January 1862, to succeed Bingham

MINNESOTA
Henry M. Rice
Morton S. Wilkinson

MISSOURI
Trusten Polk, expelled on 10 January 1862
John B. Henderson, 29 January 1862, by appointment of governor to fill Polk's vacancy
Waldo Porter Johnson, expelled 10 January 1862
Robert Wilson, 24 January 1862, by appointment of governor to fill Johnson's vacancy

NEW HAMPSHIRE
John P. Hale
Daniel Clark

NEW JERSEY
John R. Thomson, died 12 September 1862
Richard S. Field, 1 December 1862, by appointment of governor to succeed Thomson
James W. Wall, 21 January 1863, elected to succeed Thomson
John C. Ten Eyck

NEW YORK
Preston King
Ira Harris

NORTH CAROLINA
[Seceded from the Union on 20 May 1861]
Thomas L. Clingman, withdrew 28 March 1861, expelled on 11 July 1861
Thomas Bragg, withdrew 8 March 1861, expelled on 11 July 1861

OHIO
Benjamin F. Wade
Salmon P. Chase, resigned 6 March 1861 to become Sec. of the Treasury

John Sherman, 23 March 1861, elected to fill Chase's vacancy

OREGON
Edward D. Baker, killed at Ball's Bluff on 21 October 1861
Benjamin Stark, 27 February 1862, by appointment of governor to fill Baker's vacancy
Benjamin F. Harding, 1 December 1862, elected to fill Baker's vacancy
James W. Nesmith

PENNSYLVANIA
Simon Cameron, resigned 4 March 1861 to become Sec. of War
David Wilmot, 18 March 1861, elected to fill Cameron's vacancy
Edgar Cowan

RHODE ISLAND
James F. Simmons, resigned 15 August 1862
Samuel G. Arnold, 1 December 1862, elected to fill Simmons vacancy
Henry B. Anthony

TENNESSEE
[Seceded from the Union on 24 June 1861]
Andrew Johnson, resigned 4 March 1862 to become military governor of Tennessee
Alfred O. P. Nicholson, withdrew on 3 March 1861, expelled 11 July 1861

VERMONT
Solomon Foot
Jacob Collamer

VIRGINIA
[Seceded from the Union on 17 April 1861]
James M. Mason, withdrew on 28 March 1861, expelled on 11 July 1861
Waitman T. Willey, 13 July 1861, elected to fill Mason's vacancy
Robert M. T. Hunter, withdrew on 28 March 1861, expelled on 11 July 1861
John S. Carlile, 13 July 1861, elected to fill Hunter's vacancy

WISCONSIN
James R. Doolittle
Timothy O. Howe

House of Representatives

Speaker of the House of Representatives: Galusha A. Grow of Pennsylvania

ARKANSAS
[Seceded from the Union on 6 May 1861]
No delegation

CALIFORNIA
Frederick F. Low, seated on 3 June 1862 following credentials dispute
Timothy G. Phelps, 2 December 1861
Aaron A. Sargent

CONNECTICUT
Alfred A. Burnham
James E. English
Dwight Loomis
George C. Woodruff

DELAWARE
George P. Fisher

ILLINOIS
Isaac N. Arnold
Philip B. Fouke
William Kellogg
John A. Logan, resigned 2 April 1862
William J. Allen, 2 June 1862, elected to fill Logan's vacancy
Owen Lovejoy
John A. McClernand, resign 28 October 1861
Anthony L. Knapp, 12 December 1861, elected to fill McClernand's vacancy
William A. Richardson, resigned 29 January 1862 to take a seat in the Senate
James C. Robinson
Elihu B. Washburne

INDIANA
Schuyler Colfax
James A. Cravens
William McKee Dunn
William S. Julian
George W. Julian
John Law
William Mitchell
Albert G. Porter
John P. C. Shanks
Daniel W. Voorhees
Albert S. White

IOWA
Samuel B. Curtis, resigned 4 August 1861
James F. Wilson, 2 December 1861, elected to fill Curtis's vacancy
William Vandever

KANSAS
Martin Conway, at large

KENTUCKY
Henry C. Burnett, expelled on 3 December 1861
Samuel L Casey, 10 March 1862, elected to fill Burnett's vacancy
John J. Crittenden
George W. Dunlap
Henry Grider
Aaron Harding
James S. Jackson, resigned 13 December 1861 to enter army; killed at Perryville on 8 October 1862
George H. Yeaman, 1 December 1862, elected to fill Jackson's vacancy
Robert Mallory
La John W. Menzies
William H. Wadsworth
Charles A. Wickliffe

LOUISIANA
[Seceded from the Union on 26 January 1861]
Benjamin F. Flanders, 23 February 1863, by resolution of 17 February 1863 accepting his credentials
Michael Hahn, 17 February 1863, by resolution of 17 February 1863 accepting his credentials

MAINE
Samuel C. Fessenden
John N. Goodwin
Anson P. Morrill
Frederick A. Pike
John H. Rice
Charles W. Walton, resigned on 26 May 1862
Thomas A. D. Fessenden

MARYLAND
Charles B. Calvert
John W. Crisfield
Cornelius L. L. Leary
Henry May
Francis Thomas
Edwin H. Webster

MASSACHUSETTS
Charles Francis Adams, resigned on 1 May 1861 to become U.S. Minister to Great Britain
Benjamin F. Thomas, 4 July 1861, elected to fill Adams's vacancy
John B. Alley
William Appleton, resigned on 27 September 1861
Samuel Hooper, 2 December 1861, elected to fill Appleton's vacancy
Goldsmith F. Bailey, died on 8 May 1862
Amasa Walker, 1 December 1862, elected to fill Bailey's vacancy

James Buffington
Henry L. Dawes
Charles Delano
Thomas D. Eliot
Daniel W. Gooch
Alexander H. Rice
Charles R. Train

MICHIGAN
Fernando C. Beaman
Bradley F. Granger
Francis W. Kellogg
Rowland E. Trowbridge

MINNESOTA
Cyrus Aldrich, at large
William Windom, at large

MISSOURI
Francis P. Blair, resigned in July 1862
John W. Noell
Elijah H. Norton
John S. Phelps
John W. Reid, expelled on 2 December 1861
Thomas L. Price, 21 January 1862, elected to fill Reid's
    vacancy
James S. Rollins
John B. Clark, expelled on 13 July 1861
William A. Hall, 20 January 1862, elected to fill Clark's
    vacancy

NEW HAMPSHIRE
Thomas M. Edwards
Gilman Marston
Edward H. Rollins

NEW JERSEY
George T. Cobb
John T. Nixon
Nehemiah Perry
William G. Steele
J. L. N. Stratton

NEW YORK
Stephen Baker
Jacob P. Chamberlain
Ambrose W. Clark
Frederick A. Conkling
Roscoe Conkling
Erastus Coming
Isaac C. Delaplaine
Alexander S. Diven
R. Holland Duell
Alfred Ely
Reuben E. Fenton

Richard Franchot
Augustus Frank
Edward Haight
James E. Kerrigan
William E. Lansing
James B. McKean
Moses F. Odell
Abram B. Olin
Troy Theodore M. Pomeroy
Charles B. Sedgwick
Socrates N. Sherman
Edward H. Smith
Elbridge G. Spaulding
John B. Steele
Butt Van Horn
Robert B. Van Valkenburg
Charles H. Van Wyck
Chauncey Vibbard
William Wall
Elijah Ward
William A. Wheeler
Benjamin Wood

NORTH CAROLINA
[Seceded from the Union on 20 May 1861]
No delegation

OHIO
William Allen
James M. Ashley
John A. Bingham
Harrison G. O. Blake
Samuel S. Cox
William P. Cutler
Sidney Edgerton
John A. Gurley
Thomas Corwin, resigned on 12 March 1861 to
    become U.S. minister to Mexico
Richard A. Harrison, 4 July 1861, elected to fill
    Corwin's vacancy
Valentine B. Horton
John Hutchins
James R. Morris
Warren F. Noble
Robert H. Nugen
George H. Pendleton
Albert G. Riddle
Samuel Shellabarger
Carey A. Trimble
Clement L. Vallandigham
Chilton A. White
John Sherman, resigned on 21 March 1861 to take a
    seat in the Senate
Samuel T. Worcester, 4 July 1861, elected to fill
    Sherman's vacancy

OREGON

Andrew J. Thayer, at large, replaced on 30 July 1861 by Shiel who had contested election

Goerge K. Shiel, 30 July 1861

PENNSYLVANIA

Sydenham E. Ancona

Elijah Babbitt

Joseph Bailey

E. Joy Morris, resigned on 8 June 1861 to become U.S. Minister to Turkey

Charles J. Biddle, 2 December 1861, elected to fill Morris's vacancy

Samuel S. Blair

James H. Campbell

Thomas B. Cooper, died on 4 April 1862

John D. Stiles, 3 June 1862, elected to fill Cooper's vacancy

John Covode

William Morris Davis

Galusha A. Grow

James T. Hale

John Hickman

Philip Johnson

William D. Kelley

John W. Killinger

Jesse Lazear

William E. Lehman

Robert McKnight

Edward McPherson

James K. Moorhead

John Patton

Thaddeus Stevens

John P. Verree

John W. Wallace

George W. Scranton, died on 24 March 1861

Hendrick B. Wright, 4 July 1861, elected to fill Scranton's vacancy

RHODE ISLAND

George H. Browne

William P. Sheffield

TENNESSEE

[Seceded from the Union on 8 June 1861]

George W. Bridges, 25 February 1863

Andrew J. Clements, 13 January 1863

Horace Maynard, 2 December 1861

VERMONT

Portus Baxter

Justin S. Morrill

Eliakim P. Walton

VIRGINIA

[Seceded from the Union on 17 April 1861]

William G. Brown

John S. Carlile, resigned on 9 July 1861 to take a seat in the Senate

Jacob B. Blair, 2 December 1861, elected to fill Carlile's vacancy

Joseph E. Segar, 6 May 1862

Charles H. Upton, 4 July 1861, credentials revoked on 27 February 1862

Lewis McKenzie, 16 February 1863, elected to fill Upton's vacancy

Kellian V. Whaley

WISCONSIN

Luther Hanchett, died on 24 November 1862

Walter D. McIndoe, 26 January 1863, elected to fill Hanchett's vacancy

John F. Potter

A. Scott Sloan

TERRITORY OF COLORADO DELEGATE

Hiram P. Bennett

TERRITORY OF DAKOTA DELEGATE

John B. S. Todd

TERRITORY OF NEBRASKA DELEGATE

Samuel G. Daily, *Peru*

TERRITORY OF NEVADA DELEGATE

John Cradlebaugh

TERRITORY OF NEW MEXICO DELEGATE

John S. Watts

TERRITORY OF UTAH DELEGATE

John M. Bernhisel

TERRITORY OF WASHINGTON DELEGATE

William H. Wallace

Thirty–Eighth Congress
(4 March 1863–3 March 1865)

The Thirty-Eighth Congress held two sessions, and the Senate held one additional special session.

- The first session assembled on 7 December 1863 and adjourned on 4 July 1864.
- The second session assembled on 5 December 1864 and adjourned on 3 March 1865.
- The special session of the Senate was held from 4 March 1863 to 14 March 1863.

Senate

President of the Senate: Hannibal Hamlin of Maine
President Pro Tempore of the Senate: Solomon Foot of Vermont; Daniel Clark of New Hampshire, elected on 26 April 1864, 9 February 1865

CALIFORNIA
James A. McDougall
John Conness

CONNECTICUT
Lafayette S. Foster
James Dixon

DELAWARE
James A. Bayard, resigned 29 January 1864
George R. Riddle, 2 February 1864, elected to fill Bayard's vacancy
Willard Saulsbury

ILLINOIS
Lyman A. Trumbull
William A. Richardson

INDIANA
Henry S. Lane
Thomas A. Hendricks

IOWA
James Harlan
James W. Grimes

KANSAS
Samuel C. Pomeroy
James H. Lane

KENTUCKY
Lazarus W. Powell
Garrett Davis

MAINE
William Pitt Fessenden, resigned 1 July 1864 to become Sec. of the Treasury
Nathan A. Farwell, 5 December 1864, appointed and then elected to fill Fessenden's vacancy
Lot M. Morrill

MARYLAND
Thomas H. Hicks, died on 14 February 1865
Reverdy Johnson

MASSACHUSETTS
Charles Sumner
Henry Wilson

MICHIGAN
Zachariah Chandler
Jacob M. Howard

MINNESOTA
Morton S. Wilkinson
Alexander Ramsey

MISSOURI
John B. Henderson
Robert Wilson, declared not entitled to seat on 8 December 1863
B. Gratz Brown, 14 December 1863, elected to fill Waldo P. Johnson's vacancy

NEVADA
[Admitted to the Union on 31 October 1864]
William M. Stewart, 1 February 1865, term to expire on 3 March 1869 by lot
James W. Nye, 1 February 1865, term to expire on 3 March 1867 by lot

NEW HAMPSHIRE
John P. Hale
Daniel Clark

NEW JERSEY
John C. Ten Eyck
William Wright

NEW YORK
Ira Harris
Edwin D. Morgan

OHIO
Benjamin F. Wade
John Sherman

OREGON
James W. Nesmith
Benjamin F. Harding

PENNSYLVANIA
Edgar Cowan
Charles R. Buckalew

RHODE ISLAND
Henry B. Anthony
William Sprague

VERMONT
Solomon Foot
Jacob Collamer

VIRGINIA

John S. Carlile, 13 July 1861

Lemuel J. Bowden, died on 2 January 1864; seat remained vacant until 20 October 1869

WEST VIRGINIA

[Admitted to the Union on 19 June 1863 from the western portion of Virginia]

Peter G. Van Winkle, 7 December 1863, term to expire on 3 March 1869 by lot

Waitman T. Willey, 7 December 1863, term to expire on 3 March 1865 by lot

WISCONSIN

James R. Doolittle

Timothy O. Howe

House of Representatives

Speaker of the House of Representatives: Schuyler Colfax of Indiana

CALIFORNIA

Cornelius Cole, at large

William Higby, at large

Thomas B. Shannon, at large

CONNECTICUT

Augustus Brandegee

Henry C. Detains

James E. English

John H. Hubbard

DELAWARE

William Temple, never seated, died on 28 May 1863

Nathaniel B. Smithers

ILLINOIS

Isaac N. Arnold

John F. Farnsworth

Elihu B. Washburne

Charles M. Harris

Owen Lovejoy, died on 25 March 1864

Ebon C. Ingersoll, 20 May 1864, elected to fill Lovejoy's vacancy

Jesse O. Norton

John R. Eden

John T. Stuart

Lewis W. Ross

Anthony L. Knapp

James C. Robinson

William R. Morrison

William J. Allen

INDIANA

Schuyler Colfax

James A. Cravens

Ebenezer Dumont

Joseph K. Edgerton

Henry W. Harrington

William S. Holman

George W. Julian

John Law

James F. McDowell

Godlove S. Orth

Daniel W. Voorhees

IOWA

William B. Allison

Josiah B. Grinnell

Asahel W. Hubbard

John A. Kasson

Hiram Price

James F. Wilson

KANSAS

A. Carter Wilder, at large

KENTUCKY

Lucien Anderson

Brutus J. Clay

Henry Grider

Aaron Harding

Robert Mallory

La William H. Randall

Green C. Smith

William H. Wadsworth

George H. Yeoman

MAINE

James G. Blaine

Sidney Perham

Frederick A. Pike

John H. Rice

Lorenzo D. M. Sweat

MARYLAND

John A. J. Creswell

Henry Winter Davis

Benjamin G. Harris

Francis Thomas

Edwin H. Webster

MASSACHUSETTS

John B. Alley

Oakes Ames

John D. Baldwin

George S. Boutwell

Henry L. Dawes

Thomas D. Eliot
Daniel W. Gooch
Samuel Hooper
Alexander H. Rice
William B. Washburn

MICHIGAN
Augustus C. Baldwin
Fernando C. Beaman
John F. Driggs
Francis W. Kellogg
John W. Longyear
Charles Upson

MINNESOTA
Ignatius Donnelly
William Windom

MISSOURI
Francis P. Blair, Jr., replaced by Samuel Knox on 10 June 1864
Samuel Knox, 15 June 1864, after contesting Blair's election
Henry T. Blow
Sempronins H. Boyd
William A. Hall
Austin A. King
Benjamin F. Loan
Joseph W. McClurg
James S. Rollins
John W. Noell, died on 14 March 1863
John G. Scott, 7 December 1863, elected to fill Noell's vacancy

NEVADA
[Admitted to the Union on 31 October 1864]
Henry G. Worthington, 21 December 1864, at large

NEW HAMPSHIRE
Daniel Marcy
James W. Patterson
Edward H. Rollins

NEW JERSEY
George Middleton
Nehemiah Perry
Andrew J. Rogers
John F. Starr
William G. Steele

NEW YORK
James Brooks
John W. Chanler
Ambrose W. Clark
Freeman Clarke

Erastus Corning, never seated, resigned on 5 October 1863
John V. L. Pruyn, 7 December 1863, elected to fill Corning's vacancy
Thomas T. Davis
Reuben E. Fenton, resigned on 20 December 1864
Augustus Frank
John Ganson
John A. Griswold
Anson Herrick
Giles W. Hotchkiss
Calvin T. Hulburd
Martin Kalbfieisch
Orlando Kellogg
Francis Kernan
De Witt C. Littlejohn
James M. Marvin
Samuel F. Miller
Daniel Morris
Homer A. Nelson
Moses F. Oden
Theodore M. Pomerey
William Radford
Henry G. Stebbins, resigned on 24 October 1864
Dwight Townsend, 5 December 1864, elected to fill Stebbins's vacancy
John B. Steele
Robert B. Van Valkenburg
Elijah Ward
Charles H. Winfield
Benjamin Wood
Fernando Wood

OHIO
James M. Ashley
George Bliss
Samuel S. Cox
Ephraim R. Eckley
William E. Finck
James A. Garfield
Wells A. Hutchins
William Johnston
Francis C. Le Blond
Alexander Long
John F. McKinney
James R. Morris
Warren P. Noble
John O'Neill
George H. Pendleton
Robert C. Schenck
Rufus P. Spalding
Chilton A. White
Joseph W. White

OREGON
John R. McBride, at large

PENNSYLVANIA
Sydenham E. Ancona
Joseph Bailey
John M. Breomall
Alexander H. Coffroth
John L. Dawson
Charles Denison
James T. Hale
Philip Johnson
William D. Kelley
Jesse Lazear
Archibald McAllister
William H. Miller
James K. Moorhead
Amos Myers
Leonard Myers
Charles O'Neill
Samuel J. Randall
Glenni W. Schofield
Thaddeus Stevens
John D. Stiles
Myer Strouse
M. Russell Thayer
Henry W. Tracy
Thomas Williams

RHODE ISLAND
Nathan F. Dixon
Thomas A. Jenckes

VERMONT
Pertus Baxter
Justin S. Morrill
Frederick E. Woodbridge

VIRGINIA
No delegation, credentials of claimants refused

WEST VIRGINIA
Jacob B. Blair
William G. Brown
Kellian V. Whaley

WISCONSIN
James S. Brown
Amasa Cobb
Charles A. Eldridge
Walter D. McIndoe
Ithamar C. Sloan
Ezra Wheeler

TERRITORY OF ARIZONA DELEGATE
[Formed from part of New Mexico Territory on 24 February 1864]
Charles D. Poston, 5 December 1864

TERRITORY OF COLORADO DELEGATE
Hiram P. Bennett

TERRITORY OF DAKOTA DELEGATE
William Jayne, replaced on 17 June 1864 by Todd
John B. S. Todd, 17 June 1864, after contesting Jayne's election

TERRITORY OF IDAHO DELEGATE
[Formed on 3 March 1863]
William H. Wallace, 1 February 1864

TERRITORY OF MONTANA DELEGATE
[Formed on 26 May 1864]
Samuel McLean, 6 January 1865

TERRITORY OF NEBRASKA DELEGATE
Samuel G. Daily

TERRITORY OF NEVADA DELEGATE
Gordon N. Mott, occupied seat until territory admitted as a state on 31 October 1864

TERRITORY OF NEW MEXICO DELEGATE
Francisco Perea

TERRITORY OF UTAH DELEGATE
John F. Kinney

TERRITORY OF WASHINGTON DELEGATE
George E. Cole

Appendix V

CIVIL WAR BATTLEFIELD SITES

The following Civil War–related sites are administered by the National Park Service:

Andersonville National Historic Site
Andersonville, Georgia
Route 1, Box 800
Andersonville, GA 31711
(912) 924-0343

Antietam National Battlefield
Sharpsburg, Maryland
P.O. Box 158
Sharpsburg, MD 21782
(301) 432-5124 (Programs and Information)
(301) 432-7672 (Superintendent and Administration)

Appomattox Court House National Historical Park
Appomattox, Virginia
P.O. Box 218
Appomattox, VA 24522
(804) 352-8987

Arlington House, the Robert E. Lee Memorial
Arlington, Virginia
Arlington House, The Robert E. Lee Memorial
c/o National Park Service, George Washington
Memorial Parkway, Turkey Run Park
McLean, VA 22101
(703) 557-0613

Brices Cross Roads National Battlefield Site
Baldwyn, Mississippi
Natchez Trace Parkway
2680 Natchez Trace Parkway
Tupelo, MS 38804
(662) 680-4025 or (800) 305-7417

Chickamauga and Chattanooga National Military Park
Fort Oglethorpe, Georgia; Chattanooga, Tennessee
P.O. Box 2128
3370 LaFayette Road
Fort Oglethorpe, GA 30742
(706) 866-9241

Clara Barton National Historic Site
Glen Echo, Maryland
5801 Oxford Road
Glen Echo, MD 20812
(301) 492-6245

Dry Tortugas National Park
Key West, Florida
P.O. Box 6208
Key West, FL 33041
(305) 242-7700

Ford's Theatre National Historic Site
Washington, D.C.
511 10th Street NW
Washington, DC 20004
(202) 426-6924

Fort Donelson National Battlefield
Dover, Tennessee
P.O. Box 434
Dover, Tennessee 37058-0434
(931) 232-5348 (Administration)
(931) 232-5706 (Interpretive Services)

Fort Moultrie National Monument
Sullivan's Island, South Carolina
1214 Middle Street
Sullivan's Island, SC 29482
(843) 883-3123

Fort Pulaski National Monument
Savannah, Georgia
P.O. Box 30757
U.S. Highway 80 East
Savannah, GA 31410-0757
(912) 786-5787

Fort Sumter National Monument
Sullivan's Island, South Carolina
1214 Middle Street
Sullivan's Island, SC 29482
(843) 883-3123

Fort Washington Park
Fort Washington, Maryland
13551 Fort Washington Road
Fort Washington, MD 20744
(301) 763-4600

Frederick Douglass National Historic Site
Washington, D.C.
1411 W Street SE
Washington, DC 20020-4813
(202) 426-5961

Fredericksburg and Spotsylvania National Military Park
Fredericksburg, Virginia, and vicinity
120 Chatham Lane
Fredericksburg, VA 22405
(540) 373-4510 (Superintendent's Office)
(540) 371-0802 (Historians)
(540) 373-6122 (Fredericksburg Battlefield Visitor Center)
(540) 786-2880 (Chancellorsville Visitor Center)
(540) 654-5121 (Chatham Manor)
(804) 633-6076 (Jackson Shrine)

General Grant National Memorial
New York
Riverside Drive and 122nd Street
New York, NY 10003
(212) 666-1640

Gettysburg National Military Park
Gettysburg, Pennsylvania
97 Taneytown Road
Gettysburg, PA 17325
(717) 334-1124

Harpers Ferry National Historical Park
Harpers Ferry, West Virginia
P.O. Box 65
Harpers Ferry, WV 25425
(304) 535-6298

Kennesaw Mountain National Battlefield Park
Kennesaw, Georgia
900 Kennesaw Mountain Drive
Kennesaw, GA 30144
(770) 427-4686

Lincoln Boyhood National Memorial
Lincoln City, Indiana
P.O. Box 1816
Lincoln City, IN 47552
(812) 937-4541

Lincoln Home National Historic Site
Springfield, Illinois
413 South Eighth Street
Springfield, IL 62701-1905
(217) 492-4241, ext. 221 (Visitor Center)

Manassas National Battlefield Park
Prince William and Fairfax counties, Virginia
12521 Lee Highway
Manassas, VA 20109-2005
(703) 754-1861 (Headquarters)
(703) 361-1339 (Visitor Center)

Monocacy National Battlefield
Frederick, Maryland
4801 Urbana Pike
Frederick, MD 21701
(301) 662-3515

Pea Ridge National Military Park
Pea Ridge, Arkansas
P.O. Box 700
Pea Ridge, AR 72751
(501) 451-8122
(501) 451-0344 (TDD)

Petersburg National Battlefield
Petersburg, Virginia
1539 Hickory Hill Road
Petersburg, VA 23803
(804) 732-3531

Shiloh National Military Park
Shiloh, Tennessee
1055 Pittsburg Landing
Shiloh, TN 38376
(901) 689-5696

Stones River National Battlefield
Murfreesboro, Tennessee
3501 Old Nashville Highway
Murfreesboro TN 37129
(615) 893-9501

Tupelo National Battlefield
Tupelo, Mississippi
2680 Natchez Trace Parkway
Tupelo, MS 38804
(662) 680-4025

Ulysses S. Grant National Historic Site
St. Louis, Missouri
7400 Grant Road
St. Louis, MO 63123-1801
(314) 842-3298

Vicksburg National Military Park
Vicksburg, Mississippi
3201 Clay Street
Vicksburg, MS 39183-3495
(601) 636-0583 (Visitor Center)
(601) 636-2199 (Cairo Museum)

Wilson's Creek National Battlefield
Republic, Missouri
6424 W. Farm Road 182
Republic, MO 65738
(417) 732-2662

CIVIL WAR BATTLEFIELD LOCATION MAPS

Cartography by George Zirfas

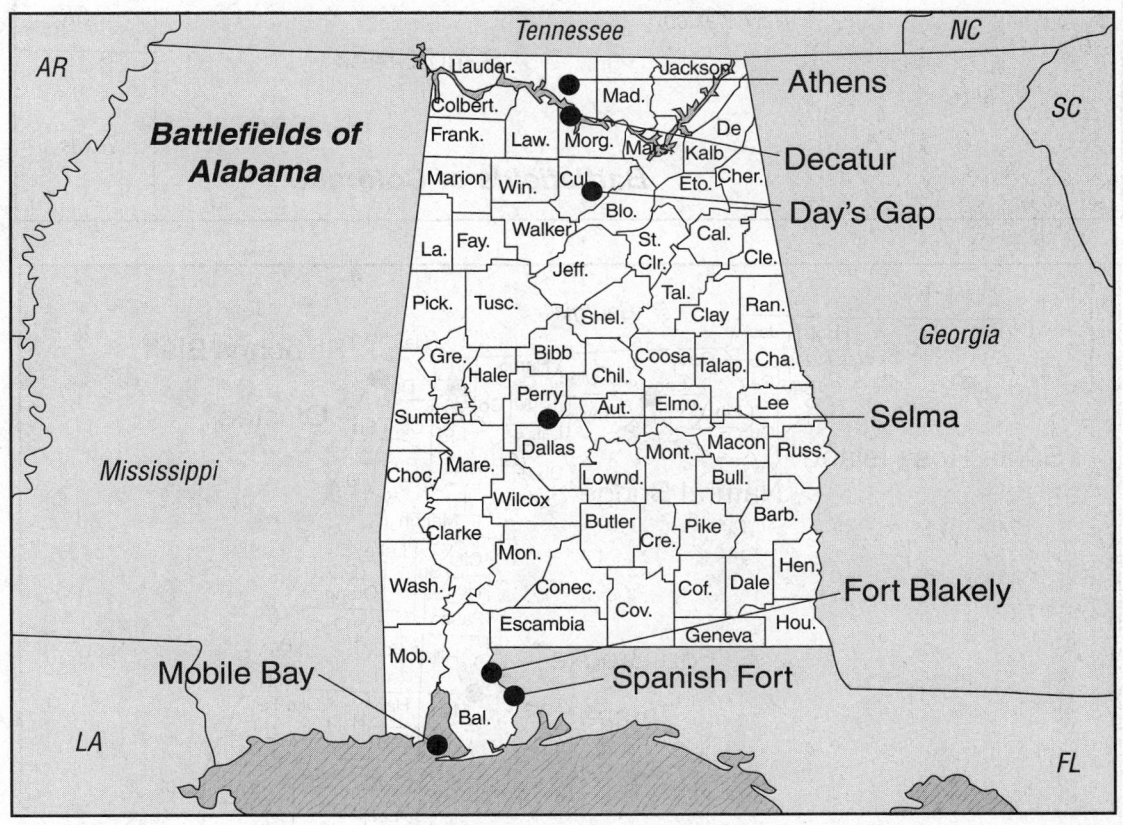

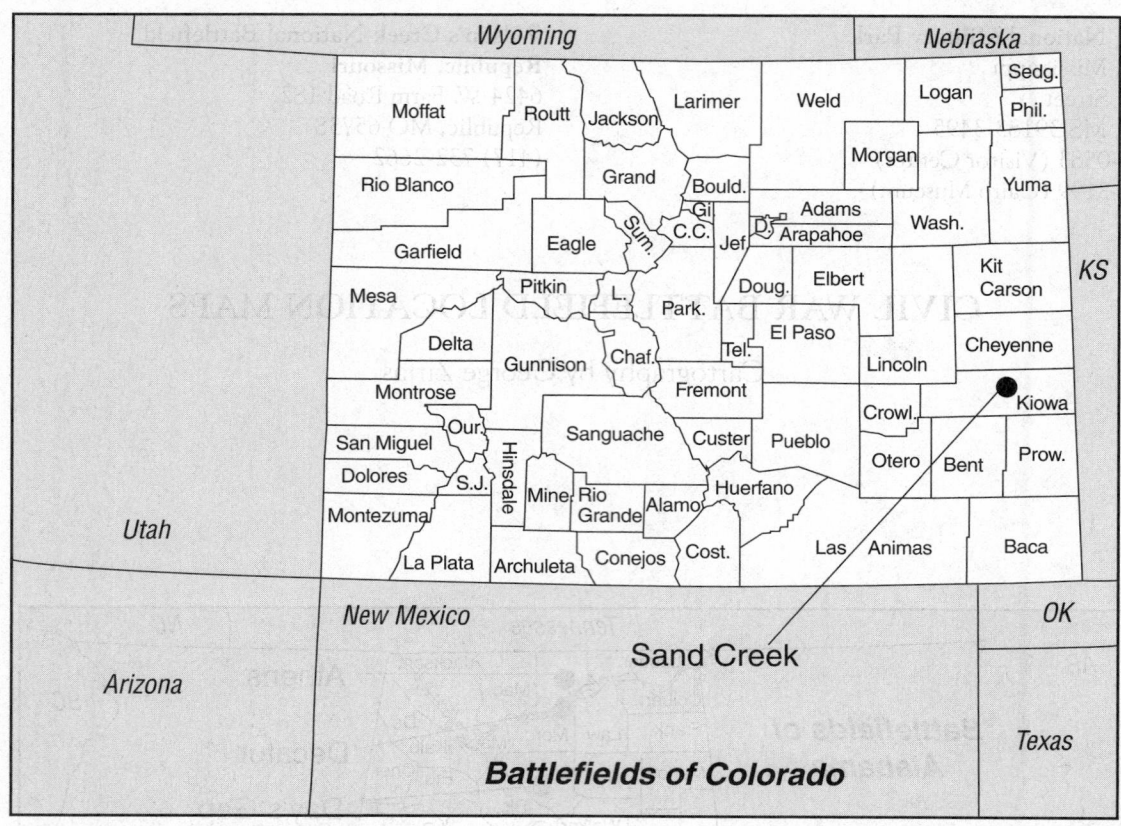

Battlefields of Colorado

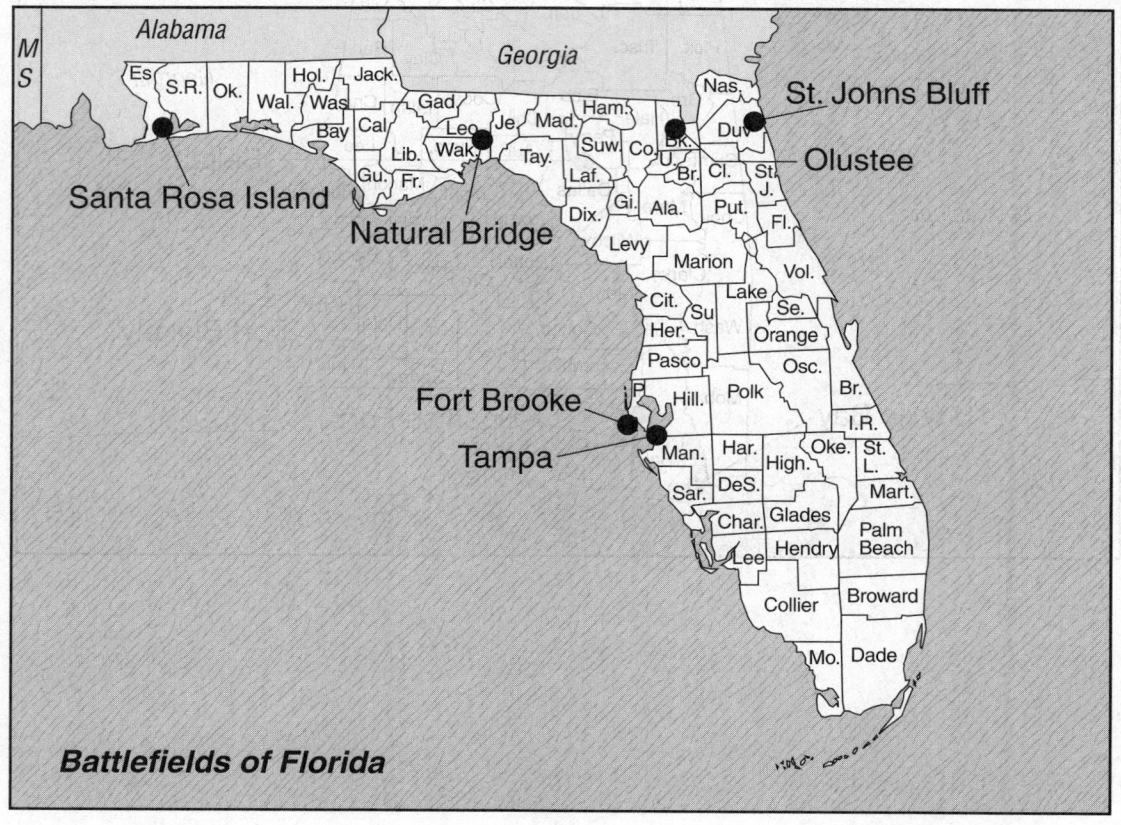

Battlefields of Florida

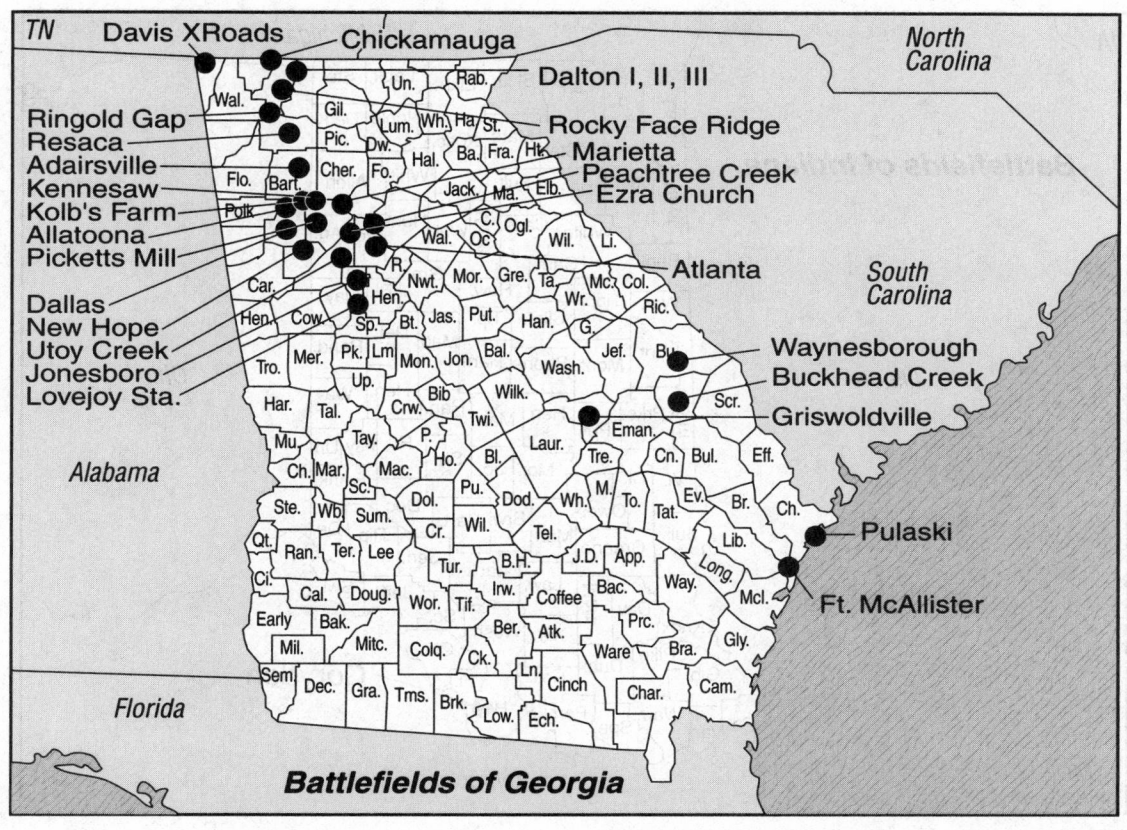

Battlefields of Georgia

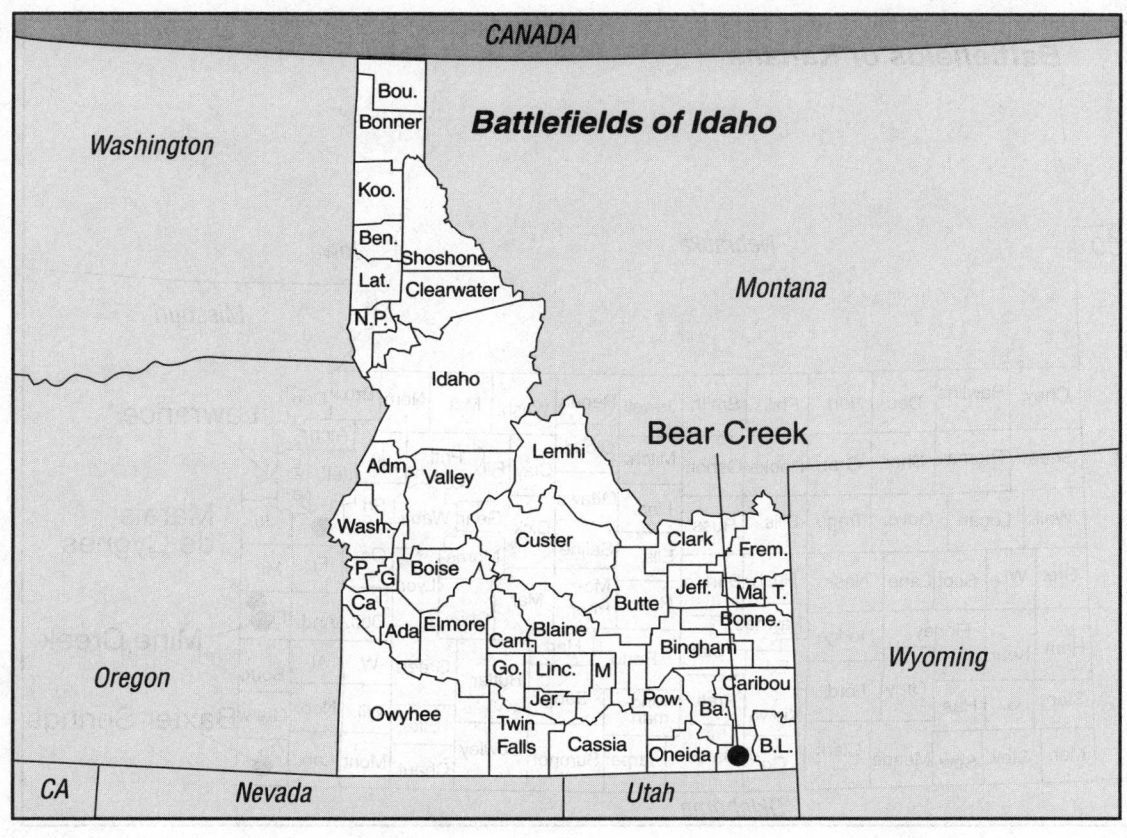

Battlefields of Idaho

Battlefields of Indiana

Corydon

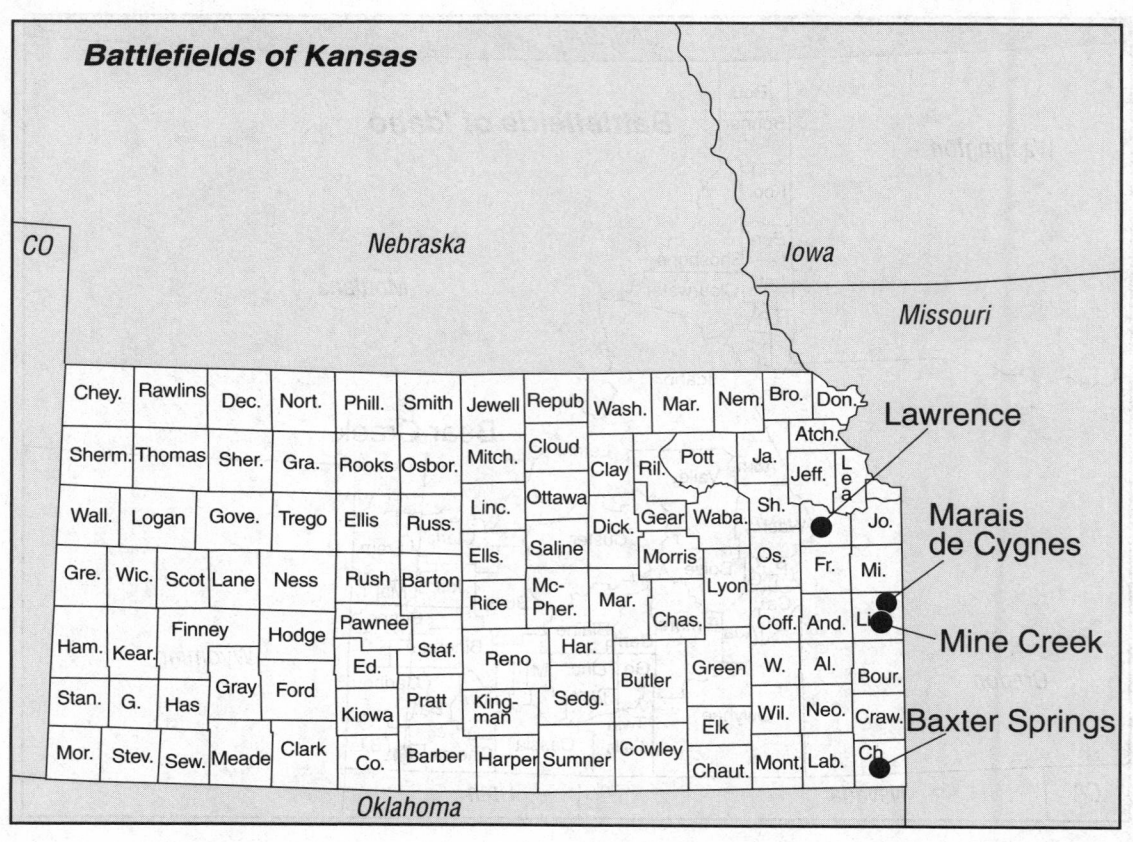

Battlefields of Kansas

Lawrence

Marais
de Cygnes

Mine Creek

Baxter Springs

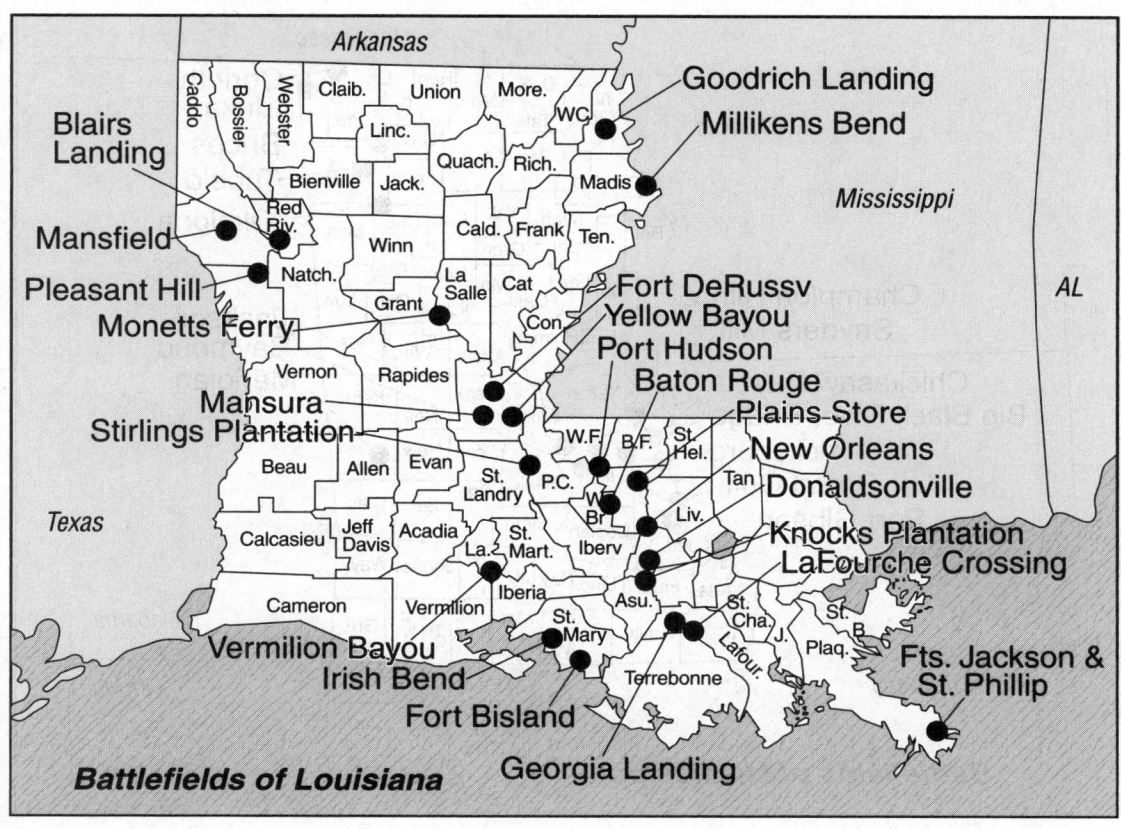

Battlefields of Louisiana

Arkansas

Caddo · Bossier · Webster · Claib. · Union · More. · WC

Goodrich Landing
Millikens Bend

Blairs Landing

Bienville · Jack. · Linc. · Quach. · Rich. · Madis

Mississippi

Mansfield

Red Riv. · Winn · Cald. · Frank · Ten.

AL

Natch.

Pleasant Hill

Grant · La Salle · Cat · Con

Monetts Ferry

Vernon · Rapides

Fort DeRussv
Yellow Bayou
Port Hudson
Baton Rouge

Mansura
Stirlings Plantation

Beau · Allen · Evan · St. Landry · P.C. · W.F. · B.F. · St. Hel.

Plains Store
New Orleans
Donaldsonville

Texas

Calcasieu · Jeff Davis · Acadia · St. Mart. · Iberv · W. Br · Tan · Liv.

Knocks Plantation
LaFourche Crossing

La.2 · Iberia

Cameron · Vermillion · Asu. · St. Cha. · J. · St. B · Plaq.

Fts. Jackson & St. Phillip

Vermilion Bayou
Irish Bend

St. Mary · Terrebonne · Lafour.

Fort Bisland

Georgia Landing

Battlefields of Minnesota

Kitts. · Roseau · Lake Woods · Kooch. · CANADA

Marshall · Beltrami · Cook

Penn. · Lake

R.L.

Polk · Itasca · St. Louis

North Dakota

Norm. · Ma. · Clwtr.

Clay · Becker · Hub. · Cass · Crow Wing · Aitkin · Carl.

Wlk. · Otter Tail · Wa. · Pine

Gr. · Doug · Todd · Morris. · ML · Kn

Wisconsin

Michigan

Tv. · St. · Pope · Stearns · Bnt. · Is. · Ch

B. · Swif. · Shb. · Ano. · W

S. · Kan. · Mkr. · Wr. · Hnp. · R

Wood Lake

L.Q. Parle · Chip. · Renv. · McL. · Cv. · Sc · Dak.

Fort Ridgely

Ln. · Ly. · Red. · Sib. · L.S. · Rice · Gdh · Wab.

Brn.

Ps · Mur. · Ctwd. · Wat. · B.E. · Wa · St. · Do. · Olm. · Win.

South Dakota

Ro. · Nob. · Jack. · Mart. · Farb. · Frbn. · Mow. · Film. · Ho.

Iowa

Battlefields of Mississippi

Battlefields of Missouri

Battlefields of New Mexico

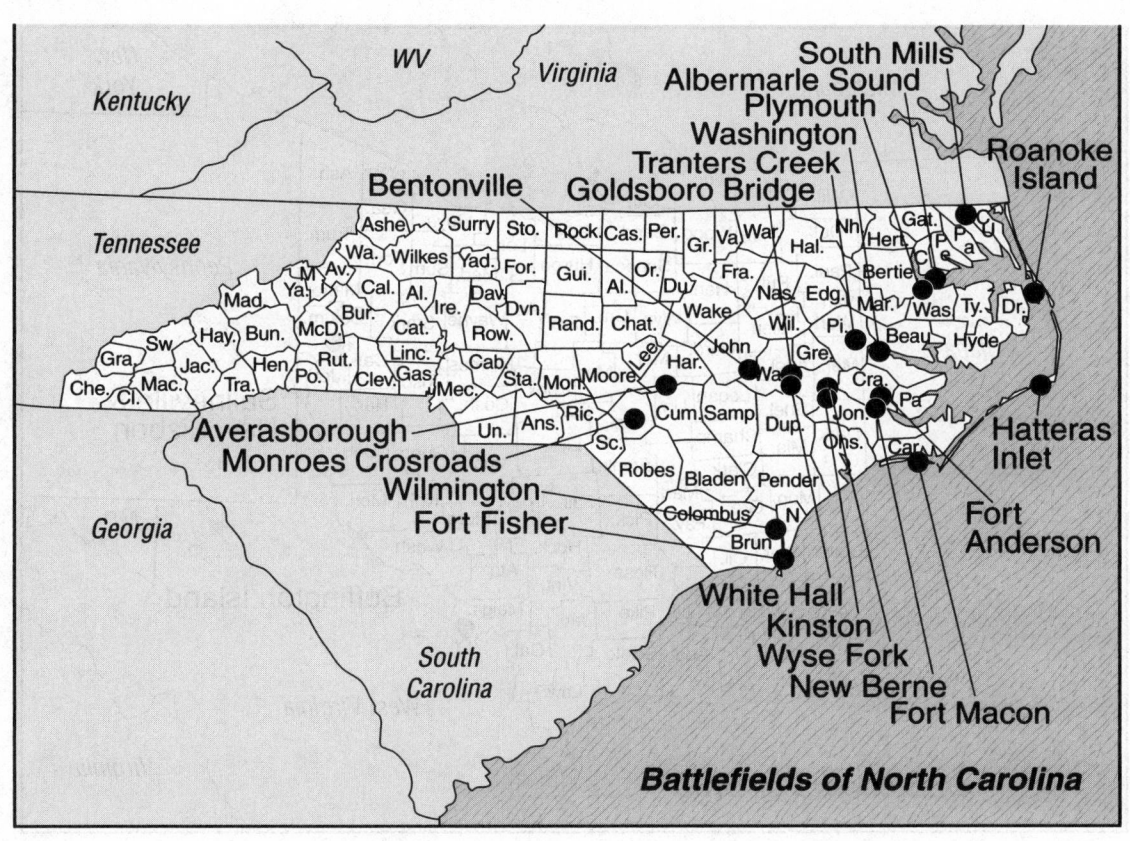

Battlefields of North Carolina

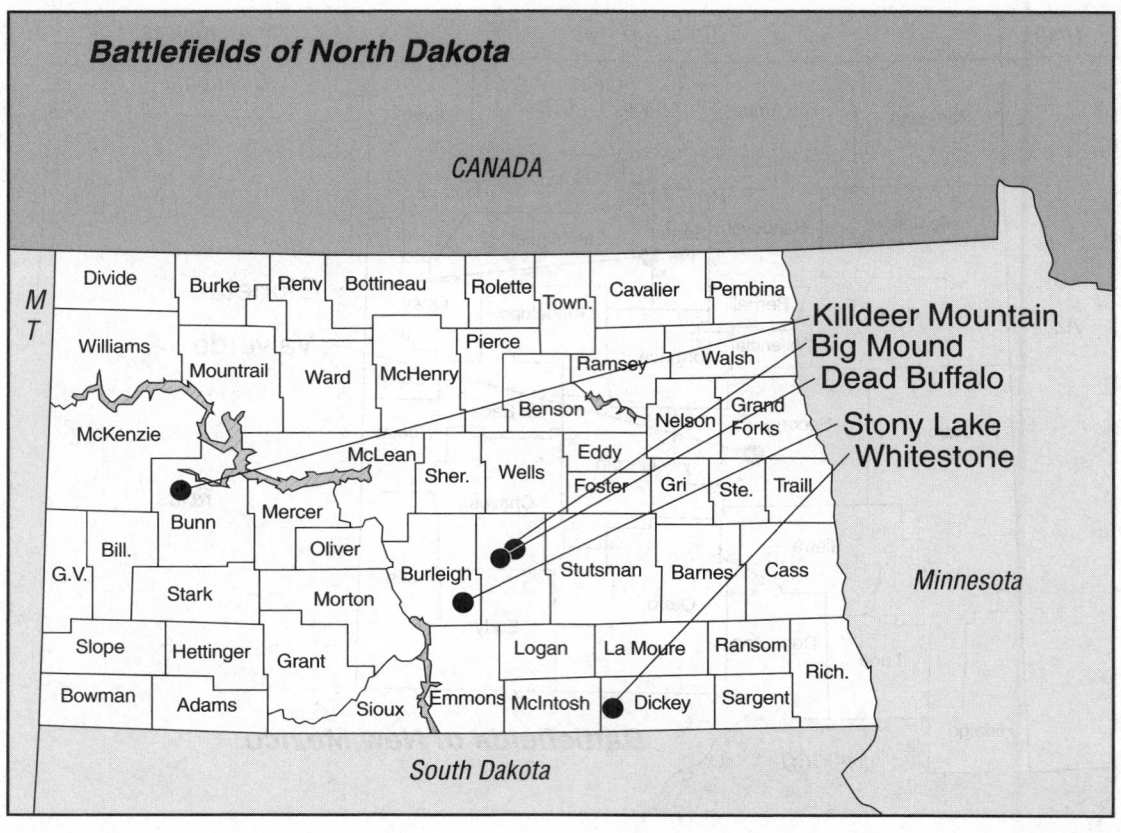

Battlefields of North Dakota

CANADA

MT

Divide | Burke | Renv | Bottineau | Rolette | Town. | Cavalier | Pembina

Williams | Mountrail | Ward | McHenry | Pierce | Ramsey | Walsh

McKenzie | McLean | Benson | Nelson | Grand Forks

Bunn | Mercer | Sher. | Wells | Eddy | Foster | Gri | Ste. | Traill

Bill. | Oliver | Burleigh | Stutsman | Barnes | Cass

G.V. | Stark | Morton | Logan | La Moure | Ransom

Slope | Hettinger | Grant | Rich.

Bowman | Adams | Sioux | Emmons | McIntosh | Dickey | Sargent

South Dakota

Minnesota

Killdeer Mountain
Big Mound
Dead Buffalo
Stony Lake
Whitestone

Michigan

New York

Wil. | Ful. | Luc. | Ott. | Lake | Ash.
Def. | Hen. | Wood | Sand. | Erie | Cuya. | Gea. | Trum.
Paul. | Put. | Han. | Seneca | Huron | Lor. | Med. | Sum | Port.
Van Wert | Allen | Wya. | Cra. | Ric. | As. | Wayne | Stark | Mahon.
Mer. | Augl. | Hard. | Mar. | Mor. | Knox | Holmes | Tusc. | Colum. | Car. | Jef.
Shel. | Logan | Un. | Del. | Lick. | Cosh. | Har.
Dark. | Mia. | Champ. | Clark | Frank. | Musk. | Guern. | Bel.
Pre. | Mon. | Gre. | Mad. | Fay. | Pick. | Fair. | Per. | Morg. | Nob. | Mon.
Butler | War. | Cli. | Ross | Hock. | Wash.
Ham. | Cl. | High. | Vint. | Ath.
Br. | Ada. | Scioto | Pike | Jac. | Gal. | Meigs.
Law.

Indiana

Pennsylvania

Salineville &
New Lisbon

MD

Buffington Island

Kentucky | West Virginia | Virginia

Battlefields of Ohio

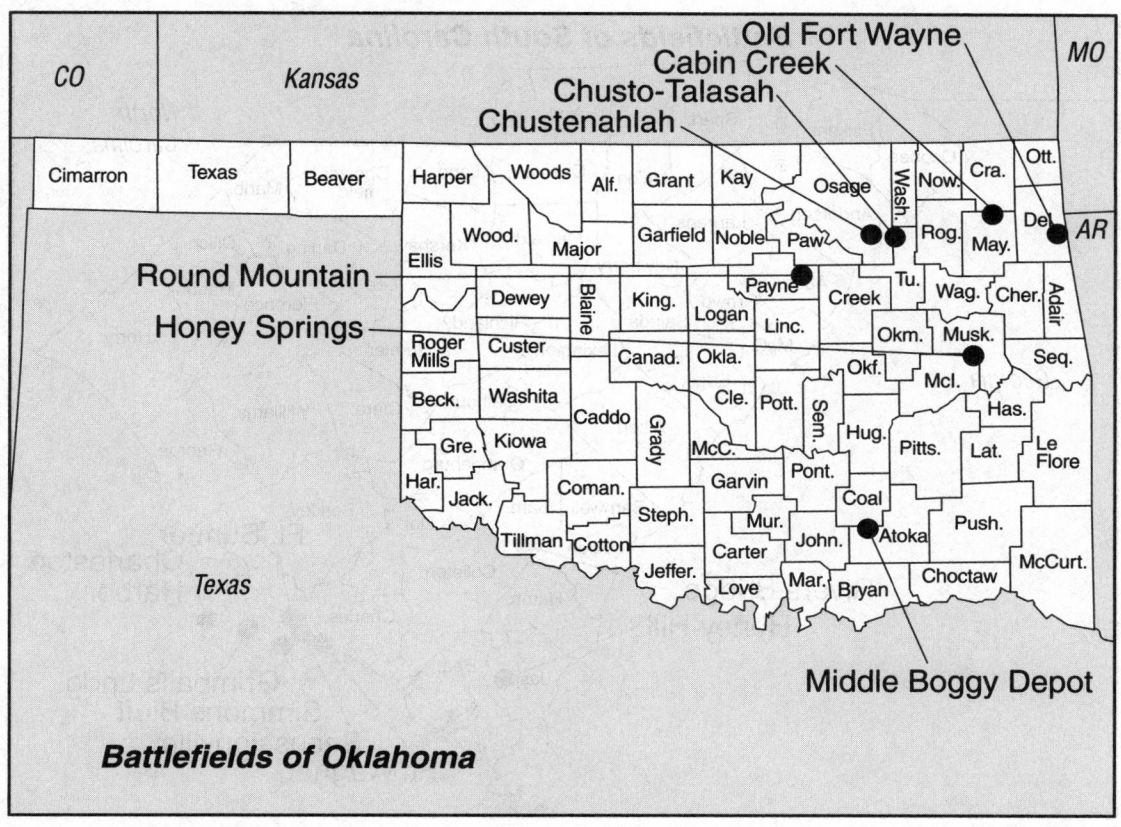

Battlefields of Oklahoma

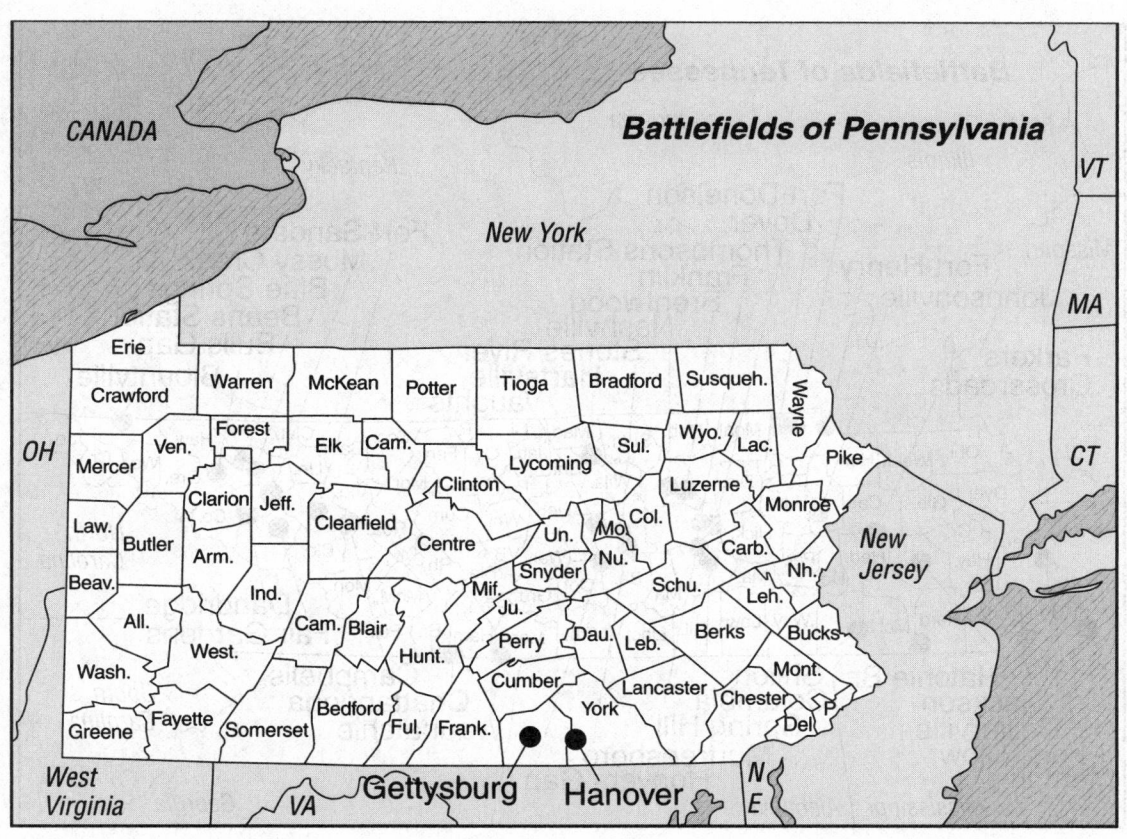

Battlefields of Pennsylvania

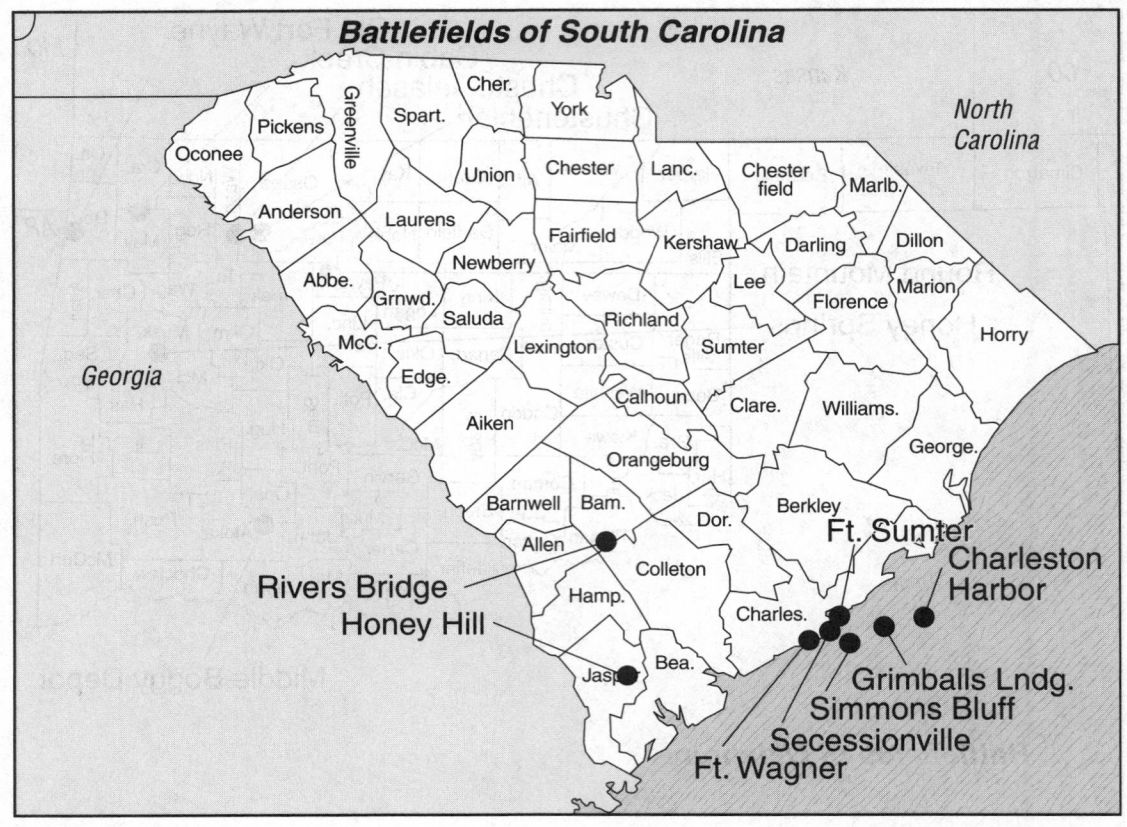

Battlefields of South Carolina

North Carolina

Oconee · Pickens · Greenville · Spart. · Cher. · York

Chester · Lanc. · Chester field · Marlb.

Anderson · Union

Laurens · Fairfield · Kershaw · Darling · Dillon

Abbe. · Newberry · Lee · Marion

Grnwd. · Saluda · Richland · Florence · Horry

McC. · Lexington · Sumter · Williams.

Edge. · Calhoun · Clare. · George.

Georgia · Aiken · Orangeburg

Barnwell · Bam. · Berkley · Ft. Sumter

Allen · Dor. · Charleston Harbor

Colleton

Hamp. · Charles. · Grimballs Lndg.

Rivers Bridge · Simmons Bluff

Honey Hill · Secessionville

Jasp. · Bea. · Ft. Wagner

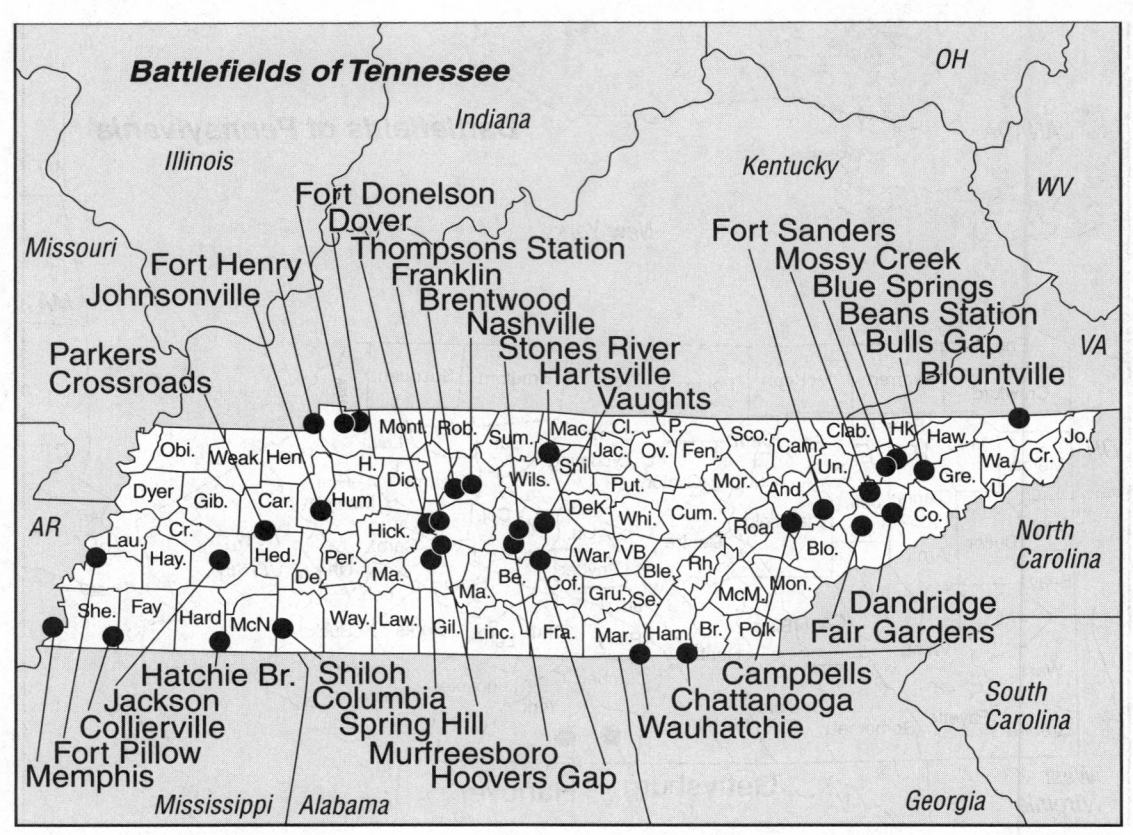

Battlefields of Tennessee

OH

Indiana · Kentucky · WV

Illinois

Missouri

Fort Donelson
Dover
Fort Henry · Thompsons Station · Fort Sanders · VA
Johnsonville · Franklin · Mossy Creek
Brentwood · Blue Springs
Nashville · Beans Station
Parkers · Stones River · Bulls Gap
Crossroads · Hartsville · Blountville
Vaughts

Obi. · Weak · Hen · Mont · Rob. · Mac. · Cl. · P. · Sco. · Cam · Clab. · Hk · Haw. · Wa · Jo.
Dyer · Gib. · Car. · H. · Dic · Sum. · Jac. · Ov. · Fen. · Mor. · Un. · Gre. · Co. · Cr.
AR · Cr. · Hum · Wils. · Snl · Put. · And · North
Lau. · Hed. · Hick. · DeK · Whi. · Cum. · Roa · Blo. · Carolina
Hay. · Per. · Ma. · War. · VB · Rh. · Mon. · Dandridge
She. · Fay · Hard · McN · Way. · Law. · Ma. · Be. · Cof. · Gru. · Se. · McM. · Fair Gardens
Hatchie Br. · Gil. · Linc. · Fra. · Mar. · Ham · Br. · Polk · South
Jackson · Shiloh · Campbells · Carolina
Collierville · Columbia · Chattanooga
Fort Pillow · Spring Hill · Wauhatchie
Memphis · Murfreesboro · Georgia
Mississippi · Alabama · Hoovers Gap

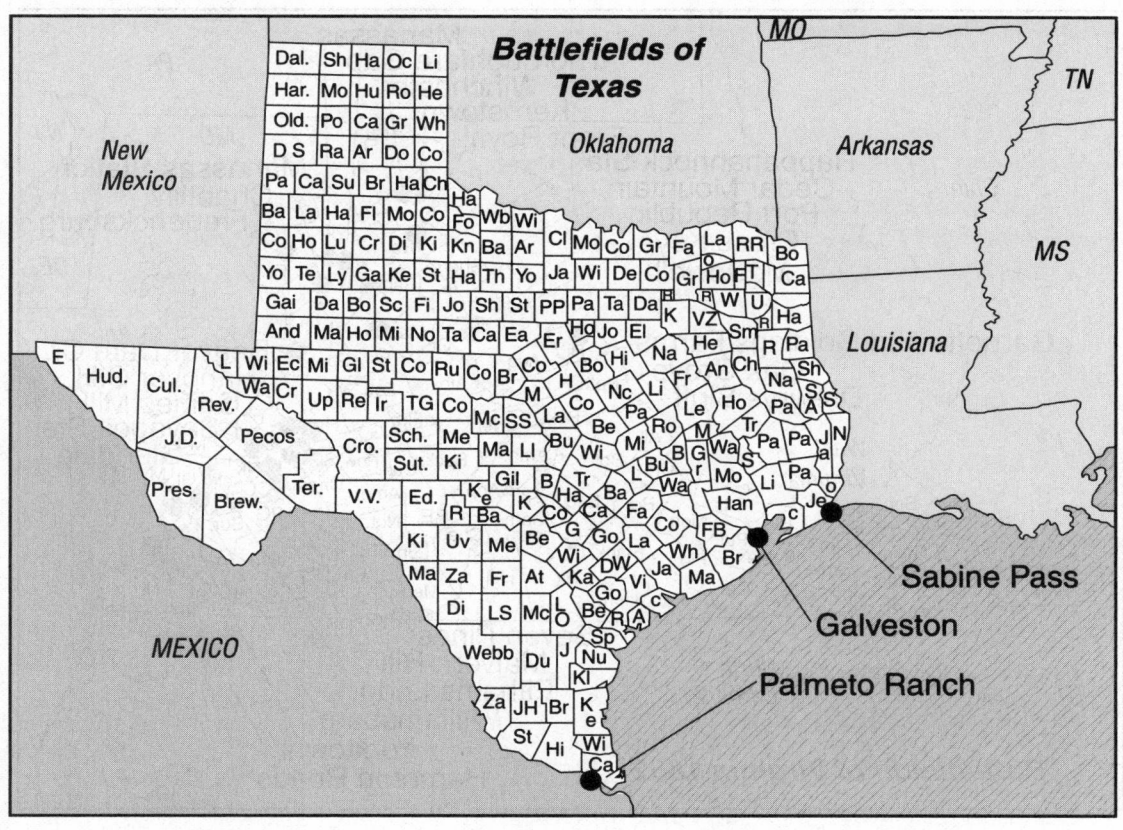

Battlefields of Texas

- Sabine Pass
- Galveston
- Palmeto Ranch

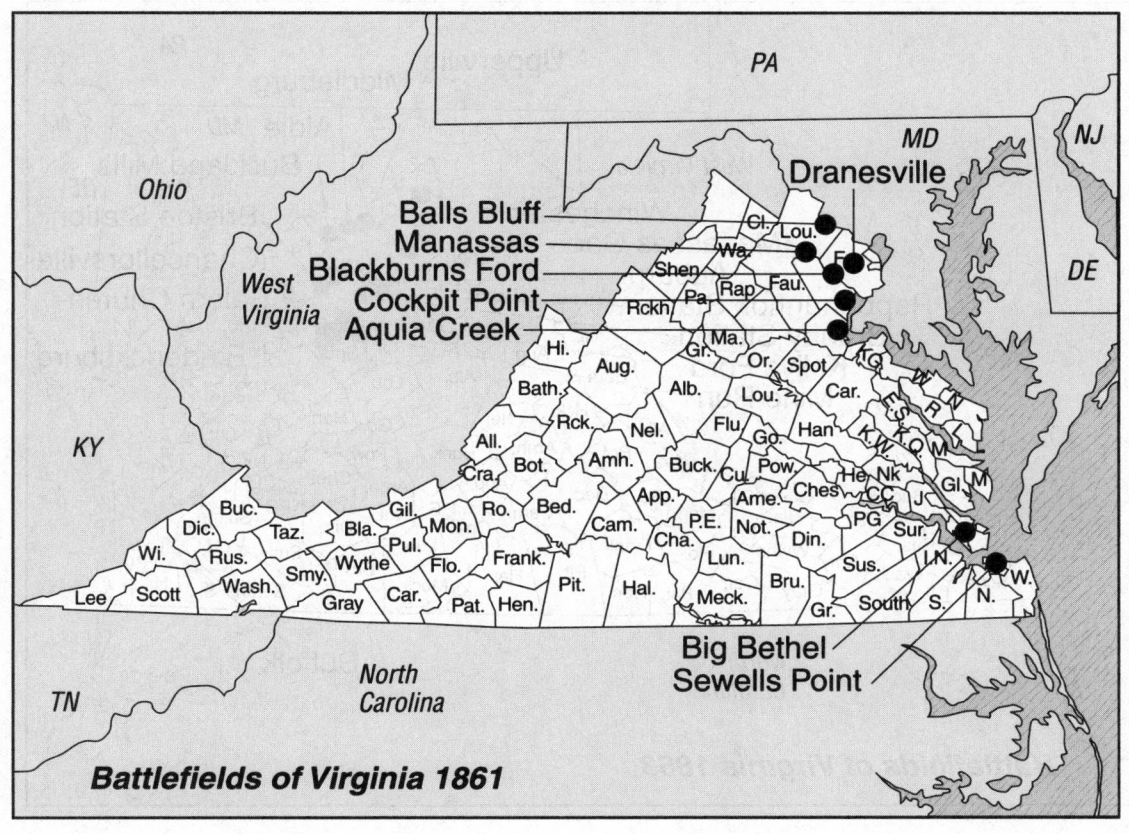

- Dranesville
- Balls Bluff
- Manassas
- Blackburns Ford
- Cockpit Point
- Aquia Creek
- Big Bethel
- Sewells Point

Battlefields of Virginia 1861

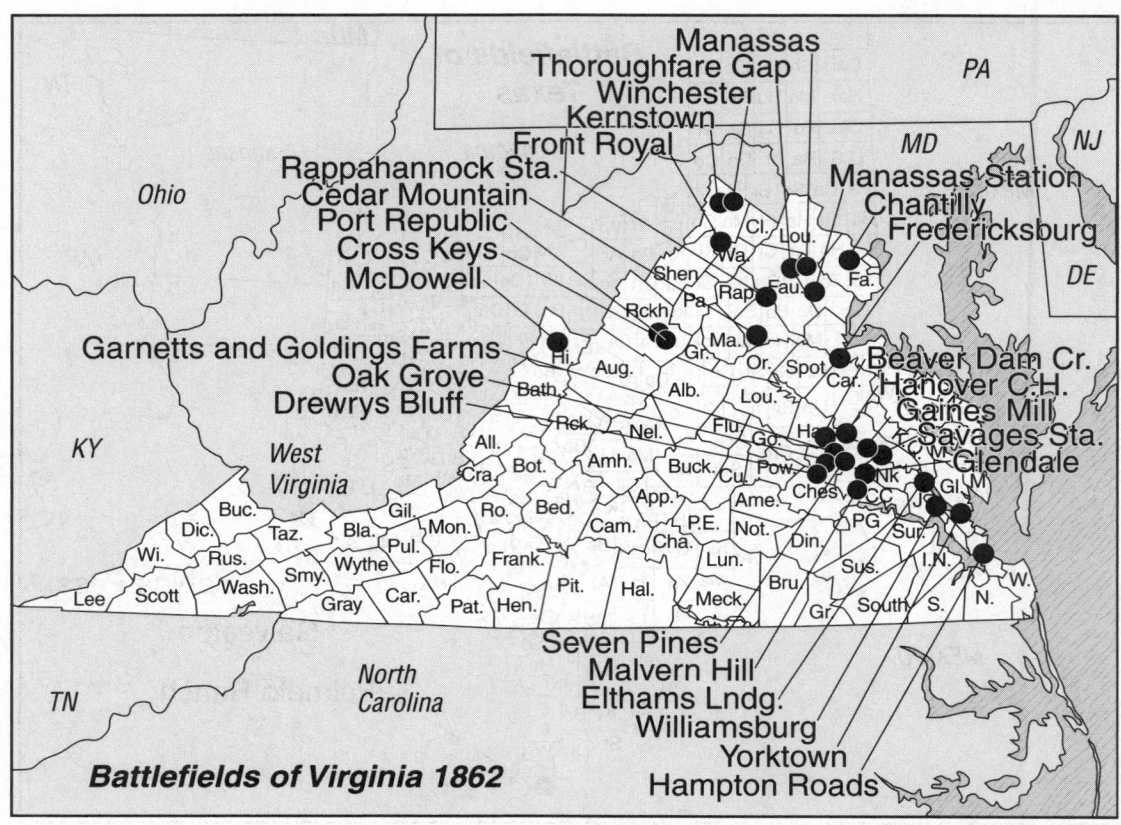

Battlefields of Virginia 1862

Manassas
Thoroughfare Gap
Winchester
Kernstown
Front Royal
Rappahannock Sta.
Cedar Mountain
Port Republic
Cross Keys
McDowell
Garnetts and Goldings Farms
Oak Grove
Drewrys Bluff

Manassas Station
Chantilly
Fredericksburg
Beaver Dam Cr.
Hanover C.H.
Gaines Mill
Savages Sta.
Glendale

Seven Pines
Malvern Hill
Elthams Lndg.
Williamsburg
Yorktown
Hampton Roads

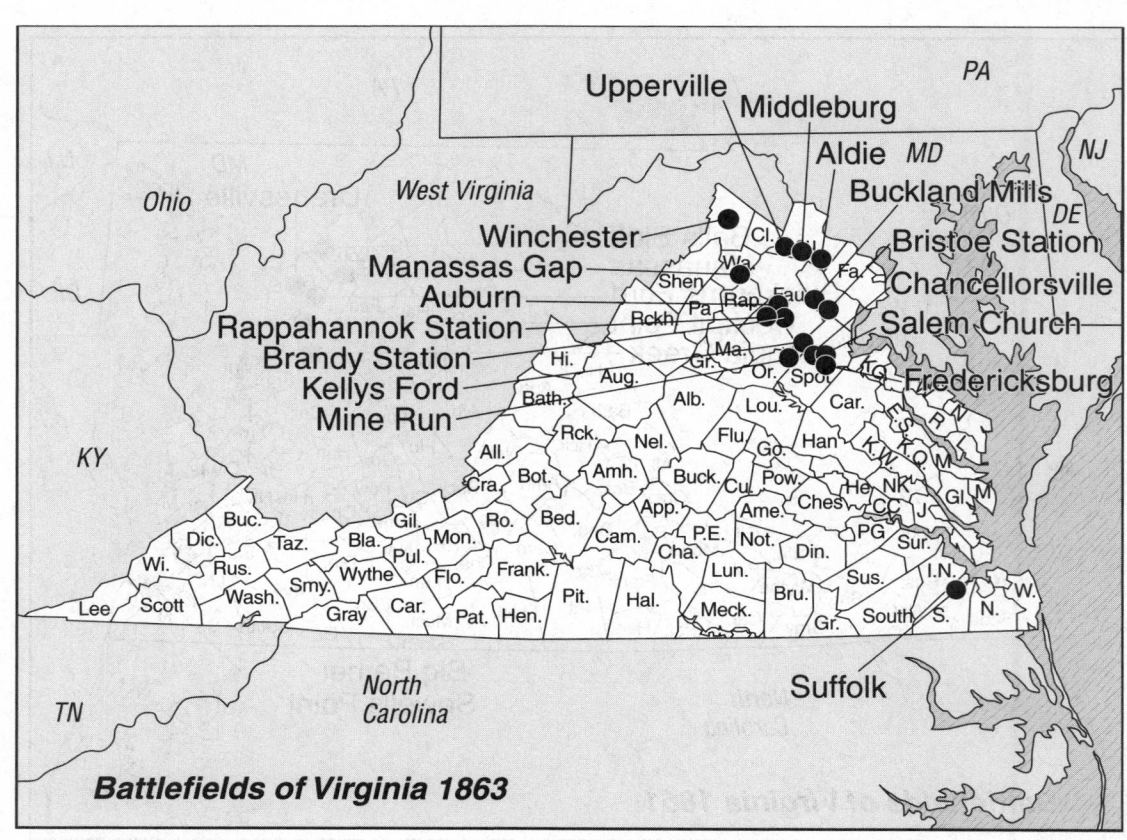

Battlefields of Virginia 1863

Upperville
Middleburg
Aldie
Buckland Mills
Bristoe Station
Chancellorsville
Salem Church
Fredericksburg

Winchester
Manassas Gap
Auburn
Rappahannok Station
Brandy Station
Kellys Ford
Mine Run

Suffolk

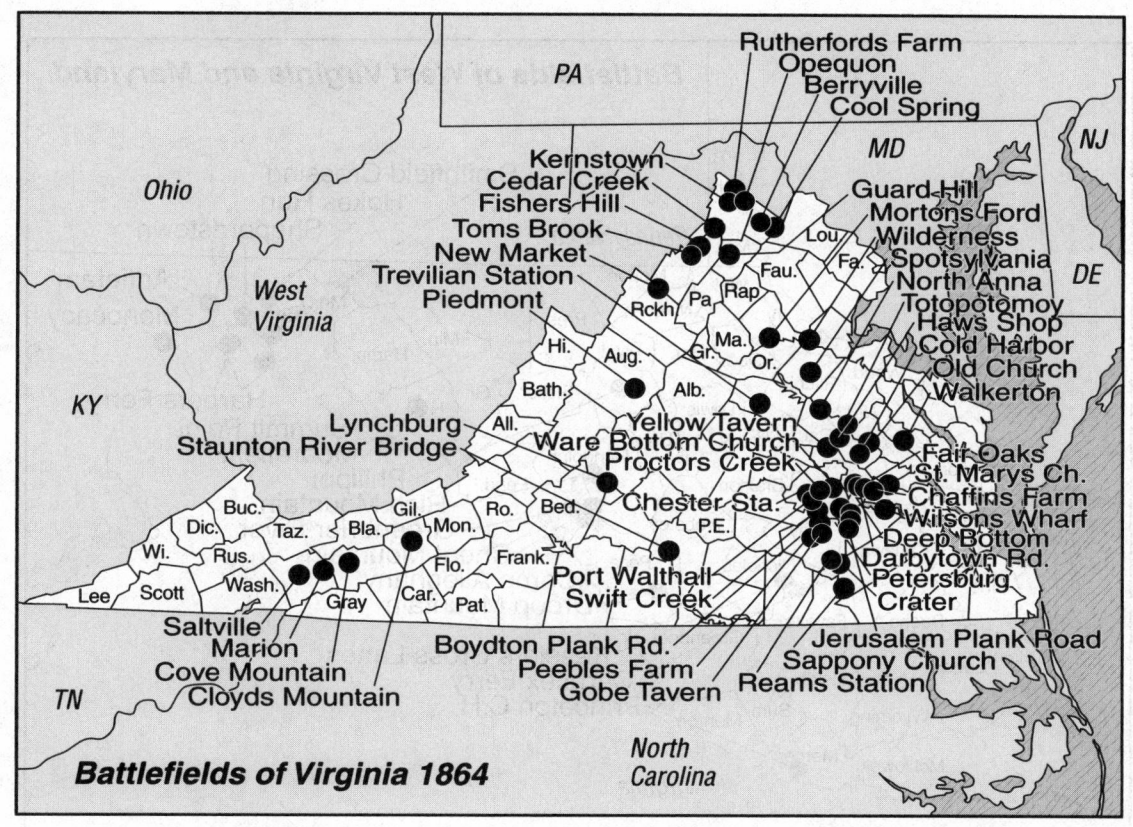

Battlefields of Virginia 1864

Rutherfords Farm
Opequon
Berryville
Cool Spring
Kernstown
Cedar Creek
Fishers Hill
Toms Brook
New Market
Trevilian Station
Piedmont
Guard Hill
Mortons Ford
Wilderness
Spotsylvania
North Anna
Totopotomoy
Haws Shop
Cold Harbor
Old Church
Walkerton
Lynchburg
Staunton River Bridge
Yellow Tavern
Ware Bottom Church
Proctors Creek
Chester Sta.
Fair Oaks
St. Marys Ch.
Chaffins Farm
Wilsons Wharf
Deep Bottom
Darbytown Rd.
Petersburg
Crater
Saltville
Marion
Cove Mountain
Cloyds Mountain
Port Walthall
Swift Creek
Boydton Plank Rd.
Peebles Farm
Gobe Tavern
Jerusalem Plank Road
Sappony Church
Reams Station

Ohio
West Virginia
KY
Lou.
Fa.
MD
NJ
DE
Fau.
Pa.
Rap
Rckh.
Hi.
Aug.
Ma.
Gr.
Or.
Bath.
Alb.
All.
Bed.
P.E.
Buc.
Dic.
Taz.
Bla.
Gil.
Mon.
Ro.
Wi.
Rus.
Wash.
Flo.
Frank.
Lee
Scott
Gray
Car.
Pat.
TN
North Carolina

Battlefields of Virginia 1865

Ohio
PA
Maryland
NJ
DE
West Virginia
KY
Waynesboro
Fr.
Cl.
Lou.
Shen
Wa.
Fau.
Fa.
Rckh.
Pa.
Rap
Cul.
Fau.
P.W.
Hi.
Ma.
Sta.
Bath.
Gr.
Or.
Spot
KG
Rck.
Nel.
Lou.
Namozine Church
Sutherlands Station
Five Forks
White Oak Road
All.
Bot.
Amh.
Buck.
Flu.
Go.
Ha.
Cra.
Bed.
Cam.
Cul.
Gl.
Buc.
Dic.
Taz.
Bla.
Gil.
Mon.
Ro.
Cha.
Not.
PG
Sur.
Wi.
Rus.
Pul.
Flo.
Frank.
I.N.
Smy.
Wythe
Lun.
Bru.
Sus.
Lee
Scott
Wash.
Gray
Car.
Pat.
Hen.
Pit.
Hal.
Meck.
Gr.
South
S. N.
W.
Appomattox Station
Appomattox C.H.
High Bridge
Rices Station
Cumberland Church
Saylers Creek
Amelia Springs
Fort Stedman
Petersburg
Hatchers Run
Lewis Farm
Dinwiddie Courthouse
TN
North Carolina

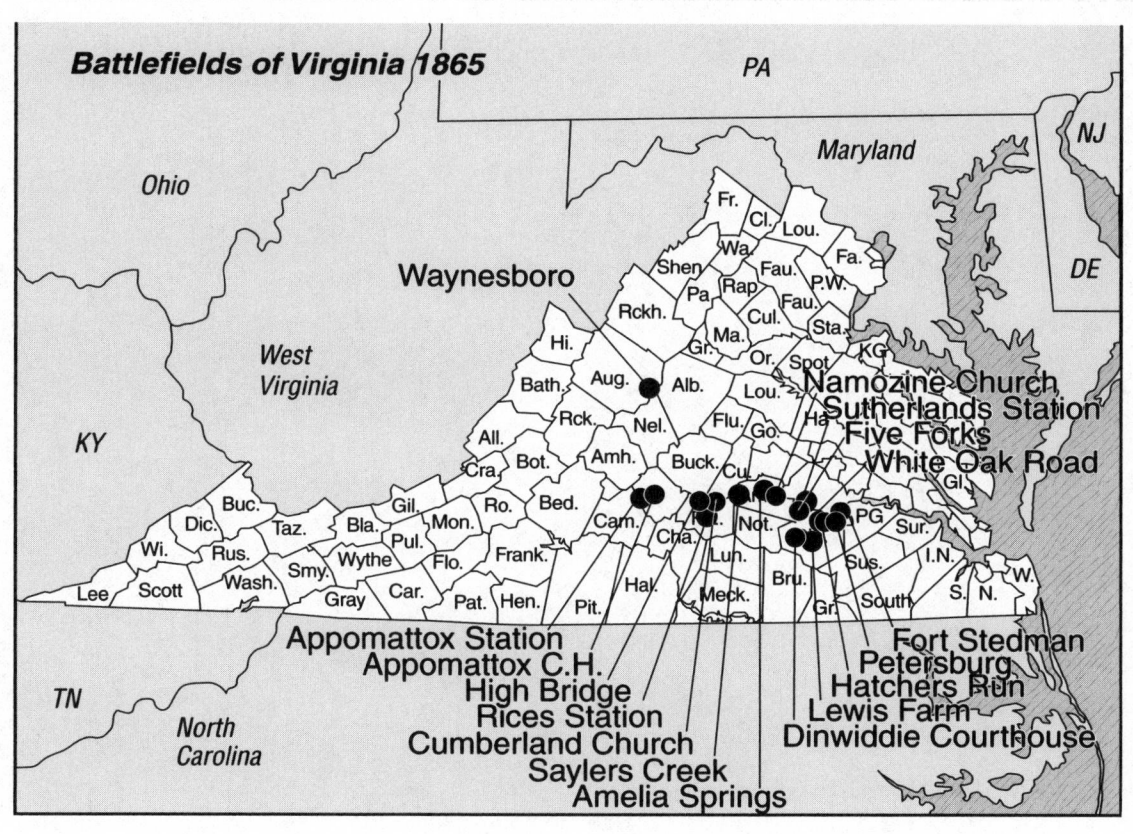

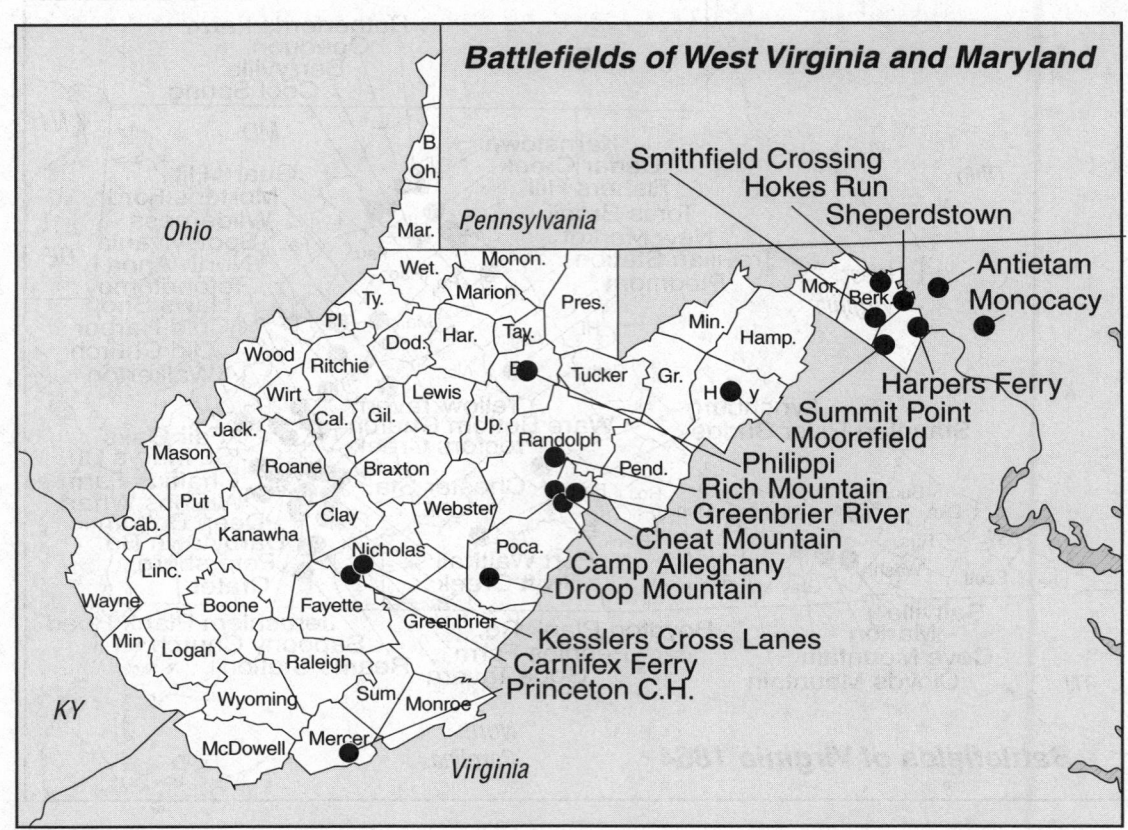

Battlefields of West Virginia and Maryland

Smithfield Crossing
Hokes Run
Sheperdstown
Antietam
Monocacy
Harpers Ferry
Summit Point
Moorefield
Philippi
Rich Mountain
Greenbrier River
Cheat Mountain
Camp Alleghany
Droop Mountain
Kesslers Cross Lanes
Carnifex Ferry
Princeton C.H.

Ohio

Pennsylvania

Virginia

KY

CHRONOLOGY OF THE AMERICAN CIVIL WAR

Military	*Political/Diplomatic/Social*
1860	
20 December	South Carolina secedes
1861	
7 January Ft. Marion, Florida, seized	
9 January *Star of the West* fired on	Mississippi secedes
10 January Louisiana forts and arsenals seized	Florida secedes
11 January	Alabama secedes
19 January	Georgia secedes
24 January Augusta Arsenal seized	
26 January	Louisiana secedes
29 January	Kansas admitted to Union
31 January New Orleans Mint seized	
1 February	Texas votes to secede
4 February	C.S.A. formed with convening of Provisional Confederate Congress
9 February	Jefferson Davis chosen Provisional CSA president
11 February	Lincoln departs for Washington
16 February	Davis arrives in Montgomery
18 February David E. Twiggs surrenders Texas posts	Davis and Stephens inaugurated
21 February	Christopher Memminger named Confederate secretary of the treasury; Robert Toombs named Confederate secretary of state; Leroy

	Pope Walker named Confederate secretary of war
23 February	Lincoln arrives in Washington
25 February	Judah P. Benjamin named Confederate attorney general
2 March	Crittenden Compromise proposed
3 March Beauregard assumes command in Charleston, South Carolina	
4 March	Lincoln and Hamlin inaugurated
5 March	William H. Seward becomes secretary of state; Salmon P. Chase becomes secretary of the treasury; Simon Cameron becomes secretary of war; Edward Bates becomes attorney general; Montgomery Blair becomes postmaster general; Gideon Welles becomes secretary of the Navy; Caleb B. Smith becomes secretary of the interior
6 March	Stephen Mallory becomes Confederate secretary of the Navy; John H. Reagan becomes Confederate postmaster general
11 March	C.S.A. Constitution adopted
16 March	First session, Confederate Provisional Congress adjourns
12 April Firing on Fort Sumter	
14 April Surrender of Fort Sumter	
15 April Lincoln's call for militia	
17 April	Virginia secedes
18 April Harper's Ferry, Virginia, evacuated	
19 April 6th Massachusetts attacked in Baltimore Lincoln declares blockade of Southern coast	
20 April Robert E. Lee resigns from United States Army	
23 April Robert E. Lee assumes command of Virginia State forces	

29 April

Second session, Confederate Provisional
Congress convenes

30 April
Colonel Thomas Jonathan Jackson occupies Harper's Ferry

6 May

Arkansas secedes
Tennessee secession ordnance passes and is
submitted to people's vote

10 May
Camp Jackson, Missouri, seized

20 May
Kentucky declares neutrality

North Carolina secedes
Confederate Congress decides to move capital to Richmond

21 May

Second session, Confederate Provisional
Congress adjourns

24 May
Union troops take Alexandria, Virginia
Colonel Elmer Ellsworth killed

30 May
Grafton, Virginia, occupied by Federal troops

3 June
Skirmish at Philippi, Virginia

Stephen A. Douglas dies

8 June
United States Sanitary Commission authorized

10 June
Battle of Big Bethel, Virginia

15 June
Confederates evacuate Harper's Ferry

17 June
Skirmish at Boonville, Missouri

30 June
CSS *Sumter* runs blockade into Gulf of Mexico

4 July

First session, Thirty-seventh Congress
convenes

11 July
Battle of Rich Mountain

13 July
Battle of Carrick's Ford

16 July
Irvin McDowell's army leaves Washington, Battle of Boonville, Missouri

Robert Toombs resigns as Confederate secretary of state

19 July

20 July

Third session, Confederate Provisional Congress convenes

21 July
Battle of First Bull Run

25 July

Robert M. T. Hunter becomes Confederate secretary of state

27 July
George McClellan assumes command of troops around Washington

1 August
Robert E. Lee sent to western Virginia

6 August

First session, Thirty-seventh Congress adjourns

10 August
Battle of Wilson's Creek

20 August
George McClellan assumes command of Army of the Potomac

24 August

Pierre A. Rost named Confederate commissioner to Spain, James M. Mason to Great Britain, and John Slidell to France

28 August
Operation against Hatteras Inlet begins

29 August
Operation against Hatteras Inlet ends

30 August
John C. Frémont issues emancipation proclamation and declares martial law in Missouri

31 August

Third session, Confederate Provisional Congress adjourns

3 September

Fourth session, Confederate Provisional Congress convenes and adjourns

6 September
Ulysses S. Grant occupies Paducah, Kentucky

10 September
Battle of Carnifex Ferry

Cheat Mountain operation begins

12 September
Battle of Lexington, Missouri

15 September
Cheat Mountain operation ends

17 September
Union forces take Ship Island, Mississippi

Judah P. Benjamin becomes Confederate secretary of war

20 September
Lexington, Missouri falls to Confederates

9 October
Confederate raid on Santa Rosa Island

12 October

Mason and Slidell leave Charleston for Cuba

21 October
Battle of Ball's Bluff

2 November
John C. Frémont relieved of command in Missouri

7 November
Battle of Port Royal Sound
Battle of Belmont, Missouri

8 November

Mason and Slidell seized from *Trent*

18 November

Fifth session Confederate Provisional Congress convenes

21 November

Thomas Bragg becomes Confederate attorney general

24 November

Mason and Slidell arrive in Boston

27 November

Trent arrives in Great Britain with news of U.S. action

2 December

Second session, Thirty-Seventh Congress convenes

9 December

Joint Committee on the Conduct of the War created

26 December

Lincoln decides to release Mason and Slidell

<u>1862</u>

1 January

Mason and Slidell released

4 January
Stonewall Jackson captures Bath, Virginia

11 January

Union secretary of war Simon Cameron resigns

15 January

Edwin M. Stanton confirmed as Union secretary of war

19 January
Battle of Logan's Cross Roads / Mill Springs

27 January
Lincoln issues General War Order No. 1

30 January

Mason and Slidell arrive in Great Britain

6 February
Fort Henry falls

7 February
Battle for Roanoke Island begins

8 February
Roanoke Island falls

14 February
Federal attack on Fort Donelson

16 February
Fort Donelson surrenders

17 February

Fifth session, Confederate Provisional Congress adjourns

18 February

First elected Confederate Congress convenes in Richmond

20 February

Tennessee government abandons Nashville

21 February
Battle of Val Verde

22 February

Davis and Stephens inaugurated

25 February
Union troops occupy Nashville

1 March
Federals evacuate Albuquerque, New Mexico

3 March
Pope arrives at New Madrid

7 March
Battle of Pea Ridge begins

8 March
Battle of Pea Ridge ends
CSS *Virginia* attacks Union ships in Hampton Roads

9 March
CSS *Virginia* vs. USS *Monitor*

13 March
Ambrose Burnside advances on New Bern, North Carolina

14 March
Burnside occupies New Bern
John Pope occupies New Madrid, Missouri

18 March

Judah Benjamin becomes Confederate secretary of state; Robert M. T. Hunter and Thomas Bragg leave cabinet

23 March
Battle of Kernstown, Virginia

George W. Randolph becomes Confederate secretary of war

26 March
Beginning of Battle of Glorieta

28 March
End of Battle of Glorieta

2 April
George McClellan arrives at Fort Monroe, Virginia

5 April
Army of the Potomac arrives at Yorktown, Virginia

6 April
Battle of Shiloh begins, Albert Sidney Johnston killed there

7 April
Battle of Shiloh ends
Island No. 10 surrenders

9 April

Confederate Congress passes conscription act

10 April
Federal bombardment of Fort Pulaski begins

11 April
Fort Pulaski surrenders

12 April
James Andrews' Raid

21 April

First session, First Confederate Congress adjourns

25 April
New Orleans falls to the Union

29 April
Halleck begins advance on Corinth, Mississippi

1 May
Benjamin Butler assumes command in New Orleans

4 May
Army of the Potomac occupies Yorktown

5 May
Battle of Williamsburg

8 May
Battle of McDowell
Union troops occupy Baton Rouge

10 May
Confederates evacuate Norfolk Navy Yard

11 May
Crew blows up CSS *Virginia*

12 May
Federal forces occupy Natchez, Mississippi

16 May
Fighting at Princeton, Virginia begins

17 May
Fighting at Princeton, Virginia ends

23 May
Battle of Front Royal

25 May
Battle of Winchester

27 May
Battle of Hanover Court House

29 May
Beauregard starts evacuation of Corinth

31 May
Battle of Seven Pines begins

1 June
Battle of Seven Pines ends
Robert E. Lee assumes command of Army of Northern Virginia

4 June
Confederates evacuate Fort Pillow

6 June
Federals occupy Memphis, Tennessee

8 June
Battle of Cross Keys

9 June
Battle of Port Republic

12 June
J. E. B. Stuart begins ride around Army of the Potomac

15 June
Stuart arrives back in Richmond

16 June
Battle of Secessionville

17 June
Stonewall Jackson departs Shenandoah Valley

25 June
Seven Days' begin with advance of Union troops at Oak Grove

26 June
Battle of Mechanicsville
Beginning of bombardment of Vicksburg

27 June
Battle of Gaines' Mill

28 June
Farragut passes Vicksburg

29 June
Battle of Savage's Station

30 June
Battle of White Oak Swamp / Glendale

1 July
Battle of Malvern Hill, end of Seven Days'
Battle of Booneville, Mississippi

2 July
McClellan completes retreat to Harrison's Landing

4 July
John Hunt Morgan begins first raid

6 July
Forrest begins raid in Tennessee

11 July
Henry Halleck made General-in-Chief of Union army

15 July
Farragut passes Vicksburg

16 July

Napoleon III meets with John Slidell

17 July

Second session, Thirty-Seventh Congress
adjourns

22 July
Prisoner exchange cartel signed

23 July
Halleck assumes his new command

1 August
Morgan's raid ends

6 August
John C. Breckinridge attacks Federal garrison at Baton Rouge

9 August
Battle of Cedar Mountain

12 August
John Hunt Morgan captures Federal garrison at
Gallatin, Tennessee

16 August
Edmund Kirby Smith invades Kentucky

17 August
Sioux begin attacking towns in Minnesota

18 August

Second session, First Confederate Congress
convenes

21 August
Federals evacuate Baton Rouge; Braxton Bragg begins
Kentucky campaign

24 August
CSS *Alabama* commissioned

26 August
Stonewall Jackson takes Federal supply depot at
Manassas Junction

28 August
Battle of Groveton

29 August
Battle of Second Bull Run begins
Battle of Richmond, Kentucky, begins

30 August
Battle of Second Bull Run ends
Battle of Richmond, Kentucky, ends

1 September
Battle of Chantilly

2 September
Confederates occupy Lexington, Kentucky

4 September
Army of Northern Virginia crosses into Maryland

6 September
Confederates enter Frederick, Maryland

9 September
Lee issues Order No. 191

13 September
McClellan enters Frederick, Maryland, and is given
lost Order No. 191

14 September
Battle of Crampton's Gap
Battle of South Mountain
Battle of Munfordville, Kentucky begins

15 September
Stonewall Jackson takes Harper's Ferry
Sterling Price occupies Iuka, Mississippi

17 September
Battle of Antietam
Munfordville, Kentucky surrenders to Braxton Bragg

19 September
Lee begins retreat into Virginia
Price retreats from Iuka, Mississippi
Battle of Blackford's Ford begins

20 September
Battle of Blackford's Ford ends

22 September

Lincoln issues preliminary Emancipation
Proclamation

25 September
Don Carlos Buell arrives at Louisville, Kentucky

1 October
John C. Pemberton given command at Vicksburg

3 October
Confederates attack Federals at Corinth, Mississippi

4 October
Battle of Corinth ends

8 October
Battle of Perryville, Kentucky

11 October
J. E. B. Stuart enters Chambersburg, Pennsylvania

13 October
Second session, First Confederate Congress adjourns

19 October
John Hunt Morgan takes Lexington, Kentucky

4 November
Federal Congressional elections, Democrats make gains

7 November
McClellan relieved as commander of the Army of the Potomac

9 November
Ambrose Burnside named commander of the Army of the Potomac

21 November
Davis appoints James A. Seddon Confederate secretary of war

28 November
Battle of Cane Hill, Arkansas

1 December
Third session, Thirty-seventh Congress convenes

4 December
Joseph E. Johnston assumes command of Confederate western armies

7 December
Battle of Prairie Grove, Arkansas

11 December
Confederate sharpshooters hamper construction of Federal pontoon bridges at Fredericksburg
Nathan Bedford Forrest begins raid from Columbia, Tennessee

12 December
Army of the Potomac enters Fredericksburg

13 December
Battle of Fredericksburg

18 December
Battle of Lexington, Tennessee

Some congressmen call for reorganization of Lincoln's cabinet

20 December
Raid on Holly Springs, Mississippi

21 December
John Hunt Morgan begins raid into Kentucky

29 December
Battle of Chickasaw Bluffs

30 December
Battle of Stones River begins

31 December
Battle of Parker Cross Roads

1863

1 January
Morgan's Raid ends
Magruder takes Galveston, Texas

Emancipation Proclamation issued

3 January
Battle of Stones River ends
Forrest returns from raid

4 January
Arkansas Post Campaign begins

8 January

John P. Usher becomes secretary of the interior

11 January
Fort Hindman (Arkansas Post) surrenders

12 January

Third session, First Confederate Congress convenes

19 January
Burnside begins moving up Rappahannock River

21 January
Naval battle of Sabine Pass, Texas

23 January
Burnside's Mud March ends

25 January
Burnside is relieved of command

26 January
Joseph Hooker assumes command of the Army
of the Potomac

3 March

Lincoln signs Conscription Act
Third session, Thirty-Seventh Congress
adjourns

17 March
Battle of Kelly's Ford
Federals withdraw from Yazoo Pass

25 March
Battle of Brentwood, Tennessee

2 April

Richmond Bread Riot

4 April
Battle of Thompson's Station, Tennessee, begins

5 April
Battle of Thompson's Station, Tennessee, ends

7 April
Federals unsuccessfully attack Charleston, South
Carolina, by sea

11 April
Operations against Suffolk, Virginia, begin

12 April
Engagements around Irish Bend begin

14 April
Engagements around Irish Bend end

16 April
David Dixon Porter makes first run past Vicksburg's
batteries

17 April
Benjamin Grierson begins his raid

19 April
Fort Huger, Virginia, falls

20 April
Jones' and Imboden's West Virginia raid begins

27 April
Army of the Potomac begins march up Rappahannock
River

28 April
Hooker begins crossing Rappahannock

30 April
Hooker at Chancellorsville
Grant crosses Mississippi to begin advance on
Vicksburg

1 May
Lee comes out of defenses of Fredericksburg to
meet Hooker
Port Gibson falls

2 May
Stonewall Jackson moves around Hooker's flank
and attacks at Chancellorsville; Jackson is shot
that night by own troops

3 May
Battle of Chancellorsville continues
Jubal Early driven out of Fredericksburg
Battle of Salem Church begins

4 May
Hooker begins withdrawal
Battle of Salem Church ends
Operations against Suffolk end

5 May

6 May
Alexandria, Louisiana, surrenders

10 May
Stonewall Jackson dies

12 May
Battle of Raymond

14 May
Battle of Jackson

16 May
Battle of Champion's Hill

17 May
Battle of Big Black River

19 May
Grant's first assault on Vicksburg

Third session, First Confederate Congress
adjourns

Clement Vallandigham arrested

22 May
Grant attacks Vicksburg's defenses

27 May
Nathaniel Banks assaults Port Hudson

3 June
Lee begins Gettysburg campaign by moving
out of area around Fredericksburg

9 June
Battle of Brandy Station

13 June
Battle of Berryville, Virginia

14 June
Engagement at Martinsburg, Virginia (WV)

15 June
Battle of Winchester II

17 June
Battle of Aldie

20 June   **West Virginia admitted to statehood**

23 June
Tullahoma Campaign begins

25 June
Stuart leaves Lee's Army

26 June
Jubal Early passes through Gettysburg

27 June
Cavalry skirmish at Hanover, Pennsylvania

28 June
George Gordon Meade relieves Hooker

30 June
Union cavalry clashes with Confederate infantry
at Gettysburg
Bragg evacuates Tullahoma

1 July
Battle of Gettysburg, day 1

2 July
Battle of Gettysburg, day 2   **Alexander Stephens goes to Hampton Roads**
John Hunt Morgan begins Ohio Raid

3 July
Battle of Gettysburg, day 3

4 July
Vicksburg surrenders
Confederates attack Helena, Arkansas

5 July
Lee retreats from Gettysburg

8 July
John Hunt Morgan crosses Ohio River

9 July
William T. Sherman advances on Jackson, Mississippi

10 July
First assault on Fort Wagner, South Carolina

13 July
New York Draft Riots begin

14 July
Skirmish at Falling Waters, Virginia

16 July
Joseph Johnston abandons Jackson, Mississippi

18 July
Second assault on Fort Wagner, South Carolina

26 July
John Hunt Morgan surrenders

16 August
Rosecrans moves on Chattanooga

21 August
Sack of Lawrence, Kansas

2 September
Ambrose Burnside occupies Knoxville, Tennessee

4 September
Sabine Pass Expedition begins

5 September

Charles Francis Adams threatens war with
Great Britain over Laird Rams

6 September
Morris Island is abandoned

8 September
Union attempts to take Sabine Pass

9 September
Bragg evacuates Chattanooga

10 September
Union forces take Little Rock, Arkansas

18 September
Fighting begins at Chickamauga

20 September
Fighting ends at Chickamauga

22 September
Siege of Chattanooga begins

1 October
Wheeler begins raid of Rosecrans's supply lines

6 October
Quantrill's attack at Baxter Springs, Kansas

14 October
A. P. Hill attacks at Bristoe Station
Skirmish at Catlett's Station

15 October
Confederate submarine *Hunley* sinks off Charleston, South Carolina, with inventor Horace Hunley in command

19 October
Cavalry battle of Buckland Mills, Virginia

23 October
Grant arrives in Chattanooga

28 October
Attack on Wauhatchie, Tennessee, begins

29 October
Attack on Wauhatchie, Tennessee, ends

4 November
Nathaniel Banks occupies Brownsville, Texas

7 November
Meade attacks at Kelly's Ford and Rappahannock Station

16 November
Banks occupies Corpus Christi, Texas
Battle of Campbell Station, Tennessee

19 November
Lincoln delivers Gettysburg Address

24 November
Battle of Lookout Mountain

25 November
Battle of Missionary Ridge

26 November
Bragg retreats from Chattanooga
Mine Run Campaign begins

27 November
John Hunt Morgan escapes from the Ohio penitentiary

29 November
Longstreet attacks at Knoxville, Tennessee, at
Fort Sanders

1 December
Mine Run Campaign ends

2 December
Braxton Bragg relieved by William Hardee

3 December
Longstreet begins withdrawal from Knoxville

7 December

Fourth session, First Confederate Congress
convenes
First session, Thirty-Eigth Congress convenes

14 December
Longstreet attacks at Bean's Station

16 December
Battle of Bean's Station ends

1864

2 January

George Davis becomes Confederate attorney
general

7 January
Federal troops land at Jacksonville, Florida

11 January

Thirteenth Amendment to free slaves is first
proposed in Congress

22 January
Rosecrans given command in Missouri

27 January
Bragg called to Richmond

1 February
Congress creates rank of lieutenant general

2 February
USS *Underwriter* destroyed in Neuse River

3 February
Sherman starts Meridian Campaign

14 February
Sherman occupies Meridian, Mississippi

15 February
Union troops occupy Gainesville, Florida

17 February
USS *Housatonic* sunk by submarine *Hunley* off
Charleston, South Carolina

Fourth session, First Confederate Congress
adjourns

20 February
Battle of Olustee, Florida
Sherman leaves Meridian

21 February
Battle of West Point, Mississippi

22 February
Federal probe at Dalton, Georgia, begins

27 February
Federal probe against Dalton ends
Andersonville prison opens
Meridian Campaign ends

28 February
Kilpatrick-Dahlgren Raid begins

1 March
Grant nominated for lieutenant general

2 March
Colonel Ulric Dahlgren killed

4 March
Kilpatrick-Dahlgren Raid ends

6 March
Confederate victory at Natural Bridge, Florida

8 March
Grant arrives in Washington

9 March
Grant receives lieutenant general's commission

10 March
Red River Campaign begins

14 March
Fort De Russy falls

16 March
Forrest begins raid in western Tennessee

25 March
Banks arrives at Alexandria, Louisiana

4 April
Philip Sheridan named head of Army of Potomac's Cavalry

8 April
Battle of Mansfield (Sabine Cross Roads)

9 April
Battle of Pleasant Hill, Louisiana

12 April
Forrest attacks Fort Pillow

18 April
Battle of Plymouth, North Carolina

25 April
Battle of Marks' Mill, Arkansas

29 April
Battle of Jenkins' Ferry, Arkansas

2 May

First session, Second Confederate Congress convenes

4 May
Army of the Potomac crosses Rapidan River; Butler takes army up James River

U.S. House of Representatives passes the Wade-Davis Bill

5 May
Battle of the Wilderness begins
Butler lands below Richmond at Bermuda Hundred
Operations at Todd's Tavern, Virginia begin

6 May
Battle of the Wilderness ends

7 May
Sherman begins Atlanta Campaign

8 May
Federals attack at Spotsylvania
Fighting at Rocky Face Ridge, Georgia
Operations at Todd's Tavern end
Operations at Ware Bottom Church, Virginia, begin

9 May
Spotsylvania continues
More attacks at Rocky Face Ridge

10 May
Major Union attack against Mule Shoe at Spotsylvania

11 May
Battle of Yellow Tavern; Stuart mortally wounded

12 May
Federals attack at Bloody Angle, Spotsylvania
Stuart dies

13 May
Johnston at Resaca, Georgia
Porter's boats make it over rapids at Alexandria,
Louisiana

14 May
Sherman attacks Resaca

15 May
Sherman begins flanking Johnston at Resaca
Battle of New Market, Virginia

16 May
Battle of Drewry's Bluff, Virginia

17 May
Butler closed off on Bermuda Hundred

19 May
Grant flanks Lee at Spotsylvania

20 May
Red River Campaign ends
Operations at Ware Bottom Church end

23 May
Fighting begins at North Anna River crossing

24 May
Fighting continues at North Anna

25 May
Fighting begins near Dallas, Georgia

26 May
Fighting continues at Dallas
Grant begins to flank Lee at the North Anna
Skirmishing at Totopotomoy Creek, Virginia

27 May

Fighting continues at Dallas
28 May
Lee moves to Cold Harbor
Fighting continues at Dallas

29 May
Cavalry battle at Haw's Shop, Virginia
30 May
Grants begins probing actions at Cold Harbor
Skirmishing along Totopotomoy Creek ends

1 June
Grant increases attacks at Cold Harbor

3 June
Sherman flanks Johnston
Major Federal attacks at Cold Harbor

5 June
Battle of Piedmont

8 June
John Hunt Morgan takes Mt. Sterling, Kentucky

9 June
Fighting at Big Shanty, Georgia

10 June
Battle of Brice's Crossroads
John Hunt Morgan enters Lexington Kentucky

11 June
David Hunter takes Lexington, Virginia
Cavalry clashes at Trevilian Station begin

12 June
Army of the Potomac begins moving across James River
Cavalry clashes at Trevilian Station end

14 June
Leonidas Polk killed at Pine Mountain, Georgia

15 June
Beauregard stops Federals at Petersburg

17 June
Hunter repulsed at Lynchburg, Virginia

19 June
CSS *Alabama* sunk by USS *Kearsarge*

27 June
Battle of Kennesaw Mountain
Early begins raid from Staunton, Virginia

Lincoln is nominated for second term

First session, Second Confederate Congress adjourns

30 June

Salmon Chase resigns, and Lincoln accepts

1 July

William Pitt Fessenden is nominated secretary of the treasury

4 July

First session, Thirty-Eighth Congress adjourns
Lincoln pocket vetoes the Wade-Davis Bill

5 July
Early crosses Potomac

6 July
Early's men take Hagerstown, Maryland

8 July
Part of Sherman's army crosses Chattahoochee

9 July
Early occupies Frederick, Maryland
Battle of Monocacy

10 July
Early moves toward Washington

11 July
Early threatens northern Washington at Fort Stevens

12 July
Early withdraws from north of Washington

13 July
Fighting begins at Tupelo, Mississippi
Sherman continues to cross the Chattahoochee

14 July
Forrest fails to defeat Federals at Tupelo
Early recrosses Potomac

15 July
Federals retreat from Tupelo

18 July
Johnston relinquishes command to John Bell Hood

George A. Trenholm becomes Confederate
secretary of the treasury

19 July
Early skirmishes with Hunter and Crook near
Berryville

20 July
Hood attacks George Thomas north of Atlanta
at Peachtree Creek

22 July

Battle of Atlanta
23 July
Fighting begins around Kernstown, Virginia

24 July
Fighting ends around Kernstown

26 July
Stoneman begins raid toward Macon, Georgia

27 July
Sherman prepares for siege of Atlanta

28 July
Battle of Ezra Church

30 July
Battle of the Crater
Early burns Chambersburg, Pennsylvania
Stoneman is captured

1 August
Sheridan given command of Army of the Shenandoah
Sherman begins shelling Atlanta

3 August
Union troops land on Dauphin Island

5 August
Battle of Mobile Bay
Fighting begins at Utoy Creek
6 August
Fighting ends at Utoy Creek

7 August
Cavalry clash at Mansfield, West Virginia

8 August
Fort Gaines surrenders

9 August
Bombardment of Fort Morgan

10 August
Wheeler begins raid of Sherman's supply lines

13 August
Deep Bottom Run Campaign begins

17 August
Deep Bottom Run ends

18 August
Globe Tavern begins

Wade-Davis Manifesto is issued

21 August
Globe Tavern ends
Forrest enters Memphis, Tennessee

23 August
Fort Morgan surrenders

25 August
Battle of Reams' Station

30 August

McClellan given Democratic nomination for president

31 August
Battle of Jonesboro begins

1 September
Battle of Jonesboro ends
People begin to evacuate Atlanta

2 September
Sherman occupies Atlanta

7 September
Sherman orders all remaining civilians out of Atlanta

16 September
Forrest begins operations against Sherman's supply lines
Sheridan and Grant meet at Charlestown, West Virginia
Wade Hampton captures over 2,000 Federal beef cattle

17 September

John C. Frémont withdraws his name from presidential consideration

19 September
Battle of Winchester
Price enters Missouri

22 September
Battle of Fisher's Hill

24 September

William Dennison becomes postmaster general

27 September
Union forces evacuate Pilot Knob, Missouri
"Bloody Bill" Anderson commits Centralia Massacre

29 September
New Market Heights

30 September
Poplar Springs Church begins

2 October
Poplar Springs Church ends

5 October
Attack at Allatoona Pass, Georgia

7 October
CSS *Florida* surrenders to the USS *Wachusett*
Engagement at Johnson Farm begins

9 October
Battle of Tom's Brook

12 October

Roger Brooke Taney dies

13 October

Maryland abolishes slavery

15 October
Shelby takes Glasgow, Missouri

18 October
St. Albans, Vermont Raid begins

19 October
Battle of Cedar Creek
St. Albans, Vermont Raid ends

23 October
Battle of Westport, Missouri

27 October
Battle of Hatcher's Run
Battle of Fair Oaks begins

28 October
Battle of Fair Oaks ends

29 October
Price fights Curtis at Newtonia
Federal forces withdraw from Johnson Farm

4 November
Forrest bombards Johnsonville, Tennessee

5 November
Forrest completes bombardment of Johnsonville, Tennessee

7 November

Second session, Second Confederate
Congress convenes

8 November

Lincoln reelected president

15 November
Much of Atlanta destroyed, and March to the Sea begins

16 November
Battle of Lovejoy, Georgia

21 November
Hood enters Tennessee
Sherman defeats Georgia Militia at Griswoldville

22 November
Sherman's forces fight at Griswoldville and begin
entering Milledgeville

23 November
Sherman's two columns join at Milledgeville

25 November
Skirmishing at Sandersville, Georgia

27 November
Skirmishing at Waynesboro, Georgia

29 November
Sand Creek Massacre

30 November
Battle of Franklin, Tennessee
Battle of Honey Hill, South Carolina

4 December
More skirmishing at Waynesboro, Georgia

5 December

James Speed becomes attorney general
Second session, Thirty-Eighth Congress
convenes

6 December

Salmon Chase nominated chief justice of the
Supreme Court

13 December
Sherman attacks Fort McAllister
First Fort Fisher expedition sails

15 December
Battle of Nashville begins

16 December
Battle of Nashville ends

18 December
Troops for Fort Fisher expedition depart

20 December
Hardee evacuates Savannah

21 December

Sherman's troops occupy Savannah

25 December
Fort Fisher assault begins

27 December
Fort Fisher expedition ends

1865

3 January
Alfred H. Terry given command of second Fort Fisher expedition

7 January
Benjamin Butler removed from command of Army of the James

13 January
Bombardment of Fort Fisher begins

15 January
Fort Fisher falls

16 January
Confederate Congress resolves that Lee should command all Confederate armies

19 January
Sherman's army begins leaving Savannah

31 January
Lee confirmed as commander of all Confederate armies

House of Representatives passes Thirteenth Amendment

1 February
Illinois ratifies Thirteenth Amendment

2 February
Lincoln leaves for Hampton Roads to meet with Confederate commissioners

3 February
Meeting at Hampton Roads

5 February
Battle of Dabney's Mills begins

6 February
Battle of Dabney's Mills continues
Sherman moves toward Columbia, South Carolina
Lee given command of all Confederate armies

John C. Breckinridge becomes Confederate secretary of war

7 February
Battle of Dabney's Mills ends

10 February
Semmes assumes command of James River Squadron

17 February
Confederate troops evacuate Charleston, South Carolina

Sherman occupies Columbia, South Carolina

21 February
Confederates begin to evacuate Wilmington,
North Carolina

22 February
Evacuation of Wilmington complete and city
occupied by Federal troops
Joseph Johnston given command of troops
opposing Sherman

2 March
Battle of Waynesboro, Virginia

3 March

U.S. Congress passes an act establishing the
Bureau of Refugees, Freedmen, and
Abandoned Lands
Second session, Thirty-Eighth Congress
adjourns

4 March

Lincoln and Johnson inaugurated

7 March

Hugh McCulloch becomes secretary of the
treasury

13 March

Confederate Congress passes authorization to
recruit African-American troops

16 March
Battle of Averasboro, North Carolina

17 March
Mobile Campaign begins

18 March

Second session, Second Confederate Congress
adjourns

19 March
Battle of Bentonville begins

21 March
Battle of Bentonville ends

22 March
Wilson begins raid on Selma, Alabama

25 March
Confederates attack Fort Stedman

28 March
Conference at City Point, Virginia, between Lincoln,
Grant, Sherman, and Porter

30 March
Battle of Five Forks begins

1 April
Battle of Five Forks ends
Battle of Blakely, Alabama, begins

Florida governor John Milton commits
suicide at his home in Marianna

2 April
A. P. Hill killed
Lee leaves lines at Petersburg
Wilson defeats Forrest at Selma

Jefferson Davis and cabinet leave Richmond

3 April
Union troops occupy Richmond and Petersburg
Cavalry clash at Namozine Church, Virginia

4 April
Lincoln tours Richmond

5 April
Skirmish at Amelia Springs
Lee at Amelia Courthouse

6 April
Battle of Sayler's Creek
Fighting at High Bridge, Virginia

7 April
Lee crosses Appomattox River and fights at Farmville

8 April
Spanish Fort and Fort Alexis at Mobile surrender

9 April
Lee surrenders at Appomattox Court House
Battle of Blakely, Alabama ends

Jefferson Davis heading south

11 April
Forts Tracy and Huger at Mobile surrender

12 April
Mobile surrenders
Surrender ceremony at Appomattox

13 April
Sherman occupies Raleigh, North Carolina

14 April

John Wilkes Booth shoots President Lincoln

15 April

President Lincoln dies
Davis heading south

17 April
Johnston and Sherman meet near Durham Station,
North Carolina

18 April
Johnston and Sherman sign armistice

19 April

Lincoln's Washington funeral

20 April
Wilson ends raid

21 April

Lincoln's body leaves Washington

26 April
Johnston and Sherman sign final surrender

John Wilkes Booth killed

27 April
Sultana explodes

3 May

Lincoln's body reaches Springfield, Illinois

4 May
Richard Taylor surrenders to Edward R. S. Canby

Lincoln laid to rest in Springfield

9 May

Accused assassination conspirators' trial begins

10 May

Jefferson Davis captured

11 May
M. Jeff Thompson surrenders in Arkansas

12 May
Fighting begins at Palmito Ranch, Texas

Andrew Johnson appoints Oliver O. Howard to head the Freedmen's Bureau

13 May
Fighting ends at Palmito Ranch, the last notable land battle of the Civil War

22 May

Jefferson Davis arrives at Fort Monroe

23 May
Army of the Potomac parades down Pennsylvania Avenue

24 May
Sherman's army parades down Pennsylvania Avenue

26 May
Simon Bolivar Buckner surrenders to Canby

29 May

President Johnson issues Pardon and Amnesty Proclamation, with qualifications

2 June
Edmund Kirby Smith surrenders to Canby

17 June   Edmund Ruffin commits suicide at Redmoor Farm, Virginia

30 June   Assassination conspirators found guilty

7 July   Conspirators hanged

6 November
CSS *Shenandoah* surrenders in Liverpool, England

<u>1866</u>

2 April   President Johnson declares insurrection at an end, except in Texas

20 August   President Johnson includes Texas in proclamation declaring the insurrection at an end, thus officially ending the Civil War

GLOSSARY

Abatis (pronounced AH-bahtee) — an obstacle placed in front of a defensive position that consists of felled trees stacked with limbs pointing toward the enemy's approach

Accouterments — a soldier's gear except for weapons or clothing; also spelled **accoutrements**

Aide-de-camp — the chief military secretary to a superior officer

Barbette — a cannon platform arranged to allow the gun to fire over a **parapet**

Bayonet — a long-bladed knife attached to the muzzle of a musket; statistics show that it caused relatively few injuries in the Civil War and likely served more often as a candle holder and an entrenching tool than a weapon

Bluecoat — a slang term for a Union soldier

Breastworks — a barricade usually about breast high that shielded defenders from enemy fire

Brevet ranks — *see* main entry

Brigade — in army organization, a grouping of three to five **regiments**; combinations of two to six brigades composed a **division**

Buck and gag — a form of tying up punishment in which a soldier was bound and gagged in a seated position with a bar placed between his arms and knees; it was usually employed for rank insubordination

Butternut — a slang term for a Confederate soldier; derived from the practice of dyeing homespun cloth in a mixture of walnuts and copper as to make a uniform of a brown, yellowish hue

Camouflet — a land mine whose reduced charge can injure its victim but is insufficient to create a crater; sometimes referred to as a stifler

Cashier — dishonorably discharge an officer

Cavalry — horse soldiers, distinct from dragoons inasmuch as their function was reconnaissance, **screening** the main army, and fighting while mounted

Contraband — by traditional rules of war, property subject to confiscation if its possession by an enemy would abet his ability to wage war; early in the Civil War the term was used to describe escaped slaves who sought asylum behind Union lines; its first such use is often attributed to General Benjamin F. Butler

Copperheads — label for Northerners who opposed the war and occasionally worked to undermine the war effort (*see* main entry)

Corps (pronounced CORE) — in an army organization, a grouping of two or more **divisions**

Cotton-clads — gunboats that used cotton bales stacked on their decks as a shield from enemy fire

Court-martial — a court that operates under military, rather than civil, law

Demonstration — in military usage, to menace but not assail an enemy to divert his attention from the location of an actual attack; a feint is distinct from a demonstration in that it entails a limited assault for the same purpose

Depot — a site for storing military equipment and provisions; also any place used for collecting soldiers to dispatch to field service

Division — in army organization, a grouping of two or more **brigades** which in combination with other divisions would form a **corps**

Doughface — a derisive term applied to a Northern politician who sympathized with Southern principles, especially in either abiding or protecting the institution of slavery

Dragoons — mounted infantry; they are distinctive from **cavalry** inasmuch as their use of horses was for mobility rather than combat

Echelon attack — a refused advance on an enemy position, meaning that the advance occurred in sequence from right to left or *vice-versa* in parallel but nonaligned formations; ideally an echelon attack would compel the reinforcement of those parts of the enemy line first assailed thereby to weaken the latter parts and increase the chances of breaching them, but more frequently such an attack became disorganized and faltered in confusion

Enfilade — to fire upon the length rather than the face of an enemy position; enfilading an enemy allows a varying range of fire to find targets while minimizing the amount of fire the enemy can return

Fascines — tightly bound bundles of wood used to construct revetments or to make temporary bridges over ditches [*see* **Revetments**]

Feint — *see* **Demonstration**

Flank — (n) also called a wing; either end of a mobile or fortified military position; a refused flank is attached to or protected by terrain, a body of water, or defended fortifications, while one that is not protected is said to be "in the air"; (v) a maneuver that seeks to avoid a frontal assault by gaining the side or rear of an enemy position

2547

Flotilla — a grouping of warships, distinctive from a fleet by its smaller size

Forced march — in military usage, a rapid movement of troops over some distance to meet a crisis such as the imperative need to reinforce positions before or during a battle; A. P. Hill's transit from Harper's Ferry to Sharpsburg during the Battle of Antietam is an example

Fraise — in fortifications, an obstacle formed by studding a **rampart** with sharpened stakes

Graycoat — slang for a Confederate soldier

Hot shot — cannon ammunition heated in a furnace to ignite the target

Infantry — foot soldiers

Interior lines — the military circumstance of either being able to move over a shorter distance to execute maneuvers and effect reinforcements or possessing a more efficient transportation method, such as a railroad, that allows for rapid deployments

Melee — hand-to-hand combat resulting from an advance that has brought a body of troops into close quarters with an enemy

Panada — mush consisting of corn meal, crackers, and boiling water, often flavored with seasoning and wine

Parapet — in fortifications, a wall on top of a **rampart** that shielded riflemen or artillery crews from enemy fire

Pickets — soldiers posted in a forward position to act as sentinels: their function was to alert the main force of an enemy's approach or proximity

Pioneers — soldiers detailed to carry out duties similar to those of modern combat engineers such as cutting roads, repairing bridges and works, and dismantling enemy artillery, fortifications, and railroads; the Pioneer Corps was a specialized unit in the Army of the Cumberland

Pontoon — a buoyant support for floating a temporary bridge

Provost marshal — chief of military police

Rampart — in fortifications, a steeply sloped earthen embankment topped by a **parapet**

Redan — in fortifications, a form of angled **breastworks** shaped like a V with its point facing the approach of the enemy

Regiment — an infantry unit usually consisting of ten companies which in combination with other regiments formed a **brigade**; cavalry or artillery regiments usually consisted of twelve companies or batteries

Retrograde — an orderly retreat usually designed to move away from an enemy

Revetments — a makeshift bulwark to brace trench walls, usually consisting of **fascines** or sand bags

Rifle — *see* main entry

Screening — a function of cavalry deployed to prevent enemy reconnaissance from determining the size or movements of the main army

Shoddy — ersatz cloth made of pressed fibers used in the early days of the Civil War for uniforms; its tendency to disintegrate became a scandal and the term came into use to describe anything inferior

Smoothbore — *see* main entry

Stand of arms — technically, the rifle musket and all its accessories for one soldier (musket, bayonet, cartridge box, and belt), but frequently the term referred to the rifle and its strap

Strategy — broadly conceived military operations that entail the application of a series of integrated **tactics**

Tactics — the maneuvering and deploying of troops before, during, and after an engagement to accomplish the objectives of **strategy**

Torpedo — term for either a land or marine mine

Wing — *see* **Flank**

Works — in military usage, standard terminology for fortifications

A Picture of Slavery Drawn from the Decisions of Southern Courts. 1863. Reprint. Louisville, KY: Lost Cause Press, 1972.

Aaron, Daniel. *The Unwritten War: American Writers and the Civil War.* Madison: University of Wisconsin Press, 1973.

Abbot, Edwin Hale. *Francis Channing Barlow.* Sanford, NC: Microfilming Corporation of America, 1983.

Abbot, Henry Larcom. *Biographical Memoir of John Gross Barnard, 1815–1882.* Washington, DC: National Academy of Sciences, 1905.

Abbott, Horace R. *My Escape from Belle Isle.* Detroit: Winn & Hammond, 1889.

Abbott, Lyman. *Henry Ward Beecher.* Cambridge, MA: Riverside Press, 1904.

Abbott, Richard H. "Cobbler in Congress; Life of Henry Wilson, 1812–1875." Ph.D. dissertation, University of Wisconsin, 1965.

———. *Ohio's War Governors.* Columbus: Ohio State University Press for the Ohio Historical Society, 1962.

Abel, Annie Heloise. *The American Indian in the Civil War, 1862–1865.* Lincoln, NE: Bison Books, 1992.

Abels, Jules. *Man on Fire: John Brown and the Cause of Liberty.* New York: Macmillan, 1971.

Abercrombie, John J. *Battle of Honey Hill, S. C.* Chicago: n. p., 1911.

Abrams, Paul R. "The Assault upon Josiah B. Grinnell by Lovell H. Rousseau." *Iowa Journal* 10 (1912): 383–402.

Abzug, Robert H. *Passionate Liberator: Theodore Dwight Weld and the Dilemma of Reform.* New York: Oxford University Press, 1980.

Adams, Charles Francis, Jr. "Address Delivered at the Dedication of Memorial Hall, Lancaster, Mass., June 17, 1868." Boston: Nichols & Noyes, 1868.

———. *Charles Francis Adams 1835–1915 An Autobiography.* Boston, Cambridge, MA: Houghton Mifflin, 1916.

———. "The Double Anniversary: '76 and '63 A Fourth of July Address Delivered at Quincy, Massachusetts by Charles F. Adams, Jr.* Boston: Wm. Parsons Lunt, 1869.

———. "Lee at Appomattox." In *Lee at Appomattox and Other Papers.* Boston: Houghton Mifflin, 1902.

———. *Richard Henry Dana.* 2 vols. With an introduction by Robert F. Lucid. *American Men and Women of Letters Series,* edited by Daniel Aaron. New York: Chelsea House, 1983.

Adams, Ephraim D. *Great Britain and the American Civil War.* 2 vols. New York: Longmans, Green, 1925.

Adams, George W. *Doctors in Blue.* New York: Collier Books, 1961.

Adams, Henry. *The Education of Henry Adams, Henry Adams: Novels, Mont Saint Michel, and the Education.* Edited by Ernest Samuels. New York: Library of America, 1983: 715–1192.

———. *Henry Adams: Selected Letters.* Edited by Ernest Samuels. Cambridge, MA: Belknap Press of Harvard University Press, 1992.

Adams, Owen E. "Confederate Major General Robert E. Rodes: A Civil War Biography." M.A. thesis, University of Southern Mississippi, 1995.

Adams, Virginia M., ed. *On the Altar of Freedom: A Black Soldier's Civil War Letters from the Front.* Amherst: University of Massachusetts Press, 1991.

Adler, Joseph Gary. "The Public Career of Senator David Levy Yulee." Ph.D. dissertation, Case Western Reserve University, 1973.

Aimone, Alan C., and Barbara Aimone. *A User's Guide to the Official Records of the American Civil War.* Shippensburg, PA: White Mane Publishing Co., 1993.

Albaugh, William A., and Edward N. Simmons. *Confederate Arms.* 1957. Reprint. Harrisburg, PA: Stackpole, 1987.

Alberts, Don E. *The Battle of Glorieta: Union Victory in the West.* College Station: Texas A&M University Press, 1998.

———. *Brandy Station to Manila Bay: A Biography of General Wesley Merritt.* Austin, TX: Presidial Press, 1980.

———. *Rebels on the Rio Grande.* Albuquerque: University of New Mexico Press, 1985.

Alcorn County Historical Association. *The History of Alcorn County Mississippi.* Dallas, TX: National ShareGraphics, 1983

Aldrich, Alfred P. *Memoir of Judge Andrew Pickens Butler.* Charleston, SC: Walker, Evans & Cogswell, 1878.

Alexander, DeAlva S. *A Political History of the State of New York.* Port Washington, NY: Ira Friedman, 1969. Vol. 3: 159–161. Reprint. New York State Historical Publications Series, No. 69, 1909.

Alexander, Edward Porter. *Fighting for the Confederacy: The Personal Recollections of General Edward Porter Alexander.* Edited by Gary W. Gallagher. Chapel Hill: University of North Carolina Press, 1989.

———. *Military Memoirs of a Confederate. A Critical Narrative.* New York: Charles Scribner's Sons, 1907.

Alexander, Ted, James Neitzel, and William P. Conrad. *Southern Revenge! Civil War History of Chambersburg, Pennsylvania.* Shippensburg, PA: White Mane Publishing Co., 1989.

Alexander, Thomas Benjamin, and Richard E. Beringer. *The Anatomy of the Confederate Congress; A Study of the Influences of Member Characteristics on Legislative Voting Behavior, 1861–1865.* Nashville, TN: Vanderbilt University Press, 1972.

Allan, William. *History of the Campaign of Gen. T. J. (Stonewall) Jackson in the Shenandoah Valley of Virginia, from November 4, 1861, to June 17, 1862.* Philadelphia: J. B. Lippincott, 1880.

Allardice, Bruce. *More Generals in Gray.* Baton Rouge: Lousiana State University Press, 1995.

Allen, Gay Wilson. *The Solitary Singer: A Critical Biography of Walt Whitman.* 1955. Rev. ed. 1967. Chicago: University of Chicago Press, 1985.

Allen, Herman R. *Open Door to Learning: The Land-Grant System Enters Its 2nd Century.* Urbana: University of Illinois Press, 1963.

Allen, Mary Bernard. "Joseph Holt, Judge Advocate General, 1862–1875." M.A. thesis, University of Chicago, 1927.

Allen, T. Harrell. *Lee's Last Major General: Bryan Grimes of North Carolina.* Mason City, IA: Savas Pub. Co., 1999.

Allen, William. *The Army of Northern Virginia in 1862.* Boston: Houghton Mifflin, 1892.

Allsopp, Frederick W. *Albert Pike; A Biography.* Little Rock: Parke-Harper, 1992.

Alvarez, David J. "The Papacy in the Diplomacy of the

American Civil War." *Catholic Historical Review* 69 (1993): 227–248.

Aman, Christopher Alan. "The Use of Field Fortifications during the American Civil War." M.A. thesis, University of Florida, 1986.

Amato, Nicholas J., and Edward Eckert, eds. *Ten Years in the Saddle: The Memoir of William Woods Averell: 1851–1862*. San Rafael, CA: Presidio Press, 1978.

Ambler, Charles H. *Francis H. Pierpont: Union War Governor of Virginia and Father of West Virginia*. Chapel Hill: University of North Carolina Press, 1937.

———, ed. *Correspondence of Robert M. T. Hunter*. New York: Da Capo Press, 1971.

Ambrose, Stephen E. *The Campaigns for Fort Donelson: A Review*. Conshohocken, PA: Eastern Acorn Press, 1983.

American Civil War Reports As Recorded in Harper's Weekly. Verplanck, NY: Historical Briefs, 1994.

Ames, Blanch Ames. *Adelbert Ames, 1835–1933: General, Senator, Governor*. New York: Argosy-Antiquarian, 1964.

Amfitheatrof, Erik. *The Children of Columbus: An Informal History of Italians in the New World*. Boston: Little, Brown, 1973.

Amos, Harriet E. "'All Absorbing Topics': Food and Clothing in Confederate Mobile." *Atlanta Historical Journal* 22 (1978): 17–28.

Anbinder, Tyler G. "Fernando Wood and New York City's Secession from the Union: A Political Reappraisal." *New York History* 68 (January 1987): 67–92.

———. *Nativism and Slavery: The Northern Know Nothings and the Politics of Slavery*. New York: Oxford University Press, 1992.

Anders, Leslie. "Fisticuffs at Headquarters: Sweeny vs. Dodge." *Civil War Times Illustrated* (August 1977): 8–15.

Anderson, Bern. *By Sea and by River: The Naval History of the Civil War*. New York: Da Capo Press, 1962.

Anderson, Eric Paul. "The Body of John Merryman: *Ex Parte Merryman*, a Case of Executive-Judicial Conflict over the Suspension of Habeas Corpus." M.A. thesis, Central Washington University, 1979.

Anderson, Gary Clayton. *Through Dakota Eyes: Narrative Accounts of the Minnesota Indian War of 1862*. St. Paul: Minnesota Historical Society Press, 1988.

Anderson, John Q., ed. *Brokenburn: The Journal of Kate Stone, 1861–1868. With a New Introduction by Drew Gilpin Faust*. Library of Southern Civilization. Edited by Lewis P. Simpson. Baton Rouge: Louisiana State University Press, 1995.

Anderson, Robert. *An Artillery Officer in the Mexican War, 1846–7 Letters of Robert Anderson, Captain 3rd Artillery, U.S.A., with a Prefatory Word*. New York: G. P. Putnam's Sons, 1911.

Anderson, William Marshall. *An American in Maximilian's Mexico, 1856–1866: The Diaries of William Marshall Anderson*. Edited by R. E. Ruiz. San Marino: California, 1959.

Andre, Richard, Stan Cohen, and Bill Wintz. *Bullets & Steel: The Fight for the Great Kanawha Valley, 1861–1865*. Charleston, WV: Pictorial Histories Publishing Companies, 1995.

Andreas, Alfred T. *History of Chicago from the Earliest Period to the Present Time*. Chicago: A. T. Andreas, 1884: 397–402.

Andrews, J. Cutler. *The North Reports the Civil War*. Pittsburgh: University of Pittsburgh Press, 1955.

———. *The South Reports the Civil War*. Princeton, NJ: Princeton University Press, 1970.

Andrews, Matthew Page. *The Women of the South in War Times.* Baltimore: Norman, Remington, 1920.

Andrews, Peter. "The Rock of Chickamauga." *American Heritage* (March 1990): 81–91.

Angell, Stephen Ward. *Bishop Henry McNeal Turner and Afro-American Religion in the South*. Knoxville: University of Tennessee Press, 1992.

Angley, Wilson, et al. *Sherman's March through North Carolina: A Chronology*. Raleigh: North Carolina Division of Archives and History, 1996.

Annual Report of the Adjutant General of the State of Maine, 1862. Augusta, GA: Stevens & Sayward, 1863.

Annual *Reports. Quartermaster General to the Secretary of War.* 1862–1866.

Anonymous. "Sharpshooting in Lee's Army." *Confederate Veteran* 3 (1895): 98.

Apltheker, Herbert. *Abolitionism: A Revolutionary Movement*. Boston: Twayne Publishers, 1989.

Arceneaux, William. *Acadian General: Alfred Mouton and the Civil War*. Lafayette, LA: Center for Louisiana Studies of the University of Southwestern Louisiana, 1981.

Armor, William C. *Lives of the Governors of Pennsylvania with the Incidental History of the State, from 1609 to 1872*. Philadelphia: James K. Simon, 1877.

Armstrong, Richard L. *Jackson's Valley Campaign: The Battle of McDowell, March 11–May 18, 1862*. Virginia Civil War Battles and Leaders Series. Lynchburg, VA: H. E. Howard, 1990.

Armstrong, Warren B. *For Courageous Fighting and Confident Dying: Union Chaplains in the Civil War*. Lawrence: University Press of Kansas, 1998.

Armstrong, William H. *Warrior in Two Camps: Ely S. Parker, Union General and Seneca Chief*. Syracuse, NY: Syracuse University, 1978.

Arnold, James R. *Grant Wins the War: Decision at Vicksburg*. New York: Wiley, 1997.

Ash, Steven V. *Middle Tennessee Society Transformed: War and Peace in the Upper South*. Baton Rouge: Louisiana State University Press, 1988.

———. *When the Yankees Came: Conflict and Chaos in the Occupied South, 1861–1865*. Chapel Hill: University of North Carolina Press, 1995.

Ashabranner, Brent. *A Grateful Nation: The Story of Arlington National Cemetery*. New York, 1990.

Ashburn, P.M. *A History of the Medical Department of the United Stated Army*. New York: Houghton Mifflin, 1929.

Ashe, Samuel A'Court. *George Davis, Attorney-General of the Confederate States*. Raleigh, NC: Edwards & Broughton Printing Co., 1916.

The Assassination of Abraham Lincoln and the Attempted Assassination of William H. Seward, Secretary of State, and Frederick W. Seward, Assistant Secretary, on the Evening of the 14th of April, 1865. Washington, DC: Government Printing Office, 1867.

Assing, Ottilie. "The Tombs—The Washington Exhibition—The Minstrels." In *Radical Passion. O. Assing's Reports on America and Letters to F. Douglass*. Edited by C. Lohmann. New York: Lang, 1999.

Athearn, Robert G. *Thomas Francis Meagher: An Irish Revolutionary in America*. Boulder: University of Colorado Press, 1949.

Atkins, John Black. *The Life of Sir William Howard Russell, the First Special Correspondent*. 2 vols. London: J. Murray, 1911.

Atkins, Jonathan M. *Parties, Politics, and the Sectional Conflict in Tennessee, 1832–1861*. Knoxville: University of Tennessee Press, 1997.

Attie, Jeanie. *Patriotic Toil: Northern Women and the American*

Civil War. Ithaca, NY: Cornell University Press, 1998.

Auchincloss, Louis, ed. *The Hone and Strong Diaries of Old Manhattan.* New York: Abbeville Press, 1989.

Auge, M. *Lives of the Eminent Dead and Biographical Notices of Prominent Living Citizens of Montgomery County, Pa.* Norristown, PA: Published by the author, 1879.

Austin, William W. *"Susanna," "Jeanie," and "The Old Folks at Home."* In *The Songs of Stephen C. Foster from His Time to Ours.* New York: Macmillan, 1975.

Ausubel, Herman. *John Bright, Victorian Reformer.* New York: Wiley, 1966.

Avery, A. C. "Memorial Address on the Life and Character of Lieutenant General D. H. Hill." *Southern Historical Society Papers* 21 (1893): 110–150.

Axelrod, Alan. *The War between the Spies: A History of Espionage during the American Civil War.* New York: Atlantic Monthly Press, 1992.

Babcock, Willoughby M., Jr. *Selections from the Letters and Diaries of Brevet-Brigadier General Willoughby Babcock of the Seventy-Fifth New York Volunteers.* New York: University of New York, 1923.

Baber, George. "James Guthrie: Lawyer, Financier, and Statesman." *Register of the Kentucky Historical Society* 10 (1912): 9–13.

Bacarella, Michael. *Lincoln's Foreign Legion: The 39th New York Infantry, The Garibaldi Guard.* Shippensburg, PA: White Mane Publishing Co., 1996.

Bacon, Margaret Hope. *Valiant Friend: The Life of Lucretia Mott.* New York: Walker, 1980.

Bailey, Anne J. "Was There a Massacre at Poison Spring?" *Military History of the Southwest* 20 (Fall 1990): 157–168.

Bailey, Fred A. *Class and Tennessee's Confederate Generation.* Chapel Hill: University of North Carolina Press, 1987.

Bailey, Fred. "The Textbooks of the Lost Cause: Censorship and the Creation of Southern State Histories." *The Georgia Historical Quarterly* 75 (Summer 1991): 507–533.

Bailey, Hugh C. *Hinton Rowan Helper: Abolitionist-Racist.* Montgomery: University of Alabama Press, 1965.

Baird, John A. *Profile of a Hero: The Story of Absalom Baird, His Family, and the American Military Tradition.* Philadelphia: Dorrance, 1977.

Baird, W. David. *Peter Pitchlynn: Chief of the Choctaws.* Norman: University of Oklahoma Press, 1972.

Bakeless, John. *Spies of the Confederacy.* Philadelphia: J. B. Lippincott Co., 1970.

Baker, Jean H. *Affairs of Party: The Political Culture of Northern Democrats in the Mid-Nineteenth Century.* Ithaca, NY: Cornell University Press, 1983.

———. *Ambivalent Americans: The Know-Nothing Party in Maryland.* Baltimore: Johns Hopkins University Press, 1977.

———. *Mary Todd Lincoln: A Biography.* New York: W. W. Norton, 1987.

———. *The Politics of Continuity: Maryland Political Parties from 1858 to 1870.* Baltimore: Johns Hopkins University Press, 1973.

Baker, Nina Brown. *Cyclone in Calico: The Story of Mary Ann Bickerdyke.* Boston: Little, Brown, 1952.

Baker, Robin E. "Class Conflict and Political Upheaval: The Transformation of North Carolina Politics during the Civil War." *North Carolina Historical Review* 69 (1992): 148–178.

Baldwin, James J. *The Struck Eagle: A Biography of Brigadier General Micah Jenkins, and a History of the Fifth South Carolina Volunteers and the Palmetto Sharpshooters.* Shippensburg, PA: Burd Street Press, 1996.

Ball, Douglas B. *Financial Failure and the Confederate Defeat.* Urbana and Chicago: University of Illinois Press, 1991.

Ballard, Michael B. *A Long Shadow: Jefferson Davis and the Final Days of the Confederacy.* Jackson: University Press of Mississippi, 1986.

———. *Pemberton: A Biography.* Jackson: University Press of Mississippi, 1991.

Baltzell, E. Digby. *Philadelphia Gentlemen.* Philadelphia: University of Pennsylvania Press, 1979.

Banasik, Michael E. *Embattled Arkansas: The Prairie Grove Campaign of 1862.* Wilmington, NC: Broadfoot Publishing Co., 1996.

Bar Association of the City of Richmond. *Proceedings in Memorium of R. C. L. Moncure and Robert Ould.* Richmond, VA: Dalton & Guthrie, 1883.

Barbee, David Rankin. "Hinton Rowan Helper." *Tyler's Historical and Genealogical Magazine* 15 (January 1934): 135–172.

Barbour, Hugh, and J. William Frost. *The Quakers.* Westport, CT: Greenwood Press, 1988.

Barefoot, Daniel W. *General Robert F. Hoke: Lee's Modest Warrior.* Winston-Salem, NC: John F. Blair, 1996.

Barker, Nancy Nichols. "Empress Eugenie and the Origins of the Mexican Venture." *The Historian,* 22 (1) (November 1959): 9–23.

Barksdale, Ethelbert. "Reconstruction in Mississippi." In *Why the Solid South?* Baltimore: R. H. Woodward, 1890: 321–348.

Barnard, George N. *Photographic Views of Sherman's Campaign. With a New Preface by Beaumont.* Newhall, NY: Dover Publications, 1977.

Barnard, John Gross. *Memoir of Joseph Gilbert Totten: 1788–1864.* Lawrence: University Press of Kansas, 1979.

Barnard, John Gross, and William F. Barry. *Report of the Engineer and Artillery Operations of the Army of the Potomac, from its Organization to the Close of the Peninsula Campaign.* New York: D. Van Nostrand, 1863.

Barnes, David M. *The Draft Riots in New York, July, 1863, The Metropolitan Police: Their Services during Riot Week, Their Honorable Record.* New York: Barker & Godwin, 1863.

Barnes, Gilbert H., and Dwight L. Dumond, eds. *Letters of Theodore Dwight Weld, Angelina Grimké Weld and Sarah Grimké, 1822–1844.* 2 vols. New York: Appleton-Century, 1934. Reprint. New York: Da Capo Press, 1970.

Barnes, J. S. *Submarine Warfare, Offensive and Defensive.* New York: D. Van Nostrand, 1869.

Barney, William. *The Secessionist Impulse.* Princeton, NJ: Princeton University Press, 1974.

Barr, Alwyn. *Polignac's Texas Brigade.* Houston: Texas Gulf Coast Historical Association, 1964.

———. "Sabine Pass, September 1863." *Texas Military History* 2 (February 1962): 17–22.

Barrett, John G. *The Civil War in North Carolina.* Chapel Hill: University of North Carolina Press, 1963.

———. *Sherman's March through the Carolinas.* 1956. Reprint. Chapel Hill: University of North Carolina Press, 1996.

Barringer, Rufus. *Civil War Diary of General Rugus Barringer, PACS from Concord, North Carolina, April 1 through August 8, 1865, from a Photocopy of the Original Manuscript given by Osmond Long "Bugs" Barringer, Jr., to the Southern Historical Collection, University of North Carolina, Chapel Hill, North Carolina.* Concord, NC: John Hanby Foard, Jr., 1998.

Barrow, Charles Kelly, J. H. Segars, and R. B. Rosenburg, eds. *Forgotten Confederates: An Anthology about Black Southerners.* 1995. Reprint. Murfreesboro, TN: Southern Heritage Press, 1998.

Bartholomees, J. Boone, Jr. *Buff Facings and Gilt Buttons. Staff and Headquarters Operations in the Army of Northern Virginia,*

1861–1865. Columbia: University of South Carolina Press, 1998.

Bartlett, Elizabeth Ann. *Letters on the Equality of the Sexes and Other Essays. By Sarah Grimké*. New Haven, CT: Yale University Press, 1988.

Bartlett, Irving H. *Wendell Phillips: Brahmin Radical*. 1961. Reprint. Westport, CT: Greenwood Press, 1973.

Bartlett, Ruhl J. *John C. Frémont and the Republican Party*. New York: Da Capo Press, 1970.

Bartman, Roger J. "Joseph Holt and Kentucky in the Civil War." *Filson Club Historical Quarterly* 40 (1966): 105–122.

Barto, William N. "James Cameron First Northern Colonel to Die in Civil War." *Milton Standard*, 28 May 1964.

Barton, Clara. Collection. Manuscript Division, Library of Congress, Washington, DC.

———. *The Red Cross*. Albany, NY: James B. Lyon, 1898.

Barton, O. S. *Three Years with Quantrill: A True Story Told by His Scout John McCorkle. With Notes by Albert Castel and Commentary by Herman Hattaway*. Norman: University of Oklahoma Press, 1992.

Barton, William E. *Lincoln at Gettysburg: What He Intended to Say; What He Said; What He Was Reported to Have Said; What He Wished He Had Said*. Indianapolis: Bobbs-Merrill, 1930.

Basler, Roy P., ed. *The Collected Works of Abraham Lincoln*. 8 vols. New Brunswick, NJ: Rutgers University Press, 1953–1955.

Basso, Hamilton. *Beauregard, The Great Creole*. New York: Charles Scribner's Sons, 1933.

Bates, David Homer. *Lincoln in the Telegraph Office: Recollections of the United States Military Telegraph Corps during the Civil War*. New York: Century Co., 1907.

Bates, Samuel P. *History of Pennsylvania Volunteers, 1861–5*. 5 vols. Harrisburg, PA: B. Singerly, State Printer, 1868– 1871. Reprint. Wilmington, NC: Broadfoot Publishing Co., 1993.

Bates, William Carver. *Adin Ballou Underwood*. Newton, MA: Tuesday Club, 1888.

"Battle of Hampton Roads—Confederate Official Reports." *Southern Historical Society Papers* 7 (1879): 305–314.

Bauer, Craig A. "The Last Effort: The Secret Mission of the Confederate Diplomat, Duncan F. Kenner." *Louisiana History* 22 (1981): 67–95.

———. *The Life and Times of Duncan Farrar Kenner*. Lafayette, LA: Center for Louisiana Studies, University of Southwestern Louisiana, 1993.

Baum, Dale. *The Civil War Party System: The Case of Massachusetts, 1848–1876*. Chapel Hill: University of North Carolina Press, 1984.

Baylies, Francis. *A Narrative of Major General Wool's Campaign in Mexico in the Years 1846, 1847 & 1848*. Albany: Little & Co., 1851.

Baylor, George Wythe. *John Robert Baylor*. Tucson: Arizona Historical Society, 1966.

Beale, George W. *A Lieutenant of Cavalry in Lee's Army*. Boston: Gorham Press, 1918.

Beale, Howard K., ed. *The Diary of Edward Bates, 1859–1866*. 1930. Reprint. New York: Da Capo Press, 1971.

Bean, W. G. *Stonewall's Man: Sandie Pendleton*. 1959. Reprint. Chapel Hill: University of North Carolina Press, 2000.

Beard, William David. "James Rood Doolittle, A Public Life: From Democrat to Demagogue." Master's thesis, University of Wisconsin—Milwaukee, 1979.

Bearss, Edwin C. "The Battle of Helena, July 4, 1863." *Arkansas Historical Quarterly* 20 (Autumn 1961): 256–297.

———. *The Battle of Wilson's Creek*. Springfield, MO: Wilson's Creek National Battlefield Foundation, 1992.

———. *The Campaign for Vicksburg*. 3 vols. Dayton, OH: Morningside, 1985–1986.

———. "Civil War Operations in and around Pensacola, Part 1." *Florida Historical Quarterly* 36 (October 1957).

———. *Decision in Mississippi: Mississippi's Important Role in the War between the States*. Jackson: Mississippi Commission on the War between the States, 1962.

———. *Forrest at Brice's Cross Roads and in North Mississippi in 1864*. Dayton, OH: Morningside Bookshop, 1979.

———. *Steele's Retreat from Camden and the Battle of Jenkins' Ferry*. Little Rock: Pioneer Press, 1967.

Bearss, Edwin C., and Arrell M. Gibson. *Fort Smith: Little Gibraltar on the Arkansas*. Norman: University of Oklahoma Press, 1988.

Bearss, Margie Riddle. *Sherman's Forgotten Campaign: The Meridian Expedition*. Baltimore: Gateway Press, 1987.

Beauregard, Pierre G. T. "Torpedo Service in the Harbor and Water Defenses at Charleston." *Southern Historical Society Papers* 5 (1878):145–161.

Beck, Brandon H., and Charles S. Grunder. *Three Battles of Winchester: A History and Guided Tour*. Berryville, VA: The Country Publishers, 1988.

Beecher, Herbert W. *History of the First Light Battery Connecticut Volunteers, 1861–1865, Volume 1*. New York: A. T. De La Mare Printing, n.d.

Beitzell, Edwin W. *Point Lookout Prison Camp for Confederates*. Leonardtown, MD: St. Mary's County Historical Society, 1991.

Belden, Thomas Graham, and Marva Robins Belden. *So Fell the Angels*. Boston: Little, Brown, 1956.

Belknap, George E. "Reminiscent of the 'New Ironsides' off Charleston." *United Service Magazine*, o.s., 1 (January 1879): 63–82.

Bell, Mark E. "A Day at the Races: The First Virginia Infantry (U.S.) at the Battle of Philippi." In *Civil War Regiments: A Journal of the American Civil War*. Vol. 5, no. 4. Savas Publishing Co., 1997: 1–19.

Bell, Rodney Ellis. "A Life of Russell Alexander Alger, 1836–1907." Ph.D. dissertation, University of Michigan, 1957.

Belz, Herman. *Abraham Lincoln, Constitutionalism, and Equal Rights in the Civil War Era*. New York: Fordham University Press, 1998.

———. *Emancipation and Equal Rights, Politics and Constitutionalism in the Civil War Era*. New York: W. W. Norton, 1978.

———. *A New Birth of Freedom: The Republican Party and Freedmen's Rights, 1861–1866*. Westport, CT: Greenwood Press, 1976.

———. *Reconstructing the Union: Theory and Policy during the Civil War*. Ithaca, NY: Cornell University Press, 1969.

Bemis, Samuel Flagg. *The American Secretaries of State and Their Diplomacy*. 10 vols. New York: Cooper Square Publishers, 1963.

Benedict, George Grenville. *History of the Seventh Regiment Vermont Volunteers*. Burlington, VT: Free Press Association, 1891.

———. *Vermont in the Civil War*. Burlington, VT: Free Press Association, 1889.

Benedict, Michael Les. *A Compromise of Principle: Congressional Republicans and Reconstruction*. New York: W. W. Norton, 1974.

Benjamin, Judah P. "The Letters of Judah Philip Benjamin to Ambrose Dudley Mann, Minister of the Confederacy to Belgium and Special Commissioner to the Vatican, together with the Correspondence with the Pope."

Louisiana Historical Quarterly 20 (1937): 738–793.

Bennett, Brian A. *Sons of Old Monroe: A Regimental History of Patrick O'Rorke's 140th New York Volunteer Infantry.* Dayton, OH: Morningside House, 1992.

Bennett, C. A. "Roswell Sabin Ripley: Charleston's Gallant Defender." *South Carolina History Magazine* 95 (July 1994): 225–242.

Bennett, Daphne. *King without a Crown.* London: Century Publishers, 1983.

Bennett, Frank M. *The Monitor and the Navy under Steam.* Boston: Houghton Mifflin, 1900.

Bennett, Whitman. *Whittier: Bard of Freedom.* Port Washington, NY: Kennikat Press, 1972.

Bennett, William W. *A Narrative of the Great Revival which Prevailed in the Southern Armies during the Late Civil War between the States of the Federal Union.* Philadelphia: Claxton, Remsen & Haffelfinger, 1877.

Bentley, George R. *A History of the Freedmen's Bureau.* 1955. Reprint. New York: Octagon Books, 1974.

Benton, Elbert J. *The Movement for Peace without Victory during the Civil War.* Cleveland: Western Reserve Historical Society Publications, No. 99, 1918.

Benton, Josiah Henry. *Voting in the Field: A Forgotten Chapter of the Civil War.* Boston: Privately printed, 1915.

Berger, Raoul. *Federalism: The Founders' Design.* Norman: University of Oklahoma Press, 1987.

Bergeron, Arthur W. *Confederate Mobile.* Jackson: University of Mississippi Press, 1991.

———, ed. *Reminiscences of Uncle Silas: A History of the Eighteenth Louisiana Infantry Regiment.* Baton Rouge: Louisiana State University Press, 1981.

Bergeron, Paul H. *Antebellum Politics in Tennessee.* Lexington: University Press of Kentucky, 1982.

———, ed. *The Papers of Andrew Johnson.* 12 vols. Knoxville: University of Tennessee Press. 1967–1995.

Bergeron, Paul, Stephen Ash, and Jeanette Keith. *Tennesseans and Their History.* Knoxville: University of Tennessee Press, 1999.

Beringer, Richard E., Herman Hattaway, Archer Jones, and William N. Still, Jr. *Why the South Lost the Civil War.* Athens: University of Georgia Press, 1986.

Berk, Joseph. *The Gatling Gun: 19th Century Machine Gun to 21st Century Vulcan.* Boulder, CO: Paladin Press, 1991.

Berlin, Ira, Joseph P. Reidy, and Leslie S. Rowland, eds. *Freedom: A Documentary History of Emancipation, 1861–1867. Series 2: The Black Military Experience.* Cambridge, UK: Cambridge University Press, 1982.

Bernard, George S., comp. *War Talks of Confederate Veterans.* Petersburg, VA: n.p., 1892.

Bernath, Stuart L. *Squall Across the Atlantic: American Civil War Prize Cases and Diplomacy.* Berkeley and Los Angeles: University of California Press, 1970.

Bernstein, Iver. *The New York City Draft Riots, Their Significance For American Society and Politics in the Age of the Civil War.* New York: Oxford University Press, 1990.

Berry, Thelma Caine. "The Life of Edmund Winston Pettus." M.A. thesis, Auburn University, Auburn, Alabama, 1941.

Berry, Thomas F. *Four Years with Morgan and Forrest.* Oklahoma City, OK: n.p., 1914.

Bettersworth, John K. *Mississippi: A History.* Austin, TX: Steck Co., 1959

Beyer, W. F., and O. F. Keydel. *Deeds of Valor: How America's Civil War Heroes Won the Congressional Medal of Honor.* Detroit: Perrien-Keydel, 1903.

Bicha, Karel D. *C. C. Washburn and the Upper Mississippi Valley.* New York: Garland Publishing, 1995.

Bickerdyke, Mary Ann Ball. Collection. Manuscript Division, Library of Congress, Washington, DC.

Bierce, Ambrose. "On a Mountain." In *Collected Works.* New York: Neale Publicating Co., 1909–1912.

Bigelow, John, Jr. *The Campaign of Chancellorsville: A Strategic and Tactical Study.* New Haven, CT: Yale University Press, 1910.

———. *The Life of Samuel J. Tilden.* New York: Harper & Brothers, 1895.

———. *Retrospections of an Active Life.* Vols. 1–2. New York: Baker & Taylor, 1909.

Bilby, Joseph G. *The Irish Brigade in the Civil War. The 69th New York and Other Irish Regiments in the Army of the Potomac.* Conshohocken, PA: Combined Publishing, 1998.

Bilby, Joseph G., and William C. Goble. *"Remember You Are Jerseymen!": A Military History of New Jersey's Troops in the Civil War.* Hightstown, NJ: Longstreet Press, 1998.

Billings, John D. *Hardtack and Coffee, or the Unwritten Story of Army Life.* 1887. Reprint. Williamstown, MA: Corner House Publishers, 1990.

Billington, Ray Allen. *The Protestant Crusade 1800–1860: A Study of the Origins of American Nativism.* New York: Macmillan, 1938.

"Biographical Annals." *The Miltonian,* 6 September 1889.

Biographical Sketches of Distinguished American Lawyers. New York: John Livingston, 1852.

Birney, Catherine H. *Sarah and Angelina Grimké: The First American Women Advocates of Abolition and Woman's Rights.* 1885. Reprint. New York: Haskell House Publishers, 1970.

Birney, William. *General William Birney's Answer to Libels Clandestinely Circulated by James Shaw, Jr., Late Colonel of the Seventh U.S. Colored Troops.* Washington, DC: Snodgrass, Printer, 1878.

Bivins, Joseph Francis. *The Life and Character of Jacob Thompson.* 1898. Reprint. New York: AMS Press, 1970.

Black, Dan Anderson. "Financing the Confederacy." M.B.A. thesis, University of Texas at Austin, 1981.

Black, Robert C., III. "The Railroads of Georgia during the War between the States, and Their Part in the Confederate War Effort." M.A. thesis, University of Denver, 1947.

———. *The Railroads of the Confederacy.* 1952. Reprint. Chapel Hill: University of North Carolina Press, 1998.

Blackburn, James Knox Polk. *Reminiscences of Terry's Texas Rangers.* 1919. Reprint. Austin, TX: Ranger Press, 1979.

Blackford, Charles M. *Campaign and Battle of Lynchburg, Virginia.* Lynchburg, VA: Warwick House Publishing, 1994.

Blackford, W. W. *War Years with Jeb Stuart.* 1945. Reprint. Baton Rouge: Louisiana State University Press. 1993.

Blackwell, Elizabeth. *Medicine & Society in America: Essays in Medical Sociology.* Vol. 1 & 2. New York: Arno Press & the New York Times, 1972.

———. *Pioneer Work in Opening the Medical Profession to Women: Autobiographical Sketches by Dr. Elizabeth Blackwell.* Introduction by Mary Roth Walsh. New York: Schocken, 1977.

Bladek, John David. "'Virginia is Middle Ground': The Know-Nothing Party and the Virginia Gubernatorial Election of 1855." *Virginia Magazine of History and Biography* 106 (Winter 1998): 35–70.

Blaine, James Gillespie. *Twenty Years of Congress.* 2 vols. Norwich, CT: Henry Bill, 1884–1886.

Blair, Harry C., and Rebecca Tarshis. *The Life of Colonel Edward D. Baker, Lincoln's Constant Ally, together with Four of His Great Orations.* Portland: Oregon Historical Society, 1960.

Blair, William. *Virginia's Private War: Feeding Body and Soul in the Confederacy, 1861–1865*. New York: Oxford University Press, 1998.

———, ed. *A Politician Goes to War: The Civil War Letters of John White Geary*. University Park: Pennsylvania State University Press, 1995.

Blake, Nelson M. *William Mahone of Virginia: Soldier and Political Insurgent*. Richmond, VA: Garret & Massie, 1935.

Blakey, Arch Fredric. *General John H. Winder, C.S.A.* Gainesville: University of Florida Press, 1990.

Blanton, DeAnne. "Women Soldiers of the Civil War." *Prologue*, 25, No. 1 (Spring 1993).

Blasio, Jose Luis. *Maximilian Emperor of Mexico. Memoirs of His Private Secretary*. Translated from the original Spanish and edited by Robert Hammond Murray. New Haven, CT: Yale University Press, 1934.

Blassingame, John W., ed. *Frederick Douglass Papers*. New Haven CT: Yale University Press, 1979.

Blay, John S. *The Civil War A Pictorial Profile*. New York: Thomas Y. Cromwell Co., 1958.

Bleser, Carol K., ed. *Secret and Sacred: The Diaries of James Henry Hammond, a Southern Slaveholder*. New York: Oxford University Press, 1988.

Blessington, Joseph P. *The Campaigns of Walker's Texas Division*. New York: Lange, Little & Co., 1875.

Blied, Benjamin J. *Catholics and the Civil War: Essays*. 1945. Reprint, microfilm. New Haven, CT: Yale University Library, 1992.

Blight, David W. *Frederick Douglass' Civil War: Keeping Faith in Jubilee*. Baton Rouge: Louisiana State University Press, 1989.

Block, Eugene B. *Above the Civil War: The Story of Thaddeus Lowe*. Berkeley, CA: Howell-North Books, 1966.

Blockson, Charles L., ed. *The Underground Railroad*. New York: Prentice-Hall, 1987.

Blue, Frederick J. *The Free Soilers: Third Party Politics, 1848–1854*. Urbana: University of Illinois Press, 1973.

———. *Salmon P. Chase: A Life in Politics*. Kent, OH: Kent State University Press, 1987.

Blustein, Bonnie Ellen. *Preserve Your Love for Science: Life of William A. Hammond, American Neurologist*. Cambridge, MA: Cambridge University Press, 1991.

Boatner, Mark Mayo, III. *Army Lore and the Customs of the Service*. New York: David McKay Co., 1954.

———. *The Civil War Dictionary*. New York: David McKay Co., 1959.

———. *Military Customs and Traditions*. New York: David McKay Co., 1956.

Bogue, Allan G. *The Earnest Men: Republicans of the Civil War Senate*. Ithaca, NY: Cornell University Press, 1981.

Bolitho, Hector. *Albert, Prince Consort*. Indianapolis: Bobbs-Merrill, 1964.

Bolt, L. T. C. *The Aeronauts: A History of Ballooning 1783–1903*. London: Longmans, Green, 1966.

Boney, F. N. *John Letcher of Virginia*. University: University of Alabama Press, 1966.

———. *Rebel Georgia*. Macon, GA: Mercer University Press, 1997.

Bonnifield, Paul. "The Choctaw Nation on the Eve of the Civil War." *Journal of the West* 12 1973 12 (3): 386–402.

Borthick, David, and Jack Britton. *Medals, Military and Civilian, of the United States*. Tulsa, OK: MCN Press, 1984.

Bosbyshell, Oliver C. *The 48th in the War, Being a Narrative of the Campaigns of the 48th Regiment, Infantry, Pennsylvania Veteran Volunteers, during the War of the Rebellion*. Philadelphia: Avil Printing Co., 1895.

Bourke, John G. *On the Border with Crook*. New York: Charles Scribner's Sons, 1891. Reprint. Lincoln: University of Nebraska Press, 1971.

Boutwell, George S. *Reminiscences of Sixty Years in Public Affairs*. 2 vols. New York: Greenwood Press, 1968. Reprint New York: McClure, Phillips & Co., 1902.

Bowers, John. *Chickamauga and Chattanooga; The Battles That Doomed the Confederacy*. New York: HarperCollins, 1994.

Boyd, Mark F. *The Federal Campaign of 1864 in East Florida*. Tallahassee, FL: Florida Boards of Parks and Historic Memorials, 1956.

———. "The Joint Operations of the Federal Army and Navy near St. Marks, Florida, March 1865." *Florida Historical Quarterly* 29 (October 1950): 96–124.

Boyden, William L. *A Bibliography of the Writings of Albert Pike: Prose, Poetry, Manuscript*. 1921. Reprint. Washington, DC: Privately printed, 1957.

Boykin, Edward. *Sea Devil of the Confederacy; the Story of the Florida and Her Captain*. New York: Funk & Wagnalls, 1959.

Bradford, James C., ed. *Captains of the Old Steam Navy: Makers of the American Naval Tradition, 1840–1880*. Annapolis, MD: Naval Institute Press, 1986.

Bradford, Ned, ed. *Battles and Leaders of the Civil War*. New York: Fairfax Press, 1957.

Bradford, Sarah E. *Harriet Tubman: The Moses of her People 1869*. Reprint. Gloucester, MA: Peter Smith, 1981.

Bradlee, Francis B. C. *Blockade Running during the Civil War and the Effect of Land and Water Transportation on the Confederacy*. Salem, MA: Essex Institute, 1925.

Bradley, Amy Morris. Diaries and Letterbooks. Perkins Library, Duke University, Durham, North Carolina.

Bradley, Erwin Stanley. *Simon Cameron; Lincoln's Secretary of War, A Political Biography*. Philadelphia: University of Pennsylvania Press, 1966.

Brady, Robert. *The Story of One Regiment the Eleventh Maine Infantry Volunteers in the War of the Rebellion*. New York: J. J. Little & Co., 1896.

Bragg, Jefferson Davis. *Louisiana in the Confederacy*. Baton Rouge: Louisiana State University Press, 1941.

Bragg, William Harris. *Joe Brown's Army: The Georgia State Line, 1862–1865*. Macon: Mercer University Press, 1987.

Brancaforte, Charlotte, ed. *The German Forty-Eighters in the United States*. New York: Peter Lang, 1989.

Brandt, Nat. *The Man Who Tried to Burn New York*. Syracuse, NY: Syracuse University Press, 1986.

Brantley, Rabun Lee. *Georgia Journalism of the Civil War Period*. Nashville, TN: George Peabody College for Teachers, 1929.

Bratton, John. Letters. Southern Historical Society Collection, University of North Carolina at Chapel Hill.

Breen, Donald J. "History of the Federal Civil War Prison on Johnson's Island, 1862–1865." M.A. thesis, Kent State University, 1962.

Brennan, Patrick. *Secessionville: Assault on Charleston*. Campbell, CA: Savas Publishing, 1996.

Brevet Major General Joseph K. Barnes, Surgeon General of the United States Army, 1864–1882. Carlisle, PA: Association of Military Surgeons, 1904.

Brewer, James D. *The Raiders of 1862*. Westport, CT: Praeger, 1997.

Brewer, James H. *The Confederate Negro: Virginia's Craftsmen and Military Laborers, 1861–1865*. Durham, NC: Duke University Press, 1969.

Bridges, Edwin C. "Juliet Opie Hopkins and Alabama's Civil

War Hospitals in Richmond, Virginia." *The Alabama Review* 53 (April 2000): 83–111.

Bridges, Hal. "D. H. Hill and Higher Education in the New South." *The Arkansas Historical Quarterly* 15, no. 2 (1956): 107–124.

———. *Lee's Maverick General: Daniel Harvey Hill.* Introduction by Gary W. Gallagher. New York: McGraw-Hill, 1961. Reprint. Lincoln: University of Nebraska Press, 1991.

Brigham, Johnson. *Iowa: Its History and Its Foremost Citizens.* 4 vols. Chicago: S. J. Clark Publishing Co., 1916.

Bright, Simeon Miller. "The McNeill Rangers: A Study in Confederate Guerrilla Warfare." *West Virginia History* 12:4 (1951): 338–394.

Brill, Ruth. "Cincinnati's 'Poet-Warrior': William Haines Lytle." *Historical and Philosophical Society of Ohio Bulletin* 21 (1963): 188–201.

Bringhurst, Newell G. *Brigham Young and the Expanding American Frontier.* Boston: Little, Brown, 1986.

Britton, James C. "Images of the Future in the *Charleston Mercury*, 1848–1860." M.A. thesis, University of North Carolina at Chapel Hill, 1980.

Britton, Wiley. *The Civil War on the Border.* 2 vols. New York: G. P. Putnam, 1890–1899.

———. *Memoirs of the Rebellion on the Border, 1863.* Lincoln: University of Nebraska Press, 1993.

———. *The Union Indian Brigade in the Civil War.* Kansas City: Franklin Hudson Publishing Co., 1922.

Brockett, Linus P., and Mary C. Vaughan. *Woman's Work in the Civil War.* Philadelphia: Zeigler, McCurdy, 1867.

Brockman, Clark. "John Beauchamp Jones." M.A. thesis, University of South Carolina, Columbia, South Carolina, 1937.

Brodie, Bernard, and Fawn M. Brodie. *From Crossbow to H-Bomb.* Bloomington: Indiana University Press, 1973.

Brodie, Fawn N. *Thaddeus Stevens, Scourge of the South.* New York: W. W. Norton, 1966.

Brooke, John M. "The *Virginia* or *Merrimac*: Her Real Projector." *Southern Historical Society Papers* 19 (1891): 3–34.

Brooks, Stewart. *Civil War Medicine.* Springfield, IL: Charles C. Thomas, 1966.

Brooksher, William R. *Bloody Hill: The Civil War Battle of Wilson's Creek.* Washington, DC: Brassey's, 1995.

———. *War along the Bayous: The 1864 Red River Campaign in Louisiana.* Washington, DC: Brasseys, 1998.

Brooksher, William R., and David K. Snider. *Glory at a Gallop: Tales of the Confederate Cavalry.* New York: Brassey's, 1993.

———. "Devil on the River." *Civil War Times Illustrated* 15 (August 1976): 12–19.

Brown, A. D. "The Battle of Pine Bluff: The Yankee View." *Jefferson County (Arkansas) Historical Quarterly* 1 (Winter 1989): 7–8.

Brown, A. F. "Van Dorn's Operations in Northern Mississippi—Recollections of a Cavalryman." *Southern Historical Society Papers*, vol. 6, July to December 1878. 1878. Reprint. Millwood, NY: Kraus Reprint Co., 1977: 151–161.

Brown, Alexander. *The Cabells and Their Kin, a Memorial Volume of History, Biography and Genealogy.* Boston: Houghton Mifflin, 1895.

Brown, Alfred Milton. "Lucius B. Northrop, Commissary-General of the Confederacy." M.A. thesis, Southern Methodist University, Dallas, Texas, 1939.

Brown, Ann. "Fort Delaware: The Most Dreaded Northern Prison." *Civil War Quarterly* 10: 36–40.

Brown, Bernard Edward. *American Conservatives: The Political Thought of Francis Lieber and John W. Burgess.* New York: Columbia University Press, 1951.

Brown, Charles H. *Agents of Manifest Destiny: The Lives and Times of the Filibusters.* Chapel Hill: University of North Carolina, 1980.

Brown, D. Alexander. "The Battle of Westport." *Civil War Times Illustrated* 5 (July 1966): 6–11, 40–43.

———. *Galvanized Yankees.* Urbana, IL: University of Illinois Press, 1963.

———. *Grierson's Raid.* Urbana: University of Illinois Press, 1962.

Brown, Francis. *Raymond of the Times.* 1950. Reprint. Westport, CT: Greenwood Press, 1970.

Brown, George W. *Reminiscences of Governor R. J. Walker; with the True Story of the Rescue of Kansas from Slavery.* Rockford: Privately published, 1902.

Brown, J. Willard *The Signal Corps, U.S.A. in the War of the Rebellion.* Boston: U.S. Veteran Signal Corps Association, 1896

Brown, James Earl. "Life of Brigadier General John McCausland." *West Virginia History* 4 (July 1943): 239–293.

Brown, John William. "Franklin Buchanan, Naval Leader." M.A. thesis, Southern Methodist University, 1948.

Brown, Josephine. *Biography of an American Bondman, by His Daughter.* Boston: R. F. Walcutt, 1856.

Brown, Joshua. "*Frank Leslie's Illustrated Newspaper*: The Pictorial Press and the Representations of America, 1855–1889." Ph.D. dissertation, Columbia University, 1993.

———. "Reconstructing Representation—Social Types, Readers, and the Pictorial Press, 1865–1877." *Radical History Review* 38 (Fall 1996): 5–38.

Brown, Kent Masterson. *Cushing of Gettysburg: The Story of a Union Artillery Commander.* Lexington: University Press of Kentucky, 1993.

Brown, Louis A. *The Salisbury Prison: A Case Study of Confederate Military Prisons, 1861–1865.* 2d ed. Wilmington, NC: Broadfoot Publishing Co., 1992.

Brown, Norman D. *Edward Stanly: Whiggery's Tarheel "Conqueror."* University: University of Alabama Press, 1974.

———, ed. *Journey to Pleasant Hill: The Civil War Letters of Captain Elijah P. Petty, Walker's Texas Division, CSA.* San Antonio: University of Texas Institute of Texan Cultures, 1982.

Brown, Richard D., ed. *Slavery in American Society.* 3d ed. Lexington, MA: D. C. Heath, 1992.

Brown, Russell K. *To the Manner Born: The Life of General William H. T. Walker.* Athens, GA: University of Georgia Press, 1994.

Brown, Thomas H. *George Sewall Boutwell, Human Rights Advocate.* Groton, MA: Groton Historical Society, 1989.

Brown, Thomas J. *Dorothea Dix, New England Reformer.* Cambridge, MA: Harvard University Press, 1998.

Brown, Walter L. *A Life of Albert Pike.* Fayetteville: University of Arkansas Press, 1997.

Brown, William Wells. *The Black Man: His Antecedents, His Genius, and His Achievements.* Savannah, GA: James M. Symms & Co., 1863.

———. *My Southern Home; or The South and Its People.* Boston: A. G. Brown & Co., 1880.

———. *The Negro in the American Rebellion.* Boston: Lee & Sheard, 1867.

Brown, William Young. *The Army Chaplain: His Office, Duties, and Responsibilities, and the Means of Aiding Him.* Philadelphia: William S. & Alfred Martin, 1863.

Browning, Robert M. *From Cape Charles to Cape Fear: The North*

Atlantic Blockading Squadron during the Civil War. Tuscaloosa: University of Alabama Press, 1993.

Brownlee, Richard S. "The Battle of Pilot Knob, Iron County, Missouri, September 27, 1864." *Missouri Historical Review* (October 1964).

———. *Gray Ghosts of the Confederacy: Guerilla Warfare in the West, 1861–1865.* Baton Rouge: Louisiana State University Press, 1958.

Bruce, Kathleen. *Virginia Iron Manufacture in the Slave Era.* 1930. Reprint. New York: A. M. Kelley, 1968.

Bruce, Robert V. *Lincoln and the Tools of War.* 1956. Reprint. Urbana: University of Illinois Press, 1989.

Bruchey, Stuart. *Cotton and the Growth of the American Economy: 1790–1860.* New York: Harcourt, Brace & World, 1967.

Brugger, Robert J. *Maryland: A Middle Temperament, 1634–1980.* Baltimore: Johns Hopkins University Press, 1988.

Brumgardt, John R. "The Confederate Career of Alexander Stephens." *Civil War History* 27 (March 1981).

Bryan, Charles Faulkner, Jr. "The Prodigal Nephew: Andrew Jackson Donelson and the Eaton Affair." *East Tennessee Historical Society Publications* 50 (1978): 92–112.

Bryan, George S. *The Great American Myth: The True Story of Lincoln's Murder.* Chicago: Americana House, 1990.

Bryan, T. Conn. *Confederate Georgia.* Athens: University of Georgia Press, 1953.

Bryan, Vernane. *Laura Keene: A British Actress on the American Stage, 1826–1873.* Jefferson, NC: McFarland, 1993 and 1997.

Buchanan, Allen. *Secession.* Boulder, CO: Westview Press, 1991.

Buck, Irving A. *Cleburne and His Command.* Wilmington: Broadfoot Publishing Co., 1995.

Buell, Thomas B. *The Warrior Generals: Combat Leadership in the Civil War.* New York: Three Rivers Press, 1997.

Buell, Walter. *Joshua R. Giddings: A Sketch.* Cleveland: W. W. Williams, 1882.

Buenger, Walter L. *Secession and the Union in Texas.* Austin: University of Texas Press, 1984.

Buker, George E. *Blockaders, Refugees, & Contrabands: Civil War on Florida's Gulf Coast, 1861–1865.* Tuscaloosa: University of Alabama Press, 1993.

Bullard, F. Lewiston. *Famous War Correspondents.* Boston: Little, Brown, 1914: 399–402.

Bulloch, James. *The Secret Service of the Confederate States in Europe, Or, How the Confederate Cruisers were Equipped.* Vols. 1 and 2. London: Richard Bentley & Son, 1883.

Burdett, Susan. "The Military Career of Brigadier-General Joseph Finegan of Florida." M.A. thesis, Columbia University, 1930.

Burgess, Lauren Cook, ed. *An Uncommon Soldier: The Civil War Letters of Sarah Rosetta Wakeman, Alias Pvt. Lyons Wakeman, 153rd Regiment, New York State Volunteers, 1862–1864.* Pasadena, MD: MINERVA Center, 1994.

Burgess, Milton V. *David Gregg; Pennsylvania Cavalryman.* State College, PA: Nittany Valley Offset, 1984.

Burke, Walter E. *Quartermaster: A Brief Account of the Life of Colonel Abraham Charles Myers, Quartermaster General, C.S.A.* Fort Myers, FL: Southwest Florida Historical Society, 1976.

Burlingame, Michael, and John R. Turner Ettlinger, eds. *Inside Lincoln's White House: The Complete Civil Diary of John Hay.* Carbondale: Southern Illinois University Press, 1997.

Burlingame, Sara Lee. "The Making of a Spoilsman: The Life and Career of Roscoe Conkling from 1829 to 1873." Ph.D. dissertation, Johns Hopkins University, 1974.

Burnett, Henry Lawrence. "Assassination of President Lincoln and the Trials of the Assassins." In *History of the Ohio Society of New York, 1885–1905.* Edited by James H. Kennedy. New York: Grafton Press, 1906.

———. *Some Incidents in the Trial of President Lincoln's Assassins. The Controversy between President Johnson and Judge Holt.* New York: D. Appleton, 1891.

Burns, Frank. *Tennessee County History Series Wilson County.* Edited by Robert E. Corlew. Memphis: Memphis State University Press, 1983.

Burns, John. File, Adams County Historical Society. Adams County, PA.

———. Vertical File V8–28, Library, Gettysburg National Military Park, Gettysburg, PA.

Burnside, William H. *The Honorable Powell Clayton.* Conway: University of Central Arkansas Press, 1991.

Burroughs, William Berrien. "A Lady Commissioned Captain in the Army of the Confederate States." *Southern Practitioner* 13 (1909), 532–534.

Burt, Jesse C. *Nashville: Its Life and Times.* Nashville: Tennessee Book Co., 1959.

Burt, Nathaniel. *The Perennial Philadelphians.* New York: Arno Press, 1975.

Burton, David H. *Clara Barton: In the Service of Humanity.* Westport: Greenwood Press, 1995.

Burton, E. Milby. *The Seige of Charleston: 1861–1865.* Columbia: University of South Carolina Press, 1970.

Burton, Matthew Wade. "The River of Blood and the Valley of Death: The Lives of Two Cousins for the Cause, Robert Selden Garnett and Richard Brooke Garnett, C.S.A." M.A. thesis, Bowling Green State University, 1996.

Burton, Theodore E. *John Sherman.* Boston: Houghton Mifflin, 1906.

Burton, William L. *Melting Pot Soldiers: The Union's Ethnic Regiments.* 1988. Reprint. New York: Fordham Unversity Press, 1998.

Busch, Francis X. *Enemies of the State.* Indianapolis: Bobbs-Merrill, 1954.

Bushong, Millard K. *Old Jube: A Biography of General Jubal A. Early.* Shippensburg, PA: White Mane, 1988.

Bushong, Millard K., and Dean M. Bushong. *Fightin' Tom Rosser, C.S.A.* Shippensburg, PA: Beidel Printing House, 1983.

Butler, Benjamin F. *Autobiography and Personal Reminiscences of Major-General Benjamin F. Butler.* Boston: A. M. Thayer & Co., 1892.

———. *Private and Official Correspondence of Benjamin F. Butler.* Norwood, MA: Plimpton Press, 1917.

Butler, Lindley S. *Pirates, Privateers, and Rebel Raiders of the Carolina Coast.* Chapel Hill: University of North Carolina Press, 2000.

Bynum, Victoria E. *Unruly Women: The Politics of Social and Sexual Control in the Old South.* Chapel Hill: University of North Carolina Press, 1992.

Byrne, Frank L. *Prophet of Prohibition: Neal Dow and His Crusade.* Madison: State Historical Society of Wisconsin, 1961.

Cain, Marvin R. *Lincoln's Attorney General: Edward Bates of Missouri.* Columbia: University of Missouri Press, 1965.

Cain, William E., ed. *William Lloyd Garrison and the Fight against Slavery: Selections from* The Liberator. Boston: St. Martin's Press, 1995.

Caldwell, Bettie D., ed. *Founders and Builders of Greensboro, 1808–1908.* Greensboro: J. J. Stone, 1925.

Caldwell, J. F. J. *The History of a Brigade of South Carolinians First Known as Gregg's and Subsequently as McGowan's*

Brigade. Philadelphia: King & Baird Printers, 1866.

Caldwell, Joshua W. *Sketches of the Bench and Bar of Tennessee.* Knoxville: Ogden Brothers & Co., 1898.

Caldwell, Martha B. "The Attitude of Kansas toward Reconstruction before 1875." Ph.D. dissertation, University of Kansas, 1933.

Caldwell, Willie Walker. *Stonewall Jim: A Biography of General James A. Walker, C.S.A.* Elliston, VA: Northcross House, 1990.

Calhoun, Charles W. *Gilded Age Cato: The Life of Walter Q. Gresham.* Lexington: University Press of Kentucky, 1988.

———. "Oliver P. Morton." *Encyclopedia of Indianapolis.* Bloomington and Indianapolis: Indiana University Press, 1994.

Calhoun, John C. *A Discourse on the Constitution and Government of the United States, in Union and Liberty: The Political Philosophy of John C. Calhoun.* Edited by Ross M. Lence. Indianapolis: Liberty Fund, 1992.

Calkins, Chris M. *The Appomattox Campaign, March 29–April 9, 1865.* Conshohocken, PA: Combined Books, 1997.

———. *From Petersburg to Appomattox: A Tour Guide to the Routes of Lee's Withdrawal and Grant's Pursuit.* Farmville, VA: Farmville Herald, 1983.

———. *Thirty-Six Hours before Appomattox.* VA: Published by the author, 1980.

Cameron, Bill. "The Signal Corps at Gettysburg." *Gettysburg Magazine* 3 (July 1990).

Camp, Vaughn, Jr. "Captain Brannan's Dilemma: Key West 1861." *Tequesta* 20 (1960): 31–33.

Campbell, Edward Christian. "James Alexander Walker: A Biography." M.A. thesis, Virginia Polytechnic Institute and State University, 1972.

Campbell, J. E. "Sumner, Brooks, Burlingame, or the Last of the Great Challenges." *Ohio Archaeological and Historical Society* 34 (1925): 435–473.

Campbell, John A. *Reminiscences and Documents Relating to the Civil War during the Year 1865.* Baltimore: John Murphy & Co., 1887.

Campbell, Stanley W. *The Slave Catchers: Enforcement of the Fugitive Slave Law, 1850–1860.* Chapel Hill: University of North Carolina Press, 1968.

Canan, Howard V. "Missouri Paw Paw Militia of 1863–1864." *Missouri Historical Review,* 62 (July 1968): 431–448.

Candela, Gregory L. "William Wells Brown." *Dictionary of Literary Biography. Vol. 50: Afro-American Writers before the Harlem Renaissance.* Edited by Trudier Harris. Detroit: Gale Research Co., 1986: 18–31.

Candler, Allen D., ed. *The Confederate Records of the State of Georgia.* 6 vols. Atlanta: Chas. P. Byrd, 1910.

Candler, Allen D., and Clement A. Evans, eds. *Cyclopedia of Georgia.* 3 vols. Atlanta: State Historical Association, 1906.

Cannan, John. *The Atlanta Campaign, May–November, 1864.* Conshohocken, PA: Combined Books, 1991.

———, ed. *War in the West: Shiloh to Vicksburg, 1862–1863: Eyewitness History of the Civil War.* New York: Gallery Books, 1990.

Canney, Donald L. *Lincoln's Navy: The Ships, Men, and Organization, 1861–1865.* Annapolis, MD: Naval Institute Press, 1998.

———. *The Old Steam Navy (Volume 2): The Ironclads, 1842–1885.* Annapolis, MD: Naval Institute Press, 1993.

———. *U.S. Coast Guard and Revenue Cutters, 1790–1935.* Annapolis, MD: Naval Institute Press, 1995.

Cannon, Devereaux D., Jr. *The Flags of the Confederacy, An Illustrated History.* Memphis: St. Lukes Press, 1988.

———. *The Flags of the Union, An Illustrated History.* Memphis: St. Luke's Press, 1993.

Cantrell, Greg. "Southern and Nativist: Kenneth Rayner and the Ideology of 'Americanism.'" *North Carolina Historical Review* 69 (April 1992).

Capers, Gerald M., Jr. "Confederates and Yankees in Occupied New Orleans, 1862–1865." *Journal of Southern History* 30 (1964): 405–426.

Capers, Henry D. *The Life and Times of C. G. Memminger.* Richmond, VA: Everett Waddey Co., 1893.

Carby, Hazel. *Reconstructing Womanhood: The Emergence of the Afro-American Woman Novelist.* New York: Oxford University Press, 1987.

Carded Service Records of Hospital Attendants, Matrons, and Nurses, 1861–1865. Record Group 94. National Archives, Washington, DC.

Cardoso, Joaquin Jose. "Hinton Rowan Helper: A Nineteenth Century Pilgrimage." Ph.D. dissertation, University of Wisconsin, 1967.

Carey, Anthony Gene. *Parties, Slavery and the Union in Antebellum Georgia.* Athens: University of Georgia Press, 1997.

Carey, Henry C. *The Harmony of Interests: Agriculture, Manufactures, and Commercial.* 1851. Reprint. New York: Augustus M. Kelley, 1976.

Carlebach, Michael L. *The Origins of Photojournalism in America.* Washington, DC: Smithsonian Institution Press, 1992

Carlesimo, Peter. "The Refugee Home Society: Its Origin, Operation and Results, 1851–1976." M.A. thesis, University of Windsor, 1973.

Carlson, David. "'The Distemper of the Time': Conscription, the Courts, and Planter Privilege in Civil War South Georgia." *The Journal of Southwest Georgia History* 13 (1999): 1–24.

Carlson, Gretchen. "Francis Jay Herron." *Palimpsest,* 11 (April 1930): 141–150.

Carlson, Oliver. *The Man Who Made the News.* New York: Sloan and Pearce, 1942.

Carlson, Paul H. *The Plains Indians.* College Station: Texas A&M University Press, 1998.

Carosso, Vincent P. *The Morgans: Private International Bankers, 1854–1913.* Cambridge, MA: Harvard University, 1987.

Carpenter, John A. *Sword and Olive Branch: Oliver Otis Howard.* Pittsburgh: University of Pittsburgh Press, 1964.

Carr, Albert Z. *The World and William Walker.* New York: Harper & Row, 1963.

Carroll, Anna Ella. *Reply to the Speech of Hon. J. C. Breckinridge.* Washington, DC: Henry Polkinhorn, 1861.

———. *The War Powers of the General Government.* Washington, DC: Henry Polkinhorn, 1861.

Carroll, Daniel B. *Henri Mercier and the American Civil War.* Princeton, NJ: Princeton University Press, 1971.

Carroll, John M. *Cyclorama of General Custer's Last Fight: A Reproduction of the Original Document Complete in All Respects, and with an Introduction.* Appendices by John M. Carroll and Brian Pohanka. El Segundo, CA: Upton & Sons, 1988.

———, ed. *Register of Officers of the Confederate States Navy, 1861–1865.* Mattituck, NY: J. M. Carroll & Co., 1983.

Carson, Christopher H. *Kit Carson's Autobiography.* Edited by Milo Milton Quaife. Lincoln: University of Nebraska Press, 1935.

Carson, James Petigru, ed. *The Life, Letters, and Speeches of James Louis Petigru, the Union Man of South Carolina.* Washington, DC: W. H. Powdermilk, 1920.

Carter, Harvey Lewis. *Dear Old Kit: The Historical Christopher*

Carson. Norman: University of Oklahoma Press, 1968.

Carter, Ruth C. *For Honor Glory and Union: The Mexican and Civil War Letters of Brig. Gen. William Haines Lytle.* Lexington: University Press of Kentucky, 1999.

Carter, Samuel, III. *The Final Fortress: The Campaign for Vicksburg, 1862–1863.* New York: St. Martin's Press, 1980.

———. *The Last Cavaliers: Confederate and Union Cavalry in the Civil War.* New York: St. Martin's Press, 1979.

Casdorph, Paul D. *Prince John Magruder: His Life and Campaigns.* New York: John Wiley & Sons, 1996.

Case, Lynn M., and Warren F. Spencer. *The United States and France: Civil War Diplomacy.* Philadelphia: University of Pennsylvania Press, 1970.

Casey, Silas. *Infantry Tactics, for the Instruction, Exercise, and Manoeuvers of The Soldier, A Company, Line of Skirmishers, Battalion, Brigade, or Corps D' Armee.* 3 vols. 1862. Reprint (3 vols. in 1). Dayton, OH: Morningside House, 1985.

Cash, W. J. *The Mind of the South.* New York: Alfred A. Knopf, 1941. Reprint. New York: Vintage, 1991.

Cashin, Joan E. "Varina Howell Davis." In *Portraits of American Women: From Settlement to The Present.* Edited by G. J. Barker-Benfield and Catherine Clinton. New York: St. Martin's Press, 1991: 259–277.

Cashman, Diane Cobb. *Headstrong: The Biography of Amy Morris Bradley.* Wilmington, NC: Broadfoot Publishing, 1990.

Casler, John O. *Four Years in the Stonewall Brigade,* 4th rev. ed. Dayton, OH: Morningside Bookshop, 1971.

Castagna, JoAnn. "Women, Sexuality, and Popular Culture: Gender Identity in Sensation Novels of the 1850s." Ph.D. dissertation, University of Iowa, 1989.

Castel, Albert E. *Civil War Kansas: Reaping the Whirlwind.* 1958. Reprint. Lawrence: University Press of Kansas, 1997.

———. *Decision in the West: The Atlanta Campaign of 1864.* Lawrence: University Press of Kansas, 1992.

———. "The Fort Pillow Massacre: A Fresh Examination of the Evidence." *Civil War History* 4 (1958): 37–50.

———. *A Frontier State at War: Kansas, 1861–1865.* Ithaca, NY: Cornell University Press, 1958.

———. *General Sterling Price and the Civil War in the West.* Baton Rouge: Louisiana State University Press, 1968.

———. "The Guerrilla War, 1861–1865." *Civil War Times Illustrated* 13 (October 1974): 3–50.

———. "A New View of the Battle of Pea Ridge." *Missouri Historical Review* 62 (January 1968): 136–151.

———. *The Presidency of Andrew Johnson.* Lawrence, KS: Regents Press of Kansas, 1979.

———. "Theophilus Holmes—Pallbearer of the Confederacy." *Civil War Times Illustrated* 16 (July 1977): 11–17.

———. *William Clarke Quantrill: His Life and Times.* New York: Frederick Fell, 1962; paperback reprint, Norman: University of Oklahoma Press, 1998.

Castel, Albert E., and Thomas Goodrich. *Bloody Bill Anderson: The Short, Savage Life of a Civil War Guerrilla.* Mechanicsburg, PA: Stackpole, 1998.

Castle, Henry A. *Opdycke's Brigade at the Battle of Franklin.* Minneapolis: A. Davis, 1908.

Cate, Wirt Armistead. *Lucius Q. C. Lamar: Secession and Reunion.* Chapel Hill: University of North Carolina Press, 1935.

Cater, Harold Dean. *Henry Adams and His Friends.* Boston: Houghton Mifflin, 1947.

Catton, Bruce. *America Goes to War: The Civil War and Its Meaning in American Culture.* Hanover, MA: Wesleyan University Press, 1986.

———. *The Army of the Potomac: Glory Road.* Garden City, NY: Doubleday, 1952.

———. *The Coming Fury. The Centennial History of The Civil War.* Vol. 1. Garden City, NY: Doubleday, 1961.

———. *Grant Moves South.* Boston and Toronto: Little, Brown, 1960.

———. *Grant Takes Command.* Boston: Little, Brown, 1968.

———. *Mr. Lincoln's Army.* New York: Doubleday, 1951.

———. *Never Call Retreat. The Centennial History of The Civil War.* Vol. 3. Garden City, NY: Doubleday, 1965.

———. *Reflections on the Civil War.* Edited by John Leekley. Garden City, NY: Doubleday, 1981.

———. *A Stillness at Appomattox.* Garden City, NY: Doubleday, 1953.

———. *Terrible Swift Sword. The Centennial History of The Civil War.* Vol. 2. Garden City, NY: Doubleday, 1963.

———. *This Hallowed Ground: The Story of The Union Side of The Civil War.* New York: Doubleday, 1961.

Cauble, Frank P. *Biography of Wilmer McLean.* Lynchburg, VA: H. E. Howard, 1987.

———. *The Surrender Proceedings: April 9, 1865, Appomattox Court House.* The Virginia Civil War Battles and Leaders Series. Lynchburg, VA: H. E. Howard, 1987.

Cauthen, Charles Edward. *South Carolina Goes to War, 1861–1865.* Chapel Hill: University of North Carolina Press, 1950.

Cavanagh, Michael. *Memoirs of General Thomas Francis Meagher.* Worcester, MA: Messenger Press, 1892.

Cavananaugh, Michael A., and William Marvel. *The Petersburg Campaign: The Battle of the Crater "The Horrid Pit," June 25–August 6, 1864.* Lynchburg, VA: H. E. Howard, Inc, 1989.

Cecchini, Bridget Theresa. "The Battle of Atlanta' Cyclorama (1885–1886) as Narrative Indicator of a National Perspective on the Civil War." M.A. thesis, Rice University, 1998.

Censer, Jane Turner, ed. *The Papers of Frederick Law Olmsted, IV, Defending the Union: The Civil War and the U.S. Sanitary Commission.* Baltimore: Johns Hopkins University Press, 1986.

Ceplair, Larry, ed. *The Public Years of Sarah and Angelina Grimké: Selected Writings 1835–1839.* New York: Columbia University Press, 1989.

Chaffin, Tom. *Fatal Glory: Narciso Lopez and the First Clandestine U.S. War against Cuba.* Charlottesville: University of Virginia Press, 1996.

Chalfant, Harry Malcolm. *These Agitators and Their Idea.* Nashville, TN: Cokesbury Press, 1931.

Chamberlain, Joshua Lawrence. *The Passing of the Armies: An Account of the Final Campaign of the Army of the Potomac, Based upon Personal Reminiscences of the Fifth Army Corps.* 1915. Reprint. Dayton, OH: Morningside Bookshop Press, 1994.

Chamberlain, Muriel E. *British Foreign Policy in the Age of Palmerston.* London: Longaman, 1980.

Chamlee, Roy. *Lincoln's Assassins: A Complete Account of their Capture, Trial, and Punishment.* Jefferson, NC: McFarland, 1990.

Chance, Joseph E., ed. *My Life in the Old Army: The Reminiscences of Abner Doubleday from the Collections of the New York Historical Society.* Fort Worth: Texas Christian University Press, 1998.

Chandler, Alfred D., Jr. *The Visible Hand: The Managerial Revolution in American Business.* Cambridge, MA: Harvard University Press, 1977.

Chandler, Peleg W. *Memoir of the Hon. John Albion Andrew.* Cambridge, MA: J. Wilson & Son, 1880.

Channing, Steven A. *Crisis of Fear: Secession in South Carolina.* New York: W. W. Norton, 1974.

Chaput, Donald. "Generals, Indian Agents, Politicians: The Doolittle Survey of 1865." *Western Historical Quarterly* 3 (July 1972): 269–282.

"Charleston Battles and Seacoast Operations in South Carolina." In *Civil War Regiments: A Journal of the American Civil War.* Vol. 5, no. 2. Campbell, CA: Regimental Studies, 1996.

Cheek, William, and Aimee Lee Cheek. *John Mercer Langston and the Fight for Black Freedom, 1829–1865.* Urbana: University of Illinois Press, 1989.

Chernow, Ron. *The House of Morgan: An American Banking Dynasty and the Rise of Modern Finance.* New York: Atlantic Monthly, 1990.

Chesnut James. *James Chesnut, Jr., Papers, 1779–1872, Camden, Kershaw District, South Carolina.* Frederick, MD: University Publications of America, 1986.

Chesson, Michael B. "Harlots or Heroines? A New Look at the Richmond Bread Riot." *Virginia Magazine of History and Biography* 92 (1984): 131–175.

Chipman, Norton Parker. *The Tragedy of Andersonville.* San Francisco: Published by the author, 1911.

Chittenden, L. E. *Report of the Peace Convention in 1861.* 1864. Reprint. New York: Da Capo Press, 1971.

Chitwood, Oliver Perry. *John Tyler: Champion of the Old South.* 2d ed. Newtown, CT: American Political Biography Press, 1996.

Christ, Mark K., ed. *Rugged and Sublime: The Civil War in Arkansas.* Fayetteville: University of Arkansas Press, 1994.

Christman, William E. *Undaunted: The History of Fort McAllister.* Darien, GA: Darien Printing and Graphics, 1996.

Christopher, Maurine. *America's Black Congressmen.* New York: Thomas Y. Crowell Co., 1971.

Churchill, Robert H. "Liberty, Conscription, and Delusions of Grandeur: The Sons of Liberty Conspiracy of 1863–64." *Prologue Quarterly* 30 (Winter 1998): 295–304.

Cikovsky, Nicolai, Jr., and Franklin Kelly. *Winslow Homer.* New Haven, CT: Yale University Press, 1995.

Cimbala, Paul A. *Under the Guardianship of the Nation: The Freedmen's Bureau and the Reconstruction of Georgia, 1865–1870.* Athens: University of Georgia Press, 1997.

Cimbala, Paul A., and Randall M. Miller, eds. *The Freedmen's Bureau and Reconstruction: Reconsiderations.* New York: Fordham University Press, 1999.

Cimprich, John, and Robert Mainfort, Jr. "The Fort Pillow Massacre: A Statistical Note." *Journal of American History* 76 (1989): 830–837.

Cimprich, John Vincent. "The Development of John Sherman's Views on Slavery and the Freedmen, 1861–1867." M.A. thesis, Ohio State University, 1973.

Cisco, Walter Brian. *States Rights Gist: A South Carolina General of the Civil War.* Shippensburg, PA: White Mane Publishing Co., 1991.

Cist, Henry M. *The Army of the Cumberland.* New York: Charles Scribner's Sons, 1882.

Civil War Naval Chronology 1861–1865: Compiled by the Naval History Division, Navy Department. Washington, DC: 1971.

Clapp, Margaret. *Forgotten First Citizen: John Bigelow.* Boston: Little, Brown, 1947.

Clark, Clifford E., Jr. *Henry Ward Beecher: Spokesman for Middle-Class America.* Chicago: University of Illinois Press, 1978.

Clark, Daniel Elbert. *Samuel Jordan Kirkwood.* Iowa City: State Historical Society of Iowa, 1917.

Clark, Walter, ed. *Histories of the Several Regiments and Battalions from North Carolina in the Great War, 1861–1865.* 5 vols. Raleigh: State of North Carolina, 1901.

Clausius, Gerhard. "The Little Soldier of the 95th: Albert D. J. Cashier." *Journal of the Illinois State Historical Society* 51 (Winter 1958): 380–387.

Clay, Cassius Marcellus. *Life of Cassius Marcellus Clay: Memoirs, Writings and Speeches.* Cincinnati: J. Fletcher Brennag & Co., 1886.

Clay-Clopton, Virginia. *A Belle of the Fifties: Memoirs of Mrs. Clay of Alabama, Covering Social and Political Life in Washington and the South, 1853–66; Put into Narrative Form by Ada Sterling.* New York: Doubleday, Page, 1905.

Cleaves, Freeman. *Meade of Gettysburg.* 1960. Reprint. Dayton, OH: Press of Morningside, 1980.

———. *Rock of Chickamauga, the Life of General George H. Thomas.* 1948. Reprint. Westport, CT: Greenwood Press, 1974.

Clements, J. B. *History of Irwin County.* Spartanburg, SC: Reprint Co., 1989.

Clifford, Deborah Pickman. *Mine Eyes Have Seen the Glory: A Biography of Julia Ward Howe.* Boston: Little, Brown, 1979.

Clift, G. Glenn. *Governors of Kentucky, 1792–1942.* Cynthiana, KY: Hobson Press, 1942.

Cline, William R. "The Ironclad Ram *Virginia.*" *Southern Historical Society Papers* 32 (1904): 243–249.

Clinton, Catherine, and Nina Silber, eds. *Divided Houses: Gender and the Civil War.* New York: Oxford University Press, 1992.

Clodfelter, Michael. *The Dakota War: The United States Army Versus the Sioux, 1862–1865.* Jefferson, NC: McFarland, 1998.

Clothier, Isaac. *Letters, 1853–1868, William Jackson Palmer.* Philadelphia: Ketterlinus, 1906.

Coburn, Jacob Osborn. *Hell on Belle Isle: Diary of a Civil War POW: Journal of Sgt. Jacob Osborn Coburn.* Bryan, OH: Faded Banner Publications, 1997.

Coburn, Mark. "The Man They Loved to Hate: Petroleum V. Nasby, America's Own Rascal." *Civil War Times Illustrated* 26 (1987): 36–43.

Cockrell, Monroe F., ed. *The Lost Account of the Battle of Corinth and the Court Martial of General Earl Van Dorn.* Jackson, TN: McCowat-Mercer Press, 1955.

Coco, Gregory A. *On the Bloodstained Field: 130 Human Interest Stories of the Campaign and Battle of Gettysburg.* Gettysburg, PA: Thomas Pub., 1987.

Coddington, Edwin B. *The Gettysburg Campaign: A Study in Command.* New York: Charles Scribner's Sons, 1968.

———. "The Strange Reputation of George G. Meade: A Lesson in Historiography." *The Historian* 23 (1962): 145–166.

Coffey, David. *John Bell Hood and the Struggle for Atlanta.* Abilene: McWhiney Foundation Press, 1998.

Coffin, Howard. *Full Duty: Vermonters in the Civil War.* Woodstock, VT: Countryman Press, 1993.

———. *Nine Months to Gettysburg: Stannard's Vermonters and the Repulse of Pickett's Charge.* New York: W. W. Norton, 1997.

Coggins, Jack. *Arms and Equipment of the Civil War.* Wilmington, NC: Broadfoot Publishing Co., 1989.

Cohen, Stan B. *The Civil War in West Virginia, a Pictorial History.* Charleston, WV: Pictorial Histories Publishing Companies, 1976.

———. *A Pictorial Guide to West Virginia's Civil War Sites and Related Information.* Charleston, WV: Pictorial Histories Publishing Companies, 1990.

Coker, Kathy R., and Carol E. Rios. *A Concise History of the U.S. Army Signal Corps.* Fort Gordon, GA: Office of the

Command Historian, 1988.

Colbert, Thomas Burnell. "Prophet of Progress: The Life and Times of Elias Cornelius Boudinot." Ph.D. dissertation, Oklahoma State University, 1982.

Cole, Birdie Hale. "The Battle of Pilot Knob." *Confederate Veteran* (September 1914).

Coleman, Ann Mary. *The Life of John J. Crittenden, with Selections from His Correspondence and Speeches.* 2 vols. Philadelphia: J. B. Lippincott, 1871.

Coleman, Charles Hubert, and Paul B. Spence. "The Charleston Riot, March 28, 1864." *Journal of the Illinois State Historical Society* 33 (1940): 7–56.

Coleman, Kenneth. "The Administration of Alfred H. Colquitt as Governor of Georgia." M.A. thesis, University of Georgia, 1940.

Coleman, S. B., and Paul Stevens. "A July Morning with the Rebel Ram *Arkansas.*" *U.S. Naval Institute Proceedings* 88 (7:1962): 84–97.

Coles, David J. "Far from Fields of Glory: Military Operations in Florida during the Civil War, 1864–1865." Ph.D. dissertation, Florida State University, 1996.

———. "Unpretending Service: The *James L. Davis,* the *Tahoma,* and the East Gulf Blockading Squadron." *Florida Historical Quarterly* 71 (July 1992): 41–62.

Collier, Mark C. *Engagement at Piedmont, Va., June 5th, 1864.* Bridgewater, VA: Collier Mapping, 1997.

Collins, Darrell L. *Jackson's Valley Campaign. The Battles of Cross Keys and Port Republic, June 8–9, 1862.* Lynchburg, VA: H. E. Howard, 1993.

Collins, George K. *Memoirs of the 149th Regt. N. Y. Vol. Inf., 3d Greene/Kuhl Brig., 2nd Div., 12th and 20th A.C.* 1891. Reprint, with a foreword by Harry W. Pfanz. Hamilton, NY: Edmonston Publishing, 1995.

Collins, Lewis. *Collins' Historical Sketches of Kentucky: History of Kentucky.* 2 vols. 1874. Reprint. Frankfort: Kentucky Historical Society, 1966.

Colton, Kenneth E., ed. "With Fremont in Missouri in 1861: Letters of Samuel Ryan Curtis." *Annals of Iowa* 24 (October 1942): 105–167.

Colton, Ray Charles. *The Civil War in the Western Territories: Arizona, Colorado, New Mexico, and Utah.* Norman: University of Oklahoma Press, 1959.

Commager, Henry S. *Theodore Parker: Yankee Crusader.* Boston: Little, Brown, 1936.

Comstock, Cyrus Ballou. *The Diary of Cyrus B. Comstock.* Dayton, OH: Morningside, 1987.

Confederate States of America, Engineering Department. *Estimate of Five Hundred Thousand Dollars Required to Meet the Just Claims Presented, or to be Presented Hereafter, for the Loss of Slaves Who Have Been Impressed in the State of Virginia.* Richmond, VA: Confederate States of America, 1864.

Confederate States of America, War Department. *Communication of the Secretary of War Relative to the Number of Able-bodied Men between the Ages of Eighteen and Forty-Five.* Richmond, VA: Confederate States of America, 1865.

Conkin, Paul K. *Prophets of Prosperity: America's First Political Economists.* Bloomington: Indiana University Press, 1980.

———. *Self-Evident Truths: Being a Discourse on the Origins and Developments of the First Principles of American Government— Popular Sovereignty, Natural Rights, and Balance and Separation of Powers.* Bloomington: Indiana University Press, 1974.

Conklin, Eileen. *Women at Gettysburg, 1863.* Gettysburg, PA: Thomas Publications, 1993.

Conkling, Alfred R. *The Life and Letters of Roscoe Conkling, Orator, Statesman, Advocate.* New York: Charles L. Webster, 1889.

Connelley, William E. *James Henry Lane: The "Grim Chieftain" of Kansas.* Topeka: Crane, 1899.

———. *Quantrill and the Border Wars.* Cedar Rapids, Iowa: The Torch Press, 1910.

Connelly, James F. *The Visit of Archbishop Bedini to the United States of America.* Rome: Serves Facultatis Historiae Ecclesiastiae Libreria Eatrice dell' Universita Gregonanci, vol. 109, 1960.

Connelly, Thomas L. *Army of the Heartland: The Army of Tennessee, 1861–1862.* Baton Rouge: Louisiana State University Press, 1967.

———. *Autumn of Glory: The Army of Tennessee, 1862–1865.* Baton Rouge: Louisiana State University Press, 1971.

———. *Civil War Tennessee: Battles and Leaders.* Knoxville: University of Tennessee Press, 1979.

Connelly, Thomas L., and Archer Jones. *The Politics of Command: Factions and Ideas in Confederate Strategy.* Baton Rouge: Louisiana State University Press, 1973.

Connor, Henry G. *George Davis.* Wilmington, NC: United Daughters of the Confederacy, North Carolina Division, 1911.

Connor, Seymour V. *Battle of Texas.* Waco: Texian Press, 1967.

Conrad, Earl. *Harriet Tubman.* Washington, DC: Associated Publishers, 1943.

Conyngham, David P. *The Irish Brigade and Its Campaigns.* Edited by Lawrence F. Kohl. 1867. Reprint. New York: Fordham University Press, 1994.

Cook, Adrian. *The Alabama Claims: American Politics and Anglo-American Relations, 1865–1872.* Ithaca, NY: Cornell University Press, 1975.

———. *The Armies of the Streets: The New York City Draft Riots of 1863.* Lexington: University Press of Kentucky, 1974.

Cook, D. P. *The North, the South, and the Powers 1861–1865.* New York: Wiley, 1974.

Cook, Harvey Toliver. *The Life Work of James Clement Furman.* Greenville, SC: Alester G. Furman, 1926.

Cook, Robert. "The Grave of All My Comforts: William Pitt Fessenden as Secretary of the Treasury, 1864–1865." *Civil War History* 41 (September 1995): 208–226.

Cook, Roy Bird. "Albert Gallatin Jenkins—A Confederate Portrait." *West Virginia Review* 11 (1934): 225–227.

Cooke, Donald E. *For Conspicuous Gallantry... Winners of the Medal of Honor.* Maplewood, NJ: C. S. Hammond, 1966.

Cooke, Philip St. George. *Cavalry Tactics: or, Regulations for the Instruction, Formations, and Movements of the Cavalry of the Army and Volunteers of the United States.* Washington, DC: Government Printing Office, 1862.

———. *The Conquest of New Mexico and California: An Historical and Personal Narrative.* New York: Putnam, 1878.

———. *Scenes and Adventures in the Army; or, Romance of Military Life.* Philadelphia, PA: Lindsay & Blakiston, 1857.

———. *William Henry Chase Whiting, and François Xavier Aubry. Exploring Southwestern Trails, 1846–1854.* Edited by Ralph P. Bieber and Averam B. Bender. Philadelphia, PA: Porcupine Press, 1974.

Cooley, Raymond K. "John M. Daniel, Editor of the Richmond Examiner and Gadfly of the Confederacy." M.A. thesis, Old Dominion University, 1973.

Cooling, Benjamin Franklin. *Forts Henry and Donelson: The Key to the Confederate Heartland.* Knoxville: University of Tennessee Press, 1987.

———. *Jubal Early's Raid on Washington, 1864.* Baltimore: Nautical & Aviation Publishing Company of America, 1989.

———. *Monocacy: The Battle that Saved Washington.* Shippensburg, PA: White Mane, 1997.

Cooper, Afua. "The Search for Mary Bibb, Black Woman Teacher in Nineteenth-Century Canada West." *Ontario History* [Canada] 1991 83 (1): 39–54.

Cooper, George. *Lost Love: A True Story of Passion, Murder, and Justice.* New York: Paragon House, 1993.

Cooper, William J., Jr. *Jefferson Davis.* New York: Knopf, 2000.

———. *The South and the Politics of Slavery, 1828–1856.* Baton Rouge: Louisiana State University Press, 1973.

Corbin, Diana Fontaine. *A Life of Matthew Fontaine Maury.* London: S. Low, Marston, Searle, and Rivington, 1888.

Corby, William. *Memoirs of Chaplain Life: Three Years in the Irish Brigade with the Army of the Potomac.* Edited by Lawrence F. Kohl. New York: Fordham University Press, 1992.

Cordley, Richard. *History of Lawrence, Kansas, from the First Settlement to the Close of the Rebellion.* Lawrence: E. F. Caldwell, 1895.

Cormier, Steven A. *The Siege of Suffolk.* Lynchburg: H. E. Howard, 1989.

Cornish, Dudley Taylor. "Kansas Negro Regiments in the Civil War." *Kansas Historical Quarterly* 21 (May 1953): 417–429.

———. *The Sable Arm: Negro Troops in the Union Army, 1861–1865.* New York: W. W. Norton, 1966.

Cornish, Dudley Taylor, and Virginia Dean Laas. *Lincoln's Lee: The Life of Samuel Phillips Lee, United States Navy, 1812–1897.* Lawrence: University Press of Kansas, 1986.

Cortissoz, Royal. *The Life of Whitelaw Reid.* 2 vols. New York: Charles Scribner's Sons, 1921.

Cortner, Richard C. *The Supreme Court and the Second Bill of Rights, the Fourteenth Amendment and the Nationalization of Civil Liberties.* Madison: University of Wisconsin Press, 1981.

Corwin, Edwin S. "National Power and State Interposition, 1787–1861." *Michigan Law Review* 10 (1912): 535–551.

Coryell, Janet L. *Neither Heroine nor Fool: Anna Ella Carroll of Maryland.* Kent, OH: Kent State University Press, 1990.

Coski, John M. *The Army of the Potomac at Berkeley Plantation: The Harrison's Landing Occupation of 1862.* Richmond, VA: J. M. Coski, 1989.

Cotham, Edward T., Jr. *Battle on the Bay: The Civil War Struggle for Galveston.* Austin: University of Texas Press, 1998.

Cotterill, Robert Spencer. "James Guthrie—Kentuckian, 1792–1869." *Register of the Kentucky Historical Society* 20 (1922): 290–296.

Cottingham, Carl D., Preston Michael Jones, and Gary W. Kent. *General John A. Logan: His Life and Times.* Carbondale: American Kestrel Books, 1989.

Cottom, Robert I., Jr., and Mary Ellen Hayward. *Maryland in the Civil War.* Baltimore: Maryland Historical Society, 1994.

Couch, Darius N. "Obituary of Cadmus Wilcox." In *Twenty-second Annual Reunion of the Association of the Graduates of the United States Military Academy.* n.p., 1891.

Coulter, E. Merton. *The Civil War and Readjustment in Kentucky.* Chapel Hill: University of North Carolina Press, 1926.

Cover, Robert M. *Justice Accused: Anti-Slavery and the Judicial Process.* New Haven, CT: Yale University Press, 1975.

Cox, George. "Sidelights on the *Chesapeake* Affair, 1863–64." *Royal Nova Scotia Historical Society Collections* 29 (1951): 124–137.

Cox, Jacob Dolson. *Atlanta.* New York: Charles Scribner's Sons, 1882.

———. *Military Reminiscences of the Civil War.* 2 vols. New York: Charles Scribner's Sons, 1900.

Cox, Karen Lynne. "Women, the Lost Cause, and the New South: The United Daughters of the Confederacy and the Transmission of Confederate Culture, 1894–1919." Ph.D. dissertation, University of Southern Mississippi, 1997.

Cox, LaWanda. *Lincoln and Black Freedom: A Study in Presidential Leadership.* Columbia: University of South Carolina Press, 1981.

———. "Negro Suffrage and Republican Politics: The Problem of Motivation in Reconstruction Historiography." *Journal of Southern History* 33 (August 1967): 317–337.

———. "The Promise of Land for the Freedmen." *Mississippi Valley Historical Review* 45 (December 1958): 429–440.

Cox, William Van Zandt. *Life of Samuel Sullivan Cox.* Syracuse, NY: M. H. Northrup, 1899.

Cozzens, Peter. *The Civil War in the West: From Stones River to Chattanooga.* 3 vols. Champagne: University of Illinois Press, 1996.

———. *The Darkest Days of the War: The Battles of Iuka and Corinth.* Chapel Hill: University of North Carolina Press, 1997

———. *No Better Place to Die: The Battle of Stones River.* Urbana: University of Illinois Press, 1991.

———. *The Shipwreck of Their Hopes: The Battles for Chattanooga.* Urbana: University of Illinois Press, 1994.

———. *This Terrible Sound: The Battle of Chickamauga.* Urbana: University of Illinois Press, 1992.

Cozzens, Peter, and Robert I. Girandi, eds. *The Military Memoirs of General John Pope.* Chapel Hill: University of North Carolina Press, 1998.

Cracknell, William H. *Warship Profile: United States Monitors of the Civil War.* Windsor, UK: Profile Publications, 1973.

Craig, David R. "James J. Archer: The Little Gamecock." M.A. thesis, Morgan State University, 1983.

Craig, Reginald S. *The Fighting Parson.* Los Angeles: Westernlore Press, 1959.

Crapol, Edward P. "John Tyler and the Pursuit of National Destiny." *Journal of the Early Republic* 17 (Fall 1997): 467–491.

Craven, Avery O. *Edmund Ruffin, Southerner.* Baton Rouge: Louisiana State University Press, 1982.

Craven, Wayne. *The Sculptures at Gettysburg.* New York: Eastern Acorn Press, 1982.

Crawford, Martin. *The Anglo-American Crisis of the Mid-Nineteenth Century: "The Times" and America, 1850–1862.* Athens: University of Georgia Press, 1987.

Crawford, Richard, comp. *The Civil War Songbook.* New York: Dover Publications, 1977.

Crawford, Samuel J. *Kansas in the Sixties.* Chicago: A. C. McClurg & Co., 1911.

Creahan, John. *Life of Laura Keene: Actress, Artist, Manager and Scholar.* Philadelphia: Rodgers Publishing Co., 1897.

Crenshaw, Ollinger. "The Knights of the Golden Circle: The Career of George Bickley." *American Historical Review* 47 (October 1941): 23–50.

Cresap, Bernarr. *Appomattox Commander: The Story of E. O. C. Ord.* South Brunswick, N. J: A. S. Barnes, 1981.

Creveld, Martin Van. *Supplying War: Logistics from Wallenstein to Patton.* New York: The Free Press, 1977.

Critchlow, Donald T. "Studebaker: Wagonmaker/Automaker." *Timeline* 4 (2):16–29 (1987).

Crittenden, H. H. *The Battle of Westport and National Military Park.* Kansas City: Lowell Press, 1938.

Crofts, Daniel W. *Reluctant Confederates: Upper South Unionists in the Secession Crisis.* Chapel Hill: University of North Carolina Press, 1989.

Crompton, James. "The Second Division of the 16th Corps

in the Atlanta Campaign." In *The Atlanta Papers*. Compiled by Sydney C. Kerksis. Dayton, OH: Press of the Morningside Bookshop, 1980: 237–257.

Cron, Frederick William. "Colonel Bailey's Red River Dams." *The Military Engineer* 29 (December 1937): 421–424.

Crook, D. P. *Diplomacy during the American Civil War*. New York: John Wiley & Sons, 1975.

———. *The North, the South, and the Powers 1861–1865*. New York: John Wiley & Sons, 1974.

Crouch, Barry A. *The Freedmen's Bureau and Black Texans*. Austin: University of Texas Press, 1992.

Crouthamel, James L. *Bennett's New York Herald and the Rise of the Popular Press*. Syracuse, NY: Syracuse University Press. 1989.

———. *James Watson Webb: A Biography*. Middletown, CT: Wesleyan University Press, 1969.

Crow, Vernon H. *Storm in the Mountains: Thomas' Confederate Legion of Cherokee Indians and Mountaineers*. Cherokee NC: Press of the Museum of the Cherokee Indian, 1982.

Crowninshield, Benjamin W. *A History of the First Regiment of Massachusetts Cavalry Volunteers*. Cambridge, MA: Houghton Mifflin, 1891.

Crozier, Emmet. *Yankee Reporters, 1861–65*. New York: Oxford University Press, 1956.

Cubbison, Douglas R. "Midnight Engagement: John Geary's White Star Division at Wauhatchie." *Civil War Regiments: A Journal of the American Civil War* 3, no. 2 (1993): 70–104.

Cullen, Joseph P. "The Battle of Chancellorsville." *Civil War Times Illustrated* 7 (special issue, May 1968).

———. *The Peninsula Campaign, 1862: McClellan and Lee Struggle for Richmond*. Harrisburg, PA: Stackpole, 1973.

Cullop, Charles P. *Confederate Propaganda in Europe, 1861–1865*. Coral Gables, FL: University of Miami Press, 1969.

———. "Edwin De Leon, Jefferson Davis' Propagandist." *Civil War History* 8 (December 1962): 386–400.

———. "English Reaction to Stonewall Jackson's Death." *West Virginia History* 36 (1967): 1–5.

Cullum, George W. *Biographical Register of the Officers and Graduates of the U.S. Military Academy at West Point, New York, from its Establishment, in 1802, to 1890; with the Early History of the United States Military Academy*. New York: Houghton Mifflin, 1891. Reprint, 1940.

Culver, Francis, "Merryman Family, Part II." *Maryland Historical Magazine* 10 (1915): 176–177.

Cumming, Kate. *A Journal of Hospital Life in the Confederate Army of Tennessee*. Louisville, KY: John Morton, 1866.

———. *Kate: The Journal of a Confederate Nurse*, edited by Richard Barksdale Harwell. Baton Rouge: Louisiana State University Press, 1959.

Cummings, Charles M. "Forgotten Man at Fort Donelson: Bushrod Rust Johnson." *Tennessee Historical Quarterly* 27 (Winter 1969): 380–397.

———. *Yankee Quaker, Confederate General; the Curious Career of Bushrod Rust Johnson*. Rutherford, NJ: Fairleigh Dickinson University Press, 1971.

Cummings v. the State of Missouri, 71 U.S. 277 (1866).

Cunningham, Edward. *The Port Hudson Campaign, 1862–1863*. Baton Rouge: Louisiana State University Press, 1963.

Cunningham, Horace Herndon. *Doctors in Gray; the Confederate Medical Service*. Baton Rouge: Louisiana State University Press, 1958.

Cuppell, Charles. *History of Durrell's Battery in the Civil War*. Philadelphia: Neale, 1904.

Curl, Donald W. *Murat Halstead and the Cincinnati Commercial*. Boca Raton: University Presses of Florida, A Florida Atlantic University Book, 1980.

Curran, Thomas F. "Acclaim, Blame, and Civil War Memory: The Case of the Kidnapping of Two Union Generals." *West Virginia History* 57 (1998): 27–45.

———. "Memory, Myth, and Musty Records: Charles Woodson's Missouri Cavalry in the Army of Northern Virginia." *Missouri Historical Review* 94 (1999–2000).

Current, Richard N. *Lincoln and the First Shot*. Philadelphia: J. B. Lippincott Co., 1963.

———. *Lincoln's Loyalists: Union Soldiers from the Confederacy*. Boston: Northeastern University Press, 1992.

———. *Old Thad Stevens*. Madison: University of Wisconsin Press, 1942.

———. *Three Carpetbag Governors*. Baton Rouge: Louisiana State University Press, 1967.

Currie, Stephen. *Music in the Civil War*. Cincinnati: Betterway Books, 1992.

Curry, Charles. *John Brown Baldwin: Lawyer, Soldier, Statesman*. Staunton, VA: n.p., 1928.

Curry, Leonard P. *Blueprint for Modern America: Nonmilitary Legislation of First Civil War Congress*. Nashville, TN: Vanderbilt University Press, 1968.

———. "Congressional Democrats: 1861–1863." *Civil War History* 12 (September 1966): 213–299.

Curry, Richard O. "Copperheadism and Continuity: The Anatomy of a Stereotype." *Journal of Negro History* 57 (1972): 29–36.

Curti, Merle. *Peace or War: The American Struggle, 1636–1936*. New York: W. W. Norton, 1936.

Curtin, Andrew G. *Annual Message of the Governor of Pennsylvania, Andrew G Curtin, to the Legislature of Pennsylvania, at Harrisburg, 7 January 1864*. Harrisburg, PA: Singerly G. Myers, State Printers. 1864.

Curtis, Earl Guy. "Biography of John Milton Thayer." M.A. thesis. University of Nebraska, 1933.

Curtis, George Ticknor. *A Memoir of Benjamin Robbins Curtis, LL.D.: With Some of His Professional and Miscellaneous Writings*. Boston: Little, Brown, 1879.

Curtis, Newton Martin. *From Bull Run to Chancellorsville, the Story of the Sixteenth New York Infantry Together with Personal Reminiscences*. New York: G. P. Putnam's Sons, 1906.

Cushing, William B. *The Journal of Lt. Comdr. William B. Cushing, 1861–1865*. Washington, DC: National Archives and Records Service, General Services Administration, 1976.

Cutler, Bruce. *The Massacre at Sand Creek*. Livingston, MT: Clark City Press, 1993.

Cutrer, Thomas W. *Ben McCulloch and the Frontier Military Tradition*. Chapel Hill: University of North Carolina Press, 1993.

———, ed. "'We are Stern and Resolved': The Civil War Letters of John Wesley Rabb, Terry's Texas Rangers." *Southwestern Historical Quarterly* 91 (October 1987): 185–226.

D'Amato, Donald A. "William Sprague: Rhode Island's Enigmatic Governor and Senator." M.A. thesis, University of Rhode Island, 1956.

Dabney, Robert Lewis. *A Defense of Virginia and through Her of the South*. New York: E. J. Hale & Son, 1867.

Dabney, Virginius. *Richmond: The Story of a City*. Revised and expanded edition. Charlottesville: University Press of Virginia, 1990.

———. *Virginia*. Garden City, NY: Doubleday, 1971.

Daddysman, James W. *The Matamoros Trade: Confederate Commerce, Diplomacy, and Intrigue*. Newark: University of Delaware Press, 1984.

Daggett, A. S. "The Battle of Rappahannock Station, Va." In *War Papers, Read before the Commandery of the State of Maine, Military Order of the Loyal Legion of the United States*. 4 vols. Portland, ME: Lefavor Tower Co., 1898–1915.

Dahlgren, John A. *Shells and Shell Guns*. Philadelphia, PA: King and Baird, 1856.

Dahlgren, Madeleine Vinton. *Memoir of John A. Dahlgren, Rear-Admiral United States Navy*. Boston, MA: James R. Osgood, 1882.

Dal Bello, Dominic J. *Parade, Inspection, and Basic Evolutions of the Infantry Battalion*. Santa Barbara, CA: AP Press, 1988.

Dale, Edward Everett, and Gaston Litton, eds. *Cherokee Cavaliers: Forty Years of Cherokee History as Told in the Correspondence of the Ridge-Watie-Boudinot Family*. Norman: University of Oklahoma Press, 1939.

Dalton, C. David. "Zollicoffer, Crittenden, and the Mill Springs Campaign: Some Persistent Questions." *The Filson Club History Quarterly* 60 (October 1986): 463–471.

Dalzel, George W. *The Flight from the Flag: The Continuing Effect of the Civil War upon the American Carrying Trade*. Chapel Hill: University of North Carolina Press, 1940.

Dana, Charles A. *Recollections of the Civil War*. New York: D. Appleton, 1898.

Dana, Napoleon Jackson Tecumseh. *"Monterrey Is Ours!": The Mexican War Letters of Lieutenant Dana, 1845–1847*. Edited by Robert H. Ferrell. Lexington: University Press of Kentucky, 1990.

Dana, Richard Henry, Jr. *Two Years before the Mast and Twenty-four Years After*. New York: P. F. Collier & Son, 1909.

Daniel, Larry J. "Manufacturing Cannon in the Confederacy." *Civil War Times Illustrated* 12 (November 1973): 4–10, 40–46.

———. *Shiloh: The Battle that Changed the Civil War*. New York: Simon & Schuster, 1997.

———. *Soldiering in the Army of the Tennessee: A Portrait of Life in a Confederate Army*. Chapel Hill: University of North Carolina Press, 1991.

Daniel, Larry J., and Lynn N. Bock. *Island No. 10: Struggle for the Mississippi Valley*. Tuscaloosa: University of Alabama Press, 1996.

Daniel, Ruth McCaskill. "William Porcher Miles, Champion of Southern Interests." M.A. thesis, University of North Carolina at Chapel Hill, 1943.

Daniels, James Douglas. "The Civil War Career of Major-General Bryan Grimes." M.A thesis, University of North Carolina at Chapel Hill, 1961.

Dannett, Sylvia G. L. *Noble Women of the North*. New York: Thomas Yoseloff, 1959.

———. *She Rode with the Generals*. New York: Thomas Nelson & Sons, 1960.

Davidson, James F. "Michigan and the Defense of Knoxville, Tennessee, 1863." *East Tennessee Historical Society's Publications* 35 (1963): 21–53.

Davies, Wallace E. *Patriotism on Parade: The Story of Veterans' and Hereditary Organizations in America, 1783–1900*. Cambridge, MA: Harvard University Press, 1955.

Davis, Archie K. *Boy Colonel of the Confederacy: The Life and Times of Henry King Burgwyn, Jr.* Chapel Hill: University of North Carolina Press, 1985.

Davis, Burke. *Sherman's March: The First Full-Length Narration of General William T. Sherman's Devastating March through Georgia and the Carolinas*. New York: Random House, 1988.

———. *To Appomattox: Nine April Days*. New York: Rinehart, 1959.

Davis, Carl L. *Arming the Union: Small Arms in the Civil War*. Port Washington, NY: Kennikat Press, 1973.

Davis, Charles H., II. *Life of Charles Henry Davis, Rear Admiral, 1807–1877*. Boston: Houghton Mifflin, 1899.

Davis, Elmer. *History of The New York Times, 1851–1921*. New York: The New York Times, 1921.

Davis, George B. "The Stoneman Raid." *Journal of the United States Cavalry Association* 24 (January 1914): 533–552.

Davis, Harold E. *Henry Grady's New South Atlanta, A Brave and Beautiful City*. Tuscaloosa: University of Alabama Press, 1990.

Davis, Jefferson. *Jefferson Davis, Constitutionalist: His Letters, Papers and Speeches*. Edited by Dunbar Rowland. 10 vols. Jackson: Mississippi Department of Archives and History, 1923.

———. *The Papers of Jefferson Davis*. Edited by Haskell M. Monroe, et al. 10 vols. to date. Baton Rouge: Louisiana State University Press, 1971.

———. *Rise and Fall of the Confederate Government*. 2 vols. New York: D. Appleton, 1881.

Davis, Keith F. *George N. Barnard: Photographer of Sherman's Campaign*. Kansas City, MS: Hallmark Cards, 1990

———. "'A Terrible Distinctness': Photography of the Civil War Era." In *Photography in Nineteenth-Century America*. Edited by Martha A. Sandweiss. Fort Worth, NY: Amon Carter Museum and Harry N. Abrams, 1991: 130–203

Davis, Lee Wright. "Robert Barnwell Rhett, Jr. and the *Charleston Mercury*, 1861–1865." Honors thesis (A.B.J.), University of Georgia, 1977.

Davis, Oliver Wilson. *Life of David Bell Birney, Major-General United States Volunteers*. Philadelphia: Sheldon & Co., 1867. Reprint. Gaithersburg, MD: Ron R. Van Sickle Military Books, 1987.

Davis, Reuben. *Recollections of Mississippi and Mississippians*. Boston: Houghton Mifflin, 1890.

Davis, Rodney O., and Terry Wilson, eds. *Herndon's Informants: Letters, Interviews, and Statements about Abraham Lincoln*. Urbana: University of Illinois Press, 1998.

Davis, Sidney Morris. *Common Soldier—Uncommon War: Life as a Cavalryman in the Civil War*. Edited by Charles F. Cooney. Baltimore: Port City Press, 1994.

Davis, Stephen. "A Georgia Firebrand: Major General William H. T. Walker, C.S.A." *Georgia Historical Quarterly* 63 (Winter 1979): 447–460.

———. "That Extraordinary Document: W. H. T. Walker and Patrick Cleburne's Emancipation Proposal." *Civil War Times Illustrated* 16 (December 1977): 14–20.

Davis, T. Frederick. *History of Jacksonville, Florida and Vicinity: 1513 to 1924*. Jacksonville: San Marco Bookstore, 1925.

Davis, Varina. *Jefferson Davis, Ex-President of the Confederate States of America, A Memoir*. 2 vols. 1890. Reprint. Baltimore: Nautical & Aviation Publishing Company of America, 1990.

Davis, William C. *Battle at Bull Run: A History of the First Major Campaign of the Civil War*. Garden City, NY: Doubleday, 1977.

———. *The Battle of New Market*. Garden City, NY: Doubleday, 1976.

———. *Breckinridge: Statesman, Soldier, Symbol*. Baton Rouge: Louisiana State University Press, 1974.

———. *The Cause Lost*. Lawrence: University Press of Kansas, 1996.

———, ed. *The Confederate General*. Harrisburg, PA: National Historical Society, 1991.

———. *Death in the Trenches: Grant at Petersburg*. Alexandria, VA: Time-Life Books, 1986.

———. *"A Government of Our Own:" The Making of the Confederacy*. New York: The Free Press, 1994.

————, ed. *The Image of War, 1861–1865*. 6 vols. Garden City, NY: National Historical Society, 1981–1984.

————. *Jefferson Davis, The Man & His Hour*. New York: HarperCollins, 1991.

————. *Lincoln's Men: How President Lincoln Became Father to an Army and a Nation*. New York: Simon & Schuster, 1999.

————. "The Massacre at Saltville." *Civil War Times Illustrated* 9 (February 1971): 4–11, 43–48.

————. *The Orphan Brigade; the Kentucky Confederates Who Couldn't Go Home*. Garden City, NY: Doubleday, 1980.

Davis, William W. *The Civil War and Reconstruction in Florida*. New York: Columbia University Press, 1913.

Dawley, Alan. *Class and Community: The Industrial Revolution in Lynn*. Cambridge, MA: Harvard University Press, 1976.

Dawson, Joseph G., III. *Army Generals and Reconstruction: Louisiana, 1862–1877*. Baton Rouge: Louisiana State University Press, 1984. Reprint (paperback). 1994.

————. "Army Generals and Reconstruction: Mower and Hancock as Case Studies." *Southern Studies* 17 (1978): 255–272.

————. "General Lovell H. Rousseau and Louisiana Reconstruction." *Louisiana History* 20 (Fall 1979): 373–391.

De Bruhl, Marshall. *Sword of San Jacinto: A Life of Sam Houston*. New York: Random House, 1993.

De Fontaine, F. G. "Death of Colonel Cameron." *Philadelphia Weekly Times*, 14 April 1883.

De Kay, James T. *Monitor: The Story of the Legendary Civil War Ironclad and the Man Whose Invention Changed the Course of History*. New York: Walker, 1997.

De Luc, William G. *Recollections of a Civil War Quartermaster: The Autobiography of William G. De Luc*. St. Paul, MN: North Central, 1963.

De Roulhac Hamilton, J. G. "The State Courts and the Confederate Constitution." *Journal of Southern History* 4 (November 1938): 425–448.

Dearing, Mary R. *Veterans in Politics: The Story of the G.A.R.* Baton Rouge: Louisiana State University Press, 1952.

DeBolt, Dean. "Life on the Front as Reflected in Soldiers' Letters." *Gulf Coast Historical Review* 4 (Winter 1988).

DeCredico, Mary A. *Mary Boykin Chesnut: A Confederate Woman's Life*. Madison, WI: Madison House, 1996.

————. *Patriotism for Profit: Georgia's Urban Entrepreneurs and the Confederate War Effort*. Chapel Hill: University of North Carolina Press, 1990.

Degler, Carl N. *The Other South: Southern Dissenters in the Nineteenth Century*. New York: Harper & Row, 1974.

Delaney, Norman C. *John McIntosh Kell of the Raider Alabama*. Tuscaloosa: University of Alabama Press, 1973.

Delaney, Robert W. "Matamoros: Port for Texas during the Civil War." *Southwestern Historical Quarterly* 58 (April 1955): 473–487.

Delauter, Roger U., Jr. *McNeill's Rangers*. Lynchburg, VA: H. E. Howard, 1986.

————. *Winchester in the Civil War*. Lynchburg, VA: H. E. Howard, Inc., 1992.

Dell, Christopher. *Lincoln and the War Democrats: The Grand Erosion of Conservative Tradition*. Madison, NJ: Fairleigh Dickinson University Press, 1975.

Dellenbaugh, Frederic S. *Frémont and '49*. New York: G. P. Putnam's Sons, 1914.

Delo, David Michael. *Peddlers and Post Traders: The Army Sutler on the Frontier*. Salt Lake City: University of Utah Press, 1992.

DeMontravel, Peter R. *A Hero to his Fighting Men: Nelson A. Miles, 1839–1925*. Kent, OH: Kent State University Press, 1998.

Denison, Frederic. *Sabres and Spurs: The First Regiment Rhode Island Cavalry in the Civil War, 1861–1865*. Providence, RI: The First Rhode Island Cavalry Association, 1876.

Dennett, Tyler. *John Hay: From Poetry to Politics*. New York: Kennikat Press, 1963.

Denney, Robert E. *Civil War Prisons and Escapes: A Day-by-Day Chronicle*. New York: Sterling, 1993.

DePeyster, J. W. "A Military Memoir of William Mahone, Major-General in the Confederate Army." *Historical Magazine* 10 (1871).

Derby, J. C. *Fifty Years among Authors, Readers, and Publishers*. New York: G. W. Carleton & Co., 1884.

DeShields, James T. *They Sat in High Places: The Presidents and Governors of Texas*. San Antonio, TX: Naylor, 1950.

Desjardin, Thomas J. *Stand Firm Ye Boys from Maine: The 20th Maine and the Gettysburg Campaign*. Gettysburg, PA: Thomas Publications, 1995.

Detroit Post and Tribune. Zachariah Chandler: An Outline of His Life and Public Service. Detroit: The Post & Tribune Co., 1880.

Deupree, J. G. "The Capture of Holly Springs, Mississippi, Dec. 20, 1862." *Publications of the Mississippi Historical Society* vol. 4: 49–61.

Deuson, Benny E. "Pendleton Murrah." In *Ten Texans in Gray*. Hillsboro, TX: Hill Junior College Press, 1968: 122–138.

Devens, Charles. *Charles Devens. Orations and Addresses on Various Occasions, Civil and Military*. Boston: Little, Brown, 1891.

Devin, Thomas Casimer. *Record of Military Service. From March 4, 1861, to January 15, 1866, of Thomas C. Devin, Brigadier and Brev. Major General U.S. Vols., Late Colonel 3rd United States Cavalry*. New York: Pliny F. Smith, 1878.

Dew, Charles B. *Ironmaker to the Confederacy: Joseph R. Anderson and the Tredegar Iron Works*. New Haven, CT: Yale University Press, 1966.

Dewey, Davis R. *Financial History of the United States*. 12th ed. New York: Longmans, Green, 1939.

DeWitt, David M. *The Judicial Murder of Mary E. Surratt*. 1895. Reprint. St. Clair Shores, Michigan: Scholarly Press, 1970.

Dickerson, Donna Lee. *The Course of Tolerance: Freedom of the Press in Nineteenth-Century America*. Westport, CT: Greenwood Press, 1990.

Dickert, D. Augustus. *History of Kershaw's Brigade, with Complete Roll of Companies, Biographical Sketches, Incidents, Anecdotes, etc.* 1899. Reprint. Dayton, OH: Morningside Bookshop, 1973.

Dickinson, Jack L. *8th Virginia Cavalry*. Lynchburg, VA: H. E. Howard, 1986.

Dickson, Paul. *War Slang American Fighting Words and Phrases from the Civil War to the Gulf War*. New York: Pocket Books, 1994.

Dictionary of American Naval Fighting Ships. Vol. 3 Washington, DC: Government Printing Office, 1976.

Diesbach, Alfred "August von Willich." *Badische Heimat* 58 (March 1978): 481–498.

Dillard, Philip D. "The Confederate Debate over Arming Slaves: Views from Macon and Augusta Newspapers." *Georgia Historical Quarterly* 79 (1995): 117–146.

Dillon, Merton Lynn. *The Abolitionists: The Growth of a Dissenting Minority*. New York: W. W. Norton, 1974.

————. *Elijah P. Lovejoy, Abolitionist Editor*. Urbana: University of Illinois Press, 1961.

————. *Slavery Attacked: Southern Slaves and their Allies, 1619–1865*. Baton Rouge: Louisiana State University Press, 1990.

Diner, Hasia. *A Time for Gathering: The Second Migration, 1820–1880. Jewish People in America, vol. 2*. Baltimore:

Johns Hopkins University Press, 1992.

Dingus, Rick. *The Photographic Artefacts of Timothy O'Sullivan.* Albuquerque: University of New Mexico Press, 1982.

Dirks, John E. *The Critical Theology of Theodore Parker.* Wesport, CT: Greenwood Press, 1970.

Dix, Dorothea. Papers. Record Group 94. National Archives and Records Administration, Washington, DC.

Dix, Morgan, comp. *Memoirs of John Adams Dix.* 2 vols. New York: Harper & Brothers, 1883.

Dodd, William Edward. *Robert J. Walker, Imperialist.* Chicago: Chicago Literary Club, 1914.

Dodge, Grenville M. *The Battle of Atlanta and Other Campaigns.* IA: Monarch Printing Co., 1911.

Dodson, W. C., ed. *Campaigns of Wheeler and His Cavalry, 1862–1865.* Jackson, TN: Guild Bindery Press, 1901.

Doenecke, Justus D. *The Presidencies of James A. Garfield and Chester A. Arthur.* Lawrence: Regents Press of Kansas, 1981.

Donald, David Herbert. *Charles Sumner and the Coming of the Civil War.* New York: Alfred A. Knopf, 1960.

———. *Charles Sumner and the Rights of Man.* New York: Alfred A. Knopf, 1970.

———, ed. *Gone for a Soldier: The Civil War memoirs of Private Alfred Bellard.* Boston: Little, Brown, 1975.

———, ed. *Inside Lincoln's Cabinet: The Civil War Diaries of Salmon P. Chase.* New York: Longman's, Green, 1954.

———. *Lincoln.* New York: Simon & Schuster, 1995.

———. *Lincoln Reconsidered: Essays on the Civil War Era.* Westport, CT: Greenwood Press, 1956.

———. *Lincoln's Herndon: A Biography.* New York: Alfred A. Knopf, 1948.

Donelly, Ralph W. *Biographival Sketches of the Commissioned Officers of the Confederate States Marine Corps.* Rev. ed. Washington, NC: Published by the author, 1983.

———. "The Confederate Lead Mines of Wythe County, Va." *Civil War History* 5 (December 1959): 402–414.

———. *The Confederate States Marine Corps: The Rebel Leathernecks.* Shippensburg, PA: White Mane Publishing Co., 1989.

Donovan, Josephine. *Uncle Tom's Cabin: Evil, Affliction, and Redemptive Love.* Boston: Twayne Publishers, 1991.

Dorsey, Florence L. *Road to the Sea: The Story of James B. Eads and the Mississippi River.* New York: Rinehart, 1947.

Doubleday, Abner. *Chancellorsville and Gettysburg.* 1882. Reprint. New York: Da Capo Press, 1994.

———. *Reminiscences of Forts Sumter and Moultrie in 1860–'61.* 1876. Reprint. Charleston, SC: Nautical & Aviation Publishing Company of America, 1998.

Douglas, Henry Kyd. *I Rode with Stonewall Being Chiefly the War Experiences of the Youngest Member of Jackson's Staff from the John Brown Raid to the Hanging of Mrs. Surratt.* Edited by Fletcher Green. Chapel Hill: University of North Carolina Press, 1940.

Dow, Neal. *The Reminiscences of Neal Dow: Recollections of Eighty Years.* Portland, ME: The Evening Express Publishing Co., 1898.

Dowdey, Clifford. *The Seven Days: The Emergence of Lee.* Boston: Little, Brown, 1964.

Downey, Fairfax Davis. *Clash of Cavalry: The Battle of Brandy Station, June 9, 1863.* New York: McKay, 1959.

———. *The Guns at Gettysburg.* New York: McKay, 1958.

———. *The Sound of the Guns: The Story of the American Artillery.* New York: McKay, 1955.

Downs, Alan Craig. "Gone Past All Redemption? The Early War Years of General Joseph Eggleston Johnston." Ph.D. dissertation, University of North Carolina at Chapel Hill, 1991.

Dowty, Alan. *The Limits of American Isolation: The United States and the Crimean War.* New York: New York University Press, 1971.

Drachman, Virginia G. "The Loomis Trial: Social Mores and Obstetrics in the Mid-Nineteenth Century." In *Women and Health in America.* Edited by Judith Walzer Leavitt. Madison: University of Wisconsin Press, 1984: 166–174.

Draughon, Ralph Brown, Jr. "William Lowndes Yancey: From Unionist to Secessionist, 1814–1852." Ph.D. dissertation, University of North Carolina at Chapel Hill, 1968.

Drew, Benjamin. *The Refugee: A North-side View of Slavery.* 1855. Reprint. Reading, MA: Addison-Wesley, 1969.

Drew, John G. *The Absorbing Power of Usury; or, Every Man His Own Actuary Prefaced by a Biographical Sketch of the Hon. F. E. Spinner.* Philadelphia: Baird, 1876.

Drinkard, Dorothy L. *Illinois Freedom Fighters: A Civil War Saga of the 29th Infantry, United States Colored Troops.* Needham Heights, MA: Simon & Schuster Custom Publishing, 1998.

Driver, Robert J. *2nd Virginia Cavalry.* Lynchburg, VA: H. E. Howard, 1995.

———. *5th Virginia Cavalry.* Lynchburg, VA: H. E. Howard, 1997.

———. *52nd Virginia Infantry.* Virginia Regimental Histories Series. Lynchburg, VA: H. E. Howard, 1986.

Dubay, Robert William. *John Jones Pettus, Mississippi Fire-eater: His Life and Times, 1813–1867.* Jackson: University of Mississippi Press, 1975.

Dubelier, Eric Alan. "Charles F. Smith: The Forgotten Soldier." Honor's thesis, Tulane University, 1977.

Duberman, Martin. *Charles Francis Adams, 1807–1886.* Stanford, CA: Stanford University Press, 1968.

———. *James Russell Lowell.* Boston: Houghton Mifflin, 1966.

DuBois, James T. *Galusha A. Grow; Father of the Homestead Law.* Boston: Houghton Mifflin, 1917.

Dubose, John Witherspoon. *General Joseph Wheeler and the Army of Tennessee.* New York: Neale Publishing Co., 1912.

———. *The Life and Times of William Lowndes Yancey: A History of Political Parties in the United States from 1834 to 1864; Especially as to the Origins of the Confederate States.* Birmingham, AL: Roberts & Son, 1892.

Dues, Michael T. "Governor Beriah Magoffin of Kentucky." *Filson Club History Quarterly* 40 (January 1966): 22–28.

———. "The Pro-Secessionists Governor of Kentucky: Beriah Magoffin's Credibility Gap." *Register of the Kentucky Historical Society* 67 (July 1969): 221–231.

Duffey, Jefferson Waite. *Two Generals Kidnapped; A Complete Account of the Capture of Federal Generals George Crook and Benjamin Kelly [sic] by McNeill's Rangers, and a Roster of Those Who Participated in the Raid, February 1865.* Moorefield, WV: The Moorefield Examiner, 1944.

Duffy, James P. *Lincoln's Admiral: The Civil War Campaigns of David Farragut.* New York: John Wiley & Sons, 1997.

Dufour, Charles L. *Gentle Tiger: The Gallant Life of Roberdeau Wheat.* Baton Rouge: Louisiana State University Press, 1957.

Dufours, Charles. *The Night the War Was Lost.* New York: Garden City, 1960.

Duke, Basil W. *History of Morgan's Cavalry.* Cincinnati: Miami Printing and Publishing Co., 1867.

———. *Reminiscences of General Basil W. Duke, CSA.* Garden City, NY: Doubleday, Page, 1911.

Dulles, Foster R. *The American Red Cross: A History.* New York: Harper & Brothers, 1950.

Dunbar, Willis Frederick. *Lewis Cass.* Grand Rapids, MI: William B. Eerdmans, 1970.

Duncan, Bingham. *Whitelaw Reid: Journalist, Politician, Diplomat*. Athens: University of Georgia Press, 1975.

Duncan, Louis C. *The Medical Department of the United States Army in the Civil War*. Gaithersburg, MD: Olde Soldiers Books, 1987.

Duncan, Richard R. *Lee's Endangered Left: The Civil War in Western Virginia, Spring of 1864*. Baton Rouge: Louisiana State University Press, 1998.

Duncan, Robert L. *Reluctant General: The Life and Times of Albert Pike*. New York, 1961.

Duncan, Russell, ed. *Blue-Eyed Child of Fortune: The Civil War Letters of Colonel Robert Gould Shaw*. Athens: University of Georgia Press, 1992.

Duncan, Ruth Henley. *The Captain and Submarine*. Memphis: S. C. Toof, 1965.

Dunn, Craig. *Iron Men Iron Will, the Nineteenth Indiana Regiment of the Iron Brigade*. Indianapolis: Guild Press, 1995.

Dunnigan, Alice Allison. *The Fascinating Story of Black Kentuckians: Their Heritage and Traditions*. Washington, DC: Association for the Study of Afro-American Life and History, 1982.

Dupree, A. Hunter, and Leslie H. Fishel, Jr., eds. "An Eyewitness Account of the New York Draft Riots, July, 1863." *Mississippi Valley Historical Review* 47 (December 1960): 472–479.

Dupuy, R. Ernest. *Sylvanus Thayer: Father of Technology in the United States*. West Point: Association of Graduates of the United States Military Academy, 1958.

Dupuy, Trevor N. *The Evolution of Weapons and Warfare*. New York: Bobbs-Merrill, 1980.

Durden, Robert F. *The Gray and the Black*. Baton Rouge: Louisiana State University Press, 1972.

Durkin, Joseph T. *Confederate Navy Chief: Stephen R. Mallory*. Columbia: University of South Carolina Press, 1954.

Durnbaugh, Donald F. "Studebaker and Stutz: The Evolution of Dunker Entrepreneurs." *Pennsylvania Folklife* 41 (1992): 118–126.

Durrill, Wayne K. *War of Another Kind: A Southern Community in the Great Rebellion*. New York: Oxford University Press, 1990.

Dvarecka, Christopher L. *Springfield Armory—Pointless Sacrifice*. Ludlow, MA: Prolitho Publishing, 1968.

Dyer, Elisha, ed. *Annual Report of the Adjutant General of the State of Rhode Island and Providence Plantations for the Year 1865*. 2 vols. Providence: E. L. Freeman & Sons, 1893–1895.

Dyer, Frederick H. *A Compendium of the War of the Rebellion*. Des Moines, IA: Dyer Publishing Co., 1908.

Dyer, John P. *"Fightin' Joe" Wheeler*. Baton Rouge: Louisiana State University Press, 1941.

———. *From Shiloh to San Juan*. Baton Rouge: Louisiana State University Press, 1961.

Dyer, Thomas G. *Secret Yankees: The Union Circle in Confederate Atlanta*. Baltimore: Johns Hopkins University Press, 1999.

Dykstra, Robert. *Bright Radical Star: Black Freedom and White Supremacy on the Hawkeye Frontier*. Cambridge, MA, 1993.

Early, Jubal A. *Autobiographical Sketch and Narrative of the War between the States*. Baltimore: Nautical and Aviation Publishing Co., 1989.

———. *Lieutenant General Jubal Anderson Early, C.S.A.: Autobiographical Sketch and Narrative of the War between the States*. With notes by R. H. Early. Philadelphia: J. B. Lippincott, 1912.

———. *The Memoirs of General Jubal A. Early*. New York: Konecky & Konecky, 1994.

Earnhart, Hugh G. "Commutation; Democratic or Undemocratic?" *Civil War History* 12 (June 1966): 132–142.

East, Sherrod D. "Montgomery C. Meigs and the Quartermaster Department." *Military Affairs* 25 (1961–1962): 183–196.

Easton, Loyd. *Hegel's First American Followers: The Ohio Hegelians*. Athens, OH: Ohio University Press, 1966.

Eaton, Clement. *Henry Clay and the Art of American Politics*. Boston: Little, Brown, 1962.

Eaton, John. *Grant, Lincoln, and the Freedmen: Reminiscences of the Civil War, with Special Reference to the Work for the Contrabands and Freedmen of the Mississippi Valley*. New York: Longmans, Green, 1907.

Ecelbarger, Gary L. *The First Battle of Kernstown*. Shippenburg, PA: White Mane Publishing Co., 1997.

Echard, William E. *Napoleon III and the Concert of Europe*. Baton Rouge: Louisiana State University Press, 1980.

Eckenrode, H. J., and Bryan Conrad. *James Longstreet: Lee's War Horse*. 1936. Reprint. Chapel Hill: University of North Carolina Press, 1986.

Eckert, Edward K., and Nicholas J. Amatos, eds. *Ten Years in the Saddle: Memoir of William Woods Averell, 1851–1862*. San Rafael, CA: Presidio Press, 1978.

Eckert, Ralph Lowell. *John Brown Gordon: Soldier, Southerner, American*. Baton Rouge: Louisiana State University Press, 1989.

Eddy, Edward Danforth, Jr. *Colleges for Our Land and Time: The Land-Grant Idea in American Education*. New York: Harper & Row, 1957.

Edgar, Walter. *South Carolina: A History*. Columbia: University of South Carolina Press, 1998.

Edmonds, Sarah Emma. *The Memoirs of a Soldier, Nurse, and Spy*. De Kalb: Northern Illinois University Press, 1999.

———. *Nurse and Spy in the Union Army: Comprising the Adventures and Experiences of a Woman in Hospitals, Camps, Battle-Fields*. Hartford, CT: W. S. Williams & Co., 1865.

Edmunds, John B. *Francis W. Pickens and the Politics of Destruction*. Chapel Hill: University of North Carolina Press, 1986.

Edrington, Thomas S. *The Battle of Glorieta Pass: A Gettysburg in the West, March 26–28, 1862*. Albuquerque: University of New Mexico Press, 1998.

Edward, Gambill. "Who Were the Senate Radicals?" *Civil War History* 11 (September 1965): 237–244.

Edwards, E. M. H. *Commander William Barker Cushing of the United States Navy*. New York: Tennyson Neely, 1896.

Edwards, William B. *Civil War Guns: The Complete Story of Federal and Confederate Small Arms: Design, Manufacture, Identification, Procurement, Issue, Employment, Effectiveness, and Postwar Disposal*. 1962. Reprint. Gettysburg, PA: Thomas Publishing, 1997.

Egan, Ferol. *Frémont, Explorer for a Restless Nation*. Garden City, NY: Doubleday, 1977.

Eggleston, John R. "Captain Eggleston's Narrative of the Battle of the *Merrimac*." *Southern Historical Society Papers* 41 (1916): 166–178.

Egle, William H., ed. *Life and Times of Andrew Gregg Curtin*. Philadelphia: Avil Printing Co., 1895.

Ehrlich, Walter. *They Have No Rights: Dred Scott's Struggle for Freedom*. Westport, CT: Greenwood Press, 1979.

Eisenhower, John S. D. *Agent of Destiny: The Life and Times of General Winfield Scott*. New York: Free Press, 1997.

———. *So Far from God: The U.S. War with Mexico, 1846–1848*.

New York: Random House, 1989.

Eisenschiml, Otto. *The Celebrated Case of Fitz John Porter, an American Dreyfuss Affair.* Indianapolis: Bobbs-Merrill, 1950.

———. *John W. Mallet, ACS President in 1882.* Washington, DC: n.p., 1951.

———. *Why Was Lincoln Murdered?* New York: Grosset & Dunlap, 1937.

Ekirch, Arthur A. *The Civilian and the Military: A Study of Antimilitarist Thought.* New York: Oxford University Press, 1956.

Eliot, William Greenleaf. Papers. Missouri Historical Society (St. Louis, Missouri).

———. Papers. Washington University (St. Louis, Missouri), Olin Library, Special Collections Division.

Ellet, Charles, Jr. *The Army of the Potomac and Its Mismanagement.* Washington, DC: L. Towers & Co., 1861.

Ellicott, John M. *The Life of John Ancrum Winslow, Rear Admiral, United States Navy.* New York: Putnam, 1902.

Elliker, Calvin. *Stephen Collins Foster. A Guide to Research.* New York: Garland, 1988.

Elliott, Charles Winslow. *Winfield Scott: The Soldier and the Man.* New York: Macmillan, 1937.

Elliott, James W. *Transport to Disaster.* New York: Holt, Rinehart, & Winston, 1962.

Elliott, Robert G. *Ironclad of the Roanoke.* Shippensburg, PA: White Mane Publishing Co., 1994.

Elliott, Sam Davis. *Soldier of Tennessee and the Civil War in the West.* Baton Rouge: Louisiana State University Press, 1999.

Ellis, John Willis. *The Papers of John Willis Ellis.* 2 vols. Raleigh, NC: State Department of Archives and History, 1964.

Ellison, Mary. *Support for Secession: Lancashire and the American Civil War.* Chicago: University of Chicago Press, 1972.

Emerson, Edward W. *Life and Letters of Charles Russell Lowell—Captain, Sixth United States Cavalry; Colonel, Second Massachusetts Cavalry; Brigadier-General, United States Volunteers.* Boston: Houghton Mifflin, 1907.

Emerson, Ralph Waldo. *Collected Works.* Edited by Robert E. Spiller, et al. 4 vols to date. Cambridge, MA: Harvard University Press, 1971.

———. *The Journals and Miscellaneous Notebooks of Ralph Waldo Emerson.* 16 vols. Edited by William H. Gilman, et al. Cambridge, MA: Harvard University Press, 1960–1982.

Emilo, Luis. *A Brave Black Regiment: The History of the Fifty-Fourth Regiment of Massachusetts Volunteer Infantry, 1863–1865.* New York: De Capo Press, 1995.

Engerud, Hal. *The History of the Siege of Munfordville, September 14–17, 1862.* Munfordville, KY: Hart County Historical Society, 1984.

Engle, Stephen D. *Don Carlos Buell: Most Promising of All.* Chapel Hill: University of North Carolina Press, 1999.

———. *Yankee Dutchman: The Life of Franz Sigel.* Fayetteville: University of Arkansas Press, 1993. Reprint. Baton Rouge: Louisiana State University Press, 1999.

Epstein, Dena J. *Publishing in Chicago before 1871: The Firm of Root & Cady, 1858–1871.* Detroit Studies in Music Bibliography, No. 14. Detroit: Information Coordinators, 1969.

Epstein, Samuel, and Beryl Epstein. *The Andrews Raid or the Great Locomotive Chase April 12, 1862.* New York: Coward-McCann, 1956.

Erkkila, Betsy. *Whitman the Political Poet.* New York: Oxford University Press, 1989.

Escott, Paul D. *After Secession: Jefferson Davis and the Failure of Confederate Nationalism.* Baton Rouge: Louisiana State University Press, 1977.

———. *Many Excellent People: Power and Privilege in North Carolina, 1850–1900.* Chapel Hill: University of North Carolina Press, 1985.

Eskew, G. L. "Our Navy's Ships and Their Builders, 1775–1883." Typescript. Bureau of Ships, U.S. Navy, 1962.

Ethel Taylor. "Discontent in Confederate Louisiana." *Louisiana History* 2 (1961): 410–428.

Ettinger, Amos A. *The Mission to Spain of Pierre Soule, 1853–1855: A Study in the Cuban Diplomacy of the United States.* New Haven, CT: Yale University Press, 1932.

Evans, Augusta J. *Beulah.* Edited by Elizabeth Fox-Genovese. Baton Rouge: Louisiana State University Press, 1992.

———. *Macaria; or, Altars of Sacrifice.* Edited by Drew G. Faust. Baton Rouge: Louisiana State University Press, 1992.

Evans, Clark. "*Maum Guinea*: Beadle's Unusual Jewel." *Dime Novel Roundup* 63 (August 1994): 7–80.

Evans, Clement A. *Intrepid Warrior: Clement Anselm Evans, Confederate General from Georgia; Life, Letters, and Diaries of the War Years.* Dayton, OH: Morningside, 1992.

———, ed. *Confederate Military History: A Library of Confederate States History.* 19 vols. extended ed. 1899. Reprint. Wilmington, NC: Broadfoot Publishing Co., 1987.

Evans, David. *Sherman's Horsemen: Union Cavalry Operations in the Atlanta Campaign.* Bloomington: Indiana University Press, 1996.

Evans, Eli N. *Judah P. Benjamin, the Jewish Confederate.* New York: The Free Press, 1988.

Evans, Frank B. *Pennsylvania Politics, 1872–1877: A Study in Political Leadership.* Harrisburg: Pennsylvania Historical and Museum Commission, 1966.

Evans, William B. *Civil War Guns.* Secaucus, NJ: Castle Books, 1962.

Ex parte Garland, 71 U.S. 333 (1866).

Ex parte Merryman, Fed. Case No. 9487.

Fahle, Michael L. *The Best the Union Could Muster: The True Story of Berdan's U.S. Sharpshooters at the Battle of Gettysburg.* Lindsey, OH: Greencoat Productions, 1998.

Fahrney, Ralph Ray. *Horace Greeley and the* Tribune *in the Civil War.* Cedar Rapids, IA: Torch Press, 1936.

Falaise, Louis De. "Gen. Stephen Gano Burbridge's Command in Kentucky." *Register of the Kentucky Historical Society* 69 (April 1971): 101–127.

Farmer, James Oscar, Jr. *The Metaphysical Confederacy: James Henley Thornwell and the Synthesis of Southern Values.* Macon, GA: Mercer University Press, 1986.

Farnum, George R. "Edward S. Bragg: Soldier, Lawyer and Diplomat." *American Bar Association Journal* 30 (January 1944): 21–22.

Farr, James. "Francis Lieber and the Interpretation of American Political Science." *Journal of Politics* 53 (1990): 1027–1049.

Farrison, William Edward. *William Wells Brown: Author and Reformer.* Chicago: University of Chicago Press, 1969.

Farwell, Byron. *Ball's Bluff: A Small Battle and Its Long Shadow.* McLean, VA: EPM Publications, 1990.

Faulk, Odie B. *General Tom Green: Fightin' Texan.* Waco, TX: Texian Press, 1963.

Faust, Drew Gilpin. "Christian Soldiers: The Meaning of Revivalism in the Confederate Army." *Journal of Southern History* 53 (February 1987): 63–90.

———. *The Creation of Confederate Nationalism: Ideology and Identity in the Civil War South.* The Walter Lynwood Fleming Lectures in Southern History. Baton Rouge: Louisiana State University, 1988.

———. *James Henry Hammond and the Old South: A Design for Mastery.* Baton Rouge: Louisiana State University Press, 1982.

———. *Mothers of Invention: Women of the Slaveholding South in the American Civil War.* New York: Vintage Books, 1996.

———. *A Sacred Circle: The Dilemma of the Intellectual in the Old South, 1840–1860.* 1977. Reprint. Philadelphia: University of Pennsylvania Press, 1986.

———. *Southern Stories: Slaveholders in Peace and War.* Columbia: University of Missouri Press, 1992.

Faust, Patricia. *Historical Times Illustrated Encyclopedia of the Civil War.* New York: Harper-Row, 1986.

Fehrenbacher, Don E. *Constitutions and Constitutionalism in the Slaveholding South.* Mercer University Lamar Memorial Lectures, No. 31. Athens: University of Georgia Press, 1989.

———. *The Dred Scott Case: Its Significance in American Law and Politics.* New York: Oxford University Press, 1978.

Feis, William B. "Intelligence Activities." *The American Civil War: A Handbook of Literature and Research.* Westport, CT: Greenwood Press, 1996.

Fellman, Michael. *Citizen Sherman: A Life of William Tecumseh Sherman.* New York: Random House, 1995.

———. *Inside War: The Guerrilla Conflict in Missouri during the American Civil War.* New York: Oxford University Press, 1989.

Ferguson, John Lewis. *Arkansas and the Civil War.* Little Rock: Pioneer Press, 1965.

Fermer, Douglas. *James Gordon Bennett and the New York Herald: A Study of Editorial Opinion in the Civil War Era, 1854–1867.* New York: St. Martin's Press, 1986.

Ferris, Norman B. *Desparate Diplomacy William H. Seward's Foreign Policy, 1861.* Knoxville: University of Tennessee Press, 1976.

———. *The Trent Affair: A Diplomatic Crisis.* Knoxville: University of Tennessee Press, 1976.

Fesler, Mayo. "Secret Political Societies in the North during the Civil War." *Indiana Magazine of History* (September 1918).

Fessenden, Francis. *The Life and Public Services of William Pitt Fessenden.* 2 vols. Boston: Houghton Mifflin, 1907.

Feuchtwanger, E. J. *Gladstone.* New York: St. Martin's Press, 1975.

Fidler, William P. *Augusta Evans Wilson, 1835–1909: A Biography.* University: University of Alabama Press, 1951.

Final Report of the Western Sanitary Commission. St. Louis: R. P. Studley, 1866.

Finan, William J. *Major General Alfred Howe Terry (1827–1890), Hero of Fort Fisher.* Hartford: Connecticut Civil War Centennial Commission, 1965.

Finch, L. Boyd. *Confederate Pathway to the Pacific: Major Sherod Hunter and Arizona Territory, C.S.A.* Tucson: Arizona Historical Society, 1996.

Finger, John R. *The Eastern Band of Cherokees.* Knoxville: University of Tennessee, 1984.

Fink, Harold S. "The East Tennessee Campaign and the Battle of Knoxville in 1863." *East Tennessee Historical Society's Publications* No. 29 (1957): 79–117.

Finkelman, Paul. *An Imperfect Union: Slavery, Federalism, and Comity.* Chapel Hill: University of North Carolina Press, 1981.

———. *Slavery in the Courtroom: An Annotated Bibliography of American Cases.* Washington, DC: Library of Congress, 1985.

Finley, Randy. *From Slavery to Uncertain Freedom: The Freedmen's Bureau in Arkansas, 1865–1869.* Fayetteville: University of Arkansas Press, 1996.

Finnegan, John P., and Romana Danysh. *Military Intelligence.* In Army Lineage Series. Washington, DC: Government Printing Office, 1998.

Fischer, LeRoy H. *Lincoln's Gadfly: Adam Gurowski.* Norman: University of Oklahoma Press, 1964.

———, ed. *The Civil War Era in Indian Territory.* Los Angeles: Lorrin L. Morrison, 1974.

Fischer, Ronald W. "A Comparative Study of Two Civil War Prisons: Old Capitol Prison and Castle Thunder Prison." M.A. thesis, Virginia Polytechnic Institute and State University, 1994.

Fishel, Edwin C. "Pinkerton and McClellan: Who Deceived Whom?" *Civil War History* 34 (June 1988): 115–142.

———. *The Secret War for the Union.* Boston: Houghton Mifflin, 1996.

Fisher, John. *Builder of the West: The Life of General William Jackson Palmer.* Caldwell, ID: Caxton Press, 1939.

Fisher, John E. *They Rode with Forrest and Wheeler: A Chronicle of Five Tennessee Brothers' Service in the Western Confederate Cavalry.* Jefferson, NC: McFarland, 1995.

Fisher, Mike. "The First Kansas Colored—Massacre at Poison Springs." *Kansas History* 2 (Summer 1979): 121–128.

Fisher, Noel. *War at Every Door: Partisan Politics and Guerilla Violence in East Tennessee, 1860–1869.* Chapel Hill: University of North Carolina Press, 1998.

Fite, Emerson D. *The Presidential Campaign of 1860.* New York: Macmillan, 1911.

———. *Social and Industrial Conditions in the North during the Civil War.* New York: Macmillan, 1910.

Fitzhugh, George. *Cannibals All! or, Slaves without Masters.* Edited by C. Vann Woodward. Cambridge, MA: Harvard University Press, 1960.

———. *Sociology for the South, or, the Failure of Free Society.* Reprint. New York: Ayer Co., n.d.

Flanagan, Vincent J. "The Life of Gouverneur Kemble Warren." Ph.D. dissertation, City University of New York, 1969.

Flanagin, Harris. *Papers of Harris Flanagin, 1862–1874.* Little Rock: Arkansas History Commission, 1965.

Flayderman, E. Norman. *Flayderman's Guide to Antique American Firearms.* 4th ed. Northbrook, IL: DBI Books, 1987.

Fleming, George T. *The Life and Letters of Alexander Hays.* Pittsburgh: Gilbert Adams Hays, 1919.

Fleming, Walter Lynwood. *Civil War and Reconstruction in Alabama.* New York: Columbia University Press, 1905.

Fletcher, Angus. "Whitman and Longfellow: Two Types of the American Poet." *Raritan* 10 (Spring 1991): 131–145.

Fletcher, Winona L. "Speech-making of the New York Draft Riots of 1863." *Quarterly Journal of Speech* 54 (April 1961): 134–139.

Flick, Alexander C., and Gustav S. Lobrano. *Samuel Jones Tilden: A Study in Political Sagacity.* New York: Dodd, Mead, 1939.

Flippin, Percy Scott. *Herschel V. Johnson of Georgia, State Rights Unionist.* Richmond, VA: Press of Dietz Printing Co., 1931.

Flynt, David. "Run the Fleet: The Career of the C.S. Ram *Arkansas.*" *Journal of Mississippi History* 51 (2: 1989):107–132.

Fogel, Robert William. *Without Consent of Contract: The Rise and Fall of American Slavery.* New York: W. W. Norton, 1989.

Fogg, Clara Newhall. *Abner Coburn.* Lewiston, ME: Journal Printshop, 1924.

Fogg, George Gilman. *A Memorial of George Gilman Fogg.* Concord, NH: Republican Press Association, 1882.

Foner, Eric. *Free Soil, Free Labor, Free Men: The Ideology of the Republican Party before the Civil War.* New York: Alfred A. Knopf, 1970.

Foner, Philip S. *History of the Labor Movement in the United States: From Colonial Times to the Founding of the American Federation of Labor.* 2d ed. New York: International Publishers, 1972.

———, ed. *The Life and Writings of Frederick Douglass.* 4 vols. New York: International Publishers, 1950–1955.

Fonvielle, Chris E. Jr. "William B. Cushing: Commando at the Cape Fear." *Blue & Gray Magazine* 14 (Summer 1997): 6–20, 53–63.

Foote, Henry Stuart. *Casket of Reminiscences.* Washington, DC: Chronicle Publishing Co., 1874.

———. *War of Rebellion; or, Scylla and Charybdis, Consisting of Observations upon the Causes, Course, and Consequences of the Late Civil War in the United States.* New York: Harper & Brothers Publishers, 1866.

Foote, Shelby. *The Civil War: A Narrative.* 3 vols. New York: Random House, 1958–1974.

Force, Manning Ferguson. *From Fort Henry to Corinth.* 1881. Reprint. Harrisburg, PA: The Archive Society, 1992.

———. *General Sherman.* New York: D. Appleton, 1899.

———. *Manning Ferguson Force Papers, 1835–1885 at the University of Washington Libraries.* Seattle: University of Washington Libraries, 1965.

———. *Personal Recollections of the Vicksburg Campaign.* Cincinnati: R. Clark, 1888.

Ford, John S. *Rip Ford's Texas.* Edited by Stephen B. Oates. Austin: University of Texas Press, 1963.

Ford, Lacy K. *Origins of Southern Radicalism: The South Carolina Upcountry, 1800–1860.* New York and Oxford: Oxford University Press, 1988.

Ford, Worthington Chauncey, ed. *A Cycle of Adams Letters, 1861–1865.* 2 vols. Boston: Houghton Mifflin, 1920.

Forman, Jacob G. *The Western Sanitary Commission; A Sketch.* St. Louis: R. P. Studley, 1864.

Formwalt, Lee W. "Planters and Cotton Production as a Cause of Confederate Defeat: Evidence from Southwest Georgia." *Georgia Historical Quarterly* 74 (1990): 269–276.

Forrest, Douglas French. *Odyssey in Gray: A Diary of Confederate Service, 1863–1865.* Edited by William N. Still, Jr. Richmond: Virginia State Library, 1979.

Foster, Colonel Frank C., and Lawrence H. Borts. *U.S. Military Medals, 1939–1994.* Fountain Inn, SC: MOA Press, 1994.

Foster, Gaines M. *Ghosts of the Confederacy: Defeat, the Lost Cause, and the Emergence of the New South, 1865–1913.* New York: Oxford University Press, 1987.

Fowler, William M., Jr. *Under Two Flags: The American Navy in the Civil War.* New York: W. W. Norton, 1990.

Fox, Fred K. "John Mohler Studebaker's 1853 Overland Journal from Indiana to California." *Overland Journal* 8 (April 1990): 12–19.

Fox, William F. *Regimental Losses in the American Civil War, 1861–1865.* Albany, NY: Albany Publishing Co., 1889.

Fox-Genovese, Elizabeth. *Within the Plantation Household: Black and White Women of the Old South.* Chapel Hill: University of North Carolina Press, 1998.

Frank, John Paul. *Justice Daniel Dissenting: A Biography of Peter V. Daniel, 1784–1860.* Cambridge, MA: Harvard University Press, 1964.

Frank, Joseph Allen. *With Ballot and Bayonet: The Political Socialization of American Civil War Soldiers.* Athens: University of Georgia Press, 1998.

Frank, Lisa Tendrich. "'To Cure Her of Her Pride and Boasting': The Gendered Implications of Sherman's March." Ph.D. dissertation, University of Florida, forthcoming.

Franke, Norman H., and Laura Webb Stone. "A History of the Association of Medical Officers of the Army and Navy of the Confederacy." *Military Medicine* 131 (April 1966): 321–333.

Frankignoul, Daniel J. *Prince Camille de Polignac Major General, C.S.A. "The La Fayette of the South."* Brussels: Confederate Historical Association of Belgium, 1996.

Franklin, John Hope. *The Emancipation Proclamation.* New York: Anchor, 1965.

———. *From Slavery to Freedom: A History of Negro Americans.* New York: Alfred A. Knopf, 1996.

———. *The Militant South, 1800–1861.* Cambridge, MA: Belknap Press, 1956.

Franklin, Robert Morris. *Battle of Galveston, January 1, 1863.* Galveston, TX: San Luis Press, 1975.

Franks, Kenny. *Stand Watie and the Agony of the Cherokee Nation.* Memphis, TN: Memphis State University Press, 1979.

Frasher, Walter J., Jr. *Charleston! Charleston!: The History of a Southern City.* Columbia: University of South Carolina Press, 1989.

Frassanito, William A. *Antietam: The Photographic Legacy of America's Bloodiest Day.* New York: Charles Scribner's Sons, 1978.

———. *Early Photography at Gettysburg.* Gettysburg, PA: Thomas Publications, 1995.

———. *Grant and Lee: The Virginia Campaigns 1864–1865.* New York: Charles Scribner's Sons, 1983.

Fraysse, Olivier. "Chicago 1860: A Mason's Wigwam?" *Lincoln Herald* (Fall 1985): 71

Frazier, Donald S. *Blood and Treasure: Confederate Empire in the Southwest.* College Station: Texas A&M Press, 1995.

———. *Cottonclads!: The Battle of Galveston and the Defense of the Texas Coast.* Abilene, TX: McWhiney Foundation Press, 1996.

Frederickson, George M. *The Inner Civil War: Northern Intellectuals and the Crisis of the Union.* New York: Harper, 1965.

Freehling, William W. "James Henley Thornwell's Mysterious Antislavery Moment." *Journal of Southern History* 57 (August 1991): 383–406.

———. *The Road to Disunion: Secessionists at Bay, 1776–1854.* New York: Oxford University Press, 1990.

Freehling, William W., and Craig M. Simpson, eds. *Secession Debated: Georgia's Showdown in 1860.* New York: Oxford University Press, 1992.

Freeman, Douglas Southall. *Lee's Lieutenants: A Study in Command.* 3 vols. New York: Charles Scribner's Sons, 1942–1944.

———. *R. E. Lee: A Biography.* 4 vols. New York: Charles Scribner's Sons, 1934.

Freidel, Frank B. *Francis Lieber, Nineteenth-Century Liberal.* Baton Rouge: Louisiana State University, 1947.

Freidel, Frank, ed. *Union Pamphlets of the Civil War, 1861–1865.* 2 vols. Cambridge, MA: Belknap Press of Harvard University Press, 1967.

Frémont, Jessie Benton. *Souvenirs of My Time.* Boston: D. Lothrop, 1887.

French, Samuel Gibbs. *Two Wars: An Autobiography of Gen. Samuel G. French.* Huntington, WV: Blue Alcorn Press, 1999.

Fribourg, Marjorie G. *The Supreme Court in American History.* Philadelphia: Macrae Smith, 1965.

Fried, Joseph P. "Story of the New York Draft Riots." *Civil War Times Illustrated* 4 (August 1965): 4–10, 28–31.

Friedman, Lawrence J. *Gregarious Saints: Self and Community in American Abolitionism, 1830–1870.* Cambridge, MA:

Cambridge University Press, 1982.

Friedman, Lawrence M. *A History of American Law*. New York: Simon & Schuster, 1985.

Friedman, Leon. *The Justices of the United States Supreme Court*. New York: Chelsea House, 1969–1978.

Frohman, Charles E. *Rebels on Lake Erie; the Piracy, the Conspiracy, Prison Life*. Columbus: Ohio Historical Society, 1975.

Frothingham, Octavius Brooks. *Gerrit Smith: A Biography*. New York: G. P. Putnam, 1878.

Fry, James B. *McDowell and Tyler in the Campaign of Bull Run, 1861*. New York: D. Van Nostrand, 1884.

———. *Operations of the Army under Buell from June 10th to October 30th, 1862 and the "Buell Commission."* New York: D. Van Nostrand, 1884.

Fuchs, Richard L. *An Unerring Fire: The Massacre at Fort Pillow*. Rutherford, NJ: Farleigh Dickinson Press, 1994.

Fulcher, Richard Carlton. *Brentwood, Tennessee: The Civil War Years*. Brentwood, TN: Fulcher Publishing Co., 1993.

Furgurson, Ernest B. *Ashes of Glory: Richmond at War*. New York: Alfred A. Knopf, 1996.

———. *Chancellorsville, 1863: The Souls of the Brave*. New York: Alfred A. Knopf, 1992.

Furlong, Patrick J., and Ann Leonard. "Schuyler Colfax, 1823–1885." In *The Vice Presidents: A Biographical Dictionary*. Edited by L. Edward Purcell. New York: Facts on File, 1998: 154–160.

Furneaux, Rupert. *The First War Correspondent: William Howard Russell of the Times*. London: Cassell & Co., 1944.

Furtwangler, Albert. *Assassin on Stage: Brutus, Hamlet, and the Death of Lincoln*. Urbana and Chicago: University of Illinois Press, 1991.

Gabler, Henry. "The Fitz John Porter Case: Politics and Military Justice." Ph.D dissertation, City University of New York, 1978.

Gaff, Alan D. *Brave Men's Tears: The Iron Brigade at Brawner Farm*. Dayton, OH: Morningside Press, 1985.

Gaines, W. Craig. *The Confederate Cherokees: John Drew's Regiment of Mounted Rifles*. Baton Rouge: Louisiana State University Press, 1989.

Galbraith, William, and Loretta Galbraith, eds. *A Lost Heroine of the Confederacy: The Diaries and Letters of Belle Edmondson*. Jackson: University Press of Mississippi, 1990.

Gale, Robert L. *Richard Henry Dana, Jr*. New York: Twayne Publishers, 1969.

Gallagher, Gary W., ed. *Antietam: Essays on the 1862 Maryland Campaign*. Kent, OH: Kent State University Press, 1989.

———, ed. *Chancellorsville: The Battle and its Aftermath*. Chapel Hill: University of North Carolina Press, 1996.

———. *The Confederate War: How Popular Will, Nationalism, and Military Strategy Could Not Stave off Defeat*. Cambridge, MA: Harvard University Press, 1997.

———, ed. *The First Day at Gettysburg: Essays in Confederate and Union Leadership*. Kent, OH: Kent State University Press, 1992.

———, ed. *The Fredericksburg Campaign: Decision on the Rappahannock*. Chapel Hill: University of North Carolina Press, 1995.

———. *Jubal A. Early, the Lost Cause, and Confederate History: A Persistent Legacy*. Milwaukee: Marquette University Press, 1995.

———. *Lee and His Generals in War and Memory*. Baton Rouge: Louisiana State University Press, 1998.

———, ed. *Lee the Soldier*. Lincoln: University of Nebraska Press, 1996.

———, ed. *The Second Day at Gettysburg: Essays on Confederate and Union Leadership*. Kent, OH: Kent State University Press, 1993.

———, ed. *The Spotsylvania Campaign*. Chapel Hill: University of North Carolina Press, 1998.

———. *Stephen Dodson Ramseur, Lee's Gallant General*. Chapel Hill: University of North Carolina Press, 1985.

———, ed. *The Third Day at Gettysburg and Beyond*. Chapel Hill: University of North Carolina Press, 1994.

———, ed. *Three Days at Gettysburg: Essays on Confederate and Union Leadership*. Kent, OH: Kent State University Press, 1999.

———, ed. *The Wilderness Campaign*. Chapel Hill: University of North Carolina, 1997.

———, ed. *Two Witnesses at Gettysburg: The Personal Accounts of Whitelaw Reid and A. J. L. Fremantle*. St. James, NY: Brandywine Press, 1994.

Gallaher, Ruth A. "Samuel Ryan Curtis." *Iowa Journal of History and Politics* 25 (July 1927): 331–358.

Gallas, Stanley. "Lord Lyons and the Civil War, 1859–1864: A British Perspective." Ph.D. dissertation, University of Illinois at Chicago Circle, 1982.

Gallman, J. Matthew. *Mastering Wartime: A Social History of Philadelphia during the Civil War*. New York: Cambridge University Press, 1990.

———. *The North Fights the Civil War: The Home Front*. Chicago: Ivan R. Dee, 1994

Gambee, Budd Leslie, Jr. *Frank Leslie and his Illustrated Newspaper 1855–1860*. Ann Arbor: University of Michigan Department of Library Science, 1964.

Gambone, Albert M. *The Life of Samuel K. Zook: Another Forgotten Union Hero*. Baltimore: Butternut and Blue, 1996.

———. *Major-General John Frederick Hartranft: Citizen Soldier and Pennsylvania Statesman*. Baltimore: Butternut and Blue, 1995.

Gammon, William Lamar, II. "Governor John Milton of Florida: Confederate States of America." M.A. thesis, University of Florida, 1948.

Gannon, James P. *Irish Rebels, Confederate Tigers: A History of the 6th Louisiana Volunteers, 1861–1865*. Campbell, CA: Savas Publishing Co., 1998.

Gannon, Michael. *Rebel Bishop: Augustin Verot, Florida's Civil War Prelate*. Gainesville: University Press of Florida, 1997.

Ganoe, William A. *The History of the United States Army, Revised Edition*. 1942. Reprint. Ashton, MD: Eric Lundberg, 1964.

Gara, Larry. *The Liberty Line: The Legend of the Underground Railroad*. Lexington: University of Kentucky Press, 1967.

———. *The Presidency of Franklin Pierce*. Lawrence: University Press of Kansas, 1991.

Gardner, Alexander. *Gardner's Photographic Sketchbook of the Civil War*. New York: Dover Publications, 1959.

Gardner, Theodore. "Andrew H. Reeder, First Territorial Governor." *Collections of the Kansas State Historical Society* 16 (1923–1925): 582–585.

Garnett, T. S. *Riding with Stuart: Reminiscences of an Aide-de-Camp*. Edited by Robert Shippensburg. Shippensburg, PA: White Mane Publishing Co.. 1994.

Garofalo, Robert, and Mark Elrod. *A Pictorial History of Civil War Era Musical Instruments and Military Bands*. Charleston, WV: Pictorial Histories, 1985.

Garrard, Kenner. *Nolan's System for Training Cavalry Horses*. New York: D. Van Nostrand, 1862.

Garrett Papers. Library of Congress, Washington, DC.

Garrison, Nancy Scripture. *With Courage and Delicacy: Civil War on the Peninsula: Women and the U.S. Sanitary Commission*. Mason City, IA: Savas Publishing, 1999.

Garrison, Webb S. *Lincoln's Little War*. Nashville, TN:

Rutledge Hill Press, 1997.

Garvan, Anthony N. B., and Carol A. Wojtowicz. *Catalogue of the Green Tree Collection*. Philadelphia: The Mutual Assurance Co., 1977.

Gaston, Paul Morton. "The New South Creed, 1865–1900." Ph.D. thesis, University of North Carolina, 1961.

Gatel, Frank Otto. "John McLean." In *The Justices of the United States Supreme Court, 1789–1969: Their Lives and Major Opinions*. Edited by Leon Friedman and Fred L. Israel, vol. I, 535–567. New York: Chelsea House, 1969.

Gates, Paul W. *Agriculture and the Civil War*. New York: Alfred A. Knopf, 1965.

———. "The Homestead Law in an Incongruous Land System." In *The Public Lands: Studies in the History of the Public Domain*. Edited by Vernon Carstensen. Madison: University of Wisconsin Press, 1962: 297–313.

Geary, James W. "Civil War Conscription in the North: A Historiographical Review." *Civil War History* 32 (September 1986): 208–228.

———. *We Need Men: The Union Draft and the Civil War*. Dekalb, IL: Northern Illinois Press, 1991.

Geary, Mary deForest. *A Giant in Those Days: A Story about the Life of John White Geary*. Brunswick, GA: Coastal Printing Co., 1980.

Geib, George. "Benjamin Harrison." *Traces of Indiana and Midwestern History* 8 (Summer 1996): 31–36.

Geier, Clarence R., Jr., and Susan E. Winter. *Look to the Earth: Historical Archaeology and the American Civil War*. Knoxville: University of Tennessee Press, 1994.

General Fry: Head of the First Federal Draft, 1863–1866. Washington, DC: Research and Statistics Division, National Headquarters, Selective Service System, 1956.

"General John R. Brooke." *Philadelphia Public Ledger*, 5 August 1898.

Genovese, Eugene D. *A Consuming Fire: The Fall of the Confederacy in the Mind of the White Christian South*. Athens: University of Georgia Press, 1998.

Gentry, Judith Fenner. "A Confederate Success in Europe: The Erlanger Loan." *Journal of Southern History* 36 (May 1970): 157–188.

George, Philip B. *Soldier Life*. Voices of the Civil War Series. Alexandria, VA: Time-Life Books, 1996.

George, Sister Mary Karl. *Zachariah Chandler: A Political Biography*. East Lansing: Michigan State University Press, 1969.

Geyer, Alejandro Bolanos. *William Walker: El Predestinado de los Ojos Grises*. St. Charles, MO: n.p., 1995.

Gibbon, John. *Personal Recollections of the Civil War*. New York: G. P. Putnam's Sons, 1928.

Gibson, Arrell. *The Chickasaws*. Norman: University of Oklahoma Press, 1971.

Gibson, Charles Dana, with E. Kay Gibson. *Assault and Logistics: Union Army Coastal and River Operations, 1861–1866*. Camden, ME: Ensign Press, 1995.

Gienapp, William. *The Origins of the Republican Party, 1852–1856*. New York: Oxford University Press, 1987.

Gilbert, Benjamin F. "California and the Civil War, Bibliographical Essay." *California Historical Society Quarterly* 40 (December 1961): 289–307.

———. "The Confederate Minority in California." *California Historical Society Quarterly* 20 (June 1941): 154–170.

———. "The Life and Writings of Hinton Rowan Helper." *The Register of the Kentucky Historical Society* 53 (January 1955).

Giles, Leonidas B. *Terry's Texas Rangers*. Austin, TX: Von Boeckmann-Jones, 1911.

Gillette, William. *Jersey Blue: Civil War Politics in New Jersey, 1854–1865*. New Brunswick, NJ: Rutgers University Press, 1994.

Gilliam, William D., Jr. "Robert J. Breckinridge." *Register of the Kentucky Historical Society*, 69 (1971): 362–385.

Gillmore, Quincy A. *Siege and Reduction of Fort Pulaski, Georgia*. 1862. Reprint. Gettysburg, PA: Thomas Publications, 1988.

Gilman, Howard. *The Constitution Besieged: The Rise and Demise of Lochner Era Police Powers Jurisprudence*. Durham, NC: Duke University Press, 1993.

Gilmore, James R. *Personal Recollections of Abraham Lincoln and the Civil War*. Boston: L. C. Page & Co., 1898.

Girardi, Robert I., and Nathaniel C. Hughes, Jr., eds. *The Memoirs of Brigadier General William Passmore Carlin USA*. Lincoln: University of Nebraska Press, 1999.

Giraud, Chester. *Embattled Maiden: The Life of Anna Dickinson*. New York: G. P. Putnam's Sons, 1951.

Gladstone, William A. *Men of Color*. Gettysburg, PA: Thomas Publications, 1993.

Glassel, William T. "Reminiscences of Torpedo Service in Charleston Harbor." *Southern Historical Society Papers* 4 (1877):225–235.

Glasson, William H. *Federal Military Pensions in the United States*. New York: Oxford University Press, 1918.

———. "The South's Care for her Confederate Veterans." *American Monthly Review of Reviews* 36 (July 1907):40–47.

Glatthaar, Joseph T. *Forged in Battle: The Civil War Alliance of Black Soldiers and White Officers*. New York: The Free Press, 1990.

———. *The March to the Sea and Beyond: Sherman's Troops in the Savannah and Carolinas Campaigns*. New York: New York University Press, 1985.

Gleeson, David. "The Irish in the Old South: 1815–1877." Ph.D. dissertation, Mississippi State University, 1997.

Gleeson, Ed. *Erin Go Gray! An Irish Rebel Trilogy*. Carmel, IN: Guild Press of Indiana, 1997.

Goas, Thomas Stewart. *The Contribution of Andrew Gregg Curtin to the Union: Honors to Andrew Gregg Curtin*. Philadelphia: King & Baird, 1869.

Godbold, E. Stanly, and Mattie U. Russell. *Confederate Colonel and Cherokee Chief: The Life of William Holland Thomas*. Knoxville: University of Tennessee, 1990.

Goff, John S. *Robert Todd Lincoln: A Man In His Own Right*. Norman: University of Oklahoma Press, 1969.

Goff, Richard D. *Confederate Supply*. Durham: Duke University Press, 1969.

Going, Charles Buxton. *David Wilmot: Free Soiler*. New York: D. Appleton & Co., 1924.

Golay, Michael. *To Gettysburg and Beyond: The Parallel Lives of Joshua Lawrence Chamberlain and Edward Porter Alexander*. New York: Crown Publishers, 1994.

Goldsmith, Adoph O. "Reporting the Civil War: Union Army Press Relations." *Journalism Quarterly* 33 (Autumn 1956): 478–487.

Gollaher, David. *Voice for the Mad: The Life of Dorothea Dix*. New York: Free Press, 1995.

Gonzales, John Edmond. "Henry Stuart Foote: A Forgotten Unionist of the Fifties." *Southern Quarterly* 1 (January 1963): 129–139.

———. "Henry Stuart Foote in Exile—1865." *Journal of Mississippi History* 15 (April 1953): 90–98.

Gooch, Brison D. *The Reign of Napoleon III*. Chicago: Rand McNally, 1969.

Goode, John. *Recollections of a Lifetime*. New York: Neale Publishing Co., 1906.

Goodman, Paul. *Of One Blood: Abolitionists and the Origins of*

Racial Equality. Berkeley and Los Angeles: University of California Press, 1998.

Goodrich, Thomas. *Black Flag: Guerrilla Warfare on the Western Border, 1861–1865.* Bloomington: Indiana University Press, 1995.

Goodstein, Anita Shafer. *Nashville: 1780–1860.* Gainesville: University of Florida Press, 1989.

Gordon, Ann D. *The Selected Papers of Elizabeth Cady Stanton and Susan B. Anthony: In the School of Anti-Slavery 1840–1866.* New Brunswick, NJ: Rutgers University Press, 1997.

Gordon, David, ed. *Secession, State and Liberty.* New Brunswick, NJ: Transaction Publishers, 1998.

Gordon, George H. *History of the Campaign of the Army of Virginia, under John Pope: From Cedar Mountain to Alexandria, 1862.* Boston: Houghton, Osgood & Co., 1879.

———. *A War Diary of Events in the War of the Great Rebellion, 1863–1865.* Boston: Houghton Mifflin, 1882.

Gordon, John B. *Reminiscences of the Civil War.* New York: Charles Scribner's Sons, 1903.

Gordon, Lesley J. *General George E. Pickett in Life and Legend.* Chapel Hill: University of North Carolina Press, 1998.

Gordon-McCutchan, R. C., ed. *Kit Carson: Indian Fighter or Indian Killer?* Boulder: University of Colorado Press, 1996.

Gorgas, Josiah. "Notes on the Ordnance Department of the Confederate Government." *Southern Historical Society Papers* 12 (1884): 66–94.

Gorman, Herbert S. *A Victorian American: Henry Wadsworth Longfellow.* New York: George H. Doran Co., 1926.

Gosnell, H. A. *Guns on the Western Waters: The Story of the River Gunboats in the Civil War.* Baton Rouge: Louisiana State University Press, 1949.

Goss, Warren Lee. *The Soldier's Story of His Captivity at Andersonville, Belle Isle and Other Rebel Prisons.* Boston: Lee & Shepard, 1867.

Gossett, Thomas F. *Uncle Tom's Cabin and American Culture.* Dallas: Southern Methodist University Press, 1985.

Gougeon, Len. *Virtue's Hero: Emerson, Anti-Slavery, and Reform.* Athens: University of Georgia Press, 1990.

Gould, John Mead. *Joseph K. F. Mansfield, Brigadier General of the U.S. Army; A Narrative of Events Connected with his Mortal Wounding at Antietam, Sharpsburg, Maryland, September 17, 1862.* 1895. Reprint. Bethesda, MD: University Publications of America, 1991.

Govan, Gilbert E., and James W. Livingood. *The Chattanooga Country, 1540–1962: From Tomahawk to TVA.* Chapel Hill: University of North Carolina Press, 1963.

———. *A Different Valor: The Story of General Joseph E. Johnston, C.S.A.* Indianapolis: Bobbs-Merrill, 1956.

Gow, June I. "Theory and Practice in Confederate Military Administration." *Military Affairs* 39 (1975): 119–123.

Grace Julian Clark. *George Washington Julian.* Indianapolis: Indiana Historical Commission, 1932.

Grace, William M. "Isaac Ridgeway Trimble, the Indefatigable and Courageous." M.A. thesis, Virginia Polytechnic Institute and State University, 1986.

Graetz, Robert Bruce. "Triumph amid Defeat: The Confederate Victory at Natural Bridge, Florida, March 1865." Bachelor honors thesis, Florida State University, 1986.

Gragg, Rod. *Confederate Goliath: The Battle of Fort Fisher.* New York: HarperCollins, 1991.

Graham, Christopher A. "Women's Revolt in Rowan County." *Columbiad* 3 (1999): 131–147.

Graham, Martin F., and George F. Skoch. *Mine Run: A Campaign of Lost Opportunities, October 21, 1863–May 1, 1864.* Lynchburg, VA: H. E. Howard, 1987.

Graham, Matthew J. *The Ninth Regiment New York Volunteers (Hawkins' Zouaves).* 1900. Reprint. Lancaster, OH: Vanberg Publishing, 1998.

Graham, Thomas. "Harriet Beecher Stowe and the Question of Race." *New England Quarterly* 46 (December 1973): 614–623.

Grant, Ulysses S. *The Papers of Ulysses S. Grant.* Edited by John Y. Simon. 24 vols. (through spring 2000). Carbondale and Edwardsville: Southern Illinois University Press, 1967–2000.

———. *Personal Memoirs of U. S. Grant.* 2 vols. New York: Charles L. Webster, 1885.

Grant, Ulysses S., and E. B. Washburne. *General Grant's Letters to a Friend, 1861–1880.* New York: AMS Press, 1997.

Gray, Elmer W. "Major General David McMurtrie Gregg, Unsung Hero of Gettysburg." *Historical Review of Berks County* 27 (1962): 67–96.

Gray, Michael P. "Elmira: A City on a Prison-Camp Contract." *Civil War History* 45 (December 1999): 322–338.

Gray, Ralph D. *Indiana's Favorite Sons, 1840–1940.* Indianapolis: Indiana Historical Society, 1988.

Gray, Wood. *The Hidden Civil War: The Story of the Copperheads.* New York: Viking Press, 1942

Grayson, Benson L. *The Unknown President: The Administration of Millard Fillmore.* Washington, DC: University Press of America, 1981.

Greeley, Horace. *Recollections of a Busy Life.* New York: J. B. Ford, 1868.

Greenbie, Sydney, and Marjorie Greenbie. *Anna Ella Carroll and Abraham Lincoln: A Biography.* ME: University of Tampa Press in cooperation with Falmouth Publishing, 1952.

Greene, Dana, ed. *Lucretia Mott: Her Complete Speeches and Sermons.* New York: Edwin Mellon Press, 1980.

———. "Quaker Feminism: The Case of Lucretia Mott." *Pennsylvania History* 48 (April 1981): 143–154.

Greene, Helen Ilone. "Politics in Georgia, 1853–54: The Ordeal of Howell Cobb." *Georgia Historical Quarterly* 30 (1946): 185–211.

Greene, Jack, and Alessandro Massignani. *Ironclads at War: The Origin and Development of the Armored Warship, 1854–1891.* Conshohocken, PA: Combined Publishing, 1998.

Greene, Jerome A. "George Crook." *Soldiers West: Biographies from the Military Frontier.* Edited by Paul Andrew Hutton. Lincoln: University of Nebraska Press, 1987.

Gregg, Frank M. *Andrews Raiders.* Chattanooga, TN: Republican Job Print, 1891.

Gregg, J. Chandler. *Life in the Army in the Department of Virginia, and the Gulf, including Observations in New Orleans: With an Account of the Author's Life and Experience in the Ministry.* Philadelphia: Perkinpine & Higgins, 1866.

Gregg, William. *Essays on Domestic Industry, an Inquiry into the Expediency of Establishing Cotton Manufactures in South Carolina.* Graniteville, SC: Graniteville Co., 1941.

Gresham, Matilda. *Life of Walter Quintin Gresham, 1832–1895.* Chicago: Rand, McNally, 1919.

Gresham, Otto. *The Greenbacks; or the Money that won the Civil War and the World War.* Chicago: Book Press, 1927.

Gretchell, Charles Munro. "Defender of the Inland Waters: The Military Career of Isaac Newton Brown, Commander, Confederate States Navy, 1861–1865." M.A. thesis, University of Mississippi, 1978.

Griffen, Lawrence E. "The Strange Story of Major General Franz Sigel: Leader and Retreater." *Missouri Historical Review* 84 (July 1990): 404–427.

Griffith, Elisabeth. *In Her Own Right: The Life of Elizabeth Cady Stanton*. New York: Oxford University Press, 1984.

Griffith, Lucille. "Mrs. Juliet Opie Hopkins and Alabama Military Hospitals." *Alabama Review* 6 (April 1953): 99–120.

Griffith, Paddy. *Battle Tactics of the Civil War*. New Haven, CT: Yale University Press, 1989.

Griggs, Walter S. *General John Pegram, C.S.A.* Lynchburg, VA: H. E. Howard, 1993.

Grimes, Bryan. *Extracts of Letters of Major-General Bryan Grimes, to His Wife: Written while in Active Service in the Army of Northern Virginia, together with Some Personal Recollections of the War*. Wilmington, NC: Broadfoot Publishing Co., 1986.

Grimsley, Mark. "The Definition of Disaster." *Civil War Times Illustrated* 28 (March 1989): 14–21.

———. *The Hard Hand of War: Union Military Policy Toward Southern Civilians, 1861–1865*. Cambridge, MA: Cambridge University Press, 1995.

———. "Modern War/Total War." In *The American Civil War: A Handbook of Literature and Research*. Edited by Steven E. Woodworth. Westport, CT: Greenwood Press, 1996.

Grinnell, George Bird. *The Fighting Cheyennes*. 1915. Reprint. Norman: University of Oklahoma Press, 1955.

Grinnell, Josiah B. *Men and Events of Forty Years: Autobiographical Reminiscences of an Active Career from 1850 to 1890*. Boston: D. Lothrop Co., 1891.

Grinstead, Marion C. *Life and Death of a Frontier Fort: Fort Craig, New Mexico, 1854–1884*. Socorro, NM: Socorro County Historical Society, 1973.

Grodzins, Dean, and Joel Myerson. "The Preaching Record of Theodore Parker." *Studies in the American Renaissance* (1994): 55–63.

Gross, George J. *The Battlefield of Gettysburg*. Philadelphia: Collins, Printer, 1866.

Grossbach, Barry Leonard. "*Harper's Weekly*: A Critique of the Editorial Viewpoints, 1860–1886." M.A. thesis, Indiana University, 1961.

Grossman, Jonathon P. *William H. Sylvis, Pioneer of American Labor: A Study of the Labor Movement during the Era of the Civil War*. New York: Columbia University Press, 1945.

Grossman, Julian. *Echo of a Distant Drum: Winslow Homer and the Civil War*. New York: Abrams, 1974.

Grot, Zdzislaw. *General Wladzimierz Kryzanowski*. Warsaw: Interpress, 1970.

Grzelonski, Bogdan. *Poles in the United States of America, 1776–1865*. Warsaw: Interpress, 1976.

Gue, Benjamin F. *A History of Iowa*. 4 vols. New York: Century History Co., 1903.

Guedalla, Philip. *Gladstone and Palmerston: Being the Correspondence of Lord Palmerston with Mr. Gladstone 1851–1865*. London: Victor Gollancz, 1928.

Guie, Heister Dean. *Bugles in the Valley: Garnett's Fort Simcoe*. Portland: Oregon Historical Society, 1977.

Guild, Thelma S. *Kit Carson: A Pattern for Heroes*. Lincoln: University of Nebraska Press, 1984.

Guilday, Peter. "Gaetano Bedini: An Episode in the Life of Archbishop John Hughes." *Historical Records and Studies* 23 (1933): 87–170.

Guilds, John Caldwell. *Simms: A Literary Life*. Fayetteville: University of Arkansas Press, 1992.

Gulley, H. E. "Women and the Lost Cause: Preserving a Confederate Identity in the American Deep South." *Journal of Historical Geography* 19 (April 1993): 125–141.

Gunderson, Robert G. *Old Gentlemen's Convention: The Washington Peace Conference of 1861*. Madison: University of Wisconsin Press, 1961.

Haberkorn, Ruth E. "Owen Lovejoy in Princeton, Illinois." *Journal of the Illinois State Historical Society* 36 (1943): 284–315.

Hacker, Barton C. "Women and Military Institutions in Early Modern Europe: A Reconnaissance." *Signs* 6 (Summer 1981): 651–652.

Hafendorfer, Kenneth A. *Perryville: Battle for Kentucky*. Owensboro, KY: McDowell Publications, 1981.

Hager, William D. "The Civilian Life and Accomplishments of John Daniel Imboden." M.A. thesis, James Madison University, 1988.

Hagerman, Edward. *The American Civil War and the Origins of Modern Warfare: Ideas, Organization, and Field Command*. Bloomington: Indiana University Press, 1988.

———. "Field Transportation and Strategic Mobility in the Union Armies." *Civil War History* 34 (1988): 143–171.

Hagerty, Edward J. *Collis' Zouaves: The 114th Pennsylvania Volunteers in the Civil War*. Baton Rouge: Louisiana State University Press, 1997.

Hake, Herbert V. "The Political Firecracker: Samuel J. Kirkwood." *Palimpsest* 56 1 (1975): 2–14.

Hall, James E. *Diary of a Confederate Soldier*. Philippi, WV: Privately printed, 1961.

Hall, Mark. "The Proslavery Thought of J. D. B. De Bow: A Practical Man's Guide to Economics." *Southern Studies* 21 (Spring 1982).

Hall, Martin H. *The Confederate Army of New Mexico*. Austin, TX: Presidial Press, 1978.

———. *Sibley's New Mexico Campaign*. Austin: University of Texas Press, 1960.

Halleck, Henry Wager. *Elements of Military Art and Science*. 1846. Reprint. Westport, CT: Greenwood Press, 1971.

Halliday, Samuel Domont. *History of the Agricultural College Land-Grant of July 2, 1862*. Ithaca, NY: Journal Book and Commercial Printing House, 1890.

Halperin, Rick. "Leroy Pope Walker and the Problems of the Confederate War Department." Ph.D. dissertation, Auburn University, 1978.

Halsell, Willie D. "Democratic Dissensions in Mississippi, 1878–1882." *Journal of Mississippi History* 2 (1940): 123–135.

———. "The Friendship of L. Q. C. Lamar and Jefferson Davis." *Journal of Mississippi History* 6 (July 1944).

Hamand, Lavern. "Ward Hill Lamon: Lincoln's 'Particular Friend.'" Ph.D. dissertation, University of Illinois, 1949.

Hamblin, Deborah. *Brevet Major-General Joseph Eldridge Hamblin, 1861–65*. Boston: Privately printed, 1902.

Hamer, Marguerite B. "Luring Canadian Soldiers into Union Lines during the War between the States." *Canadian Historical Review* 27 (June 1946): 150–162.

Hamilton, Holman. *Prologue to Conflict: The Crisis and Compromise of 1850*. Lexington: University of Kentucky Press, 1964.

Hamilton, Schuyler. *Petition of Major-General Schuyler Hamilton to the Congress of the United States: Amended Letter to Hon. John Sherman, United States Senate, President Pro Tem.* Washington, DC: n.p., 1886.

Hamilton, William Douglas. *Recollections of a Cavalryman of the Civil War after Fifty Years, 1861–1865*. Columbus, OH: F. J. Heer, 1915.

Hamlin, Charles Eugene. *The Life and Times of Hannibal Hamlin*. Cambridge, MA: Riverside Press, published by subscription, 1899.

Hamm, Thomas. *The Transformation of American Quakerism: Orthodox Friends, 1800–1907*. Bloomington: Indiana University Press, 1988.

Hammond, Bray. *Sovereignty and an Empty Purse: Banks and Politics in the Civil War.* Princeton, NJ: Princeton University, 1970.

Hammond, Charles Addison. *Gerrit Smith: The Story of a Noble Life.* Geneva, NY: Press of W. F. Humphrey, 1908.

Hamrogue, John M. "John Andrew: Abolitionist Governor, 1861–1865." Ph.D. dissertation, Fordham University, 1974.

Hanaford, Phebe A. *The Life of George Peabody.* Boston: B. B. Russell, 1870.

Hanchett, William. *Irish: Charles G. Halpine in Civil War America.* Syracuse, NY: Syracuse University Press, 1970.

———. *The Lincoln Murder Conspiracies: Being an Account of the Hatred Felt by Many Americans for President Abraham Lincoln during the Civil War and the First Complete Examination and Refutation of the Many Theories, Hypotheses, and Speculations Put Forward Since 1865 Concerning Those Presumed to Have Aided, Abetted, Controlled, or Directed the Murderous Act of John Wilkes Booth in Ford's Theater the Night of April 14.* Urbana: University of Illinois Press, 1983.

Hancock, Almira (Russell). *Reminiscences of Winfield Scott Hancock by His Wife.* New York: C. L. Webster & Co., 1887.

Hancock, Harold Bell. *Delaware during the Civil War.* Wilmington: Historical Society of Delaware, 1961.

Hankinson, Alan. *Man of War: William Howard Russell of the Times.* London: Heinemann Educational Books, 1982.

Hanna, Alfred J., and Kathryn Abby Hanna. *Confederate Exiles in Venezuela.* Tuscaloosa: University of Alabama Press, 1960.

———. *Napoleon III and Mexico: American Triumph over Monarchy.* Chapel Hill: University of North Carolina Press, 1971.

Hansen, Marcus Lee. *The Atlantic Migration, 1607–1860.* Cambridge, MA: Harvard University Press, 1951.

Harding, Bertita. *Phantom Crown. The Story of Maximilian and Carlotta of Mexico.* New York: Halcyon House, 1934.

Harding, Walter. *The Days of Henry Thoreau: A Biography.* New York: Dover Publications, 1982.

Harding, Walter and Carl Bode, eds. *The Correspondence of Henry David Thoreau.* New York: New York University Press, 1958.

Hardy, John. *Selma: Her Institutions and Her Men.* Selma, AL: Selma Times Office, 1879.

Hargrove, Hondon B. *Black Union Soldiers in the Civil War.* Jefferson, NC: McFarland, 1988.

Harley, Lewis R. *Francis Lieber: His Life and Political Philosophy.* New York: AMS Press, 1970.

Harlow, Ralph Volney. *Gerrit Smith, Philanthropist and Reformer.* New York: H. Holt, 1939.

Harper, Robert S. *Lincoln and the Press.* New York: McGraw-Hill, 1951.

Harrington, Fred Harvey. *Fighting Politician: Major General N. P. Banks.* 1948. Reprint. Westport, CT: Greenwood Press, 1970.

Harris, Nathaniel H. Report. William Mahone Collection, Virginia State Library, Richmond, VA.

Harris, Robert Charles. "Austin Blair of Michigan: A Political Biography." Ph.D dissertation, Michigan State University, 1969.

Harris, W. D. "Price's Raid through Missouri." *Confederate Veteran* (May 1905).

Harris, William C. *The Day of the Carpetbagger: Republican Reconstruction in Mississippi.* Baton Rouge: Louisiana State University Press, 1979.

———. *Leroy Pope Walker, Confederate Secretary of War.* Tuscaloosa, AL: Confederate Publishing Co., 1962.

———. "Lincoln and Wartime Reconstruction in North Carolina." *North Carolina Historical Review* 63 (1986): 149–168.

———. *With Charity for All: Lincoln and the Restoration of the Union.* Lexington: University Press of Kentucky, 1997.

Harris, William M. *Movements of the Confederate Army in Virginia and the Part Taken Therein by the Nineteenth Mississippi from the Diary of Gen. Nat H. Harris.* Duncansby, MS: Published by the author, 1901.

Harris, Wilmer C. *Public Life of Zachariah Chandler, 1851–1875.* Lansing: Michigan Historical Commission, 1917.

Harrison, John M. *The Blade of Toledo: The First 150 Years.* Toledo, OH: Toledo Blade Co., 1985.

———. *The Man Who Made Nasby, David Ross Locke.* Chapel Hill: University of North Caroline Press, 1969.

Harrison, Lowell H. *The Civil War in Kentucky.* Lexington: University Press of Kentucky, 1975.

———. "General Basil W. Duke, CSA." *Filson Club History Quarterly* 54 (January 1980): 5–31.

———. "George W. Johnson and Richard Hawes: The Governors of Confederate Kentucky." *Register of the Kentucky Historical Society* 79 (Winter 1981): 3–39.

———. "Governor Magoffin and the Secession Crisis." *Register of the Kentucky Historical Society* 72 (April 1974): 91–110.

———. "'Should I Surrender?'—A Civil War Incident." *Filson Club History Quarterly* 40 (October 1966): 297–306.

Harrison, Walter. *Pickett's Men: A Fragment of War History.* New York: D. Van Nostrand, 1870.

Harsh, Joseph L. *Confederate Tide Rising: Robert E. Lee and the Making of Southern Strategy, 1861–1862.* Kent, OH: Kent State University Press, 1998.

Hart, Herbert M. *Old Forts of the Southwest.* New York: Bonanza Books, 1956.

Harter, Dale F. "Ignored by History." *Montpelier* 15 (Spring 1992): 16–18.

Hartigan, Richard Shelly, ed. *Lieber's Code and the Law of War.* Chicago: Precedent, 1983.

Hartje, Robert G. *Van Dorn: The Life and Times of A Confederate General.* 1967. Reprint. Nashville, TN: Vanderbilt University Press, 1994.

Harvey, Charles M. "The Dime Novel in American Life." *Atlantic Monthly* 100 (July 1907).

Harwell, Richard B. *Confederate Music.* Chapel Hill: University of North Carolina Press, 1950.

Haslip, Joan. *The Crown of Mexico. Maximilian and his Empress Carlotta.* New York: Avon Books, 1971.

Hassler, Warren W. *Crisis at the Crossroads: The First Day at Gettysburg.* University: University of Alabama Press, 1970.

———. *General George B. McClellan: Shield of the Union.* Baton Rouge: Louisiana State University Press, 1957.

Hassler, William W. *A. P. Hill: Lee's Forgotten General.* Richmond, VA: Garrett & Massie, 1957.

———. *Colonel John Pelham: Lee's Boy Artillerist.* Richmond, VA: Garrett and Massie, 1960.

Hastings, Earl C., Jr., and David S. Hastings. *A Pitiless Rain: The Battle of Williamsburg, 1862.* Shippensburg, PA: White Mane Publishing Co., 1997.

Hattaway, Herman. *General Stephen D. Lee.* Jackson: University Press of Mississippi, 1976.

———. *Shades of Blue and Gray: An Introductory Military History of the Civil War.* Columbia: University of Missouri Press, 1997.

Hattaway, Herman, and Archer Jones. *How the North Won: A Military History of the Civil War.* Urbana: University of Illinois Press, 1983.

Hauptman, Laurence M. *Between Two Fires: American Indians in the Civil War.* New York: The Free Press, 1995.

Hausfeld, Eric Edward. "Catholic Involvement in Civil War Diplomacy." M.A. thesis, University of Dayton, 1965.

Hawes, Lilla Mills, ed. *Collections of the Georgia Historical Society: The Memoirs of Charles H. Olmstead.* Savannah: Georgia Historical Society, 1964.

Hawley, Joseph Roswell. Diary and Papers. Library of Congress, Washington, DC.

Hay, John M., and John G. Nicolay. *Abraham Lincoln: A History.* 10 vols. New York: Century, 1890.

Haydon, F. Stansbury. *Aeronautics in the Union and Confederate Armies With a Survey of Military Aeronautics Prior to 1861.* Baltimore: Johns Hopkins Press, 1941.

Hayes, John D. "Captain Fox—He Is the Navy Department." *United States Naval Institute Proceedings* (September 1965).

———. "The Marine Corps in the American Civil War." *Shipmate, U.S. Naval Alumni Association Monthly* 33 (November 1960): 2–4.

———, ed. *Samuel Francis Du Pont: A Selection from His Civil War Letters: Volume One, the Mission: 1860–1862.* 3 vols. Ithaca, NY: Cornell University Press, 1969.

Haynes, Fred E. *James Baird Weaver.* Iowa City: State Historical Society of Iowa, 1919.

Haynie, J. Henry. *The Nineteenth Illinois.* Chicago: M.A. Donohue, 1912.

Hays, E. Z., ed. *History of the Thirty-Second Regiment, Ohio Veteran Volunteer Infantry.* Columbus, OH: Cott & Evans, 1896.

Hays, Gilbert. *Under the Red Patch.* Pittsburgh: 63rd Pennsylvania Volunteer Regimental Association, 1908.

Hazen, William B. *A Narrative of Military Service: The Civil War through the Eyes of a Controversial Fighting General.* 1885. Reprint. Huntington, WV: Blue Acorn Press, 1993.

Headley, J. W. *Confederate Operations in Canada and N. Y.* New York: Neale Publishing Co., 1906.

Headley, Phineas C. *The Astronomer and Soldier.* New York: George A. Leavitt, 1870.

Hearn, Chester G. *Admiral Glasgow Farragut: The Civil War Years.* Annapolis, MD: Naval Institute Press, 1997.

———. *The Capture of New Orleans, 1862.* Baton Rouge: Louisiana State University Press, 1995.

———. *Companions in Conspiracy: John Brown & Gerrit Smith.* Gettysburg, PA: Thomas Publications, 1996.

———. *Gray Raiders of the Sea: How Eight Confederate Warships Destroyed the Union's High Seas Commerce.* Camden: International Marine Publishing, 1992.

———. *Mobile Bay and the Mobile Campaign: The Last Great Battles of the Civil War.* Jefferson, NC: McFarland, 1993.

———. *Six Years of Hell: Harper's Ferry during the Civil War.* Baton Rouge: Louisiana State University Press, 1999.

———. *When the Devil Came Down to Dixie: Ben Butler in New Orleans.* Baton Rouge: Louisiana State University Press, 1997.

Heath, Gary Earl. "The St. Albans Raid: Vermont Viewpoint." *Vermont History* 33 (January 1965): 250–255.

Heatwole, John L. *The Burning: Sheridan in the Shenandoah Valley.* Charlottesville, VA: Rockbridge Publishing, 1998.

Hebert, Walter H. *Fighting Joe Hooker.* New York: Bobbs-Merrill, 1944.

Heck, Frank H. *Proud Kentuckian: John C. Breckinridge, 1821–1875.* Lexington: University Press of Kentucky, 1976.

Hedges, James Blaine. *Henry Villard and the Railways of the Northwest.* New Haven, CT: Yale University Press, 1930.

Hedley, F. Y. *Marching through Georgia: Pen-Pictures of Everyday Life.* Chicago: M. A. Donohue & Co., 1884.

Hedrick, Joan. *Harriet Beecher Stowe: A Life.* New York: Oxford University Press, 1994.

———, ed. *The Oxford Harriet Beecher Stowe Reader.* New York: Oxford University Press, 1999.

Heidler, David S. *Pulling the Temple Down: The Fire-eaters and the Destruction of the Union.* Mechanicsburg, PA: Stackpole, 1994.

Heidler, Jeanne T. "The Military Career of David Emanuel Twiggs." Ph.D dissertation, Auburn University, 1988.

Heintzelman, Samuel Peter. *The Papers of Samuel Peter Heintzelman.* Washington, DC: Library of Congress, 1977.

Heisser, David C. R. "Bishop Lynch's Civil War Pamphlet on Slavery." *Catholic Historical Review* 84 (1998): 681–696.

Heitman, Francis B. *Historical Register and Dictionary of the U.S. Army.* Washington DC: Government Printing Office, 1903.

Heller, Charles E. *Portrait of an Abolitionist: A Biography of George Luther Stearns, 1809–1867.* Westport, CT: Greenwood Press, 1996.

Helm, Katherine. *The True Story of Mary, Wife of Lincoln Containing the Recollections of Mary Lincoln's Sister Emilie (Mrs. Ben Hardin Helm), Extracts from Her War-Time Diary, Numerous Letters and Other Documents Now First Published by Her Niece, Katherine Helm.* New York: Harper, 1928.

Helper, Hinton Rowan. *The Impending Crisis of the South: How to Meet It.* Edited by George M. Frederickson. 1852. Reprint. Cambridge, MA: Harvard University Press, 1968.

Helsley, Alexia J. *South Carolina's African-American Confederate Pensioners, 1923–1925.* Columbia: South Carolina Department of Archives and History, 1998.

Hemenway, Abby Maria. *The Vermont Historical Gazetteer.* Burlington, VT: Published by the author, 1868.

Henderson, G. F. R. *Stonewall Jackson and the American Civil War.* 2 vols. London: Longmans, Green, 1898.

Henderson, Harry McCorry. *Texas in the Confederacy.* San Antonio, TX: The Naylor Co., 1967.

Hendrick, Burton J. *Statesmen of the Lost Cause. Jefferson Davis and His Cabinet.* New York: Literary Guild of America, 1939.

Hendrickson, James E. *Joe Lane of Oregon: Machine Politics and the Sectional Crisis, 1849–1861.* New Haven, CT: Yale University Press, 1967.

Hendrickson, Robert. *The Road to Appomattox.* New York: J. Wiley, 1998.

Henig, Gerald S. *Henry Winter Davis: Antebellum and Civil War Congressman from Maryland.* New York: Twayne, 1973.

Henneke, Ben Graf. *Laura Keene: A Biography.* Tulsa, OK: Council Oak Books, 1990.

Hennessy, John J. *Return to Bull Run: The Campaign and Battle of Second Manassas.* New York: Simon & Schuster, 1993.

———. "The Second Battle of Manassas." *Blue & Gray Magazine* 9 (August 1992): 11–34, 46–58.

———. *Second Manassas Battlefield Map Study.* Lynchburg, VA: H. E. Howard, 1990.

Henry, Joseph O. "The United States Christian Commission in the Civil War." *Civil War History* 6 (1960): 374–388.

Henry, Robert Hiram. *Editors I Have Known since the Civil War.* Jackson, MS: Clarion-Ledger, 1922.

Henry, Robert Selph. *"First with the Most" Forrest.* Indianapolis: Bobbs-Merrill, 1944.

Hensel, Howard M. *The Anatomy of Failure: The Case of Major General George B. McClellan and the Peninsular Campaign.* Montgomery, AL: Air Command and Staff College, Maxwell Air Force Base, 1985.

Herd, Harold. *Seven Editors.* 1955. Reprint. Westport, CT:

Greenwood Press, 1977.

Herdegen, Lance J. *The Men Stood Like Iron*. Bloomington: Indiana University Press, 1997.

Hermann, Janet Sharp. *The Pursuit of a Dream*. New York: Oxford University Press, 1981

Herndon, William Henry. *The Hidden Lincoln*. New York: Viking Press, 1938.

Hernon, Joseph M., Jr. *Celts, Catholics and Copperheads: Ireland Views the American Civil War*. Columbus: Ohio State University Press, 1968.

Herr, Pamela. *Jessie Benton Frémont: A Biography*. New York: Franklin Watts, 1987.

Herr, Pamela, and Mary Lee Spence, eds. *The Letters of Jessie Benton Frémont*. Urbana: University of Illinois Press, 1993.

———. "Major General F. J. Herron." *Annals of Iowa* 5 (January 1867): 801–807.

Hess, Earl J. "Alexander Asboth: One of Lincoln's Hungarian Heroes?" *Lincoln Herald* 84 (Fall 1982): 181–191.

———. *Banners to the Breeze: The Kentucky Campaign, Corinth, and Stones River*. Lincoln: University of Nebraska Press, 2000.

———. *Liberty, Virtue, and Progress: Northerners and Their War For The Union*. 2d ed. New York: Fordham University Press, 1997.

———. "Osterhaus in Missouri: A Study of German-American Loyalty." *Missouri Historical Review* 78 (1983): 144–167.

———. "Sigel's Resignation: A Study in German-Americans and the Civil War." *Civil War History* 26 (1980): 5–17.

Hesseltine, William B., ed. *Civil War Prisons*. 1972. Reprint. Kent, OH: Kent State University Press, 1992.

———. *Civil War Prisons: A Study in War Psychology*. 1930. Reprint. Columbus: Ohio State University Press, 1998.

———, ed. *Three Against Lincoln: Murat Halsted Reports the Caucuses of 1860*. Baton Rouge: Louisiana State University Press, 1960.

———, ed. *The Tragic Conflict: The Civil War and Reconstruction*. New York: G. Braziller, 1962.

Hesseltine, William B., and Hazel C. Wolf. *The Blue and Grey on the Nile*. Chicago: University of Chicago Press, 1961.

Heth, Henry. "Letter from Major-General Henry Heth." *Southern Historical Society Papers* 4 (1877): 151–160.

Hewitt, Lawrence. *Port Hudson: Confederate Bastion on the Mississippi*. Baton Rouge: Louisiana State University Press, 1987.

Heyman, Max L. *Prudent Soldier: A Biography of Major General E. R. S. Canby, 1817–1873*. Glendale, CA: A. H. Clark, 1959.

Hibbard, Benjamin H. *A History of the Public Land Policies*. New York: Macmillan, 1924.

Hicken, Victor. "John A. McClernand and the House Speakership Battle of 1859." *Journal of the Illinois State Historical Society* (Summer 1960): 163–178.

Hidy, Muriel E. *George Peabody: Merchant and Financier, 1829–1854*. New York: Arno Press, 1978.

Higdon, Hal. *The Union vs. Doctor Mudd*. Chicago: Follett Publishing Co., 1964.

Higginson, Thomas Wentworth. *Army Life in a Black Regiment*. With notes and biographical introduction by John Hope Franklin. Boston: Beacon Press, 1962.

Hill, Benjamin Harvey, Jr. *Senator Benjamin Harvey Hill of Georgia: His Life, Speeches, and Writing*. Atlanta: H. C. Hudgins, 1891.

Hill, Daniel G. *Freedom-Seekers: Blacks in Early Canada*. Agincourt, Ontario: Book Society of Canada, 1981.

Hill, Jim Dan. *Sea Dogs of the Sixties: Farragut and Seven Contemporaries*. Minneapolis: University of Minnesota

Press, 1935.

Hill, Louise Biles. *Joseph E. Brown and the Confederacy*. Chapel Hill: University of North Carolina Press, 1939.

Hill, Richard, and Peter Hogg. *A Black Corps d'Elite*. East Lansing: Michigan State University Press, 1995.

Hindman, Biscoe. "Thomas Carmichael Hindman." *Confederate Veteran* 38:3 (March 1930): 97–104.

Hines, Thomas H. "The Northwestern Conspiracy." *Southern Bivouac: A Monthly Literary and Historical Magazine* 2 (June 1886–May 1887).

Hinkel, John Vincent. *Arlington: Monument to Heroes*. Englewood Cliffs, NJ: Prentice-Hall, 1970.

Hinton, Perry. "The Military Career of John Ellis Wool, 1812–1863." Ph.D. dissertation, University of Wisconsin, 1960.

Hinton, Richard J. *Rebel Invasion of Missouri and Kansas, and the Campaign of the Army of the Border against General Sterling Price, in October and November 1864*. Chicago: Church & Goodman; Leavenworth, KN: F. W. Marshall, 1865.

Hirsh, Edward L. *Henry Wadsworth Longfellow*. Minneapolis: University of Minnesota Press, 1964.

Hirshson, Stanley P. *Grenville M. Dodge: Soldier, Politician, Railroad Pioneer*. Bloomington: Indiana University Press, 1967.

Hitchcock, Ethan Allen. *Fifty Years in Camp and Field; Diary of Major-General Ethan Allen Hitchcock, U.S.A.* New York: G. P. Putnam's Sons, 1909.

Hitchcock, Henry. *Marching with Sherman; Passages from the Letters and Campaign Diaries of Henry Hitchcock, Major and Assistant Adjutant General of Volunteers. November 1864–May 1865*. Edited by M.A. DeWolfe Howe. New Haven, CT: Yale University Press, 1927.

Hitner, Mrs. R. K. Letter to Mrs. David Hastings 6 July 1863. Carlisle Barracks Collection, Archives of the United States Army Military History Institute, Carlisle, PA.

Hobart-Hampden, C. Augustus. *Never Caught: Personal Adventures Connected with Twelve Successful Trips in Blockade-Running during the American Civil War, 1863–4*. 1900. Reprint. Carolina Beach, NC: Blockade Runner Museum, 1967.

Hobbs, O. Kermit, Jr. *Storm over Suffolk*. Suffolk: Suffolk-Nansemond Historical Society, 1979.

Hobhouse, Hermione. *Prince Albert, His Life and Work*. London: Hamish Hamilton, 1983.

Hoffert, Sylvia. "Madame Loretta [sic] Velazquez: Heroine or Hoaxer?" *Civil War Times Illustrated* 17 (June 1978): 24–31.

Hoge, Jane Blaikie. *The Boys in Blue: Or, Heroes of the "Rank and File."* New York: E. B. Treat, 1867.

Hoig, Stan. *The Battle of the Washita*. Garden City, NY: Doubleday, 1976.

Hoke, Jacob. *Historical Reminiscences of the War or Incidents which Transpired in and about Chambersburg during the War of the Rebellion*. Chambersburg, PA: M. A. Foltz, 1884.

Holcomb, Raymond L. *The Civil War in the Choctaw Nation*. 2d ed. Atoka, OK: Atoka County Historical Society, 1997.

Holcombe, John W., and Hubert M. Skinner. *Life and Public Services of Thomas A. Hendricks*. Indianapolis: Carlon & Hollenbeck, 1886.

Holien, Kim Bernard. *Battle at Ball's Bluff*. Orange, VA: Moss Publications, 1985.

Holifield, E. Brooks. *The Gentlemen Theologians: American Theology in Southern Culture, 1795–1860*. Durham, NC: Duke University Press, 1978.

Holland, Cecil Fletcher. *Morgan and His Raiders: A Biography of the Confederate General*. New York: Macmillan, 1942.

Holland, Lynwood Mathis. *Pierce M. B. Young; the Warwick of

the South. Athens: University of Georgia Press, 1964.

Holland, Mary Gardner. *Our Army Nurses*. Boston: Lounsbery, Nichols & Worth, 1897.

Holland, Timothy J. "The Catholic Church and the Negro in the United States prior to the Civil War." Ph.D. dissertation, Fordham University, 1950.

Hollandsworth, James G. *The Louisiana Native Guards: The Black Military Experience during the Civil War*. Baton Rouge: Louisiana State University Press, 1995.

———. *Pretense of Glory: The Life of General Nathaniel P. Banks*. Baton Rouge: University of Louisiana Press, 1998.

Hollings, Celestine Caldwell. *Our Ancestors: Daughters of Union Veterans of the Civil War, 1861–1865*. Detroit: Daughters of Union Veterans of the Civil War, 1996.

Hollingsworth, Harold M. "George Andrews—Carpetbagger." *Tennessee Historical Quarterly* 28 (Fall 1969): 310–323.

Hollins, George N. "Autobiography of Commodore G. N. Hollins." *Maryland Historical Magazine* 34 (September 1939): 228.

Hollister, O. J. *Life of Schuyler Colfax*. New York: Funk & Wagnalls, 1886.

Holmes, Clayton W. *The Elmira Prison Camp, A History of the Military Prison at Elmira, N. Y.* New York: G. P. Putman's Sons, 1912.

Holmes, Torlief S. *Horse Soldiers in Blue*. Gaithersburg, MD: Butternut Press, 1985.

Holt, David A. *Mississippi Rebel in the Army of Northern Virginia: The Civil War Memoirs of Private David Holt*. Edited by Thomas D. Cockrell and Michael B. Ballard. Baton Rouge: Louisiana State University Press, 1995.

Holt, Michael F. *The Political Crisis of the 1850s*. New York: Wiley, 1978.

———. *The Rise and Fall of the American Whig Party: Jacksonian Politics and the Onset of the Civil War*. New York: Oxford University Press, 1999.

Holzer, Harold, ed. *The Lincoln-Douglas Debates*. New York: HarperCollins, 1993.

Holzer, Harold, and Mark E. Neely, Jr. *Mine Eyes Have Seen the Glory*. New York: Orion Books, 1993.

Holzman, Robert S. *Adapt or Perish: The Life of General Roger A. Pryor, C.S.A.* Hamden, CT: Archon Books, 1976.

———. "Ben Butler in the Civil War." *New England Quarterly* 30 (1957): 330–345.

———. *Stormy Ben Butler*. New York: Collier Books, 1961.

Honeywell, Roy J. *Chaplains of the United States Army*. Washington, DC: Office of the Chief of Chaplains, Department of the Army, 1958.

Hood, John Bell, General. *Advance and Retreat: Personal Experiences in the United States and Confederate States Armies*. Introduction by Richard M. McMurry. New York: Da Capo Press, 1993.

Hoogenboom, Ari. *Rutherford B. Hayes: Warrior and President*. Lawrence: University Press of Kansas, 1995.

Hopkins, Alphonso A. *The Life of Clinton Bowen Fisk*. New York: Funk & Wagnalls, 1888.

Hopkins, Juliet Opie. Collection. Alabama Department of Archives and History, Montgomery.

Horan, James D. *The Pinkertons: The Detective Dynasty that Made History*. New York: Crown Publishers, 1968.

Horn, John. *The Destruction of the Weldon Railroad: Deep Bottom, Globe Tavern, and Reams Station*. Lynchburg, VA: H. E. Howard, 1991.

———. *The Petersburg Campaign, June 1864–April 1865*. Conshohocken, PA: Combined Books, 1993.

Horn, Stanley F. *The Army of Tennessee*. Norman: University of Oklahoma Press, 1952.

———. *The Decisive Battle of Nashville*. Baton Rouge: Louisiana State University Press, 1956.

———, ed. *Tennessee's War, 1861–1865: Described by Participants*. Nashville: Tennessee Civil War Centennial Commission, 1965.

Horner, Harlan Hoyt. *Lincoln and Greeley*. Urbana: University of Illinois Press, 1953.

Horowitz, Morton J. *The Transformation of American Law*. Cambridge, MA: Harvard University Press, 1977.

Horowitz, Robert F. *The Great Impeacher: A Political Biography of James M. Ashley*. New York: Brooklyn College Press, 1979.

Horton, James O. "Links to Bondage: Free Blacks and the Underground Railroad." In *Free People of Color: Inside the African American Community*. Washington, DC: Smithsonian Institution Press, 1993: 53–74.

Horton, James O., and Lois E. Horton. *Black Bostonians: Family Life and Community Struggle in the Antebellum North*. New York: Holmes and Meier, 1979.

Horton, Louise. *Samuel Bell Maxey, A Biography*. Austin: University of Texas Press, 1974.

Hosley, William. *Colt: The Making of an American Legend*. Boston: University of Massachusetts Press, 1996.

Houston, Michael. "Edward Alfred Pollard and *The Richmond Examiner*: A Study of Journalistic Opposition In Wartime." M.A. thesis, American University, 1963.

How, Louis. *James B. Eads*. Boston: Houghton Mifflin, 1900.

Howard, Cecil Hampden Cutts. *Life and Public Services of Gen. John Wolcott Phelps; A Sketch Read before the New England Historic Genealogical Society, Dec. 1, 1886*. Frank E. Housh, 1887.

Howard, Oliver Otis. *Autobiography of Oliver Otis Howard, Major General United States Army*. 2 vols. New York: Baker & Taylor, 1908.

Howard, Victor B. *Black Liberation in Kentucky: Emancipation and Freedom, 1862–1884*. Lexington: University Press of Kentucky, 1983.

Howe, Samuel Gridley. *The Letters and Journals of Samuel Gridley Howe*. Edited by Laura E. Richards. 2 vols. Boston: Dana, Estes, 1906.

Hoyt, Edwin P. *The Peabody Influence: How A Great New England Family Helped to Build America*. New York: Dodd, Mead, 1968.

Hubbart, Henry Clyde. "'Pro-Southern' Influences in the Free West, 1840–1865." *Mississippi Valley Historical Review* 20 (June 1933), 45–62.

Hubbell, Jay B. *The Last Years of Henry Timrod*. Durham, NC: Duke University Press, 1941.

Hubell, John T., and James W. Geary, eds. *Biographical Dictionary of the Union: Northern Leaders of the Civil War*. Westport, CT: Greenwood Press, 1995.

Hudson, Frederic. *Journalism in the United States from 1690 to 1872*. 1873. Reprint. New York: Haskell House, 1968.

Hudson, Leonne M. *The Odyssey of a Southerner: The Life and Times of Gustavus Woodson Smith*. Macon, GA: Mercer University Press, 1998.

Huffstot, Robert S. "The Brief, Glorious Career of the CSS *Arkansas*." *Civil War Times Illustrated* 7 (April 1968): 20–27.

Hughes, J. Donald. *American Indians in Colorado*. Boulder, CO: Pruett, 1977.

Hughes, Nathaniel Cheairs, Jr. *The Battle of Belmont: Grant Strikes South*. Chapel Hill: University of North Carolina Press, 1991.

———. *Bentonville*. Chapel Hill: University of North Carolina Press, 1996.

———. *General William J. Hardee: Old Reliable*. Baton Rouge: Louisiana State University Press, 1965.

Hughes, Nathaniel Cheairs, Jr., and Roy P. Stonesifer, Jr. *The Life and Wars of Gideon J. Pillow*. Chapel Hill: University of North Carolina Press, 1993.

Hughes, Thomas Andrew. "The Civil War Press: Promoter of Unity or Neutral Reporter?" *American Journalism* 6 (Summer 1989): 181–201.

Hughes, W. J. *Rebellious Ranger*. Norman: University of Oklahoma Press, 1964.

Hume, Edgar Erskine. *The Golden Jubilee of the Association of Military Surgeons of the United States: A History of its First Half-Century—1891–1941*. Washington, DC: Association of Military Surgeons 7 (1941): 260–268.

Hummel, Jeffrey Rogers. *Emancipating Slaves, Enslaving Men: A History of the American Civil War*. Chicago: Open Court, 1996.

Humphreys, Andrew A. *From Gettysburg to the Rapidan. The Army of the Potomac, July 1863 to April 1864*. New York: Charles Scribner's Sons, 1883.

———. *The Virginia Campaign of 1864 and 1865. The Army of the Potomac and the Army of the James*. New York: Charles Scribner's Sons, 1883.

Humphreys, Henry H. *Andrew Atkinson Humphreys: A Biography*. Philadelphia: John C. Winston Co., 1924.

Hungerford, Edward. *Story of the Baltimore and Ohio Railroad, 1827–1927*. 2 vols. New York: G. P. Putnam's Sons, 1928.

Hunt, Aurora. *The Army of the Pacific, 1860–1866*. Glendale: A. H. Clarke Co., 1951.

Hunt, Gaillard. *Israel, Elihu and Cadwallader Washburn: A Chapter in American Biography*. New York: Macmillan, 1925.

Hunt, H. Draper. *Hannibal Hamlin of Maine: Lincoln's First Vice-President*. Syracuse, NY: Syracuse University Press, 1969.

Hunt, Roger D., and Jack R. Brown. *Brevet Brigadier Generals in Blue*. Gaithersburg, MD: Olde Soldier Books, 1990.

Hunton, Eppa. *Autobiography of Eppa Hunton*. Richmond, VA: William Byrd Press, 1933.

Hurn, Ethel Alice. *Wisconsin Women in the War between the States*. Madison: Wisconsin History Commission, 1911.

Hurst, Jack. *Nathan Bedford Forrest: A Biography*. New York: Alfred A. Knopf, 1993.

Huse, Caleb. *The Supplies of the Confederate Army*. Boston: Press of T. R. Narvin & Son, 1904.

Huston, James A. "Logistical Support of Federal Armies in the Field." *Civil War History* 7 (January 1961): 36–47.

———. *The Sinews of War: Army Logistics, 1775–1953*. Washington, DC: Office of the Chief of Military History, United States Army, 1966.

Huston, James L. "A Political Response to Industrialism: The Republican Embrace of Protectionist Labor Doctrines." *Journal of American History* 70 (June 1983): 35–57.

Hutchens, James Albert. "The Chief-Justiceship and Public Career of Richmond M. Pearson, 1861–1871." M.A. thesis.,University of North Carolina at Chapel Hill, 1960.

Hutchins, Nathan L. File. Georgia Department of Archives and History, Atlanta.

Hutton, Paul A. *Phil Sheridan and His Army*. Lincoln: University of Nebraska Press, 1985.

———, ed. *The Custer Reader*. Lincoln: University of Nebraska Press, 1992.

Hyman, Harold M. *"A More Perfect Union": The Impact of the Civil War and Reconstruction on the Constitution*. New York: Alfred A. Knopf, 1973.

———. *To Try Men's Souls: Loyalty Oaths in American History*. California: University of California Berkeley Press, 1959.

———, ed. "New Yorkers and the Civil War Draft." *New York History* 36 (April 1955): 164–171.

Hyman, Harold M., and William M. Wiecek. *Equal Justice under Law: Constitutional Development, 1835–1875*. New York: Harper & Row, 1982.

Ilisevich, Robert D. *Galusha A. Grow: The People's Candidate*. Pittsburgh, PA: University of Pittsburgh Press, 1988.

In Memoriam, Alexander Stewart Webb 1835–1911. Albany, NY: J. B. Lyon Co., 1916.

Ingraham, Charles A. *Elmer E. Ellsworth and the Zouaves of '61*. Chicago: University of Chicago Press, 1925.

Inscoe, John C. "Coping In Confederate Appalachia: Portrait of A Mountain Woman and Her Community at War." *North Carolina Historical Review* 69 (October 1992).

———. "Thomas Clingman, Mountain Whiggery, and the Southern Cause." *Civil War History* 33 (1987): 42–62.

Inscoe, John C., and Gordon B. McKinney. *The Heart of Confederate Appalachia: Western North Carolina in the Civil War*. Chapel Hill: University of North Carolina Press, 2000.

Iowa General Assembly. *Roster and Record of Iowa Soldiers in the War of the Rebellion: Together with Historical Sketches of Volunteer Organizations, 1861–1866*. 6 vols. Des Moines, IA: E. H. English, 1908–1911.

Isely, Jeter Allen. *Horace Greeley and the Republican Party, 1853–1861*. Princeton, NJ: Princeton University Press, 1947.

Isphording, Stephan M. "The House Years of John Sherman." M.A. thesis, University of Cincinnati, 1978.

Itter, William August. "Conscription in Pennsylvania during the Civil War." Ph.D. dissertation, University of Southern California, 1941.

Jackson, Harvey H., III. *Rivers of History: Life on the Coosa, Tallapoosa, Cahaba, and Alabama*. Tuscaloosa: University of Alabama Press, 1995.

Jackson, Mary Anna. *Memoirs of Stonewall Jackson by his Widow*. Louisville: Prentice Press, 1895.

Jackson, Patrick. *Education Act Forster: A Political Biography of W. E. Forster, 1818–1886*. London: Associated University Presses, 1997.

Jackson, Richard. *Popular Songs of Nineteenth Century America*. New York: Dover, 1976.

Jacob, Kathryn A. *Testament to Union: Civil War Monuments in Washington, DC*. Baltimore: Johns Hopkins University Press, 1998.

Jacobson, Doranne. *The Civil War in Art: A Visual Odyssey*. New York: Smithmark Publishers, 1996.

Jaffa, Harry V., and Robert W. Johannsen, eds. *In the Name of the People: Speeches and Writings of Lincoln and Douglas in the Ohio Campaign of 1859*. Columbus: Ohio State University Press, 1959.

Jahns, Patricia. *Matthew Fontaine Maury and Joseph Henry: Scientists of the Civil War*. New York: Hastings House, 1961.

James, D. Clayton. *Years of MacArthur: Volume I, 1880–1941*. Boston: Houghton Mifflin, 1970.

James, Marquis. *The Raven: A Biography of Sam Houston*. New York: Bobbs-Merrill, 1929.

James, Robert Rhodes. *Albert, Prince Consort: A Biography*. London: Hamish Hamilton, 1983.

Jamieson, Perry D. *Crossing the Deadly Ground: United States Army Tactics, 1865–1899*. Tuscaloosa: University of Alabama Press, 1994.

Jeffrey, Thomas E. *Thomas Lanier Clingman: Fire Eater from the Carolina Mountains*. Athens: University of Georgia Press, 1998.

Jeffries, C. C. "The Character of Terry's Texas Rangers."

Southwestern Historical Quarterly 64 (April 1961): 454–462.

Jellison, Charles A. *Fessenden of Maine: Civil War Senator.* Syracuse, NY: Syracuse University Press, 1962.

Jenkins, Brian. *Britain and the War for the Union.* 2 vols. Montreal: McGill-Queens University Press, 1974.

Jenkins, James H. *Elon J. Farnsworth: The Story of His Life.* Mount Vernon, NY: Published by the author, 1904.

Jenkins, Micah. "The Future's Promise: The Civil War Correspondence of Micah Jenkins. Edited by Ted Weaver." M.A. thesis, Clemson University, 1996.

Jenkins, Paul B. *The Battle of Westport.* Kansas City: Franklin Hudson, 1906.

Jensen, Ronald J. *The Alaska Purchase and Russian-American Relations.* Seattle: University of Washington Press, 1975.

Johannsen, Albert. *The House of Beadle and Adams.* Norman: University of Oklahoma Press, 1950.

Johannsen, Robert W. *The Frontier, The Union and Stephen A. Douglas.* Urbana: University of Illinois Press, 1989.

———. "The Lecompton Constitutional Convention: An Analysis of Its Membership." *Kansas Historical Quarterly* 23 (1957), 225–243.

———. *Stephen A. Douglas.* New York: Oxford University Press, 1973.

———, ed. *The Letters of Stephen A. Douglas.* Urbana: University of Illinois Press, 1961.

———, ed. *The Lincoln-Douglas Debates of 1858.* New York: Oxford University Press, 1965.

Johns, Jane Martin. *Personal Recollections of Early Decatur. Abraham Lincoln, Richard J. Oglesby and the Civil War.* Decatur, IL: Decatur Chapter, DAR, 1912.

Johns, John E. *Florida during the Civil War.* Gainesville: University of Florida Press, 1963.

Johnson, Adam R. *The Partisan Rangers of the Confederate States Army.* Louisville, KY: 1904.

Johnson, Angus J. *Virginian Railroads in the Civil War.* Chapel Hill: University of North Carolina Press, 1961.

Johnson, Emory R. *History of Domestic and Foreign Commerce of the United States.* Vol. 2. Washington, DC: Carnegie Institution, 1915.

Johnson, F. Roy. *The Gatling Gun and Flying Machine of Richard and Henry Gatling.* Murfreesboro, NC: Johnson Publishing, 1979.

Johnson, Flora Smith. "The War Record of Albert Gallatin Jenkins, C.S.A." *West Virginia History* 7 (1947): 392–400.

Johnson, George W. "Letters of George W. Johnson." *Register of the Kentucky Historical Society* 40 (October 1942): 336–352.

Johnson, John. *The Defense of Charleston Harbor including Fort Sumter and Adjacent Islands, 1863–1865.* Charleston: Walker, Evans & Cogswell, 1889.

Johnson, Ludwell H. *Red River Campaign: Politics and Cotton in the Civil War.* Baltimore: Johns Hopkins University Press, 1958.

Johnson, Michael P. *Toward a Patriarchal Republic: The Secession of Georgia.* Baton Rouge: Louisiana State University Press, 1977.

Johnson, Richard W. *A Soldier's Reminiscences in Peace and War.* Philadelphia: J. B. Lippincott, 1886.

Johnson, Robert E. *Rear Admiral John Rodgers, 1812–1882.* Annapolis, MD: Naval Institute Press, 1967.

Johnson, Robert Underwood, and Clarence Clough Buel, eds. *Battles and Leaders of the Civil War: Being for the Most Part Contributions by Union and Confederate Officers.* 4 vols. New York: Century Co., 1887–1888.

Johnson, Thomas Cary. *The Life and Letters of Robert Lewis Dabney.* Richmond, VA: Presbyterian Committee of Publication, 1903.

Johnson, Timothy D. *Winfield Scott: The Quest for Military Glory.* Lawrence: University Press of Kansas, 1998.

Johnson, Wait Chatterton, and Edwin S. Hartshorn. "The Development of Field Fortifications in the Civil War." In *Professional Memoirs, Corps of Engineers, U.S. Army, and Engineer Department-at-Large* 7 (1915): 570–602. Washington, DC.

Johnston, John W. *The True Story of John Burns.* Philadelphia: Privately published; William, Brown & Earle, 1916.

Johnston, Joseph E. *Narrative of Military Operations Directed during the Late War between the States.* New York: D. Appleton, 1874. Reprint. Bloomington: Indiana University Press, 1959.

Johnston, Mary Tabb. *Amelia Gayle Gorgas: A Biography.* University: University of Alabama Press, 1978.

Johnston, William Preston. *The Life of Gen. Albert Sidney Johnston.* New York: D Appleton & Co., 1878.

Jones, Archer. *Civil War Command and Strategy: The Process of Victory and Defeat.* New York: Free Press, 1992.

———. "Some Aspects of George Wythe Randolph's Service as Confederate Secretary of War." *Journal of Southern History* 26 (1960): 299–314.

Jones, Catesby ap R. "Services of the *Virginia* (*Merrimac*)." *Southern Historical Society Papers* 1 (1876): 90–91.

Jones, Charles Colcock, Jr. *The Life and Services of Commodore Josiah Tattnall.* Savannah, GA: Morning News Steam Printing House, 1878.

———. *The Siege of Savannah.* 1874. Reprint. Jonesboro, GA: Freedom Hill Press, 1988.

Jones, Charles Edgeworth. "In Memoriam Col. Charles C. Jones, Jr., LL.D., Historian, Biographer, and Archaeologist, 1831–1893." Augusta, GA: *Chronicle*, 1893.

Jones, Francis I. "Treason and Piracy in Civil War Halifax: The Second *Chesapeake* Affair Revisited." *Dalhousie Review* 71 (Winter 1991–92): 472–387.

Jones, Howard. *Mutiny on the Amistad.* Rev. ed. New York: Oxford University Press, 1987.

———. *Union in Peril. The Crisis over British Intervention in the Civil War.* Chapel Hill: University of North Carolina Press, 1992.

Jones, J. B. *A Rebel War Clerk's Diary at the Confederate States Capital.* 2 vols. Philadelphia: J. B. Lippincott, 1866.

Jones, J. William. *Christ in the Camp.* Richmond, VA: B. F. Johnson, 1887.

Jones, James Pickett. *Black Jack: John A. Logan and Southern Illinois in the Civil War Era.* Tallahassee: University Presses of Florida, 1967.

———. "Jefferson Davis in Blue: The Military Career, 1846–1866, of General Jefferson C. Davis, U.S.A." M.A. thesis, University of Florida, 1954.

———. *John A. Logan: Stalwart Republican from Illinois.* Tallahassee: University Presses of Florida, 1982.

———. "Lincoln's Courier: John L. Worden's Mission to Fort Pickens." *Florida Historical Quarterly* 41 (October 1962).

———. *Yankee Blitzkrieg: Wilson's Raid through Alabama and Georgia.* Athens: University of Georgia Press, 1976.

Jones, John Paul. *Dr. Mudd and the Lincoln Assassination: The Case Reopened.* Conshohocken, PA: Combined Books, 1995.

Jones, Lewis Hampton. *Captain Roger Jones of London and Virginia.* Albany, NY: Joel Munsell's Sons, 1891.

Jones, Maldwyn Allen. *American Immigration.* Chicago: University of Chicago Press, 1960.

Jones, Paul. *The Irish Brigade.* New York: Luce, 1969.

Jones, Robert H. *Civil War in the Northwest.* Norman:

University of Oklahoma Press, 1960.

Jones, Samuel. *The Siege of Charleston and the Operations on the South Atlantic Coast in the War among the States*. New York: Neale Publishing Co., 1911.

Jones, Terry L. *Lee's Tigers: The Louisiana Infantry in the Army of Northern Virginia*. Baton Rouge: Louisiana State University Press, 1987.

———. "The 28th Louisiana Volunteers in the Civil War." *North Louisiana Historical Association Journal* 9 (1978): 85–95.

Jones, Virgil Carrington. *The Civil War at Sea*. 3 vols. New York: Holt, Rinehart, Winston, 1961.

———. *Gray Ghosts and Rebel Raiders*. New York: Holt, 1956.

———. *Ranger Mosby*. Chapel Hill: University of North Carolina Press, 1944.

Jordan, David M. *Winfield Scott Hancock: A Soldier's Life*. Bloomington: Indiana University Press, 1988.

Jordan, Ervin L., Jr. *Black Confederates and Afro-Yankees in Civil War Virginia*. Charlottesville: University Press of Virginia, 1995.

Jordan, Thomas, and J. P. Pryor. *The Campaigns of Lieutenant General Nathan Bedford Forrest, and of Forrest's Cavalry*. 1868. Reprint. Dayton, OH: Morningside Press, 1988.

Jordan, W. T., Jr., and G. W. Thomas. "Massacre at Plymouth." *North Carolina Historical Review* (April 1995).

Joseph G. Tregle, Jr. "Thomas J. Durant, Utopian Socialism, and the Failure of Presidential Reconstruction in Louisiana." *Journal of Southern History* 45 (November 1979): 485–512.

Josephy, Alvin M. *The Civil War in the American West*. New York: Alfred A. Knopf, 1991.

Joshi, S. J., and David E. Schultz. *Ambrose Bierce: A Sole Survivor/Bits of Autobiography*. Knoxville: University of Tennessee Press, 1999.

Journal of the Congress of the Confederate States of America, 1861–1865. 7 vols. Washington, DC: Government Printing Office, 1904–1905.

Joyner, Fred B. "Robert Summing Schenck: First Citizen of the Miami Valley." *The Ohio State Archaeological and Historical Quarterly* (1949).

Julian, George W. *The Life of Joshua R. Giddings*. Chicago: A. C. McClurg, 1892.

———. *Political Recollections, 1840–1872*. Chicago: Jansen, McClurg & Co., 1884.

Kalfus, Melvin. *Frederick Law Olmsted: The Passion of a Public Artist*. New York: New York University Press, 1990.

Katcher, Philip R. N. *American Civil War Armies: Confederate Artillery, Cavalry, and Infantry*. London: Osprey Publishing, 1986.

———. "Union Captain Theodorus Bailey Faced Down an Angry Southern Mob to Take Command of New Orleans." *America's Civil War* 12 (January 2000): 8, 80–82.

Katz, D. Mark. *Witness to an Era: The Life and Photographs of Alexander Gardner: The Civil War, Lincoln, and the West*. New York: Viking, 1991.

Kaufmann, Wilhelm. *Die Deutschen im Amerikanischen Buergerkriege*. Munich and Berlin: Druck und Verlag von R. Oldenburg, 1911.

Kavanaugh, Celeste H. *David Levy Yulee: A Man and His Vision*. 2d ed. Fernandina Beach, FL: Board of Trustees of the Amelia Island Museum of History, 1995.

Kean, Robert Garlick Hill. *Inside the Confederate Government: The Diary of Robert Garlick Hill Kean*. Edited by Edward Younger. New York: Oxford University Press, 1957.

Kearney, Kevin E., ed. "Autobiography of William Marvin." *Florida Historical Quarterly* 36 (January 1958).

Kearny, Philip. *Letters from the Peninsula: The Civil War Letters of General Philip Kearny*. Kearny, NJ: Belle Grove Publishing Co., 1988.

Kearny, Thomas. *General Philip Kearny, Battle Soldier of Five Wars, including the Conquest of the West by General Stephen Watts Kearny*. New York: G. P. Putnam's Sons, 1937.

Keen, Nancy. *Confederate Prisoners of War at Fort Delaware*. Wilmington, DE: Cedar Tree Press, n.d.

Keenan, Jerry. *Wilson's Cavalry Corps; Union Campaigns in the Western Theatre, October 1864 through Spring 1865*. Jefferson, NC: McFarland, 1998.

Keene, Jesse L. *The Peace Convention of 1861*. Tuscaloosa: University of Alabama Press, 1961.

Keith, K. D. *Military Operations: Sabine Pass, 1861–63*. Austin: Texas State Historical Association, 1963.

Kell, John McIntosh. *Recollections of a Naval Life, including the Cruises of the Confederate States Steamers, Sumter and Alabama*. Washington, DC: Neale Co., 1900.

Keller, Allan. *Morgan's Raid*. Indianapolis: Bobbs-Merrill, 1961.

Kelley, Ruth E. "Robert Jefferson Breckinridge: His Political Influence and Leadership during 1849 and the Civil War." M.A. thesis, University of Kentucky, 1948.

Kellmeyer, Steven. "A Union Colonel Was the Russian Connection in the American Civil War." *Military History* (December 1993): 12–16.

Kelly, Dennis. "Second Manassas: The Battle and Campaign." *Civil War Times Illustrated* (May 1983): entire issue.

Kelly, Jack. "John J. Crittenden and the Constitutional Union Party." *Filson Club History Quarterly* 48 (July 1974): 265–276.

Kelly, Margaret Jean. *The Career of Joseph Lane, Frontier Politician*. Washington, DC: Catholic University Press, 1942.

Kelly, Michael T. *"I Will Have Justice Done": Gen. Gouverneur K. Warren, USA*. Gettysburg, PA: Farnsworth Military Impressions, 1997.

Kelly, Orr, and Mary Davies Kelly. *Dream's End: Two Iowa Brothers in the Civil War*. New York: Kodansha International, 1998.

Kemmerle, Darlene. "3,384 Who Died." *Oak Leaflets*. Maryland Forest, Park & Wildlife Service, n.d.

Kennedy, Edward F. *Lt. Darius Nash Couch in the Mexican War*. Taunton, MA: Old Colony Historical Society, 1977.

Kennedy, Frances H., ed. *The Civil War Battlefield Guide*. 2d ed. Boston: Houghton Mifflin, 1998.

Kennedy, J. C. G., Supt. of Census. *Population of the United States in 1860*. Washington, DC: U.S. Government Printing Office, 1864.

Kennerly, Dan. *The Dawn of Lightning War—General Forrest and Parker's Crossroads*. 5th ed. Houston: Published by the author, 1982.

Kennett, Lee. *Marching through Georgia: The Story of Soldiers and Civilians during Sherman's Campaign*. New York: HarperCollins, 1995.

———. "The Strange Career of the 'Stonewall'." *U.S. Naval Institute Proceedings* 94 (February 1968): 74–85.

Kerby, Robert L. *Kirby Smith's Confederacy: The Trans-Mississippi South, 1863–1865*. New York: Columbia University Press, 1972.

Kerkiss, Sydney C., comp. *The Atlanta Papers*. Dayton, OH: Press of Morningside Books, 1980.

Kerrigan, Evans. *American Medals and Decorations*. New York: Mallard Press, 1990.

Kershner, James W. *Sylvanus Thayer: A Biography*. New York: Arno Press, 1982.

Ketchum, Richard M., ed. *The American Heritage Picture History of the Civil War*. New York: American Heritage

Publishing Co., 1960.

Keyes, Erasmus D. *Fifty Years' Observations of Men and Events, Civil and Military.* New York: Charles Scribner's Sons, 1884.

Kidd, J. H. *Riding with Custer: Recollections of a Cavalryman in the Civil War.* Lincoln: University of Nebraska Press, 1997.

Kilpatrick, Arthur Roy. "Missouri's Secession Government, 1861–1865." *Missouri Historical Review* 45 (January 1951): 124–137.

Kilpatrick, Judson. *The Blue and the Gray, or, War is Hell.* Edited by J. Owen Moore and Christopher Morley. Garden City, NY: Doubleday, Doran, 1930.

Kimmel, Janice Martz. "Break Your Chains and Fly For Freedom." *Michigan History* 80:1 (1996): 20–27.

Kimmel, Stanley. *The Mad Booths of Maryland.* Indianapolis: Bobbs-Merrill, 1940.

Kincaid, Robert L. "Joshua Fry Speed—1814–1882." *Filson Club Historical Quarterly* 17 (April 1943).

Kinchen, Oscar. *Daredevils of the Confederate Army: The Story of the St. Albans Raiders.* Boston: Christopher Publishing House, 1959.

King, Alvy L. *Louis T. Wigfall, Southern Fire-eater.* Baton Rouge: Louisiana State University Press, 1970.

King, James T. "George Crook: Indian Fighter and Humanitarian." *Arizona and the West* 9 (1967): 333–348.

———. *War Eagle: A Life of General Eugene A. Carr.* Lincoln: University of Nebraska Press, 1963.

King, John H. *Three Hundred Days in a Yankee Prison; Reminiscences of War Life, Captivity, Imprisonment at Camp Chase, Ohio.* Atlanta: J. P. Davies, 1904.

King, Willard L. *Lincoln's Manager, David Davis.* Cambridge, MA: Harvard University Press, 1960.

Kiniapina, N. S. "Russia and the U.S. Civil War." In *Russian-American Dialogue on Cultural Relations, 1776–1914.* Edited by Norman E. Saul and Richard D. McKinzie. Columbia: University of Missouri Press, 1997: 93–106.

Kinsley, Philip. *The Chicago Tribune: Its First Hundred Years.* New York: Alfred A. Knopf, 1943.

Kinzer, Donald L. "Benjamin Harrison and the Politics of Availability." In *Gentlemen from Indiana: National Party Candidates, 1836–1940.* Indianapolis: Indiana Historical Bureau, 1977.

Kiper, Richard L. "Prelude to Vicksburg: The Louisiana Campaign of Major General John Alexander McClernand." *Louisiana History* (Summer 1996): 283–308.

Kirkland, Edward Chase. *Charles Francis Adams Junior 1835–1915: The Patrician at Bay.* Cambridge, MA: Harvard University Press, 1965.

———. *The Peacemakers of 1864.* New York: Macmillan, 1927.

Kirwan, Albert D. *John J. Crittenden: The Struggle for the Union.* Lexington: University Press of Kentucky, 1962.

Kitchens, Ben E., *Rosecrans Meets Price: The Battle of Iuka, Mississippi.* Florence, AL: Thornwood Book Publishers, 1987.

Klaus, Samuel, ed. *The Milligan Case.* 1929. Reprint. New York: Da Capo Press, 1970.

Klein, Maury. *Days of Defiance: Sumter, Secession, and the Coming of the Civil War.* New York: Alfred A. Knopf, 1997.

———. *Edward Porter Alexander.* Athens: University of Georgia Press, 1971.

———. *History of the Louisville & Nashville Railroad.* New York: Macmillan, 1972.

Klein, Philip Shriver. *President James Buchanan: A Biography.* University Park, PA: Pennsylvania State University, 1962.

Klement, Frank L. *The Copperheads in the Middle West.* Gloucester, MA: Peter Smith, 1972.

———. *Dark Lanterns: Secret Political Societies, Conspiracies, and Treason Trials in the Civil War.* Baton Rouge: Louisiana State University Press, 1984.

———. *The Limits of Dissent: Clement L. Vallandigham and the Civil War.* Lexington: University Press of Kentucky, 1970.

———. *Lincoln's Critics: The Copperheads of the North.* Shippensburg, PA: White Mane Books, 1999.

Kloeppel, James E. *Danger Beneath the Waves.* Orangeburg, SC: Sandlapper Publishing, 1987.

Klotter, James C. *The Breckinridges of Kentucky, 1760–1981.* Lexington: University Press of Kentucky, 1986.

Kluger, Richard. *The Paper: The Life and Death of the* New York Herald. New York: Random House, 1986.

Klunder, Willard Carl. *Lewis Cass and the Politics of Moderation.* Kent, OH: Kent State University Press, 1996.

———. "Lewis Cass and Slavery Expansion: The Father of Popular Sovereignty and Ideological Infanticide." *Civil War History* 32 (December 1986): 293–317.

Knauss, William H. *The Story of Camp Chase, a History of the Prison and Its Cemetery, Together with Other Cemeteries where Confederate Prisoners Are Buried, etc.* Nashville, TN: Methodist Episcopal Church, South, 1906.

Knetsch, Joe. "Madison Starke Perry vs. David Levy Yulee: The Fight for the Tampa Bay Route." *Sunland Tribune of the Tampa Historical Society* 23 (November 1997): 13–23.

Knight, Wilfred. *Red Fox: Stand Watie's Civil War Years in Indian Territory.* Glendale CA: Arthur H. Clark Co., 1988.

Kohl, Lawrence F., and Margeret Crosse Richards, eds. *Irish Green and Union Blue: The Civil War Letters of Peter Welsh, Color Sergeant, 28th Massachusetts.* New York: Fordham University Press, 1986.

Koistinen, Paul A. C. *Beating Plowshares into Swords: The Political Economy of American Warfare, 1606–1865.* Lawrence: University Press of Kansas, 1996.

Kolchin, Peter. *American Slavery, 1619–1877.* New York: Hill & Wang, 1993.

Korn, Bertram Wallace. *American Jewry and the Civil War.* Philadelphia: Jewish Publication Society of America, 1951.

Korn, Jerry. *Pursuit to Appomattox: The Last Battles. The Civil War.* Alexandria, VA: Time-Life Books, 1987.

Kraditor, Aileen S. *Means and Ends in American Abolitionism: Garrison and His Critics on Strategy and Tactics, 1834–1850.* New York: Vintage, 1969.

Krehbiel, Randy. "Indians in Blue and Gray." *America's Civil War* (January 1991): 30–36.

Krenkel, John H., and Catherine Yates Pickering. *Richard Yates: Civil War Governor.* Danville, IL: Interstate Printers & Publishers, 1966.

Krick, Robert K. *Conquering the Valley: Stonewall Jackson at Port Republic.* New York: William Morrow, 1996.

———. "General Nat Harris' Diary: The Rarest Army of Northern Virginia Book?" *Blue & Gray Magazine* 8 (August 1991): 30–31.

———. *Lee's Colonels: A Biographical Register of the Field Officers of the Army of Northern Virginia.* 4th ed. Dayton, OH: Morningside House, 1992.

———. *Maxcy Gregg: Political Extremist and Confederate General.* Kent, OH: Kent State University Press, 1973.

———. *Stonewall Jackson at Cedar Mountain.* Chapel Hill: University of North Carolina Press. 1990.

Krug, Kate. "Women Ovulate, Men Spermate: Elizabeth Blackwell as a Feminist Physiologist." *Journal of the History of Sexuality* 7 (1996): 51–72.

Krug, Mark M. *Lyman Trumbull: Conservative Radical.* New York: A. S. Barnes & Co., 1965.

Kruman, Marc W. *Parties and Politics in North Carolina, 1836–1865*. Baton Rouge: Louisiana State University Press, 1983.

———. "Thomas L. Clingman and the Whig Party: A Reconsideration." *North Carolina Historical Review* 64 (1987): 1–18.

Kurtz, Wilbur G. *The Atlanta Cyclorama: The Story of the Famed Battle of Atlanta*. Atlanta: City of Atlanta, 1954.

———. "The Death of Major General William H. T. Walker, July 22, 1864." *Civil War History* 6 (June 1960): 174–179.

Kushner, Howard I. "The Russian Fleet and the American Civil War: Another View." *Historian* 34 (August 1972): 633–649.

Kushner, Howard I., and Anne Hummell Sherrill. *John Hay: The Union of Poetry and Politics*. New Brunswick, NJ: Rutgers University Press, 1977.

Kutler, Stanley I. *Judicial Power and Reconstruction Politics*. Chicago: University of Chicago Press, 1968.

Laas, Virginia J., ed. *Wartime Washington: The Civil War Letters of Elizabeth Blair Lee*. Urbana: University of Illinois Press, 1991.

LaCavera, Tommie Phillips. *History of the Georgia Division, of the United Daughters of the Confederacy, 1895–1995*. Atlanta: The Georgia Division, 1995.

Ladd, Story Butler. *Halbert Eleazer Paine, February 4, 1826–April 14, 1905*. Washington, DC: Pamphlets in American History, 1920.

Lader, Lawrence. "New York's Bloodiest Week." *American Heritage* 10 (June 1959): 44–49, 95–98.

LaForce, Glen W. "The Trial of Major Henry Wirz—A National Disgrace." *The Army Lawyer* (June 1988): 3–10.

Laine, J. Gray. *Law's Alabama Brigade in the War Between the Union and the Confederacy*. Shippensburg, PA: White Mane Publisher, 1996.

Lair, John. *Songs Lincoln Loved*. New York: Duell, Sloan & Pearce, 1954.

Lambert, D. Warren. *When the Ripe Pears Fell: The Battle of Richmond, Kentucky*. Richmond, KY: Madison County Historical Society, 1995.

Lambert, Dobbie Edward. *Grumble: The W. E. Jones Brigade of 1863–1864*. Wahiawa, HA: Lambert Enterprises, 1992.

Lamers, William M. *The Edge of Glory: A Biography of General William S. Rosecrans, U.S.A.* New ed. Baton Rouge: Louisiana State University Press, 1999.

Lamon, Ward Hill. *Recollections of Abraham Lincoln, 1847–1865*. Edited by Dorothy Lamon Teillard. 1911. Reprint. Lincoln: University of Nebraska Press, 1994.

Lampe, Gregory P. *Frederick Douglass: Freedom's Voice, 1818–1845*. East Lansing: Michigan State University Press, 1998.

Landis, Merkel. "Civil War Times in Carlisle." Address delivered at the Hamilton Library, Carlisle, PA, February 12, 1931. Copy at the Cumberland County Historical Society, Carlisle, PA.

Landrith, Mark S. *The Effect of Personality of Senior Leaders on the Outcome of the Battle of Gettysburg*. Carlisle Barracks, PA: U.S. Army War College, 1997.

Lane, Wheaton Joshua. *Commodore Vanderbilt: An Epic of the Steam Age*. New York: Alfred A. Knopf, 1942.

Lang, George M. H., Raymond L. Collins, and Gerard F. White, comps. *Medal of Honor Recipients, 1863–1994*. 2 vols. New York: Facts on File, 1995.

Lang, Theodore F. *Loyal West Virginia, from 1861 to 1865*. Baltimore: Deutsch Publishing Co., 1895.

Langley, Lee M. "The Strategy and Tactics of C.S.A General Joseph E. Johnston against U.S. General William T. Sherman in North Georgia: Dalton to Kennesaw, May 4–July 3, 1864." M.A. thesis, Georgia College, 1986.

Langston, John Mercer. *From the Virginia Plantation to the National Capitol; or, The First and Only Negro Representative in Congress from the Old Dominion*. Hartford, CT: American Publishing Co., 1894.

Lapidus, Robert D. "A Southern Engima: The Unwavering Unionism of John Minor Botts." M.A. thesis, Ohio University, 1972.

Larios, Avila. "Brownsville-Matamoros: Confederate Lifeline." *Mid-America* 40 (April 1958): 67–89.

Larkin, J. L. "Battle of Santa Rosa Island." *The Florida Historical Quarterly* 37 (January–April 1959): 372–376.

Larson, Henrietta M. *Jay Cooke: Private Banker*. Cambridge, MA: Harvard University Press, 1936.

Lash, Jeffrey H. *Destroyer of the Iron Horse: General Joseph E. Johnston and the Confederate Rail Transport, 1861–1865*. Kent, OH: Kent State University Press, 1991.

Lathrop, Henry W. "The Late Gov. Wm. M. Stone." *Iowa Historical Record* 10 (January 1894): 35–39.

———. *The Life and Times of Samuel J. Kirkwood, Iowa's War Governor*. Chicago: Regan Press, 1893.

Laughlin, Sceva B. *Missouri Politics during the Civil War*. Salem, OR: Sceva B. Laughlin, 1930.

Lause, Mark. "Voting Yourself a Farm in Antebellum Iowa: Towards an Urban Working Class Prehistory of the Post Civil-War Agrarian Insurgency." *The Annals of Iowa* 49 (Winter/Spring 1988): 169–186.

Lavery, Dennis S., and Mark H. Jordan. *Iron Brigade General: John Gibbon, a Rebel in Blue*. Westport, CT: Greenwood Press, 1993.

Lawrence, Alexander A. *James Moore Wayne, Southern Unionist*. 1943. Reprint. Westport, CT: Greenwood Press, 1970.

Lawson, Lewis A. *Wheeler's Last Raid*. Greenwood, FL: Penkevil Publishing Co., 1986.

Lea, Tom. *The King Ranch*. Boston: Little, Brown, 1957.

Leach, Jack Franklin. *Conscription in the United States: Historical Background*. Tokyo: Charles B. Tuttle Co., 1960.

Leach, Margaret, and Harry J. Brown. *The Garfield Orbit*. New York: Harper & Row, 1978.

Leach, Richard H. "Benjamin R. Curtis: Case Study of a Supreme Court Justice." Ph.D. dissertation, Princeton University, 1951.

Leader, Robert Eadon, ed. *Life and Letters of John Arthur Roebuck*. New York: E. Arnold, 1897.

Leckie, Shirley Anne, ed. *The Colonel's Lady on the Western Frontier: The Correspondence of Alice Kirk Grierson*. Lincoln: University of Nebraska Press, 1989.

Leckie, William H., and Shirley A. Leckie. *Unlikely Warriors: General Benjamin H. Grierson and His Family*. Norman: University of Oklahoma Press, 1984.

Lee, Angela. "Tangling with 'Kilcavalry.'" *Civil War Times Illustrated* 37 (June 1998): 62–75.

Lee, Charles. *The Confederate Constitution*. Chapel Hill: University of North Carolina Press, 1963.

Lee, Fitzhugh. "Sketch of the Late General S. Cooper." *Southern Historical Society Papers* 3 (1877): 269–276.

Lee, R. E. *Lee's Dispatches: Unpublished Letters of General Robert E. Lee, C.S.A. to Jefferson Davis and the War Department of the Confederate States of America 1862–65*. Edited by Douglas Southall Freeman. Rev. ed. Grady McWhiney. New York: G. P. Putnam's Sons, 1957.

———. *The Wartime Papers of R. E. Lee*. Edited by Clifford Dowdey and Louis H. Manarin. Boston: Little, Brown, 1961.

Lee, Stephen D. "The Battle of Tupelo or Harrisburg, July 14, 1864." *Mississippi Valley Historical Society Publications*, 6 (1902): 39–52.

Lee, Susan Pendleton. *Memoirs of William Nelson Pendleton, D. D.* Philadelphia: J. B. Lippincott, 1893.

Leech, Margaret. *Reveille in Washington: 1860–1865.* New York: Harper & Brothers, 1941.

Leffingwell, Edward G. "'A Fine Animal': Portraits of General George Cadwalader of Philadelphia." M.A. thesis, University of Cincinnati, 1984.

Lefler, Hugh Talmadge. *Hinton Rowan Helper: Advocate of A White America.* Southern Sketches No 1. Charlottesville: University of Virginia, 1934.

LeGear, Clara E. *The Hotchkiss Map Collection: A List of Manuscript Maps.* Falls Church, VA: Sterling Press, 1977.

Lemke, William. *A Pride of Lions: Joshua Chamberlain and Other Maine Civil War Heroes.* North Attleborough, MA: Covered Bridge Press, 1997.

Leonard, Elizabeth D. *All the Daring of the Soldier: Women of the Civil War Armies.* New York: W. W. Norton, 1999.

Lerner, Eugene M. "The Monetary and Fiscal Programs of the Confederate Government, 1861–1865." *Journal of Political Economy* 62 (1954):

Lerner, Gerda. *The Grimké Sisters from South Carolina: Rebels against Slavery.* Boston: Houghton Mifflin, 1967.

Leslie, Edward E. *The Devil Knows How to Ride: The True Story of William Clarke Quantrill and His Confederate Raiders.* New York: Random House, 1996.

Leslie, James W., ed. "Arabella Lanktree Wilson's Civil War Letter." *Arkansas Historical Quarterly* 47 (Autumn 1988): 263.

Levine, Bruce. *The Spirit of 1848: German Immigrants, Labor Conflict, and the Coming of the Civil War.* Chicago: University of Illinois Press, 1992.

Levine, Peter. "Draft Evasion in the North during the Civil War, 1863–1865." *Journal of American History* 67 (1981): 816–834.

Levy, George. *To Die in Chicago; Confederate Prisoners at Camp Douglas, 1862–1865.* Evanston, IL: Evanston Publishing, 1994.

Levy, Leonard W. "Sims' Case: The Fugitive Slave Law in Boston in 1851." *Journal of Negro History* 35 (1950): 39–74.

Lewis, Charles Lee. *Admiral Franklin Buchanan Fearless Man of Action.* Baltimore: Norman, Remington Co., 1929.

———. *David Glasgow Farragut.* Annapolis, MD: Naval Institute Press, 1941–1943.

Lewis, Emmanuel. *Seacoast Fortifications of the United States: An Introductory History.* Washington, DC: Smithsonian Press, 1970.

Lewis, Gene D. *Charles Ellet, Jr.: The Engineer as Individualist.* Urbana: University of Illinois Press, 1968.

Lewis, Lloyd. *Sherman: Fighting Prophet.* New York: Harcourt, Brace, 1932.

Lewis, Oscar. *The War in the Far West: 1861–1865.* Garden City, NY: Doubleday, 1961.

Lewis, Samuel E. *Surgeon General Samuel Preston Moore and the Officers of the Medical Department of the Confederate States Army.* Washington, DC: s.n., 1911.

Lewis, Thomas A. *The Guns of Cedar Creek.* New York: Harper & Row Publishers, 1988.

Lewis, Walker. *Without Fear or Favor: A Biography of Chief Justice Roger Brooke Taney.* Boston: Houghton Mifflin, 1965.

Linderman, Gerald F. *Embattled Courage: The Experience of Combat in the Civil War.* New York: The Free Press, 1987.

Lindsey, David. *"Sunset" Cox, Irrepressible Democrat.* Detroit: Wayne State University Press, 1959.

Little, Robert Henry. *A Year of Starvation Amid Plenty, or, How a Confederate Soldier Suffered from Hunger and Cruelty in a Prison of War during the Awful Days of the Sixties.* Belton, TX: D. Kelly, 1966.

Littlefield, Daniel F., Jr. *The Chickasaw Freedmen: A People without a Country.* Westport, CT: Greenwood Press, 1980.

Lively, Donald E. *Foreshadows of the Law: Supreme Court Dissents and Constitutional Development.* Westport, CT: Praeger, 1992.

Livermore, Mary A. *My Story of the War.* Hartford: A. D. Worthington, 1887. Reprint. New York: Da Capo Press, 1995.

———. *The Story of My Life.* Hartford: A. D. Worthington, 1899. Reprint. New York: Amo, 1974.

Livermore, Thomas L. *Numbers and Losses in the Civil War in America, 1861–1865.* Carlisle, PA: John Kallman Publishers, 1996.

Livermore, William Roscoe. "Biographical Notice of George Washington Cullum." *Proceedings of the Academy of Arts and Sciences* 27: 416–421.

Lives and Speeches of Abraham Lincoln and Hannibal Hamlin. Columbus, OH: Follett, Foster & Co., 1860.

Livingston, Gary. *Fields of Gray: The Battle of Griswoldville.* New York: Caisson Press, 1996.

Livingstone, Charles B. *Charlie's Civil War: A Private's Trial by Fire in the 5th and 146th New York Zouaves.* Gettysburg, PA: Thomas Publications, 1997.

Lloyd, Mark. *Combat Uniforms of the Civil War.* New York: Mallard Press, 1990.

Logan, John A. *The Great Conspiracy, Its Origin and History.* New York: A. R. Hart, 1886.

———. *The Volunteer Soldier of America.* Chicago and New York: R. S. Peale Co., 1887.

Logan, Mary S. C. *Reminisces of a Soldier's Wife.* New York: Charles Scribner's Sons, 1913.

———. *Thirty Years in Washington.* Hartford, CT: A. D. Worthington, 1901.

Long, Armistead Lindsay. *Memoirs of Robert E. Lee; His Military and Personal History Embracing a Large Amount of Information Hitherto Unpublished.* Secaucus, NJ: Blue and Grey Press, 1983.

Long, David E. *The Jewel of Liberty: Abraham Lincoln's Re-Election and the End of Slavery.* Mechanicsburg, PA: Stackpole, 1994.

Long, E. B. *The Civil War Day by Day: An Almanac.* Garden City, NY: Doubleday, 1971.

———. *The Saints and the Union: Utah Territory during the Civil War.* Urbana: University of Illinois Press, 1981.

Long, Roger. "Copperhead Clement Vallandigham." *Civil War Times Illustrated* 20 (December 1981): 22–29.

Longacre, Edward G. *Army of Amateurs: General Benjamin F. Butler and the Army of the James, 1863–1865.* Mechanicsburg, PA: Stackpole, 1997.

———. "Brave, Radical, Wild: The Contentious Career of Brigadier General Edward A. Wild." *Civil War Times Illustrated* 19 (June 1980): 9–19.

———. *The Cavalry at Gettysburg: A Tactical Study of Mounted Operations during the Civil War's Pivotal Campaign, 9 June–14 July 1863.* 1986. Reprint. Lincoln: University of Nebraska Press, 1993.

———. *Custer and His Wolverines: The Michigan Cavalry Brigade, 1861–1865.* Conshohocken, PA: Combined Books, 1997.

———. *General John Buford: A Military Biography.* Conshohocken, PA: Combined Books, 1995.

———. *Lincoln's Cavalrymen: A History of the Mounted Forces of the Army of the Potomac.* Mechanicsburg, PA: Stackpole, 1999.

———. *The Man Behind the Guns: A Biography of General Henry Jackson Hunt, Chief of Artillery, Army of the Potomac.* New York: A. S. Barnes & Co., 1977.

———. *Mounted Raids of the Civil War.* 1975. Reprint. Lincoln: University of Nebraska Press, 1994.

Longstreet, Helen D. *Lee and Longstreet at High Tide: Gettysburg in the Light of the Official Records.* 1904. Reprint. Wilmington, NC: Broadfoot Publishing, 1989.

Longstreet, James. *From Manassas to Appomattox: Memoirs of the Civil War in America.* 1896. Reprint. Bloomington: Indiana University Press, 1960.

Longum, David J., and Howard P. Walthall. *From Maverick to Mainstream: Cumberland School of Law, 1847–1997.* Athens: University of Georgia Press, 1997.

Lonn, Ella. *Desertion during the Civil War.* 1928. Reprint. Lincoln: University of Nebraska Press, 1998.

———. *Foreigners in the Union Army and Navy.* Baton Rouge: Louisiana State University Press, 1951.

Looby, Christopher, ed. *The Complete Civil War Journal and Selected Letters of Thomas Wentworth Higginson.* Chicago: University of Chicago Press, 2000.

Looney, John Thomas. "Isham G. Harris of Tennessee: Bourbon Senator, 1877–1897." M.A. thesis, University of Tennessee, Knoxville, 1970.

Lopp, Larry G. "The Campaigns of General Robert H. Milroy, 1862–1863." M.A. thesis, Butler University, 1970.

Lord, Francis A. *Civil War Collector's Encyclopedia.* Vol. I and II. Edison: Blue & Grey Press, 1995

———. *Civil War Sutlers and Their Wares.* New York: T. Yoseloff, 1969.

———. *Lincoln's Railroad Man: Herman Haupt.* Rutherford: Farleigh Dickinson University Press, 1969.

———. *They Fought for the Union.* Harrisburg, PA: Stackpole, 1960.

Lord, Frank, "Hancock's First Veterans Corps." *Military Collector and Historian* 26 (1974): 153–158.

Lord, Walter, ed. *The Fremantle Diary: Being the Journal of Lieutenant Colonel James Arthur Lyon Fremantle, Coldstream Guards, on His Three Months in the Southern States.* Boston: Little, Brown, 1954.

Losson, Christopher. *Tennessee's Forgotten Warriors: Frank Cheatham and His Confederate Division.* Knoxville: University of Tennessee Press, 1989.

Love, William DeLoss. *Wisconsin in the War of the Rebellion: A History of All Regiments and Batteries the State Has Sent to the Field, and Deeds of Her Citizens, Governors and Other Military Officers, and State and National Legislators to Suppress the Rebellion.* Chicago: Church & Goodman, 1866.

Lovejoy, Joseph C., and Owen Lovejoy. *Memoir of the Rev. Elijah P. Lovejoy; Who Was Murdered in Defence of the Liberty of the Press, at Alton, Illinois, Nov. 7, 1837.* Introduction by John Quincy Adams. New York: John S. Taylor, 1838.

Lowe, Richard G. "Virginia's Reconstruction Convention: General Schofield Rates the Delegates." *Virginia Magazine of History and Biography* 80 (July 1972): 341–360.

Lowell, James Russell. *Letters of James Russell Lowell.* Edited by Charles Eliot Norton. 2 vols. New York: Harper, 1894.

———. *The Writings of James Russell Lowell.* 10 vols. Boston: Houghton Mifflin, 1890.

Lowry, Terry. *September Blood: The Battle of Carnifex Ferry.* Charleston, WV: Pictorial Histories Publishing Co., 1985.

Lowry, Timothy S. *And Brave Men Too.* New York: Crown Publishers, 1985.

Lubbock, Percy, ed. *Six Decades in Texas: The Memoirs of Francis R. Lubbock.* Austin, TX: Pemberton Press, 1968.

Lucas, Marion B. "Camp Nelson, Kentucky during the Civil War Cradle of Liberty or Refugee Death Camp." *The Filson Club History Quarterly* 63 (1989): 439–452.

———. *A History of Blacks in Kentucky, Vol. 1: From Slavery to Segregation, 1760–1891.* Frankfort: Kentucky Historical Society, 1992.

———. *Sherman and the Burning of Columbia.* College Station: Texas A&M University Press, 1976.

Luebke, Frederick C., ed. *Ethnic Voters and the Election of Lincoln.* Lincoln: University of Nebraska Press, 1971.

Lumpkin, Katharine Du Pre. *The Emancipation of Angelina Grimké.* Chapel Hill: University of North Carolina Press, 1974.

Luraghi, Raimondo. *A History of the Confederate Navy.* Annapolis, MD: Naval Institute Press, 1996.

Luthin, Reinhard H. "A Discordant Chapter in Lincoln's Administration: The Davis-Blair Controversy." *Maryland Historical Magazine* 39 (March 1944): 25–48.

———. *The First Lincoln Campaign.* Cambridge, MA: Harvard University Press, 1944.

Luvaas, Jay, and Wilbur S. Nye. "The Campaign that History Forgot." *Civil War Times Illustrated* 8 (November 1969).

———. *The Military Legacy of the Civil War: The European Inheritance.* 1959. Reprint. Lawrence: University Press of Kansas, 1988.

Lyman, Darryl. *The Civil War Wordbook: including Sayings, Phrases, and Slang.* Conshohocken, PA: Combined Books, 1993.

Lynch, Jeanne Hall. "Thomas Hill Watts, Civil War Governor of Alabama, 1863–1865." M.A. thesis, Auburn University, 1957.

Lyon, William H. "Claiborne Fox Jackson and the Secession Crisis in Missouri." *Missouri Historical Review* 58 (July 1964): 422–141.

Lyons, W. F. *Brigadier General Thomas Francis Meagher: His Political and Military Career.* New York: D. & J. Sadlier, 1870.

Mabee, Carleton. *Black Freedom: The Nonviolent Abolitionists from 1830 through the Civil War.* New York: Macmillan, 1970.

Mabee, Carleton, and Susan Mabee Newhouse. *Sojourner Truth: Slave, Prophet, Legend.* New York: New York University Press, 1993.

Mabry, W. S. *Brief Sketch of the Career of Captain Catesby Ap R. Jones.* Privately printed, 1912.

MacArthur, Douglas. *Reminiscences.* New York: *Time,* 1964.

Macartney, Clarence Edward. *Grant and His Generals.* New York: The McBride Co., 1953.

———. *Mr. Lincoln's Admirals.* New York: Funk & Wagnalls, 1956.

MacDonald, Cheryl. "Last Stop on the Underground Railroad." *Beaver* [Canada] 70 (1990): 32–38.

Maclay, Edgar S. *A History of American Privateers.* New York: D. Appleton & Co., 1899.

Madaus, Howard M. "Rebel Flags Afloat: A Survey of the Surviving Flags of the Confederate State Navy, Revenue Service, and Merchant Marine." *Flag Bulletin* 25 (January–April 1986): 1–79.

———. *The Battle Flags of the Confederate Army of Tennessee.* Milwaukee: Milwaukee Public Museum, 1976.

Madden, Richard C. *Catholics in South Carolina: A Record.* Lanham, MD: University Press of America, 1985.

Maddex, Jack. *The Virginia Conservatives, 1867–1879; A Study in Reconstruction Politics.* Chapel Hill: University of North Carolina Press, 1970.

Madison, James H. *The Indiana Way: A State History.* Indianapolis: Indiana Historical Society and Indiana University Press, 1986.

Madsen, Brigham D. *Glory Hunter: A Biography of Patrick Edward Connor*. Salt Lake City: University of Utah Press, 1990.

Maffitt, Emma Martin. *The Life and Services of John Newland Maffitt*. New York: Neale Publishing Co., 1906.

Magdol, Edward. *Owen Lovejoy: Abolitionist in Congress*. New Brunswick, NJ: Rutgers University Press, 1967.

———. "Owen Lovejoy's Role in the Campaign of 1858." *Journal of the Illinois State Historical Society* 51 (1958): 403–416.

Maginnes, David R. "The Case of the Court House Rioters in the Rendition of the Fugitive Slave Anthony Burns, 1854." *Journal of Negro History* 56 (1971): 31–42.

Mahan, Alfred Thayer. *Admiral Farragut: First Admiral of the United States Navy*. New York: D. Appleton, 1879.

Mahan, Harold E. "Arsenal of History: The Official Records of the Rebellion." *Civil War History* 29 (1983): 5–27.

Maher, Sr. Mary Denis, CSA. *To Bind Up the Wounds: Catholic Sister Nurses in the U.S. Civil War*. 1989. Reprint. Baton Rouge: Louisiana State University Press, 1999.

Mahon, John K. "Civil War Infantry Assault Tactics." *Military Affairs* 25 (1961): 57–68.

"Major General John R. Brooke." *New York Herald*, 18 December 1898.

Malin, James C. *The Nebraska Question, 1852–1854*. Lawrence: University Press of Kansas, 1953.

Mallison, Fred M. *The Civil War on the Outer Banks*. Jefferson, NC: McFarland, 1997.

Maness, Lonnie E. "Forrest and the Battle of Parker's Crossroads." *Tennessee Historical Quarterly* 34 (Summer 1975): 154–167.

———. *An Untutored Genius: The Military Career of General Nathan Bedford Forrest*. Oxford, MS: Guild Bindery Press, 1990.

Manigault, Arthur Middleton. *A Carolinian Goes to War: The Civil War Narrative of Arthur Middleton Manigault, Brigadier General, C.S.A.* Edited by R. Lockwood Turner. Columbia: University of South Carolina Press, 1983

Manning, Michael L. *Senseless Secrets*. New York: Birch Lane Press, 1996.

March, David D. *The History of Missouri. Vol. 2*. New York: Lewis Historical Publishing Co., 1967.

Marcot, Roy M. *Civil War Chief of Sharpshooters Hiram Berdan: Military Commander and Firearms Inventor*. Irvine, CA: Northwood Heritage Press, 1989.

Margreiter, John. "The Battle of Pilot Knob." *Civil War Times Illustrated* (November 1964).

Marino, Carl W. "General Alfred Howe Terry: Soldier from Connecticut." Ph.D. dissertation, New York University, 1968.

Markle, Donald E. *Spies and Spymasters of the Civil War*. New York: Hippocrene Books, 1994.

Marlow, Clayton Charles. *Matt W. Ransom, Confederate General from North Carolina*. Jefferson, NC: McFarland, 1996.

Marmaduke, John S. *The Battle of Chalk Bluff: An Account of General John S. Marmaduke's Second Missouri Raid*. Doniphan, MO: Ponder Books, 1994.

Marone, Biagino M. "Senator James Rood Doolittle and the Struggle against Radicalism, 1857–1866." M.A. thesis, Marquette University, 1955.

Marquis, Greg. *In Armageddon's Shadow: The Civil War and Canada's Maritime Provinces*. Toronto: University of Toronto Press, 1998.

———. "Mercenaries or Killer Angels? Nova Scotians in the American Civil War." *Collections of the Royal Nova Scotia Historical Society* 44 (1996): 83–104.

Marshall, Charles. *An Aide-de-Camp of Lee: Being the Papers of Colonel Charles Marshall Sometime Aide-de-Camp, Military Secretary, and Assistant Adjutant General on the Staff of Robert E. Lee, 1862–1865*. Edited by Major General Sir Frederick Maurice. Boston: Little, Brown, 1927.

Marshall, Humphrey. *Speeches of Hon. Humphrey Marshall & Hon. B. F. Hallett, in the City of Washington on the Nomination of Breckinridge and Lane: Speech of Hon. Humphrey Marshall, of Kentucky*. Washington, DC: National Democratic Executive Committee, 1860.

Marshall, John A. *American Bastille: A History of the Illegal Arrests and Imprisonment of American Citizens during the Late Civil War*. Philadelphia: Evans, Stoddart & Co., 1878.

Marshall, Mary Louise. "Nurse Heroines of the Confederacy." *Bulletin of the Medical Librarians' Association* 45 (July 1957): 319–336.

Marszalek, John F. *Sherman: A Soldier's Passion for Order*. New York: Vintage Books, 1994.

———. *Sherman's Other War: The General and the Civil War Press*. Rev. ed. Kent, OH: Kent State University Press, 1999.

———. "Where Did Winfield Scott Find His Anaconda?" *Lincoln Herald* (Summer 1987): 77–81.

Marten, James. *The Children's Civil War*. Chapel Hill: University of North Carolina Press, 1998.

———. *Texas Divided: Loyalty and Dissent in the Lone Star State, 1856–1874*. Lexington: University Press of Kentucky, 1990.

Martin, Bessie. *Desertion among Alabama Troops during the Civil War*. New York: Peter Smith, 1966.

Martin, David G. *Gettysburg, July 1*. Conshohocken, PA: Combined Books, 1995.

Martin, Richard A. "Defeat in Victory: Yankee Experience in Early Civil War Jacksonville." *Florida Historical Quarterly* 52 (July 1974).

Martin, Samuel J. *The Road to Glory: Confederate General Richard S. Ewell*. Indianapolis: Guild Press of Indiana, 1991.

Martin, Theodore. *The Life of His Royal Highness the Prince Consort*. 5 vols. London: Smith Elder & Co., 1880.

Marvel, William. *The* Alabama *and the* Kearsarge: *The Sailor's Civil War*. Chapel Hill: University of North Carolina Press, 1996.

———. *Andersonville: The Last Depot*. Chapel Hill: University of North Carolina Press, 1994.

———. "The Battle of Saltville: Massacre or Myth." *Blue and Gray Magazine* (August 1991): 10–19,46–60.

———. *Burnside*. Chapel Hill: University of North Carolina Press, 1991.

Massey, Mary Elizabeth. *Bonnet Brigades*. New York: Alfred A. Knopf, 1966.

———. *Women in the Civil War*. Lincoln: University of Nebraska Press, 1994.

Mathew, W. M. *Edmund Ruffin and the Crisis of Slavery*. Athens: University of Georgia Press, 1988.

Mathews, Don, "Wealth and Its Distribution in the Antebellum South: Where Do We Stand and Why Does it Matter?" *Essays in Economic and Business History* 15 (1997): 109–120.

Mathews, Joseph J. *George W. Smalley: Forty Years a Foreign Correspondent*. Chapel Hill: University of North Carolina Press, 1973.

———. *Reporting the Wars*. Minneapolis: University of Minnesota Press, 1957.

Mathis, Robert Neil. "Freedom of the Press in the Confederacy: A Reality." *Historian* 37 (1975): 633–648.

Matlock, Joseph Dixon. "The Peace Conference of 1861 in

Washington, D.C." M.A. thesis, University of Texas at Austin, 1931.

Matter, William D. *If It Takes All Summer: The Battle of Spotsylvania.* Chapel Hill: University of North Carolina Press, 1988.

Matthew, H. C. G. *Gladstone, 1809–1898.* New York: Oxford University Press, 1997.

Matthews, Byron H., Sr. *The McCook-Stoneman Raid.* Philadelphia: Dorrance & Co., 1976.

Maury, Dabney H. *Recollections of a Virginian in the Mexican, Indian, and Civil Wars.* 2d ed. New York: Charles Scribner's Sons, 1894.

Maverick, Augustus. *Henry J. Raymond and the New York Press for Thirty Years: Progress of American Journalism from 1840–1870.* Hartford, CT: A. S. Hale & Co., 1870.

Maxfield, Albert. *Roster and Statistical Record of Company D of the Eleventh Regiment Maine Infantry Volunteers: With a Sketch of its Services in the War of the Rebellion.* New York: Press of T. Humprey, 1890.

Maxwell, William Quentin. *Lincoln's Fifth Wheel: The Political History of the United States Sanitary Commission.* New York: Longmans, Green, 1956.

May, Robert E. *John A. Quitman: Old South Crusader.* Baton Rouge: Louisiana State University Press, 1985.

——. *The Southern Dream of a Caribbean Empire 1834–1861.* Baton Rouge: Louisiana State University Press, 1973.

Mayo, Bernard. *Henry Clay.* Boston: Houghton Mifflin, 1937.

Mayo, James. *War Memorials as Political Landscape: The American Experience and Beyond.* New York: Praeger, 1988.

Mays, Thomas D. *The Saltville Massacre.* Fort Worth, TX: Ryan Place Publishers, 1995.

McAfee, Michael J. *Zouaves: The First and the Bravest.* Gettysburg, PA: Thomas Publications, 1991.

McAffee, Ward M. "California's House Divided." *Civil War History* 33 (June 1987): 115–130.

McBride, Robert M., and Dan M. Robinson. *Biographical Directory of the Tennessee General Assembly.* Edited by Robert M. McBride. Vol. I. Nashville: Tennessee State Library and Archives and Tennessee Historical Commission, 1975.

McCague, James. *The Second Rebellion: The Story of the New York City Draft Riots.* New York: Dial Press, 1968.

McCann, William, ed. *Ambrose Bierce's Civil War.* Washington, DC: Regnery Gateway, 1956.

McCardell, John. *The Idea of a Southern Nation: Southern Nationalists and Southern Nationalism.* New York: W. W. Norton, 1979.

McCarthy, Carlton. *Detailed Minutiae of Soldier Life in the Army of Northern Virginia 1861–1865.* Richmond, VA: Carlton McCarthy & Co., 1882.

McCartney, Martha. *The Battle of Drewry's Bluff in Chesterfield County, Virginia: The Historical Background.* Harrisonburg, VA: James Madison University Archeological Research Center, 1988.

McCash, William B. *Thomas R. R. Cobb; The Making of a Southern Nationalist.* Macon, GA: Mercer University Press, 1983.

McCaslin, Richard B. *Portraits of Conflict. A Photographic History of South Carolina in the Civil War.* Fayetteville: University of Arkansas Press, 1994.

——. *Tainted Breeze: The Great Hanging at Gainesville, Texas.* Baton Rouge: Louisiana State University Press, 1994.

——, comp. *Andrew Johnson: A Bibliography.* Westport, CT: Greenwood Publications Group, 1993.

McClellan, George B. *The Army of the Potomac: General McClellan's Report of Its Operations While under his Command.* New York: Putnam, 1864.

——. *McClellan's Own Story: The War for the Union, the Soldiers Who Fought It, the Civilians Who Directed It, and his Relations to It and to Them.* Edited by William C. Prime. New York: Charles L. Webster, 1887.

——. *Report on the Organization of the Army of the Potomac, to Which Is Added an Account of the Campaign in Western Virginia, with Plans of Battlefields.* New York: Sheldon & Co., 1864.

McClellan, Henry B. *I Rode with Jeb Stuart: The Life and Campaigns of Major General J. E. B. Stuart.* 1885. Reprint. Millwood, NJ: Kraus Reprint.

——. *The Life and Campaigns of Major-General J. E. B. Stuart, Commander of the Cavalry of the Army of Northern Virginia.* Secaucus, NJ: Blue and Grey Press, 1993.

McCloskey, Robert G., and Sanford Levinson. *The American Supreme Court.* 2d ed. Chicago: University of Chicago Press, 1994.

McClure, Alexander K., ed. *The Annals of the War Written by Leading Participants North and South.* 1879. Reprint. Dayton, OH: Morningside Bookshop, 1988. Reprint. New York: Da Capo Press, 1994.

McConnell, Stuart. *Glorious Contentment: The Grand Army of the Republic, 1865–1900.* Chapel Hill: University of North Carolina Press, 1992.

McConnell, William F. *Remember Reno: A Biography of Major General Jesse Lee Reno.* Shippensburg, PA: White Mane Publishers, 1996.

McCormick, Robert W. "About Six Acres of Land: Camp Chase, Civil War Prison." *Timeline* 11 (1994): 34–43.

McCormick, Virginia E. "The Talented Sherwoods: Poets and Politicians." *Northwest Ohio Quarterly* 52 (Summer 1980): 244–253.

McCray, Carrie Allen. *Freedom's Child: The Life of a Confederate General's Black Daughter.* Chapel Hill, NC: Algonquin Books of Chapel Hill, 1998.

McCulloch, Hugh. *Men and Measures of Half a Century.* New York: Charles Scribner's Sons, 1888.

McDonald, Archie P., ed. *Make Me a Map of the Valley: The Civil War Journal of Stonewall Jackson's Topographer Jedediah Hotchkiss.* Dallas: Southern Methodist University Press, 1973.

McDonald, Forrest. *A Constitutional History of the United States.* New York: Franklin Watts, 1982.

McDonald, JoAnna M. *We Shall Meet Again: The First Battle of Manassas, July 18–21, 1861.* Shippensburg, PA: White Mane Publishing Co., 1999.

McDonald, Kendra Lynne. "The Creation of History and Myth in Mary Boykin Miller Chesnut's Civil War Narrative." Ph.D. dissertation, Ohio State University, 1996.

McDonald, Ronald H. "Second Chesapeake Affair." *Dalhousie Review* 54 (Winter 1974–75): 674–684.

McDonald, William N. *A History of the Laurel Brigade Originally the Ashby Cavalry of the Army of Northern Virginia and Chew's Battery.* Baltimore: Sun Job Printing, 1907.

McDonough, James L. *Chattanooga—A Death Grip on the Confederacy.* Knoxville: University of Tennessee Press, 1984.

——. *Schofield: Union General in the Civil War and Reconstruction.* Tallahassee: Florida State University Press, 1972.

——. *Shiloh—In Hell before Night.* Knoxville: University of Tennessee Press, 1997.

——. *Stones River—Bloody Winter in Tennessee.* Knoxville: University of Tennessee Press, 1980.

——. *War in Kentucky: From Shiloh to Perryville.* Knoxville: University of Tennessee Press, 1994.

McDonough, James L., and Thomas L. Connelly. *Five Tragic Hours: The Battle of Franklin.* Knoxville: University of Tennessee Press, 1983.

McDowell, Robert Emmett, ed. *Resolution of the [Confederate] Congress [in Kentucky] 1861.* Lyndon, KY: Mull-Wathen Historic Press, 1970.

McElligott, Ellen, ed. "'A Monotony Full of Sadness': The Diary of Nadine Turchin, May, 1863–April 1864." *Journal of the Illinois State Historical Society* 70 (1977): 27–89.

McFadden, Elizabeth. *The Glitter and the Gold: A Spirited Account of the Metropolitan Museum of Art's First Director, the Audacioius and High-handed Luigi Palma di Cesnola.* New York: Dial Press, 1971.

McFeely, William S. *Frederick Douglass.* New York: W. W. Norton, 1991.

———. *Grant: A Biography.* Norwalk, CT: Eastern Press, 1981.

———. *Yankee Stepfather: Genneral O. O. Howard and the Freedmen.* New Haven, CT: Yale University Press, 1968.

McGinnis, Karen Hertel. "Moving Right Along: Nineteenth Century Panorama Painting in the United States." Ph.D. dissertation, University of Minnesota, 1983.

McGlothlin, W. J. *Baptist Beginnings in Education: A History of Furman University.* Nashville, TN: Sunday School Board of the Southern Baptist Convention, 1926.

McGowen, Stanley S. *Horse Sweat and Powder Smoke: The 1st Texas Cavalry in the Civil War.* College Station: Texas A&M University Press, 1999.

McHenry, Estill, ed. *Addresses and Papers of James B. Eads, together with a Biographical Sketch.* St. Louis: Slawson & Co., 1884.

McIlwaine, H. R. "Master Surgeons of America. Samuel Preston Moore." *Surgery, Gynecology and Obstetrics* 39 (1924): 668. (Note: This article, as do several others on Moore, mistakenly uses a photograph of Brigadier General Patrick Theodore Moore, C.S.A., who commanded a brigade of General Longstreet's at First Bull Run.)

McInvale, Morton R. "'All that Devils Could Wish For': The Griswoldville Campaign, November, 1864." *Georgia Historical Quarterly* 60 (1976): 117–130.

McKay, Ernest A. *Henry Wilson: Practical Radical; A Portrait of a Politician.* Port Washington, NY: Kennikat Press, 1971.

McKee, Irving. *"Ben-Hur" Wallace: The Life of General Lew Wallace.* Berkeley: University of California Press, 1947.

McKee, W. Reid, and M. E. Mason, Jr. *Civil War Projectiles II: Small Arms & Field Artillery.* Mechanicsville, VA: Rapidan Press, 1980.

McKinney, Francis F. *Education in Violence: The Life of George H. Thomas and the History of the Army of the Cumberland.* Detroit: Wayne State University Press, 1961.

McKitrick, Eric L. *Andrew Johnson and Reconstruction.* New York: Oxford University Press. 1988.

McLendon, James. "John A. Quitman, Fire-Eating Governor." *Journal of Mississippi History* 15 (1953).

McLoughlin, William G. *After the Trail of Tears: The Cherokees' Struggle for Sovereignty, 1839–1880.* Chapel Hill: University of North Carolina Press, 1993.

McMahon, Helen Grace. "Reuben Eaton Fenton." M.A. thesis, Cornell University, 1939.

McMahon, Martin T. *In Memoriam: Maj.–Gen. John Sedgwick.* Togus, ME: Printed by the National Home, 1885.

McManus, Howard Rollins. *The Battle of Cloyd's Mountain: The Virginia and Tennessee Railroad Raid.* Lynchburg, VA: H. E. Howard, 1989.

McMillan, Malcolm C. *The Alabama Confederate Reader.* Tuscaloosa: University of Alabama Press, 1963.

———. *Constitutional Development in Alabama, 1798–1901.* Chapel Hill: University of North Carolina Press, 1955.

McMillen, James Adelbert, ed. *The Works of James D. B. De Bow.* Hattiesburg, MS: The Book Farm, 1940.

McMurray, William J. *History of the Twentieth Tennessee Volunteer Infantry C.S.A.* Nashville, TN: Publication Committee, 1904.

McMurry, Richard M. *John Bell Hood and the War for Southern Independence.* Lincoln: University of Nebraska Press, 1982.

———. *Two Great Rebel Armies: An Essay in Confederate Military History.* Chapel Hill: University of North Carolina Press, 1989.

McMurtry, Gerald. "Zollicoffer and the Battle of Mill Springs." *The Filson Club History Quarterly* 29 (October 1955): 303–319.

McMurtry, R. Gerald. *Ben Hardin Helm.* Chicago: Civil War Roundtable, 1948.

McPherson, James M. *Abraham Lincoln and the Second American Revolution.* New York: Oxford University Press, 1992.

———. *The Atlas of the Civil War.* New York: Macmillan, 1994.

———. *Battle Cry of Freedom: The Civil War Era.* New York: Oxford University Press, 1988.

———. *For Cause and Comrades: Why Men Fought in the Civil War.* New York, 1997.

———. *Lincoln and The Strategy of Unconditional Surrender.* 23d Annual Robert Fortenbaugh Memorial Lecture. Gettysburg, PA: Gettysburg College, 1984.

———. *The Negro's Civil War: How American Blacks Felt and Acted during The War for the Union.* 1965. Reprint. New York: Ballantine Books, 1991.

———. *Ordeal by Fire: The Civil War and Reconstruction.* 2d ed. New York: McGraw-Hill, 1992.

———. *The Struggle for Equality: Abolitionists and the Negro in the Civil War and Reconstruction.* Princeton, NJ: Princeton University Press, 1964.

McPherson, James M., and William J. Cooper, Jr., eds. *Writing the Civil War: The Quest to Understand.* Columbia: University of South Carolina Press, 1998.

McSeveney, Samuel T. "Re-electing Lincoln: The Union Party Campaign and the Military Vote in Connecticut." *Civil War History* 32 (1986): 139–158

McSpadden, J. Walker. *Famous Sculptors of America.* Freeport, NY: Books For Libraries Press, 1968.

McWhiney, Grady. *Braxton Bragg and Confederate Defeat.* New York: Columbia University Press, 1969.

McWhiney, Grady, and Perry Jamieson. *Attack and Die: Civil War Military Tactics and the Southern Heritage.* Tuscaloosa: University of Alabama Press, 1982.

McWhirter, A. J. "Gen. Wofford's Brigade in the Wilderness, May 6th, 1864." *Atlanta Journal,* 21 September 1901.

Meade, George G., ed. *The Life and Letters of George Gordon Meade, Major-General United States Army.* 2 vols. 1913. Reprint. Baltimore: Butternut and Blue, 1994.

Mearns, David. *The Lincoln Papers: The Story of the Collection.* New York: Doubleday, 1948.

Medical Department List of Employees, Chimborazo Hospital No. 2. Record Group 109. National Archives, Washington, DC.

Melder, Keith. "Angel of Mercy in Washington: Josephine Griffing and the Freedmen, 1864–1872." *Records of the Columbia Historical Society of Washington, D.C.* (1863–65): 243–272.

Melville, Herman. *Battle-Pieces and Aspects of the War.* Introduction by Lee Rust Brown. New York: Da Capo Press, 1995.

The Memorial to Brevet Major General Galusha Pennypacker, Youngest General of the United States Army. Philadelphia: Pennypacker Memorial Commission of Pennsylvania, 1934.

Mercer, Garry Carnell. "The Administration of Governor Henry Toole Clark, 1861–1862." M.A. thesis, East Carolina College, 1965.

Mercer, Philip. *The Gallant Pelham.* Macon, GA: J. W. Burke Co., 1929.

Merchant, John Holt. "Lawrence M. Keitt: South Carolina Fire-eater." Ph.D. dissertation, University of Virginia, 1976.

Meredith, Roy. *Storm over Sumter: The Opening Engagement of the Civil War.* New York: Simon & Schuster, 1957.

Merli, Frank. *Great Britain and the Confederate Navy, 1861–1865.* Bloomington: Indiana University Press, 1970.

Merrick, J. Vaughn. "Editorial. The U.S.S. Armored Frigate *New Ironsides.*" *Journal of the Franklin Institute of the State of Pennsylvania for the Promotion of the Mechanic Arts,* 3d ser., 53 (February 1867): 73–81.

Merrill, Catherine. *The Soldier of Indiana in the War for the Union.* 2 vols. Indianapolis: Merrill & Co., 1866, 1869.

Merrill, James M. *Du Pont, the Making of an Admiral: A Biography of Samuel Francis Du Pont.* New York: Dodd, Mead, 1986.

———. "The Hatteras Expedition, August, 1861." *North Carolina Historical Review* 29 (1952): 204–219.

———. *The Rebel Shore: The Story of Union Sea Power in the Civil War.* Boston: Little, Brown, 1957.

Meyer, Howard. *Colonel of the Black Regiment: The Life of Thomas Wentworth Higginson.* New York: W. W. Norton, 1967.

Meyers, Christopher C. "'Two Generals Cannot Command This Army': John A. McClernand and the Politics of Command in Grant's Army of the Tennessee." *Columbiad* (Spring 1998): 27–41.

———. "'The Wretch Vickery' and the Brooks County Civil War Slave Conspiracy." *Journal of Southwest Georgia History* 12 (1997): 27–38.

Michigan Women in the Civil War. Lansing: Michigan Civil War Centennial Observance Commission, 1963.

Miers, Earl Schenck. *The Web of Victory: Grant at Vicksburg.* 1955. Reprint. Baton Rouge: Louisiana State University Press, 1983.

Miles, Jim. *Paths to Victory: A History and Tour Guide of the Stone's River, Chickamauga, Chattanooga, Knoxville, and Nashville Campaigns.* Nashville, TN: Rutledge Hill Press, 1991.

Milgram, Joseph B. *George Washington Rains: Gunpowdermaker of the Confederacy.* Philadelphia: J. B. Milgram, 1961.

Milham, Charles G. *Gallant Pelham.* 1959. Reprint. Gaithersburg, MD: Olde Soldier Book, 1987.

"Military Gossip." *New York Times,* 8 September 1878.

Millard Fillmore Papers. Microfilm Collection. Buffalo Historical Society.

Miller, Clifford A. "Springfield Arms, 1794–1939: Milestones of a Great National Amory." *Army Ordnance* 20 (July–August 1939): 12–17.

Miller, Edward A., Jr. *The Black Civil War Soldiers of Illinois: The Story of the Twenty-ninth U.S. Colored Infantry.* Columbia: University of South Carolina Press, 1998.

———. *Lincoln's Abolitionist General: The Biography of David Hunter.* Columbia: University of South Carolina Press, 1997.

Miller, Edward Stokes. "The Dilemma of Commodore Craven." *Civil War Times Illustrated* 33 (May 1994): 34, 36, 38–41, 99.

Miller, Edwin Haviland. *Salem Is My Dwelling Place: A Life of Nathaniel Hawthorne.* Iowa City: University of Iowa Press, 1991.

Miller, Emily Van Dorn. *A Soldiers's Honor with Reminiscences of Major-General Earl Van Dorn.* New York: Abbey Press, 1902.

Miller, Francis Trevelyan, ed. *The Photographic History of the Civil War: Thousands of Scences Photographed 1861–1865.* 10 vols. New York: Review of Reviews, 1911.

Miller, Francis Trevelyan, and Robert S. Foster, eds. *The Photographic History of the Civil War.* 10 vols. 1911. Reprint. Secaucus, NJ: Blue and Grey Press, 1987.

Miller, Kerby A. *Emigrants and Exiles: Ireland and the Irish Exodus to North America.* New York: Oxford University Press, 1985.

Miller, Randall M., Harry S. Stout, and Charles Reagan Wilson, eds. *Religion and the American Civil War.* New York: Oxford University Press, 1998.

Miller, William J. *Battles for Richmond, 1862.* Fort Washington, PA: Eastern National, 1996.

———. *Mapping for Stonewall: The Civil War Service of Jed Hotchkiss.* Washington, DC: Elliott & Clark Publishing, 1993.

———, ed. *The Peninsula Campaign of 1862: From Yorktown to the Seven Days.* 3 vols. Mason City, IA: Savas Publishing, 1993–1996.

Millett, Allan R. *Semper Fidelis: The History of the United States Marine Corps.* New York: Macmillan, 1980.

Milligan, John D. *Gunboats Down the Mississippi.* Annapolis, MD: Naval Institute Press, 1965.

Mills, H. Sinclair. *The Vivandière: History, Tradition, Uniform and Service.* Collinswood, NJ: Civil War Historicals, 1988.

Milton, George Fort. *Abraham Lincoln and the Fifth Column.* New York: Vanguard Press, 1942.

Minor, Benjamin B. *The Southern Literary Messenger, 1834–1864.* New York: Neale Publishing Co., 1905.

Mitchel, Frederick A. *Ormsby Macknight Mitchel, Astronomer and General.* Boston: Houghton Mifflin, 1886.

Mitchell, Broadus. *William Gregg: Factory Master of the Old South.* Chapel Hill: University of North Carolina Press, 1928.

Mitchell, Memory F. *Legal Aspects of Conscription and Exemption in North Carolina, 1861–1865.* James Sprunt Studies in History and Political Science, vol. 47. Chapel Hill, NC, 1965.

Mitchell, Wesley Clair. *A History of the Greenbacks, with Special Reference to the Economic Consequence of Their Issue, 1862–1865.* 1903. Reprint. Chicago: Chicago University, 1960.

Mogelever, Jacob. *Death to Traitors; the Story of General Lafayette C. Baker, Lincoln's Forgotten Secret Service Chief.* Garden City, NY: Doubleday, 1960.

Mohr, Clarence L. *On the Threshold of Freedom: Masters and Slaves in Civil War Georgia.* Athens: University of Georgia Press, 1986.

Molar, James C., ed. *The Cormany Diaries: A Northern Family in the Civil War.* Pittsburgh: University of Pittsburgh Press, 1982.

Monaghan, Jay. *Civil War on the Western Border, 1854–1865.* Boston: Little, Brown, 1955.

———. *Swamp Fox of the Confederacy: The Life and Military Services of M. Jeff Thompson.* Tuscaloosa, AL: Confederate Publishing Co., 1956.

Moneyhon, Carl H. "Disloyalty and Class Consciousness in Southwestern Arkansas, 1852–1865." *Arkansas Historical Quarterly* 52 (1993): 223–243.

———. *The Impact of the Civil War and Reconstruction on*

Arkansas: Persistence in the Midst of Ruin. Baton Rouge: Louisiana University Press, 1994.

Monnett, Howard N. *Action before Westport 1864.* Rev. ed. Niwot: University Press of Colorado, 1995.

Monroney, Rita. *Montgomery Blair: Postmaster General.* Washington, DC: U.S. Post Office Department, 1963.

Monteiro, George. *Henry James and John Hay: The Record of A Friendship.* Providence: Brown University Press, 1965.

Monteiro, Lois A. "On Separate Roads: Florence Nightingale & Elizabeth Blackwell." *Signs: Journal of Women in Culture and Society* 9 (Spring 1984): 520–533.

Montgomery, George Jr., ed. *Georgia Sharpshooter The Civil War Diary and Letters of William Rhadamanthus Montgomery.* Macon, GA: Mercer University Press, 1997.

Montgomery, Horace. *Howell Cobb's Confederate Career.* Tuscaloosa, AL: Confederate Publishing Co., 1959.

Moore, Albert B., ed. *Conscription and Conflict in the Confederacy, Southern Classics Series.* 1924. Reprint. Columbia: University of South Carolina Press, 1996.

———. *A New Nation, a War, a Young Hero, and a Surrender.* Tuscaloosa: University of Alabama Press, 1965.

Moore, Alison. *He Died Furious.* Baton Rouge, LA: Ortlieb Press, 1983.

Moore, Claude Hunter. *Thomas Overton Moore; A Confederate Governor.* Clinton, NC: Commercial Printing Co., 1960.

Moore, Frank. *Women of the War: Their Heroism and Self-Sacrifice.* Hartford, CT: S. S. Scranton, 1866.

Moore, Guy W. *The Case of Mrs. Surratt: Her Controversial Trial and Execution.* Norman: University of Oklahoma Press, 1954.

Moore, Jerrold Northrop. *Confederate Commissary General: Lucius Bellinger Northrop and the Subsistence Bureau of the Southern Army.* Shippensburg, PA: White Mane Publishers, 1996.

Moore, John Bassett, ed. *The Works of James Buchanan: Comprising His Speeches, State Papers, and Private Correspondence.* 1908–1911. Reprint. New York: Antiquarian Press, 1960.

Moore, John H. *The Cheyenne.* Cambridge, MA: Blackwell, 1996.

Moore, Rayburn S., ed. *A Man of Letters in the Nineteenth Century South: Selected Letters of Paul Hamilton Hayne.* Baton Rouge: Louisiana State University Press, 1982.

———. *Paul Hamilton Hayne.* New York: Twayne Publishing, 1972.

Moore, Samuel Preston. "Address of the President of the Association of Medical Officers of the Confederate States Army and Navy." *Southern Practitioner* 31 (1909): 491–498.

———, ed. *"My Ever Dearest Friend"; The Letters of A. Dudley Mann to Jefferson Davis, 1869–1889.* Tuscaloosa, AL: Confederate Publishing Co., 1960.

———. "Pierre Soulé: Southern Expansionist and Promoter." *Journal of Southern History* 21 (May 1955): 203–233.

Moore, Thomas Overton. *Thomas O. Moore Papers, 1832–1865, Rapides Parish, Louisiana.* Bethesda, MD: University Publications of America, 1989.

Moorhead, James H. *American Apocalypse: Yankee Protestants and the Civil War, 1860–1869.* New Haven, CT: Yale University Press, 1978.

Morantz-Sanchez, Regina. "Feminism, Professionalism, and Germs: The Thought of Mary Putnam Jacobi and Elizabeth Blackwell." *American Quarterly* 34 (Winter 1982): 459–478.

———. "Feminist Theory and Historical Practice: Rereading Elizabeth Blackwell." *History and Theory* 31 (1992): 51–69.

Morgan, George Washington. *Reconstruction of Georgia.*

Washington, DC: F. & J. Rives & G. A. Bailey Printers, 1869.

Morgan, H. Wayne, ed. "A Civil War Diary of William McKinley." *Ohio Historical Quarterly* 69 (July 1960).

———. *William McKinley and His America.* Syracuse, NY: Syracuse University Press, 1963.

Morgan, John M. "Old Steady: The Role of General James Blair Steedman at the Battle of Chickamauga." *Northwest Ohio Quarterly* 22 (1950): 73–94.

———. "Steedman's Action at Dalton, 1864." *Northwest Ohio Quarterly* 53 (1981): 71–82.

Morison, Elting. "Election of 1860." In *History of American Presidential Elections, 1789–1968.* Edited by Arthur M. Schlesinger, Jr. 4 vols. New York: Chelsea House Publishers, 1971, 2:1097–1128.

Morley, John. *The Life of William Ewart Gladstone.* 3 vols. New York: Macmillan, 1903.

Morris, George S. *Lynchburg in the Civil War.* Lynchburg, VA: H. E. Howard, 1984.

Morris, Roy, Jr. *Ambrose Bierce: Alone in Bad Company.* Oxford, UK: Oxford University Press, 1999.

———. *Sheridan: The Life and Wars of General Phil Sheridan.* New York: Crown Publishers, 1992

Morris, Thomas D. *Free Men All: The Personal Liberty Laws of the North, 1780–1861.* Baltimore: Johns Hopkins University Press, 1974.

Morrison, James L., Jr., ed. "Getting through West Point: The Cadet Memoirs of John C. Tidball, Class of 1848." *Civil War History* 26 (1980): 304–325.

———, ed. *The Memoirs of Henry Heth.* Westport, CT: Greenwood Press, 1974.

Morrison, Michael A. *Slavery in the American West: The Eclipse of Manifest Destiny and the Coming of the Civil War.* Chapel Hill: University of North Carolina Press, 1997.

Morsberger, Robert E., and Katharine M. Morsberger. "After Andersonville: The First War Crimes Trial." *Civil War Times Illustrated* 13 (July 1974): 30–41.

———. *Lew Wallace: Militant Romantic.* New York: McGraw-Hill, 1980.

Morton, M. B. "Federal and Confederate Pensions Contrasted." *Forum* 16 (September 1893): 68–74.

Mosby, John S. *Memoirs of Colonel John S. Mosby.* Bloomington: Indiana University Press, 1959.

Moskin, J. Robert. *The U.S. Marine Corps Story.* Boston: Little, Brown, 1992.

Moss, Lemuel. *Annals of the United States Christian Commission.* Philadelphia: J. B. Lippincott & Co., 1868.

Mosser, Jeffrey S. "I Shall Make Him Remember This Insult." *Civil War Times Illustrated* 32 (March–April 1993).

Mott, Frank Luther. *American Journalism.* New York: Macmillan, 1962.

———. *A History of American Magazines.* Cambridge, MA: Belknap Press, 1938.

Motts, Wayne E. *"Trust in God and Fear Nothing": Gen. Lewis A. Armistead, CSA.* Gettysburg, PA: Farnsworth House Military Impressions, 1994.

Moulton, Gary E. *John Ross, Cherokee Chief.* Athens: University of Georgia Press, 1978.

———, ed. *The Papers of Chief John Ross.* 2 vols. Norman: University of Oklahoma Press, 1985.

Mudd, Nettie. *The Life of Dr. Samuel A. Mudd: Containing His Letters from Fort Jefferson, Dry Tortugas Island, Where He Was Imprisoned Four Years for Alleged Complicity in the Assassination of Abraham Lincoln.* New York: Neale, 1906. Reprint. Linden, TN: Continental Book Co., 1975.

Muhlenfeld, Elisabeth. *Mary Boykin Chesnut: A Biography.*

Baton Rouge: Louisiana State University Press, 1981.

Mullen, Jay Carlton. "The Turning of Columbus." *Register of the Kentucky Historical Society* 44 (1966): 209–225.

Mulligan, Thomas C. "Lest the Rebels Come to Power: The Life of William Dennison, 1815–1882." Ph.D. dissertation, Ohio State University, 1994.

Munn, Sheldon A. *Freemasons at Gettysburg.* Gettysburg, PA: Thomas Publications, 1993.

Munroe, John A. *History of Delaware.* 3d ed. Newark: University of Delaware Press, 1993.

Murdock, Eugene C. *One Million Men: The Civil War Draft in the North.* Madison: State Historical Society of Wisconsin, 1971.

——. *Patriotism Limited, 1862–1865: The Civil War Draft and the Bounty System.* Kent, OH: Kent State University Press, 1967.

Murphy, James B. *L. Q. C. Lamar: Pragmatic Patriot.* Baton Rouge: Louisiana State University Press, 1973.

Murphy, John M., and Howard M. Madaus. *Confederate Rifles & Muskets: Infantry Small Arms Manufactured in the Southern Confederacy, 1861–1865.* Newport Beach, CA: Graphic Publisher, 1996.

Murphy, Robert Joseph. "The Catholic Church in the United States during the Civil War Period: 1852–1866." *Records of the American Catholic Historical Society* 39 (December 1928): 271–346.

Mushkat, Jerome. *Fernando Wood; A Political Biography.* Kent, OH: Kent State University Press, 1990.

Musicant, Ivan. *Divided Waters. The Naval History of the Civil War.* New York: HarperCollins, 1995.

Myers, Raymond. *The Zollie Tree.* Louisville, KY: The Filson Club, 1964.

Myers, Robert Manson, ed. *The Children of Pride: A True Story of Georgia and the Civil War.* New Haven, CT: Yale University Press, 1972.

Naisawald, L. Van Loan. *Grape and Canister: The Story of the Field Artillery of the Army of the Potomac.* Washington, DC: Zenger Publishing Co., 1983.

Nalty, Bernard C. *United States Marines at Harper's Ferry and in the Civil War.* Washington, DC: Historical Branch, G–3 Division, Headquarters, U.S. Marine Corps, 1966.

Nash, Charles Edward. *Biographical Sketches of Gen. Pat Cleburne and Gen. T. C. Hindman Together with Humorous Anecdotes and Reminiscences of the Late Civil War.* 1895. Reprint. Dayton, OH: Morningside Bookshop, 1977.

Nash, Howard P., Jr. *A Naval History of the Civil War.* New York: A. S. Barnes & Co., 1972.

Nathan, Hans. *Dan Emmett and the Rise of Early Negro Minstrelsy.* Norman: University of Oklahoma Press, 1962.

Neal, Diane, and Thomas W. Kremm. *The Lion of the South: General Thomas C. Hindman.* Macon, GA: Mercer University Press, 1993.

Neely, Mark E., Jr. *The Fate of Liberty: Abraham Lincoln and Civil Liberties.* New York: Oxford University Press, 1991.

——. *The Last Best Hope of Earth: Abraham Lincoln and the Promise of America.* Cambridge, MA: Harvard University Press, 1993.

——. *Southern Rights: Political Prisoners and the Myth of Confederate Constitutionalism.* Charlottesville: University Press of Virginia, 1999.

——. "'Unbeknownst' to Lincoln: A Note on Radical Pacification in Missouri during the Civil War." *Civil War History* 44 (September 1998): 212–216.

——. "Was the Civil War a Total War?" *Civil War History* 37 (1991): 5–28.

Neely, Mark E., Jr., and Harold Holzer. *The Union Image: Popular Prints of the Civil War North.* Chapel Hill: University of North Carolina Press, 2000.

Neely, Mark E., Jr., Harold Holzer, and Gabor S. Boritt. *The Confederate: Image Prints of the Lost Cause.* Chapel Hill: University of North Carolina Press, 1987.

Nelson, Bernard H. "Confederate Slave Impressment Legislation, 1861–1865." *Journal of Negro History* 31:4 (1946): 392–410.

Nelson, Larry E. *Bullets, Ballots, and Rhetoric: Confederate Policy for the United States Presidential Contest of 1864.* University: University of Alabama Press, 1980

Nesbitt, Mark. *Saber and Scapegoat: J. E. B. Stuart and the Gettysburg Controversy.* Mechanicsburg, PA: Stackpole, 1994.

——, ed. *Through Blood and Fire: Selected Civil War Papers of Major General Joshua Lawrence Chamberlain.* Mechanicsburg, PA: Stackpole, 1996.

Nevins, Allan, ed. *A Diary of Battle: The Personal Journals of Colonel Charles S. Wainwright, 1861–1865.* Gettysburg, PA: Stan Clark Military Books, 1962.

——. *The Emergence of Lincoln.* 2 vols. New York: Charles Scribner's Sons, 1950.

——. *The Evening Post: A Century of Journalism.* New York: Boni & Liveright, 1922.

——. *Frémont: Pathmarker of the West.* New York: Longmans, Green, 1955.

——. "A Major Result of the Civil War." *Civil War History* 5 (September 1959): 237–250.

——. *Ordeal of the Union.* 4 vols. New York: Charles Scribner's Sons, 1947.

——. *The Origins of the Land-Grant Colleges and State Universities: A Brief Account of the Morrill Act of 1862 and Its Results.* Washington, DC: Civil War Centennial Commission, 1962.

Nevins, Allan, and Milton Halsey Thomas, eds. *The Diary of George Templeton Strong.* New York: Macmillan, 1952.

New York Monuments Commission. *Major General James S. Wadsworth at Gettysburg and Other Fields.* Albany: J. B. Lyon Co., 1916.

New York State Library Annual Report. *The Governor Edwin D. Morgan Papers.* Albany: University of the State of New York, 1943.

New York State Monuments Commission. *In Memoriam, Abner Doubleday, 1819–1893, and John Cleveland Robinson, 1817–1897.* Albany, NY: J. B. Lyon, 1918.

——. *In Memoriam. Francis Channing Barlow.* Albany, NY: J. B. Lyon Co., 1923.

Newell, Clayton R. *Lee vs. McClellan: The First Campaign.* Washington, DC: Regenery Publishing, 1996.

Newhall, Beaumont, and Nancy Newhall. *T. H. O'Sullivan: Photographer.* Rochester, NY: G. Eastman House, 1966.

Newmyer, R. Kent. *The Supreme Court under Marshall and Taney.* New York: Thomas Y. Crowell Co., 1968: 145–146.

Newton, Earle W. *The Vermont Story: A History of the People of the Green Mountain State, 1749–1949.* Montpelier, VT: Vermont Historical Society, 1949.

Newton, Steven H. *The Battle of Seven Pines.* Lynchburg, VA: H. E. Howard, 1993.

——. *Joseph E. Johnston and the Defense of Richmond.* Lawrence: University Press of Kansas, 1998.

Newton, Thomas Wodehouse Legh, 2d Baron. *Lord Lyons: A Record of British Diplomacy.* New York: Longmans, Green, 1913.

Nichols, David A. *Lincoln and the Indians: Civil War Policy and Politics.* Columbia: University of Missouri Press, 1978.

Nichols, George Ward. *The Story of the Great March from the Diary of a Staff Officer.* Williamstown, MA: Corner House Publishers, 1972.

Nichols, James Lynn. *Confederate Engineers.* 1957. Reprint. Gaithersburg, MD: Olde Soldier Books, 1987.

———. *General Fitzhugh Lee: A Biography.* Lynchburg, VA: H. E. Howard, 1989.

Nichols, Roy F., ed. *The Disruption of American Democracy.* New York: Macmillan, 1948.

———. "Fighting in North Carolina Waters." *North Carolina Historical Review* 40 (Winter 1963).

———. *Franklin Pierce: Young Hickory of the Granite Hills.* Philadelphia: University of Pennsylvania Press, 1958.

———. "The Kansas-Nebraska Act: A Century of Historiography." *Mississippi Valley Historical Review* 43 (1956).

Nichols, Roy F., and Philip S. Klein. "Election of 1856." In *History of American Presidential Elections, 1789–1968.* Edited by Arthur M. Schlesinger, Jr. 4 vols. New York: Chelsea House Publishers, 1971, 2:1007–1033.

[Nicholson] *Letter from Hon. Lewis Cass, of Michigan, on the War and the Wilmot Proviso.* Washington, DC: Blair & Rives, 1847.

Nicolay, Helen. *Lincoln's Secretary: A Biography of John G. Nicolay.* New York: Longmans, Green, 1949.

Nicolson, John. "New England Idealism in the Civil War: The Military Career of Joseph Roswell Hawley." Ph.D. dissertation, Claremont Graduate School, 1970.

Nieman, Donald G. "Republicanism, the Confederate Constitution, and the American Constitutional Tradition." In *An Uncertain Tradition: Constitutionalism and the History of the South.* Edited by Kermit L. Hall and James W. Ely, Jr. Athens: University of Georgia Press, 1989: 201–224.

———. *To Set the Law in Motion: The Freedmen's Bureau and the Legal Rights of Blacks, 1865–1868.* Millwood, NY: KTO Press, 1979.

Nisbet, James C. *Four Years on the Firing Line.* Edited by Bell I. Wiley. Jackson, TN: McCowat-Mercer Press, 1963.

Niven, John. *Connecticut for the Union; The Role of the State in the Civil War.* New Haven, CT: Yale University Press, 1965.

———. *Gideon Welles: Lincoln's Secretary of the Navy.* New York: Oxford University Press, 1973.

———. *Salmon P. Chase: A Biography.* New York: Oxford University Press, 1995.

———, ed. *The Salmon P. Chase Papers.* 5 vols. Kent, OH: Kent State University Press, 1993–1998.

Nixon, Raymond B. *Henry W. Grady, Spokesman of the New South.* New York: Alfred A. Knopf, 1943.

Nofi, Albert A. *The Gettysburg Campaign: June and July 1863.* Conshohocken, PA: Combined Books, 1986.

Nolan, Alan T. *The Iron Brigade: A Military History.* 3d ed. 1961. Reprint. Bloomington: Indiana University Press, 1994.

———. *Lee Considered: General Robert E. Lee and Civil War History.* Chapel Hill: University of North Carolina Press, 1991.

Nolan, Alan T., and Sharon E. Vipond. *Giants in Their Tall Black Hats: Essays on the Iron Brigade.* Bloomington: Indiana University Press, 1998.

Norris, L. David. *William H. Emory: Soldier-Scientist.* Tucson: University of Arizona Press, 1998.

Norton, Herman A. *Struggling for Recognition: The United States Army Chaplaincy, 1791–1865.* Washington, DC: Department of the Army, 1977.

Norton, Mary. Papers. Perkins Library, Duke University, Durham, North Carolina.

Nuckols, Jack Randall. "A Confederate Agent in Europe: The Life and Career of Commander James Dunwoody Bulloch." M.A. thesis, Marshall University, 1982.

Nuermberger, Ruth K. *The Clays of Alabama: A Planter-Lawyer-Politician Family.* Lexington: University of Kentucky Press, 1958.

Nulty, William H. *Confederate Florida: The Road to Olustee.* Tuscaloosa: University of Alabama Press, 1990.

Nunn, W. C. ed. *Ten More Generals in Gray.* Hillsboro, TX: Hill College Press, 1980.

Nye, Russell B. *Fettered Freedom: Civil Liberties and the Slave Controversy, 1830–1860.* East Lansing: Michigan State University Press, 1963.

O'Brien, Kevin E., ed. *My Life in the Irish Brigade. The Civil War Memoirs of Private William McCarter, 116th Pennsylvania Infantry.* Campbell, CA: Savas Publishing Co., 1996.

O'Brien, Michael and David Moltke-Hansen, eds. *Intellectual Life in Antebellum Charleston.* Knoxville: University of Tennessee Press, 1986.

O'Connell, Robert L. *Of Arms and Men: A History of War, Weapons, and Aggression.* New York: Oxford University Press, 1990.

O'Connor, Richard. *Hood: Cavalier General.* New York: Prentice-Hall, 1949.

O'Connor, Sandra Day. "Supreme Court Justices from Georgia." *The Georgia Journal of Southern Legal History* 1 (Fall/Winter 1991): 395–405.

O'Connor, Thomas H. *Civil War Boston: Homefront and Battlefield.* Boston: Northeastern University Press, 1997.

O'Flaherty, Daniel. *General Jo Shelby: Undefeated Rebel.* 1987. Reprint. Chapel Hill: University of North Carolina Press, 2000.

O'Neill, Charles. *Wild Train: The Story of the Andrews Raiders.* New York: Random House, 1956.

O'Toole, G. J. A. *Honorable Treachery: The History of U.S. Intelligence, Espionage, and Covert Action from the American Revolution to the CIA.* New York: Atlantic Monthly Press, 1991.

Oates, Stephen B. *Abraham Lincoln, the Man Behind the Myths.* New York: Penguin Books, 1984.

———. *Confederate Cavalry West of the River.* Austin: University of Texas Press, 1961.

———. "The Man at the White House Window." *Civil War Times Illustrated* 34 (May 1995): 52–62.

———. *Our Fiery Trial: Abraham Lincoln, John Brown, and the Civil War Era.* Amherst: University of Massachusetts Press, 1979.

———. *To Purge this Land with Blood: A Biography of John Brown.* New York: Harper & Row, 1970.

———. *The Whirlwind of War: Voices of the Storm, 1861–1865.* New York: HarperPerennial, 1999.

———. *With Malice toward None: The Life of Abraham Lincoln.* New York: Harper & Row, 1976.

———. *A Woman of Valor: Clara Barton and the Civil War.* New York: Free Press, 1994.

"Obituary. General Henry Pleasants." *Pottsville Weekly Miners' Journal,* 2 April 1880.

"Obsequies of the Late Col. Cameron." *Philadelphia Daily Evening Bulletin,* 19 March 1862.

Odom, Van D. "The Political Career of Thomas Overton Moore, Secession Governor of Louisiana." M.A. thesis, Louisiana State University, Baton Rouge, 1942.

Olcott, Charles S. *The Life of William McKinley.* 2 vols. Boston: Houghton Mifflin, 1916.

Oliphant, Mary C. Simms, Alfred Taylor Odell, and T. C. Duncan Eaves, eds. *The Letters of William Gilmore Simms.* 6 vols. Columbia: University of South Carolina Press,

1952–1982.

Oliver, John William. "History of Civil War Military Pensions, 1861–1885." *Bulletin of the University of Wisconsin.* 1 (1917).

Olmstead, Charles H. *Fort Pulaski.* Savannah: Georgia Historical Society, 1917.

Olmstead, Edwin, Wayne Stark, and Spencer Tucker. *The Big Guns. Civil War Siege, Seacoast and Naval Cannon.* Alexandria Bay, NY, and Bloomfield, Ontario, Canada: Museum Restoration Service, 1997.

Olson, Kenneth E. *Music and Musket: Bands and Bandsmen of the American Civil War.* Westport, CT: Greenwood Press, 1981.

Organization of the Free State Government in Kansas with the Inaugural Speech and Message of Governor Robinson. Washington, DC: Buell & Blanchard,1856.

Orrmont, Arthur. *Mr. Lincoln's Master Spy: Lafayette Baker.* New York: Messner, 1966.

Orth, Michael. "The CSS *Stonewall.*" *Civil War Times Illustrated* 5 (1) (1966): 44–48.

Osborn, Thomas. *The Fiery Trail: A Union Officer's Account of Sherman's Last Campaign.* Knoxville: University of Tennessee Press, 1986.

Osborne, Arthur Dimon. *Capture of Fort Fisher by Major General Alfred H. Terry and What It Accomplished.* New Haven, CT: Tuttle, 1911.

Osborne, Charles C. *Jubal: The Life and Times of General Jubal A. Early, CSA. Defender of the Lost Cause.* 1992. Reprint. Baton Rouge: Louisiana State University Press, 1994.

O'Toole, G. J. A. *Honorable Treachery: The History of U.S. Intelligence, Espionage, and Covert Action from the American Revolution to the CIA.* New York: Atlantic Monthly Press, 1991.

O'Toole, Patricia. *The Five of Hearts: An Intimate Portrait of Henry Adams and His Friends, 1880–1918.* New York: Random House, l990.

Owen, Henry T. "Stuart in 1861." *Philadelphia Weekly Times,* 31 October 1885.

Owen, William Miller. *In Camp and Battle with the Washington Artillery of New Orleans: A Narrative of Events during the Late Civil War from Bull Run to Appomattox and Spanish Fort.* Boston: Ticknor & Co., 1885.

Ownsbey, Betty. *Alias "Paine": Lewis Thornton Powell, The Mystery Man of the Lincoln Conspiracy.* Jefferson, NC: McFarland, 1993.

Owsley, Frank L. *King Cotton Diplomacy. Foreign Relations of the Confederate States of America.* 2d ed revised by Harriet C. Owsley. Chicago: University of Chicago Press, 1959.

Owsley, Frank Lawrence, Jr. *The C.S.S.* Florida*: Her Building and Operations.* Tuscaloosa: University of Alabama Press, 1965.

Owsley, Harriet Chappell. "Andrew Jackson and His Ward, Andrew Jackson Donelson." *Tennessee Historical Quarterly* 41 (Summer 1982): 124–139.

Pacious, Daniel M. "Seawolves of the Confederacy: The Origin, Development, and Operations of the Confederate States Marine Corps." M.A. Thesis, Southwest Texas State University, 1993.

Page, Charles P. *Letters of a War Correspondent.* Boston: L. C. Page & Co., 1899.

Paine, Charles. *The Resistant Writer; Rhetoric as Immunity, 1850 to the Present.* Boulder, CO: NetLibrary, 1999.

Painter, Nell Irvin. *Sojourner Truth: A Life, a Symbol.* New York: W. W. Norton, 1996.

Palfrey, Francis Winthrop. *Memoir of William Francis Bartlett.* Boston: Houghton Mifflin, 1881.

Palladino, Grace. *Another Civil War: Labor, Capital, and the State in the Anthracite Regions of Pennsylvania, 1840–68.* Urbana: University of Illinois Press, 1990.

Palmer, Benjamin M. *The Life and Letters of James Henley Thornwel, D.D, LL.D.: Ex-President of the South Carolina College: Late Professor of Theology in the Theological Seminary at Columbia, South Carolina.* Richmond, VA: Whittet and Shepperson, 1875.

Palmer, George T. Palmer. *A Conscientious Turncoat: The Story of John M. Palmer, 1817–1900.* New Haven, CT: Yale University Press, 1941.

Palmer, John M. *Personal Recollections of John M. Palmer: The Story of an Earnest Life.* Cincinnati: Robert Clarke, 1901.

Paludan, Phillip S. *A Covenant with Death: The Constitution, Law and Equality in the Civil War Era.* Urbana: University of Illinois Press, 1975.

———. *"A People's Contest": The Union and the Civil War, 1861–1865.* New York: Harper & Row, 1988.

———. *The Presidency of Abraham Lincoln.* Lawrence: University Press of Kansas, 1994.

Panzer, Mary. *Mathew Brady and the Image of History.* Washington, DC: Smithsonian Institution Press for the National Portrait Gallery, 1997.

Paolino, Ernest N. *The Foundations of the American Empire: William Henry Seward and U.S. Foreign Policy.* Ithaca, NY: Cornell University Press, 1973.

Paquette, Patricia. "A Bandage in One Hand and a Bible in the Other: The Story of Captain Sally L. Tompkins (CSA)." *Minerva Quarterly* 8 (Summer 1990): 47–54.

Parker, Arthur Caswell. *The Life of General Ely S. Parker.* Buffalo, NY: Buffalo Historical Society, 1919.

Parker, Daisy. "John Milton, Governor of Florida: A Loyal Confederate." *Florida Historical Quarterly* 20 (April 1942): 346–361.

Parker, David B. *Alias Bill Arp: Charles Henry Smith and the South's "Godly Heritage."* Athens: University of Georgia Press, 1991.

Parker, Foxhall A. *The Battle of Mobile Bay, and the Capture of Forts Powell, Gaines, and Morgan by the Combined Sea and Land Forces of the United States under the Command of Rear-Admiral David Glasgow Farragut, and Major-General Gordon Granger, August, 1864.* Boston: A. Williams & Co., 1878.

Parker, Franklin. *George Peabody: A Biography.* Nashville, TN: Vanderbilt University Press, 1995.

Parker, Prescott A. *Story of the Tensaw: Blakely, Spanish Fort, Jackson Oaks, Fort Mims.* Montrose, AL: P. A. Parker, 1922.

Parker, Sandra V. *Richmond's Civil War Prisons.* Lynchburg, VA: H. E. Howard, 1990.

Parker, Thomas H. *History of the 51st Regiment of P.V. and V.V.* 1869. Reprint. Baltimore: Butternut and Blue, 1998.

Parker, William Belmont. *The Life and Public Services of Justin Smith Morrill.* Boston: Houghton Mifflin, 1924.

Parks, Joseph H. *General Edmund Kirby Smith, C.S.A.* Baton Rouge: Louisiana State University Press, 1954.

———. *General Leonidas Polk, C.S.A.: The Fighting Bishop.* Baton Rouge: Louisiana State University Press, 1962.

———. *John Bell of Tennessee.* Baton Rogue: Louisiana State University Press, 1950.

———. *Joseph E. Brown of Georgia.* Baton Rouge: Louisiana State University Press, 1977.

Parrish, T. Michael. *Richard Taylor: Soldier Prince of Dixie.* Chapel Hill: University of North Carolina Press, 1992.

Parrish, Tom Z. *The Saga of the Confederate Ram* Arkansas: *The Mississippi Valley Campaign, 1862.* Hillsboro, TX: Hill College Press, 1987.

Parrish, William E. *David Rice Atchison of Missouri, Border*

Politician. Columbia: University of Missouri Press, 1961.

———. *Frank Blair: Lincoln's Conservative.* Columbia: University of Missouri Press, 1998.

———. *A History of Missouri, Volume III: 1860 to 1875.* Columbia: University of Missouri Press, 1971.

———. *Turbulent Partnership: Missouri and the Union, 1861–1865.* Columbia: University of Missouri Press, 1963.

———. "The Western Sanitary Commission." *Civil War History* 36 (March 1990): 17–35.

Parrott, Angie. "'Love Makes Memory Eternal': The United Daughters of the Confederacy in Richmond, Virginia, 1897–1920." In *The Edge of the South: Life in Nineteenth-Century Virginia.* Edited by Edward L. Ayers and John C. Willis. Charlottesville: University Press of Virginia, 1991.

Parsons, Emily Elizabeth. *Memoir of Emily Elizabeth Parsons.* Boston: Little, Brown, 1880.

Parsons, George W. *Put the Vermonters Ahead: The First Vermont Brigade in the Civil War.* Shippensburg, PA: White Mane, 1996.

Paskoff, Paul F., and Daniel J. Wilson, eds. *The Cause of the South: Selections from De Bow's Review, 1846–1867.* Baton Rouge: Louisiana State University Press, 1982.

Patrick, John J. "John Sherman: The Early Years, 1823–1865." Ph.D. dissertation, Kent State University, 1982.

Patrick, Marsena Rudolph. *Inside Lincoln's Army; the Diary of Marsena Rudolph Patrick, Provost Marshal General, Army of the Potomac.* Edited by David S. Sparks. New York: T. Yoseloff, 1964.

Patrick, Rembert W. *Jefferson Davis and His Cabinet.* Baton Rouge: Louisiana State University Press, 1944.

Patterson, Gerard. "'Allegheny' Johnson." *Civil War Times Illustrated* 5 (4):12–19.

Patterson, Robert. *A Narrative of the Campaign in the Valley of the Shenandoah, in 1861.* Philadelphia: J. Campbell, 1865.

Paul, Sherman. *The Shores of America: Thoreau's Inward Exploration.* Urbana: University of Illinois Press, 1958.

Pauley, Michael J. *Unreconstructed Rebel: The Life of General John McCausland, C.S.A.* Charleston, WV: Pictoral Historical Publishing Co., 1992.

Paulus, Margaret Babcock, comp. *Papers of General Robert Huston Milroy.* 4 vols. n.p., 1965.

Payne, Charles E. *Josiah Bushnell Grinnell.* Iowa City: State Historical Society of Iowa, 1938.

Peabody, George. Manuscripts. Essex Institute, Salem, MA.

Peacock, Virginia Tatnall. *Famous American Belles of the Nineteenth Century.* Philadelphia: J. B. Lippincott Co., 1901.

Pearce, Haywood Jefferson. *Benjamin H. Hill, Secession and Reconstruction.* Chicago: University of Chicago Press, 1928.

Pearson, Andrea G. "*Frank Leslie's Illustrated Newspaper* and *Harper's Weekly*: Innovation and Imitation in Nineteenth-Century American Pictorial Reporting." *Journal of Popular Culture* 23 (1990): 81–111.

Pearson, Edmund. *Dime Novels.* Boston: Little, Brown, 1929.

Pearson, Henry G. *James S. Wadsworth of Geneseo, Brevet Major General (U.S.V.).* New York: Scribner's, 1913.

———. *The Life of John A. Andrew, Governor of Massachusetts, 1861–1865.* 2 vols. Boston: Houghton Mifflin, 1904.

Pease, Jane H., and William H. Pease. *A Family of Women: The Carolina Pettigurs in Peace and War.* Chapel Hill: University of North Carolina Press, 1999.

———. *The Fugitive Slave Law and Anthony Burns: A Problem in Law Enforcement.* Philadelphia: J. B. Lippincott, 1975.

Pease, William H., and Jane H. Pease. *Black Utopia: Negro Communal Experiments in America.* Madison: State Historical Society of Wisconsin, 1963.

———. *James Louis Petigru: South Carolina Lawyer, Southern Unionist, and American Conservative.* Athens: University of Georgia Press, 1995.

Peckham, Howard H. "I Have Been Basely Murdered." *American Heritage* 14 (August 1963): 88–92.

Peckham, James. *General Nathaniel Lyon and Missouri in 1861.* New York: American News Co., 1866.

Pember, Phoebe Yates Levy. Letters. Southern Historical Collection. Univeristy of North Carolina, Chapel Hill, North Carolina.

———. *A Southern Woman's Story: Life in Confederate Richmond.* Edited by Bell I. Wiley. Jackson, TN: McCowat-Mercer, 1959.

Pemberton, John C. *Pemberton, Defender of Vicksburg.* Wilmington, NC: Broadfoot Publishing Co., 1987.

Pender, William Dorsey. *The General to his Lady; the Civil War Letters of William Dorsey Pender to Fanny Pender.* Edited by William W. Hassler. Chapel Hill: University of North Carolina Press, 1965.

Pennsylvania at Gettysburg: Ceremonies at the Dedication of the Monuments Erected by the Commonwealth of Pennsylvania to Major General George C. Meade, Major General Winfield S. Hancock, Major General John F. Reynolds and to Mark the Positions of the Pennsylvania Commands Engaged in the Battle. Harrisburg, PA: William Stanley Hay, State Printer, 1904.

Pennypacker, Galusha. Papers. The Historical Society of Pennsylvania.

Pennypacker, Isaac R. *Galusha Pennypacker: America's Youngest General.* Philadelphia: Christopher Sower Co., 1917.

Perkins, J. R. *Trails, Rails, and War: The Life of General G. M. Dodge.* Indianapolis: Bobbs-Merrill, 1929.

Perlman, Phillip B. "Some Maryland Lawyers in Supreme Court History." *Maryland Historical Magazine* 43 (1948): 180–196.

Perret, Geoffrey. *Ulysses S. Grant: Soldier and President.* New York: Random House, 1997.

Perry, Benjamin Franklin. *Reminiscences of Public Men.* Philadelphia: J. D. Avil & Co., 1883.

Perry, Milton F. *Infernal Machines: The Story of Confederate Submarine and Mine Warfare.* Baton Rouge: Louisiana State University Press, 1965.

Perry, Thomas S., ed. *The Life and Letters of Francis Lieber.* Boston: J. R. Osgood & Co., 1882.

Peskin, Allan. *Garfield: A Biography.* Kent, OH: Kent State University Press, 1978.

Peterson, Cyrus A., and Joseph M. Hanson. *Pilot Knob: The Thermopylae of the West.* New York: Neale Publishing Co., 1914.

Peterson, Harold L. *Round Shot and Rammers: An Introduction to Muzzle-loading Land Artillery in the United States.* South Bend, IN: South Bend Replicas, 1969.

Peterson, Merrill D. *The Great Triumvirate: Webster, Clay, and Calhoun.* New York: Oxford University Press, 1987.

Peterson, Owen. "Ethelbert Barksdale in the Democratic National Convention of 1860." *Journal of Mississippi History* 14 (1952): 257–278.

Pfanz, Donald C. *Richard S. Ewell: A Soldier's Life.* Chapel Hill: University of North Carolina Press, 1998.

Pfanz, Harry W. *Gettysburg: Culp's Hill and Cemetery Hill.* Chapel Hill: University of North Carolina Press, 1993.

———. *Gettysburg The Second Day.* Chapel Hill: University of North Carolina Press, 1987.

Phillip, Hazel Spencer. *The Governors of Ohio.* Columbus: Ohio Historical Society, 1954.

Phillips, Catherine Coffin. *Jessie Benton Frémont: A Woman*

Who Made History. Lincoln: University of Nebraska Press, 1995.

Phillips, Christopher. *Damned Yankee: The Life of General Nathaniel Lyon.* Baton Rouge: Louisiana State University Press, 1990.

Phillips, David L. *Tiger John: The Rebel Who Burned Chambersburg.* Leesburg, VA: Gauley Mount Press, 1993.

Phillips, Kenneth Edward. "James Henry Lane and the War for Southern Independence." M.A. thesis, Auburn University, 1982.

Phillips, Philip. Collection. Manuscript Division. Library of Congress, Washington, DC.

Phillips, W. F. "Wofford's Brigade at the Wilderness." *Atlanta Constitution,* 25 September 1887.

Phinney, Chester S. *Francis Lieber's Influence on American Thought and Some of His Unpublished Letters.* Philadelphia: International Print Co., 1918.

Phisterer, Frederick. *Statistical Record: A Treasury of Information About the U.S. Civil War.* Carlisle, PA: John Kallman Publishers, 1996.

Pickard, John B., ed. *The Letters of John Greenleaf Whittier, Vol. III.* Cambridge, MA: Belknap Press of Harvard University Press, 1975.

Pickenpaugh, Roger. *Rescue by Rail: Troop Transfer and the Civil War in the West, 1863.* Lincoln: University of Nebraska Press, 1998.

Pickens, Donald K. "The Republican Synthesis and Thaddeus Stevens." *Civil War History* 31 (March 1985): 57–73.

Pickett, LaSalle Corbell. *Pickett and His Men.* Atlanta: Foote & Davies Co., 1899.

Pierce, Edward L., ed. *Memoir and Letters of Charles Sumner.* 4 vols. Boston: Roberts Brothers, 1877–1894.

Pierson, William Whately. "The Committee on the Conduct of the War." *American Historical Review* 23 (1918): 550–576.

Piston, William Garrett. *Lee's Tarnished Lieutenant: James Longstreet and His Place in Southern History.* Athens: University of Georgia Press, 1987.

Piston, William Garrett, and Richard W. Hatcher. *Wilson's Creek: The Second Battle of the Civil War and the Men Who Fought It.* Chapel Hill: University of North Carolina, 2000.

Pitner, Ernst. *Maximilian's Lieutenant. A Personal History of the Mexican Campaign, 1864–67.* Translated and edited by Gordon Etherington-Smith. Albuquerque: University of New Mexico Press, 1993.

Pittenger, William. *Daring and Suffering: A History of the Great Railroad Adventure.* Philadelphia: J. W. Daughaday Publisher, 1863.

Pitts, Charles F. *Chaplains in Gray.* Nashville, TN: Broadman, 1957.

Pleasants, Henry, Jr. *The Tragedy of the Crater.* Boston: Christopher Publishing House, 1938.

Pleasants, Henry, Jr., and George H. Straley. *Inferno at Petersburg.* Philadelphia: Chilton Co., 1961.

"The Plot, Full and Minute Particulars." *New York Times,* 27 November 1864: 1.

Plummer, Mark A. *Frontier Governor: Samuel J. Crawford of Kansas.* Lawrence: University Press of Kansas, 1971.

———. "Richard J. Oglesby, Lincoln's Rail-Splitter." *Illinois Historical Journal* 80 (Spring 1987).

Poage, George R. *Henry Clay and the Whig Party.* Chapel Hill: University of North Carolina Press, 1965.

Poindexter, James E. "General Armistead's Portrait Presented." *Southern Historical Society Papers* 37 (1909): 144–151.

Poirier, Robert G. *"By the Blood of Our Alumni": Norwich

University Citizen Soldiers in the Army of the Potomac.* Mason City, IA: Savas Publishing Co., 1999.

Polk, William M. "The Hated Helper." *The South Atlantic Quarterly* 30 (April 1931).

———. *Leonidas Polk: Bishop and General.* 2 vols. New York: Longmans, Green, 1915.

Pollard, Edward A. *The Lost Cause: A New Southern History of the War of the Confederates.* New York: E. B. Treat, 1866.

———. *Southern History of the War.* 4 vols. Richmond, VA: West & Johnston, 1862–1865.

Pollard, James E. *The Presidents and the Press.* New York: Macmillan, 1947.

Pond, George E. *The Shenandoah Valley in 1864.* New York: Charles Scribner's Sons, 1883.

Pool, J. T. *Under Canvass, or, Recollections of the Fall and Summer Campaign of the 14th Regiment Indiana Volunteers, Col. Nathan Kimball, in Western Virginia, in 1861: Containing Incidents of Scouting Parties, Skirmishes, Battles, Anecdotes of the War, Life around the Camp-fires etc.* Terre Haute, IN: Oliver Barlett, 1862.

Poore, Ben Perley. *The Life and Public Services of Ambrose E. Burnside, Soldier—Citizen—Statesman.* Providence, RI: J. A. & R. A. Reid, 1882.

Poppenheim, Mary B., et al. *The History of the United Daughters of the Confederacy.* Richmond, VA: Garrett and Massie, 1938.

Porter, David D. *Incidents and Anecdotes of the Civil War.* New York: D. Appleton & Co., 1885.

———. *The Naval History of the Civil War.* 1886. Reprint. Seacaucus, NJ: Castle, 1984.

Porter, David L. "Attitudes of the Georgia Press in the Presidential Election of 1860." *Georgia Historical Quarterly* 59 (1975): 127–129.

Porter, Kenneth W. "Billy Bowlegs (Holata Micco) In the Civil War." *Florida Historical Quarterly* 45 (April 1967): 391–401.

Porter, Robert P. *Life of William McKinley, Soldier, Lawyer, Statesman.* Cleveland: N. G. Hamilton Publishing Co., 1896.

Porter, William David. *Defence of Commodore W. D. Porter before the Naval Retiring Board, Convened at Brooklyn Navy Yard, November 1863.* New York: John A. Gray & Green, 1863.

Posner, Russell M. "Thomas Starr King and the Mercy Million." *California Historical Society Quarterly* 43 (December 1964): 291–308.

Potter, David M. *The Impending Crisis, 1848–1861.* New York: Harper & Row, 1976.

———. *Lincoln and His Party in the Secession Crisis.* New Haven, CT: Yale University Press, 1942.

Potter, Jerry O. *The Sultana Tragedy: America's Greatest Maritime Disaster.* Gretna, LA: Pelican Publishing Co., 1992.

Potter, Marguerite. "Hamilton R. Gamble, Missouri's War Governor." *Missouri Historical Review* 35 (October 1940): 25–71.

Potts, William. "Biographical Sketch of the Honorable Thomas H. Dudley of Camden, New Jersey." *Proceedings of the American Philosophical Society* 34 (June 1895).

Pound, Reginald. *Albert: A Biography of the Prince Consort.* New York: Simon & Schuster, 1973.

Powell, William H. *The Fifth Army Corps (Army of the Potomac). A Record of Operations during the Civil War in the United States of America, 1861–1865.* New York: G. P. Putnam's Sons, 1896.

Powell, William S., ed. *Dictionary of North Carolina Biography.* 6 vols. Chapel Hill: University of North Carolina Press, 1979–1994.

Power, J. Tracy. *Lee's Miserables: Life in the Army of Northern Virginia from the Wilderness to Appomattox.* Chapel Hill: University of North Carolina Press, 1998.

Presbyterian Church, Gettysburg, PA. *Presentation and Unveiling of the Memorial Tablets Commemorating the Lincoln and Burns Event (November 19, 1863) Held at the Presbyterian Church, Gettysburg, Pa., Nov. 19th, 1914.* Rochester, NY: Johnston, 1916.

Prest, John. *Lord John Russell.* Columbia: University of South Carolina Press, 1972.

Preston, John S. *Address before the Washington and Jefferson Societies, of the University of Virginia. June 30, 1868.* Lynchburg, VA: Schaffter & Bryant, 1868.

Preuss, Charles. *Exploring with Frémont: The Private Diaries of Charles Preuss, Cartographer for John C. Frémont.* Translated and edited by Erwin G. and Elizabeth K. Gudde. Norman: University of Oklahoma Press, 1958.

Price, Grady Daniel. "The Secret Mission of Duncan F. Kenner, Confederate Minister Plenipotentiary to Europe in 1865." M.A. thesis, Tulane University, 1929.

Price, Isaiah. *History of the Ninety-Seventh Regiment, Pennsylvania Volunteer Infantry, during the War of the Rebellion, 1861–65.* Philadelphia: Published by the author, 1875.

Price, Richard Scott. *Nathaniel Lyon: Harbinger from Kansas.* Springfield, MO: Wilson's Creek National Battlefield Foundation, 1990.

Priest, John M. *Before Antietam: The Battle for South Mountain.* Shippensburg, PA: White Mane Publishing Co., 1992.

———. *The Soldier's Battle.* Shippensburg, PA: White Mane Publishing Co., 1989.

"Princeton." In *Southern History of the War. Official Reports of Battles, as Published by Order of the Confederate Congress at Richmond.* 1863. Reprint. New York: Kraus Reprint Co., 1970.

Prior, Leon. "Lewis Payne, Pawn of John Wilkes Booth." *Florida Historical Quarterly* 43 (July 1964).

Proceedings of the First Reunion of the Eleventh Regiment Illinois Volunteer Infantry Held at Ottawa, Ill., Oct. 27, 1875. Ottawa, IL: Osman & Hapeman, 1875.

Proft, R. J., ed. *United States of America's Congressional Medal of Honor Recipients and Their Official Citations.* Columbia Heights, MN: Highland House II, 1997.

Pryor, Elizabeth Brown. *Clara Barton, Professional Angel.* Philadelphia: University of Pennsylvania, 1987.

Pryor, Mrs. Roger A. *Reminiscences of Peace and War.* New York: Macmillan, 1905.

Pryor, Shepherd Green. *A Post of Honor: The Pryor Letters, 1861–63.* Edited by Charles R. Adams, Jr. Fort Valley, GA: Garret Publications, 1989.

Putnam, Albert D., ed. *Major General Joseph R. Hawley, Soldier and Editor (1826–1905). Civil War Military Letters.* Hartford: Connecticut Civil War Centennial Commission, 1864.

Quarles, Benjamin. "The Abduction of the *Planter.*" In *The Black Soldier: From the American Revolution to Vietnam.* Edited by Jay David and Elaine Craine. New York: William Morrow, 1971.

———. *Black Abolitionists.* New York: Oxford University Press, 1969.

———. *The Negro in the Civil War.* Boston: Little, Brown, 1953. Reprint. New York: Da Capo Press, 1989.

Quisenberry, A. C. "The Alleged Secession of Kentucky in 1861." *Register of the Kentucky Historical Society* 15 (May 1917): 13–32.

Quynn, Dorothy Mackay, and William Rogers Quynn. *Barbara Frietschie.* Baltimore: Maryland Historical Society, 1942.

Rable, George C. *Civil Wars: Women and the Crisis of Southern Nationalism.* Chicago: University of Illinois Press, 1991.

———. *The Confederate Republic: A Revolution against Politics.* Chapel Hill: University of North Carolina Press, 1994.

Raboteau, Albert J. *Slave Religion: The "Invisible Institution" in the Antebellum South.* New York: Oxford University Press, 1978.

Rabun, James Z. "Alexander Stephens and the Confederacy." *Emory University Quarterly* 6 (October 1950).

Ragan, Mark K. *The Hunley.* Miami: Narwhal Press, 1995.

Raines, Rebecca Robbins. *Getting the Message through, a Branch History of the U.S. Army Signal Corps.* Washington, DC: Center of Military History, 1996.

Rains, George Washington. *History of the Confederate States Powder Works.* Augusta, GA: Chronicle & Constitutionalist Print, 1882.

Rakes, Paul H. "The Military Career of an Ambitious Professional; Confederate General William Dorsey Pender, 1834–1863." M.A. thesis, Marshall University, 1994.

Ramage, James A. *Gray Ghost: The Life of John Singleton Mosby.* Lexington: University Press of Kentucky, 1999.

———. *Rebel Raider: The Life of John Hunt Morgan.* Lexington: University Press of Kentucky, 1986.

Ramold, Steven J. "Valuable Men for Certain Kinds of Duty: African Americans in the Civil War Navy." Ph.D. dissertation, University of Nebraska, Lincoln, 1999.

Rampp, Larry C., and Donald L. Rampp. *The Civil War in Indian Territory.* Austin, TX: Presidial Press, 1975.

Ramsdell, Charles W. "The Confederate Government and the Railroads." *American Historical Review* 22 (July 1917): 794–810.

Ramsey, Thomas R., Jr. *The Raid.* Kingsport, TN: Thomas R. Ramsey, 1973.

Ranck, James Byrne. *Albert Gallatin Brown: Radical Southern Nationalist.* New York: D. Appleton-Century Co., 1937.

Randall, James G. *Constitutional Problems under Lincoln.* Urbana: University of Illinois Press, 1951.

Randall, James G., and David Herbert Donald. *The Civil War and Reconstruction.* Lexington, MA: D. C. Heath & Co., 1969.

Randall, Ruth Painter. *Colonel Elmer Ellsworth.* Boston: Little, Brown, 1960.

———. *Lincoln's Sons.* Boston: Little, Brown, 1955.

———. *Mary Lincoln: Portrait of a Marriage.* Boston: Little, Brown, 1953.

Ransom, Roger L. *Conflict and Compromise: The Political Economy of Slavery, Emancipation, and the American Civil War.* New York: Cambridge University Press, 1989.

Rany, William F. "Recruiting and Crimping in Canada for the Northern Forces, 1861–1865." *Mississippi Valley Historical Review* 10 (June 1923): 21–33.

Raper, Horace W. "William Woods Holden and the Peace Movement in North Carolina." *North Carolina Historical Review* 31 (1954): 493–516.

Rasner, Gustav Charles. "The Effect of the Breakdown of the Prisoner Parole and Exchanve Cartel of 22 July 1862, on Conditions in Civil War Prisons." M.A. thesis, Baylor University, 1986.

Ratchford, J. W. *Some Reminiscences of Persons and Incidents of the Civil War.* 1909. Reprint. Austin, TX: Shoal Creek Publishers, 1971.

Rawley, James A. *Edwin D. Morgan, 1811–1883; Merchant in Politics.* New York: Columbia University Press, 1955.

———. *Race and Politics: "Bleeding Kansas" and the Coming of the*

Civil War. Philadelphia: University of Pennsylvania Press, 1969.

———. *Turning Points of the Civil War*. Lincoln: University of Nebraska Press, 1966.

Ray, Frederic E. *Alfred A. Waud: Civil War Artist*. New York: Viking Press, 1974.

Ray, Victor Marion. *The Life and Service of General Ben McCulloch*. Philadelphia: n.p., 1888. Reprint. Austin, TX: Speck, 1958.

Rayback, Robert J. *Millard Fillmore: Biography of a President*. Buffalo, NY: Buffalo Historical Society, 1959.

Raymond, Henry W. "Extracts from the Journal of Henry J. Raymond." *Scribner's Monthly* 19 (November 1879): 57–61; (January 1880): 419–424; (March 1880): 703–710; 20 (June 1880): 275–280.

Rea, Ralph. *Sterling Price: The Lee of the West*. Little Rock: Pioneer Press, 1959.

Read, Donald. *Cobden and Bright: A Victorian Political Partnership*. London: Edward Arnold, 1967.

Reagan, John H. *Memoirs with Special Reference to Secession and the Civil War*. New York: Neale Publishing Co., 1906.

Reardon, Carol. *Pickett's Charge in History and Memory*. Chapel Hill: University of North Carolina Press, 1997.

Records of Third Auditor's Office for 1865, Treasury Department.

Reed, Rowena. *Combined Operations in the Civil War*. Annapolis, MD: Naval Institute Press, 1963.

Reemelin, Karl. *Life of Charles Reemelin, a German: Carl Gustav Rümelin, from 1814–1892*. Cincinnati: Weier & Daiker, 1892.

Reese, Timothy J. *Sealed with Their Lives: The Battle for Crampton's Gap*. Baltimore: Butternut and Blue, 1998.

———. *Sykes' Regular Infantry Division, 1861–1864: A History of Regular United States Infantry Operations in the Civil War's Eastern Theater*. Jefferson, NC: McFarland, 1990.

Reid, Brian Holden. "Historians and the Joint Committee on the Conduct of the War." *Civil War History* 38 (1992): 319–341.

Reid, Randy L. "Howell Cobb of Georgia: A Biography." Ph.D. dissertation, Louisiana State University, 1995.

Reid, Richard J. *The Rock Riseth: George H. Thomas at Logan's Crossroads*. Central City, KY: West Kentucky Printing and Office Supply, 1988.

Reid, T. Wemyss. *Life of the Right Honourable William Edward Forster*. 2 vols. London: Chapman and Hall, 1888.

Reid, Whitelaw. *After the War: A Southern Tour*. Cincinnati: Moore, Wilsatch & Baldwin, 1866.

———. *Ohio in the War: Her Statesmen, Her Generals, and Soldiers*. 2 vols. Cincinnati: Moore, Wilstach & Baldwin, 1868.

———. "Siege of Cincinnati." In *Ohio in the War: Her Statesmen, Her Generals, and Soldiers*. 2 vols. Cincinnati: Moore, Wilstach & Baldwin, 1868.

Reiger, John F. "Deprivation, Disaffection, and Desertion in Confederate Florida." *Florida Historical Quarterly* (1970): 279–298.

Reinecke, Joseph Alfred. "Diplomatic Career of Pierre Soulé." M.A. thesis, Tulane University, 1914.

Remini, Robert V. *Daniel Webster: The Man and His Time*. New York: W. W. Norton, 1997.

———. *Henry Clay: Statesman for the Union*. New York: W. W. Norton, 1991.

Renehan, Edward J., Jr. *The Secret Six: The True Tale of the Men Who Conspired with John Brown*. New York: Crown Publishers, 1995.

Report of the Secretary of the Navy in Relation to Armored Vessels 1864 (1864).

Reynolds, Donald E. *Editors Make War*. Nashville, TN: Vanderbilt University Press, 1966.

Rezneck, Samuel. "The Civil War Role 1861–1863 of a Veteran New York Officer, Major General John E. Wool." *New York History* 44 (July 1963): 237–257.

Rhea, Gordon C. *The Battle of the Wilderness, May 5–6 1864*. Baton Rouge: Louisiana State University Press, 1994.

———. *The Battles for Spotsylvania Court House and the Road to Yellow Tavern May 7–12, 1864*. Baton Rouge: Louisiana State University Press, 1997.

Rhoades, Jeffrey L. *Scapegoat General: The Story of Major General Benjamin Huger*. Hamden, CT: Archon Books, 1985.

Rhodehamel, John, and Louise Taper, eds. *"Right or Wrong, God Judge Me": The Writings of John Wilkes Booth*. Urbana: University of Illinois Press, 1997.

Rhodes, Jane. *Mary Ann Shadd Cary: The Black Press and Protest in the Nineteenth Century*. Bloomington: Indiana University Press, 1998.

Rhodes, Steven B. "Jeremy Gilmer and the Confederate Engineers." M.A. thesis, Virginia Polytechnic Institute and State University, 1983.

Richard, J. Fraise. *The Florence Nightingale of the Southern Army: Experiences of Mrs. Ella K. Newsom, Confederate Nurse in the Great War of 1861–1865*. New York: Broadway, 1914.

Richards, Ira Don. "The Engagement at Marks' Mills." *Arkansas Historical Quarterly* 19 (Spring 1960): 51–60.

Richards, Kent D. *Isaac I. Stevens*. Pullman: Washington State University Press, 1993.

Richards, Laura E. *Samuel Gridley Howe*. New York: D. Appleton, 1935.

Richards, Laura E., and Maud Howe Elliot. *Julia Ward Howe, 1819–1910*. 2 vols. Boston and New York: Houghton Mifflin, 1915.

Richardson, Albert D. *The Secret Service, the Field, the Dungeon and the Escape*. Hartford, CT: American Publishing Co., 1865.

Richardson, H. Edward. *Cassius Marcellus Clay: Firebrand for Freedom*. Lexington: University Press of Kentucky, 1976.

Richardson, Heather Cox. *The Greatest Nation of the Earth: Republican Economic Policies during the Civil War*. Cambridge, MA: Harvard University Press, 1997.

Richardson, James H. *"Old Jack" and his Foot Cavalry; Or, a Virginian Boy's Progress to Renown*. New York: John Branburn, 1864.

Richardson, Robert D., Jr. *Henry Thoreau: A Life of the Mind*. Berkeley and Los Angeles: University of California Press, 1986.

Riddle, A. G. *The Life of Benjamin F. Wade*. Cleveland: William W. Williams, 1886.

Riddleburger, Patrick W. *George Washington Julian, Radical Republican: A Study in Nineteenth-Century Politics and Reform*. Indianapolis: Indiana Historical Bureau, 1966.

Ridley, Jasper. *Lord Palmerston*. New York: E. P. Dutton, 1971.

———. *Maximilian and Juarez*. London: Constable, 1993.

Rietti, J. C. *Military Annals of Mississippi: Military Organizations which Entered the Service of the Confederate States of America from the State of Mississippi*. Spartanburg, SC: Reprint Co., 1988.

Riggs Manuscripts. Library of Congress, Washington, DC.

Ringle, Dennis J. *Life in Mr. Lincoln's Navy*. Annapolis, MD: Naval Institute Press, 1998.

Ripley, C. Peter. "The Underground Railroad." In *Underground Railroad: Official National Park Handbook*. Washington, DC: National Park Service, 1998: 45–75.

Ripley, C. Peter, et al., eds. *The Black Abolitionist Papers*. 5 vols. Chapel Hill: University of North Carolina Press, 1985–1992.

Risch, Erna. *Quartermaster Support of the Army: A History of the Corps, 1775–1939*. Washington, DC: Center of Military History, United States Army, 1989.

Ritter, Gretchen. *Goldbugs and Greenbacks: The Antimonopoly Tradition and the Politics of Finance in America*. Cambridge, England, and New York: Cambridge University Press, 1997.

Robbins, John B. "The Confederacy and the Writ of Habeas Corpus." *Georgia Historical Quarterly* 55 (1971): 83–101.

Robbins, Keith. *John Bright*. London and Boston: Routledge & K. Paul, 1979.

Roberts, Allen E. *House Reunited: Masonry Aids Reconstruction*. 1961. Reprint. Highland Springs, VA: Anchor Communications, 1996.

Roberts, Bobby, and Carl Moneyhon. *Portraits of Conflict: A Photographic History of Arkansas in the Civil War*. Fayetteville: University of Arkansas Press, 1987.

Roberts, Gary L. "Sand Creek: Tragedy and Symbol." Ph.D. dissertation, University of Oklahoma, 1984.

Roberts, Robert B. *Encyclopedia of Historic Forts: The Military, Pioneer, and Trading Posts of the United States*. New York: Macmillan, 1988.

Roberts, William H. "The Neglected Ironclad: A Design and Constructional Analysis of the U.S.S. New Ironsides." *Warship International* 26 (1989): 109–134.

———. *New Ironsides in the Civil War*. Annapolis, MD: Naval Institute Press, 1999.

Robertson, Fred L. *Soldiers of Florida in the Seminole Indian-Civil and Spanish-American Wars*. Live Oak, FL: Democrat Book and Job Print, 1903.

Robertson Hospital Morning Reports of Patients and Attendants. Record Group 109. National Archives, Washington, DC.

Robertson, James I., Jr. *A. P. Hill: The Story of a Confederate Warrior*. New York: Random House, 1987.

———. *Civil War Virginia: Battleground for a Nation*. Charlottesville: University Press of Virginia, 1991.

———. *Soldiers Blue and Gray*. Columbia: University of South Carolina Press, 1988.

———. *The Stonewall Brigade*. Baton Rouge: Louisiana State University Press, 1963.

———. *Stonewall Jackson: The Man, the Soldier, the Legend*. New York: Simon & Schuster Macmillan, 1997.

———. *Tenting Tonight: The Soldier's Life*. Alexandria, VA: Time-Life Books, 1984.

Robertson, James Rood. *A Kentuckian at the Court of the Tsars: The Ministry of Cassius Marcellus Clay to Russia*. Berea, KY: Berea College Press, 1935.

Robertson, William Glenn. *Back Door to Richmond; The Bermuda Hundred Campaign, April–June 1864*. Newark: University of Delaware Press, 1987.

Robertson-Lorant, Laurie. *Melville: A Biography*. Amherst: University of Massachusetts Press, 1996.

Robins, Glenn M. "Leonidas Polk and Episcopal Identity: An Evangelical Experiment in the Mid-nineteenth Century South." Ph.D. dissertation, University of Southern Mississippi, 1999.

Robinson, Charles M. *Hurricane of Fire: The Union Assault on Fort Fisher*. Annapolis, MD: Naval Institute Press, 1998.

Robinson, Daniel W. "Belle Isle: Prison in the James, 1862–1865." M.A. thesis, Virginia Polytechnic Institute and State University, 1980.

Robinson, William M., Jr. *The Confederate Privateers*. n.p., 1928. Reprint. Columbia: University of South Carolina Press, 1990.

———. *Justice in Gray: A History of the Judicial System of the Confederate States of America*. Cambridge, MA: Harvard University Press, 1941.

Robinson, Vergil, comp. *Booneville, Mississippi, in the Civil War: A Compilation of Information from Many Sources*. Booneville, MS: Published by the compiler, 1998.

Robinson-Durso, Pamela. "Chaplains in the Confederate Army." *Journal of Church and State* 33 (1991): 747–763.

Robson, John S. *How a One-Legged Rebel Lives*. Durham, NC: Educator Co. Printers and Binders, 1898.

Rochelle, James Henry. *Life of Rear Admiral John Randolph Tucker*. Washington, DC: Neale Publishing Co., 1903.

Rodermyre, Edgar T. *History of Centralia, Missouri*. Centralia, MO: Press of the Centralia Fireside Guard, 1936.

Rodman, Thomas J. *Casting the 15-in. Gun: Fort Pitt, 1864*. Reprint. Port Huron, MI: Antique Ordnance Publishers, 1980.

———. "Testimony of Major T. J. Rodman, February 6, 1864." *Report of the Joint Committee on the Conduct of the War*. Reprint. Port Huron, MI: Antique Ordnance Publishers, 1980.

Rodriguez, Junius P. *Chronology of World Slavery*. Santa Barbara, CA: ABC-Clio, 1999.

———. *The Historical Encyclopedia of World Slavery*. 2 vols. Santa Barbara, CA: ABC-Clio, 1997.

Roe, Alfred S., and Charles Nutt. *History of the First Regiment of Heavy Artillery Massachusetts Volunteers, Formerly the Fourteenth Regiment of Infantry, 1861–1865*. Worcester and Boston: The Regimental Association, 1917: 114–115.

Rogers, Fred B. *Soldiers of the Overland*. San Francisco: Grabhorn Press, 1938.

Rogers, Margaret G. *Civil War Corinth, 1861–1865*. Corinth, MS: Rankin Printery, 1989.

Rogers, William Warren. *Confederate Home Front: Montgomery during The Civil War*. Tuscaloosa: University of Alabama Press, 1999.

Rogers, William W., Robert D. Ward, and Leah R. Atkins. *Alabama: The History of a Deep South State*. Tuscaloosa: University of Alabama Press, 1994.

Rohan, Jack. *Yankee Arms Maker: The Incredible Career of Samuel Colt*. New York: Harper & Brothers, 1935.

Roland, Charles P. *Albert Sidney Johnston: Soldier of Three Repubhcs*. Austin: University of Texas Press, 1964.

Rolle, Andrew F. *The Lost Cause. The Confederate Exodus to Mexico*. Norman: University of Oklahoma Press, 1965.

Rollins, Richard M., and Arthur W. Bergeron, eds. *Black Southerners in Gray: Essays on Afro-Americans in Confederate Armies*. Redondo Beach, CA: Rank and File Publications, 1994.

Rombauer, Robert J. *The Union Cause in St. Louis in 1861: An Historical Sketch*. St Louis: Nixon-Jones Print Co., 1909.

Root, George F. *The Story of a Musical Life*. n.p., 1891. Reprint. New York: Da Capo Press, 1970.

Roper, Peter W. *Jedediah Hotchkiss, Rebel Mapmaker and Virginia Businessman*. Shippensburg, PA: White Mane Publishing Co., 1992.

Ropes, John C. *The Army under Pope*. New York: Charles Scribner's Sons, 1881.

Ropp, Theodore. "Anacondas Anyone?" *Military Affairs* 27 (Summer 1963): 71–76.

Rose, Michael. *Atlanta: A Portrait of the Civil War*. Atlanta: Atlanta Historical Society and Arcadia Publishing, 1999.

Rose, Willie Lee. *Rehearsal for Reconstruction: The Port Royal Experiment*. London: Oxford University Press, 1964

Roseboom, Eugene H. *The Civil War Era: 1850–1873*. Vol 4. *The History of the State of Ohio*. Edited by Carl Wittke. Columbus: The Ohio State Archaeological and Historical Society, 1944.

Rosegarten, Joseph. *The German Soldier in the Wars of the*

United States. Philadelphia: J. B. Lippincott, 1886.

Rosenberg, Norman L. "Personal Liberty Laws and Sectional Crisis: 1850–1861." *Civil War History* 17 (1971): 25–44.

Rosenberg, R. B. *Living Monuments: Confederate Soldiers' Homes in the New South.* Chapel Hill: University of North Carolina Press, 1993.

Roske, Ralph J. *His Own Counsel: The Life and Times of Lyman Trumbull.* Reno: University of Nevada Press, 1979.

Roske, Ralph J., and Charles Van Doren. *Lincoln's Commando: The Biography of Commander William B. Cushing, U.S. Navy.* 1957. Reprint. Annapolis, MD: Naval Institute Press, 1995.

Ross, Earle Dudley. *Democracy's College: The Land-Grant Movement in the Formative Stage.* Ames: Iowa State College Press, 1942.

Rossi, Alice S., ed. *The Feminist Papers: From Adams to de Beauvoir.* New York: Columbia University Press, 1973.

Roth, Clayton D., Jr. "150 Years of Defense Activity at Key West, 1820–1970." *Tequesta* 30 (1970): 37–38.

Rowland, Dunbar, ed. *Mississippi: Comprising Sketches of Counties, Towns, Events, Institutions, and Persons, Arranged in Cyclopedic Form.* 4 vols. 1907. Reprint. Spartanburg, SC: The Reprint Co., 1972.

Rowland, Thomas J. *George B. McClellan and Civil War History: In the Shadow of Grant and Sherman.* Kent, OH: Kent State University Press, 1998.

Royster, Charles. *The Destructive War: William Tecumseh Sherman, Stonewall Jackson, and the Americans.* New York: Alfred A. Knopf, 1991.

Ruffin, Edmund. *The Diary of Edmund Ruffin.* 3 vols. Edited by William K. Scarborough. Baton Rouge: Louisiana State University Press, 1972–1989.

Russell, Charles Edward. *Blaine of Maine; His Life and Times.* New York: Cosmopolitan Book Corporation, 1931.

Russell, James Michael. *Atlanta 1847–1890: City Building in the Old South and the New.* Baton Rouge: Louisiana State University Press, 1988.

Russell, William Howard. *My Diary North and South.* Edited by Eugene H. Berwanger. New York: Alfred A. Knopf, 1988.

———. *William Howard Russell's Civil War: Private Diary and Letters, 1861–1862.* Edited by Martin Crawford. Athens: University of Georgia, 1992.

Ryan, David D. *Cornbread and Maggots—Cloak and Dagger: Union Prisoners and Spies in Civil War Richmond.* Richmond, VA: Dietz Press, 1994.

Ryan, Jeffrey T. "Some Notes on the Civil War Era Marine Corps." *Civil War Regiments* 2 (1992): 183–193.

Sacks, Howard L., and Judith Rose Sacks. *Way up North in Dixie: A Black Family's claim to the Confederate Anthem.* Washington, DC: Smithsonian Institution Press, 1993.

Sage, Leland L. *A History of Iowa.* Ames: Iowa State University Press, 1974.

Salecker, Gene Eric. *Disaster on the Mississippi: The Sultana Explosion, April 27, 1865.* Annapolis, MD: Naval Institute Press, 1996.

Sallee, Scott E. "Missouri! One Last Time: Sterling Price's 1864 Missouri Expedition, 'A Just and Holy Cause.'" *Blue and Gray Magazine* 8 (June 1991): 10–18, 20, 48–61.

Salm-Salm, Agnes Elizabeth Winona Leclerq Joy, Prinzessin zu. *Ten Years of My Life.* Detroit: Belford Bros., 1877.

Salm-Salm, Prince Felix. *My Diary in Mexico in 1867 including the Last Days of Emperor Maximilian with Leaves from the Diary of the Princess Salm-Salm.* London: R. Bently, 1868.

Salt, Henry Stephens. *Life of Henry David Thoreau.* London: Walter Scott, 1896.

Salta, Remo. "Guardians of the Coast." *America's Civil War* (March 1994).

Salter, William. "Major-General John M. Corse." *Annals of Iowa* 2 (April, July, October 1895): 1–19, 105–145, 278–304.

Samito, Christian G. *Commanding Boston's Irish Ninth: The Civil War Letters of Colonel Patrick R. Guiney, Ninth Massachusetts Volunteer Infantry.* New York: Fordham University Press, 1998.

Sampson, Robert D. "'Pretty Damned Warm Times': The 1864 Charleston Riot and 'The Inalienable Right of Revolution.'" *Illinois Historical Journal* 89 (Summer 1996): 99–116.

Samuels, Ernest. *Henry Adams.* Cambridge, MA: Belknap Press of Harvard University Press, 1989.

Sandler, Stanley. *The Emergence of the Modern Capital Ship.* Newark: University of Delaware Press, 1979.

Sanger, Donald Bridgman, and Thomas Robson Hay. *James Longstreet: I. Soldier, by Donald Bridgman Sanger; II. Politician, Officeholder, and Writer, by Thomas Robson Hay.* Baton Rouge: Louisiana State University Press, 1952.

Satterfield, Robert B. "Andrew Jackson Donelson: A Moderate Nationalist Jacksonian." Ph.D. dissertation, Johns Hopkins University, 1961.

Satterlee, Herbert L. *J. Pierpont Morgan: An Intimate Portrait.* 1939. Reprint. New York: Arno, 1975.

Sauers, Richard A. *Advance the Colors! Pennsylvania Civil War Battleflags.* 2 vols. Lebanon, PA: Sowers Printing Co. for the Pennsylvania Capitol Preservation Committee, 1987–1991.

———. *A Caspian Sea of Ink: The Meade-Sickles Controversy.* Baltimore: Butternut and Blue, 1989.

———. *The Gettysburg Campaign, June 3–August 1, 1863: A Comprehensive, Selectively Annotated Bibliography.* Westport, CT: Greenwood Press, 1982.

———. "A Succession of Honorable Victories": The Burnside Expedition in North Carolina.* Dayton, OH: Morningside House, 1996.

———. *"To Care For Him Who Has Borne the Battle": Research Guide to Civil War Material in the National Tribune, Volume 1: 1877–1884.* Jackson, KY: History Shop Press, 1995.

Sauers, Richard A., and William D. Gorges. *The Battle of New Bern and Related Sites in Craven County, N. C., 1861–1865.* New Bern, NC: Griffin & Tilghman Printers, 1994.

Saul, Norman E. *Distant Friends: The United States and Russia, 1763–1867.* Lawrence: University Press of Kansas, 1991.

Saunders, Steven. *The Music of Stephen Collins Foster. A Critical Edition.* Washington, DC: Smithsonian Institution, 1990.

Savas, Theodore P., and David A. Woodbury, eds. *The Campaign for Atlanta and Sherman's March to the Sea: Essays on the American Civil War in Georgia, 1864 Georgia.* Vols. 1 & 2. Campbell, CA: Savas & Woodbury, 1994.

Scaife, William R. *The March to the Sea.* Saline, MI: McNaughton & Gunn, 1993.

Schafer, Elizabeth D. "Jaded Mules, Twisted Rails, and Razed Depots." *Civil War* 9 (January–February 1991): 40–46.

Scharf, J. Thomas. *History of the Confederate States Navy: From Its Organization to the Surrender of Its Last Vessel.* 1877. Reprint. New York: Gramercy Books, 1996.

Scheips, Paul J. "Union Signal Communications: Innovation and Conflict." *Civil War History* 9 (December 1963).

Schenck, Martin. *Up Came Hill: The Story of the Light Division and its Leaders.* Harrisburg, PA: Stackpole, 1958.

Schenck, Reverend B. S. *The Burning of Chambersburg, Pennsylvania.* Philadelphia: Lindsay & Blakiston, 1864.

Scherer, Paul. *Lord John Russell: A Biography.* London: Associated University Presses, 1999.

Schiavo, Giovanni. *Four Centuries of Italian American History.* New York: Vigo Press, 1952.

Schiller, Herbert M. *The Bermuda Hundred Campaign.* Dayton, OH: Morningside House, 1988.

———. *Fort Pulaski and the Defense of Savannah.* National Parks Civil War Series. Eastern National, 1997.

Schmidt, James D. *Free to Work: Labor Law, Emancipation, and Reconstruction, 1815–1880.* Athens: University of Georgia Press, 1998.

Schmitt, Martin F., ed. *General George Crook: His Autobiography.* Norman: University of Oklahoma Press, 1960.

Schoeberlein, Robert W. "A Marylander at the Northwest Frontier." *Maryland Historical Magazine* 90 (Summer 1995): 229–236.

Schofield, John McAllister. *Forty Six Years in the Army.* New York: Century Co., 1897.

Scholten, Catherine M. "'On the Importance of the Obstetrick Art': Changing Customs of Childbirth in America, 1760–1825." In *Women and Health in America.* Edited by Judith Walzer Leavitt. Madison: University of Wisconsin Press, 1984: 142–154.

Schott, Thomas E. *Alexander H. Stephens of Georgia: A Biography.* Baton Rouge: Louisiana State University Press, 1988.

Schottonhamel, George Carl, "Lewis Baldwin Parsons and the Civil War Transportation." Ph.D. dissertation, University of Illinois, 1954.

Schudson, Michael. *Discovering the News: A Social History of American Newspapers.* New York: Basic Books, 1981.

Schultz, Charles R. "The Conditions at Johnson's Island Prison during the Civil War." M.A. thesis, Bowling Green State University, 1960.

Schultz, Duane P. *The Dahlgren Affair: Terror and Conspiracy in the Civil War.* New York: W. W. Norton, 1998.

Schultz, Jane. "The Inhospitable Hospital: Gender and Professionalism in Civil War Medicine." *SIGNS* (Winter 1992): 363–393.

———. *Women at the Front: Female Hospital Workers in Civil War America.* Chapel Hill: University of North Carolina, 2001.

Schuricht, Herrmann. *History of the German Element in Virginia.* 2 vols. Baltimore: Theo. Kroh & Sons, 1898–1900.

Schutz, Wallace J. *Abandoned by Lincoln: A Military Biography of Major General John Pope.* Urbana: University of Illinois Press, 1990.

———. *Major General John Pope and the Army of Virginia.* Minnesota: W. J. Schutz, 1986.

Schwab, John C. *The Confederate States of America, 1861–65; A Financial and Industrial History of the South during the Civil War.* 1901. Reprint. New York: B. Franklin, 1968.

Schwartz, Bernard. *A History of the Supreme Court.* New York: Oxford University Press, 1993.

Schwartz, Gerald, ed. *A Woman Doctor's Civil War: Esther Hill Hawks' Diary.* Columbia: University of South Carolina Press, 1984.

Schwartz, Harold. *Samuel Gridley Howe: Social Reformer, 1801–1876.* Cambridge, MA: Harvard University Press, 1956.

Schweikart, Larry. *Banking the American South from the Age of Jackson to Reconstruction.* Baton Rouge: Louisiana State University Press, 1987.

Scott, John. *Partisan Life with Col. John S. Mosby.* New York: Harper & Brothers Publishers, 1867.

Scott, Kate M. *In Honor of the National Association of Army Nurses.* Atlantic City, NJ: n. p., 1910.

Scott, Kim Allen, and Stephen Burgess. "Pursuing an Elusive Quarry: The Battle of Cane Hill, Arkansas." *Arkansas Historical Quarterly* 56 (Spring 1997): 26–55.

Scott, Quinta, and Howard S. Miller. *The Eads Bridge.* Columbia: University of Missouri Press, 1979.

Scott, Robert Garth, ed. *Fallen Leaves: The Civil War Letters of Major Henry Livermore Abbott.* Kent, OH: Kent State University Press, 1991.

———. *Into the Wilderness with the Army of the Potomac.* Bloomington: Indiana University Press, 1985.

Scott, Winfield. *Memoirs of Lieut.-General Scott, LL. D.* 2 vols. 1864. Reprint. Freeport, NY: Books for Libraries, 1970.

Scroggins, Mark. *Hannibal: The Life of Abraham Lincoln's First Vice President.* Lanham, MD: University Press of America, 1994.

Seagrave, Pia Seija, ed. *The History of the Irish Brigade: A Collection of Historical Essays.* Fredericksburg, VA: Sergeant Kirland's Museum, 1997.

Sears, Louis Martin. *John Slidell.* Durham, NC: Duke University Press, 1925.

Sears, Richard D. "*A Practical Recognition of the Brotherhood of Man;*" *John G. Fee and the Camp Nelson Experience.* Berea, KY: Berea College Press, 1986.

Sears, Stephen W. *The American Heritage Century Collection of Civil War Art.* New York: American Heritage Publishing Co., 1974.

———. *Chancellorsville.* New York: Houghton Mifflin, 1996.

———, ed. *The Civil War Papers of George B. McClellan: Selected Correspondence, 1860–1865.* New York: Ticknor & Fields, 1989.

———. *George B. McClellan: The Young Napoleon.* New York: Da Capo Press, 1999.

———. *Landscape Turned Red: The Battle of Antietam.* New Haven, CT: Ticknor & Fields, 1983.

———. "The Ordeal of General Stone." *MHQ: The Quarterly Journal of Military History* 7 (1995): 46–56.

———. *To the Gates of Richmond: The Peninsula Campaign.* New York: Ticknor & Fields, 1992.

Seddon, James A., and John Smith Preston. *Report of the Secretary of War.* Richmond, VA: n.p., 1864.

Sedgwick, John. *Correspondence of John Sedgwick, Major-General.* 2 vols. New York: De Vinne Press, 1902–1903.

Sefton, James E., ed. "Aristotle in Blue and Braid: General John M. Schofield's Essays on Reconstruction." *Civil War History* 17 (March 1971): 45–57.

Segal, David R. *Recruiting for Uncle Sam: Citizenship and Military Manpower Policy.* Lawrence: University Press of Kansas, 1989.

Segars, Ernest B. "A Study of the Charleston (S.C.) *Mercury* during Robert Barnwell Rhett, Senior's Tenure as an Editorial Writer, 1861–1863." M.A. thesis, University of South Carolina, Journalism, 1974.

Seitz, Don C. *The James Gordon Bennetts: Father and Son.* Indianapolis: Bobbs-Merrill, 1928.

Selfridge, Thomas O. *Memoirs of Thomas O. Selfridge, Jr., Rear Admiral, U.S.N.* New York: Putnam, 1900.

Semi-Annual Reports of the Ladies Aid Society of Philadelphia. Philadelphia: Sherman, 1861–1865.

Semmes, Raphael. *Memoirs of Service Afloat during the War Between the States.* 1869. Reprint. Secaucus, NJ: Blue and Gray Press, 1987.

Seward, Frederick William. *Reminiscences of A War-Time Statesman and Diplomat, 1830–1915.* New York: G. P. Putnam's Sons, 1916.

Seymour, Digby Gordon. *Divided Loyalties: Fort Sanders and the Civil War in East Tennessee.* 2d ed. Knoxville: East Tennessee Historical Society, 1982.

Seymour, William J. *The Civil War Memoirs of Captain William J. Seymour: Reminiscences of a Louisiana Tiger.* Edited by

Terry L. Jones. Baton Rouge: Louisiana State University Press, 1997.

Shackelford, George Green. *George Wythe Randolph and the Confederate Elite*. Athens: University of Georgia Press, 1988.

Shalhope, Robert E. *Sterling Price: Portrait of a Southerner*. Columbia: University of Missouri Press, 1971.

Shankman, Arnold M. *The Pennsylvania Antiwar Movement, 1861–1865*. Rutherford, PA: Fairleigh Dickinson University Press, 1980.

Shannon, Fred A. "The Homestead Act and the Labor Surplus." In *The Public Lands: Studies in the History of the Public Domain*. Edited by Vernon Carstensen. Madison: University of Wisconsin Press, 1962: 315–348.

———. *The Organization and Administration of the Union Army, 1861–1865*. 2 vols. Cleveland: Arthur H. Clark Co., 1928.

Shapack, Arnold. "Oak to Iron—Monitors in United States Naval History." M.A. thesis, University of Maryland, 1973.

Shapiro, Samuel. "The Rendition of Anthony Burns." *Journal of Negro History* 44 (1959): 34–51.

———. *Richard Henry Dana, Jr., 1815–1882*. East Lansing: Michigan State University Press, 1961.

Sharkey, Robert P. *Money, Class, and Party: An Economic Study of Civil War and Reconstruction*. Baltimore: Johns Hopkins University Press, 1959.

Sharpe, A. B. "Drainsville." *Philadelphia Weekly Times*, 9 (January 1886).

Sharpe, Henry Granville. "The Art of Supplying Armies in the Field as Exemplified during the Civil War." *Journal of the Military Service Institution of the United States* 18 (January 1896): 45–95.

Sharpe, William D. *Confederate States Medical and Surgical Journal*. Metuchen, NJ: Scarecrow Press, 1976.

Shattuck, Gardiner H. Jr. *A Shield and Hiding Place: The Religious Life of the Civil War Armies*. Macon, GA: Mercer University Press, 1985.

Shaw, Maurice. *Stonewall Jackson's Surgeon, Hunter Holmes McGuire: A Biography*. Lynchburg, VA: H. E. Howard, 1993.

Shaw, Richard. *Dagger John: The Unquiet Life and Times of Archbishop John Hughes of New York*. New York: Paulist Press, 1977.

Shea, William L. *War in the West: Pea Ridge and Prairie Grove*. Fort Worth, TX: Ryan Place, 1997.

Shea, William L., and Earl J. Hess. *Pea Ridge: Civil War Campaign in the West*. Chapel Hill: University of North Carolina Press, 1992.

Shenton, James P. *Robert John Walker: A Politician from Jackson to Lincoln*. New York: Columbia University Press, 1961.

Shepard, Richard. *The Paper's Papers: A Reporter's Journey through the Archives of the New York Times*. New York: Times Books, 1996.

Shepherd, Henry E. *Narrative of Prison Life at Baltimore and Johnson's Island, Ohio*. Baltimore: Commercial Printing & Stationery Co., 1917.

Sheridan, Don. *The Battle of Bean's Station: A Spirited Conflict, December 14–16, 1863*. Grainger County, TN: Grainger County Historic Society, 1997.

Sheridan, Philip. *Personal Memoirs of Philip Henry Sheridan, General of the U.S. Army. New and Enl. Ed. with an Account of his Life from 1871 to His Death, in 1888, by Brig.-Gen. Michael V. Sheridan*. 2 vols. New York: D. Appleton & Co., 1904.

Sherman, William T. *Memoirs of William T. Sherman*. New York: Library of America, 1990.

Sherwin, Oscar. *Prophet of Liberty: The Life and Times of Wendell Phillips*. New York: Bookman Associates, 1958.

Sherwood, Isaac Ruth. *Memories of the War*. Toledo, OH: H. J. Chittenden Co., 1923.

Shields, Richard Eugene, Jr. *Befriend and Relieve Every Brother: Freemasonry during Wartime*. Monroe, NC: Carolina Trader, 1994.

Shingleton, Royce. *High Seas Confederate: The Life and Times of John Newland Maffitt*. Columbia: University of South Carolina Press, 1994.

Shoemaker, Henry W. *The Last of the War Governors*. Altoona, PA: Altoona Tribune Publishing Co., 1916.

Shorey, Henry A. *The Story of the Maine Fifteenth*. Bridgton: Press of the Brighton News, 1890.

Shoup, Francis Asbury. *Policy of Employing Negro Troops*. Richmond, VA: n.p., 1865.

Shriver, Philip R. *Ohio's Military Prisons in the Civil War*. Columbus: Ohio State University Press, 1964.

Siebert, Wilbur H. *The Underground Railroad: From Slavery to Freedom*. New York: Macmillan, 1898.

Siegel, Martin. *The United States Supreme Court: Volume 3, The Taney Court, 1836–1864*. 10 vols. Danbury, CT: Grolier Educational Corp., 1995.

Sievers, Harry J. *Benjamin Harrison: Hoosier President, the White House and After*. Indianapolis: Bobbs-Merrill, 1968.

———. *Benjamin Harrison: Hoosier Statesman, from the Civil War to the White House, 1865–1888*. New York: University Publishers, 1959.

———. *Benjamin Harrison: Hoosier Warrior, 1833–1865*. Chicago: H. Regnery, 1952.

Silber, Irwin. *Songs of the Civil War*. New York: Columbia University Press, 1960.

Silbey, Joel H. *"A Respectable Minority": The Democratic Party in the Civil War Era, 1860–1868*. New York: W. W. Norton, 1977.

Silver, James. *Confederate Morale and Church Propaganda*. Tuscaloosa, AL: Confederate Publishing Co., 1957.

Silverman, Jerry. *Ballads and Songs of the Civil War*. Pacific, MO: Mel Bay Publications, 1993.

Silverstone, Paul H. *Warships of the Civil War Navies*. Annapolis, MD: Naval Institute Press, 1989.

Silvestro, Clement M. *Rally 'Round the Flag: The Union Leagues in the Civil War*. Ann Arbor: Historical Society of Michigan, 1966.

Simkins, Francis Butler, and James Welch Patton. *The Women of the Confederacy*. Richmond, VA: Garrett & Massie, 1936.

Simmons, Michael K. "*Maum Guinea*: or, A Dime Novelist Looks at Abolition." *Journal of Popular Culture* 10 (Summer 1976).

Simms, Henry Harrison. *Life of Robert M. T. Hunter; A Study in Sectionalism and Secession*. Richmond, VA: William Byrd Press, 1935.

Simms, William Gilmore, ed. *Sack and Destruction of the City of Columbia, S.C.* 2d ed. Edited by A. S. Salley. Atlanta: Oglethorpe University Press, 1937.

———. *War Poetry of the South*. New York: Richardson, 1866.

Simonhoff, Harry. *Jewish Participants in the Civil War*. New York: Arco Publishing Co., 1963.

Simpson, Brooks D. *Let Us Have Peace: Ulysses S. Grant and the Politics of War and Reconstruction, 1861–1868*. Chapel Hill: University of North Carolina Press, 1991.

———. *Ulysses S. Grant: Triumph over Adversity, 1822–1865*. Boston: Houghton Mifflin, 2000.

Simpson, Brooks D., and Jean V. Berlin, eds. *Sherman's Civil War: Selected Correspondence of William T. Sherman, 1860–1865*. Chapel Hill: University of North Carolina Press, 1999.

Simpson, Craig M. *A Good Southerner: The Life of Henry A. Wise of Virginia*. Chapel Hill: University of North Carolina Press, 1985.

Simpson, Marc. *Winslow Homer: Paintings of the Civil War.* San Francisco: Fine Arts Museums of San Francisco, 1988.

Sinclair, Donald A. *A Bibliography: The Civil War and New Jersey.* New Brunswick, NJ: Friends of the Rutgers University Library, 1968.

Skipper, Ottis Clark. *J. D. B. De Bow: Magazinist of the Old South.* Athens: University of Georgia Press, 1958.

Skocpol, Theda. *Protecting Soldiers and Mothers: The Political Origins of Social Policy in the United States.* Cambridge, MA: Harvard University Press, 1992.

Slade, A. D. *A. T. A. Torbert: Southern Gentleman in Union Blue.* Dayton, OH: Morningside House, 1992.

———. *That Sterling Soldier: The Life of David A. Russell.* Dayton, OH: Morningside, 1995.

Slagle, Jay. *Ironclad Captain: Seth Ledyard Phelps and the U.S. Navy, 1841–1864.* Kent, OH: Kent State University Press, 1996.

Slomovitz, Albert I. *The Fighting Rabbis: Jewish Military Chaplains and American History.* New York: New York University Press, 1999.

Smiley, David L. *Lion of White Hall: The Life of Cassius Marcellus Clay* Madison: University of Wisconsin Press, 1962.

Smith, Arthur D. Howden. *Commodore Vanderbilt: An Epic of American Achievement.* New York: Robert M. McBride, 1927.

Smith, Brier R. *Major General Mansfield Lovell and the Fall of New Orleans: The Downfall of a Career.* Memphis, TN: Memphis Pink Palace Museum, 1973.

Smith, Charles W. *Life and Military Services of Brevet-Major General Robert S. Foster.* Indianapolis: E. J. Hacker, 1915.

Smith, David P. "Conscription and Conflict on the Texas Frontier, 1863–1865." In *Lone Star Blue and Gray: Essays on Texas in the Civil War.* Austin: Texas State Historical Association, 1995: 275–287.

———. *Frontier Defense in the Civil War: Texas' Rangers and Rebels.* College Station: Texas A&M University Press, 1992.

Smith, Derek. *Civil War Savannah.* Savannah, GA: Frederic C. Beil, 1997.

Smith, Duane A. *The Birth of Colorado: A Civil War Perspective.* Norman: University of Oklahoma Press, 1989.

Smith, Elbert B. *Francis Preston Blair.* New York: Free Press, 1980.

———. *Magnificent Missourian: The Life of Thomas Hart Benton.* Philadelphia: J. B. Lippincott Co., 1958.

———. *The Presidencies of Zachary Taylor and Millard Fillmore.* Lawrence: University Press of Kansas, 1988.

Smith, Everard H. "Chambersburg: Anatomy of a Confederate Reprisal." *American Historical Review* 96 (April 1991): 432–455.

Smith, G. Judson, Jr. "The Life of Alexander Robert Lawton." M.A. thesis, Georgia Southern University, 1995.

Smith, Gene. *American Gothic: The Story of America's Legendary Theatrical Family—Junius, Edwin and John Wilkes Booth.* New York: Simon & Schuster, 1992.

———. *High Crimes and Misdemeanors: The Impeachment and Trial of Andrew Johnson.* New York: McGraw-Hill, 1976.

Smith, Gene A. *Iron and Heavy Guns: Duel between the Monitor and Merrimac.* Abilene, TX: McWhiney Foundation Press, 1996.

Smith, George W. *Henry C. Carey and the American Sectional Conflict.* Albuquerque: University of New Mexico Press, 1951.

Smith, Gerald J. *"One of the Most Daring of Men": The Life of Confederate General William Tatim Wofford.* Murfreesboro, TN: Southern Heritage Press, 1997.

Smith, Gustavus W. *Confederate War Papers.* New York: Atlantic Publishing and Engraving Co., 1884.

Smith, John David. "The Recruitment of Negro Soldiers in Kentucky, 1863–1865." *Register of the Kentucky Historical Society* 72 (1974): 364–390.

Smith, Lawrence A. "A Confederate Gentleman: George Alfred Trenholm of Charleston, South Carolina." M.A. thesis, University of New Hampshire, 1989.

Smith, Merritt Roe. *Harpers Ferry Armory and the New Technology: The Challenge of Change.* Ithaca, NY: Cornell University Press, 1977.

Smith, Philip Mason. *Confederates Down East: Confederate Operations in and around Maine.* Portland, ME: Provincial Press, 1985.

Smith, Robert Ross. "Ox Hill: The Most Neglected Battle of the Civil War, 1 September 1862." *Fairfax County and the War between the States.* Fairfax, VA: Fairfax County Civil War Centennial Commission, 1961.

Smith, Robin. *American Civil War Zouaves.* London: Osprey Military & Reed Consumer Books, 1996.

Smith, Truman. *Considerations on the Slavery Question, Addressed to the President of the United States.* New York: Published by the author, 1862.

———. *The Spoils System, The Offspring of Modern Democracy, and the Source of Numberless Evils to the Country: Crush it Out!* New York: E. Hoyt, 1876.

Smith, Vickey Dee. "The Expulsion of Jesse D. Bright from the United States Senate." M.A. thesis, California State University, Long Beach, 1974.

Smith, Walter George. *Life and Letters of Thomas Kilby Smith, Brevet Major-General, United States Volunteers, 1820–1887.* New York: G. P. Putnam's Sons, 1898.

Smith, Willard H. *Schuyler Colfax: The Changing Fortunes of a Political Idol.* Indianapolis: Indiana Historical Bureau, 1952.

Smith, William E. *The Francis Preston Blair Family in Politics.* 2 vols. 1933. Reprint. New York: Da Capo Press, 1969.

Smith, William Farrar. *Autobiography of Major General William F. Smith, 1861–1864.* Edited by Herbert O. Schiller. Dayton, OH: Morningside House, 1990.

———. *From Chattanooga to Petersburg under Generals Grant and Butler: A Contribution to the History of the War, and a Personal Vindication.* 1893. Reprint. Boston and New York: Houghton Mifflin, 1975.

Smith, William Farrus. *In Memorium of General Darius Nash Couch: Read before the Association of the Graduates of the United States Military Academy, June 10, 1897.* n.p., 1897.

Smith, William L. G. *The Life and Times of Lewis Cass.* New York: Derby & Jackson, 1856.

Smith, William Sooy. *The Mississippi Raid.* Chicago: n.p., 1907.

Snead, Claiborne. *Address by Col. Claiborne Snead at the Reunion of the Third Georgia Regiment at Union Point, on the 31st July, 1874, History of the Third Georgia Regiment, and the Career of its First Commander, Gen. Ambrose R. Wright.* Augusta, GA: Chronicle & Sentinel Job Printing Establishment, 1874.

Snell, J. G. "H. H. Emmon, Detroit's Agent in Canadian-American Relations, 1864–1866." *Michigan History* 56 (Winter 1972): 302–318.

Snell, Mark A. *William B. Franklin: A Biography.* New York: Fordham University Press, 2000.

Snow, William P. *Lee and His Generals.* New York: Fairfax Press, 1982.

Snyder, Joel. *American Frontiers: The Photographs of Timothy O'Sullivan, 1867–1874.* Millerton, NY: Aperture, 1981.

Sokoloff, Alice Hunt. *Kate Chase for the Defense.* New York: Dodd, Mead, 1971.

Soley, James R. *Admiral Porter.* New York: D. Appleton & Co., 1903.

———. *The Blockade and the Cruisers.* New York: Charles Scribner's Sons, 1887.

Solomon, Irvin D., and Grace Erhart. "The Peculiar War: Civil War Naval Operations at Charlotte Harbor, Florida, 1861–1865." *Gulf Coast Historical Review* 11 (Fall 1995): 59–78.

———. "Race and Civil War in South Florida." *Florida Historical Quarterly* 77 (Winter 1999): 320–341.

Solomon, Robert S. *The C.S.S. David: The Story of the First Successful Torpedo Boat.* 1970. Reprint (revised). Moncks Corner: Berkeley County Bicentennial Commission, 1976.

Sommers, Richard J. *Richmond Redeemed: The Siege of Petersburg.* Garden City, NY: Doubleday, 1981.

Sorrel, Gilbert Moxley. *Recollections of a Confederate Staff Officer.* Edited by Bell Irwin Wiley. Jackson, TN: McCowat-Mercer Press, 1959.

Southern Historical Society Papers. Vol. 5 (January–June 1878). Richmond, VA: J. William Jones, 1876–1884.

Southwick, Thomas P. *A Duryee Zouave.* 1930. Reprint. Brookneal, VA: Patrick A. Schroeder Publications, 1995.

Southworth, Samuel A., ed. *Great Raids in History: From Drake to Desert One.* New York: Sarpedon, 1997.

Spaulding, Elbridge G. *A Resource of War—The Credit of the Government Made Immediately Available. History of the Legal-Tender Paper Money Issued during the Great Rebellion. Being a Loan without Interest and a National Currency.* 1869. Reprint. Westport, CT: Greenwood Press, 1971.

Spear, Donald P. "The Sutler in the Union Army." *Civil War History* 16 (June 1970): 121–138.

Speer, John. *Life of Gen. James H. Lane. "The Liberator of Kansas" with Corrobative Incidents of Pioneer History.* Garden City, KS: J. Speer, 1897.

Speer, Lonnie R. *Portals to Hell: Military Prisons of the Civil War.* Mechanicsburg, PA: Stackpole, 1997.

Spencer, Warren F. *The Confederate Navy in Europe.* University: University of Alabama Press, 1983.

———. *Raphael Semmes: The Philosophical Mariner.* Tuscaloosa: University of Alabama Press, 1997.

Sperry, A. F. *History of the 33d Iowa Infantry Volunteer Regiment, 1863–6.* Edited by Gregory J. W. Urwin and Cathy Kunzinger Urwin. Fayetteville: University of Arkansas Press, 1999.

Spring, Leverett W. "The Career of a Kansas Politician." *American Historical Review* 4 (October 1898): 80–104.

Stabler, John Burgess. "A History of the Constitutional Union Party: A Tragic Failure." Ph.D. dissertation, Columbia University, 1954.

Stackpole, Edward J. *From Cedar Mountain to Antietam.* Harrisburg, PA: Stackpole, 1993.

———. *Sheridan in the Shenandoah; Jubal Early's Nemesis.* 2d ed. Harrisburg, PA: Stackpole, 1992.

Stacy, James, *History of the Midway Congregational Church, Liberty County, Georgia.* Newman, GA: S. W. Murray Printer, 1899.

Stafford, Tim, "The Abolitionists." *Christian History* 11 (Winter 1992): 21–27.

Stampp, Kenneth M. *America in 1857: A Nation on the Brink.* New York: Oxford University Press, 1990.

———. *And the War Came: The North and the Secession Crisis, 1860–1861.* Baton Rouge: Louisiana State University Press, 1950.

———. *Indiana Politics during the Civil War.* Indianapolis: Indiana Historical Bureau, 1949.

Stands in Timber, John, and Margot Liberty. *Cheyenne Memories.* New Haven, CT: Yale University Press, 1967.

Stanley, David Sloane. *Personal Memoirs of Major-General D. S. Stanley, U.S.A.* Cambridge, MA: Harvard University Press, 1917.

Stanley, F. E. V. *Sumner: Major General United States Army (1797–1863).* Borger, TX: F. Stanley, 1969.

Stanley, Gerald. "Civil War Politics in California." *Southern California Quarterly* 64 (Summer 1982): 115–132.

———. "Slavery and the Origins of the Republican Party in California." *Southern California Quarterly* 60 (Spring 1978): 1–16.

Stanly, Edward. *A Military Governor among Abolitionists. A Letter from Edward Stanly to Charles Sumner.* New York: n.p., 1865.

Stanton, Elizabeth Cady. *Eighty Years and More: Reminiscences 1815–1897.* Boston: Northeastern University Press, 1992.

Stanton, Elizabeth Cady, et al. *The History of Woman Suffrage.* 6 vols. New York: Fowler & Wells, 1970.

Starr, Louis M. *Bohemian Brigade: Civil War Newsmen in Action.* 1954. Reprint. Madison: University of Wisconsin Press, 1987.

Starr, Stephen Z. *Jennison's Jayhawkers: A Civil War Cavalry Regiment and Its Commander.* Baton Rouge: Louisiana State University Press, 1973.

———. *The Union Cavalry in the Civil War.* 3 vols. Baton Rouge: Louisiana State University Press, 1979–1985.

Steamer, Robert J. *The Supreme Court in Crisis: A History of Conflict.* Amherst: University of Massachusetts Press, 1971.

Stearns, Frank Preston. *The Life and Public Services of George Luther Stearns.* Philadelphia: J. B. Lippincott, Co., 1907.

Stearns, George Luther. *A Few Facts Pertaining to Our Currency and Banking Adapted to the Present Position of Our Finances.* Washington, DC: Gibson Brothers, 1864.

———. *Universal Suffrage and Complete Equality in Citizenship: The Safeguard of Democratic Institutions.* Boston: Press of Ran & Very, 1865.

Stearns, Merton Everett. *The Public Life of James A. Seddon.* Sugar Grove, PA: Published by the author, 1924.

Steele, Janet E. *The Sun Shines For All: Journalism and Ideology in the Life of Charles A. Dana.* Syracuse, NY: Syracuse University Press, 1993.

Steiner, Bernard C. *The Life of Reverdy Johnson.* 1914. Reprint. New York: Russel & Ussell, 1970.

Steiner, Paul E. *Disease in the Civil War.* Springfield, IL: Charles C. Thomas, 1968.

Stenberg, Richard R. "The Motivation of the Wilmot Proviso." *The Mississippi Valley Historical Review* 19 (March 1932): 535–548.

Stephens, Alexander H. *A Constitutional View of the Late War between the States.* 2 vols. 1868 and 1870. Reprint. Harrisonburg, VA: Sprinkle Publications, 1994.

Stephenson, Wendell Holmes. *The Political Career of General James H. Lane.* Topeka: Kansas State Historical Society, 1930.

Sterkx, H. E. *Partners in Rebellion: Alabama Women in the Civil War.* Rutherford, NJ: Fairleigh Dickinson University Press, 1970.

Sterling, Dorothy. *Captain of the Planter.* Garden City, NY: Doubleday, 1958.

———. *Lucretia Mott: Gentle Warrior.* Garden City, NY: Doubleday, 1964.

Sterling, Robert E. "Civil War Draft Resistance in the Middle West." Ph.D. dissertation, Northern Illinois University, 1974.

Stern, Madeleine Bettina. *Purple Passage, the Life of Mrs. Frank*

Leslie. Norman: University of Oklahoma Press, 1953.

Stern, Philip Van Doren. "Doctor Gatling and His Gun." *American Heritage* 8 (October 1957): 48–51,105,108.

Stern, Robert L. "Chief Justice Taney and the Shadow of Dred Scott." *Journal of Supreme Court History* (1992): 39–52.

Stevens, Hazard. *Life of Isaac Ingalls Stevens*. 2 vols. Boston: Houghton Mifflin, 1900.

Stevenson, David, and Theodore T. Scribner. *Indiana's Role of Honor*. 2 vols. Indianapolis: A. D. Streight, 1864, 1866.

Steward, Michelle Lee. "Robert E. Rodes: Lee's Forgotten General." M.A. thesis, University of Southwestern Louisiana, 1997.

Stewart, Charles D. "A Bachelor General." *Wisconsin Magazine of History* 17 (1933): 131–154.

Stewart, George Rippey. *Pickett's Charge; A Microhistory of the Final Attack at Gettysburg, July 3, 1863*. Boston: Houghton Mifflin, 1959.

Stewart, James B. *Holy Warriors: The Abolitionists and American Slavery*. New York: Hill & Wang, 1997.

———. *Joshua R. Giddings and the Tactics of Radical Politics*. Cleveland: Press of Case Western Reserve University, 1970.

———. *Wendell Phillips: Liberty's Hero*. Baton Rouge: Louisiana State University Press, 1986.

———. *William Lloyd Garrison and the Challenge of Emancipation*. Arlington Heights, IL: Harlan Davidson, 1992.

Stick, David. *The Outer Banks of North Carolina 1584–1958*. Chapel Hill: University of North Carolina Press, 1958.

Stickles, Arndt M. *Simon Bolivar Buckner: Borderland Knight*. Chapel Hill: University of North Carolina Press, 1940.

Stig, Förster, and Jörg Nagler, eds. *On the Road to Total War: The American Civil War and the German Wars of Unification, 1861–1871*. New York: Cambridge University Press, 1997.

Stiles, Edward H. "William M. Stone." In *Recollections and Sketches of Notable Lawyers and Public Men of Early Iowa*. Edited by Edward H. Stiles. Des Moines, IA: Homestead Publishing Co., 1916.

Still, William N., ed. *The Confederate Navy. The Ships, Men, and Organization, 1861–65*. 1997. Reprint. Annapolis, MD: Naval Institute Press, 1999.

Still, William N., Jr. "Confederate Shipbuilding in Mississippi." *Journal of Mississippi History* 30 (1968): 291–303.

———. "The Confederate States Navy at Mobile, 1861 to August 1864." *Alabama Historical Quarterly* 30 (Fall and Winter 1968): 127–144.

———. "David Glasgow Farragut: The Union's Nelson." In *Captains of the Old Steam Navy*. Edited by James C. Bradford. Annapolis, MD: Naval Institute Press, 1986.

———. *Iron Afloat: The Story of the Confederate Armorclads*. Columbia: University of South Carolina Press, 1985.

Stille, Charles J. *History of the United States Sanitary Commission*. Gansevoort, NY: Corner House Historical Publications, 1997.

Stockdale, Paul H. *The Death of an Army: The Battle of Nashville and Hood's Retreat*. Murfreesboro, TN: Southern Heritage Press, 1992.

Stoddard, William Osborn. *Inside The White House in War Times: Memoirs and Reports of Lincoln's Secretary*. Lincoln: University of Nebraska Press, 2000.

Stone, Candace. *Dana and the Sun*. New York: Dodd, Mead, 1938.

Stone, Irving. *Immortal Wife*. Garden City, NY: Doubleday, Doran, 1944.

Stouffer, Allen. *The Light of Nature and the Law of God: Anti-Slavery in Ontario 1833–1877*. Baton Rouge: Louisiana State University Press, 1992.

Stow, Mary Catherine. "Civilian General." M.A. thesis, University of California, Santa Barbara, 1956.

Stowe, Harriet Beecher. *A Key to Uncle Tom's Cabin: Presenting the Original Facts and Documents upon which the Story Is Founded*. 1853. Reprint. Port Washington, NY: Kennikat Press, 1968.

Stowell, Daniel W. *Rebuilding Zion: The Religious Reconstruction of the South, 1863–1877*. New York: Oxford University Press, 1998.

Stratton, James Newbold. *A Sketch of the Life of Major General Gershom Mott: Read before the Society of the Cincinnati in the State of New Jersey, at Princeton, July 4, 1885*. n.p., 1885.

Strevey, Tracy E. "Joseph Medill and the *Chicago Tribune* in the Nomination and Election of Lincoln." *Papers in Illinois History and Transactions for the Year 1938*. Springfield: Illinois State Historical Society, 1939: 39–63.

Strivers, Reuben E. *Privateers and Volunteers: The Men and Women of Our Reserve Naval Forces, 1766–1866*. Annapolis, MD: Naval Institute Press, 1975.

Strobel, Margaret Lynn. "A Political Biography of Senator Samuel C. Pomeroy of Kansas." M.A. thesis, Pennsylvania State University, 1962.

Strode, Hudson. *Jefferson Davis: Tragic Hero, the Last Twenty-Five Years, 1864–1889*. New York: Harcourt, Brace & World, 1964.

Strong, Edwin, Thomas Buckley, and Annetta St. Clair. "The Odyssey of the CSS *Stonewall*." *Civil War History* 30 (1984): 306–323.

Strother, David Hunter. *A Virginia Yankee in the Civil War: The Diaries of David Hunter Strother*. Edited by Cecil D. Eby, Jr. 1961. Reprint. Chapel Hill: University of North Carolina Press, 1998.

Stuart, A. A. *17th Iowa Infantry. Iowa Colonels and Regiments: Being a History of Iowa Regiments in the War of the Rebellion. Des Moines, Mills and Company, 1891. Throne, Mildred, Ed. The Civil War Diary of Cyrus F. Boyd: 15th Iowa Infantry, 1861–1863*. 1865. Reprint. New York: Krouse Reprint Co., 1977.

Stutler, Boyd Blynn. *West Virginia in the Civil War*. 2d ed. Charleston, WV: Education Foundation, 1966.

Suderow, Bryce. *Thunder in Arcadia Valley: Price's Defeat, September 27, 1864*. Cape Girardeau, MO: Southeast Missouri State University, 1986.

Sullivan, David M. *The United States Marines in the Civil War*. 3 vols. Shippensburg, PA: White Mane Publishing Co., 1997–1999.

Sullivan, George. *Mathew Brady: His Life and Photographs*. New York: L. Cobblehill Books, 1994.

Summersell, Charles G. *The Cruise of the C.S.S. Sumter*. Tuscaloosa, AL: Confederate Publishing Co., 1965.

Sumner, Helen. "Citizenship." In John R. Commons, et. al. *History of Labour in the United States*. 2d ed., 4 vols. New York: Macmillan, 1946: I.

Sunderland, Glenn W. *Lightning at Hoover's Gap: The Story of Wilder's Brigade*. New York: T. Yoseloff, 1969.

———. *Wilder's Lightening Brigade…and its Spencer Repeaters*. Washington, IL: The Book Works, 1984.

Sundquist, Eric J., ed. *Frederick Douglass: New Literary and Historical Essays*. Cambridge and New York: Cambridge University Press, 1990.

———. ed. *New Essays on Uncle Tom's Cabin*. New York: Cambridge University Press, 1986.

Sutherland, Daniel, ed. *Guerrillas, Unionists, and Violence on the Confederate Home Front*. Fayetteville: University of

Arkansas Press, 1999.

Sutherland, David. "Exiles, Emigrants, and Sojourners. The Post Civil War Confederate Exodus in Perspective." *Civil War History* 31 (September 1985): 257–256.

Swanberg, W. A. *First Blood: The Story of Fort Sumter.* New York: Charles Scribner's Sons, 1957.

Swank, Walbrook Davis. *Battle of Trevilian Station: The Civil War's Greatest and Bloodiest All Cavalry Battle.* Shippensburg, PA: Burd Street Press, 1994.

Swint, Henry L., ed. *Dear Ones at Home: Letters from Contraband Camps.* Nashville, TN: Vanderbilt University Press, 1966.

Swisher, Carl B. *History of the Supreme Court of the United States: The Taney Period, 1836–1864.* New York: Macmillan, 1974.

Swisher, Jacob A. *Iowa in Times of War.* Iowa City: State Historical Society of Iowa, 1943.

Swisher, James K. *Brigadier General Micah Jenkins, C.S.A.* Berryville, VA: Rockbridge Publishing Co., 1996.

Sword, Wiley. *Embrace an Angry Wind: The Confederacy's Last Hurrah—Spring Hill, Franklin, and Nashville.* New York: HarperCollins, 1992.

———. "Facing the Gray Wave, Alexander Webb at Gettysburg." *Civil War Times Illustrated* 19 (January 1981): 18–25.

———. *Mountains Touched with Fire: Chattanooga Besieged, 1863.* New York: St. Martin's Press, 1995.

———. *Sharpshooter: Hiram Berdan, His Famous Sharpshooters, and Their Sharps Rifles.* Lincoln, RI: A. Mowbray, 1988.

———. *Shiloh: Bloody April.* New York: William Morrow, 1974.

Sykes, E. T. "Walthall's Brigade—A Cursory Sketch with Personal Experiences of Walthall's Brigade, Army of Tennessee, C.S.A., 1862–1865." *Publications of the Mississippi Historical Society.* Edited by Dunbar Rowland. Jackson, MS: For the Society, 1917.

Sylvester, Lorna Lutes. "Oliver P. Morton and Hoosier Politics during the Civil War." Ph.D. dissertation, Indiana University, 1968.

Symonds, Craig L. *Confederate Admiral: The Life and Wars of Franklin Buchanan.* Annapolis, MD: Naval Institute Press, 1999.

———. *Joseph E. Johnston: A Civil War Biography.* New York: W. W. Norton, 1992.

———. *Stonewall of the West: Patrick Cleburne and the Civil War.* Lawrence: University Press of Kansas, 1997.

Symonds, Henry C. *Report of a Commissary of Subsistence, 1861–1865.* Sing Sing, NY: Published by the author, 1888.

Synovitz, Ronald William Jozef. "Community Conflict in the Confederacy: An Examination of Coverage by the Richmond Examiner, 1861–1864." M.A. thesis, Southern Illinois University at Carbondale, 1990.

Sypher, Josiah R. *History of the Pennsylvania Reserve Corps.* Lancaster: Elias Barr & Co., 1865.

Taliaferro, W. F. "Drainsville." *Philadelphia Weekly Times,* 24 October 1885.

Talmadge, John E. "Peace-Movement Activities in Civil War Georgia." *Georgia Review* 7 (1953): 190–203.

Tang, Edward. "Making Declarations of Her Own: Harriet Beecher Stowe as New England Historian." *New England Quarterly* 71 (March 1998): 77–96.

Tankersley, Allen P. *John B. Gordon: A Study in Gallantry.* Atlanta: Whitehall Press, 1955.

Tanner, Robert G. *Stonewall in the Valley: Thomas J. "Stonewall" Jackson's Shenandoah Valley Campaign, Spring 1862.* 1976. Reprint. Mechanicsburg, PA: Stackpole, 1996.

Tap, Bruce. *Over Lincoln's Shoulder: The Committee on the Conduct of the War.* Lawrence: University Press of Kansas, 1998.

———. "Race, Rhetoric, and Emancipation: The Election of 1862 in Illinois." *Civil War History* 39 (1993): 101–125.

Tappan, Lewis. *The Life of Arthur Tappan.* New York: Hurd & Houghton, 1870.

Tate, Gayle T. "How Antebellum Black Communities Became Mobilized: The Role of Church, Benevolent Society, and Press." *National Political Science Review* 4 (1993): 16–29.

Tatom, E. Lynn. "The Secret Six and Their Theory of Autonomous Individualism." M.A. thesis, North Texas State University, 1973.

Tatum, Georgia Lee. *Disloyalty in the Confederacy.* 1934. Reprint. New York: AMS Press, 1970.

Taylor, Edward Livingston. *Gerrit Smith.* Columbus, Ohio: F. J. Heer Printing Co., 1909.

Taylor, Emerson Gifford. *Gouverneur Kemble Warren; The Life and Letters of an American Soldier, 1830–1882.* Boston: Houghton Mifflin, 1900.

Taylor, Frank H. *Philadelphia in the Civil War, 1861–1865.* Philadelphia: Published by the city, 1913.

Taylor, James E. *The James E. Taylor Sketchbook: With Sheridan Up the Shenandoah Valley in 1864.* Dayton, OH: Morningside House, 1989.

Taylor, Jeremiah. *Memorial of Gen. J. K. F. Mansfield, United States Army, Who Fell in Battle at Sharpsburg, Md., Sept. 17, 1862.* Boston: Press of T. R. Marvin & Son, 1862.

Taylor, John. *Bloody Valverde: A Civil War Battle on the Rio Grande, February 21, 1862.* Albuquerque: University of New Mexico Press, 1995.

Taylor, John M. *William Henry Seward: Lincoln's Right Hand.* New York: HarperCollins, 1991.

Taylor, Lloyd C., Jr. "Harriet Lane—Mirror of an Age." *Pennsylvania History* 30 (April 1963): 212–225.

Taylor, M. P. "Sixth Battalion (Armory Guards)." In *Histories of the Several Regiments and Battalions from North Carolina in the Great War, 1861–'65.* Edited by Walter Clark. Goldsboro: Nash Brothers, 1901. Reprint. Wilmington: Broadfoot, 1999.

Taylor, Richard. *Destruction and Reconstruction: Personal Experiences of the Late War.* 1879. Reprint. New York: Time-Life Books, 1983.

Taylor, Robert A. *Rebel Storehouse: Florida in the Confederate Economy.* Tuscaloosa: University of Alabama Press, 1995: 44–65.

———. "Unforgotten Threat: South Florida Seminoles in the Civil War." *Florida Historical Quarterly* 69 (January 1991): 300–314.

Taylor, Rosser Howard, ed. "The Boyce-Hammond Correspondence." *Journal of Southern History* 3 (August 1937): 348–354.

Taylor, Susie King. *A Black Woman's Civil War Memoirs: Reminiscences of My Life in Camp with the 33rd U.S. Colored Troops, Late 1st South Carolina Volunteers.* New York: Markus Wiener Publishing, 1988.

Taylor, Thomas E. *Running the Blockade.* 1912. Reprint. Annapolis, MD: Naval Institute Press, 1995.

Taylor, Walter H. *Four Years with General Lee.* New York: Appleton, 1877.

———. *General Lee: His Campaigns in Virginia 1861–1865 with Personal Reminiscences.* Brooklyn, NY: Press of Braunworth & Co., 1906.

Tebbell, John, and Sarah Miles Watts. *The Press and the Presidency.* New York: Oxford University Press, 1985.

Terrell, W. H. H. *Report of the Adjutant General of Indiana.* 8 vols. Indianapolis: A. H. Connor, 1865.

Tharp, Louise Hall. *Three Saints and a Sinner: Julia Ward Howe, Louisa, Annie and Sam Ward.* Boston: Little, Brown, 1956.

Thayer, William Roscoe. *The Life and Letters of John Hay.* 2 vols. New York: Harper Brothers, 1915.

"The St. Albans Raid—A Bibliography." *Vermont History* 26 (January 1958): 44–51; 27 (April 1959): 168–169.

The Trial of John H. Surratt. 2 vols. Washington, DC: United States Government Printing Office, 1867.

Theodore, Terry. "Laura Keene and Mr. Lincoln." *Lincoln Herald* 73 (1971): 199–204.

Therry, James R. "The Life of Robert Cumming Schenck." Ph.D. dissertation, Georgetown University, 1968.

Thomas, Benjamin P. *Theodore Weld: Crusader for Freedom.* New Brunswick, NJ: Rutgers University Press, 1950.

Thomas, Benjamin P., and Harold M. Hyman. *Stanton: The Life and Times of Lincoln's Secretary of War.* New York: Alfred A. Knopf, 1962.

Thomas, Dean S. *Cannons.* Gettysburg, PA: Thomas Publications, 1985.

Thomas, Emory M. *Bold Dragoon: The Life of J. E. B. Stuart.* New York: Harper & Row, 1988.

———. *The Confederacy As A Revolutionary Experience.* 1971. Reprint. Columbia: University of South Carolina Press, 1991.

———. *The Confederate Nation.* New York: Harper & Row, 1979.

———. *The Confederate State of Richmond: A Biography of the Capitol.* 1971. Reprint. Baton Rogue: Louisiana State University Press, 1998.

———. *Robert E. Lee: A Biography.* New York: W. W. Norton, 1995.

———. *Robert E. Lee: An Album.* New York: W. W. Norton, 2000.

———. *Travels to Hallowed Ground: A Historian's Journey to the American Civil War.* Columbia: University of South Carolina Press, 1987.

Thomas, Eugene Marvin. "Prisoner of War Exchange during the American Civil War." Ph.D. dissertation, Auburn University, 1976.

Thomas, Henry W. *History of the Doles-Cook Brigade Army of Northern Virginia, C.S.A.* 1903. Reprint. Dayton, OH: Morningside, 1988.

Thomas, John L. *The Liberator: William Lloyd Garrison, A Biography.* Boston: Little, Brown, 1963.

Thomas, John Peyre. *The Career and Character of General Micah Jenkins, C.S.A.* Columbia, SC: The State Co., 1903.

Thomas, Joseph W. "The Campaigns of Generals McClellan and Rosecrans in Western Virginia, 1861–62." *West Virginia History* 5 (July 1944).

Thomas, Richard J. "Caleb Blood Smith: Whig Orator and Politician—Lincoln's Secretary of Interior." Ph.D. dissertation, Indiana University, 1969.

Thomas, Teresa A. "For Union, Not For Glory: Memory and the Civil War Volunteers of Lancaster, Massachusetts." *Civil War History Journal* (March 1994).

———. "For Union, Not For Glory: Memory and the Civil War Volunteers of Lancaster, Massachusetts." M.A. thesis, Clark University.

Thomas, Wilbur. *General George H. Thomas: The Indomitable Warrior.* New York: Exposition Press, 1964.

Thomason, John. W., Jr. *Jeb Stuart.* New York: Charles Scribner's Sons, 1930.

Thompson, Arthur W. "David Yulee: A Study of Nineteenth Century American Thought and Enterprise." Ph.D. dissertation, Columbia University, 1954.

Thompson, Jerry. *Henry Hopkins Sibley: Confederate General of the West.* Natchitoches, LA: Northwestern State University Press, 1987.

Thompson, Jerry Don. *Colonel John Robert Baylor.* Hillsboro, TX: Hill Junior College Press, 1971.

Thompson, Robert M., and Richard Wainwright, eds. *Confidential Correspondence of Gustavus Vasa Fox Assistant Secretary of the Navy, 1861–1865.* 2 vols. New York: Naval Historical Society, 1918.

Thompson, Samuel Bernard. *Confederate Purchasing Operations Abroad.* Chapel Hill: University of North Carolina Press, 1935.

Thornbrough, Emma Lou. *Indiana in the Civil War Era, 1850–1880.* Indianapolis: Indiana Historical Society, 1965.

Thornton, J. Mills, III. *Politics and Power in a Slave Society: Alabama, 1800–1860.* Baton Rouge: Louisiana State University Press, 1978.

Tidball, Eugene C. "The Fort Pickens Relief Expedition of 1861: Lt. John C. Tidball's Journals." *Civil War History* 42 (1996): 322–339.

———. "John C. Tidball: Soldier-Artist of the Great Reconnaissance." *Journal of Arizona History* 37 (1996): 107–130.

———. "The View from the Top of the Knoll: Capt. John C. Tidball's Memoir of the First Battle of Bull Run." *Civil War History* 44 (1998): 175–193.

Tidwell, William A. *April '65: Confederate Covert Action in the American Civil War.* Kent, OH: Kent State University Press, 1995.

Tidwell, William A., James O. Hall, and David Winfred Gaddy. *Come Retribution: The Confederate Secret Service and the Assassination of Abraham Lincoln.* Jackson: University Press of Mississippi, 1988.

Tilton, Robert S. *Pocahontas: The Evolution of an American Narrative.* New York: Cambridge University Press, 1994.

Tindall, George Brown. *South Carolina Negroes, 1877–1900.* Columbia: University of South Carolina Press, 1952.

Tinkcom, Harry Martin. *John White Geary: Soldier-Statesman, 1819–1873.* Philadelphia: University of Pennsylvania Press, 1940.

Todd, Frederick P. *American Military Equipage, 1851–1872.* 2 vols. New York: Charles Scribner's Sons, 1980.

Todd, Richard Cecil. *Confederate Finance.* Athens: University of Georgia Press, 1954.

Tolbert, Frank X. *Dick Dowling at Sabine Pass.* New York: McGraw-Hill, 1962.

Tompkins, Sally. Letters. Virginia State Library Archives, Richmond.

Touched with Valor: Civil War Papers and Casualty Reports of Hood's Texas Brigade. Hillsboro, TX: Hill Junior College Press, 1964.

Townsend, E. D. *Memoir of Lorenzo Thomas.* n.p., n.d.

Townsend, George Alfred. *Campaigns of a Non-Combatant.* 1966. Reprint. New York: Time-Life Books, 1982.

———. *Major General Alfred Thomas Archimedes Torbert: Delaware's Most Famous Civil War Hero.* Bowie, MD: Heritage Books, 1993.

Trachtenberg, Alan. *Reading American Photographs. Images as History—Mathew Brady to Walker Evans.* New York: Hill & Wang, 1990.

Trafzer, Clifford E. *The Kit Carson Campaign: The Last Great Navajo War.* Norman: University of Oklahoma Press, 1982.

Tredway, G. R. *Democratic Opposition to the Lincoln Administration in Indiana.* Indianapolis: Indiana Historical Bureau, 1973.

Trefousse, Hans Louis. *Andrew Johnson: A Biography.* 1957. Reprint. New York: W. W. Norton, 1997.

———. *Benjamin Franklin Wade: Radical Republican from Ohio.* New York: Twayne Publishers, 1963.

———. *Impeachment of a President; Andrew Johnson, the Blacks, Reconstruction.* Knoxville: University of Tennessee Press, 1975.

———. *The Radical Republicans, Lincoln's Vanguard for Racial Justice.* Baton Rouge: Louisiana State University Press, 1968.

———. *Thaddeus Stevens: Nineteenth-Century Egalitarian.* Chapel Hill: University of North Carolina Press, 1997.

Trevelyan, George Macaulay. *The Life of John Bright.* London: Constable & Co., 1913.

Trexler, Harrison A. *The Confederate Ironclad* Virginia (Merrimac). Chicago: University of Chicago Press, 1938.

Trindal, Mary E., and Elizabeth S. Trindal. *Mary Surratt: An American Tragedy.* Graetna: Pelican Publishing Co., 1996.

Trotter, William. *Bushwhackers: The Civil War in the North Carolina Mountains.* Winston-Salem, NC: John F. Blair, 1988.

———. *The Civil War in North Carolina, Vol. 3: Ironclads and Columbiads.* Winston-Salem, NC: John F. Blair, 1989.

Trout, Robert J. *They Followed the Plume: The Story of J. E. B. Stuart and His Staff.* Mechanicsburg, PA: Stackpole, 1993.

Trudeau, Noah Andre. *Bloody Roads South: The Wilderness to Cold Harbor, May–June 1864.* Boston: Little, Brown, 1989.

———. *The Last Citadel: Petersburg, Virginia, June 1864–April 1865.* Baton Rouge: Louisiana State University Press, 1991.

———. *Out of the Storm; The End of the Civil War, April–June 1865.* Boston: Little, Brown, 1994.

Trulock, Alice Rains. *In the Hands of Providence: Joshua L. Chamberlain and the American Civil War.* Chapel Hill: University of North Carolina Press, 1992.

Truth, Sojourner, and Olive Gilbert. *Narrative of Sojourner Truth; A Bondswoman of Olden Time, With a History of Her Labors and Correspondence, Drawn from her "Book of Life."* Edited by Nell Irvin Painter. New York: Penguin, 1998.

Tucker, Glenn. *Chickamauga: Bloody Battle in the West.* 1961. Reprint. Dayton, OH: Morningside House, 1981.

———. *Hancock the Superb.* 1960. Reprint. Dayton, OH: Press of Morningside Bookshop, 1980.

———. *High Tide at Gettysburg: The Campaign in Pennsylvania.* New York: Bobbs-Merrill, 1958.

———. *Zeb Vance: Champion of Personal Freedom.* Indianapolis: Bobbs-Merrill, 1966.

Tucker, Louis L. "The Siege of Cincinnati by a Pearl Street Rifle." *Historical and Philosophical Society of Ohio Bulletin* 20 (1962): 255–273.

Tucker, Spencer C. *Andrew Foote: Civil War Admiral on Western Waters.* Annapolis, MD: Naval Institute Press, 2000.

———. *Raphael Semmes and the* Alabama. Fort Worth, TX: Ryan Place Publishing, 1996.

Turner, Arlin. *Nathaniel Hawthorne, a Biography.* New York: Oxford University Press, 1980.

Turner, George Edgar. *Victory Rode the Rails: The Strategic Place of the Railroads in the Civil War.* Indianapolis: Bobbs-Merrill, 1953.

Turner, Justin, and Linda Levitt. *Mary Lincoln—Her Life and Letters.* New York: Alfred A. Knopf, 1972.

Turner, Thomas Reed. *Beware the People Weeping; Public Opinion and the Assassination of Abraham Lincoln.* Baton Rouge: Louisiana State University Press, 1982.

Turner, Wallace B. "The Secession Movement in Kentucky." *Register of the Kentucky Historical Society* 66 (July 1968): 259–278.

Twenty-Third Army Corps Association. *Proceedings of the Twenty-Third Army Corps Association, at Its Annual Reunion.* Cincinnati: Moore, Wilstach & Baldwin, 1865.

Tyler, Daniel. *A Concise History of the Mormon Battalion in the Mexican War, 1846–1847.* Chicago: Rio Grande Press, 1964.

Tyler, Lyon G., ed. *Encyclopedia of Virginia Biography.* 5 vols. New York: Lewis Historical Publishing Co., 1915.

Tyler, Robert Ogden. *Memoir of Brevet Major-General Robert Ogden Tyler, U.S. Army, together with His Journal of Two Months Travels in British and Farther India.* Philadelphia: J. B. Lippincott, 1878.

Tyler, Ronnie C. "Cotton on the Border, 1861–1865." *Southwestern Historical Quarterly* 73 (April 1970): 456–477.

Tyrner-Tyrnauer, A. R. *Lincoln and the Emperors.* New York: Harcourt, Brace &World, 1962.

United States Christian Commission. *Address of the Christian Commission.* New York: Office of the Christian Commission, 1862.

———. *Christian Commission for the Army and Navy of the United States of America.* Philadelphia: Ringwalt & Brown, 1862.

United States Congress. *Memorial Addresses on the Life and Character of Michael Hahn, (A Representative of Louisiana) Delivered in the House of Representatives and in the Senate, Forty-ninth Congress, First Session.* Washington, DC: Government Printing Office, 1886.

———. House. *Trial of Henry Wirz.* House Executive Doc. 23, 40th Congress, 2d Session, 1868.

———. Joint Committee on the Conduct of the War. *Supplemental Report of the Joint Committee on the Conduct of the War: Supplemental to Senate Report No. 142, 38th Congress, 2d Session.* 2 volumes. Millwood, NJ: Kraus Reprint Co., 1977.

United States Department of State. *Despatches from United States Consuls in Alexandria, 1835–1873.* National Archives, Washington, DC.

———. *Diplomatic Instructions of the Department of State to Egypt.* National Archives, Washington, DC.

United States Department of the Interior. *Bridges Across the Potomac.* Washington, DC: J. C. Greer, 1857.

United States National Archives. Bureau of Construction and Repair. Plans of ships and stations, with related records, 1794–1910. RG 19.

———. *Military Operations of the Civil War: A Guide-Index to the Official Records, 1861–65.* Compiled by Dallas D. Irvine. 5 vols. Washington, DC: Government Printing Office, 1961–1978.

United States Navy Department. *Civil War Naval Chronology, 1861–1865, Part IV, Special Studies and Cumulative Index.* Washington, DC: Office of the Chief of Naval Operations, 1961.

———. *Dictionary of American Naval Fighting Ships, Volume III.* Washington, DC: U.S. Government Printing Press, 1968.

———. Naval History Division. *Monitors of the U.S. Navy, 1861–1937.* 1969.

United States War Department. *The War of the Rebellion: A Compilation of the Official Records of the Union and Confederate Armies.* 70 vols. in 128 parts. Washington, DC: Government Printing Office, 1880–1901.

Urwin, Gregory J. W. *Custer Victorious: The Civil War Battles of General George Armstrong Custer.* Lincoln: University of Nebraska Press, 1990.

———. "'We Cannot Treat Negroes... as Prisoners of War': Racial Atrocities and Reprisals in Civil War Arkansas." *Civil War History* 42 (September 1996): 193–210.

Utley, Robert M. *Cavalier in Buckskin: George Armstrong Custer and the Western Military Frontier.* Norman: University of Oklahoma Press, 1988.

———. *Frontier Regulars: The United States Army and the Indian,*

1866–1891. New York: Macmillan, 1973.

———. *Frontiersmen in Blue: The United States Army and the Indian, 1848–1865*. New York: Macmillan, 1967.

Uya, Okon Edet. *From Slavery to Public Service: Robert Smalls, 1830–1915*. New York: Oxford University Press, 1971.

Valuska, David L. "The Negro in the Union Navy, 1861–1865." Ph.D. dissertation, Lehigh University, 1973.

Van Der Weele, Wayne J. "Jesse David Bright: Master Politician from the Old Northwest." Ph.D. dissertation, Indiana University, 1958.

Van Deusen, Glyndon G. *Horace Greeley: Nineteenth-Century Crusader*. Philadelphia: University of Pennsylvania Press, 1953.

———. *The Life of Henry Clay*. Boston: Little, Brown, 1979.

———. *William Henry Seward*. New York: Oxford University Press, 1967.

Van Horne, Thomas B. *History of the Army of the Cumberland: Its Organization, Campaigns, and Battles, Written at the Request of Major-General George H. Thomas Chiefly from His Private Military Journal and Official and Other Documents Furnished by Him*. 2 vols. Cincinnati: Robert Clarke & Co., 1875.

Van Noppen, Ina Woestemeyer. *Stoneman's Last Raid*. Raleigh: North Carolina State University, 1961.

Vanauken, Sheldon. *The Glittering Illusion. English Sympathy for the Southern Confederacy*. Worthing, England: Churhman Press, 1988.

Vanderslice, John M. *Gettysburg Then and Now. The Field of American Valor. Where and How the Regiments Fought and the Troops They Encountered. An Account of the Battle Giving Movements, Positions, and Losses of the Commands Engaged*. New York: G. W. Dillingham Co., 1899.

Vandiver, Frank E. *Jubal's Raid: General Early's Famous Attack on Washington in 1864*. New York: McGraw-Hill, 1960.

———. *Mighty Stonewall*. 1957. Reprint. College Station: Texas A&M University Press, 1988.

———. *Ploughshares into Swords: Josiah Gorgas and Confederate Ordnance*. 1952. Reprint. College Station: Texas A&M University, 1994.

———, ed. *The Civil War Diary of General Josiah Gorgas*. University: University of Alabama Press, 1947.

———, ed. *Confederate Blockade Running through Bermuda 1861–1865: Letters and Cargo Manifests*. Austin: University of Texas Press, 1947.

Varley, James F. *Brigham and the Brigadier: General Patrick Connor and his California Volunteers in Utah and along the Overland Trail*. Tucson, AZ: Westernlore Press, 1989.

Varon, Elizabeth R. *We Mean to Be Counted: White Women and Politics in Antebellum Virginia*. Chapel Hill: University of North Carolina Press, 1998.

Vasvary, Edmund. *Lincoln's Hungarian Heroes: The Participation of Hungarians in the Civil War, 1861–1865*. Washington, DC: Hungarian Reformed Federation of America, 1939.

Vaughn, J. W. *The Reynolds Campaign on Powder River*. Norman: University of Oklahoma Press, 1983.

Velazquez, Loreta Janeta. *The Woman in Battle*. Richmond, VA: Dustin, Gilman & Co., 1876.

Venet, Wendy Hamand. *Neither Ballots nor Bullets: Women Abolitionists and the Civil War*. Charlottesville: University of Virginia Press, 1991.

Victor, Orville J. *Men of the Time; Being Biographies of Generals Halleck, Pope, Siegel, Corcoran, Prentiss, Kearney, Hatch and Augur*. New York: Beadle & Co., 1862.

Villard, Henry. *Memoirs of Henry Villard*. 2 vols. 1904. Reprint. New York: Da Capo Press, 1969.

Villard, Oswald Garrison. *John Brown 1800–1859: A Biography Fifty Years After*. 1910. Reprint. Gloucester, MA: Peter Smith, 1966.

Vinovskis, Mark A., ed. *Toward a Social History of the American Civil War: Exploratory Essays*. New York: Cambridge University Press, 1990.

Von Borcke, Heros. *Memoirs of the Confederate War for Independence*. 1938. Reprint. Dayton, OH: Morningside Press, 1985.

Von Frank, Albert J. *The Trials of Anthony Burns: Freedom and Slavery in Emerson's Boston*. Cambridge, MA: Harvard University Press, 1998.

Wadley, Sarah Lois. *A Brief Record of the Life of William M. Wadley*. New York: A. S. Barnes, 1884.

Wadsworth Family Papers. Library of Congress, Washington, DC.

Wagenknecht, Edward. *John Greenleaf Whittier: A Portrait in Paradox*. New York: Oxford University Press, 1967.

Waggoner, Clark. *History of the City of Toledo and Lucas County Ohio*. New York and Toledo: Munsell & Co., 1888.

Wagner, Arthur L. *Organization and Tactics*. London: W. H. Allan & Co., 1894.

Wahl, Paul. *The Gatling Gun*. New York: Arco, 1965.

Wakelyn, Jon L., ed. *Southern Pamphlets on Secession, 1860–April 1861*. Chapel Hill: University of North Carolina Press, 1996.

———, ed. *Southern Unionist Pamphlets and the Civil War*. Columbia: University of Missouri Press, 1999.

Walker, Gary C. *Hunter's Fiery Raid through Virginia Valleys*. Roanoke, VA: A. & W. Enterprises, 1989.

Walker, John L. *Cahaba Prison and the Sultana Disaster*. Hamilton, OH: Brown & Whitaker, 1910.

Wall, Joseph Frazier. *Henry Watterson, Reconstructed Rebel*. New York: Oxford University Press, 1956.

Wallace, Lew. *Lew Wallace: An Autobiography*. Edited by Susan Elston Wallace and Mary H. Krout. 2 vols. New York: Harper & Bros., 1906.

Wallace, Margaret L. *William Henry Wallace*. New York: Published by the author, 1930.

Walpole, Spencer. *Life of Lord John Russell*. New York: Longmans, Green, 1899.

Walter, Francis X. *The Naval Battle of Mobile Bay, August 5, 1864; and Franklin Buchanan on the Tennessee, a Portrait of the Admiral of the Confederate Fleet in Mobile Bay*. Birmingham, AL: Prester Meridian Press, 1993.

Walters, Frederick Ray. "The Donelson Mission to the German Federal Government, 1848–1849." M.A. thesis, The American University, 1964.

Walters, Ronald. *The Antislavery Appeal: American Abolitionism after 1830*. Baltimore: Johns Hopkins University Press, 1978.

Walther, Eric H. *The Fire-Eaters*. Baton Rouge: Louisiana State University Press, 1992.

Ward, Geoffrey C., et al. *The Civil War: An Illustrated History*. New York: Alfred A. Knopf, 1990.

Ward, James A. *That Man Haupt: A Biography of Herman Haupt*. Baton Rouge: Louisiana State University Press, 1973.

Wardell, Morris L. *A Political History of the Cherokee Nation, 1838–1907*. Norman: University of Oklahoma Press, 1938.

Warfield, A. B. "The Quartermaster's Department, 1861–1864." 8 (1928): 43–46.

Warner, Ezra J. *Generals in Gray, Lives of the Confederate Commanders*. 1959. Reprint. Baton Rouge: Louisiana Univesity Press, 1987.

Warner, Ezra J., and W. Buck Yearns. *Biographical Register of*

the Confederate Congress. Baton Rouge: Louisiana State University Press, 1975.

Warren, Charles. *A History of the American Bar.* New York: H. Fertig, 1966.

———. *The Supreme Court in United States History.* 3 vols. Boston: Little, Brown, 1922.

Warren, Gordon H. *Fountain of Discontent: The* Trent *Affair and Freedom of the Seas.* Boston: Northeastern University Press, 1981.

Warren, Lambert, D. *When the Ripe Pears Fell: The Battle of Richmond, Kentucky.* Richmond, KY: Madison County Historical Society, 1995.

Warren, Louis A. *Lincoln's Gettysburg Dedication: "A New Birth of Freedom."* Fort Wayne, IN: Lincoln National Life Foundation, 1964.

Warren, Robert Penn. *John Greenleaf Whittier's Poetry: An Appraisal and a Selection.* Minneapolis: University of Minnesota Press, 1971.

Washburn, Cadwallader C. Collection. Washburn-Norlands Foundation Archives, Livermore, ME.

Washburn, Emory. *Memoir of the Hon. Joel Parker.* Cambridge, MA: J. Wilson & Son, 1876.

Washburn, Israel, Jr. Collection. Washburn-Norlands Foundation Archives, Livermore, ME.

Washburne, Elihu B. Collection. Washburn-Norlands Foundation Archives, Livermore, ME.

Waters, William Davis. "'Deception in the Art of War': Gabriel J. Rains, Torpedo Specialist of the Confederacy." *North Carolina Historical Review* 66 (January 1989): 26–60.

Watkins, Sam R. *Co. Aytch: A Side Show of the Big Show.* 1882. Reprint. New York: Simon & Schuster, 1997.

Watson, Charles S. *From Nationalism to Secessionism: The Changing Fiction of William Gilmore Simms.* Westport, CT: Greenwood Press, 1993.

Watters, George Wayne. "Isham Green Harris, Civil War Governor and Senator from Tennessee, 1818–1897." Ph.D. dissertation, Florida State University, 1977.

Watterson, Henry. *The Editorials of Henry Watterson; Compiled with an Introduction and Notes by Arthur Krock.* New York: George H. Doran Co., 1923.

Waugh, John C. *Reelecting Lincoln: The Battle for the 1864 Presidency.* New York: Crown Publishers, 1997.

———. *Sam Bell Maxey and the Confederate Indians.* Abilene, TX: McWhiney Foundation Press, McMurry University, 1998.

Waugh, John G. *The Class of 1846 from West Point to Appomattox: Stonewall Jackson, George McClellan and Their Brothers.* New York: Warner Books, 1994.

Wayland, John. *Robert E. Lee and His Family.* Staunton, VA: McClure Print Co., 1951.

Wayland, John W. *The Pathfinder of the Seas: The Life of Matthew Fontaine Maury.* Richmond, VA: Garret & Massie, 1930.

Wayne, Michael, "The Reshaping of Plantation Society Revisited." *Journal of Mississippi History* 54 (Fall 1992): 333–348.

Wayt DeBolt, Maragaret. *Savannah: A Historical Portrait.* Virginia Beach, VA: The Donning Co., 1974.

Weaver, Richard M. *The Southern Tradition at Bay: A History of Postbellum Thought.* New Rochelle, NY: Arlington House, 1968.

Weber, Thomas. *The Northern Railroads in the Civil War, 1861–1865.* New York: King's Crown Press of Columbia University, 1952.

Webster, Clyde Cannon. "John Minor Botts: Anti-secessionist." *Richmond College Historical Papers* 1 (1915): 9–37.

Webster, Donald B., Jr. "Rodman's Great Guns." *Ordnance* (July–August 1962): 60–62.

Weddle, Kevin J. "Ethnic Discrimination in Minnesota Volunteer Regiments during the Civil War." *Civil War History* 35 (No. 3, 1989): 239–259.

Weeks, James. "The Civil War's Greatest Scoop." *American Heritage* 40 (July/August 1989): 100–104.

Weichmann, Louis, J. *A True History of the Assassination of Abraham Lincoln and of the Confederacy of 1865.* Edited by Floyd E. Risvold. New York: Alfred A. Knopf, 1975.

Weigley, Russell F. *A Great Civil War: A Military and Political History, 1861–1865.* Bloomington: Indiana University Press, 2000.

———. *History of the United States Army.* Enlarged ed. Bloomington: Indiana University Press, 1984.

———. "The Military Thought of John M. Schofield." *Military Affairs* 23 (Summer 1959): 77–84.

———, ed. *Philadelphia, a 300-Year History.* New York: W. W. Norton, 1982.

———. *Quartermaster General of the Union Army: A Biography of M. C. Meigs.* New York: Columbia University Press, 1959.

Weinert, Richard P. *Defender of the Chesapeake: The Story of Fort Monroe.* Shippensburg, PA: White Mane, 1990.

Weintraub, Stanley. *Uncrowned King: The Life of Prince Albert.* London: John Murray, 1997.

Weisberger, Bernard A. *Reporters for the Union.* Boston: Little, Brown, 1953.

Weisenburger, Francis P. "General Isaac R. Sherwood." *Historical Society of Northwest Ohio* 14 (April 1942): 42–54.

———. *The Life of John McLean: A Politician on the United States Supreme Court.* Columbus: Ohio State University Press, 1937.

Weitz, Mark A. *A Higher Duty: Desertion among Georgia Troops during the Civil War.* Lincoln: University of Nebraska Press, 2000.

———. "Preparing For the Prodigal Son: The Development of the Union Desertion Policy during the Civil War." *Civil War History* (June 1999).

Weitzel, Godfrey. *Richmond Occupied: Entry of the United States Forces into Richmond, Va., April 3, 1865.* Richmond, VA: Richmond Civil War Centennial Committee, 1965.

Welch, Emily S. *John Sedgwick, Major-General: A Biographical Sketch.* New York: De Vinne Press, 1899.

Welcher, Frank J. *The Union Army, 1861–1865: Organization and Operations.* 2 vols. Bloomington: Indiana University Press, 1989.

Weld, Theodore D. *In Memory: Angelina Grimké Weld.* Boston: George H. Ellis, 1880.

Wellman, Manly Wade. *Giant in Gray: A Biography of Wade Hampton of South Carolina.* New York: Charles Scribner's Sons, 1949.

Wells, Tom Henderson. "Charles Augustus Lafayette Lamar." *Georgia Historical Quarterly* 47 (1963): 158–168.

———. *The Slave Ship* Wanderer. Athens: University of Georgia Press, 1967.

Wendt, Lloyd. Chicago Tribune: *The Rise of a Great American Newspaper.* Chicago: Rand McNally, 1979.

Werlich, David P. *Admiral of the Amazon: John Randolph Tucker, His Confederate Colleagues, and Peru.* Charlottesville: University of Virginia Press, 1990.

Werstein, Irving. *July, 1863.* New York: Messner, 1957.

———. *Kearny the Magnificent; the Story of General Philip Kearny, 1815–1862.* New York: John Day Co., 1962.

Wert, Jeffrey D. *Custer: The Controversial Life of George Armstrong Custer.* New York: Simon & Schuster, 1996.

———. *From Winchester to Cedar Creek: The Shenandoah Campaign of 1864.* 1987. Reprint. Mechanicsburg, PA:

Stackpole, 1997.

———. *General James Longstreet: The Confederacy's Most Controversial Soldier—A Biography.* New York: Simon & Schuster, 1993.

———. "His Unhonored Service." *Civil War Times Illustrated* 24 (June 1985).

———. "Rappahannock Station." *Civil War Times Illustrated* 25 (December 1976): 4–8, 40–46.

———. "A Single Step." *Civil War Times Illustrated* 33 (1): 29–37.

Wessels, William L. *Born to be a Soldier; the Military Career of William Wing Loring of St. Augustine, Florida.* Fort Worth: Texas Christian University Press, 1971.

Wessen, Ernest James, ed. *Papers of Brigadier General Jacob Ammen.* Mansfield, OH: Midland Rare Book Co., 1957.

West, Richard S., Jr. *Lincoln's Scapegoat General: A Life of Benjamin F. Butler, 1818–1893.* Boston: Houghton Mifflin, 1965.

———. *Mr. Lincoln's Navy.* Westport, CT: Greenwood Press, 1976.

———. *The Second Admiral: A Life of David Dixon Porter.* New York: Coward-McCann, 1937.

Whaley, Elizabeth J. *Forgotten Hero: General James B. McPherson: The Biography of a Civil War General.* New York: Exposition Press, 1955.

Wheaton, Frank. *Civil and Military Record of Frank Wheaton, Brevet major General U.S. Army, Colonel Second U.S. Infantry.* Washington, DC: Fort Omaha, 1888.

Wheeler, Francis B. "The Building of the *Monitor.*" *Magazine of American History* 13 (1895): 59–65.

Wheeler, Kenneth W., ed. *For the Union: Ohio Leaders in the Civil War.* Columbus: Ohio State University, 1998.

Wheeler, Richard. *Sword over Richmond: An Eyewitness History of McClellan's Peninsula Campaign.* New York: Harper & Row, 1986.

Wheelwright, Julie. *Amazons and Military Maids: Women Who Dressed as Men in the Pursuit of Life, Liberty and Happiness.* London: Pandora Press, 1989.

White, E. V. *The First Iron-Clad Engagement in the World.* New York: J. S. Ogilvie Publishing Co., 1906.

White, Horace. *The Life of Lyman Trumbull.* Boston: Houghton Mifflin, 1913.

White, M. E. "The Thomas G. Jordan Family during the War between the States." *Georgia Historical Quarterly* 59 (1975), 134–140.

White, Ruth. *Yankee from Sweden: The Dream and the Reality in the Days of John Ericsson.* New York: Holt, 1960.

White, William W. *The Confederate Veteran.* Tuscaloosa, AL: Confederate Publishing Co., 1962.

Whitesell, Hunter B. "Military Operations in the Jackson Purchase Area of Kentucky, 1862–1865." *Register of the Kentucky Historical Society* 63 (1965): 140–167, 240–267, 323–348.

Whitesell, Robert D. "Military and Naval Activity between Cairo and Columbus." *Register of the Kentucky Historical Society* 61 (1963): 107–121.

Whiting, William Henry Chase. *Diary of a March from El Paso to San Antonio.* Washington, DC: Publications of the Southern History Association, 1902.

———. *Whiting Diary, March from Fredericksburg to El Paso del Norte.* Washington, DC: Publications of the Southern History Association, 1906.

Whitman, Walt. *Poetry and Prose.* Edited by Justin Kaplan. New York: Library of America, 1982.

———. *Walt Whitman's Civil War.* Edited by Walter Lowenfels. New York: Alfred A. Knopf, 1960.

Wiecek, William M. *The Sources of Antislavery Constitutionalism in America, 1760–1848.* Ithaca, NY: Cornell University Press, 1977.

Wiese, E. Robert. "Life and Times of Samuel Preston Moore, Surgeon General of the Confederate States of America." *Southern Medical Journal* XXIII (October 1930): 916–922.

Wiess, William. "First Federal Defeat at Sabine Pass." *Confederate Veteran* 20 (March 1912): 108–109.

Wiggins, Sarah Woolfolk. "A Victorian Father: Josiah Gorgas and His Family." In *In Joy and in Sorrow: Women, Family, and Marriage in the Victorian Era.* Edited by Carol Bleser. New York: Oxford University Press, 1991: 233–252.

———, ed. *The Journals of Josiah Gorgas 1857–1878.* Foreword by Frank E. Vandiver. Tuscaloosa: University of Alabama Press, 1995.

Wiley, Bell I. *The Life of Billy Yank, the Common Soldier of the Union.* 1952. Reprint. Baton Rouge: Louisiana State University Press, 1993.

———. *The Life of Johnny Reb: The Common Soldier of the Confederacy.* 1943, 1978. Reprint. Baton Rouge: Louisiana State University Press, 1997.

Wiley, Bell Irwin. "Holey Joes' of the Sixties: A Study of Civil War Chaplains." *Huntington Library Quarterly* 16 (1953): 287–304.

Wilkins, Thurman. *Clarence King: A Biography.* New York: Macmillan, 1958.

Wilkinson, John. *The Narrative of a Blockade-Runner.* 1877. Reprint. Alexandria, VA: Time-Life Books, 1984.

Williams, Alfred B. *Hampton and His Redshirts.* Charleston: Walker, Evans & Cogswell Co., 1935.

Williams, Alpheus S. *From the Cannon's Mouth: The Wartime Letters of Alphesus S. Williams.* Edited by Milo M. Quaife. Detroit: Wayne State University Press, 1959.

Williams, Ames W. "Stronghold of the Straits: A Short History of Fort Zachary Taylor." *Tequesta* 15 (1954): 3–16.

Williams, Ben Ames, ed. *Mary Boykin Chesnut: A Diary from Dixie.* New York: Houghton Mifflin, 1949.

Williams, Carrington. "Samuel Preston Moore, Surgeon General of the Confederate States Army." *Virginia Medical Monthly* 88 (October 1961), 622–628.

Williams, Charles Evarts. *The Life of Abner Coburn; A Review of the Public and Private Career of the Late Ex-Governor of Maine.* Bangor, ME: T. W. Burr, 1885.

Williams, David. *Rich Man's War: Class, Caste, and Confederate Defeat in the Lower Chattahoochee Valley.* Athens: University of Georgia Press, 1998.

Williams, Edward F., III. "The Johnsonville Raid and Nathan Bedford Forrest State Park." *Tennessee Historical Quarterly* 28 (Fall 1969): 225–251.

Williams, Francis L. *Matthew Fontaine Maury: Scientist of the Sea.* New Brunswick, NJ: Rutgers University Press, 1963.

Williams, Harold A. *Robert Garrett & Sons Incorporated: Origin and Development, 1840–1865.* Baltimore: Schneidereith & Sons, 1965.

Williams, Herman Warner, Jr. *The Civil War The Artists' Record.* Boston: Beacon Press, 1961.

Williams, John Hoyt. *Sam Houston: A Biography of the Father of Texas.* New York: Simon & Schuster, 1993.

Williams, Kenneth P. *Lincoln Finds a General: A Military Study of the Civil War.* 5 vols. New York: Macmillan, 1949–1959.

———. "The Tennessee River Campaign and Anna Ella Carroll." *Indiana Magazine of History* 46 (September 1950): 221–248.

Williams, Margaret. "Henry D. Clayton: His Congressional Career." M.A. thesis, Auburn University, 1942.

Williams, Samuel Cole. *General John T. Wilder, Commander of the Lightning Brigade*. Bloomington: Indiana University Press, 1936.

Williams, T. Harry. *Hayes of the Twenty-third: The Civil War Volunteer Officer*. New York: Alfred A. Knopf, 1965.

———. *Lincoln and the Radicals*. Madison: University of Wisconsin Press, 1941.

———. *McClellan, Sherman, and Grant*. New Brunswick, NJ: Rutgers University Press, 1962.

———. *P. G. T. Beauregard: Napoleon in Gray*. Baton Rouge: Louisiana University Press, 1955.

———. "Voters in Blue." *Mississippi Valley Historical Review* 31 (1944): 187–204.

Williams, Teresa C. "'The Women Rising': Class and Gender in Civil War Georgia." M.A. thesis, Valdosta State University, 1999.

Williamson, James J. *Prison Life in the Old Capitol and Reminiscences of the Civil War*. West Orange, NJ: Published by the author, 1911.

Williamson, Joel. "The Disruption of State Government in South Carolina during the MaGrath Administration." M.A. thesis, University of South Carolina, 1951.

Wills, Brian Steel. *A Battle from the Start: The Life of Nathan Bedford Forrest*. New York: HarperCollins, 1992.

Wills, Garry. *Lincoln at Gettysburg: The Words that Remade America*. New York: Simon & Schuster, 1992.

Willson, Beckles. *John Slidell and the Confederates in Paris, 1862–1865*. New York: AMS Press, 1970.

Wilson, Angley F. *Richmond M. Pearson and the Richmond Hill Law School*. Raleigh: North Carolina Department of Cultural Resources, Division of Archives and History, 1978.

Wilson, Charles Reagan. *Baptized in Blood: The Religion of the Lost Cause, 1865–1920*. Athens: University of Georgia Press, 1980.

Wilson, Clyde N. *Carolina Cavalier: The Life and Mind of James Johnston Pettigrew*. Athens: University of Georgia Press, 1990.

———. *John C. Calhoun: A Bibliography*. Westport, CT: Meckler, 1990.

———. *The Most Promising Young Man of the South: James Johnston Pettigrew and His Men at Gettysburg*. Abilene, TX: McWhiney Foundation Press, 1998.

Wilson, Dorothy Clarke. *Lone Woman: The Story of Elizabeth Blackwell the First Woman Doctor*. Boston: Little, Brown, 1970.

———. *Stranger and Traveler: The Story of Dorothea Dix, American Reformer*. Boston: Little, Brown, 1975.

Wilson, Douglas L. *Lincoln before Washington: New Perspectives on the Illinois Years*. Urbana: University of Illinois Press, 1997.

Wilson, Douglas L., and Davis Rodney O., eds. *Herndon's Informants: Letters, Interviews, and Statements about Abraham Lincoln*. Urbana: University of Illinois Press, 1998.

Wilson, Edmund. "Justice Oliver Wendell Holmes." In *Patriotic Gore: Studies in the Literature of the American Civil War*. New York: Oxford University Press, 1962.

Wilson, Eugene K. "James H. Burton and the Development of the Confederate Small Arms Industry." M.A. thesis, Old Dominion University, 1976.

Wilson, James H. *The Life of Charles A. Dana*. New York: Harper, 1907.

———. *Life of John A. Rawlins: Lawyer, Assistant Adjutant General, Chief of Staff, Major General of Volunteers, and Secretary of War*. New York: Neale Publishing Co., 1916.

———. *Under the Old Flag: Recollections of Military Operations in the War for the Union, the Spanish War, the Boxer Rebellion, Etc.* 1912. Reprint. Westport, CT: Greenwood Press, 1971.

Wilson, John. *Chattanooga's Story*. Chattanooga: Chattanooga Free Press, 1980.

Wilson, John A. *Adventures of Alf. Wilson: A Thrilling Episode of the Dark Days of the Rebellion*. Washington, DC: National Tribune, 1897.

Wilson, R. L. *Colt: An American Legend*. New York: Abbeville Press, 1986.

Wilson, T. Paul. "Delegates of the Five Civilized Tribes to the Confederate Congress." *Chronicles of Oklahoma*, 53 (Fall 1975): 353–366.

Wilson, W. Emerson. *Fort Delaware*. Newark: University of Delaware Press, 1957.

Wiltse, Charles M. *John C. Calhoun: Sectionalist, 1840–1850*. Indianapolis: Bobbs-Merrill, 1951.

Winks, Robin. *Canada and the United States: The Civil War Years*. 1960. Reprint. Lantham, MD: University Press of America, 1988.

Winschel, Terrence J. *Triumph and Defeat, The Vicksburg Campaign*. Mason City, IA: Savas Publishing Co., 1999.

Winslow, Hattie Lou. *Camp Morton, 1861–1865: Indianapolis Prison Camp*. Indianapolis: Indiana Historical Society, 1995.

Winslow, Richard E., III. *General John Sedgwick: The Story of a Union Corps Commander*. Novato, CA: Presidio Press, 1982.

Winston, Robert. *Andrew Johnson, Plebian and Patriot*. New York: Holt, 1928.

Winter, William. *The Civil War in St. Louis*. St. Louis: Missouri Historical Society Press, 1995.

Winters, John D. *The Civil War in Louisiana*. Baton Rouge: Louisiana State University Press, 1963.

Winther, Oscar O. "Soldier Voting in the Election of 1864." *New York History* 25 (1944).

Wise, Jennings. "Field Artillery in Rearguard Actions: The Historical Incident of Dilger's Battery." *Field Artillery Journal* 13 (January 1932): 32–40.

Wise, Stephen R. *Gate of Hell: Campaign for Charleston Harbor, 1863*. Columbia: University of South Carolina Press, 1994.

———. *Lifeline of the Confederacy: Blockade Running during the Civil War*. Columbia: University of South Carolina Press, 1988.

Wish, Harvey. *George Fitzhugh, Conservative of the Old South*. Charlottesville: University of Virginia Press, 1938.

———. *George Fitzhugh, Propagandist of the Old South*. Baton Rouge: Louisiana State University Press, 1943.

Witt, Elder, ed. *Congressional Quarterly's Guide to the U.S. Supreme Court*. Washington, DC: Congressional Quarterly, 1990.

"Wofford's Brigade at Gettysburg." *Richmond Daily Enquirer*, 5 August 1863.

Woldman, Albert A. *Lincoln and the Russians*. Cleveland, OH: World Publishing Co., 1952.

Wood, Peter H., and Karen C. C. Dalton. *Winslow Homer's Images of Blacks: The Civil War and Reconstruction*. Houston: University of Texas Press, 1988.

Woodford, Frank B. *Lewis Cass: The Last Jeffersonian*. New Brunswick, NJ: Rutgers University Press, 1950.

Woodward, C. Vann, ed. *Mary Chestnut's Civil War*. New Haven, CT: Yale University Press, 1981.

———. *Origins of the New South, 1877–1913*. Baton Rouge: Louisiana University Press, 1951.

Woodward, C. Vann, and Elisabeth Muhlenfeld. *The Private Mary Chesnut: The Unpublished Civil War Diaries*. New York: Oxford University Press, 1984.

Woodward, Edward V. "Holding the Alleghany Line: Edward

Johnson, the Army of the Northwest, and the Battle of Alleghany Summit." M.A. thesis, Florida State University, 1998.

Woodward, Harold R., Jr. *Defender of the Valley. Brigadier General John Daniel Imboden, C.S.A.* Berryville, VA: Rockbridge Publishing, 1996.

Woodwell, Roland H. *John Greenleaf Whittier: A Biography.* Haverhill, MA: DBL Commercial Printers, 1985.

Woodworth, Steven E. *A Deep Steady Thunder.* Abilene, TX: McWhiney Foundation Press, 1998.

———. *Davis and Lee at War.* Lawrence: University Press of Kansas, 1995.

———. *Jefferson Davis and His Generals: The Failure of Confederate Command in the West.* Lawrence: University Press of Kansas, 1990.

———. *No Band of Brothers: Problems in the Rebel High Command.* Columbia: University of Missouri Press, 1999.

———. *Six Armies in Tennessee: The Chickamauga and Chattanooga Campaigns.* Lincoln: University of Nebraska Press, 1998.

———, ed. *The Human Tradition in the Civil War and Reconstruction.* Scholarly Resources, 2000.

———, ed. *Leadership and Command in the American Civil War.* Campbell: Savas Woodbury, 1995.

Woolsey, Ronald C. "Disunion or Dissent?" *Southern California Quarterly* 66 (Fall 1984): 185–206.

———. "The Politics of a Lost Cause." *California History* 59 (Winter 1991): 372–383.

Wooster, Ralph A., ed. *Lone Star Blue and Gray: Essays on Texas in the Civil War.* Austin: Texas State Historical Association, 1995.

———. *Texas and Texans in the Civil War.* Austin, TX: Eakin Press, 1995.

Wooster, Robert. *The Military and United States Indian Policy, 1865–1903.* New Haven, CT: Yale University Press, 1988.

———. *Nelson A. Miles and the Twilight of the Frontier Army.* Lincoln: University of Nebraska Press, 1993.

Worthington, C. J., ed. *The Woman in Battle: A Narrative of the Exploits, Adventures, and Travels of Madame Loreta Janeta Velazquez.* 1876. Reprint. New York: Arno Press, 1972.

Wright, Crafts J. *Official Journal of the Conference Convention Held at Washington City, February 1861.* Washington, DC: 1861.

Wright, David Russell. "Civil War Field Fortifications: An Analysis of Theory and Practical Application." M.A. thesis, Middle Tennessee State University, 1982.

Wright, George Bohan. *Hon. David Tod. Biography and Personal Recollections.* Columbus, OH: A. H. Smythe, 1900.

Wright, Henry H. *A History of the Sixth Iowa Infantry.* Iowa City: State Historical Society of Iowa, 1923.

Wright, L. C. *United States Policy Towards Egypt 1820–1914.* New York: Exposition Press, 1969.

Wright, Marcus J. "Colonel Elias C. Boudinot." *Southern Bivouac* 2 (June 1884): 433–440.

———. "Sketch of General Felix K. Zollicoffer." *Southern Bivouac* 2 (July 1884): 485–499.

Wubben, Hubert H. *Civil War Iowa and the Copperhead Movement.* Ames: Iowa State University Press, 1980.

———. "The Maintenance of Internal Security in Iowa, 1861–1865." *Civil War History* 10 (1964): 401–415.

Wyatt-Brown, Bertram. *Lewis Tappan and the Evangelical War on Slavery.* 1969. Reprint. Baton Rouge: Louisiana State University Press, 1997.

Wyeth, John A. *Life of General Nathan Bedford Forrest.* 1899. Reprint. Baton Rouge: Louisiana State University Press, 1989.

Wytrwal, Joseph A. *Poles in American History and Tradition.* Detroit: Endurance Press, 1969.

Yacovone, Donald, ed. *A Voice of Thunder: The Civil War Letters of George E. Stephens.* Urbana and Chicago: University of Illinois Press, 1997.

Yard, James S. *Joel Parker: "The War Governor of New Jersey": A Biographical Sketch.* Hanover, TX: F. Parker, 1962.

Yates, Richard E. *The Confederacy and Zeb Vance.* Tuscaloosa: Confederate Publishing Co., 1958.

Yearns, W. Buck. *The Confederate Congress.* Athens: University of Georgia Press, 1960.

———, ed. *The Confederate Governors.* Athens: University of Georgia Press, 1985.

Yearns, W. Buck, and John G. Barrett, eds. *North Carolina Civil War Documentary.* Chapel Hill: University of North Carolina Press, 1980.

Yelverton, Mildred. *They Also Served: Twenty-five Remarkable Alabama Women.* Dothan, AL: Ampersand Publishing, 1993.

Yonge, Julian C. "Pensacola in the War for Southern Independence." *Florida Historical Quarterly* 37 (January–April 1959).

Youmans, LeRoy Franklin. *A Sketch of the Life and Services of Francis W. Pickens of South Carolina.* Charleston, South Carolina: News Job Presses, 1989.

Young, Agatha. *The Women and the Crisis: Women of the North in the Civil War.* New York: McDowell, Obolensky, 1959.

Young, Elizabeth. "Confederate Counterfeit." *Passing and the Fictions of Identity.* Edited by Elaine K. Ginsberg. Durham, NC: Duke University Press, 1996.

Young, James Harvey. "Anna Elizabeth Dickinson and the Civil War." Ph.D. dissertation, University of Illinois, 1941.

———. "Anna Elizabeth Dickinson and the Civil War: For and against Lincoln." *Mississippi Valley Historical Review* 31 (June 1944): 59–80.

Young, John D. "A Campaign with Sharpshooters." In *Annals of War.* Philadelphia: Times Publishing, 1879: 267–287.

Young, John Russell. *Men and Memories: Personal Reminiscences.* New York: F. Tennyson Neely, 1901.

Young, Kenneth R. *General's General: The Life and Times of Arthur MacArthur.* Boulder, CO: Westview Press, 1994.

Young, Michael T. "A Study of the Activities of James Dunwoody Bulloch: Confederate Naval Agent in Great Britain." M.A. thesis, University of Nebraska at Omaha, 1968.

Young, Robert W. *Senator James Murray Mason: Defender of the Old South.* Knoxville: University of Tennessee Press, 1998.

Young, William T. *Sketch of the Life and Public Services of General Lewis Cass.* Detroit: Markham & Elwood, 1852.

Younger, Edward, ed. *Inside the Confederate Government: The Diary of Robert Garlick Hill Kean.* 1957. Reprint. New York: Greenwood Publishing Group, 1974.

Youngstrom, Gustaf Adolph. "The Official Career of Andrew Reeder in Kansas." M.A. thesis, Northwestern University, 1931.

Yulee, C. Wickliffe. "Senator Yulee." *Florida Historical Quarterly* 2 (April and July 1909): 26–43, 3–22.

Zabecki, David T. *American Artillery and the Medal of Honor.* Bennington, Vermont: Merriam Press, 1995.

———. "Father of the Rock Island Arsenal." *Field Artillery Journal* (January–February 1981): 54–56.

Zacharias, Donald W. "John J. Crittenden Crusades for the Union and Neutrality in Kentucky." *Filson Club History Quarterly* 38 (July 1964): 193–205.

Zarefsky, David. *Lincoln, Douglas and Slavery: In the Crucible of Public Debate.* Chicago: University of Chicago Press, 1990.

Zhang, Qingsong. *Mei guo Bai Nian Pal Hua Nei Mu. (A History of Chinese Exclusion in the United States)*. Shanghai: People's Publishing House, 1998.

Zinn, Jack. R. E. *Lee's Cheat Mountain Campaign*. Parsons, WV: McClain Printing Co., 1974.

Zobell, Albert L. *Sentinel in the East: A Biography of Thomas L. Kane*. Salt Lake City: N. B. Morgan, 1965.

Zornow, William Frank. *Lincoln and the Party Divided*. Norman: University of Oklahoma Press, 1954.

Zucker, A. E., ed. *The Forty-Eighters: Political Refugees of the German Revolution of 1848*. New York: Columbia University Press, 1950.

INDEX

Note: Italic page numbers indicate illustrations; bold page numbers indicate main encylopedia entries.

and Oliver O. Howard, 1009
and Philip Sheridan, 1761
and railroads, 1597
and reduction of Fort McAllister, 739–741
and Richmond campaign, 1639
Saint-Gaudens sculpture, 116
and siege of Savannah, 1707–1708
XVI Corps, 125
and Stephen Augustus Hurlbut, 1023
and Stoneman's raid (July 1864), 1871
and surrender at Bennett House, 212
targeting of Savannah, 1706–1707
and Thomas Ewing, Jr., 667
and Thomas John Wood, 2149
and Thomas Kilby Smith, 1818
and Ulysses S. Grant, 866, 868, 870, 872
use of cavalry in Georgia campaign, 380
and Vicksburg campaign, 2021–2023, 2025–2026
Washington monument, 1318
on Western Sanitary Commission, 2092
and William Farquhar Barry, 183–184
and William Sooy Smith, 1822
and William Worth Belknap, 204
and Yazoo expedition, 431–432, 2159–2160
Sherman, Willie, 1767
Sherman Antitrust Act, 938
Sherman Reservation, 783
Sherman's March to the Sea, 105, 113, 820, 1768, **1769–1773**, *1771, 1772*
    and Abraham Lincoln, 1188
    and Absalom Baird, 161
    authorized by Henry W. Halleck, 910
    bummers, 322–323
    and escaped slaves, 822
    and Fort McAllister, 739
    and Frank Blair, 239
    and George Norman Barnard, 180
    and Howell Cobb, 461
    and James Harrison Wilson, 2125
    and James Morgan, 1358–1359
    and Jefferson Columbus Davis, 572
    and Joseph Anthony Mower, 1371
    and Kate Cumming, 529
    and logistics, 1209, 1210
    and Manning Ferguson Force, 715
    map, *1770*
    and Mortimer Dormer Leggett, 1168
    and Peter J. Osterhaus, 1445
    Savannah as objective of, 1706–1707
    Sherman's planning, 771
    and Theodore Davis, 933
    and William Worth Belknap, 204
Sherwood, Daniel, 1773
Sherwood, Isaac Ruth, **1773–1774**
Shields, James, 1039, 1298, **1774–1775**, *1775*
    and battle of Cross Keys, 527
    and battle of Front Royal, 791
    and battle of Port Republic, 1550–1551
    and first battle of Kernstown, 1119
    and Shenandoah Valley campaign, 366, 1748, 1750–1751, 1753–1755
Shiloh, battle of, 12, 14, 35, 84, 1339, **1775–1780**, *1778, 1932*
    and Albert Sidney Johnston, 1082–1083
    and Alexander P. Stewart, 1865
    and Alvin Peterson Hovey, 1006–1007
    and Ambrose Bierce, 225

    and Arabella "Belle" Reynolds, 1631
    and August von Willich, 2118
    and Basil Wilson Duke, 625
    and Benjamin Prentiss, 1559
    and Bushrod Rust Johnson, 1072
    and Charles Clark, 444
    and Daniel Chevilette Govan, 856
    and Don Carlos Buell, 309
    and Francis Fessenden, 688
    and Francis Shoup, 1780
    and Franklin Gardner, 808
    and James A. Garfield, 810–811
    and James Baird Weaver, 2080
    and James Barnett Fry, 792
    and James Fleming Fagan, 673
    and James Ronald Chalmers, 389
    and Jeremy Francis Gilmer, 841
    and John A. McClernand, 1278
    and John C. Breckinridge, 278
    and John Haskell King, 1127
    and John Hunt Morgan, 1359
    and John McArthur, 1270
    and John Parker Hawkins, 950
    and John Sappington Marmaduke, 1254
    and John Stevens Bowen, 258
    and John Thomas Wilder, 2108
    and Jones Mitchell Withers, 2140
    and Joseph Wheeler, 2096
    and Kate Cumming, 528–529
    and Leonidas Polk, 1538
    and Lew Wallace, 2055–2056
    and Lovell Harrison Rousseau, 1681
    maps, *1776, 1777*
    and Marcellus M. Crocker, 525
    and Morgan Lewis Smith, 1817
    and Nathan Bedford Forrest, 720
    and Orphan Brigade, 1442
    and P. G. T. Beauregard, 199
    and Patrick Cleburne, 455–456
    and Samuel Beatty, 197
    and Thomas Kilby Smith, 1818
    and Thomas L. Crittenden, 524
    and Thomas Ransom, 1603–1604
    and Thomas Sweeny, 1912
    and Ulysses S. Grant, 866
    and Walter Quintin Gresham, 885
    Whitelaw Reid's account of, 1622
    and William Babcock Hazen, 959
    and William Grose, 897
    and William Hardee, 926
    and William Jackson Palmer, 1452
    and William Milo Stone, 1869
    and William Sooy Smith, 1822
    and William T. Sherman, 1766
    and William Worth Belknap, 204
Shirley, John T., 74, 1933
Shokokon, 536
Shorey, Henry, 1488
Shorter, John Gill, 643, 1510, **1780**, 2075
    and Andrew Moore, 1352
Shoshone Indians, 1364, 2166
Shoup, Francis Asbury, **1780–1781**
Shoup, George L., 1702
Shrapnel, Henry, 117
Shubrick, John T., 908
Shufeldt, Robert, 1393